THE STATESMAN'S YEARBOOK
2004

Statesmen are but men; and more than in any other calling, they embody the defects of their merits. The imperious leader who appears to dictate the future is at the mercy of unpredictable events and the impersonal forces of history; at the mercy too of the hesitations and doubts of those he has to trust to carry out his commands. On the other hand, the sagacious, rational conciliators see their humane plans swept aside by crude demagogues, and are unable, precisely because they appeal to reason, to defeat the emotional slogans of opponents who know how to play on the prejudice of their compatriots.

Noel Annan, *Changing Enemies.*

Editors

Frederick Martin	1864–1883
Sir John Scott-Keltie	1883–1926
Mortimer Epstein	1927–1946
S. H. Steinberg	1946–1969
John Paxton	1969–1990
Brian Hunter	1990–1997
Barry Turner	1997–

Credits

Publisher	Alison Jones (London)
	Garrett Kiely (New York)
Editor	Barry Turner
Editorial Assistants	Jill Fenner
	Jeni Giffen
Research Editor	Nicholas Heath-Brown
Research	Andrew Clarke
	Daniel Bunyard
	Nicola Varns
	Anna Brattström
	Richard German
	Clive Carpenter
	Martha Nyman
	Natasha Martin
	Daniel Smith
Index	Richard German
Production	Darren Smith
	Michael Card
Marketing	Nathan Gaw (London)
	Andrea Lansing (New York)

THE
STATESMAN'S
YEARBOOK

THE POLITICS, CULTURES AND
ECONOMIES OF THE WORLD

2004

EDITED BY

BARRY TURNER

Published annually since 1864

This edition published 2003 by
PALGRAVE MACMILLAN
Houndmills, Basingstoke, Hampshire RG21 6XS and
175 Fifth Avenue, New York, N.Y.10010
Companies and representatives throughout the world

PALGRAVE MACMILLAN is the global academic imprint of the Palgrave Macmillan division of St. Martin's Press, LLC and of Palgrave Macmillan Ltd. Macmillan® is a registered trademark in the United States, United Kingdom and other countries. Palgrave is a registered trademark in the European Union and other countries.

ISBN 0−333−98097−2
ISSN 0081−4601

This book is printed on paper suitable for recycling and made from fully managed and sustained forest sources.

A catalogue record for this book is available from the British Library.

Library of Congress Cataloging-in-Publication Data
Data available

10   9   8   7   6   5   4   3   2   1
12   11   10   09   08   07   06   05   04   03

Typeset by Penrose Typography, Maidstone

Printed and bound in Great Britain by
The Bath Press, Bath

CONTENTS

CONTENTS

CONTENTS

CONTENTS

CONTENTS

CONTENTS

CONTENTS

CONTENTS

CONTENTS

KEY WORLD FACTS

- World population in 2003 — 6,287 million (3,166 million males and 3,121 million females). The total passed 6 billion in February 1999
- World population under 30 in 2003 — 3,429 million
- World population over 60 in 2003 — 642 million
- World population over 100 in 2003 — 230,000
- World economic growth rate in 2001 — 2·2%
- Number of illiterate people — 960 million
- Number of unemployed people — 180 million
- Average world life expectancy — 69·1 years for females; 64·9 years for males
- Annual world population increase — 76·86 million people
- Number of people living outside country of birth — 185 million, or nearly 3% of the world's population
- Fertility rate — 2·8 births per woman
- Urban population — 47·2% of total population
- World defence expenditure — US$811·5 billion
- Number of TV sets — 1·36 billion
- Number of radio receivers — 2·18 billion
- Number of cigarettes smoked — 5,600 billion a year
- Number of Internet users — 606 million
- Number of mobile phone users — 1·3 billion
- Number of motor vehicles on the road — 647 million
- Number of people who cross international borders every day — 2 million
- Number of people living in poverty — 1·5 billion
- Number of malnourished people — 840 million
- Number of overweight people — 1·1 billion
- Number of obese adults — 300 million
- Number of people dying of starvation — 24,000 every day
- Number of people lacking clean drinking water — 1 billion
- Number of people lacking adequate sanitation — 3 billion
- Number of reported executions in 2001 — 3,048
- Number of people worldwide exposed to indoor air pollution that exceeds WHO guidelines — 1 billion
- Annual carbon dioxide emissions — 6·6 billion tonnes of carbon

ISO COUNTRY CODES

Below is a list of the codes of sovereign states produced by the International Organization for Standardization (ISO). There has been widespread use of these ISO codes as TLDs ('top level domains') in Internet applications (used in lower case), managed by the Internet Assigned Numbers Association (IANA), to denote 'national' domains in addition to the common TLDs such as '.com' and '.org'. There are some IANA codes used in preference to the above on the Internet (eg. '.uk' rather than '.gb').

AD	ANDORRA	DJ	DJIBOUTI
AE	UNITED ARAB EMIRATES	DK	DENMARK
AF	AFGHANISTAN	DM	DOMINICA
AG	ANTIGUA AND BARBUDA	DO	DOMINICAN REPUBLIC
AL	ALBANIA	DZ	ALGERIA
AM	ARMENIA	EC	ECUADOR
AO	ANGOLA	EE	ESTONIA
AR	ARGENTINA	EG	EGYPT
AT	AUSTRIA	ER	ERITREA
AU	AUSTRALIA	ES	SPAIN
AZ	AZERBAIJAN	ET	ETHIOPIA
BA	BOSNIA-HERZEGOVINA	FI	FINLAND
BB	BARBADOS	FJ	FIJI ISLANDS
BD	BANGLADESH	FM	MICRONESIA
BE	BELGIUM	FR	FRANCE
BF	BURKINA FASO	GA	GABON
BG	BULGARIA	GB	UNITED KINGDOM OF
BH	BAHRAIN		GREAT BRITAIN AND
BI	BURUNDI		NORTHERN IRELAND
BJ	BENIN	GD	GRENADA
BN	BRUNEI	GE	GEORGIA
BO	BOLIVIA	GH	GHANA
BR	BRAZIL	GM	THE GAMBIA
BS	BAHAMAS	GN	GUINEA
BT	BHUTAN	GQ	EQUATORIAL GUINEA
BW	BOTSWANA	GR	GREECE
BY	BELARUS	GT	GUATEMALA
BZ	BELIZE	GW	GUINEA-BISSAU
CA	CANADA	GY	GUYANA
CD	CONGO (DEMOCRATIC	HN	HONDURAS
	REPUBLIC OF)	HR	CROATIA
CF	CENTRAL AFRICAN	HT	HAITI
	REPUBLIC	HU	HUNGARY
CG	CONGO (REPUBLIC OF)	ID	INDONESIA
CH	SWITZERLAND	IE	IRELAND
CI	CÔTE D'IVOIRE	IL	ISRAEL
CL	CHILE	IN	INDIA
CM	CAMEROON	IQ	IRAQ
CN	CHINA	IR	IRAN
CO	COLOMBIA	IS	ICELAND
CR	COSTA RICA	IT	ITALY
CU	CUBA	JM	JAMAICA
CV	CAPE VERDE	JO	JORDAN
CY	CYPRUS	JP	JAPAN
CZ	CZECH REPUBLIC	KE	KENYA
DE	GERMANY	KG	KYRGYZSTAN

KH	CAMBODIA	PW	PALAU
KI	KIRIBATI	PY	PARAGUAY
KM	COMOROS	QA	QATAR
KN	ST KITTS AND NEVIS	RO	ROMANIA
KP	NORTH KOREA	RU	RUSSIA
KR	KOREA	RW	RWANDA
KW	KUWAIT	SA	SAUDI ARABIA
KZ	KAZAKHSTAN	SB	SOLOMON ISLANDS
LA	LAOS	SC	SEYCHELLES
LB	LEBANON	SD	SUDAN
LC	ST LUCIA	SE	SWEDEN
LI	LIECHTENSTEIN	SG	SINGAPORE
LK	SRI LANKA	SI	SLOVENIA
LR	LIBERIA	SK	SLOVAKIA
LS	LESOTHO	SL	SIERRA LEONE
LT	LITHUANIA	SM	SAN MARINO
LU	LUXEMBOURG	SN	SENEGAL
LV	LATVIA	SO	SOMALIA
LY	LIBYA	SR	SURINAME
MA	MOROCCO	ST	SÃO TOMÉ E PRÍNCIPE
MC	MONACO	SV	EL SALVADOR
MD	MOLDOVA	SY	SYRIA
MG	MADAGASCAR	SZ	SWAZILAND
MH	MARSHALL ISLANDS	TD	CHAD
MK	MACEDONIA	TG	TOGO
ML	MALI	TH	THAILAND
MM	MYANMAR	TJ	TAJIKISTAN
MN	MONGOLIA	TM	TURKMENISTAN
MR	MAURITANIA	TN	TUNISIA
MT	MALTA	TO	TONGA
MU	MAURITIUS	TP	EAST TIMOR
MV	MALDIVES	TR	TURKEY
MW	MALAWI	TT	TRINIDAD AND TOBAGO
MX	MEXICO	TV	TUVALU
MY	MALAYSIA	TZ	TANZANIA
MZ	MOZAMBIQUE	UA	UKRAINE
NA	NAMIBIA	UG	UGANDA
NE	NIGER	US	UNITED STATES OF
NG	NIGERIA		AMERICA
NI	NICARAGUA	UY	URUGUAY
NL	THE NETHERLANDS	UZ	UZBEKISTAN
NO	NORWAY	VA	VATICAN CITY STATE
NP	NEPAL	VC	ST VINCENT AND
NR	NAURU		THE GRENADINES
NZ	NEW ZEALAND	VE	VENEZUELA
OM	OMAN	VN	VIETNAM
PA	PANAMA	VU	VANUATU
PE	PERU	WS	SAMOA
PG	PAPUA NEW GUINEA	YE	YEMEN
PH	PHILIPPINES	YU	SERBIA AND MONTENEGRO
PK	PAKISTAN	ZA	SOUTH AFRICA
PL	POLAND	ZM	ZAMBIA
PT	PORTUGAL	ZW	ZIMBABWE

CHRONOLOGY

CHRONOLOGY

April 2002–March 2003

Week beginning 7 April 2002

In Costa Rica, a run-off for the presidency was won by Abel Pacheco of the ruling Social Christian Unity Party, with 58·0% of the vote against 42·0% for Rolando Araya.

An agreement brokered in March 2002 to create a single entity called Serbia and Montenegro was ratified by both governments.

Venezuelan president Hugo Chávez was forced to resign in a military coup led by a businessman, Pedro Carmona Estanga. The following day protests by Chávez supporters led the new president to resign and Chávez was reinstated.

Week beginning 14 April 2002

In East Timor's first democratic elections, former separatist guerrilla leader Xanana Gusmão (FRETILIN) won a landslide victory with 82·6% of votes cast against 17·3% for Xavier do Amaral, his only rival.

In the Netherlands, Prime Minister Wim Kok and his entire administration resigned after admitting that Dutch peacekeeping forces could have done more to prevent the massacre of 8,000 Bosnian Muslims at Srebrenica by Serb forces in 1995.

In Madagascar, a deal was brokered to end the power struggle between Marc Ravalomanana and Didier Ratsiraka. Both men agreed to a vote recount to determine the outcome of the disputed elections of Dec. 2001. The High Constitutional Court declared Ravalomanana the winner with 51·5% of votes against 35·9% for Ratsiraka, who refused to recognize the result. Ravalomanana was subsequently sworn in as president.

Week beginning 21 April 2002

In the first round of French presidential elections Jacques Chirac for the Rally for the Republic's came first with 19·87% of votes, with the National Front leader Jean-Marie Le Pen second with 16·86% ahead of incumbent prime minister Lionel Jospin, who received 16·17%. In the second round Jacques Chirac won a second consecutive presidential term in a landslide victory, with 82·21% of votes cast against 17·79% for Jean-Marie Le Pen.

In the second round of voting in a parliamentary election in Hungary, the Hungarian Socialist Party lost their first-round lead over the ruling party Fidesz-MPP, who won 188 seats out of a total of 386 against 178 for the Socialists.

In Chad's general election the Patriotic Salvation Movement of President Idriss Déby won a landslide victory, winning 112 out of 155 seats.

Week beginning 28 April 2002

A referendum in Pakistan confirmed Gen. Pervez Musharraf as president, giving him a further five years rule. Opposition parties boycotted the vote.

Parliamentary elections in the Bahamas were won by the Progressive Liberal Party, with 29 out of 40 seats and 50·8% of votes cast, against 7 and 41·1% for the ruling Free National Movement. Perry Christie of the PLP was sworn in as prime minister.

In Vanuatu's general election the Union of Moderate Parties won 15 out of 52 seats, while the party of Prime Minister Edward Natapei, the Party of Our Land, took 14. However, with the UMP unable to form a coalition, Prime Minster Edward Natapei remained in office.

The Palestinian leader Yasser Arafat was released after a five-month blockade of his Ramallah headquarters.

Week beginning 5 May 2002

In Burkina Faso's general elections, the ruling Congress for Democracy and Progress Party took 57 of 111 seats ahead of the coalition of Alliance for Democracy and Federation and the African Democratic Party with 17 seats.

In Comoros, after results of the April presidential elections were disputed, the Comoros Election Commission was dissolved. Its replacement, the Ratification Commission, declared Azali Assoumani president.

Week beginning 12 May 2002

In a presidential election run off in Mali, former president Amadou Toumani Touré defeated Soumaïla Cissé, with 64·4% of votes cast against 35·7%.

Presidential elections in Sierra Leone were won by incumbent president Ahmad Tejan Kabbah, with 70·1% of votes cast against 22·3% for Ernest Koroma. Kabbah's Sierra Leone People's Party was also successful in parliamentary elections, taking 83 of 112 seats.

At parliamentary elections in the Netherlands the Christian Democrat Appeal won 43 seats, ahead of the right-wing List Pim Fortuyn (the party of the murdered politician Pim Fortuyn) the People's Party for Freedom and Democracy, and the Labour Party, which had been the leading party at the 1998 election.

Parliamentary elections in the Dominican Republic were won by President Hipólito Mejía's Dominican Revolutionary Party, with 73 of 150 seats, ahead of the Dominican Liberation Party with 41 and the Social Christian Reform Party with 36.

In Ireland, parliamentary elections were won by Prime Minister Bertie Ahern's Fianna Fáil, with 81 of 166 seats, against 31 for Fine Gael.

Week beginning 19 May 2002

In parliamentary elections in Vietnam, Communist Party members won 447 of 498 seats.

East Timor became an independent country.

Kyrgyzstan's prime minister Kurmanbek Bakiyev resigned. First Deputy Prime Minister Nikolay Tanayev was named acting prime minister and was subsequently approved as prime minister.

Russian president Vladimir Putin and US president George Bush signed an arms control treaty agreeing to reduce their respective strategic nuclear warheads by two-thirds over the next ten years.

In parliamentary elections in Lesotho, the ruling Lesotho Congress for Democracy won 77 of 117 seats with 54·9% of the vote, against 21 for the Basotho National Party, with 22·4%.

Week beginning 26 May 2002

In Colombia, the independent Álvaro Uribe Vélez won an outright victory in the first round of the presidential elections. Uribe replaced Andrés Pastrana as president, winning 53·1% of votes against 31·8% for the Liberal Party's Horacio Serpa Uribe.

The Hungarian parliament elected Péter Medgyessy as the new prime minister.

In a parliamentary election in Algeria incumbent prime minister Ali Benflis' National Liberation Front won 199 out of 389 seats ahead of the National Democratic Rally with 47 seats.

Week beginning 2 June 2002

In Vanuatu, parliament re-elected Edward Natapei prime minister.

Amadou Toumani Touré was sworn in as president of Mali.

Week beginning 9 June 2002

Chad's prime minister Nagoum Yamassoum resigned. He was replaced by Haroun Kabadi.

In Afghanistan's first elections since the fall of the Taliban, the Emergency Loya Jirga (Grand Council) elected the interim leader Hamid Karzai as president with a large majority.

In elections in the Czech Republic the Social Democratic Party (ČSSD) retained power with 30·2% of votes cast. The conservative Civic Democratic Party achieved 24·5%. ČSSD leader Vladimír Špidla replaced Miloš Zeman as prime minister.

Week beginning 16 June 2002

Following the second round of French parliamentary elections, the centre right coalition Union for the Presidential Majority, comprising President Jacques Chirac's Rally for the Republic and the Liberal Democracy party, gained 357 of 577 seats in the Assemblée Nationale, with 33·7% of votes cast. President Jacques Chirac confirmed Jean-Pierre Raffarin prime minister of a majority right-wing government.

The Bangladeshi president A. Q. M. Badruddoza Chowdhury resigned. The speaker Jamiruddi Sircar was made acting president.

Week beginning 23 June 2002

The second round of the Republic of Congo's general elections took place, resulting in victory for President Denis Sassou-Nguesso's Congolese Labour Party, with 52 out of 137 seats.

The Albanian parliament elected Alfred Moisiu to succeed Rexhep Meidani as president.

Togo's prime minister, Agbeyome Messan Kodjo, was dismissed and replaced by Koffi Sama.

Week beginning 30 June 2002

Parliamentary elections in Cameroon were won by the ruling Rassemblement Démocratique du Peuple Camerounais with 133 seats, ahead of the Social-Democratic Front with 21.

In presidential elections in Bolivia, former president Gonzalo Sánchez de Lozada (Nationalist Revolutionary Movement) won 22·5% of the vote, followed by Evo Morales (Movement to Socialism) with 20·9%. Congress subsequently chose Gonzalo Sánchez de Lozada as president with 84 votes, against 43 for Evo Morales.

In parliamentary elections in Guinea the ruling Party of Unity and Progress gained 85 out of 114 seats, ahead of the Union for Progress and Revival, with 20 seats.

The International Criminal Court, set up in The Hague to try war crimes and crimes against humanity, was established.

Croatia's prime minister Ivica Račan resigned, citing differences within the five-party coalition government, but was reinstated within days and survived a vote of confidence.

Former Madagascan president Didier Ratsiraka went into exile in the Seychelles after several regions under his control were taken by troops loyal to President Marc Ravalomanana.

Week beginning 7 July 2002

Peruvian foreign minister Diego García Sayán resigned, as did the prime minister, Roberto Dañino, two days later. A new cabinet was sworn in including Luis Solari de la Fuente as prime minister and Allan Wagner Tizón as foreign minister.

In a cabinet reshuffle in Spain, Ana Palacio became foreign minister.

Turkish foreign minister Ismail Cem resigned. He was replaced by Sükrü Sina Gürel.

President Václav Havel of the Czech Republic appointed Vladimír Špidla prime minister. His cabinet included Cyril Svoboda as foreign minister with Jaroslav Tvrdík remaining as defence minister.

Week beginning 14 July 2002

German Chancellor Gerhard Schröder dismissed his defence minister, Rudolf Scharping, replacing him with Peter Struck.

In India, A. P. J. Abdul Kalam was elected president by the Indian parliament, receiving 89·6% of votes cast.

Week beginning 21 July 2002

Jan Peter Balkenende was sworn in as prime minister of the Netherlands. His coalition cabinet included Jaap de Hoop Scheffer as foreign minister and Benk Korthals as defence minister.

Alfred Moisiu took office as president of Albania. The next day Prime Minister Pandeli Majko resigned. A new government was formed with Fatos Nano as prime minister, a former prime minister Ilir Meta as foreign minister and Pandeli Majko as defence minister.

Vietnam's national assembly reappointed President Tran Duc Luong and Prime Minister Phan Van Khai to second terms.

Parliamentary elections in New Zealand were won by Prime Minister Helen Clark's Labour Party, with 52 seats and 41·3% of votes cast, ahead of the National Party, with 27 seats and 20·9% of the vote.

Week beginning 28 July 2002

In Mali, initial results following the second round of a parliamentary election indicated victory for the ruling Alliance for Democracy in Mali with 67 seats, against 47 seats for the Hope 2002 coalition. However, two weeks later the Constitutional Court ruled these results invalid and released new results giving 66 seats to the Hope Coalition 2002 against 51 for the Alliance for Democracy in Mali.

In an election in Papua New Guinea, the National Alliance Party of former prime minister Sir Michael Somare won 19 seats, ahead of the People's Democratic Movement of the incumbent prime minister Sir Mekere Morauta, with 12 seats. Parliament subsequently elected Sir Michael Somare as prime minister.

Tuvalu's parliament elected Saufatu Sopoanga prime minister.

Week beginning 4 August 2002

Gonzalo Sánchez de Lozada took office as president of Bolivia, with Carlos Diego Mesa Gilbert as vice-president. His cabinet appointments included Carlos Saavedra Bruno as foreign minister and Freddy Teodovich Ortiz as defence minister.

In Colombia, Álvaro Uribe Vélez was sworn in as president, with Francisco Santos as vice-president. His cabinet appointments included Carolina Barco as foreign minister and Marta Lucía Ramírez as defence minister.

Week beginning 11 August 2002

The new Colombian president Álvaro Uribe Vélez called a state of emergency following several days of violence.

In Bhutan, agriculture Minister Lyonpo Kinzang Dorji became prime minister.

Week beginning 18 August 2002

A cabinet reshuffle in the Republic of the Congo included the appointment of Gen. Jacques Yvon Ndolou as defence minister.

Zimbabwe's President Robert Mugabe dissolved his cabinet as the government continued to face pressure over the confiscation of white-owned farms.

Week beginning 25 August 2002

A ten-day World Development Summit opened in Johannesburg, ten years after the first earth summit took place in Rio de Janeiro.

The Namibian president Sam Nujoma replaced his prime minister Hage Geingob with Theo-Ben Gurirab.

In Kenya, President Daniel T. arap Moi dismissed his vice-president George Saitoti.

Week beginning 1 September 2002

Gibraltar's government unilaterally declared it would hold a referendum in Nov. on proposals for shared sovereignty between the UK and Spain. The British government refused to recognize the result.

The Sri Lankan government lifted the ban on the Tamil Tigers ahead of peace talks.

In Afghanistan, President Hamid Karzai survived an attempted assassination by a gunman in Kandahar.

As the sole candidate in Bangladesh's presidential elections, Iajuddin Ahmed was appointed president-elect.

Week beginning 8 September 2002

In Austria, the ruling coalition incorporating the Austrian People's Party and the Austrian Freedom Party collapsed following the resignation of the Freedom Party's leader, Susanne Riess-Passer, as vice-chancellor and those of her party colleagues, Karl-Heinz Grasser and Mathias Reichhold, at the finance and transport ministries.

Kim Suk Soo was appointed South Korean prime minister, and was subsequently confirmed by the National Assembly. The previous two prime minister-delegates appointed by the president had been rejected by the National Assembly.

Switzerland became the 190th member of the United Nations.

Week beginning 15 September 2002

In parliamentary elections in Macedonia, the 'Together for Macedonia' coalition led by the Social Democrats won 59 of 120 seats with 40·5% of votes cast, ahead of Prime Minister Ljubčo Georgievski's VMRO-DPMNE with 34 seats and 24·4% of votes cast.

In Sweden, parliamentary elections were won by the Social Democrats, led by incumbent prime minister Göran Persson, with 144 of 349 seats and 39·8% of votes cast. The opposition Moderate Alliance, second with 15·2% of the vote, had their worst election result since 1973. The Liberal Party received 13·3% of the vote, the Christian Democratic Party 9·1%, the Left Party 8·3%, the Centre Party 6·1% and the Green Party 4·6%.

After 19 years of civil war, peace talks brokered by Norwegian negotiators took place between the Sri Lankan government and Tamil rebels.

An attempted coup in Côte d'Ivoire failed, although fighting continued between the government and rebel troops. The country's former military leader and suspected coup instigator, Gen. Robert Guéï, was killed in the fighting.

In Slovakia's parliamentary elections former prime minister Vladimír Mečiar's Movement for a Democratic Slovakia (HZDS) won the largest share of the vote with 19·5%. The Slovak Democratic and Christian Union of prime minister Mikuláš Dzurinda came second with 15·1%, but with HZDS having no political allies, Dzurinda continues to lead a centre-right coalition.

Week beginning 22 September 2002

In German Bundestag elections Gerhard Schröder's Social Democrat-Green coalition government retained power with a much reduced majority of nine seats. The Social Democrats and the Christian Democratic/Social Union, the party of Schröder's main rival Edmund Stoiber, tied with 38·5% of the vote. The strong showing of the Greens (8·6%) and the weak return for Stoiber's ally, the Free Democrats (7·4%), ensured a further term for Schröder.

East Timor became the 191st member of the United Nations.

The president of São Tomé e Príncipe, Fradique de Menezes, dismissed Prime Minister Gabriel Costa's cabinet, although Costa was asked to stay on until a new government was formed.

In a parliamentary election in Morocco the ruling USFP (Union Socialiste des Forces Populaires) reduced its standing from 57 seats to 50, but took two more seats than the second place conservative PI (Istiqlal/Parti d'Indépendence).

Week beginning 29 September 2002

Maria das Neves was named the new prime minister of São Tomé e Príncipe, and subsequently appointed a government including Mateus Meira Rita as foreign minister and Fernando da Trindade Danquá as defence minister.

Nepal's King Gyanendra dismissed Prime Minister Sher Bahadur Deuba and subsequently named Lokendra Bahadur Chand prime minister for the fourth time.

In elections in Bosnia-Herzegovina the three presidential seats were all won by nationalist parties, Dragan Čović of the Croat Democratic Union being elected to the Croat seat, Mirko Šarović of the Serb Democratic Party (SDS) to the Serb seat and Sulejman Tihić of the Party for Democratic Action (SDA) to the Muslim seat.

A parliamentary election in Latvia was won by the New Times party, taking 26 out of a possible 100 seats with 23·9% of votes cast.

Week beginning 6 October 2002

In presidential elections in Brazil, Luiz Inácio Lula da Silva, 'Lula', of the Workers' Party (PT) won 46·4% of the vote, followed by José Serra of the Brazilian Social Democracy Party (PSDB) with 23·2%, thereby necessitating a second round run-off, which Lula won, taking 61·3% to 38·7% of votes won by José Serra.

In parliamentary elections in Trinidad and Tobago, Prime Minister Patrick Manning's People's National Movement won 20 of 36 seats, ahead of the United National Congress with 16.

In Morocco, Driss Jettou was named prime minister.

In parliamentary elections in Pakistan, the Pakistan Muslim League won 77 seats (24·9% of the votes), the Pakistan People's Party 62 (25·0%) and the Muttahida Majlis-e-Amal—an alliance of radical Islamists—52 (11·1%).

Former US president Jimmy Carter was awarded the Nobel Peace Prize.

A bomb explosion on the tourist island of Bali, in Indonesia, killed over 180 people including many foreign nationals.

Week beginning 13 October 2002

In Iraq, a presidential referendum extended Saddam Hussein's rule for a further seven years, with a 100% 'yes' vote.

In parliamentary elections in Jamaica, the ruling People's National Party won 52·2% of the vote (34 of 60 seats) against 26 and 47·2% for the Jamaica Labour Party.

In the Netherlands, the coalition government collapsed after two ministers resigned.

Following elections in September, Slovak Prime Minister Mikuláš Dzurinda's new cabinet took office. Eduard Kukan stayed on as foreign minister, Ivan Šimko moved from the interior to the defence ministry and Ivan Mikloš became finance minister.

Week beginning 20 October 2002

In the first round of presidential elections in Ecuador, Col. Lucio Gutiérrez received 20·4% of the vote, ahead of Álvaro Noboa with 17·4% and León Roldós with 15·4%, necessitating a run-off between Gutiérrez and Noboa.

A cabinet reshuffle in Sweden included the appointment of Leni Björklund as the country's first ever female defence minister.

A siege of a theatre in Moscow, in which 800 people were held hostage by Chechen rebels for three days, ended when Russian troops stormed the building. An anaesthetic gas, used to combat the rebels, also killed over 100 hostages.

Parliamentary elections were held in Bahrain for the first time since 1973. 21 out of 40 seats were won by secular candidates, with the remaining seats going to Sunni and Shia representatives.

Week beginning 27 October 2002

A parliamentary election in Togo was won by the ruling Rally of the Togolese People of President Gnassingbe Eyadema's, with 72 out of 81 seats. The main opposition parties boycotted the election.

Israel's coalition government collapsed when all members of the Labour Party resigned following a dispute over budget proposals.

In Macedonia, parliament voted in the new government with Branko Crvenkovski of the 'Together for Macedonia' coalition as prime minister. Ilinka Mitreva became foreign minister and Vlado Buckovski defence minister.

Week beginning 3 November 2002

In Turkey's parliamentary elections the Justice and Development Party (AKP) won 363 of the 550 seats, against 178 seats for the Republican People's Party (CHP). Prime Minister Bülent Ecevit's Democratic Left Party only took 1·2% of votes cast, failing to secure the 10% of votes needed for parliamentary representation. Ecevit subsequently resigned.

Senegal's president Abdoulaye Wade dismissed Prime Minister Madior Boye and her cabinet. Idrissa Seck was appointed her successor.

In Latvia, Einars Repše was nominated prime minister, an appointment subsequently confirmed by parliament. Other cabinet appointments included Sandra Kalniete as foreign minister and Ģirts Valdis Kristovskis as defence minister.

In US mid-term elections President George W. Bush's Republicans won control of the Senate, taking 51 of 100 seats, and consolidated their hold on the House of Representatives with 227 of 435 seats.

Week beginning 10 November 2002

In presidential elections in Slovenia, Janez Drnovšek, the Liberal Democrat nominee and favoured candidate of presidential incumbent Milan Kučan, polled 44·4%, against 30·8% for Barbara Brezigar. Since no candidate secured the 50% needed for outright victory, a run-off between the two leading candidates was required.

Chinese President Jiang Zemin and Prime Minister Zhu Rongji announced their retirements. The incumbent vice-president Hu Jintao was announced as Jiang's successor.

In Turkey, the chairman of the Justice and Development Party, Abdullah Gül, was appointed prime minister.

Ukrainian Prime Minister Anatolii Kinakh was dismissed by President Leonid Kuchma and replaced by Viktor Yanukovich.

Week beginning 17 November 2002

UN weapons inspectors returned to Iraq after a four-year absence.

Fernando da Piedade Dias dos Santos was appointed prime minister of Angola.

NATO invited Bulgaria, Estonia, Latvia, Lithuania, Romania, Slovakia and Slovenia to join the alliance in 2004.

Mir Zafarullah Khan Jamali, leader of the pro-President Musharraf Pakistan Muslim League (Quaid-e-Azam), was elected Pakistan's prime minister.

Week beginning 24 November 2002

In parliamentary elections in Austria, Chancellor Wolfgang Schüssel's People's Party took 42·3% of votes ahead of the Social Democratic Party with 36·9%, while the far right Freedom Party took 10·2%.

In Ecuador, the run-off for the presidency was won by Lucio Gutiérrez, with 54·3% of votes cast, against 45·7% for Alvaro Noboa.

US President George W. Bush signed legislation creating a Department of Homeland Security and named Tom Ridge as its secretary.

Week beginning 1 December 2002

In the run-off for the Slovenian presidency Prime Minister Janez Drnovšek won with 56·5% of votes cast against 43·5% for Barbara Brezigar. Finance Minister Anton Rop was nominated to succeed Drnovšek as prime minister.

In Switzerland, parliament elected Pascal Couchepin as president for 2003.

In parliamentary elections held in the Seychelles, President France-Albert René's Seychelles People's Progressive Front won 23 of the 34 seats with 54·3% of the vote, against 11 for the Seychelles National Party.

The US secretary of the treasury Paul O'Neill was dismissed by President Bush. The businessman John Snow was nominated his successor.

Week beginning 8 December 2002

In Serbia, presidential elections were declared invalid for a second time owing to a turn-out lower than the legally-required 50%. Yugoslav president Vojislav Koštunica took around 58% of votes to Vojislav Seselj's 36% and Borislav Pelevic's 4%. Parliamentary Speaker Nataša Micic was nominated interim president from Jan. 2003.

European Union leaders agreed to the accession of 10 new member countries on 1 May 2004—Cyprus, Czech Republic, Estonia, Hungary, Latvia, Lithuania, Malta, Poland, Slovakia and Slovenia—subject to approval in national referenda.

Week beginning 15 December 2002

Equatorial Guinea's presidential election was won by incumbent president Gen. Teodoro Obiang Nguema Mbasogo, with 99·5% of the vote. Opposition candidates withdrew within two hours of the polls opening, alleging malpractice.

I Love Madagascar, the party of President Marc Ravalomanana, dominated Madagascar's parliamentary elections, winning 103 of the 160 available seats.

Roh Moo-hyun, the candidate of the Millennium Democratic Party, won South Korea's presidential elections, with 48·9% of the vote against 46·6% for Lee Hoi Chang, candidate of the Grand National Party.

In Bosnia-Herzegovina, parliament elected Adnan Terzić as prime minister.

Week beginning 22 December 2002

In presidential elections in Lithuania, incumbent president Valdas Adamkus won 35·3% of the vote, ahead of Rolandas Paksas of the Lithuanian Liberal Union, with 19·7%. In the subsequent run-off, Paksas won with 54·9% of votes cast against 45·1% for Adamkus.

In Kenya, Mwai Kibaki of the National Rainbow Coalition won a landslide victory in the presidential election, ousting the KANU party for the first time since Kenya won independence in 1963. Kibaki defeated the KANU candidate Uhuru Kenyatta by 62·3% of votes to 31·2%.

Week beginning 29 December 2002

The Togo national assembly amended the constitution to allow President Gnassingbé Eyadéma, in power since 1967, to stand for re-election in 2004.

Pascal Couchepin was sworn in as Swiss president for a twelve-month term.

Luiz Inácio Lula da Silva of the Workers' Party was sworn in as Brazilian president.

Week beginning 5 January 2003

In Djibouti's parliamentary elections, the Union for a Presidential Majority, a coalition of RPP (People's Rally for Progress) and FRUD (Front for the Restoration of Unity and Democracy), won all 65 seats with 62·2% of votes cast, against 36·9% for the Union for a Democratic Alternative.

A cabinet reshuffle in Mexico included the appointment of economy minister Luis Ernesto Derbéz to the post of minister of foreign affairs, to replace Jorge G. Castañeda who had resigned.

Week beginning 12 January 2003

In Bosnia-Herzegovina, Adnan Terzić's government was sworn in, including Mladen Ivanić as foreign minister.

Lucio Gutiérrez took office as president of Ecuador, with Alfredo Palacio becoming vice-president, Nina Pacari foreign minister and Nelson Herrera defence minister.

Week beginning 19 January 2003

In elections to the National Assembly in Cuba all 609 candidates were from the National Assembly of People's Power and received the requisite 50% of votes for election.

In parliamentary elections in the Netherlands the ruling Christian Democrat Appeal won 44 seats, ahead of 42 for the social democratic PvdA and 28 for the VVD.

Tom Ridge became the USA's secretary of homeland security in the newly-created government department.

In Côte d'Ivoire President Laurent Gbagbo named Seydou Diarra prime minister.

Week beginning 26 January 2003

In Israel's parliamentary (Knesset) elections Prime Minister Ariel Sharon's Likud party (conservative) won 37 of 120 seats, with Avoda (social democratic) taking 19.

The US space shuttle *Columbia* broke up on its return flight to NASA's Kennedy Space Center. The aircraft exploded when entering the earth's atmosphere over Texas killing all seven astronauts.

Week beginning 2 February 2003

Václav Havel, president of the Czech Republic, left office. As parliament had failed to choose a successor, Prime Minister Vladimír Špidla took over his representative functions.

In the USA, John Snow was confirmed as the new secretary of the treasury.

The Yugoslavian parliament voted in favour of replacing the Yugoslav federation with a new single entity called Serbia and Montenegro. The parliaments of both Serbia and Montenegro also accepted the plan.

Week beginning 9 February 2003

In parliamentary elections in Monaco, the opposition Union for Monaco won 21 of 24 seats against 3 for the ruling National Democratic Union.

In Trinidad and Tobago, Maxwell Richards was elected president by parliament, with 43 votes against 25 for Ganace Ramdial.

Week beginning 16 February 2003

In presidential elections in Cyprus, Tassos Papadopoulos of the Democratic Party defeated incumbent Glafcos Clerides after the first round of voting. Papadopoulos claimed 51·5% of the vote, rendering a second round unnecessary.

Presidential elections in Armenia went to a second round as no candidate gained 50% of the vote. Incumbent Robert Kocharian received 48·3% of votes cast, Stepan Demirchyan 27·3% and Artashes Geghamyan 16·9%. In the subsequent run-off Robert Kocharian won 67·5% of the vote against 32·5% for Stepan Demirchyan.

Week beginning 23 February 2003

In presidential election in Kiribati, Teburoro Tito was re-elected with 50·4% of votes cast, ahead of Taberannang Timeon with 48·4% and Bakeua Bakeua Tekita with 1·2%.

South Korean President Roh Moo-hyun appointed former mayor of Seoul, Goh Kun, as prime minister.

Václav Klaus was elected president by the Czech parliament, defeating Jan Sokol in a run-off. It was parliament's third attempt in six weeks to choose a successor to Václav Havel, whose term of office had ended three weeks earlier.

Israeli prime minister Ariel Sharon secured the support of the Shinui Party and the National Religious Party, allowing him to form a government with an overall majority. His cabinet appointments included Ehud Olmert as acting prime minister and Silvan Shalom as foreign minister.

Week beginning 2 March 2003

In Estonia's parliamentary election the Centre Party and the newly formed opposition conservative party Res Publica each took 28 of 101 seats with 25·4% and 24·6% of votes respectively. The Reform Party of incumbent prime minister Siim Kallas secured 19 seats with 17·7%.

In parliamentary elections in Syria, the ruling National Progressive Front (led by the Baa'th Party) won 167 of 250 seats, with independents taking the remaining 83.

In parliamentary elections in Belize, the People's United Party of Prime Minister Said Musa won 22 of the 29 seats with 53·2% of votes cast, against 7 seats and 45·6% of the vote for the United Democratic Party.

In Cuba Fidel Castro was re-elected to another five-year term as president, winning 100% of the 609 parliamentary votes.

Svetozar Marović of the Democratic Party of Socialists was elected by Serbia and Montenegro's parliament to be the country's first president.

Week beginning 9 March 2003

UN-brokered talks between the leaders of the Greek and Turkish sectors of Cyprus, Tassos Papadopoulos and Rauf Denktaş, failed with neither side accepting UN proposals for the island's reunification.

Bernard Dowiyogo, the president of Nauru, died after heart surgery. Derog Gioura was appointed acting president, and was subsequently elected president by parliament.

Tayyip Erdoğan, leader of the Justice and Development Party (AK), was appointed Turkey's prime minister.

Serbian Prime Minister Zoran Djindjić was shot dead outside Belgrade's government offices.

In China, Hu Jintao was elected president with Zeng Qinghong replacing Hu as vice-president.

In the Central African Republic, rebels loyal to former army chief Gen. François Bozizé captured the capital Bangui while President Ange-Félix Patassé was out of the country. The following day Bozizé declared himself president.

Week beginning 16 March 2003

Parliamentary elections in El Salvador were won by the National Liberation Front with 31 of 84 seats, ahead of the Nationalist Republican Alliance of President Francisco Flores with 27 and the National Conciliation Party with 16.

In Finland's parliamentary election the Centre Party won 55 out of 200 seats with 24·7% of votes cast. Prime Minister Paavo Lipponen's Social Democrats came second with 53 seats and 24·5% of the vote and the National Coalition Party third with 40 seats and 18·5%.

War broke out in Iraq, as US and British forces launched the first attacks since the expiration of US President George W. Bush's ultimatum demanding the exile of Iraqi president Saddam Hussein and his sons.

Palestinian president Yasser Arafat named Mahmoud Abbas as prime minister, a newly created post.

Week beginning 23 March 2003

Abel Goumba was named prime minister of the Central African Republic.

In Kiribati, President Teburoro Tito was toppled in a no-confidence motion. Parliament was dissolved, and a caretaker government installed.

Week beginning 30 March 2003

Parliamentary elections in Benin were won by the Presidential Movement, with 52 of 83 seats ahead of the Rebirth of Benin with 15 and the Party of Democratic Renewal with 11.

In Bosnia-Herzegovina, the chairman of the Presidency, Mirko Šarović, resigned. Borislav Paravac was subsequently elected as the new Serb member (and chairman) of the Presidency.

ADDENDA

ADDENDA

ADDENDA

All dates are 2003

ARMENIA. Parliamentary elections were held on 25 May. The Republican Party of Armenia (HHK) won 23 of the 131 seats, ahead of Justice with 14, Rule of Law Country with 12 and the Armenian Revolutionary Federation with 11.

AUSTRALIA. *Governor-General* Peter Hollingworth stood down from 11 May but refused to resign after he was accused of mishandling a child abuse scandal in his time as Archbishop of Brisbane. He had also been investigated over a rape claim from the 1960s. The case was subsequently dismissed. Sir Guy Green, *Governor* of Tasmania, took over the duties of Governor-General. Hollingworth resigned on 25 May.

BENIN. After their election to parliament which precludes them from government office, *Foreign Minister* Antoine Kolawolé Idji and *Interior Minister* Daniel Tawéma were replaced by Pierre Osho and Joseph Gnonlonfoun as acting ministers on 20 May.

CANADA. In Quebec's provincial elections on 14 April, Jean Charest's Liberal Party won 76 of the 125 Assembly seats with 45·9% of the vote. The Parti Québécois won 45 seats (33·2%) and the Action Démocratique won 4 seats (18·3%). Charest was sworn in as *Premier* on 29 April.

CHAD. Abderahman Moussa became *Interior Minister* on 6 May.

DEMOCRATIC REPUBLIC OF THE CONGO. Abdoulaye Yerodia Ndombasi, a former minister, was named on 21 April as the first of four *Deputy Presidents* to *President* Joseph Kabila as part of a two-year transitional government. Jean-Pierre Bemba, the leader of the Congolese Liberation Movement (MLC), was named on 24 April. Arthur Zahidi Ngoma, of the non-military opposition, was nominated on 3 May but was rejected by other opposition elements which have nominated Etienne Tshisekedi wa Mulumba of the Union for Democracy and Social Progress (UDPS). The RCD-Goma rebel group nominated its secretary-general, Azarias Ruberwa, on 7 May.

Protestant Bishop Marini Bodo was appointed *Senate President* on 8 May.

DOMINICAN REPUBLIC. On 26 March *Foreign Minister* Hugo Tolentino Dipp resigned and was succeeded by Frank Guerrero Prats. *Finance Minister* José Lois Malkum was replaced by Rafael Calderón.

EUROPEAN UNION. On 26 May the European Union began publishing its draft constitution. Proposals included an elected president and foreign affairs minister, common foreign and security policies, closer integration of judicial and social security systems and the establishment of a single legal status for the EU. Other provisions included a charter of fundamental human rights and the election by the European Parliament of a president of a reduced European Commission. The plans were subject to ratification by each member state and, if accepted, would come into force after the EU expansion of 2004. *European Commission President* Romano Prodi described the document as lacking vision.

GEORGIA. *President* Vladislav Ardzinba of separatist Abkhazia appointed Raul Khadjimba as *Prime Minister* on 22 April.

GERMANY. Elections were held in Bremen on 25 May. The Social Democratic Party won 40 of the 83 seats with 42·3% of the vote, the Christian Democratic Union 29 seats (29·9%), the Greens 12 seats (12·8%), the Free Democratic Party

1 seat (4·2%) and the German People's Union also 1 seat (2·3%). The *Partei Rechtsstaatlicher Offensive* took 4·3% of the vote but won no seats. Turn-out was 61·4%.

GHANA. A cabinet reshuffle on 1 April saw the *Foreign Minister* Hackman Owusu-Agyeman become *Interior Minister*. He was replaced by Nana Akufo-Addo.

GIBRALTAR. Sir Francis Richards, KCMG CVO, was sworn in as *Governor* on 27 May.

GUINEA-BISSAU. On 19 April Fernando Correia Landim was appointed *Interior Minister*. On 23 April Filomena Mascarenhas Tipote was made *Defence Minister.*

INDIA. On 2 May the following state *Governors* were appointed: Gujarat, Kailashpati Mishra; Himachal Pradesh, Vishnu Sadashiv Kokje; Jammu and Kashmir, S. K. Sinha; Madhya Pradesh, Ram Prakash Gupta; Punjab, Om Prakash Verma; and Rajasthan, Nirmal Chandra Jain.

On 13 May the following *Governors* were transferred: Vinod Chandra Pande (Bihar) to Arunachal Pradesh; M. Rama Jois (Jharkhand) to Bihar; Krishna Mohan Seth (Tripura) to Chhattisgarh; Ved Prakash Marwah (Manipur) to Jharkhand; Arvind Dave (Arunachal Pradesh) to Manipur; and Dinesh Nandan Sahaya (Chhattisgarh) to Tripura.

KIRIBATI. The first of two rounds of parliamentary elections took place on 9 May. A third round will elect a president. *President* Teburoro Tito was re-elected in Feb. but lost a no-confidence vote on 28 March. The Council of State, chaired by Tion Otang, will govern until the next government is formed.

LEBANON. *Prime Minister* Rafiq al-Hariri was re-appointed on 16 April having resigned the previous day. On 17 April Jean Obeid was named *Foreign Minister* in place of Mahmoud Hammoud, who became *Defence Minister*.

LITHUANIA. *Interior Minister* Juozas Bernatonis resigned on 24 April. He was replaced with Virgilijus Vladislovas Bulovas.

A referendum was held on 10 and 11 May. Approximately 91% of voters approved accession to the European Union. Turn-out was approximately 63%.

NAURU. Parliamentary elections took place on 3 May. 15 non-partisans and three members of the Nauru First party were elected. *Speaker* Godfrey Thoma resigned on 7 May one day after his appointment.

NEPAL. *Prime Minister* Lokendra Bahadur Chand resigned on 30 May.

PAKISTAN. Shaukat Aziz was appointed *Finance Minister* on 8 April.

SLOVAKIA. Accession to the European Union was approved by 92·46% of voters in a referendum on 16 and 17 May. Turn-out was 52·15%.

TURKS AND CAICOS ISLANDS. In elections on 24 April, *Chief Minister* Derek Taylor's People's Democratic Movement won seven of the 13 Legislative Council seats. The Progressive National Party won six.

UGANDA. On 23 May Ruhakana Rugunda was appointed *Interior Minister* and *First Deputy Prime Minister* as a replacement for Eriya Kategaya.

USA. On 7 May *President* George W. Bush announced the nominations of Colin McMillan as *Secretary of the Navy* and James G. Roche, the current *Secretary of the Air Force*, as *Secretary of the Army*.

INTERNATIONAL
ORGANIZATIONS

PART I

INTERNATIONAL
ORGANIZATIONS

HAS NATO A FUTURE?

Alyson Bailes, Director of SIPRI and former British ambassador to Finland, charts the possible ways forward.

NATO has survived more supposedly fatal blows than Rasputin. Even so, the years 2001–03 have given it a bumpier ride than most people can remember from any time in modern history.

The dramatic invocation of Article 5 of the Washington Treaty in support of the USA on 12 September 2001, the day after the Al-Qaeda attacks, turned sour in retrospect when the USA failed to ask for any follow-up. Nevertheless, NATO persevered in 2002 with the effort to adapt itself to the new security challenges preoccupying the USA in particular. At the November Prague Summit the Alliance invited seven new Central European members to join, while avoiding damage (contrary to expectations) to the NATO/Russia partnership. It agreed on a streamlined command structure, a new Response Force and a new tightly-focused Capabilities Commitment, and adopted policy documents underlining that these instruments were designed (*inter alia*) to give NATO a potential role in the world-wide fight against terrorism. To crown the *annus mirabilis*, a political blockage involving Greece and Turkey, which had prevented NATO and the European Union from collaborating as they were meant to do in the development of the new EU military capacity for crisis management, was lifted in December. Yet hardly had 2003 begun than the Alliance was thrown back in turmoil by a vicious split between France, Belgium and Germany on one side and the US and other members on the other regarding contingency planning to protect Turkey in the event of fall-out from possible military action against Iraq.

As often in the past, this chain of events has exposed the mutual dependence between NATO and the course of US/European relations more generally. The last couple of years have been a time of serious strain in the latter. Not only have differences emerged, quite soon after the attacks of September 11, on the most effective way to suppress and defend against terrorism; not only have the US and some leading Europeans been at odds over the use of military force to stop weapons of mass destruction proliferation in Iraq and elsewhere; but the two sides of the Atlantic have at least temporarily lost their consensus over handling such global issues as climate change, population control and the International Criminal Court. During the twentieth century when Euro-Atlantic relations were tense elsewhere— for instance, over trade—NATO was often able to correct the balance by demonstrating Atlantic unity over issues even more critical for life and death. In present circumstances, NATO is arguably failing to function either as the principal arena for debate over new security challenges, or as a kind of corrective ballast for the turbulence arising. This should not simply be blamed on a lack of concrete NATO achievement. The problem is rather that success in the agenda of the Cold War and the 1990s tends to be already filed as 'completed business', while it is still hard to be sure that the instruments NATO is preparing for the new age will be (in material terms) *usable* or (for political reasons) *used*.

It is natural in these conditions to question whether NATO has a future and if so, in what shape and role. The considerations involved are extremely complex but may be separated into two groups. First, what are the prospects for NATO's success in its *inherited* agenda—the refinement of military capability for crisis-busting, the improvement of burden sharing between the full Alliance and Europe, and the consolidation of stability and partnership to the East? Is success on these fronts sufficient to satisfy all players, notably the US, that the Alliance is earning its keep (and justifying the resources devoted) in the new circumstances? If not—and we may already hint that the answer is No—a second set of questions comes into play about the role that NATO can play as a forum for *re-building consensus* across the Atlantic on the new global security agenda, and/or as a tool-box for pursuing joint *action* on an agenda perhaps pieced together elsewhere.

The adaptation of NATO's military plans and potential is an unfinished agenda dating back to the end of the Cold War. During the latter, most Allies were organized primarily to defend their own territory in Europe, with only the US, UK and Canada

3

having a significant part of their troops stationed abroad in peace-time (and reinforcement duties in war). In spite of the 'flexible response' doctrine, the Alliance's conventional forces were never expected to do the whole job anyway because they were backed by nuclear weapons. With the shift of prevailing demands during the 1990s towards active conflict management, and now in the 2000s to intervention in other parts of the world, the context for military planning has radically changed. Countries are judged by how much capability they can 'export' to foreign fields, how quickly they can get it there and how well they sustain it. Both the men and machines involved have to be adaptable, multi-functional, tough, self-sufficient and 'interoperable' to a degree formerly expected only from NATO elites. As a further complication, and in contrast to NATO's former multi-national forces, a national contingent will never know in advance with whom it may need to operate and under whose command. New-style intervention tasks are essentially voluntary, and are likely to draw—for both technical and political reasons—on a different 'coalition' of states each time.

Operations in the Balkans during the 1990s showed that NATO could not only cope with such tasks, but achieve a level of convincing military superiority—a 'hardness'—in doing them which no other institution could match. Ironically, however, these and other real-life preoccupations slowed down the pace of systemic change in NATO's doctrines and structures, so that a scheme (Combined Joint Task Forces) devised in 1994 for creating suitable command headquarters for coalition-based interventions was still incomplete by the century's end. Meanwhile, some nations like the US, UK and France had re-styled their own forces and equipment programmes to meet the needs of overseas deployments, while others had not. European Allies' defence spending was not only uneven, and often too low, but also ill-coordinated so that while spending in total some 60% of what the US spent the Europeans got only a fraction of the same 'bang for the buck'. The results were exposed at several points in the Balkan campaigns, notably during the bombing phase of the action over Kosovo where an overwhelming share of the air-power required had to be supplied by the US.

The Prague Summit decisions of end-2002 are NATO's most determined effort yet to dictate a transformation that actually has some chance of being carried out. The new Capabilities Commitment (PCC) tells each ally exactly what it must do to raise the quality of its assets earmarked for actions abroad, but it deliberately concentrates on these assets alone and on just four dimensions of their suitability. Meanwhile, the new NATO Response Force (NRF) is designed to intervene quickly but also finish its task quickly, leaving less capable units (and possibly other nations) to take over. It would take 20,000 men at most of which the majority could come from larger nations, allowing smaller ones to make specialized 'niche' contributions. Experts seem to agree that these are good prescriptions and capable of being fulfilled within the couple of years' deadline given—if all countries do what they are told. The main doubts remain over whether the more sluggish Europeans can squeeze out more resources even for such narrow targets: but also, over whether the US will be ready in any real emergency to place its crack troops in an NRF framework with all the institutional checks and disciplines involved. One may also wonder how far Europeans' performance will slip in those areas of their defence *not* spotlighted by the PCC and NRF. The famous 'capabilities gap'—a difference both in technological levels and fighting techniques—between the Americans and Europe may be papered over within the NRF, but can only yawn wider across the field of defence as a whole.

Since the Helsinki Summit decisions of December 1999 there has been another organization in Europe goading European States to improve their capabilities for military deployments abroad: the European Union. The EU's 'Common European Security and Defence Policy' (CESDP) aims to create a joint capacity for military crisis management tasks, ranging from military-assisted evacuations to the tougher end of the 'peace enforcement' spectrum. Since it does not involve guaranteed common defence, all the EU's members including four non-members of NATO can take part equally. The CESDP sprang from a British-French initiative in which Britain was particularly keen to find another lever to boost its neighbours' defence output; Britain and France were both interested in having a self-led option for the use of European forces especially in situations mainly affecting Europeans' interests, or playing to their comparative advantages; and France was also following a long-term dream of an autonomous European defence as an alternative (or successor) to NATO. Since Helsinki, the EU has set up politico-military and military institutions to run the new policy and has worked to develop its civilian intervention capabilities in parallel. One of the scheme's main features, however—the possibility for the EU to draw upon planning services and command structures from NATO, thus avoiding duplication—could not be activated until the end of 2002 due to the Greek/Turkish blockages mentioned earlier.

At the time of writing, the EU has its first collective police deployment under way in Bosnia, is preparing to take over a peace-keeping mission from NATO in Macedonia, and has its sights on bringing the SFOR military operation in Bosnia under an EU flag. On the face of it, this is just the kind of new burden-sharing which the CESDP was meant to achieve, offering the scope *inter alia* for NATO to focus more on the 'harder' new operational challenges outside Europe. There are, however, worries beneath the surface that the EU may be biting off more than it can chew in the still fragile state of the Balkans. Others question whether it is wise for the Europeans to hasten the withdrawal of US elements from these missions while there seems to be so little other guarantee of trans-Atlantic togetherness in defence. Beyond these specifics, there are deeper ambiguities in the NATO/CESDP relationship that are hard to banish because so much depends on the point of view. A united European defence community can be seen as a stronger pillar for NATO or as a divisive caucus within it. Equally serious conundrums apply to the place of CESDP within the EU's overall integrative enterprise. Do all the EU's members really share a common vision of what their community's strategic interests are and when and how they should contemplate using force to defend them? Can even a fragmentary common defence policy exist without a true common foreign policy, and hasn't the basis for the latter been further weakened by the latest flagrant divisions over Iraq?

Since 1989/90 there has been relative unity among all NATO members on the Alliance's new opportunity, and duty, to spread its own values of security and democracy eastward in Europe through the medium both of enlargement and partnership. During the 1990s, NATO's Partnership for Peace (later supplemented by the Euro-Atlantic Partnership Council) provided the framework both for training up and assessing prospective new members, and for pursuing stabilization and reform with those not ready or willing to join. The main difficulty lay in Russia-NATO relations, which at times grew very tense—leading at one point e.g. to a Russian boycott of PFP—due to Russia's antagonism to enlargement, but also to disagreements over the Balkans. Against this background, the Alliance's double achievement in 2002 was truly remarkable. Not only were seven new Central European members accepted for membership in 2004, but Russia quietly drew back from its former opposition and instead accepted a new format for the NATO/Russian Council, permitting a significant amount of decision-taking 'at 20'.

If NATO's self-congratulation over this feat was muted, this was not only a reflection of long-term worries that such large expansion might 'dilute' and or overstretch the Alliance. Such concerns had been somewhat blunted, by 2002, not just by the (political) reliability of the first three Central Europeans admitted in 1999, but also by the continuing strategic shifts that made the direct military contribution and 'defensibility' of new members less relevant. The problem is rather that, as hinted at above, the strategic absorption of the eastern half of Europe is the type of achievement that gets discounted as soon as (or even before) it is complete. Ironically, the less challenging the issues of European security are seen to be, the stronger the temptation for the US to shift its resources elsewhere. The trouble is that this may be, at the least, somewhat premature: conflict may be dead within Central Europe proper but democracy, including democratic defence, is a still fragile new growth. One thing that might shake it is a perception among the new allies that NATO's guarantees and values are not as solid as they seemed, or not worth the price paid to win them—which is precisely the impression left with many by the latest intra-allied spats. On top of this comes the challenge of trying to spread stability further to the areas beyond NATO's new borders where traditions of democracy and cooperation are weaker and conflict still very much alive: and on top of this comes the conundrum of Russia. President Putin's choice of rapprochement with NATO seems to be based on solid pragmatic reasoning, and to some degree also on a genuine perception of shared threats (notably terrorism). It is, however, very much a policy of the leadership rather than of the nation as a whole and is not yet backed by any significant assimilation of Russian military planning and behaviour (or indeed, Russian security behaviour in general) to western norms. Precisely because Putin's vision is a realist one, he may lose interest in cooperating with NATO—and care less about provoking it—if he sees the Alliance as starting to decline both in unity and authority. In short, NATO has problems when it looks too strong to Moscow, but also when it looks too weak.

Even if NATO could be confident of completing its military transformation, achieving fruitful symbiosis with the EU and consolidating its new eastern territories and partnerships, it would not even have started to make its mark on the issues that really matter for the US today. For some time, but especially since 9/11, US policy has seen its main challenges in those 'asymmetrical' threats that bypass traditional security structures, elude deterrence and strike at American lives even on American territory: terrorism, the spread of mass destruction weapons, and the growing arsenals and unfathomable agendas of dictators in 'rogue' States. Feeling itself so directly at risk, the administration of President Bush has been guided also by its political philosophy to adopt a forward and active stance. The US's declared strategy now proclaims that the US has and intends to maintain unrivalled power and has the will to use it on its own authority against patent threats—pre-emptively, if need be. A very difficult challenge for NATO flows from these developments, at two levels. First, in general terms the new US strategy leaves less room for alliances, attributing value to them only where they can provide backing for the US's policies and added value for its actions. Secondly, the things that the US would like to obtain from the Alliance in accord with this logic are all quite difficult for NATO to give. As a matter of observation there is no complete consensus among the 19 allies on what terrorism is or how to combat it, and even to the extent that common lines of policy development are agreed, NATO has not the right tools and competences (as compared, e.g., with the UN and EU) to execute them. Similarly on weapons of mass destruction, the relevant international legal instruments, inspection capabilities, export controls, and political sticks and carrots needed to tackle the problem all lie somewhere else than NATO. One issue of truly direct relevance, the development of missile defence shields in Europe as well as the US, was put firmly back on the NATO agenda at Prague but other WMD-related initiatives there were on a very modest scale.

What NATO does have, and aspires to develop further, are force capabilities that could be used with and in support of US forces in military actions to strike at terrorist and WMD-related targets, in 'rogue States' and elsewhere. The development of NATO doctrine in 2002 allows for such use in principle, by linking capabilities' development with 'new' as well as 'old' threats to Allied interests, and by implicitly dropping the previous geographical limitation on actions under a NATO flag. The trouble is, as suggested above, that making such capacities more *useable* is no guarantee that they will be *used*. The upheaval caused in NATO by an attempt to gear up Alliance assets for a purpose even indirectly related to a US strike on Iraq makes clear how serious the obstacles are, on both sides. The other members of NATO are uncertain and divided over the political and legal justification for using military force against 'new threats', and generally question whether NATO can do this on its own say-so. The US for its part seems increasingly impatient of acting within the harness of multilateral organizations and legal mandates, and is unlikely to pick up a NATO instrument unless it comes easily to the hand and without strings. This is why some Europeans suspect that their elite capacities identified and trained for the NRF are more likely to be 'cherry-picked' by the US for use under its own leadership in ad hoc coalitions.

Two different ways could be imagined for NATO to respond to these problems. One would be to tackle them head-on at the highest political level, by making the Alliance once more a forum for thrashing out fundamental US/European differences over the meaning of security, threat, and legitimate defence, and reaching out for a new consensus. There are just two problems about this, the first being that consensus could prove elusive and the baring of US/European divisions might then simply deepen the rift beyond healing. A more practical objection is that the essence of today's US/European arguments concerns not European security but world governance, including some completely non-defence challenges like how to handle climate change and population growth: NATO is too narrow a forum to operate both functionally and to negotiate anything like a comprehensive settlement. An alternative approach would be for NATO, as in certain kinds of therapy, to build up confidence by *doing* things and achieving a string of successes, however modest, that prove its added value in the new environment. One such test would be for NATO to make a good job of providing support to international peace-keepers in Afghanistan, where agreement has now been reached that it should co-ordinate the ISAF force directly after the next rotation. This would leave further options open, for NATO to go on building its image and capacity as a 'tool-box' for executing decisions made elsewhere, or for it to come back and tackle the big 'strategy' debate at some later point from a foundation of renewed solidarity. But given the depth of some Europeans' resistance to *any* overtly NATO-led operation outside Europe, even this step-by-step approach has real obstacles to overcome.

In NATO's history so far, the only regular feature has been the unpredictable. The organization's political, inter-governmental, non-legalistic character makes it ultimately frailer than the European Union but also far more flexible. Dramatic shifts in aim and structure have been made several times, with success, provided only that the US and leading Europeans knew what they wanted. That could still happen today, as both sides move on from their current antagonisms or try to compensate for them. Perhaps the main difference now is that NATO's fate depends more on the re-balancing of other relationships—the US and Europe in world forums, the US/Europe/Russia triangle, European unity in the EU—than any of these relationships can rely on salvation by NATO.

Alyson Bailes has been Director of the Stockholm International Peace Research Institute, SIPRI, since July 2002. She spent 33 years in the British Diplomatic Service including postings to Budapest, Bonn, Beijing, Oslo and the UK Delegation to NATO, and culminating in an appointment as HM Ambassador at Helsinki. During sabbaticals she has also worked in the UK Ministry of Defence, for the European Union and Western European Union, and for think-tanks in London and New York. She is known mainly as a writer on issues of European and Atlantic security policy, Central Europe and Nordic affairs. SIPRI was founded in 1966 as an independent international institute for research into problems of peace and conflict, especially those of arms control and disarmament. Its current main fields of research are data collection and analysis on military expenditure and armaments; arms control, export controls and non-proliferation; and trends in Euro-Atlantic and regional security.

THE UNITED NATIONS (UN)

Origin and Aims. The United Nations is an association of states which have pledged themselves to maintain international peace and security and co-operate in solving international political, economic, social, cultural and humanitarian problems towards achieving this end. The name 'United Nations' was devised by United States President Franklin D. Roosevelt and was first used in the Declaration by United Nations of 1 Jan. 1942, during the Second World War, when representatives of 26 nations pledged their Governments to continue fighting together against the Axis Powers.

The United Nations Charter, the constituting instrument of the UN, was drawn up by the representatives of 50 countries at the United Nations Conference on International Organization, which met in San Francisco from 25 April to 26 June 1945. Those delegates deliberated on the basis of proposals worked out by the representatives of China, the Soviet Union, the United Kingdom and the United States at Dumbarton Oaks (Washington, D.C.) from 21 Aug. to 28 Sept. 1944. The Charter was signed on 26 June 1945 by the representatives of the 50 countries. Poland, which was not represented at the Conference, signed it later and became one of the original 51 member states. Nothing contained in the Charter authorizes the organization to intervene in matters which are essentially within the domestic jurisdiction of any state.

The United Nations officially came into existence on 24 Oct. 1945, with the deposit of the requisite number of ratifications of the Charter with the US Department of State. United Nations Day is celebrated on 24 Oct. each year.

Today, 80% of the UN's work is devoted to helping developing countries build the capacity to help themselves. This includes promoting the creation of independent and democratic societies, which it is hoped will offer vital support for the Charter's goals in the 21st century; the protection of human rights; saving children from starvation and disease; providing relief assistance to refugees and disaster victims; countering global crime, drugs and disease; and assisting countries devastated by war and the long-term threat of landmines.

Members. New member states are admitted by the General Assembly on the recommendation of the Security Council. The Charter provides for the suspension or expulsion of a member for violation of its principles, but no such action has ever been taken. It has 191 member states. (For a list of these, see below.)

Finance. Assessments on member states constitute the main source of funds. These are in accordance with a scale specified by the Assembly, and determined primarily by the country's share of the world economy and ability to pay, in the range 22%–0·001%. The Organization is prohibited by law from borrowing from commercial institutions.

A Working Group on the Financial Situation of the United Nations was established in 1994 to address the long-standing financial crisis which has come about because of the non-payment of assessed dues by many member states, severely threatening the Organization's ability to fulfil its mandates. As of 31 Dec. 2002 member states owed the UN a total of US$1,684m., of which the USA owed US$738m. (43·8%). Total debts outstanding to the UN regular budget as of 31 Dec. 2002 were US$304·8m., of which the USA's share was US$190·3m. (62·4%).

Official languages. Arabic, Chinese, English, French, Russian and Spanish.

Structure. The UN has six principal organs established by the founding Charter. All have their headquarters in New York except the International Court of Justice, which has its seat in The Hague. These core bodies work through dozens of related agencies, operational programmes and funds, and through special agreements with separate, autonomous, intergovernmental agencies, known as Specialized Agencies, in order to provide an increasingly cohesive programme of action in the fields of peace and security, justice and human rights, humanitarian assistance, and social and economic development. The six principal UN organs are as follows:

1. **The General Assembly**, composed of all members, is the main deliberative body; each member has one vote. It meets once a year, commencing on the first Tuesday following 1 Sept., and the general debate is organized over a period of two weeks, beginning the 3rd week of Sept. (The 57th Session opened on 10 Sept. 2002.)

At the start of each session, the Assembly elects a new President, 21 vice-presidents and the chairmen of its six main committees, listed below. To ensure equitable geographical representation, the presidency of the Assembly rotates each year among the five geographical groups of states: African, Asian, Eastern European, Latin American and the Caribbean, and Western European and other States. Special sessions may be convoked by the Secretary-General if requested by the Security Council, by a majority of members, or by one member if the majority of the members concur. Emergency sessions may be called within 24 hours at the request of the Security Council on the vote of any nine Council members, or a majority of United Nations members, or one member if the majority of members concur. Decisions on important questions, such as peace and security, new membership and budgetary matters, require a two-thirds majority; other questions require a simple majority of members present and voting.

The work of the General Assembly is divided between six Main Committees, on which every member state is represented. These are: Disarmament and International Security Committee (First Committee); Economic and Financial Committee (Second Committee); Social, Humanitarian and Cultural Committee (Third Committee); Special Political and Decolonization Committee (Fourth Committee); Administrative and Budgetary Committee (Fifth Committee); Legal Committee (Sixth Committee).

There is also a General Committee charged with the task of co-ordinating the proceedings of the Assembly and its Committees, and a Credentials Committee. The General Committee consists of 28 members: the president and 21 vice-presidents of the General Assembly and the chairmen of the six main committees. The Credentials Committee consists of nine members appointed by the Assembly on the proposal of the President at each session. In addition, the Assembly has two standing committees—an Advisory Committee on Administrative and Budgetary Questions, and a Committee on Contributions; and may establish subsidiary and *ad hoc* bodies when necessary to deal with specific matters. These include: Special Committee on Peacekeeping Operations (100 members), Human Rights Committee (18 members), Committee on the Peaceful Uses of Outer Space (65 members), Conciliation Commission for Palestine (3 members), Conference on Disarmament (66 members), International Law Commission (34 members), Scientific Committee on the Effects of Atomic Radiation (21 members), Special Committee on the Situation with Regard to the Implementation of the Declaration on the Granting of Independence to Colonial Countries and Peoples (24 members), and Commission on International Trade Law (36 members).

The General Assembly has the right to discuss any matters within the scope of the Charter and, with the exception of any situation or dispute on the agenda of the Security Council, may make recommendations on any such questions or matters. Occupying a central position in the UN, the Assembly receives reports from other organs, admits new members, directs activities for development, sets policies and determines programmes for the Secretariat, appoints the Secretary-General, who reports annually to it on the work of the Organization, and approves the UN budget.

Under the 'Uniting For Peace' resolution adopted by the General Assembly in Nov. 1950, the Assembly is also empowered to take action if the Security Council, because of a lack of unanimity of its permanent members, fails to exercise its primary responsibility for the maintenance of international peace and security in any case where there appears to be a threat to the peace, breach of the peace or act of aggression. In this event, the General Assembly may consider the matter immediately with a view to making appropriate recommendations to members for collective measures, including, in the case of a breach of the peace or act of aggression, the use of armed force when necessary, to maintain or restore international peace and security.

2. **The Security Council** has primary responsibility, under the Charter, for the maintenance of international peace and security. It is so organized as to be able to function continuously. A representative of each of its members must be present at all times at UN Headquarters, but it may meet elsewhere as best facilitates its work.

The Presidency of the Council rotates monthly, according to the English alphabetical order of members' names. The Council consists of 15 members: five permanent and ten non-permanent elected for a two-year term by a two-thirds majority of the General Assembly. Each member has one vote. Retiring members are not eligible for immediate re-election. Any other member of the United Nations may participate without a vote in the discussion of questions specially affecting its interests.

Decisions on procedural questions are made by an affirmative vote of at least nine members. On all other matters, the affirmative vote of nine members must include the concurring votes of all permanent members (subject to the provision that when the Council is considering methods for the peaceful settlement of a dispute, parties to the dispute abstain from voting). Consequently, a negative vote from a permanent member has the power of veto, and all five permanent members have exercised this right at one time or other. If a permanent member does not support a decision but does not wish to veto it, it may abstain. Under the Charter, the Security Council alone has the power to take decisions which member states are obligated to carry out.

The Council has two standing committees—the Committee of Experts on Rules of Procedure and the Committee on the Admission of New Members. It may establish *ad hoc* committees and commissions, such as the Committee on Council Meetings away from Headquarters.

When a threat to peace is brought before the Council, it may undertake mediation and set out principles for a settlement, and may take measures to enforce its decisions by ceasefire directives, economic sanctions, peacekeeping missions, or in some cases, by collective military action. For the maintenance of international peace and security, the Council can, in accordance with special agreements to be concluded, call on the armed forces, assistance and facilities of the member states. It is assisted by a Military Staff Committee consisting of the Chiefs of Staff of the permanent members of the Council or their representatives.

The Council also makes recommendations to the Assembly on the appointment of the Secretary-General and, with the Assembly, elects the judges of the International Court.

In Nov. 2002 the Security Council adopted Resolution 1441, holding Iraq in 'material breach' of disarmament obligations. Weapons inspectors under the leadership of Hans Blix (Sweden) returned to Iraq four years after their last inspections, but US and British suspicion that the Iraq regime was failing to comply led to increasing tension, resulting in the USA, the UK and Spain declaring that they reserved the right to disarm Iraq without the need for a further Security Council resolution. Other Security Council members, notably China, France, Germany and Russia, opposed the proposed action, resulting in a major split in the Security Council. On 20 March 2003 US forces, supported by the UK, launched attacks on Iraq, and initiated a war aimed at bringing an end to Saddam Hussein's rule.

Permanent Members. China, France, Russian Federation, UK, USA (Russian Federation took over the seat of the former USSR in Dec. 1991).

Non-Permanent Members. Bulgaria, Cameroon, Guinea, Mexico and Syria (until 31 Dec. 2003); Angola, Chile, Germany, Pakistan and Spain (until 31 Dec. 2004).

Finance. The budget for UN peacekeeping operations in 2002–03 was US$2·6bn. The estimated total cost of operations between 1948 and 2002 was US$26bn. In Dec. 2002 outstanding contributions to peacekeeping totalled US$1·3bn.

3. **The Economic and Social Council (ECOSOC)** is responsible under the General Assembly for co-ordinating the functions of the UN with regard to international economic, social, cultural, educational, health and related matters. The year-round work of the Council is carried out by related organizations, specialized agencies, and subsidiary bodies, commissions and committees, which meet regularly and report back to it.

It consists of 54 member states elected by a two-thirds majority of the General Assembly for a three-year term. Members are elected according to the following geographic distribution: Africa, 14 members; Asia, 11; Eastern Europe, 6; Latin America and Caribbean, 10; Western Europe and other States, 13. A third of the members retire each year. Retiring members are eligible for immediate re-election. Each member has one vote. Decisions are made by a majority of the members present and voting.

The Council holds one five-week substantive session a year, alternating between New York and Geneva, and one organizational session in New York. The substantive session includes a high-level meeting attended by Ministers, to discuss economic and social issues. Special sessions may be held if required. The President is elected for one year and is eligible for immediate re-election.

The subsidiary machinery of ECOSOC is as follows:

Nine Functional Commissions. Statistical Commission; Commission on Population and Development; Commission for Social Development; Commission on Human Rights (and Subcommission on Prevention of Discrimination and Protection of Minorities); Commission on the Status of Women; Commission on Narcotic Drugs (and Subcommission on Illicit Drug Traffic and Related Matters in the Near and Middle East); Commission on Science and Technology for Development; Commission on Crime Prevention and Criminal Justice; Commission on Sustainable Development.

Five Regional Economic Commissions. ECA (Economic Commission for Africa, Addis Ababa, Ethiopia); ESCAP (Economic and Social Commission for Asia and the Pacific, Bangkok, Thailand); ECE (Economic Commission for Europe, Geneva); ECLAC (Economic Commission for Latin America and the Caribbean, Santiago, Chile); ESCWA (Economic Commission for Western Asia, Beirut, Lebanon).

Nine Standing Committees and Subsidiary Expert Bodies. Committee for Programme and Co-ordination; Commission on Human Settlements; Committee on Non-Governmental Organizations; Committee on Natural Resources; Committee for Development Planning; Committee on Economic, Social and Cultural Rights; Committee on New and Renewable Sources of Energy and on Energy for Development; Ad Hoc Group of Experts on International Co-operation in Tax Matters; Committee of Experts on the Transport of Dangerous Goods.

Other related operational programmes, funds and special bodies, which report to ECOSOC (and/or the General Assembly) include: the United Nations Children's Fund (UNICEF); Office of the United Nations High Commissioner for Refugees (UNHCR); United Nations Conference on Trade and Development (UNCTAD); United Nations Development Programme (UNDP) and Population Fund (UNFPA); United Nations Environment Programme (UNEP); World Food Programme (WFP); International Research and Training Institute for the Advancement of Women (INSTRAW); United Nations Office on Drugs and Crime (ODC).

In addition, the Council may make arrangements for consultation with international non-governmental organizations (NGOs) and, after consultation with the member concerned, with national organizations. There are over 1,600 non-governmental organizations which have consultative status with the Council. Non-governmental organizations may send observers to the Council's public meetings and those of its subsidiary bodies, and may submit written statements relevant to its work. They may also consult with the UN Secretariat on matters of mutual concern. The term of office of the members listed below expires on 31 Dec. of the year mentioned after the country.

Members. Andorra (2003), Argentina (2003), Australia (2004), Azerbaijan (2005), Benin (2005), Bhutan (2004), Brazil (2003), Burundi (2004), Chile (2004), China (2004), Congo, Republic of (2005), Cuba (2005), Ecuador (2005), Egypt (2003), El Salvador (2004), Ethiopia (2003), Finland (2004), France (2005), Georgia (2003), Germany (2005), Ghana (2004), Greece (2005), Guatemala (2004), Hungary (2004), India (2004), Iran (2003), Ireland (2005), Italy (2003), Jamaica (2005), Japan (2005), Kenya (2005), South Korea (2003), Libya (2004), Malaysia (2005), Mozambique (2005), Nepal (2003), Netherlands (2003), Nicaragua (2005), Nigeria (2003), Pakistan (2003), Peru (2003), Portugal (2005), Qatar (2004), Romania (2003), Russia (2004), Saudi Arabia (2005), Senegal (2005), South Africa (2003),

Sweden (2004), Uganda (2003), Ukraine (2004), United Kingdom (2004), USA (2003), Zimbabwe (2004).

Finance. In 2000, US$6,450m. in socio-economic development assistance grants was provided through the organizations of the UN system.

4. **The Trusteeship Council** was established to ensure that Governments responsible for administering Trust Territories take adequate steps to prepare them for self-government or independence. It consists of five permanent members of the Security Council. The task of decolonization was completed in 1994, when the Security Council terminated the Trusteeship Agreement for the last of the original UN Trusteeships (Palau), administered by the USA. All Trust Territories attained self-government or independence either as separate States or by joining neighbouring independent countries. The Council formally suspended operations on 1 Nov. 1994 following Palau's independence. By a resolution adopted on 25 May 1994 the Council amended its rules of procedure to drop the obligation to meet annually and agreed to meet as occasion required.

The proposal from UN Secretary-General Kofi Annan, in the second part of his reform programme, in July 1997, is that it should be used as a forum to exercise their 'trusteeship' for the global commons, environment and resource systems.

Members. China, France, Russia, UK, USA.

5. **The International Court of Justice** is the principal judicial organ of the UN. It has a dual role: to settle in accordance with international law the legal disputes submitted to it by States; and to give advisory opinion on legal questions referred to it by duly authorized international organs and agencies.

It operates under a Statute, which is an integral part of the United Nations Charter. Only States may apply to and appear before the Court. The Member States of the United Nations (at present numbering 191) are so entitled. The Court is composed of 15 judges, each of a different nationality elected with an absolute majority to nine-year terms of office by both the General Assembly and the Security Council. The composition of the Court must also reflect the main forms of civilization and principal legal systems of the world. Elections are held every three years for one-third of the seats, and retiring judges may be re-elected. Members do not represent their respective governments but sit as independent magistrates in the Court, and must possess the qualifications required in their respective countries for appointment to the highest judicial offices, or be jurists of recognized competence in international law.

Candidates are nominated by the national panels of jurists in the Permanent Court of Arbitration established by the Hague Conventions of 1899 and 1907. The Court elects its own President and Vice-President for a three-year term, and is permanently in session.

Decisions are taken by a majority of judges present, subject to a quorum of nine members, with the President having a casting vote. Judgement is final and without appeal, but a revision may be applied for within ten years from the date of the judgement on the ground of a new decisive factor. When the Court does not include a judge possessing the nationality of a State party to a case, that State has the right to appoint a person to sit as judge *ad hoc* for that case, on equal terms with Members.

While the Court normally sits in plenary session, it can form chambers of three or more judges to deal with specific matters. Judgements by chambers are considered as rendered by the full Court. In 1993, in view of the global expansion of environmental law and protection, the Court formed a seven-member Chamber for Environmental Matters.

Judges. The nine-year terms of office of the judges currently serving end on 5 Feb. of the year indicated next to their name: Shi Jiuyong, President (China) (2012), Raymond Ranjeva, Vice-President (Madagascar) (2009), Gilbert Guillaume (France) (2009), Abdul G. Koroma (Sierra Leone) (2012), Vladlen S. Vereshchetin (Russian Federation) (2006), Rosalyn Higgins (UK) (2009), Gonzalo Parra-Aranguren (Venezuela) (2009), Pieter H. Kooijmans (Netherlands) (2006), José F. Rezek (Brazil) (2006), Awn Shawkat Al-Khasawneh (Jordan) (2009), Thomas Buergenthal (USA) (2006), Nabil Elaraby (Egypt) (2006), Hishashi Owada (Japan) (2012), Bruno Simma (Germany) (2012), Peter Tomka (Slovakia) (2012).

Competence and Jurisdiction. In contentious cases, only States may apply to or appear before the Court, which is open only to parties to its Statute, which automatically includes all Members of the UN. The conditions under which the Court will be open to other states are laid down by the Security Council. The jurisdiction of the Court covers all matters which parties refer to it, and all matters provided for in the Charter or in treaties and conventions in force. Disputes concerning the jurisdiction of the Court are settled by the Court's own decision. The Court may apply in its decision:

(a) international conventions;

(b) international custom;

(c) the general principles of law recognized by civilized nations;

(d) as subsidiary means for the determination of the rules of law, judicial decisions and the teachings of highly qualified publicists. If the parties agree, the Court may decide a case *ex aequo et bono.*

Since 1946 the Court has delivered 76 judgments on disputes concerning *inter alia* land frontiers and maritime boundaries, territorial sovereignty, the non-use of force, non-interference in the internal affairs of States, diplomatic relations, hostage-taking, the right of asylum, nationality, guardianship, rights of passage and economic rights.

The Court may also give advisory opinions on legal questions to the General Assembly, the Security Council, certain other organs of the UN and 16 specialized agencies of the UN family.

Since 1946 the Court has given 24 advisory opinions, concerning *inter alia* admission to United Nations membership, reparation for injuries suffered in the service of the United Nations, territorial status of South-West Africa (Namibia) and Western Sahara, judgements rendered by international administrative tribunals, expenses of certain United Nations operations, the applicability of the United Nations Headquarters Agreement, the status of human rights informers and the threat or use of nuclear weapons.

Finance. The expenses of the Court are borne by the UN. No court fees are paid by parties to the Statute.

Official languages. English, French.
Headquarters: The Peace Palace, 2517 KJ The Hague, Netherlands.
Website: http://www.icj-cij.org
Registrar: Philippe Couvreur (Belgium).

6. **The Secretariat** services the other five organs of the UN, administering their programmes and carrying out the Organization's day-to-day work with its increasingly streamlined staff of some 8,900 at the UN Headquarters in New York and all over the world.

At its head is the Secretary-General, appointed by the General Assembly on the recommendation of the Security Council for a five-year, renewable term. The Secretary-General acts as chief administrative officer in all meetings of the General Assembly, Security Council, Economic and Social Council and Trusteeship Council. An Office of Internal Oversight, established in 1994 under the tenure of former Secretary-General Boutros Boutros-Ghali (Egypt), pursues a cost-saving mandate to investigate and eliminate waste, fraud and mismanagement within the system. The Secretary-General is assisted by Under-Secretaries-General and Assistant Secretaries-General. A new appointment of Deputy Secretary-General was agreed in principle by the General Assembly in 1997 and was announced in Jan. 1998.

Finance. The financial year coincides with the calendar year. The budget for the two-year period 2002–03 is US$2,890,818,700, compared to US$2,533,125,400 in 2000–01.

Headquarters: United Nations Plaza, New York, NY 10017, USA.
Website: http://www.un.org
Secretary-General: Kofi Annan (appointed 1 Jan. 1997 and re-elected 29 June 2001, Ghana). *Deputy Secretary-General:* Louise Fréchette (appointed 12 Jan. 1998, Canada).

MEMBER STATES OF THE UN

The 191 member states, with percentage scale of contributions to the Regular Budget as at 31 May 2002 and year of admission:

	% contribution	Year of admission		% contribution	Year of admission
Afghanistan	0·007	1946	France[1]	6·516	1945
Albania	0·003	1955	Gabon	0·014	1960
Algeria	0·071	1962	Gambia	0·001	1965
Andorra	0·004	1993	Georgia	0·005	1992
Angola	0·002	1976	Germany[6]	9·845	1973
Antigua and Barbuda	0·002	1981	Ghana	0·005	1957
Argentina[1]	1·159	1945	Greece[1]	0·543	1945
Armenia	0·002	1992	Grenada	0·001	1974
Australia[1]	1·640	1945	Guatemala[1]	0·027	1945
Austria	0·954	1955	Guinea	0·003	1958
Azerbaijan	0·004	1992	Guinea-Bissau	0·001	1974
Bahamas	0·012	1973	Guyana	0·001	1966
Bahrain	0·018	1971	Haiti[1]	0·002	1945
Bangladesh	0·010	1974	Honduras[1]	0·004	1945
Barbados	0·009	1966	Hungary	0·121	1955
Belarus[1, 2]	0·019	1945	Iceland	0·033	1946
Belgium[1]	1·138	1945	India[1]	0·344	1945
Belize	0·001	1981	Indonesia[7]	0·201	1950
Benin	0·002	1960	Iran[1]	0·236	1945
Bhutan	0·001	1971	Iraq[1]	0·102	1945
Bolivia[1]	0·008	1945	Ireland, Rep. of	0·297	1955
Bosnia-Herzegovina	0·004	1992	Israel	0·418	1949
Botswana	0·010	1966	Italy	5·104	1955
Brazil[1]	2·093	1945	Jamaica	0·004	1962
Brunei	0·033	1984	Japan	19·669	1956
Bulgaria	0·013	1955	Jordan	0·008	1955
Burkina Faso	0·002	1960	Kazakhstan	0·029	1992
Burundi	0·001	1962	Kenya	0·008	1963
Cambodia	0·002	1955	Kiribati	0·001	1999
Cameroon	0·009	1960	Korea (North)	0·009	1991
Canada[1]	2·579	1945	Korea (South)	1·866	1991
Cape Verde	0·001	1975	Kuwait	0·148	1963
Central African Rep.	0·001	1960	Kyrgyzstan	0·001	1992
Chad	0·001	1960	Laos	0·001	1955
Chile[1]	0·187	1945	Latvia	0·010	1991
China[1]	1·545	1945	Lebanon[1]	0·012	1945
Colombia[1]	0·171	1945	Lesotho	0·001	1966
Comoros	0·001	1975	Liberia[1]	0·001	1945
Congo,			Libya	0·067	1955
Dem. Rep. of the[3]	0·004	1960	Liechtenstein	0·006	1990
Congo, Rep. of the	0·001	1960	Lithuania	0·017	1991
Costa Rica[1]	0·020	1945	Luxembourg[1]	0·080	1945
Côte d'Ivoire	0·009	1960	Macedonia[8]	0·006	1993
Croatia	0·039	1992	Madagascar	0·003	1960
Cuba[1]	0·030	1945	Malawi	0·002	1964
Cyprus	0·038	1960	Malaysia[9]	0·237	1957
Czech Republic[4]	0·172	1993	Maldives	0·001	1965
Denmark[1]	0·755	1945	Mali	0·002	1960
Djibouti	0·001	1977	Malta	0·015	1964
Dominica	0·001	1978	Marshall Islands	0·001	1991
Dominican Republic[1]	0·023	1945	Mauritania	0·001	1961
East Timor	—	2002	Mauritius	0·011	1968
Ecuador[1]	0·025	1945	Mexico[1]	1·095	1945
Egypt[1, 5]	0·081	1945	Micronesia	0·001	1991
El Salvador[1]	0·018	1945	Moldova	0·002	1992
Equatorial Guinea	0·001	1968	Monaco	0·004	1993
Eritrea	0·001	1993	Mongolia	0·001	1961
Estonia	0·010	1991	Morocco	0·045	1956
Ethiopia[1]	0·004	1945	Mozambique	0·001	1975
Fiji Islands	0·004	1970	Myanmar[10]	0·010	1948
Finland	0·526	1955	Namibia	0·007	1990

14

	% contribution	Year of admission		% contribution	Year of admission
Nauru	0·001	1999	Slovakia[4]	0·043	1993
Nepal	0·004	1955	Slovenia	0·081	1992
Netherlands[1]	1·751	1945	Solomon Islands	0·001	1978
New Zealand[1]	0·243	1945	Somalia	0·001	1960
Nicaragua[1]	0·001	1945	South Africa[1]	0·411	1945
Niger	0·001	1960	Spain	2·539	1955
Nigeria	0·056	1960	Sri Lanka	0·016	1955
Norway[1]	0·652	1945	Sudan	0·006	1956
Oman	0·062	1971	Suriname	0·002	1975
Pakistan	0·061	1947	Swaziland	0·002	1968
Palau	0·001	1994	Sweden	1·035	1946
Panama[1]	0·018	1945	Switzerland	—	2002
Papua New Guinea	0·006	1975	Syria[1, 13]	0·081	1945
Paraguay[1]	0·016	1945	Tajikistan	0·001	1992
Peru[1]	0·119	1945	Tanzania[14]	0·004	1961
Philippines[1]	0·101	1945	Thailand	0·254	1946
Poland[1]	0·319	1945	Togo	0·001	1960
Portugal	0·466	1955	Tonga	0·001	1999
Qatar	0·034	1971	Trinidad and Tobago	0·016	1962
Romania	0·059	1955	Tunisia	0·031	1956
Russia[1, 11]	1·200	1945	Turkey[1]	0·444	1945
Rwanda	0·001	1962	Turkmenistan	0·003	1992
St Kitts and Nevis	0·001	1983	Tuvalu	0·001	2000
St Lucia	0·002	1979	Uganda	0·005	1962
St Vincent			Ukraine[1]	0·053	1945
and the Grenadines	0·001	1980	United Arab Emirates	0·204	1971
Samoa	0·001	1976	UK[1]	5·579	1945
San Marino	0·002	1992	USA[1]	22·000	1945
São Tomé e Príncipe	0·001	1975	Uruguay[1]	0·081	1945
Saudi Arabia[1]	0·559	1945	Uzbekistan	0·011	1992
Senegal	0·005	1960	Vanuatu	0·001	1981
Serbia and			Venezuela[1]	0·210	1945
Montenegro[1, 16, 17]	0·020	1945	Vietnam	0·013	1977
Seychelles	0·002	1976	Yemen[15]	0·007	1947
Sierra Leone	0·001	1961	Zambia	0·002	1964
Singapore[12]	0·396	1965	Zimbabwe	0·008	1980

[1]Original member. [2]As Byelorussia, 1945–91. [3]As Zaïre, 1960–97. [4]Pre-partition Czechoslovakia (1945–92) was an original member. [5]As United Arab Republic, 1958–71, following union with Syria (1958–61). [6]Pre-unification (1990) as two states: the Federal Republic of Germany and the German Democratic Republic. [7]Withdrew temporarily, 1965–66. [8]Pre-independence (1992), as part of Yugoslavia, which was an original member. [9]As the Federation of Malaya till 1963, when the new federation of Malaysia (including Singapore, Sarawak and Sabah) was formed. [10]As Burma, 1948–89. [11]As USSR, 1945–91. [12]As part of Malaysia, 1963–65. [13]As United Arab Republic, by union with Egypt, 1958–61. [14]As two states: Tanganyika, 1961–64, and Zanzibar, 1963–64, prior to union as one republic under new name. [15]As Yemen, 1947–90, and Democratic Yemen, 1967–90, prior to merger of the two. [16]As Yugoslavia, 1945–2003. [17]Excluded from the General Assembly in 1992; re-admitted in Nov. 2000.

The USA is the leading contributor to the Peacekeeping Operations Budget, with 27·2105% of the total at July 2002, followed by Japan (19·6690%), Germany (9·8450%), France (8·0593%), UK (6·9003%), Italy (5·1040%), Canada (2·5790%) and Spain (2·5390%). All other countries contribute less than 2%.

Publications. Yearbook of the United Nations. New York, 1947 ff.—*United Nations Chronicle. Quarterly.—Monthly Bulletin of Statistics.—General Assembly: Official Records: Resolutions.—Reports of the Secretary-General of the United Nations on the Work of the Organization.* 1946 ff.—*Charter of the United Nations and Statute of the International Court of Justice.—Official Records of the Security Council, the Economic and Social Council, Trusteeship Council and the Disarmament Commission.—Demographic Yearbook.* New York.—*Basic Facts About the United Nations.* New York, 2002.—*Statistical Yearbook.* New York, 1947 ff.—*Yearbook of International Statistics.* New York, 1950 ff.—*World Economic Survey.* New York, 1947 ff.—*Economic Survey of Asia and the Far East.* New York, 1946 ff.—*Economic Survey of Latin America.* New York, 1948 ff.—*Economic Survey of Europe.* New York, 1948 ff.—*Economic Survey of Africa.* New York, 1960 ff.—*United Nations Reference Guide in the Field of Human Rights.* UN Centre for Human Rights, 1993.

Further Reading

Arnold, G., *World Government by Stealth: The Future of the United Nations*. Macmillan, 1998

Baehr, P. R. and Gordenker, L., *The United Nations in the 1990s*. 2nd ed. London, 1994

Bailey, S. D. and Daws, S., *The United Nations: a Concise Political Guide*. 3rd ed. London, 1994

Baratta, J. P., *United Nations System* [Bibliography]. Oxford and New Brunswick (NJ), 1995

Beigbeder, Y., *The Internal Management of United Nations Organizations: the Long Quest for Reform*. London, 1996

Butler, R., *The Greatest Threat: Iraq, Weapons of Mass Destruction and the Crisis of Global Security*. Public Affairs, New York, 2000

Carnegie Commission on Preventing Deadly Conflict, *Preventing Deadly Conflict: Final Report*. New York, 1997

Cortright, D. and Lopez, G. A., *The Sanctions Decade: Assessing UN Strategies in the 1990s*, Lynne Rienner Publishers, Boulder, 2000

Durch, W. J., *The Evolution of UN Peacekeeping: Case Studies and Comparative Analysis*. New York, 1993

Ginifer, J. (ed.) *Development Within UN Peace Missions*. London, 1997

Hoopes, T., and Brinkley, D., *FDR and the Creation of the UN*. Yale Univ. Press, 1998

Luard, E., *The United Nations: How It Works and What It Does*. 2nd ed. London, 1994

Meisler, S., *United Nations: The First Fifty Years*. Atlantic Monthly Press, 1998

New Zealand Ministry of Foreign Affairs, *UN Handbook*. 1997

Osmanczyk, E., *Encyclopaedia of the United Nations*. London, 1985

Parsons, A., *From Cold War to Hot Peace: UN Interventions, 1947–94*. London, 1995

Pugh, M., *The UN, Peace and Force*. London, 1997

Ratner, S. R., *The New UN Peacekeeping: Building Peace in Lands of Conflict after the Cold War*. London, 1995

Righter, R., *Utopia Lost: the United Nations and World Order*. New York, 1995

Roberts, A. and Kingsbury, B. (eds.) *United Nations, Divided World: the UN's Roles in International Relations*. 2nd ed. Oxford, 1993

Simma, B. (ed.) *The Charter of the United Nations: a Commentary*. OUP, 1995

Williams, D., *The Specialized Agencies of the United Nations*. London, 1987

UNIVERSAL DECLARATION OF HUMAN RIGHTS

On 10 Dec. 1948 the General Assembly of the United Nations adopted and proclaimed the Universal Declaration of Human Rights.

Preamble

Whereas recognition of the inherent dignity and of the equal and inalienable rights of all members of the human family is the foundation of freedom, justice and peace in the world,

Whereas disregard and contempt for human rights have resulted in barbarous acts which have outraged the conscience of mankind, and the advent of a world in which human beings shall enjoy freedom of speech and belief and freedom from fear and want has been proclaimed as the highest aspiration of the common people,

Whereas it is essential, if man is not to be compelled to have recourse, as a last resort, to rebellion against tyranny and oppression, that human rights should be protected by the rule of law,

Whereas it is essential to promote the development of friendly relations between nations,

Whereas the peoples of the United Nations have in the Charter reaffirmed their faith in fundamental human rights, in the dignity and worth of the human person and in the equal rights of men and women and have determined to promote social progress and better standards of life in larger freedom,

Whereas Member States have pledged themselves to achieve, in co-operation with the United Nations, the promotion of universal respect for and observance of human rights and fundamental freedoms,

Whereas a common understanding of these rights and freedoms is of the greatest importance for the full realization of this pledge,

Now, Therefore THE GENERAL ASSEMBLY proclaims THIS UNIVERSAL DECLARATION OF HUMAN RIGHTS as a common standard of achievement for all peoples and all nations, to the end that every individual and every organ of society, keeping this Declaration constantly in mind, shall strive by teaching and education to promote respect for these rights and freedoms and by progressive measures, national and international, to secure their universal and effective recognition and observance, both among the peoples of Member States themselves and among the peoples of territories under their jurisdiction.

Article 1. All human beings are born free and equal in dignity and rights. They are endowed with reason and conscience and should act towards one another in a spirit of brotherhood.

Article 2. Everyone is entitled to all the rights and freedoms set forth in this Declaration, without distinction of any kind, such as race, colour, sex, language, religion, political or other opinion, national or social origin, property, birth or other status. Furthermore, no distinction shall be made on the basis of the political, jurisdictional or international status of the country or territory to which a person belongs, whether it be independent, trust, non-self-governing or under any other limitation of sovereignty.

Article 3. Everyone has the right to life, liberty and security of person.

Article 4. No one shall be held in slavery or servitude; slavery and the slave trade shall be prohibited in all their forms.

Article 5. No one shall be subjected to torture or to cruel, inhuman or degrading treatment or punishment.

Article 6. Everyone has the right to recognition everywhere as a person before the law.

Article 7. All are equal before the law and are entitled without any discrimination to equal protection of the law. All are entitled to equal protection against any discrimination in violation of this Declaration and against any incitement to such discrimination.

Article 8. Everyone has the right to an effective remedy by the competent national tribunals for acts violating the fundamental rights granted him by the constitution or by law.

Article 9. No one shall be subjected to arbitrary arrest, detention or exile.

Article 10. Everyone is entitled in full equality to a fair and public hearing by an independent and impartial tribunal, in the determination of his rights and obligations and of any criminal charge against him.

Article 11. (1) Everyone charged with a penal offence has the right to be presumed innocent until proved guilty according to law in a public trial at which he has had all the guarantees necessary for his defence.

(2) No one shall be held guilty of any penal offence on account of any act or omission which did not constitute a penal offence, under national or international law, at the time when it was committed. Nor shall a heavier penalty be imposed than the one that was applicable at the time the penal offence was committed.

Article 12. No one shall be subjected to arbitrary interference with his privacy, family, home or correspondence, nor to attacks upon his honour and reputation. Everyone has the right to the protection of the law against such interference or attacks.

Article 13. (1) Everyone has the right to freedom of movement and residence within the borders of each state.

(2) Everyone has the right to leave any country, including his own, and to return to his country.

Article 14. (1) Everyone has the right to seek and enjoy in other countries asylum from persecution.

(2) This right may not be invoked in the case of prosecutions genuinely arising from non-political crimes or from acts contrary to the purposes and principles of the United Nations.

Article 15. (1) Everyone has the right to a nationality.

(2) No one shall be arbitrarily deprived of his nationality nor denied the right to change his nationality.

Article 16. (1) Men and women of full age, without any limitation due to race, nationality or religion, have the right to marry and to found a family. They are entitled to equal rights as to marriage, during marriage and at its dissolution.

(2) Marriage shall be entered into only with the free and full consent of the intending spouses.

(3) The family is the natural and fundamental group unit of society and is entitled to protection by society and the State.

Article 17. (1) Everyone has the right to own property alone as well as in association with others.

(2) No one shall be arbitrarily deprived of his property.

Article 18. Everyone has the right to freedom of thought, conscience and religion; this right includes freedom to change his religion or belief, and freedom, either alone or in community with others and in public or private, to manifest his religion or belief in teaching, practice, worship and observance.

Article 19. Everyone has the right to freedom of opinion and expression; this right includes freedom to hold opinions without interference and to seek, receive and impart information and ideas through any media and regardless of frontiers.

Article 20. (1) Everyone has the right to freedom of peaceful assembly and association.

(2) No one may be compelled to belong to an association.

Article 21. (1) Everyone has the right to take part in the government of his country, directly or through freely chosen representatives.

(2) Everyone has the right of equal access to public service in his country.

(3) The will of the people shall be the basis of the authority of government; this will shall be expressed in periodic and genuine elections which shall be by universal and equal suffrage and shall be held by secret vote or by equivalent free voting procedures.

Article 22. Everyone, as a member of society, has the right to social security and is entitled to realization, through national effort and international co-operation and in accordance with the organization and resources of the State, of the economic, social and cultural rights indispensable for his dignity and the free development of his personality.

Article 23. (1) Everyone has the right to work, to free choice of employment, to just and favourable conditions of and to protection against unemployment.

(2) Everyone, without any discrimination, has the right to equal pay for equal work.

(3) Everyone who works has the right to just and favourable remuneration ensuring for himself and his family an existence worthy of human dignity, and supplemented, if necessary, by other means of social protection.

(4) Everyone has the right to form and to join trade unions for the protection of his interests.

Article 24. Everyone has the right to rest and leisure, including reasonable limitation of working hours and periodic holidays with pay.

Article 25. (1) Everyone has the right to a standard of living adequate for the health and well-being of himself and his family, including food, clothing, housing and medical care and necessary social services, and the right to security in the event of unemployment, sickness, disability, widowhood, old age or other lack of livelihood in circumstances beyond his control.

(2) Motherhood and childhood are entitled to special care and assistance. All children, whether born in or out of wedlock, shall enjoy the same social protection.

Article 26. (1) Everyone has the right to education. Education shall be free, at least in the elementary and fundamental stages. Elementary education shall be compulsory. Technical and professional education shall be made generally available and higher education shall be equally accessible to all on the basis of merit.

(2) Education shall be directed to the full development of the human personality and to the strengthening of respect for human rights and fundamental freedoms. It shall promote understanding, tolerance and friendship among all nations, racial or religious groups, and shall further the activities of the United Nations for the maintenance of peace.

(3) Parents have a prior right to choose the kind of education that shall be given to their children.

Article 27. (1) Everyone has the right freely to participate in the cultural life of the community, to enjoy the arts and to share in scientific advancement and its benefits.

(2) Everyone has the right to the protection of the moral and material interests resulting from any scientific, literary or artistic production of which he is the author.

Article 28. Everyone is entitled to a social and international order in which the rights and freedoms set forth in this Declaration can be fully realized.

Article 29. (1) Everyone has duties to the community in which alone the free and full development of his personality is possible.

(2) In the exercise of his rights and freedoms, everyone shall be subject only to such limitations as are determined by law solely for the purpose of securing due recognition and respect for the rights and freedoms of others and of meeting the just requirements of morality, public order and the general welfare in a democratic society.

(3) These rights and freedoms may in no case be exercised contrary to the purposes and principles of the United Nations.

Article 30. Nothing in this Declaration may be interpreted as implying for any State, group or person any right to engage in any activity or to perform any act aimed at the destruction of any of the rights and freedoms set forth herein.

NOBEL PEACE PRIZE WINNERS: 1978–2002

When the scientist, industrialist and inventor Alfred Nobel died in 1896, he made provision in his will for his fortune to be used for prizes in Physics, Chemistry, Physiology or Medicine, Literature and Peace. A prize for Economics was added later. The Norwegian Nobel Committee awards the Nobel Peace Prize, and the Nobel Foundation in Stockholm (founded 1900; Mailing address: Box 5232, SE-10245, Stockholm, Sweden) awards the other five prizes. The Prize Awarding Ceremony takes place on 10 Dec., the anniversary of Nobel's death. The last 25 recipients of the Nobel Peace Prize, worth 10m. Sw. kr. in 2002, are:

2002 – Jimmy Carter (USA) for his decades of untiring effort to find peaceful solutions to international conflicts, to advance democracy and human rights, and to promote economic and social development.

2001 – the United Nations and Kofi Annan for a better organized and more peaceful world.

2000 – Kim Dae-Jung for his work for democracy and human rights in South Korea and in East Asia in general, and for peace and reconciliation with North Korea in particular.

1999 – *Médecins Sans Frontières* (Doctors Without Borders) in recognition of the organization's pioneering humanitarian work on several continents.

1998 – John Hume and David Trimble for their efforts to find a peaceful solution to the conflict in Northern Ireland.

1997 – ICBL (*International Campaign to Ban Landmines*) and Jody Williams for their work for the banning and clearing of anti-personnel mines.

1996 – Carlos Felipe Ximenes Belo and José Ramos-Horta for their work towards a just and peaceful solution to the conflict in East Timor.

1995 – Joseph Rotblat and the *Pugwash Conferences on Science and World Affairs* for their efforts to diminish the part played by nuclear arms in international politics and eventually to eliminate such arms.

1994 – Yasser Arafat (Chairman of the Executive Committee of the PLO, President of the Palestinian National Authority), Shimon Peres (Foreign Minister of Israel) and Yitzhak Rabin (Prime Minister of Israel) for their efforts to create peace in the Middle East.

1993 – Nelson Mandela (Leader of the ANC) and Fredrik Willem De Klerk (President of the Republic of South Africa).

1992 – Rigoberta Menchú Tum (Guatemala) for his campaign work for human rights, especially for indigenous peoples.

1991 – Aung San Suu Kyi (Myanmar), opposition leader and human rights advocate.

1990 – Mikhail Sergeyevich Gorbachev (president of the USSR) for helping bring the Cold War to an end.

1989 – The 14th Dalai Lama (Tenzin Gyatso) for his religious and political leadership of the Tibetan people.

1988 – *The United Nations Peace-Keeping Forces.*

1987 – Oscar Arias Sánchez (President of Costa Rica) for initiating peace negotiations in Central America.

1986 – Elie Wiesel (USA), author and humanitarian.

1985 – *International Physicians for the Prevention of Nuclear War*, Boston, USA.

1984 – Desmond Mpilo Tutu (South Africa, Bishop of Johannesburg) for his work against apartheid.

1983 – Lech Wałęsa (Poland), founder of Solidarity and human rights campaigner.

1982 – Alva Myrdal (Sweden) and Alfonso García Robles (Mexico) for their work as delegates to the United Nations General Assembly on Disarmament.

1981 – *Office of the United Nations High Commissioner for Refugees*, Geneva, Switzerland.

1980 – Adolfo Pérez Esquivel (Argentina), human rights leader.

1979 – Mother Teresa (India), leader of the Order of the Missionaries of Charity.

1978 – Mohammad Anwar Al-Sadat (President of Egypt) and Menachem Begin (Prime Minister of Israel) for jointly negotiating peace between Egypt and Israel.

Norwegian Nobel Committee Headquarters: Det Norske Nobelinstitutt, Drammensveien 19, N-0255 Oslo, Norway.
Website: http://www.nobel.no/indexen.html

UNITED NATIONS SYSTEM

Operational Programmes and Funds. The total operating expenses for the entire UN system, including the World Bank, IMF and all the UN funds, programmes and specialized agencies, come to US\$18,200m. a year. Some 53,300 people work in the UN system, which includes the Secretariat and 28 other organizations.

Social and economic development, aimed at achieving a better life for people everywhere, is a major part of the UN system of organizations. In the forefront of efforts to bring about such progress is the United Nations Development Programme (UNDP), the world's largest agency for multilateral technical and pre-investment co-operation. It is the funding source for most of the technical assistance provided for sustainable human development by the UN system, and in 2000 helped people in 174 countries and territories, supporting some 5,000 projects, which focus on poverty elimination, environmental regeneration, job creation and the advancement of women.

UNDP assistance is provided only at the request of governments and in response to their priority needs, integrated into overall national and regional plans. Its activities are funded mainly by voluntary contributions outside the regular UN budget. 87% of the UNDP's core programme funds go to countries with an annual per capita GNP of US\$750 or less, which are home to 90% of the world's poorest peoples. Headquartered in New York, the UNDP is governed by a 36-member Executive Board, representing both developing and developed countries.

Administrator: Mark Malloch Brown (UK).

UN development programmes include the *United Nations Children's Fund (UNICEF).* It was established in 1946 by the United Nations General Assembly as the United Nations International Children's Emergency Fund, to meet the emergency needs of children of post-war Europe. Guided by the Convention on the Rights of the Child, UNICEF supports community-based programmes in immunization, nutrition, education, HIV/AIDS, water supply, environmental sanitation, gender issues and development, and child protection in more than 160 countries and territories. In 2001, with the assistance of UNICEF, WHO and other key partners, a record 575m. children were vaccinated against polio. UNICEF is the largest supplier of vaccines to developing countries, providing 40% of the world's doses of vaccine for children. UNICEF also provides relief and rehabilitation assistance in emergencies.

UNICEF served as the substantive secretariat for the UN General Assembly Special Session on Children held in New York from 8–10 May 2002, and supported a wide range of consultations and events around the world to ensure that children and young people had a voice in the process and in the Session itself. The Special Session adopted the outcome document, 'A World Fit For Children', setting 21 concrete time-bound goals for children on four key priorities: promoting healthy lives; providing quality education for all; protecting children against abuse, exploitation and violence; and combating HIV/AIDS. Over 400 young delegates participated in the Children's Forum and unanimously agreed to a message calling for a world fit for children that was delivered to world leaders at the Special Session.

UNICEF's work from 2002 to 2005 focuses on: girls' education; early childhood development; immunization 'plus' (strengthening health systems and outreach); HIV/AIDS; improved protection of children against violence, exploitation and abuse.

Executive Director: Carol Bellamy (USA).

The United Nations Population Fund (UNFPA) was established in 1969 and is the world's largest multilateral source of population assistance. About a quarter of all population assistance from donor nations to developing countries is channeled through UNFPA. The fund extends assistance to developing countries at their request to help them address reproductive health and population issues, and raises awareness of these issues in all countries.

In 2000 UNFPA provided assistance to 142 developing nations, with special emphasis on increasing the quality of reproductive health services, ending the gender discriminations and violence, formulating effective population policies and reducing the spread of HIV/AIDS.

UNFPA's three main areas of work are: to help ensure universal access to reproductive health, including family planning and sexual health, to all couples and individuals on or before the year 2015; to support population and development strategies that enable capacity-building in population programming; to promote awareness of population and development issues, and to advocate for the mobilization of the resources and political will necessary to accomplish its area of work. UNFPA's *The State of World Population* report is published annually.

Executive Director: Thoraya Obaid (Saudi Arabia).

The UN Environment Programme (UNEP), established in 1972, works to encourage sustainable development through sound environmental practices everywhere. UNEP has its headquarters in Nairobi, Kenya and other offices in Paris, Geneva, Bangkok, Washington, D.C., New York, Osaka, Manama and Mexico City. Its activities cover a wide range of issues, from atmosphere and terrestrial ecosystems, to the promotion of environmental science and information, to an early warning and emergency response capacity to deal with environmental disasters and emergencies. UNEP's present priorities include: environmental information, assessment and research; enhanced coordination of environmental conventions and development of policy instruments; fresh water; technology transfer and industry; and support to Africa. Information networks and monitoring systems established by the UNEP include: the Global Environment Information Exchange Network (INFOTERRA); Global Resource Information Database (GRID); the International Register of Potentially Toxic Chemicals (IRPTC); and the recent UNEP.net, a web-based interactive catalogue and multifaceted portal that offers access to environmentally relevant geographic, textual and pictoral information. In June 2000 the World Conservation and Monitoring Centre (WCMC) based in Cambridge, UK became UNEP's key biodiversity assessment centre. UNEP's latest state-of-the-environment report is the *Global Environment Outlook 3* (GEO-3).

Executive Director: Klaus Töpfer (Germany).

Other UN programmes working for development include: the *UN Conference on Trade and Development (UNCTAD)*, which promotes international trade, particularly by developing countries, in an attempt to increase their participation in the global economy; and the *World Food Programme (WFP)*, the world's largest international food aid organization, which is dedicated to both emergency relief and development programmes.

The *UN Centre for Human Settlements (Habitat)*, which assists over 600m. people living in health-threatening housing conditions, was established in 1978. The 58-member *UN Commission on Human Settlements (UNCHS)*, Habitat's governing body, meets every two years. The Centre serves as the focal point for human settlements action and the co-ordination of activities within the UN system.

In addition to its regular programmes, the UNDP administers various special-purpose funds, such as the *UN Capital Development Fund (UNCDP)*, a multilateral donor agency working to develop new solutions for poverty reduction in the least developed countries, the *United Nations Volunteers (UNV)* and the *UN Development Fund for Women (UNIFEM)*, whose mission is the empowerment of women and gender equality in all levels of development planning and practice. Its three areas of immediate concern are: strengthening women's economic capacity; engendering governance and leadership; and promoting women's rights. Together with the World Bank and UNEP, the UNDP is one of the managing partners of the Global Environment Facility (GEF), a US$2,000m. fund to help countries translate global concerns into national action so as to help fight ozone depletion, global warming, loss of biodiversity and pollution of international waters.

The United Nations Development Programme is active in 166 countries. At country level, it is responsible for all UN development activity. The head of each country office acts as Resident Co-ordinator for UNDP.

The United Nations Office on Drugs and Crime (ODC) educates the world about the dangers of drug abuse; strengthens international action against drug production, trafficking and drug related crime; promotes efforts to reduce drug abuse, particularly among the young and vulnerable; builds local, national and international partnership to address drug issues; provides information, analysis and expertise on the drug issue; promotes international co-operation in crime prevention and control; supports the development of criminal justice systems; and assists member states in addressing the challenges and threats posed by the changing nature of transnational organized crime.

Executive Director: Antonio Maria Costa (Italy).

The UN work in crime prevention and criminal justice aims to lessen the human and material costs of crime and its impact on socio-economic development. The UN Congress on the Prevention of Crime and Treatment of Offenders has convened every five years since 1955 and provides a forum for the presentation of policies and progress. The Tenth Crime Congress (Vienna, 2000) discussed how to promote the rule of law and to strengthen the criminal justice system and also international co-operation in combating transnational organized crime. The *Commission on Crime Prevention and Criminal Justice*, a functional body of ECOSOC, established in 1992, seeks to strengthen UN activities in the field, and meets annually in Vienna. The interregional research and training arm of the UN crime and criminal justice programme is the *United Nations Interregional Crime and Justice Research Institute (UNICRI)* in Rome. An autonomous body, it seeks through action-oriented research to contribute to the formulation of improved policies in crime prevention and control.

Humanitarian assistance to refugees and victims of natural and man-made disasters is also an important function of the UN system. The main refugee organizations within the system are the *Office of the United Nations High Commissioner for Refugees (UNHCR)* and the *United Nations Relief and Works Agency for Palestine Refugees in the Near East (UNRWA)*.

UNHCR, created in 1951, was charged primarily with resettling 1·2m. European refugees left homeless in the aftermath of the Second World War. It was initially envisioned as a temporary office with a projected lifespan of three years. Today, with some 19·8m. persons of concern in over 150 countries, it has become one of the world's principal humanitarian agencies. Its Executive Committee currently comprises 61 member states. With its Headquarters in Geneva, UNHCR has around 5,000 staff working through offices in 114 countries across the globe, and has twice been awarded the Nobel Peace Prize. The High Commissioner is elected by the UN General Assembly, to which he reports annually through ECOSOC.

The work of UNHCR is humanitarian and non-political. International protection is its primary function. Its main objective is to promote and safeguard the rights and interests of refugees. In so doing UNHCR devotes special attention to promoting a generous policy of asylum on the part of Governments and seeks to improve the legal status of refugees in their country of residence. Crucial to this status is the principle of *non-refoulement*, which prohibits the expulsion from or forcible return of refugees to a country where they may have reason to fear persecution. UNHCR pursues its objectives in the field of protection by encouraging the conclusion of intergovernmental legal instruments in favour of refugees, by supervising the implementation of their provisions and by encouraging Governments to adopt legislation and administrative procedures for the benefit of refugees. UNHCR is often called upon to provide material assistance (e.g. the provision of food, shelter, medical care and essential supplies) while durable solutions are being sought. Durable solutions generally take one of three forms: voluntary repatriation, local integration or resettlement in another country.

UNHCR works in tandem with governmental and non-governmental organizations, and within the UN framework its closest partnership is with the World Food Programme (WFP). Other partners include UNICEF, WHO, UNDP, the Office for the Coordination of Humanitarian Affairs (OCHA), the Office of the High Commissioner for Human Rights (OHCHR), the International Organization for Migration (IOM), the Red Cross Movement Institutions (ICRC and IFRC), and many non-governmental organizations (NGOs). The Office also liaises closely with the IMF, the World Bank and affiliated institutions, particularly in helping refugees to rebuild their lives and communities once they have returned home. At present, UNHCR is funded almost entirely by voluntary contributions. In 2002 UNHCR's expenditure amounted to approximately US$1bn.

High Commissioner: Ruud Lubbers (Netherlands).

UNRWA was created by the General Assembly in 1949 as a temporary, non-political agency to provide relief to the nearly 750,000 people who became refugees as a result of the disturbances during and after the creation of the State of Israel in the former British Mandate territory of Palestine. 'Palestine refugees', as defined by UNRWA's mandate, are persons or descendants of persons whose normal residence was Palestine for at least two years prior to the 1948 conflict and who, as a result of the conflict, lost their homes and means of livelihood. UNRWA has also been called upon to help persons displaced by renewed hostilities in the Middle East in 1967. The situation of Palestine refugees in south Lebanon, affected in the aftermath of the 1982 Israeli invasion of Lebanon, was of special concern to the Agency in 1984. UNRWA provides education, health, relief and social services to eligible refugees among the 3·7m. registered Palestine refugees in its five fields of operation: Jordan, Lebanon, Syria, the West Bank and the Gaza Strip. Its mandate is renewed at intervals by the UN General Assembly, and has most recently been extended until 30 June 2005. The projected budget for 2002 was US$279·3m., funded entirely by donor countries.

Commissioner-General: Peter Hansen (Denmark).

The UN's activities in the field of human rights are the primary responsibility of the *High Commissioner for Human Rights*, a post established in 1993 under the direction and authority of the Secretary-General and currently held by Sergio Vieira de Mello (Brazil). The High Commissioner is nominated by the Secretary-General for a four-year term, renewable once. The principal co-ordinating human rights organ of the UN is the *Commission on Human Rights*, set up by ECOSOC in 1946. It has 53 members elected for three-year terms, meets for six weeks in Geneva each year, and is aided in its task by a Subcommission on Prevention of Discrimination and Protection of Minorities, composed of 26 experts from all over the world. The implementation of international human rights treaties is monitored by six committees (also called treaty bodies): the Human Rights Committee; the Committee against Torture; Committee on the Rights of the Child; Committee on Economic, Cultural and Social Rights; Committee on the Elimination of Racial Discrimination; Committee on Elimination of Discrimination against Women.

Training and Research Institutes. There are six training and research institutes within the UN, all of them autonomous.

United Nations Institute for Training and Research (UNITAR). Established in 1965 to enhance the effectiveness of the UN in achieving its major objectives. Recently, its focus has shifted to training, with basic research being conducted only if extra-budgetary funds can be made available. Training is provided at various levels for agencies and institutions of UN member states, diplomatic personnel, universities, public interest groups and the private sector. By mid-2000 almost 47,000 participants from 200 countries had attended UNITAR courses, seminars or workshops.

Address: Palais des Nations, 1211 Geneva 10, Switzerland.

United Nations Institute for Disarmament Research (UNIDIR). Established in 1980 to undertake research on disarmament and security with the aim of assisting the international community in their disarmament thinking, decisions and efforts. Through its research projects, publications, small meetings and expert networks, UNIDIR promotes creative thinking and dialogue on both current and future security issues, through examination of topics as varied as tactical nuclear weapons, refugee security, computer welfare, regional confidence-building measures and small arms.

Address: Palais des Nations, 1211 Geneva 10, Switzerland.

United Nations Research Institute for Social Development (UNRISD). Established in 1963 to conduct multidisciplinary research into the social dimensions of contemporary problems affecting development, it aims to provide governments, development agencies, grassroots organizations and scholars with a better understanding of how development policies and processes of economic, social and environmental change affect different social groups.

Address: Palais des Nations, 1211 Geneva 10, Switzerland.

United Nations International Research and Training Institute for the Advancement of Women (INSTRAW). Established by ECOSOC and endorsed by the General Assembly in 1976, INSTRAW provides training, conducts research, and collects and disseminates information to promote gender equality and stimulate and assist women's advancement. Its 11-member Board of Trustees, which reports to ECOSOC, meets annually to review its programme and to formulate the principles and guidelines for INSTRAW's activities.

Address: POB 21747, Santo Domingo, Dominican Republic.

United Nations University (UNU). Sponsored jointly by the UN and UNESCO, UNU is guaranteed academic freedom by a charter approved by the General Assembly in 1973. It is governed by a 28-member Council of scholars and scientists, of whom 24 are appointed by the Secretary-General of the UN and the Director-General of UNESCO. Unlike a traditional university with a campus, students and faculty, it works through networks of collaborating institutions and individuals to undertake multidisciplinary research on problems of human survival, development and welfare; and to strengthen research and training capabilities in developing countries. It also provides postgraduate fellowships and PhD internships to scholars and scientists from developing countries. The University focuses its work within two programme areas: peace and governance, and environment and sustainable development.

Address: 53–70 Jingumae 5-chome, Shibuya-ku, Tokyo 150-8925, Japan.

University for Peace. Founded in 1980 to conduct research on, *inter alia*, disarmament, mediation, the resolution of conflicts, preservation of the environment, international relations, peace education and human rights.

Address: POB 138, Ciudad Colon, Costa Rica.
Website: http://www.upeace.org/

Information. *The UN Statistics Division* in New York provides a wide range of statistical outputs and services for producers and users of statistics worldwide, facilitating national and international policy formulation, implementation and monitoring. It produces printed publications of statistics and statistical methods in the fields of international merchandise trade, national accounts, demography and population, gender, industry, energy, environment, human settlements and disability, as well as general statistics compendiums including the *Statistical Yearbook* and *World Statistics Pocketbook*. Many of its databases are available on CD-ROM, diskette, magnetic tape and the Internet.

Website: http://www.un.org/Depts/unsd

UN Information Centres. Millbank Tower, 21st Floor, London SW1P 4QH; Public Inquiries Unit, Department of Public Information, Room GA-57, United Nations Plaza, New York, NY 10017.

Website: http://www.un.org
Website for London centre: http://www.unitednations.org.uk

SPECIALIZED AGENCIES OF THE UN

The intergovernmental agencies related to the UN by special agreements are separate autonomous organizations which work with the UN and each other through the co-ordinating machinery of the Economic and Social Council. 18 of them are 'Specialized Agencies' within the terms of the UN Charter, and report annually to ECOSOC.

FOOD AND AGRICULTURE ORGANIZATION OF THE UNITED NATIONS (FAO)

Origin. In 1943 the International Conference on Food and Agriculture, at Hot Springs, Virginia, set up an Interim Commission, based in Washington, with a remit to establish an organization. Its Constitution was signed on 16 Oct. 1945 in Quebec City. Today, membership totals 183 countries. The European Union was made a member as a 'regional economic integration organization' in 1991.

Aims and Activities. The aims of FAO are to raise levels of nutrition and standards of living; to improve the production and distribution of all food and agricultural products from farms, forests and fisheries; to improve the living conditions of rural populations; and, by these means, to eliminate hunger. Its priority objectives are to encourage sustainable agriculture and rural development as part of a long-term strategy for the conservation and management of natural resources; and to ensure the availability of adequate food supplies, by maximizing stability in the flow of supplies and securing access to food by the poor.

In carrying out these aims, FAO promotes investment in agriculture, better soil and water management, improved yields of crops and livestock, agricultural research and the transfer of technology to developing countries; and encourages the conservation of natural resources and rational use of fertilizers and pesticides; the development and sustainable utilization of marine and inland fisheries; the sustainable management of forest resources and the combating of animal disease. Technical assistance is provided in all of these fields, and in nutrition, agricultural engineering, agrarian reform, development communications, remote sensing for climate and vegetation, and the prevention of post-harvest food losses. In addition, FAO works to maintain global biodiversity with the emphasis on the genetic diversity of crop plants and domesticated animals; and plays a major role in the collection, analysis and dissemination of information on agricultural production and commodities. Finally, FAO acts as a neutral forum for the discussion of issues, and advises governments on policy, through international conferences like the 1996 World Food Summit in Rome and the World Food Summit: five years later, held in Rome in 2002.

Special FAO programmes help countries prepare for, and provide relief in the event of, emergency food situations, in particular through the setting up of food reserves. The *Special Programme for Food Security*, launched in 1994, is designed to assist target countries to increase food production and productivity as rapidly as possible, primarily through the widespread adoption by farmers of available improved production technologies, with the emphasis on high-potential areas. FAO provides support for the global co-ordination of the programme and helps attract funds. The *Emergency Prevention System for Transboundary Animal and Plant Pests and Diseases (EMPRES)*, established in 1994, strengthens FAO's existing contribution to the prevention, control and eradication of diseases and pests before they compromise food security, with locusts and rinderpest among its priorities. *The Global Information and Early Warning System (GIEWS)* provides current information on the world food situation and identifies countries threatened by shortages to guide potential donors. The interagency Food Insecurity and Vulnerability Information and Mapping System initiative (FIVIMS) was established in 1997, with FAO as its secretariat. More than 60 countries have nominated national focal points to co-ordinate efforts to collect and use statistics related to food insecurity more efficiently. Together with the UN, FAO sponsors the *World Food Programme (WFP)*.

Finance. The budget for the 2002–03 biennium is US$651·8m. FAO's Regular Programme budget, financed by contributions from member governments, covers the cost of its secretariat and Technical Co-operation Programme (TCP), and part of the costs of several special programmes.

FAO continues to provide technical advice and support through its field programmes in all areas of food and agriculture, fisheries, forestry and rural development. In the 2000–01 biennium, expenditures in the field totalled US$687·2m., of which US$325·3m. went to FAO's emergency assistance programme and US$361·9m. was spent on development and technical support. The programme was funded from FAO's regular budget, trust funds and the UN Development Programme. In addition, during 2000–01, 90 projects prepared with the FAO Investment Centre's assistance were approved for financing for total investments of US$3·7bn., including support loans from financing institutions of US$2·5bn.

Organization. The FAO Conference, composed of all members, meets every other year to determine policy and approve the FAO's budget and programme. The 49-member Council, elected by the Conference, serves as FAO's governing body between conference sessions. Much of its work is carried out by dozens of regional or specialist commissions, such as the Asia-Pacific Fishery Commission, the European Commission on Agriculture and the Commission on Plant Genetic Resources. The Director-General is elected for a renewable six-year term.

Headquarters: Viale delle Terme di Caracalla, 00100 Rome, Italy.
Website: http://www.fao.org
Director-General: Jacques Diouf (Senegal).

Publications. Unasylva (quarterly) 1947 ff.; *The State of Food and Agriculture* (annual), 1947 ff.; *Animal Health Yearbook* (annual), 1957 ff.; *Production Yearbook* (annual), 1947 ff.; *Trade Yearbook* (annual), 1947 ff.; *FAO Commodity Review* (annual), 1961 ff.; *Yearbook of Forest Products* (annual), 1947 ff.; *Yearbook of Fishery Statistics* (in two volumes); *FAO Fertilizer Yearbook; FAO Plant Protection Bulletin* (quarterly); *Environment and Energy Bulletin; Food Outlook* (monthly); *The State of World Fisheries and Aquaculture* (annual); *The State of the World's Forests; World Watch List for Domestic Animal Diversity; The State of Food Insecurity in the World.*

INTERNATIONAL BANK FOR RECONSTRUCTION AND DEVELOPMENT (IBRD) — THE WORLD BANK

Origin. Conceived at the UN Monetary and Financial Conference at Bretton Woods (New Hampshire, USA) in July 1944, the IBRD, frequently called the World Bank, began operations in June 1946, its purpose being to provide funds, policy guidance and technical assistance to facilitate economic development in its poorer member countries. The Group comprises four other organizations (see below).

Activities. The Bank obtains its funds from the following sources: capital paid in by member countries; sales of its own securities; sales of parts of its loans; repayments; and net earnings. A resolution of the Board of Governors of 27 April 1988 provides that the paid-in portion of the shares authorized to be subscribed under it will be 3%.

The Bank is self-supporting, raising most of its money on the world's financial markets. In the fiscal year ending 30 June 2002 it achieved a net income of US$2,778m. Income totalled US$7,876m. and expenditure US$5,952m.

In the fiscal year 2002 the Bank lent US$11·5bn. for 96 new operations in 40 countries. Cumulative lending had totalled US$371bn. by March 2003. 89% of borrowers took advantage of the new single-currency loans which became available in June 1996 to provide borrowers with the flexibility to select IBRD loan terms that are consistent with their debt-managing strategy and suited to their debt-servicing capacity. In order to eliminate wasteful overlapping of development assistance and to ensure that the funds available are used to the best possible effect, the Bank has organized consortia or consultative groups of aid-giving nations for many countries. These include Bangladesh, Belarus, Bolivia, Bulgaria, Egypt, Ethiopia, Jordan, Kazakhstan, Kenya, Kyrgyzstan, Macedonia, Malaŵi, Mauritania, Moldova, Mozambique, Nicaragua, Pakistan, Peru, Romania, Sierra Leone, Tanzania, the [Palestinian] West Bank and Gaza Strip, Zambia, Zimbabwe and the Caribbean Group for Co-operation in Economic Development.

For the purposes of its analytical and operational work, in 2000 the IBRD characterized economies as follows: low income (average annual *per capita* gross national income of $755 or less); lower middle income (between $756 and $2,995); upper middle income (between $2,996 and $9,265); and high income ($9,266 or more).

A wide variety of technical assistance is at the core of IBRD's activities. It acts as executing agency for a number of pre-investment surveys financed by the UN Development Programme. Resident missions have been established in 64 developing member countries and there are regional offices for East and West Africa, the Baltic States and South-East Asia which assist in the preparation and implementation of projects. The Bank maintains a staff college, the *Economic Development Institute* in Washington, D.C., for senior officials of member countries.

The Strategic Compact. Unanimously approved by the Executive Board in March 1997, the Strategic Compact set out a plan for fundamental reform to make the Bank more effective in delivering its regional programme and in achieving its basic mission of reducing poverty. Decentralizing the Bank's relationships with borrower countries is central to the reforms. The effectiveness of devolved country management and the bank's promotion of good governance and anti-corruption measures to developing countries are likely to be key policies of the new strategy.

Organization. As of March 2002 the Bank had 183 members, each with voting power in the institution, based on shareholding which in turn is based on a country's economic growth. The president is selected by the Bank's Board of Executive Directors. The Articles of Agreement do not specify the nationality of the president but by custom the US Executive Director makes a nomination, and by a long-standing, informal agreement, the president is a US national (while the managing director of the IMF is European). The initial term is five years, with a second of five years or less.

European office: 66 avenue d'Iéna, 75116 Paris, France. *London office:* New Zealand House, Haymarket, London SW1Y 4TE, England. *Tokyo office:* Kokusai Building, 1–1, Marunouchi 3-chome, Chiyoda-ku, Tokyo 100, Japan.

Headquarters: 1818 H St., NW, Washington, D.C., 20433, USA.
Website: http://www.worldbank.org
President: James D. Wolfensohn (USA).

Publications. World Bank Annual Report; Summary Proceedings of Annual Meetings; The World Bank and International Finance Company, 1986; The World Bank Atlas (annual); Catalog of Publications, 1986 ff.; World Development Report (annual); World Bank Economic Review (thrice yearly); World Bank and the Environment (annual); World Bank News (weekly); World Bank Research Observer; World Tables (annual); Social Indicators of Development (annual); ICSID Annual Report; ICSID Review: Foreign Investment Law Journal (twice yearly); Research News (quarterly).

INTERNATIONAL DEVELOPMENT ASSOCIATION (IDA)

A lending agency established in 1960 and administered by the IBRD to provide assistance on concessional terms to the poorest developing countries. Its resources consist of subscriptions and general replenishments from its more industrialized and developed members, special contributions, and transfers from the net earnings of IBRD. Officers and staff of the IBRD serve concurrently as officers and staff of the IDA at the World Bank headquarters.

In fiscal year 2002 disbursements totalled US$6,603m. for 813 operations. Pakistan was the single largest recipient of disbursements from adjustment lending.

INTERNATIONAL FINANCE CORPORATION (IFC)

Established in July 1956 to help strengthen the private sector in developing countries, through the provision of long-term loans, equity investments, guarantees, standby financing, risk management and quasi-equity instruments such as subordinated loans, preferred stock and income notes. It helps to finance new ventures and assist established enterprises to expand, improve or diversify, and provides a variety of advisory services to public and private sector clients. To be eligible for financing, projects must be profitable for investors, must benefit the economy of the country concerned, and must comply with IFC's environmental guidelines.

About 80% of its funds are borrowed from the international financial markets through public bond issues or private placements, 20% from the IBRD. Its authorized capital is US$2,450m.; total capital at 30 June 2002 was US$6,304m. IFC committed US$3·9bn. in total financing in 2001 and committed 205 new projects in 75 developing countries. It has 175 members.

Headquarters: 2121 Pennsylvania Ave., N. W., Washington, D.C., 20433, USA.
Website: http://www.ifc.org
President: James D. Wolfensohn (USA).

Publications. Annual Reports; Lessons of Experience (series); Results on the Ground (series).

MULTILATERAL INVESTMENT GUARANTEE AGENCY (MIGA)

Established in 1988 to encourage the flow of foreign direct investment to, and among, developing member countries, MIGA is the insurance arm of the World Bank. It provides investors with investment guarantees against non-commercial risk, such as expropriation and war, and gives advice to governments on improving climate for foreign investment. It may insure up to 90% of an investment, with a current limit of US$50m. per project. In March 1999 the Council of Governors adopted a resolution for a capital increase for the Agency of approximately US$850m. In addition US$150m. was transferred to MIGA by the World Bank as operating capital. By Dec. 2002 it had 160 member countries and a further 11 countries in the process of fulfilling membership requirements. It is located at the World Bank headquarters (see above).

Headquarters: 1818 H Street, NW, Washington, D.C., 20433, USA.
Website: http://www.miga.org

INTERNATIONAL CENTRE FOR SETTLEMENT OF INVESTMENT DISPUTES (ICSID)

Founded in 1966 to promote increased flows of international investment by providing facilities for the conciliation and arbitration of disputes between governments and foreign investors. It does not engage in such conciliation or arbitration. This is the task of conciliators and arbitrators appointed by the contracting parties, or as otherwise provided for in the Convention. Recourse to conciliation and arbitration by members is entirely voluntary.

In March 2003 its Convention had been signed by 153 countries. 72 cases had been concluded by it and 45 were pending. Disputes involved a variety of investment sectors: agriculture, banking, construction, energy, health, industrial, mining and tourism.

ICSID also undertakes research, publishing and advisory activities in the field of foreign investment law. Like IDA, IFC and MIGA, it is located at the World Bank headquarters in Washington (see above).

Secretary-General: Kaarina Pohto (Finland).

Publications. ICSID Annual Report; News from ICSID; ICSID Review: Foreign Investment Law Journal; Investment Laws of the World; Investment Treaties.

Further Reading

Caufield, C., *Masters of Illusion: The World Bank and the Poverty of Nations.* London, 1997
Nelson, P. J., *The World Bank and Non-Government Organizations: The Limits of Apolitical Development.* London, 1995
Salda, A. C. M., *World Bank* [Bibliography]. Oxford and New Brunswick (NJ), 1994
Wilson, C. R., *The World Bank Group: A Guide to Information Sources.* New York, 1991

INTERNATIONAL CIVIL AVIATION ORGANIZATION (ICAO)

Origin. The Convention providing for the establishment of the ICAO was drawn up by the International Civil Aviation Conference held in Chicago in 1944. A Provisional International Civil Aviation Organization (PICAO) operated for 20 months until the formal establishment of ICAO on 4 April 1947. The Convention on International Civil Aviation superseded the provisions of the Paris Convention of 1919 and the Pan American Convention on Air Navigation of 1928.

Functions. It assists international civil aviation by establishing technical standards for safety and efficiency of air navigation and promoting simpler procedures at borders; develops regional plans for ground facilities and services needed for international flying; disseminates air-transport statistics and prepares studies on aviation economics; fosters the development of air law conventions and provides technical assistance to states in developing civil aviation programmes.

Organization. The principal organs of ICAO are an Assembly, consisting of all members of the Organization, and a Council, which is composed of 33 states elected by the Assembly for three years, which meets in virtually continuous session. In electing these states, the Assembly must give adequate representation to: (1) states of major importance in air transport; (2) states which make the largest contribution to the provision of facilities for the international civil air navigation; and (3) those states not otherwise included whose election would ensure that all major geographical areas of the world were represented. The budget approved for 2002 was US$57·5m.

Headquarters: 999 University St., Montreal, PQ, Canada H3C 5H7.
Website: http://www.icao.int
President of the Council: Dr Assad Kotaite (Lebanon)
Secretary-General: Renato Claudio Costa Pereira (Brazil).

Publications. Annual Report of the Council; ICAO Journal (nine yearly; quarterly in Russian); *ICAO Training Manual; Aircraft Accident Digest; Procedures for Air Navigation Services.*

INTERNATIONAL FUND FOR AGRICULTURAL DEVELOPMENT (IFAD)

The idea for an International Fund for Agricultural Development arose at the 1974 World Food Conference. An agreement to establish IFAD entered into force on 30 Nov. 1977, and the agency began its operations the following month. IFAD's purpose is to mobilize additional funds for improved food production and better nutrition among low-income groups in developing countries through projects and programmes directly benefiting the poorest rural populations while preserving their natural resource base. In line with the Fund's focus on the rural poor, its resources are made available in highly concessional loans and grants. By March 2003 the Fund had invested US$7·7bn. in loans and US$35·4m. in grants financing 628 projects in 115 developing countries.

Organization. The highest body is the Governing Council, on which all 163 member countries are represented. Operations are overseen by an 18-member Executive Board (with 17 alternate members), which is responsible to the Governing Council. The Fund works with many co-operating institutions, including the World Bank, regional development banks and financial agencies, and other UN agencies; many of these co-finance IFAD projects.

Headquarters: 107 Via del Serafico, Rome 00142, Italy.
Website: http://www.ifad.org
President: Lennart Båge (Sweden).

Publications. Annual Report; IFAD Update (thrice yearly); *Staff Working Papers* (series); *The State of World Rural Poverty.*

INTERNATIONAL LABOUR ORGANIZATION (ILO)

Origin. The ILO was established in 1919 under the Treaty of Versailles as an autonomous institution associated with the League of Nations. An agreement establishing its relationship with the UN was approved in 1946, making the ILO the first Specialized Agency to be associated with the UN. An intergovernmental agency with a tripartite structure, in which representatives of governments, employers and workers participate, it seeks through international action to improve labour and living conditions, to promote productive employment and social justice for working people everywhere. On its fiftieth anniversary in 1969 it was awarded the Nobel Peace Prize. In Oct. 2001 it numbered 175 members.

Functions. One of the ILO's principal functions is the formulation of international standards in the form of International Labour Conventions and Recommendations. Member countries are required to submit Conventions to their competent national authorities with a view to ratification. If a country ratifies a Convention it agrees to bring its laws into line with its terms and to report periodically how these regulations are being applied. More than 6,900 ratifications of 184 Conventions had been deposited by 30 Sept. 2001. Procedures are in place to ascertain whether Conventions thus ratified are effectively applied. Recommendations do not require ratification, but member states are obliged to consider them with a view to giving effect to their provisions by legislation or other action. By 30 Sept. 2002 the International Labour Conference had adopted 193 Recommendations.

The ILO's programme and budget set out four strategic objectives for the Organization at the turn of the century: i) to promote and realize fundamental principles and rights at work; ii) to create greater opportunities for women and men to secure decent employment and income; iii) to enhance the coverage and effectiveness of social protection for all; iv) to strengthen tripartism and social dialogue.

Activities. In addition to its research and advisory activities, the ILO extends technical co-operation to governments under its regular budget and under the UN Development Programme and Funds-in-Trust in the fields of employment promotion, human resources development (including vocational and management training), development of social institutions, small-scale industries, rural development, social security, industrial safety and hygiene, productivity, etc. Technical co-operation also includes expert missions and a fellowship programme.

In 1994 the technical services offered by the ILO to its tripartite constituents came under scrutiny leading to a re-affirmation of technical co-operation as one of the principal means of ILO action. Since 1994 the process of implementing the new Active Partnership Policy made significant progress and today 16 multidisciplinary advisory teams are engaged in a dialogue with ILO constituents centred on the identification of Country Objectives to form the basis of the ILO's contribution.

In June 1998 delegates to the 86th International Labour Conference adopted a solemn ILO Declaration in Fundamental Principles and Rights at Work, committing the Organization's member states to respect the principles inherent in a number of core labour standards: the right of workers and employers to freedom of association and the effective right to collective bargaining, and to work toward the elimination of all forms of forced or compulsory labour, the effective abolition of child labour and the elimination of discrimination in respect of employment and occupation.

In June 1999 delegates to the 87th International Labour Conference adopted a new Convention banning the worst forms of child labour. The International Labour Conference 2001 adopted a budget of US$434bn. for the 2002–03 biennium. In 2001 delegates to the conference adopted the first international standard on safety in agriculture.

Field Activities. In 2000 extra-budgetary expenditure on operational activities totalled US$82·5m., compared to US$78·2m. in 1999, representing an increase of 5·5%. The leading field of activity in terms of annual expenditure (representing 46% of total expenditure) was the employment sector (US$37·7m.) and included activities in the Employment-intensive Investment Programme (US$9·9m.) and the Infocus Programme on Boosting Employment through Small Enterprise Development (US$7·4m.). The next largest field of activity was the Standards and Fundamental Principles and Rights at Work sector (representing 28% of total expenditure), which included the Infocus Programme on Child Labour (US$21·2m.). Social Protection and Social Dialogue related activities accounted for 9% and 13% respectively of total expenditure. The latter included Workers' Activities (US$4·9m.) and Employers' Activities (US$1·6m.). Interregional and global activities accounted for some US$19m. In terms of regional distribution, Africa accounted for 31% of total expenditure (US$25·5m.), Asia and the Pacific for 23% (US$19·3m.) and Latin America and the Caribbean for 15% (US$12·6m.). Expenditure in Europe showed a decrease of 14% to US$4·5m. in 2000 and the Arab States programme decreased by 49% to US$1·5m. in 2000.

The ILO's *International Institute for Labour Studies* promotes the study and discussion of policy issues. The core theme of its activities is the interaction between labour institutions, development and civil society in a global economy. It identifies emerging social and labour issues by opening up new areas for research and action; and encourages systematic dialogue on social policy between the tripartite constituency of the ILO and the international academic community, and other public opinion-makers.

The *International Training Centre* of the ILO, in Turin, was set up in 1965 to lead the training programmes implemented by the ILO as part of its technical co-operation activities. Member states and the UN system also call on its resources and experience, and a UN Staff College was established on the Turin Campus in 1996.

Organization. The International Labour Conference is the supreme deliberative organ of the ILO; it meets annually in Geneva. National delegations are composed of two government delegates, one employers' delegate and one workers' delegate. The Governing Body, elected by the Conference, is the Executive Council. It is composed of 28 government members, 14 workers' members and 14 employers' members. Ten governments of countries of industrial importance hold permanent seats on the Governing Body. These are: Brazil, China, Germany, France, India, Italy, Japan, Russia, UK and USA. The remaining 18 government members are elected every three years. Workers' and employers' representatives are elected as individuals, not as national candidates. The ILO has a branch office in London (for UK and Republic of Ireland), and regional offices in Abidjan (for Africa), Bangkok (for Asia and the Pacific), Lima (for Latin America and the Caribbean) and Beirut (for Arab States). The ILO budget for 2002–03 was US$472m.

Headquarters: International Labour Office, CH-1211 Geneva 22, Switzerland.
London Office: Vincent House, Vincent Square, London SW1P 2NB, UK.
Website: http://www.ilo.org
Director-General: Juan Somavia (Chile).
Governing Body Chairman: Alain Ludovic Tou (Burkina Faso).

Publications (available in English, French and Spanish) include: *International Labour Review; Bulletin of Labour Statistics; Official Bulletin* and *Labour Education; Yearbook of Labour Statistics* (annual); *World Labour Report* (annual); *World Employment Report* (annual); *Encyclopaedia of Occupational Health and Safety; Key Indicators of the Labour Market (KILM); World of Work* (four a year).

INTERNATIONAL MARITIME ORGANIZATION (IMO)

Origin. The International Maritime Organization (formerly the InterGovernmental Maritime Consultative Organization) was established as a specialized agency of the UN by a convention drafted in 1948 at a UN maritime conference in Geneva. The Convention became effective on 17 March 1958 when it had been ratified by 21 countries, including seven with at least 1m. gross tons of shipping each. The IMCO started operations in 1959 and changed its name to the IMO in 1982.

Functions. To facilitate co-operation among governments on technical matters affecting merchant shipping, especially concerning safety at sea; to prevent and control marine pollution caused by ships; to facilitate international maritime traffic. The IMO is responsible for convening international maritime conferences and for drafting international maritime conventions. It also provides technical assistance to countries wishing to develop their maritime activities, and acts as a depositary authority for international conventions regulating maritime affairs. *The World Maritime University (WMU),* at Malmö, Sweden, was established in 1983; the *IMO*

International Maritime Law Institute (IMLI), at Valletta, Malta and the *IMO International Maritime Academy*, at Trieste, Italy, both in 1989.

Organization. The IMO has 159 members (and three associate members). The Assembly, composed of all member states, normally meets every two years. The 40-member Council acts as governing body between sessions. There are four principal committees (on maritime safety, legal matters, marine environment protection and technical co-operation), which submit reports or recommendations to the Assembly through the Council, and a Secretariat. The budget for 2000–01 amounted to £36·6m.

Headquarters: 4 Albert Embankment, London SE1 7SR, UK.
Website: http://www.imo.org
e-mail: info@imo.org
Secretary-General: William A. O'Neil (Canada).

Publication. IMO News.

INTERNATIONAL MONETARY FUND (IMF)

The International Monetary Fund was established on 27 Dec. 1945 as an independent international organization and began financial operations on 1 March 1947; its relationship with the UN is defined in an agreement of mutual co-operation which came into force on 15 Nov. 1947. The first amendment to the IMF's Articles creating the special drawing right (SDR) took effect on 28 July 1969. The second amendment took effect on 1 April 1978. The third amendment came into force on 11 Nov. 1992; it allows for the suspension of voting and related rights of a member which persists in its failure to settle its outstanding obligations to the IMF.

Aims. To promote international monetary co-operation, the expansion of international trade and exchange rate stability; to assist in the removal of exchange restrictions and the establishment of a multilateral system of payments; and to alleviate any serious disequilibrium in members' international balance of payments by making the financial resources of the IMF available to them, usually subject to economic policy conditions to ensure the revolving nature of IMF resources.

Activities. Each member of the IMF undertakes a broad obligation to collaborate with the IMF and other members to ensure orderly exchange arrangements and to promote a system of stable exchange rates. In addition, members are subject to certain obligations relating to domestic and external policies that can affect the balance of payments and the exchange rate. The IMF makes its resources available, under proper safeguards, to its members to meet short-term or medium-term payment difficulties. The first allocation of SDRs was made on 1 Jan. 1970. A total of SDR 21·4bn. has been allocated to members in two allocations, completed in 1981.

To enhance its balance of payments assistance to its members, the IMF established a Compensatory Financing Facility on 27 Feb. 1963; temporary oil facilities in 1974 and 1975; a Trust Fund in 1976; and an Extended Fund Facility (EFF) for medium-term assistance to members with special balance of payments problems on 13 Sept. 1974. In March 1986 it established the Structural Adjustment Facility (SAF) to provide assistance to low-income countries. In Dec. 1987 it established the Enhanced Structural Adjustment Facility (ESAF) to provide further assistance to low-income countries facing high levels of indebtedness. In Oct. 1999 the ESAF was renamed as the Poverty Reduction and Growth Facility (PRGF) to reflect the increased focus on poverty reduction. Because of the importance of continuing concessional ESAF support, the IMF in 1996 endorsed proposals for a continuation of ESAF operations beyond 2000, when ESAF/PRGF resources were expected to be fully committed. There is to be an interim period of operations from 2001–04 for which new financing will be mobilized. This will be followed in 2005, or earlier, by a self-sustained PRGF. In Dec. 1997 the Supplemental Reserve Facility (SRF) was established to provide short-term assistance to countries experiencing exceptional balance of payments problems owing to a large short-term financing need resulting from a sudden disruptive loss of market confidence, reflected in pressure on the capital account and the member's reserves. Contingent Credit Lines (CCL) were established in April 1999 as instruments of crisis prevention to counter problems of international financial contagion.

Capital Resources. The capital resources of the IMF comprise SDRs and currencies that the members pay under quotas calculated for them when they join the IMF. A member's quota is largely determined by its economic position relative to other members; it is also linked to their drawing rights on the IMF under both regular and special facilities, their voting power, and their share of SDR allocations. Every IMF member is required to subscribe to the IMF an amount equal to its quota. An amount not exceeding 25% of the quota has to be paid in reserve assets, the balance in the member's own currency. The members with the largest quotas are: 1st, the USA; joint 2nd, Germany and Japan; joint 4th, France and the UK.

An increase of almost 60% in IMF quotas became effective in Nov. 1992 as a result of the 9th General Review of Quotas. Quotas were not increased under the 10th General Review. In the 11th General Review, the IMF's Executive Board adopted a resolution at its 1997 annual meeting, approving a one-time equity allocation of SDRs of SDR 21,400m., which would equalize all members' ratio of SDRs to quota at 29·3%. The Board also agreed to recommend a 45% increase in IMF quotas, which would raise total quotas from SDR 145,300m., in Sept. 1997, to SDR 209,500m.; an 85% majority of member countries is required for the quota increase to take effect. As of Jan. 1999 the 85% majority had been met. As of Feb. 2001 with an *ad hoc* quota increase for China, total quotas were SDR 212·4bn.

Borrowing Resources. The IMF is authorized under its Articles of Agreement to supplement its resources by borrowing. In Jan. 1962 a four-year agreement was concluded with ten industrial members (Belgium, Canada, France, Germany, Italy, Japan, Netherlands, Sweden, UK, USA) who undertook to lend the IMF up to US$6,000m. in their own currencies, if this should be needed to forestall or cope with an impairment of the international monetary system. Switzerland subsequently joined the group. These arrangements, known as the General Arrangements to Borrow (GAB), have been extended several times. In early 1983 agreement was reached to increase the credit arrangements under the GAB to SDR 17,000m.; to permit use of GAB resources in transactions with IMF members that are not GAB participants; to authorize Swiss participation; and to permit borrowing arrangements with non-participating members to be associated with the GAB. Saudi Arabia and the IMF have entered into such an arrangement under which the IMF will be able to borrow up to SDR 1,500m. to assist in financing purchases by any member for the same purpose and under the same circumstances as in the GAB. The changes became effective by 26 Dec. 1983.

Surveillance. In order to oversee the compliance of members with their obligations under the Articles of Agreement, the IMF is required to exercise firm surveillance over members' exchange rate policies. In conjunction with the need for up-to-date reliable data to support its surveillance activities, it encourages member countries to make available to the public and to financial markets core financial and economic data. In April 1996 the IMF established the Special Data Dissemination Standard (SDDS) to improve access to reliable economic statistical information for member countries that have, or are seeking, access to international capital markets. In Dec. 1997 it established the General Data Dissemination Standard (GDDS), which applies to all member countries and focuses on improved production and dissemination of core economic data. Information on both are available on the IMF's website.

The IMF works with the IBRD (World Bank) to address the problems of the most heavily indebted poor countries (most in Sub-Saharan Africa) through their Initiative for the Heavily Indebted Poor Countries (HIPCs). The HIPC Initiative is designed to ensure that HIPCs with a sound track record of economic adjustment receive debt relief sufficient to help them attain a sustainable debt situation over the medium term. The HIPC Initiative was enhanced in late 1999 to provide deeper and more rapid debt relief to a larger number of countries.

Organization. The highest authority is the Board of Governors, on which each member government is represented. Normally the Governors meet once a year, and may take votes by mail or other means between meetings. The Board of Governors has delegated many of its powers to the 24 executive directors in Washington, who are appointed or elected by individual member countries or groups of countries. Each appointed director has voting power proportionate to the quota of the government he or she represents, while each elected director casts all the votes of the countries represented. The managing director is selected by the executive directors and serves as chairman of the Executive Board, but may not vote except in case of a tie. The term of office is for five years, but may be extended or terminated at the discretion of the executive directors. The managing director is responsible for the ordinary business of the IMF, under the direction of the executive directors, and supervises a staff of about 2,600. Under a long-standing, informal agreement, the managing director is European (while the President of the World Bank is a US national). There are three deputy managing directors. As of Dec. 2002 the IMF had 184 members.

The *IMF Institute* is a specialized department of the IMF providing training in macroeconomic analysis and policy, and related subjects, for officials of member countries, at the Fund's headquarters in Washington, the Joint Vienna Institute, the Joint Africa Institute, the Singapore Regional Training Institute, the IMF-Arab Monetary Fund Regional Training Program, the Joint China-IMF Training Program and the Joint Regional Training Center for Latin America. In addition, the IMF operates regional training centres: the Pacific Financial Technical Assistance Center (PFTAC), the Caribbean Regional Technical Assistance Center (CARTAC) and the Regional Technical Assistance Center in Africa (AFRITAC). Since its establishment in 1964 the Institute has trained more than 10,900 officials from 181 countries.

Headquarters: 700 19th St. NW, Washington, D.C., 20431, USA. Offices in Paris and Geneva and a regional office for Asia and the Pacific in Tokyo.
Website: http://www.imf.org
Managing Director: Horst Köhler (Germany).

Publications. Annual Report; Annual Report on Exchange Arrangements and Exchange Restrictions; International Financial Statistics (monthly); *IMF Survey* (2 a month); *Balance of Payments Statistics Yearbook; Staff Papers* (4 a year); *IMF Economic Issues pamphlets; IMF Occasional Paper series; Direction of Trade Statistics* (quarterly); *Government Finance Statistics Yearbook; World Economic Outlook* (2 a year); *The International Monetary Fund, 1945–65: Twenty Years of International Monetary Co-operation,* 3 vols. Washington, 1969; de Vries, M. G., *The International Monetary Fund, 1966–1971: The System Under Stress,* 2 vols. Washington, 1976; *The International Monetary Fund 1972–1978: Co-operation on Trial.* 3 vols. Washington, 1985; *Silent Witness, International Monetary Fund 1979–89.* Washington, 2001.

Further Reading
Humphreys, N. K., *Historical Dictionary of the International Monetary Fund.* Metuchen (NJ), 1994
James, H., *International Monetary Cooperation since Bretton Woods* . OUP, 1996
Salda, A. C. M., *The International Monetary Fund.* [Bibliography] Oxford and New Brunswick (NJ), 1993

INTERNATIONAL TELECOMMUNICATION UNION (ITU)

Origin. Founded in Paris in 1865 as the International Telegraph Union, the International Telecommunication Union took its present name in 1934 and became a specialized agency of the United Nations in 1947. Therefore, the ITU is the world's oldest intergovernmental body.

Functions. To maintain and extend international co-operation for the improvement and rational use of telecommunications of all kinds, and promote and offer technical assistance to developing countries in the field of telecommunications; to promote the development of technical facilities and their most efficient operation to improve the efficiency of telecommunication services, increasing their usefulness and making them, so far as possible, generally available to the public; to harmonize the actions of nations in the attainment of these ends.

Organization. The supreme organ of the ITU is the Plenipotentiary Conference, which normally meets every four years. A 46-member Council, elected by the Conference, meets annually in Geneva and is responsible for ensuring the co-ordination of the four permanent organs at ITU headquarters: the General Secretariat; Radiocommunication Sector; Telecommunication Standardization Sector; and Telecommunication Development Sector. The Secretary-General is also elected by the Conference. ITU has 189 member countries; a further 576 scientific and technical companies, public and private operators, broadcasters and other organizations are also ITU members.

Headquarters: Place des Nations, CH-1211 Geneva 20, Switzerland.
Website: http://www.itu.int
Secretary-General: Yoshio Utsumi (Japan).

UNITED NATIONS EDUCATIONAL, SCIENTIFIC AND CULTURAL ORGANIZATION (UNESCO)

Origin. UNESCO's Constitution was signed in London on 16 Nov. 1945 by 37 countries and the Organization came into being in Nov. 1946 on the premise that: 'Since wars begin in the minds of men, it is in the minds of men that the defences of peace must be constructed'. In Jan. 2003 UNESCO had 188 members including the UK, which rejoined in 1997. They include six Associate Members with no single member status in the UN (Aruba; British Virgin Islands; Cayman Islands; Macao; Netherlands Antilles; Tokelau). In 2002 the USA announced its decision to return after an 18-year absence. East Timor has also declared its intention to join.

Aims and Activities. UNESCO's primary objective is to contribute to peace and security in the world by promoting collaboration among the nations through education, science, communication and culture in order to further universal respect for justice, the rule of the law, human rights and fundamental freedoms, affirmed for all peoples by the UN Charter.

Education. Various activities support and foster national projects to renovate education systems and develop alternative educational strategies towards a goal of lifelong education for all. The four main areas of focus, today, are: to provide basic education for all; expand access to basic education; improve the quality of basic education; and education for the 21st century. There are regional and sub-regional offices for education in 57 countries.

Science. UNESCO seeks to promote international scientific co-operation and encourages scientific research designed to improve living conditions and to protect ecosystems. Regional science co-operation offices have been set up in Cairo, Jakarta, Montevideo, Nairobi and Venice. A *Sciences in the Service of Development* programme aims to provide support to member states in the fields of higher education, advanced training and research in natural and social sciences, and in the application of these sciences to development. It focuses on questions concerning issues such as man and the biosphere, oceanography, geological correlation and hydrology.

Social and Human Sciences. UNESCO works to advance knowledge and intellectual co-operation in order to facilitate social transformations conducive to justice, freedom, peace and human dignity. It seeks to identify evolving social trends and develops and promotes principles and standards based on universal values and ethics, such as the *International Declaration on the Human Genome and Human Rights* (1997).

Communication. Activities are geared to promoting the free flow of information, freedom of expression, press freedom, media independence and pluralism. Another priority is to bridge the digital divide and help disadvantaged groups in North and South access the emerging knowledge societies created thanks to the new information and communication technologies. To this end, UNESCO promotes access to public domain information and free software, as well as encouraging the creation of local content.

Culture. In the cultural field, UNESCO's focus areas are research on the link between culture and development, and action to conserve and protect the world's cultural inheritance, by assisting member states in studying and preserving both the tangible and intangible heritage of their societies.

Organization. The General Conference, composed of representatives from each member state, meets biennially to decide policy, programme and budget. A 58-member Executive Board elected by the Conference meets twice a year and there is a Secretariat. In addition, national commissions act as liaison groups between UNESCO and the educational, scientific and cultural life of their own countries. The budget for the biennium 2002–03 was US$544·4m.

There are also seven separate UNESCO institutes: the International Bureau of Education (IBE), in Geneva; the UNESCO Institute for Education (UIE), in Hamburg; the International Institute for Educational Planning (IIEP), in Paris; the International Institute for Capacity Building in Africa (IICBA), in Addis Ababa; the International Institute for Higher Education in Latin America and the Caribbean (IESALC), in Caracas; the UNESCO Institute for Information Technologies in Education (IITE), in Moscow; and the UNESCO Institute for Statistics (UIS), in Montreal.

Headquarters: UNESCO House, 7 Place de Fontenoy, 75352 Paris 07 SP, France.
Website: http://www.unesco.org
Director-General: Koichiro Matsuura (Japan).

Periodicals. Museum International (quarterly); *International Social Science Journal* (quarterly); *The New Courier* (twice-yearly); *Prospects* (quarterly); *Copyright Bulletin* (quarterly); *World Heritage Report* (bi-monthly).

UNITED NATIONS INDUSTRIAL DEVELOPMENT ORGANIZATION (UNIDO)

Origin. UNIDO was established by the UN General Assembly in 1966 and became the 16th UN specialized agency in 1985.

Aims. UNIDO helps developing countries, and countries with economies in transition, in their fight against marginalization and poverty in today's globalized world. It mobilizes knowledge, skills, information and technology to promote productive employment, a competitive economy and a sound environment. UNIDO focuses its efforts on relieving poverty by fostering productivity growth and economic development.

Activities. As a global forum, UNIDO generates and disseminates knowledge relating to industrial matters and provides a platform for the various actors—decision makers in the public and private sectors, civil society organizations and the policy-making community in general—to enhance co-operation, establish dialogue and develop partnerships in order to address the challenges ahead. As a technical co-operation agency, UNIDO designs and implements programmes to support the industrial development efforts of its clients. It also offers tailor-made specialized support for programme development. The two core functions are both complementary and mutually supportive. On the one hand, experience gained in the technical co-operation work of UNIDO can be shared with policy makers; on the other, the Organization's analytical work shows where technical co-operation will have the greatest impact by helping to define priorities.

Organization. As part of the United Nations common system, UNIDO has the responsibility for promoting industrialization throughout the developing world, in co-operation with its 169 member states. Its headquarters are in Vienna, Austria, and with 28 smaller country and regional offices, 13 investment and technology promotion offices and a number of offices related to specific aspects of its work, UNIDO maintains an active presence in the field. The General Conference meets every two years to determine policy and approve the budget. The 53-member Industrial Development Board (membership according to constitutional lists) is elected by the General Conference. The General Conference also elects a 27-member Programme and Budget Committee for two years and appoints a Director-General for four years.

Finance. UNIDO's financial resources come from the regular and operational budgets, as well as contributions for technical co-operation activities, budgeted at US$133·7m., US$22·0m. and US$193·6m. respectively, totalling US$349·3m. for 2002–03. Administrative costs represent 7·6% of the total budget estimates. The regular budget derives from assessed contributions from member states.

Technical co-operation is funded mainly from voluntary contributions from donor countries and institutions as well as UNDP, the Multilateral Fund for the Implementation of the Montreal Protocol, the Global Environment Facility, and the Common Fund for Communities.

Headquarters: Vienna International Centre, POB 300, A-1400 Vienna, Austria.
Website: http://www.unido.org
Director-General: Carlos Alfredo Magariños (Argentina).

Publications. UNIDOScope (weekly Internet newspaper); *UNIDO Annual Report; Industry for Growth into the New Millennium, African Industry 2000: The Challenge of Going Global; Using Statistics for Process Control and Improvement: An Introduction to Basic Concepts and Techniques; Guidelines for Project Evaluation; Practical Appraisal for Industrial Project Applications—Application of Social Cost-Benefit Analysis in Pakistan; Manual for the Evaluation of Industrial Projects; Guide to Practical Project Appraisal—Social Benefit-Cost Analysis in Developing Countries; Manual for Small Industrial Businesses: Project Design and Appraisal; Manual for the Preparation of Industrial Feasibility Studies; Manual on Technology Transfer Negotiations; Guidelines for Infrastructure Development Through Build-Operate-Transfer (BOT) Projects; Gearing up for a New Development Agenda; Reforming the UN System: UNIDO's Need-Driven Model; World Directory of Industrial Information Sources; Woodworking Machinery: A Manual on Selection Options; Competition and the World Economy; The International Yearbook of Industrial Statistics 2002; Industrial Development Report 2002/2003.*

UNIVERSAL POSTAL UNION (UPU)

Origin. The UPU was established in 1875, when the Universal Postal Convention adopted by the Postal Congress of Berne on 9 Oct. 1874 came into force. It has 189 member countries.

Functions. The aim of the UPU is to assure the organization and perfection of the various postal services, and to promote the development of international collaboration in the field. To this end, UPU members are united in a single postal territory for the reciprocal exchange of correspondence. A Specialized Agency of the UN since 1948, the UPU is governed by its Constitution, adopted in 1964 (Vienna), and subsequent protocol amendments (1969, Tokyo; 1974, Lausanne; 1979, Rio de Janeiro; 1984, Hamburg; 1989, Washington; 1994, Seoul; 1999, Beijing).

Organization. It is composed of a Universal Postal Congress which meets every five years; a 41-member Council of Administration, which meets annually and is responsible for supervising the affairs of the UPU between Congresses; a 40-member Postal Operations Council; and an International Bureau which functions as the permanent secretariat, responsible for strategic planning and programme budgeting. The budget for the biennial period 2003–04 is 71·4m. Swiss francs.

Headquarters: Weltpoststrasse 4, 3000 Berne 15, Switzerland.
Website: http://www.upu.int
Director-General: Thomas E. Leavey (USA).

Publications. Beijing Postal Strategy (1999), Postal Statistics (annual), *Post 2005—Follow-up and Trends (2000), Union Postale* (quarterly), *POST*Code* (also in CD-ROM).

WORLD HEALTH ORGANIZATION (WHO)

Origin. An International Conference convened by the UN Economic and Social Council to consider a single health organization resulted in the adoption on 22 July 1946 of the Constitution of the World Health Organization, which came into force on 7 April 1948.

Functions. WHO's objective, as stated in the first article of the Constitution, is 'the attainment by all peoples of the highest possible level of health'. As the directing and co-ordinating authority on international health, it establishes and maintains collaboration with the UN, specialized agencies, government health administrations, professional and other groups concerned with health. The Constitution also directs WHO to assist governments to strengthen their health services; to stimulate and advance work to eradicate diseases; to promote maternal and child health, mental health, medical research and the prevention of accidents; to improve standards of teaching and training in the health professions, and of nutrition, housing, sanitation, working conditions and other aspects of environmental health. The Organization is also empowered to propose conventions, agreements and regulations, and make recommendations about international health matters; to revise the international nomenclature of diseases, causes of death and public health practices; to develop, establish and promote international standards concerning foods, biological, pharmaceutical and similar substances.

Methods of work. Co-operation in country projects is undertaken only on the request of the government concerned, through the six regional offices of the Organization.

Worldwide technical services are made available by headquarters. Expert committees, chosen from the 55 advisory panels of experts, meet to advise the Director-General on a given subject. Scientific groups and consultative meetings are called for similar purposes. To further the education of health personnel of all categories, seminars, technical conferences and training courses are organized, and advisors, consultants and lecturers are provided. WHO awards fellowships for study to nationals of member countries.

Activities. The main thrust of WHO's activities in recent years has been towards promoting national, regional and global strategies for the attainment of the main social target of the member states: 'Health for All in the 21st Century', or the attainment by all citizens of the world of a level of health that will permit them to lead a socially and economically productive life. Almost all countries indicated a high level of political commitment to this goal; and guiding principles for formulating corresponding strategies and plans of action were subsequently prepared.

The 50th World Health Assembly which met in 1997 adopted numerous resolutions on public health issues. *The World Health Report, 1997: Conquering suffering, enriching humanity* focused on 'non-communicable diseases'. It warned that the human and social costs of cancer, heart disease and other chronic diseases will rise unless confronted now.

The number of cancer cases was expected to double in most countries by 2020. There will be a 33% increase in lung cancers in women and a 40% increase in prostate cancers in men in European Union countries alone by 2005. The incidence of other cancers is also rising rapidly, especially in developing countries. Heart disease and stroke, the leading causes of death in richer nations, will become more common in poorer countries. Globally, diabetes will more than double by 2025, with the number of people affected rising from about 135m. to 300m., and there is likely to be a huge rise in some mental disorders, especially dementias and particularly Alzheimer's disease. Already an estimated 29m. people suffer from dementia, and at least 400m. suffer from other mental disorders ranging from mood and personality disorders to neurological conditions like epilepsy, which affects some 40m. worldwide.

These projected increases are reported to be owing to a combination of factors, not least population ageing and the rising prevalence of unhealthy lifestyles. Average life expectancy at birth globally reached 65 years in 1996. It is now well over 70 years in many countries and exceeds 80 years in some. In 1997 there were an estimated 380m. people over 65 years. By 2020 that number is expected to rise to more than 690m.

The ten leading killer diseases in the world are: coronary heart disease, 7·2m. deaths annually; cancer (all sites), 6·2m.; cerebrovascular disease, 4·6m.; acute lower respiratory infection, 3·7m.; perinatal conditions, 3·6m.; tuberculosis, 2·9m.; chronic obstructive pulmonary disease, 2·9m.; diarrhoea and dysentery, 2·5m.; HIV/AIDS, 2·3m.; malaria, 2·1m. Tobacco-related deaths, primarily from lung cancer and circulatory disease, amount to 3m. a year. Smoking accounts for one in seven cancer cases worldwide, and if the trend of increasing consumption in many countries continues, the epidemic has many more decades to run.

In response, WHO has called for an intensified and sustained global campaign to encourage healthy lifestyles and attack the main risk factors responsible for many of these diseases: unhealthy diet, inadequate physical activity, smoking and obesity.

World Health Report, 2000: The theme of the report was Health Systems: Improving Performance. It provided an expert analysis of the influence of health systems in the lives of people worldwide, debating the way in which their performance can be measured and improved. The results of the report found France to be the leading country in terms of health care, followed among major countries by Italy, Spain, Oman, Austria and Japan. The US health system was found to spend a higher portion of its GDP than any other country whilst ranking 37th out of 191 countries according to its performance.

The report stated that the main failings of many health systems were:
—Many health ministries focus on the public sector and often disregard the frequently much larger private sector health care.

—In many countries, some if not most physicians work simultaneously for the public sector and in private practice. This means the public sector ends up subsidizing unofficial private practice. Many governments fail to prevent a 'black market' in health, where widespread corruption, bribery, 'moonlighting' and other illegal practices flourish. The black markets, which themselves are caused by malfunctioning health systems, and low income of health workers, further undermine those systems.

—Many health ministries fail to enforce regulations that they themselves have created or are supposed to implement in the public interest.

Cloning in human reproduction. The 1997 Assembly adopted a resolution affirming that the use of cloning for the replication of human individuals is ethically unacceptable and contrary to human integrity and morality. In accepting the resolution delegates recognized the need to respect the freedom of ethically acceptable scientific activity and to ensure access to the benefits of its applications.

Joint UN Programme on HIV/AIDS (UNAIDS). In 1996 the Assembly reviewed implementation of the global strategy for the prevention and control of AIDS, and progress of the Joint UN Programme on HIV/AIDS (UNAIDS), which became operational in 1996. The impact of the HIV/AIDS epidemic is seen to be expanding and intensifying, particularly in developing countries, and new resource mobilization mechanisms were called for to support countries in combating HIV/AIDS. The Assembly requested WHO to facilitate the incorporation of UNAIDS-specific policies, norms and strategies into the activities of WHO at global, regional and country levels, and to collaborate in all aspects of resource mobilization for HIV/AIDS activities.

World Health Day is observed on 7 April every year. The 2003 theme for World Health Day was Healthy Environments for Children; the theme for 2002 was Move for Health. World No-Tobacco Day is held on 31 May each year; International Day Against Drug Abuse on 26 June; World AIDS Day on 1 Dec.

Organization. The principal organs of WHO are the World Health Assembly, the Executive Board and the Secretariat. Each of the 192 member states has the right to be represented at the Assembly, which meets annually in Geneva. The 32-member Executive Board is composed of technically qualified health experts designated by as many member states as elected by the Assembly. The Secretariat consists of technical and administrative staff headed by a Director-General, who is appointed for not more than two five-year terms. Health activities in member countries are carried out through regional organizations which have been established in Africa (Brazzaville), South-East Asia (New Delhi), Europe (Copenhagen), Eastern Mediterranean (Alexandria) and Western Pacific (Manila). The Pan American Sanitary Bureau in Washington serves as the regional office of WHO for the Americas. It is the oldest international health agency in the world and is the secretariat of the Pan American Health Organization (PAHO).

Finance. The global programme budget for 2002–03 submitted to the Executive Board in Jan. 2001 was US$2,222·7m.

Headquarters: Avenue Appia, CH-1211 Geneva 27, Switzerland.
Website: http://www.who.int
Director-General: Jong-Wook Lee (South Korea).

Publications. Annual Report on World Health; Bulletin of WHO (6 issues a year); *International Digest of Health Legislation* (quarterly); *Health and Safety Guides; International Statistical Classification of Diseases and Related Health Problems; WHO Technical Report Series; WHO AIDS Series; Public Health Papers; World Health Statistics Annual; Weekly Epidemiological Record; WHO Drug Information* (quarterly).

WORLD INTELLECTUAL PROPERTY ORGANIZATION (WIPO)

Origin. The roots of the World Intellectual Property Organization go back to the Paris Convention for the Protection of Industrial Property, adopted in 1883, and the Berne Convention for the Protection of Literary and Artistic Works (adopted 1886). The Convention establishing WIPO was signed at Stockholm in 1967 by 51 countries, and entered into force in April 1970. WIPO became a UN specialized agency in 1974.

Aims. To promote the protection of intellectual property throughout the world through co-operation among member states; and to ensure administrative co-operation among the intellectual property unions created by the Paris and Berne Conventions.

Intellectual property comprises two main branches: industrial property (inventions, trademarks and industrial designs) and copyright and neighbouring rights (literary, musical, artistic, photographic and audiovisual works).

Activities. There are three principal areas of activity: the progressive development of international intellectual property law; global protection systems and services; and co-operation for development. WIPO seeks to harmonize national intellectual property legislation and procedures; provide services for international applications for industrial property rights; exchange intellectual property information; provide training and legal and technical assistance to developing and other countries; facilitate the resolution of private intellectual property disputes; and marshal information technology as a tool for storing, accessing and using valuable intellectual property information.

New approaches to the progressive development of international intellectual property law. The development and application of international norms and standards is a fundamental part of WIPO's activities. It administers 21 treaties (15 on industrial property, six on copyright). The Organization plays an increasing role in making national and regional systems for the registration of intellectual property more user-friendly by harmonizing and simplifying procedures.

Global protection systems and services. The most successful and widely used treaty is the Patent Co-operation Treaty (PCT), which implements the concept of a single international patent application that is valid in many countries. Once such application is filed, an applicant has time to decide in which countries to pursue the application, thereby streamlining procedures and reducing costs. In 2001 the PCT system recorded 103,947 applications.

The treaties dealing with the international registration of marks and industrial designs are, respectively, the Madrid Agreement (and its Protocol) and the Hague Agreement. In 1999 there were more than 20,000 registrations of marks under the Madrid System, an equivalent of over 264,000 national trademark registrations. In 1999 WIPO registered 4,093 international deposits of industrial designs.

Co-operation for development. On 1 Jan. 2000 many developing and other countries, as members of the World Trade Organization, brought their national legislative and administrative structures into conformity with the Agreement on Trade-Related Aspects of Intellectual Property Rights (TRIPS). WIPO and WTO agreed, in the framework of a Co-operation Agreement which entered into force on 1 Jan. 1996, and a Joint Initiative launched in July 1998, on a joint technical co-operation initiative to provide assistance to developing countries to meet their obligations to comply with the TRIPS Agreement. This represented a major step in the international harmonization of the scope, standards and enforcement of Intellectual Property rights.

The newly created WIPO Worldwide Academy co-ordinates training activities, originates new approaches and methods to expand the scope, impact and accessibility of WIPO programmes, and creates more effective training tailored for diverse-user groups. The Academy has also launched an Internet-based distance-learning programme.

Impact of digital technology on intellectual property law. WIPO takes a range of initiatives to tackle the implications of modern digital and communications technology for copyright and industrial property law, and in electronic commerce transcending national jurisdictions. The WIPO Arbitration and Mediation Centre was established in 1994 to provide online dispute-resolution services. The Centre developed an operational and legal framework for the administration of disputes, including those relating to new technologies such as Internet Domain Name Disputes.

Organization. WIPO has three governing bodies: the General Assembly, the Conference and the Co-ordination Committee. Each treaty administered by WIPO has one or more Governing Bodies of its own, composed of representatives of the respective member states. In addition, the Paris and Berne Unions have Assemblies and Executive Committees. The executive head of WIPO is the Director-General, who is elected by the General Assembly. In March 2003 WIPO had 179 member states, with an international staff of around 850 from 86 countries. The budget for 2002–03 was 678m. Swiss francs, the majority of which was covered by revenue earned by the Organization's international registration and publication activities.

Official languages. Arabic, Chinese, English, French, Russian and Spanish.
Headquarters: 34 chemin des Colombettes, 1211 Geneva 20, Switzerland.
Website: http://www.wipo.int
Director-General: Dr Kamil Idris (Sudan).

Periodicals. Industrial Property and Copyright (monthly, bi-monthly, in Spanish); *PCT Gazette* (weekly); *PCT Newsletter* (monthly); *International Designs Bulletin* (monthly); *WIPO Gazette of International Marks* (fortnightly); *Intellectual Property in Asia and the Pacific* (quarterly).

WORLD METEOROLOGICAL ORGANIZATION (WMO)

Origin. A 1947 (Washington) Conference of Directors of the International Meteorological Organization (est. 1873) adopted a Convention creating the World Meteorological Organization. The WMO Convention became effective on 23 March 1950 and WMO was formally established. It was recognized as a Specialized Agency of the UN in 1951.

Functions. (1) To facilitate worldwide co-operation in the establishment of networks of stations for the making of meteorological observations as well as hydrological or other geophysical observations related to meteorology, and to promote the establishment and maintenance of meteorological centres charged with the provision of meteorological and related services; (2) to promote the establishment and maintenance of systems for the rapid exchange of meteorological and related information; (3) to promote standardization of meteorological and related observations and ensure the uniform publication of observations and statistics; (4) to further the application of meteorology to aviation, shipping, water problems, agriculture and other human activities; (5) to promote activities in operational hydrology and to further close co-operation between meteorological and hydrological services; and (6) to encourage research and training in meteorology and, as appropriate, to assist in co-ordinating the international aspects of such research and training.

Organization. WMO has 179 member states and six member territories responsible for the operation of their own meteorological services. Congress, which is its supreme body, meets every four years to approve policy, programme and budget, and adopt regulations. The Executive Council meets at least once a year to prepare studies and recommendations for Congress, and supervises the implementation of Congress resolutions and regulations. It has 36 members, comprising the President and three Vice-Presidents, as well as the Presidents of the six Regional Associations (Africa, Asia, South America, North and Central America, South-West Pacific, Europe), whose task is to co-ordinate meteorological activity within their regions, and 26 members elected in their personal capacity. There are eight Technical Commissions composed of experts nominated by members of WMO, whose remit includes the following areas: basic systems, climatology, instruments and methods of observation, atmospheric sciences, aeronautical meteorology, agricultural meteorology, hydrology, oceanography and marine meteorology. A permanent Secretariat is maintained in Geneva. There are three regional offices for Africa, Asia and the Pacific, and North and Central America and the Caribbean. The budget for 2000–03 is 252·3m. Swiss francs.

Headquarters: 7 bis, avenue de la Paix, Case Postale 2300, CH-1211 Geneva 2, Switzerland.
Website: http://www.wmo.ch
e-mail: wmo@gateway.wmo.ch
Secretary-General: Prof. G. O. P. Obasi (Nigeria).

Publications. WMO Bulletin (quarterly); *WMO Annual Report.*

OTHER ORGANS RELATED TO THE UN

INTERNATIONAL ATOMIC ENERGY AGENCY (IAEA)

Origin. An intergovernmental agency, the IAEA was established in 1957 under the aegis of the UN and reports annually to the General Assembly. Its Statute was approved on 26 Oct. 1956 at a conference at UN Headquarters.

Functions. To accelerate and enlarge the contribution of atomic energy to peace, health and prosperity throughout the world; and to ensure that assistance provided by it or at its request or under its supervision or control is not used in such a way as to further any military purpose. In addition, under the terms of the Non-Proliferation Treaty, the Treaty of Tlatelolco, the Treaty of Rarotonga, the Pelindaba Treaty and the Bangkok Treaty: to verify states' obligation to prevent diversion of nuclear fissionable material from peaceful uses to nuclear weapons or other nuclear explosive devices.

Activities. The IAEA gives advice and technical assistance to developing countries on nuclear power development, nuclear safety, radioactive waste management, legal aspects of atomic energy use, and prospecting for and exploiting nuclear raw materials. In addition, it promotes the use of radiation and isotopes in agriculture, industry, medicine and hydrology through expert services, training courses and fellowships, grants of equipment and supplies, research contracts, scientific meetings and publications. During 2000 there were over 1,000 operational projects for technical co-operation. These activities involved 5,600 expert assignments while 2,263 persons received training abroad.

Safeguards are the technical means applied by the IAEA to verify that nuclear equipment or materials are used exclusively for peaceful purposes. IAEA safeguards cover more than 95% of civilian nuclear installations outside the five nuclear-weapon states (China, France, Russia, UK and USA). These five nuclear-weapon states have concluded agreements with the Agency which permit the application of IAEA safeguards to all their civil nuclear activities. Installations in non-nuclear-weapon states under safeguards or containing safeguarded material at 31 Dec. 2000 were 196 power reactors, 156 research reactors and critical assemblies, 13 conversion plants, 42 fuel fabrication plants, six reprocessing plants, 11 enrichment plants and 316 other installations. In 2000, 2,467 inspections were conducted under the safeguard agreements at 900 nuclear installations in 65 non-nuclear-weapon states. By Dec. 1999 a total of 224 safeguard agreements were in force with 140 states. A programme designed to prevent and combat illicit trafficking of nuclear weapons came into force in April 1996.

Organization. The Statute provides for an annual General Conference, a 35-member Board of Governors and a Secretariat headed by a Director-General. The IAEA had 135 member states in March 2003.

There are also research laboratories in Austria and Monaco. *The International Centre for Theoretical Physics* was established in Trieste, in 1964, and is operated jointly by UNESCO and the IAEA.

Headquarters: Vienna International Centre, PO Box 100, A-1400 Vienna, Austria.
Website: http://www.iaea.org/worldatom
Director-General: Dr Mohamed ElBaradei (Egypt).

Publications. Annual Report; IAEA Bulletin (quarterly); *IAEA Newsbriefs* (bi-monthly); *IAEA Yearbook; INIS Reference Series; Legal Series; Nuclear Fusion* (monthly); *Nuclear Safety Review* (annual); *INIS Atomindex* (CD-Rom); *Technical Directories; Technical Reports Series.*

WORLD TRADE ORGANIZATION (WTO)

Origin. The WTO is founded on the General Agreement on Tariffs and Trade (GATT), which entered into force on 1 Jan. 1948. Its 23 original signatories were members of a Preparatory Committee appointed by the UN Economic and Social Council to draft the charter for a proposed International Trade Organization. Since this charter was never ratified, the General Agreement remained the only international instrument laying down trade rules. In Dec. 1993 there were 111 contracting parties, and a further 22 countries applying GATT rules on a *de facto* basis. On 15 April 1994 trade ministers of 123 countries signed the Final Act of the GATT Uruguay Round of negotiations at Marrakesh, bringing the WTO into being on 1 Jan. 1995. As of Feb. 2003 the WTO had 145 members.

The object of the Act is the liberalization of world trade. By it, member countries undertake to apply fair trade rules covering commodities, services and intellectual property. It provides for the lowering of tariffs on industrial goods and tropical products; the abolition of import duties on a variety of items; the progressive abolition of quotas on garments and textiles; the gradual reduction of trade-distorting subsidies and import barriers; and agreements on intellectual property and trade in services. Members are required to accept the results of the Uruguay Round talks in their entirety, and subscribe to all the WTO's agreements and disciplines. There are no enforcement procedures, however; decisions are ultimately reached by consensus.

Functions. The WTO is the legal and institutional foundation of the multilateral trading system. Surveillance of national trade policies is an important part of its work. At the centre of this is the *Trade Policy Review Mechanism (TPRM)*, agreed by Ministers in 1994 (Article III of the Marrakesh Agreement). The TPRM was broadened in 1995 when the WTO came into being, to cover services trade and intellectual property. Its principal objective is to facilitate the smooth functioning of the multilateral trading system by enhancing the transparency of members' trade policies. All members are subject to review under the TPRM, which mandates that four members with the largest share of world trade (European Union, USA, Japan, Canada) be reviewed every two years; the next 16, every four years; and others every six, with a longer period able to be fixed for the least-developed members. Also, in 1994, flexibility of up to six months was introduced into the review cycles, and in 1996, it was agreed that every second review of each of the first four trading entities should be an interim review. Reviews are conducted by the Trade Policy Review Body (TPRB) on the basis of a policy statement by the member under review and a report by economists in the Secretariat's Trade Policy Review Division.

The *International Trade Centre* (since 1968 operated jointly with the United Nations through UNCTAD) was established by GATT in 1964 to provide information and training on export markets and marketing techniques, and thereby to assist the trade of developing countries. In 1984 the Centre became an executing agency of the UN Development Programme, responsible for carrying out UNDP-financed projects related to trade promotion.

Organization. A two-yearly ministerial meeting is the ultimate policy-making body. The 144-member General Council has some 30 subordinate councils and committees. The *Dispute Settlement Body* was set up to deal with disputes between countries. Appeals against its verdicts are heard by a seven-member *Appellate Body*. In 2003 it was composed of representatives of Egypt, the European Union, Japan, Brazil, Australia, USA and India. Dispute panels may be set up *ad hoc*, and objectors to their ruling may appeal to the Appellate Body whose decision is binding. Refusal to comply at this stage can result in the application of trade sanctions. Each appeal is heard by three of the Appellate Body members. Before cases are heard by dispute panels, there is a 60-day consultation period. The previous GATT Secretariat now serves the WTO, which has no resources of its own other than its operating budget. The budget for 2002 was 143,129,850 Swiss francs.

Headquarters: Centre William Rappard, 154 rue de Lausanne, CH-1211 Geneva 21, Switzerland.
Website: http://www.wto.org
e-mail: enquiries@wto.org
Director-General: Supachai Panitchpakdi (Thailand).

Publications. Annual Report; International Trade: Trends and Statistics (annual); *WTO Focus* (10 a year).

Further Reading

Croome, J., *Reshaping the World Trading System.* WTO, 1996
Preeg, E., *Traders in a Brave New World.* Chicago Univ. Press, 1996

WORLD TOURISM ORGANIZATION (WTO)

Origin. Established in 1925 in The Hague as the International Congress of Official Tourist Traffic Associations. Renamed the International Union for Official Tourism Organizations after the Second World War when it moved to Geneva, it was renamed the World Tourism Organization in 1975 and moved its headquarters to Madrid the following year.

The World Tourism Organization became an executing agency of the United Nations Development Programme in 1976 and in 1977 a formal co-operation agreement was signed with the UN itself.

Aims. The World Tourism Organization exists to help nations throughout the world maximize the positive impacts of tourism, such as job creation, new infrastructure and foreign exchange earnings, while at the same time minimizing negative environmental or social impacts.

Membership. The World Tourism Organization has three categories of membership: Full membership which is open to all sovereign states; associate membership which is open to all territories not responsible for their external relations; and affiliate membership which comprises a wide range of organizations and companies working either directly in travel and tourism or in related sectors. In 2003 the World Tourism Organization had 140 full members, seven associate members and more than 350 affiliate members.

Organization. The General Assembly meets every two years to approve the budget and programme of work and to debate topics of vital importance to the tourism sector. The Executive Council is the governing board, responsible for ensuring that the organization carries out its work and keeps within its budget. The World Tourism Organization has six regional commissions—Africa, the Americas, East Asia and the Pacific, Europe, the Middle East and South Asia—which meet at least once a year. Specialized committees of World Tourism Organization members advise on management and programme content.

Headquarters: Capitán Haya 42, 28020 Madrid, Spain.
Website: http://www.world-tourism.org
Secretary-General: Francesco Frangialli (France).

Publications. Yearbook of Tourism Statistics (annual)*; Compendium of Tourism Statistics* (annual); *Travel and Tourism Barometer* (3 per year); *WTO News* (4 per year); *various others* (about 100 a year).

PREPARATORY COMMISSION FOR THE COMPREHENSIVE NUCLEAR-TEST-BAN TREATY ORGANIZATION (CTBTO)

The Preparatory Commission for the Comprehensive Nuclear-Test-Ban Treaty Organization (CTBTO Preparatory Commission) is an international organization established by the States Signatories to the Treaty on 19 Nov. 1996. It carries out the necessary preparations for the effective implementation of the Treaty, and prepares for the first session of the Conference of the States Parties to the Treaty.

The Preparatory Commission consists of a plenary body composed of all the States Signatories, and the Provisional Technical Secretariat (PTS). Upon signing the Treaty a state becomes a member of the Commission. Member states oversee the work of the Preparatory Commission and fund its activities. The Commission's main task is the establishment of the 337 facility International Monitoring System and the International Data Centre, and the development of operational manuals, including for on-site inspections. The Comprehensive Nuclear-Test-Ban Treaty prohibits any nuclear weapon test explosion or any other nuclear explosion anywhere in the world. As of March 2003, 166 States had signed the CTBT and instruments of ratification had been deposited by 98 States.

Headquarters: Vienna International Centre, PO Box 1200, A-1400 Vienna, Austria.
Website: http://www.ctbto.org
Executive Secretary: Wolfgang Herrmann (Germany).

ORGANIZATION FOR THE PROHIBITION OF CHEMICAL WEAPONS (OPCW)

The OPCW is responsible for the implementation of the Chemical Weapons Convention (CWC), which became effective on 29 April 1997. The principal organ of the OPCW is the Conference of the States Parties, composed of all the members of the Organization.

Given the relative simplicity of producing chemical warfare agents, the verification provisions of the CWC are far-reaching. The routine monitoring regime involves submission by States Parties of initial and annual declarations to the OPCW and initial visits and systematic inspections of declared weapons storage, production and destruction facilities. Verification is also applied to chemical industry facilities which produce, process or consume dual-use chemicals listed in the convention. The OPCW also when requested by any State Party conducts short-notice challenge inspections at any location under its jurisdiction or control of any other State Party.

The OPCW also co-ordinates assistance to any State Party that falls victim of chemical warfare as it fosters international co-operation in the peaceful application of chemistry.

By March 2003 a total of 151 countries were states parties to the Chemical Weapons Convention.

Headquarters: Johan de Wittlaan 32, 2517 JR The Hague, Netherlands.
Website: http://www.opcw.org
Director General: Rogelio Pfirter (Argentina).

INTERNATIONAL CRIMINAL COURT (ICC)

Origin. As far back as 1946 an international congress called for the adoption of an international criminal code prohibiting crimes against humanity and the prompt establishment of an international criminal court, but for more than 40 years little progress was made. In 1989 the end of the Cold War brought a dramatic increase in the number of UN peacekeeping operations and a world where the idea of establishing an International Criminal Court became more viable. The United Nations Conference of Plenipotentiaries on the Establishment of an International Criminal Court took place from 15 June–17 July 1998 in Rome, Italy.

Aims and Activities. The International Criminal Court is a permanent court for trying individuals who have been accused of committing genocide, war crimes and crimes against humanity, and is thus a successor to the *ad hoc* tribunals set up by the UN Security Council to try those responsible for atrocities in the former Yugoslavia and Rwanda. Ratification by 60 countries was required to bring the statute into effect. The court began operations on 1 July 2002 with 139 signatories and after ratification by 76 countries. By March 2003 the number of ratifications had increased to 89.

Judges. The International Criminal Court's first 18 judges were elected in Feb. 2003, with six serving for three years, six for six years and six for nine years. Every three years six new judges will be elected. The 18 judges elected in 2003, with the year in which their term of office is scheduled to end, were: René Blattmann (Bolivia, 2009); Maureen Harding Clark (Ireland, 2012); Fatoumata Dembele Diarra (Mali, 2012); Adrian Fulford (United Kingdom, 2012); Karl Hudson-Phillips (Trinidad and Tobago, 2012); Claude Jorda (France, 2009); Hans-Peter Kaul (Germany, 2006); Philippe Kirsch (Canada, 2009); Erkki Kourula (Finland, 2006); Akua Kuenyehia (Ghana, 2006); Elizabeth Odio Benito (Costa Rica, 2012); Georghios Pikis (Cyprus, 2009); Navanethem Pillay (South Africa, 2009); Mauro Politi (Italy, 2009); Tuiloma Neroni Slade (Samoa, 2006); Sang-hyun Song (South Korea, 2006); Sylvia Helena de Figueiredo Steiner (Brazil, 2012); Anita Usacka (Latvia, 2006).

Headquarters: Maanweg 174, 2516 AB The Hague, Netherlands.
Website: http://www.igc.org/icc

NORTH ATLANTIC TREATY ORGANIZATION (NATO)

Origin and History. On 4 April 1949 the foreign ministers of Belgium, Canada, Denmark, France, Iceland, Italy, Luxembourg, the Netherlands, Norway, Portugal, the UK and the USA signed the North Atlantic Treaty, establishing the *North Atlantic Alliance*. In 1952 Greece and Turkey acceded to the Treaty; in 1955 came the Federal Republic of Germany; in 1982 Spain; in 1999 the Czech Republic, Hungary and Poland, bringing the total to 19 member nations.

Functions. The Alliance was established as a defensive political and military alliance of independent countries in accordance with the terms of the UN Charter. It provides common security for its members through co-operation and consultation in political, military and economic as well as scientific and other non-military fields. The Alliance links the security of North America to that of Europe. NATO is the organization which enables the goals of the Alliance to be implemented.

Reform and Transformation of the Alliance. Following the demise of the Warsaw Pact in 1991, and the improved relations with Russia, NATO has undertaken a fundamental transformation of structures and policies to meet the new security challenges in Europe. Attention has focused in particular on the need to reinforce the political role of the Alliance.

An essential component of this transformation has been the establishment of close security links with the states of Central and Eastern Europe and those of the former USSR through the North Atlantic Co-operation Council (NACC), established in Dec. 1991 as an integral part of NATO's new Strategic Concept, which was adopted by heads of state and government at a summit in Rome earlier that year. The NACC was replaced by the Euro-Atlantic Partnership Council (EAPC) in 1997. The EAPC brings together NATO's 19 member countries and 27 partner countries (the 27 members of Partnership for Peace).

The Partnership for Peace (PfP) programme. The PfP builds on the momentum of co-operation created by the North Atlantic Co-operation Council. It was launched at the 1994 Brussels Summit and is expanding and intensifying political and military co-operation throughout Europe. In 1997 Allied Foreign and Defence Ministers launched a wide range of enhancement measures to PfP, which have strengthened it in political, security, military and institutional fields. Its core objectives are: the facilitation of transparency in national defence planning and budgeting processes; democratic control of defence forces; members' maintenance of capability and readiness to contribute to operations under the authority of the UN; development of co-operative military relations with NATO (joint planning, training and exercises) in order to strengthen participants' ability to undertake missions in the fields of peacekeeping, search and rescue, and humanitarian operations; development, over the longer term, of forces better able to operate with those of NATO member forces. NATO will consult with any active Partner which perceives a direct threat to its territorial integrity, political independence or security; and active participation in the Partnership is to play an important role in the process of NATO's expansion.

PfP has been a key factor in promoting the spirit of practical co-operation and commitment to the democratic principles which underpin the Alliance. One of the most tangible aspects of the PfP has been the holding of joint peacekeeping exercises. PfP exercises take place on a regular basis in both NATO and Partner countries. A large number of nationally sponsored exercises in the spirit of PfP have also been set up. In March 2003 NATO had 27 PfP partners: Albania, Armenia, Austria, Azerbaijan, Belarus, Bulgaria, Croatia, Estonia, Finland, Georgia, Ireland, Kazakhstan, Kyrgyzstan, Latvia, Lithuania, Macedonia, Moldova, Romania, Russia, Slovakia, Slovenia, Sweden, Switzerland, Tajikistan, Turkmenistan, Ukraine and Uzbekistan. Many of these countries have accepted the Alliance's invitation to send liaison officers to permanent facilities at NATO Headquarters in Brussels and to the Partnership Co-ordination Cell in Mons, Belgium, where the Supreme Headquarters Allied Powers Europe (SHAPE) is located.

Other key reforms undertaken include a reduced and more flexible force structure, development of increased co-ordination and co-operation with other international institutions (EU, UN, OSCE), development of the European Security and Defence Identity (ESDI), and the agreement to make NATO's assets and experience available to support international peace enforcement operations.

Efforts to strengthen the security and defence role of NATO's European Allies (the European Security and Defence Identity) were initially organized through the Western European Union (WEU). In 2000 the crisis management responsibilities of the WEU were increasingly assumed by the European Union (EU). A number of milestones can be identified in the development of ESDI between NATO, the WEU and the EU; the signing of the Maastricht Treaty in 1992, which allowed for the development of a common European security and defence policy; the endorsement of the concept of Combined Joint Task Forces in 1994 and of 'separable but not separate forces' that could be made available for European-led crisis response operations other than collective defence; the Berlin decisions in 1996, which included the building up of ESDI within the alliance; the EU Summits in Cologne and Helsinki in 1999, which led to important decisions on strengthening the ESDP and the development of an EU rapid reaction capability, and recent developments in NATO–EU defence co-operation, which resulted in the setting up of ad-hoc working groups in four specific areas: security arrangements, developing permanent arrangements for consultation and co-operation between the two organizations, defining modalities for EU access to NATO assets, and EU capability goals.

NATO's military capabilities and its adaptability to include forces of non-NATO countries were decisive factors in the Alliance's role in implementing the Bosnian Peace Agreement. Following the signing of the Agreement in Paris on 14 Dec. 1995, and on the basis of the UN Security Council's Resolution 1031, NATO commenced implementation of the military aspects of the accord through the NATO-led multi-national force, the Implementation Force (IFOR), under an operation code-named Joint Endeavour. Its task was to help the parties implement the peace accord to which they had freely agreed and create a secure environment for civil and economic reconstruction. IFOR was the largest-ever military operation undertaken by the Alliance. In Dec. 1996 it was replaced by the Stabilisation Force (SFOR), which is committed to contributing to peace and stability in Bosnia-Herzegovina.

In March 1999, following the collapse of negotiations with President Milošević of Yugoslavia on a settlement to the Kosovo crisis, NATO forces launched a series of attacks on Serb military targets. After an air campaign lasting 78 days these attacks were suspended and in accordance with the Military-Technical Agreement the full withdrawal of Yugoslav forces began. The deployment in Kosovo of a multinational security force, with substantial NATO participation, was synchronized with the Serb withdrawal before the end of June. The formal cessation of the air campaign was then announced by the Secretary General of NATO. Since June 1999 a NATO-led peacekeeping force (KFOR) has been deployed in Kosovo under a United Nations mandate.

Enlargement. In Dec. 1994 NATO foreign ministers initiated a study on enlargement, which was followed by intensified individual dialogues with interested partner countries and by an analysis of the relevant factors associated with the admission of new members. The conclusion was that, subject to agreed criteria, the accession of new members would enhance security and extend stability throughout the Euro-Atlantic area.

At the July 1997 meeting of Heads of State and Government in Madrid it was decided to invite three countries (Czech Republic, Hungary and Poland) to begin accession negotiations. By Dec. 1997 the three had signed accession agreements, and subsequently joined NATO in March 1999.

In April 1999 the Alliance adopted the Membership Action Plan (MAP) which is specifically designed to provide concrete advice and assistance to aspiring members with their own preparations for possible future membership. Nine partner countries are involved in this initiative: Albania, Bulgaria, Estonia, Latvia, Lithuania, Romania, Slovakia, Slovenia and the Former Yugoslavian Republic of Macedonia. At the Prague Summit in Nov. 2002 Bulgaria, Estonia, Latvia, Lithuania, Romania, Slovakia and Slovenia were invited to accession talks with NATO. They are set to join NATO officially in 2004.

On 27 May 1997, in Paris, NATO and Russia signed the Founding Act on Mutual Relations, Co-operation and Security, committing them to build together a lasting peace in the Euro-Atlantic area, and establishing a new forum for consultations and co-operation called the NATO-Russia Permanent Joint Council. NATO-Russia co-operation has since developed and a new level of partnership is being explored.

At the meeting in Sintra, Portugal, on 29 May 1997, a NATO-Ukraine charter was drawn up and initialled, to be signed in Madrid the following July. At the same time, Foreign Ministers agreed to enhance their dialogue, begun in 1995, with six countries of the Mediterranean (Egypt, Israel, Jordan, Mauritania, Morocco, Tunisia), and a new committee, the Mediterranean Co-operation Group was established to take the Mediterranean Dialogue forward. Algeria joined the Mediterranean Dialogue in March 2000.

On 12 Sept. 2001, following the attacks on New York and Washington on 11 Sept., for the first time in its history, NATO invoked articles of the Washington Treaty, declaring it considered the attack on the USA as an attack against all members of the Alliance. Actions were subsequently taken by NATO and by individual member countries in support of the US-led campaign against terrorism, in response to requests made by the USA.

Organization. The North Atlantic Council (NAC) is the highest decision-making body and forum for consultation within the Atlantic Alliance. It is composed of Permanent Representatives of all 19 member countries meeting together at least once a week. The NAC also meets at higher levels involving foreign ministers or heads of state or government, but it has the same authority and powers of decision-making, and its decisions have the same status and validity at whatever level it meets. All decisions are taken on the basis of consensus, reflecting the collective will of all member governments. The NAC is the only body within the Atlantic Alliance which derives its authority explicitly from the North Atlantic Treaty. The NAC has responsibility under the Treaty for setting up subsidiary bodies. Committees and planning groups have since been created to support the work of the NAC or to assume responsibility in specific fields such as defence planning, nuclear planning and military matters.

The *Military Committee* is responsible for making recommendations to the Council and the Defence Planning Committee on military matters and for supplying guidance to the Allied Commanders. Composed of the Chiefs-of-Staff of member countries (Iceland, which has no military forces, may be represented by a civilian), the Committee is assisted by an International Military Staff. It meets at Chiefs-of-Staff level at least twice a year but remains in permanent session at the level of national military representatives. The area covered by the North Atlantic Treaty is divided into two commands: European and the Atlantic.

Finance. The co-ordination of military plans and defence expenditures rests on detailed and comparative analysis of the capabilities of member countries. In 1997 the cost of enlargement sparked a potentially damaging dispute between the USA and European members of the Alliance following Pentagon estimates that the cost would be in the region of US$27,000m.–35,000m. over a 12-year period. Later assessments, taking into account the fact that Britain, France and Germany are already engaged in improving and increasing the mobility of their rapid-reaction or crisis forces, reduced the estimate to current members to US$1,300m. over ten years, with the cost of improved military capability in line with NATO standards in new member countries being the responsibility of new members.

Under the terms of the Partnership for Peace strategy, partner countries undertake to make available the necessary personnel, assets, facilities and capabilities to participate in the programme, and share the financial cost of any military exercises in which they participate.

Headquarters: NATO, 1110 Brussels, Belgium.
Website: http://www.nato.int
Secretary General: George Robertson (UK).

Publications. NATO Handbook; NATO Review; Extending Security; Reader's Guide to the Washington Summit; Nato Topics; NATO Update; NATO 2000; Fact Sheets.

Further Reading

Carr, F. and Infantis, K., *NATO in the New European Order.* London, 1996
Cook, D., *The Forging of an Alliance.* London, 1989
Heller, F. H. and Gillingham, J. R. (eds.) *NATO: the Founding of the Atlantic Alliance and the Integration of Europe.* London, 1992
Smith, J. (ed.) *The Origins of NATO.* Exeter Univ. Press, 1990
Williams, P., *North Atlantic Treaty Organization* [Bibliography]. Oxford and New Brunswick (NJ), 1994
Yost, David S., *NATO Transformed: The Alliance's New Roles in International Security.* United States Institute for Peace, Washington, D.C., 1999

BANK FOR INTERNATIONAL SETTLEMENTS (BIS)

Origin. Founded on 17 May 1930, the Bank for International Settlements fosters international monetary and financial co-operation and serves as a bank for central banks.

Aims. The BIS fulfils its mandate by acting as: a forum to promote discussion and facilitate decision-making processes among central banks and within the international financial community; a centre for economic and monetary research; a prime counterparty for central banks in their financial transactions; and an agent or trustee in connection with international financial operations.

Finance. Around 130 central banks and international financial institutions place deposits with the BIS. At 31 March 2002 the total of currency deposits placed with the BIS amounted to about US$154bn., representing around 7·6% of world foreign exchange reserves.

Organization and Membership. There are 50 member central banks. These are the central banks or monetary authorities of Argentina, Australia, Austria, Belgium, Bosnia-Herzegovina, Brazil, Bulgaria, Canada, China, Croatia, the Czech Republic, Denmark, Estonia, Finland, France, Germany, Greece, Hong Kong, Hungary, Iceland, India, Ireland, Italy, Japan, South Korea, Latvia, Lithuania, Macedonia, Malaysia, Mexico, the Netherlands, Norway, Poland, Portugal, Romania, Russia, Saudi Arabia, Serbia and Montenegro, Singapore, Slovakia, Slovenia, South Africa, Spain, Sweden, Switzerland, Thailand, Turkey, UK and USA, as well as the European Central Bank.

The BIS is administered by a Board of Directors, which is comprised of the governors of the central banks of Belgium, France, Germany, Italy and the UK and the Chairman of the Board of Governors of the US Federal Reserve System as *ex officio* members, each of whom appoints another member of the same nationality. The Statutes also provide for the election to the Board of not more than nine Governors of other member central banks. The Governors of the central banks of Canada, Japan, the Netherlands, Sweden and Switzerland are currently elected members of the Board.

Headquarters: Centralbahnplatz 2, CH-4002 Basle, Switzerland.
Website: http://www.bis.org
Chairman: Nout Wellink (Netherlands).
Representative Office for Asia and the Pacific: 8th Floor, Citibank Tower, 3 Garden Road, Central, Hong Kong SAR, People's Republic of China.

Further Reading

Deane, M. and Pringle, R., *The Central Banks.* London and New York, 1995
Fleming's Who's Who in Central Banking. London, 1997
Goodhart, C. A. E., *The Central Bank and the Financial System.* London, 1995

ORGANISATION FOR ECONOMIC CO-OPERATION AND DEVELOPMENT (OECD)

Origin. Founded in 1961 to replace the Organisation for European Economic Co-operation (OEEC), which was linked to the Marshall Plan and was established in 1948. The change of title marks the Organisation's altered status and functions: with the accession of Canada and USA as full members, it ceased to be a purely European body, and at the same time added development aid to the list of its priorities. The aims of the organization are to promote policies designed to achieve the highest sustainable economic growth and employment and a rising standard of living in member countries, while maintaining financial stability, and thus to contribute to the development of the world economy; to contribute to sound economic expansion in member as well as non-member countries in the process of economic development; and to contribute to the expansion of world trade on a multilateral, non-discriminatory basis in accordance with international obligations.

Members. Australia, Austria, Belgium, Canada, Czech Republic, Denmark, Finland, France, Germany, Greece, Hungary, Iceland, Ireland, Italy, Japan, South Korea, Luxembourg, Mexico, Netherlands, New Zealand, Norway, Poland, Portugal, Slovakia, Spain, Sweden, Switzerland, Turkey, UK and USA. Slovakia is the OECD's newest member, joining in Dec. 2000.

Activities. The OECD's main fields of programming are: economic policy; statistics; energy; development co-operation; sustainable development; public management; international trade; financial, fiscal and enterprise affairs; food, agriculture and fisheries; territorial development; environment; science, technology and industry; biotechnology and biodiversity; electronic commerce; initiatives to fight corruption; regulatory reform; ageing society; education, employment, labour and social affairs. Some short-term priority projects in 2003–04 include corporate governance, follow-up to the Doha development agenda, terrorism and risk.

Relations with non-member countries. Through its *Centre for Co-operation with Non-Members (CCNM)* the OECD maintains co-operative relations with a wide range of transition and emerging market economies covering topics of mutual interest. OECD member country officials and experts engage their non-member counterparts in policy dialogue and conduct peer assessments while sharing each other's rich and varied policy experiences. The year 2001 saw a major restructuring of the activities of the CNNM, grouping its work around Global Forums in eight policy areas where the OECD has particular expertise and where global dialogue can have an important impact on policy-making. The programmes for regions and countries were also reorganized. This strengthened the focus on key areas of institutional and policy reform to ensure that the benefits of globalization are fully shared worldwide. The Global Forums aim to achieve sustained results and to develop stable active networks of policy-makers in OECD member and non-member economies in eight key areas: sustainable development, the knowledge economy, governance, trade, agriculture, taxation, international investment and competition. The regional and country programmes provide for more targeted co-operation with non-members in three areas: Europe and Central Asia; Asia; and South America. There is a general programme for each region, as well as a specific programme for a particular country (Russia, China and Brazil). There are also sub-regional programmes for South Eastern Europe and the Baltic region.

Relations with developing countries. The OECD's Development Assistance Committee (DAC) is the principal body through which the Organisation deals with issues related to co-operation with developing countries. OECD member countries are major aid donors, accounting for more than 95% of total official development assistance (ODA), which amounted to US$53·7bn. worldwide in 2000. Much of the Organisation's development work is focused on how to spend and invest this aid in the most effective manner, so as to reduce poverty and ensure sustainable development in developing countries. Major new developments in 2001 included a milestone agreement on untying aid and the adoption of new guidelines on poverty reduction, conflict prevention, sustainable development and capacity building for trade. In addition, the Development Centre carries out comparative research and policy dialogue to help promote a better understanding in the OECD of the economic and social problems of developing countries and to transfer to them the knowledge, information and experience gained in the development process. The Sahel and West Africa Club (formerly the Club du Sahel) is an informal forum for reflection and exchanging views with and about African countries and working to improve development aid. It creates and facilitates links between OECD member countries and West Africa and between the public and private sectors.

Relations with other international organizations. Under a protocol signed at the same time as the OECD Convention, the European Commission generally takes part in the work of the OECD. EFTA may also send representatives to attend OECD meetings. Formal relations exist with a number of other international organizations, including the ILO, FAO, IMF, IBRD, UNCTAD, IAEA and the Council of Europe.

Relations with civil society. A few non-governmental organizations have been granted consultative status enabling them to discuss subjects of common interest and be consulted in a particular field by the relevant OECD Committee or its officers, notably the Business and Industry Advisory Committee to the OECD (BIAC) and the Trade Union Advisory Committee (TUAC). Since 2000 the OECD has organized, annually, the OECD Forum, an international public conference, offering business, labour and civil society the opportunity to discuss key issues of the 21st century with government ministers and leaders of international organizations. What is unique about the OECD Forum is that it allows participants to shape the outcome of the annual meeting of the Council at Ministerial level.

Organization. The governing body of OECD is the Council, on which each member country is represented. It meets from time to time (usually once a year) at the level of government ministers, with the chairmanship at ministerial level being rotated among member governments. The Council also meets regularly at official level, when it comprises the Secretary-General (chairman) and the Permanent Representatives to OECD (ambassadors who head resident diplomatic missions). It is responsible for all questions of general policy and may establish subsidiary bodies as required to achieve the aims of the organization. Decisions and recommendations of the Council are adopted by agreement of all its members.

The Council is assisted by an Executive Committee which prepares its work and is also called upon to carry out specific tasks where necessary. Apart from its regular meetings, the Committee meets occasionally in special sessions attended by senior governments officials. The greater part of the work of the OECD is prepared and carried out by about 200 specialized bodies (Committees, Working Parties, etc). All members are normally represented on these bodies, except those of a restricted nature. Delegates are usually officials coming either from the capitals of member states or from the Permanent Delegations to the OECD. They are serviced by an International Secretariat headed by the OECD Secretary-General. Funding is by contributions from member states, based on a formula related to their size and economy.

Three other bodies are part of the OECD system: the International Energy Agency (IEA), the Nuclear Energy Agency (NEA) and the Centre for Educational Research and Innovation (CERI).

Headquarters: 2 rue André Pascal, 75775 Paris Cedex 16, France.
Website: http://www.oecd.org
Secretary-General: Donald J. Johnston (Canada).
Deputy Secretaries-General: Richard E. Hecklinger (USA), Seiichi Kondo (Japan), Berglind Asgeirsdottir (Iceland), Herwig Schogl (Germany).

Publications. *OECD Policy Briefs* (10 a year); *Environmental Performance Reviews* (by country); *The Agricultural Outlook* (annual); *Energy Balances* (quarterly); *Financial Market Trends* (3 a year); *Foreign Trade Statistics* (monthly); *Main Developments in Trade* (annual); *Main Economic Indicators* (monthly); *OECD Economic Outlook* (2 a year); *OECD Economic Surveys* (every 18 months, by country); *OECD Employment Outlook* (annual); *Oil, Gas, Coal and Electricity Statistics* (quarterly statistics); *Quarterly Labour Force Statistics; Education at a Glance, OECD Indicators.* For a full list of OECD publications, visit the website: http://www.oecd.org/bookshop/

Further Reading

Blair, D. J., *Trade Negotiations in the OECD: Structures, Institutions and States*. London, 1993
international organizations

EUROPEAN UNION (EU)

Origin. The Union is founded on the existing European communities set up by the Treaties of Paris (1951) and Rome (1957), supplemented by revisions, the Single European Act in 1986, the Maastricht Treaty on European Union in 1992, the Treaty of Amsterdam in 1997 and the draft Treaty of Nice in 2000.

Members. (15). As at April 2003: Austria, Belgium, Denmark, Finland, France, Germany, Greece, Republic of Ireland, Italy, Luxembourg, the Netherlands, Portugal, Spain, Sweden and the UK.

History. On 19 Sept. 1946, in Zrich, Winston Churchill called for a 'united states of Europe', but neither he nor his successor pressed for British involvement. Two years later, the Congress of Europe (the meeting in The Hague of nearly 1,000 Europeans from 26 countries calling for a united Europe) resulted in the birth in 1949 of the Council of Europe, a European assembly of nations whose aim (Art. 1 of the Statute) was: 'to achieve a greater unity between its members for the purpose of safeguarding and realizing the ideals and principles which are their common heritage'.

On 18 April 1951, subsequent to a proposal by the French foreign minister Robert Schuman (Schuman Declaration), Belgium, France, the Federal Republic of Germany, Italy, Luxembourg and the Netherlands signed the Treaty of Paris establishing the *European Coal and Steel Community (ECSC)*. The treaty provided for the pooling of coal and steel production and was regarded as a first step towards a united Europe. Encouraged by the success of the ECSC, plans were laid down for the establishment of two more communities. *The European Economic Community (EEC)* and *the European Atomic Energy Community (EAEC or Euratom)* were subsequently created under separate treaties signed in Rome on 25 March 1957. The treaties provided for the establishment by stages of a common market with a customs union at its core, the approximation of economic policies, and the promotion of growth in the nuclear industries for peaceful purposes.

To this end, Euratom was awarded monopoly powers of acquisition of fissile materials for civil purposes (it is not concerned with the military uses of nuclear power). Subsequently, the various powers of the three communities (ECSC, EAEC, EEC, sometimes referred to collectively as the European Community or EC) were transferred by a treaty signed in Brussels in 1965 to a single Council and single Commission of the European Communities, today the core of the EU. The Commission is advised on matters relating to EAEC by a Scientific and Technical Committee.

Enlargement. On 30 June 1970 membership negotiations began between the European Community and the UK, Denmark, Ireland and Norway. On 22 Jan. 1972 all four countries signed a Treaty of Accession, and with the exception of Norway which later rejected membership in a referendum in Nov. that year, the UK, Denmark and Ireland became full members on 1 Jan. 1973 (though Greenland exercised its autonomy under the Danish Crown to secede in 1985). Greece joined on 1 Jan. 1981; Spain and Portugal on 1 Jan. 1986. The former German Democratic Republic entered into full membership on reunification with Federal Germany in Oct. 1990, and following referenda in favour, Austria, Finland and Sweden became members on 1 Jan. 1995. In a referendum in Nov. 1994 Norway again rejected membership.

Single European Act. The enlarging of the Community resulted in renewed efforts to promote European integration, culminating in the signing in Dec. 1985 of the Single European Act. The SEA represented the first major revision of the Treaties of Rome and provided for greater involvement of the European Parliament in the decision-making process.

Maastricht Treaty on European Union. Further amendments were agreed at the Maastricht Summit of Dec. 1991 in the draft Treaty on European Union whereby moves to a common currency were agreed subject to specific conditions (including an opt-out clause for the UK) and the social dimension was recognized in a protocol (not applicable to the UK) allowing member states to use EC institutions for this purpose. Ratification by member states of the Maastricht Treaty proved unexpectedly controversial. In June 1992 the Danish electorate in a referendum voted against it, then reversed the decision in a second referendum in May 1993. Ratification was finally completed during 1993, with the UK ratifying on 2 Aug., and the European Union (EU) officially came into being on 1 Nov. that year.

Further Enlargement. On 16 July 1997 Jacques Santer presented *Agenda 2000*, the European Commission's detailed strategy for consolidating the Union through enlargement as far eastwards as Ukraine, Belarus and Moldova. It recommended the early start of accession negotiations with Hungary, Poland, Estonia, the Czech Republic and Slovenia under the provision of Article O of the Maastricht Treaty whereby 'any European State may apply to become a member of the Union' (subject to the Copenhagen Criteria set by the European Council at its summit in 1993).

In 2002 it was announced that ten countries will be ready to join in 2004, namely: Poland, Hungary, the Czech Republic, Slovakia, Lithuania, Latvia, Estonia, Slovenia, Cyprus and Malta. Subject to the results of referenda likely to be held during 2003 they are all set to become members on 1 May 2004. A target date of 2007 is proposed for Bulgaria and Romania to join. Turkey is also hoping to become a member, but a decision on whether to start talks on a bid for membership by Turkey will not take place until Dec. 2004. Following a referendum in Ireland in Oct. 2002, all 15 EU member countries have now ratified the 2000 Nice Treaty on EU expansion. An application to join the EU has also been received by Turkey, and the Prince of Liechtenstein has made it known that he wishes his government to apply.

Objectives. The ultimate goal of the EU is 'an ever closer union among the peoples of Europe, in which decisions are taken as closely as possible to the citizen'. Priorities include the implementation of the Treaty of Amsterdam (new rights for citizens, freedom of movement, strengthening the institutions of the EU, employment); economic and monetary union; further expansion of the scope of the Communities; implementation of a common foreign and security policy; and development in the fields of justice and home affairs. At the European Summit held in Nice, France in Dec. 2000 it was agreed to concentrate on four main areas—the charter of fundamental rights, simplifying EU treaties, clarifying the balance of power between the EU and member states, and the possibility of a second chamber of parliament. In Dec. 2001 the Laeken European Conference adopted the Declaration on the Future of the European Union, committing the EU to becoming more democratic, transparent and effective, opening the way to a constitution for the people of Europe. The European Council decided to set up a convention, comprising 105 members, under the chairmanship of former French president Valéry Giscard d'Estaing, to draft an EU constitution.

Structure. The institutional arrangements of the EU provide for an independent policy-making executive with powers of proposal (European Commission), various consultative and advisory bodies, and a decision-making body drawn from the Governments (Council of Ministers).

Defence. In Nov. 2000 European Union defence ministers agreed to commit personnel and equipment to a rapid reaction force that could be deployed in tackling crises in an area up to 4,000 km from Brussels at short notice. The European Union's first ever peacekeeping force (EUFOR) officially started work in Macedonia on 1 April 2003. The rapid reaction force will ultimately have a pool of approximately 100,000 personnel, 400 combat aircraft and 100 warships, but a maximum of 60,000 personnel will be serving at any one time to allow for the rotation of forces in the event of a lengthy operation. Although final numbers have not yet been agreed, Britain, France and Germany are likely to provide the largest number of troops, at around 12,000 to 13,000 each out of the total of 60,000. Denmark has decided to opt out.

The European Union Institute for Security Studies (EUISS) was created by a Council Joint Action in July 2001 with the status of an autonomous agency. It contributes to the development of the Common Foreign and Security Policy (CFSP) through research and debate on major security and defence issues.

Major Policy Areas. The major policy areas of the EU were laid down in the Treaty of Rome of 25 March 1957 which guaranteed certain rights to the citizens of all member states, including the outlawing of economic discrimination by nationality, and equal pay for equal work as between men and women.

The single internal market. The single internal market represents the core of the process of economic integration and is characterized by the removal of obstacles to the four fundamental freedoms of movement for persons, goods, capital and services. Under the Treaty, individuals or companies from one member state may establish themselves in another country (for the purposes of economic activity) or sell goods or services there on the same basis as nationals of that country. With a few exceptions, restrictions on the movement of capital have also been ended. Under the Single European Act the member states bound themselves to achieve the suppression of all barriers to free movement of persons, goods and services by 31 Dec. 1992.

The *Schengen Accord* abolished border controls on persons and goods between certain EU states plus Norway and Iceland. It came into effect on 26 March 1995 and was signed by Austria, Belgium, Denmark, Finland, France, Germany, Greece, Iceland, Italy, Luxembourg, Netherlands, Norway, Portugal, Spain and Sweden.

Economic and Monetary Union. The establishment of the single market provided for the next phase of integration: economic and monetary union. The *European Monetary System (EMS)* was founded in March 1979 to control inflation, protect European trade from international disturbances and ultimately promote convergence between the European economies. At its heart was the *Exchange Rate Mechanism (ERM)*. The ERM is run by the finance ministries and central banks of the EU countries on a day-to-day basis; monthly reviews are carried out by the EU Monetary Committee (finance ministries) and the EU Committee of Central Bankers. Sweden is not in the ERM; the UK suspended its membership on 17 Sept. 1992. In Jan. 1995 Austria joined the ERM. Finland followed in 1996, and in Nov. that year the Italian lira, which had been temporarily suspended, was re-admitted.

With the introduction of the euro, exchange rates have been fixed for all member countries. The member countries are Austria, Belgium, Finland, France, Germany, Greece, Ireland, Italy, Luxembourg, Netherlands, Portugal and Spain. The euro became legal tender from 1 Jan. 2002 across the region. National currencies ran in parallel for certain periods depending on the country but were phased out by the end of Feb. 2002.

European Monetary Union (EMU). The single European currency with 11 member states came into operation in Jan. 1999 although it was not until 2002 that the currency came into general circulation. Greece subsequently joined in Jan. 2001. The euro-zone is the world's second largest economy after the USA in terms of output and the largest in terms of trade. EMU currency consists of the euro of 100 cents, with coins of 1, 2, 5, 10, 20 and 50 cents and 1 and 2 euros and notes of 5, 10, 20, 50, 100, 200 and 500 euros. EU member countries not in EMU will select a central rate for their currency in consultation with members of the euro bloc and the European Central Bank. The rate is set according to an assessment of each country's chances of joining the euro zone.

An agreement on the legal status of the euro and currency discipline, the Stability and Growth Pact, was reached by all member states at the Dublin summit on 13 Dec. 1996. Financial penalties will be applied to member states running a GDP deficit (negative growth) of up to 0·75%. If GDP falls between 0·75% and 2%, EU finance ministers will have discretion as to whether to apply penalties. Members running an excessive deficit will be automatically exempt from penalties in the event of a natural disaster or if the fall in GDP is at least 2% over one year.

Environment. The Single European Act made the protection of the environment an integral part of economic and social policies. Community policy aims at preventing pollution (the Prevention Principle), rectifying pollution at source, and imposing the costs of prevention or rectification upon the polluters themselves (the Polluter Pays Principle). The European Environment Agency (see below) was established to ensure that policy was based on reliable scientific data.

In March 2002 the 15 European Union member states agreed to be bound by the 1997 Kyoto Protocol to the United Nations Framework on Climate Change, which commits the EU to reduce its emissions of greenhouse gases by 8% from the 1990 levels between 2008 and 2012.

The Common Agricultural Policy (CAP). The objectives set out in the Treaty are to increase agricultural productivity, to ensure a fair standard of living for the agricultural community, to stabilize markets, to assure supplies, and to ensure reasonable consumer prices. In Dec. 1960 the Council laid down the fundamental principles on which the CAP is based: a single market, which calls for common prices, stable currency parities and the harmonizing of health and veterinary legislation; Community preference, which protects the single Community market from imports; common financing, through the European Agricultural Guidance and Guarantee Fund (EAGGF), which seeks to improve agriculture through its Guidance section, and to stabilize markets against world price fluctuations through market intervention, with levies and refunds on exports.

Following the disappearance of stable currency parities, artificial currency levels have been applied in the CAP. This factor, together with over-production owing to high producer prices, meant that the CAP consumed about two-thirds of the Community budget. In May 1992 it was agreed to reform CAP and to control over-production by reducing the price supports to farmers by 29% for cereals, 15% for beef and 5% for dairy products. In June 1995 the guaranteed intervention price for beef was decreased by 5%. In July 1996 agriculture ministers agreed a reduction in the set-aside rate for cereals from 10% to 5%. Fruit and vegetable production subsidies were fixed at no more than 4% of the value of total marketed production, rising to 4·5% in 1999. Compensatory grants are made available to farmers who remove land from production or take early retirement. The CAP reform aims to make the agricultural sector more responsive to supply and demand. Farm spending currently absorbs 46% of the EU budget but accounts for only 1·8% of Europe's GDP.

Customs Union and External Trade Relations. Goods or services originating in one member state have free circulation within the EU, which implies common arrangements for trade with the rest of the world. Member states can no longer make bilateral trade agreements with third countries; this power has been ceded to the EU. The Customs Union was achieved in July 1968.

In Oct. 1991 a treaty forming the *European Economic Area (EEA)* was approved by the member states of the then EC and European Free Trade Association (EFTA). Association agreements which could lead to accession or customs union have been made with Cyprus, Estonia, Latvia, Lithuania, Israel, Malta, Morocco and Turkey. The customs union with Turkey came into force on 1 Jan. 1996. Commercial, industrial, technical and financial aid agreements have been made with Algeria, Egypt, Jordan, Lebanon, Morocco, Russia, Serbia and Montenegro, Syria and Tunisia. In 1976 Canada signed a framework agreement for co-operation in industrial trade, science and natural resources, and a transatlantic pact was signed with the USA in Dec. 1995. Co-operation agreements also exist with a number of Latin American countries and groupings, and with Arab and Asian countries, and an economic and commercial agreement has been signed with the Association of South East Asian Nations (ASEAN). Partnership and co-operation agreements were signed with Ukraine in June 1994, Kazakhstan in Jan. 1995, Kyrgyzstan in Feb. 1995 and with Uzbekistan in June 1996. In the Development Aid sector, the EU has an agreement (the Cotonou Agreement, signed in 2000, the successor of the Lomé Convention, originally signed in 1975 but renewed and enlarged in 1979, 1984 and 1989) with some 60 African, Caribbean and Pacific (ACP) countries which removes customs duties without reciprocal arrangements for most of their imports to the Community.

The application of common duties has been conducted mainly within the framework of the *General Agreement on Tariffs and Trade (GATT),* which was succeeded in 1995 by the establishment of the World Trade Organization.

Fisheries. The Common Fisheries Policy (CFP) came into effect in Jan. 1983, according to which all EU fishermen have equal access to the waters of member countries (a zone extending up to 200 nautical miles from the shore around all its coastlines), with the total allowable catch for each species being set and shared out between member countries according to pre-established quotas, with in some cases 'historic rights' applying, as well as special rules to conserve stock, preserve marine biodiversity, and the sustainable pursuit of fishing.

A number of agreements are in place with other countries (Canada, Norway, USA and some African countries) allowing reciprocal fishing rights. When Greenland withdrew from the Community in 1985 EU boats retained their fishing rights subject to quotas and limits, which were revised in 1995 owing to concern about overfishing of Greenland halibut. Agreements were initialled with Estonia, Latvia, Lithuania and Argentina in 1992.

Transport. Under the Maastricht Treaty, the Community must contribute to the establishment and development of trans-European networks in the areas of transport, telecommunications and energy infrastructures.

Competition. The Competition (anti-trust) law of the EU is based on two principles: that businesses should not seek to nullify the creation of the common market by the erection of artificial national (or other) barriers to the free movement of goods; and against the abuse of dominant positions in any market. These two principles have led among other things to the outlawing of prohibitions on exports to other member states, of price-fixing agreements and of refusal to supply; and to the refusal by the Commission to allow mergers or takeovers by dominant undertakings in specific cases. Increasingly heavy fines are imposed on offenders.

A number of structural funds have been established in an attempt to counter specific problems within and across the Community. These include:

European Social Fund. Provides resources with the aim of combating long-term unemployment and facilitating integration into the labour market of young people and the socially disadvantaged. The 2002 budget included an allocation of around €9,402m. for the Fund's commitments.

European Regional Development Fund. Intended to compensate for the unequal rate of development among different regions of the EU by encouraging investment and improving infrastructure in 'problem regions'.

Finances. The general budget of the EU covers all EEC and Euratom expenditure, and the administrative expenditure of the ECSC.

EU revenue in €1m.:

	Financial year 2001
Agricultural duties	2,155·7
Customs duties	12,813·6
VAT	31,250·0
GNP resource	34,878·8
Miscellaneous revenue	13,492·5
Total	94,210·6

Expenditure for the financial year 2001 was €85,562·3m., of which the European Agricultural Guidance and Guarantee Fund Guarantee Section accounted for €42,184·4m.

The resources of the Community (the levies and duties mentioned above, and up to a 1·4% VAT charge) have been surrendered to it by Treaty. The Budget is made by the Council and the Parliament acting jointly as the Budgetary Authority. The Parliament has control, within a certain margin, of non-obligatory expenditure (where the amount to be spent is not set out in the legislation concerned), and can also reject the Budget. Otherwise, the Council decides.

Official languages. Danish, Dutch, English, Finnish, French, German, Greek, Italian, Portuguese, Spanish and Swedish.
Website: http://www.europa.eu.int

EU INSTITUTIONS

EUROPEAN COMMISSION

The European Commission consists of 20 members appointed by the member states (one from each small country, two from each big one) to serve for five years. The Commission President is selected by a consensus of member state heads of government and serves a five-year term. The Commission acts as the EU executive body and as guardian of the Treaties. In this it has the right of initiative (putting proposals to the Council of Ministers for action) and of execution (once the Council has decided). It can take the other institutions or individual countries before the European Court of Justice should any of these fail to comply with European Law. Decisions on legislative proposals made by the Commission are taken in the Council of the European Union. Members of the Commission swear an oath of independence, distancing themselves from partisan influence from any source. The Commission operates through 36 Directorates-General and services.

At the European Summit held in Nice in Dec. 2000 it was decided that in 2005 Germany, France, the UK, Italy and Spain would lose their second commissioner. Each new member state will have one commissioner until there are 27 EU member countries. A permanent limit of fewer than 27 will then be set, with the seats being rotated among member states.

The current Commission took office in Sept. 1999. Members, their nationality and political affiliation (S-Socialist/Social Democrat; C-Christian Democrat/Conservative; L-Liberal; G-Green; Ind-Independent) in March 2003 were as follows.

President: Romano Prodi (Italy, S); responsible for monetary and institutional affairs, foreign policy and common security.

The commissioners are:

Vice-president: Neil Kinnock (UK, S); responsible for personnel and administrative EU reform.

Vice-president: Loyola de Palacio (Spain, C); responsible for transport, energy and relations with European parliament.

Agriculture, Rural Development and Fisheries: Franz Fischler (Austria, C).
Budget: Michaele Schreyer (Germany, G).
Competition: Mario Monti (Italy, Ind).
Development and Humanitarian Aid: Poul Nielson (Denmark, S).
Economic and Monetary Affairs: Pedro Solbes Mira (Spain, S).
Education and Culture: Viviane Reding (Luxembourg, C).
Employment and Social Affairs: Anna Diamantopoulou (Greece, S).
Enlargement: Günter Verheugen (Germany, S).
Enterprise and Information Society: Erkki Liikanen (Finland, S).
Environment: Margot Wallström (Sweden, S).
External Relations: Chris Patten (UK, C).
Health and Consumer Protection: David Byrne (Ireland, C).
Internal Market, Taxation and Customs Union: Frits Bolkestein (Netherlands, L)
Justice and Home Affairs: António Vitorino (Portugal, S).
Regional Policy: Michel Barnier (France, C).
Research: Philippe Busquin (Belgium, S).
Trade: Pascal Lamy (France, S).

Headquarters: 200 rue de la Loi/Wetstraat, B-1049 Brussels, Belgium.
Secretary-General: David O'Sullivan (Ireland).

COUNCIL OF THE EUROPEAN UNION (COUNCIL OF MINISTERS)

The Council of Ministers consists of ministers from the 15 national governments and is the only institution which directly represents the member states' national interests. It is the Union's principal decision-making body. Here, members legislate for the Union, set its political objectives, co-ordinate their national policies and resolve differences between themselves and other institutions. The presidency rotates every six months. Greece had the presidency during the first half of 2003, Italy has the presidency during the second half of 2003, Ireland will have it during the first half of 2004 and the Netherlands during the second half of 2004. Meetings are held in Brussels, except in April, June and Oct. when all meetings are in Luxembourg. Around 100 formal ministerial sessions are held each year. In 1999 the final adoption of some 200 legal acts took place.

Decisions are taken either by qualified majority vote or by unanimity. Since the adoption of the Single European Act, an increasing number of decisions are by majority vote, although some areas such as taxation and social security, immigration and border controls are reserved to unanimity. At the Nice Summit in Dec. 2000 agreement was reached that a further 39 articles of the EU's treaties would move to qualified majority voting. 27 votes are needed to veto a decision, and member states carry the following vote weightings: France, Germany, Italy and the UK, 10; Spain, 8; Belgium, Greece, the Netherlands and Portugal, 5; Austria and Sweden, 4; Denmark, Finland and the Republic of Ireland, 3; Luxembourg, 2. From the accession of the new EU member countries in May 2004 until the end of 2004 these will remain unchanged but the new members will have between 2 votes (in the case of Cyprus and Malta) and 8 (in the case of Poland). At the European Council meeting in Brussels in Oct. 2002 the allocation of vote weightings from 1 Jan. 2005 was agreed. The new allocation is to be: France, Germany, Italy and the UK, 29; Poland and Spain, 27; the Netherlands, 13; Belgium, the Czech Republic, Greece, Hungary and Portugal, 12; Austria and Sweden, 10; Denmark, Finland, the Republic of Ireland, Lithuania and Slovakia, 7; Cyprus, Estonia, Latvia, Luxembourg and Slovenia, 4; Malta 3. Each member state has a national delegation in Brussels known as the Permanent Representation, headed by Permanent Representatives, senior diplomats whose committee (Coreper) prepares ministerial sessions. Coreper meets weekly and its main task is to ensure that only the most difficult and sensitive issues are dealt with at ministerial level.

The Secretariat provides the practical infrastructure of the Council at all levels. The JHA (Co-operation in the fields of Justice and Home Affairs), established in the Maastricht Treaty, brings together the ministries of justice and the interior of the 15 member states. It permits dialogue and co-operation between the police, customs, immigration services and justice departments of the member states in order to combat problems relating to both civil and criminal matters. The CFSP (the Common Foreign and Security Policy), also established by the Maastricht Treaty, came into force on 1 Nov. 1993.

Legislation. The Community's legislative process starts with a proposal from the Commission (either at the suggestion of its services or in pursuit of its declared political aims) to the Council, or in the case of co-decision, to both the Council and the European Parliament. The Council generally seeks the views of the European Parliament on the proposal, and the Parliament adopts a formal Opinion after consideration of the matter by its specialist Committees. The Council may also (and in some cases is obliged to) consult the Economic and Social Committee which similarly delivers an opinion. When these opinions have been received, the Council will decide. Most decisions are taken on a majority basis, but will take account of reservations expressed by individual member states. The text eventually approved may differ substantially from the original Commission proposal.

Provisions of the Treaties and secondary legislation may be either directly applicable in member states or only applicable after member states have enacted their own implementing legislation. Community law, adopted by the Council (or by Parliament and the Council in the framework of the co-decision procedure) may take the following forms: (1) *Regulations*, which are of general application and binding in their entirety and directly applicable in all member states; (2) *Directives,* which are binding upon each member state as to the result to be achieved within a given time, but leave the national authority the choice of form and method of achieving this result; and (3) *Decisions*, which are binding in their entirety on their addressees. In addition the Council and Commission can issue recommendations and opinions which have no binding force.

Transparency. The Council is trying to make more of its work accessible to its citizens. Votes on legislative matters, as well as the explanations of these votes, are now automatically made public and Council documents can be released to the public upon request. Other attempts to improve transparency include briefings for journalists and the provision of background notes on subjects under discussion.

Headquarters: 175 rue de la Loi, B-1048 Brussels, Belgium.
Secretary-General and High Representative for the Common Foreign and Security Policy of the European Union: Javier Solana (Spain).
Website: http://www.consilium.eu.int; www.ue.eu.int
e-mail: public.info@consilium.eu.int

THE EUROPEAN COUNCIL

Since 1974 Heads of State or Government have met at least twice a year (in the capital of the member state currently exercising the presidency of the Council of European Union) in the form of the European Council or European Summit as it is commonly known. Its membership includes the President of the European Commission, and the President of the European Parliament is invited to make a presentation at the opening session. The European Council has become an increasingly important element of the Union, setting priorities, giving political direction, providing the impetus for its development and resolving contentious issues that prove too difficult for the Council of the European Union. It has become directly responsible for common policies within the fields of foreign and security policy, justice and home affairs. Though there was no provision made for its existence in the original Treaty of Rome, its position was later acknowledged and formalized in the Single European Act.

At the European Council's Barcelona Summit in March 2002 a series of key decisions were reached, notably: free choice of supplier for non-household users of electricity and gas as from 2004; go-ahead for Galileo, the EU reply to the US dominance of global satellite positioning technology; adoption of seven financial services directives before the end of 2002, with the goal of full integration of financial services markets by 2005; research and development spending to be raised to 3% of EU GDP by 2010 from current 1·9%; widespread availability of broadband technology by 2005; implementation in 2004 of 'Single Sky' Europe-wide air traffic control area to speed air travel; labour mobility to be improved by more flexible pension and healthcare arrangements; creation of more jobs through reform of tax and benefit systems and reduced incentives for early retirement; provision of childcare for 90% of children aged between three and school age by 2010; children to be taught at least two foreign languages 'from a very early age'; one internet-connected computer to be available for every 15 school pupils by end-2003; commitment to EU average development aid of 0·39% of gross national income by 2006, with goal of member states reaching UN target of 0·7% of GDP.

EUROPEAN PARLIAMENT

The European Parliament consists of 626 members, elected in all 15 member states for five-year terms on 10 and 13 June 1999. A proportional representation system was used in Great Britain for the first time.

All EU citizens may stand or vote in their adoptive country of residence. Germany returned 99 members, France, Italy and the UK 87 each, Spain 64, the Netherlands 31, Belgium, Greece and Portugal 25 each, Sweden 22, Austria 21, Denmark and Finland 16 each, Ireland 15 and Luxembourg 6. At the EU summit held in Nice, France in Dec. 2000 the parliamentary allocation of seats after the forthcoming expansion of the EU to include the 12 candidate countries was announced. Out of a total of 732 seats, Germany would still have 99, but France, Italy and the UK would have 72 each, Poland and Spain 50 each, Romania 33, the Netherlands 25, Belgium, Greece and Portugal 22 each, the Czech Republic and Hungary 20 each, Sweden 18, Austria and Bulgaria 17 each, Denmark, Finland and Slovakia 13 each, Ireland and Lithuania 12 each, Latvia 8, Slovenia 7, Cyprus, Estonia and Luxembourg 6 each, and Malta 5.

Political groupings. Following the 1999 elections to the European Parliament the European People's Party (EPP) had 233 seats, Party of European Socialists (PES) 180, European Liberal Democratic and Reformist Group (ELDR) 51, Greens/European Free Alliance (GR/EFA) 48, European Unitary Left (EUL) 42, Union for a Europe of Nations (UEN) 31, Europe of Democracies and Diversities (EDD) 16, Independents (I) 25.

The Parliament has a right to be consulted on a wide range of legislative proposals and forms one arm of the Community's Budgetary Authority. Under the Single

European Act, it gained greater authority in legislation through the 'concertation' procedure under which it can reject certain Council drafts in a second reading procedure. Under the Maastricht Treaty, it gained the right of 'co-decision' on legislation with the Council of Ministers on a restricted range of domestic matters. The President of the European Council must report to the Parliament on progress in the development of foreign and security policy. It also plays an important role in appointing the President and members of the Commission. It can hold individual commissioners to account and can pass a motion of censure on the entire Commission, a prospect that was realized in March 1999 when the Commission, including the President, Jacques Santer, was forced to resign following an investigation into mismanagement and corruption. Parliament's seat is in Strasbourg where the one-week plenary sessions are held each month. In the Chamber, members sit in political groups, not as national delegations. All the activities of the Parliament and its bodies are the responsibility of the Bureau, consisting of the President and 14 Vice-Presidents elected for a two-and-a-half year period.

Location: Brussels, but meets at least once a month in Strasbourg.
President: Pat Cox (Ireland; ELDR).

COURT OF JUSTICE OF THE EUROPEAN COMMUNITIES

The Court of Justice of the European Communities is composed of 15 judges and eight advocates-general. It is responsible for the adjudication of disputes arising out of the application of the treaties, and its findings are enforceable in all member countries. A Court of First Instance (est. 1989) handles certain categories of cases, including cases arising under the competition rules of the EC and cases brought by Community officials.

Address: Court of Justice of the European Communities, L-2925 Luxembourg.
President of the Court of Justice: Gil Carlos Rodríguez Iglesias (Spain).
President of the Court of First Instance: Bo Vesterdorf (Denmark).

EUROPEAN COURT OF AUDITORS

The European Court of Auditors was established by a treaty of 22 July 1975 which took effect on 1 June 1977. It consists of 15 members and was raised to the status of a full EU institution by the 1993 Maastricht Treaty. It audits the accounts and verifies the implementation of the budget of the EU.

Address: 12, rue Alcide De Gasperi, L-1615 Luxembourg.
President: Juan Manuel Fabra Vallés (Spain).

EUROPEAN OMBUDSMAN

The Ombudsman was inaugurated in 1995 and deals with complaints from citizens, companies and organizations concerning maladministration in the activities of the institutions and bodies of the European Union. The present incumbent is Nikiforos Diamandouros (Greece).

Address: 1 avenue du Président Robert Schuman, B.P. 403, F-67001 Strasbourg Cedex, France.
Website: http://www.euro-ombudsman.eu.int
e-mail: euro-ombudsman@europarl.eu.int

EUROPEAN INVESTMENT BANK (EIB)

The EIB is the financing institution of the European Union, created by the Treaty of Rome in 1958 as an autonomous body set up to finance capital investment furthering European integration. To this end, the Bank raises its resources on the world's capital markets where it mobilizes significant volumes of funds on favourable terms. It directs these funds towards capital projects promoting EU economic policies. Outside the Union the EIB implements the financial components of agreements concluded under European Union development aid and co-operation policies. The members of the EIB are the member states of the European Union, who have all subscribed to the Bank's capital. Its governing body is its Board of Governors consisting of the ministers designated by each of the member states, usually the finance ministers.

Address: 100 Bd Konrad Adenauer, L-2950 Luxembourg.
Website: http://www.eib.org
President and Chairman of the Board: Philippe Maystadt (Belgium).

EUROPEAN SYSTEM OF CENTRAL BANKS (ESCB)

The ESCB is composed of the European Central Bank (ECB) and 15 National Central Banks (NCBs). The NCBs of the member states not participating in the euro area are members with special status; while they are allowed to conduct their respective national monetary policies, they do not take part in decision-making regarding the single monetary policy for the euro area and the implementation of these policies. The Governing Council of the ECB makes a distinction between the ESCB and the 'Eurosystem' which is composed of the ECB and the 12 fully participating NCBs.

Members. The 12 fully participating National Central Banks are from: Austria, Belgium, Finland, France, Germany, Greece, Ireland, Italy, Luxembourg, Netherlands, Portugal and Spain. The three members with special status are: Denmark, Sweden and the United Kingdom.

Functions. The primary objective of the ESCB is to maintain price stability. Without prejudice to this, the ESCB supports general economic policies in the Community with a view to contributing to the achievement of the objectives of the Community. Tasks to be carried out include: i) defining and implementing the monetary policy of the Community; ii) conducting foreign exchange operations; iii) holding and managing the official foreign reserves of the participating member states; iv) promoting the smooth operation of payment systems; v) supporting the policies of the competent authorities relating to the prudential supervision of credit institutions and the stability of the financial system.

The ECB has the exclusive right to issue banknotes within the Community.

Organization. The ESCB is governed by the decision-making bodies of the ECB: the Governing Council and the Executive Board. The Governing Council is the supreme decision-making body and comprises all members of the Executive Board plus the governors of the NCBs forming the Eurosystem. The Executive Board comprises the president, vice-president and four other members, appointed by common accord of the heads of state and government of the participating member states. There is also a General Council which will exist while there remain members with special status.

Address: Kaiserstrasse 29, 60311 Frankfurt am Main, Germany.
President: Willem Frederik Duisenberg (Netherlands).

The Consultative Bodies There are two main consultative committees whose members are appointed in a personal capacity and are not bound by any mandatory instruction.

1. *Economic and Social Committee.* The 222-member committee is consulted by the Council of Ministers or by the European Commission, particularly with regard to agriculture, free movement of workers, harmonization of laws and transport. It is served by a permanent and independent General Secretariat, headed by a Secretary-General.

Secretary-General: Patrick Venturini (France).

2. *Committee of the Regions.* A new advisory body established by the Maastricht Treaty and consisting of 222 full members and an equal number of alternate members appointed by the Council for a four-year term. The Committee must be consulted on matters regarding education, culture, public health, trans-European networks, economic and social cohesion, and on any issue with regional implications.

President: Sir Albert Bore (United Kingdom).

STATISTICAL OFFICE OF THE EUROPEAN COMMUNITIES (EUROSTAT)

Eurostat's mission is to provide the EU with a high-quality statistical service. It receives statistical data collected according to uniform rules from the national statistical institutes of member states, then consolidates and harmonizes the data, before making them available to the public as printed or electronic publications. The data are directly available from the Data Shop network and from EUR-OP distribution networks.

Address: Jean Monnet Building, L-2920 Luxembourg.
Data Shop: Rue de la Loi 120, B-1049 Brussels, Belgium.

EU General information. Available as free-of-charge publications. The Official Journal, other official documents, specialized publications and databases addressing professional needs can be ordered from the EUR-OP network.

Address: Jean Monnet Building, rue Alcide de Gasperi, L-2920 Luxembourg.

EU AGENCIES AND OTHER BODIES

COMMUNITY PLANT VARIETY OFFICE Launched in 1995 to administer a system of plant variety rights. The system allows Community Plant Variety Rights (CPVRs), valid throughout the European Union, to be granted for new plant varieties as sole and exclusive form of Community intellectual property rights.

Address: P.O Box 2141-3, Boulevard Maréchal Foch, F-49021 Angers Cédex 02, France.

EUROPEAN AGENCY FOR THE EVALUATION OF MEDICINAL PRODUCTS Founded in 1995 to evaluate the quality and effectiveness of health products for human and veterinary use.

Address: 7 Westferry Circus, Canary Wharf, London E14 4HB, UK.

EUROPEAN AGENCY FOR RECONSTRUCTION Founded in 2000, with responsibility for the management of the main EU assistance programmes in Serbia and Montenegro and the former Yugoslav Republic of Macedonia.

Address: Egnatia 4, Thessaloniki 54626, Greece.

EUROPEAN AGENCY FOR SAFETY AND HEALTH AT WORK Founded in 1996 in order to serve the information needs of people with an interest in occupational safety and health.

Address: Gran Via 33, E-48009 Bilbao, Spain.

EUROPEAN CENTRE FOR THE DEVELOPMENT OF VOCATIONAL TRAINING Generally known as Cedefop (Centre Européen pour le Développement de la Formation Professionnelle), it was set up to help policy-makers and practitioners of the European Commission, the member states and social partner organizations across Europe make informed choices about vocational training policy.

Address: PO Box 22427, Thessaloniki 55102, Greece.

EUROPEAN ENVIRONMENT AGENCY Launched by the EU in 1993 with a mandate to orchestrate, cross-check and put to strategic use information of relevance to the protection and improvement of Europe's environment. Based in Copenhagen, it has a mandate to ensure objective, reliable and comprehensive information on the environment at European level to enable its members to take the requisite measures to protect it. The Agency carries out its tasks through the European Information and Observation Network (EIONET). Membership is open to countries outside the EU that share the Agency's concerns. Current membership includes all EU countries, Iceland, Liechtenstein and Norway. The EU accession countries joined the EEA in 2002.

Address: Kongens Nytorv 6, 1050 Copenhagen K, Denmark.

EUROPEAN FOUNDATION FOR THE IMPROVEMENT OF LIVING AND WORKING CONDITIONS Launched in 1975 to contribute to the planning and establishment of better living and working conditions. The Foundation's role is to provide findings, knowledge and advice from comparative research managed in a European perspective, which respond to the needs of the key parties at the EU level.

Address: Wyatville Road, Loughlinstown, Dublin 18, Ireland.

EUROPEAN INVESTMENT FUND Founded in 1994 as the European Union's specialized financial institution. It has a dual mission that combines the pursuit of objectives such as innovation, the creation of employment and regional development with maintaining a commercial approach to investments. It particularly provides venture capital and guarantee instruments for the growth of small and medium-sized enterprises.

Address: 43 avenue J. F. Kennedy, L-2968 Luxembourg.

EUROPEAN MONITORING CENTRE FOR DRUGS AND DRUG ADDICTION Established in 1993 to provide the European Union and its member states with objective, reliable and comparable information on a European level concerning drugs and drug addiction and their consequences.

Address: Rua da Cruz de Santa Apolónia 23–25, PT-1149-045 Lisbon, Portugal.

EUROPEAN MONITORING CENTRE ON RACISM AND XENOPHOBIA Established in 1997 as an independent body to contribute towards the combat against racism, xenophobia and anti-semitism throughout Europe. It has the task of reviewing the extent and development of the racist, xenophobic and anti-semitic phenomena in the European Union and promoting 'best practice' among the member states.

Address: Rahlgasse 3, A-1060 Vienna, Austria.

EUROPEAN TRAINING FOUNDATION Launched in 1995 to contribute to the process of vocational education and training reform that is currently taking place within the EU's partner countries and territories.

Address: Villa Gualino, viale Settimio Severo 65, I-10133 Turin, Italy.

EUROPOL Founded on 3 Jan. 1994 to exchange criminal intelligence between EU countries. Its precursor was the Europol Drug Unit, which initially dealt with the fight against drugs, progressively adding other areas. Europol took up its full activities on 1 July 1999. Europol's current mandate includes the prevention and combat of illicit drug trafficking, crimes involving illegal immigration networks, illicit vehicle trafficking, trafficking in human beings including child pornography, forgery of money and means of payment, illicit trafficking in nuclear and radioactive substances, terrorism and associated money laundering activities. There are about 300 staff members from all member states. Of these, 44 are ELOs (Europol Liaison Officers) working for their national police, gendarmerie or customs services. The 2001 budget was €35·4m. Member countries subscribe in proportion to their GNP.

Address: Raamweg 47, The Hague, Netherlands.
Website: http://www.europol.eu.int
e-mail: info@europol.eu.int
Director: Jürgen Storbeck (Germany).

OFFICE FOR HARMONIZATION IN THE INTERNAL MARKET The Office was established in 1994, and is responsible for registering Community trade marks and designs. Both Community trade marks and Community designs confer their proprietors a uniform right, which confers all member states of the EU by means of one single application and one single registration procedure.

Address: Avenida de Europa 4, Apartado de Correos 77, E-03080 Alicante, Spain.

TRANSLATION CENTRE FOR BODIES OF THE EUROPEAN UNION
Founded in 1994 to support EU agencies and offices in the accurate translation of important communications.

Address: Bâtiment Nouvel Hémicycle 1, rue du Fort Thüngen, L-1499 Luxembourg Kirchberg, Luxembourg.

EUROPEAN FOOD SAFETY AGENCY Founded in 2002 to provide independent scientific advice on all matters with a direct or indirect impact on food safety.

Address: Rue de Genève 1, B-1140 Brussels, Belgium.

Further Reading

Official Journal of the European Communities.—General Report on the Activities of the European Communities (annual, from 1967).*—The Agricultural Situation in the Community* (annual).*—The Social Situation in the Community* (annual).*—Report on Competition Policy in the European Community* (annual).*—Bulletin of the European Community* (monthly).*— Register of Current Community Legal Instruments* (biannual).

Brittan, L., *The Europe We Need.* London, 1994.*— A Diet of Brussels: The Changing Face of Europe.* London, 2000

Burca, de, Gràinne and Scott, Joanne, *Constitutional Change in the EU: From Uniformity to Flexibility?* Hart, Oxford, 2000

Christiansen, Thomas, and Kirchner, Emil, *Europe in Charge: Committee Governance in the European Union.* Manchester Univ. Press, 2000

Chryssochoou, Dimitris, *Democracy in the European Union.* Tauris, London, 1998

Cox, A. and Furlong, P., *A Modern Companion to the European Community: a Guide to Key Facts, Institutions and Terms.* Aldershot, 1992

Crawford, M., *One Money for Europe: the Economics and Politics of EMU.* 2nd ed. London, 1996

Davies, N., *Europe: A History.* London, 1997

Delors, J., *Our Europe: the Community and National Development.* London, 1993

Dinan, D., *Ever Closer Union? An Introduction to the European Community.* London, 1994

Dod's European Companion. Hurst Green, East Sussex. Occasional

Hitiris, T., *European Community Economics: a Modern Introduction.* London, 1991

Hurwitz, L. and Lequesne, C. (eds.) *The State of the European Community: Policies, Institutions and Debates in the Transition Years.* Harlow, 1992

Kirschner, E. J., *Decision-Making in the European Community: the Council Presidency and European Integration.* Manchester Univ. Press, 1992

Leonardi, R., *Convergence, Cohesion and Integration in the European Union.* London, 1995

Lewis, D. W. P., *The Road to Europe: History, Institutions and Prospects of European Integration, 1945–1993.* Berne, 1994

Mancini, Judge G. F., *Democracy and Constitutionalism in the European Union.* Hart, Oxford, 2000

Mazower, M., *Dark Continent: Europe's 20th Century.* London, 1998

Newman, M., *Democracy, Sovereignty and the European Union.* Farnborough, 1996

Nugent, N., *The Government and Politics of the European Union.* 3rd ed. London, 1994

Nuttall, S. J., *European Political Co-operation.* Oxford, 1992

Paxton, J., *European Communities* [Bibliography]. Oxford and New Brunswick (NJ), 1992

Weigall, D. and Stirk, P., *The Origins and Development of the European Community.* Leicester Univ. Press, 1992

Westlake, M., *Modern Guide to the European Parliament.* London, 1994

Williams, A. M., *The European Community: the Contradictions of Integration.* 2nd ed. Oxford, 1994

Winters, L. and Venables, A. (eds.) *European Integration: Trade and Industry.* CUP, 1991

COUNCIL OF EUROPE

Origin and Membership. In 1948 the Congress of Europe, bringing together at The Hague nearly 1,000 influential Europeans from 26 countries, called for the creation of a united Europe, including a European Assembly. This proposal, examined first by the Ministerial Council of the Brussels Treaty Organization, then by a conference of ambassadors, was at the origin of the Council of Europe, which is, with its 45 member States, the widest organization bringing together all European democracies. The Statute of the Council was signed at London on 5 May 1949 and came into force two months later.

The founder members were Belgium, Denmark, France, Ireland, Italy, Luxembourg, the Netherlands, Norway, Sweden and the UK. Turkey and Greece joined in 1949, Iceland in 1950, the Federal Republic of Germany in 1951 (having been an associate since 1950), Austria in 1956, Cyprus in 1961, Switzerland in 1963, Malta in 1965, Portugal in 1976, Spain in 1977, Liechtenstein in 1978, San Marino in 1988, Finland in 1989, Hungary in 1990, Czechoslovakia (after partitioning, the Czech Republic and Slovakia rejoined in 1993) and Poland in 1991, Bulgaria in 1992, Estonia, Lithuania, Romania and Slovenia in 1993, Andorra in 1994, Albania, Latvia, Macedonia, Moldova and Ukraine in 1995, Croatia and Russia in 1996, Georgia in 1999, Armenia and Azerbaijan in 2001, Bosnia-Herzegovina in 2002, and Serbia and Montenegro in 2003.

Membership is limited to European states which 'accept the principles of the rule of law and of the enjoyment by all persons within [their] jurisdiction of human rights and fundamental freedoms'. The Statute provides for both withdrawal (Article 7) and suspension (Articles 8 and 9). Greece withdrew during 1969–74.

Aims and Achievements. Article 1 of the Statute states that the Council's aim is 'to achieve a greater unity between its members for the purpose of safeguarding and realizing the ideals and principles which are their common heritage and facilitating their economic and social progress'; 'this aim shall be pursued ... by discussion of questions of common concern and by agreements and common action'. The only limitation is provided by Article 1 (d), which excludes 'matters relating to national defence'.

The main areas of the Council's activity are: human rights, the media, social and socio-economic questions, education, culture and sport, youth, public health, heritage and environment, local and regional government, and legal co-operation. 188 Conventions and Agreements have been concluded covering such matters as social security, cultural affairs, conservation of European wildlife and natural habitats, protection of archaeological heritage, extradition, medical treatment, equivalence of degrees and diplomas, the protection of television broadcasts, adoption of children and transportation of animals.

Treaties in the legal field include the adoption of the European Convention on the Suppression of Terrorism, the European Convention on the Legal Status of Migrant Workers and the Transfer of Sentenced Persons. The Committee of Ministers adopted a European Convention for the protection of individuals with regard to the automatic processing of personal data (1981), a Convention on the compensation of victims of violent crimes (1983), a Convention on spectator violence and misbehaviour at sport events and in particular at football matches (1985), the European Charter of Local Government (1985), and a Convention for the Prevention of Torture and Inhuman or Degrading Treatment or Punishment (1987). The European Social Charter of 1961 sets out the social and economic rights which all member governments agree to guarantee to their citizens.

European Social Charter. The Charter defines the rights and principles which are the basis of the Council's social policy, and guarantees a number of social and economic rights to the citizen, including the right to work, the right to form workers' organizations, the right to social security and assistance, the right of the family to protection and the right of migrant workers to protection and assistance. Two committees, comprising independent and government experts, supervise the parties' compliance with their obligations under the Charter. A revised charter, incorporating new rights such as protection for those without jobs and opportunities for workers with family responsibilities, was opened for signature on 3 May 1996 and signed by 13 members.

Human rights. The promotion and development of human rights is one of the major tasks of the Council of Europe. The European Convention on Human Rights, signed in 1950, set up special machinery to guarantee internationally fundamental rights and freedoms. The European Commission of Human Rights which was set up has now been abolished and has been replaced by the new European Court of Human Rights, which came into operation on 1 Nov. 1998. The European Court of Human Rights in Strasbourg, set up under the European Convention on Human Rights as amended, is composed of a number of judges equal to that of the Contracting States (currently 41). There is no restriction on the number of judges of the same nationality. Judges are elected by the Parliamentary Assembly of the Council of Europe for a term of six years. The terms of office of one half of the judges elected at the first election expired after three years, so as to ensure that the terms of office of one half of the judges are renewed every three years. Any Contracting State (State application) or individual claiming to be a victim of a violation of the Convention (individual application) may lodge directly with the Court in Strasbourg an application alleging a breach by a Contracting State of one of the Convention rights.

President of the European Court of Human Rights: Luzius Wildhaber (Switzerland).

The Development Bank, formerly the Social Development Fund, was created in 1956. The main purpose of the Bank is to give financial aid in the spheres of housing, vocational training, regional planning and development.

The *European Youth Foundation* provides money to subsidize activities by European youth organizations in their own countries.

Structure. Under the Statute, two organs were set up: an intergovernmental *Committee of [Foreign] Ministers* with powers of decision and recommendation to governments, and an interparliamentary deliberative body, the *Parliamentary Assembly* (referred to in the Statute as the Consultative Assembly)—both served by the Secretariat. A Joint Committee acts as an organ of co-ordination and liaison between the two and gives members an opportunity to exchange views on matters of important European interest. In addition, a number of committees of experts have been established. On municipal matters the Committee of Ministers receives recommendations from the Congress of Local and Regional Authorities of Europe. The Committee usually meets twice a year and has a rotatory chair; their deputies meet for several days each month.

The *Parliamentary Assembly* consists of 313 parliamentarians elected or appointed by their national parliaments (Albania 4, Andorra 2, Armenia 4, Austria 6, Azerbaijan 6, Belgium 7, Bosnia-Herzegovina 5, Bulgaria 6, Croatia 5, Cyprus 3, the Czech Republic 7, Denmark 5, Estonia 3, Finland 5, France 18, Georgia 5, Germany 18, Greece 7, Hungary 7, Iceland 3, Ireland 4, Italy 18, Latvia 3, Liechtenstein 2, Lithuania 4, Luxembourg 3, Macedonia 3, Malta 3, Moldova 5, Netherlands 7, Norway 5, Poland 12, Portugal 7, Romania 10, Russia 18, San Marino 2, Serbia and Montenegro 7, Slovakia 5, Slovenia 3, Spain 12, Sweden 6, Switzerland 6, Turkey 12, Ukraine 12, UK 18). It meets three times a year for approximately a week. The work of the Assembly is prepared by parliamentary committees. Since June 1989 representatives of a number of central and East European countries have been permitted to attend as non-voting members ('special guests'). Armenia and Azerbaijan have subsequently become full members.

Although without legislative powers, the Assembly acts as the powerhouse of the Council, initiating European action in key areas by making recommendations to the Committee of Ministers. As the widest parliamentary forum in Western Europe, the Assembly also acts as the conscience of the area by voicing its opinions on important current issues. These are embodied in Resolutions. The Ministers' role is to translate the Assembly's recommendations into action, particularly as regards lowering the barriers between the European countries, harmonizing their legislation or introducing, where possible, common European laws, abolishing discrimination on grounds of nationality, and undertaking certain tasks on a joint European basis.

Official languages. English and French.
Headquarters: Council of Europe, F-67075 Strasbourg Cedex, France.
Website: http://www.coe.int
e-mail: infopoint@coe.int
Secretary-General: Walter Schwimmer (Austria).

Publications. *European Yearbook,* The Hague; *Yearbook on the Convention on Human Rights,* Strasbourg; *Catalogue of Publications* (annual); *Sports Information Bulletin* (quarterly); *Activities Report* (annual); *Naturopa* (3 a year); *European Heritage* (bi-annual); *Strategy Bulletin* (6 a year).

Further Reading
Cook, C. and Paxton, J., *European Political Facts of the Twentieth Century.* Macmillan, London, 2000

WESTERN EUROPEAN UNION (WEU)

Origin. In March 1948 the signing of the Brussels Treaty of Economic, Social and Cultural Collaboration and Collective Defence by Belgium, France, Luxembourg, Netherlands and the UK opened the way for the establishment of the Western European Union. Six years later, the Paris Agreements, signed in Oct. 1954, which amended the Brussels Treaty, gave birth to WEU as a new international organization and provided for the Federal Republic of Germany and Italy to join. WEU came into being in 1955. Today, as an international defence and security organization, it brings together 28 nations encompassing four types of status: member state, associate member, observer and associate partner. Only the ten member states are signatories to the modified Brussels Treaty and have full decision making rights in WEU. The other 18 countries have been increasingly associated with WEU's activities. WEU's role and operational capabilities developed considerably after 1991. This development was based on close co-operation with the European Union and NATO. WEU acquired the necessary instruments to undertake any European-led crisis management operations and worked to develop them further as preparation for the establishment within the European Union of a crisis management capability in accordance with the decisions taken at the Cologne European Council in June 1999. Following decisions taken by the European Council since its meeting in Cologne to strengthen the European Security and Defence Policy within the EU, WEU relinquished its crisis management functions to the EU on 1 July 2001.

Member states. Belgium, France, Germany, Greece, Italy, Luxembourg, Netherlands, Portugal, Spain and the UK. Associate members: Czech Republic, Hungary, Iceland, Norway, Poland and Turkey. Observers: Austria, Denmark, Finland, Ireland and Sweden. Associate partners: Bulgaria, Estonia, Latvia, Lithuania, Romania, Slovakia and Slovenia.

Reform. A joint meeting of the foreign and defence ministers within the WEU framework, held in Rome on 26–27 Oct. 1984, was marked by the adoption of the founding text of WEU's reactivation: the *Rome Declaration*. Work on the definition of a European security identity and the gradual harmonization of its members' defence policies were among the stated objectives. Ministers recognized the 'continuing necessity to strengthen western security, and that better utilization of WEU would not only contribute to the security of Western Europe but also to an improvement in the common defence of all the countries of the Atlantic Alliance'.

In 1987 WEU foreign and defence ministers adopted the *Hague Platform on European Security Interests*, defining the conditions and criteria for European security, and the responsibilities of WEU members to provide an integrated Europe with a security and defence dimension. In 1987 and 1988, following the laying of mines in the Persian Gulf during the Iran–Iraq war, minesweepers dispatched by WEU countries helped secure free movement in international waters. Operation Cleansweep helped to complete the clearance of a 480-km sea lane from the Strait of Hormuz, and was the first instance of a concerted action in WEU. During the Gulf Crisis, at the end of 1990 and early 1991, co-ordinated action took place among WEU nations contributing forces and other forms of support to the coalition forces involved in the liberation of Kuwait.

In Maastricht, on 10 Dec. 1991, WEU ministers stated that: 'WEU will be developed as the defence component of the European Union and as the means to strengthen the European pillar of the Atlantic Alliance. To this end, it will formulate common European defence policy and carry forward its concrete implementation through the further development of its own operational role'. The Declaration then proposed ways of strengthening WEU's relations with the European Union and NATO, as well as measures to develop its operational role. A number of practical decisions were taken, including the transfer of the WEU headquarters from London to Brussels, which was completed in Jan. 1993.

At a meeting in Bonn in June 1992 WEU ministers went on to adopt the *Petersberg Declaration*, agreeing that the WEU should have a military capability in order to conduct humanitarian and rescue tasks, peacekeeping tasks and tasks of combat forces in crisis management, including peacemaking (the so-called

'Petersberg tasks') at the initiative of the WEU Council or following a request by the European Union, the OSCE or the UN.

At the Alliance Summit of Jan. 1994 NATO leaders gave their full support to the development of a European Security and Defence Identity (ESDI) and to the strengthening of the WEU. They declared their readiness to make collective assets of the Alliance available for WEU operations. The Alliance leaders also endorsed the concept of Combined Joint Task Forces (CJTFs) with the objective not only of adapting Alliance structures to NATO's new missions but also of improving co-operation with the WEU, and in order to reflect the emerging ESDI. Work on the CJTF concept came to fruition at the NATO Ministerial meeting in Berlin in June 1996. One of the fundamental objectives of the Alliance adaptation process identified by NATO Ministers in Berlin was the development of the European Security and Defence Identity within the Alliance.

With the agreement on the Treaty of Amsterdam revising the Treaty on European Union, WEU has drawn closer to the EU. In particular, the European Council's guidelines for the Common Foreign Security Policy (CFSP) 'shall obtain in respect of WEU for those matters for which the Union avails itself of the WEU'; and the Petersberg tasks have been incorporated into the EU Treaty. It is stated that WEU is an integral part of the development of the European Union, giving the Union access to an operational capability, notably in the context of the Petersberg tasks. In the WEU Ministerial Declaration of 22 July 1997 responding to the Treaty of Amsterdam, WEU confirmed its readiness to develop WEU's relations with the EU and work out arrangements for enhanced co-operation.

Further to the decisions taken by the Cologne European Council in June 1999, the EU is setting up the capabilities and instruments needed to fulfil its new responsibilities in the area of conflict prevention and crisis management tasks. Following decisions taken by the European Council since its meeting in Cologne to strengthen the European Security and Defence Policy within the EU, WEU relinquished its crisis management functions to the EU. However, the organization has not disappeared. The necessary WEU functions and structures are in place to enable the WEU member states to fulfil the commitments of the modified Brussels Treaty, particularly those arising from Article V (collective defence) and Article IX (relations with the WEU Parliamentary Assembly). They also provide support to the Western European Armaments Group (WEAG), which continues to carry out its functions of reflection and co-operation in the armament field, and to the Western European Armaments Organisation (WEAO).

Operations. In the context of the Yugoslav conflict, WEU has undertaken three operations, two of them to help in the enforcement of sanctions imposed by the UN Security Council (the WEU/NATO operation SHARP GUARD in the Adriatic and the WEU Danube operation) and one to assist in the European Union administration of the town of Mostar. From 1997 to 2001 WEU deployed a Multinational Advisory Police Element (MAPE) in Albania to assist in the reorganization of the Albanian Police. A WEU Demining Assistance Mission to Croatia (WEUDAM), operating from May 1999 to Nov. 2001, provided advice, technical expertise and training support to the Croatian Mine Action Centre.

Organization. WEU comprises an intergovernmental policy-making council and an assembly of parliamentary representatives, together with a number of subsidiary bodies set up by the council to facilitate its work. Since the 1984 reforms, the Council, supreme authority of the WEU, meets twice a year at ministerial level (foreign and defence) in the capital of the presiding country. The presidency rotates biannually. The Permanent Council, chaired by the Secretary-General, meets whenever necessary at ambassadorial level, at the WEU headquarters in Brussels. The WEU Assembly, located in Paris, comprises 115 parliamentarians of member states and meets twice a year, in plenary sessions in Paris. There are Permanent Committees on: defence questions and armaments; political affairs; technological and aerospace questions; budgetary affairs and administration; rules of procedure and privileges; and parliamentary and public relations.

Headquarters: WEU, B-1000 Brussels, Belgium.
Websites: http://www.weu.int; http://www.assembly-weu.org
Secretary-General: Dr Javier Solana Madariaga (Spain).

ORGANIZATION FOR SECURITY AND CO-OPERATION IN EUROPE (OSCE)

The OSCE is a pan-European security organization of 55 participating states. It was established as a primary instrument in its region for early warning, conflict prevention, crisis management and post-conflict rehabilitation in Europe.

Origin. Initiatives from both NATO and the Warsaw Pact culminated in the first summit Conference on Security and Co-operation in Europe (CSCE) attended by heads of state and government in Helsinki on 30 July–1 Aug. 1975. It adopted the *Helsinki Final Act* laying down ten principles governing the behaviour of States towards their citizens and each other, concerning human rights, self-determination and the interrelations of the participant states. The CSCE was to serve as a multilateral forum for dialogue and negotiations between East and West.

The Helsinki Final Act comprised three main sections: 1) politico-military aspects of security: principles guiding relations between and among participating States and military confidence-building measures; 2) co-operation in the fields of economics, science and technology and the environment; 3) co-operation in humanitarian and other fields.

From CSCE to OSCE. The Paris Summit of Nov. 1990 set the CSCE on a new course. In the Charter of Paris for a New Europe, the CSCE was called upon to contribute to managing the historic change in Europe and respond to the new challenges of the post-Cold War period. At the meeting, members of NATO and the Warsaw Pact signed an important Treaty on Conventional Armed Forces in Europe (CFE) and a declaration that they were 'no longer adversaries' and did not intend to 'use force against the territorial integrity or political independence of any state'. All 34 participants adopted the Confidence and Security-Building Measures (CSBMs), which pertained to the exchange of military information, verification of military installations, objection to unusual military activities etc., and signed the Charter of Paris. The Charter sets out principles of human rights, democracy and the rule of law to which all the signatories undertake to adhere, and lays down the bases for east-west co-operation and other future action. In July 1992 member nations unanimously agreed to set up an armed peacekeeping force. The 1994 Budapest Summit recognized that the CSCE was no longer a conference and on 1 Jan. 1995 the CSCE changed its name to the Organization for Security and Co-operation in Europe (OSCE). The 1996 Lisbon Summit elaborated the OSCE's key role in fostering security and stability in all their dimensions. It also stimulated the development of an OSCE Document-Charter on European Security.

Members. Albania, Andorra, Armenia, Austria, Azerbaijan, Belarus, Belgium, Bosnia-Herzegovina, Bulgaria, Canada, Croatia, Cyprus, the Czech Republic, Denmark, Estonia, Finland, France, Georgia, Germany, Greece, Holy See, Hungary, Iceland, Ireland, Italy, Kazakhstan, Kyrgyzstan, Latvia, Liechtenstein, Lithuania, Luxembourg, Macedonia, Malta, Moldova, Monaco, Netherlands, Norway, Poland, Portugal, Romania, Russian Federation, San Marino, Serbia and Montenegro, Slovak Republic, Slovenia, Spain, Sweden, Switzerland, Tajikistan, Turkey, Turkmenistan, Ukraine, UK, USA and Uzbekistan. *Partners for co-operation:* Japan and South Korea. *Mediterranean partners for co-operation:* Algeria, Egypt, Israel, Jordan, Morocco, Tunisia.

Organization. The OSCE's regular body for political consultation and decision-making is the Permanent Council. Its members, Permanent Representatives of the OSCE participating States, meet weekly in the Hofburg Congress Center in Vienna to discuss and take decisions on all issues pertinent to the OSCE. The Forum for Security Co-operation (FSC), which deals with arms control and confidence and security-building measures, meets weekly in Vienna. There are also Summits— periodic meetings of Heads of State or Government of OSCE participating States that set priorities and provide orientation at the highest political level. During periods between these summits, decision-making and governing power lies with the *Ministerial Council*, which is made up of the Foreign Ministers of the OSCE participating States. It meets at least once a year (but not when there is a summit).

In addition, a Senior Council is convened for periodic political deliberations. It also meets once a year as the Economic Forum. The Chairman-in-Office has overall responsibility for executive action. The chair rotates annually. The Secretary-General acts as representative of the Chairman-in-Office and manages OSCE structures and operations.

The Secretariat is based in Vienna and includes a *Conflict Prevention Centre* which provides operational support for OSCE missions. There are some 270 staff employed in OSCE institutions, and about 2,500 professionals, seconded by OSCE-participating states, work at OSCE missions and other field operations.

The *Office for Democratic Institutions and Human Rights* is located in Warsaw. It is active in monitoring elections and developing national electoral and human rights institutions, providing technical assistance to national legal institutions, and promoting the development of NGOs.

The *Office of the Representative on Freedom of the Media* is located in Vienna. Its main function is to observe relevant media developments in OSCE participating States with a view to providing an early warning on violations of freedom of expression.

The *Office of the High Commissioner on National Minorities* is located in The Hague. Its function is to identify and seek early resolution of ethnic tensions that might endanger peace, stability or friendly relations between the participating States of the OSCE.

The budget for 2003 was €185·7m.

Headquarters: Kärntner Ring 5–7, A-1010 Vienna, Austria.
Website: http://www.osce.org
Chairman-in-Office: Jaap de Hoop Scheffer (Netherlands).
Secretary-General: Ján Kubiš (Slovakia).

Further Reading
Freeman, J., *Security and the CSCE Process: the Stockholm Conference and Beyond.* London, 1991

EUROPEAN BANK FOR RECONSTRUCTION AND DEVELOPMENT (EBRD)

History. The European Bank for Reconstruction and Development was established in 1991 when communism was collapsing in central and eastern Europe and ex-Soviet countries needed support to nurture a new private sector in a democratic environment.

Activities. The EBRD is the largest single investor in the region and mobilizes significant foreign direct investment beyond its own financing. It is owned by 60 countries and two intergovernmental institutions. But despite its public sector shareholders, it invests mainly in private enterprises, usually together with commercial partners. Today the EBRD uses the tools of investment to help build market economies and democracies in 27 countries from Central Europe to Central Asia.

It provides project financing for banks, industries and businesses, for both new ventures and investments in existing companies. It also works with publicly-owned companies, to support privatization, restructuring of state-owned firms and improvement of municipal services. The EBRD uses its close relationship with governments in the region to promote policies that will bolster the business environment.

The mandate of the EBRD stipulates that it must only work in countries that are committed to democratic principles. Respect for the environment is part of the strong corporate governance attached to all EBRD investments.

Organization. All the powers of the EBRD are vested in a Board of Governors, to which each member appoints a governor, generally the minister of finance or an equivalent. The Board of Governors delegates powers to the Board of Directors, which is responsible for the direction of the EBRD's general operations and policies. The President is elected by the Board of Governors and is the legal representative of the EBRD. The President conducts the current business of the Bank under the guidance of the Board of Directors.

Headquarters: 1 Exchange Square, London EC2A 2JN, UK.
Website: http://www.ebrd.com
President: Jean Lemierre (France).
Secretary-General (acting): Nigel Carter.

EUROPEAN FREE TRADE ASSOCIATION (EFTA)

History and Membership. The Stockholm Convention establishing the Association entered into force on 3 May 1960. Founder members were Austria, Denmark, Norway, Portugal, Sweden, Switzerland and the UK. With the accession of Austria, Denmark, Finland, Portugal, Sweden and the UK to the EU, EFTA was reduced to four member countries: Iceland, Liechtenstein, Norway and Switzerland. In June 2001 the Vaduz Convention was signed. It liberalizes trade further among the four EFTA States in order to reflect the Swiss–EU bilateral agreements.

Activities. Free trade in industrial goods among EFTA members was achieved by 1966. Co-operation with the EU began in 1972 with the signing of free trade agreements and culminated in the establishment of a *European Economic Area (EEA)*, encompassing the free movement of goods, services, capital and labour throughout EFTA and the EU member countries. The Agreement was signed by all members of the EU and EFTA on 2 May 1992, but was rejected by Switzerland in a referendum on 6 Dec. 1992. The agreement came into force on 1 Jan. 1994.

The main provisions of the EEA Agreement are: free movement of products within the EEA from 1993 (with special arrangements to cover food, energy, coal and steel); EFTA to assume EU rules on company law, consumer protection, education, the environment, research and development, and social policy; EFTA to adopt EU competition rules on anti-trust matters, abuse of a dominant position, public procurement, mergers and state aid; EFTA to create an EFTA Surveillance Authority and an EFTA Court; individuals to be free to live, work and offer services throughout the EEA, with mutual recognition of professional qualifications; capital movements to be free with some restrictions on investments; EFTA countries not to be bound by the Common Agricultural Policy (CAP) or Common Fisheries Policy (CFP).

The EEA-EFTA states have established a Surveillance Authority and a Court to ensure implementation of the Agreement among the EFTA-EEA states. Political direction is given by the EEA Council which meets twice a year at ministerial level, while ongoing operation of the Agreement is overseen by the EEA Joint Committee. Legislative power remains with national governments and parliaments.

EFTA has formal relations with several other states. Declarations on co-operation were signed with Hungary, former Czechoslovakia and Poland (1990), Bulgaria, Estonia, Latvia, Lithuania and Romania (1991), Slovenia and Albania (1992), Egypt, Morocco and Tunisia (1995), the former Yugoslav Republic of Macedonia and the Palestine Liberation Organization (1996), Jordan and Lebanon (1997), Croatia, the Gulf Co-operation Council, Serbia and Montenegro and Mercosur (2000). Free trade agreements have been signed with Turkey (1991), Israel and Czechoslovakia (1992, with protocols on succession with the Czech Republic and Slovakia in 1993), Poland and Romania (1992), Bulgaria and Hungary (1993), Estonia, Latvia, Lithuania and Slovenia (1995), Morocco (1997), the Former Yugoslav Republic of Macedonia and Mexico (2000) and Jordan and Croatia (2001). A draft agreement was reached with Singapore in 2001. In Dec. 1998 an interim free trade agreement was signed with the Palestinian Authority and talks on an agreement began with Egypt. Negotiations on free trade agreements are ongoing with Canada, Egypt, Tunisia, Cyprus and Chile.

Organization. The operation of the free trade area among the EFTA states is the responsibility of the EFTA Council which meets regularly at ambassadorial level in Geneva. The Council is assisted by a Secretariat and standing committees. Each EFTA country holds the chairmanship of the Council for six months. For EEA matters there is a separate committee structure.

Brussels Office (EEA matters, press and information): 74 rue de Trèves, B-1040 Brussels.

Headquarters: 9–11 rue de Varembé, 1211 Geneva 20, Switzerland.
Website: http://www.efta.int
e-mail: efta-mailbox@secrbru.efta.be
Secretary-General: William Rossier (Switzerland).
Deputy Secretary-General, Brussels: Per Mannes (Norway).

Publications. Convention Establishing the European Free Trade Association; EFTA Annual Report; EFTA Fact Sheets: Information Papers on Aspects of the EEA; EFTA Bulletin.

EUROPEAN SPACE AGENCY (ESA)

History. Established in 1975, replacing the European Space Research Organization (ESRO) and the European Launcher Development Organization (ELDO).

Members. Austria, Belgium, Denmark, Finland, France, Germany, Ireland, Italy, the Netherlands, Norway, Portugal, Spain, Sweden, Switzerland, United Kingdom. Canada takes part in some projects under a co-operation agreement.

Activities. ESA is the intergovernmental agency in Europe responsible for the exploitation of space science, research and technology for exclusively peaceful purposes. Its aim is to define and put into effect a long-term European space policy that allows Europe to remain competitive in the field of space technology. It has a policy of co-operation with various partners on the basis that pooling resources and sharing work will boost the effectiveness of its programmes. Its space plan covers the fields of science, Earth observation, telecommunications, navigation, space segment technologies, ground infrastructures, space transport systems and microgravity research.

Headquarters: 8–10 rue Mario Nikis, 75738 Paris Cedex 15, France.
Website: http://www.esa.int
Director-General: Antonio Rodotá (Italy).

CERN – THE EUROPEAN ORGANISATION FOR NUCLEAR RESEARCH

Founded in 1954, CERN is the world's leading particle physics research centre. By studying the behaviour of nature's fundamental particles, CERN aims to find out what our Universe is made of and how it works. CERN's biggest accelerator, the Large Electron Positron Collider (LEP), recreates conditions at the birth of the Universe. A yet more powerful accelerator, the Large Hadron Collider (LHC), is scheduled for completion in 2005. One of the beneficial byproducts of CERN activity is the Worldwide Web, developed at CERN to give particle physicists easy access to shared data. One of Europe's first joint ventures, CERN now has a membership of 20 member states: Austria, Belgium, Bulgaria, Czech Republic, Denmark, Finland, France, Germany, Greece, Hungary, Italy, the Netherlands, Norway, Poland, Portugal, Slovak Republic, Spain, Sweden, Switzerland, United Kingdom. Some 6,500 scientists, half of the world's particle physicists, use CERN's facilities.

Address: CH-1211 Geneva 23, Switzerland.
Website: http://www.cern.ch
Director-General: Prof. Luciano Maiani (Italy).

CENTRAL EUROPEAN INITIATIVE (CEI)

In Nov. 1989 Austria, Hungary, Italy and Yugoslavia met on Italy's initiative to form an economic and political co-operation group in the region.

Members. (2003) Albania, Austria, Belarus, Bosnia-Herzegovina, Bulgaria, Croatia, Czech Republic, Hungary, Italy, Macedonia, Moldova, Poland, Romania, Serbia and Montenegro, Slovakia, Slovenia, Ukraine.

Address: Executive Secretariat, Via Genova 9, 34132 Trieste, Italy.
Website: http://www.ceinet.org
e-mail: cei-es@cei-es.org

THE NORDIC COUNCIL

Founded in 1952 as a co-operative link between the parliaments and governments of the Nordic states. The co-operation focuses on Intra-Nordic co-operation, co-operation with Europe/EU/EEA and co-operation with the adjacent areas. The Council consists of 87 elected MPs and the committees meet several times a year, as required. Every year the Nordic Council grants prizes for literature, music, nature and environment.

Members. Denmark (including the Faroe Islands and Greenland), Finland (including Åland), Iceland, Norway, Sweden.

Address: Postboks 3043, DK-1021 Copenhagen K, Denmark.
Website: http://www.norden.org/
President: Inge Lønning (Norway).

NORDIC DEVELOPMENT FUND (NDF)

Established in 1989, the NDF is a development aid organization of the five Nordic countries, Denmark, Finland, Iceland, Norway and Sweden. NDF capital totals SDR 515m. and €330m. Credits are offered to developing countries, with poorer African, Asian and Latin American countries taking priority.

Address: Fabianinkatu 34, PO Box 185, FIN-00171 Helsinki, Finland.
Website: http://www.ndf.fi
e-mail: info.ndf@ndf.fi
President: Jens Lund Sørensen (Denmark).

NORDIC INVESTMENT BANK (NIB)

The Nordic Investment Bank, which commenced operations in August 1976, is the joint international financial institution of the Nordic countries. It finances investment projects and project exports both within and outside the Nordic area. Priority is given to investment and environmental loans for projects in the Baltic states, Poland and northwest Russia.

Address: Fabianinkatu 34, PO Box 249, FIN-00171 Helsinki, Finland.
Website: http://www.nib.int
President: Jón Sigurðsson (Iceland).

COUNCIL OF THE BALTIC SEA STATES

Established in 1992 in Copenhagen following a conference of ministers of foreign affairs.

Members. Denmark, Estonia, Finland, Germany, Iceland, Latvia, Lithuania, Norway, Poland, Russia, Sweden and the European Commission.

Aims. To promote co-operation in the Baltic Sea region in the field of trade, investment and economic exchanges, combating organized crime, civil security, culture and education, transport and communication, energy and environment, human rights and assistance to democratic institutions.

The Council meets at ministerial level once a year, chaired by rotating foreign ministers; it is the supreme decision-making body. Between annual sessions the Committee of Senior Officials and three working groups meet at regular intervals. The CBSS Commissioner on Democratic Development, Helle Degn (Denmark), appointed in Oct. 2000, acts independently to the Council, and supports and structures the promotion and consolidation of democratic development in the member states. In Oct. 1999 ministers of energy of the CBSS member states agreed to achieve the goal of creating effective, economically and environmentally sound and more integrated energy systems in the Baltic Sea region. Four summits at the level of heads of government of CBSS member states and the President of the European Commission have taken place; in 1996, 1998, 2000 and 2002. The Baltic Sea Region Energy Cooperation (BASREC) is made up of energy ministers from the region and is chaired by the energy minister from the chair country of the CBSS.

Official language: English.
CBSS Secretariat: Strömsborg, PO Box 2010, S-103 11 Stockholm, Sweden.
Website: http://www.cbss.st
Director of the Secretariat: Hannu Halinen (Finland).

EUROPEAN BROADCASTING UNION (EBU)

The EBU is the world's largest professional association of national broadcasters, with 70 active members in 51 European and Mediterranean countries and 47 associate members in 29 countries elsewhere in Africa, the Americas and Asia. One of the EBU's best-known television activities is Eurovision which has a permanent network comprising up to 30 digital satellite channels, and two satellite channels relay radio concerts and operas, sports fixtures and major news events for Euroradio.

Headquarters: 17A Ancienne Route, CP 45, CH-1218 Grand Saconnex, Geneva, Switzerland.
Website: http://www.ebu.ch

BLACK SEA ECONOMIC CO-OPERATION GROUP (BSEC)

Founded in 1992 to promote economic co-operation in the Black Sea region. Priority areas of interest include: trade and economic development; banking and finance; communications; energy; transport; agriculture and agro-industry; healthcare and pharmaceutics; environmental protection; tourism; science and technology; exchange of statistical data and economic information; combating organized crime, illicit trafficking of drugs, weapons and radioactive materials, all acts of terrorism and illegal immigration.

Members. Albania, Armenia, Azerbaijan, Bulgaria, Georgia, Greece, Moldova, Romania, Russia, Turkey, Ukraine.

Observers. Austria, Egypt, France, Germany, Israel, Italy, Poland, Slovakia, Tunisia.

The *Parliamentary Assembly of the Black Sea Economic Co-operation* is the BSEC parliamentary dimension. The *BSEC Business Council* is composed of representatives from the business circles of the member states. The *Black Sea Trade and Development Bank* is considered as the financial pillar of the BSEC. There is also an *International Center for Black Sea Studies* and a *Coordination Center for the Exchange of Statistical Data and Economic Information.*

Headquarters: İstinye Cad., Müşir Fuad Paşa Yals, Eski Tersane 80860, İstinye, İstanbul, Turkey.
Website: http://www.bsec.gov.tr
Secretary-General: Valeri Chechelashvili (Georgia).

DANUBE COMMISSION

History and Membership. The Danube Commission was constituted in 1949 according to the Convention on the regulation of shipping on the Danube signed in Belgrade on 18 Aug. 1948. The Belgrade Convention, amended by the Additional Protocol of 26 March 1998, declares that navigation on the Danube from Kelheim to the Black Sea (with access to the sea through the Sulina arm and the Sulina Canal) is equally free and open to the nationals, merchant shipping and merchandise of all states as to harbour and navigation fees as well as conditions of merchant navigation. The Commission holds annual sessions and is composed of one representative from each of its 11 member countries: Austria, Bulgaria, Croatia, Germany, Hungary, Moldova, Romania, Russia, Serbia and Montenegro, Slovakia and Ukraine.

Functions. To ensure that the provisions of the Belgrade Convention are carried out; to establish a uniform buoying system on all navigable waterways; to establish the basic regulations for navigation on the river and ensure facilities for shipping; to co-ordinate the regulations for river, customs and sanitation control as well as the hydrometeorological service; to collect relevant statistical data concerning navigation on the Danube; to propose measures for the prevention of pollution of the Danube caused by navigation; and to harmonize regulations of the Danube Commission member states with European Union regulations on inland waterway navigation.

Official languages. German, French, Russian.
Headquarters: Benczúr utca 25, H-1068 Budapest, Hungary.
e-mail: Secretariat@danubecom-intern.org
President: Dr Stanko Nick (Croatia).
Director-General: Capt. Danail Nedialkov (Bulgaria).

THE COMMONWEALTH

The Commonwealth is a free association of sovereign independent states. It numbered 54 members in 2002. With a membership of 1·7bn. people, it represents over 30% of the world's population. There is no charter, treaty or constitution; the association is expressed in co-operation, consultation and mutual assistance for which the Commonwealth Secretariat is the central co-ordinating body.

Origin. The Commonwealth was first defined by the Imperial Conference of 1926 as a group of 'autonomous Communities within the British Empire, equal in status, in no way subordinate one to another in any aspect of their domestic or external affairs, though united by a common allegiance to the Crown, and freely associated as members of the British Commonwealth of Nations'. The basis of the association changed from one owing allegiance to a common Crown, and the modern Commonwealth was born in 1949 when the member countries accepted India's intention of becoming a republic at the same time as continuing 'her full membership of the Commonwealth of Nations and her acceptance of the King as the symbol of the free association of its independent member nations and as such the Head of the Commonwealth'. In 2002 the Commonwealth consisted of 33 republics and 21 monarchies, of which 16 are Queen's realms. All acknowledge the Queen symbolically as Head of the Commonwealth. The Queen's legal title rests on the statute of 12 and 13 Will. III, c. 3, by which the succession to the Crown of Great Britain and Ireland was settled on the Princess Sophia of Hanover and the 'heirs of her body being Protestants'.

A number of territories, formerly under British jurisdiction or mandate, did not join the Commonwealth: Egypt, Iraq, Transjordan, Burma (now Myanmar), Palestine, Sudan, British Somaliland and Aden. Four countries, Ireland in 1948, South Africa in 1961, Pakistan in 1972, and Fiji (now Fiji Islands) in 1987 have left the Commonwealth. Pakistan was re-admitted to the Commonwealth in 1989, South Africa in 1994, Fiji Islands in 1997. Nigeria was suspended in 1995 for violation of human rights but was fully reinstated on 29 May 1999. Pakistan was suspended from the Commonwealth's councils following a coup in Oct. 1999. Fiji Islands was also suspended from the Commonwealth's councils in May 2000 following a coup there but was re-admitted in Dec. 2001 following the restoration of democracy. Zimbabwe was suspended from the Commonwealth's councils for a year on 19 March 2002 for a 'high level of politically motivated violence' during the vote that saw President Robert Mugabe re-elected. In March 2003 it was suspended for a further nine months. Mozambique, admitted in Nov. 1995, is the first member state not to have been a member of the former British Commonwealth or Empire. Tuvalu is a special member, with the right to participate in all functional Commonwealth meetings and activities but not to attend meetings of Commonwealth Heads of Government.

MEMBER STATES OF THE COMMONWEALTH

The 54 member states, with year of admission:

	Year of admission		Year of admission
Antigua and Barbuda	1981	Grenada	1974
Australia[1]	1931	Guyana	1966
Bahamas	1973	India	1947
Bangladesh	1972	Jamaica	1962
Barbados	1966	Kenya	1963
Belize	1981	Kiribati	1979
Botswana	1966	Lesotho	1966
Brunei[2]	1984	Malawi	1964
Cameroon	1995	Malaysia	1957
Canada[1]	1931	Maldives	1982
Cyprus	1961	Malta	1964
Dominica	1978	Mauritius	1968
Fiji Islands[3]	1997	Mozambique	1995
Gambia	1965	Namibia	1990
Ghana	1957	Nauru[4]	1968

	Year of admission		Year of admission
New Zealand[1]	1931	South Africa[7]	1994
Nigeria[5]	1960	Sri Lanka	1948
Pakistan[6]	1989	Swaziland	1968
Papua New Guinea	1975	Tanzania	1961
St Kitts and Nevis	1983	Tonga[2]	1970
St Lucia	1979	Trinidad and Tobago	1962
St Vincent and Grenadines	1979	Tuvalu	1978
Samoa	1970	Uganda	1982
Seychelles	1976	United Kingdom	1931
Sierra Leone	1961	Vanuatu	1980
Singapore	1965	Zambia	1964
Solomon Islands	1978	Zimbabwe	1980

[1]Independence given legal effect by the Statute of Westminster 1931.
[2]Brunei and Tonga had been sovereign states in treaty relationship with Britain.
[3]Fiji left 1987; but rejoined in 1997. It changed its name to Fiji Islands in 1998.
[4]Nauru was first a Mandate, then a Trust territory. It became a full member in 1999.
[5]Nigeria was suspended in 1995 but re-admitted as a full member in 1999.
[6]Left 1972, rejoined 1989. [7]Left 1961, rejoined 1994.

Aims and Conditions of Membership. Membership involves acceptance of certain core principles, as set out in the Harare Declaration of 1991, and is subject to the approval of other member states. The Harare Declaration charts a course to take the Commonwealth into the 21st century and affirms members' continued commitment to the Singapore Declarations of 1971, by which members committed themselves to the pursuit of world peace and support of the UN.

The core principles defined by the Harare Declaration are: political democracy, human rights, good governance and the rule of law, and the protection of the environment through sustainable development. Commitment to these principles was made binding as a condition of membership at the 1993 Heads of Government meeting in Cyprus.

The Millbrook Action Programme of 1995 aims to support countries in implementing the Harare Declaration, providing assistance in constitutional and judicial matters, running elections, training and technical advice. Violations of the Harare Declaration will provoke a series of measures by the Commonwealth Secretariat, including: expression of disapproval, encouragement of bilateral actions by member states, appointment of fact-finders and mediators, stipulation of a period for the restoration of democracy, exclusion from ministerial meetings, suspension of all participation and aid and finally punitive measures including trade sanctions. An eight-member *Commonwealth Ministerial Action Group on the Harare Declaration (CMAG)* may be convened by the Secretary-General as and when necessary to deal with violations. The Group held its first meeting in Dec. 1995. Its terms of reference are as set out in the Millbrook Action Programme.

The *Commonwealth Parliamentary Association* was founded in 1911. As defined by its constitution, its objectives are to 'promote knowledge of the constitutional, legislative, economic, social and cultural aspects of parliamentary democracy'. It meets these objectives by organizing conferences, meetings and seminars for members, arranging exchange visits between members, publishing books, newsletters, reports, studies and a quarterly journal and providing an information service. Its principal governing body is the General Assembly, which meets annually during the Commonwealth Parliamentary Conference and is composed of members attending that Conference as delegates. The Association elects an Executive Committee comprising a Chair, President, Vice-President, Treasurer and 27 regional representatives, which meets twice a year. The Chair is elected for three-year terms.

Commonwealth Secretariat. The Commonwealth Secretariat is an international body at the service of all 54 member countries. It provides the central organization for joint consultation and co-operation in many fields. It was established in 1965 by Commonwealth Heads of Government as a 'visible symbol of the spirit of co-operation which animates the Commonwealth', and has observer status at the UN General Assembly.

The Secretariat disseminates information on matters of common concern, organizes and services meetings and conferences, co-ordinates many Commonwealth activities, and provides expert technical assistance for economic and social development through the multilateral Commonwealth Fund for Technical Co-operation. The Secretariat is organized in divisions and sections which correspond to its main areas of operation: international affairs, economic affairs, food production and rural development, youth, education, information, applied studies in government, science and technology, law and health. Within this structure the Secretariat organizes the biennial meetings of Commonwealth Heads of Government (CHOGMs), annual meetings of Finance Ministers of member countries, and regular meetings of Ministers of Education, Law, Health, and others as appropriate. To emphasize the multilateral nature of the association, meetings are held in different cities and regions within the Commonwealth. Heads of Government decided that the Secretariat should work from London as it has the widest range of communications of any Commonwealth city, as well as the largest assembly of diplomatic missions.

Commonwealth Heads of Government Meetings (CHOGMs). Outside the UN, the CHOGM remains the largest intergovernmental conference in the world. Meetings are held every two years. The 2002 CHOGM in Coolum, Australia, scheduled for Oct. 2001 but postponed following the attacks on the United States of 11 Sept. 2001, was dominated by the Zimbabwe issue. The next meeting will be held in Abuja, Nigeria in Dec. 2003. A host of Commonwealth organizations and agencies are dedicated to enhancing interCommonwealth relations and the development of the potential of Commonwealth citizens. A list of these can be obtained from the *Commonwealth Institute* in London.

Commonwealth Day is celebrated on the second Monday in March each year. The theme for 2003 was 'Partners in Development'.

Overseas Territories and Associated States. There are 14 United Kingdom overseas territories (see pages 1717–46), six Australian external territories (see pages 234–9), two New Zealand dependent territories and two New Zealand associated states (see pages 1215–20). A dependent territory is a territory belonging by settlement, conquest or annexation to the British, Australian or New Zealand Crown.

United Kingdom Overseas Territories administered through the Foreign and Commonwealth Office comprise, in the Indian Ocean: British Indian Ocean Territory; in the Mediterranean: Gibraltar, the Sovereign Base Areas of Akrotiri and Dhekelia in Cyprus; in the Atlantic Ocean: Bermuda, Falkland Islands, South Georgia and South Sandwich Islands, British Antarctic Territory, St Helena and Dependencies (Ascension and Tristan da Cunha); in the Caribbean: Montserrat, British Virgin Islands, Cayman Islands, Turks and Caicos Islands, Anguilla; in the Western Pacific: Pitcairn Group of Islands.

The Australian external territories are: Coral Sea Islands, Cocos (Keeling) Islands, Christmas Island, Heard and McDonald Islands, Australian Antarctic Territory, and Ashmore and Cartier Islands. The New Zealand external territories are: Tokelau Islands and the Ross Dependency. The New Zealand associated states are: Cook Islands and Niue.

Headquarters: Marlborough House, Pall Mall, London SW1Y 5HX, UK.
Websites: http://www.thecommonwealth.org; www.youngcommonwealth.org
Secretary-General: Don McKinnon (New Zealand).

Selected publications. Commonwealth Yearbook; Commonwealth Currents (quarterly); *The Commonwealth at the Summit: Communiqués of Commonwealth Heads of Government Meetings.*

Further Reading
The Cambridge History of the British Empire. 8 vols. CUP, 1929 ff.
Austin, D., *The Commonwealth and Britain.* London, 1988
Ball, M., *The 'Open' Commonwealth.* Duke University Press, Durham (North Carolina), 1971
Chan, S., *Twelve Years of Commonwealth Diplomatic History: Summit Meetings, 1979–1991.* Lampeter, 1992
Hall, H. D., *Commonwealth: A History of the British Commonwealth.* London and New York, 1971
Judd, D. and Slinn, P., *The Evolution of the Modern Commonwealth.* London, 1982

Keeton, G. W. (ed.) *The British Commonwealth: Its Laws and Constitutions.* 9 vols. London, 1951 ff.

Larby, P. and Hannam, H., *The Commonwealth* [Bibliography]. Oxford and New Brunswick (NJ), 1993

Madden, F. and Fieldhouse, D., (eds.) *Selected Documents on the Constitutional History of the British Empire and Commonwealth.* Greenwood Press, New York, 1994

Mansergh, N., *The Commonwealth Experience.* Macmillan, London, 1982

McIntyre, W. D., *The Significance of the Commonwealth, 1965–90.* Macmillan, London, 1991

Moore, R. J., *Making the New Commonwealth.* Oxford, 1987

COMMONWEALTH OF INDEPENDENT STATES (CIS)

The Commonwealth of Independent States, founded on 8 Dec. 1991 in Viskuli, a government villa in Belarus, is a community of independent states which proclaimed itself the successor to the Union of Soviet Socialist Republics in some aspects of international law and affairs. The member states are the founders, Russia, Belarus and Ukraine, and nine subsequent adherents: Armenia, Azerbaijan, Georgia, Kazakhstan, Kyrgyzstan, Moldova, Tajikistan, Turkmenistan and Uzbekistan.

History. Extended negotiations in the Union of Soviet Socialist Republics (USSR) in 1990 and 1991, under the direction of President Gorbachev, sought to establish a 'renewed federation' or, subsequently, to conclude a new union treaty that would embrace all the 15 constituent republics of the USSR at that date. According to a referendum conducted in March 1991, 76% of the population (on an 80% turn-out) wished to maintain the USSR as a 'renewed federation of equal sovereign republics in which the human rights and freedoms of any nationality would be fully guaranteed'. In Sept. 1991 the three Baltic republics—Estonia, Latvia and Lithuania—were nonetheless recognized as independent states by the USSR State Council, and subsequently by the international community. Most of the remaining republics reached agreement on the broad outlines of a new 'union of sovereign states' in Nov. 1991, which would have retained a directly elected President and an all-union legislature, but which would have limited central authority to those powers specifically delegated to it by the members of the union.

A referendum in Ukraine in Dec. 1991, however, showed overwhelming support for full independence, and following this the three Slav republics (Russia, Belarus and Ukraine) concluded the Minsk Agreement on 8 Dec. 1991, establishing a Commonwealth of Independent States (CIS), headquartered in Minsk. The USSR, as a subject of international law and a geopolitical reality, was declared no longer in existence, and each of the three republics individually renounced the 1922 treaty through which the USSR had been established.

The CIS declared itself open to other former Soviet republics, and to states elsewhere that shared its objectives, and on 21 Dec. 1991 in Alma-Ata, a further declaration was signed with eight other republics: Armenia, Azerbaijan, Kazakhstan, Kyrgyzstan, Moldova, Tajikistan, Turkmenistan and Uzbekistan. The declaration committed signatories to recognize the independence and sovereignty of other members, to respect human rights including those of national minorities, and to the observance of existing boundaries. Relations among the members of the CIS were to be conducted on an equal, multilateral, interstate basis, but it was agreed to endorse the principle of unitary control of strategic nuclear arms and the concept of a 'single economic space'. In a separate agreement the heads of member states agreed that Russia should take up the seat at the United Nations formerly occupied by the USSR, and a framework of interstate and intergovernment consultation was established. Following these developments Mikhail Gorbachev resigned as USSR President on 25 Dec. 1991, and on 26 Dec. the USSR Supreme Soviet voted a formal end to the 1922 Treaty of Union, and dissolved itself. Georgia decided to join on 9 Dec. 1993 and on 1 March 1994 the national parliament ratified the act.

The Charter, adopted on 22 Jan. 1993 in Minsk, proclaims that the Commonwealth is based on the principles of the sovereign equality of all members. It is not a state and does not have supranational authority.

Activities and Institutions. The principal organs of the CIS, according to the agreement concluded in Alma-Ata on 21 Dec. 1991, are the *Council of Heads of States*, which meets twice a year, and the *Council of Heads of Government*, which meets every three months. Both councils may convene extraordinary sessions, and may hold joint sittings. There is also a *Council of Defence Ministers*, established Feb. 1992, and a *Council of Foreign Ministers* (Dec. 1993). The Secretariat is the standing working organ.

At a summit meeting of heads of states (with the exception of Azerbaijan) in July 1992, agreements were reached on a way to divide former USSR assets abroad; on the legal cessionary of state archives of former Soviet states; on the status of an Economic Court; and on collective security. In 1992 an *Inter-Parliamentary Assembly* was established by seven member states (Armenia, Belarus, Kazakhstan, Kyrgyzstan, Russia, Tajikistan and Uzbekistan).

At a subsequent meeting in Jan. 1993 Armenia, Belarus, Kazakhstan, Kyrgyzstan, Russia, Tajikistan and Uzbekistan agreed on a charter to implement co-operation in political, economic, ecological, humanitarian, cultural and other spheres; thorough and balanced economic and social development within the common economic space; interstate co-operation and integration; and to ensure human rights and freedoms. Three participants (Ukraine, Moldova and Turkmenistan) agreed only to a declaration that the decision would be open for signing in the future. For the purpose of the maintenance and development of multilateral industrial, trade and financial relations, Heads of State established an *Inter-State Bank* and adopted a Provision on it. Its charter was signed by ten Heads of State (Armenia, Belarus, Kazakhstan, Kyrgyzstan, Moldova, Russia, Tajikistan, Turkmenistan, Ukraine, Uzbekistan) on 22 Dec. 1993.

The *CIS Inter-State Bank* was set up with a starting capital of 5,000m. roubles, to facilitate multilateral clearing of CIS interstate transactions. Members' contributions (by %), based on their share of foreign trade turnover in 1990, were as follows: Russia, 50%; Ukraine, 20·7%; Belarus, 8·4%; Kazakhstan, 6·1%; Uzbekistan, 5·5%; Moldova, 2·9%; Armenia, 1·8%; Tajikistan, 1·6%; Kyrgyzstan, 1·5%; Turkmenistan, 1·5%. The bank is an international settlement and financial-credit institution, established in accordance with the rules of international public law. The authorized capital on 1 Jan. 1999 was 20,000m. roubles.

In accordance with the Agreement on Armed Forces and Border Troops, concluded on 30 Dec. 1991, it was decided to consider and solve the issue on the transference of the management of the General-Purpose Armed Forces in accordance with the national legislation of member states. On 14 Feb. 1992 the *Council of Defence Ministers* was established. In 1993 the Office of Commander-in-Chief of CIS Joint Armed Forces was reorganized in a Staff for Co-ordinating Military Co-operation. Its Chief of Staff is appointed by the Council of Heads of State. On 24 Sept. an Agreement on collective peacekeeping was concluded. Peacekeeping operations in intra-CIS conflicts could be implemented at the request of member states, and with the consent of parties to the conflict. CIS members contribute to this force in proportion to the size of their armed forces and are responsible for the conditions, training and supply of military and civil personnel to the conflict region; the commander is appointed on each occasion by the Council of Heads of State.

At the same meeting, Armenia, Azerbaijan, Belarus, Kazakhstan, Kyrgyzstan, Moldova, Russia, Tajikistan and Uzbekistan signed an agreement to form an *Economic Union*. Georgia and Turkmenistan signed later (14 and 23 Jan. 1994). Ukraine became an associated member on 15 April 1994. In Oct. 1994 a summit meeting established the *Inter-State Economic Committee (MEK)* to be based in Moscow. Members include all CIS states except Turkmenistan. The Committee's decisions are binding if voted by 80% of the membership. Russia commands 50% of the voting power; Ukraine 14%. The Committee's remit is to co-ordinate energy, transport and communications policies. A *Customs Union* to regulate payments between member states with non-convertible independent currencies and a regulatory *Economic Court* have also been established.

On 29 March 1996 Belarus, Kazakhstan, Kyrgyzstan and Russia signed an agreement increasing their mutual economic and social integration by creating a *Community of Integrated States* (Tajikistan signed in 1998). The agreement established a Supreme Inter-Governmental Council comprising heads of state and government and foreign ministers, with a rotatory Chair, an integration committee of Ministers and an Inter-Parliamentary Committee.

On 2 April 1996 the Presidents of Belarus and Russia signed a treaty providing for political, economic and military integration, creating the nucleus of a *Community of Russia and Belarus*. The agreement establishes a Supreme Council comprising the Presidents, Prime Ministers and Speakers of both countries and the Chairman of the Executive Committee. A further treaty was signed on 22 May 1997, instituting common citizenship, common deployment of military forces and the harmonization of the two economies with a view to the creation of a common currency. The Community was later renamed the *Union of Belarus and Russia* and signed subsequent agreements on equal rights for its citizens and equal conditions for state and private entrepreneurship.

In March 1994 the CIS was accorded observer status in the UN.

Headquarters: 220000 Minsk, Kirava 17, Belarus.
Website: http://www.cis.minsk.by
Executive Secretary: Yurii Yarov (Russia).

Further Reading
Brzezinski, Z. and Sullivan, P. (eds.) *Russia and the Commonwealth of Independent States: Documents, Data and Analysis.* Armonk (NY), 1996

ORGANIZATION OF AMERICAN STATES (OAS)

Origin. On 14 April 1890 representatives of the American republics, meeting in Washington at the First International Conference of American States, established an International Union of American Republics and, as its central office, a Commercial Bureau of American Republics, which later became the Pan-American Union. This international organization's object was to foster mutual understanding and co-operation among the nations of the western hemisphere. This led to the adoption on 30 April 1948 by the Ninth International Conference of American States, at Bogotá, Colombia, of the Charter of the Organization of American States. This co-ordinated the work of all the former independent official entities in the inter-American system and defined their mutual relationships. The Charter of 1948 was subsequently amended by the Protocol of Buenos Aires (1967) and the Protocol of Cartagena de Indias (1985).

Members. This is on a basis of absolute equality, with each country having one vote and there being no veto power. Members (2001): Antigua and Barbuda, Argentina, Bahamas, Barbados, Belize, Bolivia, Brazil, Canada, Chile, Colombia, Costa Rica, Cuba (suspended 1962), Dominica, Dominican Republic, Ecuador, El Salvador, Grenada, Guatemala, Guyana, Haiti, Honduras, Jamaica, Mexico, Nicaragua, Panama, Paraguay, Peru, St Kitts and Nevis, St Lucia, St Vincent and the Grenadines, Suriname, Trinidad and Tobago, USA, Uruguay, Venezuela.

Permanent Observers. Algeria, Angola, Armenia, Austria, Azerbaijan, Belgium, Bosnia-Herzegovina, Bulgaria, Croatia, Cyprus, Czech Republic, Denmark, Egypt, Equatorial Guinea, Estonia, EU, Finland, France, Georgia, Germany, Ghana, Greece, Holy See, Hungary, India, Ireland, Israel, Italy, Japan, Kazakhstan, South Korea, Latvia, Lebanon, Morocco, the Netherlands, Norway, Pakistan, Philippines, Poland, Portugal, Qatar, Romania, Russia, Saudi Arabia, Serbia and Montenegro, Slovakia, Spain, Sri Lanka, Sweden, Switzerland, Thailand, Tunisia, Turkey, UK, Ukraine, Yemen.

Aims and Activities. To strengthen the peace and security of the continent; promote and consolidate representative democracy, with due respect for the principle of non-intervention; prevent possible causes of difficulties and ensure the peaceful settlement of disputes among member states; provide for common action in the event of aggression; seek the solution of political, juridical and economic problems; promote by co-operative action economic, social and cultural development; and achieve an effective limitation of conventional weapons in order to devote maximum resources to economic and social development.

The Santiago Commitment to Democracy and the Renewal of the Inter-American System. With the emergence of democratically elected governments throughout the continent, the OAS has been increasingly concerned with the preservation, protection and promotion of democracy. At its 21st Regular Session (Santiago, Chile, 1991) the OAS General Assembly adopted the Santiago Commitment to Democracy and the Renewal of the Inter-American System as well as the Protocol of Washington (1992) to amend the Charter by provisions of the Resolution 1080 on representative democracy. The latter calls for collective action in the event of a 'sudden or irregular interruption of the democratic political institutional process or of the legitimate exercise of power by the democratically elected government in any of the Organization's member states'.

The Protocol of Washington also incorporates among the essential purposes of the OAS the eradication of extreme poverty which constitutes an obstacle to the full democratic development of the peoples of the hemisphere. This commitment was further strengthened by amendments under the Protocol of Managua the following year, with measures designed to improve the delivery of technical co-operation to such member states. At its 20th Special Session (Feb. 1994, Mexico City), the OAS General Assembly approved a resolution on a commitment to a partnership for development and struggle to overcome extreme poverty.

Declaration of Belém do Pará. At its 24th Regular Session (June 1994, Belém do Pará), the General Assembly adopted the Declaration of Belém do Pará, in which the Ministers of Foreign Affairs and Heads of Delegation of Member States declared their commitment to strengthening the OAS as the main hemispheric forum of political consensus, so that it may support: the realization of the aspirations of member states in promoting and consolidating peace, democracy, social justice, and development, in accordance with the purposes and principles of the Charter; their decision to promote and deepen co-operative relations in the economic, social, educational, cultural, scientific, technological and political fields; their commitment to continue and further the dialogue on hemispheric security in order to consolidate and strengthen mutual confidence; their determination to continue to contribute to the objective of general and complete disarmament, under effective international control; their determination to strengthen regional co-operation to increase the effectiveness of efforts to combat the illicit use of narcotic drugs and traffic therein; their decision to co-operate in a reciprocal effort towards preventing and punishing terrorist acts, methods and practices, and the development of international law in this matter; and their commitment to promote economic and social development for the indigenous populations of their countries.

Organization. Under its Charter the OAS accomplishes its purposes by means of:
(a) The General Assembly, which meets annually.
(b) The Meeting of Consultation of Ministers of Foreign Affairs, held to consider problems of an urgent nature and of common interest.
(c) The Councils: The Permanent Council, which meets on a permanent basis at OAS headquarters and carries out decisions of the General Assembly, assists the member states in the peaceful settlement of disputes, acts as the Preparatory Committee of that Assembly, submits recommendations with regard to the functioning of the Organization, and considers the reports to the Assembly of the other organs. The Inter-American Council for Integral Development (CIDI) (formed from the merger of two previous councils, the Inter-American Economic and Social Council and the Inter-American Council for Education, Science and Culture) directs and monitors OAS technical co-operation programmes.
(d) The Inter-American Juridical Committee which acts as an advisory body to the OAS on juridical matters and promotes the development and codification of

international law. 11 jurists, elected for four-year terms by the General Assembly, represent all the American States.

(e) The Inter-American Commission on Human Rights which oversees the observance and protection of human rights. Seven members elected for four-year terms by the General Assembly represent all the OAS member states.

(f) The General Secretariat, which is the central and permanent organ of the OAS.

(g) The Specialized Conferences, meeting to deal with special technical matters or to develop specific aspects of inter-American co-operation.

(h) The Specialized Organizations, intergovernmental organizations established by multilateral agreements to discharge specific functions in their respective fields of action, such as women's affairs, agriculture, child welfare, Indian affairs, geography and history, and health.

In Sept. 2001 an Inter-American Democratic Charter was adopted. It sets out a simple, clear declaration: 'The peoples of the Americas have a right to democracy and their governments have an obligation to promote and defend it.' The Charter compels the OAS to take action against any member state that disrupts its own democratic institutions.

The Secretary-General is elected by the General Assembly for five-year terms. The General Assembly approves the annual budget which is financed by quotas contributed by the member governments. The budget in 2003 amounted to US$83·17m.

Headquarters: 17th Street and Constitution Avenue, NW, Washington, D.C., 20006, USA.

Website: http://www.oas.org

Secretary-General: César Gaviria Trujillo (Colombia).

Publications. Charter of the Organization of American States. 1948.—As Amended by the Protocol of Buenos Aires in 1967 and the Protocol of Cartagena de Indias in 1985; The OAS and the Evolution of the Inter-American System; Annual Report of the Secretary-General; Status of Inter-American Treaties and Conventions (annual).

Further Reading

Sheinin, D., *The Organization of American States* [Bibliography]. Oxford and Metuchen (NJ), 1995

INTER-AMERICAN DEVELOPMENT BANK (IDB)

The IDB, the oldest and largest regional multilateral development institution, was established in 1959 to help accelerate economic and social development in Latin America and the Caribbean. The Bank's original membership included 19 Latin American and Caribbean countries and the USA. Today, membership totals 46 nations, including non-regional members.

Members. Argentina, Austria, Bahamas, Barbados, Belgium, Belize, Bolivia, Brazil, Canada, Chile, Colombia, Costa Rica, Croatia, Denmark, Dominican Republic, Ecuador, El Salvador, Finland, France, Germany, Guatemala, Guyana, Haiti, Honduras, Israel, Italy, Jamaica, Japan, Mexico, the Netherlands, Nicaragua, Norway, Panama, Paraguay, Peru, Portugal, Slovenia, Spain, Suriname, Sweden, Switzerland, Trinidad and Tobago, UK, USA, Uruguay, Venezuela.

The Bank's total lending up to 2000 has been US$106bn. for projects with a total cost of over US$263bn. Its lending has increased dramatically from the US$294m. approved in 1961 to US$6,311m. in 2002.

Current lending priorities include poverty reduction and social equity, modernization and integration, and the environment. The Bank has a Fund for Special Operations for lending on concessional terms for projects in countries classified as economically less developed. An additional facility, the Multilateral Investment Fund (MIF), was created in 1992 to help promote and accelerate investment reforms and private-sector development throughout the region.

The Board of Governors is the Bank's highest authority. Governors are usually Ministers of Finance, Presidents of Central Banks or officers of comparable rank. The IDB has country offices in each of its borrowing countries, and in Paris and Tokyo.

Official languages: English, French, Portuguese, Spanish.
Headquarters: 1300 New York Avenue, NW, Washington, D.C., 20577, USA.
Website: http://www.iadb.org
President: Enrique V. Iglesias (Uruguay).

SECRETARIAT FOR CENTRAL AMERICAN ECONOMIC INTEGRATION (SIECA)

SIECA (Secretaría de Integración Económica Centroamericana) was created by the General Treaty of Central American Economic Integration in Dec. 1960. The General Treaty incorporates the Agreement on the Regime for Central American Integration Industries. In Oct. 1993 the Protocol to the General Treaty on Central Economic Integration, known as the Guatemala Protocol, was signed.

Members. Costa Rica, El Salvador, Guatemala, Honduras, Nicaragua. *Observer:* Panama.

Official language: Spanish.
Headquarters: 4a Avenida 10–25, Zona 14, Ciudad de Guatemala, Guatemala.
Website: http://www.sieca.org.gt
Secretary-General: Haroldo Rodas Melgar.

CENTRAL AMERICAN COMMON MARKET (CACM)

In Dec. 1960 El Salvador, Guatemala, Honduras and Nicaragua concluded the General Treaty of Central American Economic Integration under the auspices of the Organization of Central American States (ODECA) in Managua. Long-standing political and social conflicts in the area have repeatedly dogged efforts to establish integration towards the establishment of a common market.

Members. Costa Rica, El Salvador, Guatemala, Honduras, Nicaragua, Panama.

A protocol to the 1960 General Treaty signed by all six members in Oct. 1993 reaffirmed an eventual commitment to full economic integration with a common external tariff of 20% to be introduced only voluntarily and gradually.

A Treaty on Democratic Security in Central America was signed by all six members at San Pedro Sula, Honduras in Dec. 1995, with a view to achieving a proper 'balance of forces' in the region, intensifying the fight against trafficking of drugs and arms, and reintegrating refugees and displaced persons.

In addition, the CACM countries signed a new framework co-operation agreement with the EC in Feb. 1993, revising the previous (1985) failing agreement between them, to provide support to CACM's integration plans.

Headquarters: 4a Avenida 10–25, Zona 14, Ciudad de Guatemala, Guatemala.
Secretary-General: Haroldo Rodas Melgar.

CENTRAL AMERICAN BANK FOR ECONOMIC INTEGRATION (BCIE)

Established in 1960, the Bank is the financial institution of the Central American Economic Integration and aims to implement the economic integration and balanced economic growth of the member states.

Members. (Regional) Costa Rica, El Salvador, Guatemala, Honduras, Nicaragua. (Non-regional) Argentina, China, Colombia, Mexico.

Official languages: Spanish, English.
Headquarters: Apartado Postal 772, Tegucigalpa, DC, Honduras.
Website: http://www.bcie.org
President: Pablo Schneider.

LATIN AMERICAN INTEGRATION ASSOCIATION (ALADI/LAIA)

The ALADI was established to promote freer trade among member countries in the region.

Members. (12) Argentina, Bolivia, Brazil, Chile, Colombia, Cuba, Ecuador, Mexico, Paraguay, Peru, Uruguay and Venezuela.

Observers. (22) Andean Development Corporation (CAF), China, Commission of the European Communities, Costa Rica, Dominican Republic, El Salvador, Guatemala, Honduras, Inter-American Development Bank, Inter-American Institute for Cooperation on Agriculture (IICA), Italy, Latin American Economic System (SELA), Nicaragua, Organization of American States, Panama, Portugal, Romania, Russia, Spain, Switzerland, UN Development Programme, UN Economic Commission for Latin America and the Caribbean (ECLAC).

Official languages: Portuguese, Spanish.
Headquarters: Calle Cebollatí 1461, Casilla de Correos 20005, 11200 Montevideo, Uruguay.
Website: http://www.aladi.org
Secretary-General: Juan Francisco Rojas Penso (Venezuela).

LATIN AMERICAN ECONOMIC SYSTEM (SELA)

Established in 1975 by the Panama Convention, SELA (Sistema Económico Latinoamericano) promotes co-ordination on economic issues and social development among the countries of Latin America and the Caribbean.

Members. Argentina, Bahamas, Barbados, Belize, Bolivia, Brazil, Chile, Colombia, Costa Rica, Cuba, Dominican Republic, Ecuador, El Salvador, Grenada, Guatemala, Guyana, Haiti, Honduras, Jamaica, Mexico, Nicaragua, Panama, Paraguay, Peru, Suriname, Trinidad and Tobago, Uruguay, Venezuela.

Official languages. English, French, Portuguese, Spanish.
Headquarters: Apartado 17035, Caracas 1010–4, Venezuela.
Website: http://www.sela.org
e-mail: difusion@sela.org
Permanent Secretary: Otto Boye Soto (Chile).

Publications. Capitulos (in Spanish and English, published thrice yearly); *SELA Antenna in the United States* (quarterly bulletin); *Integration Bulletin on Latin America and the Caribbean* (monthly).

LATIN AMERICAN RESERVE FUND

Established in 1991 as successor to the Andean Reserve Fund, the Latin American Reserve Fund assists in correcting payment imbalances through loans with terms of up to four years and guarantees extended to members, to co-ordinate their monetary, exchange and financial policies and to promote the liberalization of trade and payments in the Andean sub-region.

Members: Bolivia, Colombia, Costa Rica, Ecuador, Peru, Venezuela.

Official language. Spanish.
Headquarters: Edificio Banco de Occidente, Carrera 13, No. 27–47, Piso 10, Santafe de Bogota, DC, Colombia.
Website: http://www.flar.net
Executive President: Roberto Guarnieri.

THE ANDEAN COMMUNITY

On 26 May 1969 an agreement was signed by Bolivia, Chile, Colombia, Ecuador and Peru establishing the Cartagena Agreement (also referred to as the Andean Pact or the Andean Group). Chile withdrew from the Group in 1976. Venezuela, which was initially actively involved, did not sign the agreement until 1973. In 1997 Peru announced its withdrawal for five years; and Panama joined.

The Andean Free Trade Area came into effect on 1 Feb. 1993 as the first step towards the creation of a common market. Bolivia, Colombia, Ecuador and Venezuela have fully liberalized the trade among them, while Peru is still implementing its liberalization process, due to end by 2005. A Common External Tariff for imports from third countries has been in effect since 1 Feb. 1995.

In March 1996 at the Group's 8th summit in Trujillo in Peru, member countries (Bolivia, Colombia, Ecuador, Peru, Venezuela) signed a reform protocol to the Agreement, according to which the Group would be superseded by the Andean Community, in order to promote greater economic, commercial and political integration between member countries under a new Andean Integration System (SAI).

The member countries and bodies of the Andean Integration System are now working to establish an Andean Common Market by Dec. 2005 at the latest and to implement a Common Foreign Policy, carry out a social agenda, execute a Community policy on border integration, and devise actions for harmonizing and reaching macroeconomic targets.

Organization. The Andean Presidential Council, composed of the presidents of the member states, is the highest-level body of the Andean Integration System (SAI). The Commission and the Andean Council of Foreign Ministers are legislative bodies. The General Secretariat is the executive body and the Andean Parliament is the deliberative body of the SAI. The Court of Justice, which began operating in 1984, resolves disputes between members and interprets legislation. The SAI has other institutions: Andean Development Corporation (CAF), Latin American Reserve Fund (FLAR), Simon Bolivar Andean University, Andean Business Advisory Council, Andean Labour Advisory Council and various Social Agreements.

Official language. Spanish.
Headquarters: Avda Paseo de la República 3895, San Isidro, Lima 17, Peru.
Website: http://www.comunidadandina.org
e-mail: contacto@comunidadandina.org
Secretary-General: Guillermo Fernández de Soto (Colombia).

SOUTHERN COMMON MARKET (MERCOSUR)

Founded in March 1991 by the Treaty of Asunción between Argentina, Brazil, Paraguay and Uruguay, the treaty committed the signatories to the progressive reduction of tariffs culminating in the formation of a common market on 1 Jan. 1995. This duly came into effect as a free trade zone affecting 90% of commodities. A common external tariff averaging 14% applies to 80% of trade with countries outside Mercosur. Details were agreed at foreign minister level by the Protocol of Ouro Preto signed on 17 Dec. 1994.

In 1996 Chile negotiated a free-trade agreement with Mercosur which came into effect on 1 Oct. Two weeks later, Bolivia signed the same. In Dec. that year, an agreement conferring associate membership on Bolivia was also endorsed.

Organization. The member states' foreign ministers form a Council responsible for leading the integration process, the chairmanship of which rotates every six months. The permanent executive body is the Common Market Group of member states, which takes decisions by consensus. There is a Trade Commission and Joint Parliamentary Commission, an arbitration tribunal whose decisions are binding on member countries, and a secretariat in Montevideo.

Headquarters: Rincón 575 P12, 11000 Montevideo, Uruguay.
Website: http://www.mercosur.org.uy (Spanish and Portuguese only)
Administrative Secretary: Reginaldo Braga Arcuri (Brazil).

ASSOCIATION OF CARIBBEAN STATES (ACS)

The Convention establishing the ACS was signed on 24 July 1994 in Cartagena de Indias, Colombia, with the aim of promoting consultation, co-operation and concerted action among all the countries of the Caribbean, comprising 25 full member states and three associate members. A total of eight other non-independent Caribbean countries are eligible for associate membership.

Members. Antigua and Barbuda, Bahamas, Barbados, Belize, Colombia, Costa Rica, Cuba, Dominica, Dominican Republic, El Salvador, Grenada, Guatemala, Guyana, Haiti, Honduras, Jamaica, Mexico, Nicaragua, Panama, St Kitts and Nevis, St Lucia, St Vincent and the Grenadines, Suriname, Trinidad and Tobago, Venezuela.

Associate Members. Aruba, France (on behalf of French Guiana, Guadeloupe and Martinique) and the Netherlands Antilles.

The CARICOM Secretariat, the Latin American Economic System (SELA), the Central American Integration System (SICA) and the Permanent Secretariat of the General Agreement on Central American Economic Integration (SIECA) were declared Founding Observers of the ACS in 1996. The United Nations Economic Commission for Latin America and the Caribbean (ECLAC) and the Caribbean Tourism Organization (CTO) were admitted as Founding Observers in 2000 and 2001 respectively.

Functions. The objectives of the ACS are enshrined in the Convention and are based on the following: the strengthening of the regional co-operation and integration process, with a view to creating an enhanced economic space in the region; preserving the environmental integrity of the Caribbean Sea which is regarded as the common patrimony of the peoples of the region; and promoting the sustainable development of the Greater Caribbean. Its current focal areas are trade, transport, sustainable tourism and natural disasters.

Organization. The main organs of the Association are the Ministerial Council and the Secretariat. There are Special Committees on: Trade Development and External Economic Relations; Sustainable Tourism; Transport; Natural Disasters; Budget and Administration. There is also a Council of National Representatives of the Special Fund responsible for overseeing resource mobilization efforts and project development.

Headquarters: ACS Secretariat, 5–7 Sweet Briar Road, St Clair, PO Box 660, Port of Spain, Trinidad and Tobago.
Website: http://www.acs-aec.org
e-mail: mail@acs-aec.org
Secretary-General: Prof. Norman Girvan.

CARIBBEAN COMMUNITY (CARICOM)

Origin. The Treaty of Chaguaramas establishing the Caribbean Community and Common Market was signed by the prime ministers of Barbados, Guyana, Jamaica and Trinidad and Tobago at Chaguaramas, Trinidad, on 4 July 1973, and entered into force on 1 Aug. 1973.

Six additional countries and territories (Belize, Dominica, Grenada, St Lucia, St Vincent and the Grenadines, Montserrat) signed the Treaty on 17 April 1974, and the Treaty came into effect for those countries on 1 May 1974. Antigua acceded to membership on 4 July that year; St Kitts and Nevis on 26 July; the Bahamas on 4 July 1983 (not Common Market); Suriname on 4 July 1995.

Members. Antigua and Barbuda, Bahamas, Barbados, Belize, Dominica, Grenada, Guyana, Haiti, Jamaica, Montserrat, St Kitts and Nevis, St Lucia, St Vincent and the Grenadines, Suriname, and Trinidad and Tobago. Anguilla, the British Virgin Islands, and Turks and Caicos Islands are associate members.

Objectives. The Caribbean Community has the following objectives: improved standards of living and work; full employment of labour and other factors of production; accelerated, co-ordinated and sustained economic development and convergence; expansion of trade and economic relations with third States; enhanced levels of international competitiveness; organization for increased production and productivity; the achievement of a greater measure of economic leverage and effectiveness of member states in dealing with third States, groups of States and entities of any description; enhanced co-ordination of member states' foreign and foreign economic policies; enhanced functional co-operation.

The Civil Society 'Forward Together Conference', a historic consultation between the representatives of Civil Society in the 15 Member States of the Caribbean Community and the Heads of Government held at the Ocean View Hotel, Liliendaal, Guyana on 2–3 July 2002, agreed on several broad principles for strengthening the relationships between the Caribbean Community and the Civil Society. These included more regular engagements between the Civil Society and the Heads of Government, especially for more constructive participation of Civil Society representatives in appropriate decision-making Organs of the Community such as the Council for Trade and Economic Development (COTED), the Council for Finance and Planning (COFAP), the Council for Human and Social Development (COHSOD).

The revision of the Treaty of Chaguaramas (by means of nine protocols) was begun in the 1990s and was completed in 2001. At its 22nd Meeting in July 2001 a number of Heads signed the Revised Treaty paving the way for the implementation of the new Treaty provisions and the subsequent establishment of the CARICOM Single Market and Economy (CSME).

At its 20th Meeting, the Conference of Heads of Government of the Caribbean Community approved for signature the agreement establishing the Caribbean Court of Justice. They mandated the establishment of a Preparatory Committee comprising the Attorneys General of Barbados, Guyana, Jamaica, St Kitts and Nevis, St Lucia and Trinidad and Tobago assisted by other officials, to develop and implement a programme of public education within the Caribbean Community and to make appropriate arrangements for the inauguration of the Caribbean Court of Justice prior to the establishment of the CARICOM Single Market and Economy. To this end at its 23rd Meeting in July 2002 the Heads of Government agreed on immediate measures to inaugurate the Court by the second half of 2003. Among the measures adopted was the establishment of a Trust Fund with a one-time settlement of US$100m. to finance the Court. The President of the Caribbean Development Bank was authorized to raise the funds on international capital markets, so that member states could access these funds to meet their assessed contributions towards the financing of the Court. The agreement establishing the Regional Justice Protection Programme was also approved for signature. The agreement establishes a framework for regional co-operation in the protection of witnesses, jurors, judicial and legal officers, law enforcement personnel and their associates.

Structure. The Conference of Heads of Government is the principal organ of the Community, and its primary responsibility is to determine and provide the policy direction for the Community. It is the final authority on behalf of the Community for the conclusion of treaties and for entering into relationships between the Community and international organizations and States. It is responsible for financial arrangements to meet the expenses of the Community.

The Community Council of Ministers is the second highest organ of the Community and consists of Ministers of Government responsible for Community Affairs. The Community Council has primary responsibility for the development of Community strategic planning and co-ordination in the areas of economic integration, functional co-operation and external relations.

Ministerial Councils established by the Conference of Heads of Government to assist the principal organs are: Council for Trade and Economic Development (COTED); the Council for Foreign and Community Relations (COFCOR); the Council for Human and Social Development (COHSOD); and the Council for Finance and Planning (COFAP).

The Secretariat is the principal administrative organ of the Community. The Secretary-General is appointed by the Conference (on the recommendation of the Community Council) for a term not exceeding five years, and may be re-appointed. The Secretary-General is the Chief Executive Officer of the Community and acts in that capacity at all meetings of the Community Organs.

Institutions of the Community. Caribbean Disaster Emergency Response Agency (CDERA); Caribbean Meteorological Institute (CMI); Caribbean Meteorological Organization (CMO); Caribbean Food Corporation (CFC); Caribbean Environmental Health Institute (CEHI); Caribbean Agriculture Research and Development Institute (CARDI); Association of Caribbean Community Parliamentarians (ACCP); Caribbean Centre for Development Administration (CARICAD); Caribbean Food and Nutrition Institute (CFNI).

Associate Institutions. Caribbean Development Bank (CDB); University of Guyana (UG); University of the West Indies (UWI); Caribbean Law Institute (CLI)/ Caribbean Law Institute Centre (CLIC); Secretariat of the Organisation of Eastern Caribbean States.

Official language: English.
Headquarters: Bank of Guyana Building, PO Box 10827, Georgetown, Guyana.
Website: http://www.caricom.org
Secretary-General: Edwin W. Carrington (Trinidad and Tobago).

Publications. CARICOM Perspective (1 a year); Annual Report; Treaty Establishing the Caribbean Community; Caribbean Trade and Investment Report 2000.

Further Reading
Parry, J. H., *et. al. A Short History of the West Indies.* Rev. ed. London, 1987

CARIBBEAN DEVELOPMENT BANK (CDB)

Established in 1969 by 16 regional and two non-regional members. Membership is open to all states and territories of the region and to non-regional states which are members of the UN or its Specialized Agencies or of the International Atomic Energy Agency.

Members—regional countries and territories: Anguilla, Antigua and Barbuda, Bahamas, Barbados, Belize, British Virgin Islands, Cayman Islands, Colombia, Dominica, Grenada, Guyana, Jamaica, Mexico, Montserrat, St Kitts and Nevis, St Lucia, St Vincent and the Grenadines, Trinidad and Tobago, Turks and Caicos Islands, Venezuela. *Non-regional countries:* Canada, China, Germany, Italy, United Kingdom.

Function. To contribute to the economic growth and development of the member countries of the Caribbean and promote economic co-operation and integration among them, with particular regard to the needs of the less developed countries.

> *Headquarters:* PO Box 408, Wildey, St Michael, Barbados.
> *Website:* http://www.caribank.org
> *e-mail:* info@caribank.org
> *President:* Dr Compton Bourne (Guyana).

Publications. Annual Report; Basic Information; Caribbean Development Bank: Its Purpose, Role and Functions; Summary of Proceedings of Annual Meetings of Board of Governors; Statements by the President; Financial Policies; Guidelines for Procurement; Procedures for the Selection and Engagement of Consultants by Recipients of CDB Financing; Special Development Fund Rules; Sector Policy Papers; CDB News (newsletter).

ORGANIZATION OF EASTERN
CARIBBEAN STATES (OECS)

Founded in 1981 when seven eastern Caribbean states signed the Treaty of Basseterre agreeing to co-operate with each other to promote unity and solidarity among the members.

Members. Antigua and Barbuda, Dominica, Grenada, Montserrat, St Kitts and Nevis, St Lucia, St Vincent and the Grenadines. The British Virgin Islands and Anguilla have associate membership.

Functions. As set out in the Treaty of Basseterre: to promote co-operation among the member states and to defend their sovereignty, territorial integrity and independence; to assist member states in the realization of their obligations and responsibilities to the international community with due regard to the role of international law as a standard of conduct in their relationships; to assist member states in the realization of their obligations and responsibilities to the international community with due regard to the role of international issues; to establish and maintain, where possible, arrangements for joint overseas representation and common services; to pursue these through its respective institutions by discussion of questions of common concern and by agreement on common action.

OECS's work is carried out by four main divisions. They have responsibility for: Corporate Services, Functional Co-operation, Economic Affairs, and External Relations. These oversee the work of a number of specialized institutions, work units and projects in six countries. There is an OECS secretariat in St Lucia, which is comprised of several operating units, responsible for the following functions: Education and Human Resource Development, Export Development Unit, Legal Unit, Environment and Sustainable Development Unit, Pharmaceutical Procurement Service, Social Development Unit and OECS Sports Desk.

Official language: English.
Headquarters: Morne Fortune, PO Box 179, Castries, St Lucia.
Website: http://www.oecs.org
e-mail: oecs@oecs.org
Director-General (acting): George Goodwin Jr (Antigua and Barbuda).

EASTERN CARIBBEAN CENTRAL BANK (ECCB)

The Eastern Caribbean Central Bank was established in 1983, replacing the East Caribbean Currency Authority (ECCA). According to its Articles of Agreement, its purpose is to regulate the availability of money and credit; to promote and maintain monetary stability; to promote credit and exchange conditions and a sound financial structure conducive to the balanced growth and development of the economies of the territories of the participating Governments; and to actively promote, through means consistent with its other objectives, the economic development of the territories of the participating Governments.

Members: Anguilla, Antigua and Barbuda, Dominica, Grenada, Montserrat, St Kitts and Nevis, St Lucia, St Vincent and the Grenadines.

Official language: English.
Headquarters: PO Box 89, Bird Rock, Basseterre, St Kitts and Nevis.
Website: http://www.eccb-centralbank.org/
e-mail: eccbinfo@caribsurf.com
Governor: Sir Dwight Venner (St Vincent and the Grenadines).

AGENCY FOR THE PROHIBITION OF NUCLEAR WEAPONS IN LATIN AMERICA AND THE CARIBBEAN (OPANAL)

The Agency (Organismo para la Proscripción de las Armas Nucleares en la América Latina y el Caribe) was established following the Cuban missile crisis to guarantee implementation of the world's first Nuclear-Weapon-Free-Zone (NWFZ) in the region. Created by the Treaty of Tlatelolco (1967), OPANAL is an inter-governmental agency responsible for ensuring that the requirements of the Treaty are enforced. OPANAL has played a major role in establishing other NWFZs throughout the world.

Organization. The Agency consists of three main bodies: the General Conference which meets for biennial sessions and special sessions when deemed necessary; the Council of OPANAL consisting of five member states which meet every two months plus special meetings when necessary; and the Secretariat General.

Members of the Treaty. Antigua and Barbuda, Argentina, Bahamas, Barbados, Belize, Bolivia, Brazil, Chile, Colombia, Costa Rica, Cuba, Dominica, Dominican Republic, Ecuador, El Salvador, Grenada, Guatemala, Guyana, Haiti, Honduras, Jamaica, Mexico, Nicaragua, Panama, Paraguay, Peru, St Kitts and Nevis, St Lucia, St Vincent and the Grenadines, Suriname, Trinidad and Tobago, Uruguay, Venezuela.

Headquarters: Schiller No. 326, 5th Floor, Col. Chapultepec Morales, México, D. F. 11570, Mexico.
Website: http://www.opanal.org
e-mail: info@opanal.org
Secretary-General: Edmundo Vargas Carreño (Chile).

ASIAN DEVELOPMENT BANK

A multilateral development finance institution established in 1966 to promote economic and social progress in the Asian and Pacific region, the Bank's strategic objectives in the medium term are to foster economic growth, reduce poverty, improve the status of women, support human development (including population planning) and protect the environment.

The bank's capital stock is owned by 59 member countries, 43 regional and 16 non-regional. The bank makes loans and equity investments, and provides technical assistance grants for the preparation and execution of development projects and programmes; promotes investment of public and private capital for development purposes; and assists in co-ordinating development policies and plans in its developing member countries (DMCs).

The bank gives special attention to the needs of smaller or less developed countries, giving priority to regional, sub-regional and national projects which contribute to the economic growth of the region and promote regional co-operation. Loans from ordinary capital resources on non-concessional terms account for about 80% of cumulative lending. Loans from the bank's principal special fund, the Asian Development Fund, are made on highly concessional terms almost exclusively to the poorest borrowing countries.

Regional members. Afghanistan, Australia, Azerbaijan, Bangladesh, Bhutan, Cambodia, China, Cook Islands, East Timor, Fiji Islands, Hong Kong, India, Indonesia, Japan, Kazakhstan, Kiribati, South Korea, Kyrgyzstan, Laos, Malaysia, Maldives, Marshall Islands, Micronesia, Mongolia, Myanmar, Nauru, Nepal, New Zealand, Pakistan, Papua New Guinea, Philippines, Samoa, Singapore, Solomon Islands, Sri Lanka, Taiwan, Tajikistan, Thailand, Tonga, Turkmenistan, Tuvalu, Uzbekistan, Vanuatu and Vietnam.

Non-regional members. Austria, Belgium, Canada, Denmark, Finland, France, Germany, Italy, Netherlands, Norway, Portugal, Spain, Sweden, Switzerland, Turkey, UK, USA.

Organization. The bank's highest policy-making body is its Board of Governors, which meets annually. Its executive body is the 12-member Board of Directors (each with an alternate), eight from the regional members and four non-regional.

The ADB also has resident missions: in Bangladesh; Cambodia; China; New Delhi, India; Jakarta, Indonesia; Kazakhstan; Kyrgyzstan; Laos; Káthmandu, Nepal; Islamabad, Pakistan; the Philippines; Sri Lanka; Uzbekistan; Hanoi, Vietnam; and a regional mission in Port Vila, Vanuatu. There are also three representative offices: in Tokyo, Frankfurt and Washington, D.C.

Official language: English.
Headquarters: 6 ADB Avenue, Mandaluyong, Metro Manila, Philippines.
Website: http://www.adb.org
President: Tadao Chino (Japan).

ECONOMIC CO-OPERATION ORGANIZATION (ECO)

The Economic Co-operation Organization (ECO) is an intergovernmental regional organization established in 1985 by Iran, Pakistan and Turkey. ECO is the successor of the Regional Co-operation for Development (RCD) which was first established in 1964. ECO was later expanded in 1992 to include seven new members: Afghanistan, Azerbaijan, Kazakhstan, Kyrgyzstan, Tajikistan, Turkmenistan and Uzbekistan. The objectives of the organization, stipulated in its Charter, the Treaty of Izmir, include the promotion of conditions for sustained economic growth in the region. While transport and communications, trade and investment, and energy are the high priority areas in ECO's scheme of work, other fields of co-operation such as industry, agriculture, health, science and education, drug control and human development are also on the agenda.

While summit meetings lend reaffirmation of the high level commitment of ECO member states to the goals and objectives of the organization, the Council of Ministers (COM) remains the highest policy and decision-making body of the organization, which meets at least once a year and is chaired by rotation among the member states.

ECO Summits were instituted with the First Summit held in Tehran in 1992; the Second Summit was held in Istanbul in 1993, the Third in Islamabad in 1995, the Fourth in Ashgabat in 1996, the Fifth in Almaty in May 1999 and the Sixth in Tehran in 2000.

The long-term perspectives and priorities of ECO are defined in the form of two Action Plans: the Quetta Plan of Action, and the Istanbul Declaration and Economic Co-operation Strategy, which was adopted in 1996, with concrete targets to be achieved by 2005.

The heads of state/government of the member states and the Council of Ministers have encouraged and endorsed the establishment of co-operative arrangements between ECO and major international and regional organizations and institutions within and outside the UN system for joint efforts towards implementation of ECO's economic projects and programmes.

ECO enjoys observer status with the United Nations, World Trade Organization and the Organization of Islamic Conference. A number of resolutions have been adopted in the UN General Assembly in the context of expansion of co-operation with ECO in the 1990s, most recently in Dec. 2001.

Headquarters: 1 Goulbou Alley, Kamranieh, PO Box 14155-6176, Tehran, Islamic Republic of Iran.

Website: http://www.ecosecretariat.org

e-mail: registry@ecosecretariat.org

Secretary-General: Seyed Mojtaba Arastou (Iran).

COLOMBO PLAN

History. Founded in 1950 to promote the development of newly independent Asian member countries, the Colombo Plan has grown from a group of seven Commonwealth nations into an organization of 24 countries. Originally the Plan was conceived for a period of six years. This was renewed from time to time until the Consultative Committee gave the Plan an indefinite life span in 1980.

Members. (Permanent Member Countries) Afghanistan, Australia, Bangladesh, Bhutan, Cambodia, Fiji Islands, India, Indonesia, Islamic Republic of Iran, Japan, South Korea, Lao People's Democratic Republic, Malaysia, Maldives, Myanmar, Nepal, New Zealand, Pakistan, Papua New Guinea, Philippines, Singapore, Sri Lanka, Thailand, USA and Vietnam. *(Provisional member country)* Mongolia.

Aims. The aims of the Colombo Plan are: (1) to provide a forum for discussion, at local level, of development needs; (2) to facilitate development assistance by encouraging members to participate as donors and recipients of technical co-operation; and (3) to execute programmes to advance development within member countries. The Plan currently has the following programmes:

Programme for Public Administration (PPA). Initiated in 1995 to provide developing member country officials training in all sectors of public administration in the context of market-oriented economies, drawing on the experience of more developed economies in the region. The PPA conducts joint training programmes with member countries and sponsors participants on training courses conducted by the Asian Productivity Organization (APO) and the South East Asian Fisheries Development Centre (SEAFDEC). 1999 also saw the introduction of training programmes conducted in collaboration with the Asian Development Bank Institute (ADBI) in Tokyo.

South-South Technical Co-operation Data Bank Programme (SSTC/DB). Published a report in Dec. 1997 entitled South-South Technical Co-operation in Selected Member Countries covering technical co-operation activities of India, Indonesia, Malaysia, Pakistan, Philippines, Singapore and Thailand.

Drug Advisory Programme (DAP). Initiated in 1972, it works with governments, international bodies and NGOs in the region to deliver more effective anti-narcotics programmes. It works both in supply (controlling availability of drugs) and demand (helping counter the culture and providing assistance to addicts).

Programme for Private Sector Development (PPSD). In 1998 the PPSD conducted training programmes co-sponsored by the Asian Development Bank (ADB), the Malaysian Technical Co-operation Programme (MTCP) and the Pakistan Industrial Technical Assistance Centre (PITAC).

Colombo Plan Staff College for Technician Education (CPSC). Established in 1973, it trains management and technical staff from member countries. It is separately financed by most member countries and functions under the guidance of its own Governing Board, consisting of the heads of member countries' permanent diplomatic missions in the Philippines.

Structure. The Consultative Committee is the principal policy-making body of the Colombo Plan. Consisting of all member countries, it meets every two years to review the economic and social progress of members, exchange views on technical co-operation programmes and generally review the activities of the Plan. The Colombo Plan Council represents each member government and meets several times a year to identify development issues, recommend measures to be taken and ensure implementation.

> *Headquarters:* 12 Melbourne Avenue, PO Box 596, Colombo 4, Sri Lanka.
> *e-mail:* cplan@slt.lk
> *Website:* http://www.colombo-plan.org
> *Secretary-General:* Dr U Sarat Chandran (India).

Publications. Consultative Committee Meeting—Proceedings and Conclusions (biennial); *Report of the Colombo Plan Council* (annual); *The Colombo Plan Brochure* (annual); *The Colombo Plan Focus* (quarterly newsletter); *South-South Technical Co-operation in Selected Member Countries.*

ASIA-PACIFIC ECONOMIC CO-OPERATION (APEC)

Origin and Aims. APEC was originally established in 1989 to take advantage of the interdependence among Asia-Pacific economies, by facilitating economic growth for all participants and enhancing a sense of community in the region. Begun as an informal dialogue group, APEC is the premier forum for facilitating economic growth, co-operation, trade and investment in the Asia-Pacific region. APEC has a membership of 21 economic jurisdictions, a population of over 2·5bn. and a combined GDP of US$19trn. accounting for 47% of world trade.

APEC is working to achieve what are referred to as the 'Bogor Goals' of free and open trade and investment in the Asia-Pacific by 2010 for developed economies and 2020 for developing economies.

Members. Australia, Brunei, Canada, Chile, China, Hong Kong, Indonesia, Japan, South Korea, Malaysia, Mexico, New Zealand, Papua New Guinea, Peru, Philippines, Russia, Singapore, Taiwan, Thailand, USA and Vietnam.

Activities. APEC works in three broad areas to meet the Bogor Goals. These three broad work areas, known as APEC's 'Three Pillars', are: Trade and Investment Liberalization—reducing and eliminating tariff and non-tariff barriers to trade and investment, and opening markets; Business Facilitation—reducing the costs of business transactions, improving access to trade information and bringing into line policy and business strategies to facilitate growth, and free and open trade; Economic and Technical Co-operation—assisting member economies build the necessary capacities to take advantage of global trade and the new economy.

Official language: English.
Headquarters: 35 Heng Mui Keng Terrace, Singapore 119616.
Website: http://www.apecsec.org.sg
Executive Director: Ambassador Piamsak Milintachinda (Thailand).

SECRETARIAT OF THE PACIFIC COMMUNITY (SPC)

Until Feb. 1998 known as the South Pacific Commission, this is a regional intergovernmental organization founded in 1947 under an Agreement commonly referred to as the Canberra Agreement. It is funded by assessed contributions from its 27 members and by voluntary contributions from member and non-member countries, international organizations and other sources.

Members. American Samoa, Australia, Cook Islands, Fiji Islands, France, French Polynesia, Guam, Kiribati, Marshall Islands, Federated States of Micronesia, Nauru, New Caledonia, New Zealand, Niue, Northern Mariana Islands, Palau, Papua New Guinea, Pitcairn Islands, Samoa, Solomon Islands, Tokelau, Tonga, Tuvalu, UK, USA, Vanuatu, and Wallis and Futuna.

Functions. The SPC has three main areas of work: land resources, marine resources and social resources. It conducts research and provides technical assistance and training in these areas to member Pacific Island countries and territories of the Pacific.

Organization. The Conference of the Pacific Community is the governing body of the Community. Its key focus is to appoint the Director-General, to consider major national or regional policy issues and to note changes to the Financial and Staff Regulations approved by the CRGA, the Committee of Representatives of Governments and Administrations. It meets every two years. The CRGA meets once a year and is the principal decision-making organ of the Community. There is also a regional office in Fiji Islands.

Headquarters: BP D5, 98848 Nouméa Cedex, New Caledonia.
Website: http://www.spc.int
e-mail: spc@spc.int
Director-General: Lourdes Pangelinan (Guam).

PACIFIC ISLANDS FORUM (PIF)

In Oct. 2000 the South Pacific Forum changed its name to the Pacific Islands Forum. As the South Pacific Forum it held its first meeting of Heads of Government in New Zealand in 1971. The annual PIF provides an opportunity for discussions to be held on a wide range of issues. The Agreement Establishing the Forum Secretariat defines the membership of the Forum and the Secretariat. Decisions are reached by consensus. The administrative arm of the Forum, known officially as the Pacific Islands Forum Secretariat, is based in Suva, Fiji. In Oct. 1994 the Forum was granted observer status to the UN.

Members. (2002) Australia, Cook Islands, Fiji Islands, Kiribati, Marshall Islands, Micronesia, Nauru, New Zealand, Niue, Palau, Papua New Guinea, Samoa, Solomon Islands, Tonga, Tuvalu and Vanuatu. In 1999 the French territory of New

Caledonia was admitted to the Forum as an observer. In 2002 East Timor was admitted to the Forum as a Special Observer.

Functions. The Secretariat's mission is to provide policy options to the Pacific Islands Forum, and to promote Forum decisions and regional and international co-operation. The organization seeks to promote political stability and regional security; enhance the management of economies and the development process; improve trade and investment performance; and efficiently manage the resources of the Secretariat.

Activities. The Secretariat has four core divisions: Trade and Investment; Political and International Affairs; Development and Economic Policy; Corporate Services. The Secretariat provides policy advice to members on a wide range of social, economic and political issues. Since 1989 the Forum has held Post Forum Dialogues with key dialogue partners at ministerial level. There are currently twelve partners: Canada, China, EU, France, India, Indonesia, Japan, South Korea, Malaysia, the Philippines, the United Kingdom and the United States.

Organization. The South Pacific Bureau for Economic Cooperation (SPEC) began as a trade bureau and was established as SPEC in 1972, before being re-organized as the South Pacific Forum Secretariat in 1988. It changed its name to the Pacific Islands Forum Secretariat in 2000. The Secretariat is headed by a Secretary General and Deputy Secretary General who form the Executive. The governing body is the Forum Officials Committee, which acts as an intermediary between the Secretariat and the Forum. The Secretariat operates four Trade Offices in Auckland, Beijing, Sydney and Tokyo.

The Secretary General is the permanent Chair of the Council of Regional Organisations in the Pacific (CROP), which brings together ten main regional organizations in the Pacific region: Fiji School of Medicine (FSM); Forum Fisheries Agency (FFA); Pacific Islands Development Programme (PIDP); Pacific Islands Forum Secretariat (PIFS); Secretariat for the Pacific Community (SPC); South Pacific Applied Geoscience Commission (SOPAC); South Pacific Board for Educational Assessment (SPBEA); South Pacific Regional Environment Programme (SPREP); South Pacific Tourism Organisation (SPTO); and the University of the South Pacific (USP).

Official language: English.
Headquarters: Ratu Sukuna Road, Suva, Fiji Islands.
Website: http://www.forumsec.org.fj
Secretary-General: Noel Levi, CBE (Papua New Guinea).

ASSOCIATION OF SOUTH EAST ASIAN NATIONS (ASEAN)

History and Membership. ASEAN is a regional intergovernmental organization formed by the governments of Indonesia, Malaysia, the Philippines, Singapore and Thailand through the Bangkok Declaration which was signed by their foreign ministers on 8 Aug. 1967. Brunei joined in 1984, Vietnam in 1995, Laos and Myanmar in 1997 and Cambodia in 1999. Papua New Guinea also has observer status. In 2001 the combined GDP of member countries was estimated to be US$550,000m.

Objectives. The main objectives are to accelerate economic growth, social progress and cultural development, to promote active collaboration and mutual assistance in matters of common interest, to ensure the political and economic stability of the South East Asian region, and to maintain close co-operation with existing international and regional organizations with similar aims.

Activities. Principal projects concern economic co-operation and development, with the intensification of intra-ASEAN trade, and trade between the region and the rest of the world; joint research and technological programmes; co-operation in transportation and communications; promotion of tourism, South East Asian studies, cultural, scientific, educational and administrative exchanges. The decision to set up an *ASEAN Free Trade Area (AFTA)* was taken at the Fourth Summit meeting, in Singapore in 1992, with the aim of creating a common market in 15 years, subsequently brought forward to 2002. AFTA applies to its first six signatories, namely Brunei, Indonesia, Malaysia, Philippines, Singapore and Thailand.

In Dec. 1995 heads of government meeting in Bangkok signed a treaty establishing a South-East Asia Nuclear-Free Zone, which was extended to cover offshore economic exclusion zones. Individual signatories were to decide whether to allow port visits or transportation of nuclear weapons by foreign powers through territorial waters. The *ASEAN Regional Forum (ARF)* was proposed at a meeting of foreign ministers in July 1993 to discuss security issues in the region. Its first formal meeting took place in July 1994 attended by all seven members and its dialogue partners (Australia, Canada, the EU, Japan, South Korea, New Zealand and the USA) and observers (People's Republic of China, Laos, Papua New Guinea, Russia and Vietnam).

Organization. The highest authority is the meeting of Heads of Government, which takes place annually. The highest policy-making body is the annual Meeting of Foreign Ministers, commonly known as AMM, the ASEAN Ministerial Meeting, which convenes in each of the member countries on a rotational basis in alphabetical order. The AEM (ASEAN Economic Meeting) meets formally or informally each year to direct ASEAN economic co-operation. The AEM and AMM report jointly to the heads of government at summit meetings. Each capital has its own national secretariat. The central secretariat in Jakarta is headed by the Secretary-General, a post that revolves among the member states in alphabetical order every five years.

Official language: English.
Headquarters: POB 2072, Jakarta 12110, Indonesia.
Website: http://www.aseansec.org
Secretary-General: Ong Keng Yong (Singapore).

ASEAN MEKONG BASIN DEVELOPMENT CO-OPERATION (MEKONG GROUP)

The ministers and representatives of Brunei, Cambodia, China, Indonesia, Laos, Malaysia, Myanmar, Philippines, Singapore, Thailand and Vietnam met in Kuala Lumpur on 17 June 1996 and agreed the following basic objectives for the Group. Its principal objectives are to co-operate in the economic and social development of the Mekong Basin area and strengthen the link between it and ASEAN member countries, through a process of dialogue and common project identification.

Priorities include: development of infrastructure capacities in the fields of transport, telecommunications, irrigation and energy; development of trade and investment-generating activities; development of the agricultural sector to enhance production for domestic consumption and export; sustainable development of forestry resources and development of mineral resources; development of the industrial sector, especially small to medium enterprises; development of tourism; human resource development and support for training; co-operation in the fields of science and technology.

Further Reading

Broinowski, A., *Understanding ASEAN.* London, 1982.—(ed.) *ASEAN into the 1990s.* London, 1990
Van Hoa, Tran, (ed.) *Economic Developments and Prospects in the ASEAN.* London, 1997
Wawn, B., *The Economics of the ASEAN Countries.* London, 1982

SOUTH ASIAN ASSOCIATION FOR REGIONAL CO-OPERATION (SAARC)

SAARC was established to accelerate the process of economic and social development in member states through joint action in agreed areas of co-operation. The foreign ministers of the seven member countries met for the first time in New Delhi in Aug.

1983 and adopted the Declaration on South Asian Regional Co-operation whereby an Integrated Programme of Action (IPA) was launched. The charter establishing SAARC was adopted at the first summit meeting in Dhaka in Dec. 1985.

Members. Bangladesh, Bhutan, India, Maldives, Nepal, Pakistan, Sri Lanka.

Objectives. To promote the welfare of the peoples of South Asia; to accelerate economic growth, social progress and cultural development; to promote and strengthen collective self-reliance among members; to promote active collaboration and mutual assistance in the economic, social, cultural, technical and scientific fields; to strengthen co-operation with other developing countries, and among themselves through international forums on matters of common interest. Co-operation within the framework is based on respect for the principles of sovereign equality, territorial integrity, political independence, non-interference in the internal affairs of other states, and mutual benefit. Agreed areas of co-operation under the *Integrated Programme of Action (IPA)* include agriculture and rural development; human resource development; environment, meteorology and forestry; science and technology; transport and communications; energy; and social development.

A SAARC Preferential Trading Arrangement (SAPTA) designed to reduce tariffs on trade between SAARC member states was signed in April 1993 and entered into force in Dec. 1995. In 1998 at the Tenth Summit in Colombo, the importance of achieving a South Asian Free Trade Area (SAFTA) as mandated by the Malé Summit in 1997 was reiterated and it was decided to set up a Committee of Experts to work on drafting a comprehensive treaty regime for creating a free trade area. The Colombo Summit agreed that the text of this regulatory framework would be finalized by 2001.

Organization. The highest authority of the Association rests with the heads of state or government, who meet annually at Summit level. The Council of Foreign Ministers, which meets twice a year, is responsible for formulating policy, reviewing progress and deciding on new areas of co-operation and the mechanisms deemed necessary for that. The Council is supported by a Standing Committee of Foreign Secretaries, by the Programming Committee and by 11 Technical Committees which are responsible for individual areas of SAARC's activities. There is a secretariat in Káthmandu, headed by a Secretary-General, who is assisted in his work by seven Directors, appointed by the Secretary-General upon nomination by member states for a period of three years which may in special circumstances be extended.

Decisions at all levels are taken on the basis of unanimity. Bilateral and contentious issues are excluded from deliberations.

Official language: English.
Headquarters: PO Box 4222, Káthmandu, Nepal.
Website: http://www.saarc-sec.org
Secretary-General: Q. A. M. A. Rahim (Bangladesh).

THE LEAGUE OF ARAB STATES

Origin. The League of Arab States is a voluntary association of sovereign Arab states, established by a Pact signed in Cairo on 22 March 1945 by the representatives of Egypt, Iraq, Saudi Arabia, Syria, Lebanon, Jordan and Yemen. It seeks to promote closer ties among member states and to co-ordinate their economic, cultural and security policies with a view to developing collective co-operation, protecting national security and maintaining the independence and sovereignty of member states, in order to enhance the potential for joint Arab action across all fields.

Members. Algeria, Bahrain, Comoros, Djibouti, Egypt, Iraq, Jordan, Kuwait, Lebanon, Mauritania, Morocco, Oman, Palestine, Qatar, Saudi Arabia, Somalia, Sudan, Syria, Tunisia, United Arab Emirates and Republic of Yemen. Libya left the League of Arab States in Oct. 2002, citing its 'inefficiency' in dealing with the stand-off between Iraq and the USA and the Israeli–Palestinian conflict.

Joint Action. In the political field, the League is entrusted with defending the supreme interests and national causes of the Arab world through the implementation of joint action plans at regional and international levels, and with examining any disputes that may arise between member states with a view to settling them by peaceful means. The Joint Defence and Economic Co-operation Treaty signed in 1950 provided for the establishment of a Joint Defence Council as well as an Economic Council (renamed the Economic and Social Council in 1977). Economic, social and cultural activities constitute principal and vital elements of the joint action initiative.

Arab Common Market. An Arab Common Market came into operation on 1 Jan. 1965. The agreement, reached on 13 Aug. 1964, provided for the abolition of customs duties on agricultural products and natural resources within five years, by reducing tariffs at an annual rate of 20%. Customs duties on industrial products were to be reduced by 10% annually. However, it never became reality although it has remained the ambition of many people throughout the Arab world for many years since.

Organization. The machinery of the League consists of a Council, 11 specialized ministerial committees entrusted with drawing up common policies for the regulation and advancement of co-operation in their fields (information, internal affairs, justice, housing, transport, social affairs, youth and sports, health, environment, telecommunications and electricity), and a permanent secretariat.

The League is considered to be a regional organization within the framework of the United Nations at which its Secretary-General is an observer. It has permanent delegations in New York and Geneva for the UN, in Addis Ababa for the Organization of African Unity (OAU), as well as offices in Athens, Beijing, Berlin, Brussels, London, Madrid, Moscow, New Delhi, Paris, Rome, Vienna and Washington, D.C.

Headquarters: Al Tahrir Square, Cairo, Egypt.
Website: http://www.arableagueonline.org
Secretary-General: Amre Moussa (Egypt).

Further Reading

Clements, F. A., *Arab Regional Organizations* [Bibliography]. Oxford and New Brunswick (NJ), 1992
Gomaa, A. M., *The Foundation of the League of Arab States.* London, 1977

ARAB FUND FOR ECONOMIC AND SOCIAL DEVELOPMENT (AFESD)

Established in 1968, the Fund commenced operations in 1974.

Aims. To contribute to the financing of economic and social development in Arabic states through: financing economic and social development projects by making loans on concessionary terms to governments and public enterprises and corporations, giving preference to projects which are vital to the Arab world and to inter-Arab projects; and financing private sector projects in member states by providing all forms and loans and guarantees to corporations and enterprises processing juridical personality.

Members. Algeria, Bahrain, Djibouti, Egypt, Iraq*, Jordan, Kuwait, Lebanon, Libya, Mauritania, Morocco, Oman, Palestine, Qatar, Saudi Arabia, Somalia*, Sudan, Syria, Tunisia, United Arab Emirates, Republic of Yemen. *Membership suspended since 1993.

Headquarters: PO Box 21923, Safat 13080, Kuwait.
Website: http://www.arabfund.org
Director General and Chairman of the Board of Directors: Abdulatif Y. Al Hamad.

Publications. Annual Report; Joint Arab Economic Report.

ARAB MONETARY FUND (AMF)

Origin. The Agreement establishing the Arab Monetary Fund was approved by the Economic Council of the League of Arab States in April 1976 and the first meeting of the Board of Governors was held on 19 April 1977.

Aims. To assist member countries in eliminating payments and trade restrictions, in achieving exchange rate stability, in developing capital markets and in correcting payments imbalances through the extension of short- and medium-term loans; the co-ordination of monetary policies of member countries; and the liberalization and promotion of trade and payments, as well as the encouragement of capital flows among member countries.

Members. Algeria, Bahrain, Comoros, Djibouti, Egypt, Iraq, Jordan, Kuwait, Lebanon, Libya, Mauritania, Morocco, Oman, Palestine, Qatar, Saudi Arabia, Somalia, Sudan, Syria, Tunisia, United Arab Emirates, Republic of Yemen.

Headquarters: PO Box 2818, Abu Dhabi, United Arab Emirates.
Website: http://www.amf.org.ae
Director General and Chairman of the Board of Directors: Jassim A. Al-Mannai.

Publications (in English and Arabic): *Annual Report; The Articles of Agreement of the Arab Monetary Fund; Money and Credit in Arab Countries* (annual); *National Accounts of Arab Countries* (annual); *Foreign Trade of Arab Countries* (annual); *Cross Exchange Rates of Arab Currencies* (annual); *Arab Countries: Economic Indicators* (annual); *Balance of Payments and External Public Debt of Arab Countries* (annual); *AMF Publications Catalogue* (annual); *Arab Monetary Fund: Structure and Activities (1977–83)*. (In Arabic only): *The Joint Arabic Economic Report* (annual); *AMF Economic Bulletin; Developments in Arab Capital Markets* (quarterly).

GULF CO-OPERATION COUNCIL (GCC)

Origin. Also referred to as the Co-operation Council for the Arab States of the Gulf (CCASG), the Council was established on 25 May 1981 on signature of the Charter by Bahrain, Kuwait, Oman, Qatar, Saudi Arabia and the United Arab Emirates.

Aims. To assure security and stability of the region through economic and political co-operation; promote, expand and enhance economic ties on solid foundations, in the best interests of the people; co-ordinate and unify economic, financial and monetary policies, as well as commercial and industrial legislation and customs regulations; achieve self-sufficiency in basic foodstuffs.

Organization. The Supreme Council is formed by the heads of member states and is the highest authority. Its presidency rotates, based on the alphabetical order of the names of the member states. It holds one regular session every year, in addition to a mid-year consultation session. The Co-operation Council has a commission, called 'Commission for the Settlement of Disputes', which is attached to the Supreme Council. The Ministerial Council is formed of the Foreign Ministers of the member states or other delegated ministers and meets quarterly. The Secretariat-General is composed of Secretary-General, Assistant Secretaries-General and a number of staff as required. The Secretariat consists of the following sectors: Political Affairs, Military Affairs, Economic Affairs, Human and Environment Affairs, Information Centre, Media Department, Secretary-General's Office, GCC Delegation in Brussels, Technical Telecommunications Bureau in Bahrain. In Jan. 2003 it launched a customs union, introducing a 5% duty on foreign imports across the trade bloc.

Finance. The annual budget of the GCC Secretariat is shared equally by the six member states.

Headquarters: PO Box 7153, Riyadh-11462, Saudi Arabia.
Secretary-General: Abdulrahman bin Hamad Al-Attiyeh.

Publications. GCC News (monthly, in English); *Attaawun* (quarterly, in Arabic); *GCC Economic Bulletin* (annual).

Further Reading
Twinam, J. W., *The Gulf, Co-operation and the Council: an American Perspective.* Washington, 1992

ORGANIZATION OF THE PETROLEUM EXPORTING COUNTRIES (OPEC)

Origin and Aims. Founded in Baghdad in 1960 by Iran, Iraq, Kuwait, Saudi Arabia and Venezuela. The principal aims are: to unify the petroleum policies of member countries and determine the best means for safeguarding their interests, individually and collectively; to devise ways and means of ensuring the stabilization of prices in international oil markets with a view to eliminating harmful and unnecessary fluctuations; and to secure a steady income for the producing countries, an efficient, economic and regular supply of petroleum to consuming nations, and a fair return on their capital to those investing in the petroleum industry. It is estimated that OPEC members possess 75% of the world's known reserves of crude petroleum, of which about two-thirds are in the Middle East.

Members. (2002) Algeria, Indonesia, Iran, Iraq, Kuwait, Libya, Nigeria, Qatar, Saudi Arabia, United Arab Emirates and Venezuela. Membership applications may be made by any other country having substantial net exports of crude petroleum, which has fundamentally similar interests to those of member countries. Gabon became an associated member in 1973 and a full member in 1975, but in 1996 withdrew owing to difficulty in meeting its percentage contribution. Ecuador joined the Organization in 1973 but left in 1992.

Organization. The main organs are the Conference, the Board of Governors and the Secretariat. The Conference, which is the supreme authority meeting at least twice a year, consists of delegations from each member country, normally headed by the respective minister of oil, mines or energy. All decisions, other than those concerning procedural matters, must be adopted unanimously.

Headquarters: Obere Donaustrasse 93, A-1020 Vienna, Austria.
Website: http://www.opec.org
e-mail: prid@opec.org
Secretary-General: Álvaro Silva Calderón (Venezuela).

Publications. Annual Statistical Bulletin; Annual Report; OPEC Bulletin (monthly); OPEC Review (quarterly); OPEC General Information; Monthly Oil Market Report; OPEC Statute.

Further Reading
Al-Chalabi, F., *OPEC at the Crossroads.* Oxford, 1989
Skeet, I., *OPEC: 25 Years of Prices and Policies.* CUP, 1988

OPEC FUND FOR INTERNATIONAL DEVELOPMENT

The OPEC Fund for International Development was established in 1976 to provide financial aid on advantageous terms to developing countries (other than OPEC members) and international development agencies whose beneficiaries are developing countries. In 1980 the Fund was transformed into a permanent autonomous international agency and renamed the OPEC Fund for International Development. It is administered by a Ministerial Council and a Governing Board. Each member country is represented on the Council by its finance minister.

The initial endowment of the fund amounted to US$800m. At the start of 2003 pledged contributions totalled US$3,435m., and the Fund had extended 953 loans totalling US$5,146·1m. of which US$3,952·5m. was for project financing, US$724·2m. for balance-of-payments support, US$305·3m. for programme funding and US$164·0m. for debt relief within the context of the Highly Indebted Poor Countries Initiative. In addition, and through its private sector window, the Fund had approved financing worth a total of US$189·3m. in 40 operations in support of private sector entities in Africa, Asia, Latin America, the Caribbean and Europe. Through its grant programme the Fund had also committed a total of US$272·3m. in support of a wide range of initiatives.

Headquarters: POB 995, A-1011 Vienna, Austria.
Website: http://www.opecfund.org
e-mail: info@opecfund.org
Director-General: Dr Yesufu Seyyid Abdulai (Nigeria).

ORGANIZATION OF ARAB PETROLEUM EXPORTING COUNTRIES (OAPEC)

Established in 1968 to promote co-operation and close ties between member states in economic activities related to the oil industry; to determine ways of safeguarding their legitimate interests, both individual and collective, in the oil industry; to unite their efforts so as to ensure the flow of oil to consumer markets on equitable and reasonable terms; and to create a favourable climate for the investment of capital and expertise in their petroleum industries.

Members. Algeria, Bahrain, Egypt, Iraq, Kuwait, Libya, Qatar, Saudi Arabia, Syria, Tunisia*, United Arab Emirates. *Tunisia's membership was made inactive in 1986.

Headquarters: PO Box 20501, Safat 13066, Kuwait.
Website: http://www.oapecorg.org
Secretary-General: Abdulaziz A. Al-Turki.

Publications. Secretary General's Annual Report (Arabic and English editions); *Oil and Arab Co-operation* (quarterly; Arabic with English abstracts and bibliography); *OAPEC Monthly Bulletin* (Arabic and English editions); *Energy Resources Monitor* (Arabic); *OAPEC Annual Statistical Report* (Arabic/English).

ARAB MAGHREB UNION

The Arab Maghreb Union was founded in 1989 to promote political co-ordination, co-operation and 'complementarity' across various fields, with integration wherever and whenever possible.

Members. Algeria, Libya, Mauritania, Morocco, Tunisia.

By late 1996 joint policies and projects under way or under consideration included: the establishment of the Maghreb Investment and Foreign Trade Bank to fund joint agricultural and industrial projects; free movement of citizens within the region; joint transport undertakings, including railway improvements and a Maghreb highway; creation of a customs union; and establishment of a common market.

A Declaration committing members to the establishment of a free trade zone was adopted at the AMU's last summit in Tunis (April 1994). In Nov. 1992 members adopted a charter on protection of the environment.

Official language: Arabic.
Headquarters: 14 Rue Zalagh, Agdal, Rabat, Morocco.
Website: http://www.maghrebarabe.org
Secretary-General: Habib Boularès (Tunisia).

ARAB ORGANIZATION FOR AGRICULTURAL DEVELOPMENT (AOAD)

The AOAD was established in 1970 and commenced operations in 1972. Its aims are to develop natural and human resources in the agricultural sector and improve the means and methods of exploiting these resources on scientific bases; to increase agricultural productive efficiency and achieve agricultural integration between the Arab States and countries; to increase agricultural production with a view to achieving a higher degree of self-sufficiency; to facilitate the exchange of agricultural products between the Arab States and countries; to enhance the establishment of agricultural ventures and industries; and to increase the standards of living of the labour force engaged in the agricultural sector.

Organization. The structure comprises a General Assembly consisting of ministers of agriculture of the member states, an Executive Council, a Secretariat General, seven technical departments—Food Security, Human Resources Development, Water Resources, Studies and Research, Projects Execution, Technical Scientific Co-operation, and Financial Administrative Department—and two centres—the Arab Center for Agricultural Information and Documentation, and the Arab Bureau for Consultation and Implementation of Agricultural Projects.

Members. Algeria, Bahrain, Djibouti, Egypt, Iraq, Jordan, Kuwait, Lebanon, Libya, Mauritania, Morocco, Oman, Palestine, Qatar, Saudi Arabia, Somalia, Sudan, Syria, Tunisia, United Arab Emirates, Republic of Yemen.

Official languages: Arabic (English and French used in translated documents and correspondence).
Headquarters: Street No. 7, Al-Amarat, Khartoum, Sudan.
Director General: Salem Al-Lozi.

AFRICAN UNION (AU)

History. The Fourth Extraordinary Session of the Assembly of the Heads of State and Government of the Organization of African Unity (OAU) held in Sirté, Libya on 9 Sept. 1999 decided to establish an African Union. At Lomé, Togo on 11 July 2000 the OAU Assembly of the Heads of State and Government adopted the Constitutive Act of the African Union, which was later ratified by the required two-thirds of the member states of the Organization of African Unity (OAU); it came into force on 26 May 2001. The Lusaka Summit, in July 2001, gave a mandate to translate the transformation of the Organization of African Unity into the African Union, and on 9 July 2002 the Durban Summit, in South Africa, formally launched the African Union.

Aims. The African Union aims to promote unity, solidarity, cohesion and co-operation among the peoples of Africa and African states, and at the same time to co-ordinate efforts by African people to realize their goals of achieving economic, political and social integration.

Activities. The African Union became fully operational in July 2002, and will be working towards establishing 17 organs among which are a Pan-African parliament, the Economic, Social and Cultural Commission (ECOSOC), a Central Bank and a Court of Justice.

Official languages. Arabic, English, French, Ki-Swahili, Portuguese and Spanish.
Headquarters: POB 3243, Addis Ababa, Ethiopia.
Chairman: Thabo Mbeki (South Africa).

AFRICAN DEVELOPMENT BANK

Established in 1964 to promote economic and social development in Africa.

Regional Members. (53) Algeria, Angola, Benin, Botswana, Burkina Faso, Burundi, Cameroon, Cape Verde, Central African Republic, Chad, Comoros, Congo (Dem. Rep. of), Congo (Rep. of), Côte d'Ivoire, Djibouti, Egypt, Equatorial Guinea, Eritrea, Ethiopia, Gabon, The Gambia, Ghana, Guinea, Guinea-Bissau, Kenya, Lesotho, Liberia, Libya, Madagascar, Malaŵi, Mali, Mauritania, Mauritius, Morocco, Mozambique, Namibia, Niger, Nigeria, Rwanda, São Tomé e Príncipe, Senegal, Seychelles, Sierra Leone, Somalia, South Africa (Rep. of), Sudan, Swaziland, Tanzania, Togo, Tunisia, Uganda, Zambia, Zimbabwe.

Non-regional Members. (24) Argentina, Austria, Belgium, Brazil, Canada, China, Denmark, Finland, France, Germany, India, Italy, Japan, South Korea, Kuwait, Netherlands, Norway, Portugal, Saudi Arabia, Spain, Sweden, Switzerland, UK, USA.

Within the ADB Group is the African Development Fund, established in 1972, which provides development finance on concessional terms to low-income Regional Member Countries which are unable to borrow on the non-concessional terms of the African Development Bank. Membership of the Fund is made up of 25 non-African State Participants, the African Development Bank and the Nigerian Trust Fund.

Official languages. English, French.
Headquarters: 01 BP 1387, Abidjan 01, Côte d'Ivoire.
Website: http://www.afdb.org
e-mail: afdb@afdb.org
President: Omar Kabbaj (Morocco).

BANK OF CENTRAL AFRICAN STATES (BEAC)

The Bank of Central African States (Banque des Etats de l'Afrique Centrale) was established in 1973 when a new Convention of Monetary Co-operation with France was signed. The five original members, Cameroon, Central African Republic, Chad, Republic of the Congo and Gabon, were joined by Equatorial Guinea in 1985. Under its Convention and statutes, the BEAC is declared a 'Multinational African institution in the management and control of which France participates in return for the guarantee she provides for its currency'.

Official language: French.
Headquarters: Avenue Monseigneur Vogt, Yaoundé, Cameroon.
Website: http://www.beac.int
Governor: Jean-Félix Mamalepot.

Publications. Etudes et Statistiques (monthly bulletins); *Annual Report; Directory of Banks and Financial Establishments of BEAC Monetary Area* (annual); *Bulletin du Marché Monétaire* (monthly bulletins); *Annual Report of the Banking Commission.*

EAST AFRICAN DEVELOPMENT BANK (EADB)

Established originally under the Treaty for East African Co-operation in 1967 with Kenya, Tanzania and Uganda as signatories, a new Charter for the Bank (with the same signatories) came into force in 1980. Under the original Treaty the Bank was confined to the provision of financial and technical assistance for the promotion of industrial development in member states but with the new Charter its remit was broadened to include involvement in agriculture, forestry, tourism, transport and the development of infrastructure, with preference for projects which promote regional co-operation.

Official language: English.
Headquarters: 4 Nile Avenue, Kampala, Uganda.
Website: http://transafrica.org/eadb/
Chairman of the Board: Mwaghazi Mwachofi (Kenya).

WEST AFRICAN DEVELOPMENT BANK (BOAD)

The West African Development Bank (Banque Ouest Africaine de Développement) was established in Nov. 1973 by an Agreement signed by the member states of the West African Monetary Union (UMOA), now the West African Economic and Monetary Union (UEMOA).

Aims. To promote balanced development of the States of the Union and to achieve West African economic integration.

Members. Benin, Burkina Faso, Côte d'Ivoire, Guinea-Bissau, Mali, Niger, Senegal, Togo.

Official language: French.
Headquarters: 68 Avenue de la Libération, Lomé, Togo.
Website: http://www.boad.org
e-mail: boadsiege@boad.org
President: Boni Yayi.

CENTRAL BANK OF WEST AFRICAN STATES (BCEAO)

Established in 1962, the Central Bank of West African States (Banque Centrale des Etats de l'Afrique de l'Ouest) is the common central bank of the eight member states which form the West African Monetary Union (WAMU). It has the sole right of currency issue throughout the Union territory and is responsible for the pooling of the Union's foreign exchange reserve; the management of the monetary policy of the member states; the keeping of the accounts of the member states treasury; and the definition of the banking law applicable to banks and financial establishments.

Members. Benin, Burkina Faso, Côte d'Ivoire, Guinea-Bissau, Mali, Niger, Senegal, Togo.

Official language: French.
Headquarters: Avenue Abdoulaye Fadiga, Dakar, Senegal.
Website: http://www.bceao.int
Governor: Charles Konan Banny.

Publications. Rapport annuel (annual); *Annuaire des Banques* (annual); *Bilan des Banques U.M.O.A.* (annual); *Notes d'information et statistiques* (monthly bulletin).

AFRICAN EXPORT–IMPORT BANK (AFREXIMBANK)

Established in 1987 under the auspices of the African Development Bank to facilitate, promote and expand intra-African and extra-African trade. Membership is made up of three categories of shareholders: Class 'A' Shareholders consisting of African governments, African central banks and sub-regional and regional financial institutions and economic organizations; Class 'B' Shareholders consisting of African public and private financial institutions; and Class 'C' Shareholders consisting of international financial institutions, economic organizations and non-African states, banks, financial institutions and public and private investors.

Official languages. English, French, Arabic, Portuguese.
Headquarters: World Trade Center, 1191 Corniche El-Nil, Cairo 11221, Egypt.
Website: http//www.afreximbank.com
President and Chairman to the Board: Christopher C. Edordu.

ECONOMIC COMMUNITY OF CENTRAL AFRICAN STATES (CEEAC)

The Economic Community of Central African States (Communauté Economique des Etats de l'Afrique Centrale) was established in 1983 to promote regional economic co-operation and to establish a Central African Common Market.

Members: Burundi, Cameroon, Central African Republic, Chad, Democratic Republic of the Congo, Republic of the Congo, Equatorial Guinea, Gabon, Rwanda, São Tomé e Príncipe. *Observer:* Angola.

Headquarters: BP 2112, Libreville, Gabon.

ECONOMIC COMMUNITY OF WEST AFRICAN STATES (ECOWAS)

Founded in 1975 as a regional common market, and now aiming to operate a single currency zone by 2004, ECOWAS later also became a political forum involved in the promotion of a democratic environment and the pursuit of fundamental human rights. In July 1993 it revised its treaty to assume responsibility for the regulation of regional armed conflicts, acknowledging the inextricable link between development and peace and security. Thus it now has a new role in conflict management and prevention through its Mediation and Security Council, which monitors the moratorium on the export, import and manufacture of light weapons and ammunition. However, it still retains a military arm, ECOMOG. It is also involved in the war against drug abuse and illicit drug trafficking.

Members. Benin, Burkina Faso, Cape Verde, Côte d'Ivoire, The Gambia, Ghana, Guinea, Guinea-Bissau, Liberia, Mali, Niger, Nigeria, Senegal, Sierra Leone, Togo.

Organization. It meets at yearly summits which rotate in the different capitals of member states. The institution is governed by the Council of Ministers, and has a secretariat in Abuja which is run by an Executive Secretary.

Official languages. English, French, Portuguese.
Headquarters: 60 Yakubu Gowon Crescent, Asokoro, Abuja, Nigeria.
Website: http://www.ecowas.int
e-mail: info@ecowasmail.net
Executive Secretary: Lansana Kouyaté (Guinea).

WEST AFRICAN ECONOMIC AND MONETARY UNION (UEMOA)

Founded in 1994, the UEMOA (Union Economique et Monétaire Ouest Africaine) aims to reinforce the competitiveness of the economic and financial activities of member states in the context of an open and rival market and a rationalized and harmonized juridical environment; to ensure the convergence of the macroeconomic performances and policies of member states with the institution of a multilateral control procedure; to create a common market among member states based on the free circulation of the people, goods, services and capital and on the right of people exercising an independent or remunerated activity to establish a common external tariff as well as a common commercial policy; to institute a coordination for the national sector-based policies with the implementation of common actions and conceivably common policies, especially in the following domains: community-based land reclamation, agriculture, environment, transport, infrastructures, telecommunications, human resources, energy, industries, mines and crafts; and to harmonize the legislation, especially the fiscal system, of the member states if the necessity arose for the proper functioning of the common market.

Members. Benin, Burkina Faso, Côte d'Ivoire, Guinea-Bissau, Mali, Niger, Senegal, Togo.

Headquarters: 01 B.P. 543, Ouagadougou 01, Burkina Faso.

COMMON MARKET FOR EASTERN AND SOUTHERN AFRICA (COMESA)

COMESA is an African economic grouping of 20 member states who are committed, over the long term, to the creation of a Common Market for Eastern and Southern Africa. It was established in 1994 as a building block for the African Economic Community and replaced the Preferential Trade Area for Eastern and Southern Africa, which had been in existence since 1981.

Members. Angola, Burundi, Comoros, Democratic Republic of Congo, Djibouti, Egypt, Eritrea, Ethiopia, Kenya, Madagascar, Malawi, Mauritius, Namibia, Rwanda, Seychelles, Sudan, Swaziland, Uganda, Zambia and Zimbabwe.

Objectives. To facilitate the removal of the structural and institutional weaknesses of member states so that they are able to attain collective and sustainable development.

Activities. COMESA's Free Trade Area (FTA) was launched on 31 Oct. 2000 at a Summit of Heads of States and Government in Lusaka, Zambia. The FTA participating states shall have zero tariff on goods and services produced in these countries.

In addition to creating the policy environment for freeing trade, COMESA has also created specialized institutions like the Trade and Development Bank of Eastern and Southern Africa, the COMESA Re-Insurance Company, the Clearing House and the COMESA Court of Justice, to provide the required financial infrastructure and service support.

Official languages. English, French, Portuguese.
Headquarters: COMESA Secretariat, COMESA Centre, Ben Bella Road, PO Box 30051, 10101 Lusaka, Zambia.
Website: http://www.comesa.int
Secretary General: Erastus Mwencha (Kenya).

SOUTHERN AFRICAN DEVELOPMENT COMMUNITY (SADC)

The Southern African Development Co-ordination Conference (SADCC), the forerunner of the Southern African Development Community (SADC), was formed in Lusaka, Zambia on 1 April 1980, following the adoption of the Lusaka Declaration—*Southern Africa: Towards Economic Liberation*—by the nine founding member states.

Members. The nine founder member countries were Angola, Botswana, Lesotho, Malaŵi, Mozambique, Swaziland, Tanzania, Zambia and Zimbabwe. The Democratic Republic of the Congo, Mauritius, Namibia, the Seychelles and South Africa have since joined, bringing membership up to 14 countries.

Aims and Activities. SADC's Common Agenda includes the following: the promotion of sustainable and equitable economic growth and socio-economic development that will ensure poverty alleviation with the ultimate objective of its eradication; the promotion of common political values, systems and other shared values that are transmitted through institutions that are democratic, legitimate and effective; and the consolidation and maintenance of democracy, peace and security.

In contrast to the country-based co-ordination of sectoral activities and programmes, SADC has now adopted a more centralized approach through which the 21 Co-ordinating Units are grouped into four clusters; namely: Trade, Industry, Finance and Investment; Infrastructure and Services; Food, Agriculture, and Natural Resources; Social and Human Development and Special Programmes.

SADC has made remarkable progress in implementing its integration agenda since the 1992 Treaty came into force. Since then, 24 Protocols to spearhead the sectoral programmes and activities have been signed. The following protocols have entered into force: Immunities and Privileges; Combating Illicit Drug Trafficking; Energy; Transport, Communications and Meteorology; Shared Watercourse Systems; Mining; Trade; Education and Training.

Official languages. English, French, Portuguese.
Headquarters: Private Bag 0095, Gaborone, Botswana.
Website: http://www.sadc.int
e-mail: registry@sadc.int
Executive Secretary: Dr Prega Ramsamy (Mauritius).

LAKE CHAD BASIN COMMISSION

Established by a Convention and Statute signed on 22 May 1964 by Cameroon, Chad, Niger and Nigeria, and later by the Central African Republic and Sudan, to regulate and control utilization of the water and other natural resources in the Basin; to initiate, promote and co-ordinate natural resources development projects and research within the Basin area; and to examine complaints and promote settlement of disputes, with a view to promoting regional co-operation.

In Dec. 1977, at Enugu in Nigeria, the 3rd summit of heads of state of the commission signed the protocol for the Harmonization of the Regulations Relating to Fauna and Flora in member countries, and adopted plans for the multi-donor approach towards major integrated development for the conventional basin. An international campaign to save Lake Chad following a report on the environmental degradation of the conventional basin was launched by heads of state at the 8th summit of the Commission in Abuja in March 1994. The 10th summit, held in N'Djaména in 2000, saw agreement on a US$1m. inter-basin water transfer project.

The Commission operates an annual budget of CFA 800m., and receives assistance from various international and donor agencies including the FAO, and UN Development and Environment Programmes.

Official languages: English, French.
Headquarters: BP 727, N'Djaména, Chad.
Executive Secretary: Engr. Muhammad Sani Adamu.

NIGER BASIN AUTHORITY

As a result of a special meeting of the Niger River Commission (established in 1964), to discuss the revitalizing and restructuring of the organization to improve its efficiency, the Niger Basin Authority was established in 1980. Its responsibilities cover the harmonization and co-ordination of national development policies; the formulation of the general development policy of the Basin; the elaboration and implementation of an integrated development plan of the Basin; the initiation and monitoring of an orderly and rational regional policy for the utilization of the waters of the Niger River; the design and conduct of studies, researches and surveys; the formulation of plans, the construction, exploitation and maintenance of structure, and the elaboration of projects.

Members: Benin, Burkina Faso, Cameroon, Chad, Côte d'Ivoire, Guinea, Mali, Niger, Nigeria.

Official languages: English, French.
Website: http://www.abn.ne
Headquarters: BP 729, Niamey, Niger.
Executive Secretary: Muhammad Bello Tuga.

EAST AFRICAN COMMUNITY

The East African Community (EAC) was formally established on 30 Nov. 1999 with the signing in Arusha, Tanzania of the Treaty for the Establishment of the East African Community. The Treaty envisages the establishment of a Customs Union, as the entry point of the Community, a Common Market, subsequently a Monetary Union and ultimately a Political Federation of the East African States. The EAC partner states are aiming to sign a Protocol on the Establishment of the East African Customs Union by Nov. 2003.

Members: Kenya, Tanzania, Uganda.

Website: http://www.eachq.org
Headquarters: PO Box 1096, Arusha, Tanzania.
Secretary General: Nuwe Amanya-Mushega.

INTERGOVERNMENTAL AUTHORITY ON DEVELOPMENT

The Intergovernmental Authority on Development was created on 21 March 1996 and has its origins in the Intergovernmental Authority on Drought and Development, which had been established in 1986. It has three priority areas of co-operation: conflict prevention, management and humanitarian affairs; infrastructure development; food security and environment protection.

Members: Djibouti, Eritrea, Ethiopia, Kenya, Somalia, Sudan, Uganda.

Website: http://www.igad.org
Headquarters: PO Box 2653, Djibouti, Republic of Djibouti.
Executive Secretary: Dr Attalla Hamad Bashir (Sudan).

WORLD COUNCIL OF CHURCHES

The World Council of Churches was formally constituted on 23 Aug. 1948 in Amsterdam. Today, member churches number over 340 from more than 120 countries.

Origin. The World Council was founded by the coming together of diverse Christian movements, including the overseas mission groups gathered from 1921 in the International Missionary Council, the Faith and Order Movement founded by American Episcopal Bishop Charles Brent, and the Life and Work Movement led by Swedish Lutheran Archbishop Nathan Söderblom. On 13 May 1938, at Utrecht, a provisional committee was appointed to prepare for the formation of a World Council of Churches, under the chairmanship of William Temple, then Archbishop of York.

Membership. The basis of membership (1975) states: 'The World Council of Churches is a fellowship of Churches which confess the Lord Jesus Christ as God and Saviour according to the Scriptures and therefore seek to fulfil together their common calling to the glory of the one God, Father, Son and Holy Spirit.' Membership is open to Churches which express their agreement with this basis and satisfy such criteria as the Assembly or Central Committee may prescribe. Today, more than 340 Churches of Protestant, Anglican, Orthodox, Old Catholic and Pentecostal confessions belong to this fellowship.

Activities. The WCC's Central Committee comprises the Programme Committee and the Finance Committee. Within the Programme Committee there are advisory groups on issues relating to communication, women, justice, peace and creation, youth, ecumenical relations and inter-religious relations. Following the WCC's international assembly in Harare, Zimbabwe in 1998 the work of the WCC was restructured. Activities were grouped into four 'clusters'—Relationships; Issues and Themes; Communication; and Finance, Services and Administration. The Relationships cluster comprises four teams (Church and Ecumenical Relations, Regional Relations and Ecumenical Sharing, Inter-Religious Relations and International Relations), as well as two programmes (Action by Churches Together and the Ecumenical Church Loan Fund). The Issues and Themes cluster comprises four teams (Faith and Order; Mission and Evangelism; Justice, Peace and Creation; and Education and Ecumenical Formation).

In Aug. 1997 the WCC launched a Peace to the City campaign, as the initial focus of a programme to overcome violence in troubled cities. The Decade to Overcome Violence was launched in Feb. 2001 during the meeting of the WCC Central Committee in Berlin.

Organization. The governing body of the World Council, consisting of delegates specially appointed by the member Churches, is the Assembly, which meets every seven or eight years to frame policy. It has no legislative powers and depends for the implementation of its decisions upon the action of member Churches. The 8th Assembly, in Harare in 1998, had as its theme 'Turn to God, Rejoice in Hope'. A 154-member Central Committee meets annually to carry out the Assembly mandate, with a smaller 25-member Executive Committee meeting twice a year. The General Secretariat includes the *Ecumenical Institute* at Bossey, in Switzerland.

Headquarters: PO Box 2100, 150 route de Ferney, 1211 Geneva 2, Switzerland.
Website: http://www.wcc-coe.org
General Secretary: Rev. Dr Konrad Raiser (Germany).

Publications. Annual Reports; Dictionary of the Ecumenical Movement, Geneva, 1991; *Directory of Christian Councils,* 1985; *A History of the Ecumenical Movement,* Geneva, 1993; *Ecumenical Review* (quarterly); *Ecumenical News International* (weekly); *International Review of Mission* (quarterly).

Further Reading

Castro, E., *A Passion for Unity*. Geneva, 1992
Potter, P., *Life in all its Fullness*. Geneva, 1981
Raiser, K., *Ecumenism in Transition*. Geneva, 1994
Van Elderen, M. and Conway, M., *Introducing the World Council of Churches revised and enlarged edition*. Geneva, 1991
Vermaat, J. A. E., *The World Council of Churches and Politics*. New York, 1989
Visser 't Hooft, W. A., *The Genesis and Formation of the World Council of Churches. Geneva, 1982.—Memoirs*. Geneva, 1987

UNREPRESENTED NATIONS AND PEOPLES ORGANIZATION (UNPO)

UNPO is an international organization created by nations and peoples around the world who are not represented in the world's principal international organizations, such as the UN. Founded in 1991, UNPO now has 53 members representing over 100m. people worldwide.

Membership. Open to all nations and peoples unrepresented, subject to adherence to the five principles which form the basis of UNPO's charter: equal right to self-determination of all nations and peoples; adherence to internationally accepted human rights standards; to the principles of democracy; promotion of non-violence; and protection of the environment. Applicants must show that they constitute a 'nation or people' as defined in the Covenant.

Functions and Activities. UNPO offers an international forum for occupied nations, indigenous peoples, minorities and oppressed majorities, who struggle to regain their lost countries, preserve their cultural identities, protect their basic human and economic rights, and safeguard their environment.

It does not represent those peoples; rather it assists and empowers them to represent themselves more effectively. To this end, it provides professional services and facilities as well as education and training in the fields of diplomacy, human rights law, democratic processes, conflict resolution, and environmental protection. Members, private foundations and voluntary contributions fund the Organization.

In total six former members of UNPO (Armenia, Belau, East Timor, Estonia, Georgia and Latvia) subsequently achieved full independence and gained representation in the UN. Belau is now called Palau. Current members Bougainville and Kosovo are progressively achieving self-determination.

Headquarters: 40A Javastraat, NL-2585 AP The Hague, Netherlands.
Website: http://www.unpo.org
General Secretary: Erkin Alptekin.

Publication. UNPO News (quarterly).

INTERNATIONAL ORGANIZATION FOR MIGRATION (IOM)

Established in Brussels in 1951 to help solve European population and refugee problems through migration, and to stimulate the creation of new economic opportunities in countries lacking certain manpower. IOM is committed to the principle that humane and orderly migration benefits migrants and society.

Members (98 as of Dec. 2002). Albania, Algeria, Angola, Argentina, Armenia, Australia, Austria, Azerbaijan, Bangladesh, Belgium, Belize, Benin, Bolivia, Bulgaria, Burkina Faso, Cambodia, Canada, Cape Verde, Chile, Colombia, Congo (Democratic Republic of), Congo (Republic of), Costa Rica, Côte d'Ivoire, Croatia,

Cyprus, Czech Republic, Denmark, Dominican Republic, Ecuador, Egypt, El Salvador, Finland, France, Gambia, Georgia, Germany, Greece, Guatemala, Guinea, Guinea-Bissau, Haiti, Honduras, Hungary, Iran, Ireland, Israel, Italy, Japan, Jordan, Kazakhstan, Kenya, South Korea, Kyrgyzstan, Latvia, Liberia, Lithuania, Luxembourg, Madagascar, Mali, Mexico, Morocco, Netherlands, Nicaragua, Nigeria, Norway, Pakistan, Panama, Paraguay, Peru, Philippines, Poland, Portugal, Romania, Rwanda, Senegal, Serbia and Montenegro, Sierra Leone, Slovakia, Slovenia, South Africa, Sri Lanka, Sudan, Sweden, Switzerland, Tajikistan, United Republic of Tanzania, Thailand, Tunisia, Uganda, Ukraine, UK, USA, Uruguay, Venezuela, Yemen, Zambia and Zimbabwe. 33 governments and a large number of government agencies and NGOs have observer status.

Activities. As an intergovernmental body, IOM acts with its partners in the international community to: assist in meeting the operational challenges of migration; advance understanding of migration issues; encourage social and economic development through migration; work towards effective respect of human dignity and the well-being of migrants. Since 1952 the IOM has assisted some 11m. refugees and migrants to settle in over 125 countries. Throughout 2001 the organization assisted in the humanitarian emergency unfolding in Afghanistan by way of shelter programmes and the registration of IDPs (internally displaced persons), and by meeting the needs of the displaced brought on by drought and conflict. Those elsewhere supported by the IOM in 2001 included: India, following the earthquake affecting large areas in the west of the country; and Africa, in particular the collection and destruction of arms in the Democratic Republic of the Congo and the relocation of IDPs following continued fighting in the border region between Guinea and Sierra Leone. In 2001 IOM launched a 'Migration and Development in Africa Programme' and a 'Migration Policy and Research Programme'. IOM's operational budget in 2001 was US$360m.

Official languages. English, French, Spanish.
Headquarters: Route des Morillons 17, POB 71, 1211 Geneva 19, Switzerland.
Website: http://www.iom.int
Director-General: Brunson McKinley (USA).

INTERNATIONAL COMMITTEE OF THE RED CROSS (ICRC)

Origin. Founded in Geneva in Feb. 1863. From its outset the ICRC saw that volunteers could act effectively on the battlefield, without risking rejection by officers and soldiers, only if they could be told apart from ordinary civilians by a distinctive emblem and were protected from fighting.

The 27th International Conference of the Red Cross and Red Crescent was held in Geneva in Nov. 1999 and adopted a Plan of Action for 2000–03.

Mission Statement. The ICRC acts to help all victims of war and internal violence, attempting to ensure implementation of humanitarian rules restricting armed violence.

The ICRC's mission arises from the basic human desire, common to all civilizations, to lay down rules governing the use of force in war and to safeguard the dignity of the weak. With a mandate from the international community to help victims of war and internal violence and to promote compliance with international humanitarian law, the ICRC's activities are aimed at protecting and assisting the victims of armed conflict and internal violence so as to preserve their physical integrity and their dignity and to enable them to regain their autonomy as quickly as possible. The main treaties governing international law are the Geneva Conventions (1949) and the Additional Protocols (1977).

* The ICRC is independent of all governments and international organizations. Its work is prompted by the desire to promote humane conduct and is guided by empathy for the victims. The ICRC is impartial: its only criterion for action is the

victims' needs. The ICRC is neutral and remains detached from all political issues related to conflict.

* By applying these principles strictly, the ICRC is able to act as an intermediary between the parties to armed conflict and to promote dialogue in situations of internal violence, with a view to finding solutions for matters of humanitarian concern.

* Through its work, the ICRC helps to prevent the worsening of crises and even at times to resolve them.

* The ICRC systematically reminds all military and civilian authorities directly involved in armed conflict or internal violence of their obligations under international humanitarian law and the other humanitarian rules by which they are bound.

* The ICRC has the duty to remind all States of their collective obligation to ensure respect for international humanitarian law.

* In all societies and cultures, the ICRC endeavours to promote international humanitarian law and the fundamental human values underlying the law.

* As the founding member of the International Red Cross and Red Crescent Movement, the ICRC directs and co-ordinates the international work of the Movement's components in connection with armed conflict and internal violence.

* The ICRC gives priority to co-operation with the National Red Cross and Red Crescent Societies and their Federation. It acts in consultation with all other organizations involved in humanitarian work.

Finance. The ICRC relies for its financing on voluntary contributions from signatories to the Geneva Conventions, supranational organizations such as the European Union, and public and private sources. To obtain the necessary funding the ICRC launches annual appeals.

In 2001 the ICRC maintained a permanent presence in 69 countries with a total staff of around 11,000, and conducted operations in around 80 countries.

Headquarters: 19 Avenue de la Paix, 1202 Geneva, Switzerland.
Website: http://www.icrc.org
President: Jakob Kellenberger (Switzerland).

Further Reading
Moorehead, Caroline, *Dunant's Dream: War, Switzerland and the History of the Red Cross.* HarperCollins, London, 1998

MÉDECINS SANS FRONTIÈRES (MSF)

Origin. Médecins sans Frontières was established on 20 Dec. 1971 by a group of French doctors. MSF has offices in 20 countries and provides emergency medical assistance to more than 80 countries.

Functions. MSF was the first non-military, non-governmental organization to specialize in international humanitarian aid and emergency medical assistance. MSF is dedicated to rectifying what it perceives as the shortcomings of international aid agencies who, it believes, offer too little medical assistance and are overly reticent in the face of legal and administrative obstacles. MSF works in countries where health structures are insufficient, collaborating with authorities such as the Ministry of Health to provide assistance. MSF works in rehabilitation of hospitals and dispensaries, vaccination programmes and water and sanitation projects. MSF also works in remote health care centres, slum areas and provides training of local personnel with the objective of rebuilding health structures to acceptable levels.

Headquarters: MSF International Office, Rue de la Tourelle 39, B–1040 Brussels, Belgium.
Website: http://www.msf.org
Secretary-General: Rafael Vilasan Juan.
President: Dr Morten Rostrup (Norway).

AMNESTY INTERNATIONAL (AI)

Origin. Founded in 1961 by British lawyer Peter Beneson as a one-year campaign for the release of prisoners of conscience, Amnesty International has grown to become a worldwide organization, winning the Nobel Peace Prize in 1977. As defined by AI, 'prisoners of conscience' are people imprisoned solely because of their political or religious beliefs, gender, or their racial or ethnic origin, who have neither used nor advocated violence. The organization's mandate is based on the United Nations Universal Declaration of Human Rights.

AI has over 1m. members, subscribers and regular donors in more than 100 countries. The organization is governed by a nine-member International Executive Committee (IEC). It comprises eight volunteer members elected every two years by an International Council comprising representatives of the worldwide movement, and an elected member of the International Secretariat. During the 12 months to 31 March 1998 the International Secretariat had expenditure of £16,312,000.

Each year, AI produces a global report detailing human rights violations in all regions of the world. The 2001 report, which detailed abuses during 2000, included the fact that executions were carried out in 61 countries, people were arbitrarily arrested and detained, or in detention without charge or trial in 72 countries, and in 125 countries people were reportedly tortured or ill-treated by security forces, police or other state authorities.

International Secretariat: 99–119 Rosebery Avenue, London EC1R 3RE, UK.
Website: http://www.amnesty.org
Secretary-General: Irene Khan (Bangladesh).

INTERNATIONAL SEABED AUTHORITY (ISA)

The ISA is an autonomous international organization established under the UN Convention on the Law of the Sea (UNCLOS) of 1982 and the 1994 Agreement relating to the implementation of Part XI of the above Convention. It came into existence on 16 Nov. 1994 and became fully operational in June 1996.

The administrative expenses are met from assessed contributions from its members. Membership currently numbers 138 and the budget for the biennium 2003–04 is US$10,509,700.

The Convention on the Law of the Sea covers almost all ocean space and its uses: navigation and overflight, resource exploration and exploitation, conservation and pollution, fishing and shipping. It entitles coastal states and inhabited islands to proclaim a 200-mile exclusive economic zone or continental shelf (which may be larger). Its 320 Articles and nine Annexes constitute a guide for behaviour by states in the world's oceans, defining maritime zones, laying down rules for drawing sea boundaries, assigning legal rights, duties and responsibilities to States, and providing machinery for the settlement of disputes.

Organization. The Assembly, consisting of representatives from all member states, is the supreme organ. The 36-member Council, elected by the Assembly, includes the four largest importers or consumers of seabed minerals, four largest investors in seabed minerals, four major exporters of the same, six developing countries representing special interests and 18 members from all the geographical regions. The Council is the executive organ of the Authority. There are also two subsidiary bodies: the Legal and Technical Commission (currently 24 experts) and the Finance Committee (currently 15 experts). The Secretariat serves all the bodies of the Authority and under the 1994 Agreement is performing functions of the Enterprise (until such time as it starts to operate independently of the Secretariat). The Enterprise is the organ through which the ISA carries out deep seabed activities directly or through joint ventures.

Activities. In July 2000 the ISA adopted the Regulations for Prospecting and Exploration for Polymetallic Nodules in the Area. Pursuant thereto, it signed exploration contracts with seven contractors who have submitted plans of work for deep seabed exploration. These are: Institut Français de Recherche pour l'Exploitation de la Mer (IFREMER) and Association Française pour l'Etude de la Recherche des Nodules (AFERNOD), France; Deep Ocean Resources Development Co. Ltd (DORD), Japan; State Enterprise Yuzhmorgeologiya, Russian Federation; China Ocean Minerals Research and Development Association (COMRA); Interoceanmetal Joint Organization (IOM), a consortium sponsored by Bulgaria, Cuba, Czech Republic, Poland, Russian Federation and Slovakia; the government of South Korea; and the government of India.

Between 1998 and 2002 the ISA organized five workshops: the development of guidelines for the assessment of the possible environmental impacts arising from exploration for polymetallic nodules; proposed technologies for deep seabed mining of polymetallic nodules; the available knowledge on mineral resources other than polymetallic nodules in the deep seabed; a standardized system of data interpretation; prospects for international collaboration in marine environmental research. The workshop to be convened in 2003 will have as its objective the establishment of a programme to develop a geologic model of the Clarion-Clipperton Fracture Zone in the Pacific Ocean. While continuing to develop a database on polymetallic nodules (POLYDAT), the Authority has also made significant progress towards the establishment of a central data repository for all marine minerals in the deep seabed.

The *International Tribunal for the Law of the Sea (ITLOS)*, founded in Oct. 1996 and based in Hamburg, adjudicates on disputes relating to the interpretation and application of the United Nations Convention on the Law of the Sea. The Convention gives the Tribunal jurisdiction to resolve a variety of international law of the sea disputes such as the delimitation of maritime zones, fisheries, navigation and the protection of the marine environment. Its Seabed Disputes Chamber has compulsory jurisdiction to resolve disputes amongst States, the International Seabed Authority, companies and private individuals, arising out of the exploitation of the deep seabed. The Tribunal also has compulsory jurisdiction in certain instances to protect the rights of parties to a dispute or to prevent serious harm to the marine environment, and over the prompt release of arrested vessels and their crews upon the deposit of a security. The jurisdiction of the Tribunal also extends to all matters specifically provided for in any other agreement which confers jurisdiction on the Tribunal. The Tribunal is composed of 21 judges, elected by signatories from five world regional blocs: five each from Africa and Asia; four from Western Europe and other States; four from Latin America and the Caribbean; and three from Eastern Europe. The judges serve a term of nine years, with one third of the judges' terms expiring every three years.

Headquarters: 14–20 Port Royal St., Kingston, Jamaica.
Website: http://www.isa.org.jm
Secretary-General: Satya N. Nandan (Fiji Islands).

Publications. Handbook 2002; plus selected decisions and documents from the Authority's sessions; various others.

ANTARCTIC TREATY

Antarctica is an island continent some 15·5m. sq. km in area which lies almost entirely within the Antarctic Circle. Its surface is composed of an ice sheet over rock, and it is uninhabited except for research and other workers in the course of duty. It is in general ownerless: for countries with territorial claims, *see* ARGENTINA; AUSTRALIA: Australian Antarctic Territory; CHILE; FRANCE: Southern and Antarctic Territories; NEW ZEALAND: Ross Dependency; NORWAY: Queen Maud Land; UNITED KINGDOM: British Antarctic Territory.

12 countries which had maintained research stations in Antarctica during International Geophysical Year, 1957–58 (Argentina, Australia, Belgium, Chile,

France, Japan, New Zealand, Norway, South Africa, the USSR, the UK and the USA) signed the Antarctic Treaty (Washington Treaty) on 1 Dec. 1959. Austria, Brazil, Bulgaria, Canada, China, Colombia, Cuba, Czech Republic, Denmark, Ecuador, Estonia, Finland, Germany, Greece, Guatemala, Hungary, India, Italy, South Korea, North Korea, the Netherlands, Papua New Guinea, Peru, Poland, Romania, Slovakia, Spain, Sweden, Switzerland, Turkey, Ukraine, Uruguay and Venezuela subsequently acceded to the Treaty. The Treaty reserves the Antarctic area south of 60° S. lat. for peaceful purposes, provides for international co-operation in scientific investigation and research, and preserves, for the duration of the Treaty, the *status quo* with regard to territorial sovereignty, rights and claims. The Treaty entered into force on 23 June 1961. The 45 nations party to the Treaty (27 full voting signatories and 18 adherents) meet biennially.

An agreement reached in Madrid in April 1991 and signed by all 39 parties in Oct. imposes a ban on mineral exploitation in Antarctica for 50 years, at the end of which any one of the 27 voting parties may request a review conference. After this the ban may be lifted by agreement of three quarters of the nations then voting, which must include the present 27.

Website: http://www.nsf.gov/od/opp/antarct/anttrty.htm

Further Reading

Elliott, L. M., *International Environmental Politics: Protecting the Antarctic*. London, 1994
Jørgensen-Dahl, A. and Østreng, W., *The Antarctic Treaty System in World Politics*. London, 1991
Meadows, J. *et al.*, *The Antarctic* [Bibliography]. Oxford and New Brunswick (NJ), 1994

INTER-PARLIAMENTARY UNION (IPU)

Founded in 1889 by William Randal Cremer (UK) and Frédéric Passy (France), the Inter-Parliamentary Union was the first permanent forum for political multilateral negotiations. The Union is a centre for dialogue and parliamentary diplomacy among legislators representing every political system and all the main political leanings in the world. It was instrumental in setting up what is now the Permanent Court of Arbitration in The Hague.

Activities. The IPU fosters contacts, co-ordination and the exchange of experience among parliaments and parliamentarians of all countries; considers questions of international interest and concern, and expresses its views on such issues in order to bring about action by parliaments and parliamentarians; contributes to the defence and promotion of human rightsan essential factor of parliamentary democracy and development; contributes to better knowledge of the working and development of representative institutions and to the strengthening of representative democracy.

Membership. The IPU had 144 members and five associate members in Nov. 2002.

Headquarters: Chemin du Pommier 5, C.P. 330, 1218 Le Grand Saconnex, Geneva 19, Switzerland.
Website: http://www.ipu.org
Secretary-General: Anders B. Johnsson (Sweden).

INTERNATIONAL INSTITUTE FOR DEMOCRACY AND ELECTORAL ASSISTANCE (IDEA)

Created in 1995, the International IDEA is an intergovernmental organization that seeks to promote and develop sustainable democracy worldwide. Global in membership and independent of specific national interests, IDEA works with both new and long-established democracies, helping to develop the institutions and culture of democracy. It operates at international, regional and national levels, working in partnership with a range of institutions.

Aims and Activities. The International IDEA aims to: help countries build capacity to develop democratic institutions; provide a meeting-place for and facilitate dialogue between democracy practitioners around the world; increase knowledge and expertise about elections and election observation; promote transparency, accountability, professionalism and efficiency in elections in the context of democratic development; develop and promote norms, rules and guidelines relating to multi-party pluralism and broader democratic processes. The principal areas of activity include: electoral systems and management; political participation, including women in politics; political parties, management and financing; post-conflict democracy building and reconciliation; democracy at local level; democracy indicators and assessment.

Membership. The International IDEA had 19 members in Dec. 2002.

Headquarters: Strömsberg, 103 34 Stockholm, Sweden.
Website: http://www.idea.int
Secretary-General: Karen Fogg (UK).

ORGANIZATION OF THE ISLAMIC CONFERENCE (OIC)

Founded in 1969, the objectives of the OIC are to promote Islamic solidarity among member states; to consolidate co-operation among member states in the economic, social, cultural, scientific and other vital fields of activities, and to carry out consultations among member states in international organizations; to endeavour to eliminate racial segregation, discrimination and to eradicate colonialism in all its forms; to take the necessary measures to support international peace and security founded on justice; to strengthen the struggle of all Muslim peoples with a view to safeguarding their dignity, independence and national rights; to create a suitable atmosphere for the promotion of co-operation and understanding among member states and other countries.

Members (57 as of March 2003). Afghanistan, Albania, Algeria, Azerbaijan, Bahrain, Bangladesh, Benin, Brunei, Burkina Faso, Cameroon, Chad, Comoros, Côte d'Ivoire, Djibouti, Egypt, Gabon, The Gambia, Guinea, Guinea-Bissau, Guyana, Indonesia, Iran, Iraq, Jordan, Kazakhstan, Kuwait, Kyrgyzstan, Lebanon, Libya, Malaysia, Maldives, Mali, Mauritania, Morocco, Mozambique, Niger, Nigeria, Oman, Pakistan, Palestine, Qatar, Saudi Arabia, Senegal, Sierra Leone, Somalia, Sudan, Suriname, Syria, Tajikistan, Togo, Tunisia, Turkey, Turkmenistan, Uganda, United Arab Emirates, Uzbekistan, Yemen. *Observer states:* Bosnia-Herzegovina, Central African Republic, Thailand.

Headquarters: PO Box 5925, Jeddah, Saudi Arabia.
Website: http://www.oic-un.org
Secretary-General: Dr Abdelouahed Belkeziz (Morocco).

ISLAMIC DEVELOPMENT BANK

The Agreement establishing the IDB (Banque islamique de développement) was adopted at the Second Islamic Finance Ministers' Conference held in Jeddah, Saudi Arabia in Aug. 1974. The Bank, which is open to all member countries of the

Organization of the Islamic Conference, commenced operations in 1975. Its main objective is to foster economic development and social progress of member countries and Muslim communities individually as well as jointly in accordance with the principles of the Sharia. It is active in the promotion of trade and the flow of investments among member countries, and maintains a Special Assistance Fund for member countries suffering natural calamities. The Fund is also used to finance health and educational projects aimed at improving the socio-economic conditions of Muslim communities in non-member countries. A US$1·5bn. IDB Infrastructure Fund was launched in 1998 to invest in projects such as power, telecommunications, transportation, energy, natural resources, petro-chemical and other infrastructure-related sectors in member countries.

Members (54 as of March 2003). Afghanistan, Albania, Algeria, Azerbaijan, Bahrain, Bangladesh, Benin, Brunei, Burkina Faso, Cameroon, Chad, Comoros, Côte d'Ivoire, Djibouti, Egypt, Gabon, The Gambia, Guinea, Guinea-Bissau, Indonesia, Iran, Iraq, Jordan, Kazakhstan, Kuwait, Kyrgyzstan, Lebanon, Libya, Malaysia, Maldives, Mali, Mauritania, Morocco, Mozambique, Niger, Oman, Pakistan, Palestine, Qatar, Saudi Arabia, Senegal, Sierra Leone, Somalia, Sudan, Suriname, Syria, Tajikistan, Togo, Tunisia, Turkey, Turkmenistan, Uganda, United Arab Emirates, Yemen.

Official language. Arabic. *Working languages.* English, French.
Headquarters: PO Box 5925, Jeddah 21432, Saudi Arabia.
Website: http://www.isdb.org
President: Ahmed Mohamed Ali (Saudi Arabia).

WORLD CUSTOMS ORGANIZATION

Established in 1952 as the Customs Co-operation Council, the World Customs Organization is an intergovernmental body with worldwide membership, whose mission it is to enhance the effectiveness and efficiency of customs administrations throughout the world. It has 161 member countries or territories.

Headquarters: Rue de l'Industrie 26–38, B-1040 Brussels, Belgium.
Website: http://www.wcoomd.org
Secretary-General: Michel Danet (France).

INTERPOL (INTERNATIONAL CRIMINAL POLICE ORGANIZATION)

Organization. Interpol was founded in 1923, disbanded in 1938 and reconstituted in 1946. The International Criminal Police Organization—Interpol was founded to ensure and promote the widest possible mutual assistance between all criminal police authorities within the limits of the law existing in the different countries worldwide and the spirit of the Universal Declaration of Human Rights, and to establish and develop all institutions likely to contribute effectively to the prevention and suppression of ordinary law crimes.

Aims. Interpol provides a co-ordination centre (General Secretariat) for its 181 member countries. Its priority areas of activity concern criminal organizations, public safety and terrorism, drug-related crimes, financial crime and high-tech crime, trafficking in human beings, and tracking fugitives from justice. Interpol centralizes records and information on international offenders; it operates a worldwide communication network.

Interpol's General Assembly is held annually. The General Assembly is the body of supreme authority in the organization. It is composed of delegates appointed by the members of the organization.

Interpol's Executive Committee, which meets four times a year, supervises the execution of the decisions of the General Assembly. The Executive Committee is composed of the president of the organization, the three vice-presidents and nine delegates.

Interpol's General Secretariat is the centre for co-ordinating the fight against international crime. Its activities, undertaken in response to requests from the police services and judicial authorities in its member countries, focus on crime prevention and law enforcement.

As of March 2003 Interpol's Sub-Regional Bureaus are located in Abidjan, Buenos Aires, El Salvador, Harare and Nairobi. The Interpol's Liaison Office for Asia is located in Bangkok.

Headquarters: 200 Quai Charles de Gaulle, 69006 Lyon, France.
Website: http://www.interpol.int
e-mail: cp@interpol.int
Secretary-General: Ronald K. Noble (USA).

INTERNATIONAL MOBILE SATELLITE ORGANIZATION (IMSO)

Founded in 1979 as the International Maritime Satellite Organization (Inmarsat) to establish a satellite system to improve maritime communications for distress and safety and commercial applications. Its competence was subsequently expanded to include aeronautical and land mobile communications. Privatization, which was completed in April 1999, transferred the business to a newly created company and the Organization remains as a regulator to ensure that the company fulfils its public services obligations. The company has taken the Inmarsat name and the Organization uses the acronym IMSO. In Oct. 1999 the Organization had 86 member parties.

Organization. The Assembly of all Parties to the Convention meets every two years. There is also a 22-member Council of representatives of national telecommunications administrations as well as an executive Directorate.

Headquarters: 99 City Road, London EC1Y 1AX, UK.
Director of the Secretariat, IMSO: Jerzy Vonau.
Chief Executive, Inmarsat Ltd: Michael Storey.

INTERNATIONAL TELECOMMUNICATIONS SATELLITE ORGANIZATION (ITSO)

Founded in 1964 as Intelsat, the organization was the world's first commercial communications satellite operator. Today, with capacity on a fleet of geostationary satellites and expanding terrestrial network assets, Intelsat continues to provide highly reliable connectivity for telephony, corporate network, broadcast and Internet services.

Organization. In 2001 the member states of the organization implemented restructuring by transferring certain assets to Intelsat Ltd, a new Bermuda-based commercial company under the supervision of the International

Telecommunications Satellite Organization, now known as ITSO. The Intelsat Global Service Corporation is located in Washington, D. C., and Intelsat Global Services & Marketing Ltd, the sales arm of the international firm, has its headquarters in London. Intelsat also has offices in Australia, Brazil, China, France, Germany, Hawaii, India, Peru and South Africa. There were 148 member countries in March 2003.

Headquarters: 3400 International Drive, NW, Washington, D.C., 20008–3006, USA.
Website: http://www.itso.int
Director-General: Ahmed Toumi (Morocco).

INTERNATIONAL AIR TRANSPORT ASSOCIATION (IATA)

Founded in 1945 for inter-airline co-operation in promoting safe, reliable, secure and economical air services, IATA has over 230 members from more than 130 nations worldwide. IATA is the successor to the International Air Traffic Association, founded in the Hague in 1919, the year of the world's first international scheduled services.

Main offices: IATA Centre, Route de l'Aéroport 33, PO Box 416, CH-1215 Geneva, Switzerland. 800 Place Victoria, PO Box 113, Montreal, Quebec, Canada H4Z 1M1. 77 Robinson Road, #05-00 SIA Building, Singapore 068896.
Website: http://www.iata.org
Director-General: Giovanni Bisignani (Italy).

INTERNATIONAL ROAD FEDERATION (IRF)

The IRF is a non-profit, non-political service organization whose purpose is to encourage better road and transportation systems worldwide and to help apply technology and management practices to give maximum economic and social returns from national road investments.

Founded following the Second World War, over the years the IRF has led major global road infrastructure developments, including achieving 1,000 km of new roads in Mexico in the 1950s, and promoting the Pan-American Highway linking North and South America. It publishes *World Road Statistics*, as well as road research studies, including a 140-country inventory of road and transport research in co-operation with the US Bureau of Public Roads.

Headquarters: 2 chemin de Blandonnet, CH-1214 Vernier/GE, Switzerland.
Website: http://www.irfnet.org
Director-General (Geneva): Wim Westerhuis (Netherlands).
Director-General (Washington, D.C.): C. Patrick Sankey (USA).

INTERNATIONAL CONFEDERATION OF FREE TRADE UNIONS (ICFTU)

Origin. The founding congress of the ICFTU was held in London in Dec. 1949 following the withdrawal of some Western trade unions from the World Federation of Trade Unions (WFTU), which had come under Communist control. The constitution, as amended, provides for co-operation with the UN and the ILO, and for regional organizations to promote free trade unionism, especially in developing countries. By Nov. 2002 the ICFTU represented 158m. workers across 231 national trade union centres in 150 countries and territories.

Aims. The ICFTU aims to promote the interests of working people and to secure recognition of workers' organizations as free bargaining agents; to reduce the gap between rich and poor; and to defend fundamental human and trade union rights. In 1996 it campaigned for the adoption by the WTO of a social clause, with legally binding minimum labour standards.

Organization. The Congress meets every four years. The 17th Annual World Congress was held in Durban in April 2000. The next Congress will be held in 2004 in Japan. It elects the General Secretary and an Executive Board of 53 members nominated on an area basis for a four-year period. Five seats are reserved for women, nominated by the Women's Committee, and one reserved for a representative of young workers. The Board meets at least once a year. Various committees cover economic and social policy, violation of trade union and other human rights, trade union co-operation projects and also the administration of the International Solidarity Fund. There are joint ICFTU–Global Union Federations for co-ordinating activities.

The ICFTU has branch offices in Geneva and New York, and regional organizations in Latin America (Caracas), Asia (Singapore) and Africa (Nairobi).

Headquarters: Bd. du Roi Albert II, N° 5, bte 1, Brussels 1210, Belgium.
Website: http://www.icftu.org
General Secretary (acting): Guy Ryder (UK).
President: Fackson Shamenda (Zambia).

Publications. Trade Union World (monthly); *Annual Survey of Violations of Trade Union Rights* (annual); *ICFTU On-Line* (daily electronic news bulletin). Other publications available; contact the press department.

WORLD FEDERATION OF TRADE UNIONS (WFTU)

Origin and History. The WFTU was founded on a worldwide basis in 1945 at the international trade union conferences held in London and Paris, with the participation of all the trade union centres in the countries of the anti-Hitler coalition. The aim was to reunite the world trade union movement at the end of the Second World War. The acute political differences among affiliates, especially the east–west confrontation in Europe on ideological lines, led to a split. A number of affiliated organizations withdrew in 1949 and established the ICFTU. The WFTU now draws its membership from the industrially developing countries like India, Vietnam and other Asian countries, Brazil, Peru, Cuba and other Latin American countries, Syria, Lebanon, Kuwait and other Arab countries, and it has affiliates and associates in more than 20 European countries. It has close relations with the International Confederation of Arab Trade Unions, the Organization of African Trade Union Unity as well as the All-China Federation of Trade Unions, all of which participated at its Congress in New Delhi, India in 2000. Its Trade Unions Internationals (TUIs) have affiliates in Russia, the Czech Republic, Poland and other East European countries, Portugal, France, Spain, Japan and other OECD countries.

The headquarters of the TUIs are situated in Helsinki, New Delhi, Budapest, Mexico, Paris and Moscow. The WFTU and its TUIs have 130m. members, organized in 92 affiliated or associated national federations and six Trade Unions Internationals, in 130 countries. It has regional offices in New Delhi, Havana, Dakar, Damascus and Moscow and Permanent Representatives accredited to the UN in New York, Geneva and Rome.

Headquarters: Branicka 112, CZ-14701 Prague 4, Czech Republic.
Website: http://www.wftu.cz
President: K. L. Mahendra (India).
General Secretary: Aleksander Zharikov (Russia).

Publications. Flashes From the Trade Unions (fortnightly, published in English, French, Spanish and Arabic), reports of Congresses, etc.

EUROPEAN TRADE UNION CONFEDERATION (ETUC)

Established in 1973, the ETUC is recognized by the EU, the Council of Europe and EFTA as the only representative cross-sectoral trade union organization at a European level. It has grown steadily with a membership of 78 National Trade Union Confederations from 34 countries and 11 European Industry Federations with a total of 60m. members. The Congress meets every four years, with the 10th Statutory Congress scheduled to meet in Prague in May 2003.

Address: 5 Boulevard Roi Albert II, B-1210 Brussels, Belgium.
Website: http://www.etuc.org
e-mail: etuc@etuc.org
General Secretary: Emilio Gabaglio (Italy).

WORLD CONFEDERATION OF LABOUR (WCL)

Founded in 1920 as the International Federation of Christian Trade Unions, it went out of existence in 1940 as a large proportion of its $3·4m$. members were in Italy and Germany, where affiliated unions were suppressed by the Fascist and Nazi regimes. Reconstituted in 1945 and declining to merge with the WFTU or ICFTU, its policy was based on the papal encyclicals *Rerum novarum* (1891) and *Quadragesimo anno* (1931), and in 1968 it became the WCL and dropped its openly confessional approach.

Today, it has Christian, Buddhist and Muslim member confederations, as well as organizations without religious reference. The WCL defines itself as pluralist and humanist. In its concern to defend trade union freedoms and assist trade union development, the WCL differs little in policy from the ICFTU above. A membership of 26m. in 116 countries is claimed. The biggest group is the Confederation of Christian Trade Unions (CSC) of Belgium (1·6m.).

Organization. The WCL is organized on a federative basis which leaves wide discretion to its autonomous constituent unions. Its governing body is the Congress, which meets every four years. The Congress appoints (or re-appoints) the Secretary-General at each four-yearly meeting. The General Council which meets at least once a year, is composed of the members of the Confederal Board (at least 22 members, elected by the Congress) and representatives of national confederations, international trade federations, and trade union organizations where there is no confederation affiliated to the WCL. The Confederal Board is responsible for the general leadership of the WCL, in accordance with the decisions and directives of the Council and Congress. There are regional organizations in Latin America (Caracas), Africa (Lomé) and Asia (Manila), and three liaison offices (Bucharest, Geneva and Washington).

Headquarters: 33 rue de Trèves, Brussels 1040, Belgium.
Website: http://www.cmt-wcl.org
Secretary-General: Willy Thys (Belgium).
President: Basile Mahan Gahé (Côte d'Ivoire).

Publications. Annual Report on Workers Rights; Teleflash (20 a year), *Labor Magazine* (4 a year).

THE INTERNATIONAL ORGANIZATION OF THE FRANCOPHONIE

The International Organization of the Francophonie represents 56 countries and provinces/regions (including five with observer status) using French as an official language. Objectives include the promotion of peace, democracy, and economic and social development, through political and technical co-operation. The Secretary-General is based in Paris.

Members. Albania, Belgium, Benin, Bulgaria, Burkina Faso, Burundi, Cambodia, Cameroon, Canada, Canada–New Brunswick, Canada–Quebec, Cape Verde, Central African Republic, Chad, Comoros, Republic of the Congo, Democratic Republic of the Congo, Côte d'Ivoire, Djibouti, Dominica, Egypt, Equatorial Guinea, France, French Community of Belgium, Gabon, Guinea, Guinea-Bissau, Haïti, Laos, Lebanon, Luxembourg, Macedonia, Madagascar, Mali, Mauritania, Mauritius, Moldova, Monaco, Morocco, Niger, Romania, Rwanda, St Lucia, São Tomé e Príncipe, Senegal, Seychelles, Switzerland, Togo, Tunisia, Vanuatu, Vietnam. *Observers.* Czech Republic, Lithuania, Poland, Slovakia, Slovenia.

Headquarters: 28 rue de Bourgogne, 75007 Paris, France.
Website: http://www.francophonie.org
Secretary-General: Boutros Boutros-Ghali (Egypt).

INTERNATIONAL ORGANIZATION FOR STANDARDIZATION (ISO)

Established in 1947, the International Organization for Standardization is a non-governmental federation of national standards bodies from some 145 countries worldwide, one from each country. ISO's work results in international agreements which are published as International Standards. The first ISO standard was published in 1951 with the title 'Standard reference temperature for industrial length measurement'.

Some 14,000 ISO International Standards are available on subjects in such diverse fields as information technology, textiles, packaging, distribution of goods, energy production and utilization, building, banking and financial services. ISO standardization activities include the widely recognized ISO 9000 family of quality management system and standards and the ISO 14000 series of environmental management system standards. Standardization programmes are now being developed in completely new fields, such as advanced materials, life sciences, urbanization and the service sector.

Mission. To promote the development of standardization and related activities in the world with a view to facilitating the international exchange of goods and services, and to developing co-operation in the spheres of intellectual, scientific, technological and economic activity.

Headquarters: 1 rue de Varembé, Case postale 56, CH-1211 Geneva 20, Switzerland.
Website: http://www.iso.org
e-mail: central@iso.org
Secretary-General: Alan Bryden.

WORLD WIDE FUND FOR NATURE (WWF)

Origin. WWF was officially formed and registered as a charity on 11 Sept. 1961. The first National Appeal, with HRH The Duke of Edinburgh as President, was launched in the United Kingdom on 23 Nov. 1961, shortly followed by the United States and Switzerland.

Organization. WWF is the world's largest and most experienced independent conservation organization with over 4·7m. supporters and a global network of 27 National Organizations, five Associates and 24 Programme Offices.

The National Organizations carry out conservation activities in their own countries and contribute technical expertise and funding to WWF's international conservation programme. The Programme Offices implement WWF's fieldwork, advise national and local governments, and raise public understanding of conservation issues.

Mission. WWF has as its mission preserving genetic, species and ecosystem diversity; ensuring that the use of renewable natural resources is sustainable now and in the longer term, for the benefit of all life on Earth; promoting actions to reduce to a minimum pollution and the wasteful exploitation and consumption of resources and energy. WWF's ultimate goal is to stop, and eventually reverse, the accelerating degradation of our planet's natural environment, and to help build a future in which humans live in harmony with nature.

Address: Avenue du Mont-Blanc, CH–1196 Gland, Switzerland.
Website: http://www.panda.org
Director General: Dr Claude Martin (Switzerland).
President Emeritus: HRH The Prince Philip, Duke of Edinburgh.
President: Chief Emeka Anyaoku (Nigeria).

INTERNATIONAL OLYMPIC COMMITTEE (IOC)

Founded in 1894 by French educator Baron Pierre de Coubertin, the International Olympic Committee is an international non-governmental, non-profit organization whose members act as the IOC's representatives in their respective countries, not as delegates of their countries within the IOC. The Committee's main responsibility is to supervise the organization of the summer and winter Olympic Games. It owns all rights to the Olympic symbols, flag, motto, anthem and Olympic Games.

Aims. 'To contribute to building a peaceful and better world by educating youth through sport, practised without discrimination of any kind and in the Olympic Spirit, which requires mutual understanding with a spirit of friendship, solidarity and fair play.'

Finances. The IOC receives no public funding. Its only source of funding is from private sectors, with the substantial part of these revenues coming from television broadcasters and sponsors.

Address: Château de Vidy, Case Postale 356, CH–1007 Lausanne, Switzerland.
Website: http://www.olympic.org
President: Jacques Rogge (Belgium).

INTERNATIONAL UNION AGAINST CANCER (UICC)

Founded in 1933, the UICC is an international non-governmental association of 291 member organizations in 87 countries.

Objectives. The UICC is devoted exclusively to all aspects of the worldwide fight against cancer. Its objectives are to advance scientific and medical knowledge in research, diagnosis, treatment and prevention of cancer, and to promote all other aspects of the campaign against cancer throughout the world. Particular emphasis is placed on professional and public education.

Membership. The UICC is made up of voluntary cancer leagues, associations and societies as well as cancer research and treatment centres and, in some countries, ministries of health.

Activities. The UICC creates and carries out programmes around the world in collaboration with several hundred volunteer experts, most of whom are professionally active in UICC member organizations. It promotes co-operation between cancer organizations, researchers, scientists, health professionals and cancer experts, with a focus in four key areas: building and enhancing cancer control capacity, tobacco control, population-based cancer prevention and control, and transfer of cancer knowledge and dissemination. The International Cancer Congress is held by the UICC every four years; the most recent took place in 2002 in Oslo and the next is scheduled to take place in Washington, D.C. in 2006.

Address: 3 rue du Conseil-Général, 1205-Geneva, Switzerland.
Website: http://www.uicc.org
President: Dr Eliezer Robinson (Israel).
Executive Director: Isabel Mortara (Switzerland).
Secretary-General: Dr Stener Kvinnsland (Norway).

PART II

COUNTRIES OF THE WORLD
A—Z

AFGHANISTAN

Islamic State of Afghanistan

Capital: Kabul
Population estimate, 2000: 21·77m.
GDP per capita: not available

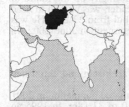

KEY HISTORICAL EVENTS

For much of the 19th century Afghanistan was part of the power struggle between Britain, as the dominant power in India, and the Russian empire. While the country achieved independence after the First World War, tribal wars and banditry restricted economic and social development. Stability came in the period of Záhir Shah who ruled for 40 years. In 1964 he was able to overcome opposition and put through a constitution establishing parliamentary democracy. In 1973 there was a military coup led by his cousin and brother-in-law, and a former prime minister, Mohammed Daoud, who abolished the 1964 constitution and declared a republic. Záhir Shah abdicated on 24 Aug. 1973.

The republic inherited pressure for tribal autonomy and economic crises mainly brought about by drought and famine. In April 1978 President Daoud was overthrown and killed in a further coup which installed a pro-Soviet government. The new president, Noor Mohammad Taraki, was overthrown in Sept. 1979, whereupon the Soviet Union invaded Afghanistan in Dec., deposed his successor and placed Babrak Karmal at the head of government.

In Dec. 1986 Sayid Mohammed Najibullah became president amid continuing civil war between government and rebel Muslim forces. Whereas in the 1960s both the USSR and the USA had financed government projects, in 1987 the USSR provided considerable military support and development aid to the pro-Soviet administration while the USA extended more limited support to the rebels. In the mid-1980s the UN began negotiations on the withdrawal of Soviet troops and the establishment of a government of national unity. Soviet troops began withdrawing from Afghanistan in early 1988.

After talks in Nov. 1991 with Afghan opposition movements ('mujahideen'), the Soviet government transferred its support from the Najibullah regime to an 'Islamic Interim Government'. As mujahideen insurgents closed in on Kabul, President Najibullah stepped down on 16 April 1992 but fighting continued.

In 1994 a newly formed militant Islamic movement, 'Taliban' (i.e. 'students of religion'), took Kabul, apparently with Pakistani support. The Taliban, most of whose leaders were Pashtuns, were in turn defeated by the troops of President Rabbani but in Sept. 1996 Taliban forces recaptured Kabul and set up an interim government under Mohamed Rabbani. Afghanistan was declared a complete Islamic state under Sharia law.

Government forces which had retreated to the north of Kabul counter-attacked but a new Taliban offensive, launched on 27 Dec. 1996, gave Taliban control of 90% of the country. The opposition Northern Alliance controlled the remaining 10% in the northeast of the country. Under the Taliban, irregular forces were disarmed and roads cleared of bandits. Rebuilding of towns and villages started. But the strict application of Islamic law ran counter to western sensitivities with the result that only three countries—Pakistan, Saudi Arabia and the United Arab Emirates—recognized the Taliban as the legal government.

In March 2001 Afghanistan was widely condemned for the destruction of ancient monuments that the Taliban deemed un-Islamic, including the world's tallest Buddhas. In May 2001 the ruling Taliban refused to extradite Osama bin Laden, a Saudi militant, to the USA to face charges connected to the bombing of American embassies in Kenya and Tanzania during 1998. In Sept. 2001 Ahmed Shah Masood, leader of the Northern Alliance, was killed after being attacked by two suicide bombers.

Following the attacks on the USA on 11 Sept. 2001 Osama bin Laden became the chief suspect. Within two weeks of the attacks on the USA both Saudi Arabia and the United Arab Emirates had broken off diplomatic relations. The USA put pressure on the ruling Taliban to hand over Osama bin Laden, but without success. Consequently the USA launched air strikes on Afghanistan on 7 Oct. During the following month the Taliban's control over Afghanistan gradually dwindled. On 13 Nov. the Northern Alliance took the capital Kabul, effectively bringing an end to Taliban rule, and with the surrender of Kandahar the Taliban lost control of their last stronghold. On 27 Nov. representatives of rival factions, but excluding the Taliban, took part in United Nations-sponsored talks in Germany on the future of their country. As a result Hamid Karzai, a Pashtun tribal leader, was chosen to head an interim power-sharing council, which took office in Kabul from 22 Dec. He was subsequently appointed president of the transitional government in June 2002. In Sept. 2002 he survived an assassination attempt.

TERRITORY AND POPULATION
Afghanistan is bounded in the north by Turkmenistan, Uzbekistan and Tajikistan, east by China, east and south by Pakistan and west by Iran.

The area is 251,773 sq. miles (652,090 sq. km). The estimated population in 2001 was 26·8m. The UN gives a projected population for 2010 of 31·18m. In 1995 an estimated 19·9% of the population lived in urban areas.

According to humanitarian agencies in Jan. 2002 there were almost 1·2m. internally displaced persons in Afghanistan. An estimated 4m. sought asylum outside Afghanistan including 2m. in Pakistan, 1·5m. in Iran, 26,000 in Turkmenistan, Tajikistan and Uzbekistan, and several hundred thousand in western European countries, Australia and North America. Approximately half of the internally displaced persons in Afghanistan moved prior to the events of Sept. 2001, for reasons such as drought and food scarcity. As a consequence of the US war in Afghanistan, numbers of refugees to Pakistan and Iran increased dramatically. Pakistan took more than 70,000 Afghan refugees in the months following 11 Sept. 2001 while Iran admitted some 60,000. In the meantime more than 1·6m. Afghans have returned to their country since a UN-sponsored programme began in early 2002, and in Dec. 2002 Pakistan and Afghanistan agreed to repatriate the remaining refugees, lodged in various camps in Pakistan, within three years.

The country is divided into 30 regions *(velayat)*. Area and estimated population in 1990:

Region	Area (sq. km)	Population (1,000)	Region	Area (sq. km)	Population (1,000)
Badakhshan	45,556	554	Kunar	10,153	308
Badghis	22,136	318	Kunduz	8,576	577
Baghlan	18,144	484	Laghman	7,147	379
Balkh	12,319	629	Logar	4,853	265
Bamyan	18,033	317	Nangarhar	7,650	1,003
Farah	58,900	378	Nimroz	40,902	140
Faryab	20,331	674	Paktika	19,101	251
Ghazni	22,059	771	Paktiya	9,709	524
Ghowr	40,247	318	Parwan	6,365	531
Helmand	61,420	542	Samangan	12,902	313
Herat	43,334	870	Saripul[1]	24,484	–
Jawzjan	10,456	678	Takhar	12,939	558
Kabul	4,685	2,280	Uruzgan	28,522	502
Kandahar	48,630	738	Vardak	9,762	399
Kapisa	5,407	433	Zabul	17,503	186

[1]Saripul did not exist at the time of the 1990 population estimates.

The capital, Kabul, had a population of 2·45m. in 1999. Other towns (with UN population estimates, 1988): Kandahar (225,500), Herat (177,300), Mazar i Sharif, (130,600), Jalalabad (55,000).

Main ethnic groups: Pashtuns, 38%; Tajiks, 25%; Hazaras, 19%; Uzbeks, 6%; Others, 12%. The official languages are Pashto and Dari.

SOCIAL STATISTICS
Based on 2001 estimates: birth rate, 41 per 1,000 population; death rate, 18 per 1,000; infant mortality, 147 per 1,000 live births; annual population growth rate, 3·5%. Life expectancy at birth, 47 years for men and 45 for women.

The maternal mortality rate is among the highest in the world with some 16,000 pregnancy-related deaths every year.

CLIMATE
The climate is arid, with a big annual range of temperature and very little rain, apart from the period Jan. to April. Winters are very cold, with considerable snowfall, which may last the year round on mountain summits. Kabul, Jan. 27°F (–2·8°C), July 76°F (24·4°C). Annual rainfall 13" (338 mm).

CONSTITUTION AND GOVERNMENT
Following UN-sponsored talks in Bonn, Germany in Nov. 2001, on 22 Dec. 2001 power was handed over to an Interim Authority, designed to oversee the restructuring of the country until a second stage of government, the Transitional Authority, could be put into power. This second stage resulted from a Loya Jirga (Grand Council), which convened between 10–16 June 2002. A Constitutional Commission has been established, with UN assistance, to help the Constitutional Loya Jirga prepare a new constitution. In the meantime the 1964 constitution has been reintroduced with some modifications.

RECENT ELECTIONS
Elections were held by the Loya Jirga on 13 June 2002. Hamid Karzai was elected president with 1,295 out of 1,575 votes cast, against 171 for Masooda Jalal and 89 for Mir Mohammad Mahfoz Nadai.

CURRENT ADMINISTRATION
In March 2003 the Transitional Government was composed as follows:

President of the Transitional Government: Hamid Karzai; b. 1957 (Pashtun; sworn in 19 June 2002).

Vice Presidents: Mohammad Fahim Khan (Tajik; also *Minister of Defence*); Karim Khalili (Hazara Shia); Hedayat Amin Arsala (Pashtun); Niamatullah Shahrani (Uzbek).

Presidential Adviser on Security Affairs and Minister of Education: Younis Qanooni. *Minister of Foreign Affairs:* Dr Abdullah Abdullah. *Economy and Finance:* Ashraf Qani Ahmadzai. *Interior:* Taj Mohammad Wardak. *Planning:* Haji Mohammad Mohaqeq. *Commerce:* Seyyed Mustafa Kazemi. *Mines and Industries:* Vacant. *Small Industries:* Alim Razim. *Information and Culture:* Rahin Makhdoom. *Communications:* Masoum Stanakzai. *Labour and Social Affairs:* Noor Ahmed Qarqeen. *Hajj (Pilgrimage) and Awqaf:* Mohammad Amin Nasiryar. *Martyrs and Disabled:* Abdullah Wardak. *Higher Education:* Dr Sharif Faez. *Public Health:* Suhaila Seddiqi. *Public Works:* Abdullah Ali. *Rural Development:* Hanif Atmar. *Urban Development:* Mohammad Yousuf Pashtun. *Reconstruction:* Mohammad Amin Farhang. *Transport:* Syed Ali Jawed. *Return of Refugees:* Enayatullah Nazeri. *Agriculture:* Seyyed Hussein Anwar. *Water and Power:* Ahmed Shakar Kargar. *Irrigation and Environment:* Yousuf Nuristani. *Justice:* Abbas Karimi. *Air Transport and Tourism:* Mir Wais Sadeq. *Department of Border Affairs:* Arif Noorzai. *Women's Affairs:* Habiba Sorabi.

DEFENCE
In 2000 military expenditure totalled US$245m. (US$10 per capita), representing 13·0% of GDP. In 1998 Afghanistan was estimated to have 108,000 soldiers and rebels under the age of 18—more than twice as many young soldiers as any other country.

The threat of chemical and biological weapons development by al-Qaeda forces stimulated opposition to the Taliban regime during the US campaign following the attacks on New York and Washington of 11 Sept. 2001, although no such weapons capability was proved to exist.

Casualties from landmines and unexploded munitions total 150–300 per month, a figure exacerbated by the crisis of late 2001.

Army. The decimation of the Taliban's armed forces left Afghanistan without an army. There are now plans for a multi-ethnic Afghan National Army, under the command of President Hamid Karzai, ultimately with a strength of 70,000.

Air Force. Afghanistan's air forces have been severely damaged, but there are now plans for a new air force with a strength of 8,000.

INTERNATIONAL RELATIONS

UN sanctions were imposed in 1999 but were withdrawn following the collapse of the Taliban regime.

Afghanistan is a member of the UN, Asian Development Bank, ECO, Colombo Plan and OIC.

ECONOMY

Following the military campaign in Afghanistan pledges of economic aid came from many countries, totalling more than US$4·5bn., of which the USA pledged US$1·8bn. An Implementation Group has been established to oversee the allocation of funding and the implementation of international assistance. Donor organizations working in co-operation with the Afghan Interim Authority, and subsequently the Transitional Government, for fund allocation include the World Bank, UNDP, Asian Development Bank and the Islamic Development Bank.

Currency. A new currency was introduced in Oct. 2002. Called the *afghani* (as was its predecessor), one of the new notes is worth 1,000 of the old ones. The old *afghani* had been trading at around 46,000 to the US$.

Performance. Real GDP growth was estimated at 6% in both 1997 and 1998.

Banking and Finance. The Afghan State Bank is the largest of the three main banks and also undertakes the functions of a central bank, holding the exclusive right of note issue.

The UN sanctions placed on Afghanistan in 1999 extended to the Afghan State Bank and to Bank Millie Afghan (Afghan National Bank) but have now been lifted. The Afghanistan Central Bank (Da Afghanistan Bank) was founded in 1939. Its *Governor* is Anwarulhaq Ahadi. There are no commercial banks in the country. Money is exchanged in bazaars.

Weights and Measures. The metric system is in increasingly common use. Local units include: one *khurd* = 0·244 lb; one *pao* = 0·974 lb; one *charak* = 3·896 lb; one *sere* = 16 lb; one *kharwar* = 1,280 lb or 16 maunds of 80 lb each; one *gaz* = 40 inches; one *jarib* = 60 x 60 kabuli yd or ½ acre; one *kulba* = 40 jaribs (area in which 2½ kharwars of seed can be sown); one jarib yd = 29 inches.

The Afghan Interim Authority replaced the lunar calendar with the traditional Afghan solar calendar. The solar calendar was used in Afghanistan until 1999 when it was changed by the Taliban authorities who wanted the country to adopt the system used in Saudi Arabia. The change means the current year switches from 1424 to 1382.

ENERGY AND NATURAL RESOURCES

Electricity. In 2000 there were six generating plants, four of which were hydro-electric. Installed capacity was 494,000 kW in 1995. Production was 430m. kWh in 1998; consumption in 1996 was 660m. kWh.

Oil and Gas. Natural gas reserves were 99bn. cu. metres in 1997. Production in 1996 was 7 petajoules. A consortium of oil and gas companies ('CentGas') was planning a US$2bn. natural gas pipeline from Turkmenistan through Afghanistan to Pakistan, although the withdrawal from the project of the US oil company Unocal in April 1998 led to doubts over the viability of the project. Since the installation of the Interim Authority, and now the Transitional Government, both the CentGas project and other major oil and gas ventures within the region from US, Chinese and Iranian companies seem likely to proceed.

Minerals. There are deposits of coal, copper, barite, lapis-lazuli, emerald, talc and salt.

Agriculture. The greater part of Afghanistan is mountainous but there are many fertile plains and valleys. In 1998 there were 7·91m. ha of arable land and 0·14m. ha of permanent cropland; 2·39m. ha were irrigated in 1998. 69·2% of the economically active population were engaged in agriculture in 1995. Principal crops include grains, rice, fresh and dried fruits, vegetables, cottonseed and potatoes.

Production, 2000, in 1,000 tonnes: wheat, 1,469; grapes, 330; potatoes, 235; rice, 233; maize, 115. Opium production in 2001 was just 200 tonnes (down from 4,581 tonnes in 1999), but in 2002 it rose again to 3,400 tonnes. In 1998 the harvest was worth an estimated US$69m. The area under cultivation in 2002 was 55,000 ha, up from 7,606 ha in 2001 but down from 90,983 ha in 1999. For several years Afghanistan's annual narcotics production was more than twice that of the second largest producer, Myanmar. In Feb. 2001 the United Nations Drug Control Programme reported that opium production had been almost totally eradicated after the Taliban outlawed the cultivation of poppies. As a result in 2001 Myanmar became the largest producer of opium, but in 2002 Afghanistan was again the leading producer. Despite a renewed clampdown on opium production and trafficking since the fall of the Taliban Afghanistan's farmers are being forced by poverty to revive the industry.

Livestock (2000): cattle, 3·5m.; sheep, 18·0m.; goats 7·4m.; asses, 920,000; camels, 290,000; horses, 104,000; chickens, 7m.

Forestry. In 1995 forests covered 2·1% of the total land area (3·1% in 1990). Timber production in 1999 was 8·28m. cu. metres.

Fisheries. In 2000 the total catch was estimated to be 1,000 tonnes, exclusively from inland waters.

INDUSTRY

Major industries include natural gas, fertilizers, cement, coalmining, small vehicle assembly plants, building, carpet weaving, cotton textiles, clothing and footwear, leather tanning, sugar manufacturing and fruit canning.

Labour. The workforce was 8,851,000 in 1996 (65% males). In 1995 the unemployment rate was estimated at 8%.

INTERNATIONAL TRADE

Imports and Exports. Total exports (1995), US$153m.; imports US$344m. Main exported products: non-edible crude materials (excluding fuels), manufactured goods (raw material intensive), machinery and transport equipment, fruits, nuts, hand-woven carpets, wool, hides, precious and semi-precious gems. Main imports: foodstuffs and live animals, beverages and tobacco, mineral fuels, manufactured goods, chemicals and related products, machinery and transport equipment. Main trading partners: Kyrgyzstan, Pakistan and Russia.

Imports and exports were largely unaffected by the sanctions imposed during the Taliban regime.

COMMUNICATIONS

Roads. There were 20,720 km of roads in 2001, of which 3,120 km were paved. Approximately half of all road surfaces are in a poor state of repair as a result of military action, but rebuilding is underway. In Jan. 2003 women regained the right to drive after a 10-year ban. Approximately 31,000 passenger cars (1·4 per 1,000 inhabitants) and 25,000 trucks and vans were in use in 1996.

Rail. There are two short stretches of railway in the country, extensions of the Uzbek and Turkmen networks. A Trans-Afghan Railway was proposed in an Afghan-Pakistan-Turkmen agreement of 1994.

Civil Aviation. There is an international airport at Kabul (Khwaja Rawash Airport). The national carrier is Ariana Afghan Airlines, which in 1998 operated direct flights from Kabul to Amritsar, Dubai and Jeddah. In 1999 scheduled airline traffic of Afghanistan-based carriers flew 2·7m. km, carrying 140,000 passengers (36,000 on international flights). The UN sanctions imposed on 14 Nov. 1999 included the cutting off of Afghanistan's air links to the outside world. In Jan. 2002 Ariana Afghan Airlines resumed services and Kabul airport was reopened. The airport was heavily bombed during the US campaign and is still under repair.

Shipping. There are practically no navigable rivers. A port has been built at Qizil Qala on the Oxus and there are three river ports on the Amu Darya, linked by road to Kabul. The container port at Kheyrabad on the Amu Darya river has rail connections to Uzbekistan.

Telecommunications. In 2000 there were 29,000 telephone main lines, or 1·3 per 1,000 inhabitants—the lowest penetration rate of any country outside Africa.

Postal Services. In 1995 there were 352 post offices.

SOCIAL INSTITUTIONS

Justice. A Supreme Court was established in June 1978. It retained its authority under the Taliban regime.

Under the Taliban, a strict form of Sharia law was followed. This law, which was enforced by armed police, included prohibitions on alcohol, television broadcasts, internet use and photography, yet received its widest condemnation for its treatment of women. Public executions and amputations were widely used as punishment under the regime.

A Judicial Commission is being instituted that will create a civil justice system in accordance with Islamic principles, international standards, the rule of law and Afghan legal traditions.

Religion. The predominant religion is Islam. An estimated 84% of the population are Sunni Muslims, and 15% Shias.

The Taliban provoked international censure in May 2001 by forcing the minority population of Afghan Hindus and Sikhs to wear yellow identification badges.

Education. Adult literacy was 31·5% in 1995 (male, 46·2%; female, 16·1%).

The primary enrolment ratio in 1999 was 38% for boys and 3% for girls. Enrolment at secondary and tertiary levels was even lower. In Jan. 2002 there were an estimated 3,600 primary schools, two-thirds of which were government-supported.

In 1995–96 there were 5 universities, 1 university of Islamic studies, 1 state medical institute and 1 polytechnic. Kabul University had 9,500 students and 500 academic staff. Formerly one of Asia's finest educational institutes, Kabul University lost many of its staff during the Taliban regime, and following the US bombing attacks it was closed down.

In areas controlled by the Taliban education was forbidden for girls. Boys' schools taught only religious education and military training. Female teachers and pupils are now returning to education after five years of exclusion.

Health. Afghanistan is one of the least successful countries in the battle against undernourishment. Between 1980 and 1996 the proportion of undernourished people rose from 33% of the population to 62%. Half of all Afghan children suffer from chronic malnutrition. One in four children die before reaching the age of five, largely as a result of diarrhoea, pneumonia, measles and other similar illnesses.

The bombing of Afghanistan beginning in Oct. 2001 severely disrupted the supply of aid to the country and left much of the population exposed to starvation.

In the period 1990–98 only 6% of the population had access to safe drinking water (the lowest percentage of any country).

CULTURE

Broadcasting. In 1997 there were 2·75m. radio receivers and 270,000 television receivers (colour by PAL).

Under the Taliban television stations were closed down—only one remained in operation, in a Northern Alliance-controlled area. Television sets were smashed or even publicly hanged. The single radio broadcasting station to remain in operation, Radio Afghanistan, was renamed Voice of Shariah and was used to broadcast official propaganda and religious sermons. It proclaimed itself as the only radio station in the world where music of any kind was banned. Since the collapse of the regime Radio Afghanistan has resumed services, as have Kabul TV and a number of other broadcasters.

Cinema. Cinemas were banned under the Taliban but have since reopened. The Afghan Film Institute is responsible for censorship.

Press. In 1996 there were 12 daily newspapers with a combined circulation of 113,000, at a rate of 5·6 per 1,000 inhabitants.

Under Taliban control there was only one, tightly-controlled, newspaper named *Shariat*. Other newspapers in circulation in Jan. 2002 were *Hewad*, *Anis* and the English-language *Kabul Times*.

Tourism. In 1998 there were 4,000 foreign tourists bringing in receipts of US$1m.

DIPLOMATIC REPRESENTATIVES

Of Afghanistan in the United Kingdom (31 Prince's Gate, London, SW7 1QQ)
Ambassador: Vacant.
Chargé d'Affaires a.i.: Ahmad Wali Masud.

Of the United Kingdom in Afghanistan
Ambassador: Ronald Nash.

Of Afghanistan in the USA (2341 Wyoming Avenue, NW, Washington, D.C., 20008)
Ambassador: Ishaq Shahryar.

Of the USA in Afghanistan
Ambassador: Robert Finn.

Of Afghanistan to the United Nations
Ambassador: Abdallah Baali.

Of Afghanistan to the European Union
Ambassador: Umayun Tandar.

FURTHER READING

Amin, S. H., *Law, Reform and Revolution in Afghanistan*. London, 1991
Arney, G., *Afghanistan*. London, 1990
Ewans, Martin, *Afghanistan, A New History*. Curzon Press, Richmond, 2001
Goodson, Larry, *Afghanistan's Endless War: State Failure, Regional Politics and the Rise of the Taliban*. University of Washington Press, 2001
Griffiths, John, *Afghanistan: A History of Conflict*. Andre Deutsch, London, 2001
Hyman, A., *Afghanistan under Soviet Domination, 1964–1991*. 3rd ed. London, 1992
Jones, Schuyler, *Afghanistan*. [Bibliography] ABC-Clio, Oxford and Santa Barbara (CA), 1992
Margolis, Eric, *War at the Top of the World: The Struggle for Afghanistan, Kashmir and Tibet*. Routledge, New York, 2001
Nojumi, Neamatollah, *The Rise of the Taliban in Afghanistan*. Palgrave Macmillan, Basingstoke, 2001
Roy, O., *Islam and Resistance in Afghanistan*. 2nd ed. CUP, 1990
Rubin, B. R., *The Fragmentation of Afghanistan: State Formation and Collapse in the International System*. Yale Univ. Press, 1995.—*The Search for Peace in Afghanistan: from Buffer State to Failed State*. Yale Univ. Press, 1996
Vogelsang, Willem, *The Afghans*. Blackwell, Oxford, 2002

ALBANIA

Republika e Shqipërisë

Capital: Tirana
Population estimate, 2000: 3·13m.
GDP per capita, 2000: (PPP$) 3,506
HDI/world rank: 0·733/92

KEY HISTORICAL EVENTS

After the Russo-Turkish war of 1877–78, demands grew for independence from Turkey. After the defeat of Turkey in the Balkan war of 1912, Albanian nationalists proclaimed Albania's independence and set up a provisional government.

During the First World War Albania became a battlefield for warring occupation forces. Albania was admitted to the League of Nations on 20 Dec. 1920. In Nov. 1921 the conference of ambassadors confirmed her 1913 frontiers with minor alterations. Italian influence grew from the mid-1920s. A friendship pact was signed with Italy in 1926 and a defence treaty in 1927. In April 1939 Mussolini invaded Albania and set up a puppet state. During the Second World War Albania suffered first Italian and then German occupation. Resistance was carried on by royalist, nationalist republican and communist movements, often at odds with each other. The latter enjoyed the support of Tito's partisans, who were instrumental in forming the Albanian Communist Party on 8 Nov. 1941. Communists dominated the Anti-Fascist National Liberation Committee which became the Provisional Democratic Government on 22 Oct. 1944 after the German withdrawal, with Enver Hoxha, a French-educated school teacher and member of the Communist Party Central Committee, at its head. Large estates were broken up and the land distributed, though full collectivization was not brought in until 1955–59. Close ties were forged with the USSR but following Khrushchev's reconciliation with Tito in 1956 China replaced the Soviet Union as Albania's powerful patron from 1961 until the end of the Maoist phase in 1977. The regime then adopted a policy of 'revolutionary self-sufficiency'. Following the collapse of the Soviet empire the People's Assembly adopted a decree legalizing opposition parties. A non-Communist government was elected in March 1992.

In 1997 Albania was disrupted by financial crises caused by the collapse of fraudulent pyramid finance schemes. A period of violent anarchy led to the fall of the administration and to fresh elections which returned a Socialist-led government. A UN peacekeeping force withdrew in Aug. 1997 but sporadic violence continued. In April 1999 the Kosovo crisis which led to NATO air attacks on Yugoslavian military targets set off a flood of refugees into Albania.

TERRITORY AND POPULATION

Albania is bounded in the north by Serbia and Montenegro, east by Macedonia, south by Greece and west by the Adriatic. The area is 28,748 sq. km (11,101 sq. miles). At the census of April 2001 the population was 3,087,159; density, 107 per sq. km.

The UN gives a projected population for 2010 of 3·31m.

In 2001, 57·9% of the population lived in rural areas. The capital is Tirana (population in 2001, 343,078); other large towns (population in 2001) are Durrës (99,546), Elbasan (87,797), Shkodër (82,445), Vlorë (77,691), Fier (56,297), Korçë (55,130), Berat (40,112), Lushnjë (32,580), Kavajë (24,817) and Gjirokastër (Argyrocastro) (20,630).

The country is administratively divided into 12 prefectures, 36 districts, 306 communes and 65 municipalities.

Districts	Area (sq. km)	Population (2001)	Districts	Area (sq. km)	Population (2001)
Berat	938	128,410	Durrës	433	182,988
Bulqizë	469	42,985	Elbasan	1,372	224,974
Delvinë	348	10,859	Fier	785	200,154
Devoll	429	34,744	Gjirokastër	1,137	55,991
Dibër	1,088	86,144	Gramsh	695	35,723

Districts	Area (sq. km)	Population (2001)	Districts	Area (sq. km)	Population (2001)
Has	393	19,842	Mat	1,029	61,906
Kavajë	414	78,415	Mirditë	867	37,055
Kolonjë	805	17,179	Peqin	109	32,920
Korçë	1,752	143,499	Permet	930	25,837
Krujë	333	64,357	Pogradec	725	70,900
Kuçovë	84	35,571	Pukë	1,034	34,454
Kukës	938	64,054	Sarandë	749	35,235
Kurbin	273	54,519	Shkodër	1,973	185,794
Lezhë	479	68,218	Skrapar	775	29,874
Librazhd	1,023	72,520	Tepelenë	817	32,465
Lushnjë	712	144,351	Tirana	1,238	523,150
Mallakastër	393	39,881	Tropojë	1,043	28,154
Malsi e Madhe	555	36,770	Vlorë	1,609	147,267

In most cases districts are named after their capitals. Exceptions are: Devoll, capital—Bilisht; Dibër—Peshkopi; Has—Krume; Kolonjë—Ersekë; Kurbin—Laç; Mallakastër—Ballsh; Malsi e Madhe—Koplik; Mat—Burrel; Mirditë—Rrëshen; Skrapar—Çorovodë; Tropojë—Bajram Curri.

At the 1989 census, members of ethnic minorities totalled 64,816, including 58,758 Greeks and 4,697 Macedonians.

The official language is Albanian.

SOCIAL STATISTICS
2000: births, 50,077; deaths, 16,421. Rates in 2000 (per 1,000): births, 16·2; deaths, 5·3. Infant mortality, 1999, was 29 per 1,000 live births. Fertility rate (number of births per woman), 2·1 in 2000. Annual population growth rate, 1990–99, –0·6%. Life expectancy at birth, 1999, 71·7 years for males and 76·4 years for females. Abortion was legalized in 1991.

CLIMATE
Mediterranean-type, with rainfall mainly in winter, but thunderstorms are frequent and severe in the great heat of the plains in summer. Winters in the highlands can be severe, with much snow. Tirana, Jan. 44°F (6·8°C), July 75°F (23·9°C). Annual rainfall 54" (1,353 mm). Shkodër, Jan. 39°F (3·9°C), July 77°F (25°C). Annual rainfall 57" (1,425 mm).

CONSTITUTION AND GOVERNMENT
A new constitution was adopted on 28 Nov. 1998. The supreme legislative body is the single-chamber *People's Assembly* of 140 deputies, 100 directly elected and 40 elected by proportional representation, for four-year terms, Where no candidate wins an absolute majority, a run-off election is held. The *President* is elected by Parliament for a five-year term.

National Anthem. 'Rreth Flamurit të për bashkuar' ('The flag that united us in the struggle'); words by A. S. Drenova, tune by C. Porumbescu.

RECENT ELECTIONS
Parliamentary elections took place on 24 June and 8 July 2001. The ruling Socialist Party of Albania (PSS) won 73 of the 140 seats with 42·0% of votes cast, the Union for Victory coalition 46 with 37·1%, the Democratic Party 6 with 5·1%, and the Social Democratic Party 4 with 3·6%. Other parties won three seats or fewer.

Parliament chose Alfred Moisiu (ind.) as president on 24 June 2002.

CURRENT ADMINISTRATION
President: Alfred Moisiu; b. 1929 (in office since 24 July 2002).

In March 2003 the government comprised:

Prime Minister: Fatos Nano (PSS; sworn in 31 July 2002, having previously held office from Feb.–June 1991 and July 1997–Oct. 1998).

Deputy Prime Minister and Minister for Foreign Affairs: Ilir Meta. *Minister for Labour and Social Affairs:* Valentina Leskaj. *Public Order:* Luan Rama. *Defence:* Pandeli Majko. *Justice:* Spiro Peçi. *Local Government and Decentralization:* Ben Blushi. *Finance:* Kastriot Islami. *Economy:* Arben Malaj. *Transport and*

Telecommunications: Spartak Poçi. *Education and Science:* Luan Memushi. *Health:* Mustafa Xhani. *Culture, Youth and Sports:* Arta Dade. *Environment:* Lufter Xhuveli. *Minister of State for European Integration:* Sokol Nako. *Industry and Energy:* Viktor Doda. *Agriculture:* Agron Duka. *Public Works and Tourism:* Besnik Dervishi. *Minister of State for Anti-Corruption:* Blendi Klosi.

Albanian Parliament: http://www.parlament.al/

DEFENCE
Conscription is for 15 months. In 2000 defence expenditure totalled US$111m. (US$36 per capita), representing 3·0% of GDP.

Army. The Army is to consist of seven divisions under Plan 2000. Strength in 1996 was 60,000 (including 20,000 conscripts). There is an internal security force, and frontier guards number 500.

Navy. Navy personnel in 1999 totalled 2,500 officers and ratings. Of the 30 vessels in the navy there were 11 torpedo craft. There are naval bases at Durrës, Sarandë, Shëngjin and Vlorë.

Air Force. The Air Force, controlled by the Army, had (1999) about 2,500 personnel, and operated 98 combat aircraft including Chinese built MiG-15s, MiG-17s and MiG-19s.

INTERNATIONAL RELATIONS
Albania is a member of the UN, WTO, the Council of Europe, OSCE, the Central European Initiative, BSEC, IOM, OIC and the NATO Partnership for Peace.

ECONOMY
In 1998 agriculture accounted for 54·4% of GDP (among the highest percentages of any country), services 21·0% and industry 24·6%.

Overview. Priority is given to the development of agriculture and the exploitation of tourism and natural resources. Privatization of land, small businesses and housing was achieved in 1991–93. A privatization programme for large enterprises was initiated in 1995 under the aegis of the National Privatization Agency. Sales are at auction or through vouchers.

Towards the end of 1997 Prime Minister Fatos Nano succeeded in raising US$600m. from foreign donors (more than had been requested) to help rebuild the country's economy.

Currency. The monetary unit is the *lek* (ALL), notionally of 100 *qindars*. In Sept. 1991 the lek (plural, *lekë* or leks) was pegged to the ecu at a rate of 30 leks = one ecu. In June 1992 it was devalued from 50 to 110 to US$1. After several years of high inflation (225% in 1992), in 2001 there was inflation of 3·1%. Foreign exchange reserves were US$319m. in June 2002, total money supply was 156,469m. leks and gold reserves totalled 111,000 troy oz.

Budget. The fiscal year is the calendar year.
Government revenue and expenditure (in 1m. leks):

	1995	1996	1997	1998
Revenue	49,068	47,551	53,205	89,145
Expenditure	69,687	83,553	97,472	137,254

Performance. Total GDP in 2001 was US$4·1bn. GDP contracted by 7·0% in 1997 after the collapse of pyramid finance schemes, but then grew by 8·0% in 1998. In 1999 growth was 7·3%, followed by 7·8% in 2000 and 7·3% in 2001.

Banking and Finance. The central bank and bank of issue is the Bank of Albania, founded in 1925 with Italian aid as the Albanian State Bank and renamed in 1993. Its *Governor* is Shkëlqim Cani. In 1996 there were 3 state-owned commercial banks, 1 foreign bank and 2 joint ventures. Albania's largest bank, the Savings Bank of Albania, is currently 100% owned by the government but is set to be privatized. It has total assets of US$1·4bn., approximately 60% of the total assets of the Albanian banking sector.

A stock exchange opened in Tirana in 1996.

Weights and Measures. The metric system is in force.

ENERGY AND NATURAL RESOURCES

Environment. According to the *World Bank Atlas* Albania's carbon dioxide emissions in 1998 were the equivalent of 0·5 tonnes per capita.

Electricity. Albania is rich in hydro-electric potential. Although virtually all of the electricity is generated by hydro-electric power plants only 30% of potential hydro-electric sources are currently being used. Electricity capacity was 1·67m. kW in 2000. Production was 5·40bn. kWh in 2000 and consumption per capita 776 kWh.

Oil and Gas. Offshore exploration began in 1991. Oil has been produced onshore since 1920. Oil reserves are some 165m. bbls. Crude oil production in 1999, 323,000 tonnes. Natural gas is extracted. Reserves in 1997 totalled 2,000m. cu. metres; output in 1996 was one petajoule. Oil investment includes the building of a 40 km pipeline to the Adriatic coast. A consortium led by Premier Oil, an independent UK company, signed an agreement in Dec. 1997 to develop Albania's biggest onshore oilfield, Patos Merinze, by investing US$250m. Production was to increase from 6,000 bbls. a day to more than 25,000 within four years as a result of the venture, which represents the largest single foreign investment made in Albania.

Minerals. Mineral wealth is considerable and includes lignite, chromium, copper and nickel. Production (in 1,000 tonnes): iron-nickel ore (1991), 931; copper ore (1995), 258; chromium ore (1994), 223; lignite (1999), 33. Nickel reserves are 60m. tonnes of iron containing 1m. tonnes of nickel, but extraction had virtually ceased by 1996. A consortium of British and Italian companies is modernizing the chrome industry with the aim of making Albania the leading supplier of ferrochrome to European stainless steel producers.

Agriculture. In 2000, 53% of the population depended upon agriculture, which contributed 54·4% of GDP in 1998. The country is mountainous, except for the Adriatic littoral and the Korçë Basin, which are fertile. Only 24% of the land area is suitable for cultivation; 15% of Albania is used for pasture. In 2000 there were 578,000 ha of arable land and 121,000 ha of permanent cropland. 129,000 ha were irrigated in 2000.

A law of Aug. 1991 privatized co-operatives' land. Families received allocations, according to their size, from village committees. In 1998 there were 466,659 private agricultural holdings with a total area of 451,917 ha; average 0·96 ha. Since 1995 owners have been permitted to buy and sell agricultural land. In 2000 there were 7,691 tractors in use.

Production (in 1,000 tonnes), 2000: total grains, 566 (including wheat 341 and maize 206); tomatoes, 162; potatoes, 161; grapes, 79; sugarbeet, 42; wine, 7,413 hectolitres.

Livestock, 2000: cattle, 728,000; sheep, 1,939,000; goats, 1,106,000; pigs 81,000; asses, 113,000; horses, 63,000; chickens, 4,087,000. Livestock products, 2000 (in 1,000 tonnes): beef and veal, 35; mutton and lamb, 19; goat meat, 16; pork, bacon and ham, 7; poultry meat, 6; cheese, 8; milk, 948; 530m. eggs.

Forestry. Forests covered 1,026,000 ha in 2000 (36·9% of the total land area), mainly oak, elm, pine and birch. Timber production in 2000 was 190,000 cu. metres.

Fisheries. The total catch in 2000 amounted to 3,290 tonnes (1,613 tonnes from sea fishing).

INDUSTRY

Output is small, and the principal industries are agricultural product processing, textiles, oil products and cement. Closures of loss-making plants in the chemical and engineering industries built up in the Communist era led to a 60% decline in production by 1993. Output (1994) (in 1,000 tonnes): cement, 100; rolled steel, 17; phosphate fertilizer, 11; ammonium nitrate, 6; vegetable oil, 6; soap, 3; sugar (1998), 3; washing powder and detergents (1997), 2; beer (1997), 15·1m. litres; wine, 0·5m. litres; 40m. bricks; 414m. cigarettes (1997); 3m. articles of knitwear.

Labour. In 2000 the workforce was 1,283,000, of which 1,068,000 were employed (877,000 in the private sector). Unemployment was 16·8% at the end of 2000.

The average monthly wage in 1999 was 12,708 leks; the official minimum wage was 6,380 leks. Minimum wages may not fall below one-third of maximum. Retirement age is 60 for men and 55 for women.

Trade Unions. Independent trade unions became legal in Feb. 1991.

INTERNATIONAL TRADE

Foreign investment was legalized in Nov. 1990. Foreign debt was US$784m. in 2000.

Imports and Exports. Exports in 2000 totalled US$255·7m.; imports, US$1,070·0m. In 2000 exports included manufactures (85·2%) and agriculture and food (10·9%); imports included capital goods (21·5%) and food (20·3%).

Main export markets, 2000 (% of total trade): Italy, 70·6%; Greece, 12·7%; Germany, 6·6%. Main import suppliers: Italy, 35·2%; Greece, 26·4%; Germany, 6·1%.

COMMUNICATIONS

Roads. In 2000 there were 3,221 km of main roads, 4,278 km of secondary roads and 10,500 km of other roads. There were 114,531 passenger cars in 2000, as well as 16,806 buses and coaches and 43,301 lorries and vans. There were 428 road accidents in 2000 (280 fatalities).

Rail. Total length in operation in 2000 was 400 km. Passenger-km travelled in 2000 came to 124m. and freight tonne-km to 28m.

Civil Aviation. The national carrier is Albanian Airlines, a joint venture with a Kuwaiti firm. It began operations in Oct. 1995. In 2002 it flew services to Bologna, Frankfurt, Istanbul, Priština and Rome. Air civil transportation is carried out by 12 airlines, of which 10 are foreign airlines and 2 are joint ventures. In 1999 scheduled airline traffic of Albania-based carriers flew 0·3m. km, carrying 20,000 passengers (all on international flights). The main airport is Mother Teresa International Airport at Rinas, 25 km from Tirana, which handled 356,823 passengers in 1999.

Shipping. In 2000 merchant shipping totalled 24,105 GRT. The main port is Durrës, with secondary ports being Vlorë, Sarandë and Shëngjin.

Telecommunications. By the end of 2002 there were 220,000 telephone main lines. Albtelecom, the fixed-line operator, is set to be privatized. A state-owned mobile telephone network was set up in 1996, initially serving 8,000 subscribers. In 2000 there were 25,000 PCs in use (6·4 for every 1,000 persons) and 20,000 mobile phone subscribers. There were 12,000 Internet users in Dec. 2000.

Postal Services. In 1995 there were 698 post offices. The volume of postal traffic in 2000 was 2,095,000 pieces of ordinary mail and 892,000 pieces of registered post.

SOCIAL INSTITUTIONS

Justice. A new criminal code was introduced in June 1995. The administration of justice (made up of First Instance Courts, The Courts of Appeal and the Supreme Court) is presided over by the *Council of Justice*, chaired by the President of the Republic, which appoints judges to courts. A Ministry of Justice was re-established in 1990 and a Bar Council set up. In Nov. 1993 the number of capital offences was reduced from 13 to six and the death penalty was abolished for women. In 2000 the death penalty was abolished for peacetime offences. The prison population in 1999 was 3,083, including 306 minors.

Religion. The population is 70% of Muslim origin, mainly Sunni with some Belaktashi, 7% Albanian Orthodox, 5% Roman Catholic and 18% others. The Albanian Orthodox Church is autocephalous; it is headed by an Exarch and three metropolitans. In 2001 there were 118 priests. The Roman Catholic cathedral in Shkodër has been restored. In 2000 there were one Roman Catholic archbishop and three bishops. Percentages of the population actively practising were estimated in 1996 as Muslims, 20%; Orthodox, 6%; Roman Catholics, 3%.

Education. Primary education is free and compulsory in eight-year schools from seven to 15 years. Secondary education is also free and lasts four years. Secondary education is divided into three categories: general; technical and professional; vocational. There were, in 2000–01, 2,002 nursery schools with 80,443 pupils and 3,749 teachers; 28,293 primary school teachers with 535,238 pupils; and 108,173 pupils and 5,760 teachers at secondary schools. In 2000–01 there were 5 universities,

1 agricultural university, 1 technological university, 1 polytechnic, 1 academy of fine arts and 1 higher institute of physical education. There were 40,859 university students registered and 1,683 academic staff in 2000–01; Tirana is the largest university, with 14,683 students in 1999–2000. Adult literacy in 1999 was 84·0% (90·9% among males and 76·9% among females).

In 2000 total expenditure on education came to 3% of GNP.

Health. Medical services are free, though medicines are charged for. In 1999 there were 51 hospitals, 4,325 doctors and 12,674 nurses or midwives. In 1999 there were 10,237 hospital beds. The expenditure for health in 1999 was 12,077m. leks (7·3% of total government expenditure).

CULTURE

Broadcasting. Broadcasting is regulated by the National Council for Radio-Television (NCRT), one member of which is appointed by the president, and the other six by the permanent Commission on the Media, which is composed equally of representatives of government and opposition parties. In Dec. 2000 the NCRT licensed two national television stations, 45 local television stations, 31 local radio stations and one national radio station. There are also a number of privately owned television broadcasting stations. In 1997 there were 810,000 radio and 405,000 TV receivers (colour by SECAM H).

Cinema. In 2002 there were 25 cinemas, compared to 65 in 1991.

Press. In 1996 there were 5 national dailies (combined circulation of 116,000, at a rate of 37 per 1,000 inhabitants).

Tourism. In 1999 26,000 foreign tourists stayed in 102 Albanian hotels.

The Greek colony of Butrint, Sarandë is a UNESCO world heritage site.

Libraries. The National Library in Tirana contains over 1m. items.

Theatre and Opera. The National Albanian Theatre, Tirana, is the most prestigious, with a capacity of 540. The Opera and Ballet Theatre, Tirana, is the home of the Albanian Philharmonic Orchestra.

Museums and Galleries. The largest museum is the National Historical Museum in Tirana.

DIPLOMATIC REPRESENTATIVES

Of Albania in the United Kingdom (2nd Floor, 24 Buckingham Gate, London SW1E 6LB)
Ambassador: Kastriot Robo.

Of the United Kingdom in Albania (Rruga Skenderberg 12, Tirana)
Ambassador: Dr David Landsman.

Of Albania in the USA (1150 18th St., NW, Washington, D.C., 20036)
Ambassador: Dr Fatos Tarifa.

Of the USA in Albania (Tirana Rruga Elbasanit 103, Tirana)
Ambassador: James Jeffrey.

Of Albania to the United Nations
Ambassador: Agim Nesho.

Of Albania to the European Union
Ambassador: Artur Kuko.

FURTHER READING
Fischer, Bernd, *Albania at War 1939–45.* Hurst, London, 1999
Hutchings, R., *Historical Dictionary of Albania.* Lanham (MD), 1997
Sjoberg, O., *Rural Change and Development in Albania.* Boulder (CO), 1992
Vickers, M., *The Albanians: a Modern History.* London, 1997
Vickers, M. and Pettifer, J., *Albania: from Anarchy to a Balkan Identity.* Farnborough, 1997
Winnifrith, T. (ed.) *Perspectives on Albania.* London, 1992
Young, A., *Albania.* [Bibliography] 2nd ed. ABC-Clio, Oxford and Santa Barbara (CA), 1997

National statistical office: Albanian Institute of Statistics, Tirana. *Director General:* Milva Ekonomi.
Website: http://www.instat.gov.al/

ALGERIA

Jumhuriya al-Jazairiya
ad-Dimuqratiya ash-Shabiya
(People's Democratic Republic
of Algeria)

Capital: Algiers
Population estimate, 2000: 30·3m.
GDP per capita, 2000: (PPP$) 5,308
HDI/world rank: 0·697/106

KEY HISTORICAL EVENTS

Algeria came under French control in the 1850s. The French settlers who subsequently arrived developed political and economic power at the expense of the indigenous Muslim population. In Nov. 1954 the *Front de Libération Nationale* (FLN), representing the Muslim majority, declared open warfare against the French administration and armed forces. There was extensive loss of life and property during the fighting which continued unabated until March 1962 when a ceasefire was agreed between the French government and the nationalists. Against the wishes of the French in Algeria, Gen. de Gaulle conceded Algerian independence on 3 July 1962.

The Political Bureau of the FLN took over the functions of government, a National Constituent Assembly was elected and the Republic was declared on 25 Sept. 1962. The founder of the FLN, Ahmed Ben Bella, became prime minister, and president the following year. On 15 June 1965 the government was overthrown by a junta of army officers, who established a Revolutionary Council under Col. Houari Boumédienne. After 10 years of rule, Boumédienne proposed that elections should be held for a president and a National Assembly. The proposed new constitution was accepted in a referendum in Nov. 1976 and Boumédienne was elected president unopposed. A National Assembly was elected in Feb. 1977, only FLN members being allowed as candidates.

On the death of the president in Dec. 1978 the Revolutionary Council again took over the government. The Islamic Salvation Front (FIS) was banned in March 1992. The head of state, Mohamed Boudiaf, was assassinated on 29 July 1992, and a campaign of terrorism was launched by fundamentalists which has continued to the present day. It is estimated that over 100,000 lives have been lost, although Algeria has emerged from the worst of the war, with most of the guerrilla activity now restricted to the countryside. Unrest among Berbers, Algeria's main ethnic community, erupted into violence in May 2001, resulting in 60 people losing their lives in the Berber region of Kabylie. In March 2002 President Bouteflika agreed to grant the Berber language official status alongside Arabic.

TERRITORY AND POPULATION

Algeria is bounded in the west by Morocco and Western Sahara, southwest by Mauritania and Mali, southeast by Niger, east by Libya and Tunisia, and north by the Mediterranean Sea. It has an area of 2,381,741 sq. km (919,595 sq. miles). Population (census 1998) 29,2767,767; density, 12·3 per sq. km. In 1999, 59·5% of the population lived in urban areas.

The UN gives a projected population for 2010 of 35·6m.

2·5m. Algerians live in France.

83% of the population speak Arabic, 17% Berber; French is widely spoken. A law of Dec. 1996 made Arabic the sole official language, but in March 2002 Tamazight, the Berber language, was given official status and also made a national language.

The 1998 census populations of the 48 *wilayat* (provincial councils) were as follows:

Adrar	311,952	Annaba	555,485
Ain Defla	659,182	Batna	968,820
Ain Témouchent	326,611	al-Bayadh	226,528
Algiers	2,561,992	Béchar	230,482

Béjaia	848,560	Ouahran (Oran)	1,155,464
Biskra	588,648	Ouargla	438,831
Blida	787,069	al-Oued	529,842
Bordj Bou Arreridj	559,928	Oum al-Bouaghi	533,711
Bouira	626,586	Qacentina (Constantine)	815,032
Boumerdes	645,497	Relizane	639,253
Chlef	884,978	Saida	280,752
Djelfa	860,981	Sétif	1,315,940
Ghardaia	296,926	Sidi-bel-Abbès	529,704
Guelma	432,721	Skikda	787,118
Illizi	33,960	Souk Ahras	373,033
Jijel	574,336	Tamanrasset	151,814
Khenchela	348,122	at-Tarf	354,213
Laghouat	327,634	Tébessa	550,021
Mascara	677,099	Tiaret	728,513
Médéa	721,861	Tindouf	32,004[1]
Mila	680,815	Tipaza	505,382
Mostaganem	629,445	Tissemsilt	261,298
M'Sila	815,045	Tizi-Ouzou	1,101,059
Naâma	165,578	Tlemcen	846,942

[1]Excluding Saharawi refugees (170,000 in 1988) in camps.

The capital is Algiers (1998 population, 1,519,570). Other major towns (with 1998 census populations): Oran, 655,852; Constantine, 462,187; Batna, 242,514; Annaba, 215,083; Sétif, 211,859; Sidi-bel-Abbès, 180,260; Biskra, 170,956; Djelfa, 154,265; Tébassa, 153,246; Blida, 153,083; Skikda, 152,335; Béjaia, 147,076; Tiaret, 145,332; Chlef, 133,874; al-Buni, 133,471; Béchar, 131,010.

SOCIAL STATISTICS
1998 estimates: births, 806,000; deaths, 164,000; marriages, 151,467; stillbirths, 17,190. Rates (1998): births, 27·5 per 1,000; deaths, 5·6 per 1,000; growth, 2·14%. Infant mortality in 1998 was 53·3 per 1,000 live births. Expectation of life (1999), 70·8 years for females and 67·9 years for males. Annual population growth rate, 1990–99, 2·4%. Fertility rate, 1999, 3·7 births per woman.

CLIMATE
Coastal areas have a warm temperate climate, with most rain in winter, which is mild, while summers are hot and dry. Inland, conditions become more arid beyond the Atlas Mountains. Algiers, Jan. 54°F (12·2°C), July 76°F (24·4°C). Annual rainfall 30" (762 mm). Biskra, Jan. 52°F (11·1°C), July 93°F (33·9°C). Annual rainfall 6" (158 mm). Oran, Jan. 54°F (12·2°C), July 76°F (24·4°C). Annual rainfall 15" (376 mm).

CONSTITUTION AND GOVERNMENT
A referendum was held on 28 Nov. 1996. The electorate was 16,434,527; turn-out was 79·6%. The electorate approved by 85·81% of votes cast a new Constitution which defines the fundamental components of the Algerian people as Islam, Arab identity and Berber identity. It was signed into law on 7 Dec. 1996. Political parties are permitted, but not if based on a separatist feature such as race, religion, sex, language or region. The terms of office of the President are limited to two, but the President's powers of nomination are widened (General-Secretary of the government, governor of the national bank, judges, chiefs of security organs and prefects). Parliament is bicameral: a 380-member *National Assembly* elected by direct universal suffrage using proportional representation, and a 144-member *Council of the Nation*, one-third nominated by the President and two-thirds indirectly elected by the 48 local authorities. The Council of the Nation debates bills passed by the National Assembly which become law if a three-quarters majority is in favour.

In a referendum on 16 Sept. 1999 voters were asked 'Do you agree with the president's approach to restore peace and civilian concord?' Turn-out was 85·1% and 98·6% of the votes cast were in favour.

National Anthem. 'Qassaman bin nazilat Il-mahiqat' ('We swear by the lightning that destroys'); words by M. Zakaria, tune by Mohamed Fawzi.

RECENT ELECTIONS
In presidential elections on 15 April 1999 Abdelaziz Bouteflika (National Democratic Rally) gained 73·8% of the votes cast; turn-out was 60·3%. All of the other candidates had withdrawn the previous day alleging fraud.

Parliamentary elections were held on 30 May 2002. Prime Minister Ali Benflis' National Liberation Front won 199 out of 389 seats with 34·3% of votes cast; the National Democratic Rally, 47 seats with 8·2%; the Movement for National Reform, 43 with 9·5%; the Movement of the Society for Peace, 38 with 7·0%; and the Workers' Party, 21 with 3·3%. Turn-out was 46·2%.

CURRENT ADMINISTRATION
President: Abdelaziz Bouteflika; b. 1937 (sworn in 27 April 1999).

In May 2003 the government comprised:

Prime Minister: Ahmed Ouyahia; b. 1952 (RND; appointed 5 May 2003, having previously held office from Dec. 1995 to Dec. 1998).

Minister of State, Interior Minister: Noureddine Yazid Zerhouni. *Minister of State, Foreign Affairs Minister:* Abdelaziz Belkhadem. *Minister of Agriculture and Rural Development:* Saïd Berkat. *Commerce:* Noureddine Boukrouh. *Culture and Communication:* Khalida Toumi. *Energy and Mines:* Chakib Khelil. *Finance:* Abdelatif Benachenhou. *Fisheries and Marine Resources:* Smaïl Mimoune. *Health and Population:* Abdelhamid Aberkane. *Higher Education and Scientific Research:* Rachid Harraoubia. *Housing and Urban Planning:* Mohamed Nadir Hamimid. *Industry:* El-Hachemi Djaaboub. *Information Technology:* Zine Eddine Youbi. *Justice and Lord Chancellor:* Mohammed Charfi. *Labour and Social Security:* Tayeb Louh. *War Veterans:* Mohamed Cherif Abbes. *National and Regional Development and Environment:* Chérif Rahmani. *National Education:* Boubekeur Benbouzid. *National Solidarity and Employment:* Tayeb Belaiz. *Participation and Investment Promotion:* Karim Djoudi. *Vocational Training:* Abdelhamid Abad. *Public Works:* Omar Ghoul. *Relations with Parliament:* Noureddine Taleb. *Religious Affairs:* Bouabdellah Ghlamallah. *Small and Medium-Sized Businesses:* Mustapha Benbada. *Tourism:* Lakhdar Dorbani. *Transport:* Abdelmalek Sellal. *Water Resources:* Abdelmadjid Attar. *Youth and Sports:* Mohamed Allalou.

President of the Republic: http://www.elmouradia.dz

DEFENCE
Conscription is for 18 months (six months basic training and 12 months civilian tasks) at the age of 19.

Military expenditure totalled US$2,930m. in 2000 (US$97 per capita), representing 6·8% of GDP.

Army. There are six military regions. The Army had a strength of 105,000 (75,000 conscripts) in 1999. The Ministry of the Interior maintains National Security Forces of 20,000. The Republican Guard numbers 1,200 personnel and the Gendarmerie 60,000. There were in addition legitimate defence groups (self-defence militia and communal guards) numbering around 100,000.

Navy. Naval personnel in 1999 totalled 7,000. The Navy's 41 vessels included two submarines and three frigates. There are naval bases at Algiers, Annaba, Mers el Kebir and Jijel.

Air Force. The Air Force in 1999 had 10,000 personnel, 181 combat aircraft and 65 armed helicopters.

INTERNATIONAL RELATIONS
Algeria is a member of the UN, the African Union, the League of Arab States, Arab Maghreb Union, OPEC, African Development Bank, IOM and the OIC.

ECONOMY
In 1998 agriculture accounted for 12·1% of GDP, services 40·6% and industry 47·3%.

Overview. A law on privatization of July 1995 envisages the creation of small- and medium-size businesses in commerce, tourism and transport. Strategic industries (gas and oil) and large industrial complexes are to remain state-owned. Some 1,200 small and 50 large businesses were offered for sale to Algerian citizens; 30% of the shares are reserved for employees (5% free of charge).

Currency. The unit of currency is the *Algerian dinar* (DZD) of 100 *centimes*. Foreign exchange reserves were US$21,133m. in June 2002, with gold reserves 5·58m. troy oz. Total money supply was 1,287bn. dinars in March 2002. Inflation was 4·2% in 2001. The dinar was devalued by 28·6% in April 1994.

Budget. The fiscal year starts on 1 Jan. In 1999 revenue totalled 950,496m. dinars and expenditure 961,682m. dinars.

Performance. Total GDP was US$53·0bn. in 2001. GDP growth was 2·5% in 2000 and 2·8% in 2001.

Banking and Finance. The central bank and bank of issue is the Banque d'Algérie. The *Governor* is Mohammed Laksaci. In 1996 there were five state-owned commercial banks. Private banking recommenced in Sept. 1995.

Weights and Measures. The metric system is in use.

ENERGY AND NATURAL RESOURCES

Environment. According to the *World Bank Atlas* Algeria's carbon dioxide emissions in 1998 were the equivalent of 3·6 tonnes per capita.

Electricity. Installed capacity was 6m. kW in 1997. 7% is hydro-electric. Production in 1998 was 21·38bn. kWh, with consumption per capita 563 kWh.

Oil and Gas. A law of Nov. 1991 permits foreign companies to acquire up to 49% of known oil and gas reserves. Oil and gas production accounted for 23·2% of GDP in 1994. Oil production in 1996 was 298m. bbls.; oil reserves in 1999 totalled 9·2bn. bbls. Production of natural gas in 1999 was 83,189m. cu. metres (the fifth highest in the world); proven reserves in 2000 were 3,700bn. cu. metres.

Minerals. Output in 1999 (in metric tonnes): iron ore, 1,336,000; phosphate rock, 1,096,000; salt, 163,748; zinc, 9,808; lead, 1,215. There are also deposits of mercury, silver, copper, antimony, kaolin, marble, onyx, salt and coal.

Agriculture. Much of the land is unsuitable for agriculture. The northern mountains provide grazing. There were 7·65m. ha of arable land in 1998 and 0·51m. ha of permanent crops. 0·56m. ha were irrigated in 1998. In 1987 the government sold back to the private sector land which had been nationalized on the declaration of independence in 1962; a further 0·5m. ha, expropriated in 1973, were returned to some 30,000 small landowners in 1990. In 1995 the agricultural population was 6·57m. There were 92,800 tractors and 9,200 harvester-threshers in 1998.

The chief crops in 2000 were (in 1,000 tonnes): potatoes, 950; tomatoes, 800; wheat, 800; melons and watermelons, 540; dates, 430; barley, 400; onions, 380; olives, 350; oranges, 310; grapes, 180; chillies and green peppers, 155; carrots, 135.

Livestock, 2000: sheep, 18·2m.; goats, 3·4m.; cattle, 1·65m.; asses, 202,000; camels, 151,000; mules, 72,000; horses, 55,000; chickens, 110m. Livestock products, 2000 (in 1,000 tonnes): poultry meat, 200; lamb and mutton, 170; beef and veal, 117; eggs, 120; cow's milk, 1,000; sheep's milk, 220; goat's milk, 150.

Forestry. Forests covered 1·86m. ha. in 1995, or 0·8% of the total land area. The greater part of the state forests are brushwood, but there are large areas with cork-oak trees, Aleppo pine, evergreen oak and cedar. The dwarf-palm is grown on the plains, alfalfa on the tableland. Timber is cut for firewood and for industrial purposes, and for bark for tanning. Timber production in 1999 was 2·79m. cu. metres.

Fisheries. There are extensive fisheries for sardines, anchovies, sprats, tuna and shellfish. The total catch in 1999 amounted to 105,693 tonnes, exclusively from marine waters.

INDUSTRY

1997 output (in 1,000 tonnes): pig iron, 700; rolled steel, 439; crude steel, 427; steel tubes (1992), 106; concrete bars (1992), 134; cement (1995), 6,200; bricks (1992), 1,776; ammonitrates (1992), 193; phosphate fertilizers (1992), 154; tobacco (1992), 24; (in units) tractors (1992), 3,009; lorries (1994), 1,230 (assembled); TV sets (1994), 165,000.

Labour. In 1996 the workforce numbered about 5·4m. (75% males) of whom 1m. were engaged in agriculture. Some 1·2m. non-agricultural workers were employed in the private sector; 2m. workers were unemployed. By 2001 unemployment was approaching 30%.

INTERNATIONAL TRADE

Foreign debt was US$25,002m. in 2000. Foreign investors are permitted to hold 100% of the equity of companies, and to repatriate all profits.

Imports and Exports. In 1999 exports (f.o.b.) were valued at US$12,525m. and imports (c.i.f.) at US$9,162m. Main export markets in 1999 (in US$1m.): Italy, 2,942; USA, 1,755; France, 1,719; Spain, 1,329; Netherlands, 1,021. Main import suppliers (in US$1m.): France, 2,086; Italy, 907; USA, 770; Germany, 679; Spain, 508. Main imports (in US$1m.): machinery and transport equipment, 3,035; food and live animals, 2,222; manufactured goods, 1,667; chemicals and related products, 1,073. Main exports (in US$1m.): petroleum and products, 6,940; gas, 5,227.

COMMUNICATIONS

Roads. There were, in 1996, an estimated 25,840 km of motorways and national highways, 23,900 km of regional roads and 53,700 km of other roads. There were approximately 1,505,000 vehicles registered in 1996, of which 725,000 were passenger cars (24·8 cars per 1,000 inhabitants). In 1991, 55m. passengers and 6·2m. tonnes of freight were conveyed by public transport.

Rail. In 1995 there were 3,210 km of 1,432 mm route (301 km electrified) and 1,156 km of 1,055 mm gauge. In 1995 the railways carried 8·6m. tonnes of freight and 44·2m. passengers.

Civil Aviation. The main international airport is at Algiers (Houari Boumédienne), with some international services also using Annaba, Constantine and Oran. The national carrier is the state-owned Air Algérie. In 2000 Houari Boumédienne International Airport handled 2,754,689 passengers (1,392,438 on domestic flights) and, in 1999, 14,757 tonnes of freight. In 1999 scheduled airline traffic of Algerian-based carriers flew 32·2m. km, carrying 2,937,000 passengers (1,663,000 on international flights).

Shipping. In 1997 vessels totalling 103,138,000 NRT entered ports and vessels totalling 10,187,000 NRT cleared. The state shipping line, Compagnie Nationale Algérienne de Navigation, owned 47 vessels in 2001. The merchant shipping fleet totalled 1,005,000 GRT in 1998, including oil tankers, 33,000 GRT.

Telecommunications. In 2000 there were 1,761,300 telephone main lines, or 57·0 per 1,000 inhabitants, and 200,000 PCs in use (6·5 per 1,000 persons). In March 2001 there were approximately 180,000 Internet users and in Dec. 1998 mobile phone subscribers numbered 9,900. There were 7,000 fax machines in 1999.

Postal Services. There were 3,223 post offices in 1997.

SOCIAL INSTITUTIONS

Justice. The judiciary is constitutionally independent. Judges are appointed by the Supreme Council of Magistrature chaired by the President of the Republic. Criminal justice is organized as in France. The Supreme Court is at the same time Council of State and High Court of Appeal. The death penalty is in force for terrorism.

The population in penal institutions in 1996 was 35,737 (125 per 100,000 of national population).

Religion. The 1996 Constitution made Islam the state religion, established a consultative *High Islamic Council*, and forbids practices 'contrary to Islamic morality'. Over 98% of the population are Sunni Muslims. There are also around 110,000 Ibadiyah Muslims and 150,000 Christians, mainly Roman Catholics. The Armed Islamic Group (GIA) vowed in 1994 to kill 'Jews, Christians and polytheists' in Algeria. Hundreds of foreign nationals, including priests and nuns, have since been killed. Signalling an increasing tolerance amongst the Muslim community, the Missionaries of Africa's house at Ghardaia Oasis was re-opened in 2000.

Education. Adult literacy in 1999 was 66·6% (77·4% among males and 55·7% among females). In 1996–97 there were 33,503 children in pre-primary education. There were 15,426 state primary schools with 170,956 teachers and 4,674,947 pupils; 3,934 middle and secondary schools (1995) with 151,948 teachers and 2,618,242 pupils, of whom 48% were female.

In 1995–96 there were 6 universities, 2 universities of science and technology, 5 university centres, 1 agronomic institute, 1 telecommunications institute, 1 veterinary institute, 1 school of architecture and town planning and 1 *école normale supérieure*. In 1996 there were 160,000 university students and 7,947 academic staff.

In 1996 expenditure on education came to 5·1% of GNP and represented 16·4% of total government expenditure.

Health. In 1994 there were 25,796 doctors, 7,763 dental surgeons and 3,425 pharmacists. In 1990 there were 284 hospitals (with 60,124 beds), 1,309 health centres, 510 polyclinics, 475 maternity clinics and 3,344 care centres.

Welfare. Welfare payments to 7·4m. beneficiaries on low incomes were introduced in March 1992.

CULTURE

Broadcasting. The state-controlled Radiodiffusion Algérienne and Entreprise Nationale de Télévision broadcast home services in Arabic, Kabyle (Berber) and French, and an external service. There are 18 TV transmitting stations (colour by PAL). In 1997 there were 7·1m. radio and 3·1m. TV receivers.

Press. Algeria had five daily newspapers in 1996, with a combined circulation of 1·1m.

Tourism. In 1998 there were 678,000 foreign tourists, spending US$20m.

DIPLOMATIC REPRESENTATIVES
Of Algeria in the United Kingdom (54 Holland Park, London, W11 3RS)
Ambassador: Ahmed Attaf.

Of the United Kingdom in Algeria (6 Avenue Souidani Boudjemaa, BP08 Alger-Gare 16000, Algiers)
Ambassador: Graham Hand.

Of Algeria in the USA (2118 Kalorama Rd., NW, Washington, D.C., 20008)
Ambassador: Idriss Jazairy.

Of the USA in Algeria (4 Chemin Cheich Bachir Ibrahimi, Algiers)
Ambassador: Janet Sanderson.

Of Algeria to the United Nations
Ambassador: Abdallah Baali.

Of Algeria to the European Union
Ambassador: Halim Benattallah.

FURTHER READING
Ageron, C.-R., *Modern Algeria: a History from 1830 to the Present.* London, 1991
Eveno, P., *L'Algérie.* Paris, 1994
Heggoy, A. A. and Crout, R. R., *Historical Dictionary of Algeria.* Metuchen (NJ), 1995
Lawless, R. I., *Algeria.* [Bibliography] 2nd ed. ABC-Clio, Oxford and Santa Barbara (CA), 1995
Ruedy, J., *Modern Algeria: the Origins and Development of a Nation.* Indiana Univ. Press, 1992
Stone, M., *The Agony of Algeria.* Columbia University Press, 1997
Stora, B., *Histoire de l'Algérie depuis l'Indépendance.* Paris, 1994
Willis, M., *The Islamist Challenge in Algeria: A Political History.* New York, 1997

National statistical office: Office National des Statistiques, 8 rue des Moussebiline, Algiers.
Website: http://www.ons.dz/

ANDORRA

Principat d'Andorra

Capital: Andorra la Vella
Population estimate, 2000: 66,000
GDP per capita: not available

KEY HISTORICAL EVENTS

The political status of Andorra was regulated by the *Paréage* of 1278 which placed Andorra under the joint suzerainty of the Comte de Foix and of the Bishop of Urgel. The rights vested in the house of Foix passed by marriage to that of Bearn and, on the accession of Henri IV, to the French crown. A democratic constitution was adopted in 1993.

TERRITORY AND POPULATION

The co-principality of Andorra is situated in the eastern Pyrenees on the French–Spanish border. The country is mountainous and has an average altitude of 1,996 metres. Area, 468 sq. km. In lieu of a census, a register of population is kept. The registered population on 31 Dec. 2000 was 65,844; density, 141 per sq. km.

In 1995, 95·4% of the population lived in urban areas.

The chief towns are Andorra la Vella, the capital (population, 25,000 in 1999) and its suburb Escaldes-Engordany (13,177). 36·0% of the residential population are Andorran, 40·6% Spanish, 10·2% Portuguese and 6·5% French. Catalan is the official language, but Spanish and French are widely spoken.

SOCIAL STATISTICS

Births in 2000 numbered 747 (rate of 11·3 per 1,000 inhabitants) and deaths 259 (3·9 per 1,000 inhabitants). Life expectancy (2000): male, 89·8 years; female, 91·1 years. Annual population growth rate, 1990–99, 4·3%. Fertility rate, 1999, 1·3 births per woman.

CLIMATE

Escaldes-Engordany, Jan. 35·8°F (2·1°C), July 65·8°F (18·8°C). Annual rainfall 34·9" (886 mm).

CONSTITUTION AND GOVERNMENT

The joint heads of state are the President of the French Republic and the Bishop of Urgel, the co-princes.

A new democratic constitution was approved by 74·2% of votes cast at a referendum on 14 March 1993. The electorate was 9,123; turn-out was 75·7%. The new Constitution, which came into force on 4 May 1993, makes the co-princes a single constitutional monarch and provides for a parliament, the *General Council of the Andorran Valleys*, with 28 members, two from each of the seven parishes and 14 elected by proportional representation from the single national constituency, for four years. In 1982 an *Executive Council* was appointed and legislative and executive powers were separated. The General Council elects the President of the Executive Council, who is the head of the government.

There is a *Constitutional Court* of four members who hold office for eight-year terms, renewable once.

National Anthem. 'El Gran Carlemany, mon pare' ('Great Charlemagne, my father'); words by Enric Marfany, tune by D. J. Benlloch i Vivò.

RECENT ELECTIONS

Elections to the General Council were held on 4 March 2001. The Liberal Party of Andorra won 15 seats, the Social Democratic Party 6, the Democratic Party 5, and the Lauredian Union 2. Turn-out was 81·6%.

CURRENT ADMINISTRATION
In March 2003 the government comprised:

President, Executive Council: Marc Forné Molné; b. 1946 (Liberal Party of Andorra; sworn in 7 Dec. 1994 and re-elected in Feb. 1997 and March 2001).

Minister for Foreign Affairs: Juli Minoves Triquell. *Economy:* Miquel Alvarez Marfany. *Finance:* Mireia Maestre Cortadella. *Interior and Justice:* Jordi Visent Guitart. *Territorial Planning:* Jordi Malleu Serra. *Health and Social Affairs:* Mónica Tort Codina. *Culture:* Xavier Montane Atero. *Education, Youth and Sports:* Pere Cervós Cardona. *Presidency and Tourism:* Enric Pujal Areny. *Agriculture and Environment:* Olga Adellach Coma.

Government Website (Catalan only): http://www.govern.ad/

INTERNATIONAL RELATIONS
The 1993 Constitution empowers Andorra to conduct its own foreign affairs, with consultation on matters affecting France or Spain.

Andorra is a member of the UN, UNESCO, WIPO, the Council of Europe and the OSCE.

ECONOMY
Currency. Since 1 Jan. 2002 Andorra has been using the euro.

Budget. 2001: revenue, €234,705,780; expenditure, €250,775,790.

Performance. Real GDP growth was 3·3% in 1999 and averaged 2·4% between 1995 and 2000.

Banking and Finance. The banking sector, with its tax-haven status, contributes substantially to the economy.

ENERGY AND NATURAL RESOURCES
Electricity. Installed capacity was 26,500 kW in 2000. Production in 1998 was 116m. kWh. 60% of Andorra's electricity comes from Spain.

Agriculture. In 1998 there were some 1,000 ha of arable land (2% of total). Tobacco and potatoes are principal crops. The principal livestock activity is sheep raising.

INDUSTRY
Labour. Only 1% of the workforce is employed in agriculture, the rest in tourism, commerce, services and light industry. Manufacturing consists mainly of cigarettes, cigars and furniture.

INTERNATIONAL TRADE
Andorra is a member of the EU Customs Union for industrial goods, but is a third country for agricultural produce. There is a free economic zone.

Imports and Exports. 1997 exports, US$46·2m.; imports, US$920·2m. Main export markets (2000): Spain, 60·9%; France, 26·1%. Leading import suppliers (2000): Spain, 48·5%; France, 26·6%. The European Union accounted for 92·3% of exports in 2000 and 89·2% of imports.

COMMUNICATIONS
Roads. In 1994 there were 269 km of roads (198 km paved). Motor vehicles (2000) totalled 60,287, including 46,421 cars and 6,029 trucks and vans.

Civil Aviation. There is an airport at Seo de Urgel.

Telecommunications. In 2000 there were 34,215 telephone main lines, or 519·6 per 1,000 inhabitants. There were 25,099 mobile phone subscribers in Dec. 2000 and 24,500 Internet users in April 2001. In 1996 there were 3,000 fax machines.

SOCIAL INSTITUTIONS
Justice. Justice is administered by the High Council of Justice, comprising five members appointed for single six-year terms. The independence of judges is

constitutionally guaranteed. Judicial power is exercised in civil matters in the first instance by Magistrates' Courts and a Judge's Court. Criminal justice is administered by the *Corts*, consisting of the judge of appeal, a *raonador* (ombudsman) elected by the General Council of the Valleys, a general attorney and an attorney nominated for five years alternately by each of the co-princes.

Religion. The Roman Catholic is the established church, but the 1993 Constitution guarantees religious liberty. In 1997 around 79% of the population were Catholics.

Education. Free education in French- or Spanish-language schools is compulsory: six years primary starting at six years, followed by four years secondary. A Roman Catholic school provides education in Catalan. In 1996–97 there were 18 schools altogether with 8,079 pupils.

Health. In 2000 there were two hospitals (one private, one public); in 1994 there were 132 doctors.

CULTURE

Broadcasting. Servei de Telecomunicacions d'Andorra relays French and Spanish programmes. Radio Andorra is a commercial public station; Radio Valira is commercial. Number of receivers: radio (1997), 16,000; TV (1997), 27,000. Colour is by PAL.

Press. In 1996 there were three daily newspapers with a combined circulation of 4,000, at a rate of 60 per 1,000 inhabitants.

Tourism. Tourism is the main industry, averaging 11m. visitors a year and accounting for 80% of GDP.

DIPLOMATIC REPRESENTATIVES

Of Andorra in the United Kingdom (63 Westover Road, London, SW18 2RF)
Ambassador: Albert Pintat (resides in Andorra).

Of the United Kingdom in Andorra
Ambassador: Stephen J. L. Wright, CMG (resides at Madrid).

Of Andorra in the USA (2 United Nations Plaza, 25th Floor, N.Y. 10017)
Ambassador: Vacant.
Chargé d'Affaires a.i.: Jelena V. Pia-Comella.

Of USA in Andorra
Ambassador: George L. Argyros (resides in Spain).

Of Andorra to the United Nations
Ambassador: Vacant.
Deputy Permanent Representative: Jelena V. Pia-Comella.

Of Andorra to the European Union
Ambassador: Meritxell Mateu i Pi.

FURTHER READING

Taylor, Barry, *Andorra.* [Bibliography] ABC-Clio, Oxford and Santa Barbara (CA), 1993.

National statistical office: Servie d'Estudi Ministeri de Finances.
Website: http://estudis-estadistica.finances.ad

ANGOLA

República de Angola

Capital: Luanda
Population estimate, 2000: 13·13m.
GDP per capita, 2000: (PPP$) 2,187
HDI/world rank: 0·403/161

KEY HISTORICAL EVENTS

The Portuguese were dominant from the late 19th century. Angola remained a Portuguese colony until 11 June 1951, when it became an Overseas Province of Portugal.

A guerrilla war broke out in 1961 when the People's Movement for the Liberation of Angola launched a military offensive to end Portuguese colonial rule. After the coup d'état in Portugal in April 1974, negotiations with Portugal, the MPLA (People's Movement for the Liberation of Angola), the FNLA (National Front for the Liberation of Angola) and UNITA (National Union for the Total Liberation of Angola) led to independence on 11 Nov. 1975. The FNLA tried to seize power by force but was driven out of the capital. As independence approached, invasion from the north was combined with a South African invasion in support of UNITA. The MPLA declared independence and, subsequently, with the help of Cuban troops, defeated the FNLA in the north and drove the invading South African army out of the country. South African invasions and the occupation of large areas of Angola continued until the signing of the New York Agreement in Dec. 1988, under which South Africa agreed to withdraw its forces from Angola and Namibia (and grant independence to Namibia), while Angola and Cuba agreed to the phased withdrawal of Cuban troops.

After many abortive attempts to end the internal conflict with UNITA, a peace agreement was signed on 31 May 1991 under which a single national army was to be formed and multi-party elections held. In Sept. 1992 the MPLA won the elections and José Eduardo dos Santos was re-elected president against UNITA leader Jonas Savimbi. But the latter rejected the election results, withdrew his generals from the unified army and went back to war, seizing an estimated 70% of the country.

On 20 Nov. 1994 a peace agreement was signed in Lusaka, allowing for UNITA to share in government.

On 9 Jan. 1998 a breakthrough in negotiations between the government and UNITA rebels was announced. Jonas Savimbi, UNITA's leader, met with President dos Santos but talks soon foundered and serious fighting resumed in the north, raising fears of a major new offensive by the Angolan Armed Forces against the UNITA rebels. Meanwhile, Angolan troops fought in the Democratic Republic of the Congo alongside the forces of President Kabila in his efforts to quash a Rwandan-backed rebellion in the east of his country. They remained after the assassination of Kabila in Jan. 2001 but renewed hopes of peace resulted in their withdrawal in Jan. 2002. In Feb. 2002 Jonas Savimbi was killed in fighting with government troops. On 4 April 2002 commanders of the Angolan army and UNITA signed a ceasefire agreement aimed at ending the civil war. More than half a million Angolans died in the civil unrest that plagued their country for over a quarter of a century.

TERRITORY AND POPULATION

Angola is bounded in the north by the Republic of the Congo, north and northeast by the Democratic Republic of the Congo, east by Zambia, south by Namibia and west by the Atlantic Ocean. The area is 1,246,700 sq. km (481,354 sq. miles) including the province of Cabinda, an exclave of territory separated by 30 sq. km of the Democratic Republic of the Congo's territory. The population at census, 1970, was 5,646,166, of whom 14% were urban. Official estimate, 1995, 11·5m.; density, 9·2 per sq. km. In 1999, 66·5% of the population were living in rural areas. Population figures are rough estimates because the civil war has led to huge movements of population.

There were 0·3m. Angolan refugees in the Democratic Republic of the Congo, Zambia and the Republic of the Congo in 1995.

The UN gives a projected population for 2010 of 17·77m.

Area, population and chief towns of the provinces:

Province	Area (in sq. km)	Population estimate, 1992 (in 1,000)	Chief town
Bengo	31,371	196·1	Caxito
Benguela	31,788	656·6	Benguela
Bié	70,314	1,119·8	Kuito
Cabinda	7,270	152·1	Cabinda
Cuando-Cubango	199,049	139·6	Menongue
Cuanza Norte	24,190	385·2	Ndalatando
Cuanza Sul	55,660	694·5	Sumbe
Cunene	89,342	241·2	Ondjiva
Huambo	34,274	1,521·0	Huambo
Huíla	75,002	885·1	Lubango
Luanda	2,418	1,588·6	Luanda
Lunda Norte	102,783	305·9	Lucapa
Lunda Sul	45,649	169·1	Saurimo
Malanje	97,602	906·0	Malanje
Moxico	223,023	319·3	Luena
Namibe	58,137	107·3	Namibe
Uíge	58,698	802·7	Uíge
Zaire	40,130	237·5	Mbanza Congo

The most important towns (populations) are Luanda, the capital (1999, 2·55m.), Huambo (1995, 400,000), Benguela (1983, 155,000), Lobito (1983, 150,000), Lubango (1984, 105,000), Malanje (1970, 31,559) and Namibe (formerly Moçâmedes, 1981, 100,000).

The main ethnic groups are Umbundo (Ovimbundo), Kimbundo, Bakongo, Chokwe, Ganguela, Luvale and Kwanyama.

Portuguese is the official language. Bantu and other African languages are also spoken.

SOCIAL STATISTICS

Life expectancy at birth, 1999, 43·6 years for males and 46·3 years for females. 1995 births (estimates), 567,000; deaths, 217,000. Birth rate in 1995 was 49·3 per 1,000 population; death rate, 18·9. Annual population growth rate, 1990–99, 3·4%. Fertility rate, 1999, 6·6 births per woman; infant mortality, 1999, 172 per 1,000 live births. Angola has one of the highest rates of child mortality in the world, at nearly 300 deaths among children under 5 per 1,000 live births in 1999.

CLIMATE

The climate is tropical, with low rainfall in the west but increasing inland. Temperatures are constant over the year and most rain falls in March and April. Luanda, Jan. 78°F (25·6°C), July 69°F (20·6°C). Annual rainfall 13" (323 mm). Lobito, Jan. 77°F (25°C), July 68°F (20°C). Annual rainfall 14" (353 mm).

CONSTITUTION AND GOVERNMENT

Under the Constitution adopted at independence, the sole legal party was the MPLA. In Dec. 1990, however, the MPLA announced that the Constitution would be revised to permit opposition parties. The supreme organ of state is the 220-member *National Assembly.* There is an executive *President* elected for renewable terms of five years, who appoints a *Council of Ministers.*

In Dec. 2002 Angola's ruling party and the UNITA party of former rebels agreed on a new constitution. The president would keep key powers, including the power to name and to remove the prime minister. The president will also appoint provincial governors, rather than letting voters elect them, but the governor must be from the party that received a majority of votes in that province. The draft constitution has been submitted to the Angolan parliament for consideration, and a referendum is likely to be held before the end of 2003.

National Anthem. 'O Pátria, nunca mais esqueceremos' ('Oh Fatherland, never shall we forget'); words by M. R. Alves Monteiro, tune by R. A. Dias Mingas.

RECENT ELECTIONS

At the presidential and parliamentary elections of 29–30 Sept. 1992 the electorate was 4,862,748. Turn-out was about 90%. Eduardo dos Santos (MPLA) was re-elected as president with 49·5% of votes cast against 40·5% for his single opponent, Jonas Savimbi (UNITA). The latter refused to accept the result. The MPLA gained 129 seats in the National Assembly with 53·74% of votes cast, and UNITA 77 with 34·1%. 10 other parties gained 6 seats or fewer.

On 11 April 1997 a Government of National Unity was installed, with 3 ministerial posts going to UNITA. Jonas Savimbi, UNITA's leader, received the specially created position of Chief of the Principal Opposition Party.

CURRENT ADMINISTRATION
President: José Eduardo dos Santos; b. 1943 (MPLA; since 10 Sept. 1979; re-elected 9 Dec. 1985 and 29–30 Sept. 1992).

Prime Minister and Minister of the Interior: Fernando Dias dos Santos da Piedade 'Nando'; b. 1952 (MPLA; since 6 Dec. 2002).

In March 2003 the government comprised:

Minister for Agriculture and Rural Development: Gilberto Lutucuta. *Assistance and Social Reintegration:* Joao Kussumua. *Commerce:* Victorino Domingos Hossi. *Education and Culture:* António Burity da Silva Neto. *Energy and Water:* Luis Filipe da Silva. *External Relations:* João Bernardo de Miranda. *Family and Women's Affairs:* Candida Celeste da Silva. *Finance:* Julio Bessa. *Fisheries and Environment:* Maria de Fatima Monteiro Jardim. *Geology and Mines:* Manuel António Africano. *Health:* Albertina Julia Hamukuya. *Hotels and Tourism:* Jorge Alicerces Valentim. *Industry:* Joaquim Duarte da Costa David. *Justice:* Paulo Tjipilica. *National Defence:* Kundi Paihama. *Petroleum:* José Maria Botelho de Vasconcelos. *Planning:* Ana Dias Lourenco. *Posts and Telecommunications:* Licinio Tavares Ribeiro. *Public Administration, Employment and Social Welfare:* António Domingos Pitra Costa Neto. *Public Works and Urban Affairs:* António Henriques da Silva. *Science and Technology:* João Baptista Nganda Gina. *Social Communication:* Pedro Hendrick Vaal Neto. *Territorial Administration:* Fernando Faustino Muteka. *Transport:* André Luis Brandão. *War Veterans:* Pedro José van Dunem. *Youth and Sports:* José Marcos Barrica.

Government Website: http://www.angola.org

DEFENCE
Conscription is for two years. Defence expenditure totalled US$1,250m. in 2000 (US$97 per capita), representing 19·2% of GDP.

Army. In 1999 the Army had 35 regiments. Total strength was estimated at 100,000. In addition the paramilitary Rapid Reaction Police numbered 15,000.

Navy. Naval personnel in 1999 totalled about 1,500 with nine operational vessels. There is a naval base at Luanda.

Air Force. The Angolan People's Air Force (FAPA) was formed in 1976 and has about 11,000 personnel. Since the elections in 1992 and the relative calm, the Air Force has been run down and serviceability of combat aircraft is low. In 1999 there were 85 combat aircraft and 28 armed helicopters.

INTERNATIONAL RELATIONS
Angola is a member of the UN, WTO, the African Union, African Development Bank, COMESA, SADC, IOM and is an ACP member state of the ACP-EU relationship.

ECONOMY
In 1998 agriculture accounted for 12·2% of GDP, services 36·4% and industry 51·4%.

Overview. Reforms are under way to introduce a market economy and restore private property. In April 2000 Angola signed a far-reaching agreement with the International Monetary Fund which stipulates economic reforms. In July 2000 the World Bank also signed an agreement approving a series of reforms in return for help with the country's huge foreign debt. During 2000 there were plans to privatize at least ten large- and medium-sized companies. It is hoped to complete the privatization process before the end of 2003.

Currency. The unit of currency is the *kwanza* (AOA), introduced in Dec. 1999, replacing the *readjusted kwanza* at a rate of 1 kwanza = 1m. readjusted kwanzas. Foreign exchange reserves were US$902m. in June 2002. Gold reserves were 46,500 troy oz in 1990. Inflation was 4,146% in 1996. It has slowed since then, and in 2001 was 153%.

Budget. Revenues in 1997 were KZr694·6m. and expenditure KZr521·3m.

Performance. Total GDP was US$9·5bn. in 2001. The civil war meant GDP growth in 1993 was negative, at −24·0%, but a recovery followed and in 2000 and 2001 it was 3·0% and 3·2% respectively, mainly thanks to booming diamond exports and post-war rebuilding.

Banking and Finance. Banking was re-opened to commercial competition in 1991. The Banco Nacional de Angola is the central bank and bank of issue (*Governor*, Aguinaldo Jaime). All banks remain state-owned, though the government is progressively reducing its stake in them. An agricultural bank and a commercial and industrial bank were founded in 1991. Five Portuguese banks have branches, as well as the French Banque Paribas, Citibank, the Equator Bank, and the African Development Bank.

Angola received US$1·8bn. in foreign direct investment in 2000, approximately 90% of which was in the oil sector.

Weights and Measures. The metric system is in force.

ENERGY AND NATURAL RESOURCES

Environment. In 1998 Angola's carbon dioxide emissions were the equivalent of 0·5 tonnes per capita according to the *World Bank Atlas*.

Electricity. Installed capacity was 1m. kW in 1997. Production in 1998 was 1·89bn. kWh, with consumption per capita 60 kWh.

Oil and Gas. Oil is produced mainly offshore and in the Cabinda exclave. Oil production and supporting activities contribute some 45% of Angolan GDP and provide the government with approximately US$3·5bn. annually. The oil industry is expected to invest US$3·5bn. a year in offshore Angola in the early part of the 21st century, and it is hoped that by 2005 output may be double the 750,000 bbls. a day produced in 2000. There are plans for a new US$3·3bn. oil refinery near Lobito which is scheduled to begin operations in 2006. Only Nigeria among sub-Saharan African countries produces more oil. It is believed that there are huge oil resources yet to be discovered. Proven resources in 2001 were 5·4bn. bbls. Total production (1996) 258m. bbls. Natural gas production, 1996, 57 petajoules.

Minerals. Mineral production in Angola is dominated by diamonds, and 90% of all workers in the mining sector work in the diamond industry. Production in 1998 totalled 2,764,000 carats. Angola has billions of dollars worth of unexploited diamond fields. In 2000 the government regained control of the nation's richest diamond provinces from UNITA rebels. Other minerals produced include (1991) granite, 635,000 cu. metres; marble, 244,000 cu. metres; salt, 6,600 tonnes. Iron ore, phosphate, manganese and copper deposits exist.

Agriculture. In 1998 there were 3m. ha of arable land and 0·5m. ha of permanent crops. The agricultural population in 1995 was 8·17m., of whom 3·78m. were economically active. There were 10,300 tractors in 1998. Principal crops (with 2000 production, in 1,000 tonnes): cassava (3,130); maize (428); sugarcane (330); bananas (290); sweet potatoes (182); millet (102); citrus fruits (75); dry beans (68).

Livestock (2000): 4·0m. cattle, 350,000 sheep, 2·15m. goats, 800,000 pigs.

Forestry. In 1995, 222,000 sq. km, or 17·8% of the total land area, was covered by forests (18·8% in 1990), including mahogany and other hardwoods. Timber production in 1999 was 6·68m. cu. metres.

Fisheries. In 1993 the fishing fleet had 73 vessels over 100 GRT totalling 17,332 GRT. Total catch in 2000 came to 238,351 tonnes, mainly from sea fishing.

INDUSTRY

The principal manufacturing branches are foodstuffs, textiles and oil refining. Output, 1998 (in tonnes): sugar, 32,000; 1997 (in tonnes): residual fuel oil, 640,000; distillate fuel oil, 325,000; jet fuels, 160,000; petrol, 110,000; 1994 (in tonnes): bread, 15,082; wheat flour, 4,496; corn flour, 2,513; soap, 530; beer, 12·33m. litres; fabric, 3,038,000 sq. metres. Output, 1991 (in tonnes): maize flour, 21,200; plate glass, 6,900; plastic bags, 1,600; zinc sheets, 6,012; 52,000 radio sets; 15,600 TV sets.

Labour. In 1996 the total labour force numbered 5,144,000 (54% males).

INTERNATIONAL TRADE
In 2000 total foreign debt was US$10,146m.

Imports and Exports. Imports and exports for calendar years in US$1m.:

	1996	1997	1998	1999	2000
Imports	2,040	2,477	2,079	3,267	3,281
Exports	5,169	5,007	3,543	5,344	6,602

Main exports, 1994 (in US$1m.): crude oil, 2,821; diamonds, 96; refined oil, 61; gas, 14. Chief import suppliers (1991 trade in US$1m.): Portugal, 587; USA, 207; France, 194; Japan, 153; Brazil, 144. Chief export markets: USA, 1,751; France, 328; Germany, 174; Brazil, 152; Netherlands, 131.

COMMUNICATIONS

Roads. There were, in 1997, 76,626 km of roads (7,955 km highways; 25% of all roads surfaced), and in 1996 approximately 207,000 passenger cars and 25,000 commercial vehicles. Many roads remain mined as a result of the civil war; a programme of de-mining and rehabilitation is under way.

Rail. The length of railways open for traffic in 1987 was 2,952 km, comprising 2,798 km of 1,067 mm gauge and 154 km of 600 mm gauge, but much of the network was severely damaged in the civil war. Restoration and redevelopment of the network is under way, notably the Benguela Railway, linking the port city of Lobito with Huambo in Angola's rich farmlands and neighbouring Democratic Republic of the Congo and Zambia.

Civil Aviation. There is an international airport at Luanda (Fourth of February). The national carrier is Linhas Aéreas de Angola (TAAG). In 1999 scheduled airline traffic of Angola-based carriers flew 6·5m. km, carrying 531,000 passengers (120,000 on international flights).

Shipping. There are ports at Luanda, Lobito and Namibe, and oil terminals at Malongo, Lobito and Soyo. In 1998 the merchant fleet totalled 74,000 GRT, including oil tankers 3,000 GRT.

Telecommunications. There were 69,700 telephone main lines in 2000, or 5·3 per 1,000 inhabitants, and 15,000 PCs in use. It is intended to privatize Angola Telecom, although no date has been set. In Dec. 2000 there were approximately 30,000 Internet users, and in Dec. 1998, 9,700 mobile phone subscribers.

Postal Services. In 1997 there were 80 post offices, or 1 for every 145,000 persons.

SOCIAL INSTITUTIONS

Justice. The Supreme Court and Court of Appeal are in Luanda. The death penalty was abolished in 1992.

Religion. In 1997 there were 5·39m. Roman Catholics, 1·56m. Protestants, 460,000 African Christians, and most of the remainder follow traditional animist religions.

Education. The education system provides three levels of general education totalling eight years, followed by schools for technical training, teacher training or pre-university studies. Enrolment (in 1,000) in 1991–92: pre-school, 214; general education first level, 989; second level, 141; third level, 42; technical training, 12·7; teacher training, 109; pre-university studies (1990–91), 6·1. There is one university. Private schools have been permitted since 1991. The University of Luanda has campuses at Luanda, Huambo and Lubango. It had 8,954 students in 1991–92. The adult literacy rate was 42·0% in 1998.

Health. In 1990 there were 662 doctors, 10 dentists, 9,334 nurses, 4,165 medical auxiliaries and 266 hospitals and health centres with 11,857 beds. There were 1,339 medical posts.

In the period 1990–98 only 31% of the population had access to safe drinking water. In 2000 it was estimated that 60% of the 3·9m. displaced people were suffering from malnutrition.

CULTURE

Broadcasting. In 1997 there were 150,000 TV receivers and 630,000 radio receivers in Angola. The government-controlled Rádio Nacional de Angola broadcasts three programmes and an international service. There are also regional stations. Televisão Popular de Angola transmits from seven stations (colour by PAL).

Press. Angola had five daily newspapers in 1996, with a combined circulation of 128,000. The government daily is the *Jornal de Angola*. The *Diário da República* is the official gazette. There is an independent weekly, *Agora*, and there are around 100 specialized and independent publications.

Tourism. In 1999 there were 45,000 foreign tourists, bringing revenue of US$13m.

DIPLOMATIC REPRESENTATIVES

Of Angola in the United Kingdom (98 Park Lane, London, W1K 3TQ)
Ambassador: António da Costa Fernandes.

Of the United Kingdom in Angola (Rua Diogo Cão 4, Luanda)
Ambassador: John Thompson, MBE.

Of Angola in the USA (2108 16th Street, NW 20009, Washington, D.C., 20036)
Ambassador: Josefina Pitra Diakite.

Of the USA in Angola (32 rua Houari Boumédienne, Miramar, Luanda)
Ambassador: Christopher William Dell.

Of Angola to the United Nations
Ambassador: Ismael Gaspar Martins.

Of Angola to the European Union
Ambassador: Armando Mateus Cadete.

FURTHER READING

Anstee, M. J., *Orphan of the Cold War: the Inside Story of the Collapse of the Angolan Peace Process, 1992–93*. London, 1996
Black, Richard, *Angola*. [Bibliography] ABC-Clio, Oxford and Santa Barbara (CA), 1992
Brittain, Victoria, *Death of Dignity: Angola's Civil War*. Pluto, London, 1999
Guimarães, Fernando Andersen, *The Origins of the Angolan Civil War: Foreign Intervention and Domestic Political Conflict*. Palgrave, Basingstoke, 2001
Hodges, Tony, *Angola From Afro-Stalinism to Petro-Diamond Capitalism*. James Currey, Oxford, 2001
James, W. M., *Political History of the War in Angola*. New York, 1991
Roque, F., *Económia de Angola*. Lisbon, 1991

National statistical office: Instituto Nacional de Estatística, Luanda.

ANTIGUA AND BARBUDA

Capital: St John's
Population estimate, 2000: 67,000
GDP per capita, 2000: (PPP$) 10,541
HDI/world rank: 10,541

KEY HISTORICAL EVENTS
Antigua and Barbuda make up the island nation of the Lesser Antilles in the Eastern Caribbean. Most of the population is descended from African slaves brought in during colonial times to work on sugar plantations.

As British colonies Antigua and Barbuda formed part of the Leeward Islands Federation from 1871 until 30 June 1956 when Antigua and Barbuda became a separate Crown Colony. It was part of the West Indies Federation from 3 Jan. 1958 until 31 May 1962 and became an Associated State of the UK on 27 Feb. 1967. Antigua and Barbuda gained independence on 1 Nov. 1981.

TERRITORY AND POPULATION
Antigua and Barbuda comprises three islands of the Lesser Antilles situated in the eastern Caribbean with a total land area of 442 sq. km (171 sq. miles); it consists of Antigua (280 sq. km), Barbuda, 40 km to the north (161 sq. km) and uninhabited Redonda, 40 km to the southwest (one sq. km). The population in July 2002 was 67,448 (1,400 on Barbuda); density, 153 per sq. km. Urban population (1998), 36·3%.

The chief towns are St John's, the capital on Antigua (25,000 inhabitants in 1999) and Codrington (1,400), the only settlement on Barbuda.

English is the official language; local dialects are also spoken.

SOCIAL STATISTICS
Expectation of life, 1996: males, 71·5 years, females, 75·8. Annual population growth rate, 1995–2001, 0·7%. Births, 1997, 1,448; deaths, 1999, 508. Infant mortality in 1998 was 17 per 1,000 live births; fertility rate, 1999, 1·7 births per woman.

CLIMATE
A tropical climate, but drier than most West Indies islands. The hot season is from May to Nov., when rainfall is greater. Mean annual rainfall is 40" (1,000 mm).

CONSTITUTION AND GOVERNMENT
H.M. Queen Elizabeth, as Head of State, is represented by a Governor-General appointed by her on the advice of the Prime Minister. There is a bicameral legislature, comprising a 17-member Senate appointed by the Governor-General and a 17-member House of Representatives elected by universal suffrage for a five-year term. The Governor-General appoints a Prime Minister and, on the latter's advice, other members of the Cabinet.

Barbuda is administered by a nine-member directly-elected council.

National Anthem. 'Fair Antigua and Barbuda'; words by N. H. Richards, tune by W. G. Chambers.

RECENT ELECTIONS
At the elections to the House of Representatives of 9 March 1999 the Antigua Labour Party (ALP) gained 12 seats, the United Progressive Party 4, and the Barbuda People's Movement 1.

CURRENT ADMINISTRATION
Governor-General: Sir James Beethoven Carlisle, GCMG.
In March 2003 the government comprised:

Prime Minister and Minister of External Affairs, Finance, Defence, Caricom and OECS Affairs, Justice and Legal Affairs, Legislature, Privatization, Printing and Electoral Affairs, Public Works, Sewage, Energy, and Telecommunications and Gaming: Lester Bird; b. 1938 (ALP; in office since 9 March 1994).

Deputy Prime Minister and Public Utilities, Aviation, International and Local Transportation, and Housing: Robin Yearwood.

Minister of Health and Social Improvement, Home Affairs, Urban Development, Renewal and Social Development: John St Luce. *Education, Culture and Technology:* Rodney Williams. *Labour, Co-operatives and Public Safety:* Steadroy Benjamin. *Tourism and Environment:* Molwyn Joseph. *Planning, Implementation and Public Service, Trade, Industry and Business Development:* Gaston Browne. *Information and Public Broadcasting, Youth Empowerment, Sports, Community Development and Carnival:* Guy Yearwood. *Agriculture, Lands and Fisheries:* Vere Bird, Jr.

Government Website: http://www.antiguagov.com/

DEFENCE
The Antigua and Barbuda Defence Force numbers 150. There are some 75 reserves. A coastguard service has been formed.

In 2000 defence expenditure totalled US$4m. (US$59 per capita), representing 0·6% of GDP.

Army. The strength of the Army section of the Defence Force was 125 in 1999.

Navy. There was a naval force of 25 operating two patrol craft in 1999.

INTERNATIONAL RELATIONS
Antigua and Barbuda is a member of the UN, the World Bank, ILO, IMO, IMF, UNESCO, WHO, WIPO, WTO, the Commonwealth, OAS, ACS, CARICOM, OECS and is an ACP member state of the ACP-EU relationship.

ECONOMY
In 2001 services accounted for approximately 77·0% of GDP, industry 19·1% and agriculture 3·9%.

Currency. The unit of currency is the *Eastern Caribbean dollar* (ECD), issued by the Eastern Caribbean Central Bank. Foreign exchange reserves in May 2002 were US$84m. and total money supply was EC$334m. Inflation in 2001 was 1·0%.

Budget. The budget for 2002 envisaged recurrent revenue of EC$571·1m. and recurrent expenditure of EC$599·2m.

Performance. Real GDP growth was 2·5% in 2000, but the general downturn in the world economy resulted in negative growth of 0·6% in 2001. GDP was US$0·7bn. in 2001.

Banking and Finance. The East Caribbean Central Bank based in St Kitts functions as a central bank. The *Governor* is Sir Dwight Venner. In 1999, nine commercial banks were operating (six foreign). There is also the Antigua Co-operative Bank and a government savings bank. Total national savings were EC$1,357m. in Dec. 2001.

In 1981 Antigua established an offshore banking sector which in 2002 had 21 banks registered and operating. The offshore sector is regulated by the Financial Services Regulatory Commission, a statutory body.

ENERGY AND NATURAL RESOURCES

Environment. In 1998 Antigua and Barbuda's carbon dioxide emissions were the equivalent of 5·0 tonnes per capita according to the *World Bank Atlas*.

Electricity. Capacity in 1995 was 26,000 kW. Production was 90m. kWh in 1998 and consumption per capita an estimated 1,509 kWh in 1997.

Water. There is a desalination plant with a capacity of 0·6m. gallons per day, sufficient to meet the needs of the country.

Agriculture. In 1998 there were 8,000 ha of arable land and land under permanent crops. Cotton and fruits are the main crops. Production (2000) of fruits, 8,000 tonnes (notably melons and mangoes).

Livestock (2000): cattle, 16,000; pigs, 2,000; sheep, 12,000; goats, 12,000.

Forestry. Forests covered 9,000 ha, or 20·5% of the total land area, in 1995.

Fisheries. Total catch in 2000 came to approximately 1,481 tonnes, exclusively from sea fishing.

INDUSTRY

Manufactures include beer, cement, toilet tissue, stoves, refrigerators, blenders, fans, garments and rum (molasses imported from Guyana).

Labour. The unemployment rate in 1998 was the lowest in the Caribbean, at 4·5%. Between 1994 and 1998, 2,543 jobs were created. The average annual salary in 1998 was US$8,345 per head of population.

INTERNATIONAL TRADE

Imports and Exports. Imports in 2000 were estimated at US$357m. and exports US$40m. The main trading partners were CARICOM, the USA, the UK and Canada.

COMMUNICATIONS

Roads. In 1995 there were 384 km of main roads, 164 km of secondary roads, 320 km of rural roads and 293 km of other roads. 15,100 passenger cars and 5,700 commercial vehicles were in use in 1995. More than EC$64m. was spent to rebuild major roads and highways in the three years following damage caused by hurricanes Luis and Marilyn in 1995.

Civil Aviation. V. C. Bird International Airport is near St John's. There are flights to Anguilla, Barbados, Dominica, Georgetown, Grenada, Guadeloupe, Kingston, London, Martinique, Miami, the Netherlands Antilles, New York, Paris, Puerto Rico, St Kitts and Nevis, St Lucia, St Vincent, Toronto, Trinidad, the British and US Virgin Islands and Washington, D.C. A domestic flight links the airports on Antigua and Barbuda.

Shipping. The main port is St John's Harbour. The merchant shipping fleet of 762 vessels totalled 4,541,940 GRT in Dec. 2001. In 1997 vessels totalling 94,907,000 NRT entered ports and vessels totalling 667,126,000 NRT cleared.

Telecommunications. There were 38,300 main telephone lines in 2000, or 499·5 per 1,000 inhabitants. There is a mobile phone system, with approximately 8,500 subscribers in 1999. There were 8,000 Internet users in April 2000.

Postal Services. The main Post Office is located in St John's. There is another one at the airport.

SOCIAL INSTITUTIONS

Justice. Law is based on UK common law as exercised by the Eastern Caribbean Supreme Court (ECSC) on St Lucia. There are Magistrates' Courts and a Court of Summary Jurisdiction. Appeals lie to the Court of Appeal of ECSC, or ultimately to the UK Privy Council. Antigua and Barbuda was one of ten countries to sign an agreement in Feb. 2001 establishing a Caribbean Court of Justice to replace the British Privy Council as the highest civil and criminal court. The Court of Justice is expected to sit for the first time in the second half of 2003.

The population in penal institutions in Nov. 1995 was 225 (equivalent to 345 per 100,000 of national population).

Religion. In 1997, 73% of the population were Protestants and 11% Roman Catholics.

Education. Adult literacy was 95% in 1998. In 1994–95 there were 11,506 pupils and 439 teachers at primary schools, and 4,294 pupils and 277 teachers at secondary schools. In 1992–93 there were 72 government primary and secondary schools. Other schools were run by religious organizations. The Antigua State College offers technical and teacher training. Antigua is a partner in the regional University of the West Indies.

Health. There is one general hospital, a private clinic, seven health centres and 17 associated clinics. A new medical centre at Mount St John's is set to open during 2003.

ANTIGUA AND BARBUDA

Welfare. The state operates a Medical Benefits Scheme providing free medical attention, and a Social Security Scheme, providing age and disability pensions and sickness benefits.

CULTURE

Broadcasting. Radio and television services are provided by the government-owned Antigua and Barbuda Broadcasting Service (ABS). Other radio and/or TV stations are Observer Radio, Caribbean Radio Lighthouse (Baptist Mission), Rado ZDK (commercial), Caribbean Relay (BBC and Deutsche Welle), CTV Entertainment Systems (12 US cable channels). In 1997 there were 36,000 radio and 31,000 TV receivers.

Press. The main newspapers are The Antigua Sun and The Daily Observer. The Outlet Newspaper, the National Informer and the Worker's Voice are published weekly. The Chamber of Commerce has a monthly publication.

Tourism. Tourism is the main industry, contributing about 90% of GDP and 80% of foreign exchange earnings and related activities. In 2001 there were 193,126 staying visitors and 429,406 cruise ship arrivals. Income from tourism amounted to US$275m. in 1998.

Festivals. Of particular interest are the International Sailing Week (April–May); Annual Tennis Championship (May); Mid-Summer Carnival (July–Aug.).

Museums and Galleries. The main attractions are the Museum of Antigua and Barbuda; Coates Cottage; Aiton Place; Harmony Hall; Cedars Pottery; SOFA (Sculpture Objects Functional Art); Pigeon Point Pottery; Harbour Art Gallery; Nelson's Dockyard; Shirley Heights.

DIPLOMATIC REPRESENTATIVES
Of Antigua and Barbuda in the United Kingdom (15 Thayer St., London, W1U 3JT)
High Commissioner: Sir Ronald M. Sanders KCMG, KCN.

Of the United Kingdom in Antigua and Barbuda (Price Waterhouse Centre, 11 Old Parham Rd, St John's, Antigua)
High Commissioner: John White (resides at Bridgetown, Barbados).

Of Antigua and Barbuda in the USA (3216 New Mexico Av., NW, Washington, D.C., 20016)
Ambassador: Lionel Alexander Hurst.

Of the USA in Antigua and Barbuda
Ambassador: Earl Norfleet Phillips, Jr (resides at Bridgetown).

Of Antigua and Barbuda to the United Nations
Ambassador: Dr Patrick Albert Lewis.

Of Antigua and Barbuda to the European Union
Ambassador: Edwin Laurent.

FURTHER READING
Berleant-Schiller, Riva, *et al.*, *Antigua and Barbuda.* [Bibliography] ABC-Clio, Oxford and Santa Barbara (CA), 1995
Nicholson, Desmond, *Antigua, Barbuda and Redonda: A Historical Sketch.* St John's, 1991

ARGENTINA

República Argentina

Capital: Buenos Aires
Population estimate, 2000: 37·03m.
GDP per capita, 2000: (PPP$) 12,377
HDI/world rank: 0·844/34

KEY HISTORICAL EVENTS

Argentina gained its independence from Spain in 1816. Civil wars and anarchy followed until, in 1853, stable government was established.

In 1943 when Gen. Juan Domingo Perón led a military coup his regime was autocratic but popularist. His wife Eva (Evita), played a major role, giving the regime an almost cult-like following. She died in 1955 and a civilian administration followed until 1966 when the next military coup led to seven years of government by the military. However, a political party had established itself around the Peróns and when elections were held in 1973 Gen. Perón was elected president. When he died in 1974, his widow Isobel succeeded him as president. She was deposed in 1976 following another military coup, which established a three-man junta with Gen. Jorge Videla, C.-In-C. of the army, as president. The new government instituted a savagely repressive regime.

Videla was succeeded by Gen. Leopoldo Galtieri, the army C.-in-C. In April 1982 Galtieri, in an effort to distract attention from domestic failings, invaded the Falkland Islands (Islas Malvinas). The subsequent military defeat helped to precipitate the fall of Galtieri and the junta in July 1982. Return to civilian rule took place on 10 Dec. 1983. A new Constitution was adopted in Aug. 1994.

On 4 July 2001 former President Carlos Menem, who had been placed under house arrest a month earlier, was formally charged in connection with his alleged role in illegal arms deals, but he was released by a federal court four months later and announced that he would again run for the presidency. A state of emergency was introduced in Dec. 2001 as Argentina verged on bankruptcy in the face of an ever-worsening economic crisis. President Fernando de la Rua resigned on 20 Dec. 2001 after days of rioting, protests and looting across the country. During a period of 11 days there were three different acting or interim presidents before Eduardo Duhalde was elected president by congress until elections in 2003.

TERRITORY AND POPULATION

The second largest country in South America, the Argentine Republic is bounded in the north by Bolivia, in the northeast by Paraguay, in the east by Brazil, Uruguay and the Atlantic Ocean, and the west by Chile. The republic consists of 23 provinces and one federal district with the following areas and estimated populations in 2000 (in 1,000):

Provinces	Area (sq. km)	Population 2000	Capital	Population (1991 census)
Buenos Aires	307,571	14,215	La Plata	542,567
Catamarca	102,602	318	Catamarca	132,626
Chaco	99,633	952	Resistencia	292,350
Chubut	224,686	448	Rawson	19,161
Córdoba	165,321	3,091	Córdoba	1,208,713
Corrientes	88,199	922	Corrientes	258,103
Entre Ríos	78,781	1,113	Paraná	277,338
Formosa	72,066	504	Formosa	148,074
Jujuy	53,219	604	San Salvador de Jujuy	180,102
La Pampa	143,440	306	Santa Rosa	80,592
La Rioja	89,680	280	La Rioja	103,727
Mendoza	148,827	1,608	Mendoza	121,696
Misiones	29,801	995	Posadas	210,755
Neuquén	94,078	561	Neuquén	243,803
Río Negro	203,013	618	Viedma	57,473
Salta	155,488	1,067	Salta	370,904
San Juan	89,651	579	San Juan	352,691
San Luis	76,748	363	San Luis	110,136

Provinces	Area (sq. km)	Population 2000	Capital	Population (1991 census)
Santa Cruz	243,943	207	Río Gallegos	64,640
Santa Fé	133,007	3,099	Santa Fé	406,388
Santiago del Estero	136,351	726	Santiago del Estero	263,471
Tierra del Fuego	21,571	116	Ushuaia	29,166
Tucumán	22,524	1,293	San Miguel de Tucumán	622,324
Federal Capital	200	3,047	Buenos Aires	–

Buenos Aires: Buenos Aires was first founded in 1536 with the foundation of a Spanish settlement and fort, 'Puerto de Nuestra Señora de Santa Maria del Buen Ayre', by Pedro de Mendoza. Rising from the Rio Plata it is situated on the east coast of Argentina, covering an area of 194 sq. km. It is South America's second largest city after São Paulo.

Argentina also claims territory in Antarctica.

The area is 2,780,400 sq. km excluding the claimed Antarctic territory, and the population at the 1991 census was 32,615,528 (16,677,548 females); 2000 estimate, 37·03m. giving a density of 13 per sq. km.

The UN gives a projected population for 2010 of 41·47m.

In 1999, 89·6% of the population were urban.

In April 1990 the National Congress declared that the Falklands and other British-held islands in the South Atlantic were part of the new province of Tierra del Fuego formed from the former National Territory of the same name. The 1994 Constitution reaffirms Argentine sovereignty over the Falkland Islands.

The population of the principal metropolitan areas in 1995 was: Buenos Aires, 11,802,000; Córdoba, 1,294,000; Rosario, 1,155,000; Mendoza, 851,000; La Plata, 676,128 (1992); Tucumán, 642,473 (1992).

95% speak the national language, Spanish, while 3% speak Italian, 1% Guaraní and 1% other languages. In 1999, 12,989 immigrants were granted permanent residency, down from 18,463 in 1996.

SOCIAL STATISTICS

1999 births, 688,000; deaths, 289,000. Rates, 1999 (per 1,000 population): birth, 18·8; death, 7·9. Infant mortality, 1999, 19 per 1,000 live births. Estimated life expectancy at birth, 1999, 69·9 years for males and 77·0 years for females. Annual population growth rate, 1995–2000, 1·3%; fertility rate, 1999, 2·6 births per woman.

CLIMATE

The climate is warm temperate over the pampas, where rainfall occurs in all seasons, but diminishes towards the west. In the north and west, the climate is more arid, with high summer temperatures, while in the extreme south conditions are also dry, but much cooler. Buenos Aires, Jan. 74°F (23·3°C), July 50°F (10°C). Annual rainfall 37" (950 mm). Bahía Blanca, Jan. 74°F (23·3°C), July 48°F (8·9°C). Annual rainfall 21" (523 mm). Mendoza, Jan. 75°F (23·9°C), July 47°F (8·3°C). Annual rainfall 8" (190 mm). Rosario, Jan. 76°F (24·4°C), July 51°F (10·6°C). Annual rainfall 35" (869 mm). San Juan, Jan. 78°F (25·6°C), July 50°F (10°C). Annual rainfall 4" (89 mm). San Miguel de Tucumán, Jan. 79°F (26·1°C), July 56°F (13·3°C). Annual rainfall 38" (970 mm). Ushuaia, Jan. 50°F (10°C), July 34°F (1·1°C). Annual rainfall 19" (475 mm).

CONSTITUTION AND GOVERNMENT

On 10 April 1994 elections were held for a 230-member constituent assembly to reform the 1853 constitution. The Justicialist National Movement (Peronist) gained 38·8% of votes cast and the Radical Union 20%. On 22 Aug. 1994 this assembly unanimously adopted a new Constitution. This reduces the presidential term of office from six to four years, but permits the President to stand for two terms. The President is no longer elected by an electoral college, but directly by universal suffrage. A presidential candidate is elected who gains more than 45% of votes cast, or 40% if at least 10% ahead of an opponent; otherwise there is a second round. The Constitution attenuates the President's powers by instituting a *Chief of Cabinet*. The *National Congress* consists of a Senate and a Chamber of Deputies: the Senate comprises 72 members, three nominated by each provincial legislature and three from the Federal District for nine years (one-third retiring every three years). The Chamber of Deputies comprises 257 members directly elected by universal suffrage (at age 18).

National Anthem. 'Oid, mortales, el grito sagrado Libertad' ('Hear, mortals, the sacred cry of Liberty'); words by V. López y Planes, 1813; tune by J. Blas Parera.

RECENT ELECTIONS

On 1 Jan. 2002 Congress elected Eduardo Duhalde as the country's new president after Fernando de la Rúa and three acting or interim presidents had all resigned.

In the first round of presidential elections held on 27 April 2003, Carlos Menem (Peronist) won 24·4% of the vote, followed by Néstor Kirchner (Peronist) with 22·0%, Ricardo López Murphy (ind.) with 16·3%, Elisa Carrió (ind.) with 14·1% and Adolfo Rodriguez Saá (Peronist) with 14·1%. There were three other candidates. Turn-out was 77·6%. On 14 May Menem pulled out of the second round, leaving Kirchner as winner by default.

Following the elections to the Chamber of Deputies of 24 Oct. 1999, the Alliance (consisting of the Radical Union and the centre-left Frepaso) held 122 seats; the Justicialist Party (JP/Peronists), 100; Action for the Republic, 12. Other parties held 23 seats. In the elections of 14 Oct. 2001 for the 127 seats not contested in 1999 the Justicialist Party won 66 seats with 37·4% of votes cast, the Alliance 35 with 23·1%, Alternative for a Republic of Equals 8 with 7·2%, and Front for Change 4 with 4·1%. Other parties won 2 seats or fewer. Turn-out was 73·7%. As a result of the election the JP had 116 of the 257 seats, the Alliance 88, Alternative for a Republic of Equals 17 and the Action for the Republic 9.

CURRENT ADMINISTRATION

President: Néstor Carlos Kirchner; b. 1950 (Peronist; sworn in 27 May 2003).

In May 2003 the cabinet comprised:

Chief of the Cabinet: Alberto Fernandez. *Minister of Defence:* José Pampuro. *Foreign Affairs:* Rafael Bielsa. *Education and Culture:* Daniel Filmus. *Federal Planning:* Julio De Vido. *Interior:* Dr Aníbal Fernandez. *Justice:* Gustavo Beliz. *Health:* Ginés Gonzáléz García. *Economy and Production:* Roberto Lavagna. *Labour:* Carlos Tomada. *Social Development:* Alicia Kirchner. *Secretary General of the Presidency:* Oscar Parilli. *Secretary of State Intelligence:* Sergio Acevedo.

Office of the President (Spanish only): http://www.presidencia.gov.ar

DEFENCE

Conscription was abolished in 1995. In 2000 defence expenditure totalled US$4,658m. (US$126 per capita), representing 1·7% of GDP (compared to over 8% in 1981).

Army. There are five military regions. In 1999 the Army was 40,000 strong. The trained reserve numbers about 250,000, of whom 200,000 belong to the National Guard and 50,000 to the Territorial Guard.

There is a paramilitary gendarmerie of 18,000 run by the Ministry of Defence.

Navy. The Argentinian Fleet (1999) included three diesel submarines, six destroyers and seven frigates. Total personnel was 20,000 including 2,000 in Naval Aviation and 2,800 marines. Main bases are at Buenos Aires, Puerto Belgrano (HQ and Dockyard), Mar del Plata and Ushuaia.

The Naval Aviation Service had some 31 combat aircraft in 1999 including Super-Etendard strike aircraft and eight armed helicopters.

Air Force. The Air Force is organized into Air Operations, Air Regions, Logistics and Personnel Commands. There were (1999) 10,500 personnel and 125 combat aircraft including Mirage 5 and Mirage III jet fighters. In addition there were 27 armed helicopters.

INTERNATIONAL RELATIONS

Argentina is a member of the UN, WTO, BIS, OAS, Inter-American Development Bank, LAIA, Mercosur, IOM and the Antarctic Treaty, and is set to apply for membership of the OECD. Diplomatic relations with Britain, broken since the 1982 Falklands War, were re-opened in 1990. Praising Argentina's 'call to peace', in Nov.

1997 US President Clinton announced his intention to give the country 'major non-NATO ally' status. The alignment with US foreign policy came after years of anti-American sentiment and a policy of neutrality.

ECONOMY

Services contributed 65·6% of GDP in 1998, industry 28·7% and agriculture 5·7%.

Overview. Argentina suffers from the world's largest debt default, a severe recession and a freeze on bank savings. At the root of the crisis lie failures in fiscal policy. Governments have raised spending so high that it cannot be financed in an orderly way. By mid-2002 the debt burden was US$140bn. while dollar reserves dropped by nearly a third to US$10bn. Owing to the external debt position, the government has been unable to use fiscal policy to boost the economy. Inflation is accelerating and confidence in public finances is undermined.

Currency. The monetary unit is the *peso* (ARP), which replaced the austral on 1 Jan. 1992 at a rate of one peso = 10,000 australs. For nearly a decade the peso was pegged at parity with the US dollar, but it was devalued by nearly 30% in Jan. 2002 and floated in Feb. 2002. There was deflation in 2000 of 0·9% and 2001 of 1·1%, but in early 2002 there was high inflation. Gold reserves were 9,000 troy oz in June 2002 (4·4m. troy oz in 1995); foreign exchange reserves were US$9,621m. (US$20,780m. in June 2001). Total money supply was 15,701m. pesos in Dec. 2001.

Budget. The financial year commences on 1 Jan.

Government revenue and expenditure (in 1m. pesos):

	1997	1998	1999	2000
Revenue	39,842·8	41,188·6	39,765·2	40,346·0
Expenditure	44,697·0	45,930·4	48,056·6	48,224·7

Performance. The economy grew in 1998 by 3·8% but shrank by 3·4% and 0·5% in 1999 and 2000 respectively, mainly as a result of the recession in Brazil, which started in 1998, and the devaluation of the Brazilian *real* in Jan. 1999. In 2001 the economy contracted by 4·5%. As Argentina's economic crisis worsened, in the first quarter of 2002 the economy contracted by 16·3%. Total GDP was US$268·8bn. in 2001. In March 2001 the economy minister, José Luis Machinea, resigned after a turbulent 15 months in which he had failed to revive a stagnant economy. As the economic situation deteriorated Argentina had a further five economy ministers in the space of just over a year. In Nov. 2001 the government tried to persuade creditors to accept a restructuring of the US$132bn. public debt, but on 23 Dec. 2001 interim President Adolfo Rodríguez Saá announced that Argentina would default on the debt payments—the biggest debt default in history. One in five Argentines now live in extreme poverty and more than half the population lives below the official poverty line.

Banking and Finance. In 2000 there were 15 government banks, 74 private banks and 24 other financial institutions. The total assets of the Argentine Central Bank (BCRA) in Feb. 2001 were 41·90bn. pesos. The *President* of the Central Bank is Alfonso de Prat-Gay. In early 2002 banks and financial markets were temporarily closed as an emergency measure in response to the economic crisis that made the country virtually bankrupt.

There is a stock exchange at Buenos Aires. Some analysts predict that it may close down before long, with activity in 2000 at its lowest level since the late 1980s.

Weights and Measures. The metric system is legal.

ENERGY AND NATURAL RESOURCES

Environment. According to the *World Bank Atlas* Argentina's carbon dioxide emissions in 1998 were the equivalent of 3·8 tonnes per capita.

Electricity. Electric power production (1999) was 78,493m. kWh (7,106m. kWh nuclear). In 2001 there were two nuclear reactors. Installed capacity in 1998 was 21·76m. kW; consumption per capita was 1,891 kWh. The electricity market is almost entirely under private ownership, much of it in foreign hands.

Oil and Gas. Crude oil production (2000) was 44·68m. cu. metres. Reserves were estimated at some 2·7bn. bbls in 1999. The oil industry was privatized in 1993.

Natural gas extraction in 2000 was 44,870m. cu. metres. Reserves were about 775,500m. cu. metres in 2000. The main area in production is the Neuquen basin in western Argentina, with over 40% of the total oil reserves and nearly half the gas reserves. Natural gas accounts for approximately 45% of all the energy consumed in Argentina.

Minerals. An estimated 250,000 tonnes of hard coal were produced in 1997. Other minerals (with estimated production in 2000) include clays (2·3m. tonnes), salt (1m. tonnes), borates (580,000 tonnes), bentonite (122,000 tonnes), zinc (33,761 tonnes of metal), lead (14,115 tonnes of metal), iron ore (3,388 tonnes of metal in 1996), beryllium (10 tonnes of metal), silver (78,271 kg), gold (25,954 kg), granite, marble and tungsten. Production from the US$1·1bn. Alumbrera copper and gold mine, the country's biggest mining project, in Catamarca province in the northwest, started in late 1997. In 1993 the mining laws were reformed and state regulation was swept away creating a more stable tax regime for investors. In Dec. 1997 Argentina and Chile signed a treaty laying the legal and tax framework for mining operations straddling the 5,000 km border, allowing mining products to be transported out through both countries.

Agriculture. In 1998 there were 25·0m. ha of arable land and 2·2m. ha of permanent crops. The agricultural population was 3·82m. in 1995, of whom 1·49m. were economically active. 1·25m. ha were irrigated in 1998.

Livestock (2000): cattle, 48,674,400; sheep, 13,703,400; goats, 3,490,200. In 1998 there were 3,341,652 pigs and 1,994,241 horses. In 1997 wool production was 45,120 tonnes; milk (in 2000, provisional), 9,658m. litres; eggs (in 2000, provisional), 484m. dozen.

Crop production (in 1,000 tonnes) in 1999–2000, provisional: soybeans, 20,207; sugarcane, 18,193 (1998–99); maize, 16,817; wheat, 15,303; sunflower seed, 6,098; potatoes, 3,412 (1997–98). Cotton, vine, citrus fruit, olives and *yerba maté* (Paraguayan tea) are also cultivated. Wine is fast becoming a major product. Argentina is the world's leading producer of sunflower seeds, and is now the fifth largest wine producer after Italy, France, Spain and the USA; the value of wine exports has grown from US$19m. in 1995 to a predicted US$200m. in 2000.

Forestry. The woodland area was 44,975,115 ha in 1994. Production in 1999 (preliminary) included 1·82m. cu. metres of sawn wood, 5·58m. tonnes of round logs, 1·01m. tonnes of paper and cardboard, 382,000 cu. metres of chipboard. Timber production totalled 5·74m. cu. metres in 1999.

Fisheries. Fish landings in 2000 amounted to 917,725 tonnes, almost exclusively from sea fishing. Hake and squid are the most common catches.

INDUSTRY

The leading companies by market capitalization in Argentina, excluding banking and finance, in Jan. 2002 were: YPF SA (23bn. pesos), an integrated oil company; Siderca SAIC (6bn. pesos), a manufacturer of steel pipe for the energy industry; Pecom Energía SA (5bn. pesos), an energy conglomerate.

Production (2000 in tonnes): Portland cement, 6,114,000; crude steel, 4,472,000; crude iron, 3,605,000; sugar, 1,462,000; paper, 1,214,000; polyethylene, 286,500; primary aluminium, 261,895; synthetic rubber, 54,402; distillate oil, 10,394,000 (1997); petrol, 4,815,000 (1997); residual fuel oil, 2,555,000 (1997); jet fuel, 1,235,000 (1997). Motor vehicles produced in 2000 totalled 238,706; tyres, 8,519,000; motorcycles, 20,537.

Labour. In 2000 the economically active population totalled 9·72m.; there were 1·46m. unemployed in 2000. The unemployment rate, which had been 18·4% in 1995, was down to 11·0% of the workforce in 1998, but had risen to 19·0% by Dec. 2001.

INTERNATIONAL TRADE

External debt was US$146,172m. in 2000 (the fifth highest in the world).

Imports and Exports. Foreign trade (in US$1m.):

	1995	1996	1997	1998	1999	2000
Imports	20,122	23,762	30,450	31,377	25,508	23,851
Exports	20,963	23,811	26,431	26,434	23,309	26,409

Principal exports in 2000 (in US$1m., provisional) were food products and live animals (8,404); fuels, mineral lubricants and related products (4,678); animal and vegetable oils (3,173); machinery and transportation equipment (3,107); and manufactured goods (2,982).

Principal imports in 2000 (in US$1m., provisional) were machinery and transportation equipment (9,005); manufactured goods (5,518); food products and live animals (4,928); and chemical products (4,025).

In 2000 imports (in US$1m.) were mainly from Brazil (6,443); USA (4,785); Germany (1,262); China, including Hong Kong (1,222); Italy (1,014); and Japan (1,006). Exports went mainly to Brazil (6,990); USA (3,156); Chile (2,670); Spain (915); China, including Hong Kong (884); and Uruguay (808).

COMMUNICATIONS

Roads. In 1998 there were 38,371 km of motorways and national and provincial highways. The four main roads constituting Argentina's portion of the Pan-American Highway were opened in 1942. Vehicles in use in 1997 totalled 6,280,650, of which 4,901,600 were passenger cars, 1,338,400 trucks and vans, and 40,650 buses and coaches. In 2000, 3,686 people were killed in road accidents. In 2000, 352,641 new vehicles were registered.

Rail. Much of the 33,000 km state-owned network (on 1,000 mm, 1,435 mm and 1,676 mm gauges; 210 km electrified) was privatized in 1993–94. 30-year concessions were awarded to five freight operators; long-distance passenger services are run by contractors to the requirements of local authorities. Metro, light rail and suburban railway services are also operated by concessionaires.

In 2000 railways carried 16,265,000 tonnes of freight and 480,150,000 passengers.

The metro and light rail network in Buenos Aires extends to 46 km.

Civil Aviation. The main international airports are Buenos Aires Aeroparque, which handled 7,038,000 passengers in 2000, and Buenos Aires Ezeiza, which handled 5,690,600 passengers in 2000. The national carrier, Aerolíneas Argentinas, is 15% state-owned.

In 2000 a total of 13·63m. passengers and 203,606 tonnes of freight were carried on domestic and international airlines. In 1998 Aerolíneas Argentinas flew 83·2m. km, carrying 4,024,600 passengers (2,060,000 on international flights).

Shipping. The merchant shipping fleet totalled 499,000 GRT in 1998, including oil tankers totalling 102,000 GRT.

Telecommunications. The telephone service Entel was privatized in 1990. The sell-off split Argentina into two monopolies, operated by Telefonica Internacional de España, and a holding controlled by France Telecom and Telecom Italia. In Nov. 2000 the industry was opened to unrestricted competition. The number of lines in service in 2000 totalled 7,894,200 (213·2 per 1,000 inhabitants). There are two independent cellular operators; mobile phone subscribers numbered 4,434,000 in 1999. There were 1,900,000 PCs in use in 2000 (51·3 per 1,000 persons) and 70,000 fax machines in 1997. Argentina had 3·88m. Internet users in July 2001.

Postal Services. In 1995 there were 5,676 post offices.

SOCIAL INSTITUTIONS

Justice. Justice is administered by federal and provincial courts. The former deal only with cases of a national character, or those in which different provinces or inhabitants of different provinces are parties. The chief federal court is the Supreme Court, with five judges whose appointment is approved by the Senate. Other federal courts are the appeal courts, at Buenos Aires, Bahía Blanca, La Plata, Córdoba, Mendoza, Tucumán and Resistencia. Each province has its own judicial system, with a Supreme Court (generally so designated) and several minor chambers. The death penalty was re-introduced in 1976 for the killing of government, military police and judicial officials, and for participation in terrorist activities. The population in penal institutions in Dec. 1996 was 43,174 (120 per 100,000 of national population). In 1997 there were 816,340 crimes reported; and in 2000, 18,377 guilty verdicts were passed.

The police force is centralized under the Federal Security Council.

Religion. The Roman Catholic religion is supported by the State; affiliation numbered 31·06m. in 1997. In Feb. 2001 there were four Cardinals. There were 2·66m. Protestants of various denominations in 1997 and 520,000 Muslims. There were 275,000 Latter-day Saints (Mormons) in 1998.

Education. Adult literacy was 96·7% in 1999 (males, 96·8%; females, 96·7%). In 1999, 1,180,733 children attended pre-school institutions, 6,595,923 were in basic general education, 1,294,666 in 'multimodal' secondary schooling and 391,010 in higher non-universities.

In 1996, in the public sector, there were 33 universities; one technical university; and university institutes of aeronautics, military studies, naval and maritime studies and police studies. In the private sector, there were 15 universities; 7 Roman Catholic universities; 1 Adventist university; universities of business administration, business and social science, the cinema, notarial studies, social studies, and theology; and university institutes of biomedical science, health and the merchant navy. In 1999 there were 994,788 students attending public universities and 171,783 private universities. In 1996 there was a total of 128,478 academic staff.

In 1997 total expenditure on education came to 3·5% of GNP and 12·6% of total government spending.

Health. Free medical attention is obtainable from public hospitals. In 1999 there were 7,428 public health care institutions which had an average of 76,363 available beds.

Welfare. Until the end of 1996 trade unions had a monopoly in the handling of the compulsory social security contributions of employees, but private insurance agencies are now permitted to function alongside them.

Unique Social Security System Expenditure (in 1m. pesos):

	1999	2000
Retirement and pensions	17,508	17,386
Healthcare assistance and other forms of social insurance	5,249	5,440
Family allowances	1,879	1,920
Unemployment insurance, employment and training programmes	519	484
Work risks insurance	323	367
Other	2,201	2,361
Total	27,679	27,958

CULTURE

Broadcasting. There are state-owned, provincial, municipal and private radio stations overseen by the Secretaria de Comunicaciones, the Comité Federal de Radiodifusión, the Servicio Oficial de Radiodifusión (which also operates an external service and a station in Antarctica) and the Asociación de Teleradiodifusoras Argentinas. There were 24·3m. radio sets and 8m. TV receivers (colour by PAL N) in 1997. In Dec. 2000 there were 2·88m. cable TV subscribers.

Cinema. In 2000 there were 1,007 cinemas with an audience of approximately 20,864,000.

Press. In 1996 there were 181 daily newspapers with a combined circulation of 4,320,000, a rate of 123 per 1,000 inhabitants. In 1996 a total of 9,850 book titles were published in 39·66m. copies.

Tourism. In 2000 (provisional), 2,949,139 tourists visited Argentina, including 567,967 from Chile, 499,831 from Paraguay, 488,007 from Uruguay and 466,016 from Brazil. Receipts in 1999 totalled US$2·81bn. In 2000 there were 7,190 hotels providing 397,037 beds.

Libraries. In 1995 there were 2,700 public libraries. They held a combined 13,496,000 volumes.

DIPLOMATIC REPRESENTATIVES
Of Argentina in the United Kingdom (65 Brook St., London, W1Y 1YE)
Ambassador: Vicente Berasategui.

Of the United Kingdom in Argentina (Dr Luis Agote 2141/52, 1425 Buenos Aires)
Ambassador: Sir Robin Christopher KBE, CMG.

Of Argentina in the USA (1600 New Hampshire Ave., NW, Washington, D.C., 20009)
Ambassador: Eduardo Amadeo.

Of the USA in Argentina (4300 Colombia, 1425 Buenos Aires)
Ambassador: James Donald Walsh.

Of Argentina to the United Nations
Ambassador: Arnoldo M. Listre.

Of Argentina to the European Union
Ambassador: D. Jorge Remes Lenicov.

FURTHER READING

Bethell, L. (ed.) *Argentina since Independence.* CUP, 1994
Biggins, Alex, *Argentina.* [Bibliography] ABC-Clio, Oxford and Santa Barbara (CA), 1991
Lewis, P., *The Crisis of Argentine Capitalism.* North Carolina Univ. Press, 1990
Manzetti, L., *Institutions, Parties and Coalitions in Argentine Politics.* Univ. of Pittsburgh Press, 1994
Romero, Luis Alberto, *A History of Argentina in the Twentieth Century;* translated from Spanish. Pennsylvania State Univ. Press, 2002
Shumway, N., *The Invention of Argentina.* California Univ. Press, 1992
Turner, Barry, (ed.) *Latin America Profiled.* Macmillan, London, 2000
Wynia, G. W., *Argentina: Illusions and Realities.* 2nd ed. Hoddesdon, 1993

National statistical office: Instituto Nacional de Estadística y Censos (INDEC). Av. Presidente Julio A. Roca 609, 1067 Buenos Aires. *Director:* Juan Carlos del Bello.
Website (Spanish only): http://www.indec.mecon.ar

ARMENIA

Hayastani Hanrapetoutiun
(Republic of Armenia)

Capital: Yerevan
Population estimate, 2000: 3·80m.
GDP per capita, 2000: (PPP$) 2,559
HDI/world rank: 0·754/76

KEY HISTORICAL EVENTS

According to tradition, the kingdom was founded in the region of Lake Van by Haig, or Haik, a descendant of Noah. Historically, the region and former kingdom that was Greater Armenia lay east of the Euphrates River; Little, or Lesser, Armenia was west of the river. In 189 BC the Armenians split away from the Syrians to found a native dynasty, the Artashesids. The imperialistic ambitions of King Tigranes led to war with Rome and defeated Armenia became a tributary kingdom. In the 3rd century AD it was overrun by Sassanian Persia. Armenia was the first country to adopt Christianity as its state religion, in the early 4th century. The persecution of Christians under Persian rule created martyrs and kindled nationalism among the Armenians, particularly after the partition (387) of the kingdom between Persia and Rome. However, because of its strategic location, attempts at independence were short-lived, as Armenia was the constant prey of the Persians, Byzantines and Arabs, and later of the Turkish and Russian Empires.

In the early part of the 20th century the Armenians under Turkish rule suffered brutal persecution. An estimated 1·75m. were massacred or deported to present-day Syria from their homeland in Anatolia. Armenia enjoyed a brief period of independence after the First World War but in 1920 the country was proclaimed a Soviet Socialist Republic. After the collapse of Communism, 99% of voters supported a breakaway from the Soviet Union. A declaration of independence in Sept. 1991 was followed by presidential elections after which President Ter-Petrosyan came to an agreement on economic co-operation with the other Soviet republics and joined the CIS. A new constitution adopted in July 1995 led to National Assembly elections. President Ter-Petrosyan was re-elected in Sept. 1996. OSCE observers noted 'very serious irregularities' in the conduct of the election and there were demonstrations of protest in Yerevan, leading to several deaths.

Hostilities with Azerbaijan over the enclave of Nagorno-Karabakh were brought to an end with a 1994 ceasefire. Resigning over Nagorno-Karabakh in Feb. 1998, President Ter-Petrosyan was succeeded by Robert Kocharyan, who was sworn in as president in April 1998. On 27 Oct. 1999, five men burst into the parliamentary chamber, killing the Prime Minister, Vazgen Sarkisian, and seven other officials. Aram Sarkisian, brother of the slain prime minister, was named as his successor. In April 2001 a first round of high-level talks on the settlement of the Nagorno-Karabakh conflict was held in Florida. Armenia and Azerbaijan have agreed to continue talks in principle, without specifying when.

TERRITORY AND POPULATION

Armenia covers an area of 29,743 sq. km (11,484 sq. miles). It is bounded in the north by Georgia, in the east by Azerbaijan and in the south and west by Turkey and Iran.

The population in 2001 was estimated at 3,802,400 (1,848,500 males; 1,953,900 females), of which 2,532,400 (66·6%) lived in urban areas; population density is 128 per sq. km. Armenians account for 97%, Kurds 1·6% and Russians 0.8%—in 1989, 2·6% of the population were Azeris, prior to the Nagorno-Karabakh conflict.

The UN gives a projected population for 2010 of 3·81m.

According to the Second Armenia-Diaspora Conference in May 2002 there are approximately 10m. Armenians worldwide.

The capital is Yerevan (1·25m. population in 2000). Other large towns are Gyumri (formerly Leninakan) (211,600 in 2000) and Vanadzor (formerly Kirovakan) (172,500 in 2000).

The official language is Armenian.

SOCIAL STATISTICS

2000 births, 34,276; deaths, 24,025; marriages, 10,986; divorces, 1,349. Rates, 2000 (per 1,000 population): births, 9·0; deaths, 6·3; marriage, 2·9; divorce, 0·4. Infant mortality, 1998, 14·7 per 1,000 live births. Annual population growth rate, 1990–2000, 0·7%. Life expectancy at birth, 2000, 70·5 years for men and 74·5 years for women; fertility rate, 2000, 1·1 births per woman.

CLIMATE

Summers are very dry and hot although nights can be cold. Winters are very cold, often with heavy snowfall. Yerevan, Jan. −9°C, July 28°C. Annual rainfall 318 mm.

CONSTITUTION AND GOVERNMENT

The head of state is the *President*, directly elected for five-year terms. Parliament is a 190-member *National Assembly*, of which 150 members are directly elected on a first-past-the-post system, and 40 by proportional representation, distributed among those parties gaining more than 5% of votes cast. The government is nominated by the President.

National Anthem. 'Mer Hayrenik azat, ankakh' ('Land of our fathers, free and independent'); words by M. Nalbandyan, tune by B. Kanachyan.

RECENT ELECTIONS

In presidential elections held on 19 Feb. 2003 incumbent president Robert Kocharian received 48·3% of votes cast, ahead of Stepan Demirchyan with 27·4% and Artashes Geghamyan 16·9%. Turn-out was 61·2%. The Organisation for Security and Co-operation in Europe said that the election process 'fell short of international standards in several key respects'. In the run-off on 5 March 2003 between the two leading candidates Robert Kocharian won 67·5% of the vote against 32·5% for Stepan Demirchyan. Again observers claimed the elections failed to meet international standards for a democratic poll.

Parliamentary elections were held on 30 May 1999. The Miasnutyun (Unity) alliance won 55 of the 131 seats available with 41·2% of the vote. The Communists (HKK) were second with 11 seats and 12·1% of the vote.

CURRENT ADMINISTRATION

President: Robert Kocharian, formerly President of Nagorno-Karabakh, the Armenian-inhabited enclave in Azerbaijan; b. 1954 (in office since 4 Feb. 1998).

In March 2003 the government comprised:

Prime Minister: Andranik Markaryan; b. 1951 (Republican Party of Armenia; appointed 12 May 2000).

Minister of Foreign Affairs: Vardan Oskanian. *Defence:* Serge Sargsian. *Justice:* Davit Harutyunian. *Education and Science:* Levon Mkrtchyan. *Health:* Ararat Mkrtchyan. *Culture, Sports and Youth Affairs:* Roland Sharoyan. *Industry and Trade:* Karen Chshmaritian. *Transportation and Telecommunications:* Andranik Manukian. *Agriculture:* Davit Zadoyan. *Environment:* Vardan Ayvazian. *Finance and Economy:* Vardan Khachatrian. *Energy:* Armen Movsisyan. *National Security:* Karlos Petrosian. *Urban Development:* Davit Lokian. *Regional Government and Co-ordinating the Operation of Infrastructures:* Hovik Abrahamian. *State Property Management:* Davit Vardanian. *State Revenues:* Yervand Zakharian. *Social Welfare:* Razmik Martirosian. *Cabinet Chief of Staff:* Manook Topuzian.

Government Website: http://www.gov.am

DEFENCE

There is conscription for 18 months. Paramilitary forces at the disposal of the Ministry of the Interior are estimated at 30,000.

Defence expenditure in 2000 totalled US$149m. (US$42 per capita), representing 8·0% of GDP.

Army. Current troop levels are 52,000 including a special forces regiment and an independent helicopter squadron. There are approximately 300,000 Armenians who have received some kind of military service experience within the last 15 years. The Defence Ministry is aiming for a standing army of 70,000.

INTERNATIONAL RELATIONS

There is a dispute over the mainly Armenian-populated enclave of Nagorno-Karabakh, which lies within Azerbaijan's borders—Armenia and Azerbaijan are technically still at war.

Armenia is a member of the UN, NATO Partnership for Peace, Council of Europe, CIS, OSCE, BSE and the IOM. It is the biggest recipient of US government aid, per head of population, after Israel.

ECONOMY

In 2000 agriculture contributed 30·8% of GDP, industry 19·9% and services 42·2%. Net taxes made up the remaining 7·1%.

Overview. A privatization scheme was launched on 1 March 1995 under the auspices of a Privatization Commission.

Currency. In Nov. 1993 a new currency unit, the *dram* (AMD) of 100 *lumma*, was introduced to replace the rouble. Inflation, which had been 5,273% in 1994, was just 3·2% in 2001. Foreign exchange reserves were US$323m. in June 2002, gold reserves were 28,000 troy oz and total money supply was 74,904m. drams.

Budget. In 2000 total revenue was 172,132·8m. drams and total expenditure 222,886·4m. drams.

Performance. Real GDP growth was 3·3% in 1999, 6·0% in 2000 and 9·6% in 2001. Total GDP in 2001 was US$2·0bn.

Banking and Finance. The *Chairman* of the Central Bank (founded in 1993) is Tigran Sargsyan. In 1997 there were 33 commercial banks (one state-owned).

ENERGY AND NATURAL RESOURCES

Environment. According to the *World Bank Atlas* Armenia's carbon dioxide emissions in 1998 were the equivalent of 0·9 tonnes per capita.

Electricity. Output of electricity in 2000 was 5,567m. kWh. Capacity was 3m. kW in 1997. Consumption per capita was 1,464 kWh in 2000. A nuclear plant closed in 1989 was re-opened in 1995 because of the blockade of the electricity supply by Azerbaijan; it was anticipated that domestic supply would be raised from four to 12 hours daily.

Minerals. There are deposits of copper, zinc, aluminium, molybdenum, marble, gold and granite.

Agriculture. The chief agricultural area is the valley of the Arax and the area round Yerevan. Here there are cotton plantations, orchards and vineyards. Almonds, olives and figs are also grown. In the mountainous areas the chief pursuit is livestock raising. In 1998 there were 494,000 ha of arable land and 65,000 ha of permanent crops. Major agricultural production (in tonnes in 2000): potatoes, 290,300; wheat, 177,800; tomatoes, 143,700; grapes, 115,800; barley, 32,900. Livestock (2000): cattle, 497,306; sheep, 539,992; pigs, 68,912; horses, 11,400; chickens, 4m.

Forestry. In 1995 forests covered 334,000 ha, or 11·8% of the total land area (10·4% in 1990). Timber production in 1998 was 36,000 cu. metres.

Fisheries. Total catch in 2000 came to an estimated 389 tonnes, exclusively from inland waters.

INDUSTRY

Among the chief industries are chemicals, producing mainly synthetic rubber and fertilizers, the extraction and processing of building materials, ginning- and textile-mills, carpet weaving and food processing, including wine-making.

Labour. In 2000 the population of working age was 2·35m., of whom 1·3m. were employed: 44% in agriculture, 14% in industry. The registered unemployment rate was 11·7% of the workforce in 2000 (11·5% in 1999). The official average monthly salary in Jan. 2001 was 20,612 drams.

INTERNATIONAL TRADE

External debt was US$898m. in 2000.

Imports and Exports. Imports and exports for calendar years in US$1m.:

	1996	1997	1998	1999	2000
Imports	855·8	892·3	902·4	811·3	884·7
Exports	290·3	232·5	229·5	231·7	300·5

The main import suppliers in 2000 were Russia (14·9%), USA (11·6%), Belgium (9·5%) and Iran (9·4%). Principal export markets were Belgium (25·2%), Russia (15·0%), USA (12·7%) and Iran (9·3%). Cut diamonds and jewellery from precious metals and stones account for 45% of Armenia's exports, non-precious metals 15% and mineral products 13%. Foodstuffs account for 26% of Armenia's imports, mineral products 19%, and equipment and machinery 15%.

COMMUNICATIONS

Roads. There were 12,072 km of road network in 2000. There were also 7,527 km of motorway. In 1996 there were 5,760 passenger cars, buses, coaches, lorries and vans as well as 7,200 motorcycles and mopeds. There were 316 fatalities as a result of road accidents in 1998.

Rail. Total length in 2000 was 711 km of 1,000 mm gauge. Passenger-km travelled in 2000 came to 52m. and freight tonne-km to 354m.
There is a tramway in Yerevan.

Civil Aviation. There is an international airport at Yerevan (Zvartnots). The state-owned Armenian Airlines has been operational since 1995. In 1998 it operated services to Adler/Sochi, Aleppo, Amman, Amsterdam, Anapa, Ashgabat, Athens, Beirut, Delhi, Dubai, Ekaterinburg, Istanbul, Kharkiv, Krasnodar, Kyiv, London, Milan, Mineralnye Vody, Moscow, Nizhny Novgorod, Novosibirsk, Odesa, Paris, Rostov, St Petersburg, Samara, Saratov, Simferopol, Sofia, Stavropol, Tashkent, Tbilisi, Tehran, Vladikavkaz and Volgograd. In 1999 scheduled airline traffic of Armenian-based carriers flew 8·2m. km, carrying 343,000 passengers (all on international flights).

Telecommunications. Telephone main lines numbered 527,000 in 2000 (138·6 per 1,000 inhabitants) and there were 25,000 PCs in use (7·1 for every 1,000 persons). In 1996 there were 350 fax machines. Armenia had 17,400 mobile phone subscribers in Dec. 1998 and 30,000 Internet users in July 2000.

SOCIAL INSTITUTIONS

Justice. In 2000, 12,048 crimes were reported, including 127 murders or attempted murders. The population in penal institutions in Feb. 2000 was 6,789 (178 per 100,000 of national population).

Religion. Armenia adopted Christianity in AD 301, thus becoming the first Christian nation in the world. The Armenian Apostolic Church is headed by its Catholicos (Karekin II, b. 1932) whose seat is at Etchmiadzin, and who is head of all the Armenian (Gregorian) communities throughout the world. In 1995 it numbered 7m. adherents (4m. in diaspora). The Catholicos is elected by representatives of parishes. The Catholicos of the diaspora is Kachechyan of Cilicia, with seat at Antelias. In 1997, 70% of the population belonged to the Armenian Apostolic Church.

Education. Armenia's literacy rate was 98·3% in 1999 (99·2% among males and 97·5% among females). At the end of 2000, 46,300 children (17% of those eligible) attended pre-school institutions. In 2000–01 there were 176,302 pupils in primary schools (and 13,620 teachers in 1996–97) and 292,368 pupils in secondary schools. In 2000–01 there were 25 technical colleges with 26,870 students and 19 higher educational institutions with 43,615 students. Yerevan houses the National Academy of Sciences of the Republic of Armenia (NAS RA), 43 scientific institutes, a medical institute and other technical colleges, and a state university. NAS RA is composed of more than 50 institutions and organizations with a staff of 4,500.
In 2000–01 there were seven universities (including the Yerevan State University and the American University), with 22,400 students, out of a total of 19 public higher education establishments.

Health. In 2000 there were some 12,270 doctors, 22,672 junior medical personnel and 146 hospitals with 20,795 beds.

Welfare. In 2000 there were 501,711 old age, and 58,371 other, pensioners.

CULTURE

Broadcasting. The state-owned Armenian Radio broadcasts two national programmes and relays of Radio Moscow and Voice of America, and a foreign service, Radio Yerevan (Armenian, English, French, Spanish, Arabic, Kurdish, Russian). Television broadcasting is by the state-controlled Armenian Television (colour by SECAM H). In 1997 there were 825,000 TV receivers and 850,000 radio receivers.

Cinema. 3 full-length films were made in 1995.

Press. In 2000 there were 91 daily publications.

Tourism. In 1999 there were 41,000 foreign tourists bringing in receipts of US$27m.

Libraries. There were 1,138 libraries in 2000, which lent 5·1m. items.

Theatre and Opera. 360,000 people attended 21 theatres in 2000.

Museums and Galleries. In 2000 there were 93 museums with 874,100 visitors.

DIPLOMATIC REPRESENTATIVES

Of Armenia in the United Kingdom (25A Cheniston Gdns, London, W8 6TG)
Ambassador: Vacant.
Chargé d'Affaires a.i.: Karine Khoudaverdian.

Of the United Kingdom in Armenia (28 Charents St., Yerevan 375010)
Ambassador: Thorda Abbott-Watt.

Of Armenia in the USA (2225 R St., NW, Washington, D.C., 20008)
Ambassador: Arman Kirakossian.

Of the USA in Armenia (18 Gen. Bagramian, Yerevan 375019)
Ambassador: John Malcolm Ordway.

Of Armenia to the United Nations
Ambassador: Dr Movses Abelian.

Of Armenia to the European Union
Ambassador: Viguen Tchitetchian.

FURTHER READING

Brook, S., *Claws of the Crab: Georgia and Armenia in Crisis*. London, 1992
Hovannisian, R. G., *The Republic of Armenia*. 4 vols. Univ. of California Press, 1996
Malkasian, M., *Gha-Ra-Bagh: the Emergence of the National Democratic Movement in Armenia*. Wayne State Univ. Press, 1996
Nersessian, V. N., *Armenia*. [Bibliography] ABC-Clio, Oxford and Santa Barbara (CA), 1993
Walker, C. J., *Armenia: The Survival of a Nation*. 2nd ed. London, 1990

National statistical office: National Statistical Service of the Republic of Armenia. *President:* Stepan L. Mnatsakanyan.
Website: http://www.armstat.am

AUSTRALIA

Commonwealth of Australia

Capital: Canberra
Population estimate, 2000: 19·14m.
GDP per capita, 2000: (PPP$) 25,693
HDI/world rank: 0·939/5

KEY HISTORICAL EVENTS

Various dates are given for the discovery of Australia, including 1522 in which year it was sighted by Magellan's followers. Capt. Cook discovered the east coast in 1770 and initially the British planned to establish a colony there; instead, however, the government decided to set up a penal settlement.

The appointment of Lachlan Macquarie as Governor in 1809 began a period of development in which Australia ceased primarily to be a penal settlement. The crossing of the Blue Mountains in 1813 was the first of many expeditions which led to discovery and use of vast areas of good grazing land.

On 1 Jan. 1901 the six separately constituted colonies of New South Wales, Victoria, Queensland, South Australia, Western Australia and Tasmania were federated under the name of the Commonwealth of Australia, the designation of 'colonies' being at the same time changed into that of 'states'—except in the case of Northern Territory which was transferred from South Australia to the Commonwealth as a 'territory' on 1 Jan. 1911.

In 1911 the Commonwealth acquired from the State of New South Wales the Canberra site for the Australian capital. Building began in 1923 and a Federal Parliament was opened at Canberra in 1927.

Since the Second World War, Australia has played an increasingly important role in Asia and the Pacific. For much of this period central government has been in the hands of the Liberal–National Party coalition, including 23 years consecutively between 1949 and 1972. The Australian Labor Party (ALP) has held power for some 20 years in three spells since 1945 and during its third period of rule, between 1983 and 1996, shifted its stance on state control and economic planning to allow for an ambitious programme of privatization. In March 1986 the Australia Act abolished the remaining legislative, executive and judicial controls of the British Parliament.

A referendum to decide whether Australia should become a republic was held on 6 Nov. 1999. 54·87% of votes cast were in favour of remaining a monarchy with Queen Elizabeth II as head of state, against 45·13% in favour of a republic with a president chosen by parliament.

TERRITORY AND POPULATION

Australia, excluding external territories, covers an estimated land area of 7,692,030 sq. km, extending from Cape York (10° 41' S) in the north some 3,680 km to South East Cape, Tasmania (43° 39' S), and from Cape Byron, New South Wales (153° 39' E) in the east some 4,000 km west to Steep Point, Western Australia (113° 9' E). External territories under the administration of Australia comprise the Ashmore and Cartier Islands, Australian Antarctic Territory, Christmas Island, the Cocos (Keeling) Islands, the Coral Sea Islands, the Heard and McDonald Islands and Norfolk Island. For these *see below.*

Growth in census population has been:

1901	3,774,310	1966	11,599,498	1986	15,763,000
1911	4,455,005	1971	12,755,638	1991	16,852,258
1921	5,435,734	1976	13,915,500	1996	17,892,423
1947	7,579,358	1981	15,053,600	2001	18,972,350
1961	10,508,186				

Of the 2001 census population, 9,618,981 were females.

The UN gives a projected population for 2010 of 21·03m.

At the census in 1996 density was 2·3 per sq. km. In 1999, 84·7% of the population lived in urban areas.

Areas and populations of the States and Territories at the 1996 census:

States and Territories	Area (sq. km)	Population	Per sq. km
New South Wales (NSW)	800,640	6,038,696	7·6
Victoria (Vic.)	227,420	4,373,520	19·2
Queensland (Qld.)	1,730,650	3,368,850	1·9
South Australia (SA)	983,480	1,427,936	1·4
Western Australia (WA)	2,529,880	1,726,095	0·7
Tasmania (Tas.)	68,400	459,659	6·7
Northern Territory (NT)	1,349,130	195,101	0·1
Australian Capital Territory (ACT)	2,360	299,243	126·8

Population at 31 Dec. 2001: New South Wales, 6,642,900; Victoria, 4,854,100; Queensland, 3,670,500; South Australia, 1,518,900; Western Australia, 1,918,800; Tasmania, 473,300; Northern Territory, 199,900; Australian Capital Territory, 322,600.

Resident population (estimate) in capitals and other statistical districts with more than 150,000 population at 30 June 2000:

Capital	State	Population	Capital	State	Population
Canberra	ACT	310,500	Darwin	NT	90,000
Sydney	NSW	4,085,600	Statistical district		
Melbourne	Vic.	3,466,000	Newcastle	NSW	483,300
Brisbane	Qld.	1,626,900	Wollongong	NSW	264,400
Adelaide	SA	1,096,100	Gold Coast[1]	Qld.	404,300
Perth	WA	1,381,100	Geelong	Vic.	157,900
Hobart	Tas.	194,200	Sunshine Coast[2]	Qld.	178,000

[1]Includes part of Tweed Shire (in NSW). [2]Includes Caloundra, Maroochy and Noosa.

The median age of the 2001 census population was 35 years.

Australians born overseas (census 2001), 4,105,444, of whom 1,036,245 (5·5%) were from the UK. In 1998 it was estimated that 23·4% of the population was born overseas.

Aboriginals have been included in population statistics only since 1967. At the 2001 census 410,003 people identified themselves as being of indigenous origin (2·2% of the total population). A 1992 High Court ruling that the Meriam people of the Murray Islands had land rights before the European settlement reversed the previous assumption that Australia was *terra nullius* before that settlement. The Native Title Act setting up a system for deciding claims by Aborigines came into effect on 1 Jan. 1994.

Overseas arrivals and departures:

	Settler arrival numbers[1]	Permanent departure numbers	Net permanent migration
1995–96	99,100	28,600	70,500
1996–97	85,800	29,900	55,900
1997–98	77,300	32,000	45,300
1998–99	84,100	35,200	49,000

[1]Equals the total number of people entitled to permanent residence actually arriving.

Under the Migration Program, the planning level for 1998–99 was 68,000. The Migration Act of Dec. 1989 sought to curb illegal entry and ensure that annual immigrant intakes were met but not exceeded. Provisions for temporary visitors to become permanent were restricted. According to the 1996 census, 68% of the population born overseas have become Australian citizens.

The national language is English.

SOCIAL STATISTICS
Life expectancy at birth, 1999, 76·2 years for males and 81·8 years for females. A World Health Organization report published in June 2000 put Australians in second place in a 'healthy life expectancy' list, with an expected 73·2 years of healthy life for babies born in 1999.

Statistics for years ended 30 June:

	Births	Deaths	Marriages	Divorces
1997	252,718	128,428	106,701	51,334
1998	249,726	127,270	110,392	51,603
1999	249,282	127,200	114,300	52,600
2000	249,600	128,100	113,400	49,900

In 2000 the median age for marrying was 30 years for males and 28 for females. Infant mortality, 1999, was 5·7 per 1,000 live births. Fertility rate, 2000, 1·8 births per woman.

Suicide rates (per 100,000 population, 1997): 14·6 (men, 23·4; women, 6·1).

CLIMATE
Over most of the continent, four seasons may be recognized. Spring is from Sept. to Nov., summer from Dec. to Feb., autumn from March to May and winter from June to Aug., but because of its great size there are climates that range from tropical monsoon to cool temperate, with large areas of desert as well. In northern Australia there are only two seasons, the wet one lasting from Nov. to March, but rainfall amounts diminish markedly from the coast to the interior. Central and southern Queensland are subtropical, north and central New South Wales are warm temperate, as are parts of Victoria, Western Australia and Tasmania, where most rain falls in winter. Canberra, Jan. 68°F (20°C), July 42°F (5·6°C). Annual rainfall 25" (635 mm). Adelaide, Jan. 73°F (22·8°C), July 52°F (11·1°C). Annual rainfall 21" (528 mm). Brisbane, Jan. 77°F (25°C), July 58°F (14·4°C). Annual rainfall 45" (1,153 mm). Darwin, Jan. 83°F (28·3°C), July 77°F (25°C). Annual rainfall 59" (1,536 mm). Hobart, Jan. 62°F (16·7°C), July 46°F (7·8°C). Annual rainfall 23" (584 mm). Melbourne, Jan. 67°F (19·4°C), July 49°F (9·4°C). Annual rainfall 26" (659 mm). Perth, Jan. 74°F (23·3°C), July 55°F (12·8°C). Annual rainfall 35" (873 mm). Sydney, Jan. 71°F (21·7°C), July 53°F (11·7°C). Annual rainfall 47" (1,215 mm).

CONSTITUTION AND GOVERNMENT
Federal Government. Under the Constitution legislative power is vested in a Federal Parliament, consisting of the Queen, represented by a Governor-General, a Senate and a House of Representatives. Under the terms of the constitution there must be a session of parliament at least once a year.

The Senate (Upper House) comprises 76 Senators (12 for each State voting as one electorate and, as from Aug. 1974, 2 Senators respectively for the Australian Capital Territory and the Northern Territory). Senators representing the States are chosen for six years. The terms of Senators representing the Territories expire at the close of the day next preceding the polling day for the general elections of the House of Representatives. In general, the Senate is renewed to the extent of one-half every three years, but in case of disagreement with the House of Representatives, it, together with the House of Representatives, may be dissolved, and an entirely new Senate elected. Elections to the Senate are on the single transferable vote system; voters list candidates in order of preference. A candidate must reach a quota to be elected, otherwise the lowest-placed candidate drops out and his or her votes are transferred to other candidates.

The *House of Representatives* (Lower House) consists, as nearly as practicable, of twice as many Members as there are Senators, the numbers chosen in the several States being in proportion to population as shown by the latest statistics, but not less than 5 for any original State. The 148 membership is made up as follows: New South Wales, 50; Victoria, 37; Queensland, 26; South Australia, 12; Western Australia, 14; Tasmania, 5; ACT, 3; Northern Territory, 1. Elections to the House of Representatives are on the alternative vote system; voters list candidates in order of preference, and if no one candidate wins an overall majority, the lowest-placed drops out and his or her votes are transferred. The Northern Territory has been represented by one Member in the House of Representatives since 1922; the Australian Capital Territory by one Member since 1949 and two Members since May 1974. The Member for the Australian Capital Territory was given full voting rights as from the Parliament elected in Nov. 1966. The Member for the Northern Territory was given full voting rights in 1968. The House of Representatives continues for three years from the date of its first meeting, unless sooner dissolved.

Every Senator or Member of the House of Representatives must be a subject of the Queen, be of full age, possess electoral qualifications and have resided for three years within Australia. The franchise for both Houses is the same and is based on universal (males and females aged 18 years) suffrage. Compulsory voting was introduced in 1925. If a Member of a State Parliament wishes to be a candidate in a federal election, he must first resign his State seat.

Executive power is vested in the *Governor-General*, advised by an Executive Council. The Governor-General presides over the Council, and its members hold office at his pleasure. All Ministers of State, who are members of the party or parties commanding a majority in the lower House, are members of the Executive Council under summons. A record of proceedings of meetings is kept by the Secretary to the Council. At Executive Council meetings the decisions of the Cabinet are (where necessary) given legal form, appointments made, resignations accepted, proclamations, regulations and the like made.

The policy of a ministry is, in practice, determined by the Ministers of State meeting without the Governor-General under the chairmanship of the Prime Minister. This group is known as the *Cabinet*. There are 11 Standing Committees of the Cabinet comprising varying numbers of Cabinet and non-Cabinet Ministers. In Labour governments all Ministers have been members of Cabinet; in Liberal and National Country Party governments, only the senior ministers. Cabinet meetings are private and deliberative, and records of meetings are not made public. The Cabinet does not form part of the legal mechanisms of government; the decisions it takes have, in themselves, no legal effect. The Cabinet substantially controls, in ordinary circumstances, not only the general legislative programme of Parliament but the whole course of Parliamentary proceedings. In effect, though not in form, the Cabinet, by reason of the fact that all Ministers are members of the Executive Council, is also the dominant element in the executive government of the country.

The legislative powers of the Federal Parliament embrace trade and commerce, shipping, etc.; taxation, finance, banking, currency, bills of exchange, bankruptcy, insurance, defence, external affairs, naturalization and aliens, quarantine, immigration and emigration; the people of any race for whom it is deemed necessary to make special laws; postal, telegraph and like services; census and statistics; weights and measures; astronomical and meteorological observations; copyrights; railways; conciliation and arbitration in disputes extending beyond the limits of any one State; social services; marriage, divorce, etc.; service and execution of the civil and criminal process; recognition of the laws, Acts and records, and judicial proceedings of the States. The Senate may not originate or amend money bills. Disagreement with the House of Representatives may result in dissolution and, in the last resort, a joint sitting of the two Houses. The Federal Parliament has limited and enumerated powers, the several State parliaments retaining the residuary power of government over their respective territories. If a State law is inconsistent with a Commonwealth law, the latter prevails.

The Constitution also provides for the admission or creation of new States. Proposed laws for the alteration of the Constitution must be submitted to the electors, and they can be enacted only if approved by a majority of the States and by a majority of all the electors voting.

The Australia Acts 1986 removed residual powers of the British government to intervene in the government of Australia or the individual states.

In Feb. 1998 an Australian Constitutional Convention voted for Australia to become a republic. In a national referendum, held on 6 Nov. 1999, 54·87% voted against Australia becoming a republic.

State Government. In each of the six States (New South Wales, Victoria, Queensland, South Australia, Western Australia, Tasmania) there is a State government whose constitution, powers and laws continue, subject to changes embodied in the Australian Constitution and subsequent alterations and agreements, as they were before federation. The system of government is basically the same as that described above for the Commonwealth—i.e., the Sovereign, her representative (in this case a Governor), an upper and lower house of Parliament (except in Queensland, where the upper house was abolished in 1922), a cabinet led by the Premier and an Executive Council. Among the more important functions of the State governments are those relating to education, health, hospitals and charities, law, order and public safety, business undertakings such as railways and tramways, and public utilities such as water supply and sewerage. In the domains of education, hospitals, justice, the police, penal establishments, and railway and tramway operation, State government activity predominates. Care of the public health and recreative activities are shared with local government authorities and the Federal government; social services other than those referred to above are now primarily the concern of the

Federal government; the operation of public utilities is shared with local and semi-government authorities.

Administration of Territories. Since 1911 responsibility for administration and development of the Australian Capital Territory (ACT) has been vested in Federal Ministers and Departments. The ACT became self-governing on 11 May 1989. The ACT House of Assembly has been accorded the forms of a legislature, but continues to perform an advisory function for the Minister for the Capital Territory.

On 1 July 1978 the Northern Territory of Australia became a self-governing Territory with expenditure responsibilities and revenue-raising powers broadly approximating those of a State.

National Anthem. 'Advance Australia Fair' (adopted 19 April 1984; words and tune by P. D. McCormick). The 'Royal Anthem' (i.e. 'God Save the Queen') is used in the presence of the British Royal Family.

RECENT ELECTIONS

The 40th Parliament was elected on 10 Nov. 2001.

House of Representatives. Liberal Party (LP), 68 seats and 37·1% of votes cast; Australian Labor Party (ALP), 65 seats but 37·8% of votes cast; National Party of Australia (NP), 13 (3·6%); Northern Territory Country Liberal Party, 1; independents and others, 3.

Senate. Following elections of 10 Nov. 2001 the make-up of the Senate was Liberal Party, 31; Australian Labor Party, 28; Australian Democratic Party, 8; National Party of Australia, 3; Greens, 2, Northern Territory Country Liberal Party, 1; One Nation, 1; Country Labor Party, 1; ind., 1.

CURRENT ADMINISTRATION

Governor-General: Dr Peter Hollingworth, AO, OBE (assumed office 29 June 2001).

An LP–NP coalition government was formed on 21 Oct. 1998. In March 2003 it comprised:

Prime Minister: John Winston Howard; b. 1939 (LP; in office since 11 March 1996).

Deputy Prime Minister and Minister for Transport and Regional Services: John Anderson (NP). *Treasurer:* Peter Costello (LP). *Defence and Leader of the Government in the Senate:* Robert Hill (LP). *Communications and Information Technology, Arts, and Deputy Leader of the Government in the Senate:* Richard Alston (LP). *Employment and Workplace Relations, Leader of the House of Representatives and Minister Assisting the Prime Minister for the Public Service:* Tony Abbott (LP). *Foreign Affairs:* Alexander Downer (LP). *Environment and Heritage:* David Kemp (LP). *Industry, Tourism and Resources:* Ian Macfarlane (LP). *Immigration, Multicultural and Indigenous Affairs, and Minister Assisting the Prime Minister for Reconciliation:* Philip Ruddock (LP). *Agriculture, Fisheries and Forestry:* Warren Truss (NP). *Health and Ageing:* Kay Patterson (LP). *Education, Science and Training:* Brendan Nelson (LP). *Finance and Administration:* Nick Minchin (LP). *Family and Community Services, and Minister Assisting the Prime Minister for the Status of Women:* Amanda Vanstone (LP). *Trade:* Mark Vaile (NP). *Attorney-General:* Daryl Williams AM, QC (LP).

Outer Ministry: Minister for Revenue and Assistant Treasurer: Helen Coonan (LP). *Regional Services, Territories and Local Government:* Wilson Tuckey (LP). *Science and Deputy Leader of the Government in the House of Representatives:* Peter McGauran (NP). *Justice and Customs:* Chris Ellison (LP). *Veterans' Affairs, Minister Assisting the Minister for Defence:* Danna Vale (LP). *Small Business and Tourism:* Joe Hockey (LP). *Special Minister of State:* Eric Abetz (LP). *Fisheries, Forestry and Conservation:* Ian MacDonald (LP). *Children and Youth Affairs:* Larry Anthony (NP). *Arts and Sport:* Rod Kemp (LP). *Employment Services:* Mal Brough (LP). *Citizenship and Multicultural Affairs:* Gary Hardgrave (LP). *Ageing:* Kevin Andrews (LP).

The *Speaker* is Neil Andrew (LP).

The *President* of the Senate is Paul Calvert (LP).

Leader of the Opposition: Simon Crean (ALP). *Deputy Leader of the Opposition:* Jenny Macklin (ALP).

Government: http://www.gov.au/

DEFENCE
The Minister for Defence has responsibility under legislation for the control and administration of the Defence Force. The Chief of Defence Force Staff is vested with command of the Defence Force. He is the principal military adviser to the Minister. The Chief of Naval Staff, the Chief of the General Staff and the Chief of the Air Staff command the Navy, Army and Air Force respectively. They have delegated authority from the Chief of Defence Force Staff and the Secretary to administer matters relating to their particular Service.

2001 defence expenditure was US$6,752m., amounting to US$350 per capita and representing 1·9% of GDP (which, along with 1999 and 2000, was the lowest proportion since 1939).

Army. The strength of the Army was 25,150, including 2,500 women, in 2002. The effective strength of the Army Reserve was 16,200.

Women have been eligible for combat duties since 1993.

Navy. The all-volunteer Navy in 2002 was 12,750 including 990 in the Fleet Air Arm and 1,900 women. The Fleet included 6 diesel-powered submarines and 9 frigates.

The fleet main base is at Sydney, with subsidiary bases at Cockburn Sound (Western Australia), Cairns and Darwin.

Air Force. The Royal Australian Air Force (RAAF) operated 156 combat aircraft including 35 F-111 and 71 F-18 'Hornets' in 2002. Personnel numbered 13,200, including 1,964 women. There is also an Australian Air Force Reserve, 2,000-strong.

INTERNATIONAL RELATIONS
Australia is a member of the UN, WTO, BIS, the Commonwealth, OECD, Asian Development Bank, Colombo Plan, APEC, IOM, the Pacific Islands Forum, the Pacific Community and the Antarctic Treaty.

ECONOMY
In 1999–2000 service industries accounted for around 64% of GDP and goods-producing industries around 19%.

According to the anti-corruption organization *Transparency International*, Australia ranked 11th in the world in a 2002 survey of the countries with the least corruption in business and government. It received 8·6 out of 10 in the annual index.

Overview. Thanks to a combination of liberalization, increased competition and technological advance, the economy has changed radically in recent years. The reforms undertaken since the mid-1980s have led to a more competitive and outward-looking economy. This, together with flexible macroeconomic policies, enabled Australia to weather the Asian financial crisis. In 2000 the economy suffered from higher world energy prices and a slowing American economy. Monetary policy is expansionary. Performance in research and development suggests there are barriers to innovation. In 2001 the Backing Australia's Ability programme was launched to boost infrastructure and research funding.

Currency. On 14 Feb. 1966 Australia adopted a system of decimal currency. The currency unit, the Australian dollar (AUD), is divided into 100 *cents*.

Foreign exchange reserves were US$18,515m. in June 2002 and gold reserves 2·56m. troy oz. Total money supply was $A166,978m. in March 2002.

Inflation during the late 1990s remained under the Reserve Bank's 2%–3% headline inflation target, increasing by 1·2% in 1998–99, 2·4% in 1999–2000 and 6·0% in 2000–01.

Budget. In 1929, under a financial agreement between the Federal government and States, approved by a referendum, the Federal government took over all State debts existing on 30 June 1927 and agreed to pay $A15·17m. a year for 58 years towards interest charges, and to make substantial contributions towards a sinking fund on State debt. The Sinking Fund arrangements were revised under an amendment to the agreement in 1976. After 1942 the Federal government alone has levied income taxes. State expenditure was backed by federal grants.

In Aug. 1998 the Commonwealth government introduced a tax reform package including, from 2000, the introduction of a Goods and Services Tax (GST) at a 10%

rate, with all the revenues going to the states in return for the abolition of a range of other indirect taxes; the abolition of Financial Assistance Grants to states; the abolition of wholesale sales tax (which is levied by the Commonwealth government); cuts in personal income tax; and increases in social security benefits, especially for families. In all, the underlying cash balance is expected to be in surplus by \$A2·1bn. (0·3% of GDP) in the financial year 2002–03. In accrual terms, a fiscal deficit of \$A0·5bn. (0·1% of GDP) is expected in 2002–03. The economy is forecast to grow by around 3% in 2002–03, following growth of around 4% in 2001–02.

General expenses and revenue of the Commonwealth government for years ending 30 June (in \$A1m.):

	2001–02	2002–03[1]
Total expenses (by function)	166,482	170,666
including		
General public services	10,241	10,379
Defence	12,017	13,250
Public order and safety	1,856	2,078
Education	11,761	12,324
Health	27,614	29,377
Social security and welfare	69,081	72,561
Housing and community amenities	2,210	1,901
Recreation and culture	2,036	2,108
Fuel and energy	3,052	3,523
Agriculture, fisheries and forestry	1,691	1,814
Mining and mineral resources (other than fuels), manufacturing and construction	1,686	1,621
Transport and communications	2,647	2,238
Other economic affairs	3,899	4,023
Other purposes	16,693	13,380
Total revenue (by source)	162,370	169,623
including		
Income tax		
Individuals and other witholding	86,422	91,980
Companies	27,133	29,240
Superannuation funds	4,171	4,480
Petroleum resource rent tax	1,306	1,650
Indirect tax		
Excise duty—Petroleum products and crude oil	12,793	13,100
Other excise	6,837	7,060
Total excise duty	19,630	20,160
Customs duty	5,214	5,330
Other indirect taxes	791	810
Fringe benefit tax	3,675	3,360
Other taxes	1,506	1,517
Non-tax revenue	12,522	11,096

[1]Estimate as at Nov. 2002.

Performance. Real domestic demand increased by 5·2% in year average terms in 1999–2000, the 9th consecutive year of growth, and 5·6% in the calendar year 1999. GDP was \$A631,810m. for 1999–2000, nominal terms (\$A595,417m. in 1998–99); and GDP growth was 4·3% in 1999–2000 (real terms), the 9th consecutive year of real GDP growth, averaging 3·9% per annum since 1991–92 (3·8% growth in the calendar year 2000, real terms). During much of the 1990s the real GDP growth rate, along with inflation being brought down and kept low, made the Australian economic performance one of the best in the OECD area.

Banking and Finance. From 1 July 1998 a new financial regulatory framework based on three agencies was introduced by the Australian government, following recommendations by the Financial System Inquiry. The framework included changes in the role of the Reserve Bank of Australia and creation of the Australian Prudential Regulation Authority (APRA) with responsibility for the supervision of deposit-taking institutions (comprising banks, building societies, credit unions and friendly societies), life and general insurance companies and superannuation funds. It further involved replacement of the Australian Securities Commission with the Australian Securities and Investments Commission (ASIC) with responsibility for the regulation of financial services and Australia's 1·2m. companies.

The banking system comprises:

(a) The Reserve Bank of Australia is the central bank. It has two broad responsibilities—monetary policy and the maintenance of financial stability, including stability of the payments system. It also provides selected banking and registry services to Federal and State Government customers and some overseas official institutions. A wholly owned subsidiary of the Reserve Bank (Note Printing Australia Limited) manufactures Australia's currency notes (all polymer) and other security products. The *Governor* is a statutory appointee (present incumbent, Ian Macfarlane, appointed 1996 for a seven-year term). Within the Reserve Bank there are two Boards: the Reserve Bank Board and the Payments System Board; the *Governor* is the Chairman of each.

At 30 June 2001 total assets of the Reserve Bank of Australia were \$A58,113m., including gold, \$A1,381m., foreign exchange, \$A35,786m. and Australian dollar securities, \$A19,814m. Main liability items were capital and reserves, \$A9,431m.; Australian notes on issue, \$A27,168m.; and deposits, \$A16,864m. Responsibilities derive principally from the Reserve Bank Act 1959, the Payment Systems (Regulation) Act 1998 and the Payment Systems and Netting Act 1998.

(b) Four major banks: (i) The Commonwealth Bank of Australia; (ii) the Australia and New Zealand Banking Group Ltd; (iii) Westpac Banking Corporation; (iv) National Australia Bank.

(c) The Commonwealth Bank of Australia has two subsidiaries—Colonial State Bank and Commonwealth Development Bank. There are eight other Australian-owned banks—Adelaide Bank Ltd, AMP Bank Ltd, Bank of Queensland Ltd, Bendigo Bank Ltd, Elders Rural Bank (50% owned by Bendigo Bank Ltd), Macquarie Bank Ltd, St George Bank Ltd and Suncorp-Metway Ltd.

(d) There are 12 banks incorporated in Australia which are owned by foreign banks and 27 branches of foreign banks (these figures include four foreign banks which have both a subsidiary and a branch presence in Australia).

(e) At 30 June 2000 there were 51 authorized banks with Australian banking assets of \$A730bn., with 5,000 branches and similar number of agencies, almost 11,000 ATMs and 320,000 EFTPOS terminals. As at 30 June 2000 there were 19 building societies with assets of \$A13bn. and 215 credit unions with assets of \$A22bn.

There is an Australian Stock Exchange (ASX) in Sydney.

Weights and Measures. The metric system is in use.

ENERGY AND NATURAL RESOURCES

Environment. According to the *World Bank Atlas* Australia's carbon dioxide emissions were the equivalent of 17·7 tonnes per capita in 1998. An *Environmental Sustainability Index* compiled for the World Economic Forum meeting in Feb. 2002 ranked Australia 16th in the world, with 60·3%. The index measured the ability of countries to maintain favourable environmental conditions and examined various factors including pollution levels and the use or abuse of natural resources.

Electricity. Electricity supply is the responsibility of the State governments. At 30 June 1997 total installed plant capacity was 39,017m. kW; production (1999), 186,252m. kWh (15% hydro-electric). In the year ended 30 June 1999 total consumption stood at 161,762m. kWh, including 48,334m. kWh by residential customers.

Oil and Gas. The main fields are Gippsland (Vic.) and Carnarvon (WA). Crude oil and condensate production was 34,000m. litres in 1997–98; natural gas, 30,323m. cu. metres. Oil reserves in 1999 totalled 2·9bn. bbls. and natural gas reserves 1,260bn. cu. metres. Australia's most productive oilfield in 2000 was Laminaria in Northern Territory with peak production of around 180,000 bbls. and average production at Nov. 2000 of around 167,000 bbls. per day.

Minerals. Australia is the world's largest producer of bauxite (38% of total world production) and diamonds (28% of world production, mostly for industrial use). It is also the third-largest gold producer and the fifth-largest silver producer. Black coal is Australia's major source of energy. Reserves are large (1997: 95bn. recoverable tonnes) and easily worked. The main fields are in New South Wales and Queensland. Brown coal (lignite) reserves are mainly in Victoria. Coal production, 1998–99, was 225m. tonnes; lignite production, 68·6m. tonnes.

Production of other major minerals (preliminary figures) in 1999–2000 (in tonnes): aluminium, 14·9m.; manganese, 2·1m.; zinc, 1·3m.; copper concentrate, 752,000; uranium, 8,223; silver, 1,894; gold, 296. Diamond production, 1999–2000 (preliminary figure): 29·7m. carats.

Agriculture. In the year ended 30 June 2000 there were 146,371 establishments mainly engaged in agriculture, of which an estimated 12,300 farm businesses (12%) had a turnover of $A500,000 or more. Farm business turnover in 1999–2000 was estimated to total $A28·5bn. In 1999–2000 the estimated total area of land under agricultural use was 456m. ha (about 59% of total land area) with farm holdings of over 2,500 ha representing 10% of all establishments. Beef cattle farming represents the largest sector, accounting for 24% of farming establishments. Important crops (1999–2000): wheat (24·8m. tonnes from 12·2m. ha); barley (5·0m. tonnes from 2·6m. ha); oats (1·1m. tonnes from 0·58m. ha); canola (2·5m. tonnes from 1·9m. ha); grain sorghum (2·1m. tonnes from 0·62m. ha); sugarcane, 1998–99 total, (38·5m. tonnes from 0·4m. ha). In 1999–2000, 1·3m. tonnes of grapes were harvested from 140,000 ha of vines.

Livestock totals (1999–2000): beef cattle, 24·4m.; dairy cattle, 3·1m.; sheep and lambs, 118·6m.; pigs, 2·5m.; chicken for meat, 72·9m.; chicken for egg production, 12·0m. Gross value of agricultural production in 1999–2000, $A30·2bn., including (in $A1bn.) cattle and calves slaughtering, 5·1; wheat, 4·8; wool, 2·1; milk, 2·8.

Fruit and vegetable production in 1999–2000 (in 1,000 tonnes): potatoes, 1,200; oranges, 510; apples, 320; carrots, 283; bananas, 257.

Figures compiled by the Soil Association, a British organization, show that in 1999 organic crops were grown in an area covering 1·7m. ha (the largest area of any country in the world), representing 1·4% of all farmland.

Australia is the world's leading wool producer; only China has more sheep.

Livestock products (in 1,000 tonnes), 1999–2000: beef, 1,952; lamb and mutton, 680; pigmeat, 363; poultry meat, 593; veal, 36; wool, 695; milk, 10,847m. litres.

Forestry. The Federal government is responsible for forestry at the national level. Each State is responsible for the management of publicly owned forests. Estimated total native forest cover was 164·41m. ha at June 2001 (1997, 155·84m. ha), made up of (in 1,000 ha): public forest, 124,468 (112,631); privately owned, 37,299 (42,018). (The changes in area since 1997 are primarily down to improvements in mapping and do not necessarily reflect the establishment of new forests.) The major part of wood supplies derives from coniferous plantations, of which there were 972,164 ha at 30 June 2000. Australia also had 502,620 ha of hardwood plantation at that date. Timber production in 1999–2000 was 24·01m. cu. metres.

Fisheries. The Australian Fishing Zone covers an area 16% larger than the Australian land mass and is the third largest fishing zone in the world, but fish production is insignificant by world standards owing to low productivity of the oceans. The major commercially exploited species are prawns, rock lobster, abalone, tuna, other fin fish, scallops, oysters and pearls. Total fisheries production in 1999–2000 came to 221,405 tonnes with a gross value of $A2·3bn. In the same year aquaculture production was 40,632 tonnes with a gross value of $A678m., which represented 30% of the total value of fisheries production.

INDUSTRY

The leading companies by market capitalization in Australia, excluding banking and finance, in Jan. 2002 were: Telstra Corporation Ltd ($A71bn.), a telecommunications company; The News Corporation Ltd ($A68bn.); and Rio Tinto Ltd ($A54bn.), the metal and mining sister enterprise of Rio Tinto plc.

Manufacturing industries at 30 June 2000: persons employed, 933,000; salaries paid, $A35,482m.; turnover, $A231,145m. (excludes small single-establishment enterprises employing fewer than four persons).

Manufacturing by sector, 1999–2000:

	Persons Employed	Salaries in $1m.	Turnover in $A1m.
Food, beverages and tobacco	168,100	6,140	51,089
Textiles, clothing, footwear and leather products	65,300	1,895	9,337
Wood and paper products	64,800	2,276	14,060

	Persons Employed	Salaries in $1m.	Turnover in $A1m.
Printing, publishing and recording media	99,600	3,879	17,256
Chemical, petroleum, coal and associated products	97,500	4,321	36,002
Non-metallic mineral products	35,600	1,517	10,560
Metal products	144,600	5,789	41,304
Machinery and equipment	200,700	8,149	44,350
Other manufacturing	56,600	1,516	7,188

Manufactured products in 1999–2000 included: clay bricks, 1,735m.; portland cement, 7·9m. tonnes; ready-mixed concrete, 20·6m. cu. metres; basic iron, spiegeleisen and sponge iron, 6·5m. tonnes; tobacco and cigarettes, 20,688 tonnes; newsprint, 381m. tonnes; tin, 600m. tonnes; aviation turbine fuel, 5,538m. litres; beer, 1,768m. litres.

Labour. In June 2001 the total workforce (persons aged 15 and over) numbered 9,461,000 (4,169,600 females). In June 2001 there were 8,839,500 employed persons (51·8% females). In Feb. 2001 the labour force included 329,700 employers, 7,326,400 wage and salary earners and 866,900 self-employed. The majority of wage and salary earners have had their minimum wages and conditions of work prescribed in awards by the Industrial Relations Commission. In Oct. 1991 the Commission decided to allow direct employer-employee wage bargaining, provided agreements reached are endorsed by the Commission. In some States, some conditions of work (e.g., weekly hours of work, leave) are set down in State legislation. Average weekly wage, May 2001, $A662·60 (men, $A789·40; women, $A524·70). Average working week, 2000–01: 34·0 hours. Four weeks annual leave is standard. In 2000–01 part-time work accounted for 26·7% of all employment in Australia and persons born overseas made up 58·0% of the total labour force.

Employees in all States are covered by workers' compensation legislation and by certain industrial award provisions relating to work injuries.

During 2000 there were 698 industrial disputes recorded which accounted for 469,100 working days lost (28% decrease on 1999). In these disputes 325,400 workers were involved.

The following table shows the distribution of employed persons by industry in 2000–01, by sex and average weekly hours worked:

Industry	Numbers (in 1,000)		Hours worked	
	Persons	(Females)	Per person	(Females)
Agriculture, forestry, fishing	428·8	(134·8)	42·2	(30·5)
Mining	78·3	(9·1)	45·8	(40·1)
Manufacturing	1,129·8	(302·0)	38·7	(33·0)
Electricity, gas and water supply	65·7	(11·0)	38·0	(32·0)
Construction	681·3	(85·5)	38·7	(22·8)
Wholesale trade	438·7	(132·8)	39·2	(32·7)
Retail trade	1,331·2	(694·2)	30·5	(25·1)
Transport and storage	421·2	(103·4)	40·1	(33·0)
Property and business services	1,081·0	(482·3)	36·9	(31·1)
Education	621·1	(417·5)	34·2	(32·0)
Cultural and recreation services	225·2	(105·2)	31·3	(27·7)
Accommodation, cafés and restaurants	469·0	(254·3)	32·9	(28·4)
Communication services	182·6	(55·6)	37·8	(32·7)
Finance and insurance	337·3	(190·7)	36·5	(32·8)
Government administration and defence	365·8	(173·3)	34·5	(31·7)
Health and community services	874·8	(677·6)	30·7	(28·8)
Personal and other services	342·5	(167·7)	33·6	(28·7)
Totals	9,074·3	(3,997·0)	35·6	(29·6)

In Feb. 2001, 1,427,500 wage and salary earners worked in the public sector and 5,898,900 in the private sector.

The following table shows the estimated distribution of employed persons in 2000–01 according to the *Australian Standard Classification of Occupations (2nd edition)*:

Occupation	Employed persons (in 1,000)	
	Persons	(Females)
Managers and administrators	653·2	(162·3)
Professionals	1,662·1	(822·8)

Occupation	Employed persons (in 1,000) Persons	(Females)
Associate professionals	1,042·5	(398·0)
Tradespersons and related workers	1,178·2	(114·1)
Advanced clerical and service workers	409·1	(361·1)
Intermediate clerical, sales and service workers	1,575·6	(1,126·5)
Labourers and related workers	869·9	(320·2)
Intermediate production and transport workers	777·2	(95·2)
Elementary clerical, sales and service workers	906·5	(596·7)

In 2000–01, 625,500 persons were unemployed, of whom 552,400 persons were seeking full-time work; 23·0% had been unemployed for more than one year. The unemployment rate in Jan. 2003 was 6·1%.

Trade Unions. In Aug. 2001, 24·5% of all full-time employees (22·7% females) were members of a trade union. In 1999 there were 11 unions with fewer than 1,000 members and 14 unions with 50,000 or more members. Many of the larger trade unions are affiliated with central labour organizations, the oldest and by far the largest being the Australian Council of Trade Unions (ACTU) formed in 1927. In 2002, 46 unions were affiliated to ACTU, representing approximately 1·8m. workers. In July 1992 the Industrial Relations Legislation Amendment Act freed the way for employers and employees to negotiate enterprise-based awards and agreements.

INTERNATIONAL TRADE

In 1990 Australia and New Zealand completed a Closer Economic Relations agreement (initiated in 1983) which establishes free trade in goods. Net foreign debt was \$A268·1bn. as at 30 June 2000 (an increase of 16% on the previous year). In 1998 the effect of the Asian meltdown on exports resulted increasingly in shipments of commodities and exports of manufactures and some services being redirected to other destinations, notably the USA and Europe. Merchandise exports rose by 23% in 2000–01 against the previous year while imports rose by 7%. Australia is the world's largest exporter of black coal, bauxite, lead, diamonds and mineral sands.

Imports and Exports. Merchandise imports and exports for years ending 30 June (in \$A1m.):

	Imports	Exports
1997–98	90,684	87,768
1998–99	97,611	85,991
1999–2000	110,078	97,286
2000–01	118,264	119,062

The Australian customs tariff provides for preferences to goods produced in and shipped from certain countries as a result of reciprocal trade agreements. These include the UK, New Zealand, Canada and Ireland.

Merchandise exports and imports, 2000–01 (in \$A1m.):

	Exports	Imports
Live animals	871	61
Meat and preparations	5,772	131
Dairy products and eggs	2,383	306
Fish, shellfish and their preparations	1,538	871
Cereals and preparations	5,405	304
Vegetables and fruit	1,505	775
Sugar, sugar preparations and honey	218	126
Coffee, tea, cocoa, spices and their manufactures	250	592
Animal feed (excl. unmilled cereal)	976	182
Miscellaneous edible products	439	887
Beverages	1,931	680
Tobacco and manufactures	61	227
Raw hides and skins	794	2
Oil seeds and oleaginous fruit	725	82
Crude rubber (incl. synthetic and reclaimed)	10	132
Cork and wood	888	494
Pulp and waste paper	44	329
Textile fibres and their wastes	5,590	140
Crude fertilizers, minerals (not coal, petroleum, gems)	507	197
Metal ores and scrap	14,761	279

	Exports	Imports
Crude animal and vegetable materials	273	269
Coal, coke and briquettes	10,840	10
Petroleum and products	10,868	10,295
Gas, natural and manufactured	3,504	167
Animal oils and fats	214	11
Fixed vegetable oils and fats	37	240
Processed oils and fats, waxes thereof	49	34
Organic chemicals	118	2,854
Inorganic chemicals	547	911
Dyeing, colouring and tanning materials	660	566
Medicinal and pharmaceutical products	2,231	4,371
Essential oils, perfume and cleansing preparations	396	1,070
Manufactured fertilizers	134	836
Plastics in primary forms	224	1,209
Plastics in non-primary forms	202	976
Chemical materials and products	634	1,406
Leather and manufactures, dressed furskins	552	193
Rubber manufactures	172	1,412
Cork and wood manufactures (not furniture)	219	521
Paper, board and pulp	587	2,444
Textile yarn, fabrics, made-up articles and related products	596	2,607
Non-metallic mineral goods	1,022	1,871
Iron and steel	741	1,430
Non-ferrous metals	9,398	863
Metal manufactures	724	2,714
Power generators	887	2,701
Special machinery, industrial	1,339	3,835
Metalworking machinery	206	436
General machinery and parts, industrial	1,215	5,729
Office machines and data-processing equipment	1,557	8,317
Telecommunications and sound recording equipment	1,455	7,938
Electrical machinery and parts	1,718	6,782
Road vehicles (inc. air-cushion vehicles)	3,833	14,346
Other transport equipment	1,197	3,409
Sanitary, plumbing, heating and lighting fittings, pre-fabricated buildings	88	378
Furniture and parts	135	1,130
Travel goods, handbags etc.	14	477
Clothing and accessories	348	3,188
Footwear	64	932
Professional, scientific and controlling instruments	1,250	2,740
Photographic and optical goods, watches and clocks	1,107	1,628
Miscellaneous manufactured articles	1,448	6,332
Other commodities and transactions	1,860	53
Gold and other coin	69	10
Non-monetary gold	5,110	1,688
Confidential items of trade	4,330	137

Trade by bloc or country in 2000–01 (in $A1m.):

	Exports	Imports
APEC	87,353	83,540
ASEAN	15,390	17,477
EU	13,963	25,509
OPEC	8,605	6,504
China	6,846	9881
Japan	23,479	15,371
South Korea	9,209	4,710
New Zealand	6,872	4,565
Singapore	5,997	3,898
Taiwan	5,871	3,327
Indonesia	3,119	3,277
Malaysia	2,506	4,177
Germany	1,490	6,174
UK	4,639	6,321
USA	11,654	22,356

COMMUNICATIONS

Roads. As at June 1999 controlled access roads (motorways excluding tolled roads) totalled 1,563 km; national highways, 18,620 km; rural arterial, 94,854 km; urban arterial, 12,398 km; rural local, 600,725 km; urban local, 84,845 km.

In Dec. 2001 there were 10,101,441 passenger vehicles, 1,819,993 light commercial vehicles, 424,185 trucks, 70,196 buses, 370,982 motorcycles and 35,164 campervans. New registrations in 2001 included 646,010 passenger vehicles, 104,770 light commercial vehicles, 17,707 trucks, 2,969 buses and 34,762 motorcycles.

In 2001, 1,756 persons were killed in road accidents (1,819 in 2000).

Rail. Privatization of government railways began in Victoria in 1994 with West Coast Railway and Hoys Transport being granted seven-year franchises. A three-year extension was granted to West Coast Railway in 2001. Specialised Container Transport (SCT) won the first private rail freight franchise in 1995 followed by TNT (now Toll Holdings). Australian National Railway Commission was sold by the Commonwealth Government in Nov. 1997 and in Feb. 1999 V/Line Freight Corporation, owned by the Victorian Government, was sold to Freight Australia. Rail passenger services in Victoria were franchised in mid-1999. The Australian Railroad Group acquired Western Australia's government rail freight operation, Westrail, in Nov. 2000. Agreement has been reached by the Federal, New South Wales and Victorian Governments that the sale of freight operator National Rail Corporation (NRC) should go ahead and the New South Wales Government is proceeding with the privatization of FreightCorp. These two sales leave QR as the only government-owned rail freight operator in Australia.

The total length of track in 1998–99 was 4,010 km (broad gauge, 1,600 mm); 16,380 km (standard, 1,435 mm); 15,120 km (narrow, 1,067 mm); 4,150 km (610 mm gauge); and 265 km (dual gauge). In the financial year 1999–2000 a total of 508m. tonnes of freight were carried with a total revenue of $A3bn.; passengers carried totalled 618·7m. urban (including train and tram); 10·5m. non-urban.

Under various Commonwealth–State standardization agreements, all the State capitals are now linked by standard gauge track. Work is under way on the 'AustralAsia Rail Project', which involves the construction of 1,410 km standard gauge railway between Alice Springs and Darwin. It is due for completion before the end of 2003.

There are also private industrial and tourist railways, and tramways in Adelaide, Melbourne and Sydney.

Civil Aviation. Qantas Airways is Australia's principal international airline. In 1992 Qantas merged with Australian Airlines, and in 1993, 25% of the company was purchased by British Airways. The remainder is government-owned. Qantas relaunched Australian Airlines in Oct. 2002 to connect Asia-Pacific with Cairns and the Gold Coast. In 1999 Qantas flew 292·7m. km, carrying 16,347,800 passengers (6,222,200 on international flights). A total of 54 international airlines operated air services to and from Australia in 2000–01. There are 13 international airports, the main ones being Adelaide, Brisbane, Cairns, Darwin, Melbourne, Perth and Sydney. International passenger traffic increased from 4·12m. in 1980 to 16·49m. in 2000, an average annual growth of 7·2%. International cargo (freight and mail) increased from 133,000 tonnes in 1980 to 709,000 tonnes in 2000, an average annual growth of 8·7%.

Sydney (Kingsford Smith) handled the most traffic in Australia in 2000 (22,393,629 passengers, of which 14,195,306 on domestic flights), followed by Melbourne International and Brisbane.

Internal airlines (domestic and regional) carried 31,356,096 passengers in 1999–2000. Domestic airlines were deregulated in Oct. 1990.

At 31 March 1999 there were 278 licensed aerodromes in Australia and its external territories.

Shipping. The chief ports are Sydney, Botany Bay, Newcastle, Port Kembla, Melbourne, Geelong, Adelaide, Hastings, Gladstone, Brisbane, Hobart, Fremantle, Dampier, Pt Hedland, Hay Point, Pt Walcott and Townsville. At 30 June 2000 the trading fleet comprised 77 vessels totalling 2,283,336 DWT, 1,729,770 GRT.

Coastal cargo handled at Australian ports in 1999–2000 (in gross weight tonnes): loaded, 51·3m.; unloaded, 50·7m. International trade loaded, 462·2m. tonnes;

unloaded, 56·6m. tonnes. Calls to ports made by commercial ships in 1999–2000 totalled 24,600 with 230 made by passenger vessels.

Telecommunications. Australian telecommunications are in the latter stages of an evolution from a state-owned monopoly. In 1989 the domestic market became a regulated monopoly with Telstra as the government-owned company providing all services and, in 1991, a duopoly (with Optus) in fixed network services. In 1993 Vodafone joined Telstra and Optus in the provision of mobile phone services. A new regulatory regime was created by the introduction of the Telecommunications Act 1997 and both markets were opened to wholesale and retail competition. There is no limit to the number of carriers that can hold licences under the new arrangements and by June 2000 a total of 72 licences had been issued. The Australian Communications Authority (ACA) and the Australian Competition and Consumer Commission (ACCC) are the primary regulators with responsibility for the industry's development.

Telephone main lines numbered 10,050,000 in 2000 (524·6 per 1,000 inhabitants), and there were 8,900,000 PCs in use, or 464·6 per 1,000 persons. In Feb. 2002 there were 12·87m. mobile phone subscribers (the largest supplier being Optus, with 4·59m. subscribers) and 10·63m. Internet users.

Three telecommunications satellites are in orbit covering the entire continent.

Postal Services. Postal services are operated by Australia Post, operating under the Australian Postal Corporation Act 1989 as a government business enterprise. Revenue was $A3,732·6m. in 2000–01, expenditure $A3,300·5m. There were 4,787 post offices and other agencies in 2000–01, and 4,761·1m. postal items were handled.

SOCIAL INSTITUTIONS

Justice. The judicial power of the Commonwealth of Australia is vested in the High Court of Australia (the Federal Supreme Court), in the Federal courts created by the Federal Parliament (the Federal Court of Australia and the Family Court of Australia) and in the State courts invested by Parliament with Federal jurisdiction.

High Court. The High Court consists of a Chief Justice and six other Justices, appointed by the Governor-General in Council. The Constitution confers on the High Court original jurisdiction, *inter alia*, in all matters arising under treaties or affecting consuls or other foreign representatives, matters between the States of the Commonwealth, matters to which the Commonwealth is a party and matters between residents of different States. Federal Parliament may make laws conferring original jurisdiction on the High Court, *inter alia*, in matters arising under the Constitution or under any laws made by the Parliament. It has in fact conferred jurisdiction on the High Court in matters arising under the Constitution and in matters arising under certain laws made by Parliament.

The High Court may hear and determine appeals from its own Justices exercising original jurisdiction, from any other Federal Court, from a Court exercising Federal jurisdiction and from the Supreme Courts of the States. It also has jurisdiction to hear and determine appeals from the Supreme Courts of the Territories. The right of appeal from the High Court to the Privy Council in London was abolished in 1986.

Other Federal Courts. Since 1924, four other Federal courts have been created to exercise special Federal jurisdiction, i.e. the Federal Court of Australia, the Family Court of Australia, the Australian Industrial Court and the Federal Court of Bankruptcy. The Federal Court of Australia was created by the Federal Court of Australia Act 1976 and began to exercise jurisdiction on 1 Feb. 1977. It exercises such original jurisdiction as is invested in it by laws made by the Federal Parliament including jurisdiction formerly exercised by the Australian Industrial Court and the Federal Court of Bankruptcy, and in some matters previously invested in either the High Court or State and Territory Supreme Courts. The Federal Court also acts as a court of appeal from State and Territory courts in relation to Federal matters. Appeal from the Federal Court to the High Court will be by way of special leave only. The State Supreme Courts have also been invested with Federal jurisdiction in bankruptcy.

State Courts. The general Federal jurisdiction of the State courts extends, subject to certain restrictions and exceptions, to all matters in which the High Court has jurisdiction or in which jurisdiction may be conferred upon it.

Industrial Tribunals. The chief federal industrial tribunal is the Australian Conciliation and Arbitration Commission, constituted by presidential members (with the status of judges) and commissioners. The Commission's functions include settling industrial disputes, making awards, determining the standard hours of work and wage fixation. Questions of law, the judicial interpretation of awards and imposition of penalties in relation to industrial matters are dealt with by the Industrial Division of the Federal Court.

In June 2000 the daily prison population averaged 21,714.

Each State has its own individual police service which operates almost exclusively within its State boundaries. State police investigations include murder, robbery, street-level drug dealing, kidnapping, domestic violence and motor vehicle offences. State police activities are broadly known as community policing.

The role of the Australian Federal Police (AFP) is to enforce Commonwealth criminal law and protect Commonwealth and national interests from crime in Australia and overseas. Responsibilities include combating organized crime, transnational crime, money laundering, illicit drug trafficking, e-crime, the investigation of fraud against the Australian Government, and handling special references from Government. The AFP also provides a protection service to dignitaries and crucial witnesses as well as community policing services to the people of the Australian Capital Territory, Jervis Bay and Australia's External Territories.

Total Australian Federal Police personnel as at 30 June 2002 was 3,051, of which 2,043 were sworn employees (police members) and 1,008 unsworn employees. There are approximately 45,000 police officers in Australia.

Religion. Under the Constitution the Commonwealth cannot make any law to establish any religion, to impose any religious observance or to prohibit the free exercise of any religion. The following percentages refer to those religions with the largest number of adherents at the census of 1996. Answering the census question on religious adherence was not obligatory, however.

Christian, 71% of population: Catholic, 27·0%; Anglican, 22·0%; Uniting Church, 7·5%; Presbyterian and Reformed, 3·8%; Orthodox, 2·8%; Baptist, 1·7%; Lutheran, 1·4%; Pentecostal, 1·0%; Churches of Christ, 0·4%; Jehovah's Witnesses, 0·5%; Salvation Army, 0·4%; other Christian, 2·4%. Religions other than Christian 3·4%; no religion, 16·6%; no statement, 9·0%.

The Anglican Synod voted for the ordination of 10 women in Nov. 1992.

Thompson, R. C., *Religion in Australia, a History.* OUP, 1995

Education. The governments of the Australian States and Territories have the major responsibility for education, including the administration and substantial funding of primary, secondary, and technical and further education. In most States, a single Education Department is responsible for these three levels but in Queensland, Western Australia and the Northern Territory, separate departments deal with school-based and technical and further education issues.

The Australian government provides supplementary finance to the States for government schools, provides the bulk of the public funding that goes to non-government schools and is responsible for direct funding of the higher education sector. It has special responsibilities for student assistance, education programmes for indigenous people and children from non-English-speaking backgrounds, and for international relations in education.

The Australian Constitution empowers the Federal government to make grants to the States and Territories and to place conditions upon such grants. The Commonwealth has worked with the States and Territories to put in place a new set of National Goals for Schooling in the Twenty-First Century, and to develop national performance measures in key areas of schooling including literacy, numeracy, science and information technology.

School attendance is compulsory between the ages of six and 15 years (16 years in Tasmania), at either a government school or a recognized non-government educational institution. Many children attend pre-schools for a year before entering school (usually in sessions of two–three hours, for two–five days per week).

Government schools are usually co-educational and comprehensive. Non-government schools have been traditionally single-sex, particularly in secondary schools, but there is a trend towards co-education. Tuition is free at government schools, but fees are normally charged at non-government schools.

In Aug. 2001 there were 6,942 government (and 2,654 non-government) primary and secondary schools with 152,138 (69,789) full-time teachers and 2,248,481 (1,019,660) full-time pupils.

Vocational education and training (VET) in Australia is essentially a partnership between the Commonwealth, the States and Territories and industry. The Commonwealth is involved in VET through an agreed set of national arrangements for sharing responsibility with the States and Territories. The current mechanism for giving effect to this is the Australian National Training Authority (ANTA) Agreement, which sets out the roles and responsibilities for VET: they provide two-thirds of the funding and have all of the regulatory responsibility for the sector. They are also the 'owners' of the network of public Technical and Further Education (TAFE) institutes. In 2000 publicly-funded VET programmes were provided by some 86 TAFEs and other government institutions, 1,139 community education providers, and by some 3,388 other providers including registered training organizations. In 2000 there were 1·75m. people participating in VET.

In 2000, 45 higher education institutions received Commonwealth Government funding. Most of these institutions operate under State and Territory legislation although several operate under Commonwealth legislation. There is also a completely privately-funded university and numerous private higher education providers in a range of specialist fields. Institutions established by appropriate legislation are autonomous and have the authority to accredit their own programmes and are primarily responsible for their own quality assurance. There were 695,445 university students in 2000, of which 95,607 were overseas students. The total revenue of the higher education system was estimated at around $A9bn. in 2000. Fields of university study with the largest number of award course students in 1999 were administration, business, economics and law (26%); arts, humanities and social sciences (24%); and science (16%).

The higher education sector contributes a significant proportion of the research and research training undertaken in Australia. The Australian Research Council provides advice on research issues and administers the allocation of some research grants to higher education sector researchers and institutions.

The Commonwealth Government offers a number of programmes which provide financial assistance to students. The Youth Allowance is available for eligible full-time students aged 16 to 24, depending on the circumstances of study. Austudy is available to eligible full-time students aged over 25. Abstudy provides financial assistance for eligible Aboriginal and Torres Strait Islanders who undertake full-time or part-time study. AIC—the Assistance for Isolated Children scheme—provides special support to families whose children are isolated from schooling or who have physical disabilities.

Most Australian students contribute to the cost of their higher education through the Higher Education Contribution Scheme (HECS). Most students can choose to make an upfront contribution (with a 25% discount) or to defer all or part of their payment until their income reaches a certain level when they must begin repaying their contribution through the taxation system. Overseas students generally pay full tuition fees. Universities are also able to offer full-fee places in postgraduate courses and to a limited number of domestic undergraduate students. In 2000 Australia hosted approximately 150,000 international students, mostly from Asia, who contributed around $A3·7bn. to the local economy in fees and expenditure on goods and services.

National bodies with a co-ordinating, planning or funding role include: the Australian National Training Authority (ANTA); the ANTA Ministerial Council, comprising the Federal and State and Territory Ministers for training; the Conference of Directors-General of Education, the Australian Council for Educational Research and advisory bodies, the National Aboriginal Education Committee, Australian Research Council—Department of Education, Training and Youth Affairs; Australian Education International; Australian Qualifications Framework Advisory Board; Ministerial Council on Education, Employment, Training and Youth Affairs; and National Office of Overseas Skills Recognition and Open Learning Australia.

Total operating expenses of Australian Government on education in 1999–2000 were \$A34,036m. (5·4% of GDP). Private expenditure on education amounted to \$A9,575m. (1·5% of GDP). The figures include government grants to the private sector which are also included in the operating expenses of Australian governments.

The adult literacy rate in 1999 was at least 99%.

Health. In 1999–2000 there were 748 public hospitals, including 24 psychiatric hospitals and 509 private hospitals, including 24 psychiatric hospitals; there were an average 2·8 public hospital beds per 1,000 population (down from 3·3 in 1995–96). In 1999–2000 there were 163,200 registered nurses, 34,600 general medical practitioners, 12,400 physiotherapists and 6,800 dentists. The Royal Flying Doctor Service serves remote areas. Estimated total government expenditure on health services (public and private sectors) in 1999–2000 was \$A53·7bn. (\$A51·0bn in 1998–99), representing 8·5% of GDP.

At 31 Dec. 2000 there were estimated to be 20,955 HIV cases, 8,616 AIDS diagnoses and 6,017 deaths following AIDS.

By 1999, 20·8% of the adult population were considered obese (having a body mass index over 30), compared to 8·7% in 1990 and 7·1% in 1980.

Welfare. All Commonwealth government social security pensions, benefits and allowances are financed from the Commonwealth government's general revenue. In addition, assistance is provided for welfare services.

Age Pensions—age pensions are payable to men 65 years of age or more who have lived in Australia for a specified period and, unless permanently blind, also satisfy an income and assets test. The minimum age for women's eligibility was raised by six months on 1 July 2001 and is being lifted in six-month increments every two years until 1 July 2013 when it will be 65 years. The qualifying age at 1 July 2001 was 62 years. In the year ending 30 June 2001, 1,785,554 age pensioners received a total of \$A15,616·5m.

Disability Support Pension (DSP)—payable to persons aged 16 years or over with a physical, intellectual or psychiatric impairment of at least 20%, assessed as being unable to work for at least 30 hours a week. DSP for those of 21 years or over is paid at the same rate as Age Pensions and is subject to the same means test except for those who are permanently blind. In the year ending 30 June 2001, 623,926 disability support pensioners received a total of \$A5,849·8m.

Carer Payment—payable to a person without other means of support who is providing constant care and attention at home for a severely disabled person aged 16 or over, or a person who is frail aged, either permanently or for an extended period. Since 1 July 1998 Carer Payment has been extended to carers of children under 16 years of age with profound disabilities. The rate of Carer Payment is the same as for other pensions. In the year ending 30 June 2001, 57,190 carers received a total of \$A480·9m.

Sickness Allowance—paid to those over school-leaving age but below Age Pension age who are unable to work or continue full-time study temporarily owing to illness or injury. Eligibility rests on the person having a job or study course to which they can return. In the year ending 30 June 2001 a total of \$A95·6m. was paid to beneficiaries.

Family Tax Benefit—replaced *Family Allowance* and *Family Tax Payment* on 1 July 2000. Family Tax Benefit Part A is paid to assist families with children under 21 years of age or dependent full-time students aged 21–24 years; Family Tax Benefit Part B provides additional assistance to families with only one income earner and children under 16 years of age or dependent full-time students aged 16–18 years. Both benefits are subject to an income and assets test. In the year ending 30 June 2001, 2,980,746 families comprising 5,758,423 children received a total of \$A6,391·5m.

Parenting Payment (Single) and (Partnered)—is paid to assist those who care for children under 16, with income and assets under certain amounts, and have been an Australian resident for at least two years or a refugee or have become a lone parent while an Australian resident. Parenting Payment (Single) is paid to lone parents under pension rates and conditions; Parenting Payment (Partnered) is paid to one of the parents in the couple. [Since 1 July 2000 the basic component of

Parenting Payment (Partnered) was incorporated into Family Tax Benefit with 375,233 beneficiaries transferring to Family Tax Benefit Part B.] In the year ending 30 June 2001, 424,616 Parenting Payment (Single) beneficiaries and 214,721 Parenting Payment (Partnered) beneficiaries received a total of $A5,325·7m.

Maternity Allowance—was introduced from 1 Feb. 1996 to assist families with the costs associated with a new baby (including foregone income). It is paid for each new child to families meeting the Family Tax Benefit A residence, income and assets criteria. Since 1 Jan. 1998 Maternity Allowance is paid in two stages as part of the initiative to boost immunization rates. A lump sum of $A780 (1 July 2001) is paid within 13 weeks of the birth and an additional $A208 (1 July 2001) is paid when the specific immunization or exemption requirements have been met. Families are not disadvantaged in cases where children are not immunized for medical reasons, or where parents conscientiously object to immunization. In the year ended 30 June 2001 a total of $A217·9m. was paid.

Newstart Allowance (NSA)—payable to those who are unemployed and are over 21 years of age but less than Age Pension age. Eligibility is subject to income and assets tests and recipients must satisfy the 'activity test' whereby they are actively seeking and willing to undertake suitable paid work, including casual and part-time work. To be eligible for benefit a person must have resided in Australia for at least 12 months preceding his or her claim or intend to remain in Australia permanently; unemployment must not be as a result of industrial action by that person or by members of a union to which that person is a member. In the year ended 30 June 2001 a total of $A4,885·4m. was paid to NSA beneficiaries.

Youth Allowance—replaced five former schemes for young people, including the Youth Training Allowance. In the year ending 30 June 2001 a total of $A2,101·9m. was paid to YA beneficiaries.

Mature Age Allowance (MAA)—paid to older long-term unemployed, over 60 years of age but less than Age Pension age. MAA is non-activity tested. In the year ended June 2001 a total of $A352·6m. was paid.

Service Pensions—are paid by the Department of Veterans' Affairs. Male veterans who have reached the age of 60 years or are permanently unemployable, and who served in a theatre of war, are eligible subject to an income and assets test. The minimum age for female veterans' eligibility is being lifted from 55 to 60 years in six-month increments every two years over the period 1995–2013. The qualifying age at 1 July 2001 was 57 years. Wives of service pensioners are also eligible, provided that they do not receive a pension from the Department of Social Security. Disability pension is a compensatory payment in respect of incapacity attributable to war service. It is paid at a rate commensurate with the degree of incapacity and is free of any income test. In the year ended 30 June 2001, $A2,832·3m. of service pensions and $A2,314·1m. of disability and dependants' pensions were paid out; at 30 June 2001 there were 290,695 eligible veterans.

In addition to cash benefits, welfare services are provided, either directly or through State and local government authorities and voluntary agencies, for people with special needs.

Medicare—covers: automatic entitlement under a single public health fund to medical and optometrical benefits of 85% of the Medical Benefits Schedule fee, with a maximum patient payment for any service where the Schedule fee is charged; access without direct charge to public hospital accommodation and to inpatient and outpatient treatment by doctors appointed by the hospital; the restoration of funds for community health to approximately the same real level as 1975; a reduction in charges for private treatment in shared wards of public hospitals, and increases in the daily bed subsidy payable to private hospitals.

The Medicare programme is financed in part by a 1·5% levy on taxable incomes, with low income cut-off points, which were $A13,807 p.a. for a single person in 2000–01 and $A23,299 p.a. for a family with an extra allowance of $A2,140 for each child. A levy surcharge of 1% was introduced from 1 July 1997 for single individuals with taxable incomes in excess of $A50,000 p.a. and couples and families with combined taxable incomes in excess of $A100,000 who do not have private hospital cover through private health insurance.

Medicare benefits are available to all persons ordinarily resident in Australia. Visitors from the UK, New Zealand, Italy, Sweden, the Netherlands and Malta have immediate access to necessary medical treatment, as do all visitors staying more than six months.

CULTURE

Broadcasting. Broadcasting is regulated by the Australian Broadcasting Authority (ABA), established under the Broadcasting Services Act 1992. Foreign ownership of commercial radio and TV companies is restricted to 20%. The national broadcasting service is provided by the Australian Broadcasting Corporation (ABC) (established 1932), an independent statutory corporation receiving 82% of its funding from the Federal Government and the remainder from independent sources, and the Special Broadcasting Service (established 1978). The latter provides radio and TV services in more than 100 languages. The transmission system is PAL. There are also commercial radio and TV services operated by companies under licence, subscription TV services, community radio services operated on a non-profit basis and a parliamentary radio service to state capitals, Canberra and Newcastle. The international service Radio Australia broadcasts via short-wave to Papua New Guinea and the Pacific and also via satellite to the Asia-Pacific regions in English and other languages. Digital television broadcasting commenced in the five mainland metropolitan areas on 1 Jan. 2001. As at 30 June 2001 the ABA had licensed 48 commercial television TV services, 255 commercial radio services and 286 community radio services. The ABA had allocated licences for six new commercial radio and 10 community radio services in 2000–01.

In 2000 there were estimated to be 7·0m. TV households and 14·13m. TV sets (99% of households had at least one set). As at Sept. 2000 it was estimated there were 1·32m. pay-TV subscribers, representing 18·86% of households.

Cinema. At 30 June 2000 there were 326 cinema sites with a total of 1,514 screens, 374,000 seats and paid admissions of $A79·4m.

Press. There were 49 daily metropolitan newspapers in 2000 (2 national, 10 metropolitan and 37 regional). The papers with the largest circulations are the *Sunday Telegraph* (New South Wales), with an average of 724,000 per issue in 1999; the *Sunday Mail* (Queensland), with an average of 594,000 per issue; and the *Sun-Herald* (New South Wales), with an average of 591,000 per issue. At least 30 magazines have a circulation of over 85,000 copies per issue.

Tourism. As at 30 Nov. 2000 the total number of overseas visitors for the year stood at 4·4m. (a 9·5% increase on 1999) and an estimated $A13·2bn. had been spent. The top source countries for visitors in 1999 were Japan (662,500); New Zealand (660,800); UK (508,900); USA (392,500); Singapore (234,100); and Germany (140,000). Tourism is Australia's largest single earner of foreign exchange.

Festivals. There are around 1,300 festivals annually.

Libraries. In the year ended 30 April 1999, almost 5·7m. people visited a national, State or local library at least once. Total government funding for libraries in 1998–99 was $A756·2m.

Theatre and Opera. Opera Australia is the largest performing arts organization in the country with almost 250 performances staged annually. The last major survey, held in March 1995, revealed that 2,722,100 people aged 15 years and over had attended at least one performance of musical theatre in the previous year; 2,336,300 people, other theatre; 2,634,400 people, other performing arts; 1,407,500 people, dance performances.

Museums and Galleries. In 2000 there were some 2,000 museums, including 250 art museums and 400 historic properties, with a total of 61·6m. artworks and artefacts. Australian museums employ around 37,500 people and receive 27·5m. visitors annually. The majority (68%) of their $A716m. income comes from the government.

DIPLOMATIC REPRESENTATIVES

Of Australia in the United Kingdom (Australia House, Strand, London, WC2B 4LA) *High Commissioner:* Michael L'Estrange.

Of the United Kingdom in Australia (Commonwealth Ave., Yarralumla, Canberra)
High Commissioner: Sir Alastair Goodlad, KCMG.

Of Australia in the USA (1601 Massachusetts Ave., NW, Washington, D.C., 20036)
Ambassador: Michael J. Thawley.

Of the USA in Australia (Moonah Pl., Canberra, A.C.T. 2600)
Ambassador: John Thomas Schieffer.

Of Australia to the United Nations
Ambassador: John Dauth, LVO.

Of Australia to the European Union
Ambassador: Joanna Hewitt.

FURTHER READING

Australian Bureau of Statistics (ABS). *Year Book Australia.—Pocket Year Book Australia.—
   Monthly Summary of Statistics.* ABS also publish numerous specialized statistical digests.
Australian Encyclopædia. 12 vols. Sydney, 1983
Blainey, G., *A Short History of Australia.* Melbourne, 1996
The Cambridge Encyclopedia of Australia. CUP, 1994
Clark, M., *Manning Clark's History of Australia*; abridged by M. Cathcart. London, 1994
Concise Oxford Dictionary of Australian History. 2nd ed. OUP, 1995
Davison, Graeme, *et al.*, (eds.) *The Oxford Companion to Australian History.* 2nd ed. OUP,
   2002
Docherty, J. D., *Historical Dictionary of Australia.* Metuchen (NJ), 1993
Foster, S. G., Marsden, S. and Russell, R. (compilers), *Federation. A guide to records.*
   Australian Archives, Canberra, 2000
Gilbert, A. D. and Inglis, K. S. (eds.) *Australians: a Historical Library.* 5 vols. CUP, 1988
Hirst, John, *The Sentimental Nation: The Making of the Australian Commonwealth.* OUP,
   2000.—*Australia's Democracy: A Short History.* Allen and Unwin, Sydney, 2002
Irving, H. (ed.) *The Centenary Companion to Australian Federation.* CUP, 2000
Kepars, I., *Australia.* [Bibliography] 2nd ed. ABC-Clio, Oxford and Santa Barbara (CA), 1994
Knightley, Phillip, *Australia: A biography of a Nation.* Cape, London, 2000
Macintyre, S., *A Concise History of Australia.* CUP, 2000
Oxford History of Australia. vol 2: 1770–1860. OUP, 1992. vol 5: 1942–88. OUP, 1990
The Oxford Illustrated Dictionary of Australian History. OUP, 1993
Turnbull, M., *The Reluctant Republic.* London, 1994
Ward, Stuart, *Australia and the British Embrace: The Demise of the Imperial Ideal.* Melbourne
   Univ. Press, 2002

A more specialized title is listed under RELIGION, *above*

National library: The National Library, Canberra, ACT.
National statistical office: Australian Bureau of Statistics (ABS), Belconnen, ACT. The
   statistical services of the states are integrated with the Bureau.
ABS Website: http://www.abs.gov.au/

AUSTRALIAN TERRITORIES AND STATES

AUSTRALIAN CAPITAL TERRITORY

KEY HISTORICAL EVENTS

The area, now the Australian Capital Territory (ACT), was explored in 1820 by
Charles Throsby who named it Limestone Plains. Settlement commenced in 1824.
Until its selection as the seat of government, it was a quiet pastoral and agricultural
community with a few large holdings and a sprinkling of smaller settlers.

In 1901 the Commonwealth constitution stipulated that a land tract of at least 260
sq. km in area and not less than 160 km from Sydney be set aside from New South
Wales and reserved as a capital district. The Canberra site was adopted by the Seat
of Government Act 1908. The present site, together with an area for a port at Jervis

Bay, was surrendered by New South Wales and accepted by the Commonwealth in 1909. By subsequential proclamation the Territory became vested in the Commonwealth from 1 Jan. 1911. In 1911 an international competition held for the city plan was won by W. Burley Griffin of Chicago but construction was delayed by the First World War. It was not until 1927 that Canberra became the seat of government. Located on the Molonglo River surrounding an artificial lake, it was built as a compromise capital in order to stop squabbling between Melbourne and Sydney following the 1901 Federation of Australian States. Canberra's population has risen since its formal inauguration in 1927 owing to the continual expansion of government offices and the establishment of the National University.

In 1989 self-government was proclaimed and the first ACT assembly was elected in May of that year.

TERRITORY AND POPULATION

The total area is 2,360 sq. km, of which 60% is hilly or mountainous. Timbered mountains are located in the south and west, and plains and hill country in the north. The ACT lies within the upper Murrumbidgee River catchment, in the Murray-Darling Basin. The Murrumbidgee flows throughout the Territory from the south, and its tributary, the Molonglo, from the east. The Molonglo was dammed in 1964 to form Lake Burley Griffin. As at 31 Dec. 2001 the resident population was 322,600, an increase of 0·1% from Dec. 2000. Population (1996 census), 299,243.

SOCIAL STATISTICS

2000: births, 4,065, deaths, 1,300; marriages, 1,735; divorces, 1,561. Infant mortality (per 1,000 live births), 4·2.

CLIMATE

ACT has a continental climate, characterized by a marked variation in temperature between seasons, with warm to hot summers and cold winters.

CONSTITUTION AND GOVERNMENT

The ACT became self-governing on 11 May 1989. It is represented by 2 members in the Commonwealth House of Representatives and 2 senators.

The parliament of the ACT, the *Legislative Assembly*, consists of 17 members elected for a 3-year term. Its responsibilities are at State and Local government level. The Legislative Assembly elects a Chief Minister and a 4-member cabinet.

RECENT ELECTIONS

At the elections of 20 Oct. 2001 the Labor party won 8 seats (41·7% of the vote) against the Liberal party with 7 seats (31·6%). The Green party and the Australian Democrats party won 1 seat each with 9·1% and 8% of the vote respectively.

CURRENT ADMINISTRATION

The ACT Australian Labor Party Ministry was as follows in Feb. 2003:

Chief Minister, Attorney-General, Minister for Community Affairs, Corrections and the Environment: Jon Stanhope.

Deputy Chief Minister, Treasurer, Minister for Economic Development, Business and Tourism, Sport, Racing and Gaming: Ted Quinlan. *Health and Planning:* Simon Corbell. *Disability, Housing and Community Services, Urban Services, Arts and Heritage and Police and Emergency Services:* Bill Wood. *Education, Youth and Family Services, Women and Industrial Relations:* Katy Gallagher.

Speaker: Wayne Berry.

ACT Government website: http://www.act.gov.au

ECONOMY

Budget. The ACT is treated equitably with the States and the Northern Territory regarding revenue raising, expenditure and assistance from the Commonwealth government. The Territory was one of the first governments to introduce accrual budgeting and accounting, and financial management reforms in Australia. In 2001–02 the Territory received revenues of $A2,369m. and had expenditure of $A2,294m. achieving a surplus of $A75m. on an accrual basis.

Banking and Finance. Bank Deposits as at March 2002: deposits, $A6,597m.; loans, $A7,962m.; Housing Finance for Owner Occupation (all lenders), total commitments 2000–01, $A1,159m.

ENERGY AND NATURAL RESOURCES

Electricity. See NEW SOUTH WALES.

Water. ACTEW (Australian Capital Territory, Electricity & Water) provides more than 100m. litres of water each day to Canberra residents. The Cotter River catchment includes the Cotter (4,700m. litre) storage capacity, Bendora (10,700m.) and Corin Dams (75,400m.). Googong Dam (124,500m. litres), developed on the Queanbeyan River in New South Wales, is used to meet peaks in demand in summer or during extensive dry periods. There were 44 reservoirs in 2000–01 with a capacity of 912m. litres.

Agriculture. Sheep and/or beef cattle farming is the main agricultural activity. In the year ended June 2000 there were 96 farming establishments with a total area of 47,000 ha. The gross value of commodities produced rose by 2% to $A15·1m. over the previous financial year. Increases in the value of crop production were partially offset by a decrease in the value of livestock products.

Forestry. There is about 23,838 ha of plantation forest in the ACT (approximately 10% of the land area). Most of the area is managed for the production of softwood timber. The established pine forests, such as Kowen, Stromlo, Uriarra and Pierces Creek, are in the northern part of the Territory. After harvesting, 500–1,000 ha of land are planted with new pine forest each year. No native forests or woodlands have been cleared for plantation since the mid-1970s.

INDUSTRY

Turnover in manufacturing industries in 1999–2000 increased by 6% over the previous year to a total of $A640m.

Labour. In May 2002 there were an estimated 170,300 employed persons and in 1999–2000, 9,100 unemployed persons. The annual average unemployment rate in the ACT has fallen since 1996–97 (7·5%) to an average of 4·9% in 2000–01.

In the year ending May 2002, 22% of the ACT labour force was employed in public administration and defence; 15% in property and business services; 14% in retail trade.

Trade Unions. As at Aug. 2001 there were 32,600 people belonging to a trade union (22% of total employees).

INTERNATIONAL TRADE

Imports and Exports. In 2000–01 imports were valued at $A4·8m. (54% decrease on 1999–2000); exports at $A21·6m. (35% decrease on 1999–2000). Manufactured goods accounted for 57% of total imports; optical instruments and apparatus, 86% of total exports.

COMMUNICATIONS

Roads. At April 2002 there were 2,610 km of road. At 31 March 2001 there were 232,057 vehicles registered in the ACT. In 2000–01, 20 fatalities were caused by traffic accidents.

Civil Aviation. In 2000–01 Canberra International Airport handled an estimated 2,114,173 passengers. Figures for 2001–02 are expected to be 13% down on this.

Telecommunications. In 2001 there were 175,305 people with home computer access (59% of the population) and 123,178 with home Internet access (51%).

Postal Services. See NEW SOUTH WALES.

SOCIAL INSTITUTIONS

Justice. In the year ending June 2001 there were 48,715 criminal incidents recorded by police, representing a decrease of 9% on the previous year. During 2000–01 there were 590 full-time sworn police officers in the ACT and 184 unsworn police staff.

The proportion of women in the ACT police force grew to 29% during 2000–01. Operational budget for the same financial year was $A65·7m.

Religion. At the 2001 census, 63% of the population were Christian. Of these, 45% were Roman Catholic and 29% Anglican. Non-Christian religions accounted for 5%, the largest groups being Buddhism, Islam and Hinduism.

Education. In Feb. 2002 there were 221 schools comprising 80 pre-schools, 136 primary and secondary schools (including colleges) and 5 special schools. Of these 175 were government schools. There was a total of 64,064 full-time students. There were four higher education institutions in 2001: the Signadou Campus of the Australian Catholic University (ACU) had 624 students enrolled; the Australian National University, 9,636 students; the University of Canberra, 8,675; and the Australian Defence Force Academy, 1,624.

Health. The ACT is serviced by three public and nine private hospitals (six of the private hospitals are day surgery only). At June 2001 there were 199 dental practitioners.

Welfare. At June 2000 there were 14,747 age pensioners (4·7% of ACT population); 5,948 persons received disability support pension (1·9%).

CULTURE
For the year ended 30 June 1998 total funding on culture by the ACT Government was $A28·1m.

Cinema. In the year to April 1999 cinemas attracted an attendance rate of 73·5%.

Tourism. In the year ended 30 June 2000 an estimated 182,400 international visitors came to the ACT, 7% of all international tourists to Australia. 14% of visitors were from the UK. At Dec. 2000 there were 60 tourist accommodation establishments with 15 rooms or more.

Libraries. At Jan. 2003 there were 8 government-operated libraries and 1 mobile service with 2 special libraries (the ACT Heritage Library and the Government and Assembly Library). 1·75m. people visited these libraries and borrowed a total of 2·5m. books.

Theatre and Opera. The renovated Canberra Playhouse opened in 1998.

Museums and Galleries. The Canberra Museum and Gallery opened in 1998.

FURTHER READING
Regional Statistics (Cat. no. 1362.8), Australian Capital Territory.
Australian Capital Territory in Focus (formerly *Statistical Summary*). Australian Bureau of Statistics. Annual.
Wigmore, L., *Canberra: A History of Australia's National Capital.* 2nd ed. Canberra, 1971

Sources: ACT in Focus 1307.8, Labour Force, Australia 6203.0 and *Labour Force, New South Wales and Australian Capital Territory 6201.1.*

NORTHERN TERRITORY

KEY HISTORICAL EVENTS
The Northern Territory, after forming part of New South Wales, was annexed on 6 July 1863 to South Australia and in 1901 entered the Commonwealth as a corporate part of South Australia. The Commonwealth Constitution Act of 1900 having made provision for the surrender to the Commonwealth of any territory by any state, an agreement was entered into on 7 Dec. 1907 for the transfer of the Northern Territory to the Commonwealth. It formally passed under the control of the Commonwealth government on 1 Jan. 1911. On 1 Feb. 1927 the Northern Territory was divided for administrative purposes into two territories but in 1931 it was again administered as a single territory under the control of an Administrator in Darwin. The Legislative Council for the Northern Territory, constituted in 1947, was reconstituted in 1959. In that year, citizenship rights were granted to Aboriginal people of 'full descent'. On 1 July 1978 self-government was granted to the Northern Territory.

TERRITORY AND POPULATION

The Northern Territory is bounded by the 26th parallel of S. lat. and 129° and 138° E. long. Its total area is 1,346,200 sq. km and includes adjacent islands. It has 5,100 km of mainland coastline and 2,100 km of coast around the islands. The greater part of the interior consists of a tableland rising gradually from the coast to a height of about 700 metres. On this tableland there are large areas of excellent pasturage. The southern part of the Territory is generally sandy and has a small rainfall, but water may be obtained by means of sub-artesian bores.

The population of the Territory at Dec. 2001 was 199,900. The 1996 census was 181,843. The capital, seat of government and principal port is Darwin, on the north coast; estimated population 69,698 at 30 June 2001. Other main centres include Katherine (8,965), 330 km south of Darwin; Alice Springs (26,990), in Central Australia; Tennant Creek (3,065), a rich mining centre 500 km north of Alice Springs; Nhulunbuy (3,918), a bauxite mining centre in the Gove Peninsula Province in eastern Arnhem Land; and Jabiru (1,161), a model town built to serve the rich Uranium Province in eastern Arnhem Land. Palmerston is a Darwin satellite town and Yulara is a resort village serving Uluru National Park and Ayers Rock. There also are a number of large self-contained Aboriginal communities. People identifying themselves as indigenous numbered 50,785 at the 2001 census. This includes people of Aboriginal and Torres Strait Islanders.

SOCIAL STATISTICS

2001 estimated totals: births, 3,822; deaths, 872; marriages, 781; divorces, 447. Infant mortality per 1,000 live births (2001 estimate), 9·9. Life expectancy, 1996: 69·2 years for males, 75·0 for females. The estimated annual rates per 1,000 population in 2001 were: births, 19·1; deaths, 4·4; marriages, 3·9; divorces, 2·2.

CLIMATE

See AUSTRALIA: Climate.

The highest temperature ever recorded in the NT was 118·9°F (48·3°C) at Finke in 1960, while the lowest recorded temperature was 18·5°F (−7·5°C) at Alice Springs in 1976.

CONSTITUTION AND GOVERNMENT

The Northern Territory (Self-Government) Act 1978 established the Northern Territory as a body politic as from 1 July 1978, with Ministers having control over and responsibility for Territory finances and the administration of the functions of government as specified by the Federal government. Regulations have been made conferring executive authority for the bulk of administrative functions. At 31 Dec. 1979 the only important powers retained by the Commonwealth related to rights in respect of Aboriginal land, some significant National Parks and the mining of uranium and other substances prescribed in the Atomic Energy Act. Proposed laws passed by the Legislative Assembly require the assent of the Administrator. The Governor-General may disallow any law assented to by the Administrator within six months of the Administrator's assent.

The Northern Territory has federal representation, electing 1 member to the House of Representatives and two members to the Senate.

The Legislative Assembly has 25 members, directly elected for a period of four years. The Chief Minister, Deputy Chief Minister and Speaker are elected by, and from, the members. The *Administrator* (John Anictomatis) appoints Ministers on the advice of the Leader of the majority party.

RECENT ELECTIONS

In parliamentary elections held in Aug. 2001 the Australian Labor Party won 13 seats against 10 for the Country Liberal Party.

CURRENT ADMINISTRATION

Administrator: John Anictomatis, AO.

The NT Territory Labor Party Cabinet was as follows in Feb. 2003:

Chief Minister, Treasurer, Minister for Territorial Development, Indigenous Affairs, Arts and Museums, Young Territorians, Senior Territorians and Women's Policy: Clare Martin.

AUSTRALIA

Deputy Chief Minister, Treasurer, Minister for Employment, Education and Training, and Racing, Gaming and Licensing: Syd Stirling. *Attorney General, Minister for Justice, Corporate and Information Services, Communications and Central Australia:* Peter Toyne. *Business, Industry and Resource Development, Asian Relations and Trade and Police, Fire and Emergency Services and Defence Support:* Paul Henderson. *Community Development, Housing, Sport and Recreation, Local Government and Regional Development:* John Ah Kit. *Health and Community Services:* Jane Aagaard. *Transport and Infrastructure, Lands and Planning, Ethnic Affairs, and Parks and Wildlife:* Kon Vatskalis. *Tourism, Primary Industry and Fisheries, Environment and Heritage, and Essential Services:* Chris Burns.

NT Government website: http://www.nt.gov.au/

ECONOMY

Budget. Revenue and expenditure in $A1m.:

	1999–2000	2000–01	2001–02
Revenue	1,883	2,003	2,099
Expenditure	1,888	1,873	1,892

Using uniform presentation standards, total revenue in 2001–02 was $A1,892m. of which $A1,691m. were grants to the Northern Territory from the Commonwealth, and $A408m. was raised by the Northern Territory government, which included $A218m. through state-like taxes.

Expenditure during 2001–02 included $A428m. for education; $A397m. for health; $A208m. for public order and safety; $A246m. for community services; and $A192m. for general public services.

General Government net debt increased by $A15m. to $A1,455m. in 2002.

Banking and Finance. At Sept. 2001 there were 11 banks operating in the Territory with total deposits, $A1,509m.; loans, $A3,463m.

ENERGY AND NATURAL RESOURCES

Environment. There are 93 parks and reserves covering 43,709 sq. km. Twelve of the parks are classified as national parks, including the Kakadu and Uluru-Kata Tjuta National Park which are included on the World Heritage List.

Electricity. The majority of electric power is supplied by the Power and Water Authority (PAWA). There is one other electricity generator in the Territory—NT Power Generation, with 6% of the market. At 30 June 2001 total electricity generated was 1,513 GWh.

Oil and Gas. The Timor Sea is a petroleum producing province with oil produced from five fields. Also containing more than 22m. cu. ft of known gas reserves, the Timor Sea is well on its way to becoming a significant gas province. The Territory is on the verge of a major development phase for gas reserves and gas-based manufacturing. Gas is currently supplied from the Palm Valley and Mereenie fields in the onshore Amadeus Basin to the Channel Island Power Station in Darwin via one of Australia's longest onshore gas pipelines. The value of energy mineral production in the Territory increased by 77·3% in 2000–01. The total value of oil and gas production in 2000–01 was $A2,622m., an increase of $A1,192m. over 1999–2000. This is largely a result of an increase in crude oil production which rose by 86·3% in 2000–01 with the first full production year at Laminaria and Corallina in the Timor Sea. The Territory produced 5,316 megalitres of crude oil and 458m. cu. metres of natural gas in 2000–01.

Water. The Power and Water Authority (PAWA) is responsible for providing water supply (also electric power and sewerage services) throughout the NT. The Aboriginal Essential Services Branch of PAWA maintains water supply to the 85 remote communities and Aboriginal outstations.

Minerals. Mining is the major contributor to the Territory's economy. Compared to 1999–2000 the overall value of production in the mining industry increased by 43·6% in 2000–01. This represents a $A1,256m. increase from $A2,884m. in 1999–2000 to $A4,138m. in 2000–01. Value of major mineral commodities production in 2000–01 (in $A1m.): bauxite/alumina, 682; gold, 323; uranium, 195; manganese, 152; lead/zinc concentrate, 126; diamonds, 20.

Agriculture. In the year ended June 2000 there were 367 agricultural establishments with a total area under holding of 67·5m. ha. Beef cattle production constitutes the largest farming industry with a total value for slaughter and products in the year ended 30 June 2000 of $A230·0m. During 2000–01 the value of fruit increased by 3·4% to $A70·8m. Fruit production consists mainly of bananas and mangoes. The banana crop has increased significantly from 625 tonnes in 1989 to 7,600 tonnes in 1999–2000. There were eight crocodile farms in 2001 producing a total of 16,335·25 kg of meat in the period Jan.–June 2001.

Forestry. In 2001 there were 35m. ha of native forest, accounting for 26% of the Territory's total land area. Of the total native forest cover, 1% is rainforest, 23% open forest and 76% woodland. Total area of plantation forest is around 5,500 ha, consisting mainly of softwoods. Hardwood plantations of fast growing Acacia Mangium have been established on the Tiwi Islands north of Darwin for the production of woodchip for paper pulp. In addition, a number of operations for the production of sandalwood oil and neem products have been established near Batchelor, south of Darwin. Teak plantations are planned for designated farmland in the Katherine/Daly development region.

Fisheries. The value of the fishing industry in 2000–01 decreased by 1·4% to $A142m. with significant decreases in trepang (41·3%), aquaculture (37·3%), and mud crabs (14·2%) compared with the previous year. Significant gains were made in the value of barramundi (22·3%), sea perch (10·7%) and prawns (28·5%).

INDUSTRY
At 30 June 2000 the manufacturing industry turnover was $A1,020·2m.; 3,300 persons were employed and salaries totalled $A144·9m. In Nov. 2001, 15,102 persons were employed in the wholesale and retail trade.

Labour. The labour force totalled 103,141 in Dec. 2001, of whom 97,100 were employed. The unemployment rate was 8·3%, up from 4·6% in Dec. 1999. Around 4,500 were estimated to have been employed at mines and on oil and gas projects in late 2000.

Trade Unions. In June 1996, 26 trade unions had 19,300 members.

INTERNATIONAL TRADE

Imports and Exports. In 2001–02 the value of the Territory's exports decreased by around 30·2% to $A2,972m. Major export destinations (figures in $A1m.): Singapore (1,001), Japan (497), China (414), Korea (298), Indonesia (175), USA (130). 2001–02 imports totalled $A782m. Major sources of imports for 2000–01 (figures in $A1m.): Singapore (189), Kuwait (137), USA (114), Japan (74), Norway (20).

COMMUNICATIONS

Roads. At 30 June 2001 there were 20,627 km of sealed and unsealed roads. Registered motor vehicles at 31 Dec. 2002 numbered 126,562, including 93,002 passenger vehicles, 3,216 motorcycles and 1,420 buses. There were 51 road accident fatalities in 2000.

Rail. In 1980 Alice Springs was linked to the Trans-continental network by a standard (1,435 mm) gauge railway to Tarcoola in South Australia (830 km). Construction began in 2001 on a new 1,410 km standard gauge line between Darwin and Alice Springs. This will create the AustralAsia Railway, linking Darwin and Adelaide and creating a new trade route between Asia and southern Australia. The $A1·3bn. project is being funded by $A165m. from the Northern Territory Government, $A165m. from the Commonwealth Government, $A150m. from the South Australian Government and $A750m. from the Asia Pacific Transport Company, which will build, own and operate the railway. The project is scheduled to be completed by the end of 2004 together with completion of Stage Two of Darwin's $A73m. East Arm Port, which will include a railway embankment and intermodal container terminal.

Civil Aviation. Darwin and most regional centres in the Territory are serviced by daily flights to all State capitals and major cities. In 1998 there were direct international services connecting Darwin to Bali, Brunei, Kuala Lumpur, Kupang and Singapore. In 2001 Darwin airport handled around 950,000 domestic and 450,00 international passengers, and Alice Springs around 750,000 domestic passengers.

Shipping. Regular freight shipping services connect Darwin with both the east and west coasts of Australia, Southeast Asia and the rest of the world. In 2001 there were nine shipping lines making regular calls, and cruise ships and naval vessels also include Darwin as a port of call.

A $90m. development of deepwater port facilities is nearing completion. The Port of Darwin is equipped to handle bulk, container and roll-on-roll-off traffic. 895 vessels visited the port in 2000–01 and it handled 904,783 tonnes of cargo in 1999–2000 (excluding fishing). There is a sheltered mooring basin which provides 85 non-tidal berths.

Commercial and pleasure vessels also call at the ports of Melville Bay (Gove) and Milner Bay (Groote Eylandt), and at Seven Spirit Bay on a regular basis.

Telecommunications. In 2001 there were 63,480 households with home computer access and 26,801 households with home Internet access.

Postal Services. At 30 June 1999 there were 548 Australia Post retail facilities in South Australia and Northern Territory.

SOCIAL INSTITUTIONS

Justice. Voluntary euthanasia for the terminally ill was legalized in 1995. However, the federal Prime Minister stated that the High Court of Australia would consider cases of euthanasia as murder, and the law was overturned by the Federal Senate on 24 March 1997. The first person to have recourse to legalized euthanasia died on 22 Sept. 1996.

Police personnel at 31 Dec. 2001, 896. In addition there were 49 Aboriginal community police officers. At June 2001 the Territory had three prisons with a daily average of 717 prisoners held.

Education. Education is compulsory from the age of 6 to 15 years. There were (Aug. 2001) 32,717 full-time students enrolled in 149 government schools and 8,692 enrolled in 32 non-government schools with an additional 3,392 in preschools. There were a total of 3,178 teaching staff including preschools, a decrease of 73 teachers from 2000. The proportion of Indigenous students in the Territory is high, comprising 34·7% all primary and secondary students (38,017) in 2001. Schools range from single classrooms and transportable units catering for the needs of small Aboriginal communities and pastoral properties to urban high schools and secondary colleges (years 11–12), catering for about 7,500 students. Bilingual programmes operate in some Aboriginal communities where traditional Aboriginal culture prevails. Secondary education extends from school years 8 to 12 (7 to 12 in Alice Springs).

The Northern Territory University (NTU) was founded in 1989 by amalgamating the existing University College of the Northern Territory and the Darwin Institute of Technology, with the technical and further education courses hitherto offered by the latter to be conducted by an Institute of Technical and Further Education within the new University. In 2001, 1,934 students were enrolled at the NTU of whom 5·3% were identified as Indigenous. The Batchelor Institute of Indigenous Tertiary Education, which provides higher and vocational education and training for Aboriginal and Torres Straits Islanders, had 451 students enrolled in higher education courses in 2000. In 1997 there were 107 registered Vocational Education and Training (VET) course providers in the Territory, offering 101 courses. At 31 Dec. 1997, 22,321 students were enrolled in VET courses. In 2000 there were 22,797 enrolled in VET courses and of these 33·2% were registered as Indigenous.

Health. In 2002 there were five public hospitals with a total of 569 beds. Community health services are provided from urban and rural Health Centres including mobile units. Remote communities are served by resident nursing staff, aboriginal health workers and in larger communities, resident GPs. Each community receives visiting services from specialist physicians, allied health professionals, public health staff and District Medical Officers. Emergency services are supported by the Aerial Medical Services throughout the Territory.

Welfare. The Aged and Disability Program administers NT and Commonwealth funds ($A32m. in 1999–2000) to provide a number of services for senior Territorians and those with a disability. At June 2002 the numbers of pensioners receiving concessions was 16,252. Concessions include allowances on electricity; water, sewerage and property rates; vehicle registrations; spectacles; urban bus travel; and interstate travel. In 2001–02 disability services expenditure was $A14,618m.

CULTURE

Broadcasting. Darwin's radio services include 4 ABC stations, 1 SBS station, 2 commercial stations and a community station. Darwin has 2 commercial, 1 ABC and 1 SBS TV service. Alice Springs radio services include 4 ABC stations, 2 commercial and 2 community stations. It has 2 commercial, 1 ABC and 1 SBS TV service. Most other Northern Territory centres have 1 commercial and 1 national radio service, with 1 each of ABC, SBS and commercial television, many of these being provided by self-help projects.

Tourism. In 2001 tourist expenditures were $A973·5m. An estimated 1·58m. people visited the Northern Territory, an increase of 29,000 over 2000. Of these 569,000 were international visitors. Tourism is the second largest revenue earner after the mining industry.

FURTHER READING
Profile of Australia's Northern Territory—1997/98. Protocol and Public Affairs Branch, Dept. of the Chief Minister, GPO Box 4396, Darwin
The Northern Territory: Annual Report. Dept. of Territories, Canberra, from 1911. Dept. of the Interior, Canberra, from 1966–67. Dept. of Northern Territory, from 1972
Australian Territories, Dept. of Territories, Canberra, 1960 to 1973. Dept. of Special Minister of State, Canberra, 1973–75. Department of Administrative Services, 1976
Northern Territory in Focus (formerly *Statistical Summary*). Australian Bureau of Statistics, Canberra, from 1960
Donovan, P. F., *A Land Full of Possibilities: A History of South Australia's Northern Territory 1863–1911*, 1981.—*At the Other End of Australia: The Commonwealth and the Northern Territory 1911–1978*. Univ. of Queensland Press, 1984
Heatley, A., *Almost Australians: the Politics of Northern Territory Self-Government*. Australian National Univ. Press, 1990
Powell, A., *Far Country: A Short History of the Northern Territory*. Melbourne Univ. Press, 1996

NEW SOUTH WALES

KEY HISTORICAL EVENTS

The name New South Wales was applied to the entire east coast of Australia when Capt. James Cook claimed the land for the British Crown on 23 Aug. 1770. The separate colonies of Tasmania, South Australia, Victoria and Queensland were proclaimed in the 19th century. In 1911 and 1915 the Australian Capital Territory around Canberra and Jervis Bay was ceded to the Commonwealth. New South Wales was thus gradually reduced to its present area. The first settlement was made at Port Jackson in 1788 as a penal settlement. A partially elective council was established in 1843 and responsible government in 1856.

Gold discoveries from 1851 had brought a large influx of immigrants, and responsible government was at first unstable, with seven ministries holding office in the five years after 1856. The times were somewhat lawless and bitter conflict arose from loose land laws enacted in 1861. Lack of transport hampered agricultural expansion.

New South Wales federated with the other Australian states to form the Commonwealth of Australia in 1901.

TERRITORY AND POPULATION
New South Wales is situated between the 29th and 38th parallels of S. lat. and 141st and 154th meridians of E. long., and comprises 800,640 sq. km, inclusive of Lord Howe Island, 17 sq. km, but exclusive of the Australian Capital Territory (2,360 sq. km) and 70 sq. km at Jervis Bay.

Lord Howe Island, 31' 33' 4" S., 159° 4' 26" E., which is part of New South Wales, is situated about 702 km northeast of Sydney; area, 1,654 ha, of which only about 120 ha are arable; resident population, estimate (1996 census), 369. The Island, which was discovered in 1788, is of volcanic origin. Mount Gower, the highest point, reaches a height of 866 metres.

The Lord Howe Island Board manages the affairs of the Island and supervises the Kentia palm-seed industry.

Census population of New South Wales (including full-blood Aboriginals from 1966):

	Males	Females	Persons	Population per sq. km	Average annual increase % since previous census
1901	710,264	645,091	1,355,355	2	1·86
1911	857,698	789,036	1,646,734	2	1·97
1921	1,071,501	1,028,870	2,100,371	3	2·46
1933	1,318,471	1,282,376	2,600,847	3	1·76
1947	1,492,211	1,492,627	2,984,838	4	0·99
1954	1,720,860	1,702,669	3,423,529	4	1·98
1961	1,972,909	1,944,104	3,917,013	5	1·94
1971	2,307,210	2,293,970	4,601,180	6	1·66
1981	2,548,984	2,577,233	5,126,217	6	1·42
1986	2,684,570	2,717,311	5,401,881	7	1·05
1991	2,844,532	2,886,415	5,730,947	7	1·22
1996	2,983,447	3,055,249	6,038,696	8	1·07

At 31 Dec. 2001 the estimated resident population was 6,642,900 (annual growth rate, 1·1%). Although NSW comprises only 10·4% of the total area of Australia, over 33·7% of the Australian population live there. Of the 84,100 immigrants to Australia in 1998–99, 35,141, or 42%, settled in New South Wales—nearly twice as many as any other state.

The state is divided into 12 *Statistical Divisions.* The estimated population of these (in 1,000) at 30 June 2001 was: Sydney, 4,140·8; Hunter, 582·0; Illawarra, 393·3; Mid-North Coast, 275·1; Richmond-Tweed, 212·8; Murrumbidgee, 184·4; South Eastern, 184·4; Central West, 173·2; Northern, 172·2; North Western, 116·4; Murray, 110·1; Far West, 23·2. Population of the Statistical Subdivisions Newcastle (within Hunter) and Wollongong (within Illawarra) was 487·8 and 266·7 respectively.

SOCIAL STATISTICS
Statistics for calendar years:

	Live births	Deaths	Marriages	Divorces
1997	87,156	45,641	36,679	14,655
1998	85,499	44,741	39,136	14,987
1999	86,784	45,215	41,016	14,470
2000	86,752	45,409	39,323	14,756

The annual rates per 1,000 of mean estimated resident population in 2000 were: births, 13·4; deaths, 7·0; marriages, 6·1; divorce, 2·3; infant mortality, 5·2 per 1,000 live births. Expectation of life in 1999: males, 76·4 years, females, 82·0.

CLIMATE
See AUSTRALIA: Climate.

CONSTITUTION AND GOVERNMENT
Within the State there are three levels of government: the Commonwealth government, with authority derived from a written constitution; the State government with residual powers; the local government authorities with powers

based upon a State Act of Parliament, operating within incorporated areas extending over almost 90% of the State.

The Constitution of New South Wales is drawn from several diverse sources; certain Imperial statutes such as the Commonwealth of Australia Constitution Act (1900); the Australian States Constitution Act (1907); an element of inherited English law; amendments to the Commonwealth of Australia Constitution Act; the (State) Constitution Act; the Australia Acts of 1986; the Constitution (Amendment) Act 1987 and certain other State Statutes; numerous legal decisions; and a large amount of English and local convention.

The Parliament of New South Wales may legislate for the peace, welfare and good government of the State in all matters not specifically reserved to the Commonwealth government.

The State Legislature consists of the Sovereign, represented by the Governor, and two Houses of Parliament, the Legislative Council (upper house) and the Legislative Assembly (lower house).

Australian citizens aged 18 and over, and other British subjects who were enrolled prior to 26 Jan. 1984, men and women aged 18 years and over, are entitled to the franchise. Enrolment and voting is compulsory. The optional preferential method of voting is used for both houses.

The Legislative Council has 42 members elected for a term of office equivalent to two terms of the Legislative Assembly, with 21 members retiring at the same time as the Legislative Assembly elections. The whole State constitutes a single electoral district.

The Legislative Assembly has 93 members elected in single-seat electoral districts for a maximum period of four years.

RECENT ELECTIONS

In elections held on 22 March 2003 the Labor Party won 56 of 93 seats, the Liberal Party 18, the National Party 12 and ind. 7.

CURRENT ADMINISTRATION

In Feb. 2003 the Legislative Council consisted of the following parties: Australian Labor Party (ALP), 8; Liberal Party of Australia (Lib), 4; National Party (NP), 2; Christian Democratic Party (Fred Nile Group), 1; Greens, 1; Australian Democrats (AD), 1; Outdoor Recreation Party, 1; One Nation Party, 1; Reform the Legal System, 1; Unity, 1.

The Legislative Assembly, which was elected in 1999, consisted of the following parties in Feb. 2003: ALP, 55 seats; Lib, 20; NP, 13; ind., 5.

Governor: Prof. Marie Bashir, AC.

The New South Wales ALP Ministry was as follows in April 2003:

Premier, Minister for the Arts and for Citizenship: Robert Carr (b. 1947).

Deputy Premier, Minister for Education and Training and for Aboriginal Affairs: Dr Andrew Refshauge. *Treasurer, Minister for State Development and Vice-President of Executive Council:* Michael Egan. *Attorney General and Minister for the Environment:* Bob Debus. *Special Minister of State, Assistant Treasurer, Minister for Commerce, for Industrial Relations and for the Central Coast:* John Della Bosca. *Infrastructure and Planning, and Natural Resources:* Craig Knowles. *Transport Services, and Minister for the Hunter:* Michael Costa. *Roads and Housing:* Carl Scully. *Police:* John Watkins. *Health:* Morris Iemma. *Community Services, Ageing, Disability Services and Youth:* Carmel Tebbutt. *Tourism, Sport and Recreation, and Women:* Sandra Nori. *Energy and Utilities, and Science and Medical Research:* Frank Sartor. *Rural Affairs, Local Government and Emergency Services:* Tony Kelly. *Regional Development, Illawarra and Small Business:* David Campbell. *Agriculture and Fisheries:* Ian Macdonald. *Juvenile Justice and Western Sydney:* Diane Beamer. *Fair Trading:* Reba Meagher. *Justice:* John Hatzistergos. *Gaming and Racing:* Grant McBride. *Mineral Resources:* Kerry Hickey.

Speaker of the Legislative Assembly: John Murray.

NSW Government website: http://www.nsw.gov.au/

ECONOMY

Budget. State government outlays (in $A1m.) for financial years ending 30 June:

	1997–98	1998–99	1999–2000
General public services	1,578	1,989	1,499
Public order and safety	2,105	2,502	2,626
Education	6,356	7,154	7,433
Health	5,535	6,423	6,598
Social security and welfare	1,764	1,831	1,873
Housing and community amenities	1,119	1,016	2,387
Recreation and culture	1,529	728	1,683
Fuel and energy	545	146	3,450
Agriculture, forestry and fishing	366	877	966
Mining, manufacturing and construction	61	97	88
Transport and communications	3,133	2,524	4,569
Other economic affairs	480	1,344	1,296
Public debt transactions	–	1,888	2,714
Other purposes	2,856	404	354
Total	27,427	28,923	37,536

State government receipts for 1999–2000 included taxes, $A14,547m., and Commonwealth government grant, $A10,934m.

State government taxes, by type:

	1997–98	1998–99	1999–2000
Employers' payroll taxes	3,374	3,605	3,769
Taxes on property—			
Taxes on immovable property	884	974	924
Taxes on financial and capital transactions	3,296	3,512	4,193
Taxes on provision of goods and services—			
Excises and levies	34	–	–
Taxes on gambling	1,338	1,419	1,570
Taxes on insurance	943	850	902
Taxes on goods and performance of activities—			
Motor vehicle taxes	1,321	1,499	1,468
Franchise taxes	1,530	1,981	2,023
Other taxes on use of goods, etc.	187	303	343
Total	12,907	14,143	15,191

Performance. In 1998–99 the gross state product of New South Wales represented 36% of Australia's total GDP.

Banking and Finance. Banking business is transacted chiefly by the Commonwealth Bank of Australia, the State Bank of New South Wales (government banks) and three private banks. At June 1998 there were 45 banking groups (comprised of 52 banking companies, of which 16 were domestic owned and 36 foreign owned).

Lending activity of financial institutions in New South Wales in 2000–01 comprised (in $A1m.): commercial, 95,469; personal, lease financing, 2,778.

ENERGY AND NATURAL RESOURCES

Electricity. In the year ended 30 June 1999 total consumption (including ACT total consumption) stood at 57,168m. kWh, of which 17,720m. kWh was by residential customers. In 1998–99, 60,058m. kWh were produced, an increase of 4·4% on the previous year. Coal is the main fuel source for electricity generation in the state, accounting for 58,975m. kWh in the year ended 30 June 1999. Total installed capacity at 30 June 2000 was 12,687 MW.

Oil and Gas. No natural gas is produced in NSW. Almost all gas is imported from the Moomba field in South Australia plus, since 2001, a small amount from Bass Strait.

Water. Ground water represents the largest source with at least 130 communities relying on it for drinking water.

Minerals. New South Wales contains extensive mineral deposits. For the year ended 30 June 2000, turnover from 123 mining establishments in the coal and metal ore mining industries, employing 10,461 people, was $A5,660m. The value of metallic minerals produced in 1999–2000 was $A1·28bn.; industrial minerals, $A116·3m.; construction materials, $A444·4m. Output of principal products:

	1997–98	1998–99	1999–2000
Antimony (tonnes)	1,711	1,784	1,585
Coal (1,000 tonnes)	107,708	103,421	105,000
Copper (tonnes)	118,000	93,000	124,000
Gold (tonnes)	12	19	20
Lead (tonnes)	166,000	162,000	151,000
Construction sand (1,000 tonnes)	9,428	10,378	10,498
Zinc (tonnes)	270,000	273,000	266,000

Agriculture. NSW accounts for around 27% of Australia's total agricultural production and 20% of total agricultural exports. In 1998–99 GDP at factor income for agriculture, forestry, hunting and fishing was $A4,716m. Farm income (including Australian Capital Territory) was $A1,570m. In the year ended June 2000 there were 43,654 farming establishments. These had an area of 62·1m. ha, of which 6·11 m. ha were used for cropping.

Principal crops in 1999–2000 with production in 1,000 tonnes: wheat for grain, 8,600; sugarcane, 1,977; canola, 827; oats for grain, 284. Estimated value of crops, 1999–2000, came to $A4·9bn. with wheat totalling $A1·4bn. and cotton $A1·1bn. (Data relates to farms whose estimated value of agricultural operations was $A5,000 or more at the census.)

The total area under vines at 1999–2000 was 32,300 ha; grape production totalled 327,000 tonnes.

In 2000 there were 3,899·69 ha of banana plantations, with production of 34,400 tonnes; 4,162,000 citrus fruit trees, with production of 200,269 tonnes.

1999–2000 estimated gross value of livestock products was $A1·4bn., including wool produced, $A833m.; and milk, $A467m. In 1999–2000 production (in tonnes) of butter was 3,912; cheese, 26,140; beef and veal, 445,001; mutton, 118,943; lamb, 79,961; pig meat, 103,232.

Forestry. The area of forests managed by State Forests of NSW in 1999–2000 totalled 2·7m. ha of native forest; 267,000 ha of softwood and 46,000 ha of hardwood plantation with a total yield of 2·78m. cu. metres of sawlogs and veneer logs.

Fisheries. Gross value of fisheries production, including crustaceans and molluscs, in 1998–99, came to $A121·5m.; total volume of fisheries production, 21,777 tonnes.

INDUSTRY

A wide range of manufacturing is undertaken in the Sydney area, and there are large iron and steel works near the coalfields at Newcastle and Port Kembla. Around one-third of Australian manufacturing takes place in NSW.

Manufacturing establishments' operations, 1999–2000:

Industry	No. of persons employed	Wages and salaries ($A1m.)	Turnover ($A1m.)	Industry gross product ($A1m.)
Food, beverages and tobacco	47,620	1,880·9	14,982·1	4,438·8
Textiles, clothing, footwear and leather	17,497	532·7	2,812·9	882·9
Wood and paper products	19,563	691·9	4,067·3	1,472·8
Printing, publishing and recorded media	40,841	1,662·7	7,834·3	3,137·0
Petroleum, coal, chemical and associated products	32,434	1,499·4	12,561·9	3,388·4
Non-metallic mineral products	10,856	491·8	3,499·7	1,229·0
Metal products	48,107	2,011·8	14,126·5	3,934·3
Machinery and equipment	58,399	2,442·7	11,306·9	3,928·6
Other manufacturing	16,613	446·3	2,067·4	691·4
Total manufacturing	291,930	11,660·1	73,259·1	23,103·1

Labour. In May 2001 the labour force was estimated to number 3,244,700 persons, of whom 3,057,700 were employed: 533,900 as intermediate clerical, sales and service workers; 593,700 as professionals; 274,900 as labourers and related workers; 375,300 as tradespersons and related workers; 239,800 as managers and administrators; 256,500 as intermediate production and transport workers; and

154,000 as advanced clerical and service workers. There were 186,900 unemployed (a rate of 5·8%) in May 2001.

Industrial tribunals are authorized to fix minimum rates of wages and other conditions of employment. Their awards may be enforced by law, as may be industrial agreements between employers and organizations of employees, when registered.

During 2000, 150,800 workers were directly involved in 268 industrial disputes. A total of 166,800 working days were lost.

Trade Unions. Registration of trade unions is effected under the New South Wales Trade Union Act 1881, which follows substantially the Trade Union Acts of 1871 and 1876 of England. Registration confers a quasi-corporate existence with power to hold property, to sue and be sued, etc., and the various classes of employees covered by the union are required to be prescribed by the constitution of the union. For the purpose of bringing an industry under the review of the State industrial tribunals, or participating in proceedings relating to disputes before Commonwealth tribunals, employees and employers must be registered as industrial unions, under State or Commonwealth industrial legislation respectively. Trade union membership was held by 26% of employees in Aug. 2000.

INTERNATIONAL TRADE

Imports and Exports. External commerce, exclusive of interstate trade, is included in the statement of the commerce of Australia. Overseas commerce of New South Wales in $A1m. for years ending 30 June:

	Imports	Exports		Imports	Exports
1995–96	34,917	16,683	1998–99	42,142	17,950
1996–97	34,227	17,731	1999–2000	47,945	18,951
1997–98	38,481	19,680	2000–01	52,506	22,749

The major commodities exported in 2000–01 (in $A1m.) were coal, not agglomerated (3,829), aluminium (1,636), cotton (1,157), wool and other animal hair (1,051), medicaments (including veterinary) (1,021), wheat (including spelt) and meslin (unmilled) (1,005), and meat (960). Principal imports were telecommunications equipment (4,447), computers (4,143) and private motor vehicles (3,060).

Principal destinations of exports in 2000–01 (in $A1m.) were Japan (4,799), USA (2,378), New Zealand (1,777), South Korea (1,395), Taiwan (1,277) and China (948). Major sources of supply were USA (10,787), Japan (5,894), China (4,353), UK (3,550), Germany (2,501), South Korea (2,445) and Malaysia (2,019).

COMMUNICATIONS

Roads. At June 2001 there were 181,840 km of public roads of all sorts. The Roads and Traffic Authority of New South Wales is responsible for the administration and upkeep of major roads. In 2001 there were 20,542 km of roads under its control, comprising 3,105 km of national highways, 14,550 km of state roads and 2,887 km of regional and local roads.

The number of registered motor vehicles (excluding tractors and trailers) at 31 March 2001 was 3,745,500, including 3,007,300 passenger vehicles, 501,700 light commercial vehicles, 128,700 trucks, 17,200 buses and 90,700 motorcycles. There were 556 fatalities in road accidents in 2000–01.

Rail. In 1996 the Rail Access Corporation was formed to own and maintain the railway infrastructure. It leases trackage rights to the State Rail Authority (consisting of CityRail and Countrylink), which operates passenger trains, and to the FreightCorp. In 2000–01, 285·7m. passengers were carried on CityRail and 2·1m. on Countrylink. In 2000–01, 89·0m. tonnes of freight were transported. Also open for traffic are 325 km of Victorian government railways which extend over the border, 68 km of private railways (mainly in mining districts), and 53 km of Commonwealth government-owned track.

A tramway opened in Sydney in 1996. There is also a small overhead railway in the city centre.

Civil Aviation. Sydney Airport (Kingsford Smith) is the major airport in New South Wales and Australia's principal international air terminal. In 2000 it handled a total of 22,393,629 passengers (14,195,306 on domestic flights). It is also the leading airport for freight, handling 428,704 tonnes in 2000. At 31 Aug. 2001 registered aircraft totalled 3,513.

Shipping. The main ports are at Sydney, Newcastle, Port Kembla and Botany Bay. 4,612 commercial and 84 passenger vessels called at ports in New South Wales in 1999–2000.

Telecommunications. At 30 June 2001 there were 11·2m. mobile telephone subscribers (8·6m. in 2000). In 2000 there were 1·25m. households with home computer access (53% of all households) and 785,000 households home Internet access (33%).

Postal Services. At June 2000 a total of 1,303 post offices, post office agencies and community mail agencies provided Australia Post services throughout NSW and the ACT.

SOCIAL INSTITUTIONS

Justice. Legal processes may be conducted in Local Courts presided over by magistrates or in higher courts (District Court or Supreme Court) presided over by judges. There is also an appellate jurisdiction. Persons charged with more serious crimes must be tried before a higher court.

Children's Courts remove children as far as possible from the atmosphere of a public court. There are also a number of tribunals exercising special jurisdiction, e.g. the Industrial Commission and the Compensation Court.

As at 25 June 2000 there were 7,328 persons held in prison (including 1,521 on remand). Police personnel as at 30 June 2001, 17,501.

Religion. At the 1996 census of those who stated a religion, 29% were Roman Catholic and 25% Anglican. These two religions combined had almost 3·3m. followers.

Education. The State government maintains a system of free primary and secondary education, and attendance at school is compulsory from 6 to 15 years of age. Non-government schools are subject to government inspection.

In 2000 there were 2,187 government schools with 759,623 pupils (455,914 primary and 303,709 secondary) and 49,768 teachers, and 901 non-government schools with 334,693 pupils (173,046 primary and 161,647 secondary) and 22,437 teachers.

There were 223,459 students in higher education in 2000, with the largest numbers enrolled in arts, humanities and social sciences, and business, administration and economics, each with 25% of total enrolments.

Student enrolments in 2000: University of Sydney (founded 1850), 35,121; University of New England at Armidale (incorporated 1954), 14,809; University of New South Wales (founded 1949), 31,498; University of Newcastle (granted autonomy 1965), 18,249; University of Wollongong, 12,657; Macquarie University in Sydney (founded 1964), 20,621; University of Technology, Sydney, 23,807; University of Western Sydney, 28,874; Charles Sturt University, 27,909.

Colleges of advanced education were merged with universities in 1990.

Post-school technical and further education is provided at State TAFE colleges. Enrolments in 2000 totalled 544,096.

Health. In 1999–2000 there were 24,401 medical practitioners, 3,975 dentists and 76,162 registered nurses. There were 16,469 beds in public hospitals and 6,222 private hospitals.

Welfare. The number of income support payments in June 2000 included: age, 577,924; disability support, 200,071; single parent, 130,114; child care assistance, 128,861; carer, 16,860.

Direct State government social welfare services are limited, for the most part, to the assistance of persons not eligible for Commonwealth government pensions or benefits, and the provision of certain forms of assistance not available from the Commonwealth government. The State also subsidizes many approved services for needy persons.

CULTURE

Broadcasting. In addition to national broadcasting, at Sept. 2001 there were 22 commercial television services (including stations whose licence covers part of NSW as well as remote satellite services) and a total of 36 AM and 48 FM commercial radio services. The first cable-pay television service commenced in Sept. 1995, and satellite-delivered services in Nov. 1995.

Cinema. A major film studio development for Fox Studios, valued at $A120m., opened to the public in Nov. 1999. At 30 June 2000 there was a total of 456 cinema screens in New South Wales.

Tourism. In the year ended 30 June 1999, 1·75m. overseas visitors arrived for short-term visits. At 30 June 2000 there were 1,314 hotels, motels, guest houses and serviced apartments providing 63,153 rooms.

Libraries. In the year ended 30 June 1997 there were 406 public libraries processing 44·9m. loans of books and other materials. In 1998–99, 1·8m. people visited a library.

FURTHER READING

Statistical Information: The NSW Government Statistician's Office was established in 1886, and in 1957 was integrated with the Commonwealth Bureau of Census and Statistics (now called the Australian Bureau of Statistics). Its principal publications are:

New South Wales Year Book (1886/87–1900/01 under the title *Wealth and Progress of New South Wales*). Annual.—*Regional Statistics.—New South Wales Pocket Year Book.—Monthly Summary of Statistics.—New South Wales in Brief.*

State Library: The State Library of NSW, Macquarie St., Sydney.

QUEENSLAND

KEY HISTORICAL EVENTS

Queensland was first visited by Capt. Cook in 1770. From 1778 it was part of New South Wales and was formed into a separate colony, with the name of Queensland, by letters patent of 8 June 1859, when responsible government was conferred. Although by 1868 gold had been discovered, wool was the colony's principal product. The first railway line was opened in 1865. Queensland federated with the other Australian states to form the Commonwealth of Australia in 1901.

TERRITORY AND POPULATION

Queensland comprises the whole northeastern portion of the Australian continent, including the adjacent islands in the Pacific Ocean and in the Gulf of Carpentaria. Estimated area 1,730,650 sq. km.

The increase in the population as shown by the censuses since 1901 has been as follows (including Aboriginals from 1966):

| | Census counts | | | Intercensal increase | |
Year	Males	Females	Total	Numerical	Rate per annum %
1901	277,003	221,126	498,129	—	—
1911	329,506	276,307	605,813	107,684	1·98
1921	398,969	357,003	755,972	150,159	2·24
1933	497,217	450,317	947,534	191,562	1·86
1947	567,471	538,944	1,106,415	158,881	1·11
1954	676,252	642,007	1,318,259	211,844	2·53
1961	774,579	744,249	1,518,828	200,569	2·04
1966	849,390	824,934	1,674,324	144,857	1·84
1971	921,665	905,400	1,827,065	152,741	1·76
1976	1,024,611	1,012,586	2,037,197	210,132	2·20
1981	1,153,404	1,141,719	2,295,123	257,926	2·41
1986	1,295,630	1,291,685	2,587,315	292,192	2·43
1991	1,482,406	1,495,404	2,977,810	390,495	2·60
1996	1,673,220	1,695,630	3,368,850	391,040	2·63

At the 1996 census there were 95,518 Aboriginals and Torres Strait Islanders.

Since the 1981 census, official population estimates are according to place of usual residence and are referred to as estimated resident population. Estimated resident population at 30 June 2000, 3,512,356 (annual growth rate, 1·7%).

Statistics on birthplaces from the 1996 census are as follows: Australia, 78·4% (83·6% in 1986); UK and Ireland, 5·6% (6·1%); other countries, 12·4% (14·4%); at sea and not stated, 3·6% (1·4%).

Brisbane, the capital, had at 30 June 1999 (estimate) a resident population of 1,601,417 (Statistical Division). The estimated resident populations of the other major centres (Statistical Districts) at 30 June 1999 (preliminary) were: Gold Coast-Tweed, (including that part in New South Wales) 391,236; Sunshine Coast, 172,928; Townsville, 127,174; Cairns, 113,954; Mackay, 64,916; Rockhampton, 64,344; Bundaberg, 55,781; Gladstone, 39,100.

SOCIAL STATISTICS

Statistics (including Aboriginals) for calendar years:

	Births	Deaths	Marriages	Divorces
1996	47,769	22,281	20,913	10,996
1997	46,965	21,945	20,868	11,744
1998	47,046	22,321	21,257	11,349
1999	46,953	22,409	21,535	11,467

The annual rates per 1,000 population in 1999 were: births, 13·4; deaths, 6·4; marriages, 6·1. The infant mortality rate was 6·4 per 1,000 live births. Life expectancy, 1998: 74·0 years for males, 80·3 for females.

CLIMATE

A typical subtropical to tropical climate. High daytime temperatures during Oct. to March give a short spring and long summer. Centigrade temperatures in the hottest inland areas often exceed the high 30s before the official commencement of summer on 1 Dec. Daytime temperatures in winter are quite mild, in the low- to mid-20s. Average rainfall varies from about 150 mm in the desert in the extreme southwestern corner of the State to about 4,000 mm in parts of the sugar lands of the wet northeastern coast, the latter being the wettest part of Australia.

CONSTITUTION AND GOVERNMENT

Queensland, formerly a portion of New South Wales, was formed into a separate colony in 1859, and responsible government was conferred. The power of making laws and imposing taxes is vested in a parliament of one house—the *Legislative Assembly*—which comprises 89 members, returned from four electoral zones for three years, elected from single-member constituencies by compulsory ballot.

Queensland elects 26 members to the Commonwealth House of Representatives.

The Elections Act, 1983, provides franchise for all males and females, 18 years of age and over, qualified by six months' residence in Australia and three months in the electoral district.

RECENT ELECTIONS

Legislative Assembly representation following the State general election in Feb. 2001: Australian Labor Party (ALP), 66 seats; National Party (NP), 12; Liberal Party (LP), 3; ind. 5; One Nation, 3. The NP/LP coalition forms the opposition.

CURRENT ADMINISTRATION

Governor of Queensland: Maj.-Gen. Peter Arnison, AC, CVO.

In Feb. 2003 the ALP administration was as follows:

Premier and Minister for Trade: Peter Beattie (appointed 29 June 1998).

Deputy Premier, Treasurer and Minister for Sport: Terry Mackenroth. *Education:* Anna Bligh. *Employment, Training and Youth and Arts:* Matt Foley. *Health:* Wendy Edmond. *State Development:* Tom Barton. *Police and Corrective Services:* Tony McGrady. *Transport and Main Roads:* Steve Bredhauer. *Attorney General, Justice:* Rod Welford. *Environment:* Dean Wells. *Public Works and Housing:* Rob Schwarten. *Families, Aboriginal and Torres Strait Islander Policy, Disability Services and Seniors:* Judy Spence. *Primary Industries and Rural Communities:* Henry Palaszczuk. *Tourism and Racing, Fair Trading:* Merri Rose. *Natural Resources, Mines:* Stephen Robertson. *Local Government and Planning:* Nita Cunningham. *Emergency Services:* Mike Reynolds. *Industrial Relations:* Gordon Nuttall. *Innovation and Information Economy:* Paul Lucas.

QLD Government website: http://www.qld.gov.au/

ECONOMY

Budget. In 1998–99 current outlays by the state totalled $A16,345m.; revenue and grants received totalled $A16,488m.

Banking and Finance. In Sept. 2001 deposits at all banks in Queensland totalled $A62,844m. Other lending totalled $A85,632m.

ENERGY AND NATURAL RESOURCES

Electricity. The government-owned sector of the state's electricity industry has been restructured, and since Dec. 1998 it has operated as part of the wholesale national electricity market. Part of the restructuring was the formation of a single corporation, Ergon Energy, by the amalgamation of the six former regional distribution corporations. In the year ended 30 June 1999 total consumption stood at 32,210m. kWh by 1,532,034 customers, including 9,638m. kWh by residential customers. Coal is the main fuel source for electricity generation in the state, producing 37,379m. kWh in the year ended 30 June 1999. In Feb. 1999 installed generation capacity stood at 7,415 MW.

Water. In the western portion of the State water is comparatively easily found by sinking artesian bores. Monitoring of water quality in Queensland is carried out by the Department of the Environment (estuarine and coastal waters) and the Department of Natural Resources (fresh water).

Minerals. There are large reserves of coal, bauxite, gold, copper, silver, lead, zinc, nickel, phosphate rock and limestone. Most of the coal produced comes from the Bowen Basin coalfields in central Queensland. Copper, lead, silver and zinc are mined in the northwest and the State's largest goldmines are in the north. The total value of metallic minerals in 1999–2000 was $A2·52bn. In 1999–2000 there were 43 coal mines in operation producing 124,348,239 tonnes of saleable coal (an increase of 10·3% on the previous year); and at 30 June 2000, 7,972 persons were employed in mining.

Agriculture. Queensland is Australia's leading beef-producing state and its chief producer of fruit and vegetables. In the year ended June 2000 there were 30,698 agricultural establishments farming 145·4m. ha. Livestock on farms and stations numbered 10,748,000 cattle, 10,600,000 sheep and lambs and 621,000 pigs. Total wool production, 45,686 tonnes. The total area under crops during 1998–99 was 3,014,000 ha.

| | Area (1,000 ha) | | Production (1,000 tonnes) | |
Crop	1997–98	1998–99	1997–98	1998–99
Sugarcane, crushed	394	379	36,790	36,966
Wheat	1,001	1,139	1,392	1,941
Maize	34	37	97	145
Sorghum	379	367	690	1,059
Barley	135	163	204	320
Soybeans	11	24	16,000	46,000
Sunflower seed	77	113	66,000	115,000
Potatoes	5	5	122	108
Pumpkins	3	4	35	38
Tomatoes	3	3	97	88
Peanuts	18	20	30	45
Bananas[1]	7	8	166	175
Pineapples[1]	3	3	123	131
Cotton (raw)	137	154	424	481

[1]Bearing area only.

The gross value of agricultural commodity production in 1999–2000 was estimated to be $A6·5bn. (1·5% increase on the previous year) which comprised crops, $A3·3bn.; livestock disposals, $A2·6bn.; and livestock products, $A544m.

Forestry. Of a total of 54m. ha of forests and woodlands in 1999, 6% was in national parks and World Heritage areas while 7% was in State forests and timber reserves outside World Heritage sites. Queensland's plantation forests supply around 40% of Australia's wood and paper products. The forestry industry is an important part of the state's economy, employing around 17,000 people with a gross output of $A1,700m.

Fisheries. Gross value of fisheries production, including crustaceans and molluscs, in 1998–99 came to $A241·6m.; total volume of fisheries production, 29,652 tonnes.

INDUSTRY

In 1999–2000 manufacturing industry turnover was $A34,109m. At 30 June 2000, 142,100 people were employed in manufacturing and a total of $A4,987m. wages and salaries were paid. The largest manufacturing sector was food, beverages and tobacco.

Labour. In May 2000 the labour force numbered 1,823,600, of whom 1,680,500 (736,000 females) were employed. Unemployment stood at 8·0% in 1999–2000, the lowest total for a decade.

Trade Unions. In Aug. 1999, 332,373 employees were members of a trade union (25·0% of total employment).

INTERNATIONAL TRADE

Imports and Exports. Total value of direct overseas imports and exports (in $A1m.) f.o.b. port of shipment for both imports and exports:

	1996–97	1997–98	1998–99
Imports	8,636·8	9,751·0	10,809·9
Exports	13,566·6	16,288·2	15,900·2

In 1998–99 interstate exports totalled $A5,840·7m. and imports $A14,203·8m. Chief sources of imports in 1998–99 (in $A1m.): Japan, 2,227·8; EU, 1,989·4; USA, 1,921; Papua New Guinea, 629·3; New Zealand, 627·8. Exports went chiefly to: Japan, 4,446·0; EU, 2,319·0; South Korea, 1,473·0; USA, 1,024·2; Taiwan, 745·5. The chief exports overseas in 1998–99 (in $A1m.) were: coal, 5,508·3; meat and meat preparations, 1,906·5; non-ferrous metals, 1,514·7; metalliferous ores and metal scrap, 1,018·2; machinery and transport equipment, 678·3. Principal overseas imports were: road vehicles, 2,379·8; petroleum and petroleum products, 1,068·5; machinery, specialized for particular industries, 805·5; general industrial machinery and equipment, 741·7; power generating machinery and equipment, 375·9.

COMMUNICATIONS

Roads. At 30 June 2001 there were 178,295 km of roads open to the public. Of these, 68,076 km were surfaced with sealed pavement. At 31 Oct. 1999 motor vehicles registered (in 1,000) totalled 2,242·4, comprising 1,741·1 passenger vehicles, 396·3 light commercial vehicles, 85·7 trucks, 73·2 motorcycles, 14·1 buses and 5·2 campervans. There were 313 fatalities in road accidents in 1999.

Rail. Queensland Rail is a State government-owned corporation. Total length of line at 30 June 1999 was 9,500 km, of which 1,875 km were electrified. In 1998–99, 42·0m. passengers and 111·9m. tonnes of freight were carried.

Civil Aviation. Queensland is well served with a network of air services, with overseas and interstate connections. Subsidiary companies provide planes for taxi and charter work, and the Flying Doctor Service operates throughout western Queensland. In 1997–98 all Federal airports were leased to private sector operators—Brisbane, Archerfield, Coolangatta, Mount Isa and Townsville Airports (the latter is operated jointly with the Department of Defence). In 2000 Brisbane handled 10,534,293 passengers (8,084,979 on domestic flights); Cairns, 2,506,218 passengers (1,834,386 on domestic flights). The number of aircraft registered at 30 June 1999 was 2,423.

Shipping. Queensland has 14 modern trading ports, 2 community ports and a number of non-trading ports. In 1999–2000 general cargo imported through Queensland ports was 1,012,441 mass tonnes and general cargo exported was 1,264,913 mass tonnes. There were 6,377 commercial ship calls during 1999–2000.

Telecommunications. In 2000 there were 668,000 households with home computer access (50% of all households) and 408,000 households with home Internet access (31%).

Postal Services. At 1 July 1997 there were 446 post offices and postal agencies.

SOCIAL INSTITUTIONS

Justice. Justice is administered by Higher Courts (Supreme and District), Magistrates' Courts and Children's Courts. The Supreme Court comprises the Chief Justice and 21 judges; the District Courts, 34 district court judges. Stipendiary magistrates preside over the Magistrates' and Children's Courts, except in the smaller centres, where justices of the peace officiate. A parole board may recommend prisoners for release.

In 1998–99 the Queensland Police Service recorded 409,722 offences, an average annual increase of 6·0% since 1989–90. As at 30 June 2000 the average daily number of prisoners stood at 4,482.

Religion. Religious affiliation at the 1996 census: Roman Catholic, 25·2%; Anglican, 23·6%; Uniting Church, 9·5%; Presbyterian, 4·7%; Lutheran, 2·2%; Baptist, 1·9%; other Christian, 6·8%; non-Christian, 1·5%; no religion, 15·3%; not stated, 9·0%.

Education. Education is compulsory between the ages of 6 and 15 years and is provided free in government schools.

Primary and secondary education comprises 12 years of full-time formal schooling, and is provided by both the government and non-government sectors. In 1999 the State administered 1,300 schools with 273,710 primary students and 152,166 secondary students. In 1999 there were 29,164 teachers in government schools. There were 420 private schools in 1999 with 85,278 primary students and 83,430 secondary students. Educational programmes at private schools were provided by 11,109 teachers in 1999.

In 1999 there were 27,687 full-time students at TAFE institutes. The seven publicly funded universities had 125,185 full-time students in 2000.

Health. In 1998–99 there were 151 public acute hospitals with over 9,800 beds and 4 public psychiatric hospitals; 47 private acute hospitals and 5 private psychiatric hospitals. At 30 June 1999 there were 7,571 doctors, 3,614 specialists, 1,953 dentists and 35,329 registered nurses.

Welfare. Welfare institutions providing shelter and social care for the aged, the handicapped and children are maintained or assisted by the State. A child health service is provided throughout the State. Age, invalid, widows', disability and war service pensions, family allowances, and unemployment and sickness benefits are paid by the Federal government. The number of age and disability pensions (including wives' and carers' pensions) at 30 June 1999 was: age, 284,852; disability support, 105,276; carer, 7,770. There were 5,879 widows' and 80,318 single parent payments current at 30 June 1999, and basic family payment was being paid for 654,363 children under 16 years.

CULTURE

Broadcasting. In addition to the national networks Queensland is served by 13 public radio stations (non-profit-making), 44 commercial radio stations and 3 commercial TV channels.

Tourism. Overseas visitors to Australia who specified Queensland as their primary destination numbered 1,309,800 in 1999, with the main source being from Asia with 52·7% of the State visitor total, of which Japanese made up 30·8%. Visitors from New Zealand accounted for 19·9%; Europe 14·0% (including UK and Ireland, 5·5%); and North America 6·3%.

Libraries. The State Library of Queensland received about 113,000 requests for information during 1998–99 and was visited by more than 309,000 people.

Theatre and Opera. The Queensland Performing Arts Complex at South Bank comprises a Concert Hall, Lyric Theatre, the Cremorne Theatre and a drama theatre, the Southbank Playhouse.

Museums and Galleries. In 1996–97 there were 37 museums at over 46 locations throughout Queensland with admissions totalling 2,114,100. The Queensland Museum focuses on science and human achievement. The Queensland Art Gallery is located at South Bank and during 1998–99 held 26 special exhibitions which attracted a total of 336,090 visitors.

FURTHER READING
Statistical Information: The Statistical Office (now Australian Bureau of Statistics, 313 Adelaide St., Brisbane) was set up in 1859. *A Queensland Official Year Book* was issued in 1901, the annual *ABC of Queensland Statistics* from 1905 to 1936 with exception of 1918 and 1922. Present publications include: *Queensland Year Book.* Annual, from 1937 (omitting 1942, 1943, 1944, 1987, 1991). —*Queensland Pocket Year Book.* Annual from 1950.— *Monthly Summary of Statistics, Queensland.* From Jan. 1961. Selected statistics available at *website:* http://www.abs.gov.au

Australian Sugar Year Book. Brisbane, from 1941
Johnston, W. R., *A Bibliography of Queensland History. Brisbane,* 1981.—*The Call of the Land: A History of Queensland to the Present Day.* Brisbane, 1982
Johnston, W. R. and Zerner, M., *Guide to the History of Queensland.* Brisbane, 1985

State Library: The State Library of Queensland, Queensland Cultural Centre, South Bank, South Brisbane.
Website: http://www.slq.qld.gov.au

SOUTH AUSTRALIA

KEY HISTORICAL EVENTS
South Australia was surveyed by Tasman in 1644 and charted by Flinders in 1802. It was formed into a British province by letters of patent of Feb. 1836, and a partially elective legislative council was established in 1851. From 6 July 1863 the Northern Territory was placed under the jurisdiction of South Australia until the establishment of the Commonwealth of Australia in 1911.

TERRITORY AND POPULATION
The total area of South Australia is 983,480 sq. km. The settled part is divided into counties and hundreds. There are 49 counties proclaimed, and 536 hundreds, covering 23m. ha, of which 19m. ha are occupied. Outside this area there are extensive pastoral districts, covering 76m. ha, 49m. of which are under pastoral leases.

The resident population at 31 Dec. 2001 was 1,518,900 (annual growth rate, 0·5%); at 31 Dec. 1999 the population was 1,496,207. The 1996 census population was 1,427,936 (22,051 Aboriginal and Torres Strait Islanders).

At the 1996 census the Adelaide Statistical Division had 1,045,854 persons (73·2% of South Australia's total population) in 25 councils and 4 municipalities and other districts. Urban centres outside this area (with 1996 census populations) are Whyalla (23,382), Mount Gambier (22,037), Port Augusta (13,914), Port Pirie (13,633) and Port Lincoln (11,678).

SOCIAL STATISTICS
Statistics for calendar years:

	Live Births	Deaths	Marriages	Divorces
1997	18,849	11,668	7,945	4,115
1998	17,979	11,432	8,022	4,159
1999	18,261	11,684	8,240	4,300
2000	18,018	17,439	–	–

The rates per 1,000 population in 2000 were: births, 11·9; deaths, 7·9; marriages, 5·5; divorces, 2·7. The infant mortality rate in 2000 was 4·6 per 1,000 live births. Life expectancy for 1999–2000 was 76·6 years for men and 82·3 years for women.

CONSTITUTION AND GOVERNMENT
The present Constitution dates from 24 Oct. 1856. It vests the legislative power in an elected Parliament, consisting of a Legislative Council and a House of Assembly. The former is composed of 22 members. Eleven members are elected at alternate elections for a term of at least six years and are elected on the basis of proportional representation with the State as one multi-member electorate. The House of Assembly consists of 47 members elected by a preferential system of voting for the term of a Parliament (approximately four years). Election of members of both

Houses takes place by preferential secret ballot. Voting is compulsory for those on the Electoral Roll. The qualifications of an elector are to be an Australian citizen, or a British subject who was, at some time within the period of three months commencing on 26 Oct. 1983, enrolled under the Repealed Act as an Assembly elector or enrolled on an electoral roll maintained under the Commonwealth or a Commonwealth Territory, must be at least 18 years of age and have lived in the subdivision for which the person is enrolled for at least one month. By the Constitution Act Amendment Act, 1894, the franchise was extended to women, who voted for the first time at the general election of 25 April 1896. Certain persons are ineligible for election to either House.

Electors enrolled (30 Dec. 2002) numbered 1,050,000.

The executive power is vested in a Governor appointed by the Crown and an Executive Council, consisting of the Governor and the Ministers of the Crown. The Governor has the power to dissolve the House of Assembly but not the Legislative Council, unless that Chamber has twice consecutively with an election intervening defeated the same or substantially the same Bill passed in the House of Assembly by an absolute majority.

RECENT ELECTIONS
The House of Assembly, elected on 9 Feb. 2002, consisted of the following members: Australian Labor Party (ALP), 23; Liberal Party (LIB), 20; Independent (ind.), 2; National, 1; CLIC, 1.

CURRENT ADMINISTRATION
Governor: Marjorie Jackson-Nelson, AC, CVO, MBE.

In Feb. 2003 the Labor Ministry was as follows:

Premier, Minister for Economic Development, the Arts and Volunteers: Mike Rann.

Deputy Premier, Treasurer, Minister for Industry and Investment and Federal/State Relations: Kevin Foley. *Agriculture, Food and Fisheries, and Mineral Resources Development:* Paul Holloway. *Government Enterprises, Energy, Police and Emergency Services:* Patrick Conlon. *Attorney-General, Justice, Consumer Affairs and Multicultural Affairs:* Michael Atkinson. *Aboriginal Affairs and Reconciliation and Correctional Services:* Terry Roberts. *Health:* Lea Stevens. *Education and Children's Services:* Trish White. *Environment and Conservation, River Murray and Southern Suburbs:* John Hill. *Social Justice, Housing, Youth and the Status of Women:* Stephanie Key. *Transport, Industrial Relations, Recreation, Sport and Racing:* Michael Wright. *Tourism, Small Business, Science and Information Technology, and Employment, Training and Further Education:* Jane Lomax-Smith. *Urban Development and Planning, Gambling and Administrative Services:* Jay Weatherill. *Trade and Regional Development and Local Government:* Rory McEwen (ind.).

Speaker: Peter Lewis (ind.).

SA Government website: http://www.sa.gov.au/

ECONOMY
Budget. Non-financial public sector revenue and expenses (in $A1m.):

	1998–99	1999–2000	2000–01
Revenue	9,417	9,300	9,051
Expenditure	9,618	9,638	9,279

Performance. South Australia's 2000–01 gross state product represented 6·49% of Australia's total GDP. Economic growth was expected to slow to 2·5% in 2001–02 following growth of 2·75% in 2000–01.

Banking and Finance. In Sept. 2001 total deposits held by banks was $A21,633m. and loans totalled $A28,670m.

ENERGY AND NATURAL RESOURCES
Electricity. In the year ended 30 June 1999 total consumption stood at 10,456m. kWh, including 3,814m. kWh by residential customers.

Minerals. The principal metallic minerals produced are copper, iron ore, uranium oxide, gold and silver. The total value of minerals produced in 2000–01 was $A2,152·3m. including copper, $A702·9m.; natural gas, $A426·6m.; uranium oxide, $A227·7m.; opals (estimate), $A38·3m.

Agriculture. In the year ended 31 March 2000 there were 15,905 establishments mainly engaged in agriculture with a total area under holding of 59·9m. ha. The gross value of agricultural commodities in 1999–2000 was $A2,999·7m. Total value of wool production, $A204·1m. The area of cereal crops in 1999–2000 totalled 2,853,000 ha. Estimated value (in $A1m.) of the chief crops in 1999–2000: wheat, 492·3; barley, 245·0; winegrapes, 484·3 (vineyards' total area, 61,141 ha, including 12,729 ha not yet bearing, representing 41·8% of Australia's total). Fruit culture is extensive with citrus and orchard fruits. The most valuable vegetable crops are potatoes, onions and carrots.

Livestock, 30 June 2000 preliminary figures: 1,152,000 cattle, 13,675,000 sheep and 402,000 pigs. Value of livestock products for 1999–2000, $A504·3m.

Irrigation. For the year ended 31 March 1999, 137,500 ha were under irrigated culture, being used as follows: vineyards, 44,700; fruit (excluding grapes) and nuts, 15,300; vegetables, 10,500; and pasture, 58,900.

Forestry. Total area of plantations at 30 June 2001 totalled 81,262 ha.

Fisheries. Gross value of fisheries production, including crustaceans and molluscs, in 1998–99 came to $A348·1m.; total volume of fisheries production, 26,862 tonnes.

INDUSTRY

The turnover for manufacturing industries for 1999–2000 was $A21,442·0m.; wages and salaries totalled $A3,084·8m.

Industry sub-division	Persons employed (1,000)	Turnover ($A1m.)
Food, beverages and tobacco	15·3	4,881·2
Textiles, clothing, footwear and leather manufacturing	3·4	716·1
Wood and paper products manufacturing	6·6	1,374·3
Printing, publishing and recorded media	5·4	833·3
Chemical, petroleum, coal and associated products	6·4	1,614·0
Non-metallic mineral products	2·8	710·1
Metal products manufacturing	11·0	2,827·4
Machinery and equipment	28·1	7,814·0
Other manufacturing	5·1	671·2
Total	84·0	21,442·0

Practically all forms of secondary industry are to be found, the most important being motor vehicle manufacture, saw-milling and the manufacture of household appliances, basic iron and steel, meat and meat products, and wine and brandy.

Labour. Two systems of industrial arbitration and conciliation for the adjustment of industrial relations between employers and employees are in operation—the State system, which operates when industrial disputes are confined to the territorial limits of the State, and the Federal system, which applies when disputes involve other parts of Australia as well as South Australia.

The industrial tribunals are authorized to fix minimum rates of wages and other conditions of employment, and their awards may be enforced by law. Industrial agreements between employers and organizations of employees, when registered, may be enforced in the same manner as awards.

As at Feb. 2001 the labour force stood at 674,400. There were 57,300 unemployed, a rate of 7·5%, down from 9·3% in Feb. 2000.

INTERNATIONAL TRADE

Imports and Exports. Overseas imports and exports in $A1m. (year ending 30 June):

	1997–98	1998–99	1999–2000
Imports	3,942·4	3,717·0	4,319·4
Exports	4,983·5	5,301·0	6,179·5

Principal exports in 1999–2000 were (with values in $A1m.): wine, 898·4; road vehicles, parts and accessories, 883·9; metals and metal manufacture, 804·2; wheat, 473·1; fish and crustaceans, 393·6; petroleum and petroleum products, 218·5; wool and sheepskins, 179·0; meat and meat preparations, 160·1.

Principal imports in 1999–2000 were (with values in $A1m.): machinery, 1,164·7; road vehicles, parts and accessories, 838·9; petroleum and petroleum products, 515·5.

In 1999–2000 the leading suppliers of imports were (with values in $A1m.): Japan (831·4), USA (572·6), Saudi Arabia (240·9), UK (208·6), other European Union (678·1), New Zealand (120·9). Main export markets were USA (953·5), Japan (785·9), UK (624·9), other European Union (446·8), New Zealand (445·8), China (314·5), Hong Kong (255·6).

COMMUNICATIONS

Roads. At 30 June 1999 there were 27,117 km of sealed and 69,335 km of unsealed roads. Motor vehicles registered as at 30 June 1999: passenger vehicles, 838,485; other motor vehicles, 167,922; motorcycles, 26,129. In 1999 there were 153 road accident fatalities.

Rail. In Aug. 1997 the passenger operations of Australian National Railways were sold to Great Southern Railway and the freight operations to Australian Southern Railroad. At 30 June 1996 Australian National Railways operated 4,415 km of railway in country areas. TransAdelaide operates 120 km of railway in the metropolitan area of Adelaide.

There is a tramway in Adelaide that runs from the city centre to the coast. A planned joint South Australia and Northern Territory project 'The AustralAsia Rail Project' is a major infrastructure project involving the construction of 1,410 km standard gauge railway between Alice Springs and Darwin.

Civil Aviation. The main airport is Adelaide International Airport, which handled 3,868,854 passengers (3,599,032 on domestic flights) in 2000.

Shipping. There are 10 state and 5 private deep-sea ports. In 1999–2000, 1,714 commercial vessels arrived in South Australia. General cargo imported in 1999–2000 was 212,719 mass tonnes and general cargo exported was 626,266 mass tonnes.

Telecommunications. In 1998 residential telephone penetration was 98·0% (93·6% in 1986). In 2000 there were 295,000 households with home computer access (50% of all households) and 176,000 households with home Internet access (30%).

Postal Services. At 30 June 1999 there were 548 Australia Post retail facilities in South Australia and Northern Territory.

SOCIAL INSTITUTIONS

Justice. There is a Supreme Court, which incorporates admiralty, civil, criminal, land and valuation, and testamentary jurisdiction; district criminal courts, which have jurisdiction in many indictable offences; and magistrates courts, which include the Youth Court. Circuit courts are held at several places. At 1 July 2001 the police force numbered 3,808. The average daily number of prisoners in June 2001 was 1,389.

Religion. Religious affiliation at the 1996 census: Catholic, 296,048; Anglican, 228,151; Uniting Church, 180,604; Lutheran, 70,970; Orthodox, 42,053; Baptist, 26,251; Presbyterian, 23,994; other Christians, 74,868; non-Christians, 25,236; indefinite, 4,885; no religion, 310,908; not stated, 138,554.

Education. Education is compulsory for children between the ages of 6 and 15 years although most children are enrolled at age 5 or soon after. Primary and secondary education at government schools is secular and free. In Aug. 2001 there were 812 schools operating, of which 611 were government and 201 non-government schools. There were 114,287 children in government and 43,500 in non-government primary schools, and 61,935 children in government and 31,800 in non-government secondary schools. In 2000 there were eight Training and Further Education (TAFE) institutes delivering through 54 separate campuses across the state to 97,061 students. There were 24,738 students enrolled at the University of South Australia in 2000; University of Adelaide, 12,885; and Flinders University, 11,404.

Health. As at 30 June 2001 there were 80 public hospitals, 52 private hospitals. Beds available in public and private hospitals totalled 6,675.

Welfare. The number of age and disability pensions (including wives' and carers' pensions) on 30 June 2001 was: age, 169,370; disability support, 59,794. There were 57,588 Newstart and Mature Age allowances and 34,312 single parent payments current at 30 June 2001.

CULTURE

Broadcasting. There are 131 radio stations (24 AM and 107 FM) and 4 commercial TV stations, 1 community service TV station and the national ABC service.

Tourism. In the year ended 30 June 2000 international visitors totalled 350,100 (over 50% from Europe), an increase of 12%. At 30 June 2001 there were 234 hotels, motels, guest houses and serviced apartments with 10,596 rooms.

Festivals. Over 400 festivals, carnivals and special events take place each year. The Adelaide Festival Arts, founded in 1960, is held biennially in the Adelaide Festival Centre.

Libraries. In the year ending April 1999, 492,400 people visited a library. In June 1997, 83 authorities were operating 136 public libraries, including 46 school/community libraries and 9 mobile libraries.

FURTHER READING

Statistical Information: The State office of the Australian Bureau of Statistics is at 55 Currie St., Adelaide (GPO Box 2272). Although the first printed statistical publication was the *Statistics of South Australia, 1854*, with the title altered to *Statistical Register* in 1859, there is a manuscript volume for year back to 1838. These contain simple records of trade, demography, production, etc. and were prepared only for the information of the Colonial Office; one copy was retained in the State.

The publications of the State office include the *South Australian Year Book* (now discontinued), a monthly *South Australian Economic Indicators*, a quarterly bulletin of building activity, and approximately 40 special bulletins issued each year as particulars of various sections of statistics become available.

Gibbs, R. M., *A History of South Australia: from Colonial Days to the Present.* 3rd ed. revised, Adelaide, 1995

Prest, Wilfred, Round, Kerrie and Fort, Carol, (eds.) *The Wakefield Companion to South Australian History.* Wakefield Press, Kent Town, 2002

Whitelock, D., *Adelaide from Colony to Jubilee: a Sense of Difference.* Adelaide, 1985

State Library: The State Library of S.A., North Terrace, Adelaide.

TASMANIA

KEY HISTORICAL EVENTS

Abel Janszoon Tasman discovered Van Diemen's Land (Tasmania) on 24 Nov. 1642. The island became a British settlement in 1803 as a dependency of New South Wales; in 1825 its connection with New South Wales was terminated; in 1851 a partially elected Legislative Council was established; and in 1856 responsible government came into operation. On 1 Jan. 1901 Tasmania was federated with the other Australian states into the Commonwealth of Australia.

TERRITORY AND POPULATION

Tasmania is a group of islands separated from the mainland by Bass Strait with an area (including islands) of 68,400 sq. km, of which 63,447 sq. km form the area of the main island. The population at 11 consecutive censuses (including full-blood Aboriginals from 1966) was:

	Population		Population
1947	257,078	1981	418,957
1954	308,752	1986	436,353
1961	350,340	1991	452,837
1966	371,435	1996	459,659
1971	390,413	2001	456,652
1976	402,868		

At the census of 7 Aug. 2001, 21,910 were born in the UK or Ireland, 11,120 in other European countries and 386,036 in Australia. The resident population at 31 Dec. 2001 was 473,300 (annual growth rate, 0·2%).

The largest cities and towns (with populations at the 2001 census) are: Hobart (191,169), Launceston (95,604), Devonport (23,030) and Burnie (18,145).

SOCIAL STATISTICS
Statistics for calendar years:

	Births	Deaths	Marriages	Divorces
1997	6,007	3,809	2,672	1,321
1998	5,978	3,605	2,599	1,322
1999	6,032	3,783	2,499	1,391
2000	5,692	3,711	2,589	1,329

CLIMATE
Mostly a temperate maritime climate. The sea, never more than 115 km distant, suppresses temperature extremes. The prevailing westerly airstream leads to a marked variation of cloudiness, rainfall and temperature. The result is a west coast and highlands that are cool, wet and cloudy, and an east coast and lowlands that are milder, drier and sunnier.

CONSTITUTION AND GOVERNMENT
Parliament consists of the Governor, the Legislative Council and the House of Assembly. The Council has 15 members, elected by adults with 6 months' residence. Members sit for six years, with either two or three retiring annually. There is no power to dissolve the Council. Vacancies are filled by by-elections. The House of Assembly has 25 members; the maximum term for the House of Assembly is four years. Women received the right to vote in 1903. Proportional representation was adopted in 1907, the method now being the single transferable vote in five member constituencies. Casual vacancies in the House of Assembly are determined by a transfer of the preference of the vacating member's ballot papers to consenting candidates who were unsuccessful at the last general election.

A Minister must have a seat in one of the two Houses.

RECENT ELECTIONS
At the elections of July 2002 the Australian Labor Party won 14 seats in the House of Assembly, the Liberal Party 7 and the Tasmanian Greens 4.

CURRENT ADMINISTRATION
The Legislative Council is predominantly independent without formal party allegiance; four members are Labor-endorsed.

Governor: Sir Guy Green, AC, KBE.

A majority Labor government was re-elected in July 2002, which in Feb. 2003 comprised:

Premier, Minister for Arts, Tourism, Parks and Heritage: Jim Bacon.

Deputy Premier, Minister for Economic Development, Energy and Resources, Racing, Sport and Recreation: Paul Lennon. *Infrastructure:* Jim Cox. *Primary Industries, Water and Environment:* Bryan Green. *Cabinet Secretary and Treasury Spokesperson in Lower House:* Steven Kons. *Attorney General, Minister for Justice and International Relations:* Judy Jackson. *Health and Human Services, Police and Public Safety:* David Llewellyn. *Treasurer and Minister for Employment:* David Crean. *Minister for Education, Women:* Paula Wriedt. *Parliamentary Secretary to the Premier:* Kathryn Hay. *Parliamentary Secretary to the Deputy Premier:* Lara Giddings.

Speaker of the House of Assembly: Michael Polley.

TAS Government website: http://www.service.tas.gov.au/

ECONOMY

Budget. Revenue is derived chiefly from taxation (pay-roll, motor, lottery and land tax, business franchises and stamp duties), and from grants and reimbursements from the Commonwealth government. General Purpose Payments (GPPs) are made to States from the Commonwealth and can be spent at the State's discretion.

Other Specific Purpose Payment (SPP) Grants from the Commonwealth are mainly used to provide essential services such as hospitals, housing, roads and educational services.

Consolidated Revenue Fund receipts and expenditure, in $A1m., for financial years ending 30 June:

	2000–01	2001–02
Revenue	2,301	2,420
Expenditure	2,297	2,416

Total State Government Sector Debt as at 30 June 2001 was, in real terms, $A2,036m. (2000, $A2,458m.).

In 2000–01 State government revenue from taxes amounted to $A547m., of which pay-roll tax provided $A165m.; motor tax, $A96m.; taxes on property, $A161m.; taxes on gambling, insurance and levies on statutory corporations, $A234m.; and franchise taxes, $A6m.

Banking and Finance. The total value of deposits at 30 June 2001 was $A3,489m. The value of loans at 30 June 2001 was $A5,327m.

ENERGY AND NATURAL RESOURCES

Electricity. Installed capacity is 2,502 MW. In the year ended 30 June 2000 total consumption stood at 9,563m. kWh, including 1,759m. kWh by residential customers. The disaggregation process has created the new Hydro-Electric Commission, Aurora Energy and Transend Networks.

Minerals. Output of principal metallic minerals in 2000–01 was (in tonnes): zinc, 143,200; iron ore pellets, 2,027,300; copper, 105,400; lead, 40,600; tin, 14,800.

Agriculture. There were 4,286 agricultural establishments at 30 March 2000 occupying a total area of 1·7m. ha. Principal crops (1999–2000): wheat (19,800 tonnes from 6,300 ha); barley (22,200 tonnes from 9,100 ha); oats (9,700 tonnes from 6,300 ha); peas (28,500 tonnes from 4,500 ha); potatoes (267,200 tonnes from 5,700 ha); hay (222,200 tonnes from 50,600 ha). The estimated gross value of recorded production from agriculture in 1999–2000 was (in $A1m.): livestock products, 217·2; livestock slaughterings and other disposals, 153·6; crops, 320·4; total gross value, 691·2. Livestock at 31 March 2001: cattle, 682,300; sheep, 3,483,700; pigs, 22,200. Wool produced during 2000–01 was 15,218 tonnes, valued at $A85·0m. In 2000–01, 5,949 tonnes of butter and 32,355 tonnes of cheese, were produced.

Forestry. Indigenous forests cover a considerable part of the State, and the sawmilling and woodchipping industries are very important. Production of sawn timber in 2000–01 was 339,000 cu. metres. Newsprint and paper are produced from native hardwoods, principally eucalypts.

Fisheries. The gross value of production from Tasmania's fisheries in 2000–01 was $A311·9m., a 12·7% increase on 1999–2000 figures.

INDUSTRY

The most important manufactures for export are refined metals, woodchips, newsprint and other paper manufactures, pigments, woollen goods, fruit pulp, confectionery, butter, cheese, preserved and dried vegetables, sawn timber, and processed fish products. The electrolytic-zinc works at Risdon near Hobart treat large quantities of local and imported ore, and produce zinc, sulphuric acid, superphosphate, sulphate of ammonia, cadmium and other by-products. At George Town, large-scale plants produce refined aluminium and manganese alloys. During

1999–2000, 5,145,300 tonnes (green weight) of woodchips were produced. In 1999–2000 employment in manufacturing establishments was 20,200; wages and salaries totalled $A745m.; turnover, $A5,490·3m.

Labour. There were an estimated 217,100 persons (based on trend estimates) in the labour force in Nov. 2002 and an estimated 374,900 civilian Tasmanians aged 15 and over, yielding a workforce participation rate of 57·9% compared to 58·7% in Nov. 2001.

Trade Unions. In 2000 Tasmania had the highest rate of trade union membership of any Australian State, at 31·3%. This compared with 34·6% in Aug. 1998 and 39·3% in Aug. 1996.

INTERNATIONAL TRADE

Imports and Exports. In 2000–01 exports totalled $A2,435·6m. to overseas countries. The principal countries of destination in 2000–01 (with values in $A1m.) for overseas exports were: Japan, 573·3; Hong Kong, 252·8; USA, 229·8; Taiwan, 214·0; Korea, 184·0. Exports to the European Community totalled $A154·0m. In 2000–01 direct imports into Tasmania totalled $A524·0m. from overseas countries.

Commodities by value (in $A1m.) exported to overseas countries in 1999–2000 included: non-ferrous metals, 793·2; metallic ores and metal scrap, 242·7; fish, crustaceans and molluscs, 176·7; road vehicles and transport equipment, 107·3; dairy products, 101·0; meat and meat preparations, 88·7; vegetables and fruit, 44·7.

COMMUNICATIONS

Roads. In 2001 there were approximately 24,000 km of roads open to general traffic, of which 370 km were National Highway and 3,350 km were arterial State roads. Motor vehicles registered at 31 Oct. 2001 comprised 246,367 passenger vehicles, 76,432 commercial vehicles and 8,469 motorcycles. In 2001 there were 61 road accident fatalities.

Rail. Tasmania's rail network, incorporating 867 km of railways, is primarily a freight system with no regular passenger services. There are some small tourist railways, notably the newly rebuilt 34 km Abt Wilderness Railway on the west coast.

Civil Aviation. Regular passenger and freight services connect the south, north and northwest of the State with the mainland. During 1999–2000 the six main airports handled 1,736,000 passengers and 5,470 tonnes of freight.

Shipping. There are four major commercial ports, Burnie, Devonport, Launceston and Hobart. Total tonnage through these ports in 2000–01 was 13·6m. mass tonnes. Passenger ferry services connect Tasmania with the mainland and offshore islands.

In 2000–01 passenger/vehicle services carried 330,961 people, 127,124 motor vehicles and 21,771 Twenty-Foot Equivalent Units (TEUs).

Telecommunications. In April 1999 there were 34 post offices and 152 licensees. In 2000 there were 84,000 households with home computer access (45% of all households) and 48,000 households with home Internet access (26%). In 2000, 49% of all households had access to a mobile phone.

SOCIAL INSTITUTIONS

Justice. The Supreme Court of Tasmania, with civil, criminal, ecclesiastical, admiralty and matrimonial jurisdiction, established by Royal Charter on 13 Oct. 1823, is a superior court of record, with both original and appellate jurisdiction, and consists of a Chief Justice and five puisne judges. There are also inferior civil courts with limited jurisdiction, licensing courts, mining courts, courts of petty sessions and coroners' courts.

In 2000–01 there were 58,295 recorded offences, of which 51,339 were against property; 3,660 against the person; and 2,879 fraud and similar offences. The total police force at 30 June 2001 was 1,131. There are three prisons and one detention centre which received a combined total of 347 prisoners at 30 June 2001.

Religion. At the census of 2001 the following numbers of adherents of the principal religions were recorded:

Anglican Church	147,413	Other Christian	10,526
Roman Catholic	87,691	Indefinite and not stated	47,430
Uniting Church	30,376	No religion	78,672
Presbyterian	12,508	Non-Christian	2,975
Baptist	8,984		
		Total	456,652

Education. Education is controlled by the State and is free, secular and compulsory between the ages of 6 and 16. In 2001 government schools had a total enrolment of 61,976 pupils, including 25,571 at secondary level; 67 private schools had a total enrolment of 20,821 pupils, including 10,354 at secondary level.

Vocational Education and Training is mostly provided by TAFE Tasmania through five state-wide product-aligned institutes. In 2001 there were 45,727 enrolments in Vocational Education and Training activities.

Tertiary education is offered at the University of Tasmania in Hobart and Launceston and the Australian Maritime College in Launceston. In 2001 the University (established 1890) had 12,820 students and 1,556 academic staff.

Health. In 2000–01 there were 109 public hospitals with 1,090 beds and nine private hospitals with 831 beds. There were 1,814 nurses employed in public hospitals.

Welfare. The number of age and disability pensions (including wives' and carers' pensions) on 30 June 2001 was: age, 48,499; disability support, 21,655; carer, 2,005. There were 976 widows' and 20,217 single parent payments current at 30 June 2001, and basic family payment was being paid for 83,433 children under 16 years.

CULTURE

Broadcasting. In 2002 there were four TV broadcasters and 21 radio stations.

Press. There are three daily papers with a combined circulation of 120,710 at March 2001. The largest circulation for a Tasmanian daily is for the Saturday edition of *The Mercury*, with a circulation of 65,097.

Tourism. In 2000–01 there was an estimated 531,000 adult visitors arrived to Tasmania.

Festivals. The Taste of Tasmania is a seven-day food and wine festival held on Hobart's waterfront over the New Year. The annual festival attracts approximately 200,000 patrons.

Libraries. The State Library of Tasmania delivers its services through a Statewide network of 49 public libraries and seven reference specialist libraries. These include the Tasmaniana Library, the W. L. Crowther Library, and the Allport Library and Museum of Fine Arts.

Theatre and Opera. The Theatre Royal in Hobart, established in 1834, has resumed its pre-eminent position in the city's cultural scene following extensive renovation.

Museums and Galleries. The Tasmanian Museum and Art Gallery (TMAG) houses collections in the fields of fine and applied art, zoology, geology, botany, history, anthropology and applied science. The Queen Victoria Museum and Art Gallery was established in 1891.

FURTHER READING
Statistical Information: The State Government Statistical Office (200 Collins St., Hobart), established in 1877, became in 1924 the Tasmanian Office of the Australian Bureau of Statistics, but continues to serve State statistical needs as required.
Main publications: Annual Statistical Bulletins (e.g., *Demography, Agriculture, Government Finance, Manufacturing Industry* etc.).—*Tasmanian Pocket Year Book.* Annual (from 1913).—*Tasmanian Year Book.* Annual (from 1967; biennial from 1986).—Monthly *Tasmanian Statistical Indicators* (from July 1945).
E-mail address: Sales and Inquiries: client.services@abs.gov.au
Website: http://abs.gov.au

Kepars, I., *Tasmania.* [Bibliography] ABC-Clio, Oxford and Santa Barbara (CA), 1997
Robson, L., *A History of Tasmania. Vol. 1: Van Diemen's Land from the Earliest Times to 1855.* Melbourne, 1983.—*A History of Tasmania. Vol. 2: Colony and State from 1856 to the 1980s.* Melbourne, 1990

State library: The State Library of Tasmania, 91 Murray St., Hobart.
Website: http://statelibrary.tas.gov.au

VICTORIA

KEY HISTORICAL EVENTS

The first permanent settlement in the area was formed at Portland Bay in 1834. Regular government was first established in 1839. Victoria, formerly a portion of New South Wales, was proclaimed a separate colony in 1851 at much the same time as gold was discovered. A new constitution giving responsible government to the colony was proclaimed on 23 Nov. 1855. This event had far-reaching effects, as the population increased from 76,162 in 1850 to 589,160 in 1864. By this time the main impetus behind the search for gold had waned and the new arrivals availed themselves of the opening of the pastoral and agricultural lands to smaller holders and the gradual development of manufacturing industries. Victoria federated with the other Australian states to form the Commonwealth of Australia in 1901.

TERRITORY AND POPULATION

The State has an area of 227,420 sq. km, and, at 31 Dec. 2001, a resident population of 4,854,100 (annual growth rate, 1·3%). The 1996 census population was 4,373,520. Victoria has the greatest proportion of people from non-English-speaking countries of any State or Territory, with (1996) 2·3% from Italy, 1·4% from Greece and 1·3% from Vietnam. Of the 84,150 immigrants to Australia in 1998–99, 17,290, or 20·5%, settled in Victoria—second only to New South Wales.

Estimated population at 30 June 1999, within 11 'Statistical Divisions': Melbourne, 3,413,894; Barwon, 245,343; Goulburn, 186,500; Loddon, 161,263; Gippsland, 152,943; Central Highlands, 137,221; Western District, 98,954; Ovens-Murray, 90,452; Mallee, 88,118; East Gippsland, 80,652; Wimmera, 51,453.

Population of urban centres with over 10,000 inhabitants at the 1996 census: Melbourne, 2,865,329; Geelong, 125,382; Ballarat, 64,831; Bendigo, 59,936; Shepparton-Mooroopna, 31,945; Melton, 30,304; Warrnambool, 26,052; Albury-Wodonga (Wodonga Part), 25,825; Cranbourne, 24,752; Mildura, 24,142; Sunbury, 22,126; Traralgon, 18,993; Wangaratta, 15,527; Moe-Yallourn, 15,512; Morwell, 13,823; Sale, 13,366; Craigieburn, 12,919; Horsham, 12,591; Bacchus Marsh, 11,279; Ocean Grove-Barwon Heads, 11,272; Bairnsdale, 10,890; Echuca-Moama (Echuca part), 10,014.

SOCIAL STATISTICS

Statistics for calendar years:

	Births	Deaths	Marriages	Divorces
1997	60,732	33,261	25,456	12,463
1998	60,492	32,007	26,372	12,307
1999	58,875	31,918	27,252	12,742
2000	59,171	32,018	26,852	12,401

The annual rates per 1,000 of the mean resident population (estimate) in 2000 were: births, 12·4; deaths, 6·7; marriages, 5·6; divorces, 2·6. Infant mortality rate, 2000, 4·5 per 1,000 live births. Expectation of life, 2000: males, 77·1 years; females, 82·3 years.

CLIMATE

See AUSTRALIA: Climate.

CONSTITUTION AND GOVERNMENT

Victoria, formerly a portion of New South Wales, was, in 1851, proclaimed a separate colony, with a partially elective Legislative Council. In 1856 responsible government was conferred, the legislative power being vested in a parliament of two Houses, the Legislative Council and the Legislative Assembly. At present the Council consists of 44 members who are elected for two terms of the Assembly, one-half retiring at each election. The Assembly consists of 88 members, elected for four years from the date of its first meeting unless sooner dissolved by the Governor. Members and electors of both Houses must be aged 18 years and Australian citizens or those British subjects previously enrolled as electors, according to the Constitution Act 1975. No property qualification is required, but judges, members of the Commonwealth Parliament, undischarged bankrupts and persons convicted of an offence which is punishable by life imprisonment, may not be members of either House. Single voting (one elector one vote) and compulsory preferential voting apply to Council and Assembly elections. Enrolment for Council and Assembly electors is compulsory. The Council may not initiate or amend money bills, but may suggest amendments in such bills other than amendments which would increase any charge. A bill shall not become law unless passed by both Houses.

In the exercise of the executive power the Governor is advised by a Cabinet of responsible Ministers. Section 50 of the Constitution Act 1975 provides that the number of Ministers shall not at any one time exceed 22, of whom not more than 6 may sit in the Legislative Council and not more than 17 may sit in the Legislative Assembly.

RECENT ELECTIONS

In elections to the Legislative Assembly held on 18 Sept. 1999 the Labor Party won 41 seats with 45·5% of votes cast; the Liberal Party, 36 (42·2%); the National Party, 7 (4·9%); others, 3 (7·4%). Turn-out was 76·3%.

In the simultaneous elections to the Legislative Council the Liberal Party won 25 seats; the Labor Party, 13; and the National Party, 6.

CURRENT ADMINISTRATION

Governor: John Landy, AC, MBE.

The Labor Cabinet was as follows in Feb. 2003:

Premier, Minister for Multicultural Affairs: Stephen Bracks.

Deputy Premier, Minister for the Environment, Water and Victorian Communities: John Thwaites. *Transport and Major Projects:* Peter Batchelor. *Local Government and Housing:* Candy Broad. *State and Regional Development, Innovation and Treasurer:* John Brumby. *Agriculture:* Bob Cameron. *Health:* Bronwyn Pike. *Education and Training:* Lynne Kosky. *Community Services:* Sherryl Garbutt. *Finance and Consumer Affairs:* John Lenders. *Police and Emergency Services, Corrections:* Andre Haermeyer. *Planning, Arts, Women's Affairs:* Mary Delahunty. *Education Services, Youth Affairs and Employment:* Jacinta Allan. *Small Business, Information and Communication Technology:* Marsha Thomson. *Attorney General, Minister for Industrial Relations and Workcover:* Rob Hulls. *Sport and Recreation, Commonwealth Affairs:* Justin Madden. *Gaming and Racing, and Tourism:* John Pandazopoulos. *Aged Care, Aboriginal Affairs:* Gavin Jennings. *Manufacturing and Export, Financial Services Industry:* Tim Holding.

Speaker of the Legislative Assembly: Judy Maddigan.

VIC Government website: http://www.vic.gov.au/

ECONOMY

Budget. State expenditure 1999–2000: total outlay (in $A1m.), 20,321, including education, 5,629; health, 5,027; transport and communications, 2,029; public order and safety, 1,956; general public services, 838. State revenue 1999–2000: 22,027.

Local expenditure 1999–2000: total outlay (in $A1m.), 3,175, including transport and communications, 844; housing and community amenities, 579; recreation and culture, 569; social security and welfare, 430; general public services, 322. Local revenue 1999–2000: 3,123.

Performance. In 1999–2000 Victoria's gross state product represented 25·43% of Australia's total GDP.

Banking and Finance. The State Bank of Victoria, the largest bank in the State, provides domestic and international services for business and personal customers and is the largest supplier of housing finance in Victoria. In 1990 it ran into debt and was acquired by the Commonwealth from the Victorian government in Sept. 1990.

The 11 major trading banks in Victoria are the Commonwealth Bank of Australia, the Australia and New Zealand Banking Group, the Westpac Banking Corporation, the National Australia Bank, the Bank of Melbourne, the St George Bank, the Challenge Bank, the Metway Bank, the State Bank of New South Wales, Bendigo Bank and Citibank. Banks had a total of 1,217 branches and 1,262 agencies between them at 30 June 2000.

In Sept. 2001 bank deposits repayable totalled $A105,770m. and loans $A132,832m.

ENERGY AND NATURAL RESOURCES

Electricity. In the year to 30 June 1999 total production was 39,767m. kWh; total consumption stood at 36,314m. kWh, including 10,631m. kWh by residential customers.

In 1993 the State government began a major restructure of the government-owned electricity industry along competitive lines. The distribution sector was privatized in 1995, and four generator companies in 1997.

About 90% of power generated is supplied by four brown-coal fired generating stations. There are two other thermal stations and three hydro-electric stations in northeast Victoria. Victoria is also entitled to approximately 30% of the output of the Snowy Mountains hydro-electric scheme and half the output of the Hume hydro-electric station, both of which are in New South Wales.

Oil and Gas. Crude oil in commercially recoverable quantities was first discovered in 1967 in two large fields offshore, in East Gippsland in Bass Strait, between 65 and 80 km from land. These fields, with 20 other fields since discovered, have been assessed as containing initial recoverable oil reserves of 4,063·4m. bbls. Estimated remaining oil reserves as at 30 June 2001 is 432·0m. bbls. Production of crude oil (2000–01), 59m. bbls.

Natural gas was discovered offshore in East Gippsland in 1965. The initial recoverable gas reserves were 272·0m. cu. metres. Estimated remaining gas reserves (30 June 2001), 117·68m. cu. metres. Production of natural gas (2000–01), 6·43m. cu. metres. Natural gas is distributed to residential and industrial consumers through a network of 23,400 km of mains.

Liquefied petroleum gas is produced after extraction of the propane and butane fractions from the untreated oil and gas.

Brown Coal. Major deposits of brown coal are located in the Central Gippsland region and comprise approximately 94% of the total resources in Victoria. In 1993 the resource was estimated to be 0·2m. megatonnes, of which about 52,000 megatonnes was economically recoverable. It is young and soft with a water content of 60% to 70%. In the Latrobe Valley section of the region, the thick brown coal seams underlie an area from 10 to 30 km wide extending over approximately 70 km from Yallourn in the west to the south of Sale in the east. It can be won continuously in large quantities and at low cost by specialized mechanical plant.

The primary use of these reserves is to fuel electricity generating stations. Production of brown coal in 1999–2000 was 67·4m. tonnes.

Minerals. Production, 1999–2000: gold, 4,791 kg; (in 1,000 tonnes) basalt, 13,074; sand for concrete, 4,977.

Land Settlement. Of the total area of Victoria (22·76m. ha), 13,973,915 ha on 30 June 1984 were either alienated or in the process of alienation. The remainder (8,786,085) constituted Crown land as follows: perpetual leases, grazing and other leases and licences, 2,160,352; reservations including forest and timber reserves, water, catchment and drainage purposes, national parks, wildlife reserves, water frontages and other reserves, plus unoccupied and unreserved including areas set aside for roads, 6,625,733.

Agriculture. In the year ended June 2000 there were 37,304 agricultural establishments (excluding those with an estimated value of agricultural operations less than $A5,000) with a total area of 13·3m. ha. The estimated gross value of agricultural production in 1999–2000 was $A6·8m. Principal crops produced in 1999–2000 (in 1,000 tonnes): wheat, 2,642; oats, 296; barley, 1,189; potatoes, 295.

Preliminary estimated value of livestock production in 2000–01 totalled $A2·1bn., including wool production $A409m.

Grape growing, particularly for winemaking, is an important crop. In 1999–2000, 449,000 tonnes of grapes were produced from 36,300 ha of vineyards. Other produce (estimate, in tonnes), 1999–2000: tomatoes, 249,200; apples, 98,200; oranges, 84,200.

Forestry. Commercial timber production is an increasingly important source of income. As at Sept. 2000 there were 318,633 ha of plantation. Of Victoria's 7·3m.

ha of native forest (June 1997), 6·2m. ha (85%) were publicly owned (2·7m. ha in conservation reserves).

Fisheries. The total catch in 2000–01 was 9,666 tonnes and was worth $A130·2m. Of this, crustaceans totalled 895 tonnes with a value of $A24·7m.

INDUSTRY
Total turnover in the manufacturing industry in 2000–01 was $A74,311·9m. At 30 June 2000 there were 292,100 persons employed in the manufacturing sector.

Labour. At Aug. 2001 there were 2,455,100 persons in the labour force (63·2% of the civilian population aged 15 years and over), of whom 2,303,100 were employed: wholesale and retail trade, 463,300; finance, insurance, property and business services, 349,800; manufacturing, 361,100; health and community services, 221,200; construction, 158,100; education, 165,700; culture, recreation, personal and other services, 143,600; transport and storage, 103,900; accommodation, cafes and restaurants, 91,000; agriculture, forestry and fishing, 91,300; government administration and defence, 80,600; communication services, 49,200; electricity, gas and water supply, 20,500; mining, 3,800. There were 152,000 unemployed persons in Aug. 2001 (6·2% of the labour force).

Trade Unions. There were 57 trade unions with a total membership of 680,000 at 30 June 1996.

INTERNATIONAL TRADE
Imports and Exports. The total value of the overseas imports and exports of Victoria, including bullion and specie, was as follows (in $A1m.):

	1998–99	1999–2000	2000–01
Imports	31,014	33,717	36,485
Exports[1]	16,484	19,034	22,510

[1]Includes re-exports.

The chief exports in 2000–01 (in $A1m.) were: food and live animals chiefly for food, 5,772; machinery and transport equipment, 4,083; manufacturing goods, 2,901; crude materials, inedible (except fuels), 2,164; minerals, fuels, lubricants and related materials, 1,393. Exports in 2000–01 (in $A1m.) went mainly to Japan, 2,248; USA, 2,073; New Zealand, 1,876; Singapore, 1,518; China, 1,430; Republic of Korea, 1,308; Saudi Arabia, 1,206; Hong Kong, 1,062; Taiwan, 816; UK, 696.

The chief imports in 2000–01 (in $A1m.) were: machinery and transport equipment, 15,435; miscellaneous manufactured articles, 6,205; manufacturing goods, 4,773; chemical and related products, 3,885; minerals, fuels, lubricants and related materials, 2,309; food and live animals chiefly for food, 1,430. Imports in 2000–01 (in $A1m.) came mainly from the USA, 7,377; Japan, 4,828; China, 3,890; Germany, 2,585; UK, 1,842; New Zealand, 1,535; Republic of Korea, 1,065; Indonesia, 1,049; Malaysia, 1,037; Italy, 1,028.

COMMUNICATIONS
Roads. There are over 150,000 km of roads open for general traffic, consisting of (at 31 Oct. 2000) 1,004 km of National Highways, 6,524 km of state highways and freeways, 14,710 km of main, tourist and forest roads, and (at 30 June 1999) 133,960 km of other roads and streets. The number of registered motor vehicles (other than tractors and motor cycles) at 31 March 2001 was 3,222,941. There were 407 road accident fatalities in 2000.

Rail. The railways are the property of the State and the land is owned and managed by the Victorian Rail Track Corporation (VicTrack). The railway land and infrastructure was transferred from the Public Transport Corporation (PTC) to VicTrack during privatization in 1996–99. In 1999 the non-electrified intra-State railway was leased (for a total of 45 years) to Freight Victoria (trading as Freight Australia), a private company which in May 1999 purchased the business of V/Line Freight Corporation from the State. The passenger rail businesses were franchised to the following private operators in Aug. 1999: National Express, Melbourne Transport Enterprises Pty Ltd, and Metrolink Victoria Pty Ltd.

Victoria's rail network consists of over 5,000 km of track, comprising 1,274 km of standard gauge (1,435 mm). There are 3,745 km of broad gauge (1,600 mm) of which 336 km are electrified. 849 km of standard gauge lines form part of the interstate rail network from Brisbane to Perth and are under the control of the Australian Rail Track Corporation. In 2000–01, 7·7m. tonnes of freight were carried by Freight Australia and there was a total of 139·4m. passenger boardings (11·5m. non-urban). Melbourne's tramway and light rail network extends to 241 km and is the tenth longest in the world. There were 131·4m. boardings in 2000–01.

Civil Aviation. There were 12,939,135 domestic and regional passenger movements and 3,043,169 international passenger movements in 2000 at Melbourne (Tullamarine) airport (Australia's second busiest airport after Sydney). Total freight handled in 2000 was 271,605 tonnes (international, 199,437; domestic, 72,168).

Shipping. The four major commercial ports are at Melbourne, Geelong, Portland and Hastings. Together, these ports serviced 4,045 ships (Melbourne, 3,019; Geelong, 555; Portland, 278; Hastings, 193) with a total trade of 44·8m. mass tonnes in 2001–02.

Telecommunications. In May 1998, 93·5% of households had a fixed telephone connected; 44·3% had mobile phones. In 2000 there were 973,000 households with home computer access (56% of all households) and 598,000 households with home Internet access (34%).

Postal Services. At June 2001 there were 1,055 retail outlets including 842 licensed post offices. Postal items handled by Australia Post in Victoria (1999–2000) totalled 1,637·2m.

SOCIAL INSTITUTIONS

Justice. There is a Supreme Court with a Chief Justice and 21 puisne judges. There are a county court, magistrates' courts, a court of licensing and a bankruptcy court.

During 1996–97 the State's prisons were replaced with new facilities developed, owned and operated by the private sector. During 1999–2000 approximately 45% of Victoria's prison population was accommodated in the three private prisons. There are 10 public prisons remaining.

At 30 June 2000 the daily average of prisoners held stood at 3,153. Police personnel at 30 June 2001, 9,744.

Religion. There is no State Church, and no State assistance has been given to religion since 1875. At the 1991 census the following were the enumerated numbers of the principal religions: Catholic, 1,237,399; Anglican, 772,632; Uniting, 342,493 (including Methodist); Orthodox, 199,063; Presbyterian, 193,300; other Christian, 255,375; Muslim, 49,617; Jewish, 33,882; Buddhist, 42,350; no religion, 612,074; not stated, 474,921.

Education. In 2000 there were 1,629 government schools with 528,189 pupils and 35,660 full-time teaching staff plus full-time equivalents of part-time teaching staff: 313,369 pupils were in primary schools and 214,820 in secondary schools. As from 1990 students attending special schools have not been identified separately and have been allocated to either primary or secondary level of education. They are integrated where possible into mainstream education. There were, in 2000, 695 non-government schools, excluding commercial colleges, with 18,830 teaching staff and 273,506 pupils; 138,351 pupils at primary schools; and 135,155 pupils at secondary schools.

All higher education institutions, excluding continuing education and technical and further education (TAFE), now fall under the Unified National System, and can no longer be split into universities and colleges of advanced education. In addition, a number of institutional amalgamations and name changes occurred in the 12 months prior to the commencement of the 1992 academic year. There are ten publicly funded higher education institutions including eight State universities, Marcus Oldham College and the Australian Catholic University (partly privately funded), and the Melbourne University Private, established in 1998. At 31 March 2000 there were 185,978 students in higher education.

Health. In 1999–2000 there were 142 public hospitals with 12,072 beds, and 86 private hospitals; 17,660 nurses were employed in public hospitals. Total government outlay on health in 1999–2000 was $A5,027m.

Welfare. Victoria was the first State of Australia to make a statutory provision for the payment of Age Pensions. The Act came into operation on 18 Jan. 1901, and continued until 1 July 1909, when the Australian Invalid and Old Age Pension Act came into force. The Social Services Consolidation Act, which came into operation on 1 July 1947, repealed the various legislative enactments relating to age and invalid pensions, maternity allowances, child endowment, unemployment and sickness benefits and, while following in general the Acts repealed, considerably liberalized many of their provisions.

The number of age and disability pensions (including wives' and carers' pensions) on 30 June 1999 was: age, 439,595; disability support, 136,218; carer, 10,266. There were 7,680 widows' and 84,368 single parent payments current at 30 June 1999, and basic family payment was being paid for 789,899 children under 16 years.

CULTURE

Cinema. During the year ended April 1999, 2·6m. (68·3% of Victoria's population) people attended cinema screenings.

Tourism. In 1999–2000 the number of short-term overseas visitors to Australia who specified Victoria as their main destination was 685,950 (14·7% of total overseas visitors to Australia), with 466,480 nominating 'holiday' or 'visiting friends/ relatives' as purpose of their visit. New Zealand represented the major source of international visitors with 19·9%; followed by the UK and Ireland (11·7%), USA (11·3%), Singapore (7·5%) and Japan (6·8%).

Libraries. During the year ended April 1999, 37·5% of Victoria's population visited national, State or local libraries.

FURTHER READING

Australian Bureau of Statistics Victorian Office. *Victorian Year Book.—Summary of Statistics (annual).*

State library: The State Library of Victoria, 328 Swanston St., Melbourne 3000.
State statistical office: Victorian Office, Australian Bureau of Statistics, 525 Collins Street, Melbourne 3000. *Deputy Commonwealth Statistician:* Stuart Jackson.

WESTERN AUSTRALIA

KEY HISTORICAL EVENTS

In 1791 the British navigator George Vancouver took formal possession of the country around King George Sound. In 1826 the government of New South Wales sent 20 convicts and a detachment of soldiers to King George Sound and formed a settlement then called Frederickstown. The following year, Capt. James Stirling surveyed the coast from King George Sound to the Swan River, and in May 1829 Capt. Charles Fremantle took possession of the territory. In June 1829 Capt. Stirling founded the Swan River Settlement (now the Commonwealth State of Western Australia) and the towns of Perth and Fremantle and was appointed Lieut.-Governor.

Large grants of land were made to the early settlers and agricultural and pastoral occupations were pursued by a small population with varying success until, in 1850, with the colony languishing, the inhabitants' successfully petitioned for the colony to be made a penal settlement. Between 1850 and 1868 (in which year transportation ceased), 9,668 convicts were sent out. In 1870 partially representative government was instituted, and in 1890 the administration was vested in the Governor, a legislative council and a legislative assembly. The legislative council was, in the first instance, nominated by the Governor but in 1893 it became elective. Western Australia federated with the other Australian states to form the Commonwealth of Australia in 1901.

In the 1914–18 war Western Australia provided more volunteers for overseas military service in proportion to population than any other State (possibly because Western Australia had a higher proportion of British migrants and single men).

The worldwide depression of 1929 brought widespread unemployment (30% of trade union membership), and in 1933 over two-thirds voted to leave the Federation.

While there were modest improvements in the standard of living through the 1930s, it was the 1939–45 war which brought regular employment for all.

Japanese aircraft attacked the Western Australia coast in 1942. Talk of a 'Brisbane line', which would abandon the West to invasion, only served to reinforce Western Australia's sense of isolation from the rest of the nation. The post-war years saw increasing demand for wheat and wool but the 1954–55 decline in farm incomes led to diversification. Work began in the early 1950s on steel production and oil processing. Oil was discovered in 1953 but it was not until 1966 that it was commercially exploited. The discovery of deposits of iron ore in the Pilbara, bauxite in the Darling scarp, nickel in Kambalda and ilmenite from mineral sands led to the State becoming a major world supplier of mineral exports by 1965.

TERRITORY AND POPULATION

Western Australia lies between 113° 09' and 129° E. long. and 13° 44' and 35° 08' S. lat.; its area is 2,529,880 sq. km and it has 12,500 km of coastline.

The population at each census from 1947 was as follows[1]:

	Males	Females	Total		Males	Females	Total
1947	258,076	244,404	502,480	1976	599,959	578,383	1,178,342
1954	330,358	309,413	639,771	1981	659,249	642,807	1,300,056
1961	375,452	361,177	736,629	1986	736,131	722,888	1,459,019
1966	432,569	415,531	848,100	1991	793,626	792,767	1,586,393
1971	539,332	514,502	1,053,834	1996	862,645	863,450	1,726,095

[1]1961 and earlier exclude persons of predominantly Aboriginal descent; from 1966 figures refer to total population (*i.e.*, including Aborigines). Figures from 1971 are based on estimated resident population.

Of the total 1996 census population, 1,178,331 were born in Australia. Married persons numbered 710,468 (355,594 males and 354,874 females); widowers, 13,656; widows, 59,635; divorced, 39,624 males and 48,986 females; never married, 233,048 males and 186,081 females. The resident population at 31 Dec. 2001 was 1,918,800 (annual growth rate of 1·3%).

Perth, the capital, had an estimated resident population of 1,400,500 at 30 June 2001.

Principal local government areas outside the metropolitan area, with population at 30 June 2000: Mandurah, 45,580; Kalgoorlie-Boulder, 32,042; Albany, 29,873; Bunbury, 28,779; Busselton, 22,751; Geraldton, 19,510; Roebourne, 14,320; Port Hedland, 13,171.

SOCIAL STATISTICS

Statistics for calendar years[1]

	Births	Deaths	Marriages	Divorces
1996	24,793	11,027	10,294	4,895
1997	25,702	10,905	10,450	5,022
1998	24,864	10,741	10,501	5,210
1999	24,849	10,877	10,197	5,317
2000	25,093	10,668	11,000	5,276

[1]Figures are on state of usual residence basis.

CLIMATE

Western Australia is a region of several climate zones, ranging from the tropical north to the semi-arid interior and Mediterranean-style climate of the southwest. Most of the State is a plateau between 300 and 600 metres above sea level. Except in the far southwest coast, maximum temperatures in excess of 40°C have been recorded throughout the State. The normal average number of sunshine hours per day is 8·0.

CONSTITUTION AND GOVERNMENT

In 1870 partially representative government was instituted, and in 1890 the administration was vested in the Governor, a Legislative Council and a Legislative Assembly. The Legislative Council was, in the first instance, nominated by the Governor, but it was provided that in the event of the population of the colony reaching 60,000, it should be elective. In 1893 this limit of population being reached, the Colonial Parliament amended the Constitution accordingly.

The *Legislative Council* consists of 34 members elected for a term of four years. There are six electoral regions for Legislative Council elections. Four electoral regions return five members and the other two electoral regions seven members. Each member represents the entire region.

There are 57 members of the *Legislative Assembly*, each member representing one of the 57 electoral districts of the State. Members are elected for the duration of the Assembly which may be for a period of up to four years. The qualifications applying to candidates and electors are identical for the Legislative Council and the Legislative Assembly. A candidate must be at least 18 years of age and free from legal incapacity, be an Australian citizen, and be enrolled, or qualified for enrolment, as an elector. A member of the Commonwealth Parliament or of the legislature of a territory or another state, an undischarged bankrupt or a debtor against whose estate there is a subsisting receiving order in bankruptcy, or a person who has been attainted or convicted of treason or felony, is disqualified from membership of the legislature. No person may hold office as a member of the Legislative Assembly and the Legislative Council at the same time. An elector must be at least 18 years of age, be an Australian citizen (or a British subject who was at some time within the three months preceding 26 Jan. 1984 an elector of the Assembly or the Commonwealth parliament), be free from legal incapacity, and must have resided in Western Australia for three months continuously, and in the electoral district for which he or she claims enrolment for a continuous period of one month immediately preceding the date of his or her claim. Enrolment is compulsory for all qualified persons. Voting at elections is on the preferential system and is compulsory for all enrolled persons. A system of proportional representation is used to elect members of the Legislative Council.

Ordinary members of the legislature were paid (with effect from 1 Sept. 2001) a salary of $A100,000 a year with an electorate allowance of $A21,000 a year. They also receive an additional electorate allowance ranging from $A400 to $A17,500 a year according to location of the electorate.

The Premier receives a salary of $A232,000 and other ministers $A180,000. No additional allowances are paid.

RECENT ELECTIONS

Legislative Assembly representation in Feb. 2003: Australian Labor Party, 32; Liberal Party, 16; National Party of Australia, 5; Independent Liberal Party, 2; ind., 2. Legislative Council following the State general election in Feb. 2001: Australian Labor Party, 13; Liberal Party, 12; Greens (WA), 5; One Nation, 3; National Party of Australia, 1.

CURRENT ADMINISTRATION

Governor: Lieut.-Gen. John M. Sanderson, AC.

Lieut.-Governor and Chief Justice: David Kingsley Malcolm, AC.

In Feb. 2003 the Cabinet comprised:

Premier, Minister for Public Sector Management, Federal Affairs, Science, Citizenship and Multicultural Interests: Dr Geoff Gallop.

Deputy Premier, Treasurer, Minister for Energy: Eric Ripper. *Agriculture, Forestry and Fisheries, the Midwest, Wheatbelt and Great Southern:* Kim Chance. *Housing and Works, Local Government and Regional Development, the Kimberley, Pilbara and Gascoyne:* Tom Stephens. *Consumer and Employment Protection:* John Kobelke. *Attorney General, Minister for Justice and Legal Affairs, Electoral Affairs, Peel and the South West:* Jim McGinty. *Environment and Heritage:* Dr Judy Edwards. *Police and Emergency Services:* Michelle Roberts. *Planning and Infrastructure:* Alannah MacTiernan. *State Development, Tourism, Small Business:* Clive Brown. *Education and Training, Sport and Recreation, Indigenous Affairs:* Alan Carpenter. *Community Development, Women's Interests, Seniors and Youth, Disability Services, Culture and the Arts:* Sheila McHale. *Health:* Bob Kucera, APM. *Racing and Gaming, Government Enterprises, Goldfields-Esperance:* Nick Griffiths.

Speaker of the Legislative Assembly: Fred Riebeling.

WA Government website: http://www.wa.gov.au/

ECONOMY

Budget. Revenue and expenditure (in $A1m.) in years ending 30 June:

	1998–99	1999–2000	2000–01	2001–02[1]
Revenue	8,984·3	9,692·8	10,531·5	10,713·5
Expenditure	9,119·3	9,723·0	10,276·4	10,661·9

[1]Projected.

The general government net operating surplus of $A51·6m. projected for 2001–02 indicates that the State's finances have returned to a more sustainable path following the deficits of 1998–99 and 1999–2000.

Banking and Finance. In Sept. 2001 bank deposits totalled $A31,407m., and loans $A51,887.

ENERGY AND NATURAL RESOURCES

Electricity. The Office of Energy was established to administer energy policy and regulatory functions previously managed by the State Electricity Commission of Western Australia (SECWA), which was split into two corporate utilities in 1995 (Western Power and AlintaGas). The Office of Energy reports directly to the Minister of Energy and provides advice on policy and co-ordinates economic and commercial issues in the Western Australian energy sector. Deregulation of the energy industry was passed by the Office of Energy during 1996–97. The gradual introduction of the Electricity Transmission Open Access Plan commenced on 1 July 1997, allowing independent generators to supply associated loads by utilizing Western Power's transmission system. Electricity users now have the option of obtaining power from Western Power or private sector operators. In the year ended 30 June 1999 total Western Power customer consumption stood at 11,407m. kWh, including 3,605m. kWh by residential customers.

Oil and Gas. Petroleum continued to be the State's largest resource sector with a sales increase of $A2·9bn. to $A10·6bn. in 2000–01. During the same year crude oil was the most valuable product with a 16% increase in the quantity of sales to 14bn. litres and value of sales at 52% to $A4·8bn. The State accounts for around 48% of Australia's oil and condensate production.

Western Australia has significant natural gas resources and, with a $A2·4bn. expansion of the North West Shelf liquefied natural gas (LNG) project, production will increase with exports forecast to rise by around $A1bn. when full production takes place in 2004. Total natural gas production, 2000–01: 18,641 gigalitres.

Source: Western Australian Department of Mineral and Petroleum Resources

Water. The administration of Western Australia's water resources is the responsibility of the Water and Rivers Commission, and the Water Corporation is the primary provider of services. The operation and activities of the Water Corporation are monitored by the Office of Water Regulation.

Minerals. Mining is a significant contributor to the Western Australia economy. Until the mid-1960s the major mineral produced was gold. It was then replaced by iron ore in terms of value, and has at various times fallen behind nickel concentrates, bauxite, oil, mineral sands and salt. The State is the world's third largest producer of iron ore and accounts for around 97% of Australia's iron ore production.

Principal minerals produced in 2000–01 were: gold, 206,700 kg; iron ore, 170·6m. tonnes; diamonds, 22·4m. carats; crude oil, 18,812 megalitres. Most of the State's coal production (6·2m. tonnes in 2000) is used by Western Power's electricity generation.

Source: Western Australian Department of Mineral and Petroleum Resources

Agriculture. In the year ended June 2000 there were 13,917 establishments mainly engaged in agriculture with a total area of 105·6m. ha of which 7·69m. ha were under crops. Estimated gross value of agricultural commodities in 1999–2000 totalled $A3,459·8m.

The State is Australia's biggest producer of wheat with 4·6m. ha planted which, in 1999–2000, yielded a record crop of 9·0m. tonnes valued at $A1·8bn. Other crop production in 1999–2000 (in tonnes), barley, 1·4m.; lupins for grain, 1·2m.; canola, 963,000; oats, 439,000; sugarcane, 460,556; onions, 91,900; potatoes, 82,100; apples, 41,823; bananas, 7,700; oranges, 5,400.

Value of livestock products in 1999–2000 totalled $A638·1m. (estimated wool production, $A486m.).

Total wool produced in 1999–2000 was 153,000 tonnes.

Forestry. The area of State forests and timber reserves at 30 June 1997 was 1,725,036 ha; production of sawn timber was 1,036,466 cu. metres in 1994–95. Jarrah and Karri hardwoods account for 69·0% and pine accounts for 28·9% of sawn timber production.

Fisheries. The total fisheries production in 1998–99 was 39,652 tonnes and was worth $A592·2m. Of this, crustaceans totalled 18,667 tonnes with a value of $A331·1m. Pearling was also a significant contributor, producing $A171·4m. worth of pearls, or 30% of the total value of Western Australia's fishing production.

INDUSTRY

Heavy industry is concentrated in the southwest, and is largely tied to export-orientated mineral processing, especially alumina and nickel. Other significant manufacturing industries include meat and seafood processing, production of timber and wood products, metal fabrication and production of industrial and mining machinery. The North West Shelf development has stimulated recent growth in industries involved in providing materials and equipment during the construction phase, as well as in new and existing industries using gas in processing.

The following table shows manufacturing industry statistics for 1999–2000:

Industry sub-division	Persons employed 1,000	Wages and salaries $A1m.	Turnover $A1m.
Food, beverages and tobacco	13·6	447·0	3,508·5
Textiles, clothing and leather products	3·2	86·2	386·6
Wood and paper products	4·3	144·0	834·9
Printing and publishing and recorded media	7·0	232·0	958·0
Petroleum, coal, chemical products	6·7	301·1	3,847·3
Non-metallic mineral products	4·6	199·4	1,250·9
Metal products	15·7	634·8	4,960·3
Machinery and equipment	12·9	468·3	2,202·1
Other manufacturing	6·3	142·6	703·0

Labour. The labour force comprised 943,900 employed and 66,100 unemployed persons in Nov. 2001 (an unemployment rate of 6·5%). The average weekly wage in Nov. 2001 was $A651·50 (males $A812·80, females $A486·10).

Trade Unions. In 1996 there were 54 trade unions with a total of 135,200 male members and 86,500 female members.

INTERNATIONAL TRADE

Imports and Exports. Foreign commerce is comprised in the statement of the commerce of the Commonwealth of Australia.

Value of foreign imports and exports (i.e. excluding inter-state trade) for years ending 30 June (in $A1m.):

	1998–99	1999–2000	2000–01
Imports	9,012	9,517	9,302
Exports	21,777	25,424	30,862

Selected overseas exports (in $A1m.) for 2000–01: iron ore and concentrates, 4,840; petroleum, petroleum products and related materials, 5,176; gold bullion, 3,166; wheat, 1,379; wool, 519.

The chief countries exporting to Western Australia in 2000–01 were (in $A1m.): USA, 1,383; Japan, 1,209; UK, 470. Main export markets in 2000–01 (in $A1m.): Japan, 8,186; Singapore, 1,768; UK, 363.

COMMUNICATIONS

Roads. At 30 June 2001 there were 173,970 km of sealed and unsealed roads comprising 10,815 km of National and State highways, 6,859 km of main roads and 125,962 km of unclassified local roads. In addition, there were 29,289 km of roads in forests and national parks and 1,045 km of private roads.

New motor vehicles registered during the year ended 30 June 2001 were 77,642. In 1999 there were 217 fatalities in road accidents.

Rail. The Western Australian Government Railways Commission (WAGR) operates urban passenger services over 95 km of electrified track with country passenger services operating between Perth and regional centres at Kalgoorlie, Northam and

Bunbury. In 1999–2000, 29·5m. passenger journeys were made on WAGR urban services. In 1999–2000, 31·1m. tonnes of freight were carried with grain accounting for around 35% of the total. In Dec. 2000 State-owned Westrail's freight business was sold to the Australian Railroad Group (ARG) with a 49-year lease of the rail freight network.

Civil Aviation. An extensive system of regular air services operates for passengers, freight and mail. In 2000 Perth International Airport handled 4,763,250 passengers (3,183,938 on domestic flights).

Shipping. In 1999–2000, 5,423 commercial vessels called at Western Australian ports (1,675 at Fremantle). General cargo imported in 1999–2000 was 334,989 mass tonnes and general cargo exported was 612,025 mass tonnes.

Telecommunications. In 2000 there were 390,000 households with home computer access (56% of all households) and 241,000 households with home Internet access (34%).

Postal Services. In 1995 the Australia Post Corporation had 441 outlets and 722,114 delivery points in Western Australia.

SOCIAL INSTITUTIONS

Justice. Justice is administered by a Supreme Court, consisting of a Chief Justice, 16 other judges and 2 masters; a District Court comprising a chief judge and 20 other judges; a Magistrates Court, a Chief Stipendiary Magistrate, 37 Stipendiary Magistrates and Justices of the Peace. All courts exercise both civil and criminal jurisdiction except Justices of the Peace who deal with summary criminal matters only. Juvenile offenders are dealt with by the Children's Court. Overall responsibility for the Children's Court is vested in a President, who has the status of a District Court Judge. A children's court may be constituted by a judge, a magistrate or two lay members. Each has different sentencing powers. For certain offences involving first offenders under the age of 16 years who have pleaded guilty, such cases may be dealt with by the Children's (suspended Proceedings) Panel which comprises a representative from the Department for Community Services and one from the Police Department. The Family Court also forms part of the justice system and comprises a Chief Judge, four other judges, seven magistrates/registrars, and exercises both State and Federal jurisdictions.

At June 2000 there was a daily average of 3,124 prisoners held. At 1 July 1999 police personnel stood at 4,676.

Religion. At the census of 6 Aug. 1996 the principal denominations were: Catholic, 427,848; Anglican, 410,233; Uniting, 87,549; Presbyterian and Reformed, 45,761; Baptist, 27,618; other Christian, 126,041. There were 48,294 persons practising non-Christian religions and 367,491 persons had no religion.

Education. School attendance is compulsory from the age of six until the end of the year in which the child attains 15 years. A non-compulsory year of education is available to children from the beginning of the year in which they reach five years of age, at pre-primary centres attached to most government primary schools, or at community-based and privately owned pre-school centres, and at some non-government schools. Children may be enrolled during their fourth year where vacancies exist. In Aug. 2002 there were 775 government primary and secondary schools (with 15,136 full-time equivalent teaching staff, excluding pre-primary teaching staff) providing free education to 250,096 primary and secondary students; in Aug. 2002 there were 308 non-government schools, providing education, for which fees are charged, to 108,629 kindergarten, pre-primary, primary and secondary students (with 7,745 full-time equivalent teaching staff in Aug. 2000, excluding pre-primary teaching staff).

Technical and Further Education (TAFE) is offered by the Department of TAFE, a sub-department of the Ministry of Education, and by three independent regional colleges. The latter also provide higher education facilities. Additionally, higher education is available through four state universities and one private (Notre Dame).

In 2002 there was a total of 70,932 students in tertiary education at the University of Western Australia, Murdoch University, the University of Notre Dame Australia, Curtin University of Technology and the Edith Cowan University.

Health. In Jan. 1999 there were 91 acute public hospitals, 28 acute private hospitals and 11 day hospitals.

Welfare. The Department for Community Development is responsible for the provision of welfare and community services throughout the State. Operations and planning are managed through a decentralized structure of 5 regions and 21 districts. There are 8 directorates (2 support, 1 special services and 5 regional).

Direct services provided to the community include emergency financial assistance, family and substitute care, and counselling and psychological services. The Department supervises children's Day Care Centres. There is a 24-hour emergency welfare service provided through the Crisis Care Unit. Specialist units work in the areas of child abuse, adoptions, youth activities and Family Court counselling.

The Department provides residential facilities for the temporary accommodation, care and training of children, is responsible for young offenders recommended for detention or remand by a Court, and also supervises young offenders subject to non-custodial court orders.

Age, invalid, widows', disability and service pensions, and unemployment benefits, are paid by the Federal government. The number of age and disability pensions (including wives' and carers' pensions) on 30 June 1999 was: age, 140,033; disability support, 47,768; carer, 2,602. There were 2,473 widows' and 38,694 single parent payments current at 30 June 1999, and basic family payment was being paid for 326,692 children under 16 years.

CULTURE

Tourism. In 1999–2000 there were 441,090 short-term overseas visitors. Of these, 96,050 were from the UK and Ireland, 73,230 from Singapore and 40,670 from Japan.

Festivals. The Festival of Perth is the oldest and largest annual international arts festival in the southern hemisphere. It is held annually for 3½ weeks in Feb. and March.

Libraries. The Libraries and Information Service of Western Australia (LISWA) within the Ministry for Culture and the Arts is responsible for delivering library archival and information services to the people of Western Australia. The State Reference Library is situated in the Alexander Library in the Perth Cultural Centre. Also located in the Alexander Library Building is the J. S. Battye Library of Western Australian History.

The provision of public library services is a partnership between LISWA and local government authorities. Through its Public Library Services Program, LISWA provides and maintains the bookstock and other resource materials for public libraries throughout the State.

Museums and Galleries. The Western Australian Museum was established in the early 1890s, and its headquarters and principal exhibition centre is located in the Perth Cultural Centre, with branches in Fremantle (Fremantle History Museum including Samson House, and the Western Australian Maritime Museum incorporating the Historic Boats Museum), Albany, Geraldton and Kalgoorlie. The Art Gallery of Western Australia is the oldest visual arts organization in the State, having acquired its first work of art in 1895. The Gallery is located in the Perth Cultural Centre and is housed in two buildings: the Main Galleries and the adjoining Centenary Galleries. The Gallery collects for, and maintains, the State Art Collection, comprising Western Australian, Australian and international works, with a particular emphasis on Western Australian and Aboriginal art.

FURTHER READING

Statistical Information: The State Government Statistician's Office was established in 1897 and now functions as the Western Australian Office of the Australian Bureau of Statistics (Level 16 Exchange Plaza, 2 The Esplanade, Perth). *Deputy Commonwealth Statistician and Government Statistician:* William McLennan. Its principal publications are: *Western Australia: Facts and Figures* (from 1989). *Monthly Summary of Statistics* (from 1958)

Broeze, F. J. A. (ed.) *Private Enterprise, Government and Society.* Univ. of Western Australia, 1993

Crowley, F. K., *Australia's Western Third: A History of Western Australia from the First Settlements to Modern Times.* (Rev. ed.) Melbourne, 1970
Stannage, C. T. (ed.) *A New History of Western Australia.* Perth, 1980

State library: Alexander Library Building, Perth.

AUSTRALIAN EXTERNAL TERRITORIES

AUSTRALIAN ANTARCTIC TERRITORY

An Imperial Order in Council of 7 Feb. 1933 placed under Australian authority all the islands and territories other than Adélie Land situated south of 60° S. lat. and lying between 160° E. long. and 45° E. long. The Order came into force with a Proclamation issued by the Governor-General on 24 Aug. 1936 after the passage of the Australian Antarctic Territory Acceptance Act 1933. The boundaries of Adélie Land were definitively fixed by a French Decree of 1 April 1938 as the islands and territories south of 60° S. lat. lying between 136° E. long. and 142° E. long. The Australian Antarctic Territory Act 1954 declared that the laws in force in the Australian Capital Territory are, so far as they are applicable and are not inconsistent with any ordinance made under the Act, in force in the Australian Antarctic Territory.

The area of the territory is estimated at 6,119,818 sq. km (2,362,875 sq. miles).

There is a research station on MacRobertson Land at lat. 67° 37' S. and long. 62° 52' E. (Mawson), one on the coast of Princess Elizabeth Land at lat. 68° 34' S. and long. 77° 58' E. (Davis), and one at lat. 66° 17' S. and long. 110° 32' E. (Casey). The Antarctic Division also operates a station on Macquarie Island.

COCOS (KEELING) ISLANDS

GENERAL DETAILS

The Cocos (Keeling) Islands are two separate atolls comprising some 27 small coral islands with a total area of about 14·2 sq. km, and are situated in the Indian Ocean at 12° 05' S. lat. and 96° 53' E. long. They lie 2,768 km northwest of Perth and 3,685 km west of Darwin.

The main islands are West Island (the largest, about 10 km from north to south), on which there is an airport and an animal quarantine station, and most of the European community; Home Island, occupied by the Cocos Malay community; Direction, South and Horsburgh Islands, and North Keeling Island, 24 km to the north of the group.

The islands were discovered in 1609 by Capt. William Keeling but remained uninhabited until 1826. In 1857 the islands were annexed to the Crown; in 1878 responsibility was transferred from the Colonial Office to the government of Ceylon, and in 1886 to the government of the Straits Settlement. By indenture in 1886, Queen Victoria granted all land in the islands to George Clunies-Ross and his heirs in perpetuity (with certain rights reserved to the Crown). In 1903 the islands were incorporated in the Settlement of Singapore and in 1942–46 were temporarily placed under the Governor of Ceylon. In 1946 a Resident Administrator, responsible to the Governor of Singapore, was appointed.

On 23 Nov. 1955 the Cocos Islands were placed under the authority of the Australian government as the Territory of Cocos (Keeling) Islands. An Administrator, appointed by the Governor-General, is the government's representative in the Territory and is responsible to the Minister for Territories and Local Government. The Cocos (Keeling) Islands Council, established as the elected body of the Cocos Malay community in July 1979, advises the Administrator on all issues affecting the Territory.

In 1978 the Australian government purchased the Clunies-Ross family's entire interests in the islands, except for the family residence. A Cocos Malay co-operative was established to take over the running of the Clunies-Ross copra plantation and to engage in other business with the Commonwealth in the Territory, including construction projects. In 1993 the Australian government took control of the Clunies-Ross family residence also.

The population of the Territory (1994) was 670, distributed between Home Island (75%) and West Island (25%).

The islands are low-lying, flat and thickly covered by coconut palms, and surround a lagoon in which ships drawing up to 7 metres may be anchored, but which is extremely difficult for navigation.

There is an equable and pleasant climate, affected for much of the year by the southeast trade winds. Temperatures range over the year from 68° F (20° C) to 88° F (31·1° C) and rainfall averages 80" (2,000 mm) a year.

The Cocos (Keeling) Islands Act 1955 is the basis of the Territory's administrative, legislative and judicial systems. Under section 8 of this Act, those laws which were in force in the Territory immediately before the transfer continued in force there.

CURRENT ADMINISTRATION
Administrator: William Leonard Taylor (appointed Feb. 1999).

COMMUNICATIONS
Roads. There are 15 km of roads.

Civil Aviation. In 1998 National Jet operated scheduled flights to Christmas Island and Perth.

Telecommunications. In 1992 there were 190 radio receivers and 287 telephones.

SOCIAL INSTITUTIONS
Religion. About 85% are Muslims and 15% Christians.

Education. In 1992 there were two primary schools (on Home Island and West Island) with 98 pupils and seven teachers and one teaching assistant, two secondary schools with 70 pupils and nine teachers and one teaching assistant, and 29 students in a technical school.

Health. In 1992 there was one doctor and seven nursing personnel, with five beds in clinics.

CHRISTMAS ISLAND

GENERAL DETAILS
Christmas Island is an isolated peak in the Indian Ocean, lat. 10° 25' 22" S., long. 105° 39' 59" E. It lies 360 km S. 8° E. of Java Head, and 417 km N. 79° E. from Cocos Islands, 1,310 km from Singapore and 2,623 km from Fremantle. Area about 135 sq. km. The climate is tropical with temperatures varying little over the year at 27° C. The wet season lasts from Nov. to April with an annual total of about 2,673 mm. The island was formally annexed by the UK on 6 June 1888, placed under the administration of the Governor of the Straits Settlements in 1889, and incorporated with the Settlement of Singapore in 1900. Sovereignty was transferred to the Australian government on 1 Oct. 1958. The population at the 1991 census was 1,275; 1994 estimate, 2,500, of whom 1,300 were of Chinese, 400 of Malay and 800 of Australian/European origin.

The legislative, judicial and administrative systems are regulated by the Christmas Island Act, 1958–73. They are the responsibility of the Commonwealth government and are operated by an Administrator. The Territory underwent major changes to its legal system when the Federal Parliament passed the Territories Law Reform Bill of 1992; Commonwealth and State laws applying in the state of Western Australia now apply in the Territory as a result, although some laws have been repealed to take into account the unique status of the Territory. The first Island Assembly was elected in Sept. 1985, and is now replaced by the elected members of the Christmas Island Shire Council.

Extraction and export of rock phosphate dust is the main industry. The government is also encouraging the private sector development of tourism.

CONSTITUTION AND GOVERNMENT

The Christmas Island Assembly has nine annually-elected members. The last elections were in Dec. 1999. Only non-partisans were elected and no parties exist.

CURRENT ADMINISTRATION

Administrator: William Leonard Taylor (appointed Feb. 1999).

ECONOMY

Banking and Finance. Australian currency is legal tender.

ENERGY AND NATURAL RESOURCES

Electricity. Annual energy consumption is around 25m. kWh with a maximum loading of 4·0 MW.

COMMUNICATIONS

Roads. The Shire of Christmas Island has responsibility for approximately 140 km of roads with the remaining 100 km of haul roads and tracks maintained by Christmas Island Phosphates and Park Australia North. In 1999 there were 1,398 registered vehicles.

Civil Aviation. In 1998 National Jet operated scheduled flights to Perth and Cocos Island.

Shipping. In 1999 there were up to seven ships a month collecting phosphate products from the island.

Postal Services. There was one post office in 1999, operated by Australia Post licensees.

SOCIAL INSTITUTIONS

Religion. About 50% of the population are Buddhists or Taoists, 16% Muslims and 30% Christians.

Education. In 1999 there were 530 students at the Christmas Island District High School of whom 15% were pre-primary, 60% primary and 25% secondary level pupils.

Health. There is a nine-bed hospital, the island's only one, which was completed in 1994. There are two doctors, one dentist, a director of nursing and 20 locally engaged staff. Specialists visit about every three months.

CULTURE

Broadcasting. A local radio and television station operate 24 hours per day. Local Radio VLU2 broadcasts in English, Malay and Chinese.

NORFOLK ISLAND

KEY HISTORICAL EVENTS

The island was formerly part of the colony of New South Wales and then of Van Diemen's Land (now known as Tasmania). It was a penal colony between 1788–1814 and 1825–55. In 1856 it was separated from the state of Tasmania and established as a distinct settlement and placed under the jurisdiction of the Australian State of New South Wales. Soon thereafter, 194 descendants of the *Bounty* mutineers were transferred to Norfolk Island from Pitcairn Island.

Following the passage of the Norfolk Island Act 1913 (Cth), the Island was accepted as a Territory of Australia with the Australian Federal Government having jurisdiction for the Island. In 1976 the High Court of Australia confirmed that Norfolk Island is part of the Commonwealth of Australia and that the Australian Federal Parliament had broad law-making power in respect of Norfolk Island under the Australian Constitution. The Norfolk Island Act 1979 (Cth)—an Act passed by the Australian Federal Parliament—provides the basis of the Island's legislative, administrative and judicial systems.

TERRITORY AND POPULATION

Situated 29° 02' S. lat. 167° 57' E. long.; area 3,455 ha; permanent population (Aug. 1996), 1,470.

Descendants of the *Bounty* mutineer families constitute the 'original' settlers and are known locally as 'Islanders', while later settlers, mostly from Australia and New Zealand, are identified as 'mainlanders'. 80% of the Island's permanent population are Australian citizens with 16% being New Zealand citizens. Descendants of the Pitcairn Islanders make up about 46% of the permanent resident population. Over the years the Islanders have preserved their own lifestyle and customs, and their language remains a mixture of West Country English, Gaelic and Tahitian.

CLIMATE

Sub-tropical. Summer temperatures (Dec.–March) average about 75°F (25°C), and 65°F (18°C) in winter (June–Sept.). Annual rainfall is approximately 50" (1,200 mm), most of which falls in winter.

CONSTITUTION AND GOVERNMENT

An Administrator, appointed by the Governor-General and responsible to the Minister for Territories and Local Government, is the senior government representative in the Territory.

The Norfolk Island Act 1979 gives Norfolk Island responsible legislative and executive government to enable it to run its own affairs to the greatest practicable extent. Wide powers are exercised by the Norfolk Island Legislative Assembly of nine members, elected for a period of three years, and by an Executive Council, comprising the executive members of the Legislative Assembly, who have ministerial-type responsibilities. The seat of administration is Kingston. The Norfolk Island Act confers wide-ranging powers on the Legislative Assembly. It can pass any law with respect to 'the peace, order and good government' of Norfolk Island. The only exceptions in the Act are laws with respect to euthanasia, the unjust acquisition of property, the raising of a military force or authorizing the coining of money. In effect, this means that the Norfolk Island Legislative Assembly can enact laws on virtually any topic that it wishes. Once the Legislative Assembly enacts a law, the Act also equips the Norfolk Island Government with broad executive powers and responsibilities to administer and enforce that law.

The Norfolk Island Act also provides for consultation with the Federal Government in respect of certain types of laws proposed by Norfolk Island's Legislative Assembly. Laws on topics that are not listed in schedule 2 of the Act must be referred to the Governor-General or to the Federal Minister responsible for Australia's Territories for consideration and advice prior to receiving royal assent. This is to ensure consistency with any relevant Federal Government policies or programmes and with national obligations under international law. The range of matters on which consultation is required has reduced since self-government was granted in 1979, with some 61 topics—some very broad in scope—having been added to Schedule 2 of the Norfolk Island Act to date.

RECENT ELECTIONS

At the last elections, on 29 Nov. 2001, only non-partisans were elected.

CURRENT ADMINISTRATION

Administrator: Anthony J. Messner (since 1997).
  Chief Minister: Geoffrey Robert Gardner (since 2001).

ECONOMY

The office of the Administrator is financed from Commonwealth expenditure which in 1999–2000 was $A560,000; local revenue for 1999–2000 totalled $A10,300,000; expenditure, $A10,400,000.

Public revenue is derived mainly from tourism, the sale of postage stamps, customs duties, liquor sales, telecommunications and electricity generation charges, company registration and licence fees. Residents are not liable for income tax on earnings within the Territory, nor are death and personal stamp duties levied.

Currency. Australian notes and coins are the legal currency.

Banking and Finance. There are two banks, Westpac and the Commonwealth Bank of Australia.

COMMUNICATIONS

Roads. There are 100 km of roads (53 km paved), some 2,800 passenger cars and 200 commercial vehicles.

Civil Aviation. In 1999 there were scheduled flights to Auckland, Brisbane and Sydney.

Telecommunications. In 1999 there were 1,920 telephones.

Postal Services. There is one post office located in Burnt Pine.

SOCIAL INSTITUTIONS

Justice. The Island's Supreme Court sits as required and a Court of Petty Sessions exercises both civil and criminal jurisdiction. Appeals from decisions of the Norfolk Island Supreme Court are heard by the Federal Court of Australia and by the High Court of Australia.

Religion. 40% of the population are Anglicans.

Education. A school is run by the New South Wales Department of Education covering pre-school to Year 12. It had 320 pupils at 30 June 1999.

Health. In 1999 there were two doctors, one dentist, a pharmacist and a hospital with 24 beds. Visiting specialists attend the Island on a regular basis.

CULTURE

Broadcasting. In 1999 there were 1,500 television receivers and 1,600 radio receivers.

Press. There is one weekly with a circulation of 1,200.

Tourism. In 1998–99, 35,000 visitors travelled to Norfolk Island.

HEARD AND McDONALD ISLANDS

These islands, about 2,500 miles southwest of Fremantle, were transferred from UK to Australian control as from 26 Dec. 1947. Heard Island is about 43 km long and 21 km wide; Shag Island is about 8 km north of Heard. The total area is 412 sq. km (159 sq. miles). The McDonald Islands are 42 km to the west of Heard. Heard is an active stratovolcano that has erupted eight times since 1910, most recently in 1993. In 1985–88 a major research programme was set up by the Australian National Antarctic Research Expeditions to investigate the wildlife as part of international studies of the Southern Ocean ecosystem. Subsequent expeditions followed from June 1990 through to 1992.

TERRITORY OF ASHMORE AND CARTIER ISLANDS

By Imperial Order in Council of 23 July 1931, Ashmore Islands (known as Middle, East and West Islands) and Cartier Island, situated in the Indian Ocean, some 320 km off the northwest coast of Australia (area, 5 sq. km), were placed under the authority of the Commonwealth. Under the Ashmore and Cartier Islands Acceptance Act, 1933, the islands were accepted by the Commonwealth as the Territory of Ashmore and Cartier Islands. It was the intention that the Territory should be administered by the State of Western Australia but owing to administrative difficulties the Territory was deemed to form part of the Northern Territory of Australia (by amendment to the Act in 1938). On 16 Aug. 1983 Ashmore Reef was declared a National Nature Reserve. The islands are uninhabited but Indonesian fishing boats fish within the Territory and land to collect water in accordance with an agreement between the governments of Australia and Indonesia. It is believed that the islands and their waters may house considerable oil reserves.

TERRITORY OF CORAL SEA ISLANDS

The Coral Sea Islands, which became a Territory of the Commonwealth of Australia under the Coral Sea Islands Act 1969, comprises scattered reefs and islands over a sea area of about 1m. sq. km. The Territory is uninhabited apart from a meteorological station on Willis Island.

FURTHER READING

Australian Department of Arts, Sport, the Environment, Tourism and Territories. *Christmas Island: Annual Report.—Cocos (Keeling) Islands: Annual Report.—Norfolk Island: Annual Report.*

AUSTRIA

Republik Österreich

Capital: Vienna
Population estimate, 2000: 8·08m.
GDP per capita, 2000: (PPP$) 26,765
HDI/world rank: 0·926/15

KEY HISTORICAL EVENTS

Governed by the Hapsburgs from 1282, Austria served thereafter as the centre of their expanding power and empire, an empire which lasted until 1918. At their greatest extent under Charles V (1519–55), the Hapsburg dominions included part of Hungary (wholly conquered from the Turks in 1688), Belgium, Italian territories, Spain and its vast empire. It remained the major power in Central Europe till defeated in 1866 by Prussia and her German allies, a position confirmed by the unification of Germany in 1870–71 under Prussian leadership. Empire politics turned increasingly on national rivalries and aspirations. Tension was particularly high among the Serbs of Bosnia (annexed 1908) who looked to the independent state of Serbia. It was at Sarajevo in Bosnia on 28 June 1914 that the heir to the throne, Archduke Franz Ferdinand, was assassinated by Serbian nationalists, an event that triggered the First World War. In 1918 the Empire disintegrated into its national units.

Christian Socialists dominated the governments of Austria (except for 1929–30) until 1938. But the Socialists were strong and the general strike of July 1927 and the rising of Feb. 1934 induced Chancellor Dolfuss to end parliamentary democracy and introduce Fatherland Front backed by the paramilitary Heimwehr. The Nazis who assassinated Dolfuss on 25 July 1934 helped to bring about the *Anschluss* or Union with Germany, which was achieved by a German invasion on 12 March 1938. Until 1945 Austria was Ostmark, a province of the Third Reich.

Although the 1943 Moscow Conference of Allied Foreign Ministers regarded Austria as the first victim of German aggression, Austria was occupied by Britain, France, USA and USSR (and paid reparations over a ten-year period). Independence came with the Austrian State Treaty of 15 May 1955. Austria became a member of the European Union on 1 Jan. 1995.

In Jan. 2000 the Freedom Party headed by the far-right leader Jörg Haider joined the government. Although Haider, described as a 'dangerous extremist' by EU leaders, did not take a post in the government, he continued to exercise political influence and remained popular with the Austrian electorate. However, in May 2000 he was succeeded as party leader by deputy-chancellor Susanne Riess-Passer. Meanwhile sanctions against Austria were imposed by the European Union in Feb. 2000, but lifted in Sept. 2000. In the parliamentary elections of Oct. 2002 the Freedom Party received less than half the number of votes that it had obtained in 1999. Nevertheless Chancellor Schüssel again asked the Freedom Party to join a coalition government.

TERRITORY AND POPULATION

Austria is bounded in the north by Germany and the Czech Republic, east by Slovakia and Hungary, south by Slovenia and Italy, and west by Switzerland and Liechtenstein. It has an area of 83,858 sq. km (32,378 sq. miles). Population (2001 census) 8,065,166; density, 96·2 per sq. km. Previous population censuses: (1923) 6·53m., (1934) 6·76m., (1951) 6·93m., (1971) 7·49m., (1981) 7·56m., (1991) 7·80m. In 1999, 64·6% of the population lived in urban areas.

In 1991, 93·4% of residents were of Austrian nationality and 94% were German-speaking, with linguistic minorities of Slovenes (29,000), Croats (60,000), Hungarians (33,000) and Czechs (19,000). Between 1986 and 1996 the number of foreigners living in Austria more than doubled, from just over 4% to just over 9%.

The UN gives a projected population for 2010 of 7·95m.

The areas, populations and capitals of the nine federal states:

Federal States	Area (sq. km)	Population at censuses (1991)	(2001)	State capitals
Vienna (Wien)	415	1,539,848	1,562,676	Vienna
Lower Austria (Niederösterreich)	19,174	1,473,813	1,549,640	St Pölten

Federal States	Area (sq. km)	Population at censuses (1991)	(2001)	State capitals
Burgenland	3,965	270,880	278,600	Eisenstadt
Upper Austria (Oberösterreich)	11,980	1,333,480	1,382,017	Linz
Salzburg	7,154	482,365	518,580	Salzburg
Styria (Steiermark)	16,388	1,184,720	1,185,911	Graz
Carinthia (Kärnten)	9,533	547,798	561,114	Klagenfurt
Tyrol	12,648	631,410	675,063	Innsbruck
Vorarlberg	2,601	331,472	351,565	Bregenz

The populations of the principal towns at 1 Jan. 2000 (and at the census of 1991): Vienna, 1,608,144 (1,539,848); Graz, 240,967 (237,810); Linz, 188,022 (203,044); Salzburg, 144,247 (143,978); Innsbruck, 111,752 (118,112); Klagenfurt, 91,141 (89,415); Villach, 57,422 (54,640); Wels, 56,894 (52,594); St Pölten, 49,352 (50,026).

The official language is German. For orthographical changes agreed in 1996 *see* GERMANY: Territory and Population.

SOCIAL STATISTICS

Statistics, 1999: live births, 78,138 (rate of 9·7 per 1,000 population); deaths, 78,200 (rate of 9·7 per 1,000 population); infant deaths, 341; stillborn, 316; marriages, 39,485; divorces, 18,512. In 1999 there were 1,555 suicides (rate of 19·2 per 100,000 population), of which 1,126 males and 429 females. Annual population growth rate, 1999, 0·17%. Life expectancy at birth, 1999, 80·94 years for women and 75·06 years for men. In 1999 the most popular age range for marrying was 25–29 for both males and females. Infant mortality, 1999, was 4·4 per 1,000 live births; fertility rate, 1999, 1·3 children per woman. In 1999 some 364,000 Austrians resided permanently abroad: 185,000 lived in Germany, 28,000 in Switzerland, and 16,000 in both Australia and the USA. In 2001 Austria received 20,135 asylum applications (including 12,975 Afghans, 2,113 Iraqis and 1,874 Turks), equivalent to 2·50 per 1,000 inhabitants.

CLIMATE

The climate is temperate and from west to east in transition from marine to more continental. Depending to the elevation, the climate is also predominated by alpine influence. Winters are cold with snowfall. In the eastern parts summers are warm and dry.

Vienna, Jan. 0·0°C, July 20·2°C. Annual rainfall 624 mm. Graz, Jan. −1·0°C, July 19·4°C. Annual rainfall 825 mm. Innsbruck, Jan. −1·7°C, July 18·1°C. Annual rainfall 885 mm. Salzburg, Jan. −0·9°C, July 18·6°C. Annual rainfall 1,174 mm.

CONSTITUTION AND GOVERNMENT

The Constitution of 1 Oct. 1920 was restored on 27 April 1945. Austria is a democratic federal republic comprising nine states *(Länder)*, with a federal *President (Bundespräsident)* directly elected for not more than two successive six-year terms, and a bicameral National Assembly which comprises a National Council and a Federal Council.

The National Council *(Nationalrat)* comprises 183 members directly elected for a four-year term by proportional representation in a three-tier system by which seats are allocated at the level of 43 regional and nine state constituencies, and one federal constituency. Any party gaining 4% of votes cast nationally is represented in the National Council.

The Federal Council *(Bundesrat)* has 64 members appointed by the nine states for the duration of the individual State Assemblies' terms; the number of deputies for each state is proportional to that state's population. In April 2001 the ÖVP held 28 of the 64 seats, the SPÖ 23, the FPÖ 12 and the Greens 1.

The head of government is a *Federal Chancellor*, who is appointed by the President (usually the head of the party winning the most seats in National Council elections). The *Vice-Chancellor*, the *Federal Ministers* and the *State Secretaries* are appointed by the President at the Chancellor's recommendation.

National Anthem. 'Land der Berge, Land am Strome' ('Land of mountains, land on the river'); words by Paula Preradovic; tune attributed to Mozart.

RECENT ELECTIONS

Elections were held on 24 Nov. 2002. The Austrian People's Party (ÖVP) won 79 seats with 42·3% of votes cast (52 with 26·9% in 1999); the Social Democratic Party (SPÖ), 69 with 36·9% (65 with 33·2%); the Freedom Party (FPÖ), 18 with 10·2% (52 with 26·9%); and the Greens, 17 with 9·0% (14 with 7·4%). Turn-out was 80·5%.

In the presidential election held on 19 April 1998 Thomas Klestil (ÖVP) was re-elected for a second six-year term, obtaining 63·5% of the votes cast, with his nearest rival, Gertraud Knoll, polling 13·5% of votes cast. There were five candidates in total.

European Parliament. Austria has 21 representatives. At the June 1999 elections turn-out was 49·0%. The SPÖ won 7 seats with 31·7% of votes cast (political affiliation in European Parliament: Party of European Socialists); the ÖVP, 7 with 30·6% (European People's Party); the FPÖ, 5 with 23·5% (Non-attached); the Greens, 2 with 9·2% (Greens). Other small parties received 5% of the votes cast between them.

CURRENT ADMINISTRATION

President: Dr Thomas Klestil; b. 1933 (ÖVP; re-elected 19 April 1998; previously elected 24 May 1992 and sworn in 8 July 1992).

Following the elections of Nov. 1999, the ÖVP and the right-wing FPÖ agreed in Feb. 2000 to form a coalition government, with Dr Wolfgang Schüssel (ÖVP) as chancellor. In Sept. 2002 the coalition collapsed in the wake of a bitter power struggle within the FPÖ. Chancellor Schüssel called for new elections, held on 24 Nov 2002 and won by the ÖVP, which revived the coalition with the FPÖ. In March 2003 the government comprised:

Chancellor: Dr Wolfgang Schüssel; b. 1945 (ÖVP; sworn in 4 Feb. 2000).

Deputy-Chancellor and Minister for Social Security and Generations: Herbert Haupt (FPÖ).

Minister for Foreign Affairs: Benita Maria Ferrero-Waldner (ÖVP). *Economic Affairs and Labour:* Martin Bartenstein (ÖVP). *Finance:* Karl-Heinz Grasser (ind.). *Interior:* Ernst Strasser (ÖVP). *Justice:* Dieter Böhmdorfer (FPÖ). *Defence:* Günther Platter (ÖVP). *Agriculture, Forestry and Environment:* Josef Pröll (ÖVP). *Health Affairs and Women's Issues:* Maria Rauch-Kallat (ÖVP). *Education, Science and Culture:* Elisabeth Gehrer (ÖVP). *Transport, Innovation and Technology:* Hubert Gorbach (FPÖ). *State Secretary in the Ministry for Finance:* Alfred Finz (ÖVP). *State Secretary in the Federal Chancellery:* Franz Morak (ÖVP); Karl Schweitzer (FPÖ). *State Secretary in the Ministry for Social Security and Generations:* Ursula Hubner (FPÖ); Reinhart Waneck (FPÖ). *State Secretary in the Ministry for Transport, Innovation and Technology:* Herbert Kukacka (ÖVP).

Government Website: http://www.austria.gv.at

DEFENCE

The Federal President is C.-in-C. of the armed forces. Conscription is for a seven-month period, with liability for at least another 30 days' reservist refresher training spread over eight to ten years. Since 1992 the total 'on mobilization strength' of the forces has been reduced from approximately 200,000 to 110,000 troops. In 2002 approximately 1,000 personnel from so-called 'prepared units' were deployed in peace support operations in places such as Afghanistan, Bosnia, Cyprus, the Golan Heights and Syria.

Defence expenditure in 2000 totalled US$1,609m. (US$196 per capita), representing 0·8% of GDP.

Army. The army is structured in five brigades and nine provincial military commands. Two brigades are mechanized, the rest infantry brigades. The mechanized brigades are equipped with Leopard 2/A4 main battle tanks. One of three infantry brigades is earmarked for airborne operations, the second is equipped with Pandur wheeled armoured personnel carriers and the third infantry brigade is specialized in mountain operations. The artillery units are brigade-directed. M-109 armoured self-propelled guns equip the artillery battalions. In addition to these standing units, some 20 infantry battalions under the direction of the provincial military commands are available on mobilization. Active personnel, 2000, 45,500 (to be 26,100) including 16,600 conscripts. Women started to serve in the armed forces on 1 April 1998.

Air Force. The Air Force Command comprises three aviation and three air-defence regiments with about 6,500 personnel, more than 150 aircraft and a number of fixed- and mobile radar stations. Some 23 Draken interceptors equip a surveillance wing responsible for the defence of the Austrian air space and a fighter-bomber wing operates SAAB 105s. Helicopters including the S-70 Black Hawk equip six squadrons for transport/support, communication, observation, and search and rescue duties. Fixed-wing aircraft including PC-6s, PC-7s, Skyvans and in the near future C-130 Hercules are operated as trainers and for transport. The procurement of a fourth generation fighter is also planned for the near future.

INTERNATIONAL RELATIONS

Austria is a member of the UN, WTO, BIS, NATO Partnership for Peace, OECD, EU, Council of Europe, OSCE, CERN, CEI, Danube Commission, Inter-American Development Bank, Asian Development Bank, IOM and the Antarctic Treaty. Austria is a signatory to the Schengen Accord abolishing border controls between Austria, Belgium, Denmark, Finland, France, Germany, Greece, Iceland, Italy, Luxembourg, Netherlands, Norway, Portugal, Spain and Sweden.

ECONOMY

Trade and services account for about two-thirds of value added, and the industrial sector about one-third.

According to the anti-corruption organization *Transparency International*, Austria ranked 15th in the world in a 2002 survey of the countries with the least corruption in business and government. It received 7·8 out of 10 in the annual index.

Overview. The government aimed for a balanced budget in 2002, the first in 28 years, but this is not likely to be achieved until 2003. The most important sector in the economy is the service sector, accounting for 62% of economic output. Tourism plays an important role. EU membership has led to a more liberal market and many companies have been taken over by foreign, particularly German, companies. Lower taxes are planned for 2003 and the focus is on regulatory reform, the liberalization of public utilities and privatization. Monetary conditions have tightened owing to higher interest rates. The pension system, absorbing around 14·5% of GDP, is one of the most expensive in Europe. A major goal of the government is to reduce Austria's tax burden to 40% of GDP by 2010.

Currency. On 1 Jan. 1999 the euro (EUR) became the legal currency in Austria; irrevocable conversion rate 13·7603 schillings to one euro. The euro, which consists of 100 cents, has been in circulation since 1 Jan. 2002. There are seven euro notes in different colours and sizes denominated in 500, 200, 100, 50, 20, 10 and 5 euros, and eight coins denominated in 2 and 1 euros, then 50, 20, 10, 5, 2 and 1 cents. On the introduction of the euro there was a 'dual circulation' period before the schilling ceased to be legal tender on 28 Feb. 2002. Euro banknotes in circulation on 1 Jan. 2002 had a total value of €30·7bn.

Inflation was 2·3% in 2000 and 2·7% in 2001, with a forecast for 2002 of 1·8%. Foreign exchange reserves were US$12,020m. in June 2002 and gold reserves were 10·21m. troy oz. Total money supply was €9,258m. in June 2002.

Budget. The federal budget for calendar years provided revenue and expenditure as follows (in €1m.):

	2000	2001	2002[1]
Revenue	58,247	60,403	61,748
Expenditure	55,393	58,988	59,350

[1]Provisional.

VAT is 20% (10% reduced rate).

Performance. Real GDP growth was 2·7% in 1999 and 3·5% in 2000, but only 0·7% in 2001, with a forecast for 2002 of 0·9%. Total GDP was US$188·7bn. in 2001.

Banking and Finance. The Oesterreichische Nationalbank, central bank of Austria, opened on 1 Jan. 1923 but was taken over by the German Reichsbank on 17 March 1938. It was re-established on 3 July 1945. Its *Governor* is Klaus Liebscher.

In 2001 banking and insurance accounted for 6·8% of gross domestic product at current prices. In 2001 an average of 110,161 individuals were engaged in banking and insurance (banking 75,816 and insurance 29,276), representing 3·5% of Austria's wage and salary earners.

By the end of 2002, 906 credit institutions and branch offices from banks located in the European Union were active in Austria. 40 credit institutions from countries outside the EU have established representative offices. The leading banks with total assets in 2001 (in €1bn.) were: Bank Austria Group of Companies, 140·03; Erste Bank der Oesterreichischen Sparkassen AG, 55·94; Bank für Arbeit und Wirtschaft AG, 39·71; Raiffeisenzentralbank Österreich AG, 33·17; Oesterreichische Kontrollbank AG, 24·64.

There is a stock exchange in Vienna (VEX). It is one of the oldest in Europe and one of the smallest.

Weights and Measures. The metric system is in force.

ENERGY AND NATURAL RESOURCES

Environment. According to the *World Bank Atlas* Austria's carbon dioxide emissions were the equivalent of 7·9 tonnes per capita in 1998. An *Environmental Sustainability Index* compiled for the World Economic Forum meeting in Feb. 2002 ranked Austria seventh in the world, with 64·2%. The index measured the ability of countries to maintain favourable environmental conditions and examined various factors including pollution levels and the use or abuse of natural resources.

Austria is one of the world leaders in recycling. In 1996, 48% of all household waste was recycled.

Electricity. The Austrian electricity market was fully liberalized on 1 Oct. 2001. Installed capacity was 18·0m. kW in 1998. Production in 1999 was 60·35bn. kWh. Consumption per capita: 6,895 kWh (1998).

Oil and Gas. The commercial production of petroleum began in the early 1930s. Production of crude oil (in tonnes): 1998, 959,285.

The Austrian gas market was fully liberalized on 1 Oct. 2002. Production of natural gas (in 1,000 cu. metres): 1999, 1,740,652.

Minerals. The most important minerals are limestone and marble (1999 production, 26,408,576 tonnes), dolomite (1999 production, 7,968,072 tonnes), quartz and arenacious quartz, lignite, basalt, clay and kaolin.

Agriculture. In 1998, 149,600 persons were employed in agriculture as their main occupation. In 1998 the total cultivated area amounted to 3,422,449 ha. There were 252,110 farms in 1999. Figures compiled by the Soil Association, a British organization, show that in 1999 Austria set aside 345,000 ha (10·1% of its agricultural land—one of the highest proportions in the world) for the growth of organic crops. Agriculture accounted for 1·4% of GDP, 4·9% of exports and 7·0% of imports in 1999.

The chief products (area in 1,000 ha, yield in tonnes) were as follows:

	1997		1998		1999	
	Area	Yield	Area	Yield	Area	Yield
Barley	260·6	1,257,800	265·6	1,211,557	244·0	1,152,801
Oats	46·1	196,684	40·5	164,204	35·5	152,381
Potatoes	23·5	676,872	22·9	646,915	23·2	711,730
Rye	57·8	207,238	59·3	236,356	56·0	218,183
Sugarbeets	51·6	3,011,921	49·6	3,314,143	46·5	3,216,731
Wheat	259·8	1,352,281	264·4	1,341,820	260·6	1,416,200

Other important agricultural products include apples (410,000 tonnes in 1999) and pears (70,000 tonnes in 1999). Wine production in 1999 totalled 2,803,383 hectolitres.

Livestock (1999): cattle, 2,152,800; pigs, 3,433,000; sheep, 352,300; goats, 58,000; horses, 81,600; poultry, 14,498,000.

Forestry. Forested area in 1998, 3·9m. ha (47% of the land area), of which 76% was coniferous. Felled timber, in 1,000 cu. metres: 1996, 15,010·2; 1997, 14,725·8; 1998, 14,033·5; 1999, 14,083·9.

Fisheries. Total catch in 2000 came to 859 tonnes, exclusively from inland waters.

INDUSTRY

The leading companies by market capitalization in Austria, excluding banking and finance, in Jan. 2002 were: Telekom Austria AG (€5bn.); Österreichische Elektrizitätswirtschaft AG (€3bn.), a hydro-electric and thermal energy producer; and ÖMV AG (€3bn.), an energy, chemicals and plastics producer.

Output (in tonnes if not stated otherwise):

	1997	1998
Raw steel	1,349,687	1,424,599
Rolled steel	3,206,794	3,315,715
Cellulose	742,902	786,415
Paper and cardboard	3,793,664	3,893,220
Sawnwood (1,000 cu. metres)	7,334	6,629
Synthetic fibre yarn	46,939	45,138
Glass (flat) (1,000 sq. metres)	1,885	1,763
Sugar (refined)	501,421	473,945
Milk (1,000 litres)	1,360,597	1,367,806
Fertilizers	773,348	817,736

In 1998, 7,657 industrial establishments employed 571,048 persons, producing a value of 1,167bn. schillings (excluding VAT).

Labour. Austria has the second highest per capita income among the euro-12 countries and one of the lowest unemployment rates (4·1% in Jan. 2003). During 2000 Austria experienced its biggest fall in joblessness since the mid 1950s. Youth unemployment, at 4·5% in May 2000, was also one of the lowest in the world.

In Sept. 2000 there were 3,157,932 employed persons. In 1998, 890,000 people worked in personal social and public services, 617,000 in manufacturing, 482,000 in trade, 298,000 in finance, insurance and real estate, 265,000 in construction and 225,000 in transport and communications. In Sept. 2000 the number of registered jobseekers was 153,000.

The number of foreigners who may be employed in Austria is limited to 9% of the potential workforce. There were two strikes in 1997, with 25,800 participants (total strike hours, 153,000). There were no strikes in 1996 or 1998. Between 1989 and 1998 strikes cost Austria an average of just four days per 1,000 employees a year (the lowest in the European Union), compared to the EU average of 85 per 1,000.

Austria has one of the lowest average retirement ages but reforms passed in 1997 now make it less attractive to retire before 60. Only 15% of men and 6% of women in the 60–65 age range work, although the legal retirement ages are 60 for women and 65 for men.

Trade Unions. The 14 unions in the Austrian Trade Union Confederation (Österreichischer Gewerkschaftsbund, ÖGB) had 1,465,000 members in Dec. 1999.

INTERNATIONAL TRADE

The budgetary external debt was 393,400m. schillings in 1998.

Imports and Exports. Trade in US$1m.:

	1996	1997	1998	1999	2000
Imports f.o.b.	65,252	62,936	66,983	68,051	67,415
Exports f.o.b.	57,937	58,662	63,299	64,422	64,684

Main export markets (% of total exports) in 1999: Germany, 34·8%; Italy, 8·4%; Switzerland, 6·1%; Hungary, 5·0%. Main import suppliers: Germany, 41·7%; Italy, 7·6%; USA, 5·4%; France, 5·0%. Other EU-member countries accounted for 62·6% of exports and 68·4% of imports. The value of exports to eastern Europe increased from 35bn. schillings in 1988 to 128·5bn. schillings in 1998. Imports amounted to 56,991 tonnes in 1999 (56,311 tonnes in 1998) and exports amounted to 36,064 tonnes (34,759 tonnes in 1998).

In 1999 principal exports were: machinery and transport equipment, 40·5%, including vehicles, 10·3%; manufactured goods, 23·6%; chemicals and related products, 7·1%. Principal imports were: machinery and transport equipment, 41·2%, including vehicles, 12·4%; manufactured goods, 17·6%; chemicals and related products, 10·0%.

Trade Fairs. Austria's largest trade fairs are the Graz International Autumn Fair (Oct.), with 1,159 exhibitors and 204,947 visitors in 1999; the Graz International Spring Fair (May), with 1,139 exhibitors and 194,607 visitors in 1999; and Aufgetischt—International Fair for the Food and Catering Trade, in Vienna (Feb.), with 925 exhibitors and 125,500 visitors in 1999. Vienna ranked as the fourth most popular convention city behind Paris, London and Brussels in 2001 according to the Union des Associations Internationales (UAI).

COMMUNICATIONS

Roads. On 31 Dec. 1998 federal roads had a total length of 10,276 km: Autobahn, 1,613 km; provincial roads, 23,472 km. On 31 Dec. 1999 motor vehicles registered numbered 5,470,948, including 4,009,604 passenger cars, 318,757 trucks, 9,834 buses and 622,927 motorcycles. There were 976 fatalities in road accidents in 2000.

Rail. The major railways are nationalized. Length of route in 1999, 5,643 km, of which 3,456 km were electrified. There are also 19 private railways with a total length of 598 km. In 1999, 181·7m. passengers and 78·0m. tonnes of freight were carried by Federal Railways.

There is a metro and tramway in Vienna, and tramways in Gmunden, Graz, Innsbruck and Linz.

Civil Aviation. The national airline is Austrian Airlines, which is 51·9% state-owned. There are international airports at Vienna (Schwechat), Linz, Salzburg, Graz, Klagenfurt and Innsbruck. In 1999 services were provided by 64 other airlines. In 1999, 244,438 commercial aircraft and 14,281,758 passengers arrived and departed (11·1m. at Vienna); 116,604 tonnes of freight and 7,451 tonnes of mail were handled. In 2000 Vienna handled 11,790,504 passengers (11,293,186 on international flights) and 124,403 tonnes of freight. In 1998 Austrian Airlines carried 3,821,387 passengers (1,758,369 on international flights) and Lauda Air 743,243 passengers (all on international flights).

Shipping. The Danube is an important waterway. Goods traffic (in 1,000 tonnes): 9,303 in 1996; 9,204 in 1997; 10,236 in 1998; 9,987 in 1999 (including the Rhine-Main-Danube Canal). The merchant shipping fleet totalled 68,000 GRT in 1998.

Telecommunications. In 1998 postal, telegraph and telephone services were mainly state-owned. In Nov. 2000 approximately 25% of Austria Telekom was placed on the international and national equity markets (the majority of Austria Telekom is now in private hands). There were 3,832,900 telephone main lines in 2000 (466·8 per 1,000 inhabitants). Mobile phone subscribers numbered 5·35m. in Nov. 2000, up from 4·03m. in 1999. There were 2·3m. PCs in use in 2000 (276·5 per 1,000 persons). The number of Internet users in June 2002 was approximately 3·7m.

Postal Services. The Postal Savings Bank was privatized in 2000. In 2002 there were 1,669 post offices and 120 post-agencies, the so-called 'Post-Partner'. A total of 4,541m. postal items were handled in 2000.

SOCIAL INSTITUTIONS

Justice. The Supreme Court of Justice *(Oberster Gerichtshof)* in Vienna is the highest court in civil and criminal cases. In addition, in 2000 there were four Courts of Appeal *(Oberlandesgerichte)*, 21 High Courts *(Landesgerichte)* and 192 District Courts *(Bezirksgerichte)*. There is also a Supreme Constitutional Court *(Verfassungsgerichtshof)* and a Supreme Administrative Court *(Verwaltungs-gerichtshof)*, both seated in Vienna.

In 2000 a total of 516,929 criminal offences were reported to the police and 41,624 people were convicted of offences.

Religion. In 2001 there were 5,920,000 Roman Catholics (73·6%), 376,000 Evangelical Lutherans (4·7%), 339,000 Muslims (4·2%), 963,000 without religious allegiance (12·0%) and 439,000 others (5·5%). The Roman Catholic Church has two archbishoprics and seven bishoprics. In Feb. 2001 there were four Cardinals.

Education. In 1999–2000 there were 5,011 general compulsory schools (including special education) with 75,857 teachers and 689,906 pupils. Secondary schools totalled 1,680 in 1998–99 with 519,882 pupils.

In 1999–2000 there were also 122 commercial academies with 41,048 pupils and 5,558 teachers, 72 higher schools of economic professions (secondary level) with 22,463 pupils, and 13 training colleges of social workers with 1,255 pupils; and in 1998–99, 296 schools of technical and industrial training (including schools of hotel management and catering) with 7,321 teachers and 68,884 pupils, and 124 trade schools with 14,819 pupils.

The dominant institutions of higher education are the 12 universities and six colleges of arts, which are publicly financed. In 1994 Higher Technical Study Centres (*Fachhochschul-Studiengänge*, FHS) were established, which are private, but government-dependent, institutions. In the winter term 1998–99 there were 226,115 students enrolled at the universities, 8,777 at the colleges of arts and 7,869 at 46 FHS. About 15,000 teachers (full-time equivalent) provide tertiary-level education.

In 1996 expenditure on education came to 5·4% of GNP and 10·4% of total government spending.

The adult literacy rate in 1998 was at least 99%.

Health. In 1999 there were 29,855 doctors, 3,666 dentists, 37,007 nurses and 1,553 midwives. In 1998 there were 330 hospitals and 74,810 hospital beds.

Welfare. Maternity/paternity leave is for 18 months. A new parenting allowance was introduced on 1 Jan 2002, replacing the maternity/paternity allowance. The new system is based on family benefit financed from the Family Fund instead of the insurance principle. The basic allowance is €436 per month for a maximum of three years. In 1996, 29·6% of GNP was spent on social security. Total expenditure in 1997 on social security schemes came to 273·3bn. schillings.

CULTURE

Graz is the European Capital of Culture for 2003. The title attracts large European Union grants.

Broadcasting. The 'Österreichische Rundfunk' (Austrian Broadcasting Corporation) is state-controlled. It transmits four national and nine regional radio programmes. An additional programme in English and French can be received all over the country; there is also a 24-hour foreign service (short wave). There were 2·77m. registered listeners and 2·67m. television licenses (colour by PAL) issued in Dec. 1999. There were also 991,000 cable TV subscribers in Dec. 1999.

Cinema. In 1999 there were 528 fixed cinemas, one drive-in cinema and 23 mobile units. Audience numbers totalled 15,219,008 in 1998. In 1995 gross box office receipts came to 847m. schillings and 22 full-length films were made.

Press. There were 17 daily newspapers (seven of them in Vienna), 159 non-daily newspapers and 2,774 other periodicals in 1999. The most popular newspaper is the mass-market tabloid *Kronen-Zeitung*, which is read on a daily basis by 42% of the population. In 1999 a total of 18,719 books were published, including 6,487 new titles.

Tourism. Tourism is an important industry. In 1999, 17,582 hotels and boarding houses had a total of 628,940 beds available. In 1999, 17,467,000 foreigners visited Austria and tourist receipts were US$11·09bn. Tourist arrivals reached 27·3m. in 2002. Tyrol is the most popular province for visits, recording more than a third of all overnight stays in 1999. Of 112,733,040 overnight stays in tourist accommodation in 1999, 30,309,286 were by Austrians and 53,091,546 by Germans.

Festivals. The main festivals are Salzburger Festspiele, held every July–Aug. (231,432 visitors in 2002), and Bregenzer Festspiele, also held in July–Aug. (197,090 visitors in 2002). The Haydn Days in Eisenstadt, held every Sept., is also considered to be one of the leading annual festivals. The Vienna Festival (Wiener Festwochen), which takes place in May–June, is the major arts festival in the country and attracted 96,900 visitors in 1998.

Libraries. In 1997 there were 5,642,000 library users and 26,123,000 volumes in scientific and special libraries, and 1,149,300 users and 11,252,800 volumes in public libraries.

Theatre and Opera. The attendance at federal theatres was 1,354,200 in 1998–99.

Museums and Galleries. In 1998 there were 23,312,000 visitors to museums, exhibitions and similar attractions (10,133,000 in Vienna).

DIPLOMATIC REPRESENTATIVES

Of Austria in the United Kingdom (18 Belgrave Mews West, London, SW1X 8HU)
Ambassador: Dr Alexander Christiani.

Of the United Kingdom in Austria (Jaurèsgasse 12, 1030 Vienna)
Ambassador: Sir Anthony Ford, CMG.

Of Austria in the USA (3524 International Court, NW, Washington, D.C., 20008)
Ambassador: Peter Moser.

Of the USA in Austria (Boltzmanngasse 16, A-1091 Vienna)
Ambassador: Lyons Brown, Jr.

Of Austria to the United Nations
Ambassador: Dr Gerhard Pfanzelter.

FURTHER READING

Austrian Central Statistical Office. *Main publications: Statistisches Jahrbuch für die Republik Österreich.* New Series from 1950. Annual.—*Statistische Nachrichten.* Monthly.—*Beiträge zur österreichischen Statistik.—Statistik in Österreich 1918–1938.* [Bibliography] 1985.— *Veröffentlichungen des Österreichischen Statistischen Zentralamtes 1945–1985.* [Bibliography], 1990.—*Republik Österreich, 1945–1995.*

Brook-Shepherd, G., *The Austrians: a Thousand-Year Odyssey.* London, 1997
Peniston-Bird, C. M., *Vienna.* [Bibliography] ABC-Clio, Oxford and Santa Barbara (CA), 1997
Pick, Hella, *Guilty Victim: Austria from the Holocaust to Haider.* I. B. Tauris, London, 2000
Sully, M. A., *A Contemporary History of Austria.* London, 1990
Wolfram, H. (ed.) *Österreichische Geschichte.* 10 vols. Vienna, 1994

National library: Österreichische Nationalbibliothek, Josefsplatz, 1015 Vienna.
National statistical office: Austrian Central Statistical Office, POB 9000, A-1033 Vienna.
Website: http://www.statistik.at

AZERBAIJAN

Azarbaijchan Respublikasy

Capital: Baku
Population estimate, 2000: 8·04m.
GDP per capita, 2000: (PPP$) 2,936
HDI/world rank: 0·741/88

KEY HISTORICAL EVENTS

In 1920 Azerbaijan was proclaimed a Soviet Socialist Republic. From 1922, with Georgia and Armenia, it formed the Transcaucasian Soviet Federal Socialist Republic. Conflict with Armenia over the enclave of Nagorno-Karabakh escalated in 1988, leading to violent expulsions of Armenians in Azerbaijan and Azeris in Armenia. In 'Black January' 1990 Soviet tanks moved in to react to rioting in Baku, and over 100 civilians were killed. War broke out between the two countries in 1992, with a ceasefire agreed in 1994. The dispute over territory remains unsettled, although negotiations in Florida in 2001 promised a peaceful solution. In 1990 it adopted a declaration of republican sovereignty and on 18 Aug. 1991 the Supreme Soviet of Azerbaijan declared independence. Under the presidency of Heydar Aliyev, elected in Oct. 1993, parliament ratified association with the CIS on 20 Sept. 1993. A treaty of friendship and co-operation was signed with Russia on 3 July 1997 and Aliyev was re-elected in Oct. 1998, although the administration of the election was criticized by international observers.

TERRITORY AND POPULATION

Azerbaijan is bounded in the west by Armenia, in the north by Georgia and the Russian Federation (Dagestan), in the east by the Caspian sea and in the south by Turkey and Iran. Its area is 86,600 sq. km (33,430 sq. miles), and it includes the Nakhichevan Autonomous Republic and the largely Armenian-inhabited Nagorno-Karabakh.

The population at the 1999 census was 7,953,000 (4,119,000 females); density, approximately 92 per sq. km. In 1999, 56·9% of the population lived in urban areas. There are 65 towns (one in each region), eight of which have over 50,000 people. The population breaks down into 82·7% Azerbaijanis, 5·6% Armenians, 5·6% Russians and 2·4% Lezgis (1989 census).

The UN gives a projected population for 2010 of 8·50m.

Chief cities: Baku (1999 census population, 1,786,700), Gandja (298,600) and Sumgait (281,600).

The official language is Azeri. On 1 Aug. 2001 Azerbaijan abolished the use of the Cyrillic alphabet and switched to using Latin script.

SOCIAL STATISTICS

In 1999: births, 117,500; deaths, 46,295; marriages, 37,400; divorces, 5,000. Rates, 1999 (per 1,000 population): births, 14·7; deaths, 5·8; infant mortality (per 1,000 live births), 16·2. Life expectancy in 1999: 74·8 years for women and 67·7 years for men. Annual population growth rate, 1990–99, 0·8%; fertility rate, 1999, 2·0 children per woman.

CLIMATE

The climate is almost tropical in summer and the winters slightly warmer than in regions north of the Caucasus. Cold spells do occur, however, both on the high mountains and in the enclosed valleys. There are nine climatic zones. Baku, Jan. –6°C, July 25°C. Annual rainfall 318 mm.

CONSTITUTION AND GOVERNMENT

Parliament is the 125-member *Melli-Majlis*. 100 seats are contested on a majority basis, and 25 distributed proportionally among political parties. For the majority seats there is a minimum 50% turn-out requirement. There is an 8% threshold. A constitutional referendum and parliamentary elections were held on 12 Nov. 1995.

Turn-out for the referendum was 86%. The new Constitution was approved by 91·9% of votes cast.

National Anthem. 'Azerbaijan! Azerbaijan!'; words by A. Javad, tune by U. Hajibayov.

RECENT ELECTIONS

At elections on 3 Oct. 1993 Heydar Aliyev was elected president unopposed, with 98·8% of votes cast; he was re-elected on 11 Oct. 1998 with 76·1% of votes cast and again on 11 Aug. 2002 with 88·4% of the vote.

At the parliamentary elections held on 5 Nov. 2000 and 7 Jan. 2001 the New Azerbaijan Party (NAP) gained 75 seats with 62·3% of votes cast; Popular Front Party gained 6 seats with 10·8%; the Party of Citizen's Solidarity, 3 seats with 6·3%; the Communist Party of Azerbaijan, 2 seats with 6·3%.

CURRENT ADMINISTRATION

President: Heydar Aliyev; b. 1923 (NAP; sworn in 10 Oct. 1993, re-elected Oct. 1998).

In March 2003 the government comprised:

Prime Minister: Artur Rasizade; b. 1935 (NAP; in office since 20 July 1996).

First Deputy Prime Minister: Abbas Abbasov. *Deputy Prime Ministers:* Elchin Efendiyev, Yagub Eyyubov, Ali Hasanov, Abid Sharifov.

Minister of Foreign Affairs: Vilayat Guliyev. *Interior:* Ramil Usubov. *Culture:* Polad Byul-Byul. *Education:* Misir Mardanov. *National Security:* Namig Abbasov. *Defence:* Lt.-Gen. Safar Abiyev. *Communications:* Nadir Ahmedov. *Agriculture and Food:* Ershad Aliyev. *Justice:* Fikret Mamedov. *Health:* Ali Insanov. *Finance:* Avaz Alekperov. *Labour and Social Protection:* Ali Nagiyev. *Youth and Sport:* Abulfaz Karaev. *Economic Development:* Farhad Aliyev. *Ecology and Natural Resources:* Huseyngulu Bagirov. *Fuel and Energy Development:* Macid Karimov. *Taxation:* Fazil Mamedov. *Transport:* Ziya Mammadov.

Chairman of the National Assembly (Melli-Majlis): Murtuz Aleskerov.

Office of the President: http://www.president.az

DEFENCE

Conscription is for 17 months. Defence expenditure in 2000 totalled US$213m. (US$28 per capita), representing 4·5% of GDP.

Army. Personnel, 1999, 69,900. In addition there is a reserve force of 575,700 Azerbaijanis who have received some kind of military service experience within the last 15 years. There is also a paramilitary Ministry of the Interior militia of about 10,000 and a border guard of approximately 5,000.

Navy. The flotilla is based at Baku on the Caspian Sea and numbered about 2,200 in 1999 including two small frigates.

Air Force. How many ex-Soviet aircraft are usable is not known but there are 49 combat aircraft and 15 armed helicopters. Personnel, 8,100 in 1999.

INTERNATIONAL RELATIONS

Azerbaijan is a member of the UN, the NATO Partnership for Peace, Council of Europe, OSCE, CIS, IMO, the World Bank, IMF, EBRD, BSEC, ECO, IOM, OIC and OEC. There is a dispute with Armenia over the status of the chiefly Armenian-populated Azerbaijani enclave of Nagorno-Karabakh. A ceasefire was negotiated from 1994 with 20% of Azerbaijan's land in Armenian hands and with 1m. Azeri refugees and displaced persons.

ECONOMY

In 1998 agriculture accounted for 20·3% of GDP, services 41·0% and industry 38·7%.

Currency. The *manat* (AZM) of 100 *gyapiks* replaced the rouble in Jan. 1994. Inflation was 1·8% in 2000 and 1·5% in 2001. Foreign exchange reserves were US$763m. in June 2002 and total money supply was 1,729·57bn. manats.

Budget. Government revenue and expenditure (in 1m. manats):

	1995	1996	1997	1998
Revenue	1,920,245	1,881,015	2,350,032	3,076,024
Expenditure	2,254,334	2,283,635	3,028,574	3,993,139

Profits tax accounted for 498,000m. manats of the 1998 budget revenue and VAT accounted for 800,000m. manats. Of the 1998 expenditure, education accounted for 825,842·9m. manats, social protection 340,000m. manats, health 290,143m. manats and social welfare 88,275m. manats.

Performance. Total GDP was US$5·7bn. in 2001. Azerbaijan has one of the fastest growing economies in the world. Real GDP growth was 10·0% in 1998, 7·4% in 1999, 11·1% in 2000 and 9·9% in 2001. This was largely thanks to foreign investment into the country in anticipation of the forthcoming oil boom. Between 1990 and 1996 the average annual real growth in GNP per capita was –18·7%.

Banking and Finance. The central bank and bank of issue is the National Bank (*Chairman*, Dr Elman Rustamov). In 1996 there were 112 commercial and four state-owned banks. With capital requirements increasing, the number of commercial banks is rapidly decreasing.

ENERGY AND NATURAL RESOURCES

Environment. According to the *World Bank Atlas* Azerbaijan's carbon dioxide emissions were the equivalent of 4·9 tonnes per capita in 1998.

Electricity. Capacity in 1997 was 5m. kW. Output was 18,062m. kWh in 1998; consumption per capita was 1,584 kWh.

Oil and Gas. The most important industry is crude oil extraction. Baku is at the centre of oil exploration in the Caspian. Partnerships with Turkish, western European and US companies have been forged.

In 1999 oil reserves totalled 7bn. bbls. A century ago Azerbaijan produced half of the world's oil, but production today is less than 1% of the total. An estimated average of 9·0m. tonnes of oil are produced annually (1997). In July 1999 BP Amoco announced a major natural gas discovery in the Shakh Deniz offshore field, with reserves of at least 700bn. cu. metres and perhaps as much as 1,000bn. cu. metres. There were proven reserves of 850bn. cu. metres. Natural gas production in 1999 amounted to 5·6bn. cu. metres.

Accords for the construction of an oil pipeline from Baku, the Azerbaijani capital, on the Caspian Sea through Georgia to Ceyhan in southern Turkey, and a gas pipeline from Turkmenistan through Azerbaijan and Georgia, to Erzurum in northeastern Turkey, were signed in Nov. 1999. Work on the oil pipeline, which is expected to become operational in 2005, began in Sept. 2002.

Minerals. The republic is rich in natural resources: iron, bauxite, manganese, aluminium, copper ores, lead, zinc, precious metals, sulphur pyrites, nepheline syenites, limestone and salt. In 1995, 1·0m. tonnes of iron ore were produced. Cobalt ore reserves have been discovered in Dashkasan, and Azerbaijan has the largest iodine-bromine ore reserves of the former Soviet Union (the Neftchala region has an iodine-bromine mill).

Agriculture. In 1997 the total area devoted to agriculture was 4·5m. ha, of which 1·7m. ha was under crop and 223,747 ha were orchards and vineyards. In 1997, 34% of the economically active population was engaged in agriculture. Principal crops include grain, cotton, rice, grapes, citrus fruit, vegetables, tobacco and silk.

Output of main agricultural products (in 1,000 tonnes) in 2000: wheat, 1,198; potatoes, 450; tomatoes, 331; barley, 202; apples, 180; watermelons, 180.

Livestock (2000): cattle, 1·94m.; sheep, 5·39m.; goats, 400,000; chickens, 14m. Livestock products (2000, in 1,000 tonnes): beef and veal, 53; lamb and mutton, 36; cow's milk, 1,011; eggs, 29.

Forestry. In 1995 forests covered 990,000 ha, or 11·4% of the total land area.

Fisheries. About ten tonnes of caviar from the Caspian sturgeon are produced annually. Total catch in 2000 came to approximately 18,797 tonnes, exclusively from inland waters.

INDUSTRY

There are oil extraction and refining, oil-related machinery, iron and steel, aluminium, copper, chemical, cement, building materials, timber, synthetic rubber, salt, textiles, food and fishing industries. Output (1997) was, in tonnes: residual fuel oil, 3,868,000; distillate fuel oil, 2,157,000; jet fuel, 579,000; cement, 315,000; rolled ferrous metals, 200,000 (1993); mineral fertilizers, 30,000 (1993); processed meat, 16,500 (1993); milk products, 48,000 (1993); fabrics, 116m. sq. metres (1993); footwear, 4·1m. pairs (1993); 17,000 drilling and boring machines; 1,000 TV sets.

Labour. In 1997 the population of working age was 4·5m. of whom 2·9m. were employed. The unemployment rate in 1999 was 13·9%. The average monthly salary in 1997 was 125,500 manats.

INTERNATIONAL TRADE

Total external debt was US$1,184m. in 2000.

Imports and Exports. In 2000 imports (f.o.b.) were valued at US$1,539·0m. and exports (f.o.b.) at US$1,858·3m.

Petroleum and related products accounted for approximately 75% of exports in 1999. Cotton, chemicals, tobacco, beverages, air conditioners, wool and refrigerators are also important exports. Principal imports are machinery, power, cereals, steel tubes, sugar and sweets.

The main export markets in 1999 were Italy (34%), Russia (9%), Georgia (8%) and Turkey (7%). Leading import suppliers were Russia (21%), Turkey (13%), US (8%) and UK (6%).

COMMUNICATIONS

Roads. There were 24,981 km of roads (6,879 km highways and main roads) in 1998. Passenger cars in use in 1998 totalled 281,320 (36 per 1,000 inhabitants). In addition, there were 79,934 trucks and vans and 13,666 buses and coaches. There were 594 fatalities as a result of road accidents in 1998.

Rail. Total length in 1994 was 2,118 km of 1,520 mm gauge (1,310 km electrified). Passenger-km travelled in 1998 came to 550m. and freight tonne-km to 4,613m.

There is a metro and tramway in Baku and a tramway in Sumgait.

Civil Aviation. There is an international airport at Baku. Azerbaijan Airlines had international flights in 1998 to Aleppo, Ankara, Antalya, Ashgabat, Chelyabinsk, Delhi, Ekaterinburg, Istanbul, Kazan, Kharkov, Kyiv, London, Moscow, Nakhichevan, Nizhny Novgorod, Orenburg, Perm, St Petersburg, Samara, Tbilisi, Tehran, Tel Aviv, Trabzon, Turkmanbashi, Volgograd, Voronezh and Zaporozhye. In 1999 Azerbaijan Airlines flew 10·4m. km, carrying 571,700 passengers (187,500 on international flights).

Shipping. In 1998 merchant shipping totalled 651,000 GRT (including oil tankers, 176,000 GRT). In 1998 vessels totalling 3,967,000 NRT entered ports and vessels totalling 1,483,000 NRT cleared.

Telecommunications. Telephone main lines numbered 801,200 in 2000 (103·6 per 1,000 inhabitants). In 1999 there were 180,000 mobile phone subscribers and (1995) 2,500 fax machines. There were 12,000 Internet users in Dec. 2000.

Postal Services. There were 1,857 post offices in 1995.

SOCIAL INSTITUTIONS

Justice. The number of reported crimes in 1997 was 16,402 (compared to 18,533 in 1994), including 449 murders or attempted murders (605 in 1994). There were 219 crimes per 1,000 inhabitants (249 in 1994) and 80% of crimes were solved (69·3% in 1994).

The population in penal institutions in July 1997 was 24,881 (325 per 100,000 of national population).

The death penalty was abolished in 1998.

Religion. In 1997 the population was 92% Muslim (mostly Shia), the balance being mainly Russian Orthodox, Armenian Apostolic and Judaism.

Education. In 1996–97 there were 719,013 pupils and 35,514 teachers at 4,454 primary schools, and 819,625 pupils at secondary schools. There were 103,608 children enrolled at pre-school institutions. In 1997 there were 111,382 students at 25 institutes of higher education and 73 specialized secondary schools. There is a state university at Baku, with 94,300 students in 1993–94 (including correspondence students). The Azerbaijan Academy of Sciences, founded in 1945, has 30 research institutes. Adult literacy was estimated to be 99% in 1998.

In 1997 total expenditure on education came to 3·0% of GNP and represented 18·8% of total government expenditure.

Health. In 1997 there were 29,300 doctors, 65,500 paramedics and 762 hospitals with 72,000 beds.

Welfare. In Jan. 1994 there were 797,000 age pensioners and 454,000 other pensioners.

CULTURE

Broadcasting. The government-controlled Azerbaijan Radio broadcasts two national and one regional programme, a relay of Radio Moscow and a foreign service, Radio Baku (Azeri, Arabic, Iranian and Turkish). There are a number of private TV and radio stations. In 1997 there were 170,000 TV receivers and 175,000 radio receivers.

Cinema. In 1997 there were 696 cinemas.

Press. In 1997 Azerbaijan published 270 different newspapers and 45 magazines. In 1995, 422 newspapers were registered with the Ministry of Justice, but only about 50 were actually appearing. There is one daily, published by parliament, with a circulation of 5,000, and two independent thrice-weeklies with a combined circulation of 30,000. 73 journals were registered in 1995, but only 12 were appearing.

Tourism. In 1998 there were 170,000 foreign tourists, spending US$125m.

Libraries. There are 4,647 public libraries (1997).

Theatre and Opera. Azerbaijan had 26 professional theatres in 1997.

Museums and Galleries. There were 145 museums including a National Museum of History in 1997.

DIPLOMATIC REPRESENTATIVES

Of Azerbaijan in the United Kingdom (4 Kensington Court, London, W8 5DL)
Ambassador: Rafael Ibrahimov.

Of the United Kingdom in Azerbaijan (2 Izmir St., Baku 370065)
Ambassador: Andrew Tucker.

Of Azerbaijan in the USA (2741 34th Street, Washington, D.C., NW, 20008)
Ambassador: Hafiz Mir Jalal Pashayev.

Of the USA in Azerbaijan (83 Azadliq Prospekt, Baku 37007)
Ambassador: Ross Wilson.

Of Azerbaijan to the United Nations
Ambassador: Yashar Aliyev.

Of Azerbaijan to the European Union
Ambassador: Arif Mamedov.

FURTHER READING
Swietochowski, T., *Russia and a Divided Azerbaijan.* Columbia University Press, 1995
Van Der Leeuw, C., *Azerbaijan.* Saint Martin's Press, New York, 1999

State Statistical Committee Website: http://www.azeri.com/goscomstat/

NAKHICHEVAN

This territory, on the borders of Turkey and Iran, forms part of Azerbaijan although separated from it by the territory of Armenia. Its population in 1989 was 95·9% Azerbaijani. It was annexed by Russia in 1828. In June 1923 it was constituted as an Autonomous Region within Azerbaijan. On 9 Feb. 1924 it was elevated to the status of Autonomous Republic. The 1996 Azerbaijani Constitution defines it as an Autonomous State within Azerbaijan.

Area, 5,500 sq. km (2,120 sq. miles); population (Jan. 1994), 315,000. Capital, Nakhichevan (66,800).

70% of the people are engaged in agriculture, of which the main branches are cotton and tobacco growing. Fruit and grapes are also produced.

In 1989–90 there were 219 primary and secondary schools with 60,200 pupils, and 2,200 students in higher educational institutions.

In Jan. 1990 there were 381 doctors and 2,445 junior medical personnel.

NAGORNO-KARABAKH

Established on 7 July 1923 as an Autonomous Region within Azerbaijan, in 1989 the area was placed under a 'special form of administration' subordinate to the USSR government. In Sept. 1991 the regional Soviet and the Shaumyan district Soviet jointly declared a Nagorno-Karabakh republic, which declared itself independent with a 99·9% popular vote (only the Armenian community took part in this vote as the Azeri population had already been expelled from Nagorno-Karabakh) in Dec. 1991. The autonomous status of the region was meanwhile abolished by the Azerbaijan Supreme Soviet in Nov. 1991, and the capital renamed Khankendi. A presidential decree of Jan. 1992 placed the region under direct rule. Azeri-Armenian fighting for possession of the region culminated in its occupation by Armenia in 1993 (and the occupation of seven other Azerbaijani regions outside it), despite attempts at international mediation. Since May 1994 there has been a ceasefire. Negotiations on settlements are conducted within the OSCE Minsk Group.

Area, 4,400 sq. km (1,700 sq. miles); population (Jan. 1990), 192,400. Capital, Khankendi (33,000). Populated by Armenians (76·9% at the 1989 census) and Azerbaijanis (21·5%).

In presidential elections held on 11 Aug. 1997 the hard-line independence candidate Arkady Gukasyan received more than 89% of votes cast, and was sworn in on 8 Sept. He was re-elected on 11 Aug. 2002 with 88·4% of votes cast. Legislative elections were held on 18 June 2000. The Democratic Artsakh Party, which supports President Gukasyan, won 13 seats; the Armenian Revolutionary Federation 9; the Armenakan Party 1; and independents 10. The *Prime Minister* is Anushavan Danielyan.

Main industries are silk, wine, dairying and building materials. Crop area is 67,200 ha; cotton, grapes and winter wheat are grown. There are 33 collective and 38 state farms.

In 1989–90, 34,200 pupils were studying in primary and secondary schools, 2,400 in colleges and 2,100 in higher educational institutions.

BAHAMAS

Commonwealth of
The Bahamas

Capital: Nassau
Population estimate, 2000: 304,000
GDP per capita, 2000: (PPP$) 17,012
HDI/world rank: 0·826/41

KEY HISTORICAL EVENTS
For most of the period from the 17th century, the Bahamas were governed by Britain. Internal self-government with cabinet responsibility was introduced on 7 Jan. 1964 and full independence achieved on 10 July 1973.

TERRITORY AND POPULATION
The Commonwealth of The Bahamas consists of over 700 islands and inhabited cays off the southeast coast of Florida extending for about 260,000 sq. miles. Only 22 islands are inhabited. Land area, 5,382 sq. miles (13,939 sq. km).

The areas and populations of the major islands in 1990 were as follows:

	Area (in sq. km)	Population		Area (in sq. km)	Population
New Providence	207	172,196	Bimini Islands	23	1,639
Grand Bahama	1,373	40,898	Inagua Islands	1,671	985
Eleuthera, Harbour Island			Berry Islands	31	628
and Spanish Wells	518	10,584	San Salvador	163	465
Abaco	1,681	10,003	Crooked Island	238	412
Andros	5,957	8,177	Acklins Island	389	405
Exuma Islands	290	3,556	Mayaguana	285	312
Long Island	448	2,949	Ragged Island	23	89
Cat Island	388	1,698	Rum Cay	78	53

Census population for 2000 was 303,611.

The UN gives a projected population for 2010 of 341,000.

In 1999, 87·9% of the population were urban. The capital is Nassau on New Providence Island (212,432 in 2000); the other large town is Freeport (45,000 in 1999) on Grand Bahama.

English is the official language. Creole is spoken among Haitian immigrants.

SOCIAL STATISTICS
1997 estimates: births, 6,300; deaths, 1,600. Rates, 1997 (per 1,000 population): birth, 21·47; death, 5·45; marriage (1996), 9·3; infant mortality (per 1,000 live births), 1999, 18. Expectation of life was 64·9 years for males and 73·6 years for females in 1999. Annual population growth rate, 1990–99, 1·9%; fertility rate, 1999, 2·6 children per woman.

CLIMATE
Winters are mild and summers pleasantly warm. Most rain falls in May, June, Sept. and Oct., and thunderstorms are frequent in summer. Rainfall amounts vary over the islands from 30" (750 mm) to 60" (1,500 mm). Nassau, Jan. 71°F (21·7°C), July 81°F (27·2°C). Annual rainfall 47" (1,179 mm).

CONSTITUTION AND GOVERNMENT
The Commonwealth of The Bahamas is a free and democratic sovereign state. Executive power rests with Her Majesty the Queen, who appoints a Governor-General to represent her, advised by a Cabinet whom he appoints. There is a bicameral legislature. The *Senate* comprises 16 members all appointed by the Governor-General, nine on the advice of the Prime Minister, four on the advice of the Leader of the Opposition, and three after consultation with both of them. The *House of Assembly* consists of 40 members elected from single-member constituencies for a maximum term of five years.

National Anthem. 'Lift up your head to the rising sun, Bahamaland'; words and tune by T. Gibson.

RECENT ELECTIONS
In parliamentary elections held on 2 May 2002 the Progressive Liberal Party (PLP) won 50·8% of votes cast and 29 out of 40 seats, the Free National Movement (FNM) 41·1% (7) and ind. 5·2% (4). Turn-out was 82·4%.

CURRENT ADMINISTRATION
Governor-General: Dame Ivy Dumont; b. 1930 (appointed 13 Nov. 2001).

In March 2003 the cabinet was composed as follows:

Prime Minister and Minister of Finance: Perry Christie; b. 1943 (PLP; sworn in 3 May 2002).

Deputy Prime Minister and Minister of National Security: Cynthia Pratt. *Agriculture, Fisheries and Local Government:* Alfred Grey. *Transportation and Aviation:* Glenys Hanna-Martin. *Foreign Affairs and Public Service:* Fred Mitchell. *Education:* Alfred Sears. *Financial Services and Investments:* Allyson Maynard-Gibson. *Health and Environment:* Marcus Bethel. *Housing and National Insurance:* Shane Gibson. *Labour and Immigration:* Vincent Peet. *Social Services and Community Development:* Melanie Griffin. *Youth, Sports and Culture:* Neville Wisdom. *Tourism:* Obie Wilchcombe. *Justice:* Vacant.

Office of the Prime Minister: http://www.opm.gov.bs

DEFENCE
The Royal Defence Force is a primarily maritime force tasked with naval patrols and protection duties in the extensive waters of the archipelago. Personnel in 1999 numbered 860, and the base is at Coral Harbour on New Providence Island.

In 2000 defence expenditure totalled US$25m. (US$94 per capita), representing 0·6% of GDP.

Navy. The Navy operates 19 vessels including seven patrol craft.

INTERNATIONAL RELATIONS
The Commonwealth of The Bahamas is a member of the UN, OAS, Inter-American Development Bank, the Commonwealth, ACS, CARICOM, FAO, IBRD, ICAO, ILO, IMF, Intelsat, ITU, UNESCO, UNIDO, WHO, WIPO and is an ACP member state of the ACP-EU relationship.

ECONOMY
Services contributed an estimated 92% of GDP in 1997.

Overview. The government of the Commonwealth of The Bahamas is committed to building an economic environment in which free enterprise can flourish, where the government assumes its proper role as regulator and facilitator of economic development. The National Investment Policy is designed to support an investment-friendly climate; guarantees the complementarity of Bahamian and overseas investments; fosters appropriate links with all sectors of the economy, in particular, the tourism and financial services sectors.

Currency. The unit of currency is the *Bahamian dollar* (BSD) of 100 *cents.* American currency is generally accepted. Inflation was 2·0% in 2001. Foreign exchange reserves were US$461m. in June 2002 and total money supply was B$812m.

Budget. Government revenue and expenditure (in B$1m.):

	1996	1997	1998	1999	2000
Revenue	685·9	729·0	761·3	869·1	940·8
Expenditure	719·7	829·3	807·2	884·5	916·6

The main sources of revenue are import duties, stamp duty from land sales, work permits and residence fees, and accommodation tax. There is no direct taxation.

Performance. The Bahamas experienced a recession during the period 1988–94; this was mainly due to the recession in the USA leading to a fall in the number of American tourists. The economy has been growing since, and there are continuing efforts to diversify. Freeport's tax-free status was extended by 25 years in 1995, and import duties were reduced in the 1996–97 budget. 1996 saw an increase in growth but the budget deficit is increasing; an overall deficit of US$190m. was projected for 1997–98, 3 times the 1996–97 deficit, and 5% of GDP.

Real GDP growth was 5·0% in 2000 but the general downturn in the world economy resulted in negative growth of 0·5% in 2001. Total GDP in 2000 was US$4·8bn.

Banking and Finance. The Central Bank of The Bahamas was established in 1974. Its *Governor* is Julian Francis. The Bahamas is an important centre for offshore banking. Financial business produces about 20% of GDP. In Dec. 1996, 425 banks and trust companies were licensed, about half being branches of foreign companies.

The Bahamas was one of 15 countries and territories named in a report in June 2000 as failing to co-operate in the fight against international money laundering. The Financial Action Task Force on Money Laundering was set up by the G7 group of major industrialized nations.

A stock exchange, the Bahamas International Securities Exchange (BISX), was inaugurated in May 2000.

Weights and Measures. The Bahamas follows the USA in using linear, dry and liquid measure.

ENERGY AND NATURAL RESOURCES

Environment. According to the *World Bank Atlas* the carbon dioxide emissions of the Bahamas in 1998 were the equivalent of 6·1 tonnes per capita.

Electricity. In 1996 installed capacity was 424 MW, all thermal. Output, 1998, 1·34bn. kWh; consumption per capita was 4,859 kWh in 1997.

Oil and Gas. The Bahamas does not have reserves of either oil or gas, but oil is refined in the Bahamas. The Bahamas Oil Refining Company (BORCO), in Grand Bahama, operates as a terminal which trans-ships, stores and blends oil.

Minerals. Aragonite is extracted from the seabed.

Agriculture. In 1998 there were some 6,000 ha of arable land and 4,000 ha of permanent crops. Production (in 1,000 tonnes), 2000: sugarcane, 45; fruit, 22 (notably grapefruit, lemons and limes); vegetables, 21.

Livestock (2000): cattle, 1,000; sheep, 6,000; goats, 15,000; pigs, 6,000; chickens, 5m.

Forestry. In 1995 forests covered 158,000 ha or 15·8% of the total land area (18% in 1990). Timber production in 1999 was 17,000 cu. metres.

Fisheries. The estimated total catch in 2000 amounted to 10,500 tonnes, mainly lobsters, and exclusively from sea fishing. Total value in 1995 of fish landings was B$59·7m.

INDUSTRY

Tourism and offshore banking are the main industries. Two industrial sites, one in New Providence and the other in Grand Bahama, have been developed as part of an industrialization programme. The main products are pharmaceutical chemicals, salt and rum.

Labour. The workforce was estimated at 146,600 in 1996. Around 30% of the economically active population work in trade, restaurants and hotels. Unemployment was 6·9% in 2001.

Trade Unions. In 1996 there were 43 unions, the largest being The Bahamas Hotel Catering and Allied Workers' Union (5,000 members).

INTERNATIONAL TRADE

Public-sector foreign debt was US$372,862 in Dec. 1997. There is a freeport zone of Grand Bahama. Although a member of CARICOM, the Bahamas is not a signatory to its trade protocol.

Imports and Exports. Imports and exports for calendar years in US$1m.:

	1996	1997	1998	1999	2000
Imports f.o.b.	1,287·4	1,410·7	1,737·1	1,808·1	1,905·0
Exports f.o.b.	273·3	295·0	362·9	379·9	549·8

The principal exports are oil products and trans-shipments, chemicals, fish, rum and salt. In 1997 the main export markets were USA (77%) and France (12%); the USA was the source of 91% of imports.

COMMUNICATIONS

Roads. There were about 2,500 km of roads in 1996 (1,450 km paved). In 1996 there were around 46,000 passenger cars and 12,000 lorries and vans.

Civil Aviation. There are international airports at Nassau, Freeport (Grand Bahama Island) and Moss Town (Andros). The national carrier is the state-owned Bahamasair, which in 1998 flew to Fort Lauderdale, Miami, Newark, Orlando and West Palm Beach as well as providing services between different parts of the Bahamas. In 1999 scheduled airline traffic of Bahamas-based carriers flew 6·8m. km, carrying 1,719,000 passengers (944,000 on international flights).

Shipping. The Bahamas' shipping registry consists of a fleet of 27·7m. GRT, a figure exceeded only by the fleets of Panama and Liberia. There were nearly 1,300 vessels in 1998, including 255 tankers.

Telecommunications. New Providence and most of the other major islands have automatic telephone systems in operation, interconnected by a radio network, while local distribution within the islands is by overhead and underground cables. In 2000 there were 114,300 telephone main lines in use or 375·9 per 1,000 inhabitants. International telecommunications service is provided by a submarine cable system to Florida, USA, and an INTELSAT Standard 'A' Earth Station and a Standard 'F2' Earth Station. International operator-assisted and direct dialling telephone services are available to all major countries. There is an automatic Telex system and a packet switching system for data transmission, and land mobile and marine telephone services. In 2001 there were 120,000 mobile phone subscribers and (1995) 500 fax machines. There were 13,100 Internet users in Dec. 2000.

Postal Services. In 1997 there were over 120 post offices.

SOCIAL INSTITUTIONS

Justice. English Common Law is the basis of the Bahamian judicial system, although there is a large volume of Bahamian Statute Law. The highest tribunal in the country is the Court of Appeal. New Providence has 15 Magistrates' Courts and Grand Bahama has three.

The strength of the police force (1995) was 2,223 officers.

There were 64 murders in 1999 (a rate of 21·5 per 100,000 population). The death penalty is in force, the most recent execution being carried out in Jan. 2000. The population in penal institutions in Jan. 1998 was 1,401 (485 per 100,000 of national population).

Religion. Religious adherents at the 1996 census: Baptist, 32%; Anglican/Episcopalian, 20%; Roman Catholic, 19%; Protestant, 12%; Church of God, 6%; Methodist, 6%.

Education. Education is compulsory between five and 16 years of age. The adult literacy rate in 1999 was 95·7% (94·9% among males and 96·4% among females). In 1996 there were 210 schools (49 independent). Total school enrolment, Sept. 1996, 61,118. Courses lead to The Bahamas General Certificate of Secondary Education (BGCSE). Independent schools provide education at primary, secondary and high school levels.

The four institutions offering higher education are: the government-sponsored College of The Bahamas, established in 1974; the University of the West Indies (regional), affiliated with the Bahamas since 1960; The Bahamas Hotel Training College, sponsored by the Ministry of Education and the hotel industry; and The Bahamas Technical and Vocational Institute, established to provide basic skills. Several schools of continuing education offer secretarial and academic courses.

Health. In 1996 there was a government general hospital (436 beds) and a psychiatric/geriatric care centre (502 beds) in Nassau, and a hospital in Freeport (82 beds). The Family Islands, comprising 20 health districts, had 13 health centres and 107 main clinics in 1996. There were two private hospitals (86 beds) in New Providence in 1993.

Welfare. Social Services are provided by the Department of Social Services, a government agency which grants assistance to restore, reinforce and enhance the capacity of the individual to perform life tasks, and to provide for the protection of children in the Bahamas.

The Department's divisions comprise: community support services, child welfare, family services, senior citizens, Family Island and research planning, training and community relations.

CULTURE

Broadcasting. The Broadcasting Corporation of the Bahamas is a government-owned company which operates five radio broadcasting stations and a TV service with one channel, ZNS TV 13. In 1998, five independent radio stations were operating. In 1997 there were 67,000 television and 215,000 radio receivers. TV colour is by NTSC. There is cable TV on Grand Bahama, New Providence and the majority of the Family Islands.

Cinema. In 1998 there were four cinemas.

Press. There were three national dailies and one weekly in 1998.

Tourism. Tourism is the most important industry, accounting for about 70% of GDP. In 1998 there were 1,590,000 stop-over and 1,730,000 cruise-ship visitors. Tourist expenditure was US$1,415m. in 1998.

Festivals. Junkanoo is the quintessential Bahamian celebration, a parade or 'rush-out', characterized by colourful costumes, goatskin drums, cowbells, horns and a brass section. It is staged in the early hours of 26 Dec. and the early hours of 1 Jan.

Libraries. There were eight libraries in the Bahamas in 1998.

Theatre and Opera. The Bahamas had one National Theatre in 1998, the Dundas Centre for the Performing Arts.

Museums and Galleries. In 1998 there were four museums and 13 art galleries.

DIPLOMATIC REPRESENTATIVES
Of the Bahamas in the United Kingdom (10 Chesterfield St., London, W1X 8AH)
High Commissioner: Basil G. O'Brien, CMG.

Of the United Kingdom in the Bahamas (3rd Floor, Ansbacher House, East St., Nassau)
High Commissioner: Peter Heigl.

Of the Bahamas in the USA (2220 Massachusetts Ave., NW, Washington, D.C., 20008)
Ambassador: Joshua Sears.

Of the USA in the Bahamas (Mosmar Bldg., Queen St., Nassau)
Ambassador: Richard J. Blakenship.

Of the Bahamas to the United Nations
Ambassador: Anthony Charles Rolle.

Of the Bahamas to the European Union
Ambassador: Basil G. O'Brien, CMG.

FURTHER READING
Cash, P., *et al.*, *Making of Bahamian History.* London, 1991
Craton, M. and Saunders, G., *Islanders in the Stream: a History of the Bahamian People.* 2 vols. Univ. of Georgia Press, 1998

BAHRAIN

Al-Mamlaka Al-Bahrayn
(Kingdom of Bahrain)

Capital: Manama
Population estimate, 2000: 640,000
GDP per capita, 2000: (PPP$) 15,084
HDI/world rank: 0·831/39

KEY HISTORICAL EVENTS
Bahrain was controlled by the Portuguese from 1521 until 1602. The Khalifa family gained control in 1783 and has ruled since that date. British assistance was sought to retain independence and from 1861 until 1971 Bahrain was in all but name a British protectorate. Bahrain declared its independence in 1971. Shaikh Isa bin Salman Al-Khalifa became the Amir. A constitution was ratified in June 1973 providing for a National Assembly of 30 members, popularly elected for a four-year term, together with all members of the cabinet (appointed by the Amir). However, in 1975 the National Assembly was dissolved and the Amir began ruling by decree. In 1987 the main island was joined to the Saudi mainland by a causeway. In Feb. 2002 Bahrain became a kingdom, with the Amir proclaiming himself king.

TERRITORY AND POPULATION
The Kingdom of Bahrain forms an archipelago of 36 low-lying islands in the Arabian (Persian) Gulf, between the Qatar peninsula and the mainland of Saudi Arabia. The total area is 706·6 sq. km.

The island of Bahrain (578 sq. km) is connected by a 1·5-mile causeway to the second largest island, Muharraq to the northeast, and by a causeway with the island of Sitra to the east. A causeway links Bahrain with Saudi Arabia. From Sitra, oil pipelines and a causeway carrying a road extend out to sea for 3 miles to a deep-water anchorage.

Population (1996 est.) 598,600 (males, 349,100; females, 249,500), of which 369,200 were Bahraini and 229,400 non-Bahraini. The population density was 850 per sq. km. In 1999, 91·8% of the population were urban.

The UN gives a projected population for 2010 of 744,000.

There are 12 regions: Central, Eastern, Hamad Town, Hidd Town, Isa Town, Jidhafs, Manama, Muharraq, Northern, Rifa'a, Sitra, Western. Manama, the capital and commercial centre, had a 1999 population of 162,000. Other towns (1991 census population) are Muharraq (74,254), Rifa'a (45,596), Jidhafs (44,769), Sitra (36,755) and Isa Town (34,509).

Arabic is the official language. English is widely used in business.

SOCIAL STATISTICS
Statistics 1999: births, 14,280 (Bahraini, 11,269); deaths, 1,920 (Bahraini, 1,557). Rates (per 1,000) for Bahrainis in 1999: birth, 28·0; death, 3·87; natural increase, 24·13; infant mortality (per 1,000 live births), 8·7 (1999). For non-Bahrainis: birth, 11·4; death, 1·4; natural increase, 10. Life expectancy at birth, 1999, was 71·4 years for men and 75·6 years for women. Annual population growth rate, 1990–99, 2·4%; fertility rate, 1999, 2·7 children per woman. In 1999 there were 3,673 marriages and 834 divorces.

The Shia make up 70% of the national population, half of whom are under 15.

CLIMATE
The climate is pleasantly warm between Dec. and March but from June to Sept. the conditions are very hot and humid. The period June to Nov. is virtually rainless. Bahrain, Jan. 66°F (19°C), July 97°F (36°C). Annual rainfall 5·2" (130 mm).

CONSTITUTION AND GOVERNMENT
The ruling family is the Al-Khalifa who have been in power since 1783.

BAHRAIN

The constitution changing Bahrain from an Emirate to a Kingdom dates from 14 Feb. 2002. The new constitutional hereditary monarchy has a bicameral legislature, inaugurated on 14 Dec. 2002. National elections for a legislative body took place on 24 and 31 Oct. 2002 (the first for 27 years). One chamber is a directly elected assembly while the second (upper) chamber, a *Shura* consultative council of experts, is appointed by the government. Both chambers have 40 members. All Bahraini citizens over the age of 21—men and women—are able to vote for the elected assembly. In the Oct. 2002 national elections women stood for office for the first time.

National Anthem. 'Bahrain ona, baladolaman' ('Our Bahrain, secure as a country'); words by M. S. Ayyash, tune anonymous.

RECENT ELECTIONS
On 24 and 31 Oct. 2002 the first national elections since Dec. 1973 were held. Despite a call from opposition parties for the election to be boycotted, turn-out was over 50%. 21 out of 40 seats were won by secular candidates, with the remaining seats going to Sunni and Shia representatives. There were eight women among a total of 177 candidates running for the legislature, although males won all of the seats.

CURRENT ADMINISTRATION
The present king (formerly Amir), HH Shaikh Hamad bin Isa Al-Khalifa, KCMG (b. 1950), succeeded on 6 March 1999 and became king on 14 Feb. 2002.

In March 2003 the cabinet was composed as follows:

Prime Minister: Shaikh Khalifa bin Salman Al-Khalifa; b. 1936. He is currently the longest-serving prime minister of any sovereign country, having been Bahrain's Prime Minister since it became independent in Aug. 1971.

Deputy Prime Minister and Minister of Foreign Affairs: Shaikh Mohammed bin Mubarak Al-Khalifa. *Deputy Prime Minister and Minister of Islamic Affairs:* Shaikh Abdullah bin Khalid Al-Khalifa.

Minister of Cabinet Affairs: Mohammed bin Ibrahim Al-Mutawa. *Commerce:* Ali Saleh Abdullah Al-Saleh. *Defence:* Shaikh Khalifa bin Ahmed Al-Khalifa. *Electricity and Water:* Shaikh Abdulla bin Salman Al-Khalifa. *Finance and National Economy:* Abdullah Hasan Al-Saif. *Health:* Khalil Ibrahim al-Hasan. *Housing:* Fahmi bin Ali al-Jowdar. *Industry:* Hasan Abdallah al-Fakhru. *Information:* Nabil bin Yacoub Al-Hamer. *Interior:* Shaikh Mohammed bin Khalifa bin Hamad Al-Khalifa. *Justice:* Jawad al-Arrayed. *Labour and Social Affairs:* Majid Muhsin al-Alawi. *Municipalities and Agriculture:* Muhammad Ali al-Sitri. *Oil:* Shaikh Isa bin Ali Hamad Al-Khalifa. *Prime Minister's Court:* Shaikh Khalid bin Abdulla Al-Khalifa. *Transport and Communications:* Shaikh Ali bin Khalifa bin Salman Al-Khalifa. *Works and Education:* Majid Ali al-Nuaymi.

Government Website: http://www.bahrain.gov.bh

DEFENCE
The Crown Prince is C.-in-C. of the armed forces. An agreement with the USA in Oct. 1991 gave port facilities to the US Navy and provided for mutual manoeuvres.

Military expenditure totalled US$435m. in 2000 (US$706 per capita), representing 6·4% of GDP.

Army. The Army consists of one infantry brigade, one artillery brigade and one air defence battalion. Personnel, 1999, 8,500. In addition there is a National Guard of approximately 900 and a paramilitary police force of 9,000.

Navy. The Naval force based at Mina Sulman numbered 1,000 in 1999.

Air Force. Personnel (1999), 1,500. Equipment includes 24 combat aircraft and 26 armed helicopters.

INTERNATIONAL RELATIONS
Bahrain is a member of the UN, WTO, the League of Arab States, the Gulf Co-operation Council, OAPEC (Organization of Arab Petroleum Exporting Countries) and OIC.

In March 2001 the International Court of Justice ruled on a long-standing dispute between Bahrain and Qatar over the boundary between the two countries and ownership of certain islands. Both countries accepted the decision.

ECONOMY

In 1996 services accounted for an estimated 53% of GDP and industry 46%.

Currency. The unit of currency is the *Bahraini dinar* (BHD), divided into 1,000 *fils*. In June 2002 foreign exchange reserves were US$1,675m., total money supply was BD602m. and gold reserves were 150,000 troy oz. There was deflation of 1·2% in 2001.

In 2001 the six Gulf Arab states—Bahrain, along with Kuwait, Oman, Qatar, Saudi Arabia and the United Arab Emirates—signed an agreement to establish a single currency by 2010.

Budget. Government revenue and expenditure (in BD1m.):

	1995	1996	1997	1998	1999	2000
Revenue	526·6	615·2	633·2	516·5	653·5	1,065·9
Expenditure	594·1	581·3	620·0	644·6	699·3	777·0

Bahrain is suffering from low oil prices, as it relies on oil for 50% of government revenue.

Performance. Total GDP in 2000 was US$8·0bn. Real GDP growth was 5·3% in 2000 and 4·8% in 2001.

Banking and Finance. The Bahrain Monetary Agency (*Governor*, Ahmed bin Mohammed Al-Khalifa) has central banking powers. In 1998 Bahrain hosted 180 different financial institutions including 46 offshore banking units. In 1994, 38 foreign banks had representative offices. Offshore banking units may not engage in local business; their assets totalled US$62,503m. in March 1996.

There is a stock exchange linked with those of Kuwait and Oman.

Weights and Measures. The metric system is in use.

ENERGY AND NATURAL RESOURCES

Environment. According to the *World Bank Atlas* Bahrain's carbon dioxide emissions in 1998 were the equivalent of 29·1 tonnes per capita.

Electricity. In 1997 installed capacity was 1m. kW; 4·77bn. kWh were produced in 1998. Electricity consumption per capita was 7,645 kWh in 1998.

Oil and Gas. In 1931 oil was discovered. Operations were at first conducted by the Bahrain Petroleum Co. (BAPCO) under concession. In 1975 the government assumed a 60% interest in the oilfield and related crude oil facilities of BAPCO. Oil reserves in 1997 were 210m. bbls. Crude oil runs to refinery in 1996 amounted to 14·2m. bbls. Production (1996) was around 39,000 bbls. a day.

There were known natural gas reserves of 110bn. cu. metres in 1999. Production in 1999 was 8·5bn. cu. metres. Gas reserves are government-owned.

Water. Water is obtained from artesian wells and desalination plants and there is a piped supply to Manama, Muharraq, Isa Town, Rifa'a and most villages.

Agriculture. There are about 900 farms and smallholdings (average 2·5 ha) operated by about 2,500 farmers who produce a wide variety of fruits (22,000 tonnes in 2000) including dates (17,000 tonnes). In 2000 an estimated 12,000 tonnes of vegetables were produced. The major crop is alfalfa for animal fodder.

Livestock (2000): cattle, 11,000; camels, 1,000; sheep, 18,000; goats, 16,000.

In 2000 an estimated 5,000 tonnes of lamb and mutton, 5,000 tonnes of poultry meat, 3,000 tonnes of eggs and 14,000 tonnes of fresh milk were produced. Agriculture contributed 1% of GDP in 1997.

Fisheries. In 1990 the government operated a fleet of two large and five smaller trawlers totalling 1,004 GRT. The total catch in 2000 was 11,718 tonnes, exclusively from sea fishing.

INDUSTRY

Industry is being developed with foreign participation: aluminium smelting (and ancillary industries), shipbuilding and repair, petrochemicals, electronics assembly and light industry. Aluminium production was 480,000 tonnes in 1997.

Traditional crafts include boatbuilding, weaving and pottery.

BAHRAIN

Labour. The workforce (estimate 1996) was 272,100 of which 103,500 were Bahraini. There were 5,100 unemployed persons in 1995.

INTERNATIONAL TRADE
Totally foreign-owned companies have been permitted to register since 1991.

In 2001 Bahrain, along with Kuwait, Oman, Qatar, Saudi Arabia and the United Arab Emirates agreed to the complete implementation of a customs union by 2003.

Imports and Exports. In 2000 imports (f.o.b.) totalled US$4,373·4m. and exports (f.o.b.) US$5,700·5m. In 1999 mineral fuels and related materials made up 62% of exports and 35% of imports. In 1999 the main export markets were Saudi Arabia, USA and India; the main import sources were Australia (6%), Saudi Arabia (6%), USA (6%) and UK (5%).

COMMUNICATIONS

Roads. A 25-km causeway links Bahrain with Saudi Arabia. In 1998 there were 3,164 km of roads (76·9% paved), including 414 km of main roads and 450 km of secondary roads. Bahrain has one of the densest road networks in the world. In 1998 there were 196,143 vehicles in use, including 157,208 passenger cars (244·5 per 1,000 inhabitants). The average distance covered by a passenger car in the course of 1998 was 25,725 km (18,280 km in 1992).

Civil Aviation. Bahrain has a 25% share (with Oman, Qatar and UAE) in Gulf Air. In 2000 Bahrain International Airport handled 3·38m. passengers (all on international flights) and 146,800 tonnes of freight. In 1999 scheduled airline traffic of Bahrain-based carriers flew 20·8m. km, carrying 1,307,000 passengers (all on international flights).

Shipping. In 1998 the merchant fleet totalled 284,000 GRT, including oil tankers 54,000 GRT. The port of Mina Sulman is a free transit and industrial area; about 800 vessels are handled annually. In 1994, 3,864 passengers arrived and 3,963 departed by sea.

Telecommunications. The government has a 37% stake in Bahrain Telecommunications (BATELCO). In 2000 there were 171,000 telephone lines (249·7 per 1,000 inhabitants) and 95,000 PCs were in use (138·7 for every 1,000 persons). In 1997 there were 6,620 fax machines. Bahrain had 94,000 mobile phone subscribers in Dec. 1998 and 105,000 Internet users in March 2001.

Postal Services. There were 12 post offices in 1995.

SOCIAL INSTITUTIONS

Justice. The new constitution which came into force in Feb. 2002 includes the creation of an independent judiciary. The State Security Law and the State Security Court were both abolished in the lead-up to the change to a constitutional monarchy.

Religion. Islam is the state religion. In 1997, 84% of the population were Muslim (63% Shia and 21% Sunni). There are also Christian, Jewish, Bahai, Hindu and Parsee minorities.

Education. Adult literacy was 87·1% in 1999 (male, 90·5%; female, 82·2%). Government schools provide free education from primary to technical college level. Schooling is in three stages: primary (six years), intermediate (three years) and secondary (three years). Secondary education may be general or specialized.

Government school statistics for 1993–94:

	Pupils		Schools		Teachers	
	Boys	Girls	Boys	Girls	Male	Female
Primary	29,533	29,148	50	47	1,203	1,343
Intermediate	13,380	13,143	22	25	944	1,143
Secondary	10,413	10,982	12	11	1,120	799

In 1993–94 there were also in the private sector 86 nurseries; and 33 schools with 4,046 Bahraini and 19,554 non-Bahraini pupils, and 144 Bahraini and 1,435 non-Bahraini teachers. There were two universities (1994–95) with 7,019 students in attendance; as well as 3,711 persons attending adult education centres.

Health. There is a free medical service for all residents. In 1994 there were 278 doctors in government service and 96 in private practice, and 49 dentists. In 1996 there were 7 general hospitals (4 government; 3 private), 5 maternity hospitals, 19 health centres, and a total of 669 physicians.

Welfare. In 1976 a pensions, sickness benefits and unemployment, maternity and family allowances scheme was established. Employers contribute 7% of salaries and Bahraini employees 11%. In 1994, 36,612 persons received state benefit payments totalling BD3,715,158. A total of BD5,975,700 was paid out to pensioners, and BD306,600 to recipients of social insurance.

CULTURE

Broadcasting. Radio Bahrain is government-controlled, Bahrain Television part-commercial. In 1997 there were 338,000 radio and 275,000 TV receivers (colour by PAL).

In 1998 there were six television channels—two in English and four in Arabic—as well as a satellite channel.

Cinema. There were ten cinemas in 1998, three of which screened English films. In 1996 the total attendance was 833,000.

Press. In 1996 there were four daily newspapers with a combined circulation of 67,000, at a rate of 117 per 1,000 inhabitants.

Tourism. In 1998 there were 1,750,000 foreign tourists, spending US$366m. In 1994 there were 44 hotels with 5,175 beds.

Libraries. In 1996 there were ten public libraries; a total of 242,573 books were borrowed in that year.

DIPLOMATIC REPRESENTATIVES
Of Bahrain in the United Kingdom (98 Gloucester Rd., London, SW7 4AU)
Ambassador: Shaikh Khalid bin Ahmed Al Khalifa.

Of the United Kingdom in Bahrain (21 Government Ave., Manama 306, P.O. Box 114, Bahrain)
Ambassador: Peter Ford.

Of Bahrain in the USA (3502 International Dr., NW, Washington D.C., 20008)
Ambassador: Khalifa Ali Al-Khalifa.

Of the USA in Bahrain (Building No. 979, Road No. 3119, Block 331, Zinj District, Manama)
Ambassador: Ronald E. Neumann.

Of Bahrain to the United Nations
Ambassador: Tawfeeq Ahmed Khalil Almansoor.

FURTHER READING
Bahrain Monetary Authority. *Quarterly Statistical Bulletin.*
Central Statistics Organization. *Statistical Abstract.* Annual.

Al-Khalifa, A. and Rice, M. (eds.) *Bahrain through the Ages.* London, 1993
Al-Khalifa, H. bin I., *First Light: Modern Bahrain and its Heritage.* London, 1995

National statistical office: Central Statistics Organization, Council of Ministers, Manama.

BANGLADESH

Gana Prajatantri Bangladesh
(People's Republic of
Bangladesh)

Capital: Dhaka
Population estimate, 2000: 137·44m.
GDP per capita, 2000: (PPP$) 1,602
HDI/world rank: 0·478/145

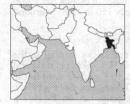

KEY HISTORICAL EVENTS

When the Indian sub-continent gained independence from Britain in 1947, it was partitioned according to religion. West Bengal became part of India while East Bengal elected to join Pakistan as East Pakistan. The province, however, was separated from West Pakistan physically and ethnically. Differences became unmanageable when East Pakistan's Awami League, campaigning for greater autonomy, won the majority of seats in the federal parliament in Dec. 1970. There was civil war from March to Dec. 1971. With the help of Indian troops, the Pakistani forces were defeated and the East broke away as an independent state to become the Republic of Bangladesh. The constitution of 1972 provided parliamentary democracy but in Jan. 1975 the president banned political parties. There followed a succession of coups until 1991 when democratic parliamentary elections were held. Continuing unrest reflected the increasing strength of Islamic fundamentalism.

TERRITORY AND POPULATION

Bangladesh is bounded in the west and north by India, east by India and Myanmar and south by the Bay of Bengal. The area is 57,295 sq. miles (148,393 sq. km). In 1992 India granted a 999-year lease of the Tin Bigha corridor linking Bangladesh with its enclaves of Angarpota and Dahagram. At the 1991 census the population was 111,455,000 (54,141,000 females). Estimate, July 1997: 125,430,000. Population density, 845 per sq. km. The most recent census took place in Jan. 2001; population (provisional), 129,247,233 (65,841,419 males).

The UN gives a projected population for 2010 of 167·93m.

In 2001, 76·6% of the population lived in rural areas. The country is administratively divided into five divisions, subdivided into 64 *zila*. Area (in sq. km) and population (in 1,000) in 1994 of the five divisions:

	Area	Population
Barisal division	13,297	7,757
Chittagong division	46,367	29,015
Dhaka division	31,119	33,940
Khulna division	22,274	13,243
Rajshahi division	34,513	27,500

The populations of the chief cities (1991 census) were as follows:

Dhaka[1]	3,397,187	Mymensingh	185,517	Nawabganj	121,205
Chittagong[2]	1,363,998	Barisal	163,481	Pabna	104,479
Khulna[3]	545,849	Jessore	160,198	Tangail	104,387
Rajshahi[4]	299,671	Tongi	154,175	Saidpur	102,030
Narayanganj	268,952	Comilla	143,282	Jamalpur	101,242
Rangpur	203,931	Dinajpur	126,189	Naogaon	100,794

[1]Metropolitan area 11,726,000 in 1999. [2]Metropolitan area 2,477,000 in 1995.
[3]Metropolitan area 1,071,000 in 1995. [4]Metropolitan area 756,000 in 1995.

The official language is Bengali. English is also in use for official, legal and commercial purposes.

Dhaka: The capital of Bangladesh, Dhaka is in the south of the country. It grew in stature when it became the seat of Moghul rule in the Bengal province (1608–39, 1660–1704). It was part of the British empire from 1765 until the partition in 1947, when it became the capital of East Bengal province. In 1956 it was named as the capital of East Pakistan. During the war of independence in 1971 it suffered great damage but has since risen to prominence as an important industrial centre and seat of learning.

SOCIAL STATISTICS

1998 births, 2,625,000; deaths, 633,000. In 1998 the birth rate was 19·9 per 1,000 population; death rate, 4·8; marriage rate, 1994, 10·7; infant mortality, 1999, 58 per 1,000 live births. Life expectancy at birth, 1999, 58·9 years for females and 59·0 years for males. The annual population growth rate by the late 1990s was almost half the 3·1% of the early 1970s. The fertility rate dropped from 6·2 births per woman in 1980–85 to 3·4 births per woman in 1990–95. By 1999 it had declined still further to 3·0 births. Bangladesh has had one of the largest reductions in its fertility rate of any country in the world over the past 20 years. It has also made some of the best progress in recent years in reducing child mortality. The number of deaths per 1,000 live births among children under five was reduced from nearly 150 in 1990 to around 90 in 1999.

CLIMATE

A tropical monsoon climate with heat, extreme humidity and heavy rainfall in the monsoon season, from June to Oct. The short winter season (Nov.–Feb.) is mild and dry. Rainfall varies between 50" (1,250 mm) in the west to 100" (2,500 mm) in the southeast and up to 200" (5,000 mm) in the northeast. Dhaka, Jan. 66°F (19°C), July 84°F (28·9°C). Annual rainfall 81" (2,025 mm). Chittagong, Jan. 66°F (19°C), July 81°F (27·2°C). Annual rainfall 108" (2,831 mm). In mid-1998 the Ganges and other rivers flowing into Bangladesh burst their banks causing a deluge that covered two-thirds of the country. More than 22m. were made homeless and 700 died in the floods.

CONSTITUTION AND GOVERNMENT

Bangladesh is a unitary republic. The Constitution came into force on 16 Dec. 1972 and provides for a parliamentary democracy. The head of state is the *President*, elected by parliament every five years, who appoints a *Vice-President*. A referendum of Sept. 1991 was in favour of abandoning the executive presidential system and opted for a parliamentary system. Turn-out was low. The most recent amendment to the constitution was in 1996 and allowed for a caretaker government, which the president may instal to supervise elections should the parliament be dissolved. There is a *Council of Ministers* to assist and advise the President. The President appoints the government ministers.

Parliament has one chamber of 300 members directly elected every five years by citizens over 18. There are additionally 30 seats reserved for women members elected by Parliament.

National Anthem. 'Amar Sonar Bangla, ami tomay bhalobashi' ('My golden Bengal, I love you'); words and tune by Rabindranath Tagore.

RECENT ELECTIONS

Iajuddin Ahmed was declared president-elect on 5 Sept. 2002 after the opposition Bangladesh Awami League failed to put forward a rival candidate.

In parliamentary elections of 1 Oct. 2001 the Bangladesh Jatiyatabadi Dal (BJD) and its coalition partners gained 47% of votes cast. The BJD itself gained 191 seats, with allies the Jamaat-e-Islami Bangladesh (JIB) gaining 18, the Jatiya Dal–Naziur (JD-N) 4 and the Islami Oikya Jote (IOJ) 2. The Bangladesh Awami League (BAL) gained 62 seats (40%), the Jatiya Dal–Ershad (JD-E) 14 (7·5%) with remaining seats going to other parties. Turn-out was 74·9%.

CURRENT ADMINISTRATION

President: Iajuddin Ahmed; b. 1931 (since 6 Sept. 2002).

In March 2003 the government included:

Prime Minister and Minister of Defence, Chittagong Hill Tracts Affairs, Cabinet Affairs, Special Affairs, Energy and Mineral Resources, Primary and Mass Education, and Establishment: Khaleda Zia; b. 1945 (BJD; sworn in 10 Oct. 2001).

Minister of Foreign Affairs: Morshed Khan. *Finance and Planning:* Saifur Rahman. *Textiles:* Abdul Matin Chowdhury. *Health and Family Welfare:* Dr Khandaker Mosharraf Hossain. *Law, Justice and Parliamentary Affairs:* Moudud Ahmed. *Agriculture:* Matiur Rahman Nizami. *Communications:* Nazmul Huda. *Land:* Shamsul Islam. *Disaster Management and Relief:* Chowdhury Kamal Ibne

BANGLADESH

Yusuf. *Industries:* M. K. Anwar. *Local Government, Rural Development and Co-operatives:* Abdul Mannan Bhuiyan. *Food:* Abdullah Al-Noman. *Environment and Forestry:* Shahjahan Siraj. *Shipping:* Akbar Hossain. *Women and Children's Affairs:* Khurshid Jahan Haq. *Labour and Employment:* Lutfar Rahman Khan. *Water Resources:* L. K. Siddiqui. *Information:* Tariqul Islam. *Housing and Public Works:* Mirza Abbas. *Fisheries and Livestock:* Sadek Hossain Khoka. *Commerce:* Amir Khasru Mahmud Chowdhury. *Post and Telecommunications:* Amunul Haq. *Science and Technology:* Abdul Moyeen Khan. *Home Affairs:* Altaf Hossain Chowdhury. *Jute:* Hafizuddin Ahmed. *Education:* Osman Faruq. *Social Welfare:* Ali Ahsan Mohammed Mujahid. *Without Portfolio:* Harunur Rashid Khan Monno.

Government Website: http://www.bangladeshgov.org/

DEFENCE
The supreme command of defence services is vested in the President. Defence expenditure in 2000 totalled US$670m. (US$5 per capita), representing 1·8% of GDP.

Army. Strength (1999) 120,000. There is also an armed police reserve, 5,000 strong, 20,000 security guards (Ansars) and the Bangladesh Rifles (border guard) numbering 30,000. There is a further potential reserve Ansar force of 180,000.

Navy. Naval bases are at Chittagong, Kaptai, Khulna and Dhaka. The fleet includes one new Chinese-built missile-armed frigate and three old ex-British frigates. Personnel, 1999, 10,500.

Air Force. There are 11 squadrons. Personnel strength (1999) 6,500. There were 65 combat aircraft in 1999.

INTERNATIONAL RELATIONS
Bangladesh is a member of the UN, WTO, the Commonwealth, Asian Development Bank, Colombo Plan, IOM, D-8, Organization of the Islamic Conference, SAARC and the Non-Aligned Movement.

ECONOMY
In 1998 agriculture accounted for 22·2% of GDP, services 49·9% and industry 27·9%.

Overview. The National Economic Council is responsible for policy. The prospective development of large natural gas reserves is expected to push up annual growth to 7–8%.

Currency. The unit of currency is the *taka* (BDT) of 100 *poisha*, which was floated in 1976. Foreign exchange reserves in June 2002 were US$1,543m. and gold reserves 112,000 troy oz. Inflation was 1·9% in 2001. Total money supply was Tk.231,658m. in May 2002.

Budget. The fiscal year ends on 30 June. Budget, 1996–97: revenue, US$3·6bn.; expenditure, US$5·3bn.

Performance. Real GDP growth was 5·6% in 2000 and 4·7% in 2001. Total GDP was US$46·7bn. in 2001. Corporate earnings grew by 9% in 1997. Trade liberalization measures were introduced 1994–96.

Banking and Finance. Bangladesh Bank is the central bank (*Governor*, Dr Fakhruddin Ahmed). There are three nationalized commercial banks, 11 private commercial banks, four specialized banks and seven foreign commercial banks. In May 1992 the Bangladesh Bank had Tk.22,402m. deposits, Tk.33,612m. foreign liabilities and Tk.57,619m. assets. The scheduled banks had Tk.244,533m. deposits, Tk.53,442m. assets and Tk.36,289m. borrowings from the Bangladesh Bank. Post office savings deposits were Tk.6,265·7m. in 1994.

There is a stock exchange in Dhaka.

Weights and Measures. The metric system was introduced from July 1982, but some imperial and traditional measures are still in use. One *maund* = 37·32 kg = 40 *seers*; one *seer* = 0·93 kg.

ENERGY AND NATURAL RESOURCES

Environment. According to the *World Bank Atlas* Bangladesh's carbon dioxide emissions in 1998 were the equivalent of 0·2 tonnes per capita.

Electricity. Installed capacity, 1997, 3m. kW; electricity generated, 1997, 11·5bn. kWh. Consumption per capita was 81 kWh in 1998.

Oil and Gas. In May 2000 it was estimated that Bangladesh had proven natural gas reserves of 311,000m. cu. metres in about 20 mainly onshore fields. Some international companies believe the actual figure to be very much higher. Total natural gas production in 1999 amounted to 8·1bn. cu. metres.

Water. A Ganges water-sharing accord was signed with India in 1997, ending a 25-year dispute which had hindered and dominated relations between the two countries.
By 2000 it was estimated that 85m. people out of the total population of 128m. had been accidentally poisoned over the previous 30 years through arsenic-contaminated drinking water. A World Health Organization report has described it as 'the largest mass poisoning of a population in history'.

Minerals. The principal minerals are lignite, limestone, china clay and glass sand. There are reserves of good-quality coal of 300m. tonnes. Production, 1992–93: limestone, 23,209m. tonnes (value Tk.13·93m.); china clay, 1,637m. tonnes (Tk.12·48m.).

Agriculture. In 1995 the agricultural population was 74·13m., of whom 37·18m. were economically active. There were 7·9m. ha of arable land in 1998 and 0·34m. ha of permanent crops. 3·84m. ha were irrigated in 1998. Bangladesh is a major producer of jute: production, 2000, 1·53m. tonnes. Rice is the most important food crop; production in 2000 (in 1m. metric tonnes), 35·82. Other major crops (1m. tonnes): sugarcane, 6·95; wheat, 1·90; potatoes, 1·70; bananas, 0·56.
Livestock in 2000: cattle, 23,652,000; goats, 33,800,000; sheep, 1,121,000; buffalo, 828,000; chickens, 139,000,000. Livestock products in 2000 (tonnes): beef and veal, 170,000; goat meat, 127,000; poultry meat, 112,000; goat milk, 1,296,000; cow milk, 755,000; buffalo milk, 22,000; sheep milk, 22,000; eggs, 132,000. Bangladesh is the second largest producer of goat milk, after India.

Forestry. In 1995 the area under forests was 10,000 sq. km, or 7·8% of the total land area (8·1% in 1990). Timber production in 1999 was 33·63m. cu. metres.

Fisheries. Bangladesh is a major producer of fish and fish products. There are 500,000 sea- and 800,000 inland-fishermen, with 1,249 mechanized boats, including 52 trawlers, and 3,317 motor boats. The total catch in 2000 amounted to 1,004,264 tonnes, of which 670,465 tonnes came from inland waters. Only China and India have larger annual catches of freshwater fish.

INDUSTRY

Manufacturing contributes around 11% of GDP. The principal industries are jute and cotton textiles, tea, paper, newsprint, cement, chemical fertilizers and light engineering. Production, 1994–95 (in 1,000 tonnes unless otherwise stated): jute goods, 550,000; cotton (1997), 63m. sq. metres; cement (1997), 610; sugar (1998), 159; vegetable oil, 13; fertilizer, 1,981; paper and paperboard, 46; bicycles (1997), 13,000; television sets (1997), 94,000; cigarettes (1997), 18·6bn. (units).

Labour. In 1996 the labour force totalled 60·4m. (58% males). In 1990–91 it was 51·2m. (20·1m. females), of whom 50·2m. (19·7m.) were employed (5·7m. children between ten and 14 years were also employed). Employment (in 1,000) by industry: agriculture, forestry and fishing, 33,303; manufacturing, 5,925; trade and catering, 4,285; services, 1,909; transport and communications, 1,611. On average, wage rates (US$0·23 an hour, 1997) are among the lowest of developing countries. Labour unrest was widespread in 1996.

INTERNATIONAL TRADE

Foreign companies are permitted wholly to own local subsidiaries. Tax concessions are available to foreign firms in the export zones of Dhaka and Chittagong. Foreign debt was US$15,609m. in 2000.

Imports and Exports. The main exports are jute and jute goods, tea, hides and skins, newsprint, fish and garments, and the main imports are machinery, transport equipment, manufactured goods, minerals, fuels and lubricants.

Imports and exports for calendar years in US$1m.:

	1996	1997	1998	1999	2000
Imports f.o.b.	6,284·6	6,550·7	6,715·7	7,535·5	8,052·9
Exports f.o.b.	4,009·3	4,839·9	5,141·4	5,458·3	6,399·2

In 1998, 39% of exports went to the USA, 9% to France, 9% to Germany and 7% to the UK. 15% of imports in 1998 came from India, 10% from China, 7% from Japan and 6% from Singapore.

Since the early 1980s the garment industry has developed from virtually nothing to earn some 70% of the country's hard currency. Garment exports in 1997 earned US$3·5bn.

COMMUNICATIONS

Roads. In 1997 the total road network was 201,182 km with 34,850 km of main roads and 27,023 km of secondary roads, but some 10,000 km of roads were destroyed in the floods of 1998. In 1998 there were 30,361 buses and coaches, 42,425 trucks and lorries, 2,235 taxis (1995), 46,561 motorized rickshaws (1995) and 57,068 passenger cars. In 1995 there were also 411,000 rickshaws and 727,000 bullock carts. There were 5,453 road accidents in 1997, resulting in 3,162 fatalities.

Rail. In 1993 there were 2,706 km of railways, comprising 884 km of 1,676 mm gauge and 1,822 km of metre gauge. Passenger-km travelled in 1995–96 came to 4·04bn. and freight tonne-km to 760m.

Civil Aviation. There are international airports at Dhaka (Zia) and Chittagong, and eight domestic airports. Biman Bangladesh Airlines is state-owned. In addition to domestic routes, in 1998 it operated international services to Abu Dhabi, Bahrain, Bangkok, Bombay, Brussels, Calcutta, Delhi, Doha, Dubai, Frankfurt, Hong Kong, Jeddah, Karachi, Káthmandu, Kuala Lumpur, Kuwait, London, Manchester, Muscat, New York, Paris, Rangoon (Yangon), Riyadh, Rome, Singapore and Tokyo. In 2000 Dhaka's Zia International Airport handled 2,585,317 passengers (2,101,201 on international flights) and 113,333 tonnes of freight. In 1999 Biman Bangladesh Airlines flew 21·0m. km, carrying 1,215,400 passengers (891,600 on international flights).

Shipping. There are sea ports at Chittagong and Mongla, and inland ports at Dhaka, Chandpur, Barisal, Khulna and five other towns. There are 8,000 km of navigable inland waterways. The Bangladesh Shipping Corporation owned 18 ships in 1994. Total tonnage registered, 1998, 0·41m. GRT (including oil tankers, 59,000 GRT). In 1993–94 the two sea ports handled 8·20m. tonnes of imports and 1·66m. tonnes of exports. In 1996 vessels totalling 5,928,000 NRT entered ports and vessels totalling 3,136,000 NRT cleared. The Bangladesh Inland Water Transport Corporation had 288 vessels in 1994. 70·29m. passengers were carried in 1992–93.

Telecommunications. Telephone main lines numbered 491,300 in 2000 (3·6 per 1,000 inhabitants). International communications are by the Indian Ocean Intelsat IV satellite. There were 200,000 PCs in use in 2000 (1·5 for every 1,000 persons), 75,000 mobile phone subscribers in 1998 and 4,000 fax machines in 1995. Bangladesh had 30,000 Internet users in Dec. 1999.

Postal Services. There were 8,312 post offices in 1994.

SOCIAL INSTITUTIONS

Justice. The Supreme Court comprises an Appellate and a High Court Division, the latter having control over all subordinate courts. Judges are appointed by the President and retire at 65. There are benches at Comilla, Rangpur, Jessore, Barisal, Chittagong and Sylhet, and courts at District level.

The population in penal institutions in 1995 was 44,111 (35 per 100,000 of national population).

Religion. Islam is the state religion. In 1997 the population was 88% Muslim and 11% Hindu.

Education. In 1993–94 there were 95,886 primary schools, with 16·7m. pupils and 312,186 teachers. In 1992–93 there were 11,382 secondary schools, with 4·7m. pupils and 129,655 teachers; 1,031 colleges of further education (797 private), with 912,895 students and 26,263 teachers. In 1993–94 there were 80 professional colleges with 43,503 students and 2,752 teachers.

In 1995–96 there were five universities, an Islamic university, an open university and universities of agriculture, engineering and technology, and science and technology; there were 5 teacher training colleges, 5 medical, 3 law and 2 fine arts colleges, an institute of ophthalmology and a rehabilitation institute. In 1994–95 there were 92,654 university students and 2,217 academic staff. Adult literacy was 40·8% in 1999 (51·7% among males and 29·3% among females).

Health. In 1994 there were 639 state and 280 private hospitals with a total of 35,795 beds, equivalent to just three beds for every 10,000 persons. There were 24,911 doctors, 9,630 nurses, 7,713 midwives and 75,567 other medical personnel.

CULTURE

Broadcasting. The government-controlled Bangladesh Betam and part-commercial Bangladesh Television transmit a home service and an external service radio programmes, and a TV programme (colour by PAL). In 1997 there were 6·15m. radio and 770,000 TV receivers.

Cinema. In 1994 there were 946 cinemas with 420,000 seats. 130 full-length films were made.

Press. In 1996 there were 37 daily newspapers with a combined circulation of 1·1m., at a rate of 9·3 per 1,000 inhabitants. In 1994, 1,258 book titles were published (122 in English).

Tourism. In 1999 there were 173,000 foreign tourists. Receipts totalled US$50m.

Libraries. Dhaka is home to The United States Information Centre, The British Council, and The Central Public Library (which also has branches outside the capital).

Theatre and Opera. The principal theatres are the Dhaka Theatre and the Nagorik Theatre.

Museums and Galleries. The main museums are: The National Museum; Muktijuddha Judughar (War of Liberation Museum); and The Bangabandhu Memorial Museum.

DIPLOMATIC REPRESENTATIVES
Of Bangladesh in the United Kingdom (28 Queen's Gate, London, SW7 5JA)
High Commissioner: Sheikh Razzak Ali.
(There are also Assistant High Commissioners in Birmingham and Manchester)

Of the United Kingdom in Bangladesh (United Nations Rd, Baridhara, Dhaka 12)
High Commissioner: Dr David Carter, CVO.

Of Bangladesh in the USA (3510 International Drive, NW, Washington, D.C., 20008)
Ambassador: Syed Hasan Ahmed.

Of the USA in Bangladesh (Madani Ave., Baridhara, Dhaka 1212)
Ambassador: Mary Ann Peters.

Of Bangladesh to the United Nations
Ambassador: Iftekhar Ahmed Chowdhury.

Of Bangladesh to the European Union
Ambassador: Muhammed Zamir.

FURTHER READING
Bangladesh Bureau of Statistics. *Statistical Yearbook of Bangladesh.—Statistical Pocket Book of Bangladesh.*

BANGLADESH

Ahmed, A. F. S., *Bangladesh: Tradition and Transformation.* Dhaka, 1987
Hajnoczy, R., *Fire of Bengal.* Bangladesh Univ. Press, 1993
Muhith, A. M. A., *Issues of Governance in Bangladesh.* Mowla Brothers, Dhaka, 2000
Rashid, H. U., *Foreign Relations of Bangladesh.* Rishi Publications, Varanasi, 2001
Tajuddin, M., *Foreign Policy of Bangladesh: Liberation War to Sheikh Hasina.* National Book Organisation, New Delhi, 2001
Ziring, L., *Bangladesh from Mujib to Ershad: an Interpretive Study.* OUP, 1993

National statistical office: Bangladesh Bureau of Statistics, Ministry of Planning, Dhaka
Website: http://www.bbsgov.org/

BARBADOS

Capital: Bridgetown
Population estimate, 2000: 269,000
GDP per capita, 2000: (PPP$) 15,494
HDI/world rank: 0·871/31

KEY HISTORICAL EVENTS
Barbados was settled by the British during the 1620s and developed as a sugar plantation economy, initially on the basis of slavery until its abolition in the 1840s. In 1951 universal suffrage was introduced, followed in 1954 by cabinet government. Full internal self-government was attained in Oct. 1961. On 30 Nov. 1966 Barbados became an independent sovereign state within the Commonwealth.

TERRITORY AND POPULATION
Barbados lies to the east of the Windward Islands. Area 166 sq. miles (430 sq. km). In 2000 the census population was 268,792, giving a density of 625·1 per sq. km.

The UN gives a projected population for 2010 of 277,000.

In 1999, 50·5% of the population were rural. Bridgetown is the principal city: population (including suburbs), 133,000 in 1999.

The official language is English.

SOCIAL STATISTICS
In 2001: births, 4,051; deaths, 2,047; birth rate, 15·0 per 1,000 population; death rate, 8·9; infant mortality, 16·3 per 1,000 live births. Expectation of life, 1999, males 73·9 years and females 78·9. Annual population growth rate, 1990–2000, 0·2%; fertility rate, 1999, 2·3 children per woman.

CLIMATE
An equable climate in winter, but the wet season, from June to Nov., is more humid. Rainfall varies from 50" (1,250 mm) on the coast to 75" (1,875 mm) in the higher interior. Bridgetown, Jan. 76°F (24·4°C), July 80°F (26·7°C). Annual rainfall 51" (1,275 mm).

CONSTITUTION AND GOVERNMENT
The head of state is the British sovereign, represented by an appointed Governor-General. Parliament consists of a Senate and a House of Assembly. The *Senate* comprises 21 members appointed by the Governor-General, 12 being appointed on the advice of the Prime Minister, two on the advice of the Leader of the Opposition and seven at the Governor-General's discretion. The *House of Assembly* comprises 30 members elected every five years. In 1963 the voting age was reduced to 18.

The *Privy Council* is appointed by the Governor-General after consultation with the Prime Minister. It consists of 12 members and the Governor-General as chairman. It advises the Governor-General in the exercise of the royal prerogative of mercy and in the exercise of his disciplinary powers over members of the public and police services.

Following the victory of the Barbados Labour Party in the Jan. 1999 elections, the severing of links with Britain is expected to proceed, with amendments to the constitution allowing for the replacement of the Queen as head of state by a Barbadian president.

National Anthem. 'In plenty and in time of need'; words by Irvine Burgie, tune by V. R. Edwards.

RECENT ELECTIONS
In the general election of 21 May 2003 the Barbados Labour Party (BLP) gained 23 seats (55·8% of the total vote) and the Democratic Labour Party (DLP) seven seats (44·1%).

CURRENT ADMINISTRATION

Governor-General: Sir Clifford Husbands, GCMG, KA; b. 1926.
In May 2003 the government comprised:
Prime Minister, Minister of Finance, Culture, Information, Defence and Security: Owen S. Arthur; b. 1950 (BLP; appointed 7 Sept. 1994).
Deputy Prime Minister, Attorney-General, Minister of Home Affairs: Mia Amor Mottley. *Minister of Foreign Affairs and Foreign Trade:* Billie A. Miller. *Physical Development and Environment:* Elizabeth Thompson. *Education, Youth Affairs and Sports:* Rudolph N. Greenidge. *Health:* Dr Jerome Walcott. *Labour and Social Security:* Rawle C. Eastmond. *Tourism and International Transport:* Noel Anderson Lynch. *Commerce, Consumer Affairs and Business Development:* Ronald Toppin. *Economic Development, Industry and International Business:* Reginald R. Farley. *Transport and Public Works:* Rommel Marshall. *Housing and Lands:* Gline Arley Clarke. *Social Transformation:* Hamilton Lashley. *Agriculture and Rural Development:* Anthony Wood. *Minister of State:* Glyne Murray.

Government of Barbados Information Network: http://www.barbados.gov.bb/

DEFENCE

The Barbados Defence Force has a strength of about 600. In 2000 defence expenditure totalled US$13m. (US$48 per capita), representing 0·5% of GDP.

Army. Army strength was 500 with reserves numbering 430.

Navy. A small maritime unit numbering 110 (1999) operates five patrol vessels. The unit is based at St Ann's Fort Garrison, Bridgetown.

INTERNATIONAL RELATIONS

Barbados is a member of the UN, WTO, OAS, Inter-American Development Bank, ACS, CARICOM, the Commonwealth and is an ACP member state of the ACP-EU relationship.

ECONOMY

In 2001 agriculture accounted for 4·7% of GDP, industry 16·0% and services 79·3%.

Currency. The unit of currency is the *Barbados dollar* (BDS$) of 100 *cents*, which is pegged to the US dollar at BDS$2=US$1. Inflation was 2·2% in 2001. Total money in circulation was BDS$1,309m. in April 2002. Foreign exchange reserves were US$734m. in May 2002.

Budget. The financial year runs from April. Capital expenditure (provisional) for 2001–02 was BDS$305·8m.; current expenditure for the same period (provisional) was BDS$1,705·4m. The budget for 2002–03 put total revenue at an estimated BDS$1,795·4m. and recurrent expenditure at BDS$1,928·4m.
VAT at 15% was introduced in Jan. 1997.

Performance. Total GDP in 2000 was US$2·6bn. Real GDP growth 3·1% in 2000, but in 2001 the economy contracted by 2·1%.

Banking and Finance. The central bank and bank of issue is the Central Bank of Barbados (*Governor,* Dr Marion Williams), which had total assets of BDS$1,291·1m. in Dec. 2001. The provisional figures for the total assets of commercial banks in Dec. 2001 were BDS$5,417·3m. and savings banks' deposits BDS$4,397·7m. Barbados is of growing importance as an offshore banking centre. In 2001 there were 4,065 international business companies, 2,975 foreign sales corporations, 383 exempt insurance companies and 58 offshore banks.
There is a stock exchange which participates in the regional Caribbean exchange.

Weights and Measures. Both Imperial and metric systems are in use.

ENERGY AND NATURAL RESOURCES

Environment. According to the *World Bank Atlas* carbon dioxide emissions in Barbados in 1998 were the equivalent of 5·9 tonnes per capita.

Electricity. Production in 2001, 828·2m. kWh. Capacity in 1995 was 153,000 kW. Consumption per capita was an estimated 2,726 kWh in 2001.

Oil and Gas. Crude oil production in 2001 was 463,669 bbls. and reserves in 1998 were 2·3m. bbls. (3·2m. bbls. in 1994). Output of gas (2001) 32·2m. cu. metres, and reserves (1997) 200m. cu. metres. Production of Liquid Petroleum Gas (LPG) was 17,587 bbls. in 2001.

Water. In 2001 water consumption was 32·5m. cu. metres (metered), 21·9m. cu. metres (non-metered). The number of metered consumers was 84,459; non-metered, 8,244.

Agriculture. The agricultural sector accounted for 4·7% of GDP in 2001 (24% in 1967). Of the total labour force in 2001, 5·4% were employed in agriculture. Of the total area of Barbados (42,995 ha), about 16,000 ha are arable land, which is intensively cultivated. In 2001, 8,500 ha were under sugarcane cultivation. Cotton was successfully replanted in 1983. Production, 2001 (in tonnes): sugarcane, 49,800; sweet potatoes, 2,898; yams, 1,818; carrots, 1,346; cucumbers, 679; cabbages, 664; tomatoes, 663; okra, 420; sweet peppers, 180; onions, 54.

Meat and dairy products, 2001 (in tonnes): poultry, 11,360; cow milk, 8,140; eggs, 1,465; pork, 632; beef, 148.

Livestock (2000): cattle, 23,000; sheep, 41,000; pigs, 33,000; chickens, 4m.

Forestry. Timber production in 1999 was 5,000 cu. metres.

Fisheries. In 2001 there were 954 fishing vessels employed during the flying-fish season. Large numbers of these boats are laid up from July to Oct. The catch in 2001 was 2,708 tonnes, exclusively from sea fishing.

INDUSTRY
Industrial establishments in 1994 numbered 442 and ranged from the manufacture of processed food to small specialized products such as garment manufacturing, furniture and household appliances, electrical components, plastic products and electronic parts. In 1998, 48,000 tonnes of raw sugar were produced.

Labour. In 2001 the workforce was 144,900, of whom 124,100 were employed. Unemployment stood at 9·8%, down from 24% in 1993.

Trade Unions. About one-third of employees are unionized. The Barbados Workers' Union was founded in 1938 and has the majority of members. There are also a National Union of Public Workers and two teachers' unions.

INTERNATIONAL TRADE
External debt was BDS$1,588m. in 2001.

Imports and Exports. In 2002 (provisional figures, excluding petroleum products) exports were valued at BDS$430m. (BDS$518m. in 2001), and imports at BDS$1,994m. (BDS$2,137m. in 2001). The main import suppliers in 2002 were the USA (44·5%), Trinidad and Tobago (16·2%), UK (7·9%), Jamaica (7·0%) and Canada (3·7%). Principal export markets in 2001 were USA (15·4%), Trinidad and Tobago (14·4%), UK (13·4%) and Jamaica (7·6%).

The main exports are electrical components, sugar, chemicals and petroleum products. Main imports are foodstuffs, cars, chemicals, mineral fuels, and machinery and equipment.

COMMUNICATIONS
Roads. There were 1,600 km of roads in 1998. In 2001 there were 55,479 cars; 10,017 lorries, vans and pickups; 5,134 buses, coaches and taxis; 1,128 other commercial vehicles. There were 31 deaths as a result of road accidents in 1997.

Civil Aviation. The Grantley Adams International Airport is 16 km from Bridgetown. In 2000 it handled 1,772,200 passengers (all on international flights) and 11,391 tonnes of freight.

Shipping. There is a deep-water harbour at Bridgetown. 665,595 tonnes of cargo were handled in 1994. Shipping registered in 1998 totalled 688,000 GRT, including oil tankers 350,000 GRT. The number of merchant vessels entering in 2000 was 2,279 of 15·9m. net tonnes.

Telecommunications. In Dec. 2001 there were 127,632 telephone main lines (474·8 per 1,000 inhabitants), 39,789 of which were business lines. In 2000 there were 15,900 mobile phone subscribers, 22,000 PCs in use (82·2 per 1,000 inhabitants) and 12,000 Internet users. In 1995 there were 1,800 fax machines.

Postal Services. There is a general post office in Bridgetown and 16 branches on the island.

SOCIAL INSTITUTIONS

Justice. Justice is administered by the Supreme Court and Justices' Appeal Court, and by magistrates' courts. All have both civil and criminal jurisdiction. There is a Chief Justice, three judges of appeal, five puisne judges of the Supreme Court and nine magistrates. The death penalty is authorized. Final appeal lies to the Privy Council in London. Barbados was one of ten countries to sign an agreement in Feb. 2001 establishing a Caribbean Court of Justice to replace the British Privy Council as the highest civil and criminal court. The Court of Justice is expected to sit for the first time in the second half of 2003.

In 1996 the police force numbered 1,221 and the population in penal institutions in Jan. 1998 was 772 (295 per 100,000 of national population).

Religion. In 1997, 65% of the population were Protestants, 4% Roman Catholics and the remainder other religions.

Education. The adult literacy rate was 97·0% in 1998. In 2000–01 there were 26,066 primary and 21,181 secondary school pupils in government schools and 3,733 primary and 1,293 secondary pupils in private schools. There were 22 secondary schools altogether in 1994–95. Education is free in all government-owned and government-maintained institutions from primary to university level.

In 2000–01 the University of the West Indies in Barbados (founded 1963) had 3,938 students, the Community College had 3,844, the Samuel Jackman Prescod Polytechnic had 2,821 and Erdiston Teachers' College had 108 students.

Health. In 1999 there was one general hospital, one psychiatric hospital, five district hospitals, eight health centres and two private hospitals with 35 beds. There were 1,916 hospital beds and 306 doctors in the same year.

Welfare. The National Insurance and Social Security Scheme provides contributory sickness, age, maternity, disability and survivors benefits. Sugar workers have their own scheme.

CULTURE

Broadcasting. The Caribbean Broadcasting Corporation is a government-owned commercial TV and radio service. There are two other commercial services. In 1997 there were 237,000 radios and 76,000 television sets (colour by NTSC).

Cinema. In 2001 there were two cinemas and one drive-in cinema for 600 cars.

Press. In 2003 there were two daily newspapers, the *Barbados Advocate* (est. 1895) and the *Daily Nation* (est. 1973), and a weekly business publication, the *Broad Street Journal*. The *Daily Nation* has an average daily circulation of 25,000; the *Barbados Advocate*, 15,000.

Tourism. There were 507,078 foreign tourists in 2001, plus 527,594 cruise ship arrivals, bringing revenue of BDS$1,373·5m. and contributing 11·2% of the country's GDP.

DIPLOMATIC REPRESENTATIVES

Of Barbados in the United Kingdom (1 Great Russell St., London, WC1B 3JY)
High Commissioner: Peter Patrick Simmons.

Of the United Kingdom in Barbados (Lower Collymore Rock, Bridgetown)
High Commissioner: John White.

Of Barbados in the USA (2144 Wyoming Ave., NW, Washington, D.C. 20008)
Ambassador: Michael I. King.

Of the USA in Barbados (PO Box 302, Bridgetown)
Ambassador: Earl Norfleet Phillips, Jr.

Of Barbados to the United Nations
Ambassador: June Yvonne Clarke.

Of Barbados to the European Union
Ambassador: Errol Humphrey.

FURTHER READING

Beckles, H., *A History of Barbados: from Amerindian Settlement to Nation-State.* Cambridge Univ. Press, 1990

Hoyos, F. A., *Tom Adams: a Biography.* London, 1988.—*Barbados: A History from the Amerindians to Independence.* 2nd ed. London, 1992

National statistical office: Barbados Statistical Service, Fairchild Street, Bridgetown.

BELARUS

Respublika Belarus

Capital: Minsk
Population estimate, 2000: 10·00m.
GDP per capita, 2000: (PPP$) 7,544
HDI/world rank: 0·788/56

KEY HISTORICAL EVENTS
Belarus was fully integrated with Russia until the Gorbachev reforms of the mid-1980s encouraged demands for greater freedom. On 25 Aug. 1991 Belarus declared its independence and in Dec. it became a founder member of the CIS. The Communists retained power in Belarus despite formidable opposition and it was not until a new constitution was adopted in March 1994 that the economic reformers began to influence events. Alexander Lukashenka was elected president in July 1994. By 1996, only 11% of state enterprises had been privatized and the government remains pro-Russian, striving for eventual unification with Russia within the Russia–Belarus Union. A referendum held over 9–24 Nov. 1996 extended the President's term of office from three to five years and increased his powers to rule by decree. The last parliamentary elections were criticized by the OSCE for a lack of transparency.

TERRITORY AND POPULATION
Belarus is situated along the western Dvina and Dnieper. It is bounded in the west by Poland, north by Latvia and Lithuania, east by Russia and south by Ukraine. The area is 207,600 sq. km (80,134 sq. miles). The capital is Minsk. Other important towns are Homel, Vitebsk, Mahilyou, Bobruisk, Hrodno and Brest. On 2 Nov. 1939 western Belorussia was incorporated with an area of over 108,000 sq. km and a population of 4·8m. Census population, 1999, 10,045,237; density, 48·4 per sq. km.

The UN gives a projected population for 2010 of 9·82m.

In 1999, 70·7% of the population lived in urban areas. Major ethnic groups: 78% Belorussians, 13% Russians, 4% Poles, 3% Ukrainians, 1% Jews, 1% others.

Belarus comprises 6 provinces. Areas and estimated populations:

Province	Area sq. km	Population 1995	Capital	Population 1999
Brest	32,300	1,508,000	Brest	300,400
Homel	40,400	1,594,000	Homel	503,700
Hrodno	25,000	1,209,000	Hrodno	308,900
Mahilyou	29,000	1,259,000	Mahilyou	371,300
Minsk	40,800	3,288,000	Minsk	1,729,000
Vitebsk	40,100	1,439,000	Vitebsk	358,800

Belorussian is the national language. Russian is also spoken.

SOCIAL STATISTICS
1999 births, 93,102 (rate of 9·2 per 1,000 population); deaths, 141,805 (rate of 14·0 per 1,000 population). In 1999 abortions totalled 1,451 per 1,000 live births—one of the highest rates in the world. In 1996 there were 68 divorces per 100 marriages, also one of the highest rates in the world. Annual population growth rate, 1990–99, 0·0%. Life expectancy at birth, 1999, was 62·8 years for men and 74·4 years for women. Infant mortality, 1999, 11·4 per 1,000 live births; fertility rate, 1999, 1·4 children per woman.

CLIMATE
Moderately continental and humid with temperatures averaging 20°F (–6°C) in Jan. and 64°F (18°C) in July. Annual precipitation is 22–28" (550–700 mm).

CONSTITUTION AND GOVERNMENT
A new Constitution was adopted on 15 March 1994. It provides for a *President* who must be a citizen of at least 35 years of age, have resided for 10 years in Belarus and whose candidacy must be supported by the signatures of 70 deputies or 100,000 electors.

There is an 11-member *Constitutional Court*. The chief justice and five other judges are appointed by the President.

Four referendums held on 14 May 1995 gave the President powers to dissolve parliament; work for closer economic integration with Russia; establish Russian as an official language of equal status with Belorussian; and introduce a new flag.

At the referendum of 9–24 Nov. 1996 turn-out was 84·05%. 79% of votes cast were in favour of the creation of an upper house of parliament nominated by provincial governors and 70% in favour of extending the presidential term of office by two years to five years. The Supreme Soviet was dissolved and a 110-member lower *House of Representatives* established.

National Anthem. 'Magutny Bozha' ('Mighty God'); words by Natalla Arsiennieva, tune by Mikola Revienski.

RECENT ELECTIONS

Parliamentary elections were held on 15 and 29 Oct. 2000. Non-partisans (pro-government) won 81 of the 110 seats, the Communist Party of Belarus 6, the Agrarian Party of Belarus 5, the Republican Party of Labour and Justice 2, and the Liberal Democratic Party, the Social Democratic Party of People's Accord and the Social and Sporting Party 1 each. 13 seats remained vacant. Observers claimed the elections failed to meet international standards for a democratic poll; many opposition candidates boycotted the second round. A partial re-run of the elections was held on 18 March 2001.

Presidential elections were held on 9 Sept. 2001. Alyaksandr Lukashenka was re-elected with 75·6% of votes cast against 15·4% for Uladzimir Hancharyk and 2·5% for Syarhey Haydukevich. The election took place amid accusations of vote rigging. No independent observers were allowed to watch the count. However, experts estimated that the opposition actually gained between 30% and 40% of the votes. Turn-out was 83·9%.

CURRENT ADMINISTRATION

President: Alyaksandr Lukashenka; b. 1955 (sworn in 20 July 1994 and re-elected in 2001).

In March 2003 the government comprised:

Prime Minister: Gennady Novitsky; b. 1949 (appointed 1 Oct. 2001).

First Deputy Prime Minister: Sergei Sidorsky. *Deputy Prime Ministers:* Andrei Kobyakov (*also Minister of Economy*); Vladimir Drahzin; Alexander Popkov; Anatoly Tyuyunov.

Minister for Architecture and Construction: Gennady Kurochkin. *Internal Affairs:* Vladimir Naumov. *Housing and Communal Services:* Aleksandr Milkota. *Health:* Ludmila Postoyalko. *Foreign Affairs:* Sergei Martynov. *Information:* Mikhail Podgainy. *Culture:* Leonid Gulyako. *Defence:* Leonid Maltsev. *Education:* Pyotr Brigadin. *Revenues:* Konstantin Sumar. *Emergencies:* Valery Astapov. *Natural Resources and Environmental Protection:* Leonty Khoruzhik. *Industry:* Anatoly Kharlap. *Communication:* Vladimir Goncharenko. *Agriculture and Food:* Mikhail Rusy. *Sports and Tourism:* Yevgeny Vorsin. *Statistics and Analysis:* Vladimir Zinovsky. *Trade:* Aleksandr Kulichkov. *Transport and Communications:* Mikhail Borovoy. *Labour and Social Protection:* Antonina Morova. *Finance:* Nikolai Korbut. *Energy:* Vladimir Semashko. *Justice:* Viktor Golovanov.

Government of Belarus: http://www.government.by

DEFENCE

Conscription is for 18 months. A treaty with Russia of April 1993 co-ordinates their military activities. All nuclear weapons had been transferred to Russia by Dec. 1996. Total active armed forces in 1999 numbered 80,900.

Defence expenditure in 2000 totalled US$366m. (US$36 per capita), representing 4·0% of GDP.

Army. In 1999 ground forces numbered 43,350, including 40,000 conscripts and 2,100 women. In addition there were 289,500 reserves.

Air Force. In 1999 the Air Force operated 152 combat aircraft, including MiG-23s, MiG-29s, Su-24s, Su-25s and Su-27s, and 44 attack helicopters. Personnel, 1999, 22,450 including 10,000 in Air Defence.

INTERNATIONAL RELATIONS

A treaty of friendship with Russia was signed on 21 Feb. 1995. A further treaty signed by the respective presidents on 2 April 1997 provided for even closer integration.

Belarus is a member of the UN, CIS, IMF, the World Bank, European Bank, OSCE, CEI and the NATO Partnership for Peace.

ECONOMY

In 1998 industry contributed 46·1% of GDP, services 40·5% and agriculture 13·4%. In 1999 an estimated 20% of economic output was being produced by the private sector.

Currency. The rouble was retained under an agreement of Sept. 1993 and a treaty with Russia on monetary union of April 1994. Foreign currencies ceased to be legal tender in Oct. 1994. In Nov. 2000 President Lukashenka and President Putin of Russia agreed the introduction of a single currency, with the Russian rouble to be introduced in Belarus by 2005 and a single currency in 2008. The draft agreement has to be ratified by the parliaments of the two countries. The inflation rate in 1994 was 2,434%. By 2000 it was down to 169% before falling in 2001 to 61%. Foreign exchange reserves in June 2002 were US$392m. and total money supply was 1,047·53bn. roubles.

Budget. Government revenue and expenditure (in 1bn. roubles):

	1995	1996	1997	1998	1999	2000
Revenue	37·10	58·99	117·83	206·59	876·23	2,646·02
Expenditure	40·33	62·51	121·79	213·23	933·88	2,639·80

In 1995 VAT constituted 28·4% of revenue, profits tax 23·8%, income tax 9·4% and excise tax 8·0%. Main items of expenditure in 1995 were education (17·5%), health (15·2%), subsidies (10·8%) and transfers (9·4%).

Performance. Real GDP growth was 5·8% in 2000 and 3·0% in 2001. Total GDP in 1998 was US$22·6bn. It was predicted in 2000 that GDP would increase by between 24% and 33% by 2005.

Banking and Finance. The central bank is the National Bank (*Chairman*, Petr P. Prokopovich). In 1996 there were 36 commercial banks (three specialized), one development bank and one commercial savings bank.

In early 1998 Belarus experienced a major currency collapse, and within the space of a month the value of the rouble dropped from around 45,000 to the dollar to 67,000 to the dollar.

ENERGY AND NATURAL RESOURCES

Environment. According to the *World Bank Atlas* carbon dioxide emissions in Belarus were the equivalent of 6·0 tonnes per capita in 1998.

Electricity. Installed capacity was 7m. kW in 1997. Production was 21·89bn. kWh in 1998. Consumption per capita in 1998 was 2,762 kWh.

Oil and Gas. In 1996 output of crude petroleum totalled 37m. bbls. Natural gas production in 1996 was nine petajoules.

Minerals. Particular attention has been paid to the development of the peat industry with a view to making Belarus as far as possible self-supporting in fuel. There are over 6,500 peat deposits. There are rich deposits of rock salt and of iron ore.

Agriculture. Belarus is hilly, with a general slope towards the south. It contains large tracts of marshland, particularly to the southwest.

Agriculturally, it may be divided into three main sections—Northern: growing flax, fodder, grasses and breeding cattle for meat and dairy produce; Central: potato growing and pig breeding; Southern: good natural pasture land, hemp cultivation and cattle breeding for meat and dairy produce. In 1997 agriculture employed 19·6% of the workforce.

Output of main agricultural products (in 1m. tonnes) in 2000: potatoes, 8·5; barley, 1·70; rye, 1·45; sugarbeet, 1·50; wheat, 0·95; cabbage, 0·52; oats, 0·52; milk, 4·32; eggs, 0·19. In 2000 there were 4·33m. cattle; 3·57m. pigs; 221,000 horses; and 30m. chickens.

Since 1991 individuals may own land and pass it to their heirs, but not sell it. In 1997 there were 6·18m. ha of arable land and 144,000 ha of permanent crops. There were 2,700 farms in 1993. The private and commercial sectors accounted for 38% of the value of agricultural output in 1993 (particularly potatoes and vegetables). It was predicted in 2000 that agricultural output would increase by between 20% and 30% by 2005.

Forestry. Forests occupied 74,000 sq. km, or 35·5% of the land area, in 1995 (33·9% in 1990). There are valuable reserves of oak, elm, maple and white beech. Timber production in 1999 was 17·75m. cu. metres.

Fisheries. Fish landings in 2000 amounted to 553 tonnes, exclusively from inland waters.

INDUSTRY
There are food-processing, chemical, textile, artificial silk, flax-spinning, motor vehicle, leather, machine-tool and agricultural machinery industries. Output in 1997 (in 1,000 tonnes): fertilizers (1995), 3,350; cement, 1,876; wheat flour (1995), 1,417; crude steel, 1,220; footwear (1995), 13m. pairs; 13,002 lorries; 26,500 tractors (1995); 454,000 TV sets; 795,000 refrigerators; 6,787m. cigarettes; linen fabrics (1995), 41·5m. sq. metres; woven cotton, 48m. sq. metres. Machine-building equipment and chemical products are also important.

Most industry is still state-controlled. It was predicted in 2000 that industrial output would increase by between 24% and 28% by 2005.

Labour. In 1998 the labour force totalled 4,558,000. In 1994, out of 4,696,000 economically active people, 1,245,600 were in manufacturing and 1,099,700 in community, social and personal services. In 1998 there were 108,000 unemployed persons, or 2·4% of the workforce. It was predicted in 2000 that labour productivity and wages would rise by between 20% and 30% by 2005.

Trade Unions. Trade unions are grouped in the Federation of Trade Unions of Belarus.

INTERNATIONAL TRADE
Foreign debt was US$850m. in 2000.

Imports and Exports. In 2000 imports f.o.b. were valued at US$7,824·9m. and exports f.o.b. at US$6,986·8m. The main import suppliers in 1999 were Russia (56%), Germany (10%), Ukraine (6%) and Poland (3%). Principal export markets were Russia (55%), Ukraine (5%), Latvia (4%) and Poland (4%). Main import commodities are petroleum, natural gas, rolled metal and coal. Export commodities include machinery and transport equipment, diesel fuel, synthetic fibres and consumer goods.

COMMUNICATIONS
Roads. In 1998 there were 63,355 km of motor roads (over 95% paved). There were estimated to be 1,279,208 passenger cars in use in 1998 (126 per 1,000 inhabitants). In 1993, 1,702m. passengers and 209m. tonnes of freight were carried. There were 1,843 fatalities as a result of road accidents in 1998.

Rail. In 1995 there were 5,523 km of 1,520 mm gauge railways (889 km electrified). Passenger-km travelled in 1998 came to 13·3bn. and freight tonne-km to 30·4bn.

Civil Aviation. The main airport is Minsk International 2, which handled 400,000 passengers (all international) and 2,600 tonnes of freight in 2000. The national carriers are Belavia and Minskavia. In 1998 Belavia flew on domestic routes and operated international services to Adler/Sochi, Beijing, Berlin, Chelyabinsk, Chişinau, Ekaterinburg, Frankfurt, Istanbul, Krasnodar, Kyiv, Larnaca, London, Moscow, Nizhnevartovsk, Prague, Rome, Samara, Shannon, Stockholm, Tashkent, Tbilisi, Tel Aviv, Vienna, Warsaw and Yerevan. Minskavia flew to Chişinau, Kyiv,

Moscow and Stockholm. In 1999 scheduled airline traffic of Belarus-based carriers flew 8·0m. km, carrying 212,000 passengers (all on international flights).

Shipping. In 1993, 0·3m. passengers and 8·9m. tonnes of freight were carried on inland waterways.

Telecommunications. In 2000 there were 2,751,900 telephone main lines (268·8 per 1,000 inhabitants). There are plans to privatize Beltelecom, the state monopoly, in 2007. There were 23,500 mobile phone subscribers in 1999 and 15,200 fax machines in 1997. Belarus had 180,000 Internet users in Dec. 2000.

Postal Services. In 1994 there were 3,894 post offices.

SOCIAL INSTITUTIONS

Justice. The death penalty is retained following the constitutional referendum of Nov. 1996 and was used in 2000.

120,254 crimes were reported in 1994. In 1996 there were 52,200 prisoners, giving Belarus one of the highest rates of imprisonment in the world, with 505 prisoners per 100,000 population.

Religion. The Orthodox is the largest church. There is a Roman Catholic archdiocese of Minsk and Mahilyou, and five dioceses embracing 455 parishes. In 1997, 31% of the population were Belorussian Orthodox and 18% Roman Catholics.

Education. Adult literacy rate in 1999 was 99·5% (male, 99·7%; female, 99·4%). There were 335,400 children and 54,100 teachers at 4,494 pre-school institutions in 1996–97, 625,000 pupils at primary schools, 1,064,700 pupils in secondary schools, and 328,746 students and 40,300 teachers at institutions of higher education.

In 1999 there were 57 state higher educational establishments including: four universities; specialized universities of agriculture, culture, economics, information technology and radio-electronics, linguistics, teacher training and transport; academies of agriculture, arts, music, physical culture and sport, and a polytechnical academy; 4 medical, 3 polytechnical and 3 teacher training institutes, and institutes of agriculture, co-operation, light industry technology, machine-building and veterinary science. In 1999–2000 there were 262,100 people enrolled at state higher education establishments.

In 1996 total expenditure on education came to 5·9% of GNP and represented 17·8% of total government expenditure.

Health. In 1999 there were 45,900 doctors (45·8 per 10,000 population). In 1995 there were 117,000 nurses and midwives, and 880 hospitals. In 1995 there were 122 beds per 10,000 population.

Welfare. In Jan. 1994 there were 1,987,000 age, and 0·6m. other, pensioners.

CULTURE

Broadcasting. The government-controlled Belarus Radio broadcasts two national programmes and various regional programmes, a foreign service (Belorussian, German) and a shared relay with Radio Moscow. Belarus Television broadcasts on one channel (colour by SECAM H). In 1997 there were 2·5m. TV receivers and 3·02m. radio receivers.

Cinema. In 1995 there were 3,780 cinemas with an annual attendance of 12·5m.; gross box office receipts came to 19,290m. roubles. Two full-length films were made in 1995.

Press. There were 10 dailies in 1995, with a combined circulation of 1,800,000, a ratio of 174 per 1,000 inhabitants. In 1996 a total of 3,809 book titles were published in 59·07m. copies.

Tourism. In 1997 there were 250,000 foreign tourists. Receipts totalled US$49m.

DIPLOMATIC REPRESENTATIVES
Of Belarus in the United Kingdom (6 Kensington Court, London, W8 5DL)
Ambassador: Dr Alyaksei Mazhukhou.

Of the United Kingdom in Belarus (37 Karl Marx St., Minsk 220030)
Ambassador: Iain Kelly.

Of Belarus in the USA (1619 New Hampshire Avenue, NW, Washington, D.C., 20009)
Ambassador: Vacant.
Chargé d'Affaires a.i.: Valentin Rybakov.

Of the USA in Belarus (46 Starovilenskaya, Minsk 220002)
Ambassador: Michael G. Kozak.

Of Belarus to the United Nations
Ambassador: Sergei Ling.

Of Belarus to the European Union
Ambassador: Sergei N. Martynov.

FURTHER READING

Marples, D. R., *Belarus: from Soviet Rule to Nuclear Catastrophe.* London, 1996
Zaprudnik, J., *Belarus at the Crossroads in History.* Boulder (CO), 1993

National Statistical Office: Ministry of Statistics and Analysis of the Republic of Belarus, Minsk.
Website: http://www.president.gov.by/Minstat/en/main.html

BELGIUM

Royaume de Belgique
Koninkrijk België
(Kingdom of Belgium)

Capital: Brussels
Population estimate, 2000: 10·25m.
GDP per capita, 2000: (PPP$) 27,178
HDI/world rank: 0·939/4

KEY HISTORICAL EVENTS

The War of the Spanish Succession (1701–14) ended with the cession of Belgium to the Austrian Hapsburgs. Briefly annexed to France during the Napoleonic war, Belgium and Holland were reunited by the Treaty of Paris (1815) to form one state. The Belgians rose in revolt and the kingdom of Belgium was formed as an independent state in 1830. By the Treaty of London, 15 Nov. 1831, the neutrality of Belgium was guaranteed by Austria, Russia, Great Britain and Prussia. In 1914 Belgian neutrality was violated and, as a consequence, Britain declared war on Germany. In the Second World War Belgium was again invaded by Germany. In the post-war years, linguistic rivalry between the Flemish (Dutch)-speaking north of the country and the French-speaking Walloons of the south led to bitter political divisions. Belgium's sole colony, the Belgian Congo, gained independence in 1960. Following constitutional reforms voted by Parliament in May 1993, Belgium became a federal state.

TERRITORY AND POPULATION

Belgium is bounded in the north by the Netherlands, northwest by the North Sea, west and south by France, and east by Germany and Luxembourg. Its area is 30,528 sq. km. The Belgian exclave of Baarle-Hertog in the Netherlands has an area of 7 sq. km and a population (1996) of 2,702. Population (1991 census), 9,978,681. Population (2001 estimate) 10,263,414, (5,245,395 females); density, 336·2 per sq. km. There were 845,700 resident foreign nationals as at 1 Jan. 2002. In 1999, 97·3% of the population lived in urban areas.

The UN gives a projected population for 2010 of 10·30m.

Dutch (Flemish) is spoken by the Flemish section of the population in the north, French by the Walloon south. The linguistic frontier passes south of the capital, Brussels, which is bilingual. Some German is spoken in the east. Each language has official status in its own community. (Bracketed names below signify French or Dutch alternatives.)

Area, population and chief towns of the ten provinces on 1 Jan. 2001:

Province	Area (sq. km)	Population	Chief Town
Flemish Region			
Antwerp	2,867	1,645,652	Antwerp (Anvers)
Flemish Brabant	2,106	1,018,403	Leuven (Louvain)
East Flanders	2,982	1,363,672	Ghent (Gand)
West Flanders	3,144	1,130,040	Bruges (Brugge)
Limbourg	2,422	794,785	Hasselt
Walloon Region			
Walloon Brabant	1,091	352,018	Wavre
Hainaut (Henegouwen)	3,786	1,279,823	Mons (Bergen)
Liège (Luik)	3,862	1,020,042	Liège (Luik)
Luxembourg	4,440	248,750	Arlon (Aarlen)
Namur (Namen)	3,666	445,824	Namur (Namen)

Population of the regions on 1 Jan. 2001: Brussels Capital Region, 964,405; Flemish Region, 5,952,552; Walloon Region, 3,346,457 (including the German-speaking Region, 71,036).

The most populous towns, with population on 1 Jan. 2001:

Brussels (19 communes)	964,405	Charleroi	200,233
Antwerp (Anvers)	445,570	Liège (Luik)	184,550
Ghent (Gand)	224,685	Bruges (Brugge)	116,559

Namur (Namen)	105,248	St Niklaas (St Nicolas)	68,364
Mons (Bergen)	91,123	Tournai (Doornik)	67,227
Leuven (Louvain)	88,581	Ostend	67,279
La Louvière	76,497	Genk	62,860
Aalst (Alost)	76,470	Seraing	60,271
Mechelen (Malines)	75,560	Roeselare (Roulers)	54,376
Kortrijk (Courtrai)	74,543	Verviers	52,760
Hasselt	68,373	Mouscron (Moeskroen)	52,475

Brussels: Formerly capital of the Netherlands and under control, at varying times, of the French, Spanish, Austrians and the Germans, Brussels is now one of the administrative focal points for Europe. It houses the headquarters of both the EU and NATO. Capital of Belgium since its creation as a kingdom in 1831, it is a notable manufacturer of chemicals and machinery. Constitutional changes since 1970 have consolidated its status as the seat of Belgium's federal government.

SOCIAL STATISTICS
Statistics for calendar years:

	Births	Deaths	Marriages	Divorces	Immigration[1]	Emigration[1]
1996	115,214	104,140	50,552	28,402	511,095	486,247
1997	115,864	103,802	47,759	26,748	511,934	492,405
1998	114,276	104,583	44,393	26,503	513,025	491,995
1999	114,164	104,929	44,171	26,423	521,684	509,432
2000	114,883	104,903	45,123	27,002	511,180	486,051

[1]Including internal.

In 2000 Belgium received 42,690 asylum applications, equivalent to 4·20 per 1,000 inhabitants. Annual population growth rate, 1990–99, 0·2%. Life expectancy at birth, 2000, was 75·1 years for men and 81·4 years for women. 1999 birth rate (per 1,000 population): 11·2; death rate: 10·3. Infant mortality, 1999, 6 per 1,000 live births; fertility rate, 1999, 1·6 children per woman.

A UNICEF report published in 2000 showed that 4·4% of children in Belgium live in poverty (in households with income below 50% of the national median).

CLIMATE
Cool temperate climate influenced by the sea, giving mild winters and cool summers. Brussels, Jan. 36°F (2·2°C), July 64°F (17·8°C). Annual rainfall 33" (825 mm). Ostend, Jan. 38°F (3·3°C), July 62°F (16·7°C). Annual rainfall 31" (775 mm).

CONSTITUTION AND GOVERNMENT
According to the constitution of 1831, Belgium is a constitutional, representative and hereditary monarchy. The legislative power is vested in the King, the federal parliament and the community and regional councils. The King convokes parliament after an election or the resignation of a government, and has the power to dissolve it in accordance with Article 46 of the Constitution.

The reigning King is **Albert II,** born 6 June 1934, who succeeded his brother, Baudouin, on 9 Aug. 1993. Married on 2 July 1959 to Paola Ruffo di Calabria, daughter of Don Fuleo and Donna Luisa Gazelli de Rossena. *Offspring:* Prince Philippe, Duke of Brabant, b. 15 April 1960; Princess Astrid, b. 5 June 1962; Prince Laurent, b. 19 Oct. 1963. Prince Philippe married Mathilde d'Udekem d'Acoz, 4 Dec. 1999. *Offspring:* Princess Elizabeth, b. 25 Oct. 2001. Princess Astrid married Archduke Lorenz of Austria, 22 Sept. 1984. *Offspring:* Prince Amedeo, b. 21 Feb. 1986; Princess Maria Laura, b. 26 Aug. 1988; Prince Joachim, b. 9 Dec. 1991; Princess Luisa Maria, b. 11 Oct. 1995. Prince Laurent married Claire Coombs, 12 April 2003.

The Dowager Queen. Queen Fabiola de Mora y Aragón, daughter of the Conde de Mora y Aragón and Marqués de Casa Riera; married to King Baudouin on 15 Dec. 1960. *Sister of the King.* Josephine Charlotte, Princess of Belgium, b. 11 Oct. 1927; married to Prince Jean of Luxembourg, 9 April 1953. *Half-brother and half-sisters of the King.* Prince Alexandre, b. 18 July 1942; Princess Marie Christine, b. 6 Feb. 1951; Princess Maria-Esmeralda, b. 30 Sept. 1956.

A constitutional amendment of June 1991 permits women to accede to the throne.

The King receives a basic annual tax-free sum from the civil list of €6,048,000 for the duration of his reign; Queen Fabiola receives €1,115,000; Prince Philippe,

€768,400; Princess Astrid and Prince Laurent, €272,000 each. These figures are adapted annually in accordance with the general price index.

Constitutional reforms begun in Dec. 1970 culminated in May 1993 in the transformation of Belgium from a unitary into a 'federal state, composed of communities and regions'. The communities are three in number and based on language: Flemish, French and German. The regions also number three, and are based territorially: Flemish, Walloon and the Capital Brussels.

Since 1995 the federal parliament has consisted of a 150-member *Chamber of Representatives*, directly elected by obligatory universal suffrage from 20 constituencies on a proportional representation system for four-year terms; and a *Senate* of 71 members (excluding senators by right, i.e. certain members of the Royal Family). 25 senators are elected by a Flemish, and 15 by a French, electoral college; 21 are designated by community councils (10 Flemish, 10 French and 1 German). These senators co-opt a further 10 senators (6 Flemish and 4 French).

The federal parliament's powers relate to constitutional reform, federal finance, foreign affairs, defence, justice, internal security, social security and some areas of public health. The Senate is essentially a revising chamber, though it may initiate certain legislation, and is equally competent with the Chamber of Representatives in matters concerning constitutional reform and the assent to international treaties.

The number of ministers in the federal government is limited to 15. The Council of Ministers, apart from the Prime Minister, must comprise an equal number of Dutch- and French-speakers. Members of parliament, if appointed ministers, are replaced in parliament by the runner-up on the electoral list for the minister's period of office. Community and regional councillors may not be members of the Chamber of Representatives or Senate.

National Anthem. 'La Brabançonne'; words by C. Rogier, tune by F. van Campenhout. The Flemish version is 'O Vaderland, o edel land der Belgen' ('Oh Fatherland, noble land of the Belgians').

RECENT ELECTIONS

Elections to the 150-member Chamber of Representatives were held on 18 May 2003. The Flemish Liberal and Democratic Party (VLD) won 25 seats with 15·4% of votes cast; The Socialist Party (PS) won 25 seats (13·0%); the Reformist Movement (MR) won 24 seats (11·4%); SPA (Socialist Party Different)-Spirit coalition won 23 seats (14·9% of the vote); the Christian Democratic and Flemish Party (CD&V) won 21 seats (13·3%); the Vlaams Blok (Flemish Block, VB) won 18 seats (11·6%); the Humanist Democratic Centre (CDH) won 8 seats (5·5%); Ecolo won 4 seats (3·1%); the New Flemish Alliance (N-VA) won 1 seat (3·1%); and the National Front (FN) won 1 seat (2·0%). Agalev (2·5%) and Vivant (1·2%) won no seats. Prime Minister Guy Verhofstadt's VLD won two more seats than in the 1999 elections.

Voting for the 40 electable seats in the Senate took place on the same day. SPA-Spirit and VLD both won 7 seats; CD&V and PS won 6; MR and VB, 5; CDH, 2; and Ecolo and FN 1. There are also 31 indirectly elected senators.

European Parliament. Belgium has 25 representatives. At the June 1999 elections turn-out was 95·0%. The Flemish Liberal and Democratic Party won 3 seats with 13·6% (group in European Parliament: European Liberal, Democrat and Reform Party); the CVP, 3 with 13·5% of votes cast (European People's Party); the PRL, 3 with 10·0% (European Liberal, Democrat and Reform Party; European People's Party); the PS, 3 with 9·6% (Party of European Socialists); Ecolo, 3 with 8·4% (Greens); the Vlaams Blok, 2 with 9·4% (non-affiliated); the SP, 2 with 9·0% (Party of European Socialists); Agalev, 2 with 7·5% (Greens); VU-ID21, 2 with 7·6% (European Radical Alliance); the PSC, 1 with 5·0% (European People's Party); the CSP, 1 with 0·2% (European People's Party).

CURRENT ADMINISTRATION

In March 2003 the coalition government ('rainbow coalition' of liberals, socialists and environmentalists) comprised:

Prime Minister: Guy Verhofstadt; b. 1953 (VLD; in office since 12 July 1999).

Deputy Prime Ministers: Laurette Onkelinx (also *Minister of Employment*); Louis Michel (also *Minister of Foreign Affairs*); Johan Vande Lanotte (also *Minister of*

Budget, Social Integration and Social Economy); Isabelle Durant (also *Minister of Transportation*).
 Minister of Agriculture: Annemie Neyts. *Defence:* André Flahaut. *Health, Environment and Consumer Affairs:* Jef Tavernier. *Social Affairs and Pensions:* Frank Vandenbroucke. *Economics and Research:* Charles Picqué. *Finance:* Didier Reynders. *Interior:* Antoine Duquesne. *Public Administration:* Luc van den Bossche. *Justice:* Marc Verwilghen. *Telecommunications and State-owned Companies:* Rik Daems.

Government Website: http://www.belgium.fgov.be

DEFENCE
Conscription was abolished in 1995 and the Armed Forces were restructured, with the aim of progressively reducing the size and making more use of civilian personnel. The Interforces Territorial Command is responsible for assignments to assure the safety of the National Territory and for logistic support in those fields which are mutual for the different forces.

In 2000 defence expenditure totalled US$3,335m. (US$328 per capita), representing 1·4% of GDP. The budget for 1999 was BEF100·8bn. (US$2,700m.).

Army. The Army consists of three divisions: the Intervention Force, the Combat Support Division and the Logistical Support Division. Total strength (1999) 26,400 including 1,500 women. In addition there is a reserve force of 105,000 personnel.

Navy. The naval forces, based at Ostend and Zeebrugge, include three frigates. Naval personnel (1999) totalled 2,600.

The naval air arm comprises three general utility helicopters.

Air Force. The Belgian Royal Air Force has a strength of (1999) 11,500 personnel and comprises a Tactical Air Force and a Training and Support Command (schools and logistical units). The Tactical Air Force operates 90 combat aircraft including F-16s.

INTERNATIONAL RELATIONS
Belgium is a member of the UN, WTO, NATO, BIS, OECD, EU, Council of Europe, WEU, OSCE, CERN, Inter-American Development Bank, Asian Development Bank, IOM, Antarctic Treaty and the International Organization of the Francophonie. Belgium is a signatory to the Schengen Accord abolishing border controls between Austria, Belgium, Denmark, Finland, France, Germany, Greece, Iceland, Italy, Luxembourg, the Netherlands, Norway, Portugal, Spain and Sweden.

ECONOMY
Services contributed 71·2% of GDP in 1997, with industry accounting for 27·6% and agriculture just 1·1%.

According to the anti-corruption organization *Transparency International*, Belgium ranked equal 20th in the world in a 2002 survey of the countries with the least corruption in business and government. It received 7·1 out of 10 in the annual index.

Currency. On 1 Jan. 1999 the euro (EUR) became the legal currency in Belgium; irrevocable conversion rate BEF40·3399 to EUR1. The euro, which consists of 100 cents, has been in circulation since 1 Jan. 2002. There are seven euro notes in different colours and sizes denominated in 500, 200, 100, 50, 20, 10 and 5 euros, and eight coins denominated in 2 and 1 euros, then 50, 20, 10, 5, 2 and 1 cents. On the introduction of the euro there was a 'dual circulation' period before the Belgian franc ceased to be legal tender on 28 Feb. 2002. Euro banknotes in circulation on 1 Jan. 2002 had a total value of €24·0bn.

In June 2002 gold reserves were 8·29m. troy oz (20·54m. troy oz in 1995) and foreign exchange reserves US$8,517m. Total money supply was €10,626m. in June 2002. Inflation was 2·7% in 2000, falling to 2·4% in 2001.

Budget. Federal government receipts and expenditure in BEF1m.:

	1997	1998	1999	2000
Revenue	2,520,834	2,801,700	2,889,828	2,981,437
Expenditure	2,736,305	2,656,545	2,739,332	2,935,352

VAT is 21% (reduced rate, 6%).

Performance. Real GDP growth was 4·0% in 2000 but only 1·0% in 2001. Total GDP was US$227·6bn. in 2001.

Wage-price performance has remained relatively stable during this upswing. According to the Jan. 1999 *OECD Economic Survey*: 'The end of the 1995–96 real wage freeze was followed by modest acceleration in wage increases and compensation per employee. Contributing factors to this include the introduction of the law on employment and competitiveness, which limits on an *ex ante* basis the maximum increase in compensation per employee in the private sector to the expected weighted average increase in Germany, France and the Netherlands.'

Banking and Finance. The National Bank of Belgium was established in 1850. The *Governor*—in 2003, Guy Quaden—is appointed for a five-year period. Its shares are listed on Euronext (Brussels); half of them are nominative held by the state.

The law of 22 Feb. 1998 has adapted the status of the National Bank of Belgium in view of the realization of the Economic and Monetary Union.

The National Bank of Belgium is within the ESCB-framework in charge of the issue of banknotes, the execution of exchange rate policy and monetary policy. Furthermore, it is the Bank of banks and the cashier of the federal state.

The law of 22 March 1993 defines the legal provisions governing banking activity. It transposes into Belgian legislation the European Directive of 15 Dec. 1989 on the co-ordination of laws, regulations and administrative provisions relating to the taking up and pursuit of the business of credit institutions; and the Directive of 6 April 1992 on the supervision of credit institutions on a consolidated basis.

The term 'credit institutions' covers the Belgian credit institutions and those which come under the law of another country, be it a member of the European Union or not, with a registered office in Belgium. The activity of credit institutions must consist of receiving deposits and other repayable funds from the public, and granting credit on their own account.

The law of 4 Dec. 1990 on financial transactions and financial markets defines the legal framework for collective investment institutions, the sole object of which is the collective investment of capital raised from the public. It transposes into Belgian legislation the European Directive of 20 Dec. 1985 on the co-ordination of laws, regulations and administrative provisions relating to undertakings for collective investment in transferable securities.

The law of 6 April 1995 relating to secondary markets, status and supervision of investment firms, intermediaries and investment consultants, provides the credit institutions with direct access to securities' stock exchanges. Stock exchange legislation was also subject to an important reform. The law fundamentally modifies the competitive environment and strengthens exercise conditions for securities' dealers.

On 31 Dec. 2001, 113 credit institutions with a balance sheet totalling €846bn. were established in Belgium: 67 governed by Belgian law and 46 by foreign law. 431 collective investment institutions (157 Belgian and 274 foreign) were marketed in Belgium and supervised by the Banking and Finance Commission; and 85 investment firms were operating in Belgium with the approval of the Banking and Finance Commission.

There is a stock exchange (a component of Euronext) in Brussels. Euronext was created in Sept. 2000 through the merger of the Amsterdam, Brussels and Paris bourses.

Weights and Measures. The metric system is in force.

ENERGY AND NATURAL RESOURCES

Environment. According to the *World Bank Atlas* Belgium's carbon dioxide emissions were the equivalent of 9·9 tonnes per capita in 1998.

Electricity. The production of electricity amounted to 79,792m. kWh in 1998; consumption per capita was 7,249 kWh. 56% of production in 1998 was nuclear-produced. Belgium had seven nuclear reactors in 2001. Capacity (1997) was 13m. kW.

Oil and Gas. Production of gas in 1998 was 379,373m. cu. metres.

Water. Total capacity for 1998 was 1,038·18m. cu. metres.

Minerals. Output (in tonnes) for four calendar years:

	1995	1996	1997	1998
Coke	3,696,076	3,549,789	3,401,431	3,003,744
Cast iron	9,198,831	8,626,651	8,076,475	8,618,117
Wrought steel	11,539,883	10,751,711	10,717,603	11,103,848
Finished steel	11,035,293	10,962,985	12,044,923	12,194,290

Agriculture. There were, in 2001, 1,390,191 ha under cultivation, of which 845,779 ha were arable land. There were 62,000 farms in 2000. The agricultural sector employs 2·7% of the workforce.

Chief	Area in ha		Produce in tonnes		
crops	2000	2001	1998	1999	2000
Wheat	204,022	173,270	1,733,046	1,490,247	1,633,854
Barley	48,570	51,504	374,500	387,564	333,381
Oats	5,341	—	28,468	42,552	28,887
Rye	1,098	—	7,130	3,971	4,781
Potatoes	65,845	62,157	2,455,777	3,059,162	2,921,871
Beet (sugar)	90,858	95,553	5,364,649	7,112,021	6,151,978
Beet (fodder)	6,713	5,970	676,396	738,315	670,224
Tobacco	388	380	1,308	1,314	1,166

In 2001 there were 29,767 horses, 3,037,757 cattle, 156,132 sheep, 12,631 goats and 6,833,721 pigs.

Forestry. In 1996 forest covered 608,151 ha (19·9% of the total land area).

Fisheries. In 2000 the fishing fleet had a total tonnage of 22,975 GRT. Total catch, 2000, 29,800 tonnes, almost totally from marine waters.

INDUSTRY

The leading companies by market capitalization in Belgium, excluding banking and finance, in Jan. 2002 were: Tractebel SA (€18bn.), a global energy and service business; Interbrew SA (€13bn.); and Electrabel (€13bn.), Belgium's leading energy producer.

Output (1998) of sugar factories and refineries, 995,053 tonnes; 11 distilleries, 320,000 litres of alcohol; breweries, 1,481·6m. litres of beer; mineral water (1997), 822·8m. litres; cigarettes (1997), 18bn. (units); margarine factories, 304,321 tonnes. Output, 1997, in 1,000 tonnes: distillate oil, 12,520; crude steel, 10,780; cement, 8,052; residual fuel oil, 7,444; petrol, 6,103.

Labour. Retirement age is flexible for men and 60–65 years for women. In 2001 (Labour Force Survey), 66,305 persons worked in the primary sector (agriculture, fishing and mining), 1,055,186 in the secondary sector (industry and construction) and 2,934,119 in the tertiary sector (services). The unemployment rate was 7·6% in Dec. 2002. In French-speaking Wallonia the rate is more than double that in Flemish-speaking Flanders. In Oct. 1999 the participation rate of the active population in the labour market was one of the lowest in the EU, at 56·8%.

Trade Unions. The main trade union organizations are the Confederation of Christian Trade Unions (CSC/ACV), the Belgian Socialist Confederation of Labour (FGTB/ABVV) and the Federation of Liberal Trade Unions of Belgium (CGSLB/ACLVB).

INTERNATIONAL TRADE

In 1922 the customs frontier between Belgium and Luxembourg was abolished; their foreign trade figures are amalgamated.

Imports and Exports. Imports and exports for three calendar years (in €1m.):

	Imports	Exports
1999	154,635	168,091
2000	192,195	203,953
2001	197,402	209,933

Leading imports and exports (in €1m.):

	Imports		Exports	
	2000	2001	2000	2001
Machinery and appliances	36,778	35,859	33,850	32,530
Chemicals and pharmaceutical products	25,154	30,336	30,492	33,968

	Imports		Exports	
	2000	2001	2000	2001
Transport equipment	24,072	25,564	27,718	32,070
Mineral products	18,757	18,682	10,892	10,261
Precious stones and				
precious metals	14,657	13,455	15,555	14,419
Base metals	14,216	13,434	17,039	16,255
Plastics and rubber	11,204	11,327	16,647	16,597
Textile and textile articles	9,265	9,385	11,230	11,511
Food industry	6,903	7,510	10,892	10,261
Paper and applications	5,694	5,467	5,705	5,471

Trade by selected countries (in €1m.):

	Imports from		Exports to	
	2000	2001	2000	2001
China	1,340	1,675	4,011	4,307
France	35,846	36,491	24,354	26,424
Germany	34,531	38,157	32,553	31,900
India	3,467	3,009	1,732	1,679
Ireland	1,619	1,679	4,301	6,602
Israel	3,805	3,066	2,373	2,153
Italy	11,285	12,098	7,515	8,289
Japan	2,420	2,196	5,949	5,630
Luxembourg	4,144	4,095	1,080	1,141
Netherlands	25,753	25,444	33,584	33,417
Spain	7,339	8,051	3,488	3,784
Sweden	3,194	2,891	4,395	4,500
Switzerland	3,081	3,025	1,678	1,733
UK	20,230	21,160	16,500	15,196
USA	11,919	11,749	14,392	13,701

In 2000 other EU-member countries accounted for 74·0% of exports and 68·1% of imports.

Trade Fairs. Brussels ranked as the third most popular convention city behind Paris and London in 2001 according to the Union des Associations Internationales (UAI).

COMMUNICATIONS

Roads. Length of roads, 1999: motorways, 1,691 km; other state roads, 12,542 km; provincial roads, 1,349 km; local roads, about 130,900 km. Belgium has one of the densest road networks in the world. The number of motor vehicles registered on 1 Aug. 2001 was 5,542,964, including 4,739,850 passenger cars, 14,676 buses, 526,344 trucks, 46,302 non-agricultural tractors, 293,630 motorcycles and 54,513 special vehicles. Road accidents caused 1,470 fatalities in 2000.

Rail. The main Belgian lines were a State enterprise from their inception in 1834. In 1926 the *Société Nationale des Chemins de Fer Belges (SNCB)* was formed to take over the railways. The State is sole holder of the ordinary shares of SNCB, which carry the majority vote at General Meetings. The length of railway operated in 2000 was 3,471 km (electrified, 2,705 km). Revenue in 1998 was BEF81,715m.; expenditure, BEF75,441m. In 2000, 61·28m. tonnes of freight and 153·3m. passengers were carried.

The regional transport undertakings *Société Régionale Wallonne de Transport* and *Vlaamse Vervoermaatschappij* operate electrified light railways around Charleroi (19 km) and from De Panne to Knokke (68 km). There is also a metro and tramway in Brussels (165 km), and tramways in Antwerp (180 km) and Ghent (29 km).

Civil Aviation. The former national airline SABENA (*Société anonyme belge d'exploitation de la navigation aérienne*) was set up in 1923. In 1997 its fleet comprised 33 aircraft. In 1999 SABENA flew 179·1m. km, carrying 9,965,200 passengers. However, in Nov. 2001 it filed for bankruptcy after failing to secure financial assistance from its part-owner Swissair, which itself was on the verge of collapse. Its successor, Delta Air Transport (DAT), a former SABENA subsidiary, was given a new identity in Feb. 2002 as SN Brussels Airlines. Some 60 other airlines operate services. In 2000 Brussels National Airport handled 21,521,000 passengers (21,515,000 on international flights) and 676,400 tonnes of freight. Antwerp is the second busiest airport in terms of passenger numbers and Charleroi the third busiest.

Shipping. On 1 Jan. 1999 the merchant fleet was composed of 19 vessels of 345,058 tonnes. There were eight shipping companies in 1997. In 1997 vessels totalling 337,862,000 NRT entered ports and vessels totalling 333,694,000 NRT cleared. In 1996, 14,628 vessels entered, and 14,653 cleared, the port of Antwerp.

The length of navigable inland waterways was 1,493·3 km in 1995. 104m. tonnes of freight were carried on inland waterways in 1998.

Telecommunications. In 2000 telephone main lines numbered 5,060,900 (502·4 per 1,000 inhabitants) and there were 3·5m. PCs in use (344·5 for every 1,000 persons). Belgium had 4·0m. mobile phone subscribers in Nov. 2000 and 3·76m. Internet users in Aug. 2002. There were 190,000 fax machines in 1996.

Postal Services. In 1995 there were 1,635 post offices, with a gross revenue totalling BEF50,540m.

SOCIAL INSTITUTIONS

Justice. Judges are appointed for life. There is a court of cassation, five courts of appeal and assize courts for political and criminal cases. There are 27 judicial districts, each with a court of first instance. In each of the 222 cantons is a justice and judge of the peace. There are also various special tribunals. There is trial by jury in assize courts. The death penalty, which had been in abeyance for 45 years, was formally abolished in 1991.

The Gendarmerie ceased to be part of the army in Jan. 1992.

The population in penal institutions in Sept. 1997 was 8,342 (80 per 100,000 of national population).

Religion. There is full religious liberty, and part of the income of the ministers of all denominations is paid by the State. In 1997 there were 8·96m. Roman Catholics. Numbers of clergy, 1996: Roman Catholic, 3,899; Protestant, 84; Anglican, 9; Jews, 26; Greek Orthodox, 39. There are eight Roman Catholic dioceses subdivided into 260 deaneries. The Protestant (Evangelical) Church is under a synod. There is also a Central Jewish Consistory, a Central Committee of the Anglican Church and a Free Protestant Church.

Education. Following the constitutional reform of 1988, education is the responsibility of the Flemish and Walloon communities. There were (1996–97) 4,107 pre-primary schools, with 424,521 pupils; 4,401 primary schools, with 737,823 pupils and 82,168 teachers; and 1,727 secondary schools, with 796,945 pupils and 115,262 teachers. In higher education, there were 229,749 students and 38,014 teachers in 17 university and 134 non-university colleges and institutes. There are five royal academies of fine arts and five royal conservatoires at Brussels, Liège, Ghent, Antwerp and Mons.

Total expenditure on education in 1996 amounted to 3·3% of GNP and represented 7·0% of total government expenditure.

The adult literacy rate in 1998 was at least 99%.

Health. On 1 Jan. 1998 there were 39,240 physicians, 7,360 dentists and 14,597 pharmacists. Hospital beds numbered 75,360 in 1995. Total health spending accounted for 8·7% of GDP in 2000. In Jan. 2000 the Belgian government agreed to decriminalize the use of cannabis. Euthanasia became legal on 24 Sept. 2002. The Belgian Chamber of Representatives had given its approval on 16 May 2002 to a measure adopted by the Senate on 26 Oct. 2001. Belgium was the second country to legalize euthanasia, after the Netherlands.

Welfare. Expenditure in 2000: social security (wage earners) €39,114·47m., (self employed) €3,315·46m.; pensions €5,712·17m.

CULTURE

Broadcasting. Broadcasting is organized according to the language communities. VRT, RTBF and BRF fulfil the public service of broadcasting in Dutch, French and German respectively. TV colour is by PAL.

VRT (*Vlaamse Radio- en Televisieomroep*) is organized by decree as a public-sector public-limited company. It has seven radio and three TV services: Radio 1, Radio 2, Klara, Studio Brussel, Radio Donna, DAB klassiek and RVi; TV1, Canvas and Ketnet. In July 2000 VRT started a new branch, e-VRT, which is responsible for the organization and development of a truly multimedia e-service platform and e-service network in Flanders.

RTBF has five radio and three TV services: La Première, FW, Musique 3, Bruxelles Capitale, Radio 21; RTBF International, La Une, La Deux.

BRF transmits a radio programme from three stations.

There are also four commercial networks: VTM (Dutch, cable only), VT4 (under British licence; Dutch, cable only), RTL-TVI (French, one station), Canal Plus (pay TV; French, three channels; Dutch, two channels).

Number of receivers (1997): radios, 8·07m., including car radios, 2,952,832; TVs, 4·7m.

Cinema. In 1998 there were 463 cinemas, with an annual attendance of 19·2m.; gross box office receipts came to BEF3,526m. Eight full-length films were made in 1995.

Press. In 1996 there were 30 daily newspapers with a combined circulation of 1,625,000, at a rate of 161 per 1,000 inhabitants.

Tourism. *Internal Tourism.* In 2001, 28,693,963 tourist nights were spent in 3,550 establishments in accommodation for 619,413 persons. The number of overnight stays accounted for by leisure, holiday and recreation was 22,033,903, with 2,932,483 for congresses and conferences, and 3,408,532 for other business purposes. Total number of tourists reached 10,641,144 (7,520,461 leisure, 1,465,996 conference, 1,654,687 for other business purposes).

National Tourism. In 1998, 10,972,140 Belgians went on holiday. They spent 6,799,990 nights abroad and 4,172,150 in Belgium. 6,883,752 Belgians went on holiday for four nights or more spending 5,262,232 nights abroad and 1,626,884 in Belgium. Belgian tourists tend to organize holidays themselves. They prefer to travel by car to France for long holidays and stay in hotels. In 1996 they spent on average BEF19,651 per holiday of four nights and more.

Libraries. In 1997 there were 1,490 public libraries, one National library and 117 Higher Education libraries. They held a combined 53,832,000 volumes for 2,464,000 registered users.

DIPLOMATIC REPRESENTATIVES

Of Belgium in the United Kingdom (103 Eaton Sq., London, SW1W 9AB)
Ambassador: Baron Thierry de Gruben.

Of the United Kingdom in Belgium (Rue d'Arlon 85, 1040 Brussels)
Ambassador: Gavin Hewitt, CMG.

Of Belgium in the USA (3330 Garfield St., NW, Washington, D.C., 20008)
Ambassador: Franciskus Van Daele.

Of the USA in Belgium (Blvd. du Régent 27, 1000 Brussels)
Ambassador: Stephen F. Brauer.

Of Belgium to the United Nations
Ambassador: Jean de Ruyt.

FURTHER READING

The Institut National de Statistique. *Statistiques du commerce extérieur* (monthly). *Bulletin de Statistique.* Bi-monthly. *Annuaire Statistique de la Belgique* (from 1870).—*Annuaire statistique de poche* (from 1965).
Service Fédéral d'Information. *Guide de l'Administration Fédérale.* Occasional

Deprez, K., and Vos, L., *Nationalism in Belgium—Shifting Identities, 1780–1995*, London 1998
Fitzmaurice, J., *The Politics of Belgium: a Unique Federalism.* Farnborough, 1996
Hermans, T. J., *et al.*, (eds.) *The Flemish Movement: a Documentary History.* London, 1992

National statistical office: Institut National de Statistique, Rue de Louvain 44, 1000 Brussels.
Service Fédérale d'Information: POB 3000, 1040 Brussels 4.
Website: http://statbel.fgov.be

BELIZE

Capital: Belmopan
Population estimate, 2000: 240,000
GDP per capita, 2000: (PPP$) 5,606
HDI/world rank: 0·784/58

KEY HISTORICAL EVENTS
From the 17th century, British settlers, later joined by British soldiers and sailors disbanded after the capture of Jamaica from Spain in 1655, governed themselves under a form of democracy by public meeting. A constitution was granted in 1765 and, with some modification, continued until 1840 when an executive council was created. In 1862 what was then known as British Honduras was declared a British colony with a legislative assembly and a Lieut.-Governor under the Governor of Jamaica. The administrative connection with Jamaica was severed in 1884. Universal suffrage was introduced in 1964 and thereafter the majority of the legislature were elected rather than appointed. In June 1974 British Honduras became Belize. Independence was achieved on 21 Sept. 1981 and a new constitution introduced.

TERRITORY AND POPULATION
Belize is bounded in the north by Mexico, west and south by Guatemala and east by the Caribbean. Fringing the coast there are three atolls and some 400 islets (cays) in the world's second longest barrier reef (140 miles), which was declared a world heritage site in 1997. Area, 22,965 sq. km.

There are six districts as follows, with area, population estimates and chief city:

District	Area (in sq. km)	Population 2000	Chief City	Population 2000
Belize	4,307	68,197	Belize City	49,050
Cayo	5,196	52,564	San Ignacio	13,260
Corozal	1,860	32,708	Corozal	7,888
Orange Walk	4,636	38,890	Orange Walk	13,483
Stann Creek	2,554	24,548	Dangriga	8,814
Toledo	4,413	23,297	Punta Gorda	4,329

Population (2000 census), 240,204 (121,278 males); density, 10·5 per sq. km.
The UN gives a projected population for 2010 of 268,000.

In 1999 an estimated 53·6% of the population were urban. The proportion of the population considered as rural had been 52·5% in 1990. No other country saw such a considerable percentage swing away from urbanization over the same period. In 1995 some 45,000 Belizeans were working abroad.

The capital is Belmopan (1996 population, 6,490).

English is the official language. Spanish is widely spoken. In 1996 the main ethnic groups were Mestizo (Spanish-Maya), 44%; Creole (African descent), 30%; Mayans, 11%; and Garifuna (Caribs), 7%.

SOCIAL STATISTICS
1996 births, 7,200; deaths, 1,250. In 1996 (est.) the birth rate per 1,000 was 32·8 and the death rate 5·7; infant mortality in 1999 was 35 per 1,000 births and there were 1,138 marriages. Life expectancy in 1999 was 72·6 years for males and 75·3 for females. Annual population growth rate, 1990–99, 2·6%; fertility rate, 1999, 3·5 children per woman.

CLIMATE
A tropical climate with high rainfall and small annual range of temperature. The driest months are Feb. and March. Belize City, Jan. 74°F (23·3°C), July 81°F (27·2°C). Annual rainfall 76" (1,890 mm).

CONSTITUTION AND GOVERNMENT
The head of state is the British sovereign, represented by an appointed Governor-General. The Constitution, which came into force on 21 Sept. 1981, provided for a

National Assembly, with a five-year term, comprising a 29-member *House of Representatives* elected by universal suffrage, and a *Senate* consisting of eight members, five appointed by the Governor-General on the advice of the Prime Minister, two on the advice of the Leader of the Opposition and one on the advice of the Belize Advisory Council.

National Anthem. 'O, Land of the Free'; words by S. A. Haynes, tune by S. W. Young.

RECENT ELECTIONS
In parliamentary elections held on 5 March 2003 the People's United Party (PUP) of Prime Minister Said Musa won 22 of the 29 seats in the National Assembly with 53·2% of votes cast against 7 and 45·6% for the United Democratic Party. Turn-out was 78·9%.

CURRENT ADMINISTRATION
Governor-General: Sir Colville Young, GCMG; b. 1932 (sworn in 17 Nov. 1993).
   In March 2003 the cabinet comprised as follows:
   Prime Minister and Minister for Education: Said Musa; b. 1944 (PUP; sworn in 28 Aug. 1998).
   Minister of Finance and Home Affairs: Ralph Fonseca. *Housing:* Cordel Hyde. *Foreign Affairs and Attorney General:* Godfrey Smith. *Economic Development, Tourism and Culture:* Mark Espat. *Natural Resources, Commerce, Industry and Environment:* John Briceño. *Works, Transport and Communications:* Vildo Marin. *Health:* José Coye. *Human Development, Local Government and Labour:* Marcial Mes. *Agriculture and Fisheries:* Servulo Baeza. *Defence and National Emergency Management:* Sylvia Flores. *Investment and Foreign Trade:* Eamon Courtenay. *Office of the Prime Minister:* Francis Fonseca.

Government Website: http://www.belize.gov.bz/

DEFENCE
The Belize Defence Force numbers 1,050 (1999) with a reserve militia of 700. There is an Air Wing and a Maritime Wing.
   In 2000 defence expenditure totalled US$17m. (US$69 per capita), representing 2·4% of GDP.

INTERNATIONAL RELATIONS
While asserting a longstanding territorial claim on Belize, Guatemala recognized Belize's independence in Sept. 1991. In return Belize reduced its maritime zones to 3 miles in the south, subject to final agreement on a maritime boundary.
   Belize is a member of the UN, WTO, the Commonwealth, OAS, Inter-American Development Bank, ACS, CARICOM, IOM and is an ACP member state of the ACP-EU relationship.

ECONOMY
In 1998 agriculture accounted for 18·7% of GDP, industry 25·5% and services 55·8%.

Overview. The National Social and Economic Council was set up in 1993 to provide a forum for discussion between the public and private sectors. There are national economic plans.

Currency. The unit of currency is the *Belize dollar* (BZD) of 100 *cents*. Since 1976 $B2 has been fixed at US$1. Total money supply was $B352m. in June 2002 and foreign exchange reserves were US$91m. There was inflation of 1·2% in 2001.

Budget. Government revenue and expenditure ($B1,000):

	1993–94	1994–95	1995–96[1]	1996–97[1]
Revenue	258,978	261,658	288,256	283,357
Expenditure	348,953	306,090	317,781	362,261

[1]Estimate.

Performance. Real GDP growth was 9·7% in 2000 and 2·5% in 2001. Total GDP in 2001 was US$0·8bn.

Banking and Finance. A Central Bank was established in 1981 (*Governor*, Jorge Meliton Auil). There were (1993) four commercial banks of which two were locally owned, and a Government Savings Bank.

ENERGY AND NATURAL RESOURCES

Environment. According to the *World Bank Atlas* carbon dioxide emissions in Belize were the equivalent of 1·8 tonnes per capita in 1998.

Electricity. Installed capacity in 1995 was 34,000 kW. Production was 175m. kWh in 1998 and consumption per capita in 1997 was 857 kWh. Supply, 110 and 220 volts; 60 Hz. A rural electrification unit was set up in 1991.

Agriculture. In 1998 there were 64,000 ha of arable land and 25,000 ha of permanent crops. Agriculture accounted for 23% of GDP in 1997. Production, 2000 (in 1,000 tonnes): sugarcane, 1,181; oranges, 190; bananas, 75; grapefruit, 42. Livestock (1996): cattle, 59,000; pigs, 24,000; horses, 5,000; mules, 4,000; chickens, 1m.

Forestry. In 1995, 1,962,000 ha (86·1% of the total land area) were under forests, which include mahogany, cedar, Santa Maria, pine and rosewood and many secondary hardwoods, as well as woods suitable for pulp. Timber production in 1999 was 188,000 cu. metres.

Fisheries. There were (1995) 13 registered fishing co-operatives. The total catch in 2000 amounted to 61,059 tonnes, exclusively from sea fishing.

INDUSTRY

Manufacturing is mainly confined to processing agricultural products and timber. There is also a clothing industry. Sugar production was 123,100 tonnes in 1998; molasses, 46,500 (1995).

Labour. The labour market alternates between full employment, often accompanied by local shortages in the citrus and sugarcane harvesting (Jan.–July), and under-employment during the wet season (Aug.–Dec.), aggravated by the seasonal nature of the major industries. In 1996 the labour force totalled 73,000 (78% males), of whom 13% were unemployed.

Trade Unions. There were 14 accredited unions in 1997.

INTERNATIONAL TRADE

External debt was US$499m. in 2000.

Imports and Exports. Imports and exports for calendar years in US$1m.:

	1996	1997	1998	1999	2000
Imports f.o.b.	229·5	282·9	290·9	337·5	403·7
Exports f.o.b.	171·3	193·4	186·2	213·2	212·3

Main exports in 1999 were: sugar (23%), shellfish (18%), orange juice (18%), clothes (11%) and bananas (9%); main imports were machinery and transport equipment (27%), manufactured goods (16%), food and live animals (15%) and petroleum and related products (14%).

Main export markets in 1999: USA (48%), UK (25%), Denmark (7%) and Mexico (4%). Main import suppliers were USA (52%), Mexico (12%), Cuba (10%) and UK (4%).

COMMUNICATIONS

Roads. In 1998 there were 543 km of main roads and 2,329 km of other roads. In 1998 there were 9,930 passenger cars in use and 11,440 trucks and vans. There were 49 deaths as a result of road accidents in 1998.

Civil Aviation. There is an international airport (Philip S. W. Goldson) in Belize City. The national carrier is Maya Airways, which in 1998 operated domestic services and international flights to Flores (Guatemala). In 2000 Philip S. W. Goldson International handled 492,385 passengers (363,811 on international flights).

Shipping. The main port is Belize City, with a modern deep-water port able to handle containerized shipping. There are also ports at Commerce Bight and Big

Creek. In 1998 the merchant marine totalled 2,382,000 GRT, including oil tankers 360,000 GRT. Nine cargo shipping lines serve Belize, and there are coastal passenger services to the offshore islands and Guatemala.

Telecommunications. In 2000 telephone main lines numbered 35,800 (about half in Belize City) or 148·8 per 1,000 inhabitants. Belize Telecommunications Ltd has instituted a countrywide fully automatic telephone dialling facility. There were 6,200 mobile telephone subscribers and, in 2000, 30,000 PCs in use (124·9 per 1,000 inhabitants). In 1995 there were 1,000 paging users, 300 voice mail users and 500 fax machines. In Dec. 1999 there were 15,000 Internet users.

Postal Services. In 1995 there were 113 post offices.

SOCIAL INSTITUTIONS

Justice. Each of the six judicial districts has summary jurisdiction courts (criminal) and district courts (civil), both of which are presided over by magistrates. There is a Supreme Court, a Court of Appeal and a Family Court. There is a Director of Public Prosecutions, a Chief Justice and two Puisne Judges. Belize was one of ten countries to sign an agreement in Feb. 2001 establishing a Caribbean Court of Justice to replace the British Privy Council as the highest civil and criminal court. The Court of Justice is expected to sit for the first time in the second half of 2003.

In 1995 the police force was 450 strong. The population in penal institutions in Jan. 1998 was 1,118 (490 per 100,000 of national population).

Religion. In 1997, 59% of the population was Roman Catholic and 37% Protestant.

Education. The adult literacy rate rose from 70·3% in 1991 to 93·1% in 1999 (93·2% among males and 92·9% among females). Education is in English. State education is managed jointly by the government and the Roman Catholic and Anglican Churches. It is compulsory for children between six and 14 years and primary education is free. In 1996–97, 245 primary schools had 52,994 pupils; and there were 10,648 pupils at 30 secondary schools. There are two government-maintained special schools for disabled children. There is a teachers' training college. The University College of Belize opened in 1986. The University of the West Indies maintains an extramural department in Belize City.

Health. In 1995 there were seven government hospitals (1 in Belmopan, 1 in Belize City and 1 in each of the other five districts) and an infirmary for geriatric and chronically ill patients, with 139 doctors and (1993) 300 nurses and 233 midwives. Medical services in rural areas are provided by health care centres and mobile clinics.

CULTURE

Broadcasting. The Broadcasting Corporation of Belize operates a national broadcasting service. Proportion of programmes, 60% in English, the remainder in Spanish and the Amerindian languages. There is also a commercial radio station. There are two commercial TV channels (colour by NTSC). There are satellite links with Bermuda, the USA and the UK, and radio links with Central America. In 1997 there were some 133,000 radio and 41,000 TV sets in use.

Press. There were four weekly newspapers and several monthly magazines in 1995.

Tourism. In 1998 there were 157,000 foreign tourists. Receipts totalled US$99m.

DIPLOMATIC REPRESENTATIVES
Of Belize in the United Kingdom (22 Harcourt House, 19 Cavendish Sq., London, W1M 9AD)
High Commissioner: Alexis Rosado.

Of the United Kingdom in Belize (P.O. Box 91, Belmopan, Belize)
High Commissioner: Philip J. Priestly, CBE.

Of Belize in the USA (2535 Massachusetts Av., NW, Washington, D.C., 20008)
Ambassador: Lisa M. Shoman.

Of the USA in Belize (Gabourel Lane, Belize City)
Ambassador: Russell F. Freeman.

Of Belize to the United Nations
Ambassador: Stuart M. Leslie.

Of Belize to the European Union
Ambassador: Yvonne Hyde.

FURTHER READING

Leslie, R., *A History of Belize: Nation in the Making.* 2nd ed. Cubola Productions, Benque Viejo, 1995
Wright, P. and Coutts, B. E., *Belize.* [Bibliography] 2nd ed. ABC-Clio, Oxford and Santa Barbara (CA), 1993

National statistical office: Central Statistical Office, Belmopan.
Website: http://www.cso.gov.bz/

BENIN

République du Bénin

Capital: Porto-Novo
Population estimate, 2000: 6·17m.
GDP per capita, 2000: (PPP$) 990
HDI/world rank: 0·420/158

KEY HISTORICAL EVENTS
The People's Republic of Benin is the former Republic of Dahomey. Dahomey was a powerful, well-organized state from the 17th century, trading extensively in slaves through the port of Whydah with the Portuguese, British and French. On the coast an educated African elite grew up in the 19th century.

After the defeat of Dahomey, whose monarchy was abolished, the French occupied territory inland up to the River Niger and created the colony of Dahomey as part of French West Africa. The African elite protested frequently at French rule and, as African nationalism blossomed after the Second World War, Dahomey saw lively political activity.

After Dahomey became independent on 1 Aug. 1960 civilian government was interrupted by long periods of military rule. In Oct. 1972 Gen. Mathieu Kérékou seized power and installed a new left-wing regime committed to socialist policies. A constitution was adopted in 1977, based on a single Marxist-Leninist party, the *Parti de la Révolution Populaire du Bénin* (PRPB). Benin is beset with economic problems, factional fighting and frequent plots to overthrow the regime.

TERRITORY AND POPULATION
Benin is bounded in the east by Nigeria, north by Niger and Burkina Faso, west by Togo and south by the Gulf of Guinea. The area is 112,622 sq. km, and the population, census 1992, 4,855,349. Estimate (1996) 5·71m.; density, 50·7 per sq. km.

The UN gives a projected population for 2010 of 8·28m.

In 1999, 58·5% of the population were rural.

The areas, populations and capitals of the six provinces are as follows:

Province	Sq. km	Census 1992	Capital	Census 1992
Atakora	31,200	648,330	Natitingou	57,535
Atlantique	3,200	1,060,310	Cotonou	533,212[1]
Borgou	51,000	816,278	Parakou	106,708
Mono	3,800	646,954	Lokossa	52,909
Ouéme	4,700	869,492	Porto-Novo	177,660
Zou	18,700	813,985	Abomey	65,725

[1]1999 population, 716,000.

Other large towns (with 1992 census population): Djougou (132,192), Bohicon (81,121), Kandi (74,169), Ouidah (64,068).

In 1992 the main ethnic groups numbered (in 1,000): Fon, 1,930; Yoruba, 590; Adja, 540; Aizo, 420; Bariba, 420; Somba, 320; Fulani, 270. The official language is French. Over half the people speak Fon.

SOCIAL STATISTICS
1997 (estimates) births, 267,000; deaths, 76,000. Rates, 1997 (per 1,000 population): births, 46·0; deaths, 13·0. Infant mortality, 1999 (per 1,000 live births), 99. Expectation of life in 1999 was 52·0 years for males and 55·4 for females. Annual population growth rate, 1990–99, 3·3%. Fertility rate, 1999, 5·7 children per woman.

CLIMATE
In coastal parts there is an equatorial climate, with a long rainy season from March to July and a short rainy season in Oct. and Nov. The dry season increases in length from the coast, with inland areas having rain only between May and Sept. Porto-Novo, Jan. 82°F (27·8°C), July 78°F (25·6°C). Annual rainfall 52" (1,300 mm). Cotonou, Jan. 81°F (27·2°C), July 77°F (25°C). Annual rainfall 53" (1,325 mm).

CONSTITUTION AND GOVERNMENT

The Benin Party of Popular Revolution (PRPB) held a monopoly of power from 1977 to 1989.

In Feb. 1990 a 'National Conference of the Active Forces of the Nation' proclaimed its sovereignty and appointed Nicéphore Soglo Prime Minister of a provisional government. At a referendum in Dec. 1990, 93·2% of votes cast were in favour of the new constitution, which has introduced a presidential regime. The *President* is directly elected for renewable five-year terms. Parliament is the 83-member *National Assembly*, elected by proportional representation for four-year terms.

A 30-member advisory *Social and Economic Council* was set up in 1994. There is a *Constitutional Court.*

National Anthem. 'L'Aube Nouvelle' ('New Dawn'); words and tune by Gilbert Dagnon.

RECENT ELECTIONS

Presidential elections were held in two rounds on 4 and 22 March 2001. There were four candidates for the first round, won by President Mathieu Kérékou with 45·4% of votes cast, ahead of former president Nicéphore Soglo with 27·1%. Following the withdrawal of both Nicéphore Soglo and the third-placed candidate, both of whom claimed that the election had been flawed, President Kérékou was re-elected with 84·06% of votes cast in the run-off against the fourth-placed candidate, Bruno Amoussou. Turn-out in the first round was 87·7% and in the second round 53·4%.

Parliamentary elections were held on 30 March 2003. The Presidential Movement won 52 of 83 seats (of which the Union for the Benin of the Future 31, the African Movement for Development and Progress 9, the Key Force 5 and smaller parties 7), the Rebirth of Benin 15, the Party of Democratic Renewal 11 and the Star Alliance 2, with 2 results unavailable.

CURRENT ADMINISTRATION

President: Mathieu Kérékou; b. 1933 (Action Front for Renewal and Development; sworn in 4 April 1996 and re-elected 22 March 2001, having previously been president from 26 Oct. 1972 to 4 April 1991).

In March 2003 the government comprised:

Minister of Foreign Affairs and African Integration: Antoine Kolawolé Idji. *Justice, Legislation and Human Rights:* Joseph Gnonlonfoun. *Communications, Promotion of New Technologies and Information:* Gaston Zossou. *Technical and Vocational Education:* Dominique Codjo Sohounloué. *Higher Education and Scientific Research:* Dorothée Sossa. *Primary and Secondary Education:* Jean Chabi Orou. *Mines, Energy, Mines and Water Resources:* Kamarou Fassassi. *Environment, Housing and Urban Affairs*: Luc Gnacadja. *Finance and Economy:* Abdoulaye Bio Tchané. *Public Health:* Yvette-Celine Seignon Kandissounon. *Family Affairs, Social Welfare and Solidarity:* Claire H. Ayémona. *Interior, Security and Territorial Administration:* Daniel Tawéma. *Commerce, Industry, Community Development and Promotion of Employment:* Lazarre Sèhouéto. *Public Works and Transport:* Joseph Sourou Attin. *Agriculture, Husbandry and Fisheries:* Théophile Nata. *Youth, Sports and Leisure:* Valentin Aditi Houdé. *Civil Service and Administrative Reform:* Ousmane Batoko. *Culture, Artisanry and Tourism:* Amos Elègbè. *Relations with Institutions, Civil Society and Beninese Abroad:* Sylvain Akindès Adékpédjou. *Minister of State for National Defence:* Pierre Osho. *Minister of State for Co-ordination of Government Actions, Economic Development and Planning:* Bruno Amoussou.

Government Website (French only): http://www.gouv.bj/

DEFENCE

There is selective conscription for 18 months. Defence expenditure totalled US$36m. in 2000 (US$6 per capita), representing 1·4% of GDP.

Army. The Army Strength (1999) was 4,500, with an additional 2,500-strong paramilitary gendarmerie.

Navy. Personnel in 1999 numbered 150; the force is based at Cotonou.

Air Force. The Air Force has suffered a shortage of funds and operates no combat aircraft. Personnel, 1999, 150.

INTERNATIONAL RELATIONS

Benin is a member of the UN, WTO, the African Union African Development Bank, ECOWAS, IOM, OIC, International Organization of the Francophonie and is an ACP member state of the ACP-EU relationship.

ECONOMY

Agriculture accounted for 38·6% of GDP in 1998, industry 13·5% and services 47·9%.

Overview. The Second Structural Adjustment Programme began in 1991; it seeks to provide resources for priority social and economic goals by economies, reforms and rationalization. An action plan envisages some privatization. Price controls were imposed in 1994.

Currency. The unit of currency is the *franc CFA* (XOF) with a parity of 655·957 francs CFA to one euro. Total money supply was 351,786m. francs CFA in May 2002 and foreign exchange reserves were US$563m. Gold reserves in June 2000 were 11,000 troy oz. Inflation was 4·0% in 2001.

Budget. The fiscal year is the calendar year. In 1997 revenue was 183,984m. francs CFA and expenditure 295,547m. francs CFA.

Performance. Real GDP growth was 5·8% in 2000 and 5·0% in 2001. Total GDP was US$2·3bn. in 2001.

Banking and Finance. The bank of issue and the central bank is the regional Central Bank of West African States (BCEAO). The *Governor* is Charles Konan Banny. There are five private commercial banks. Total deposits were 182,000m. francs CFA in May 1995.

ENERGY AND NATURAL RESOURCES

Environment. According to the *World Bank Atlas* Benin's carbon dioxide emissions in 1998 were the equivalent of 0·1 tonnes per capita.

Electricity. Installed capacity in 1995 was 15,000 kW. In 1998 production was 6m. kWh; in 1996 Benin imported 245m. kWh. A solar energy programme was initiated in 1993. Consumption per capita in 1998 was 46 kWh.

Oil and Gas. The Semé oilfield, located 10 miles offshore, was discovered in 1968. Production commenced in 1982 and was 70,000 bbls. in 1996. Crude petroleum reserves in 1997 were 29m. bbls.

Agriculture. Benin's economy is underdeveloped, and is dependent on subsistence agriculture. In 1998, 3·23m. persons depended on agriculture, of whom 1·47m. were economically active. Small independent farms produce about 90% of output. In 1998, 1·69m. ha were arable and 0·15m. ha permanent crops. There were 182 tractors in 1998. The chief agricultural products, 2000 (in 1,000 tonnes) were: cassava, 2,026; yams, 1,773; maize, 663; seed cotton, 435; cottonseed, 240; sorghum, 136; groundnuts, 81.

Livestock, 2000: cattle, 1,438,000; sheep, 645,000; goats, 1,183,000; pigs, 470,000; poultry, 23m.

Forestry. In 1995 there were 4·62m. ha of forest (41·8% of the total land area), mainly in the north. In 1990 the area under forests had been 4·92m. ha. Timber production in 1999 was 6·14m. cu. metres.

Fisheries. In 1991 there were eight fishing boats totalling 1,078 GRT. Total catch, 2000, 32,324 tonnes, of which fresh fish approximately 82% and marine fish 18%.

INDUSTRY

Only about 2% of the workforce is employed in industry. The main activities include palm-oil processing, brewing and the manufacture of cement, sugar and textiles. Also important are cigarettes, food, construction materials and petroleum. Firms by product in 1994: printing, paper, publishing, 33; chemicals, 22; wood, 16; foodstuffs, 11.

Labour. The labour force numbered 2,490,000 in 1996 (52% males). Approximately half of the economically active population is engaged in agriculture, fishing and forestry.

Trade Unions. In 1973 all trade unions were amalgamated to form a single body, the *Union Nationale des Syndicats des Travailleurs du Bénin*. In 1990 some unions declared their independence from this Union, which itself broke its links with the PRPB. In 1992 there were three trade union federations.

INTERNATIONAL TRADE
Commercial and transport activities, which make up 36% of GDP, are extremely vulnerable to developments in neighbouring Nigeria, with which there is a significant amount of illegal trade. Foreign debt was US$1,599m. in 2000.

Imports and Exports. Imports f.o.b. in 1999, US$635·2m.; exports f.o.b., US$421·5m.

Principal export markets, 1998: France, 20%; Brazil, 16%; Niger, 9%; Thailand, 5%. Principal import suppliers: France, 21%; Côte d'Ivoire, 11%; UK, 7%; USA, 6%.

Main imports in 1998 were: manufactured goods (19%), including textiles (9%); refined oil (19%); food and live animals (18%); machinery and transport equipment (17%). The main exports were: cotton (47%); uranium ores (30%); cigarettes (6%).

COMMUNICATIONS
Roads. There were 6,787 km of roads in 1996, of which 20% were surfaced. Passenger cars in use in 1996 totalled 37,772, and there were also 7,554 buses and coaches plus approximately 250,000 motorcycles and mopeds. In 1996, 412 people died in road accidents.

Rail. There are 578 km of metre-gauge railway. In 1994, 0·6m. passengers were carried and, in 1995, 388·4m. tonne-km of freight.

Civil Aviation. The international airport is at Cotonou (Cadjehoun), which in 2000 handled 250,000 passengers (all on international flights) and 4,100 tonnes of freight. Benin is a member of Air Afrique. In 1999 scheduled airline traffic of Benin-based carriers flew 3·0m. km, carrying 84,000 passengers (all on international flights).

Shipping. There is a port at Cotonou. In 1998 the merchant fleet totalled 1,000 GRT. In 1994 vessels entering totalled 1,163,000 NRT.

Telecommunications. In 2000 there were 51,600 main telephone lines (8·5 per 1,000 persons) and 10,000 PCs in use. There were 6,300 mobile phone subscribers in 1998 and 1,000 fax machines in 1996. Benin had approximately 10,000 Internet users in July 2000.

Postal Services. In 1995 there were 159 post offices.

SOCIAL INSTITUTIONS
Justice. The Supreme Court is at Cotonou. There are Magistrates Courts and a *tribunal de conciliation* in each district. The legal system is based on French civil law and customary law.

Religion. Some 62% of the population follow traditional animist beliefs. In 1997 there were 1·24m. Roman Catholics and 710,000 Muslims.

Education. Adult literacy rate was 39% in 1999 (55·4% among males and 23·6% among females). There were, in 1996–97, 779,329 pupils in 3,072 primary schools with 13,957 teachers and 146,135 pupils in secondary schools with 5,352 teachers. The University of Benin (Cotonou) had 9,000 students and 240 academic staff in 1994–95.

Health. In 1993 there were 363 doctors and 1,236 nurses. Hospital bed provision was just 2 for every 10,000 persons in 1993.

CULTURE

Broadcasting. The media are overseen by the nine-member Haute Autorité de l'Audiovisuel et de la Communication. The government-controlled Office de Radiodiffusion et Télévision du Bénin broadcasts a radio programme from Cotonou and a regional programme from Parakou, and a TV service (colour by SECAM V) from Cotonou. In 1997 there were 620,000 radio and some 60,000 TV receivers.

Press. In 1996 there was one daily newspaper with a circulation of 12,000, at a rate of 2·2 per 1,000 inhabitants.

Tourism. In 1998 there were 152,000 foreign tourists. Receipts totalled US$33m.

DIPLOMATIC REPRESENTATIVES

Of Benin in the United Kingdom
Ambassador: André-Guy Ologoudou (resides at Paris).
Honorary Consul: Lawrence Landau (Dolphin House, 16 The Broadway, Stanmore, Middlesex HA7 4DW)

Of the United Kingdom in Benin
Ambassador: Philip Thomas, CMG (resides at Abuja, Nigeria).

Of Benin in the USA (2124 Kalorama Road., NW, Washington, D.C., 20008)
Ambassador: Segbe Cyrille Oguin.

Of the USA in Benin (Rue Caporal Bernard Anani, Cotonou)
Ambassador: Pamela Bridgewater.

Of Benin to the United Nations
Ambassador: Joël Wassi Adechi.

Of Benin to the European Union
Ambassador: Euloge Hinvi.

FURTHER READING

Bay, E., *Wives of the Leopard: Gender, Politics, and Culture in the Kingdom of Dahomey.* University Press of Virginia, 1998
Eades, Jerry S. and Allen, Christopher, *Benin.* [Bibliography] ABC-Clio, Oxford and Santa Barbara (CA), 1996

BHUTAN

Druk-yul

(Kingdom of Bhutan)

Capital: Thimphu
Population estimate, 2000: 2·09m
GDP per capita, 2000: (PPP$) 1,412
HDI/world rank: 0·494/140

KEY HISTORICAL EVENTS
A sovereign kingdom in the Himalayas, Bhutan was governed by a spiritual ruler and a temporal ruler—the Dharma and Deb Raja—from the 17th century. The interior was organized into districts controlled by governors and fort commanders. These officials formed the electoral council appointing the Deb Raja. During the 19th century civil wars were fought between district governors for the office of the Deb Raja. The election became a formality and the governors of Tongsa and Paro were the most frequently chosen because they were the strongest. In 1863 a British attempt to bring stability to Bhutan led to war on the frontier with India.

In 1907 the office of Dharma Raja came to an end. The governor of Tongsa, Ugyen Wangchuk, was then chosen Maharajah of Bhutan, the throne becoming hereditary in his family (the title is now King of Bhutan). He concluded a treaty with the British in 1910 allowing internal autonomy but British control of foreign policy. The treaty was renewed with the Government of India in 1949. In the early 1990s, tens of thousands of 'illegal immigrants', mostly Nepali-speaking Hindus, were forcibly expelled. Some ten years on, there are still nearly 90,000 people claiming to be Bhutanese refugees in camps set up by the UNHCR in eastern Nepal.

TERRITORY AND POPULATION
Bhutan is situated in the eastern Himalayas, bounded in the north by Tibet and on all other sides by India. In 1949 India retroceded 32 sq. miles of Dewangiri, annexed in 1865. Area about 18,000 sq. miles (46,500 sq. km); population estimate, 1997, 1·87m.; density, 40 per sq. km.

The UN gives a projected population for 2010 of 2·71m.

In 1999, 93·1% of the population lived in rural areas. Only Rwanda has a larger proportion of its population living in rural areas. A Nepalese minority makes up 30–35% of the population, mainly in the south. The capital is Thimphu (1999, 28,000 population).

The official language is Dzongkha.

SOCIAL STATISTICS
1995 (estimates) births, 74,000 (rate of 41·4 per 1,000 population); deaths, 25,000 (rate of 14·4 per 1,000 population). Life expectancy at birth, 1999, was 60·3 years for men and 62·8 years for women. Infant mortality, 1999, 80 per 1,000 live births. Annual population growth rate, 1990–99, 2·2%; fertility rate, 1999, 5·4 children per woman.

CLIMATE
The climate is largely controlled by altitude. The mountainous north is cold, with perpetual snow on the summits, but the centre has a more moderate climate, though winters are cold, with rainfall under 40" (1,000 mm). In the south, the climate is humid sub-tropical and rainfall approaches 200" (5,000 mm).

CONSTITUTION AND GOVERNMENT
There is no formal constitution. The monarchy acts in consultation with a National Assembly (*Tshogdu*), which was reinstituted in 1953. But King Wangchuck is leaning towards democracy. In July 1998 the National Assembly was given the right to dismiss him. This has 150 members and meets at least once a year. Two-thirds are representatives of the people and are elected for a three-year term. All Bhutanese over 30 years may be candidates.

The reigning King is **Jigme Singye Wangchuck** (b. 1955), who succeeded his father Jigme Dorji Wangchuck (died 21 July 1972).

In 1907 the Trongsa Penlop (the governor of the province of Trongsa in central Bhutan), Sir Ugyen Wangchuk, GCIE, KCSI, was elected as the first hereditary Maharaja of Bhutan. The Bhutanese title is *Druk Gyalpo*, and his successor is now addressed as King of Bhutan. Educated in Britain, King Wangchuk is opposed to certain western influences such as television and jeans. The stated goal is to increase Gross National Happiness.

12 monastic representatives are elected by the central and regional ecclesiastical bodies, while the remaining members are nominated by the King, and include members of the Council of Ministers (the Cabinet) and the Royal Advisory Council.

National Anthem. 'Druk tsendhen koipi gyelknap na' ('In the Thunder Dragon Kingdom'); words by Dasho Shinkar Lam, tune by A. Tongmi.

CURRENT ADMINISTRATION
In March 2003 the government comprised:

Prime Minister and Minister of Agriculture: Lyonpo Kinzang Dorji; b. 1951 (in office since 14 Aug. 2002).

Minister of Education and Health: Sanjay Nedup. *Finance:* Hishey Zimba. *Foreign Affairs:* Jigme Thinley. *Home Affairs:* Thinley Gyamtso. *Law:* Sonam Tobgye. *Trade and Industry:* Khandu Wangchuck. *Chairman, Royal Advisory Council:* Vacant.

DEFENCE
In 2000 defence spending totalled US$20m. (US$10 per capita), representing 5·6% of GDP.

Army. In 1996 there was an army of 6,000 men. Three to five weeks militia training was introduced in 1989 for senior students and government officials, and three months training for some 10,000 volunteers from the general population in 1990 and 1991. Since 1992 only refresher training has been implemented.

INTERNATIONAL RELATIONS
Bhutan is a member of the UN, Asian Development Bank, Colombo Plan and SAARC.

ECONOMY
Agriculture accounted for 38·2% of GDP in 1998, with services accounting for 25·3% and industry 36·5%.

Overview. The 8th development plan (1997–2002) allowed for expenditure of Nu35,169m. Hydro-electric power and industries were stressed. The 9th development plan (2003–07) focuses on decentralization, and aims to bring electricity to 15,000 rural households as part of a plan to make Bhutan fully electrified by 2020, supported by the Asian Development Bank.

Currency. The unit of currency is the *ngultrum* (BTN) of 100 *chetrum*, at parity with the Indian rupee. Indian currency is also legal tender. Foreign exchange reserves were US$273m. in May 2002. Total money supply in May 2002 was Nu4,922m. In 2001 inflation was 5·0%.

Budget. Current provincial revenue and expenditure in Nu1m. for fiscal years ending 30 June:

	1996–97	1997–98	1998–99	1999–2000	2000–01[1]
Revenue	2,424·2	3,133·0	3,656·9	4,585·4	4,777·0
Expenditure	4,630·6	4,588·4	7,284·0	8,334·2	9,081·2

[1]Provisional.

Performance. Real GDP growth was 6·1% in 2000 and 5·9% in 2001. Total GDP in 2001 was US$0·5bn.

Banking and Finance. The Bank of Bhutan was established in 1968. The headquarters are at Phuentsholing with 26 branches throughout the country. The Royal Monetary Authority (founded 1982) acts as the central bank. Deposits (Dec. 1995) Nu2,816·3m. Foreign exchange reserves in 1997: US$120m.

ENERGY AND NATURAL RESOURCES

Environment. According to the *World Bank Atlas* Bhutan's carbon dioxide emissions in 1998 were the equivalent of 0·5 tonnes per capita.

Electricity. Installed capacity at June 1995 was 342,000 kW (of which 336,000 kW were hydro-electric). Production (1998) was 1,788m. kWh. In 1995, 38 towns and 297 villages had electricity. Consumption per capita in 1997 was 213 kWh. Bhutan exports electricity to India.

Minerals. Large deposits of limestone, marble, dolomite, slate, graphite, lead, copper, coal, talc, gypsum, beryl, mica, pyrites and tufa have been found. Most mining activity (principally limestone, coal, slate and dolomite) is on a small-scale. Output, 1998 estimates: limestone, 272,000 tonnes; dolomite, 255,000 tonnes; cement, 150,000 tonnes; coal, 69,000 tonnes.

Agriculture. The area under cultivation in 1996 was 0·36m. ha. The chief products (2000 production in 1,000 tonnes) are maize (70), oranges (58), rice (50), potatoes (34), wheat (20), sugarcane (13), millet, barley, apples, handloom cloth, timber and cardamom.

Livestock (2000): cattle, 435,000; pigs, 75,000; sheep, 59,000; goats, 42,000; horses, 30,000.

Forestry. In 1996, 2·98m. ha were forested. Timber production in 1999 was 1·75m. cu. metres.

Fisheries. The total catch in 2000 amounted to an estimated 300 tonnes, exclusively from inland waters.

INDUSTRY

In 1995 there were 3,206 licensed industrial establishments, of which 1,785 were service, 1,085 construction and 336 manufacturing industries. Of the latter, 167 were forest-based, 81 agriculture-based and 35 mineral-based.

Labour. In 1996 the labour force totalled 888,000 (60% males).

INTERNATIONAL TRADE

External debt in 2000 amounted to US$198m. and cumulative debt service payments in 1999 totalled US$7m.

Financial support is received from India, the UN and other international aid organizations.

Imports and Exports. Trade with India dominates but oranges and apples, timber, cardamom and liquor are also exported to the Middle East, Singapore and Europe. Exports in 1997 amounted to US$117·9m. and imports to US$137·4m.

COMMUNICATIONS

Roads. In 1996 there were about 3,285 km of roads, of which 1,543 km were highways and main roads, and 10,384 cars, buses, coaches, trucks and vans plus 5,959 motorcycles and mopeds. A number of sets of traffic lights were installed during the late 1990s but all have subsequently been removed as they were considered to be eyesores. There had previously been just one set.

Civil Aviation. In 1998 Druk-Air made two weekly flights to Delhi via Káthmandu and four weekly services to Bangkok via Dhaka and Rangoon (Yangon) or Calcutta. In 1999 scheduled airline traffic of Bhutan-based carriers flew 1·0m. km, carrying 31,000 passengers (all on international flights).

Telecommunications. In 2000 there were 13,300 telephone main lines (19·7 per 1,000 inhabitants).

An international microwave link connects Thimphu to the Calcutta and Delhi satellite connections. A telecommunications link between Thimphu and London by Intelsat-satellite was inaugurated in 1990. Thimphu and Phuentsholing are connected by telex to Delhi. There were 1,000 fax machines in 1997 and 4,000 PCs (5·2 for every 1,000 persons) were in use in 2000. The country's first Internet cafe was opened in March 2000 in the capital Thimphu. There were 500 Internet users in Dec. 1999.

Postal Services. In 1995 there were 103 post offices. Prior to the opening of the country to tourism in 1974 the main source of foreign exchange was the sale of commemorative postage stamps.

SOCIAL INSTITUTIONS

Justice. The High Court consists of eight judges appointed by the King. There is a Magistrate's Court in each district, under a *Thrimpon*, from which appeal is to the High Court at Thimphu.

Religion. Government estimates, 1995: 70% of the population are Mahayana Buddhists, 25% Hindu and 5% Muslim.

Education. In April 1996 there were 9,257 pupils and 225 teachers in community schools, 53,097 pupils and 1,374 teachers in primary schools, 18,762 pupils and 650 teachers in 20 junior high and 10 high schools, and 1,795 pupils and 203 teachers in technical, vocational and tertiary-level schools. There were 1,248 students and 61 teachers in seven private schools. Many students receive higher technical training in India, as well as under the UN Development Programme and the Colombo Plan, in Australia, Germany, New Zealand, Japan, Singapore, the USA and the UK. Adult literacy was 42% in 1998.

Health. There were (1996) 27 hospitals, 32 dispensaries, 97 basic health units, 10 indigenous dispensaries, 454 outreach clinics, 19 malaria centres and 3 training institutes. In 1994 beds totalled 970; there were 100 doctors and 578 paramedics in 1994. Free health facilities are available to 90% of the population.

CULTURE

Broadcasting. In 1994 there were 52 radio stations for internal administrative communications, and 13 hydro-met stations. Bhutan Broadcasting Service (autonomous since 1992) broadcasts a daily programme in English, Sharchopkha, Dzongkha and Nepali. The first television station was launched in 1999. Satellite and cable television are illegal. In 1997 there were 11,000 TV receivers and 37,000 radio receivers.

Cinema. There are two cinemas in Thimphu and four others.

Press. There is one weekly newspaper, published in English, Dzongkha and Nepali. Total circulation (1996) about 12,000.

Tourism. Bhutan was not formally opened to foreign tourists until 1974, but tourism is now the largest source of foreign exchange. In 1999, 7,000 tourists visited Bhutan, bringing revenue of US$9m.

DIPLOMATIC REPRESENTATIVES
Of Bhutan to the United Nations
Ambassador: Om Pradhan.

Of Bhutan to the European Union
Ambassador: Bap Kesang.

FURTHER READING
Das, B. N., *Mission to Bhutan: a Nation in Transition*. New Delhi, 1995
Hutt, M., *Bhutan: Perspectives on Conflict and Dissent*. London, 1994
Savada, A. M. (ed.) *Nepal and Bhutan: Country Studies*. Washington, D.C., 1993

National statistical office: Central Statistical Organization, Thimphu

BOLIVIA

República de Bolivia

Capital: Sucre
Seat of government: La Paz
Population estimate, 2000: 8·33m
GDP per capita, 2000: (PPP$) 2,424
HDI/world rank: 0·653/114

KEY HISTORICAL EVENTS
Bolivia was part of the Inca Empire until conquered by the Spanish in the 16th century. Independence was won and the Republic of Bolivia was proclaimed on 6 Aug. 1825. During the first 154 years of its independence, Bolivia had 189 governments, many of them installed by coups. In the 1960s the Argentinian revolutionary and former minister of the Cuban government, Ernesto 'Che' Guevara, was killed in Bolivia while fighting with a left-wing guerrilla group. In 1971 Bolivian instability reached a peak with the brief establishment of a revolutionary Popular Assembly during the regime of Gen. Torres. Later repression under Gen. Hugo Banzer took a heavy toll on the left-wing parties. Banzer was followed by a succession of military-led governments until civilian rule was restored in Oct. 1982 when Dr Siles Zuazo became president. He introduced a period of economic reform embracing free markets and open trade, since when 'Bolivia has been a model of democratic stability'. (*The Economist*, 24 June 2000).

TERRITORY AND POPULATION
Bolivia is a landlocked state bounded in the north and east by Brazil, south by Paraguay and Argentina, and west by Chile and Peru, with an area of some 424,165 sq. miles (1,098,581 sq. km). A coastal strip of land on the Pacific passed to Chile after a war in 1884. In 1953 Chile declared Arica a free port and Bolivia has certain privileges there.

Population estimate, 2000: 8,328,700 (63·7% urban); density, 7·6 per sq. km.

The UN gives a projected population for 2010 of 10·23m.

Area and population of the departments (capitals in brackets) at the 1992 census and as estimated in 2000:

Departments	Area (sq. km)	Census 1992	Estimate 2001
Beni (Trinidad)	213,564	276,174	362,521
Chuquisaca (Sucre)	51,524	453,756	531,522
Cochabamba (Cochabamba)	55,631	1,110,205	1,455,711
La Paz (La Paz)	133,985	1,900,786	2,350,466
Oruro (Oruro)	53,588	340,114	391,870
Pando (Cobija)	63,827	38,072	52,525
Potosí (Potosí)	118,218	645,889	709,013
Santa Cruz (Santa Cruz)	370,621	1,364,389	2,029,471
Tarija (Tarija)	37,623	291,407	391,226
Total	1,098,581	6,420,792	8,274,325

Population (2000 estimates, in 1,000) of the principal towns: Santa Cruz, 1,034; La Paz, 1,004; Cochabamba, 616; El Alto, 569; Oruro, 248; Sucre, 223; Tarija, 163; Potosí, 162.

Spanish is the official and commercial language. The Amerindian languages Aymará and Quechua are spoken exclusively by 22% and 5·2% of the population respectively; Tupi Guaraní is also spoken.

SOCIAL STATISTICS
The annual population growth rate has been estimated at 2·74% for the years 1992–2001; in 1999 births totalled an estimated 265,000 (birth rate of 32·4 per 1,000 population); deaths totalled an estimated 72,000 (rate, 8·8 per 1,000); infant mortality (1999), 63 per 1,000 live births, the highest in South America. Expectation of life (1999) was 60·4 years for men and 63·8 years for women. Fertility rate, 1999, 4·2 children per woman, also the highest in South America.

CLIMATE

The varied geography produces different climates. The low-lying areas in the Amazon Basin are warm and damp throughout the year, with heavy rainfall from Nov. to March; the Altiplano is generally dry between May and Nov. with sunshine but cold nights in June and July, while the months from Dec. to March are the wettest. La Paz, Jan. 55·9°F (13·3°C), July 50·5°F (10·3°C). Annual rainfall 20·8" (529 mm). Sucre, Jan. 58·5°F (14·7°C), July 52·7°F (11·5°C). Annual rainfall 20·1" (510 mm).

CONSTITUTION AND GOVERNMENT

Bolivia's first constitution was adopted on 19 Nov. 1826. The *President* is elected by universal suffrage for a five-year term. If 50% of the vote is not obtained, the result is determined by a secret ballot in Congress amongst the leading two candidates. The President appoints the members of his Cabinet. There is a bicameral legislature; the *Senate* comprises 27 members, three from each department, and the *Chamber of Deputies* 130 members, all serving terms of five years. A constitutional amendment of 1996 introduced direct elections for 65 deputies; the remainder are nominated by party leaders. Voting is compulsory.

National Anthem. 'Bolivianos, el hado propicio' ('Bolivians, the propitious fate'); words by I. de Sanjinés, tune by B. Vincenti.

RECENT ELECTIONS

Presidential elections were held on 30 June 2002. Former president Gonzalo Sánchez de Lozada (the Nationalist Revolutionary Movement) won 22·5% of votes cast against 20·9% for Evo Morales (Movement Towards Socialism), 20·91% for Manfred Reyes Villa (New Republican Force) and 16·3% for former president Jaime Paz Zamora (Movement of the Revolutionary Left). Turn-out was 63·4%. In the run-off held on 4 Aug. 2002 Gonzalo Sánchez de Lozada was elected president by parliament with 84 votes against 43 for Evo Morales.

CURRENT ADMINISTRATION

President: Gonzalo Sánchez de Lozada; b. 1930 (Nationalist Revolutionary Movement; in office since 6 Aug. 2002, having previously been president from 1993 to 1997).

Vice-President: Carlos Diego Mesa Gilbert.

In March 2003 the cabinet was composed as follows:

Minister of Foreign Affairs and Worship: Carlos Saavedra Bruno. *Treasury:* Javier Comboni Salinas. *Economic Development:* Jorge Torres Obleas. *Sustainable Development and Planning:* Moira Paz Cortéz. *Presidency:* José Guillermo Justiniano Sandoval. *Health:* Javier Torréz Goitia Caballero. *Defence:* Freddy Teodovic Ortiz. *Government:* Yerko Kukoc del Carpio. *Labour:* Juan Subirana Suárez. *Education:* Hugo Carvajal. *Housing and Basic Services:* Carlos Morales Landívar. *Agriculture, Livestock and Rural Development:* Arturo Liebers Valdivieso. *Ministers Without Portfolio:* Fernando Illanes; Hernán Paredes Muñóz; Francisco Javier Suárez Ramírez; Silvia Amparo Velarde Olmos.

Government Website (Spanish only): http://www.bolivia.gov.bo/

DEFENCE

There is selective conscription for 12 months at the age of 18 years. There has been optional pre-military training for high school pupils since 1998.

In 2000 defence expenditure totalled US$128m. (US$16 per capita), representing 1·4% of GDP.

Army. There are six military regions. Strength (1999): 25,000 (18,000 conscripts), including a Presidential Guard infantry regiment under direct headquarters command.

Navy. A small force exists for river and lake patrol duties. Personnel in 1999 totalled 4,500, including 1,700 marines and 1,800 conscripts. There were three Naval Areas and six Naval Districts, covering Lake Titicaca and the rivers.

Air Force. The Air Force, established in 1923, has 50 combat aircraft and 10 armed helicopters. Personnel strength (1999) about 3,000 (2,000 conscripts).

INTERNATIONAL RELATIONS
Bolivia is a member of the UN, WTO, OAS, Inter-American Development Bank, LAIA, the Andean Group, IOM and the Amazon Pact, and is an associate member of Mercosur.

ECONOMY
In 1998 agriculture accounted for 15·4% of GDP, industry 28·7% and services 55·9%.

Overview. Following the collapse of the international tin market in 1985 and severe inflation, a New Economic Policy was introduced liberalizing foreign trade, ending price controls and subsidies and freezing public-sector wages. A privatization programme affecting some 60 state-owned enterprises was instituted in June 1992. A programme of capitalization aims to attract foreign investment into state enterprises in oil, telephones, electricity supply, railways, airlines and smelters, while distributing 50% of the shares to adult citizens, to be held in retirement accounts.

Currency. The unit of currency is the *boliviano* (BOB) of 100 *centavos*, which replaced the *peso* on 1 Jan. 1987 at a rate of one boliviano = 1m. pesos. Inflation was 4·6% in 2000 and 1·6% in 2001. In June 2002 foreign exchange reserves were US$557m., total money supply was 4,163m. bolivianos and gold reserves totalled 911,000 troy oz.

Budget. Government revenue and expenditure (in 1m. bolivianos):

	1995	1996	1997	1998	1999	2000
Revenue	5,336·5	6,564·7	7,092·3	8,300·8	8,638·3	9,278·7
Expenditure	6,801·6	8,627·4	9,193·7	10,339·8	11,166·9	12,314·4

Performance. Real GDP growth was 2·4% in 2000 and 1·2% in 2001. Total GDP was US$8·0bn. in 2001.

Banking and Finance. The Central Bank (*President*, Juan Antonio Morales Anaya) is the bank of issue. In 1998 there were 14 commercial banks operating, including five foreign and eight specialized development banks.

There are stock exchanges in La Paz and Santa Cruz.

Weights and Measures. The metric system is legal, but the old Spanish system is also employed.

ENERGY AND NATURAL RESOURCES

Environment. In 1998 Bolivia's carbon dioxide emissions were the equivalent of 1·5 tonnes per capita according to the *World Bank Atlas*.

Electricity. Installed capacity was estimated to be 1,010,520 kW in 1997. Production from all sources (1998), 2·58bn. kWh; consumption per capita was 409 kWh in 1998.

Oil and Gas. There are petroleum and natural gas deposits in the Santa Cruz–Camiri areas. Production of oil in 2000 was 11,424,058 bbls. Work has begun on a US$1·9bn. pipeline from eastern Bolivia to São Paulo in Brazil. Natural gas output was 2·6bn. cu. metres in 2001 with proven reserves of 120bn. cu. metres.

Minerals. Mining accounts for 5·76% of GDP (1996 estimate). Tin-mining had been the mainstay of the economy until the collapse of the international tin market in 1985. Estimated production, 2000 (in tonnes): zinc, 141,983; tin, 12,039; lead, 9,090; antimony, 2,072; wolfram, 671; silver, 410; gold, 12,374 fine kg.

Agriculture. The rural population was estimated at 3,012,260 in 1996, 39·70% of total population. There were 1·87m. ha of arable land in 1998 and 0·23m. ha of permanent crops. Output in 1,000 tonnes in 2000 was: sugarcane, 3,602; soybeans, 1,232; potatoes, 927; bananas, 695; maize, 653; cassava, 515; rice, 310; plantains, 187. In 1992, 77,000 tonnes of coca (the source of cocaine) were grown. Since 1987 Bolivia has received international (mainly US) aid to reduce the amount of coca grown, with compensation for farmers who co-operate.

Livestock, 2000: cattle, 6,725,000; sheep, 8,752,000; pigs, 2,793,000; goats, 1,500,000; asses and mules, 712,000; horses, 322,000; chickens, 74m.

Forestry. Forests covered 48·3m. ha (44·6% of the land area) in 1995, down from 51·2m. ha in 1990. Tropical forests with woods ranging from the 'iron tree' to the light balsa are exploited. Timber production in 1999 was 1·91m. cu. metres.

Fisheries. In 2000 the total catch was 6,106 tonnes, exclusively from inland waters.

INDUSTRY
In 1998 it was estimated that the industrial sector employed a total of 51,214 persons. The principal manufactures are mining, petroleum, smelting, foodstuffs, tobacco and textiles.

Labour. Out of 3,884,251 people (54·8% male) in employment in 2001, 44·1% were in agriculture, ranching and hunting, 14·0% in retail and repair, 9·2% in industrial manufacturing, 4·9% in construction and 4·6% in transport, storage and communications. The unemployment rate in 1997 was 11·4%. In 1998 the minimum wage was 300 bolivianos a month.

Trade Unions. Unions are grouped in the Confederación de Obreros Bolivianos.

INTERNATIONAL TRADE
An agreement of Jan. 1992 with Peru gives Bolivia duty-free transit for imports and exports through a corridor leading to the Peruvian Pacific port of Ilo from the Bolivian frontier town of Desaguadero, in return for Peruvian access to the Atlantic via Bolivia's roads and railways. The mining code of 1991 gives tax incentives to foreign investors. Foreign debt was US$5,762m. in 2000.

Imports and Exports. In 2000 imports (f.o.b.) amounted to US$1,610·1m. (US$1,539·0m. in 1999); exports (f.o.b.) US$1,229·6m. (US$1,051·2m. in 1999). Main exports (2001 provisional, in US$1m.): soybeans and products, 272·9; natural gas, 237·4; zinc, 120·7; gold, 89·9; food products, 58·1; tin, 51·1; silver ore, 48·9; other fuels, 47·4; wood and products, 41·1. Main import commodities are road vehicles and parts, machinery for specific industries, cereals and cereal preparations, general industrial machinery, chemicals, petroleum, food, and iron and steel.

Main export markets, 2001 (provisional, in US$1m.): Brazil, 286·7; Colombia, 186·0; Switzerland, 175·4; USA, 156·8; Venezuela, 96·1; UK, 72·3. Main import suppliers, 2001 (provisional, in US$1m.): Argentina, 289·1; USA, 281·7; Brazil, 277·3; Chile, 142·6; Peru, 107·1; China, 69·7.

Imports and exports pass chiefly through the ports of Arica and Antofagasta in Chile, Mollendo-Matarani in Peru, through La Quiaca on the Bolivian-Argentine border, and through river-ports on the rivers flowing into the Amazon.

COMMUNICATIONS

Roads. The total length of the road system was 49,400 km in 1996, of which 3,660 km were national roads. Estimated total vehicles in use in 1997 was 397,112.

Rail. In 1994 the state railway ENFE network totalled 3,697 km of metre gauge, comprising unconnected Eastern (1,423 km) and Andina (2,274 km) systems. Passenger-km travelled in 1998 came to 270m. and freight tonne-km to 908m.

Civil Aviation. The two international airports are La Paz (El Alto) and Santa Cruz (Viru Viru). The national airlines are the state-owned Aerosur (domestic services only) and Lloyd Aéreo Boliviano (97·5% state-owned), which in 1998 ran scheduled services between La Paz and Arica, Buenos Aires, Guayaquil, Lima, Miami, Montevideo and Trinidad, as well as many internal services. In 1999 Lloyd Aéreo Boliviano flew 18·8m. km, carrying 1,525,900 passengers (658,800 on international flights).

Shipping. Lake Titicaca and about 19,000 km of rivers are open to navigation.

Telecommunications. In 2000 there were 504,200 telephone main lines (60·5 per 1,000 persons) and 140,000 PCs in use (16·8 per 1,000 persons). In 1999 Bolivia had 420,300 mobile phone subscribers. There were five Internet Service Providers in 1999; Internet users numbered 78,000 in Dec. 1999.

Postal Services. In 1995 there were 159 post offices, or 1 for every 46,600 persons.

SOCIAL INSTITUTIONS

Justice. Justice is administered by the Supreme Court, superior department courts (of five or seven judges) and courts of local justice. The Supreme Court, with headquarters at Sucre, is divided into two sections, civil and criminal, of five justices each, with the Chief Justice presiding over both. Members of the Supreme Court are chosen on a two-thirds vote of Congress. The death penalty was abolished for ordinary crimes in 1997.

The population in penal institutions in Dec. 1996 was 5,412 (70 per 100,000 of national population).

Religion. The Roman Catholic church was disestablished in 1961. It is under a cardinal (in Sucre), an archbishop (in La Paz), six bishops and vicars apostolic. It had 6·87m. adherents in 1997. There were also 700,000 Evangelical Protestants and 200,000 followers of other faiths.

Education. Adult literacy was 85·2% in 1999 (male, 92·5%; female, 78·3%). Primary instruction is free and obligatory between the ages of six and 14 years. In 1999 there were 13,365 schooling facilities. In 1998 state schools were attended by 2,056,084 pupils and employed 15,132 teachers. The national rate of school attendance (6–19-year-olds) reaches 74·3%.

In 1994–95 there were 7 universities, 2 technical universities, 1 Roman Catholic university, 1 musical conservatory, and colleges in the following fields: business, 6; teacher training, 4; industry, 1; nursing, 1; technical teacher training, 1; fine arts, 1, rural education, 1; physical education, 1. In 1997 state universities had 162,538 students and 7,490 teaching staff. In 1998 there were 35 private universities with 32,253 students and 3,538 teaching staff.

In 1999 total expenditure on education came to 8·0% of GNP.

Health. In 1998 there were 2,561 doctors and 5,077 nurses, and 230 hospitals and 9,185 hospital beds (1 per 897 persons).

Welfare. The pensions and social security systems in Bolivia were reformed in 1996. Instead of a defined-benefit publicly managed pension system, a defined-contribution system based on privately managed individual capitalization accounts was introduced. There are now two funds: the Collective Capitalization Fund, made up of 50% of the shares of capitalized companies formerly owned by the state, and the Individual Capitalization Fund, made up of contributions of those associated to the new system with a monthly income of above US$50. A solidarity bonus, BONOSOL—worth approximately US$250 a year—is paid to all Bolivians over the age of 65.

CULTURE

Broadcasting. The broadcasting authority is the Dirección General de Telecomunicaciones. In 1999 there were 321 radio stations. Broadcasts are in Spanish, Aymará and Quechua. There were 5·25m. radios in 1997. There were 48 television stations in 1997 and 900,000 televisions (colour by NTSC) in 1997.

Cinema. 4 full-length films were made in 1995.

Press. There were 18 daily newspapers in 1996 with a combined circulation of 420,000, at a rate of 55 per 1,000 inhabitants.

Tourism. In 1999 there were 410,000 foreign tourists. Receipts totalled US$170m.

DIPLOMATIC REPRESENTATIVES

Of Bolivia in the United Kingdom (106 Eaton Sq., London, SW1W 9AD)
Ambassador: Vacant.
Chargé d'Affaires a.i.: Roberto Calzadilla Sarmiento.

Of the United Kingdom in Bolivia (Avenida Arce 2732, La Paz)
Ambassador: William Sinton, OBE.

Of Bolivia in the USA (3014 Massachusetts Ave, NW, Washington, D.C., 20008)
Ambassador: Jaime Aparicio Otero.

Of the USA in Bolivia (Avenida Arce 2780, La Paz)
Ambassador: Vacant.
Chargé d'Affaires a.i.: Daniel Santos Jr.

Of Bolivia to the United Nations
Ambassador: Javier Murillo de la Rocha.

Of Bolivia to the European Union
Ambassador: Carlos Rios Dabdoub.

FURTHER READING
Fifer, J. V., *Bolivia*. [Bibliography] ABC-Clio, Oxford and Santa Barbara (CA), 2000
Klein, H., *Bolivia: The Evolution of a Multi-Ethnic Society*. OUP, 1982

National statistical office: Instituto Nacional de Estadistica, Casilla Postal 6129, La Paz.
Website (Spanish only): http://www.ine.gov.bo/

BOSNIA-HERZEGOVINA

Republika Bosna i
Hercegovina

Capital: Sarajevo
Population estimate, 2000: 3·98m.
GDP per capita: not available
GNP per capita: $1,210

KEY HISTORICAL EVENTS

Settled by Slavs in the 7th century, Bosnia was conquered by the Turks in 1463 when much of the population was gradually converted to Islam. At the Congress of Berlin (1878) the territory was assigned to Austro-Hungarian administration under nominal Turkish suzerainty. Austria-Hungary's outright annexation in 1908 generated international tensions which contributed to the outbreak of the First World War. After 1918 Bosnia Hercegovina became part of a new kingdom of Serbs, Croats and Slovenes under the Serbian monarchy. Its name was changed to Yugoslavia in 1929. (See SERBIA AND MONTENEGRO for developments up to and beyond the Second World War.)

On 15 Oct. 1991 the National Assembly adopted a 'Memorandum on Sovereignty', the Serbian deputies abstaining. This envisaged Bosnian autonomy within a Yugoslav federation. Though boycotted by Serbs, a referendum in March 1992 supported independence. In March 1992 an agreement was reached by Muslims, Serbs and Croats to set up three autonomous ethnic communities under a central Bosnian authority.

Bosnia-Herzegovina declared itself independent on 5 April 1992. Fighting broke out between the Serb, Croat and Muslim communities, with particularly heavy casualties and destruction in Sarajevo, leading to extensive Muslim territorial losses and an exodus of refugees. UN-sponsored ceasefires were repeatedly violated.

On 13 Aug. 1992 the UN Security Council voted to authorize the use of force if necessary to ensure the delivery of humanitarian aid to besieged civilians. Internationally sponsored peace talks were held in Geneva in 1993, but Serb-Muslim-Croat fighting continued.

In Dec. 1994 Bosnian Serbs and Muslims signed a countrywide interim ceasefire. Bosnian Croats also signed in Jan. 1995. However, Croatian Serbs and the Muslim secessionist forces under Fikret Abdić did not sign the agreement, and fighting continued. On 16 June 1995 Bosnian government forces launched an attack to break the Bosnian Serb siege of Sarajevo. On 11 July Bosnian Serb forces began to occupy UN security zones despite retaliatory NATO air strikes, and on 28 Aug. shelled Sarajevo.

To stop the shelling of UN safe areas, more than 60 NATO aircraft attacked Bosnian Serb military installations on 30–31 Aug. On 26 Sept. in Washington the foreign ministers of Bosnia, Croatia and Yugoslavia (the latter negotiating for the Bosnian Serbs) agreed a draft Bosnian constitution under which a central government would handle foreign affairs and commerce and a Serb Zone, and a Muslim-Croat Federation would run their internal affairs. A ceasefire came into force on 12 Oct. 1995.

In Dayton (Ohio) on 21 Nov. 1995 the prime ministers of Bosnia, Croatia and Yugoslavia initialled a US-brokered agreement to end hostilities. The Bosnian state was divided into a Croat-Muslim Federation containing 51% of Bosnian territory and a Serb Republic containing 49%. A central government authority representing all ethnic groups with responsibility for foreign and monetary policy and citizenship issues was established, and free elections held. On 20 Dec. 1995 a NATO contingent (IFOR) took over from UN peacekeeping forces to enforce the Paris peace agreements and set up a 4-km separation zone between the Serb and Muslim-Croat territories. There are still some 15,000 NATO troops in Bosnia-Herzegovina.

'Bosnia is not now a failed state, but it is a center for the trafficking of women and narcotics, a hide-out for war criminals and a steady drain on Western aid and defense budgets. It's not likely to collapse soon, but neither will foreign troops and administrators likely be able to safely pull out for many years to come'. (*International Herald Tribune*, 13 Nov. 2002).

TERRITORY AND POPULATION

The republic is bounded in the north and west by Croatia and in the east and southeast by Serbia and Montenegro. It has a coastline of only 20 km with no harbours. Its area is 51,129 sq. km. The capital is Sarajevo.

Population at the 1991 census: 4,377,033 (34·2% urban), of which the predominating ethnic groups were Muslims (1,905,829), Serbs (1,369,258) and Croats (755,892). Population of the principal cities in 1991: Sarajevo, 415,631 (est. 1999, 522,000); Banja Luka, 142,644; Zenica, 96,238. By 1996, following the civil war, 1,319,250 Bosnians had taken refuge abroad, including 0·45m. in Serbia and Montenegro, 0·32m. in Germany, 0·17m. in Croatia and 0·12m. in Sweden.

The UN gives a projected population for 2010 of 4·27m.

In 1999 Bosnia-Herzegovina had the fastest-growing population in Europe, with a rise of 4·6% on the 1998 figure. In 1995 an estimated 58·9% of the population lived in rural areas.

The official language is Serbo-Croat.

SOCIAL STATISTICS

1996 births, 36,000; deaths, 69,000. Rates per 1,000, 1996: birth, 7·9; death, 15·4. Annual population growth rate, 1990–99, –1·3%. Life expectancy at birth, 1996, was 51·2 years for men and 61·4 years for women. Infant mortality, 1990–95, 15 per 1,000 live births; fertility rate, 1999, 1·4 children per woman.

CLIMATE

The climate is generally continental with steady rainfall throughout the year, although in areas nearer the coast it is more Mediterranean.

CONSTITUTION AND GOVERNMENT

On 18 March 1994, in Washington, Bosnian Muslims and Croats reached an agreement for the creation of a federation of cantons with a central government responsible for foreign affairs, defence and commerce. It was envisaged that there would be a president elected by a two-house legislature alternating annually between the nationalities.

On 31 May 1994 the National Assembly approved the creation of the Muslim Croat federation. Alija Izetbegović remained the unitary states' President. An interim government with Hasan Muratović as Prime Minister was formed on 30 Jan. 1996.

The Dayton Agreement including the new constitution was signed and came into force on 14 Dec. 1995. The government structure was established in 1996 as follows:

Heading the state is a three-member *Presidency* (one Croat, one Muslim, one Serb) with a rotating president. The Presidency is elected by direct universal suffrage, and is responsible for foreign affairs and the nomination of the prime minister. There is a two-chamber parliament: the *Chamber of Representatives* (which meets in Sarajevo) comprises 42 directly elected deputies, two-thirds Croat and Muslim and one-third Serb; and the *Chamber of Peoples* (which meets in Lukavica) comprises five Croat, five Muslim and five Serb delegates.

Below the national level the country is divided into two self-governing entities along ethnic lines.

The **Federation of Bosnia and Herzegovina** is headed by a President and Vice-President, alternately Croat and Muslim, a 140-member Chamber of Representatives and a 74-member Chamber of Peoples. The **Serb Republic** is also headed by an elected President and Vice-President, and there is a National Assembly of 83 members, elected by proportional representation.

Central government is conducted by a *Council of Ministers*, which comprises Muslim and Serb Co-Prime Ministers and a Croat Deputy Prime Minister. The Co-Prime Ministers alternate in office every week.

National Anthem. 'Intermezzo'; tune by Dusan Sestić; no words.

313

RECENT ELECTIONS

Elections were held on 5 Oct. 2002 for the Presidium and the federal parliament. Seats for the three-member rotating presidency went to Serb, Croat and Muslim nationalist parties. The elected members were as follows: Sulejman Tihić (Muslim; Party of Democratic Action—SDA); Dragan Čović (Croat; Croatian Democratic Community—HDZ); and Mirko Šarović (Serb; Social Democratic Party—SDS). In the parliamentary elections, the Party for Democratic Action won ten seats with 32·5% of the vote, against five seats for both the Croat Democratic Union and the Serb Democratic Party.

CURRENT ADMINISTRATION

Presidency Chairman: Borislav Paravac (Serb; SDS). *Presidency Members:* Sulejman Tihić (Muslim; SDA); Dragan Čović (Croat; HDZ). Mirko Šarović was sworn in as presidency chairman on 28 Oct. 2002, but resigned on 2 April 2003. He was replaced by Borislav Paravac, also of the Social Democratic Party.

In March 2003 the cabinet comprised:

Prime Minister and Minister of European Integration: Adnan Terzić (Muslim; SDA); b. 1960 (sworn in 23 Dec. 2002).

Minister of Civil Affairs: Safet Halilović. *Finance and Treasury:* Ljerka Marić. *Foreign Affairs:* Mladen Ivanić. *Foreign Trade and Economic Relations:* Mila Gadžić. *Human Rights and Refugees:* Mirsad Kebo. *Justice:* Slobodan Kovać. *Security:* Bariša Čolak. *Transportation and Communications:* Branko Dokić.

UN High Representative: Lord Ashdown (UK); b. 1941 (sworn in 27 May 2002).

Office of the High Representative: http://www.ohr.int/

DEFENCE

Defence expenditure in 2000 totalled US$183m. (US$46 per capita), representing 3·7% of GDP.

Army. In 1999 the Army numbered some 40,000 with reserves of 150,000. The Croatian Defence Council also had personnel of some 16,000 active in the country, with 50 main battle tanks, while the forces of the Serb Republic were estimated at up to 30,000, with 500 main battle tanks. The Croatian Defence Council is to merge with the Army to form the armed forces of a Muslim-Croat Federation. The USA is assisting in training and equipping the armed forces.

INTERNATIONAL RELATIONS

Bosnia-Herzegovina is a member of the UN, BIS, OSCE and the Central European Initiative.

The Serb Republic and Yugoslavia (now Serbia and Montenegro) signed an agreement on 28 Feb. 1997 establishing 'special parallel relations' between them. The agreement envisages co-operation in cultural, commercial, security and foreign policy matters, allows visa-free transit of borders and includes a non-aggression pact. A customs agreement followed on 31 March.

ECONOMY

Overview. Privatization is under way but extremely slowly. The private sector only generates approximately 40% of GDP.

Currency. A new currency, the *konvertiblna marka* (BAM) consisting of 100 *pfening*, was introduced in June 1998. Initially trading at a strict 1-to-1 against the Deutsche Mark, it is now pegged to the euro at a rate of 1·95583 convertible marks to the euro. Inflation was 3·3% in 2001. Total money supply was 3,117m. convertible marks in June 2002.

Budget. Revenue in 1997 was 618m. Deutsche Marks; expenditure 598·5m. Deutsche Marks.

Performance. Bosnia-Herzegovina had one of the fastest growing economies in the world during the second half of the 1990s. Real GDP growth was 10·0% in both 1998 and 1999, but then 4·5% in 2000 and 2·3% in 2001. Total GDP was US$4·8bn. in 2001.

Banking and Finance. The Dayton agreement stipulated that the governor of the Central Bank must not be a Bosnian citizen. The present *Governor* is Peter Nicholl (New Zealand). In 1998 there were 59 commercial banks.

ENERGY AND NATURAL RESOURCES

Environment. According to the *World Bank Atlas* Bosnia-Herzegovina's carbon dioxide emissions in 1998 were the equivalent of 1·2 tonnes per capita.

Electricity. Capacity was 2·41m. kW in 1995. Production in 1998 was 2·22bn. kWh. In 1996 consumption per capita was 772 kWh.

Minerals. Output, 1995: iron ore, 150,000 tonnes; bauxite, 75,000 tonnes; lignite, 1,640,000 tonnes (1997).

Agriculture. In 1998 there were 500,000 ha of arable land and 150,000 ha of permanent crops. 2000 yields (in 1,000 tonnes): maize, 900; potatoes, 365; wheat, 275; cabbages, 120; plums, 90; barley, 64. Livestock in 2000: cattle, 462,000; sheep, 672,000; pigs, 150,000; poultry, 3m.

Forestry. In 1995 forests covered 27,100 sq. km, or 53·1% of the total land area. Timber production in 1999 was 40,000 cu. metres.

Fisheries. Estimated total fish catch in 2000: 2,500 tonnes (exclusively freshwater).

INDUSTRY

In 1991 there were 7,823 enterprises (4,563 private, 1,882 social, 655 limited companies, 322 co-operatives and 157 public). Production (in 1,000 tonnes) 1995: cement, 150; aluminium (1994), 89; crude steel (1990), 1,421. Cars (1990), 38,000 units; tractors (1990), 34,000 units; lorries (1990), 16,000 units; televisions (1990), 21,000 sets.

Labour. The labour force totalled 1,719,000 in 1996 (62% males). Unemployment in 2001 was nearly 40%.

INTERNATIONAL TRADE

External debt was US$2,828m. in 2000.

Imports and Exports. 2000 external trade (in US$1m.): exports f.o.b., 1,066·2; imports f.o.b., 2,896·0. In 2000 main export markets were Italy, 31·5%; Germany, 13·8%; Slovenia, 7·6%. Principal import sources in 2000 were Slovenia, 16·1%; Germany, 13·6%; Italy, 13·0%. In 2000 the EU accounted for 65·4% of Bosnia-Herzegovina's exports and 43·8% of imports.

COMMUNICATIONS

Roads. In 1996 there were 21,846 km of roads, 3,722 km of which were highways or main roads. There were 96,182 passenger cars in use in 1996 (23 per 1,000 inhabitants) and 9,783 vans and trucks. There were 199 road accident fatalities in 1996.

Rail. There were 1,021 km of railways in 1991 (795 km electrified); they carried 554m. passenger-km and 1,946m. tonne-km of freight. It is estimated that up to 80% of the rail network was destroyed in the civil war, and it was not until July 2001 that the first international services were resumed. There are three state-owned rail companies—the Bosnia and Herzegovina railway company (ZBH), the Herzeg-Bosnia Railway company (ZHB), and the Serb Republic Railway and Transport Company (ZTP).

Civil Aviation. There are international airports at Sarajevo (Butmir) and Banja Luka. In 1998 there were direct flights to Belgrade, Istanbul, Ljubljana, Munich, Tivat, Vienna, Zagreb and Zürich. In 2000 Sarajevo handled 355,000 passengers (all international) and 1,200 tonnes of freight

Telecommunications. Telephone main lines numbered 408,800 in 2000, equivalent to 102·9 per 1,000 inhabitants. There were 52,600 mobile phone subscribers in 1999 and 45,000 Internet users in 2001. Three state-owned companies run the telephone networks in different parts of the country, the largest of which is the Saravevo-based PTT Bih.

Postal Services. In 1995 there were 159 post offices.

SOCIAL INSTITUTIONS

Justice. The population in penal institutions in Jan. 1998 was 769 (30 per 100,000 of national population).

Police. The European Union Police Mission (EUPM) in Bosnia and Herzegovina, the EU's first civilian crisis management operation, took over from the UN's International Police Task Force on 1 Jan. 2003. It aims to help the authorities develop their police forces to the highest European and international standards.

Religion. In 1998 there were estimated to be 1,350,000 Sunni Muslims, 960,000 Serbian Orthodox, 460,000 Roman Catholics and 600,000 followers of other religions.

Education. In 1990–91 there were 543,500 pupils in 2,205 primary schools (23,400 teachers), 173,100 in 238 secondary schools (9,000 teachers) and 37,500 in 44 tertiary schools (2,800 teachers). In 1995 there were four universities.

Health. In 1996 there were 4,500 doctors, 550 dentists and 11,900 nurses.

Welfare. There were 380,000 pensions in 1990 (including 140,000 old age).

CULTURE

Broadcasting. In 1997 there were 940,000 radio receivers and 1,000 TV receivers.

Press. There were two daily newspapers in 1995 with a combined circulation of 520,000, at a rate of 146 per 1,000 inhabitants.

Tourism. In 1999 there were 89,000 foreign tourists, bringing revenue of US$13m.

DIPLOMATIC REPRESENTATIVES

Of Bosnia-Herzegovina in the United Kingdom (4th Floor, Morley House, 320 Regent St., London, W1R 5AB)
Ambassador: Elvira Begović.

Of the United Kingdom in Bosnia-Herzegovina (8 Tina Ujevića, Sarajevo)
Ambassador: Ian Cliff, OBE.

Of Bosnia-Herzegovina in the USA (2109 E Street, NW, Washington, D.C., 20037)
Ambassador: Igor Davidović.

Of the USA in Bosnia-Herzegovina (Alipasina 43, 71000, Sarajevo)
Ambassador: Clifford G. Bond.

Of Bosnia-Herzegovina to the United Nations
Ambassador: Mirza Kušljugić.

Of Bosnia-Herzegovina to the European Union
Ambassador: Zdenko Martinović.

FURTHER READING

Bert, W., *The Reluctant Superpower: United States Policy in Bosnia, 1991–1995.* New York, 1997
Burg, Steven L. and Shoup, Paul S., *The War in Bosnia-Herzegovina.* New York, 1999
Cigar, N., *Genocide in Bosnia: the Policy of Ethnic Cleansing.* Texas Univ. Press, 1995
Fine, J. V. A. and Donia, R. J., *Bosnia-Hercegovina: a Tradition Betrayed.* Farnborough, 1994
Friedman, F., *The Bosnian Muslims: Denial of a Nation.* Boulder (CO), 1996
Garde, P., *Journal de Voyage en Bosnie-Herzégovine.* Paris, 1995
Holbrooke, R., *To End a War.* Random House, London, 1998
Malcolm, N., *Bosnia: a Short History.* 2nd ed. London, 1996
O'Ballance, E., *Civil War in Bosnia, 1992–94.* London, 1995
Rieff, D., *Slaughterhouse: Bosnia and the Failure of the West.* New York, 1997
Sells, M. A., *The Bridge Betrayed: Religion and Genocide in Bosnia.* California Univ. Press, 1996

National statistical office: Institute of Statistics, Zelenih Beretki 26, 71000 Sarajevo. *Director:* Dervis Djurdjevic.

BOTSWANA

Republic of Botswana

Capital: Gaborone
Population estimate, 2000: 1·54m.
GDP per capita, 2000: (PPP$) 7,184
HDI/world rank: 0·572/126

KEY HISTORICAL EVENTS
The Tswana or Batswana people are the principal inhabitants of the country formerly known as Bechuanaland. The territory was declared a British protectorate in 1895. Britain ruled through her High Commissioner in South Africa until the post was abolished in 1964. Frequent suggestions for the addition of Bechuanaland and the other two High Commission Territories to South Africa were rejected, the Africans being strongly against the idea. Economically, however, the country was very closely tied to that of South Africa and has remained so. In Dec. 1960 Bechuanaland received its first constitution. Further constitutional change brought full self-government in 1965 and full independence on 30 Sept. 1966. For years Botswana had great difficulties with the neighbouring settler regime in Rhodesia, until that country became Zimbabwe in 1980. Relations with South Africa were also strained until the ending of apartheid. Today the country enjoys stability and a fast-growing economy.

TERRITORY AND POPULATION
Botswana is bounded in the west and north by Namibia, northeast by Zambia and Zimbabwe, and east and south by South Africa. The area is 581,730 sq. km. Population (1991 census), 1,326,796 (45·7% urban). Estimate, 2000, 1,540,000; density, 2·6 per sq. km.

The UN gives a projected population for 2010 of 1·63m.

In 1999, 50·3% of the population were rural. Between 1990 and 1995 there was a 10% rise in the urban population every year, the largest percentage increase anywhere in the world in the same period.

The country is divided into town districts (Central, Chobe, Ghanzi, Kgalagadi, Kgatleng, Kweneng, Ngamiland, Ngwaketse, North East and South East).

The main towns (with population, 1998) are Gaborone (192,845), Francistown (92,516), Selebi-Phikwe (46,766), Molepolole (44,564), Kanye (35,515); 1991: Serowe (30,260), Mahalapye (28,079), Maun (26,769), Lobatse (26,052) and Mochudi (25,542).

The official languages are Setswana and English. Setswana is spoken by over 90% of the population and English by approximately 40%. More than ten other languages, including Shona, San and Hottentot, are spoken in various tribal areas.

SOCIAL STATISTICS
1996 (estimates) births, 49,000; deaths, 25,000. Rates, 1996 estimates (per 1,000 population): births, 33·3; deaths, 17·0. Infant mortality, 1999 (per 1,000 live births), 46. As a result of the impact of AIDS, expectation of life in 1999 was 41·6 years for males and 41·9 for females, down from an overall average of 65 years in 1993. Approximately 36% of all adults are infected with HIV, the highest percentage of any country, with well over half of those aged between 25 and 29 having the disease. Annual population growth rate, 1990–99, 2·5% per annum. Fertility rate, 1999, 4·2 children per woman.

CLIMATE
In winter, days are warm and nights cold, with occasional frosts. Summer heat is tempered by prevailing northeast winds. Rainfall comes mainly in summer, from Oct. to April, while the rest of the year is almost completely dry with very high sunshine amounts. Gaborone, Jan. 79°F (26·1°C), July 55°F (12·8°C). Annual rainfall varies from 650 mm in the north to 250 mm in the southeast. The country is prone to droughts.

317

CONSTITUTION AND GOVERNMENT

The Constitution adopted on 30 Sept. 1966 provides for a republican form of government headed by the President with three main organs: the Legislature, the Executive and the Judiciary. The executive rests with the President who is responsible to the National Assembly. The President is elected for five-year terms by the National Assembly.

The *National Assembly* consists of 47 members, 40 elected by universal suffrage, and seven elected by itself. Elections are held every five years. Voting is on the first-past-the-post system.

The President is an *ex officio* member of the Assembly.

There is also a *House of Chiefs* to advise the government. It consists of the Chiefs of the eight tribes who were autonomous during the days of the British protectorate, plus four members elected by and from among the sub-chiefs in four districts; these 12 members elect a further three politically independent members.

National Anthem. 'Fatshe leno la rona' ('Blessed be this noble land'); words and tune by K. T. Motsete.

RECENT ELECTIONS

At the National Assembly elections of 16 Oct. 1999 the Botswana Democratic Party (BDP) gained 33 seats with 54·2% of the vote (27 in 1994), the Botswana National Front 6 with 24·6% (13 in 1994) and the Botswana Congress Party 1 with 11·3% (0 in 1994).

CURRENT ADMINISTRATION

President: Festus Mogae; b. 1939 (BDP; sworn in on 1 April 1998).

Vice-President: Lieut.-Gen. Seretse Ian Khama.

In March 2003 the cabinet was as follows:

Minister of Finance and Development Planning: Baledzi Goalathe. *Foreign Affairs:* Mompati Merahfe. *Communications, Science and Technology:* Boyce Sebetela. *Health:* Joy Phumaphi. *Works, Transport and Communications:* Tebelelo Seretse. *Conservation, Wildlife and Tourism:* Venson Pelonomi. *Mineral Resources, Energy and Water Affairs:* Boometswe Mokgothu. *Education:* Pontashego Kedikilwe. *Labour and Home Affairs:* Thebe Mogami. *Agriculture:* Johnny Swarts. *Lands and Housing:* Margaret Nasha. *Local Government:* Michael Tshipinare. *Trade and Industry:* Jacob Nkate. *Presidential Affairs and Public Administration:* Daniel Kwelagobe.

Government Website: http://www.gov.bw

DEFENCE

In 2000 defence expenditure totalled US$245m. (US$151 per capita), representing 5·5% of GDP.

Army. The Army personnel (2000) numbered more than 11,000, including the air wing and a commando unit.

Air Force. The Air Wing operated 50 combat aircraft in 2000 and numbered more than 2,000.

INTERNATIONAL RELATIONS

Botswana is a member of the UN, WTO, the Commonwealth, the African Union, African Development Bank, SADC and is an ACP member state of the ACP-EU relationship.

ECONOMY

Agriculture accounted for 3·6% of GDP in 1998, industry 46·1% and services 50·4%.

Overview. The Eighth National Development Plan is running from 1997 to 2003. It is intended to stimulate industries and economic activities that can take over from mines and create jobs.

Currency. The unit of currency is the *pula* (BWP) of 100 *thebe*. Inflation was 7·2% in 2001. Foreign exchange reserves were US$5,683m. in June 2002. Total money supply was P2,409m. in May 2002.

Budget. The fiscal year begins in April. Government finance for recent years (in P1m.):

	1997–98	1998–99	1999–2000
Revenue	8,218·2	7,677·6	11,921·7
Expenditure	7,406·1	9,065·4	11,411·9

1993–94 revenue (in P1m.) included: mineral taxes, 2,456; customs pool, 830; other revenue, 1,858. Expenditure: recurrent, 3,470; development and capital transfer, 1,735.

Performance. In 2001 real GDP growth was 4·9% (8·6% in 2000). In 2001 total GDP was US$5·1bn.

Banking and Finance. There were four commercial banks at 1 Jan. 1996 with 46 branches. Total assets were P3,729m. at 30 Nov. 1995. The Bank of Botswana (*Governor*, Linah Mohohlo), established in 1976, is the central bank. The National Development Bank, founded in 1964, has six regional offices, and agricultural, industrial and commercial development divisions. The Botswana Co-operative Bank is banker to co-operatives and to thrift and loan societies. The government-owned Post Office Savings Bank operates throughout the country.

There is a stock exchange.

Weights and Measures. The metric system is in use.

ENERGY AND NATURAL RESOURCES

Environment. According to the *World Bank Atlas* Botswana's carbon dioxide emissions in 1998 were the equivalent of 2·4 tonnes per capita.

Electricity. Installed capacity was 197,000 kW in 1993. Production in 1998 was 1bn. kWh. Consumption per capita was an estimated 747 kWh in 1993. The coal-fired power station at Morupule supplies cities and major towns.

Water. Surface water resources are about 18,000m. cu. metres a year. Nearly all flows into northern districts from Angola through the Okavango and Kwando river systems. The Zambezi, also in the north, provides irrigation in the Chobe District. In the southeast, there are dams to exploit the ephemeral flow of the tributaries of the Limpopo. 80% of the land has no surface water, and must be served by some 6,000 boreholes.

Minerals. Botswana is the world's biggest diamond producer in terms of value; in 2000 the total value was estimated to be US$2·1bn. Debswana, a partnership between the government and De Beers, runs three mines producing around 17·5m. carats a year, with plans to double the capacity of the largest mine from 6m. to 12m. carats a year. Coal reserves are estimated at 17,000m. tonnes. There is also copper, salt and soda ash. Mineral production, 2000: diamonds, 24,700,000 carats (the second largest quantity after Australia); copper (1997), 18,350 tonnes; nickel ore (1996), 17,461 tonnes; coal (1997), 776,000 tonnes.

Agriculture. 70–80% of the total land area is desert. 80% of the population is rural, 71% of all land is 'tribal', protected and allocated to prevent over-grazing, maintain small farmers and foster commercial ranching. Agriculture provides a livelihood for over 80% of the population, but accounts for only 3% of GDP (1997). In 1998, 343,000 ha were arable and 3,000 ha permanent crops. There were 6,000 tractors in 1998 and 95 harvester-threshers. Cattle-rearing is the chief industry after diamond-mining, and the country is more a pastoral than an agricultural one, crops depending entirely upon the rainfall. In 2000, 300,000 persons were economically active in agriculture. In 2000 there were: cattle, 2·5m.; goats, 2·2m.; sheep, 350,000; asses, 330,000; chickens, 4m. In 1995, 80% of cattle were owned by traditional farmers, about half owning fewer than 20 head. A serious outbreak of cattle lung disease in 1995–96 led to the slaughter of around 300,000 animals.

Production (2000, in 1,000 tonnes): pulses, 17; vegetables, 17; sorghum, 14; roots and tubers, 13; sunflower seeds, 7; maize, 6; seed cotton, 3.

17% of the land is set aside for wildlife conservation and 20% for wildlife management areas, with four national parks and game reserves.

Forestry. Forests covered 139,000 sq. km, or 24·6% of the total land area, in 1995 (25·2% in 1990). There are forest nurseries and plantations. Concessions have been granted to harvest 7,500 cu. metres in Kasane and Chobe Forestry Reserves, and up to 2,500 cu. metres in the Masame area. In 1999, 1·70m. cu. metres of roundwood were cut.

Fisheries. In 2000 the total catch was 166 tonnes, exclusively from inland waters.

INDUSTRY
Meat is processed, and textiles, foodstuffs and soap manufactured. 565 companies were registered at the end of 1992. Rural technology is being developed and traditional crafts encouraged.

Labour. In 1999, 255,607 persons were in formal employment. At the 1991 census there were 276,950 paid employees (including informal employment) and 28,764 self-employed. A further 76,101 persons worked on a non-cash basis, e.g. as family helpers. 60,757 were seeking work. In March 1994 there were 12,342 Botswana nationals employed in the mines of South Africa. In 1991 there were 57,001 building workers, 34,322 in trade and 29,325 in domestic service. Botswana's biggest individual employer is the Debswana Diamond Company, with a workforce (1997) of nearly 6,000. In April 1998 the unemployment rate was 21%.

INTERNATIONAL TRADE
Botswana is a member of the Southern African Customs Union (SACU) with Lesotho, Namibia, South Africa and Swaziland. There are no foreign exchange restrictions. External debt in 2000 totalled US$413m.

Imports and Exports. In 1999 imports (f.o.b.) totalled US$1,996·5m. More than three-quarters of all imports are from the SACU countries, the main commodities being machinery and electrical equipment, foodstuffs, vehicles and transport equipment, textiles and petroleum products.

In 1999 exports (f.o.b.) totalled US$2,671·0m., including diamonds (74·6% of exports in 1998), vehicles, copper, nickel and beef.

In addition to the SACU countries, other significant trading partners are the UK, Zimbabwe and the USA for exports; and South Korea, Zimbabwe and the UK for imports.

COMMUNICATIONS
Roads. In 1996 some 4,600 km of road were bitumen-surfaced out of a total of 18,482 km. In 1996 there were 66,330 motor vehicles in use (22,540 cars and 44,000 trucks and vans). In 1995 there were 410 deaths in road accidents.

Rail. The main line from Mafeking in South Africa to Bulawayo in Zimbabwe traverses Botswana. With three branches the total length was 971 km in 1994. Passenger-km travelled in 1998 came to 71m. and freight tonne-km to 1,278m.

Civil Aviation. There are international airports at Gaborone (Sir Seretse Khama) and at Maun and six domestic airports. The national carrier is the state-owned Air Botswana. Direct flights are operated to the UK, South Africa and Zimbabwe. In 1998 Air Botswana flew 2·6m. km, carrying 123,700 passengers (92,500 on international flights). In Oct. 1999 an Air Botswana pilot who had been suspended two months earlier crashed an empty passenger plane into the airline's two serviceable aeroplanes at Gaborone Airport, killing himself and destroying the airline's complete fleet in the process. In 2000 Gaborone handled 224,794 passengers (170,186 on international flights).

Telecommunications. There were 150,300 main telephone lines in 2000 (92·7 per 1,000 inhabitants), and 60,000 PCs were in use (37·0 per 1,000 persons). In 1996 there were 3,500 fax machines. In July 2000 Internet users numbered 12,000 and in Sept. 2000 there were 140,000 mobile phone subscribers, compared to just 23,000 in 1998.

Postal Services. There are 109 post offices and 65 agencies.

SOCIAL INSTITUTIONS
Justice. Law is based on the Roman-Dutch law of the former Cape Colony, but judges and magistrates are also qualified in English common law. The Court of Appeal has jurisdiction in respect of criminal and civil appeals emanating from the

High Court, and in all criminal and civil cases and proceedings. Magistrates' courts and traditional courts are in each administrative district. As well as a national police force there are local customary law enforcement officers. The death penalty is still in force and was used in 2001.

Religion. Freedom of worship is guaranteed under the Constitution. About 50% of the population is Christian. Non-Christian religions include Bahais, Muslims and Hindus.

Education. Adult literacy rate in 1999 was 76·4% (male, 73·8%; female, 78·9%). Basic free education, introduced in 1986, consists of 7 years of primary and 3 years of junior secondary schooling. In 1994 enrolment in 670 primary schools was 310,128 with 11,371 teachers, and 93,250 pupils at secondary level with 5,678 teachers. In 1993 there were 1,261 students in teacher training colleges. 'Brigades' (community-managed private bodies) provide lower-level vocational training. The Department of Non-Formal Education offers secondary-level correspondence courses and is the executing agency for the National Literacy Programme. There is 1 university (6,673 students in 1995–96).

In 1997 expenditure on education came to 8·6% of GNP and 20·6% of total government spending.

Health. In 1994 there were 16 general hospitals, a mental hospital, 13 health centres, 200 clinics and 310 health posts. There were also 701 stops for mobile health teams. In 1994 there were 339 doctors and 3,329 nurses.

CULTURE

Broadcasting. The government-controlled Radio Botswana broadcasts daily on two channels in English and Setswana. A commercial television company transmits on a 50 km-radius from Gaborone (colour by PAL). There were 237,000 radio and 31,000 TV sets in 1997.

Press. The government owned *Daily News* is distributed free. There are also four weekly independent newspapers. *The Gazette, The Botswana Guardian* and *The Mid-Week Sun* are middle-of-the-road politically. For a more distinctive political slant there is the left-wing *Mmegi* (The Reporter). The press in Botswana is free from censorship.

Tourism. There were 740,000 foreign visitors in 1998 and receipts totalled US$175m.

DIPLOMATIC REPRESENTATIVES
Of Botswana in the United Kingdom (6 Stratford Pl., London, W1C 1AY)
High Commissioner: Roy Warren Blackbeard.

Of the United Kingdom in Botswana (Private Bag 0023, Gaborone)
High Commissioner: David Merry, CBE.

Of Botswana in the USA (1531–1533 New Hampshire Ave., NW, Washington, D.C., 20037)
Ambassador: Lapolang Caeser Lekoa.

Of the USA in Botswana (PO Box 90, Gaborone)
Ambassador: Vacant.
Chargé d'Affaires a.i.: Leslie Bassett.

Of Botswana to the United Nations
Ambassador: Alfred M. Dube.

Of Botswana to the European Union
Ambassador: Sasara George.

FURTHER READING
Central Statistics Office. *Statistical Bulletin* (Quarterly).
Ministry of Information and Broadcasting. *Botswana Handbook.—Kutlwano* (Monthly).
Molomo, M. G. and Mokopakgosi, B. (eds.) *Multi-Party Democracy in Botswana.* Harare, 1991
Perrings, C., *Sustainable Development and Poverty Alleviation in Sub-Saharan Africa: the Case of Botswana.* London, 1995
Wiseman, John, *Botswana.* [Bibliography] ABC-Clio, Oxford and Santa Barbara (CA), 1992

National statistical office: Central Statistics Office, Private Bag 0024, Gaborone.

BRAZIL

República Federativa do
Brasil

Capital: Brasília (Federal District)
Population estimate, 2000: 166·80m.
GDP per capita, 2000: (PPP$) 7,625
HDI/world rank: 0·757/73

KEY HISTORICAL EVENTS

Brazil, South America's largest country, was colonized by the Portuguese in the 16th century and remained under Portuguese rule until independence in 1822. Bursts of economic growth were interspersed by periods of intense political rivalry which held up development. Brasília, supposed to be the catalyst for development of Brazil's huge interior, was built in the late 1950s when there was massive inflation. In 1964 the military took power, inaugurating 20 years of single party rule and censored press.

Brazil's military regime was not as brutal as those of Chile or Argentina, but at its height, around 1968 and 1969, the use of torture was widespread. The generals benefited from the Brazilian economic miracle in the late '60s and '70s when the economy was growing more than 10% every year. Brazil became one of the biggest industrial nations in the world, but unco-ordinated growth spawned corruption and inflation. By the 1980s Brazil had descended into economic chaos. Efforts to bring order to the economy climaxed in 1994 when Fernando Henrique Cardoso, a former finance minister responsible for the 'Plano Real', the economic plan to end inflation, was elected president. He instituted a radical privatization programme, a lowering of trade barriers and tight financial control, a programme which met with success up to 1997 when Brazil was hit by economic turbulence spreading from the Far East. In Oct. 2002 Luiz Inácio Lula da Silva ('Lula'), a left-wing former union leader, came to power on a wave of popular support.

TERRITORY AND POPULATION

Brazil is bounded in the east by the Atlantic and on its northern, western and southern borders by all the South American countries except Chile and Ecuador. The total area (including inland water) is 8,514,215 sq. km. Population as at censuses of 1996 and 2000:

Federal Unit and Capital	Area (sq. km)	Census 1996	Census 2000
North	3,852,968		
Rondônia (Porto Velho)	237,565	1,229,306	1,379,787
Acre (Rio Branco)	152,522	483,593	557,526
Amazonas (Manaus)	1,570,947	2,389,279	2,812,557
Roraima (Boa Vista)	224,118	247,131	324,397
Pará (Belém)	1,247,703	5,510,849	6,192,307
Amapá (Macapá)	142,816	379,459	477,032
Tocantins (Palmas)	277,298	1,048,642	1,157,098
North-East	1,553,917[1]		
Maranhão (São Luís)	331,918	5,222,183	5,651,475
Piauí (Teresina)	251,312	2,673,085	2,843,278
Ceará (Fortaleza)	145,712	6,809,290	7,430,661
Rio Grande do Norte (Natal)	53,077	2,558,660	2,776,782
Paraíba (João Pessoa)	56,341	3,305,616	3,443,825
Pernambuco (Recife)	98,527	7,399,071	7,918,344
Alagoas (Maceió)	27,819	2,633,251	2,822,621
Sergipe (Aracajú)	21,962	1,624,020	1,784,475
Bahia (Salvador)	564,273	12,541,675	13,070,250
South-East	924,574		
Minas Gerais (Belo Horizonte)	586,552	16,672,613	17,891,494
Espírito Santo (Vitória)	46,047	2,802,707	3,097,232
Rio de Janeiro (Rio de Janeiro)	43,797	13,406,308	14,391,282
São Paulo (São Paulo)	248,177	34,119,110	37,032,403

Federal Unit and Capital	Area (sq. km)	Census 1996	Census 2000
South	576,301		
Paraná (Curitíba)	199,282	9,003,804	9,563,458
Santa Catarina (Florianópolis)	95,285	4,875,244	5,356,360
Rio Grande do Sul (Porto Alegre)	281,734	9,634,688	10,187,798
Central West	1,606,446		
Mato Grosso (Cuiabá)	903,386	2,235,832	2,504,353
Mato Grosso do Sul (Campo Grande)	357,140	1,927,834	2,078,001
Goiás (Goiânia)	340,118	4,514,967	5,003,228
Distrito Federal (Brasília)	5,802	1,821,946	2,051,146
Total	8,514,215	157,070,163	169,799,170

[1]Including disputed areas between states of Piauí and Ceará.

Population density, 19·9 per sq. km. The 2000 census showed 83,576,015 males and 86,576,015 females. The urban population comprised 81·2% of the population in 2000.

The UN gives a projected population for 2010 of 191·44m.

The official language is Portuguese.

Population of principal cities (2000 census):

São Paulo	10,434,252	São Luis	870,028	Contagem	538,017
Rio de Janeiro	5,857,904	Maceió	797,759	Ribeirão Preto	504,923
Salvador	2,443,107	Duque de Caxias	775,456	Uberlândia	501,214
Belo Horizonte	2,238,526	Teresina	715,360	Sorocaba	493,468
Fortaleza	2,141,402	Natal	712,317	Cuiabá	483,346
Brasília	2,051,146	São Bernardo do Campo	703,177	Feira de Santana	480,949
Curitíba	1,587,315			Aracajú	461,949
Recife	1,422,905	Campo Grande	663,216	Niterói	459,451
Manaus	1,405,835	Osasco	652,593	Juiz de Fora	456,796
Porto Alegre	1,360,590	Santo André	649,331	São João de Meriti	449,476
Belém	1,280,614	João Pessoa	597,934	Londrina	447,065
Goiânia	1,093,007	Joboatão dos Guararapes	581,556	Joinville	429,604
Guarulhos	1,072,717			Santos	417,983
Campinas	969,396	São José dos Campos	539,313	Campos dos Goytacazes	406,279
Nova Iguaçu	920,599				
São Gonçalo	891,119				

The principal metropolitan areas (census, 1996) were São Paulo (16,583,234), Rio de Janeiro (10,192,097), Belo Horizonte (3,803,249), Porto Alegre (3,246,869), Recife (3,087,967), Salvador (2,709,084), Fortaleza (2,582,820), Curitíba (2,425,361) and Belém (1,485,569).

Approximately 54% of the population of Brazil is white, 40% mixed white and black, and 5% black. There are some 260,000 native Indians, compared to nearly 5m. when the country was discovered in 1500.

Rio de Janeiro: Although situated on the southeast coast and deprived of status as national capital since 1960, Rio is still the pulsing heart of Brazil. Backed by mountains and possessing the famed Copacabana beach, many colonial buildings remain as a reminder of the Portuguese arrival in 1502. A major port for the export of sugar, iron ore and coffee, Rio's roads and city centre buckle and bend under the weight of the teeming population.

São Paulo: Founded by Jesuit missionaries on 25 Jan. 1554, the city is Brazil's biggest and is one of the largest in the world. It is 55 km from the Atlantic coast, southwest of Rio de Janeiro, and is Latin America's foremost industrial centre, accounting for a third of Brazil's total exports. It has an international airport and is served by the nation's busiest port, Santos.

Brasília: The idea of a centralized Brazilian capital to replace vulnerable, coastal Rio was first mooted in 1789 but the site was not selected until 1956. After four years of construction Brasília was inaugurated as the new capital in 1960. Crammed with fascinating modern architecture, original plans to house 500,000 occupants have been outstripped by rapid population growth, necessitating the building of satellite towns.

SOCIAL STATISTICS

1999 estimates: births, 3,295,000 (rate of 20·1 per 1,000 population); deaths, 1,102,000 (6·7 per 1,000 population). Life expectancy in 1999 was 63·9 for males and 71·8 for females. 1999 growth rate, 1·3%; infant mortality (1999), 38 per 1,000 live births; fertility rate, 1999, 2·2 children per woman.

CLIMATE
Because of its latitude, the climate is predominantly tropical, but factors such as altitude, prevailing winds and distance from the sea cause certain variations, though temperatures are not notably extreme. In tropical parts, winters are dry and summers wet, while in Amazonia conditions are constantly warm and humid. The northeast *sertão* is hot and arid, with frequent droughts. In the south and east, spring and autumn are sunny and warm, summers are hot, but winters can be cold when polar air-masses impinge. Brasília, Jan. 72°F (22·3°C), July 68°F (19·8°C). Annual rainfall 60" (1,512 mm). Belém, Jan. 78°F (25·8°C), July 80°F (26·4°C). Annual rainfall 105" (2,664 mm). Manaus, Jan. 79°F (26·1°C), July 80°F (26·7°C). Annual rainfall 92" (2,329 mm). Recife, Jan. 80°F (26·6°C), July 77°F (24·8°C). Annual rainfall 75" (1,907 mm). Rio de Janeiro, Jan. 83°F (28·5°C), July 67°F (19·6°C). Annual rainfall 67" (1,758 mm). São Paulo, Jan. 75°F (24°C), July 57°F (13·7°C). Annual rainfall 62" (1,584 mm). Salvador, Jan. 80°F (26·5°C), July 74°F (23·5°C). Annual rainfall 105" (2,669 mm). Porto Alegre, Jan. 75°F (23·9°C), July 62°F (16·7°C). Annual rainfall 59" (1,502 mm).

CONSTITUTION AND GOVERNMENT
The present Constitution came into force on 5 Oct. 1988, the eighth since independence. The *President* and *Vice-President* are elected for a four-year term. To be elected candidates must secure 51% of the votes, otherwise a second round of voting is held to elect the President between the two most voted candidates. Voting is compulsory for men and women between the ages of 18 and 70, and optional for illiterates, persons from 16 to 18 years old and persons over 70. A referendum on constitutional change was held on 21 April 1993. Turn-out was 80%. 66·1% of votes cast were in favour of retaining a republican form of government, and 10·2% for re-establishing a monarchy. 56·4% favoured an executive presidency, 24·7% parliamentary supremacy.

A constitutional amendment of June 1997 authorizes the re-election of the President for one extra term of four years.

Congress consists of an 81-member *Senate* (three Senators per federal unit) and a 513-member *Chamber of Deputies*. The Senate is two-thirds directly elected (50% of these elected for eight years in rotation) and one-third indirectly elected. The Chamber of Deputies is elected by universal franchise for four years. There is a *Council of the Republic* which is convened only in national emergencies.

Baaklini, A. I., *The Brazilian Legislature and Political System*. London, 1992
Martinez-Lara, J., *Building Democracy in Brazil: the Politics of Constitutional Change*. London, 1996

National Anthem. 'Ouviram do Ipiranga. . .' ('They hear the river Ipiranga'); words by J. O. Duque Estrada, tune by F. M. da Silva.

RECENT ELECTIONS
In the first round of presidential elections held on 6 Oct. 2002, Luiz Inácio Lula da Silva (Workers' Party) won 46·4% of votes cast, twice as many votes as his nearest opponent, José Serra (Brazilian Social Democracy Party), who won 23·2%. The two other candidates, Anthony Garotinho and Ciro Gomes, won 17·9% and 12% respectively. In the run-off held on 27 Oct. 2002 Luiz Inácio Lula da Silva won 61·3% against 38·7% for José Serra, the biggest ever winning margin in a Brazilian presidential election.

Parliamentary elections were also held on 6 Oct. 2002 for both the Chamber of Deputies and the Senate.

In the elections to the 513-seat Chamber of Deputies, the Workers' Party (PT) won 91 seats; the Liberal Front Party (PFL), 84; the Brazilian Democratic Movement Party (PMDB), 74; the Brazilian Social Democracy Party (PSDB), 71; the Brazilian Progressive Party (PPB), 49; the Liberal Party (PL), 26; the Brazilian Labour Party (PTB), 26; the Brazilian Socialist Party (PSB), 22; the Democratic Labour Party (PDT), 21; the Socialist People's Party (PPS), 15; the Communist Party of Brazil (PCdoB), 12; others, 22.

Following the Senate elections the Brazilian Democratic Movement Party had 19 seats; the Liberal Front Party, 19; the Worker's Party, 14; the Brazilian Social Democracy Party, 11; the Democratic Labour Party, 5; the Brazilian Socialist Party, 4; the Liberal Party, 3; the Brazilian Labour Party, 3; the Socialist People's Party, 1; the Democratic Socialist Party, 1; and the Brazilian Progressive Party, 1.

CURRENT ADMINISTRATION
President: Luiz Inácio Lula da Silva 'Lula'; b. 1945 (Workers' Party; sworn in on 1 Jan. 2003).

Vice-President: José Alencar.

In March 2003 the cabinet was composed as follows:

Minister of Agrarian Development: Miguel Rossetto. *Agriculture:* João Roberto Rodrigues. *Communications:* Miro Teixeira. *Culture:* Gilberto Gil. *Defence:* José Viegas Filho. *Development, Industry and Foreign Trade:* Luiz Fernando Furlan. *Education:* Cristovam Buarque. *Environment:* Marina Silva. *Finance:* Antônio Palocci. *Foreign Relations:* Celso Amorim. *Health:* Humberto Costa. *Justice:* Márcio Tomaz Bastos. *Labour:* Jaques Wagner. *Mines and Energy:* Dilma Rousseff. *National Integration:* Ciro Gomes. *Planning and Administration:* Guido Mantega. *Science and Technology:* Roberto Amarral. *Sport:* Agnelo Queiroz. *Tourism:* Walfrido Mares Guia. *Transport:* Anderson Adauto. *Urban Affairs:* Olívio Dutra. *Social Assistance:* Benedita da Silva. *Social Welfare:* Ricardo Berzoini.

Government Website: http://www.brasil.gov.br

DEFENCE
Conscription is for 12 months, extendable by six months.

In 2001 defence expenditure totalled US$10,511m. (US$61 per capita), representing 2·1% of GDP. In 1985 expenditure was just US$5,854m.

Army. There are seven military commands and 12 military regions. Strength, 2002, 189,000 (40,000 conscripts). There is an additional potential first-line 1,115,000 of whom 400,000 are subject to immediate recall. There is a second-line reserve of 225,000 and a paramilitary Public Police Force of some 385,600.

Navy. The principal ship of the Navy and Brazil's only aircraft carrier is the 32,700-tonne *São Paulo* (formerly the French *Foch*), commissioned in 1963 and purchased in 2000. There are also four diesel submarines and 14 frigates including four bought from the UK in 1995 and 1996. Fleet Air Arm personnel only fly helicopters.

Naval bases are at Rio de Janeiro, Recife, Belém, Floriancholis and Salvador, with river bases at Ladario and Manaus.

Active personnel, 2002, totalled 48,600 (3,200 conscripts), including 13,900 Marines and 1,150 in Naval Aviation.

Air Force. The Air Force has an air defence command, tactical command, maritime command, transport command and training command. Personnel strength (2002) 50,000 (5,000 conscripts). There were 264 combat aircraft in 2002, including Mirage F-103s and F-5Es, and 29 armed helicopters.

INTERNATIONAL RELATIONS
Brazil is a member of the UN, WTO, BIS, OAS, Inter-American Development Bank, LAIA, Mercosur and the Antarctic Treaty.

ECONOMY
Agriculture accounted for 8·4% of GDP in 1998, industry 46·1% and services 50·3%.

Overview. With strong performance in 2002, economic policy for 2003 includes major pension reforms and measures to combat poverty. In 2002 the IMF approved a US$30·4bn. stand-by credit agreement. The government aims for a budget surplus of 4·25% for 2003 to cut its public debt of 56% of GDP. Since 1999 there has been a free-floating exchange rate and monetary policy has been led by a 4% inflation target. However, in 2003 inflation reached double figures for the first time since 1995. There are plans to make the central bank autonomous.

Currency. The unit of currency is the *real* (equal to 100 *centavos*), which was introduced on 1 July 1994 to replace the former *cruzeiro real* at a rate of 1 real

(R$1) = 2,750 cruzeiros reais (CR$2,750). The *real* was devalued in Sept. 1994, March 1995, June 1995 and Jan. 1999. Inflation fell from nearly 2,076% in 1994 to 3·2% in 1998, before rising to 6·8% in 2001. In June 2002 foreign exchange reserves were US$41,838m.; gold reserves totalled 0·46m. troy oz (4·57m. troy oz in 1995). Total money supply in May 2002 was R$74,988m.

Budget. 2000 (in R$1m.): revenue was 235,062 (158,781 in 1999) and expenditure 247,253 (163,709 in 1999). Internal federal debt, July 1996, was R$176,478m. Internal states and municipalities (main securities outstanding), R$49,672m.

Performance. Real GDP growth was 4·5% in 2000 but only 1·5% in 2001. In March 1999 an IMF agreement introduced a tight monetary policy with an emphasis on reducing the ratio of debt to GDP. Total GDP in 2001 was US$502·5bn.

Banking and Finance. On 31 Dec. 1964 the Banco Central do Brasil (*President*, Henrique Meirelles) was founded as the national bank of issue.

The Bank of Brazil (founded in 1853 and reorganized in 1906) is a state-owned commercial bank; it had 2,927 branches in 2000 throughout the country. The largest private banks are Banco Bradesca, Banco Itaú and Unibanco. On 31 Dec. 1996 deposits were R$33,604m. In 2000 there were 190 banking establishments with 14,892 branches (26 commercial banks with 3,352 branches and 164 multiple banks with 11,540 branches), plus 19 investment banks with 45 branches.

In Nov. 1998 the IMF announced a US$41·5bn. financing package to help shore up the Brazilian economy. In Aug. 2001 it gave approval for a new US$15bn. stand-by credit, and in Aug. 2002 granted an additional US$30bn. loan to try to prevent a financial meltdown that was threatening to devastate the region.

Brazil received US$22·5bn. worth of foreign direct investment in 2001, down from a record US$33·5bn. in 2000. Spain was the leading investor in 2000, providing 21·3% of foreign capital, ahead of the USA.

There are nine stock exchanges of which Rio de Janeiro and São Paulo are the most important. All except São Paulo are linked in the National Electronic Trading System (Senn).

Weights and Measures. The metric system has been compulsory since 1872.

ENERGY AND NATURAL RESOURCES

Environment. According to the *World Bank Atlas* Brazil's carbon dioxide emissions in 1998 were the equivalent of 1·8 tonnes per capita.

Brazil has the world's biggest river system and about a quarter of the world's primary rainforest. Current environmental issues are deforestation in the Amazon Basin, air and water pollution in Rio de Janeiro and São Paulo (the world's fourth largest city), and land degradation and water pollution caused by improper mining activities. Contaminated drinking water causes 70% of child deaths.

Electricity. Hydro-electric power accounts for over 90% of Brazil's total electricity output. Although Brazil was only the 10th largest electricity producer overall in the world in 1998, it was the 3rd largest producer of hydro-electric power. Installed electric capacity (1998) 61,312 MW, of which 55,857 MW were hydro-electric. In July 2001 the government announced that supply would be increased by 20,000 MW by the end of 2003 to help solve the country's worst energy crisis in modern times. There are two nuclear power plants, supplying some 1·5% of total output. Production (2000) 348,000 GWh (95% hydro-electric). Consumption per capita in 1998 was 1,846 kWh.

Oil and Gas. There are 13 oil refineries, of which 11 are state-owned. Crude oil production (2000), 71,843,896 cu. metres. Crude oil reserves were estimated at 7·3bn. bbls. in 1999. Brazil began to open its markets in 1999 by inviting foreign companies to drill for oil, and in 2000 the monopoly of the state-owned Petrobrás on importing oil produucts was removed.

Gas production (2000), 13,327,562,000 cu. metres with reserves (in 1997) of 230bn. cu. metres. One of the most significant developments has been the construction of the 3,150-km Bolivia–Brazil gas pipeline, one of Latin America's biggest infrastructure projects, costing around US$2bn. (£1·2bn.). The pipeline runs from the Bolivian interior across the Brazilian border at Puerto Suárez-Corumbá to the far southern port city of Porto Alegre. Gas from Bolivia began to be pumped to São Paulo in 1999.

Minerals. The chief minerals are bauxite, gold, iron ore, manganese, nickel, phosphates, platinum, tin and uranium. Output figures, 1999 (in tonnes): phosphate rock, 27,000,000; bauxite, 12,880,000; salt, 5,958,000; hard coal (1996), 5,647,000; asbestos (crude ore), 3,950,000; manganese ore, 1,674,000; aluminium, 1,245,000; magnesite, 868,604; graphite, 650,000; chrome (crude ore), 420,000; barytes, 48,789; zirconium, 29,448; tin (tin content), 13,202; lead (lead content in concentrate), 10,281; mica, 5,000; quartz crystal, 1,470. Deposits of coal exist in Rio Grande do Sul, Santa Catarina and Paraná. Total reserves were estimated at 11,950m. tonnes in 2000.

Iron is found chiefly in Minas Gerais, notably the Cauê Peak at Itabira. The government is opening up iron-ore deposits in Carajás, in the northern state of Pará, with estimated reserves of 35,000m. tonnes, representing a 66% concentration of high-grade iron ore. Total output of iron ore, 1999, mainly from the Vale do Rio Doce mine at Itabira, was 194m. tonnes. Brazil is the second largest producer of iron ore after China.

Gold is chiefly from Pará, Mato Grosso and Minas Gerais; total production (1999), 48·7 tonnes. Silver output (1999), 42 tonnes. Diamond output in 1998 was 900,000 carats, with the principal output coming from Minas Gerais and Mato Grosso.

Agriculture. In 1995, 30·22m. people depended on agriculture. There were 4·86m. farms in 1995. There were 53·3m. ha of arable land in 1998 and 12·0m. ha of permanent crops. 2·66m. ha were irrigated.

Production (in tonnes):

	1999	2000		1999	2000
Apples	4,724,062	5,800,627	Onions	990,093	1,136,505
Bananas			Oranges		
(1,000 bunches)	552,778	630,149	(1,000 fruits)	113,841,460	108,552,006
Beans	2,817,348	3,005,591	Pineapples	1,175,199	1,348,702
Cassava	20,891,531	23,203,442	Potatoes	2,843,273	2,608,173
Coconut			Rice	11,782,662	11,144,123
(1,000 fruits)	1,148,556	1,233,191	Soya	30,901,142	32,679,270
Coffee	3,267,892	3,651,331	Sugarcane	337,165,474	317,601,477
Cotton	1,413,920	1,922,997	Tomatoes	3,251,046	3,072,788
Grapes	894,965	978,578	Wheat	2,438,197	1,669,839
Maize	32,037,624	31,717,126			

Brazil is the world's leading producer of sugarcane, oranges and coffee (and the second largest consumer of coffee after the USA). Harvested coffee area, 1998, 2,081,591 ha, principally in the states of Minas Gerais, Espírito Santo, São Paulo and Paraná. Harvested cocoa area, 1998, 709,997 ha. Bahia furnished 84% of the output in 1998. Two crops a year are grown. Harvested castor-bean area, 1998, 60,979 ha. Tobacco is grown chiefly in Rio Grande do Sul and Santa Catarina.

Rubber is produced chiefly in the states of Acre, Amazonas, Rondônia and Pará. Output, 1997 (preliminary), 32,959 tonnes (natural). Brazilian consumption of rubber in 1996 was 150,676 tonnes. Plantations of tung trees were established in 1930; output, 1995, 993 tonnes.

Livestock, 2000: cattle, 169·9m.; pigs, 31·6m.; sheep, 14·8m.; goats, 9·3m.; horses, 5·8m.; mules, 1·35m.; asses, 1·24m.; chickens, 843m. Livestock products, 2000 (in 1,000 tonnes): beef and veal, 6,460; pork, bacon and ham, 1,804; poultry meat, 6,020; cow's milk, 22,134; hen's eggs, 1,400; wool, 24; honey, 18.

Forestry. With forest lands covering 5,439,053 sq. km in 2000, only Russia had a larger area of forests. In 1995, 65·2% of the total land area of Brazil was under forests, down from 66·7% in 1990. In 1990 the total area under forests was 5,639,000 sq. km. The loss of 128,000 sq. km of forests between 1990 and 1995 was the biggest in any country in the world over the same period, and more than twice the area lost in Indonesia, the country with the second biggest reduction in forest area. Nevertheless, an independent study commissioned by NASA found that the rate of deforestation was on the decline and stated that the government had been extremely active since 1990 in reducing the rate of illegal deforestation. In 1996 the government ruled that Amazonian landowners could log only 20% of their holdings, instead of 50%, as had previously been permitted. Timber production in 1999 totalled 197·90m. cu. metres. In 1997 the government's environmental agency,

Ibama, levied fines of nearly US$11m. on illicit loggers. In 2001 Ibama seized 25,600 cu. metres (US$40m. worth) of illegally-cut mahogany.

Fisheries. In 2000 the fishing industry had a catch of 693,710 tonnes (74% sea fishing and 26% inland).

INDUSTRY

The leading companies by market capitalization in Brazil, excluding banking and finance, in Jan. 2002 were: Petróleo Brasileiro SA (Petrobras), R$56bn.; Companhia Vale do Rio Doce, the world's largest iron ore producer (R$23bn.); and Centrais Elétricas Brasileiras SA (Eletrobrás), the electricity holding company (R$19bn.).

The main industries are textiles, shoes, chemicals, cement, lumber, iron ore, tin, steel, aircraft, motor vehicles and parts, and other machinery and equipment. The National Iron and Steel Co. at Volta Redonda, State of Rio de Janeiro, furnishes a substantial part of Brazil's steel. Total output, 2000: crude steel, 27,763,000 tonnes; rolled steel, 18,201,000 tonnes; cast iron, 27,854,000 tonnes; cement, 39,559,000 tonnes; paper, 7·1m. tonnes. Production of rubber tyres for motor vehicles (1994), 33,820,000 units; motor vehicles (2000), 1,667,985 units; TV sets (2000), 5,289,000 units; refrigerators (2000), 3,239,000 units; distillate fuel oil (1997), 24,236,000 tonnes; residual fuel oil (1997), 14,993,000 tonnes; beer (1997), 6,658·2m. litres; soft drinks (1997), 5,460·2m. litres.

Labour. The workforce in 1998 numbered 69,963,113, of whom 16,338,100 worked in agriculture and 13,210,555 worked in industry (including the construction industry). A constitutional amendment of Oct. 1996 prohibits the employment of children under 14 years. However, in 2000 more than 14% of children between 10 and 14 were working. In 1999 there was a minimum monthly wage of R$136. In 2000, 7·1% of the workforce was unemployed (7·5% in 1999).

Trade Unions. The main union is the United Workers' Centre (CUT).

INTERNATIONAL TRADE

In 1990 Brazil repealed most of its protectionist legislation. Import tariffs on some 13,000 items were reduced in 1995. Since 1991 direct foreign investment on equal terms with domestic has been permitted. Foreign investment reached an annual average of US$21·6bn. in 1997–98, much of it as a result of the privatization programme. In 1991 the government permitted an annual US$100m. of foreign debt to be converted into funds for environmental protection. Total foreign debt in 2000 was US$237,953m. (the highest in the world).

Imports and Exports. Imports and exports for calendar years (in US$1m.):

	1997	1998	1999	2000
Imports	61,347	57,733	49,272	55,783
Exports	52,987	51,140	48,011	55,086

Principal imports in 1999 were: machinery and transport equipment, 42·9%; chemicals, 18·4%; manufactured goods, 10·0%; petroleum and related products, 9·0%; and food and live animals, 6·9%.

Principal exports in 1999 were: machinery and transport equipment, 23·7%; food and live animals, 21·6%, including coffee (5·1%), oilcake (3·1%), orange juice (2·6%) and sugar (2·4%); iron ore, 5·7%; footwear, 2·7%; and aluminium, 2·5%. Brazil is the world's leading sugar exporter.

Main export markets, 1999: USA, 23%; Argentina, 11%; Netherlands, 5%; Germany, 5%; Japan, 5%; Italy, 4%. Main import suppliers: USA, 24%; Argentina, 12%; Germany, 9%; Japan, 5%; Italy, 5%; France, 4%.

COMMUNICATIONS

Roads. In 2000 there were 1,724,929 km of roads, of which 164,988 km were paved. In 2000 there were 33,707,640 vehicles registered. Some 56% of freight is carried by truck.

Rail. The Brazilian railways have largely been privatized: all six branches of the large RFFSA network were under private management by the end of Aug. 1997. In 2000 RFFSA (Rede Ferroviária Federal S.A.) had a route-length of 21,316 km and FERROBAN (Ferrovias Bandeirantes S.A.) a route-length of 4,235 km. Total route-length nationwide was 29,283 km in 2000. Two-thirds is narrow (1·0 metre) gauge, the rest either broad (1·60) or a mix of the two. Passenger-km travelled in 1996 came to 13,999m. and freight tonne-km to 128·79bn.

There are several important independent freight railways, including the Vitoria à Minas (898 km in 1993), the Ferroeste (238 km), the Carajas (1,076 km in 1991) and the Amapa (194 km). There are metros in São Paulo (44 km), Rio de Janeiro (23 km), Belo Horizonte (14 km), Porto Alegre (28 km) and Brasília (38·5 km).

Civil Aviation. There are major international airports at Rio de Janeiro-Galeão (Antonio Carlos Jobim International) and São Paulo (Guarulhos) and some international flights from Brasília, Porto Alegre, Recife and Salvador. The three main airlines are Viação Aérea Rio Grande do Sul (Varig), with 33% of the market, TAM and Viação Aérea São Paulo (Vasp). In 1999 Varig carried 10,064,000 passengers, TAM carried 4,775,000 passengers and VASP 4,190,000 passengers.

Brazil's busiest airport is Guarulhos (São Paulo), which handled 13,163,000 passengers in 2000 (up from 6·45m. in 1992) and 348,200 tonnes of freight, followed by Congonhas (São Paulo) with 7,757,514 passengers (in 1998), and Rio de Janeiro with 5,416,000 passengers and 117,900 tonnes of freight in 2000.

Shipping. Inland waterways, mostly rivers, are open to navigation over some 43,000 km. Santos and Rio de Janeiro are the two leading ports; there are 19 other large ports. During 1997, 28,973 vessels entered and cleared the Brazilian ports; vessels totalling 82,593,000 NRT entered ports and vessels totalling 192,889,000 NRT cleared. In 1997 Santos handled 0·85m. container units. In 1995 the merchant fleet comprised 249 vessels totalling 10·22m. DWT, representing 1·55% of the world's total fleet tonnage. 16 vessels (14·67% of tonnage) were registered under foreign flags. In 1998, total tonnage registered, 4·17m. GRT, including oil tankers 1·83m. GRT.

Telecommunications. The state-owned telephone system was privatized in 1998. There were 30,926,300 telephone main lines in 2000 (181·8 per 1,000 inhabitants). Mobile phone services were opened to the private sector in 1996. By March 2001 there were 24·4m. mobile phone subscribers, with Telefónica/Portugal Telecom having 41·4% of the market share, Bell South 17·6% and Telecom Italia Mobile 16·8%. There were 13·98m. Internet users in Sept. 2002, up from 3·1m. in July 1999. In 2000 PCs numbered 7·5m. (44·1 per 1,000 persons) and in 1997 there were 500,000 fax machines. There were still 28,000 telex subscribers in 1996, although telex usage has declined considerably in recent years.

Postal Services. In 2000 there were 25,957 post offices. A total of 6,009,791,111 items were handled in 1996.

SOCIAL INSTITUTIONS

Justice. There is a Supreme Federal Court of Justice at Brasília composed of 11 judges, and a Supreme Court of Justice; all judges are appointed by the President with the approval of the Senate. There are also Regional Federal Courts, Labour Courts, Electoral Courts and Military Courts. Each state organizes its own courts and judicial system in accordance with the federal Constitution.

In Dec. 1999 President Cardoso created the country's first intelligence agency (the Brazilian Intelligence Agency) under civilian rule. It replaced informal networks which were a legacy of the military dictatorship, and will help authorities crack down on organized drug gangs.

The prison population was 167,000 in Dec. 1997 (105 per 100,000 of national population). Brazil's annual murder rate, in excess of 25 per 100,000 population, is on the increase and is more than five times that of the USA.

Religion. In 1997 there were estimated to be 115,500,000 Roman Catholics (including syncretic Afro-Catholic cults having spiritualist beliefs and rituals) and 37,000,000 Evangelical Protestants, with 7,200,000 followers of other religions. Roman Catholic estimates in 1991 suggest that 90% were baptized Roman Catholic but only 35% were regular attenders. In 1991 there were 338 bishops and some 14,000 priests. In Feb. 2001 there were eight Cardinals. There are numerous sects, some evangelical, some African-derived (e.g. *Candomble*).

Education. Elementary education is compulsory from seven to 14. Adult literacy in 1999 was 84·9 % (male, 84·8%; female, 84·9%). There were 50,646 literacy classes in 1993 with 1,584,147 students and 75,413 teachers. In 2000 there were 84,617 pre-primary schools, with 4,421,332 pupils and 228,335 teachers; 181,504 primary schools, with 35,717,948 pupils and 1,538,011 teachers; 19,456 secondary schools, with 8,192,948 pupils and 430,467 teachers; and 1,097 higher education institutions, with 2,369,945 students and 173,836 teachers. In 1999, 95·7% of children between the ages of 7 and 14 were enrolled at schools. However, only a third of Brazilian teenagers attend school. In Jan. 2001 President Cardoso announced a National Education Plan that involves teaching 10m. young people and adults to read and write within five years and eradicating illiteracy within a decade.

The tertiary education sector includes 114 universities (53 private, 37 federal, 20 state and 4 municipal), 85 private and 3 municipal college faculty federations, and 671 other higher education institutions (514 private, 80 municipal, 57 state and 20 federal).

In 1995 total expenditure on education came to 5·2% of GNP.

Health. In 1999 there were 48,815 hospitals and clinics (26,209 private), of which 7,806 were for in-patients (5,193 private). There were a total of 484,945 hospital beds in 1999 (341,871 private). In 1997 there were 205,828 doctors, 160,000 dentists (1993) and (1992) 57,047 pharmacists.

Brazil has been one of the most successful countries in the developing world in the campaign against AIDS. It is reported to have reduced AIDS-related deaths by 40% between 1996 and 2000.

CULTURE

Broadcasting. In 1995 there were 2,033 radio and 119 television stations (colour by PAL M). In 1997 there were 71m. radio and 36·5m. television receivers.

Press. In 1996 there were 380 daily newspapers with a combined circulation of 6,472,000, at a rate of 40 per 1,000 inhabitants.

Tourism. In 1999, 5,107,000 tourists visited Brazil. Argentina is the country of origin of the largest number of visitors, ahead of the USA, Uruguay and Paraguay. Receipts in 1999 totalled US$3·99bn.

Festivals. New Year's Eve in Rio de Janeiro is always marked with special celebrations, with a major fireworks display over the bay at Copacabana Beach. Immediately afterwards, preparations start for Carnival, which in 2004 will begin on 21 Feb., when the parade of samba schools takes place.

Libraries. In 1993 Brazil had a National Library with 5·28m. volumes, and in 1994 a total of 2,739 public libraries.

DIPLOMATIC REPRESENTATIVES
Of Brazil in the United Kingdom (32 Green St., London, W1Y 4AT)
Ambassador: Vacant.
Chargé d'Affaires a.i.: Piragibe Tarragô.

Of the United Kingdom in Brazil (Setor De Embaixadas Sul, Quadro 801, Conjunto K, CP70.408-900, Brasília, DF *or* Av. das Nações, CP07-0586, 70.359, Brasília, DF)
Ambassador: Sir Roger Bridgland Bone, KCMG.

Of Brazil in the USA (3006 Massachusetts Ave., NW, Washington, D.C. 20008)
Ambassador: Rubens Antônio Barbosa.

Of the USA in Brazil (Av. das Nações, Lote 03, Quadra 801, CEP: 70403-900, Brasília, D.F.)
Ambassador: Donna Jean Hrinak.

Of Brazil to the United Nations
Ambassador: Ronaldo Mota Sardenberg.

Of Brazil to the European Union
Ambassador: José Alfredo Graca Lima.

FURTHER READING
Instituto Brasileiro de Geografia e Estatística. *Anuário Estatístico do Brasil.—Censo Demográfico de 1991.—Indicadores IBGE.* Monthly

BRAZIL

Boletim do Banco Central do Brasil. Banco Central do Brasil. Brasília. Monthly

Baer, W., *The Brazilian Economy: Growth and Development.* 4th ed. New York, 1995

Dickenson, John, *Brazil.* [Bibliography] 2nd ed. ABC-Clio, Oxford and Santa Barbara (CA), 1997

Eakin, Marshall C., *Brazil: The Once and Future Country.* New York, 1997

Fausto, Boris, *A Concise History of Brazil.* CUP, 1999

Font, M. A., *Coffee, Contention and Change in the Making of Modern Brazil.* Oxford, 1990

Guirmaraes, R. P., *Politics and Environment in Brazil: Ecopolitics of Development in the Third World.* New York, 1991

Stepan, A. (ed.) *Democratizing Brazil: Problems of Transition and Consolidation.* OUP, 1993

Turner, Barry, (ed.) *Latin America Profiled.* Macmillan, London, 2000

Welch, J. H., *Capital Markets in the Development Process: the Case of Brazil.* London, 1992

For other more specialized titles see under CONSTITUTION AND GOVERNMENT *above.*

National library: Biblioteca Nacional, Avenida Rio Branco 21939, Rio de Janeiro, RJ.

National statistical office: Instituto Brasileiro de Geografia e Estatística (IBGE), Rua General Canabarro 666, 20.271-201 Maracanã, Rio de Janeiro, RJ.

Website: http://www.ibge.gov.br

BRUNEI

Negara Brunei Darussalam—
State of Brunei Darussalam

Capital: Bandar Seri Begawan
Population estimate, 2000: 328,000
GDP per capita, 2000: (PPP$) 16,779
HDI/world rank: 0·856/32

KEY HISTORICAL EVENTS
Brunei became an independent Sultanate in the 15th century, controlling most of Borneo, its neighbouring islands and the Suhi Archipelago. By the end of the 16th century, however, the power of Brunei was on the wane. By the middle of the 19th century the State had been reduced to its present limits. Brunei became a British protectorate in 1888. The discovery of major oilfields in the western end of the State in the 1920s brought economic stability to Brunei and created a new style of life for the population. Brunei was occupied by the Japanese in 1941 and liberated by the Australians in 1945. Self-government was introduced in 1959 but Britain retained responsibility for foreign affairs. In 1965 constitutional changes were made which led to direct elections for a new Legislative Council. Full independence and sovereignty were gained in Jan. 1984.

TERRITORY AND POPULATION
Brunei, on the coast of Borneo, is bounded in the northwest by the South China Sea and on all other sides by Sarawak (Malaysia), which splits it into two parts, the smaller portion forming the Temburong district. Area, 2,226 sq. miles (5,765 sq. km). Population (1991 census) 260,482; 1996 estimate, 299,900, giving a density of 52 per sq. km.

The UN gives a projected population for 2010 of 388,000.

In 1999, 71·7% of the population lived in urban areas. The four districts are Brunei/Muara (1995: 195,000), Belait (60,000), Tutong (32,500), Temburong (8,500). The capital is Bandar Seri Begawan (estimate 1999: 85,000); other large towns are Kuala Belait (1991: 21,163) and Seria (1991: 21,082). Ethnic groups include Malays 64% and Chinese 20%.

The official language is Malay but English is in use.

SOCIAL STATISTICS
1999 births, 7,360; deaths, 871. Rates, 1999: birth per 1,000 population, 22·3; death, 2·6. There were 1,874 marriages in 1993. Life expectancy in 1999: males, 73·6 years; females, 78·3. Annual population growth rate, 1990–99, 2·5%. Infant mortality, 1999, 6·0 per 1,000 live births; fertility rate, 1999, 2·9 children per woman.

CLIMATE
The climate is tropical marine, hot and moist, but nights are cool. Humidity is high and rainfall heavy, varying from 100" (2,500 mm) on the coast to 200" (5,000 mm) inland. There is no dry season. Bandar Seri Begawan, Jan. 80°F (26·7°C), July 82°F (27·8°C). Annual rainfall 131" (3,275 mm).

CONSTITUTION AND GOVERNMENT
The Sultan and Yang Di Pertuan of Brunei Darussalam is HM Paduka Seri Baginda Sultan Haji Hassanal Bolkiah Mu'izzadin Waddaulah. He succeeded on 5 Oct. 1967 at his father's abdication and was crowned on 1 Aug. 1968. On 10 Aug. 1998 his son, Oxford-graduate Prince Al-Muhtadee Billah, was inaugurated as Crown Prince and heir apparent.

On 29 Sept. 1959 the Sultan promulgated a Constitution, but parts of it have been in abeyance since Dec. 1962. There is no legislature and supreme power is vested in the Sultan.

National Anthem. 'Ya Allah, lanjutkan lah usia' ('O God, long live His Majesty'); words by P. Rahim, tune by I. Sagap.

CURRENT ADMINISTRATION
In March 2003 the Council of Ministers was composed as follows:
Prime Minister, Minister of Defence and of Finance: The Sultan.
Minister of Foreign Affairs: Prince Haji Mohammad Bolkiah. *Home Affairs:* Pehin Dato Haji Isa bin Ibrahim. *Education:* Pehin Dato Haji Abdul Aziz bin Umar. *Health:* Ahmed bin Jumaat. *Industry and Primary Resources:* Pehin Dato Haji Abdul Rahman bin Mohammad Taib. *Religious Affairs:* Pehin Dato Dr Haji Mohammad Zain bin Serudin. *Development:* Pengiran Dato Dr Haji Ismail bin Damit. *Culture, Youth and Sports:* Pehin Dato Haji Hussain bin Mohammad Yusof. *Communications:* Dato Haji Zakaria bin Sulaiman.

Government Website: http://www.brunei.gov.bn/

DEFENCE
In 2000 military expenditure totalled US$348m. (US$1,060 per capita), representing 5·8% of GDP.

Army. The armed forces are known as the Task Force and contain the naval and air elements. Only Malays are eligible for service. Strength (1999) 3,900.

There is a 2,000-strong paramilitary Gurkha reserve unit.

Navy. The Royal Brunei Armed Forces Flotilla includes three fast missile-armed attack craft. Personnel in 1999 numbered 700. The Flotilla is based at Muara.

Air Wing. The Air Wing of the Royal Brunei Armed Forces was formed in 1965. Personnel (1999), 400. There are no combat aircraft.

INTERNATIONAL RELATIONS
Brunei is a member of the UN, WTO, the Commonwealth, APEC, Mekong Group, ASEAN and the OIC.

ECONOMY
In 1998 agriculture accounted for 2·8% of GDP, industry 44·5% and services 52·7%. The fall in oil prices in 1997–98 led to the setting up of an Economic Council to advise the Sultan on reforms. An investigation was mounted into the affairs of the Amedeo Corporation, Brunei's largest private company run by Prince Jefri, the Sultan's brother.

Currency. The unit of currency is the *Brunei dollar* (BND) of 100 cents, which is at parity with the Singapore dollar (also legal tender). Inflation in 2001 was 1·1%.

Budget. Revenues in 1995 were an estimated US$2·5bn. Expenditure in 2000 was put at US$3·2bn.

Performance. Real GDP growth was 2·8% in 2000 but the general downturn in the world economy resulted in negative growth of 0·4% in 2001. Total GDP in 1998 was US$4·9bn.

Banking and Finance. The Brunei Currency Board is the note-issuing monetary authority. In 1993 there were seven banks (one incorporated in Brunei), with a total of 33 branches. Savings deposits totalled B$999·3m. in 1993 and fixed time deposits B$1,935·4m. Total bank assets in 1993 were B$6,567·7m.

ENERGY AND NATURAL RESOURCES
Environment. According to the *World Bank Atlas* Brunei's carbon dioxide emissions were the equivalent of 17·1 tonnes per capita in 1998.

Electricity. Installed capacity was 344,000 kW in 1995. Production in 1998 was 2·56bn. kWh and consumption per capita was 7,676 kWh.

Oil and Gas. The Seria oilfield, discovered in 1929, has passed its peak production. The high level of crude oil production is maintained through the increase of offshore oilfields production. Production was 55m. bbls. in 1996. The crude oil is exported directly, and only a small amount is refined at Seria for domestic uses. There were proven oil reserves of 1·4bn. bbls. in 1999.

Natural gas is produced (11·3bn. cu. metres in 1999) at one of the largest liquefied natural gas plants in the world and is exported to Japan. There were proven reserves of 390bn. cu. metres in 1999.

Agriculture. In 1998 there were 3,000 ha of arable land and 4,000 ha of permanent crops. The main crops produced in 2000 were (estimates, in 1,000 tonnes) vegetables, 9; fruit, 6 (notably bananas and pineapples); cassava, 2.

Livestock in 2000: cattle, 2,000; buffaloes, 6,000; pigs, 6,000; goats, 4,000; chickens, 6m.

Forestry. Forests covered 448,000 ha, or 82·4% of the total land area, in 1995 (down from 85% in 1990). Most of the interior is under forest, containing large potential supplies of serviceable timber. Timber production in 1999 was 296,000 cu. metres.

Fisheries. The 2000 catch totalled 2,487 tonnes, almost exclusively from marine waters.

INDUSTRY

Brunei depends primarily on its oil industry. Other minor products are rubber, pepper, sawn timber, gravel and animal hides. Local industries include boatbuilding, cloth weaving and the manufacture of brass- and silverware.

Labour. The labour force totalled 131,000 in 1996 (66% males).

INTERNATIONAL TRADE

Imports and Exports. In 1998 (and 1997) imports totalled US$1,566·0m. (US$2,110·4m.); exports US$2,306·8m. (US$2,657·1m.). In 1998 liquefied natural gas accounted for 52·6% of exports, and crude oil 33·7%. In 1998 Singapore supplied 23% of imports, Malaysia 17% and the USA 15%. Japan took 53% of all exports, South Korea 18%, and USA 9%.

COMMUNICATIONS

Roads. There were in 1996, 1,712 km of roads, of which 75% were surfaced. The main road connects Bandar Seri Begawan with Kuala Belait and Seria. In 1998 there were 94,136 private cars and 13,803 vans and trucks. There were 50 fatalities in road accidents in 1998.

Civil Aviation. Brunei International Airport handled 949,000 passengers (all international) in 1999. The national carrier is the state-owned Royal Brunei Airlines (RBA). In 1998 RBA operated services to Abu Dhabi, Balikpapan, Bangkok, Beijing, Brisbane, Calcutta, Darwin, Denpasar Bali, Dubai, Frankfurt, Hong Kong, Jakarta, Jeddah, Kota Kinabalu, Kuala Lumpur, Kuching, Labuan, London, Manila, Miri, Mulu, Osaka, Perth, Singapore, Surabaya and Taipei. In 1997 RBA flew 35·3m. km, carrying 876,800 passengers (all on international flights).

Shipping. Regular shipping services operate from Singapore, Hong Kong, Sarawak and Sabah to Bandar Seri Begawan, and there is a daily passenger ferry between Bandar Seri Begawan and Labuan. 97 sea-going vessels were licensed in 1993. In 1995 merchant shipping totalled 366,000 GRT.

Telecommunications. There is a telephone network (80,500 telephone main lines in 2000, or 245·2 per 1,000 inhabitants) linking the main centres. In 1999 mobile phone subscribers numbered 49,100 (142 per 1,000 persons), and in 2000 there were 23,000 PCs (70·1 for every 1,000 persons). There were 4,000 Internet users in Dec. 1999 and 2,000 fax machines in 1995.

Postal Services. There were 17 post offices in 1993.

SOCIAL INSTITUTIONS

Justice. The Supreme Court comprises a High Court and a Court of Appeal and the Magistrates' Courts. The High Court receives appeals from subordinate courts in the districts and is itself a court of first instance for criminal and civil cases. The Judicial Committee of the Privy Council in London is the final court of appeal. Shariah Courts deal with Islamic law. 25,310 crimes were reported in 1993.

The Royal Brunei Police numbers 1,750 officers and men (1997). In addition, there are 500 additional police officers mostly employed on static guard duties. The population in penal institutions in Oct. 1998 was 285 (90 per 100,000 of national population).

Religion. The official religion is Islam. In 1991, 67% of the population were Muslim (mostly Malays), 13% Buddhists and 10% Christian.

Education. The government provides free education to all citizens from pre-school up to the highest level at local and overseas universities and institutions. In 1994 there were 165 kindergartens and schools, with 10,717 children and 506 teachers in kindergartens. In 1996 there were 43,291 pupils at primary schools. There were 2,961 teachers in secondary schools for 30,470 pupils; and 6 technical and vocational colleges (one teacher training college) with 1,966 students and 370 teachers.

In 1993 the University of Brunei Darussalam (founded 1985) had 1,138 students and 207 teachers. An institute of advanced education had 310 students and 71 teachers.

Adult literacy rate, 1999, 91·0% (male, 94·3%; female, 87·3%).

Health. Medical and health services are free to citizens and those in government service and their dependants. Citizens are sent overseas, at government expense, for medical care not available in Brunei. Flying medical services are provided to remote areas. In 1995 there were ten hospitals; there were 251 doctors, 38 dentists, 15 pharmacists, 278 midwives and 1,228 nursing personnel.

CULTURE

Broadcasting. Radio Television Brunei operates on medium- and shortwaves in Malay, English, Chinese and Nepali. Number of receivers (1997): radio 93,000 and television 77,000 (colour by PAL).

Press. In 1996 there was one local newspaper with a circulation of 21,000.

Tourism. In 1998 there were 964,000 foreign tourists. Receipts totalled US$37m.

DIPLOMATIC REPRESENTATIVES

Of Brunei in the United Kingdom (19/20 Belgrave Sq., London, SW1X 8PG)
High Commissioner: Penigran Haji Yunus.

Of the United Kingdom in Brunei (2/01 2nd Flr. Block D, Komplexs Bangunan Yayasan, Sultan Haji Hassanal Bolkiah, Jalan Pretty, Bandar Seri Begawan 1921)
High Commissioner: Andrew Caie.

Of Brunei in the USA (3520 International Court, NW, Washington, D.C., 20008)
Ambassador: Pengiran Anak Dato Puteh.

Of the USA in Brunei (3rd Floor, Teck Guan Plaza, Jalan Sultan, Bandar Seri Begawan 2085)
Ambassador: Vacant.
Chargé d'Affaires a.i.: Robert Pons.

Of Brunei to the United Nations
Ambassador: Vacant.
Deputy Permanent Representative: Joham Tham Abdullah.

Of Brunei to the European Union
Ambassador: Penigran Mashor Penigran Ahmad.

FURTHER READING

Ministry of Finance Statistics Department. *Brunei Darussalam Statistical Yearbook.*

Cleary, M. and Wong, S. Y., *Oil, Economic Development and Diversification in Brunei.* London, 1994
Horton, A. V. M., *A Critical Guide to Source Material Relating to Brunei with Special Reference to the British Residential Era, 1906–1959.* Bordesley, 1995
Saunders, G., *History of Brunei.* OUP, 1996

National statistical office: Ministry of Finance Statistics Department.

BULGARIA

Republika Bulgaria

Capital: Sofia
Population estimate, 2000: 7·95m.
GDP per capita, 2000: (PPP$) 5,710
HDI/world rank: 0·779/62

KEY HISTORICAL EVENTS

The Bulgarians take their name from an invading Asiatic horde (Bulgars) and their language from the Slav population, with whom they merged after 680. The Bulgarians carved out empires against a background of conflict with Byzantium and Serbia but after the Serb-Bulgarian defeat at Kosovo in 1389 Bulgaria finally succumbed to Ottoman encroachment. The Ottoman empire's decline, however, engendered rebellion which met with brutal repression, provoking great power intervention. By the Treaty of Berlin (1878), Macedonia and Thrace reverted to Turkey, Eastern Rumelia became semi-autonomous and Bulgaria proper became a principality under Turkish suzerainty.

After Austria annexed Bosnia in 1908, Bulgaria declared itself independent. To block Austrian expansion into the Balkans, Russia encouraged Greece, Serbia, Montenegro and Bulgaria to attack Turkey (First Balkan War, 1912), but in the dispute which followed over the territorial spoils Bulgaria failed to secure her claims against her formal allies by force (Second Balkan War, 1913). Territorial aspirations led Bulgaria to join the First World War on the German side.

Economic decline caused by the war produced social unrest. Ferdinand was forced to abdicate in favour of his son, Boris III, in Oct. 1918. Bedevilled by Macedonian terrorism and the effects of the world economic depression, parliamentary government was ended by a military coup in May 1934. In 1935 Boris established a royal dictatorship under which political parties were banned. Boris died in 1943 and was succeeded by a regency.

Increasingly drawn into the German economic orbit, Bulgaria joined the Nazis against Britain in March 1941. In Sept. 1944 the Soviet Union declared war and sent its troops across the frontiers. The Communist-dominated Fatherland Front formed a government and a referendum in 1946 abolished the monarchy. Demonstrations in Sofia in Nov. 1989, occasioned by the Helsinki Agreement ecological conference, broadened into demands for political reform. In Dec. the National Assembly approved 21 measures of constitutional reform, including the abolition of the Communist Party's sole right to govern. But attempts at economic reform led to strikes and unrest. In 1996 Petar Stoyanov was elected as an anti-Communist pro-reform President. In the election the following April the anti-Communist Union of Democratic Forces (UDF) coalition, led by Ivan Kostov and Alexander Bozhkov, swept back to power.

In 2002 Bulgaria was one of seven countries invited to join NATO in 2004. Its EU membership target date is 2007.

TERRITORY AND POPULATION

The area of Bulgaria is 110,994 sq. km (42,855 sq. miles). It is bounded in the north by Romania, east by the Black Sea, south by Turkey and Greece, and west by Serbia and Montenegro and the Republic of Macedonia. The country is divided into nine regions.

Area and population in 2001 (census):

Region	Area (sq. km)	Population	Region	Area (sq. km)	Population
Bourgas	14,724	802,932	Rousse	10,843	702,292
Haskovo	13,824	816,874	Sofia (city)	1,311	1,173,811
Lovech	15,150	924,505	Sofia (region)	19,021	930,958
Montana	10,607	559,449	Varna	11,929	887,222
Plovdiv	13,585	1,175,628	*Total*	*110,994*	*7,973,671*

The capital, Sofia, has regional status.

The population of Bulgaria at the census of 1992 was 8,472,724 (females, 4,515,936); population density 76·3 per sq. km. Bulgaria's population has been declining since the mid-1980s. It has been falling at such a rate that by 2000 it was the same as it had been in the early 1960s. In 1999, 69·3% of the population were urban.

The UN gives a projected population for 2010 of 7·19m.

Population of principal towns (2001 census): Sofia, 1,096,389; Plovdiv, 340,638; Varna, 314,539; Bourgas, 193,316; Rousse, 162,128; Stara Zagora, 143,989; Pleven, 122,149; Sliven, 100,695; Dobrich, 100,379.

Ethnic groups at the 1992 census: Bulgarians, 7,271,185; Turks, 800,052; Gypsies, 313,396.

Bulgarian is the official language.

SOCIAL STATISTICS

1999: live births, 72,291; deaths, 111,786; marriages, 34,300; divorces (1998), 10,409. Rates per 1,000 population, 1999: birth, 8·8; death, 13·6; marriage, 4·2; divorce (1998), 1·3; infant mortality, 14·5 per 1,000 live births (1999). Abortions totalled 72,382 in 1999. In 1997 the most popular age range for marrying was 20–24 for both males and females. Expectation of life in 1999 was 67·1 years among males and 74·8 years among females. Annual population growth rate, 1990–99, –0·6%; fertility rate, 1999, 1·2 children per woman.

CLIMATE

The southern parts have a Mediterranean climate, with winters mild and moist and summers hot and dry, but further north the conditions become more Continental, with a larger range of temperature and greater amounts of rainfall in summer and early autumn. Sofia, Jan. 28°F (–2·2°C), July 69°F (20·6°C). Annual rainfall 25·4" (635 mm).

CONSTITUTION AND GOVERNMENT

A new constitution was adopted at Turnovo in July 1991. The *President* is directly elected for not more than two five-year terms. Candidates for the presidency must be at least 40 years old and have lived for the last five years in Bulgaria. American-style primary elections were introduced in 1996; voting is open to all the electorate.

The 240-member *National Assembly* is directly elected by proportional representation. The President nominates a candidate from the largest parliamentary party as Prime Minister.

National Anthem. 'Gorda stara planina' ('Proud and ancient mountains'); words and tune by T. Radoslavov.

RECENT ELECTIONS

Presidential elections were held in two rounds on 11 and 18 Nov. 2001. Georgi Parvanov won the first round against five opponents with 36·4% of votes cast; turn-out was 39·2%. He also won the run-off round against the incumbent president Petar Stoyanov, with 54·1% of votes cast; turn-out was 54·4%.

At the elections of 17 June 2001 the National Movement Simeon II, the party of former King Simeon II, won 120 of the 240 seats with 42·7% of the vote; incumbent prime minister Ivan Kostov's United Democratic Forces coalition (consisting of the Union of Democratic Forces, the Bulgarian Agrarian People's Union-PU, the Democratic Party, the Bulgarian Social Democratic Party and the National Democratic Party) won 51 seats with 18·2%; the Coalition for Bulgaria (headed by the Bulgarian Socialist Party) won 48 seats with 17·1%; and the Movement for Rights and Freedoms (consisting of the Movement for Rights and Freedoms, the Liberal Union and Euroroma) won 21 seats with 7·5%. Turn-out was 66·7%.

CURRENT ADMINISTRATION

President: Georgi Parvanov; b. 1957 (Bulgarian Socialist Party; in office since 22 Jan. 2002).

Vice-President: Angel Marin.

In March 2003 the government comprised:

Chairman of the Council of Ministers: Simeon Borisov Sakskoburggotski (former King Simeon II); b. 1937 (National Movement Simeon II; sworn in 24 July 2001).

Deputy Prime Ministers: Nikolay Vasilev, Kostadin Paskalev, Lidiya Shuleva. *Minister of Agriculture and Forests:* Mehmed Dikme. *Culture:* Bozhidar Abrashev. *Defence:* Nikolay Svinarov. *Economy:* Nikolay Vasilev. *Education and Science:* Vladimir Atanasov. *Energy:* Milko Kovachev. *Environment and Water:* Dolores Arsenova. *Finance:* Milen Velchev. *Foreign Affairs:* Solomon Passy. *Health:* Bozhidar Finkov. *Interior:* Georgi Petkanov. *Justice:* Anton Stankov. *Labour and Social Policy:* Lidiya Shuleva. *Regional Development and Public Works:* Kostadin Paskalev. *State Administration:* Dimitur Kalchev. *Transportation and Communications:* Plamen Petrov. *Without Portfolio:* Nezhdet Mollov.

Government Website: http://www.government.bg/

DEFENCE

Conscription was reduced from 18 to 12 months in 1992.

Defence expenditure in 2000 totalled US$347m. (US$42 per capita), representing 2·8% of GDP. In 1985 the total had been US$2,425m., equivalent to US$288 per capita and representing 14·0% of GDP.

Army. There are three military districts based around Sofia, Plovdiv and Sliven. In 1999 the Army had a strength of 43,400, including 33,300 conscripts. In addition there are reserves of 303,000, 12,000 border guards and 18,000 railway and construction troops.

Navy. The Navy, all ex-Soviet or Soviet-built, includes one old diesel submarine and one small frigate. The Naval Aviation Wing operates nine armed helicopters. The naval headquarters is at Varna, and there are bases at Atiya and at Vidin on the Danube. Personnel in 1999 totalled 5,260 (2,000 conscripts).

Air Force. The Air Force had (1999) 18,300 personnel (14,500 conscripts). There are 227 combat aircraft, including MiG-21s, MiG-23s and Su-25s, and 43 attack helicopters.

INTERNATIONAL RELATIONS

Bulgaria is a member of the UN, WTO, BIS, NATO Partnership for Peace, Council of Europe, OSCE, CEI, BSEC, Danube Commission, IOM, Antarctic Treaty and the International Organization of the Francophonie, and is an Associate Member of the EU and an Associate Partner of the WEU. At the European Union's Helsinki Summit in Dec. 1999 Bulgaria, along with five other countries, was invited to begin full negotiations for membership in Feb. 2000. Entry into the EU is unlikely before 2007.

ECONOMY

Agriculture accounted for 18·8% of GDP in 1998, industry 25·5% and services 55·7%.

Overview. A Centre for Mass Privatization was set up in 1994; by mid-1999 nearly 2,000 privatization deals had been completed. Privatized firms enjoy a five-year tax exemption.

Currency. The unit of currency is the *lev* (BGN) of 100 *stotinki.* In May 1996 the lev was devalued by 68%. A new *lev* was introduced on 5 July 1999, at 1 new *lev* = 1,000 old *leva.* Runaway inflation (123·0% in 1996 rising to 1,061% in 1997) forced the closure of 14 banks in 1996. However, by 2001 the rate was down to 7·5%. In June 1997 the new government introduced a currency board financial system which stabilized the lev and renewed economic growth. Under it, the lev is pegged to the euro at one euro = 1·95583 new leva. Foreign exchange reserves were estimated to be US$3,835m. in June 2002; gold reserves were 513,000 troy oz. Total money supply was 4,603m. leva in April 2002.

Budget. The fiscal year is the calendar year.

Government revenue and expenditure (in 1m. new leva):

	1996	1997	1998	1999	2000
Revenue	5,269·5	6,530·1	8,913·1	9,678·6	11,087·1
Expenditure	7,722·9	6,731·4	8,689·2	9,901·3	11,356·1

VAT was first introduced in 1995. In 1996 there was an increase in VAT from 18% to 22%. The current account deficit was estimated to be US$-161m. in 1998.

Performance. Total GDP in 2001 was US$12·7bn. Real GDP growth was 5·8% in 2000 and 4·5% in 2001. In 1997–98 the country pulled itself back from economic and financial disaster. Its success in stabilizing the economy, in the wake of the collapse of the banking system and the lurch into hyperinflation in early 1997, has exceeded expectations.

Banking and Finance. The National Bank (*Governor*, Svetoslav Gavriiski) is the central bank and bank of issue. There is a commercial bank, Bulbank (founded 1964) and a State Savings Bank, the latter serving local enterprises as well as the public. In 1996 there were savings accounts totalling 81,606m. leva. There were 41 commercial banks in 1996.

There is a stock exchange in Sofia.

Weights and Measures. The metric system is in general use. On 1 April 1916 the Gregorian calendar came into force.

ENERGY AND NATURAL RESOURCES

Environment. According to the *World Bank Atlas* Bulgaria's carbon dioxide emissions were the equivalent of 5·7 tonnes per capita in 1998.

Electricity. Bulgaria has little oil, gas or high-grade coal, and energy policy is based on the exploitation of its low-grade coal and hydro-electric resources. But the country is a major distribution centre for energy in the Black Sea region, a fact underlined by the 1997 deal with Russia which guarantees gas supplies to Bulgaria, while clearing the way for the construction of a transit gas pipeline between Russia and western Turkey. In 2001 there were six nuclear reactors in use, at the country's sole nuclear power plant in Kozloduy (dating from the 1970s). In Dec. 2002 it was announced that the two oldest reactors would close in 2003, with a further two to follow by 2006. The closure of the oldest reactor is a condition for the country's EU membership, proposed for 2007. To compensate, the government plans to complete a nuclear plant in Belene, started in the 1980s but suspended in 1990 because of lack of funds and environmental protests. Installed electrical capacity was 12m. kW in 1997. Output, 1998, 38·42bn. kWh (53% thermal, 40% nuclear and 7% hydro-electric). Consumption per capita: 3,166 kWh (1998).

Oil and Gas. Oil is extracted in the Balchik district on the Black Sea, in an area 100 km north of Varna, and at Dolni Dubnik near Pleven. There are refineries at Bourgas (annual capacity 5m. tonnes) and Dolni Dubnik (7m. tonnes). Crude oil production (1996) was 32,000 tonnes; natural gas (1996), 2 petajoules.

Minerals. Production in 1996: manganese ore, 13,100 tonnes; iron ore, 282,000 tonnes; lignite, 26·93m. tonnes. There are also deposits of gold, silver and copper.

Agriculture. Agricultural land covered 6,164,000 ha in 1996, of which 4,693,000 ha were arable. In 1996 sown area was 2,902,000 ha; there were 277,000 ha of meadows and 1,471,000 ha of commons and pastures. By 1999, 60% of Bulgarian households worked a plot of land, often on a part-time basis. In 2000 around 25% of the labour force was employed in agriculture.

Legislation of 1991 and 1992 provided for the redistribution of collectivized land to its former owners up to 30 ha. There were 2,073 agricultural collectives and firms in 1992 and 2,435 private farms in 1996.

Production in 2000 (in 1,000 tonnes): wheat, 2,800; maize, 937; barley, 684; potatoes, 566; grapes, 450; tomatoes, 446; sunflower seeds, 438; melons and watermelons, 384; chillies and green peppers, 207; cucumbers and gherkins, 170; cabbages, 140. Bulgaria is a leading producer of attar of roses (rose oil). Bulgaria produced 139,000 tonnes of wine in 2000. Other products (in 1,000 tonnes) in 2000: meat, 445; cow milk, 1,200; goat milk, 200; sheep milk, 106; eggs, 90.

Livestock (2000, in 1,000): cattle, 682; sheep, 2,549; pigs, 1,512; goats, 1,046; poultry, 14,000.

There were 25,000 tractors in use in 1998.

Forestry. Forest area, 1996, was 3,878,000 ha, or nearly 35% of the total land area (1·29m. ha coniferous, 2·58m. ha broad-leaved). 16,000 ha were afforested in 1997. Timber production in 1999 totalled 3·04m. cu. metres.

Fisheries. In 2000 total catch was 6,998 tonnes, mainly from sea fishing. As recently as 1988 the catch amounted to 106,000 tonnes.

INDUSTRY

In 1996 there were 342,261 registered economic units. Units by ownership: state, 9,682; municipal, 9,820; joint-stock companies, 3,588; co-operatives, 5,410; social organizations, 6,306; associations, 2,483; foreign ventures, 9,005; resident, 307,448. In 1996 the private sector accounted for 45·9% of production.

Production, 1997 (in 1,000 tonnes): crude steel, 2,628; rolled steel (1996), 1,898; cement, 1,654; pig iron, 1,643; artificial fertilizers (1996), 559; sulphuric acid, 556; paper (1998), 150; cotton, 98m. sq. metres; woven wool, 17m. sq. metres; cigarettes, 43·3bn. (units); 6,000 TV sets; and 21,000 refrigerators.

Labour. In Nov. 1996, 646,600 employees worked in the private sector. There is a 42½-hour five-day working week. Retirement is at 55 for women and 60 for men, or 52 and 57 after 25 years in the last employment. The average wage (excluding peasantry) was 13,269 leva per month in 1996; minimum wage was 1,200 leva per month. Population of working age (males 16–59; females 16–54), 1996, 4,746,790 (47·6% females). At the end of 1996 the economically active population was 3,576,200 (1,681,000 females), of whom 3,085,400 were employed. Unemployment was 17·9% in 2000.

Trade Unions. An independent white-collar trade union movement, Podkrepa, was formed in 1989. It claimed 100,000 members in July 1990. The former official Central Council of Trade Unions reconstituted itself in 1990 as the Confederation of Independent Trade Unions.

INTERNATIONAL TRADE

Legislation in force as of Feb. 1992 abolished restrictions imposed in 1990 on the repatriation of profits and allows foreign nationals to own and set up companies in Bulgaria. Western share participation in joint ventures may exceed 50%. Total foreign debt was US$10,026m. in 2000.

Imports and Exports. Imports and exports (f.o.b.) for calendar years in US$1m.:

	1996	1997	1998	1999	2000
Imports	4,702·6	4,559·3	4,574·2	5,087·4	5,987·6
Exports	4,890·2	4,939·6	4,193·5	4,006·4	4,812·2

Leading export commodities are non-precious metals and articles, textile materials and articles, mineral products and chemical industry produce. Leading import commodities are mineral products, machinery and apparatus, electrical equipment and parts, textile materials and articles, and transportation facilities.

Main export markets in 1997: Italy, 12·0%; Turkey, 9·2%; Germany, 8·9%; Greece, 8·0%; Russia, 7·8%. Main import suppliers: Russia, 24·9%; Germany, 10·6%; Italy, 6·6%; Greece, 3·8%; Ukraine, 3·4%. Trade with the EU has been steadily growing, with exports to the EU increasing from 39% of all exports in 1996 to 56% in 2000, and imports from the EU rising from 35% of the total in 1996 to 51% in 2000.

COMMUNICATIONS

Roads. In 1998 there were 36,759 km of roads, including 319 km of motorways and 3,080 km of main roads. 817m. passengers and 40·67m. tonnes of freight were carried in 1996. In 1998 there were 1,809,350 passenger cars (219·8 per 1,000 inhabitants) and 515,70 motorcycles or mopeds. There were 6,905 road accidents in 1998 with 1,003 fatalities.

Rail. In 1998 there were 4,290 km of 1,435 mm gauge railway (2,655 km electrified). Passenger-km travelled in 1998 came to 4·74bn. and freight tonne-km to 6·15bn.

There is a tramway in Sofia.

Civil Aviation. There is an international airport at Sofia (Vrazhdebna), which handled 1,128,000 passengers (1,049,000 on international flights) and 9,400 tonnes of freight in 2000. The state-owned Balkan is the national carrier. In 1999 it flew 18·5m. km, carrying 695,400 passengers (627,400 on international flights).

Shipping. In 1998 the merchant fleet totalled 1,091,000 GRT, including oil tankers 145,000 GRT. Bourgas is a fishing and oil-port. Varna is the other important port. There is a rail ferry between Varna and Ilitchovsk (Ukraine). In 1996, 20,000 passengers and 17·07m. tonnes of cargo were carried. There were 74,000 km of inland waterways in 1996. 11,000 passengers and 1m. tonnes of freight were carried.

Telecommunications. The Bulgarian Telecommunications Company is in the process of being privatized. Only about 15% of local exchanges had been digitalized by early 1999. In 2000 there were 2,881,800 telephone main lines (350·4 per 1,000 inhabitants) and 361,000 PCs in use (43·9 per 1,000 persons). Bulgaria had approximately 585,000 Internet users in April 2001. There were 2·5m. mobile phone subscribers in 2002 and 15,000 fax machines in 1995.

Postal Services. In 1996 there were 3,502 post and telecommunications offices.

SOCIAL INSTITUTIONS

Justice. A law of Nov. 1982 provides for the election (and recall) of all judges by the National Assembly. There are a Supreme Court, 28 provincial courts (including Sofia) and regional courts. Jurors are elected at the local government elections. The Prosecutor General and judges are elected by the Supreme Judicial Council established in 1992.

The population in penal institutions in July 1998 was 11,814 (140 per 100,000 of national population). The maximum term of imprisonment is 20 years. The death penalty was abolished for all crimes in 1998.

Religion. 'The traditional church of the Bulgarian people' (as it is officially described) is that of the Eastern Orthodox Church. It was disestablished under the 1947 Constitution. In 1953 the Bulgarian Patriarchate was revived. The Patriarch is Maksim (enthroned 1971). The seat of the Patriarch is at Sofia. There are 11 dioceses (each under a Metropolitan), 10 bishops, 2,600 parishes, 1,700 priests, 400 monks and nuns, 3,700 churches and chapels, one seminary and one theological college.

Anti-Maksim schismatics set up a rival synod in 1992 and elected Pimen as Patriarch in 1996.

In 1992 there were some 70,000 Roman Catholics with 53 priests, in three bishoprics. At the 1992 census, 7,349,544 Christians were recorded and 1,110,295 Muslims (Pomaks). There is a Chief Mufti elected by regional muftis.

Education. Adult literacy rate in 1999 was 98·3% (male, 98·9%; female, 97·7%). Education is free, and compulsory for children between the ages of 7 and 16.

In 1996 there were 3,713 kindergartens with 247,000 children and 23,353 teachers; 3,286 primary schools with 71,431 teachers and 944,733 pupils; 129 special needs schools with 2,336 teachers and 13,849 pupils; 7 vocational technical schools with 125 teachers and 3,384 pupils; 203 secondary vocational technical schools with 5,113 teachers and 77,299 pupils; 337 technical colleges and schools of art with 13,943 teachers and 125,887 students; 46 post-secondary institutions with 3,018 teachers and 24,981 students; 42 institutes of higher education with 23,285 teachers and 235,701 students. There are four state universities, an American university, and universities of mining and geology, architecture, civil engineering and geodesy. The Academy of Sciences was founded in 1869.

There were also 62 private schools with 5,874 pupils in 1996–97.

In 1996 total expenditure on education came to 3·1% of GNP and 7·0% of total government spending.

Health. All medical services are free. Private medical services were authorized in Jan. 1991. In 1996 there were 289 hospitals and clinics with 86,160 beds. There were 29,529 doctors, 5,467 dentists, 1,736 pharmacists, 6,576 midwives, 6,910 medical auxiliaries and 51,269 nurses. In 2000 health spending represented 4·3% of GDP.

Welfare. Retirement and disability pensions and temporary sick pay are calculated as a percentage of previous wages (respectively 55–80%, 35–100%, 69–90%) and according to the nature of the employment. Free medical treatment is available to all, but private practice also exists. Medicines are free to people with chronic conditions or on low incomes.

In 1996 there were 2,381,128 recipients of pensions; disbursements were 121,191m. leva. The average annual pension was 49,681 leva.

CULTURE

Broadcasting. Broadcasting is under the aegis of the state-controlled Bulgarian National Radio and Bulgarian Television. There are four national and six regional radio programmes. A service for tourists is broadcast from Varna. There are two TV programmes; Bulgaria also receives transmissions from the French satellite channel TV5. There are two independent TV channels—Nova TV (New Television) and 7 Dni (7 Days). Colour programmes are by the SECAM V system. Radio receivers in 1997, 4·5m.; televisions, 3·3m.

Cinema. There were 219 cinemas in 1996 (attendance, 3·69m.). In 1995 gross box office receipts came to 219m. leva; 11 full-length films were made.

Press. In 1996 there were 1,053 newspapers with an annual circulation of 454m., and 635 other periodicals. 5,100 book titles were published in 22·9m. copies in 1996.

Tourism. There were 2,036,000 foreign tourists in 2000. Most came from Russia and Ukraine as well as traditional western markets such as Germany, Britain and Scandinavia. 3,006,292 Bulgarians made visits abroad in 1996. Earnings from tourism were US$963m. in 2000.

Libraries. In 1997 there were 4,237 public libraries, 1 National library and 92 Higher Education libraries. They held a combined 51,525,000 volumes for 1,111,000 registered users.

DIPLOMATIC REPRESENTATIVES

Of Bulgaria in the United Kingdom (186–188 Queen's Gate, London, SW7 5HL)
Ambassador: Valentin Dobrev.

Of the United Kingdom in Bulgaria (38 Blvd. Vassil Levski, Sofia)
Ambassador: Ian Soutar.

Of Bulgaria in the USA (1621 22nd St., NW, Washington, D.C., 20008)
Ambassador: Elena Borislavova Poptodorova.

Of the USA in Bulgaria (1 Saborna St., Sofia)
Ambassador: James Pardew.

Of Bulgaria to the United Nations
Ambassador: Stefan Tafrov.

Of Bulgaria to the European Union
Ambassador: Stanislav Daskalov.

FURTHER READING

Central Statistical Office. *Statisticheski Godishnik.—Statisticheski Spravochnik* (annual).— *Statistical Reference Book of Republic of Bulgaria* (annual).

Crampton, Richard J., *A Concise History of Bulgaria.* CUP, 1997
Melone, A., *Creating Parliamentary Government: The Transition to Democracy in Bulgaria.* Ohio State Univ. Press, 1998
National statistical office: Natsionalen Statisticheski Institut, Sofia. *President:* Alexander Hadjiiski.

Website: http://www.nsi.bg/

BURKINA FASO

République Démocratique
du Burkina Faso

Capital: Ouagadougou
Population estimate, 2000: 11·54m.
GDP per capita, 2000: (PPP$) 976
HDI/world rank: 0·325/169

KEY HISTORICAL EVENTS
Formerly known as Upper Volta, the country's name was changed in 1984 to Burkina Faso, meaning 'the land of honest men'. The area it covers was settled by farming communities until their invasion by the Mossi people in the 11th century, who successfully resisted Islamic crusades and attacks by neighbouring empires for seven centuries until conquered by the French between 1895 and 1903.

France made Upper Volta a separate colony in 1919, only to abolish it as such in 1932, dividing its territory between the Ivory Coast (now Côte d'Ivoire), French Sudan (now Mali) and Niger. In 1947 the territory of Upper Volta was reconstituted. Upper Volta remained a desperately poor country often hit by drought, particularly in 1972–74 and again in 1982–84. The military has held power for most of the period after independence. In Aug. 1983 a coup brought to power Capt. Thomas Sankara, a leading radical, who headed a left-wing regime. Sankara was overthrown and killed in a coup on 15 Oct. 1987, the fifth since 1960, led by his friend Capt. Blaise Compaoré.

TERRITORY AND POPULATION
Burkina Faso is bounded in the north and west by Mali, east by Niger and south by Benin, Togo, Ghana and Côte d'Ivoire. Area: 274,122 sq. km; 1996 census population, 10,312,609 (82·1% rural in 1999), giving a density of 37·6 per sq. km.

The UN gives a projected population for 2010 of 15·76m.

The largest cities are Ouagadougou, the capital (1999 estimate, 1,026,000), Bobo-Dioulasso (300,000 in 1993), Koudougou (105,000 in 1993), Ouahigouya (38,604 in 1985), Banfora (35,204 in 1985 and Kaya (25,799 in 1985).

Areas and populations of the 45 provinces:

Province	Sq. km	Population 1998	Province	Sq. km	Population 1998
Bale	4,614	149,925	Mouhoun	6,740	239,063
Bam	4,092	216,098	Nahouri	3,842	131,557
Banwa	5,955	204,386	Namentenga	6,379	275,226
Bazéga	3,946	214,367	Nayala	3,851	143,454
Bougouriba	2,879	73,538	Noumbiel	2,881	51,424
Boulgou	6,693	411,418	Oubritenga	2,775	204,935
Boulkiemdé	4,288	423,779	Oudalan	9,864	110,185
Comoé	15,621	243,082	Passoré	3,907	281,317
Ganzourgou	4,203	289,464	Poni	7,531	201,371
Gnagna	8,578	357,097	Sanguié	5,172	236,740
Gourma	11,868	298,801	Sanmatenga	9,328	497,188
Houet	11,639	354,417	Séno	6,953	214,436
Ioba	2,879	163,874	Sissili	7,186	147,842
Kadiogo	2,857	189,813	Soum	12,285	263,028
Kénédougou	8,289	196,236	Sourou	5,852	195,724
Komondjari	5,058	54,487	Tapoa	14,707	250,798
Kompienga	7,281	44,190	Tuy	5,664	165,072
Kossi	7,464	233,129	Yagha	6,512	127,156
Koulpelogo	4,611	192,861	Yatenga	6,786	421,975
Kourritenga	2,739	256,957	Ziro	5,208	11,680
Kourweogo	1,593	118,239	Zondoma	2,018	134,590
Leraba	3,059	94,377	Zoundwéogo	3,538	190,686
Loroum	3,588	113,153			

The principal ethnic groups are the Mossi (49%), Fulani (8%), Mandé (7%), Bobo (7%), Gourmantché (7%), Gourounsi (7%), Bissa (4%), Lobi-Dagari (4%), Sénoufo (2%).

French is the official language.

SOCIAL STATISTICS

Births, 1996, 499,000; deaths, 212,000. Birth rate (1996) per 1,000 population, 47·0; death, 20·0. Annual population growth rate, 1990–99, 2·8%. Expectation of life at birth, 1999, 47·0 years for females and 45·1 for males. Infant mortality, 1999 (per 1,000 live births), 106. Fertility rate, 1999, 6·4 children per woman.

CLIMATE

A tropical climate with a wet season from May to Nov. and a dry season from Dec. to April. Rainfall decreases from south to north. Ouagadougou, Jan. 76°F (24·4°C), July 83°F (28·3°C). Annual rainfall 36" (894 mm).

CONSTITUTION AND GOVERNMENT

At a referendum in June 1991 a new constitution was approved; there is an executive presidency. Parliament consists of the 111-member *Assembly of People's Deputies*, elected by universal suffrage, and the 178-member *Chamber of Representatives*, a consultative body representing social, religious, professional and political organizations. There is also a 90-member *Economic and Social Council*. In April 2000 parliament passed a law reducing presidential terms from seven to five years, with a maximum of two terms. The new law will not affect President Blaise Compaoré's current seven-year term, which expires in 2005.

National Anthem. 'Contre la férule humiliante' ('Against the shameful fetters'); words by T. Sankara, tune anonymous.

RECENT ELECTIONS

At the presidential elections of 15 Nov. 1998 Blaise Compaoré was re-elected by 87·5% of votes cast against two other candidates.

Parliamentary elections were held on 5 May 2002. The Congress for Democracy and Progress (CDP) won 57 out of 111 seats, the Alliance for Democracy and the Federation-African Democratic Rally (ADF-RDA) 17, and the Party for Democracy and Progress (PDP) 10. Turn-out was 64·1%.

CURRENT ADMINISTRATION

President: Capt. Blaise Compaoré; b. 1951 (CDP; in office since 1987, most recently re-elected on 15 Nov. 1998).

In March 2003 the government comprised:

Prime Minister: Paramanga Ernest Yonli; b. 1956 (CDP; sworn in 7 Nov. 2000).

Minister of Agriculture, Water and Water Resources: Salif Diallo. *Animal Resources:* Alphonse Bonou. *Civil Service and State Reform:* Lassané Sawadogo. *Arts, Tourism and Culture:* Mahamoudou Ouédraogo. *Defence:* Kouame Lougue. *Economy and Development:* Seydou Bouda. *Employment, Labour and Youth:* Alain Lodovic Tou. *Energy and Mines:* Abdoulaye Abdulkader Cisse. *Environment:* Djiri Dakar. *Finance and Budget:* Jean-Baptiste Compaoré. *Foreign Affairs:* Youssouf Ouédraogo. *Health:* Bedouma Alain Yoda. *Trade, Industry and Crafts:* Bénoît Ouattara. *Justice, Keeper of the Seals:* Boureima Badini. *Human Rights Promotion:* Monique Ilboudo. *Basic Education and Mass Literacy:* Matthieu Ouédraogo. *Infrastructure, Housing and Transport:* Hippolyte Lingani. *Information:* Raymond Edouard Ouédraogo. *Post and Telecommunications:* Justin Tiéba Thombiano. *Relations with Parliament:* Adama Fofana. *Security:* Djibril Yipéné Bassolet. *Secondary and Higher Education and Scientific Research:* Laya Sawadogo. *Social Affairs and National Solidarity:* Miriam Lamizana. *Territorial Administration and Decentralization:* Moumouni Fabre. *Sports and Leisure:* Tioudoun Sessouma. *Promotion of Women:* Gisèle Guigma.

Government Website: http://www.primature.gov.bf/republic/fgouvernement.htm

DEFENCE

There are six military regions. All forces form part of the Army. Defence expenditure totalled US$68m. in 2000 (US$6 per capita), representing 1·8% of GDP.

Army. Strength (1999), 5,600 with a paramilitary Gendarmerie of 4,200. In addition there is a Peoples' Militia of 45,000.

Air Force. Personnel total (1999), 200 with five combat aircraft.

INTERNATIONAL RELATIONS

Burkina Faso is a member of the UN, WTO, the African Union, African Development Bank, ECOWAS, IOM, OIC, International Organization of the Francophonie and is an ACP member state of the ACP-EU relationship.

ECONOMY

In 1998 agriculture accounted for 33·3% of GDP, industry 27·2% and services 39·5%.

Overview. A development programme for 1994–96, based mainly on agriculture and costing 62,000m. francs CFA, was financed largely by foreign aid. It is proposed to privatize and restructure the banking and industrial sectors. 11 enterprises had been privatized by Nov. 1994. A second phase of privatization was then initiated.

Currency. The unit of currency is the *franc CFA* (XOF) with a parity of 655·957 francs CFA to one euro. Foreign exchange reserves were US$260m. in May 2002 and total money supply was 256,913m. francs CFA. Gold reserves were 11,000 troy oz in June 2000. There was deflation in 2000, of 0·3%, but then inflation in 2001, of 4·9%.

Budget. Total revenues in 1995 were an estimated US$277m. and expenditure US$492m.

Performance. Real GDP growth was 2·2% in 2000 and 5·7% in 2001. Total GDP was US$2·3bn. in 2001.

Banking and Finance. The bank of issue which functions as the central bank is the regional Central Bank of West African States (BCEAO; *Governor*, Charles Konan Banny). There are 3 commercial banks, 4 specialized development institutions, a savings bank, 5 non-bank credit institutions and an investment company.

Weights and Measures. The metric system is in use.

ENERGY AND NATURAL RESOURCES

Environment. According to the *World Bank Atlas* Burkina Faso's carbon dioxide emissions in 1998 were the equivalent of 0·1 tonnes per capita.

Electricity. Production of electricity (1998) was 225m. kWh. There are five thermal power stations with a total capacity in 1995 of 38·9 MW. Hydro-electric capacity in 1994 was 15 MW. Consumption per capita was 27 kWh in 1997.

Minerals. There are deposits of manganese, zinc, limestone, phosphate and diamonds. Gold production was 1·5 tonnes in 1997.

Agriculture. In 1998 there were 3·40m. ha of arable land and 50,000 ha of permanent crops. 25,000 ha were irrigated in 1998. 9·54m. persons depended on agriculture in 1994, of whom 5m. were economically active. Production (2000, in 1,000 tonnes): sorghum, 1,100; millet, 900; sugarcane, 400; maize, 350; seed cotton, 300; cottonseed, 175; groundnuts, 205; cotton lint, 125; rice, 88.

Livestock (2000): cattle, 4·70m.; sheep, 6·59m.; goats, 8·40m.; pigs, 610,000; asses, 491,000; chickens, 22m. Livestock products, 2000 (in 1,000 tonnes): beef and veal, 52; goat meat, 22; poultry meat, 26; cow's milk, 163; eggs, 18.

Forestry. In 1995 forests covered 42,700 sq. km, or 15·6% of the total land area (down from 16·2% in 1990). Timber production in 1999 was 11·10m. cu. metres.

Fisheries. In 2000 total catch was approximately 8,500 tonnes, exclusively from inland waters. There is some fish farming.

INDUSTRY

In 1994 manufacturing contributed 14% of GDP, mainly food-processing and textiles. Plant is primitive, and employs only about 1% of the workforce. There are about 100 firms, most publicly owned. Output of major products, 1995, in tonnes: sugar (1998), 30,200; flour, 31,046; soap, 5,787; edible oils, 4,286; soft drinks and beer, 28·7m. litres; printed fabric, 5,297,000 sq. metres.

Labour. In 1996 the labour force was 5,419,000 (53% males). Over 80% of the economically active population are engaged in agriculture, fishing and forestry.

Trade Unions. There were six federations in 1999: Confédération Générale de Travailleurs de Burkina (CGTB), Union syndicale des travailleurs du Burkina (USTB), Union générale des travailleurs du Burkina (UGTB), Confédération syndicale Burkinabe (CSB), Confédération nationale des travailleurs Burkinabe (CNTB) and Organisation nationale des syndicats libres (ONSL).

INTERNATIONAL TRADE

Foreign debt was US$1,332m. in 2000.

Imports and Exports. In 1997 imports totalled US$529·9m. and exports US$194·1m. Principal export markets, 1998: Switzerland, 21%; France, 16%; Côte d'Ivoire, 11%; Belgium-Luxembourg, 10%. Principal import suppliers: France, 29%; Côte d'Ivoire, 16%; Japan, 5%. Cotton is the main export, accounting for about half of the country's export income.

COMMUNICATIONS

Roads. The road system comprised an estimated 12,100 km in 1996, of which 5,720 km were national, 3,030 km regional and 3,290 km other roads. Only 1,900 km are asphalted. There were an estimated 56,430 vehicles in use in 1996, including 38,220 passenger cars (3·6 per 1,000 inhabitants).

Rail. The railway from Abidjan in Côte d'Ivoire to Kaya (622 km of metre gauge within Burkina Faso) is operated by the mixed public-private company Sitarail, a concessionaire to both governments. The railways carried 0·6m. passengers and 0·2m. tonnes of freight in 1993.

Civil Aviation. The international airports are Ouagadougou (which handled 188,000 passengers in 2000) and Bobo-Dioulasso. The national carrier is Air Burkina (66% state-owned), which in 1998 flew to Abidjan, Bamako, Cotonou, Lomé and Niamtougou in addition to operating on domestic routes. Burkina Faso is also a member of Air Afrique. In 1999 scheduled airline traffic of Burkina Faso-based carriers flew 3·9m. km, carrying 147,000 passengers (132,000 on international flights).

Telecommunications. There were 53,200 telephone main lines in 2000, equivalent to 4·5 per 1,000 inhabitants, and 15,000 PCs were in use (1·3 per 1,000 persons). There were 10,000 Internet users in 2000 and 5,000 mobile phone subscribers in 1999.

SOCIAL INSTITUTIONS

Justice. Civilian courts replaced revolutionary tribunals in 1993. A law passed in April 2000 split the supreme court into four separate entities—a constitutional court, an appeal court, a council of state and a government audit office.

Religion. In 1999 there were 5·79m. Muslims and 1·16m. Christians (mainly Roman Catholic). Many of the remaining population follow traditional animist religions.

Education. In 1999 adult literacy was 23·1% (male, 33·0%; female, 13·3%), the second lowest in the world after Niger. The 1994–96 development programme established an adult literacy campaign, and centres for the education of 10–15-year-old non-school-attenders. In 1994–95 there were 3,233 primary schools with 14,037 teachers (1995–96) and 700,995 pupils (1995–96). During the period 1990–95 only 24% of females of primary school age were enrolled in school. In 1993–94 there were 116,033 pupils in secondary schools, and in 1994 there were 9,452 students in higher education. There is a university at Ouagadougou, with over 8,000 students.

Health. In 1993 there were 78 hospitals.

Burkina Faso has made more progress in the reduction of undernourishment in the past 20 years than any other country in the world apart from Ghana. Between 1980 and 1996 the proportion of undernourished people declined by 34%.

CULTURE

Broadcasting. Radio and television services (colour by NTSC) are provided by the state-controlled Radiodiffusion-Télévision Burkina. Radio Bobo is a regional service and there is a commercial radio station. In 1997 there were 370,000 radio and 100,000 television receivers.

Press. There were four dailies (one government-owned) with a combined circulation of 14,000 in 1996. There were nine non-dailies and periodicals in 1995.

Tourism. In 1998 there were 140,000 foreign tourists. Receipts totalled US$39m.

DIPLOMATIC REPRESENTATIVES
Of Burkina Faso in the United Kingdom
Ambassador: Kadré Désiré Ouedraogo (resides at Brussels).
Honorary Consul: Stuart Singer (5 Cinnamon Row, Plantation Wharf, London SW11 3TW)

Of the United Kingdom in Burkina Faso
Ambassador: Jean François Gordon, CMG (resides at Abidjan, Côte d'Ivoire).

Of Burkina Faso in the USA (2340 Massachusetts Ave., NW, Washington, D.C., 20008)
Ambassador: Tertius Zongo.

Of the USA in Burkina Faso (PO Box 35, Ouagadougou)
Ambassador: J. Anthony Holmes.

Of Burkina Faso to the United Nations
Ambassador: Michel Kafando.

Of Burkina Faso to the European Union
Ambassador: Kadré Désiré Ouedraogo.

FURTHER READING
Decalo, Samuel, *Burkina Faso.* [Bibliography] ABC-Clio, Oxford and Santa Barbara (CA), 1994
Nnaji, B. O., *Blaise Compaoré: Architect of the Burkina Faso Revolution.* Lagos, 1991

BURUNDI

Republika y'Uburundi

Capital: Bujumbura
Population estimate, 2000: 6·36m.
GDP per capita, 2000: (PPP$) 591
HDI/world rank: 0·313/171

KEY HISTORICAL EVENTS

From 1890 Burundi was part of German East Africa and from 1919 part of Ruanda-Urundi administered by Belgium as a League of Nations mandate. Internal self-government was granted on 1 Jan. 1962, followed by independence on 1 July 1962. In April 1972 fighting broke out between rebels from both Burundi and neighbouring countries and the ruling Tutsi, apparently with the intention of destroying the Tutsi hegemony. Up to 120,000 died. On 1 Nov. 1976 President Micombero was deposed by the Army, as was President Bagaza on 3 Sept. 1987. Pierre Buyoya assumed the presidency on 1 Oct. 1987.

On 1 June 1993 President Buyoya was defeated in elections by Melchior Ndadaye, who thus became the country's first elected president and the first Hutu president, but on 21 Oct. President Ndadaye and six ministers were killed in an attempted military coup. A wave of Tutsi-Hutu massacres broke out, costing thousands of lives. On 6 April 1994 the new president, Cyprien Ntaryamira, was also killed, possibly assassinated, together with the President of Rwanda.

On 25 July 1996 the army seized power, installing Maj. Pierre Buyoya, a Tutsi, as president for the second time. In June 1998 Maj. Buyoya drew up a settlement for a power-sharing transitional government and the replacement of the prime minister by two vice-presidents, one Hutu and one Tutsi. Extremists on both sides denounced the agreement. An attempted coup in April 2001 failed. In July 2001 it was agreed that a three-year transitional government should be installed with Pierre Buyoya as president and Domitien Ndayizeye, a Hutu, as vice-president for the first 18 months, after which the roles would be reversed. A further attempted coup shortly after the announcement of the agreement also failed, although fighting continued. A ceasefire was eventually signed in Dec. 2002 by the government and the Forces for the Defence of Democracy, the country's principal rebel movement. More than 200,000 people have been killed in civil conflict since 1993.

TERRITORY AND POPULATION

Burundi is bounded in the north by Rwanda, east and south by Tanzania and west by the Democratic Republic of the Congo, and has an area of 27,834 sq. km (10,759 sq. miles). The population at the 1990 census was 5,292,793; estimate (1996) 5,356,000; population density, 192·4 per sq. km. Only 8·7% of the population was urban in 1998 (91·3% rural).

The UN gives a projected population for 2010 of 8·66m.

There are 15 regions, all named after their chief towns. Area and population:

Region	Area (in sq. km.)	Population (1990 census)
Bubanza	1,093	222,953
Bujumbura	1,334	608,931
Bururi	2,515	385,490
Cankuzo	1,940	142,707
Cibitoke	1,639	279,843
Karuzi	1,459	287,905
Kayanza	1,229	443,116
Kirundo	1,711	401,103
Kitega	1,989	596,174
Makamba	1,972	223,799
Muhinga	1,825	373,382
Muramuya	1,530	441,653
Ngozi	1,468	482,246
Rutana	1,898	195,834
Ruyigi	2,365	238,567

The capital, Bujumbura, had an estimated population of 321,000 in 1999. The second largest town, Gitega, had a population in 1990 of 102,000.

There are three ethnic groups—Hutu (Bantu, forming over 83% of the total); Tutsi (Nilotic, less than 15%); Twa (pygmoids, less than 1%). The local language is Kirundi. French is also an official language. Kiswahili is spoken in the commercial centres.

SOCIAL STATISTICS
1995 births, 268,000; deaths, 111,000. Rates, 1995 (per 1,000 population): birth, 44·2; death, 18·3. Life expectancy at birth, 1999, was 39·6 years for men and 41·5 years for women. Infant mortality, 1999, 106 per 1,000 live births. Annual population growth rate, 1990–99, 2·1%; fertility rate, 1999, 6·1 children per woman.

CLIMATE
An equatorial climate, modified by altitude. The eastern plateau is generally cool, the easternmost savanna several degrees hotter. The wet seasons are from March to May and Sept. to Dec. Bujumbura, Jan. 73°F (22·8°C), July 73°F (22·8°C). Annual rainfall 33" (825 mm).

CONSTITUTION AND GOVERNMENT
The Constitution of 1981 provided for a one-party state. In Jan. 1991 the government of President Buyoya, leader of the sole party, the Party of Unity and National Progress (Uprona), proposed a new constitution which was approved by a referendum in March 1992 (with 89% of votes cast in favour), legalizing parties not based on ethnic group, region or religion and providing for presidential elections by direct universal suffrage.

There used to be a National Assembly with 81 members elected from 16 constituencies by proportional representation. There was a 5% threshold. On 16 July 1998 the National Assembly was reformed into a National Transition Assembly, whereby 40 additional members were appointed from a mix of political parties and civil society. In July 2001 agreement was reached on President Pierre Buyoya's presidency for the first 18 months of a three-year transition period of multi-ethnic broad-based government. In accordance with the terms of the Arusha peace accord, initially he was being assisted by Hutu Vice-President Domitien Ndayizeye, after which the roles were to be reversed for the second 18 months. The transitional government was established on 1 Nov. 2001. On 30 April 2003 Domitien Ndayizeye became president but Alphonse Marie Kadege, like Pierre Buyoya a Tutsi from the Party of Unity and National Progress, became the vice-president.

National Anthem. 'Uburundi Bwacu' ('Dear Burundi'); words by a committee, tune by M. Barengayabo.

RECENT ELECTIONS
At the presidential elections of 1 June 1993 the electorate was 2·36m.; turn-out was 97·18%. Melchior Ndadaye was elected against former President Buyoya and one other opponent with 64·79% of votes cast, and was sworn in on 10 July 1993.

Following Ndadaye's assassination Cyprien Ntaryamira was elected President by the National Assembly on 13 Jan. 1994 to serve out President Ndadaye's five-year term of office. After Ntaryamira's death and possible assassination, Sylvestre Ntibantunganya (b. 1956; Frodebu) was elected *President* by the National Assembly on 5 Sept. 1994 against five opponents.

At the parliamentary elections of 29 June 1993, 740 candidates stood representing 6 parties. The Front for Democracy in Burundi (Frodebu) gained 65 seats with 71·4% of votes cast, and Uprona, 16 with 21·4%. A number of Frodebu MPs elected in June 1993 have been killed in the meantime. 40 additional members were elected on 16 July 1998.

CURRENT ADMINISTRATION
On 30 April 2003 Domitien Ndayizeye (b. 1953; Frodebu) was installed as *President* in accordance with the agreement reached in July 2001 on a three-year transition period of multi-ethnic broad-based government. The *Vice-President* is Alphonse Marie Kadege (Uprona).

In May 2003 the transitional government also comprised:

Minister of Foreign Affairs and Co-operation: Thérence Sinunguruza. *Interior and National Security:* Salvator Nthabose. *Justice:* Fulgence Dwima Bakana. *National Defence:* Maj.-Gen. Vincent Niyungeko. *Planning, Development and Reconstruction:* Séraphine Wakana. *Local Development:* Casimir Ngendanganya. *Reintegration:* Françoise Ngendahayo. *Peace Mobilization and National Reconciliation:* Luc Rukingama. *Country Planning, Environment and Tourism:* Barnabé Muteragiranwa. *Agriculture and Livestock:* Pierre Ndikumagenge. *Handicrafts, Professional Training and Adult Literacy:* Godefroy Hakizimana. *Employment and Social Security:* Dismas Nditabiriye. *Public Service:* Cyrille Hicintuka. *Finance:* Athanase Gahungu. *Governance and Privatization:* Didace Kiganahe. *Commerce and Industry:* Charles Karikurubu. *National Education:* Prosper Mpawenayo. *Welfare and Promotion of Women:* Marie Goreth Nduwimana. *Youth, Sports and Culture:* Rodolphe Baranyizigiye. *Health:* Jean Kamana. *Communication and Government Spokesperson:* Albert Mbonerane. *Minister in the Presidency responsible for the fight against AIDS:* Génévière Sindabizera. *Public Works and Equipment:* Gaspard Kobako. *Transport and Telecommunications:* Séverin Ndikumugongo. *Energy and Mining:* André Nkundikije. *Institutional Reforms, Human Rights, and Parliamentary Relations:* Alphonse Barancira.

Government Website: http://www.burundi.gov.bi/

DEFENCE
Armed forces personnel, including the Gendarmerie, totalled 45,500 in 1999.

Defence expenditure totalled US$65m. in 2000 (US$10 per capita), representing 5·6% of GDP.

Army. The Army had a strength (1999) of 40,000 including a small naval flotilla and an air wing. In addition there is a People's Militia of 45,000.

Air Force. There were 200 air wing personnel in 1999 with four combat aircraft.

INTERNATIONAL RELATIONS
Burundi is a member of the UN, WTO, the African Union, African Development Bank, COMESA, International Organization of the Francophonie, and is an ACP member state of the ACP-EU relationship.

ECONOMY
Agriculture accounted for 54·1% of GDP in 1998, services 29·5% and industry 16·4%.

Currency. The unit of currency is the *Burundi franc* (BIF) of 100 *centimes*. The inflation rate in 2001 was 9·3%. In June 2002 gold reserves were 1,000 troy oz and foreign exchange reserves US$26m. Total money supply was 481,193m. Burundi francs in April 2002.

Budget. Government revenue and expenditure (in 1m. Burundi francs):

	1995	1996	1997	1998	1999
Revenue	48,397	46,401	46,253	66,333	72,047
Expenditure	76,403	75,405	80,800	98,061	105,181

Performance. In 2000 real GDP growth was negative, at –0·1%, but there was then growth of 2·4% in 2001. Total GDP in 2001 was US$0·7bn.

Banking and Finance. The Bank of the Republic of Burundi is the central bank and bank of issue. There are three commercial banks; a state development bank, a savings bank and a property investment bank.

Weights and Measures. The metric system operates.

ENERGY AND NATURAL RESOURCES
Electricity. Installed capacity was 55,000 kW in 1991. Production was 127m. kWh in 1998. Consumption per capita in 1997 was 24 kWh.

Minerals. Gold is mined on a small scale. Deposits of nickel (280m. tonnes) and vanadium remain to be exploited. There are proven reserves of phosphates of 17·6m. tonnes.

Agriculture. The main economic activity is agriculture, which contributed 53% of GDP in 1997. In 1998, 0·77m. ha were arable and 0·33m. ha permanent crops. Beans, cassava, maize, sweet potatoes, groundnuts, peas, sorghum and bananas are grown according to the climate and the region.

The main cash crop is coffee, of which about 95% is arabica. It accounts for 90% of exports, and taxes and levies on coffee constitute a major source of revenue. A coffee board (OCIBU) manages the grading and export of the crop. Production (2000) 19,000 tonnes. The main agricultural crops (2000 production, in 1,000 tonnes) are bananas (1,514), sweet potatoes (687), cassava (657), dry beans (187), sugarcane (174), maize (118), taro (81), sorghum (61), rice (52), peas (30) and potatoes (24).

Livestock (2000): 550,000 goats, 390,000 cattle, 120,000 sheep, 50,000 pigs and 4m. chickens.

Forestry. Forests covered 317,000 ha, or 12·3% of the total land area, in 1995 (324,000 ha and 12·6% in 1990). Timber production in 1999 was 1·8m. cu. metres, the majority of it for fuel.

Fisheries. There is a small commercial fishing industry on Lake Tanganyika. In 2000 the estimated total catch was 10,000 tonnes, exclusively from inland waters.

INDUSTRY
In 1994 manufacturing contributed 20% of GDP. Textile and leather industries constituted 20% of production, foodstuffs 13% and agricultural industries 9%. In 1998 production of sugar totalled 24,000 tonnes. Other major products (1994 figures) are beer (138·3m. litres), cigarettes (584,580,000 units) and blankets (248,438 units).

Labour. In 1996 the labour force was 3,337,000 (51% males).

INTERNATIONAL TRADE
With Rwanda and the Democratic Republic of the Congo, Burundi forms part of the Economic Community of the Great Lakes. Foreign debt was US$1,100m. in 2000.

Imports and Exports. Imports and exports for calendar years in US$1m.:

	1996	1997	1998	1999	2000
Imports f.o.b.	100·0	96·1	123·5	97·3	107·9
Exports f.o.b.	40·4	87·5	64·0	55·0	49·1

Main exports are coffee, manufactures and tea. Main export markets, 1999: Belgium, 31%; Switzerland, 18%; UK, 14%. Main import suppliers, 1999: Belgium, 15%; Saudi Arabia, 13%; Italy, 12%; Zambia, 5%.

COMMUNICATIONS

Roads. In 1996 there were 14,480 km of roads of which approximately 1,030 km were paved. An estimated 37,240 vehicles were in use in 1996, including 19,200 passenger cars (2·8 per 1,000 inhabitants).

Civil Aviation. There are regular services to Johannesburg and Sharjah. In 1998 scheduled airline traffic of Burundi-based carriers flew 800,000 km, carrying 12,000 passengers (all on international flights). Bujumbura International airport handled 52,257 passengers and 3,898 tonnes of freight in 2000.

Shipping. There are lake services from Bujumbura to Kigoma (Tanzania) and Kalémie (Democratic Republic of the Congo). The main route for exports and imports is via Kigoma, and thence by rail to Dar es Salaam.

Telecommunications. In 2000 there were 20,000 main telephone lines (3·0 per 1,000 inhabitants). In 1995 there were 4,000 fax machines, and in 1999, 800 mobile phone subscribers. The number of Internet users in July 2000 was 2,000.

Postal Services. In 1994 there were 27 post offices, equivalent to one for every 219,000 persons.

SOCIAL INSTITUTIONS

Justice. There is a Supreme Court, an appeal court and a court of first instance at Bujumbura, and provincial courts in each provincial capital.

The population in penal institutions in 1997 was 9,411 (145 per 100,000 of national population). The death penalty is in force.

Religion. In 1993 there were 3·69m. Roman Catholics with an archbishop and three bishops. About 3% of the population are Pentecostal, 1% Anglican and 1% Muslim, while the balance follow traditional tribal beliefs.

Education. Adult literacy rate was 46·9% in 1999 (55·6% among males and 39·0% among females). In 1995–96 there were 518,144 pupils in 1,501 primary schools with 10,316 teachers; in 1994–95 there were 47,636 pupils in secondary schools. In 1992–93 there were 4,256 students in eight higher education institutes with 556 teachers. In 1995–96 there were 3,750 students and 170 academic staff at the university.

Health. In 1993 there were 354 doctors and 1,270 nurses.

CULTURE

Broadcasting. Broadcasting is provided by the state-controlled *Radiodiffusion et Télévision du Burundi*. In 1997 there were 440,000 radio and 25,000 TV (colour by SECAM V) receivers.

Press. There was (1996) one daily newspaper *(Le Renouveau)* with a circulation of 20,000.

Tourism. There were 14,000 foreign tourists in 1998. Receipts totalled US$1m.

DIPLOMATIC REPRESENTATIVES

Of Burundi in the United Kingdom (26 Armitage Road, London, NW11 8RD)
Ambassador: Vacant.
Chargé d'Affaires a.i.: Salvator Kaburundi (resides at Brussels).

Of the United Kingdom in Burundi
Ambassador: Sue Hogwood, MBE (resides at Kigali, Rwanda).

Of Burundi in the USA (2233 Wisconsin Ave., NW 212, Washington, D.C., 20007)
Ambassador: Antoine Ntamobwa.

Of the USA in Burundi (PO Box 1720, Ave. des Etats-Unis, Bujumbura)
Ambassador: James Yellin.

Of Burundi to the United Nations
Ambassador: Marc Nteturuye.

Of Burundi to the European Union
Ambassador: Vacant.
First Counsellor: Philippe Ntahonkuriye.

FURTHER READING
Daniels, Morna, *Burundi.* [Bibliography] ABC-Clio, Oxford and Santa Barbara (CA), 1992
Lemarchand, R., *Burundi: Ethnic Conflict and Genocide.* CUP, 1996

National statistical office: Service des Etudes et Statistiques, Ministère du Plan, Bujumbura.

CAMBODIA

Preah Reach Ana Pak Kampuchea
(Kingdom of Cambodia)

Capital: Phnom Penh
Population estimate, 2000: 13·10m.
GDP per capita, 2000: (PPP$) 1,446
HDI/world rank: 0·543/130

KEY HISTORICAL EVENTS

Cambodia was made a French protectorate in 1863. A nationalist movement began in the 1930s, and anti-French feeling strengthened in 1940–41 when the French submitted to Japanese demands for bases in Cambodia. Anti-French guerrillas, active from 1945, gave the impetus to a communist-led revolution. A fragile peace was established before Cambodia gained independence in 1953 but in 1967 the Khmer Rouge took up arms to support peasants against a rice tax. Their aim was to establish a communist rice-growing dynasty, a combination of Maoism and ancient xenophobic nationalism. From 1970 hostilities extended throughout most of the country involving US and North Vietnamese forces. During 1973 direct US and North Vietnamese participation came to an end, leaving a civil war which continued with large-scale fighting between the Khmer Republic, supported by US arms, and the United National Cambodian Front including 'Khmer Rouge' communists, supported by North Vietnam and China. After unsuccessful attempts to capture Phnom Penh in 1973 and 1974, the Khmer Rouge defeated the American backed leader Lon Nol in April 1975, when the remnants of the republican forces surrendered the city.

From 1975 the Khmer Rouge instituted a harsh and highly centralized regime. All cities and towns were forcibly evacuated and the citizens set to work in the fields. In 1978, in response to repeated border attacks, Vietnam invaded Cambodia. On 7 Jan. 1979 Phnom Penh was captured by the Vietnamese, and the Prime Minister, Pol Pot, fled. Over 2m. Cambodian lives were lost from 1975 to 1979. On 23 Oct. 1991 the warring factions and 19 countries signed an agreement in Paris instituting a ceasefire in Cambodia to be monitored by UN troops. Following the election of a constituent assembly in May 1993, a new constitution was promulgated on 23 Sept. 1993 restoring parliamentary monarchy. The Khmer Rouge continued hostilities, refusing to take part in the 1993 elections. By 1996 the Khmer Rouge had split into two warring factions. The leader of one, Ieng Sary, who had been sentenced to death in his absence for genocide, was pardoned by the King in Sept. 1996. In early Nov. 1996 Ieng Sary and some 4,000 of his forces threw in their lot with government forces.

In July 1997 Hun Sen, the second prime minister, engineered a coup which led to the exiling of first prime minister, Prince Norodom Ranariddh. However, on 30 March 1998 he returned as guest of a Japanese-brokered plan to ensure 'fair and free' elections. These took place on 26 July 1998 against a background of violence and general intimidation. Hun Sen's Cambodian People's Party declared victory.

TERRITORY AND POPULATION

Cambodia is bounded in the north by Laos and Thailand, west by Thailand, east by Vietnam and south by the Gulf of Thailand. It has an area of about 181,035 sq. km (69,898 sq. miles).

Population, 11,437,656 (1998 census), of whom 5,926,248 were females. In 1994, 88·6% of the population were Khmer, 5·5% Vietnamese and 3·1% Chinese. In 1999, 77·8% of the population lived in rural areas.

The UN gives a projected population for 2010 of 16·63m.

The capital, Phnom Penh, had an estimated population of 938,000 in 1999. Other cities are Kompong Cham and Battambang. Ethnic composition, 1994: Khmer, 89%; Vietnamese, 5%; Chinese, 3%; Cham, 2%; Lao-Thai, 1%.

Khmer is the official language.

SOCIAL STATISTICS

1996 estimated births, 429,000; deaths, 156,000. Rates, 1996 estimates (per 1,000 population): births, 43·5; deaths, 15·8. Infant mortality, 1999 (per 1,000 live births), 86. Expectation of life in 1999 was 54·1 years for males and 58·6 for females. Annual population growth rate, 1990–99, 2·8%. Fertility rate, 1999, 4·5 children per woman.

CLIMATE

A tropical climate, with high temperatures all the year. Phnom Penh, Jan. 78°F (25·6°C), July 84°F (28·9°C). Annual rainfall 52" (1,308 mm).

CONSTITUTION AND GOVERNMENT

A parliamentary monarchy was re-established by the 1993 constitution. Prince Norodom Sihanouk (b. 31 Oct. 1922) regained the throne (which had been abolished in 1955) as King on 23 Sept. 1993. He had previously reigned from 1941 to 1955. The protocol of succession is to be determined by a Throne Council consisting of the Speaker and two Deputy Speakers, the First and Second Prime Ministers and two Buddhist patriarchs. In Jan. 1996 King Sihanouk's wife, Queen Monineath, was dubbed 'First Lady'.

There is a 122-member constituent assembly, which on 14 June 1993 elected Prince Sihanouk head of state. On 21 Sept. it adopted a constitution (promulgated on 23 Sept.) by 113 votes to five with two abstentions making him monarch of a parliamentary democracy. The constitution converted the constituent assembly into a legislature sitting for a five-year term.

National Anthem. 'Nokoreach' ('Royal state'); words by Chuon Nat, tune adapted from a Cambodian folk song.

RECENT ELECTIONS

Parliamentary elections were held on 27 July 1998. Under the UN-brokered constitution, a party had to win two-thirds of seats in the 122-member Parliament in order to form a government. With a 90% turn-out, the Cambodian People's Party (KPK) won 64 seats with 41·4% of the vote, the royalist FUNCINPEC party of Prince Norodom Ranariddh won 43 seats with 31·7%, and the party of the government critic Sam Rainsy won 15 seats with 14·1%. Opposition parties claimed a wide range of irregularities and there were re-counts in a number of districts.

Parliamentary elections are scheduled to take place on 27 July 2003.

CURRENT ADMINISTRATION

In March 2003 the cabinet comprised:

Prime Minister: Hun Sen; b. 1951 (KPK; sworn in on 30 Nov. 1998).

Deputy Prime Ministers: Sar Kheng, Tol Lah. *National Defence, Co-ministers:* Gen. Tea Banh, Prince Sisowath Sirirath. *Interior, Co-ministers:* Sar Kheng, You Hockry. *Parliamentary Affairs and Inspection:* Khun Haing. *Foreign Affairs and International Co-operation:* Hor Nam Hong. *Economy and Finance:* Keat Chhon. *Information and Press:* Lu Lay Sreng. *Health:* Dr Hong Sun Huot. *Industry, Mines and Energy:* Suy Sem. *Planning:* Chhay Than. *Commerce:* Cham Prasidh. *Education, Youth and Sports:* Tol Lah. *Agriculture, Forestry and Fisheries:* Chan Sarun. *Culture and Fine Arts:* Princess Norodom Bopha Devi. *Environment:* Dr Mok Mareth. *Rural Development:* Ly Thuch. *Social Affairs, Labour, Vocational Training and Youth Rehabilitation:* Ith Sam Heng. *Post and Telecommunications:* So Khun. *Religious Affairs:* Chea Savoeun. *Women's Affairs and War Veterans:* Mov Sok Huor. *Public Works and Transport:* Khy Taing Lim. *Justice:* Neav Sithong. *Tourism:* Veng Sereyvuth. *Urbanization and Construction:* Im Chhun Lim. *Water Resources and Meteorology:* Lim Kean Hor. *Minister in the Council of Ministers:* Sok An.

Government Website: http://www.camnet.com.kh/ocm/

DEFENCE

The King is C.-in-C. of the armed forces. Defence expenditure in 2000 totalled US$192m. (US$17 per capita), representing 6·1% of GDP.

Army. Strength (1999) 99,000. There are also provincial forces numbering some 45,000 (although perhaps only 19,000 are combat capable) and paramilitary local forces organized at village level.

Navy. Naval personnel in 1999 totalled about 3,000 including a naval infantry of 1,500.

Air Force. Aviation operations were resumed in 1988 under the aegis of the Army. Personnel (1999), 2,000. Of the 24 combat aircraft operated only 8 MiG-21s are serviceable.

INTERNATIONAL RELATIONS

Cambodia is a member of the UN, Asian Development Bank, ASEAN, Colombo Plan, Mekong Group, IOM, and the International Organization of the Francophonie.

ECONOMY

Agriculture accounted for 50·6% of GDP in 1998, industry 14·8% and services 34·6%.

Currency. The unit of currency is the *riel* (KHR) of 100 *sen*. Inflation was 14·7% in 1998. Foreign exchange reserves were US$718m. in June 2002. Total money supply in May 2002 was 713,831m. riels. Inflation in 2001 was 0·2%.

Budget. In 1996 revenues were 797·5bn. riels and expenditure 1,395·1bn. riels.

Performance. Real GDP growth was 7·7% in 2000 and 6·3% in 2001. Total GDP in 2001 was US$3·4bn.

Banking and Finance. The banking system consists of the National Bank of Cambodia, which is the bank of issue; the Central Bank and 28 commercial banks (2 state-owned, 17 privately-owned, 6 foreign and 3 joint venture banks). The National Bank of Cambodia is studying the possibility of setting up a stock market and a capital market for stimulating the flow of capital from foreign countries.

ENERGY AND NATURAL RESOURCES

Environment. According to the *World Bank Atlas* Cambodia's carbon dioxide emissions in 1998 were the equivalent of 0·1 tonnes per capita.

Electricity. Installed capacity was 100,000 kW in 1995. Production (1998) was 210m. kWh. Consumption per capita in 1997 was 20 kWh. A long-term plan for hydro-electricity has been issued by the government.

Water. In 1995, 65% of the urban and 26% of the rural population had access to safe water.

Minerals. There are phosphates and high-grade iron-ore deposits. Some small-scale gold panning and gem (mainly zircon) mining is carried out.

Agriculture. The majority of the population is engaged in agriculture, fishing or forestry. In 1998 there were 3·7m. ha of arable land and 107,000 ha of permanent crops. Before the spread of war, the high productivity provided for a low but well-fed standard of living for the peasant farmers, the majority of whom owned the land they worked before agriculture was collectivized. A relatively small proportion of the food production entered the cash economy. The war and unwise pricing policies led to a disastrous reduction in production, so much so that the country became a net importer of rice. Private ownership of land was restored by the 1989 Constitution.

A crop of 3·76m. tonnes of rice was produced in 2000. Production of other crops, 2000 (in 1,000 tonnes): bananas, 147; sugarcane, 140; maize, 95; cassava, 68; oranges, 63; coconuts, 56.

Livestock (2000): cattle, 3·0m.; pigs, 2·60m.; buffaloes, 710,000; poultry, 13m.

Forestry. Some 9·8m. ha, or 55·7% of the land area, were covered by forests in 1995, nearly half of which is reserved by the government to be awarded to concessionaires. Such areas are not at present worked to any extent. The remainder is available for exploitation by the local residents, and as a result some areas are over-exploited and conservation is not practised. Timber exports have been banned since Dec. 1996. In 1990 the area under forests was 10·65m. ha. There are substantial reserves of pitch pine. Rubber plantations are a valuable asset with production at around 40,000 tonnes per year. There are plans to expand the area under rubber cultivation from 50,000 ha to 800,000 ha. Timber production in 1999 was 8·16m. cu. metres. In 1997 forestry represented 43% of foreign trade.

Fisheries. 1999 catch, 269,100 tonnes (231,000 tonnes from inland waters).

INDUSTRY
Some development of industry had taken place before the spread of open warfare in 1970, but little was in operation by the 1990s except for rubber processing, seafood processing, jute sack making and cigarette manufacture. In the private sector small family concerns produce a wide range of goods. Apart from rice mills, about 70 factories were functioning in 1994. Light industry is generally better developed than heavy industry.

Labour. In 1996 the labour force was 5,322,000. Females constituted 52% of the labour force in 1999—the highest proportion of women in the workforce anywhere in the world. More than 60% of the economically active population are engaged in agriculture, fishing and forestry.

INTERNATIONAL TRADE
Foreign investment has been encouraged since 1989. Legislation of 1994 exempts profits from taxation for eight years, removes duties from various raw and semi-finished materials and offers tax incentives to investors in tourism, energy, the infrastructure and labour-intensive industries. External debt was US$2,357m. in 2000.

Imports and Exports. Imports and exports for calendar years in US$1m.:

	1996	1997	1998	1999	2000
Imports f.o.b.	1,071·8	1,064·0	1,073·2	1,211·5	1,525·1
Exports f.o.b.	643·6	736·0	899·9	979·9	1,327·1

The main exports are timber, rubber, soybeans and sesame. Main imports include cigarettes, construction materials, petroleum products, machinery and motor vehicles. Principal export destinations, 1998: USA (37%), Singapore (17%), Thailand (10%) and Germany (9%). Major import sources, 1998: Thailand (16%), Hong Kong (12%), Singapore (9%) and Mainland China (9%).

COMMUNICATIONS
Roads. There were 35,769 km of roads in 1997, of which 2,700 km were paved. 52,919 passenger cars were in use in 1997 (up from 20,085 in 1992) and 456,800 motorcycles and mopeds. There were 172 fatalities in road accidents in 1997.

Rail. Main lines link Phnom Penh with Sisophon near the Thai border and the port of Kompong Som (total 603 km, metre gauge). After a long period of disruption due to political unrest, limited services were restored on both lines in 1992. Passengers carried, 1994, 500,000; freight carried, 1994, 100,000 tonnes.

Civil Aviation. Pochentong airport is 8 km from Phnom Penh and handled 861,000 passengers (641,000 on international flights) in 2000. Royal Air Cambodge was reconstituted in Jan. 1995 with 60% of the equity government-owned. There are regular domestic services, and in 1998 there were international flights to Bangkok, Chongqing, Guangzhou, Ho Chi Minh City, Kuala Lumpur, Singapore, Taipei and Vientiane.

Shipping. There is an ocean port at Kompong Som; the port of Phnom Penh can be reached by the Mekong (through Vietnam) by ships of between 3,000 and 4,000 tonnes. In 1995 merchant shipping totalled 60,000 GRT.

Telecommunications. There are telephone exchanges in all the main towns. Number of telephone main lines in 2000 totalled 30,900 (2·4 per 1,000 persons). In 1997 mobile phone subscribers numbered 33,500 and there were 3,000 fax machines. In 1999, 76·3% of all telephone subscribers were mobile phone subscribers—the highest ratio of mobile to fixed-line subscribers of any country in the world. In 2000, 15,000 PCs were in use (1·1 for every 1,000 persons). In Dec. 2000 there were 6,000 Internet users.

Postal Services. In 1995 there were 30 post offices, or one for every 328,000 persons.

SOCIAL INSTITUTIONS

Justice. The population in penal institutions in 1997 was 2,909. In March 2003 the government announced plans to establish a special court in partnership with the UN to try leaders of the former Khmer Rouge regime.

Religion. The Constitution of 1989 reinstated Buddhism as the state religion; it had 8·2m. adherents in 1994. About 2,800 monasteries were active in 1994. There are small Roman Catholic and Muslim minorities.

Education. In 1997–98 there were 2,011,772 pupils and 43,282 teachers in 5,026 primary schools, and in general secondary education 19,135 teachers for 312,934 pupils. In 1994–95 there were 16,350 students in vocational establishments. There is a university (with 8,400 students and 350 academic staff in 1995–96) and a fine arts university. Adult literacy in 1999 was 68·9% (male, 80·1%; female, 57·7%).

Health. In 1993 there were 5,642 doctors, 9,950 nurses and 3,235 midwives.

Cambodia has made great progress in the reduction of undernourishment in the past 20 years. Between 1980 and 1996 the proportion of undernourished people declined from 62% of the population to 33%—the biggest reduction outside of Africa.

CULTURE

Broadcasting. Broadcasting is provided by the state-owned Voice of the People of Cambodia and Cambodian Television (colour by PAL). In 1997 there were an estimated 94,000 TV and 1·34m. radio sets.

Press. There are 21 newspapers, two of which are in English.

Tourism. In 1999 there were 368,000 foreign visitors, up from 25,000 in 1991. Tourist numbers in the 1990s increased at a faster rate in Cambodia than in any other country. Receipts in 1999 totalled US$190m.

DIPLOMATIC REPRESENTATIVES

Of the United Kingdom in Cambodia (29 Street 75, Phnom Penh)
Ambassador: Stephen Bridges.

Of Cambodia in the USA (4500 16th Street, NW, Washington, D.C., 20011)
Ambassador: Ronald Eng.

Of the USA in Cambodia (27 EO Street 240, Phnom Penh)
Ambassador: Vacant.
Chargé d'Affaires a.i.: Arvizu Alexander.

Of Cambodia to the United Nations
Ambassador: Ouch Borith.

Of Cambodia to the European Union
Ambassador: Prak Sokhonn.

FURTHER READING

Chandler, D. P., *A History of Cambodia*. 2nd ed. Boulder (CO), 1996
Jarvis, Helen, *Cambodia*. [Bibliography] ABC-Clio, Oxford and Santa Barbara (CA), 1997
Martin, M. A, *Cambodia: A Shattered Society*. California Univ. Press, 1994
Peschoux, C., *Le Cambodge dans la Tourmente: le Troisième Conflit Indochinois, 1978–1991*. Paris, 1992.—*Les 'Nouveaux' Khmers Rouges*. Paris, 1992

National statistical office: National Institute of Statistics, Ministry of Planning, 386 Monivong Boulevard, Phnom Penh.
Website: http://www.nis.gov.kh/

CAMEROON

Capital: Yaoundé
Population estimate, 2000: 14·88m.
GDP per capita, 2000: (PPP$) 1,703
HDI/world rank: 0·512/135

République du Cameroun—
Republic of Cameroon

KEY HISTORICAL EVENTS

The name Cameroon derives from *camaráes* (prawns), introduced by Portuguese navigators. Called Kamerun in German and Cameroun in French, the estuary was later called the Cameroons River by British navigators. The Duala people living there were important traders, selling slaves and later palm oil to Europeans. On 12 July 1884 they signed a treaty establishing German rule over Kamerun. Originally covering the Duala's territory on the Wouri, this German colony later expanded to cover a large area inland, home to a number of African peoples. In the First World War Allied forces occupied the territory which was partitioned between France and Britain. British Cameroons consisted of British Southern Cameroons and British Northern Cameroons, adjoining Nigeria. France's mandated territory of Cameroun occupied most of the former German colony. The Dualas continued to take the lead in anti-colonial protest.

In 1946 the French and British territories became Trust Territories of the UN. In French Cameroun the *Union des Populations du Cameroun* (UPC), founded in 1948, became the major nationalist party, calling for independence and 'reunification' with British Cameroons. In Dec. 1956, when elections were held prior to self-government, the UPC began a guerrilla war against the French and the new Cameroonian government. On 1 Jan. 1960 French Cameroun gained independence. The UPC guerrillas were largely defeated by 1963. On 11 Feb. 1961 British Southern Cameroons voted in a referendum to join ex-French Cameroun, while British Northern Cameroons chose to join Nigeria. The country's name was changed to the Republic of Cameroon in 1984.

TERRITORY AND POPULATION

Cameroon is bounded in the west by the Gulf of Guinea, northwest by Nigeria, east by Chad and the Central African Republic, and south by the Republic of the Congo, Gabon and Equatorial Guinea. The total area is 475,440 sq. km. On 29 March 1994 Cameroon asked the International Court of Justice to confirm its sovereignty over the oil-rich Bakassi Peninsula, occupied by Nigerian troops. The dispute continued for eight years, with Equatorial Guinea also subsequently becoming involved. In Oct. 2002 the International Court of Justice rejected Nigeria's claims and awarded the peninsula to Cameroon. All parties agreed to accept the Court's judgment. Population (1987 census) 10,494,000. Estimate (July 1996) 14,261,600 (7,150,400 females); density, 30·0 per sq. km. In 1999, 52% of the population were rural.

The UN gives a projected population for 2010 of 18·35m.

The areas, populations and chief towns of the 10 provinces were:

Province	Sq. km	Census 1987	Chief town	Estimate 1981
Adamaoua	63,691	495,185	Ngaoundéré	47,508
Centre	68,926	1,651,600	Yaoundé	1,120,000[1]
Est	109,011	517,198	Bertoua	18,254
Extrême-Nord	34,246	1,855,695	Maroua	124,000[2]
Littoral	20,239	1,354,833	Douala	1,320,000[3]
Nord (Bénoué)	65,576	832,165	Garoua	142,000[2]
Nord-Ouest	17,810	1,237,348	Bamenda	110,000[2]
Ouest	13,872	1,339,791	Bafoussam	113,000[2]
Sud	47,110	373,798	Ebolowa	22,222
Sud-Ouest	24,471	838,042	Buéa	29,953[2]

[1]1999. [2]1991. [3]1995.

The population is composed of Sudanic-speaking people in the north (Fulani, Sao and others) and Bantu-speaking groups, mainly Bamileke, Beti, Bulu, Tikar,

358

Bassa and Duala, in the rest of the country. The official languages are French and English.

SOCIAL STATISTICS

1995 births, 526,000 (rate of 39·9 per 1,000 population); deaths, 164,000 (rate of 12·4 per 1,000 population). Annual population growth rate, 1990–99, 2·9%. Infant mortality, 1999, 95 per 1,000 live births. Life expectancy in 1999: males, 49·1 years; females, 50·8. Fertility rate, 1999, 5·2 children per woman.

CLIMATE

An equatorial climate, with high temperatures and plentiful rain, especially from March to June and Sept. to Nov. Further inland, rain occurs at all seasons. Yaoundé, Jan. 76°F (24·4°C), July 73°F (22·8°C). Annual rainfall 62" (1,555 mm). Douala, Jan. 79°F (26·1°C), July 75°F (23·9°C). Annual rainfall 160" (4,026 mm).

CONSTITUTION AND GOVERNMENT

The 1972 Constitution, subsequently amended, provides for a *President* as head of state and government. The President is directly elected for a five-year term, and there is a *Council of Ministers* whose members must not be members of parliament.

The *National Assembly*, elected by universal adult suffrage for five years, consists of 180 representatives. After 1966 the sole legal party was the Cameroon People's Democratic Movement (RDPC), but in Dec. 1990 the National Assembly legalized opposition parties.

National Anthem. 'O Cameroon, Thou Cradle of our Fathers'/'O Cameroun, Berceau de nos Ancêtres'; words by R. Afame, tune by R. Afame, S. Bamba and M. Nko'o.

RECENT ELECTIONS

Presidential elections were held on 12 Oct. 1997. The electorate in 1992 was 4,195,687. Paul Biya was elected against two opponents by 92·6% of votes cast.

The most recent National Assembly elections were held on 30 June 2002. The conservative Rassemblement Démocratique du Peuple Camerounais (RDPC) won 133 seats, the Social-Democratic Front (SDF) 21, the Union Démocratique du Cameroun (UDC) 5, the Union des Populations du Cameroun (UPC) 3, and others won 18 seats.

CURRENT ADMINISTRATION

President: Paul Biya; b. 1933 (RDPC; assumed office 6 Nov. 1982, elected 14 Jan. 1984, re-elected 24 April 1988, also 10 Oct. 1992, and once again re-elected 12 Oct. 1997).

In March 2003 the cabinet comprised:

Prime Minister: Peter Mafany Musonge; b. 1942 (RDPC; in office since 19 Sept. 1996).

Minister of State for Justice, Guardian of the Seals: Amadou Ali. *Culture:* Ferdinand Léopold Oyono. *Agriculture:* Augustin Frederick Kodock. *Territorial Administration and Decentralization (Interior):* Marafa Hamidou Yaya. *Industrial and Commercial Development:* Bello Bouba Maigari. *Secretary General at the Presidency:* Jean Marie Atangana Mebara. *External Relations:* François-Xavier Ngoubeyou.

Minister for National Education: Jospeh Owona. *Health:* Urbain Olanguena Awono. *Technical Education and Vocational Training:* Louis Bapes Bapes. *Scientific and Technical Research:* Zachary Perevet. *Youth and Sports:* Bidounng Mkwpatt. *Livestock, Fisheries and Animal Industries:* Hamadjoda Adjoudji. *Environment and Forests:* Tanyi Mbianyor Oben. *Housing:* Adji Abdoulaye Haman. *Town Planning:* Lekene Donfack. *Higher Education:* Maurice Tchuente. *Tourism:* Pierre Hélé. *Public Service and Administrative Reform:* René Ze Nguele. *Communication:* Jacques Fame Ndongo. *Social Affairs:* Cecile Mbomba Nkolo. *Women's Affairs:* Cathérine Bakang Mbock. *Public Works:* Dieudonne Ambassa. *Transport:* Ndeh John Bengheni. *Employment, Labour and Social Insurance:* Robert Nkili. *Mines, Water Resources and Energy:* Joseph Aoudou. *Communications:* Maximin N'Koue Nkongo. *Relations with the Assemblies:* Gregoire Owona. *Economic Affairs, Programming and*

Regional Development: Martin Okouda. *Finance and Budget:* Michel Meva'a Meboutou. *Minister Delegate to the President for Defence:* Laurent Esso.

DEFENCE

The President of the Republic is C.-in-C. of the armed forces. Defence expenditure totalled US$154m. in 2000 (US$10 per capita), representing 1·4% of GDP.

Army. Total strength (1999) is 11,500 and includes a Presidential Guard; there is a Gendarmerie 9,000 strong.

Navy. Personnel in 1999 numbered 1,300. There are bases at Douala (HQ), Limke and Kribi.

Air Force. Aircraft availability is low because of funding problems. Personnel (1999), 300. There are 15 combat aircraft.

INTERNATIONAL RELATIONS

Cameroon is a member of the UN, WTO, the Commonwealth, the African Union, African Development Bank, OIC, International Organization of the Francophonie, the Lake Chad Basin Commission and is an ACP member state of the ACP-EU relationship.

ECONOMY

In 1998 agriculture accounted for 42·4% of GDP, industry 21·7% and services 35·9%.

Overview. The Technical Commission for the Rehabilitation of Public Enterprises is overseeing both privatization and the restructuring of all state-owned companies.

Currency. The unit of currency is the *franc CFA* (XAF) with a parity of 655·957 francs CFA to one euro. In April 2002 foreign exchange reserves were US$508m. (negligible in 1997) and total money supply was 644,230m. francs CFA. Gold reserves were 30,000 troy oz in June 2002. Inflation in 2001 was 2·8%.

Budget. The financial year ends on 30 June. In 1998–99 revenues totalled 867·46bn. francs CFA (862·31bn. francs CFA in 1997–98) and expenditure 859·80bn. francs CFA (777·60bn. francs CFA in 1997–98).

VAT, introduced in 1999, is 17%.

Performance. Real GDP growth was 4·2% in 2000 and 5·3% in 2001. Total GDP in 2001 was US$8·6bn.

Banking and Finance. The *Banque des Etats de l'Afrique Centrale* (*Governor,* Jean-Félix Mamalepot) is the sole bank of issue. There are ten, including three foreign, commercial banks.

Weights and Measures. The metric system is in use.

ENERGY AND NATURAL RESOURCES

Environment. According to the *World Bank Atlas* Cameroon's carbon dioxide emissions in 1998 were the equivalent of 0·1 tonnes per capita.

Electricity. Installed capacity in 1997 was 1m. kW. Total production in 1998 was 3·28bn. kWh (97% hydro-electric), with consumption per capita 185 kWh.

Oil and Gas. Oil production (1996), mainly from Kole oilfield, was 33m. bbls. In 1999 there were proven reserves of 0·4bn. bbls. In June 2000 the World Bank approved funding for a 1,000-km US$4bn. pipeline to run from 300 new oil wells in Chad through Cameroon to the Atlantic Ocean.

Minerals. Tin ore and limestone are extracted. There are deposits of bauxite, uranium, nickel, gold, cassiterite and kyanite.

Agriculture. In 1998 there were 5·96m. ha of arable land and 1·20m. ha of permanent crops. 33,000 ha were irrigated in 1998. Main agricultural crops (with 2000 production in 1,000 tonnes): cassava, 2,067; plantains, 1,403; sugarcane, 1,350; bananas, 850; maize, 850; sorghum, 500; yams, 260; seed cotton, 220; sweet potatoes, 180; dry beans, 170; groundnuts, 160; palm oil, 140; cocoa beans, 120; pumpkins and squash, 120.

Livestock (2000): 5·9m. cattle; 3·88m. sheep; 3·85m. goats; 1·43m. pigs; 30m. chickens.

Livestock products (in 1,000 tonnes), 2000: beef and veal, 90; pork, bacon and ham, 18; lamb and mutton, 17; goat meat, 15; poultry meat, 24; cow's milk, 125; goat's milk, 42; eggs, 14.

Forestry. Forests covered 19·6m. ha in 1995 (42·1% of the total land area), ranging from tropical rain forests in the south (producing hardwoods such as mahogany, ebony and sapele) to semi-deciduous forests in the centre and wooded savannah in the north. The area under forests in 1990 had been 20·3m. ha (43·5% of the land area). Timber production in 1999 was 15·28m. cu. metres.

Fisheries. In 2000 the total catch was 112,109 tonnes (57,109 tonnes from sea fishing).

INDUSTRY
Manufacturing is largely small-scale, with only some 30 firms employing more than 10 workers. Aluminium production in 1997 was 91,000 metric tonnes. 1997 output included: petrol, 303,000 tonnes; distillate fuel oil, 291,000 tonnes; kerosene, 247,000 tonnes; residual fuel oil, 155,000 tonnes; sugar (1998), 46,100 tonnes; cigarettes (1993), 5m. There are also factories producing shoes, beer, soap, oil and food products.

Labour. In 1996 the workforce numbered 5,500,000 (62% males), of whom over 50% were occupied in agriculture.

Trade Unions. The principal trade union federation is the *Organisation des syndicats des travailleurs camerounais* (OSTC), established on 7 Dec. 1985 to replace the former body, the UNTC.

INTERNATIONAL TRADE
Foreign debt was US$9,241m. in 2000.

Imports and Exports. In 1999 total imports amounted to US$1,315·8m. and exports to US$1,587·7m. Principal exports (in US$1m.), 1999: crude oil, 552·1; sawn wood, 191·1; cocoa, 162·5; coffee, 121·0; aluminium, 94·5.

Main export markets, 1999: Italy, 22%; France, 18%; Spain, 13%; Netherlands, 9%. Main import suppliers: France, 28%; Nigeria, 12%; Germany, 6%.

COMMUNICATIONS

Roads. There were about 64,626 km of classified roads in 1997, of which 2,666 km were paved. In 1996 there were 98,000 passenger cars and 64,350 commercial vehicles.

Rail. Cameroon Railways (*Regifercam*), 1,104 km in 1995, link Douala with Nkongsamba and Ngaoundéré, with branches from M'Banga to Kumba and Makak to M'Balmayo. In 1992–93 railways carried 1·9m. passengers and 1·2m. tonnes of freight.

Civil Aviation. There are 45 airports including three international airports at Douala, Garoua and Yaoundé (Nsimalen). In 2000 Douala handled 419,000 passengers (339,000 on international flights). In 1998 Cameroon Airlines (Camair), the national carrier, operated on domestic routes and provided international services to Abidjan, Brazzaville, Cotonou, Harare, Jeddah, Johannesburg, Kigali, Lagos, Libreville, Lomé, London, Malabo, Nairobi, N'Djaména and Paris. In 1999 scheduled airline traffic of Cameroon-based carriers flew 6·0m. km, carrying 293,000 passengers (204,000 on international flights).

Shipping. In 1998 the merchant marine totalled 13,000 GRT. In 1993 vessels totalling 5,279,000 net registered tons entered. The main port is Douala; other ports are Bota, Campo, Garoua (only navigable in the rainy season), Kribi and Limbo-Tiko.

Telecommunications. In 1999 there were 94,600 telephone main lines, or 6·4 per 1,000 inhabitants. There were 4,200 mobile phone subscribers in 1997 and 50,000 PCs were in use in 2000 (3·3 per 1,000 persons). Cameroon had 20,000 Internet users in July 2000.

Postal Services. There were 261 post offices in 1995.

SOCIAL INSTITUTIONS

Justice. The Supreme Court sits at Yaoundé, as does the High Court of Justice (consisting of nine titular judges and six surrogates all appointed by the National Assembly). There are magistrates' courts situated in the provinces.

The population in penal institutions in 1997 was 15,903 (115 per 100,000 of national population).

Religion. In 1992 there were 4·43m. Roman Catholics, 2·79m. Muslims and 2·23m. Protestants. Some of the population follow traditional animist religions.

Education. In 1996–97 there were 1,109 pre-primary schools with 4,545 teachers for 87,318 pupils and 8,514 primary schools with 39,384 teachers for 1,921,186 pupils. In 1994–95 there were 459,068 secondary level pupils at general secondary and tertiary schools and technical schools.

In 1991, 33,177 students were in higher education at 33 teacher training colleges and 5 new institutions of higher education. Total staff: 1,086. In 1994–95 there were 6 universities and 1 Roman Catholic university, 4 specialized *Ecoles Nationales*, an *Ecole Supérieure* for posts and telecommunications, 6 specialized institutes, a national school of administration and magistracy and a faculty of Protestant theology. In 1995–96 there were 15,220 university students and 830 academic staff. The adult literacy rate in 1999 was 74·8% (81·2% among males and 68·6% among females).

Health. In 1988 there were 629 hospitals. In 1989 there were 945 doctors, 55 dentists, 206 pharmacists and 6,053 nurses.

CULTURE

Broadcasting. The state-controlled Cameroon Radio Television provides home, national, provincial and urban radio programmes and a TV service (colour by PAL). In 1997 there were about 2·3m. radio and 450,000 TV receivers.

Press. There was (1997) one national government-owned daily newspaper with a circulation of 66,000 and about 100 other periodicals, including 20 weeklies.

Tourism. In 1998 there were 135,000 foreign tourists, bringing revenue of US$40m.

DIPLOMATIC REPRESENTATIVES

Of Cameroon in the United Kingdom (84 Holland Park, London, W11 3SB)
High Commissioner: Dr Samuel Libock Mbei.

Of the United Kingdom in Cameroon (Ave Winston Churchill, BP 547, Yaoundé)
High Commissioner: Richard Wildash, LVO.

Of Cameroon in the USA (2349 Massachusetts Ave., NW, Washington, D.C., 20008)
Ambassador: Jérôme Mendouga.

Of the USA in Cameroon (Rue Nachtigal, BP 817, Yaoundé)
Ambassador: George M. Staples.

Of Cameroon to the United Nations
Ambassador: Martin Belinga-Eboutou.

Of Cameroon to the European Union
Ambassador: Isabelle Bassong.

FURTHER READING

National statistical office: Direction de la Statistique et de la Comptabilité Nationale, Ministère du Plan et de l'Aménagement du Territoire, Yaoundé

Ardener, E., *Kingdom on Mount Cameroon: Studies in the History of the Cameroon Coast 1500–1970.* Berghahn Books, Oxford, 1996
DeLancey, M. W., *Cameroon: Dependence and Independence.* London, 1989

CANADA

Capital: Ottawa
Population estimate, 2000: 30·76m.
GDP per capita, 2000: (PPP$) 24,277
HDI/world rank: 0·941/2

KEY HISTORICAL EVENTS

The first European in Canada was John Cabot in 1497. France claimed possession in 1534. The territories which now constitute Canada came under British power at various times by settlement, conquest or cession. For the most part such efforts were directed at gaining advantage over the indigenous Indian and Eskimo communities as well as displacing French colonial rule. Conflict also broke out, however, with the fledgling United States in the Anglo-American war of 1812–14. Since then, Canada and the USA have maintained the world's longest undefended border. Nova Scotia was occupied in 1628 by settlement at Port Royal, was ceded back to France in 1632 and was finally ceded by France in 1713 by the Treaty of Utrecht. The Hudson's Bay Company's charter, conferring rights over all the territory draining into Hudson Bay, was granted in 1670. Canada, with all its dependencies, including New Brunswick and Prince Edward Island, was formally ceded to Great Britain by France in 1763; Vancouver Island was acknowledged to be British by the Oregon Boundary Treaty of 1846; and British Columbia was established as a separate colony in 1858. As originally constituted, Canada was composed of the provinces of Upper and Lower Canada (now Ontario and Quebec), Nova Scotia and New Brunswick. They were united under the British North America Act, 1867. The Act provided that the constitution of Canada should be 'similar in principle to that of the United Kingdom'; that the executive authority should be vested in the Sovereign and carried out by a Governor-General and Privy Council; and that the legislative power should be exercised by a Parliament of two Houses: the Senate, membership of which is by appointment, and the House of Commons, whose members are elected.

In 1931 the Statute of Westminster emancipated the Provinces as well as the Dominion from the operation of the Colonial Laws Validity Act, thus removing any remaining limitations on Canada's legislative autonomy.

Provision was made in the British North America Act for the admission of British Columbia, Prince Edward Island, the Northwest Territories and Newfoundland into the Union. In 1869 Rupert's Land, or the Northwest Territories, was purchased from the Hudson's Bay Company; the province of Manitoba was erected from this territory and admitted into the confederation on 15 July 1870. On 20 July 1871 the province of British Columbia was admitted and Prince Edward Island on 1 July 1873. The provinces of Alberta and Saskatchewan were formed from the provisional districts of Alberta, Athabaska, Assiniboia and Saskatchewan, and were admitted on 1 Sept. 1905. Newfoundland formally joined Canada as its 10th province on 31 March 1949. In Feb. 1931 Norway formally recognized the Canadian title to the Sverdrup group of Arctic islands. Canada thus holds sovereignty in the whole Arctic sector north of the Canadian mainland.

In 1982 an amended constitution replaced the British North America Act to give Canada prerogative over all future constitutional changes. At the same time a charter of Rights and Freedoms was introduced recognizing the nation's multi-cultural heritage, affirming the existing rights of native peoples and the principle of equality of benefits to the provinces.

In April 1999 the predominantly-Inuit territory of Nunavut came into existence.

TERRITORY AND POPULATION

Canada is bounded in the northwest by the Beaufort Sea, north by the Arctic Ocean, northeast by Baffin Bay, east by the Davis Strait, Labrador Sea and Atlantic Ocean, south by the USA and west by the Pacific Ocean and USA (Alaska). The area is 9,984,670 sq. km, of which 891,163 sq. km are fresh water. 2001 census population, 30,007,094 (15,693,393 females), giving a density of 3·0 per sq. km. In 2001, 79·7% of the population were urban.

The UN gives a projected population for 2010 of 33·22m.
Population at previous censuses:

1851	2,436,297	1911	7,206,643	1971	21,568,311
1861	3,229,633	1921	8,787,949	1976[1]	22,992,604
1871	3,689,257	1931	10,376,786	1981	24,343,181
1881	4,324,810	1941	11,506,655	1986[1]	25,309,331
1891	4,833,239	1951	14,009,429	1991	27,296,859[2]
1901	5,371,315	1961	18,238,247	1996[1]	28,848,761[2]

[1]It became a statutory requirement to conduct a census every five years in 1971.
[2]Excludes data from incompletely enumerated Indian reserves and Indian settlements.

Of the total population in 2001, 80·9% were Canadian-born. Alberta had the biggest population increase between 1996 and 2001 with 10·3%, whilst Newfoundland had the biggest population reduction with −7·0%, more than double the 2·9% rate of decline recorded between 1991 and 1996.

The population (2001) born outside Canada in the provinces was in the following ratio (%): Alberta, 14·9; British Columbia, 26·1; Manitoba, 12·1; New Brunswick, 3·1; Newfoundland, 1·6; Northwest Territories, 6·4; Nova Scotia, 4·6; Nunavut, 1·7; Ontario, 26·8; Prince Edward Island, 3·1; Quebec, 9·9; Saskatchewan, 5·0; Yukon, 10·6.

Figures for the 2001 census population according to ethnic origin (leading categories), were[1]:

Canadian	11,682,680	Chinese	1,094,700
English	5,978,875	Ukrainian	1,071,060
French	4,668,410	North American Indian	1,000,890
Scottish	4,157,210	Dutch	923,310
Irish	3,822,660	Polish	817,085
German	2,742,765	East Indian	713,330
Italian	1,270,370		

[1]Census respondents who reported multiple ethnic origins are counted for each origin they reported.

The aboriginal population (those persons identifying with at least one aboriginal group, and including North American Indian, Métis or Inuit) numbered 976,305 in 2001. In 2001, 59·1% of the population gave their mother tongue as English and 22·9% as French (English and French are both official languages); Chinese was reported as the third most common language, accounting for 2·9% of the total population. In 2001, 1·8m. residents were immigrants who arrived between 1991 and 2001, accounting for 6·2% of the total population; 58% came from Asia (including the Middle East), 20% from Europe, 11% from the Caribbean, Central and South America, 8% from Africa, and 3% from the USA.

Populations of Census Metropolitan Areas (CMA) and Cities (proper), 2001 census:

	CMA	City proper		CMA	City proper
Toronto	4,682,897	2,481,494	Halifax	359,183	119,292
Montreal	3,426,350	1,039,534	Victoria	311,902	74,125
Vancouver	1,986,965	545,671	Windsor	307,877	208,402
Ottawa-Hull	1,063,664	—	Oshawa	296,298	139,051
Ottawa	—	774,072	Saskatoon	225,927	196,811
Hull	—	66,246	Regina	192,800	178,225
Calgary	951,395	878,866	St John's	172,918	99,182
Edmonton	937,845	616,014	Sudbury	155,601	85,354
Quebec	682,757	169,076	Chicoutimi-		
Winnipeg	671,274	619,544	Jonquière	154,938	—
Hamilton	662,401	490,268	Chicoutimi	—	60,008
London	432,451	336,539	Jonquière	—	54,842
Kitchener	414,284	190,399	Sherbrooke	153,811	75,916
St Catharines-			Abbotsford	147,370	115,463
Niagara	377,009	—	Kingston	146,838	114,195
St Catharines	—	129,170	Trois Rivières	137,507	46,295
Niagara Falls	—	78,815	Saint John	122,678	69,661

Ottawa: Situated in the southeast of the province of Ontario, Ottawa has a population of just over 1m., with two-thirds English speaking and one-third French speaking. The city lies on the Ottawa River, which has been used by native Canadians as a highway for thousands of years. As well as being the seat of Canadian federal government, Ottawa is an important centre for health and life science research and the development of space and environmental technology.

SOCIAL STATISTICS
Statistics for period from July–June:

	Live births	Deaths
1998–99	338,963	222,538
1999–2000	333,954	229,138
2000–01	329,791	227,076
2001–02	327,187	231,232

Annual population growth rate, 1990–99, 1·2%. Birth rate, 2000–01 (per 1,000 population), 10·7; death rate, 7·3. Marriages, 2001, numbered 153,234; divorces, 70,292. In 1997 the most popular age range for marrying was 25–29 for both males and females, followed by 30–34 for males and 20–24 for females. Suicides, 1997, 3,681 (12·3 per 100,000 population). Life expectancy at birth, 1999, was 75·9 years for men and 81·4 years for women. Infant mortality, 1999, 6 per 1,000 live births; fertility rate, 1999, 1·6 children per woman.

CLIMATE
The climate ranges from polar conditions in the north to cool temperate in the south, but with considerable differences between east coast, west coast and the interior, affecting temperatures, rainfall amounts and seasonal distribution. Winters are very severe over much of the country, but summers can be very hot inland. See individual provinces for climatic details.

CONSTITUTION AND GOVERNMENT
In Nov. 1981 the Canadian government agreed on the provisions of an amended constitution, to the end that it should replace the British North America Act and that its future amendment should be the prerogative of Canada. These proposals were adopted by the Parliament of Canada and were enacted by the UK Parliament as the Canada Act of 1982. This was the final act of the UK Parliament in Canadian constitutional development. The Act gave to Canada the power to amend the Constitution according to procedures determined by the Constitutional Act 1982. The latter added to the Canadian Constitution a charter of Rights and Freedoms, and provisions which recognize the nation's multi-cultural heritage, affirm the existing rights of native peoples, confirm the principle of equalization of benefits among the provinces, and strengthen provincial ownership of natural resources.

Under the Constitution legislative power is vested in Parliament, consisting of the Queen, represented by a Governor-General, a Senate and a House of Commons. The members of the *Senate* are appointed until age 75 by summons of the Governor-General under the Great Seal of Canada. Members appointed before 2 June 1965 may remain in office for life. The Senate consists of 105 senators: 24 from Ontario, 24 from Quebec, 10 from Nova Scotia, 10 from New Brunswick, 6 from Manitoba, 6 from British Columbia, 6 from Alberta, 6 from Saskatchewan, 6 from Newfoundland, 4 from Prince Edward Island, 1 from the Yukon Territory, 1 from the Northwest Territories, and 1 from Nunavut. Each senator must be at least 30 years of age and reside in the province for which he or she is appointed. The *House of Commons* is elected by universal secret suffrage, by a first-past-the-post system, for five-year terms. Representation is based on the population of all the provinces taken as a whole with readjustments made after each census.

The Special Joint Committee of the Senate and the House of Commons on a Renewed Canada released a unanimous report on 28 Feb. 1992 (Beaudoin-Dobbie Report). Another constitutional document was released on 16 July 1992 by the provincial premiers which summarized the multilateral meetings on the Constitution. A final constitutional accord was arrived at by the provinces and the federal government in Aug. 1992. At a national referendum on 26 Oct. 1992 proposed constitutional reforms were rejected by 54·4% of votes cast.

Indians have representation in the *Assembly of First Nations* (Chief, Matthew Coon Come).

The office and appointment of the Governor-General are regulated by letters patent of 1947. In 1977 the Queen approved the transfer to the Governor-General

of functions discharged by the Sovereign. The Governor-General is assisted by a
Privy Council composed of Cabinet Ministers.

Canadian Parliamentary Guide. Annual. Ottawa
Bejermi, J., *Canadian Parliamentary Handbook.* Ottawa, 1993
Cairns, A. C., *Charter versus Federalism: the Dilemmas of Constitutional Reform.* Montreal, 1992
  Canada: The State of the Federation. Queen's Univ., annual
Forsey, E. A., *How Canadians Govern Themselves.* Ottawa, 1991
Fox, P. W. and White, G., *Politics Canada.* 7th ed. Toronto, 1991
Hogg, P. W., *Constitutional Law of Canada.* 3rd ed. Toronto, 1992
Kaplan, W. (ed.) *Belonging: the Meaning and Future of Canadian Citizenship.* McGill-Queen's Univ. Press, 1993
Kernaghan, K., *Public Administration in Canada: a Text.* Scarborough, 1991
Mahler, G., *Contemporary Canadian Politics, 1970–1994: an Annotated Bibliography.* 2 vols. Westport (CT), 1995
Osbaldston, G. F., *Organizing to Govern.* Toronto, 1992
Reesor, B., *The Canadian Constitution in Historical Perspective.* Scarborough, 1992
Tardi, G., *The Legal Framework of Government: a Canadian Guide.* Aurora, 1992

National Anthem. 'O Canada, our home and native land'/'O Canada, terre de nos aïeux'; words by A. Routhier, tune by C. Lavallée.

RECENT ELECTIONS
At the elections of 27 Nov. 2000 the Liberal Party (Lib.) gained 172 seats (155 in 1997) with 40·78% of votes cast; the Canadian Reform Conservative Alliance 66 (60, as the Reform Party) with 25·51%; the Bloc Québécois (BQ) 38 (44) with 10·68%; the New Democratic Party 13 (21) with 8·53%; the Progressive Conservative Party 12 (20) with 12·21%. Turn-out was a record low 62·9%.

CURRENT ADMINISTRATION
Governor-General: Adrienne Clarkson (b. 1939; term of office 1999–2004).

The thirty-seventh Parliament, elected on 27 Nov. 2000, comprised 301 members.

State of the parties in the Senate (March 2002): Liberals, 62; Progressive Conservatives, 30; independents, 5; Canadian Reform Conservative Alliance, 1; vacant, 7.

In March 2003 the Liberal cabinet comprised:

Prime Minister: The Rt. Hon. Jean Chrétien; b. 1934 (sworn in 4 Nov. 1993; re-elected in 1997 and 2000).

Deputy Prime Minister and Minister of Finance and Infrastructure: John Manley. *Minister of Foreign Affairs:* Bill Graham. *Transport:* David Michael Collenette. *Fisheries and Oceans:* Robert Thibault. *Natural Resources:* Herb Dhaliwal. *Public Works and Government Services:* Ralph E. Goodale. *Canadian Heritage:* Sheila Copps. *International Trade:* Pierre Pettigrew. *Industry:* Allan Rock. *International Co-operation:* Susan Whelan. *National Defence:* John McCallum. *President of the Treasury Board:* Lucienne Robillard. *Justice and Attorney General of Canada:* Martin Cauchon. *Health:* Anne McLellan. *Labour:* Claudette Bradshaw. *Environment:* David Anderson. *Citizenship and Immigration:* Denis Coderre. *Veterans Affairs:* Rey Pagtakhan. *Agriculture:* Lyle Vanclief. *National Revenue:* Elinor Caplan. *Indian Affairs and Northern Development:* Robert Nault. *President of the Queen's Privy Council for Canada and Intergovernmental Affairs:* Stéphane Dion. *Human Resources Development:* Jane Stewart. *Leader of the Government in the Senate:* Sharon Carstairs. *Solicitor General of Canada:* Wayne Easter.

The *Leader of the Opposition* is Stephen Harper.

Office of the Prime Minister: http://www.pm.gc.ca/

DEFENCE
The armed forces are unified and organized in functional commands: Land Forces (army), Air Command (air forces) and Maritime Command (naval and naval air forces). In 2002 the armed forces numbered 52,300 (6,100 women); reserves, 35,400.

Military expenditure totalled US$7,745m. in 2001 (US$250 per capita), representing 1·1% of GDP.

Army. The Land Forces numbered 19,300 in 2002 including 1,600 women. Reserves include a Militia of 14,000 and 3,500 Canadian Rangers.

Navy. The naval combatant force, which forms part of the Maritime Command of the unified armed forces, is headquartered at Halifax (Nova Scotia), and includes 2 diesel submarines, 4 destroyers and 12 helicopter-carrying frigates. Naval personnel in 2002 numbered about 9,000, with 4,000 reserves. The main bases are Halifax, where about two-thirds of the fleet is based, and Esquimalt (British Columbia).

Air Force. The air forces numbered 13,500 in 2002 (1,700 women) with 140 combat aircraft.

INTERNATIONAL RELATIONS

Canada is a member of the UN, WTO, NATO, the Commonwealth, OAS, OECD, OSCE, APEC, BIS, Inter-American Development Bank, Asian Development Bank, IOM, Antarctic Treaty and the International Organization of the Francophonie.

ECONOMY

Agriculture accounted for 3% of GDP in 1998, industry 31% and services 66%.

According to the anti-corruption organization *Transparency International*, Canada ranked equal 7th in the world in a 2002 survey of the countries with the least corruption in business and government. It received 9·0 out of 10 in the annual index.

Overview. The economy expanded strongly until late 2000, but is now suffering from the weaker US economy. Greater integration of the two economies follows a relaxation of trade barriers throughout the 1990s. The Bank of Canada has relaxed its monetary policy. In 2001, with interest rates at a 40-year low, the stock market fell and the currency was depressed. Growth in employment and disposable income together with lower tax and interest rates supported consumer spending. In Feb. 2000 the government introduced the largest tax cuts in Canadian history. Budget 2000 introduced a five-year programme to improve the infrastructure.

Currency. The unit of currency is the *Canadian dollar* (CAD) of 100 *cents*. In June 2002 gold reserves were 0·86m. troy oz and foreign exchange reserves totalled US$32,831m. Total money supply was $258,252m. CDN in June 2002. Inflation was 2·7% in 2000 and 2·5% in 2001.

Budget. Consolidated federal, provincial, territorial and local government revenue and expenditure for fiscal years ending 31 March (in $1m. CDN):

	1997–98	1998–99	1999–2000	2000–01
Revenue	373,531	382,797	409,884	436,631
Expenditure	372,695	386,147	398,406	416,646

In 2000–01 revenue included (in $1m. CDN): income taxes, 187,683; consumption taxes, 85,422; sales of goods and services, 32,753; contributions to Social Insurance Plans, 30,633. Expenditure included social services, 107,437; health, 69,384; education, 61,742; debt charges, 61,568.

On 1 Jan. 1991 a 7% Goods and Services Tax (GST) was introduced, superseding a 13·5% Manufacturers' Sales Tax.

Performance. Total GDP was US$677,178m. in 2001. Real GDP growth was 4·5% in 2000 and 1·5% in 2001, rising to an estimated 3·3% in 2002.

Banking and Finance. The Bank of Canada (established 1935) is the central bank and bank of issue. The *Governor* (David Dodge) is appointed by the Bank's directors for seven-year terms. The Minister of Finance owns the capital stock of the Bank on behalf of Canada. Banks in Canada are chartered under the terms of the Bank Act, which imposes strict conditions on capital reserves, returns to the federal government, types of lending operations, ownership and other matters. In June 2000 there were 50 chartered banks, 11 domestic and 39 foreign, with 8,267 branches in all provinces and both territories in Canada. The total assets owned by the domestic banks in 1999 came to $1,277bn. CDN. The First Nations Bank was founded in Dec. 1996 to provide finance to Inuit and Indian entrepreneurs.

Bank charters expire every 10 years which gives the federal government an opportunity to review and amend sections of the Bank Act. Extensive changes were brought into force in June 1992. As a result of the substantial revision, bank charters were only renewed for five years. The chartered banks make regular detailed returns to and are subject to periodic inspection by the Superintendent of Financial Institutions, an official appointed by the government.

The Bank Act of 1980 required chartered banks to maintain a statutory primary reserve of 10% on demand deposits, 3% on foreign-currency deposits and 2% on notice deposits, with an additional 1% on the portion of notice deposits exceeding $500m. CDN. This reserve is required to be maintained in the form of notes and deposits with the Bank of Canada. A secondary reserve of 4% in the form of treasury bills, government bonds, etc., is also required.

There are stock exchanges at Calgary (Alberta Stock Exchange), Montreal, Toronto, Vancouver and Winnipeg.

Weights and Measures. The legal weights and measures are in transition from the Imperial to the International system of units. The Metric Commission, established in June 1971, co-ordinates Canada's conversion to the metric system.

ENERGY AND NATURAL RESOURCES

Environment. According to the *World Bank Atlas* Canada's carbon dioxide emissions in 1998 were the equivalent of 15·4 tonnes per capita. An *Environmental Sustainability Index* compiled for the World Economic Forum meeting in Feb. 2002 ranked Canada fourth in the world, with 70·6%. The index measured the ability of countries to maintain favourable environmental conditions and examined various factors including pollution levels and the use or abuse of natural resources.

Electricity. Generating capacity, 1997, 112m. kW. Net electricity generation in 1995 was 544m. MWh, of which 503m. MWh was to meet domestic demand. Of the total generated, 62% was from hydrogeneration, 21% from thermal generation and 17% from nuclear generation. In 2001 there were 14 nuclear reactors in use. Production, 1998, 550·85bn. kWh; consumption per capita was 15,071 kWh in 1998.

Oil and Gas. Oil reserves in 1999 were 6·8bn. bbls.; gas (1999), 1,810,000m. cu. metres. Production of crude petroleum, 1998, 128·4m. cu. metres; natural gas (1999), 176,797m. cu. metres. Canada is the third largest producer of natural gas, after Russia and the USA. Canada's first off-shore field, 250 km off Nova Scotia, began producing in June 1992.

Water. Annual average water usage in Canada is 1,600 cu. metres per person—less than in the USA but nearly twice the average for an industrialized nation.

Minerals. Mineral production in 1998 (in 1,000 tonnes): sand and gravel, 225,338; coal, 75,360; iron ore, 36,586; lignite, 37,434 (1997); salt, 13,034; aluminium, 2,370; peat, 1,125; zinc, 992; copper, 691; asbestos, 321; nickel, 198; lead, 150; uranium, 9·99 (the highest of any country in the world); silver, 1·14; gold, 155 (2000); cobalt, 2; cadmium, 1·5 (1994); lime, 2,461; gypsum, 7,974 (1995); diamonds, 2·3m. carats (1999).

Agriculture. According to the census of 1991 the total land area was 9,221,175 sq. km, of which 677,444 sq. km was agricultural.

Grain growing, dairy farming, fruit farming, ranching and fur farming are all practised. In 2000, 2·4% of the economically active population was engaged in agriculture. Total farm cash receipts (2000) $38,298,728,817 CDN. There were 711,335 tractors in 1998 and 132,453 harvester-threshers.

The following table shows the value of farm cash receipts for 1997, for selected agricultural commodities, in $1m. CDN:

Crops		Livestock and products	14,581
Wheat	3,593	Beef	5,222
Barley	732	Hogs	2,985
Canola	2,038	Poultry	1,298
Oats	274	Dairy	3,710
Deferred grain receipts	102		
Other cereals and oilseeds	1,962		
Other crops	4,507		

Crops total 13,933.

Average farm size, 598 acres. In 1996, 252,839 farms (of which 67,531 were beef cattle farms; 24,411 dairy; 29,526 wheat; 51,577 other grain and oilseed) reported total gross farm receipts of $2,500 CDN or more.

Output (in 1,000 tonnes) and harvested area (in 1,000 ha) of crops:

	Output		Harvested Area	
	1999	2000	1999	2000
Wheat	26,900	26,804	10,367	10,963
Barley	13,196	13,468	4,069	4,551
Rapeseeds	8,798	7,119	5,564	4,816
Maize	9,161	6,827	1,141	1,088
Potatoes	4,268	4,569	157	158
Oats	3,641	3,389	1,398	1,299
Peas	2,252	2,864	835	1,220
Soybeans	2,781	2,703	1,004	1,061
Lentils	724	914	497	688
Sugarbeets	744	821	17	15
Linseeds	1,022	693	777	591
Tomatoes	683	670	9	8
Chickpeas	197	387	139	283
Carrots	294	279	9	8
Beans	294	261	150	158
Rye	387	260	169	115
Onions	181	189	5	5
Cabbages	180	167	9	8
Sunflower seeds	122	119	79	69

Canada is the world's leading barley and rapeseed producer and the second largest producer of oats.

Livestock. In parts of Saskatchewan and Alberta, stockraising is still carried on as a primary industry, but the livestock industry of the country at large is mainly a subsidiary of mixed farming. The following table shows the numbers of livestock (in 1,000) by provinces in 2001:

Provinces	Milch cows	Total cattle and calves	Sheep and lambs	Pigs
Newfoundland and Labrador	4·7	9·5	7·9	2·7
Prince Edward Island	14·6	84·8	3·6	126·1
Nova Scotia	23·9	108·4	24·9	124·9
New Brunswick	19·0	91·2	9·6	137·0
Quebec	407·2	1,362·8	254·1	4,267·4
Ontario	363·5	2,140·7	337·6	3,457·3
Manitoba	42·4	1,424·4	84·8	2,540·2
Saskatchewan	30·1	2,899·5	149·4	1,109·8
Alberta	84·0	6,615·2	307·3	2,027·5
British Columbia	71·4	814·9	83·3	165·8
Total	1,061·0	15,551·4	1,262·4	13,958·8

Other livestock totals (2000): horses, 385,000; chickens, 158m.; turkeys, 5m.

Livestock products. Slaughterings in 2000: pigs, 19·96m.; cattle, 3·77m.; sheep, 0·53m. Production, 2000 (in 1,000 tonnes): pork, bacon and ham, 1,675; beef and veal, 1,260; poultry meat, 1,065; horsemeat, 18; lamb and mutton, 11; cow's milk, 8,090; hens' eggs, 357; cheese, 351; honey, 32; tallow, 94.

Fruit production in 2000, in 1,000 tonnes: apples, 532; grapes, 61; peaches and nectarines, 27; strawberries, 24; pears, 20; raspberries, 14.

Forestry. Forestry is of great economic importance, and forestry products (pulp, newsprint, building timber) constitute Canada's most valuable exports. As of 1986, the total area of land covered by forests was estimated at 453·3m. ha. In 1995 the area classed as productive forest land was estimated at 2,446 sq. km, or 26·5% of the total land area, up from 2,437 sq. km in 1990 as a result of afforestation.

In 1999, 185·66m. cu. metres of roundwood was produced.

Fur Trade. In 1996, 1,467,500 wildlife pelts valued at $34,541,000 CDN, and 948,800 ranch-raised pelts valued at $41,265,300 CDN were produced.

Fisheries. In 1993 the fishing fleet comprised 432 vessels totalling 169,900 GRT.

In 2000 the total catch was 993,605 tonnes (952,938 tonnes from sea fishing). In 1997 Atlantic landings totalled 679,283 tonnes and Pacific landings 226,183 tonnes. Value of sea fisheries landed in 1996 totalled $1,536m. CDN.

INDUSTRY

The leading companies by market capitalization in Canada, excluding banking and finance, in Jan. 2002 were: The Thomson Corporation ($28bn. CDN), a media and photography company; BCE Inc. ($28bn. CDN), a telecommunications company; and Nortel Networks Corporation ($26bn. CDN), a telecom equipment manufacturer.

Principal manufactures in 1998 (in 1,000 tonnes): petrol, 28,353 (1997); distillate oil, 27,541 (1997); mechanical wood pulp (1992), 22,830; paper and cardboard (1997), 18,969; cement, 12,124; crude steel, 10,819 (1999); crude iron and alloys, 8,640 (1996); newsprint, 8,623; residual fuel oil, 6,792 (1997); jet fuel, 4,140 (1997); sulphuric acid, 4,100 (1997); aluminium, 2,390 (1999); kerosene, 2,177 (1997); synthetic rubber, 191; sugar, 103; motor vehicles (1997), 2·58m. units; cigarettes (1996), 49·4bn. units; sawn timber (1997), 64·8m. cu. metres; plywood (1997), 1·83m. cu. metres; chipboard (1992), 3·26m. cu. metres.

Labour. In 1997 there were (in 1,000), 13,940·5 (6,291·7 females) in employment, distributed as follows: community, social and personal services, 4,191·2; trade, restaurants and hotels, 3,283·9; manufacturing, 2,166·2; finance, insurance and real estate, 1,799·8; transport, storage and communication, 897·1; construction, 747·3; agriculture, forestry, hunting and fishing, 537·5; utilities, 139·9. In Jan. 2003 the unemployment rate stood at 7·4%.

In 1995, 1,607,000 working days were lost in industrial disputes.

Trade Unions. Union membership in early 2000 was 3·7m., of whom nearly 70% belonged to the Canadian Labour Congress. Newfoundland is the most unionized province, with 40% of all paid employees being union members.

It is generally established by legislation, both federal and provincial, that a trade union to which the majority of employees in a unit suitable for collective bargaining belong, is given certain rights and duties. An employer is required to meet and negotiate with such a trade union to determine wage rates and other working conditions of employees. The employer, the trade union and the employees affected are bound by the resulting agreement. If an impasse is reached in negotiation, conciliation services provided by the appropriate government board are available. Generally, work stoppages do not take place until an established conciliation or mediation procedure has been carried out, and are prohibited while an agreement is in effect.

INTERNATIONAL TRADE

A North American Free Trade Agreement (NAFTA) between Canada, Mexico and the USA was signed on 7 Oct. 1992 and came into force on 1 Jan. 1994.

Imports and Exports. Trade in US$1m.:

	1996	1997	1998	1999	2000
Imports f.o.b.	174,352	200,516	204,631	220,064	244,538
Exports f.o.b.	205,443	217,739	217,406	242,820	281,148

Canada is heavily dependent on foreign trade, with exports and imports equivalent to 82% of GDP. Exports to the USA accounted for over 30% of GDP in 1998. Main export markets, 1998 (in $1m. CDN): USA, 270,560·5; Japan, 9,635·5; EU, 17,837·3; other OECD countries, 7,487·0; other countries, 17,879·9. Main import suppliers (in $1m. CDN): USA, 234,177·3; Japan, 9,657·0; EU, 25,424·0; other OECD countries, 11,377·3; other countries, 23,348·2.

Main categories of exports, 1998 (in $1m. CDN): vehicles and parts, 79,246·8 (of which passenger cars and chassis, 43,599·9; motor vehicle parts, 21,621·4); machinery and equipment, 78,770·2 (industrial and agricultural machinery, 16,598·1; aircraft and other transport equipment, 16,245·6); industrial goods and materials, 57,356·1 (metals and alloys, 19,720·2; chemicals, plastics and fertilizers, 17,513·7); forestry products, 35,464·6 (lumber and sawmill products, 16,569·6; newsprint and other paper and paperboard products, 12,761·9). Imports (in $1m. CDN): machinery and equipment, 101,599·2 (of which industrial and agricultural machinery, 28,200·9; office machines and equipment, 16,037·9); vehicles and parts, 66,753·0 (motor vehicle parts, 39,459·5); industrial goods and materials, 60,295·6 (chemicals and plastics, 21,502·0; metals and metal ores, 15,344·6).

COMMUNICATIONS

Roads. In 1998 there were 901,903 km of roads. In 1995, 16,571 km were motorways, 123,187 km highways and main roads, 178,161 km secondary roads and 583,983 km other roads.

In general, highways are controlled and maintained by the provinces, who also have the responsibility of providing assistance to their municipalities and townships. Federal expenditures are directed largely to the maintenance of national park highways, Indian Reserve roads and designated provincial/territorial highway construction projects. The Alaska Highway is part of the Canadian highway system.

In 1991 intercity and rural bus services carried 15·3m. passengers 163·6m. vehicle-km, earning $408·2m. CDN.

Motor vehicles registered totalled 17,988,000 in 1998; they included 13,887,000 passenger cars, 3,626,000 trucks and truck tractors, 68,000 buses and 334,000 motorcycles and mopeds.

There were 3,064 fatalities in road accidents in 1997.

Rail. Canada has two great trans-continental systems: the Canadian National Railway system (CN), a body privatized in 1995 which operated 31,764 km (2000) of routes, and the Canadian Pacific Railway (CP), operating 22,590 km (2000). A government-funded organization, VIA Rail, operates passenger services; 4·0m. passengers were carried in 2000. There are several provincial and private railways operating 17,528 km (2000),

There are metros in Montreal, Toronto and Vancouver, and tram/light rail systems in Calgary, Edmonton and Toronto.

Civil Aviation. Civil aviation is under the jurisdiction of the federal government. The technical and administrative aspects are supervised by Transport Canada, while the economic functions are assigned to the National Transportation Agency.

The busiest Canadian airport is Toronto (Lester B. Pearson International), which in 2000 handled 28,930,000 passengers (16,612,000 on international flights), ahead of Vancouver International, with 16,007,000 passengers (8,306,000 on domestic flights) and Montreal (Dorval International), with 8,493,000 passengers (5,751,000 on domestic flights). Toronto is also the busiest airport for freight, handling 392,000 tonnes in 2000.

Air Canada (privatized in July 1989) took over its main competitor, Canadian Airlines, in April 2000. In 1999 Air Canada flew 356·6m. km and carried 16,520,600 passengers, and Canadian Airlines International flew 211·9m. km and carried 7,496,900 passengers (3,667,300 on international flights).

Shipping. In 1998 the merchant marine comprised 835 vessels over 100 GRT including 27 oil tankers. Total tonnage, 1998, 2·5m. GRT, including oil tankers, 0·3m. GRT. In 1997 vessels totalling 74,422,000 net registered tons entered ports and vessels totalling 124,999,000 NRT cleared.

The major canals are those of the St Lawrence-Great Lakes waterway. Main commodities moved along the seaway are grain, iron ore, coal, other bulk and steel. Total traffic on the Montreal-Lake Ontario (MLO) section of the seaway was 39,246,000 tonnes in 1998; on the Welland Canal section, 40,657,000 tonnes. There were 4,366 vessel transits in 1998, of which 1,438 were ocean vessels.

Telecommunications. In 2000 there were 20,802,900 telephone main lines in use (676·5 per 1,000 persons); telephone provision was delivered in 1996 by about 100 companies to 98·7% of households. Canada had 16·84m. Internet users in March 2002. There were 12m. PCs in 2000 (390·2 for every 1,000 persons), 7m. mobile phone subscribers in 1999 (229·6 for every 1,000 persons) and 1·1m. fax machines in 1997.

Postal Services. The Canada Post Corporation processed 10bn. pieces of mail in 2000–01. Revenue from operations reached $5·9bn. CDN, an increase of $305m. CDN over 1999–2000. Consolidated net income for the year was $84m. CDN, an increase of $9m. CDN from the $75m. CDN reported for 1999–2000. The Corporation has some 20,000 retail locations.

SOCIAL INSTITUTIONS

Justice. There is a Supreme Court in Ottawa, having general appellate jurisdiction in civil and criminal cases throughout Canada. The Exchequer Court (established in 1875) was replaced by the Federal Court in 1971. This has a Trial Division, consisting of the Associate Chief Justice and nine other judges, and an Appeal Division, consisting of the Chief Justice and three other judges. Its seat is in Ottawa, but each Division may sit in any place in Canada. There is a Superior Court in each province and county courts, with limited jurisdiction, all the judges being appointed by the Governor-General. Police, magistrates and justices of the peace are appointed by the provincial governments.

There were 2,353,926 Criminal Code Offences (excluding traffic) reported in 2000. There were 269 violent crimes per 100,000 population in 1996 (598 per 100,000 in the USA). In 2001 there were 554 homicides in Canada, giving a rate of 1·8 homicides per 100,000 population (the same as 1999, which was the lowest rate for 32 years). The population in penal institutions in 1998 was 34,166 (115 per 100,000 of national population). The death penalty was abolished for all crimes in 1998.

Royal Canadian Mounted Police (RCMP). The RCMP is a civil force maintained by the federal government. Established in 1873 as the North-West Mounted Police, it became the Royal North-West Mounted Police in 1904. Its sphere of operations was expanded in 1918 to include all of Canada west of Thunder Bay. In 1920 the force absorbed the Dominion Police, its headquarters was transferred from Regina to Ottawa, and its title was changed to Royal Canadian Mounted Police. The force is responsible to the Solicitor-General of Canada and is controlled by a Commissioner who is empowered to appoint peace officers in all the provinces and territories of Canada.

The responsibilities of the RCMP are national in scope. The administration of justice within the provinces, including the enforcement of the Criminal Code of Canada, is the responsibility of provincial governments, but all the provinces except Ontario and Quebec have entered into contracts with the RCMP to enforce criminal and provincial laws under the direction of the respective Attorneys-General. In addition, in these eight provinces the RCMP is under agreement to provide police services to municipalities. The RCMP is also responsible for all police work in the Yukon, Northwest Territories and Nunavut, enforcing federal law and territorial ordinances. The 14 Divisions, alphabetically designated, make up the strength of the RCMP across Canada; they comprise 52 sub-divisions which include 800 detachments. Headquarters Division, as well as the Office of the Commissioner, is located in Ottawa.

Assisting the criminal investigation work of the RCMP is the Directorate of Identification Services. Its services, together with those of divisional and sub-divisional units, and of six Forensic Laboratories, are available to police forces throughout Canada. The Canadian Police Information Centre (CPIC) at RCMP Headquarters, a national computer network, is staffed and operated by the RCMP. Law Enforcement agencies throughout Canada have access to information on stolen vehicles, licences and wanted persons.

In Feb. 2001 the Force had a total strength of 20,000 including regular members, special constables, civilian members and public service employees. It maintained 8,677 motor vehicles, 92 police service dogs and 156 horses.

The Force has 14 divisions actively engaged in law enforcement, one Headquarters Division and one training division. Marine services are divisional responsibilities and the Force currently has 402 boats at various points across Canada. The Air Directorate has stations throughout the country and maintains a fleet of 21 fixed-wing aircraft and eight helicopters.

Total police personnel in Canada in June 2000 numbered 56,020. There were 7,658 female police officers, up from 3,573 in June 1990. Policing costs in 1999 totalled $6·4bn. CDN.

Religion. Most recent statistics available (1997):

Religious body	Inclusive membership	Number of churches	Number of clergy
Anglican Church of Canada	780,897	2,499	3,240
Canadian Baptist Ministries	138,000	1,136	1,107
Evangelical Lutheran Church	290,846	1,006	1,230
Pentecostal Assemblies of Canada	226,678	1,075	. . .
Presbyterian Church	152,425	1,026	1,169
Roman Catholic Church	12,498,605	5,878	11,838
Ukrainian Greek Orthodox	120,000	270	. . .
United Church of Canada	2,018,808	4,044	3,939

Membership of other denominations: Jews (1996), 0·35m.; Muslims (1996), 0·35m.; Latter-day Saints (Mormons) (2001), 161,000; Mennonites (1995), 114,000; Jehovah's Witnesses (1996), 110,659; Salvation Army (1996), 92,330. In Feb. 2001 the Roman Catholic church had five Cardinals.

Education. Under the Constitution the provincial legislatures have powers over education. These are subject to certain qualifications respecting the rights of denominational and minority language schools. School board revenues derive from local taxation on real property, and government grants from general provincial revenue.

In 1996–97 there were 16,096 elementary and secondary public and private schools and 198 community colleges. There were 541,650 children in pre-elementary institutions; 4,969,317 children in elementary and secondary schools with 306,498 teachers; and 388,976 students in community colleges.

Enrolment for Indian and Inuit children in elementary/secondary schools for 1999–2000: federal schools, 1,708; band-operated schools, 71,823; provincial/private schools, 45,839; giving a total of 119,370 students funded by the Department of Indian and Northern Affairs (DIAND). However, this total represents only a portion of Indian and Inuit students attending elementary/secondary schools.

In 1995–96 there were 48 universities, 1 technical university, 4 university colleges, 10 colleges, 1 Dominican college, 1 college of agriculture, 1 college of art and design, 2 open universities, 2 polytechnics, higher schools of business, public administration, and technology, and institutes of education, microbiology and virology, and scientific research. In 1996–97 there were 572,179 full-time and 248,231 part-time university students with 36,035 teachers. In 1995–96 there were 6,984 tertiary-level students per 100,000 population, the highest proportion of any country.

The adult literacy rate in 1998 was at least 99%.

In 1996 public education expenditure represented 7% of GDP.

Health. Constitutional responsibility for healthcare services rests with the provinces and territories. Accordingly, Canada's national health insurance system consists of an interlocking set of provincial and territorial hospital and medical insurance plans conforming to certain national standards rather than a single national programme. These national standards, which are set out in the Canada Health Act, include: provision of a comprehensive range of hospital and medical benefits; universal population coverage; access to necessary services on uniform terms and conditions; portability of benefits; and public administration of provincial and territorial insurance plans.

Provinces and territories satisfying these national standards are eligible for federal financial transfer payments. The provinces and territories are entitled to receive equal-per-capita federal health contributions escalated annually by the 3-year average increase in nominal GNP. These federal contributions are paid in the form of a combination of tax point and cash transfers. Over and above these health transfers, the federal government also provides financial support for such provincial and territorial extended healthcare service programmes as nursing-home care, certain home care services, ambulatory healthcare services and adult residential care services.

The national health insurance programmes were introduced in stages. The Hospital Insurance and Diagnostic Services Act was passed in 1957, providing prepaid coverage to all Canadians for in-patient and, at the option of each province and territory, out-patient hospital services. The Medical Care Act was introduced in 1968 to extend universal coverage to all medically equipped services provided by medical practitioners. The Canada Health Act, which took effect on 1 April 1984, consolidated the original federal health insurance legislation and clarified the national standards that provinces and territories are required to meet in order to qualify for full federal health contributions.

The approach taken by Canada is one of state-sponsored health insurance. Accordingly, the advent of insurance programmes produced little change in the ownership of hospitals, almost all of which are owned by non-government non-profit corporations, or in the rights and privileges of private medical practice. Patients are free to choose their own general practitioner. Except for a small percentage of the population whose care is provided for under other legislation (such as serving members of the Canadian Armed Forces and inmates of federal penitentiaries), all residents are eligible, regardless of whether they are in the workforce. Benefits are available without upper limit so long as they are medically necessary, provided any registration obligations are met.

In addition to the benefits qualifying for federal contributions, provinces and territories provide additional benefits at their own discretion. Most fund their portion of health costs out of general provincial and territorial revenues. There are no co-charges for medically necessary short-term hospital care or medical care. Most provinces and territories have charges for long-term chronic hospital care geared, approximately, to the room and board portion of the OAS-GIS payment mentioned under Welfare. Public sector spending accounts for about 72·2% of total national health expenditure. Health spending accounted for 9·1% of GDP in 2000.

In 1997 there were estimated to be 66,600 doctors, giving a rate of 455 persons per doctor.

Welfare. The social security system provides financial benefits and social services to individuals and their families through programmes administered by federal, provincial and municipal governments, and voluntary organizations. Federally, Human Resources and Labour is responsible for research into the areas of social issues, provision of grants and contributions for various social services, and the administration of income security programmes, including the Old Age Security programme, the Guaranteed Income Supplement, the Spouse's Allowance, and the Canada Pension Plan and Canada Assistance Plan.

The Old Age Security (OAS) pension is payable to persons 65 years of age and over who satisfy the residence requirements stipulated in the Old Age Security Act. The amount payable, whether full or partial, is also governed by stipulated conditions, as is the payment of an OAS pension to a recipient who absents himself from Canada. OAS pensioners with little or no income apart from OAS may, upon application, receive a full or partial supplement known as the Guaranteed Income Supplement (GIS). Entitlement is normally based on the pensioner's income in the preceding year, calculated in accordance with the Income Tax Act. The spouse of an OAS pensioner, aged 60 to 64, meeting the same residence requirements as those stipulated for OAS, may be eligible for a full or partial Spouse's Allowance (SPA). SPA is payable, on application, depending on the annual combined income of the couple (not including the pensioner spouse's basic OAS pension or GIS). In 1979 the SPA programme was expanded to include a spouse, who is eligible for SPA in the month the pensioner spouse dies, until the age of 65 or until remarriage (Extended Spouse's Allowance). Since Sept. 1985 SPA has also been available to low income widow(er)s aged 60–64 regardless of the age of their spouse at death. In Aug. 1999 the basic OAS pension was $396·80 CDN monthly; the maximum Guaranteed Income Supplement was $496·07 CDN monthly for a single pensioner or a married pensioner whose spouse was not receiving a pension or a Spouse's Allowance, and $323·12 CDN monthly for each spouse of a married couple where both were pensioners. The maximum Spouse's Allowance for the same quarter was $740·54 CDN monthly (equal to the basic pension plus the maximum GIS married rate), and $817·57 CDN for widow(er)s.

The Canada Pension Plan (CPP) is designed to provide workers with a basic level of income protection in the event of retirement, disability or death. Benefits may be payable to a contributor, a surviving spouse or an eligible child. Actuarially adjusted retirement benefits may begin as early as age 60 or as late as age 70. Benefits are determined by the contributor's earnings and contributions made to the Plan. Contribution is compulsory for most employed and self-employed Canadians 18 to 65 years of age. The CPP does not operate in Quebec, which has exercised its constitutional prerogative to establish a similar plan. In 1999 the maximum retirement pension payable under CPP was $751·67 CDN; the maximum disability pension was $903·55 CDN; and the maximum surviving spouse's pension was $451·00 CDN (for survivors 65 years of age and over) or 60% of the retirement pension which the deceased contributor would have received at age 65. The survivor pension payable to a surviving spouse under 65 (maximum of $414·46 CDN in 1999) is composed of two parts: a flat-rate component and an earnings-related portion. In 1999 CPP was funded by equal contributions of 3·5% of pensionable earnings from the employer and 3·5% from the employee (self-employed persons contribute the full 7%), in addition to the interest on the investment of excess funds. In 1999 the range of yearly pensionable earnings was from $3,500 CDN to $37,400 CDN. A person who earned and contributed at less than the maximum level generally receives monthly benefits at rates lower than the maximum allowable under CPP. There are, however, drop-out provisions that offer some protection as a result of child rearing, periods of disablement, unemployment or other periods of no or low earnings. In June 1999 over 5m. Canadians received Canada or Quebec Pension Plan benefits.

Social security agreements co-ordinate the operation of the Old Age Security and the CPP with the comparable social security programmes of certain other countries.

In Nov. 1992 the Federal government replaced the Family Allowances programme with a new Child Tax Benefit, administered jointly by Human Resources and Labour and Revenue Canada. The programme delivered Canada its first payments in Jan. 1993.

CULTURE

Broadcasting. The Canadian Radio-Television and Telecommunications Commission is an independent authority established by parliament in 1968 to regulate public and private radio and television. The Canadian Broadcasting Corporation operates two national TV networks, one in English and one in French, and there are three private TV networks (colour by NTSC). In 1995 there were 2,245 cable TV systems, and in 1997 there were 7,867,000 subscribers to cable television—approximately 69% of all households with TV licences in 1997 had cable TV. There were 21·5m. TV receivers and 32·3m. radio receivers in 1997.

There were 841 originating radio stations operating in 1996, of which 333 were AM and 508 FM. There were also 968 radio re-broadcasters.

Press. In 1996 there were 107 daily papers (total circulation, 4·72m., giving a rate of 159 per 1,000 inhabitants). There were 1,071 non-daily papers with a circulation of 21,235,000, or 715 per 1,000 inhabitants. In 1996 a total of 19,900 book titles were published.

Tourism. In 1999 there were 19,557,000 foreign tourists, around 90% of whom were from the USA. Revenue from visitors was US$10,025m.

Festivals. The Calgary Stampede in July is not only the world's largest rodeo, but also a series of concerts and a carnival. The Toronto International Film Festival in Sept. is second only to Cannes.

Libraries. In 1995 there was one National Library and 3,672 public libraries with 76,464,000 volumes.

Museums and Galleries. In 1997–98 there were 1,368 museums with over 26m. visitors. Revenue totalled $651m. CDN.

DIPLOMATIC REPRESENTATIVES

Of Canada in the United Kingdom (Macdonald House, 1 Grosvenor Sq., London, W1X 0AB)
High Commissioner: Mel Cappe.

Of the United Kingdom in Canada (80 Elgin St., Ottawa, K1P 5K7)
High Commissioner: Sir Andrew Burns, KCMG.

Of Canada in the USA (501 Pennsylvania Ave., NW, Washington, D.C., 20001)
Ambassador: Michael Kergin.

Of the USA in Canada (490 Sussex Drive, Ottawa, K1N 1G8)
Ambassador: Argeo Paul Cellucci.

Of Canada to the United Nations
Ambassador: Paul Heinbecker.

Of Canada to the European Union
Ambassador: Vacant.
Chargé d'Affaires a.i.: Laurette Glasgow.

FURTHER READING
Canadian Annual Review. From 1960
Canadian Encyclopedia. 2nd ed. 4 vols. Edmonton, 1988

Brown, R. C., *An Illustrated History of Canada*. Toronto, 1991
Cook, C., *Canada after the Referendum of 1992*. McGill-Queens Univ. Press, 1994
Dawson, R. M. and Dawson, W. F., *Democratic Government in Canada*. 5th ed. Toronto Univ. Press, 1989
Ingles, E., *Canada*. [Bibliography] ABC-Clio, Oxford and Santa Barbara (CA), 1990
Jackson, R. J., *Politics in Canada: Culture, Institutions, Behaviour and Public Policy*. 2nd ed. Scarborough (Ont.), 1990
Longille, P., *Changing the Guard: Canada's Defence in a World in Transition*. Toronto Univ. Press, 1991
Silver, A. I. (ed.) *Introduction to Canadian History*. London, 1994

Other more specialized titles are listed under CONSTITUTION AND GOVERNMENT *above.*

National library: The National Library of Canada, Ottawa, Ontario. *Librarian:* Roch Carrier.
National statistical office: Statistics Canada, Ottawa, K1A 0T6.
Website: http://www.statcan.ca/

CANADIAN PROVINCES

GENERAL DETAILS

The ten provinces each have a separate parliament and administration, with a Lieut.-Governor, appointed by the Governor-General in Council at the head of the executive. They have full powers to regulate their own local affairs and dispose of their revenues, provided only that they do not interfere with the action and policy of the central administration. Among the subjects assigned exclusively to the provincial legislatures are: the amendment of the provincial constitution, except as regards the office of the Lieut.-Governor; property and civil rights; direct taxation for revenue purposes; borrowing; management and sale of Crown lands; provincial hospitals, reformatories, etc.; shop, saloon, tavern, auctioneer and other licences for local or provincial purposes; local works and undertakings, except lines of ships, railways, canals, telegraphs, etc., extending beyond the province or connecting with other provinces, and excepting also such works as the Canadian Parliament declares are for the general good; marriages, administration of justice within the province; education. On 18 July 1994 the federal and provincial governments signed an agreement easing inter-provincial barriers on government procurement, labour mobility, transport licences and product standards. Federal legislation of Dec. 1995 grants provinces a right of constitutional veto.

For the administration of the three territories *see* Northwest Territories, Nunavut, Yukon Territory *below.*

Areas of the ten provinces and three territories (Northwest Territories, Nunavut and Yukon) (in sq. km) and population at recent censuses:

Province	Land area	Total land and fresh water area	Population, 1991[1, 2]	Population, 1996	Population, 2001[1]
Newfoundland (Nfld.)	373,872	405,212	568,474	551,792	512,930
Prince Edward Island (PEI)	5,660	5,660	129,765	134,557	135,294
Nova Scotia (NS)	53,338	55,284	899,942	909,282	908,007
New Brunswick (NB)	71,450	72,908	723,900	738,133	729,498
Quebec (Que.)	1,365,128	1,542,056	6,895,963	7,138,795	7,237,479
Ontario (Ont.)	917,741	1,076,395	10,084,885	10,753,573	11,410,046
Manitoba (Man.)	553,556	647,797	1,091,942	1,113,898	1,119,583
Saskatchewan (Sask.)	591,670	651,036	988,928	990,237	978,933
Alberta (Alta.)	642,317	661,848	2,545,553	2,696,826	2,974,807
British Columbia (BC)	925,186	944,735	3,282,061	3,724,500	3,907,738
Nunavut (Nvt.)	1,936,113	2,093,190			26,745[3]
Northwest Territories (NWT)	1,183,085	1,346,106	57,649	64,402	37,360[4]
Yukon Territory (YT)	474,391	482,443	27,797	30,766	28,674

[1]Excludes data from incompletely enumerated Indian reserves and Indian settlements.
[2]Comparison of the 1991 census data with data from earlier censuses is affected by a change in the definition of the 1991 census population. Persons in Canada on student authorizations, Minister's permits, and as refugee claimants were enumerated in the 1991 census but not in previous censuses. These persons are referred to as non-permanent residents.
[3]Nunavut only came into existence in 1999.
[4]The population of the Northwest Territories declined so steeply between 1996 and 2001 because of the formation of Nunavut, previously part of the Northwest Territories, in 1999.

Local Government. Under the terms of the British North America Act the provinces are given full powers over local government. All local government institutions are, therefore, supervised by the provinces, and are incorporated and function under provincial acts.

The acts under which municipalities operate vary from province to province. A municipal corporation is usually administered by an elected council headed by a mayor or reeve, whose powers to administer affairs and to raise funds by taxation and other methods are set forth in provincial laws, as is the scope of its obligations to, and on behalf of, the citizens. Similarly, the types of municipal corporations, their official designations and the requirements for their incorporation vary between provinces. The following table sets out the classifications as at the 1996 census:

	Federal electoral districts	*Economic regions*	*Census divisions*
Nfld.	7	4	10
PEI	4	1	3[1]
NS	11	5	18[1]
NB	10	5	15[1]
Que.	75	16	99[2]
Ont.	103	11	49[3]
Man.	14	8	23
Sask.	14	6	18
Alta.	26	8	19
BC	34	8	28[4]
YT	1	1	1[5]
NWT	2	1	5[6]

[1]Counties.
[2]3 Census divisions, 3 communautés urbaines, 93 municipalités régionales de comté. [3]24 counties, 10 districts, 1 district municipality, 1 metropolitan municipality, 10 regional municipalities, 3 united counties. [4]1 region, 27 regional districts. [5]Territory. [6]Regions.

Following the creation of Nunavut (part of the Northwest Territories) on 1 April 1999, both the Northwest Territories and Nunavut have one federal electoral district. The Northwest Territories has two census divisions and Nunavut has three.

Justice. The administration of justice within the provinces, including the enforcement of the Criminal Code of Canada, is the responsibility of provincial governments, but all the provinces except Ontario and Quebec have entered into contracts with the Royal Canadian Mounted Police (RCMP) to enforce criminal and provincial law. In addition, in these eight provinces the RCMP is under agreement to provide police services to municipalities.

ALBERTA

KEY HISTORICAL EVENTS

The southern half of Alberta was administered from 1670 as part of Rupert's land by the Hudson's Bay Company. Trading posts were set up after 1783 when the North West Company took a share in the fur trade. In 1869 Rupert's land was transferred from the Hudson's Bay Company (which had absorbed its rival in 1821) to the new Dominion and in the following year this land was combined with the former Crown land of the North Western Territories to form the Northwest Territories. In 1882 'Alberta' first appeared as a provisional 'district', consisting of the southern half of the present province. In 1905 the Athabasca district to the north was added when provincial status was granted to Alberta.

TERRITORY AND POPULATION

The area of the province is 661,848 sq. km, 642,317 sq. km being land area and 16,531 sq. km water area. The population at the 2001 census was 2,974,807. Alberta has the fastest growing population of any Canadian province, with a 10·3% increase since the 1996 census. The urban population (2001), centres of 1,000 or over, was 80·9% and the rural 19·1%. Population (15 May 2001) of the 14 cities, as well as the 2 specialized municipalities: Calgary, 878,866; Edmonton, 616,104; Red Deer, 67,707; Lethbridge, 67,374; St Albert, 53,081; Medicine Hat, 51,249; Grande Prairie, 36,983; Airdrie, 20,382; Leduc, 15,032; Spruce Grove, 15,983; Camrose,

14,854; Fort Saskatchewan, 13,121; Lloydminster (Alberta portion), 13,148; Wetaskiwin, 11,154; Specialized Municipality of Wood Buffalo (Fort McMurray), 41,466; Specialized Municipality of Strathcona County (Sherwood Park), 71,986.

SOCIAL STATISTICS
Births in 2001 numbered 37,006 (a rate of 11·5 per 1,000 population), and deaths 18,068 (rate of 5·9 per 1,000 population). There were 18,717 marriages in 2001 and 7,922 divorces in 2000.

CLIMATE
Alberta has a continental climate of warm summers and cold winters—extremes of temperature. For the capital city, Edmonton, the hottest month is usually July (mean 17·5°C), while the coldest are Dec. and Jan. (−12°C). Rainfall amounts are greatest between May and Sept. In a year, the average precipitation is 461 mm (19·6") with about 129·6 cm of snowfall.

CONSTITUTION AND GOVERNMENT
The constitution of Alberta is contained in the British North America Act of 1867, and amending Acts; also in the Alberta Act of 1905, passed by the Parliament of the Dominion of Canada, which created the province out of the then Northwest Territories. All the provisions of the British North America Act, except those with respect to school lands and the public domain, were made to apply to Alberta as they apply to the older provinces of Canada. On 1 Oct. 1930 the natural resources were transferred from the Dominion to provincial government control. The province is represented by five members in the Senate and 26 in the House of Commons of Canada.

The executive is vested nominally in the Lieut.-Governor, who is appointed by the federal government, but actually in the Executive Council or the Cabinet of the legislature. Legislative power is vested in the Assembly in the name of the Queen.

Members of the Legislative Assembly are elected by the universal vote of adults, 18 years of age and older.

RECENT ELECTIONS
There are 83 members in the legislature. In March 2003 there were 74 Progressive Conservatives, 7 Liberals and 2 New Democrats.

CURRENT ADMINISTRATION
Lieut.-Governor: Lois Hole, CM (sworn in 10 Feb. 2000).

As of Feb. 2003 the members of the Ministry were as follows:

Premier, President of Executive Council: Ralph Klein (b. 1942; Progressive Conservative).

Deputy Premier, Minister of Agriculture, Food and Rural Development: Shirley McClellan. *Finance:* Patricia Nelson. *International and Intergovernmental Relations:* Halvar Jonson. *Infrastructure:* Ty Lund. *Health and Wellness:* Gary Mar. *Energy:* Murray Smith. *Seniors:* Stan Woloshyn. *Transportation:* Ed Stelmach. *Human Resources and Employment:* Clint Dunford. *Learning:* Lyle Oberg. *Children's Services:* Iris Evans. *Justice and Attorney General, and Government House Leader:* David Hancock. *Environment:* Lorne Taylor. *Sustainable Resource Development:* Mike Cardinal. *Aboriginal Affairs and Northern Development:* Pearl Calahasen. *Community Development:* Gene Zwozdesky. *Gaming:* Ron Stevens. *Revenue:* Greg Melchin. *Municipal Affairs:* Guy Boutilier. *Innovation and Science:* Victor Doerksen. *Government Services:* David Coutts. *Solicitor General:* Heather Forsyth. *Economic Development:* Mark Norris.

Office of the Premier: http://www.gov.ab.ca/premier/

ECONOMY
GDP per person in 2000 was $47,402 CDN.

Budget. The budgetary revenue and expenditure (in $1m. CDN) for years ending 31 March were as follows:

	1997–98	*1998–99*	*1999–2000*	*2000–01*	*2001–02*
Revenue	17,815	16,882	20,168	25,597	22,027
Expenditure	15,156	15,788	17,377	19,024	20,919

Performance. Real GDP growth was 5·4% in 2000.

Banking and Finance. Personal income *per capita* (2001), $30,993 CDN.

ENERGY AND NATURAL RESOURCES

Environment. There are five national parks in Alberta totalling 63,045 sq. km, the largest area of any province in Canada. There are also 518 parks and protected areas in Alberta covering 2,752,969 ha.

Oil and Gas. Oil sands underlie some 60,000 sq. km of Alberta, the four major deposits being: the Athabasca, Cold Lake, Peace River and Buffalo Head Hills deposits. Some 7% (3,250 sq. km) of the Athabasca deposit can be exploited through open-pit mining. The rest of the Athabasca, and all the deposits in the other areas, are deeper reserves which must be developed through in situ techniques. These reserves reach depths of 760 metres. In 2001, 86,679,000 cu. metres of crude oil were produced with gross sales value of $18,234·8m. CDN. Alberta produced 69% of Canada's crude petroleum output in 2001. 18,608,000 cu. metres of synthetic crude oil were produced in 2000.

Natural gas is found in abundance in numerous localities. In 2001, 133,283,000 cu. metres valued at $26,303·7m. CDN were produced in Alberta.

Minerals. Coal production in 2001 was 30,911,020 tonnes with 6,893,677 tonnes of coal being exported.

Value of total mineral production was $49,832·5m. CDN in 2001.

Agriculture. There were 53,652 farms in Alberta in 2001 with a total area of 21,067,486 ha. About 9,728,181 ha are land in crop (2001 census). The majority of farms are made up of cattle, followed by grains and oilseed, and wheat. For particulars of livestock *see* CANADA: Agriculture.

Farm cash receipts in 2001 totalled $8,322·0m. CDN of which crops contributed $2,299·4m. CDN, livestock and products $5,186·7m. CDN, and direct payments $835·9m. CDN.

Forestry. Forest land in 1999 covered some 38,210,000 ha. In 1999, 42,210 ha of forest was harvested.

Fisheries. The largest catch in commercial fishing is whitefish. Perch, tullibee, walley, pike and lake trout are also caught in smaller quantities. Commercial fish production in 2000–01 was 2,023 tonnes, value $3·27m. CDN.

INDUSTRY

The leading manufacturing industries are food and beverages, petroleum refining, metal fabricating, wood industries, primary metal, chemical and chemical products and non-metallic mineral products.

Manufacturing shipments had a total value of $42,552·0m. CDN in 2001. Greatest among these shipments were (in $1m. CDN): food, 9,143; refined petroleum and coal products, 7,449; chemicals and chemical products, 7,010; machinery, 3,363; fabricated metal products, 2,716; wood products, 2,200; computer and electronic products, 2,004; paper and allied products, 1,503; non-metal mineral products, 1,202; and primary metal, 1,008.

Total retail sales in 2001 were $34,602m. CDN, as compared with $31,712·3m. CDN in sales. Main sales in 2001 were (in $1m. CDN): automobiles, 9,309·4; food, 7,316·0; general merchandise, 3,859·4; fuel 2,638·5; and automotive parts, accessories and services, 2,068·0.

Labour. In 2001 the labour force was 1,710,700 (771,600 females), of whom approximately 1,632,100 (736,900) were employed. In 2001 a total of 44,100 new jobs were created. Alberta's unemployment rate dropped to 4·6% in 2001, compared to the national average of 7·2%.

INTERNATIONAL TRADE

Imports and Exports. Alberta's domestic commodity exports were valued at $56·9bn. CDN in 2001. The largest export markets were the USA, Japan, China, Mexico and South Korea, which together accounted for approximately 94% of Alberta's international exports. Mining and energy accounted for 71% of exports in 2001.

COMMUNICATIONS

Roads. In 2002 there were 16,012 km of primary highways, 14,717 km secondary highways and 137,298 km of local municipal roads.

On 31 March 2002 there were 2,296,748 motor vehicles registered, including 1,067,625 passenger vehicles.

Rail. In 2002 the length of main railway lines was 7,067 km. There are light rail networks in Edmonton (12·3 km) and Calgary (32·7 km).

Civil Aviation. Calgary International is a major international airport. It handled 8,090,000 passengers (5,751,000 on domestic flights) in 2000.

Telecommunications. The primary telephone system is owned and operated by the Telus Corporation. Telus Corporation had 1,998,366 telephone subscriber lines (including residential and business lines) in service in 2002.

SOCIAL INSTITUTIONS

Justice. The Supreme Judicial authority of the province is the Court of Appeal. Judges of the Court of Appeal and Court of Queen's Bench are appointed by the Federal government and hold office until retirement at the age of 75. There are courts of lesser jurisdiction in both civil and criminal matters. The Court of Queen's Bench has full jurisdiction over civil proceedings. A Provincial Court which has jurisdiction in civil matters up to $2,000 CDN is presided over by provincially appointed judges. Youth Courts have power to try boys and girls 12–17 years old inclusive for offences against the Young Offenders Act.

The jurisdiction of all criminal courts in Alberta is enacted in the provisions of the Criminal Code. The system of procedure in civil and criminal cases conforms as nearly as possible to the English system. In 2001, 276,860 Criminal Code offences were reported, including 70 homicides.

Education. Schools of all grades are included under the term of public school (including those in the separate school system, which are publicly supported). The same board of trustees controls the schools from kindergarten to university entrance. In 2001–02 there were approximately 547,830 pupils enrolled in grades 1–12, including private schools and special education programmes. The University of Alberta (in Edmonton), founded in 1907, had, in 2001–02, 32,248 students; the University of Calgary had 26,654 students; Athabasca University had 24,136 students; the University of Lethbridge had 6,217 students. Alberta has 30 post-secondary institutions including four universities and two technical colleges.

CULTURE

Alberta has several annual festivals. Heritage Days in Edmonton (Aug.) is a celebration of multiculturalism. There are various music festivals around Alberta (rock, folk, country, jazz) throughout the summer. The Fringe Festival in Edmonton (Aug.) is ten days of performance art and theatre shows. The Calgary Stampede (July) is a rodeo, agricultural exhibits, parade and carnival. Klondike Days (July) is a celebration of gold rush heritage including a carnival and parade in Edmonton.

Tourism. Alberta attracted more than 5,067,000 visitors from outside the province in 2000. It is known for its mountains, museums, parks and festivals. Total tourism receipts in 2000 were $4·9bn. CDN.

FURTHER READING

Savage, H., Kroetsch, R., Wiebe, R., *Alberta.* NeWest Press, 1993

Economic Development Edmonton, *Edmonton Info: Edmonton's Official Fact Book 1999.* Edmonton, 1999

Statistical office: Alberta Finance, Statistics, Room 259, Terrace Bldg, 9515–107 St., Edmonton, AB T5K 2C3.

Websites: http://www.alberta-canada.com; http://www.discoveralberta.com

BRITISH COLUMBIA

KEY HISTORICAL EVENTS

British Columbia, formerly known as New Caledonia, was first administered by the Hudson's Bay Company. In 1849 Vancouver Island was given crown colony status and in 1853 the Queen Charlotte Islands became a dependency. The discovery of gold on the Fraser river and the following influx of population resulted in the creation in 1858 of the mainland crown colony of British Columbia, to which the Strikine Territory (established 1862) was later added. In 1866 the two colonies were united.

TERRITORY AND POPULATION

British Columbia has an area of 944,735 sq. km of which land area is 926,492 sq. km. The capital is Victoria. The province is bordered westerly by the Pacific Ocean and Alaska Panhandle, northerly by the Yukon and Northwest Territories, easterly by the Province of Alberta and southerly by the USA along the 49th parallel. A chain of islands, the largest of which are Vancouver Island and the Queen Charlotte Islands, affords protection to the mainland coast.

The population at the 2001 census was 3,907,738; 2002 estimate, 4·1m.

The principal metropolitan areas and cities and their population census for 2001 are as follows: Metropolitan Vancouver, 1,986,965; Metropolitan Victoria, 325,754; Abbotsford (amalgamated with Matsqui), 115,463; Kelowna, 96,298; Kamloops, 77,281; Prince George, 72,406; Nanaimo, 73,000; Chilliwack, 62,927; Vernon, 33,494; Mission, 31,272; Penticton, 30,985; Campbell River, 29,465; North Cowichan, 26,148; Cranbrook, 18,476; Port Alberni, 17,743.

SOCIAL STATISTICS

Births in 1999–2000 numbered 41,667 (a rate of 10·3 per 1,000 population), and deaths 30,418 (rate of 7·5 per 1,000 population). There were 21,749 marriages and 9,827 divorces in 1998.

CLIMATE

The climate is cool temperate, but mountain influences affect temperatures and rainfall considerably. Driest months occur in summer. Vancouver, Jan. 36°F (2·2°C), July 64°F (17·8°C). Annual rainfall 58" (1,458 mm).

CONSTITUTION AND GOVERNMENT

The British North America Act of 1867 provided for eventual admission into Canadian Confederation, and on 20 July 1871 British Columbia became the sixth province of the Dominion.

British Columbia has a unicameral legislature of 79 elected members. Government policy is determined by the Executive Council responsible to the Legislature. The Lieut.-Governor is appointed by the Governor-General of Canada, usually for a term of five years, and is the head of the executive government of the province.

The Legislative Assembly is elected for a maximum term of five years. There are 79 electoral districts. Every Canadian citizen 18 years and over, having resided a minimum of six months in the province, duly registered, is entitled to vote. The province is represented in the Federal Parliament by 33 members in the House of Commons, and six Senators.

RECENT ELECTIONS

At the Legislative Assembly elections of 16 May 2001 the Liberal Party won 58% of the vote and 77 of the 79 available seats. The other two seats went to the New Democratic Party.

CURRENT ADMINISTRATION

Lieut.-Governor: Iona Campagnolo, PC, OM, OBC (sworn in 25 Sept. 2001).

The Liberal Executive Council comprised in Jan. 2003:

Premier, President of the Executive Council: Gordon Campbell.

Deputy Premier and Minister for Education: Christy Clark. *Attorney General and Minister Responsible for Treaty Negotiations:* Geoff Plant. *Solicitor General and*

Minister of Public Safety: Rich Coleman. *Intergovernmental Relations:* Greg Halsey-Brandt. *Finance:* Gary Collins. *Children and Family Development:* Gordon Hogg. *Early Childhood Development:* Linda Reid. *Community, Aboriginal Affairs and Women's Services:* George Abbott. *Women's Equality:* Lynn Stephens. *Community Charter:* Ted Nebbeling. *Advanced Education:* Shirley Bond. *Skills Development and Labour:* Graham Bruce. *Agriculture, Food and Fisheries:* John van Dongen. *Energy and Mines:* Richard Neufeld. *Water, Land and Air Protection:* Joyce Murray. *Forests:* Michael de Jong. *Health Services:* Colin Hansen. *Health Planning:* Sindi Hawkins. *Intermediate, Long Term and Home Care:* Katherine Whittred. *Mental Health:* Gulzar Cheema. *Transportation:* Judith Reid. *Provincial Revenue:* Bill Barisoff. *Human Resources:* Murray Coell. *Sustainable Resource Management:* Stan Hagen. *Management Services:* Sandy Santori. *Competition, Science and Enterprise:* Rick Thorpe. *Deregulation:* Kevin Falcon.

Office of the Premier: http://www.gov.bc.ca/prem/

ECONOMY
GDP per person in 2001 was $30,252 CDN.

Budget. Current provincial revenue and expenditure in $1m. CDN for fiscal years ending 31 March:

	1998–99	1999–2000[1]	2000–01[1]	2001–02	2002–03[2]
Revenue	20,306	21,385	21,500	23,125	22,266
Expenditure	20,771	22,593	22,300	25,255	25,366

[1]Estimate. [2]Forecast.

The main sources of current revenue are income taxes, sales taxes, contributions from the federal government, licences and fees, and natural resource taxes and royalties.

The main items of expenditure in 2002–03 (forecast) were as follows: health, $10,390m. CDN; education, $6,871m. CDN; social services, $3,090m. CDN; protection of persons and property, $1,200m. CDN; natural resources and economic development, $1,065m. CDN; transportation, $734m. CDN; general government, $379m. CDN.

Banking and Finance. At Oct. 1997 Canadian chartered banks maintained 925 branches and had total assets of $146·3bn. CDN in British Columbia. In 1997 credit unions at 96 locations had total assets of $20·4bn. CDN. Several foreign banks have Canadian head offices in Vancouver and several others have branches.

ENERGY AND NATURAL RESOURCES
Electricity. Generation in 2001 totalled 57,870 GWh (48,338 GWh from hydroelectric sources), of which 6,408 GWh were delivered outside the province. Available within the province were 61,616 GWh (with imports of 10,154 GWh).

Oil and Gas. In 2001 natural gas production, from the northeastern part of the province, was valued at $5·18bn. CDN.

Water. Canada accounts for a quarter of the world's fresh water supply, a third of which is located in British Columbia. An extensive hydro-electric generation system has been developed in the province.

Minerals. Coal, copper, gold, zinc, silver and molybdenum are the most important minerals produced but natural gas amounts to approximately half of the value of mineral and fuel extraction. The value of mineral and petroleum products production in 2001 was estimated at $9·6bn. CDN. Coal production (from the northeastern and southeastern regions) was valued at $1·1bn. CDN. Copper was the most valuable metal with production totalling $679m. CDN in 2001; gold production amounted to $322m. CDN.

Agriculture. Only 3% of the total land area is arable or potentially arable. Farm holdings (20,290 in 2001) cover 2·6m. ha. with an average size of 127 ha. Farm cash receipts in 2001 were estimated at $2·3bn. CDN, led by floriculture and nursery products valued at $410m. CDN, dairy products valued at $364m. CDN and vegetables valued at $362m. CDN.

Forestry. Around 49·9m. ha are considered productive forest land of which 48·0m. ha are provincial crown lands managed by the Ministry of Forests. Approximately

96% of the forested land is coniferous. The total timber harvest in 2001 was 72m. cu. metres. Output of forest-based products, 2001: lumber, 30·15m. cu. metres; plywood, 1·57m. cu. metres; pulp, 4·70m. tonnes; newsprint, paper and paperboard, 2·88m. tonnes.

Fisheries. In 2001 the total landed value of the catch was $643m. CDN; wholesale value $1bn. CDN. Salmon (wild and farmed) generated 45% of the wholesale value of seafood products, followed by shellfish, groundfish and herring. The seafood sector supported 11,200 jobs in 2001.

INDUSTRY
The value of shipments from all manufacturing industries reached $34bn. CDN in 2001 and accounted for around 10·5% of the province's GDP.

Labour. In 2001 the labour force averaged 2,103,000 persons (47% female) with 1,942,000 employed and 161,000 unemployed (7·7%). Of the employed workforce 1·55m. were in service industries and 392,000 in goods production. There were 309,000 employed in trade, 204,000 in healthcare and social assistance, 196,000 in manufacturing, 171,000 in accommodation and food industries, 116,000 in finance and related business, 115,000 in construction, 107,000 in transportation and warehousing, 89,000 in public administration, 26,000 in forestry, 26,000 in agriculture, 12,000 in mining and 5,000 in fishing and trapping.

Trade Unions. In 2001, 34% of the province's paid workers were unionized. The largest unions are: Canadian Union of Public Employees (63,999 members in early 2003); B.C. Government and Service Employees' Union and affiliates (approximately 60,000); and B.C. Teachers' Federation (43,876 in 1997).

INTERNATIONAL TRADE
Imports and Exports. Exports in 2001 totalled $31,304m. CDN in value, while imports amounted to $31,657m. CDN. The USA is the largest market for products exported through British Columbia customs ports ($22,092m. CDN in 2001), followed by Japan ($3,882m. CDN) and South Korea ($753m. CDN).

The leading exports in 2001 were: wood products, $10,327m. CDN; paper and allied products, $5,421m. CDN; food, $4,149m. CDN; fabricated metal products, $1,577m. CDN; machinery, $1,467m. CDN.

COMMUNICATIONS
Roads. In 2001 there were 42,440 km of provincial highway, of which 23,710 km were paved. In 2001, 1,765,000 passenger cars and 581,000 commercial vehicles were registered.

Rail. The province is served by two transcontinental railways, the Canadian Pacific Railway and the Canadian National Railway. Passenger service is provided by VIA Rail, a Crown Corporation, and the publicly owned British Columbia Railway. In 1995 the American company Amtrak began operating a service between Seattle and Vancouver after a 14-year hiatus. British Columbia is also served by the freight trains of the B.C. Hydro and Power Authority, the Northern Alberta Railways Company and the Burlington Northern and Southern Railways Inc. The combined route-mileage of mainline track operated by the CPR, CNR and BCR totals 6,800 km. The system also includes CPR and CNR wagon ferry connections to Vancouver Island, between Prince Rupert and Alaska, and interchanges with American railways at southern border points. A metro line was opened in Vancouver in 1986 (29 km). A commuter rail service linking Vancouver and the Fraser Valley was established in 1995 (69 km).

Civil Aviation. International airports are located at Vancouver and Victoria. Total passenger arrivals and departures on scheduled services made by 33 foreign and domestic airlines were 15·5m. in 2001 at Vancouver and 1·1m. in 1997 at Victoria. Daily interprovincial and intraprovincial flights serve all main population centres. Small public and private airstrips are located throughout the province.

Shipping. The major ports are Vancouver (the largest dry cargo port on the North American Pacific coast), Prince Rupert and ports on the Fraser River. Other deep-sea ports include Nanaimo, Port Alberni, Campbell River, Powell River, Kitimat, Stewart and Squamish. Total cargo shipped through the port of Vancouver during 2001 was 72·9m. tonnes. 1,060,000 cruise passengers visited Vancouver in 2001.

British Columbia Ferries—one of the largest ferry systems in the world— connect Vancouver Island with the mainland and also provide service to other coastal points; in 2000–01, 21·4m. passengers and 7·9m. vehicles were carried. Service by other ferry systems is also provided between Vancouver Island and the USA. The Alaska State Ferries connect Prince Rupert with centres in Alaska.

Telecommunications. The British Columbia Telephone Company had (1997) approximately 2·5m. customers. In 2000 there were 800,000 cellular phone subscribers in the province.

SOCIAL INSTITUTIONS

Justice. The judicial system is composed of the Court of Appeal, the Supreme Court, County Courts, and various Provincial Courts, including Magistrates' Courts and Small Claims Courts. The federal courts include the Supreme Court of Canada and the Federal Court of Canada.

In 1998, 486,804 Criminal Code offences were reported, including 90 homicides.

Education. Education, free up to Grade XII level, is financed jointly from municipal and provincial government revenues. Attendance is compulsory from the age of five to 16. There were approximately 632,024 pupils enrolled in 1,779 public schools from kindergarten to Grade 12 in Sept. 2001.

The universities had a full-time enrolment of approximately 73,527 for 1998–99. Non-vocational enrolment at leading institutions: the University of British Columbia, 35,382 (2000–01); Simon Fraser University, 21,684 (autumn 2002); University of Victoria, 18,036 (Nov. 2002); University of Northern British Columbia, 3,582 (autumn 2001); Royal Roads University, 2,300 (2001–02). The regional colleges in 1996 were: Camosun College, Victoria; Capilano College, North Vancouver; Cariboo College, Kamloops; College of New Caledonia, Prince George; Douglas College, New Westminister; East Kootenay Community College, Cranbrook; Fraser Valley College, Chilliwack/Abbotsford; Kwantlen College, Surrey; Malaspina College, Nanaimo; North Island College, Comox; Northern Lights College, Dawson Creek/Fort St John; Northwest Community College, Terrace/Prince Rupert; Okanagan College, Kelowna with branches at Salmon Arm and Vernon; Selkirk College, Castlegar; Vancouver Community College, Vancouver; Langara College, Vancouver.

There are also the British Columbia Institute of Technology, Burnaby; Emily Carr College of Art and Design, Vancouver; Open Learning Institute, Richmond. A televised distance education and special programmes through KNOW, the Knowledge Network of the West, is provided.

Health. The government operates a hospital insurance scheme giving universal coverage after a qualifying period of three months' residence in the province. The province has come under a national medicare scheme which is partially subsidized by the provincial government and partially by the federal government. In March 2001 there were approximately 8,500 acute care and 500 rehabilitation hospital beds. The provincial government spent $9·8bn. CDN on health programmes during 2001–02. 40% of the government's total expenditure was for health care.

CULTURE

Broadcasting. In 2001 there were ten television broadcasting stations in operation, with 84% of households subscribing to cable television. In July 1997 there were 130 radio stations originating in British Columbia.

Tourism. British Columbia's greatest attractions are Vancouver, and the provincial parks and ecological reserves that make up the Protected Areas System. The entire Tatshenshini-Alsek region, almost 1m. ha in northwestern B.C., has been protected as a Class A provincial park and nominated as a World Heritage Site. In 2002 there were 13,302 campsites and 3,000 km of hiking trails. In 2001, 22·36m. tourists spent $9·2bn. CDN in the province.

FURTHER READING

Barman, J., *The West beyond the West: a History of British Columbia*. Toronto Univ. Press, 1991

Statistical office: BC STATS, Ministry of Finance and Corporate Relations, P.O. Box 9410, Stn. Prov. Govt., Victoria V8W 9V1.

MANITOBA

KEY HISTORICAL EVENTS

Manitoba was known as the Red River Settlement before it entered the dominion in 1870. During the 18th century its only inhabitants were fur-trappers, but a more settled colonization began in the 19th century. The area was administered by the Hudson's Bay Company until 1869 when it was purchased by the new dominion. In 1870 it was given provincial status. It was enlarged in 1881 and again in 1912 by the addition of part of the Northwest Territories.

TERRITORY AND POPULATION

The area of the province is 250,114 sq. miles (647,797 sq. km), of which 213,728 sq. miles are land and 36,386 sq. miles water. From north to south it is 1,225 km, and at the widest point it is 793 km.

Population estimate, 1 July 2002, was 1,150,848. The 2001 census showed the following figures for areas of population of over 10,000 people: Winnipeg, the province's capital and largest city, 671,274; City of Brandon, 39,716; City of Thompson, 13,256; City of Portage la Prairie, 12,978; Rural Municipality of Springfield, 12,602; Rural Municipality of Hanover, 10,789; Rural Municipality of St Andrews, 10,695.

SOCIAL STATISTICS

Births in 2001–02 numbered 14,170 (a rate of 12·3 per 1,000 population) and deaths 10,304 (rate of 8·9 per 1,000 population). There were 6,410 marriages and 2,457 divorces in 2000.

CLIMATE

The climate is cold continental, with very severe winters but pleasantly warm summers. Rainfall amounts are greatest in the months May to Sept. Winnipeg, Jan. –3°F (–19·3°C), July 67°F (19·6°C). Annual rainfall 21" (539 mm).

CONSTITUTION AND GOVERNMENT

The provincial government is administered by a *Lieut.-Governor* assisted by an *Executive Council* (Cabinet), which is appointed from and responsible to a *Legislative Assembly* of 57 members elected for five years. Women were enfranchised in 1916. The Electoral Division Act, 1955, created 57 single-member constituencies and abolished the transferable vote. There are 26 rural electoral divisions, and 31 urban electoral divisions. The province is represented by six members in the Senate and 14 in the House of Commons of Canada.

RECENT ELECTIONS

In elections to the Legislative Assembly held on 21 Sept. 1999 the New Democratic Party won 32 out of 57 seats (44·8% of the vote), the Progressive Conservative Party 24 seats (40·7%) and the Liberal Party 1 seat (13·3%). The Progressive Conservative Party had held office for the previous 11 years.

CURRENT ADMINISTRATION

Lieut.-Governor: Peter M. Liba, CM, OM (appointed 1999).

The members of the New Democratic Party Ministry in Feb. 2003 were:

Premier, President of the Executive Council, Minister of Federal-Provincial Relations: Gary A. Doer.

Minister of Conservation: Steve Ashton. *Labour and Immigration:* Becky Barrett. *Health:* Dave Chomiak. *Deputy Premier, Minister of Intergovernmental Affairs:* Jean

CANADA

Friesen. *Aboriginal and Northern Affairs:* Oscar Lathlin. *Agriculture and Food:*
Rosann Wowchuk. *Justice and Attorney General, Keeper of the Great Seal,
Government House Leader:* Gord Mackintosh. *Culture, Heritage and Tourism:* Eric
Robinson. *Advanced Education and Training, Responsibility for the Status of
Women, and Seniors:* Diane McGifford. *Industry, Trade and Mines:* MaryAnn
Mihychuk. *Energy, Science and Technology:* Tim Sale. *Family Services and
Housing, Responsibility for Persons with Disabilities:* Drew Caldwell. *Education
and Youth:* Ron Lemieux. *Finance, Responsibility for French Language Services
and the Civil Service:* Greg Selinger. *Transportation and Government Services,
Responsibility for Emergency Measures:* Scott Smith.

Manitoba Government Website: http://www.gov.mb.ca

ECONOMY
Real GDP for Manitoba in 2001 was $33·16bn. CDN, or $28,835 CDN per person.

Performance. Manitoba's economy grew 1·6% in real terms in 2001, down from
3% in 2000.

Banking and Finance. Provincial revenue and expenditure (current account,
excluding capital expenditures, debt/pension repayment and transfers from/to the
Fiscal Stabilization Fund) for fiscal years ending 31 March (in $1m. CDN):

	1999–2000	2000–01	2001–02[1]	2002–03[2]
Revenue	6,337	6,752	6,900	6,941
Expenditure	6,436	6,615	6,779	6,928

[1]Forecast. [2]Budgeted figure.

ENERGY AND NATURAL RESOURCES
Electricity. In the year ending 31 March 2002 the province's two electrical utilities,
which had normal winter generating capacity at system peak of 5,175,000 kW,
produced 32,633m. kWh of electricity. Most of this was produced by the
provincially-owned Manitoba Hydro, with 1,106m. kWh produced by City of
Winnipeg owned Winnipeg Hydro. In 2001–02 power purchases from elsewhere in
Canada and the USA totalled 968m. kWh. Manitoba provided 20,529m. kWh to its
domestic customers. Manitoba Hydro revenues from extra-provincial power sales
increased $108m. CDN in the 2001–02 fiscal year to $588m. CDN. Energy sold
outside Manitoba was 11,800m. kWh. Of the total extra-provincial revenue, $495m.
CDN was derived from the US market and $93m. CDN came from sales to other
Canadian provinces.

Oil and Gas. The value of oil production in 2001 was $135m. CDN, down 18%
from 2000.

Minerals. Principal minerals mined are zinc, nickel, copper, gold and small
quantities of silver. The value of mineral production declined 15% in 2001 to $1bn.
CDN. Zinc accounted for 13% of the value of mineral production in 2001, down
only slightly from 2000. In 2001 zinc prices dropped 21% but the volume of
production increased by 17%.

Agriculture. Rich farmland is the main primary resource, although the area in farms
is only about 14% of the total land area. In 2001 better prices and growth in livestock
farm production volumes combined to boost total farm cash receipts by 17% to a
new record level of $3·7bn. CDN. Market receipts rose 15·8%, receipts from
livestock increased 16·4% and receipts from crops rose 14·9%. Various forms of
income assistance to producers including crop insurance, income stabilization and
adjustment programmes increased 32% in 2001 to $376m. CDN. The Manitoba
Bureau of Statistics estimates that total accrued net income of farm operators
increased 41·7% in 2001. Net cash income increased 46·4% to $917m. CDN.

Forestry. About 53% of the province is classified as forest zone, which includes
142,696 sq. km of productive forest land. In 2001 there were 211 primary roundwood
producers with 3,317 direct employees. Primary wood producers were responsible
for $1·1bn. CDN of shipments, of which $593·4m. CDN was the value of exports.

Fisheries. From about 57,000 sq. km of rivers and lakes, the value of fisheries
production to fishers was about $32·2m. CDN in 2001–02 representing about 14,800

386

tonnes of fish. Whitefish, sauger, pickerel and pike are the principal varieties of fish caught.

INDUSTRY
Manitoba's diverse manufacturing sector is the province's largest industry, accounting for approximately 13% of total GDP, about 64% of total foreign exports and about 69% of exports to the US. The value of manufacturing shipments grew 1·1% in 2001 to $11·5bn. CDN.

Labour. Employment in Manitoba increased 0·6% or 3,500 to a total of 557,000 jobs in 2001. Part-time employment increased 2·5% while full-time employment increased 0·2%. Labour force growth outstripped the increase in employment, pushing unemployment rates up slightly by 0·1% to 5%, the second lowest rate among Canadian provinces. The labour force participation rate reached a record high of 68·1%, the second highest among Canadian provinces.

INTERNATIONAL TRADE
Products grown and manufactured in Manitoba find ready markets in other parts of Canada, in the USA, particularly the upper Midwest region, and in other countries.

Imports and Exports. Value of exports in 2001 totalled $9·36bn. CDN, up 7·4% from $8·71bn. CDN in 2000. Exports to the USA, which accounted for 80% of total merchandise exports, increased by 7·3% while non-US exports rose 7·9%. After the USA, the largest volume of exports went to Japan, Mexico, China, Belgium and Hong Kong respectively. In 2001 all major commodity industries posted merchandise export gains. Agriculture products, which equalled 19·8% of provincial exports, increased 15·4%, while other primary commodities, which accounted for 7·6% of exports, grew by 10·8%. Manufacturing exports, which comprised almost two-thirds of foreign commodity exports, rose 4·2%.

COMMUNICATIONS
Roads. Highways and provincial roads total 18,500 km, with 2,800 bridges and other structures. As of July 2002 there were 489,574 passenger vehicles (including taxis), 117,541 trucks, 51,625 farm trucks, 25,727 off-road vehicles and 8,834 motorcycles registered in the province.

Rail. The province has about 5,650 km of commercial track, not including industrial track, yards and sidings. Most of the track belongs to the country's two national railways. Canadian Pacific owns about 1,950 km and Canadian National about 2,400 km. The Hudson Bay Railway, operated by Denver-based Omnitrax, has about 1,300 km of track. Fort Worth-based Burlington Northern's railcars are moved in Manitoba on CN and CP tracks and trains.

Civil Aviation. There are 56 domestic commercial aviation operators flying from bases in Manitoba. Four are designated private; 47 air taxi companies are licensed to carry fewer than 10 passengers; and five commuter operations are licensed to carry up to 19 passengers. Fourteen national airlines are licensed to carry more than 19 passengers. Nine foreign airlines land in the province (cargo and passenger). In addition, 38 aerial services are licensed (largely for agricultural chemical spraying).

Telecommunications. In 2001 Manitoba Telecom Services provided 685,314 access lines to its network. It also had 206,447 cellular subscribers and 97,089 Internet access customers.

SOCIAL INSTITUTIONS
Justice. In 2001, 130,700 Criminal Code offences were reported in Manitoba (a ratio of 11,365 per 100,000 people), including 34 homicides (a ratio of 2·96 per 100,000 people).

Education. Education is controlled through locally elected school divisions. There were 206,653 students enrolled in the province's public, independent (private) and home schools in the 2001–02 school year. Student teacher ratios (including all instructors but excluding school-based administrators) averaged one teacher for every 18·5 students.

Manitoba has four universities with a total full- and part-time undergraduate and graduate enrolment for the 2002–03 academic year of 38,000. They are the University of Manitoba, founded in 1877; the University of Winnipeg; Brandon University; and the Collège universitaire de Saint Boniface.

Community colleges in Brandon, The Pas and Winnipeg offer 2-year diploma courses in a number of fields, as well as specialized training in many trades. They also give a large number and variety of shorter courses, both at their campuses and in many communities throughout the province. Provincial government expenditure on education and training for the 2002–03 fiscal year is budgeted at $1·52bn. CDN.

CULTURE

Tourism. In 2001 total tourism expenditure in Manitoba increased by 7·8% to $1,287m. CDN, including $775·6m. CDN (and 5,609,639 person visits) from elsewhere in Manitoba; $253m. CDN (868,385 visits) from the remainder of Canada; $183·5m. CDN (773,412 visits) from the USA; and $75·2m. CDN (95,200 visits) from overseas.

Festivals. Folklorama is a celebration of Canadian culture that takes place in over 40 multicultural pavilions each July. The Festival du Voyageur takes place in St Boniface each Feb. and is western Canada's biggest winter festival. Canada's National Ukrainian Festival takes place over a long weekend each Aug., and in mid-July there is the four-day Manitoba Stampede and Exhibition, one of Canada's largest rodeos.

Theatre and Opera. The Royal Winnipeg Ballet is Canada's oldest ballet company.

Museums and Galleries. The Manitoba Museum has seven galleries showing the inter-relationship between man and the environment.

FURTHER READING

General Information: Inquiries may be addressed to Information Services, Room 29, Legislative Building, 450 Broadway, Winnipeg, Manitoba R3C 0V8.

NEW BRUNSWICK

KEY HISTORICAL EVENTS

Visited by Jacques Cartier in 1534, New Brunswick was first explored by Samuel de Champlain in 1604. With Nova Scotia, it originally formed one French colony called Acadia. It was ceded by the French in the Treaty of Utrecht in 1713 and became a permanent British possession in 1759. It was first settled by British colonists in 1764 but was separated from Nova Scotia, and became a province in June 1784 as a result of the great influx of United Empire Loyalists. Responsible government came into being in 1848 and consisted of an executive council, a legislative council (later abolished) and a House of Assembly. In 1867 New Brunswick entered the Confederation.

TERRITORY AND POPULATION

The area of the province is 28,150 sq. miles (72,908 sq. km), of which 27,587 sq. miles (71,450 sq. km) is land area. The population at the 2001 census was 729,498. Based on the 2001 census, 30% were of 'Canadian' origin, 18% of New Brunswick's total population were of British Isles only ancestry and 16% had French only ancestry. Other significant ethnic groups were German, Dutch, Scottish and Irish. In 2001 there were 15,940 North American Indian, Métis or Inuit people in New Brunswick. Census 2001 population of urban centres: Saint John, 122,678; Moncton, 117,727; Fredericton (capital), 81,346; Bathurst, 23,935; Edmundston, 22,173; Campbellton, 16,265. The official languages are English and French.

SOCIAL STATISTICS

Births in 2002 numbered 7,179 (a rate of 9·8 per 1,000 population), and deaths 6,427 (rate of 8·8 per 1,000 population). There were 4,003 marriages and 1,482 divorces in 2000.

CLIMATE

A cool temperate climate, with rain in all seasons but temperatures modified by the influence of the Gulf Stream. Annual average total precipitation in Fredericton: 1,131 mm. Warmest month, July (average high) 25·6°C.

CONSTITUTION AND GOVERNMENT

The government is vested in a Lieut.-Governor, appointed by the Queen's representative in New Brunswick, and a Legislative Assembly of 55 members, each of whom is individually elected to represent the voters in one constituency or riding. The political party with the largest number of elected representatives, after a Provincial election, forms the government. A simultaneous translation system is used in the Assembly. Any Canadian subject of full age and six months' residence is entitled to vote.

RECENT ELECTIONS

The last provincial election was held on 7 June 1999. As of Dec. 2002 the Legislative Assembly consisted of 47 Progressive Conservatives, seven Liberals and one from the New Democratic Party. The province has ten appointed members in the Canadian Senate and elects ten members in the House of Commons.

CURRENT ADMINISTRATION

Lieut.-Governor: Dr Marilyn Trenholme Counsell (appointed in April 1997).

The members of the Cabinet were as follows in Jan. 2003:

Premier, Executive Council, Intergovernmental Affairs, Regional Development Corporation and eNB: Bernard Lord. *Deputy Premier, Supply and Services:* Dale Graham. *Justice, Attorney General and Aboriginal Affairs:* Bradley Green, QC. *Finance, NB Liquor Corp., Investment Management, Atlantic Lotto:* Peter Mesheau. *Transportation:* Percy Mockler. *Natural Resources and Energy:* Jeannot Volpé. *Agriculture, Fisheries and Aquaculture:* Rodney Western. *Health and Wellness, Office of Human Resources:* Elvy Robichaud. *Public Safety, Status of Women:* Margaret-Ann Blaney. *Training and Employment Development:* Norman McFarlane. *Education, Culture and Sport Secretariat:* Dr Dennis Furlong. *Family and Community Services:* Joan MacAlpine. *Environment and Local Government:* Kimberly Jardine. *Services New Brunswick, Business New Brunswick:* Norman Betts. *Tourism and Parks, La Francophonie:* Paul Robichaud.

Government of New Brunswick Website: http://www.gnb.ca

ECONOMY

GDP per capita in 2001 was $27,090 CDN. Personal income was $18,138m. CDN; personal income per capita was $23,960 CDN; personal disposable income was $14,327 CDN. The Consumer Price Index in 2002 was 118·6 (100 in 1992); and retail sales in 2001 were $7,070m. CDN.

Budget. The ordinary budget (in $1m. CDN) is shown as follows (financial years ended 31 March):

	1998	1999	2000	2001	2002
Gross revenue	4,474·1	4,486·4	4,366·6	4,707·2	4,707·2
Gross expenditure	4,439·2	4,650·7	4,297·6	4,488·0	4,725·2

Funded debt and capital loans outstanding (exclusive of Treasury Bills) as of 31 March 1998 was $6,685·1m. CDN. Sinking funds held by the province at 31 March 1999, $2,693·2m. CDN. The ordinary budget excludes capital spending.

ENERGY AND NATURAL RESOURCES

Electricity. Hydro-electric, thermal and nuclear generating stations of NB Power had an installed capacity of 3,769 MW at 31 March 2002, consisting of 15 generating stations. The Mactaquac hydro-electric development near Fredericton has a name plate capacity of 672 MW. The largest thermal generating station, Coleson Cove, near Saint John, has 998 MW of installed capacity. Atlantic Canada's first nuclear generating station, a 635 MW plant on a promontory in the Bay of Fundy, near Saint John, went into operation in 1983. New Brunswick is electrically interconnected with utilities in neighbouring provinces of Quebec, Nova Scotia and

Prince Edward Island, as well as the New England States of the USA. The sale of out-of-province power accounted for 27·2% of revenue in 2001–02. Total revenue amounted to $1,319m. CDN.

Oil and Gas. In 2001 major construction projects were the natural gas pipeline and the oil refinery expansion. Construction continues on the natural gas pipeline.

Minerals. In 2001 approximately 18 different metals, minerals and commodities were produced. These included lead, zinc, copper, cadmium, bismuth, gold, silver, antimony, potash, salt, lime, stone, gas, coal, sand and gravel, peat and marl. The total value of minerals produced in 2001 reached $789·2m. CDN. The top four contributors to mineral production are zinc, silver, lead and peat accounting for 73·5% of total value in 2001. In 2000 New Brunswick ranked first in Canada for the production of zinc, bismuth and lead, and second for silver and fifth for copper. Not all of the province's minerals have been explored sufficiently and research continues.

Agriculture. The total area under crops is estimated at 135,008 ha. Farms numbered 3,034 and averaged 149 ha each (census 2001). Potatoes accounted for 25·3% of total farm cash receipts in 2001. Mixed farming is common throughout the province. Dairy farming is centred around the larger urban areas, and is located mainly along the Saint John River Valley and in the southeastern sections of the province. Income from dairy products provides 16·6% of farm cash receipts. New Brunswick is self-sufficient in fluid milk and supplies a processing industry. For particulars of livestock, *see* CANADA: Agriculture. Farm cash receipts in 2001 were $411·7m. CDN.

Forestry. New Brunswick contains some 6m. ha of productive forest lands. The value of manufacturing shipments for the wood-related industries in 2001 was just over $3·7bn. CDN, representing 33% of total shipments in the province. The paper and allied industry group is the largest component of the industry, contributing 58·4% of forestry output. In 2001 nearly 16,000 people were employed in all aspects of the forest industry, including harvesting, processing and transportation. Practically all forest products are exported from the province's numerous ports and harbours, near which many of the mills are located, or sent by road or rail to the USA.

Fisheries. Commercial fishing is one of the most important primary industries of the province, employing 7,123 in 1999. Nearly 50 commercial species of fish and shellfish are landed, including scallop, shrimp, crab, herring and cod. Landings in 2000 (121,576 tonnes) amounted to $177m. CDN. In 2001 molluscs and crustaceans ranked first with a value of $153m. CDN, 87·6% of the total landed value; pelagic fish second, 10·7%; and groundfish third, 1·3%. Exports in 2001 totalled $655·8m. CDN, and went mainly to the USA and Japan.

INDUSTRY

New Brunswick's location, with deepwater harbours open throughout the year and container facilities at Saint John, makes it ideal for exporting. Some of the main industries include food and beverages, paper and allied industries, and timber products. Nearly 20% of the industrial labour force work in Saint John.

Labour. New Brunswick's labour force increased by 2·4% in 2002 to 385,700 while employment increased to 345,000. Goods producing industries employed 79,700 and the service-producing industries employed 253,700. In 2002 the participation rate rose to 63·5% and the unemployment rate was 10·4%.

INTERNATIONAL TRADE

Imports and Exports. The main exports of New Brunswick include lumber, woodpulp, newsprint, refined petroleum products and electricity. In 2001 the major trading partners of the province were the USA with 88·9% of total exports, followed by Japan with 2·1% and the UK with 1% of total exports. Exports reached $8,295·8m. CDN while imports totalled $5,626m. CDN in 2001.

COMMUNICATIONS

Roads. There are 21,380 km of roads in the Provincial Highway system, of which 8,320 km consists of arterial, collector and local roads that provide access to most areas. The main highway system, including approximately 516 km of the Trans-Canada Highway, links the province with the principal roads in Quebec, Nova Scotia and Prince Edward Island, as well as the Interstate Highway System in the eastern seaboard states of the USA. A new four-lane access highway between Fredericton and Moncton was completed in 2001. At 31 March 2001 total road motor vehicle registrations numbered 545,668 of which 372,680 were passenger automobiles, 155,195 were truck and truck tractors, 13,406 motorcycles and mopeds, and 4,387 other vehicles.

Rail. Brunswick is served by the Canadian National Railways, Springfield Terminal Railway, Van Buren Bridge Railway Company, New Brunswick Southern Railway, New Brunswick East Coast Railway, Le Chemin de fer de la Matapédia et du Golfe and VIA Rail. The Salem-Hillsborough rail and The Acadian Railway Company are popular with tourists.

Civil Aviation. There are three major airports at Fredericton, Moncton and Saint John. There are also a number of small regional airports.

Shipping. New Brunswick has five ports which provide a leading role in international trade. The Port of Saint John handles approximately 20m. tonnes of cargo each year including forest products, steel, potash and petroleum. In 2001, 52 cruise ships visited Saint John. The Port of Belledune is a deep-water port and open all year round. Other ports are Dalhousie, Bayside/St Andrews and Miramichi.

Telecommunications. In 1996 the New Brunswick Telephone Co. Ltd had 542,887 access lines in service.

SOCIAL INSTITUTIONS

Justice. In 2001, 52,900 Criminal Code offences were reported, including eight homicides.

Education. Public education is free and non-sectarian.

There were, in 2001–02, 122,792 students (including kindergarten) and 7,481 full-time equivalent/professional educational staff in the province's 349 schools. There are 14 school districts.

There are four universities. The University of New Brunswick at Fredericton (founded 13 Dec. 1785 by the Loyalists, elevated to university status in 1823, and reorganized as the University of New Brunswick in 1859) had 6,839 full-time students at the Fredericton campus and 2,292 full-time students at the Saint John campus (2002–03); the Université de Moncton at Moncton, 4,793 full-time students; St Thomas University at Fredericton, 2,750 full-time students; Mount Allison University at Sackville had 2,250 full-time students.

CULTURE

Broadcasting. The province is served by 37 radio stations and a number of television stations, the majority of which broadcast exclusively in English; the remainder broadcast in French (some radio stations are bilingual).

Press. In 2002 New Brunswick had four daily newspapers (one in French), and 17 weekly newspapers, five in French and two bilingual.

Tourism. New Brunswick has a number of historic buildings as well as libraries, museums and other cultural sites. Tourism is one of the leading contributors to the economy. In 2002 tourism revenues reached $985m. CDN. Popular attractions include Magnetic Hill (Moncton), the Reversing Falls (Saint John) and the Hopewell Rocks Formation. There are two national parks (Fundy and Kouchibouguac) as well as a number of provincial parks and two historic settlements, Kings Landing (west of Fredericton) and an Acadian settlement.

Festivals. Festivals include: the Lobster Festival in Shediac, Fredericton Jazz and Blues Festival, Festival by the Sea in Saint John, the Irish Festival held in Miramichi and *Le Festival Acadien de Caraquet*.

Libraries. Fredericton's libraries include The Harriet Irving Library (located on the university campus) and Legislative Library (established 1841). There are also a number of regional libraries.

Theatre and Opera. Theatre New Brunswick is based at the Playhouse in Fredericton, and Symphony New Brunswick and Imperial Theatre are located in Saint John.

Museums and Galleries. The Beaverbrook Art Gallery and the Provincial Archives (both located in Fredericton) are two of the most notable galleries and museums. The New Brunswick Museum (one of the oldest) and Loyalist House are located in Saint John.

FURTHER READING

Industrial Information: Dept. of Economic Development and Tourism, Fredericton. *Economic Information:* Dept. of Finance, New Brunswick Statistics Agency, Fredericton. *General Information:* Communications New Brunswick, Fredericton.

NEWFOUNDLAND AND LABRADOR

KEY HISTORICAL EVENTS

Archaeological finds at L'Anse-au-Meadow in northern Newfoundland show that the Vikings established a colony here in about AD 1000. This site is the only known Viking colony in North America. Newfoundland was discovered by John Cabot on 24 June 1497, and was soon frequented in the summer months by the Portuguese, Spanish and French for its fisheries. It was formally occupied in Aug. 1583 by Sir Humphrey Gilbert on behalf of the English Crown but various attempts to colonize the island remained unsuccessful. Although British sovereignty was recognized in 1713 by the Treaty of Utrecht, disputes over fishing rights with the French were not finally settled till 1904. By the Anglo-French Convention of 1904, France renounced her exclusive fishing rights along part of the coast, granted under the Treaty of Utrecht, but retained sovereignty of the offshore islands of St Pierre and Miquelon. Self-governing from 1855, the colony remained outside of the Canadian confederation in 1867 and continued to govern itself until 1934, when a commission of government appointed by the British Crown assumed responsibility for governing the colony and Labrador. This body controlled the country until union with Canada in 1949.

TERRITORY AND POPULATION

Area, 405,212 sq. km (156,452 sq. miles), of which freshwater, 31,340 sq. km (12,100 sq. miles). In March 1927 the Privy Council decided the boundary between Canada and Newfoundland in Labrador. This area, now part of the Province of Newfoundland and Labrador, is 294,330 sq. km (113,641 sq. miles) of land area.

Newfoundland island's coastline is punctuated with numerous bays, fjords and inlets, providing many good deep water harbours. The interior is a plateau of moderate elevation. The highest peak of Long Range reaches 815 metres. Approximately one-third of the area is covered by water. Grand Lake, the largest body of water, has an area of about 530 sq. km. The principal rivers flow towards the northeast. Good agricultural land is generally found in the valleys of the Terra Nova River, the Gander River, the Exploits River and the Humber River, which are also heavily timbered. The Strait of Belle Isle separates the island from Labrador to the north. Bordering on the Canadian province of Quebec, Labrador is a vast, pristine wilderness and extremely sparsely populated (approximately 10 sq. km per person). Labrador's Lake Melville is 2,934 sq. km and its highest peak, Mount Caubvick, is 5,577 ft.

The population at the 2001 census was 512,930. The population is declining at a faster rate than any other Canadian province, with a drop of 7·0% between the censuses of 1996 and 2001.

The capital of the province is the City of St. John's (2001 population, 172,918 metropolitan area). The other cities are Mt Pearl (24,964 in 2001) and Corner Brook (20,103); important towns are Conception Bay South (19,772), Grand Falls-Windsor (13,340), Gander (9,651), Paradise (9,598), Happy Valley-Goose Bay (7,969), Labrador City (7,744), Stephenville (7,101), Marystown (5,908), Portugal Cove-St

Philip's (5,866), Bay Roberts (5,237), Clarenville (5,104), Channel-Port aux Basques (4,637).

SOCIAL STATISTICS
Births in 2001–02 numbered 4,689 (a rate of 8·8 per 1,000 population), and deaths 4,420 (rate of 8·3 per 1,000 population). There were 3,025 marriages and 936 divorces in 2000.

CLIMATE
The cool temperate climate is marked by heavy precipitation, distributed evenly over the year, a cool summer and frequent fogs in spring. St. John's, Jan. –4°C, July 15·8°C. Annual rainfall 1,240 mm.

CONSTITUTION AND GOVERNMENT
Until 1832 Newfoundland was ruled by the Governor under instructions of the Colonial Office. In that year a Legislature was brought into existence, but the Governor and his Executive Council were not responsible to it. Under the constitution of 1855, which lasted until its suspension in 1934, the government was administered by the Governor appointed by the Crown with an Executive Council responsible to the House of Assembly of 27 elected members, and a Legislative Council of 24 members nominated for life by the Governor in Council. Women were enfranchised in 1925. At the Imperial Conference of 1917 Newfoundland was constituted as a Dominion.

In 1933 the financial situation had become so critical that the government of Newfoundland asked the government of the UK to appoint a Royal Commission to investigate conditions. On the strength of their recommendations, the parliamentary form of government was suspended and Government by Commission was inaugurated on 16 Feb. 1934.

A National Convention, elected in 1946, made recommendations to H. M. government in Great Britain in 1948 as to the possible forms of future government to be submitted to the people at a national referendum. Two referenda were held. In the first referendum (June 1948) the three forms of government submitted to the people were: commission of government for five years; confederation with Canada; and responsible government as it existed in 1933. No one form of government received a clear majority of the votes polled, and commission of government, receiving the fewest votes, was eliminated. In the second referendum (July 1948) confederation with Canada received 78,408 and responsible government 71,464 votes.

In the Canadian Senate on 18 Feb. 1949 Royal Assent was given to the terms of union of Newfoundland and Labrador with Canada, and on 23 March 1949, in the House of Lords, London, Royal assent was given to an amendment to the British North America Act, made necessary by the inclusion of Newfoundland and Labrador as the tenth Province of Canada.

Under the terms of union of Newfoundland and Labrador with Canada, which was signed at Ottawa on 11 Dec. 1948, the constitution of the Legislature of Newfoundland and Labrador as it existed immediately prior to 16 Feb. 1934 shall, subject to the terms of the British North America Acts, 1867 to 1946, continue as the constitution of the Legislature of the Province of Newfoundland and Labrador until altered under the authority of the said Acts.

The House of Assembly (Amendment) Act, 1979, established 52 electoral districts and 52 members of the Legislature. The province is represented by six members in the Senate and by seven members in the House of Commons of Canada. The franchise was in 1965 extended to all male and female residents who have attained the age of 19 years and are otherwise qualified as electors.

RECENT ELECTIONS
Elections were held on 9 Feb. 1999. In Jan. 2003 there were 27 Liberals, 19 Progressive Conservatives and 2 New Democrats.

CURRENT ADMINISTRATION
Lieut.-Governor: Edward M. Roberts (assumed office 1 Nov. 2002).

In Feb. 2003 the Liberal Cabinet was composed as follows:
Premier: Roger Grimes.
Minister of Education: Gerry Reid. *Environment:* Robert Mercer. *Finance:* Joan Marie Aylward. *Fisheries and Aquaculture, and Responsible for Status of Women:* Yvonne Jones. *Forest Resources and Agrifoods:* Rick Woodford. *Government Services and Lands:* George Sweeney. *Health and Community Services:* Gerald Smith. *Human Resources and Employment:* Ralph Wiseman. *Industry, Trade and Rural Development:* Judy Foote. *Intergovernmental Affairs and Government House Leader:* Tom Lush. *Justice and Attorney General:* Kelvin Parsons. *Labour:* Percy Barrett. *Labrador and Aboriginal Affairs:* Wally Andersen. *Mines and Energy:* Walter Noel. *Municipal and Provincial Affairs:* Oliver Langdon. *Tourism, Culture and Recreation:* Julie Bettney. *Works, Services and Transportation:* James Walsh. *Youth Services and Post-Secondary Education:* Anna Thistle.
Speaker of the House of Assembly: Lloyd Snow.

Office of the Premier: http://www.gov.nf.ca/premier/

ECONOMY

GDP growth for 2002 was expected to be 7·5%.

Budget. Government budget in $1,000 CDN in fiscal years ending 31 March:

	2000–01	2001–02	2002–03[1]
Gross Revenue	3,595,106	3,800,799	3,840,165
Gross Expenditure	3,475,062	3,684,975	3,826,879

[1]Estimate.

ENERGY AND NATURAL RESOURCES

Electricity. Newfoundland and Labrador is currently served by two physically independent electrical systems with a total of 7,401 MW of operational electrical generating capacity. The island of Newfoundland is served by an isolated system of approximately 1,890 MW of electrical capacity, of which about 64% is hydro-electric. Of the total provincial generating capacity, 5,511 MW are located in Labrador, with the majority from the Churchill Falls hydro-electric facility rated at 5,428 MW. In 2001 total provincial electricity generation equalled 40·9bn. kWh, of which about 95% was from hydro-electric sources. Of this total, 29·7bn. kWh (or 73%), from the Churchill Falls hydro-electric facility, was exported and sold to Hydro-Québec. During 2001 total electrical energy load was 11·2bn. kWh (including system losses), with about 71% of this demand located on the island portion of the province and 29% in Labrador. The province is currently reviewing options for the development of a 2,000 MW hydroelectric generating facility at the Gull Island site located on the Lower Churchill River in Labrador.

Oil and Gas. Since 1965, 140 wells have been drilled on the Continental Margin of the Province. Only the Hibernia discovery had commercial capability with production starting in the early 1990s. In 2001 oil production from Hibernia reached 54·3m. bbls. 2002 production was expected to increase to around 60m. bbls. The Terra Nova development produced oil in Jan. 2002 and is permitted to produce almost 55m. bbls. annually.

Minerals. The mineral resources are vast but only partially documented. Large deposits of iron ore, with an ore reserve of over 5,000m. tonnes at Labrador City, Wabush City and in the Knob Lake area, are supplying approximately half of Canada's production. Other large deposits of iron ore are known to exist in the Julienne Lake area. There are a variety of other minerals being produced in more limited amounts. The Central Mineral Belt, which extends from the Smallwood Reservoir to the Atlantic coast near Makkovik, holds uranium, copper, beryllium and molybdenite potential. Staking activity has increased since 2000 because of exploration for nickel and platinum-palladium in Labrador and gold in central Newfoundland.

The percentage share of mineral shipment value in 2001 stood at 92·6% for iron ore; 2·2%, gold; 5·2%, structural metals. The value of mineral shipments in 2001 totalled $819m. CDN, a drop of 16% owing to reduced demand in key markets.

NEWFOUNDLAND AND LABRADOR

Agriculture. The value of farm production in 2001 was $81·3m. CDN, an increase of 11·9% on 2000.

Forestry. The forestry economy in the province is mainly dependent on the operation of three newsprint mills—Corner Brook Pulp and Paper and Abitibi-Consolidated (which operates two mills). In 2002 the estimated value of newsprint exported totalled $541m. CDN, a decrease of 20% over 2001. Lumber mills and saw-log operations produced 144m. flat bd ft in 2001–02.

Fisheries. Closure of the northern cod and other groundfish fisheries has resulted in changes to the structure of the fishing industry. New resource opportunities, secondary seafood production and aquaculture are the main focus today with over 100 commercial or developing aquaculture operations generating $20m. CDN in exports in 2001. The Newfoundland and Labrador fishery registered a production value of $883m. CDN. The total catch in 2001 decreased by 4% to 257,000 tonnes valued at $496m. CDN.

INDUSTRY

The total value of manufacturing shipments in 2001 was $2·2bn. CDN. This consisted largely of fish products, refined petroleum and newsprint.

Labour. In 2002 those in employment numbered 213,900 with 12,400 workers employed in manufacturing. The unemployment rate was 16·9% in 2002 (16·1% in 2001).

Trade Unions. In 2001 union membership was 40% of the employed workforce, the highest in any Canadian province. The Newfoundland and Labrador Federation of Labour (NLFL) has 50,000 members; the Newfoundland and Labrador Association of Public and Private Employees (NAPE) has 19,000.

COMMUNICATIONS

Roads. In 2001 there were 8,938 km of roads, of which 6,990 were paved. In 2001 there were 360,375 motor vehicles registered, including 226,292 passenger cars.

Rail. In 1997 the Quebec North Shore and Labrador Railway operated both freight and passenger services on its 588 km main line from Sept-Iles, Quebec, to Shefferville, Quebec and its 58 km spur line from Ross Bay Junction to Labrador City, Newfoundland. In 1996 freight totalled 20·8m. tonnes (iron ore, 20·0m. tonnes).

Civil Aviation. The province is linked to the rest of Canada by regular air services provided by Air Canada, Quebecair and a number of smaller air carriers.

Shipping. At Jan. 2003 there were 1,799 ships on register in Newfoundland. Marine Atlantic, a federal crown corporation, provides a freight and passenger service all year round from Channel-Port aux Basques to North Sydney, Nova Scotia; and seasonal ferries connect Argentia with North Sydney, and Lewisporte with Goose Bay, Labrador.

Telecommunications. There were 459 full service post office outlets in March 1996. Telephone access lines numbered 262,856 in 1993 (193,987 private). There were 3,384 public pay phones.

SOCIAL INSTITUTIONS

Justice. In 2001, 33,079 Criminal Code offences were reported, including one homicide.

Education. In 2001–02 total enrolment for elementary and secondary education was 86,898; full time teachers numbered 6,264; total number of schools was 326. The Memorial University, offering courses in arts, science, engineering, education, nursing and medicine, had 14,000 full-time students in 1999–2000.

CULTURE

Tourism. In 2001, 427,700 non-resident tourists (408,500 in 1999) spent approximately $289m. CDN in the province. In 2001 the 100th anniversary of Marconi's transatlantic transmission from St John's was celebrated.

FURTHER READING
Statistical office: Newfoundland Labrador Statistics Agency, POB 8700, St. John's, NL A1B 4J6.
Website: http://www.nfstats.gov.nf.ca/

NOVA SCOTIA

KEY HISTORICAL EVENTS
Nova Scotia was visited by John and Sebastian Cabot in 1497–98. In 1605 a number of French colonists settled at Port Royal. The old name of the colony, Acadia, was changed in 1621 to Nova Scotia. The French were granted possession of the colony by the Treaty of St-Germain-en-Laye (1632). In 1654 Oliver Cromwell sent a force to occupy the settlement. Charles II, by the Treaty of Breda (1667), restored Nova Scotia to the French. It was finally ceded to the British by the Treaty of Utrecht in 1713. In the Treaty of Paris (1763) France resigned all claims and in 1820 Cape Breton Island united with Nova Scotia. Representative government was granted as early as 1758 and a fully responsible legislative assembly was established in 1848. In 1867 the province entered the dominion of Canada.

TERRITORY AND POPULATION
The area of the province is 21,345 sq. miles (55,284 sq. km), of which 20,594 sq. miles are land area and 751 sq. miles water area. The population at the 2001 census was 908,007.

Population of the principal cities (2001 census): Halifax, 119,292; Dartmouth, 65,741. Principal towns (2001 estimates): Bedford, 16,603; Truro, 12,264; New Glasgow, 10,060; Amherst, 9,718; Bridgewater, 7,778; Yarmouth, 7,565; Kentville, 5,536.

SOCIAL STATISTICS
Births in 2001–02 numbered 8,918 (a rate of 9·4 per 1,000 population), and deaths 8,104 (rate of 8·6 per 1,000 population). There were 5,035 marriages in 2001 and 1,949 divorces in 2000.

CLIMATE
A cool temperate climate, with rainfall occurring evenly over the year. The Gulf Stream moderates the temperatures in winter so that ports remain ice-free. Halifax, Jan. 23·7°F (–4·6°C), July 63·5°F (17·5°C). Annual rainfall 54" (1,371 mm).

CONSTITUTION AND GOVERNMENT
Under the British North America Act of 1867 the legislature of Nova Scotia may exclusively make laws in relation to local matters, including direct taxation within the province, education and the administration of justice. The legislature of Nova Scotia consists of a Lieut.-Governor, appointed and paid by the federal government, and holding office for five years, and a House of Assembly of 52 members, chosen by popular vote at least every five years. The province is represented in the Canadian Senate by ten members, and in the House of Commons by 11.

The franchise and eligibility to the legislature are granted to every person, male or female, if of age (18 years), a British subject or Canadian citizen, and a resident in the province for six months before the date of the writ of election in the county or electoral district of which the polling district forms part, and if not by law otherwise disqualified.

RECENT ELECTIONS
At the provincial elections of 27 July 1999 the Progressive Conservatives won 30 seats (57·7% of the vote), the New Democratic Party 11 seats (21·2%) and the Liberals 11 (21·2%). Turn-out was 68·8%. As of Oct. 2002 the standings were: 31 Progressive Conservatives, 11 New Democratic Party and 10 Liberals.

CURRENT ADMINISTRATION
Lieut.-Governor: Myra Freeman, ONS.

The members of the Progressive Conservative Ministry in Feb. 2003 were:
Premier, President of the Executive Council and Minister of Intergovernmental Affairs: John F. Hamm.

Deputy Premier, Deputy President of the Executive Council, Minister of Environment and Labour and Government House Leader: Ronald Russell. *Minister of Agriculture and Fisheries and of the Public Service Commission:* Gordon Balser. *Justice and Attorney General:* Jamie Muir. *Transportation and Public Works, Responsible for Aboriginal Affairs:* Michael Baker, QC. *Tourism and Culture, Minister of the Office of Health Promotion:* Rodney MacDonald. *Energy:* Ernest Page. *Minister of Service Nova Scotia and Municipal Relations:* Peter Christie. *Finance and Responsible for Acadian Affairs:* Neil LeBlanc. *Education:* Angus MacIsaac. *Health, Chair of the Senior Citizens' Secretariat:* Jane Purves. *Community Services:* David Morse. *Economic Development:* Cecil Clarke. *Natural Resources:* Timothy Olive.

Speaker of the House of Assembly: Murray Scott.

Government of Nova Scotia Website: http://www.gov.ns.ca/

ECONOMY

Budget. Summary of operations and net funding requirements for the consolidated entity (in $1m. CDN) for fiscal years ending 31 March:

	2000[1]	2001[2]	2002[3]
Revenues	5,090·9	5,147·6	5,306·7
Net Programme Expenditures/Expenses	4,250·6	4,478·4	4,512·7
Net Debt Servicing Costs	872·8	862·4	865·1
Pension Valuation Adjustment	(76·2)	(60·0)	(50·0)
Total Net Expenditures/Expenses	5,047·3	5,280·7	5,327·9
Consolidation Adjustment	(322·2)	–	–
Net Income from Government Business Enterprises	246·1	26·8	22·5
Unusual Item	179·8	–	–
Surplus (Deficit)	147·3	(106·3)	1·3

[1]Actual. [2]Forecast. [3]Estimate.

Performance. GDP (market prices) was $25,203m. CDN in 2001, an increase of just over 4% on 2000. GDP per person in 2001 was $26,726 CDN.

Banking and Finance. Revenue is derived from provincial sources, payments from the federal government under the equalization agreements and the Canada Health and Social Transfer (CHST). Recoveries consist generally of amounts received under various federal cost-shared programmes. Main sources of provincial revenues include income and sales taxes.

In the fourth quarter of 2001 total deposits with chartered banks totalled $7,688m. CDN.

Weights and Measures. The metric system was officially adopted in 1983, but measurement in the imperial system is still widespread.

ENERGY AND NATURAL RESOURCES

Electricity. In 2001 production was 11,824,531 kWh, of which 94% came from thermal sources and the rest from hydro-electric, wind and tidal sources.

Oil and Gas. Significant finds of offshore natural gas are currently under development. Gas is flowing to markets in Canada and the USA (the pipeline was completed in 1999). Total marketable gas receipts for the first quarter of 2002 was 1·3bn. cu. metres.

Minerals. Principal minerals in 2001 were: coal, 1·1m. tonnes, valued at $53·6m. CDN; gypsum, 6·7m. tonnes, valued at $76·0m. CDN; stone, 8·4m. tonnes, valued at $51·9m. CDN. Total value of mineral production in 2001 was $1·4bn. CDN.

Agriculture. Dairying, poultry and egg production, livestock and fruit growing are the most important branches. Farm cash receipts for 2001 were $418·4m. CDN. Cash receipts from sale of dairy products were $95·9m. CDN, with total milk and cream sales of 176,052,000 litres. The production of poultry meat in 2001 was 36,066 tonnes, of which 32,302 tonnes were chicken and 3,764 tonnes were turkey. Egg production in 2001 was 17·8m. dozen.

The main fruit crops in 2001 were apples, 35,385 tonnes; blueberries, 13,032 tonnes; strawberries, 1,449 tonnes.

Forestry. The estimated forest area of Nova Scotia is 15,830 sq. miles (40,990 sq. km), of which about 28% is owned by the province. The principal trees are spruce, balsam fir, hemlock, pine, larch, birch, oak, maple, poplar and ash. 6,182,686 cu. metres of roundforest products were produced in 2001.

Fisheries. The fisheries of the province in 2001 had a landed value of $753m. CDN of sea fish; including scallop fishery, $111·9m. CDN; and lobster fishery, $362m. CDN. In 1999 there were 8,700 employees in the fish-processing industry; the value of shipment of goods was $755m. CDN. In 2000 there were 14,005 fishermen and 4,984 vessels.

INDUSTRY
The number of manufacturing establishments was 634 in 1999; the number of employees was 37,617; wages and salaries, $1,279m. CDN. The value of shipments in 1999 was $7,915m. CDN, and the leading industries were food, paper production, and plastic and rubber products.

Labour. In 2001 the labour force was 468,900 (221,600 females), of whom 423,200 (201,700) were employed.

Trade Unions. Total union membership in 2001 was 107,800. In 1997 there were 78 unions comprised of 653 individual locals. The largest union membership was in the service sector, followed by public administration and defence.

INTERNATIONAL TRADE
Imports and Exports. Total of imports and exports to and from Nova Scotia (in $1m. CDN):

	1998	1999	2000	2001
Imports	5,099	4,524	5,429	5,502
Exports	3,440	3,985	4,710	4,710

COMMUNICATIONS
Roads. In 2001 there were 26,000 km of highways, of which 13,600 km were paved. The Trans Canada and 100 series highways are limited access, all-weather, rapid transit routes. The province's first toll road opened in Dec. 1997. Acadian Lines provides a bus link to most major communities in the province and there are also a number of regional and local bus services. In the fiscal year 2000–01 total road vehicle registrations numbered 544,407 and over 632,027 persons had road motor vehicle operators licences.

Rail. The province has a 700 km network of mainline track operated predominantly by Canadian National Railways. The Cape Breton and Central Nova Scotia Railway operates between Truro and Cape Breton Island. The Windsor and Hantsport Railway operates in the Annapolis Valley region. VIA Rail operates the Ocean for six days a week, a transcontinental service between Halifax and Montreal.

Civil Aviation. There is direct air service to all major Canadian points, and international scheduled services to Boston, New York, Bermuda, London, Glasgow and Amsterdam. There are winter charter services to Florida and the Caribbean. Halifax International Airport is the largest airport, and there are also major airports at Yarmouth and Sydney.

Shipping. Ferry services connect Nova Scotia to the provinces of Newfoundland, Prince Edward Island and New Brunswick as well as to the USA. The deep-water, ice-free Port of Halifax handles about 14m. tonnes of cargo annually. Direct container service is provided to the USA, Europe, Asia, Australia/New Zealand and the Caribbean. There are numerous smaller ports.

Telecommunications. In 1996 there were 565,874 access lines (372,794 residential and 193,080 business). There were 59·8 access lines per 100 population and 98·3% of households had telephones.

Postal Services. The postal service is provided by the Federal Crown Corporation Canada Post.

SOCIAL INSTITUTIONS

Justice. The Supreme Court (Trial Division and Appeal Division) is the superior court of Nova Scotia and has original and appellate jurisdiction in all civil and criminal matters unless they have been specifically assigned to another court by Statute. An appeal from the Supreme Court, Appeal Division, is to the Supreme Court of Canada. The other courts in the Province are the Provincial Court, which hears criminal matters only, the Small Claims Court, which has limited monetary jurisdiction, Probate Court, County Court, which has jurisdiction in criminal matters as well as original jurisdiction over actions not exceeding $50,000 CDN, and Family Court. Young offenders are tried in the Family Court or the Provincial Court.

For the year ending 31 March 2001 there were 1,624 admissions to provincial sentenced custody. In 2001, 71,990 Criminal Code offences were reported, including nine homicides.

Religion. The population is predominantly Christian. In 1991, 37·2% were Roman Catholic, 17·2% were United Church, 14·4% Anglicans, 11·1% Baptist and 3·5% Presbyterian.

Education. Public education in Nova Scotia is free, compulsory and undenominational through elementary and high school. Attendance is compulsory to the age of 16. There were 511 elementary-secondary public schools, with 9,444 full-time teachers and 149,111 pupils, in 2000–01, plus the Nova Scotia Youth Centres for young offenders in Shelburne and in Waterville. The province has ten degree-granting institutions. The Nova Scotia Agricultural College is located at Truro. The Technical University of Nova Scotia, which grants degrees in engineering and architecture, amalgamated with Dalhousie University and is now known as DalTech. Through the Nova Scotia Community College, the Department of Education administers 13 college campuses, including two vocational training centres, two institutes of technology, a nautical institute, plus the College de l'Acadie, the French component of the Nova Scotia Community College. There are also seven teaching hospitals.

The Nova Scotia government offers financial support and organizational assistance to local school boards for provision of weekend and evening courses in academic and vocational subjects, and citizenship for new Canadians.

Health. A provincial retail sales tax of 8% provides funds for free hospital in-patient care up to ward level and free medically required services of physicians. Health service programmes in the province are administered by the Department of Health and operated in conjunction with Maritime Medical Care Inc. Prescription service is available to those over 65 years for a minimum fee. The Queen Elizabeth II Hospital in Halifax is the overall referral hospital for the province and, in many instances, for the Atlantic region. The Izaak Walton Killam Hospital provides similar regional specialization for children.

Welfare. General and specialized welfare services in the province are under the jurisdiction of the Department of Community Services. The provincial government funds all of the costs. The Employment Support and Income Assistance Act provides financial assistance to individuals or families where the cause of need is likely to be of a prolonged nature. Qualifying groups include the aged, disabled, unemployable, foster parents and disabled parents.

CULTURE

Broadcasting. Nova Scotia has 26 radio stations and nine television stations. In 1996 there were 85 operating cable television systems with 243,683 subscribers.

Press. Nova Scotia has approximately 50 newspapers, including eight dailies. Daily newspapers with the largest circulations are *The Chronicle Herald and Mail-Star* of Halifax, *The Daily News* of Dartmouth, and *The Cape Breton Post* of Sydney.

Tourism. Tourism revenues were $1·2bn. CDN in 2001. Total number of visitors in 2001 was 2,143,700.

Festivals. Main festivals include the International Buskers Festival and the Atlantic Jazz Festival in Halifax, the Apple Blossom Festival in the Annapolis Valley and the Celtic Colours Festival in Cape Breton.

Libraries. The Halifax Regional Municipality is serviced by the Halifax Regional Library system. There is also a comprehensive university library system which connects the many university and community college libraries in the province.

Museums and Galleries. Nova Scotia has a large number of museums and galleries, including the Nova Scotia Museum and the Nova Scotia Art Gallery in Halifax, and the Fisheries Museum in Lunenburg.

FURTHER READING
Nova Scotia Fact Book. N. S. Department of Economic Development, Halifax, 1993
Nova Scotia Statistical Review. N. S. Department of Finance, Halifax, 2002
Nova Scotia Facts at a Glance. N. S. Department of Finance, Halifax, 2002

Statistical office: Statistics Division, Department of Finance, POB 187, Halifax, Nova Scotia B3J 2N3.
Website: http://www.gov.ns.ca/finance/statisti/

ONTARIO

KEY HISTORICAL EVENTS
The French explorer Samuel de Champlain explored the Ottawa River from 1613. The area was governed by the French, first under a joint stock company and then as a royal province, from 1627 and was ceded to Great Britain in 1763. A constitutional act of 1791 created there the province of Upper Canada, largely to accommodate loyalists of English descent who had immigrated after the United States war of independence. Upper Canada entered the Confederation as Ontario in 1867.

TERRITORY AND POPULATION
The area is 415,596 sq. miles (1,076,395 sq. km), of which some 354,340 sq. miles (917,741 sq. km) are land area and some 61,256 sq. miles (158,654 sq. km) are lakes and fresh water rivers. The province extends 1,050 miles (1,690 km) from east to west and 1,075 miles (1,730 km) from north to south. It is bounded in the north by the Hudson and James Bays, in the east by Quebec, in the south by Manitoba, and in the south by the USA, the Great Lakes and the St Lawrence Seaway.

The census population in 2001 was 11,410,046. Population of the principal cities (2001 census):

Toronto[1]	2,481,494	Markham	208,615	Richmond Hill	132,030
Ottawa	774,072	Windsor	208,402	St Catharines	129,170
Mississauga	612,925	Kitchener	190,399	East York[1]	115,185
North York[1]	608,288	Thunder Bay	190,016	Cambridge	110,372
Scarborough[1]	593,297	Vaughan	182,022	Gloucester	110,264
Hamilton	490,286	Burlington	150,836	Guelph	106,170
Etobicoke[1]	338,117	York[1]	150,255	Barrie	103,710
London	336,539	Oakville	144,738	Brantford	86,417
Brampton	325,428	Oshawa	139,051	Sudbury	85,354

[1]The new City of Toronto was created on 1 Jan. 1998 through the amalgamation of seven municipalities: Metropolitan Toronto and six local area municipalities of Toronto, North York, Scarborough, Etobicoke, East York and York.

There are over 1m. French-speaking people and 0·25m. native Indians. An agreement with the Ontario government of Aug. 1991 recognized Indians' right to self-government.

SOCIAL STATISTICS
Births in 2000–01 numbered 130,672 (a rate of 11·1 per 1,000 population), and deaths 87,565 (a rate of 7·4 per 1,000 population). In 2000 there were 65,043 marriages and 25,786 divorces; in 1998 life expectancy was 76·3 years for males and 81·5 years for females.

CLIMATE
A temperate continental climate, but conditions can be quite severe in winter, though proximity to the Great Lakes has a moderating influence on temperatures. Ottawa,

average temperature, Jan. –10·8°C, July 20·8°C. Annual rainfall (including snow) 911 mm. Toronto, average temperature, Jan. –4·5°C, July 22·1°C. Annual rainfall (including snow) 818 mm.

CONSTITUTION AND GOVERNMENT
The provincial government is administered by a *Lieut.-Governor*, a cabinet and a single-chamber 103-member *Legislative Assembly* elected by a general franchise for a period of no longer than five years. The minimum voting age is 18 years.

RECENT ELECTIONS
At the elections on 3 June 1999 to the *Legislative Assembly*, the Progressive Conservative Party won 59 of a possible 103 seats, the Liberal Party 35 and the New Democratic Party (NDP) 9.

CURRENT ADMINISTRATION
Lieut.-Governor: James K. Bartleman, OOnt; b. 1939 (in office since March 2002).
In March 2003 the Executive Council comprised:
Premier, President of the Council and Minister of Intergovernmental Affairs: Ernie Eves.
Deputy Premier and Minister of Education: Elizabeth Witmer. *Energy, Responsible for Francophone Affairs and Deputy House Leader:* John Baird. *Labour:* Brad Clark. *Health and Long-Term Care:* Tony Clement. *Tourism and Recreation:* Brian Coburn. *Training, Colleges and Universities, Responsible for Women's issues:* Dianne Cunningham. *Citizenship, Responsible for Seniors:* Carl DeFaria. *Finance:* Janet Ecker. *Community, Family and Children's Services:* Brenda Elliot. *Enterprise, Opportunity and Innovation:* Jim Flaherty. *Consumer and Business Services:* Tim Hudak. *Agriculture and Food:* Helen Johns. *Transportation:* Frank Klees. *Municipal Affairs and Housing:* Tina Molinari. *Natural Resources:* Jerry Ouellette. *Public Safety and Security:* Bob Runciman. *Attorney General:* Norman Sterling. *Environment and Government House Leader:* Chris Stockwell. *Culture and Chair of the Management Board of Cabinet:* David Tsubouchi. *Northern Development and Mines:* Jim Wilson. *Municipal Affairs and Housing:* David Young. *Minister Without Portfolio and Chief Government Whip:* Doug Gait. *Associate Minister of Municipal Affairs and Housing, Rural Affairs:* Ernie Hardeman. *Associate Minister of Health and Long-Term Care:* Dan Newman. *Associate Minister of Enterprise, Opportunity and Innovation:* David Turnbull.

Office of the Premier: http://www.premier.gov.on.ca

ECONOMY
GDP per person in 2000 was $29,333 CDN.

Budget. Provincial revenue and expenditure (in $1m. CDN) for years ending 31 March:

	1997–98	1998–99	1999–2000	2000–01	2001–02[1]
Gross revenue	52,488	55,786	62,931	64,682	66,544
Gross expenditure	56,454	57,788	61,909	61,101	63,336

[1]Estimate.

Gross revenue and expenditure figures reflect accrual and consolidation accounting as recommended by the Public Sector Accounting and Auditing Board of the Canadian Institute of Chartered Accountants. Transactions on behalf of Ontario Hydro are excluded.

Performance. In 2000 real GDP grew at a rate of 5·3% (5·7% in 1999).

ENERGY AND NATURAL RESOURCES
Electricity. Ontario Hydro recorded for the calendar year 1999 an installed generating capacity of 31,000 MW. Primary energy made available (1998), 139bn. kWh. In 1999 there were 69 hydro-electric, six fossil fuel and five nuclear stations operating. The industry has since been deregulated and Ontario Power Generation now has the province's 80 generating stations. In 1999 Ontario Hydro served 108 direct industrial customers, almost 1m. retail customers (homes, farms and small businesses) and 255 municipal utilities, who in turn serve over 3m. customers.

Oil and Gas. Ontario is Canada's leading petroleum refining region. The province's five refineries have an annual capacity of 170m. bbls. (27m. cu metres).

Minerals. The total value of mineral production in 1998 was $5,126,995,000 CDN. In 1999 the most valuable commodities (production in $1m. CDN) were: nickel, 1,139·9; gold, 1,016·4; cement, 511·2; copper, 485·8; sand and gravel, 408·3; stone, 385·7. Total direct employment in the mining industry was 10,667 (9,609, metals; 1,061 non-metals) in 1999.

Agriculture. In 2001, 59,728 census farms operated on 5,466,256 ha, with total farm receipts of $8·49bn. CDN.

Forestry. The forested area totals 69·1m. ha, approximately 65% of Ontario's total area. Composition of Ontario forests: conifer, 56%; mixed, 26%; deciduous, 18%. The total growing stock (62% conifer, 38% hardwood) equals 5·3bn. cu. metres with an annual harvest level of 23m. cu. metres.

INDUSTRY
Ontario is Canada's most industrialized province, with GDP in 2000 at $429,530m. CDN, or 41·8% of the Canadian total. Manufacturing accounts for 20·1% of Ontario's GDP.

Leading manufacturing industries include: motor vehicles and parts; office and industrial electrical equipment; food processing; chemicals; and steel.

In 1998 Ontario was responsible for about 54% ($171,870m. CDN) of Canada's merchandise exports; motor vehicles and parts accounted for about 45%.

Labour. In 2000 the labour force was 6,288,000, of whom 5,872,000 were employed. The major employers were: manufacturing, 1,098·7; trade, 874·3 (wholesale, 209·1; retail, 665·3); health care and social assistance, 544·4; professional, scientific and technical services, 423·5; finance and insurance, 385·3. The unemployment rate in 2000 was 5·7%. In 1999 total labour income was $185,099m. CDN.

INTERNATIONAL TRADE

Imports and Exports. Ontario's exports rose by 11·2% in 1998 following a rise of 10·6% in 1997. Imports rose by 10·3% in 1998 following a rise of 17·8% in 1997. In 2000 exports totalled $314,752m. and imports totalled $267,352m.

COMMUNICATIONS

Roads. Almost 40% of the population of North America is within one day's drive of Ontario. There were, in 1998, 159,456 km of roads (municipal, 143,000; provincial MTO, 16,456). Motor licences (on the road) numbered (1999) 8,961,741, of which 5,521,803 were passenger cars, 1,189,414 commercial vehicles, 27,938 buses, 1,616,152 trailers, 103,469 motorcycles and 361,292 snow vehicles.

Rail. In 1999 there were 14 provincial short lines plus the provincially-owned Ontario Northland Railway and 12 federal railways. The Canadian National and Canadian Pacific Railways operate in Ontario. Total track miles, approximately 12,500 km. There is a metro and tramway network in Toronto.

Civil Aviation. Toronto's Lester B. Pearson International Airport is Canada's busiest, serving approximately 29m. passengers annually.

Shipping. The Great Lakes/St. Lawrence Seaway, a 3,747 km system of locks, canal and natural water connecting Ontario to the Atlantic Ocean, has 95,000 sq. miles of navigable waters and serves the water-borne cargo needs of 4 Canadian provinces and 17 American States.

Telecommunications. The telephone service in 1998 was provided by 30 independent systems and Bell Canada.

SOCIAL INSTITUTIONS
Justice. In 2000 there were 6,421 criminal code offences per 100,000 population, compared to a national average of 7,655 per 100,000 population.

Education. There is a provincial system of publicly financed elementary and secondary schools as well as private schools. In 1997–98 publicly financed elementary and secondary schools had a total enrolment of 2,103,586 pupils. In 2001–02, of the $64,270m. CDN total expenditure, 18·5% was on education.

There are 18 universities (Brock, Carleton, Dominicain, Guelph, Lakehead, Laurentian, McMaster, Nipissing, Ottawa, Queen's, Ryerson, Toronto, Trent, Waterloo, Western Ontario, Wilfred Laurier, Windsor and York) and 1 institute of equivalent status (Ontario College of Art and Design) with full-time enrolment for 1998–99 of 229,241. All receive operating grants from the Ontario government. There are also 25 publicly financed Colleges of Applied Arts and Technology (CAAT), with a full-time enrolment of 136,170 in 1998–99.

Operating expense (including capital expense) by the Ontario government on education for 1997–98 was $9,470m. CDN.

Health. Ontario Health Insurance Plan healthcare services are available to eligible Ontario residents at no cost. The Ontario Health Insurance Plan (OHIP) is funded, in part, by an Employer Health Tax.

FURTHER READING
Statistical Information: Annual publications of the Ontario Ministry of Finance include:
Ontario Statistics; Ontario Budget; Public Accounts; Financial Report.

PRINCE EDWARD ISLAND

KEY HISTORICAL EVENTS
The first recorded European visit was by Jacques Cartier in 1534, who named it Isle St-Jean. In 1719 it was settled by the French, but was taken from them by the English in 1758, annexed to Nova Scotia in 1763, and constituted a separate colony in 1769. Named Prince Edward Island in honour of Prince Edward, Duke of Kent, in 1799, it joined the Canadian Confederation on 1 July 1873.

TERRITORY AND POPULATION
The province lies in the Gulf of St Lawrence, and is separated from the mainland of New Brunswick and Nova Scotia by Northumberland Strait. The area of the island is 2,185 sq. miles (5,660 sq. km). The population at the 2001 census was 135,294. Population of the principal cities (2001): Charlottetown (capital), 32,245; Summerside, 14,654.

SOCIAL STATISTICS
Births in 1999–2000 numbered 1,473 (a rate of 10·7 per 1,000 population), and deaths 1,255 (rate of 9·1 per 1,000 population). There were 866 marriages and 279 divorces in 1998.

CLIMATE
The cool temperate climate is affected in winter by the freezing of the St. Lawrence, which reduces winter temperatures. Charlottetown, Jan. –3°C to –11°C, July 14°C to 23°C. Annual rainfall 853·5 mm.

CONSTITUTION AND GOVERNMENT
The provincial government is administered by a Lieut.-Governor-in-Council (Cabinet) and a Legislative Assembly of 27 members who are elected for up to five years.

RECENT ELECTIONS
At elections on 17 April 2000 the Progressive Conservatives won 26 of the available 27 seats and the Liberals took the other seat.

CURRENT ADMINISTRATION
Lieut.-Governor: J. Léonce Bernard, OPEI (sworn in 28 May 2001).
The Executive Council was composed as follows in Feb. 2003:
Premier, President of the Executive Council and Minister Responsible for Intergovernmental Affairs: Patrick G. Binns.

Provincial Treasurer: Patricia Mella. *Minister for Development and Technology:* Michael Currie. *Agriculture and Forestry:* P. Mitchell Murphy. *Education and Environment:* Chester Gillan. *Health and Social Services:* Jamie Ballem. *Fisheries, Aquaculture:* Greg Deighan. *Attorney General and Tourism:* Jeff Lantz. *Transportation and Public Works:* Gail Shea. *Community and Cultural Affairs:* Elmer MacFadyen.

Office of the Premier: http://www.gov.pe.ca/premier/

ECONOMY

Banking and Finance. Revenue and expenditure (in $1,000 CDN) for five financial years ending 31 March:

	1993–94	1994–95	1995–96	1996–97	1997–98
Revenue	738,855	812,461	802,579	801,143	804,387
Expenditure	810,199	821,422	797,937	818,747	821,156

Per capita personal income was $18,713 CDN in 1999.

ENERGY AND NATURAL RESOURCES

Electricity. Prince Edward Island's electricity consumption in 1998 reached a provincial record of 948,890 MWh, an increase of 2·7% over the preceding year. All but 1% was accessed from other provinces, via an underwater cable which spans the Northumberland Strait.

Oil and Gas. In 1999 Prince Edward Island had more than 400,000 ha under permit for oil and natural gas exploration.

Agriculture. Total area of farmland occupies approximately half of the total land area of 566,177 ha. Farm cash receipts in 1996 were $294m. CDN, with cash receipts from potatoes accounting for about 50% of the total. Cash receipts from dairy products, cattle and hogs followed in importance. For particulars of livestock, *see* CANADA: Agriculture.

Forestry. Total forested area is 280,000 ha. Of this 87% is owned by 12,000 woodlot owners. Most of the harvest takes place on private woodlots. The forest cover is 23% softwood, 29% hardwood and 48% mixed wood. In 1998 harvesting and processing had a delivered value of around $29m. CDN plus $7·5m. CDN in value added processing by the sawmill industry. Secondary processing contributed another $10m. CDN or so in 1998.

Fisheries. The total catch of 130m. lb in 1998 had a landed value of $122m. CDN. Lobsters accounted for $81m. CDN, around two-thirds of the total value; other shellfish, $30m. CDN; pelagic and estuarial, $9·2m. CDN; groundfish, $0·8m. CDN; seaplants, $1·1m. CDN.

INDUSTRY

Value of manufacturing shipments for all industries in 1998 was $885·6m. CDN. In 1997 provincial GDP in constant prices for manufacturing was $273·5m. CDN; construction, $132·0m. CDN. In 1996 the total value of retail trade was $1,003·0m. CDN.

Labour. The average weekly wage (industrial aggregate) fell from $491·04 CDN in 1997 to $475·13 CDN in 1998. The labour force averaged 71,000 in 1997, while employment averaged 60,100 in 1995.

COMMUNICATIONS

Roads. In 1999 there were 3,500 km of paved highway and 1,900 km of unpaved road as well as 1,200 bridge structures. The Confederation Bridge, a 12·9 km two-lane bridge that joins Borden-Carleton with Cape Jourimain in New Brunswick, was opened in June 1997. A bus service operates twice daily to the mainland.

Civil Aviation. In 1998 Air Canada provided daily services between Charlottetown and Boston, Fredericton, Halifax and Toronto. Canadian Airlines International operated daily services to Boston and Halifax, and there were also services to Moncton, Montreal and St John.

Shipping. Modern car ferries link the Island to New Brunswick and Nova Scotia. Service is provided year-round to New Brunswick on schedules which vary from 14 to 20 return crossings daily, with ice-breaking ferries maintaining the service during the winter months. Ferry service is operated to Nova Scotia from late April to mid-Dec. on schedules ranging from nine to 19 return crossings daily. A third ferry service, to the Magdalen Islands (Quebec), operates from 1 April to 31 Jan. There is also a substantial water movement of certain commodities, primarily through the ports of Summerside and Charlottetown, with additional capacity provided at the Souris and Georgetown ports.

Telecommunications. In 1999 there were 88,577 telephone lines in service.

SOCIAL INSTITUTIONS

Justice. In 1998, 8,561 Criminal Code offences were reported, including no homicides.

Education. Under the regional school boards there were in 1998 a total of 65 public schools, 1,427 teaching positions and 24,365 students. There is one undergraduate university (2,401 full-time and 7,477 part-time students), a veterinary college (197 students), and a Master of Science programme (25 students), all in Charlottetown. Holland College provides training for employment in business, applied arts and technology, with approximately 2,300 full-time students in post-secondary and vocational career programmes. The college offers extensive academic and career preparation programmes for adults.

Estimated government expenditure on education, 2000–01, $183·4m. CDN.

CULTURE

Tourism. The value of the tourist industry was estimated at $245·9m. CDN in 1997, with 371,500 tourist parties.

FURTHER READING
Baldwin, D. O., *Abegweit: Land of the Red Soil.* Charlottetown, 1985

QUEBEC—QUÉBEC

KEY HISTORICAL EVENTS
Quebec was known as New France from 1534 to 1763; as the province of Quebec from 1763 to 1790; as Lower Canada from 1791 to 1846; as Canada East from 1846 to 1867, and when, by the union of the four original provinces, the Confederation of the Dominion of Canada was formed, it again became known as the province of Quebec (Québec).

The Quebec Act, passed by the British Parliament in 1774, guaranteed to the people of the newly conquered French territory in North America security in their religion and language, their customs and tenures, under their own civil laws.

In a referendum on 20 May 1980, 59·5% voted against 'separatism'. At a further referendum on 30 Oct. 1995, 50·6% of votes cast were against Quebec becoming 'sovereign in a new economic and political partnership' with Canada. The electorate was 5m.; turn-out was 93%.

On 20 Aug. 1998 Canada's supreme court ruled that Quebec was prohibited by both the constitution and international law from seceding unilaterally from the rest of the country, but that a clear majority in a referendum would impose a duty on the Canadian government to negotiate. Both sides claimed victory.

TERRITORY AND POPULATION
The area of Quebec (as amended by the Labrador Boundary Award) is 1,542,056 sq. km (595,388 sq. miles), of which 1,365,128 sq. km is land area (including the Territory of Ungava, annexed in 1912 under the Quebec Boundaries Extension Act). The population at the 2001 census was 7,237,479.

Principal cities (2001 census populations): Montreal, 1,039,534; Laval, 343,005; Quebec (capital), 169,076; Longueuil, 128,016; Gatineau 103,207; Montreal North,

82,408 (1999 estimate); Saint-Laurent, 77,391; Sherbrooke, 75,916; Saint-Hubert, 75,912; LaSalle, 73,983; Beauport, 72,813; Sainte-Foy, 72,547; Charlesbourg, 70,310; Saint-Léonard 69,604; Hull, 66,246; Brossard, 65,026; Verdun, 60,564; Chicoutimi, 60,008; Jonquière, 54,842

SOCIAL STATISTICS
Births in 1999–2000 numbered 73,536 (a rate of 10·0 per 1,000 population), and deaths 52,527 (rate of 7·1 per 1,000 population). There were 23,746 marriages and 16,916 divorces in 1998.

CLIMATE
Cool temperate in the south, but conditions are more extreme towards the north. Winters are severe and snowfall considerable, but summer temperatures are quite warm. Quebec, Jan. –12·5°C, July 19·1°C. Annual rainfall 1,123 mm. Montreal, Jan. –10·7°C, July 20·2°C. Annual rainfall 936 mm.

CONSTITUTION AND GOVERNMENT
There is a Legislative Assembly consisting of 125 members, elected in 125 electoral districts for four years.

RECENT ELECTIONS
At the elections of 30 Nov. 1998 the Parti Québécois won 75 seats with 42·7% of votes cast, the Liberal Party 48 with 43·7%.

CURRENT ADMINISTRATION
Lieut.-Governor: Lise Thibault (took office on 30 Jan. 1997).
Members of the Cabinet in March 2003:
Premier and President of Executive Council: Bernard Landry (b. 1937).
Deputy Premier and Minister of State for the Economy and Finance: Pauline Marois. *Minister of State for International Relations:* Louise Beaudoin. *Municipal Affairs and Greater Montréal, the Environment and Water, and Government House Leader:* André Boisclair. *Administration and the Public Service:* Joseph Facal. *Social Solidarity and Child and Family Welfare:* Linda Goupil. *Health and Social Services:* François Legault. *Culture and Communications:* Diane Lemieux. *Human Resources and Labour:* Jean Rochon. *Education and Employment:* Sylvain Simard. *Population, Regions and Nature Affairs:* Rémy Trudel.
In addition to the above, the Cabinet also includes 'Ministers of' and 'Ministers responsible for' (both of secondary rank), and 'Ministers for' (full ministers who assist senior ministers).
Minister of Justice and Attorney General: Normand Jutras.

Government of Quebec Website: http://www.gouv.qc.ca/

ECONOMY
GDP per person in 1999 was $27,767 CDN.

Budget. Ordinary revenue and expenditure (in $1,000 CDN) for fiscal years ending 31 March:

	1995–96	1996–97	1997–98	1998–99	1999–2000
Revenue	38,704,000	37,820,000	41,689,000	46,572,000	47,279,000
Expenditure	42,661,000	41,032,000	43,846,000	46,446,000	47,249,000

The total net debt at 31 March 2000 was $88,886m. CDN.

ENERGY AND NATURAL RESOURCES
Electricity. Water power is one of the most important natural resources of Quebec. Its turbine installation represents about 40% of the aggregate of Canada. At the end of 1997 the installed generating capacity was 34,972 MW. Production, 1997, was 166,255 MWh.

Water. There are 4,500 rivers and 500,000 lakes in Quebec, which possesses 3% of the world's freshwater resources.

Minerals. For 1999 the value of mineral production (metal only) was $2,224m. CDN. Chief minerals: iron ore (confidential); copper, $314·0m. CDN; gold, $495·5m. CDN; zinc, $294·7m. CDN.

Non-metallic minerals produced include: asbestos ($160·8m. CDN), titanium-dioxide (confidential), industrial lime, dolomite and brucite, quartz and pyrite. Among the building materials produced were: sand and gravel, $834·0m. CDN; cement, $246·6m. CDN; stone, $218·4m. CDN; lime (confidential).

Agriculture. In 1995 the agricultural area was 3,445,000 ha. The yield of the principal crops was (1998 in 1,000 tonnes):

Crops	Yield	Crops	Yield
Tame hay	4,300	Barley	425
Corn for grain	2,690	Soya	390
Fodder corn	1,520	Oats for grain	197
Potatoes	475	Mixed grains	111

About 38,000 farms were operating in 1995. Cash receipts, 1998, $4,882m. CDN (dairy products, 30·8%; livestock, 21·9%; crops, 24·6%; poultry and eggs, 10·7%). In 1996, 33,906 census farms reported total gross farm receipts of $2,500 CDN or more.

Forestry. Forests cover an area of 757,900 sq. km. 518,164 sq. km are classified as productive forests, of which 448,929 sq. km are provincial forest land and 66,198 sq. km are privately owned. Quebec leads the Canadian provinces in pulp and paper production, having nearly half of the Canadian estimated total.

In 1999 production of lumber was: softwood and hardwood, 17,897,000 cu. metres; pulp and paper, 10,092,000 tonnes.

Fisheries. The principal fish are cod, herring, red fish, lobster and salmon. Total catch of sea fish, 1999, 55,257 tonnes, valued at $134m. CDN.

INDUSTRY

In 1999 there were 10,176 industrial establishments in the province; employees, 500,906; salaries and wages, $17,769m. CDN; cost of materials, $63,702m. CDN; value of shipments, $113,079m. CDN. Among the leading industries are petroleum refining, pulp and paper mills, smelting and refining, dairy products, slaughtering and meat processing, motor vehicle manufacturing, women's clothing, sawmills and planing mills, iron and steel mills, commercial printing.

Labour. In 1999 there were 3,357,400 persons (1,507,500 female) in employment.

INTERNATIONAL TRADE

Imports and Exports. In 1999 the value of Canadian exports through Quebec custom ports was $45,404m. CDN; value of imports, $43,656m. CDN.

COMMUNICATIONS

Roads. In 1998 there were 29,140 km of roads and 4,496,376 registered motor vehicles.

Rail. There were (1998) 6,621 km of railway. There is a metro system in Montreal (64 km).

Civil Aviation. There are two international airports, Dorval (Montreal) and Mirabel (Laurentides).

Telecommunications. In 1997, 3,028,318 households (98·9%) had telephones.

SOCIAL INSTITUTIONS

Justice. In 1998, 467,530 Criminal Code offences were reported. In 1997 there were 110 homicides.

Education. Education is compulsory for children aged 6–16. Pre-school education and elementary and secondary training are free in some 2,527 public schools. In July 1998 the number of school boards was reduced to 72. These were organized along linguistic lines, 60 French, nine English and three special school boards that served native students in the Cote-Nord and Nord-du-Quebec regions. Just under 10% of the student population attends private schools: in 1999–2000, 272 establishments were authorized to provide pre-school, elementary and secondary education. After six years of elementary and five years of secondary school education, students enter Cegeps, a post-secondary educational institution. In 1999–2000 college, pre-university and technical training for young and adult students was provided by 48 Cegeps, 11 government schools and 77 private establishments.

In 1999–2000 in pre-kindergartens there were 15,174 pupils; in kindergartens, 89,223; in primary schools, 573,102; in secondary schools, 674,964; in colleges (post-secondary, non-university), 219,144; and in classes for children with special needs, 135,838. In 1998–99 the school boards had a total of 92,746 teachers (57,456 full-time and 32,290 part-time).

Expenditure of the Departments of Education for 1999–2000, $9,521·1m. CDN net. This included $1,511·2m. CDN for universities, $5,450·1m. CDN for public primary and secondary schools, $272·1m. CDN for private primary and secondary schools and $1,255·6m. CDN for colleges.

In 1999–2000 the province had nine universities: six French-language universities: Laval (Quebec, founded 1852), Montreal University (opened 1876 as a branch of Laval, independent 1920), Sherbrooke University (founded 1954), University of Quebec (founded 1968) and two others; and three English-language universities, McGill (Montreal, founded 1821), Bishop (Lennoxville, founded 1845) and the Concordia University (Montreal, granted a charter 1975). In 1999 there were 137,183 full-time university students and 94,691 part-time.

Health. Quebec's socio-health network consisted of 478 public and private establishments in 2001, of which 348 were public.

CULTURE

Broadcasting. In 1998 there were 50 television and 171 radio stations.

Press. In 2000 there were 11 French- and three English-language daily newspapers.

FURTHER READING
Dickinson, J. A. and Young, B., *A Short History of Quebec.* 2nd ed. Harlow, 1994
Gagnon, A.- G., *Québec.* [Bibliography] ABC-Clio, Oxford and Santa Barbara (CA), 1998
Young, R. A., *The Secession of Quebec and the Future of Canada.* McGill-Queen's Univ. Press, 1995

Statistical office: Bureau de la Statistique du Québec, 117 rue Saint-André, Québec G1K 3Y3

SASKATCHEWAN

KEY HISTORICAL EVENTS
Saskatchewan derives its name from its major river system, which the Cree Indians called 'Kis-is-ska-tche-wan', meaning 'swift flowing'. It officially became a province when it joined the Confederation on 1 Sept. 1905.

In 1670 King Charles II granted to Prince Rupert and his friends a charter covering exclusive trading rights in 'all the land drained by streams finding their outlet in the Hudson Bay'. This included what is now Saskatchewan. The trading company was first known as The Governor and Company of Adventurers of England; later as the Hudson's Bay Company. In 1869 the Northwest Territories was formed, and this included Saskatchewan. In 1882 the District of Saskatchewan was formed. By 1885 the North-West Mounted Police had been inaugurated, with headquarters in Regina (now the capital), and the Canadian Pacific Railway's transcontinental line had been completed, bringing a stream of immigrants to southern Saskatchewan. The Hudson's Bay Company surrendered its claim to territory in return for cash and land around the existing trading posts.

TERRITORY AND POPULATION
Saskatchewan is bounded in the west by Alberta, in the east by Manitoba, in the north by the Northwest Territories and in the south by the USA. The area of the province is 251,365 sq. miles (651,036 sq. km), of which 228,444 sq. miles is land area and 22,921 sq. miles is water. The population at the 2001 census was 978,933; it was estimated at 1,011,808 in July 2002. Population of cities, 2001 census: Regina

(capital), 178,225; Saskatoon, 196,811; Prince Albert, 34,291; Moose Jaw, 32,131; Yorkton, 15,105; Swift Current, 14,821; North Battleford, 13,692; Estevan, 10,242; Weyburn, 9,534; Lloydminster, 7,840; Melfort, 5,559; Humboldt, 5,161.

SOCIAL STATISTICS
Births in 1999–2000 numbered 12,632 (a rate of 12·3 per 1,000 population), and deaths 9,320 (rate of 9·1 per 1,000 population). There were 5,730 marriages and 2,246 divorces in 1998.

CLIMATE
A cold continental climate, with severe winters and warm summers. Rainfall amounts are greatest from May to Aug. Regina, Jan. 0°F (−17·8°C), July 65°F (18·3°C). Annual rainfall 15" (373 mm).

CONSTITUTION AND GOVERNMENT
The provincial government is vested in a Lieut.-Governor, an Executive Council and a Legislative Assembly, elected for five years. Women were given the franchise in 1916 and are also eligible for election to the legislature.

RECENT ELECTIONS
In elections on 16 Sept. 1999 the New Democrat Party won 29 of 58 seats (39·6% of the vote); Saskatchewan Party, 25 (38·7%); the Liberal Party, 3 (20·2%); and one seat was subject to recount. State of parties in Feb. 2003: New Democratic Party, 28; Saskatchewan Party, 24; ind., 3; vacant, 3.

CURRENT ADMINISTRATION
Lieut.-Governor: Dr Lynda M. Haverstock, SOM (took office 21 Feb. 2000).

The New Democratic Party ministry in Feb. 2003 comprised as follows:

Premier, President of the Executive Council: Lorne Calvert.

Deputy Premier, Minister of Agriculture and Food and Rural Revitalization: Clay Serby. *Labour and Minister Responsible for the Status of Women:* Debra Higgins. *Intergovernmental Affairs, Aboriginal Affairs and Government House Leader:* Eldon Lautermilch. *Learning:* Judy Junor. *Social Services and Minister Responsible for Disability Issues and Gaming, and Deputy Government House Leader:* Glenn Hagel. *Corrections and Public Safety, and Minister Responsible for Information Technology:* Andrew Thompson. *Northern Affairs and Environment:* Buckley Belanger. *Culture, Youth and Recreation, and Provincial Secretary:* Joanne Crofford. *Government Relations and Minister Responsible for Saskatchewan Property Management Corporation:* Ron Osika. *Finance:* Jim Melenchuk. *Industry and Resources, Justice and Attorney General:* Eric Cline, QC. *Health and Minister Responsible for Seniors:* John Nilson. *Highways and Transportation:* Mark Wartman. *Minister Responsible for Crown Investments Corporation:* Maynard Sonntag.

Office of the Premier: http://www.gov.sk.ca/govinfo/premier/

ECONOMY
GDP per capita in 2001 was $32,653 CDN.

Budget. Budget and net assets (years ending 31 March) in $1,000 CDN:

	1998–99	1999–200	2000–01	2001–02
Budgetary revenue	5,339,100	6,629,490	6,382,400	6,041,700
Budgetary expenditure	5,233,413	6,785,466	5,967,986	6,302,624

ENERGY AND NATURAL RESOURCES
Agriculture used to dominate the history and economics of Saskatchewan, but the 'prairie province' is now a rapidly developing mining and manufacturing area. It is a major supplier of oil, has the world's largest deposits of potash and the net value of its non-agricultural production accounted for (2001 estimate) 84·6% of the provincial economy.

Electricity. The Saskatchewan Power Corporation generated 16,899m. kWh in 2001.

Minerals. In 2001 mineral sales were valued at $7,507m. CDN, including (in $1m. CDN): petroleum, 3,706·4; potash, 1,601·0; natural gas, 1,285·2; coal and others,

871·5; sodium sulphate, 22·0; salt, 21·1. Other major minerals included copper, zinc, potassium sulphate, ammonium sulphate, bentonite, coal, uranium, gold and base metals.

Agriculture. Saskatchewan normally produces about two-thirds of Canada's wheat. Wheat production in 2001 (in 1,000 tonnes) was 10,188 (13,533 in 2000) from 16·1m. acres; oats, 1,033 from 2·1m. acres; barley, 3,697 from 4·8m. acres; canola, 2,109 from 4·8m. acres; flax, 483 from 1·2m. acres. Livestock (1 July 2002): cattle and calves, 2·9m.; swine, 1·2m.; sheep and lambs, 155,000. Poultry in 2001: chickens, 20·2m.; turkeys, 793,000. Cash income from the sale of farm products in 2001 was $6,550m. CDN. At the June 2001 census there were 50,598 farms in the province, each being a holding of one acre or more with sales of $250 CDN or more during the previous year.

The South Saskatchewan River irrigation project, the main feature of which is the Gardiner Dam, was completed in 1967. It will ultimately provide for an area of 0·2m. to 0·5m. acres of irrigated cultivation in Central Saskatchewan. As of 2001, 240,178 acres were intensively irrigated. Total irrigated land in the province, 334,386 acres.

Forestry. Half of Saskatchewan's area is forested, but only 115,000 sq. km are of commercial value at present. Forest products valued at $356m. CDN were produced in 2001–02.

Fur Production. In 2000–01 wild fur production was estimated at $1,910,908 CDN. Ranch-raised fur production amounted to $31,226 CDN in 2000 and $11,426 CDN in 2001.

Fisheries. The lakeside value of the 2001–02 commercial fish catch of 3·3m. kg was $5·3m. CDN.

INDUSTRY
In 1999 there were 698 manufacturing establishments, employing 19,307 persons. In 2001 manufacturing contributed $2,003·4m. CDN and construction $1,297·1m. CDN to total GDP at basic prices of $23,886·2m. CDN.

Labour. In 2002 the labour force was 511,100 (232,000 females), of whom 482,000 (220,500) were employed.

COMMUNICATIONS
Roads. In 2001 there were 26,219 km of provincial highways and 196,869 km of municipal roads (including prairie trails). Motor vehicles registered totalled 713,000 (2001). Bus services are provided by two major lines.

Rail. In 2001 there were approximately 9,908 km of railway track.

Civil Aviation. There were two major airports and 147 airports and landing strips in 2000.

Telecommunications. There were 626,421 telephone network access services to the Saskatchewan Telecommunications system in 2001.

Postal Services. In 2001 there were 477 post offices (excluding sub-post offices).

SOCIAL INSTITUTIONS
Justice. In 2001, 136,699 Criminal Code offences were reported, including 27 homicides.

Education. The Saskatchewan education system in 2001–02 consisted of 99 school divisions and 5 comprehensive school boards, of which 1 is Protestant and 19 are Roman Catholic Separate School Divisions, serving 118,985 elementary pupils, 59,278 high-school students and 2,755 students enrolled in special classes. In addition, the Saskatchewan Institute of Applied Science and Technology (SIAST) had 11,307 full-time and 29,096 part-time and extension course registration students in 2001–02. There are also eight regional colleges with an enrolment of approximately 30,126 students in 2001–02.

The University of Saskatchewan was established at Saskatoon in 1907. In 2001–02 it had 15,368 full-time students, 4,101 part-time students and 961 full-time academic staff. The University of Regina, established in 1974, had 8,975 full-time and 3,205 part-time students and 388 full-time academic staff in 2001–02.

CULTURE

Broadcasting. In 2001 there were 50 TV and re-broadcasting stations, and 30 AM and FM radio stations.

Tourism. An estimated 1·5m. out-of-province tourists spent $449m. CDN in 2001.

FURTHER READING

Archer, J. H., *Saskatchewan: A History*. Saskatoon, 1980
Arora, V., *The Saskatchewan Bibliography*. Regina, 1980

Statistical office: Bureau of Statistics, 5th Floor, 2350 Albert St., Regina, SK, S4P 4A6.

THE NORTHWEST TERRITORIES

KEY HISTORICAL EVENTS

The Territory was developed by the Hudson's Bay Company and the North West Company (of Montreal) from the 17th century. The Canadian government bought out the Hudson's Bay Company in 1869 and the Territory was annexed to Canada in 1870. The Arctic Islands lying north of the Canadian mainland were annexed to Canada in 1880.

A plebiscite held in March 1992 approved the division of the Northwest Territories into two separate territories. (For the new territory of Nunavut *see* CONSTITUTION AND GOVERNMENT, *below*, and NUNAVUT on page 414).

TERRITORY AND POPULATION

The total area of the Territories was 3,426,320 sq. km, but since the formation of Nunavut is now 1,346,106 km. Of its five former administrative regions—Fort Smith, Inuvik, Kitikmeot, Keewatin and Baffin—only Fort Smith and Inuvik remain in the Northwest Territories. The population at the 1991 census was 57,649, 37% of whom were Inuit (Eskimo), 16% Dene (Indian) and 7% Metis. The formation of Nunavut in 1999 out of the Northwest Territories resulted in a large decline in the population. The population at the 2001 census was 37,360. The capital is Yellowknife, population (2001); 16,541. Other main centres (with population in 2001): Hay River (3,510), Inuvik (2,894), Fort Smith (2,185), Rae-Edzo (1,552). Iqaluit and Rankin Inlet, formerly in the Northwest Territories, are now in Nunavut.

SOCIAL STATISTICS

Births in 1999–2000 numbered 758 (a rate of 18·2 per 1,000 population), and deaths 160 (rate of 3·8 per 1,000 population). There were 142 marriages and 93 divorces in 1998.

CLIMATE

Conditions range from cold continental to polar, with long hard winters and short cool summers. Precipitation is low. Yellowknife, Jan. mean high –24·7°C, low –33°C; July mean high 20·7°C, low 11·8°C. Annual rainfall 26·7 cm.

CONSTITUTION AND GOVERNMENT

The Northwest Territories comprises all that portion of Canada lying north of the 60th parallel of N. lat. except those portions within Nunavut, the Yukon Territory and the provinces of Quebec and Newfoundland.

The Northwest Territories is governed by a Premier, with a cabinet (the Executive Council) of eight members including the Speaker, and a Legislative Assembly, who choose the premier and ministers by consensus. There are no political parties. The Assembly is composed of 19 members elected for a four-year term of office. A Commissioner of the Northwest Territories acts as a Lieut.-Governor and is the federal government's senior representative in the Territorial government. The seat of government was transferred from Ottawa to Yellowknife when it was named

Territorial Capital on 18 Jan. 1967. On 10 Nov. 1997 the governments of Canada and the Northwest Territories signed an agreement so that the territorial government could assume full responsibility to manage its elections.

Legislative powers are exercised by the Executive Council on such matters as taxation within the Territories in order to raise revenue, maintenance of justice, licences, solemnization of marriages, education, public health, property, civil rights and generally all matters of a local nature.

The Territorial government has assumed most of the responsibility for the administration of the Northwest Territories but political control of Crown lands and non-renewable resources still rests with the Federal government. On 6 Sept. 1988 the Federal and Territorial governments signed an agreement for the transfer of management responsibilities for oil and gas resources, located on- and off-shore, in the Northwest Territories to the Territorial government. In a Territory-wide plebiscite in April 1982, a majority of residents voted in favour of dividing the Northwest Territories into two jurisdictions, east and west. In a plebiscite held in March 1992 residents voted in favour of an east-west boundary line. Constitutions for an eastern and western government have been under discussion since 1992. A referendum was held in Nov. 1992 among the Inuit on the formation of a third territory, **Nunavut** ('Our Land'), in the eastern Arctic, and comprising the administrative regions of Kitikmeot, Keewatin and Baffin. The electorate was 9,648; turn-out was 80%. 69% of votes cast were in favour. An agreement was signed on 25 May 1993 by the federal Prime Minister beginning the process of establishing this territory. Nunavut became Canada's 3rd territory on 1 April 1999.

RECENT ELECTIONS

On 6 Dec. 1999, 19 non-partisan members (MLAs) were returned to the Legislative Assembly. Elections are due to take place in Nov. 2003.

CURRENT ADMINISTRATION

Commissioner: Glenna F. Hansen, b. 1956 (took office 31 March 2000).

Members of the Executive Council of Ministers in Feb. 2003:

Premier, Chairman of the Executive Council, Minister Responsible for Intergovernmental Affairs and for the Status of Women: Stephen Kakfwi.

Deputy Premier and Minister of Aboriginal Affairs, Intergovernmental Forum, Resources, Wildlife and Economic Development: Jim Antoine. *Finance, Transportation, Energy and Hydro Secretariats, and Government House Leader:* Joseph Handley. *Education, Culture and Employment:* Jake Ootes. *Public Works and Services, and Municipal and Community Affairs:* Vince Steen. *Justice, Youth, NWT Housing Corporation, and NWT Public Utilities Board:* Roger Allen. *Health and Social Services, Responsible for Persons with Disabilities and Senior Citizens:* J. Michael Miltenberger.

Speaker: Tony Whitford.

Government of the Northwest Territories Website: http://www.gov.nt.ca/

ECONOMY

GDP per person in 1997 was $43,000 CDN, the highest of any Canadian province or territory.

Budget. The 2000–01 budget anticipates operating expenditures of $763·6m. CDN and total revenues of $751·3m. CDN.

ENERGY AND NATURAL RESOURCES

Oil and Gas. Oil production was 1,535,000 cu. metres in 2000, down from 1,640,000 cu. metres in 1999. Natural gas production in 2000 was 541m. cu. metres, up from 110m. cu. metres in 1999.

Minerals. Mineral production in 2000: gold, 4,372 kg (valued at $58,148,000 CDN); silver, 1 tonne ($248,000 CDN); diamonds, 2,558 carats ($638,161,000 CDN); sand and gravel, 539,000 tonnes ($4,805,000 CDN); stone, 184,000 tonnes ($2,848,000 CDN). Total mineral production in 2000 was valued at $1·14bn. CDN.

Forestry. Forest land area in the Northwest Territories consists of 61·4m. ha, about 18% of the total land area. The principal trees are white and black spruce, jack-pine, tamarack, balsam poplar, aspen and birch. In 1996, 202,000 cu. metres of timber were produced.

Trapping and Game. Wildlife harvesting is the largest economic activity undertaken by aboriginal residents in the Northwest Territories. The value of the subsistence food harvest is estimated at $28m. CDN annually in terms of imports replaced. Fur-trapping (the most valuable pelts being white fox, wolverine, beaver, mink, lynx, and red fox) was once a major industry, but has been hit by anti-fur campaigns. In 1999–2000, 37,124 pelts worth $842,049 CDN were sold.

Fisheries. Fish marketed through the Freshwater Fish Marketing Corporation in 1996–97 totalled 1,742,700 kg at a value of $1,725,000 CDN, principally whitefish, northern pike and trout.

INDUSTRY

Co-operatives. There are 37 active co-operatives, including two housing co-operatives and two central organizations to service local co-operatives, in the Northwest Territories. They are active in handicrafts, furs, fisheries, retail stores, hotels, cable TV, post offices, petroleum delivery and print shops. Total revenue in 2000 was about $97m. CDN.

COMMUNICATIONS

Roads. The Mackenzie Route connects Grimshaw, Alberta, with Hay River, Pine Point, Fort Smith, Fort Providence, Rae-Edzo and Yellowknife. The Mackenzie Highway extension to Fort Simpson and a road between Pine Point and Fort Resolution have both been opened.

Highway service to Inuvik in the Mackenzie Delta was opened in spring 1980, extending north from Dawson, Yukon as the Dempster Highway. The Liard Highway connecting the communities of the Liard River valley to British Columbia opened in 1984.

In 2000 there were 27,703 vehicle registrations, including 21,630 passenger cars and 1,881 trucks and 2,841 trailers.

Rail. There is one small railway system in the north which runs from Hay River, on the south shore of Great Slave Lake, 435 miles south to Grimshaw, Alberta, where it connects with the Canadian National Railways, but it is not in use.

Civil Aviation. In 2000 there were 132,775 take-offs and landings in the Northwest Territories.

Shipping. A direct inland-water transportation route for about 1,700 miles is provided by the Mackenzie River and its tributaries, the Athabasca and Slave rivers. Subsidiary routes on Lake Athabasca, Great Slave Lake and Great Bear Lake total more than 800 miles. Communities in the eastern Arctic are resupplied by ship each summer via the Atlantic and Arctic Oceans or Hudson Bay.

Telecommunications. Telephone service is provided to nearly all communities in the Northwest Territories. Those few communities without service have high frequency or very high frequency radios for emergency use.

Postal Services. There is a postal service in all communities.

SOCIAL INSTITUTIONS

Education. The Education System in the Northwest Territories is comprised of eight regional bodies (boards) that have responsibilities for the K–12 education programme. Three of these jurisdictions are located in Yellowknife; a public school authority, a catholic school authority and a Commission scolaire francophone that oversees a school operating in Yellowknife, and one in Hay River.

For the 2000–01 school year there were 49 public plus two (small) private schools operating in the NWT. Within this system there were 667 teachers, including Aboriginal Language Specialists, for 9,855 students. 98% of students have access to high school programmes in their home communities. There is a full range of courses available in the school system, including academic, French immersion, Aboriginal language, cultural programmes, technical and occupational programmes.

A range of post secondary programmes are available through the Northwest Territories' Aurora College. The majority of these programmes are offered at the three main campus locations: Inuvik, Yellowknife and Fort Smith.

Health. In 2000 there were nine separate regional boards. An independent review of the Northwest Territories' health and social services system in June 2001 recommended the reduction of the number of regional health boards from nine to four. Each board would take on a greater degree of power and accountability, three of which would act as regional service authorities. Expenditure on health totalled $159·4m. CDN in 1999–2000.

Welfare. Welfare services are provided by professional social workers. Facilities included (1993) for children: seven group homes and two residential treatment centres.

CULTURE

Broadcasting. In 2000 CBC operated radio stations at Yellowknife and Inuvik. There is an English language CBC-owned television station at Yellowknife. There are also two other television broadcasting stations based in Yellowknife.

FURTHER READING
Annual Report of the Government of the Northwest Territories
Government Activities in the North, 1983–84. Indian and Northern Affairs, Canada
NWT Data Book 90/91. Yellowknife, 1991

Zaslow, M., *The Opening of the Canadian North 1870–1914.* Toronto, 1971

NUNAVUT

KEY HISTORICAL EVENTS
Inuit communities started entering and moving around what is now the Canadian Arctic between 4500 BC and AD 1000 . By the 19th century these communities were under the jurisdiction of the Northwest Territories. In 1963 the Canadian government first introduced legislation to divide the territory, a proposal that failed at the order paper stage. In 1973 the Comprehensive Land Claims Policy was established which sought to define the rights and benefits of the Aboriginal population in a land claim settlement agreement. The Northwest Territories Legislative Assembly voted in favour of dividing the territory in 1980, and in a public referendum of 1982, 56% of votes cast were also for the division. In 1992 the proposed boundary was ratified in a public vote and the Inuit population approved their land claim settlement. A year later, the Nunavut Act (creating the territory) and the Nunavut Land Claim Agreement Act were passed by parliament. Iqaluit was selected as the capital in 1995.

On 15 Feb. 1999 Nunavut held elections for its Legislative Assembly and on 1 April 1999 the territory was officially designated and the government inaugurated.

TERRITORY AND POPULATION
The total area of the region is 2,093,190 sq. km or about 21% of Canada's total mass, making Nunavut Canada's largest territory. It contains seven of Canada's 12 largest islands and two thirds of the country's coastline. The territory is divided into three regions: Qikiqtaaluk (Baffin), Kivalliq (Keewatin) and Kitikmeot. The total population at the 1996 census was 24,720 (12,910 males, 11,810 females) or 97 persons per 10,000 sq. km; at the 2001 census the population was 26,745. 85% of the population are Inuit. The population is divided up into 28 communities of which the largest is in the capital Iqaluit, numbering 4,500.

The native Inuit language is Inuktitut.

SOCIAL STATISTICS
Births in 1999–2000 numbered 779 (a rate of 28·5 per 1,000 population), and deaths 141 (rate of 5·2 per 1,000 population). Nunavut's birth rate is the highest in Canada

and is more than twice the national average of 10·9 per 1,000 births. Life expectancy, 1996: males, 67 years; females, 72. 56% of the population are under 25 years of age.

CLIMATE
Conditions range from cold continental to polar, with long hard winters and short cool summers. In Iqaluit there can be as little as four hours sunshine per day in winter and up to 21 hours per day at the summer solstice. Iqaluit, Jan. mean high –22°C; July mean high, 15°C.

CONSTITUTION AND GOVERNMENT
Government is by a Legislative Assembly of 19 elected members, who then choose a leader and ministers by consensus. There are no political parties. The government is being established in evolutionary stages, a process which began in 1993 and is scheduled for completion in 2009. It is intended that government be highly decentralized, consisting of ten departments spread over 11 different communities.

Inuktitut will be the working language of government but government agencies will also offer services in English and French. Although the Inuits will be the dominant force in public government, non-Inuit citizens have the same voting rights.

RECENT ELECTIONS
The first Legislative Assembly elections were held on 15 Feb. 1999 and the government was inaugurated on 1 April. Turn-out was 99%.

CURRENT ADMINISTRATION
Commissioner: Peter T. Irniq (took office in 2000).

In Feb. 2003 the cabinet was as follows:

Premier and Minister of Executive and Intergovernmental Affairs and of Justice and Responsible for Aboriginal Affairs: Paul Okalik (b. 1964).

Deputy Premier, Minister of Finance and Government House Leader: Kelvin Ng. *Minister of Education and Human Resources:* Peter Kilabuk. *Health and Social Services and Energy:* Ed Picco. *Community Government and Transportation:* Manitok Thompson. *Sustainable Development, and Culture, Language, Elders and Youth:* Olayuk Akesuk. *Public Works and Services:* Peter Kattuk. *Minister without Portfolio:* Jack Anawak.

Government of Nunavut Website: http://www.gov.nu.ca

ECONOMY
While the cost of living in Nunavut is around 160 to 200% that of southern Canadians, the average household income is $31,471 CDN compared to $45,251 CDN for Canada as a whole. With unemployment running high, transport costs expensive and education limited, Nunavut has many challenges to face in its quest for self-sufficiency.

Overview. Nunavut is looking to capitalize on its wealth of natural resources and also develop its existing industries such as tourism, and arts and crafts.

Currency. The Canadian dollar is the standard currency.

Banking and Finance. Few banks have branches in the province. Iqaluit has two automated cash machines and stores are increasingly installing debit card facilities.

ENERGY AND NATURAL RESOURCES
Water. Nunavut's major rivers are on the mainland.

Minerals. There are two lead and zinc mines operating in the High Arctic region. There are also known deposits of copper, gold, silver and diamonds.

Hunting and Trapping. Most communities still rely on traditional foodstuffs such as caribou and seal. The Canadian government now provides meat inspections so that caribou and musk ox meat can be sold across the country.

Fisheries. Fishing is still very important in Inuit life. The principal catches are shrimp, scallop and arctic char.

INDUSTRY
The main industries are mining, tourism, fishing, hunting and trapping, arts and crafts production.

Labour. Unemployment was running at 20·7% in 1999.

COMMUNICATIONS
Roads. There is one 21-km government-maintained road between Arctic Bay and Nanisivik. There are a few paved roads in Iqaluit and Rankin Inlet, but most are unpaved. Some communities have local roads and tracks but Kivalliq has no direct land connections with southern Canada.

Civil Aviation. There are air connections between communities and a daily air connection between Iqaluit and Montreal/Ottawa.

Shipping. There is an annual summer sea-lift by ship and barge for transport of construction materials, dry goods, non-perishable food, trucks and cars, etc.

Telecommunications. There are telephone services in all communities except for Bathurst Inlet and Umingmaktok. Because of the wide distances between communities, there is a very high rate of Internet use in Nunavut. However, line speeds are slow and there is a problem with satellite bounce.

Postal Services. There is no door-to-door delivery service, so correspondence has to be retrieved from post offices.

SOCIAL INSTITUTIONS
Justice. A territorial court has been put in place. Policing is by the Royal Canadian Mounted Police (RCMP).

Education. Approximately one third of Nunavut's population aged over 15 have less than Grade 9 schooling. Training and development is seen as central to securing a firm economic foundation for the province. The Canadian government has pledged $40m. CDN for recruiting and training Inuit employees into Nunavut public service.

Courses in computer science, business management and public administration may be undertaken at Arctic College. In 1997–98 there were 39 schools with 7,770 students.

Health. There is one hospital in Iqaluit. 26 health centres provide nursing care for communities. For more specialized treatment, patients of Qikiqtaaluk may be flown to Montreal, patients in Kivalliq to Churchill or Winnipeg and patients in Kitikmeot to Yellowknife's Stanton Regional Hospital.

CULTURE
Broadcasting. The Canadian Broadcasting Corporation (CBC) North transmits television to Iqaluit and other communities. The Inuit Broadcasting Corporation (IBC) transmits in Inuktitut and Television Northern Canada (TVNC) is devoted to programming by and for northerners and native citizens. There are 5½ hours of Inuktitut television programming per week. Cable satellite television is also widely available.

CBC is the only local radio station accessible in all Nunavut communities.

Tourism. Auyuittuq National Park is one of the principal tourist attractions, along with the opportunity of seeing Inuit life first-hand. Under the terms of the land claim settlement, three more national parks are planned. It is also hoped that the publicity surrounding the new territory will encourage visitors.

FURTHER READING
The Nunavut Handbook, Raincoast Books, Vancouver, 1999

YUKON TERRITORY

KEY HISTORICAL EVENTS

The territory owes its fame to the discovery of gold in the Klondike at the end of the 19th century. Formerly part of the Northwest Territories, the Yukon was joined to the Dominion as a separate territory on 13 June 1898.

Yukon First Nations People lived a semi-nomadic subsistence lifestyle in the region long before it was established as a territory. The earliest evidence of human activity was found in caves containing stone tools and animal bones estimated to be 20,000 years old. The Athapaskan cultural linguistic tradition to which most Yukon First Nations belong is more than 1,000 years old. The territory's name comes from the native 'Yu-kun-ah' for the great river that drains most of this area.

The Yukon was created as a district of the North West Territories in 1895. The Klondike Gold Rush in the late 1890s saw the invasion of thousands of stampeders pouring into the gold fields of the Canadian northwest. Population at the peak of the rush reached 40,000. This event spurred the federal government to set up basic administrative structures in the Yukon. The territory was given the status of a separate geographical and political entity with an appointed legislative council in 1898.

In 1953 the capital was moved south from Dawson City to Whitehorse, where most of the economic activity was centred.

The federal government granted the Yukon responsible government in 1979.

TERRITORY AND POPULATION

The territory consists of one city, three towns, four villages, two hamlets, 13 unincorporated communities and 8 rural communities. It is situated in the northwestern region of Canada and comprises 482,443 sq. km of which 8,052 sq. km is fresh water.

The population at the 2001 census was 28,674.

Principal centres in 2001 were Whitehorse, the capital, 19,058; Dawson City, 1,251; Watson Lake, 912; Haines Junction, 531; Faro, 313.

The Yukon represents 4·8% of Canada's total land area.

SOCIAL STATISTICS

Births in 2000 numbered 378 (a rate of 12·3 per 1,000 population), and deaths 153 (rate of 5·0 per 1,000 population). There were 161 marriages and 117 divorces in 1998.

CLIMATE

Temperatures in the Yukon are usually more extreme than those experienced in the southern provinces of Canada. A cold climate in winter with moderate temperatures in summer provide a considerable annual range of temperature and moderate rainfall.

Whitehorse, Jan. −18·7°C (−2·0°F), July 14°C (57·2°F). Annual precipitation 268·8 mm. Dawson City, Jan. −30·7°C (−23·3°F), July 15·6°C (60·1°F). Annual precipitation 182·7 mm.

CONSTITUTION AND GOVERNMENT

The Yukon was constituted a separate territory on 13 June 1898.

The Yukon Legislative Assembly consists of 17 elected members and functions in much the same way as a provincial legislature. The seat of government is at Whitehorse. It consists of an executive council with parliamentary powers similar to those of a provincial cabinet. A federally appointed commissioner acts on the recommendations made by the legislative assembly, and serves in a similar capacity to Lieut.-Governor in the provinces.

The Yukon government consists of 12 departments, as well as a Women's Directorate and four Crown corporations. Government departments and agencies are responsible for a similar range of activities as found in Canadian provinces, including education, economic development, tourism, renewable resources, justice, community and transportation services and finance.

The administration of certain programmes, mostly in the natural resources field, remains under federal control. The Yukon government is, however, involved in negotiations with the federal government on the transfer of further responsibilities to its jurisdiction.

RECENT ELECTIONS

At elections held on 4 Nov. 2002 the Yukon Party took 12 of the available 18 seats; the New Democratic Party 5; and the Liberals 1.

CURRENT ADMINISTRATION

Commissioner: Jack Cable; b. 1934 (took office on 1 Oct. 2000).

In March 2003 the Yukon Party Ministry comprised:

Premier, Minister responsible for Executive Council Office, including Devolution, Land Claims, Women's Directorate and Youth Directorate, and Minister of Finance: Dennis Fentie.

Minister of Health and Social Services: Peter Jenkins. *Education:* John Edzerza. *Justice and Business, Tourism and Culture:* Elaine Taylor. *Energy, Mines and Resources:* Archie Lang. *Infrastructure and Community Services:* Glenn Hart. *Environment:* Jim Kenyon.

Government of Yukon Website: http://www.gov.yk.ca/

ECONOMY

The key sectors of the economy are government, tourism, finance, insurance and real estate.

Budget. The Territorial government's revenue and expenditure (in $1,000 CDN) for years ended 31 March was:

	1999–2000	2000–01[1]	2002–03[2]
Revenue	482,759	509,276	513,934
Expenditure	499,714	541,593	535,530

[1]Forecast. [2]Estimate.

Performance. GDP at market prices in 2000 was $1,124m. CDN. Mining, oil and gas production was estimated at $72·8m. CDN in 1998 and revenue from agriculture, forestry, hunting and fishing was estimated at $4m. CDN. In the manufacturing sector, shipments were valued at $2·3m. CDN in 2000. GDP per person in 2000 was $36,258 CDN.

ENERGY AND NATURAL RESOURCES

Environment. The Yukon is recognized as a critical habitat for many species of rare and endangered flowers, big game animals, birds of prey and migratory birds. There are 278 species of birds and 38 species of fish. The vegetation is classified as sub-arctic and alpine.

Three national parks (total area 36,572 sq. km), five territorial parks (7,861 sq. km), two ecological reserves (181 sq. km), eight wildlife management areas (10,651 sq. km) and one wildlife sanctuary (6,450 sq. km) have been established to protect fragile and significant areas for the future.

Electricity. The Yukon currently depends on imported refined petroleum products for about 16% of the energy it uses. At the same time, 94·6% (2000 figure) of the territory's electrical supply comes from four utility-owned hydro-electrical facilities. There are also several microhydro facilities and studies indicate a number of sites that could support new developments.

Hydro-generated power is supplemented with diesel power plants which are located in most communities. Current capacity is 130·2 MW combined hydrodiesel-generated power. Total generation for 2000 was 268 GWh. There are over 100 known occurrences of coal in the Yukon and potential local markets include power generation and industrial heating.

Fuel wood represents approximately $4m. CDN to $5m. CDN in direct employment and petroleum substitution in the Yukon annually.

A number of Yukon homes and businesses use solar energy for heating water and to supply electricity in remote locations. Wind energy is an option being explored by both private interests and the crown-owned utility. A number of sites have been identified with wind regimes on the verge of commercial viability.

Oil and Gas. In 1997 the Yukon Oil and Gas Act was passed, replacing the federal legislation. This Act provides for the transfer of responsibility for oil and gas resources to Yukon jurisdiction. Five unexplored oil and gas basins with rich potential exist. Modest exploration has been conducted in three basins. Current net production is about 1·7m. cu. metres of natural gas per day.

Minerals. Gold and silver are the chief minerals. There are also deposits of lead, zinc, copper, tungsten and iron ore. Gold deposits, both hard rock and placer, are being mined. In addition, several important occurrences of asbestos, barite and coal have been discovered.

Estimates for 2000 mineral production: gold, $51·6m. CDN; and silver, $0·3m. CDN. Total: $51·9m. CDN.

Agriculture. Many areas have suitable soils and climate for the production of forages, cereal grains and vegetables, domestic livestock and game farming. The territory also has arctic char fish farms. The greenhouse industry is the Yukon's largest horticulture sector.

In 1996 there were 160 farms operating full- and part-time. The total area of farms was 9,890 ha of which 2,248 ha are in field crop.

Farm receipts in 1996 were estimated at $3·5m. CDN. Total farm capital, 1996, was $45m. CDN.

Forestry. The forests, covering 275,000 sq. km of the territory, are part of the great Boreal forest region of Canada, which covers 57% of the Yukon. Vast areas are covered by coniferous stands in the southern region of Yukon, with white spruce and lodgepole pine forming on wet sites, and in northern aspects. Deciduous species form pure stands or occur mixed with conifers throughout forest areas. Yukon forestry products include posts and beams for the construction industry, roof trusses, niche products and timber.

Production from forestry was 145·0m. cu. metres in 1999–2000.

Game and Furs. The country abounds with big game, such as moose, goat, caribou, mountain sheep and bear (grizzly and black). The fur-trapping industry is considered vital to rural and remote residents and especially First Nations people wishing to maintain a traditional lifestyle. Preliminary fur production in 2000 (mostly marten, muskrat, beaver, lynx and wolverine) was valued at $296,896 CDN.

Fisheries. Commercial fishing concentrates on chinook salmon, chum salmon, lake trout and whitefish.

INDUSTRY

The key sectors of the economy are tourism and government.

Labour. The 2000 labour force was 15,242, of whom 13,475 were employed.

INTERNATIONAL TRADE

Imports and Exports. In 2000 exports made up 35·2% of Yukon goods and services produced. In 2000 exports were valued at $396m. CDN.

COMMUNICATIONS

Roads. The Alaska Highway and branch highway systems connect Yukon's main communities with Alaska, the Northwest Territories, southern Canada and the United States. The year round highway system is built and maintained to accommodate loads up to 77,000 kg. The 735-km Dempster Highway north of Dawson City connects with Inuvik, on the Arctic coast; this highway, the first public road to be built to the Arctic Ocean, was opened in Aug. 1979. The South Klondike Highway links the tidewater port of Skagway, Alaska with the Yukon. It was opened in May 1979, providing a new access to the Pacific Ocean. In 2000 there were 4,712·5 km of roads maintained by the Yukon Territorial government: 3,178·1 km, Alaska Highway; 1,534·4 km is secondary. The major roads, including the Alaska Highway, have received a new surface treatment which resembles pavement, and the rest are all-weather gravel, of which 700 km are accessible during the summer months only. Vehicles registered in 2000 totalled 23,915 (excluding buses, motorcycles and trailers), including 21,149 passenger vehicles.

Rail. The 176-km White Pass and Yukon Railway connected Whitehorse with year-round ocean shipping at Skagway, Alaska, but was closed in 1982. A modified passenger service was restarted in 1988 to take cruise ship tourists from Skagway to Carcross, Yukon, over the White Pass summit.

Civil Aviation. Whitehorse has an international airport with direct daily flights from Vancouver, Alaska and the Northwest Territories. In the summer there are regular scheduled flights from Europe. There are ten airports throughout the territory, with many smaller airstrips and aerodromes in remote areas. Commercial airlines offering charter services are located throughout the territory.

Shipping. The majority of goods are shipped into the territory by truck over the Alaska and Stewart-Cassiar Highways. Some goods are shipped through the ports of Skagway and Haines, Alaska, and then trucked to Whitehorse for distribution throughout the territory. Skagway, 160 km south of Whitehorse, is a commercial shipping outlet for goods destined for Asia and the west coast of North America. The majority of goods are transported by road within the territory, while a modest amount is shipped by air.

Telecommunications. All telephone and telecommunications, including Internet access in most communities, are provided by Northwestel, a subsidiary of Bell Canada Enterprises. Microwave stations, satellite ground stations and radio-telephone facilities provide most of the telephone transmission services to the communities.

SOCIAL INSTITUTIONS

Education. The Yukon Department of Education operates (with the assistance of elected school boards) the territory's 28 schools, both public and private, from kindergarten to grade 12. In 2001 there were 5,579 pupils. There are also one French First Language school and one Roman Catholic school. The total enrolment figure for 1999–2000 was 5,332. The Whitehorse campus is the administrative and programme centre for 13 other campuses located throughout the territory. In 1999–2000 a total of 664 full-time and 4,668 part-time students enrolled in programmes and courses. The Yukon government provides financial assistance to students for post-secondary education whether they study at Yukon College or outside the territory.

Health. In 2000 there were two hospitals with 61 staffed beds, four nursing stations, nine health treatment centres, 55 resident doctors and 15 dentists. The territorial government operates a medical travel programme to send patients to nearby provinces for specialized treatment not available in the territory.

CULTURE

Broadcasting. There are three radio stations in Whitehorse and 15 low-power relay radio transmitters operated by CBC, and six operated by the Yukon government. CHON-FM, operated by Northern Native Broadcasting, is broadcast to virtually all Yukon communities by satellite. Dawson City has its own community-run radio station, CFYT-FM. There are also 27 basic and 36 extended pay-cable TV channels in Whitehorse, and private cable operations in some communities. Live CBC national television and TVNC is provided by satellite and relayed to all communities.

Press. In 2000 there were one daily and one semi-weekly newspaper in Whitehorse, and a semi-weekly (summer only) and a monthly newspaper in Dawson City. Other communities with local newspapers include Stewart Crossing, Haines Junction and Faro. There is also a monthly newspaper for francophones. In total, the territory publishes 10 newspapers which range in publication from daily to annual.

Tourism. In 1999 there were about 280,500 visitors, generating revenues of $160m. CDN. Primary tourist activities are related to highway travel, wilderness adventure and historical and cultural interests. Major markets for Yukon tourism include North America, German-speaking European nations and the United Kingdom. Emerging markets include Japan, Taiwan, New Zealand and Australia. Enhanced airport infrastructure has stimulated direct flights from Europe and increased flights by national charter companies.

Tourism is the largest private sector employer. In 1999, 66% of employed Yukon people were working for businesses that reported some level of tourism revenue. 20% of businesses generate more than 33% of gross revenues from tourism.

Festivals. Yukon festivals include the Yukon Sourdough Rendezvous in Feb. (outdoor winter activities) and the Yukon International Storytelling Festival in May.

FURTHER READING
Annual Report of the Government of the Yukon.
Yukon Executive Council, *Annual Statistical Review.*

Berton, P., *Klondike.* (Rev. ed.) Toronto, 1987
Coates, K. and Morrison, W., *Land of the Midnight Sun: A History of the Yukon.* Edmonton, 1988

There is a Yukon Archive at Yukon College, Whitehorse.

Website: http://www.gov.yk.ca/

CAPE VERDE

República de Cabo Verde

Capital: Praia
Population estimate, 2000: 434,000
GDP per capita, 2000: (PPP$) 4,863
HDI/world rank: 0·715/100

KEY HISTORICAL EVENTS

During centuries of Portuguese rule the islands were gradually peopled with Portuguese, slaves from Africa, and people of mixed African-European descent who became the majority. While retaining some African culture, the Cape Verdians spoke Portuguese or the Portuguese-derived Crioulo (Creole) language and became Catholics. In 1956 nationalists from Cape Verde and Portuguese Guinea formed the *Partido Africano da Independência da Guiné e Cabo Verde* (PAIGC). In the 1960s the PAIGC waged a successful guerrilla war. On 5 July 1975 Cape Verde became independent, ruled by the PAIGC, which was already the ruling party in ex-Portuguese Guinea-Bissau. But resentment at Cape Verdians' privileged position in Guinea-Bissau led to the end of the ties between the two countries' ruling parties. Although the PAIGC retained its name in Guinea-Bissau, in Jan. 1981 it was renamed the *Partido Africano da Independência do Cabo Verde* (PAICV) in Cape Verde. The Constitution of 1981 made the PAICV the sole legal party but in Sept. 1990 the National Assembly abolished its monopoly and free elections were permitted.

TERRITORY AND POPULATION

Cape Verde is situated in the Atlantic Ocean 620 km off west Africa and consists of ten islands (Boa Vista, Brava, Fogo, Maio, Sal, Santa Luzia, Santo Antão, São Nicolau, São Tiago and São Vicente) and five islets. The islands are divided into two groups, named Barlavento (windward) and Sotavento (leeward). The total area is 4,033 sq. km (1,557 sq. miles). The population was 341,491 at the census of 1990. The 2000 census population (provisional) was 434,812, giving a density of 107·8 per sq. km. In 1999, 60·4% of the population lived in urban areas.

The UN gives a projected population for 2010 of 522,000.

About 600,000 Cape Verdeans live abroad.

Areas and populations of the islands:

Island	Area (sq. km)	Population Census 1980	Population Census 1990
Santo Antão	779	43,321	43,845
São Vicente[1]	227	41,594	51,277
São Nicolau	388	13,572	13,665
Sal	216	5,826	7,715
Boa Vista	620	3,372	3,452
Barlavento	*2,230*	*107,685*	*119,954*
Maio	269	4,098	4,969
São Tiago	991	145,957	175,691
Fogo	476	30,978	33,902
Brava	67	6,985	6,975
Sotavento	*1,803*	*188,018*	*221,537*

[1]Including Santa Luzia island, which is uninhabited.

The main towns are Praia, the capital, on São Tiago (76,000, 1999 estimate) and Mindelo on São Vicente (47,109, 1990 census). Ethnic groups: Mixed, 71%; Black, 28%; White, 1%. The official language is Portuguese; a creole (Crioulo) is in ordinary use.

SOCIAL STATISTICS

1998 births, 15,460; 1996 deaths, 2,786. 1998 birth rate, 37·1 per 1,000 population; 1996 death rate, 7·0. Annual population growth rate, 1990–99, 2·3%. Annual emigration varies between 2,000 and 10,000. Life expectancy at birth, 1999, was 66·0 years for men and 71·8 years for women. Infant mortality, 1999, 54 per 1,000 live births; fertility rate, 1999, 3·5 children per woman.

CLIMATE
The climate is arid, with a cool dry season from Dec. to June and warm dry conditions for the rest of the year. Rainfall is sparse, rarely exceeding 5" (127 mm) in the northern islands or 12" (304 mm) in the southern ones. There are periodic severe droughts. Praia, Jan. 72°F (22·2°C), July 77°F (25°C). Annual rainfall 10" (250 mm).

CONSTITUTION AND GOVERNMENT
The Constitution was adopted in Sept. 1992.

A constitutional referendum was held on 28 Dec. 1994; turn-out was 45%. 82·06% of votes cast favoured a reform extending the powers of the presidency and strengthening the autonomy of local authorities. The President is elected for five-year terms by universal suffrage.

The National Assembly is elected for five-year terms.

National Anthem. 'Sol, suor, o verde e mar' ('Sun, sweat, the green and the sea'); words and tune by A. Lopes Cabral.

RECENT ELECTIONS
Elections for the *National Assembly* of 72 members were held on 14 Jan. 2001. Turn-out was 57·8%. Three parties stood. The PAICV won 40 seats with 49·9% of votes cast, the Movement for Democracy (MPD) won 30 seats with 40·8%, and the Democratic Alliance for Change won 2 with 6·2%.

In the presidential elections which took place on 11 Feb. 2001 Pedro Pires won 46·5% of the vote and Carlos Veiga 45·9%, with 2 other candidates winning less than 4% each, qualifying the two former prime ministers for a run-off. Turn-out was 50%. After the 25 Feb. 2001 run-off, Pires was confirmed as the victor with 75,828 votes (49·43%) against Veiga's 75,811 (49·42%), a difference of just 17 votes. Turn-out was 59%.

CURRENT ADMINISTRATION
President: Pedro Pires; b. 1934 (PAICV; sworn in 22 March 2001).

In March 2003 the government comprised:
Prime Minister: José Maria Neves; b. 1959 (PAICV; sworn in 1 Feb. 2001).

Minister for Foreign Affairs, Co-operation and Communities: Fátima Veiga. *Health:* Basílio Mosso Ramos. *Defence and Parliamentary Affairs:* Armindo Cipriano Maurício. *Education:* Víctor Borges. *Environment, Agriculture and Fisheries:* Maria Madalena Brito Neves. *Justice and Internal Administration:* Maria Cristina Lopes Almeida Fontes Lima. *Culture and Sport:* Jorge Homero Tolentino Araújo. *Infrastructure and Transport:* Manuel Inocêncio Sousa. *Finance and Economic Planning:* Carlos Augusto Duarte Burgo. *Labour and Solidarity:* Júlio Correira. *Presidency of the Council of Ministers:* Arnaldo Andrade Ramos. *Economy and Growth:* Avelino Bonifácio Fernandes Lopes.

Government Website (Portuguese only): http://www.governo.cv/

DEFENCE
There is selective conscription. Defence expenditure totalled US$7m. in 2000 (US$17 per capita), representing 2·7% of GDP.

Army. The Army is composed of two battalions and had a strength of 1,000 in 1999.

Navy. There is a coast guard of 50 (1999).

Air Force. The Air Force had under 100 personnel and no combat aircraft in 1999.

INTERNATIONAL RELATIONS
Cape Verde is a member of the UN, the African Union, African Development Bank, ECOWAS, IOM, the International Organization of the Francophonie and is an ACP member state of the ACP-EU relationship.

ECONOMY
Services accounted for 68·7% of GDP in 1998, industry 19·1% and agriculture 12·2%.

Currency. The unit of currency is the *Cape Verde escudo* (CVE) of 100 *centavos*. Foreign exchange reserves were US$63m. in June 2002 and total money supply was 20,893m. escudos. There was inflation in 2001 of 3·7%. In 2000 there had been deflation of 2·4%.

Budget. The budget for 1996 envisaged revenue of 21,110m. escudos and expenditure of 21,020m. escudos.

Performance. Real GDP growth was 6·8% in 2000 and 2·9% in 2001. Total GDP in 2001 was US$0·6bn.

Banking and Finance. The Banco de Cabo Verde is the central bank (*Governor*, Amaro Alexandre da Luz) and bank of issue, and was also previously a commercial bank. Its latter functions have been taken over by the Banco Comercial do Atlântico, mainly financed by public funds. The Caixa Econômica de Cabo Verde (CECV) has been upgraded into a commercial and development bank. Two foreign banks have also been established there.

Weights and Measures. The metric system is in use.

ENERGY AND NATURAL RESOURCES

Environment. According to the *World Bank Atlas* Cape Verde's carbon dioxide emissions in 1998 were the equivalent of 0·3 tonnes per capita.

Electricity. Installed capacity is 17,000 kW. Production was 40m. kWh in 1998. Consumption per capita in 1997 was 103 kWh.

Minerals. Salt is obtained on the islands of Sal, Boa Vista and Maio. Volcanic rock (pozzolana) is mined for export. There are also deposits of kaolin, clay, gypsum and basalt.

Agriculture. Some 10–15% of the land area is suitable for farming. In 1998, 39,000 ha were arable and 2,000 ha permanent crops, mainly confined to inland valleys. 3,000 ha were irrigated in 1998. The chief crops (production, 2000, in 1,000 tonnes) are: sugarcane, 13; maize, 11; bananas, 6; cabbages, 6; coconuts, 6; mangoes, 5; sweet potatoes, 4; tomatoes, 4.

Livestock (2000): 640,000 pigs, 110,000 goats, 22,000 cattle, 14,000 asses.

Forestry. In 1995 the woodland area was 47,000 ha, or 31% of the total land area (16,000 ha and 11·7% in 1990). Cape Verde is one of only two developing countries to have increased its area under forests between 1990 and 1995, the other being India.

Fisheries. In 1993 there were 64 large and 1,400 small fishing vessels. In 1999 the total catch was 10,371 tonnes (mainly tuna), exclusively from marine waters. About 200 tonnes of lobsters are caught annually.

INDUSTRY

The main industries are the manufacture of paint, beer, soft drinks, rum, flour, cigarettes, canned tuna and shoes.

Labour. In 1996 the workforce was 157,000 (62% males).

INTERNATIONAL TRADE

Foreign debt was US$327m. in 2000.

Imports and Exports. Imports and exports (f.o.b.) for calendar years in US$1m.:

	1994	1995	1996	1997	1998
Imports	195·3	233·6	207·5	215·1	218·3
Exports	14·2	16·6	23·9	43·2	32·7

Main exports in 1997: road vehicles (43%), refined petroleum (29%), footwear (7%) and fish and shellfish (4%). Main export markets, 1997: Portugal, 45%; Guinea-Bissau, 6%; Netherlands, 3%. Main import suppliers: Portugal, 40%; USA, 10%; France, 9%; Netherlands, 6%. Approximately 90% of food is imported.

COMMUNICATIONS

Roads. In 1996 there were 1,100 km of roads (858 km paved) and there were 3,280 private cars and 820 commercial vehicles.

424

Civil Aviation. Amilcar Cabral International Airport, at Espargos on Sal, is a major refuelling point on flights to Africa and Latin America. A new airport, Francisco Mendes Airport, has been built at Praia, and was scheduled to open in April 2003. Transportes Aéreos de Cabo Verde (TACV), the national carrier, provided services to most of the other islands in 1998, and internationally to Amsterdam, Basle, Bissau, Bologna, Lisbon, Munich, Paris and Vienna. In 2000 Amilcar Cabral International Airport handled 489,000 passengers (254,000 on international flights) and 3,500 tonnes of freight. In 1999 scheduled airline traffic of Cape Verde-based carriers flew 5·5m. km, carrying 252,000 passengers (114,000 on international flights).

Shipping. The main ports are Mindelo and Praia. In 1998 the merchant marine totalled 20,000 GRT. There is a state-owned ferry service between the islands.

Telecommunications. There were 54,900 telephone main lines in 2000 (126·2 per 1,000 persons). In 1996 there were approximately 1,000 fax machines. The number of Internet users in Dec. 2000 was 8,000, up from 150 in 1999. There were 8,100 mobile phone subscribers in 1999, up from 1,000 in 1998. This represented an increase of 710% over the year—the highest in the world.

Postal Services. In 1995 there were 55 post offices.

SOCIAL INSTITUTIONS

Justice. There is a network of People's Tribunals, with a Supreme Court in Praia. The Supreme Court is composed of a minimum of five Judges, of whom one is appointed by the President, one elected by the National Assembly, and the other by the Supreme Council of Magistrates.

The population in penal institutions in 1997 was approximately 600 (150 per 100,000 of national population).

Religion. At the 1990 census 93·2% of the population were Roman Catholic and 6·8% were mainly Protestant (Nazarene Church).

Education. Adult literacy in 1999 was 73·6% (male, 84·5%; female, 65·1%). Primary schooling is followed by lower (13–15 years) and upper (16–18 years) secondary education options. In 1997–98 there were 3,219 primary school teachers for 91,777 pupils; and 1,372 teachers for 31,602 pupils at secondary schools. In 1990 there were 531 students and 52 teachers at a technical school, 211 students and 53 teachers in three teacher-training colleges and about 500 students at foreign universities.

Health. Medical provision, 1992: one doctor per 4,270 inhabitants, one nurse per 670 inhabitants. In 1996 there were 2 central and 3 regional hospitals, 15 health centres, 22 dispensaries and 60 community health clinics.

CULTURE

Broadcasting. There are two national radio stations and a national TV service. Portuguese and French international radio and TV services also broadcast to Cape Verde. There were (1997) 73,000 radio receivers and 2,000 television receivers.

Press. In 1996 there were three national newspapers—a state-owned bi-weekly, and a weekly and a fortnightly, owned by political parties. Total circulation approximates 12,000, but publication is suspended from time to time due to shortage of paper.

Tourism. Tourism is in the initial stages of development. In 1998 there were 52,000 foreign tourists, bringing revenue of US$20m. Some 50% of tourists originate from Portugal, 15% from Germany and 7% from France.

DIPLOMATIC REPRESENTATIVES
Of Cape Verde in the United Kingdom
Ambassador: Vacant (resides at The Hague).
2nd Secretary: Clara Manuela da Luz Delgado.

Of the United Kingdom in Cape Verde
Ambassador: Alan Burner (resides at Dakar, Senegal).

Of Cape Verde in the USA (3415 Massachusetts Ave., NW, Washington, D.C., 20007)
Ambassador: José Brito.

Of the USA in Cape Verde (Rua Abilio Macedo 81, Praia)
Ambassador: Donald C. Johnson.

Of Cape Verde to the United Nations
Ambassador: Luis da Fonseca.

Of Cape Verde to the European Union
Ambassador: Fernando Jorge Wahnon Ferreira.

FURTHER READING

Lobban, R., *Cape Verde: Crioulo Colony to Independent Nation.* Westview Press, Boulder (CO), 1998

Meintel, D., *Race, Culture, and Portuguese Colonialism in Cabo Verde.* Syracuse Univ. Press, 1984

Shaw, Caroline E., *Cape Verde Islands.* [Bibliography] ABC-Clio, Oxford and Santa Barbara (CA), 1991

National statistical office: Instituto Nacional de Estatística, Praia.
Website (Portuguese only): http://www.ine.cv/

CENTRAL AFRICAN REPUBLIC

Capital: Bangui
Population estimate, 2000: 3·72m..
GDP per capita, 2000: (PPP$) 1,172
HDI/world rank: 0·375/165

République Centrafricaine

KEY HISTORICAL EVENTS

Central African Republic became independent on 13 Aug. 1960, after having been one of the four territories of French Equatorial Africa. A Constitution of 1976 provided for the country to be a parliamentary democracy to be known as the Central African Empire. President Bokassa became Emperor Bokassa I. He was overthrown in 1979. In 1981 General André Kolingba took power, initiating a gradual return to constitutional rule.

On 5 June 1996, following an army mutiny, President Patassé accepted an agreement brokered by France which led to the formation of a government of national unity. But mutineers demanded the replacement of President Patassé and killed two French soldiers. France chaired a mediation committee of various neighbouring French-speaking states, and an agreement to end the mutiny was signed in 1997 and a peacekeeping force of neighbouring states, MISAB, was set up. Conflicts between the mutineers and MISAB continued until a ceasefire was concluded on 2 July 1997. There was an attempted coup on 28 May 2001, allegedly led by Gen. André Kolingba, who had been the country's military ruler from 1981 to 1993. However, it failed following several days of fighting in and around the capital, Bangui. Fighting erupted once more in Oct. 2002 after another coup attempt. In March 2003 a further coup saw Gen. François Bozizé, a former army chief, seize power.

TERRITORY AND POPULATION

The republic is bounded in the north by Chad, east by Sudan, south by the Democratic Republic of the Congo and the Republic of the Congo, and west by Cameroon. The area covers 622,436 sq. km (240,324 sq. miles). The population at the 1988 census was 2,568,426; estimate, 1996, 3,274,000, giving a density of 5 per sq. km. In 1999, 59·2% of the population were rural.

The UN gives a projected population for 2010 of 4·43m.

The areas, populations and capitals of the prefectures are as follows:

Prefecture	Sq. km	1988 census	Capital
Bamingui-Bangoran	58,200	28,643	Ndele
Bangui[1]	67	451,690	Bangui
Basse-Kotto	17,604	194,750	Mobaye
Haute-Kotto	86,650	58,838	Bria
Haut-M'bomou	55,530	27,113	Obo
Kemo	17,204	82,884	Sibut
Lobaye	19,235	169,554	M'baiki
Mambere Kadéi	30,203	230,364	Berbérati
M'bomou	61,150	119,252	Bangassou
Nana Gribizi	19,996	95,497	Kaga-Bandoro
Nana-Mambere	26,600	191,970	Bouar
Ombella-M'poko	31,835	180,857	Bimbo
Ouaka	49,900	208,332	Bambari
Ouham	50,250	262,950	Bossangoa
Ouham-Pendé	32,100	287,653	Bozoum
Sangha M'baéré	19,412	65,961	Nola
Vakaga	46,500	32,118	Birao

[1]Autonomous commune.

The capital, Bangui, had an estimated population in 1999 of 622,000. Other main towns, with 1994 populations, are Bebérati (47,000), Bouar (43,000), Bambari (43,000) and Carnot (41,000).

There are a number of ethnic groups, the main ones being Baya (34%) and Banda (27%).

French and Sango are the official languages.

SOCIAL STATISTICS
1996 births, 131,000; deaths, 58,000. Rates, 1996 estimates (per 1,000 population): births, 40·0; deaths, 17·6. Infant mortality, 1999 (per 1,000 live births), 113. Expectation of life in 1999 was 42·7 years for males and 46·0 for females. Annual population growth rate, 1990–99, 2·1%. Fertility rate, 1999, 4·8 children per woman.

CLIMATE
A tropical climate with little variation in temperature. The wet months are May, June, Oct. and Nov. Bangui, Jan. 31·9°C, July 20·7°C. Annual rainfall 1,289·3 mm. Ndele, Jan. 36·3°C, July 30·5°C. Annual rainfall 203·6 mm.

CONSTITUTION AND GOVERNMENT
Under the Constitution adopted by a referendum on 21 Nov. 1986, the sole legal political party was the *Rassemblement Démocratique Centrafricaine*. In Aug. 1992 the Constitution was revised to permit multi-party democracy. Further constitutional reforms followed a referendum in Dec. 1994, including the establishment of a *Constitutional Court*. The President is elected by popular vote for not more than two terms of six years, and appoints and leads a Council of Ministers. There is a 109-member *National Assembly.* Following the coup of March 2003 Gen. François Bozizé suspended the constitution and dissolved parliament.

National Anthem. 'La Renaissance' ('Rebirth'); words by B. Boganda, tune by H. Pepper.

RECENT ELECTIONS
At the presidential elections held on 19 Sept. 1999 there were ten presidential candidates. Incumbent president Ange-Félix Patassé gained 51·6% of votes cast in the first round making a second round of voting unnecessary. Former president Andre Kolingba, standing as a candidate for the Central African Democratic Rally, came second with 19·3%.

In National Assembly elections on 22 Nov. and 13 Dec. 1998 the Central African People's Liberation Movement (MLPC) gained 47 seats, the Central African Democratic Rally (RDC) 20, the Movement for Democracy and Development (MDD) 8, Patriotic Front for Progress 7, Social Democratic Party 6, Alliance for Democracy and Progress 5, National Unity Party 3, the Liberal Democratic Party 2, FODEM 2, ind. 7. 2 other parties gained 1 seat each.

CURRENT ADMINISTRATION
Former army chief Gen. François Bozizé seized power on 15 March 2003 in a coup and the following day declared himself president, saying that he had dissolved the National Assembly and government. He subsequently named Abel Goumba prime minister. A transitional government was formed comprising representatives of civil society and all political parties. Gen. Bozizé has said that a transition period will last between one and three years, after which elections would be held to decide on a new government.

DEFENCE
Selective national service for a two-year period is in force. Some 1,200 French military personnel were stationed in 1993.

Defence expenditure totalled US$43m. in 2000 (US$12 per capita), representing 3·7%of GDP.

Army. The Army consisted (1999) of about 2,500 personnel, including the Republican Guard. In addition there are some 2,300 personnel in the paramilitary Gendarmerie.

Navy. The Army includes a small naval wing operating a handful of patrol craft.

Air Force. Personnel strength (1999) about 150. There are no combat aircraft.

INTERNATIONAL RELATIONS

The Central African Republic is a member of the UN, WTO, the African Union, African Development Bank, Lake Chad Commission, the International Organization of the Francophonie, and is an ACP member state of the ACP-EU relationship.

ECONOMY

Agriculture accounted for 52·6% of GDP in 1998, industry 18·6% and services 28·8%.

Currency. The unit of currency is the *franc CFA* (XAF) with a parity of 655·957 francs CFA to one euro. Total money supply in April 2002 was 103,991m. francs CFA and foreign exchange reserves were US$123m. Gold reserves were 11,000 troy oz in June 2002. In 2001 there was inflation of 3·8%.

Budget. In 1996 expenditure totalled 114,400m. francs CFA, and revenue 45,800m. francs CFA.

Performance. Total GDP in 2001 was US$1·0bn. Real GDP growth was 0·6% in 2000 (0·5% in 1999).

Banking and Finance. The *Banque des Etats de l'Afrique Centrale* (*BEAC*) acts as the central bank and bank of issue. The *Governor* is Jean-Félix Mamalepot.

Weights and Measures. The metric system is in use.

ENERGY AND NATURAL RESOURCES

Environment. According to the *World Bank Atlas* the Central African Republic's carbon dioxide emissions in 1998 were the equivalent of 0·1 tonnes per capita.

Electricity. Installed capacity was 40,000 kW in 1991. Production in 1998 totalled 105m. kWh (approximately 80% hydro-electric). Consumption per capita in 1997 was 30 kWh.

Minerals. In 1998, 330,000 carats of gem diamonds, 200,000 carats of industrial diamonds and, in 1997, 90 kg of gold were mined. There are also oil, uranium and other mineral deposits which are for the most part unexploited.

Agriculture. In 1998 the agricultural population numbered 2·59m. persons, of whom 1·24m. were economically active. In 1998, 1·93m. ha were arable and 0·09m. ha permanent crops. The main crops (production 2000, in 1,000 tonnes) are cassava, 500; yams, 360; bananas, 115; groundnuts, 105; maize, 101; taro, 100; plantains, 82; seed cotton, 35.

Livestock, 2000: cattle, 2·95m.; goats, 2·60m.; sheep, 210,000; pigs, 650,000; chickens, 4m.

Forestry. There were 29·9m. ha of forest in 1995, or 48% of the total land area (down from 49·1% in 1990). The extensive hardwood forests, particularly in the southwest, provide mahogany, obeche and limba. Timber production in 1999 was 3·55m. cu. metres.

Fisheries. The catch in 2000 was approximately 15,000 tonnes, exclusively from inland waters.

INDUSTRY

The small industrial sector includes factories producing cotton fabrics, footwear, beer and radios. Output in 1995: beer, 26·9m. litres; cotton fabrics (1992), 5·32m. metres; soap (1994), 1,896 tonnes; leather (1994), 19 tonnes.

Labour. In 1996 the labour force was 1,623,000 (53% males).

INTERNATIONAL TRADE

External debt was US$827m. in 2000.

Imports and Exports. Exports in 2000 totalled US$181m. (US$178m. in 1999); imports in 2000 totalled US$247m. (US$253m. in 1999).

Main export markets, 1996: Belgium-Luxembourg, 60·1%; France, 30·9%; UK, 3·5%; Democratic Republic of the Congo, 1·7%. Main import suppliers, 1996: France, 39·5%; Japan, 8·7%; Cameroon, 3·9%; Republic of the Congo, 1·9%. Main exports are coffee, diamonds, timber and cotton. Main imports include food, textiles, petroleum products, machinery, electrical equipment and motor vehicles.

COMMUNICATIONS

Roads. There were 24,307 km of roads in 1998, including 5,398 km of highways or main roads. In 1997 there were 966 passenger cars and 662 commercial vehicles. There were 52 road accident deaths in 1996.

Civil Aviation. There is an international airport at M'Poko, near Bangui, which handled 56,000 passengers (52,000 on international flights) in 2000. The country is a member of Air Afrique, the regional carrier, with services to Paris and African capitals. In 1999 scheduled airline traffic of Central African Republic-based carriers flew 3·0m. km, carrying 84,000 passengers (all on international flights).

Shipping. Timber and barges are taken to Brazzaville (Republic of the Congo).

Telecommunications. There were 9,500 main telephone lines in 2000 (equivalent to 2·6 per 1,000 persons), around 500 mobile phone subscribers, 6,000 PCs in use (1·4 per 1,000 persons), and 250 fax machines. The number of Internet users in July 2000 was 1,000.

Postal Services. In 1995 there were 31 post offices.

SOCIAL INSTITUTIONS

Justice. The Criminal Court and Supreme Court are situated in Bangui. There are 16 high courts throughout the country.

Religion. In 1999 there were 880,000 Protestants and 580,000 Roman Catholics. Traditional animist beliefs are still widespread.

Education. A national education plan was initiated in 1994 to fund capital educational projects. Adult literacy rate was 45·4% in 1999 (58·6% among males and 33·3% among females). In 1991–92 there were 277,961 pupils at primary schools and 43,740 at secondary schools. The pupil/teacher ratio at primary school level was 77 pupils per teacher in 1990–91, the highest ratio in any country in the world. There is a university at Bangui. It had 3,590 students and 140 academic staff in 1995–96.

Health. In 1990 there were 255 hospitals and health centres with 4,120 beds; in 1992 there were 157 doctors; in 1990, 8 dentists, 1,353 nurses and 166 midwives.

In the period 1990–98 only 38% of the population had access to safe drinking water.

CULTURE

Broadcasting. Broadcasting is provided by the state-controlled Radiodiffusion-Télévision Centrafricaine. There were 283,000 radio and 18,000 TV (colour by SECAM V) sets in 1997.

Press. In 1996 there were three daily newspapers with a circulation of 6,000, giving a rate of 1·8 per 1,000 inhabitants.

Tourism. In 1998 there were 20,000 foreign tourists, bringing revenue of US$6m.

DIPLOMATIC REPRESENTATIVES
Of Central African Republic in the United Kingdom
Ambassador: Vacant.
First Counsellor: Germain Gresenguet (resides at Paris).

Of the United Kingdom in Central African Republic
Ambassador: Richard Wildash, LVO (resides at Yaoundé, Cameroon).

Of Central African Republic in the USA (1618 22nd St., NW, Washington, D.C., 20008)
Ambassador: Emmanuel Touaboy.

Of the USA in Central African Republic (Ave. David Dacko, Bangui)
Ambassador: Mattie R. Sharpless.

Of Central African Republic to the United Nations
Ambassador: Vacant.
First Counsellor: Fernand Poukré-Kono.

Of Central African Republic to the European Union
Ambassador: Armand-Guy Zounguere-Sokambi.

FURTHER READING

Kalck, P., *Historical Dictionary of the Central African Republic.* Scarecrow Press, Metuchen, (NJ), 1992.—*Central African Republic.* [Bibliography] ABC-Clio, Oxford and Santa Barbara (CA), 1993
Titley, B., *Dark Age: The Political Odyssey of Emperor Bokassa.* McGill-University Press, Montreal, 1997

CHAD

République du Tchad

Capital: N'Djaména
Population estimate, 2000: 7·89m.
GDP per capita, 2000: (PPP$) 871
HDI/world rank: 0·365/166

KEY HISTORICAL EVENTS

France proclaimed a protectorate over Chad in 1900 and in July 1908 the territory was incorporated into French Equatorial Africa. It became a separate colony in 1920, and in 1946 one of the four constituent territories of French Equatorial Africa. It achieved full independence on 11 Aug. 1960. Conflicts between the government and secessionist groups, particularly in the Muslim north and centre, began in 1965 and developed into civil war. In 1982 forces led by Hissène Habré gained control of the country. In June 1983 Libyan-backed forces re-occupied some territory but a ceasefire took effect in Sept. 1987. Rebel forces of the Popular Salvation Movement led by Idriss Déby entered Chad from Sudan in Nov. 1990. On 4 Dec. 1990 Déby declared himself President. In Feb. 2000 Hissène Habré was charged with torture and barbarity in Senegal, where he had lived since being toppled in 1990, and placed under house arrest.

TERRITORY AND POPULATION

Chad is bounded in the west by Cameroon, Nigeria and Niger, north by Libya, east by Sudan and south by the Central African Republic. In Feb. 1994 the International Court of Justice ruled that the Aozou Strip along the Libyan border, occupied by Libya since 1973, was part of Chad. Area, 1,284,000 sq. km. At the 1993 census the population was 6,279,931 (5,929,192 settled, of whom 1,327,570 were urban and 359,069 nomadic). 1996 population estimate, 6,977,000; density, 5 per sq. km.

The UN gives a projected population for 2010 of 10·69m.

In 1999, 76·5% of the population were rural. The capital is N'Djaména with 998,000 inhabitants (1999 estimate), other large towns being (1993 census figures) Moundou (282,103), Sarh (193,753), Bongor (196,713), Abéché (187,936) and Doba (185,461).

The areas, populations and chief towns of the 14 prefectures were:

Prefecture	Area sq. km	Population (1993 census)	Capital
Batha	88,800	288,458	Ati
Biltine	46,850	184,807	Biltine
Borkou-Ennedi-Tibesti	600,350	73,185	Faya (Largeau)
Chari-Baguirmi	82,910	1,251,906	N'Djaména
Guéra	58,950	306,253	Mongo
Kanem	114,520	279,927	Mao
Lac	22,320	252,932	Bol
Logone Occidental	8,695	455,489	Moundou
Logone Oriental	28,035	441,064	Doba
Mayo-Kebbi	30,105	825,158	Bongor
Moyen-Chari	45,180	738,595	Sarh
Ouaddaï	76,240	543,900	Abéché
Salamat	63,000	184,403	Amtiman
Tandjilé	18,045	453,854	Laï

The official languages are French and Arabic, but more than 100 different languages and dialects are spoken. The largest ethnic group is the Sara of southern Chad (27·7% of the total population), followed by the Sudanic Arabs (11·5%).

SOCIAL STATISTICS

1996 births, 308,000; deaths, 121,000. Rates, 1996 estimates (per 1,000 population): births, 44·2; deaths, 17·4. Annual rate of growth, 1990–99, 2·9%. Expectation of life in 1999 was 44·2 years among males and 46·7 among females. Infant mortality, 1999 (per 1,000 live births), 118. Fertility rate, 1999, 5·9 children per woman.

CLIMATE
A tropical climate, with adequate rainfall in the south, though Nov. to April are virtually rainless months. Further north, desert conditions prevail. N'Djaména, Jan. 75°F (23·9°C), July 82°F (27·8°C). Annual rainfall 30" (744 mm).

CONSTITUTION AND GOVERNMENT
After overthrowing the regime of Hissène Habré, Idriss Déby proclaimed himself *President* and was sworn in on 4 March 1991.

A law of Oct. 1991 permits the formation of political parties provided they are not based on regionalism, tribalism or intolerance. There were 59 parties in 1996.

At a referendum on 31 March 1997 a new Constitution was approved by 63·5% of votes cast. It defines Chad as a unitary state. The head of state is the *President*, elected by universal suffrage.

The *National Assembly* has 125 members, elected for a four-year term in 25 single-member constituencies and 34 multi-member constituencies.

National Anthem. 'Peuple tchadien, debout et à l'ouvrage' ('People of Chad, arise and to the task'); words by L. Gidrol, tune by P. Villard.

RECENT ELECTIONS
Presidential elections were held on 20 May 2001. Turn-out was 80·9%. Incumbent Idriss Déby won re-election, with 67·4% of the vote, against 13·9% for Ngarlejy Yorongar, 6·5% for Saleh Kabzabo and 5·1% for Wadal Abdelkader Kamougue.

In parliamentary elections held on 21 April 2002 the Patriotic Salvation Movement of President Idriss Déby won 102 seats, the Rally for Democracy and Progress 12, the Federation Action for the Republic 11, the National Rally for Development and Progress 5, the National Union for Democracy and Renewal 5 and the Union for Renewal and Democracy 3. Turn-out was 52·8%.

CURRENT ADMINISTRATION
President: Lt. Gen. Idriss Déby; b. 1954 (Patriotic Salvation Movement; in office since 1990 and re-elected 3 July 1996).

In March 2003 the government comprised:

Prime Minister: Haroun Kabadi (Patriotic Salvation Movement; sworn in 12 June 2002).

Minister of Agriculture: David Houdeingar Ngarimaden. *Civil Service, Labour and Employment:* Abakaka Moustapha Lopa. *Commerce, Industry and Handicrafts:* Mahamat Abdoulaye. *Communications:* Moctar Wawa Dabab. *Culture, Youth and Sports:* Mahamat Zene Bada. *Economic Promotion and Development:* Mahamat Ali Hassan. *Education:* Yokabdjim Mandigui. *Environment and Water Resources:* Oumar Kadjallami Boukar. *Finance:* Idriss Ahamat Idriss. *Foreign Affairs and Co-operation:* Mahamat Saleh Annadif. *Health:* Maina Touka Sahanaye. *Higher Education, Scientific Research and Vocational Training:* Adoum Guemessou. *Interior, Security and Decentralization:* Abderaman Moussa. *Justice:* Djimnaye Koudji Gaou. *Livestock:* Mahamat Allahou Taher. *Mines and Energy:* Lawal Adji Grema. *National Administration:* Abderahman Moussa. *National Defence and Reintegration:* Mahamat Nouri. *National Development, Urban Planning and Housing:* Djimrangar Dadnadji. *Oil Resources:* Ousmane Mahamat Nour Elimi. *Post and Telecommunications:* Routouang Yoma Golom. *Public Security and Immigration:* Mahamat Ali Abdallah. *Public Works and Transport:* Moussa Faki Mahamat. *Social Affairs and Family Affairs:* Agnes Alafi Maimouna. *Tourism:* Akia Abouna.

President's Website (French only): http://www.tit.td/presidence.html

DEFENCE
There are eight military regions. Conscription is for three years. Defence expenditure totalled US$47m. in 2000 (US$6 per capita), representing 2·8% of GDP.

Army. In 1999 the strength was 25,000. In addition there was a paramilitary Gendarmerie of 4,500, and a Republican Guard of 5,000.

Air Force. Personnel (1999) about 350 including four combat aircraft.

INTERNATIONAL RELATIONS

Chad is a member of the UN, WTO, the African Union, African Development Bank, Lake Chad Basin Commission, OIC, the International Organization of the Francophonie, and is an ACP member state of the ACP-EU relationship.

ECONOMY

Agriculture accounted for 39·8% of GDP in 1998, industry 14·3% and services 45·9%.

Currency. The unit of currency is the *franc CFA* (XAF) with a parity of 655·957 francs CFA to one euro. Inflation in 2001 was 12·4%, up from 3·7% in 2000. Foreign exchange reserves were US$154m. in April 2002 and total money supply was 161,104m. francs CFA. Gold reserves were 11,000 troy oz in June 2002.

Budget. Revenues in 1998 were an estimated US$198m. and expenditure US$218m.

Performance. Real GDP growth was 1·0% in 2000 but then 8·5% in 2001, thanks mainly to the acceleration of the construction of an oil pipeline from Chad to Cameroon. The pipeline will allow Chad to export its oil riches to the world market. In 2001 total GDP was US$1·6bn.

Banking and Finance. The *Banque des Etats de l'Afrique Centrale* (*Governor,* Jean-Félix Mamalepot) is the bank of issue, and the principal commercial banks are the *Banque de Développement du Tchad*, the *Banque Tchadienne de Crédit et de Dépôts* and the *Banque Commerciale du Chari*.

ENERGY AND NATURAL RESOURCES

Electricity. Installed capacity was 40,000 kW in 1991. Production in 1998 amounted to 100m. kWh. Consumption per capita was 13 kWh—the lowest in the world—in 1997.

Oil and Gas. The oilfield in Kanem préfecture has been linked by pipeline to a new refinery at N'Djaména but production has remained minimal. There is a larger oilfield in the Doba Basin. In June 2000 the World Bank approved funding for a 1,000-km US$4bn. pipeline to run from 300 new oil wells in Chad through Cameroon to the Atlantic Ocean. With construction well under way, oil revenues are expected to reach US$80m. by 2004 when the first oil from the Doba oilfield is scheduled to flow through the pipeline.

Minerals. Salt (about 4,000 tonnes per annum) is mined around Lake Chad, and there are deposits of uranium, gold, iron ore and bauxite. There are small-scale workings for gold and iron.

Agriculture. Some 80% of the workforce is involved in subsistence agriculture and fisheries. In 1998, 3·50m. ha were arable and 0·03m. ha permanent crops. Cotton growing (in the south) and animal husbandry (in the central zone) are the most important branches. Production, 2000 (in 1,000 tonnes): sorghum, 567; groundnuts, 372; millet, 321; sugarcane, 315; cassava, 255; seed cotton, 235; yams, 230; rice, 131; cottonseed, 125; cotton lint, 90; maize, 87.

Livestock, 2000: cattle, 5,595,000; goats, 5,050,000; sheep, 2,500,000; camels, 715,000; chickens, 5m.

Forestry. In 1995 the area under forests was 11·02m. ha, or 8·8% of the total land area (11·5m. ha and 9·1% in 1990). Timber production in 1999 was 1·97m. cu. metres.

Fisheries. Total catches, from Lake Chad and the Chari and Logone rivers, were approximately 84,000 tonnes in 1999.

INDUSTRY

Output, 1996: cotton fibre, 61,670 tonnes; edible oil, 12·55m. litres; sugar (1998), 31,100 tonnes; beer, 1·17m. litres; cigarettes, 35m. packets; soap, 2,958 tonnes; bicycles, 3,444.

Labour. In 1996 the labour force was 3,145,000 (56% males). In 1994 approximately 70% of the economically active population were engaged in agriculture, fishing and forestry.

INTERNATIONAL TRADE

External debt was US$1,116m. in 2000.

Imports and Exports. Exports in 2000 totalled US$233m. (US$242m. in 1999); imports in 2000 totalled US$450m. (US$474m. in 1999).

The main export markets are Portugal, Germany, Costa Rica and the USA. In 1995 the main import suppliers were France, Cameroon, Nigeria and the USA. Cotton exports in 1994, 28,857m. francs CFA; cattle, 15,401 francs CFA. Apart from cotton and cattle, other important exports are textiles and fish. The principal imports are machinery and transportation equipment, industrial goods, petroleum products and foodstuffs.

COMMUNICATIONS

Roads. In 1996 there were 33,400 km of roads, of which 0·82% were surfaced. Approximately 10,560 passenger cars were in use in 1996, plus 14,550 trucks and vans, and 3,640 motorcycles and mopeds.

Civil Aviation. There is an international airport at N'Djaména, from which there were direct flights in 1998 to Abidjan, Abu Dhabi, Addis Ababa, Bamako, Bangui, Bissau, Brazzaville, Douala, El Fasher, Garoua, Jeddah, Khartoum, Lomé, Niamey, Paris and Yaoundé. In 1999 scheduled airline traffic of Chad-based carriers flew 2·9m. km, carrying 84,000 passengers (all on international flights). In 2000 N'Djaména handled 17,000 passengers and 2,300 tonnes of freight.

Telecommunications. In 1999 telephone main lines numbered 9,700 (1·3 per 1,000 persons). Only the Democratic Republic of the Congo had a lower penetration rate. There were 10,000 PCs in use in 1999 (1·3 per 1,000 persons). Internet users numbered 1,000 in July 2000 and there were 185 fax machines in use in Dec. 1997.

Postal Services. In 1994 there were 34 post offices, or one for every 200,000 persons.

SOCIAL INSTITUTIONS

Justice. There are criminal courts and magistrates courts in N'Djaména, Moundou, Sarh and Abéché, with a Court of Appeal situated in N'Djaména.

The population in penal institutions in 1996 was 2,521 (40 per 100,000 of national population).

Religion. The northern and central parts of the country are predominantly Muslim. In 1999 there were estimated to be 4,070,000 Muslims, 1,540,000 Roman Catholics and 1,090,000 Protestants. Some 560,000 people follow traditional beliefs.

Education. In 1996–97 there were 680,909 pupils in primary schools with 10,151 teachers and there were 99,789 pupils in secondary schools with 2,792 teachers. In 1994–95 there were 2,108 pupils in technical schools and 2,000 at the university, with 120 academic staff. Adult literacy rate was 41·0% in 1999 (male, 50·1%; female, 32·3%).

Health. In 1994 there were 3,962 hospital beds, 217 doctors, 878 nurses, 130 midwives and 10 pharmacists.

Chad has made significant progress in the reduction of undernourishment in the past 20 years. Between 1980 and 1997 the proportion of undernourished people declined from 70% of the population to 38%.

CULTURE

Broadcasting. The state-controlled Radiodiffusion Nationale Tchadienne broadcasts a national and three regional services in French, Arabic and Sara. There were estimated to be 1·7m. radio sets in 1997. Television is being developed (colour by SECAM V) by the state-controlled Télé-Tchad, and there were 10,000 TV receivers in 1997.

Press. In 1996 there was one daily newspaper with a circulation of 2,000, giving a rate of one per 2,500 inhabitants.

Tourism. There were 11,000 foreign tourists in 1998, bringing revenue of US$10m.

DIPLOMATIC REPRESENTATIVES
Of Chad in the United Kingdom
Ambassador: Abderahim Yacoub Ndiaye (resides at Brussels).

Of the United Kingdom in Chad
Ambassador: Richard Wildash, LVO (resides at Yaoundé, Cameroon).

Of Chad in the USA (2002 R. St., NW, Washington, D.C., 20009)
Ambassador: Hassaballah Ahmat Soubiane.

Of the USA in Chad (Ave. Felix Eboue, N'Djaména)
Ambassador: Christopher E. Goldthwait.

Of Chad to the United Nations
Ambassador: Koumtog Laotegguelnodji.

Of Chad to the European Union
Ambassador: Abderahim Yacoub Ndiaye.

FURTHER READING
Joffe, Emille and Day-Viaud, Valerie (eds.) *Chad.* [Bibliography] ABC-Clio, Oxford and Santa Barbara (CA), 1995

National statistical office: Direction de la Statistique des Etudes Economiques et Démographiques, Ministère du Plan et de la Cooperation, N'Djaména.

CHILE

República de Chile

Capital: Santiago (Administrative),
Valparaíso (Legislative)
Population estimate, 2000: 15·21m.
GDP per capita, 2000: (PPP$) 9,417
HDI/world rank: 0·831/38

KEY HISTORICAL EVENTS

Magellan sighted what is now Chile in 1520. Subsequently Spaniards colonized the land in the 1530s and 1540s, defeating the Incas in the north and subjugating the Araucanian Indians in the South. In 1810 the Republic of Chile threw off allegiance to the Spanish crown. However, there were seven years of fighting before Chile was recognized as an independent republic. A constitution was adopted in 1883, and the country enjoyed stable government. In 1925 the constitution was amended to strengthen the executive at the expense of the legislature. In 1970 Dr Salvador Allende Gossens was elected president as the Marxist leader of a left-wing coalition. This government was overthrown in 1973 by a military junta headed by Gen. Augusto Pinochet Ugarte. President Allende died in the course of the coup and tens of thousands of his supporters were murdered. A new constitution came into force on 11 March 1981 providing for a return to democracy. Gen. Pinochet continued as head of state until 1989 and army commander until March 1998 when he claimed his constitutional right to become a senator for life (and hence immune from prosecution). While clearing the way for much-needed economic reforms, the Pinochet regime was responsible for wholesale human rights abuses, a legacy which had its consequences in 1999 when Pinochet, in Britain for medical treatment, was held on human rights charges instigated by Spain. On 2 March 2000 he returned to Chile after the British government ruled he was too ill to be extradited to Spain to face torture charges.

TERRITORY AND POPULATION

Chile is bounded in the north by Peru, east by Bolivia and Argentina, and south and west by the Pacific Ocean. The area is 756,096 sq. km (291,928 sq. miles) excluding the claimed Antarctic territory. Many islands to the west and south belong to Chile: the Islas Juan Fernández (147 sq. km with 488 inhabitants in 1992) lie about 600 km west of Valparaíso, and the volcanic Isla de Pascua (Easter Island or Rapa Nui, 164 sq. km with 2,764 inhabitants in 1992), lies about 3,000 km west-northwest of Valparaíso. Small uninhabited dependencies include Sala y Gomez (400 km east of Easter Is.), San Félix and San Ambrosio (1,000 km northwest of Valparaíso, and 20 km apart) and Islas Diego Ramírez (100 km southwest of Cape Horn).

In 1940 Chile declared, and in each subsequent year has reaffirmed, its ownership of the sector of the Antarctic lying between 53° and 90° W. long., and asserted that the British claim to the sector between the meridians 20° and 80° W. long. overlapped the Chilean by 27°. Seven Chilean bases exist in Antarctica. A law of 1955 put the governor of Magallanes in charge of the 'Chilean Antarctic Territory' which has an area of 1,250,000 sq. km and a population (1992) of 1,945.

The population at the census of 1992 was 13,348,401 (6,795,147 females). Estimate, 2002, 15,773,504 (86·2% urban in 2002; 7,869,161 females in 2002); density, 21 per sq. km.

The UN gives a projected population for 2010 of 17·01m.

Area, population and capitals of the 13 regions:

Region	Sq. km	Population (June 2002)	Capital	Population (June 2002)
Aisén del Gral. Carlos Ibáñez del Campo	108,494	87,789	Coihaique	43,044
De Antofagasta	126,049	436,744	Antofagasta	257,207
De La Araucanía	31,842	826,308	Temuco	287,326
De Atacama	75,176	250,163	Copiapó	127,504
Del Bíobío	37,063	1,830,651	Concepción	391,733

Region	Sq. km	Population (June 2002)	Capital	Population (June 2002)
De Coquimbo	40,580	536,216	La Serena	135,526
Del Libertador Gral B. O'Higgins	16,387	737,047	Rancagua	221,881
De Los Lagos	67,013	1,004,929	Puerto Montt	144,880
De Magallanes y de la Antártica Chilena	132,297	151,355	Punta Arenas	126,586
Del Maule	30,296	872,011	Talca	187,513
Metropolitana de Santiago	15,403	5,641,811	Santiago	4,886,629
De Tarapacá	59,099	366,257	Iquique	175,677
De Valparaíso	16,396	1,469,148	Valparaíso	285,389

Other large towns (June 2002 populations) are: Puente Alto (458,906), Viña del Mar (350,221), Talcahuano (288,666), San Bernardo (262,623), Arica (189,743), Chillán (176,863), Coquimbo (141,796), Osorno (135,204) and Calama (135,526). 69·7% of the population is mixed or mestizo, 20% are of European descent and 10·3% declared themselves to be indigenous Amerindians of the Araucanian, Fuegian and Chango groups. Language and culture remain of European origin, with 998,385 Araucanian-speaking (mainly Mapuche) Indians the only sizeable minority.

The official language is Spanish.

SOCIAL STATISTICS
2000 births, 248,893; deaths, 78,814; marriages, 66,607. Rates, 2000 (per 1,000 population): birth, 17·2; death, 5·2. Divorce is illegal, as is abortion. Annual population growth rate, 1990–99, 1·25%. Infant mortality, 2000 (per 1,000 live births), 8·9. In 2000 the most popular age range for marrying was 25–29 for males and 20–24 for females. Expectation of life at birth (1999): males 72·5 years, females 78·5 years. Chile has the highest life expectancy in South America. Fertility rate, 2000, 2·1 children per woman.

CLIMATE
With its enormous range of latitude and the influence of the Andean Cordillera, the climate of Chile is very complex, ranging from extreme aridity in the north, through a Mediterranean climate in Central Chile, where winters are wet and summers dry, to a cool temperate zone in the south, with rain at all seasons. In the extreme south, conditions are very wet and stormy. Santiago, Jan. 67°F (19·5°C), July 46°F (8°C). Annual rainfall 15" (375 mm). Antofagasta, Jan. 69°F (20·6°C), July 57°F (14°C). Annual rainfall 0·5" (12·7 mm). Valparaíso, Jan. 64°F (17·8°C), July 53°F (11·7°C). Annual rainfall 20" (505 mm).

CONSTITUTION AND GOVERNMENT
A new Constitution was approved by 67·5% of the voters on 11 Sept. 1980 and came into force on 11 March 1981. It provided for a return to democracy after a minimum period of eight years. Gen. Pinochet would remain in office during this period after which the government would nominate a single candidate for President. At a plebiscite on 5 Oct. 1988 President Pinochet was rejected as a presidential candidate by 54·6% of votes cast.

The *President* is directly elected for a non-renewable six-year term. Parliament consists of a 120-member *Chamber of Deputies* and a *Senate* of 48 members.

Santiago is the administrative capital of Chile, but since 11 March 1990 Valparaíso has been the legislative capital.

National Anthem. 'Dulce patria, recibe los votos' ('Sweet Fatherland, receive the vows'); words by E. Lillo, tune by Ramón Carnicer.

RECENT ELECTIONS
In the presidential run-off held on 16 Jan. 2000 leftist Ricardo Lagos (Party for Democracy/PPD) polled 51·3%, defeating the conservative Joaquín Lavin (Independent Democratic Union/UDI). Four other candidates had participated in the first round of voting on 12 Dec. 1999.

In elections to the Chamber of Deputies on 16 Dec. 2001 the Independent Democratic Union (UDI) won 35 seats, the Christian Democratic Party (PDC) 24,

National Renewal 22, Party for Democracy 21, the Socialist Party (PS) 11 and the Social Democratic Radical Party 6. Member parties of the Concertation of Parties for Democracy/CPD (PDC, PPD, PS and PRSD) won 62 of the 120 seats (with 47·9% of votes cast) against 57 seats (44·3%) for the Alliance for Chile/APC (UDI, RN). After partial elections to the Senate on the same day the composition in the Senate was: PDC, 12; UDI, 11; RN, 7; PS, 5; PPD, 3; appointed members, 10.

CURRENT ADMINISTRATION

In March 2003 the CPD government comprised:

President: Ricardo Lagos; b. 1938 (PPD; sworn in 11 March 2000).

Minister of Agriculture: Jaime Campos Quiroga. *Defence:* Michelle Bachelet Jeria. *Economy and Energy:* Jorge Rodríguez Grossi. *Education:* Sergio Bitar Chacra. *Finance:* Nicolás Eyzaguire Guzmán. *Foreign Affairs:* María Soledad Alvear Valenzuela. *Health:* Pedro García Aspillaga. *Housing and National Assets:* Jaime Ravinet de la Fuente. *Interior:* José Miguel Insulza Salinas. *Justice:* Luis Bates Hidalgo. *Mining:* Alfonso Dulanto Rencoret. *Labour and Social Security:* Ricardo Solari Saaverdra. *Planning and Co-operation:* Andrés Palma Irarrazabal. *Public Works, Transportation and Telecommunications:* Javier Etcheberry Celhay. *National Women's Service:* Cecilia Pérez Díaz. *General Secretary of the Government:* Francisco Vidal Salinas. *General Secretary of the Presidency:* Francisco Huenchumilla Jaramillo.

Government Website (Spanish only): http://www.gobiernodechile.cl/

DEFENCE

Military service is for one year in the Army and two in the Navy and Air Force. Plans for weapons' modernization amounting to nearly US$2bn., which would benefit both the army and the air force, were announced in April 1998.

In 2000 defence expenditure totalled US$2,891m. (US$190 per capita), representing 3·4% of GDP. In 1985 defence spending had accounted for 10·6% of GDP.

Army. A modernization plan of 1995 provided for the transformation of the seven Army divisions into three garrisons—North, Centre-South and Austral—independent and adapted to the terrains in which they operate. Strength (1999): 51,000 (27,000 conscripts) with 50,000 reserves. There is a 29,500-strong paramilitary force of Carabineros.

Navy. The principal ships of the Navy are three ex-British destroyers, four diesel submarines and three frigates. There is a Naval Air Service numbering 600 personnel with no combat aircraft.

Naval personnel in 1999 totalled 29,000 (2,100 conscripts) including 2,700 marines and 1,300 Coast Guard. There are HQ's at Valaparaíso, Talacahuano, Puerto Montt, Punta Arenas, Puerto Williams and Iquique.

Air Force. Strength (1999) was 13,000 personnel (1,500 conscripts). There are 90 combat aircraft made up largely of Mirage jets.

INTERNATIONAL RELATIONS

Chile is a member of the UN, WTO, OAS, Inter-American Development Bank, LAIA, APEC, IOM and the Antarctic Treaty, and has a free trade agreement with Mercosur.

ECONOMY

Agriculture and fisheries accounted for 5·6% of GDP in 1998, mining 8·4%, industry 27·1% and services 58·9%.

According to the anti-corruption organization *Transparency International*, Chile ranked 17th in the world in a 2002 survey of the countries with the least corruption in business and government. It received 7·5 out of 10 in the annual index, making it Latin America's least corrupt nation.

Currency. The unit of currency is the *Chilean peso* (CLP) of 100 *centavos.* The peso was revalued 3·5% against the US dollar in Nov. 1994. In Sept. 1999 the managed exchange-rate system was abandoned and the peso allowed to float. Inflation was 2·8% in 2002. In June 2002 gold reserves were 12,000 troy oz (1·22m.

troy oz in Jan. 2000); foreign exchange reserves were US$14,612m. Total money supply in June 2002 was 3,722·29bn. pesos.

Budget. The fiscal year is the calendar year.
Central government revenue and expenditure (in 1bn. pesos):

	1997	1998	1999	2000	2001
Revenue	7,525·4	7,907·0	7,910·1	9,114·5	9,795·6
Expenditure	6,902·2	7,775·2	8,412·4	9,058·1	9,908·2

VAT is 16–18%.

Performance. Real GDP growth averaged 7·7% between 1991 and 1997, leading to Chile being labelled the 'tiger of South America'. In 1998 GDP growth was 3·2%. In 1999 the economy contracted by 1·0%, but there was then growth of 4·4% in 2000 and 2·8% in 2001. Total GDP in 2001 was US$63·5bn.

Banking and Finance. Banking is regulated by legislation of 1995. There is a Central Bank and a State Bank. The Central Bank was made independent of government control in March 1990. The *President* is Carlos Massad Abud. There were 13 domestic and 23 foreign banks in 20016. In Dec. 2001 deposits in domestic banks totalled 17,440,672m. pesos; in foreign banks, 6,062,888m. pesos, and in other finance companies, 184,226m. pesos.

There are stock exchanges in Santiago and Valparaíso.

Weights and Measures. The metric system has been legally established since 1865, but the old Spanish weights and measures are still in use to some extent.

ENERGY AND NATURAL RESOURCES

Environment. According to the *World Bank Atlas* Chile's carbon dioxide emissions in 1998 were the equivalent of 4·1 tonnes per capita.

Electricity. Installed capacity was 10·4m. kW in 2000. Production of electricity was 41·3bn. kWh in 2000, of which just over 46% was hydro-electric. Consumption per capita in 2000 was 2,406 kWh.

Oil and Gas. Production of crude oil, 2000, was 270,000 tonnes. Gas production, 2000, was 106 petajoules.

Minerals. The wealth of the country consists chiefly in its minerals. Chile is the world's largest copper producer; copper is the most important source of foreign exchange and government revenues. Production, 2000, 4,617,885 tonnes. Coal is low-grade and difficult to mine, and mining is made possible by state subsidies. Production, 2000, 503,350 tonnes.

Output of other minerals, 2000 (in tonnes): iron, 8,728,927; limestone, 5,395,215; iron pellets, 4,502,456; manganese, 41,716; lignite (1997), 36,000; zinc (1995), 34,457; molybdenum, 33,639; salt, 5,082,911; gold, 39,407 kg; silver, 1,239 tonnes. Lithium, nitrate, iodine and sodium sulphate are also produced.

Agriculture. In 1998, 1·98m. ha of land was arable and 0·32m. ha permanent crops. 1·8m. ha were irrigated in 1998. Some 54,000 tractors were in use in 1998.
Principal crops were as follows:

Crop	Area harvested, 1,000 ha 2000	Production, 1,000 tonnes 2000	Crop	Area harvested, 1,000 ha 2000	Production, 1,000 tonnes 2000
Sugarbeets	46	2,882	Oats	89	344
Wheat	407	1,746	Onions	6	282
Tomatoes	22	1,267	Rice	28	143
Potatoes	63	1,210	Pumpkins	5	100
Maize	82	778	Carrots	4	97

Fruit production, 2000 (in 1,000 tonnes): apples, 1,135; grapes, 935; peaches and nectarines, 250; pears, 230; plums, 205; lemons and limes, 120; oranges, 92. 660,000 tonnes of wine were produced in 2000.

Livestock, 2000: cattle, 3,900,000; sheep, 3,800,000; pigs, 1,900,000; goats, 760,000; horses, 400,000; poultry, 42m. Livestock products, 2000 (in 1,000 tonnes): pork, bacon and ham, 265; beef and veal, 226; poultry meat, 378; milk, 1,990; eggs, 95.

Since 1985 agricultural trade has been consistently in surplus. Wine exports rose from US$52m. in 1990 to US$593m. in 2001.

Forestry. In 1997, 20·7% of the total land area was under forests. There were 13·4m. ha of natural forest and woodland (larch, araucaria, lenga, coihue, oak are important species) and 2·1m. ha of planted forest. Deforestation between 1990 and 1995 had resulted in an average loss of 29,000 ha each year. Timber production in 2001 was 25·7m. cu. metres.

Fisheries. Chile has 4,200 km of coastline and exclusive fishing rights to 1·6m. sq. km. There are 220 species of edible fish. In 1990 the fishing fleet comprised 250 vessels over 100 GRT, totalling 111,140 GRT. The catch in 2001 was 4,150,966 tonnes and came entirely from sea fishing. Exports of fishery commodities in 2000 were valued at US$1·78bn., against imports of US$47·96m. Fish farms produced 99,300 tonnes of salmon in 2001.

INDUSTRY

The leading companies by market capitalization in Chile, excluding banking and finance, in Jan. 2002 were: Compañía de Petróleos de Chile SA (COPEC), 3trn. pesos; Compañía de Telecomunicaciones de Chile SA (Telefónica CTC Chile), 2trn. pesos; and Endesa Chile (Empresa Nacional de Electricida SA), 2trn. pesos.

Output of major products in 2001 (in 1,000 tonnes): cement, 2,832·7; cellulose, 1,373·4; fishmeal, 503·4; sugar, 476·3; iron or steel plates, 403·1; newsprint, 225·4; paper and cardboard, 112·6; beer, 337·4m. litres; motor vehicles, 21,574 items (1995); motor tyres, 3·25m. units.

Labour. In 2001 there were 5,326,370 people in employment (1,738,120 women). In Dec. 2001, 1,497,620 persons were employed in social or personal services, 1,011,360 in trade, 756,830 in manufacturing, 704,390 in agriculture, forestry and fisheries, 413,380 in building and 427,080 in transport and communications. In 2001 there was a monthly minimum wage of 105,500 pesos. In Jan. 2001, 9·1% of the workforce was unemployed, up from 6·1% in 1997 although down from a peak of 11·4% in Aug. 1999.

Trade Unions. Trade unions were established in the mid-1880s.

INTERNATIONAL TRADE

In Sept. 1991 Chile and Mexico signed the free trade Treaty of Santiago envisaging annual tariff reductions of 10% from Jan. 1992. On 1 Oct. 1996 Chile joined the Mercosur free trade zone, but continues to act unilaterally in trade with third countries.

Foreign debt was US$38,032m. in 2001.

Imports and Exports. Trade in US$1m.:

	1997	1998	1999	2000	2001
Imports	19,663·4	18,780·5	15,147·8	18,089·9	17,180·8
Exports	16,654·1	15,076·3	16,255·7	18,425·8	17,658·7

In 2001 the principal exports were (in US$1m.): manufactures, 8,304·9; minerals, 7,510·2 (of which copper, 6,673·4, equivalent to 37·8% of all exports); agricultural products, 1,710·8. Major export markets (in US$1m.), 2001: USA, 3,451·4; Japan, 2,140·2; UK, 1,231·4; China, 1,069·6; Brazil, 834·6; Mexico, 828·1; Italy, 800·8. Major import suppliers (in US$1m.), 2001: Argentina, 3,063·8; USA, 2,888·7; Brazil, 1,498·6; China, 1,052·9; Germany, 699·2.

COMMUNICATIONS

Roads. In 2001 there were 79,605 km of roads, but only 20·2% were hard-surfaced. There were 2,132 km of motorways and 16,056 km of main roads. In 2001 there were 1,172,572 private cars, 747,311 trucks and vans, 160,586 buses and coaches and 41,271 motorcycles and mopeds.

Rail. The total length of state railway (EFE) lines was (2001) 4,024 km, including 1,051 km electrified, of broad- and metre-gauge. EFE is now mainly a passenger carrier, and carried 16·1m. passengers in 2001. Freight operations are in the hands of the semi-private companies Ferronor, which carried 5·9m. tonnes in 2001, and

Pacifico, which carried 5·5m. tonnes in 2001. The Antofagasta (Chili) and Bolivia Railway (973 km, metre-gauge) links the port of Antofagasta with Bolivia and Argentina, and carried 3·5m. tonnes in 2001. Passenger-km travelled in 2001 came to 1,105m. and freight tonne-km to 925m.

There is a metro in Santiago (40·4 km).

Civil Aviation. There are 389 airports, with an international airport at Santiago (Comodoro Arturo Merino Benítez). The largest airline is Línea Aérea Nacional Chile (Lan-Chile), which in 2001 flew 70·3m. km and carried 5,046,600 passengers, followed by Línea Aérea de Colore (Ladeco), which in 1998 flew 15·1m. km and carried 1,148,100 passengers. In 2000 Santiago handled 5,778,000 passengers (3,187,000 on international flights) and 292,800 tonnes of freight.

Shipping. The mercantile marine in 2001 totalled 647,820 GRT, including oil tankers 160,179 GRT. The five major ports, Valparaíso, San Antonio, Antofagasta, Arica and Iquique, are state-owned; there are 11 smaller private ports. Valparaíso, the largest port, handled 4,469,302 tonnes of freight in 2001.

Telecommunications. In 2001 there were 3,505,000 telephone main lines, equivalent to 227·6 for every 1,000 persons, and there were 1·5m. PCs in use (97·4 for every 1,000 persons). There were approximately 1·8m. Internet users in Feb. 2001. Mobile phone subscribers numbered 4·2m. in 2001 and there were 40,000 fax machines in 1997.

Postal Services. In 2002 there were 752 post offices.

SOCIAL INSTITUTIONS

Justice. There are a High Court of Justice in the capital, 17 courts of appeal distributed over the republic, courts of first instance in the departmental capitals and second-class judges in the sub-delegations.

The population in penal institutions in Dec. 2002 was 36,214 (232 per 100,000 of national population).

The death penalty for ordinary crimes was abolished in 2001.

Religion. In 1997 Chile had an estimated 11·37m. Roman Catholics. In Jan. 2002 there were 3 cardinal archbishops, 5 archbishops, 25 bishops and 2 vicars apostolic. 13·2% of the population defined themselves as evangelical. There were 478,000 Latter-day Saints in 1998 and 130,000 Jews in 1991.

Education. In 2001 there were 287,196 pupils at pre-primary schools; 146,918 teachers (imparting primary and/or secondary education) for 2·36m. primary school pupils; and 850,713 pupils at secondary level. Adult literacy rate in 2000 was 95·8% (male, 95·9%; female, 95·6%).

In 2001 there were 479,487 students in higher education. There were 60 universities with 339,200 students, 51 professional institutes with 86,392 students and 111 technical education centres with 53,895 students.

In 1998 total expenditure on education came to 3·5% of GNP and represented 15·3% of total government expenditure.

Health. There were 846 hospitals and 19,000 doctors in 2002, and 1,012 dentists in the national health service and 3,677 university nurses in 2000.

Welfare. The Pension Fund Administration was founded in 1981. Employees are required to save 13% of their pay. In May 2002 it had 6,477,244 members and assets of 24,016,805m. pesos. In 1995 about 25% of adults had private health insurance.

CULTURE

Broadcasting. In 2002 there were 1,341 radio broadcasting stations (including repeaters), 1,173 FM and 168 AM. In Sept. 1999 there were five television channels operating in UHF frequencies on the national territory. 18 other channels were operating on VHF through 400 frequencies. Both data included four university channels (3 VHF and 1 UHF frequency). In Dec. 2002 the Televisión Nacional de Chile covered the whole of the country through 170 transmitters. In 1997 there were 5·18m. radio and 3·15m. TV sets.

Press. In 2002 there were 76 national daily newspapers; in 1996 Chile's newspapers had a combined circulation of 1·4m.

Tourism. There were 1,723,107 foreign visitors in 2001. Tourist receipts were US$788m. in 2001.

DIPLOMATIC REPRESENTATIVES
Of Chile in the United Kingdom (12 Devonshire St., London, W1G 7DS)
Ambassador: Mariano Fernández.

Of the United Kingdom in Chile (Av. El Bosque Norte 0125, Piso 2, Las Condes, Santiago)
Ambassador: Greg Faulkner.

Of Chile in the USA (1732 Massachusetts Ave., NW, Washington, D.C., 20036)
Ambassador: Andrés Bianchi Larre.

Of the USA in Chile (Av. Andrés Bello 2800, Las Condes, Santiago)
Ambassador: William R. Brownfield.

Of Chile to the United Nations
Ambassador: Juan Gabriel Valdés Soublette.

Of Chile to the European Union
Ambassador: Alberto Van Klaveren Stork.

FURTHER READING
Banco Central de Chile. *Boletín Mensual.*
Bethell, L. (ed.) *Chile since Independence.* CUP, 1993
Collier, S. and Sater, W. F., *A History of Chile, 1808–1994.* CUP, 1996
Hickman, J., *News From the End of the Earth: A Portrait of Chile.* Hurst, London, 1998
Hojman, D. E., *Chile: the Political Economy of Development and Democracy in the 1990s.* London, 1993.—(ed.) *Change in the Chilean Countryside: from Pinochet to Aylwin and Beyond.* London, 1993
Oppenheim, L. H., *Politics in Chile: Democracy, Authoritarianism and the Search for Development.* Boulder (CO), 1993

National statistical office: Instituto Nacional de Estadísticas (INE), Santiago.
Website (Spanish only): http://www.ine.cl/

CHINA

Zhonghua Renmin Gonghe Guo
(People's Republic of China)

Capital: Beijing (Peking)
Population estimate, 2000: 1,275·1m
GDP per capita, 2000: (PPP$) 3,976
HDI/world rank: 0·726/96

KEY HISTORICAL EVENTS

An embryonic Chinese state emerged in the fertile Huang He (Yellow River) basin before 4000 BC. Chinese culture reached the Chang Jiang (Yangtze) basin by 2500 BC and within 500 years the far south was also within the Chinese orbit. About 1500 BC writing developed using recognizable Chinese characters. Around 1000 BC under the Zhou dynasty, a centralized administration developed. In about 500 BC a court official, Kongfuzi (Confucius), outlined his vision of society. Confucianism, which introduced a system of civil service recruitment through examination, remained the principal Chinese belief system until the mid-20th century.

In 221 BC the ruler of the Warring State of Qin became the first emperor of China. He built an empire extending from the South China Sea to the edge of Central Asia, where work was begun on the Great Wall of China. The Qin dynasty standardized laws, money and administration throughout the empire but it was short-lived. By 206 BC the state had divided into three.

Reunification came gradually under the Han dynasty (202 BC–AD 200), then the Jin (265–316) and Sui (589–612) dynasties, interspersed by a period of inter-state war and anarchy. Reunification was achieved by the Tang dynasty, whose rule brought new prosperity to China from 618–917. Eventually the Tang empire too collapsed as separatism grew.

In 1126 nomads from Manchuria invaded the north, defeating the Song dynasty (960–1127) north of the Chang Jiang. The northern invaders were overthrown by the Mongols, led by Genghis Khan (c. 1162–1227), who went on to claim the rest of China. In 1280 their ruler Kublai Khan (1251–94), who had founded the Yuan dynasty in 1271, swept into southern China. The Mongol Yuan dynasty adopted Chinese ways but was overthrown by a nationalist uprising in 1368 which established the Ming dynasty.

The Ming empire collapsed in a peasants' revolt in 1644. Within months the peasants' leader was swept aside by the invasion of the Manchus, whose Qing dynasty ruled China until 1911.

Preoccupied with threats from the north, China neglected its southern coastal frontier where European traders were attempting to open up the country. The Portuguese, who landed on the Chinese coast in 1516, were followed by the Dutch in 1622 and the English in 1637. In the two Opium Wars (1838–42; 1856–58), Britain forced China to allow the import of opium from India into China, while Britain, France, Germany and other European states gained concessions in 'treaty ports' that virtually came under foreign rule. In 1860 British and French forces invaded Beijing and burnt the imperial palace. Defeat in the Sino-Japanese War (1894–95) resulted in the loss of Taiwan and Korea.

The xenophobic Boxer Rebellion, led by members of a secret society called the Fists of Righteous Harmony, broke out in 1900. The Guangxu emperor (1875–1908) attempted modernization in the Hundred Days Reform, but was taken captive by the conservative dowager empress who harnessed the Boxer Rebellion to her own ends. The rebellion was put down by European troops in 1901. China was then divided into zones of influence between the major European states and Japan.

The turning point came in 1911 when a revolution led by the Kuomintang (Guomintang or Nationalist movement) of Sun Yet-sen (Sun Zhong Shan; 1866–1925) overthrew the emperor. In 1916 Sun founded a republic in southern China on Soviet lines. After Sun's death the nationalist movement was taken over by his ally Chiang Kai-shek (Jiang Jie Shi; 1887–1976). In April 1927 he tried to suppress the Chinese Communist Party in a bloody campaign in which thousands of Communists were slaughtered. The remains of the party fled to the far western province of Jiangxi, beyond the reach of the Nationalists. In 1928 Chiang's army entered Beijing. With the greater part of the country reunited under Chiang's rule, he formed a government in Nanjing, which became the capital of China.

In 1934 the Communists were forced to retreat from Jiangxi province. Led by Mao Zedong (Mao Tse-tung; 1893–1976) they trekked for more than a year on the 5,600-mile Long March. Harried during their journey, they were besieged by the Nationalists when they eventually took refuge in Shaanxi province.

Against this backdrop of civil unrest, the Japanese invaded Manchuria in 1931, and by 1937 they had seized Beijing and most of coastal China. At the end of the World War II, the Soviet sponsored Communist Party marched into Manchuria beginning a civil war. On 1 Oct. 1949 Mao declared the People's Republic of China in Beijing. Chiang fled with the remains of his Nationalist forces to the island of Taiwan, where he established a rival Chinese administration. It was not until 1978 that the USA recognized the People's Republic of China.

In 1950 China invaded Tibet. China posted 'volunteers' to fight alongside Communist North Korea during the Korean War (1950–53). There were clashes on the Soviet border in the 1950s and the Indian border in the 1960s. A Soviet-style five-year plan was put into action in 1953, but the two Communist powers fell out over their different interpretations of Marxist orthodoxy. Chinese research into atomic weapons culminated in the testing of the first Chinese atomic bomb in 1964.

Mao introduced the collectivization of farms in 1955. In 1956 he encouraged intellectual debate letting a 'hundred flowers bloom'. However, the new freedoms led to the questioning of the role of the party. Strict controls were reimposed and free-thinkers were sent to work in the countryside to be 're-educated'. In May 1958 Mao launched another ill-fated policy, the Great Leap Forward. To promote rapid industrialization and socialism, the collectives were reorganized into larger units. Neither the resources nor trained labour were available for this huge task. As relations with the Soviet Union cooled, a rapprochement with the United States was achieved in the early 1970s.

By the mid-1960s, Mao became the centre of a personality cult. Mao's 'Thoughts' were published in the 'Little Red Book'. In 1964 Mao set the Cultural Revolution in motion. Anyone who lacked enthusiasm for Mao Zedong Thought was denounced. After Mao's death in 1976, the Gang of Four, led by Mao's widow Chang Ch'ing, attempted to seize power. After these hard-liners were denounced and arrested, China came under the control of Deng Xiaoping, who emphasized economic reform. The country was opened to Western investment. Special Economic Zones and 'open cities' were designated and private enterprise gradually returned.

Greatly improved standards of living and a thriving economy increased expectations for civil liberties. The demand for political change climaxed in demonstrations by workers and students in April 1989, following the funeral of Communist Party leader Hu Yaobang. In Beijing the demonstrators were evicted from Tiananmen Square by the military who opened fire, killing more than 1,500. Hard-liners took control of the government, and martial law was imposed from May 1989 to Jan. 1990. Since then a more liberal regime has focused on economic development. Hong Kong was returned to China from British rule in 1997 and Macao from Portuguese rule in 1999. The late 1990s saw a cautious extension of civil liberties.

For the background to the handover of Hong Kong in 1997, see p. 459.

TERRITORY AND POPULATION

China is bounded in the north by Russia and Mongolia; east by North Korea, the Yellow Sea and the East China Sea, with Hong Kong and Macao as enclaves on the southeast coast; south by Vietnam, Laos, Myanmar, India, Bhutan and Nepal; west by India, Pakistan, Afghanistan, Tajikistan, Kyrgyzstan and Kazakhstan. The total area (including Taiwan, Hong Kong and Macao) is estimated at 9,574,000 sq. km (3,696,500 sq. miles). A law of Feb. 1992 claimed the Spratly, Paracel and Diaoyutasi Islands. An agreement of 7 Sept. 1993 at prime ministerial level settled Sino-Indian border disputes which had first emerged in the war of 1962.

At the 1990 census the population was 1,130,510,638 (548,690,231 females). Population estimate, 1998: 1,248·10m. (611·81m. female); density, 143 per sq. km.

In 1999, 68·4% of the population were rural. The most recent census took place in Oct.–Nov. 2000, involving 6m. census officials.

The UN gives a projected population for 2010 of 1,366·2m.

China is set to lose its status as the world's most populous country to India by 2040, and according to UN projections its population will begin to decline between 2035 and 2040.

1979 regulations restricting married couples to a single child, a policy enforced by compulsory abortions and economic sanctions, have been widely ignored, and it was admitted in 1988 that the population target of 1,200m. by 2000 would have to be revised to 1,270m. Since 1988 peasant couples have been permitted a second child after four years if the first born is a girl, a measure to combat infanticide. In 1999 China started to implement a more widespread gradual relaxation of the one-child policy.

43·2m. persons of Chinese origin lived abroad in 1993.

A number of widely divergent varieties of Chinese are spoken. The official 'Modern Standard Chinese' is based on the dialect of North China. Mandarin in one form or another is spoken by 800m. people in China, or around 63% of the population. The Wu language and its dialects has some 90m. native speakers and Cantonese 70m. The ideographic writing system of 'characters' is uniform throughout the country, and has undergone systematic simplification. In 1958 a phonetic alphabet (*Pinyin*) was devised to transcribe the characters, and in 1979 this was officially adopted for use in all texts in the Roman alphabet. The previous transcription scheme (Wade) is still used in Taiwan and Hong Kong.

China is administratively divided into 22 provinces, five autonomous regions (originally entirely or largely inhabited by ethnic minorities, though in some regions now outnumbered by Han immigrants) and four government-controlled municipalities. These are in turn divided into 335 prefectures, 666 cities (of which 218 are at prefecture level and 445 at county level), 2,142 counties and 717 urban districts.

Government-controlled municipalities	Area (in 1,000 sq. km)	Population (1990 census, in 1,000)	Density per sq. km (in 1987)	Population (1997 estimate, in 1,000)	Capital
Beijing	16·8	10,870	644	12,400	—
Chongqing	82·4	...	...	30,420	—
Shanghai	6·2	13,510	2,152	14,570	—
Tianjin	11·3	8,830	777	9,530	—
Provinces					
Anhui	139·9	52,290	402	61,270	Hefei
Fujian	123·1	30,610	244	32,820	Fuzhou
Gansu[1]	366·5	22,930	61	24,940	Lanzhou
Guangdong[1]	197·1	63,210	319	70,510	Guangzhou
Guizhou[1]	174·0	32,730	186	35,550	Guiyang
Hainan[1]	34·3	6,420	191	7,430	Haikou
Hebei[1]	202·7	60,280	301	65,250	Shijiazhuang
Heilongjiang[1]	463·6	34,770	76	37,510	Harbin
Henan	167·0	86,140	512	92,430	Zhengzhou
Hubei[1]	187·5	54,760	288	58,730	Wuhan
Hunan[1]	210·5	60,600	288	64,650	Changsha
Jiangsu	102·6	68,170	654	71,480	Nanjing
Jiangxi	164·8	38,280	229	41,500	Nanchang
Jilin[1]	187·0	25,150	132	26,280	Changchun
Liaoning[1]	151·0	39,980	261	41,380	Shenyang
Qinghai[1]	721·0	4,430	6	4,960	Xining
Shaanxi	195·8	32,470	168	36,060	Xian
Shandong	153·3	83,430	551	87,850	Jinan
Shanxi	157·1	28,180	183	31,410	Taiyuan
Sichuan[1]	546·0	106,370	188	114,300[2]	Chengdu
Yunnan[1]	436·2	36,750	85	40,420	Kunming
Zhejiang[1]	101·8	40,840	407	44,350	Hangzhou
Autonomous regions					
Guangxi Zhuang	220·4	42,530	192	46,330	Nanning
Inner Mongolia	1,177·5	21,110	18	23,260	Hohhot
Ningxia Hui	66·4	4,660	70	5,300	Yinchuan

Autonomous regions	Area (in 1,000 sq. km)	Population (1990 census, in 1,000)	Density per sq. km (in 1987)	Population (1997 estimate, in 1,000)	Capital
Tibet[3]	1,221·6	2,220	2	2,480	Lhasa
Xinjiang Uighur	1,646·9	15,370	9	17,180	Urumqi

[1]Also designated minority nationality autonomous area.
[2]1996 figure. [3]See also Tibet below.

Population of largest cities in 1995: Shanghai, 12·91m. (1999 figure); Beijing (Peking), 10·82m. (1999 figure); Tianjin, 8·97m.; Shenyang, 4·74m.; Wuhan, 4·45m.; Chongqing, 4·07m.; Guangzhou (Canton), 3·91m.; Chengdu, 3·12m.; Xian, 2·99m.; Harbin, 2·96m.; Nanjing, 2·67m.; Changchun, 2·60m.; Zibo, 2·58m.; Dalian, 2·55m.; Jinan, 2·48m.; Taiyuan, 2·32m.; Qingdao, 2·21m.; Linyi, 2·08m.; Guiyang, 2·05m.; Jinxi, 1·93m.; Liupanshui, 1·93m.; Zaozhuang, 1·92m.; Zhengzhou, 1·90m.; Handan, 1·88m.; Lanzhou, 1·67m.; Kunming, 1·66m.; Liuan, 1·64m.; Tianmen, 1·62m.; Hangzhou, 1·62m.; Tangshan, 1·57m.; Wanxian, 1·57m.; Changsha, 1·54m.; Xinghua, 1·53m.; Shijiazhuang, 1·48m.; Xiantao, 1·48m.; Nanchang, 1·47m.; Taian, 1·46m.; Anshan, 1·45m.; Yancheng, 1·45m.; Pingxiang, 1·44m.; Yulin, 1·44m.; Qiqihar, 1·42m.; Fushun, 1·40m.; Fuzhou, 1·40m.; Heze, 1·39m.; Jilin, 1·38m.; Neijiang, 1·34m.; Suining, 1·34m.; Luoyang, 1·32m.; Yantai, 1·32m.; Xintai, 1·31m.; Xuzhou, 1·30m.; Huainan, 1·29m.; Urumqi (Wulumuqi), 1·28m.; Baotou, 1·27m.; Changde, 1·27m.; Nanning, 1·23m.; Datong, 1·22m.; Weifang, 1·22m.; Zhanjiang, 1·20m.; Yiyang, 1·19m.; Huaian, 1·17m.; Hefei, 1·17m.; Ningbo, 1·16m.; Yueyang, 1·14m.; Suqian, 1·12m.; Xiaoshan, 1·12m.; Yuzhou, 1·12m.; Tianshui, 1·11m.; Leshan, 1·10m.; Yixing, 1·09m.; Jingmen, 1·08m.; Wuxi, 1·07m.; Huzhou, 1·05m.; Chifeng, 1·04m.; Zaoyang, 1·04m.; Daqing, 1·03m.; Shantou, 1·02m.; Suzhou, 1·02m.; Yongzhou, 1·02m.; Zigong, 1·02m. Yantai (1995 population of 1·32m.) is currently the fastest-growing city in the world, with a population increase of 253·4% projected for the period 1995–2015, by when it is expected to have 4·66m. inhabitants.

Beijing: Located in the northeast of China, Beijing (Peking) is the capital of China and its second largest city. China's traditional cultural heartland, it has also been at the centre of the country's political life for over 800 years. Since Chairman Mao proclaimed it capital of the People's Republic in 1949 the city has grown massively both in area and population. Beijing was the launch pad for Mao's Cultural Revolution when much of its rich heritage was destroyed. Today, though, it is the showpiece of 21st century China.

Shanghai: Situated on the Huangpu River on the coast of the East China Sea, Shanghai is China's biggest city and one of the world's largest seaports. Before the Communist Party came to power in 1947 the city was notorious for its corruption and huge social inequalities. Today, however, Shanghai is a central part of the country's drive for modernization. With huge financial backing it has become the major industrial and commercial centre in China.

The autonomous regions and provinces (*see table above*) have non-Han components in their populations, ranging from 97·2% (in 1994) in Tibet to 9·9% in Zhejiang. Total minority population, 1994, 72,818,100. 55 ethnic minorities are identified. At the 1990 census the largest were: Zhuang, 15,555,820; Manchu, 9,846,776; Hui, 8,612,001; Miao, 7,383,622; Uighur, 7,207,024; Yi, 6,578,524; Tujia, 5,725,049; Mongolian, 4,802,407; Tibetan, 4,593,072.

Li Chengrui, *The Population of China*. Beijing, 1992

Tibet

After the 1959 revolt was suppressed, the Preparatory Committee for the Autonomous Region of Tibet (set up in 1955) took over the functions of local government, led by its Vice-Chairman, the Banqen Lama, in the absence of its Chairman, the Dalai Lama, who had fled to India in 1959. In Dec. 1964 both the Dalai and Banqen Lamas were removed from their posts and on 9 Sept. 1965 Tibet became an Autonomous Region. 301 delegates were elected to the first People's Congress, of whom 226 were Tibetans. The Chief of Government is Gyaincain Norbu. The senior spiritual leader, the Dalai Lama, is in exile. He was awarded the Nobel Peace Prize in 1989. The Banqen Lama died in Jan. 1989. The borders were opened for trade with neighbouring countries in 1980. In July 1988 Tibetan was reinstated as a 'major official language', competence in which is required of all administrative officials. Monasteries and shrines have been renovated and reopened. There were some 15,000 monks and nuns in 1987. In 1984 a Buddhist seminary in Lhasa opened with 200 students. A further softening of Beijing's attitude towards Tibet was shown during President Bill Clinton's visit to China in June 1998. Jiang Zemin, China's president, said he was prepared to meet the Dalai Lama provided he acknowledged Chinese sovereignty over Tibet and Taiwan. In Sept. 2002 direct contact between the exiled government and China was re-established after a nine-year gap.

In 1996 the population was 2·49m. In 1994 there were 2·22m. Tibetans living in Tibet out of a total population of 2·36m. Birth rate (per 1,000), 1996, 24·7; death rate, 8·5; growth rate, 16·2. Population of the capital, Lhasa, in 1992 was 124,000. Expectation of life was 65 years in 1990. 2m. Tibetans live outside Tibet, in China, and in India and Nepal.

Chinese efforts to modernize Tibet include irrigation, road-building and the establishment of light industry. In 1991 there were 328 township and 123 village enterprises employing 21,168 persons; 12,000 persons worked in heavy industry, 16,000 in state-owned enterprises. 1990 output included 136,300 metres of woollen fabrics, 1,000 tonnes of salt, 1,900 tonnes of vegetable oil, 208,200 cu. metres of timber and 132,300 tonnes of cement. In 2000 plans were announced to build a railway of some 900 km to link Lhasa with the town of Golmud, which already has a link with the city of Xining. It would be the highest railway in the world. The Chinese government approved the plan on 8 Feb. 2001 with the aim of completing the link by 2008.

Electricity production in 1990 was 330m. kWh, of which 323m. kWh were hydro-electric.

In 1996 there were 953,000 rural labourers, including 886,000 in farming, forestry and fisheries. The total sown area was 220,100 ha, including 52,500 ha sown to wheat, 18,300 ha to rapeseed, 18,300 ha to oil-bearing crops and 14,500 ha to soya beans. Output (in 1,000 tonnes), 1996: wheat, 261; soya beans, 41; oil-bearing crops, 35; rapeseed, 35. There were 5·10m. cattle, 1·21m. draught animals, 0·36m. horses, 0·22m. pigs, 11·10m. sheep and 5·83m. goats in 1996.

In 1991 there were 21,842 km of roads, of which 6,240 km were paved. There are airports at Lhasa and Bangda providing external links. 30,000 tourists visited Tibet in 1986.

In 1988 there were 2,437 primary schools, 67 secondary schools, 14 technical schools and 3 higher education institutes. The total number of primary school pupils in 1990–91 was 101,000. A university was established in 1985.

In 1990 there were some 9,000 medical personnel and 1,006 medical institutions, with a total of about 5,000 beds.

Barnett, R. and Akiner, S. (eds.) *Resistance and Reform in Tibet*. Farnborough, 1994

Margolis, Eric, *War at the Top of the World: The Struggle for Afghanistan, Kashmir and Tibet*. Routledge, New York, 2001

Pinfold, John, *Tibet* [Bibliography]. Oxford and Santa Barbara (CA), 1991

Schwartz, R. D., *Circle of Protest: Political Ritual in the Tibetan Uprising*. Farnborough, 1994

Smith, W. W., *A History of Tibet: Nationalism and Self-Determination*. Oxford, 1996

SOCIAL STATISTICS

Births, 1998, 20,010,000 (more than the total population of Australia); deaths, 8,110,000. 1998 birth rate (per 1,000 population), 16·03; death rate, 6·50. The birth rate in 1998 declined for the 12th successive year. There were 9,339,615 marriages and 1,132,215 divorces in 1996. In April 2001 parliament passed revisions to the marriage law prohibiting bigamy and cohabitation outside marriage. The suicide rate in China in 1994 was 14·3 per 100,000 population among men but 17·9 per 100,000 among women. China is the only major country in which the suicide rate is higher among females—over half the world's women suicides occur in China. In 1996 the most popular age for marrying was 25–29 for both men and women. Life expectancy at birth, 1999, was 68·3 years for men and 72·5 years for women. Annual population growth rate, 1990–99, 1·0%. Infant mortality, 1999, 33 per 1,000 live births. Fertility rate, 1999, 1·8 births per woman.

CLIMATE

Most of China has a temperate climate but, with such a large country, extending far inland and embracing a wide range of latitude as well as containing large areas at high altitude, many parts experience extremes of climate, especially in winter. Most rain falls during the summer, from May to Sept., though amounts decrease inland. Beijing (Peking), Jan. 24°F (−4·4°C), July 79°F (26°C). Annual rainfall 24·9" (623 mm). Chongqing, Jan. 45°F (7·2°C), July 84°F (28·9°C). Annual rainfall 43·7" (1,092 mm). Shanghai, Jan. 39°F (3·9°C), July 82°F (27·8°C). Annual rainfall 45·4" (1,135 mm). Tianjin, Jan. 24°F (−4·4°C), July 81°F (27·2°C). Annual rainfall 21·5" (533·4 mm).

CONSTITUTION AND GOVERNMENT

On 21 Sept. 1949 the *Chinese People's Political Consultative Conference* met in Beijing, convened by the Chinese Communist Party. The Conference adopted a 'Common Programme' of 60 articles and the 'Organic Law of the Central People's Government' (31 articles). Both became the basis of the Constitution adopted on 20 Sept. 1954 by the 1st National People's Congress, the supreme legislative body. The Consultative Conference continued to exist after 1954 as an advisory body. Its 10th session was convened in March 2003.

New Constitutions were adopted in 1975, 1978, 1982 and 1993, the latter embodying the principles of a 'Socialist market economy'. The constitution was amended in 1999 to endorse formally the concept of private ownership.

The *National People's Congress* can amend the Constitution and nominally elects and has power to remove from office the highest officers of state. The Congress elects a *Standing Committee* (which supervises the State Council) and the *President* and *Vice-President* for a five-year term. Congress has 2,979 deputies and is elected for a five-year term, and meets once a year for two or three weeks. When not in session, its business is carried on by its *Standing Committee.*

The *State Council* is the supreme executive organ and comprises the Prime Minister, Deputy Prime Ministers and State Councillors.

National Anthem. 'March of the Volunteers'; words by Tien Han, tune by Nieh Erh.

RECENT ELECTIONS

The 10th *National People's Congress* was elected in March 2003.

CURRENT ADMINISTRATION

President and Chairman of Central Military Commission: Hu Jintao; b. 1942 (Chinese Communist Party; elected 15 March 2003).

Deputy President: Zeng Qinghong.

In March 2003 the government comprised:

Prime Minister: Wen Jiabao; b. 1942 (Chinese Communist Party; elected 16 March 2003).

Deputy Prime Ministers: Huang Ju, Wu Yi (also *Minister of Health*), Zeng Peiyan, Hui Liangyu.

Minister of Agriculture: Du Qinglin. *Civil Administration:* Li Xueju. *Construction:* Wang Guangtao. *Commerce:* Lu Fuyuan. *Culture:* Sun Jiazheng. *Education:* Zhouji. *Finance:* Jin Renqing. *Foreign Affairs:* Li Zhaoxing. *Information Industry:* Wang Xudong. *Justice:* Zhang Fusen. *Labour and Social Security:* Zheng Silin. *National Land Resources:* Tian Fengshan. *National Defence:* Cao Gangchuan. *National Security:* Xu Yongyue. *Personnel:* Zhang Bolin. *Public Security:* Zhou Yongkang. *Railways:* Liu Zhijun. *Science and Technology:* Xu Guanhua. *Supervision:* Li Zhilun. *Transportation:* Zhang Chunxian. *Water Resources:* Wang Shucheng.

Ministers heading State Commissions: *Family Planning*, Zhang Weiqing. *Nationalities Affairs*, Li Dezhu. *Development and Reform*, Ma Kai. *Science, Technology and Industry for National Defence*, Zhang Yunchuan.

De facto power is in the hands of the Communist Party of China, which had 66m. members in 2002. There are eight other parties, all members of the Chinese People's Political Consultative Conference.

The members of the Standing Committee of the Politburo in Nov. 2002 were Hu Jintao (*General Secretary*), Wen Jiabao, Luo Gan, Wu Bangguo, Zeng Qinghong, Huang Ju, Jia Qinglin, Li Changchun, Wu Guanzheng.

Government Website (Chinese only): http://www.gov.cn

DEFENCE

The Chinese president is chairman of the State and Party's Military Commissions. China is divided into seven military regions. The military commander also commands the air, naval and civilian militia forces assigned to each region.

Conscription is compulsory but for organizational reasons selective: only some 10% of potential recruits are called up. Service is for two years. A military academy to train senior officers in modern warfare was established in 1985.

Defence expenditure in 2001 totalled US$46,049m. (US$36 per capita) and represented 4·0% of GDP, down from 7·9% of GDP in 1985. In the period 1997–2001 China spent US$7·1bn. on defence imports, making it the world's second largest buyer of arms, after Taiwan. In 2001 China's expenditure was the highest of any country, at US$3,100m.

Nuclear Weapons. Having carried out its first test in 1964, there have been 45 tests in all at Lop Nur, in Xinjiang (the last in 1996). The nuclear arsenal consisted of approximately 402 warheads in Jan. 2002 according to the Stockholm International Peace Research Institute. China has been helping Pakistan with its nuclear efforts. Despite China's official position, *Deadly Arsenals*, published by the Carnegie Endowment for International Peace, alleges that the Chinese government is secretly pursuing chemical and biological weapons programmes.

Army. The Army (PLA: 'People's Liberation Army') is divided into main and local forces. Main forces, administered by the seven military regions in which they are stationed, but commanded by the Ministry of Defence, are available for operation anywhere and are better equipped. Local forces concentrate on the defence of their own regions. There are 21 Integrated Group Armies comprising 44 infantry divisions, 9 armoured divisions, 12 armoured brigades, 1 mechanized infantry, 22 motorized infantry brigades, 6 artillery divisions, 15 artillery brigades, 1 anti-tank brigade, 8 surface-to-air missile brigades, 13 anti-aircraft artillery brigades and 3 army aviation regiments. Total strength in 2002 was 1·60m. including some 800,000 conscripts. Reserve forces are undergoing major reorganization on a provincial basis but are estimated to number some 500–600,000.

There is a paramilitary People's Armed Police force estimated at 1·5m. under PLA command.

Navy. The naval arm of the PLA comprises 1 nuclear-powered ballistic missile armed submarine, 5 nuclear-propelled fleet submarines, 1 diesel-powered cruise missile submarine and some 61 patrol submarines. Surface combatant forces include 21 missile-armed destroyers, 42 frigates and some 93 missile craft.

There is a land-based naval air force of about 472 combat aircraft, primarily for defensive and anti-submarine service. The force includes H-5 torpedo bombers, Q-5 fighter/ground attack aircraft J-6 (MiG-19) and J-7 (MiG-21) fighters.

The naval arm is split into a North Sea Fleet, an East Sea Fleet and a South Sea Fleet.

In 2002 naval personnel were estimated at 250,000, including 26,000 in the naval air force and 40,000 conscripts.

Air Force. There are 5 air corps and 32 air divisions. Up to four squadrons make up an air regiment and three air regiments form an air division. The Air Force has an estimated 1,900 combat aircraft.

Equipment includes J-7 (MiG-21) interceptors and fighter-bombers, H-5 (Il-28) jetbombers, H-6 Chinese-built copies of Tu-16 strategic bombers, Q-5 fighter-bombers (evolved from the MiG-19) and Su-27 fighters supplied by Russia. About 100 of a locally-developed fighter designated J-8 (known in the West as 'Finback') are in service.

Total strength (2002) was 420,000 (160,000 conscripts), including 220,000 in air defence organization. The Air Force headquarters are in Beijing.

INTERNATIONAL RELATIONS

The People's Republic of China is a member of UN (and its Security Council), WTO, BIS, the Asian Development Bank, APEC, Mekong Group and the Antarctic Treaty. China joined the WTO in Dec. 2001.

China is heavily dependent on foreign aid. In 2000 it received US$1·7bn., more than any other country.

ECONOMY

In 1998 industry accounted for 48·7% of GDP, services 32·9% and agriculture 18·4%.

It has been estimated that corruption cost China US$150bn. in the 1990s, or between 13% and 16% of the country's GDP.

Overview. A tenth five-year plan covers 2001–2005; there is also a 15-year strategic plan 'Long-Term Target for 2010'. The five-year plan has as its guiding principles economic restructuring, making technological progress the driving force for economic growth, improving living standards, and co-ordinating economic development and social development.

A Communist Party statement of Nov. 1993 declared that public ownership should remain the mainstay of the economy, but alongside a modern enterprise system suited to the demands of a market economy in which government control is separated from management. Private enterprise, which did not exist until the late 1970s, now accounts for over 30% of national output.

Ongoing reforms aim to complete the transition from a closed, agriculture-based command economy to an open, manufacturing- and service-based market economy. Growth has been led on the supply side by increased industrial output which until 1978 was dominated by state-owned enterprises. Since then, much of the increase in manufacturing has been produced by collective enterprises, e.g., by private entrepreneurs working with foreign investors. However, the state sector contains the most capital-intensive industries. Government revenue is strong thanks to high industrial profits and improvements in tax administrations. This has enabled the government to increase social security spending and to cope with public investment, interest costs and civil service wage bills. Monetary developments have been steady and WTO membership is expected to have a positive effect on investment.

Currency. The currency is called Renminbi (*i.e.*, People's Currency). The unit of currency is the *yuan* (CNY) which is divided into ten *jiao*, the *jiao* being divided into ten *fen*. The yuan was floated to reflect market forces on 1 Jan. 1994 while remaining state-controlled, and the official rate of exchange was abolished. It became convertible for current transactions from 1 Dec. 1996. Total money supply in June 2002 was 6,565·77bn. yuan and gold reserves were 16·08m. troy oz. Foreign exchange reserves were US$242,763m. in June 2002 (US$73,579m. in 1995). Only Japan, with US$428,850m., had more. Inflation, which had been 24·1% in 1994, was 0·4% in 2000 and 0·7% in 2001.

Budget. Government revenue and expenditure (in 1bn. yuan):

	1994	1995	1996	1997	1998	1999
Revenue	297·75	330·56	372·98	432·27	496·68	590·05
Expenditure	440·01	482·21	540·65	601·72	730·85	890·88

Of the total revenue in 1996, local government revenue accounted for 374,692m. yuan, and local government expenditure 578,628m. yuan. Total debt incurred, 1996, 196,728m. yuan, of which 119,510m. yuan were foreign debts. The current account surplus was running at US$29,718m. in 1997.

Sources of revenue, 1996 (in 1m. yuan): taxes, 690,982; industrial and commercial taxes, 527,004. Expenditure: economic construction, 285,578 (1995); culture and education, 175,672 (1995); national defence, 63,672 (1995); government administration, 99,654 (1995); agriculture, 51,007; pensions and social welfare, 12,803; debt payments, 131,191.

Performance. GDP totalled US$1,159bn. in 2001. GDP growth was 7·1% in 1999 (the slowest rate for a decade), but then 8·0% in 2000. In 2001 there was 7·3% growth. Between 1990 and 1996 the average annual real growth in GNP per capita was 11%—the second highest in the world after Equatorial Guinea.

Banking and Finance. The People's Bank of China is the central bank and bank of issue (*Governor*, Zhou Xiaochuan). There are a number of other banks, the largest of which are Agricultural Bank of China, Industrial and Commercial Bank of China, China Construction Bank, Bank of China, Bank of Communications and Agricultural Development Bank of China. Legislation of 1995 permitted the establishment of commercial banks; credit co-operatives may be transformed into banks, mainly to provide credit to small businesses. Insurance is handled by the

People's Insurance Company. There were (1994) 350,813 credit co-operatives. The Bank of China is responsible for foreign banking operations.

Savings bank deposits were 2,151,880m. yuan in 1994.

611,566m. yuan was loaned from State Banks in 1996. It is estimated that up to 20% of outstanding loans are bad debts (about US$145bn. at the end of 1996).

There are stock exchanges in the Shenzhen Special Economic Zone and in Shanghai. The Shanghai B Index (for foreign investors) was the best performing stock exchange in the world in 2000, gaining 136% in the course of the year. A securities trading system linking six cities (Securities Automated Quotations System) was inaugurated in 1990 for trading in government bonds.

In 2001 China received a record $47bn. worth of foreign direct investment.

Weights and Measures. The metric system is in general use alongside traditional units of measurement.

ENERGY AND NATURAL RESOURCES

Environment. China's carbon dioxide emissions in 1998 accounted for 12·9% of the world total (the second highest after the USA), and according to the *World Bank Atlas* were equivalent to 2·5 tonnes per capita. An *Environmental Sustainability Index* compiled for the World Economic Forum meeting in Feb. 2002 ranked China 129th in the world out of 142 countries analysed, with 38·5%. The index measured the ability of countries to maintain favourable environmental conditions and examined various factors including pollution levels and the use or abuse of natural resources.

Electricity. Installed capacity, 1997, 254m. kW. In 1998 electricity output was 1,160,000 MWh. Consumption per capita was 746 kWh in 1998. Sources of energy in 1996 as percentage of total energy production: coal, 74·8%; crude oil, 17·1%; hydro-electric power, 6·2%; natural gas, 1·9%. In 2001 there were three nuclear reactors in use, with two more set to be opened in 2002. Generating electricity is not centralized; local units range between 30 and 60 MW of output. In Dec. 2002 China formally broke up its state power monopoly, creating instead five generating and two transmission firms.

Oil and Gas. There are on-shore fields at Daqing, Shengli, Dagang and Karamai, and ten provinces south of the Yangtze River have been opened for exploration in co-operation with foreign companies. Crude oil production was 161m. tonnes in 1999. Proven reserves in 1999 were 24bn. bbls.

Natural gas is available from fields near Canton and Shanghai, and in Sichuan province. Production was 24·3bn. cu. metres in 1999 with proven reserves of 1,370bn. cu. metres.

Minerals. Most provinces contain coal, and there are 70 major production centres, of which the largest are in Hebei, Shanxi, Shandong, Jilin and Anhui. Recoverable coal reserves were estimated at 118bn. tonnes in 1997. Coal production was 1,409m. tonnes in 1997.

Iron ore reserves were 47,560m. tonnes in 1996. Deposits are abundant in the anthracite field of Shanxi, in Hebei and in Shandong, and are found in conjunction with coal and worked in the northeast. Production in 1998 was 210m. tonnes, making China the world's leading iron ore producer.

Tin ore is plentiful in Yunnan, where the tin-mining industry has long existed. Tin production was 54,076 tonnes in 1994.

China is a major producer of wolfram (tungsten ore). Mining of wolfram is carried on in Hunan, Guangdong and Yunnan.

Salt production was 30·8m. tonnes in 1998; gold production was 162 tonnes in 2000. Output of other minerals (in 1,000 tonnes) in 1998: bauxite, 8,500; aluminium, 2,100; zinc (1997), 1,400; lead (1997), 650; copper, 476; diamonds, 1,130,000 carats. Other minerals produced: nickel, barite, bismuth, graphite, gypsum, mercury, molybdenum, silver. Reserves (in tonnes) of phosphate ore, 15,766m.; sylvite, 458m.; salt, 402,400m.

Agriculture. Agriculture accounted for approximately 19% of GDP in 1997, compared to over 50% in 1949 at the time of the birth of the People's Republic of China and over 30% in 1980. In 2000 areas harvested for major crops were (in 1m.

ha): rice, 30·50; wheat, 26·65; maize, 22·54; soybeans, 9·03; rapeseed, 7·80; sweet potatoes, 6·21. Intensive agriculture and horticulture have been practised for millennia. Present-day policy aims to avert the traditional threats from floods and droughts by soil conservancy, afforestation, irrigation and drainage projects, and to increase the 'high stable yields' areas by introducing fertilizers, pesticides and improved crops. In spite of this, 18·1m. ha of land were flooded in 1996 and 20·1m. ha were covered by drought. 52·58m. ha were irrigated in 1998. In Aug. 1998 more than 21m. ha, notably in the Yangtze valley, were under water as China experienced its worst flooding in recent times.

'Township and village enterprises' in agriculture comprise enterprises previously run by the communes of the Maoist era, co-operatives run by rural labourers and individual firms of a certain size. There were 24·95m. such enterprises in 1994, employing 120·18m. persons. There were 2,157 state farms in 1994 with 5·18m. employees. In 1996 there were 234·38m. rural households. The rural workforce was 452·88m., of whom 322·6m. were employed in agriculture, fishing or land management. Net per capita annual peasant income, 1996: 1,926 yuan. Around 44% of the total workforce is engaged in agriculture, down from 68% in 1980. The percentage of the total population living in rural areas remains around 70%, however, as it was in 1980.

In 1992 there were 25,023 agricultural technical stations. There were 704,066 tractors in 1998.

Agricultural production of main crops (in 1m. tonnes), 2000: rice, 190·17; sweet potatoes, 121·02; maize, 105·23; wheat, 99·37; sugarcane, 70·20; potatoes, 62·04; watermelons, 38·38; cabbages, 20·21; tomatoes, 19·31; cucumbers and gherkins, 17·18; soybeans, 15·40; groundnuts, 15·07; seed cotton, 13·05; onions, 12·18; aubergines, 11·91; rapeseeds, 11·55; cottonseed, 8·70; pears, 8·62; chillies and green peppers, 8·14; sugarbeets, 7·70; tangerines and mandarins, 7·61; garlic, 6·47. Tea production in 2000 was just 721,000 tonnes. China is the world's leading producer of a number of agricultural crops, including rice, sweet potatoes, wheat, potatoes, watermelons, groundnuts and honey (256,000 tonnes). The gross value of agricultural output in 1996 was 2,342,866m. yuan. Agricultural production during the period 1990–97 grew on average by 4·4% every year. Only Vietnam among Asian countries achieved higher annual agricultural growth over the same period.

Livestock, 2000: pigs, 437,551,000; goats, 148,401,000; sheep, 131,095,000; cattle, 104,582,000; buffaloes, 22,599,000; horses, 8,916,000; chickens, 3·62bn.; ducks, 612m. China has more sheep, goats, pigs, horses and chickens than any other country. China also has more than two-thirds of the world's ducks. Meat production in 2000 was 64·44m. tonnes; milk, 7·84m. tonnes; eggs, 19·24m. tonnes; honey, 256,000 tonnes. China is the world's leading producer of meat and eggs.

Powell, S. G., *Agricultural Reform in China: from Communes to Commodity Economy, 1978–1990.* Manchester Univ. Press, 1992

Forestry. In 1995 the area under forests was 133·32m. ha, or 14·3% of the total land area (133·76m. ha in 1990). Total roundwood production in 1999 was 582·66m. cu. metres, making China the world's largest timber producer (18% of the world total in 1999). It is the world's leading importer of roundwood, accounting for 21% of world timber imports in 1999. It is also the leading producer of wood fuel.

Fisheries. Total catch, 1999: 17,240,032 tonnes, of which 14,954,668 tonnes were from marine waters. China's annual catch is the largest in the world, and currently accounts for approximately 20% of the world total. In 1989 the annual catch had been just 5·3m. tonnes.

INDUSTRY

Industry accounts for approximately 49% of GDP, up from 21% in 1949 when the People's Republic of China came into existence. Cottage industries persist into the 21st century. Modern industrial development began with the manufacture of cotton textiles, and the establishment of silk filatures, steel plants, flour mills and match factories. In 1996 there were 7,986,500 industrial enterprises. 113,800 were state-owned, 1,591,800 were collectives and 6,210,700 were individually owned. A law of 1988 ended direct state control of firms and provided for the possibility of bankruptcy.

Output of major products, 1997 (in tonnes): cement, 492·6m. (nearly a third of the world total); crude steel (1999), 123·7m.; rolled steel, 94·9m.; distillate fuel oil

(1997), 49·2m.; residual fuel oil (1997), 23·1m.; chemical fertilizers, 29·11m.; paper and paperboard (1998), 31·6m.; sulphuric acid, 19·46m.; sugar (1998), 8·9m.; cotton yarn, 5·31m.; aluminium, 2·2m.; silk (1996), 94,900; woollen fabrics (1996), 459·5m. metres; bicycles, 30m. units; motorcycles (and scooters), 10·3m. units; TV sets, 26·43m. units; radios (1996), 56·50m. units; watches, 295m. units; clocks, 81·8m. units; cameras, 46·87m. units; washing machines, 12,571,000 units; refrigerators, 9·86m. units; motor vehicles, 1·62m. units; locomotives (1996), 1,050 units; beer, 18,889·4m. litres. China is the world's leading steel producer.

The gross value of industrial output in 1996 was 9,959,500m. yuan.

Labour. The employed population at the 1990 census was 647·2m. (291·1m. female). By 1997 it was estimated to have risen to 696·0m., of whom 71% were in rural areas and 29% in urban areas. In 1997 there were 330·1m. people working in agriculture, 96·1m. in manufacturing, 47·1m. in commerce, 44·8m. in construction and 18·0m. in community and social services. In 1996, 109·4m. worked in state-owned enterprises, 29·5m. in urban collectives and 50·2m. were self-employed. In 1994 there were 446·54m. working as individual rural labourers or in rural collectives and there were 15·57m. individual urban labourers.

By 2001 China had more than 2m. private companies employing 22m. people. It was not until the late 1970s that the private sector even came into existence in China.

At the 1990 census there was a floating population of 21m. internal migrants who tour the country seeking seasonal employment. There were 5·53m. urban unemployed in 1996 (3% of the urban population). Almost one-third of unemployed people had not worked for a year. Only a quarter of the unemployed in 1996 were registered at employment services and only 1·7% received unemployment relief payments. In April 1998 the official unemployment rate was 5%, but Prime Minister Zhu Rongji admitted that 10% of the workforce were unemployed.

The average non-agricultural annual wage in 1996 was 6,210 yuan: 4,302 yuan, urban collectives; 6,280 yuan, state-owned enterprises; 8,261 yuan, other enterprises. There is a 6-day 48-hour working week. Minimum working age was fixed at 16 in 1991. There were 120,000 labour disputes in 1999, up from 8,000 in 1989.

Trade Unions. The All-China Federation of Trade Unions, founded in 1925, is headed by Wang Zhaoguo. In 2003 there were 103m. members. It consists of 31 federations of trade unions. Its National Congress convenes every five years.

INTERNATIONAL TRADE

Foreign debt was US$149,800m. in 2000 (the fourth highest in the world). Actual foreign investment totalled US$33,800m. in 1994. Direct foreign investment (in US$1m.) in 1995 by major countries of origin: Taiwan, 11,600; USA, 10,900; Japan, 10,500; Singapore, 3,900; South Korea, 2,300; UK, 2,200.

There are six Special Economic Zones at Shanghai and in the provinces of Guangdong and Fujian, in which concessions are made to foreign businessmen. The Pudong New Area in Shanghai is designated a special development area. Since 1979 joint ventures with foreign firms have been permitted. A law of April 1991 reduced taxation on joint ventures to 33%. There is no maximum limit on the foreign share of the holdings; the minimum limit is 25%.

In May 2000 the US granted normal trade relations to China, a progression after a number of years when China was accorded 'most favoured nation' status. China subsequently joined the World Trade Organization on 11 Dec. 2001.

Imports and Exports. Trade in US$1m.:

	1995	1996	1997	1998	1999	2000
Imports f.o.b.	110,060	131,542	136,448	136,915	158,734	214,657
Exports f.o.b.	128,110	151,077	182,670	183,529	194,716	249,131

Major exports in 1999 (in US$1bn.): electrical machinery and equipment, 32·9; textiles and clothing, 27·3; power generation equipment, 19·1; footwear and parts thereof, 8·7; toys and games, 7·7; iron and steel, 6·4. Imports: electrical machinery and equipment, 35·2; power generation equipment, 27·8; plastics and articles thereof, 11·6; mineral fuels and oil, 8·9; iron and steel, 8·8; inorganic and organic chemicals, 6·5. Chinese exports have doubled in just over five years. China is now the world's largest importer of steel, having overtaken the USA in 2002.

Main export markets in 2000: USA, 33·2%; Hong Kong, 26·7%; Japan, 17·9%; Germany, 5·0%. Main import suppliers, 2000; Hong Kong, 21·8%; Japan, 18·6%; South Korea, 10·3%; USA, 9·6%. Customs duties with Taiwan were abolished in 1980.

Pearson, M. M., *Joint Ventures in the People's Republic of China: the Control of Foreign Direct Investment under Socialism.* Princeton Univ. Press, 1991

COMMUNICATIONS

Roads. The total road length was 1,526,389 km in 1996. Of these, 24,474 km were motorways and 156,154 were main roads. In 1996 there were 6,127,000 trucks and 3,894,000 passenger vehicles. 2·89m. vehicles were privately owned. The use of bicycles is very widespread and there are also 9,760,000 motorcycles and mopeds. In 1996, 9,838m. tonnes of freight and 11,221m. persons were transported by road.

There were 253,537 traffic accidents in 1994, with 66,362 fatalities.

Rail. In 1996 there were 56,700 km of railway including 10,100 km electrified. Gauge is standard except for some 600 mm track in Yunnan. Passenger-km travelled in 1997 came to 354·8bn. and freight tonne-km to 1,309·7bn.

Civil Aviation. There are major international airports at Beijing, Shanghai (Hongqiao and Pu Dong airports) and Guangzhou (Baiyun). Altogether there were 142 civil airports in 1996, 106 of which can accommodate Boeing 737s or larger aircraft. The national and major airlines are state-owned, except Shanghai Airlines (75% municipality-owned, 25% private) and Shenzhen Airlines (private). The leading Chinese airlines operating scheduled services in 1999 were China Southern Airlines (13,266,700 passengers), China Eastern Airlines (8,253,100), Air China (6,521,200), China Southwest Airlines (4,507,600), China Northern Airlines (4,034,000), China Yunnan Airlines (3,018,500), China Northwest Airlines (2,882,500) and Xinjiang Airlines (1,361,400). Other Chinese airlines include Changan Airlines, China National Aviation, Fujian Airlines, Hainan Airlines, Shandong Airlines, Shanghai Airlines, Shanxi Airlines, Shenzhen Airlines, Sichuan Airlines and Xiamen Airlines.

In 1999 the busiest airport was Beijing, with 21,691,000 passengers (16,073,000 on domestic flights), followed by Guangzhou (Baiyun), with 12,791,000 passengers (11,527,000 on domestic flights) and Shanghai (Hongqiao), with 12,139,000 passengers (7,481,000 on domestic flights).

Shipping. In 1998 the merchant fleet consisted of 3,214 vessels (523 oil tankers) totalling 16·5m. GRT (tankers, 2·03m. GRT).

Cargo handled by the major ports in 1996 (in tonnes): Shanghai, 164m.; Qinhuangdao, 83m.; Ningbo, 76m.; Guangzhou (Canton), 75m.; Dalian, 64m.; Tianjin, 62m.; Qingdao, 60m. In 1993, 125·08m. tonnes of freight were carried. Shanghai handled 6·33m. 20-ft equivalent units (TEUs) in 2001, making it the world's fifth busiest container port in terms of number of containers handled. Construction began in 2002 on the 14·31bn. yuan Yangshan deep-water port that should make Shanghai the world's third busiest port. On completion in 2020 it is estimated that it will have a capacity of 13m. TEUs.

In Jan. 2001 the first legal direct shipping links between the Chinese mainland and Taiwanese islands in more than 50 years were inaugurated.

Inland waterways totalled 110,593 km in 1994. 1,070·91m. tonnes of freight and 261·65m. passengers were carried.

Telecommunications. In 2000 there were 144,829,000 telephone main lines (111·8 per 1,000 persons) and 20·6m. PCs were in use (15·9 per 1,000 inhabitants). In Nov. 2002 there were 200m. mobile phone subscribers, making China the biggest market for mobile phones in the world. There were 45·8m. Internet users in July 2002. At the beginning of 1998 there had only been around 500,000 users. By 2007 Chinese is expected to have overtaken English as the most-used language on the Internet. There were 2m. fax machines in 1997.

Postal Services. There were 72,496 post offices in 1996. The use of *Pinyin* transcription of place names has been requested for mail to addresses in China (*e.g.*, 'Beijing' *not* 'Peking').

SOCIAL INSTITUTIONS

Justice. Six new codes of law (including criminal and electoral) came into force in 1980, to regularize the legal unorthodoxy of previous years. There is no provision for *habeas corpus*. The death penalty has been extended from treason and murder to include rape, embezzlement, smuggling, fraud, theft, drug-dealing, bribery and robbery with violence. There were 2,468 reported executions in 2001—more than in any other country. 'People's courts' are divided into some 30 higher, 200 intermediate and 2,000 basic-level courts, and headed by the Supreme People's Court. The latter tries cases, hears appeals and supervises the people's courts. People's courts are composed of a president, vice-presidents, judges and 'people's assessors' who are the equivalent of jurors. 'People's conciliation committees' are charged with settling minor disputes. There are also special military courts. Procuratorial powers and functions are exercised by the Supreme People's Procuracy and local procuracies.

The population in penal institutions in 1997 was 1,410,000 (115 per 100,000 of national population).

Religion. The government accords legality to five religions only: Buddhism, Islam, Protestantism, Roman Catholicism and Taoism. Confucianism, Buddhism and Taoism have long been practised. Confucianism has no ecclesiastical organization and appears rather as a philosophy of ethics and government. Taoism—of Chinese origin—copied Buddhist ceremonial soon after the arrival of Buddhism two millennia ago. Buddhism in return adopted many Taoist beliefs and practices. A more tolerant attitude towards religion had emerged by 1979, and the government's Bureau of Religious Affairs was reactivated.

Ceremonies of reverence to ancestors have been observed by the whole population regardless of philosophical or religious beliefs.

A new quasi-religious movement, Falun Gong, was founded in 1992, but has since been banned by the authorities. The movement claims it has some 100m. adherents, although the Chinese government has maintained the real number is closer to 2m.

Muslims are found in every province of China, being most numerous in the Ningxia-Hui Autonomous Region, Yunnan, Shaanxi, Gansu, Hebei, Honan, Shandong, Sichuan, Xinjiang and Shanxi. They totalled 18m. in 1997.

Roman Catholicism has had a footing in China for more than three centuries. In 1992 there were about 3·5m. Catholics who are members of the Patriotic Catholic Association, which declared its independence from Rome in 1958. Protestants are members of the All-China Conference of Protestant Churches. In 1997 there were an estimated 73,000,000 Christians in total.

In 1997 there were also estimated to be 247,000,000 Chinese folk-religionists, 147,000,000 atheists, 104,000,000 Buddhists, 1,000,000 advocates of traditional beliefs and 637,000,000 non-religious persons.

Legislation of 1994 prohibits foreign nationals from setting up religious organizations.

Education. Adult literacy in 1999 was 83·5% (male, 91·2%; female, 75·5%). In 1994, 98·4% of school-age children attended school. In 1993 maximum school fees were 10 yuan a term, to which other charges might be added. In 1996 there were 187,324 kindergartens with 26·66m. children and 889,000 teachers. An educational reform of 1985 planned to phase in compulsory 9-year education consisting of 6 years of primary schooling and 3 years of secondary schooling, to replace a previous 5-year system. In 1997 there were 628,840 primary schools with 5,794,000 teachers and 139·95m. pupils; and 78,642 secondary schools with 3,587,000 teachers and 60·18m. pupils. In 1996 there were 10,049 vocational schools with 308,000 teachers and 4·73m. students. There were 1,032 institutes of higher education, including universities, with 403,000 teachers and 3·02m. students. One-third of all higher education students study engineering.

There is an Academy of Sciences with provincial branches. An Academy of Social Sciences was established in 1977.

In 1995–96 in the private sector there were 3 general universities and 9 specialized universities (aeronautics and astronautics; agricultural engineering; agriculture; chemical technology; foreign studies; labour; medicine; traditional Chinese medicine; polytechnic). In the public sector there were 60 general universities, 2 for ethnic minorities and the following specialized universities: agriculture, 12; agriculture and land reclamation, 1; land reclamation, 1; architecture, 2; architecture and technology, 1; chemical technology, 1; coal and chemical technology, 1; electronic science and technology, 1; engineering, 1; fisheries, 1; foreign languages, 1; forestry, 1; hydraulic and electrical engineering, 1; international business and economics, 1; international studies, 1; iron and steel technology, 1; maritime studies, 1; medicine, 11; traditional Chinese medicine, 2; mining and technology, 1; petroleum, 1; pharmacology, 1; political science and law, 1; polytechnic, 8; radio and television, 1; science and technology, 5; surveying and mapping, 1; teaching, 4; technology, 6; textiles, 1.

In 1996 there were also 893 teacher training schools. In 1994, 19,000 students were studying abroad. Fees were introduced for university students in 1996–97.

In 1996 total expenditure on education came to 155,611m. yuan (2·3% of GNP), around 11·9% of total government expenditure.

Health. Medical treatment is free only for certain groups of employees, but where costs are incurred they are partly borne by the patient's employing organization. In 1996 there were 1·94m. doctors, of whom 0·35m. practised Chinese medicine, and 1·16m. nurses. About 10% of doctors are in private practice.

In 1996 there were 67,964 hospitals (with 2·87m. beds), 528 sanatoria (with 109,000 beds) and 103,472 clinics. There were 24 beds per 10,000 population in 1996.

Approximately 1m. Chinese were HIV-infected in 2002. Some suggestions indicate that there may be as many as 10m. HIV-positive people by 2010.

In 1996 some 62% of males smoked, but fewer than 4% of females. The rate among males has been gradually rising over the past 15 years whilst that among females has gradually gone down.

In 1997 approximately 164m. people, representing 13% of the population, were undernourished. In 1979, 22% of the population had been undernourished.

Welfare. In 1996 there were 42,821 social welfare institutions with 769,348 inmates. Numbers (in 1,000) of beneficiaries of relief funds: persons in poor rural households, 30,790; in poor urban households, 2,610; persons in rural households entitled to 'the 5 guarantees' (food, clothing, medical care, housing, education for children or funeral expenses), 2,675; retired, laid-off or disabled workers, 535. The major relief funds (in 1,000 yuan) in 1996 were: families of deceased or disabled servicemen, 5,187,970; poor households, 712,270; orphaned, disabled, old and young persons, 1,856,680; welfare institutions, 1,551,000.

CULTURE

Broadcasting. In 1994 there were 1,107 radio and 766 TV stations. The Central People's Broadcasting Station provides two central programmes, regional services, special services, a Taiwan service and external services. China Central Television (colour by PAL) transmits three programmes from Beijing, a programme from Shanghai, and an English-language programme. There are 29 regional programmes transmitted from 361 local stations. By 1995 about 600 cable TV systems had been licensed. There were 50m. cable TV subscribers in 1997. In 1996 there were 240·1m. radio receivers (only the USA has more), and in 1999, 450m. TV receivers (the greatest number in any country in the world). In 1980 there had been just 9m., representing an increase of 441m. between 1980 and 1999, or more TV sets than were in use in the USA (the country with the second highest number of sets) in 1999. In urban areas 96%, and in rural areas 48·5%, of households possessed a TV set in 1994. The use of satellite receiving dishes was prohibited in 1993.

Cinema. There were 4,639 cinemas in 1995. 148 feature films were made in 1994.

Press. In 1994 there were 1,635 newspapers with a combined circulation of 125,200m. and 7,325 periodicals with 2,210m. The Party newspaper is *Renmin Ribao* (People's Daily), which had a daily circulation of 3m. in 1994. 110,283 book titles were published in 1996. There were 2,596 public libraries in 1993.

Tourism. 27,047,000 tourists visited in 1999. The World Tourism Organization predicts that China will overtake France as the world's most visited destination by

2020 and become the world's 4th most important source of tourists to other countries. Income from tourists in 1999 was US$14,098m.

Festivals. The lunar New Year, also known as the 'Spring Festival', is a time of great excitement for the Chinese people. The festivities get under way 22 days prior to the New Year date and continue for 15 days afterwards. Dates of the lunar New Year: Year of the Monkey, 22 Jan. 2004; Year of the Rooster, 9 Feb. 2005. Lantern Festival, or Yuanxiao Jie, is an important, traditional Chinese festival, which is on the 15th of the first month of the Chinese New Year. Guanyin's Birthday is on the 19th day of the second month of the Chinese lunar calendar. Guanyin is the Chinese goddess of mercy. Tomb Sweeping Day, as the name implies, is a day for visiting and cleaning the ancestral tomb and usually falls on 5 April. Dragon Boat Festival is called Duan Wu Jie in Chinese. The festival is celebrated on the 5th of the 5th month of the Chinese lunar calendar. The Moon Festival is on the 15th of the 8th lunar month. It is sometimes called Mid-Autumn Festival. The Moon Festival is an occasion for family reunion.

Libraries. In 1995 there were 2,600 public libraries with a combined 328,500,000 volumes and 5,400,000 registered users.

DIPLOMATIC REPRESENTATIVES

Of China in the United Kingdom (49–51 Portland Pl., London W1N 4JL)
Ambassador: Zha Peixin.

Of the United Kingdom in China (11 Guang Hua Lu, Jian Guo Men Wai, Beijing 100600)
Ambassador: Sir Christopher Hum, CMG.

Of China in the USA (2300 Connecticut Ave., NW, Washington, D.C. 20008)
Ambassador: Yang Jiechi.

Of the USA in China (Xiu Shui Bei Jie 3, 100600 Beijing)
Ambassador: Clark T. Randt, Jr.

Of China to the United Nations
Ambassador: Wang Ying-Fan.

Of China to the European Union
Ambassador: Guan Chengyuan.

FURTHER READING

State Statistical Bureau. *China Statistical Yearbook*
China Directory [in Pinyin and Chinese]. Tokyo, annual
Adshead, S. A. M., *China in World History.* Macmillan, London, 1999
Baum, R., *Burying Mao: Chinese Politics in the Age of Deng Xiaoping.* Princeton Univ. Press, 1994
Becker, Jasper, *The Chinese.* John Murray, London, 2000
Brown, Raj, *Overseas Chinese Merchants.* Macmillan, London, 1999
Brugger, B. and Reglar, S., *Politics, Economics and Society in Contemporary China.* London, 1994
The Cambridge Encyclopaedia of China. 2nd ed. CUP, 1991
The Cambridge History of China. 14 vols. CUP, 1978 ff.
Chang, David Wen-Wei and Chuang, Richard Y., *The Politics of Hong Kong's Reversion to China.* Macmillan, London, 1999
Cook, Sarah, Yao, Shujie and Zhuang, Juzhong, (eds.) *The Chinese Economy Under Transition.* Macmillan, London, 1999
De Crespigny, R., *China This Century.* 2nd ed. OUP, 1993
Dixin, Xu and Chengming, Wu, (eds.) *Chinese Capitalism, 1522–1840.* Macmillan, London, 1999
Dreyer, J. T., *China's Political System: Modernization and Tradition.* 2nd ed. London, 1996
Evans, R., *Deng Xiaoping and the Making of Modern China.* London, 1993
Fairbank, J. K., *The Great Chinese Revolution 1800–1985.* London, 1987.—*China: a New History.* Harvard Univ. Press, 1992
Glassman, R. M., *China in Transition: Communism, Capitalism and Democracy.* New York, 1991
Goldman, M., *Sowing the Seeds of Democracy in China: Political Reform in the Deng Xiaoping Era.* Harvard Univ. Press, 1994
Hayford, C. W., *China.* [Bibliography] ABC-Clio, Oxford and Santa Barbara (CA), 1997

Ho, Samuel P. S. and Kueh, Y. Y. (eds.) *Sustainable Economic Development in South China.* Macmillan, London, 1999

Huang, R., *China: a Macro History.* 2nd ed. Armonk (NY), 1997

Hunter, A. and Sexton, J., *Contemporary China.* Macmillan, London, 1999

Lieberthal, K. G., *From Revolution through Reform.* New York, 1995.—and Lampton, D. M. (eds.) *Bureaucracy, Politics and Decision-Making in Post-Mao China.* California Univ. Press, 1992

Lu, Aiguo, *China and the Global Economy Since 1840.* Macmillan, London, 1999

Ma, Jun, *Chinese Economy in the 1990s.* Macmillan, London, 1999

MacFarquhar, R. (ed.) *The Politics of China: the Eras of Mao and Deng.* 2nd ed. CUP, 1997.— *The Origins of the Cultural Revolution.* 3 vols. Columbia Univ. Press, 1998

Mackerras, C. and Yorke, A., *The Cambridge Handbook of Contemporary China.* CUP, 1991

Mok, Ka-Ho, *Social and Political Development in Post-Reform China.* Macmillan, London, 1999

Nolan, Peter, *China and the Global Economy.* Palgrave, Basingstoke, 2001

Phillips, R. T., *China Since 1911.* London, 1996

Roberts, J. A. G., *A History of China.* Palgrave, Basingstoke, 2001

Saich, Tony, *Governance and Politics of China.* Palgrave, Basingstoke, 2001

Schram, S. (ed.) *Mao's Road to Power: Revolutionary Writings 1912–1949.* 4 vols. Harvard, 1998

Shen, Xiobai, *The Chinese Road to High Technology.* Macmillan, London, 1999

Sheng Hua, *et al., China: from Revolution to Reform.* London, 1992

Shirk, S. L., *The Political Logic of Economic Reform in China.* Univ. of California Press, 1993

Short, Philip, *Mao: A Life.* Henry Holt, New York and Hodder and Stoughton, London, 2000

Spence, Jonathan, D., *The Chan's Great Continent: China in Western Minds.* Norton, New York, 1998.—*Mao Zedong.* Viking, New York and Weidenfeld & Nicolson, London, 2000

Suyin, H., *Eldest Son, Zhou Enlai and The Making of Modern China.* Kodansha Globe, 1995

Turner, Barry, (ed.) *China Profiled.* Macmillan, London, 1999

Womack, B. (ed.) *Contemporary Chinese Politics in Historical Perspective.* CUP, 1992

Yan, Yanni, *International Joint Ventures in China.* Macmillan, London, 1999

Yeung, Henry Wai-Cheung and Olds, Kristopher, (eds.) *The Globalisation of Chinese Business Firms.* Macmillan, London, 1999

Zhang, Xiao-Guang, *China's Trade Patterns and International Comparative Advantage.* Macmillan, London, 1999

Other more specialized titles are listed under TERRITORY AND POPULATION; TIBET; AGRICULTURE; INTERNATIONAL TRADE.

National statistical office: National Bureau of Statistics, 38 Yuetan Nanjie, Beijing.
Website: http://www.stats.gov.cn/

HONG KONG
Xianggang

KEY HISTORICAL EVENTS

Hong Kong island and the southern tip of the Kowloon peninsula were leased to Britain for 99 years in 1898. Talks began in Sept. 1982 between Britain and China over the future of Hong Kong after the lease expiry in 1997. On 19 Dec. 1984 the two countries signed a Joint Declaration by which Hong Kong became, with effect from 1 July 1997, a Special Administrative Region of the People's Republic of China enjoying a high degree of autonomy, and vested with executive, legislative and independent judicial power, including that of final adjudication. The existing social and economic systems were to remain unchanged for another 50 years. This 'one country, two systems' principle, embodied in the Basic Law, became the constitution for the Hong Kong Special Administrative Region of the People's Republic of China.

TERRITORY AND POPULATION

Hong Kong ('Xianggang' in Mandarin *Pinyin*) island is situated off the southern coast of the Chinese mainland 32 km east of the mouth of the Pearl River. The area of the island is 79·99 sq. km. It is separated from the mainland by a fine natural harbour. On the opposite side is the peninsula of Kowloon (46·27 sq. km). Total area of the Territory is 1,091 sq. km, a large part of it being steep and unproductive hillside. Country parks and special areas cover over 40% of the land area. Since 1945 the government has reclaimed over 5,400 ha from the sea, principally from the seafronts of Hong Kong and Kowloon, facing the harbour. The 'New Territories' are on the mainland, north of Kowloon.

Based on the results of the 2001 population census Hong Kong's resident population in March 2001 was 6,708,389 and the population density 6,237 per sq. km. 59·7% of the population was born in Hong Kong, 33·7% in other parts of China and 6·6% in the rest of the world.

In 2001, 100% of the population lived in urban areas. Some 10,600 persons emigrated in 2001. The British Nationality Scheme enables persons to acquire citizenship without leaving Hong Kong. There were 53,655 legal entrants (one-way permit holders) from the mainland of China in 2001. The population is projected to increase to 8·7m. by 2031.

The official languages are Chinese and English.

SOCIAL STATISTICS

Annual population growth rate, 2001, 0·9%. Vital statistics, 2001: known births, 48,200; known deaths, 33,400; registered marriages, 32,800. Rates (per 1,000): birth, 7·2; death, 5·0; marriage, 4·8; infant mortality, 2001, 2·6 per 1,000 live births (one of the lowest rates in the world). Expectation of life at birth, 2001: males, 78·4 years; females, 84·6. The median age for marrying in 2001 was 31·3 years for males and 28·1 for females. Total fertility rate, 2001, 0·9 child per woman.

CLIMATE

The climate is sub-tropical, tending towards temperate for nearly half the year, the winter being cool and dry and the summer hot and humid, May to Sept. being the wettest months. Normal temperatures are Jan. 60°F (15·8°C), July 84°F (28·8°C). Annual rainfall 87" (2,214·3 mm).

THE BRITISH ADMINISTRATION

Hong Kong used to be administered by the Hong Kong government. The Governor was the head of government and presided over the *Executive Council*, which advised the Governor on all important matters. The last British Governor was Chris Patten. In Oct. 1996 the Executive Council consisted of three ex officio members and ten appointed members, of whom one was an official member. The chief functions of the *Legislative Council* were to enact laws, control public expenditure and put questions to the administration on matters of public interest. The Legislative Council elected in Sept. 1995 was, for the first time, constituted solely by election. It comprised 60 members, of whom 20 were elected from geographical constituencies, 30 from functional constituencies encompassing all eligible persons in a workforce of 2·9m., and ten from an election committee formed by members of 18 district boards. A president was elected from and by the members.

At the elections on 17 Sept. 1995 turn-out for the geographical seats was 35·79%, and for the functional seats (21 of which were contested), 40·42%. The Democratic Party and its allies gained 29 seats, the Liberal Party 10 and the pro-Beijing Democratic Alliance 6. The remaining seats went to independents.

CONSTITUTION AND GOVERNMENT

In Dec. 1995 the Standing Committee of China's National People's Congress set up a Preparatory Committee of 150 members (including 94 from Hong Kong) to oversee the retrocession of Hong Kong to China on 1 July 1997. In Nov. 1996 the Preparatory Committee nominated a 400-member Selection Committee to select the Chief Executive of Hong Kong and a provisional legislature to replace the Legislative Council. The Selection Committee was composed of Hong Kong residents, with 60 seats reserved for delegates to the National People's Congress and appointees of the People's Political Consultative Conference. On 11 Dec. 1996 Tung Chee Hwa was elected Chief Executive by 80% of the Selection Committee's votes.

On 21 Dec. 1996 the Selection Committee selected a provisional legislature which began its activities in Jan. 1997 while the Legislative Council was still functioning. In Jan. 1997 the provisional legislature started its work by enacting legislation which would be applicable to the Hong Kong Special Administrative Region and compatible with the Basic Law.

Constitutionally Hong Kong is a Special Administrative Region of the People's Republic of China. The Basic Law enables Hong Kong to retain a high degree of autonomy. It provides that the legislative, judicial and administrative systems which were previously in operation are to remain in place. The Special Administrative Region Government is also empowered to decide on Hong Kong's monetary and economic policies independent of China.

In July 1997 the first-past-the-post system of returning members from geographical constituencies to the Legislative Council was replaced by proportional representation.

In July 2002 a new accountability or 'ministerial' system was introduced, under which the Chief Executive nominates for appointment 14 policy secretaries, who report directly to the Chief Executive. The Chief Executive is aided by the Executive Council, consisting of the three senior Secretaries of Department (the Chief Secretary, the Financial Secretary and the Secretary for Justice) and eleven other secretaries plus five non-officials.

RECENT ELECTIONS

In the Legislative Council election held on 10 Sept. 2000 turn-out was just 43%, a drop of nearly 10% on the 1998 vote. 24 of the 60 seats were directly elected, the other 36 being returned by committees and professional associations. The Democratic Party gained 12 seats, the pro-Beijing Democratic Alliance for the Betterment of Hong Kong 11, Liberals 8, Progressives 4, Frontier 3, New Century 2 and others 20. The Democrats saw their share of the vote in the directly-elected seats fall, from 42·6% of votes cast in 1998 to 34·7% of votes cast in 2000, while the Democratic Alliance for the Betterment of Hong Kong saw their share rise, from 25·2% of votes cast in 1998 to 29·7% of votes cast in 2000.

CURRENT ADMINISTRATION

Chief Executive: Tung Chee Hwa; b. 1937 (elected 11 Dec. 1996; re-elected unopposed for a second term 28 Feb. 2002).

Chief Secretary for Administration: Donald Tsang, OBE, JP. *Financial Secretary:* Antony Leung. *Secretary for Justice:* Elsie Leung, JP.

Secretary for Commerce, Industry and Technology: Henry Tang. *Housing, Planning and Lands:* Michael Suen. *Education and Manpower:* Arthur Li. *Health, Welfare and Food:* Yeoh Eng-kiong. *Civil Service:* Joseph Wong. *Home Affairs:* Patrick Ho. *Security:* Regina Ip. *Economic Development and Labour:* Stephen Ip. *Environment, Transport and Works:* Sarah Liao. *Financial Services and the Treasury:* Frederick Ma. *Constitutional Affairs:* Stephen Lam.

Government Website: http://www.info.gov.hk

ECONOMY

Services accounted for 84% of GDP in 1997 and industry 15%.

According to the anti-corruption organization *Transparency International*, Hong Kong ranked 14th in the world in a 2002 survey of the countries and regions with the least corruption in business and government. It received 8·2 out of 10 in the annual index.

Income tax is a flat 15% and only 25% of the population pay any tax at all. 6% of the population pays 80% of the total income tax bill. Hong Kong represents 20% of China's total worth.

Currency. The unit of currency is the *Hong Kong dollar* (HKD) of 100 *cents.* Banknotes are issued by the Hongkong and Shanghai Banking Corporation and the Standard Chartered Bank, and, from May 1994, the Bank of China. Total money supply was HK$216,760m. in May 2002. In June 2002 gold reserves were 67,000 troy oz and in Feb. 1998 foreign exchange reserves US$112,335m. (US$55,398m. in 1995). Inflation was negative in 1999, at −5·4%.

Budget. The total government revenue and expenditure for financial years ending 31 March were as follows (in HK$1m.):

	1998	1999	2000	2001	2002
Revenue[1]	281,226	216,115	232,995	225,060	175,559
Expenditure[2]	194,241	218,811	214,533	224,791	238,585

[1]Including the change in the net worth of investments up to 31 Oct. 1998.
[2]Excluding Capital Investment Fund.

Public expenditure in 2002 (based on revised estimates 2001–02) was divided as follows (HK$1bn.): education, 52·6; support, 35·7; health, 34·0; housing, 33·2;

social welfare, 30·7; security, 28·1; infrastructure, 24·7; economic, 14·1; environment and food, 11·3; community and external affairs, 8·5.

The final reserve balance as at 31 March 2002 was HK$372·5bn.

Performance. Total GDP was US$163,995m. in 2001. Following real GDP growth of 5·1% in 1997, the economy contracted in 1998 by 5·0%, representing Hong Kong's most severe recession since the 1970s. There was then growth of 3·4% in 1999 and 10·2% in 2000, including 14·1% in the first quarter of 2000. GDP growth was only 0·6% in 2001. The third quarter of 2002 saw growth of 3·3% after contracting at the end of 2001.

Banking and Finance. The Hong Kong Monetary Authority acts as a central bank. The *Chief Executive* is Joseph Yam. As at Dec. 1995 there were 185 banks licensed under the Banking Ordinance, of which 31 were locally incorporated, 63 restricted licence banks and 154 representative offices of foreign banks. Licensed bank deposits were HK$2,601,971m. in June 1997; restricted licence bank deposits were HK$62,033m. There were 132 deposit-taking companies registered under the Banking Ordinance with total deposits of HK$18,419m. as at Nov. 1995.

In March 2000 the stock exchange, the futures exchange and the clearing settlement merged into Hong Kong Exchanges and Clearing (HKEx). The summer of 1997 saw record highs on the Hang Seng index (16,365 in July 1997 compared with 10,681 in July 1996). In July 1997 the average daily turnover was HK$19,500m.

Weights and Measures. Metric, British Imperial, Chinese and US units are all in current use in Hong Kong. However, government departments have now effectively adopted metric units; all new legislation uses metric terminology and existing legislation is being progressively metricated. Metrication is also proceeding in the private sector.

ENERGY AND NATURAL RESOURCES

Environment. According to the *World Bank Atlas* Hong Kong's carbon dioxide emissions in 1998 were the equivalent of 5·4 tonnes per capita.

Electricity. Installed capacity was 11m. kW in 1997. Production in 1998 was 31·41bn. kWh. Consumption in 1998 was 34·85bn. kWh.

Water. Reservoirs are needed to store the summer rainfall in order to meet supply requirements. There are 17 impounding reservoirs with a total capacity of 586m. cu. metres. Raw water is also purchased from the Guangdong Province of China (729m. cu. metres in 2001). Consumption in 2001 was 940m. cu. metres.

Agriculture. The local agricultural industry is directed towards the production of high quality fresh food through intensive land use and modern farming techniques. Out of the territory's total land area of 1,097 sq. km, only 27 sq. km is currently farmed. In 1999 local production accounted for 11·7% of fresh vegetables, 18·2% of live poultry and 22·2% of live pigs consumed. Pig production increased by about 17% compared with the previous year. Crop production continued to fall as vegetable prices fell and land was redeveloped for other uses. The common crops cultivated are leafy vegetables, high value cut flowers and ornamental plants. In 1999, 48,000 tonnes of vegetables were produced. Poultry production was 12,650 tonnes. There were 415,400 pigs in 1999.

Forestry. Timber production in 1995 was 200,000 cu. metres.

Fisheries. In 1999 the capture and mariculture fisheries supplied about 36% of seafood consumed in Hong Kong and pond fish farm produced about 10% of the freshwater fish consumed. The capture fishing industry employs some 5,170 fishing vessels and some 12,900 local fishermen. In 1999 the industry produced an estimated 127,800 tonnes of fisheries produce. Some 75,000 tonnes were supplied for local consumption and the remainder landed or exported outside Hong Kong. On the other hand, there are 26 fish culture zones occupying a total sea area of 209 ha with some 1,450 licensed operators. The estimated production in 1999 was 1,250 tonnes, or 7% of local consumption of live marine fish. The inland fish ponds, covering a total of 1,094 ha, produced 4,500 of freshwater fish in 1999. The first phase of the artificial reefs programme was successfully completed in 1999 with more than 110 species of fish recorded on the reefs.

INDUSTRY

The leading companies by market capitalization in Hong Kong, excluding banking and finance, in Jan. 2002 were: China Mobile Hong Kong Ltd (HK$439bn.), formerly China Telecom; Hutchison Whampoa (HK$288bn.), a diversified industrial conglomerate; and Cheung Kong Holdings (HK$160bn.), an investment holding company.

An economic policy based on free enterprise and free trade, a skilled workforce, an efficient commercial infrastructure, the modern and efficient sea-port (including container shipping terminals) and airport facilities, a geographical position relative to markets in North America and traditional trading links with the UK all contribute to Hong Kong's success as a modern industrial territory. Links with China have been growing increasingly strong in recent years and will remain so.

In Sept. 2001 there were 19,801 manufacturing establishments employing 209,329 persons. Other establishment statistics by product type (and persons engaged) were: printing, publishing and allied industries, 4,778 (42,963); textiles and clothing, 3,696 (58,821); plastics, 973 (5,938); electronics, 748 (20,939); watches and clocks, 347 (2,945); shipbuilding, 325 (3,173); electrical appliances, 49 (390).

Labour. In 2001 the size of the labour force (synonymous with the economically active population) was 3,427,100 (1,461,900 females). The persons engaged in Sept. 2001 included 1,027,000 people in wholesale, retail and import/export trades, restaurants and hotels, 437,000 in finance, insurance, real estate and business services, 209,000 in manufacturing, 177,000 in the civil service and 77,000 in construction sites (manual workers only).

The seasonally-adjusted unemployment rate for July–Sept. 2002 was 7·4%, compared to the equivalent rate for July–Sept. 1997 of 2·1%.

EXTERNAL ECONOMIC RELATIONS

Imports and Exports. Industry is mainly export-oriented. In 2001 the total value of imports (c.i.f.) was HK$1,586·2bn. and total exports (f.o.b.) HK$1,481·0bn. In 2001, 36·9% of total exports went to the mainland of China, 22·3% to the USA, 5·9% to Japan, 3·7% to the United Kingdom and 3·5% to Germany. The main suppliers of imports were the mainland of China (43·5%), Japan (11·3%), Taiwan (6·9%), USA (6·7%) and Singapore (4·6%).

In 2001 domestic exports included (in HK$1m.): clothing and accessories, 72,240; electrical machinery and parts, 20,322; textiles and fabrics, 8,193; parts and accessories suitable for use solely with office machines and automatic data processing machines, 4,705. The chief import items were consumer goods (537,967), raw materials and semi-manufactures (511,367), capital goods (428,147) and foodstuffs (60,353).

Visible trade normally carries an adverse balance which is offset by a favourable balance of invisible trade, in particular transactions in connection with air transportation, shipping, tourism and banking services.

Hong Kong has a free exchange market. Foreign merchants may remit profits or repatriate capital. Import and export controls are kept to the minimum, consistent with strategic requirements.

COMMUNICATIONS

Roads. In 1998 there were 1,865 km of roads, more than 900 km of which were in the New Territories. There are eight major road tunnels, including two under Victoria Harbour. In 1998 there were 501,000 licensed motor vehicles, including 318,000 private cars, 115,000 goods vehicles and 23,000 motorcycles. There were 14,014 road accidents in 1998, 221 fatal. A total of 14·8m. tonnes of cargo were transported by road in 1996.

Rail. The railway network covers around 143 km. The electrified Kowloon-Canton Railway runs for 34 km from the terminus at Hung Hom in Kowloon to the border point at Lo Wu. It carried 255m. passengers in 1998. In 1996, 939,000 tonnes of cargo were transported by rail. A light rail system (32 km and 57 stops) is operated by the Kowloon-Canton Railway Corporation in Tuen Mun, Yuen Long and Tin Shui Wai; it carried 105m. passengers in 1998.

The electric tramway on the northern shore of Hong Kong Island commenced operating in 1904 and has a total track length of 16 km. The Peak Tram, a funicular railway connecting the Peak district with the lower levels in Victoria, has a track length of 1,365 metres and a capacity of 120 passengers per trip.

A metro, the Mass Transit Railway system, comprises 74 km with 43 stations and carried 2·3m. passengers per weekday in 1998.

The Airport Express Line (35 km) opened in 1998 and carried a total of 3·9m. passengers in that year.

In 1996 a total of 3·9m. passenger journeys were made on public transport (including local railways, buses, etc.).

Civil Aviation. The new Chek Lap Kok airport, built on reclaimed land off Lantau Island to the west of Hong Kong, opened on 6 July 1998, replacing Hong Kong International Airport (Kai Tak), which was situated on the north shore of Kowloon Bay. More than 70 airlines now operate scheduled services to and from Hong Kong. Cathay Pacific Airways, one of the three Hong Kong-based airlines, operates more than 530 passenger and cargo services weekly to Europe (including 18 passenger and 10 cargo services per week to the UK), the Far and Middle East, South Africa, Australasia and North America. Cathay Pacific flew 197·6m. km in1999 and carried 12,321,256 passengers in 2002. Hong Kong Dragon Airlines provides scheduled services to 19 cities in Mainland China and nine other destinations in Asia plus 14 cargo services per week to seven destinations (including six weekly services to the UK). AHK Air Hong Kong Ltd., an all-cargo operator, provides seven weekly scheduled services to and from Hong Kong with Incheon, Tokyo and Osaka as destinations. In 2002 (provisional figures), 206,640 aircraft arrived and departed and 33m. passengers and 2·48m. tonnes of freight were carried on aircraft. Hong Kong International Airport handled more international freight in 2001 than any other airport.

Hong Kong–Taipei and vice-versa is the most flown airline route in the world, with 5·43m. passengers flying between the two cities in 2001.

Shipping. The port of Hong Kong handled 17·8m. 20-ft equivalent units in 2001, making it the world's busiest container port. The Kwai Chung Container Port has 18 berths with 5,754 metres of quay backed by 217 ha of cargo handling area. Merchant shipping in 2001 totalled 13,726,000 GRT, including oil tankers 1,593,000 GRT. In 2001, 37,350 ocean-going vessels, 116,190 river cargo vessels and 61,200 river passenger vessels called at Hong Kong. In 2001, 178m. tonnes of freight were handled. In 2001 vessels totalling 340,027,000 NRT entered ports and vessels totalling 340,163,000 NRT cleared.

Telecommunications. In Dec. 2001 there were 4,940,525 telephones (731 per 1,000 population), of which 1,764,623 were for business use and 2,161,151 were residential lines. There were also 411,099 fax lines.

The local fixed telecommunications network services (FTNS) market in Hong Kong was liberalized in 1995. Apart from the incumbent FTNS operator at that time, three new local FTNS operators were licensed. In July 1999 the Government invited the industry to apply for licences to operate local wireless fixed networks. On 18 Jan. 2000 the Government announced that five licences for the local fixed wireless FTNS services would be provided. This would further increase the choice of consumers in the local fixed market.

In Dec. 2000 there were six mobile phone operators providing 11 networks in Hong Kong. There were only 687,600 mobile phone subscribers in 1995, since when the sector has expanded substantially. By Dec. 2001 there were approximately 5·70m. mobile phone subscribers (84% of Hong Kong's population). In addition there were 29 radio paging operators in Nov. 2000 serving 333,990 users. The Internet market has also seen considerable growth. In April 2002 there were 4·35m. Internet users, up from 1·85m. in June 2000.

The external telecommunications services market has been fully liberalized since 1 Jan.1999, and the external telecommunications facilities market was also liberalized starting from 1 Jan. 2000.

In 2000 there were 2·4m. PCs in use (350·6 per 1,000 persons).

Postal Services. In Dec. 2002 there were 131 post offices. In 2001 Hongkong Post handled 1,360m. letters and 923,000 parcels.

SOCIAL INSTITUTIONS

Justice. The Hong Kong Act of 1985 provided for Hong Kong ordinances to replace English laws in specified fields.

The courts of justice comprise the Court of Final Appeal (inaugurated 1 July 1997) which hears appeals on civil and criminal matters from the High Court; the High Court (consisting of the Court of Appeal and the Court of First Instance); the Lands Tribunal which determines on statutory claims for compensation over land and certain landlord and tenant matters; the District Court (which includes the Family Court); the Magistracies (including the Juvenile Court); the Coroner's Court; the Labour Tribunal, which provides a quick and inexpensive method of settling disputes between employers and employees; the Small Claims Tribunal deals with monetary claims involving amounts not exceeding HK$50,000; and the Obscene Articles Tribunal.

While the High Court has unlimited jurisdiction in both civil and criminal matters, the District Court has limited jurisdiction. The maximum term of imprisonment it may impose is seven years. Magistracies exercise criminal jurisdiction over a wide range of offences, and the powers of punishment are generally restricted to a maximum of two years' imprisonment or a fine of HK$100,000.

After being in abeyance for 25 years, the death penalty was abolished in 1992.

71,962 crimes were reported in 1998, of which 14,682 were violent crimes. 40,422 people were arrested in 1998, of whom 9,207 were for violent crimes. The prison population was 11,637 in 1997 (190 per 100,000 of national population).

Religion. In 1997 there were 4,790,000 Buddhists and Taoists, 280,000 Protestants, 270,000 Roman Catholics and 1,150,000 people of other beliefs.

Education. Adult literacy was 93·5% in 1999 (96·4% among males and 89·7% among females). Universal basic education is available to all children aged from 6 to 15 years. In around three-quarters of the ordinary secondary day schools teaching has been in Cantonese since 1998–99, with about a quarter of ordinary secondary day schools still using English. In 1998 there were 175,073 pupils in 744 kindergartens (all private), 476,802 full-time students in 832 ordinary primary day schools (some 10·7% in private schools) and 455,872 in 37 government, 352 aided and 82 private ordinary secondary day schools.

There were 15,204 full-time and 32,543 part-time students enrolled in the seven Technical Institutes in the academic year 1998–99, and 5,220 full-time and 9,454 part-time students enrolled in the two Technical Colleges. The Hong Kong Technical Institutes and the Hong Kong Technical Colleges were renamed the Hong Kong Institute of Vocational Education in 1999.

The University of Hong Kong (founded 1911) had 10,687 full-time and 2,985 part-time students in the academic year of 1998–99, the Chinese University of Hong Kong (founded 1963), 10,271 full-time and 2,224 part-time students, the Hong Kong University of Science and Technology (founded 1991), 6,446 full-time and 710 part-time students, the Hong Kong Polytechnic University (founded 1972 as the Hong Kong Polytechnic), 11,646 full-time and 6,778 part-time students, the City University of Hong Kong (founded 1984 as the City Polytechnic of Hong Kong), 11,123 full-time and 5,241 part-time students, the Hong Kong Baptist University (founded 1956 as the Hong Kong Baptist College), 4,185 full-time and 517 part-time students, the Lingnan University (founded 1967 as the Lingnan College), 2,133 full-time and three part-time students, and the Hong Kong Institute of Education (founded 1997), 3,037 full-time and 5,954 part-time students.

Estimated total government expenditure on education in 1999–2000 was HK$55·2bn., 19% of total public expenditure.

Health. The Department of Health (DH) is the Government's health adviser and regulatory authority. The Hospital Authority (HA) is an independent body responsible for the management of all public hospitals. In 2002 there were 9,021 doctors on the local list, equivalent to 1·5 doctors per 1,000 population. In 2001 there were 1,900 dentists, 42,000 nurses and 136 midwives. In 2002 the total number of hospital beds was 35,100, including 29,432 beds in 41 public hospitals under the

HA and 2,928 beds in 12 private hospitals. The bed-population ratio was 5·2 beds per thousand population.

The Chinese Medicine Ordinance was passed by the Legislative Council in July 1999 to establish a statutory framework to control the practice, use, manufacture and trading of Chinese medicine.

Recurrent spending on health amounts to US$4·15bn. (HK$324bn.), an increase of 4% in real terms over the latest estimated spending for 2001–02.

Welfare. Social welfare programmes include social security, family services, child care, services for the elderly, medical social services, youth and community work, probation, and corrections and rehabilitation. 181 non-governmental organizations are subsidized by public funds.

The government gives non-contributory cash assistance to needy families, unemployed able-bodied adults, the severely disabled and the elderly. Caseload as at 31 Dec. 2002 totalled 266,571. Victims of natural disasters, crimes of violence and traffic accidents are financially assisted. Estimated total government expenditure on social welfare for 2002–03 is HK$32·1bn.

CULTURE

Broadcasting. Broadcasting is regulated by the Broadcasting Authority, a statutory body comprising three government officers and nine non-official members.

There is a public broadcasting station, Radio Television Hong Kong (colour by PAL), which broadcasts 7 channels (3 Chinese, 1 English, 1 bilingual and 1 Putonhua service, and 1 for the relay of the BBC World Service), 6 of which provide a 24-hour service. Hong Kong Commercial Broadcasting Co. Ltd and Metro Broadcast Co. Ltd transmit commercial sound programmes on six channels. Television Broadcasts Ltd and Asia Television Ltd transmit domestic free television programme services in English and Chinese on four channels. Hong Kong Cable Television Ltd offers over 30 TV channels on a subscription basis. The PCCW VOD Ltd launched the world's first commercial scale video-on-demand programme service in March 1998. Four new domestic pay television service licences have been granted respectively to Hong Kong Network TV Ltd, Galaxy Satellite Broadcasting Ltd, Yes Television (Hong Kong) Ltd and Pacific Digital Media (HK) Corp. Ltd. These new services are expected to bring in over 100 television channels. There are four non-domestic television programme services in Hong Kong. Hutchvision Hong Kong broadcasts by satellite to the entire Asian region on 30 TV channels. Galaxy Satellite Broadcasting Ltd offers by satellite two channels covering Asia, Australia, Middle East, South Africa and part of Europe. The 3rd and 4th non-domestic television programme service licensees are APT Satellite Glory Ltd and Starbucks (HK) Ltd.

In 1997 there were 1·84m. TV receivers and 4·45m. radio receivers.

Cinema. In 2000 there were 63 cinemas (with 178 screens); some 151 local films and 299 foreign films were screened, generating box office receipts of HK$383m. and HK$532m. respectively. In 1995 gross box office receipts came to HK$1,368m. 150 full-length films were made in 2000.

Press. In 1999 there were 45 newspapers including 22 Chinese-language dailies, three English dailies, six other Chinese and eight other English papers, one bilingual paper and five other language papers. The newspapers with the highest circulation figures are all Chinese-language papers—*The Sun, Apple Daily* and *Oriental Daily*. In 1999 there were 722 periodicals of which 452 were Chinese, 152 English, 106 bilingual and 12 in other languages. Circulation of dailies in 1996 was 5m. At 800 newspapers per 1,000 inhabitants, Hong Kong has one of the highest rates of circulation in the world. A number of news agency bulletins are registered as newspapers.

Tourism. There were 11,328,000 visitor arrivals in 1999. Receipts totalled US$7·21bn.

Libraries. In 1995 there were two public libraries and in 1990 there were 17 higher education libraries. These libraries held 8,336,000 volumes for 2,119,383 registered users.

FURTHER READING

Statistical Information: The Census and Statistics Department is responsible for the preparation and collation of government statistics. These statistics are published mainly in the *Hong Kong Monthly Digest of Statistics.* The Department also publishes monthly trade statistics, economic indicators and an annual review of overseas trade, etc. *Website:* http://www.info.gov.hk/censtatd/

Hong Kong [various years] Hong Kong Government Press

Brown, J. M. (ed.) *Hong Kong's Transitions, 1842–1997.* London, 1997

Buckley, R., *Hong Kong: the Road to 1997.* CUP, 1997

Cameron, N., *An Illustrated History of Hong Kong.* OUP, 1991

Cottrell, R., *The End of Hong Kong: the Secret Diplomacy of Imperial Retreat.* London, 1993

Courtauld, C. and Holdsworth, M., *The Hong Kong Story.* OUP, 1997

Flowerdew, J., *The Final Years of British Hong Kong: the Discourse of Colonial Withdrawal.* Hong Kong, 1997

Keay, J., *Last Post: the End of Empire in the Far East.* London, 1997

Lo, C. P., *Hong Kong.* London, 1992

Lo, S.-H., *The Politics of Democratization in Hong Kong.* London, 1997

Morris, J., *Hong Kong: Epilogue to an Empire.* 2nd ed. [of *Hong Kong: Xianggang*]. London, 1993

Roberti, M., *The Fall of Hong Kong: China's Triumph and Britain's Betrayal.* 2nd ed. Chichester, 1997

Roberts, E. V., *et al., Historical Dictionary of Hong Kong and Macau.* Metuchen (NJ), 1993

Scott, Ian, *Hong Kong.* [Bibliography] ABC-Clio, Oxford and Santa Barbara (CA), 1990

Shipp, S., *Hong Kong, China: a Political History of the British Crown Colony's Transfer to Chinese Rule.* Jefferson (NC), 1995

Tsang, S. Y., *Hong Kong: an Appointment with China.* London, 1997

Wang, G. and Wong, S. L. (eds.) *Hong Kong's Transition: a Decade after the Deal.* OUP, 1996

Welsh, F., *A History of Hong Kong.* 3rd ed. London, 1997

Yahuda, M., *Hong Kong: China's Challenge.* London, 1996

MACAO

KEY HISTORICAL EVENTS

Macao was visited by Portuguese traders from 1513 and became a Portuguese colony in 1557. Initially sovereignty remained vested in China, with the Portuguese paying an annual rent. In 1848–49 the Portuguese declared Macao a free port and established jurisdiction over the territory. On 6 Jan. 1987 Portugal agreed to return Macao to China on 20 Dec. 1999 under a plan in which it would become a special administrative zone of China, with considerable autonomy.

TERRITORY AND POPULATION

The territory, which lies at the mouth of the Pearl River, comprises a peninsula (7·84 sq. km) connected by a narrow isthmus to the People's Republic of China, on which is built the city of Santa Nome de Deus de Macao, and the islands of Taipa (5·79 sq. km), linked to Macao by a 2-km bridge, and Colôane (7·82 sq. km) linked to Taipa by a 2-km causeway. The total area of Macao is 21·45 sq. km. Land is being reclaimed from the sea. The population (1991 census) was 339,464 (174,858 females). Population on 31 Dec. 1999, 437,500 (206,600 females), a growth rate of 1·6%; density (1997), 19,387 people per sq. km. An estimated 98·8% of the population lived in urban areas in 1995. The official languages are Chinese and Portuguese, with the majority speaking the Cantonese dialect. The UN gives a projected population for 2010 of 481,000.

In Dec. 1999, 24,290 foreigners were legally registered for residency in Macao. There were 4,984 legal immigrants from the People's Republic of China.

SOCIAL STATISTICS

1999: births, 4,148 (9·5 per 1,000 population); marriages, 1,367 (3·1); deaths, 1,374 (3·1); divorces, 283 (0·6). Infant mortality, 1999 (per 1,000 live births), 3·6%. Life expectancy at birth (1994–97) 76·79 years.

CLIMATE

Sub-tropical tending towards temperate. The number of rainy days is more than a third of the year. Average annual rainfall varies from 39–79" (1,000–2,000 mm). It is very humid from May to Sept.

CONSTITUTION AND GOVERNMENT

Macao's constitution is the 'Basic Law', promulgated by China's National People's Congress on 31 March 1993 and in effect since 20 Dec. 1999. It is a Special Administrative Region (SAR) of the People's Republic of China, and is directly under the Central People's Government while enjoying a high degree of autonomy.

RECENT ELECTIONS

At the elections held on 23 Sept. 2001 pro-Beijing candidates and pro-business candidates each won four seats, with the pro-democracy New Democratic Macau Association winning two. Turn-out was 52%.

CURRENT ADMINISTRATION

Chief Executive: Hau-wah (Edmund) Ho; b. 1955 (appointed 20 Dec. 1999).

Government Website: http://www.macau.gov.mo/

ECONOMY

Gambling is of major importance to the economy of Macao. Casino takings account for a quarter of total GDP and provide billions of dollars in taxes. 5% of the workforce is directly employed by the casinos.

Currency. The unit of currency is the *pataca* (MOP) of 100 *avos* which is tied to the Hong Kong dollar at parity. Inflation was 8·6% in 1995 and an estimated 6·5% in 1996. Foreign exchange reserves were US\$3,670m. in June 2002. Total money supply was 6,468m. patacas in May 2002.

Budget. Provisional figures for 1999 were: revenue, 9,859·0m. patacas; expenditure, 9,552·6m. patacas.

Performance. Real GDP growth was an estimated −7·1% in 1998 and −5·2% in 1999.

Banking and Finance. There are two note-issuing banks in Macao—the Macao branch of the Bank of China and the Macao branch of the Banco Nacional Ultramarino. The Monetary Authority of Macao functions as a central bank (*Director,* Teng Ling Seng). Commercial business is handled (1999) by 22 banks, 11 of which are local and 11 foreign. Total deposits, 1999 (including non-resident deposits), 98,267·9m. patacas.

ENERGY AND NATURAL RESOURCES

Environment. According to the *World Bank Atlas* Macao's carbon dioxide emissions in 1998 were the equivalent of 3·8 tonnes per capita.

Electricity. Installed capacity was 351·6 MW in 1999; production, 1·43bn. kWh; net import, 194·4m. kWh.

Oil and Gas. 306,836,000 litres of fuel oil were imported in 1999.

Fisheries. The catch in 1999 was approximately 1,500 tonnes.

INDUSTRY

Although the economy is based on gambling and tourism there is a light industrial base of textiles and toy-making. In 1998 the number of manufacturing establishments was 1,381 (textiles and clothing, 575; metal products, 171; foods, 160; furniture, 109).

Labour. In 1999 a total of 202,480 people were in employment of which 56,433 (27·9%) were employed in public, social and private services; 52,961 (26·2%), wholesale and retail trade, hotels, restaurants and similar activities; 44,507 (22·0%), manufacturing; 16,300 (8·1%), construction; 15,697 (7·8%), financial activities, real estate, leasing and commercial services; 15,016 (7·4%), transport, storage and communications; and 366 (0·6%) in other employment. Employment in 1999 totalled 64·7% (65·3% in 1998); unemployment stood at 6·4% (4·6%).

INTERNATIONAL TRADE

Imports and Exports. In 1999 imports were valued at 16,300m. patacas, of which the main products were consumer goods, raw materials and semi-manufactured goods, capital goods, fuels and lubricants. Main markets for imports (in MOP1m.): 5,808·9, mainland China; 2,945·0, Hong Kong; 2,102·8, European Union.

1999 exports were valued at 17,580m. patacas, of which the main products were textiles and garments, machinery and apparatus, footwear, cement and toys. Main markets for exports (in MOP1m.): 8,249·1, USA; 5,303·7, European Union.

COMMUNICATIONS

Roads. In 1999 there were 321·2 km of roads; 114,247 vehicles were in circulation (55,144 automobiles; 58,116 motorcycles); and 8,333 vehicles were registered, of which 5,034 were motorcycles. There are 126 cars per 1,000 inhabitants. 2,024 people were injured or killed in 7,950 traffic accidents in 1999.

Civil Aviation. An international airport opened in Dec. 1995. In 2000 Macau International Airport handled 1,793,824 passengers and 51,635 tonnes of freight. In 1998 Air Macau flew to Bangkok, Beijing, Chongqing, Fuzhou, Kaohsiung, Manila, Nanjing, Shanghai, Taipei, Wuhan, Xiamen and Zhengzhou, and flew a total of 11·5m. km. In 1999 it carried 1,270,600 passengers.

Shipping. Macao is served by Portuguese, British and Dutch steamship lines. Regular services connect Macao with Hong Kong, 65 km to the northeast. In 1998 merchant shipping totalled 2,000 GRT.

Telecommunications. In 2000 there were 176,800 main line telephones (403·8 per 1,000 inhabitants) and 70,000 PCs in use (159·9 for every 1,000 persons). In early 2000 Macao had 122,000 mobile phone subscribers and in Dec. 2000 there were 60,000 Internet subscribers. There were 7,300 fax machines in 1997.

Postal Services. 14,278,000 letters and parcels were posted in 1999.

SOCIAL INSTITUTIONS

Justice. There is a judicial district court, a criminal court and an administrative court with 13 magistrates in all.

In 1999 (1998) there were 8,582 (8,058) crimes, of which 5,503 (5,769) were against property. There were 788 persons in prison in 1999 (711 in 1998).

Religion. The majority of the Chinese population is Buddhist. About 6% are Roman Catholic.

Education. There are three types of schools: public, church-run and private. In 1998–99 there were 221 schools and colleges with 107,419 students and 4,750 teachers. Numbers of schools and colleges by category (number of students at the end of the 1998–99 academic year): pre-primary, 62 (17,354); primary, 83 (48,269); secondary, 41 (28,543); technical/professional secondary, 9 (3,239); higher, 26 (10,014). In 1998–99 there were 112 adult education institutions with a total of 47,504 students enrolled.

Health. In 1995 there were 467 doctors, 22 dentists, 861 nurses and 41 pharmacists. In 1999 there were 488 inhabitants per doctor and 415 per hospital bed.

CULTURE

Broadcasting. One government and a private commercial radio station are in operation on medium-waves broadcasting in Portuguese and Chinese. Number of receivers (1996), 160,000. Macao receives television broadcasts from Hong Kong and in 1984 a public bilingual TV station began operating. There were, in 1997, 49,000 receivers (colour by PAL).

Press. In 1999 there were 11 daily newspapers (three in Portuguese and eight in Chinese) and seven weekly newspapers (two in Portuguese and five in Chinese), plus 16 periodicals (five in Portuguese and 11 in Chinese).

Tourism. Tourism is one of the mainstays of the economy. In 1999 there were 7·4m. visitors of which 1·6m. were from mainland China, 4·2m. from Japan, and 1·65m. from Hong Kong. Receipts totalled US$2,466m.

Libraries. There are 14 public and seven university/college libraries.

FURTHER READING

Direcção de Serviços de Estatística e Censos. *Anuário Estatístico/Yearbook of Statistics Macau in Figures*. Macao, Annual.

Porter, J., *Macau, the Imaginary City: Culture and Society, 1557 to the Present*. Oxford, 1996
Roberts, E. V., *Historical Dictionary of Hong Kong and Macau*. Metuchen (NJ), 1993

Statistics and Census Service Website: http://www.dsec.gov.mo/

TAIWAN[1]

KEY HISTORICAL EVENTS

Taiwan, christened Ilha Formosa (beautiful island) by the Portuguese, was ceded to Japan by China by the Treaty of Shimonoseki in 1895. After the Second World War the island was surrendered to Gen. Chiang Kai-shek who made it the headquarters for his crumbling Nationalist Government. Until 1970 the US fully supported Taiwan's claims to represent all of China. Only in 1971 did the government of the People's Republic of China manage to replace that of Chiang Kai-shek at the UN. In Jan. 1979 the UN established formal diplomatic relations with the People's Republic of China, breaking off all formal ties with Taiwan. Taiwan itself has continued to reject all attempts at reunification, and although there have been frequent threats from mainland China to precipitate direct action (including military manoeuvres off the Taiwanese coast) the prospect of confrontation with the USA supports the status quo.

In July 1999 President Lee Teng-hui repudiated Taiwan's 50-year-old One China policy—the pretence of a common goal of unification—arguing that Taiwan and China should maintain equal 'state to state' relations. This was a rejection of Beijing's view that Taiwan is no more than a renegade Chinese province which must be reunited with the mainland, by force if necessary. In the Presidential election of 18 March 2000 Chen Shui-bian, leader of the Democratic Progressive Party, was elected, together with Annette Lu Hsiu-bien as his Vice-President. Both support independence although Chen Shui-bian has made friendly gestures towards China and has distanced himself from colleagues who want an immediate declaration of independence.

TERRITORY AND POPULATION

Taiwan lies between the East and South China Seas about 100 miles from the coast of Fujian. The territories currently under the control of the Republic of China include Taiwan, Penghu (the Pescadores), Kinmen (Quemoy), and the Matsu Islands, as well as the archipelagos in the South China Sea. Off the Pacific coast of Taiwan are Green Island and Orchid Island. To the northeast of Taiwan are the Tiaoyutai Islets. The total area of Taiwan Island, the Penghu Archipelago and the Kinmen area (including the fortified offshore islands of Quemoy and Matsu) is 13,973 sq. miles (36,188 sq. km). Population (2001), 22,405,568. The ethnic composition is 84% native Taiwanese (including 15% of Hakka), 14% of Mainland Chinese, and 2% aborigine of Malayo-Polynesian origin. There are also 420,892 aboriginals of Malay origin. Population density: 619 per sq. km.

Taiwan's administrative units comprise (with 2001 populations): two special municipalities: Taipei, the capital (2·69m.) and Kaohsiung (1·48m.); five cities outside the county structure: Chiayi (265,109), Hsinchu (361,958), Keelung (390,966), Taichung (983,694), Tainan (740,846); 16 counties (*hsien*): Changhwa (1,313,994), Chiayi (563,365), Hsinchu (446,300), Hualien (353,139), Ilan (465,799), Kaohsiung (1,236,958), Miaoli (560,640), Nantou (541,818), Penghu (92,268), Pingtung (909,364), Taichung (1,502,274), Tainan (1,109,397), Taipei (3,610,252), Taitung (244,612), Taoyuan (1,792,962), Yunlin (743,562).

SOCIAL STATISTICS

In 2001 the birth rate was 11·65 per 1,000 population; death rate, 5·71 per 1,000; rate of growth, 0·56% per annum. Life expectancy: males, 72·87 years; females, 78·79 years. Infant mortality, 6·62 per 1,000 live births.

[1]See note on transcription of names in CHINA: Territory and Population.

CLIMATE

The climate is subtropical in the north and tropical in the south. The typhoon season extends from July to Sept. The average monthly temperatures of Jan. and July in Taipei are 59·5°F (15·3°C) and 83·3°F (28·5°C) respectively, and average annual rainfall is 84·99" (2,158·8 mm). Kaohsiung's average monthly temperatures of Jan. and July are 65·66°F (18·9°C) and 83·3°F (28·5°C) respectively, and average annual rainfall is 69·65" (1,769·2 mm).

CONSTITUTION AND GOVERNMENT

The ROC Constitution is based on the Principles of Nationalism, Democracy and Social Wellbeing formulated by Dr Sun Yat-sen, the founding father of the Republic of China. The ROC government is divided into three main levels: central, provincial/municipal and county/city each of which has well-defined powers.

The central government consists of the Office of the President, the National Assembly, which is specially elected only for constitutional amendment, and five governing branches called '*yuan*', namely the Executive Yuan, the Legislative Yuan, the Judicial Yuan, the Examination Yuan and the Control Yuan. The additional Article 4 of the Constitution stipulates that, beginning with the fourth Legislative Yuan (1999), the Legislative Yuan shall have 225 members.

At the provincial level, the provincial governments exercise administrative responsibility. Since the ROC government administers only Taiwan Province and two counties in Fukien Province, only two provincial governments are currently operational—the Taiwan Provincial Government and the Fukien Provincial Government. Taipei and Kaohsiung are special municipalities which are under the direct jurisdiction of the central government. At the local level, under the Taiwan Provincial Government are five city governments: Keelung, Hsinchu, Taichung, Chiayi and Tainan; and 16 county governments with the governments of their subordinate cities. The Fukien Provincial Government oversees the regional affairs of Kinmen County and Lienchiang County. From 5 May to 23 July 1997 the *Additional Articles of the Constitution of the Republic of China* underwent yet another amendment. The roles of the provincial government and the Control Yuan have taken on drastic changes. Under the newest revision:

- The provincial government is to be streamlined and the popular elections of the governor and members of the provincial council are suspended.
- A resolution on the impeachment of the President or Vice President is no longer to be instituted by the Control Yuan but rather by the Legislative Yuan.
- The Legislative Yuan has the power to pass a no-confidence vote against the premier of the Executive Yuan, while the president of the Republic has the power to dissolve the Legislative Yuan.
- The premier of the Executive Yuan is to be directly appointed by the president of the Republic. Hence the consent of the Legislative Yuan is no longer needed.
- Educational, scientific and cultural budgets, especially the compulsory education budget, will be given priority, but no longer restricted by Article 164 of the Constitution to remain at least 15% of the total national budget.

National Anthem. 'San Min Chu I'; words by Dr Sun Yat-sen, tune by Cheng Mao-yun.

RECENT ELECTIONS

Presidential elections took place on 18 March 2000. Chen Shui-bian (Democratic Progressive Party) emerged victorious with 39·3% of the vote, against independent James Soong (36·8%), Nationalist Lien Chan (23·1%) and two other opponents. Turn-out was 82·7%. Chen Shui-bian's victory ended more than 50 years of uninterrupted Nationalist (Kuomintang) rule.

Elections to the Legislative Yuan were held on 1 Dec. 2001. The Democratic Progressive Party won 87 seats with 36·6% of votes cast; the Nationalist Party, 68 seats (31·3%); the People First Party, 46 seats (20·3%); the Taiwan Solidarity Union, 13 seats (8·5%); and non-partisans and others, 11 seats (3·4%).

CURRENT ADMINISTRATION

President: Chen Shui-bian; b. 1951 (Democratic Progressive Party; sworn in 20 May 2000).

Vice President: Hsiu-lien Annette Lu.

In March 2003 the cabinet comprised:

Prime Minister and *President of the Executive Yuan:* Yu Shyi-kun; b. 1948 (Democratic Progressive Party; sworn in 1 Feb. 2002). There are eight ministries under the Executive Yuan: Interior; Foreign Affairs; National Defence; Finance; Education; Justice; Economic Affairs; Transport and Communications.

Vice-President of the Executive Yuan and Chairman of the Council for Economic Planning and Development: Lin Hsin-i. *President, Control Yuan:* Frederick Chien. *President, Examination Yuan:* Yao Chia-wen. *President, Judicial Yuan:* Yueh-sheng Weng. *President, Legislative Yuan:* Jin-ping Wang. *Secretary General, Executive Yuan:* Liu Shyh-fang. *Minister of Foreign Affairs:* Eugene Chien. *Defence:* Tang Yian-min. *Interior:* Yu Cheng-hsien. *Finance:* Lin Chuan. *Education:* Huang Jong-tsun. *Economic Affairs:* Lin Yi-fu. *Justice:* Chen Ding-nan. *Transport and Communications:* Lin Ling-san. *Ministers without Portfolio:* Tsay Ching-yen; Hu Sheng-cheng; Chen Chi-nan; Huang Hwei-chen; Lin Sheng-feng; Kuo Yao-chi (also *Chairwoman of the Public Construction Commission*); Yeh Jiunn-rong.

In addition to the Mongolian and Tibetan Affairs Commission and the Overseas Chinese Affairs Commission, a number of commissions and subordinate organizations have been formed with the resolution of the Executive Yuan Council and the Legislature to meet new demands and handle new affairs. Examples include the Environmental Protection Administration, which was set up in 1987 as public awareness of pollution control rose; the Mainland Affairs Council, which was established in 1990 to handle the thawing of relations between Taiwan and the Chinese mainland; and the Fair Trade Commission, which was established in 1992 to promote a fair trade system. Since 1995 even more commissions have been set up to provide a wider scope of services: the Public Construction Commission was set up in July 1995, the Council of Aboriginal Affairs in Dec. 1996, and the National Council on Physical Fitness and Sports in July 1997.

These commissions and councils are headed by:

Aboriginal Affairs Council: Chen Chien-nien. *Agricultural Council:* Lee Ching-lung. *Atomic Energy Council:* Ouyang Min-shen. *Council for Hakka Affairs:* Yeh Chu-lan. *Coast Guard Administration:* Wang Chun. *Cultural Affairs:* Chen Yu-chiou. *Environmental Protection Administration:* Hau Lung-bin. *Fair Trade Commission:* Hwang Tzong-leh. *Health Department:* Twu Shiing-jer. *Labour Affairs Council:* Chen Chu. *Mainland Affairs Council:* Tsai Ing-wen. *Mongolian and Tibetan Affairs Commission:* Hsu Chih-hsiung. *National Council on Physical Fitness and Sports:* Lin Te-fu. *National Palace Museum:* Tu Cheng-sheng. *National Science Council:* Wei Che-ho. *National Youth Commission:* Lin Fang-mei. *Overseas Chinese Affairs Commission:* Chang Fu-mei. *Research, Development and Evaluation Commission:* Lin Chia-cheng. *Vocational Assistance for Retired Veterans Affairs Commission:* Yang Teh-chih.

Government Website: http://www.gio.gov.tw

DEFENCE

Conscription is for two years. Defence expenditure in 2000 totalled US$17,248m. (US$785 per capita), representing 5·6% of GDP. Between 1997 and 2001 Taiwan spent US$11·4bn. on defence imports, making it the world's largest buyer of arms, although expenditure in 2000 and 2001 was greatly reduced.

Army. The Army was estimated to number about 190,000 in 2000, including military police. Army reserves numbered 2·7m. In addition the Ministry of Justice, Ministry of Interior and the Ministry of Defence each command paramilitary forces totalling 25,000 personnel in all. The Army consists of Army Corps, Defence Commands, Airborne Cavalry Brigades, Armoured Brigades, Motorized Rifle Brigades, Infantry Brigades, Special Warfare Brigades and Missile Command.

Navy. Active personnel in the Navy in 2000 totalled 50,000. There are 425,000 naval reservists. The operational and land-based forces consist of four submarines, 16 destroyers and 21 frigates. There is a naval air wing operating 31 combat aircraft and 21 armed helicopters.

Air Force. Units in the operational system are equipped with aircraft that include locally developed IDF, F-16, Mirage 2000-5 and F-5E fighter-interceptors. There were 50,000 Air Force personnel in 2000 and 334,000 reservists.

INTERNATIONAL RELATIONS

By a treaty of 2 Dec. 1954 the USA pledged to defend Taiwan, but this treaty lapsed one year after the USA established diplomatic relations with the People's Republic of China on 1 Jan. 1979. In April 1979 the Taiwan Relations Act was passed by the US Congress to maintain commercial, cultural and other relations between USA and Taiwan through the American Institute in Taiwan and its Taiwan counterpart, the Coordination Council for North American Affairs in the USA, which were accorded quasi-diplomatic status in 1980. The People's Republic took over the China seat in the UN from Taiwan on 25 Oct. 1971. In May 1991 Taiwan ended its formal state of war with the People's Republic. Taiwan became a member of the World Trade Organization on 1 Jan. 2002.

In Nov. 2000 Taiwan had formal diplomatic ties with 29 countries and maintained substantive relations with over 100 countries and territories around the globe.

ECONOMY

Overview. The government launched a Global Logistics Development Plan in 2000 in order to strengthen the technology base of Taiwan's industries. This plan exploits Taiwan's advantage in high-tech manufacturing to develop e-commerce and a complete range of supply-chain services, with the goal of making Taiwan a major international procurement and logistics base.

From 2002 to 2007, the government will implement the new national development plan, *Challenge 2008*, which will pave the way for Taiwan's emergence as a Green Silicon Island in the 21st century.

Currency. The unit of currency is the *New Taiwan dollar* (TWD) of 100 *cents*. Gold reserves were 13·55m. oz in Oct. 2000. There was deflation in both 1999 and 2000, of 1·4% and 1·6% respectively. Foreign exchange reserves were US$109,056m. in Oct. 2000.

Budget. As a result of the constitutional amendment to abolish the provincial government from the fiscal year 2000 the central government budget has been enlarged to include the former provincial government. The central government's general budget for the fiscal year 2002 (beginning on 1 Jan.) was NT$1,518,724m. Expenditure planned: 18·1% on education, science and culture; 17·6% on economic development; 17·5% on social security; 15% on defence.

Performance. Taiwan sustained rapid economic growth at an annual rate of 9·2% from 1960 up to 1990. The rate slipped to 6·4% in the 1990s and 5·9% in 2000; Taiwan suffered from the Asian financial crisis, though less than its neighbours. Consumer prices showed increasing stability, rising at an average annual rate of 6·3% from 1960 to 1989, 2·9% in the 1990s and 1·3% in 2000. In 2001 global economic sluggishness and the events of 11 Sept. in the USA severely affected Taiwan's economy, which contracted by 2·2%. Per capita GNP stood at US$12,876, while consumer prices remained almost unchanged.

Banking and Finance. The Central Bank of China (reactivated in 1961) regulates the money supply, manages foreign exchange and issues currency. The *Governor* is Perng Fai-nan. The Bank of Taiwan is the largest commercial bank and the fiscal agent of the government. There are two stock exchanges in Taipei.

ENERGY AND NATURAL RESOURCES

Electricity. Output of electricity in 2001 was 188·5m. MWh; total installed capacity was 35,568 MW, of which 77·1% is held by the Taiwan Power Company. There were six units in three nuclear power stations in 2002. Consumption per capita stood at 4,257 litres of oil equivalent in 2001.

Oil and Gas. Crude oil production in 2001 was 40·6m. litres; natural gas, 849m. cu. metres.

Minerals. Coal production ceased by 2001 because of competitive imports and increasing local production costs.

Agriculture. In 2001 the cultivated area was 848,743 ha, of which 438,974 ha were paddy fields. Rice production totalled 1,396,274 tonnes. Livestock production was valued at more than NT$101,205m., accounting for 28·67% of Taiwan's total agricultural production value.

Forestry. Forest area, 2001: 2,101,719 ha. Forest reserves: trees, 357,492,423 cu. metres; bamboo, 1,109m. poles. Timber production, 26,401 cu. metres.

Fisheries. In 2001 Taiwan's fishing fleet totalled 27,018 vessels (12,942 were powered craft); the catch was approximately 1·32m. tonnes. NT$89,813m. worth of fish was produced. Of this, 52% came from far-sea fishing, 26% from inland aquaculture, 14% from offshore fishing and 5% from coastal fishing. More than 40% of the catch was exported, with the biggest items being big eye tuna and albacore (long-finned tuna).

INDUSTRY
According to the Financial Times Survey (FT500), the largest companies in Taiwan by market capitalization on 28 March 2002 were Taiwan Semicon. Mnfg (US$46,445·2m.) and United Micro Electronics (US$19,987·9m.).

Output (in tonnes) in 1999: steel bars, 1·4m.; sugar, 0·28m.; cement, 18·2m.; pulp, 0·30m.; cotton fabrics, 1,061m. sq. metres; portable computers, 9·95m. units; desktop computers 3·01m. units. Taiwan is the 3rd largest information technology producer after the USA and Japan. The IT sector has replaced traditional industries as the engine for growth.

Labour. In Sept. 2002 the total labour force was 9·97m., of whom 9·44m. were employed. Of the employed population, 55·09% worked in the service sector (including 22·70% in trade and 16·11% in accommodation and eating and drinking establishments); 37·28% in industry (including 27·05% in manufacturing and 7·64% in construction); and 7·63% in agriculture, forestry and fisheries. The unemployment rate was 5·32%.

INTERNATIONAL TRADE
Restrictions on the repatriation of investment earnings by foreign nationals were removed in 1994.

Imports and Exports. Total trade, in US$1m.:

	1996	1997	1998	1999	2000	2001
Imports	102,370	114,425	104,665	110,690	140,011	107,237
Exports	115,942	122,081	110,582	121,591	148,321	122,866

In 2001 the main export markets were the USA (22·5%), Hong Kong (21·9%), Japan (10·4%) and Germany (3·6%). The main import suppliers were Japan (24·1%), the USA (17·0%), South Korea (6·3%) and Germany (4·0%).

Principal exports, in US$1bn.: machinery and electrical equipment, 66·85; textiles, 12·63; basic metals and articles, 11·33; plastic and rubber products, 7·99; vehicles and transport equipment, 4·44; toys, games and sports equipment, 1·79; footwear, headwear and umbrellas, 0·79. By 2001 high-tech products were responsible for more than 54% of exports.

Principal imports, in US$1bn.: machinery and electrical equipment, 47·55; minerals, 12·76; chemicals, 10·23; basic metals and articles, 7·78; precision instruments, clocks and watches, and musical instruments, 6·21; vehicles and transport equipment, 4·24; textile products, 2·36.

COMMUNICATIONS
Roads. In 2001 there were 36,698 km of roads. 17·5m. motor vehicles were registered including 4·8m. passenger cars, 24,053 buses, 830,673 trucks and 12m. motorcycles. 1,091m. passengers and 301m. tonnes of freight were transported (including urban buses). There were 64,264 road accidents, resulting in 3,344 fatalities.

Rail. In 2001 freight traffic amounted to 16·9m. tonnes and passenger traffic to 165m. Total route length was 2,363 km.

Civil Aviation. There are currently two international airports: Chiang Kai-shek International at Taoyuan near Taipei, and Kaohsiung International in the south. In addition there are 14 domestic airports: Taipei, Hualien, Taitung, Taichung, Tainan, Chiayi, Pingtung, Makung, Chimei, Orchid Island, Green Island, Wangan, Kinmen and Matsu (Peikan). A second passenger terminal at Chiang Kai-shek International Airport opened in July 2000 as part of a US$800m. expansion project, which included aircraft bays, airport connection roads, a rapid transit link with Taipei, car parks and the expansion of air freight facilities, begun in 1989. The planned facilities are designed to allow the airport to handle an additional 14m. passengers annually by the year 2010.

In June 2002, 38 airlines including code-share airlines provided flights to destinations in Taiwan, of which 32 foreign and six Taiwanese carriers—China Airlines (CAL), EVA Airways, Far Eastern Air Transport Corp., Mandarin Airlines (MDA; CAL's subsidiary), Trans Asia Airways (TNA) and UNI Airways—operated international services. In 2001, 44·1m. passengers and 1·3m. tonnes of freight were flown.

Taipei–Hong Kong and vice-versa is the most flown airline route in the world, with 5·43m. passengers flying between the two cities in 2001.

Shipping. Maritime transportation is vital to the trade-oriented economy of Taiwan. At the end of 2001 Taiwan's shipping fleet totalled 249 national-flagged ships (over 100 GRT), amounting to 4·7m. GRT and 7·4m. DWT. There are six international ports: Kaohsiung, Keelung, Hualien, Taichung, Anping and Suao. The first two are container centres, Kaohsiung handling 7·54m. 20-ft equivalent units in 2001, making it the world's fourth busiest container port in terms of number of containers handled. Suao port is an auxiliary port to Keelung. In Jan. 2001 the first legal direct shipping links between Taiwanese islands and the Chinese mainland in more than 50 years were inaugurated.

Telecommunications. In 2000 there were 12,642,200 main telephone lines (567·5 per 1,000 inhabitants) and PCs numbered 4·96m. (222·8 per 1,000 inhabitants). Taiwan's biggest telecommunications firm, the state-owned Chunghwa Telecom, lost its fixed-line monopoly in Aug. 2001. There were approximately 11·6m. Internet users in July 2001 and some 13m. mobile phone subscribers in March 2001, more than half of the total population. In 1997 there were 2,496,090 radio pager subscribers.

SOCIAL INSTITUTIONS

Justice. The Judicial Yuan is the supreme judicial organ of state. Comprising 15 grand justices, from 2003 these are nominated and, with the consent of the Legislative Yuan, appointed by the President of the Republic. The grand justices hold meetings to interpret the Constitution and unify the interpretation of laws and orders. There are three levels of judiciary: district courts and their branches deal with civil and criminal cases in the first instance; high courts and their branches deal with appeals against judgments of district courts; the Supreme Court reviews judgments by the lower courts. There is also the Supreme Administrative Court, high administrative courts and a Commission on the Disciplinary Sanctions of Public Functionaries. Criminal cases relating to rebellion, treason and offences against friendly relations with foreign states are handled by high courts as the courts of first instance.

The death penalty is still in force. There were 4 executions in 2002 (as of 30 Sept.). The population in penal institutions on 30 Sept. 2002 was approximately 39,000 (135 per 100,000 of national population).

Religion. According to the registered statistics of Municipality, County and City Government there were 827,135 Taoists in 2001 (and 7,714 temples), 382,437 Protestants (and 2,387 churches), 216,495 Buddhists (and 1,966 temples) and 182,814 Catholics (and 728 churches).

Education. Since 1968 there has been compulsory education for six to 15 year olds with free tuition. The illiteracy rate dropped to 4·21% in 2001 and is still falling. In 2001 there were 2,611 elementary schools with 103,501 teachers and 1,925,491 pupils; 1,181 secondary schools with 98,609 teachers and 1,684,499 students; 154 schools of higher education, including 57 universities, 78 colleges and 19 junior colleges, with 44,769 teachers and 1,189,225 students. Almost one-quarter of the total population attend an educational institution.

Health. In 2001 there was one physician serving every 733 persons, one doctor of Chinese medicine per 5,631 persons and one dentist per 2,505 persons. Some 114,179 beds were provided by the 92 public and 501 private hospitals, averaging nearly 57 beds per 10,000 persons. In addition to the 492 public and 17,136 private clinics, there were 369 health stations and 503 health rooms serving residents in the sparsely populated areas. Acute infectious diseases were no longer the number one killer. Malignant neoplasms, cerebrovascular diseases, heart diseases and accidents and adverse effects were the first four leading causes of death.

Welfare. A universal health insurance scheme came into force in March 1995 as an extension to 13 social insurance plans which cover only 59% of Taiwan's population. Premium shares among the government, employer and insured are varied according to the insured statuses. By the end of 2001 about 21·65m. people or 96% of the population were covered by the National Health Insurance programme.

CULTURE

Broadcasting. At Oct. 2002 there were 174 radio stations, 1 public and 4 commercial TV services and 65 cable systems. June 1997 saw the inauguration of a fourth over-the-air television station—The Kaohsiung-based Formosa Television—which is affiliated with the Democratic Progressive Party and telecasts on VHF low-band. A Public Television Law was promulgated on 18 June 1997. In 2000 there were 9·5m. TV receivers (colour by NTSC).

Cinema. In 2001 cinemas numbered 186; 17 full-length films were made.

Press. There were 267 domestic news agencies, 454 newspapers and 7,236 periodicals in 2001.

Tourism. In 2002, 2,617,137 tourists visited Taiwan and 7,189,334 Taiwanese made visits abroad.

Libraries. There is a national library in Taipei (established in 1986).

FURTHER READING
Statistical Yearbook of the Republic of China. Taipei, annual. *The Republic of China Yearbook.* Taipei, annual. *Taiwan Statistical Data Book.* Taipei, annual. *Annual Review of Government Administration, Republic of China.* Taipei, annual.

Arrigo, L. G., *et al.*, *The Other Taiwan: 1945 to the Present Day.* New York, 1994
Cooper, J. F., *Historical Dictionary of Taiwan.* Metuchen (NJ), 1993
Hughes, C., *Taiwan and Chinese Nationalism: National Identity and Status in International Society.* London, 1997
Lee, W.-C., *Taiwan.* [Bibliography] ABC-Clio, Oxford and Santa Barbara (CA), 1990
Long, S., *Taiwan: China's Last Frontier.* London, 1991
Moody, P. R., *Political Change in Taiwan: a Study of Ruling Party Adaptability.* New York, 1992
Smith, H., *Industry Policy in Taiwan and Korea in the 1980s.* Edward Elgar, Cheltenham, 2000
Tsang, S. (ed.) *In the Shadow of China: Political Developments in Taiwan since 1949.* Farnborough, 1994

National library: National Central Library, Taipei (established 1986).
National Statistics Website: http://www.stat.gov.tw/

KEY

1.	Afghanistan	74.	Honduras	147.	Samoa
2.	Albania	75.	Hungary	148.	San Marino
3.	Algeria	76.	Iceland	149.	São Tomé and Príncipe
4.	Andorra	77.	India	150.	Saudi Arabia
5.	Angola	78.	Indonesia	151.	Senegal
6.	Antigua and Barbuda	79.	Iran	152.	Seychelles
7.	Argentina	80.	Iraq	153.	Sierra Leone
8.	Armenia	81.	Ireland	154.	Singapore
9.	Australia	82.	Israel	155.	Slovakia
10.	Austria	83.	Italy	156.	Slovenia
11.	Azerbaijan	84.	Jamaica	157.	Solomon Islands
12.	Bahamas	85.	Japan	158.	Somalia
13.	Bahrain	86.	Jordan	159.	South Africa
14.	Bangladesh	87.	Kazakhstan	160.	Spain
15.	Barbados	88.	Kenya	161.	Sri Lanka
16.	Belarus	89.	Kiribati	162.	Sudan
17.	Belgium	90.	Korea (South)	163.	Suriname
18.	Belize	91.	Korea (North)	164.	Swaziland
19.	Benin	92.	Kuwait	165.	Sweden
20.	Bhutan	92.	Kyrgyzstan	166.	Switzerland
21.	Bolivia	94.	Laos	167.	Syria
22.	Bosnia-Hercegovina	95.	Latvia	168.	Tajikistan
23.	Botswana	96.	Lebanon	169.	Tanzania
24.	Brazil	97.	Lesotho	170.	Thailand
25.	Brunei	98.	Liberia	171.	Togo
26.	Bulgaria	99.	Libya	172.	Tonga
27.	Burkina Faso	100.	Liechtenstein	173.	Trinidad and Tobago
28.	Burundi	101.	Lithuania	174.	Tunisia
29.	Cambodia	102.	Luxembourg	175.	Turkey
30.	Cameroon	103.	Macedonia	176.	Turkmenistan
31.	Canada	104.	Madagascar	177.	Tuvalu
32.	Cape Verde	105.	Malawi	178.	Uganda
33.	Central African Republic	106.	Malaysia	179.	Ukraine
34.	Chad	107.	Maldives	180.	United Arab Emirates
35.	Chile	108.	Mali	181.	United Kingdom
36.	China, People's Republic of	109.	Malta	182.	United States of America
37.	Colombia	110.	Marshall Islands	183.	Uruguay
38.	Comoros	111.	Mauritania	184.	Uzbekiston
39.	Congo, Democratic	112.	Mauritius	185.	Vanuatu
	Republic of (former Zaïre)	113.	Mexico	186.	Vatican City
40.	Congo, Republic of	114.	Micronesia	187.	Venezuela
41.	Costa Rica	115.	Moldova	188.	Vietnam
42.	Côte d'Ivoire	116.	Monaco	189.	Yemen
43.	Croatia	117.	Mongolia	190.	Yugoslavia*
44.	Cuba	118.	Morocco	191.	Zambia
45.	Cyprus	119.	Mozambique	192.	Zimbabwe
46.	Czech Republic	120.	Myanmar		
47.	Denmark	121.	Namibia		*Now Serbia and Montenegro.
48.	Djibouti	122.	Nauru		New flag to be confirmed.
49.	Dominica	123.	Nepal		
50.	Dominican Republic	124.	Netherlands		
51.	East Timor	125.	New Zealand		**FLAGS OF INTERNATIONAL**
52.	Ecuador	126.	Nicaragua		**ORGANIZATIONS**
53.	Egypt	127.	Niger	A.	Arab League
54.	El Salvador	128.	Nigeria	B.	Association of South East
55.	Equatorial Guinea	129.	Norway		Asian Nations (ASEAN)
56.	Eritrea	130.	Oman	C.	Caricom
57.	Estonia	131.	Pakistan	D.	Commonwealth of
58.	Ethiopia	132.	Palau		Independent States (CIS)
59.	Fiji Islands	133.	Panama	E.	Commonwealth
60.	Finland	134.	Papua New Guinea	F.	Danube Commission
61.	France	135.	Paraguay	G.	Europe
62.	Gabon	136.	Peru	H.	North Atlantic Treaty
63.	The Gambia	137.	Philippines		Organization (NATO)
64.	Georgia	138.	Poland	I.	Organization of American
65.	Germany	139.	Portugal		States (OAS)
66.	Ghana	140.	Qatar	J.	Organization of African
67.	Greece	141.	Romania		Unity (OAU)
68.	Grenada	142.	Russia	K.	Organization of Oil
69.	Guatemala	143.	Rwanda		Exporting Countries
70.	Guinea	144.	St Kitts and Nevis		(OPEC)
71.	Guinea-Bissau	145.	St Lucia	L.	Red Crescent
72.	Guyana	146.	St Vincent and the	M.	Red Cross
73.	Haiti		Grenadines	N.	United Nations
					Organization (UNO)

COLOMBIA

República de Colombia

Capital: Bogotá
Population estimate, 2000: 42·3m.
GDP per capita, 2000: (PPP$) 6,248
HDI/world rank: 0·772/68

KEY HISTORICAL EVENTS

In 1564 the Spanish Crown appointed a President of New Granada, which included the territories of Colombia, Panama and Venezuela. In 1718 a viceroyalty of New Granada was created. This viceroyalty gained its independence from Spain in 1819, and together with the present territories of Panama, Venezuela and Ecuador was officially constituted as the state of 'Greater Colombia'. This new state lasted only until 1830 when it split up into Venezuela, Ecuador and the republic of New Granada, later renamed *Estados Unidos de Colombia*. The constitution of 5 Aug. 1886, forming the Republic of Colombia, abolished the sovereignty of the states, converting them into departments with governors appointed by the President of the Republic. The department of Panama, however, became an independent country in 1903. Conservatives and Liberals fought a civil war from 1948 to 1957 (*La Violencia*) during which some 300,000 people were killed. Subsequently, powerful drugs lords have made violence endemic. Two Marxist guerrilla forces are active, the Colombian Revolutionary Armed Forces (FARC), and the smaller National Liberation Army (ELN). They are opposed by a well-armed paramilitary organization which emerged after the setting up of rural self-defence groups. Killings and other abuses by paramilitary squads, guerrillas and the military in 1996 made it the most infamous year in the nation's history for human rights violations. On average, ten Colombians were killed every day for political or ideological reasons, while one person disappeared every two days.

There were hopes of a fresh start in 1998 when Andrés Pastrana was elected president. Offers to talk peace were taken up by the rebels and by their paramilitary enemies. But political differences are wide, with FARC demanding sweeping agrarian reform and a redistribution of wealth. FARC controls around 40% of the country including areas which produce the bulk of illegal drugs. Approximately 80% of the cocaine and 60% of the heroin sold in the USA originates in Colombia. In Feb. 2002, following the kidnapping of a prominent senator, President Pastrana broke off three years of peace talks. In May 2002 Álvaro Uribe Vélez became president, but within days of his inauguration, amidst mounting violence, he called a state of emergency.

TERRITORY AND POPULATION

Colombia is bounded in the north by the Caribbean Sea, northwest by Panama, west by the Pacific Ocean, southwest by Ecuador and Peru, northeast by Venezuela and southeast by Brazil. The estimated area is 1,141,815 sq. km (440,855 sq. miles). Population census (1993), 33,109,840; density, 29·0 per sq. km.

The UN gives a projected population for 2010 of 49·16m.

In 1999, 73·5% lived in urban areas. Bogotá, the capital (estimate 1999): 6,276,000.

The following table gives population estimates for departments and their capitals for 1999:

Departments	Area (sq. km)	Population	Capital	Population
Amazonas	109,665	69,000	Leticia	30,000[2]
Antioquia	63,612	5,300,000	Medellín	1,958,000
Arauca	23,818	232,000	Arauca	69,000[2]
Atlántico	3,388	2,081,000	Barranquilla	1,226,000
Bogotá[1]	—	6,276,000	—	—
Bolívar	25,978	1,951,000	Cartagena	877,000
Boyacá	23,189	1,355,000	Tunja	118,000[2]
Caldas	7,888	1,094,000	Manizales	362,000
Caquetá	88,965	410,000	Florencia	115,000[2]

477

Departments	Area (sq. km)	Population	Capital	Population[2]
Casanare	44,640	278,000	Yopal	69,000[2]
Cauca	29,308	1,234,000	Popayán	218,000[2]
César	22,905	944,000	Valledupar	297,000[2]
Chocó	46,530	406,000	Quibdó	123,000[2]
Córdoba	25,020	1,308,000	Montería	321,000
Cundinamarca	24,275	2,099,000	Bogotá[1]	—
Guainía	72,238	36,000	Puerto Inírida	20,000[2]
Guaviare	53,460	114,000	San José del Guaviare	54,000[2]
Huila	19,890	911,000	Neiva	322,000
La Guajira	20,848	475,000	Riohacha	115,000[2]
Magdalena	23,188	1,260,000	Santa Marta	343,000[2]
Meta	85,635	686,000	Villavicencio	314,000
Nariño	33,268	1,603,000	Pasto	379,000
Norte de Santander	21,659	1,316,000	Cúcuta	624,000
Putumayo	24,885	324,000	Mocoa	30,000[2]
Quindío	1,845	552,000	Armenia	284,000[2]
Risaralda	4,140	928,000	Pereira	457,000
San Andrés y Providencia	44	71,000	San Andrés	61,000[2]
Santander	30,537	1,939,000	Bucaramanga	521,000
Sucre	10,917	779,000	Sincelejo	214,000[2]
Tolima	23,562	1,293,000	Ibagué	420,000[2]
Valle del Cauca	22,140	4,104,000	Cali	2,111,000
Vaupés	54,135	29,000	Mitú	14,000[2]
Vichada	100,242	80,000	Puerto Carreño	12,000[2]

[1]Capital District. [2]1997.

Ethnic divisions (1996): mestizo 58%, white 20%, mulatto 14%, black 4%, mixed black-Indian 3%, Indian 1%.

The official language is Spanish.

Bogotá: Situated in the centre of Columbia, Bogotá was established by the Spanish conquistador, Gonzalo Jiménez de Quesada, who took the land from the Chibcha Indians in 1538. After achieving independence from the Spanish in 1810, Bogotá was made the nation's capital in 1821. Today Bogotá is an important producer of chemicals and pharmaceutical goods as well as being Colombia's commercial centre with a stock exchange and large financial community.

SOCIAL STATISTICS
1997 births, 988,000; deaths, 191,000. 1997 birth rate (per 1,000 population) 26·4; death rate, 5·1. Annual population growth rate, 1990–99, 1·9%. Life expectancy at birth, 1999, was 67·8 years for men and 74·6 years for women. Infant mortality, 1999, 28·1 per 1,000 live births; fertility rate, 1999, 2·7 children per woman.

CLIMATE
The climate includes equatorial and tropical conditions, according to situation and altitude. In tropical areas, the wettest months are March to May and Oct. to Nov. Bogotá, Jan. 58°F (14·4°C), July 57°F (13·9°C). Annual rainfall 42" (1,052 mm). Barranquilla, Jan. 80°F (26·7°C), July 82°F (27·8°C). Annual rainfall 32" (799 mm). Cali, Jan. 75°F (23·9°C), July 75°F (23·9°C). Annual rainfall 37" (915 mm). Medellín, Jan. 71°F (21·7°C), July 72°F (22·2°C). Annual rainfall 64" (1,606 mm).

CONSTITUTION AND GOVERNMENT
Simultaneously with the presidential elections of May 1990, a referendum was held in which 7m. votes were cast for the establishment of a special assembly to draft a new constitution. Elections were held on 9 Dec. 1990 for this 74-member 'Constitutional Assembly' which operated from Feb. to July 1991. The electorate was 14·2m.; turn-out was 3·7m. The Liberals gained 24 seats, M19 (a former guerrilla organization), 19. The Assembly produced a new constitution which came into force on 5 July 1991. It stresses the state's obligation to protect human rights, and establishes constitutional rights to healthcare, social security and leisure. Indians are allotted two Senate seats. Congress may dismiss ministers, and representatives may be recalled by their electors.

The *President* is elected by direct vote for a term of four years, and is not eligible for re-election until four years afterwards. A vice-presidency was instituted in July 1991.

The legislative power rests with a *Congress* of two houses, the *Senate*, of 102 members, and the *House of Representatives*, of 165 members, both elected for four years by proportional representation. Congress meets annually at Bogotá on 20 July.

National Anthem. 'O! Gloria inmarcesible' ('Oh unfading Glory!'); words by R. Núñez, tune by O. Síndici.

RECENT ELECTIONS

Presidential elections were held on 26 May 2002, in which Álvaro Uribe Vélez (independent) won with 53·1% of votes cast, against 31·8% for his nearest rival, Horacio Serpa Uribe (Liberal Party). Turn-out was 46·8%.

Congressional elections were held on 10 March 2002. Unlike the 1998 elections, which were marred by vote-buying, fraud, kidnapping and violence, the balloting process was largely peaceful. This was in spite of warnings of violence from FARC and their apparent involvement in the kidnapping of a presidential candidate and the assassination of an opposition-member senator in the weeks prior to the ballot. In the elections to the Senate candidates from the two largest parties, the Colombian Conservative Party and the Liberal Party, were routed by independents. The Liberal Party won 28 seats, down from 56, the Colombian Conservative Party won 13, down from 17, with independent candidates accounting for the remainder. In elections to the House of Representatives the Liberal Party won 54 seats, the Colombian Conservative Party 21, the Coalition Party 17, the Radical Change Party 7 and the Liberal Opening Party 5, with the remaining seats going to smaller parties.

CURRENT ADMINISTRATION

President: Álvaro Uribe Vélez; b. 1952 (ind.; sworn in 7 Aug. 2002).

Vice President: Francisco Santos.

In March 2003 the government comprised:

Minister of Interior and Justice: Fernando Londoño Hoyos. *Finance:* Roberto Junguito Bonnet. *Defence:* Marta Lucía Ramírez. *Agriculture and Livestock:* Carlos Gustavo Cano Sanz. *Social Welfare:* Diego Palacio Betancourt. *Mines and Energy:* Luis Ernesto Mejía Castro. *National Education:* Cecilia María Vélez White. *Communications:* Martha Elena Pinto de De Hart. *Foreign Trade:* Jorge Humberto Botero. *Foreign Relations:* Carolina Barco. *Environment:* Cecilia Rodríguez González-Rubio. *Transport:* Andrés Uriel Gallego. *Culture:* María Consuelo Araújo.

Office of the President (Spanish only): http://www.presidencia.gov.co

DEFENCE

Selective conscription at 18 years varies from one to two years of service. In 2000 defence expenditure totalled US$1,955m. (US$46 per capita), representing 2·4% of GDP. In 1985 expenditure had been US$628m.

Army. Personnel (1999) 121,000 (conscripts, 63,800), including a Presidential Guard division and Mobile Counter Guerilla Forces; reserves number 54,700. The national police numbered (1999) 87,000.

Navy. The Navy has 2 diesel powered submarines, 2 midget submarines and 4 small frigates. Naval personnel in 1999 totalled 15,000. There are also two brigades of marines numbering 8,500. An air arm operates light reconnaissance aircraft.

The Navy's main ocean base is Cartagena with Pacific bases at Buenaventura and Malaga. There are in addition numerous river bases.

Air Force. The Air Force has been independent of the Army and Navy since 1943, when its reorganization began with US assistance. It has 72 combat aircraft, including two fighter-bomber squadrons (one with Mirage 5s and one with Kfirs) and 72 armed helicopters. There are several dozen light transports, confiscated from drug smugglers, in use. Total strength (1999) 8,000 personnel (3,900 conscripts).

INTERNATIONAL RELATIONS

Colombia is a member of the UN, WTO, OAS, Inter-American Development Bank, the Andean Group, ALADI/LAIA, ACS, IOM and the Antarctic Treaty.

It was announced in Aug. 2000 that Colombia would receive US$1·3bn. in anti drug-trafficking aid (mostly of a military nature) from the USA as part of 'Plan

Colombia', a series of projects intended to serve as a foundation for stability and peace of which the focal point is the fight against drugs.

ECONOMY

In 1998 agriculture accounted for 13·5% of GDP, industry 25·1% and services 61·4%.

Currency. The unit of currency is the *Colombian peso* (COP) of 100 *centavos*. Inflation was 8·0% in 2001, the lowest rate in more than 30 years. In June 2002 gold reserves were 327,000 troy oz and foreign exchange reserves were US$10,188m. Total money supply was 17,289bn. pesos in June 2002.

Budget. Government revenue and expenditure (in 1bn. pesos):

	1995	1996	1997	1998	1999
Revenue	9,524	12,048	15,283	16,592	18,760
Expenditure	11,290	15,363	19,584	23,492	28,536

Performance. In 1999 Colombia experienced its worst recession since the 1930s, with GDP shrinking by 4·2%. In 2000 there was a recovery, with growth at 2·7%, and in 2001 the economy grew by 1·4%. Total GDP in 2001 was US$83·4bn.

Banking and Finance. In 1923 the Bank of the Republic (*Governor*, Miguel Montoya Urrutia) was inaugurated as a semi-official central bank, with the exclusive privilege of issuing banknotes. Its note issues must be covered by a reserve in gold of foreign exchange of 25% of their value. Interest rates of 40% plus are imposed.

There are 24 commercial banks, of which 18 are private or mixed, and six official. There is also an Agricultural, Industrial and Mining Credit Institute, a Central Mortgage Bank and a Social Savings Bank. Bank deposits totalled 1,446,686 pesos in May 1991.

There are stock exchanges in Bogotá, Medellín and Cali.

Weights and Measures. The metric system was introduced in 1857, but Spanish weights and measures are generally used, *e.g., botella* (750 grammes), *galón* (5 *botellas*), *vara* (70 cm), *arroba* (25 lb, of 500 grammes; 4 *arrobas* = 1 quintal).

ENERGY AND NATURAL RESOURCES

Environment. In 1998 Colombia's carbon dioxide emissions were the equivalent of 1·7 tonnes per capita according to the *World Bank Atlas*.

Electricity. Capacity of electric power (1997) was 15m. kW. In 1998 production was 45·02bn. kWh and consumption per capita 866 kWh.

Oil and Gas. Production (1998): crude oil, 275·5m. bbls.; fuel oil, 18·76m. bbls.; diesel oil, 23·2m. bbls.; gasoline 38·35m. bbls.; kerosene, 1·02m. bbls.; propane gas, 7·5m. bbls. Natural gas production in 1999 totalled 5·2bn. cu. metres. In 1999 there were proven oil reserves of 2·6bn. bbls and proven gas reserves of 200bn. cu. metres.

Minerals. Production (1998): gold, 598,035 troy oz; silver, 167,730 troy oz; platinum, 14,016 troy oz. Other important minerals include: copper, lead, steel, mercury, manganese and emeralds (of which Colombia accounts for about half of world production).

Salt production (1998): 159,621 tonnes. Coal production (1997): 32·6m. tonnes; iron ore (1996): 605,716 tonnes.

Agriculture. There is a wide range of climate and, consequently, crops. In 1998 there were 1·98m. ha of arable land and 2·03m. ha of permanent crops.

Production, 2000 (in 1,000 tonnes): sugarcane, 37,000; potatoes, 2,705; plantains, 2,689; rice, 2,100; cassava, 1,956; bananas, 1,570; maize, 1,010; coffee, 630. Colombia is the third largest coffee producer in the world after Brazil and Vietnam. Coca was cultivated in 2000 on approximately 135,000 ha, up from 40,000 ha in 1992. Coca leaf production in 2000 totalled 88,000 tonnes, making Colombia the world's largest producer of coca leaves, the raw material for cocaine.

Livestock (2000): 26,000,000 cattle; 2,800,000 pigs; 2,200,000 sheep; 2,450,000 horses; 100m. chickens. Meat production, 2000: beef and veal, 754,000 tonnes; poultry meat, 520,000 tonnes; pork, bacon and ham, 152,000 tonnes.

Forestry. In 1995 the area under forests was 52·98m. ha, or 51% of the total land area (down from 52·3% in 1990). Timber production in 1999 was 17·85m. cu. metres.

Fisheries. Total catch (1999), 117,949 tonnes, of which about 76% was from marine waters.

INDUSTRY

Production (1998): steel ingots, 264,466 tonnes; cement, 8,463,995 tonnes; motor cars, 49,807; industrial vehicles, 14,162; sugar, 2,125,575 tonnes; beer (1997), 1,829m. litres.

Labour. The economically active workforce (1998 estimate) was 7,828,397, of which 6,586,668 were employed and 1,241,729 unemployed; the rate of unemployment was estimated to be 15·8%. In 1999 the rate was 18%.

INTERNATIONAL TRADE

Foreign companies are liable for basic income tax of 30% and surtax of 7·5%. Since 1993 tax on profit remittance has started at 12%, reducing (except for oil companies) to 7% after three years. Foreign debt was US$34,081m. in 2000.

The Group of Three (G-3) free trade pact with Mexico and Venezuela came into effect on 1 Jan. 1995.

Imports and Exports. In US$1m.:

	1998	1999	2000
Exports f.o.b.	11,480	12,030	13,620
Imports f.o.b.	13,930	10,255	11,077

Main export markets, 1999: USA (50·3%), Venezuela (7·9%), Germany (4·2%), Peru (3·1%), Ecuador (2·8%). Main import suppliers: USA (37·4%), Venezuela (8·2%), Japan (4·9%), Germany (4·7%). Main exports in 1999 were (in US$1m.): crude oil (3,334·4), chemicals and related products (1,163·7), coal (835·2), bananas (559·5), cut flowers (550·4) and clothing (426·6).

COMMUNICATIONS

Roads. Total length of roads was estimated to be 115,564 km in 1997, of which 12% were paved. Of the 2,300-mile Simón Bolívar highway, which runs from Caracas in Venezuela to Guayaquil in Ecuador, the Colombian portion is complete. Motor vehicles in 1996 numbered 1,434,000, of which 762,000 were passenger cars and 672,000 vans and trucks.

Rail. The National Railways (2,532 km of route, 914 mm gauge) went into liquidation in 1990 prior to takeover of services and obligations by three new public companies in 1992. Freight tonne-km performed in 1998 came to 658m. Total rail track, 3,386 km.

Civil Aviation. There are international airports at Barranquilla, Bogotá (Eldorado), Cali, Cartagena, Medellín and San Andrés. The national carriers are Avianca and ACES. In 1998 Avianca flew 48·5m. km and carried 3,924,100 passengers; ACES flew 20·1m. km and carried 2,078,500 passengers in 1997. The busiest airport is Bogotá, which in 2000 handled 7,154,312 passengers (5,234,807 on domestic flights) and 372,957 tonnes of freight.

Shipping. Vessels entering Colombian ports in 1995 unloaded 13,806,000 tonnes of imports and loaded 26,284,000 tonnes of exports. In 1997 vessels totalling 40,863,000 NRT entered ports and vessels totalling 39,562,000 NRT cleared. The merchant marine totalled 112,000 GRT in 1998, including oil tankers 6,000 GRT.

The Magdalena River is subject to drought, and navigation is always impeded during the dry season, but it is an important artery of passenger and goods traffic. The river is navigable for 900 miles; steamers ascend to La Dorada, 592 miles from Barranquilla.

Telecommunications. In 2000 there were 7,185,600 telephone main lines in use (169·2 for every 1,000 inhabitants) and 1·5m. PCs (35·4 for every 1,000 persons). The number of Internet users was 878,000 in Dec. 2000. Mobile phone subscribers numbered 3,133,700 in 1999 and there were 173,000 fax machines in 1997.

Postal Services. In 1995 there were 1,655 post offices.

SOCIAL INSTITUTIONS

Justice. The July 1991 constitution introduced the offices of public prosecutor and public defence. There is no extradition of Colombians for trial in other countries. The Supreme Court, at Bogotá, of 20 members, is divided into three chambers—civil cassation (six), criminal cassation (eight), labour cassation (six). Each of the 61 judicial districts has a superior court with various sub-dependent tribunals of lower juridical grade.

In 2002 there were 32,000 murders (a rate of around 76 per 100,000 persons). Colombia's murder rate is the highest in the world. In 2001 the reported number of kidnappings numbered 3,041, down on the 2000 total but up from around 1,000 in 1993. Colombia accounts for two-thirds of reported kidnappings worldwide.

The police force numbered 73,176 in 1989. Colombia abolished the death penalty in 1997. The population in penal institutions in 1998 was 43,000 (115 per 100,000 of national population).

Religion. The religion is Roman Catholic (33·27m. adherents in 1997), with the Cardinal Archbishop of Bogotá as Primate of Colombia and nine other archbishoprics. There are also 44 bishops, 8 apostolic vicars, 5 apostolic prefects and 2 prelates. In 1990 there were 1,546 parishes and 4,020 priests. In Feb. 2001 there were three Cardinals. Other forms of religion are permitted so long as their exercise is 'not contrary to Christian morals or the law'. In 1997 there were 2·93m. followers of other religions.

Education. Primary education is free but not compulsory. Schools are both state and privately controlled. In 1997 there were 22,994 pre-primary schools with 43,356 teachers for 835,409 pupils; 51,411 primary schools with 181,521 teachers for 4,561,198 pupils; and 10,869 secondary schools for 3,162,583 pupils with 165,818 teachers. In 1995 there were 235 higher education establishments with 562,716 students.

In 1995–96 in the public sector there were 20 universities, one open university, three technological universities, and universities of education, educational technology and industry. There were also 2 colleges of public administration, 1 school of police studies, 1 institute of fine art, 1 polytechnic and 1 conservatory. In the private sector there were 25 universities, 4 Roman Catholic universities, 1 college of education and 1 school of administration. There were 8 public, and 44 private, other institutions of higher education. In 1994–95 there were 208,394 university students.

Adult literacy in 1999 was 91·5% (91·5% among both males and females).

In 1996 total expenditure on education came to 4·4% of GNP and represented 19·0% of total government expenditure.

Health. In 1997 there were 1,165 hospitals with 47,236 beds. Medical personnel was as follows: doctors, 40,355; dentists, 22,121; nurses, 13,558; auxiliaries, 38,723.

CULTURE

Broadcasting. There are five radio companies overseen by the Dirección General de Radiocomunicaciones. Instituto Nacional de Radio y Televisión transmits on three networks (colour by NTSC) and rents air time to 26 commercial companies. In 1997 there were 21m. radio and 4·6m. TV sets. There are 33 television broadcast stations.

Press. There were 37 daily newspapers in 1996, with daily circulation totalling 1·8m.

Tourism. In 1998 there were 841,000 foreign tourists, bringing revenue of US$939m.

DIPLOMATIC REPRESENTATIVES

Of Colombia in the United Kingdom (Flat 3a, 3 Hans Cres., London, SW1X 0LN)
Ambassador: Dr Alfonso Lopez-Cabellero.

Of the United Kingdom in Colombia (Edificio Ing. Barings, Carrera 9 No 76–49, Piso 9, Bogotá)
Ambassador: Tom Duggin.

Of Colombia in the USA (2118 Leroy Pl., NW, Washington, D.C., 20008)
Ambassador: Luis Alberto Moreno.

Of the USA in Colombia (Calle 220-BIS, No. 47–51, Aparteado Aereo 3831, Bogotá)
Ambassador: Anne Woods Patterson.

Of Colombia to the United Nations
Ambassador: Luis Guillermo Giraldo.

Of Colombia to the European Union
Ambassador: Roberto Arenas Bonilla.

FURTHER READING
Departamento Administrativo Nacional de Estadística. *Boletín de Estadística.* Monthly.

Davis, Robert H., *Historical Dictionary of Colombia.* 2nd ed. Metuchen (NJ), 1994.—*Colombia.* [Bibliography] ABC-Clio, Oxford and Santa Barbara (CA), 1990

Thorp, R., *Economic Management and Economic Development in Peru and Colombia.* London, 1991

National statistical office: Departamento Administrativo Nacional de Estadística (DANE), Avenida Eldorado, Bogotá.
Website (Spanish only): http://www.dane.gov.co/

COMOROS

Union des Iles Comores

Capital: Moroni
Population estimate, 2000: 706,000
GDP per capita, 2000: (PPP$) 1,588
HDI/world rank: 0·511/137

KEY HISTORICAL EVENTS

The three islands forming the present state became French protectorates at the end of the 19th century and were proclaimed colonies in 1912. With neighbouring Mayotte they were administratively attached to Madagascar from 1914 until 1947 when the four islands became a French Overseas Territory, achieving internal self-government in Dec. 1961. In referendums held on each island on 22 Dec. 1974, the three western islands voted overwhelmingly for independence, while Mayotte voted to remain French. There have been more than 20 coups or attempted takeovers since independence, with recent years being marked by political disruption. In 1997 the islands of Anjouan and Mohéli attempted to secede from the federation.

TERRITORY AND POPULATION

The Comoros consist of three islands in the Indian Ocean between the African mainland and Madagascar with a total area of 1,862 sq. km (719 sq. miles). The population at the 1991 census was 446,817; estimate, 1996, 569,200; density, 306 per sq. km.

The UN gives a projected population for 2010 of 925,000.

In 1999, 67·3% of the population were rural.

	Area (sq. km)	Population (1995 estimate)	Chief town
Njazídja (Grande Comore)	1,148	250,500	Moroni
Nzwani (Anjouan)	424	211,900	Mutsamudu
Mwali (Mohéli)	290	27,600	Fomboni

Estimated population of the chief towns: Moroni, 44,000 (1999); Mutsamudu, 20,000 (1991); Domoni, 8,000 (1990); Fomboni, 5,600 (1990).

The indigenous population are a mixture of Malagasy, African, Malay and Arab peoples; the vast majority speak Comorian, an Arabized dialect of Swahili, but a small proportion speak Makua (a Bantu language) or one of the official languages, French and Arabic.

SOCIAL STATISTICS

1996 births, 26,100; deaths, 5,900. Birth rate per 1,000 population, 1996, 45·8; death, 10·3. Annual population growth rate, 1990–99, 2·58%. Infant mortality, 64 per 1,000 live births (1999). Expectation of life in 1999 was 58·0 years among men and 60·8 among females. Fertility rate, 1999, 4·7 children per woman.

CLIMATE

There is a tropical climate, affected by Indian monsoon winds from the north, which gives a wet season from Nov. to April. Moroni, Jan. 81°F (27·2°C), July 75°F (23·9°C). Annual rainfall, 113" (2,825 mm).

CONSTITUTION AND GOVERNMENT

At a referendum on 23 Dec. 2001, 77% of voters approved a new constitution that keeps the three islands as one country while granting each one greater autonomy.

The *President of the Union* is Head of State.

National Anthem. 'Udzima wa ya Masiwa' ('The union of the islands'); words by S. H. Abderamane, tune by K. Abdallah and S. H. Abderamane.

RECENT ELECTIONS

Presidential elections were held on 14 April 2002. Turn-out was 39·1%. The elections were marred by violence and were boycotted by two of the three candidates and by most of the voters of Anjouan. On 22 April the results, which indicated 75% of votes cast for Col. Azaly Assoumani, were cancelled, although on 8 May a newly-appointed electoral commission confirmed Assoumani as president-elect.

CURRENT ADMINISTRATION

President of the Union: Col. Azaly Assoumani; b. 1959 (sworn in 26 May 2002).
President of Anjouan: Mohamed Bacar. *President of Grande Comore:* Mze Soule El Bak. *President of Mohéli:* Mohamed Fazul.

In March 2003 the cabinet comprised:
Vice President of the Union and Minister of Finance: Caambi El Yachourtu. *Vice President of the Union and Minister of Justice, Information, Religious Affairs, Human Rights and Parliamentary Relations:* Rachidi Ben Massoundi. *Minister of Foreign Affairs and Environment:* Soeuf Mohamed Elamine. *Social Affairs, Decentralization, Post, Telecommunications and Transport:* Solihi Ali Mohamed.

Office of the President: http://www.presidence-uniondescomores.com/

DEFENCE

Army. The Army was reorganized after the failed coup of Sept. 1995.

Navy. One landing craft with ramps was purchased in 1981. Two small patrol boats were supplied by Japan in 1982. Personnel in 1996 numbered about 200.

INTERNATIONAL RELATIONS

Comoros is a member of the UN, the League of Arab States, African Development Bank, COMESA, OIC and the International Organization of the Francophonie, and an ACP member state of the ACP-EU relationship.

ECONOMY

Agriculture accounted for 38·7% of GDP in 1998, industry 12·8% and services 48·5%.

Currency. The unit of currency is the *Comorian franc* (KMF) of 100 *centimes*. It is pegged to the euro at 491·96775 *Comorian francs* to the euro. Foreign exchange reserves were US$76m. in June 2002 and total money supply was 24,586m. Comorian francs. There was inflation of 5·0% in 2001.

Budget. Revenues were an estimated US$48m. and expenditure an estimated US$53m. in 1997.

Performance. Real GDP growth was negative in 2000, at −1·1%, but in 2001 the economy grew by 1·9%. In 2001 total GDP was US$0·2bn.

Banking and Finance. The Central Bank is the bank of issue. The chief commercial banks are the Banque Internationale des Comores and the Banque de Développement des Comores.

Weights and Measures. The metric system is in force.

ENERGY AND NATURAL RESOURCES

Environment. According to the *World Bank Atlas* carbon dioxide emissions were the equivalent of 0·1 tonnes per capita in 1998.

Electricity. In 1991 installed capacity was 16,000 kW. Production was 15m. kWh in 1998; consumption per capita was 27 kWh in 1997.

Agriculture. 80% of the economically active population depends upon agriculture, which (including fishing, hunting and forestry) contributed 39% to GDP in 1997. There were 78,000 ha of arable land in 1998 and 40,000 ha of permanent crops. The chief product was formerly sugarcane, but now vanilla, copra, maize and other food crops, cloves and essential oils (citronella, ylang-ylang, lemon grass) are the most important products. Production (2000 in 1,000 tonnes): coconuts, 75; bananas, 59; cassava, 53; rice, 17; copra, 9; taro, 9; sweet potatoes, 6.

Livestock (2000): goats, 140,000; cattle, 52,000; sheep, 20,000; asses, 5,000.

Forestry. In 1995 the area under forest was 9,000 ha, or 4% of the total land area (12,000 ha and 5·4% in 1990). The forested area has been severely reduced because of the shortage of cultivable land and ylang-ylang production.

Fisheries. Fishing is on an individual basis, without modern equipment. The catch was estimated to be 12,200 tonnes in 1999.

INDUSTRY
Branches include perfume distillation, textiles, furniture, jewellery, soft drinks and the processing of vanilla and copra.

Labour. The workforce in 1996 was 286,000 (58% males).

INTERNATIONAL TRADE
Total foreign debt was US$232m. in 2000.

Imports and Exports. In 1998 imports amounted to US$47·8m. (US$62·6m. in 1995); exports to US$4m. (US$11·4m.).

Main export markets, 1998: France, 60%; USA, 17%; Germany, 12%. Main import suppliers: France, 38%; Pakistan, 12%; Saudi Arabia, 9%. The main exports are vanilla (US$6·2m. in 1995), cloves, ylang-ylang, essences, cocoa, copra and coffee. Principal imports are rice (US$14·1m. in 1995), petroleum products (US$7·7m. in 1995), cement, meat, vehicles, and iron and steel.

COMMUNICATIONS

Roads. In 1996 there were estimated to be 900 km of classified roads (440 km highways and main roads, 230 km secondary and 230 km other roads). The number of cars in use has increased dramatically in recent years, from 2,910 in 1992 to 9,100 in 1996.

Civil Aviation. There is an international airport at Moroni (International Prince Said Ibrahim). In 2000 it handled 103,000 passengers (79,000 on international flights).

Shipping. In 1998 the merchant marine totalled 1,000 GRT.

Telecommunications. There were 7,000 telephone main lines in 2000 (10·0 per 1,000 persons) and 3,000 PCs in use (4·3 per 1,000 persons). In 1995 there were 100 fax machines. Internet users numbered 1,500 in Dec. 2000.

Postal Services. In 1993 there were 36 post offices.

SOCIAL INSTITUTIONS

Justice. French and Muslim law is in a new consolidated code. The Supreme Court comprises seven members, two each appointed by the President and the Federal Assembly, and one by each island's Legislative Council. The death penalty is authorized for murder. The last execution was in 1996.

Religion. Islam is the official religion: 86% of the population are Sunni Muslims; 14% are Roman Catholics. Following the coup of April 1999 the federal government discouraged the practice of religions other than Islam, with Christians especially facing restrictions on worship.

Education. After two pre-primary years at Koran school, which 50% of children attend, there are six years of primary schooling for seven- to 13-year-olds followed by a four-year secondary stage attended by 25% of children. Some 5% of 17- to 20-year-olds conclude schooling at *lycées*. In 1995–96 there were 327 primary schools with 78,527 pupils. 17,637 pupils attended secondary schools in 1993–94. There were 348 students in higher education in 1995–96.

The adult literacy rate in 1999 was 59·2% (66·3% among males and 52·1% among females).

Health. In 1993 there were 77 doctors; in 1990, 6 dentists, 6 pharmacists, 86 midwives and 155 nursing personnel. In 1980 there were 17 hospitals and clinics with 763 beds.

CULTURE

Broadcasting. The state-controlled Radio Comoro broadcasts in French and Comorian. In 1997 there were 90,000 radio and 1,000 television receivers.

Press. There was one weekly newspaper in 1997.

Tourism. In 1999 there were 24,000 foreign tourists (around a third from France), bringing revenue of US$17m.

DIPLOMATIC REPRESENTATIVES
Of the United Kingdom in the Comoros
Ambassador: Brian Donaldson (resides at Antananarivo, Madagascar).

Of the Comoros in the USA (Temporary: c/o the Permanent Mission of the Union of the Comoran Islands to the United Nations, 430 E 50th Street, N.Y. 10022)
Ambassador: Vacant.

Of the USA in the Comoros
Ambassador: John Price (resides at Port Louis, Mauritius).

Of the Comoros to the United Nations
Ambassador: Vacant.
Chargé d'Affaires a.i.: Mahmoud M. Aboud.

Of the Comoros to the European Union
Ambassador: Vacant.
Chargé d'Affaires a.i.: Amoïss Assoumani.

FURTHER READING
Ottenheimer, M. and Ottenheimer, H. J., *Historical Dictionary of the Comoro Islands.* Metuchen (NJ), 1994

CONGO, DEMOCRATIC REPUBLIC OF THE (FORMERLY ZAÏRE)

Capital: Kinshasa
Population estimate, 2000: 50·95m
GDP per capita, 2000: (PPP$) 765
HDI/world rank: 0·431/155

République Démocratique du Congo

KEY HISTORICAL EVENTS

King Leopold II of the Belgians took the lead in exploring and exploiting the Congo Basin. In 1908 the country was annexed to Belgium as the Belgian Congo. In 1961, a year after the country gained independence, the radical nationalist former Prime Minister Patrice Lumumba was assassinated. Only in 2002 did Belgium admit to participating in his murder. Mobutu Sésé Séko, a puppet of Western interests, came to power in a coup in 1965. At first he was seen as a strongman who could hold together a huge, unstable country comprising hundreds of tribes and language groups. He changed the country's name to Zaïre in 1971. In the 1970s he was feted by the USA which used Zaïre as a springboard for operations into neighbouring Angola where western-backed Unita rebels were locked in civil war with a Cuban and Soviet backed government. Because Mobutu was useful in the fight against Communism the brutality and repressiveness of his regime was ignored.

After armed insurrection by Tutsi rebels in the province of Kivu, the government alleged pro-Tutsi intervention by the armies of Burundi and Rwanda and on 25 Oct. 1996 declared a state of emergency. By Dec. the secessionist forces of Laurent-Désiré Kabila, the Alliance of Democratic Forces for the Liberation of Congo-Zaïre (ADFL), had begun to drive the regular Zaïrean army out of Kivu and an attempt was made to establish a rebel administration, called 'Democratic Congo'. In the face of continuing rebel military successes and the disaffection of the army, the Government accepted a UN resolution demanding the immediate cessation of hostilities. The Security Council asked the rebels also to make a public declaration of their acceptance. However, the latter continued in their victorious advance westwards, capturing Kisangani on 15 March 1997, then Kasai and Shaba, giving Kabila control of eastern Zaïre, and crucially the country's mineral wealth. After a futile attempt to deploy Serbian mercenaries, Mobutu succumbed to pressure—particularly from the USA and South Africa—and agreed to meet Kabila. Little happened but the meeting had all the trappings of a symbolic surrender. Mobutu fled without warning or conditions on the night of 15–16 May 1997. He died of cancer four months later. Described as one of the most destructive tyrants of the African independence era, it is said that his personal fortune, if ever recovered, could wipe out his country's national debt.

On coming to power Kabila changed the name of the country to the Democratic Republic of the Congo. Hopes for democratic and economic renewal were soon disappointed. The Kabila regime relied too closely on its military backup, mainly Rwandans and eastern Congolese from the Tutsi minority. Those supporters seemed more interested in eliminating tribal enemies in eastern border areas than in establishing democracy. As a result, Rwanda and Uganda switched support to rebel forces. When Zimbabwe and Angola sent in troops to help President Kabila, full-scale civil war threatened. A ceasefire was negotiated at a Franco-African summit in Nov. 1998 but the military build-up continued into the new year and violence intensified.

A ceasefire agreement was signed by leaders from more than a dozen African countries in July 1999 to bring the civil war between the government of President Kabila and rebel forces to an end. Rival factions of the Rally for Congolese Democracy, the main rebel group opposed to the president, also signed the accord, but not until Sept. The threat remained of an early return to outright civil war.

'On the third anniversary of Kabila's assumption of power, a dispatch from the Panafrican News Agency reviewed the Democratic Republic of the Congo's condition:– Basic infrastructure is in total decay. Major sections of trunk "A" roads ... are not usable. Proposals for the rehabilitation of other facilities, such as hospitals, industries, manufacturing, and other structures, have also been stalled. On the social front, dirt and environmental decay have spewed all sorts of diseases. Smallpox, diarrhoea, sleeping sickness, among others, have come back in force while AIDS, malaria and poliomyelitis continue to devastate a population already weakened by under-nourishment... More than 60 per cent of the country's working population is not at work...' (*The New Yorker*, 25 Sept. 2000).

On 16 Jan. 2001 President Kabila was assassinated, allegedly by one of his own bodyguards. Kabila was succeeded by his son Joseph.

Prospects for peace improved dramatically in Feb. 2001 when the UN Security Council approved a plan for the disengagement of the warring factions that would allow the eventual deployment of 3,000 UN-supported peacekeepers. In early 2002 talks between the government and rebels on how to end the conflict ended without a satisfactory agreement embracing all factions. However, talks were resumed and in July 2002 the presidents of the Democratic Republic of the Congo and neighbouring Rwanda signed a peace deal that was expected to be the first stage towards ending the war which has claimed more than 3m. lives. In Oct. 2002 Rwanda completed the withdrawal of its forces. The Democratic Republic of the Congo and Uganda also signed a peace agreement. The conflict, which was described as Africa's first continental war, drew in Zimbabwe, Angola and Namibia (and, for a time, Sudan and Chad) on the side of the government, which controls the west of the country, while Rwanda and Uganda backed different rival factions. The Rally for Congolese Democracy, which controls areas in the east, was backed by Rwanda, while Uganda supported the Movement for the Liberation of Congo, based in the north and northeast of the country. Burundi also had troops in the country, allied to the Rwandans, although they stayed close to the border with Burundi. In addition to the vast numbers of deaths in the conflict, large numbers of people were displaced and sought asylum in Tanzania and Zambia. Since the end of the war relative peace and economic stability have returned to the Democratic Republic of the Congo.

TERRITORY AND POPULATION

The Democratic Republic of the Congo is bounded in the north by the Central African Republic, northeast by Sudan, east by Uganda, Rwanda, Burundi and Lake Tanganyika, south by Zambia, southwest by Angola and northwest by the Republic of the Congo. There is a 37-km stretch of coastline which gives access to the Atlantic Ocean, with the Angolan exclave of Cabinda to the immediate north, and Angola itself to the south. Area, 2,344,885 sq. km (905,365 sq. miles). At the 1988 census the population was 34·7m. Estimate (1997) 47,440,000 (70% rural, 1999); density, 20 per sq. km.

The UN gives a projected population for 2010 of 71·27m.

More than 200,000 refugees who escaped the fighting between Hutus and Tutsis in Rwanda and Burundi in 1994 are still in the Democratic Republic of the Congo (out of 1m. who came originally), and there are also 100,000 Angolan and 100,000 Sudanese refugees in the country.

Area, populations (1994 estimate) and chief towns of the regions in 1994:

Region	Area (sq. km)	Population (in 1,000)	Chief town	Population
Bandundu	295,658	4,907	Bandundu	. . .
Bas-Zaïre	53,920	2,578	Matadi	172,730
Equateur	403,293	4,789	Mbandaka	169,841
Haut-Zaïre	503,239	5,432	Kisangani	417,517
Kasai Occidental	154,742	3,117	Kananga	393,030
Kasai Oriental	170,302	3,778	Mbuji-Mayi	806,475
Kinshasa City	9,965	4,655	Kinshasa	4,885,000[1]
Maniema[2]	132,250	—	Kindu	. . .
Nord-Kivu[2]	59,483	—	Goma	109,094
Sud-Kivu[2]	65,130	—	Bukavu	201,569
Shaba	496,965	5,602	Lubumbashi	851,381

[1]1999 figure. [2]Combined population of Maniema, Nord-Kivu and Sud-Kivu, 7,687,000.

Other large cities (with estimated 1994 population): Kolwezi (417,810), Likasi (299,118), Kikwit (182,142), Tshikapa (180,860).

The population is Bantu, with minorities of Sudanese (in the north), Nilotes (northeast), Pygmies and Hamites (in the east). French is the official language, but of more than 200 languages spoken, four are recognized as national languages: Kiswahili, Tshiluba, Kikongo and Lingala. Lingala has become the *lingua franca* after French.

SOCIAL STATISTICS

1997 births, 2,263,000; deaths, 788,000. Rates (1997 estimates, per 1,000 population); birth, 47·7; death, 16·6. Annual population growth rate, 1990–99, 3·4%. Infant mortality in 1999 was 128 per 1,000 live births. Expectation of life in 1999 was 49·7 years for men and 52·3 for females. Fertility rate, 1999, 6·3 children per woman.

CLIMATE

The climate is varied, the central region having an equatorial climate, with year-long high temperatures and rain at all seasons. Elsewhere, depending on position north or south of the Equator, there are well-marked wet and dry seasons. The mountains of the east and south have a temperate mountain climate, with the highest summits having considerable snowfall. Kinshasa, Jan. 79°F (26·1°C), July 73°F (22·8°C). Annual rainfall 45" (1,125 mm). Kananga, Jan. 76°F (24·4°C), July 74°F (23·3°C). Annual rainfall 62" (1,584 mm). Kisangani, Jan. 78°F (25·6°C), July 75°F (23·9°C). Annual rainfall 68" (1,704 mm). Lubumbashi, Jan. 72°F (22·2°C), July 61°F (16·1°C). Annual rainfall 50" (1,237 mm).

CONSTITUTION AND GOVERNMENT

Gen. Laurent-Désiré Kabila seized power on 17 May 1997 after the military defeat of Marshal Mobutu Sésé Séko and his government, and until his death in 2001 was both chief of state and head of government. Although parties other than the ADFL have been dissolved, a constitutional referendum was due to be held in Dec. 1998, and presidential and parliamentary elections in April 1999. However, these did not take place as scheduled.

National Anthem. 'Debout Congolais' ('Stand up, Congolese'); words and tune by J. Lutumba and S. Boka.

RECENT ELECTIONS

The Democratic Republic of the Congo's first elections since independence in 1960 are set to take place in 2005.

CURRENT ADMINISTRATION

President and Minister of Defence: Joseph Kabila; b. 1971 (in office since 17 Jan. 2001).

In March 2003 the government comprised:

Minister of Agriculture: Salomon Banamuhere. *Communications and Press:* Kkiaya bin Karubi. *Culture and Arts:* Matuka Kavokisa. *Defence:* Irung Awan. *Economy:* André-Philippe Futa. *Education:* Kutumisan Kyota. *Energy:* Georges Buse Falay. *Finance (acting):* Léonard Luhongwe. *Foreign Affairs and International Co-operation:* Léonard She Okitundu. *Health:* Mashako Mamba. *Human Rights:* Ntumba Luaba. *Industry and Commerce:* Ngalula Wafwana. *Interior:* Théophile Mbemba. *Justice and Guardian of the Seals:* Me Masudi Ngele. *Labour and Social Security:* Marie Ange Lukiana Mufwankol. *Lands:* Yuma Moota. *Mining and Petroleum:* Nkulu Kikuku. *Post, Telephone and Telecommunications:* Mutombo Kyamakosa. *Public Administration:* Benjamin Mukulungu. *Public Works:* Kimbembe Mazunga. *Social Affairs:* Jeanne Ebamba Moboto. *Transport:* Pauni Kamanzi. *Youth and Sports:* Timothée Moleka Nzulama.

DEFENCE

Following the overthrow of the Mobutu regime in May 1997, the former Zaïrean armed forces were in disarray. The insurgent Congo Liberation Army has between 20,000 and 40,000 fighters, equipped with small arms and some SA-7 SAMs. Much of this equipment is believed to be non-operational.

Defence expenditure totalled US$392m. in 2000 (US$8 per capita), representing 8·4% of GDP.

Army. The total strength of the Army was estimated at 55,000 (1999). There is an additional paramilitary National Police Force of unknown size.

Navy. Naval strength is estimated at 900. The main coastal base is at Banana.

INTERNATIONAL RELATIONS

Following an invasion in Aug. 1998, in June 1999 the Democratic Republic of the Congo instituted proceedings against Burundi, Uganda and Rwanda before the International Court of Justice for 'acts of armed aggression committed in flagrant breach of the United Nations Charter and of the Organization of African Unity'.

The Democratic Republic of the Congo is a member of the UN, WTO, the African Union, African Development Bank, COMESA, IOM, International Organization of the Francophonie and is an ACP member state of the ACP-EU relationship.

ECONOMY

Agriculture accounted for 57·9% of GDP in 1997 (the second highest percentage in the world), services 25·2% and industry 16·9%.

Following the end of the civil war in 2002, several donor countries and institutions agreed to a development aid package worth US$2·5bn.

Currency. The unit of currency is the *Congo franc* which replaced the former *zaïre* in July 1998. The value of the new currency fell by two-thirds in the six months following its launch. Foreign exchange reserves were US$83m. in Dec. 1996. Gold reserves were 54,000 troy oz in 1997. Inflation, which reached 23,760% in 1994, had declined to 358% by 2001. In May 2001 the franc was floated in an effort to overcome the economic chaos caused by three years of state control and inter-regional war.

Budget. Total revenue was 604m. francs and total expenditure was 1,086m. francs in 1998. International economic aid has been made dependent on a coherent plan to revive the economy and progress on democracy and human rights.

Performance. GDP growth was –4·3% in 1999, –6·2% in 2000 and –4·4% in 2001. However, following the end of the five-year long war the economy was estimated to have grown by 3% in 2002. In Feb. 1998 GDP was reported to be 65% lower than it was in 1960, when the country gained independence. Total GDP in 1998 was US$7·0bn.

Banking and Finance. The central bank, the Banque Centrale du Congo (*Governor*, Jean-Claude Masangu), achieved independence in May 2002. The largest bank is the Banque Commerciale Congolaise, in which the Société Générale of Belgium has a 25% stake through its subsidiary, Belgolaise. Other banks include Citibank and Stanbic. A 40% state-owned investment bank, Société Financière de Développement (Sofide) lends mainly to agriculture and manufacturing.

Weights and Measures. The metric system is in force.

ENERGY AND NATURAL RESOURCES

Environment. According to the *World Bank Atlas* carbon dioxide emissions in 1998 were the equivalent of 0·1 tonnes per capita.

Electricity. Production (1998), 5·74bn. kWh. A dam at Inga, on the River Congo near Matadi, has a potential capacity of 39,600 MW. Installed capacity was 3m. kW in 1998. Consumption per capita was 110 kWh in 1998.

Oil and Gas. Offshore oil production began in Nov. 1975; estimated crude production (1996) was 11m. bbls. There is an oil refinery at Kinlao-Muanda.

Minerals. Production in 2001 (in 1,000 tonnes): copper, 23 (down from 450,000 tonnes in 1989); zinc, 19; cobalt, 5; gold (1997), 394 kg; diamonds (2000), 16·5m. carats. Only Australia, Botswana and Russia produce more diamonds. Coal, tin and silver are also found. The most important mining area is in the region of Shaba (formerly Katanga).

Agriculture. There were, in 1998, 6·7m. ha of arable land and 1·18m. ha of permanent crops. The main agricultural crops (2000 production in 1,000 tonnes) are: cassava, 15,959; plantains, 1,800; sugarcane, 1,669; maize, 1,184; rice, 383; groundnuts, 382; sweet potatoes, 370; bananas, 312; yams, 255; papayas, 213; mangoes, 206; pineapples, 196; oranges, 185; palm oil, 157; dry beans, 122; palm kernels, 63; taro, 62.

Livestock (2000): goats, 4,131,000; pigs, 1,049,000; sheep, 925,000; cattle, 882,000; poultry, 22m.

Forestry. Equatorial rainforests covered 1,092,000 sq. km in 1995, or 48·2% of the land area, down from 1,129,000 sq. km and 49·8% in 1990. The reduction of 37,000 sq. km in the area under forests between 1990 and 1995 was the biggest in any African country over the same period, and was only exceeded worldwide in Brazil and Indonesia. Timber production in 1999 was 50·75m. cu. metres.

Fisheries. The catch for 2000 was 208,448 tonnes, almost entirely from inland waters.

INDUSTRY

The main manufactures are foodstuffs, beverages, tobacco, textiles, rubber, leather, wood products, cement and building materials, metallurgy and metal extraction, metal items, transport vehicles, electrical equipment and bicycles. Main products, 1995, in 1,000 tonnes included: iron and steel, 965; cement, 140 (1997); sugar, 51 (1998); soap, 47; tyres, 50,000 units; printed fabrics, 15·73m. sq. metres; shoes, 1·6m. pairs; beer, 178m. litres.

Labour. In 1996 the workforce was 19·62m. (56% males). Agriculture employs around 65% of the total economically active population.

INTERNATIONAL TRADE

With Burundi and Rwanda, the Democratic Republic of the Congo forms part of the Economic Community of the Great Lakes. External debt was US$11,645m. in 2000.

Imports and Exports. Exports in 2001 were US$868·2m. (US$823·5m. in 2000); imports were US$703·9m. (US$697·1m. in 2000). Main commodities for export are diamonds, copper, coffee, cobalt and crude oil; and for import: consumer goods, foodstuffs, mining and other machinery, transport equipment and fuels. Principal export markets are Belgium, USA, France, Germany, Italy, UK, Japan and South Africa. Principal import suppliers are Belgium, South Africa, USA, France, Germany, Italy, Japan and China.

COMMUNICATIONS

Roads. In 1996 there were approximately 33,130 km of motorways and main roads, 40,500 km of secondary roads and 83,400 km of other roads. There were an estimated 787,000 passenger cars in use in 1996 (16·9 per 1,000 inhabitants) plus 538,000 trucks and vans.

Rail. There was 5,138 km of track on three gauges in 1995, of which 858 km was electrified. However, the length of track in use was severely reduced by the civil strife in late 1996 and the early part of 1997.

Civil Aviation. There is an international airport at Kinshasa (Ndjili). Other major airports are at Lubumbashi (Luano), Bukavu, Goma and Kisangani. The national carrier is Congo Airlines. In 1996 Kinshasa handled 344,000 passengers (192,000 on domestic flights) and 96,300 tonnes of freight.

Shipping. The River Congo and its tributaries are navigable to 300-tonne vessels for about 14,500 km. Regular traffic has been established between Kinshasa and Kisangani as well as Ilebo, on the Lualaba (*i.e.*, the river above Kisangani), on some tributaries and on the lakes. The Democratic Republic of the Congo has only 37 km of sea coast. In 1998 merchant shipping totalled 13,000 GRT. Matadi, Kinshasa and Kalemie are the main seaports; in 1993 Matadi handled 0·6m. tonnes of freight.

Telecommunications. There is a ground satellite communications station outside Kinshasa. Telephone main lines numbered 20,000 in 2000, or 0·4 per 1,000 inhabitants—the lowest penetration rate of any country in the world. In 1995 there were 5,000 fax machines; and in 1998, 10,000 mobile phone subscribers. In May 1999 there were 1,500 Internet users.

Postal Services. In 1995 there were 304 post offices.

SOCIAL INSTITUTIONS

Justice. There is a Supreme Court at Kinshasa, 11 courts of appeal, 36 courts of first instance and 24 'peace tribunals'. The death penalty is in force.

Religion. In 1996 there were 21·9m. Roman Catholics, 13·1m. Protestants, 7·74m. Kimbanguistes (African Christians) and 0·63m. Muslims. Animist beliefs persist.

Education. In 1994–95 there were 14,885 primary schools with 121,054 teachers for 5·4m. pupils, and 1·5m. pupils in secondary schools. In 1994–95 there were 93,266 students at university level. In higher education there were three universities (Kinshasa, Kisangani and Lubumbashi) in 1994–95, 14 teacher training colleges and 18 technical institutes in the public sector; and 13 university institutes, four teacher training colleges and 49 technical institutes in the private sector. Adult literacy rate was 60·3% in 1999 (male, 72·4%; female, 48·7%).

Health. In 1990 there were 2,469 doctors, 41 dentists and 27,601 nurses. In 1995 government expenditure on health totalled 25,000m. zaïres.

The Democratic Republic of the Congo has been one of the least successful countries in the battle against undernourishment in the past decade. The proportion of the population classified as undernourished increased from 35% in 1990–92 to 64% by 1997–99.

CULTURE

Broadcasting. Broadcasting is provided by government-controlled radio and television stations (colour by SECAM V). There is also an educational radio station. In 1997 there were 18m. radio and 6·48m. TV receivers.

Press. In 1996 there were nine daily newspapers with a combined circulation of 124,000.

Tourism. In 1998 there were 32,000 foreign tourists, spending US$2m.

DIPLOMATIC REPRESENTATIVES

Of the Democratic Republic of the Congo in the United Kingdom (26 Chesham Pl., London, SW1X 8HH)
Ambassador: Vacant.
Chargé d'Affaires a.i.: Henri N'Swana.

Of the United Kingdom in the Democratic Republic of the Congo (83 Ave. du Roi Baudouin, Kinshasa)
Ambassador: Jim Atkinson.

Of the Democratic Republic of the Congo in the USA (1800 New Hampshire Ave., NW, Washington, D.C., 20009)
Ambassador: Faïda Mitifu.

Of the USA in the Democratic Republic of the Congo (310 Ave. des Aviateurs, Kinshasa)
Ambassador: Aubrey Hooks.

Of the Democratic Republic of the Congo to the United Nations
Ambassador: Ileka Atoki.

Of the Democratic Republic of the Congo to the European Union
Ambassador: Vacant.
Second Counsellor: Tshibola-tshia-Kadiebue.

FURTHER READING
Hochschild, Adam, *King Leopold's Ghost: A Study of Greed, Terror and Heroism in Colonial Africa.* Macmillan, London, 1999
Leslie, W. J., *Zaïre: Continuity and Political Change in an Oppressive State.* Boulder (CO), 1993
Williams, D. B., *et al.*, *Zaïre.* [Bibliography] 2nd ed. ABC-Clio, Oxford and Santa Barbara (CA), 1995
Wrong, Michaela, *In the Footsteps of Mr Kurtz: Living on the Brink of Disaster in the Congo.* Fourth Estate, London, 2000

CONGO, REPUBLIC OF THE

République du Congo

Capital: Brazzaville
Population estimate, 2000: 3·02m.
GDP per capita, 2000: (PPP$) 825
HDI/world rank: 0·512/136

KEY HISTORICAL EVENTS

First occupied by France in 1882, the Congo became a territory of French Equatorial Africa from 1910–58, and then a member state of the French Community. Between 1940 and 1944, thanks to Equatorial Africa's allegiance to General de Gaulle, he named Brazzaville the capital of the Empire and Liberated France. Independence was granted in 1960. A Marxist-Leninist state was introduced in 1970. Free elections were restored in 1992 but violence erupted when in June 1997 President Lissouba tried to disarm opposition militia ahead of a fresh election. There followed four months of civil war with fighting concentrated on Brazzaville which became a ghost town. In Oct. Gen. Sassou-Nguesso proclaimed victory, having relied upon military support from Angola. President Lissouba went into hiding in Burkina Faso. A peace agreement signed in Nov. 1999 between President Sassou-Nguesso and the Cocoye and Ninja militias brought a period of relative stability.

TERRITORY AND POPULATION

The Republic of the Congo is bounded by Cameroon and the Central African Republic in the north, the Democratic Republic of the Congo to the east and south, Angola and the Atlantic Ocean to the southwest and Gabon to the west, and covers 341,821 sq. km. At the census of 1984 the population was 1,909,248.

Estimated population in 1997, 2,769,000; density, 8·1 per sq. km.

The UN gives a projected population for 2010 of 4·08m.

In 1999, 61·7% of the population were urban. Estimated population of major cities in 1995: Brazzaville, the capital, 937,579 (1,187,000 in 1999); Pointe-Noire, 576,206; Loubomo (Dolisie), 83,605; N'Kayi, 42,465; Mossendjo, 16,405; Ouesso, 16,171.

Area, estimated population and county towns of the regions in 1992 were:

Region	Sq. km	Population	County town
Bouenza	12,266	219,822	Madingou
Capital District	100	937,579	Brazzaville
Cuvette	74,850	151,839	Owando
Kouilou	13,694	665,502	Pointe-Noire
Lékoumou	20,950	74,420	Sibiti
Likouala	66,044	70,675	Impfondo
Niari	25,940	220,087	Loubomo (Dolisie)
Plateaux	38,400	119,722	Djambala
Pool	33,955	182,671	Kinkala
Sangha	55,800	52,132	Ouesso

Main ethnic groups are: Kongo (48%), Sangha (20%), Teke (17%) and M'Bochi (12%).

French is the official language. Kongo languages are widely spoken. Monokutuba and Lingala serve as lingua francas.

SOCIAL STATISTICS

1997 births, 100,000; deaths, 45,000. Rates, 1997 estimates (per 1,000 population): births, 38·8; deaths, 17·3. Infant mortality, 1999 (per 1,000 live births), 81. Expectation of life in 1999 was 49·0 years for males and 53·3 for females. Annual population growth rate, 1990–99, 2·9%. Fertility rate, 1999, 5·9 children per woman.

CLIMATE

An equatorial climate, with moderate rainfall and a small range of temperature. There is a long dry season from May to Oct. in the southwest plateaus, but the

Congo Basin in the northeast is more humid, with rainfall approaching 100" (2,500 mm). Brazzaville, Jan. 78°F (25·6°C), July 73°F (22·8°C). Annual rainfall 59" (1,473 mm).

CONSTITUTION AND GOVERNMENT

A new constitution was approved in a referendum held in Jan. 2002. Under the new constitution the president's term of office is increased from five to seven years. The constitution abolished the position of prime minister, and provides for a new two-chamber assembly consisting of a house of representatives and a senate. The president may also appoint and dismiss ministers. 84·3% of voters were in favour of the draft constitution and 11·3% against. Turn-out was 78%, despite calls from opposition parties for a boycott. The new constitution came into force in Aug. 2002.

National Anthem. 'La Congolaise'; words and tune by Jean Royer and others.

RECENT ELECTIONS

Presidential elections were held on 10 March 2002. Incumbent Denis Sassou-Nguesso won with 89·4% of votes cast, against 2·7% for Joseph Kignoumbi Kia Mboungou. The turn-out was 74·7%. The election represented the first time that Sassou-Nguesso was elected to the presidency, having seized power in 1979 and again in 1997.

Parliamentary elections were held on 26 May and 22 June 2002. President Denis Sassou-Nguesso's Congolese Labour Party won 52 out of 137 seats; his allies, 31; the Pan-African Union for Social Development, 4; and the Union for Democracy and Republic, 6.

CURRENT ADMINISTRATION

President: Denis Sassou-Nguesso; b. 1943 (sworn in 25 Oct. 1997 for a second time and re-elected in March 2002, having previously held office 1979–92).

In March 2003 the government comprised:

Minister of Transport and Privatization, in Charge of Coordinating Government Action: Isidore Mvouba. *Economic Integration and Territorial Development:* Pierre Moussa. *Foreign Affairs, Co-operation and Francophonie Affairs:* Rodolphe Adada. *Justice, Guardian of the Seals and Human Rights:* Martin Mbémba. *Oil:* Jean-Baptiste Taty Loutard. *Economy, Finance and Budget:* Roger Rigobert Andely. *Security and Police:* Pierre Oba. *Equipment and Public Works:* Florent Ntsiba. *Presidential Affairs, in Charge of State Control:* Simon Mfoutou. *Agriculture, Livestock, Fisheries and the Promotion of Women:* Jeanne Dambedzet. *Forestry and the Environment:* Henri Djombo. *Construction, Urbanism, Housing and Land Reform:* Claude Alphonse Nsilou. *Territorial Administration and Decentralization:* François Ibovi. *Labour, Employment and Social Security:* André Okombi Salissa. *Posts and Telecommunications, in Charge of Technological Development:* Jean Dellot. *Technical and Vocational Training:* Pierre Michel Nguimbi. *Higher Education and Scientific Research:* Henri Ossebi. *Industrial Development, Small and Medium-Sized Businesses, and Handicrafts:* Emile Mabondzot. *Commerce, Consumer Affairs and Supplies:* Adélaïde Moundélé-Ngollo. *Social Affairs, Solidarity, Humanitarian Action, Disabled War Veterans and Family Affairs:* Emilienne Eaoul. *Civil Service and State Reform:* Gabriel Entcha Ebia. *Mines, Energy and Water Resources:* Philippe Mvouo. *Health and Population:* Dr Alain Moka. *Primary Education and Literacy:* Rosalie Kama. *Culture and Tourism:* Jean Claude Gakosso. *Communications, in Charge of Relations with Parliament and Government Spokesperson:* Alain Akoualat. *Sports and Youth Affairs:* Marcel Mbani.

DEFENCE

In 2000 military expenditure totalled US$72m. (US$24 per capita), representing 2·5% of GDP.

Army. Total personnel (1999) 8,000. There is a Gendarmerie of 2,000. The 'People's Militia', numbering some 3,000, is being absorbed into the Army.

Navy. Personnel in 1999 totalled about 800. The navy is based at Pointe Noire.

Air Force. The Air Force had (1999) about 1,200 personnel and 12 combat aircraft, most of which are in store.

INTERNATIONAL RELATIONS

The Republic of the Congo is a member of the UN, WTO, the African Union, African Development Bank, IOM, International Organization of the Francophonie and is an ACP member state of the ACP-EU relationship.

ECONOMY

Agriculture produced 11·5% of GDP in 1998, industry 49·9% and services 38·6%.

Overview. An economic and social recovery plan (Paséco) was launched in 1994.

Currency. The unit of currency is the *franc CFA* (XAF) with a parity of 655·957 francs CFA to one euro. Total money supply in April 2002 was 238,885m. francs CFA and foreign exchange reserves were US$51m. Gold reserves were 11,000 troy oz in June 2002. In 2001 there was deflation of 0·5%.

Budget. Total revenue in 2000 was 604·52bn. francs CFA (637·40bn. forecast for 2001) and total expenditure was 584·80bn. francs CFA (524·90bn. forecast for 2001).

Performance. Total GDP in 2001 was US$2·8bn. Real GDP growth was 2·9% in 2001.

Banking and Finance. The *Banque des États de l'Afrique Centrale* (BEAC) is the bank of issue. There are three commercial banks and a development bank, in all of which the government has majority stakes.

Weights and Measures. The metric system is in use.

ENERGY AND NATURAL RESOURCES

Environment. According to the *World Bank Atlas* carbon dioxide emissions in 1998 were the equivalent of 0·6 tonnes per capita.

Electricity. Installed capacity was 165,000 kW in 1995. Total production in 1998 was 503m. kWh and consumption per capita 83 kWh.

Oil and Gas. Oil was discovered in the mid-1960s when Elf Aquitaine was given exclusive rights to production. Elf still has the lion's share but Agip Congo is also involved in oil exploitation. In 1997 production was averaging 230,000 bbls. a day. Proven reserves in 1999 were 1·5bn. bbls. in 1999, including major off-shore deposits. Oil provides about 90% of government revenue and exports. There is a refinery at Pointe-Noire, the second largest city. Gas reserves are estimated at 91,000m. cu. metres.

Minerals. A government mine produces several metals; gold and diamonds are extracted by individuals. There are reserves of potash (4·5m. tonnes), iron ore (1,000m. tonnes), and also clay, bituminous sand, phosphates, zinc and lead.

Agriculture. In 1998 there were 170,000 ha of arable land and 45,000 ha of permanent crops. Production (2000, in thousand tonnes): cassava, 790; sugarcane, 450; plantains, 78; bananas, 52; avocados, 25; groundnuts, 22; sweet potatoes, 22; palm oil, 17; yams, 14.

Livestock (2000): cattle, 77,000; pigs, 46,000; sheep, 116,000; goats, 285,000; poultry, 2m. There were some 700 tractors and 85 thresher-harvesters in use in 1998.

Forestry. In 1995 equatorial forests covered 19·54m. ha (57·2% of the total land area), down from 19·74m. ha in 1990. In 1999, 3·24m. cu. metres of timber were produced, mainly okoumé from the south and sapele from the north. Timber companies are required to replant, and to process at least 60% of their production locally. Before the development of the oil industry, forestry was the mainstay of the economy.

Fisheries. The catch for 2000 was an estimated 49,980, of which approximately half was from inland waters and half from marine waters.

INDUSTRY

There is a growing manufacturing sector, located mainly in the four major towns, producing processed foods, textiles, cement, metal goods and chemicals. Industry produced 37·4% of GDP in 1991, including 7·6% from manufacturing. Production (1997): residual fuel oil, 262,000 tonnes; distillate fuel oil, 95,000 tonnes; petrol,

55,000 tonnes; jet fuel, 17,000 tonnes; cigarettes (1994), 655m. cartons; beer (1994), 50·7m. litres; cement (1995), 100,000 tonnes; veneer sheets (1993), 35,000 cu. metres; cotton textiles (1993), 1·8m. metres; footwear (1990), 300,000 pairs.

Labour. In 1996 the labour force was 1,105,000 (57% males). More than 50% of the economically active population were engaged in agriculture.

Trade Unions. In 1964 the existing unions merged into one national body, the Confédération Syndicale Congolaise. The 40,000-strong *Confédération Syndicale des Travailleurs Congolais* split off from the latter in 1993.

INTERNATIONAL TRADE
Foreign debt was US$4,887m. in 2000.

Imports and Exports. Imports and exports for calendar years in US$1m.:

	1993	1994	1995	1996	1997
Imports	500	612	650	1,361	802
Exports	1,119	958	1,167	1,554	1,744

Apart from crude oil, other significant commodities for export are lumber, plywood, sugar, cocoa, coffee and diamonds. Principal imported commodities are intermediate manufactures, capital equipment, construction materials, foodstuffs and petroleum products. Main export markets are the USA (which accounts for some 23% of exports), Belgium/Luxembourg, Taiwan, Netherlands, France and Italy. Main import suppliers are France (accounting for some 31% of imports), Netherlands, Italy and the USA.

COMMUNICATIONS
Roads. In 1996 there were 12,800 km of roads, of which 1,240 km were surfaced. Vehicles in use in 1996 numbered 53,000, including approximately 37,240 passenger cars (14 per 1,000 inhabitants). There were 124 deaths in road accidents in 1994.

Rail. A railway (510 km, 1,067 mm gauge) connects Brazzaville with Pointe-Noire via Loubomo and Bilinga, and a 285 km branch links Mont-Belo with Mbinda on the Gabon border. Total length is 795 km. In 1995 railways carried 302m. passenger-km and 267m. tonne-km of freight.

Civil Aviation. The principal airports are at Brazzaville (Maya Maya) and Pointe-Noire. The Republic of the Congo is a member of the multinational Air Afrique, which absorbed the former national carrier Lina-Congo in 1992. In 2000 Brazzaville handled 412,000 passengers (335,000 on domestic flights) and 57,400 tonnes of freight.

Shipping. The only seaport is Pointe-Noire, which handled 2·59m. tonnes of freight in 1990. The merchant marine totalled 4,000 GRT in 1998. There are some 5,000 km of navigable rivers, and river transport is an important service for timber and other freight as well as passengers. There are hydrofoil connections from Brazzaville to Kinshasa.

Telecommunications. There were 22,000 telephone main lines in 2000 (7·5 per 1,000 persons). In 1999 there were 3,400 mobile phone subscribers and 10,000 PCs were in use (3·5 per 1,000 persons). There were 500 Internet users in July 2000. In 1995 there were 100 fax machines.

Postal Services. There were 114 post offices in 1995.

SOCIAL INSTITUTIONS
Justice. The Supreme Court, Court of Appeal and a criminal court are situated in Brazzaville, with a network of *tribunaux de grande instance* and *tribunaux d'instance* in the regions.

Religion. In 1999 there were 1·11m. Roman Catholics and 0·66m. Protestants. Traditional animist beliefs are still practised by nearly 900,000 people.

Education. In 1995–96 there were 1,162 primary schools with 7,060 teachers for 497,305 pupils; 7,173 secondary school teachers for 214,650 pupils; and there were 13,806 students at university level in 1992–93. Adult literacy rate in 1999 was 79·5% (male, 86·6%; female, 73·0%).

Health. In 1990 there were 613 doctors, 35 dentists, 1,624 nurses and 498 midwives.

CULTURE

Broadcasting. Broadcasting is under the aegis of the government-controlled Radiodiffusion-Télévision Congolaise, which transmits a national and a regional radio programme and a programme in French. There were 341,000 radio and 33,000 TV receivers in 1997.

Press. In 1996 there were six daily newspapers with a combined circulation of 20,000.

Tourism. There were 44,000 foreign tourists in 1998, bringing revenue of US$3m.

DIPLOMATIC REPRESENTATIVES

Of the Republic of the Congo in the United Kingdom
Ambassador: Henri Marie Joseph Lopes (resides at Paris).
Honorary Consul: Louis Muzzu (4 Wendle Court, 131–137 Wandsworth Road, London SW8 2LH).

Of the United Kingdom in the Republic of the Congo
Ambassador: Jim Atkinson (resides at Kinshasa).

Of the Republic of the Congo in the USA (4891 Colorado Ave., NW, Washington, D.C., 20011)
Ambassador: Serge Mombouli.

Of the USA in the Republic of the Congo (PO Box 1015, Brazzaville)
Ambassador: David H. Kaeuper.

Of the Republic of the Congo to the United Nations
Ambassador: Basile Ikouebe.

Of the Republic of the Congo to the European Union
Ambassador: Jacques Obia.

FURTHER READING

Fegley, Randall, *Congo.* [Bibliography] ABC-Clio, Oxford and Santa Barbara (CA), 1993
Thompson, V. and Adloff, R., *Historical Dictionary of the People's Republic of the Congo.* 2nd ed. Metuchen (NJ), 1984

COSTA RICA

República de Costa Rica

Capital: San José
Population estimate, 2000: 3·81m.
GDP per capita, 2000: (PPP$) 8,650
HDI/world rank: 0·820/43

KEY HISTORICAL EVENTS

Discovered by Columbus in 1502 on his last voyage, Costa Rica (Rich Coast) was part of the Spanish viceroyalty of New Spain from 1540 to 1821. It was part of the Central American Federation until 1838 when it achieved full independence. Coffee was introduced in 1808 and became a mainstay of the economy, helping to create a peasant land-owning class. In 1948 accusations of election fraud led to a six-week civil war, at the conclusion of which José Figueres Ferrer won power at the head of a revolutionary junta. A new constitution was promulgated with, amongst other changes, the abolition of the army. In 1986 Oscar Arias Sánchez was elected president. He promised to prevent Nicaraguan anti-Sandinista (*contra*) forces using Costa Rica as a base. In 1987 he received the Nobel Peace Prize as recognition of his Central American peace plan, agreed to by the other Central American states. Costa Rica was beset with economic problems in the early 1990s when several politicians, including President Calderón, were accused of profiting from drug trafficking.

TERRITORY AND POPULATION

Costa Rica is bounded in the north by Nicaragua, east by the Caribbean, southeast by Panama, and south and west by the Pacific. The area is estimated at 51,100 sq. km (19,730 sq. miles). The population at the census of July 2000 was 3,810,179; density, 71·4 per sq. km. In 2000, 58·9% of the population were urban.

The UN gives a projected population for 2010 of 4·53m.

There are seven provinces (with 2000 population): Alajuela (716,286); Cartago (432,395); Guanacaste (264,238); Heredia (354,732); Limón (339,295); Puntarenas (357,483); San José (1,345,750). The largest cities, with estimated 2000 populations, are San José (346,600); Limón (62,000); and Alajuela (53,900).

The population is mainly of Spanish (85%) and mixed (8%) descent. About 3% are Afro-Caribbean (including some 70,000 speakers of an English Creole along the Caribbean coast). There is a residual Amerindian population of about 10,000.

Spanish is the official language.

SOCIAL STATISTICS

Statistics for calendar years:

	Marriages	Births	Deaths
1996	23,574	78,203	13,993
1997	24,300	78,018	14,260
1998	24,831	76,982	14,708
1999	25,613	78,526	15,052

1999 rates per 1,000 population: births, 21·8; deaths, 4·2. Annual population growth rate, 1990–99, 2·9%. Life expectancy at birth, 2000, was 74·8 years for men and 80·3 years for women. Infant mortality, 2000, 10·2 per 1,000 live births; fertility rate, 2000, 2·4 children per woman.

CLIMATE

The climate is tropical, with a small range of temperature and abundant rain. The dry season is from Dec. to April. San José, Jan. 66°F (18·9°C), July 69°F (20·6°C). Annual rainfall 72" (1,793 mm).

CONSTITUTION AND GOVERNMENT

The Constitution was promulgated in Nov. 1949. The legislative power is vested in a single-chamber *Legislative Assembly* of 57 deputies elected for four years. The President and two Vice-Presidents are elected for four years; the candidate receiving the largest vote, provided it is over 40% of the total, is declared elected, but a second ballot is required if no candidate gets 40% of the total. Elections are normally held on the first Sunday in Feb.

The President may appoint and remove members of the cabinet.

National Anthem. 'Noble patria, tu hermosa bandera' ('Noble fatherland, thy beautiful banner'); words by J. M. Zeledón Brenes, tune by M. M. Gutiérrez.

RECENT ELECTIONS
In the first round of presidential elections held on 3 Feb. 2002 Abel Pacheco (Social Christian Unity Party/PUSC) won 38·6% of votes cast against 31·0% for Rolando Araya Monge (National Liberation Party) and 26·2% for Ottón Solís Fallas (Citizen's Action Party). Turn-out was 68·9%. In the presidential run-off held on 7 April 2002 Abel Pacheco won with 58·0% of votes cast against 42·0% for Rolando Araya Monge.

At the parliamentary elections held on 3 Feb. 2002 the Social Christian Unity Party (PUSC) won 19 seats with 29·8% of the vote, the National Liberation Party 17 (27·1%), the Citizen's Action Party 14 (21·9%), Libertarian Movement 6 (9·3%) and Costa Rican Renewal Party 1 (3·6%). Turn-out was 66·6%.

CURRENT ADMINISTRATION
President: Abel Abel Pacheco; b. 1933 (PUSC; sworn in 8 May 2002).

In March 2003 the government comprised:

First Vice President: Lineth Saborío. *Second Vice President:* Luis Fishman. *Minister of Agriculture and Livestock:* Rodolfo Coto. *Culture, Youth and Sports:* Guido Sáenz González. *Economy and Industry:* Vilma Villalobos. *Education:* Astrid Fischel Volio. *Environment and Energy:* Carlos Manuel Rodríguez. *Finance:* Jorge Bolaños. *Foreign Relations and Religion:* Roberto Tovar Faja. *Foreign Trade:* Alberto Trejos. *Health:* María del Rocio Sáenz. *Housing:* Helio Fallas Venegas. *Justice:* José Miguel Villalobos. *Labour and Social Security:* Ovidio Pacheco Salazar. *Planning:* Danilo Chaverri Soto. *Presidency:* Rina Contreras López. *Public Security, Government and Police:* Rogelio Vicente Ramos Martínez. *Public Works and Transportation:* Javier Chávez. *Science and Technology:* Rogelio Pardo Evans. *Tourism:* Ruben Pacheco. *Women's Affairs:* Gloria Valerin. *Minister Without Portfolio:* Rosalia Gil.

Government Website (Spanish only): http://www.casapres.go.cr/

DEFENCE
In 2000 defence expenditure totalled US$84m. (US$21 per capita), representing 0·8% of GDP.

Army. The Army was abolished in 1948, and replaced by a Civil Guard numbering 5,500 in 1999. In addition there is a Border Security Police of 509 and a Rural Guard of 8,221.

Navy. The paramilitary Maritime Surveillance Unit numbered (1999) 245.

Air Wing. The Civil Guard operates a small air wing equipped with three light planes and helicopters.

INTERNATIONAL RELATIONS
Costa Rica is a member of the UN, WTO, OAS, Inter-American Development Bank, CACM, ACS and IOM.

ECONOMY
Services accounted for 60·5% of GDP in 1998, industry 24·5% and agriculture 15·2%.

Currency. The unit of currency is the *Costa Rican colón* (CRC) of 100 *céntimos*. The official rate is used for all imports on an essential list and by the government and autonomous institutions, and a free rate is used for all other transactions. In June 2002 total money supply was 641,189m. colones, foreign exchange reserves were US$1,426m. and gold reserves were 2,000 troy oz. Inflation was 11·3% in 2001.

Budget. In 2000 total revenue was 1,025·90bn. colones (899·52bn. in 1999) and total expenditure 1,095·16bn. colones (966·89bn. in 1999).

Performance. Costa Rica, said to be the most stable country in Central America, experienced GDP growth of 8·4% in 1998 and 9·4% in 1999, although then only 2·2% in 2000 and 0·9% in 2001. Total GDP in 2001 was US$16·2bn.

Banking and Finance. The bank of issue is the Central Bank (founded 1950) which supervises the national monetary system, foreign exchange dealings and banking operations. The bank has a board of seven directors appointed by the government, including *ex officio* the Minister of Finance and the Planning Office Director. The *Governor* is Francisco de Paula Gutiérrez Gutiérrez.

There is a stock exchange, which in 2000 was the second most successful market in the world after China's Shanghai B Index, gaining in value by nearly 34% in the course of the year.

Weights and Measures. The metric system is legally established, but in country districts the following old Spanish weights and measures may be found: *Libra* = 1·014 lb avoirdupois; *arroba* = 25·35 lb avoirdupois; *quintal* = 101·40 lb avoirdupois, and *fanega* = 11 Imperial bushels.

ENERGY AND NATURAL RESOURCES

Environment. According to the *World Bank Atlas* Costa Rica's carbon dioxide emissions in 1998 were the equivalent of 1·4 tonnes per capita. An *Environmental Sustainability Index* compiled for the World Economic Forum meeting in Feb. 2002 ranked Costa Rica ninth in the world, with 63·2%. The index measured the ability of countries to maintain favourable environmental conditions and examined various factors including pollution levels and the use or abuse of natural resources.

Electricity. Installed capacity was 1,487,000 kW in 1999. Production was 6·20bn. kWh in 1999. Consumption per capita was 1,450 kWh in 1998.

Minerals. Gold output is about 500 kg per year. Salt production was 23,000 tonnes in 1998.

Agriculture. Agriculture is a key sector, with 263,000 people being economically active in 1995. There were 0·23m. ha of arable land in 1998 and 0·28m. ha of permanent crops. The principal agricultural products are coffee, bananas and sugar. Cattle are also of great importance. Production figures for 2000 (in 1,000 tonnes): sugarcane, 4,000; bananas, 2,700; rice, 264; melons, 177; coffee, 164; palm oil, 134; oranges, 126; plantains, 90; watermelons, 77; potatoes, 74; pineapples, 43; papayas, 36.

Livestock (2000): cattle, 1·71m.; pigs, 390,000; horses, 115,000; chickens, 17m.

Forestry. The forest area is being depleted, having been 1·45m. ha and 28·5% of the total land area in 1990, but only 1·25m. ha and 24·4% of the land area in 1995. Timber production in 1999 was 5·40m. cu. metres.

Fisheries. Total catch in 1999 amounted to 25,679 tonnes, mostly from sea fishing.

INDUSTRY

The main manufactured goods are foodstuffs, palm oil, textiles, fertilizers, pharmaceuticals, furniture, cement, tyres, canning, clothing, plastic goods, plywood and electrical equipment.

Labour. In July 2000 there were 1,318,625 people in employment. There were 71,935 unemployed persons, or 5·2% of the workforce. The main area of employment is community, social and personal services (337,000 people in 2000), followed by agriculture (269,000 in 2000).

Trade Unions. There are two main trade unions, *Rerum Novarum* (anti-Communist) and *Confederación General de Trabajadores Costarricenses* (Communist).

INTERNATIONAL TRADE

A free trade agreement was signed with Mexico in March 1994. Some 2,300 products were freed from tariffs, with others to follow over ten years. External debt was US$3,011m. in June 2000.

Imports and Exports. The value of imports and exports in US$1m. was:

	1997	1998	1999
Imports	3,503	4,377	5,962
Exports	2,995	3,614	4,914

Chief exports: manufactured goods and other products, coffee, bananas, sugar, cocoa. Main export markets, 1996: USA, 39·0%; Germany, 7·2%; Italy, 5·2%; Belgium-Luxembourg, 4·4%. Main import suppliers, 1996: USA, 49·9%; Mexico, 6·5%; Venezuela, 6·5%; Guatemala, 3·0%.

COMMUNICATIONS

Roads. In 1999 there were 35,876 km of roads. On the Costa Rica section of the Inter-American Highway it is possible to motor to Panama during the dry season. The Pan-American Highway into Nicaragua is metalled for most of the way and there is now a good highway open almost to Puntarenas. Motor vehicles, 1999, numbered 507,796 (294,100 passenger cars in 1997). There were 324 fatalities as a result of road accidents in 1998.

Rail. The nationalized railway system *(Incofer)* was closed in 1994.

Civil Aviation. There is an international airport at San José (Juan Santamaria). The national carrier is Líneas Aéreas Costarriquenses (LACSA), which in 1999 flew 23·9m. km and carried 922,600 passengers. In 2000 San José handled 2,159,215 passengers (1,994,829 on international flights) and 77,137 tonnes of freight.

Shipping. The chief ports are Limón on the Atlantic and Caldera on the Pacific. The merchant marine totalled 6,000 GRT in 1998. In 1996 vessels totalling 4,135,000 NRT entered ports and vessels totalling 2,992,000 NRT cleared.

Telecommunications. There were 1,003,400 telephone main lines in 2000 (249·4 per 1,000 inhabitants) and 600,000 PCs in use (149·1 for every 1,000 persons). The government has 202 telegraph offices and 88 official telephone stations. In 1999 mobile phone subscribers numbered 143,000 and in 1997 there were 8,500 fax machines. Costa Rica had 250,000 Internet users in Dec. 2000, up from 30,000 a year earlier.

SOCIAL INSTITUTIONS

Justice. Justice is administered by the Supreme Court and five appeal courts divided into five chambers—the Court of Cassation, the Higher and Lower Criminal Courts, and the Higher and Lower Civil Courts. There are also subordinate courts in the separate provinces and local justices throughout the republic. Capital punishment may not be inflicted.

The population in penal institutions in Dec. 1996 was 5,495 (155 per 100,000 of national population).

Religion. Roman Catholicism is the state religion; it had 2·82m. adherents in 1997. There is entire religious liberty under the constitution. The Archbishop of Costa Rica has four bishops at Alajuela, Limón, San Isidro el General, Tilarán and Puntarenas. Followers of other faiths number about 650,000.

Education. The adult literacy rate in 1999 was 95·5% (95·4% among males and 95·5% among females). Primary instruction is compulsory and free from six to 15 years; secondary education (since 1949) is also free. Primary schools are provided and maintained by local school councils, while the national government pays the teachers, besides making subventions in aid of local funds. In 1999 there were 3,780 public and private primary schools with 25,208 teachers and administrative staff and 536,490 enrolled pupils, and 454 public and private secondary schools with 17,636 teachers and 235,425 pupils. In 1999 there was 1 university and 1 technological institute in the public sector, and 8 universities, 1 Adventist university and 1 university of science and technology in the private sector. There were also four other institutions of higher education. In 1999 there were 59,947 university students.

In 1999 total expenditure on education came to 5·2% of GNP and represented 23·0% of total government expenditure.

Health. In 2000 there were 3,333 doctors, 346 dentists, 1,214 nurses, 272 pharmacists and (1999) 29 hospitals.

CULTURE

Broadcasting. There were 980,000 radio sets and 525,000 television receivers in 1997 (colour by NTSC).

Cinema. There were 39 cinemas in 1995, with a total attendance for the year of 1·7m.; gross box office receipts came to 1,058m. colones.

Press. There were six daily newspapers in 1996 with a combined circulation of 320,000, at a rate of 88 per 1,000 inhabitants.

Tourism. In 1999 there were 1,027,000 foreign tourists, bringing revenue of US$1,002m.

Theatre and Opera. There are eight national theatres.

Museums and Galleries. Costa Rica has three museums.

DIPLOMATIC REPRESENTATIVES

Of Costa Rica in the United Kingdom (Flat 1, 14 Lancaster Gate, London, W2 3LH)
Ambassador: Rodolfo Gutiérrez.

Of the United Kingdom in Costa Rica (Edificio Centro Colón, 11th Floor, Apartado 815, San José 1007)
Ambassador: Georgina Butler.

Of Costa Rica in the USA (2114 S Street, NW, Washington, D.C., 20008)
Ambassador: Jaime Daremblum.

Of the USA in Costa Rica (Pavas, Frente Centro Comercial, San José)
Ambassador: John J. Danilovich.

Of Costa Rica to the United Nations
Ambassador: Bruno Stagno.

Of Costa Rica to the European Union
Ambassador: Vacant.
Chargé d'Affaires a.i.: Maria Salvadora Ortiz Ortiz.

FURTHER READING

Biesanz, R., *et al.*, *The Costa Ricans.* Hemel Hempstead, 1982
Bird, L., *Costa Rica: Unarmed Democracy.* London, 1984
Creedman, T. S., *Historical Dictionary of Costa Rica.* 2nd ed. Metuchen (N.J.), 1991
Stansifer, Charles L., *Costa Rica.* [Bibliography] ABC-Clio, Oxford and Santa Barbara (CA), 1991

National statistical office: Instituto Nacional de Estadística y Censos, San José.

Website (Spanish only): http://www.inec.go.cr/

CÔTE D'IVOIRE

République de la
Côte d'Ivoire
(Republic of the Ivory Coast)

Capital: Yamoussoukro
Seat of government: Abidjan
Population estimate, 2000: 16·01m.
GDP per capita, 2000: (PPP$) 1,630
HDI/world rank: 0·428/156

KEY HISTORICAL EVENTS

France obtained rights on the coast in 1842 but did not occupy the territory until 1882. In the early 1870s a French offer to exchange Côte d'Ivoire with the British for the Gambia, which bisected the French colony of Senegal, was refused. Rumours of gold later rekindled French interest and in 1889 Côte d'Ivoire was declared a French protectorate. Governors appointed from France administered the colony using a system of centralized rule that allowed little room for local participation. In 1946 Côte d'Ivoire's first political party, the Democratic Party of Côte d'Ivoire, was created under the leadership of Félix Houphouët-Boigny who eventually adopted a policy of co-operation with the French authorities. By the mid-1950s the country had become the wealthiest in French West Africa and in 1958 Côte d'Ivoire became an autonomous republic within the French Community. Côte d'Ivoire achieved full independence on 7 Aug. 1960, with Félix Houphouët-Boigny as its first president.

On 23 Dec. 1999 President Henri Konan Bédié was ousted in a military coup led by Gen. Robert Guéï, the country's military chief from 1990 to 1995. On 6 Oct. 2000 a state of emergency was declared ahead of a Supreme Court announcement on the candidates allowed to stand for the presidential election on 22 Oct. 2000. After Robert Guéï declared himself the winner in the election, a violent uprising in which over 2,000 people were killed resulted in Gen. Guéï fleeing to Benin. The veteran opposition candidate Laurent Gbagbo was then declared the rightful winner. In Sept. 2002 there was a failed coup attempt by mutinous soldiers that claimed more than 20 lives, including those of both Gen. Guéï and the interior minister. Since then, Côte d'Ivoire has descended further into civil war involving different rebel factions.

TERRITORY AND POPULATION

Côte d'Ivoire is bounded in the west by Liberia and Guinea, north by Mali and Burkina Faso, east by Ghana, and south by the Gulf of Guinea. It has an area of 320,783 sq. km and a population at the 1988 census of 10,812,782 (54·3% rural in 1999). Estimate (1996) 14·76m.; density, 46·0 per sq. km.

The UN gives a projected population for 2010 of 19·63m.

Since 1991 the country has been divided into ten regions (North-West, North, North-East, West, Centre-West, Centre-North, Centre, Centre-East, South-West, South) comprising 50 departments. Departments are named after their chief towns.

The areas and populations (1988 census) of the departments:

	Area (in sq. km)	Population		Area (in sq. km)	Population
Abengourou	5,200	214,162	Boundiali	7,895	127,231
Abidjan	8,550	2,492,513	Dabakala	9,670	82,094
Aboisso	6,250	225,882	Daloa	5,450	361,472
Adzopé	5,230	237,265	Danané	4,600	222,045
Agboville	3,850	203,730	Daoukro[4]	3,610	86,425
Agnibilekrou[1]	1,700	84,404	Dimbokro	4,920	141,934
Bangolo[2]	2,060	80,374	Divo	7,920	389,530
Béoumi[3]	2,860	91,062	Duékoué[5]	2,930	101,451
Biankouma	4,950	99,431	Ferkessedougou	17,728	172,850
Bondoukou	10,040	175,632	Gagnoa	4,500	275,765
Bongouanou	5,570	225,432	Grand-Lahou[6]	2,280	52,645
Bouaflé	3,980	163,917	Guiglo	11,220	169,660
Bouaké	4,700	453,074	Issia	3,590	194,974
Bouna	21,470	134,459	Katiola	9,420	131,221

CÔTE D'IVOIRE

	Area (in sq. km)	Population		Area (in sq. km)	Population
Korhogo	12,500	387,947	Sinfra[8]	1,690	120,301
Lakota	2,730	115,948	Soubré	8,270	309,307
Man	4,990	286,860	Tabou[7]	5,440	59,708
Mankono	10,660	123,723	Tanda[9]	6,490	203,129
M'bahiakro[3]	5,460	102,774	Tiassalé[6]	3,370	132,626
Odiénné	20,600	169,433	Tingréla	2,200	55,251
Oumé	2,400	140,166	Touba	8,720	109,155
Sakassou[3]	1,880	59,494	Toumodi[3]	2,780	80,909
San Pédro[7]	6,900	168,174	Vavoua[10]	6,160	169,454
Sassandra	5,190	107,616	Yamoussoukro[3]	6,160	284,613
Séguéla	11,240	121,120	Zuénoula	2,830	114,440

[1]Formerly part of Abengourou. [2]Formerly part of Man. [3]Formerly parts of Bouaké.
[4]Formerly part of Dimbokro. [5]Formerly part of Guiglo. [6]Formerly parts of Abidjan.
[7]Formerly parts of Sassandra. [8]Formerly part of Bouaflé. [9]Formerly part of Bondoukou.
[10]Formerly part of Daloa.

In 1999 the population of Abidjan stood at 3,199,000. Other major towns (with 1988 census population): Bouaké, 329,850; Daloa, 121,842; Korhogo, 109,445; Yamoussoukro, 106,786.

There are about 60 ethnic groups, the principal ones being the Baoulé (23%), the Bété (18%) and the Sénoufo (15%).

Approximately 30% of the population are immigrants.

French is the official language.

SOCIAL STATISTICS
1996 births, 627,000; deaths, 232,000. Rates, 1996 estimates (per 1,000 population): births, 42·5; deaths, 15·7. Infant mortality (per 1,000 live births), 102 (1999). Expectation of life in 1999 was 47·5 years for males and 48·1 for females. Annual population growth rate, 1990–99, 2·95%. Infant mortality, 1999, 102 per 1,000 live births; fertility rate, 1999, 4·9 births per woman. 29% of the population are migrants.

CLIMATE
A tropical climate, affected by distance from the sea. In coastal areas, there are wet seasons from May to July and in Oct. and Nov., but in central areas the periods are March to May and July to Nov. In the north, there is one wet season from June to Oct. Abidjan, Jan. 81°F (27·2°C), July 75°F (23·9°C). Annual rainfall 84" (2,100 mm). Bouaké, Jan. 81°F (27·2°C), July 77°F (25°C). Annual rainfall 48" (1,200 mm).

CONSTITUTION AND GOVERNMENT
The 1960 Constitution was amended in 1971, 1975, 1980, 1985, 1986, 1990 and 1998. The sole legal party was the Democratic Party of Côte d'Ivoire, but opposition parties were legalized in 1990. There is a 225-member *National Assembly* elected by universal suffrage for a five-year term. The President is also directly elected for a five-year term (renewable). He appoints and leads a Council of Ministers.

In Nov. 1990 the National Assembly voted that its Speaker should become President in the event of the latter's incapacity, and created the post of Prime Minister to be appointed by the President. Following the death of President Houphouët-Boigny on 7 Dec. 1993, the speaker, Henri Konan Bédié, proclaimed himself head of state till the end of the presidential term in Sept. 1995.

Following the coup of Dec. 1999 a referendum was held on 23 July 2000 on the adoption of a new constitution, which set eligibility conditions for presidential candidates (the candidate and both his parents must be Ivorian), reduced the voting age from 21 to 18, and abolished the death penalty. It also offered an amnesty to soldiers who staged the coup and the junta, but committed the junta to hand over power to an elected civilian head of state and parliament within six months of the proclamation of the text. Approximately 87% of votes cast were in favour of the new constitution.

National Anthem. 'L'Abidjanaise'; words by M. Ekra and others, tune by P. M Pango.

RECENT ELECTIONS
Presidential elections were held on 22 Oct. 2000, but were boycotted by the former ruling Democratic Party and the Rally of the Republicans. Laurent Gbagbo (Front Populaire Ivorienne/FPI) obtained 59·4% of votes cast against 32·7% for Robert Guéï, who had seized power in a coup in Dec. 1999. Initially Robert Guéï claimed victory but following a violent uprising accepted defeat (the first time in Africa that a popular rising had succeeded in toppling a military regime). There were three other candidates.

The National Assembly elections were held on 10 Dec. 2000 and 14 Jan. 2001. The Ivorian People's Front (FPI) won 96 seats; the Democratic Party (PDCI) won 94 seats; Rally of the Republicans, 5. There were also two vacant seats.

CURRENT ADMINISTRATION
President: Laurent Gbagbo; b. 1945 (FPI; assumed office 26 Oct. 2000).

In March 2003 a power-sharing unity government was formed with the hope of bringing to an end six months of civil war. It included:
Prime Minister: Seydou Diarra; b. 1933 (ind.; sworn in on 10 Feb. 2003 for a second time, having previously been prime minister for five months in 2000).

Minister of State for Economic Infrastructure: Patrick Achi (PDCI). *Economy and Finance:* Paul Bohoun Bouabré (FPI). *Environment:* Angèle Gnonsoa (Parti Ivorien des Travailleurs). *Foreign Affairs:* Bamba Mamadou (PDCI). *Health and Population:* Toiqueuse Mabri (Union pour la Démocratie et la Paix en Côte d'Ivoire). *Mines and Energy:* Léon Monnet (FPI). *Regional Integration and African Union:* Théodore Mel Eg (Union Démocratique Citoyenne). *Transport:* Anaki Kobenan (Mouvement des Forces de l'Avenir).

Minister of Administrative Reform: Eric Kahé (Union pour la Démocratie et la Paix en Côte d'Ivoire). *Animal Production and Fishery Resources:* Kouassi Adjoumani (PDCI). *Culture and Francophonie:* Messaou Malan (PDCI). *Fight Against AIDS:* Christine Adjobi (FPI). *Housing and Town Planning:* Raymond N'Doli (FPI). *Human Rights:* Victorine Wodié (Parti Ivorien des Travailleurs). *Industry and Promotion of the Private Sector:* Kouadio Jeannot Ahoussou (PDCI). *Labour and Civil Service:* Hubert Oulaye (FPI). *National Education:* Amani N'Guessan Michel (FPI). *National Reconciliation:* Sébastien Danon Djédjé (FPI). *Planning and Development:* Boniface Britto (PDCI). *Relations with the Institutions of the Republic:* Alfonse Douaty (FPI). *Religion:* Désiré Gnonkonté (PDCI). *Solidarity, Health and Social Security:* Clotilde Ohouochi (FPI). *Water and Forests:* Assoa Adou (FPI).

Office of the President (French only): http://www.presidence.gov.ci/

DEFENCE
There is selective conscription for six months. Defence expenditure totalled US$132m. in 2000 (US$9 per capita), representing 0·9% of GDP.

Army. Total strength (1999), 6,800. In addition there is a Presidential Guard of 1,100, a Gendarmerie of 4,400 and a Militia of 1,500.

Navy. Personnel in 1999 totalled 900 and the force is based at Locodjo (Abidjan).

Air Force. There are five Alpha Jet light strike combat aircraft, although only one or two are operational. Personnel (1999) 700.

INTERNATIONAL RELATIONS
Côte d'Ivoire is a member of the UN, WTO, the African Union, African Development Bank, UEMOA, ECOWAS, IOM, OIC, International Organization of the Francophonie and is an ACP member state of the ACP-EU relationship.

ECONOMY
Agriculture accounted for 26·0% of GDP in 1998, industry 22·7% and services 51·3%.

Overview. Austerity measures were introduced in May 1990. A privatization programme, concentrating on the agro-industrial sectors, was introduced in 1992. 54 companies from an initial list of 60 had been privatized by mid-1999, when 20 additional companies were listed.

Daniel Kablan Duncan, then Prime Minister, stated in 1999: 'We are a middle-income country and are striving to become a new industrialized nation within a generation—to quit the list of developing countries within 25 to 30 years'.

Currency. The unit of currency is the *franc CFA* (XOF) with a parity of 655·957 francs CFA to one euro. Foreign exchange reserves were US$1,273m. in May 2002 and total money supply was 1,338·30bn. francs CFA. In 2000 gold reserves were 45,000 troy oz. Inflation was 4·4% in 2001.

Budget. Government revenue and expenditure (in 1bn. francs CFA):

	1996	1997	1998	1999[1]
Revenue	1,230·0	1,330·1	1,392·2	1,442·1
Expenditure	1,385·2	1,494·5	1,557·3	1,533·1

[1]Estimate.

VAT is 25%.

Performance. Real GDP growth was negative in 2000, at –2·3%, and in 2001 there was growth of just 0·1%. Total GDP in 2001 was US$10·4bn.

Banking and Finance. The regional *Banque Centrale des Etats de l'Afrique de l'Ouest* is the central bank and bank of issue. The *Governor* is Charles Konan Banny. In 1994 there were 12 commercial banks; three other banks maintained representative offices. The African Development Bank is based in Abidjan. There is a stock exchange in Abidjan.

ENERGY AND NATURAL RESOURCES

Environment. According to the *World Bank Atlas* carbon dioxide emissions in 1998 were the equivalent of 0·9 tonnes per capita.

Electricity. The electricity industry was privatized in 1990. Installed capacity was 1m. kW in 1997. Production in 1998 amounted to 3·36bn. kWh. Consumption per capita in 1997 was an estimated 196 kWh.

Oil and Gas. Petroleum has been produced (offshore) since Oct. 1977. Production (1996), 7m. bbls. Gas reserves, 1997, 23bn. cu. metres. Daily output, 1997, 2·12m. cu. metres.

Minerals. Côte d'Ivoire has large deposits of iron ores, bauxite, tantalite, diamonds, gold, nickel and manganese, most of which are untapped. Gold production has steadily increased with 2·4 tonnes being produced in 1997. In 1998 diamond production totalled 307,000 carats.

Agriculture. In 1995 the agricultural population was 14·25m., of whom 2·97m. were economically active. In 1998 agriculture accounted for 66% of exports. There were 2·95m. ha of arable land in 1998 and 4·40m. ha of permanent crops. Côte d'Ivoire is the world's largest producer and exporter of cocoa beans, with an output of 1·30m. tonnes in 2000 (more than 41% of the world total) and the fifth largest coffee producer, with 365,000 tonnes in 2000. The cocoa and coffee industries have for years relied on foreign workers, but tens of thousands have left the country since the 1999 coup resulting in labour shortages. Other main crops, with 2000 production figures in 1,000 tonnes, are: yams (2,923), cassava (1,673), plantains (1,405), rice (1,162), sugarcane (1,155), maize (571), taro (365), seed cotton (270), palm oil (242), bananas (241), pineapples (226), coconuts (193), groundnuts (144), cottonseed (140), cotton lint (130), tomatoes (130), natural rubber (119).

Livestock, 2000: 1·35m. cattle, 1·39m. sheep, 1·09m. goats, 280,000 pigs and 30m. chickens.

Forestry. In 1995 the rainforest covered 5·47m. ha, or 17·72% of the total land area, down from 5·62m. ha in 1990 and 13m. ha in 1900. Products include teak, mahogany and ebony. In 1999, 13·40m. cu. metres of roundwood were produced. Côte d'Ivoire is the biggest producer of rubber in Africa.

Fisheries. In 1989 the fishing fleet comprised 32 vessels over 100 GRT totalling 9,386 GRT. The catch in 2000 amounted to 80,332 tonnes, of which 69,820 tonnes were from marine waters.

INDUSTRY

Industrialization has developed rapidly since independence, particularly food processing, textiles and sawmills. Output in 1997 (in 1,000 tonnes): distillate fuel oil, 706; residual fuel oil, 482; petrol, 434; cement (1995), 500; sawn wood (1997), 613,000 cu. metres; veneer sheets (1995), 252,000 cu. metres; centrifugal sugar (1998), 126.

Labour. In 1996 the workforce was 5·7m. (67% males).

Trade Unions. The main trade union is the *Union Générale des Travailleurs de Côte d'Ivoire*, with over 100,000 members.

INTERNATIONAL TRADE

External debt was US$12,138m. in 2000.

Imports and Exports. Imports and exports for calendar years in US$1m.:

	1996	1997	1998	1999	2000
Imports f.o.b.	2,622·4	2,658·4	2,886·5	2,766·1	2,175·5
Exports f.o.b.	4,446·1	4,451·2	4,606·5	4,661·4	3,972·9

Principal exports, 1994 (in 1,000m. francs CFA): cocoa beans, 424; sawnwood, 113; petroleum products (1992), 85; coffee, 78; tinned tuna, 65; cotton, 64. Principal imports: petroleum products, 204; non-electrical machinery, 68; fish, 54; rice, 44, pharmaceuticals, 44; electrical plant, 41; vehicles, 36. Main export markets, 1994: France, 16·1%; Germany, 9·8%; Netherlands, 8·9%; Italy, 7·1%. Main import suppliers, 1994: France, 28·2%; Nigeria, 26·8%; USA, 5·9%; Germany, 3·3%.

Trade Fairs. A major international farming and livestock trade show, SARA, takes place every other year in Nov. and attracts exhibitors from around the world.

COMMUNICATIONS

Roads. In 1998 roads totalled 70,000 km, of which 6,000 km were paved. There were about 456,000 motor vehicles in 1996 (293,000 cars, or 18·1 per 1,000 inhabitants, and 163,000 trucks and vans).

Rail. From Abidjan a metre-gauge railway runs to Leraba on the border with Burkina Faso (655 km), and thence through Burkina Faso to Ouagadougou and Kaya. Operation of the railway in both countries is franchised to the mixed public-private company Sitarail. Abidjan is to have an underground railway system.

Civil Aviation. There is an international airport at Abidjan (Felix Houphouet Boigny Airport), which in 2000 handled 946,000 passengers (all on international flights) and 20,900 tonnes of freight. The national carrier is the state-owned Air Ivoire, which in 1997 flew 1·3m. km and carried 72,100 passengers. It provides domestic services and in 1998 operated international flights to Burkina Faso, Ghana, Guinea, Liberia and Mali.

Shipping. The main ports are Abidjan and San Pédro. Abidjan handled 15m. tonnes of cargo for the first time in 1998 and has become the biggest container port in West Africa. Some US$200m. have been earmarked for continued expansion of the port. In 1998 the merchant marine totalled 10,000 GRT, including oil tankers 1,000 GRT.

Telecommunications. In 2000 there were 263,700 telephone main lines, or 17·8 per 1,000 inhabitants, and there were 90,000 PCs in use (6·1 per 1,000 persons). Since liberalization in 1995 the telecommunications sector has quickly progressed to become the West African leader and second only to that in South Africa in the continent as a whole. Mobile phone subscribers numbered 342,000 in Sept. 2000. In July 2000 there were 20,000 Internet users.

Postal Services. In 1995 there were 364 post offices.

SOCIAL INSTITUTIONS

Justice. There are 28 courts of first instance and three assize courts in Abidjan, Bouaké and Daloa, two courts of appeal in Abidjan and Bouaké, and a supreme court in Abidjan. Côte d'Ivoire abolished the death penalty in 2000.

Religion. In 1994 there were 5·2m. Muslims (mainly in the north) and 3·8m. Christians (chiefly Roman Catholics in the south). Traditional animist beliefs are also practised.

Education. The adult literacy rate in 1999 was 45·7% (53·8% among males and 37·2% among females). There were, in 1996–97, 1,735,814 pupils in 7,599 primary schools and 534,214 pupils at secondary schools. In 1993–94 there were 51,215 students at higher education institutions. In 1995–96 there was one university with 21,000 students and 730 academic staff, and three university centres. There were six other institutions of higher education.

In 1997 expenditure on education came to 5·0% of GNP and 24·9% of total government spending.

Health. In 1990 there were 2,020 doctors, 219 dentists, 3,691 nurses, 135 pharmacists and 1,533 midwives. There were 93 hospitals and 669 health centres in 1984. In 1982 there were 10,062 hospital beds.

CULTURE

Broadcasting. The government-controlled Radiodiffusion Télévision Ivoirienne is responsible for broadcasting. There were 900,000 television sets (colour by SECAM V) and 2·26m. radio receivers in 1997.

Press. In 1996 there were 12 daily newspapers with a combined circulation of 231,000, at a rate of 17 per 1,000 inhabitants.

Tourism. Efforts are being made by the government to revive the tourist industry which has declined over recent years as a result of the decade-long recession. Tourist development centres in the regions and 11,000 hotel bedrooms are planned. There were 301,000 foreign tourists in 1998, spending US$108m.

DIPLOMATIC REPRESENTATIVES

Of Côte d'Ivoire in the United Kingdom (2 Upper Belgrave St., London, SW1X 8BJ)
Ambassador: Yousoufou Bamba.

Of the United Kingdom in Côte d'Ivoire (3rd Floor, Immeuble 'Les Harmonies', angle Blvd. Carde et Ave. Dr Jamot, Plateau, Abidjan)
Ambassador: Jean François Gordon, CMG.

Of Côte d'Ivoire in the USA (3421 Massachusetts Ave., NW, Washington, D.C., 20007)
Ambassador: Pascal Dago Kokora.

Of the USA in Côte d'Ivoire (5 Rue Jesse Owens, Abidjan)
Ambassador: Arlene Render.

Of Côte d'Ivoire to the United Nations
Ambassador: Vacant.
Chargé d'Affaires a.i.: Ahipeaud Guebo Noël Emmanuel.

Of Côte d'Ivoire to the European Union
Ambassador: Marie Gosset.

FURTHER READING
Direction de la Statistique. *Bulletin Mensuel de Statistique.*
Daniels, Morna, *Côte d'Ivoire.* [Bibliography] ABC-Clio, Oxford and Santa Barbara (CA), 1996

National statistical office: Direction de la Statistique, Ministère du Plan, Abidjan.

CROATIA

Republika Hrvatska

Capital: Zagreb
Population estimate, 2000: 4·65m.
GDP per capita, 2000: (PPP$) 8,091
HDI/world rank: 0·809/48

KEY HISTORICAL EVENTS

Croatia was united with Hungary in 1091 and remained under Hungarian administration until the end of the First World War. On 1 Dec. 1918 Croatia became a part of the new Kingdom of Serbs, Croats and Slovenes, which was renamed Yugoslavia in 1929. During the Second World War an independent fascist (Ustaša) state was set up under the aegis of the German occupiers. During the Communist period Croatia became one of the six 'Socialist Republics' constituting the Yugoslav federation led by Marshal Tito. With the collapse of Communism, an independence movement gained momentum.

In a referendum on 19 May 1991, 94·17% of votes cast were in favour of Croatia becoming an independent sovereign state with the option of joining a future Yugoslav confederation as opposed to remaining in the existing Yugoslav federation. The Krajina and other predominantly Serbian areas of Croatia wanted union with Serbia and seized power by force of arms. Croatian forces and Serb insurgents backed by federal forces became embroiled in a conflict throughout 1991 until the arrival of a UN peace-keeping mission at the beginning of 1992 and the establishment of four UN peace-keeping zones ('pink zones'). In early May 1995 Croatian forces re-took Western Slavonia from the Serbs and opened the Zagreb-Belgrade highway. In a 60-hour operation mounted on 4 Aug. 1995 the former self-declared Serb Republic of Krajina was occupied, provoking an exodus of 180,000 Serb refugees. Croats who had left the area in 1991 began to return. On 12 Nov. 1995 the Croatian government and Bosnian Serbs reached an agreement to place Eastern Slavonia, the last Croatian territory still under Bosnian Serb control, under UN administration.

TERRITORY AND POPULATION

Croatia is bounded in the north by Slovenia and Hungary and in the east by Serbia and Montenegro and Bosnia-Herzegovina. It includes the areas of Dalmatia, Istria and Slavonia which no longer have administrative status. Its area is 56,542 sq. km. Population at the 2001 census was 4,437,460 (4,784,265 in 1991), of whom the predominating ethnic groups were Croats (90%) and Serbs (5%); population density, 78·5 per sq. km. The significant population decrease, popularly called 'the white plague', is seen as a serious social problem.

The UN gives a projected population for 2010 of 4·65m.

In 1999, 57·3% of the population lived in urban areas. Zagreb, the capital, had a 1999 population of 1,047,000. Other major towns (with 1991 census population): Split (189,388), Rijeka (167,964), Osijek (104,761).

At the beginning of 1991 there were some 0·6m. resident Serbs. A law of Dec. 1991 guaranteed the autonomy of Serbs in areas where they are in a majority after the establishment of a permanent peace.

The official language is Croatian.

SOCIAL STATISTICS

2000: births, 43,746; deaths, 50,246; marriages (1999), 23,778; divorces (1998), 3,962. Suicides (1996), 1,002. 1999 rates: birth, 9·9 per 1,000 population; death, 11·4; marriage, 5·2; divorce (1998), 0·9. Suicide rate, 1996, 22·3 per 100,000 population. Infant mortality, 1999, 7·7 per 1,000 live births. Annual population growth rate, 1990–99, –0·1%. In 1997 the most popular age range for marrying was 25–29 for males and 20–24 for females. Life expectancy at birth, 1999, was 69·6 years for males and 77·6 years for females. Fertility rate, 1999, 1·6 children per woman.

CLIMATE

Inland Croatia has a central European type of climate, with cold winters and hot summers, but the Adriatic coastal region experiences a Mediterranean climate with mild, moist winters and hot, brilliantly sunny summers with less than average rainfall. Average annual temperature and rainfall: Dubrovnik, 16·6°C and 1,051 mm. Zadar, 15·6°C and 963 mm. Rijeka, 14·3°C and 1,809 mm. Zagreb, 12·4°C and 1,000 mm. Osijek, 11·3°C and 683 mm.

CONSTITUTION AND GOVERNMENT
A new constitution was adopted on 21 Dec. 1990. The *President* is elected for renewable five-year terms. There is a unicameral Parliament (*Hrvatski Sabor*), consisting of 151 deputies. It has 140 members elected from multi-seat constituencies for a four-year term, 5 seats are reserved for national minorities and 6 members representing Croatians abroad are chosen by proportional representation. The upper house, the *Chamber of Counties*, was abolished in 2001.

National Anthem. 'Lijepa nasva domovino' ('Beautiful our homeland'); words by A. Mihanović, tune by J. Runjanin.

RECENT ELECTIONS
Following Franjo Tudjman's death, presidential elections took place on 24 Jan. 2000 with a second round on 7 Feb. Mate Granić, the candidate from Tudjman's HDZ party, was heavily defeated in the first round in which there were nine candidates. In the run-off centrist Stipe Mesić won 56·2% of the vote against Social Liberal Dražen Budiša's 43·8%. Turn-out in the first round was approximately 64·0% and in the second round 61·5%.

Elections to the Sabor were held on 3 Jan. 2000. An alliance of the Social Democratic Party/SDP and the Social Liberal Party/HSLS (along with the regionalist Primorian Goranian Union and the Slavonian-Baranian Croatian Party) claimed 71 seats with 38·7% of the vote. The Croatian Democratic Union (HDZ) won 40 seats with 26·7%, the United List (an alliance between the Croatian Peasant Party, the Istrian Democratic Assembly, the Liberal Party and the Croatian People's Party) won 24 with 14·7%, and the Croatian Rights Party/Croatian Christian Democratic Union coalition won 5 with 5·2%. A further five seats went to national minorities and six to representatives of Croatians abroad.

CURRENT ADMINISTRATION
President: Stipe Mesić; b. 1934 (Croatian People's Party; sworn in 18 Feb. 2000).

Following the election of 3 Jan. 2000 a coalition government was formed between the SDP/HSLS and the United List. The Istrian Democratic Assembly, one of the parties in the United List, left the coalition in June 2001. In March 2003 the government comprised:

Prime Minister: Ivica Račan; b. 1944 (Social Democratic Party; sworn in 27 Jan. 2000).

Deputy Prime Ministers: Goran Granić; Slavko Linić; Željca Antunović (also *Minister of Defence*); Ante Simonić.

Minister of Public Works, Development and Reconstruction: Radimir Čačić. *Finance:* Mato Crkvenac. *Foreign Affairs:* Tonino Picula. *Interior:* Šime Lučin. *Agriculture and Forestry:* Božidar Pankretić. *Culture:* Antun Vujić. *Economy:* Ljubo Jurčić. *Education and Sport:* Vladimir Strugar. *Health:* Andro Vlahusić. *Homeland War Veterans:* Ivica Pančić. *Justice, Administration and Local Government:* Ingrid Antičević-Marinović. *Labour and Social Welfare:* Davorko Vidović. *Maritime Affairs, Transportation and Communications:* Roland Žuvanić. *Science and Technology:* Gvozden Flego. *Environmental Protection:* Božo Kovačević. *European Integration:* Neven Mimica. *Handicrafts, Small and Medium Businesses:* Željco Pecek. *Tourism:* Pave Župan Rusković. *Minister Without Portfolio:* Godana Sobol.

The *Speaker* is Zlatko Tomčić.

Government Website: http://www.vlada.hr/

DEFENCE
Conscription is for ten months. Defence expenditure in 2000 totalled US$509m. (US$114 per capita), representing 2·7% of GDP.

Army. The country is divided into six operations zones. Personnel, 1999, 53,000 (around 20,000 conscripts). Paramilitary forces include an armed police of 40,000.

There are 70,000 reserves in 27 Home Defence regiments and 150,000 regular Army reservists.

Navy. In 1999 the fleet included one submarine for special operations and one missile-armed corvette. Total personnel in 1999 numbered about 3,000 including two companies of marines.

Air Force. Personnel, 1999, 5,000 (including Air Defence and 1,320 conscripts). There are over 44 combat aircraft including 25 MiG-21s and 15 armed helicopters.

INTERNATIONAL RELATIONS
Croatia is a member of the UN, WTO, BIS, NATO Partnership for Peace, the Council of Europe, OSCE, the Central European Initiative, the Danube Commission, the Inter-American Development Bank and the IOM.

ECONOMY
Services contributed an estimated 58·7% of GDP in 1998, industry 32·4% and agriculture 8·9%.

Overview. A process of privatization is under way. Between 1991 and 1999 a total of 2,650 formerly state-owned companies had been privatized, 667 of which were industrial.

Currency. On 30 May 1994 the *kuna* (HRK; a name used in 1941–45) of 100 *lipa* replaced the Croatian dinar at one kuna = 1,000 dinars. Foreign exchange reserves were US$5,506m. in June 2002. Gold reserves have been negligible since Sept. 2001. Inflation was 4·9% in 2001. Total money supply was 26,715m. kuna in May 2002.

Budget. Government revenue and expenditure (1m. kuna):

	1996	1997	1998	1999	2000	2001[1]
Revenue	47,696	52,945	63,173	61,358	63,817	64,928
Expenditure	48,407	54,362	63,079	68,889	73,269	73,978

[1]Provisional.

Expenditure by function (1997): education, 3,558·52; health, 7,837·70; social security and welfare, 17,916·79. VAT at 22% was introduced in 1997.

Performance. Real GDP growth was 3·7% in 2000 and 4·1% in 2001. Total GDP was US$19·8bn. in 2001.

Banking and Finance. The National Bank of Croatia (*Governor*, Zeljko Rohatinski) is the bank of issue. In 2001 there were 43 registered banks. The largest banks are Zagrebačka Banka, with assets in 2000 of US$2·8bn., and Privredna Banka Zagreb. There are stock exchanges in Zagreb and Varaždin.

Total foreign direct investments from 1993 to Sept. 2001 amounted to US$5,927·5m., principally from Austria (US$1,739m.), Germany (US$1,199m.) and the USA (US$1,189m).

Weights and Measures. The metric system is in use.

ENERGY AND NATURAL RESOURCES
Environment. According to the *World Bank Atlas* Croatia's carbon dioxide emissions in 1998 were the equivalent of 4·5 tonnes per capita. An *Environmental Sustainability Index* compiled for the World Economic Forum meeting in Feb. 2002 ranked Croatia 12th in the world, with 62·5%. The index measured the ability of countries to maintain favourable environmental conditions and examined various factors including pollution levels and the use or abuse of natural resources.

Electricity. Installed capacity in 1997 was 4m. kW. Output was 9·51bn. kWh in 1998, with consumption per capita 2,463 kWh.

Oil and Gas. In 1996, 12m. bbls. of crude oil were produced. Natural gas output in 1998 totalled 1,570m. cu. metres.

Minerals. Production, 1998 (in 1,000 tonnes): coal, 54; salt (1997), 17.

Agriculture. Agriculture and fishing generate approximately 8% of GDP. At the 1993 census 409,647 persons subsisted on agriculture. Agricultural land totals

3·15m. ha (63·4% is cultivated). In 1998, 3,000 ha were irrigated. Production (in 1,000 tonnes, 2000): wheat, 1,080; maize, 800; sugarbeets, 770; potatoes, 500; grapes, 394; wine, 209; barley, 125.

Livestock, 2000: cattle, 427,000; sheep, 528,000; pigs, 1,233,000; chickens, 11m. Animal products, 2000: milk, 641,000 tonnes; meat, 125,000 tonnes; eggs, 49,000 tonnes; cheese, 19,000 tonnes.

Forestry. Forests covered 1·96m. ha in 2002, of which 80% are state owned. In 1999, 3·49m. cu. metres of roundwood were produced.

Fisheries. In 2002 there were 15 fish-processing factories. The 2000 output of fresh-water fish amounted to 4,800 tonnes, and salt-water fish and other sea food to 24,000 tonnes.

INDUSTRY

The largest company in Croatia in Jan. 2003 was Pliva (market capitalization of 9,360·3m. kuna), a pharmaceuticals company.

In 2001 industrial production growth totalled 6% in comparison with 2000. Production, 1998: cement, 2·29m. tonnes; cotton fabrics and blankets, 16·75m. sq. metres; wool fabrics and blankets, 6·55m. sq. metres; beer, 375m. litres; distilled alcoholic beverages, 24·1m. litres.

Labour. In 2001 the estimated number of employees was 1,033,000 and unemployment was 22·3%.

INTERNATIONAL TRADE

Croatia has accepted responsibility for 29·5% of the US$4,400m. commercial bank debt of the former Yugoslavia. Total foreign debt was US$12,120m. in 2000.

Imports and Exports. Exports in 2001 were valued at US$4,659·3m. Imports for 2001 came to US$9,043·7m.

The main exports are machinery and transport equipment, clothing, food and live animals, mineral fuels and lubricants, and plastics. Principal imports are machinery and transport equipment, mineral fuels and lubricants, chemicals and foodstuffs. In 2001 the main export markets were (in US$1m.): Italy (1,104); Germany (689); Bosnia-Herzegovina (560); Slovenia (426); Austria (268). Main import suppliers (in US$1m.): Germany (1,547); Italy, (1,524); Slovenia (712); Russia (654); Austria (630).

COMMUNICATIONS

Roads. There were 27,840 km of roads in 1998 (as well as 330 km of motorways), of which 84·4% were paved. In 1998 there were 1m. passenger cars, 5,000 buses and coaches, and 115,000 vans and trucks. 84m. passengers and 5·69m. tonnes of freight were carried by public transport in 1998. There were 646 deaths in road accidents in 1998.

Rail. There are 2,726 km of 1,435 mm gauge rail (1,213 km electrified). In 1998 railways carried 17·10m. passengers and 12·64m. tonnes of freight.

Civil Aviation. There are international airports at Zagreb (Pleso), Split and Dubrovnik. The national carrier is Croatia Airlines. In 1999 scheduled airline traffic of Croatian-based carriers flew 9·6m. km, carrying 838,000 passengers (503,000 on international flights). In 2000 Zagreb handled 1,139,000 passengers (784,000 on international flights) and 5,300 tonnes of freight, Split handled 514,000 passengers (353,000 on international flights) and Dubrovnik 387,000 passengers (276,000 on international flights).

Shipping. The main port is Rijeka, which handled 8·9m. tonnes of freight in 2000 (2·6m. dry cargo). There were 168 ocean-going vessels in 1995, totalling 3·29m. DWT. 132 of the vessels (94·09% of tonnage) were registered under foreign flags. In 1998 total GRT was 896,000, including oil tankers 11,000 GRT. Provisional figures for 1998 show that 12·75m. passengers and 15·71m. tonnes of cargo were transported. In 1996 vessels totalling 86,065,000 NRT entered ports and vessels totalling 81,757,000 NRT cleared.

Telecommunications. The repair and expansion of the telecommunications industry has been made a high priority in the development process of the country. In 1999 Deutsche Telekom acquired a 35% stake in Croatian Telecom from the Croatian government. The telephone density (the number of lines per 1,000 population) rose from 17·2% in 1990 to 35% in 1998.

In 2000 there were 2,881,800 telephone main lines in use, equivalent to 360·4 per 1,000 persons, and 361,000 PCs (80·7 per 1,000 persons). Mobile phone subscribers numbered 295,000 in 1999, and in 1997 there were 50,200 fax machines. The number of Internet users in Sept. 2001 was 480,000.

Postal Services. In 1995 there were 1,190 post offices.

SOCIAL INSTITUTIONS

Justice. The population in penal institutions in Dec. 1997 was 2,119 (45 per 100,000 of national population).

Religion. At the 1991 census the population was 76·5% Roman Catholic, 11·1% Orthodox and 12·4% other (mainly Old Catholics and Muslims).

Education. In 1997–98 there were 980 pre-school institutions with 84,467 children and 6,201 childcare workers; 2,127 primary schools with 420,860 pupils and 25,802 teachers; 605 secondary schools with 199,515 pupils and 17,294 teachers. In 1998–99 there were 94 institutes of higher education with 91,810 students and 6,748 academic staff. In 2002 there were four universities (Zagreb, Osijek, Rijeka and Split). Adult literacy rate in 1999 was 98·2% (male, 99·3%; female, 97·1%).

In 1995 total expenditure on education came to 5·3% of GNP.

Health. In 1994 there were 9,138 doctors and 1,798 dentists. There were 84 hospitals with 28,230 beds.

Welfare. The health insurance scheme covered 4,591,341 persons in 1994, of whom 1,354,146 were contributing and 755,644 were pensioners.

CULTURE

Broadcasting. Broadcasting is controlled by the state Croatian Radio-Television (colour by PAL). In 1998 there were 108 radio and ten television stations. In 1997 there were 1·5m. radio and 1·22m. television receivers.

Cinema. There were 147 cinemas with a total attendance of 2·74m in 1998. Gross box office receipts in 1995 came to 75m. kuna. In 1998, three feature films made in 1998.

Press. In 1996 there were ten daily newspapers with a combined circulation of 515,000, at a rate of 115 per 1,000 inhabitants. An amendment of March 1996 to the criminal code makes it an offence for the press to defame the government. In 1996 a total of 1,718 book titles were published.

Tourism. The following are UNESCO World Heritage Sites: Diocletian's Palace, Split; the Plitvice Lakes National Park; the Episcopal Complex of Euphrasius' Basilica; the historical core of Trogir; Sibenik's cathedral.

In 2000 there were a total of 6·62m tourists (5·34m foreign tourists, including 920,000 Germans and 886,000 Italians) staying 38·41m. tourist nights. In 2002 there were 160,000 hotel beds and 306,000 beds in private accommodation. The tourist industry is now recovering following the 1991–95 war, although the events in neighbouring Yugoslavia in 1999 resulted in the number of tourists for the year declining to 4·75m. In 2000 tourism accounted for more than 15% of GDP. The industry directly employs about 10% of the population.

Festivals. Croatia has a number of cultural and traditional festivals, including the Zagreb Summer Festival (July–Aug.); the International Folk Dance Festival in Zagreb (July); Dubrovnik Summer Festival (July–Aug.); Split Summer (July–Aug.); Alka Festival (traditional medieval tilting), Sinj (Aug.).

Libraries. In 1995 there were 232 public libraries, one National library and 134 Higher Education libraries. They held a combined 12,683,000 volumes for 1,233,600 registered users.

DIPLOMATIC REPRESENTATIVES
Of Croatia in the United Kingdom (21 Conway St., London, W1P 5HL)
Ambassador: Josip Paro.

Of the United Kingdom in Croatia (Ivana Lucica 4, 10000 Zagreb)
Ambassador: Nicholas Jarrold.

Of Croatia in the USA (2343 Massachusetts Ave., NW, Washington, D.C., 20008)
Ambassador: Dr Ivan Grdesić.

Of the USA in Croatia (Andrije Hebranga 2, 10000 Zagreb)
Ambassador: Lawrence Rossin.

Of Croatia to the United Nations
Ambassador: Dr Ivan Šimonović.

Of Croatia to the European Union
Ambassador: Vladimir Drobnjak.

FURTHER READING
Central Bureau of Statistics. *Statistical Yearbook, Monthly Statistical Report, Statistical Information, Statistical Reports.*

Carmichael, Cathie, *Croatia.* [Bibliography] ABC-Clio, Oxford and Santa Barbara (CA), 1999
Jovanovic, Nikolina, *Croatia: A History.* Translated from Croatian. Hurst, London, 2000
Stallaerts, R. and Laurens, J., *Historical Dictionary of the Republic of Croatia.* Metuchen (NJ), 1995
Tanner, M. C., *A Nation Forged in War.* Yale, 1997

National statistical office: Central Bureau of Statistics, 3 Ilica, Zagreb. *Director:* Marijan Gredelj.
Website: http://www.dzs.hr/

CUBA

República de Cuba

Capital: Havana
Population estimate, 2000: 11·2m.
GDP per capita, 2000: (PPP$) 3,967
HDI/world rank: 0·795/55

KEY HISTORICAL EVENTS

Cuba was a Spanish possession for four hundred years until sovereignty was relinquished in 1898 at the end of the Spanish-American War. Cuba became an independent republic in 1901. In 1933 Fulgencio Batista Zladivar led a successful military revolution. He ruled the country for most of the period up to 1959. A revolutionary movement, led by Dr Fidel Castro from 26 July 1953, was eventually successful and Batista fled the country on 1 Jan. 1959. Under Castro, Cuba's relationship with the USA deteriorated while relations with the USSR became closer. In Jan. 1961 the USA severed diplomatic relations after US business interests in Cuba had been expropriated without compensation. On 17 April an invasion force of émigrés and adventurers, encouraged by the USA, landed in Cuba but was defeated at the Bay of Pigs. At the end of 1961 Castro declared Cuba to be a Communist state. The US Navy imposed a blockade on Cuba from 22 Oct. until 22 Nov. 1962 to force the USSR to withdraw Soviet missile bases. Cuba continued to receive financial aid and technical advice from the USSR until the early 1990s when subsidies were suspended. This led to a 40% drop in GDP between 1989 and 1993. The USA has maintained an economic embargo against the island and relations between Cuba and the USA have remained embittered, although contact between the two countries has been growing in recent years. Starting from Jan. 2002 the Americans brought suspected al-Qaeda and Taliban prisoners from Afghanistan to the military prison at their naval base at Guantánamo Bay.

TERRITORY AND POPULATION

The island of Cuba forms the largest and most westerly of the Greater Antilles group and lies 135 miles south of the tip of Florida, USA. The area is 110,860 sq. km, and comprises the island of Cuba (104,945 sq. km.); the Isle of Youth (Isla de la Juventud, formerly the Isle of Pines; 2,200 sq. km); and some 1,600 small isles ('cays'; 3,715 sq. km). Population, census (1981), 9,723,605; 1998 estimate, 11·1m., giving a density of 100·5 per sq. km. In 1998, 77·1% of the population were urban.

The UN gives a projected population for 2010 of 11·51m.

The area, population and density of population of the 14 provinces and the special Municipality of the Isle of Youth (Isla de la Juventud) were as follows (1998):

	Area sq. km	*Population*		*Area sq. km*	*Population*
Ciudad de La Habana	727	2,192,300	Matanzas	11,669	654,500
Santiago de Cuba	6,343	1,027,900	Las Tunas	6,373	525,000
Holguín	9,105	1,024,900	Guantánamo	6,366	510,800
Villa Clara	8,069	833,400	Sancti Spíritus	6,737	458,800
Granma	8,452	827,600	Ciego de Avila	6,485	403,900
Camagüey	14,134	782,200	Cienfuegos	4,149	392,400
Pinar del Río	10,860	731,300			
La Habana	5,671	696,200	Isla de la Juventud	2,199	78,700

The capital city, Havana, had a population in 1999 of 2,242,000. Other major cities (1997 population estimate in 1,000): Santiago de Cuba (435), Camagüey (301), Holguín (254), Santa Clara (209), Guantánamo (205), Bayamo (144), Las Tunas (134), Pinar del Río (133), Cienfuegos (130) and Matanzas (124).

The official language is Spanish.

SOCIAL STATISTICS

1999 births, 150,871; deaths, 79,337; marriages, 57,300; divorces, 39,500; suicides (1996), 2,015. Rates, 1999: birth, 13·5 per 1,000 population; death, 6·4; marriage, 5·1; divorce, 3·5; suicide (1996), 18·3. Infant mortality rate, 1999, 6 per 1,000 live births. Annual population growth rate, 1996 39, 0·4%. Life expectancy in 1998 was 74·3 years for males and 78·0 for females. The fertility rate in 1999 was 1·6 births per woman.

CLIMATE
Situated in the sub-tropical zone, Cuba has a generally rainy climate, affected by the Gulf Stream and the N.E. Trades, although winters are comparatively dry after the heaviest rains in Sept. and Oct. Hurricanes are liable to occur between June and Nov. Havana, Jan. 72°F (22·2°C), July 82°F (27·8°C). Annual rainfall 48" (1,224 mm).

CONSTITUTION AND GOVERNMENT
A Communist Constitution came into force on 24 Feb. 1976. It was amended in July 1992 to permit direct parliamentary elections and in June 2002 to make the country's socialist system 'irrevocable'.

Legislative power is vested in the *National Assembly of People's Power*, which meets twice a year and consists of 609 deputies elected for a five-year term by universal suffrage. Lists of candidates are drawn up by mass organizations (trade unions, etc.). The National Assembly elects a 31-member *Council of State* as its permanent organ. The Council of State's President, who is head of state and of government, nominates and leads a Council of Ministers approved by the National Assembly.

National Anthem. 'Al combate corred bayameses' ('Run, Bayamans, to the combat'); words and tune by P. Figueredo.

RECENT ELECTIONS
Elections to the National Assembly were held on 19 Jan. 2003. All 609 candidates were from the National Assembly of People's Power and received the requisite 50% of votes for election. No other parties are allowed.

CURRENT ADMINISTRATION
President: Dr Fidel Castro Ruz (b. 1927) became *President* of the Council of State on 3 Dec. 1976; re-elected for five years on 24 Feb. 1998 and again on 6 March 2003. He is also First Secretary of the Cuban Communist Party, President of the Council of Ministers and C.-in-C. of the National Defence Council.

In March 2003 the government comprised:

First Vice-President of the Council of State and of the Council of Ministers, Minister of the Revolutionary Armed Forces: Gen. Raúl Castro Ruz (Fidel Castro's younger brother and his designated successor).

Vice-Presidents of the Council of Ministers: Osmani Cienfuegos Gorriarán, José Ramón Fernández Alvárez, José Luis Rodríguez García (also Minister of Economy and Planning), Adolfo Díaz Suárez, Pedro Miret Prieto. *Secretary of the Council of Ministers:* Carlos Lage Dávila.

Minister of Agriculture: Alfredo Jordán Morales. *Auditing and Control:* Lina Olinda Pedraza Rodríguez. *Basic Industries:* Marcos Portal León. *Construction:* Fidel Figueroa de la Paz. *Culture:* Abel Prieto Jiménez. *Domestic Trade:* Barbara Castillo Cuesta. *Education:* Luis Gómez Gutiérrez. *Finance and Prices:* Manuel Millares Rodríguez. *Fishing Industry:* Alfredo López Valdes. *Food Industry:* Alejandro Roca Iglesias. *Foreign Investment and Economic Co-operation:* Marta Lomas Morales. *Foreign Relations:* Felipe Pérez Roque. *Foreign Trade:* Raúl de la Nuez. *Higher Education:* Fernando Vecino Alegret. *Information Science and Communications:* Ignacio González Planas. *Interior:* Gen. Abelardo Colomé Ibarra. *Justice:* Roberto Díaz Sotolongo. *Labour and Social Security:* Alfredo Morales Cartaya. *Light Industry:* Jesús Pérez Othón. *Public Health:* Damodar Peña Pentón. *Science, Technology and Environment:* Rosa Elena Simeón Negrín. *Steelworking Industry:* Fernando Acosta Santana. *Sugar Industry:* Div. Gen. Ulises Rosales del Toro. *Tourism:* Ibrahim Ferradaz. *Transport:* Alvaro Perez Morales. *Ministers without Portfolio:* Wilfredo López Rodríguez; Ricardo Cabrisas Ruiz.

The Congress of the Cuban Communist Party (PCC) elects a Central Committee of 225 members, which in turn appoints a Political Bureau comprising 26 members.

Government Website: http://www.cubagob.cu/

DEFENCE

The National Defence Council is headed by the president of the republic. Conscription is for two years.

In 2000 defence expenditure totalled US$735m. (US$66 per capita), representing 4·5% of GDP. Defence expenditure in 1985 was US$2,366m.

Army. The strength was estimated at 45,000 (including conscripts and Ready Reservists) in 1999. Border Guard and State Security forces total 26,500. The Territorial Militia is estimated at 1m. (reservists), all armed. In addition there is a Youth Labour Army of 65,000 and a Civil Defence Force of 50,000.

Navy. Naval combatants, all ex-Soviet, include one diesel submarine and two frigates. Personnel in 1999 totalled about 5,000 conscripts including about 550 marines. Main bases are at Cienfuegos, Havana and Mariel. The USA still occupies the Guantánamo naval base.

Air Force. The Air Force has been extensively re-equipped with aircraft supplied by USSR and in 1999 had a strength of some 10,000 and about 130 combat aircraft of which only around 25 are thought to be operational. They include MiG-29, MiG-23 and MiG-21 jet fighters.

INTERNATIONAL RELATIONS

Cuba is a member of the UN, WTO, OAS, LAIA, ACS, Antarctic Treaty and SELA (Latin American Economic System).

ECONOMY

Agriculture accounted for an estimated 6·4% of GDP in 1998, industry 36·9% and services 56·7%.

Overview. After the economic crisis of the early 1990s, growth has picked up through the legalization of the use of the US dollar and the promotion of dollar-based tourism with a parallel dollar economy. Over 50% of the population now have access to dollars, but there remains 50% who have to survive in the more limited pesos economy.

Currency. The unit of currency is the *Cuban peso* (CUP) of 100 *centavos*, which is not convertible, although an official exchange rate is announced daily reflecting any changes in the strength of the US dollar. The US dollar has been legal tender since 1993. 9,710m. pesos were in circulation in 1998. Inflation was negative in 1999, at –0·5%.

Budget. The 1998 budget envisaged revenue of 12,502bn. pesos and expenditure of 13,061bn. pesos. Hard-currency earners and the self-employed became liable to a 10–50% income tax in Nov. 1995.

Performance. A combination of poor commodity export prices and a poor sugar harvest slowed down Cuba's economic growth in 1998 to 1·2%, below the government's original target of 2·5–3·5%. In 1999, however, growth was an impressive 6·2%. GDP in 1997 was estimated to be only 80% of that in 1984.

Banking and Finance. The Central Bank of Cuba (*Governor*, Francisco Soberón Valdés) replaced the National Bank of Cuba as the central bank in June 1997. On 14 Oct. 1960 all banks were nationalized. Changes to the banking structure beginning in 1996 divested the National Bank of its commercial functions, and created new commercial and investment institutions. There were seven commercial banks in March 1999 and nine local non-banking financial institutions. In addition, 17 foreign financial institutions, including 14 foreign banks, had representative offices in 1999; foreign branches are not permitted. All insurance business was nationalized in Jan. 1964. A National Savings Bank was established in 1983.

Weights and Measures. The metric system is legally compulsory, but the American and old Spanish systems are much used. The sugar industry uses the Spanish long ton (1·03 tonnes) and short ton (0·92 tonne). Cuba sugar sack = 329·59 lb or 149·49 kg. Land is measured in *caballerías* (of 13·4 ha or 33 acres).

ENERGY AND NATURAL RESOURCES

Environment. According to the *World Bank Atlas* Cuba's carbon dioxide emissions were the equivalent of 2·2 tonnes per capita in 1998.

Electricity. Installed capacity was 4m. kW in 1997. Production was 14·1bn. kWh in 1998; consumption per capita in 1997 was 1,273 kWh.

Oil and Gas. Crude oil production (1998), 1,678,000 tonnes. Raw gas production (1998), 120m. cu. metres.

Minerals. Iron ore abounds, with deposits estimated at 3,500m. tonnes. Output of copper concentrate (1997) was 1,000 tonnes; refractory chrome (1987), 52,400 tonnes. Other minerals are nickel (1999, 64,407 tonnes), cobalt, silica and barytes. Nickel is Cuba's second largest foreign exchange earner, after tourism. Gold and silver are also worked. Salt output in 1998 was 180,000 tonnes. Sulphuric acid production (1989), 381,500 tonnes.

Agriculture. In 1959 all land over 30 *caballerías* was nationalized and eventually turned into state farms. In 1998 there were 3·63m. ha of arable land and 0·84m. ha of permanent crops. Under legislation of 1993, state farms were re-organized as 'units of basic co-operative production'. Unit workers select their own managers, and are paid an advance on earnings. 294,700 persons were employed in these units in 1995. In 1963 private holdings were reduced to a maximum of 5 *caballerías*. In 1994 farmers were permitted to trade on free market principles after state delivery quotas had been met.

The most important product is sugar and its by-products, but in 1998 the harvest suffered a series of weather disasters reducing production to 3·2m. tonnes (3·4m. tonnes in 1995–96), the smallest crop for 50 years. By 2000 production had risen again to 3·6m. tonnes. Production of other important crops in 2000 was (in 1,000 tonnes): oranges, 441; rice, 369; potatoes, 344; plantains, 329; grapefruit and pomelos, 233; cassava, 210; sweet potatoes, 195; maize, 185; bananas, 133; tomatoes, 129.

In 2000 livestock included 4·7m. cattle; 2·8m. pigs; 450,000 horses; 310,000 sheep; 140,000 goats; 15m. chickens.

Forestry. Cuba had 1·84m. ha of forests in 1995, representing 16·8% of the land area (1·96m. ha and 17·8% in 1990). These forests contain valuable cabinet woods, such as mahogany and cedar, besides dye-woods, fibres, gums, resins and oils. Cedar is used locally for cigar boxes, and mahogany is exported. In 1999, 1·59m. cu. metres of roundwood were produced.

Fisheries. Fishing is the third most important export industry, after sugar and nickel. The total catch was 67,262 tonnes in 1999, of which 62,638 tonnes were from marine waters.

INDUSTRY

The gross value of the manufacturing industry in 1998 was 4,290·7m. pesos. All industrial enterprises had been state-controlled, but in 1995 the economy was officially stated to comprise state property, commercial property based on activity by state enterprises, joint co-operative and private property. 1998 production (in 1,000 tonnes) was: sugar, 3,291·3; cement, 1,713·4; steel, 278·0; complete fertilizers, 156·7; tobacco, 40·0; cotton yarn, 4·5. Also in 1998, petroleum, 1,678·2 tonnes; charcoal, 87m. tonnes; cigars, 160m. units; textiles, 54m. sq. metres. The sugar industry, the backbone of the country's economy for much of its history, is being restructured. Up to half of Cuba's sugar mills are facing closure.

Labour. In 1998 the labour force was 6,621,522, with 3,753,600 in employment. Self-employment was legalized in 1993. Under legislation of Sept. 1994 employees made redundant must be assigned to other jobs or to strategic social or economic tasks; failing this, they are paid 60% of former salary.

Trade Unions. The Workers' Central Union of Cuba groups 23 unions.

INTERNATIONAL TRADE

Foreign debt to non-communist countries was US$11,208m. in 1998. Since July 1992 foreign investment has been permitted in selected state enterprises, and Cuban companies have been able to import and export without seeking government permission. Foreign ownership is recognized in joint ventures. A free-trade zone opened at Havana in 1993. In 1994 the productive, real estate and service sectors were opened to foreign investment. Legislation of 1995 opened all sectors of the economy to foreign investment except defence, education and health services. 100% foreign-owned investments and investments in property are now permitted.

The Helms-Burton Law of March 1996 gives US nationals the right to sue foreign companies investing in Cuban estate expropriated by the Cuban government.

Imports and Exports. In 1997 exports fell by 11% while imports grew by 6%. In 1998 exports totalled US$1,616m., and imports US$4,084m. The principal exports are sugar, minerals, tobacco, fish and coffee. Sugar accounts for more than half of Cuba's export revenues, but revenues have been gradually declining are now only a tenth of the 1990 total.

In 1998 the chief export markets (as % of total) were: Russia, 17·6; Canada, 14·0; Netherlands, 13·2; Spain, 6·2. The chief import sources (as % of total) were: Spain, 8·1; Russia, 6·9; Canada, 6·1; France, 4·5.

COMMUNICATIONS

Roads. In 1997 there were some 60,858 km of roads, of which 29,820 km were paved. Vehicles in use in 1997 included 172,500 passenger cars (15·6 per 1,000 inhabitants) and 156,600 trucks and vans. There were 1,309 fatalities as a result of road accidents in 1997.

Rail. There were (1994) 4,807 km of public railway (1,435 mm gauge), of which 147 km was electrified. Passenger-km travelled in 1996 came to 2,156m. and freight tonne-km to 871m. In addition, the large sugar estates have 7,773 km of lines in total on 1,435 mm, 914 mm and 760 mm gauges.

Civil Aviation. There is an international airport at Havana (Jose Martí). The state airline Cubana operates all services internally, and in 1998 had international flights from Havana to Barcelona, Berlin, Bogotá, Brussels, Buenos Aires, Cancún, Caracas, Cologne, Copenhagen, Curaçao, Fort de France, Frankfurt, Guayaquil, Istanbul, Kingston, Las Palmas, Lima, Lisbon, London, Madrid, Manchester, Maracaibo, Mendoza, Mexico City, Montego Bay, Montreal, Moscow, Paris, Pointe-à-Pitre, Quito, Rio de Janeiro, Rome, St Maarten, San José (Costa Rica), Santa Cruz, Santiago, Santiago de Compostela, Santo Domingo, São Paulo, Toronto and Vitoria. Cubana flew 26·2m. km in 1999 and carried 1,259,000 passengers (683,000 on international flights). In 2000 Havana Jose Martí International handled 2,425,000 passengers (2,001,200 on international flights) and 20,526 tonnes of freight.

Shipping. There are 11 ports, the largest being Havana, Cienfuegos and Mariel. The merchant marine in 1998 totalled 158,000 GRT, of which 8,000 GRT were oil tankers.

Telecommunications. There were 488,600 telephone main lines in 2000 (43·6 for every 1,000 persons). In 1999 there were 80,000 PCs in use (7·2 for every 1,000 persons) and mobile phone subscribers numbered 5,100; in 1995 there were 400 fax machines. There were 60,000 Internet users in Dec. 2000.

Postal Services. In 1993 there were 1,545 post offices, or one for every 7,150 persons.

SOCIAL INSTITUTIONS

Justice. There is a Supreme Court in Havana and seven regional courts of appeal. The provinces are divided into judicial districts, with courts for civil and criminal actions, and municipal courts for minor offences. The civil code guarantees aliens the same property and personal rights as those enjoyed by nationals.

The 1959 Agrarian Reform Law and the Urban Reform Law passed on 14 Oct. 1960 have placed certain restrictions on both. Revolutionary Summary Tribunals have wide powers.

The death penalty is still in force and was used in April 2003. The population in penal institutions in 1997 was approximately 33,000 (300 per 100,000 of national population).

Religion. Religious liberty was constitutionally guaranteed in July 1992. 60% of the population were estimated to be Roman Catholics in 1996. In 1994 Cardinal Jaime Ortega (b. 1936) was nominated Primate by the Pope. In 2002 there were 180 Roman Catholic priests, approximately half of them foreign nationals. There is a seminary in Havana which had 61 students in 1996. There is a bishop of the American Episcopal Church in Havana; there are congregations of Methodists in Havana and in the provinces as well as Baptists and other denominations. Cults of African origin still persist.

Education. Education is compulsory (between the ages of 6 and 14), free and universal. In 1996–97 there were 154,520 pre-primary pupils with 6,970 teachers; 9,926 primary schools with 92,820 teachers for 1·09m. pupils; and 712,897 secondary level pupils with 70,628 teachers. There were 122,346 students at university level.

There are four universities, and ten teacher training, two agricultural, four medical and ten other higher educational institutions.

The adult literacy rate was 96·4% in 1998 (96·5% among males and 96·3% among females).

Health. In 1992 there were 46,860 doctors, 8,057 dentists, 73,943 nurses and (1993) 244 hospitals. There were 65 beds per 10,000 population in 1993.

Free medical services are provided by the state polyclinics, though a few doctors still have private practices.

CULTURE

Broadcasting. Broadcasting is the responsibility of the state-controlled Instituto Cubano de Radio y Televisión. There are five national radio networks, provincial and local stations and an external service, Radio Habana (Spanish, Arabic, Creole, English, Esperanto, French, Guaraní, Portuguese and Quechua). There are two TV channels (colour by NTSC). There were 3·9m. radio receivers and 2·64m. TV sets in 1997.

Press. There were (1998) 17 daily newspapers with a combined circulation of 1·3m.

Tourism. Tourism is Cuba's largest foreign exchange earner, and for some years was growing by nearly 20% per year. Ironically, with Cuba's sympathy for rebel causes, the country was one of the most seriously affected by the huge drop in visitors following the attacks on New York and Washington of 11 Sept. 2001. There were 1,561,000 foreign tourists in 1999. Total receipts from tourism in 1999 amounted to US$1,714m., more than the total exports of goods.

DIPLOMATIC REPRESENTATIVES
Of Cuba in the United Kingdom (167 High Holborn, London, WC1 6PA)
Ambassador: José Fernandez de Cossío.

Of the United Kingdom in Cuba (Calle 34, No. 702/4, entre 7 ma Avenida y 17 Miramar, Havana)
Ambassador: Paul Hare, LVO.

Of Cuba to the United Nations
Ambassador: Bruno Rodríguez Parrilla.

Of Cuba to the European Union
Ambassador: René Mujica Cantelar.

The USA broke off diplomatic relations with Cuba on 3 Jan. 1961 but Cuba has an Interests Section in the Swiss Embassy in Washington, D.C., and the USA has an Interests Section in the Swiss Embassy in Havana.

FURTHER READING
Bethell, L. (ed.) *Cuba: a Short History.* CUP, 1993
Bunck, J. M., *Fidel Castro and the Quest for a Revolutionary Culture in Cuba.* Pennsylvania State Univ. Press, 1994
Cabrera Infantye, G., *Mea Cuba*; translated into English from Spanish. London, 1994
Cardoso, E. and Helwege, A., *Cuba after Communism.* Boston (Mass.), 1992
Eckstein, S. E., *Back from the Future: Cuba under Castro.* Princeton Univ. Press, 1994

CUBA

Fursenko, A. and Naftali, T., *'One Hell of a Gamble': Khrushchev, Castro and Kennedy, 1958–1964*. New York, 1997

Levine, Robert, *Secret Missions to Cuba: Fidel Castro, Bernardo Benes, and Cuban Miami.* Palgrave Macmillan, Basingstoke, 2002

May, E. R. and Zelikow, P. D., *The Kennedy Tapes: Inside the White House during the Cuban Missile Crisis*. Belknap Press/Harvard Univ. Press, 1997

Mesa-Lago, C. (ed.) *Cuba: After the Cold War*. Pittsburgh Univ. Press, 1993

Stubbs, J., *et al.*, *Cuba*. [Bibliography] ABC-Clio, Oxford and Santa Barbara (CA), 1996

Sweig, Julia, *Inside the Cuban Revolution*. Harvard Univ. Press, 2002

Thomas, Hugh, *Cuba, or the Pursuit of Freedom*. Eyre & Spottiswoode, London, 1971; Picador, London, 2001

CYPRUS

Kypriaki Dimokratia—
Kibris Çumhuriyeti
(Republic of Cyprus)

Capital: Nicosia
Population estimate, 2000: 759,000
GDP per capita, 2000: (PPP$) 20,824
HDI/world rank: 0·883/26

KEY HISTORICAL EVENTS

In 1193 the island became a Frankish kingdom, in 1489 a Venetian dependency, and in 1751 was conquered by the Turks. In 1914 the island was annexed by Great Britain and on 1 May 1925 it was given the status of a Crown Colony. In the 1930s the Greek Cypriots began to agitate for ENOSIS (Union with Greece). In 1955 they started a guerrilla movement (EOKA) against the British, with Archbishop Makarios, the head of the Greek Orthodox Church in Cyprus, as leader. In 1959 the Greek and Turkish Cypriots agreed on a constitution for an independent Cyprus and Makarios was elected President. On 16 June 1960 Cyprus became an independent state. In Dec. 1963 the Turkish Cypriots withdrew from the government. Fighting between Turkish and Greek Cypriots led to a UN peacekeeping force being sent in. Turkey invaded the island on 20 July 1974, eventually occupying the northern part. 0·2m. Greek Cypriots fled to live as refugees in the south. In 1975 a Turkish Cypriot Federated State was proclaimed. Rauf Denktaş was appointed President. In 1983 the Turkish state unilaterally proclaimed itself the 'Turkish Republic of Northern Cyprus' (TRNC). In 1991 the UN rejected Rauf Denktaş' demands for the recognition of sovereignty for the TRNC, including a right to secession. In 1998 a proposal by Rauf Denktaş that the Greek and Turkish communities should join in a federation that recognizes 'the equal and sovereign status of Cyprus' Greek and Turkish parts' was rejected by the Greek and Cypriot governments. Greece is threatening to block progress on Turkey's application for EU membership until the Cyprus question is resolved. In 2002 Cyprus was nominated as one of ten countries eligible for EU membership in 2004, although the TRNC will only be accepted if UN-brokered talks to reunify the country succeed. Otherwise the south will accede alone. Turkey has warned that it might annexe north Cyprus if the Greek Cypriot south is admitted to the EU. In Nov. 2002 the UN presented a peace plan to the Greek Cypriot and Turkish Cypriot leaders for a 'common' state with two 'component' states, along the lines of Switzerland and its cantons. In March 2003 UN-brokered talks to pave the way for the reunification of Cyprus collapsed. As a result it is likely that only the southern, Greek Cypriot part of the island will join the European Union in 2004.

TERRITORY AND POPULATION

The island lies in the Mediterranean, about 60 km off the south coast of Turkey and 90 km off the coast of Syria. Area, 3,572 sq. miles (9,251 sq. km). The Turkish-occupied area is 3,335 sq. km. Population by ethnic group:

Ethnic group	1960 census	1973 census	1992	2000
Greek Cypriot	452,291	498,511	599,200	647,100
Turkish Cypriot	104,942	116,000	94,500	87,800
Others	16,333	17,267	20,000	24,200
Total	573,566	631,778	713,700	759,100

Estimated population, 2000, 759,100; density, 82 per sq. km.

The UN gives a projected population for 2010 of 841,000.

70·1% of the population lived in urban areas in 2000. Principal towns with populations (2000 estimate): Nicosia (the capital), 199,100; Limassol, 159,800; Larnaca, 70,500; Paphos, 40,900.

As a result of the Turkish occupation of the northern part of Cyprus, 0·2m. Greek Cypriots were displaced and forced to find refuge in the south. The urban centres of Famagusta, Kyrenia and Morphou were completely evacuated. *See below* for details on the 'Turkish Republic of Northern Cyprus'. (The 'TRNC' was unilaterally declared as a 'state' in 1983 in the area of the Republic of Cyprus, which has been under Turkish occupation since 1974, when Turkish forces invaded the island. The establishment of the 'TRNC' was declared illegal by UN Security Resolutions 541/83 and 550/84. The 'TRNC' is not recognized by any country in the world except Turkey). Nicosia is a divided city, with the UN-patrolled Green Line passing through it.

Greek and Turkish are official languages. English is widely spoken.

SOCIAL STATISTICS

2000 births, 9,557; deaths, 6,059; marriages, 9,775; divorces, 1,337. Rates, 2000 (per 1,000 population): birth, 12·6; death, 8·0; marriage, 12·6; divorce, 1·8. Life expectancy at birth, 1999, was 75·7 years for males and 80·2 years for females. Annual population growth rate, 1990–99, 1·5%; infant mortality, 2000, 5·6 per 1,000 live births; fertility rate, 2000, 1·8 children per woman. In 2000 the average age of first marriage was 28·9 years for men and 26·1 years for women.

CLIMATE

The climate is Mediterranean, with very hot, dry summers and variable winters. Maximum temperatures may reach 112°F (44·5°C) in July and Aug., but minimum figures may fall to 22°F (−5·5°C) in the mountains in winter, when snow is experienced. Rainfall is generally between 10" and 27" (250 and 675 mm) and occurs mainly in the winter months, but it may reach 48" (1,200 mm) in the Troodos mountains. Nicosia, Jan. 50°F (10·0°C), July 83°F (28·3°C). Annual rainfall 19·6" (500 mm).

CONSTITUTION AND GOVERNMENT

Under the 1960 Constitution executive power is vested in a *President* elected for a 5-year term by universal suffrage, and exercised through a Council of Ministers appointed by him or her. The *House of Representatives* exercises legislative power. It is elected by universal suffrage for five-year terms, and consists of 80 members, of whom 56 are elected by the Greek Cypriot and 24 by the Turkish Cypriot community. Voting is compulsory, and is by preferential vote in a proportional representation system with reallocation of votes at national level. As from Dec. 1963 the Turkish Cypriot members have ceased to attend.

National Anthem. 'Segnoriso apo tin kopsi' ('Always shall I know you'); words by D. Solomos, tune by N. Mantzaros.

RECENT ELECTIONS

Parliamentary elections were held on 27 May 2001. The Communist Progressive Party of the Working People won 34·7% of the vote and 20 seats, the Democratic Rally won 34·0% and 19 seats, the Democratic Party 14·8% and 9 seats and the Social Democrats Movement 6·5% and 4 seats. Four other parties won a single seat each. The electorate was 467,182 and turn-out 91·8%. For the first time in a parliamentary election those aged 18 to 21 were able to vote.

Presidential elections held on 16 Feb. 2003 were won by Tassos Papadopoulos, with 51·5% of the vote, against 38·8% for incumbent Glafcos Clerides and 6·6% for Alekos Markidis. Turn-out was 95·9%.

CURRENT ADMINISTRATION

President: Tassos Papadopoulos; b. 1934 (Democratic Party; sworn in on 28 Feb. 2003).

In March 2003 the Council of Ministers consisted of:

Minister of Foreign Affairs: George Iacovou. *Interior:* Andreas Christou. *Defence:* Kyriacos Mavronicolas. *Agriculture, Natural Resources and Environment:* Efthimios Efthimiou. *Commerce, Industry and Tourism:* George Lillikas. *Health:* Constantia Akkelidou. *Communications and Works:* Kyriacos Kazamias. *Finance:* Marcos Kyprianou. *Education and Culture:* Pefkios Georgiades. *Labour and Social*

Insurance: Iacovos Keravnos. *Justice and Public Order:* Doros Thedorou. *Government Spokesman:* Kypros Chrysostomides. *Undersecretary to the President:* Christodoulos Pashiardis.

Government Website: http://www.cyprus.gov.cy/

DEFENCE
Conscription is for 26 months. Defence expenditure in 2000 totalled US$453m. (US$577 per capita), representing 4·8% of GDP. At the end of 1998 the President cancelled a US$450m. contract with Russia for the deployment of S-300 anti-aircraft missiles on the island and negotiated to place them on Crete instead.

National Guard. Total strength (1998) 10,000 (8,700 conscripts). There is also a paramilitary force of 500 armed police.

There are two British bases (Army and Royal Air Force) and some 3,200 personnel. Greek (1,250) and UN peacekeeping (1,228; UNFICY) forces are also stationed on the island.

There are approximately 35,000 Turkish troops stationed in the occupied area of Cyprus. The Turkish Cypriot army amounts to 5,000 troops, with 26,000 reservists and a paramilitary armed police of approximately 150.

Navy. The Maritime wing of the National Guard operates two vessels. In the Turkish-occupied area of Cyprus the Coast Guard operates five patrol craft.

Air Force. The Air Wing of the National Guard operates a handful of aircraft and helicopters.

INTERNATIONAL RELATIONS
Cyprus is a member of the UN, WTO, the Commonwealth, Council of Europe, OSCE and IOM. In March 1998 Cyprus entered into accession negotiations with the EU, and is scheduled to become a member on 1 May 2004.

ECONOMY
Currency. The *Cyprus pound* (CYP) is divided into 100 *cents*. Inflation was 4·1% in 2000, but only 2·1% in 2001. In June 2002 gold reserves were 465,000 troy oz and foreign exchange reserves were US$2,539m. In Dec. 2001 total money supply was £C1,081m.

Budget. Revenue in 2000 (1999) was £C1·87bn. (£C1·59bn.) and expenditure £C2·02bn. (£C1·79bn.). Main sources of revenue in 2000 (in £C1m.) were: direct taxes, 558·1; indirect taxes, 653·5; social security contributions, 244·0.

Main divisions of expenditure in 2000 (in £C1m.): wages and salaries, 526·3; social security payments, 304·0; education, 233·7; goods and services, 160·9; health, 127·6; pensions and gratuities, 112·0; commodity subsidies, 79·5.

Development expenditure for 2000 (in £C1m.) included 42·3 for roads, 16·9 for water development, 12·7 for rural development and 11·9 for agriculture, forests and fisheries.

The outstanding domestic debt at 31 Dec. 2000 was £C2,457·7m. and the foreign debt was £C825·6m.

VAT is 15%.

Performance. Real GDP growth was 5·1% in 2000 and 4·5% in 2001. Total GDP in 2001 was US$9·1bn. GDP per capita in 2000 was 83% of the European Union average, the highest percentage of any of the EU candidate countries.

Banking and Finance. The Central Bank of Cyprus, established in 1963, is the bank of issue. It regulates money supply, credit and foreign exchange and supervises the banking system. The *Governor* is Christodoulos Christodoulou.

In 1997 there were nine commercial banks (three foreign) and three specialized banks (co-operative, development and mortgage). The leading banks are Bank of Cyprus and Cyprus Popular Bank.

At 31 Dec. 1997 total deposits in banks were £C6,483m. Cyprus has a fast-growing offshore sector—in 2000 there were more than 40,000 offshore companies registered on the island.

There is a stock exchange, which opened in 1996 and which in 1999 recorded spectacular gains of around 700%.

Weights and Measures. The metric (SI) system was introduced in 1986 and is now widely applied.

ENERGY AND NATURAL RESOURCES

Environment. According to the *World Bank Atlas* carbon dioxide emissions in Cyprus were the equivalent of 7·9 tonnes per capita in 1998.

Electricity. Installed capacity is 997,300 kW. Production in 2000 was 3,370m. kWh and consumption 3,011m. kWh.

Water. In 1997, £C16·6m. was spent on water dams, water supplies, hydrological research and geophysical surveys. Existing dams had (1997) a capacity of 299m. cu. metres.

Minerals. The principal minerals extracted in 2000 were (in tonnes): gypsum, 138,000; bentonite, 125,000; umber and other ochres, 12,000; copper, 5,000.

Agriculture. 28% of the government-controlled area is cultivated. There were 93,400 ha of arable land in 2000 and 41,800 ha of permanent crops. About 8·7% (2000) of the economically active population were engaged in agriculture.

Chief agricultural products in 2000 (1,000 tonnes): milk, 193·8; citrus fruit, 127·2; potatoes, 117·0; grapes, 108·0; meat, 100·6; cereals (wheat and barley), 47·6; fresh fruit, 37·3; olives, 21·0; carrots, 1·9; other vegetables, 134·0; eggs, 14·0m. dozen.

Livestock in 2000: cattle, 54,200; sheep, 246,000; goats, 378,600; pigs, 408,400; poultry, 3,660,000.

Forestry. Total forest area in 1995 was 1,400 sq. km (15·2% of the land area). In 2000, 25,000 cu. metres of timber were produced.

Fisheries. The total catch in 2000 amounted to 3,535 tonnes.

INDUSTRY

The most important industries in 2000 were: food, beverages and tobacco, textiles, wearing apparel and leather, chemicals and chemical petroleum, rubber and plastic products, metal products, machinery and equipment, wood and wood products including furniture. Manufacturing industry in 2000 contributed about 11·0% of the GDP.

Labour. Out of 302,700 people in employment in 2000, 54,200 were in wholesale and retail trade, 36,700 in manufacturing and 33,000 in hotels and restaurants. The unemployment rate was 3·9% at the end of 2001, down from 4·9% at the end of 2000.

Trade Unions. About 80% of the workforce is organized and the majority of workers belong either to the Pancyprian Federation of Labour or the Cyprus Workers Confederation.

INTERNATIONAL TRADE

Imports and Exports. Trade figures for calendar years were (in £C1,000):

	1997	1998	1999	2000
Imports[1]	1,899,339	1,904,738	1,970,905	2,401,826
Exports	640,015	551,134	542,919	591,864

[1]Excludes military goods.

Chief imports, 2000 (in £C1m.):

Live animals and animal products	35·5	Machinery, electrical equipment, sound and television recorders	408·6
Vegetable products	76·4		
Prepared foodstuffs, beverages and tobacco	331·2	Vehicles, aircraft, vessels and equipment	270·7
Mineral products	313·9	Optical, photographic, medical, musical and other instruments, clocks and watches	48·5
Products of chemical or allied industries	174·7		
Plastics and rubber and articles thereof	84·2	Base metal and articles of base metal	122·4
Pulp, waste paper and paperboard and articles thereof	80·1	Wood and articles, charcoal, cork, etc.	31·1

Textiles and textile articles	172·3	Pearls, precious stones and	
Footwear, headgear, umbrellas,		metals, semi-precious stones	
prepared leathers, etc.	33·1	and articles	29·1
Articles of stone, plaster, cement,			
etc., ceramic and glass products	50·6		

Chief domestic exports, 2000 (in £C1,000):

Citrus fruit	12,795	Cement	10,911
Potatoes	12,328	Clothing	22,456
Wine	6,232	Footwear	6,126
Cheese	8,717	Medicinal and pharmaceutical	
Cigarettes	16,192	products	30,859
Fruit, preserved and juices	6,741		

Main export markets, 2001: UK, 16·6%; Greece 9·2%; Russia, 9·0%; Syria, 7·5%; Lebanon, 5·8%. Main import suppliers, 2001: UK, 10·7%; USA, 10·5%; Italy, 8·9%; Greece, 8·7%; Germany, 7·1%.

COMMUNICATIONS

Roads. In 2000 the total length of roads in the government-controlled area was 11,141 km. The asphalted roads maintained by the Ministry of Communications and Works (Public Works Department) by the end of 2000 totalled 2,359 km. Construction of new asphalted roads in 2000 totalled 240 km. In 2000 there were 267,589 passenger cars, 2,949 buses and coaches, 114,666 trucks and vans and 43,315 motorcycles and mopeds. There were 98 deaths as a result of road accidents in 2001.

The area controlled by the government of the Republic and that controlled by the 'TRNC' are now served by separate transport systems, and there are no services linking the two areas.

Civil Aviation. Nicosia airport has been closed since the Turkish invasion in 1974. It is situated in the UN controlled buffer zone. There are international airports at Larnaca (the main airport) and Paphos. In 2000, 6,125,211 passengers and 33,477 tonnes of commercial freight went through these airports. Both are set to be expanded with a view to increasing annual capacity by 3m. In 2000 Larnaca handled 4,745,249 passengers (all on international flights) and 32,077 tonnes of freight. In 2000 Paphos handled 1,379,962 passengers (all on international flights) and 1,396 tonnes of freight. The national carrier is Cyprus Airways, which is 69·62% state-owned. Cyprus Airways flew 21·1m. km in 2000, carrying 1,452,608 passengers (all on international flights).

Shipping. The two main ports are Limassol and Larnaca. In 2000, 5,289 ships of 20,570,975 net registered tons entered Cyprus ports carrying 6,901,088 tonnes of cargo from, to and via Cyprus. In 2000 the merchant marine totalled 27·2m. GRT, including oil tankers 5·35m. GRT. The fleet consisted of 1,735 vessels (185 tankers). In 2000 vessels totalling 20,570,975 NRT entered ports. The port in Famagusta has been closed to international traffic since the Turkish invasion in 1974.

Telecommunications. Main telephone lines numbered 440,100 in 2000 (647·2 for every 1,000 inhabitants) and there were 150,000 PCs in use (220·6 per 1,000 persons). There were 218,000 mobile phone subscribers and 150,000 Internet users in Dec. 2001. In 1995 there were 7,000 fax machines. The Cyprus Tele-communications Authority provides telephone and data transmission services nationally, and to 253 countries automatically. The European Union is insisting on the privatization of the telecommunications sector as a condition of accession.

Postal Services. In 2000 there were 51 post offices and 992 postal agencies.

SOCIAL INSTITUTIONS

Justice. There is a Supreme Court, Assize Courts and District Courts. The Supreme Court is composed of 13 judges, one of whom is the President of the Court. The Assize Courts have unlimited criminal jurisdiction, and may order the payment of compensation up to £C3,000. The District Courts exercise civil and criminal jurisdiction, the extent of which varies with the composition of the Bench.

A Supreme Council of Judicature, consisting of the President and Judges of the Supreme Court, is entrusted with the appointment, promotion, transfers, termination of appointment and disciplinary control over all judicial officers, other than the Judges of the Supreme Court. The Attorney-General (Alecos Markides) is head of the independent Law Office and legal advisor to the President and his Ministers.

The population in penal institutions in 1996 was 235 (35 per 100,000 of national population).

The death penalty was abolished for all crimes in 2002.

Religion. The Greek Cypriots are Greek Orthodox Christians, and the Turkish Cypriots are Muslims (mostly Sunnis of the Hanafi sect). There are also small groups of the Armenian Apostolic Church, Roman Catholics (Maronites and Latin Rite) and Protestants (mainly Anglicans). *See also* CYPRUS: Territory and Population.

Education. *Greek-Cypriot Education.* Elementary education is compulsory and is provided free in six grades to children between 5 years 8 months and 11 years 8 months. There are also schools for the deaf and blind, and eight schools for handicapped children. In 1999–2000 the Ministry of Education and Culture ran 223 kindergartens for children in the age group 2½–5; there were also 115 communal and 89 private kindergartens. There were 366 primary schools with 63,715 pupils and 3,711 teachers in 1999–2000.

Secondary education is also free and attendance for the first cycle is compulsory. The secondary school is six years—three years at the gymnasium followed by three years at the *lykeion* (lyceum) or three years at one of the technical schools which provide technical and vocational education for industry. In 1999–2000 there were 130 secondary schools with 5,313 teachers and 69,043 pupils.

Post-secondary education is provided at seven public institutions: the University of Cyprus, which admitted its first students in Sept. 1992 and had 2,589 students by 1999–2000; the Higher Technical Institute, which provides courses lasting three to four years for technicians in civil, electrical, mechanical and marine engineering; a two-year Forestry College (administered by the Ministry of Agriculture, Natural Resources and Environment); the Higher Hotel Institute (Ministry of Labour and Social Insurance); the Mediterranean Institute of Management (Ministry of Labour and Social Insurance); the School of Nursing (Ministry of Health) which runs courses lasting two to three years; the Cyprus Police Academy which provides a three-year training programme.

There are also various public and private institutions which provide courses at various levels. These include the Apprenticeship Training Scheme and Evening Technical Classes, and other vocational and technical courses organized by the Industrial Training Authority.

In 1999 the adult literacy rate was 96·9% (98·7% among males, 95·1% among females). The percentage of the population aged 20 years and over that has attended school was 95·9% in 1997.

Health. In 2000 there were 1,800 doctors, 619 dentists, 2,931 nurses and 584 pharmacists. There were 115 hospitals and clinics (excluding psychiatric hospitals) in 2000.

Welfare. The administration of social security services is in the hands of the Ministry of Labour and Social Insurance, with the Ministry of Health providing medical services through public clinics and hospitals on a means test. The exception is for medical treatment for employment accidents, which is given free to all insured employees and financed by the Social Insurance Scheme.

CULTURE

Broadcasting. Cyprus Broadcasting Corporation has three radio channels and broadcasts mainly in Greek, but also in Turkish, English and Armenian. The Corporation also broadcasts on two TV channels (colour by SECAM H). A law of June 1990 permits the operation of commercial radio and TV stations. In 1994 there were two independent radio stations broadcasting nationwide and numerous radio stations broadcasting locally. There were also two private TV stations operating and one private Pay-TV. There are also two foreign broadcasting stations. In 1997 there were 310,000 radio and 248,000 TV sets.

Cinema. In the government-controlled area there were 24 cinemas and 28 screens in 1999. In 1999 gross box office receipts came to £C2·6m.

Press. In 2000 there were eight daily newspapers with a circulation of 87,000; and 38 other newspapers with a circulation of 200,000.

Tourism. There were 2,696,732 tourist arrivals in 2001, an increase of 0·4% on 2000. Visitors from the UK account for some 50% of all tourist arrivals. Tourist spending in 2001 totalled £C1,277m.

Libraries. In 1995 there were 117 public libraries, 1 National library and 1 non-specialized library, holding a combined 454,000 volumes for 30,051 registered users.

Museums and Galleries. In 1999 there were 29 museums which received 764,319 visitors.

DIPLOMATIC REPRESENTATIVES
Of Cyprus in the United Kingdom (93 Park St., London, W1K 7ET)
High Commissioner: Myrna Kleopas.

Of the United Kingdom in Cyprus (Alexander Pallis St., Nicosia)
High Commissioner: Lyn Parker.

Of Cyprus in the USA (2211 R. St., NW, Washington, D.C., 20008)
Ambassador: Erato Kozakou Marcoullis.

Of the USA in Cyprus (Metochiou and Ploutarchou Streets, Engomi, Nicosia)
Ambassador: Michael Klosson.

Of Cyprus to the United Nations
Ambassador: Sotirios Zackheos.

Of Cyprus to the European Union
Ambassador: Theophilos Theophilou.

FURTHER READING
Calotychos, V., *Cyprus and Its People: Nation, Identity and Experience in an Unimaginable Community 1955–1997*, Westview, Oxford, 1999
Christodolou, D., *Inside the Cyprus Miracle: the Labours of an Embattled Mini-Economy.* Univ. of Minnesota Press, 1992
Kitromilides, P. M. and Evriviades, M. L., *Cyprus.* [Bibliography] 2nd ed. ABC-Clio, Oxford and Santa Barbara (CA), 1995
Salem N. (ed.) *Cyprus: a Regional Conflict and its Resolution.* London, 1992

Statistical Information: Statistics and Research Department, Nicosia.

'TURKISH REPUBLIC OF NORTHERN CYPRUS (TRNC)'

KEY HISTORICAL EVENTS
See CYPRUS: Key Historical Events.

TERRITORY AND POPULATION
The Turkish Republic of Northern Cyprus occupies 3,355 sq. km (about 33% of the island of Cyprus) and its population in 1999 was estimated to be 190,000. Distribution of population by districts (1994): Nicosia, 82,424; Famagusta, 67,167; Kyrenia, 27,529.

CONSTITUTION AND GOVERNMENT
The Turkish Republic of Northern Cyprus was proclaimed on 15 Nov. 1983.

RECENT ELECTIONS
Presidential elections were held on 15 April 2000. Rauf Denktaş won 43·7% against seven opponents. His nearest rival, Derviş Eroğlu, claimed 30·2% but subsequently pulled out of the run-off.

A 50-seat Legislative Assembly was elected on 6 Dec. 1998. Prime Minister Derviş Eroğlu's National Unity Party (UBP) won 24 seats, Democratic Party (DP) 13, Communal Liberation Party (TKP) 7 and Republican Turkish Party (CTP) 6.

CURRENT ADMINISTRATION

President: Rauf Denktaş; b. 1924 (first appointed 13 Feb. 1975).
In March 2003 the Council of Ministers consisted of:
Prime Minister: Derviş Eroğlu (UBP).
Minister of State in Charge of Economy and Deputy Prime Minister: Salih Coşar (DP). *Foreign Affairs and Defence:* Tahsin Ertuğruloğlu (UBP). *Internal Affairs, Rural Affairs and Housing:* Mehmet Albayrak (UBP). *Finance:* Mehmet Bayram (UBP). *National Education and Culture:* İlkay Kamil (UBP). *Agriculture and Forestry:* İrsen Küçük (UBP). *Public Works and Transport:* Salih Miroğlu (UBP). *Labour, Social Security, Youth and Sports:* Ahmet Kaşif (DP). *Health and Social Aid:* Mustafa Arabacıoğlu (DP). *Tourism and Environment:* Serdar Denktaş (DP).
President of Legislative Assembly: Ertuğrul Hasipoğlu.

Government Website: http://www.trncgov.com

DEFENCE

In 1997, 30,000 members of Turkey's armed forces were stationed in the TRNC with 465 main battle tanks. TRNC forces comprise seven infantry battalions and three patrol boats with a total personnel strength of 4,000. Conscription is for two years.

ECONOMY

Currency. The Turkish lira is used.

Budget. Revenue (in 1,000m. Turkish lira) in 1995 was 8,463·4; expenditure, 13,655·4.

Banking and Finance. 50 banks, including offshore banks, were operating in 1995. Control is exercised by the Central Bank of the TRNC.

ENERGY AND NATURAL RESOURCES

Agriculture. Agriculture accounted for 10·9% of GDP in 1994.

INTERNATIONAL TRADE

Exports earned US$67·3m. in 1995. Imports cost US$366·1m. Customs tariffs with Turkey were reduced in July 1990. There is a free port at Famagusta.

COMMUNICATIONS

Civil Aviation. There is an international airport at Ercan. In 1998 there were flights to İstanbul with Turkish Airlines.

SOCIAL INSTITUTIONS

Education. In 1995–96 there were 15,526 pupils and 1,103 teachers in primary schools; 14,816 pupils and 1,107 teachers in secondary and general high schools; 2,477 students and 348 teachers in technical and vocational schools; and 8,932 students in higher education. There are three private colleges and six universities.

Health. In 1995 there were 353 doctors, 120 dentists, 116 other specialists and 1,214 beds in state hospitals and private clinics.

CULTURE

Broadcasting. The local radio, Radio Bayrak (BRTK), broadcasts in several languages including Greek, Arabic and English. BRT Television broadcasts for an average of ten hours a day (colour by PAL). In 1994 there were 108,800 TV and radio sets.

Press. In 1995 there were seven daily and four weekly newspapers.

Tourism. There were 385,759 tourists in 1995. Tourist earnings totalled US$388·3m.

FURTHER READING

North Cyprus Almanack, London, 1987

Dodd, C. H. (ed.) *The Political, Social and Economic Development of Northern Cyprus.* Huntingdon, 1993

Hanworth, R., *The Heritage of Northern Cyprus.* Nicosia, 1993

Ioannides, C. P., *In Turkey's Image: the Transformation of Occupied Cyprus into a Turkish Province.* New Rochelle (N.Y.), 1991

CZECH REPUBLIC

Česká Republika

Capital: Prague
Population estimate, 2000: 10·28m.
GDP per capita, 2000: (PPP$) 13,991
HDI/world rank: 0·849/33

KEY HISTORICAL EVENTS

The Czech tribe rose to dominance in Bohemia in the 8th century. In 1212 Otakar I received a hereditary kingship from the Holy Roman Emperor. Wenceslas II was elected king of Poland in 1300. Wenceslas was succeeded in 1310 by John of Luxemburg whose son, Charles (1346–78), became Holy Roman Emperor as Charles IV in 1355. Bohemia attained a high degree of prosperity and civilization at this time. In 1527 the diet elected the Hapsburg Ferdinand as king. The Hapsburgs gradually encroached upon Czech rights and religious freedom. The Czech nobility were replaced by German-speaking adventurers; the burgesses lost their rights; burdens were piled on to the peasantry; and Catholicism was enforced.

The increasingly political aspirations of Czech nationalists were not for the resuscitation of the old Bohemia but for the formation of a new Czechoslovakia, an idea fostered by Thomáš Masaryk. Male suffrage was granted in 1906 but the chamber of deputies was constantly bypassed by the emperor. The First World War brought a complete estrangement between Czech and German sectors of the population, the latter supporting the German war effort. Masaryk and other leaders went into exile. In 1918 he secured the support of US president Woodrow Wilson for Czech and Slovak unity (*see* Slovakia). Austria accepted President Wilson's terms on 27 Oct. 1918 and the next day a republic was proclaimed with Masaryk as president and Edvard Beneš as foreign minister. On 29 Oct. the Slovak leaders declared Slovakia part of the Czechoslovak nation. Czechoslovakia developed into a prosperous democracy but was hard hit by the economic depression of the 1930s. Nationalist agitation amongst the Sudeten Germans was fomented by Hitler. Czechoslovakia relied on France for her defence against German aggression but France sided with Britain in the Munich agreement of 29 Sept. 1938 which stipulated that all districts with a German population of more than 50% should be ceded to Germany. Beneš resigned the presidency and went into exile. On 14 March 1939 Slovakia declared itself independent under German hegemony, and the next day the German army occupied the rest of the country. Czechoslovaks who managed to escape joined Beneš to form a government in exile. Liberation by the Soviet Army and US Forces was completed by May 1945 and territories taken by Germans, Poles and Hungarians were restored to Czechoslovak sovereignty. Elections were held in May 1946, at which the Communist Party obtained about 38% of the votes. A coalition government under a Communist Prime Minister, Klement Gottwald, remained in power until 20 Feb. 1948, when a predominantly Communist government was formed by Gottwald. In May elections resulted in an 89% majority for the government, and President Beneš resigned.

In 1968 pressure for liberalization culminated in the overthrow of the Stalinist leader, Antonín Novotný. Under Alexander Dubček's leadership the 'Prague Spring' began to take shape, with an 'Action Programme' of far-reaching reforms. Soviet pressure to abandon this programme was exerted between May and Aug. 1968, when Warsaw Pact forces occupied Czechoslovakia.

Mass demonstrations demanding political reform began in Nov. 1989. On 30 Nov. the Federal Assembly abolished the Communist Party's sole right to govern. On 10 Dec. Gustáv Husák resigned as President and was replaced by Václav Havel.

On 25 Nov. 1992 the Federal Assembly voted the dissolution of the Czech and Slovak Federal Republic. Economic property was divided in accordance with a federal law of 13 Nov. 1992. Government real estate became the property of the republic in which it was located. Other property was divided by specially constituted commissions in the proportion of two (Czech Republic) to one (Slovakia) on the basis of population size. Czechoslovakia split into the Czech Republic and Slovakia on 1 Jan. 1993.

In 1998 a new minority Social Democratic government was sworn in, headed by Miloš Zeman, the country's first left-wing prime minister since the fall of socialism. The Czech Republic joined NATO in 1999 and is scheduled to join the EU in 2004.

TERRITORY AND POPULATION

The Czech Republic is bounded in the west by Germany, north by Poland, east by Slovakia and south by Austria. Minor exchanges of territory to straighten their mutual border were agreed between the Czech Republic and Slovakia on 4 Jan. 1996, but the Czech parliament refused to ratify them on 24 April 1996. Its area is 78,864 sq. km. At the 2001 census (provisional) the population was 10,292,933 (51·2% female); density, 130·5 per sq. km. In 1999, 74·7% of the population lived in urban areas.

The UN gives a projected population for 2010 of 10·14m.

There are 14 administrative regions *(Kraj)*, one of which is the capital, Prague (Praha).

Region	Chief city	Area in sq. km	Population 2001 census (provisional)
Brněnský	Brno	7,067	1,133,916
Budějovický	České Budějovice	10,056	630,168
Jihlavský	Jihlava	6,925	521,212
Karlovarský	Karlovy Vary	3,315	306,779
Královéhradecký	Hradec Králové	4,757	554,348
Liberecký	Liberec	3,163	430,769
Olomoucký	Olomouc	5,139	642,465
Ostravský	Ostrava	5,555	1,277,095
Pardubický	Pardubice	4,519	510,079
Plzeňský	Plzeň (Pilsen)	7,560	553,741
Praha (Prague)	—	496	1,178,567
Středočeský	Praha (Prague)	11,014	1,129,627
Ústecký	Ústí nad Labem	5,335	856,380
Zlínský	Zlín	3,965	597,758

The estimated population of the principal towns in 1997 (in 1,000):

Prague (Praha)	1,178[1]	Liberec	100	Havířov	88
Brno	379[1]	Hradec Králové	100	Zlín	83
Ostrava	319[1]	České Budějovice	100	Most	71
Plzeň	166[1]	Ústí nad Labem	97	Karlovy Vary	55
Olomouc	104	Pardubice	93	Jihlava	53

[1]2000 figure.

Prague: Dating back to 870 with the foundation of Prague Castle, Prague lies at the centre of Bohemia. Early in the 19th century it acquired the name of the 'City of 100 Spires', the latest estimate being 500 spires and towers. In 1784 Emperor Joseph II merged the four historic towns (Old Town, New Town, Lesser Town and Hradčany) into one unified Capital City of Prague.

At the 1991 census 81·2% of the population was Czech, 13·2% Moravian and 3·1% Slovak. There were also (in 1,000): Poles, 59; Germans, 48; Silesians, 44; Roma (Gypsies), 34; Hungarians, 21.

The official language is Czech.

SOCIAL STATISTICS

1999 births, 89,471; deaths, 109,768; marriages, 53,523; divorces, 23,657. Rates (per 1,000 population), 1999: birth, 8·7; death, 10·7; marriage, 5·2; divorce, 2·3. Life expectancy at birth, 1999, 71·2 years for males and 78·0 years for females. In 1997 the most popular age range for marrying was 20–24 for both males and females. Annual population growth rate, 1990–99, 0·0%. Infant mortality, 1999, 4·6 per 1,000 live births; fertility rate, 1999, 1·2 children per woman.

CLIMATE

A humid continental climate, with warm summers and cold winters. Precipitation is generally greater in summer, with thunderstorms. Autumn, with dry clear weather, and spring, which is damp, are each of short duration. Prague, Jan. 29·5°F (–1·5°C), July 67°F (19·4°C). Annual rainfall 19·3" (483 mm). Brno, Jan. 31°F (–0·6°C), July 67°F (19·4°C). Annual rainfall 21" (525 mm).

CONSTITUTION AND GOVERNMENT

The Constitution of 1 Jan. 1993 provides for a parliament comprising a 200-member *Chamber of Deputies*, elected for four-year terms by proportional representation, and an 81-member *Senate* elected for six-year terms in single-member districts, 27 senators being elected every two years. The main function of the Senate is to scrutinize proposed legislation. Senators must be at least 40 years of age, and are elected on a first-past-the-post basis, with a run-off in constituencies where no candidate wins more than half the votes cast. For the House of Representatives there is a 5% threshold; votes for parties failing to surmount this are redistributed on the basis of results in each of the eight electoral districts.

There is a *Constitutional Court* at Brno, whose 15 members are nominated by the President and approved by the Senate for ten-year terms.

The *President* of the Republic is elected for a five-year term by both chambers of parliament. He or she must be at least 40 years of age. The President names the Prime Minister at the suggestion of the Speaker.

National Anthem. 'Kde domov můj?' ('Where is my homeland?'); words by J. K. Tyl, tune by F. J. Škroup.

RECENT ELECTIONS

Former prime minister Václav Klaus (Civic Democratic Party/ODS) was elected president on 28 Feb. 2003 by parliament. He won the lower house 115–81 over Jan Sokol (Czech Social Democratic Party), but Sokol won the Senate 47–32. A second round was also inconclusive. In the third round, in which votes from both chambers were counted together, Klaus won a majority with 142 votes against 124 for Sokol. Previous attempts to elect a president on 15 Jan. and 24 Jan. 2003 had both failed.

Elections to the National Assembly were held on 14 and 15 June 2002; turn-out was 58·0%. The Czech Social Democratic Party (ČSSD) gained 70 seats with 30·2% of votes cast; the Civic Democratic Party (ODS) gained 58 with 24·5%; the Communist Party of Bohemia and Moravia (KSČM), 41 with 18·5%; and Koalice, the coalition of the Christian and Democratic Union, the Czechoslovak People's Party, the Freedom Union and the Democratic Union, 31 with 14·3%.

Elections for the Senate were held on 25 and 26 Oct. 2002. As a result Čtyřkoalice (the coalition of four) had 31 seats in the Senate; ODS, 26; ČSSD, 11; KSČM, 3; and a number of parties held either one or two seats.

CURRENT ADMINISTRATION

President: Václav Klaus; b. 1941 (ODS; sworn in on 7 March 2003).

In March 2003 the government comprised:

Prime Minister: Vladimír Špidla; b. 1951 (ČSSD; sworn in 12 July 2002).

Deputy Prime Minister and Minister of Internal Affairs: Stanislav Gross. *Deputy Prime Minister and Minister of Justice:* Pavel Rychetský. *Deputy Prime Minister and Minister of Foreign Affairs:* Cyril Svoboda. *Deputy Prime Minister:* Petr Mareš.

Minister of Agriculture: Jaroslav Palas. *Culture:* Pavel Dostál. *Defence:* Jaroslav Tvrdík. *Education:* Petra Buzková. *Environment:* Libor Ambrozek. *Finance:* Bohuslav Sobotka. *Health:* Marie Součková. *Industry and Trade:* Milan Urban. *Labour and Social Affairs:* Zdeněk Škromach. *Local Development:* Pavel Němec. *Transport and Communications:* Milan Šimonovský. *Minister Without Portfolio for Information Technology:* Vladimír Mlynář.

Government Website: http://www.vlada.cz

DEFENCE

Conscription is for 12 months. Defence expenditure in 2000 totalled US$1,133m. (US$111 per capita), representing 2·2% of GDP.

Army. Strength (1999) 25,300 (15,500 conscripts). There are also paramilitary Border Guards (4,000-strong) and Internal Security Forces (1,600).

Air Force. The Air Force has a strength of some 15,400 (including air defence troops) and operates a regiment of MiG-21s and MiG-23s. The Tactical Air Corps has a regiment of L-39, Su-22 and Su-25 strike aircraft, and a helicopter regiment. There are 94 combat aircraft and 34 attack helicopters in all.

INTERNATIONAL RELATIONS

In 1974 the Federal Republic of Germany and the then Czechoslovakia annulled the Munich agreement of 1938. On 14 Feb. 1997 the Czech parliament ratified a declaration of German–Czech reconciliation, with particular reference to the Sudeten German problems.

The Czech Republic is a member of the UN, WTO, BIS, NATO, OECD, Council of Europe, OSCE, CEFTA, CERN, CEI, IOM, and the Antarctic Treaty, and is an associate member of the EU and an associate partner of the WEU. The Czech Republic became a member of NATO on 12 March 1999. In Jan. 1996 the Czech Republic applied to join the EU and is scheduled to become a member on 1 May 2004. In 2000 a visa requirement for Russians entering the country was introduced as one of the conditions for EU membership.

ECONOMY

Agriculture accounted for 4·2% of GDP in 1998, industry 39·2% and services 56·6%. In 1999 an estimated 80% of economic output was produced by the private sector.

Currency. The unit of currency is the *koruna* (CEK) or crown of 100 *haler*, introduced on 8 Feb. 1993 at parity with the former Czechoslovakian koruna. Gold reserves were 443,000 troy oz in June 2002; foreign currency reserves were US$21,136m. Inflation, which reached 10·6% in 1998, was brought down to 3·9% in 2000, before rising to 4·7% in 2001. The koruna became convertible on 1 Oct. 1995. In May 1997 the koruna was devalued 10% and allowed to float. Total money supply was Kč. 583,548m. in Dec. 2001.

Budget. Revenue and expenditure in Kč. 1m.:

	1995	1996	1997	1998	1999	2000
Revenue	486,347	536,135	560,146	594,027	624,630	649,388
Expenditure	500,109	556,269	591,839	637,413	670,717	730,012

Expenditure by category, 1996: defence, 30,604; education, 64,964; health, 95,416; social security and welfare, 139,433.

VAT, introduced on 1 Jan. 1993, is 22% (reduced rate, 5%).

Performance. The Czech Republic is coming out of a recession which saw three years of negative growth in 1997, 1998 and 1999. In 2000 growth was 2·9%, rising to 3·6% in 2001. Total GDP was US$56·4bn. in 2001.

Banking and Finance. The central bank and bank of issue is the Czech National Bank (*Governor*, Zdeněk Tůma), which also acts as banking supervisor and regulator. Decentralization of the banking system began in 1991, and private banks began to operate. The Commercial Bank and Investment Bank are privatized nationwide networks with a significant government holding. Specialized banks include the Czech Savings Bank and the Czech Commercial Bank (for foreign trade payments). Private banks tend to be on a regional basis, many of them agricultural banks. There are also subsidiaries of foreign banks, joint ventures with foreign participation, and branches and representative offices of foreign banks. In Nov. 1997 the cabinet agreed to sell off large stakes in three of the largest state-held banks to individual foreign investors through tenders, in preparation for European Union entry. In June 2000 the country's 4th largest bank, Československá obchodní banka (CSOB), acquired the operations of the 3rd largest bank, Investiční a Poštovní banka (IPB). The newly-formed institution became the country's largest bank, with assets of US$16·6bn. in Dec. 1999. Other major banks are Komerční banka (assets of US$10·8bn. in Dec. 1999) and Česká Spořitelna (assets of US$9·6bn.). Foreign investors own 95% of bank assets.

Foreign direct investment, which was only US$1·3bn. in 1997, more than doubled to US$2·72bn. in 1998 and rose to US$5·11bn. in 1999.

Savings deposits were Kč. 289,163m. in 1993.

A stock exchange was founded in Prague in 1992.

Weights and Measures. The metric system is in force.

ENERGY AND NATURAL RESOURCES

Environment. According to the *World Bank Atlas* the Czech Republic's carbon dioxide emissions in 1998 were the equivalent of 11·5 tonnes per capita.

Electricity. Installed capacity was 13·96m. kW in 1998. Production in 1998 was 61·5bn. kWh. 75% of electricity was produced by thermal power stations (mainly using brown coal), 20% was nuclear and the rest was from hydro-electric generation and autoproduction. In 2001 there were five nuclear reactors in operation. Consumption per capita in 1998 was 5,331 kWh.

Oil and Gas. Natural gas reserves in 1997 totalled 4bn. cu. metres. Production in 1996 was eight petajoules. In 1997 crude petroleum reserves were 6m. bbls.

Minerals. There are hard coal and lignite reserves (chief fields: Most, Chomutov, Kladno, Ostrava and Sokolov). Lignite production in 1997 was 57·4m. tonnes; coal production in 1996 was 16·5m. tonnes.

Agriculture. In 1997 there were 4,282,000 ha of agricultural land. In 1998 there were 3·1m. ha of arable land and 0·24m. ha of permanent crops. Approximately 24,000 ha were irrigated in 1998. 31·1% of agricultural land was state-owned, 61% co-operative, 4·4% private and 2·2% public. Agriculture employs just 5% of the workforce—the smallest proportion of any of the ex-Communist countries in eastern Europe.

A law of May 1991 returned land seized by the Communist regime to its original owners, to a maximum of 150 ha of arable to a single owner.

Main agricultural production figures, 2000 (1,000 tonnes): wheat, 4,084; sugarbeets, 2,809; barley, 1,629; potatoes, 1,476; rapeseed, 844; apples, 339; maize, 304; rye, 150.

Livestock, 2000: cattle, 1·57m.; pigs, 3·69m.; sheep, 84,000; chickens, 30m. In 2000 production of meat was 715,000 tonnes; milk, 2,708,000 tonnes; eggs, 176,000 tonnes; cheese, 146,000 tonnes.

Forestry. In 1995 forests covered 2,630,000 ha (34% of the total land area). Timber production in 1999 was 14·20m. cu. metres.

Fisheries. Ponds created for fish-farming number 21,800 and cover about 101,311 acres, the largest of them being two lakes in southern Bohemia. Fish landings in 1999 amounted to 4,190 tonnes, entirely from inland waters.

INDUSTRY

The leading companies by market capitalization in the Czech Republic, excluding banking and finance, in Jan. 2002 were: Český Telecom a.s. (Kč. 111bn.); ČEZ (České Energetické Závody a.s.), Kč. 45bn.; and Philip Morris CR a.s. (Kč. 23bn.), a tobacco company.

In 1996 there were 1,123,804 small private businesses (of which 15,072 were incorporated), 117,040 companies (of which 8,002 were joint-stock companies), 6,332 co-operatives and 2,185 state enterprises. Output, 1998, included: crude steel, 6·49m. tonnes; pig iron, 4·98m. tonnes; cement, 4·61m. tonnes; motor cars (1997), 358,000; beer (1997), 1,854·4m. litres.

Labour. In 1997 the economically active population numbered 5,469,500. The major areas of activity were 1·47m. persons employed in mining and manufacturing; 822,500 in trade; 743,200 in services; 470,600 in construction; 384,700 in transport and communications; 345,500 in finance; and 317,500 in public administration and defence. In Jan. 2003 the unemployment rate was 6·8%. Workers in the Czech Republic put in among the longest hours of any country in the world. In 1996, 95% of male workers and 83% of female workers worked more than 40 hours a week. The average monthly wage was Kč. 8,500 in 1996. Pay increases are regulated in firms where wages grow faster than production. Fines are levied if wages rise by more than 15% over four years. In 1996, 11,500 employees were involved in industrial disputes resulting in a loss of 16,400 working days.

INTERNATIONAL TRADE

A memorandum envisaging a customs union and close economic co-operation was signed with Slovakia in Oct. 1992. An agreement of Dec. 1992 with Hungary, Poland and Slovakia abolished tariffs on raw materials and goods, where exports do not compete directly with locally produced items, and envisaged tariff reductions on agricultural and industrial goods in 1995–97.

Foreign debt was US$21,299m. in 2000. There were 10,599 joint ventures in June 1993.

Imports and Exports. Trading with EU and EFTA countries has increased significantly while trading with all post-communist states has decreased.

Trade, 2000, in US$1m. (1999 in brackets): imports f.o.b., 32,115 (28,161); exports f.o.b., 29,019 (26,259). Main export markets, 1997: Germany, 35·7%; Slovakia, 12·9%; Austria, 6·4%; Poland, 5·7%; Italy, 3·7%. Main import suppliers: Germany, 31·9%; Slovakia, 8·4%; Russia, 6·8%; Austria, 6·1%; Italy 5·5%. The EU accounts for 69% of Czech exports and 62% of imports.

COMMUNICATIONS

Roads. In 1998 there were 498 km of motorways, 20,653 km of highways and main roads, 34,242 km of secondary roads and 72,300 km of other roads, forming a total network of 127,693 km. Passenger cars in use in 1998 numbered 3,687,451 (358 per 1,000 inhabitants), and there were also 423,434 trucks and vans and 20,505 buses and coaches. Motorcycles and mopeds numbered 1,092,272. In 1995 passenger transport totalled 16,777m. passenger-km and freight 8,713m. tonne-km. There were 1,360 deaths as a result of road accidents in 1998.

Rail. In 1998 Czech State Railways had a route length of 9,341 km (1,435 mm gauge), of which 2,946 km were electrified. Passenger-km travelled in 1998 came to 7·0bn. and freight tonne-km to 19·53bn. There is a metro (44 km) and tram/light rail system (496 km) in Prague, and tram/light rail networks in Brno, Liberec, Most, Olomouc, Ostrava, Plzeň and Teplice-Trecianské.

Civil Aviation. There are international airports at Prague (Ruzyné), Ostrava (Mosnov) and Brno (Turany). The national carrier is Czech Airlines, which is 68·1% state-owned. In 1999 it flew 36·2m. km and carried 1,852,600 passengers (all on international flights). In 2000 Prague handled 5,527,524 passengers (5,476,067 on international flights) and 30,284 tonnes of freight, Ostrava handled 107,387 passengers and Brno 106,009 passengers.

Shipping. 4·9m. tonnes of freight were carried by inland waterways in 1993. Merchant shipping totalled 16,000 GRT in 1997.

Telecommunications. In 2000 there were 3,871,700 telephone main lines in use, or 377·9 for every 1,000 inhabitants, and 1·3m. PCs (122·0 per 1,000 persons). Český Telecom and České Radiokomunikace, the two main telecommunications companies, are partly privatized. The government plans to privatize Český Telecom fully by 2005. Mobile phone subscribers numbered 1·9m. in 1999 and in 1997 there were 103,000 fax machines. There were 2·69m. Internet users in June 2001.

Postal Services. In 1995 there were 3,511 post offices.

SOCIAL INSTITUTIONS

Justice. The post-Communist judicial system was established in July 1991. This provides for a unified system of civil, criminal, commercial and administrative courts. Commercial courts arbitrate in disputes arising from business activities. Administrative courts examine the legality of the decisions of state institutions when appealed by citizens. In addition, there are military courts which operate under the jurisdiction of the Ministry of Defence. There is a Supreme Court, and a hierarchy of courts under the Ministry of Justice at republic, region and district level. District courts are courts of first instance. Cases are usually decided by senates comprising a judge and two associate judges, though occasionally by a single judge. (Associate judges are citizens in good standing over the age of 25 who are elected for four-year terms). Regional courts are courts of first instance in more serious cases and also courts of appeal for district courts. Cases are usually decided by a senate of two judges and three associate judges, although occasionally by a single judge. There is also a Supreme Administrative Court. The Supreme Court interprets law as a guide to other courts and functions also as a court of appeal. Decisions are made by senates of three judges. Judges are appointed for life by the National Council.

There is no death penalty. In 1993, 398,505 crimes were reported, of which 31·7% were solved. The population in penal institutions in Oct. 1998 was 22,138 (215 per 100,000 of national population).

Religion. In 2003 there were 25 registered churches and religious societies. In 1997 church membership was estimated to be: Roman Catholic, 4,020,000; Evangelical Church of the Czech Brethren, 200,000; Hussites, 180,000; Silesian Evangelicals, 30,000; Eastern Orthodox, 20,000. 4,120,000 persons were classified as atheist or non-religious, and there were 1,740,000 adherents of other religions.

Miloslav Vlk (b. 1932) was installed as Archbishop of Prague and Primate of Czechoslovakia in 1991. The national Czech church, created in 1918, took the name 'Hussite' in 1972. In 1991 it had a patriarch, five bishops and 300 pastors (40% women). In 1991 there were also around a dozen other Protestant churches, the largest being the Evangelical which unites Calvinists and Lutherans, and numbered about 200,000.

Education. Elementary education up to age 15 is compulsory. 52% of children continue their education in vocational schools and 48% move on to secondary schools.

In 1997–98 there were 9 universities, 4 technical universities, 1 university for economics, 1 for agriculture, 1 for agriculture and forestry, 1 for veterinary and pharmaceutical sciences and 1 for chemical technology. There were also 4 academies (for performing arts, music and dramatic arts, fine arts and arts, architecture and industrial design) and a higher school of teacher training. Together, these 23 higher education institutions had 165,754 students in 1997–98 and 13,216 teaching staff.

In 1996 total expenditure on education came to Kč. 80,079m., or 5·4% of GNP. The adult literacy rate in 1999 was at least 99%.

Health. In 1997 there were 39,831 doctors (one per 259 persons); and in 1995, 6,267 dentists and 4,032 pharmacists. There were 299 hospitals in 1995, with a provision of 89 beds per 10,000 population.

CULTURE

Broadcasting. Broadcasting is the responsibility of the independent Board for Radio and Television. Czech Television (CTV, colour by SECAM H) and Czech Radio are public corporations. The former Czechoslovakian broadcasting stations in the Czech Republic have become a second service. There is also a nationwide private TV company and two radio companies as well as local private stations. There were 5·5m. TV receivers and 8·27m. radio receivers in 1997.

Cinema. In 1995 there were 940 cinemas; attendance for the year was 9·3m.; gross box office receipts came to Kč. 255m. and 22 full-length films were made in 1995.

Press. There were 21 daily newspapers in 1996 with a total readership of 2,620,000 (256 per 1,000 inhabitants). There were also 181 non-dailies with total readership 4,200,000 (410 per 1,000 inhabitants).

Tourism. There were 16,031,000 foreign tourists in 1999; foreign currency income from tourism was US$3,035m. Tourism accounted for 6·5% of GDP in 1996.

Libraries. In 1997 there were 1,403 public libraries, 1 National library and 4,041 Higher Education libraries. They held a combined 68,534,000 volumes for 5,473,000 registered users.

Museums and Galleries. In 2000 there were 325 museums hosting a combined 7,851,000 visitors.

DIPLOMATIC REPRESENTATIVES

Of the Czech Republic in the United Kingdom (26 Kensington Palace Gdns., London, W8 4QY)
Ambassador: Štefan Füle.

Of the United Kingdom in the Czech Republic (Thunovská 14, 118 00 Prague 1)
Ambassador: Anne Pringle.

Of the Czech Republic in the USA (3900 Spring of Freedom St., NW, Washington, D.C., 20008)
Ambassador: Martin Palous.

Of the USA in the Czech Republic (Tržiste 15, 118 01 Prague 1)
Ambassador: Craig Roberts Stapleton.

Of the Czech Republic to the United Nations
Ambassador: Hynek Kmonicek.

Of the Czech Republic to the European Union
Ambassador: Libor Secka.

FURTHER READING

Czech Statistical Office. *Statistical Yearbook of the Czech Republic.*
Havel, V., *Disturbing the Peace.* London, 1990.—*Living in Truth: Twenty-Two Essays.* London, 1990.—*Summer Meditations.* London, 1992
Kalvoda, J., *The Genesis of Czechoslovakia.* New York, 1986
Krejci, Jaroslav and Machonin, Pavel, *Czechoslovakia 1918–1992: A Laboratory for Social Change.* Macmillan, London, 1996
Leff, C. S., *National Conflict in Czechoslovakia: The Making and Remaking of a State, 1918–1987.* Princeton, 1988
Lunt, Susie, *Prague.* [Bibliography] ABC-Clio, Oxford and Santa Barbara (CA), 1997
Simmons, M., *The Reluctant President: a Political Life of Vaclav Havel.* London, 1992
Turner, Barry, (ed.) *Central Europe Profiled.* Macmillan, London, 2000

National statistical office: Czech Statistical Office, Sokolovská 142, 186 04 Prague 8.
Website: http://www.czso.cz

DENMARK

Kongeriget Danmark
(Kingdom of Denmark)

Capital: Copenhagen
Population estimate, 2000: 5·33m.
GDP per capita, 2000: (PPP$) 27,627
HDI/world rank: 0·926/14

KEY HISTORICAL EVENTS

Denmark was first organized as a unified state in the 10th century with a Christian monarchy. King Canute was also King of England and King of Norway in the 11th century, but the union of the three countries was soon dissolved. In 1363 a royal marriage united Denmark and Norway and these two countries joined with Sweden in 1397. Sweden separated herself in 1523 and thereafter was in conflict with Denmark until the Peace of Copenhagen in 1660. Denmark acquired approximately its present boundaries in 1815 at the end of the Napoleonic Wars. Having supported Napoleon, it was forced to cede Norway to Sweden by the Treaty of Kiel (1814); it lost its north-German territory to Prussia 1864–66 and only in 1920 was North Schleswig returned to Denmark.

After 1815 there was much pressure for a more liberal form of government in preference to the traditional absolute monarchy, and on 5 June 1849 the royal assent was given to a new constitution. A parliament, the *Rigsdag*, was created, divided into an upper house, the *Landsting*, and a lower house, the *Folketing*. The franchise was granted to men over 30 years old.

During the First World War (1914–18) Denmark remained neutral and in 1939, at the commencement of the Second World War, it again declared its neutrality. On this occasion, however, it was soon overwhelmed by the German forces which invaded on 9 April 1940. Throughout the war there was a considerable Danish resistance movement to which the Germans responded by imposing direct rule. Immediately after the Second World War, Denmark recognized the independence of Iceland. Home rule was granted to the Faroes in 1948 and to Greenland in 1979. Denmark became a member of the European Union on 1 Jan. 1973.

TERRITORY AND POPULATION

Denmark is bounded in the west by the North Sea, northwest and north by the Skagerrak and Kattegat straits (separating it from Norway and Sweden), and south by Germany. A 16-km long fixed link with Sweden was opened in July 2000 when the Øresund motorway and railway bridge between Copenhagen and Malmö was completed.

Administrative divisions		Area (sq. km) 2002	Population 1 Jan. 2002	Population per sq. km 2002
København (Copenhagen)	(city)	88	500,531	5,671·7
Frederiksberg	(borough)	9	91,332	10,413·0
Københavns	(county)	528	617,336	1,168·6
Frederiksborg	,,	1,347	370,555	275·0
Roskilde	,,	891	234,820	263·4
Vestsjælland	,,	2,984	298,731	100·1
Storstrøm	,,	3,398	260,498	76·7
Bornholm	,,	589	44,197	75·1
Fyn	,,	3,486	472,504	135·5
Sønderjylland	,,	3,939	253,166	64·3
Ribe	,,	3,132	224,444	71·7
Vejle	,,	2,997	351,328	117·2
Ringkøbing	,,	4,854	274,385	56·5
Aarhus	,,	4,561	644,666	141·3
Viborg	,,	4,123	2334,323	56·8
Nordjylland	,,	6,173	495,548	80·3
Total		43,098	5,368,354	124·6

Statistics Denmark gives a projected population for 2010 of 5·51m.

In 2002 an estimated 85·2% of the population lived in urban areas. In 2001, 93·1% of the inhabitants were born in Denmark, including the Faroe Islands and Greenland.

On 1 Jan. 2002 the population of the capital, Copenhagen (comprising Copenhagen, Frederiksberg and Gentofte municipalities), was 660,066; Aarhus, 220,217; Odense, 144,636; Aalborg, 120,359; Esbjerg, 72,665; Randers, 56,102; Kolding, 54,137; Vejle, 49,339; Horsens, 49,057; Roskilde, 43,343.

Copenhagen: Bishop Absalom built his 'Castle at Havn' (Harbour) in 1167 and from this salt marsh on the coast of Øresund (The Sound) the capital city of Copenhagen grew. Approximately 11% of the Danish population live in Copenhagen. The image most often associated with the city, 'The Little Mermaid', was based on the fairy-tale by Hans Christian Andersen. The sculptor was Edvard Eriksen and the model was his wife.

The official language is Danish.

SOCIAL STATISTICS
Statistics for calendar years:

	Live births	Marriages	Divorces	Deaths	Emigration	Immigration
1998	66,170	34,733	13,141	58,453	40,340	51,372
1999	66,232	35,439	13,537	59,156	41,340	50,236
2000	67,081	38,388	14,381	57,986	43,417	52,915
2001	65,450	36,567	14,597	58,388	43,980	55,984

2001 rates per 1,000 population: birth, 12·2; death, 10·9. Single-parent births: 1997, 45·1%; 1998, 44·8%; 1999, 44·9%; 2000, 44·6%; 2001, 44·6%. Denmark is the only west European country in which the percentage of births out of wedlock has declined in the past 10 years. Annual population growth rate, 1990–2001, 0·4%. Suicide rate, 1990–98 (per 100,000 population) was 19·3 (men, 26·4; women, 12·5). Life expectancy at birth, 2000–01, was 74·5 years for males and 79·2 years for females. In 2001 the most popular age range for marrying was 25–29 for both males and females. Infant mortality, 2001, 4·9 per 1,000 live births. Fertility rate, 2001, 1·7 births per woman. In 2001 Denmark received 8,535 asylum applications, equivalent to 1·93 per 1,000 inhabitants. In July 2002 a controversial new immigration law was introduced in an attempt to deter potential asylum seekers.

CLIMATE
The climate is much modified by marine influences and the effect of the Gulf Stream, to give winters that may be both cold or mild and often cloudy. Summers may be warm and sunny or chilly and rainy. Generally the east is drier than the west. Long periods of calm weather are exceptional and windy conditions are common. Copenhagen, Jan. 33°F (0·5°C), July 63°F (17°C). Annual rainfall 650 mm. Esbjerg, Jan. 33°F (0·5°C), July 61°F (16°C). Annual rainfall 800 mm. In general 10% of precipitation is snow.

CONSTITUTION AND GOVERNMENT
The present constitution is founded upon the Basic Law of 5 June 1953. The legislative power lies with the Queen and the *Folketing* (parliament) jointly. The executive power is vested in the monarch, who exercises authority through the ministers.

The reigning Queen is **Margrethe II,** b. 16 April 1940; married 10 June 1967 to Prince Henrik, b. Count de Monpezat. She succeeded to the throne on the death of her father, King Frederik IX, on 14 Jan. 1972. *Offspring:* Crown Prince Frederik, b. 26 May 1968; Prince Joachim, b. 7 June 1969; married 18 Nov. 1995 Alexandra Manley, b. 30 June 1964 (*Offspring:* Prince Nikolai William Alexander Frederik, b. 28 Aug. 1999; Prince Felix Henrik Valdemar Christian, b. 22 July 2002).

Sisters of the Queen; Princess Benedikte, b. 29 April 1944; married 3 Feb. 1968 to Prince Richard of Sayn-Wittgenstein-Berleburg; Princess Anne-Marie, b. 30 Aug. 1946; married 18 Sept. 1964 to King Constantine of Greece.

The crown was elective from the earliest times but became hereditary by right in 1660. The direct male line of the house of Oldenburg became extinct with King Frederik VII on 15 Nov. 1863. In view of the death of the king, without direct heirs, the Great Powers signed a treaty at London on 8 May 1852, by the terms of which the succession to the crown was made over to Prince Christian of Schleswig-Holstein-Sonderburg-Glücksburg, and to the direct male descendants of his union with the Princess Louise of Hesse-Cassel. This became law on 31 July 1853. Linked to the constitution of 5 June 1953, a new law of succession, dated 27 March 1953, has come into force, which restricts the right of succession to the descendants of King Christian X and Queen Alexandrine, and admits the sovereign's daughters to the line of succession, ranking after the sovereign's sons.

The Queen receives a tax-free annual sum of 57·0m. kroner from the state (2002).

The judicial power is with the courts. The monarch must be a member of the Evangelical-Lutheran Church, the official Church of the State, and may not assume major international obligations without the consent of the Folketing. The Folketing consists of one chamber. All men and women of Danish nationality of more than 18 years of age and permanently resident in Denmark possess the franchise, and are eligible for election to the Folketing, which is at present composed of 179 members; 135 members are elected by the method of proportional representation in 17 constituencies. In order to attain an equal representation of the different parties, 40 additional seats are divided among such parties which have not obtained sufficient returns at the constituency elections. Two members are elected for the Faroe Islands and two for Greenland. The term of the legislature is four years, but a general election may be called at any time. The Folketing convenes every year on the first Tuesday in Oct. Besides its legislative functions, every six years it appoints judges who, together with the ordinary members of the Supreme Court, form the *Rigsret*, a tribunal which can alone try parliamentary impeachments.

National Anthem. 'Kong Kristian stod ved højen mast' ('King Christian stood by the lofty mast'); words by J. Ewald, tune by J. E. Hartmann.

RECENT ELECTIONS

Parliamentary elections were held on 20 Nov. 2001; turn-out was 89·3%. The Liberal Party won 56 seats, with 31·3% of votes cast (42 seats with 24% in 1998); the Social Democratic Party 52 with 29·1% (63 with 35·9%); the Danish People's Party 22 with 12·0% (13 with 7·4%); the Conservative Party 16 with 9·1% (16 with 8·9%); and the Socialist People's Party 12 with 6·4% (13 with 7·6%). The 21 remaining seats went to the Radical Left-Social Liberal Party (9); the Unity List (4); the Christian People's Party (4); and four seats to representative parties from the Faroe Islands and Greenland. The election was the first since 1920 at which a party other than the Social Democrats won the highest number of seats. In Feb. 2000, 37·4% of the seats in parliament were held by women.

European Parliament. Denmark has 16 representatives. At the June 1999 elections turn-out was 49·9%. The Liberal Party won 5 seats with 23·3% of votes cast (group in European Parliament: Liberal, Democrat and Reform Party); the SD, 3 with 16·5% (Party of European Socialists); the June Movement, 3 with 16·1% (Independents for a Europe of Nations); the Radical Liberal Party, 1 with 9·1% (Liberal, Democrat and Reform Party); the Conservative Party, 1 with 8·6% (European People's Party); the People's Anti-EU Movement, 1 with 7·3% (Independents for a Europe of Nations); the Socialist People's Party, 1 with 7·1% (Greens); DF (Danish People's Party), 1 with 5·8% (Union for a Europe of Nations Group).

CURRENT ADMINISTRATION

Following the 2001 election a coalition government of the Liberal Party (V) and Conservatives (KF) was formed. The government relies on the support of the far-right, anti-immigrant Danish People's Party, although it is not represented in the cabinet. In March 2003 the government comprised:

Prime Minister: Anders Fogh Rasmussen; b. 1953 (V; sworn in 27 Nov. 2001).

Minister of Economic Affairs, Business and Trade: Bendt Bendtsen (KF). *Defence:* Svend Aage Jensby (V). *Foreign Affairs:* Per Stig Møller (KF). *Finance:* Thor Pedersen (V). *Cultural Affairs:* Brian Mikkelsen (KF). *Ecclesiastical Affairs:* Tove Fergo (V). *Education:* Ulla Tørnæs (V). *Employment:* Claus Hjort Frederiksen (V). *Environment:* Hans Christian Schmidt (V). *Food, Agriculture and Fisheries:*

Mariann Fischer Boel (V). *Interior Affairs and Health:* Lars Løkke Rasmussen (V).
Justice: Lene Espersen (KF). *Refugees, Immigration and Integration, and European
Affairs:* Bertel Haarder (V). *Science, Technology and Innovation:* Helge Sander (V).
Social Affairs and Gender Equality: Henriette Kjær (KF). *Taxation:* Svend Erik
Hovmand (V). *Transport:* Flemming Hansen (KF).

Office of the Prime Minister: http://www.statsministeriet.dk

DEFENCE
The Danish military defence is organized in accordance with 'The Act on the Aims,
Tasks and Organization etc. of the Armed Forces' from 27 Feb. 2001. According to
the Act the Danish Armed Forces shall (1) as an integral part of NATO in co-
operation with allied forces be able to participate in the prevention of conflicts,
crisis management and the defence of NATO's territory in accordance with the
strategy of the Alliance; (2) be able to ascertain and repulse violations of Danish
sovereignty and to exercise authority in the Danish sovereign area; (3) be able to
participate in confidence-building and stability-promoting tasks as well as dialogues
and co-operation in the defence-related area with countries outside NATO, with a
particular emphasis on the countries of Central and Eastern Europe; (4) by military
means be able to contribute to conflict prevention, peace-keeping, peace-
enforcement, humanitarian and other similar tasks; (5) in accordance with the
Minister of Defence's more detailed determination and negotiations with the
Ministers concerned, be able to perform other tasks.

The overall organization of the Danish Armed Forces includes the Ministry of
Defence (MoD), the Danish Defence Command, the Army, the Navy, the Air Force
and several joint service institutions and authorities; to this should be added the
Home Guard, which is an integral part of Danish military defence. The Chief of
Defence (CHOD), answering to the Minister of Defence, is in full command of the
Army, the Navy and the Air Force.

Denmark has a compulsory military service with mobilization based on The
Constitution of 1849. This states that it is the duty of every fit man to contribute to
the national defence. In 2000 defence expenditure totalled US$2,394m. (US$448
per capita), representing 1·5% of GDP.

Army. The Danish Army is comprised of field army formations and local defence
forces. The peacetime strength of the Danish Army is approximately 15,800
(including about 5,100 conscripts and 3,300 civilians). The Army's military wartime
establishment would be about 46,000. The Danish Army is organized in one
division, four brigades, and two regimental combat groups, headquarters units and
support elements.

Navy. The peacetime strength of the Royal Danish Navy is approximately 5,400
(including some 500 conscripts and 1,500 civilians). The naval wartime
establishment would be about 7,300. The two main naval bases are located at
Frederikshavn and Korsør.

Air Force. The peacetime strength of the Royal Danish Air Force is approximately
6,500 (including approximately 125 conscripts and 2,000 civilians). The wartime
establishment would be about 11,600. The Royal Danish Air Force consists of
Tactical Air Command Denmark and the Danish Air Materiel Command.

Home Guard (Hjemmeværnet). The overall Home Guard organization comprises
the Home Guard Command, the Army Home Guard, the Naval Home Guard, the
Air Force Home Guard and supporting institutions. The personnel are recruited on
a voluntary basis. The personnel establishment of the Home Guard is approximately
61,000 soldiers.

INTERNATIONAL RELATIONS
In a referendum in June 1992 the electorate voted against ratifying the Maastricht
Treaty for closer political union within the EU. Turn-out was 82%. 50·7% of votes
were against ratification, 49·3% in favour. However, a second referendum on 18 May
1993 reversed this result, with 56·8% of votes cast in favour of ratification and 43·2%
against. Turn-out was 86·2%. In a referendum held on 28 Sept. 2000 Danish voters
rejected their country's entry into the common European currency, 53·2% opposing
membership of the euro against 46·8% voting in favour. Turn-out was 87·6%.

Denmark gave US$1·7bn. in international aid in 2000, which at 1·06% of GNP made it the world's most generous country as a percentage of its gross national product.

Denmark is a member of the UN, WTO, BIS, NATO, OECD, the EU, Council of Europe, OSCE, CERN, Nordic Council, Council of the Baltic Sea States, Inter-American Development Bank, Asian Development Bank, IOM and the Antarctic Treaty. On 19 Dec. 1996 Denmark acceded to the Schengen Accord of June 1990 which abolishes border controls between Denmark, Austria, Belgium, Finland, France, Germany, Greece, Iceland, Italy, Luxembourg, the Netherlands, Norway, Portugal, Spain and Sweden.

ECONOMY
In 1997 services accounted for 69% of GDP, industry 27% and agriculture 4%.

According to the Berlin-based organization *Transparency International*, in 2002 Denmark ranked equal second behind Finland in having the least corruption in business and government of any country in the world. It received 9·5 out of 10 in a corruption perceptions index.

Overview. Consumer prices and wage rates have risen slightly faster than the EU average. The size of the public sector is falling but the state sector is one of the most efficient and transparent in the world and there is little public pressure for reducing the role of the state. The EU Commission, the IMF and the OECD all urge Denmark to lower its tax level to stimulate labour supply. Generous student grants, early retirement benefits and disability compensation have resulted in 25% of the working age population living on some form of social welfare assistance. Monetary policy for the euro area has been appropriate for the Danish economy.

Currency. The monetary unit is the *Danish krone* (DKK) of 100 øre. Inflation was 2·5% in 1999 and 2·8% in 2000. Foreign exchange reserves were US$22,565m. in June 2002 and gold reserves 2·14m. troy oz. In June 2000 the money supply was 387,135m. kroner.

While not participating directly in EMU, the Danish krone is pegged to the new currency in ERM-2, the successor to the exchange rate mechanism.

Budget. The following shows the actual revenue and expenditure in central government accounts for the calendar years 2000 and 2001, the approved budget figures for 2002 and the budget for 2003 (in 1,000 kroner):

	2000	2001	2002	2003
Revenue[1]	432,865,000	436,231,900	432,748,000	440,131,100
Expenditure[1]	398,012,300	409,968,300	412,310,600	424,678,100

[1]Receipts and expenditures of special government funds and expenditures on public works are included.

The 2003 budget envisaged revenue of 119,093·5m. kroner from income and property taxes and 220,857·5m. from consumer taxes. The central government debt on 31 Dec. 2001 amounted to 545,688m. kroner.

VAT is 25%.

Performance. Real GDP growth averaged 3% in the period 1995–97. For 1998 a growth rate of 2·8% was recorded, followed by 2·1% in 1999 and 3·2% in 2000. For 2001 growth of 1·8% was forecast. The current account has moved into deficit and was unlikely to return to surplus before 2000. As stated in the *OECD's Economic Survey of Denmark (1998–99)*, assessing recent economic performance as a whole, it is evident that fiscal consolidation, monetary policy credibility and the structural reform programme have together been highly successful in creating the conditions for long-term growth. Total GDP in 2001 was US$162·8bn.

Banking and Finance. On 31 Dec. 2001 the accounts of the National Bank (*Chairman of the Board of Governors*, Bodil Nyboe Andersen) balanced at 295,286m. kroner. The assets included official net foreign reserves of 148,427m. kroner. The liabilities included notes and coins totalling 47,299m. kroner. On 31 Dec. 2000 there were 97 commercial banks and savings banks, with deposits of 757,625m. kroner.

The two largest commercial banks are Den Danske Bank and Unibank, which merged with MeritaNordbanken in 2000 and now forms part of the Stockholm-based Nordea group.

There is a stock exchange in Copenhagen.

ENERGY AND NATURAL RESOURCES

Environment. According to the *World Bank Atlas* Denmark's carbon dioxide emissions in 1998 were the equivalent of 10·1 tonnes per capita.

Electricity. Installed capacity is 13·08m. kW. Production (2000), 36,005m. kWh. Consumption per capita in 2000 was 6,707 kWh. In 2001 some 6,445 wind turbines produced 12% of output.

Oil and Gas. Oil production was (2000) 17·4m. tonnes with 184m. tonnes of proven reserves. Production of natural gas was (2001) 8·2bn. cu. metres with 94bn. cu. metres of proven reserves.

Wind. Denmark is one of the world's largest wind-power producers, with an installed capacity of 2,556 MW at the end of 2001. Denmark generates 18% of its electricity from wind, the highest proportion of any country.

Minerals. 23,000 tonnes of hard coal were produced in 1997.

Agriculture. Agriculture accounted for 11·0% of exports and 2·6% of imports in 2001. Land ownership is widely distributed. In May 2001 there were 53,489 holdings with at least 5 ha of agricultural area (or at least a production equivalent to that from 5 ha of barley). There were 10,421 small holdings (with less than 10 ha), 25,405 medium-sized holdings (10–50 ha) and 17,663 holdings with more than 50 ha. Approximately 5·0% of all agricultural land is used for organic farming. There were 25,596 agricultural workers in 1999.

In 2001 the cultivated area was (in 1,000 ha): grain, 1,537; green fodder and grass, 611; set aside, 202; root crops, 108; other crops, 186; pulses, 32; total cultivated area, 2,676.

Chief crops	Area (1,000 ha)				Production (in 1,000 tonnes)			
	1998	1999	2000	2001	1998	1999	2000	2001
Wheat	680	619	619	633	4,928	4,471	4,693	4,886
Barley	686	701	731	737	3,565	3,675	3,980	4,068
Potatoes	36	38	39	39	1,456	1,502	1,645	1,543
Rye	105	49	50	65	538	248	262	338
Oats	31	26	44	59	161	130	233	291
Other root crops	98	86	77	69	5,606	5,042	4,498	4,048

Livestock, 2001 (in 1,000): pigs, 12,608; cattle, 1,907; sheep, 152; horses, 43; poultry, 21,237.

Production (in 1,000 tonnes) in 2001: pork and bacon, 1,836; beef, 169; milk, 4,418; cheese, 315; eggs, 77; butter, 36.

In 2000 tractors numbered 123,221 and combine harvesters 23,272.

Forestry. The area under forests in 2000 was 486,000 ha, or 11·3% of the total land area. Timber production in 2001 was 1·79m. cu. metres.

Fisheries. The total value of the fish caught was (in 1m. kroner): 1950, 156; 1955, 252; 1960, 376; 1965, 650; 1970, 854; 1975, 1,442; 1980, 2,888; 1985, 3,542; 1990, 3,485; 1995, 3,020; 2000, 3,141.

In 2000 the total catch was 1,421,164 tonnes, almost exclusively from sea fishing. Denmark is the leading fishing nation in the EU.

INDUSTRY

The leading companies by market capitalization in Denmark, excluding banking and finance, in Jan. 2002 were: Novo Nordisk A/S (116bn. kroner), a healthcare company; the A.P. Møller Group companies D/S 1912 and D/S Svendborg (54 bn. kroner and 49 bn. kroner respectively in mid-2002), which trade as the shipping company Mærsk; and TDC A/S (58bn. kroner), formerly Tele Danmark.

The following table is of gross value added by kind of activity (in 1m. kroner; 1995 constant prices):

	1999[1]	*2000*[1]	*2001*[1]
Total	963,651	998,214	1,010,038
Agriculture, fishing and quarrying	47,684	49,779	49,227
Manufacturing	158,964	169,650	174,012
Electricity, gas and water supply	21,634	19,357	18,793
Construction	45,077	47,615	45,794
Trade, hotels and restaurants	154,728	157,570	159,421
Transport, storage and communications	84,725	90,282	90,959
Financial intermediation, business activities	234,508	247,538	256,917
Public and personal services	252,482	253,447	253,306
Financial intermediation services indirectly measured	−36,150	−37,024	−38,392

[1]Provisional or estimated figures.

In the following table 'number of jobs' refers to 22,006 local activity units including single-proprietor units (Nov. 2000):

Branch of industry	Number of employees
Food, beverages and tobacco	85,873
Textiles, wearing apparel, leather	15,910
Wood and wood products	16,598
Paper products	61,669
Refined petroleum products	628
Chemicals and man-made fibres	28,406
Rubber and plastic products	23,162
Non-metallic mineral products	22,322
Basic metals	58,325
Machinery and equipment	71,314
Electrical and optical equipment	53,153
Transport equipment	16,826
Furniture, other manufactures	34,531
Total manufacturing	488,717

Labour. In 2001 the labour force was 2,891,388. 34·6% of the working population in 2001 worked in public and personal services; 18·0% in wholesale and retail trade, hotels and restaurants; 16·7% in manufacturing; 13·0% in financial intermediation, commerce etc.; 6·6% in transport, storage and telecommunications; 6·3% in construction; 3·8% in agriculture, fisheries and quarrying; and 0·5% in electricity, gas and water supply. In 2001, 464,098 persons were employed in manufacturing. Retirement age is 67. In Dec. 2002 the unemployment rate was 4·7%. In 2001 Denmark lost 23 working days to strikes per 1,000 employees.

INTERNATIONAL TRADE

Imports and Exports. In 2001 imports totalled 336,337·69m. kroner and exports 421,744·88m. kroner.

Imports and exports (in 1m. kroner) for calendar years:

	2000[1]		*2001*[1]	
Leading commodities	Imports	Exports	Imports	Exports
Live animals, meat and meat preparations	4,011	28,313	3,720	32,610
Dairy products, eggs	2,112	10,546	2,437	10,885
Fish, crustaceans, etc. and preparations	9,068	15,177	10,248	16,644
Cereals and cereal preparations	2,635	5,077	2,925	5,235
Fodder for animals	5,070	4,029	5,499	4,166
Wood and cork	4,833	1,250	4,457	1,038
Textile fibres, yarns, fabrics, etc.	8,945	8,319	9,204	8,522
Mineral fuels, lubricants, etc.	19,365	32,935	17,312	27,929
Chemicals and plastics	16,990	12,519	17,687	12,916
Medicine and pharmaceutical products	7,674	24,075	9,138	28,214
Metals, manufacture of metals	27,700	18,794	27,824	19,453
Machinery, electrical, equipment, etc.	95,638	95,586	96,746	102,143
Transport equipment	35,645	14,989	34,430	15,341
Furniture, etc.	5,568	15,192	5,600	15,419
Clothing and clothing accessories	17,926	13,943	18,503	14,741

[1]Excluding trade not distributed.

Distribution of foreign trade (in 1,000 kroner) according to countries of origin and destination for 2001:

Countries	Imports[1]	Exports[1]
Austria	4,041,871	3,658,836
Belgium	12,494,370	6,869,640
Canada	2,167,983	3,051,709
China	10,918,296	3,617,735
Faroe Islands	1,516,003	1,901,286
Finland	9,865,792	12,520,132
France	21,396,895	21,536,535
Germany	80,575,226	83,235,137
Greece	833,607	3,353,740
Greenland	1,916,109	2,117,045
Hong Kong	1,868,331	3,753,808
Ireland	4,430,292	5,920,363
Italy	16,117,523	14,242,233
Japan	5,210,014	14,766,945
Lithuania	1,875,738	1,970,098
Netherlands	25,704,283	18,977,588
Norway	16,791,414	23,573,643
Poland	7,669,085	7,199,730
Portugal	2,431,688	2,011,737
Russia	3,474,978	5,856,496
South Korea	2,685,913	2,509,468
Spain	5,802,251	9,492,345
Sweden	43,966,351	48,100,164
Switzerland	4,704,299	5,305,984
Taiwan	2,659,017	1,578,480
Turkey	2,328,593	1,344,942
UK	27,974,323	40,391,574
USA	16,311,175	29,323,114

[1]Excluding trade not distributed.

In 2001 other European Union member countries accounted for 65·3% of exports and 70·5% of imports.

COMMUNICATIONS

Roads. Denmark proper had (1 Jan. 2002) 971 km of motorways, 701 km of other state roads, 9,976 km of other provincial roads and 60,240 km of commercial roads. Motor vehicles registered at 1 Jan. 2002 comprised 1,872,631 passenger cars, 36,801 trucks, 343,450 vans, 16,181 taxi cabs (including 10,085 for private hire), 13,954 buses and 78,390 motorcycles. There were 6,861 road accidents in 2001, resulting in 431 fatalities.

Rail. In 2001 there were 2,273 km of State railways of 1,435 mm gauge (624 km electrified), which carried 156m. passengers and 7·29m. tonnes of freight. There were also 495 km of private railways.

Civil Aviation. The main international airport is at Copenhagen (Kastrup), and there are also international flights from Aalborg, Aarhus, Billund and Esbjerg. The Scandinavian Airlines System (SAS) resulted from the 1950 merger of the three former Scandinavian airlines.

On 1 Jan. 2001 Denmark had 1,089 aircraft with a capacity of 23,110 seats. In 2001 there were 305,636 take-offs and landings to and from abroad, and 335,392 to and from Danish airports, including local flights. Copenhagen (Kastrup) handled 9,124,447 departing passengers in 2001, Billund 849,761, Aalborg 348,390 and Aarhus 327,399.

Shipping. On 1 Jan. 2002 the merchant fleet consisted of 705 vessels (above 20 GRT) totalling 6·6m. GRT. In 2001, 40m. tonnes of cargo were unloaded and 31m. tonnes were loaded in Danish ports; traffic by passenger ships and ferries is not included.

Telecommunications. On 31 Dec. 2001 there were 3·86m. telephone subscribers (720 per 1,000 persons). On 31 Dec. 2001 there were 3·96m. mobile phone subscribers (630 per 1,000 persons). In June 2002 there were 3·37m. Internet users (62·73% of the population) and approximately 70% of Danish households had access to PCs.

Postal Services. In 2001 there were 1,083 post offices.

SOCIAL INSTITUTIONS

Justice. The lowest courts of justice are organized in 82 tribunals *(byretter)*, where minor cases are dealt with by a single judge. The tribunal at Copenhagen has one president and 49 other judges; and Aarhus one president and 15 other judges; the other tribunals have one to 11 judges. Cases of greater consequence are dealt with by the two High Courts *(Landsretterne)*; these courts are also courts of appeal for minor cases. The Eastern High Court in Copenhagen has one president and 63 other judges; and the Western in Viborg one president and 38 other judges. From these an appeal lies to the Supreme Court in Copenhagen, composed of a president and 15 other judges. Judges under 65 years of age can be removed only by judicial sentence.

In 2001, 20,344 men and 2,144 women were convicted of violations of the criminal code, fines not included. In 2001 the daily average population in penal institutions was 3,236·1 (60·5 per 100,000 of national population), of whom 849·1 were on remand.

Religion. There is complete religious liberty. The state church is the Evangelical-Lutheran to which about 85% of the population belong. It is divided into ten dioceses, each with a Bishop. The Bishop together with the Chief Administrative Officer of the county make up the diocesan-governing body, responsible for all matters of ecclesiastical local finance and general administration. Bishops are appointed by the Crown after an election by the clergy and parish council members. Each diocese is divided into a number of deaneries (111 in the whole country), each with its Dean and Deanery Committee, who have certain financial powers.

Education. Education has been compulsory since 1814. The first stage of the Danish education system is the basic school (education at first level). This starts with an optional pre-school year (education preceding the first level) and continues up to and including the optional 10th year in the *folkeskole* (municipal primary and lower secondary school). In 2000, 671,634 pupils attended education at first level and second level, first stage. Of this group, 69,983 began their education at pre-school, while 145,075 attended grades 8 to 10. Owing to the changes in the age distribution in the population, the number of pupils attending pre-school has increased by 4% since 1999, whereas the number of students attending grades 8 to 10 (education at second level, first stage) has fallen by 19% since 1991.

Of all students leaving basic school in 1997–98, 76·1% had commenced further education after a period of three months. Almost half the students had elected to attend general upper-secondary education (general programmes of education at secondary level, second stage), while 27% opted for a vocational education at secondary level, second stage.

Education that qualifies students for education at third level is called general upper-secondary education and comprises general upper-secondary education (general programmes of education at second level, second stage), such as *gymnasium* (upper-secondary school), higher preparatory examination, and adult upper-secondary level courses as well as general/vocational upper secondary education at the vocational education institutions. In 2000, 63,972 students attended general upper-secondary education.

Higher education is divided into three levels: short-cycle higher education involves two years of training, sometimes practical, after completion of upper-secondary education (23,521 students in 2000); medium-cycle higher education involves two–four years of mainly theoretical training (67,122 students in 2000); long-cycle higher education requires more than four years of education, mainly theoretical, divided between a bachelors' degree and a candidate programme (44,535 students in bachelors' programmes in 2000 and 53,667 in the candidate programme). Universities, 1997–98: the University of Copenhagen (founded 1479), 29,389 students; the University of Aarhus (founded in 1928), 17,901 students; the University of Odense (founded in 1964), 9,127 students; the University of Aalborg (founded in 1974), 8,927 students; Roskilde University Centre (founded in 1972), 5,719 students. The Technical University of Denmark had 6,372 students in 1997–98. 8 engineering colleges had 6,126 students.

Other types of post-secondary education (1996–97): the Royal Veterinary and Agricultural University has 3,054 students; The Danish School of Pharmacy, 1,137 students; 7 colleges of economics, business administration and modern languages, 22,276 students; 2 schools of architecture, 2,065 students; 7 academies of music, 1,291 students; 2 schools of librarianship, 929 students; The Royal Danish School of Educational Studies, 3,024 students; 5 schools of social work, 1,733 students; The Danish School of Journalism, 998 students; 10 colleges of physical therapy, 2,768 students; 2 schools of Midwifery Education, 255 students; 2 colleges of home economics, 537 students; The School of Visual Arts, 196 students; 27 schools of nursing, 9,402 students; 3 military academies, 601 students.

In 1996 total expenditure on education came to 8·1% of GNP.

The adult literacy rate in 1998 was at least 99%.

Health. In 1999 there were 15,102 doctors (284 per 100,000 persons), 4,629 dentists, 74,106 nurses and 1,032 midwives. There were 76 hospitals in 2000 (provision of 1 bed per 210 population in 1996).

In 2000 an estimated 37% of men and 34% of women smoked. The rate among women is one of the highest in the world.

Welfare. The main body of Danish social welfare legislation is consolidated in seven acts concerning: (1) public health security, (2) sick-day benefits, (3) social pensions (for early retirement and old age), (4) employment injuries insurance, (5) employment services, unemployment insurance and activation measures, (6) social assistance including assistance to handicapped, rehabilitation, child and juvenile guidance, daycare institutions, care of the aged and sick, and (7) family allowances.

Public health security, covering the entire population, provides free medical care, substantial subsidies for certain essential medicines together with some dental care, and a funeral allowance. Hospitals are primarily municipal and treatment is normally free. All employed workers are granted daily sickness allowances; others can have limited daily sickness allowances. Daily cash benefits are granted in the case of temporary incapacity because of illness, injury or childbirth to all persons in paid employment. The benefit is paid up to the rate of 100% of the average weekly earnings. There is, however, a maximum rate of 3,016 kroner a week.

Social pensions cover the entire population. Entitlement to the old-age pension at the full rate is subject to the condition that the beneficiary has been ordinarily resident in Denmark for 40 years. For a shorter period of residence, the benefits are reduced proportionally. The basic amount of the old-age pension in Jan. 2002 was 154,392 kroner a year to married couples and 105,396 to single persons. Various supplementary allowances, depending on age and income, may be payable with the basic amount. Depending on health and income, persons aged 60–66 may apply for an early retirement pension. Persons over 67 years of age are entitled to the basic amount. The pensions to a married couple are calculated and paid to the husband and the wife separately. Early retirement pension to a disabled person is payable at ages 18–66 years, having regard to the degree of disability (physical as well as otherwise), at a rate of up to 166,212 kroner to a single person. Early retirement pensions may be subject to income regulation. The same applies to the basic amount of the old-age pension to persons aged 67–69.

Employment injuries insurance provides for disability or survivors' pensions and compensations. The scheme covers practically all employees.

Employment services are provided by regional public employment agencies. Insurance against unemployment provides daily allowances and covers about 85% of the unemployed. The unemployment insurance system is based on state subsidized insurance funds linked to the trade unions. The unemployment insurance funds had a membership of 2,170,853 in Aug. 2002.

The *Social Assistance Act* applies to individual benefits in contrast to the other fields of social legislation which apply to fixed benefits. Total social expenditure, including hospital and health services, statutory pensions, etc. amounted in the financial year 2001 to 370,661·9m. kroner.

CULTURE

Broadcasting. *Danmarks Radio* is the government broadcasting station and is financed by household licence fees. Television is broadcast by *Danmarks Radio* and *TV2* with colour programmes by PAL system. Number of licences (2001): TV,

2·16m., including 2·15m. colour sets. Denmark had 1·26m. cable TV subscribers in 1997. There were 6·02m. radio receivers and 3·1m. television receivers in 1997.

Cinema. In 2001 there were 361 auditoria. Total attendance in 2001 was 11·9m.; in 2001 net box office receipts came to 517m. kroner. 24 full-length films were made in 2001.

Press. In 2001 there were 32 daily newspapers with a combined circulation of 1·45m. The newspaper with the largest average circulation in the period Jan.–June 2001 was *Jyllands-Posten* (180,000 on weekdays and 243,000 on Sundays), followed by *Berlingske Tidende* (152,000 on weekdays and 188,000 on Sundays).

Tourism. In 2001, 3,304,000 foreign tourists visited Denmark, spending some 39,078m. kroner. Foreigners spent 5,978,000 nights in hotels and 3,379,000 nights at camping sites in 2001.

Libraries. In 2001 there were 797 public libraries, 1 National library and 43 Higher Education libraries. They held a combined 103,655,000 volumes.

DIPLOMATIC REPRESENTATIVES
Of Denmark in the United Kingdom (55 Sloane St., London, SW1X 9SR)
Ambassador: Tom Risdahl Jensen.

Of the United Kingdom in Denmark (Kastelsvej 36–40, DK-2100, Copenhagen Ø)
Ambassador: Philip Astley, LVO.

Of Denmark in the USA (3200 Whitehaven St., NW, Washington, D.C., 20008)
Ambassador: Ulrik Andreas Federspiel.

Of the USA in Denmark (Dag Hammarskjölds Allé 24, DK-2100, Copenhagen Ø)
Ambassador: Stuart A Bernstein.

Of Denmark to the United Nations
Ambassador: Ellen Margrethe Løj.

FURTHER READING
Statistical Information: Danmarks Statistik (Sejrøgade 11, DK-2100 Copenhagen Ø. *Website:* http://www.dst.dk/) was founded in 1849 and reorganized in 1966 as an independent institution; it is administratively placed under the Minister of Economic Affairs. Its main publications are: *Statistisk Årbog* (Statistical Yearbook). From 1896: *Statistiske Efterretninger* (Statistical News). *Konjunkturstatistik* (Main indicators); *Statistisk tiårsoversigt* (Statistical Ten-Year Review).

Dania polyglotta. Annual Bibliography of Books . . . in Foreign Languages Printed in Denmark. State Library, Copenhagen. Annual
Kongelig Dansk Hof og Statskalender. Copenhagen. Annual
Petersson, O., *The Government and Politics of the Nordic Countries.* Stockholm, 1994
Turner, Barry, (ed.) *Scandinavia Profiled.* Macmillan, London, 2000

National library: Det kongelige Bibliotek, P.O.B. 2149, DK-1016 Copenhagen K. *Director:* Erland Kolding Nielsen.
National statistical office: Statistics Denmark, Copenhagen. *Director General:* Jan Plovsing.
Website: http://www.dst.dk/

THE FAROE ISLANDS
Føroyar/Færøerne

KEY HISTORICAL EVENTS
A Norwegian province till the peace treaty of 14 Jan. 1814, the islands have been represented by two members in the Danish parliament since 1851. In 1852 they obtained an elected parliament of their own which in 1948 secured a certain degree of home-rule. The islands are not included in the EU but left EFTA together with Denmark on 31 Dec. 1972. Recently, negotiations for independence were given a push by the prospect of exploiting offshore oil and gas.

TERRITORY AND POPULATION
The archipelago is situated due north of Scotland, 300 km from the Shetland Islands, 675 km from Norway and 450 km from Iceland, with a total land area of 1,399 sq.

km (540 sq. miles). There are 17 inhabited islands (the main ones being Streymoy, Eysturoy, Vágoy, Suðuroy, Sandoy and Borðoy) and numerous islets, all mountainous and of volcanic origin. Population in Jan. 2000 was 45,409; density, 32 per sq. km. In 1995 an estimated 67·9% of the population lived in rural areas. The capital is Tórshavn (16,000 residents in 1999) on Streymoy.

The official languages are Faroese and Danish.

SOCIAL STATISTICS
Birth rate per 1,000 inhabitants (1996 est.), 13·91; death rate, 8·69. Life expectancy at birth for total population (1996 est.), 77·83.

CONSTITUTION AND GOVERNMENT
The parliament comprises 32 members elected by proportional representation by universal suffrage at age 18. Parliament elects a government of at least three members which administers home rule. Denmark is represented in parliament by the chief administrator. A referendum was to be held on 26 May 2001 on the government's plan to move towards full sovereignty, but it was called off after the Danish prime minister at the time Poul Nyrup Rasmussen stated that subsidies would cease after four years if the islanders voted for independence.

RECENT ELECTIONS
Parliamentary elections were held on 30 April 2002. The Union Party (SF) and the Party for People's Government (TF) each won 8 seats with 26·0% and 23·7% respectively, the Equality Party (JF) 7 seats with 20·9%, the People's Party (FF) 7 seats with 20·8%, the Self Government Party (SSF) 1 seat with 4·4%, and the Centre Party 1 seat with 4·2%.

CURRENT ADMINISTRATION
Prime Minister: Anfinn Kallsberg (FF).

Following the 1998 elections, a coalition government was formed comprising FF, TF and SSF members.

High Commissioner: Birgit Kleis (appointed 2001).

ECONOMY
Currency. Since 1940 the currency has been the Faroese *króna* (kr.) which remains freely interchangeable with the Danish krone.

Budget. The 1995 budget balanced at 2,805m. kr. As a result of an economic crash in the early 1990s, Denmark restructured the banks and lent money to the government to meet its international obligations. Since then the economy has improved, but 5·5bn. Danish kroner (£480m.) is still owed to the Danish state. Meanwhile, subsidies from Copenhagen are worth at least 1bn. Danish kroner a year.

Banking and Finance. The largest bank is the state-owned Føroya Banki.

ENERGY AND NATURAL RESOURCES
Electricity. Installed capacity is 91,000 kW. Total production in 1998 was 180m. kWh, of which approximately 50% was hydro-electric. There are five hydro-electric stations at Vestmanna on Streymoy and one at Eiði on Eysturoy. Consumption per capita was 4,043 kWh in 1995.

Agriculture. Only 2% of the surface is cultivated; it is chiefly used for sheep and cattle grazing. Potatoes are grown for home consumption. Livestock (1996): sheep, 68,000; cattle, 2,000.

Fisheries. Deep-sea fishing now forms the most important sector (90%) of the economy, primarily in the 200-mile exclusive zone, but also off Greenland, Iceland, Svalbard and Newfoundland and in the Barents Sea. Total catch (1999) 358,044 tonnes, primarily cod, coalfish, redfish, mackerel, blue whiting, capelin, prawns and herring.

INTERNATIONAL TRADE

Imports and Exports. Exports, mainly fresh, frozen, filleted and salted fish, amounted to 2,026m. kr. in 1995; imports to 1,776m. kr. In 1995 Denmark supplied 35% of imports, Norway 16% and UK 8%; exports were mainly to UK (26%), Denmark (22%), Germany (10%), France (8%) and Spain (5%).

COMMUNICATIONS

Roads. In 1995 there were 458 km of highways, 11,528 passenger cars and 2,901 commercial vehicles.

Civil Aviation. The airport is on Vágoy, from which there are regular services to Aberdeen, Billund, Copenhagen, Reykjavík and Glasgow (in summer).

Shipping. The chief port is Tórshavn, with smaller ports at Klaksvik, Vestmanna, Skálafjørður, Tvøroyri, Vágur and Fuglafjørður. In 1998 merchant shipping totalled 103,000 GRT, including oil tankers 2,000 GRT.

Telecommunications. In 2000 there were 25,000 telephone main lines in use (554·5 for every 1,000 inhabitants). There were 10,300 mobile phone subscribers in Dec. 1999 and 3,000 Internet users.

SOCIAL INSTITUTIONS

Religion. About 80% are Evangelical Lutherans and 20% are Plymouth Brethren, or belong to small communities of Roman Catholics, Pentecostal, Adventists, Jehovah's Witnesses and Bahai.

Education. In 1994–95 there were 4,898 primary and 3,041 secondary school pupils with 554 teachers.

Health. In 1994 there were 90 doctors, 38 dentists, 10 pharmacists, 17 midwives and 355 nursing personnel. In 1994 there were three hospitals with 297 beds.

CULTURE

Broadcasting. Radio and TV broadcasting (colour by PAL) are provided by Utvarp Føroya and Sjónvarp Føroya respectively. In 1997 there were 26,000 radio and 15,000 TV receivers registered.

Press. In 1996 there was one daily newspaper with a circulation of 6,000.

FURTHER READING

Árbók fyri Føroyar. Annual.
Rutherford, G. K. (ed.) *The Physical Environment of the Færoe Islands.* The Hague, 1982
Wylie, J., *The Faroe Islands: Interpretations of History.* Lexington, 1987

National statistical office: Hagstova Føroya, Statistics Faroe Islands.
Website: http://www.hagstova.fo/Welcome_uk.html

GREENLAND

Grønland/Kalaallit Nunaat

KEY HISTORICAL EVENTS

A Danish possession since 1380, Greenland became an integral part of the Danish kingdom on 5 June 1953. Following a referendum in Jan. 1979, home rule was introduced from 1 May 1979.

TERRITORY AND POPULATION

Area, 2,166,086 sq. km (840,000 sq. miles), made up of 1,755,437 sq. km of ice cap and 410,449 sq. km of ice-free land. The population, 1 Jan. 2000, numbered 56,124; density, 0·03 sq. km. In 2000, 45,714 persons were urban (81%); 49,369 were born in Greenland and 6,755 were born outside Greenland. 2000 population of West Greenland, 51,069; East Greenland, 3,462; North Greenland (Thule/Qaanaaq), 864; and 729 not belonging to any specific municipality. The capital is Nuuk (Godthåb), with a population in 1999 of 13,445.

The predominant language is Greenlandic. Danish is widely used in matters relating to teaching, administration and business.

SOCIAL STATISTICS
Registered live births (1999), 947. Number of abortions (1999): 842. Death rate per 1,000 population (1999), 8·6. In 1999 suicide was the cause of death in 11% of all deaths. Annual growth rate (2000), 0·1%.

CONSTITUTION AND GOVERNMENT
There is a 31-member Home Rule Parliament, which is elected for four-year terms and meets two to three times a year. The seven-member cabinet is elected by parliament. Ministers need not be members of parliament. In accordance with the Home Rule Act, the Greenland Home Rule government is constituted by an elected parliament, *Landstinget* (The Greenland Parliament), and an administration headed by a local government, *Landsstyret* (The Cabinet).

Greenland elects two representatives to the Danish parliament (*Folketing*). Denmark is represented by an appointed High Commissioner.

RECENT ELECTIONS
At parliamentary elections held on 3 Dec. 2002 Siumut (Social Democratic) won 10 of 31 seats and 28% of votes cast, Inuit Ataqatigiit (leftist) 8 and 25%, Atássut (Liberal) 7 and 20%, and the Democrats 5 and 16%. Turn-out was 75%.

CURRENT ADMINISTRATION
The government is currently a coalition between Siumut and Atássut.
Prime Minister: Hans Enoksen; b. 1956 (Siumut; in office since 14 Dec. 2002).
High Commissioner: Gunnar Martens (appointed 1995).

Greenland Homerule Website: http://www.nanoq.gl

INTERNATIONAL RELATIONS
Greenland has two representatives, appointed by the Greenland Parliament, in the Council for European Politics.

ECONOMY
Currency. The Danish krone is the legal currency.

Budget. The budget (*finanslovsforslag*) for the following year must be approved by the Home Rule Parliament (*Landstinget*) no later than 31 Oct.

The following table shows the actual revenue and expenditure as shown in Home Rule government accounts for the calendar years 1997–99 and the approved budget figures for 2000 and 2001. Figures are in 1,000 kroner.

	1997	1998	1999	2000	2001
Revenue	4,178	4,304	4,511	4,646	4,687
Expenditure	4,089	4,366	4,393	4,342	4,652

Performance. Following a period of recession between 1990–93, the economy has been growing since 1994, although at a rate well below the OECD average in recent years. In 1998 the real GNP growth rate was 7·8%, GNP at market prices was 7,706m. kroner and gross national disposable income at market prices was 10,695m. kroner.

Banking and Finance. There are two private banks, Grønlandsbanken and Sparbank Vest.

Weights and Measures. The metric system is in use.

ENERGY AND NATURAL RESOURCES
Environment. According to the *World Bank Atlas* Greenland's carbon dioxide emissions in 1998 were the equivalent of 9·4 tonnes per capita.

Electricity. Installed capacity is 92,500 kW. Production in 1999 was 295·2m. GWh.

Oil and Gas. Imports of fuel and fuel oil (1999), 171,523 tonnes worth 256m. kroner.

Water. Production of water in tonnes (1999), 5·38m. cu. metres, of which 2·74m. cu. metres were for industry.

Minerals. Exploitation of minerals (1999): number of licences, 26; area, 11,459 sq. km.

Agriculture. Livestock, 1999: sheep, 21,007; reindeer, 2,106. There are approximately 57 sheep-breeding farms in southwest Greenland.

Fisheries. Fishing and product-processing are the principal industry. The total catch in 1999 was 117,500 tonnes. In 1999 prawns accounted for almost 64% of the country's economic output. Greenland halibut and other fish made up around 26%. In 1999, 190 large whales were caught and 3,981 smaller cetacean mammals, such as porpoise (subject to the International Whaling Commission's regulations); and in 1998, 167,506 seals.

INDUSTRY

Six shipyards repair and maintain ships and produce industrial tanks, containers and steel constructions for building.

Labour. At 1 Jan. 2000 the potential labour force was 36,434.

INTERNATIONAL TRADE

Imports and Exports. Principal commodities (1999 provisional figures, in 1m. kroner):

Imports (c.i.f.), 2,856·2, including: food and live animals, 378·3 (meat and meat preparations 97·4); beverages and tobacco, 113·8 (beverages 86·6); minerals, fuels, lubricants, etc., 247·4 (petroleum products 247·1); chemicals, 120·2; basic manufactures, 456·6; machinery and transport equipment, 762·8 (machinery, 519·4; transport equipment, 243·4); miscellaneous manufactured articles, 340·1.

Exports (f.o.b.), 1,932·4, including: prawns, 1,238·4; Greenland halibut, 385·9; cod, 43·4; other fish products, 152·5.

Principal trading partners (provisional, 1m. kroner, 1999): imports (c.i.f.): Denmark, 1,965·8; Norway, 153·7; Japan, 90·2. Exports (f.o.b.): Denmark, 1,616·9; Japan, 160·8; UK, 16·0.

COMMUNICATIONS

Roads. There are no roads between towns. Registered vehicles (1999): passenger cars, 2,226; lorries and trucks, 1,332; total (including others), 4,026.

Rail. There is no railway system.

Civil Aviation. Number of passengers to/from Greenland (1999): 100,094. Domestic flights—number of passengers (1999): aeroplanes, 169,732; helicopters, 62,155. Greenland Air operates services to Denmark, Iceland and Iqaluit/Frobisher Bay (Nunavut, Canada). There are international airports at Kangerlussuaq (Søndre Strømfjord), Narsarsuaq and Kulusuk and 18 local airports/heliports with scheduled services. There are cargo services to Denmark, Iceland and Canada.

Shipping. There are no overseas passenger services. In 1998, 100,969 passengers were carried on coastal services. There are cargo services to Denmark, Iceland and St John's (Canada).

Telecommunications. In 1998 there were 25,006 telephone main lines and 4,008 Internet dial-ups. There were 13,600 mobile phone subscribers in Dec. 1999. In Dec. 2000 there were 17,800 Internet users.

SOCIAL INSTITUTIONS

Justice. The High Court in Nuuk comprises one professional judge and two lay magistrates, while there are 18 district courts under lay assessors.

The population in penal institutions in Aug. 1998 was 78 (140 per 100,000 of national population).

Religion. About 99% of the population are Evangelical Lutherans. In 1998 there were 17 parishes with 81 churches and chapels, and 22 ministers.

Education. Education is compulsory from six to 15 years. A further three years of schooling are optional. Pre-primary and primary schools (1999–2000), 11,164 pupils and 1,109 teachers; secondary schools, three with 571 pupils.

Health. The medical service is free to all citizens. There is a central hospital in Nuuk and 15 smaller district hospitals. In 1998 there were 83 doctors.

Non-natural death occurred in approximately one-fifth of all deaths in 1999. Suicide is the most dominant non-natural cause of death. There were 63 reported cases of tuberculosis in 1999 and 633 cases of venereal disease. Reported cases of syphilis had decreased from 37 in 1991 to 1 in 1999. In 1998, 17 cases of HIV were reported while a total of eight new HIV-positive cases were reported in 1999.

Welfare. Pensions are granted to persons who are 63 or above. The right to maternity leave has been extended to two weeks before the expected birth and up to 20 weeks after birth against a total of 21 weeks in earlier regulations. The father's right to one week's paternity leave in connection with the birth has been extended to three weeks as from 1 Jan. 2000. Wage earners who are members of SIK (The National Workers' Union) receive financial assistance (unemployment benefit) according to fixed rates, in case of unemployment or illness.

CULTURE

Broadcasting. The government Kalaallit Nunaata Radioa provides broadcasting services, and there are also local services. In 1997 there were estimated to be 27,000 radio and 22,000 TV sets (colour by NTSC). Several towns have local television stations.

Cinema. There is one cinema in Nuuk at the Cultural Centre Katuaq. Video is widely used.

Press. There are two national newspapers.

Tourism. In 1999 visitors stayed 205,573 nights in hotels (including 105,227 Greenlandic visitors) at 31 hotels.

Libraries. There are 17 municipal libraries and the National Library, Nunatta Atuagaateqarfia, which is administered by the Home Rule authorities.

Museums and Galleries. There are museums in most towns. The Greenland National Museum is in Nuuk. 17,815 persons visited the museum in 1999.

FURTHER READING
Greenland 19xx and *Greenland 20xx: Statistical Yearbook* has been published annually since 1989 by Statistics Greenland in Greenlandic/Danish. *Greenland 2001–2002* in English
Gad, F., *A History of Greenland*. 2 vols. London, 1970–73
Miller, K. E., *Greenland*. [Bibliography] ABC-Clio, Oxford and Santa Barbara (CA), 1991
Greenland National Library, P.O. Box 1011, DK-3900 Nuuk

National statistical office: Statistics Greenland, PO Box 1025, DK-3900 Nuuk.
Website: http://www.statgreen.gl

DJIBOUTI

Jumhouriyya Djibouti
(Republic of Djibouti)

Capital: Djibouti
Population estimate, 2000: 632,000
GDP per capita, 2000: (PPP$) 2,377
HDI/world rank: 0·445/149

KEY HISTORICAL EVENTS
At a referendum held on 19 March 1967, 60% of the electorate voted for continued association with France rather than independence. France affirmed that the Territory of the Afars and the Issas was destined for independence but no date was fixed. Independence as the Republic of Djibouti was achieved on 27 June 1977. Afar rebels in the north, belonging to the Front for the Restoration of Unity and Democracy (FRUD), signed a 'Peace and National Reconciliation Agreement' with the government on 26 Dec. 1994, envisaging the formation of a national coalition government, the redrafting of the electoral roll and the integration of FRUD militants into the armed forces and civil service.

TERRITORY AND POPULATION
Djibouti is in effect a city-state surrounded by a semi-desert hinterland. It is bounded in the northwest by Eritrea, northeast by the Gulf of Aden, southeast by Somalia and southwest by Ethiopia. The area is 23,200 sq. km (8,958 sq. miles). The population was estimated in 1995 at 601,000 (83·0% urban in 1999), of whom about half were Somali (Issa, Gadaboursi and Issaq), 35% Afar, and some Europeans (mainly French) and Arabs. 1995 density, 26 per sq. km.

The UN gives a projected population for 2010 of 679,000.

There are five administrative districts (areas in sq. km): Ali-Sabieh (2,600); Dikhil (7,800); Djibouti (600); Obock (5,700); Tadjoura (7,300). The capital is Djibouti (1999 population, 523,000).

French and Arabic are official languages; Somali and Afar are also spoken.

SOCIAL STATISTICS
1995 births, 23,500; deaths, 9,500. Birth rate in 1995, 38·8 per 1,000 population; death rate, 15·6. Annual population growth rate, 1990–99, 2·2%. Infant mortality, 1999, 104 per 1,000 live births. Expectation of life, 1999: 42·6 years for men, 45·3 for women. Fertility rate, 1999, 5·2 children per woman.

CLIMATE
Conditions are hot throughout the year, with very little rain. Djibouti, Jan. 78°F (25·6°C), July 96°F (35·6°C). Annual rainfall 5" (130 mm).

CONSTITUTION AND GOVERNMENT
After a referendum at which turn-out was 70%, a new constitution was approved on 4 Sept. 1992 by 96·63% of votes cast, which permits the existence of up to four political parties. Parties are required to maintain an ethnic balance in their membership. The *President* is directly elected for a renewable six-year term. Parliament is a 65-member *Chamber of Deputies* elected for five-year terms.

National Anthem. 'Hinjinne u sara kaca' ('Arise with strength'); words by A. Elmi, tune by A. Robleh.

RECENT ELECTIONS
In the presidential election on 9 April 1999 Ismail Omar Guelleh won with 74·1% of the votes cast against one opponent.

At the parliamentary elections of 10 Jan. 2003—the first free multi-party general elections since independence—the Union for a Presidential Majority, a coalition of RPP (People's Rally for Progress) and FRUD (Front for the Restoration of Unity and Democracy), won all 65 seats with 62·2% of votes cast, against 36·9% for the Union for a Democratic Alternative. Turn-out was 48%.

CURRENT ADMINISTRATION
President: Ismail Omar Guelleh; b. 1947 (RPP; sworn in 8 May 1999).
In March 2003 the Council of Ministers comprised:
Prime Minister: Dilleita Mohamed Dilleita; b. 1958 (RPP; sworn in 7 March 2001).
Minister of Agriculture, Fisheries and Livestock: Dini Abdallah Bililis. *Commerce and Industry:* Saleban Omar Oudine. *Communications, Culture, Post and Telecommunications, Government Spokesperson:* Rifki Abdoulkader Bamakhrama. *Defence:* Ougoureh Kifleh Ahmed. *Economy, Finance and Privatization:* Yacin Elmi Bouh. *Education:* Abdi Ibrahim Absieh. *Employment and National Solidarity:* Mohamed Barkat Abdillahi. *Energy and Natural Resources:* Mohamed Ali Mohamed. *Foreign Affairs, International Co-operation and Parliamentary Relations:* Ali Abdi Farah. *Health:* Dr Banoita Tourab Saleh. *Housing, Town Planning, Environment and Territorial Administration:* Abdallah Adillahi Miguil. *Interior and Decentralization:* Abdoulkader Doualeh Waïs. *Justice, Penal and Muslim Affairs, and Human Rights:* Ismail Ibrahim Houmed. *Presidential Affairs:* Osman Ahmed Moussa. *Transport:* Elmi Obsieh Waïs. *Youth, Sports, Leisure and Tourism:* Otban Goïta Moussa.

Government Website: http://www.presidence.dj/

DEFENCE
France maintains a naval base and forces numbering 3,900 under an agreement renewed in Feb. 1991. Defence expenditure totalled US$23m. in 2000 (US$30 per capita), representing 5·0% of GDP.

Army. There are three Army commands: North, Central and South. The strength of the Army in 1999 was 8,000. There is also a paramilitary Gendarmerie of some 1,200, and an Interior Ministry National Security Force of 3,000.

Navy. A coastal patrol is maintained. Personnel (1999), 200.

Air Force. There is a small air force with no combat aircraft. Personnel (1999), 200.

INTERNATIONAL RELATIONS
Djibouti is a member of the UN, WTO, the African Union, African Development Bank, COMESA, OIC, the League of Arab States, the Intergovernmental Authority on Development, the International Organization of the Francophonie and is an ACP member state of the ACP-EU relationship.

ECONOMY
Services accounted for 75·8% of GDP in 1997, industry 20·5% and agriculture 3·6%.

Currency. The currency is the *Djibouti franc* (DJF), notionally of 100 *centimes.* Foreign exchange reserves were US$72m. in June 2002 and total money supply was 31,286m. Djibouti francs. Inflation was 1·8% in 2001.

Budget. Revenues in 1997 were an estimated US$156m. and expenditure US$175m.

Performance. Real GDP growth was 0·7% in 2000 and 1·9% in 2001. Total GDP in 2001 was US$0·6bn.

Banking and Finance. The Banque Nationale de Djibouti is the bank of issue (*Governor,* Djama Mahamoud Haid). There are six commercial banks.

Weights and Measures. The metric system is in use.

ENERGY AND NATURAL RESOURCES
Environment. According to the *World Bank Atlas* Djibouti's carbon dioxide emissions in 1998 were the equivalent of 0·6 tonnes per capita.

Electricity. Installed capacity in 1991 was 115,000 kW. Production in 1998 was 177m. kWh; consumption per capita was 303 kWh in 1997.

Agriculture. Approximately 1·3m. ha were permanent pasture in 1994. Production is dependent on irrigation which in 1998 covered 1,000 ha. There were six tractors in 1998. Vegetable production (2000) 24,000 tonnes. The most common crops are tomatoes and dates. Livestock (2000): cattle, 269,000; sheep, 465,000; goats, 513,000; camels, 67,000. Livestock products, 2000: meat, 9,000 tonnes; milk, 8,000 tonnes.

Forestry. In 1995 the area under forests was 22,000 ha, or 0·9% of the total land area.

Fisheries. In 1995 there were 140 individual fishing boats. In 1999 the catch was about 350 tonnes, entirely from sea fishing.

INDUSTRY

Labour. In 1991 the estimated labour force totalled 282,000, with 75% employed in agriculture, 14% in services and 11% in industry. A 40-hour working week is standard. Unemployment in 1994 was estimated at 30%.

INTERNATIONAL TRADE

Foreign debt totalled US$262m. in 2000.

Imports and Exports. The main economic activity is the operation of the port; in 1990 only 36% of imports were destined for Djibouti. Exports are largely re-exports. In 1996 imports totalled US$200m. and exports US$40m. The chief imports are cotton goods, sugar, cement, flour, fuel oil and vehicles; the chief exports are hides, cattle and coffee (transit from Ethiopia).

Main export markets, 1996 (% of total trade): Ethiopia, 44·8%; Somalia, 38·2%; Yemen, 8·2%; Saudi Arabia, 3·3%. Main import suppliers, 1996: France, 15·0%; Ethiopia, 10·9%; Italy, 7·8%; Saudi Arabia, 7·5%.

COMMUNICATIONS

Roads. In 1996 there were 2,890 km of roads, of which 364 km were hard-surfaced. An estimated 9,200 passenger cars were in use in 1996 (17·2 per 1,000 inhabitants), plus 2,040 vans and trucks.

Rail. For the line from Djibouti to Addis Ababa, of which 97 km lie within Djibouti, see ETHIOPIA: Communications. Traffic carried is mainly in transit to and from Ethiopia.

Civil Aviation. There is an international airport at Djibouti (Ambouli), 5 km south of Djibouti. Djibouti-based carriers are Air Djibouti, Daallo Airlines and Djibouti Airlines. Flights operated in 1998 to Addis Ababa, Aden, Asmara, Assab, Berbera, Borama, Bossaso, Burao, Cairo, Dire Dawa, Dubai, Erigavo, Hargeisa, Jeddah, Johannesburg, Karachi, Khartoum, Mogadishu, Mombasa, Muscat, Paris, Rome, Sana'a, Sharjah and Ta'iz.

Shipping. Djibouti is a free port and container terminal. 950 ships berthed in 1989 (including 177 warships), totalling 3·87m. NRT. 3,211 passengers embarked or disembarked, and 0·87m. tonnes of cargo were handled (1·48m. tonnes in 1992). In 1998 the merchant marine totalled 4,000 GRT.

Telecommunications. There were 9,700 telephone main lines in 2000 (15·2 for every 1,000 inhabitants) and 7,000 PCs in use. In 1997 there were 300 fax machines and 200 mobile phone subscribers. Djibouti had 1,000 Internet users in July 2000.

Postal Services. There were ten post offices in 1995.

SOCIAL INSTITUTIONS

Justice. There is a Court of First Instance and a Court of Appeal in the capital. The judicial system is based on Islamic law. The death penalty was abolished for all crimes in 1994.

The population in penal institutions in 1997 was approximately 650 (115 per 100,000 of national population).

Religion. In 1995, 96% of the population were Muslim, with about 12,000 Roman Catholics and 10,000 Protestant and Orthodox.

Education. Adult literacy in 1999 was 63·4% (74·9% of men; 52·8% of women). In 1996–97 there were 72 primary schools with 36,896 pupils and 1,096 teachers, and in 1995–96, 11,860 pupils and 628 teachers in secondary schools. In 1995–96 there were 130 students at higher education institutions.

Health. In 1993 there were 2 hospitals, 6 medical centres and 21 dispensaries. There were 97 doctors, 10 dentists and 14 pharmacists in 1989.

CULTURE

Broadcasting. The state-run *Radiodiffusion-Télévision de Djibouti* broadcasts in French, Somali, Afar and Arabic. There is a television transmitter in Djibouti, broadcasting for 35 hours a week. Number of receivers in 1997: radio, 52,000; TV, 28,000 (colour by SECAM V).

Tourism. There were 20,000 foreign tourists in 1998, spending US$4m.

DIPLOMATIC REPRESENTATIVES
Of Djibouti in the United Kingdom
Ambassador: Mohamed Gomaneh Guirreh (resides at Paris).

Of the United Kingdom in Djibouti
Ambassador: Myles Wickstead (resides at Addis Ababa, Ethiopia).

Of the USA in Djibouti (Plateau du Serpent Blvd., Djibouti)
Ambassador: Donald Y. Yamamoto.

Of Djibouti to the United Nations and in the USA (1156 15th Street, NW, Suite 515, Washington, D.C., 20005)
Ambassador: Roble Olhaye.

Of Djibouti to the European Union
Ambassador: Mohamed Moussa Chehem.

FURTHER READING
Direction Nationale de la Statistique. *Annuaire Statistique de Djibouti*
Schraeder, Peter J., *Djibouti.* [Bibliography] ABC-Clio, Oxford and Santa Barbara (CA), 1991

National statistical office: Direction Nationale de la Statistique, Ministère du Commerce, des Transports et du Tourisme, BP 1846, Djibouti.

DOMINICA

Commonwealth of Dominica

Capital: Roseau
Population estimate, 2000: 72,000
GDP per capita, 2000: (PPP$) 5,880
HDI/world rank: 0·779/61

KEY HISTORICAL EVENTS

Dominica was discovered by Columbus on Sunday (hence the island's name), 3 Nov. 1493. But it was French settlers who began to create plantations on the island. Recognizing the island's strategic position, control was contested between the British and French until it was awarded to the British in 1783. In March 1967 Dominica became an Associated State of the UK, with internal self-government, and an independent republic as the Commonwealth of Dominica on 3 Nov. 1978.

TERRITORY AND POPULATION

Dominica is an island in the Windward group of the West Indies situated between Martinique and Guadeloupe. It has an area of 748·5 sq. km (289·5 sq. miles) and a provisional population at the 2001 census of 71,727, down from 71,794 in 1991 (mainly as a result of overseas migration). The population density in 2001 was 95·8 per sq. km.

In 1998, 70·3% of the population were urban. The chief town, Roseau, had 24,000 inhabitants in 1999.

The population is mainly of African and mixed origins, with small white and Asian minorities. There is a Carib settlement of about 500, almost entirely of mixed blood.

The official language is English, although 95% of the population speak a French Creole.

SOCIAL STATISTICS

Births, 1998, 1,230 (rate of 16·2 per 1,000 population); deaths, 595 (rate of 7·8); marriages, 336 (rate of 4·4); divorces, 71 (rate of 0·9). Life expectancy, 1996, 77·4 years; male 74·55, female 80·4. Annual population growth rate, 1990–96, 0·3%. Infant mortality rate, 1998, 17 per 1,000 live births.

CLIMATE

A tropical climate, with pleasant conditions between Dec. and March, but there is a rainy season from June to Oct., when hurricanes may occur. Rainfall is heavy, with coastal areas having 70" (1,750 mm) but the mountains may have up to 225" (6,250 mm). Roseau, Jan. 76°F (24·2°C), July 81°F (27·2°C). Annual rainfall 78" (1,956 mm).

CONSTITUTION AND GOVERNMENT

The head of state is the *President*, nominated by the Prime Minister and the Leader of the Opposition, and elected for a five-year term (renewable once) by the House of Assembly. The *House of Assembly* has 21 elected and nine members nominated by the President.

National Anthem. 'Isle of beauty, isle of splendour'; words by W. Pond, tune by L. M. Christian.

RECENT ELECTIONS

Elections were held on 31 Jan. 2000. The Dominica Labour Party (DLP) won 10 of the 21 available seats (5 in 1995), the United Workers Party (UWP) won 9 seats (11 in 1995) and the Dominica Freedom Party (DFP) 2 (5 in 1995). The DLP and DFP formed the government. It was the first time that the DLP had been in power for 20 years. Around 60,000 people were registered to vote.

CURRENT ADMINISTRATION

President: Vernon Shaw; b. 1930 (UWP; elected 6 Oct. 1998).

In March 2003 the cabinet comprised:

Prime Minister, Minister of Finance, Caribbean Affairs, and Labour: Pierre Charles; b. 1954 (DLP; sworn in 3 Oct. 2000).

Minister of Foreign Affairs: Osborne Riviere. *Communications, Works and Physical Planning:* Reginald Austrie. *Tourism, Industry and Enterprise Development:* Charles Savarin. *Health and Social Security:* John Toussaint. *Community Development and Gender Affairs:* Matthew Walter. *Agriculture, Fisheries and the Environment:* Vince Henderson. *Education, Youth and Sports:* Roosevelt Skerritt. *Legal Affairs:* David Bruney.

Government Website: http://www.government.dm/

INTERNATIONAL RELATIONS

Dominica is a member of the UN, WTO, the Commonwealth, OAS, ACS, CARICOM, OECS, the International Organization of the Francophonie and is an ACP member state of the ACP-EU relationship.

ECONOMY

Agriculture accounted for 20·2% of GDP in 1998, industry 22·5% and services 57·3%.

Currency. The *East Caribbean dollar* and the US dollar are legal tender. Foreign exchange reserves were US$34m. in May 2002 and total money supply was EC$113m. Inflation in 2001 was 1·8%.

Budget. Revenues for the fiscal year 1995–96 were US$77m. and expenditure US$78m.

Performance. Real GDP growth was 0·5% in 2000 and 1·0% in 2001. In 2001 total GDP was US$0·3bn.

Banking and Finance. The East Caribbean Central Bank based in St Kitts and Nevis functions as a central bank. The *Governor* is Sir Dwight Venner. In 1996 there were 4 foreign banks, 1 domestic bank, a development bank and a credit union.

ENERGY AND NATURAL RESOURCES

Environment. According to the *World Bank Atlas* carbon dioxide emissions in 1997 were the equivalent of 1·1 tonnes per capita.

Electricity. Installed capacity was 13,500 kW in 1995. Production in 1998 was 40m. kWh. Consumption per capita in 1997 was 535 kWh. There is a hydro-electric power station.

Agriculture. Agriculture employs 26% of the labour force. Production (2000, in 1,000 tonnes): bananas, 31; grapefruit and pomelos, 21; coconuts, 12; taro, 11; oranges, 8; plantains, 8; yams, 8. Livestock (2000): cattle, 13,000; goats, 10,000; sheep, 8,000; pigs, 5,000.

Forestry. In 1995 forests covered 46,000 ha, or 61·3% of the total land area.

Fisheries. In 1999 fish landings were estimated at 1,200 tonnes, exclusively from sea fishing.

INDUSTRY

Manufactures include soap (12,413 tonnes in 1995), clothing, shampoo, cream, footwear, mineral water, fruit juice, rum, electronic assemblies, candles and paint.

Labour. Around 25% of the economically active population are engaged in agriculture, fishing and forestry. In 1994 the minimum wage was US$0·75 an hour.

INTERNATIONAL TRADE

Total foreign debt was US$108m. in 2000.

Imports and Exports. In 1998 imports f.o.b. were worth US$98·81m. and exports f.o.b. US$62·25m. Main exports: bananas, soap, fruit juices, essential oils, coconuts, vegetables, fruit and fruit preparations, and alcoholic drinks. Main export markets, 1996: UK, 35·6%; Jamaica, 20·8%; USA, 7·3%; Antigua and Barbuda, 5·0%. Main imports: machine and transport equipment, basic manufactures, food, chemicals and chemical products. Main import suppliers, 1996: USA, 40·9%; UK, 13·0%; Trinidad and Tobago, 12·5%; Japan, 5·6%.

COMMUNICATIONS

Roads. In 1996 it was estimated there were 780 km of road, of which 393 km were paved. Approximately 7,000 passenger cars and 2,800 commercial vehicles were in use in 1994.

Civil Aviation. There are international airports at Melville Hall and Cane Field. In 1998 there were direct flights to Antigua, Barbados, Guadeloupe, Martinique, Puerto Rico, St Lucia, St Maarten and St Vincent.

Shipping. There are deep-water harbours at Roseau and Woodbridge Bay. Roseau has a cruise ship berth. In 1998 merchant shipping totalled 3,000 GRT. In 1998 vessels totalling 2,218,000 NRT entered ports.

Telecommunications. There were 22,700 telephone main lines in 2000, equivalent to 294·3 per 1,000 inhabitants, and the number of PCs in use totalled 6,000 (71·3 for every 1,000 persons). In 1995 approximately 300 fax machines were in use and in 1998 there were 700 mobile phone subscribers. Dominica had 2,000 Internet users in Dec. 1999.

Postal Services. In 1994 there were 131 post offices, or one for every 566 persons. Only Nauru, with 1 for every 406 persons in 1995, had an even better provision of post offices.

SOCIAL INSTITUTIONS

Justice. There is a supreme court and 12 magistrates courts. Law is based on UK common law as exercised by the Eastern Caribbean Supreme Court on St Lucia. Final appeal lies to the UK Privy Council.

The police force, numbering 439, has a residual responsibility for defence. The population in penal institutions in Dec. 1997 was 243 (equivalent to 330 per 100,000 of national population).

Religion. 77% of the population was Roman Catholic in 1995.

Education. In 1998 adult literacy was 94%. Education is free and compulsory between the ages of 5 and 15 years. In 1994–95 there were 64 primary schools with 641 teachers and 12,627 pupils, and 6,493 pupils in general secondary level education. In 1992–93 there were 484 students and 34 teachers at higher education institutions.

Health. In 1994 there were 54 hospitals and health centres with 312 beds, 23 doctors, 6 dentists, 27 pharmacists and 265 nursing personnel.

CULTURE

Broadcasting. Radio and television broadcasting is provided by the part government-controlled, part-commercial Dominica Broadcasting Corporation. There are also two religious radio networks, two commercial TV channels (colour by NTSC) and a commercial cable service. In 1997 there were 46,000 radio and 6,000 TV sets.

Cinema. There is one cinema with a seating capacity of 1,000.

Press. In 1994 there were three newspapers, including one government and one independent weekly.

Tourism. There were 66,000 foreign tourists in 1998, plus 239,000 cruise ship arrivals. Tourism receipts in 1998 totalled US$42m.

DIPLOMATIC REPRESENTATIVES

Of Dominica in the United Kingdom (1 Collingham Gdns., South Kensington, London, SW5 0HW)
Acting High Commissioner: Brian Richard Bellevue.

Of the United Kingdom in Dominica
High Commissioner: John White (resides at Bridgetown, Barbados).

Of Dominica in the USA (3216 New Mexico Ave., NW, Washington, D.C., 20016)
Ambassador: Vacant.

Of the USA in Dominica
Ambassador: Earl Norfleet Phillips, Jr (resides at Bridgetown).

Of Dominica to the United Nations
Ambassador: Crispin Gregoire.

Of Dominica to the European Union
Ambassador: Edwin Laurent.

FURTHER READING
Baker, P. L., *Centring the Periphery: Chaos, Order and the Ethnohistory of Dominica*. McGill-Queen's Univ. Press, 1994
Honychurch, L., *The Dominica Story: a History of the Island*. 2nd ed. London, 1995
Myers, R. A., *Dominica*. [Bibliography] ABC-Clio, Oxford and Santa Barbara (CA), 1987

National statistical office: Central Statistical Office, Kennedy Avenue, Roseau.

DOMINICAN REPUBLIC

República Dominicana

Capital: Santo Domingo
Population estimate, 2000: 8·37m.
GDP per capita, 2000: (PPP$) 6,033
HDI/world rank: 0·727/94

KEY HISTORICAL EVENTS

Columbus discovered the island of Santo Domingo, which he called La Isla Española, and which for a time was also known as Hispaniola. The city of Santo Domingo, founded by his brother, Bartholomew, in 1496, is the oldest city in the Americas. The western third of the island—now the Republic of Haiti—was later occupied and colonized by the French, to whom the Spanish colony of Santo Domingo was also ceded in 1795. In 1808 the Dominican population routed the French at the battle of Palo Hincado. Eventually, with the aid of a British naval squadron, the French were forced to return the colony to Spanish rule, from which it declared its independence in 1821. It was invaded and held by the Haitians from 1822 to 1844, when the Dominican Republic was founded and a constitution adopted.

Thereafter the rule was dictatorship interspersed with brief democratic interludes. Between 1916 and 1924 the country was under US military occupation. From 1930 until his assassination in 1961, Rafael Trujillo was one of Latin America's legendary dictators. The conservative pro-American Joaquin Balaguer was president from 1966 to 1978. In 1986 Balaguer returned to power at the head of the Socialist Christian Reform Party, leading the way to economic reforms. But there was violent opposition to spending cuts and general austerity. The 1996 elections brought in a reforming government pledged to act against corruption.

TERRITORY AND POPULATION

The Dominican Republic occupies the eastern portion (about two-thirds) of the island of Hispaniola, the western division forming the Republic of Haiti. The frontier with Haiti is closed. The area is 48,671 sq. km (18,800 sq. miles). The area and 1993 census populations of the 29 provinces and National District (Santo Domingo area) were:

	Area (in sq. km)	Population		Area (in sq. km)	Population
La Altagracia	3,010	115,685	Pedernales	2,077	18,054
Azua	2,532	199,684	Peravia	1,648	201,851
Bahoruco	1,283	105,206	Puerto Plata	1,857	261,485
Barahona	1,739	164,835	La Romana	654	166,550
Dajabón	1,021	68,606	Salcedo	440	101,810
Distrito Nacional			Samaná	854	75,253
(Santo Domingo area)	1,401	2,193,046	Sánchez Ramírez	1,196	163,166
Duarte	1,605	281,879	San Cristóbal	1,265	420,820
Elías Piña	1,424	64,461	San Juan	3,571	252,637
Espaillat	838	202,376	San Pedro de Macorís	1,255	212,368
Hato Mayor	1,329	80,074	Santiago	2,836	710,803
Independencia	2,008	39,541	Santiago Rodríguez	1,112	62,144
María Trinidad Sánchez	1,271	124,957	El Seíbo	1,786	96,770
Monseñor Nouel	992	149,318	Valverde	823	152,257
Monte Cristi	1,925	95,705	La Vega	2,286	344,721
Monte Plata	2,633	167,148			

Census population (1993), 7,293,390 (3,742,593 females). Estimate (1996), 8,088,900 (64·4% urban in 1999).

The UN gives a projected population for 2010 of 9·62m.

Population of the main towns (1991 estimate, in 1,000): Santo Domingo, the capital, 3,523 (1999); Santiago de los Caballeros, 1,289 (1995); La Vega, 189; San Francisco de Macorís, 162; San Pedro de Macorís, 137; La Romana, 136.

The population is mainly composed of a mixed race of European (Spanish) and African blood. The official language is Spanish; about 0·15m. persons speak a Haitian-French Creole.

SOCIAL STATISTICS

1996 births, 190,000; deaths, 46,000. Rates, 1996: birth, 23·5 (per 1,000 population); death, 5·7. Annual population growth rate, 1990–99, 1·8%. Life expectancy, 1999, 65·0 years for males and 70·0 for females. Infant mortality, 1999, 10·2 per 1,000 live births. Fertility rate, 1999, 2·7 children per woman.

CLIMATE

A tropical maritime climate with most rain falling in the summer months. The rainy season extends from May to Nov. and amounts are greatest in the north and east. Hurricanes may occur from June to Nov. Santo Domingo, Jan. 75°F (23·9°C), July 81°F (27·2°C). Annual rainfall 56" (1,400 mm).

CONSTITUTION AND GOVERNMENT

The constitution dates from 28 Nov. 1966. The *President* is elected for four years, by direct vote, and has executive power. A constitutional amendment of Aug. 1994 prohibits the president from serving consecutive terms. In 1994 the constitution was amended to allow for a second round of voting in a presidential election, when no candidate secures an absolute majority in the first ballot. There is a bicameral legislature, the *Congress*, comprising a 30-member Senate (one member for each province and one for the National District of Santo Domingo) and a 149-member *Chamber of Deputies*, both elected for four-year terms. Citizens are entitled to vote at the age of 18, or less when married.

National Anthem. 'Quisqueyanos valientes, alcemos' ('Valiant Quisqueyans, Let us raise our voices'); words by E. Prud'homme, tune by J. Reyes.

RECENT ELECTIONS

Presidential elections were held on 16 May 2000. Turn-out was 76·1%. The Partido Revolucionario Dominicana (Dominican Revolutionary Party/PRD) candidate, Hipólito Mejía, won 49·9% of the vote, the Partido de la Liberación Domincana (Dominican Liberation Party/PLD) candidate Danilo Medina 30·4% and the Partido Reformista Social Cristiano (Social Christian Reform Party/PRSC) candidate 92-year-old former president Joaquín Balaguer 24·6%. Medina withdrew from the run-off, paving the way for Mejía to take office.

Parliamentary elections were held on 16 May 2002. In the election to the Chamber of the Deputies the PRD won 73 seats, the PLD 41 and the PRSC 36. In the Senate elections on the same day, the PRD won 29 seats, the PLD 1 and the PRSC 1.

CURRENT ADMINISTRATION

President: Hipólito Mejía; b. 1941 (PRD; sworn in 16 Aug. 2000).

Vice-President and Secretary of State for Education, Fine Arts and Public Worship: Milagros Ortíz Bosch.

In March 2003 the government comprised:

Secretary of State for Agriculture: Eligio Jáquez. *Armed Forces:* José Miguel Jímenez Soto. *Culture:* Tony Raful. *Environment:* Frank Pons Moya. *Finance:* José Lois Malkun. *Foreign Relations:* Hugo Dipp Tolentino. *Industry and Commerce:* Sonia Guzman. *Interior and Police:* Pedro Franco Badia. *Labour:* Milton Guevara Ray. *Presidency:* Sergio Grullon. *Public Health:* José Soldevilla Rodríguez. *Public Works and Communications:* Miguel Vargas. *Sports, Physical Education and Recreation:* César Cedeño. *Tourism:* Rafael Suverbí Bonilla. *Women:* Yadira Henríquez. *Youth:* Antonio Peña Guaba.

Office of the President: http://www.presidencia.gov.do

DEFENCE

In 2000 defence expenditure totalled US$112m. (US$13 per capita), representing 0·8% of GDP.

Army. There are three defence zones. The Army has a strength (1999) of about 15,000 and includes a special forces unit and a Presidential Guard. There is a paramilitary National Police 15,000-strong.

Navy. The Navy is equipped with former US vessels. Personnel in 1999 totalled 4,000, based at Santo Domingo and Calderas.

Air Force. The Air Force, with HQ at San Isidoro, has 10 combat aircraft. Personnel strength (1999), 5,500.

INTERNATIONAL RELATIONS

The Dominican Republic is a member of the UN, WTO, OAS, Inter-American Development Bank, ACS, IOM and is an ACP member state of the ACP-EU relationship.

ECONOMY

In 1998 agriculture accounted for 11·6% of GDP, industry 32·8% and services 55·6%.

Overview. In Jan. 1995 subsidies to the 33 state companies were discontinued. 20 state companies were put up for sale in Nov. 1995.

Currency. The unit of currency is the *peso* (DOP) of 100 *centavos*. Gold reserves were 18,000 troy oz in June 2002 and foreign exchange reserves US$876m. Total money supply was RD$37,826m. in March 2002. Inflation was 8·9% in 2001.

Budget. Central government budgetary revenue and expenditure in RD$1m. for calendar years:

	1995	1996	1997	1998	1999
Revenue	26,096·6	27,945·0	36,646·3	40,520·1	45,535·5
Expenditure	24,984·1	28,653·1	35,864·3	39,419·0	47,234·2

Tax revenue in 1995 was RD$22,642·7m.; non-tax revenue, RD$2,079·6m.; capital revenue, RD$59·4m.

Performance. Real GDP growth was 2·8% in 2001, down from 7·2% in 2000. Total GDP in 2001 was US$21·2bn.

Banking and Finance. In 1947 the Central Bank was established (*Governor*, Francisco Guerrero Prats). Its total assets were RD$34,958·7m. in 1993. In 1993 there were 20 commercial banks (two foreign); total assets, RD$30,765·5m.

The Santo Domingo Securities Exchange is a member of the Association of Central American Stock Exchanges (Bolcen).

The Dominican Republic was one of 15 countries and territories named in a report in June 2000 as failing to co-operate in the fight against international money laundering. The Financial Action Task Force on Money Laundering was set up by the G7 group of major industrialized nations.

Weights and Measures. The metric system was adopted on 1 Aug. 1913, but English and Spanish units have remained in common use.

ENERGY AND NATURAL RESOURCES

Environment. According to the *World Bank Atlas* carbon dioxide emissions in 1998 were the equivalent of 2·5 tonnes per capita.

Electricity. Installed capacity was 2,450 MW in 1995. Production was 8·48bn. kWh in 1998; consumption per capita was 627 kWh.

Minerals. Bauxite output in 1988 was 167,800 tonnes, but had declined to nil by 1992. Output, 1998: nickel, 41,600 tonnes; gold (1997), 2,349 kg; silver (1997), 12 tonnes.

Agriculture. Agriculture and processing are the chief sources of income, sugar cultivation being the principal industry. In 1998 there were 1·02m. ha of arable land and 0·48m. ha of permanent cropland.

Production, 2000 (in 1,000 tonnes): sugarcane, 4,785; rice, 527; bananas, 422; plantains, 343; tomatoes, 286; mangoes, 180; coconuts, 173; oranges, 131; cassava, 125; avocados, 82; pineapples, 64.

DOMINICAN REPUBLIC

Livestock in 2000: 1·90m. cattle; 539,000 pigs; 330,000 horses; 170,000 goats; 46m. chickens. Livestock products, 2000 (in 1,000 tonnes): poultry meat, 254; beef and veal, 69; pork, bacon and ham, 61; eggs, 61; milk, 398.

Forestry. Forests and woodlands covered 1·58m. ha in 1995, representing 32·7% of the total land area (down from 1·71m. ha and 35·4% in 1990). In 1999, 562,000 tonnes of timber were cut.

Fisheries. The total catch in 1999 was 8,521 tonnes, mainly from sea fishing.

INDUSTRY
Production, 1998 (in tonnes): sugar, 516,184; cement (1997), 1,835,000; paint (1992), 16,328; beer (1995–96), 201m. litres; rum (1995–96), 395·6m. litres; cigarettes (1995–96), 201,800,000 packets (of 20).

Labour. In 1996 the labour force was 3,379,000 (71% males). Of the total workforce, 24·6% work in public administration, services and defence, 21·2% in trade and restaurants, 17·5% in manufacturing and 12·9% in agriculture.

INTERNATIONAL TRADE
In 1994 there were 38 industrial free zones (employing 164,296 persons), which enjoy duty-free imports of raw materials and various tax exemptions. Legislation of 1995 allows foreign investments of 100% in all sectors except industries affecting the environment and arms production. Profits may be repatriated. Foreign debt was US$4,598m. in 2000.

Imports and Exports. Total imports and exports in US$1m.:

	1996	1997	1998	1999	2000
Imports f.o.b.	5,727·0	6,608·7	7,597·3	8,041·1	9,478·5
Exports f.o.b.	4,052·8	4,613·7	4,980·5	5,136·7	5,736·7

Main exports, 1995: ferronickel, 31·6%; raw sugar, 13·3%; coffee, 10·6%; cocoa, 7·1%; gold, 5·4%. Main imports (in US$1m.): oil and products, 21·7%; agricultural products, 17·2%.

Main export markets (% of trade), 1995: USA, 47·6%; Netherlands, 14·1%; Puerto Rico, 6·5%; South Korea, 4·6%; Canada, 4·4%. Main import suppliers: USA, 44%; Venezuela, 11%; Mexico, 6%; Japan, 5%.

COMMUNICATIONS

Roads. The road network in 1996 totalled 12,600 km, of which 6,225 km were surfaced. In 1996 there were 224,000 passenger cars (29·8 per 1,000 inhabitants), 137,000 trucks and vans, and 14,550 buses and coaches.

Rail. In 1995 the total length was 757 km, comprising 375 km of the Central Romana Railroad, 142 km of the Dominican Republic Government Railway between Guayubin and the port of Pepillo, and 240 km operated by the sugar industry.

Civil Aviation. There are international airports at Santo Domingo (Las Americas), Puerto Plata, La Romana and Punta Cana. Dominican Airlines ceased operations in 1995 and was put up for privatization. Aerolíneas Santo Domingo and Air Atlantic Dominicana operate scheduled domestic and international services. In 2000 Santo Domingo was the busiest airport, handling 4,652,000 passengers, followed by Puerto Plata (estimated at 2,023,000 passengers) and Punta Cana (1,745,000).

Shipping. The main ports are Santo Domingo, Puerto Plata, La Romana and Haina. In 1998 the merchant marine totalled 9,000 GRT. In 1994 vessels totalling 10,821,000 net registered tons entered and vessels totalling 10,683,000 NRT cleared.

Telecommunications. In 2000 there were 894,200 telephone main lines in use (104·5 for every 1,000 inhabitants). Mobile phone subscribers numbered 255,900 in 1998 and there were 2,500 fax machines in 1995. The number of Internet users in April 1999 was 25,000.

Postal Services. In 1995 there were 215 post offices.

SOCIAL INSTITUTIONS

Justice. The judicial power resides in the Supreme Court of Justice, the courts of appeal, the courts of first instance, the communal courts and other tribunals created by special laws, such as the land courts. The Supreme Court, consisting of a president and eight judges chosen by the Senate, and the procurator-general, appointed by the executive, supervises the lower courts. Each province forms a judicial district, as does the National District, and each has its own procurator fiscal and court of first instance; these districts are subdivided, in all, into 97 municipalities, each with one or more local justices. The death penalty was abolished in 1924.

The population in penal institutions in June 1997 was 11,114 (135 per 100,000 of national population).

Religion. The religion of the state is Roman Catholic; there were 6·65m. adherents in 1999.

Education. Primary instruction is free and compulsory for children between seven and 14 years of age; there are also secondary, normal, vocational and special schools, all of which are either wholly maintained by the State or state-aided. In 1996–97 there were 1·36m. primary school pupils, and 313,840 pupils at secondary level. There are 4 universities, 3 Roman Catholic universities, 1 Adventist university, 3 technological universities and 1 Roman Catholic university college, and 5 other higher education institutions. Adult literacy was 83·2% in 1999 (83·2% among both males and females).

In 1997 expenditure on education came to 2·3% of GNP and 13·8% of total government spending.

Health. In 1992 there were 11,130 doctors, 1,898 dentists and 6,035 nurses. There were 723 government hospitals in 1992.

CULTURE

Broadcasting. There were (1994) more than 170 broadcasting stations in Santo Domingo and other towns; this includes the two government stations. There were seven television stations (colour by NTSC). In 1997 there were 1·44m. radio and 770,000 television receivers.

Press. In 1996 there were 12 dailies with a combined circulation of 416,000.

Tourism. There were 2,649,000 foreign tourists in 1999 (394,000 cruise ship arrivals in 1998). Tourism receipts in 1999 totalled US$2,524m. For some 15 years the Dominican Republic has been experiencing annual growth of 10% or more in both tourist arrivals and hotel capacity. In Dec. 1998 there were 41,600 hotel rooms (11,400 in 1987).

Festivals. The Festival Presidente de Música Latina, featuring musicians from all over Latin America, is held in June.

DIPLOMATIC REPRESENTATIVES

Of the Dominican Republic in the United Kingdom (139 Inverness Terrace, London, W2 6JF)
Ambassador: Rafael Ludovino Fernández.

Of the United Kingdom in the Dominican Republic (Edificio Corominas Pepin, Ave. 27 de Febrero 233, Santo Domingo)
Ambassador: Andy Ashcroft.

Of the Dominican Republic in the USA (1715 22nd St., NW, Washington, D.C., 20008)
Ambassador: Hugo Guiliani Cury.

Of the USA in the Dominican Republic (Calle Cesar Nicolas Penson, Santo Domingo)
Ambassador: Hans H. Hertell.

Of the Dominican Republic to the United Nations
Ambassador: Pedro L. Padilla R. Tonos.

Of the Dominican Republic to the European Union
Ambassador: Clara Quiñones.

FURTHER READING
Black, J. K., *The Dominican Republic: Politics and Development in an Unsovereign State.* London, 1986
Schoenhals, K., *Dominican Republic.* [Bibliography] ABC-Clio, Oxford and Santa Barbara (CA), 1990

National statistical office: Oficina Nacional de Estadística, Av. México esq. Leopoldo Navarro, Edificio Oficinas Gubernamentales 'Juan Pablo Duarte' Pisos 8 y 9 Gazcue, Santo Domingo.
Website (Spanish only): http://www.one.gov.do/

EAST TIMOR

República Democrática de
Timor-Leste
(Democratic Republic of
East Timor)

Capital: Dili
Population estimate, 2000: 983,000
GDP per capita: not available

KEY HISTORICAL EVENTS

Portugal abandoned its former colony, with its largely Roman Catholic population, in 1975, when it was occupied by Indonesia and claimed as the province of Timor Timur. The UN did not recognize Indonesian sovereignty over the territory. An independence movement, the Revolutionary Front for an Independent East Timor (FRETILIN), maintained a guerrilla resistance to the Indonesian government which resulted in large-scale casualties and alleged atrocities. On 24 July 1998 Indonesia announced a withdrawal of troops from East Timor and an amnesty for some political prisoners, although no indication was given of how many of the estimated 12,000 troops and police would pull out. On 5 Aug. Indonesia and Portugal reached agreement on the outlines of an autonomy plan which would give the Timorese the right to self-government except in foreign affairs and defence.

In a referendum on the future of East Timor held on 30 Aug. 1999 the electorate was some 450,000 and turn-out was nearly 99%. 78·5% of voters opted for independence, but pro-Indonesian militia gangs wreaked havoc both before and after the referendum. The militias accused the UN of rigging the poll. There was widespread violence in and around Dili, the provincial capital, with heavy loss of life, and thousands of people were forced to take to the hills after intimidation. East Timor's first democratic election took place on 30 Aug. 2001 in a ballot run by the UN, with FRETILIN winning 57% of the vote and 55 of the 88 seats in the new constituent assembly. East Timor became an independent country on 20 May 2002 but unrest continues.

TERRITORY AND POPULATION

East Timor has a total land area of 17,222 sq. km (6,649 sq. miles), consisting of the mainland (14,609 sq. km), the enclave of Oscússu-Ambeno in West Timor (2,461 sq. km), and the islands of Ataúro to the north (144 sq. km) and Jaco to the east (8 sq. km). The mainland area incorporates the eastern half of the island of Timor. Oscússu-Ambeno lies westwards, separated from the main portion of East Timor by a distance of some 100 km. The island is bound to the south by the Timor Sea and lies approximately 500 km from the Australian coast.

The UN population estimate for mainland East Timor in 1999 was 920,000; Oscússu-Ambeno has an estimated population of 55,000 and Ataúro an estimated population of 8,000. Population density for East Timor, 53 per sq. km.

The largest city is Dili, East Timor's capital. In 1999 its population was an estimated 180,000.

The ethnic East Timorese form the majority of the population. Non-East Timorese, comprising Portuguese and West Timorese as well as persons from Sumatra, Java, Sulawesi and other parts of Indonesia, are estimated to constitute approximately 20% of the total population.

During Indonesian occupation the official language was Bahasa Indonesia. East Timor's new constitution designates Portuguese and Tetum (the region's *lingua franca*) as the official languages, and English and Bahasa Indonesia as working languages.

Dili: East Timor's capital is located on the north coast of the island on the Ombai Strait. Historically it is the chief port and commercial centre of East Timor although much of the city was burnt to the ground during the violence ensuing from the 1999 referendum.

SOCIAL STATISTICS

Based on UN figures for the period 1995–2000: birth rate, 32 per 1,000; death rate, 15 per 1,000; fertility rate, 4·3 births per woman; annual population growth rate, 1·7%; life expectancy at birth, 48 years.

From having the world's highest rate of infant mortality in the early 1980s, East Timor's infant mortality rate has dropped to around 60 per 1,000 live births in 1999, although the figure varies widely between urban and rural areas.

CLIMATE

In the north there is an average annual temperature of over 24°C (75°F), weak precipitation—below 1,500 mm (59") annually—and a dry period lasting five months. The mountainous zone, between the northern and southern parts of the island, has high precipitation—above 1,500 mm (59")—and a dry period of four months. The southern zone has precipitation reaching 2,000 mm (79") and is permanently humid. The monsoon season extends from Nov. to May.

CONSTITUTION AND GOVERNMENT

The 88-seat *Constituent Assembly* is formed from a national and district assembly, which have 75 and 13 seats respectively. The *President*, who is elected for a period of five years, is appointed by the *Constituent Assembly*.

National Anthem. 'Eh! Foho Ramelau, Foho Ramelau !' ('Hey, Mount Ramelau, Mount Ramelau!'); words by F. Borja da Costa, tune by A. Araujo.

RECENT ELECTIONS

Presidential elections were held on 14 April 2002. Former separatist guerrilla leader Xanana Gusmão (FRETILIN) won a landslide victory with 82·6% of votes cast against 17·3% for Xavier do Amaral, his single rival. Turn-out was 86%. Amaral, who served as president of East Timor for nine days in 1975, in the short period between Portuguese withdrawal and Indonesian occupation, declared that his intention to run for the presidency was solely to provide the electorate with a choice of candidates.

Elections to the 75-member national assembly took place on 30 Aug. 2001, the anniversary of the referendum for independence two years earlier. The Frente Revolucionária do Timor Leste Independente (FRETILIN; Revolutionary Front for an Independent East Timor) won 57·37% of the vote and took 43 seats with 208,531 votes. The Partido Democrático (PD; Democratic Party) won 8·72% of votes cast and 7 seats; the Partido Social Democrata (PSD; Social Democratic Party) won 8·18% and 6 seats; the Associação Social-Democrata Timorense (ASDT) 7·84% and 6 seats; the União Democrática Timorense (UDT) 2·36% and 2 seats; the Partido do Povo de Timor (PPT) 2·01% and 2 seats. Other parties won less than 2% of the vote. In elections to the district assembly, held on the same day, FRETILIN secured 12 of the 13 seats, giving them a total of 55 seats in the 88-seat constituent assembly. Turn-out for the elections was 91·3%. 23 of the seats went to women.

CURRENT ADMINISTRATION

President: Xanana Gusmão; b. 1946 (ind.; sworn in 20 May 2002).

In March 2003 the government was comprised as follows:

Prime Minister and Minister for Development and the Environment: Marí Bim Amude Alkatiri (FRETILIN).

Deputy Prime Minister: Ana Maria Pessoa Pereira da Silva Pinto.

Minister for Foreign Affairs and Co-operation: José Ramos Horta. *Justice:* Domingos Maria Sarmento. *Finance:* Madalena Brites Boavida. *Internal Administration:* Rogerio Tiago Lobato. *Health:* Rui Maria de Araujo. *Education, Culture and Youth:* Armindo Maia. *Agriculture and Fisheries:* Estanislau Aleixo da Silva. *Transportation, Communications and General Employment:* Ovidio Amaral.

UN Transitional Administration: http://www.un.org/peace/etimor/etimor.htm

INTERNATIONAL RELATIONS

East Timor is a member of the UN, the IMF and the Asian Development Bank.

ECONOMY

Currency. The official currency is the US dollar. The Australian dollar and the Indonesian rupiah, both previously used, no longer serve as legal tender.

ENERGY AND NATURAL RESOURCES

Electricity. In 1996 only a quarter of households in East Timor had electricity.

Oil and Gas. Although current production is small, the Timor Gap, an area of offshore territory between East Timor and Australia, is one of the richest oil fields in the world outside the Middle East. Potential revenue from the area is estimated at US$11bn. The area is split into three zones with a central 'zone of occupation' (occupying 61,000 sq. km). Royalties on oil discovered within the central zone were split equally between Indonesia and Australia following the Timor Gap Treaty which came into force on 9 Feb. 1991. Questions over East Timor's rights to oil revenue from the area have arisen following the 1999 independence referendum.

Minerals. Gold, iron sands, copper and chromium are present.

Agriculture. Although the presence of sandalwood was one of the principal reasons behind Portuguese colonization, its production has declined in recent years. Coffee is grown extensively.

Fisheries. The total fish catch in 1999 was estimated at 513 tonnes.

INDUSTRY

Labour. In 2000 the unemployment rate exceeded 80% of the labour force.

INTERNATIONAL TRADE

Imports and Exports. All basic goods such as rice, sugar and flour are imported. Coffee and cattle are important exports.

COMMUNICATIONS

Civil Aviation. There is an international airport at Dili.

SOCIAL INSTITUTIONS

Religion. Over 90% of East Timor's population are Roman Catholic, with Protestants, Muslims, Hindus and Buddhists accounting for the remainder.

DIPLOMATIC REPRESENTATIVES

Of the United Kingdom in East Timor (Pantai Kelapa, PO Box 194, The Post Office, Dili)
Ambassador: Hamish Daniel.

Of the USA in East Timor (Avenido do Portugal, Farol, Dili)
Ambassador: Grover Joseph Rees III.

Of East Timor to the United Nations
Ambassador: José Luis Guterres.

FURTHER READING

Carey, P. and Bentley, G. C. (eds.) *East Timor at the Crossroads: the Forging of a Nation.* London, 1995

Kohen, Arnold S., *From the Place of the Dead: Bishop Belo and the Struggle for East Timor.* Lion, Oxford, 2000

Rowland, Ian, *Timor.* [Bibliography] ABC-Clio, Oxford and Santa Barbara (CA), 1992

ECUADOR

República del Ecuador

Capital: Quito
Population estimate, 2000: 12·65m.
GDP per capita, 2000: (PPP$) 3,203
HDI/world rank: 0·732/93

KEY HISTORICAL EVENTS

In 1532 the Spaniards founded a colony in Ecuador, then called Quito. In 1821 a revolt led to the defeat of the Spaniards at Pichincha and thus independence from Spain. On 13 March 1830, Quito became the Republic of Ecuador. Political instability was endemic. From the mid-1930s, President José Maria Velasco Ibarra gave more continuity to the presidential regimes, although he was deposed by military coups from four of his five presidencies.

From 1963 to 1966 and from 1976 to 1979 military juntas ruled the country. The second of these juntas produced a new constitution which came into force on 10 Aug. 1979. Since then presidencies have been more stable but civil unrest continued in the wake of economic reforms and attempts to combat political corruption.

In Jan. 2000 President Mahaud declared a state of emergency as protesters demanded his resignation over his handling of the country's economic crisis. There was a coup on 21 Jan., but after five hours in control the military junta handed power to the former vice-president, Gustavo Noboa.

TERRITORY AND POPULATION

Ecuador is bounded in the north by Colombia, in the east and south by Peru and in the west by the Pacific ocean. The frontier with Peru has long been a source of dispute. It was delimited in the Treaty of Rio, 29 Jan. 1942, when, after being invaded by Peru, Ecuador lost over half her Amazonian territories. Ecuador unilaterally denounced this treaty in Sept. 1961. Fighting between Peru and Ecuador began again in Jan. 1981 over this border issue but a ceasefire was agreed in early Feb. Following a confrontation of soldiers in Aug. 1991 the foreign ministers of both countries signed a pact creating a security zone, and took their cases to the UN in Oct. 1991. On 26 Jan. 1995 further armed clashes broke out with Peruvian forces in the undemarcated mutual border area ('Cordillera del Cóndor'). On 2 Feb. talks were held under the auspices of the guarantor nations of the 1942 Protocol of Rio de Janeiro (Argentina, Brazil, Chile and the USA), but fighting continued. A ceasefire was agreed on 17 Feb., which was broken, and again on 28 Feb. On 25 July 1995 an agreement between Ecuador and Peru established a demilitarized zone along their joint frontier. The frontier was re-opened on 4 Sept. 1995. Since 23 Feb. 1996 Ecuador and Peru have signed three further agreements to regulate the dispute. The dispute was settled in Oct. 1998. Confirming the Peruvian claim that the border lies along the high peaks of the Cóndor, Ecuador gained navigation rights on the Amazon within Peru.

No definite figure of the area of the country can yet be given. One estimate of the area of Ecuador is 275,830·0 sq. km, excluding the litigation zone between Peru and Ecuador, which is 190,807 sq. km, but including the **Galápagos** Archipelago (8,010 sq. km), situated in the Pacific ocean about 960 km west of Ecuador, and comprising 13 islands and 19 islets. These were discovered in 1535 by Fray Tomás de Berlanga and had a population of 10,207 in 1996. They constitute a national park, and had about 80,000 visitors in 1995.

The population is an amalgam of European, Amerindian and African origins. Some 40% of the population is Amerindian: Quechua, Swiwiar, Achuar and Zaparo. In May 1992 they were granted title to the 1m. ha of land they occupy in Pastaza.

The official language is Spanish. Quechua and other languages are also spoken.

Census population in 1990, 9,648,189. Estimate, 1996, 11,698,400; density, 42 per sq. km.

The UN gives a projected population for 2010 of 14·90m.

In 1999, 64·3% lived in urban areas.

The population was distributed by provinces as follows in 1996:

Province	Sq. km	Population	Capital	Population[2]
Azuay	8,124·7	529,177	Cuenca	194,981
Bolívar	3,939·9	166,957	Guaranda	15,730
Cañar	3,122·1	194,529	Azogues	21,060
Carchi	3,605·1	146,343	Tulcán	37,069
Chimborazo	6,569·3	378,111	Riobamba	94,505
Cotopaxi	6,071·9	289,774	Latacunga	39,882
El Oro	5,850·1	441,025	Machala	144,197
Esmeraldas	15,239·1	327,931	Esmeraldas	98,558
Guayas	20,502·5	2,689,745	Guayaquil	2,205,000
Imbabura	4,559·3	286,155	Ibarra	80,991
Loja	11,026·5	392,877	Loja	94,305
Los Ríos	7,175·0	553,479	Babahoyo	50,285
Manabí	18,878·8	1,076,966	Portoviejo	132,937
Morona-Santiago	25,690·0	104,737	Macas	8,246
Napo	33,930·9	114,380	Tena	7,873
Orellana[1]	...	...	Francisco de Orellana	...
Pastaza	29,773·7	46,095	Puyo	14,438
Pichincha	12,914·7	1,893,744	Quito	1,376,000
Sucumbíos	18,327·5	90,222	Nueva Loja	13,165
Tungurahua	3,334·8	383,460	Ambato	124,166
Zamora-Chinchipe	23,110·8	73,383	Zamora	8,048
Galápagos	8,010·0	10,207	Puerto Baquerizo Moreno	3,023
Non-delimited zones	2,288·8	74,842		

[1]Split off from Napo in 1998. [2]1990 census population, except Guayaquil (1999 figure) and Quito (1995 figure).

SOCIAL STATISTICS
1995: births, 408,983; deaths, 50,867; marriages, 70,480. Rates, 1995 (per 1,000 population): birth, 35·7; death, 4·4; marriage, 6·2. Life expectancy at birth, 1999, was 67·6 years for males and 72·8 years for females. Annual population growth rate, 1990–99, 2·1%. Infant mortality, 1999, 24·6 per 1,000 live births; fertility rate, 1999, 3·0 children per woman. In 1998 the most popular age for marrying was 20–24 for both men and women.

CLIMATE
The climate varies from equatorial, through warm temperate to mountain conditions, according to altitude, which affects temperatures and rainfall. In coastal areas, the dry season is from May to Dec., but only from June to Sept. in mountainous parts, where temperatures may be 20°F colder than on the coast. Quito, Jan. 59°F (15°C), July 58°F (14·4°C). Annual rainfall 44" (1,115 mm). Guayaquil, Jan. 79°F (26·1°C), July 75°F (23·9°C). Annual rainfall 39" (986 mm).

CONSTITUTION AND GOVERNMENT
A new constitution came into force on 10 Aug. 1998. It provides for an executive president and a vice-president to be directly elected by universal suffrage. The president appoints and leads a *Council of Ministers*, and determines the number and functions of the ministries that comprise the executive branch. The new constitution strengthened the executive branch by eliminating mid-term congressional elections and by restricting congress' power to challenge and remove cabinet ministers.

Legislative power is vested in a 125-member *National Congress*, 105 members in two- or multi-seat constituencies and 20 members elected at large by proportional representation. Voting is obligatory for all literate citizens of 18–65 years.

National Anthem. 'Salve, Oh Patria, mil veces, Oh Patria' ('Hail, Oh Fatherland, a thousand times, Oh Fatherland'); words by J. L. Mera, tune by A. Neumane.

RECENT ELECTIONS
Dissatisfaction with President Fabián Alarcón led to presidential elections in 1998. Jamil Mahuad, candidate of the centre-right Popular Democracy party (DP), won in the second round of the presidential election on 12 July 1998, with 51·3% of the votes, against 48·7% for Alvaro Noboa, a populist businessman. In the first round on 31 May he had defeated five other candidates to win 35·3% of the vote. After a

coup in Jan. 2000 Noboa (who was elected vice-president) replaced Jamil Mahuad as president. In the first round of presidential elections held on 20 Oct. 2002 Col. Lucio Gutiérrez (the instigator of the coup) won 20·3% of the vote, against 17·4% for Alvaro Noboa. In the run-off held on 24 Nov. 2002 Gutiérrez won 54·3% against 45·7% for Noboa.

In *National Congress* elections on 31 May 1998 the People's Democracy–Christian Democrat Union (DP–UDC) won 35 seats, the Social Christian Party (PSC) 26, Ecuadorian Roldosist Party (PRE) 25, the Party of the Democratic Left (ID) 17 and Pluri–National Pachakutik Movement–New Country (MUPP–NP) 6. No other party won more than three seats.

Elections to the 70-member *Constitutional Assembly* (members of the *National Congress*) were held on 30 Nov. 1997. The Social Christian Party won 20 seats and the People's Democracy–Christian Democrat Union 10 seats, with the remaining 40 seats going to 15 other parties.

CURRENT ADMINISTRATION
President: Col. Lucio Gutiérrez; b. 1957 (sworn in on 15 Jan. 2003, having previously been in power as one of the leaders of the coup that deposed democratically-elected president Jamil Mahuad on 21 Jan. 2000 only to be forced to stand down less than a day later).

Vice-President: Alfredo Palacio.

In March 2003 the cabinet comprised:

Minister of Agriculture and Livestock: Luis Macas. *Defence:* Nelson Herrera. *Economy:* Mauricio Pozo. *Education:* Rosa María Torres. *Energy and Mines:* Carlos Arboleda. *Environment:* Edgar Isch. *Foreign Relations:* Nina Pacari. *Foreign Trade:* Ivonne A-Baki. *Government:* Mario Canessa. *Housing:* Nelson Alvarez. *Labour:* Felipe Mantilla. *Public Health:* Francisco Andino. *Public Works:* Estuardo Peñaherrera. *Social Welfare:* Patricio Ortiz. *Tourism:* Doris Solís.

Office of the President: http://www.presidencia.gov.ec

DEFENCE
Military service is selective, with a one-year period of conscription. The country is divided into four military zones, with headquarters at Quito, Guayaquil, Cuenca and Pastaza.

In 2000 defence expenditure totalled US$314m. (US$25 per capita), representing 1·6% of GDP.

Army. Strength (1999) 50,000, with about 100,000 reservists.

Navy. Navy combatant forces include two diesel submarines and two ex-UK frigates. The Maritime Air Force has 11 aircraft but no combat aircraft. Naval personnel in 1999 totalled 3,000 including some 1,500 marines.

Air Force. The Air Force had a 1999 strength of about 3,000 personnel and 78 combat aircraft, and includes Jaguars, Mirage F-1s and Kfirs.

INTERNATIONAL RELATIONS
Ecuador is a member of the UN, WTO, OAS, Inter-American Development Bank the Andean Group, LAIA, IOM and the Antarctic Treaty.

ECONOMY
Agriculture accounted for 12·9% of GDP in 1998, industry 35·2% and services 50·2%.

Overview. A reform programme was announced in 1992, including the privatization of 20 state-owned enterprises. A new economic plan was promulgated in Nov. 1996, envisaging privatization of the oil and electricity sectors, but in 1998 privatization was put on hold as the sale of 35% of state telecommunications companies was suspended in April 1998 owing to a lack of serious bidders. Congress approved the Economic Transformation Law on 1 March 2000 to introduce flexibility into the labour market and encourage further private investment in the oil, electrical and telecommunications sectors.

Currency. The monetary unit is the US dollar. Inflation was 96·2% in 2000 but was brought down to 37·7% in 2001. In March 2000 the government passed a law to phase out the former national currency, the *sucre*, to be replaced by the US dollar, and in April bank cash machines began dispensing dollars instead of sucres. On 11 Sept. 2000 the dollar became the only legal currency. Foreign exchange reserves were US$880m. in June 2002 and gold reserves 845,000 troy oz.

Budget. Total revenue and total expenditure from 1991 to 1995 (in 1bn. sucres) was as follows:

	1991	1992	1993	1994	1995
Revenue	1,907	3,096	4,371	5,374	8,030
Expenditure	1,739	3,145	4,166	5,717	8,451

The budget deficit in 1998 was nearly 6% of GDP.

In 2000 VAT was increased from 10% to 12% and corporate tax from 15% to 25%.

Performance. Real GDP growth was negative in 1999, at −7·3%, partly owing to years of mismanagement and partly to El Niño. There was a recovery in 2000, however, with the growth rate reaching 2·3%. In 2001 growth was 5·4%, the highest in Latin America. Total GDP in 2001 was US$18·0bn.

Banking and Finance. The Central Bank of Ecuador (*President of the Directorate*, Mauricio Yépez Najas), the bank of issue, with a capital and reserves of US$1,557m. at 31 Dec. 1995, is modelled after the Federal Reserve Banks of the USA; through branches opened in 16 towns, it now deals in mortgage bonds. All commercial banks must be affiliated to the Central Bank. Legislation of May 1994 liberalized the financial sector.

There are stock exchanges in Quito and Guayaquil.

Weights and Measures. The metric system is the legal standard but English and old Spanish measures are still in use. A case (*caja*) of bananas = 18·14 kg.

ENERGY AND NATURAL RESOURCES

Environment. According to the *World Bank Atlas* Ecuador's carbon dioxide emissions were the equivalent of 2·2 tonnes per capita in 1998.

Electricity. Installed capacity was 2·75m. kW in 1996. Production was 9·66bn. kWh in 1998; consumption per capita was 625 kWh.

Oil and Gas. Production of crude oil in 1996 was 141m. bbls. Estimated reserves, 1999, 2,100m. bbls. In 1996 natural gas production was 45 petajoules.

Minerals. Main products are silver, gold, copper and zinc. The country also has some iron, uranium, lead, coal, cobalt, manganese and titanium.

Agriculture. There were 1·57m. ha of arable land in 1998 and 1·43m. ha of permanent crops. In 1995, 28·8% of the economically active population worked in agriculture.

50,000 ha of rich virgin land in the Santo Domingo de los Colorados area has been set aside for settlement by medium and large landowners. A law of 1994 restricts the redistribution of land to small farmers to land which has lain fallow for more than three years.

The staple export products are bananas and coffee. Main crops, in 1,000 tonnes, in 2000: bananas, 6,816; sugarcane, 6,200; rice, 1,520; potatoes, 788; maize, 747; plantains, 476; palm oil, 268; cassava, 184; soybeans, 170; oranges, 157; coffee, 133. Ecuador's annual banana crop is exceeded only by that of India.

Livestock, 2000: cattle, 5·11m.; sheep, 2·13m.; pigs, 2·87m.; horses, 521,000; goats, 284,000; asses, 269,000; chickens, 130m.

Forestry. Excepting the agricultural zones and a few arid spots on the Pacific coast, Ecuador is a vast forest. 11·13m. ha, or 40·2% of the land area, was forested in 1995, but much of the forest is not commercially accessible. In 1990, 12·08m. ha and 43·6% of the land area had been under forests. In 1999, 11·34m. cu. metres of roundwood were produced.

Fisheries. In 1993 primary sea export products were valued at US$498·9m. Fish landings in 1999 were 497,872 tonnes (almost entirely from sea fishing).

INDUSTRY

Manufacturing showed an annual average increase of 3·2% from 1991 to 1996, accounting for around 15·4% of GDP in 1997. Service industries accounted for 46·1% of GDP in 1996. Main products include (1997, in 1,000 tonnes): residual fuel oil, 3,728; cement, 2,688; distillate fuel oil, 1,912; petrol, 1,324.

Labour. Out of 2,697,000 people in urban employment in 1997, 983,200 were in community, social and personal services, 870,900 in trade, restaurants and hotels, and 475,300 in manufacturing industries. In June 2001, 10·4% of the workforce was unemployed, down from 14·1% in June 2000.

Trade Unions. The main trade union federation is the United Workers' Front.

INTERNATIONAL TRADE

Most restrictions on foreign investment were removed in 1992 and the repatriation of profits was permitted. Foreign debt was US$13,281m. in 2000.

Imports and Exports. Imports and exports for calendar years, in US$1m.:

	1995	1996	1997	1998	1999
Imports f.o.b.	4,057	3,680	4,666	5,198	2,786
Exports f.o.b.	4,381	4,873	5,264	4,203	4,451

Ecuador is the world's leading exporter of bananas (US$845m. in 1995). Other major exports (1995, in US$1m.): shrimps, 673; coffee beans, 244; cocoa beans and products, 133; cut flowers, 79. Main export markets, 1995 (in US$1m.): USA, 1,847 (42%); Colombia, 246; Chile, 193; Germany, 166; Spain, 149. Main import suppliers: USA, 1,290 (32%); Colombia, 396; Japan, 328; Germany, 192; Brazil, 187.

COMMUNICATIONS

Roads. In 1998 there were estimated to be 43,197 km of roads. A trunk highway through the coastal plain, currently under construction, will link Machala in the extreme southwest with Esmeraldas in the northwest, and with Quito and the northern section of the Pan-American Highway. In 1997 there were 483,900 passenger cars (40·5 per 1,000 inhabitants) and 41,330 lorries and vans. There were 1,258 fatalities in road accidents in 1997.

In 1998 storms and floods on the coast, caused by El Niño, resulted in 2,000 km of roads being damaged or destroyed.

Rail. The railway was closed in 1995.

Civil Aviation. There are international airports at Quito (Mariscal Sucre) and Guayaquil (Simon Bolivar). The national carriers are Tame Linea Aerea del Ecuador (955,200 passengers in 1999), SAETA (274,500 passengers in 1999) and Ecuatoriana (157,000 passengers in 1999). In 2000 Quito handled 1,953,859 passengers (1,036,578 on domestic flights) and 111,867 tonnes of freight, and Guayaquil handled 1,285,583 passengers (686,964 on domestic flights) and 38,471 tonnes of freight.

Shipping. Ecuador has three major seaports, of which Guayaquil is the most important, and six minor ones. In 1998 the merchant navy totalled 171,000 GRT of ocean-going vessels, including oil tankers 93,000 GRT. In 1997 vessels totalling 3,263,000 NRT entered ports and vessels totalling 18,277,000 NRT cleared.

Telecommunications. In 2000 there were 1,265,200 main telephone lines, equivalent to 100·0 for every 1,000 persons, and 275,000 PCs were in use (21·7 for every 1,000 persons). Mobile phone subscribers numbered 383,200 in 1999 and there were 30,000 fax machines in 1995. Ecuador had approximately 180,000 Internet users in Dec. 2000.

Postal Services. In 1995 there were 267 post offices.

SOCIAL INSTITUTIONS

Justice. The Supreme Court in Quito, consisting of a President and 30 Justices, comprises six chambers each of five Justices. It is also a Court of Appeal. There is a Superior Court in each province, comprising chambers (as appointed by the Supreme Court) of three magistrates each. The Superior Courts are at the apex of a hierarchy of various tribunals. There is no death penalty.

The population in penal institutions in Dec. 1996 was 9,961 (85 per 100,000 of national population).

Religion. The state recognizes no religion and grants freedom of worship to all. In 1997 there were 11·04m. Roman Catholics and 0·9m. followers of other faiths.

Education. In 1997–98 there were 167,582 pre-primary pupils with 10,992 teachers. Primary education is free and compulsory. Private schools, both primary and secondary, are under some state supervision. In 1996–97 there were 17,367 primary schools with 1·88m. pupils; and, in 1995, 2,965 secondary schools. In the public sector in 1995–96 there were: 9 universities, 3 Roman Catholic, 12 technical, 1 agricultural and 2 polytechnical universities, 2 institutes of technology and 1 military polytechnic; and in the private sector: 2 universities, 1 Roman Catholic and 1 technological university. Adult literacy was 91·0% in 1999 (male, 92·8%; female, 89·1%).

Health. In 1993 there were 12,149 doctors and 433 hospitals, 1,542 dentists and 906 pharmacists.

CULTURE

Broadcasting. There were 4·15m. radio sets and 1·55m. TV receivers in 1997 (colour by NTSC).

Press. There were 29 daily newspapers in 1996, with a circulation of 820,000.

Tourism. Foreign tourists numbered 509,000 in 1999, with spending of US$343m.

DIPLOMATIC REPRESENTATIVES

Of Ecuador in the United Kingdom (Flat 3b, 3 Hans Cres., London, SW1X 0LS)
Ambassador: Vacant.
Chargé d'Affaires a.i.: Ricardo Falconi-Puig.

Of the United Kingdom in Ecuador (Citiplaza Bldg., Naciones Unidas Ave., & Republica de El Salvador, 14th Floor, Quito)
Ambassador: Ian Gerken, LVO.

Of Ecuador in the USA (2535 15th St., NW, Washington, D.C., 20009)
Ambassador: Carlos A. Jativa.

Of the USA in Ecuador (Avenida 12 de Octubre y Avenida Patria, Quito)
Ambassador: Kristie A. Kenney.

Of Ecuador to the United Nations
Ambassador: Luis Gallegos Chiriboga.

Of Ecuador to the European Union
Ambassador: Méntor Villagomez Merino.

FURTHER READING
Hidrobo, J. A., *Power and Industrialization in Ecuador.* Boulder (CO), 1993
Pineo, R. F., *Social and Economic Reform in Ecuador.* Univ. Press of Florida, 1996
Roos, W. and van Renterghem, O., *Ecuador in Focus: A Guide to the People, Politics and Culture.* Interlink Publishing Group, Northanpton (MA), 1997
Selverston-Scher, M., *Ethnopolitics in Ecuador: Indigenous Rights and the Strengthening of Democracy.* Lynne Rienner Publishers, 2001

National statistical office: Instituto Nacional de Estadistica y Censos (INEC), Juan Larrea 534 y Riofrío, Quito.
Website (Spanish only): http://www.inec.gov.ec/

EGYPT

Jumhuriyat Misr al-Arabiya
(Arab Republic of Egypt)

Capital: Cairo
Population estimate, 2000: 67·88m.
GDP per capita, 2000: (PPP$) 3,635
HDI/world rank: 0·642/115

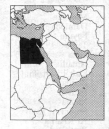

KEY HISTORICAL EVENTS

There is evidence of Neolithic habitation along the Nile and there was agricultural activity by 6000 BC. Around 3100 BC Menes united Upper and Lower Egypt and so began the rule of 31 successive pharaonic dynasties. This period may be divided into three broad phases. The Old Kingdom, which lasted from c. 2575–2150 BC, was governed centrally from Memphis and saw the construction of the Giza pyramids. The Middle Kingdom (c. 2050–1650 BC) saw Egypt reach its zenith culturally and intellectually. The era finished with the incursions of the Hyksos, a nomadic Asiatic tribe. The New Kingdom came into being with the expulsion of the Hyksos around 1550 BC and lasted until 1050 BC. It saw Egypt achieve its greatest territorial dominance, with Syria, Palestine and northern Iraq all under Egyptian jurisdiction.

The last Pharaoh was ousted by Persian invading forces under Cambyses in 525 BC. The Persians remained in power until overrun by Alexander the Great around 330 BC. He founded the port city of Alexandria, including its great lighthouse, and made it the commercial and cultural centre of the Greek world. On his death in 305 BC, Ptolemy of Macedonia seized power, establishing a dynasty which lasted until 30 BC and the suicide of Cleopatra. Egypt then became a province of the Roman empire until Islamic forces took control in AD 642.

Under the successive rule of Turkish, Arabic and Mameluke leaders, Egypt gained an increasingly Arabic Islamic culture. In 1517 it was absorbed into the Ottoman empire. Napoleonic forces seized the country between 1798 and 1801, but were forced to flee by a combined Anglo-Ottoman force. Muhammad Ali (1805–40) succeeded in establishing a hereditary dynasty of Khedives but with the opening of the Suez Canal in 1869 and Britain's purchase of the Khedives' shares, Egypt's strategic importance paved the way for foreign intervention and domination.

In the Second World War (1939–45) Egypt supported the Allies. Following a revolution in July 1952 led by Gen. Neguib, King Farouk abdicated in favour of his son but in 1953 the monarchy was abolished. Neguib became president but encountered opposition from the military when he attempted to move towards a parliamentary republic. Col. Gamal Abdel Nasser became head of state on 14 June 1954 (president from 1956), and remained in office until he died on 28 Sept. 1970. In 1956 Egypt nationalized the Suez Canal, a move which led Britain, France and Israel to mount military attacks against Egypt until forced by the UN and the USA to withdraw.

The 1960s and 1970s saw constant conflict with Israel until President Muhammad Anwar Sadat, who succeeded Nasser, made a dramatic peace treaty with Israel in March 1979. Sadat was assassinated on 6 Oct. 1981, and was succeeded by the vice-president, Lieut.-Gen. Muhammad Hosni Mubarak.

TERRITORY AND POPULATION

Egypt is bounded in the east by Israel and Palestine, the Gulf of Aqaba and the Red Sea, south by Sudan, west by Libya and north by the Mediterranean. The total area is 997,739 sq. km, but the cultivated and settled area, that is the Nile Valley, Delta and oases, covers only 35,189 sq. km. A number of new desert cities are being developed to entice people away from the overcrowded Nile valley. Population density in this latter, 1992, 1,557·9 per sq. km. In 1999, 55% of the population were rural. In 1997 the population was 61,404,000.

The UN gives a projected population for 2010 of 79·26m.

2·3m. Egyptians were living abroad in 1997.

Area, population and capitals of the governorates (1986 and 1996 censuses):

Governorate	Area (in sq. km)	Population (1986 census)	(1996 census)	Capital
Alexandria	2,679·36	2,917,327	3,328,196	Alexandria
Aswan	678·50	801,408	973,671	Aswan
Asyut	1,553·00	2,223,034	2,802,185	Asyut
Behera	10,129·49	3,257,168	3,981,209	Damanhur
Beni Suef	1,321·65	1,442,981	1,860,180	Beni Suef
Cairo	214·20	6,052,836	6,789,497	Cairo
Dakahlia	3,470·90	3,500,470	4,223,665	Mansura
Damietta	589·17	741,264	914,614	Damietta
Fayum	1,827·15	1,544,047	1,989,881	Fayum
Gharbia	1,942·21	2,870,960	3,404,827	Tanta
Giza	85,153·20	3,700,054	4,779,865	Giza
Ismailia	1,441·59	544,427	715,009	Ismailia
Kafr El Shaikh	3,437·12	1,800,129	2,222,920	Kafr El Shaikh
Kalyubia	1,001·09	2,514,244	3,302,860	Benha
Matruh	212,112·00	160,567	211,866	Matruh
Menia	2,261·72	2,648,043	3,308,875	Menia
Menufia	1,532·13	2,227,087	2,758,499	Shibin Al Kom
New Valley	376,505·00	113,838	141,737	Al Kharija
Port Said	72·01	399,793	469,553	Port Said
Qena	1,850·70	2,252,315	2,441,420	Qena
Red Sea	203,685·00	90,491	155,695	El Gurdakah
Sharkia	4,179·55	3,420,119	4,287,848	Zagazig
North Sinai	27,574·00	171,505	252,750	Al Arish
South Sinai	33,140·00	28,988	54,495	At Tur
Suez	17,840·42	326,820	417,610	Suez
Suhag	1,547·21	2,455,134	3,125,000	Suhag

Principal cities, with estimated 1998 populations (in 1,000): Cairo, 7,109; Alexandria, 3,485; Giza, 2,326; Shubra Al Khayma, 912; Port Said, 492; Suez, 437.

Smaller cities, with 1996 populations (in 1,000): Mahalla Al Kubra, 395; Hulwan, 372; Tanta, 371; Mansura, 369; Luxor (Uqsur), 361; Asyut, 343; Zagazig, 267; Fayum, 261; Ismailia, 254; Kafr Ad Dawwar, 232; Aswan, 219; Damanhur, 212; Menia, 201; Beni Suef, 172; Qena, 171; Suhag, 170; Shibin Al Kom, 160.

Cairo: The Romans occupied a town called Babylon (now the Misrah al-Qadimar quarter) on the site of Cairo and contemporary Cairo sprang from the town of Al-Fustat. Successive dynasties added royal suburbs until 969 when the Fatmids established a rectangular walled city initially named al-Mausuriyah, re-named al-Qahira in 973–974. In Greater Cairo is one of the Seven Wonders of the World, the Great Pyramids, and not far away on the Giza platform is the Sphynx.

The official language is Arabic, although French and English are widely spoken.

SOCIAL STATISTICS

Births, 1997, 1,654,695 (27·5 per 1,000 population); deaths, 389,301 (6·5). Marriages, 1994, 530,000 (rate per 1,000 population, 9·1); divorces, 90,000 (1·5). Annual population growth rate, 1990–99, 2·0%. In 1991 the average family size was 4·3 and 40% of the population was under 40 years. Life expectancy at birth, 1999, was 65·3 years for males and 68·5 years for females. Fertility rate, 1999, 3·2 births per woman; infant mortality, 1999, 41 per 1,000 live births. Egypt has made some of the best progress in recent years in reducing child mortality. The number of deaths per 1,000 live births among children under five was reduced from more than 100 in 1990 to only just over 50 in 1999.

In the Human Development Index, or HDI (measuring progress in countries in longevity, knowledge and standard of living), Egypt's index achieved the second largest improvement during the last quarter of the 20th century, rising from 0·430 in 1975 to 0·635 in 1999. Only Indonesia recorded a greater increase.

CLIMATE

The climate is mainly dry, but there are winter rains along the Mediterranean coast. Elsewhere, rainfall is very low and erratic in its distribution. Winter temperatures are comfortable everywhere, but summer temperatures are very high, especially in the south. Cairo, Jan. 56°F (13·3°C), July 83°F (28·3°C). Annual rainfall 1·2" (28 mm). Alexandria, Jan. 58°F (14·4°C), July 79°F (26·1°C). Annual rainfall 7" (178 mm). Aswan, Jan. 62°F (16·7°C), July 92°F (33·3°C). Annual rainfall (trace). Giza, Jan. 55°F (12·8°C), July 78°F (25·6°C). Annual rainfall 16" (389 mm). Ismailia, Jan. 56°F (13·3°C), July 84°F (28·9°C). Annual rainfall 1·5" (37 mm). Luxor, Jan. 59°F (15°C), July 86°F (30°C). Annual rainfall (trace). Port Said, Jan. 58°F (14·4°C), July 78°F (27·2°C). Annual rainfall 3" (76 mm).

CONSTITUTION AND GOVERNMENT
The Constitution was approved by referendum on 11 Sept. 1970. It defines Egypt as 'an Arab Republic with a democratic, socialist system' and the Egyptian people as 'part of the Arab nation'. The *President* is nominated by the People's Assembly and confirmed by plebiscite for a six-year term. The President may appoint one or more *Vice-Presidents*. The *People's Assembly* is a unicameral legislature consisting of 444 members directly elected from 222 constituencies for a five-year term, and ten members appointed by the President. There is a *Constitutional Court*.

The President appoints the Prime Minister and a Council of Ministers. It is traditional for two ministers to be Coptic Christians.

A 210-member consultative body, the *Shura Council*, was established in 1980. Two-thirds of its members are elected and one-third appointed by the President.

National Anthem. 'Biladi' ('My homeland'); words and tune by S. Darwish.

RECENT ELECTIONS
Elections for the People's Assembly were held in three rounds on 18 and 29 Oct. and 13 Nov. 2000. Turn-out was low. The National Democratic Party (NDP) gained 388 seats (including 35 'independents'); non-partisans, 37; Wafd, 7; Al-Tagamu, 6; Nasserites, 3; Liberal Party, 1.

On 26 Sept. 1999 a referendum was held to confirm the People's Assembly's nomination of Hosni Mubarak for a fourth term as president. Turn-out was 79% with Mubarak gaining 93·97% support.

CURRENT ADMINISTRATION
President: Hosni Mubarak; b. 1928 (NDP; first sworn in 14 Oct. 1981 and most recently re-elected in Sept. 1999).

In March 2003 the cabinet comprised:
Prime Minister: Atef Ebeid; b. 1932 (NDP; sworn in 5 Oct. 1999).

Deputy Prime Minister and Minister of Agriculture and Land Reclamation: Dr Youssouf Amin Wali. *Transport:* Ibrahim El-Demeri. *Electricity and Energy:* Hassan Ahmed Younis. *Defence and Military Production:* Fld. Mar. Mohamed Hussein Tantawi. *Environment:* Mamdouh Riyadh Tadros. *Information:* Mohamed Safwat El-Sherief. *Foreign Affairs:* Ahmed Maher. *Public Business Sector:* Mokhtar Khattab. *Justice:* Farouk Self El-Nasr. *Culture:* Farouk Abdel Aziz Hosni. *Finance:* Muhammad Medhat Hassaneen. *Religious Affairs (Awqaf):* Mahmoud Hamdi Zakzouk. *Industry and Technology Development:* Ali al-Saidi. *Health and Population:* Dr Mohammad Awad Tag El-Din. *Foreign Trade:* Dr Youssef Boutros Ghali. *Education:* Dr Hussein Kamal Baha'eddin. *Petroleum:* Amin Sameh Fahmy. *Interior:* Habib Ibrahim Al-Adly. *Tourism:* Mohammad Ahmed Mamdouh El-Beltagui. *Water Resources and Irrigation:* Mahmoud Abd Al-Halim Abu-Zeid. *Housing, Construction and New Urban Communities:* Dr Mohammad Ibrahim Soliman. *Higher Education:* Moufed Mahmoud Shehab. *Telecommunications and Information Technology:* Ahmad Mahmoud Nazif. *Insurance and Social Affairs:* Almina al-Guindi. *Manpower and Immigration:* Ahmed El-Amawy. *Planning:* Osman Mohammed Osman. *Supply and Internal Trade:* Hassan Ali Khedr. *Youth:* Ali al-Din Hillal Dessouki.

DEFENCE
Conscription is selective, and for three years. Military expenditure totalled US$2,821m. in 2000 (US$45 per capita), representing 3·2% of GDP. According to *Deadly Arsenals*, published by the Carnegie Endowment for International Peace, Egypt has a chemical and biological weapons programme.

Army. Strength (1999) 320,000 (250,000 conscripts). In addition there were 150,000 reservists, a Central Security Force of 150,000, a National Guard of 60,000 and 20,000 Border Guards.

Navy. Major surface combatants include one destroyer and ten frigates. A small shore-based naval aviation branch operates 24 helicopters. There are naval bases at Alexandria, Port Said, Mersa Matruh, Port Tewfik, Hurghada and Safaqa. Naval personnel in 1999 totalled 20,000.

Air Force. Until 1979 the Air Force was equipped largely with aircraft of USSR design, but subsequent re-equipment involves aircraft bought in the West, as well as some supplied by China. Strength (1999) is about 30,000 personnel (10,000 conscripts), 129 attack helicopters and 523 combat aircraft including F-16s, F-4 Phantoms, MiG-21s, F-7s (Chinese MiG-21s) and Mirages.

INTERNATIONAL RELATIONS
Egypt is a member of the UN, WTO, the League of Arab States, OAPEC (Organization of Arab Petroleum Exporting Countries), the African Union, African Development Bank, COMESA, IOM, OIC and the International Organization of the Francophonie.

ECONOMY
In 1998 services accounted for 50·2% of GDP, industry 32·3% and agriculture 17·5%.

Overview. With slowing growth since 2000, conditions have worsened with the fall in tourism revenues since 11 Sept. 2001. The service sector dominates the economy, and the tourism sector and the Suez Canal are important revenue earners. Egypt is chiefly a cash economy with basic banking services. There is a large informal market. Each year Egypt receives US$2bn. in military and civilian assistance from the USA. In Feb. 2002 foreign donors agreed US$10·3bn. in aid over three years. Excessive bureaucracy is a concern. Following reforms since the early 1990s, by 2000 around 50% of state-owned enterprises were fully privatized. By the end of 2000 a total of 172 state-owned enterprises had been sold, generating US$3·9bn. However, privatization has stalled. Foreign investment has financed a development project in the Sinai Peninsula and Upper Egypt that aims to increase the inhabited area of the country from 6% to 20% in 20 years.

Currency. The monetary unit is the *Egyptian pound* (EGP) of 100 *piastres*. Inflation was 2·4% in 2001. Faced with slowing economic activity, the country devalued the Egyptian pound four times in 2001. In Jan. 2003 the Egyptian pound was allowed to float against the dollar after years of a government-controlled foreign exchange regime. In May 2002 foreign exchange reserves were US$12,587m. and gold reserves 2·43m. troy oz. Total money supply in May 2002 was £E70,345m.

Budget. The financial year runs from 1 July. Revenues in 1997–98 were £E69,084m. and expenditure £E71,703m. Main sources of revenue were income and profits taxes, 22·7%; sales taxes, 18·3%; customs duties, 17·8%; oil revenue, 7·0%. Main items of expenditure were salaries and pensions, 31·0%; public debt interest, 21·5%.

Performance. Real GDP growth was 5·1% in 2000 and 3·3% in 2001. Total GDP in 2001 was US$98·5bn.

Banking and Finance. The Central Bank of Egypt (founded 1960) is the central bank and bank of issue. The *Governor* is Dr Mahmoud I. Abul-Eyoun.

In 1999, four major public-sector commercial banks accounted for some 70% of all banking assets: the National Bank of Egypt (the largest bank, with assets of nearly £E74bn.), the Banque Misr, the Bank of Alexandria and the Banque du Caïre. There were 40 other domestic commercial banks, 15 investment banks and 30 regional development banks, as well as foreign banks, branches and joint ventures. Foreign banks have only been allowed to operate since 1996.

There are stock exchanges in Cairo and Alexandria.

Weights and Measures. In 1951 the metric system was made official with the exception of the feddan and its subdivisions. However, other traditional measures are still in use: *Kadah* = 1/96th ardeb = 3·36 pints. *Rob* = 4 kadahs = 1·815 gallons. *Keila* = 8 kadahs = 3·63 gallons. *Ardeb* = 96 kadahs = 43·555 gallons, or 5·44439 bu., or 198 cu. decimetres. *Rotl* = 144 dirhems = 0·9905 lb. *Oke* = 400 dirhems = 2·75137 lb. *Qantar* or 100 rotls or 36 okes = 99·0493 lb. 1 *Qantar* of unginned cotton = 315 lb. 1 *Qantar* of ginned cotton = 99·05 lb. The approximate weight of the ardeb is as follows: wheat, 150 kg; beans, 155 kg; barley, 120 kg; maize, 140 kg; cotton seed, 121 kg. *Feddan,* the unit of measure for land = 4,200·8 sq. metres = 7,468·148 sq. pics = 1·03805 acres. 1 sq. pic = 6·0547 sq. ft = 0·5625 sq. metre.

ENERGY AND NATURAL RESOURCES

Environment. According to the *World Bank Atlas* Egypt's carbon dioxide emissions in 1998 were the equivalent of 1·7 tonnes per capita.

Electricity. Installed capacity was 17m. kW in 1997. Electricity generated in 1998 was 57·8bn. kWh. Egypt now exports electricity to Jordan and Syria. Consumption per capita was 861 kWh in 1998. Electricity sector investments reached approximately £E25bn. in 1996–97. The use of solar energy is expanding.

Oil and Gas. Oil was discovered in 1909. Oil policy is controlled by the state-owned Egyptian General Petroleum Corporation, whole or part-owner of the production and refining companies. Oil reserves in 2000 were 8·2bn. bbls. Production of crude oil has been declining from a record 992,000 bbls. a day in 1996 to an estimated 770,000 bbls. a day in 1999.

As a result of a series of new discoveries in 1999 and 2000 gas reserves are thought to be as high as 3,400bn. cu. metres. Annual revenue from future natural gas exports could exceed US$1·5bn. 1999 total production amounted to 14·7bn. cu. metres. By 1995, 75% of power was gas-generated.

Water. The Aswan High Dam, completed in 1970, allows for a perennial irrigation system.

The Mubarak Pumping Station, the world's largest, has been operational since Jan. 2003. Located behind the Aswan High Dam at Lake Nasser, since its inauguration it has been pumping 14·5m. cu. metres of water per day into a 67 km canal to irrigate approximately 540,000 feddans of desert land in Toshka.

Minerals. Production (1993–94, in tonnes): phosphate, 0·86m.; iron ore (1995), 2·44m.; salt (1996), 1·53m.; kaolin (1995–96), 0·26m.; quartz (1995–96), 90,393; asbestos (1996), 1,836. Mining for uranium ore began near Aswan in May 1991.

Agriculture. There were 2·83m. ha of arable land in 1998 and 0·47m. ha of permanent crops. In 1996, of the total cultivated area 18·4% was reclaimed desert. Irrigation is vital to agriculture and is being developed by government programmes; it now reaches most cultivated areas and in 1998 covered 3·3m. ha. The Nile provides 85% of the water used in irrigation, some 55,000m. cu. metres annually. There were 90,000 tractors in 1998 and 2,370 harvester-threshers.

In 1994 there were 5,214 agricultural co-operatives. 0·71m. feddan of land had been distributed by 1991 to 0·35m. families under an agrarian reform programme. In 1995, 33·1% of the workforce were engaged in agriculture. Cotton, sugarcane and rice are subject to government price controls and procurement quotas.

Output (in 1,000 tonnes), 2000: sugarcane, 15,668; wheat, 6,564; maize, 6,395; tomatoes, 6,354; rice, 5,597; sugarbeets, 2,560; melons and watermelons, 2,225; potatoes, 1,784; oranges, 1,550; grapes, 1,008; dry onions, 1,000; sorghum, 950; dates, 890; pumpkins and squash, 650; seed cotton 644; bananas, 620; aubergines, 562; cabbages, 500; tangerines and mandarins, 450; apples, 410; peaches and nectarines, 400; cottonseed, 389; chillies and green peppers, 369; broad beans, 354; garlic, 301. Egypt is Africa's largest producer of a number of crops, including wheat, rice, tomatoes, potatoes and oranges.

Livestock, 2000: cattle, 3·18m.; sheep, 4·45m.; buffaloes, 3·20m.; goats, 3·30m.; asses, 3·05m.; camels, 120,000; chickens, 88m. Livestock products in 2000 (in 1,000 tonnes): buffalo milk, 2,079; cow milk, 1,645; meat, 1,391; eggs, 170. 464,000 tonnes of cheese were produced in 2000, making Egypt the largest cheese producer in Africa.

Forestry. In 1999, 2·88m. cu. metres of roundwood were produced.

Fisheries. The catch in 1999 was 380,504 tonnes, of which 225,300 tonnes were freshwater fish.

INDUSTRY

According to the Financial Times Survey (FT 500), the largest companies by market capitalization in Egypt on 4 Jan. 2001 were MobiNil (US$1,860·4m.), the Egyptian mobile phone provider; and Orascom Telecom (US$1,375·3m.).

Almost all large-scale enterprises are in the public sector, and these account for about two-thirds of total output. The private sector, dominated by food processing and textiles, consists of about 150,000 small and medium businesses, most employing fewer than 50 workers. Industrial production in 1997–98 showed a growth rate of 9% compared to 1996–97. Production during 1995–96 totalled £E74·1bn., compared to £E69·98bn. in 1994–95.

Production in 1997–98 (in 1,000 tonnes) included: fertilizers, 4,634; paper and paperboard (1998), 221; refined sugar, 1,352·5; tobacco, 595; cotton yarn, 275; cement (1997), 18,100. Cars, 36,713 units; refrigerators, 495,000 units; washing machines, 316,100 units.

Labour. In 1996–97 the workforce was 17·4m. (from 16·9m. in 1995–96). In 1995, 29·4% of the workforce were employed in agriculture; 22·5% in services, public administration and defence; 12·3% in manufacturing; 9·0% in trade; 5·5% in construction; 5·1% in transport and communications; and 1·6% in finance. Unemployment was to be 11·5% in 2000. The high birth rate of the 1980s has meant that there are now some 800,000 new entrants into the job market annually.

INTERNATIONAL TRADE
Foreign debt totalled US$28,957m. in 2000. Foreign direct investment in 1999 was US$1·5bn.

Imports and Exports. In 2000 exports (f.o.b.) were valued at US$7,061m.; imports (f.o.b.) were valued at US$15,382m. Services accounted for 64·1% of exports in 1998—mainly from travel and tourism—the highest percentage of any country.

Export of principal commodities in 1995–96: petroleum and petroleum products, 48·5%; cotton yarn, textiles and clothing, 12·5%; basic metals and manufactures, 5·4%. Imports: machinery and transport equipment, 29·7%; foodstuffs, 20·9%; iron and steel products, 9·5%; chemical products, 3·9%. Egypt exports less than 20% of its manufactured goods. Much higher exports are deemed necessary to accelerate growth and job creation.

Main export markets, 1998 (percentage share of total trade): Italy, 13·5%; USA, 13·0%; UK, 8·9%; Turkey, 7·3%. Main import suppliers in 1998: USA, 15·2%; Germany, 9·5%; Italy, 8·0%; France, 7·4%. Trade between Egypt and the European Union, which has been continuously increasing in recent years, now represents 42% of Egypt's foreign trade.

COMMUNICATIONS
Roads. In 1996 there were 26,000 km of highways and main roads, 25,000 km of secondary roads and 13,000 km of other roads. The road link between Sinai and the mainland across the Suez Canal was opened in 1996. Vehicles (in 1,000), 1996: passenger cars, 1,354 (22 per 1,000 inhabitants); trucks and vans, 397; motorcycles, 418; buses, 38.

Rail. In 1994 there were 5,024 km of state railways (1,435 mm gauge), of which 42 km were electrified. Passenger-km travelled in 1996 came to 55·6bn. and freight tonne-km to 4·1bn.

There are tramway networks in Cairo and Alexandria, and a metro (11 km) opened in Cairo in 1996.

Civil Aviation. There are international airports at Cairo, Luxor, Alexandria and a new one which opened at Marsa Alam in 2001. The national carrier is Egyptair, which flew 67·7m. km in 1999 and carried 4,620,100 passengers (3,064,000 on international flights). In 2000 Cairo handled 8,633,307 passengers (6,384,961 on international flights) and 170,329 tonnes of freight. Luxor was the second busiest in 2000, with 2,313,000 passengers.

Shipping. In 1998 the merchant marine totalled 1,368,000 GRT, including oil tankers 210,000 GRT. In 1997 vessels totalling 48,856,000 NRT entered ports and vessels totalling 40,924,000 NRT cleared. Dockyards for containerized shipping were constructed in Alexandria, Dekheila, Damietta and Port Said in 1995–96, with two more planned for Adabeya and the Suez Canal. Egypt's largest port is Damietta, which handles 14m. tonnes of cargo annually.

Suez Canal. The Suez Canal was opened for navigation on 17 Nov. 1869 and nationalized in June 1956. By the convention of Constantinople of 29 Oct. 1888, the canal is open to vessels of all nations and is free from blockade, except in time of war. It is 173 km long (excluding 11 km of approach channels to the harbours), connecting the Mediterranean with the Red Sea. It is being deepened from 16 to 17 metres and widened from 365 to 415 metres to permit the passage of vessels of 180,000 DWT.

In 1999, 13,490 vessels (net tonnage, 385m.) went through the canal. In 1995, 293m. tonnes of cargo were transported and in 1994 a total of 15,800 passengers were carried. Toll revenue in 1999 was US$1,824m. Tolls for tankers were reduced by 20% after Jan. 1996.

Telecommunications. In 2000 there were 5,483,600 telephone main lines (86·4 per 1,000 persons) and 1·4m. PCs were in use (22·1 per 1,000 persons). The planned privatization of Telecom Egypt remains on hold. In April 2001 mobile phone subscribers numbered 2·7m. (shared between Mobinil and Click Vodafone) and in Dec. 2001 Egypt had 600,000 Internet users. There were 31,000 fax machines in 1996.

Postal Services. There were, in 1993–94, 2,035 postal agencies, 1,972 mobile offices, 2,655 government and 2,472 private post offices.

SOCIAL INSTITUTIONS

Justice. The court system comprises: a Court of Cassation with a bench of five judges which constitutes the highest court of appeal in both criminal and civil cases; five Courts of Appeal with three judges; Assize Courts with three judges which deal with all cases of serious crime; Central Tribunals with three judges which deal with ordinary civil and commercial cases; Summary Tribunals presided over by a single judge which hear minor civil disputes and criminal offences. Contempt for religion and what is judged to be a false interpretation of the Koran may result in prison sentences.

The population in penal institutions in 1996 was approximately 40,000 (60 per 100,000 of national population). The death penalty is in force. There were two confirmed executions in 2002.

Religion. Islam is constitutionally the state religion. In 1999 there were 57·5m. Muslims, mostly of the Sunni sect. Some 7% of the population are Coptic Christians, the remainder being Roman Catholics, Protestants or Greek Orthodox, with a small number of Jews. A Patriarch heads the Coptic Church, and there are 25 metropolitans and bishops in Egypt; 4 metropolitans for Ethiopia, Jerusalem, Khartoum and Omdurman, and 12 bishops in Ethiopia. The Copts use the Diocletian (or Martyrs') calendar, which begins in AD 284.

Education. The adult literacy rate in 1999 was 54·6% (66·1% among males and 42·8% among females). Free compulsory education is provided in primary schools (eight years). Secondary and technical education is also free. Approximately 98% of girls and 90% of boys are enrolled in the primary school system. In 1996–97 there were 2,367 pre-primary schools with 289,995 pupils and 12,050 teachers. In 1997–98 there were 7,499,303 primary school pupils and 310,116 teachers; and, in 1996–97, 6,726,738 secondary school pupils with 424,586 teachers.

Al Azhar institutes educate students who intend enrolling at Al Azhar University, one of the world's oldest universities and Sunni Islam's foremost seat of learning. In 1993–94 in the Al Azhar system there were 1,912 primary schools with 704,446 pupils, 1,030 preparatory schools with 147,762 pupils and 587 secondary schools with 165,829 pupils.

In 1993–94 there were 49,703 students in commerce institutes (24,906 women) and 31,259 in technical institutes (9,401 women). In 1995–96 there were 13 state universities, 1 American university and 1 academy of science and technology. There were 612,844 students (231,065 women) and 33,100 academic staff in 1993–94. Four private universities opened in 1996.

Education expenditure in 1998 was between 6% and 7% of GDP.

Health. In 1996 there were 129,000 doctors, and in 1992, 15,150 dentists, 34,700 pharmacists and 98,500 other medical personnel. In 1994 there were 6,332 treatment units (including 330 general hospitals) with 113,020 beds.

CULTURE

Broadcasting. Broadcasting is conducted by the government-controlled Egyptian Radio and TV Union. Number of radio receivers in 1997, 20·5m.; TV sets, 7·7m. Colour is by SECAM V.

Cinema. In 1994 there were 138 cinemas. 72 films were made in 1995.

Press. In 1996 there were 17 dailies with a total circulation of 2·4m. To set up a newspaper requires permission from the prime minister. In 1995 a total of 2,215 book titles were published in 92·35m. copies.

Tourism. There were a record 5,116,000 foreign tourists in 2000, spending US$4·34bn. As a consequence of the attacks on the US, however, 2001 saw a decline in numbers, with only 4·6m. visitors. Tourism is the leading source of foreign revenue and employs nearly 150,000 people. Expenditure by Egyptian tourists abroad in 1995 was US$1·28bn., up from US$52m. in 1986. No other country increased its overseas tourist expenditure at such a rate over the same 10-year period.

Libraries. In 1995 there were 187 public libraries and 60 National libraries. They held a combined 2,654,000 volumes.

DIPLOMATIC REPRESENTATIVES

Of Egypt in the United Kingdom (26 South Street, London, W1K 1DW)
Ambassador: Adel El-Gazzar.

Of the United Kingdom in Egypt (Ahmed Ragheb St., Garden City, Cairo)
Ambassador: John Sawers, CMG.

Of Egypt in the USA (3521 International Court, NW, Washington, D.C., 20008)
Ambassador: Nabil Fahmy.

Of the USA in Egypt (8 Kamal el-Din Salah St., Garden City, Cairo)
Ambassador: C. David Welch.

Of Egypt to the United Nations
Ambassador: Ahmed Aboulgheit.

Of Egypt to the European Union
Ambassador: Soliman Awaad.

FURTHER READING

CAPMAS, *Statistical Year Book, Arab Republic of Egypt*
Abdel-Khalek, G., *Stabilization and Adjustment in Egypt.* Edward Elgar, Cheltenham, 2001
Daly, M. W. (ed.) *The Cambridge History of Egypt.* 2 vols. CUP, 2000
Hopwood, D., *Egypt: Politics and Society 1945–1990.* 3rd ed. London, 1992
Ibrahim, Fouad N. and Ibrahim, Barbara, *Egypt: An Economic Geography.* I. B. Tauris, London, 2001
King, J. W., *Historical Dictionary of Egypt.* 2nd ed. Revised by A. Goldschmidt. Metuchen (NJ), 1995
Malek, J. (ed.) *Egypt.* Univ. of Oklahoma Press, 1993
Raymond, André, *Cairo.* Harvard Univ. Press, 2001
Rodenbeck, M., *Cairo—the City Victorious.* Picador, London, 1998
Rubin, Barry, *Islamic Fundamentalism in Egyptian Politics.* Palgrave Macmillan, Basingstoke, 2002
Vatikiotis, P. J., *History of Modern Egypt: from Muhammad Ali to Mubarak.* London, 1991

National statistical office: Central Agency for Public Mobilization and Statistics (CAPMAS), Nasr City, Cairo.

EL SALVADOR

República de El Salvador

Capital: San Salvador
Population estimate, 2000: 6·28m.
GDP per capita, 2000: (PPP$) 4,497
HDI/world rank: 0·706/104

KEY HISTORICAL EVENTS

Conquered by Spain in 1526, El Salvador remained under Spanish rule until 1821. Thereafter, El Salvador was a member of the Central American Federation comprising the states of El Salvador, Guatemala, Honduras, Nicaragua and Costa Rica until this federation was dissolved in 1839. In 1841 El Salvador declared itself an independent republic.

The country's history has been marked by political violence. The repressive dictatorship of President Maximiliano Hernandez Martínez lasted from 1931 to 1944 when he was deposed as were his successors in 1948 and 1960. The military junta that followed gave way to more secure presidential succession although left-wing guerrilla groups were fighting government troops in the late 1970s. As the guerrillas grew stronger and gained control over a part of the country, the USA sent economic aid and assisted in the training of Salvadorean troops. A new constitution was enacted in Dec. 1983 but the presidential election was boycotted by the main left-wing organization, the Favabundo Marti National Liberation Front (FMLN). Talks between the government and the FMLN in April 1991 led to constitutional reforms in May, envisaging the establishment of civilian control over the armed forces and a reduction in their size. On 16 Jan. 1992 the government and the FMLN signed a peace agreement.

TERRITORY AND POPULATION

El Salvador is bounded in the northwest by Guatemala, northeast and east by Honduras and south by the Pacific Ocean. The area (including 247 sq. km of inland lakes) is 21,041 sq. km. Population (1992 census), 5,047,925 (female 52%); 1996 est., 5·79m., giving a population density of 275 per sq. km.

The UN gives a projected population for 2010 of 7·44m.

In 1999, 53·7% of the population were rural. In 1995, 1m. Salvadoreans were living abroad, mainly in the USA.

The republic is divided into 14 departments. Areas (in sq. km) and 1992 census populations:

Department	Area	Population	Chief town	Population
Ahuachapán	1,240	260,563	Ahuachapán	83,885
Cabañas	1,140	136,293	Sensuntepeque	38,073
Chalatenango	2,017	180,627	Chalatenango	27,600
Cuscatlán	756	167,290	Cojutepeque	43,564
La Libertad	1,653	522,071	Nueva San Salvador	116,575
La Paz	1,224	246,147	Zacatecoluca	57,032
La Unión	2,074	251,143	La Unión	36,927
Morazán	1,447	166,772	San Francisco	20,497
San Miguel	2,077	380,442	San Miguel	182,817
San Salvador	886	1,477,766	San Salvador	422,570[1]
San Vicente	1,184	135,471	San Vicente	45,842
Santa Ana	2,023	451,620	Santa Ana	202,337
Sonsonate	1,226	354,641	Sonsonate	76,200
Usulatán	2,130	317,079	Usulután	62,967

[1]Greater San Salvador conurbation, 1,522,126.

The official language is Spanish.

SOCIAL STATISTICS

1995 births, 164,000; deaths, 35,000. Rates (1995, per 1,000 population): births, 28·9; deaths, 6·1. Life expectancy at birth in 1999 was 66·8 years for males and 72·9 years for females. Annual population growth rate, 1990–99, 2·1%. Infant mortality, 1999, 35 per 1,000 live births; fertility rate, 1999, 3·1 births per woman.

CLIMATE

Despite its proximity to the equator, the climate is warm rather than hot, and nights are cool inland. Light rains occur in the dry season from Nov. to April, while the rest of the year has heavy rains, especially on the coastal plain. San Salvador, Jan. 71°F (21·7°C), July 75°F (23·9°C). Annual rainfall 71" (1,775 mm). San Miguel, Jan. 77°F (25°C), July 83°F (28·3°C). Annual rainfall 68" (1,700 mm).

CONSTITUTION AND GOVERNMENT

A new Constitution was enacted in Dec. 1983. Executive power is vested in a *President* and *Vice-President* elected for a non-renewable term of five years. There is a *Legislative Assembly* of 84 members elected by universal suffrage and proportional representation: 64 locally and 20 nationally, for a term of three years.

National Anthem. 'Saludemos la patria orgullosos' ('We proudly salute the Fatherland'); words by J. J. Cañas, tune by J. Aberle.

RECENT ELECTIONS

Presidential elections were held on 7 March 1999. Francisco Guillermo Flores Pérez (Alianza Republicana Nacionalista, ARENA) won with 51·4% against six other candidates. Turn-out was 35% (compared to 55% at the previous presidential election in 1994).

In parliamentary elections on 16 March 2003 the FMLN (National Liberation Front) gained 31 of a possible 84 seats in the Legislative Assembly, the Nationalist Republican Alliance of President Flores 27, the National Conciliation Party 16, the Democratic United Centre 5 and the Christian Democrat Party 5.

CURRENT ADMINISTRATION

President: Francisco Guillermo Flores Pérez; b. 1959 (ARENA; sworn in 1 June 1999).

In March 2003 the cabinet comprised:

Vice-President: Carlos Quintanilla.

Minister of Agriculture and Livestock: Salvador Urrutia Loucel. *Economy:* Miguel Ernesto Lacayo. *Defence:* Maj. Gen. Juan Antonio Martínez Varela. *Environment and Natural Resources:* Walter Jokisch. *Foreign Affairs:* María Eugenia Brizuela de Avila. *Health:* José Francisco López Beltran. *Governance:* Conrado Lopez Andreu. *Labour and Social Security:* Jorge Isidoro Nieto Menéndez. *Education:* Rolando Marín. *Public Works:* José Angel Quiros. *Treasury:* Juan José Daboub.

Office of the President: http://www.casapres.gob.sv/

DEFENCE

There is selective conscription for two years. In 2000 defence expenditure totalled US$168m. (US$27 per capita), representing 1·6% of GDP.

Army. Strength (1999): 22,300 (4,000 conscripts). The National Civilian Police numbers 12,000 and is due to be increased to 16,000.

Navy. A small coastguard force based largely at Acajutla, with 700 (1999) personnel. There was also (1999) one company of Naval Infantry numbering 150.

Air Force. Strength (1999): 1,600 personnel (200 conscripts). There are 31 combat aircraft and 17 armed helicopters.

INTERNATIONAL RELATIONS

El Salvador is a member of the UN, WTO, OAS, Inter-American Development Bank, CACM, ACS and IOM.

ECONOMY

Agriculture accounted for 12·1% of GDP in 1998, industry 28·0% and services 59·9%.

Overview. An economic liberalization programme aims at raising exports, foreign investment and domestic savings.

Currency. The monetary unit is the *colón* (SVC) of 100 *centavos*. Since the beginning of 2001 the US dollar may also be used for salaries and pensions, and savings can be held in dollars. The colón is expected to disappear completely by the end of 2003. Inflation was 0·1% in 2001. Foreign exchange reserves were US$1,669m. and gold reserves 469,000 troy oz in June 2002. Total money supply was ₡9,608m. in Dec. 2000.

Budget. Central government budgetary revenue and expenditure in ₡1m. for calendar years:

	1998	1999	2000
Revenue	11,963·6	12,015·8	13,493·1
Expenditure	9,532·1	10,979·5	11,452·2

Performance. Real GDP growth was 2·2% in 2000 and 1·8% in 2001. Total GDP in 2001 was US$14·0bn.

Banking and Finance. The bank of issue is the Central Reserve Bank (*President*, Luz María Serpas de Portillo), formed in 1934 and nationalized in 1961. There are 15 commercial banks (two foreign). Individual private holdings may not exceed 5% of the total equity.

There is a stock exchange in San Salvador, founded in 1992.

Weights and Measures. The metric system is standard but other units are still commonly in use, of which the principal ones are as follows: *Libra* = 1·014 lb; *quintal* = 100 lb; *arroba* = 25·35 lb; *fanega* = 1·5745 bushels.

ENERGY AND NATURAL RESOURCES

Environment. According to the *World Bank Atlas* El Salvador's carbon dioxide emissions were the equivalent of 1·0 tonnes per capita in 1998.

Electricity. Installed capacity in 1996 was 900,000 kW, around half of it hydro-electric. Production in 1996 was 3,340m. kWh; consumption per capita was 559 kWh in 1998.

Minerals. El Salvador has few mineral resources. Production (1993, in tonnes): limestone, 3·6m.; gypsum (1987), 4,500. Annual marine salt production averages 30,000 tonnes.

Agriculture. 27% of the land surface is given over to arable farming. In 1995, 32·4% of the working population was engaged in agriculture. Large landholdings have been progressively expropriated and redistributed in accordance with legislation initiated in 1980. By 1994 some 12,000 individuals had received plots of 4–5 ha.

Since the mid-19th century El Salvador's economy has been dominated by coffee. Cotton is the second main commercial crop. Production, in 1,000 tonnes (2000): sugarcane, 5,145; maize, 588; sorghum, 157; coffee, 138; coconuts, 86; dry beans, 71; bananas, 70; rice, 48.

Livestock (2000): 1,212,000 cattle, 300,000 pigs, 96,000 horses, 8m. chickens. Livestock products (2000, in 1,000 tonnes): beef and veal, 34; pork, bacon and ham, 8; poultry, 48; milk, 401; eggs, 53.

Forestry. Forest area was 105,000 ha (5·1% of the land area) in 1995, down from 124,000 ha and 6% in 1990. In the national forests, dye woods are found, and valuable hardwoods including mahogany, cedar and walnut. Balsam trees abound: El Salvador is the world's principal source of this medicinal gum. In 1999, 5·17m. cu. metres of roundwood were cut.

Fisheries. The catch in 1999 was 15,232 tonnes (84% from marine waters).

INDUSTRY

Production (1998, in 1,000 tonnes): cement, 1,020; sugar, 487; residual fuel oil (1997), 378; distillate fuel oil (1997), 126; petroleum (1997), 152; paper and paperboard, 56. Traditional industries include food processing and textiles.

Labour. Out of 2,076,000 people in employment in 1997, 546,000 were in agriculture, forestry and fishing, 467,100 in community, social and personal services, and 445,100 in trade, restaurants and hotels. There were 163,400 unemployed persons, or 7·7% of the workforce, in 1995.

INTERNATIONAL TRADE

In May 1992 El Salvador, Guatemala and Honduras agreed to create a free trade zone for almost all goods and capital. External debt was US$4,023m. in 2000.

Imports and Exports. Imports and exports in calendar years (in US$1m.):

	1996	1997	1998	1999	2000
Imports f.o.b.	3,029·7	3,580·3	3,765·2	3,879·4	4,690·2
Exports f.o.b.	1,787·4	2,437·1	2,459·5	2,534·3	2,971·6

Principal import suppliers, 1996: USA, 40·0%; Guatemala, 10·5%; Panama, 6·6%; Mexico, 6·5%. Principal export markets, 1996: Guatemala, 20·6%; USA, 19·3%; Germany, 15·5%; Honduras, 9·5%. Main import commodities are chemicals and chemical products, transport equipment, and food and beverages; main export commodities are coffee, paper and paper products, and clothing.

COMMUNICATIONS

Roads. In 1997 there were 10,029 km of roads, including 327 km of motorways. Vehicles in use in 1997: passenger cars, 177,500; trucks and vans, 151,800. There were 656 fatalities in road accidents in 1997.

Rail. The railways are run by the National Railways of El Salvador. Route length (1994): 564 km. There is a link to the Guatemalan system. Passenger-km travelled in 1998 came to 6m. and freight tonne-km to 24m.

Civil Aviation. The international airport is El Salvador International. The national carrier is Taca International Airlines, which flew 27·6m. km in 1999, carrying 1,624,100 passengers. It flies to various destinations in the USA, Mexico and all Central American countries. In 2000 El Salvador International handled 1,256,347 passengers on international flights and 32,397 tonnes of international freight.

Shipping. The main ports are Acajutla and Cutuco. Merchant shipping totalled 1,000 GRT in 1998. In 1998 vessels totalling 7,969,000 NRT entered ports and vessels totalling 490,000 NRT cleared.

Telecommunications. The telephone system has been privatized and is owned by two international telephone companies. In 2000 there were 625,800 telephone main lines (99·7 per 1,000 inhabitants) and 120,000 PCs in use (19·1 for every 1,000 persons). There were 382,600 mobile phone subscribers in 1999. Internet users numbered 40,000 in Dec. 1999.

Postal Services. In 1995 there were 297 post offices.

SOCIAL INSTITUTIONS

Justice. Justice is administered by the Supreme Court (six members appointed for three-year terms by the Legislative Assembly and six by bar associations), courts of first and second instance, and minor tribunals.

Following the disbanding of security forces in Jan. 1992 a new National Civilian Police Force was created which numbered 10,500 by 1997.

The population in penal institutions in Dec. 1996 was 8,725 (150 per 100,000 of national population).

Religion. In 1997 there were 4,430,000 Roman Catholics. Under the 1962 Constitution, churches are exempted from the property tax; the Catholic Church is recognized as a legal person, and other churches are entitled to secure similar recognition. There is an archbishop in San Salvador and bishops at Santa Ana, San Miguel, San Vicente, Santiago de María, Usulután, Sonsonate and Zacatecoluca. There were about 400,000 Protestants in 1997 and 830,000 followers of other religions.

Education. The adult literacy rate in 1999 was 78·3% (81·3% among males and 75·6% among females). Education, run by the state, is free and compulsory. In 1995 there were 134,000 pupils in nursery schools, 1,191,000 in primary (1996–97) and 143,600 in secondary schools (1997). In 1995–96 in the public sector there were three universities; in the private sector there were 21 universities and 14 specialized universities (1 American, 3 Evangelical, 1 Roman Catholic, 1 Open and 1 each for business, integrated education, polytechnic, science and development, teaching, science and technology, technical studies and technology). In 1994–95 there were 63,413 university students and 3,983 academic staff.

Health. In 1993 there were 4,525 doctors, 1,182 dentists, 5,094 nurses and 78 hospitals.

Welfare. The Social Security Institute now administers the sickness, old age and death insurance, covering industrial workers and employees earning up to ₡700 a month. Employees in other private institutions with higher salaries are included but are excluded from the medical and hospital benefits.

CULTURE

Broadcasting. Broadcasting is under the control of the Administración Nacional de Telecomunicaciones. There are six commercial television channels, a government-owned channel and two educational channels sponsored by the Ministry of Education. In 1997 there were 2·75m. radio receivers and 4m. television sets (colour by NTSC).

Press. In 1996 there were five daily newspapers with a combined circulation of 278,000, at a rate of 48 per 1,000 inhabitants.

Tourism. There were 658,000 foreign tourists in 1999, spending US$211m.

DIPLOMATIC REPRESENTATIVES

Of El Salvador in the United Kingdom (Mayfair House, 39 Great Portland St., London, W1W 7JZ)
Ambassador: Eduardo Ernesto Vilanova-Molina.

Of the United Kingdom in El Salvador (89 Av. Norte y Calle Del Mirador, World Trade Center, Torre 1, 6th Floor, Colonia Escalon, San Salvador)
Ambassador and Consul General: Patrick Morgan.

Of El Salvador in the USA (2308 California St., NW, Washington, D.C., 20008)
Ambassador: Rene A. León Rodríguez.

Of the USA in El Salvador (Urbanización Santa Elena, Antiguo Cuscatlán, San Salvador)
Ambassador: Rose M. Likins.

Of El Salvador to the United Nations
Ambassador: José Roberto Andino Salazar.

Of El Salvador to the European Union
Ambassador: Hector Gonzalez-Urrutia.

FURTHER READING
Kufeld, A., *El Salvador.* NY, 1991
Montgomery, T. S., *Revolution in El Salvador: Origins and Evolution.* Boulder (CO), 1982

National statistical office: Dirección General de Estadística y Censos, Calle Arce, San Salvador.

EQUATORIAL GUINEA

Capital: Malabo
Population estimate, 2000: 457,000
GDP per capita, 2000: (PPP$) 15,073
HDI/world rank: 0·679/111

República de Guinea
Ecuatorial

KEY HISTORICAL EVENTS

Equatorial Guinea consists of the island of Bioko, for centuries called Fernando Po; other smaller islands and the mainland territory of Rio Muni. Fernando Po was named after the Portuguese navigator Fernão do Po. The island was then ruled for three centuries by Portugal until 1778 when it was ceded to Spain. For some decades after taking possession of Fernando Po, Spain did not effectively occupy it and allowed Britain to establish a naval base at Clarence (later Santa Isabel), which was important for the suppression of slave trading over a wide area. Spain asserted its rule from the 1840s. On Fernando Po the Spanish grew cocoa on European-owned plantations using imported African labour. This traffic led to an international scandal in 1930 when Liberians were found to be held in virtual slavery. Later many Nigerians were employed, often in poor conditions.

African nationalist movements began in the 1950s. Internal self-government was granted in 1963. In 1969 Spain suspended the constitution but then, under pressure to grant independence, agreed on condition of its approval by a referendum, which was given on 11 Aug. 1969. The two parts of Equatorial Guinea were united under Macías Nguema who established single-party rule. Up to a third of the population was killed or else left the country. Macías was declared President-for-Life in July 1972 but was overthrown by a military coup on 3 Aug. 1979.

A constitution approved by a referendum on 3 Aug. 1982 restored some institutions but a Supreme Military Council remained the sole political body until constitutional rule was resumed on 12 Oct. 1982.

TERRITORY AND POPULATION

The mainland part of Equatorial Guinea is bounded in the north by Cameroon, east and south by Gabon, and west by the Gulf of Guinea, in which lie the islands of Bioko (formerly Macías Nguema, formerly Fernando Póo) and Annobón (called Pagalu from 1973 to 1979). The total area is 28,051 sq. km (10,831 sq. miles) and the population at the 1983 census was 304,000. Estimate (July 1997), 443,000; density, 16 per sq. km. Another 110,000 are estimated to remain in exile abroad.

The UN gives a projected population for 2010 of 605,000.

In 1999, 54·1% of the population were rural.

The seven provinces are grouped into two regions—Continental (C), chief town Bata; and Insular (I), chief town Malabo—with areas and populations as follows:

	Sq. km	Census 1983	Chief town
Annobón (I)	17	2,006	San Antonio de Palea
Bioko Norte (I)	776	46,221	Malabo
Bioko Sur (I)	1,241	10,969	Luba
Centro Sur (C)	9,931	52,393	Evinayong
Kié-Ntem (C)	3,943	70,202	Ebebiyin
Litoral (C)	6,665[1]	66,370	Bata
Wele-Nzas (C)	5,478	51,839	Mongomo

[1]Including the adjacent islets of Corisco, Elobey Grande and Elobey Chico (17 sq. km).

In 1995 the capital, Malabo, had a population of 30,000.

The main ethnic group on the mainland is the Fang, which comprises 85% of the total population; there are several minority groups along the coast and adjacent islets. On Bioko the indigenous inhabitants (Bubis) constitute 60% of the population there, the balance being mainly Fang and coast people. On Annobón the indigenous inhabitants are the descendants of Portuguese slaves and still speak a Portuguese patois. The official language is Spanish.

SOCIAL STATISTICS
1997 births, 17,400; deaths, 6,100. Birth rate (per 1,000 population, 1997 estimate): 39·3; death, 13·7. Life expectancy (1999): male, 49·0 years; female, 52·2. Annual population growth rate, 1990–99, 2·6%. Infant mortality, 1999, 105 per 1,000 live births; fertility rate, 1999, 5·5 births per woman.

CLIMATE
The climate is equatorial, with alternate wet and dry seasons. In Rio Muni, the wet season lasts from Dec. to Feb.

CONSTITUTION AND GOVERNMENT
A Constitution was approved in a plebiscite in Aug. 1982 by 95% of the votes cast. It provided for an 11-member Council of State, and for a 41-member House of Representatives of the People, the latter being directly elected on 28 Aug. 1983 for a five-year term and re-elected on 10 July 1988. The President appointed and leads a Council of Ministers.

On 12 Oct. 1987 a single new political party was formed as the *Partido Democrático de Guinea Ecuatorial*.

A referendum on 17 Nov. 1991 approved the institution of multi-party democracy, and a law to this effect was passed in Jan. 1992. The electorate is restricted to citizens who have resided in Equatorial Guinea for at least ten years. A parliament created as a result, the *National Assembly*, has 80 seats.

National Anthem. 'Caminemos pisando las sendas' ('Let us journey treading the pathways'); words by A. N. Miyongo, tune anonymous.

RECENT ELECTIONS
At the *National Assembly* elections on 6 March 1999 the main opposition parties called for a boycott. 75 of the 80 seats went to the ruling Democratic Party of Equatorial Guinea (PDGE), 4 to the Popular Union and 1 to the Convergence for the Social Democracy.

Presidential elections were held on 15 Dec. 2002. President Nguema Mbasogo was re-elected with 97·1% of votes cast, against 2·2% for Celestino Bonifacio Bacalé. Opposition parties withdrew their candidates during polling, citing irregularities.

CURRENT ADMINISTRATION
President of the Supreme Military Council: Brig.-Gen. Teodoro Obiang Nguema Mbasogo; b. 1943 (PDGE; in office since 1979, most recently re-elected in 2002).

In March 2003 the government comprised:

Prime Minister and Head of Government: Cándido Muatetema Rivas; b. 1961 (PDGE; sworn in 4 March 2001).

First Deputy Prime Minister, Minister of Civil Service and Administrative Co-ordination: Ignacio Milam Tang. *Minister of Economy and Finance:* Marcelino Owono Edu. *Foreign Affairs and International Co-operation:* Micha Ondo Bile. *Agriculture, Fisheries and Animal Husbandry, Industry, Commerce, and Small and Medium Enterprises:* Constantino Ekong Nsue. *Interior and Local Corporations:* Clemente Engonga Nguema Onguene. *Justice and Religion:* Ruben Maye Nsue. *Mines and Energy:* Cristobal Menana Ela. *Planning and Economic Development:* Fortunato Ofa Mbo. *Public Works, Housing and Urban Affairs:* Florentino Nkogo Ndong. *Social Affairs and Women's Development:* Teresa Efua Asangono. *Youth and Sports:* Juan Antonio Ntutumu. *Minister of State at the Presidency in Charge of Special Duties, Minister of State for Missions:* Alejandro Evuna Owono Asangono. *At the Presidency in Charge of Relations with Assemblies and Legal Matters, Planning:* Miguel Abia Biteo Boriko. *Education, Science and Government Spokesman:* Antonio Fernando Nve Ngu. *Forestry and Environment:* Teodoro Nguema Obiang. *Health and Social Welfare:* Dr Marcelino Nguema Onguene. *Information, Tourism and Culture:* Lucas Nguema Esono. *Labour and Social Promotion:* Ricardo Mangue Obama Nfube. *Transport and Communications:*

Marcelino Oyono Ntutumu. *Secretary General of the Government:* Francisco Pascual Eyegue Obama Asue.

DEFENCE
In 2000 defence expenditure totalled US$12m. (US$24 per capita), representing 1·7% of GDP.

Army. The Army consists of three infantry battalions with (1999) 1,100 personnel. There is also a paramilitary Guardia Civil.

Navy. A small force, numbering 120 in 1999 and based at Malabo, operates four inshore patrol craft.

Air Force. There are no combat aircraft or armed helicopters. Personnel (1999), 100.

INTERNATIONAL RELATIONS
Equatorial Guinea is a member of the UN, the African Union, African Development Bank and the International Organization of the Francophonie, and is an ACP member state of the ACP-EU relationship.

ECONOMY
Industry accounted for 66·4% of GDP in 1998 (the highest percentage of any country), agriculture 21·8% and services 11·8%.

Overview. Overseas investment, particularly in the oil industry, has transformed the economy.

Currency. On 2 Jan. 1985 the country joined the Franc Zone and the *ekpwele* was replaced by the *franc CFA* (XAF) which now has a parity value of 655·957 francs CFA to one euro. Foreign exchange reserves were US$77m. in April 2002 and total money supply was 68,514m. francs CFA. Inflation in 2001 was 12·0%.

Budget. In 1995 the estimated total revenue was 13,542m. francs CFA and expenditure 13,400m. francs CFA, of which 12,170m. francs CFA were current expenditure.

Performance. Equatorial Guinea is the world's fastest growing economy thanks to the rapid expansion of its oil sector. The economy grew by more than nearly 30% in 1996 and by a record 71·2% in 1997. In 2001 the growth rate was 45·5%. Since 1997, except for 2000, Equatorial Guinea's real GDP growth has been the highest in the world. Between 1990 and 1996 the average annual real growth in GNP per capita was 15·9%—the highest of any country in the world over the same period. In 2001 total GDP was US$1·8bn.

Banking and Finance. The *Banque des Etats de l'Afrique Centrale* became the bank of issue in Jan. 1985. There is 1 commercial bank.

ENERGY AND NATURAL RESOURCES
Environment. According to the *World Bank Atlas* carbon dioxide emissions in 1998 were the equivalent of 0·6 tonnes per capita.

Electricity. There are two hydro-electric plants. Installed capacity was 23,000 kW in 1995. Production was 21m. kWh in 1998; consumption per capita in 1997 was 48 kWh.

Oil and Gas. Oil production started in 1992, and by 2002 had reached 200,000 bbls. a day. Mobil is the biggest operator in the country but other US-based oil companies are investing heavily. Since oil in commercial quantities was discovered in 1995 Equatorial Guinea has attracted more than US$1bn. in foreign direct investment.
  Natural gas reserves were 37bn. cu. metres in 1997.

Minerals. There is some small-scale alluvial gold production.

Agriculture. There were 130,000 ha of arable land in 1998 and 100,000 ha of permanent crops. Subsistence farming predominates, and in 1995 approximately 73% of the economically active population were engaged in agriculture. Production (in 1,000 tonnes, in 2000): cassava, 45; sweet potatoes, 36; bananas, 20; coconuts,

6; cocoa beans, 4; coffee, 4. Plantations in the hinterland have been abandoned by their Spanish former owners and, except for cocoa and coffee, commercial agriculture is under serious difficulties. Livestock (2000): cattle, 5,000; goats, 8,000; pigs, 5,000; sheep, 36,000.

Forestry. In 1995 forests covered 1·78m. ha, or 63·5% of the total land area (down from 65·2% of the land area in 1990). Timber production in 1999 totalled 811,000 cu. metres.

Fisheries. The total catch in 1999 was estimated to be 7,001 tonnes (84% from sea fishing). Tuna and shellfish are caught.

INDUSTRY

The once-flourishing light industry collapsed under the Macías regime. Oil production is now the major activity; production, 1996, 3m. bbls. Production of veneer sheets, 1997, 9,000 cu. metres. Food processing is also being developed.

Labour. In 1996 the labour force was 171,000 (65% males). The wage-earning non-agricultural workforce is small. The average monthly wage was 14,000 francs CFA in 1992.

INTERNATIONAL TRADE

Foreign debt was US$248m. in 2000.

Imports and Exports. Imports and exports for calendar years in US$1m.:

	1992	1993	1994	1995	1996
Imports f.o.b.	56·0	51·0	37·0	120·6	292·0
Exports f.o.b.	49·5	61·1	62·0	89·9	175·3

Main export markets, 1995: USA, 34%; Japan, 16%; China, 12%. Main import suppliers: Spain, 51%; Cameroon, 21%; France, 6%; USA, 4%. Principal export commodities are petroleum, cocoa and timber; principal import commodities are machinery and transport equipment, and petroleum and petroleum products.

COMMUNICATIONS

Roads. Length of network, 1996, 2,880 km. Most roads are in a state of disrepair. Vehicles in use numbered 2,040 (1,520 passenger cars, or 3·3 per 1,000 inhabitants, and 540 vans and trucks) in 1996.

Civil Aviation. There is an international airport at Malabo. There were international flights in 1998 to Abidjan, Brazzaville, Cotonou, Douala, Lagos, Libreville, Madrid, Paris, Pointe Noire, São Tomé, Yaoundé and Zürich. In 1998 Malabo handled 54,000 passengers.

Shipping. Bata is the main port, handling mainly timber. The other ports are Luba, formerly San Carlos (bananas, cocoa), in Bioko, and Malabo, Evinayong and Mbini on the mainland. Ocean-going shipping totalled 59,000 GRT in 1998.

Telecommunications. Telephone services are rudimentary. In 2000 there were 6,100 main telephone lines in use (13·5 for every 1,000 persons) and in 1995 around 100 fax machines. In May 1999 there were 600 Internet users; the number of PCs in use in 1999 was 1,000 (2·3 per 1,000 persons).

Postal Services. There were 23 post offices in 1994.

SOCIAL INSTITUTIONS

Justice. The Constitution guarantees an independent judiciary. The Supreme Tribunal, the highest court of appeal, is located at Malabo. There are Courts of First Instance and Courts of Appeal at Malabo and Bata.

Religion. Christianity was proscribed under President Macías but reinstated in 1979. In 1999 there were 430,000 Roman Catholics and 30,000 followers of other religions.

Education. In 1993–94 there were 85 pre-primary schools with 171 teachers for 3,788 pupils; 781 primary schools with 1,381 teachers for 75,751 pupils; and 16,616 secondary pupils with 588 teachers. In 1993 there were 2 teacher training colleges, 2 post-secondary vocational schools and 1 agricultural institute. Adult literacy was

82·2% in 1999 (male, 91·9%; female, 73·3%). The rate for males is second only to Zimbabwe among African countries.

Health. In 1990 there were 99 doctors, 154 nurses and 55 midwives.

CULTURE

Broadcasting. Two radio programmes are broadcast by the state-controlled Radio Nacional de Guinea Ecuatorial and Televisión Nacional. There is also a commercial radio network, and a cultural programme produced with Spanish collaboration. In 1997 there were 180,000 radio and 4,000 TV receivers (colour by SECAM).

Press. In 1996 there was one daily newspaper with a circulation of 2,000, at a rate of 4·9 per 1,000 inhabitants.

Tourism. Foreign tourists brought in revenue of US$2m. in 1998.

DIPLOMATIC REPRESENTATIVES
Of Equatorial Guinea in the United Kingdom
Ambassador: Vacant (resides at Paris).
Chargé d'Affaires a.i.: Moises Mba Sima Nchama.

Of the United Kingdom in Equatorial Guinea
Ambassador: Richard Wildash, LVO (resides at Yaoundé, Cameroon).

Of Equatorial Guinea in the USA (2020 16th St., NW, Washington, D.C., 20009)
Ambassador: Teodoro Biyogo Nsue Okomo.

Of Equatorial Guinea to the United Nations
Ambassador: Teodoro Biyogo Nsue Okomo.

Of Equatorial Guinea to the European Union
Ambassador: Vacant.
Chargé d'Affaires a.i.: Mari-Cruz Evuna Andeme.

The USA does not have an embassy in Equatorial Guinea; US relations with Equatorial Guinea are handled through the US Embassy in Yaoundé, Cameroon.

FURTHER READING
Fegley, Randall, *Equatorial Guinea, an African Tragedy.* New York, 1989
Liniger-Goumaz, M., *Guinea Ecuatorial: Bibliografía General.* Geneva, 1974–91
Molino, A. M. del, *La Ciudad de Clarence.* Madrid, 1994

ERITREA

Capital: Asmara
Population estimate, 2000: 3·66m.
GDP per capita, 2000: (PPP$) 837
HDI/world rank: 0·421/157

KEY HISTORICAL EVENTS
Italy was the colonial ruler from 1890 until 1941 when Eritrea fell to British forces and a British protectorate was set up. This ended in 1952 when the UN sanctioned federation with Ethiopia. In 1962 Ethiopia became a unitary state and Eritrea was incorporated as a province. Eritreans began an armed struggle for independence under the leadership of the Eritrean People's Liberation Front (EPLF) which culminated successfully in the capture of Asmara on 24 May 1991. Thereafter the EPLF maintained a *de facto* independent administration recognized by the Ethiopian government. Sovereignty was proclaimed on 24 May 1993. In 1999 fighting broke out along the border with Ethiopia. After the failure of international mediation, the 13-month long-truce between Eritrea and Ethiopia ended in May 2000. Ethiopia launched a major offensive in the ongoing war over territorial disputes and claimed victory. In June both sides agreed to an Organization of African Unity peace deal to end the two-year border war.

TERRITORY AND POPULATION
Eritrea is bounded in the northeast by the Red Sea, southeast by Djibouti, south by Ethiopia and west by Sudan. Some 300 islands form the Dahlak Archipelago, most of them uninhabited. For the dispute with Yemen over the islands of Greater and Lesser Hanish *see* YEMEN: Territory and Population. Its area is 93,679 sq. km (36,171 sq. miles). Population, 1995, 3,434,500 (81·6% rural in 1999); density, 27·6 per sq. km.

The UN gives a projected population for 2010 of 5·03m.

1m. Eritreans lived abroad in 1995, 0·5m. as refugees in Sudan. A UN Programme for Refugee Reintegration and Rehabilitation of Resettlement Areas in Eritrea (PROFERI) is in operation.

There are ten provinces: Akele Guzai, Asmara, Barka, Denkel, Gash-Setir, Hamasien, Sahel, Semhar, Senhit and Seraye. The capital is Asmara (1999 population, 514,000). Other large towns (with 1992 populations) are Assab (50,000), Keren (40,000) and Massawa (40,000). An agreement of July 1993 gives Ethiopia rights to use the ports of Assab and Massawa.

48% of the population speak Tigrinya and 31% Tigré, and there are seven other indigenous languages. Arabic is spoken on the coast and along the Sudanese border, and English is used in secondary schools. Arabic and Tigrinya are the official languages.

SOCIAL STATISTICS
Births, 1995, 131,000; deaths, 48,000. Rates, 1995 (per 1,000 population): birth, 41·4; death, 15·2. Annual population growth rate, 1990–99, 2·8%. Life expectancy at birth, 1999, was 50·4 years for males and 53·2 years for females. Infant mortality, 1999, 66 per 1,000 live births; fertility rate, 1999, 5·6 births per woman.

CLIMATE
Massawa, Jan. 78°F (25·6°C), July 94°F (34·4°C). Annual rainfall 8" (193 mm).

CONSTITUTION AND GOVERNMENT
A referendum to approve independence was held on 23–25 April 1993. The electorate was 1,173,506. 99·8% of votes cast were in favour.

The transitional government has a four-year term and consists of the *President* and a 130-member *National Assembly.* The latter consists of the members of the People's Front for Democracy and Justice (PFDJ; until Feb. 1994 EPLF) Central Committee and 60 other deputies (including 11 seats reserved for women). It elects the President, who in turn appoints the *State Council* made up of 14 ministers and the governors of the ten provinces. The President chairs both the State Council and the National Assembly.

National Anthem. 'Ertra, Ertra, Ertra' ('Eritrea, Eritrea, Eritrea'); words by S. Beraki, tune by I. Meharezghi and A. Tesfatsion.

RECENT ELECTIONS
In the presidential and legislative elections in May 1997, President Afewerki was re-elected to office. National assembly elections, postponed in 1998, are set to take place before the end of 2003. In the meantime several dissident politicians have been jailed.

CURRENT ADMINISTRATION
President: Issaias Afewerki; b. 1945 (PFDJ; elected 22 May 1993 and re-elected in May 1997).
   In March 2003 the ministers in the State Council were:
   Minister of Agriculture: Arefaine Berhe. *Construction:* Abraha Asfaha. *Defence:* Sebhat Ephrem. *Education:* Osman Saleh. *Energy and Mining:* Tesfai Ghebreselassie. *Finance:* Berhane Abrehe. *Fisheries and Maritime Resources:* Ahmed Haj Ali. *Foreign Affairs:* Ali Said Abdella. *Health:* Saleh Meki. *Information:* Naizghi Kiflu. *Justice:* Fozia Hashim. *Labour and Human Welfare:* Askalu Menkerios. *Land, Water and Environment:* Woldemichael Ghebremariam. *Tourism:* Amna Nur Husayn. *Trade and Industry:* Giorgis Teklemikael. *Transport and Communications:* Woldemikael Abraha.

DEFENCE
Conscription for 18 months was introduced in 1994 for all Eritreans between the ages of 18 and 40, with some exceptions. The total strength of all forces was estimated at 180,000–200,000 in 1999.
   Defence expenditure totalled US$173m. in 2001 (US$45 per capita and 20·9% of GDP—the highest percentage of any country in the world).

Army. The army had a strength of around 180,000 in 1999. There were an additional 120,000 reservists available.

Navy. Most of the former Ethiopian Navy is now in Eritrean hands. The main bases and training establishments are at Massawa and Assab. Personnel numbered 1,100 in 1999.

Air Force. Personnel numbers were estimated at 1,000 in 1999. There were over 19 combat aircraft including MiG-23s, MiG-21s and MiG-29s.

INTERNATIONAL RELATIONS
A border dispute between Eritrea and Ethiopia broke out in May 1998. Eritrean troops took over the border town of Badame after a skirmish between Ethiopian police units and armed men from Eritrea. Ethiopia maintained that Badame and Sheraro, a nearby town, had always been part of Ethiopia and called Eritrea's action an invasion. An agreement ending hostilities was signed in June 2000, followed by a peace accord in Dec. A buffer zone has been created to separate the armies.
   Eritrea is a member of the UN, the African Union, African Development Bank, COMESA, the Intergovernmental Authority on Development and is an ACP member state of the ACP-EU relationship.

ECONOMY
In 1997 agriculture accounted for 9·3% of GDP, services 61·2% and industry 29·5%.
   Eritrea's resources are meagre, the population small and poorly-educated; communications are difficult and there is a shortage of energy.

Currency. A new currency, the *nakfa*, has replaced the Ethiopian currency, the *birr*. However, its introduction led to tensions with Ethiopia, adversely affecting cross-border trade. Inflation was 14·6% in 2001.

Budget. Revenues in 1996 were US$226m. and expenditure US$453m. Over 40 enterprises are scheduled for privatization.

Performance. Total GDP in 2001 was US$0·7bn. The economy contracted by 12·1% in 2000, as a result of the conflict with neighbouring Ethiopia, but then expanded by 9·7% in 2001 following the end of hostilities.

Banking and Finance. The central bank is the National Bank of Eritrea (*Governor*, Tequie Beyene). All banks and financial institutions are state-run. There is a Commercial Bank of Eritrea with 15 branches, an Eritrean Investment and Development Bank with 13 branches, a Housing and Commercial Bank of Eritrea with seven branches and an Insurance Corporation.

ENERGY AND NATURAL RESOURCES

Electricity. Installed capacity was 73 MW in 1995. Electricity is provided to only some 10% of the population.

Minerals. There are deposits of gold, silver, copper, zinc, sulphur, nickel, chrome and potash. Basalt, limestone, marble, sand and silicates are extracted. Oil exploration is taking place in the Red Sea. Salt production totals 200,000 tonnes annually.

Agriculture. Agriculture engaged approximately 79% of the economically active population in 1997. Several systems of land ownership (state, colonial, traditional) co-exist. In 1994 the PFDJ proclaimed the sole right of the state to own land. There were 391,000 ha of arable land in 1998 and 2,000 ha of permanent crops. Main agricultural products, 2000 (in 1,000 tonnes): sorghum, 100; potatoes, 35; barley, 25; millet, 25; maize, 12; wheat, 10. Livestock, 2000: cattle, 1·80m.; sheep, 1·54m.; goats 1·50m.; camels, 73,000; chickens, 1m.

Forestry. In 1995 forests covered 282,000 ha, or 2·8% of the total land area. Timber production in 1999 was 2·29m. cu. metres.

Fisheries. The total catch in 1999 was 7,042 tonnes, exclusively from marine waters, but a joint French–Eritrean project to assess fish stocks in the Red Sea suggests a sustainable yield of up to 70,000 tonnes a year.

INDUSTRY

Light industry was well developed in the colonial period but capability has declined. Processed food, textiles, leatherwear, building materials, glassware and oil products are produced. Industrial production accounted for nearly 30% of GDP in 1997, with the manufacturing sector providing over 15%.

Labour. In 1996 the labour force was 1,649,000 (53% males).

INTERNATIONAL TRADE

Eritrea is dependent on foreign aid for most of its capital expenditure. Total external debt in 2000 was US$311m.

Imports and Exports. In 1996 exports were valued at 520·4m. birr and imports at 3,062·8m. birr. The main exports are drinks, leather and products, textiles and oil products. The leading imports are machinery and transport equipment, basic manufactures, and food and live animals. Principal import suppliers: Saudi Arabia, Italy, UAE, Germany. Principal export markets: Ethiopia, Sudan, Yemen, Saudi Arabia. Until the outbreak of hostilities, Ethiopia had been Eritrea's leading trading partner, followed by Sudan.

COMMUNICATIONS

Roads. There were some 4,010 km of roads in 1996, around 875 km of which were paved. A tarmac road links the capital Asmara with one of the main ports, Massawa. In 1996 passenger cars in use numbered 5,940 (1·5 per 1,000 inhabitants). About 500 buses operate regular services.

Rail. In Jan. 2000 the reconstruction of the 117 km Massawa–Asmara line reached Embatkala, thus opening up an 80 km stretch from Massawa on the coast.

Civil Aviation. There are international airports at Asmara (Yohannes IV Airport) and Assab. In 1998 there were flights to Cairo, Djibouti, Dubai, Frankfurt, Jeddah and Riyadh. In 2000 Asmara handled 103,000 passengers (88,000 on international flights) and 7,300 tonnes of freight.

Shipping. Massawa is the main port; Assab used to be the main port for imports to Ethiopia. Both were free ports for Ethiopia until the onset of hostilities. Merchant shipping totalled 7,000 GRT in 1998.

Telecommunications. International telephone links were restored in 1992. In 2000 there were 30,600 telephone main lines (8·0 for every 1,000 inhabitants) and some 1,300 fax machines. In Dec. 2000 there were 5,000 Internet users. There were 6,000 PCs in use (1·6 per 1,000 inhabitants) in 2000.

Postal Services. In 1995 there were 35 post offices, equivalent to one for every 95,000 persons.

SOCIAL INSTITUTIONS

Justice. The legal system derives from a decree of May 1993.

Religion. Half the population are Sunni Muslims (along the coast and in the north), and half Coptic Christians (in the south).

Education. Adult literacy was about 52·7% in 1999 (66·5% among males and 39·4% among females). In 1996–97 there were 549 primary schools with 240,737 pupils and 5,476 teachers, and 89,087 pupils at secondary schools with 2,071 teachers. There is one university, with 3,200 students and 250 academic staff in 1994–95.

Health. In 1993 there were 10 small regional hospitals, 32 health centres, 65 medical posts, 68 doctors (equivalent to one for every 46,200 persons), 488 nurses, 33 midwives and 850 auxiliary medical personnel.

CULTURE

Broadcasting. There is daily radio and TV broadcasting. In 1997 there were 1,000 TV receivers and 345,000 radio receivers.

Press. There is a government daily in Arabic and Tigrinya. In Sept. 2001 the government closed down the country's eight independent newspapers. A number of journalists have been jailed.

Tourism. There were 57,000 foreign tourists in 1999. Receipts totalled US$28m.

DIPLOMATIC REPRESENTATIVES

Of Eritrea in the United Kingdom (96 White Lion Street, London, N1 9PF)
Ambassador: Ghirmai Ghebremariam.

Of the United Kingdom in Eritrea (Emperor Yohannes Avenue, House No. 24, PO Box 5584, Asmara)
Ambassador: Mike Murray.

Of Eritrea in the USA (1708 New Hampshire Avenue, NW, Washington, D.C., 20009)
Ambassador: Girma Asmerom.

Of the USA in Eritrea (Franklin D. Roosevelt St., POB 211, Asmara)
Ambassador: Donald J. McConnell.

Of Eritrea to the United Nations
Ambassador: Ahmed Tahir Badun.

Of Eritrea to the European Union
Ambassador: Tesfai Ghermazien.

FURTHER READING
Connel, D., *Against All Odds: a Chronicle of the Eritrean Revolution.* Trenton (NJ), 1993
Fegley, Randall, *Eritrea.* [Bibliography] ABC-Clio, Oxford and Santa Barbara (CA), 1995
Henze, Paul, *Eritrea's War: Confrontation, International Response, Outcome, Prospects.* Shama, Addis Ababa, 2001
Lewis, R., *Eritrea: Africa's Newest Country.* London, 1993
Negash, Tekeste and Tronvoll, Kjetil, *Brothers at War: Making Sense of the Eritrean–Ethiopian War.* Ohio Univ. Press and James Currey, Oxford, 2001

ESTONIA

Eesti Vabariik
(Republic of Estonia)

Capital: Tallinn
Population estimate, 2000: 1·37m.
GDP per capita, 2000: (PPP$) 10,066
HDI/world rank: 0·826/42

KEY HISTORICAL EVENTS

Estonia was part of the Holy Roman Empire until it became a Swedish possession in the 17th century. On Sweden's defeat by Peter the Great, Estonia passed to the Russian Empire in 1721. The workers' and soldiers' Soviets, which came to prominence in 1917, were overthrown with the assistance of British naval forces in May 1919 and a democratic republic proclaimed. In March 1934 this regime was, in turn, overthrown by a fascist coup. The secret protocol of the Soviet-German agreement of 23 Aug. 1939 assigned Estonia to the Soviet sphere of interest. An ultimatum (16 June 1940) led to the formation of the Estonian Soviet Socialist Republic. At a referendum in March 1991, 77·8% of votes cast were in favour of independence. A fully independent status was conceded by the USSR State Council on 6 Sept. 1991. Estonia was admitted to the Council of Europe in 1993, and in 2002 was invited to join both NATO and the EU in 2004.

TERRITORY AND POPULATION

Estonia is bounded in the west and north by the Baltic Sea, east by Russia and south by Latvia. There are 1,541 offshore islands, of which the largest are Saaremaa and Hiiumaa, but only 14 are permanently inhabited. Area, 45,227 sq. km (17,462 sq. miles); population, 1,370,052 (2000 census), giving a density of 30·3 per sq. km.

The UN gives a projected population for 2010 of 1·25m.

As of 1 Jan. 2000, 69·1% of the population lived in urban areas. Of the whole population, Estonians accounted for 67·9%, Russians 25·6%, Ukrainians 2·1%, Belorussians 1·3% and Finns 0·9%. The capital is Tallinn (population, 408,329 or 29·2%). Other large towns are Tartu (101,169), Narva (68,680), Kohtla-Järve (47,679) and Pärnu (45,500). There are 15 counties, 47 towns and 207 rural municipalities.

The official language is Estonian.

SOCIAL STATISTICS

2001 births 12,720; deaths, 18,627. Rates (per 1,000 population): birth, 9·6, death, 13·5. There were 12,743 induced abortions in 2000. Expectation of life in 2000 was 65·1 years for males and 76·0 for females. Infant mortality in 2000 was 8·4 per 1,000 births. Total fertility rate was 1·39 births per women.

CLIMATE

Because of its maritime location Estonia has a moderate climate, with cool summers and mild winters. Average daily temperatures in 2000: Jan. –2·5°C; July 16·3°C. Rainfall is heavy, 500–700 mm per year, and evaporation low.

CONSTITUTION AND GOVERNMENT

A draft constitution drawn up by a constitutional assembly was approved by 91·1% of votes cast at a referendum on 28 June 1992. Turn-out was 66·6%. The constitution came into effect on 4 July 1992. It defines Estonia as a 'democratic state guided by the rule of law, where universally recognized norms of international law are an inseparable part of the legal system.' It provides for a 101-member national assembly (*Riigikogu*) elected for four-year terms. There are 11 electoral districts with eight to 11 mandates each. Candidates may be elected: a) by gaining more than 'quota', i.e. the number of votes cast in a district divided by the number of its mandates; b) by standing for a party which attracts for all of its candidates more than the quota, in order of listing; c) by being listed nationally for parties which clear a 5% threshold

601

and eligible for the seats remaining according to position on the lists. The head of state is the *President*, elected by the Riigikogu for five-year terms. Presidential candidates must gain the nominations of at least 20% of parliamentary deputies. If no candidate wins a two-thirds majority in any of three rounds, the Speaker convenes an electoral college, composed of parliamentary deputies and local councillors. At this stage any 21 electors may nominate an additional candidate. The electoral college elects the President by a simple majority.

Citizenship requirements are two years residence and competence in Estonian for existing residents. For residents immigrating after 1 April 1995, five years qualifying residence is required.

National Anthem. 'Mu isamaa, mu õnn ja rõõm' ('My native land, my pride and joy'); words by J. V. Jannsen, tune by F. Pacius (same as Finland).

RECENT ELECTIONS
Parliamentary elections were held on 2 March 2003; turn-out was 58·2%. The Estonian Centre Party (K) won 28 of the 101 seats (with 25·4% of the total votes); Res Publica (RESP), 28 seats (24·6%); Estonian Reform Party (RE), 19 seats (17·7%); Estonian People's Union, 13 (13·3%); Pro Patria Union (I), 7 seats (7·3%); Mõõdukad (M), 6 seats (7·0%).

A special government assembly elected the president after two rounds of votes on 21 Sept. 2001. There were four candidates. In the run-off for the presidency Arnold Rüütel won with 186 votes against 155 for Toomas Savi.

CURRENT ADMINISTRATION
President: Arnold Rüütel; b. 1928 (sworn in 8 Oct. 2001).

A new government was formed in April 2003 comprising:

Prime Minister: Juhan Parts; b. 1966 (RESP; in office since 10 April 2003).

Minister of Agriculture: Tiit Tammsaar. *Culture:* Urmas Paet. *Defence:* Margus Hanson. *Economic Affairs and Communications:* Meelis Atonen. *Education:* Toivo Maimets. *Environment:* Villu Reiljan. *Finance:* Tõnis Palts. *Foreign Affairs:* Kristiina Ojuland. *Internal Affairs:* Margus Leivo. *Justice:* Ken-Marti Vaher. *Population and Ethnic Affairs:* Paul-Eerik Rummo. *Regional Affairs:* Jaan Õunapuu. *Social Affairs:* Marko Pomerants.

Government Website: http://www.riik.ee

DEFENCE
The President is the head of national defence. Conscription is eight to 11 months for men and voluntary for women. Conscientious objectors may opt for 16 months civilian service instead.

Defence expenditure in 2001 totalled 1,639bn. krooni, representing 1·8% of GDP.

The Estonian Defence Forces (EDF) regular component is divided into the Army, the Air Force and the Navy.

Army. The army consists of 9 army-training battalions (6 for infantry, 1 for air defence, 1 for artillery and 1 for peace operations). Annually around 3,000 conscripts are trained for reserve. The total number of personnel in the Army in 2000 was 4,535 (1,420 officers and NCOs and contract soldiers; 2,290 conscripts and 825 civilians).

Navy. The Navy consists of the Naval Staff (Naval HQ), the Naval Base, and the Mine Countermeasures (MCM) Squadron. The total number of personnel in the Navy in 2000 was 385 (110 officers and NCOs and contract soldiers, 220 conscripts and 55 civilians).

Air Force. The Air Force consists of an Air Force Staff, Air Force Base, and Air Surveillance Battalion. The total number of personnel in the Air Force is 200 (120 officers and NCOs and contract soldiers, 50 conscripts and 30 civilians).

INTERNATIONAL RELATIONS
Estonia is a member of the UN, WTO, BIS, the NATO Partnership for Peace, the Council of Europe, OSCE and Council of the Baltic Sea States, is an associate member of the EU and is an associate partner of the WEU. Estonia applied to join the EU in Nov. 1995, and is scheduled to become a member on 1 May 2004, subject to a referendum.

ECONOMY

Services contributed 69% of GDP in 1999, industry 25% and agriculture 6%.

Overview. Privatization is managed by the Estonian Privatization Agency under the jurisdiction of the Ministry of Finance. It has now entered its final phase with only large-scale infrastructure companies left to be sold. By June 1997, 456 enterprises had been privatized, realizing 3,300m. krooni.

Currency. The unit of currency is the *kroon* (EKR) of 100 *sents*. The kroon is pegged to the euro at a rate of 15·6466 *krooni* to one euro. Foreign exchange reserves were US$914m. in June 2002 and gold reserves 8,000 troy oz. Inflation was 5·8% in 2001. Total money supply in June 2002 was 25,936m. krooni.

Budget. Government budgetary revenue and expenditure in 1m. krooni for calendar years:

	1996	1997	1998	1999	2000
Revenue	17,544·8	22,360·5	24,006·5	23,397·4	26,474·5
Expenditure	17,713·7	20,551·8	24,103·3	26,815·5	27,373·3

In 2000 estimated sources of revenue included value added tax, 8,159m. krooni; and personal and corporate income tax, 3,605m. krooni. Items of expenditure: social welfare, 9,269m. krooni; health service, 4,458m. krooni; education, 3,057m. krooni; and recreational, cultural and arts affairs, 1,005m. krooni. VAT is 18%.

Performance. GDP growth rate was 6·9% in 2000 and 5·4% in 2001. Growth was supported by the increasing import demand of the European Union. Total GDP in 2001 was US$5·3bn.

Banking and Finance. A central bank, the Bank of Estonia, was re-established in 1990 (*Governor*, Vahur Kraft). The Estonian Investment Bank was established in 1992 to provide financing for privatized and private companies. Since 1 Jan. 1996 banks have been required to have an equity of at least 50m. krooni. As of Nov. 2000 there were 6 Estonian authorized commercial banks, 1 foreign bank's branch and 3 foreign bank's representative offices. As a result of a wave of mergers the two largest groups, Hansabank and the Union Bank of Estonia, control 80% of the market. Total assets and liabilities of commercial banks at Oct. 2000 were 55bn. krooni.

A stock exchange opened in Tallinn in 1996.

Weights and Measures. The metric system is in use.

ENERGY AND NATURAL RESOURCES

Environment. According to the *World Bank Atlas* Estonia's carbon dioxide emissions in 1998 were the equivalent of 12·1 tonnes per capita.

Electricity. In 1999, 92% of electricity was produced by burning oil shale (down from 98% in 1996). Installed capacity was 3·3m. kW in 1999 and production was 8·52bn. kWh. Consumption per capita was 3,531 kWh in 1998. A pilot wind-turbine project was set up in 1996. Electricity production in power plants in 1999 was 8,265 GWh (9,217 GWh in 1997).

Oil and Gas. There are rich oil shale deposits estimated at 3,972m. tonnes in 1997. A factory for the production of gas from shale and a 208 km-pipeline from Kohtla-Järve supplies shale gas to Tallinn, and exports to St Petersburg. Natural gas is imported from Russia.

Water. A total of six isolated underground water complexes provide 75% of the water consumed.

Minerals. Oil shale is the most valuable mineral resource. Production volume has decreased (from 21·2m. tonnes in 1990 to 12m. tonnes in 1999) because of falls in exports and domestic electricity consumption, and an increase in the use of natural gas. There are extensive peat deposits, estimated at 1·5bn. tonnes in 1997. Phosphorites and super-phosphates are found and refined, and lignite, limestone, dolomite, clay, sand and gravel are mined.

Agriculture. In the course of the 1990s the proportion of agriculture in the gross national product decreased from 15% to 3·3%. Farming employs around 6% of the population. At 1 Jan. 1999 there were 11,700 private farms and 680 agricultural enterprises averaging 490 ha cultivable land. In 2000 there were 1·43m. ha of agricultural land of which 1·12m. ha were arable and 0·3m. ha were natural grassland. In 1995, 13·1% of the labour force was employed in agriculture. Minimum prices and the quantity of state purchases of agricultural produce were guaranteed by the government for 1997, along with agricultural supports of 332·81m. krooni. Gross agricultural output in 1999 was 5·6bn. krooni.

At 1 Jan. 2000 there were 267,300 cattle (138,400 milch cows), 28,200 sheep, 285,700 pigs and 2,461,800 poultry.

Output of main agricultural products (in 1,000 tonnes) in 2000: potatoes, 457; barley, 293; wheat, 149; oats, 129; rye, 62. Livestock products (in 1,000 tonnes), 2000: meat, 59; milk, 600; eggs, 17. Export of dairy products in 1999 comprised 35% of the year's volume.

Forestry. In 1999, 2·14m. ha were covered by forests, which provide material for sawmills, furniture, and the match and pulp industries, as well as wood fuel. Private, municipal and state ownership of forests is allowed. In 1999 there were 600,000 ha of privately owned forests out of a total of 2,143,000 ha. In 1999 the annual timber cut was 6·7m. cu. metres, of which 3·7m. cu. metres was from private forests.

Fisheries. Some 4,670 people are employed in the active fishing section of the industry and 4,870 in the fish-processing section. The total catch in 1999 was 86,008 tonnes, mainly from sea fishing. Export volumes of fishing products in 1999 was 71,760 tonnes.

INDUSTRY

The leading companies by market capitalization in Estonia, excluding banking and finance, in Jan. 2002 were: Eesti Telekom (12b. krooni); Norma (830m. krooni), a car seatbelt producer; and Merko Ehitus (719m. krooni), a construction company.

In Estonia the share of manufacturing in the GDP has been decreasing in recent years. The share of value added by the sectors of service activities and finance has grown more rapidly in comparison with the industrial sector.

Labour. The workforce in 2000 totalled 705,100, of whom 608,600 were employed. The monthly average wage in the 1st quarter of 2001 was 5,098 krooni. The unemployment rate was 9·1% in the third quarter of 2002, compared to 13·7% in 2000.

Retirement age was 63 years for both men and women in 1998.

Trade Unions. The main trade union organization in Estonia is the Estonian Association of Trade Unions, which represents the interests of industrial, service, trade, public and agricultural employees.

INTERNATIONAL TRADE

Free Trade agreements are in force with the EU, EFTA, Latvia, Lithuania, Czech Republic, Slovakia, Slovenia, Ukraine, Poland, Hungary, Faroe Islands and Turkey.

Direct investment position in Estonia by countries as of 30 Sept. 2000: Sweden, 39·2%; Finland, 31·1%; USA, 4·5%; Norway, 4·3%; Denmark, 4·1%; Germany, 2·7%; UK, 2·6%.

Estonia's direct investment position abroad by countries as of 30 June 2000: Latvia, 59·1%; Lithuania, 23·7%; Cyprus, 7·9%; Ukraine, 1·4%; and Sweden, 0·5%. Direct foreign investment in Estonia as at Sept. 2000 totalled 41,929·8m. krooni (14,454·4m. as at March 1997). Estonia's direct investment abroad as at Sept. 2000 totalled 6,542m. krooni. The foreign trade balance in 1999 was 17,192·9m. krooni. External debt was US$3,280m. in 2000.

Imports and Exports. Exports (in 1m. krooni) in 2000 (and 1999) were valued at 53,911·1 (43,173·7); imports, 72,215·4 (60,488·8). Main export markets, 1999: Finland, 8,378·5 (19·4% of the total); Sweden, 8,103·6 (18·8%); Russia, 3,969·8 (9·2%); Latvia, 3,766·3 (8·7%); Germany, 3,237·2 (7·5%); UK, 1,930·9 (4·5%); Denmark, 1,696·6 (3·9%); Lithuania, 1,675·2 (3·9%); Netherlands, 1,441·5 (3·3%); Ukraine, 1,234·4 (2·9%); USA, 1,056·6 (2·5%).

Main import suppliers, 1999: Finland, 13,769·9 (22·8% of total); Russia, 8,171·2 (13·5%); Germany, 5,621·9 (9·3%); Sweden, 5,603·8 (9·3%); Japan, 2,855·3 (4·7%); USA, 2,680·7 (4·4%); Italy, 1,915·9 (3·2%); Denmark, 1,505·8 (2·5%); Netherlands, 1,486·1 (2·4%); UK, 1,437·5 (2·4%); Latvia, 1,313·2 (2·2%).

Around 65% of Estonian trade is w member countries, and 50% with Finland and Sweden alone.

COMMUNICATIONS

Roads. As of 1 Jan. 2000 there were 16,43(road network is being developed under a 10-f state roads (50·8% paved). The there were 458,700 passenger cars in use (31an inaugurated in 1995. In 1999 trucks and vans, 6,196 buses and coaches, and 61,000 inhabitants), plus 81,030 were 284 fatalities in road accidents in 1998. notorcycles and mopeds. There

Rail. Length of railways on 1 Jan. 2000 was 968 132 km was electrified. In 1999, 6·76m. passeng(1,520 mm gauge), of which were carried. Domestic total volume of goods transpnd 37·4m. tonnes of freight international total volume (in tonnes), 29·9m. l in 1999 (in tonnes), 7·5m.;

Civil Aviation. There is an international airport at TallUlemiste), which handled 554,898 passengers (550,255 on international flighte) in 2000. Estonian aviation companies handled 336,200 l 2,4?7 tonnes of freight of goods in 1999. The national carrier is Estonian Air, 3?engers and 5,500 tonnes Estonian Aviation also provides international service I tate-owned. The smaller services to Amsterdam, Copenhagen, Frankfurt, Hambur9 Estonian Air operated Minsk, Moscow, Oslo, Riga, Stockholm and Vilnius, withlsinki, Kyiv, London, to Riga and Turku. In 1999 Estonian Air flew 6·0m. km, carrynian Aviation flying (all on international flights). In Jan. 2000 there were 124 air?91,300 passengers in Estonia.

Shipping. There are six major shipping companies, all of w are privatized. There were 542 registered vessels totalling 445,470 DWT at 1 Ja?000. There are ice-free, deep-water ports at Tallinn and Muuga (state-owned). Tall handled 85% of the total turnover of goods in Estonia in 2000. Central Port se?s about 6m. passengers a year.

Telecommunications. Estonia had 522,800 telephone main lines in 20? (363·3 per 1,000 persons) and 220,000 PCs (152·9 per 1,000 persons). There we 500,000 mobile phone subscribers in 1999 and 13,000 fax machines in 1995. In eb. 2000 the Estonian parliament voted to guarantee Internet access to its citizns. The number of Internet users in Dec. 2001 was 429,700.

Postal Services. There were 12 postal service providers in 2000, the main provider being the state-owned Eesti Post. In 1999 there were 534 post offices.

SOCIAL INSTITUTIONS

Justice. A post-Soviet criminal code was introduced in 1992. There is a three-tier court system with the State Court at its apex, and there are both city and district courts. The latter act as courts of appeal. The State Court is the final court of appeal, and also functions as a constitutional court. There are also administrative courts for petty offences. Judges are appointed for life. City and district judges are appointed by the President; State Court judges are elected by Parliament.

In 1999, 51,539 crimes were reported (including 200 murders), of which 34·5% were solved. The murder rate, at 13·9 per 100,000 population in 1999, is one of the highest in Europe. There are nine prisons; in Dec. 1999, 4,712 persons were in custody.

The death penalty was abolished for all crimes in 1998.

Religion. There are about 0·35m. Lutherans and a Methodist Church. The Estonian Orthodox Church owed allegiance to Constantinople until it was forcibly brought under Moscow's control in 1940; a synod of the free Estonian Orthodox Church was established in Stockholm. Returning from exile, it registered itself in 1993 a the Estonian Apostolic Orthodox Church. By an agreement in 1996 between Moscow and Constantinople Orthodox Patriarchates, there are now two Orth jurisdictions in Estonia. In 2000 there were some 209,300 Christians of v denominations in 311 congregations, including the Estonian Evangelical L Church (membership: 180,000) and the Estonian Apostolic Orthodox Church (membership: 18,000).

Education. Adult literacy rate in 1998 was at least 99%. There are n comprehensive school starting at age six, followed by three years seco

ONIA

In 1999 pupils in 706 primary, ...ry and special schools numbered 215,841; of these general education ...386 were Estonian-language, 104 Russian-language and 16 mixed-langua...1999, 64% of children between one and six years attended pre-school inst...a total of 46,409 students, and 86 secondary institutes of higher education...dents. vocational schools with 31,1...ication came to 7·2% of GNP and 25·5% of total In 1997 total expenditure ... government spending.

In 2000 central governm... ...penditure on education came to 3,333·9m. krooni.

Health. There were 78 s... ...nd 28 private hospitals in 1999, and 71·9 hospital beds per 10,000 populatio... ...1999 there were 4,426 state and 1,788 private doctors (in 1996, 4,457 state and ... private doctors).

Welfare. In 1999 there ... 0·37m. pensioners. The average monthly pension was 1,453 krooni in 1999 ... official poverty line was introduced in 1993 (then 280 krooni per mont... Persons receiving less are entitled to state benefit. Unemployment benefi... ...as 400 krooni a month in 1999.

CULTURE

Broadcasting. There w... ...over 30 radio stations in Estonia in 2000. Public service radio, Estonian Radi... ...perates four channels, three in Estonian and one in languages of natio... ...inorities, mainly Russian. In 2000 there were four TV channels with nati... ...le networks (colour by PAL): Estonian State Television and three commercial... ...annels. The Broadcasting Council is the regulatory body for public service ... ...dcasting and has nine members nominated by Riigikogu (the Estonian Parlia... ...nt). There were 605,000 TV receivers and 1·01m. radio receivers in 1997.

Cinema. In ...95 there were 220 cinemas, three full-length films were made and gross box o...ce receipts came to 16m. krooni. Attendances were 1m. in 1996.

Press. In ...000 there were 109 officially registered newspapers, including 82 in Estonian...and 956 periodicals, including 778 in Estonian. *The Baltic Times* is an English...anguage weekly.

Tourism. There were 3·18m. foreign visitors in 1999 who spent US$667·8m., 18% of Estonia's GDP.

Festivals. Festivals include: International Folklore Festival, BALTICA, which is staged every three years; Festival of Baroque Music; Jazz festival, JAZZKAAR; Pärnu International Documentary and Anthropology Film Festival and the Viljandi Folk Music Festival. Estonia's Song Festival, which was first held in 1869, is held every five years and is next scheduled to take place in 2004.

Baltoscandal, an international theatre festival which takes place every two years, celebrated its 7th staging in June 2002.

Libraries. The Eesti Rahvusraamatukogu (National Library of Estonia), opened in 1993, hosts exhibitions of local and international art. Other libraries include the Tallinn Tartu University Library (1802); Technical University Library (1919); and the Estonian Academic Library (1946). In 1997 there were 743 public libraries, 2 National libraries and 33 Higher Education libraries. They held a combined 18,116,000 volumes for 1,073,000 registered users.

Theatre and Opera. Most performances are in the Estonian language with the exception of the Russian Drama Theatre, and the Estonia Opera and Ballet Theatre which sometimes performs operas in their original language. There were nine state ...atres and one municipal in 2000.

...OMATIC REPRESENTATIVES
...nia in the United Kingdom (16 Hyde Park Gate, London, SW7 5DG)
...dor: Kaja Tael.

...ted Kingdom in Estonia (Wismari 6, 10136 Tallinn)
...: Sarah Squire.

606

Of Estonia in the USA (2131 Massachusetts Ave., NW, Washington, D.C., 20008)
Ambassador: Sven Jürgenson.

Of the USA in Estonia (Kentmanni 20, 15099 Tallinn)
Ambassador: Joseph M. DeThomas.

Of Estonia to the United Nations
Ambassador: Merle Pajula.

Of Estonia to the European Union
Ambassador: Priit Kolbre.

FURTHER READING

Statistical Office of Estonia. *Statistical Yearbook.*
Ministry of the Economy. *Estonian Economy.* Annual
Hood, N., *et al.*, (eds.) *Transition in the Baltic States.* London, 1997
Lieven, A., *The Baltic Revolution: Estonia, Latvia, Lithuania and the Path to Independence.* 2nd ed. Yale Univ. Press, 1994
Misiunas, R.-J. and Taagepera, R., *The Baltic States: Years of Dependence 1940–1991.* 2nd ed., Farnborough, 1993
Smith, I. A. and Grunts, M. V., *The Baltic States.* [Bibliography] ABC-Clio, Oxford and Santa Barbara (CA), 1993
Taagepera, R., *Estonia: Return to Independence.* Boulder (CO), 1993

National statistical office: Statistical Office of Estonia, Tallinn.
Website: http://www.stat.ee/

ETHIOPIA

Federal Democratic Republic of Ethiopia

Capital: Addis Ababa
Population estimate, 2000: 62·91m.
GDP per capita, 2000: (PPP$) 668
HDI/world rank: 0·327/168

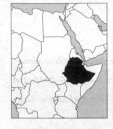

KEY HISTORICAL EVENTS

The ancient empire of Ethiopia has its legendary origin in the meeting of King Solomon and the Queen of Sheba. The empire developed at Askum in the north in the centuries before and after the birth of Christ as a result of Semitic immigration from South Arabia. Ethiopia's subsequent history is one of sporadic expansion southwards and eastwards, checked from the 16th to early 19th centuries by devastating wars with Muslims and Gallas. Modern Ethiopia dates from the reign of the Emperor Theodore (1855–68). Menelik II (1889–1913) defeated the Italians in 1896 and thereby safeguarded the empire's independence in the scramble for Africa.

In 1923 the heir to the throne, Ras Tafari (crowned Emperor Haile Selassie five years later), succeeded in getting Ethiopia admitted as an independent country to the League of Nations. However, the League was ineffective in preventing a second Italian invasion in 1936. The emperor fled the country, only returning when the Allied forces defeated the Italians in 1941.

In 1950 the former Italian colony of Eritrea, from 1941 under British military administration, was handed over to Ethiopia. Thereafter, a secessionist movement fought a guerrilla war for independence under the Eritrean Peoples' Liberation Front (EPLF). A military government, known as the Dirgue, assumed power on 12 Sept. 1974 under the leadership of Lieut. Col. Mengistu Haile Miriam. It deposed the emperor, abolished the monarchy and mounted an agricultural collectivization programme. In 1977 Somalia invaded Ethiopia and took control of the Ogaden region. After a counter offensive with Soviet and Cuban support the area was recaptured. Following ever-increasing territorial gains by the insurgent Ethiopian People's Revolutionary Democratic Front (EPRDF) and the EPLF, Mengistu fled the country. In July 1991 a conference of 24 political groups, called to appoint a transitional government, agreed a democratic charter. Eritrea seceded, and became independent, on 24 May 1993. In 1999 fighting broke out along Ethiopia's border with Eritrea. After the failure of international mediation, the 13-month long-truce between Ethiopia and Eritrea ended in May 2000. Ethiopia launched a major offensive in the ongoing war over territorial disputes and claimed victory. In June both sides agreed to an Organization of African Unity peace deal to end the two-year border war. Economic progress, including market-led reforms, raised hopes of higher living standards until three successive years of drought left food resources seriously depleted. Widespread malnutrition was alleviated by international aid.

TERRITORY AND POPULATION

Ethiopia is bounded in the northeast by Eritrea, east by Djibouti and Somalia, south by Kenya and west by Sudan. It has a total area of 1,104,300 sq. km. The secession of Eritrea in 1993 left Ethiopia without a coastline. An Eritrean–Ethiopian agreement of July 1993 gives Ethiopia rights to use the Eritrean ports of Assab and Massawa.

The first census was carried out in 1984: population, 42,019,418 (without Eritrea, 39,570,266). 1994 census population: 49,218,178. Estimate (1995), 56·68m. (82·8% rural in 1999); density, 51 per sq. km.

The UN gives a projected population for 2010 of 79·85m.

The 1994 Constitution provides for a federation of nine regions: Afar, Amhara, Benshangi, Gambella, Harar, Oromia, the Peoples of the South, Somalia and Tigre.

The population of the capital, Addis Ababa, was 2,534,000 in 1999. Other large towns (1994 populations): Dire Dawa, 164,851; Nazret, 127,842; Harar, 122,932; Mekele, 119,779; Jimma, 119,717.

There are six major ethnic groups (in % of total population in 1996): Oromo, 31%; Amhara, 30%; Tigrinya, 7%; Gurage, 4·7%; Somali, 4·1%; Sidamo, 3·2%. There are also some 60 minor ethnic groups and 286 languages are spoken. The *de facto* official language is Amharic (which uses its own alphabet), though Oromo-speakers form the largest group.

SOCIAL STATISTICS

Births, 1995, 2,741,000; deaths, 965,000. Rates per 1,000 population, 1995: births, 48·6; deaths, 17·1. Expectation of life at birth in 1999 was 43·3 years for males and 44·9 years for females. Annual population growth rate, 1990–99, 2·7%; infant mortality, 1999, 118 per 1,000 live births; fertility rate, 1999, 6·2 births per woman.

CLIMATE

The wide range of latitude produces many climatic variations between the high, temperate plateaus and the hot, humid lowlands. The main rainy season lasts from June to Aug., with light rains from Feb. to April, but the country is very vulnerable to drought. Addis Ababa, Jan. 59°F (15°C), July 59°F (15°C). Annual rainfall 50" (1,237 mm). Harar, Jan. 65°F (18·3°C), July 64°F (17·8°C). Annual rainfall 35" (897 mm). Massawa, Jan. 78°F (25·6°C), July 94°F (34·4°C). Annual rainfall 8" (193 mm).

CONSTITUTION AND GOVERNMENT

A 548-member constituent assembly was elected on 5 June 1994; turn-out was 55%. The EPRDF gained 484 seats. On 8 Dec. 1994 it unanimously adopted a new federal Constitution which provides for the creation of a federation of nine regions based (except the capital and the southern region) on a predominant ethnic group. These regions have the right of secession after a referendum. The *President*, a largely ceremonial post, is elected by parliament, the 548-member *Council of People's Representatives*. There is also an upper house, the 108-member *Federal Council*.

National Anthem. 'Yazegennat keber ba-Ityop yachchen santo' ('In our Ethiopia our civic pride is strong'); words anonymous, tune by S. Lulu.

RECENT ELECTIONS

Elections to the Council of People's Representatives took place on 14 May 2000. The Oromo People's Democratic Organization (OPDO) took 177 seats; Amhara National Democratic Movement (ANDM) 134; Tigray People's Liberation Front (TPLF) 38; Walayta, Gamo, Gofa Dawro Konta People's Democratic Organization 27; Ethiopian People's Revolutionary Democratic Front (EPRDF) 19; Sidama People's Democratic Organization 18; Gurage Nationalities Democratic Movement 15. 19 other parties won 10 seats or fewer. Non-partisans took 8 seats. The main parliamentary parties belong to the Ethiopian People's Revolutionary Front.

CURRENT ADMINISTRATION

President: Girma Wolde-Giyorgis; b. 1925 (elected 8 Oct. 2001).

In March 2003 the government comprised:

Prime Minister: Meles Zenawi; b. 1955 (TPLF; appointed 22 Aug. 1995).

Deputy Prime Ministers: Kassu Ilala (also *Minister of Infrastructure*), Adisu Legesse (also *Minister of Rural Development*).

Minister of Agriculture: Mulatu Teshome. *Defence:* Abadula Gemeda. *Capacity Building:* Tefera Walwa. *Education:* Genet Zewdie. *Federal Affairs:* Abay Tsehay. *Finance and Economic Development:* Sufyan Ahmad. *Foreign Affairs:* Seyoum Mesfin. *Health:* Kebede Tadesse. *Information:* Bereket Simon. *Justice:* Harika Haroye. *Labour and Social Affairs:* Hassan Abdella. *Mines and Energy:* Mohammed Dirir. *Revenue:* Getachew Belay. *Trade and Industry:* Girma Birru. *Water Resources:* Shiferaw Jarso. *Youth, Sports and Culture:* Teshome Toga.

DEFENCE

In 2000 defence expenditure totalled US$448m. (US$8 per capita), representing 6·8% of GDP.

Army. Following the overthrow of President Mengistu's government Ethiopian armed forces were constituted from former members of the Tigray Peoples' Liberation Front. The strength of the armed forces is estimated at 350,000 (1999).

Air Force. Due to its role in the war with Eritrea aircraft operability has improved. There were over 70 combat aircraft in 1999, including MiG-21s and MiG-23s, and 24 armed helicopters; and Russia has agreed to supply Su-27s. Personnel estimated at 2,500 in 1999. There were airfields at Debre Zeit, Asmara, Gode, Dire Dawa and Deke.

INTERNATIONAL RELATIONS

A border dispute between Ethiopia and Eritrea broke out in May 1998. Eritrean troops took over the border town of Badame after a skirmish between Ethiopian police units and armed men from Eritrea. Ethiopia maintained that Badame and Sheraro, a nearby town, had always been part of Ethiopia and called Eritrea's action an invasion. An agreement ending hostilities was signed in June 2000, followed by a peace accord in Dec. A buffer zone has been created to separate the armies.

Ethiopia is a member of the UN, the African Union, African Development Bank, COMESA, the Intergovernmental Authority on Development and is an ACP member state of the ACP-EU relationship.

ECONOMY

Agriculture accounted for 49·8% of GDP in 1998, industry 6·7% and services 43·5%.

Overview. Following a long period of stagnation, the Ethiopian economy came to a turning point in 1991 when peace was restored. An Economic Reform Programme, instituted in 1992, aimed at stabilizing the economy and deregulating economic activities to prepare the ground for a free-market economy. Also in 1992, a government agency, the Ethiopian Investment Authority, was created to promote, facilitate and co-ordinate foreign investment in the country. An Economic Rehabilitation and Reconstruction Programme (ERRP), launched in 1991–92, eased foreign exchange regulations to allow for imports of raw materials and capital equipment. But economic growth has been hampered by three years of drought leading to widespread food shortages.

A privatization programme began in 1995. Since then more than 200 companies have been privatized, yielding some US$360m. In total around 300 companies are to be privatized.

Currency. The *birr* (ETB), of 100 *cents*, is the unit of currency. The birr was devalued in Oct. 1992. In May 2002 total money supply was 12,976m. birr, foreign exchange reserves were US$638m. and gold reserves 205,000 troy oz. There was deflation in 2001, of 7·1%.

Budget. The fiscal year ends on 6 July. Revenue, 1996–97, US$1bn.; expenditure, US$1·5bn.

Performance. Real GDP growth was 5·4% in 2000, rising to 7·7% in 2001. Total GDP was US$6·4bn. in 2001.

Banking and Finance. The central bank and bank of issue is the National Bank of Ethiopia (founded 1964; *Governor*, Teklewold Atnafu). The country's largest bank is the state-owned Commercial Bank of Ethiopia. The complete monopoly held by the bank ended with deregulation in 1994, but it still commands about 90% of the market share. On 1 Jan. 1975 the government nationalized all banks, mortgage and insurance companies.

Weights and Measures. The metric system is officially in use. Traditional units include the *frasilla* (= approximately 37½ lb), and the *gasha*, which can vary between 80 and 300 acres. The Julian calendar remains in use; the year has 13 months, and is seven years behind the Gregorian calendar.

ENERGY AND NATURAL RESOURCES

Electricity. Installed capacity in 1991 was 630,000 kW. Production in 1998 was 1·36bn. kWh. Hydro-electricity accounts for 98% of generation. Consumption per capita was estimated to be 22 kWh in 1998. Supply: 220 volts; 50 Hz.

Oil and Gas. The Calub gas field in the southeast of Ethiopia has reserves estimated at 75bn. cu. metres.

Minerals. Gold and salt are produced. Lege Dembi, an open-pit gold mine in the south of the country, has proven reserves of over 62 tonnes and produces more than 3 tonnes a year.

Agriculture. Small-scale farmers make up about 85% of Ethiopia's population. There were 9·90m. ha of arable land in 1998 and 0·65m. ha of permanent crops. By 1993, 96% of agricultural land was worked by smallholdings averaging 0·5–1·5 ha. Land remains the property of the state, but individuals are granted rights of usage which can be passed to their children, and produce may be sold on the open market instead of compulsorily to the state at low fixed prices.

Coffee is by far the most important source of rural income. Main agricultural products (2000, in 1,000 tonnes): maize, 2,600; sugarcane, 2,300; wheat, 1,220; sorghum, 1,190; barley, 750; potatoes, 340; millet, 320; broad beans, 280; yams, 250; coffee, 230. Teff (*Eragrastis abyssinica*) and durra are also major products.

Livestock, 2000: cattle, 35·0m.; sheep, 21·0m.; goats, 16·8m.; asses, 5·20m.; horses, 2·75m.; camels, 1·06m.; chickens, 56m.

Forestry. In 1995 forests covered 13·58m. ha, representing 13·6% of the land area (13·89m. ha and 13·9% of the land area in 1990). Timber production in 1999 was 51·27m. cu. metres.

Fisheries. The catch in 1999 was approximately 15,858 tonnes, entirely from inland waters.

INDUSTRY

Most public industrial enterprises are controlled by the state. Industrial activity is centred around Addis Ababa. Processed food, cement, textiles and drinks are the main commodities produced.

In 1998 Ethiopia signed a US$500m. deal with the World Bank for power and road development projects.

Labour. The labour force in 1996 was 25,392,000 (59% males); it was estimated by the UN that 30% were unemployed. Coffee provided a livelihood to a quarter of the population.

INTERNATIONAL TRADE

Foreign debt was US$5,481m. in 2000.

Imports and Exports. Imports and exports for calendar years in US$1m.:

	1996	1997	1998	1999	2000
Imports f.o.b.	1,002·2	1,001·6	1,309·8	1,387·2	1,131·4
Exports f.o.b.	417·5	588·3	560·3	467·4	486·0

Principal exports (1994): coffee (64%); raw hides and skins (16%). Principal imports: refined petroleum products (12%); crude petroleum oils (9%); wheat and meslin (8%); motor vehicles for goods transport (7%).

Coffee accounts for about half of the country's export earnings. In 1997, 103,000 tonnes of coffee were exported, earning around US$360m. (£220m.) compared to just US$160m. (£100m.) in 1993. Other important exports include hides and skins, sugar, pulses and cattle.

Main export markets, 1997: Germany, 22%; Japan, 12%; Italy, 9%; UK, 5%. Main import suppliers, 1997: Italy, 10%; USA, 9%; Japan, 8%; Jordan, 5%.

COMMUNICATIONS

Roads. There were 28,500 km of roads in 1996, only about 4,275 km of which are paved. Passenger cars in use in 1998 numbered 55,644 (less than one per 1,000 inhabitants) and there were also 28,170 trucks and vans, and 14,622 buses and coaches.

In 1998 a US$500m. deal was signed with the World Bank for road and power development projects.

Rail. The Ethiopian-Djibouti Railway Corp. (782 km, metre-gauge) in 1993 carried 0·24m. tonnes of freight and 0·71m. passengers.

Civil Aviation. There are international airports at Addis Ababa (Bole) and Dire Dawa. The national carrier is the state-owned Ethiopian Airlines.

In 1998 Ethiopian Airlines served 44 international and 35 domestic destinations. In 1999 scheduled airline traffic of Ethiopian-based carriers flew 28·5m. km, carrying 861,000 passengers (617,000 on international flights). In 2000 Addis Ababa (Bole) handled 1,040,623 passengers and 27,237 tonnes of freight.

Shipping. Merchant shipping totalled 83,000 GRT in 1998.

Telecommunications. All the main centres are connected with Addis Ababa by telephone or radio telegraph. In 2000 there were 231,900 telephone main lines (3·7 per 1,000 persons), three-quarters of which are in Addis Ababa. There were 60,000 PCs in use in 2000 (0·9 per 1,000 persons) and 2,000 fax machines in 1997. In Dec. 2000 Ethiopia had 10,000 Internet users.

Postal Services. In 1995 there were 570 post offices, or one for every 97,000 persons.

SOCIAL INSTITUTIONS

Justice. The legal system is based on the Justinian Code. A new penal code came into force in 1958 and Special Penal Law in 1974. Codes of criminal procedure, civil, commercial and maritime codes have since been promulgated. Provincial and district courts have been established, and High Court judges visit the provincial courts on circuit. The Supreme Court at Addis Ababa is presided over by the Chief Justice.

Religion. About 53% of the population are Christian, mainly belonging to the Ethiopian Orthodox Church, and 30% Sunni Muslims. Amhara, Tigreans and some Oromos are Christian. Somalis, Afars and some Oromos are Muslims. About 12% of the population follow traditional animist beliefs.

Education. The adult literacy rate in 1999 was 37·4% (42·8% among males and 31·8% among females). Primary education commences at seven years and continues with optional secondary education at 13 years. Up to the age of 12, education is in the local language of the federal region. Pupil/teacher ratio: 33. In 1996–97 there were 4,007,694 pupils at 10,256 primary schools with 92,775 teachers, and (1995–96) 819,242 pupils with 25,984 teachers at secondary schools. During the period 1990–95 only 19% of females of primary school age were enrolled in school. In 1994–95 there was one university with 19,200 students and 900 academic staff, and one agricultural university with 1,551 students and 324 academic staff. There were two institutes of health sciences and water technology; and two colleges—one of teacher training and one of town planning.

In 1996 expenditure on education came to 4·0% of GNP and 13·7% of total government spending.

Health. Population per hospital bed, 1994–95, 293,787; population per health centre, 22,242. In the period 1990–98 only 25% of the population had access to safe drinking water.

CULTURE

Broadcasting. The government-run Voice of Ethiopia broadcasts a national programme and an external service in English. Ethiopian Television (colour by PAL) transmits about 28 hours a week. In 1997 there were 11·75m. radio and 320,000 TV receivers.

Press. In 1996 there were four government-controlled daily newspapers with a combined circulation of about 86,000. In 1995 there were 17 non-dailies and periodicals.

Tourism. In 1998 there were 91,000 foreign visitors. Revenue from tourists in 1998 totalled US$11m.

DIPLOMATIC REPRESENTATIVES

Of Ethiopia in the United Kingdom (17 Prince's Gate, London, SW7 1PZ)
Ambassador: Fisseha Adugna.

Of the United Kingdom in Ethiopia (Fikre Mariam Abatechan St., Addis Ababa)
Ambassador: Myles Wickstead.

Of Ethiopia in the USA (3506 International Drive, NW, Washington, D.C., 20008)
Ambassador: Ayele Kassahun.

Of the USA in Ethiopia (Entoto St., Addis Ababa)
Ambassador: Aurelia B. Brazeal.

Of Ethiopia to the United Nations
Ambassador: Abdulmejid Hussein.

Of Ethiopia to the European Union
Ambassador: Ato Berhane Gebre-Christos.

FURTHER READING

Alemneh Dejene. *Environment, Famine and Politics in Ethiopia: a View from the Village.* Boulder (Colo.), 1991

Araia, G., *Ethiopia: the Political Economy of Transition.* Univ. Press of America, 1995

Crummey, Donald, *Land and Society in the Christian Kingdom of Ethiopia: From the Thirteenth to the Twentieth Century.* Univ. of Illinois Press and James Currey, Oxford, 2000

Marcus, H. G., *A History of Ethiopia.* California Univ. Press, 1994

Mekonnen, T. (ed.) *The Ethiopian Economy: Structure, Problems and Policy Issues.* Addis Ababa, 1992

Munro-Hay, Stuart and Pankhurst, Richard, *Ethiopia.* [Bibliography] ABC-Clio, Oxford and Santa Barbara (CA), 1995

Negash, Tekeste and Tronvoll, Kjetil, *Brothers at War: Making Sense of the Eritrean–Ethiopian War.* Ohio Univ. Press and James Currey, Oxford, 2001

Pankhurst, Richard, *The Ethiopians.* Oxford, 1999

Tiruneh, A., *The Ethiopian Revolution: a Transformation from an Aristocratic to a Totalitarian Autocracy.* CUP, 1993

National statistical office: Central Statistical Office, Addis Ababa.

FIJI ISLANDS

Capital: Suva
Population estimate, 2000: 814,000
GDP per capita, 2000: (PPP$) 4,668
HDI/world rank: 0·758/72

KEY HISTORICAL EVENTS

The Fiji Islands were first recorded in detail by Capt. Bligh after the mutiny of the Bounty (1789). In the 19th century the demand for sandalwood attracted merchant ships. Deserters and shipwrecked men stayed. Tribal wars were bloody and general until Fiji was ceded to Britain on 10 Oct. 1874. Fiji gained independence on 10 Oct. 1970. It remained an independent state within the Commonwealth with a Governor-General appointed by the Queen until 1987. In the general election of 12 April 1987 a left-wing coalition came to power with the support of the Indian population who outnumbered the indigenous Fijians by 50% to 44%. However, it was overthrown in a military coup. A month later, Fiji declared itself a Republic and Fiji's Commonwealth membership lapsed.

In 1990 a new coalition restored civilian rule but made it impossible for Fijian Indians to hold power. A rapprochement with Indian leaders led to an agreement to restore multi-racial government in 1998. Fiji rejoined the Commonwealth in 1997. On 27 July 1998 a new constitution changed the country's name from Fiji to Fiji Islands.

A coup was staged in May 2000 under the leadership of George Speight, a failed businessman. His main aim was to exclude Indians from the government. An interim government, excluding Speight supporters, was appointed on 3 July 2000 to rule for 18 months. On 26 July George Speight and 400 of his supporters were arrested. On 18 Feb. 2002 Speight was sentenced to death although this was subsequently commuted to life imprisonment.

TERRITORY AND POPULATION

The Fiji Islands comprise 332 islands and islets (about one-third are inhabited) lying between 15° and 22° S. lat. and 174° E. and 177° W. long. The largest is Viti Levu, area 10,429 sq. km (4,027 sq. miles); next is Vanua Levu, area 5,556 sq. km (2,145 sq. miles). The island of Rotuma (47 sq. km, 18 sq. miles), about 12° 30' S. lat., 178° E. long., was added to the colony in 1881. Total area, 7,078 sq. miles (18,333 sq. km). Total population (1996 census), 775,077 (females, 381,146); ethnic groups: Fijian, 393,575; Indian, 338,818; part-European/European, 14,788; Chinese, 4,939; other Pacific islanders, 10,463; Rotuman, 9,727; other, 2,767. Population density (1996), 42·4 per sq. km. Of the total population, 51·4% lived in urban areas in 1999.

The UN gives a projected population for 2010 of 896,000.

Population estimate of the capital, Suva, in 1999 was 196,000. Other large towns, with 1996 populations, are Lautoka (42,917), Nadi (30,791) and Labasa (24,187).

English is the official language; Fijian and Hindustani are also spoken.

SOCIAL STATISTICS

Births, 1998, 17,944; deaths, 5,241; marriages, 8,058. 1998 birth rate per 1,000 population, 22·5; death rate per 1,000 population, 6·6. Annual population growth rate, 1990–99, 1·2%. Life expectancy at birth in 1999 was 67·1 years for males and 70·7 years for females. Infant mortality, 1999, 18 per 1,000 live births; fertility rate, 1999, 2·7 births per woman.

CLIMATE

A tropical climate, but oceanic influences prevent undue extremes of heat or humidity. The S. E. Trades blow from May to Nov., during which time nights are cool and rainfall amounts least. Suva, Jan. 80°F (26·7°C), July 73°F (22·8°C). Annual rainfall 117" (2,974 mm).

CONSTITUTION AND GOVERNMENT

The executive authority of the State is vested in the President, who is appointed by the Bose Levu Vakaturaga (Great Council of Chiefs). The Prime Minister is appointed by the President. The Prime Minister must establish a multi-party cabinet. The President's term of office is five years.

The Upper House or Senate consists of 32 members of whom 14 are appointed by the President on the advice of Bose Levu Vakaturaga. Nine are appointed by the President on the advice of the Leader of the Opposition and one appointed by the President on the advice of the Council of Rotuma.

A new Constitution unanimously passed by Parliament and assented to by H.E. the President came into force on 27 July 1998. The country's name was changed from Fiji to Fiji Islands and the people were to be known as Fiji Islanders instead of Fijians. The new Constitution also does away with an indigenous Prime Minister and has a 71-seat *House of Representatives* (Lower House), with 46 elected on a communal role and 25 from an open electoral roll. Of the 46, 23 will be elected from a roll of voters registered as Fijians, 19 from a roll of voters registered as Indians, 1 from a roll of voters registered as Rotumans, and 3 from a roll of voters registered who are none of these. Parliament was reopened in Oct. 2001, having been suspended following the May 2000 coup.

National Anthem. 'Blessing grant, oh God of Nations, on the isles of Fiji'; words by M. Prescott, tune anonymous.

RECENT ELECTIONS

Mahendra Chaudhry, the Labour Party leader, became the country's first Indian prime minister in 1999, but was ousted in the coup of May 2000 after just over a year in office. In parliamentary elections held between 25 Aug.–2 Sept. 2001 Soqosoqo Duavata ni Leweniavanua (Fiji United Party) won 32 out of 71 seats ahead of the Fiji Labour Party with 27. Other parties won six seats or fewer.

CURRENT ADMINISTRATION

President: Ratu Josefa Iloilo; b. 1920 (appointed as interim president on 18 July 2000; re-appointed as president for a five-year term on 15 March 2001).

Vice President: Jope Seniloli.

In March 2003 the government comprised:

Prime Minister, Minister for National Reconciliation and Unity, Information and Media Relations, Fijian Affairs, Culture and Heritage: Laisenia Qarase (sworn in 10 Sept. 2001, having previously been interim prime minister from 4 July 2000 to 14 March 2001 and from 16 March 2001 until officially taking office). He named a cabinet that did not include any members of the Indian-dominated Labour party in defiance of the constitution, which states that any party with eight or more seats is entitled to ministerial positions.

Minister of Agriculture, Sugar and Land Resettlement: Jonetani Galuinadi. *Commerce, Business Development and Investment:* Tomasi Vuetilovoni. *Education:* Ro Teimumu Kepa. *Finance and National Planning, and Communications:* Jone Kubuabola. *Fisheries and Forests:* Konisi Yabaki. *Foreign Affairs and External Trade:* Kaliopate Tavola. *Health:* Solomone Naivalu. *Home Affairs and Immigration:* Joketani Cokanasiga. *Justice and Attorney-General:* Qoriniasi Bale. *Labour and Industrial Relations:* Kenneth Zinck. *Lands and Mineral Resources:* Ratu Naiqama Lalabalavu. *Local Government, Housing, Squatter Settlement and Environment:* Mataiasi Ragigia. *Multi-Ethnic Affairs:* George Shiu Raj. *Public Enterprises and Public Sector Reform:* Irami Matairavula. *Regional Development:* Ilaitia Tuisese. *Tourism:* Pita Nacuva. *Transportation and Civil Aviation:* Josefa Vosanibola. *Women, Social Welfare and Poverty Alleviation:* Adi Asenaca Caucau. *Works and Energy:* Savenaca Draunidalo. *Youth, Employment Opportunities and Sports:* Isireli Leweniqila.

Fiji Government Online: http://www.fiji.gov.fj/

DEFENCE

In 2000 defence expenditure totalled US$32m. (US$39 per capita), representing 2·1% of GDP.

Army. Personnel in (1999) numbered close to 3,200 including 300 recalled reserves. More than 800 of these are actively involved in peacekeeping duties with the United Nations in the Middle East. There was an additional reserve force of 6,000.

Navy. A small naval division of the armed forces numbered 300 in 1999.

INTERNATIONAL RELATIONS

The Fiji Islands is a member of the UN, WTO, the Commonwealth, the Asian Development Bank, the Colombo Plan, the Pacific Community, the Pacific Islands Forum, and is an ACP member state of the ACP-EU relationship.

ECONOMY

Agriculture accounted for 19·5% of GDP in 1998, industry 31·0% and services 49·5%.

Operating revenue (1997), $F700·00m. Operating expenditure (1997), $F550·00m.

Currency. The unit of currency is the *Fiji dollar* (FJD) of 100 *cents*. In June 2002 total money supply was $F661m., foreign exchange reserves were US$332m. and gold reserves 1,000 troy oz. Inflation in 2001 was 2·3%. The Fiji dollar was devalued by 20% in Jan. 1998.

Budget. The financial year corresponds with the calendar year. Government revenue and expenditure (in $F1m.):

	1994	1995	1996	1997	1998
Revenue	689·02	710·18	736·18	794·09	848·65
Expenditure	786·20	801·14	881·44	770·30	1,029·46

VAT of 10% was introduced in 1992.

Performance. There was a recession in 2000, with the economy shrinking by 2·8%, although 2001 saw a recovery, with growth of 2·6%. Total GDP in 2001 was US$1·7bn.

Banking and Finance. The central bank and bank of issue is the Reserve Bank of Fiji (*Governor*, Savenaca Narube). Total assets were $F493·07m. in June 1996. The National Bank is a government-owned commercial bank. The Fiji Development Bank has assets totalling $F356·01m. There are six foreign banks in the country. Total assets of commercial banks were $F1,797·92m. in June 1996.

ENERGY AND NATURAL RESOURCES

Environment. According to the *World Bank Atlas* carbon dioxide emissions in 1998 were the equivalent of 0·9 tonnes per capita.

Electricity. The Fiji Electricity Authority is responsible for the generation, transmission and distribution of electricity in the country. It operates six separate supply systems. The largest energy project is one of hydro-electricity generating 95% of the main island's electric needs. Two rural hydro schemes have been completed, one generating 100 kW and the other 800 kW. In 1994 there were seven thermal and one hydro-electric power stations.

Installed capacity in 1993 was 200,000 kW; production was 550m. kWh in 1998. Consumption per capita in 1997 was 693 kWh.

Minerals. The main gold-mine accounts for almost one tenth of the country's exports and employs about 1,700 people. Since the beginning of 1997 gold prices have been falling. However, a total of 2,000 tonnes have been sold since 1991. Net sales in 1996 were 239 tonnes (gross sales were 588 tonnes). Gold is likely to overtake sugar as the Fiji Islands' main export by 2005. Gold production, 1996, was 4,452 kg; silver production, 1995, 1,572 kg.

Agriculture. With a total land area of 1·8m. ha, only 16% is suitable for farming. Arable land: 24% sugarcane, 23% coconut, 53% other crops. Production figures for 2000 (in 1,000 tonnes): sugarcane, 2,250; coconut, 215; cassava, 30; taro, 27; rice, 18; copra, 14; sweet potatoes, 8. Ginger is the most successful diversification crop to date—1995 showed an increase of 1,000 tonnes; total export value for the 1995 crop was $F1,445,000. Fruits and vegetables were valued at $F1m. in 1995 for 1,000 tonnes of export.

Livestock (2000): cattle, 350,000; horses, 44,000; goats, 235,000; pigs, 115,000; chickens, 4m. Products, 2000 (in 1,000 tonnes): beef and veal, 10; pork, bacon and ham, 4; poultry meat, 8; eggs, 4. Total production of milk was 58,000 tonnes in 2000.

Forestry. Forests covered 835,000 ha—45·7% of the land area—in 1995 (most of it natural forest), compared to 853,000 ha and 46·7% in 1990. Forestry contributed around 1·2% of GDP in 1998. It is the fifth most important export commodity, valued at $F34m. in 1996. Hardwood plantations covered over 48,000 ha in 1996. In 2000 Fiji Pine Ltd had nearly 42,000 ha of softwood plantations, and aims eventually to have 52,000 ha. Log production in 1999 was 483,000 cu. metres.

Fisheries. The catch in 1999 was 36,713 tonnes, of which 31,091 tonnes came from sea fishing. Fisheries accounts for 2% of GDP. Mainstay of export fisheries are the skipjack and albacore tuna for canning. There was an increase in export of fresh and chilled tuna from 53 tonnes in 1989 to over 3,000 tonnes in 1995.

INDUSTRY
The Tax Free Factory scheme was instituted in 1987 as an encouragement to industry. A total of 133 Tax Free Factories (TFF) were in operation in 1996, a decline from 144 in 1995. Of the total, 68 factories were engaged in garment manufacturing. The garment industry earned $F141m. in 1996.

Output (in tonnes): sugar (1998), 277,900; coconut oil (1993), 6,017; flour (1994), 26,933; butter (1994), 1,477; cigarettes (1996), 481m. (units); animal feed (1994), 25,377; cement (1996), 84,000; soap, washing powder and detergents (1995), 7,000; beer (1995), 15m. litres.

Labour. Approximately 301,500 persons were in paid employment in 1996. There were 17,700 unemployed persons in 1998, or 5·4% of the workforce.

INTERNATIONAL TRADE
The Tax Free Factory/Tax Free Zone Scheme was introduced in 1987 to stimulate investment and encourage export-oriented businesses.

Foreign debt was US$136m. in 2000.

Imports and Exports. Imports and exports for calendar years in US$1m.:

	1995	1996	1997	1998	1999
Imports f.o.b.	761·4	839·9	818·9	614·6	653·3
Exports f.o.b.	519·6	672·2	535·6	428·9	537·7

Chief exports are sugar, prepared and preserved fish, timber, ginger and molasses. Main export markets, 1996: Australia, 27·9%; UK, 14·4%; New Zealand, 12·4%; USA, 8·5%. Main import suppliers, 1996: Australia, 44·4%; New Zealand, 14·8%; USA, 9·3%; Japan, 5·7%.

COMMUNICATIONS
Roads. Total road length in 1996 was 3,440 km, of which almost half were sealed. There were a total of 30,000 passenger cars and 29,000 lorries and vans in 1996. In 1997, 73 fatalities were caused by road accidents.

Rail. Fiji Sugar Cane Corporation runs 600 mm gauge railways at four of its mills on Viti Levu and Vanua Levu, totalling 595 km.

Civil Aviation. There are international airports at Nadi and Suva. The national carrier is Air Pacific (78% government-owned). In 1998 it provided services to Australia, Japan, New Zealand, USA and a number of Pacific island nations. Air Fiji only operates on domestic routes. In 2000 Nadi handled 816,000 passengers (700,000 on international flights).

Shipping. The three ports of entry are Suva, Lautoka and Levuka. Ocean-going shipping totalled 29,000 GRT in 1998, including oil tankers 3,000 GRT. Inter-island shipping fleet is a mix of private and government vessels. A total of 620 foreign vessels called into the Suva port in 1995, 318 and 109 respectively in Lautoka and Levuka. Altogether 7,189 ships including local ships, yachts and foreign vessels called into the three major ports.

Telecommunications. The national telephone service had 86,400 telephone main lines in 2000 (106·2 for every 1,000 population). In 1998, 40% of subscribers were business customers and 60% residential. There were over 500 cardphones located around the country in 1998 and approximately 80 in rural areas. There were 3,800 fax machines in use in 1997, 8,000 mobile phone subscribers in 1998 and 45,000 PCs in use in 2000 (55·3 per 1,000 persons). Internet users numbered 7,500 in Dec. 1999.

Postal Services. In 1995, 19·6m. items were posted in the Fiji Islands for delivery to local addresses in addition to 4·76m. items posted for overseas destinations, making total posting of 24·45m. items. There are currently 50 major post offices and 108 postal agencies.

SOCIAL INSTITUTIONS

Justice. An independent Judiciary is guaranteed under the constitution. A High Court has unlimited original jurisdiction to hear and determine any civil or criminal proceedings under any law. The High Court also has jurisdiction to hear and determine constitutional and electoral questions including the membership of the House of Representatives. The Chief Justice of the Fiji Islands is appointed by the President after consultation with the Prime Minister.

The Fiji Islands' Court of Appeal, of which the Chief Justice is *ex officio* President, is formed by three specially appointed Justices of Appeal, appointed by the President after consultation with the Judicial and Legal Services Commission. Generally, any person convicted of an offence has a right of appeal from the High Court of Appeal. The final appellant court is the Supreme Court. Most matters coming before the Superior Courts originate in Magistrates' Courts.

The population in penal institutions in 1997 was 1,091 (140 per 100,000 of national population).

Police. In 1997 the Royal Fiji Police Force had a total strength of 1,915.

Religion. In 1996 the population consisted of 52% Christians, 39·4% Hindus, 7·8% Muslims, 0·7% Sikhs and 0·1% others.

Education. Adult literacy rate was 92·6% in 1999 (94·7% among males and 90·5% among females). Total enrolment in 1996: primary schools, 142,781 (with 5,011 teachers); secondary schools, 70,098 (with 3,519 teachers); teacher training, 903 (with 92 teachers); vocational/technical education, 1,876. The number of registered schools totalled 1,261. Of these there were 391 pre-schools, 16 special schools, 698 primary schools, 151 secondary schools and 5 post secondary schools.

The University of the South Pacific, which is located in Suva, serves 12 countries in the South Pacific region. The Fiji Islands also has a college of agriculture, school of medicine and nursing, an institute of technology, a primary school teacher training college and an advanced college of education.

Health. In 1997 there were 25 hospitals with 1,805 beds; 409 doctors, 36 dentists and 1,742 nurses.

Through its national health service system, the government continues to provide the bulk of health services both in the curative and public health programmes. In 1998, 41% of adults in the Fiji Islands aged 15 and over smoked—the second highest percentage of any country, after Russia.

CULTURE

Broadcasting. There are two major radio stations, Island Network Corporation Ltd and Communications Fiji Ltd. Each has its own unique programmes to suit the culture, age and taste of the nation's radio audience. Fiji Television Company is a commercial network that has one free to air and two pay channels (colour by NTSC). In 1997 there were 21,000 TV receivers and 500,000 radio receivers.

Press. There are two daily newspapers, *Fiji Times and Herald* and *The Daily Post*. Vernacular newspapers are also published by these two, including *Nai Lalakai, Nai Volasiga* and *Shanti Dut*. Other locally produced periodicals are the *Review, Island's Business, Fiji First, Pacific Islands Monthly* and *Marama Vou*.

Tourism. Visitor arrivals in 1999 totalled a record high 409,955, earning US$541m. The inauguration of new flight routes and their associated promotions contributed to an increase in visitors.

DIPLOMATIC REPRESENTATIVES
Of the Fiji Islands in the United Kingdom (34 Hyde Park Gate, London, SW7 5DN)
High Commissioner: Emitai Lausiki Boladuadua.

Of the United Kingdom in the Fiji Islands (Victoria House, 47 Gladstone Rd., Suva)
High Commissioner: Charles Mochan.

Of the Fiji Islands in the USA (2233 Wisconsin Ave., NW, Washington, D.C., 20007)
Ambassador: Anare Jale.

Of the USA in the Fiji Islands (31 Loftus St., Suva)
Ambassador: David Lyon.

Of the Fiji Islands to the United Nations
Ambassador: Amraiya Naidu.

Of the Fiji Islands to the European Union
Ambassador: Isikeli Uluinairai Mataitoga.

FURTHER READING
Bureau of Statistics. *Annual Report; Current Economic Statistics*, Quarterly
Reserve Bank of Fiji. *Quarterly Review*
Gorman, G. E. and Mills, J. J., *Fiji.* [Bibliography] ABC-Clio, Oxford and Santa Barbara (CA), 1994
Lal, B. J., *Broken Waves: a History of the Fiji Islands in the Twentieth Century.* Univ. of Hawaii Press, 1992
Sutherland, W., *Beyond the Politics of Race: an Alternative History of Fiji to 1992.* Australian National Univ. Press, 1992

National statistical office: Bureau of Statistics, POB 2221, Government Buildings, Suva.
Website: http://www.statsfiji.gov.fj

FINLAND

Suomen Tasavalta—
Republiken Finland

Capital: Helsinki
Population estimate, 2000: 5·17m.
GDP per capita, 2000: (PPP$) 24,996
HDI/world rank: 0·930/10

KEY HISTORICAL EVENTS

Finland was part of Sweden until the 18th century when the southeast territory was conquered by Russia. The rest of the country was ceded to Russia by the treaty of Hamina in 1809 when Finland became an autonomous grand-duchy retaining its laws and institutions under a grand duke, the Emperor of Russia. The Diet, elected since 1906 on universal suffrage, produced in 1916 a social democrat majority, the first in Europe. After the Russian revolution Finland declared itself independent but civil war broke out in Jan. 1918 between the 'whites' and 'reds', the latter supported by Russian Bolshevik forces. The defeat of the red guards led to a peace treaty with Soviet Russia, signed in 1920. On 30 Nov. 1939 a Soviet invasion compelled Finland to cede 32,806 sq. km including the Carelian Isthmus, Viipuri and the shores of Lake Ladoga. When the German attack on the USSR was launched in June 1941 Finland was again involved in war against the USSR. On 19 Sept. 1944 an armistice was signed in Moscow. Finland agreed to cede more territory and to pay reparations. To pacify the USSR, the post-war premier and later president Juho Passikivi pursued a policy of neutralism favourable to the Russians. This policy, known as Finlandization, was continued under Presidents Urho Kekkonen (1956–81) and Mauno Koivisto (1981–94). With the collapse of the Soviet Union, Finland was able to adopt an independent foreign policy which led to EU admission in 1995.

TERRITORY AND POPULATION

Finland, a country of lakes and forests, is bounded in the northwest and north by Norway, east by Russia, south by the Baltic Sea and west by the Gulf of Bothnia and Sweden. The most recent 10-yearly census took place on 31 Dec. 2000. The area and the population of Finland on 31 Dec. 2001 (Swedish names in brackets):

Region	Area (sq. km)[1]	Population	Population per sq. km
Uusimaa (Nyland)	6,366	1,318,324	207·1
Itä–Uusimaa (Östra Nyland)	2,747	90,201	32·8
Varsinais–Suomi (Egentliga Finland)	10,624	449,293	42·3
Satakunta	8,289	236,308	28·5
Kanta–Häme (Egentliga Tavastland)	5,204	165,509	31·8
Pirkanmaa (Birkaland)	12,272	450,745	36·7
Päijät–Häme (Päijänne–Tavastland)	5,133	197,656	38·5
Kymenlaakso (Kymmenedalen)	5,106	186,707	36·6
Etelä–Karjala (Södra Karelen)	5,618	137,019	24·4
Etelä–Savo (Södra Savolax)	14,137	164,471	11·6
Pohjois–Savo (Norra Savolax)	16,808	252,842	15·0
Pohjois–Karjala (Norra Karelen)	17,782	170,793	9·6
Keski–Suomi (Mellersta Finland)	16,582	264,762	16·0
Etelä–Pohjanmaa (Södra Österbotten)	13,458	194,542	14·5
Pohjanmaa (Österbotten)	7,675	173,083	22·6
Keski–Pohjanmaa (Mellersta Österbotten)	5,286	70,848	13·4
Pohjois–Pohjanmaa (Norra Österbotten)	35,290	368,029	10·4
Kainuu (Kajanaland)	21,567	88,473	4·1

FINLAND

Region	Area (sq. km)[1]	Population	Population per sq. km
Lappi (Lappland)	93,004	189,288	2·0
Ahvenanmaa (Åland)	1,527	26,008	17·0
Total	304,473	5,194,901	17·1

[1]Excluding inland water area which totals 33,672 sq. km.

The growth of the population, which was 421,500 in 1750, has been:

End of year	Urban[1]	Semi-urban[2]	Rural	Total	Percentage urban
1800	46,600	. . .	786,100	832,700	5·6
1900	333,300	. . .	2,322,600	2,655,900	12·5
1950	1,302,400	. . .	2,727,400	4,029,800	32·3
1970	2,340,300	. . .	2,258,000	4,598,300	50·9
1980	2,865,100	. . .	1,922,700	4,787,800	59·8
1990	2,846,220	803,224	1,349,034	4,998,500	56·9
1998	3,101,104	853,571	1,204,971	5,159,646	60·1
1999	3,123,190	853,084	1,195,028	5,171,302	60·4
2000	3,167,668	898,860	1,114,587	5,181,115	61·1
2001	3,190,897	899,120	1,104,884	5,194,901	61·4

The classification urban/rural has been revised as follows:

[1]Urban—at least 90% of the population lives in urban settlements, or in which the population of the largest settlement is at least 15,000.

[2]Semi-urban—at least 60% but less than 90% live in urban settlements, or the population of the largest settlement is more than 4,000 but less than 15,000.

The population on 31 Dec. 2001 by language spoken: Finnish, 4,793,199; Swedish, 290,771; other languages, 109,197; Lappish, 1,734.

The projected population for 2010 is 5·27m.

The principal towns with resident population, 31 Dec. 2000, are (Swedish names in brackets):

Helsinki (Helsingfors)—capital	555,474	Kajaani	36,088
Espoo (Esbo)	213,271	Järvenpää	35,915
Tampere (Tammerfors)	195,468	Kokkola (Karleby)	35,539
Vantaa (Vanda)	178,471	Rovaniemi	35,427
Turku (Åbo)	172,561	Lohja (Lojo)	35,243
Oulu (Uleåborg)	120,753	Kouvola	31,364
Lahti	96,921	Imatra	30,663
Kuopio	86,651	Seinäjoki	30,290
Jyväskylä	78,996	Kerava (Kervo)	30,270
Pori (Björneborg)	75,994	Savonlinna (Nyslott)	27,796
Lappeenranta (Villmanstrand)	58,041	Nokia	26,905
Vaasa (Vasa)	56,737	Riihimäki	26,173
Kotka	54,846	Salo	24,561
Joensuu	51,758	Kemi	23,689
Mikkeli (St Michel)	46,727	Varkaus	23,246
Hämeenlinna (Tavastehus)	46,108	Raisio (Reso)	23,149
Porvoo (Borgå)	44,969	Iisalmi	23,113
Hyvinkää (Hyvinge)	42,545	Tornio (Torneå)	22,617
Rauma (Raumo)	37,190	Heinola	21,178

In 2000, 59·0% of the population lived in urban areas. Nearly one-fifth of the total population lives in the Helsinki metropolitan region.

Finnish and Swedish are the official languages. Sami is spoken in Lapland.

SOCIAL STATISTICS

Statistics in calendar years:

	Living births	Of which outside marriage	Still-born	Marriages	Deaths (exclusive of still-born)	Emigration
1994	65,231	20,439	249	24,898	48,000	8,672
1995	63,067	20,886	293	23,737	49,280	8,957
1996	60,723	21,484	231	24,464	49,167	10,587
1997	59,329	21,659	221	23,444	49,108	9,854
1998	57,108	21,244	211	24,023	49,262	10,817
1999	57,574	22,273	177	24,271	49,345	11,966
2000	56,742	22,247	231	26,150	49,339	14,311
2001	56,189	22,222	185	24,830	48,550	13,153

In 2001 the rate per 1,000 population was: births, 11; deaths, 9; marriages, 5; infant deaths (per 1,000 live births), 3·2. Annual population growth rate, 1992–2001, 0·3%. In 2001 the suicide rate per 100,000 population was 36·8 among men and 10·2 among women, giving Finland the highest suicide rate in the European Union. Life expectancy at birth, 2001, 74·6 years for males and 81·5 years for females. In 2001 the most popular age range for marrying was 25–29 for both males and females. Fertility rate, 2000, 1·7 births per woman. In 2001 Finland received 1,651 asylum applications, equivalent to 0·3 per 1,000 inhabitants.

A UNICEF report published in 2000 showed that 4·3% of children in Finland live in poverty (in households with income below 50% of the national median), the third lowest percentage of any country behind Sweden and Norway.

CLIMATE
A quarter of Finland lies north of the Arctic Circle. The climate is severe in winter, which lasts about six months, but mean temperatures in the south and southwest are less harsh, 21°F (–6°C). In the north, mean temperatures may fall to 8·5°F (–13°C). Snow covers the ground for three months in the south and for over six months in the far north. Summers are short but quite warm, with occasional very hot days. Precipitation is light throughout the country, with one third falling as snow, the remainder mainly as rain in summer and autumn. Helsinki (Helsingfors), Jan. 30·2°F (–1·0°C), July 68·4°F (20·2°C). Annual rainfall 27·9" (708·7 mm).

CONSTITUTION AND GOVERNMENT
Finland is a republic governed by the constitution of 1 March 2000 (which replaced the previous constitution dating from 1919). Although the president used to choose who formed the government, under the new constitution it is the responsibility of parliament to select the prime minister. The government is in charge of domestic and EU affairs with the president responsible for foreign policy 'in co-operation with the government'.

Parliament consists of one chamber (*Eduskunta*) of 200 members chosen by direct and proportional election by all citizens of 18 or over. The country is divided into 15 electoral districts, with a representation proportional to their population. Every citizen over the age of 18 is eligible for parliament, which is elected for four years, but can be dissolved sooner by the president.

The *president* is elected for six years by direct popular vote. In the event of no candidate winning an absolute majority, a second round is held between the two most successful candidates.

National Anthem. 'Maamme'/'Vårt land' ('Our land'); words by J. L. Runeberg, tune by F. Pacius (same as Estonia).

RECENT ELECTIONS
Presidential elections were held on 16 Jan. 2000 with a second round on 6 Feb. In the first round SDP candidate Tarja Halonen came first with 40·0%, followed by Esko Aho (KESK) with 34·4%. There were five other candidates. In the run-off Halonen won with 51·6% against 48·4% for Aho. Turn-out was around 80%.

At the elections for the 200-member parliament on 16 March 2003, turn-out was 69·6%. The Centre Party (KESK) won 55 seats with 24·7% of votes cast (48 seats in 1999), the ruling Social Democratic Party (SDP) 53 with 24·5% (51 seats in 1999), the National Coalition Party 40 with 18·5%, the Left Alliance 19 with 9·9% (19), the Greens 14 with 8·0%, the Christian Democrats 7 with 5·3% and the Swedish People's Party 8 with 4·6%. Turn-out was 69·6%. In Feb. 2002, 37·5% of the seats in parliament were held by women.

European Parliament. Finland has 16 representatives. At the June 1999 elections turn-out was 30·1%. The National Rally won 4 seats with 25·3% of votes cast (political affiliation in European Parliament: European Liberal, Democrat and Reform Party); Centre Party, 4 with 21·3% (European People's Party); Social Democratic Party, 3 with 17·8% (Party of European Socialists); Green League, 2 with 13·4% (Greens); Left Wing League, 1 with 9·1% (Confederal Group of the European United Left/Nordic Green Left); Swedish People's Party in Finland, 1 with 6·8% (European Liberal, Democrat and Reform Party); Christian League of Finland, 1 with 2·4% (European People's Party).

CURRENT ADMINISTRATION

President: Tarja Halonen; b. 1943 (Social Democrat; sworn in 1 March 2000).

The Council of State (Cabinet) is composed of a coalition of the Centre Party (KESK), the Social Democratic Party (SDP) and the Swedish People's Party (SFP). The 18-member cabinet consists of nine men and nine women. In April 2003 it comprised:

Prime Minister: Anneli Jäätteenmäki; b. 1955 (KESK; sworn in 17 April 2003). *Deputy Prime Minister and Minister of Finance:* Antti Kalliomäki (SDP). *Foreign Affairs:* Erkki Tuomioja (SDP). *Justice:* Johannes Koskinen (SDP). *Education:* Tuula Haatainen (SDP). *Culture:* Tanja Karpela (KESK). *Interior:* Kari Rajamäki (SDP). *Trade and Industry:* Mauri Pekkarinen (KESK). *Transport and Communications:* Leena Luhtanen (SDP). *Social Affairs and Health:* Sinikka Mönkäre (SDP). *Health and Social Services:* Liisa Hyssälä (KESK). *Labour:* Tarja Filatov (SDP). *Defence:* Matti Vanhanen (KESK). *Environment:* Jan-Erik Enestam (SFP). *Regional and Municipal Affairs:* Hannes Manninen (KESK). *Foreign Trade and Development:* Paula Lehtomäki (KESK). *Agriculture and Forestry:* Juha Korkeaoja (KESK). *Minister at the Ministry of Finance:* Ulla-Maj Wideroos (SFP).

The *Speaker* is Riitta Uosukainen.

Government Website: http://www.valtioneuvosto.fi

DEFENCE

Conscript service is 6–12 months. Total strength of trained and equipped reserves is about 490,000 (to be 350,000).

Defence expenditure in 2001 totalled US$1,757m. (US$338 per capita), representing 1·2% of GDP.

Army. The Army consists of 1 armoured training brigade, 3 readiness brigades, 3 infantry training brigades, 3 jaeger regiments, 1 artillery brigade, 3 brigade artillery regiments, 2 air defence regiments, 1 engineer regiment (including ABC school), 3 brigade engineer battalions, 1 signals regiment, 4 brigade signals battalions and a reserve officer school. Total strength of 27,300 (21,600 conscripts).

Frontier Guard. This comes under the purview of the Ministry of the Interior, but is militarily organized to participate in the defence of the country. It is in charge of border surveillance and border controls. It is also responsible for conducting maritime search and rescue operations. Personnel, 2002, 3,200 (professional) with a potential mobilizational force of 22,000.

Navy. The organization of the Navy was changed on 1 July 1998. The Coastal Defence, comprising the coast artillery and naval infantry, was merged into the navy.

About 50% of the combatant units are kept manned, with the others on short-notice reserve and re-activated on a regular basis. Naval bases exist at Upinniemi (near Helsinki), Turku and Kotka. Naval Infantry mobile troops are trained at Tammisaari. Total personnel strength (2001) was 7,400, of whom 5,000 were conscripts.

Air Force. Personnel (2002), 4,300 (1,500 conscripts). Equipment included 63 F-18 Hornets.

INTERNATIONAL RELATIONS

Finland is a member of the UN, WTO, BIS, NATO Partnership for Peace, OECD, EU, Council of Europe, OSCE, CERN, Nordic Council, Council of the Baltic Sea States, Inter-American Development Bank, Asian Development Bank, IOM and the Antarctic Treaty. Finland has acceded to the Schengen Accord, which abolishes border controls between Finland, Austria, Belgium, Denmark, France, Germany, Greece, Iceland, Italy, Luxembourg, the Netherlands, Norway, Portugal, Spain and Sweden.

ECONOMY

Services accounted for 63% of GDP in 2001, industry 34% and agriculture 3%.

According to the Berlin-based organization *Transparency International*, Finland has the least corruption in business and government of any country in the world. It received 9·7 out of 10 in a corruption perceptions index published in 2002.

Overview. Sound macroeconomic policies and economic openness have led the recovery from the recession of the early 1990s. A surplus in central government finances has been achieved by cutting taxes to boost the economy and by a tight control of expenditure. Fiscal policy in 2002 promoted growth in domestic demand. Income tax paid by households, pensioners' social security contribution and employers' national pension contributions have been reduced. In the last decade there has been a structural shift from a resource-based to a knowledge-based economy. The basic metals and forestry industry have given way to ICT (Information and Communications Technology). Finland ranks as one of the world's leading ICT producers.

Currency. On 1 Jan. 1999 the euro (EUR) became the legal currency in Finland; irrevocable conversion rate 5·94573 marks to one euro. The euro, which consists of 100 cents, has been in circulation since 1 Jan. 2002. There are seven euro notes in different colours and sizes denominated in 500, 200, 100, 50, 20, 10 and 5 euros, and eight coins denominated in 2 and 1 euros, then 50, 20, 10, 5, 2 and 1 cents. On the introduction of the euro there was a 'dual circulation' period before the mark ceased to be legal tender on 28 Feb. 2002. Euro banknotes in circulation on 1 Jan. 2002 had a total value of €8·0bn.

Inflation in 2001 was 2·6%, declining to 1·6% in 2002. Foreign exchange reserves were US$7,904m. in June 2002 and gold reserves 1·58m. troy oz. Total money supply was €5,189m. in June 2002.

Budget. Revenue and expenditure for the calendar years 1999–2003 in 1m. euros:

	1999	2000	2001	2002	2003[1]
Revenue	35,845	37,756	35,426	35,326	35,722
Expenditure	35,602	38,472	36,072	35,326	35,722

[1]Proposed figure.

Of the total revenue in 2001, 36% derived from income and property tax, 29% from value added tax, 13% from excise duties, 5% from other taxes and similar revenue and 13% from miscellaneous sources. Of the total expenditure, 2001, 21% went to health and social security, 14% to education and culture, 7% to agriculture and forestry, 5% to defence, 5% to transport and 49% to other expenditure according to the budget.

VAT is 22% (reduced rates, 12% and 8%).

At the end of Dec. 2001 the central government debt totalled €61,760m. Domestic debt amounted to €5,323m.; foreign debt, 9,082m. marks.

Performance. Real GDP growth was 5·6% in 2000, but only 0·7% in 2001. It was forecast to be 1·6% in 2002. Total GDP was US$120·9bn. in 2001.

In 2000 the OECD reported that 'After expanding vigorously for several years, the Finnish economy experienced a temporary and mild slowdown in 1999 prompted by the global downturn in the wake of the financial crisis in Asia and Russia... Despite the slowdown in 1999, output growth outpaced the euro area average for the sixth successive year by a wide margin. Indeed, the rebound since the end of the deep recession of the early 1990s has been remarkably strong...' The report referred to the 'skilful macroeconomic management, moderate wage agreements, labour market reforms, the take-off of the electronic equipment industry (with output increasing by 25 per cent per year), rapid restructuring in other industries and a favourable international economic climate' as instrumental in economic growth. The report also cited the urgent need for reforms in the pension system and the need to lighten the Finnish tax burden (among the highest in the OECD).

Finland was placed second in the world in both the Growth Competitiveness Ranking and the Microeconomic Competitiveness Ranking in the World Economic Forum's *Global Competitiveness Report 2002–03*. In the 2002 *World Competitiveness Yearbook*, compiled by the International Institute for Management Development, Finland came second in the world ranking behind the USA.

Banking and Finance. The central bank is the Bank of Finland (founded in 1811), owned by the State and under the guarantee and supervision of Parliament. The *Governor* is Matti Vanhala. It is the only bank of issue, and the limit of its right to issue notes is fixed equal to the value of its assets of gold and foreign holdings plus 1,500m. marks.

At the end of 2001 the deposits in banking institutions totalled 359,474m. marks and the loans granted by them 408,416m. marks.

The most important groups of banking institutions in 2001 were:

	Number of institutions	Number of offices	Deposits (1m. marks)	Loans (1m. marks)
Commercial banks	9	724	209,346	252,063
Savings banks	40	254	29,520	27,328
Co-operative banks	287	626	110,555	104,678
Foreign banks	7	28	7,486	24,347

The three largest banks are Nordea Bank Finland (formed in 1997 as MeritaNordbanken when Nordbanken of Sweden merged with Merita of Finland), Sampo Bank (formerly Leonia) and OKO Bank. In March 2000 MeritaNordbanken acquired Denmark's Unidanmark, thereby becoming the Nordic region's biggest bank in terms of assets. It has also become Europe's leading Internet bank, by July 2000 having 1·4m. Internet banking clients. By early 2001 approximately 40% of the Finnish population were using e-banking, the highest percentage in any country.

There is a stock exchange in Helsinki, which is one of the best performers among small industrialized nations. In 1999 share prices rose by 125%.

In 1998 Finland received US$11bn. worth of foreign direct investment, equivalent to 8·9% of GDP. No other country received foreign investment totalling such a high proportion of its GDP.

Weights and Measures. The metric system is in use.

ENERGY AND NATURAL RESOURCES

Environment. Finland's carbon dioxide emissions in 2001 were the equivalent of 11·6 tonnes per capita. An *Environmental Sustainability Index* compiled for the World Economic Forum meeting in Feb. 2002 ranked Finland first in the world, with 73·9%. The index measured the ability of countries to maintain favourable environmental conditions and examined various factors including pollution levels and the use or abuse of natural resources.

Electricity. Installed capacity was 17·24m. kW at the beginning of 2001. Production was 66,655m. kWh in 1999 (19% hydro-electric) and 67,278m. kWh in 2000 (21%). Consumption per capita in 2000 was an estimated 15,279 kWh. In 2001 there were four nuclear reactors, which contributed 32% of production. In May 2002 parliament approved the construction of a fifth reactor. Supply: 220 volts; 50 Hz.

Oil and Gas. There is no oil and gas production.

Water. Finland has abundant surface water and groundwater resources relative to its population and level of consumption. The total groundwater yield is estimated to be 10–30m. cu. metres a day, of which some 6m. is suitable for water supplies. Approximately 15% of this latter figure is made use of at the present time. A total of 2–4% of Finland's exploitable water resources are utilized each year.

Minerals. Notable of the mines are Pyhäsalmi (zinc–copper), Orivesi (gold ore), Hitura (nickel) and Keminmaa (chromium). In 2001 the metal content (in tonnes) of the output of copper ore was 11,600; of zinc ore, 20,100; of nickel ore, 2,000; and of chromium, 236,710.

Agriculture. The cultivated area covers only 7% of the land, and of the economically active population 6% were employed in agriculture and forestry in 2001. The arable area was divided in 2001 into 77,320 farms (including 1,001 farms with under one hectare of arable land). The distribution of this area by the size of the farms was: less than 5 ha cultivated, 6,605 farms; 5–20 ha, 29,758 farms; 20–50 ha, 29,474 farms; 50–100 ha, 9,651 farms; over 100 ha, 1,832 farms.

Agriculture accounted for 7·8% of exports and 8·6% of imports in 1997.

The principal crops (area in 1,000 ha, yield in 1,000 tonnes) were in 2001:

Crop	Area	Yield	Crop	Area	Yield
Barley	547·2	1,786·0	Hay	156·0	565·5
Oats	422·7	1,287·1	Wheat	144·6	488·9
Potatoes	30·0	732·8	Rye	29·0	64·1

The total area under cultivation in 2000 was 2,005,731 ha. Approximately 6·7% of all agricultural land is used for organic farming. Production of dairy butter in 2001 was 61,026 tonnes; and of cheese, 97,846 tonnes.

Livestock (2001): horses, 58,600 (including trotting and riding horses, and ponies); cattle, 1,037,400; pigs, 1,260,800; poultry, 4,244,700; reindeer (1998), 292,000.

Forestry. The total forest land amounts to 23·0m. ha. The productive forest land covers 20·2m. ha. Timber production in 1999 was 53·85m. cu. metres. Finland is one of the largest producers of roundwood in Europe. Finland's per capita consumption of roundwood is the highest in the world, at 11·5m. cu. metres per person in 2000.

Fisheries. The catch in 2000 was 115,400 tonnes, of which 110,041 tonnes came from sea fishing. In 2001 there were 247 food fish production farms in operation, of which 74 were freshwater farms. Their total production amounted to 15,739 tonnes. In addition there were 126 fry-farms and 301 natural food rearers, most of these in freshwater.

INDUSTRY

The leading companies by market capitalization in Finland, excluding banking and finance, in Jan. 2002 were: Nokia Oyj (€106bn.), the world's leading mobile phone producer; and Stora Enso Oyj (€14bn.) and UPM-Kymmene Corporation (€10bn.) world-class forest products companies.

Finland originally became industrialized by harnessing its forest resources. Over a century later, forests are still Finland's most crucial raw material resource, although the metal and engineering industry has long been Finland's leading branch of manufacturing, both in terms of value added and as an employer. Today Finland is a typical advanced industrial economy: two-thirds of its total output is generated in the service sector.

In 1999 there were 29,614 establishments in industry (of which 27,168 were manufacturing concerns) with 436,565 personnel (of whom 414,252 were in manufacturing). Gross value of industrial production in 1999 was 528,824m. marks, of which manufacturing accounted for 499,398m. marks.

Labour. In 2001 the labour force was 2,605,000 (52% males). In 2001, 66·8% of the economically active population worked in services, 21·0% in manufacturing and 15·1% in trade and restaurants. In 2001 unemployment was 9·1%, up from 3·2% in 1990, but down from 16·6% in 1994. In Jan. 2003 the rate dropped further still to 9·0%.

Trade Unions. There are three labour organizations: the Confederation of Unions for Academic Professionals—Akateemisten Toimihenkilöiden Keskusjarjesto (AKAVA); the Finnish Confederation of Salaried Employees—Toimihenkilokeskusjarjesto (STTK); and the Central Organization of Finnish Trade Unions (SAK). According to an incomes policy agreement reached by the central labour market organizations in Nov. 2002, which is in force until Feb. 2005, wages and salaries were to be raised by 1·8% in March 2003 and by 1·7% in March 2004. The government has undertaken to cut taxes on wages and salaries to support moderate pay increases.

INTERNATIONAL TRADE

At the start of the 1990s a collapse in trade with Russia led to the worst recession in the country's recent history. Today, exports to Russia are about 6% of the total.

In 1960 wood and paper industry dominated exports with their 69% contribution, but today the metal and engineering industry is the largest export sector.

Region	Exports 2001	Imports 2001
European Union	54%	56%
Other Europe	18%	21%
Developing Countries	14%	10%
EFTA	4%	5%
Other Countries	10%	8%

Industry	Exports 2001
Metal, Engineering, Electronics	55%
Forest Industry	27%
Chemical Industry	6%
Other	12%

Use of Goods	Imports 2001
Raw materials, production necessities	39%
Investment goods	24%
Durable consumer goods	10%
Energy	12%
Other	15%

Imports and Exports. Imports and exports for calendar years, in €1m.:

	1998	1999	2000	2001
Imports	29,066	29,691	36,837	35,891
Exports	38,779	39,246	49,484	47,800

Trade with principal partners in 2001 was as follows (in 1,000 marks):

	Imports	Exports		Imports	Exports
Australia	1,470,900	2,244,356	Italy	7,520,598	10,240,938
Austria	2,414,211	2,984,062	Japan	9,088,816	5,326,589
Belgium	4,896,729	7,014,950	Netherlands	7,753,303	11,083,327
Brazil	1,204,550	2,556,553	Norway	6,995,100	7,197,343
Canada	1,125,667	2,322,072	Philippines	367,146	2,217,503
China	6,500,265	7,474,511	Poland	2,136,522	5,295,445
Czech Republic	1,672,579	1,391,468	Republic of Korea	1,414,402	2,297,642
Denmark	7,715,878	6,911,342	Russia	20,343,755	16,640,555
Estonia	6,994,462	6,277,090	Spain	3,941,075	7,108,112
France	9,529,927	13,089,747	Sweden	21,543,530	23,689,474
Germany	30,690,952	35,078,718	Switzerland	3,018,266	3,784,749
Greece	479,020	2,162,891	Taiwan	1,853,350	1,392,963
Hong Kong	712,090	2,811,421	Thailand	731,233	2,344,559
Hungary	1,087,881	1,896,258	UK	13,601,580	27,331,736
Ireland	2,285,907	2,232,810	USA	14,516,339	27,586,986

COMMUNICATIONS

Roads. In Jan. 2002 there were 78,059 km of public roads, of which 50,301 km were paved. At the end of 2001 there were 2,160,103 registered cars, 68,569 lorries, 243,988 vans and pick-ups, 9,769 buses and coaches, and 16,225 special automobiles. Road accidents caused 433 fatalities in 2001.

Rail. On 31 Dec. 2001 the total length of the line operated was 5,850 km (2,400 km electrified), all of it owned by the State. The gauge is 1,524 mm. In 2001, 55·0m. passengers and 41·7m. tonnes of freight were carried. There is a metro (17 km) and tram/light rail network (75·8 km) in Helsinki.

In 1995 the Finnish State Railways was transformed into a joint-stock company. Operations continue under the VR Group, the largest transport services group in Finland.

Civil Aviation. The main international airport is at Helsinki (Vantaa), and there are also international airports at Turku, Tampere, Rovaniemi and Oulu. The national carrier is Finnair. Scheduled traffic of Finnish airlines covered 83m. km in 2001. The number of passengers was 8·0m. and the number of passenger-km 13,211,000; the air transport of freight and mail amounted to 198·1m. tonne-km. Helsinki-Vantaa handled 10,030,918 passengers in 2001 (7,031,246 on international flights) and 84,850 tonnes of freight and mail. Oulu is the second busiest airport, handling 717,244 passengers in 2001, and Turku the third busiest, with 352,131 in 2001.

Shipping. The total registered mercantile marine on 31 Dec. 2001 was 611 vessels of 1,675,964 GRT. In 2001 the total number of vessels arriving in Finland from abroad was 29,246 and the goods discharged amounted to 44·9m. tonnes. The goods loaded for export from Finnish ports amounted to 37·1m. tonnes.

The lakes, rivers and canals are navigable for about 6,300 km. Timber floating has some importance, and there are about 8,894 km of floatable inland waterways. In 2000 bundle floating was about 1·0m. tonnes.

Telecommunications. In 2001 there were 2,806,000 telephone main lines in use and 4,175,600 mobile telephones. According to a survey conducted in Nov. 2002 around 90% of Finnish households own a mobile phone. The rate among 18- and 19-year-olds is almost 100%. Mobile subscribers account for 60% of all telephone subscribers—a percentage only exceeded in Cambodia. In mid-1999 approximately 19% of Finnish households only had a mobile phone and did not have a fixed-line phone at all. The Finnish company Nokia is the world's biggest manufacturer of mobile phones, making 41m. of the 163m. phones sold in 1998. It is by far the biggest company in Finland, accounting for 4·5% of the country's GDP in 2000 and more than half the value of its stock exchange. The biggest operator is Sonera (formerly Telecom Finland). Approximately 50% of all voice and data traffic streams through the company's networks, and approximately 60% of all mobile users are Sonera customers. In March 2002 Sonera and the Swedish telecommunications operator Telia announced merger plans. Finland has the lowest rates in Europe for both fixed and mobile phone calls.

There were 2·2m. PCs in use in 2001 (424·1 per 1,000 persons) and 198,000 fax machines in 1997. Finland had 2·55m. Internet users in June 2002. According to the World Economic Forum's *Global Information Technology Report 2002–2003* Finland is the country best placed to reap the economic and social benefits of the Internet.

Postal Services. In 2001 there were 322 primary post offices and 1,102 agents providing postal services in Finland. Finland Post Group is now exposed to competition in its business operations, with the exception of addressed letter mail for which it holds a licence for nationwide delivery.

SOCIAL INSTITUTIONS

Justice. The lowest court of justice is the District Court. In most civil cases a District Court has a quorum of three legally qualified members. In criminal cases as well as in some cases related to family law the District Court has a quorum with a chair and three lay judges. In the preliminary preparation of a civil case and in a criminal case concerning a minor offence, a District Court is composed of the chair only. From the District Court an appeal lies to the courts of appeal in Turku, Vaasa, Kuopio, Helsinki, Kouvola and Rovaniemi. The Supreme Court sits in Helsinki. Appeals from the decisions of administrative authorities are in the final instance decided by the Supreme Administrative Court, also in Helsinki. Judges can be removed only by judicial sentence. Two functionaries, the Chancellor of Justice and the Ombudsman or Solicitor-General, exercise control over the administration of justice. The former acts also as counsel and public prosecutor for the government; the latter is appointed by Parliament.

At the end of 2001 the daily average number of prisoners was 3,135 of which 159 were women. The number of convictions in 2001 was 303,053, of which 236,448 were for minor offences with a maximum penalty of fines, and 26,082 with penalty of imprisonment. 11,740 of the prison sentences were unconditional.

Religion. Liberty of conscience is guaranteed to members of all religions. National churches are the Lutheran National Church and the Greek Orthodox Church of Finland. The Lutheran Church is divided into eight bishoprics (Turku being the archiepiscopal see), 80 provostships and 595 parishes. The Greek Orthodox Church is divided into three bishoprics (Kuopio being the archiepiscopal see) and 27 parishes, in addition to which there are a monastery and a convent.

Percentage of the total population at the end of 2001: Lutherans, 84·9; Greek Orthodox, 1·6; others, 0·6; not members of any religion, 12·9.

Education. Number of institutions, teachers and students (2001).

Primary and Secondary Education:

	Number of institutions	Teachers[1]	Students
First-level Education (Lower sections of the comprehensive schools, grades I–VI)			405,880[2]
Second-level Education General education (Upper sections of the comprehensive schools, grades VII–IX, and upper secondary general schools)	4,394	49,592	318,489
Vocational and Professional Education	291[3]	12,606[3, 4]	157,545

[1]Data for teachers refers to 2000.
[2]Including pre-primary education (12,613 pupils) in comprehensive schools.
[3]Numbers of institutions for vocational and professional education refer to secondary and tertiary education.
[4]Number of teachers for vocational and professional education refer to secondary and tertiary education.

Tertiary Education. Vocational and professional education at tertiary education level was provided for 2,570 students in 2001. Polytechnic education was provided at 30 permanent and 1 experimental polytechnics with 118,013 students and 5,300 teachers (the latter only at permanent polytechnics). In 2001, 23·7% of the population aged 15 years or over had been through tertiary education.

University Education. Universities with the number of teachers and students in 2001:

	Founded[1]	Teachers	Students Total	Women
Universities				
Helsinki	1640	1,573	37,338	23,664
Turku (Swedish)	1918	329	6,667	4,037
Turku (Finnish)	1922	801	14,708	9,278
Tampere	1925	573	14,358	9,479
Jyväskylä	1934	658	13,332	8,534
Oulu	1958	842	14,494	7,058
Vaasa	1968	157	4,514	2,445
Joensuu	1969	374	6,876	4,407
Kuopio	1972	307	5,288	3,531
Lapland	1979	170	3,807	2,517
Universities of Technology				
Helsinki	1849	490	14,432	2,960
Tampere	1965	333	10,485	2,044
Lappeenranta	1969	178	4,749	1,214
Schools of Economics and Business Administration				
Helsinki (Swedish)	1909	95	2,337	999
Helsinki (Finnish)	1911	150	3,963	1,685
Turku (Finnish)	1950	87	2,087	1,076
Universities of Art				
Academy of Fine Arts	1848	23	227	135
University of Art and Design	1871	133	1,666	1,035
Sibelius Academy	1882	239	1,453	803
Theatre Academy	1943	47	358	189
Total		7,559	162,939	87,090

[1]Year when the institution was founded regardless of university status.

Adult Education. Adult education provided by educational institutions in 2001.

Type of institution	Participants[1]
General education institutions[2]	1,891,300
Vocational and professional education institutions	592,900
Permanent polytechnics	96,200
Universities[3]	160,600
Summer universities	73,500
	2,814,500

[1]Participants are persons who have attended adult education courses run by educational institutions in the course of the calendar year. The same person may have attended a number of different courses and has been recorded as a participant in each one of them.
[2]Including study centres.
[3]Adult education at continuing education centres of universities.

In 1999 total expenditure on education came to 5·8% of GDP and represented 12·5% of total government expenditure.

The adult literacy rate in 2002 was almost 100%.

Health. In 2001 there were 16,115 physicians, 4,731 dentists and, in 2000, 43,250 hospital beds. The average Finnish adult smokes 2·2 cigarettes a day, compared to a European Union average of 4·5, and drinks 8·4 litres of alcohol a year, compared to a European Union average of 11·1 litres.

Welfare. The Social Insurance Institution administers general systems of old-age pensions (to all persons over 65 years of age and disabled younger persons) and of health insurance. An additional system of compulsory old-age pensions paid for by the employers is in force and works through the Central Pension Security Institute. Systems for other public aid are administered by the communes and supervised by the National Social Board and the Ministry of Social Affairs and Health.

The total cost of social security amounted to €33,068m. in 2000. Out of this €14,653m. (44%) was spent on old age and disability, €7,637m. (23%) on health, €5,283m. (16%) on family allowances and child welfare, €3,345m. (10%) on unemployment and €2,150m. (7%) on general welfare purposes and administration. Out of the total expenditure, 24·0% was financed by the State, 19·2% by local authorities, 37·7% by employers, 12·1% by the insured and 7·1% by property income.

CULTURE

Broadcasting. The Finnish Broadcasting Company, YLE, is the biggest national radio and television service provider. YLE operates two television channels (colour by PAL) with full national coverage. The second biggest television broadcaster, the privately owned Commercial MTV3, has one nationwide channel. A new private TV channel, Ruutunelonen, started in 1997. Television programmes from TV Sweden are transmitted over YLE's channel 4. There are some 30 local TV stations that mainly relay foreign and domestic programmes over cable and radio waves, in addition to locally produced material. The only radio broadcaster with full nationwide coverage is YLE. It transmits three national channels in Finnish and one in Swedish, as well as various regional channels, including one in Sami in Lapland. At the end of 2001 there were 57 local radio stations. Two of them, the news and music stations Nova and Classic, cover almost 60% of the population. There were 3·3m. TV receivers in 1999 and 7·7m. radio receivers in 1996. On 31 Dec. 2001 the number of television licences was 2,008,486.

Cinema. In Dec. 2001 there were 339 cinema halls with a seating capacity of 58,359. In 2001 total attendance was 6·5m. In 2000 gross box office receipts came to 277m. marks and nine full-length films were made.

Press. Finland has 54 newspapers that are published 4 to 7 times a week, 9 of which are in Swedish, and 154 with 1 to 3 issues per week. The total circulation of all newspapers is 2·3m. There are 5,158 registered periodicals with a total circulation of over 21m. In terms of total circulation of dailies relative to population, Finland ranks second in Europe after Norway. Most newspapers are bought on subscription rather than from newsstands. Only two newspapers depend entirely on newsstand sales. The five bestselling newspapers in 2001 were: *Helsingin Sanomat* (average daily circulation, 446,380 copies), *Ilta-Sanomat* (218,829), *Aamulehti* (135,478), *Iltalehti* (134,777) and *Turun Sanomat* (115,142). The bestselling newspaper in the Swedish language is *Hufvudstadsbladet*, 52,523. In 2001 a total of 12,090 book titles were published.

Tourism. There were 1,999,000 foreign tourists in 2001; the income from tourism was €1,609m. and the expenses were €2,070m.

Theme and amusement parks are popular tourism destinations for the Finns, while international tourists visit the country's nature attractions. Major international tourist attractions include Santa Park on the Polar Circle, the Kemi Snow Castle, and the Bomba House and Carelian Village in Nurmes. Helsinki's churches, the Sampo icebreaker in Kemi and the Sámi Museum in Inari are particularly popular among foreigners, who account for the majority of their visitors.

Festivals. Major festivals are Helsinki's Festival of Light, the Helsinki Festival Week, the Savonlinna Opera Festival, the Kuhmo Chamber Music Festival, Pori Jazz, Kaustinen Folk Music Festival, Tampere Theatre Festival, Kuopio Dance Festival and the Sodankylä Film Festival.

Libraries. The Helsinki University Library doubles as a National Library. The collections of the university libraries and major research libraries comprise in total 43·9m. volumes (of which the university libraries have 18·9m.). In total, they issued 10·4m. loans (university libraries 9·9m.) in 2001.

The revised Public Library Act, which came into force on 1 Jan. 1999, requires each municipality to provide basic library services free of charge. The public library network is comprehensive with 989 libraries altogether. These are complemented by 199 mobile units with over 16,000 service stops. The Helsinki City Library doubles as a Central Library in this sector. Additionally the country is divided into 19 regions with a Regional Central Library providing supplementary services. In 2001 there were over 2·4m. registered borrowers, who represent 47% of the population. The number of loans issued totalled 103·4m.

Theatre and Opera. A new Opera House and a new 14,000-seat Arena Show Hall opened in 1999 in Helsinki. The city hosts both the National Theatre and the National Opera. All major cities have theatres and showhalls. In the summer season open air theatres are very popular. In 2001 there were 13,460 performances in total with over 2·7m. tickets sold.

Museums and Galleries. The National Museum as well as the National Gallery (the Atheneum) are located in Helsinki. The new Museum of Modern Art (Kiasma) was opened in Helsinki in 1998 and a new Ethnographic Museum and a media centre, also in Helsinki, opened in 1999. Major cities all host their own art galleries and local museums. The Alvar Aalto Museum is located in Jyväskylä in central Finland. In 2001 there were 157 museums with full-time personnel. The number of exhibitions was 1,192 and there were 4·7m. visitors.

DIPLOMATIC REPRESENTATIVES

Of Finland in the United Kingdom (38 Chesham Pl., London, SW1X 8HW)
Ambassador: Pertti Salolainen.

Of the United Kingdom in Finland (Itäinen Puistotie 17, 00140 Helsinki)
Ambassador: Matthew Kirk.

Of Finland in the USA (3301 Massachusetts Ave., NW, Washington, D.C., 20008)
Ambassador: Jukka Valtasaari.

Of the USA in Finland (Itäinen Puistotie 14B, Helsinki 00140)
Ambassador: Bonnie McElveen-Hunter.

Of Finland to the United Nations
Ambassador: Marjatta Rasi.

FURTHER READING

Statistics Finland. *Statistical Yearbook of Finland* (from 1879).—*Bulletin of Statistics* (monthly, from 1924).
Constitution Act and Parliament Act of Finland. Helsinki, 1984
Suomen valtiokalenteri—Finlands statskalender (State Calendar of Finland). Helsinki. Annual
Facts About Finland. Helsinki. Annual (Union Bank of Finland)
Finland in Figures. Helsinki, Annual
Jakobson, M., *Myth and Reality.* Helsinki, 1987
Kirby, D. G., *Finland in the Twentieth Century.* 2nd ed. London, 1984
Klinge, M., *A Brief History of Finland.* Helsinki, 1987
Petersson, O., *The Government and Politics of the Nordic Countries.* Stockholm, 1994
Screen, J. E. O., *Finland.* [Bibliography] 2nd ed. ABC-Clio, Oxford and Santa Barbara (CA), 1997
Singleton, F., *The Economy of Finland in the Twentieth Century.* Univ. of Bradford Press, 1987.—*A Short History of Finland*, 2nd edition. CUP, 1998
Tillotson, H. M., *Finland at Peace and War, 1918–1993.* London, 1993
Turner, Barry, (ed.) *Scandinavia Profiled.* Macmillan, London, 2000

National statistical office: Statistics Finland, Tilastokeskus, FIN-00022.
Website: http://www.stat.fi/

FRANCE

République Française

Capital: Paris
Population estimate, 2000: 58·74m.
GDP per capita, 2000: (PPP$) 24,223
HDI/world rank: 0·928/12

KEY HISTORICAL EVENTS

Gaul, the area that is now France, was conquered by Julius Caesar in the 1st century BC and became a part of the Roman Empire. In the 3rd and 4th centuries it was overrun by Germanic tribes and in the 10th century Norsemen invaded. There was a long period of conflict with England, typified by the Hundred Years' War (1337–1453); and this was followed by rivalry with Spain in the latter part of the 15th and in the 16th century. The Reformation caused a long religious civil war between 1562 and 1598, at the end of which the Huguenot leader Henry of Navarre was converted to Catholicism and reigned as the first Bourbon king, Henry IV. The two powerful ministers of the 17th century, Cardinal Richelieu and Mazarin, successively ensured that France, and not Spain, established itself as the dominant country in Europe. Militarily, this was achieved by the treaties of Westphalia (which ended the Thirty Years' War in 1648) and of the Pyrenees (1659).

The second half of the 18th century saw France defeated by England in the Seven Years' War (1756–63). The French Revolution began in 1789 when the 'Third Estate' assumed power as a National Assembly and overthrew the government. Riots and the storming of the Bastille were followed by the proclamation of a republic (1792) and the execution of the king, Louis XVI (1793). A Reign of Terror followed during which thousands were guillotined. After these excesses the Directory ruled from 1795 until 1799 when it was overthrown by Napoleon Bonaparte, who became First Consul and then Emperor (1804) of the first French Empire. Napoleon went on to gain control of most of Europe until he was finally defeated at the Battle of Waterloo in 1815. The monarchy was restored, with the Bourbon family reigning (officially from 1814). A revolution in 1830 brought Louis Philippe, son of the Duke of Orleans, to the throne as a constitutional monarch. This 'July Monarchy' was overthrown in 1848 and superseded by the Second Republic, with Louis Napoleon (nephew of Napoleon I) elected president. In 1852 he took the title of Emperor Napoleon III, and hence began the Second Empire. However, the early military failures of France in the Franco-Prussian War (1870–71) led to Napoleon being deposed and the proclamation of the Third Republic in 1870. This survived both the First World War, which was fought chiefly on French soil, and also 44 successive governments from the end of the war in 1918 until 1940. In 1940 German troops invaded France, the French government capitulated, and a pro-German government was established at Vichy. Gen. Charles de Gaulle headed a Free French government in London, while in France the Resistance continued to harass the German Army of Occupation.

When France was liberated in 1944 a provisional government under de Gaulle ruled the country until the Fourth Republic was established in 1946 and de Gaulle retired. The country now faced problems in Algeria and in Indo-China. There were many changes of government up to 1958. In that year de Gaulle was recalled as prime minister and then president of the Fifth Republic. He granted independence to Algeria (1962) and was successful in establishing a firm and stable government until rioting and strikes by students and workers led to his resignation in 1969. He was succeeded by Georges Pompidou, who died in 1974 and then by Giscard d'Estaing. Both presidents continued Gaullist policies but in 1981 François Mitterrand, a socialist, was elected to the presidency. For a time he had to govern in an uneasy relationship with a right-wing premier, Jacques Chirac. Mitterrand's period of office was clouded by charges of corruption. In 1995 Chirac was elected President in succession to the ailing Mitterrand, who died the following year. An ill-judged general election called by Chirac led to a socialist government headed by Lionel Jospin, who was frequently at odds with his right-wing President. In the 2002 presidential election the extreme right-wing National Front leader Jean-Marie Le Pen caused a sensation by pushing the socialist candidate, Prime Minister Lionel

Jospin, into third place in the first round, thereby qualifying for the second round run-off against incumbent president Jacques Chirac. However, Chirac easily won a further term in the second round on 5 May 2002.

TERRITORY AND POPULATION
France is bounded in the north by the English Channel *(La Manche)*, northeast by Belgium and Luxembourg, east by Germany, Switzerland and Italy, south by the Mediterranean (with Monaco as a coastal enclave), southwest by Spain and Andorra, and west by the Atlantic Ocean. The total area is 549,090 sq. km. Paris is the most populous agglomeration in Europe, with a population of over 9·6m. More than 14% of the population of Paris are foreign and 19% are foreign born.

Population (1999 census), 58·52m.; density, 108 persons per sq. km.

The UN gives a projected population for 2010 of 59·94m.

In 1999, 75·4% of the population lived in urban areas.

The growth of the population has been as follows:

Census	Population	Census	Population	Census	Population
1801	27,349,003	1946	40,506,639	1975	52,655,802
1861	37,386,313	1954	42,777,174	1982	54,334,871
1901	38,961,945	1962	46,519,997	1990	56,615,155
1921	39,209,518	1968	49,778,540	1999	58,518,748
1931	41,834,923				

According to the 1999 census, there were 3·26m. people of foreign extraction in France (5·6% of the population). The largest groups of foreigners with residence permits in 1999 were: Portuguese (573,000), Algerians (545,000) and Moroccans (445,000). 116,194 persons were naturalized in 1997 (71,596 in 1992). France's Muslim population, at 5m., is the highest in Europe.

Controls on illegal immigration were tightened in July 1991. Automatic right to citizenship for those born on French soil was restored in 1997 by the new left-wing coalition government. New immigration legislation, which came into force in 1998, brought in harsher penalties for organized traffic in illegal immigrants and extended asylum laws to include people whose lives are at risk from non-state as well as state groups. It also extended nationality at the age of 18 to those born in France of non-French parents, provided they have lived a minimum of five years in France since the age of 11.

The areas, populations and chief towns of the 22 metropolitan regions at the 1999 census were as follows:

Regions	Area (sq. km)	Population	Chief town
Alsace	8,280	1,734,145	Strasbourg
Aquitaine	41,308	2,908,359	Bordeaux
Auvergne	26,013	1,308,878	Clermont-Ferrand
Basse-Normandie	17,589	1,422,193	Caen
Bourgogne (Burgundy)	31,582	1,610,067	Dijon
Bretagne (Brittany)	27,208	2,906,197	Rennes
Centre	39,151	2,440,329	Orléans
Champagne-Ardenne	25,606	1,342,363	Reims
Corse (Corsica)	8,680	260,196	Ajaccio
Franche-Comté	16,202	1,117,059	Besançon
Haute-Normandie	12,317	1,780,192	Rouen
Île-de-France	12,012	10,925,011	Paris
Languedoc-Roussillon	27,376	2,295,648	Montpellier
Limousin	16,942	710,939	Limoges
Lorraine	23,547	2,310,376	Nancy
Midi-Pyrénées	45,348	2,551,687	Toulouse
Nord-Pas-de-Calais	12,414	3,996,588	Lille
Pays de la Loire	32,082	3,222,061	Nantes
Picardie	19,399	1,857,834	Amiens
Poitou-Charentes	25,810	1,640,068	Poitiers
Provence-Alpes-Côte d'Azur	31,400	4,506,151	Marseilles
Rhône-Alpes	43,698	5,645,407	Lyons

The 22 regions are divided into 96 metropolitan *départements*, which, in 1999, consisted of 36,565 communes.

Populations of the principal conurbations (in descending order of size) and towns at the 1999 census:

	Conurbation	Town		Conurbation	Town
Paris	9,644,507[1]	2,147,857	Mulhouse	234,445	112,002
Marseilles-Aix-			Angers	226,843	156,327
en-Provence	1,349,772[2]	807,071	Reims	215,581	191,325
Lyons	1,348,832[3]	453,187	Brest	210,055	156,217
Lille	1,000,900[4]	191,164	Caen	199,490	117,157
Nice	888,784	345,892	Le Mans	194,825	150,605
Toulouse	761,090	398,423	Dunkerque	191,173	72,333
Bordeaux	753,931	218,948	Pau	181,413	80,610
Nantes	544,932	277,728	Bayonne	178,965	41,778
Toulon	519,640	166,442	Limoges	173,299	137,502
Douai–Lens	518,727	. . [5]	Perpignan	162,678	107,241
Strasbourg	427,245	267,051	Amiens	160,815	139,210
Grenoble	419,334	156,203	Nîmes	148,889	137,740
Rouen	389,862	108,758	Saint-Nazaire	136,886	68,616
Valenciennes	357,395	42,343	Annecy	136,815	52,100
Nancy	331,363	105,830	Besançon	134,376	122,308
Metz	322,526	127,498	Thionville	130,480	42,205
Tours	297,631	137,046	Troyes	128,945	62,612
Saint-Étienne	291,960	183,522	Poitiers	119,371	87,012
Montpellier	287,981	229,025	Valence	117,448	66,568
Rennes	272,263	212,494	Lorient	116,174	61,844
Orléans	263,292	116,559	La Rochelle	116,157	80,055
Béthune	259,198	28,522	Chambéry	113,457	57,592
Clermont-Ferrand	258,541	141,004	Montbéliard	113,059	28,766
Avignon	253,580	88,312	Genève–Annemasse	106,673	. . [6]
Le Havre	248,547	193,259	Calais	104,852	78,170
Dijon	236,953	153,815	Angoulême	103,746	46,324

[1]Including Boulogne-Billancourt (107,042), Montreuil (91,146), Argenteuil (95,416), Versailles (88,476), Saint-Denis (86,871), Nanterre (86,219), Vitry-sur-Seine (79,322), Aulnay-sous-Bois (80,315), Créteil (82,630).
[2]Including Aix-en-Provence (137,067).
[3]Including Villeurbanne (127,299), Vénissieux (56,487).
[4]Including Roubaix (98,039), Tourcoing (94,204).
[5]Including Douai (44,742), Lens (36,823).
[6]Including Annemasse (27,659).

Paris: The capital of France since 987, Paris flowered as a centre of medieval commerce and scholasticism. Rebellion has marked its history, especially the revolutions of 1789, 1830 and 1848 and the Commune of 1871. Paris' reputation as a centre for the intellectual and artistic avant-garde was cemented during the Belle Epoque of the late 19th century. The Eiffel Tower, the Arc de Triomphe, the Louvre and the Cathedral of Notre Dame de Paris are among its most famous monuments.

France has 6 national parks, 35 regional national parks and 132 nature reserves.

Languages. The official language is French. Breton and Basque are spoken in their regions. The *Toubon* legislation of 1994 seeks to restrict the use of foreign words in official communications, broadcasting and advertisements (a previous such decree dated from 1975). The Constitutional Court has since ruled that imposing such restrictions on private citizens would infringe their freedom of expression.

SOCIAL STATISTICS

Statistics for calendar years:

	Births	Deaths	Marriages	Divorces
1997	726,768	530,319	283,984	118,284
1998	738,080	534,005	271,361	. . .
1999	744,791	537,661	286,191	. . .
2000[1]	774,782	536,300	305,000	. . .
2001[1]	774,800	528,000	303,500	. . .

[1]Provisional.

Live birth rate (1999) was 12·7 per 1,000 population; death rate, 9·2; marriage rate, 4·9; divorce rate (1997), 2·0. 40·7% of births in 1998 were outside marriage. In 1995 the most popular age range for marrying was 25–29 for both males and females. Abortions were legalized in 1975; there were an estimated 220,000 in 1995. Life expectancy at birth, 1999, 74·5 years for males and 82·3 years for females (the highest in the EU). Annual population growth rate, 1990–99, 0·4%. From 1990–95 the suicide rate per 100,000 population was 20·1 (men, 29·6; women, 11·1). Infant mortality, 1999, 4·8 per 1,000 live births; fertility rate, 1999, 1·7 births per woman. In 2000 France received 38,590 asylum applications, equivalent to 0·65 per 1,000 inhabitants.

CLIMATE
The northwest has a moderate maritime climate, with small temperature range and abundant rainfall; inland, rainfall becomes more seasonal, with a summer maximum, and the annual range of temperature increases. Southern France has a Mediterranean climate, with mild moist winters and hot dry summers. Eastern France has a continental climate and a rainfall maximum in summer, with thunderstorms prevalent. Paris, Jan. 37°F (3°C), July 64°F (18°C). Annual rainfall 22·9" (573 mm). Bordeaux, Jan. 41°F (5°C), July 68°F (20°C). Annual rainfall 31·4" (786 mm). Lyons, Jan. 37°F (3°C), July 68°F (20°C). Annual rainfall 31·8" (794 mm).

CONSTITUTION AND GOVERNMENT
The Constitution of the Fifth Republic, superseding that of 1946, came into force on 4 Oct. 1958. It consists of a preamble, dealing with the Rights of Man, and 92 articles.

France is a republic, indivisible, secular, democratic and social; all citizens are equal before the law (Art. 1). National sovereignty resides with the people, who exercise it through their representatives and by referendums (Art. 3). Constitutional reforms of July 1995 widened the range of issues on which referendums may be called. Political parties carry out their activities freely, but must respect the principles of national sovereignty and democracy (Art. 4).

A constitutional amendment of 4 Aug. 1995 deleted all references to the 'community' (*communauté*) between France and her overseas possessions, representing an important step towards the constitutional dismantling of the former French colonial empire.

The head of state is the President, who sees that the Constitution is respected; ensures the regular functioning of the public authorities, as well as the continuity of the state; is the protector of national independence and territorial integrity (Art. 5). As a result of a referendum held on 24 Sept. 2000 the President is elected for five years by direct universal suffrage (Art. 6). Previously the term of office had been seven years. The President appoints (and dismisses) a Prime Minister and, on the latter's advice, appoints and dismisses the other members of the government (*Council of Ministers*) (Art. 8); presides over the Council of Ministers (Art. 9); may dissolve the National Assembly, after consultation with the Prime Minister and the Presidents of the two Houses (Art. 12); appoints to the civil and military offices of the state (Art. 13). In times of crisis, the President may take such emergency powers as the circumstances demand; the National Assembly cannot be dissolved during such a period (Art. 16).

Parliament consists of the National Assembly and the Senate. The National Assembly is elected by direct suffrage by the second ballot system (by which candidates winning 50% or more of the vote in their constituencies are elected, candidates winning less than 12·5% are eliminated and other candidates go on to a second round of voting); the Senate is elected by indirect suffrage (Art. 24). Since 1996 the National Assembly has convened for an annual nine-month session. It comprises 577 deputies, elected by a two-ballot system for a five-year term from single-member constituencies (555 in Metropolitan France, 22 in the overseas departments and dependencies), and may be dissolved by the President.

The *Senate* comprises 321 senators elected for nine-year terms (one-third every three years) by an electoral college in each Department or overseas dependency, made up of all members of the Departmental Council or its equivalent in overseas dependencies, together with all members of Municipal Councils within that area. The *Speaker* of the Senate deputizes for the President of the Republic in the event of the latter's incapacity. Senate elections were last held on 23 Sept. 2001.

The *Constitutional Council* is composed of nine members whose term of office is nine years (non-renewable), one-third every three years; three are appointed by the President of the Republic, three by the President of the National Assembly, three by the President of the Senate; in addition, former Presidents of the Republic are, by right, life members of the Constitutional Council (Art. 56). It oversees the fairness of the elections of the President (Art. 58) and Parliament (Art. 59), and of referendums (Art. 60), and acts as a guardian of the Constitution (Art. 61). Its *President* is Yves Guéna (app. 2000).

The *Economic and Social Council* advises on Government and Private Members' Bills (Art. 69). It comprises representatives of employers', workers' and farmers' organizations in each Department and Overseas Territory.

Ameller, M., *L'Assemblée Nationale*. Paris, 1994

Duhamel, O. and Mény, Y., *Dictionnaire Constitutionnel*. Paris, 1992

Elgie, R. (ed.) *Electing the French President: the 1995 Presidential Election*. Macmillan, London, 1996

National Anthem. 'La Marseillaise'; words and tune by C. Rouget de Lisle.

RECENT ELECTIONS

At the first round of presidential elections on 21 April 2002 Jacques Chirac gained the largest number of votes (19·87% of those cast) against 15 opponents. His nearest rivals were the National Front leader Jean-Marie Le Pen, who came second with 16·86% of votes cast, and incumbent prime minister Lionel Jospin, with 16·17%. The result caused a series of anti-Le Pen protest rallies across France. Socialist leaders urged their supporters to vote for Chirac in the second round run-off between Chirac and Le Pen in order that the extreme right-wing leader might be kept from gaining power. In the second round of voting, held on 5 May 2002, Jacques Chirac won a second consecutive presidential term in a landslide victory, with 82·21% of votes cast against 17·79% for Le Pen. Turn-out was 79·7%.

Elections to the National Assembly were held on 9 and 16 June 2002. The Union for the Presidential Majority (UMP), the allies of President Jacques Chirac, gained an overwhelming parliamentary majority with 357 seats, winning 33·7% of votes cast; the Socialist Party (PS), 140 seats with 24·1%; the Union for French Democracy (UDF), 29 seats with 4·8%; the Communist Party (PCF), 21 seats with 4·8%; the Greens, 3 seats with 4·5%. Despite winning 11·3% of votes cast, the National Front (FN) failed to gain a single seat. The result brought to an end five years of 'cohabitation', with a right-wing president and a socialist prime minister.

In March 2002 only 55 out of 564 deputies were women. The proportion of women deputies, at 9·8%, is the lowest of any EU-member country.

Following the election held on 23 Sept. 2001, the Senate was composed of (by group, including affiliates): RPR, 95; PS, 83; Union Centriste (UC), 53; Républicains et Indépendants (RI), 40; Rassemblement Démocratique et Europeén Social (RDES), 19; Républicain, Communiste et Citoyen (RCC), 23; Unattached, 6. In Oct. 1998 Christian Poncelet (RPR) was elected *Speaker* for a 3-year term. He was re-elected for a further term in Oct. 2001.

European Parliament. France has 87 representatives. At the June 1999 elections turn-out was 47·0%. The PS won 22 seats with 22·0% of votes cast (political affiliation in European Parliament: Party of European Socialists); RPFIE (Euro Sceptics RPF), 13 with 13·0% (Independents for a Europe of Nations); the RPR-DL (Gaullists), 12 with 12·8% (European People's Party); the Greens, 9 with 9·7% (Greens); UDF, 9 with 9·3% (European People's Party); PCF-Ind, 6 with 6·8% (Confederal Group of the European United Left); CPTN (Pro-Hunting Party), also 6 with 6·8% (Group for a Europe of Democracies and Diversities); the National Front, 5 with 5·7% (non-affiliated); LO-LCR (Communists), 5 with 5·2% (Confederal Group of the United European Left/Nordic Green Left).

CURRENT ADMINISTRATION

President: Jacques Chirac; b. 1932 (RPR; sworn in 17 May 1995 and re-elected 5 May 2002).

After the second round of the presidential election on 5 May 2002 the Socialist Prime Minister Lionel Jospin formally resigned and an interim centre-right government was installed. Following the parliamentary elections of June 2002 all of the cabinet members were confirmed in their posts. In March 2003 the cabinet was composed as follows:

Prime Minister: Jean-Pierre Raffarin; b. 1948 (Liberal Democracy Party; sworn in 6 May 2002). *Minister of Interior, Domestic Security and Local Freedoms:* Nicolas Sarkozy. *Social Affairs, Employment and Solidarity:* François Fillon. *Justice and Keeper of the Seals:* Dominique Perben. *Foreign Affairs, Co-operation and Francophony:* Dominique Galouzeau de Villepin. *Defence and Veterans' Affairs:* Michèle Alliot-Marie. *National Education, Youth and Research:* Luc Ferry. *Economy, Finance and Industry:* Francis Mer. *Capital Works, Transportation, Housing, Tourism and Maritime Affairs:* Gilles de Robien. *Environment and Sustainable Development:* Roselyne Bachelot-Narquin. *Health, Family and the Disabled:* Jean-François Mattei. *Agriculture, Food, Fisheries and Rural Affairs:* Hervé Gaymard. *Culture and Communication:* Jean-Jacques Aillagon. *Civil Service, Administrative Reform and Land Management:* Jean-Paul Delevoye. *Overseas Departments and Territories:* Brigitte Girardin. *Sport*: Jean-François Lamour.

President of the National Assembly: Raymond Forni.

Office of the Prime Minister: http://www.premier-ministre.gouv.fr/

DEFENCE

The President of the Republic is the supreme head of defence policy and exercises command over the Armed Forces. He is the only person empowered to give the order to use nuclear weapons. He is assisted by the Council of Ministers, which studies defence problems, and by the Defence Council and the Restricted Defence Committee, which formulate directives.

Legislation of 1996 inaugurated a wide-ranging reform of the defence system over 1997–2002, with regard to the professionalization of the armed forces (brought about by the ending of military conscription and consequent switch to an all-volunteer defence force), the modification and modernization of equipment and the restructuring of the defence industry. In 2001 defence expenditure totalled US$33,765m. (equivalent to US$570 per capita). Defence spending as a proportion of GDP has fallen from 4·0% in 1985 to 2·6% in 2001.

French forces are not formally under the NATO command structure, although France signed the NATO strategic document on eastern Europe in Nov. 1991. The Minister of Defence attends informal NATO meetings which have an agenda of French interest, but not the formal twice-yearly meetings. Since Dec. 1995 France has taken a seat on the NATO Military Committee. In 2001, 2,230 service personnel were stationed in Germany, 16,344 in the overseas departments and territories, 6,096 on UN peacekeeping missions and 977 constituted the 'French maritime presence' abroad.

Conscription was for ten months, but France officially ended its military draft on 27 June 2001 with a reprieve granted to all conscripts (barring those serving in civil positions) on 30 Nov. 2001.

Nuclear Weapons. Having carried out its first test in 1960, there have been 210 tests in all. The last French test was in 1996 (this compares with the last UK test in 1991 and the last US test in 1993). The nuclear arsenal consisted of approximately 348 warheads in Jan. 2002 according to the Stockholm International Peace Research Institute.

Arms Trade. France was the world's third largest exporter after the USA and the UK in 1999, with sales worth US$6,630m., or 12·4% of the world total). In 1987 sales had been worth US$8·3bn., but had only represented 9·0% of the world total.

Army. The Army comprises the Logistic Force (CFLT), based in Montlhéry with two logistic brigades, and the Land Force Command (CFAT), based in Lille. Apart from the Franco-German brigade, there are 12 brigades, each made up of between four and seven battalions, including 1 airmobile brigade.

Personnel numbered (2002) 168,126 (5,544 volunteers and 11,240 women) including 16,500 marines and a Foreign Legion of 8,000. There were 242,500 reserves in 2002. The 1997–2002 Programming Act provided for the following force at the end of the transitional period: 16,000 officers, 50,000 NCOs, 66,500 army enlistees, 5,500 volunteers, 34,000 civilians and 30,000 reservists. Equipment levels in 2001 included 809 main battle tanks and 410 helicopters.

Gendarmerie. The paramilitary police force exists to ensure public security and maintain law and order, as well as participate in the operational defence of French territory as part of the armed forces. It consisted in 2002 of 98,135 personnel including 15,203 volunteers, 5,705 women and 2,020 civilians. It comprises a territorial force of 69,000 personnel throughout the country, a mobile force of 17,025 personnel and specialized formations including the Republican Guard, the Air Force and Naval Gendarmeries, and an anti-terrorist unit.

Navy. The missions of the Navy are to provide the prime element of the French independent nuclear deterrent through its force of strategic submarines; to assure the security of the French offshore zones; to contribute to NATO's missions; and to provide on-station and deployment forces overseas in support of French territorial interests and UN commitments. French territorial seas and economic zones are organized into two maritime districts (with headquarters in Brest and Toulon).

The strategic deterrent force comprises four nuclear-powered strategic-missile submarines, including two of four new-generation ships of a new, much larger, class, *Le Triomphant* and *Le Téméraire*, which entered service in 1997 and 1999.

Until it was withdrawn from service in 2000, the *Foch*, of 33,000 tonnes, was the principal surface ship. The 40,000-tonne nuclear-powered replacement *Charles de Gaulle*, which was launched at Brest in 1994, commissioned in Oct. 2000. There is 1 cruiser, the *Jeanne d'Arc*, completed in 1964 and used in peacetime as a training vessel. Other surface combatants include four destroyers and 26 frigates.

The naval air arm, *Aviation Navale*, numbers some 6,800 personnel. Operational aircraft include Super-Etendard nuclear-capable strike aircraft, Etendard reconnaissance aircraft and US-built Crusader F-8P all-weather fighters. The maritime Rafale combat aircraft was scheduled to enter service on board the *Charles de Gaulle*. A small Marine force of 1,700 *Fusiliers Marins* provides assault groups.

Personnel in 2002 numbered 54,433, including 1,613 volunteers, 3,328 women and 10,157 civilians. There were 97,000 reserves in 2002.

Air Force. Created in 1934, the Air Force was reorganized in June 1994. The Conventional Forces in Europe (CFE) Agreement imposes a ceiling of 800 combat aircraft. In 2002 there were 355 combat aircraft, 100 transport aircraft and 290 aircraft for training purposes.

Personnel (2002) 69,667 (1,942 volunteers; 8,210 women; 6,003 civilians). Air Force reserves in 2002 numbered 79,500.

INTERNATIONAL RELATIONS

France is a member of the UN, WTO, BIS, the Council of Europe, WEU, EU, OSCE, OECD, CERN, Inter-American Development Bank, Asian Development Bank, the Pacific Community, IOM, Antarctic Treaty and the International Organization of the Francophonie. France is a signatory to the Schengen Accord, which abolishes border controls between France, Austria, Belgium, Denmark, Finland, Germany, Greece, Iceland, Italy, Luxembourg, the Netherlands, Norway, Portugal, Spain and Sweden.

At a referendum in Sept. 1992 to approve the ratification of the Maastricht treaty on European union of 7 Feb. 1992, 12,967,498 votes (50·81%) were cast for and 12,550,651 (49·18%) against.

France is the focus of the *Communauté Francophone* (French-speaking Community) which formally links France with many of its former colonies in Africa. A wide range of agreements, both with members of the Community and with other French-speaking countries, extend to economic and technical matters, and in particular to the disbursement of overseas aid.

ECONOMY

Agriculture accounted for 2·3% of GDP in 1998, industry 26·2% and services 71·5%.

Overview. Between 1992 and 1998 privatization proceeds amounted to US$49bn. As monetary policy is set for the euro area as a whole, the government has only the budget as an instrument to influence domestic demand. The introduction of the euro stabilized the financial system and made it more efficient. The government is involved or directly responsible for many services, such as healthcare, education, telecommunications and the railways. Public expenditure has been put under pressure with healthcare and pensions running above budget.

Currency. On 1 Jan. 1999 the euro (EUR) became the legal currency in France; irrevocable conversion rate 6·55957 francs to one euro. The euro, which consists of 100 cents, has been in circulation since 1 Jan. 2002. There are seven euro notes in different colours and sizes denominated in 500, 200, 100, 50, 20, 10 and 5 euros, and eight coins denominated in 2 and 1 euros, then 50, 20, 10, 5, 2 and 1 cents. On the introduction of the euro there was a 'dual circulation' period before the franc ceased to be legal tender on 17 Feb. 2002. Euro banknotes in circulation on 1 Jan. 2002 had a total value of €84·2bn.

Foreign exchange reserves were US$23,338m. in June 2002 and gold reserves 97·25m. troy oz (81·89m. troy oz in 1997). Inflation was 1·7% in 2001. Total money supply was €62,266m. in June 2002.

Franc Zone. 13 former French colonies (Benin, Burkina Faso, Cameroon, Central African Republic, Chad, Comoros, the Republic of the Congo, Côte d'Ivoire, Gabon, Mali, Niger, Senegal and Togo), the former Spanish colony of Equatorial Guinea and the former Portuguese colony of Guinea-Bissau are members of a Franc Zone, the CFA (*Communauté Financière Africaine*). Comoros uses the Comorian franc. The *franc CFA* is pegged to the euro at a rate of 655·957 francs CFA to one euro. The franc CFP *(Comptoirs Français du Pacifique)* is the common currency of French Polynesia, New Caledonia and Wallis and Futuna. It is pegged to the euro at 119·3317422 francs CFP to the euro.

Budget. Receipts and expenditure in 1bn. francs:

	1998	1999	2000	2001
Revenue	1,420·6	1,494·5	1,508·4	1,537·6
Expenditure	1,672·9	1,709·8	1,700·9	1,745·0

The standard rate of VAT is 19·6% (reduced rate, 5·5%). In Aug. 2000 a series of tax cuts was announced, including the gradual reduction of the top rate of income tax from 54% to 52·5% by 2003 and of corporate tax from 36·6% to 33·3%.

Ministère de l'Economie, des Finances et du Plan. *Le Budget de l'Etat: de la Préparation à l'Exécution.* Paris, 1995

Performance. Real GDP growth averaged 3·3% annually between 1998 and 2000, but was only 1·8% in 2001. Total GDP in 2001 was US$1,303bn.

The OECD reported in 2000 that 'France has not enjoyed such a favourable economic situation for ten years. After performing poorly during 1990–96, the French economy benefited from rapidly growing activity, low inflation and growth that was richer in jobs, and entered the new millennium with an effervescent stock market and favourable prospects. After a temporary pause in the wake of the Asian and Russian crises, activity picked up again, and the outturn for 1999 as a whole exceeded most forecasts, with real GDP growing by 2·9 per cent.'

Banking and Finance. The central bank and bank of issue is the *Banque de France* (*Governor*, Jean-Claude Trichet, appointed 1993), founded in 1800, and nationalized on 2 Dec. 1945. In 1993 it received greater autonomy in line with EU conditions. The Governor is appointed for a six-year term (renewable once) and heads the nine-member Council of Monetary Policy.

The National Credit Council, formed in 1945 to regulate banking activity and consulted in all political decisions on monetary policy, comprises 45 members nominated by the government; its president is the Minister for the Economy; its Vice-President is the Governor of the Banque de France.

In 1996 there were 1,445 banks and other credit institutions, including 400 shareholder-owned banks and 342 mutual or savings banks. Four principal deposit banks were nationalized in 1945, the remainder in 1982; the latter were privatized in 1987. The banking and insurance sectors underwent a flurry of mergers, privatizations, foreign investment, corporate restructuring and consolidation in 1997, in both the national and international fields. The largest banks in 1998 (with assets in 1bn. francs) were: Crédit Agricole (2,565), Socété Générale (2,519), Banque Nationale de Paris (2,132), Groupe Paribas (1,627), Crédit Lyonnais (1,371). On 28 Aug. 1999 Banque Nationale de Paris merged with Paribas to create the BNP-Paribas Group, now the largest French bank both by market capitalization and assets.

The state savings organization *Caisse Nationale d'Epargne* is administered by the post office on a giro system. There are also commercial savings banks (*caisses d'epargne et de prévoyance*). Deposited funds are centralized by a non-banking body, the *Caisse de Dépôts et Consignations*, which finances a large number of local authorities and state-aided housing projects, and carries an important portfolio of transferable securities.

There is a stock exchange (Bourse) in Paris; it is a component of Euronext, which was created in Sept. 2000 through the merger of the Paris, Brussels and Amsterdam bourses.

Weights and Measures. The metric system is in general use.

ENERGY AND NATURAL RESOURCES

Environment. According to the *World Bank Atlas* France's carbon dioxide emissions in 1998 were the equivalent of 6·3 tonnes per capita. According to an *Environmental Sustainability Index* compiled for the World Economic Forum meeting in Feb. 2002 France ranked 33rd in the world, with 55·5%. The index measured the ability of countries to maintain favourable environmental conditions and examined various factors including pollution levels and the use or abuse of natural resources.

Electricity. The state-owned monopoly Electricité de France is responsible for power generation and supply under the Ministry of Industry. Installed capacity was 108,000 MW in 1997. Electricity production in 1998: 480·97bn. kWh, of which 76·2% was nuclear. Hydro-electric power contributes about 12·5% of total electricity output. Consumption per capita in 1998 was 6,287 kWh. In 1997 France was the European Union's biggest exporter of electricity with 71·4bn. kWh. Electricité de France is Europe's leading electricity producer, generating more than twice as much in 1998 (460bn. kWh) as the second largest producer.

France, not rich in natural energy resources, is at the centre of Europe's nuclear energy industry. In 2001 there were 59 nuclear reactors in operation—more than in any other country in the world apart from the USA—with a generating capacity in 1999 of 61,723 MW. Only Lithuania has a higher percentage of its electricity generated through nuclear power.

Oil and Gas. In 1996, 16m. bbls. of crude oil were produced. The greater part came from the Parentis oilfield in the Landes. Reserves in 1997 totalled 117m. bbls. The importation and distribution of natural gas is the responsibility of the government monopoly Gaz de France. Production of natural gas (1995) was 33,395m. cu. metres. Gas reserves were 19bn. cu. metres in 1997.

Minerals. France is a significant producer of nickel, uranium, iron ore, bauxite, potash, pig iron, aluminium and coal. Société Le Nickel extracts in New Caledonia and is the world's third largest nickel producer; France is the world's seventh largest uranium producer. The mining sector contributed 1% of GDP in 1994, and employed 0·8% of the workforce.

Coal production (1997): 7m. tonnes. Coal power generators contributed 6·2% of total energy consumption in 1994. Coal reserves in Jan. 1996: 139m. tonnes. Production of other principal minerals and metals (1994, in 1,000 tonnes): salt (1998), 7,000; iron ore (metal content), 708; aluminium (1998), 400; potash salts, 936; gold (1997), 4,350 kg.

Agriculture. France has the highest agricultural production in Europe, accounting for more than a fifth of the European Union total. In 2000 the agricultural sector employed about 885,000 people, down from 1,869,000 in 1980. Agriculture accounts for 14·5% of exports and 11·4% of imports.

In 2000 there were 664,000 holdings (average size 42 ha), down from over 1m. in 1988. Co-operatives account for between 30–50% of output. There were 1,270,000 tractors and 110,000 harvester-threshers in 1998. Although the total number of tractors has been declining steadily in recent years, increasingly more powerful ones are being used. In 1997, 368,000 tractors in use were of 80 hp or higher, compared to 96,000 in 1979.

Of the total area of France (54·9m. ha), the utilized agricultural area comprised 29·63m. ha in 2001. 18·45m. ha were arable, 10·05m. ha were under pasture, and 1·14m. ha were under permanent crops including vines (0·90m. ha).

Area under cultivation and yield for principal crops:

	Area (1,000 ha)			Production (1,000 tonnes)		
	1998	1999	2000	1998	1999	2000
Wheat	5,235	5,114	5,266	39,809	37,002	37,529
Sugarbeets	456	442	414	31,156	32,919	31,454
Maize	1,797	1,759	1,834	15,191	15,656	16,469
Barley	1,631	1,534	1,573	10,591	9,539	9,927
Potatoes	164	171	169	6,053	6,645	6,652
Rapeseeds	1,145	1,369	1,225	3,734	4,469	3,572
Peas	640	510	465	3,775	3,179	2,507
Sunflower seeds	782	799	720	1,713	1,868	1,824

Production of principal fruit crops (in 1,000 tonnes) as follows:

	1998	1999	2000
Apples	2,210	2,643	2,537
Peaches	202	280	272
Melons	324	322	314
Pears	260	300	271
Plums	205	185	214

Total fruit and vegetable production in 2000 was 19,075,000 tonnes. Other important vegetables include tomatoes (898,000 tonnes in 2000), carrots (450,000 tonnes), cauliflowers (412,000 tonnes) and onions (361,000 tonnes). France is the world's leading producer of sugarbeets. Total area under cultivation and yield of grapes from the vine (2000): 745,000 ha; 7·63m. tonnes. Wine production (2000): 5,880,000 tonnes. France and Italy are by far the largest wine producers in the world. Italy was the leading producer in 1998, but France produced more in 1999 and 2000. Consumption in France has declined dramatically in recent times, from nearly 120 litres per person in 1966 to 60 litres per person in 1997.

Figures compiled by the Soil Association, a British organization, show that in 1999 France set aside 220,000 ha (1% of its agricultural land) for the growth of organic crops, compared to the EU average of 2·2%.

Livestock (2000, in 1,000): cattle, 20,527; pigs, 14,635; sheep, 10,004; goats, 1,191; horses, 349; asses and mules, 37; chickens, 233,000; turkeys, 42,000; ducks, 24,000. Livestock products (2000, in 1,000 tonnes): pork, bacon and ham, 2,315; beef and veal, 1,590; lamb and mutton, 130; poultry, 2,022; horse, 10; eggs, 1,050. Milk production, 2000: cow, 24,890; sheep, 247; goat, 483. Cheese production, 1,668,000 tonnes. France is the second largest cheese producer in the world after the USA.

Source: SCEES/Agreste

Forestry. Forestry is France's richest natural resource and employs 550,000 people. In 2000 forest covered 15·05m. ha (27·4% of the land area). In 1990 the area under forests had been 14·23m. ha, or 25·9% of the land area, 73% of forest is private; 26% state-owned. Timber production in 1999 was 36·38m. cu. metres.

Fisheries. In 1998 there were 6,074 fishing vessels totalling (in 1996) 176,356 GRT, and 16,556 fishermen. Catch in 1999 was 578,071 tonnes, of which 573,571 tonnes were from marine waters.

INDUSTRY

The leading companies by market capitalization in France, excluding banking and finance, in Jan. 2002 were: Total Fina Elf SA (€115bn.), an integrated oil company; Aventis SA (€60bn.), a pharmaceutical and biotechnology company; and Sanofi-Synthélabo (€52bn.), a pharmaceutical group.

The industrial sector employs about 27% of the workforce. In Nov. 1997 capacity utilization in industry was approaching 85%. Chief industries: steel, chemicals, textiles, aircraft, machinery, electronic equipment, tourism, wine and perfume.

Industrial production (1997, in 1,000 tonnes): distillate fuel oil, 35,172; crude steel, 20,200 (1999); cement, 19,780; petrol, 18,894; pig iron, 13,428; residual fuel oil, 11,073; sulphuric acid, 2,382 (1995); caustic soda, 1,561 (1994). France is one of the biggest producers of mineral water, with output of 6,123m. litres in 1996.

Engineering production (1999, in 1,000 units): cars, 4,200; car tyres, 59,700; television sets (1994), 2,796.

Labour. Out of an economically active population of 23,529,000 in March 2000, 44·7% were women. By sector, 71·5% worked in services (58·1% in 1980), 24·4% in industry and construction (33·1% in 1980) and 4·1% in agriculture (8·8% in 1980). Some 5m. people work in the public sector at national and local level. It was estimated in 1997 that 51% of households have no-one working in the private sector.

A new definition of 'unemployed' was adopted in Aug. 1995, omitting persons who had worked at least 78 hours in the previous month. In Jan. 2003 the unemployment rate was 9·0%. In the year to March 2000 a total of 430,000 jobs were created, representing the biggest jump in employment for 30 years.

Conciliation boards (*Conseils de Prud'hommes*) mediate in labour disputes. They are elected for five-year terms by two colleges of employers and employees. Between 1989 and 1998 strikes cost France an average of 45 days per 1,000 employees a year, compared to the EU average of 85 per 1,000. In Jan. 2002 the minimum wage (SMIC) was €6·67 an hour (€1,126·40 a month); in Jan. 2000 it affected about 2·5m. wage-earners. The net average annual wage was 130,790 francs (€19,938) in 1999. Retirement age is 60, although in 1995 the average actual age for retirement among males was 59. A five-week annual holiday is statutory.

In May 1998 the national assembly approved a reduction in the working week from 39 to 35 hours. The main provisions obliged all companies employing more than 20 people to introduce the shorter working week from Feb. 2000 and all the rest from 2002.

Trade Unions. The main trade union confederations are as follows: the Communist-led CGT (Confédération Générale du Travail), founded 1895; the CGT-FO (Confédération Générale du Travail–Force Ouvrière) which broke away from the CGT in 1948; the CFTC (Confédération Française des Travailleurs Chrétiens), founded in 1919 and divided in 1964, with a breakaway group retaining the old name and the main body continuing under the new name of CFDT (Confédération Française Démocratique du Travail); and the CGC-CFE (Confédération Générale des Cadres-Confédération Française de l'Encadrement) formed in 1946, which represents managerial and supervisory staff. The main haulage confederation is the FNTR; the leading employers' association is the CNPF, often referred to as the *Patronat*. Unions are not required to publish membership figures, but in 1993 the two largest federations, the CGT and CFDT, had an estimated 0·63m. and 0·65m. members respectively.

Although France has the lowest rate of trade union membership in Europe (9% in 2000, compared to 29% in the UK, 30% in Germany and over 90% in Sweden), its trade unionists have considerable clout: they run France's welfare system; staff the country's dispute-settling industrial tribunals (*conseils de prud'hommes*); and fix national agreements on wages and working conditions. A union call to strike is invariably answered by more than a union's membership.

INTERNATIONAL TRADE

Imports and Exports. In 2000 imports (f.o.b.) totalled US$294·40bn.; exports (f.o.b.), US$295·53bn. Principal imports include: oil, machinery and equipment, chemicals, iron and steel, and foodstuffs. Major exports: metals, chemicals, industrial equipment, consumer goods and agricultural products.

Foreign trade by sector (1999, as % of total trade):

	% Imports	% Exports
Agriculture and foodstuffs	10·1	13·1
Energy	7·1	2·7
Cars	10·9	13·4
Producer durables	23·4	25·5
Intermediate goods	32·9	31·5
Consumer goods	15·6	13·8

In 1999 the chief import sources (as % of total imports) were as follows: Germany, 17·2%; Italy, 9·6%; USA, 8·8%; UK, 8·4%; Spain, 7·1%. The chief export markets (as % of total) were: Germany, 15·7%; UK, 10·3%; Italy, 9·4%; Spain, 9·1%; USA, 7·8%. Exports to other European Union members constituted 64·2% of the total, and imports from fellow European Union members accounted for 61·5% of all imports.

Trade Fairs. Paris ranked as the world's leading major convention city in 2001 by the Union des Associations Internationales (UAI).

COMMUNICATIONS

Roads. In 1998 there were 893,300 km of road, including 10,300 km of motorway. France has the longest road network in the EU. Around 90% of all freight is transported by road. In 1998 there were 26,800,000 private cars and 5,418,000 lorries, 82,000 buses, and 870,000 motorcycles and scooters (1996). The average distance travelled by a passenger car in 1997 was 14,000 km. Road passenger traffic in 1998 totalled 753·1bn. passenger-km. In 2001 there were 8,160 road deaths, up from 8,079 in 2000.

Rail. In 1938 all the independent railway companies were merged with the existing state railway system in a Société Nationale des Chemins de Fer Français (SNCF), which became a public industrial and commercial establishment in 1983. Legislation came into effect in 1997 which vested ownership of the railway infrastructure (track and signalling) in a newly established public corporation, the National Railway Network (RFN). The RFN is funded by payments for usage from the SNCF, government and local subventions and authority capital made available by the state derived from the proceeds of privatization. The SNCF remains responsible for maintenance and management of the rail network. The legislation also envisages the establishment of regional railway services which receive funds previously given to the SNCF as well as a state subvention. These regional bodies negotiate with SNCF for the provision of suitable services for their area. SNCF is the most heavily indebted and subsidized company in France.

In 1997 SNCF totalled 33,769 km of track (one third of it electrified). High-speed TGV lines link Paris to the south and west of France, and Paris and Lille to the Channel Tunnel (Eurostar). The high-speed TGV line appeared in 1983; it had 2,110 km of track in 2001, and another 4,000 km planned by 2015. Services from London through the Channel Tunnel began operating in 1994. Rail passenger traffic in 1999 totalled 66·6bn. passenger km.

The Paris transport network consisted in 2000 of 211·3 km of metro (297 stations), 115 km of regional express railways and 20 km of tramway. There are metros in Lille (45·0 km), Lyons (29·4 km), Toulouse (10·0 km) and Marseilles (19·5 km), and tram/light railway networks in Grenoble (20·6 km), Lille (23·0 km), Lyons (18·7 km), Marseilles (3·1 km), Montpellier (15·2 km), Nantes (38·5 km), Orléans (17·9 km), Rouen (15·4 km), St Étienne (9·3 km) and Strasbourg (28·0 km).

Civil Aviation. The main international airports are at Paris (Charles de Gaulle), Paris (Orly), Bordeaux (Mérignac), Lyons (Satolas), Marseilles-Provence, Nice-Côte d'Azur, Strasbourg (Entzheim), Toulouse (Blagnac) and Nantes (Atlantique). The following had international flights to only a few destinations in 1998: Beauvais, Brest, Caen, Carcassonne, Clermont-Ferrand, Deauville, Le Havre, Le Touquet, Lille, Pau, Rennes, Rouen and Saint-Étienne. The national airline, Air France, is 54·4% state-owned, although there are plans to reduce this to under 20%. In 1999 it flew 636·8m. km, carrying 37,027,900 passengers (19,141,000 on international flights). In 2000 Charles de Gaulle airport handled 47,800,726 passengers (42,505,503 on international flights) and 1,019,311 tonnes of freight. Only Heathrow handled more international passengers in 2000. Orly was the second busiest airport, handling 25,378,013 passengers (19,285,061 on domestic flights) and 87,063 tonnes of freight. Nice was the third busiest for passengers, with 9,363,952 (4,934,161 on domestic flights).

Shipping. In 1998 the merchant fleet comprised 808 vessels (of 100 gross tons or more) totalling 4·85m. GRT, including 69 tankers of 2·83m. GRT. In 1997 vessels totalling 1,989·8m. NRT entered ports. In 1993 from a total of 215 vessels (all sizes; GRT: 3,928,000), 212m. tonnes of cargo were unloaded, including 130m. tonnes of crude and refined petroleum products, 93m. tonnes were loaded; total passenger traffic was 29·2m. Chief ports: Marseilles, Le Havre, Nantes, Bordeaux and Rouen.

France has extensive inland waterways. Canals are administered by the public authority France Navigable Waterways (FVN). In 1993 there were 8,500 km of navigable rivers, waterways and canals (of which 1,647 km were accessible to vessels over 3,000 tons), with a total traffic of 59·8m. tonnes.

Telecommunications. France Télécom became a limited company on 1 Jan. 1997. In 2000 there were 34·1m. telephone main lines, or 579·3 for every 1,000 inhabitants, and there were 18m. PCs in use (equivalent to 304·3 per 1,000 persons). In Nov. 2001 mobile phone subscribers numbered 33·72m. In 1997 there were 2·8m. fax machines in use. There were still 39,000 telex subscribers in 1996, although telex usage has declined considerably in recent years. France had 16·97m. Internet users in May 2002—just over 28% of the population.

Postal Services. There were 16,919 post offices in 1994. In 1995 a total of 24,391m. pieces of mail were processed, or 419 items per person. La Poste is a public enterprise under autonomous management responsible for mail delivery and financial services.

SOCIAL INSTITUTIONS

Justice. The system of justice is divided into two jurisdictions: the judicial and the administrative. Within the judicial jurisdiction are common law courts including 473 lower courts (*tribunaux d'instance*, 11 in overseas departments), 181 higher courts (*tribunaux de grande instance*, 5 *tribunaux de première instance* in the overseas territories), and 454 police courts (*tribunaux de police*, 11 in overseas departments).

The *tribunaux d'instance* are presided over by a single judge. The *tribunaux de grande instance* usually have a collegiate composition, but may be presided over by a single judge in some civil cases. The *tribunaux de police*, presided over by a judge on duty in the *tribunal d'instance*, deal with petty offences (*contraventions*); correctional chambers (*chambres correctionelles*, of which there is at least one in each *tribunal de grande instance*) deal with graver offences (*délits*), including cases involving imprisonment up to five years. Correctional chambers normally consist of three judges of a *tribunal de grande instance* (a single judge in some cases). Sometimes in cases of *délit*, and in all cases of more serious *crimes*, a preliminary inquiry is made in secrecy by one of 569 examining magistrates (*juges d'instruction*), who either dismisses the case or sends it for trial before a public prosecutor.

Within the judicial jurisdiction are various specialized courts, including 191 commercial courts (*tribunaux de commerce*), composed of tradesmen and manufacturers elected for two years initially, and then for four years; 271 conciliation boards (*conseils de prud'hommes*), composed of an equal number of employers and employees elected for five years to deal with labour disputes; 437 courts for settling rural landholding disputes (*tribunaux paritaires des baux ruraux*, 11 in overseas departments); and 116 social security courts (*tribunaux des affaires de sécurité sociale*).

When the decisions of any of these courts are susceptible of appeal, the case goes to one of the 35 courts of appeal (*cours d'appel*), composed each of a president and a variable number of members. There are 104 courts of assize (*cours d'assises*), each composed of a president who is a member of the court of appeal, and two other magistrates, and assisted by a lay jury of nine members. These try crimes involving imprisonment of over five years. The decisions of the courts of appeal and the courts of assize are final. However, the Court of Cassation (*cour de cassation*) has discretion to verify if the law has been correctly interpreted and if the rules of procedure have been followed exactly. The Court of Cassation may annul any judgment, following which the cases must be retried by a court of appeal or a court of assizes.

The administrative jurisdiction exists to resolve conflicts arising between citizens and central and local government authorities. It consists of 35 administrative courts (*tribunaux administratifs*, 7 in overseas departments and territories) and 7 administrative courts of appeal (*cours administratives d'appel*). The Council of State is the final court of appeal in administrative cases, though it may also act as a court of first instance.

Cases of doubt as to whether the judicial or administrative jurisdiction is competent in any case are resolved by a *Tribunal de conflits* composed in equal measure of members of the Court of Cassation and the Council of State. In 1997 the government restricted its ability to intervene in individual cases of justice.

Penal code. A revised penal code came into force on 1 March 1994, replacing the *Code Napoléon* of 1810. Penal institutions consist of: (1) *maisons d'arrêt*, where persons awaiting trial as well as those condemned to short periods of imprisonment are kept; (2) punishment institutions – (a) central prisons (*maisons centrales*) for those sentenced to long imprisonment, (b) detention centres for offenders showing promise of rehabilitation, and (c) penitentiary centres, establishments combining (a) and (b); (3) hospitals for the sick. Special attention is being paid to classified treatment and the rehabilitation and vocational re-education of prisoners including work in open-air and semi-free establishments. Juvenile delinquents go before special judges in 139 (11 in overseas departments and territories) juvenile courts (*tribunaux pour enfants*); they are sent to public or private institutions of supervision and re-education.

The first Ombudsman (*Médiateur*) was appointed for a six-year period in Jan. 1973. The present incumbent is Bernard Stasi (app. 1998).

Capital punishment was abolished in Aug. 1981. In metropolitan France the detention rate in July 2001 was 84·3 prisoners per 100,000 population, up from 50 per 100,000 in 1975. The average period of detention in 1998 was 8·3 months. The principal offences committed were: theft, 27·2%; rape and other sexual assaults, 21·0%; drug-related offences, 16·8%. The population of the 186 penal establishments (3 for women) in July 2001 was 49,718 including 1,746 women.

Weston, M., *English Reader's Guide to the French Legal System.* Oxford, 1991

Religion. A law of 1905 separated church and state. In 1996 there were 95 Roman Catholic dioceses in metropolitan France and 112 bishops. In Feb. 2001 there were six Cardinals. In 1997 there were 44·86m. Roman Catholics (over 75% of the population), 3·24m. Muslims, 1·08m. Protestants and 0·61m. Jews. An estimated 6·26m. people were non-religious and there were 2m. atheists.

Education. The primary, secondary and higher state schools constitute the 'Université de France'. Its Supreme Council of 84 members has deliberative, administrative and judiciary functions, and as a consultative committee advises respecting the working of the school system; the inspectors-general are in direct communication with the Minister. For local education administration France is divided into 25 academic areas, each of which has an Academic Council whose members include a certain number elected by the professors or teachers. The Academic Council deals with all grades of education. Each is under a Rector, and each is provided with academy inspectors, one for each department.

Compulsory education is provided for children of 6–16. The educational stages are as follows:

1. Non-compulsory pre-school instruction for children aged 2–5, to be given in infant schools or infant classes attached to primary schools.

2. Compulsory elementary instruction for children aged 6–11, to be given in primary schools and certain classes of the *lycées*. It consists of three courses: preparatory (one year), elementary (two years), intermediary (two years). Physically or mentally handicapped children are cared for in special institutions or special classes of primary schools.

3. Lower secondary education (*Enseignement du premier cycle du Second Degré*) for pupils aged 11–15, consists of four years of study in the *lycées* (grammar schools), *Collèges d'Enseignement Technique* or *Collèges d'Enseignement Général*.

4. Upper secondary education (*Enseignement du second cycle du Second Degré*) for pupils aged 15–18: (1) *Long, général* or *professionel* provided by the *lycées* and leading to the *baccalauréat* or to the *baccalauréat de technicien* after three years; and (2) *Court*, professional courses of 3, 2 and 1 year are taught in the *lycées d'enseignement professionel*, or the specialized sections of the *lycées*, CES or CEG.

The following table shows the number of schools in 1994–95 and the numbers of teachers and pupil in 1995–96:

	Number of Schools[1]	Teachers	Pupils
Nursery	18,989	105,925	2,500,867
Primary	41,244	216,938	4,065,005
Secondary	11,212	478,592	5,980,518

[1]Includes vocational education institutions.

Higher education is provided by the state free of charge in the universities and in special schools, and by private individuals in the free faculties and schools. Legislation of 1968 redefined the activities and workings of universities. Bringing several disciplines together, 780 units for teaching and research (*UER—Unités d'Enseignement et de Recherche*) were formed which decided their own teaching activities, research programmes and procedures for checking the level of knowledge gained. They and the other parts of each university must respect the rules designed to maintain the national standard of qualifications. The UERs form the basic units of the 69 state universities and three national polytechnic institutes (with university status), which are grouped into 25 *Académies*. There are also five Catholic universities in Paris, Angers, Lille, Lyons and Toulouse; and private universities. There were 2,107,600 students at universities in 1994–95.

Outside the university system, higher education (academic, professional and technical) is provided by over 400 schools and institutes, including the 177 *Grandes Écoles*, which are highly selective public or private institutions offering mainly technological or commercial curricula. These have an annual output of about 17,000 graduates, and in 1994–95 there were also 71,271 students in preparatory classes leading to the *Grandes Écoles;* in 1993–94, 232,844 were registered in the Sections de Techniciens Supérieurs, 71,273 in the Écoles d'Ingénieurs.

Adult literacy rate in 1998 was at least 99%.

In 1995 total expenditure on education came to 6·1% of GNP and represented 11·1% of total government expenditure.

Health. Ordinances of 1996 created a new regional regime of hospital administration and introduced a system of patients' records to prevent abuses of public health benefits. In 1995 there were 160,235 doctors (equivalent to 1 for every 362 persons), 39,284 dentists, 53,085 pharmacists, 330,943 nurses and 11,957 midwives; and 3,810 hospitals, with a provision of 118 beds per 10,000 population.

In 2000 France spent 9·5% of its GDP on health, public spending amounting to 76·0% of the total. A survey published by the World Health Organization in June 2000 to measure health systems in all of the sovereign countries and find which country has the best overall health care ranked France in first place.

The average French adult smokes 4·0 cigarettes a day, compared to a European Union average of 4·5, and drinks 14·1 litres of alcohol a year, compared to a European Union average of 11·1 litres. France has the highest alcohol consumption per person of any EU member country. It has the lowest rate of cardiovascular disease in the EU, but the highest rate of cancer among men.

Welfare. An order of 4 Oct. 1945 laid down the framework of a comprehensive plan of Social Security and created a single organization which superseded the various laws relating to social insurance, workmen's compensation, health insurance, family allowances, etc. All previous matters relating to Social Security are dealt with in the Social Security Code, 1956; this has been revised several times. The Chamber of Deputies and Senate, meeting as Congress on 19 Feb. 1996, adopted an important revision of the Constitution giving parliament powers to review annually the funding of social security (previously managed by the trade unions and employers' associations), and to fix targets for expenditure in the light of anticipated receipts.

In 1997, 6m. people were dependent on the welfare system, which accounted for more than a quarter of GDP (US$333,000m.). The Social Security budget had a deficit of some 17,000m. francs in 1996, and a cumulative debt (1992–96) of 250,000m. francs. A special levy, the new social debt repayment tax (RDS), at 0·5% on all incomes including pensions and unemployment benefit, has been introduced to clear the cumulative debt.

Contributions. The general social security contribution (CSG) introduced in 1991 was raised by 4% to 7·5% in 1997 by the Jospin administration in an attempt to dramatically reduce the deficit on social security spending, effectively almost doubling the CSG. All wage-earning workers or those of equivalent status are insured regardless of the amount or the nature of the salary or earnings. The funds for the general scheme are raised mainly from professional contributions, these being fixed within the limits of a ceiling and calculated as a percentage of the salaries. The calculation of contributions payable for family allowances, old age and industrial injuries relates only to this amount; on the other hand, the amount payable for sickness, maternity expenses, disability and death is calculated partly within the limit of the 'ceiling' and partly on the whole salary. These contributions are the responsibility of both employer and employee, except in the case of family allowances or industrial injuries, where they are the sole responsibility of the employer.

Self-employed Workers. From 17 Jan. 1948 allowances and old-age pensions were paid to self-employed workers by independent insurance funds set up within their own profession, trade or business. Schemes of compulsory insurance for sickness were instituted in 1961 for farmers, and in 1966, with modifications in 1970, for other non-wage-earning workers.

Social Insurance. The orders laid down in Aug. 1967 ensure that the whole population can benefit from the Social Security Scheme; at present all elderly persons who have been engaged in the professions, as well as the surviving spouse, are entitled to claim an old-age benefit.

Sickness Insurance refunds the costs of treatment required by the insured and the needs of dependants.

Maternity Insurance covers the costs of medical treatment relating to the pregnancy, confinement and lying-in period; the beneficiaries being the insured person or the spouse.

Insurance for Invalids is divided into three categories: (1) those who are capable of working; (2) those who cannot work; (3) those who, in addition, are in need of the help of another person. According to the category, the pension rate varies from 30 to 50% of the average salary for the last ten years, with additional allowance for home help for the third category.

Old-Age Pensions for workers were introduced in 1910 and are now fixed by the Social Security Code of 28 Jan. 1972. Since 1983 people who have paid insurance for at least 37½ years (150 quarters) receive at 60 a pension equal to 60% of basic salary. People who have paid insurance for less than 37½ years but no less than 15 years can expect a pension equal to as many 1/150ths of the full pension as their quarterly payments justify. In the event of death of the insured person, the husband or wife of the deceased person receives half the pension received by the latter. Compulsory supplementary schemes ensure benefits equal to 70% of previous earnings.

Family Allowances. A controversial programme of means-testing for Family Allowance was introduced in 1997 by the new administration. The Family Allowance benefit system comprises: (a) Family allowances proper, equivalent to 25·5% of the basic monthly salary for two dependent children, 46% for the third child, 41% for the fourth child, and 39% for the fifth and each subsequent child; a supplement equivalent to 9% of the basic monthly salary for the second and each subsequent dependent child more than ten years old, and 16% for each dependent child over 15 years. (b) Family supplement for persons with at least three children or one child aged less than three years. (c) Ante-natal grants. (d) Maternity grant is equal to 260% of basic salary. Increase for multiple births or adoptions, 198%; increase for birth or adoption of third or subsequent child, 457%. (e) Allowance for specialized education of handicapped children. (f) Allowance for orphans. (g) Single parent allowance. (h) Allowance for opening of school term. (i) Allowance for accommodation, under certain circumstances. (j) Minimum family income for those with at least three children. Allowances (b), (g), (h) and (j) only apply to those whose annual income falls below a specified level.

Workmen's Compensation. The law passed by the National Assembly on 30 Oct. 1946 forms part of the Social Security Code and is administered by the Social Security Organization. Employers are invited to take preventive measures. The application of these measures is supervised by consulting engineers (assessors) of the local funds dealing with sickness insurance, who may compel employers who do not respect these measures to make additional contributions; they may, in like manner, grant rebates to employers who have in operation suitable preventive measures. The injured person receives free treatment, the insurance fund reimburses the practitioners, hospitals and suppliers chosen freely by the injured. In cases of temporary disablement, the daily payments are equal to half the total daily wage received by the injured. In case of permanent disablement, the injured person receives a pension, the amount of which varies according to the degree of disablement and the salary received during the past 12 months.

Unemployment Benefits vary according to circumstances (full or partial unemployment) which are means-tested.

Ambler, J. S. (ed.) *The French Welfare State: Surviving Social and Ideological Change*. New York Univ. Press, 1992

CULTURE

Lille, along with Genoa in Italy, will be one of the European Capitals of Culture for 2004. The title attracts large European Union grants.

Broadcasting. The broadcasting authority (an independent regulatory commission) is the *Conseil Supérieur de l'Audiovisuel (CSA)*. Public radio is provided by Radio France which broadcasts nationwide on *France Info, France Inter, France Musique, France Culture, Radio Bleue* and *Le Mouv'* and, locally, via 39 radio stations. In Oct. 1998 there were 3,229 private local radio stations. An external service, *Radio-France Internationale*, was founded in 1931 (as 'Poste Coloniale'), and broadcasts in 20 languages. Two of the state-owned TV channels are partly financed by advertising—*FR2* and *FR3*—and there are four private terrestrial channels. Colour is by SECAM H. TV broadcasts must contain at least 60% EU-generated programmes and 50% of these must be French.

There are three state controlled national TV channels. Until the mid-1990s, French state controlled television was protected from competition by legislation but under pressure from the private sector and cable companies, the two public channels were re-named and France Television was created to manage them. The third channel, La Cinquième, started up in 1994, mainly as an education service. The four main terrestrial private channels broadcasting nationwide are: TF1, a former state channel privatized in 1987; M6, established in 1987; Arte, a joint Franco-German cultural channel; and Canal Plus, a subscription channel. There were 116 TV channels altogether in 1997, up from 32 in 1980.

France has been broadcasting via satellite since 1984 with a combined service relaying programmes from Belgian and Swiss as well as French satellites. More satellites have been added including TDF1and TDF2 broadcasting for Arte, Canal Plus and Radio France. Télécom A and Télécom B transmit for the principal TV stations and from 1995, Astra, Eutelsat and Télécom satellites have been broadcasting to the majority of households able to receive television. Digital Television arrived in 1996 and three new satellites, Canal Satellite, Télévision par Satellite and AB Sat, were launched. In 1999 there were 3·5m. satellite and cable TV subscribers.

In addition to specialized French national channels, foreign channels are also transmitted to approximately 1·5m. French households via cable.

There were about 58m. radio receivers in use in 1997 and 35·5m. TV sets.

Cinema. There were 4,762 cinemas in 1998. Attendances totalled 170m. in 1998 (130m. in 1995); gross box office receipts came to 4,523m. francs in 1995. A record 204 full-length films were made in 2001. In 1996 French films took 37% of the national market, but in 1998 this dropped to 27%. Around 360 new screens were to be opened between 1998 and 2000.

Press. There were about 80 daily papers (10 nationals, 70 provincials) in 1997. The leading dailies are: *L'Équipe; Le Monde; Le Parisien-Aujourd'hui; Le Figaro-L'Aurore; Libération; France-Soir; Ouest France; Le Progrès; Centre France; Sud Ouest; Voix du Nord*. The *Journal de Dimanche* is the only national Sunday paper. In 1995 total daily press circulation was 13·6m. copies, up from 10·3m. in 1980. In 1995 a total of 34,766 book titles were published.

Tourism. There were 75,000,000 foreign tourists in 2000; tourism receipts in 1999 were US$31·70bn. France is the most popular tourist destination in the world, and receipts from tourism in 1999 were exceeded only in the USA and Spain. The most visited tourist attractions in 1998 were Disneyland Paris (12·1m.), the Eiffel Tower (6·1m.) and the Louvre (5·7m.). Around 11m. foreigners a year visit Paris. Countries of origin (visitors, in 1,000) in 1993: Germany, 12,900; UK, 8,000; Netherlands, 7,100; Italy, 6,300; Spain, 3,000; Belgium, 2,000; USA, 1,900; Switzerland, 1,900;

Portugal, 1,700. There were 583,578 classified hotel rooms in 18,563 hotels in 2000. 39,000 new jobs were created in 2000 through tourism.

Festivals. *Religious Festivals.* Assumption of the Blessed Virgin Mary (15 Aug.) and All Saints Day (1 Nov.) are both Public Holidays.

Cultural Festivals. The Grande Parade de Montmartre, Paris (1 Jan.); the Carnival of Nice (Feb.–March); the Fête de la Victoire (8 May), celebrates victory in World War Two; the May Feasts take place in Nice regularly throughout May; the prestigious Cannes Film Festival, which has been running since 1946, lasts two weeks in mid-May; the Avignon Festival is a celebration of theatre that attracts average attendances of 140,000 each year and runs for most of July; Bastille Day (14 July) sees celebrations, parties and fireworks across the country. The Festival International d'Art Lyrique, focusing on classical music, opera and ballet, takes place in Aix-en-Provence every July. There are also annual festivals of opera at Orange (July–Aug.) and baroque music at Ambronay (Sept.–Oct.).

Libraries. In 1997 there were 2,577 public libraries, 2 National libraries and 186 Higher Education libraries; they held a combined 125,772,000 volumes. There were 295,229,000 visits to the libraries in 1997.

DIPLOMATIC REPRESENTATIVES

Of France in the United Kingdom (58 Knightsbridge, London, SW1X 7JT)
Ambassador: Gérard Errera.

Of the United Kingdom in France (35 rue du Faubourg St Honoré, 75383 Paris Cedex 08)
Ambassador: Sir John Eaton Holmes, KBE, CVO, CMG.

Of France in the USA (4101 Reservoir Rd., NW, Washington, D.C., 20007)
Ambassador: Jean-David Levitte.

Of the USA in France (2 Ave. Gabriel, Paris)
Ambassador: Howard H. Leach.

Of France to the United Nations
Ambassador: Jean-Marc de la Sablière.

FURTHER READING

Institut National de la Statistique et des Études Économiques: *Annuaire statistique de la France* (from 1878); *Bulletin mensuel de statistique* (monthly); *Documentation économique* (bi-monthly); *Economie et Statistique* (monthly); *Tableaux de l'Économie Française* (biennially, from 1956); *Tendances de la Conjoncture* (monthly).

Agulhon, Maurice, *De Gaulle: Histoire, Symbole, Mythe.* Plon, Paris, 2000
Agulhon, M., and Nevill, A., *The French Republic, 1879–1992.* Blackwell, Oxford, 1993
Ardagh, John, *France in the New Century: Portrait of a Changing Society.* Viking, London, 1999
Ardant, P., *Les Institutions de la Ve République.* Paris, 1992
Balladur, E., *Deux Ans à Matignon.* Paris, 1995
Bell, David, *Presidential Power in Fifth Republic France.* Berg, Oxford, 2000.—*Parties and Democracy in France: Parties under Presidentialism.* Ashgate, Aldershot, 2000
Chafer, Tony and Sackur, Amanda, (eds.) *French Colonial Empire and the Popular Front.* Macmillan, London, 1999
Chazal, C., *Balladur.* [in French] Paris, 1993
Cubertafond, A., *Le Pouvoir, la Politique et l'État en France.* Paris, 1993
L'État de la France. Paris, annual
Friend, Julius W., *The Long Presidency: France in the Mitterrand Years, 1981–95.* Westview, Oxford, 1999
Gildea, R., *France since 1945.* OUP, 1996
Guyard, Marius-François, (ed.) *Charles de Gaulle: Mémoires.* Gallimard, Paris, 2000
Guyomarch, Alain, Machin, Howard, Hall, Peter and Hayward, Jack, (eds.) *Developments in French Politics.* Palgrave, Basingstoke, 2001
Hollifield, J. F. and Ross, G., *Searching for the New France.* Routledge, London, 1991
Hudson, G. L., *Corsica.* [World Bibliographic Series, vol. 202] Oxford, 1997
Jack, A., *The French Exception.* Profile Books, London, 1999
Jones, C., *The Cambridge Illustrated History of France.* CUP, 1994
Lacoutre, Jean, *Mitterrand: Une histoire de Français.* 2 vols. Seuil, Paris, 1999
MacLean, Mairi, *The Mitterrand Years: Legacy and Evaluation.* Macmillan, London, 1999
McMillan, J. F., *Twentieth-Century France: Politics and Society in France, 1898–1991.* 2nd ed. [of *Dreyfus to De Gaulle*]. Arnold, London, 1992

Menon, Anand, *France, NATO and the Limits of Independence, 1918–97.* Macmillan, London, 1999

Noin, D. and White, P., *Paris.* John Wiley, Chichester, 1998

Peyrefitte, Alain, *C'était de Gaulle.* Fayard, Paris, 2000

Popkin, J. D., *A History of Modern France.* New York, 1994

Price, Roger, *A Concise History of France.* CUP, 1993

Raymond, Gino G. (ed.) *Structures of Power in Modern France.* Macmillan, London, 1999

Tiersky, Ronald, *Mitterrand in Light and Shadow.* Macmillan, London, 1999.—*François Mitterrand: The Last French President.* St Martin's Press, New York, 2000

Tippett-Spiritou, Sandy, *French Catholicism.* Macmillan, London, 1999

Turner, Barry, (ed.) *France Profiled.* Macmillan, London, 1999

Zeldin, T., *The French.* Harvill Press, London, 1997

(Also see specialized titles listed under relevant sections, above.)

National statistical office: Institut National de la Statistique et des Études Économiques (INSEE), 75582 Paris Cedex 12.

Website: http://www.insee.fr/

DEPARTMENTS AND TERRITORIES OVERSEAS

Départements (DOM) et Territoires (TOM) d'outre-Mer

GENERAL DETAILS

These fall into five categories: *Overseas Departments* (French Guiana, Guadeloupe, Martinique, Réunion); *Departmental Collectivities* (Mayotte); *Territorial Collectivities* (New Caledonia, St Pierre and Miquelon); *Overseas Territories* (French Polynesia, Southern and Antarctic Territories, Wallis and Futuna); and *Dependencies* (Bassas da India, Clipperton Island, Europa Island, Glorieuses Islands, Juan de Nova Island and Tromelin Island).

FURTHER READING

Aldrich, R. and Connell, J., *France's Overseas Frontier: Départements et Territoires d'Outre-Mer.* CUP, 1992

OVERSEAS DEPARTMENTS

FRENCH GUIANA

Guyane Française

KEY HISTORICAL EVENTS

A French settlement on the island of Cayenne was established in 1604 and the territory between the Maroni and Oyapock rivers finally became a French possession in 1817. Convict settlements were established from 1852, that on Devil's Island being the most notorious; all were closed by 1945. On 19 March 1946 the status of French Guiana was changed to that of an Overseas Department.

TERRITORY AND POPULATION

French Guiana is situated on the northeast coast of Latin America, and is bounded in the northeast by the Atlantic Ocean, west by Suriname, and south and east by Brazil. It includes the offshore Devil's Island, Royal Island and St Joseph, and has an area of 85,534 sq. km. Population at the 1999 census: 157,213. The UN gives a projected population for 2010 of 223,000. In 1995, 76·4% lived in urban areas. The chief towns are (with 1999 census populations): the capital, Cayenne (50,594 inhabitants), Saint-Laurent-du-Maroni (19,210) and Kourou (19,107). About 58% of inhabitants are of African descent.

The official language is French.

SOCIAL STATISTICS

1998 estimates (per 1,000 population): birth rate, 23·7; death rate, 4·5. 49% of the population are migrants. Annual growth rate, 1995–99, 4·3%.

CLIMATE

Equatorial type climate with most of the country having a main rainy season between April and July and a fairly dry period between Aug. and Dec. Both temperatures and humidity are high the whole year round. Cayenne, Jan. 26°C, July 29°C. Annual rainfall 3,202 mm.

CONSTITUTION AND GOVERNMENT

French Guiana is administered by a General Council of 19 members directly elected for five-year terms, and by a Regional Council of 31 members. It is represented in the National Assembly by two deputies; in the Senate by one senator. The French government is represented by a Prefect. There are two *arrondissements* (Cayenne and Saint Laurent-du-Maroni) sub-divided into 22 communes and 19 cantons.

CURRENT ADMINISTRATION

Prefect: Ange Mancini.
   President of the General Council: Stéphan Phinera-Horth (PS).
   President of the Regional Council: Antoine Karam (PS).

ECONOMY

Currency. Since 1 Jan. 2002 the euro has been the official currency as in metropolitan France.

Performance. In 1993 GDP was 7,989m. French francs. GDP per capita (1993) was 54,516 French francs. Real GDP growth was 20·9% in both 1994 and 1995.

Banking and Finance. The Caisse Centrale de Coopération Economique is the bank of issue. In 2001 commercial banks included the Banque Nationale de Paris-Guyane, Crédit Populaire Guyanais and Banque Française Commerciale.

ENERGY AND NATURAL RESOURCES

Electricity. Installed capacity was 228,000 kW in 1995. Production in 1998 was 430m. kWh.

Minerals. Placer gold mining is the most important industry in French Guiana. In 1999, 3,000 kg of gold were produced.

Agriculture. There were 10,000 ha of arable land in 1998 and 3,000 ha of permanent crops. Principal crops (1998 estimates, in 1,000 tonnes): rice, 31; cassava, 10; cabbages, 5; sugarcane, 5; bananas, 4.

   Livestock (1996): 8,000 cattle; 9,000 pigs; 3,000 sheep; 220,000 poultry (1993).

Forestry. The country has immense forests which are rich in many kinds of timber. In 1995 forests covered 79,900 sq. km, or 90·6% of the total land area. Roundwood production (1999) 120,000 cu. metres. The trees also yield oils, essences and gum products.

Fisheries. The catch in 1999 was an estimated 7,700 tonnes. Shrimps account for nearly 55% of the total catch.

INDUSTRY

Important products include rum, rosewood essence and beer. The island has sawmills and one sugar factory.

Labour. The economically active population (1993) was 46,300. In Jan. 2002 the minimum wage (SMIC) was €6·67 an hour (€1,126·40 a month). 8,324 persons were registered unemployed in 1994.

INTERNATIONAL TRADE

Imports and Exports. Total trade (1995); imports, US$752m.; exports, US$131m.

COMMUNICATIONS

Roads. There were (1996) 356 km of national and 366 km of departmental roads. In 1993 there were 29,100 passenger cars and 10,600 commercial vehicles.

Civil Aviation. In 2000 Rochambeau International Airport (Cayenne) handled 435,421 passengers and 6,053 tonnes of freight. The base of the European Space Agency (ESA) is located near Kourou and has been operational since 1979.

Shipping. 359 vessels arrived and departed in 1993; 249,160 tonnes of petroleum products and 230,179 tonnes of other products were discharged, and 69,185 tonnes of freight loaded. Chief ports: Cayenne, St-Laurent-du-Maroni and Kourou. There are also inland waterways navigable by small craft.

Telecommunications. In 1999 there were 49,200 telephone main lines (282·6 per 1,000 population), 23,000 PCs in use (132·2 for every 1,000 persons) and 18,000 mobile phone subscribers. In Dec. 1999 there were 2,000 Internet users

SOCIAL INSTITUTIONS

Justice. At Cayenne there is a *tribunal d'instance* and a *tribunal de grande instance*, from which appeal is to the regional *cour d'appel* in Martinique.

The population in penal institutions in Oct. 1998 was 3,471 (240 per 100,000 of national population).

Religion. In 1997 approximately 52% of the population was Roman Catholic.

Education. Primary education is free and compulsory. There were 24,000 children at primary schools in 1993; 12,000 at secondary schools; and (1988) a further 2,224 registered at private schools. In 1993, 644 students from French Guiana attended the Henri Visioz Institute, which forms part of the University of Antilles-Guyana (8,290 students in 1993).

Health. In 1995 there were 2 hospitals with 567 beds, 3 private clinics and a care centre. There were (1994) 213 doctors, 38 dentists, 47 pharmacists, 40 midwives and 495 nursing personnel.

CULTURE

Broadcasting. *Radiodiffusion Française d'Outre-Mer-Guyane* broadcasts for 133 hours each week on medium- and short-waves, and FM in French. Television is broadcast for 60 hours each week on two channels. In 1997 there were 104,000 radio and 30,000 TV receivers; colour is by SECAM.

Press. There was (1996) one daily newspaper with a circulation of 1,000, and a second paper published four times a week has a circulation of 5,500.

Tourism. Total number of visitors (1993), 54,000.

FURTHER READING

Crane, Janet, *French Guiana*. [Bibliography] ABC-Clio, Oxford and Santa Barbara (CA), 1998

GUADELOUPE

KEY HISTORICAL EVENTS

The islands were discovered by Columbus in 1493. The Carib inhabitants resisted Spanish attempts to colonize. A French colony was established on 28 June 1635, and apart from short periods of occupancy by British forces, Guadeloupe has since remained a French possession. On 19 March 1946 Guadeloupe became an Overseas Department.

TERRITORY AND POPULATION

Guadeloupe consists of a group of islands in the Lesser Antilles with a total area of 1,705 sq. km. The two main islands, Basse-Terre (to the west) and Grande-Terre (to the east), are joined by a bridge over a narrow channel. Adjacent to these are the islands of Marie-Galante (to the southeast), La Désirade (to the east), and the

Îles des Saintes (to the south); the islands of St Martin and St Barthélemy lie 250 km to the northwest.

Island	Area (sq. km)	1999 populations	Chief town
St Martin[1]	53[2]	29,078	Marigot
St Barthélemy	21	6,852	Gustavia
Basse-Terre	848	172,693	Basse-Terre
Grande-Terre	590	196,767	Pointe-à-Pitre
Îles des Saintes	13	2,998	Terre-de-Bas
La Désirade	22	1,620	Grande Anse
Marie-Galante	158	12,488	Grand-Bourg

[1]Northern part only; the southern third is Dutch. [2]Includes uninhabited Tintamarre.

Population at the last census (1999), 422,496. The UN gives a projected population for 2010 of 460,000. An estimated 99·4% of the population were urban in 1995. Population of principal towns (1999): Les Abymes, 63,054; Saint-Martin, 29,078; Pointe-à-Pitre, 20,948; Basse-Terre, 12,410. Basse-Terre is the seat of government, while larger Pointe-à-Pitre is the department's main economic centre and port; Les Abymes is a 'suburb' of Pointe-à-Pitre.

French is the official language, but Creole is spoken by the vast majority, except on St Martin.

SOCIAL STATISTICS
1998: live births, 6,507; deaths, 2,514; marriages, 3,510. 1998 estimates (per 1,000 population): birth rate, 15·5; death rate, 6·0. Annual growth rate, 1995–99, 1·5%. Life expectancy at birth, 1990–95, 71·1 years for males and 78·0 years for females.

CLIMATE
Warm and humid. Pointe-à-Pitre, Jan. 74°F (23·4°C), July 80°F (26·7°C). Annual rainfall 71" (1,814 mm).

CONSTITUTION AND GOVERNMENT
Guadeloupe is administered by a General Council of 42 members directly elected for six-year terms (assisted by an Economic and Social Committee of 40 members) and by a Regional Council of 41 members. It is represented in the National Assembly by four deputies; in the Senate by two senators; and on the Economic and Social Council by one councillor. There are four *arrondissements*, sub-divided into 42 cantons and 34 communes, each administered by an elected municipal council. The French government is represented by an appointed Prefect.

CURRENT ADMINISTRATION
Prefect: Dominique Vian.
President of the General Council: Jacques Gillot.
President of the Regional Council: Lucette Michaux-Chevry.

ECONOMY
Currency. Since 1 Jan. 2002 the euro has been the official currency as in metropolitan France.

Performance. In 1995 GDP was 28,186m. French francs. GDP per capita (1995) was 68,850 French francs. Real GDP growth was –2·9% in 1995 and 1·9% in 1994.

Banking and Finance. The Caisse Française de Développement is the official bank of the department. The main commercial banks in 1995 (with number of branches) were: Banque des Antilles Françaises (6), Banque Régionale d'Escompte et de Depôts (5), Banque Nationale de Paris (8), Crédit Agricole (18), Banque Française Commerciale (8), Société Générale de Banque aux Antilles (5), Crédit Lyonnais (6), Crédit Martiniquais (3), Banque Inschauspé et Cie (1).

ENERGY AND NATURAL RESOURCES
Electricity. Total production (1998): 1·22bn. kWh.

Agriculture. Chief products (1998 estimates, in 1,000 tonnes): sugarcane, 638; bananas, 141; pineapples, 7; plantains, 6; melons and watermelons, 4. Other fruits and vegetables are also grown for both export and domestic consumption.

Livestock (1996): cattle, 60,000; goats, 63,000 (1995); sheep, 3,000; pigs, 14,000.

Forestry. In 1995 forests covered 89,000 ha, or 47·3% of the total land area (down from 51·5% in 1990). Timber production in 1999 was 15,000 cu. metres.

Fisheries. Total catch in 1999 amounted to an estimated 9,150 tonnes, exclusively from sea fishing.

INDUSTRY

The main industries are sugar refining, food processing and rum distilling, carried out by small and medium-sized businesses. Other important industries are cement production and tourism.

Labour. The economically active population in 1997 was approximately 125,900. In Jan. 2002 the minimum wage (SMIC) was €6·67 an hour (€1,126·40 a month). 46,360 persons were registered unemployed in 1994.

INTERNATIONAL TRADE

Imports and Exports. Total imports (1997): US$1,700m.; total exports: US$140m. Main export commodities are bananas, sugar and rum. Trade with France (1997): 63% of all imports; 60% of exports.

COMMUNICATIONS

Roads. In 1996 there were 3,200 km of roads. In 1993 there were 101,600 passenger cars and 37,500 commercial vehicles. There were 83 road-related fatalities in 1996.

Civil Aviation. Air France and a dozen or so other airlines call at Guadeloupe airport. In 2000 there were 35,245 arrivals and departures of aircraft, and 1,974,350 passengers, at Le Raizet (Pointe-à-Pitre) airport. There are also airports at Marie-Galante, La Désirade, St Barthélemy and St Martin. Most domestic services are operated by Société Nouvelle Air Guadeloupe.

Shipping. In 1996 Port Autonome was visited by 2,014 cargo vessels carrying 2·9m. tonnes of freight and by 1,328 passenger ships.

Telecommunications. Guadeloupe had 204,900 main telephone lines in 2000, or 449·3 per 1,000 inhabitants, and there were 90,000 PCs in use (197·4 for every 1,000 persons). There were 3,400 fax machines in 1995 and 88,000 mobile phone subscribers in 1999. Internet users numbered 4,000 in Dec. 1999.

Postal Services. In 1984 there were 47 post offices.

SOCIAL INSTITUTIONS

Justice. There are four *tribunaux d'instance* and two *tribunaux de grande instance* at Basse-Terre and Pointe-à-Pitre; there is also a court of appeal and a court of assizes.

The population in penal institutions in Oct. 1998 was 706 (160 per 100,000 of national population).

Religion. The majority of the population are Roman Catholic.

Education. Education is free and compulsory from six to 16 years. In 1994 there were 54,493 pupils at 321 pre-elementary and primary schools, and 46,176 at 20 *lycées* and 40 *collèges* at secondary level. In 1993 there were 4,308 students from Guadeloupe at the University of Antilles-Guyana (out of total number of 8,290).

Health. In 1995 there were 13 public hospitals and 16 private clinics. In 1993 there were 590 doctors, 119 dentists, 1,470 nurses, 206 pharmacists and 108 midwives.

CULTURE

Broadcasting. *Radiodiffusion Française d'Outre-Mer* broadcasts for 17 hours a day in French. There is a local region radio station, and several private stations. There are two television channels (one regional; one satellite) broadcasting for six hours a day (colour by SECAM V). There were (1997) 113,000 radio and 118,000 TV receivers.

Press. There was (1996) 1 daily newspaper with a circulation of 30,000.

Tourism. Tourism is the chief economic activity. In 1998 there were 693,000 tourists plus 334,000 cruise ship arrivals. Tourism receipts in 1998 totalled US$583m.

MARTINIQUE

KEY HISTORICAL EVENTS
Discovered by Columbus in 1502, Martinique became a French colony in 1635 and apart from brief periods of British occupation the island has since remained under French control. On 19 March 1946 its status was altered to that of an Overseas Department.

TERRITORY AND POPULATION
The island, situated in the Lesser Antilles between Dominica and St Lucia, occupies an area of 1,128 sq. km. Population at last census (1999), 381,427; density, 338 per sq. km. The UN gives a projected population for 2010 of 402,000. An estimated 93·3% of the population were urban in 1995. Population of principal towns (1999 census): the capital and main port Fort-de-France, 94,049; Le Lamentin, 35,460; Schoelcher, 20,845; Sainte-Marie, 20,098; Rivière-Pilote, 13,057; La Trinité, 12,890.

French is the official language but the majority of people speak Creole.

SOCIAL STATISTICS
1998: live births, 5,793; deaths, 2,518. 1998 estimates per 1,000 population: birth rate, 15·3; death rate, 6·6. Annual growth rate, 1995–99, 0·2%. Life expectancy at birth, 1990–95, 73·0 years for males and 79·5 years for females.

CLIMATE
The dry season is from Dec. to May, and the humid season from June to Nov. Fort-de-France, Jan. 74°F (23·5°C), July 78°F (25·6°C). Annual rainfall 72" (1,840 mm).

CONSTITUTION AND GOVERNMENT
The island is administered by a General Council of 45 members directly elected for six-year terms and by a Regional Council of 42 members. The French government is represented by an appointed Prefect. There are four *arrondissements*, sub-divided into 45 cantons and 34 communes, each administered by an elected municipal council. Martinique is represented in the National Assembly by four deputies, in the Senate by two senators and on the Economic and Social Council by one councillor.

CURRENT ADMINISTRATION
Prefect: Michel Cadot.
  President of the General Council: Claude Lise.
  President of the Regional Council: Alfred Marie-Jeanne.

ECONOMY
Main sectors of activity: tradeable services, distribution, industry, building and public works, transport and telecommunications, agriculture and tourism.

Currency. Since 1 Jan. 2002 the euro has been the official currency as in metropolitan France.

Performance. In 1994 GDP was 24,500m. French francs. GDP per capita was 64,286 French francs. Real GDP growth was –2·9% in 1995 and 1·9% in 1994.

Banking and Finance. The Agence Française de Développement is the government's vehicle for the promotion of economic development in the region. There were 5 commercial banks, 4 co-operative banks, 1 savings bank, 5 investment companies and 2 specialized financial institutions in 1999.

Weights and Measures. The metric system is in use.

ENERGY AND NATURAL RESOURCES
Electricity. A network of 4,262 km of cables covers 98% of Martinique and supplies more than 142,000 customers. Electricity is produced by two fuel-powered electricity stations. Total production (1998): 1·08bn. kWh.

Agriculture. In 1997 there were 3,035 ha under sugarcane, 11,200 ha under bananas and 600 ha under pineapples. Production (1997 in tonnes): bananas, 318,155; sugarcane, 188,827; pineapples, 20,000; plantains, 13,000.

Livestock (1997): 25,600 cattle, 16,500 sheep, 12,000 pigs, 11,200 goats and 295,000 poultry.

Forestry. In 1995 there were 38,000 ha of forest, or 35·8% of the total land area (down from 37·7% in 1990). Timber production in 1999 was 12,000 cu. metres.

Fisheries. The catch in 1999 was approximately 5,000 tonnes, exclusively from sea fishing.

INDUSTRY

Some food processing and chemical engineering is carried out by small and medium-size businesses. There were 14,839 businesses in 2000. There is an important cement industry; 11 rum distilleries and an oil refinery, with an annual treatment capacity of 0·75m. tonnes. Martinique has five industrial zones.

Labour. In 1998, 6·6% of the working population were in agriculture; 15·1% in industry; 23·8% in retail; 34·1% in services; 16·9% in distribution. In Jan. 2002 the minimum wage (SMIC) was €6·67 an hour (€1,126·40 a month). The economically active population in 1999 was 166,800. In 1999, 48,667 persons were unemployed.

INTERNATIONAL TRADE

Imports and Exports. Martinique has a structural trade deficit owing to the nature of goods traded. It imports high-value-added goods (foodstuffs, capital goods, consumer goods and motor vehicles) and exports agricultural produce (bananas) and refined oil.

In 1999 imports were valued at 10·6bn. French francs; exports at 1·7bn. French francs. Main trading partners: France, EU, French Guiana and Guadeloupe. Trade with France accounted for 63% of imports and 61% of exports in 1995.

COMMUNICATIONS

Roads. Martinique has 2,176 km of roads. In 1995, 106m. French francs were spent on improving them. In 1993 there were 108,300 passenger cars and 32,200 commercial vehicles.

Civil Aviation. There is an international airport at Fort-de-France (Lamentin). In 2000 it handled 1,645,468 passengers and 15,755 tonnes of freight.

Shipping. The island is visited regularly by French, American and other lines. The main sea links to and from Martinique are ensured by CGM Sud. It links Martinique to Europe and some African and American companies. Since 1995 new scheduled links have been introduced between Martinique, French Guiana, Haiti and Panama. These new links facilitate exchanges between Martinique, Latin America and the Caribbean, especially Cuba. In 1993, 2,856 vessels called at Martinique and discharged 80,605 passengers and 1,612,000 tonnes of freight, and embarked 82,119 passengers and 789,000 tonnes of freight.

Telecommunications. In 2000 there were 171,600 main telephone lines, or 434·4 per 1,000 inhabitants, and 50,000 PCs in use (equivalent to 126·6 for every 1,000 persons). There were 102,000 mobile phone subscribers in 1999 and 20,000 fax machines in 1995. The main operator is France Télécom. In Dec. 1999 there were 5,000 Internet users.

SOCIAL INSTITUTIONS

Justice. Justice is administered by two lower courts (*tribunaux d'instance*), a higher court (*tribunal de grande instance*), a regional court of appeal, a commercial court and an administrative court.

The population in penal institutions in Oct. 1998 was 547 (140 per 100,000 of national population).

Religion. In 1997, 95% of the population was Roman Catholic.

Education. Education is compulsory between the ages of 6 and 16 years. In 1994 there were 51,824 pupils in 263 nursery and primary schools, and 43,384 pupils in 61 secondary schools. There were 29 institutes of higher education. In 1993, 3,670 students from Martinique were registered at the University of Antilles-French Guyana (out of a total of 8,290).

Health. In 1995 there were 8 hospitals, 3 private clinics and 7 nursing homes. Total number of beds, 2,100. There were 680 doctors, 230 pharmacists, 123 dentists, 1,700 nurses, 147 midwives, 141 physiotherapists and 48 speech therapists.

CULTURE

Broadcasting. *Radio Diffusion Française d'Outre-Mer* broadcasts on FM wave, and operates two channels (one satellite). There are also two commercial TV stations. In 1997 there were 82,000 radio and 66,000 TV receivers (colour by SECAM V).

Cinema. There is a ten-screen cinema and convention centre complex.

Press. In 1996 there was one daily newspaper with a circulation of 30,000.

Tourism. In 1999 there were 564,303 tourists plus 339,086 cruise ship arrivals. Tourism receipts totalled US$415m. in 1998. In 1999 there were 122 hotels, with 6,051 rooms.

FURTHER READING

Crane, Janet, *Martinique*. [Bibliography] ABC-Clio, Oxford and Santa Barbara (CA), 1995

RÉUNION

KEY HISTORICAL EVENTS

Réunion (formerly Île Bourbon) became a French possession in 1638 and remained so until 19 March 1946, when its status was altered to that of an Overseas Department.

TERRITORY AND POPULATION

The island of Réunion lies in the Indian Ocean, about 880 km east of Madagascar and 210 km southwest of Mauritius. It has an area of 2,507 sq. km. Population on 1 Jan. 2001: 728,400, giving a density of 291 per sq. km. An estimated 67·7% of the population were rural in 1995. The capital is Saint-Denis (population, 1999: 132,338); other large towns are Saint-Pierre (69,358), Saint-Paul (88,254) and le Tampon (60,701).

The UN gives a projected population for 2010 of 809,000.

French is the official language, but Creole is also spoken.

SOCIAL STATISTICS

2000: births, 14,587; deaths, 3,832 (1999); marriages, 3,510 (1999). Birth rate per 1,000 population (1999), 20·0; death rate, 5·4. Annual growth rate, 1995–99, 1·3%. Life expectancy at birth, 2000, 70·6 years for males and 78·7 years for females. Infant mortality, 1998, 8·0 per 1,000 live births; fertility rate, 1998, 2·8 births per woman.

CLIMATE

There is a sub-tropical maritime climate, free from extremes of weather, although the island lies in the cyclone belt of the Indian Ocean. Conditions are generally humid and there is no well-defined dry season. Saint-Denis, Jan. 80°F (26·7°C), July 70°F (21·1°C). Annual rainfall 56" (1,400 mm).

CONSTITUTION AND GOVERNMENT

Réunion is administered by a General Council of 47 members directly elected for six-year terms, and by a Regional Council of 45 members. Réunion is represented in the National Assembly in Paris by five deputies; in the Senate by three senators; and in the Economic and Social Council by one councillor. There are 4 *arrondissements* sub-divided into 47 cantons and 24 communes, each administered by an elected municipal council. The French government is represented by an appointed Commissioner.

CURRENT ADMINISTRATION
Prefect: Gonthier Friederici.
President of the General Council: Jean-Luc Poudroux.
President of the Regional Council: Paul Vergès.

ECONOMY
Currency. Since 1 Jan. 2002 the euro has been the official currency as in metropolitan France. Owing to its geographical location, Réunion was by two hours the first territory to introduce the euro.

Performance. GDP was 42,577m. French francs in 1995. Real GDP growth was 2·7% in 1995. GDP per capita (1995) was 64,303 French francs.

Banking and Finance. The Institut d'Émission des Départements d'Outre-mer has the right to issue bank-notes. Banks operating in Réunion are the Banque de la Réunion (Crédit Lyonnais), the Banque Nationale de Paris Intercontinentale, the Crédit Agricole de la Réunion, the Banque Française Commerciale (BFC) CCP, Trésorerie Générale, and the Banque de la Réunion pour l'Économie et le Développement (BRED).

ENERGY AND NATURAL RESOURCES
Electricity. Production (2001), 1,871m. kWh. Consumption per capita (2000), 2,208 kWh.

Oil and Gas. Production (1999), 212,641 tonnes.

Water. Production (2000), 116·7m. cu. metres.

Agriculture. There were 43,692 ha of arable land in 2000 and 4,000 ha of permanent crops in 1997. Main agricultural products: sugarcane, 1,675,000 (1998 estimate); maize, 17,000 (1998 estimate); cabbages, 14,000 (1998 estimate); pineapples, 12,000 (1999); tomatoes, 12,000 (1998 estimate); potatoes, 8,100 (1999); onions, 1,776 (1999).

Livestock (1999): 84,500 pigs, 28,100 cattle, 1,730 sheep, 11,835 poultry (1997) and 29,050 goats. Meat production (1999, in tonnes): pork, 11,810; beef and veal, 1,660; poultry, 13,550. Milk production (1999), 19,726 hectolitres.

Forestry. There were 100,916 ha of forest in 1998, or 40·3% of the total land area. Timber production in 1999 was 100,000 cu. metres.

Fisheries. In 2001 the catch was 5,406 tonnes, almost entirely from marine waters. Deep-sea fishing (1999) is mainly for blue marlin, sail-fish, blue-fin tuna and sea bream.

INDUSTRY
The major industries are electricity and sugar. Food processing, chemical engineering, printing and the production of perfume, textiles, leathers, tobacco, wood and construction materials are carried out by small and medium-sized businesses. At the beginning of 1994 there were 9,465 craft businesses employing about 20,000 persons. Production of sugar was 215,600 tonnes in 1999; rum, 74,154 hectolitres (pure alcohol) in 1999.

Labour. The workforce was 284,300 in 2000. In Jan. 2002 the minimum wage (SMIC) was €6·67 an hour (€1,126·40 a month). In 2000, 130,400 persons were registered unemployed, a rate of 42·1%. Among the under 25s the unemployment rate is nearly 60%

INTERNATIONAL TRADE
Imports and Exports. Trade in 1m. French francs:

	1996	1997	1998	1999	2000	2001
Imports	14,214	14,262	15,310	15,828	17,908	18,728
Exports	1,071	1,250	1,215	1,267	1,489	1,502

The chief export is sugar, accounting for 53·7% of total exports (1999). In 1999, 62·2% of trade was with France.

COMMUNICATIONS

Roads. There were, in 2001, 2,914 km of roads and 258,400 registered vehicles. In 1999 the County Council was operating bus services to all towns.

Civil Aviation. In 2000, 736,499 passengers and 17,206 tonnes of freight arrived at, and 730,980 passengers and 8,934 tonnes of freight departed from, Roland Garros Saint-Denis airport.

Shipping. 753 vessels visited the island in 2000, unloading 2,783,700 tonnes of freight and loading 482,300 tonnes at Port-Réunion.

Telecommunications. There were 269,500 telephone main lines in 1999, or 388·6 per 1,000 inhabitants, and 32,000 PCs in use (46·3 per 1,000 persons). There were 197,000 mobile phone subscribers in Sept. 2000, up from 26,700 in 1997. In 1995 there were 1,900 fax machines. Internet users numbered 10,000 in July 2000.

Postal Services. In 1996 there were 824 post offices.

SOCIAL INSTITUTIONS

Justice. There are 3 lower courts (*tribunaux d'instance*), 2 higher courts (*tribunaux de grande instance*), 1 appeal, 1 administrative court and 1 conciliation board.
The population in penal institutions in Oct. 1998 was 1,019 (150 per 100,000 of national population).

Religion. In 1990, 95% of the population was Roman Catholic.

Education. In 1999–2000 there were 501 primary schools with 111,845 pupils. Secondary education was provided in 27 *lycées*, 73 colleges, and 13 technical *lycées*, with, altogether, 96,168 pupils. The *Université Française de l'Océan Indien* (founded 1971) had 13,371 students in 1999–2000.

Health. In 2000 there were 17 hospitals with 2,734 beds, 1,595 doctors, 364 dentists, 342 pharmacists, 221 midwives and 2,906 nursing personnel.

CULTURE

Broadcasting. *Radiodiffusion Française d'Outre-Mer* broadcasts in French on medium- and short-waves for more than 18 hours a day. There are two national television channels (*RFDI, Tempo*) and three independent channels (*Antenne Réunion, Canal Réunion/Canal +* and *Parabole Réunion*). Colour transmission is by SECAM V. In 1997 there were 127,000 TV receivers and 173,000 radio receivers.

Cinema. In 2000 there were 18 cinemas.

Press. There were (2000) 3 daily newspapers (*Quotidien, Journal de l'Île, Témoignages*), 2 weekly (*Visu, Télé Magazine*), 3 monthly (*Memento, Via, l'Eco Austral*) and 2 fortnightly magazines (*Leader* and *Attitude*), with a combined circulation of 57,000.

Tourism. Tourism is a major resource industry. There were 430,000 visitors in 2000 (81·6% French). Receipts (2000) totalled €276m. In Jan. 2001 accommodation included 60 hotels, 126 country lodges (*gîtes ruraux*), 269 bed and breakfast houses, 22 stopover lodges (*gîtes d'étape*) and 22 mountain huts.

Libraries. There were 58 libraries in 1999.

Theatre and Opera. There were six theatres in 2000.

FURTHER READING
Institut National de la Statistique et des Etudes Économiques: *Tableau Économique de la Réunion*. Paris (annual)
Bertile, W., *Atlas Thématique et Régional*. Réunion, 1990

DEPARTMENTAL COLLECTIVITIES

MAYOTTE

KEY HISTORICAL EVENTS
Mayotte was a French colony from 1843 until 1914 when it was attached, with the other Comoro islands, to the government-general of Madagascar. The Comoro group was granted administrative autonomy within the French Republic and became an Overseas Territory. When the other three islands voted to become independent (as the Comoro state) in 1974, Mayotte voted against this and remained a French dependency. In Dec. 1976 it became (following a further referendum) a Territorial Collectivity. On 11 July 2001 Mayotte became a Departmental Collectivity—a constitutional innovation—as a result of a referendum. This was denounced by the Comorian authorities, who claim Mayotte as part of the Union of the Comoro Islands.

TERRITORY AND POPULATION
Mayotte, east of the Comoro Islands, had a total population at the 2002 census of 160,265 (population density of 426 persons per sq. km). The estimated population for 2003 is 183,400. The whole territory covers 376 sq. km (144 sq. miles). It consists of a main island (362 sq. km) with (2003 estimate) 158,500 inhabitants, containing the chief town, Mamoudzou (45,485 inhabitants in 2002); and the smaller island of Pamanzi (11 sq. km) lying 2 km to the east (24,900 estimated for 2003) containing the old capital of Dzaoudzi (12,066 in 2002).

The spoken language is Shimaoré (akin to Comorian, an Arabized dialect of Swahili), but French remains the official, commercial and administrative language.

CLIMATE
The dry and sunniest season is from May to Oct. The hot but rainy season is from Nov. to April. Average temperatures are 27°C from Dec. to March and 24°C from May to Sept.

CONSTITUTION AND GOVERNMENT
The island is administered by a General Council of 17 members, directly elected for a six-year term. The French government is represented by an appointed Prefect. The legislation of 11 July 2001 stipulates that executive powers will be transferred from the prefect to the president of the General Council in March 2004. Mayotte is represented by one deputy in the National Assembly and by one member in the Senate. There are 17 communes, including two on Pamanzi.

RECENT ELECTIONS
At the General council elections on 23 March 1997 the Mouvement Populaire Mahorais (MPM) won 8 seats, the Rassemblement Mahorais pour la République (RPR) 5, the Parti Socialiste (PS) 1 and others 5.

CURRENT ADMINISTRATION
Prefect: Jean-Jacques Brot; b. 1956 (took office on 3 July 2002).
President of the General Council: Younoussa Bamana (MPM); since 1977.

ECONOMY
Currency. Since 1 Jan. 2002 the euro has been the official currency as in metropolitan France.

Banking and Finance. The Institut d'Emission d'Outre-mer and the Banque Française Commerciale both have branches in Dzaoudzi and Mamoudzou.

ENERGY AND NATURAL RESOURCES

Agriculture. The area under cultivation in 1998 was 14,400 ha. Mayotte is the world's second largest producer of ylang-ylang essence. The chief cash crops (1997) were: cinnamon 27,533 kg, ylang-ylang 14,300 kg, vanilla 4,417 kg, coconut 2,060 kg. The main food crops (1997) were bananas (30,200 tonnes) and cassava (10,000 tonnes). Livestock (1997): cattle, 17,000; goats, 25,000; sheep, 2,000.

Forestry. There are some 19,750 ha of forest, of which 1,150 is primary, 15,000 secondary and 3,600 badlands (uncultivable or eroded).

Fisheries. A lobster and shrimp industry has been created. Fish landings in 1999 totalled approximately 1,500 tonnes.

INDUSTRY

Labour. In 1994, 18·5% of the active population was engaged in public building and works. Unemployment rate, 1997, 41%.

INTERNATIONAL TRADE

Imports and Exports. In 1997 exports of ylang-ylang totalled 5·5m. French francs; vanilla 763,023 French francs; coconut 2,075 French francs; cinnamon 201,319 French francs. Imports (1993–94) totalled 573·6m. French francs.

COMMUNICATIONS

Roads. In 2002 there were 224 km of main roads, all of which are paved, and 1,528 motor vehicles.

Civil Aviation. There is an airport at Pamandzi, with scheduled services in 2002 provided to the Comoros, Kenya, Madagascar, Mozambique, Réunion, Seychelles and South Africa.

Shipping. There are services provided by Tratringa and Ville de Sima to Anjouan (Comoros) and Moroni (Comoros).

Telecommunications. In 1999 there were 9,700 telephone main lines, or 72·7 per 1,000 inhabitants.

SOCIAL INSTITUTIONS

Justice. There is a *tribunal de première instance* and a *tribunal supérieur d'appel*.

Religion. The population is 97% Sunni Muslim, with a small Christian (mainly Roman Catholic) minority.

Education. In 1994 there were 25,805 pupils in nursery and primary schools, and 6,190 pupils at seven *collèges* and one *lycée* at secondary level. There were also 1,922 pupils enrolled in pre-professional classes and professional *lycées*. There is a teacher training college.

Health. There were two hospitals with 100 beds in 1994. In 1985 there were 9 doctors, 1 dentist, 1 pharmacist, 2 midwives and 51 nursing personnel.

CULTURE

Broadcasting. Broadcasting is conducted by *Radio-Télévision Française d'Outre-Mer* (RFO-Mayotte) with one hour a day in Shimaoré. *Télé Mayotte RFO* on Petite Terre transmits from 6 a.m. to around midnight every day. There are two private radio stations. In 2000 there were an estimated 40,000 radio and 5,000 TV receivers; colour is by SECAM. Since 1999, two satellite TV programmes have been available.

Press. There are two newspapers: *Kwezi*, published twice a week, and *Mayotte Hebdo*, published once a week.

Tourism. In 2001 there were 23,000 visitors. In 1999, 44% came from Réunion, 42% from mainland France and 14% from other countries. The average length of stay was 11 to 14 days.

TERRITORIAL COLLECTIVITIES

NEW CALEDONIA
Nouvelle Calédonie et Dépendances

KEY HISTORICAL EVENTS
New Caledonia was discovered by James Cook on 4 Sept. 1774. The first settlers (English Protestants and French Catholics) came in 1840. New Caledonia was annexed by France in 1853 and, together with most of its former dependencies, became an Overseas Territory in 1958. In 1998 it became a Territorial Collectivity.

TERRITORY AND POPULATION
The territory comprises the New Caledonia mainland and various outlying islands, all situated in the southwest Pacific (Melanesia) with a total land area of 18,575 sq. km (7,172 sq. miles). The population (1996 census) was 196,836, including 67,151 Europeans (majority French), 86,788 Melanesians (Kanaks), 7,825 Vietnamese and Indonesians, 5,171 Polynesians, 17,763 Wallisians and Futunians, 1,318 others. Density, 10 per sq. km. In 1996 an estimated 60·4% of the population lived in urban areas. The estimated population at 1 Jan. 2001 was 212,709. The capital, Nouméa, had 76,293 inhabitants in 1996.

There are four main islands (or groups of):

New Caledonia mainland An area of 16,372 sq. km (about 400 km long, 50 km wide) with a population (1996 census) of 170,365. The east coast is predominantly Melanesian; the Nouméa region predominantly European; and the rest of the west coast is of mixed population.

Loyalty Islands 100 km (60 miles) east of New Caledonia, consisting of four large islands: Maré, Lifou, Uvéa and Tiga. It has a total area of 1,981 sq. km and a population (1996) of 20,877, nearly all Melanesians, except on Uvéa which is partly Polynesian. The chief culture in the islands is coconuts; the chief export is copra.

Isle of Pines A tourist and fishing centre 50 km (30 miles) to the southeast of Nouméa, with an area of 152 sq. km and a population (1996) of 1,671.

Bélep Archipelago About 50 km northwest of New Caledonia, with an area of 70 sq. km and a population (1996) of 923.

The remaining islands are very small and have no permanent inhabitants. The largest are the Chesterfield Islands, a group of 11 well-wooded coral islets with a combined area of 10 sq. km, about 550 km west of the Bélep Archipelago. The Huon Islands, a group of four barren coral islets with a combined area of just 65 ha, are 225 km north of the Bélep Archipelago. Walpole, a limestone coral island of 1 sq. km, lies 150 km east of the Isle of Pines; Matthew Island (20 ha) and Hunter Island (2 sq. km), respectively 250 km and 330 km east of Walpole, are spasmodically active volcanic islands. There are also Surprise and Beautemps-Beaupré Islands.

At the 1996 census there were 341 tribes (which have legal status under a high chief) living in 160 reserves, covering a surface area of 392,550 ha (21% of total land), and representing about 28·7% of the population. 80,443 Melanesians belong to a tribe.

New Caledonia has a remarkable diversity of Melanesian languages (29 vernacular), divided into four main groups (Northern, Central, Southern and Loyalty Islands). There were 53,556 speakers (1996). The three most spoken forms are Drehu (11,338), Nengone (6,377) and Paicî (5,498). A ministerial decision in 1991 introduced local languages into the baccalauréat system. In 2000 six Melanesian languages were taught in schools.

SOCIAL STATISTICS
2000: live births, 4,564; deaths, 1,075; marriages, 995; divorces, 159. Annual growth rate, 1·65%. Life expectancy at birth, 1990–95, 69·7 years for males and 74·7 years for females. Infant mortality, 1990–95, 22 per 1,000 live births; fertility rate, 2·7 births per woman.

CLIMATE
2000: Nouméa, Jan. 25·8°C, July 20·4°C (average temperature, 23·8°C; max. 33·5°C, min. 14·3°C). Annual rainfall 1,294 mm.

CONSTITUTION AND GOVERNMENT
Subsequent to the referendum law of 9 Nov. 1988, the organic and ordinary laws of 19 March 1999 define New Caledonia's new statute. Until then an 'Overseas Territory', New Caledonia became a Territorial Collectivity with specific status endowed with wide autonomy. New Caledonia's institutions comprise the congress, government, economic and social council (CES), the customary senate and customary councils. The three provinces and 33 municipalities are territorial collectivities of the French Republic, freely administrating themselves in assemblies elected by direct universal suffrage.

The congress is made up of 54 members called 'Councillors of New Caledonia', from the provincial assemblies. Each year it elects the members of its executive, standing committee, and internal committees.

The 11-member government is elected by congress on a proportional ballot from party lists. The president is elected by majority vote of all members. Each member is allocated to lead and control a given sector in the administration. The government's mandate ends when the mandate of the Congress that elected it comes to an end.

The economic and social council comprises 39 members, including 28 representatives directly involved in economic, social and cultural activities designated in the provinces (16 for the South, 8 for the North, and 4 for the Loyalty Islands), 2 members designated by the customary senate and 9 personalities designated by the government. CES is completely renewed every five years.

RECENT ELECTIONS
On 8 Nov. 1998 there was a referendum for the agreement of the Nouméa accords. The electorate was 106,716; turn-out was 74·2%. Nearly 71·9% of those who voted said 'Yes' to the question 'Do you approve the agreement on New Caledonia, signed in Nouméa on May 5 1998?' Voting was restricted to those people resident in New Caledonia before 1998.

In elections to the Territorial Congress on 9 May 1999, the conservative Rally for Caledonia in the Republic (RPCR) won 24 seats and the National Liberation Front of the Socialist Kanaks 18, with other parties and independents winning 4 seats or fewer.

CURRENT ADMINISTRATION
High Commissioner: Daniel Constantin.
  President: Pierre Frogier (RPCR).
  President of the Territorial Congress: Simon Loueckhote (RPCR).

ECONOMY
Currency. The unit of currency is the franc CFP (XPF), with a parity of 119·3317422 francs CPF to the euro. 211,396m. francs CFP were in circulation in Dec. 2000.

Budget. The budget for 2000 balanced at 74,904m. francs CFP.

Performance. In 1997 GDP was 349,260m. francs CFP; GDP per capita was 1·74m. francs CFP.

Banking and Finance. In 2000 the banks were: Banque Calédonienne d'Investissement (BCI), the Bank of Hawaii-Nouvelle-Calédonie (BoH-NC), the Banque Nationale de Paris/Nouvelle-Calédonie (BNP/NC), the Société Générale Calédonienne de Banque (SGCB) and the Caisse d'Epargne.

ENERGY AND NATURAL RESOURCES
Environment. According to the *World Bank Atlas* carbon dioxide emissions in 1998 were the equivalent of 8·5 tonnes per capita.

Electricity. Production (2000): 1,645m. kWh.

Minerals. A wide range of minerals have been found in New Caledonia including: nickel, copper and lead, gold, chrome, gypsum and platinum metals. The nickel deposits are of special value, being without arsenic, and constitute between 20–40% of the world's known nickel resources located on the mainland.

Production of nickel ore (2000): 128,289 tonnes, of which garnieritic ore (108,302 tonnes) and lateritic ore (19,987). In 2000 the furnaces produced 57,463 tonnes, of which ferro-nickels (43,914 tonnes) and mattes (13,549 tonnes).

Agriculture. According to the 1996 census, 4,663 persons worked in the agricultural sector. In 1998 there were an estimated 7,000 ha of arable land and 6,000 ha of permanent crops. In 1999 livestock numbered: pigs, 38,252; goats, 16,498; horses, 11,245; deer, 12,523; poultry, 877,364; cattle (1994), 105,000. The chief products are beef, pork, poultry, coffee, copra, maize, fruit and vegetables. Production (1998 estimates, in 1,000 tonnes): coconuts, 17; yams, 11; cassava, 3; sweet potatoes, 3; maize, 2; potatoes, 2; taro, 2.

Livestock (1996): cattle, 113,000; pigs, 39,000; goats (1995), 17,000; poultry (1995), 1m.

Forestry. There were 698,000 ha of forest in 1995, or 38·2% of the total land area (down from 38·3% in 1990). Timber production (1999), 5,000 cu. metres.

Fisheries. In 1998 there were 291 fishing boats (1,950 GRT) and a catch (1999) of 3,152 tonnes. Aquaculture (consisting mainly of saltwater prawns) provides New Caledonia's second highest source of export income after nickel.

INDUSTRY

Up until the end of the 1970s the New Caledonia economy was almost totally dependent on the nickel industry. Subsequently transformation or processing industries gained in importance to reach levels similar to those in metallurgic industries.

However, small to medium size businesses are still absent in many sectors, in particular the majority of primary and capital goods industries. Among local production for consumption goods, the agri-foods industry is the most widely represented. Small in size, the production units largely work to satisfy the local market, through processing of imported raw materials, with only marginal production for exports.

Labour. The employed population (1996) was 64,377. In July 2001 the guaranteed monthly minimum wage was 100,000 francs CFP. In 1996 there were 30 industrial disputes and 13,826 working days were lost. There were 15,018 registered unemployed in 1997 (66% under 30 years of age).

INTERNATIONAL TRADE

Imports and Exports. In 2000 the balance of trade showed a deficit of 41,312m. francs CFP. Imports and exports in 1m. francs CFP:

	1997	1998	1999	2000
Imports	97,700	99,531	112,887	119,766
Exports	55,912	40,621	52,387	78,454

In 2000, 38·8% of imports came from France, 16·8% from Australia and 14·9% from other countries of European Union. In 2000, 20·6% of exports went to France and 26·6% to Japan. Mining and metallurgic products accounted for 92·4% of exports: nickel ore, 21·1%; ferro-nickels, 57·2%; mattes, 14·1%.

COMMUNICATIONS

Roads. In 2000 there were 5,432 km of road and 83,554 vehicles. In 1999 road accidents inured 983 and killed 58 persons.

Civil Aviation. New Caledonia is connected by air routes with France, Australia, New Zealand, Japan, Vanuatu, Wallis and Futuna, Fiji Islands and French Polynesia. Regular domestic air services are provided by Air Calédonie from Magenta aerodrome in Nouméa. In 2000 there were 288,322 passengers recorded at Magenta Aerodrome. Internal services with Air Calédonie link Nouméa to a number of domestic airfields.

In 2000, 359,381 passengers and 5,243 tonnes of freight were carried via La Tontouta International Airport, near Nouméa.

Shipping. In 1999, 510 vessels entered New Caledonia, unloading 1,254,662 tonnes of freight, loading 4,007,049 tonnes (including 3·8m. tonnes of nickel ore).

Telecommunications. In 2000 there were 51,000 telephone main lines (236·9 per 1,000 inhabitants); in 1997, 5,100 mobile phone subscribers; and in 1995, 2,200 fax machines. New Caledonia has had Internet access since 1995. In Dec. 2000 there were 24,000 Internet users.

Postal Services. In 2000 there were 36 post offices.

SOCIAL INSTITUTIONS

Justice. There are courts at Nouméa, Koné and Wé (on Lifou Island), a court of appeal, a labour court and a joint commerce tribunal. There were 4,054 cases judged in the magistrates courts in 1999; 280 went before the court of appeal, 26 were sentenced in the court of assizes.

The population in penal institutions in Oct. 1998 was 303 (155 per 100,000 of national population).

Religion. There were about 0·1m. Roman Catholics in 1994.

Education. In 1999 there were 36,667 pupils and 1,628 teachers in 284 primary schools; 27,877 pupils and 2,212 teachers in 85 secondary schools; and 1,866 students at university with 89 teaching staff. By decree of 1999 the New Caledonia campus of the French University of the Pacific (UFP), established in 1987, was separated from the campus, to become University of New Caledonia (UNC), a public establishment under shared authority of the French State and New Caledonia with responsibilities in tertiary education, research and international co-operation.

Health. In 1999 there were 418 doctors, 106 dentists, 91 pharmacists and 1,209 paramedical personnel. There were 26 socio-medical districts, with 4 hospitals, 3 private clinics for a total of 838 beds.

Welfare. There are two main forms of social security cover: Free Medical Aid provides total sickness cover for non-waged persons and low-income earners; the Family Benefit, Workplace Injury and Contingency Fund for Workers in New Caledonia (CAFAT). There are also numerous mutual benefit societies. In 1999 Free Medical Aid had 56,894 beneficiaries; CAFAT had approximately 150,000 beneficiaries.

CULTURE

Broadcasting. Television broadcasting was, for a long time, limited to one or two state-owned stations (today Télé Nouvelle-Calédonie and Tempo). A private channel (Canal+) began broadcasting in 1994, and in late 1999 a digital selection of 13 pay-channels (Canal'Sat) was launched. By the end of 2001 Canal Calédonie had 17,000 Canal'Sat and 18,000 Canal+ subscribers.

There were 90,000 TV sets and 107,000 radio receivers in 1997.

Cinema. In 1999 there were seven cinemas in New Caledonia including three in Nouméa and one drive-in in the Greater Nouméa.

Press. In 2001 there was one daily newspaper, Les Nouvelles Calédoniennes.

Tourism. In 2000 New Caledonia welcomed 109,587 tourists (Japan, 23·8%; France, 16·4%; Australia, 16·4%; New Zealand, 8·7%). In 1999 there were 82 hotels providing 2,398 beds.

Festivals. New Caledonia has been host to the Pacific Arts Festival and holds numerous cultural events including a biennial contemporary art exhibition and the Equinox Festival.

Museums and Galleries. In 1996 there were nine museums, including three in Nouméa.

FURTHER READING

Institut de la Statistique et des Etudes Économiques: *Tableaux de l'Économie Calédonienne/New Caledonia: Facts & Figures (TEC 2000)* (every 3 years); *Informations Statistiques Rapides de Nouvelle-Calédonie* (monthly).

Imprimerie Administrative, Nouméa: *Journal Officiel de la Nouvelle Calédonie.*

Dommel, D., *La Crise Calédonienne: Démission ou Guérison?* Paris, 1993

Local statistical office: Institut Territorial de la Statistique et des Études Économiques, BP 823, 98845 Nouméa.

ST PIERRE AND MIQUELON

Îles Saint-Pierre et Miquelon

KEY HISTORICAL EVENTS

The only remaining fragment of the once-extensive French possessions in North America, the archipelago was settled from France in the 17th century. It was a French colony from 1816 until 1976, an overseas department until 1985, and is now a Territorial Collectivity.

TERRITORY AND POPULATION

The archipelago consists of two islands off the south coast of Newfoundland, with a total area of 242 sq. km, comprising the Saint-Pierre group (26 sq. km) and the Miquelon-Langlade group (216 sq. km). The population (1999 census) was 6,316 of whom 3,169 were female. This total population figure represents a decrease of 76 from the 1990 census. Approximately 88% of the population lives on Saint-Pierre. The chief town is St Pierre.

The official language is French.

SOCIAL STATISTICS

2000: births, 51; deaths, 35; marriages, 24; divorces, 7.

CONSTITUTION AND GOVERNMENT

The Territorial Collectivity is administered by a General Council of 19 members directly elected for a six-year term. It is represented in the National Assembly in Paris by one deputy, in the Senate by one senator and in the Economic and Social Council by one councillor. The French government is represented by a Prefect.

RECENT ELECTIONS

At the General Council elections on 19 and 26 March 2000, 11 seats went to Défense des Intérêts de l'Archipel, 3 to Volonté Insulaire, 2 to Expérience et Innovation, 2 to Cap sur l'Avenir and 1 to Miquelon 2000.

CURRENT ADMINISTRATION

Prefect: Claude Valleix.

President of the General Council: Marc Plantegenest.

ECONOMY

Currency. Since 1 Jan. 2002 the euro has been the official currency as in metropolitan France.

Budget. The budget for 2000 balanced at 270m. French francs.

Banking and Finance. Banks include the Banque des Îles Saint-Pierre et Miquelon, the Crédit Saint-Pierrais and the Caisse d'Épargne.

A Development Agency was created in 1996 to help with investment projects.

Weights and Measures. The metric system is in use.

ENERGY AND NATURAL RESOURCES

Electricity. Production (2000): 39m. kWh.

Agriculture. The islands, being mostly barren rock, are unsuited for agriculture, but some vegetables are grown and livestock is kept for local consumption.

Fisheries. In June 1992 an international tribunal awarded France a 24-mile fishery and economic zone around the islands and a 10·5-mile-wide corridor extending for 200 miles to the high seas. The 2000 catch amounted to 1,261 tonnes, chiefly snow crab, cod, lumpfish, shark and scallops. A Franco-Canadian agreement regulating fishing in the area was signed in Dec. 1994. The total annual catch has declined dramatically in the past 15 years.

INDUSTRY

In 1994 there were 351 businesses (including 144 services, 69 public works, 45 food trade, 8 manufacturing and 2 agriculture). The main industry, fish processing, resumed in 1994 after a temporary cessation due to lack of supplies in 1992. Diversification activities are in progress (aquaculture, sea products processing, scallops plant).

Labour. The economically active population in 2000 was 3,261. In Jan. 2002 the minimum wage (SMIC) was €6·67 an hour (€1,126·40 a month). In 1996, 11% of the labour force was registered as unemployed.

INTERNATIONAL TRADE

Imports and Exports. Trade in 1m. French francs (2000): imports, 371 (51% from Canada); exports, 50.

COMMUNICATIONS

Roads. In 2000 there were 117 km of roads, of which 80 km were surfaced. There were 2,508 passenger cars and 1,254 commercial vehicles in use.

Civil Aviation. Canadian Airlines International connects St Pierre with Montreal, Halifax, Sydney (Nova Scotia) and St John's (Newfoundland). In addition, a new airport capable of receiving medium-haul aeroplanes was opened in 1999.

Shipping. St Pierre has regular services to Fortune and Halifax in Canada. In 1999, 893 vessels called at St Pierre; 17,067 tonnes of freight were unloaded and 3,020 tonnes were loaded.

Telecommunications. There were 4,900 telephones in 2000.

SOCIAL INSTITUTIONS

Justice. There is a court of first instance and a higher court of appeal at St Pierre.

Religion. The population is chiefly Roman Catholic.

Education. Primary instruction is free. In 2000 there were three nursery and five primary schools with 799 pupils; three secondary schools with 564 pupils; and two technical schools with 199 pupils.

Health. In 2000 there was one hospital with 45 beds, one convalescent home with 20 beds, one retirement home with 40 beds; 15 doctors and 1 dentist.

CULTURE

Broadcasting. *Radio Télévision Française d'Outre Mer* (RFO) broadcasts in French on medium waves and on two television channels (one satellite). In 2000 there were 35 cable television channels from Canada and USA. In 2000 there were also approximately 4,900 radio and 4,500 television sets in use.

Tourism. In 2000 there were 10,090 visitors.

Libraries. There is one municipal library in Saint-Pierre.

OVERSEAS TERRITORIES

FRENCH POLYNESIA
Territoire de la Polynésie Française

KEY HISTORICAL EVENTS
French protectorates since 1843, these islands were annexed to France 1880–82 to form 'French Settlements in Oceania', which opted in Nov. 1958 for the status of an overseas territory within the French Community.

TERRITORY AND POPULATION
The total land area of these five archipelagoes, comprising 130 volcanic islands and coral atolls (76 inhabited) scattered over a wide area in the eastern Pacific, is 4,167 sq. km. The population (1996 census) was 219,521 (105,587 females); density, 53 per sq. km. At Dec.1998 French forces stationed in Polynesia numbered 2,119 (based mostly on Tahiti and the Hao atoll) and employed 1,162 Polynesian citizens. In 1995 an estimated 56·4% of the population lived in urban areas.

The UN gives a projected population for 2010 of 271,000.

The official languages are French and Tahitian.

The islands are administratively divided into five *circonscriptions* as follows:

Windward Islands (Îles du Vent) (162,398 inhabitants, 1996) comprise Tahiti with an area of 1,042 sq. km and 150,707 inhabitants; Moioréa with an area of 132 sq. km and 11,682 inhabitants; Maiao (Tubuai Manu) with an area of 9 sq. km; and the smaller Mehetia and Tetiaroa. The capital is Papeete, Tahiti (79,024 inhabitants in 1996, including suburbs).

Leeward Islands (Îles sous le Vent) comprise the five volcanic islands of Raiatéa, Tahaa, Huahine, Bora-Bora and Maupiti, together with four small atolls (Tupai, Mopelia, Scilly, Bellinghausen), the group having a total land area of 404 sq. km and 26,838 inhabitants in 1996. The chief town is Uturoa on Raiatéa. The Windward and Leeward Islands together are called the Society Archipelago (Archipel de la Société). Tahitian, a Polynesian language, is spoken throughout the archipelago and used as a *lingua franca* in the rest of the territory.

Marquesas Islands 12 islands lying north of the Tuamotu Archipelago, with a total area of 1,049 sq. km and 8,064 inhabitants in 1996. There are six inhabited islands: Nuku Hiva, Ua Pou, Ua Uka, Hiva Oa, Tahuata, Fatu Hiva; and six smaller (uninhabited) ones; the chief centre is Taiohae on Nuku Hiva.

Austral or Tubuai Islands lying south of the Society Archipelago, comprise a 1,300 km chain of volcanic islands and reefs. There are five inhabited islands (Rimatara, Rurutu, Tubuai, Raivavae and, 500 km to the south, Rapa), with a combined area of 148 sq. km (6,563 inhabitants in 1996); the chief centre is Mataura on Tubuai.

Tuamotu Archipelago consists of two parallel ranges of 76 atolls (53 inhabited) lying north and east of the Society Archipelago, and has a total area of 690 sq. km, with 15,370 inhabitants in 1996. The most populous atolls are Rangiroa (1,913 inhabitants), Hao (1,356) and Manihi (769).

The Mururoa and Fangataufa atolls in the southeast of the group were ceded to France in 1964 by the Territorial Assembly, and were used by France for nuclear tests from 1966–96. The cessation of nuclear testing marked the end of activities of the Pacific Testing Centre (CEP) in French Polynesia. The CEP was entirely dismantled during 1998. A small military presence remains to ensure permanent radiological control.

The *circonscription* also includes the Gambier Islands further east, with an area of 36 sq. km; the chief centre is Rikitea on the group's only inhabited island, Mangareva.

SOCIAL STATISTICS
Annual population growth rate, 2·2%. Birth rate (1996) was 22·1 per 1,000 inhabitants; death rate, 4·7; marriage rate, 5·5. Life expectancy at birth, 1990–95,

68·3 years for males and 73·8 years for females. Infant mortality, 1990–95, 11 per 1,000 live births; fertility rate, 3·1 births per woman.

CLIMATE
Papeete. Jan. 81°F (27·1°C), July 75°F (24°C). Annual rainfall 83" (2,106 mm).

CONSTITUTION AND GOVERNMENT
Under the 1984 Constitution, the Territory is administered by a Council of Ministers, whose President is elected by the Territorial Assembly from among its own members; the President appoints a Vice-President and 14 other ministers (16 ministers in total in 1999). There is an advisory Economic and Social Committee. French Polynesia is represented in the French Assembly by two deputies, in the Senate by one senator, in the Economic and Social Council by one councillor. The French government is represented by a High Commissioner. The Territorial Assembly comprises 41 members elected every five years from five constituencies by universal suffrage, using the same proportional representation system as in metropolitan French regional elections. To be elected a party must gain at least 5% of votes cast. The Assembly elects a head of local government.

A statute drafted at the end of 1995 proposes to create French Polynesia as an Autonomous Overseas Territory in which the President of the Council of Ministers will become the President of the territory.

RECENT ELECTIONS
Elections were held on 6 May 2001. The People's Front-Rally for the Republic, the party of President Gaston Flosse, won 28 seats. People's Servant won 13 and New Fatherland took 7 seats. In the presidential vote held on 18 May 2001 Flosse was re-elected, defeating Oscar Temaru by 29 votes to 13.

CURRENT ADMINISTRATION
High Commissioner: Michel Mathieu.
President of the Council of Ministers: Gaston Flosse (RPR).

ECONOMY
In decline since 1993, the economy has shown signs of recovery since 1997.

Currency. The unit of currency is the franc CFP (XPF). Up to 31 Dec. 1998, its parity was to the French franc: 1 franc CFP = 0·055 French francs; from 1 Jan. 1999 parity was linked to the euro: 119·3317422 francs CPF = one euro.

Budget. Total expenditure (1997), 10,416m. French francs, of which 6,744m. French francs comes directly from France.

Performance. In 1997 GDP was 21,600m. French francs (5·5% up on 1996); GDP per capita was 96,964 French francs.

Banking and Finance. There are four commercial banks: Banque de Tahiti, Banque de Polynésie, Société de Crédit et de Développement de l'Océanie, and the Banque Westpac. There are also 22 credit institutions, including SOFOTOM and the Agence Française de Développement (AFD).

ENERGY AND NATURAL RESOURCES
French Polynesia is heavily dependent on external sources for its energy. Since the early 1980s efforts have been made to reduce this, which have included the development of solar energy. By 1999 it was estimated that production of solar energy was in the region of 2,700 hours a year.

Environment. According to the *World Bank Atlas* carbon dioxide emissions in 1998 were the equivalent of 2·5 tonnes per capita.

Electricity. Production (1998) was 360m. kWh, of which approximately 35% was hydro-electric. Consumption per capita (1995) was estimated to be 1,409 kWh. Between 1988 and 1997, 14,212 solar photovoltaic modules were installed in Polynesia.

Oil and Gas. In 1997 over 236,000 tonnes of combustible products were imported (with a value of 346m. French francs), mainly from Australia and Hawaii; 8,600 tonnes of gas was imported.

Agriculture. Agriculture used to be the primary economic sector but now accounts for only a modest 8% (1997) of GDP. An important product is copra (coconut trees cover the coastal plains of the mountainous islands and the greater part of the low-lying islands). A new and increasingly successful crop is the nono fruit, which has medicinal value. Production in 1,000 tonnes (1998 estimates): coconuts, 87; copra, 11; cassava, 6; potatoes, 5. Exports of the nono reached 15m. French francs in 1998. Tropical fruits, such as bananas, pineapples and oranges, are grown for local consumption.

Livestock (1996): cattle 7,000; pigs 42,000; goats (1995) 27,286; poultry (1995) 297,700.

Forestry. In 1999 there was between 4,000 and 5,000 ha of forest, around half of it exploitable. The industry remains embryonic.

Fisheries. Polynesia has an exclusive zone of 5·2m. sq. km, one of the largest in the world. The industry employs some 2,000 people, including 700 traditional fishermen. Catch (1997): 12,336 tonnes, almost exclusively from sea fishing. Subject to annual agreement, a Korean fleet of 70 ships operates in the Polynesian waters; it had a quota of 3,000 tonnes in 1998–99.

INDUSTRY

Some 2,218 industrial enterprises employ 5,800 people. Principal industries include food and drink products, cosmetics, clothing and jewellery, furniture-making, metalwork and shipbuilding. Commerce is an important sector of the economy, employing (1997) some 7,400 persons in 2,448 enterprises across 1,752 retail and 696 manufacturing businesses.

INTERNATIONAL TRADE

Imports and Exports. The trade balance is precarious: Polynesia imports a great deal and exports very little. The trade deficit in 1997 was 4·15m. French francs. Total imports (1997), 5·46m. French francs; total exports, 1·31m. French francs.

The chief exports are coconut oil, fish, nono juice, mother of pearl and cultured pearls. Pearl production in recent years has doubled, with 794m. French francs worth of pearls exported in 1998. Representing 27% of the world market, Polynesia is the world's second largest producer of pearls after Australia. It is the second largest industry in Polynesia after tourism, and employs some 4,000 islanders.

Major trading partners: France, Japan (66% of pearl exports), Hong Kong, the USA and the EU, with France accounting for over 38% of total imports and around 25% of exports in 1997, and the EU as a whole 52% of imports.

COMMUNICATIONS

Roads. There were estimated to be 2,590 km of roads in 1999, 67% bitumenized.

Civil Aviation. The main airport is at Papeete (Tahiti-Faa'a). Air France and eight other international airlines (including Air France, Air New Zealand and AOM French Airlines) connect Tahiti International Airport with Paris, Auckland, Honolulu, Los Angeles, Santiago, Sydney, Tokyo and many Pacific islands. Local companies, including Air Tahiti, connect the islands with services from 48 secondary airfields, including those at Bora-Bora, Rangiroa and Raiatea. In 2000 Papeete handled 1,553,132 passengers (849,540 on domestic flights) and 11,429 tonnes of freight.

Shipping. Ten shipping companies connect France, San Francisco, New Zealand, Japan, Australia, southeast Asia and most Pacific locations with Papeete. In 1997, 727,000 tonnes of cargo were unloaded and 28,000 tonnes loaded at Papeete's main port. Around 1·4m. people pass through the port each year.

Telecommunications. Number of telephone main lines in 2000 was 51,500 (220·7 per 1,000 inhabitants); mobile phones (1999), 21,900. In 1997 there were 2,900 fax machines. In Dec. 1999 there were 5,000 Internet users.

Postal Services. In 1999 there were 56 post offices, handling some 700 tonnes of post a year.

SOCIAL INSTITUTIONS

Justice. There is a *tribunal de première instance* and a *cour d'appel* at Papeete. The population in penal institutions in Oct. 1998 was 280 (125 per 100,000 of national population).

Religion. In 1997 there were approximately 110,000 protestants (about 50% of the population) and 55,000 Roman Catholics (25%).

Education. In 1998–99 there were 77,300 pupils and 5,200 teachers in 316 schools (46,800 in 255 primary schools; 30,500 in secondary school). The French University of the Pacific (UFP), founded in 1987, has a campus on Tahiti. The South Pacific University Institute for Teacher Training, founded in 1992 (part of UFP), has three colleges: in French Polynesia, Wallis and Futuna, and in Nouméa (New Caledonia), where it is headquartered. In 1997–98, 2,200 students followed university courses.

Health. In 1999 there were 1 territorial hospital centre, 4 general hospitals, 1 specialist hospital and 2 private clinics, with a total of 855 beds. Medical personnel numbered 1,590 persons, including 384 doctors (175 per 100,000 inhabitants), 94 dentists and 51 pharmacists. Health spending accounted for 10·2% of GDP in 1997.

Welfare. In 1997, 202,760 people benefited from social welfare.

CULTURE

Broadcasting. There are three TV broadcasters (one public, two independent): *Radio Télévision Française d'Outre-mer* (RFO) which broadcasts on two channels in French, Tahitian and English; *Canal + Polynésie*; and *Telefenua* which broadcasts across 16 channels. There are also 11 private radio stations. Number of receivers (1999): radio, 40,350; TV, 40,000 (colour by SECAM H).

Cinema. There are four cinemas in Papeete.

Press. In 1999 there were two daily newspapers.

Tourism. Tourism is the main industry. There were 189,000 tourist arrivals in 1998. Total revenue (1997) 2m. French francs.

FURTHER READING

Local statistical office: Institut Statistique de Polynésie Française, Papeete.
Website (French only): http://www.ispf.pfl

SOUTHERN AND ANTARCTIC TERRITORIES

Terres Australes et Antarctiques Françaises (TAAF)

The Territory of the TAAF was created on 6 Aug. 1955. It comprises the Kerguelen and Crozet archipelagoes, the islands of Saint Paul and Amsterdam (formerly Nouvelle Amsterdam), all in the southern Indian ocean, and Terre Adélie. Since 2 April 1997 the administration has had its seat in Saint-Pierre, Réunion; before that it was in Paris. The Administrator is assisted by a seven-member consultative council which meets twice yearly in Paris; its members are nominated by the government for five years. The 15-member Polar Environment Committee, which in 1993 replaced the former Consultative Committee on the Environment (est. 1982), meets at least once a year to discuss all problems relating to the preservation of the environment.

The French Institute for Polar Research and Technology was set up to organize scientific research and expeditions in Jan. 1992. The staff of the permanent scientific stations of the TAAF (120 in 1998) is renewed every 6 or 12 months and forms the only population.

Administrateur Supérieur. François Garde.

Kerguelen Islands Situated 48–50° S. lat., 68–70° E. long.; consists of one large and 85 smaller islands, and over 200 islets and rocks, with a total area of 7,215 sq. km (2,786 sq. miles) of which Grande Terre occupies 6,675 sq. km (2,577 sq. miles). It was discovered in 1772 by Yves de Kerguelen, but was effectively occupied by France only in 1949. Port-aux-Français has several scientific research stations (56 members). Reindeer, trout and sheep have been acclimatized.

Crozet Islands Situated 46° S. lat., 50–52° E. long.; consists of five larger and 15 tiny islands, with a total area of 505 sq. km (195 sq. miles). The western group includes Apostles, Pigs and Penguins islands; the eastern group, Possession and Eastern islands. The archipelago was discovered in 1772 by Marion Dufresne, whose first mate, Crozet, annexed it for Louis XV. A meteorological and scientific station (17 members) at Base Alfred-Faure on Possession Island was built in 1964.

Amsterdam and **Saint-Paul Islands** Situated 38–39° S. lat., 77° E. long. Amsterdam, with an area of 54 sq. km (21 sq. miles) was discovered in 1522 by Magellan's companions; Saint-Paul, lying about 100 km to the south, with an area of 7 sq. km (2·7 sq. miles), was probably discovered in 1559 by Portuguese sailors. Both were first visited in 1633 by the Dutch explorer, Van Diemen, and were annexed by France in 1843. They are both extinct volcanoes. The only inhabitants are at Base Martin de Vivies (est. 1949 on Amsterdam Island), including several scientific research stations, a hospital, communication and other facilities (20 members). Crayfish are caught commercially on Amsterdam.

Terre Adélie Comprises that section of the Antarctic continent between 136° and 142° E. long., south of 60° S. lat. The ice-covered plateau has an area of about 432,000 sq. km (166,800 sq. miles), and was discovered in 1840 by Dumont d'Urville. A research station (27 members) is situated at Base Dumont d'Urville, which is maintained by the French Institute for Polar Research and Technology.

WALLIS AND FUTUNA

KEY HISTORICAL EVENTS
French dependencies since 1842, the inhabitants of these islands voted on 22 Dec. 1959 by 4,307 votes out of 4,576 in favour of exchanging their status to that of an overseas territory, which took effect from 29 July 1961.

TERRITORY AND POPULATION
The territory comprises two groups of islands in the central Pacific (total area 240 sq. km, census population 14,166 in 1996). The projected population for 2000 was 15,000. The Îles de Hoorn lie 255 km northeast of the Fiji Islands and consist of two main islands: Futuna (64 sq. km, 5,000 inhabitants) and uninhabited Alofi (51 sq. km). The Wallis Archipelago lies another 160 km further northeast, and has an area of 159 sq. km (9,000 inhabitants). It comprises the main island of Uvéa (60 sq. km) and neighbouring uninhabited islands, with a surrounding coral reef. The capital is Mata-Utu (over 1,000 inhabitants in 1996) on Uvéa. Wallisian and Futunian are distinct Polynesian languages.

SOCIAL STATISTICS
Estimates per 1,000 population, 1998: birth rate, 23·0; death rate, 4·8.

CONSTITUTION AND GOVERNMENT
A Prefect represents the French government and carries out the duties of head of the territory, assisted by a 20-member Territorial Assembly directly elected for a five-year term, and a six-member Territorial Council, comprising the three traditional chiefs and three nominees of the Prefect agreed by the Territorial Assembly. The territory is represented by one deputy in the French National Assembly, by one senator in the Senate, and by one member on the Economic and Social Council. There are three districts: Singave and Alo (both on Futuna), and

Wallis; in each, tribal kings exercise customary powers assisted by ministers and district and village chiefs.

RECENT ELECTIONS

Territorial Assembly elections were held on 16 March 1997 and 6 Sept. 1998. In three of the five constituencies, elections had to be repeated after allegations of fraud. Official results are unavailable but it is generally agreed that right-wing candidates won around 14 seats while socialist and left-wing candidates won around 6.

CURRENT ADMINISTRATION

Chief Administrator: Christian Job.
President of the Territorial Assembly: Victor Brial (RPR).

ECONOMY

Currency. The unit of currency is the franc CFP (XPF), with a parity of 119·3317422 francs CPF to the euro.

Budget. The budget for 1997 balanced at 120,100m. French francs.

Banking and Finance. There is a branch of Banque Indosuez at Mata-Utu.

ENERGY AND NATURAL RESOURCES

Electricity. There is a thermal power station at Mata-Utu.

Agriculture. The chief products are bananas, coconuts, copra, cassava, yams and taro.

Livestock (1996): 25,000 pigs; 7,000 goats.

Fisheries. The catch in 1999 was estimated at 206 tonnes.

COMMUNICATIONS

Roads. There are about 100 km of roads on Uvéa.

Civil Aviation. There is an airport on Wallis, at Hihifo, and another near Alo on Futuna. Five flights a week link Wallis and Futuna. Air Calédonie International operates two flights a week to Nouméa and one a week to French Polynesia.

Shipping. A regular cargo service links Mata-Utu (Wallis) and Singave (Futuna) with Nouméa (New Caledonia). In 1998 merchant shipping totalled 111,000 GRT.

Telecommunications. There were 1,400 main telephone lines in 1997.

Postal Services. There were six post offices in 1986.

SOCIAL INSTITUTIONS

Justice. There is a court of first instance, from which appeals can be made to the court of appeal in New Caledonia.

Religion. The majority of the population is Roman Catholic.

Education. In 1993 there were 3,624 pupils in primary schools and 1,777 in secondary schools. The South Pacific University Institute for Teacher Training, founded in 1992 (part of the French University of the Pacific, UFP) has three colleges: in Wallis and Futuna, French Polynesia and Nouméa (New Caledonia), where it is headquartered.

Health. In 1991 there was 1 hospital with 60 beds, and 4 dispensaries.

CULTURE

Broadcasting. There were two radio stations in 1986.

DEPENDENCIES

BASSAS DA INDIA

Île Bassas da India

KEY HISTORICAL EVENTS
The island was annexed by France in 1897. Its present status, an entity administered by France but not part of any other French territory, was established in 1960. The island is claimed by Madagascar.

TERRITORY AND POPULATION
Bassas da India is an uninhabited Indian Ocean atoll surrounded by reefs. It lies 380 km west of Madagascar and 460 km from the African mainland, and covers an area of 0·2 sq. km. The entire surface of the atoll is made of volcanic rock. Most of the island is submerged under water at high tide.

CONSTITUTION AND GOVERNMENT
The island is administered from St Denis, in Réunion, although it is not legally part of that territory.

CLIPPERTON ISLAND

Île Clipperton

KEY HISTORICAL EVENTS
In the 18th century the island was the hideout of a pirate, John Clipperton, for whom it was named. In 1855 it was claimed by France, and in 1897 by Mexico. It was awarded to France by international arbitration in 1935.

TERRITORY AND POPULATION
Clipperton Island is a Pacific atoll, 3 km long, some 1,120 km south-west of the coast of Mexico. It covers an area of 7 sq. km and is uninhabited.

CONSTITUTION AND GOVERNMENT
The island is administered from Papeete, in French Polynesia, although it is not legally part of that territory.

ECONOMY
The island is occasionally visited by tuna fishermen.

EUROPA ISLAND

Île Europa

KEY HISTORICAL EVENTS
The island was annexed by France in 1897. Its present status, an entity administered by France but not part of any other French territory, was established in 1960. The island is claimed by Madagascar.

TERRITORY AND POPULATION
The island, which lies 350 km west of Madagascar, is low and flat. It covers an area of 28 sq. km. There is no permanent population, although there is a small French military garrison and a meteorological station.

CONSTITUTION AND GOVERNMENT
The island is administered from St Denis, in Réunion, although it is not legally part of that territory.

GLORIEUSES ISLANDS
Îles Glorieuses

KEY HISTORICAL EVENTS
The islands were claimed by France in 1892. Their present status, an entity administered by France but not part of any other French territory, was established in 1960. The islands are claimed by Madagascar.

TERRITORY AND POPULATION
The Glorieuses Islands (also known as Glorioso) are two lush tropical islands, Ile du Lys and Grande Glorieuse, plus a number of rocky outcrops, Les Rochers. The group lies between Madagascar and Mayotte and have an area of 5 sq. km. There is no permanent population although there is a French military garrison, a meteorological station and a radio station on Grande Glorieuse.

CONSTITUTION AND GOVERNMENT
The islands are administered from St Denis, in Réunion, although they are not legally part of that territory.

JUAN DE NOVA ISLAND
Île Juan de Nova

KEY HISTORICAL EVENTS
The island was discovered by a 15th century Spanish navigator for whom it was named. In 1897 it was claimed by France. Its present status, an entity administered by France but not part of any other French territory, was established in 1960. The island is claimed by Madagascar.

TERRITORY AND POPULATION
Situated in the Mozambique Channel between Madagascar and Mozambique, the island has an area of 4·4 sq. km. There is no permanent population although there is a small French military garrison that runs a meteorological station. There is also a small civilian workforce to mine the island's guano.

CONSTITUTION AND GOVERNMENT
The island is administered from St Denis, in Réunion, although it is not legally part of that territory.

ECONOMY
About 12,000 tonnes of guano are mined annually and are taken to the jetty on what is probably the world's shortest railway system.

TROMELIN ISLAND
Île Tromelin

KEY HISTORICAL EVENTS
The island was explored by French navigators in 1776. In 1814 it was claimed by France and annexed to Réunion. Its present status, an entity administered by France but not part of any other French territory, was established in 1960. The island is claimed by Madagascar.

TERRITORY AND POPULATION
Tromelin, which is 535 km north-west of Réunion, covers an area of 1 sq. km. There is no permanent population although there is a meteorological station.

CONSTITUTION AND GOVERNMENT
The island is administered from St Denis, in Réunion, although it is not legally part of that territory.

GABON

República Gabonaise

Capital: Libreville
Population estimate, 2000: 1·23m.
GDP per capita, 2000: (PPP$) 6,237
HDI/world rank: 0·637/117

KEY HISTORICAL EVENTS

Between the 16th and 18th centuries, the Fang and other peoples in the region of present-day Gabon were part of a federation of chiefdoms. The country's capital, Libreville, grew from a settlement of slaves who were rescued from captivity by the French in 1849. Colonized by France around this period, the territory was annexed to French Congo in 1888. There was resistance by the indigenous people between 1905 and 1911 to the depredations of colonial rule, but the country became a separate colony in 1910 as one of the four territories of French Equatorial Africa. Gabon became an autonomous republic within the French Community on 28 Nov. 1958 and achieved independence on 17 Aug. 1960.

TERRITORY AND POPULATION

Gabon is bounded in the west by the Atlantic Ocean, north by Equatorial Guinea and Cameroon and east and south by the Republic of the Congo. The area covers 267,667 sq. km. Its population at the 1993 census was 1,014,976; density, 3·8 per sq. km. In 1999, 80·3% of the population were urban. 1997 estimate, 1,190,000; density, 4·4 per sq. km.

The UN gives a projected population for 2010 of 1·57m.

The capital is Libreville (523,000 inhabitants, 1999 estimate), other large towns (1993 census) being Port-Gentil (80,841), Franceville (30,246), Oyem (22,669) and Moanda (21,921).

Provincial areas, populations (in 1,000) and capitals:

Province	Area in Sq. km	Population 1993 census	Capital
Estuaire	20,740	463,187	Libreville
Haut-Ogooué	36,547	104,301	Masuku
Moyen-Ogooué	18,535	42,316	Lambaréné
Ngounié	37,750	77,781	Mouila
Nyanga	21,285	39,430	Tchibanga
Ogooué-Ivindo	46,075	48,862	Makokou
Ogooué-Lolo	25,380	43,915	Koulamoutou
Ogooué-Maritime	22,890	97,913	Port-Gentil
Woleu-Ntem	38,465	97,271	Oyem

The largest ethnic groups are the Fang (25%) and Bapounou (24%) in the north. There are some 40 smaller groups. French is the official language.

SOCIAL STATISTICS

1995 births, 39,000; deaths, 16,000. Birth rate (per 1,000 population), 1995: 36·5; death rate, 14·8. Annual population growth rate, 1990–99, 2·8%. Expectation of life at birth, 1999, 51·4 years for males and 53·8 years for females. Infant mortality, 1999, 85 per 1,000 live births; fertility rate, 1999, 5·3 births per woman.

CLIMATE

The climate is equatorial, with high temperatures and considerable rainfall. Mid-May to mid-Sept. is the long dry season, followed by a short rainy season, then a dry season again from mid-Dec. to mid-Feb., and finally a long rainy season once more. Libreville, Jan. 80°F (26·7°C), July 75°F (23·9°C). Annual rainfall 99" (2,510 mm).

CONSTITUTION AND GOVERNMENT

On 21 March 1997 the government presented to the Parliament legislation aimed at reforming the constitution in a number of key areas: notably, the bill mandated the creation of a Vice-President of the Republic, the extension of the presidential term

676

of office from five to seven years, and the transformation of the Senate into an Upper Chamber of Parliament. The bicameral Chambers of Parliament consist of 120 members of the National Assembly and 91 members of the Senate. At a referendum on electoral reform on 23 July 1995, 96·48% of votes cast were in favour; turn-out was 63·45%. The 1991 Constitution provides for an Executive President directly elected for a five-year term (renewable once only). The head of government is the Prime Minister who appoints a Council of Ministers. The unicameral *National Assembly* consists of 120 members, directly elected for a five-year term. There is constitutional provision for the formation of an upper house.

National Anthem. 'Uni dans la concorde' ('United in concord'); words and tune by G. Damas.

RECENT ELECTIONS

Presidential elections were held on 6 Dec. 1998. President Bongo was re-elected against eight opponents with 66·6% of votes cast.

Elections for the National Assembly were held in two rounds on 9 and 23 Dec. 2001. The Gabonese Democratic Party (PDG) won 85 seats, the National Woodcutters' Rally 6, the Gabonese Party of Progress 3, the Social Democratic Party 2, and the People's Unity Party 1. Non-partisans took 11 seats.

CURRENT ADMINISTRATION

President: El Hadj Omar Bongo; b. 1935 (PDG; succeeded 2 Dec. 1967, re-elected in 1973, 1979, 1986, 1993 and 1998).

Vice President: Didjob Divungi Di Ndinge.

In March 2003 the Council of Ministers comprised:

Prime Minister: Jean-François Ntoutoume-Emane; b. 1939 (sworn in 23 Jan. 1999).

Deputy Prime Ministers: Emmanuel Ondo-Metogho (also *Minister of Town and Country Planning*); Antoine de Padoue Mboumbou Miyakou (also *Minister of the City*).

Minister for Civil Service, Administrative Reform and State Modernization: Pascal Désiré Missongo. *Communications, Postal Services and Information Technologies:* André Dieudonné Berre. *Culture and Arts:* Pierre Amoughe Mba. *Defence:* Ali-Ben Bongo. *Family, Child Welfare and Women's Affairs:* Angélique Ngoma. *Forest Economy, Water, Fishing, in charge of the Environment:* Émile Doumba. *Higher Education and Scientific Research:* Vincent Moulengui Boukossou. *Interior, Public Security and Decentralization:* Gen. Idriss Ngari. *Justice:* Honorine Dossou Naki. *Labour and Employment:* Clotaire Christian Ivala. *Merchant Navy:* Félix Siby. *Mines, Energy, Oil and Hydraulic Resources:* Richard Onouviet. *National Education:* Daniel Ona-Ondo. *Minister in Charge of Relations with Parliament and Government Spokesperson:* René Ndemezo Obiang. *Public Health:* Faustin Boukoubi. *Public Works, Equipment and Construction:* Egide Boundono-Simangoye. *Small and Medium-Sized Enterprises:* Paul Biyoghé-Mba. *Social Affairs and National Solidarity:* André Mba Obame. *Tourism and Handicrafts:* Jean Massima. *Vocational Training and Social Rehabilitation:* Barnabé Ndaki. *Youth and Sports:* Alfred Mabicka. *Minister of State for Agriculture, Livestock and Rural Development:* Pierre Claver Maganga Moussavou. *Minister of State for Commerce and Regional Development:* Jean-Rémy Pendy-Bouyiki. *Minister of State for Economy, Finance, Budget and Privatization:* Paul Toungui. *Minister of State for Foreign Affairs, Co-operation and Francophonie Affairs:* Jean Ping. *Minister of State for Housing, Town Planning and Land Register:* Jacques Adiahénot. *Minister of State for Human Rights:* Paul Mba Abessole. *Minister of State for Planning and Development Programmes:* Casimir Oyé Mba. *Minister of State for Transportation and Civil Aviation:* Paulette Missambo.

DEFENCE

In 2000 military expenditure totalled US$123m. (US$81 per capita), representing 2·2% of GDP.

Army. The Army totalled (1999) 3,200. A referendum of 23 July 1995 favoured the transformation of the Presidential Guard into a republican guard. There is also a paramilitary Gendarmerie of 2,000. France maintains a 700-strong marine infantry battalion.

Navy. There is a small naval flotilla, 500 strong in 1999.

Air Force. Personnel (1999) 1,000. There are 16 combat aircraft including nine Mirage 5s and five armed helicopters.

INTERNATIONAL RELATIONS

Gabon is a member of the UN, WTO, IMF, World Bank, African Development Bank, the African Union, Islamic Development Bank, Central African Customs and Economic Union (UDEAC), Economic Community of the Central African States (CEEAC), Islamic Conference, International Organization of the Francophonie, Movement of Non-Aligned Countries and is an ACP member state of the ACP-EU relationship.

ECONOMY

Agriculture accounted for 7·2% of GDP in 1998, industry 60·3% and services 32·5%. Only in Equatorial Guinea did industry contribute a greater share.

Overview. The *Economic and Social Council* was established in 1993 to advise the Council of Ministers. It comprises representatives of central government, local government, employers' groups, trade unions and other interest groups. Five-year development plans, of which there were five after 1966, have been replaced by three-year rolling investment plans.

Currency. The unit of currency is the *franc CFA* (XAF) with a parity of 655·957 francs CFA to one euro. Foreign exchange reserves were US$38m. in April 2002 and total money supply was 343,048m. francs CFA. Gold reserves were 13,000 troy oz in June 2002. Inflation was 2·1% in 2001.

Budget. In 1996 revenue was an estimated US$1·5bn. and expenditure US$1·3bn.

Performance. Gabon experienced a recession in 1999 and 2000, with the economy shrinking by 8·9% and 1·9% respectively. A slight recovery followed in 2001, with growth of 2·4%. Total GDP in 2001 was US$4·3bn.

Banking and Finance. The *Banque des États de l'Afrique Centrale* (*Governor,* Jean-Félix Mamalepot) is the bank of issue. There are nine commercial banks. The *Banque Gabonaise de Développement* and the *Union Gabonaise de Banque* are Gabonese-controlled.

ENERGY AND NATURAL RESOURCES

Environment. According to the *World Bank Atlas* Gabon's carbon dioxide emissions in 1998 were the equivalent of 2·4 tonnes per capita.

Electricity. Installed capacity was 301,000 kW in 1992. The semi-public *Société d'energie et d'eau du Gabon* produced 1·02bn. kWh in 1998 (approximately 72% of which was from hydro-electric). Consumption per capita was 749 kWh in 1998.

Oil and Gas. Proven oil reserves (2001), 2·5bn. bbls. Production, 1996, 135m. bbls. Natural gas production (1997) was 26 petajoules.

Minerals. There are an estimated 200m. tonnes of manganese ore and 850m. tonnes of iron ore deposits; proven reserves of uranium, 35,000 tonnes. Gold, zinc and phosphates also occur. Output, 1996: manganese ore, 1·98m. tonnes; uranium (1999), 294 tonnes.

Agriculture. There were 325,000 ha of arable land in 1998 and 170,000 ha of permanent crops. The major crops (estimated production, 2000, in 1,000 tonnes) are: plantains, 280; cassava, 225; sugarcane, 176; yams, 150; taro, 59; maize, 31; groundnuts, 17; bananas, 12. Other important products include palm oil, sweet potatoes and soybeans.

Livestock (2000): 36,000 cattle, 198,000 sheep, 91,000 goats, 213,000 pigs.

Forestry. Equatorial forests covered 17·86m. ha in 1995, or 69·3% of the total land area (down from 71·1% in 1990). Timber production in 1999 was 5·4m. cu. metres.

In 2002 President Bongo announced that a tenth of the country would be transformed into 13 national parks covering nearly 30,000 sq. km. Gabon is likely to need US$85m. over a seven-year period to build the national parks.

Fisheries. In 1992 there were 14 fishing vessels over 100 GRT, totalling 2,141 GRT. Industrial fleets account for about 25% of the catch. The catch in 1999 was 52,882 tonnes, of which 44,882 tonnes were from marine waters.

INDUSTRY

Most manufacturing is based on the processing of food (particularly sugar), timber and mineral resources, cement and chemical production and oil refining. Production figures (1997) in 1,000 tonnes: residual fuel oil, 285; distillate fuel oil, 230; kerosene, 81; cement (1996), 185; sugar (1998), 17; beer (1995), 81·6m. litres; soft drinks (1995), 41·6m. litres.

Labour. The workforce in 1996 numbered 519,000 (56% males). Around 60% of the economically active population are engaged in agriculture. In 1993 the legal minimum monthly wage was 1,200 francs CFA. There is a 40-hour working week.

INTERNATIONAL TRADE

Foreign debt was US$3,995m. in 2000. The government retains the right to participate in foreign investment in oil and mineral extraction.

Imports and Exports. In 1999 imports (f.o.b.) totalled US$910·5m. and exports (f.o.b.) US$2,498·8m. The main exports in 1994 were worth, in millions of francs CFA: crude oil and natural gas, 1,004,387 (accounting for 74% of exports); timber and wood products, 195,677; manganese, 62,434; uranium, 20,069. Imports are mainly industrial goods. Main export markets, 1996: USA, 64·1%; France, 7·6%; China, 4·3%. Main import suppliers, 1996: France, 42·8%; USA, 10·4%; Japan, 6·0%.

COMMUNICATIONS

Roads. There were, in 1996, 7,670 km of roads (629 km asphalted) and some 24,750 passenger cars plus 16,490 trucks and vans. There were 854 road accidents in 1993 with 116 fatalities.

Rail. The 657-km standard gauge Transgabonais railway runs from the port of Owendo to Franceville. Total length of railways, 1995, 683 km. In 1995, 175,000 passengers and 3m. tonnes of freight were transported.

Civil Aviation. There are international airports at Libreville (Léon M'Ba Airport) and Port-Gentil; scheduled internal services link these to a number of domestic airfields. The national carrier is Air Gabon (80% state-owned). Libreville handled 745,000 passengers (421,000 on domestic flights) and 14,900 tonnes of freight in 2000. In 1999 scheduled airline traffic of Gabonese-based carriers flew 8·0m. km, carrying 423,000 passengers (226,000 on international flights).

Shipping. In 1998 the merchant marine totalled 27,000 GRT, including oil tankers 1,000 GRT. Owendo (near Libreville), Mayumba and Port-Gentil are the main ports. In 1994, 19·8m. tonnes of cargo were handled at the ports. Rivers are an important means of inland transport.

Telecommunications. In 2000 Gabon had 39,000 telephone main lines (31·8 per 1,000 population) and 12,000 PCs were in use (9·8 per 1000 persons). There were 9,500 mobile phone subscribers and 500 fax machines in 1997. In Dec. 2000 there were 15,000 Internet users.

Postal Services. There were 60 post offices in 1995.

SOCIAL INSTITUTIONS

Justice. There are *tribunaux de grande instance* at Libreville, Port-Gentil, Lambaréné, Mouila, Oyem, Masuku and Koulamoutou, from which cases move progressively to a central Criminal Court, Court of Appeal and Supreme Court, all three located in Libreville. Civil police number about 900.

Religion. In 1993 there were 0·66m. Roman Catholics, 0·19m. Protestants and 0·12m. followers of African Christian sects. The majority of the remaining population follow animist beliefs. There are about 10,000 Muslims.

Education. The adult literacy rate in 1998 was 63·0%. Education is compulsory between 6–16 years. In 1995–96 there were 250,693 pupils and 4,943 teachers in

1,147 primary schools and 80,552 pupils with 3,094 teachers at secondary schools; in 1993 there were 8,414 students with 421 teachers in 12 technical schools and 780 students with 43 teachers in 8 teacher-training establishments.

In 1994–95 there was one university and one university of science and technology, with a total of 2,950 students and 410 academic staff.

Health. In 1989 there were 448 doctors, 32 dentists, 71 pharmacists, 240 midwives and 759 nurses. In 1988 there were 27 hospitals and 633 medical centres, with a total of 5,329 beds.

CULTURE

Broadcasting. Broadcasting is the responsibility of the state-controlled Radiodiffusion Télévision Gabonaise, which transmits two national radio programmes and provincial services. There is also a commercial radio station and two TV channels. In 1997 there were 208,000 radio and 63,000 TV sets (colour by SECAM).

Press. In 1996 there were two daily newspapers with a circulation of 33,000, at a rate of 30 per 1,000 inhabitants.

Tourism. There were 194,000 foreign tourists in 1999, spending US$11m.

DIPLOMATIC REPRESENTATIVES

Of Gabon in the United Kingdom (27 Elvaston Place, London, SW7 5NL)
Ambassador: Alain Mansah-Zoguelet.

Of the United Kingdom in Gabon
Ambassador: Richard Wildash, LVO (resides at Yaoundé, Cameroon).

Of Gabon in the USA (2034 20th St., NW, Suite 200, Washington, D.C., 20009)
Ambassador: Jules M. Ogouebandja.

Of the USA in Gabon (Blvd de la Mer, Libreville)
Ambassador: Kenneth P. Moorefield.

Of Gabon to the United Nations
Ambassador: Denis Dangue Réwaka.

Of Gabon to the European Union
Ambassador: René Makongo.

FURTHER READING

Barnes, J. F. G., *Gabon: Beyond the Colonial Legacy.* Boulder (Colo.), 1992
Gardinier, David E. (ed.) *Historical Dictionary of Gabon.* 2nd ed. Metuchen (NJ), 1994.— *Gabon.* [Bibliography] ABC-Clio, Oxford and Santa Barbara (CA), 1992
Saint Paul, M. A., *Gabon: the Development of a Nation.* London, 1989

National statistical office: Direction Générale de la Statistique et des Études Économiques, Ministère de la Planification, de l'Économie et de l'Aménagement du Territoire, Libreville.

THE GAMBIA

Republic of The Gambia

Capital: Banjul
Population estimate, 2000: 1·30m.
GDP per capita, 2000: (PPP$) 1,649
HDI/world rank: 0·405/160

KEY HISTORICAL EVENTS
The Gambia was discovered by the early Portuguese navigators, but they did not settle. During the 17th century companies of merchants obtained trading charters and established a settlement on the river, which, from 1807, was controlled from Sierra Leone. The Gambia became an independent member of the Commonwealth on 18 Feb. 1965 and a republic within the Commonwealth on 24 April 1970.

TERRITORY AND POPULATION
The Gambia takes its name from the River Gambia, and consists of a strip of territory never wider than 10 km on both banks. It is bounded in the west by the Atlantic Ocean and on all other sides by Senegal. The area is 10,689 sq. km, including 2,077 sq. km of inland water. Population (census, 1993), 1,025,867. Estimate, 1995, 1,087,000; density, 102 per sq. km. In 1999, 68·2% of the population were rural.

The UN gives a projected population for 2010 of 1·63m.

The largest ethnic group is the Mandingo, followed by the Wolofs, Fulas, Jolas and Sarahuley. The country is administratively divided into the capital, Banjul (1999 estimate, 229,000), and the surrounding urban area, Kombo St Mary (1993 census, 228,214), plus five other administrative divisions in the rural areas.

The five rural divisions, with their areas, populations and chief towns are (listed west to east, or upriver):

Division	Area in sq. km	Population 1993 census	Chief town
Western	1,764	234,917	Brikama
North Bank	2,256	156,462	Kerewan/Farafenni
Lower River	1,618	65,146	Soma
Central River	2,894	156,021	Jangjangbureh
Upper River	2,069	155,059	Basse

The official language is English.

SOCIAL STATISTICS
1995 births, 46,000; deaths, 20,000. 1995 birth rate per 1,000 population, 41·6; death rate, 18·3. Annual population growth rate, 1990–99, 3·6%. Expectation of life, 1999, was 44·5 years for males and 47·3 for females. Fertility rate, 1999, 5·1 births per woman; infant mortality, 1999, 61 per 1,000 live births. The Gambia has made some of the best progress in recent years in reducing child mortality. The number of deaths per 1,000 live births among children under five was reduced from around 130 in 1990 to approximately 80 in 1999.

CLIMATE
The climate is characterized by two very different seasons. The dry season lasts from Nov. to May, when precipitation is very light and humidity moderate. Days are warm but nights quite cool. The SW monsoon is likely to set in with spectacular storms and produces considerable rainfall from July to Oct., with increased humidity. Banjul, Jan. 73°F (22·8°C), July 80°F (26·7°C). Annual rainfall 52" (1,295 mm).

CONSTITUTION AND GOVERNMENT
The 1970 constitution provided for an executive *President* elected directly for renewable five-year terms. The then President appoints a *Vice-President* who is the government's chief minister. The single-chamber *House of Assembly* has 51 members: 36 elected, 8 nominated (these are from different fields of work and are selected by the Head of State), 5 Head Chief members (nominated by the Head of State), the Attorney-General and the Speaker (both of whom are nominated).

A referendum of 8 Aug. 1996 approved a new constitution by 70·4% of votes cast. Under this the number of seats in parliament, now the *National Assembly*, is increased to 45 directly elected members and four nominated MPs, and the ban on political parties imposed in July 1994 is lifted. Members of the ruling Military Council resigned from their military positions before joining the Alliance for Patriotic Reorientation and Construction (APRC).

National Anthem. 'For The Gambia, our homeland'; words by V. J. Howe, tune traditional.

RECENT ELECTIONS

Presidential elections were held on 18 Oct. 2001. President Jammeh was re-elected against four opponents with 53·0% of votes cast. Turn-out was 89·9%.

Parliamentary elections were held on 17 Jan. 2002. The Alliance for Patriotic Reorientation and Construction (APRC) won 45 seats (33 of which were unopposed because of boycotting by opposition parties), the People's Democratic Organization for Independence and Socialism 2, and the National Reconciliation Party 1.

CURRENT ADMINISTRATION

President: Rtd Col. Yahya Jammeh; b. 1965 (APRC; seized power 22 July 1994; elected 26 Sept. 1996 and re-elected in 2001).

In March 2003 the government comprised:

Vice-President: Isatou Njie Saidy.

Secretary of State for Public Works, Construction and Infrastructure Development: Capt. Edward Singhatey. *Communications, Information and Technology:* Bakary Njie. *Local Government and Lands:* Malafi Jarju. *Finance and Economic Affairs:* Famara Jatta. *Foreign Affairs:* Baboucarr-Blaise Ismaila Jagne. *Interior and Religious Affairs:* Ousman Badjie. *Trade, Industry and Employment:* Musa Sillah. *Education:* Ann Therese Ndong-Jatta. *Fisheries, Natural Resources and the Environment:* Susan Waffa-Ogoo. *Health and Social Affairs:* Yankuba Gassama. *Justice and Attorney General:* Joseph Joof. *Agriculture and Natural Resources:* Hassan Sallah. *Tourism:* Yankuba Touray. *Youth, Sports and Culture:* Samba Faal.

DEFENCE

The Gambia National Army, 800 strong, has two infantry battalions and one engineer squadron.

The marine unit of the Army consisted in 1996 of 70 personnel operating two ex-Chinese and two British-built inshore patrol craft and some boats, based at Banjul.

Defence expenditure totalled US$15m. in 2000 (US$11 per capita), representing 3·2% of GDP.

INTERNATIONAL RELATIONS

The Gambia is a member of the UN, WTO, the Commonwealth, the African Union, African Development Bank, ECOWAS, IOM, OIC and is an ACP member state of the ACP-EU relationship.

ECONOMY

Services accounted for 58·9% of GDP in 1998, agriculture 27·4% and industry 13·7%.

Currency. The unit of currency is the *dalasi* (GMD), of 100 *butut.* Inflation was 4·0% in 2001. Foreign exchange reserves were US$94m. in May 2002. Total money supply in May 2002 was 1,343m. dalasis.

Budget. The fiscal year starts on 1 July. In 1996–97 revenues were estimated to be US$88·6m. and expenditures US$98·2m.

Performance. Real GDP growth was 5·5% in 2001 (5·6% in 2000). Total GDP was US$0·4bn. in 2001.

Banking and Finance. The Central Bank of The Gambia (founded 1971) is the bank of issue. There are five commercial banks: Standard Chartered, BICI Trust Bank, Western Union Monetary Transfer, Arab Gambian Islamic Bank, Continent Bank.

Weights and Measures. The UK imperial system is in common use, but the metric system is being introduced.

ENERGY AND NATURAL RESOURCES

Environment. According to the *World Bank Atlas* carbon dioxide emissions in 1998 were the equivalent of 0·2 tonnes per capita.

Electricity. Installed capacity was 30,000 kW in 1995. Production was 75m. kWh in 1998; consumption per capita in 1997 was 65 kWh.

Minerals. Heavy minerals, including ilmenite, zircon and rutile, have been discovered in Sanyang, Batokunku and Kartong areas.

Agriculture. About 75% of the population depend upon agriculture. There were 0·2m. ha of arable land in 1998 and 5,000 ha of permanent crops. Almost all commercial activity centres upon the marketing of groundnuts, which is the only export crop of financial significance; in 2000 an estimated 126,000 tonnes were produced. Cotton is also exported on a limited scale. Rice is of increasing importance for local consumption; production (2000) 29,000 tonnes. Major products (2000 estimates, in 1,000 tonnes), are: groundnuts, 126; millet, 76; rice, 29; maize, 21; sorghum, 18; cassava, 6; palm oil, 3; palm kernels, 2.

Livestock (2000): 370,000 cattle, 270,000 goats, 195,000 sheep and 1m. poultry.

Forestry. In 1995 forests covered 91,000 ha, or 9·1% of the land area. Timber production in 1999 was 618,000 cu. metres.

Fisheries. The total catch in 1999 was estimated at 30,000 tonnes, of which 27,500 tonnes were from marine waters.

INDUSTRY

Labour. The labour force in 1996 totalled 579,000 (55% males). Nearly 80% of the economically active population in 1994 were engaged in agriculture, fisheries and forestry.

INTERNATIONAL TRADE
Foreign debt was US$471m. in 2000.

Imports and Exports. Imports and exports in US$1m.:

	1995	1996	1997
Imports f.o.b.	162·5	217·1	207·1
Exports f.o.b.	123·0	118·8	119·6

Chief items of export: groundnuts, groundnut oil, groundnut cake, cotton lint, fish and fish preparations, hides and skins. Chief items of import: manufactured goods, food and live animals, machinery and transport equipment.

Main export markets, 1994: Belgium-Luxembourg, 50·4%; Japan, 21·5%; Guinea, 6·2%; UK, 3·6%. Main import suppliers, 1994: China, 24·7%; Belgium-Luxembourg, 10·1%; UK, 8·5%; Hong Kong, 7·7%.

COMMUNICATIONS

Roads. There were 2,700 km of roads in 1996, of which 950 km were paved. Number of vehicles (1996): 8,640 passenger cars; 9,000 trucks and vans.

Civil Aviation. There is an international airport at Banjul (Yundum). The national carrier is Gambia Airways. Banjul handled 301,756 passengers in 2000 (all on international flights) and 2,236 tonnes of freight.

Shipping. The chief port is Banjul. Ocean-going vessels can travel up the Gambia River as far as Kuntaur. The merchant marine totalled 2,000 GRT in 1998.

Telecommunications. The Gambia had 30,300 main telephone lines in 2000, or 25·6 per 1,000 population, and there were 15,000 PCs in use (11·5 per 1,000 persons). Mobile phone subscribers numbered 4,700 in 1997 and there were 1,100 fax machines. In July 2000 there were 4,000 Internet users.

Postal Services. There are several post offices and agencies; postal facilities are also afforded to all towns.

SOCIAL INSTITUTIONS

Justice. Justice is administered by a Supreme Court consisting of a chief justice and puisne judges. The High Court has unlimited original jurisdiction in civil and criminal matters. The Supreme Court is the highest court of appeal and succeeds the judicial committee of the Privy Council in London. There are Magistrates Courts in each of the divisions plus one in Banjul and two in nearby Kombo St Mary's Division—eight in all. There are resident magistrates in provincial areas. There are also Muslim courts, district tribunals dealing with cases concerned with customary law, and two juvenile courts.

The death penalty was abolished in 1993 but restored by decree in 1995.

Religion. About 90% of the population is Muslim. Banjul is the seat of an Anglican and a Roman Catholic bishop. There is a Methodist mission. A few sections of the population retain their original animist beliefs.

Education. The adult literacy rate in 1999 was 35·7% (43·1% among males and 28·5% among females). In 1995–96 there were 124,513 pupils at primary schools and 80,552 pupils at secondary schools. In 1993–94 there were 1,591 students at 155 institutions of higher education, which comprise The Gambia College, a technical training institute, a management development institute, a multi-media training institute, a hotel training school, and centres for self-development and skills training, and continuing education.

Health. In 1994 there were 2 hospitals, 1 clinic, 10 health centres and some 60 dispensaries.

CULTURE

Broadcasting. Gambia Radio and Television Services (GRTS) broadcasts radio and television programmes in English and some other local languages. There are four private commercial radio stations and three community radio stations. TV operations started in 1995 and programmes are transmitted countrywide and beyond (colour by PAL). In 1997 there were 196,000 radio receivers and 4,000 television receivers.

Cinema. In 1992 there were 15 cinemas.

Press. There is a government-owned daily; an independent newspaper appears five times a week, there are two weeklies and several news-sheets and a monthly.

Tourism. Tourism is The Gambia's biggest foreign exchange earner. In 1998, 91,000 foreign tourists visited bringing in receipts of US$33m.

DIPLOMATIC REPRESENTATIVES
Of The Gambia in the United Kingdom (57 Kensington Ct., London, W8 5DG)
High Commissioner: Gibril Seman Joof.

Of the United Kingdom in The Gambia (48 Atlantic Rd., Fajara, Banjul)
High Commissioner: Eric Jenkinson.

Of The Gambia in USA (1155 15th St, Suite 1000, NW, Washington, D.C., 20005)
Ambassador: Essa Bokarr Sey.

Of the USA in The Gambia (Fajara (East), Kairaba Ave., Banjul)
Ambassador: Jackson McDonald.

Of The Gambia to the United Nations
Ambassador: Crispin Grey-Johnson.

Of The Gambia to the European Union
Ambassador: Alieu M. Ngum.

FURTHER READING
Hughes, A. and Perfect, D., *Political History of The Gambia, 1816–1992.* Farnborough, 1993

GEORGIA

Sakartvelos Respublika
(Republic of Georgia)

Capital: Tbilisi
Population estimate, 2000: 5·26m.
GDP per capita, 2000: (PPP$) 2,664
HDI/world rank: 0·748/81

KEY HISTORICAL EVENTS

The independent Georgian Social Democratic Republic was declared on 26 May 1918 and was recognized by the Russian Soviet Federal Socialist Republic on 7 May 1920. In 1936 the Georgian Soviet Socialist Republic became one of the constituent republics of the USSR. Following nationalist successes at elections in Oct. 1990, the Supreme Soviet resolved on a transition to full independence and on 9 April 1991 unanimously declared the republic an independent state. President Zviad Gamsakhurdia was deposed by armed insurrection on 6 Jan. 1992 and a military council took control. After elections in which he gained 95% of votes cast, Eduard Shevardnadze became *de facto* head of state in Oct. 1992. On 22 Oct. 1993 Georgia joined the CIS. Supporters of the deposed president Gamsakhurdia were in intermittent conflict with the government, mainly in Mingrelia, but suffered heavy defeats once Russian support became available via the CIS. Ethnic conflict has been rife in the two autonomous republics of South Ossetia and Abhkazia. Civil war broke out with South Ossetia in 1990 and Abhkazia in 1992 and 1998, leading to thousands of refugees. Georgia has since moved closer to the West but economic reforms have been slow in coming and industry and agriculture are both in need of investment.

TERRITORY AND POPULATION

Georgia is bounded in the west by the Black Sea and south by Turkey, Armenia and Azerbaijan. Area, 69,700 sq. km (26,900 sq. miles). Its population in 1997 was estimated to be 5,316,000 (2,536,000 male); density, 76 per sq. km.

The UN gives a projected population for 2010 of 4·96m.

In 1999, 60·2% of the population lived in urban areas. The capital is Tbilisi (1999 population estimate, 1·31m.). Other important towns are Kutaisi (240,000; 1997), Rustavi (158,000; 1997), Batumi (136,000; 1991), Sukhumi (121,000; 1991), Poti (54,000; 1991), Gori (59,000; 1991).

Georgians accounted for 70·1% of the 1989 census population of 5,400,841; others included 8·1% Armenians, 6·3% Russians, 5·7% Azerbaijanis, 3% Ossetians, 1·9% Greeks, 1·8% Abkhazians and 1% Ukrainians. Georgia includes the Autonomous Republics of Abkhazia and Adjaria and the former Autonomous Region of South Ossetia.

Georgian is the official language. Armenian, Russian and Azeri are also spoken.

SOCIAL STATISTICS

1998 births, 57,300; deaths, 41,600. Rates, 1998 estimates: birth, 11·3 per 1,000 population; death, 8·2 per 1,000. Annual population growth rate, 1990–99, –1·0%. Life expectancy, 1999, 68·8 years for males and 77·0 years for females. Infant mortality, 1999, 19 per 1,000 live births; fertility rate, 1999, 1·9 births per woman.

CLIMATE

The Georgian climate is extremely varied. The relatively small territory covers different climatic zones, ranging from humid sub-tropical zones to permanent snow and glaciers. In Tbilisi summer is hot: 25–35°C. Nov. sees the beginning of the Georgian winter and the temperature in Tbilisi can drop to –8°C; however, average temperature ranges from 2–6°C.

CONSTITUTION AND GOVERNMENT

A new Constitution of 24 Aug. 1995 defines Georgia as a presidential republic with federal elements. The head of state is the *President*, elected by universal suffrage for not more than two five-year terms. The 235-member parliament is elected by a system combining 85 single-member districts with proportional representation based on party lists. There is a 5% threshold.

National Anthem. 'Dideba zetsit kurtheuls' ('Praise be to the Heavenly Bestower of Blessings'); words anonymous, tune by K. Potskhverashvili.

RECENT ELECTIONS
At the presidential election held on 9 April 2000 incumbent Eduard Shevardnadze was re-elected *President* with 79·8% of votes cast against five opponents. His nearest rival was Dzhumber Patiashvili who polled 16·7%.

At the parliamentary elections of 31 Oct. and 14 Nov. 1999 the ruling Citizens' Union won 41·7% of the vote (130 of the 235 seats) while Revival, the main opposition, obtained 25·2% (64 seats). Turn-out was 67·6%.

CURRENT ADMINISTRATION
President: Eduard Shevardnadze; b. 1928 (Citizens' Union of Georgia; sworn in 10 March 1992).

In March 2003 the government comprised:

Minister of Education: Aleksandre Kartozia. *Environmental Protection and Natural Resources:* Nino Chkhobadze. *Trade, Economy and Industry:* Giorgi Gachechiladze. *Defence:* David Tevzadze. *Culture:* Sesili Gogiberidze. *Refugees (acting):* Otar Keinashvili. *Foreign Affairs:* Irakli Menagharishvili. *State Security:* Valeri Khaburdzania. *Agriculture:* Davit Kirvalidze. *Labour, Health and Social Affairs:* Amiran Gamkrelidze. *Internal Affairs:* Koba Narchemashvili. *Fuel and Energy:* David Mirtskhulava. *Justice:* Roland Giligashvili. *Transport and Communication:* Merab Adeishvili. *Finance and Revenue:* Mirian Gogiashvili. *Minister of State:* Avtandil Djorbenadze. *Minister Without Portfolio:* Malkhaz Kakabadze.

The *Speaker* is Nino Burjanadze.

Press Office of the President: http://www.presidpress.gov.ge/

DEFENCE
The total strength of the Armed Forces consists of 26,300 personnel. In 1999 some 5,000 Russian troops and 1,500 peacekeeping forces were stationed in Georgia. The UN has some 100 observers from 22 countries.

Defence expenditure in 2000 totalled US$116m. (US$23 per capita), representing 2·5% of GDP.

Army. The Army totals 12,600 although a force of 24,000 is planned. In addition there are 250,000 reservists and a paramilitary border guard estimated at 6,500.

Navy. Former Soviet facilities at Poti have been taken over. Personnel, 1999, 750.

Air Force. Personnel, 1999, 2,400. Equipment includes Su-17 and Su-25 fighter-bombers.

INTERNATIONAL RELATIONS
Georgia is a member of the UN, WTO, CIS, NATO Partnership for Peace, Council of Europe, OSCE, WTO, BSEC and IOM.

ECONOMY
In 1998 agriculture accounted for 26·0% of GDP in 1998, industry 15·8% and services 58·2%.

Overview. A privatization programme was inaugurated in 1995.

Currency. The unit of currency is the *lari* (GEL) of 100 *tetri*, which replaced coupons at 1 lari = 1m. coupons on 25 Sept. 1995. Inflation was 4·7% in 2001, having been 163% in 1995 and 15,606% in 1994. Gold reserves are negligible. Total money supply was 394m. laris in June 2002.

Budget. Government revenue and expenditure (in 1m. laris):

	1997	1998	1999	2000
Revenue	568·8	591·4	674·6	625·9
Expenditure	788·7	761·5	849·1	737·7

Performance. Real GDP growth was 3·0% in 1999, 2·0% in 2000 and 4·5% in 2001. In both 1996 and 1997 growth had exceeded 10%, but prior to that the economy had suffered a sharp downturn, contracting by 45% in 1992, 29% in 1993 and 10% in 1994. Total GDP was US$3·1bn. in 2001.

Between 1990 and 1996 the average annual real growth in GNP per capita was −19·3% (the lowest of any country in the world).

Banking and Finance. The *Governor* of the Central Bank is Irakli Managadze. In 1996 there were 65 commercial banks. One foreign bank had a representative office.

ENERGY AND NATURAL RESOURCES

Environment. According to the *World Bank Atlas* carbon dioxide emissions in Georgia were the equivalent of 1·0 tonnes per capita in 1998.

Electricity. The many fast-flowing rivers provide an important hydro-electric resource. Installed capacity was 5m. kW in 1997. Production in 1998 was 6·96bn. kWh; consumption per capita in 1998 was 1,257 kWh.

Oil and Gas. Output (1996) of crude petroleum, 3m. bbls.; natural gas (1995 estimate), 3·3m. cu. metres (excluding Abkhazia and South Ossetia). A 920 km long oil pipeline is under construction from an offshore Azerbaijani oil field in the Caspian Sea across Azerbaijan and Georgia to a new oil terminal at Supsa, near Poti, on the Black Sea Coast. The US$600m. pipeline started pumping oil in early 1999 and will have an ultimate capacity of some 15m. tonnes of oil a year. The pipeline allowed Georgia to create 25,000 new jobs. However, Georgia is still heavily dependent on Russia for natural gas. Accords for the construction of a second oil pipeline through Georgia and a gas pipeline were signed in Nov. 1999, to take oil from Azerbaijan to Turkey via Georgia and gas from Turkmenistan to Turkey via Azerbaijan and Georgia. Work on the oil pipeline, which is expected to become operational in 2005, began in Sept. 2002.

Minerals. Manganese deposits are calculated at 250m. tonnes. Other important minerals are coal, barytes, clays, gold, diatomite shale, agate, marble, alabaster, iron and other ores, building stone, arsenic, molybdenum, tungsten and mercury. Output of coal in 1996 was estimated to be 20,000 tonnes (excluding Abkhazia and South Ossetia).

Agriculture. Agriculture plays an important part in Georgia's economy, contributing 26·1% of GDP in 1998. In 1998 there were 781,000 ha of arable land and 285,000 ha permanent crops.

Output of main agricultural products (in 1,000 tonnes) in 2000: potatoes, 480; tomatoes, 325; maize, 225; grapes, 200; cabbages, 125; wine, 116; apples, 115; wheat, 84; watermelons (including melons, pumpkins and squash), 70.

Livestock, 2000: cattle, 1,122,000; sheep, 560,000; pigs, 411,000; chickens, 8m. Livestock products, 2000 (in 1,000 tonnes): meat, 105; milk, 721; eggs, 24.

Forestry. There were 2·99m. ha of forest in 1995, or 42·9% of the total land area.

Fisheries. The catch in 1999 was 1,500 tonnes, down from 147,688 tonnes in 1989.

INDUSTRY

Industry accounted for 9·8% of GDP in 1998. There is a metallurgical plant and a motor works. There are factories for processing tea, creameries and breweries. There are also textile and silk industries.

Production in 1995 (in tonnes): steel (1997), 103,000; fertilizer (1993), 60,000; cement (1997), 91,000; processed meat (1993), 700,000; textiles (1993), 16·6m. cu. metres; footwear (1994), 200,000 pairs; cigarettes (1997), 918m. units.

Labour. The total labour force in 1996 was 2·2m. (54% males). The unemployment rate was 5·6% in 1999. Approximately 500,000 Georgians, or a tenth of the population, work in Russia, but in Dec. 2000 Russia began requiring Georgians to have a visa to visit the country.

INTERNATIONAL TRADE

Total foreign debt was US$1,633m. in 2000. The debt was mainly as a result of the importing of natural gas from Turkmenistan.

Imports and Exports. In 2000 Georgian exports (f.o.b.) amounted to US$459·0m. and imports (f.o.b.) US$970·5m. Major commodities imported are fuel, grain and other foods, machinery and parts, and transport equipment. Major commodities for export are iron and steel products, food and beverages, machinery, textiles and chemicals. Main export markets, 1997: Russia, 27·4%; Turkey, 20·0%; Azerbaijan, 10·0%; Armenia, 7·6%. Main import suppliers, 1997: Russia, 15·2%; Azerbaijan, 12·3%; Turkey, 11·9%; USA, 7·4%.

COMMUNICATIONS

Roads. There were 20,700 km of roads in 1996 (19,355 km hard-surfaced). An estimated 427,000 passenger cars were in use in 1996 (79·7 per 1,000 inhabitants).

Rail. Total length is 1,583 km of 1,520 mm gauge (1,483 km electrified). In 1994 railways carried 2·7m. tonnes of freight and 9·8m. passengers.

Civil Aviation. The main airport is at Tbilisi (Novo-Alexeyevka). There are four Georgian air carriers—Georgian Airlines, Georgian Airways, Airzena Georgian Airlines and Air Georgia. In 1998 Georgian Airlines operated international flights to Adler/Sochi, Athens, Frankfurt, Kyiv, Moscow, Prague, Rostov, St Petersburg, Tel Aviv, Thessaloniki and Volgograd; Georgian Airways had international flights to Atyrau, Delhi, London and Tehran; Airzena Georgian Airlines had flights to Dubai, Tashkent and Vienna; Air Georgia had flights to Frankfurt and Moscow. In 2000 Tbilisi airport handled 271,820 passengers (270,011 on international flights) and 7,529 tonnes of freight.

Shipping. In 1998 sea-going shipping totalled 118,000 GRT, of which oil tankers accounted for 73,000 GRT.

Telecommunications. There were 757,500 telephone main lines in 2000, or 138·6 per 1,000 persons. Mobile phone subscribers numbered 60,000 in 1998 and there were 500 fax machines in 1995. In Dec. 1999 there were 20,000 Internet users.

SOCIAL INSTITUTIONS

Justice. The population in penal institutions in May 1997 was 7,900 (145 per 100,000 of national population). The death penalty was abolished in 1997.

Religion. The Georgian Orthodox Church has its own organization under Catholicos (patriarch) Ilya II who is resident in Tbilisi.

Education. In 1996 there were 1,332 pre-primary schools with 10,491 teachers for 81,938 pupils. In 1996–97 there were 3,201 primary schools with 16,542 teachers for 293,325 pupils. There were 444,058 pupils at secondary level and, in 1996, 155,033 students at 76 technical colleges and 23 institutions of higher education. There is one university and one technical university, with a total of 34,590 students and 6,464 academic staff. Adult literacy rate in 1998 was over 99%.

Health. Georgia had 29,900 doctors and 57,100 hospital beds in 1994.

Welfare. In 1994 there were 804,000 age and 355,000 other pensioners.

CULTURE

Broadcasting. The government-controlled Georgian Radio broadcasts two national and three regional programmes, and a foreign service, Radio Georgia (English, Russian). There are local independent TV stations in ten towns (colour by SECAM V). In 1997 there were 3·02m. radio receivers and 2·57m. TV receivers.

Press. In 1995 there were 25 dailies and weeklies.

Tourism. Investment in tourism has increased substantially in recent years, and large numbers of hotels have been built. In 1999 there were 384,000 foreign tourists bringing in receipts of US$400m.

DIPLOMATIC REPRESENTATIVES

Of Georgia in the United Kingdom (3 Hornton Pl., Kensington Place, London, W8 4LZ)

Ambassador: Teimuraz Mamatsashvili.

Of the United Kingdom in Georgia (Sheraton Metechi Palace Hotel, 380003 Tbilisi)

Ambassador: Deborah Barnes Jones.

Of Georgia in the USA (1615 New Hampshire Ave., NW, Suite 300, Washington, D.C., 20009)
Ambassador: Levan Mikeladze.

Of the USA in Georgia (25 Antoneli Street, 380026 Tbilisi)
Ambassador: Richard M. Miles.

Of Georgia to the United Nations
Ambassador: Revaz Adamia.

Of Georgia to the European Union
Ambassador: Konstantin Zaldastanishvili.

FURTHER READING
Brook, S., *Claws of the Crab: Georgia and Armenia in Crisis.* London, 1992
Gachechiladze, R., *The New Georgia: Space, Society, Politics.* London, 1995
Nasmyth, P., *Georgia: a Rebel in the Caucasus.* London, 1992
Suny, R. G., *The Making of the Georgian Nation.* 2nd ed. Indiana Univ. Press, 1994

State Department for Statistics Website: http://www.statistics.ge/

ABKHAZIA

Area, 8,600 sq. km (3,320 sq. miles); population (Jan. 1990), 537,500. Capital Sukhumi (1990 population, 121,700). This area, the ancient Colchis, saw the establishment of a West Georgian kingdom in the 4th century and a Russian protectorate in 1810. In March 1921 a congress of local Soviets proclaimed it a Soviet Republic, and its status as an Autonomous Republic, within Georgia, was confirmed on 17 April 1930 and again by the Georgian Constitution of 1995.

Ethnic groups (1989 census) Georgians, 45·7%; Abkhazians, 17·8%; Armenians, 14·6%; and Russians, 14·3%.

In July 1992 the Abkhazian parliament declared sovereignty under the presidency of Vladislav Ardzinba and the restoration of its 1925 constitution. Fighting broke out as Georgian forces moved into Abkhazia. On 3 Sept. and on 19 Nov. ceasefires were agreed, but fighting continued into 1993 and by Sept. Georgian forces were driven out. On 15 May 1994 Georgian and Abkhazian delegates under Russian auspices signed an agreement on a ceasefire and deployment of 2,500 Russian troops as a peacekeeping force. On 26 Nov. 1994 parliament adopted a new Constitution proclaiming Abkhazian sovereignty. CIS economic sanctions were imposed in Jan. 1996. Parliamentary elections were held on 23 Nov. 1996. Neither the constitution nor the elections were recognized by the Georgian government or the international community. Fighting flared up between rival militia forces again in May 1998 after Abkhazian forces ejected thousands of ethnic Mingrelian and Georgian refugees who had returned to the southern Abkhazian region of Gali. After the fighting in 1998, the worst in five years, both sides declared a ceasefire. Up to 20,000 Georgians lost their homes. Abkhazia has expressed a desire to join the Russian Federation, but Russia is wary of the request.

Abkhazia, and notably Sukhumi, the capital, have seen living standards plunge dramatically. There are no Internet links, no mobile phones and no hotels. There is very little work and practically no money.

Head of the Separatist Government. Vladislav Ardzinba (elected by parliament on 26 Nov. 1994).

The republic has coal, electric power, building materials and light industries. In 1985 there were 89 collective farms and 56 state farms; main crops are tobacco, tea, grapes, oranges, tangerines and lemons. Crop area 43,900 ha.

Livestock, 1 Jan. 1987: 147,300 cattle, 127,900 pigs, 28,800 sheep and goats.

In 1990–91 there were 16,700 children attending pre-school institutions. There is a university at Sukhumi with 3,000 students and 270 academic staff in 1995–96. In 1990 there were 2,100 students at colleges and 7,700 students at other institutions of higher education.

In Jan. 1990 there were 2,500 doctors and 6,600 junior medical personnel.

ADJARIA

Area, 2,900 sq. km (1,160 sq. miles); population: 396,400. Capital, Batumi (1990 population, 137,300). Adjaria fell under Turkish rule in the 17th century, and was annexed to Russia (rejoining Georgia) after the Berlin Treaty of 1878. On 16 July 1921 the territory was constituted as an Autonomous Republic within the Georgian SSR, a status confirmed by the Georgian Constitution of 1995.

Ethnic groups (1989 census): Georgians, 82·8%; Russians, 7·7%; and Armenians 4%.

Chairman of the Supreme Council of Adjaria. Aslan Abashidze.

Elections were held in Sept. 1996. A coalition of the Citizens' Union of Georgia and the All-Georgian Union of Revival gained a majority of seats.

Adjaria specializes in sub-tropical agricultural products. These include tea, citruses, bamboo, eucalyptus, tobacco, etc. Livestock (Jan. 1990): 112,300 cattle, 6,200 pigs, 7,000 sheep and goats. In 1980 there were 69 collective farms and 21 state farms.

There is a port and a shipyard at Batumi, oil-refining, food-processing and canning factories, clothing, building materials, pharmaceutical factories, etc.

The population is almost exclusively Sunni Muslim.

In 1990–91, 77,239 pupils were engaged in study at all levels.

In Jan. 1990 there were 1,700 doctors and 4,400 junior medical personnel.

SOUTH OSSETIA

Area, 3,900 sq. km (1,505 sq. miles); population (Jan. 1990), 99,800 (ethnic groups at the 1989 census; Ossetians 66·2% and Georgians 29%). Capital, Tskhinvali (34,000). This area was populated by Ossetians from across the Caucasus (North Ossetia), driven out by the Mongols in the 13th century. The region was set up within the Georgian SSR on 20 April 1922. Formerly an Autonomous Region, its administrative autonomy was abolished by the Georgian Supreme Soviet on 11 Dec. 1990, and it has been named the Tskhinvali Region.

Fighting broke out in 1990 between insurgents wishing to unite with North Ossetia (in the Russian Federation) and Georgian forces. By a Russo-Georgian agreement of July 1992 Russian peacekeeping forces moved into a seven-km buffer zone between South Ossetia and Georgia pending negotiations. An OSCE peacekeeping force has been deployed since 1992.

At elections not recognized by the Georgian government on 10 Nov. 1996, Lyudvig Chibirov was elected president. Though maintaining a commitment to independence, President Chibirov came to a political agreement with the Georgian government in 1996 that neither force nor sanctions should be applied.

Presidential elections in Dec. 2001 were won by Eduard Kokoev.

Main industries are mining, timber, electrical engineering and building materials. Crop area, chiefly grains, was 21,600 ha in 1985; other pursuits are sheep-farming (128,500 sheep and goats on 1 Jan. 1987) and vine-growing. There were 14 collective farms and 18 state farms in 1985.

In 1989–90 there were 21,200 pupils in elementary and secondary schools. There were 6,525 children in pre-school institutions.

In Jan. 1987 there were 511 doctors and 1,400 hospital beds.

GERMANY

**Bundesrepublik Deutschland
(Federal Republic of Germany)**

Capital: Berlin
Seat of Government: Berlin/Bonn
Population estimate, 2000: 82·02m.
GDP per capita, 2000: (PPP$) 25,103
HDI/world rank: 0·925/17

KEY HISTORICAL EVENTS

At the outbreak of the Napoleonic wars Germany consisted of many small states, independent but loosely bound by a common allegiance to the Holy Roman Emperor, a title which for most of its history fell to the Austrian royal house of Hapsburg. In 1806 the Holy Roman Empire was destroyed by Napoleon who then combined 16 German states as the Confederation of the Rhine. Following Napoleon's defeat in 1815, a larger Confederation was formed with 38 members (39 after 1817). Austria remained the dominant power with a permanent right to the presidency. Prussia held the vice-presidency.

In 1848–50 attempts were made to draw up a constitution but the parliament which sat from 20 March to 29 April 1850 was neither recognized by Austria nor powerful enough to control the other dominant state, Prussia. The Federal Diet therefore resumed power and held it until 1866. In 1866 Prussia defeated Austria and formed the North German Confederation under her own control.

In 1870 Prussia went to war with France, rallied the German states in support and, following German victory, went on to the creation of the German Empire in 1871. The Empire included all German states except Austria and had, therefore, deep North-South, Protestant-Catholic divisions. It was dominated by Prussia, whose king became emperor. The imperial government led Germany into the First World War in 1914 and when defeated, national unity collapsed. The emperor abdicated on 28 Nov. 1918.

After an anarchic period a republican government attempted to restore the economy and political stability. But the onset of world depression and the loss of resources and territory through warfare were too much for the fledgling government to manage. In 1933 the National Socialist leader Adolf Hitler was appointed Chancellor. The National Socialist ('Nazi') party appealed to national pride and offered a return to self-respect after humiliation. Hitler became president of the Third Reich in 1934. Hitler's expansionism led to his annexation of Austria and of German-speaking Czechoslovakia (the Sudetenland) in 1938. In March 1939 he invaded Poland, attempting to restore the authority exercised there by Prussia before 1918. This precipitated the Second World War.

The War ended in German defeat in 1945. The Allied forces occupied Germany; the UK, the USA and France holding the west and the USSR the east. By the Berlin Declaration of 5 June 1945 these governments assumed authority; each was given a zone of occupation, and the zone commanders-in-chief together made up the Allied Control Council in Berlin. The area of Greater Berlin was also divided into four sectors.

By 1948 it had become clear that there would be no agreement between the occupying powers as to the future of Germany. Accordingly, the western allies united their zones into one unit. In protest, the USSR withdrew from the Allied Control Council, blockaded Berlin until May 1949, and consolidated control of eastern Germany, establishing the German Democratic Republic. A People's Council appointed in 1948 drew up a constitution which came into force in Oct. 1949, providing for a communist state of five Länder with a centrally-planned economy. In 1952 the government made a division between its own territory and that of the Federal Republic, with a three-mile cordon fenced and guarded along the frontier. Berlin was closed as a migration route by the construction of a concrete boundary wall in 1961. In 1954 the USSR ceased to collect reparation payments, and sovereignty was granted. The GDR signed the Warsaw Pact in 1955. Socialist policies were stepped up in 1958, leading to flight to the West of skilled workers.

Meanwhile, a constituent assembly met in Bonn in Sept. 1948 to draft a Basic Law which brought the Federal Republic of Germany into existence. The occupation forces retained some powers, however, and the Republic did not become a sovereign state until 1955.

Even before sovereignty the Republic had begun negotiations for a measure of European unity and joined in creating the European Coal and Steel Community in 1951 and the European Economic Community in 1957. In Jan. 1957 the Saarland was returned to full German control. In 1973 the Federal Republic entered the UN.

In the autumn of 1989 movements for political liberalization in the GDR and re-unification with Federal Germany gathered strength. Erich Honecker and other long-serving Communist leaders were replaced in Oct.–Nov. The Berlin Wall was opened on 9 Nov. Following the reforms in the GDR in Nov. 1989 the Federal Chancellor Helmut Kohl issued a plan for German confederation. On 18 May 1990 Federal Germany and the GDR signed a treaty extending Federal Germany's currency, its economic, monetary and social legislation to the GDR as of 1 July. German reunification took place on 3 Oct. 1990.

The Federal Assembly (*Bundestag*) moved from Bonn to the renovated *Reichstag* in Berlin in 1999.

TERRITORY AND POPULATION

Germany is bounded in the north by Denmark and the North and Baltic Seas, east by Poland, east and southeast by the Czech Republic, southeast and south by Austria, south by Switzerland and west by France, Luxembourg, Belgium and the Netherlands. Area: 357,023 sq. km. Population estimate, 31 Dec. 2000: 82,259,500 (42,103,700 females). Of the total population, 67,019,000 lived in the former Federal Republic of Germany (up from 66,834,000 in 1999) and 15,169,000 in the former German Democratic Republic (down from 15,253,000 in 1999); density, 230 per sq. km. In 1999, 87·3% of the population lived in urban areas. There were 37·80m. households in April 1999; 13·49m. were single-person, and 11·37m. had a female principal breadwinner.

The UN gives a projected population for 2010 of 81·35m.

On 14 Nov. 1990 Germany and Poland signed a treaty confirming Poland's existing western frontier and renouncing German claims to territory lost as a result of the Second World War.

The capital is Berlin; the Federal German government moved from Bonn to Berlin in 1999.

The Federation comprises 16 Länder (states). Area and population:

Länder	Area in sq. km	Population (in 1,000) 1987 census	Population (in 1,000) 2001 estimate	Density per sq. km (2001)
Baden-Württemberg (BW)	35,751	9,286	10,631[1]	297[1]
Bavaria (BY)	70,550	10,903	12,330	175
Berlin (BE)[2]	892	· · ·	3,388	3,800
Brandenburg (BB)[3]	29,476	· · ·	2,593	88
Bremen (HB)	404	660	660	1,634
Hamburg (HH)	755	1,593	1,726	2,286
Hessen (HE)	21,115	5,508	6,076	288
Lower Saxony (NI)	47,616	7,162	7,956	167
Mecklenburg-West Pomerania (MV)[2]	23,171	· · ·	1,760	76
North Rhine-Westphalia (NW)	34,082	16,712	18,052	530
Rhineland-Palatinate (RP)	19,853	3,631	4,099	206
Saarland (SL)	2,570	1,056	1,066	415
Saxony (SN)[2]	18,413	· · ·	4,384	238
Saxony-Anhalt (ST)[2]	20,447	· · ·	2,581	126
Schleswig-Holstein (SH)	15,761	2,554	2,804	178
Thuringia (TH)[2]	16,172	· · ·	2,411	149

[1]June 2002. [2]1987 census population of West Berlin: 2,013,000.
[3]Reconstituted in 1990 in the Federal Republic.

On 31 Dec. 2000 there were 7,296,800 resident foreigners, including 1,998,500 Turks, 662,500 Yugoslavs, 619,100 Italians and 365,400 Greeks. More than 1·6m. of these were born in Germany. Germany's Muslim population, at 3·2m., is the second highest in Europe after that of France. In 2001 Germany received 88,287 asylum applications (the highest number of any European country), compared to

438,200 in 1992. The main countries of origin in 2001 were Iraq, Turkey, Yugoslavia and Afghanistan. 186,688 persons were naturalized in 2000, of whom 82,861 were from Turkey and 4,583 from the former USSR (170,381 in 1998). In 2000 there were 674,000 emigrants and 841,200 immigrants. New citizenship laws were introduced on 1 Jan. 2000, whereby a child of non-Germans will have German citizenship automatically if the birth is in Germany, if at the time of the birth one parent has made Germany his or her customary legal place of abode for at least eight years, and if this parent has had an unlimited residence permit for at least three years. Previously at least one parent had to hold German citizenship for the child to become a German national.

Populations of the 82 towns of over 100,000 inhabitants in Dec. 2000 (in 1,000):

Town (and Land)	Population (in 1,000)	Ranking by population	Town (and Land)	Population (in 1,000)	Ranking by population
Aachen (NW)	244·4	30	Krefeld (NW)	239·9	31
Augsburg (BY)	255·0	27	Leipzig (SN)	493·2	13
Bergisch Gladbach (NW)	105·7	77	Leverkusen (NW)	161·0	49
Berlin (BE)	3,382·2	1	Lübeck (SH)	213·4	35
Bielefeld (NW)	321·8	18	Ludwigshafen am Rhein		
Bochum (NW)	391·1	16	(RP)	162·2	48
Bonn (NW)	302·2	20	Magdeburg (ST)	231·5	33
Bottrop (NW)	120·6	62	Mainz (RP)	182·9	42
Braunschweig (NI)	245·8	29	Mannheim (BW)	306·7	19
Bremen (HB)	539·4	10	Moers (NW)	107·1	76
Bremerhaven (HB)	120·8	61	Mönchengladbach (NW)	263·0	25
Chemnitz (SN)	259·2	26	Mülheim a. d. Ruhr		
Cologne (NW)	962·9	4	(NW)	172·9	45
Cottbus (BB)	108·5	73=	Munich (BY)	1,210·2	3
Darmstadt (HE)	138·2	54	Münster (NW)	265·6	24
Dortmund (NW)	589·0	7	Neuss (NW)	150·0	51
Dresden (SN)	477·8	15	Nuremberg (BY)	488·4	14
Duisburg (NW)	514·9	12	Oberhausen (NW)	222·2	34
Düsseldorf (NW)	569·4	9	Offenbach am Main (HE)	117·5	65
Erfurt (TH)	200·6	38	Oldenburg (NI)	154·8	50
Erlangen (BY)	100·8	82	Osnabrück (NI)	164·1	47
Essen (NW)	595·2	6	Paderborn (NW)	139·1	53
Frankfurt am Main (HE)	646·6	5	Pforzheim (BW)	117·2	66=
Freiburg im Breisgau (BW)	205·1	36	Potsdam (BB)	129·3	55
Fürth (BY)	110·5	72	Recklingshausen (NW)	124·8	58
Gelsenkirchen (NW)	278·7	21	Regensburg (BY)	125·7	57
Gera (TH)	112·8	69	Remscheid (NW)	119·3	63=
Göttingen (NI)	124·1	59	Reutlingen (BW)	110·7	71
Hagen (NW)	203·2	37	Rostock (MV)	200·5	39
Halle (ST)	247·7	28	Saarbrücken (SL)	183·3	41
Hamburg (HH)	1,715·4	2	Salzgitter (NI)	112·3	70
Hamm (NW)	182·4	43	Schwerin (MV)	101·3	81
Hanover (NI)	515·0	11	Siegen (NW)	108·5	73=
Heidelberg (BW)	140·3	52	Solingen (NW)	165·0	46
Heilbronn (BW)	119·3	63=	Stuttgart (BW)	583·9	8
Herne (NW)	174·5	44	Ulm (BW)	117·2	66=
Hildesheim (NI)	103·9	78	Wiesbaden (HE)	270·1	23
Ingolstadt (BY)	115·7	68	Witten (NW)	103·2	79
Karlsruhe (BW)	278·6	22	Wolfsburg (NI)	121·8	60
Kassel (HE)	194·8	40	Wuppertal (NW)	366·4	17
Kiel (SH)	232·6	32	Würzburg (BY)	128·0	56
Koblenz (RP)	108·0	75	Zwickau (SN)	103·0	80

Berlin: From a fishing village on the River Spree Berlin grew, and, in 1307, formed a union with its sister town of Cölln. After the founding of the German Empire in 1871 it became the capital of the new Germany. It had a turbulent history culminating in the building of the Wall dividing East and West in 1961. The Wall fell in 1989 and after re-unification of East and West Germany in 1990, Berlin was declared the capital. Berlin was immortalized in Christopher Isherwood's novel *Goodbye To Berlin* about his experiences in the twenties and thirties and on which the film *Cabaret* was based.

The official language is German. Minor orthographical amendments were agreed in 1995. An agreement between German-speaking countries in Vienna on 1 July

1996 provided for minor orthographical changes and established a Commission for German Orthography in Mannheim. There have been considerable objections within Germany, particularly in the North, and many Länder are to decide their own language programmes for schools. Generally, both old and new spellings are acceptable.

SOCIAL STATISTICS

Calendar years:

	Marriages	Live births	Of these to single parents	Deaths	Divorces
1996	427,297	796,013	135,700	882,843	175,550
1997	422,776	812,173	145,833	860,389	187,802
1998	417,420	785,034	157,117	852,382	192,416
1999	430,674	770,744	170,634	846,330	190,590
2000	418,550	766,999	179,574	838,797	194,630
2001	389,591	734,475	183,816	828,541	197,498

Of the 418,550 marriages in 2000, 31,324 were between foreign males and German females, and 33,433 vice-versa. The average age of bridegrooms in 2000 was 35·0 years, and of brides 31·9. The average first-time marrying age for men was 31·2 and for women 28·4.

Rates (per 1,000 population), 2000: birth, 9·3; marriage, 5·1; death, 10·2; infant mortality, 4·4 per 1,000 births; stillborn rate, 4·0 per 1,000 births. Life expectancy, 1999: men, 74·3 years; women, 80·6. Suicide rates, 2000, per 100,000 population, 13·5 (men, 20·3; women, 7·0). Annual population growth rate, 1990–99, 0·4%; fertility rate, 1999, 1·3 births per woman.

Legislation of 1995 categorizes abortions as illegal, but stipulates that prosecutions will not be brought if they are performed in the first three months of pregnancy after consultation with a doctor. The annual abortion rate, at under ten per 1,000 women aged 15–44, is among the lowest in the world.

Since 1 Aug. 2001 same-sex couples have been permitted to exchange vows at registry offices. The law also gives them the same rights as heterosexual couples in inheritance and insurance law.

A UNICEF report published in 2000 showed that 10·7% of children in Germany live in poverty (in households with income below 50% of the national median). The report also showed that the poverty rate of children in lone-parent families was 51·2%, compared to 6·2% in two-parent families.

CLIMATE

Oceanic influences are only found in the northwest where winters are quite mild but stormy. Elsewhere a continental climate is general. To the east and south, winter temperatures are lower, with bright frosty weather and considerable snowfall. Summer temperatures are fairly uniform throughout. Berlin, Jan. 31°F (–0·5°C), July 66°F (19°C). Annual rainfall 22·5" (563 mm). Cologne, Jan. 36°F (2·2°C), July 66°F (18·9°C). Annual rainfall 27" (676 mm). Dresden, Jan. 30°F (–0·1°C), July 65°F (18·5°C). Annual rainfall 27·2" (680 mm). Frankfurt, Jan. 33°F (0·6°C), July 66°F (18·9°C). Annual rainfall 24" (601 mm). Hamburg, Jan. 31°F (–0·6°C), July 63°F (17·2°C). Annual rainfall 29" (726 mm). Hanover, Jan. 33°F (0·6°C), July 64°F (17·8°C). Annual rainfall 24" (604 mm). Munich, Jan. 28°F (–2·2°C), July 63°F (17·2°C). Annual rainfall 34" (855 mm). Stuttgart, Jan. 33°F (0·6°C), July 66°F (18·9°C). Annual rainfall 27" (677 mm).

CONSTITUTION AND GOVERNMENT

The Basic Law (*Grundgesetz*) was approved by the parliaments of the participating Länder and came into force on 23 May 1949. It is to remain in force until 'a constitution adopted by a free decision of the German people comes into being'. The Federal Republic is a democratic and social constitutional state on a parliamentary basis. The federation is constituted by the 16 Länder (states). The Basic Law decrees that the general rules of international law form part of the federal law. The constitutions of the Länder must conform to the principles of a republican, democratic and social state based on the rule of law. Executive power is vested in the Länder, unless the Basic Law prescribes or permits otherwise. Federal law takes precedence over state law.

Legislative power is vested in the *Bundestag* (Federal Assembly) and the *Bundesrat* (Federal Council). The Bundestag is currently composed of 603 members and is elected in universal, free, equal and secret elections for a term of four years. A party must gain 5% of total votes cast in order to gain representation in the Bundestag, although if a party has three candidates elected directly, they may take their seats even if the party obtains less than 5% of the national vote. The electoral system combines relative-majority and proportional voting; each voter has two votes, the first for the direct constituency representative, the second for the competing party lists in the Länder. All directly elected constituency representatives enter parliament, but if a party receives more 'indirect' than 'direct' votes, the first name in order on the party list not to have a seat becomes a member—the number of seats is increased by the difference ('overhang votes'). Thus the number of seats in the Bundestag varies, but is 598 regular members (for the 2002 election, down from 656 for the previous elections since reunification) plus the 'overhang votes'. The Bundesrat consists of 69 members appointed by the governments of the Länder in proportions determined by the number of inhabitants. Each *Land* has at least three votes.

The Head of State is the Federal *President,* who is elected for a five-year term by a *Federal Convention* specially convened for this purpose. This Convention consists of all the members of the Bundestag and an equal number of members elected by the Länder parliaments in accordance with party strengths, but who need not themselves be members of the parliaments. No president may serve more than two terms. Executive power is vested in the Federal government, which consists of the Federal *Chancellor,* elected by the Bundestag on the proposal of the Federal President, and the Federal Ministers, who are appointed and dismissed by the Federal President upon the proposal of the Federal Chancellor.

The Federal Republic has exclusive legislation on: (1) foreign affairs; (2) federal citizenship; (3) freedom of movement, passports, immigration and emigration, and extradition; (4) currency, money and coinage, weights and measures, and regulation of time and calendar; (5) customs, commercial and navigation agreements, traffic in goods and payments with foreign countries, including customs and frontier protection; (6) federal railways and air traffic; (7) post and telecommunications; (8) the legal status of persons in the employment of the Federation and of public law corporations under direct supervision of the Federal government; (9) trade marks, copyright and publishing rights; (10) co-operation of the Federal Republic and the Länder in the criminal police and in matters concerning the protection of the constitution, the establishment of a Federal Office of Criminal Police, as well as the combating of international crime; (11) federal statistics.

In the field of finance the Federal Republic has exclusive legislation on customs and financial monopolies and concurrent legislation on: (1) excise taxes and taxes on transactions, in particular, taxes on real-estate acquisition, incremented value and on fire protection; (2) taxes on income, property, inheritance and donations; (3) real estate, industrial and trade taxes, with the exception of the determining of the tax rates.

Federal laws are passed by the Bundestag and after their adoption submitted to the Bundesrat, which has a limited veto. The Basic Law may be amended only upon the approval of two-thirds of the members of the Bundestag and two-thirds of the votes of the Bundesrat.

Die Bundesrepublik Deutschland: Staatshandbuch. Cologne, annual

National Anthem. 'Einigkeit und Recht und Freiheit' ('Unity and right and freedom'); words by H. Hoffmann, tune by J. Haydn.

RECENT ELECTIONS

On 23 May 1999 Johannes Rau was elected President by the Federal Convention against two opponents, Dagmar Schipanski and Uta Ranke-Heinemann.

Bundestag elections were held on 22 Sept. 2002. The Social Democratic Party (SPD) of Chancellor Gerhard Schröder won 251 seats with 38·5% of votes cast (298 seats with 40·9% in 1998); the Christian Democratic Union/Christian Social Union (CDU/CSU; the CSU is a Bavarian party where the CDU does not stand) won 248 with 38·5% (245 with 35·2%); the Greens/Alliance 90, 55 with 8·6% (47 with 6·6%); the Free Democratic Party (FDP), 47 with 7·4% (44 with 6·2%); and the Party for

Democratic Socialism (PDS; former Communists), 2 with 4·3% (35 with 5·2%). Turn-out was 79·1%. With the SPD renewing its alliance with the Greens, the new government had a 9-seat majority in the Bundestag.

European Parliament. Germany has 99 representatives. At the June 1999 elections turn-out was 45·2%. The CDU won 43 seats with 39·3% of votes cast (group in European Parliament: European People's Party); the SPD, 33 with 30·7% (Party of European Socialists); the CSU, 10 with 9·4% (European People's Party); the Greens, 7 with 6·4% (Greens); PDS, 6 with 5·8% (Confederal Group of the European United Left).

CURRENT ADMINISTRATION

Federal President: Johannes Rau; b. 1931 (SPD; sworn in 1 July 1999).

Speaker of the Bundestag: Wolfgang Thierse (elected Oct. 1998).

In Oct. 1998 an SPD–Green party coalition was formed, the first time that the Green party had entered national government in Germany. Following elections in Sept. 2002 a new SPD–Green cabinet was formed. In March 2003 the cabinet was composed as follows:

Chancellor: Gerhard Schröder; b. 1944 (SPD; sworn in on 27 Oct. 1998 and re-elected in Sept. 2002).

Vice-Chancellor and Foreign Minister: Joschka Fischer (Greens/Alliance 90). *Interior:* Otto Schily (SPD). *Justice:* Brigitte Zypries (SPD). *Finance:* Hans Eichel (SPD). *Economy and Labour:* Wolfgang Clement (SPD). *Consumer Protection, Food and Agriculture:* Renate Künast (Greens/Alliance 90). *Defence:* Peter Struck (SPD). *Family Affairs, Senior Citizens, Women and Youth:* Renate Schmidt (SPD). *Health and Social Security:* Ulla Schmidt (SPD). *Transport, Housing and Construction:* Manfred Stolpe (SPD). *Environment, Nature Conservation and Nuclear Safety:* Jürgen Trittin (Greens/Alliance 90). *Education and Research:* Edelgard Bulmahn (SPD). *Economic Co-operation and Development:* Heidemarie Wieczorek-Zeul (SPD).

The leader of the opposition Christian Democratic Union (CDU) is Angela Merkel, an East German liberal, who was elected to succeed Wolfgang Schäuble in March 2000 in the wake of the financial scandal which had previously brought down Helmut Kohl. However, Edmund Stoiber of the Christian Social Union (the CDU's sister party in Bavaria) was chosen instead of Angela Merkel as the conservative challenger to Gerhard Schröder for the federal election of Sept. 2002.

Government Website: http://www.bundesregierung.de/

DEFENCE

Conscription was reduced from ten months to nine months from Jan. 2002. In July 1994 the Constitutional Court ruled that German armed forces might be sent on peacekeeping missions abroad. Germany has increased the number of professionals available for military missions abroad and sent troops to Afghanistan as part of the international alliance against terrorism in the aftermath of 11 Sept. 2001. The first time that German armed forces have been deployed in this way since the Second World War, the move has provoked controversy in Germany. Germany has 10,000 troops on international missions, a figure exceeded only by the USA. Since Jan. 2001 women have been allowed to serve in all branches of the military on the same basis as men.

In 2001 defence expenditure totalled US$26,902m. (US$328 per capita), representing 1·5% of GDP.

Army. The Army is organized in the Army Forces Command. The equipment of the former East German army is in store. Total strength was (2002) 203,200 (conscripts 85,900, women 4,600). There are Army reserves of 317,050.

The Territorial Army is organized into five Military Districts, under three Territorial Commands. Its main task is to defend rear areas and remains under national control even in wartime.

Navy. The Fleet Commander operates from a modern Maritime Headquarters at Glücksburg, close to the Danish border.

The fleet includes 14 diesel coastal submarines, 2 destroyers and 12 frigates. The main naval bases are at Wilhelmshaven, Olpenitz, Kiel, Eckernförde and Warnemünde.

The Naval Air Arm, 3,700 strong, is organized into three wings and includes 66 combat aircraft (Tornados and Atlantics) and 43 armed helicopters.

Personnel in 2002 numbered 25,500, including 5,000 conscripts and 1,000 women.

Air Force. Since 1970 the *Luftwaffe* has comprised the following commands: German Air Force Tactical Command, German Air Force Support Command (including two German Air Force Regional Support Commands—North and South) and General Air Force Office. Personnel in 2002 was 67,300 (16,100 conscripts). There were 446 combat aircraft, including Tornados, F-4Fs and MiG-29s.

INTERNATIONAL RELATIONS

A treaty of friendship with Poland signed on 17 June 1991 recognized the Oder-Neisse border and guaranteed minorities' rights in both countries.

Germany is a member of the UN, WTO, NATO, BIS, OECD, EU, Council of Europe, WEU, OSCE, CERN, Council of the Baltic Sea States, Danube Commission, Inter-American Development Bank, Asian Development Bank, IOM and the Antarctic Treaty. Germany is a signatory to the Schengen Accord which abolishes border controls between Germany, Austria, Belgium, Denmark, Finland, France, Greece, Iceland, Italy, Luxembourg, the Netherlands, Norway, Portugal, Spain and Sweden.

ECONOMY

Germany is the third largest economy in the world after the USA and Japan.

Services accounted for 68·7% of GDP in 2000, industry 30·1% and agriculture 1·2%.

According to the anti-corruption organization *Transparency International*, Germany ranked equal 18th in the world in a 2002 survey of the countries with the least corruption in business and government. It received 7·3 out of 10 in the annual index.

Overview. The German economy is described as a 'social market', in that it embraces industrial relations and company management, as well as social welfare and other aspects of government policy. The European Central Bank determines interest rates for the entire euro-zone, including Germany. The US economic slowdown has reduced demand for German exports. High inflation has been caused by high world oil prices. In 2001 a major income and business tax reform was introduced, the most ambitious in German post-war history.

Currency. On 1 Jan. 1999 the euro (EUR) became the legal currency in Germany; irrevocable conversion rate 1·95583 DM (deutschemark) to one euro. The euro, which consists of 100 cents, has been in circulation since 1 Jan. 2002. There are seven euro notes in different colours and sizes denominated in 500, 200, 100, 50, 20, 10 and 5 euros, and eight coins denominated in 2 and 1 euros, then 50, 20, 10, 5, 2 and 1 cents. It was still possible to make cash transactions in German marks until 28 Feb. 2002, although formally the mark had ceased to be legal tender on 31 Dec. 2001. Euro banknotes in circulation on 1 Jan. 2002 had a total value of €254·2bn.

Foreign exchange reserves were US$42,260m. in June 2002 and gold reserves were 110·79m. troy oz (95·18m. troy oz in 1997). Only the USA, with 262·00m. troy oz, had more in June 2002. Total money supply was €93,977m. in June 2002. Inflation was 1·3% in 2002, down from 2·5% in 2001.

Budget. In 2002 the budget deficit exceeded 3%, the target set by the European Stability and Growth Pact.

In July 2000 Chancellor Schröder pushed through the largest tax-cutting package in Germany's history. From 2001 corporation tax was cut from 40%/30% to 25%. The top rate of income tax was gradually to be reduced from 51% to 42% in 2005. In March 2003 Schröder announced 'Agenda 2010', a major economic reform package. It includes cuts in unemployment benefits, enhanced legislation to ease job protection rules and trimmed state pensions. The health system, among the world's most expensive, is also a core target. The boldest reform package in German post-war history, 'Agenda 2010' has encountered criticism from trade unionists and left-wingers within the SPD.

Since 1 Jan. 1979 tax revenues have been distributed as follows: *Federal government.* Income tax, 42·5%; capital yield and corporation tax, 50%; turnover tax, 67·5%; trade tax, 15%; capital gains, insurance and accounts taxes, 100%; excise duties (other than on beer), 100%. *Länder.* Income tax, 42·5%; capital yield and corporation tax, 50%; turnover tax, 32·5%; trade tax, 15%; other taxes, 100%. *Local authorities.* Income tax, 15%; trade tax, 70%; local taxes, 100%.

VAT is 16% (reduced rate, 7%).

Budget for 2001 (in €1m.):

Revenue	All public authorities	Federal portion
	Current	
Taxes	464,464	216,341
Economic activities	18,107	4,680
Interest	4,557	1,615
Current allocations and subsidies	130,916	3,786
Other receipts	29,524	2,940
minus equalising payments	117,251	. . .
	530,317	229,362
	Capital	
Sale of assets	20,339	8,508
Allocations for investment	25,824	2
Repayment of loans	10,217	3,288
Public sector borrowing	612	. . .
minus equalising payments	21,351	. . .
	35,641	11,798
Totals	565,099	241,160
Expenditure	*Current*	
Staff	169,984	27,002
Materials	78,665	26,089
Interest	69,001	39,369
Allocations and subsidies	325,561	141,480
minus equalising payments	117,251	. . .
	525,960	233,940
	Capital	
Construction	30,402	5,916
Acquisition of property	9,250	1,265
Allocations and subsidies	47,357	18,269
Loans	12,417	4,123
Acquisition of shares	2,682	683
Repayments in the public sector	833	. . .
minus equalising payments	21,351	. . .
	81,592	30,256
Totals	605,838	263,580

Performance. Real GDP growth was 1·8% in 1999 and 3·0% in 2000, the highest rate since reunification. However, this was followed by growth of just 0·6% in 2001, and at the end of 2001 Germany went into a recession for the first time since 1993 following two successive quarters of negative growth. In 2002 growth was down to 0·2%. Growth in the Länder of the former German Democratic Republic was estimated to be around 0·6% lower than the overall national average in both 1997 and 1998, and GDP per capita in the former GDR is only two-thirds of that in the former West Germany. Total GDP in 2001 was US$1,873·9bn., the third highest behind the USA and Japan.

Banking and Finance. The Deutsche Bundesbank (German Federal Bank) is the central bank and bank of issue. Its duty is to protect the stability of the currency. It is independent of the government but obliged to support the government's general policy. Its Governor is appointed by the government for eight years. The *President* is Ernst Welteke. Its assets were US$874,706m. in June 2001. Ranked by total assets it is the third largest bank in the world. Its market capitalization in June 2001 was

US\$45·7bn. The largest private banks are the Deutsche Bank, HypoVereinsbank, Dresdner Bank and Commerzbank. The former GDR central bank Staatsbank has become a public commercial bank. In April 2001 Dresdner Bank accepted a takeover offer from Allianz, the country's largest insurance company.

In 2001 there were 2,521 credit institutes, including 279 banks, 537 savings banks, 28 mortgage lenders and 1,619 credit societies. They are represented in the wholesale market by the 13 public sector Länder banks. Total assets, 2001, €6,386,110m. Savings deposits were €586,530m. in 2001. By Oct. 2000 approximately 6% of the German population were using e-banking.

A single stock exchange, the Deutsche Börse, was created in 1992, based on the former Frankfurt stock exchange in a union with the smaller exchanges in Berlin, Bremen, Düsseldorf, Hamburg, Hanover, Munich and Stuttgart. Share turnover on the Frankfurt stock exchange rose from 900bn. DM in 1992 to 2,200bn. DM in 1997, while trading on the other seven exchanges only rose from 340bn. DM in 1992 to 430bn. DM in 1997. Frankfurt processes 90% of equities trading in the country.

Germany attracted a record amount of foreign capital in 1999. The total of 96·2bn. DM was more than twice the 1998 total. France was the largest investor in 1999, with 50·9bn. DM, followed by Luxembourg with 17·8bn. DM and the USA with 17·4bn. DM. Investment abroad from Germany in 1999 was also a record high, at 172·1bn. DM, up from 146bn. DM in 1998, with Britain the leading target for investors (81·9bn. DM), followed by the USA (41·5bn. DM) and Sweden (10·4bn. DM).

Gull, L. *et al.*, *The Deutsche Bank, 1870–1995*. London, 1996

Weights and Measures. The metric system is in force.

ENERGY AND NATURAL RESOURCES

Environment. According to the *World Bank Atlas* Germany's carbon dioxide emissions were the equivalent of 10·1 tonnes per capita in 1998. An *Environmental Sustainability Index* compiled for the World Economic Forum meeting in Feb. 2002 ranked Germany 50th in the world, with 52·5%. The index measured the ability of countries to maintain favourable environmental conditions and examined various factors including pollution levels and the use or abuse of natural resources.

Germany is one of the world leaders in recycling. In 1996, 48% of all household waste was recycled. In 1998 recycling included 81% of glass, 81% of steel and 86% of aluminium cans.

Electricity. Installed capacity in 2000 was 120·86m. kW. In 2001 there were 19 nuclear reactors in operation, but in Dec. 2001 the German parliament decided to decommission the country's nuclear reactors over the next two decades. Production of electricity was 564·45bn. kWh in 2000, of which about 19% was nuclear. There is a moratorium on further nuclear plant construction. Consumption per capita was 5,681 kWh in 1998. In April 1998 the electricity market was liberalized, leading to huge cuts in bills for both industrial and residential customers. In June 2000 Veba and Viag merged to form E.ON, which became the world's largest private energy service provider.

By 2010 it is hoped that renewable energy sources, which currently account for 6% of electric power, will constitute 10% of the total.

Oil and Gas. The chief oilfields are in Emsland (Lower Saxony). In 2000, 3·12m. tonnes of crude oil were produced. Natural gas production was 16·9bn. cu. metres in 2000. Natural gas reserves were 330bn. cu. metres in 2000 and crude petroleum reserves 385m. bbls in 1997.

Wind. Germany is the world's leading producer of wind-power. By the end of 2001 there were 11,438 wind turbines with a total rated power of 8,753·8 MW.

Minerals. The main production areas are: North Rhine-Westphalia (for coal, iron and metal smelting-works), Central Germany (for lignite) and Lower Saxony (Salzgitter for iron ore; the Harz for metal ore).

Production (in tonnes), 2001: lignite, 175,360,537; coal, 27,361,098; salt, 6,537,000. In 2000 recoverable coal reserves were estimated at 67bn. tonnes. Germany is the world's largest lignite producer and the third largest salt producer after the USA and China.

Agriculture. In 1999 there were 11·82m. ha of arable land and 228,000 ha of permanent crops. Sown areas in 2001 (in 1,000 ha) included: wheat, 2,897·2; barley, 2,111·8; fodder, 1,538·7; rape, 1,138·0; rye, 837·0; sugarbeets, 447·7; maize, 396·5; potatoes, 282·1; oats, 233·3. Crop production, 2001 (and 1994) (in 1,000 tonnes): fodder, 53,968·1 (52,187·9); sugarbeets, 24,729·9 (24,211·3); wheat, 22,837·8 (16,480·5); barley, 13,494·6 (10,902·5); potatoes, 11,502·8 (9,668·6); rye, 5,132·3 (3,450·6); rapeseed, 4,160·1 (2,895·5); maize, 3,504·5 (2,446·0); oats, 1,151·0 (1,663·0). Germany is the world's largest producer of hops (30,000 tonnes in 2000) and the second largest producer of both barley and rye.

Figures compiled by the Soil Association, a British organization, show that in 1999 Germany set aside 422,000 ha (3% of its agricultural land) for the growth of organic crops. Organic food sales for Germany in 2000 were valued at US$2·4bn. (the second highest in the world behind the USA).

In 2001 there were 448,936 farms, of which 75,677 were between 2 and 5 ha and 26,324 over 100 ha. In 2001 there were 413,400 farmers assisted by 446,600 household members and 462,700 hired labourers (274,000 of them seasonal). In the former GDR in 1990 state farms were leased to farmers until 2004 and will then be sold. Collective farms have continued operating as co-operatives or been turned over to their former members.

In 2000 wine production was 9,852,000 hectolitres.

Livestock, 2001 (in 1,000): beef cattle, 14,603·1; milch cows, 4,548·6; sheep, 2,771·1; pigs, 25,783·9; horses, 506·2; poultry, 109,992·9. Livestock products, 2001 (in 1,000 tonnes): milk, 28,191; meat, 5,362; cheese, 1,015,819; eggs 134,607.

Forestry. Forest area in 2001 was 8,984,600 ha, of which about half was owned by the State. Timber production was 49·11m. cu metres in 2000. In recent years depredation has occurred through pollution with acid rain.

Fisheries. The total catch in 2000 was 217,300 tonnes (204,100 tonnes from marine waters). In 2000 the fishing fleet consisted of 44 ocean-going vessels and 2,247 coastal cutters.

INDUSTRY

The leading companies by market capitalization in Germany, excluding banking and finance, in Jan. 2002 were: Vodafone AG, formerly the Mannesmann AG (€108bn.); SAP AG (Systeme Anwendungen Produkte in der Datenverarbeitung), a software and computer services company (€76bn.); and Siemens AG, an electronic and electric equipment producer (€63bn.).

In 2001 a total of 728,978 firms were registered, 563,305 of which were classified as sole traders.

Output of major industrial products, 2001 (in 1,000 tonnes): cement, 38,099 (1999); rolled steel, 23,757; household plastics, 12,665 (1999); crude steel, 12,072 (2000); paper, 9,177; flour, 4,383; nitrogenous fertilizers, 1,079; aluminium, 1,000; refined copper, 544; synthetic fibre, 112; cotton yarn, 89; passenger cars, 5,487,000 (units); refrigerators, 3,059,000 (units); glass bottles, 11,913m. (units); beer, 10,637m. litres; soft drinks (excluding milk-based beverages), 18,975m. litres.

Labour. Retirement age is normally 65 years. At April 2001 the workforce was 40·55m. (17·86m. females), of whom 36·82m. (16·19m. females) were working and 3·74m. (1·78m. females) were unemployed. In April 2001 there were 27·7m. employees, 4·07m. self-employed or helping other family members and 2·26m. civil servants. 2·81m. foreign workers were employed in 2001. Of the 2001 workforce the year average for the number of employees in each industry was as follows: 10,974,000 in the public and private service sector, 9,583,000 in the retail, hotel and catering industries, 8,522,000 in the mining, processing and manufacturing industries, 4,429,000 in real estate and corporate services, 2,736,000 in the civil service (2000), 2,582,000 in the construction industry, 2,098,000 in transport and communications, 1,281,000 in banking and insurance, 940,000 in agriculture, forestry and fisheries (2000) and 300,000 in energy and water services (2000). In April 2001 there were 506,141 job vacancies. By 2000 there was a shortfall of 75,000 people in the information technology industry. In Aug. 2000 Germany launched a 'Green Card' project, aimed at attracting 20,000 telecommunication and information technology specialists from non-European Union countries in a bid to make up for the shortfall in qualified personnel. The card will authorize the holder to unrestricted employment in Germany for five years. By Aug. 2001 more than 8,000 recruits had found work. The standardized unemployment rate was 8·6% in Jan. 2003; the rate in the former GDR is more than double that in the states of the former Federal Republic of Germany. In June 2001, 47% of those unemployed were women and 34·3% were long-term unemployed. The number of people in employment in March 2002 was 38,340,000.

Trade Unions. Germany's largest trade union is *Vereinigte Dienstleistungs-gewerkschaft*, or *ver.di*, created in March 2001 as a result of the merger of five smaller unions. Representing 3m. workers in the service industry, it is the largest trade union outside of China.

The majority of trade unions belong to the *Deutscher Gewerkschaftsbund* (DGB, German Trade Union Federation), which had 8,310,783 (2,534,063 women) members in 1998, including 4,960,852 (980,078) manual workers, 2,431,727 (1,283,369) white-collar workers and 622,765 (178,392) civil servants. It functions as an umbrella organization for its eight member unions. DGB unions are organized in industrial branches such that only one union operates within each enterprise. The official GDR trade union organization (FDGB) was merged in the Deutscher Gewerkschaftsbund. Trade union membership declined significantly during the 1990s, from 11·8m. in 1991 to 8·3m. in 1999. Strikes are not legal unless called by a union with the backing of 75% of members. Certain public service employees are contractually not permitted to strike. 26,833 days were lost through strikes in 2001, up from 16,102 in 1998 but down from 247,460 in 1995. Between 1989 and 1998 strikes cost Germany an average of 11 days per 1,000 employees a year, compared to the EU average of 85 per 1,000.

INTERNATIONAL TRADE

In 2001 Germany had its highest ever annual trade surplus, at €95·5bn. for the year compared to €59·1bn. a year earlier.

Imports and Exports. Imports and exports in €1m.:

Imports				Exports			
1998	1999	2000	2001	1998	1999	2000	2001
423,452	444,797	538,311	542,774	488,371	510,008	597,440	638,268

Most important trading partners in 2001 (trade figures in €1m.). Imports: France, 51,671; Netherlands, 46,280; USA, 45,454; UK, 38,204; Italy, 35,677; Belgium, 28,446; Japan, 22,599. Exports: France, 70,672; USA, 67,307; UK, 53,271; Italy, 47,516; Netherlands, 39,297; Austria, 32,645; Belgium, 31,386; Switzerland, 27,611.

Distribution of imports and exports by commodities in 2001 (in €1m.): finished goods, 384,657 and 545,512; semi-finished goods, 48,603 and 28,686; foodstuffs, 40,030 and 27,259; raw materials, 29,405 and 4,076; drinks and tobacco, 6,423 and 4,874; live animals, 440 and 460.

Germany is the second largest trading nation in the world after the USA.

Trade Fairs. Germany has a number of major annual trade fairs, among the most important of which are Internationale Grüne Woche Berlin (International Green Week Berlin—Exhibition for the Food Industry, Agriculture and Horticulture), held in Berlin in Jan.; Ambiente (for high quality consumer goods and new products), held in Frankfurt in Feb.; ITB Berlin (International Tourism Exchange), held in Berlin in March; CeBit (World Business Fair for Office Automation, Information Technology and Telecommunications), held in Hanover in March; Hannover Messe (the World's Leading Fair for Industry, Automation and Innovation), held in Hanover, in April; Internationale Funkausstellung Berlin (Your World of Consumer Electronics), held in Berlin in late Aug./early Sept.; and Frankfurter Buchmesse (Frankfurt Book Fair) held in Frankfurt in Oct. Hanover's trade fair site is the largest in Europe and Frankfurt's the second largest.

COMMUNICATIONS

Roads. In 2001 the total length of the road network was 230,774 km, including 11,712 km of motorway *(Autobahn)*, 41,282 km of federal highways and 86,303 km of secondary roads. The motorway network is the largest in Europe. On 1 Jan.

2002 there were 53,305,900 motor vehicles, including: passenger cars, 44,383,300 (approximately one car for every two persons); trucks, 2,649,100; buses, 86,500; motorcycles, 3,557,400. In 2000, 7,943m. passengers were transported by long-distance road traffic. The estimated average distance travelled by a passenger car in the year 1997 was 12,700 km. In 2001, 336,625 motorists were arrested at the scene of an accident for driving offences, of which 16,151 were alcohol related and 68,063 for exceeding speed limits. Road casualties in 2001 (and 2000) totalled 501,752 (511,577), with 494,775 injured (504,074) and 6,977 killed (7,503).

Rail. Legislation of 1993 provides for the eventual privatization of the railways, but in 2001 DB Regio, part of Deutsche Bahn, still had more than 90% of the market. On 1 Jan. 1994 West German Bundesbahn and the former GDR Reichsbahn were amalgamated as the Deutsche Bahn, a joint-stock company in which track, long-distance passenger traffic, regional passenger traffic and goods traffic are run as four separate administrative entities. These were intended after 3–5 years to become themselves companies, at first under a holding company, and ultimately independent. Initially the government will hold all the shares. Length of railway in 2000 was 44,730 km (1,435 mm gauge) of which 19,518 km were electrified. There were 5,317 stations. 2,001m. passengers were carried in 2001 and 288·2m. tonnes of freight.

There are metros in Berlin (136 km), Hamburg (95 km), Frankfurt am Main (51 km), Munich (63 km) and Nuremberg (23 km), and tram/light rail networks in 56 cities.

Civil Aviation. Lufthansa, the largest carrier, was set up in 1953 and was originally 75% state-owned. The government sold its final shares in 1997. Other airlines include Condor, Deutsche-British Airways, Hapag Lloyd, Eurowings and LTU International Airways. Lufthansa flew 629·9m. km in 1999, carrying 41,892,700 passengers (27,276,400 on international flights). In 2001 civil aviation had 633 aircraft over 20 tonnes (583 jets).

In 2001 there were 71·41m. passenger arrivals and 71·50m. departures. Main international airports: Bremen, Cologne-Bonn, Düsseldorf, Frankfurt am Main, Hamburg (Fuhlsbüttel), Hanover, Leipzig, Munich, Nuremberg, Stuttgart and three at Berlin (Tegel, Tempelhof and Schönefeld). Airports at Dortmund, Dresden, Frankfurt (Hahn), Lübeck, Paderborn, Rostock and Saarbrücken are used for only a few scheduled international flights in addition to domestic flights.

In 2001 Frankfurt am Main handled 48,197,000 passengers (37,087,000 on international flights in 1999) and 1,466,455 tonnes of freight. It is the busiest airport in Europe in terms of freight handled. Munich was the second busiest German airport in terms of passenger traffic in 2001 (23·41m.) but third for freight. Cologne-Bonn was the second busiest in 2001 for freight, with 439,518 tonnes, but only seventh for passenger traffic.

Shipping. At 31 Dec. 2001 the mercantile marine comprised 1,114 ocean-going vessels of 6,530,000 GRT. Sea-going ships in 2001 carried 246·05m. tonnes of cargo. Navigable rivers and canals have a total length of 7,472 km. The inland-waterways fleet on 31 Dec. 2001 included 984 motor freight vessels totalling 1·16m. tonnes and 313 tankers of 460,060 tonnes. 236·10m. tonnes of freight were transported in 2001. In 1999 vessels totalling 320,033,000 NRT entered ports and vessels totalling 318,498,000 NRT cleared.

Telecommunications. Telecommunications were deregulated in 1989. On 1 Jan. 1995, three state-owned joint-stock companies were set up: Deutsche Telekom, Postdienst and Postbank. The partial privatization of Deutsche Telekom began in Nov. 1996.

In 2000 there were 50·2m. telephone main lines, equivalent to 610·5 per 1,000 population. In 2001, 96·4% of all households had a private telephone. There were 27·6m. PCs in use in 2000 (336 per 1,000 persons). In Nov. 2001 Germany had 55·06m. mobile phone subscribers, the highest number in any European country. Over 80% of users subscribe with either T-Mobile or D2 Vodafone. With 22·30m. subscribers in Nov. 2001 T-Mobile has the largest number of subscribers of any mobile telephone company in Europe. D2 Vodafone has the second highest number of subscribers, with 21·84m. Germany is the country with the second highest number of Internet users in Europe after the UK, with approximately 32·1m. in Aug. 2002 (nearly 39% of the population). In 1997 there were 5·6m. fax transmitters.

Postal Services. In 2000 there were 13,663 post offices and 8,073 affiliated agents. A total of 21,760m. pieces of mail were processed during the year.

SOCIAL INSTITUTIONS

Justice. Justice is administered by the federal courts and by the courts of the Länder. In criminal procedures, civil cases and procedures of non-contentious jurisdiction the courts on the *Land* level are the local courts *(Amtsgerichte)*, the regional courts *(Landgerichte)* and the courts of appeal *(Oberlandesgerichte)*. Constitutional federal disputes are dealt with by the Federal Constitutional Court *(Bundesverfassungsgericht)* elected by the Bundestag and Bundesrat. The Länder also have constitutional courts. In labour law disputes the courts of the first and second instance are the labour courts and the *Land* labour courts, and in the third instance the Federal Labour Court *(Bundesarbeitsgericht)*. Disputes about public law in matters of social security, unemployment insurance, maintenance of war victims and similar cases are dealt with in the first and second instances by the social courts and the *Land* social courts and in the third instance by the Federal Social Court *(Bundessozialgericht)*. In most tax matters the finance courts of the Länder are competent, and in the second instance the Federal Finance Court *(Bundesfinanzhof)*. Other controversies of public law in non-constitutional matters are decided in the first and second instance by the administrative and the higher administrative courts *(Oberverwaltungsgerichte)* of the Länder, and in the third instance by the Federal Administrative Court *(Bundesverwaltungsgericht)*.

For the inquiry into maritime accidents the admiralty courts *(Seeämter)* are competent on the *Land* level and in the second instance the Federal Admiralty Court *(Bundesoberseeamt)* in Hamburg.

The death sentence was abolished in the Federal Republic of Germany in 1949 and in the German Democratic Republic in 1987.

The population in penal institutions in 2001 was 60,421. 1,658 prisoners were serving life sentences.

Religion. In 2000 there were 26,614,000 Protestants in 16,896 parishes, 26,817,000 Roman Catholics in 13,214 parishes; and in 2001, 93,326 Jews with 27 rabbis (in 2000) and 70 synagogues (in 2000).

There are five Roman Catholic archbishoprics (Bamberg, Cologne, Freiburg, Munich and Freising, Paderborn) and 23 bishoprics. Chairman of the German Bishops' Conference is Cardinal Karl Lehmann, Bishop of Mainz. A concordat between Germany and the Holy See dates from 10 Sept. 1933. In Feb. 2001 there were nine Cardinals.

The Evangelical (Protestant) Church (EKD) consists of 24 member-churches including 7 Lutheran Churches, 8 United-Lutheran-Reformed, 2 Reformed Churches and 1 Confederation of United member Churches: 'Church of the Union'. Its organs are the Synod, the Church Conference and the Council under the chairmanship of Rev. Manfred Kock. There are also some 12 Evangelical Free Churches.

Education. Education is compulsory for children aged 6 to 15. After the first four (or six) years at primary school *(Grundschulen)* children attend post-primary *(Hauptschulen)*, secondary modern *(Realschulen)*, grammar *(Gymnasien)*, or comprehensive schools *(Integrierte Gesamtschulen)*. Secondary modern school lasts six years and grammar school nine. Entry to higher education is by the final Grammar School Certificate *(Abitur*—Higher School Certificate). There are also schools for physically disabled children and those with other special needs *(Sonderschulen)*.

In 2000–01 there were 3,649 kindergartens with 64,704 pupils and 4,619 teachers; 17,275 primary schools with 3,552,935 pupils and 191,102 teachers; 3,123 special schools with 420,427 pupils and 67,232 teachers; 11,402 secondary modern schools with 2,771,455 pupils and 174,832 teachers; 3,166 grammar schools with 2,256,861 pupils and 152,775 teachers; 964 comprehensive schools with 619,458 pupils and 47,841 teachers.

In 2000–01 there were 671,569 working teachers, of whom 441,250 were female. The adult literacy rate in 1998 was at least 99%.

In 1998 total expenditure on education came to 155,049m. DM. In 1995 total expenditure on education came to 4·8% of GNP and represented 9·5% of total government expenditure.

Vocational education is provided in part-time, full-time and advanced vocational schools (*Berufs-, Berufsaufbau-, Berufsfach-* and *Fachschulen,* including *Fachschulen für Technik* and *Schulen des Gesundheitswesens).* Occupation-related, part-time vocational training of 6 to 12 hours per week is compulsory for all (including unemployed) up to the age of 18 years or until the completion of the practical vocational training. Full-time vocational schools comprise courses of at least one year. They prepare for commercial and domestic occupations as well as specialized occupations in the field of handicrafts. Advanced full-time vocational schools are attended by pupils over 18. Courses vary from six months to three or more years.

In 2000–01 there were 9,773 full- and part-time vocational schools with 2,681,837 students and 113,481 teachers.

Higher Education. In the winter term of the 2001–02 academic year there were 355 institutes of higher education *(Hochschulen)* with 1,860,698 students, including 91 universities (1,186,778 students), 7 polytechnics *(Gesamthochschulen;* 141,522 students), 6 teacher training colleges (15,029), 16 theological seminaries (2,408), 50 schools of art (30,646), 156 technical colleges (451,593) and 29 management schools (32,722). Only 290,530 students (15·6%) were in their first year.

Health. In 2000 there were 294,676 doctors (359 doctors for every 100,000 people), 63,156 dentists and 53,223 pharmacists. In 2000 there were 2,252 hospitals with 565,268 beds. In 2000 Germany spent 10·6% of its GDP on health, public spending amounting to 75·1% of the total.

Welfare. *Social Health Insurance* (introduced in 1883). Wage-earners and apprentices, salaried employees with an income below a certain limit and social insurance pensioners are compulsorily insured within the state system. Voluntary insurance is also possible.

Benefits: medical treatment, medicines, hospital and nursing care, maternity benefits, death benefits for the insured and their families, sickness payments and out-patients' allowances. Economy measures of Dec. 1992 introduced prescription charges related to recipients' income.

51·99m. persons were insured in 2001 (29·04m. compulsorily). Number of cases of incapacity for work (2000) totalled 37·18m., and the number of working days lost were 283·57m. (men) and 227·88m. (women). Total disbursements in 2000 were €125,943m.

Accident Insurance (introduced in 1884). Those insured are all persons in employment or service, apprentices and the majority of the self-employed and the unpaid family workers.

Benefits in the case of industrial injuries and occupational diseases: medical treatment and nursing care, sickness payments, pensions and other payments in cash and in kind, surviving dependants' pensions.

Number of insured in 2000, 57·96m.; number of current pensions, 1,143,131; total disbursements, €9,682m.

Workers' and Employees' Old-Age Insurance Scheme (introduced in 1889). All wage-earners and salaried employees, the members of certain liberal professions and—subject to certain conditions—self-employed craftsmen are compulsorily insured. The insured may voluntarily continue to insure when no longer liable to do so or increase the insurance.

Benefits: measures designed to maintain, improve and restore the earning capacity; pensions paid to persons incapable of work, old age and surviving dependants' pensions.

Number of insured in May 2000, 43·13m. (20·28m. women); number of current pensions (in July 2001), 23·26m.; pensions to widows and widowers, 5·44m. Total disbursements in 2000, €213,471m.

There are also special retirement and unemployment pension schemes for miners and farmers, assistance for war victims and compensation payments to members of German minorities in East European countries expelled after the Second World War and persons who suffered damage because of the war or in connection with the currency reform.

Family Allowances. €25,941m. were dispensed to 8·94m. recipients (0·96m. foreigners) in 2001 on behalf of 14·94m. children. Paid child care leave is available for three years to mothers or fathers.

Unemployment Allowances. In 2001, 1·72m. persons (0·73m. women) were receiving unemployment benefit and 1·48m. (0·63m. women) earnings-related benefit. Total expenditure on these and similar benefits (e.g. short-working supplement, job creation schemes) was 98,700m. DM in 2000.

Public Welfare (introduced in 1962). In 2000, €23·32m. were distributed to 2·68m. recipients (1·51m. women).

Public Youth Welfare. For supervision of foster children, official guardianship, assistance with adoptions and affiliations, social assistance in juvenile courts, educational assistance and correctional education under a court order. A total of €18,465m. was spent on recipients in 1999.

Pension Reform. A major reform of the German pension system became law on 11 May 2001. The changes entail a cut in the value of the average state pension from 70% to approximately 67% of average final earnings by 2030. There will be incentives in the form of tax concessions and direct payments to encourage individuals to build up supplementary provision by contributing up to 4% of their earnings into private-sector personal pensions. In the long term these could supply up to 40% of overall pension income, with 60% coming from the state as opposed to 85% prior to the changes.

CULTURE

Broadcasting. There are two public service broadcasting companies—ARD (*Arbeitsgemeinschaft der öffentlich-rechtlichen Rundfunkanstalten der Bundesrepublik Deutschland*) and ZDF (*Zweites Deutsches Fernsehen*)—plus many private and regional stations, notably RTL and SAT1. ARD is the co-ordinating body for television and radio. It represents public-right broadcasters and organizes co-operation between them. Deutsche Welle Fernsehen (DW-tv) is the foreign service broadcaster. Most German households now subscribe to cable television. In 2001 there were 35·50m TV licences. There were 17·3m. cable TV subscribers in 1997—52% of all households with licences had cable TV, compared to 67% in the USA and 11% in the UK.

Public service radio is provided by ARD and ZDF via DeutschlandRadio. Private radio stations also broadcast in the regions. Deutsche Welle (DW-radio) broadcasts overseas. In 2001 there were 40·25m. radio licences.

Cinema. In 2000 there were 4,612 cinemas with a total seating capacity of 870,150. In 2000, 75 feature films were made. A total of 152·5m. visits to the cinema were made in 2000; gross box office receipts came to €824·5m. in 2000. In 2001 German films took 18% of the national market, up from 10% in 1998.

Press. The daily press is mainly regional. The dailies with the highest circulation are (average figures for Jan.–March 2001): the tabloid *Bild* (Hamburg, 4·40m. copies per day); *Westdeutsche Allgemeine Zeitung* (Essen, 0·56m.); *Süddeutsche Zeitung* (Munich, 0·44m.); and *Frankfurter Allgemeine Zeitung* (0·41m.). Other important opinion leaders are the weeklies *Die Zeit, Die Woche* and *Rheinischer Merkur. Bild* has the highest circulation of any paper in Europe. In 2000, 355 newspapers and 408 newsstand magazines were published with respective circulations of 24m. and 127m. The seven main Sunday papers sold 4·5m. copies. The total circulation of daily newspapers in Germany is the highest in Europe. 78% of the population over the age of 14 regularly read a daily newspaper. There are also 230 online newspapers. Among magazines the most widely read are *stern* (7·51m. copies per issue according to figures published in July 2001), *Focus* and *Der Spiegel*. In 2001 a total of 68,399 book titles were published.

Tourism. In 2001 there were 54,553 places of accommodation with 2,494,462 beds (including 13,092 hotels with 923,787 beds). 16,886,643 foreign visitors and 90,506,261 tourists resident in Germany spent a total of 326,633,155 nights in holiday accommodation. Berlin is the most visited city with 4,929,578 visitors in 2001, and Bavaria the most visited Land with 22,748,035. More foreign visitors were from the Netherlands (2,053,500) than any other country. In 2001 tourism brought in €19,216m.

Festivals. The Munich Opera Festival takes place annually in June–July, and the Wagner Festspiele (the Wagner Festival) in Bayreuth is held from late July to the end of Aug. The Oberammergau Passion Play, which takes place every ten years, was last held in 2000. Karneval (Fasching in some areas), in Jan./Feb./March, is a major event in the annual calendar in cities such as Cologne, Munich, Düsseldorf and Mainz. The Berlin Love Parade, which takes place in mid-July, is Europe's second largest street party. Oktoberfest, Munich's famous beer festival which first began in 1810, takes place each year in late Sept. and early Oct. and regularly attracts 7m. visitors.

Libraries. In 2000 there were 11,332 public libraries, 7 national libraries and 237 Higher Education libraries; they and other libraries held a combined 322,636,000 volumes. There were 12,313,000 active users in 2000, with 375,108,000 loans.

Theatre and Opera. In 1999–2000 there were 153 theatre companies, performing on 731 stages. Audiences totalled 20·19m.

Museums and Galleries. In 2000 there were 4,716 museums which attracted 99,560,000 visitors.

DIPLOMATIC REPRESENTATIVES

Of Germany in the United Kingdom (23 Belgrave Sq., 1 Chesham Place, London, SW1X 8PZ)
Ambassador: Thomas Matussek.

Of the United Kingdom in Germany (Wilhelmstrasse 70, 10117 Berlin)
Ambassador: Peter J. Torry.

Of Germany in the USA (4645 Reservoir Rd, NW, Washington, D.C., 20007)
Ambassador: Wolfgang Ischinger.

Of the USA in Germany (Neustädtische Kirchstr. 4, 10117 Berlin)
Ambassador: Daniel Coats.

Of Germany to the United Nations
Ambassador: Gunter Pleuger.

FURTHER READING

Statistisches Bundesamt. *Statistisches Jahrbuch für die Bundesrepublik Deutschland; Wirtschaft und Statistik* (monthly, from 1949); *Das Arbeitsgebiet der Bundesstatistik* (latest issue 1997; Abridged English version: *Survey of German Federal Statistics*).

Ardagh, J., *Germany and the Germans.* 3rd ed. London, 1996
Balfour, M., *Germany: the Tides of Power.* Routledge, London, 1992
Bark, D. L. and Gress, D. R., *A History of West Germany, 1945–1991.* 2nd ed. 2 vols. Oxford, 1993
Betz, H. G., *Postmodern Politics in Germany.* London, 1991
Blackbourn, D., *Fontana History of Germany, 1780–1918: The Long Nineteenth Century.* Fontana, London, 1997
Blackbourn, D. and Eley, G., *The Peculiarities of German History.* Oxford University Press, 1985
Carr, W., *A History of Germany, 1815–1990.* 4th ed. Edward Arnold, London, 1995
Childs, D., *Germany in the 20th Century.* London, 1991.—*The Stasi: The East German Intelligence and Security Service.* Macmillan, London, 1999
Dennis, M., *The German Democratic Republic: Politics, Economics and Society.* Pinter, London, 1987

Edinger, L. J., *West German Politics*. Columbia Univ. Press, New York, 1986

Fulbrook, Mary, *A Concise History of Germany*. CUP, 1991.—*The Divided Nation: A History of Germany, 1918–1990*. CUP, 1992.—*German National Identity After the Holocaust*. Polity, Oxford, 1999.—*Interpretation of the Two Germanies, 1945–1997*. Macmillan, London, 1999

Glees, A., *Reinventing Germany: German Political Development since 1945*. Berg, Oxford, 1996

Heneghan, Tom, *Unchained Eagle: Germany After the Wall*. Reuters, London, 2000

Huelshoff, M. G., *et al.*, (eds.) *From Bundesrepublik to Deutschland: German Politics after Reunification*. Michigan Univ. Press, 1993

Kielinger, T., *Crossroads and Roundabouts, Junctions in German-British Relations*. Bonn, 1997

Langewiesche, Dieter, *Liberalism in Germany*. Macmillan, London, 1999

Loth, W., *Stalin's Unwanted Child—The Soviet Union, the German Question and the Founding of the GDR*. St Martin's Press, New York, 1998

Maier, C. S., *Dissolution: The Crisis of Communism and the End of East Germany*. Princeton Univ. Press, N.J., 1997

Marsh, D., *The New Germany: At the Crossroads*. London, 1990

Merkl, Peter H. (ed.) *The Federal Republic of Germany at Fifty: The End of a Century of Turmoil*. Macmillan, London, 1999

Müller, Jan-Werner, *Another Country: German Intellectuals, Unification and National Identity*, Yale, New Haven (CT) and London, 2000

Neville, P., *Appeasing Hitler: The Diplomacy of Sir Neville Henderson*. Macmillan, London, 1999

Nicholls, A. J., *The Bonn Republic: West German Democracy, 1945–1990*. Addison-Wesley, Harlow, 1998

Olsen, Jonathan, *Nature and Nationalism: Right-wing Ecology and the Politics of Identity in Contemporary Germany*. Macmillan, London, 2000

Orlow, D., *A History of Modern Germany, 1871 to the Present*. 4th ed. Prentice Hall, New York, 1994

Parkes, K. S., *Understanding Contemporary Germany*. Routledge, London, 1996

Pulzer, P., *German Politics, 1945–1995*. OUP, 1995

Sa'adah, Anne, *Germany's Second Chance: Trust, Justice and Democratization*. Harvard Univ. Press, 1999

Schmidt, H., *Handeln für Deutschland*. Berlin, 1993

Schwartz, H-P., translator, Willmot, L., *Konrad Adenauer Vol 1: From the German Empire to the Federal Republic, 1876–1952*. Berghahn Books, Oxford and New York, 1995

Schwartz, H-P., translator, Willmot, L., *Konrad Adenauer Vol 2: The Statesman: 1952–1967*. Berghahn Books, Oxford and New York, 1997

Schweitzer, C.-C., Karsten, D., Spencer, R., Cole, R. T., Kommers, D. P. and Nicholls, A. J. (eds.) *Politics and Government in Germany, 1944–1994: Basic Documents*. 2nd ed. Berghahn Books, Oxford, 1995

Sereny, Gitta, *The German Trauma: Experiences and Reflections, 1938–99*. Penguin Press, London, 2000

Sinn, G. and Sinn, H.-W., *Jumpstart: the Economic Reunification of Germany*. MIT Press, Boston (MA), 1993

Smyser, W. R., *The Economy of United Germany: Colossus at the Crossroads*. New York, 1992.—*From Yalta to Berlin: The Cold War Struggle over Germany*. St Martin's, New York and Macmillan, London, 1999

Stürmer, M., *Die Grenzen der Macht*. Berlin, 1992

Taylor, R., *Berlin and its Culture*. Yale Univ. Press, 1997

Thompson, W. C., *et al.*, *Historical Dictionary of Germany*. Scarecrow Press, Metuchen (NJ), 1995

Turner, Barry, (ed.) *Germany Profiled*. Macmillan, London, 1999

Turner, H. A., *Germany from Partition to Reunification*. 2nd ed. [of *Two Germanies since 1945*]. Yale Univ. Press, 1993

Tusa, A., *The Last Division – A History of Berlin, 1945–1989*. Perseus Books, Reading, Mass., 1997

Wallace, I., *East Germany: the German Democratic Republic*. [Bibliography] ABC-Clio, Oxford and Santa Barbara (CA), 1987

Watson, A., *The Germans: Who Are They Now?* 2nd ed. London, 1994

Williams, C., *Adenauer: The Father of the New Germany*. Little, Brown, London, 2000

Other more specialized titles are listed under CONSTITUTION AND GOVERNMENT *and* BANKING AND FINANCE, *above*.

National statistical office: Statistiches Bundesamt, D-65189 Wiesbaden, Gustav Stresemann Ring 11. *President:* Johann Hahlen. *Website:* http://www.destatis.de

National libraries: Deutsche Bibliothek, Zeppelinallee 4–8; Frankfurt am Main. *Director:* Elisabeth Niggemann; (Berliner) Staatsbibliothek Preussischer Kulturbesitz, Potsdamer Str. 33, Postfach 1407, D-10785 Berlin. *Director:* Vacant.

THE LÄNDER

BADEN-WÜRTTEMBERG

KEY HISTORICAL EVENTS

The *Land* is a combination of former states. Baden (the western part of the present *Land*) became a united margravate in 1771, after being divided as Baden-Baden and Baden-Durlach since 1535; Baden-Baden was predominantly Catholic, and Baden-Durlach predominantly Protestant. The margrave became an ally of Napoleon, ceding land west of the Rhine and receiving northern and southern territory as compensation. In 1805 Baden became a grand duchy and in 1806 a member state of the Confederation of the Rhine, extending from the Main to Lake Constance. In 1815 it was a founder-state of the German Confederation. A constitution was granted by the grand duke in 1818, but later rulers were less liberal and there was revolution in 1848, put down with Prussian help. The grand Duchy was abolished and replaced by a *Land* in 1919.

In 1949 Baden was combined with Württemberg to form three states; the three were brought together as one in 1952.

Württemberg, having been a duchy since 1495, became a kingdom in 1805 and joined the Confederations as did Baden. A constitution was granted in 1819 and the state remained liberal. In 1866 the king allied himself with Austria against Prussia, but in 1870 joined Prussia in war against France. The liberal monarchy came to an end with the abdication of William II in 1918, and Württemberg became a state of the German Republic. In 1945 the state was divided between Allied occupation authorities but the divisions ended in 1952.

TERRITORY AND POPULATION

Baden-Württemberg comprises 35,751 sq. km, with a population (at 30 June 2002) of 10,630,723 (5,415,363 females, 5,215,505 males).

The *Land* is divided into 4 administrative regions, 9 urban and 35 rural districts, and numbers 1,111 communes. The capital is Stuttgart.

SOCIAL STATISTICS

Statistics for calendar years:

	Live births	Marriages	Divorces	Deaths
1998	111,056	55,693	21,833	96,810
1999	107,973	56,437	21,697	96,933
2000	106,182	55,422	22,050	95,354
2001	101,366	51,382	22,774	94,096

CONSTITUTION AND GOVERNMENT

The *Land* Baden-Württemberg is a merger of the three *Länder*, Baden, Württemberg-Baden and Württemberg-Hohenzollern. The merger was approved by a plebiscite held on 9 Dec. 1951, when 70% of the population voted in its favour. It has six votes in the Bundesrat.

RECENT ELECTIONS

At the elections to the 128-member Diet of 25 March 2001, turn-out was 62·6%. The Christian Democrats won 63 seats with 44·8% of the vote, the Social Democrats 45 with 33·3%, the Free Democrats 10 with 8·1% and the Greens 10 with 7·7%. The Republicans only received 4·4% of the vote, and therefore won no seats.

CURRENT ADMINISTRATION

Erwin Teufel (CDU) is *Prime Minister* (Minister President).

Government Website: http://www.baden-wuerttemberg.de

ECONOMY

Performance. GDP in 2001 was €302,542m., which amounted to 14·7% of Germany's total GDP. Manufacturing industries (*Verarbeitendes Gewerbe*) provide around 32·4% of GDP (36·6% in 1991). Real GDP growth in 2001 was 2·0%. Services enterprises account for nearly 28·4% of GDP, compared to 23·3% as recently as 1991.

Banking and Finance. There is a stock exchange in Stuttgart. Turnover of shares and bonds in 2001 was €65·3bn.

ENERGY AND NATURAL RESOURCES

Electricity. Hydro-electric power is a significant source of electricity in the Land.

Oil and Gas. The amount of oil and gas produced in Baden-Württemberg was insignificant and ceased altogether in Sept. 1997.

Agriculture. Area and yield of the most important crops:

	Area (in 1,000 ha)			Yield (in 1,000 tonnes)		
	1999	2000	2001	1999	2000	2001
Wheat	210·6	233·5	218·4	1,323·5	1,617·5	1,623·9
Sugarbeet	22·7	21·1	20·9	1,371·0	1,427·5	1,266·0
Barley	199·0	187·8	201·5	1,004·1	1,061·0	1,121·2
Potatoes	8·1	7·8	6·8	233·5	309·3	240·2
Oats	40·3	41·6	42·8	200·5	223·0	235·9
Rye	10·5	11·3	10·3	55·1	60·6	57·3

Livestock in May 2002 (in thousands): cattle, 1,171·3 (including 410·0 milch cows); pigs, 2,288·6; sheep, 319·7; poultry, 5,185·6 (May 2001).

INDUSTRY

Baden-Württemberg is one of Germany's most industrialized states. In 2001, 8,794 establishments (with 20 or more employees) employed 1,273,644 persons; of these, 273,627 were employed in machine construction (excluding office machines, data processing equipment and facilities); 234,229 in car manufacture; 211,870 in electrical engineering; 23,158 in the textile industry.

Labour. Economically active persons totalled 4,976,800 at the 1%-EU-sample survey of May 2001: 4·42m. were employees and 556,600 were self-employed (including family workers); 2,008,800 were engaged in power supply, mining, manufacturing and building; 973,200 in commerce and transport; 109,500 in agriculture and forestry; 1,885,400 in other industries and services. There were 264,213 unemployed in 2001, a rate of 5·5%.

INTERNATIONAL TRADE

Imports and Exports. Total imports (2001): €78,117·1m. Total exports: €101,342·3m., of which €48,789·3m. went to the EU. Machinery exports totalled €24,519m. and automotive exports €26,540m.

COMMUNICATIONS

Roads. On 1 Jan. 2001 there were 27,455 km of 'classified' roads, comprising 1,029 km of Autobahn, 4,433 km of federal roads, 9,937 km of first-class and 12,056 km of second-class highways. Motor vehicles, at 1 Jan. 2002, numbered 7,258,549, including 5,975,963 passenger cars, 9,706 buses, 307,203 lorries, 336,156 tractors and 531,388 motorcycles.

Rail. Railway track operated by Deutsche Bahn AG covered 3,819 km in 1998. In addition, 488 km of track was operated by private railway companies.

Civil Aviation. The largest airport in Baden-Württemberg is at Stuttgart, which in 2000 handled 7,977,651 passengers (5,378,319 on international flights) and 19,489 tonnes of freight. There are two further regional airports, 14 helicopter landing fields and numerous smaller airstrips.

Shipping. The harbour in Mannheim is the largest in Baden-Württemberg. In 2001 it handled 8·3m. tonnes of freight, compared to 6·2m. tonnes in Karlsruhe.

SOCIAL INSTITUTIONS

Justice. There are a constitutional court *(Staatsgerichtshof)*, 2 courts of appeal, 17 regional courts, 108 local courts, a *Land* labour court, 9 labour courts, a *Land* social court, 8 social courts, a finance court, a higher administrative court *(Verwaltungs-gerichtshof)* and 4 administrative courts.

Religion. On 1 Jan. 2000, 38·7% of the population were Protestants and 43·2% were Roman Catholics.

Education. In 2001–02 there were 2,719 primary schools *(Grund- und Hauptschulen)* with 35,760 teachers and 678,398 pupils; 571 special schools with 10,436 teachers and 53,501 pupils; 461 intermediate schools with 12,275 teachers and 237,855 pupils; 421 high schools with 19,649 teachers and 300,906 pupils; 44 *Freie Waldorf* schools with 1,442 teachers and 20,587 pupils. Other general schools had 574 teachers and 8,840 pupils in total; there were also 746 vocational schools with 391,734 pupils. There were 37 *Fachhochschulen* (colleges of engineering and others) with 63,480 students in winter term 2001–02.

In the winter term 2001–02 there were nine universities (Freiburg, 18,906 students; Heidelberg, 21,009; Konstanz, 7,573; Tübingen, 19,300, Karlsruhe, 14,914; Stuttgart, 16,411; Hohenheim, 4,729; Mannheim, 10,993; Ulm 5,961); six teacher-training colleges with 16,432 students; five colleges of music with 2,652 students; and three colleges of fine arts with 1,404 students.

CULTURE

Cinema. In 2001 there were 606 cinema screens and 109,789 seats.

Tourism. In 2001, 13,448,740 visitors spent a total of 39,290,097 nights in Baden-Württemberg. Only Bavaria of the German *Länder* recorded more overnight stays.

Libraries. Baden-Württemberg had 814 libraries and 14,183,000 books in 2001.

Theatre and Opera. Opera at the Württembergische Staatstheater enjoys a high international reputation. In 2002 the opera choir was chosen as German choir of the year for the fourth year running. The ballet is also very highly regarded. The Nationaltheater in Mannheim is Germany's oldest theatre. In 1998 the Baden-Baden Festival Hall opened with seating for 2,500 persons.

Museums and Galleries. In 1999 there were 990 museums putting on 1,152 exhibitions for 13,540,290 visitors.

FURTHER READING
Statistical Information: Statistisches Landesamt Baden-Württemberg (P.O.B. 10 60 33, 70049 Stuttgart) *(President:* Dr Gisela Meister-Scheufelen), publishes: *Statistisches Monatsheft* (monthly); *Statistisch-prognostischer Bericht* (latest issue 2002); *Statistisches Taschenbuch* (latest issue 2002).

State libraries: Württembergische Landesbibliothek, Konrad-Adenauer-Str. 8, 70173 Stuttgart. Badische Landesbibliothek Karlsruhe, Erbprinzenstr. 15, 76133 Karlsruhe.

BAVARIA
Bayern

KEY HISTORICAL EVENTS
Bavaria was ruled by the Wittelsbach family from 1180. The duchy remained Catholic after the Reformation, which made it a natural ally of Austria and the Hapsburg Emperors.

The present boundaries were reached during the Napoleonic wars, and Bavaria became a kingdom in 1805. Despite the granting of a constitution and parliament, radical feeling forced the abdication of King Ludwig I in 1848. Maximilian II was followed by Ludwig II who allied himself with Austria against Prussia in 1866, but was reconciled with Prussia and entered the German Empire in 1871. In 1918 the King Ludwig III abdicated. The first years of republican government were filled with unrest, attempts at the overthrow of the state by both communist and right-wing groups culminating in an unsuccessful coup by Adolf Hitler in 1923.

The state of Bavaria included the Palatinate from 1214 until 1945, when it was taken from Bavaria and added to the Rhineland. The present *Land* of Bavaria was formed in 1948. Munich became capital of Bavaria in the reign of Albert IV (1467–1508) and remains capital of the *Land*.

TERRITORY AND POPULATION

Bavaria has an area of 70,550 sq. km. The capital is Munich. There are 7 administrative regions, 25 urban districts, 71 rural districts, 233 unadopted areas and 2,056 communes, 1,003 of which are members of 319 administrative associations (as of 31 Dec. 2001). The population (31 Dec. 2001) numbered 12,329,714 (6,029,762 males, 6,299,952 females).

SOCIAL STATISTICS

Statistics for calendar years:

	Live births	Marriages	Divorces	Deaths
1998	126,529	64,065	26,553	120,447
1999	123,244	65,489	25,438	119,519
2000	120,765	63,038	27,250	118,846
2001	115,964	60,226	28,347	117,930

CONSTITUTION AND GOVERNMENT

The Constituent Assembly, elected on 30 June 1946, passed a constitution on the lines of the democratic constitution of 1919, but with greater emphasis on state rights; this was agreed upon by the Christian Social Union (CSU) and the Social Democrats (SPD). Bavaria has six seats in the Bundesrat. The CSU replaces the Christian Democratic Party in Bavaria.

RECENT ELECTIONS

At the Diet elections on 13 Sept. 1998 the CSU won 123 seats with 52·9% of votes cast, the SPD 67 with 28·7%, and Alliance '90/The Greens 14 with 5·7%. Turn-out was 70%. The next Diet elections will take place on 21 Sept. 2003.

CURRENT ADMINISTRATION

The *Prime Minister* is Dr Edmund Stoiber (CSU).

Government Website: http://www.bayern.de

ECONOMY

Performance. Real GDP growth in 2001 was 0·9%, compared to the national growth rate of 0·6%.

ENERGY AND NATURAL RESOURCES

Agriculture. Area and yield of the most important products:

	Area (in 1,000 ha)			Yield (in 1,000 tonnes)		
	2000	2001	2002	2000	2001	2002
Sugarbeet	72·1	71·6	74·1	5,183·1	4,460·9	5,272·8
Wheat	478·5	465·8	468·1	3,317·8	3,269·4	3,103·0
Barley	434·6	458·2	451·2	2,379·3	2,579·7	2,382·6
Potatoes	55·4	50·0	51·6	2,417·2	1,811·1	2,094·6
Oats	54·7	51·9	51·4	254·2	249·4	217·0
Rye	50·7	49·5	42·4	255·3	249·2	212·1

Livestock, 2002: 3,895,800 cattle (including 1,384,600 milch cows); 82,200 horses (2001); 467,300 sheep; 3,720,800 pigs; 9,599,700 poultry (2001).

INDUSTRY

In 2001, 8,013 establishments (with 20 or more employees) employed 1,218,867 persons; of these, 197,374 were employed in the manufacture of machinery and equipment, 175,377 in the manufacture of motor vehicles and 41,836 in the manufacture of textiles and textile products.

Labour. The economically active persons totalled 5,921,000 at the 1% sample survey of the microcensus of 2002. Of the total, 5,139,000 were employees, 685,000 were self-employed, 97,000 were unpaid family workers; 2,069,000 worked in power supply, mining, manufacturing and building; 1,311,000 in commerce, hotels and restaurants, and transport; 199,000 in agriculture and forestry; 2,342,000 in other services.

COMMUNICATIONS

Roads. There were, on 1 Jan. 2002, 41,761 km of 'classified' roads, comprising 2,283 km of Autobahn, 6,785 km of federal roads, 13,972 km of first-class and 18,721 km of second-class highways. Number of motor vehicles on 1 Jan. 2002 was 8,865,295, including 7,046,089 passenger cars, 384,621 lorries, 14,544 buses and 696,518 motorcycles.

Civil Aviation. Munich airport handled 22,869,447 passengers (14,600,358 on international flights) and 125,256 tonnes of freight in 2000. Nuremberg handled 3,052,717 (1,895,293 on international flights) and 18,541 tonnes of freight in 2000.

SOCIAL INSTITUTIONS

Justice. There are a constitutional court *(Verfassungsgerichtshof)*, a supreme *Land* court *(Oberstes Landesgericht)*, 3 courts of appeal, 22 regional courts, 72 local courts, 2 *Land* labour courts, 11 labour courts, a *Land* social court, 7 social courts, 2 finance courts, a higher administrative court *(Verwaltungsgerichtshof)* and 6 administrative courts.

Religion. At the census of 25 May 1987 there were 67·2% Roman Catholics and 23·9% Protestants.

Education. In 2001–02 there were 2,862 primary schools with 48,130 teachers and 846,372 pupils; 374 special schools with 7,835 teachers and 63,210 pupils; 334 intermediate schools with 10,680 teachers and 182,583 pupils; 402 high schools with 22,228 teachers and 329,076 pupils; 234 part-time vocational schools with 8,200 teachers and 299,621 pupils, including 49 special part-time vocational schools with 994 teachers and 14,161 pupils; 633 full-time vocational schools with 4,990 teachers and 62,642 pupils including 272 schools for public health occupations with 1,638 teachers and 18,478 pupils; 365 advanced full-time vocational schools with 2,014 teachers and 25,481 pupils; 117 vocational high schools *(Berufsoberschulen, Fachoberschulen)* with 2,201 teachers and 34,550 pupils.

In 2001–02 there were 12 universities with 154,882 students (Augsburg, 12,055; Bamberg, 7,004; Bayreuth, 7,541; Eichstätt, 3,909; Erlangen-Nürnberg, 20,432; München, 42,253; Passau, 7,342; Regensburg, 14,892; Würzburg, 16,165; the Technical University of München, 19,776; München, University of the Federal Armed Forces *(Universität der Bundeswehr)*, 2,889; the college of politics, München, 624; plus the college of philosophy, München, 375, and 2 philosophical-theological colleges with 236 students in total (Benediktbeuern, 104; Neuendettelsau, 132). There were also 4 colleges of music, 2 colleges of fine arts and 1 college of television and film, with 3,198 students in total; 20 vocational colleges *(Fachhochschulen)* with 61,129 students including 1 for the civil service *(Bayerische Beamtenfachhochschule)* with 3,151 students.

Welfare. In Dec. 2001 there were 215,412 persons receiving benefits of all kinds.

CULTURE

Cinema. Bavaria had 710 cinema screens with 118,724 seats in 2001.

Tourism. In June 2001 there were 14,207 places of accommodation (with nine beds or more) providing beds for 573,996 people. In 2001 they received 22,748,035 guests of whom 4,277,982 were foreigners. They stayed an average of 3·3 nights each, totalling 74,508,396 nights (9,108,562 nights stayed by foreign visitors).

Festivals. Oktoberfest, Munich's famous beer festival, takes place each year from the penultimate Saturday in Sept. through to the first Sunday in Oct. (extended to 3 Oct. if the last Sunday of the festival falls on 1 or 2 Oct.).

Libraries. In 2001 there were 2,001 public libraries holding approximately 21·5m. volumes (printed and other media).

Theatre and Opera. There are 32 theatre companies and opera houses with their own ensembles in Bavaria.

Museums and Galleries. Bavaria had more than 1,150 museums in 2001. There are approximately 20m. visits per year on average.

FURTHER READING
Statistical Information: Bayerisches Landesamt für Statistik und Datenverarbeitung, Neuhauser Str. 8, 80331 Munich. *President:* Dr Peter Bauer. It publishes: *Statistisches Jahrbuch für Bayern.* 1894 ff.—*Bayern in Zahlen.* Monthly (from Jan. 1947).—*Zeitschrift des Bayerischen Statistischen Landesamts.* July 1869–1943; 1948 ff.—*Beiträge zur Statistik Bayerns.* 1850 ff.—*Statistische Berichte.* 1951 ff.—*Kreisdaten.* 1972 ff.—*Gemeindedaten.* 1973 ff.

State Library: Bayerische Staatsbibliothek, Munich. *Director General:* Dr Hermann Leskien.

BERLIN

KEY HISTORICAL EVENTS
After the end of World War II, Berlin was divided into four occupied sectors, each with a military governor from one of the victorious Allied Powers (the USA, the Soviet Union, Britain and France). On 30 Nov. 1948 a separate municipal government was set up in the Soviet sector which led to the political division of the city. In contravention of the special Allied status agreed for the entire city, East Berlin became 'Capital of the GDR' in 1949 and thus increasingly integrated into the GDR as a whole. In West Berlin, the formal supreme authority of the western allies endured until 1990.

On 17 June 1953 the protest by workers in East Berlin against political oppression and economic hardship was suppressed by Soviet military forces. To stop refugees, the east German government erected the Berlin Wall to seal off West Berlin's borders on 13 Aug. 1961.

The Berlin Wall unexpectedly collapsed on 9 Nov. 1989 as the regime in the GDR bowed to the internal pressure which had been building for months. East and West Berlin were amalgamated on the re-unification of Germany in Oct. 1990. In April 1994 the *Land* governments of Berlin and Brandenburg agreed to merge the two *Länder* in 1999 or 2002, subject to the approval of their respective parliaments, and of their electorates in referendums held in May 1996. In Berlin 53·4% of votes were cast in favour, but in Brandenburg 62·8% were against. A further referendum on the proposed merger is likely to take place in the next few years.

With the move of the national government, the parliament (Bundestag), and the federal organ of the Länder (Bundesrat) in 1999, Berlin is once again a capital city.

TERRITORY AND POPULATION
The area is 891·76 sq. km. Population, 31 Dec. 2001, 3,388,434 (1,740,265 females), including 440,777 foreign nationals; density, 3,800 per sq. km.

SOCIAL STATISTICS
Statistics for calendar years:

	Live births	Marriages	Divorces	Deaths
1998	29,612	14,526	9,677	35,224
1999	29,856	14,635	10,001	34,996
2000	29,695	14,119	9,631	33,335
2001	28,624	12,903	8,734	32,826

CONSTITUTION AND GOVERNMENT
According to the constitutions of Sept. 1950 and Oct. 1995, Berlin is simultaneously a *Land* of the Federal Republic and a city. It is governed by a House of Representatives (of at least 130 members); executive power is vested in a Senate, consisting of the Governing Mayor, two Mayors and not more than eight senators. Since 1992 adherence to the constitution has been watched over by a Constitutional Court.

After a proposed merger was rejected by Brandenburg in the 1996 referendum, a Joint Berlin-Brandenburg Co-operation Council was set up.

Berlin has 4 seats in the Bundesrat.

RECENT ELECTIONS

In Dec. 1999 a CDU–SPD coalition government was formed, but the 'grand coalition' that had held power for more than ten years collapsed on 7 June 2001. The Social Democrats announced their withdrawal after the authorities had accumulated huge debts. At the elections of 21 Oct. 2001 turn-out was 68·1%. The Social Democratic Party (SPD) won 44 seats with 29·7% of votes cast; the Christian Democratic Union (CDU) 35, with 23·8%; the Party of Democratic Socialism (former Communists) 33, with 22·6%; the Free Democratic Party 15, with 9·9%; and the Greens 14, with 9·1%. Initially the SPD had coalition talks with the Free Democratic Party and the Greens, but these broke down. Thus the SPD formed a coalition with the Party of Democratic Socialism, the successor to the former German Democratic Republic's Communist Party, who thereby had their first share of power in Berlin since the fall of the Wall.

CURRENT ADMINISTRATION

The *Governing Mayor* is Klaus Wowereit (SPD).

Government Website: http://www.berlin.de

ECONOMY

Berlin's real GDP growth was –0·1% in 2001.

INDUSTRY

In 2001 there were 898 industrial concerns employing 111,889 people. The main industries in terms of percentage of the labour force employed were: electronics, 27·8%; paper, printing and publishing, 13·8%; food and tobacco, 12·6%; machine-building, 11·0%; chemicals, 9·2%; metallurgy, 8·7%; vehicle production, 8·5%.

Labour. In 2001 the workforce was 1,557,700. There were 272,307 persons registered unemployed in 2001 and 3,599 on short time. An average of 7,005 jobs were available at any one time in 2001. The unemployment rate in 2001 was 16·1%.

COMMUNICATIONS

Roads. In 2002 there were 5,317·4 km of roads (251·4 km of 'classified' roads, made up of 68·6 km of Autobahn and 182·8 km of federal roads). In Jan. 2001, 1,425,278 motor vehicles were registered, including 1,225,588 passenger cars, 87,853 lorries, 2,497 buses and 85,319 motorcycles. There were 142,078 road accidents in 2001 of which 16,109 involved badly damaged vehicles or injured persons, of whom there were 17,913.

Civil Aviation. 189,474 flights were made from Berlin's three airports—Tegel, Tempelhof and Schönefeld—in 2001, carrying a total of 12,387,959 passengers.

SOCIAL INSTITUTIONS

Justice. There are a court of appeal *(Kammergericht)*, a regional court, nine local courts, a *Land* Labour court, a labour court, a *Land* social court, a social court, a higher administrative court, an administrative court and a finance court.

Religion. In 2001 membership and number of places of worship for major religions was as follows:

Religion	Members	Places of Worship
Protestant	792,925	461[1]
Roman Catholic	309,563	171
Jewish	12,207	7
Muslim	206,308	106

[1]2000.

Education. In the autumn of 2001 there were 365,613 pupils attending schools. There were 480 primary schools with 163,069 pupils, 61 schools for practical education with 15,124 pupils, 99 special schools with 13,769 pupils, 88 secondary modern schools with 31,661 pupils, 124 grammar schools with 86,617 pupils and 66 comprehensive schools with 52,018 pupils. In 2001–02 there were 2 universities and 1 technical university, 4 arts colleges and 10 technical colleges. There was a total of 138,394 students in higher education.

Health. In 2001 there were 70 hospitals with 22,620 beds, 6,545 doctors and 3,067 dentists.

CULTURE

Cinema. In 2001 there were 289 cinemas with 61,396 seats.

Tourism. In 2001 Berlin had 543 places of accommodation providing 62,024 beds for 4,929,578 visitors.

Libraries. In 2001 there were 146 libraries holding 7,596,357 volumes.

Theatre and Opera. In 2000–01 Berlin had 41 theatres and concert halls putting on 8,657 productions for audiences numbering 2,927,382.

Museums and Galleries. There were 114 museums in 2000, visited by a total of 8,117,435 people. There were 303 special exhibitions in 2000.

FURTHER READING

Statistical Information: The Statistisches Landesamt Berlin was founded in 1862 (Alt-Friedrichsfelde 60, 10315 Berlin (Lichtenberg)). *Director:* Dr Eckart Elsner. It publishes: *Statistisches Jahrbuch* (from 1867): *Berliner Statistik* (monthly, from 1947).—*100 Jahre Berliner Statistik* (1962).

Read, A., and Fisher, D., *Berlin, Biography of a City.* London, 1994

Taylor, R., *Berlin and its Culture.* London, 1997

Wallace, Ian, *Berlin.* [Bibliography] ABC-Clio, Oxford and Santa Barbara (CA), 1993

State Library: Amerika-Gedenkbibliothek-Berliner Zentralbibliothek, Blücherplatz 1, D-10961 Berlin. *Director:* Dr Klaus Bock.

Website: http://www.statistik-berlin.de

BRANDENBURG

KEY HISTORICAL EVENTS

For the proposed merger with Berlin *see* BERLIN: Key Historical Events.

Brandenburg surrounds the new capital city of Germany, Berlin, but the people of the state voted against the recommendations of the Berlin House of Representatives and the Brandenburg State Parliament that the two states should merge around the year 2000. The state capital, Potsdam, is the ancient city of the Emperor Frederic II 'The Great' who transformed the garrison town of his father Frederic I 'The Soldier' into an elegant city.

TERRITORY AND POPULATION

The area is 29,476 sq. km. Population on 31 Dec. 2001 was 2,593,040 (1,312,548 females). There are 4 urban districts, 14 rural districts and 1,092 communes. The capital is Potsdam.

SOCIAL STATISTICS

Statistics for calendar years:

	Live births	Marriages	Divorces	Deaths
1998	17,146	9,266	5,540	26,327
1999	17,928	10,219	5,559	26,016
2000	18,444	9,804	6,010	26,068
2001	17,692	9,774	6,043	25,889

CONSTITUTION AND GOVERNMENT

The *Land* was reconstituted on former GDR territory on 14 Oct. 1990. Brandenburg has 4 seats in the Bundesrat and 16 in the Bundestag.

After a proposed merger was rejected by Brandenburg in the 1996 referendum, a Joint Berlin-Brandenburg Co-operation Council was set up.

At a referendum on 14 June 1992, 93·5% of votes cast were in favour of a new constitution guaranteeing direct democracy and the right to work and housing.

RECENT ELECTIONS

At the Diet elections on 5 Sept. 1999 the Social Democrats (SPD) won 37 seats with 39·3% of the vote; the Christian Democrats (CDU) 25, with 26·6%; the Party of Democratic Socialism (PDS, former Communists) 22, with 23·3%; the extreme right German People's Union (DVU) 5, with 5·3%.

CURRENT ADMINISTRATION

The *Prime Minister* is Matthias Platzeck (SPD).

Government Website: http://www.brandenburg.de

ECONOMY

Performance. GDP in 2001 was €42,333m. (nominal).

ENERGY AND NATURAL RESOURCES

Electricity. Power stations in Brandenburg produced 38,190m. kWh in 2000. A minimal amount was produced from hydro-electric power.

Agriculture. Area and yield of the most important crops:

	Area (in 1,000 ha)			Yield (in 1,000 tonnes)		
	1999	2000	2001	1999	2000	2001
Rye	233·2	250·7	253·2	1,116·6	926·9	1,350·8
Wheat	115·6	132·8	131·5	753·4	693·9	858·8
Sugarbeet	11·9	12·4	11·3	488·8	594·5	561·0
Barley	89·8	87·6	84·9	521·2	391·4	547·8
Potatoes	14·5	13·8	12·3	371·5	365·7	380·2
Rape	...	...	99·6	...	...	330·0
Oats	15·5	16·7	15·8	68·3	41·2	63·8

Livestock on 3 May 2001: cattle, 649,389 (including 189,597 milch cows); pigs, 732,943; sheep, 156,473; horses, 17,710; poultry, 7,452,804.

INDUSTRY

In 2001, 1,169 establishments (20 or more employees) in the mining and manufacturing industries employed 89,527 persons, the main areas being: vehicle construction (11,843); the food industry (10,594); machine construction (7,746); glassworks, ceramics, processing stones and earthenware (7,074); mining and quarrying (5,204); and chemical industries (4,871). There were 1,033 companies (with 20 or more employees) in the building industry, employing 43,774 persons.

Labour. In May 2001 at the 1%-sample of the microcensus, 1,143,000 persons were economically active, of which 568,000 white-collar and 397,900 manual workers, 111,300 self-employed and family assistants, and 65,800 civil servants. In Dec. 2001 there were 231,552 unemployed persons (18·6%).

INTERNATIONAL TRADE

Imports and Exports. Total imports (2001): €5,770·2m. Total exports: €4,536·4m.

COMMUNICATIONS

Roads. On 1 Jan. 2002 there were 1,639,823 registered vehicles including 1,385,324 passenger cars.

SOCIAL INSTITUTIONS

Education. In 2001–02 there were 1,052 schools providing general education (including special schools) with 314,894 pupils and 53 vocational schools with 77,479 pupils.

In the winter term 2001–02 there were three universities and eight colleges with 34,654 students.

CULTURE

Cinema. In 2001 Brandenburg had 146 screens (including 'rambler-cinemas') with 26,222 seats and 4·6m. visitors.

Tourism. In 2001 there were 1,514 places of accommodation (with nine or more beds), including 501 hotels, providing a total of 79,358 beds. 3,117,756 visitors spent a total of 8,828,846 nights in Brandenburg in 2001.

Libraries. In 2001 there were 268 public libraries with 265,691 active users and 2,980,033 visitors, who borrowed a total of 9,945,139 items.

Theatre and Opera. There were 30 theatres and venues which put on 2,361 performances for audiences totalling 428,152 persons in 2000–01.

Museums and Galleries. Brandenburg had 233 museums in 1999, with 2,893,751 visitors during the year.

BREMEN
Freie Hansestadt Bremen

KEY HISTORICAL EVENTS
The state is dominated by the Free City of Bremen and its port, Bremerhaven. In 1815, when it joined the German Confederation, Bremen was an autonomous city and Hanse port with important Baltic trade. In 1827 the expansion of trade inspired the founding of Bremerhaven on land ceded by Hanover at the confluence of the Geest and Weser rivers. Further expansion followed the founding of the Norddeutscher Lloyd Shipping Company in 1857. Merchant shipping, associated trade and fishing were dominant until 1940 but there was diversification in the post-war years. In 1939 Bremerhaven was absorbed by the Hanoverian town of Wesermünde. The combined port was returned to the jurisdiction of Bremen in 1947.

TERRITORY AND POPULATION
The area of the *Land*, consisting of the two urban districts and ports of Bremen and Bremerhaven, is 404 sq. km. Population, 31 Dec. 2001, 660,253 (318,637 males and 341,616 females).

SOCIAL STATISTICS
Statistics for calendar years:

	Live births	Marriages	Divorces	Deaths
1996	6,623	3,509	1,870	8,080
1997	6,644	3,553	2,003	8,036
1998	6,360	3,477	1,996	7,838
1999	6,096	3,438	1,906	7,670

CONSTITUTION AND GOVERNMENT
Political power is vested in the 100-member House of Burgesses *(Bürgerschaft)* which appoints the executive, called the Senate. Bremen has three seats in the Bundesrat.

RECENT ELECTIONS
At the elections of 6 June 1999 the Social Democratic Party won 47 seats with 42·6% of votes cast (37 with 33·4% in 1995); the Christian Democrats 42 with 37·1% (37 with 32·6%); the Alliance '90/Greens 10 with 8·9% (14 with 13·1%); the nationalist Deutsche Volksunion (DVU) 1 with 3·0% (0 with 2·5%); the Party of Democratic Socialism (PDS) no seats with 2·9% (no seats with 2·4%); the Free Democrats (FDP) no seats with 2·5% (none with 3·4% in 1995); and the Arbeit für Bremen (AFB) no seats with 2·4% (12 with 10·7%).

CURRENT ADMINISTRATION
The Burgomaster is Dr Henning Scherf (Social Democrat).

Government Website: http://www.bremen.de

ENERGY AND NATURAL RESOURCES
Agriculture. Agricultural area comprised (1999) 8,554 ha. Livestock (2 May 1999): 12,612 cattle (including 3,502 milch cows); 1,792 pigs; 301 sheep; 1,099 horses; 10,866 poultry.

INDUSTRY
In 1999, 359 establishments (20 or more employees) employed 64,986 persons; of these, 24,404 were employed in the production of cars and car parts and other vehicles; 1,767 were employed in shipbuilding (except naval engineering); 5,464 in machine construction; 3,295 in electrical engineering; 1,380 in coffee and tea processing.

Labour. The economically active persons totalled 276,300 at the microcensus of April 1999. Of the total, 25,100 were self-employed, 251,200 employees; 72,400 in production industries, 85,000 in commerce, trade and communications, 115,400 in other industries and services.

COMMUNICATIONS
Roads. On 1 Jan. 1999 there were 98 km of 'classified' roads, of which 48 km were Autobahn and 50 km federal roads. Registered motor vehicles on 1 Jan. 2000 numbered 329,366, including 285,270 passenger cars, 17,623 lorries, 552 buses, 2,835 tractors and 18,087 motorcycles.

Civil Aviation. Bremen airport handled 1,887,318 passengers (1,014,117 on international flights) in 2000.

Shipping. Vessels entered in 1999, 8,034 of 50,346,023 net tons; cleared, 8,808 of 50,045,092 net tons. Sea traffic, 1999, incoming 21,066,000 tonnes; outgoing, 14,970,000 tonnes.

SOCIAL INSTITUTIONS
Justice. There are a constitutional court *(Staatsgerichtshof)*, a court of appeal, a regional court, three local courts, a *Land* labour court, two labour courts, a *Land* social court, a finance court, a higher administrative court and an administrative court.

Religion. On 25 May 1987 (census) there were 61% Protestants and 10% Roman Catholics.

Education. In 1999 there were 386 new system schools with 4,906 teachers and 70,597 pupils; 27 special schools with 668 teachers and 2,709 pupils; 24 part-time vocational schools with 18,482 pupils; 25 full-time vocational schools with 4,572 pupils; 5 advanced vocational schools (including institutions for the training of technicians) with 728 pupils; 10 schools for public health occupations with 788 pupils.

In the winter term 1999–2000, 17,443 students were enrolled at the university. In addition to the university there were four other colleges in 1999–2000 with 8,329 students.

CULTURE
Cinema. In 1998 there were 45 cinema screens with 9,538 seats.

Tourism. Bremen had 81 places of accommodation providing 8,346 beds for 600,593 visitors in 1998.

Libraries. In 1998 there were 30 libraries with 889,000 volumes.

Theatre and Opera. Bremen had nine concert halls and theatres in 1997–98. There were 1,064 productions and audiences numbered 403,000.

Museums and Galleries. In 1999 there were 942,703 visitors to the 30 museums in Bremen.

FURTHER READING
Statistical Information: Statistisches Landesamt Bremen (An der Weide 14–16, P. B. 101309, D-28195 Bremen), founded in 1850. *Director:* Reg. Dir. Jürgen Dinse. Its current publications include: *Statistisches Jahrbuch Bremen* (from 1992).—*Statistische Mitteilungen* (from 1948).—*Statistische Monatsberichte* (from 1954).—*Statistische Berichte* (from 1956).—*Statistisches Handbuch Bremen (1950–60*, 1961; *1960–64*, 1967; *1965–69*, 1971; *1970–74*, 1975; *1975–80*, 1982; *1981–85*, 1987).—*Bremen im statistischen Zeitvergleich 1950–1976.* 1977.—*Bremen in Zahlen*, 2000.

State and University Library: Bibliotheksstr., D-28359 Bremen. *Director:* Annette Rath-Beckmann.

HAMBURG

Freie und Hansestadt Hanburg

KEY HISTORICAL EVENTS

Hamburg was a free Hanse town owing nominal allegiance to the Holy Roman Emperor until 1806. In 1815 it became part of the German Confederation, sharing a seat in the Federal Diet with Lübeck, Bremen and Frankfurt. During the Empire it retained its autonomy. By 1938 it had become the third largest port in the world and its territory was extended by the cession of land (3 urban and 27 rural districts) from Prussia. After World War II, Hamburg became a *Land* of the Federal Republic with its 1938 boundaries.

TERRITORY AND POPULATION

Total area, 755·3 sq. km (2001), including the islands Neuwerk and Scharhörn (7·6 sq. km). Population (31 Dec. 2001), 1,726,400 (837,700 males, 888,700 females). The Land forms a single urban district (*Stadtstaat*) with seven administrative subdivisions.

SOCIAL STATISTICS

Statistics for calendar years:

	Live births	Marriages	Divorces	Deaths
1998	16,235	7,994	4,968	19,228
1999	16,034	8,298	4,341	18,561
2000	16,159	7,865	4,645	18,210
2001	15,786	7,020	4,328	17,869

CONSTITUTION AND GOVERNMENT

The constitution of 6 June 1952 vests the supreme power in the House of Burgesses *(Bürgerschaft)* of 121 members. The executive is in the hands of the Senate, whose members are elected by the Bürgerschaft. Hamburg has three seats in the Bundesrat.

RECENT ELECTIONS

The elections of 23 Sept. 2001 had the following results: Social Democrats, 46 seats with 36·5% of votes cast; Christian Democrats, 33 with 26·2%; Schill-Party, 25 with 19·4%; the Greens, 11 with 8·6%; Free Democrats, 6 with 5·1%.

CURRENT ADMINISTRATION

The First Burgomaster is Ole von Beust (Christian Democrat).

Government Website: http://www.hamburg.de

ENERGY AND NATURAL RESOURCES

Agriculture. The agricultural area comprised 14,019 ha in 2001. Yield in 1997, in tonnes: of cereals, 16,700; potatoes, 700.

Livestock (3 May 2001): cattle, 8,239 (including 1,190 milch cows); pigs, 2,478; horses, 3,268; sheep, 3,740; poultry, 7,507.

INDUSTRY

In June 2001, 572 establishments (with 20 or more employees) employed 100,570 persons; of these, 22,922 were employed in manufacturing transport equipment (including motor vehicles, aircraft and ships), 14,587 in manufacturing machinery, 11,991 in manufacturing electrical and optical equipment, 6,875 in manufacturing chemical products and 6,363 in mineral oil industry.

Labour. The economically active persons totalled 813,000 at the 1%-sample survey of the microcensus of April 2001. Of the total, 711,000 were employees and 102,000 were self-employed or unpaid family workers; 239,000 were engaged in commerce and transport, 168,000 in power supply, mining, manufacturing and building, 6,000 in agriculture and forestry, 401,000 in other industries and services.

COMMUNICATIONS

Roads. In 2001 there were 3,947 km of roads, including 82 km of Autobahn, 150 km of federal roads. Number of motor vehicles (1 Jan. 2001), 942,158, of which

822,612 were passenger cars, 55,406 lorries, 1,418 buses, 36,609 motorcycles and 26,113 other motor vehicles.

Civil Aviation. Hamburg airport handled 9,824,979 passengers (5,553,935 on international flights) and 31,162 tonnes of freight in 2000.

Shipping. Hamburg is the largest sea port in Germany.

Vessels		1999	2000	2001
Entered:	Number	11,626	11,630	12,333
	Tonnage (gross)	66,246,840[1]	101,333,291	115,383,156
Cleared:	Number	11,724	11,678	12,344
	Tonnage (gross)	66,194,343[1]	101,570,627	115,135,138

[1]Tonnage for 1999 is net.

SOCIAL INSTITUTIONS

Justice. There is a constitutional court *(Verfassungsgericht)*, a court of appeal *(Oberlandesgericht)*, a regional court *(Landgericht)*, six local courts *(Amtsgerichte)*, a *Land* labour court, a labour court, a *Land* social court, a social court, a finance court, a higher administrative court and an administrative court.

Religion. In 2001, 34·0% of the population went to the Evangelical Church and Free Churches, whilst 10·4% were Roman Catholic.

Education. In 2001 there were 416 schools of general education (not including *Internationale Schule*) with 178,197 pupils (13,670 teachers in 1998); 46 special schools with 7,526 pupils; 43 part-time vocational schools with 35,182 pupils; 41 schools with 5,448 pupils in manual instruction classes; 48 full-time vocational schools with 9,966 pupils; 9 economic secondary schools with 2,034 pupils; 2 technical *Gymnasien* with 414 pupils; 17 advanced vocational schools with 2,733 pupils; 30 schools for public health occupations with 2,150 pupils; and 20 technical superior schools with 2,020 pupils.

In the winter term 2001–02 there was 1 university with 38,269 students; 1 technical university with 4,901 students; 1 college of music and 1 college of fine arts with 1,573 students in total; 1 university of the *Bundeswehr* with 1,771 students; 1 university of economics and political sciences with 2,548 students; 4 professional colleges with a total of 17,244 students.

Health. In 2001 there were 35 hospitals with 12,732 beds, 9,118 doctors and 1,735 dentists.

CULTURE

Broadcasting. In 2001 there was one public broadcasting service as well as seven private broadcasters.

Cinema. In Dec. 2001 there were 94 cinemas (including one drive-in) with a total of 25,160 seats. There were 5,583,002 tickets sold in 2001.

Tourism. At Dec. 2001 there were 270 places of accommodation with 28,726 beds. Of the 2,554,029 visitors in 2001, 20·9% were foreigners.

Libraries. In 2001 there were 113 branches of the Hamburg Public Library which held 1,792,041 books and other forms of media. 9,448,941 items were borrowed in 2001. The city and university library held 3,024,255 books, and lent 1,069,766 items.

Theatre and Opera. In the 2001 season the three national theatre and opera houses put on 1,608 performances, attracting 754,876 visitors. The two largest stages in Hamburg, the *Neue Flora* and *Operettenhaus*, are both private. The former put on 414 performances during 1999–2000 for a total audience of 432,613 whilst *Operettenhaus* had 416 performances for 317,500 persons.

Museums and Galleries. The seven national museums were visited by 1,367,043 people in 2001. There are a further 40 or so private and public museums and about 100 art galleries in Hamburg as well as a *Planetarium*, which received 129,474 visits in 2001.

FURTHER READING

Statistical Information: The Statistisches Landesamt der Freien und Hansestadt Hamburg (Steckelhörn 12, D-20457 Hamburg) publishes: *Hamburg in Zahlen, Statistische Berichte, Statistisches Jahrbuch, Hamburger Statistische Porträts, Statistik Magazin.*

Hamburger Sparkasse, *Hamburg: von Altona bis Zollspieker.* Hamburg, 2002
Hamburgische Gesellschaft für Wirtschaftsförderung mbH, *Hamburg.* Oldenburg, 1993
Klessmann, E., *Geschichte der Stadt Hamburg.* 7th ed. Hamburg, 1994
Kopitzsch, F. and Brietzke, D., *Hamburgische Biografie, Personenlexikon.* Vol. 1. Hamburg, 2001
Kopitzsch, F. and Tilgner, D., *Hamburg Lexikon.* Hamburg, 1998
Möller, I., *Hamburg.* 2nd ed. Stuttgart, 1999
Schubert, D. and Harms, H., *Wohnen am Hafen.* Hamburg, 1993
Schütt, E. C., *Die Chronik Hamburgs.* Hamburg, 1991

State Library: Staats- und Universitätsbibliothek, Carl von Ossietzky, Von-Melle-Park 3, D-20146 Hamburg. *Director:* Prof. Dr Peter Rau.

HESSEN

KEY HISTORICAL EVENTS

The *Land* consists of the former states of Hesse-Darmstadt and Hesse-Kassel, and Nassau. Hesse-Darmstadt was ruled by the Landgrave Louis X from 1790. He became grand duke in 1806 with absolute power, having dismissed the parliament in 1803. However, he granted a constitution and bicameral parliament in 1820. Hesse-Darmstadt lost land to Prussia in the Seven Weeks' War of 1866, but retained its independence, both then and as a state of the German Empire after 1871. In 1918 the grand duke abdicated and the territory became a state of the German Republic. In 1945 areas west of the Rhine were incorporated into the new *Land* of Rhineland-Palatinate, areas east of the Rhine became part of the *Land* of Greater Hesse.

Hesse-Kassel was ruled by the Landgrave William IX from 1785 until he became Elector in 1805. In 1807 the Electorate was absorbed into the Kingdom of Westphalia (a Napoleonic creation), becoming independent again in 1815 as a state of the German Confederation. In 1831 a constitution and parliament were granted but the Electors remained strongly conservative.

In 1866 the Diet approved alliance with Prussia against Austria; the Elector nevertheless supported Austria. He was defeated by the Prussians and exiled and Hesse-Kassel was annexed to Prussia. In 1867 it was combined with Frankfurt and some areas taken from Nassau and Hesse-Darmstadt to form a Prussian province (Hesse-Nassau). In 1801 Nassau west of the Rhine passed to France; Napoleon also took the northern state in 1806. The remnant of the southern states allied in 1803 and three years later they became a duchy. In 1866 the duke supported Austria against Prussia and the duchy was annexed by Prussia as a result. In 1944 the Prussian province of Hesse-Nassau was split in two: Nassau and Electoral Hesse, also called Kurhessen. The following year these were combined with Hesse-Darmstadt as the *Land* of Greater Hesse which became known as Hessen.

TERRITORY AND POPULATION

Area, 21,115 sq. km. The capital is Wiesbaden. There are three administrative regions with 5 urban and 21 rural districts and 426 communes. Population, 31 Dec. 2001, was 6,077,826 (2,977,832 males, 3,099,994 females).

SOCIAL STATISTICS

Statistics for calendar years:

	Live births	Marriages	Divorces	Deaths
1998	60,567	31,992	14,676	60,980
1999	58,996	32,621	15,256	61,054
2000	58,817	32,516	14,905	60,345
2001	56,228	29,832	15,078	59,370

CONSTITUTION AND GOVERNMENT

The constitution was put into force by popular referendum on 1 Dec. 1946. Hessen has five seats in the Bundesrat.

RECENT ELECTIONS

At the Diet elections on 2 Feb. 2003 the Christian Democratic Union (CDU) won 56 of 110 seats, with 48·8% of votes cast (up from 43·4% in 1999), the Social Democratic Party (SPD) 33 with 29·1% (down from 39·4% in 1999), the Greens 12 with 10·1% and the Free Democratic Party (FDP) 9 with 7·9%.

CURRENT ADMINISTRATION

The cabinet is headed by *Prime Minister* Roland Koch (Christian Democrats; CDU).

Government Website: http://www.hessen.de

ECONOMY

Performance. In 2001 the gross domestic product at market prices (GDP) increased by 1·5% at 1995 constant prices in comparison with the previous year. The total amount was €181·8bn. in 2001. The GDP per person engaged in labour productivity was €60,219 in 2001 (€59,967 in 2000).

ENERGY AND NATURAL RESOURCES

Electricity. Electricity production in 2000 was 25,542m. kWh (gross) and 23,013m. kWh (net). Total electricity consumption in 1999 was 34,740m. kWh.

Oil and Gas. Gas consumption in 2000 was 64,592m. kWh. All gas was imported from other parts of Germany.

Water. Public water production in 1998 totalled 549,607,000 cu. metres.

Agriculture. Area and yield of the most important crops:

	Area (in 1,000 ha)			Yield (in 1,000 tonnes)		
	2000	2001	2002	2000	2001	2002
Wheat	147·8	146·4	148·9	1,056·3	1,180·2	1,075·3
Sugarbeet	18·7	18·4	18·8	1,218·1	1,001·6	1,029·8
Barley	105·9	109·6	105·0	655·3	670·2	597·2
Potatoes	5·4	4·7	4·7	226·8	172·6	180·5
Rape	51·9	51·3	53·5	170·1	178·2	176·5
Rye	21·2	20·1	17·5	124·6	121·7	98·9
Oats	18·3	17·5	16·9	89·2	83·3	72·1

Livestock, May 2002: cattle, 511,238 (including 160,560 milch cows); pigs, 851,386; May 2001: sheep, 181,194; horses, 34,479; poultry, 1·85m.

INDUSTRY

In Sept. 2002, 3,181 establishments (with 20 or more employees) employed 444,496 persons; of these, 63,291 were employed in the chemical industry; 61,524 in machine construction; 56,741 in car building; 37,178 in production of metal products.

Labour. The economically active persons totalled 2,806,500 at the 1% sample survey of the microcensus of April 2001. Of the total, 2,474,500 were employees, 300,700 self-employed, 31,400 unpaid family workers; 850,600 were engaged in power supply, mining, manufacturing and building, 678,100 in commerce, transport, hotels and restaurants, 46,700 in agriculture and forestry, 1,231,100 in other services.

COMMUNICATIONS

Roads. On 1 Jan. 2002 there were 15,938 km of 'classified' roads, comprising 956 km of Autobahn, 3,127 km of federal highways, 7,190 km of first-class highways and 4,665 km of second-class highways. Motor vehicles licensed on 1 Jan. 2002 totalled 4,161,427, including 3,496,251 passenger cars, 6,337 buses, 187,947 lorries, 137,531 tractors and 281,858 motorcycles.

Civil Aviation. Frankfurt/Main airport is one of the most important freight airports in the world. In 2001, 456,452 aeroplanes took off and landed, carrying 48,568,918 passengers, 1,494,125 tonnes of air freight and 141,011 tonnes of air mail.

Shipping. Frankfurt/Main harbour and Hanau harbour are the two most important harbours. In 2001, 12·4m. tonnes of goods were imported into the *Land* and 2·6m. tonnes were exported.

SOCIAL INSTITUTIONS

Justice. There are a constitutional court *(Staatsgerichtshof)*, a court of appeal, 9 regional courts, 58 local courts, a *Land* labour court, 12 labour courts, a *Land* social court, 7 social courts, a finance court, a higher administrative court *(Verwaltungsgerichtshof)* and 5 administrative courts.

Religion. In 2000 the churches in Hessen reported 2,654,000 Protestants and 1,615,000 Roman Catholics.

Education. In 2001 there were 1,250 primary schools with 289,093 pupils (including *Förderstufen*); 157 intermediate schools with 52,030 pupils; 19,564 teachers in primary and intermediate schools; 228 special schools with 3,809 teachers and 24,217 pupils; 163 high schools with 8,910 teachers and 135,406 pupils; 215 *Gesamtschulen* (comprehensive schools) with 12,421 teachers and 193,596 pupils; 119 part-time vocational schools with 135,547 pupils; 265 full-time vocational schools with 41,934 pupils; 107 advanced vocational schools with 10,420 pupils; 8,307 teachers in the vocational schools.

In the winter term 2001–02 there were three universities (Frankfurt/Main, 38,133 students; Giessen, 19,898; Marburg/Lahn, 17,268); 1 technical university in Darmstadt (17,412); 1 private *Wissenschaftliche Hochschule* (1,104); 1 *Gesamthochschule* (16,698); 17 *Fachhochschulen* (44,132); 2 Roman Catholic theological colleges and 1 Protestant theological college with a total of 328; 1 college of music and 2 colleges of fine arts with 1,441 students in total.

CULTURE

Cinema. In 2001 there were 334 cinemas with 63,983 seats in total.

Press. In 2001 there were 87 newspapers published in Hessen with a combined circulation of 2·0m.

Tourism. In 2001, 9·8m. visitors stayed 25·6m. nights in Hessen.

Libraries. In 2000 there were 897 public libraries which lent out 8,583,154 books. There were also nine academic and scientific libraries.

Theatre and Opera. In 1999–2000 there were 3,608 productions put on in 43 theatres and concert halls for audiences totalling 1,291,000.

Museums and Galleries. Hessen had 327 museums in 2000. A total of 4,825,000 visitors came to 716 exhibitions.

FURTHER READING
Statistical Information: The Hessisches Statistisches Landesamt (Rheinstr. 35–37, D-65175 Wiesbaden). *President:* Eckart Hohmann. Main publications: *Statistisches Handbuch für das Land Hessen* (biannual).—*Staat und Wirtschaft in Hessen* (monthly).—*Beiträge zur Statistik Hessens.*—*Statistische Berichte.*—*Hessische Gemeindestatistik* (annual, 1980 ff.).

State Library: Hessische Landesbibliothek, Rheinstr. 55–57, D-65185 Wiesbaden. *Director:* Dr Dieter Wolf.

LOWER SAXONY
Niedersachsen

KEY HISTORICAL EVENTS
The *Land* consists of the former states of Hanover, Oldenburg, Schaumburg-Lippe and Brunswick. It does not include the cities of Bremen or Bremerhaven. Oldenburg,

Danish from 1667, passed to the bishopric of Lübeck in 1773; the Holy Roman Emperor made it a duchy in 1777. As a small state of the Confederation after 1815 it supported Prussia, becoming a member of the Prussian Zollverein (1853) and North German Confederation (1867). The grand duke abdicated in 1918 and was replaced by an elected government.

Schaumburg-Lippe was a small sovereign principality. As such it became a member of the Confederation of the Rhine in 1807 and of the German Confederation in 1815. Surrounded by Prussian territory, it also joined the Prussian-led North German Confederation in 1867. Part of the Empire until 1918, it then became a state of the new republic.

Brunswick, a small duchy, was taken into the Kingdom of Westphalia by Napoleon in 1806 but restored to independence in 1814. In 1830 the duke, Charles II, was forced into exile and replaced in 1831 by his more liberal brother, William. The succession passed to a Hanoverian claimant in 1913 but the duchy ended in 1918 with the Empire.

As a state of the republican Germany, Brunswick was greatly reduced under the Third Reich. Its boundaries were restored by the British occupation forces in 1945.

Hanover was an autonomous Electorate of the Holy Roman Empire whose rulers were also kings of Great Britain from 1714 to 1837. From 1762 they ruled almost entirely from England. After Napoleonic invasions Hanover was restored in 1815. A constitution of 1819 made no radical change and had to be followed by more liberal versions in 1833 and 1848. Prussia annexed Hanover in 1866; it remained a Prussian province until 1946. On 1 Nov. 1946 all four states were combined by the British military administration to form the *Land* of Lower Saxony.

TERRITORY AND POPULATION

Lower Saxony has an area of 47,616 sq. km, and is divided into 4 administrative regions, 8 urban districts, 38 rural districts and 1,023 communes; capital, Hanover.

Population, on 31 Dec. 2001, was 7,956,416 (3,893,308 males, 4,063,108 females).

SOCIAL STATISTICS

Statistics for calendar years:

	Live births	Marriages	Divorces	Deaths
1998	82,207	46,532	18,176	83,677
1999	80,483	47,568	18,106	82,652
2000	79,436	45,233	18,367	82,901
2001	75,239	41,781	19,485	82,517

CONSTITUTION AND GOVERNMENT

The *Land* Niedersachsen was formed on 1 Nov. 1946 by merging the former Prussian province of Hanover and the *Länder* Brunswick, Oldenburg and Schaumburg-Lippe. Lower Saxony has seven seats in the Bundesrat.

RECENT ELECTIONS

At the Diet elections on 2 Feb. 2003 the Christian Democratic Union won 91 of 183 seats, receiving 48·3% of votes cast (up from 35·9% in 1998), the Social Democratic Party 63 with 33·4% (down from 47·9% in 1998), the Free Democrats 15 with 8·1% and the Greens 14 with 7·6%.

CURRENT ADMINISTRATION

The *Prime Minister* is Christian Wulff (CDU).

Government Website: http://www.niedersachsen.de

ECONOMY

Banking and Finance. 249 credit institutions were operating in 2001. Deposits totalled €49,308m.

ENERGY AND NATURAL RESOURCES

Electricity. Electricity production in 2001 was 59,420m. kWh. Consumption in 2000 was 47,528m. kWh.

Agriculture. Area and yield of the most important crops:

	Area (in 1,000 ha)			Yield (in 1,000 tonnes)		
	1999	2000	2001	1999	2000	2001
Sugarbeet	125	114	115	6,971	6,554	6,289
Potatoes	132	129	122	5,548	5,979	5,529
Wheat	328	391	390	2,834	3,214	3,463
Barley	362	313	306	2,294	1,843	2,016
Rye	125	154	156	806	857	1,114
Oats	35	24	23	177	110	113

Livestock, 3 May 2001: cattle, 2,827,016 (including 762,780 milch cows); pigs, 7,501,953; sheep, 272,087; horses, 98,636; poultry, 54,269,193.

Fisheries. In 1999 the yield of sea and coastal fishing was 32,117 tonnes valued at 66·5m. DM.

INDUSTRY

In Sept. 2001, 4,139 establishments employed 561,758 persons; of these 59,135 were employed in electrical engineering; 52,241 in machine construction.

Labour. The economically active persons totalled 3,424,500 in April 2001. Of the total, 3,043,800 were employees, 325,500 self-employed, 55,300 unpaid family workers; 1,058,600 were engaged in power supply, mining, manufacturing and building, 835,700 in commerce and transport, 115,600 in agriculture and forestry, 1,414,700 in other industries and services.

COMMUNICATIONS

Roads. At 1 Jan. 2002 there were 28,103 km of 'classified' roads, comprising 1,351 km of Autobahn, 4,823 km of federal roads, 8,324 km of first-class and 13,604 km of second-class highways. Number of motor vehicles, 1 Jan. 2002, was 5,301,616 including 4,373,403 passenger cars, 249,464 lorries, 8,582 buses, 236,176 tractors and 360,208 motorcycles.

Rail. In 2001, 25·9m. tonnes of freight came into the *Land* by rail and 20·9m. tonnes left by rail.

Civil Aviation. 77,853 planes landed at Hanover airport in 2001, which saw 2,528,608 passenger arrivals and 2,503,510 departures. 3,579 tonnes of freight left by air and 2,079 tonnes came in.

SOCIAL INSTITUTIONS

Justice. There are a constitutional court *(Staatsgerichtshof)*, 3 courts of appeal, 11 regional courts, 79 local courts, a *Land* labour court, 15 labour courts, a *Land* social court, 8 social courts, a finance court, a higher administrative court and 4 administrative courts.

Religion. On 25 May 1987 (census) there were 66·12% Protestants and 19·6% Roman Catholics.

Education. In 2001–02 there were 1,879 primary schools with 353,128 pupils; 952 post-primary schools with 245,676 pupils; 286 special schools with 38,204 pupils; 418 secondary modern schools with 115,200 pupils; 235 grammar schools with 153,108 pupils; 33 comprehensive schools with 33,849 pupils.

In the winter term 2001–02 there were seven universities (Göttingen, 22,574 students; Hanover, 26,241; Hildesheim, 3,748; Lüneburg, 6,913; Oldenburg, 11,476; Osnabrück, 10,544; Vechta, 1,769); two technical universities (Braunschweig, 14,166; Clausthal, 2,761); the medical college of Hanover (3,228); the veterinary college in Hanover (1,718).

Health. At Dec. 2000 there were 24,724 doctors and 216 hospitals with 6·0 beds per 1,000 population.

CULTURE

Broadcasting. Norddeutscher Rundfunk is the public broadcasting service for Lower Saxony.

Cinema. In 2001 there were 457 screens with 83,432 seats.

Tourism. In 2001, 9,620,917 guests spent 33,880,736 nights in Lower Saxony.

Libraries. In 2000 there were 1,183 public libraries and (1997) 98 academic libraries.

Theatre and Opera. 47 theatres and concert halls hosted 4,494 productions for audiences of 1,460,000 in 1998–99.

Museums and Galleries. 7,911,772 people visited the 620 museums in 2000.

FURTHER READING
Statistical Information: The Niedersächsisches Landesamt für Statistik, Postfach 910764, D-30427 Hanover. *Head of Division:* President Karl-Ludwig Strelen. Main publications are: *Statistisches Jahrbuch Niedersachsen* (from 1950).—*Statistische Monatshefte Niedersachsen* (from 1947).—*Statistische Berichte Niedersachsen.*—*Statistisches Taschenbuch Niedersachsen 2002* (biennial).

State Libraries: Niedersächsische Staats- und Universitätsbibliothek, Prinzenstr. 1, D-37073 Göttingen. *Director:* Helmut Vogt; Niedersächsische Landesbibliothek, Waterloostr. 8, D-30169 Hanover. *Director:* Dr Wolfgang Dittrich.

MECKLENBURG-WEST POMERANIA
Mecklenburg-Vorpommern

KEY HISTORICAL EVENTS
Pomerania was at one time under Swedish control while Mecklenburg was an independent part of the German Empire. The two states were not united until after the Second World War, and after a short period when it was subdivided into three districts under the GDR, it became a state of the Federal Republic of Germany in 1990. The people of the region speak a dialect known as Plattdeutsch (Low German). The four main cities of this state are Hanseatic towns from the period when the area dominated trade with Scandinavia. Rostock on the North Sea coast became the home of the GDR's biggest shipyards.

TERRITORY AND POPULATION
The area is 23,171 sq. km. It is divided into 6 urban districts, 12 rural districts and 989 communes. Population on 31 Dec. 2001 was 1,759,877 (898,648 females). It is the most sparsely populated of the German Länder, with a population density of 76 per sq. km in 2001. The capital is Schwerin.

SOCIAL STATISTICS
Statistics for calendar years:

	Live births	Marriages	Divorces	Deaths
1998	12,246	6,903	3,891	17,619
1999	12,589	8,029	3,456	17,458
2000	13,319	8,083	3,951	17,460
2001	12,968	7,869	4,021	17,179

CONSTITUTION AND GOVERNMENT
The *Land* was reconstituted on former GDR territory in 1990. It has three seats in the Bundesrat.

RECENT ELECTIONS
At the Diet elections of 22 Sept. 2002 the Social Democrats (SPD) won 33 seats with 40·6% of the vote; the Christian Democrats (CDU), 25, with 31·3%; and the Party of Democratic Socialism (PDS, former Communists), 13, with 16·4%.

CURRENT ADMINISTRATION
The *Prime Minister* is Dr Harald Ringstorff (SPD).

Government Website: http://www.mecklenburg-vorpommern.de

ENERGY AND NATURAL RESOURCES

Agriculture. Area and yield of the most important crops:

	Area (in 1,000 ha)			Yield (in 1,000 tonnes)		
	1999	2000	2001	1999	2000	2001
Wheat	275·2	310·4	297·2	2,108·0	2,131·7	2,333·5
Sugarbeet	31·2	28·9	27·9	1,444·9	1,420·2	1,334·0
Barley	160·9	151·8	148·8	1,140·9	969·6	1,151·3
Rape	196·3	190·4	207·9	777·1	726·4	858·8
Rye	99·0	107·1	111·0	651·0	563·3	737·1
Potatoes	16·3	16·4	15·9	493·3	640·2	580·9
Oats	12·0	12·0	12·0	63·7	43·1	58·9

Livestock in 2001: cattle, 591,948 (including 190,103 milch cows); pigs, 632,626; sheep, 111,988; horses, 12,549; poultry, 7,394,398.

Fisheries. Sea catch, 2000: 14,686 tonnes (535 tonnes frozen, 14,150 tonnes fresh). Freshwater catch, 2000: 847 tonnes (mainly carp, trout and eels). Fish farming, 2001: 553 tonnes.

INDUSTRY

In 2001 there were 662 enterprises (with 20 or more employees) employing 48,573 persons.

Labour. 747,400 persons (337,600 females) were employed at the 1%-sample survey of the microcensus of April 2001, including 356,200 white-collar workers, 287,700 manual workers and 63,900 self-employed and family assistants. 39,500 persons were employed as officials. Employment by sector (on average for the year 2001): public and private services, 250,500; trade, guest business, transport and communications, 191,500; financing, leasing and services for enterprises, 88,300; construction, 84,000; manufacturing, 77,200; agriculture, forestry and fisheries, 32,500; mining, energy and water resources, 6,900; total, 731,000.

COMMUNICATIONS

Roads. In 2001 there were 9,805 km of 'classified' roads, comprising 354 km of Autobahn, 2,081 km of federal roads, 3,246 km of first-class and 4,124 km of second-class highways. Number of motor vehicles at 1 Jan. 2002 was 1,051,961, including 889,928 passenger cars, 75,353 lorries, 2,001 buses and 45,605 motorcycles.

Shipping. There is a lake district of some 660 lakes. The ports of Rostock, Stralsund and Wismar are important for ship-building and repairs. In 2001 the cargo fleet consisted of 87 vessels (including 1 tanker) of 1,191,000 GT. Sea traffic, 2001, incoming 13,681,629 tonnes; outgoing 10,609,714 tonnes.

SOCIAL INSTITUTIONS

Justice. There is a court of appeal (*Oberlandesgericht*), 4 regional courts (*Landgerichte*), 21 local courts (*Amtsgerichte*), a *Land* labour court, 4 labour courts, a *Land* social court, 4 social courts, a finance court, a higher administrative court and 2 administrative courts.

Religion. In 2001 the Evangelical Lutheran Church of Mecklenburg had 226,000 adherents, 214 pastors and 336 parishes. Roman Catholics numbered 69,800, with 62 priests and 68 parishes. The Pomeranian Evangelical Church had 115,700 adherents, 144 pastors and 279 parishes in 2001.

Education. In 2001 there were 265 primary schools, 17 comprehensives, 401 secondary schools and 96 special needs schools. There are universities at Rostock and Greifswald with (in 2001–02) 19,110 students and 4,366 academic staff, and 5 institutions of equivalent status with 9,431 students and 1,148 academic staff.

CULTURE

Cinema. 4·1m. people visited 112 cinemas in 2001.

Tourism. In July 2001 there were 2,615 places of accommodation (with nine or more beds) providing a total of 160,961 beds. 4,534,825 guests stayed an average of 4·4 nights each in 2001.

Libraries. In 2000 there were 193 public libraries with 222,920 active users, who borrowed around 6·6m. items.

Theatre and Opera. In 2000 there were seven theatre companies. 575,797 people attended 2,968 productions during the year.

Museums and Galleries. 3,275,718 visitors saw 399 exhibitions in 159 museums in 2000.

FURTHER READING

Statistical Office: Statistisches Landesamt Mecklenburg-Vorpommern, Postfach 120135, D-19018 Schwerin. Main publications are: *Statistische Monatshefte Mecklenburg-Vorpommern* (since 1991); *Gemeindedaten Mecklenburg-Vorpommern* (since 1999; electronic); *Statistische Berichte* (since 1991; various); *Statistisches Jahrbuch Mecklenburg-Vorpommern* (since 1991); *Statistische Sonderhefte* (since 1992; various).

NORTH RHINE-WESTPHALIA

Nordrhein-Westfalen

KEY HISTORICAL EVENTS

Historical Westphalia consisted of many small political units, most of them absorbed by Prussia and Hanover before 1800. In 1807 Napoleon created a Kingdom of Westphalia for his brother Joseph. This included Hesse-Kassel, but was formed mainly from the Prussian and Hanoverian lands between the rivers Elbe and Weser.

In 1815 the kingdom ended with Napoleon's defeat. Most of the area was given to Prussia, with the small principalities of Lippe and Waldeck surviving as independent states. Both joined the North German Confederation in 1867, Lippe remained autonomous after the end of the Empire in 1918; Waldeck was absorbed into Prussia in 1929.

In 1946 the occupying forces combined Lippe with most of the Prussian province of Westphalia to form the *Land* of North Rhine-Westphalia. On 1 March 1947 the allied Control Council formally abolished Prussia.

TERRITORY AND POPULATION

The *Land* comprises 34,082 sq. km. It is divided into 5 administrative regions, 23 urban districts, 31 rural districts and 396 communes. Capital: Düsseldorf. Population, 31 Dec. 2001, 18,052,092 (8,782,352 males, 9,269,740 females).

SOCIAL STATISTICS

Statistics for calendar years:

	Live births	Marriages	Divorces	Deaths
1998	182,287	97,679	45,246	189,147
1999	176,578	99,645	45,105	188,851
2000	175,144	97,508	45,201	187,736
2001	167,752	89,529	46,913	184,824

CONSTITUTION AND GOVERNMENT

Since Oct. 1990 North Rhine-Westphalia has had six seats in the Bundesrat.

RECENT ELECTIONS

The Diet elected on 14 May 2000 consisted of 102 Social Democrats (42·8% of votes cast), 88 Christian Democrats (37·0%), 24 Free Democrats (9·8%) and 17 Greens (7·1%). Turn-out was 56·7%.

CURRENT ADMINISTRATION

North Rhine-Westphalia is governed by Social Democrats (SPD) and the Greens.
Prime Minister: Peer Steinbrück (SPD).

Government Website: http://www.nrw.de

ECONOMY

North Rhine-Westphalia has the highest GDP of any German *Land*—€459·6bn. in 2001 out of a total of €2,063·0bn. Foreign direct investment is also higher than in any other *Land*.

Budget. The predicted total revenue for 2002 was €48,558·4m. and the predicted total expenditure was also €48,558·4m.

ENERGY AND NATURAL RESOURCES

Agriculture. Area and yield of the most important crops:

	Area (in 1,000 ha)			Yield (in 1,000 tonnes)		
	1999	2000	2001	1999	2000	2001
Sugarbeet	75·3	70·5	71·1	4,530·9	4,377·3	3,939·1
Wheat	239·5	262·4	257·1	2,023·6	2,095·5	2,356·4
Barley	200·3	190·6	193·1	1,322·4	1,203·3	1,420·1
Potatoes	31·0	32·9	30·1	1,294·2	1,584·9	1,282·9
Rye	21·3	26·2	25·3	209·1	160·9	184·1
Oats	31·4	23·5	22·2	167·7	115·0	122·4

Livestock, 3 May 2001: cattle, 1,513,783 (including 404,110 milch cows); pigs, 6,119,904; sheep, 225,079; poultry, 10,772,733.

INDUSTRY

In Sept. 2001, 10,927 establishments (with 20 or more employees) employed 1,453,761 persons: 315,443 were employed in metal production and manufacture of metal goods; 226,335 in machine construction; 159,682 in manufacture of office machines, computers, electrical and precision engineering and optics; 131,508 in the chemical industry; 114,962 in production of food and tobacco; 102,514 in motor vehicle manufacture. 64% of the workforce is now employed in the services industry. Of the total population, 8·1% were engaged in industry.

Labour. The economically active persons totalled 7,686,000 at the 1%-sample survey of the microcensus of May 2001. Of the total, 6,910,000 were employees, 700,000 self-employed and 76,000 unpaid family workers; 2,486,000 were engaged in power supply, mining, manufacturing, water supply and building, 1,858,000 in commerce, hotel trade and transport, 123,000 in agriculture, forestry and fishing, and 3,218,000 in other industries and services.

COMMUNICATIONS

Roads. There were (1 Jan. 2002) 29,629 km of 'classified' roads, comprising 2,180 km of Autobahn, 5,045 km of federal roads, 12,582 km of first-class and 9,808 km of second-class highways. Number of motor vehicles (1 Jan. 2002): 11,183,116, including 9,518,936 passenger cars, 509,195 lorries, 17,948 buses and 783,285 motorcycles.

Civil Aviation. In 2001, 89,611 aircraft landed at Düsseldorf, bringing 7,649,449 incoming passengers; and 65,909 aircraft landed at Cologne-Bonn, bringing 2,833,572 incoming passengers.

SOCIAL INSTITUTIONS

Justice. There are a constitutional court *(Verfassungsgerichtshof)*, 3 courts of appeal, 19 regional courts, 130 local courts, 3 *Land* labour courts, 30 labour courts, 1 *Land* social court, 8 social courts, 3 finance courts, a higher administrative court and 7 administrative courts.

Religion. On 25 May 1987 (census) there were 35·2% Protestants and 49·4% Roman Catholics.

Education. In 2001 there were 4,213 primary schools with 61,753 teachers and 1,086,391 pupils; 705 special schools with 16,058 teachers and 98,460 pupils; 545 intermediate schools with 18,084 teachers and 334,439 pupils; 264 *Gesamtschulen* (comprehensive schools) with 17,769 teachers and 234,481 pupils; 628 high schools with 33,561 teachers and 536,299 pupils; there were 304 part-time vocational schools with 382,551 pupils; 195 vocational preparatory year schools with 17,531 pupils; 301 full-time vocational schools with 101,647 pupils; 189 full-time vocational schools leading up to vocational colleges with 17,626 pupils; 264 advanced full-time vocational schools with 40,504 pupils; 552 schools for public health occupations with 16,062 teachers and 41,503 pupils.

In the winter term 2001–02 there were eight universities (Bielefeld, 19,353 students; Bochum, 33,482; Bonn, 37,462; Cologne (Köln), 59,114; Dortmund, 24,361; Düsseldorf, 25,111; Münster, 42,565; Witten, 911); the Technical University of Aachen (28,462); 3 Roman Catholic and 2 Protestant theological colleges with a total of 535 students. There were also 4 colleges of music, 4 colleges of fine arts and the college for physical education in Cologne with 10,346 students in total; 23 *Fachhochschulen* (vocational colleges) with 97,407 students, and 6 *Universitäten-Gesamthochschulen* with a total of 119,518 students.

Health. In 2001 there were 462 hospitals in North Rhine-Westphalia with 134,883 beds, which had an average occupancy rate of 79·3%.

CULTURE

Cinema. In 1998 there were 930 screens with 186,151 seats.

Tourism. At Dec. 2001 there were 5,664 places of accommodation (nine beds or more) providing 281,931 beds altogether. In 2001, 14,488,057 visitors (2,479,528 foreigners) spent 36,987,064 nights in North Rhine-Westphalia.

Libraries. In 2001 there were 2,083 public libraries lending a total of 64,268,293 items.

Theatre and Opera. 19,849 productions were put on in 160 theatres and concert halls for audiences totalling 6,495,090 in 2000–01.

Museums and Galleries. In 2000 there were 655 museums which had 12,545,769 visitors.

FURTHER READING

Statistical Information: The Landesamt für Datenverarbeitung und Statistik Nordrhein-Westfalen (Mauerstr. 51, D-40476 Düsseldorf) was founded in 1946, by amalgamating the provincial statistical offices of Rhineland and Westphalia. *President:* Jochen Kehlenbach. The Landesamt publishes: *Statistisches Jahrbuch Nordrhein-Westfalen.* From 1949. More than 550 other publications yearly.

Land Library: Universitätsbibliothek, Universitätsstr. 1, D-40225 Düsseldorf. *Director:* Dr Irmgard Siebert.

RHINELAND-PALATINATE

Rheinland-Pfalz

KEY HISTORICAL EVENTS

The *Land* was formed from the Rhenisch Palatinate and the Rhine valley areas of Prussia, Hesse-Darmstadt, Hesse-Kassel and Bavaria.

From 1214 the Palatinate was ruled by the Bavarian house of Wittelsbach, with its capital as Heidelberg. In 1797 the land west of the Rhine was taken into France, and Napoleon divided the eastern land between Baden and Hesse. In 1815 the territory taken by France was restored to Germany and allotted to Bavaria. The area and its neighbours formed the strategically important Bavarian Circle of the Rhine. The rule of the Wittelsbachs ended in 1918 but the Palatinate remained part of Bavaria until the American occupying forces detached it in 1946. The new *Land*, incorporating the Palatinate and other territory, received its constitution in April 1947.

TERRITORY AND POPULATION

Rhineland-Palatinate has an area of 19,853 sq. km. It comprises 12 urban districts, 24 rural districts and 2,306 other communes. The capital is Mainz. Population (at 31 Dec. 2001), 4,099,066 (2,063,389 females).

SOCIAL STATISTICS

Statistics for calendar years:

	Live births	Marriages	Divorces	Deaths
1998	39,639	21,763	10,148	42,708
1999	38,190	22,641	9,860	42,524
2000	37,826	22,129	10,416	42,088
2001	35,781	20,608	10,301	42,222

CONSTITUTION AND GOVERNMENT

The constitution of the *Land* Rheinland-Pfalz was approved by the Consultative Assembly on 25 April 1947 and by referendum on 18 May 1947, when 579,002 voted for and 514,338 against its acceptance. It has four seats in the Bundesrat.

RECENT ELECTIONS

At the elections of 25 March 2001 the Social Democratic Party won 49 seats of the 101 in the state parliament with 44·7% of votes cast; the Christian Democrats 38 with 35·3% (their worst result ever in Rheinland-Pfalz); the Free Democrats 8 with 7·8%; and the Greens 6 with 5·2%; turn-out was 62·1%.

CURRENT ADMINISTRATION

The coalition cabinet is headed by Kurt Beck (b. 1949; Social Democrat).

Government Website: http://www.rlp.de

ENERGY AND NATURAL RESOURCES

Agriculture. Area and yield of the most important products:

	Area (1,000 ha)			Yield (1,000 tonnes)		
	1999	2000	2001	1999	2000	2001
Sugarbeet	23·3	22·3	19·8	1,310·9	1,633·7	1,094·2
Wheat	82·5	100·0	84·2	556·1	664·6	603·9
Barley	117·6	106·2	121·2	632·2	549·6	582·9
Potatoes	10·4	9·7	8·7	339·5	368·1	267·9
Rye	12·8	14·4	11·3	74·7	85·1	66·6
Oats	13·7	11·9	11·9	63·9	57·4	45·9
Wine	64·7	64·6	62·7	7,954·81[1]	6,786·3[1]	5,959·4[1]

[1]1,000 hectolitres.

Livestock (2001, in 1,000): cattle, 446·2 (including milch cows, 131·9); sheep, 138·2; pigs, 361·9; horses, 23·9 (1999); poultry, 1,732·9 (1999).

Forestry. Total area covered by forests in Dec. 2001 was 8,103·5 sq. km or 40·8% of the total area.

INDUSTRY

In 2001, 2,390 establishments (with 20 or more employees) employed 302,652 persons; of these 61,071 were employed in the chemical industry; 35,723 in machine construction; 22,412 in processing stones and earthenware; 19,896 in electrical equipment manufacture; 5,317 in leather goods and footwear.

Labour. The economically active persons totalled 1,795,400 in 2002. Of the total, 1,507,600 were employees, 186,300 were self-employed, 25,100 were unpaid family workers; 579,300 were engaged in power supply, mining, manufacturing and building, 407,300 in commerce, transport, hotels and restaurants, 48,900 in agriculture and forestry, 760,000 in other industries and services.

COMMUNICATIONS

Roads. In 2002 there were 18,403 km of 'classified' roads, comprising 839 km of Autobahn, 2,985 km of federal roads, 7,175 km of first-class and 7,405 km of second-class highways. Number of motor vehicles, 1 Jan. 2002, was 2,861,809, including 2,351,407 passenger cars, 126,429 lorries, 5,628 buses, 137,705 tractors and 205,864 motorcycles.

SOCIAL INSTITUTIONS

Justice. There are a constitutional court *(Verfassungsgerichtshof)*, 2 courts of appeal, 8 regional courts, 46 local courts, a *Land* labour court, 5 labour courts, a *Land* social court, 4 social courts, a finance court, a higher administrative court and 4 administrative courts.

Religion. On 25 May 1987 (census) there were 37·7% Protestants and 54·5% Roman Catholics.

Education. In 2001 there were 995 primary schools with 8,996 teachers and 177,518 pupils; 631 secondary schools with 17,360 teachers and 293,809 pupils; 144 special schools with 2,361 teachers and 16,951 pupils; 109 vocational and advanced vocational schools with 5,065 teachers and 123,876 pupils.

In higher education, in the winter term 2002–03 (provisional figures) there were the University of Mainz (31,212 students), the University of Kaiserslautern (8,425 students), the University of Trier (11,821 students), the University of Koblenz-Landau (9,537 students), the *Deutsche Hochschule für Verwaltungswissenschaften* in Speyer (538 students), the *Wissenschaftliche Hochschule für Unternehmens-führung* (Otto Beisheim Graduate School) in Vallendar (445 students), the Roman Catholic Theological College in Trier (266 students) and the Roman Catholic Theological College in Vallendar (114 students). There were also 9 *Fach-hochschulen* with 26,024 students and 3 *Verwaltungsfachhochschulen* with 2,139 students.

CULTURE

Cinema. There were 178 screens in 1996 with 32,855 seats.

Tourism. In 1997, 3,776 places of accommodation provided 150,906 beds for 5,396,000 visitors.

Libraries. In 1996 there were 5,052 volumes held in 909 libraries.

Theatre and Opera. There were 15 theatres and concert halls in 1998–99. 542,000 people attended 1,617 productions.

Museums and Galleries. In 1999, 335 exhibitions took place in 386 museums, visited by 3,756,281 people.

FURTHER READING

Statistical Information: Statistisches Landesamt Rheinland-Pfalz (Mainzer Str., 14–16, D-56130 Bad Ems). *President:* Klaus Maxeiner. Its publications include: *Statistisches Taschenbuch Rheinland-Pfalz* (from 1948); *Statistische Monatshefte Rheinland-Pfalz* (from 1958); *Statistik von Rheinland-Pfalz* (from 1949) 381 vols. to date; *Rheinland-Pfalz im Spiegel der Statistik* (from 1968); *Rheinland-Pfalz—seine kreisfreien Städte und Landkreise* (1992); *Rheinland-Pfalz heute* (from 1973).

SAARLAND

KEY HISTORICAL EVENTS

Long disputed between Germany and France, the area was occupied by France in 1792. Most of it was allotted to Prussia at the close of the Napoleonic wars in 1815. In 1870 Prussia defeated France and when, in 1871, the German Empire was founded under Prussian leadership, it was able to incorporate Lorraine. This part of France was the Saar territory's western neighbour so the Saar was no longer a vulnerable boundary state. It began to develop industrially, exploiting Lorraine coal and iron.

In 1919 the League of Nations took control of the Saar until a plebiscite of 1935 favoured return to Germany. In 1945 there was a French occupation, and in 1947 the Saar was made an international area, but in economic union with France. In 1954 France and Germany agreed that the Saar should be a separate and autonomous state, under an independent commissioner. This was rejected by referendum and France agreed to return Saarland to Germany; it became a *Land* of the Federal Republic on 1 Jan. 1957.

TERRITORY AND POPULATION

Saarland has an area of 2,570 sq. km. Population, 31 Dec. 2001, 1,066,470 (517,432 males, 549,038 females). It comprises 6 rural districts and 52 communes. The capital is Saarbrücken.

SOCIAL STATISTICS

Statistics for calendar years:

	Live births	Marriages	Divorces	Deaths
1998	9,111	5,857	2,996	12,450
1999	8,941	6,150	2,902	12,775
2000	8,783	5,856	3,066	12,311
2001	8,196	5,417	3,100	12,316

CONSTITUTION AND GOVERNMENT

Saarland has three seats in the Bundesrat.

RECENT ELECTIONS

At the elections to the Saar Diet of 5 Sept. 1999 the Christian Democrats (CDU) won 26 seats with 45·5% of votes cast and the Social Democrats (SDP) 25 with 44·4%.

CURRENT ADMINISTRATION

Saarland is governed by Christian Democrats in Parliament. The *Prime Minister* is Peter Müller (Christian Democrat).

Government Website: http://www.saarland.de

ENERGY AND NATURAL RESOURCES

Electricity. In 2001 electricity production was 11,300m. kWh. End-user consumption totalled 7,569m. kWh in 2001.

Oil and Gas. 9,211m. kWh of gas was used in 2001.

Agriculture. The cultivated area (2001) occupied 114,618 ha or 44·6% of the total area.

Area and yield of the most important crops:

	Area (in 1,000 ha)			Yield (in 1,000 tonnes)		
	1999	2000	2001	1999	2000	2001
Wheat	6·3	8·8	7·3	39·0	56·7	44·6
Barley	8·9	7·0	7·7	44·6	35·8	37·0
Rye	3·6	4·5	3·7	20·0	26·5	19·0
Oats	3·9	2·7	3·2	18·3	12·6	12·4
Potatoes	0·2	0·2	0·2	6·8	7·7	7·3

Livestock, May 2001: cattle, 62,157 (including 15,611 milch cows); pigs, 22,524; sheep, 16,381; horses, 5,142; poultry, 207,017.

Forestry. The forest area comprises nearly 33·4% of the total (256,929 ha).

INDUSTRY

In June 2002, 515 establishments (with 20 or more employees) employed 102,459 persons; of these 24,925 were engaged in manufacturing of motor vehicles, parts and accessories, 12,812 in machine construction, 10,656 in iron and steel production, 8,862 in coalmining, 4,020 in steel construction, 3,437 in electrical engineering. In 2001 the coalmines produced 5·3m. tonnes of coal. Two blast furnaces and nine steel furnaces produced 4·0m. tonnes of pig-iron and 4·8m. tonnes of crude steel.

Labour. The economically active persons totalled 443,000 at the 1%-sample survey of the microcensus of April 2001. Of the total, 403,000 were employees and 37,000 self-employed; 107,600 were engaged in commerce and transport, 105,400 in power supply, mining, manufacturing and building, 4,600 in agriculture and forestry, and 108,400 in other industries and services.

COMMUNICATIONS

Roads. At 1 Jan. 2002 there were 2,031 km of classified roads, comprising 236 km of Autobahn, 348 km of federal roads, 827 km of first-class and 620 km of second-class highways. Number of motor vehicles, 31 Dec. 2001, 741,922, including 629,244 passenger cars, 34,411 lorries, 1,395 buses, 14,889 tractors and 54,122 motorcycles.

Shipping. During 2001, 1,272 ships docked in Saarland ports, bringing 2·5m. tonnes of freight. In the same period 453 ships left the ports, carrying 820,049 tonnes of freight.

SOCIAL INSTITUTIONS

Justice. There are a constitutional court *(Verfassungsgerichtshof)*, a regional court of appeal, a regional court, 10 local courts, a *Land* labour court, 3 labour courts, a *Land* social court, a social court, a finance court, a higher administrative court and an administrative court.

Religion. In 2000, 67·7% of the population were Roman Catholics and 20·0% were Protestants.

Education. In 2002–03 there were 269 primary schools with 41,402 pupils; 40 special schools with 3,827 pupils; 54 *Realschulen, Erweiterte Realschulen* and *Sekundarschulen* with 31,075 pupils; 37 high schools with 30,4684 pupils; 15 comprehensive high schools with 10,612 pupils; 4 *Freie Waldorfschulen* with 1,240 pupils; 2 evening intermediate schools with 277 pupils; 1 evening high school and 1 Saarland College with 250 pupils; 38 part-time vocational schools with 22,029 pupils; year of commercial basic training: 57 institutions with 2,619 pupils; 18 advanced full-time vocational schools and schools for technicians with 1,989 pupils; 52 full-time vocational schools with 5,104 pupils; 32 *Fachoberschulen* (full-time vocational schools leading up to vocational colleges) with 4,837 pupils; 38 schools for public health occupations with 2,162 pupils. The number of pupils attending the vocational schools amounts to 38,683.

In the winter term 2001–02 there was the University of the Saarland with 16,270 students; 1 academy of fine art with 255 students; 1 academy of music and theatre with 325 students; 1 vocational college (economics and technics) with 2,661 students; 1 vocational college for social affairs with 250 students; and 1 vocational college for public administration with 389 students.

Health. In 2001 the 28 hospitals in the Saarland contained 7,540 beds and treated 259,448 patients. The average occupancy rate was 84·8%. There were also 22 out-patient and rehabilitation centres which treated 37,300 patients in 2001. On average they were using 84·9% of their capacity.

CULTURE

Cinema. Saarland had 79 cinema screens in 2001 with 2,232,000 visitors.

Tourism. In 2001, 15,101 beds were available in 311 places of accommodation (of nine or more beds). 646,917 guests spent 2,160,632 nights in the Saarland, staying an average of 3·3 days each.

Libraries. In 1998, 162 libraries held 1,041,000 volumes.

Theatre and Opera. In 1997–98 there were five theatres and concert halls. 237,000 people attended a total of 606 productions.

Museums and Galleries. 62 museums hosted 91 exhibitions in 1999. Attendances were 569,030 for the year.

FURTHER READING

Statistical Information: Statistisches Landesamt Saarland (Virchowstrasse 7, D-66119 Saarbrücken). *Chief:* Michael Sossong. The most important publications are: *Statistisches Jahrbuch Saarland,* from 1999.—*Saarland in Zahlen* (special issues).—*Einzelschriften zur Statistik des Saarlandes,* from 1950.—*Statistik-Journal* (monthly), from 1996. *Website:* http://www.statistik.saarland.de
Born, M., *Geographische Inselkunde des Saarlandes.* Saarbrücken, 1980
Herrmann, H.-W., *et al., Das Saarland: Politische, wirtschaftliche und kulturelle Entwicklung.* Saarbrücken, 1989
Matthias, K., *Wirtschaftsgeographie des Saarlandes.* Saarbrücken, 1980.—*Wirtschaftsraum Saarland* (published in collaboration with the Industrie- und Handelskammer des Saarlandes). Oldenburg, 1990
Staerk, D., *Das Saarlandbuch.* Saarbrücken, 1981

SAXONY
Freistaat Sachsen

KEY HISTORICAL EVENTS
The former kingdom of Saxony was a member state of the German Empire from 1871 until 1918, when it became the state of Saxony and joined the Weimar Republic. After the Second World War it was one of the five states in the German Democratic Republic until German reunification in 1990. It has been home to much of Germany's cultural history. In the 18th century, the capital of Saxony, Dresden, became the cultural capital of northern Europe earning the title 'Florence of the North', and the other great eastern German city, Leipzig, was a lively commercial city with strong artistic trends. The three cities of Dresden, Chemnitz and Leipzig formed the industrial heartland of Germany which, after World War II, was the manufacturing centre of the GDR.

TERRITORY AND POPULATION
The area is 18,413 sq. km. It is divided into 3 administrative regions, 7 urban districts, 22 rural districts and 537 communes. Population on 31 Dec. 2001 was 4,384,192 (2,257,469 females, 2,126,723 males); density, 238 per sq. km. The capital is Dresden.

SOCIAL STATISTICS
Statistics for calendar years:

	Live births	Marriages	Divorces	Deaths
1998	30,190	15,648	9,337	51,883
1999	31,383	17,145	8,748	50,562
2000	33,139	16,482	8,775	50,428
2001	31,943	15,421	8,430	49,244

CONSTITUTION AND GOVERNMENT
The *Land* was reconstituted as the Free State of Saxony on former GDR territory in 1990. It has four seats in the Bundesrat.

RECENT ELECTIONS
At the Diet elections of 19 Sept. 1999 the Christian Democrats won 76 seats, with 56·9% of the vote; the Party of Democratic Socialism (former Communists), 30, with 22·2%; the Social Democrats, 14, with 10·7%.

CURRENT ADMINISTRATION
The *Prime Minister* is Georg Milbradt (b. 1945; Christian Democrat).

Government Website: http://www.sachsen.de

ENERGY AND NATURAL RESOURCES
Agriculture. Area and yield of the most important crops:

	Area (in 1,000 ha)			Yield (in 1,000 tonnes)		
	2000	2001	2002	2000	2001	2002
Maize	65·9	70·5	69·5	2,396·8	2,477·6	2,528·1
Fodder	188·3	187·7	183·7	1,474·2	1,488·2	1,504·2
Wheat	171·5	167·5	172·9	1,107·1	1,202·5	1,070·8
Barley	149·0	149·1	138·8	844·3	988·1	715·7
Potatoes	8·8	8·1	8·3	315·7	317·7	284·2
Rye	50·6	48·8	41·9	256·6	289·0	204·0

Livestock in May 2002 (in 1,000): cattle, 529 (including milch cows, 208); pigs, 613; sheep, 138.

INDUSTRY
In Sept. 2002, 2,807 establishments (with 20 or more employees) employed 224,769 persons.

Labour. The unemployment rate was 18·9% in Dec. 2002.

COMMUNICATIONS

Roads. On 1 Jan. 2002 there were 454·3 km of autobahn and 2,467 km of main roads. On 1 Jan. 2002 there were 2,622,529 registered motor vehicles, including 2,253,592 motor cars, 232,759 lorries and tractors, 4,402 buses and 109,875 motorcycles.

Civil Aviation. Leipzig airport handled 2,194,000 passengers (1,399,000 on international flights) in 2000.

SOCIAL INSTITUTIONS

Religion. In 2001, 22·9% of the population belonged to the Evangelical Church and 4·4% were Roman Catholic.

Education. In 2002–03 there were 885 primary schools (*Grundschulen*) with 95,195 pupils and 10,062 teachers; 581 secondary schools (*Mittelschulen*) with 176,660 pupils and 12,914 teachers; 172 grammar schools (*Gymnasien*) with 119,945 pupils and 8,855 teachers; and 183 high schools (*Förderschulen*) with 22,834 pupils and 3,615 teachers. There were 805 professional training schools with 167,923 students and 6,967 teachers and three *Freie Waldorfschulen* (private) with 1,135 pupils and 94 teachers. In 2001–02 there were six universities with 63,671 students, 11 polytechnics with 23,145 students, seven art schools with 2,564 students and one management college with 782 students.

Health. In 2001 there were 92 hospitals with 29,619 beds. There were 13,833 doctors and 3,777 dentists.

CULTURE

Cinema. In 2001 there were 79 cinemas with seating for 42,671 persons. 8·1m. tickets were sold for performances.

Tourism. In 2001 there were 114,434 beds in places of accommodation (totalling 2,235 in 2000). There were 5,146,341 visitors during the year.

Libraries. In 2000, 772 public libraries, with 481,000 active users, lent 21,293,000 items.

Theatre and Opera. During the 2000–01 season there were 65 stages and seating for 22,385 persons. Audiences totalled 1,900,804.

Museums and Galleries. In 1999 there were 348 museums which received 8,097,459 visits.

FURTHER READING

Statistical office: Statistisches Landesamt des Freistaates Sachsen, Postfach 105, D-01911 Kamenz. It publishes *Statistisches Jahrbuch des Freistaates Sachsen* (since 1990).

SAXONY-ANHALT

Sachsen-Anhalt

KEY HISTORICAL EVENTS

Saxony-Anhalt has a short history as a state in its own right. Made up of a patchwork of older regions ruled by other states, Saxony-Anhalt existed between 1947 and 1952 and then, after reunification in 1990, it was re-established. Geographically, it lies at the very heart of Germany and despite the brevity of its federal status, the region has some of the oldest heartlands of German culture.

TERRITORY AND POPULATION

The area is 20,447 sq. km. It is divided into 3 administrative regions, 3 urban districts, 21 rural districts and 1,270 communes. Population in 2001 was 2,580,626 (1,324,898 females). The capital is Magdeburg.

SOCIAL STATISTICS

Statistics for calendar years:

	Live births	Marriages	Divorces	Deaths
1997	17,194	9,285	4,494	30,892
1998	17,513	9,485	5,274	31,011
1999	18,176	10,667	6,080	30,059
2000	18,723	10,310	5,823	30,175
2001	18,073	9,359	5,829	29,621

CONSTITUTION AND GOVERNMENT

The *Land* was reconstituted on former GDR territory in 1990. It has four seats in the Bundesrat.

RECENT ELECTIONS

At the Diet election on 21 April 2002 the CDU received 38·2% of votes cast giving them 48 of 115 seats, the PDS (former Communists) 21·8% (25 seats), the SPD 21·3% (25 seats), the Free Democratic Party 13·1% (17), the Law and Order Offensive Party 4·3% and the Green Party 2·1%.

CURRENT ADMINISTRATION

The *Prime Minister* is Wolfgang Böhmer (CDU).

Government Website: http://www.sachsen-anhalt.de

ENERGY AND NATURAL RESOURCES

Agriculture. Area and yield of the most important crops:

	Area (in 1,000 ha)			Yield (in 1,000 tonnes)		
	1999	2000	2001	1999	2000	2001
Cereals	565·2	605·7	608·1	4,203·4	3,903·3	4,362·8
Sugarbeet	56·5	50·9	50·2	2,711·3	2,673·7	2,546·6
Maize	59·3	56·8	55·7	2,097·4	2,074·1	2,125·0
Potatoes	15·7	15·9	14·0	554·0	630·2	584·3

Livestock in 2000 (in 1,000): cattle, 391·8 (including milch cows, 149·3); pigs, 816·1; sheep, 137·6.

INDUSTRY

In 2001, 1,326 establishments (with 20 or more employees) employed 106,747 persons; of these, 49,590 were employed in basic industry, 31,399 in capital goods industry and 18,778 in the food industry. Major sectors are extraction of metal, metal working, metal articles, the nutrition industry, mechanical engineering and the chemical industry.

Labour. The economically active persons totalled 1,060,000 in April 2001. Of the total, 980,000 were employees, 74,000 self-employed, 6,000 unpaid family workers; 319,000 were engaged in power supply, mining, manufacturing and building, 243,000 in commerce and transport, 41,000 in agriculture and forestry, 456,000 in other industries and services.

COMMUNICATIONS

Roads. In 2001 there were 320 km of motorways, 2,429 km of main and 3,821 km of local roads. In 2001 there were 1,522,925 registered motor vehicles, including 1,305,906 passenger cars, 102,794 lorries, 2,644 buses and 63,772 motorcycles.

SOCIAL INSTITUTIONS

Religion. There are Saxon and Anhalt branches of the Evangelical Church. There were some 0·2m. Roman Catholics in 1990.

Education. In 2001–02 there were 1,317 schools with 290,470 pupils. There were 10 universities and institutes of equivalent status with 40,709 students in 2001–02.

CULTURE

Cinema. There were 78 screens with 19,675 seats in 1996.

738

Tourism. 1,051 places of accommodation provided 50,537 beds in Dec. 2001. There were 2,214,457 visitors during the year.

Libraries. In 1996 there were 540 libraries holding 5,925,000 books.

Theatre and Opera. There were 69 theatres and concert halls in 1998–99. 794,000 people attended 5,041 productions during the year.

Museums and Galleries. In 1999 there were 207 museums which put on 487 exhibitions for 2,425,022 visitors.

FURTHER READING
Statistical office: Statistisches Landesamt Sachsen-Anhalt, Postfach 20 11 56, D-06012 Halle (Saale). It publishes *Statistisches Jahrbuch des Landes Sachsen-Anhalt* (since 1991).

SCHLESWIG-HOLSTEIN

KEY HISTORICAL EVENTS
The *Land* is formed from two states formerly contested between Germany and Denmark.

Schleswig was a Danish dependency ruled since 1474 by the King of Denmark as Duke of Schleswig. He also ruled Holstein, its southern neighbour, as Duke of Holstein, but he did so recognizing that it was a fief of the Holy Roman Empire. As such, Holstein joined the German Confederation which replaced the Empire in 1815.

Disputes between Denmark and the powerful German states were accompanied by rising national feeling in the duchies, where the population was part-Danish and part-German. There was war in 1848–50 and in 1864, when Denmark surrendered its claims to Prussia and Austria. Following her defeat of Austria in 1866 Prussia annexed both duchies.

North Schleswig (predominately Danish) was awarded to Denmark in 1920. Prussian Holstein and south Schleswig became the present *Land* in 1946.

TERRITORY AND POPULATION
The area of Schleswig-Holstein is 15,761 sq. km. It is divided into 4 urban and 11 rural districts and 1,132 communes. The capital is Kiel. The population (estimate, 31 Dec. 2001) numbered 2,804,249 (1,370,626 males, 1,433,623 females).

SOCIAL STATISTICS
Statistics for calendar years:

	Live births	Marriages	Divorces	Deaths
1998	27,729	17,949	7,139	30,042
1999	27,351	18,936	7,175	30,110
2000	26,920	17,849	7,641	29,821
2001	25,681	16,773	7,604	29,667

CONSTITUTION AND GOVERNMENT
The *Land* has four seats in the Bundesrat.

RECENT ELECTIONS
At the elections of 27 Feb. 2000 the Social Democrats won 41 of the 89 available seats with 43·1% of votes cast, the Christian Democrats 33 with 35·2%, the Free Democrats 7 with 7·6%, the Greens 5 with 6·2% and the (Danish) South Schleswig Voters Association 3 with 4·1%. Turn-out was 69·5%.

CURRENT ADMINISTRATION
The *Prime Minister* is Heide Simonis (b. 1943; SPD).

Government Website: http://www.schleswig-holstein.de

ENERGY AND NATURAL RESOURCES

Agriculture. Area and yield of the most important crops:

	Area (in 1,000 ha)			Yield (in 1,000 tonnes)		
	1999	2000	2001	1999	2000	2001
Wheat	195	191	195	1,543	1,842	1,911
Sugarbeet	15	14	13	790	753	715
Barley	80	76	76	552	593	618
Rye	28	36	34	189	243	245
Potatoes	6	6	6	220	212	218
Oats	10	7	9	58	40	51

Livestock, Nov. 2001: 1,290,868 cattle (including 373,002 milch cows); 1,383,085 pigs. In May 2001: 365,831 sheep; 14,430 horses; 2,885,719 poultry.

Fisheries. In 2001 the yield of small-scale deep-sea and inshore fisheries was 26,622 tonnes valued at 97·5m. DM.

INDUSTRY

In 2001 (average), 1,479 mining, quarrying and manufacturing establishments (with 20 or more employees) employed 139,341 persons; of these, 22,897 were employed in machine construction; 19,235 in food and related industries; 10,795 in electrical engineering; 7,299 in shipbuilding (except naval engineering).

Labour. The economically active persons totalled 1,245,000 in 2001. Of the total, 1,090,000 were employees, 138,000 were self-employed, 18,000 unpaid family workers; 328,000 were engaged in commerce and transport, 301,000 in power supply, mining, manufacturing and building, 42,000 in agriculture and forestry, and 574,000 in other industries and services.

COMMUNICATIONS

Roads. There were (1 Jan. 2002) 9,888 km of 'classified' roads, comprising 485 km of Autobahn, 1,673 km of federal roads, 3,631 km of first-class and 4,098 km of second-class highways. Number of motor vehicles was 1,859,272, including 1,531,853 passenger cars, 95,524 lorries, 2,937 buses, 71,622 tractors and 125,437 motorcycles.

Shipping. The Kiel Canal (*Nord-Ostsee-Kanal*) is 98·7 km (51 miles) long; in 2001, 38,406 vessels of 48m. NRT passed through it.

SOCIAL INSTITUTIONS

Justice. There are a court of appeal, 4 regional courts, 27 local courts, a *Land* labour court, 5 labour courts, a *Land* social court, 4 social courts, a finance court, an upper administrative court and an administrative court.

Religion. At the census of 25 May 1987, 73% of the population were Protestants and 6% Roman Catholics.

Education. In 2001–02 there were 626 primary schools with 7,233 teachers and 122,769 pupils; 247 elementary schools with 3,095 teachers and 44,638 pupils; 172 intermediate schools with 4,062 teachers and 63,170 pupils; 105 grammar schools (*Gymnasien*) with 5,351 teachers and 70,042 pupils; 24 comprehensive schools with 1,335 teachers and 16,255 pupils; 152 other schools (including special schools) with 2,342 teachers and 16,981 pupils; 398 vocational schools with 4,183 teachers and 87,857 pupils.

In the winter term of the academic year 2001–02 there were 24,456 students at the three universities (Kiel, Flensburg and Lübeck) and 18,010 students at 11 further education colleges.

CULTURE

Cinema. In 2002 there were 166 cinema screens with 28,344 seats.

Tourism. 4,827 places of accommodation provided 176,028 beds in 2001 for 4,344,310 visitors.

Libraries. In 2001 there were 179 libraries (6 academic).

Theatre and Opera. 1,890 productions were staged at 19 venues for 601,000 visitors in 1999–2000.

Museums and Galleries. In 1999 there were 204 museums that put on 424 exhibitions for 2,827,138 visitors.

FURTHER READING
Statistical Information: Statistisches Landesamt Schleswig-Holstein (Fröbel Str. 15–17, D-24113 Kiel). *Director:* Dr Hans-Peter Kirschner. Publications: *Statistisches Taschenbuch Schleswig-Holstein,* since 1954.—*Statistisches Jahrbuch Schleswig-Holstein,* since 1951.— *Statistische Monatshefte Schleswig-Holstein,* since 1949.—*Statistische Berichte,* since 1947.—*Beitrage zur historischen Statistik Schleswig-Holstein,* from 1967.—*Lange Reihen,* from 1977.

Baxter, R. R., *The Law of International Waterways.* Harvard Univ. Press, 1964
Brandt, O., *Grundriss der Geschichte Schleswig-Holsteins.* 5th ed. Kiel, 1957
Handbuch für Schleswig-Holstein. 28th ed. Kiel, 1996

State Library: Schleswig-Holsteinische Landesbibliothek, Kiel, Schloss. *Director:* Prof. Dr Dieter Lohmeier.
State Website: http://www.statistik-sh.de

THURINGIA
Thüringen

KEY HISTORICAL EVENTS
Thuringia with its capital Erfurt is criss-crossed by the rivers Saale, Werra and Weisse Elster and dominated in the south by the mountains of the Thuringian Forest. Martin Luther spent his exile in Eisenach where he translated the New Testament into German while he lived in protective custody in the castle. Weimar became the centre of German intellectual life in the 18th century. In 1919 Weimar was the seat of a briefly liberal Republic. Only ten miles from Weimar lies Buchenwald, the site of a war-time Nazi concentration camp, which is now a national monument to the victims of fascism.

TERRITORY AND POPULATION
The area is 16,172 sq. km. Population on 31 Dec. 2001 was 2,411,387 (1,229,210 females); density, 149 per sq. km. It is divided into 6 urban districts, 17 rural districts and 1,017 communes. The capital is Erfurt.

SOCIAL STATISTICS
Statistics for calendar years:

	Live births	Marriages	Divorces	Deaths
1998	16,607	8,591	4,988	26,991
1999	16,926	9,296	4,960	26,590
2000	17,577	9,067	4,878	26,081
2001	17,351	8,575	4,748	25,499

CONSTITUTION AND GOVERNMENT
The *Land* was reconstituted on former GDR territory in 1990. It has four seats in the Bundesrat.

RECENT ELECTIONS
At the Diet elections of 12 Sept. 1999 the Christian Democrats (CDU) won 49 seats, with 51·0% of the vote; the Party of Democratic Socialism (PDS) 21, with 21·3%; and the Social Democrats (SPD) 18, with 18·5%.

CURRENT ADMINISTRATION
The *Prime Minister* is Dr Bernhard Vogel (CDU).
Government Website: http://www.thueringen.de

ENERGY AND NATURAL RESOURCES

Agriculture. Area and yield of the most important crops:

	Area (in 1,000 ha)			Yield (in 1,000 tonnes)		
	1999	2000	2001	1999	2000	2001
Wheat	185·2	218·1	215·3	1,344·9	1,503·0	1,624·3
Barley	137·0	126·9	126·1	863·7	741·3	814·0
Sugarbeet	12·5	11·0	10·8	662·1	613·1	562·7
Rye	16·7	17·1	16·4	113·4	114·4	118·7
Potatoes	4·0	3·7	2·8	160·1	134·7	110·0
Oats	7·0	6·7	6·7	41·0	32·0	37·7

Livestock, 3 May 2001: 390,421 cattle (including 134,859 milch cows); 686,860 pigs; 238,597 sheep; 8,618 horses; 4,777,989 poultry.

INDUSTRY

In 2001, 1,752 establishments (with 20 or more employees) employed 137,927 persons; of these, 65,658 were employed by producers of materials and supplies, 35,745 by producers of investment goods, 10,363 by producers of durables and 26,161 by producers of non-durables.

Labour. The economically active persons totalled 1,079,200 in April 2001, including 519,500 professional workers, 418,400 manual workers and 92,100 self-employed. 365,400 were engaged in production industries, 236,700 in commerce, transport and communications, 37,400 persons in agriculture and forestry, and 439,700 in other sectors. There were 194,579 persons registered unemployed in Dec. 2001 (100,858 females) and 7,667 on short time; the unemployment rate was 16·6%.

COMMUNICATIONS

Roads. In 2002 there were 299 km of motorways, 1,940 km of federal roads, 5,646 km of first-class and 2,365 km of second-class highways. Number of motor vehicles, Jan. 2002, 1,491,978, including 1,263,597 private cars, 104,121 lorries, 2,871 buses, 38,593 tractors and 68,982 motorcycles.

SOCIAL INSTITUTIONS

Religion. In 2000, 206,335 persons were Roman Catholic and 678,593 persons were Protestant. In 2001, 550 were Jewish.

Education. In 2001–02 there were 509 primary schools with 55,321 pupils, 335 core curriculum schools with 102,293 pupils, 113 grammar schools with 78,123 pupils and 100 special schools with 17,635 pupils; there were 86,936 pupils in technical and professional education, and 4,481 in professional training for the disabled.

In the winter term 2001–02 there were 12 universities and colleges with 43,302 students enrolled.

Health. In 2001 there were 53 hospitals with 17,250 beds. There were 7,660 doctors (1 doctor per 315 population).

Welfare. 2001 expenditure on social welfare was €414m.

CULTURE

Cinema. In 2000 there were 130 cinema screens with 20,195 seats.

Tourism. In July 2001, 1,482 places of accommodation (with nine or more beds) received 2,946,000 visitors who stayed 8,785,400 nights.

Libraries. There were 440 public libraries in 2000 with 280,300 active users who borrowed 5,731,600 items.

Theatre and Opera. In 1999–2000 there were 48 theatres and concert halls. 852,500 people attended 3,804 different productions.

Museums and Galleries. There were 179 museums in 2000 putting on 479 exhibitions for 4,730,500 visitors.

FURTHER READING

Statistical information: Thüringer Landesamt für Statistik (Postfach 900163, D-99104 Erfurt; Europaplatz 3, D-99091 Erfurt). *President:* Gerhard Scheuerer. Publications: *Statistisches Jahrbuch Thüringen,* since 1993. *Kreiszahlen für Thüringen,* since 1995. *Gemeindezahlen für Thüringen,* since 1998. *Thüringen-Atlas,* since 1999. *Statistische Monatshefte Thüringen,* since 1994. *Statistische Berichte,* since 1991. *Faltblätter,* since 1991.

State library: Thüringer Universitäts- und Landesbibliothek, Jena.
Website: http://www.tls.thueringen.de

GHANA

Republic of Ghana

Capital: Accra
Population estimate, 2000: 18·80m.
GDP per capita, 2000: (PPP$) 1,964
HDI/world rank: 0·548/129

KEY HISTORICAL EVENTS

By the 17th century, strong chiefdoms and warrior states, notably the Ashanti, dominated the territory. The Ashanti state was strengthened by its collaboration with the slave trade but by 1874 it had been conquered by Britain and made a colony. The hinterland became a protectorate in 1901. British rule was challenged after the Second World War by Kwame Nkrumah and the Convention People's Party (CPP), formed in 1949. The state of Ghana came into existence on 6 March 1957 when the former Colony of the Gold Coast with the Trusteeship Territory of Togoland attained Dominion status. The country was declared a Republic within the Commonwealth on 1 July 1960 with Dr Kwame Nkrumah as the first President.

In 1966 the Nkrumah regime was overthrown by the military who ruled until 1969 when they handed over to a civilian regime under a new constitution. On 13 Jan. 1972 the armed forces regained power. In 1979 the Supreme Military Council (SMC) was toppled in a coup led by Flight-Lieut. J. J. Rawlings. The new government permitted elections already scheduled and these resulted in a victory for Dr Hilla Limann and his People's National Party. However, on 31 Dec. 1981 another coup led by Flight-Lieut. Rawlings dismissed the government and Parliament, suspended the constitution and established a Provisional National Defence Council to exercise all government powers. A new pluralist democratic constitution was approved by referendum in April 1992. The Fourth Republic was proclaimed on 7 Jan. 1993.

TERRITORY AND POPULATION

Ghana is bounded west by Côte d'Ivoire, north by Burkina Faso, east by Togo and south by the Gulf of Guinea. The area is 238,537 sq. km; the 2000 census population was 18,800,000, giving a density of 78·8 persons per sq. km.

The UN gives a projected population for 2010 of 23·94m.

In 1999, 62·6% of the population was rural. 1m. Ghanaians lived abroad in 1995. Ghana is divided into 10 regions:

Regions	Area (sq. km)	Population census 1984	Capital
Ashanti	24,390	2,090,100	Kumasi
Brong-Ahafo	39,557	1,206,608	Sunyani
Central	9,826	1,142,335	Cape Coast
Eastern	19,977	1,680,890	Koforidua
Greater Accra	2,593	1,431,099	Accra
Northern	70,383	1,164,583	Tamale
Upper East	8,842	772,744	Bolgatanga
Upper West	18,477	438,008	Wa
Volta	20,572	1,211,907	Ho
Western	23,921	1,157,807	Sekondi-Takoradi

In 1999 the capital, Accra, had a population of 1,904,000. Other major cities with 1988 estimated populations: Kumasi, 385,192; Tamale, 151,069; Tema, 109,975; Sekondi-Takoradi, 103,653.

About 44% of the population are Akan. Other tribal groups include Moshi-Dagomba (16%), Ewe (13%) and Ga (8%). About 75 languages are spoken; the official language is English.

SOCIAL STATISTICS

1995 births, 676,000; deaths, 191,000. Birth rate (per 1,000 population), 1995: 39·3; death rate, 11·0. 1999 life expectancy, 55·3 years for men and 57·9 for women. Infant mortality, 63 per 1,000 live births (1999). Annual population growth rate, 1990–99, 3·0%; fertility rate, 1999, 5·0 births per woman.

CLIMATE
The climate ranges from the equatorial type on the coast to savannah in the north and is typified by the existence of well-marked dry and wet seasons. Temperatures are relatively high throughout the year. The amount, duration and seasonal distribution of rain is very marked, from the south, with over 80" (2,000 mm), to the north, with under 50" (1,250 mm). In the extreme north, the wet season is from March to Aug., but further south it lasts until Oct. Near Kumasi, two wet seasons occur, in May and June and again in Oct., and this is repeated, with greater amounts, along the coast of Ghana. Accra, Jan. 80°F (26·7°C), July 77°F (25°C). Annual rainfall 29" (724 mm). Kumasi, Jan. 77°F (25°C), July 76°F (24·4°C). Annual rainfall 58" (1,402 mm). Sekondi-Takoradi, Jan. 77°F (25°C), July 76°F (24·4°C). Annual rainfall 47" (1,181 mm). Tamale, Jan. 82°F (27·8°C), July 78°F (25·6°C). Annual rainfall 41" (1,026mm).

CONSTITUTION AND GOVERNMENT
After the coup of 31 Dec. 1981, supreme power was vested in the Provisional National Defence Council (PNDC), chaired by Flight-Lieut. Jerry John Rawlings.

A new constitution was approved by 92·6% of votes cast at a referendum on 28 April 1992. The electorate was 8,255,690; turn-out was 43·8%. The constitution sets up a presidential system on the US model, with a multi-party parliament and an independent judiciary. The *President* is elected by universal suffrage for a four-year term renewable once.

National Anthem. 'God bless our Homeland, Ghana'; words by the government, tune by P. Gbeho.

RECENT ELECTIONS
Presidential elections were held on 7 and 28 Dec. 2000. Turn-out was 61·8%. In the first round, John Agyekum Kufuor gained 48·4% of votes cast and John Atta Mills gained 44·8% against five other candidates. In the second round, John Agyekum Kufuor was elected by 57·2% of votes cast.

Parliamentary elections were held on 7 Dec. 2000 and 3 Jan. 2001. The New Patriotic Party (NPP) won, gaining 100 seats; the National Democratic Congress (NDC) gained 92 seats; two other parties and independents gained four seats or fewer.

John Kufuor's victory marked the first occasion in African history that power was being transferred from a Marxist to a free-market liberal.

CURRENT ADMINISTRATION
In March 2003 the government comprised the following:
President: John Agyekum Kufuor; b. 1938 (NPP; sworn in 7 Jan. 2001).
Vice-President: Aliu Mahama.
Secretary for Foreign Affairs: Hackman Owusu-Agyeman. *Justice and Attorney-General:* Nana Akufo Addo. *Defence:* Dr Kwame Addo Kufuor. *Finance:* Yaw Osafu-Marfo. *Interior:* Malik Alhassan Yakubu. *Trade and Industries:* Dr Kofi Konadu Apraku. *Agriculture:* Major Courage Quarshigah. *Forestry and Lands:* Kasim Kasanga. *Local Government and Rural Development:* Kwadwo Baah-Wiredu. *Health:* Dr Kweku Afriyie. *Environment, Science and Technology:* Dominic Fobih. *Parliamentary Affairs:* Papa Owusu-Ankoma. *Information and Presidential Affairs:* Jake Obetsebi-Lamptey. *Women's Affairs:* Gladys Asmah. *Communication and Technology:* Owusu Agyapong. *Education:* Christopher Ameyaw-Akumfi. *Energy:* Albert Kan-Dapaah. *Roads and Transportation:* Dr Richard Anane. *Economic Planning and Regional Co-operation:* Dr Kwesi Nduom. *Mines:* Kwadwo Adjei-Dako. *Tourism:* Hawa Yakubu. *Manpower Development and Employment:* Cecilia Bannerman. *Works and Housing:* Yah Barimah. *Youth and Sport:* Edward Osel Kwaku. *Minister of the Northern Region:* Imoro Andani. *Minister Without Portfolio:* Elizabeth Ohene.

Government Website: http://www.ghana.gov.gh

DEFENCE
Defence expenditure totalled US$95m. in 2000 (US$5 per capita), representing 0·9% of GDP.

Army. Total strength (1999), 5,000.

Navy. The Navy, based at Sekondi and Tema, numbered 1,000 in 1999 including support personnel.

Air Force. There are air bases at Takoradi and Tamale. Personnel strength (1999), 1,000. There were 19 combat aircraft.

INTERNATIONAL RELATIONS
In March 1998 the IMF removed barriers to the offer of financial support from aid donors totalling US$1·6bn. in 1998 and 1999.

Ghana is a member of the UN, WTO, the Commonwealth, the African Union, African Development Bank, ECOWAS and is an ACP member state of the ACP-EU relationship.

ECONOMY
Agriculture accounted for 10·4% of GDP in 1998, industry 6·9% and services 82·7%.

Overview. Ghana is committed to the reform programmes of the IMF and World Bank and is one of Africa's biggest borrowers. In 1996 aid amounted to 11% of GDP, or four times the value of Ghana's exports. A privatization programme was inaugurated in 1988. By April 2000, 132 state-owned enterprises had been sold off to become 232 privately-owned companies. A further 168 were set to be privatized. Privatization deals raised US$804m. between 1990 and 1996, including the Ashanti Goldfields sell-off worth more than US$400m. Only South Africa among sub-Saharan African nations has raised more from privatization. Building, tourism, technology and financial services account for more than 46% of national income.

Currency. The monetary unit is the *cedi* (GHC) of 100 *pesewas* (P). In 1995 inflation was running at nearly 60%. It was brought down to 12·4% in 1999, but rose again to 32·9% in 2001. Foreign exchange reserves were US$238m. in April 2002 and gold reserves 281,000 troy oz in May 2002. Total money supply in Sept. 2001 was ₵3,867·83bn.

Budget. The 1996 budget provided for (in ₵1,000m.): revenue, 2,328·3; expenditure, 2,169·5.

Performance. Average GDP growth in the 10 years to 1998 was 4·5%—almost twice the African average. Real GDP growth was 3·7% in 2000 and 4·2% in 2001. Total GDP was US$5·3bn. in 2001.

Banking and Finance. The Bank of Ghana (*Governor,* Dr Paul Acquah) was established in 1957 as the central bank and bank of issue. At Dec. 1995 its total assets were ₵3,272,946·6m. There are 3 large commercial banks, 7 secondary banks, 3 merchant banks and 100 rural banks. There are two discount houses. Banks are required to have a capital base of at least 6% of net assets. At Dec. 1995 assets of commercial banks totalled ₵1,900,327·1m.

Foreign investment is actively encouraged with the Ghana Free Zone Scheme offering particular incentives such as full exemption of duties and levies on all imports for production and exports from the zones, full exemption on tax on profits for ten years, and no more than 8% after ten years. It is a condition of the scheme that at least 70% of goods made within the zones must be exported. Within 18 months of the scheme being set up in 1995, 50 projects had been registered.

Ghana's stock exchange, which opened in 1990, was one of the world's best performing stock markets in 1998.

ENERGY AND NATURAL RESOURCES
Ghana is facing an energy crisis, with power cuts of up to 12 hours a day because drought has caused the level of Lake Volta to drop to below the danger level.

Environment. Ghana's carbon dioxide emissions in 1998 were the equivalent of 0·2 tonnes per capita according to the *World Bank Atlas.*

Electricity. Installed capacity was 1m. kW in 1997. Production (1998) 6·21bn. kWh, mainly from two hydro-electric stations operated by the Volta River Authority, Akosombo (six units) and Kpong (four units). Consumption per capita was 289 kWh in 1998. A drought in 1998 caused power cuts, with over 99% of electricity being hydro-electric. It is planned that electricity production will become less dependent on hydro-electric stations and more so on gas, with the construction of a 600 km pipeline forming part of the proposed West African Gas Pipeline Project.

Oil and Gas. Ghana is pursuing the development of its own gas fields and plans to harness gas at the North and South Tano fields located off the western coast. Natural gas reserves, 1997, totalled 6bn. cu. metres. Oil reserves in 1997 were 129·6m. bbls.

Minerals. Gold is one of the mainstays of the economy; Ghana ranks second only to South Africa among African gold producers. Production in 1998 was 2·3m. troy oz (1997, 1·6m. troy oz; 1996, 1·5m. troy oz). In 1998 diamond production was 800,000 carats; bauxite (1998), 443,000 tonnes; manganese (1993), 362,000 tonnes.

Agriculture. The rural poor earn little and many small farmers have reverted to subsistence farming. Around 2·5m. households were engaged in the agricultural sector in 1998. There were 3·60m. ha of arable land in 1998 and 1·70m. ha of permanent crops. In southern and central Ghana main food crops are maize, rice, cassava, plantains, groundnuts, yam and taro, and in northern Ghana groundnuts, rice, maize, sorghum, millet and yams. Agriculture presently operates at only 20% of its potential and is an area that is to be a major focus of investment.

Production of main food crops, 2000 (in 1,000 tonnes): cassava, 7,845; yams, 3,249; plantains, 2,046; taro, 1,707; maize, 1,014; cocoa beans, 398; coconuts, 305; sorghum, 302; chillies and green peppers, 270; oranges, 270. Cocoa is the main cash crop. The government estimates that more than 40% of the population relies either directly or indirectly on cocoa as a source of income. It contributes approximately 13% of GDP. Ghana is the second largest cocoa bean producer in the world after Côte d'Ivoire, and the second largest producer of both yams and taro, after Nigeria.

Livestock, 2000: cattle, 1·28m.; sheep, 2·56m.; pigs, 350,000; goats, 2·80m.; chickens, 18m.

Forestry. There were 9·02m. ha of forest in 1995, or 39·7% of the total land area (down from 42·2% in 1990). Reserves account for some 30% of the total forest lands. Timber production in 1999 was 21·9m. cu. metres.

Fisheries. In 1999 total catch was 492,776 tonnes, of which 418,276 tonnes came from sea fishing.

INDUSTRY
Ghana's industries include mining, lumbering, light manufacturing, aluminium and food processing.

Production of aluminium (1997) 151,600 tonnes.

Labour. In 1996 the labour force was 8,393,000. Females constituted 51% of the workforce in 1999. Only Cambodia had a higher percentage of females in its workforce.

In 1994 there were 37,000 persons registered as unemployed.

INTERNATIONAL TRADE
Foreign debt was US$6,657m. in 2000.

Imports and Exports. In 2000 exports (f.o.b.) totalled US$1,898·4m.; imports (f.o.b.) were valued at US$2,741·3m. Principal exports, 1995: gold, 1,539,000m. oz valued at US$635·90m.; cocoa and products, 236,255 tonnes valued at US$364·63m.; timber valued at US$190m.; plus tuna, bauxite, aluminium, manganese ore and diamonds. The value of gold exports has risen since 1995, being worth US$710m. in 1999. Principal imported commodities: capital equipment, petroleum, consumer goods, food. Main export markets, 1997: Togo, 13·0%; UK, 12·0%; Germany, 10·0%; USA, 9·0%. Main import suppliers: UK, 15·0%; Nigeria, 14·0%; USA, 10·0%; Germany, 6·0%.

COMMUNICATIONS
Roads. In 1996 there were approximately 30 km of motorway, 5,230 km of primary roads, 9,620 km of secondary roads and 22,900 km of other roads. About 24·1% of

all roads, including 21 km of expressway, are hard-surfaced. A Road Sector Strategy and Programme to develop the road network ran from 1995 to 2000. There were 90,000 passenger cars in use in 1996, equivalent to 4·7 per 1,000 inhabitants.

Rail. Total length of railways in 1993 was 953 km of 1,067 mm gauge. In 1994 railways carried 0·7m. tonnes of freight and 2·3m. passengers.

Civil Aviation. There is an international airport at Accra (Kotoka). The national carrier is the state-owned Ghana Airways. In 1999 scheduled airline traffic of Ghana-based carriers flew 9·1m km, carrying 304,000 passengers (all on international flights). Accra handled 602,000 passengers (592,000 on international flights) in 2000.

Shipping. The chief ports are Takoradi and Tema. In 1995, 1·2m. tonnes of cargo were unloaded at Takoradi and 3·9m. tonnes at Tema. There is inland water transport on Lake Volta. In 1998 the merchant marine totalled 115,000 GRT. The Volta, Ankobra and Tano rivers provide 168 km of navigable waterways for launches and lighters.

Telecommunications. Ghana Telecom was privatized in 1996. In 2000 Ghana had 237,200 telephone main lines, or 11·7 for every 1,000 inhabitants, and there were 60,000 PCs in use (3·0 per 1,000 persons). Mobile phone subscribers numbered 132,000 in Sept. 2000 and there were 30,000 Internet users in Dec. 2000. In 1995 there were 4,500 fax machines.

Postal Services. In 1995 there were 1,001 post offices.

SOCIAL INSTITUTIONS

Justice. The Courts are constituted as follows:

Supreme Court. The Supreme Court consists of the Chief Justice who is also the President, and not less than four other Justices of the Supreme Court. The Supreme Court is the final court of appeal in Ghana. The final interpretation of the constitution is entrusted to the Supreme Court.

Court of Appeal. The Court of Appeal consists of the Chief Justice with not less than five other Justices of the Appeal court and such other Justices of Superior Courts as the Chief Justice may nominate. The Court of Appeal is duly constituted by three Justices. The Court of Appeal is bound by its own previous decisions and all courts inferior to the Court of Appeal are bound to follow the decisions of the Court of Appeal on questions of law. Divisions of the Appeal Court may be created, subject to the discretion of the Chief Justice.

High Court of Justice. The Court has jurisdiction in civil and criminal matters as well as those relating to industrial and labour disputes including administrative complaints. The High Court of Justice has supervisory jurisdiction over all inferior Courts and any adjudicating authority and in exercise of its supervisory jurisdiction has power to issue such directions, orders or writs including writs or orders in the nature of habeas corpus, certiorari, mandamus, prohibition and quo qarrantto. The High Court of Justice has no jurisdiction in cases of treason. The High Court consists of the Chief Justice and not less than 12 other judges and such other Justices of the Superior Court as the Chief Justice may appoint.

Under the Provisional National Defence Council which ruled from 1981 to 2001 public tribunals were established in addition to the traditional courts of justice.

The population in penal institutions in 1996 was 7,076 (40 per 100,000 of national population).

Religion. An estimated 30% of the population are Muslim and 24% Christian, with 38% adherents to indigenous beliefs and 8% other religions.

Education. Schooling is free and compulsory, and consists of six years of primary, three years of junior secondary and three years of senior secondary education. In 1990, 75% of eligible children attended primary, and 39% secondary, school. In 1994–95 there were 2·15m. pupils in 12,134 primary schools with 71,863 teachers; in 1990–91, 768,603 in general education at secondary schools. University education is free. There are two universities, one university each for development studies, and science and technology. In 1994–95 there were 11,225 university students and 779 academic staff. There were also 6 polytechnics, 7 colleges and 38 teacher training colleges. Adult literacy in 1999 was 70·3% (79·4% among men and 61·5% among women). In 1970 adult literacy was just 31%.

Health. Provision of doctors, 1994: one per 22,970 population. Provision of hospital beds, 1994: one per 638 population. At the end of 1995 there were 15,890 cases of AIDS, mainly women.

Ghana has made more progress in the reduction of undernourishment in the past 20 years than any other country in the world. Between 1980 and 1996 the proportion of undernourished people declined from 61% of the population to just 11%. The proportion of the population with access to safe water increased from 35% in 1980 to 65% in 1996.

CULTURE

Broadcasting. The Ghana Broadcasting Corporation is an autonomous statutory body. There are five national radio programmes. There were 1·73m. TV receivers (colour by PAL) and 4·4m. radio receivers in 1997.

Press. There were (1996) four daily newspapers with a combined circulation of 250,000.

Tourism. There were 335,000 foreign tourists in 1998, spending US$274m. A Ministry of Tourism was established in 1994. A five-year Tourism Development Plan was instituted in 1996. Many new hotels are planned including two five-star 400-room hotels.

DIPLOMATIC REPRESENTATIVES

Of Ghana in the United Kingdom (13 Belgrave Sq., London, SW1X 8PN)
High Commissioner: Isaac Osei.

Of the United Kingdom in Ghana (Osu Link, off Gamel Abdul Nasser Ave., Accra)
High Commissioner: Dr Rod Pullen.

Of Ghana in the USA (3512 International Dr., NW, Washington, D.C., 20008)
Ambassador: Alan Kyerematen.

Of the USA in Ghana (Ring Rd. East, Accra)
Ambassador: Vacant.
Chargé d'Affaires a.i.: Gary Pergl.

Of Ghana to the United Nations
Ambassador: Nana Effah-Apentang.

Of Ghana to the European Union
Ambassador: Kobina Wudu.

FURTHER READING

Carmichael, J., *Profile of Ghana.* London, 1992.—*African Eldorado: Ghana from Gold Coast to Independence.* London, 1993
Herbst, J., *The Politics of Reform in Ghana, 1982–1991.* California Univ. Press, 1993
Myers, Robert A., *Ghana.* [Bibliography] ABC-Clio, Oxford and Santa Barbara (CA), 1991
Petchenkine, Y., *Ghana in Search of Stability, 1957–1992.* New York, 1992
Rathbone, R., *Nkrumah and the Chiefs: The Politics of Chieftaincy in Ghana.* Currey, Oxford, 2000
Ray, D. I., *Ghana: Politics, Economics and Society.* London, 1986
Rimmer, D., *Staying Poor: Ghana's Political Economy, 1950–1990.* Oxford, 1993
Rothchild., D. (ed.) *Ghana: the Political Economy of Recovery.* Boulder (Colo.), 1991

National statistical office: Statistical Service, Accra.

GREECE

Elliniki Dimokratia
(Hellenic Republic)

Capital: Athens
Population estimate, 2000: 10·61m.
GDP per capita, 2000: (PPP$) 16,501
HDI/world rank: 0·885/24

KEY HISTORICAL EVENTS

The land which is now Greece was first inhabited between 2000–1700 BC by tribes from the North. This period was followed by the Mycenaean Civilization which was overthrown by the Dorians at the end of the 12th century BC. Its dominant citadels were at Tiryns and Mycenae. What little is known about this period is from stories such as those by Homer written in the 9th or 8th century BC.

The following period, known as the Greek Dark Ages, ended by the 6th century BC when the *polis*, or city state, was formed. Built mainly on coastal plains, the two principal cities were Sparta and Athens. Based on ideas of democracy and meritocracy, and rich in theatre, art and philosophy, the *polis* was the pinnacle of the Greek Classical Age. It was the era of Euripydes, Theusidades and Socrates. With strong trade links, Greece also had territories in Southern Italy, Sicily, Southern France and Asia Minor.

Two Persian invasions in the 5th century were checked at Marathon (490 BC) and Thermopylae (480 BC) where Spartans held off a great force of Persian soldiers. In 431 BC rivalry between the dominant city states erupted into the Peloponnesian War. Eventually in 404 BC Sparta emerged victorious against Athens, but in the next century Sparta itself fell to Thebes (371 BC).

Led by Philip II of Macedon, the Macedonians defeated the city states in 338 BC. The *poleis* were forced to unify under his rule. With Plato and Aristotle active at this time, the latter serving as a tutor to Philip's son Alexander, this was a period of rich cultural heritage. When Philip was assassinated in 336 BC, Alexander succeeded him at the age of 20. He spent the next thirteen years on a relentless campaign to expand the Macedonian territories. The Greek Empire stretched to the edge of India and encompassed most of the known civilized world.

Following Alexander's death in 323 BC, the empire gradually disintegrated. By the end of the 2nd century AD, the Romans had defeated the Macedonians and Greece was incorporated into the Roman Empire. It remained in Roman hands until it became part of the Byzantine Empire in the 4th century AD. Byzantium was populated with Greek-speaking Christians with its power base in Constantinople.

Over the next six centuries Greece was invaded by Franks, Normans and Arabs but remained part of the Byzantine Empire. Following the Empire's decline in the 11th century, Greece was incorporated into the Ottoman Empire in 1460. Apart from a period under Venetian control between 1686–1715, Greece was part of Turkey until the Greek War of Independence.

Greece broke away from the Ottoman Empire in the 1820s and was declared a kingdom under the protection of Great Britain, France and Russia. Many Greeks were left outside the new state but Greece's area increased by 70%, the population growing from 2·8m. to 4·8m., after the Treaty of Bucharest (1913) recognized Greek sovereignty over Crete.

King Constantine opted for neutrality in the First World War, while Prime Minister Venezelos favoured the Entente powers. This National Schism led to British and French intervention which deposed Constantine on 11 June 1917. When his son Alexander died on 25 Oct. 1920, he returned and reigned until 1922. He was forced to abdicate by a coup after defeat by Turkey and the loss of Smyrna. The Treaty of Lausanne (1923) recognized Smyrna as Turkish with Eastern Thrace and the islands of Imvros and Tenedos, all of which had been ceded to Greece by the 1920 Treaty of Sevres. An exchange of Christian and Muslim populations followed. Resistance to Italian demands brought Greece into the Second World War when Germany had to come to the aid of the hard-pressed Italians. Athens was occupied on 27 April 1941. The occupation lasted until 15 Oct. 1944.

A communist led insurrection in 1946–47 was put down with the help of British and, later, US troops. Peace came after 1949.

The late 1950s saw the emergence of the Left, capitalizing on the movement for union with Cyprus and unease over NATO membership (1952). A military coup in 1967 led to the authoritarian rule of the 'Colonels' headed by George Papadopoulos. A republic was declared on 29 July 1973. The dictatorship collapsed in 1974 giving way to a civilian government of national unity. The monarchy was abolished by a referendum on 8 Dec. 1974. The 1981 election brought Andreas Papandreou to power and the head of a socialist government. Earlier that year Greece had become the tenth member of the EU. Re-elected in 1985, Papandreou imposed economic austerity to combat inflation and soaring budgets but industrial unrest and evidence of widespread corruption led to his fall and a succession of weak governments. Papandreou returned to power in Oct. 1993 but ill-health forced his resignation two years later. His successor Constantinos Simitis took a more pro-European stance instituting economic reforms to prepare the way for entry into European Monetary Union (EMU).

TERRITORY AND POPULATION

Greece is bounded in the north by Albania, the Former Yugoslav Republic of Macedonia (FYROM) and Bulgaria, east by Turkey and the Aegean Sea, south by the Mediterranean and west by the Ionian Sea. The total area is 131,957 sq. km (50,949 sq. miles), of which the islands account for 25,042 sq. km (9,669 sq. miles).

The population was 10,259,900 (5,204,492 females) according to the census of March 1991. 1998 estimate: 10,516,000; density, 80 per sq. km.

The UN gives a projected population for 2010 of 10·58m.

In 1999, 59·9% of the population lived in urban areas. There were 166,031 resident foreign nationals in 1991. A further 5m. Greeks are estimated to live abroad.

In 1987 the territory of Greece was administratively reorganized into 13 *regions* comprising in all 51 *departments*. Areas and populations according to the 1991 census:

Region/Department	Area in sq. km	Population	Chief town
Attica[1]	*3,808*	*3,523,407*	*Athens*
Aegean North	*3,836*	*199,231*	*Mytilene*
Chios	904	52,184	Chios
Lesbos	2,154	105,082	Mytilene
Samos	778	41,965	Samos
Aegean South	*5,286*	*257,481*	*Hermoupolis*
Cyclades	2,572	94,005	Hermoupolis
Dodecanese	2,714	163,476	Rhodes
Crete	*8,336*	*540,054*	*Heraklion*
Canea	2,376	133,774	Canea
Heraklion	2,641	264,906	Heraklion
Lassithi	1,823	71,279	Aghios Nikolaos
Rethymnon	1,496	70,095	Rethymnon
Epirus	*9,203*	*339,728*	*Ioannina*
Arta	1,662	78,719	Arta
Ioannina	4,990	158,193	Ioannina
Preveza	1,036	58,628	Preveza
Thesprotia	1,515	44,188	Hegoumenitsa
Greece Central[2]	*15,549*	*582,280*	*Lamia*
Boeotia	2,952	134,108	Levadeia
Euboea	4,167	208,408	Chalcis
Evrytania	1,869	24,307	Karpenissi
Phocis	2,120	44,183	Amphissa
Phthiotis	4,441	171,274	Lamia
Greece West	*11,350*	*707,687*	*Patras*
Achaia	3,271	300,078	Patras
Aetolia and Acarnania	5,461	228,180	Messolonghi
Elia	2,618	179,429	Pyrgos
Ionian Islands	*2,307*	*193,734*	*Corfu*
Cephalonia	904	32,474	Argostoli
Corfu	641	107,592	Corfu

Region/Department	Area in sq. km	Population	Chief town
Leucas	356	21,111	Leucas
Zante	406	32,557	Zante
Macedonia Central	*19,147*	*1,710,513*	*Thessaloniki*
Chalcidice	2,918	92,117	Polygyros
Imathia	1,701	139,934	Veroia
Kilkis	2,519	81,710	Kilkis
Mount Athos	336	1,536	—
Pella	2,506	138,761	Edessa
Pieria	1,516	116,763	Katerini
Serres	3,968	192,828	Serres
Thessaloniki (Salonika)	3,683	946,864	Thessaloniki
Macedonia East and Thrace	*14,157*	*570,496*	*Comotini*
Cavalla	2,111	135,937	Cavalla
Drama	3,468	96,554	Drama
Evros	4,242	143,752	Alexandroupolis
Rhodope	2,543	103,190	Comotini
Xanthi	1,793	91,063	Xanthi
Macedonia West	*9,451*	*293,015*	*Kozani*
Florina	1,924	53,147	Florina
Grevena	2,291	36,797	Grevena
Kastoria	1,720	52,685	Kastoria
Kozani	3,516	150,386	Kozani
Peloponnese	*15,490*	*607,428*	*Tripolis*
Arcadia	4,419	105,309	Tripolis
Argolis	2,154	97,636	Nauplion
Corinth	2,290	141,823	Corinthos
Laconia	3,636	95,696	Sparti
Messenia	2,991	166,964	Calamata
Thessaly	*14,037*	*734,846*	*Larissa*
Karditsa	2,636	126,854	Karditsa
Larissa	5,381	270,612	Larissa
Magnesia	2,636	198,434	Volos
Trikala	3,384	138,946	Trikala

[1]Attica is both region and department. [2]Without Attica.

The largest cities (1991 census populations) are Athens (the capital), 772,072 (total agglomeration of Greater Athens, 3,072,922; up to 3,112,000 in 1999); Thessaloniki (agglomeration), 749,048 (768,000 in 1995); Piraeus (municipality), 182,671; Patras (agglomeration), 170,452; Peristerion (municipality), 137,288; Heraklion (agglomeration), 126,907; Larissa, 112,777; Kallithea, 114,233. Greater Athens, composed of the capital city, the port of Piraeus and a number of suburbs, contains about one third of the Greek population. It also contains about 50% of the country's industry and is the principal commercial, financial and diplomatic centre. Efforts have, however, been made to decentralize the economy. The second city, Thessaloniki, with its major port, has grown rapidly in population and industrial development. Other important towns are Patras (agglomeration, 170,452 inhabitants; department, 300,078), Larissa (city, 112,777 inhabitants; department, 270,612), Volos (agglomeration, 116,031 inhabitants) and Heraklion on the island of Crete.

The Monastic Republic of **Mount Athos** (or Agion Oros, i.e. 'Holy Mountain'), the easternmost of the three prongs of the peninsula of Chalcidice, is a self-governing community composed of 20 monasteries. The peninsula is administered by a Council of four members and an Assembly of 20 members, one deputy from each monastery. The Constitution of 1927 gives legal sanction to the Charter of Mount Athos, drawn up by representatives of the 20 monasteries on 20 May 1924, and its status is confirmed by the 1952 and 1975 Constitutions. Women are not permitted to enter. Population, 1991, 1,536.

The modern Greek language had two contesting literary standard forms, the archaizing *Katharevousa* ('purist'), and a version based on the spoken vernacular, 'Demotic'. In 1976 Standard Modern Greek was adopted as the official language, with Demotic as its core.

SOCIAL STATISTICS
1999: 116,038 live births; 104,190 deaths; 67,623 marriages; 9,500 divorces (1998); 597 still births (1998); 3,842 births to unmarried mothers (1998). 1999 rates: birth

(per 1,000 population), 10·9; death, 9·8; marriage, 6·4; divorce (1998), 0·9. Annual population growth rate, 1990–99, 0·4%. With only 3·8% of births to unmarried mothers, Greece has the lowest percentage of births out of wedlock of any EU member country. Over 1990–98 the suicide rate per 100,000 population was 3·8 (men, 6·1; women, 1·6). Expectation of life at birth, 1999, 75·5 years for males and 80·8 years for females. In 1998 the most popular age range for marrying was 25–29 for both males and females. Infant mortality, 1998, 5·5 per 1,000 live births; fertility rate, 1999, 1·3 births per woman. In 1998 Greece received 2,950 asylum applications, equivalent to 0·28 per 1,000 inhabitants.

CLIMATE
Coastal regions and the islands have typical Mediterranean conditions, with mild, rainy winters and hot, dry, sunny summers. Rainfall comes almost entirely in the winter months, though amounts vary widely according to position and relief. Continental conditions affect the northern mountainous areas, with severe winters, deep snow cover and heavy precipitation, but summers are hot. Athens, Jan. 48°F (8·6°C), July 82·5°F (28·2°C). Annual rainfall 16·6" (414·3 mm).

CONSTITUTION AND GOVERNMENT
Greece is a presidential parliamentary democracy. A new Constitution was introduced in June 1975. The 300-member *Chamber of Deputies* is elected for four-year terms by proportional representation. There is a 3% threshold. Extra seats are awarded to the party which leads in an election. The Chamber of Deputies elects the head of state, the *President*, for a five-year term.

National Anthem. 'Imnos eis tin Eleftherian' ('Hymn to Freedom'); words by Dionysios Solomos, tune by N. Mantzaros.

RECENT ELECTIONS
Parliamentary elections were held on 9 April 2000. Turn-out was 75%. Seats gained (and % of vote): Pasok (Panhellenic Socialist Movement), 158 (43·8%); New Democracy, 125 (42·7%); Communist Party, 11 (5·5%); Coalition of the Left and Progress, 6 (3·2%).

European Parliament. Greece has 25 representatives. At the June 1999 elections turn-out was 70·1%. New Democracy won 9 seats with 36·0% of votes cast (group in European Parliament: European People's Party); Pasok, 9 with 32·8% (Party of European Socialists); Communist Party, 3 with 8·7% (Confederal Group of the European United Left); Dikki, 2 with 6·9% (European United/Nordic Green Left); SYN, 2 with 5·2% (Confederal Group of the European United Left).

CURRENT ADMINISTRATION
President: Konstantinos 'Kostis' Stephanopoulos; b. 1926 (elected 8 March 1995; re-elected 8 Feb. 2000).
    In March 2003 the government comprised:
    Prime Minister: Constantinos Simitis; b. 1937 (Pasok; in office since 22 Jan. 1996).
    Minister of Foreign Affairs: Yeoryios Papandreou. *Foreign Affairs (Alternate):* Anastasios Yiannitsis. *Interior, Public Administration and Decentralization:* Costas Skandalidis. *Defence:* Yiannis Papantoniou. *National Economy and Finance:* Nikos Khristodhoulakis. *Agriculture:* Yeoryios Drys. *Labour and Social Security:* Dimitris Reppas. *Health and Welfare:* Konstandinos Stephanis. *Justice:* Philippos Petsalnikos. *Education and Religious Affairs:* Petros Efthimiou. *Culture:* Evangelos Venizelos. *Merchant Marine:* Yeoryios Anomeritis. *Public Order:* Mikhail Khrisokhoidhis. *Macedonia and Thrace:* Yeoryios Paskhalidhis. *Aegean:* Nikolaos Sifounakis. *Environment, Town Planning and Public Works:* Vasso Papandreou. *Transport and Communications:* Khristos Varelis. *Press and Mass Media:* Christos Protopapas. *Development:* Apostolos-Athanasios 'Akis' Tsohatsopulos.

Office of the Prime Minister: http://www.primeminister.gr/

DEFENCE
Prior to 2001 conscription was generally: (Army) 18 months, (Navy) 21 months, (Air Force) 20 months. However, a gradual shortening of military service is now

taking place and during 2003 conscription is set to be reduced to 12 months in the Army, 14 in the Air Force and 16 in the Navy. There are plans for 50% of the armed forces to be professional by 2005.

In 2000 defence expenditure totalled US$5,457m. (US$513 per capita), representing 4·9% of GDP (the highest percentage in the EU).

Army. The Field Army is organized in 3 military regions, with 1 Army, 5 corps and 4 divisional headquarters. Total Army strength (1999) 116,000 (88,500 conscripts, 2,700 women). There is also a Territorial Defence Force/National Guard of 35,000 whose role is internal security.

Navy. The current strength of the Hellenic Navy includes 8 diesel submarines, 4 destroyers and 11 frigates. Main bases are at Salamis, Patras and Soudha Bay (Crete). Personnel in 1999 totalled 19,500 (9,800 conscripts, 1,300 women).

Air Force. The Hellenic Air Force (HAF) had a strength (1999) of 30,170 (7,521 conscripts, 1,520 women). There were 458 combat aircraft including F-4s, F-5s, F-16s, Mirage F-1s and Mirage 2000s. The HAF is organized into Tactical and Air Support Commands.

INTERNATIONAL RELATIONS
Greece is a member of the UN, WTO, BIS, NATO, OECD, EU, WEU, Council of Europe, OSCE, CERN, BSEC, IOM and the Antarctic Treaty. Greece is a signatory to the Schengen Accord which abolishes border controls between Greece, Austria, Belgium, Denmark, Finland, France, Germany, Iceland, Italy, Luxembourg, the Netherlands, Norway, Portugal, Spain and Sweden.

ECONOMY
Agriculture accounted for 10·6% of GDP in 1998 (the highest percentage in the EU), industry 17·7% and services 71·7%.

Overview. In the late 1990s Greek growth rates were among the highest in the EU. Besides a restrictive incomes policy, the government has announced a number of structural reforms, including measures to enhance the flexibility of the labour market, improve the social security system, restructure public sector enterprises and speed up privatization.

Currency. In June 2000 EU leaders approved a recommendation for Greece to join the European single currency, the euro, and on 1 Jan. 2001 the euro (EUR) became the legal currency; irrevocable conversion rate 340·750 drachmas to 1 euro. The euro, which consists of 100 cents, has been in circulation since 1 Jan. 2002. There are seven euro notes in different colours and sizes denominated in 500, 200, 100, 50, 20, 10 and 5 euros, and eight coins denominated in 2 and 1 euros, then 50, 20, 10, 5, 2 and 1 cents. On the introduction of the euro there was a 'dual circulation' period before the drachma ceased to be legal tender on 28 Feb. 2002. Euro banknotes in circulation on 1 Jan. 2002 had a total value of €13·4bn.

Inflation was 2·9% in 2000. Foreign exchange reserves were US$6,509m. and gold reserves 3·86m. troy oz in June 2002. Total money supply in June 2002 was €7,683m.

Budget. Estimated revenue 1999 (in 1,000m. drachmas): 11,090; expenditure: 13,489.

VAT is 18% (reduced rate, 8%).

Performance. Real GDP growth was 4·1% in both 2000 and 2001. Greece has had economic growth above the EU average every year since 1996. Total GDP in 2001 was US$116·3bn.

Banking and Finance. The central bank and bank of issue is the Bank of Greece. Its *Governor* is Nicholas Garganas. There were 25 domestic banks in 1994, 8 private and the remainder in 4 state groupings. Total assets of all banks were 41,819bn. drachmas in 1999. The six leading banks in 2000 accounted for nearly 80% of assets of all Greek banks. Ranked by size of assets the largest banks were National Bank of Greece, Alpha Bank, Agricultural Bank, Commercial Bank of Greece, EFG Eurobank and Piraeus Bank.

There is a stock exchange in Athens.

Weights and Measures. The metric system was made obligatory in 1959; the use of other systems is prohibited. The Gregorian calendar was adopted in Feb. 1923.

ENERGY AND NATURAL RESOURCES

Environment. According to the *World Bank Atlas* carbon dioxide emissions in Greece were the equivalent of 8·1 tonnes per capita in 1998.

Electricity. Installed capacity in 1997 was 9m. kW. 72% of power is supplied by lignite-fired power stations. A national grid supplies the mainland, and islands near its coast. Power is produced in remoter islands by local generators. Total production in 1998 was 43·68bn. kWh, with consumption per capita 3,739 kWh. Electricity supply is: domestic, 220v, 50 cycles AC; industrial, 280v, AC 3 phase.

Oil and Gas. Output of crude petroleum, 1996, 3m. bbls.; proven reserves, 1996, 12m. bbls. The oil sector plays a critical role in the Greek economy, accounting for more than 70% of total energy demand. Supply is mostly imported but oil prospecting is intensifying. Natural gas was introduced in Greece in 1997 through a pipeline from Russia, and an additional source of supply is liquefied natural gas from Algeria. Demand for natural gas is in its infancy. The public monopoly in natural gas, DEPA, has developed only a few sales contracts to some large industrial groups, outside a large contract with DEH.

Minerals. Greece produces a variety of ores and minerals, including (with production, 1995, in tonnes) asbestos (4,920,650), nickel ore (2,069,466), bauxite (1,823,000 in 1998), magnesite (532,500 in 1996), caustic magnesia (206,532), iron-pyrites (18,737), chromite (5,650 in 1993), marble (white and coloured) and various other earths. There is little coal, and the lignite is of indifferent quality (59·78m. tonnes, 1996). Salt production (1997) 150,000 tonnes.

Agriculture. In 1998 there were 2·85m. ha of arable land and 1·1m. ha of permanent crops.

The Greek economy was traditionally based on agriculture, with small-scale farming predominating, except in a few areas in the north. There were 819,000 farms in 1998. However, there has been a steady shift towards industry and although agriculture still employs nearly 17% of the population, it accounted for only 9% of GDP in 1997. Nevertheless, Greece has a higher percentage of its population working in agriculture than any other EU member country. Agriculture accounts for 33·1% of exports (the highest proportion of any EU member country) and 17·9% of imports.

Production (2000, in 1,000 tonnes):

Sugarbeets	2,906	Oranges	950
Olives	2,000	Peaches and nectarines	900
Tomatoes	1,960	Potatoes	890
Maize	1,850	Cottonseed	650
Wheat	1,770	Watermelons	650
Seed cotton	1,250	Olive oil	443
Grapes	1,200	Wine	430

Livestock (2000, in 1,000): 590 cattle, 9,041 sheep, 5,293 goats, 906 pigs, 78 asses, 37 mules, 33 horses, 28,000 poultry. Livestock products, 2000 (in 1,000 tonnes): milk, 1,990; meat, 499; cheese, 240.

Forestry. Area covered by forests in 1995 was 29,400 sq. km. Timber production in 1999 was 2·22m. cu. metres.

Fisheries. Total catch in 1999 was 136,699 tonnes, mainly from sea fishing. In 1998, 17,093 fishermen were active. 10,000 kg of sponges were produced in 1998.

INDUSTRY

The leading companies by market capitalization in Greece, excluding banking and finance, in Jan. 2002 were: Hellenic Telecommunications Organization SA (OTE) (€8bn.); Coca-Cola HBC SA (CCHBC), formerly the Hellenic Bottling Company (€3bn.); and Cosmote Mobile Telecommunications SA (€3bn.).

The main products are canned vegetables and fruit, fruit juice, beer, wine, alcoholic beverages, cigarettes, textiles, yarn, leather, shoes, synthetic timber, paper, plastics, rubber products, chemical acids, pigments, pharmaceutical products, cosmetics, soap, disinfectants, fertilizers, glassware, porcelain sanitary items, wire and power coils and household instruments.

Production, 1998 (provisional) in 1,000 tonnes: cement, 25,832; petroleum, 3,455 (1997); chemical acids, 1,364; fertilizers, 1,030; crude steel, 1,020 (1997); iron (concrete-reinforcing bars), 835; alumina, 648; packing materials, 302; soap, washing powder, detergents, 241; aluminium, 169; textile yarns, 149; beer, 370·5m. litres; bottled wine, 146,466 litres; cigarettes (1,000 units), 31,063; glass, 230,351 sq. metres.

Although manufacturing accounts for more than 21% of GDP, Greece's performance is hampered by the proliferation of small, traditional, low-tech firms, often run as family businesses. Food, drink and tobacco processing are the most important sectors, but there are also some steel mills and several shipyards. Shipping is of prime importance to the economy. In addition, there are major programmes under way in the fields of power, irrigation and land reclamation.

Labour. Of the total workforce of 4,445,702 in the period April–June 1998, 3,967,167 persons were employed. 704,204 were engaged in the primary sector (agriculture, animal breeding, etc.), 913,848 in the secondary sector (manufacturing, construction, etc.) and 2,349,115 in the tertiary sector. Automatic index-linking of wages was abolished at the end of 1990. Since 1989 a statutory minimum of wage-bills must be spent on training (0·45%). Retirement age is 65 years for men and 60 for women, although most men retire before the age of 60. Unemployment was 9·9% in Sept. 2002, with youth unemployment nearly 30%.

Greeks work an average of 44·9 hours a week, the longest working week in the European Union.

Trade Unions. The status of trade unions is regulated by the Associations Act 1914. Trade union liberties are guaranteed under the Constitution, and a law of June 1982 altered the unions' right to strike.

The national body of trade unions is the Greek General Confederation of Labour.

INTERNATIONAL TRADE

Following the normalization of their relations, Greece lifted its trade embargo (imposed in Feb. 1994) on Macedonia on 13 Oct. 1995. There are quarrels with Turkey over Cyprus, oil rights under the Aegean and ownership of uninhabited islands close to the Turkish coast.

Imports and Exports. In 2000 exports (f.o.b.) were valued at US$10,202m. and imports (f.o.b.) at US$30,440m. In 1998 principal exports (in 1m. drachmas) were: manufactured goods, 676,015·3; food and live animals, 589,712·3; machinery and transport equipment, 346,476·4; mineral fuels, lubricants and related minerals, 216,722·4; chemicals and related products, 209,031·7. Principal imports were: machinery and transport equipment, 2,764,327·5; manufactured goods, 1,536,599·3; chemicals and related products, 1,095,265·3; food and live animals, 976,668·9; mineral fuels, lubricants and related minerals, 654,467·0.

Services accounted for 63·1% of exports in 1998—mainly from travel and tourism—the second highest percentage of any country after Egypt.

In 2001 Germany was the leading export market (12·3% of the total), followed by Italy (9·2%), UK (6·4%) and USA (5·3%). Italy was the principal supplier of imports (13·5% of the total), ahead of Germany (13·4%), France (7·1%) and the Netherlands (5·7%). Fellow EU member countries accounted for 46·7% of exports in 2001 and 54·8% of all imports.

COMMUNICATIONS

Roads. There were, in 1996, 117,000 km of roads, including 470 km of motorways, 9,100 km of national roads, 31,300 km of secondary and 75,600 km of other roads. Number of motor vehicles in 1999: 2,928,881 passenger cars, 1,023,987 trucks and vans, 710,775 motorcycles and 26,769 buses. There are approximately 278 passenger cars per 1,000 population. There were 2,131 road deaths in 1999. Greece has among the highest death rates in road accidents of any industrialized country. Road projects include improved links to Turkey and Bulgaria.

Rail. In 1997 the state network, Hellenic Railways (OSE), totalled 2,503 km including 1,565 km of 1,435 mm gauge, 887 km of 1,000 mm gauge, and 51 km of 750 mm gauge. Railways carried 2·17m. tonnes of freight and 11·75m. passengers in 1998. The Greek Railways Organization is investing US$23bn. in the link from Athens to the northern Bulgarian border. An 18-km long metro opened in Athens in Jan. 2000.

Civil Aviation. There are international airports at Athens (Spata 'Eleftherios Venizelos') and Thessaloniki-Makedonia. The airport at Spata opened in March 2001 and is Europe's newest airport. The old airport at Hellenikon has now closed down. The national carrier is Olympic Airways, serving some 30 towns and islands. Currently state-owned, Olympic Airways is set to be privatized but a second attempt to sell the carrier failed in Feb. 2003. Apart from the international airports, there are a further 25 provincial airports all connected by regular services operated by Olympic Airways. 6·27m. passengers were carried in 1999, of whom 3·64m. were on domestic and 2·63m. on international flights. Olympic Airways operates routes from Athens to all important cities of the country, Europe, the Middle East and USA. In 1999 Athens airport (Hellenikon) handled 10,335,000 passengers (6,164,000 on international flights).

Shipping. In 1998 the merchant navy totalled 25,225,000 GRT. Greek-owned ships under foreign flags numbered 127 of 2,785,865 GRT in 1997. In 1995 vessels totalling 38,573,000 NRT entered ports and vessels totalling 21,940,000 NRT cleared.

There is a canal (opened 9 Nov. 1893) across the Isthmus of Corinth (about 4 miles). The principal seaports are Piraeus, Thessaloniki, Patras, Volos, Igoumenitsa and Heraklion. Greece has 123 seaports with cargo and passenger handling facilities. Container terminals at the port of Piraeus are to be expanded to 1m. TEUs (twenty-foot equivalent units).

Telecommunications. In 2000 Greece had 5,659,300 telephone main lines (equivalent to 531·6 per 1,000 inhabitants) and 750,000 PCs were in use (or 70·5 per 1,000 persons). Mobile phone subscribers numbered 4·8m. in Nov. 2000 and there were 1·4m. Internet users in Dec. 2001. In 1996 there were 40,000 fax machines.

Postal Services. In 1996 there were 963 post offices with a staff of 11,520. A total of 465,274,000 letters and 3,186,000 parcels were dispatched worldwide in 1996. Total receipts were valued at 78,550m. drachmas and expenses at 92,515m. drachmas

SOCIAL INSTITUTIONS

Justice. Judges are appointed for life by the President after consultation with the judicial council. Judges enjoy personal and functional independence. There are three divisions of the courts—administrative, civil and criminal—and they must not give decisions which are contrary to the Constitution. Final jurisdiction lies with a Special Supreme Tribunal.

The first Ombudsman (*Synigoros*), Nikiforos Diamandouros, was appointed for a five-year term in Sept. 1998. In the two years from Oct. 1998–Sept. 2000 a total of 15,726 complaints were submitted, relating to: State–Citizen Relations (33·21%), Social Welfare (28·63%), Quality of Life (24·88%) and Human Rights (13·28%).

The population in penal institutions in Sept. 1997 was 5,577 (55 per 100,000 of national population). The death penalty was abolished for ordinary crimes in 1993.

Religion. The Christian Eastern (Greek) Orthodox Church is the established religion to which 98% of the population belong. It is under an archbishop and 67 metropolitans, 1 archbishop and 7 metropolitans in Crete, and 4 metropolitans in the Dodecanese. The head of the Greek Orthodox Church is Archbishop Christodoulos Paraskevaides of Athens and All Greece (b. 1939). Roman Catholics have 3 archbishops (in Naxos and Corfu and, not recognized by the State, in Athens) and 1 bishop (for Syra and Santorin). The Exarchs of the Greek Catholics and the Armenians are not recognized by the State. There were 0·15m. Muslims in 1995.

Complete religious freedom is recognized by the Constitution of 1974, but proselytizing from, and interference with, the Greek Orthodox Church is forbidden.

Education. Public education is provided in nursery, primary and secondary schools, starting at 5½–6½ years of age and free at all levels. Adult literacy rate, 1999, 97·1% (male 98·5%; female 95·8%).

In 1998–99 there were 5,576 nursery schools with 8,607 teachers and 141,658 pupils; 6,549 primary schools with 45,876 teachers and 646,559 pupils; 1,923 high schools with 31,662 teachers and 380,109 pupils; 1,244 general lycea with 18,206 teachers and 255,403 pupils; 48 multibranch lycea with 2,312 teachers and 10,388 pupils; 18 technical and ecclesiastical secondary schools of the first cycle with 52 teachers and 968 pupils; and 619 technical and ecclesiastical secondary schools of the second cycle with 11,218 teachers and 138,454 pupils. There was also 1 teacher training school with 159 teachers and 895 students; 14 technical education institutions (TEI) with 7,808 teachers and 64,671 students; 41 vocational and ecclesiastical schools with 710 teachers and 4,358 students. In 1998–99 there were 18 universities with 9,435 academic staff and 119,580 students.

In 1996 total expenditure on education came to 3·1% of GNP.

Health. Doctor and hospital treatment within the Greek national health system is free, but patients have to pay 25% of prescription charges. Those living in remote areas can reclaim a proportion of private medical expenses. In 1998 there were 341 hospitals and sanatoria with a total of 52,495 beds and 174 health centres. There were 43,030 doctors and 11,638 dentists (1997).

Greeks smoke on average 3,020 cigarettes a year—nearly twice the average for the European Union.

Welfare. The majority of employees are covered by the Social Insurance Institute, financed by employer and employee contributions. Benefits include pensions, medical expenses and long-term disability payments.

CULTURE

Greece will host the Olympic Games in 2004, from 13–29 Aug.

Broadcasting. *Elliniki Radiophonia Tileorasis* (ERT), the Hellenic National Radio and Television Institute, is the government broadcasting station. There are four national and regional programmes, and an external service, Voice of Greece (16 languages). ERT broadcasts two TV programmes (colour by SECAM H). Number of receivers: radio (1997), 5·02m.; television (1997), 2·5m. 97% of households have a radio, 75% have a colour TV set and 33% have a video recorder.

Cinema. There were 322 screens in 1995 and 8·5m. admissions. 17 full-length films were made.

Press. There were 31 daily newspapers published in Athens, 7 in Piraeus and 119 elsewhere in 1996. In 1996 a total of 4,225 book titles were published.

Tourism. Tourism is Greece's biggest industry with an estimated revenue for 1999 of US$8·77bn., contributing approximately 7% of GDP. Tourists in 1999 numbered 12·0m. There were 597,855 hotel beds in 1999 (285,956 in 1981). A total of 60,257,000 nights were spent in hotels in 1999 (provisional), 45,803,000 by foreigners and 14,454,000 by nationals.

Festivals. There are many festivals throughout the year, notably: The feast of St. Basil (1 Jan.); Gynaecocracy (8 Jan., female dominion); Carnival Season (mid-Feb. to mid-March); Independence Day (25 March); Feast of St George (23 April); Anastenaria (21–23 May, firewalking); Navy Week (end of June/beginning of July); Athens Lycabettus Theatre artistic performances (June–Aug.); Athens Festival (June–Sept.); Epidaurus Festival (July–Sept.); Philipi and Thasos Festival (July–Sept.); Dodoni Festival (July–Sept.); Athens Wine Festival and Ithaca Music Festival (end of July); Olympus Festival (Aug.); Epirotika Festival (Aug.); Kos Hippokrateia Festival (Aug.); Thessaloniki Film Festival and Festival of Popular Song (Sept.–Oct.); National Anniversary Procession (28 Oct.).

Libraries. In 1997 there were 829 public libraries, 2 National libraries and 64 Higher Education libraries; they held a combined 18,159,000 volumes. There were 7,521,000 visits to the libraries in 1997.

Theatre and Opera. There are two National Theatres and one Opera House.

Museums and Galleries. Amongst Greece's most important museums are the Acropolis Museum, the Museum of the City of Athens, the National Archaeological Museum and the National Historical Museum. In 1999 there were 89 museums and 182 galleries visited by 1,814,823 guests.

DIPLOMATIC REPRESENTATIVES
Of Greece in the United Kingdom (1A Holland Park, London, W11 3TP)
Ambassador: Alexandros Sandis.

Of the United Kingdom in Greece (1 Ploutarchou St., 106 75 Athens)
Ambassador: David C. A. Madden, CMG.

Of Greece in the USA (2221 Massachusetts Ave., NW, Washington, D.C., 20008)
Ambassador: George Savvaides.

Of the USA in Greece (91 Vasilissis Sophias Blvd., 101 60 Athens)
Ambassador: Thomas J. Miller.

Of Greece to the United Nations
Ambassador: Adamantios Th. Vassilakis.

FURTHER READING
Clogg, Richard, *A Concise History of Greece.* 2nd ed. CUP, 2002
Jougnatos, G. A., *Development of the Greek Economy, 1950–91: an Historical, Empirical and Econometric Analysis.* London, 1992
Legg, K. R. and Roberts, J. M., *Modern Greece: A Civilization on the Periphery.* Oxford, 1997
Pettifer, J., *The Greeks: the Land and the People since the War.* London, 1994
Sarafis, M. and Eve, M. (eds.) *Background to Contemporary Greece.* London, 1990
Tsakalotos, E., *Alternative Economic Strategies: the Case of Greece.* Aldershot, 1991
Veremis, T., *The Military in Greek Politics: From Independence to Democracy.* C. Hurst, London, 1997
Woodhouse, C. M., *Modern Greece: a Short History.* rev. ed. London, 1991

National statistical office: National Statistical Service; 14–16 Lycourgou St., Athens.
Website: http://www.statistics.gr/

GRENADA

Capital: St George's
Population estimate, 2000: 99,700
GDP per capita, 2000: (PPP$) 7,580
HDI/world rank: 0·747/83

KEY HISTORICAL EVENTS
Grenada became an independent nation within the Commonwealth on 7 Feb. 1974. The 1973 Constitution was suspended in 1979 following a revolution. On 19 Oct. 1983 the army took control after a power struggle led to the killing of the prime minister. At the request of a group of Caribbean countries, Grenada was invaded by US-led forces on 25–28 Oct. On 1 Nov. a State of Emergency was imposed which ended with the restoration of the 1973 Constitution.

TERRITORY AND POPULATION
Grenada is the most southerly island of the Windward Islands with an area of 133 sq. miles (344 sq. km); the state also includes the Southern Grenadine Islands to the north, chiefly Carriacou (58·3 sq. km) and Petit Martinique. The total population at the 2001 census (provisional) was 100,895; density, 293 per sq. km.

In 1998, 63·0% of the population were rural. The Borough of St George's, the capital, had 35,559 inhabitants in 2001. 85% of the population is of African descent, 11% of mixed origins, 3% Indian and 1% white.

The official language is English. A French-African patois is also spoken.

SOCIAL STATISTICS
Births, 1996, 2,096; deaths, 782. Rates per 1,000 population, 1996: birth, 22·8; death, 8·5. Life expectancy, 1994, 72·0 years. Infant mortality, 1998, 23 per 1,000 live births. Annual population growth rate, 1990–99, 0·3%; fertility rate, 1999, 3·6 births per woman.

CLIMATE
The tropical climate is very agreeable in the dry season, from Jan. to May, when days are warm and nights quite cool, but in the wet season there is very little difference between day and night temperatures. On the coast, annual rainfall is about 60" (1,500 mm) but it is as high as 150–200" (3,750–5,000 mm) in the mountains. Average temperature, 27°C.

CONSTITUTION AND GOVERNMENT
The head of state is the British sovereign, represented by an appointed Governor-General. There is a bicameral legislature, consisting of a 13-member *Senate,* appointed by the Governor-General, and a 15-member *House of Representatives,* elected by universal suffrage.

National Anthem. 'Hail Grenada, land of ours'; words by I. M. Baptiste, tune by L. A. Masanto.

RECENT ELECTIONS
At the elections of 14 Jan. 1999 for the House of Representatives the New National Party (NNP) won all 15 seats, with 62·4% of the votes cast.

CURRENT ADMINISTRATION
Governor-General: Sir Daniel Williams.

In March 2003 the government comprised:
Prime Minister, Minister of Information and National Security: Dr Keith Mitchell; b. 1946 (NNP; in office since 22 June 1995).

Minister of Health and the Environment: Clarice Modeste-Curwen. *Foreign Affairs, International Trade, Carriacou and Petit Martinique Affairs, and Legal Affairs:* Elvin Nimrod. *Finance, Industry, Trade and Planning:* Anthony Boatswain. *Agriculture, Lands, Forestry and Fisheries:* Claris Charles. *Education:* Augustine

John. *Labour and Local Government:* Lawrence Joseph. *Implementation:* Joslyn Whiteman. *Tourism, Civil Aviation, Gender and Family Affairs, Social Security and Culture:* Brenda Hood. *Social Services, Housing and Co-operatives:* Brian McQueen. *Youth, Sports and Community Development:* Adrian Mitchell. *Communications, Works and Public Utilities:* Gregory Bowen. *Attorney General:* Raymond Anthony.

DEFENCE

Royal Grenada Police Force. Modelled on the British system, the 730-strong police force includes an 80-member paramilitary unit and a 30-member coastguard.

INTERNATIONAL RELATIONS

Grenada is a member of the UN, WTO, OAS, ACS, CARICOM, OECS, IOM, the Commonwealth and is an ACP member state of the ACP-EU relationship.

ECONOMY

Agriculture accounted for 8·4% of GDP in 1998, industry 22·2% and services 69·4%.

Currency. The unit of currency is the *Eastern Caribbean dollar* (EC$). Foreign exchange reserves were US$69m. in May 2002. Total money supply in May 2002 was EC$228m. Inflation was 2·5% in 2001.

Budget. In 1996 recurrent revenue was US$74·1m. and recurrent expenditure US$68·8m. Capital expenditure was US$25·7m. Income tax has been abolished. VAT is 25% (reduced rate, 5%).

Performance. Real GDP growth was 3·5% in 2001 (6·4% in 2000). Total GDP in 2001 was US$0·4bn.

Banking and Finance. Grenada is a member of the Eastern Caribbean Central Bank. The *Governor* is Sir Dwight Venner. In 1995 there were five commercial banks (two foreign). The Grenada Agricultural Bank was established in 1965 to encourage agricultural development; in 1975 it became the Grenada Agricultural and Industrial Development Corporation. In 1995 bank deposits were EC$666·8m. (US$249·7m.). Total foreign currency deposits in 1995 amounted to US$11·8m.

ENERGY AND NATURAL RESOURCES

Environment. According to the *World Bank Atlas* Grenada's carbon dioxide emissions in 1998 were the equivalent of 1·9 tonnes per capita.

Electricity. Installed capacity in 1995 was 17,300 kW. Production in 1998 was 105m. kWh, with consumption per capita 1,161 kWh in 1997.

Agriculture. There were 2,000 ha of arable land in 1998 and 9,000 ha of permanent crops. Principal crop production (2000, in 1,000 tonnes): coconuts 7; sugarcane, 7; bananas, 5; avocados, 2; grapefruit and pomelos, 2; mangoes, 2. Nutmeg, corn, pigeon peas, citrus, root-crops and vegetables are also grown, in addition to small scattered cultivations of cotton, cloves, cinnamon, pimento, coffee and fruit trees. Grenada is the second largest producer of nutmeg in the world, after Indonesia.

Livestock (2000): cattle, 4,000; sheep, 13,000; goats, 7,000; pigs, 5,000.

Forestry. In 1995 the area under forests was 4,000 ha, or 11·8% of the total land area.

Fisheries. The catch in 1999 was 1,631 tonnes, entirely from marine waters.

INDUSTRY

Main products are wheat flour, soft drinks, beer, animal feed, rum and cigarettes.

Labour. In 1993 the labour force was estimated at 27,820. Unemployment was 16·7%.

INTERNATIONAL TRADE

Total external debt amounted to US$207m. in 2000.

Imports and Exports. Imports and exports for calendar years in US$1m.:

	1994	1995	1996
Imports f.o.b.	115·6	125·4	147·5
Exports f.o.b.	26·5	25·9	24·9

The principal exports are nutmeg, cocoa, bananas, mace and textiles. Exports are mainly to the UK, Trinidad and Tobago, the Netherlands and Germany. Main import suppliers are the USA, the UK, Barbados and Japan.

COMMUNICATIONS

Roads. In 1996 there were 1,040 km of roads, of which 638 km were hard-surfaced.

Civil Aviation. The main airport is Point Salines International. Union Island and Carriacou have smaller airports. There were direct flights from Point Salines in 1998 to Antigua, Barbados, the British Virgin Islands, London, Miami, the Netherlands Antilles, New York, Puerto Rico, St Lucia, St Vincent, Tobago and Trinidad. In 1998 Point Salines handled 330,000 passengers (317,000 on international flights) and 1,700 tonnes of freight.

Shipping. The main port is at St George's; there are eight minor ports. Total number of containers handled in 1991 was 5,161; cargo landed, 187,039 tonnes; cargo loaded, 24,786 tonnes. Sea-going shipping totalled 1,000 GRT in 1998.

Telecommunications. Telephone main lines numbered 31,400 in 2000 (332·0 per 1,000 persons) and there were 12,000 PCs in use (127·1 for every 1,000 persons). There were 2,000 mobile phone subscribers in 1999 and 300 fax machines in 1995. In Dec. 2000 Grenada had 4,100 Internet users.

Postal Services. In 1994 there were 58 post offices.

SOCIAL INSTITUTIONS

Justice. The Grenada Supreme Court, situated in St George's, comprises a High Court of Justice, a Court of Magisterial Appeal (which hears appeals from the lower Magistrates' Courts exercising summary jurisdiction) and an Itinerant Court of Appeal (to hear appeals from the High Court). Grenada was one of ten countries to sign an agreement in Feb. 2001 establishing a Caribbean Court of Justice to replace the British Privy Council as the highest civil and criminal court. The Court of Justice is expected to sit for the first time in the second half of 2003. For police *see* DEFENCE, *above*.

The population in penal institutions in Jan. 1998 was 327 (equivalent to 330 per 100,000 of national population).

Religion. At the 1991 census 53% of the population were Roman Catholic, 14% Anglican, 8·5% Seventh Day Adventists and 7·2% Pentecostal.

Education. Adult literacy was 96% in 1998. In 1994 there were 74 pre-primary schools with 3,499 pupils; in 1995 there were 57 primary schools with 23,256 pupils and 19 secondary schools with 7,260 pupils. In 1991 there were 10 schools for special education and 12 day-care centres caring for 249 children. The Grenada National College was established in 1988. There is also a branch of the University of the West Indies.

Health. In 1990 there was one main hospital with two subsidiaries. In 1995 there were 64 doctors, 8 dentists, 28 pharmacists (1990), 36 midwives (1990) and 365 nursing personnel.

CULTURE

Broadcasting. The government-owned Grenada Broadcasting Corporation operates Radio Grenada and Grenada Television. There are also four independent radio stations. Grenada Television transmits on three channels (colour by NTSC). A private cable TV company provides services on 25 channels, and there is a religious TV service. In 1997 there were 57,000 radio and 33,000 TV sets.

Press. In 1993 there were 5 weekly, 1 monthly and 2 bi-monthly newspapers.

Tourism. In 1999 there were 125,000 visitors to the country, plus (in 1998) 266,000 cruise ship arrivals. Tourism receipts totalled US$63m. in 1999.

DIPLOMATIC REPRESENTATIVES
Of Grenada in the United Kingdom (Lauderdale House, 8 Queen Street, London, W1X 7PH)
High Commissioner: Ruth Elizabeth Rouse.

Of the United Kingdom in Grenada
High Commissioner: John White (resides at Bridgetown, Barbados).

Of Grenada in the USA (1701 New Hampshire Ave., NW, Washington, D.C., 20009)
Ambassador: Denis Antoine.

Of the USA in Grenada
Ambassador: Earl Norfleet Phillips, Jr (resides at Bridgetown).

Of Grenada to the United Nations
Ambassador: Dr Lamuel A. Stanislaus.

Of Grenada to the European Union
Ambassador: Joan Marie Coutain.

FURTHER READING
Ferguson, J., *Grenada: Revolution in Reverse.* London, 1991
Heine, J. (ed.) *A Revolution Aborted: the Lessons of Grenada.* Pittsburgh Univ. Press, 1990

Air Force. There is a small Air Force with 10 combat aircraft and 12 armed helicopters (although less than half were operational). Strength was (1999) 700.

INTERNATIONAL RELATIONS

Guatemala is a member of the UN, WTO, OAS, Inter-American Development Bank, CACM, ACS and IOM.

ECONOMY

In 1998 agriculture accounted for 23·2% of GDP, industry 20·0% and services 56·8%.

Overview. Partial privatization of utilities, telecommunications and railways began in 1997.

Currency. The unit of currency is the *quetzal* (CTQ) of 100 *centavos*, established on 7 May 1925. In June 2002 foreign exchange reserves were US$2,222m., total money supply was Q.20,561m. and gold reserves were 222,000 troy oz. Inflation was 8·7% in 2001.

Budget. Government revenue and expenditure (in Q.1m.):

	1996	1997	1998	1999	2000
Revenue	8,445·1	9,627·7	11,856·2	13,967·1	15,205·8
Expenditure	8,612·7	10,418·7	13,486·0	16,373·7	18,220·8

VAT is 10%.

Performance. Real GDP growth was 3·6% in 2000, but only 1·8% in 2001. Total GDP in 2001 was US$20·6bn.

Banking and Finance. The Banco de Guatemala is the central bank and bank of issue (*President*, Lizardo Sosa López). Constitutional amendments of 1993 placed limits on its financing of government spending. In 1996 there were 21 private banks, 3 state banks, 4 international banks and 18 foreign banks. The international banks and the foreign banks are authorized to operate as commercial banks.

There are two stock exchanges.

Weights and Measures. The metric system has been officially adopted, but traditional measures are still used locally.

ENERGY AND NATURAL RESOURCES

Environment. According to the *World Bank Atlas* carbon dioxide emissions in 1998 were the equivalent of 0·9 tonnes per capita.

Electricity. Installed capacity in 1995 was 973,500 kW, of which around half was hydro-electric. Production, 1998, 3·08bn. kWh. Consumption per capita in 1998 was 322 kWh.

Oil and Gas. There were proven natural gas reserves in 1997 of 3m. cu. metres. Production (1995), 8m. cu. metres. In 1997 crude petroleum reserves were 200m. bbls. and in 1995 output was 5m. bbls.

Minerals. There are deposits of gold, silver and nickel.

Agriculture. There were 1·36m. ha of arable land in 1998 and 0·55m. ha of permanent crops. Production, 2000 (in 1,000 tonnes): sugarcane, 17,150; maize, 1,109; bananas, 733; coffee, 295; tomatoes, 150; lemons and limes, 117; melons, 115. Rubber development schemes are under way, assisted by US funds. Guatemala is one of the largest sources of essential oils (citronella and lemongrass). Arable land: 12%; permanent crops: 4%; meadows and pastures: 12%; forest and woodland: 40%; other: 32%.

Livestock (2000): cattle, 2·30m.; pigs, 825,000; sheep, 551,000; horses, 120,000; goats, 110,000; chickens, 24m.

Forestry. In 1995 the area under forests was 3·84m ha, or 35·4% of the total land area (4·25m. ha and 39·2% in 1990). Mahogany and cedar are grown, and chick, a chewing gum base, is produced. Timber production in 1999 was 13·30m. cu. metres.

Fisheries. In 1999 the total catch was 11,028 tonnes (6,976 tonnes from inland waters), up from 3,614 tonnes in 1989.

INDUSTRY
Manufacturing contributed 14·1% of GDP in 1995. The principal industries are food and beverages, tobacco, chemicals, hides and skins, textiles, garments and non-metallic minerals. Cement production in 1997 was 1,280,000 tonnes; raw sugar production was 1,682,000 tonnes in 1998. New industries include electrical goods, plastic sheet and metal furniture.

Labour. In 1995 the workforce totalled 3,316,723 including: agriculture, 1,513,600; commerce, 572,011; services, 439,719; manufacturing, 439,121; building, 214,102; transport and communications, 77,476; finance, 40,474.

The working week is 44 hours, with a 12-day paid holiday annually.

Trade Unions. There are three federations for private sector workers.

INTERNATIONAL TRADE
In May 1992 Guatemala, El Salvador and Honduras agreed to create a free trade zone and standardize import duties. External debt was US$4,622m. in 2000.

Imports and Exports. Values in US$1m. were:

	1996	1997	1998	1999	2000
Imports f.o.b.	2,880·3	3,542·7	4,255·7	4,225·7	4,508·2
Exports f.o.b.	2,236·9	2,602·9	1,846·9	2,780·6	3,082·3

In 1995 the principal exports were (in US$1m.): coffee, 550; sugar, 237; bananas, 138; cardamom, 41. Main export markets, 1995: USA, 31%; El Salvador, 13·8%; Honduras, 6·4%; Germany, 5·8%; Costa Rica, 5·2%. Main import suppliers: USA, 43%; Mexico, 9·3%; El Salvador, 5·0%; Venezuela, 4·6%; Japan, 3·7%.

COMMUNICATIONS

Roads. In 1998 there were 13,856 km of roads, of which 2,087 km were highways or national roads. There is a highway from coast to coast via Guatemala City. There are two highways from the Mexican to the Salvadorean frontier: the Pacific Highway serving the fertile coastal plain and the Pan-American Highway running through the highlands and Guatemala City. Passenger cars numbered about 102,000 in 1996 (8·8 per 1,000 inhabitants); vans and trucks, 97,000.

Rail. The state-owned Ferrocarriles de Guatemala operated 953 km of railway in 1996, linking east and west coast seaports to Guatemala City, with branch lines to the north and south borders. Passenger-km travelled in 1995 came to 16·58bn. and freight tonne-km to 85·61bn.

Civil Aviation. There are international airports at Guatemala City (La Aurora) and Flores. The 25%-government-owned airline, Aviateca, furnishes both domestic and international services, as does Mayan World Airlines. In 2000 La Aurora handled 1,258,919 passengers and 58,118 tonnes of freight. In 1999 scheduled airline traffic of Guatemalan-based carriers flew 5·3m. km, carrying 506,000 passengers (472,000 on international flights).

Shipping. The chief ports on the Atlantic coast are Puerto Barrios and Santo Tomás de Castilla: on the Pacific coast, Puerto Quetzal and Champerico. Merchant shipping totalled 1,000 GRT in 1998. In 1997 vessels totalling 4,505,000 NRT entered ports and vessels totalling 3,815,000 NRT cleared.

Telecommunications. The government own and operate the telecommunications services. In 2000 there were 649,800 telephone main lines, or 57·1 for every 1,000 persons, and 130,000 PCs were in use in 2000 (11·4 for every 1,000 persons). There were 351,200 mobile phone subscribers in 1999 and 10,000 fax machines in 1995. Guatemala had 65,000 Internet users in Dec. 1999.

Postal Services. There were 540 post offices in 1994.

SOCIAL INSTITUTIONS

Justice. Justice is administered in a Constitution Court, a Supreme Court, 6 appeal courts and 28 courts of first instance. Supreme Court and appeal court judges are elected by Congress. Judges of first instance are appointed by the Supreme Court.

The death penalty is authorized for murder and kidnapping. Two executions were carried out in 2000.

There are three police forces (strengths in 1996) controlled respectively by the Ministry of the Interior (12,000), the Ministry of Finance (2,100) and the Ministry of Defence (4,000).

The population in penal institutions in Dec. 1996 was 6,931 (65 per 100,000 of national population).

Religion. Roman Catholicism is the prevailing faith (8·4m. adherents in 1999) and there is a Roman Catholic archbishopric. Membership of the approximately 100 evangelical Protestant churches was estimated at 2·4m. in 1999 (75% Pentecostalist).

Education. In 1997 there were 1,544,709 pupils at primary schools and 384,729 pupils at secondary level. The adult literacy rate in 1999 was 68·1% (male, 75·6%; female, 60·5%). In 1994–95 there were five universities with 70,233 students and 4,450 academic staff.

Health. Guatemala had 7,601 doctors and 14,401 nurses in 1992 and 1,065 dentists in 1990. There were 60 state hospitals and 100 dispensaries in 1990.

Welfare. A comprehensive system of social security was outlined in a law of 30 Oct. 1946.

CULTURE

Broadcasting. There are 5 government, 6 educational and 84 commercial radio broadcasting services. There are 4 commercial TV stations and 1 government station. There is also reception by US television satellite. There were 640,000 TV receivers (colour by NTSC) and 835,000 radio sets in 1997.

Press. In 1996 there were 4 independent dailies and 1 evening newspaper, 1 government daily and 2 weeklies.

Tourism. Tourism is an important source of foreign exchange (US$570m. in 1999). There were 823,000 foreign tourists in 1999.

DIPLOMATIC REPRESENTATIVES
Of Guatemala in the United Kingdom (13 Fawcett St., London, SW10 9HN)
Ambassador: Vacant.
Chargé d'Affaires a.i.: Manuel Estuardo Roldán Barillas.

Of the United Kingdom in Guatemala (Avenida La Reforma 16-00, Zona 10, Edificio Torre Internacional, Nivel 11, Guatemala City)
Ambassador: Richard Lavers.

Of Guatemala in the USA (2220 R. St., NW, Washington, D.C., 20008)
Ambassador: Antonio Arenales Forno.

Of the USA in Guatemala (7–01 Avenida de la Reforma, Zone 10, Guatemala City)
Ambassador: John R. Hamilton.

Of Guatemala to the United Nations
Ambassador: Gert Rosenthal.

Of Guatemala to the European Union
Ambassador: Edmond Mulet-Lesieur.

FURTHER READING
Jonas, Susanne, *Of Centaurs and Doves: Guatemala's Peace Process.* Westview Press, Boulder (CO), 2001
Woodward, R. L., *Guatemala.* [Bibliography] 2nd ed. ABC-Clio, Oxford and Santa Barbara (CA), 1992

National library: Biblioteca Nacional, 5a Avenida y 8a Calle, Zona 1, Guatemala City.
National Institute of Statistics Website: http://www.segeplan.gob.gt/ine/

GUINEA

République de Guinée

Capital: Conakry
Population estimate, 2000: 8·15m.
GDP per capita, 2000: (PPP$) 1,982
HDI/world rank: 0·414/159

KEY HISTORICAL EVENTS
In 1888 Guinea became a French protectorate, in 1893 a colony, and in 1904 a constituent territory of French West Africa. Forced labour and other colonial depredations ensued, although a form of representation was introduced in 1946. The independent Republic of Guinea was proclaimed on 2 Oct. 1958, after the territory of French Guinea had decided to leave the French community. Guinea became a single-party state.

In 1980 the armed forces staged a coup and dissolved the National Assembly. Following popular disturbances a multi-party system was introduced in April 1992.

In 2000 fierce fighting broke out between Guinean government troops and rebels, believed to be a mix of Guinean dissidents and mercenaries from Liberia and Sierra Leone. More than 250,000 refugees were caught up in what the United Nations High Commissioner for Refugees described as the world's worst refugee crisis.

TERRITORY AND POPULATION
Guinea is bounded in the northwest by Guinea-Bissau and Senegal, northeast by Mali, southeast by Côte d'Ivoire, south by Liberia and Sierra Leone, and west by the Atlantic Ocean.

The area is 245,857 sq. km (94,926 sq. miles). In 1996 the census population was 7,164,823 (density 29·1 per sq. km).

The UN gives a projected population for 2010 of 9·96m.

The capital is Conakry. In 1999, 68% of the population were rural.

The areas, populations and chief towns of the major divisions in 1991 were:

	Sq. km	1991 population	Chief town	Population (in year)
Conakry (city)	308	1,320,000	Conakry	1,764,000 (1999)
Guinée-Forestière	57,324	1,033,000	Nzérékoré	55,356 (1983)
Guinée-Maritime	43,980	975,000	Kindia	80,000 (1986)
Haute-Guinée	92,535	1,147,000	Kankan	70,000 (1992)
Moyenne-Guinée	51,710	1,262,000	Labé	110,000 (1986)

The country has since been divided into seven administrative regions: Boké, Faranah, Kankan, Kindia, Labé, Mamou and Nzérékoré.

The ethnic composition is Fulani (40·3%, predominant in Moyenne-Guinée), Malinké (or Mandingo, 25·8%, prominent in Haute-Guinée), Susu (11%, prominent in Guinée-Maritime), Kissi (6·5%) and Kpelle (4·8%) in Guinée-Forestière, and Dialonka, Loma and others (11·6%).

The official language is French.

SOCIAL STATISTICS
Births, 1997, 311,000; deaths, 135,000. Rates, 1997: birth, 42·0 per 1,000 population; death, 18·2; infant mortality, 115 per 1,000 live births (1999). Life expectancy, 1999, 46·6 years for males and 47·6 for females. Annual population growth rate, 1990–99, 2·8%; fertility rate, 1999, 5·4 births per woman.

CLIMATE
A tropical climate, with high rainfall near the coast and constant heat, but conditions are a little cooler on the plateau. The wet season on the coast lasts from May to Nov., but only to Oct. inland. Conakry, Jan. 80°F (26·7°C), July 77°F (25°C). Annual rainfall 172" (4,293 mm).

CONSTITUTION AND GOVERNMENT
There is a 114-member *National Assembly*, 38 of whose members are elected on a first-past-the-post system, and the remainder from national lists by proportional representation.

On 11 Nov. 2001 a referendum was held in which 98·4% of votes cast were in favour of President Conté remaining in office for a third term, requiring an amendment to the constitution (previously allowing a maximum two presidential terms). The referendum, which also increased the presidential mandate from five to seven years, was boycotted by opposition parties.

National Anthem. 'Peuple d'Afrique, le passé historique' ('People of Africa, the historic past'); words anonymous, tune by K. Fodeba.

RECENT ELECTIONS

Presidential elections were held on 14 Dec. 1998. President Conté was re-elected against four opponents by 54·1% of votes cast.

Parliamentary elections took place on 30 June 2002. The Party of Unity and Progress (PUP) gained 85 out of 114 seats with 61·6% of votes cast and the Union for Progress and Revival gained 20 seats with 26·6%. The turn-out was 72·5%.

CURRENT ADMINISTRATION

President: Gen. Lansana Conté; b. 1934 (PUP; seized power 3 April 1984, most recently re-elected 14 Dec. 1998).

In March 2003 the cabinet comprised:

Prime Minister: Lamine Sidimé; b. 1944 (PUP; sworn in 8 March 1999).

Minister of Agriculture and Animal Husbandry: Jean-Paul Sarr. *Commerce, Industry and Small- and Medium-Scale Enterprise:* Adama Balde. *Communication:* Mamadi Condé. *Defence:* Vacant. *Economy and Finance:* Sheik Amadou Camara. *Employment and Public Administration:* Lamine Kamara. *Mining, Geology and Environment:* Dr Alpha Mady Souma. *Fishing and Aquaculture:* Oumare Kouyate. *Foreign Affairs:* François Lonseny Fall. *Justice and Keeper of the Seals:* Abou Camara. *Higher Education and Scientific Research:* Eugène Camara. *Planning:* Fassou Niankoye Sagno. *Public Works and Transport:* Cellou Dalein Diallo. *Pre-University and Civic Education:* Germain Doualamou. *Public Health:* Dr Mamadou Saliou Diallo. *Security:* Moussa Sampil. *Social Affairs and Promotion of Women and Children:* Mariama Aribot. *Technical Teaching and Professional Training:* Ibrahima Souma. *Territorial Administration and Decentralization:* Moussa Solano. *Tourism, Hotels and Handicrafts:* Sylla Koumba Diakité. *Urban Planning and Housing:* Blaise Foromo. *Water Power and Energy:* Mory Kaba. *Youth, Sports and Culture:* Abdel Kadr Sangaré.

Government Website (French only): http://www.guinee.gov.gn/

DEFENCE

Conscription is for two years. Defence expenditure totalled US$57m. in 2000 (US$8 per capita), representing 1·5% of GDP.

Army. The Army of 9,700 (1999) includes 7,500 conscripts. There are also three paramilitary forces: People's Militia (7,000), Gendarmerie (1,000) and Republican Guard (1,600).

Navy. A small force of 400 (1999) operate from bases at Conakry and Kakanda.

Air Force. Personnel (1997) 800. There were eight combat aircraft including MiG-17s and MiG-21s.

INTERNATIONAL RELATIONS

Guinea is a member of the UN, WTO, the African Union, African Development Bank, ECOWAS, IOM, OIC, International Organization of the Francophonie and is an ACP member state of the ACP-EU relationship.

ECONOMY

Agriculture produced 22·4% of GDP in 1998, industry 35·5% and services 42·1%.

Currency. The monetary unit is the *Guinean franc* (GNF). Inflation in 2001 was 5·4%. In June 2002 foreign exchange reserves were US$192m. and total money supply was 600,100m. Guinean francs.

Budget. Estimated government revenue for 1999 was 574,901m. Guinean francs (497,293m. in 1998) and expenditure in 1999 was 1,010,060m. Guinean francs (792,554m. in 1998).

Of total government revenue in 1997, current revenues accounted for 494·1bn. Guinean francs and foreign aid accounted for 134·5bn. Guinean francs. The mining sector accounted for 18·8% of current revenues in 1997. Expenditure (in 1,000m. Guinean francs): 754·7, of which current expenditure, 383·3. VAT was applied to non-essential goods in July 1996.

Performance. Real GDP growth in 2001 was 3·6% (2·1% in 2000). Total GDP in 2001 was US$2·9bn.

Banking and Finance. In 1986 the Central Bank (*Governor*, Ibrahim Cherif Bah) and commercial banking were restructured, and commercial banks returned to the private sector. There were six commercial banks in 1993.

ENERGY AND NATURAL RESOURCES

Environment. According to the *World Bank Atlas* Guinea's carbon dioxide emissions in 1998 were the equivalent of 0·2 tonnes per capita.

Electricity. In 1996 installed capacity was 176 MW. Production was 535m. kWh in 1998. Consumption per capita was 74 kWh in 1997.

Minerals. Mining produced 19·1% of GDP in 1994. Guinea possesses over 25% of the world's bauxite reserves and is the second largest producer after Australia. 1997 output: bauxite, 18,392,000 tonnes; alumina (1996), 564,237 tonnes; diamonds (1998), 205,000 carats; gold (1996), 2,100 kg. There are also deposits of granite, iron ore, chrome, copper, lead, manganese, molybdenum, nickel, platinum, uranium and zinc.

Agriculture. Subsistence agriculture supports about 70% of the population. There were 885,000 ha of arable land in 1998 and 600,000 ha of permanent crops. The chief crops (production, 2000, in 1,000 tonnes) are: cassava, 870; rice, 750; plantains, 429; sugarcane, 220; groundnuts, 182; bananas, 150; sweet potatoes, 135; maize, 90; yams, 88; mangoes, 83; pineapples, 72; palm kernels, 52; palm oil, 50; seed cotton, 50; taro, 29; coffee, 21; cotton lint, 21.

Livestock (2000): cattle, 2·37m.; goats, 864,000; sheep, 687,000; pigs, 54,000; chickens, 9m.

Forestry. The area under forests in 1995 was 6·37m. ha, or 25·9% of the total land area (6·74m. ha and 27·4% in 1990). In 1999, 8·65m. cu. metres of roundwood were cut.

Fisheries. In 1999 the total catch was 87,314 tonnes, almost entirely from sea fishing.

INDUSTRY
Manufacturing accounted for 4·6% of GDP in 1994. Cement, corrugated and sheet iron, beer, soft drinks and cigarettes are produced.

Labour. In 1996 the labour force was 3,565,000 (53% males). The agricultural sector employs 80% of the workforce.

INTERNATIONAL TRADE
Foreign debt was US$3,388m. in 2000. Imports require authorization and there are restrictions on the export of capital.

Imports and Exports. Imports and exports for calendar years in US$1m.:

	1995	1996	1997	1998	1999
Imports f.o.b.	621·7	525·3	512·5	572·0	583·4
Exports f.o.b.	582·8	636·5	630·1	693·0	677·9

Main exports by value (US$1m.), 1994: bauxite, 272; alumina, 103; gold, 84; coffee, 58. Main export markets, 1994: Belgium, 26·7%; USA, 15·1%; Ireland, 10·0%; Spain, 9·6%; Germany, 5·8%; Brazil, 5·4%. Main import suppliers: France, 19·5%; Côte d'Ivoire, 16·0%; USA, 7·1%; Belgium, 6·9%; Hong Kong, 6·3%.

COMMUNICATIONS

Roads. In 1996 there were about 4,300 km of main and national roads, 7,960 km of secondary roads and 18,200 km of other roads of which 16·5% were hard-surfaced. In 1996 there were 14,100 passenger cars, or two per 1,000 inhabitants, and 21,000 trucks and vans.

Rail. A railway connects Conakry with Kankan (662 km) and is to be extended to Bougouni in Mali. A line 134 km long linking bauxite deposits at Sangaredi with Port Kamsar was opened in 1973 (carried 12·5m. tonnes in 1993), a third line links Conakry and Fria (144 km; carried 1m. tonnes in 1993) and a fourth, the Kindia Bauxite Railway (102 km) linking Débéle with Conakry, carried 3m. tonnes in 1994.

Civil Aviation. There is an international airport at Conakry (Gbessia). In 1998 there were scheduled flights to Abidjan, Accra, Bamako, Banjul, Bissau, Brazzaville, Brussels, Casablanca, Dakar, Freetown, Johannesburg, Lagos, Libreville, Monrovia, Moscow, Paris and Praia. In 2000 Conakry handled 243,000 passengers (227,000 on international flights) and 4,600 tonnes of freight. In 1999 scheduled airline traffic of Guinean-based carriers flew 800,000 km, carrying 59,000 passengers (all on international flights).

Shipping. There are ports at Conakry and for bauxite exports at Kamsar (opened 1973). Merchant shipping totalled 11,000 GRT in 1998.

Telecommunications. The Société des Télécommunications de Guinée is 40% state-owned. In 2000 there were 62,400 main telephone lines, equivalent to 7·9 per 1,000 population, and 29,000 PCs in use (3·7 per 1,000 persons). There were 22,200 mobile phone subscribers in 1999 and 2,800 fax machines in 1998. In Dec. 2000 Guinea had 8,000 Internet users.

Postal Services. In 1995 there were 83 post offices, or one for every 86,000 persons.

SOCIAL INSTITUTIONS

Justice. There are *tribunaux du premier degré* at Conakry and Kankan, and a *juge de paix* at Nzérékoré. The High Court, Court of Appeal and Superior Tribunal of Cassation are at Conakry. The death penalty is in force, and was used in 2001 for the first time in 17 years.

The population in penal institutions in 1997 was approximately 4,000 (55 per 100,000 of national population).

Religion. 85% of the population are Muslim, 5% Christian. Traditional animist beliefs are still found.

Education. In 1998 adult literacy was 36·0%. In 1997–98 there were 674,732 pupils and 13,883 teachers in 3,723 primary schools and 5,099 teachers for 153,661 pupils in general education in secondary schools. In 1995 there were 28,311 pupils (6,143 girls) and 1,407 teachers in 61 *lycées* and 8,569 pupils (3,013) and 1,268 teachers in 55 institutions of professional education. In 1996 there were two universities with 5,735 students and 525 academic staff.

Besides French, there are eight official languages taught in schools: Fulani, Malinké, Susu, Kissi, Kpelle, Loma, Basari and Koniagi.

Health. In 1991 there were 375 hospitals and dispensaries. In 1988 there were 3,382 beds; there were also 920 doctors (1991), 22 dentists (1988), 197 pharmacists (1991), 371 midwives (1991) and 1,243 trained nursing personnel (1988).

CULTURE

Broadcasting. Broadcasting is the responsibility of the state-controlled Radiodiffusion Télévision Guinéenne. There were 85,000 TV receivers (colour by SECAM H) and 357,000 radio receivers in 1997.

Press. There is one daily newspaper (circulation 20,000).

Tourism. There were 27,000 foreign tourists in 1999 bringing in revenue of US$7m.

DIPLOMATIC REPRESENTATIVES
Of Guinea in the United Kingdom
Ambassador: Vacant.
Chargé d'Affaires a.i.: Ibrahima Kalil Toure (resides at Paris).
Honorary Consul: Alexander Harper (20 Upper Grosvenor St., London, W1X 9PB).

Of the United Kingdom in Guinea
Ambassador: David Alan Jones (resides in Freetown, Sierra Leone).

Of Guinea in the USA (2112 Leroy Pl., NW, Washington, D.C., 20008)
Ambassador: Alpha Oumar Rafiou Barry.

Of the USA in Guinea (Rue KA 038, Conakry)
Ambassador: R. Barrie Walkley.

Of Guinea to the United Nations
Ambassador: Mamady Traore.

Of Guinea to the European Union
Ambassador: Vacant.
Chargé d'Affaires a.i.: Ousmane Tolo Thiam.

FURTHER READING
Bulletin Statistique et Economique de la Guinée. Monthly. Conakry

Binns, Margaret, *Guinea.* [Bibliography] ABC-Clio, Oxford and Santa Barbara (CA), 1996

GUINEA-BISSAU

Republica da Guiné-Bissau

Capital: Bissau
Population estimate, 2000: 1·20m.
GDP per capita, 2000: (PPP$) 755
HDI/world rank: 0·349/167

KEY HISTORICAL EVENTS

Portugal was the major power in the area throughout the colonial period. In 1974, after the Portuguese revolution, Portugal abandoned the struggle to keep Guinea-Bissau and independence was formally recognized on 10 Sept. 1974. In 1975 Cape Verde also became independent but the two countries remained separate sovereign states. On 14 Nov. 1980 a coup d'état was in part inspired by resentment in Guinea-Bissau over the privileges enjoyed by Cape Verdians. Guineans obtained a more prominent role under the new government. On 16 May 1984 a new constitution was approved based on Marxist principles but after 1986 there was a return to private enterprise in an attempt to solve critical economic problems and to lift the country out of poverty. A year-long civil war broke out in 1998 between army rebels and the country's long-time ruler. Neighbouring Senegal and Guinea sent troops in to aid the government. On 7 May 1999 President João Bernardo Vieira was ousted in a military coup led by former chief of staff Gen. Ansumane Mané, whom the president had dismissed in 1998. Following the coup Mané briefly headed a military junta before National Assembly speaker Malam Bacai Sanhá took power as acting president. After presidential elections in Nov. 1999 and Jan. 2000 Kumba Ialá gained the presidency in a landslide victory. Marking a change towards a democratic future in Guinea-Bissau's politics, Ialá rejected a demand made by the outgoing junta for special consultative status following the elections.

TERRITORY AND POPULATION

Guinea-Bissau is bounded by Senegal in the north, the Atlantic Ocean in the west and by Guinea in the east and south. It includes the adjacent archipelago of Bijagós. Area, 36,125 sq. km (13,948 sq. miles). Population (1991 census), 983,367. Population estimate, 1997: 1,178,600 (606,800 female); density, 32·6 per sq. km. The capital, Bissau, had an estimated 274,000 inhabitants in 1999. In 1999, 76·7% of the population were rural.

The UN gives a projected population for 2010 of 1·53m.

The area, population, and chief town of the capital and the eight regions:

Region	Area in sq. km	Population (1991 census)	Chief town
Bissau City	78	197,610	—
Bafatá	5,981	143,377	Bafatá
Biombo	838	60,420	Bissau
Bolama	2,624	26,691	Bolama
Cacheu	5,175	146,980	Cacheu
Gabú	9,150	134,971	Gabú
Oio	5,403	156,084	Farim
Quinara	3,138	44,793	Fulacunda
Tombali	3,736	72,441	Catió

The main ethnic groups were (1998) the Balante (30%), Fulani (20%), Manjaco (14%), Mandingo (13%) and Papeis (7%). Portuguese remains the official language, but Crioulo is spoken throughout the country.

SOCIAL STATISTICS

Births, 1997, 46,000; deaths, 19,000. 1997 birth rate, 39·2 per 1,000 population; death rate, 15·9. Annual population growth rate, 1990–99, 2·3%. Life expectancy in 1999 was 45·9 years for women and 43·1 for men. Infant mortality, 1999, 128 per 1,000 live births; fertility rate, 1999, 5·6 births per woman.

CLIMATE
The tropical climate has a wet season from June to Nov., when rains are abundant, but the hot, dry Harmattan wind blows from Dec. to May. Bissau, Jan. 76°F (24·4°C), July 80°F (26·7°C). Annual rainfall 78" (1,950 mm).

CONSTITUTION AND GOVERNMENT
A new Constitution was promulgated on 16 May 1984. The Revolutionary Council, established following the 1980 coup, was replaced by a 15-member Council of State, while in April 1984 a new National People's Assembly was elected comprising 150 representatives elected by and from the directly-elected regional councils for five-year terms. The sole political movement was the *Partido Africano da Independência da Guiné e Cabo Verde* (PAIGC), but in Dec. 1990 a policy of 'integral multi-partyism' was announced, and in May 1991 the National Assembly voted unanimously to abolish the law making the PAIGC the sole party. The *President* is Head of State and Government and is elected for a five-year term. The *National Assembly* has 100 members.

National Anthem. 'Sol, suor, o verde e mar' ('Sun, sweat, the green and the sea'); words and tune by A. Lopes Cabral.
  (Same as Cape Verde.)

RECENT ELECTIONS
Presidential elections were held in two rounds on 28 Nov. 1999 and 16 Jan. 2000. After the first round Kumba Ialá (Party for Social Renewal) and Malam Bacai Sanhá (African Party for the Independence of Guinea and Cape Verde) out-polled four opponents and went into a run-off. At the second round turn-out was 69%. Ialá won with 72% of the vote.
  At the parliamentary elections on 28 Nov. 1999 turn-out was 80%. The Party for Social Renewal (PRS) gained 36·6% of the vote (38 of 102 seats), the Resistance of Guinea-Bissau (RGB) 25·7% (28 seats) and the African Party for the Independence of Guinea and Cape Verde (PAIGC) 24·8% (24 seats). Five other parties gained four seats or fewer.

CURRENT ADMINISTRATION
President: Kumba Ialá; b. 1953 (PRS; sworn in 17 Feb. 2000).
  In March 2003 the government comprised:
  Prime Minister: Mário Pires; b. 1949 (sworn in 16 Nov. 2002).
  Minister of Economy and Finance: Augusto Ussumane So. *Agriculture, Forestry and Livestock:* Daniel Suleimane Embalo. *Commerce, Industry, Small and Medium-Scale Enterprise:* Botché Candé. *Council of Ministers:* José de Pina. *Defence:* Marcelino Simoes Lopes Cabral. *Employment and Public Administration:* Tibna Sambé Na Wana. *Public Works:* Domingos Simoes Perreira. *Foreign Affairs and International Co-operation:* Joãozinho Vieira Có. *Justice and Keeper of the Seals:* Vençã Gomes Naluak. *Public Health:* Antonio Serifo Embalo. *Interior:* António Sedja Man. *National Education:* Filomena Lopes.

DEFENCE
There is selective conscription. Defence expenditure totalled US$6m. in 2000 (US$5 per capita), representing 1·7% of GDP.

Army. Army personnel in 1999 numbered 6,800. There is a paramilitary Gendarmerie 2,000 strong.

Navy. The naval flotilla, based at Bissau, numbered 350 in 1999.

Air Force. Formation of a small Air Force began in 1978. Personnel (1999) 100 with three combat aircraft (MiG-17s).

INTERNATIONAL RELATIONS
Guinea-Bissau is a member of the UN, WTO, the African Union, African Development Bank, ECOWAS, IOM, OIC, International Organization of the Francophonie and is an ACP member state of the ACP-EU relationship.

ECONOMY

In 1998 agriculture accounted for 62·4% of GDP (the highest proportion in the world), industry 12·7% and services 24·9%.

Currency. On 2 May 1997 Guinea-Bissau joined the French Franc Zone, and the *peso* was replaced by the franc CFA at 65 pesos = one franc CFA. The *franc CFA* (XOF) has a parity rate of 655·957 francs CFA to one euro. Foreign exchange reserves were US$84m. in May 2002. Inflation was 3·3% in 2001. Total money supply in May 2002 was 77,011m. francs CFA.

Budget. Revenue in 1996 (in 1m. pesos) was 899,500; expenditure (also in 1m. pesos) totalled 2,188,200.

Performance. GDP growth was 9·5% in 2000, but only 0·2% in 2001. Total GDP in 2001 was US$0·2bn.

Banking and Finance. The bank of issue and the central bank is the regional Central Bank of West African States (BCEAO). The *Governor* is Charles Konan Banny. A commercial bank was set up in 1990, with 51% of the capital held by the state and local companies and 49% by Portuguese banks. There is also a commercial bank.

ENERGY AND NATURAL RESOURCES

Environment. According to the *World Bank Atlas* carbon dioxide emissions in 1998 were the equivalent of 0·8 tonnes per capita.

Electricity. Installed capacity in 1991 was 22,000 kW. Production was 40m. kWh in 1998; consumption per capita in 1997 was 47 kWh.

Minerals. Mineral resources are not exploited. There are estimated to be 200m. tonnes of bauxite and 112m. tonnes of phosphate.

Agriculture. Agriculture employs 80% of the labour force. There were 300,000 ha of arable land in 1998 and 50,000 ha of permanent crops. Chief crops (production, 2000, in 1,000 tonnes) are: rice, 138; coconuts, 46; cashew nuts, 42; plantains, 38; millet, 35; sorghum, 26; groundnuts, 19; cassava, 17; maize, 10; copra, 9; palm kernels, 9; sugarcane, 6.

Livestock (2000): cattle, 530,000; pigs, 345,000; goats, 325,000; sheep, 285,000; chickens, 1m.

Forestry. The area covered by forests in 1995 was 2·31m. ha, or 82·1% of the total land area (2·36m. ha and 84% in 1990). In 1999, 592,000 cu. metres of roundwood were cut.

Fisheries. Total catch in 1999 came to approximately 5,000 tonnes, of which 96% was from sea fishing. Revenue from fishing licences may be worth as much as 40% of government revenue.

INDUSTRY

Output of main products: vegetable oils (35·8m. litres in 1994), soap (2,900 tonnes in 1995) and animal hides (1,277 tonnes in 1993).

Labour. The labour force in 1996 was 514,000 (60% males).

INTERNATIONAL TRADE

Foreign debt totalled US$942m. in 2000.

Imports and Exports. Imports (f.o.b.) in 1997, US$62·49m.; exports (f.o.b.), US$48·86m. Main exports in 1994 (in US$1m.) were: cashew nuts, 31·0; saw timber, 0·3; frozen shrimps, 0·1; frozen fish, 0·1. Imports: food, 16·4; transport equipment, 14·5; machines, 6·5; fuel, 6·3.

Main export markets, 1994: India, 48·1%; Portugal, 35·7%; China, 8·8%; Cape Verde, 5·5%. Main import suppliers: Portugal, 40·5%; Netherlands, 16·6%; Japan, 14·8%.

COMMUNICATIONS

Roads. In 1996 there were about 4,400 km of roads of which 453 km were paved; and 7,120 passenger cars (5·7 per 1,000 inhabitants) and 5,640 trucks.

Civil Aviation. The national carrier is Transportes Aéreos de Guiné-Bissau. There is an international airport serving Bissau (Osvaldo Vieira). In 1998 there were scheduled flights to Abidjan, Banjul, Conakry, Dakar, Lisbon, Nouakchott, Praia and Sal.

Shipping. The main port is Bissau; minor ports are Bolama, Cacheu and Catió. In 1998 the merchant marine totalled 6,000 GRT.

Telecommunications. Telephone main lines numbered 11,100 in 2000 (9·3 per 1,000 persons) and there were 500 fax machines in 1995. In July 2000 there were 1,500 Internet users.

Postal Services. In 1995 there were 26 post offices.

SOCIAL INSTITUTIONS

Justice. The death penalty was abolished for all crimes in 1993.

Religion. In 1998 about 30% of the population were Muslim and about 5% Christian (mainly Roman Catholic). The remainder held traditional animist beliefs.

Education. Adult literacy was 37·7% in 1999 (male, 58·3%; female, 18·3%). Some 60% of children of primary school age attend school. In 1994–95 there were 100,369 pupils at primary schools.

Health. In 1993 there were 10 private, 2 national and 4 regional hospitals with a total of 1,300 beds. There were 125 dispensaries.

CULTURE

Broadcasting. In 1997 there were 49,000 radio receivers. A television service started in 1989 (colour by SECAM V).

Press. In 1996 there were three newspapers, including one privately owned.

DIPLOMATIC REPRESENTATIVES
Of Guinea-Bissau in the United Kingdom
Chargé d'affaires a.i.: Fali Embalo (resides at Paris).
Honorary Consul: Mabel Figueirdo da Fonseca Smith (Pine Ridge Cottage, Little London Rd, Cross-in-Hand, Heathfield, East Sussex, TN21 0LT).

Of the United Kingdom in Guinea-Bissau
Ambassador: Alan Burner (resides at Dakar, Senegal).

Of Guinea-Bissau in the USA (15929 Yukon Lane, Rockville, MD 20855).
Ambassador: Vacant.
Chargé d'Affaires a.i.: Henrique Adriano Da Silva.
The US embassy in Guinea-Bissau has been closed since 1998.

Of Guinea-Bissau to the United Nations
Ambassador: Luzeria Dos Santos Jalo.

Of Guinea-Bissau to the European Union
Ambassador: Vacant.
Chargé d'Affaires a.i.: José Francisco Da Costa.

FURTHER READING

Forrest, J. A., *Guinea-Bissau: Power, Conflict and Renewal in a West African Nation.* Boulder (CO), 1992
Galli, Rosemary, *Guinea-Bissau.* [Bibliography] ABC-Clio, Oxford and Santa Barbara (CA), 1990

GUYANA

Co-operative Republic of Guyana

Capital: Georgetown
Population estimate, 2000: 761,000
GDP per capita, 2000: (PPP$) 3,963
HDI/world rank: 0·708/103

KEY HISTORICAL EVENTS
First settled by the Dutch West Indian Company about 1620, the territory was captured by Britain to whom it was ceded in 1814 and named British Guiana. To work the sugar plantations African slaves were transported to Guyana in the 18th century and East Indian and Chinese indentured labourers in the 19th century. From 1950 the anti-colonial struggle was spearheaded by the People's Progressive Party (PPP) led by Cheddi Jagan and Forbes Burnham. By the time internal autonomy was granted in 1961 Burnham had split with Jagan to form the more moderate People's National Congress (PNC). Guyana became an independent member of the Commonwealth in 1966 with Burnham as the first prime minister, later president. By the 1980s, desperate economic straits had forced Guyana to seek outside help which came on condition of restoring free elections. Dr Jagan returned to power in 1992. Following his death in March 1997 his wife, Janet Jagan, was sworn in as President.

TERRITORY AND POPULATION
Guyana is situated on the northeast coast of Latin America on the Atlantic Ocean, with Suriname on the east, Venezuela on the west and Brazil on the south and west. Area, 83,000 sq. miles (214,969 sq. km). In 1991 the census population was 723,800; density 3·4 per sq. km. Estimated population (1997), 750,000.

The UN gives a projected population for 2010 of 783,000.

Guyana has the highest proportion of rural population in South America, with only 37·6% living in urban areas in 1999. Ethnic groups by origin: 49% Indian, 36% African, 7% mixed race, 7% Amerindian and 1% others. The capital is Georgetown (1999 population, 275,000); other towns are Linden, New Amsterdam, Rose Hall and Corriverton.

Venezuela demanded the return of the Essequibo region in 1963. It was finally agreed in March 1983 that the UN Secretary-General should mediate. There was also an unresolved claim (1984) by Suriname for the return of an area between the New River and the Corentyne River.

The official language is English.

SOCIAL STATISTICS
Births, 1997, 29,000; deaths, 7,000. 1997 birth rate per 1,000 population, 34·7; death rate, 8·6. Life expectancy at birth in 1999, male 59·3 years and female 67·5 years. Annual population growth rate, 1990–99, 0·8%. Infant mortality, 1999, 56 per 1,000 live births; fertility rate, 1999, 2·3 births per woman.

CLIMATE
A tropical climate, with rainy seasons from April to July and Nov. to Jan. Humidity is high all the year but temperatures are moderated by sea-breezes. Rainfall increases from 90" (2,280 mm) on the coast to 140" (3,560 mm) in the forest zone. Georgetown, Jan. 79°F (26·1°C), July 81°F (27·2°C). Annual rainfall 87" (2,175 mm).

CONSTITUTION AND GOVERNMENT
A new Constitution was promulgated in Oct. 1980. There is an *Executive Presidency*, and a *National Assembly* which consists of 53 elected members and 12 members appointed by the regional authorities. Elections for five-year terms are held under the single-list system of proportional representation, with the whole of the country forming one electoral area and each voter casting a vote for a party list of candidates.

National Anthem. 'Dear land of Guyana'; words by A. L. Luker, tune by R. Potter.

778

RECENT ELECTIONS
Bharrat Jagdeo and the People's Progressive Party (PPP) won the presidential and parliamentary elections of 19 March 2001. In the presidential election incumbent Bharrat Jagdeo received 209,031 votes (53·1% of the vote), with former president Desmond Hoyte of the People's National Congress (PNC) receiving 164,074 (41·7%). The PPP won 35 seats with 52·6% of votes in the parliamentary election, compared to 27 and 41·5% for the PNC.

CURRENT ADMINISTRATION
President: Bharrat Jagdeo; b. 1964 (PPP; sworn in 11 Aug. 1999 and re-elected in March 2001).

In March 2003 the government comprised:

Prime Minister and Minister of Public Works: Samuel Hinds; b. 1943 (PPP; first sworn in 9 Oct. 1992 and now in office for the third time).

Minister in the Office of the President with Responsibility for Parliamentary Affairs: Reepu Daman Persaud. *Attorney-General and Minister of Legal Affairs:* Doodnauth Singh. *Cabinet Secretary:* Roger Luncheon. *Minister of Finance:* Sasenarine Kowlessar. *Foreign Affairs:* Samuel Rudolph Insanally. *Foreign Trade:* Clement Rohee. *Health:* Leslie Ramsammy. *Education:* Henry Jeffrey. *Home Affairs:* Ronald Gajraj. *Trade, Industry and Tourism:* Manzoor Nadir. *Amerindian Affairs:* Carolyn Rodrigues. *Housing and Water:* Shaik Baksh. *Culture, Youth and Sports:* Gail Teixeira. *Information:* Vacant. *Local Government:* Harripersaud Nokta. *Human Services, Social Security and Labour:* Dale Bisnauth. *Public Service:* Jennifer Westford. *Agriculture:* Navin Chandarpal. *Fisheries, Crops and Livestock:* Satyadeow Sawah. *Transport and Hydraulics:* Carl Anthony Xavier.

Government Information Agency Website: http://www.gina.gov.gy/

DEFENCE
In 2000 defence expenditure totalled US$7m. (US$8 per capita), representing 0·8% of GDP.

Army. The Guyana Army had (1999) a strength of 1,400 including 500 reserves. There is a paramilitary Guyana People's Militia 1,500 strong.

Navy. The Maritime Corps is an integral part of the Guyana Defence Force. In 1999 it had 100 personnel and two armed boats based at Georgetown and New Amsterdam.

Air Force. The Air Command has no combat aircraft. It is equipped with light aircraft and helicopters. Personnel (1999) 100.

INTERNATIONAL RELATIONS
In June 2000 a maritime dispute arose between Guyana and Suriname over offshore oil exploration.

Guyana is a member of the UN, WTO, the Commonwealth, OAS, Inter-American Development Bank, ACS, CARICOM, OIC and is an ACP member state of the ACP-EU relationship.

ECONOMY
Agriculture accounted for 34·7% of GDP in 1998, industry 32·5% and services 32·8%.

Overview. State control was reduced during the 1990s, with some privatization.

Currency. The unit of currency is the *Guyana dollar* (GYD) of 100 *cents*. Inflation was 2·7% in 2001. Foreign exchange reserves were US$280m. in June 2002 and total money supply was G$26·31bn.

Budget. Revenues in 1996–97 totalled G$36,293m. (current revenue, 94·3%) and expenditures G$42,305m. (current expenditure, 61·3%).

Performance. GDP growth in 2000 was negative, at −1·3%, but was followed by a slight recovery with growth in 2001 of 1·4%. Total GDP was US$0·7bn. in 2001.

Banking and Finance. The bank of issue is the Bank of Guyana (*Governor,* Dolly Singh), established 1965. Of the six commercial banks operating, two are foreign-owned. At March 1996 the total assets of commercial banks were G$62,587,892,000. Savings deposits were G$26,564·2m.

ENERGY AND NATURAL RESOURCES

Environment. According to the *World Bank Atlas* Guyana's carbon dioxide emissions were the equivalent of 2·2 tonnes per capita in 1998.

Electricity. Capacity in 1995 was estimated at 157,000 kW; in 1998 production was 325m. kWh. Consumption per capita was 479 kWh in 1997.

Minerals. Placer gold mining commenced in 1884, and was followed by diamond mining in 1887. Output of bauxite in 1997 was 2,467,000 tonnes, and of gold 13,521 kg. Other minerals include copper, tungsten, iron, nickel, quartz and molybdenum.

Agriculture. Agricultural production, 2000 (in 1,000 tonnes): sugarcane, 3,000; rice, 600; coconuts, 56; cassava, 26; plantains, 14; bananas, 12; pineapples, 7.

Livestock (2000): cattle, 220,000; sheep, 130,000; goats, 79,000; pigs, 20,000; chickens, 13m. Livestock products, 2000 (in 1,000 tonnes): meat, 17; milk, 13; eggs, 7.

Forestry. In 1995 the area under forests totalled 18·58m. ha (94·4% of the land area), down from 18·62m. ha and 94·6% in 1990. In terms of percentage coverage, Guyana and Suriname were the world's most heavily forested countries in 1995. 25% of the country's energy needs are met by wood fuel. Timber production in 1999 was 467,000 cu. metres.

Fisheries. Fish landings in 1999 came to 53,844 tonnes, of which 99% was from sea fishing.

INDUSTRY

The main industries are agro-processing (sugar, rice, timber and coconut) and mining (gold and diamonds). There is a light manufacturing sector, and textiles and pharmaceuticals are produced by state and private companies. Production: sugar (1998), 263,010 tonnes; rum (1996), 237,200 hectolitres; beer (1995), 8·47m. litres; soft drinks (1996), 4,253,000 cases; textiles (1995), 322m. metres; footwear (1995), 54,132 pairs; margarine (1995), 1,262,420 kg; edible oil (1995), 2,388,120 litres; refrigerators (1995), 2,763 units; paint (1995), 923,847 litres.

Labour. In 1996 the labour force was 353,000 (67% males).

INTERNATIONAL TRADE

Guyana's external debt in 2000 was US$1,455m.

Imports and Exports. In 1998 exports were valued at US$547·0m. and imports at US$601·2m. Principal commodities exported, 1996 (in US$1m.): sugar, 150·7; gold, 105·9; rice, 93·7; bauxite, 86·0. Other important export commodities included shrimps, timber and rum. Exports by volume, 1995: bauxite, 1,971,063 tonnes; sugar, 225,421 tonnes; rice, 200,544 tonnes; gold, 275,305 oz; shrimps, 827 tonnes; timber, 35,873 cu. metres. Major import suppliers: USA, Trinidad and Tobago, Netherlands Antilles; main export markets: Canada, UK, USA.

COMMUNICATIONS

Roads. In 1996 it was estimated there were 7,970 km of roads, of which 590 km were paved. Passenger cars numbered 24,000 in 1993 and commercial vehicles 9,000.

Rail. There is a government-owned railway in the North West District, while the Guyana Mining Enterprise operates a standard gauge railway of 133 km from Linden on the Demerara River to Ituni and Coomacka.

Civil Aviation. There is an international airport at Georgetown (Timehri). The national carrier is the state-owned Guyana Airways Corporation. In 1998 there were direct flights to Antigua, Barbados, Miami, New York, Paramaribo, Port of Spain and Toronto. In 1999 scheduled airline traffic of Guyana-based carriers flew 1·7m. km, carrying 70,000 passengers.

Shipping. The major port is Georgetown; there are two other ports. In 1995 sea-going shipping totalled 13,925 GRT. There are 217 nautical miles of river navigation. There are ferry services across the mouths of the Demerara, Berbice and Essequibo rivers.

Telecommunications. The inland public telegraph and radio communication services are operated by the Guyana Telephone and Telegraph Company Ltd. In 2000 there were 68,400 telephone main lines, equivalent to 79·4 per 1,000 population, and 22,000 PCs in use (or 25·6 for every 1,000 persons). Mobile phone subscribers numbered 1,500 in 1998. There were 3,000 Internet users in Dec. 1999.

Postal Services. In 1995 there were 85 post offices.

SOCIAL INSTITUTIONS

Justice. The law, both civil and criminal, is based on the common and statute law of England, save that the principles of the Roman–Dutch law have been retained for the registration, conveyance and mortgaging of land.

The Supreme Court of Judicature consists of a Court of Appeal, a High Court and a number of courts of summary jurisdiction. Guyana was one of ten countries to sign an agreement in Feb. 2001 establishing a Caribbean Court of Justice to replace the British Privy Council as the highest civil and criminal court. The Court of Justice is expected to sit for the first time in the second half of 2003.

In 1996 there were 4,563 reported serious crimes, including 88 homicides. The population in penal institutions in Jan. 1998 was 1,697 (200 per 100,000 of national population).

Religion. In 1997, 57% of the population were Protestant and Roman Catholic, 33% Hindu, 9% Muslim and 1% other.

Education. In 1996–97 there were 365 pre-primary schools with 1,831 teachers for 30,736 pupils; 420 primary schools with 3,461 teachers for 102,000 pupils; and 62,043 pupils at secondary level. In 1995 there were 6,945 students at university level.

Adult literacy in 1999 was 98·4% (male, 98·8%; female, 97·9%). The rate of 98·4% is the highest in South America.

Health. In 1994 there were 30 hospitals (5 private), 162 health centres and 14 health posts. In 1997 there were 38·8 hospital beds per 10,000 population. There were (1993) 244 doctors, 34 dentists, 22 pharmacists, 172 midwives (1989) and 681 nursing personnel.

CULTURE

Broadcasting. The Guyana Broadcasting Corporation has two radio programmes. There were 46,000 TV receivers (colour by PAL) and 420,000 radio receivers in 1997. The Guyana Television Broadcasting Company (GTV) is state-owned and there are 12 private stations relaying US satellite services.

Cinema. In 1997 there were 18 cinemas.

Press. In 1996 there were two daily newspapers with a combined circulation of 42,000.

Tourism. There were 80,000 foreign visitors in 1998. Receipts totalled US$60m.

Festivals. There are a number of Christian, Hindu and Muslim festivals throughout the year.

Libraries. There is a National Library in Georgetown.

Museums and Galleries. The Guyana National Museum contains a broad selection of animal life and Guyanese heritage. Castellani House, the National Gallery, is home to the finest art collection in Guyana.

DIPLOMATIC REPRESENTATIVES
Of Guyana in the United Kingdom (3 Palace Ct., London, W2 4LP)
High Commissioner: Laleshwar K. N. Singh.

Of the United Kingdom in Guyana (44 Main St., Georgetown)
High Commissioner: Stephen Hiscock.

Of Guyana in the USA (2490 Tracy Pl., NW, Washington, D.C., 20008)
Ambassador: Mohammed Ali Odeen Ishmael.

Of the USA in Guyana (99–100 Young and Duke Streets, Kingston, Georgetown)
Ambassador: Ronald D. Godard.

Of Guyana to the United Nations
Ambassador: Samuel Rudolph Insanally.

Of Guyana to the European Union
Ambassador: Kenneth F. S. King.

FURTHER READING

Braveboy-Wagner, J. A., *The Venezuela-Guyana Border Dispute: Britain's Colonial Legacy in Latin America.* London, 1984
Daly, V. T., *A Short History of the Guyanese People.* 3rd. ed. London, 1992
Williams, B. F., *Stains on My Name, War in My Veins: Guyana and the Politics of Cultural Struggle.* Duke Univ. Press, 1992

National statistical office: Bureau of Statistics, Avenue of the Republic and Brickdam, Georgetown.

HAITI

République d'Haïti

Capital: Port-au-Prince
Population estimate, 2000: 8·14m.
GDP per capita, 2000: (PPP$) 1,467
HDI/world rank: 0·471/146

KEY HISTORICAL EVENTS

In the 16th century, Spain imported large numbers of African slaves whose descendants now populate the country. The colony subsequently fell under French rule. In 1791 a slave uprising led to the 13-year-long Haitian Revolution. In 1801 Toussaint Louverture, one of the leaders of the revolution, succeeded in eradicating slavery. He proclaimed himself governor-general for life over the whole island. He was captured and sent to France, but Jean-Jacques Dessalines, one of his generals, led the final battle that defeated Napoleon's forces. The newly-named Haiti declared its independence on 1 Jan. 1804, becoming the first independent black republic in the world. Ruled by a succession of self-appointed monarchs, Haiti became a republic in the mid-19th century. From 1915 to 1934 Haiti was under United States occupation.

A corrupt regime was dominated by François Duvalier from 1957 to 1964 when he was succeeded by his son, Jean-Claude Duvalier. He fled the country on 7 Feb. 1986. After a period of military rule, Father Jean-Bertrand Aristide was elected president in Dec. 1990.

On 30 Sept. 1991 President Aristide was deposed by a military junta and went into exile. Under international pressure, parliament again recognized Aristide as president in June 1993. However, despite a UN led naval blockade, the junta showed no sign of stepping down. 20,000 US troops moved into Haiti on 19 Sept. in an uncontested occupation. President Aristide returned to office on 15 Oct. 1994 and on 1 April 1995 a UN peacekeeping force (MANUH) took over from the US military mission. Aristide was succeeded by René Préval who was generally assumed to be a stand-in for his predecessor. Jean-Bertrand Aristide subsequently won the presidential elections held in Nov. 2000. In Dec. 2001 there was an unsuccessful coup led by former police and army officers.

TERRITORY AND POPULATION

Haiti is bounded in the east by the Dominican Republic, to the north by the Atlantic and elsewhere by the Caribbean Sea. The area is 27,750 sq. km (10,714 sq. miles). The Île de la Gonave, some 40 miles long, lies in the gulf of the same name. Among other islands is La Tortue, off the north peninsula. Population (1996 est.), 7·3m. Population density, 263 per sq. km. In 1999, 64·9% of the population were rural.

The UN gives a projected population for 2010 of 9·50m.

Areas, populations (1995 estimates) and chief towns of the nine departments:

Department	Area (in sq. km)	Population	Chief town
Artibonite	4,895	1,013,800	Gonaïves
Centre	3,597	460,800	Hinche
Grande Anse	3,100	641,400	Jérémie
Nord	2,175	759,300	Cap Haïtien
Nord-Est	1,698	248,800	Fort-Liberté
Nord-Ouest	2,094	421,000	Port-de-Paix
Ouest	4,595	2,494,900	Port-au-Prince
Sud	2,602	653,400	Les Cayes
Sud-Est	2,077	457,000	Jacmel

The capital is Port-au-Prince (1999 population, 1,699,000); other towns are Cap Haïtien (100,638 in 1995); Gonaïves (63,291 in 1992), Les Cayes (45,904 in 1992) and Jérémie (43,277 in 1992). Most of the population is of African or mixed origin.

The official languages are French and Créole. Créole is spoken by all Haitians; French by only a small minority.

SOCIAL STATISTICS

1995 births, 247,000; deaths, 92,000. Birth rate (per 1,000 population), 1995, 34·7; death rate, 12·9. Annual population growth rate, 1990–99, 1·8%. Expectation of life at birth, 1999, 49·4 years for males and 55·4 years for females. Infant mortality, 1999, 83 per 1,000 live births; fertility rate, 1999, 4·3 births per woman.

In the Human Development Index, or HDI (measuring progress in countries in longevity, knowledge and standard of living), Haiti is the lowest-ranked country outside of Africa.

CLIMATE
A tropical climate, but the central mountains can cause semi-arid conditions in their lee. There are rainy seasons from April to June and Aug. to Nov. Hurricanes and severe thunderstorms can occur. The annual temperature range is small. Port-au-Prince, Jan. 77°F (25°C), July 84°F (28·9°C). Annual rainfall 53" (1,321 mm).

CONSTITUTION AND GOVERNMENT
The 1987 Constitution, ratified by a referendum, provides for a bicameral legislature (an 83-member *Chamber of Deputies* and a 27-member *Senate*), and an executive *President*, directly elected for a five-year term. The President can stand for a second term but only after a five-year interval.

National Anthem. 'La Dessalinienne'; words by J. Lhérisson, tune by N. Geffrard.

RECENT ELECTIONS
Presidential elections were held on 26 Nov. 2000. There were seven candidates. Jean-Bertrand Aristide was elected with 91·8% of votes cast. However, most opposition parties refused to recognize the result, with doubts being cast over the accuracy of the counting process.

Much delayed parliamentary elections were held on 21 May and 30 July 2000. In the vote for the Chamber of Deputies, Fanmi Lavalas (Water Fall Family/FL) won 72 of the available 82 seats, Mouvement Chrétien National (Christian National Movement/Mochrena) 3, Parti Louvri Baryé (Open the Gate Party/PLB), 2, Espace (Space/E) 2, Eskanp-Korega (EK) 1, Organisation de Peuple en Lutte (Organization of Struggling People/OPL) 1 and 1 seat went to a non-partisan. In elections for the Senate, FL claimed 18 of the 27 available seats, PLD took 1 and 9 seats were to be contested on 26 Nov. 2000.

CURRENT ADMINISTRATION
President: Jean-Bertrand Aristide; b. 1953 (FL; sworn in 7 Feb. 2001 for the fourth time).

In March 2003 the government comprised:

Prime Minister: Yvon Neptune; b. 1946 (FL; sworn in 15 March 2002).

Minister of Agriculture and Natural Resources and Rural Development: Sébastien Hilaire. *Commerce and Industry:* Leslie Gouthier. *Culture and Communication:* Lilas Desquiron. *Economy and Finance:* Faubert Gustave. *Environment:* Webster Pierre. *Foreign Affairs and Religion:* Joseph Philippe Antonio. *Haitians Living Abroad:* Leslie Voltaire. *Interior and Territorial Collectivities:* Jocelerme Privert. *Justice:* Delatour Calixte. *National Education:* Marie Carmelle Paul-Austin. *Planning and External Co-operation:* Paul Duret. *Public Health and Population:* Dr Henri Claude Voltaire. *Public Works, Transport and Communications:* Harry Clinton. *Social Affairs:* Eudes St Preux Craan. *Tourism:* Martine Deverson. *Women's Affairs and Rights:* Ginette Rivière Lubin.

DEFENCE
After the restoration of civilian rule in 1994 the armed forces and police were disbanded and a 3,000-strong Interim Public Security Force formed in 1995. In 2000 defence expenditure totalled US$48m. (US$6 per capita), representing 1·5% of GDP. For Police, *see* JUSTICE, *below*.

Army. The Army has effectively, although not formally, been disbanded. An Interim Public Security Force of 3,000 has been formed.

Navy. A small Coast Guard, based at Port-au-Prince, is being developed.

Air Force. The air force was disbanded in 1995.

INTERNATIONAL RELATIONS

Although foreign aid has been promised, political infighting and corruption have held up US$340m. worth of aid. However, EU aid continues to arrive.

Haiti is a member of the UN, WTO, OAS, Inter-American Development Bank, ACS, CARICOM, IOM, International Organization of the Francophonie and is an ACP member state of the ACP-EU relationship.

ECONOMY

Agriculture accounted for 30·4% of GDP in 1998, industry 20·1% and services 49·6%.

Currency. The unit of currency is the *gourde* (HTG) of 100 *centimes*. Total money supply in June 2002 was 10,763m. gourdes. Inflation in 2001 was 16·7%. In April 2002 foreign exchange reserves were US$185m.

Budget. In 1996–97 revenues were US$284bn. and expenditure US$308m. No budget was voted for in the fiscal years 1997–98 or 1998–99 because of the absence of a prime minister or government.

Performance. Real GDP growth was 0·9% in 2000, but there was then a recession in 2001, with the economy contracting by 1·7%. Total GDP in 2001 was US$3·7bn.

Banking and Finance. The Banque Nationale de la République d'Haïti is the central bank and bank of issue (*Governor*, Fritz Jean). In 1999 there were 12 commercial banks.

Weights and Measures. The metric system and British imperial and US measures are in use.

ENERGY AND NATURAL RESOURCES

Environment. According to the *World Bank Atlas* carbon dioxide emissions in 1998 were the equivalent of 0·2 tonnes per capita. An *Environmental Sustainability Index* compiled for the World Economic Forum meeting in Feb. 2002 ranked Haiti 137th in the world out of the 142 countries analysed, with 34·8%. The index measured the ability of countries to maintain favourable environmental conditions and examined various factors including pollution levels and the use or abuse of natural resources.

Electricity. Most of the country is only provided with around four hours of electricity a day, supplied by the state-owned Electricité d'Haiti. Installed capacity was 216,500 kW in 1995. Production in 1998 was 728m. kWh, with consumption per capita 33 kWh.

Minerals. Until the supply was exhausted in the 1970s, a small quantity of bauxite was mined.

Agriculture. There were 560,000 ha of arable land in 1998 and 350,000 ha of permanent crops. 65% of the workforce, mainly smallholders, make a living by agriculture carried on in seven large plains, from 0·2m. to 25,000 acres, and in 15 smaller plains down to 2,000 acres. Irrigation is used in some areas and in 1998 covered 75,000 ha. The main crops are (2000 production, in 1,000 tonnes): sugarcane, 800; cassava, 338; bananas, 323; plantains, 290; mangoes, 250; maize, 203; yams, 200; sweet potatoes, 180; rice, 130; sorghum, 98. Livestock (2000): cattle, 1·43m.; goats 1·94m.; pigs, 1·0m.; horses, 500,000; chickens, 6m.

Forestry. The area underforests in 1995 was 21,000 ha, or 0·8% of the total land area (25,000 ha and 0·9% in 1990). In 1999, 6·5m. cu. metres of roundwood were cut.

Fisheries. The total catch in 1999 was estimated to be 5,000 tonnes, of which 90% was from marine waters.

INDUSTRY

Manufacturing is largely based on the assembly of imported components: toys, sports equipment, clothing, electronic and electrical equipment. Textiles, steel, soap, chemicals, paint and shoes are also produced. Many jobs were lost to other Central American and Caribbean countries during the 1991–94 trade embargo, after President Aristide was deposed.

Labour. In 1996 the labour force was 3,209,000 (57% males). The unemployment rate in July 1998 was around 60%.

Trade Unions. Whilst at least six unions exist, their influence is very limited.

INTERNATIONAL TRADE
Foreign debt was US$1,169m. in 2000.

Imports and Exports. In 1998 exports (f.o.b.) totalled US$299·3m. and imports (f.o.b.) US$640·7m. The leading imports are petroleum products, foodstuffs, textiles, machinery, animal and vegetable oils, chemicals, pharmaceuticals, raw materials for transformation industries and vehicles. The USA is by far the leading trading partner, accounting for over 60% of both exports and imports. France, Germany and Italy are also important for exports and Japan, France and Germany for imports.

COMMUNICATIONS

Roads. Total length of roads was estimated at 4,160 km in 1996, of which 1,010 km were surfaced. There were 32,000 passenger cars in 1996 (4·4 per 1,000 inhabitants), plus 21,000 trucks and vans.

Civil Aviation. There is an international airport at Port-au-Prince. Cap Haïtien also has scheduled flights to the Turks and Caicos Islands and the Bahamas. In 1998 there were flights to Aruba, Cayenne, Curaçao, Fort de France, Miami, Montreal, New York, Panama City, Paris, Pointe-à-Pitre, St Maarten, St Martin, San Juan and Santo Domingo. In 2000 Port-au-Prince handled 924,000 passengers (781,000 on international flights) and 15,300 tonnes of freight.

Shipping. Port-au-Prince and Cap Haïtien are the principal ports, and there are 12 minor ports. In 1998 the merchant marine totalled 1,000 GRT. In 1997 vessels totalling 1,304,000 NRT entered ports.

Telecommunications. The state telecommunications agency is Teleco. Main telephone lines in 2000 numbered 72,500 (8·9 for every 1,000 inhabitants), and in 1999 there were 25,000 mobile phone subscribers. In Dec. 1999 there were approximately 6,000 Internet users.

Postal Services. There were 121 post offices in 1995. The postal service is fairly reliable in the capital and major towns. Many businesses, however, prefer to use express courier services (DHL and Federal Express).

SOCIAL INSTITUTIONS

Justice. The Court of Cassation is the highest court in the judicial system. There are four Courts of Appeal and four Civil Courts. Judges are appointed by the President. The legal system is basically French. In 1995 a new police force—Police Nationale d'Haiti (PNH)—was recruited from former military personnel and others not implicated in human rights violations. The PNH currently has about 5,000 members; there are plans to increase the size of the force in the near future.

The population in penal institutions in Feb. 1996 was 2,300 (30 per 100,000 of national population).

Religion. Since the Concordat of 1860 Roman Catholicism has been given special recognition, under an archbishop with nine bishops. The Episcopal Church has one bishop. 90% of the population are nominally Roman Catholic, while other Christian churches number perhaps 10%. Probably two-thirds of the population to some extent adhere to Voodoo, recognized as an official religion in 2003.

Education. The adult literacy rate in 1999 was 48·8% (51·1% among males and 46·8% among females). Haiti has the lowest literacy rate among males outside of Africa. Education is divided into nine years 'education fondamentale', followed by four years to 'Baccalaureate' and university/higher education. The school system is based on the French system and instruction is in French and Créole. About 20% of education is provided by state schools; the remaining 80% by private schools, including Church and Mission schools.

There are 360 primary schools (221 state, 139 religious), 21 public lycées, 123 private secondary schools, 18 vocational training centres and 42 domestic science centres.

There is a state university, several private universities and an Institute of Administration and Management.

Health. In 1994 there were 641 doctors, 95 dentists and 2,725 nurses, and 50 hospitals. There were ten beds per 10,000 population in 1994. In the period 1990–98 only 37% of the population had access to safe drinking water.

CULTURE

Broadcasting. Under the aegis of the Conseil National des Télécommunications, radio and TV programmes (colour by SECAM V) are broadcast by Radio Nationale and Télévision Nationale. There is a privately-owned cable TV company, and several privately-owned radio stations. There were 415,000 radio and 38,000 TV sets in 1997.

Cinema. There are ten cinemas in Port-au-Prince.

Press. There were two daily newspapers in 1998. In 1995 the press had a combined circulation of 45,000, at a rate of six per 1,000 inhabitants.

Tourism. In 1998 there were 150,000 foreign tourists, spending US$80m. Cruise ship arrivals numbered 246,000. There are only about 1,000 hotel rooms in the whole country.

Libraries. There is a public library, Bibliothèque Nationale, in Port-au-Prince. A private library open to scholars, Bibliothèque des Frères de l'Instruction Chrétienne, is nearby.

Theatre and Opera. The Théâtre National is in Port-au-Prince.

Museums and Galleries. The main museums are MUPANAH and the Musée de l'Art Haïtien, both in Port-au-Prince. There are at least 20 private art shops in Port-au-Prince and major towns.

DIPLOMATIC REPRESENTATIVES
Of Haiti in the United Kingdom. The Embassy closed on 30 March 1987.

Of the United Kingdom in Haiti
Ambassador: Andy Ashcroft (resides at Santo Domingo, Dominican Republic).

Of Haiti in the USA (2311 Massachusetts Ave., NW, Washington, D.C., 20008)
Ambassador: Vacant.
Chargé d'Affaires a.i.: Louis Harold Joseph.

Of the USA in Haiti (Harry Truman Blvd., Port-au-Prince)
Ambassador: Brian Curran.

Of Haiti to the United Nations
Ambassador: Dr Jean C. Alexandre.

Of Haiti to the European Union
Ambassador: Yolette Azor-Charles.

FURTHER READING
Chambers, F., *Haiti.* [Bibliography] 2nd ed. ABC-Clio, Oxford and Santa Barbara (CA), 1994
Heinl, Robert & Nancy, revised by Michael Heinl, *Written in Blood.* Univ. Press of America, 1996
Nicholls, D., *From Dessalines to Duvalier: Race, Colour and National Independence in Haiti.* 2nd ed. CUP, 1992.
Thomson, I., *Bonjour Blanc: a Journey through Haiti.* London, 1992
Weinstein, B. and Segal, A., *Haiti: the Failure of Politics.* New York, 1992

National library: Bibliothèque Nationale, Rue du Centre, Port-au-Prince.

HONDURAS

República de Honduras

Capital: Tegucigalpa
Population estimate, 2000: 6·42m.
GDP per capita, 2000: (PPP$) 2,453
HDI/world rank: 0·638/116

KEY HISTORICAL EVENTS
Discovered by Columbus in 1502, Honduras was ruled by Spain until independence in 1821. Political instability was endemic throughout the 19th and most of the 20th century. The end of military rule seemed to come in 1981 when a general election gave victory to the more liberal and non-military party, PLH (Partido Liberal de Honduras). Considerable power, however, remained with the armed forces. Internal unrest continued into the 1990s with politicians and military leaders at loggerheads, particularly over attempts to investigate violations of human rights. In Oct. 1998 Honduras was devastated by Hurricane Mitch, the worst natural disaster to hit the area in modern times.

TERRITORY AND POPULATION
Honduras is bounded in the north by the Caribbean, east and southeast by Nicaragua, west by Guatemala, southwest by El Salvador and south by the Pacific Ocean. The area is 112,492 sq. km (43,433 sq. miles). In 1988 the census population was 4,248,561. The estimated population in 1997 was 5,751,400 (2,870,700 female), giving a density of 51 per sq. km. In 1999, 51·6% of the population were urban.

The UN gives a projected population for 2010 of 7·96m.

The chief cities (populations in 1,000, 1994) were Tegucigalpa, the capital (919, in 1999), San Pedro Sula (368·5), El Progreso (81·2), Choluteca (72·8), Danlí (43·3) and the Atlantic coast ports of La Ceiba (86·0), Puerto Cortés (33·5) and Tela (24·8); other towns include Comayagua (52·3), Siguatepeque (37·5), Juticalpa (25·6), Santa Rosa de Copán (23·4) and Olanchito (17·9).

Areas and 1991 populations estimates of the 18 departments and the Central District (Tegucigalpa):

Department	Area (in sq. km)	Population	Department	Area (in sq. km)	Population
Atlántida	4,251	255,000	Islas de la Bahía	261	24,000
Choluteca	4,211	309,000	La Paz	2,331	112,000
Colón	8,875	164,000	Lempira	4,290	180,000
Comayagua	5,196	257,000	Ocotepeque	1,680	77,000
Copán	3,203	226,000	Olancho	24,350	309,000
Cortés	3,954	706,000	Santa Bárbara	5,115	291,000
El Paraíso	7,218	277,000	Valle	1,565	121,000
Francisco Morazán	6,298	268,000	Yoro	7,939	355,000
Gracias a Dios	16,630	37,000	Central District	1,648	610,000
Intibucá	3,072	130,000			

The official language is Spanish. The Spanish-speaking population is of mixed Spanish and Amerindian descent (90%), with 7% Amerindians.

SOCIAL STATISTICS
Births, 1997 estimates, 187,000; deaths, 32,000. 1997 birth rate, 32·6 per 1,000 population; death rate 5·6. 1999 life expectancy, 63·2 years for men and 68·8 for women. Annual population growth rate, 1990–99, 2·59%. Infant mortality, 1999, 33 per 1,000 live births; fertility rate, 1999, 4·1 births per woman.

CLIMATE
The climate is tropical, with a small annual range of temperature but with high rainfall. Upland areas have two wet seasons, from May to July and in Sept. and Oct. The Caribbean Coast has most rain in Dec. and Jan. and temperatures are generally higher than inland. Tegucigalpa, Jan. 66°F (19°C), July 74°F (23·3°C). Annual rainfall 64" (1,621 mm).

CONSTITUTION AND GOVERNMENT
The present Constitution came into force in 1982. The *President* is elected for a four-year term. Members of the *National Congress* (total 128 seats) and municipal mayors are elected simultaneously on a proportional basis, according to combined votes cast for the Presidential candidate of their party.

National Anthem. 'Tu bandera' ('Thy Banner'); words by A. C. Coello, tune by C. Hartling.

RECENT ELECTIONS
Presidential and parliamentary elections took place on 25 Nov. 2001. In the presidential elections Ricardo Maduro won with 52·9% of votes cast, against 43·4% for his chief rival, Rafael Piñeda Ponce. In the elections to the National Congress, the Partido Nacional (PN) of Ricardo Madura won 61 seats with 46·6% of the vote, while the Partido Liberal (PL) won 55 seats with 39·3%. The remaining seats went to the Partido de Unificación Democrática (PUD), 5 seats; the Partido de Inovación y Unidad-Social Democracia (PINU), 4; and the Partido Demócrata Cristiano de Honduras (PDCH), 3.

CURRENT ADMINISTRATION
President: Ricardo Maduro; b. 1946 (PN; sworn in 27 Jan. 2002).

First Vice-President: Vicente Williams. *Second Vice-President:* Armida de López Contreras. *Third Vice-President:* Alberto Díaz Lobo.

In March 2003 the government consisted of:

Minister of Agriculture and Livestock: Mariano Jiménez. *Culture, Arts and Sports:* Mireya Batres Mejía. *Defence:* Federico Brevé Travieso. *Education:* Carlos Alberto Avila Molina. *Finance:* José Arturo Alvarado Sánchez. *Foreign Relations:* Guillermo Augusto Pérez Arias. *Industry and Commerce:* Norman Garcia. *Interior and Justice:* Jorge Ramón Hernández Alcerro. *Labour and Social Security:* German Leitzelar Vidaurreta. *Natural Resources and Environment:* Patricia Panting. *Presidency:* Luis Consenza Jiménez. *Public Employee's Retirement and Pensions (INJUPEMP):* David Mendoza Lupiac. *Public Health:* Elías Lizardo Zelaya. *Public Works, Transportation and Housing:* Jorge Carranza Díaz. *Security:* Oscar Alvarez. *Tourism:* Thiery Pierrefeu Midence. *Ministers without Portfolio:* Carlos Vargas; Johnny Roberto Káfaty; Camilo Atala; Eduardo Kafaty; Ramón Medina Luna.

DEFENCE
Conscription was abolished in 1995. In 2000 defence expenditure totalled US$93m. (US$14 per capita), representing 1·6% of GDP.

Army. The Army numbered (1999) 5,500. There is also a paramilitary Public Security Force of 6,000.

Navy. Personnel (1999), 1,000 including 400 marines. Bases are at Puerto Cortés and Amapala.

Air Force. There were 49 combat aircraft in 1999 including F-5E/F Tiger II fighters. Total strength was (1999) about 1,800 personnel.

INTERNATIONAL RELATIONS
Honduras is a member of the UN, WTO, OAS, Inter-American Development Bank, CACM, ACS and IOM.

ECONOMY
Agriculture accounted for 20·3% of GDP in 1998, industry 30·9% and services 48·8%.

Currency. The unit of currency is the *lempira* (HNL) of 100 *centavos*. Foreign exchange reserves were US$1,526m. and gold reserves 21,000 troy oz in June 2002. Inflation was 9·7% in 2001. Total money supply in May 2002 was 11,610m. lempiras.

Budget. 1998 estimate: expenditure was US$1,152m. (including capital expenditures of US$150m.); revenues (1997) totalled US$655m.

Performance. Real GDP growth was 4·9% in 2000 and 2·6% in 2001. Total GDP in 2001 was US$6·4bn.

Banking and Finance. The central bank of issue is the Banco Central de Honduras (*President,* Maria Elena Mondragón de Villar). There is an agricultural development bank, Banadesa, for small grain producers, a state land bank and a network of rural credit agencies managed by peasant organizations. The Central American Bank for Economic Integration (BCIE) has its head office in Tegucigalpa. In 1999 there were 40 private banks, including four foreign.

There are stock exchanges in Tegucigalpa and San Pedro Sula.

Weights and Measures. The metric system has been legal since 1 April 1897, although there are still some minor traces of the Imperial and old Spanish systems.

ENERGY AND NATURAL RESOURCES

Environment. Carbon dioxide emissions in 1998 were the equivalent of 0·8 tonnes per capita according to the *World Bank Atlas*.

Electricity. Installed capacity was 605,900 kW in 1995. Production in 1998 was 2·9bn. kWh (mainly hydro-electric); consumption per capita was 446 kWh.

Minerals. Output in 1998 (in 1,000 tonnes): lead, 10·4; zinc, 8·5. Silver, 15·3 tonnes. Small quantities of gold are mined, and there are also deposits of tin, iron, copper, coal, antimony and pitchblende.

Agriculture. There were 1·70m. ha of arable land in 1998 and 0·35m. ha of permanent crops. Legislation of 1975 provided for the compulsory redistribution of land, but in 1992 the grounds for this were much reduced, and a 5-ha minimum area for land titles abolished. Members of the 2,800 co-operatives set up in 1975 received individual shareholdings which can be broken up into personal units. Since 1992 women may have tenure in their own right. The state monopoly of the foreign grain trade was abolished in 1992. In 1996 the Agricultural Incentive Program was created (Ley de Incentivo Agrícola, LIA) which involves the redistribution of land for agricultural development.

Crop production in 2000 (in 1,000 tonnes): sugarcane, 3,896; maize, 534; bananas, 453; plantains, 250; coffee, 196; palm oil, 150; melons, 102; dry beans, 85; oranges, 80; pineapples, 71; sorghum, 65.

Livestock (2000): cattle, 1·95m.; pigs, 800,000; horses, 179,000; mules, 70,000; chickens, 18m.

Forestry. In 1995 forests covered 4·11m. ha, or 36·8% of the total land area (down from 41·3% of the land area in 1990). In 1999, 7·41m. cu. metres of roundwood were cut.

Fisheries. Shrimps and lobsters are important catches. The total catch in 1999 was 7,215 tonnes, almost entirely from sea fishing.

INDUSTRY

Industry is small-scale and local. 1995 output (in 1,000 tonnes): cement (1996), 952; raw sugar, 406; wheat flour, 216; fabrics, 11,641 metres; beer, 7,989,000 hectolitres; rum, 2·37m. litres.

Labour. The workforce was 1·9m. in 1999. In 1997, 36·9% of those in employment were in agriculture, forestry and fishing, 17·9% in community, social and personal services and 17·3% in manufacturing industries. Unemployment rate (1998 estimate): 6·5%.

Trade Unions. About 346,000 workers were unionized in 1994.

INTERNATIONAL TRADE

In May 1992 Honduras, El Salvador and Guatemala agreed to create a free trade zone. Import duties are to be standardized. Foreign debt was US$5,487m. in 2000.

Imports and Exports. Imports (f.o.b.) in 2000 were valued at US$2,697·6m. and exports (f.o.b.) at US$2,039·2m.

Main exports are bananas, coffee, shrimps and lobsters, fruit, lead and zinc, timber, and refrigerated meats. Main imports are machinery and electrical equipment, industrial chemicals, and mineral products and lubricants. Principal export markets, 1995: USA, 42·7%; Germany, 19·3%; Japan, 6·7%; Spain, 3·9%. Principal import suppliers, 1995: USA, 46·6%; Netherlands, 7·5%; Guatemala, 6·8%; Mexico, 4·2%.

COMMUNICATIONS

Roads. Honduras is connected with Guatemala, El Salvador and Nicaragua by the Pan-American Highway. Out of a total of 15,400 km of roads (1996), 3,110 km were paved. In 1996 there were 201,000 vehicles registered.

Rail. The small government-run railway was built to serve the banana industry and is confined to the northern coastal region and does not reach Tegucigalpa. In 1995 there were 595 km of track in three gauges, which in 1994 carried 1m. passengers and 1·2m. tonnes of freight.

Civil Aviation. There are four international airports: San Pedro Sula (Ramon Villeda) and Tegucigalpa (Toncontín) are the main ones, plus Roatán and La Ceiba, with over 80 smaller airstrips in various parts of the country. The Honduras-based carriers are Aero Lineas Sosa and Caribbean Air. In addition to domestic flights and services to other parts of central America and the Caribbean, there were flights in 1998 to Barcelona, Dallas/Fort Worth, Houston, Madrid, Miami, New Orleans, New York, Orlando and Quito. In 2000 San Pedro Sula handled 636,000 passengers (507,000 on international flights) and 20,500 tonnes of freight, and Tegucigalpa handled 499,000 passengers (281,000 on international flights) and 8,400 tonnes of freight.

Shipping. The largest port is Puerto Cortés on the Atlantic coast. There are also ports at Henecán (on the Pacific) and Puerto Castilla and Tela (northern coast). In 1998 the merchant marine totalled 1,083,000 GRT, including oil tankers 108,000 GRT. Honduras is a flag of convenience registry.

Telecommunications. In 2000 there were 298,700 telephone main lines, or 46·1 for every 1,000 persons, and 70,000 PCs were in use (10·8 for every 1,000 persons). There were 78,600 mobile phone subscribers in 1999. Honduras had 40,000 Internet users in Dec. 1999.

Postal Services. There were 435 post offices in 1995.

SOCIAL INSTITUTIONS

Justice. Judicial power is vested in the Supreme Court, with nine judges elected by the National Congress for four years; it appoints the judges of the courts of appeal, and justices of the peace.

The population in penal institutions in Dec. 1996 was 9,457 (160 per 100,000 of national population).

Religion. Roman Catholicism is the prevailing religion (5,050,000 followers in 1997), but the constitution guarantees freedom to all creeds, and the State does not contribute to the support of any. In 1997 there were 600,000 Evangelical Protestants and 170,000 followers of other faiths.

Education. Adult literacy in 1999 was 74·0% (male, 73·9%; female, 74·1%). Education is free, compulsory (from 7 to 12 years) and secular. There is a high drop-out rate after the first years in primary education. In 1995 the 8,168 primary schools had 1,008,092 children (28,978 teachers); the 661 secondary, normal and technical schools had 184,589 pupils (12,480 teachers). There were eight universities or specialized colleges, with a total of 54,293 students and 3,676 academic staff. In addition, 73,491 children attended pre-primary school.

In 1995 expenditure on education came to 3·6% of GNP and 16·5% of total government spending.

Health. In 1993 there were 3,803 doctors, 622 dentists, 6,288 nurses and 975 pharmacists. In 1994 there were 29 public hospitals and 32 private, with 4,737 beds, and 849 health centres.

CULTURE

Broadcasting. There were six commercial TV channels in 1993 (colour by NTSC) and various radio stations (mostly local). There were 570,000 TV sets and 2·45m. radio receivers in 1997.

Press. Honduras had eight national daily papers in 1998, with a combined circulation of 240,000.

Tourism. In 1999 there were 371,000 foreign tourists, spending US$165m.

DIPLOMATIC REPRESENTATIVES

Of Honduras in the United Kingdom (115 Gloucester Pl., London, W1H 3PJ)
Ambassador: Hernán Antonio Bermúdez-Aguilar.

Of the United Kingdom in Honduras (Edificio Palmira, 3er Piso, Colonia Palmira, Tegucigalpa)
Ambassador: Kay Coombs.

Of Honduras in the USA (3007 Tilden St., NW, Washington, D.C., 20008)
Ambassador: Mario Miguel Canahuati.

Of the USA in Honduras (Av. La Paz, Tegucigalpa)
Ambassador: Larry L. Palmer.

Of Honduras to the United Nations
Ambassador: Manuel Acosta Bonilla.

Of Honduras to the European Union
Ambassador: Vacant.
Chargé d'Affaires a.i.: Doris Garcia Paredes.

FURTHER READING

Banco Central de Honduras. *Honduras en Cifras 1990–92.* Tegucigalpa, 1993
Howard-Reguindin, Pamela F., *Honduras.* [Bibliography] ABC-Clio, Oxford and Santa Barbara (CA), 1992
Meyer, H. K. and Meyer, J. H., *Historical Dictionary of Honduras.* 2nd ed. Metuchen (NJ), 1994

HUNGARY

Magyar Köztársaság
(Hungarian Republic)

Capital: Budapest
Population estimate, 2000: 10·04m.
GDP per capita, 2000: (PPP$) 12,416
HDI/world rank: 0·835/35

KEY HISTORICAL EVENTS

The Hungarians call themselves 'Magyars'; 'Hungarian' derives from the Turkic name ('On ogur', i,e. ten arrows) of the tribal federation on the Don which Árpád and his horde left in order to settle the sparsely inhabited middle Danubian basin in 896. As nomadism gave way to agriculture a feudal society developed led by nobility descended from the original conquerors. In 1301 Árpád's line died out. Henceforth, with two exceptions, the throne was held by foreigners, sometimes holding other thrones simultaneously. In the 15th century the expansionist Ottoman empire reached the southern borders of Hungary. This first incursion was repelled but in 1526 the Turks annexed southern and central Hungary. The western rump came under Hapsburg rule which was extended to most of Hungary with the expulsion of the Turks in 1699. After a national rising in 1703, Emperor Charles IV restored the constitution and the Hungarian assembly recognized the Emperor's claim to the Hungarian throne. Nationalist sentiments supported the radical democracy of Lájos Kossuth who set up a breakaway government. Ruthless repression followed but Austria's military defeats in Italy (1859) and against Prussia (1866) forced the emperor to moderate his absolutism. Under the Compromise (*Ausgleich*) of 1867 a Dual Monarchy was constituted; Hungary gained internal autonomy while foreign affairs and defence became joint Austro-Hungarian responsibilities.

Hungary entered World War I on Austria's side but after the armistice of 3 Nov. 1918 a National Council proclaimed an independent republic. Political and social unrest, however, were compounded by a Romanian invasion. After Béla Kun's Soviet republic antagonized most of the population, a counter-revolutionary government appointed Admiral Horthy as regent.

Hungary's desire to revise the Versailles peace settlements brought her into alignment with Germany in the 1930s. In 1940 Hungary adhered to the Tripartite pact and in June 1941 sent a force to join the German invaders of the Soviet Union. But pro-German sentiment was never wholehearted. In Oct. 1944 Horthy was forced to abdicate in favour of a fascist 'Arrow Cross' government but by then Soviet forces were well inside the frontiers. At the elections of Nov. 1945 the Communists polled only 17% of the vote; their way to power was to lie in their leader Rákosi's 'salami tactics' of divide and purge, backed up by their acquisition of key ministries under Soviet pressure. A Soviet-type constitution was adopted in Aug. 1949 and Rákosi embarked on a programme of ruthless collectivization. Removed from the premiership by the post-Stalin Soviet leadership, he intrigued against his successor Imre Nagy's more liberal 'new course'. In 1956 the attempted suppression of a student demonstration sparked off a 13-day revolution. Nagy became prime minister and János Kádár party leader. Nagy declared Hungary's neutrality and withdrawal from the Warsaw pact. The Soviet army crushed the revolt on 4 Nov. and installed Kádár in power. Nagy was arrested and later executed; the gains of the uprising were harshly suppressed. Cautious economic reforms were introduced in the mid-60s when liberalization brought higher living standards. A gathering reformist tendency within the Hungarian Socialist Workers' (i.e. Communist) Party culminated in its self-dissolution in Oct. 1989 and reconstitution as the Hungarian Socialist Party. The People's Republic was abolished on 23 Oct. 1989. The following year a multi-party democracy, committed to political and economic reforms, was instituted.

Hungary gained membership to NATO in 1999 and is scheduled to join the EU in 2004.

TERRITORY AND POPULATION
Hungary is bounded in the north by Slovakia, northeast by Ukraine, east by Romania, south by Croatia and Serbia and Montenegro, southwest by Slovenia and west by Austria. The peace treaty of 10 Feb. 1947 restored the frontiers as of 1 Jan. 1938. The area of Hungary is 93,036 sq. km (35,921 sq. miles).

At the census of 1 Jan. 1990 the population was 10,374,823 (5,389,919 females); 1 Feb. 2001 census population, 10,197,119.

The UN gives a projected population for 2010 of 9·49m.

Hungary's population has been falling at such a steady rate since 1980 that its 2000 population was the same as that in the mid 1960s.

63·8% of the population was urban (18·7% of the urban population lived in Budapest in 1996) in 1999; population density, 1996, 109·8 per sq. km. Ethnic minorities, 1995: Roma (Gypsies), 4%; Germans, 2·6%; Serbs, 2%; Slovaks, 0·8%; Romanians, 0·7%. A law of 1993 permits ethnic minorities to set up self-governing councils. There is a worldwide Hungarian diaspora of nearly 2·5m. (1·5m. in the USA; 200,000 in Israel; 140,000 in Canada; 140,000 in Germany), and Hungarian minorities (3·2m. in 1992) in Romania (1·7m.), Slovakia (0·6m.), Yugoslavia (0·35m., mainly in Vojvodina) and Ukraine (0·16m.).

Hungary is divided into 19 counties (*megyék*) and the capital, Budapest, which has county status.

Area (in sq. km) and population (in 1,000) of counties and county towns:

Counties	Area	2002 population	Chief town	2000 population
Bács-Kiskun	8,362	546	Kecskemét	105
Baranya	4,487	406	Pécs	158
Békés	5,631	399	Békéscsaba	65
Borsod-Abaúj-Zemplén	7,247	749	Miskolc	182
Csongrád	4,263	428	Szeged	164
Fejér	4,373	429	Székesfehérvár	106
Győr-Moson-Sopron	4,062	435	Győr	127
Hajdú-Bihar	6,211	552	Debrecen	210
Heves	3,637	327	Eger	58
Jász-Nagykún-Szolnok	5,607	419	Szolnok	78
Komárom-Esztergom	2,251	317	Tatabánya	72
Nógrád	2,544	221	Salgótarján	45
Pest	6,394	1,089	Budapest	1,852[1]
Somogy	6,036	337	Kaposvár	67
Szabolcs-Szatmár-Bereg	5,937	588	Nyíregyháza	113
Tolna	3,704	250	Szekszárd	36
Vas	3,336	269	Szombathely	83
Veszprém	4,639	375	Veszprém	66
Zala	3,784	299	Zalaegerszeg	63
Budapest	525	1,740	(has county status)	

[1]1999 figure.

The official language is Hungarian. 96·6% of the population have Hungarian as their mother tongue. Ethnic minorities have the right to education in their own language.

SOCIAL STATISTICS
2001: births, 97,047; deaths, 132,183; marriages, 43,583; divorces, 26,000 (1999). In 2000 the number of births rose for the first time in a decade. There were 3,328 suicides in 1999. Rates (per 1,000 population), 2001: birth, 9·5; death, 13·0; marriage, 4·3; divorce, 2·6 (1999). Annual population growth rate, 1990–99, –0·3%. In 1999 the suicide rate per 100,000 population was 33·1, with the rate among men nearly three times as high as that among women. In 1998 the most popular age range for marrying was 20–24 for both males and females. Expectation of life at birth, 1999, 66·8 years for males and 75·4 years for females (the lowest of any OECD member country). Infant mortality, 2001, 8 per 1,000 live births. Fertility rate, 1999, 1·3 births per woman.

CLIMATE
A humid continental climate, with warm summers and cold winters. Precipitation is generally greater in summer, with thunderstorms. Dry, clear weather is likely in

autumn, but spring is damp and both seasons are of short duration. Budapest, Jan. 32°F (0°C), July 71°F (21·5°C). Annual rainfall 25" (625 mm). Pécs, Jan. 30°F (−0·7°C), July 71°F (21·5°C). Annual rainfall 26·4" (661 mm).

CONSTITUTION AND GOVERNMENT
On 18 Oct. 1989 the National Assembly approved by an 88% majority a constitution which abolished the People's Republic, and established Hungary as an independent, democratic, law-based state.

The head of state is the *President*, who is elected for five-year terms by the National Assembly.

The single-chamber *National Assembly* has 386 members, made up of 176 individual constituency winners, 152 allotted by proportional representation from county party lists and 58 from a national list. It is elected for four-year terms. A *Constitutional Court* was established in Jan. 1990 to review laws under consideration.

National Anthem. 'Isten áldd meg a magyart' ('God bless the Hungarians'); words by Ferenc Kölcsey, tune by Ferenc Erkel.

RECENT ELECTIONS
Ferenc Mádl was elected President by the National Assembly on 6 June 2000 by 243 votes to 96. In two previous rounds he had failed to achieve the required two-thirds majority.

In the Hungarian parliamentary elections on 7 and 21 April 2002 the centre-right coalition of Fidesz-Hungarian Civic Party (Fidesz-MPP) and the Hungarian Democratic Forum (MDF) won 188 seats with 41·1% of the votes, against 178 seats and 42·1% for the Hungarian Socialist Party (MSzP). The remaining 20 seats in the 386-seat National Assembly went to the Alliance of Free Democrats (SzDSz) who received 5·5% of votes cast. Parties which failed to win seats included the Hungarian Justice and Life Party (4·4%), the Centre Party (3·9%), the Worker's Party (2·8%) and the Independent Party of Smallholders, Agrarian Workers and Citizens (0·8%). Turn-out was 70·5%. Following the elections, a coalition was formed between the Hungarian Socialist Party and the Alliance of Free Democrats, giving them a total of 198 seats. Fidesz-MPP leader Viktor Orbán conceded defeat and a government was subsequently formed with Péter Medgyessy as prime minister.

CURRENT ADMINISTRATION
President: Ferenc Mádl; b. 1931 (sworn in 4 Aug. 2000).

In March 2003 the MSzP-SzDSz coalition government consisted of:

Prime Minister: Péter Medgyessy; b. 1942 (sworn in 27 May 2002).

Head of Prime Minister's Office: Péter Kiss. *Minister of Agriculture and Regional Development:* Imre Németh. *Defence:* Ferenc Juhász. *Economic Affairs and Transport:* István Csillag. *Education:* Bálint Magyar. *Employment and Labour:* Sándor Burány. *Environment and Water Management:* Mária Koródi. *Finance:* Csaba László. *Foreign Affairs:* László Kovács. *Health, Social and Family Affairs:* Judit Csehák. *Information Technology and Telecommunications:* Kálmán Kovács. *Interior:* Mónika Lamperth. *Justice:* Péter Bárándy. *Cultural Heritage:* Gábor Görgey. *Children, Youth and Sport:* György Jánosi.

Office of the Prime Minister: http://www.kancellaria.gov.hu/

DEFENCE
The President of the Republic is C.-in-C. of the armed forces.

Men between the ages of 18 and 23 are liable for nine months' conscription, or two years of civilian service.

Defence expenditure in 2000 totalled US$777m., compared to US$3,517m. in 1985. Per capita spending in 2000 was US$77, down from US$330 in 1985. The 2000 expenditure represented 1·7% of GDP, compared to 7·2% in 1985.

Army. Hungary is divided into four army districts: Budapest, Debrecen, Kiskunfélegyháza and Pécs. The strength of the Army was (1999) 23,500 (including 17,800 conscripts). There is an additional force of 12,000 border guards and 2,000 paramilitary police.

Navy. The Danube Flotilla, the maritime wing of the Army, consisted of some 290 personnel in 1999. It is based at Budapest.

Air Force. The Air Force is under the control of the Army General Staff, with a strength (1999) of 11,500 (5,100 conscripts). There were 136 combat aircraft including MiG-21s, MiG-23s, MiG-29s, Su-22s and 86 attack helicopters.

INTERNATIONAL RELATIONS
Hungary is a member of the UN, WTO, BIS, NATO, OECD, Council of Europe, OSCE, CEFTA, CERN, CEI, Danube Commission, IOM, Antarctic Treaty, and is an Associate Member of the EU and an Associate Partner of the WEU. In April 1994 Hungary applied to join the EU and is expected to become a member by 2004. A European Commission report endorsed in Dec. 1999 named Hungary (along with Poland) as the country from central and eastern Europe most likely to be the first to join the EU. Hungary held a referendum on EU membership on 12 April 2003, in which 83·8% of votes cast were in favour of accession, with 16·2% against, although turn-out was less than 46%. Hungary is scheduled to become a member of the EU on 1 May 2004. Hungary became a member of NATO on 12 March 1999. In 2000 Hungary introduced a visa requirement for Russians entering the country as one of the conditions for EU membership.

Hungary has had a long-standing dispute with Slovakia over the Gabčíkovo-Nagymaros Project, involving the building of dam structures in both countries for the production of electric power, flood control and improvement of navigation on the Danube as agreed in a treaty signed in 1977 between Hungary and Czechoslovakia. In late 1998 Slovakia and Hungary signed a protocol easing tensions between the two nations and settling differences over the dam.

ECONOMY
Agriculture accounted for 6% of GDP in 1997, industry 34% and services 60%. In 1999 the private sector was responsible for an estimated 80% of economic output.

Overview. Free market principles have been at the centre of economic policy since 1990. In 1995 the State Property Agency and the State Holding Company were merged in a new body charged with extending the private sector's share of former state assets to 80%. Legislation of June 1991 compensates former owners or their descendants for property nationalized after May 1939. A Small Shareholder Programme of Privatization was launched in April 1994.

The OECD reported in 1998 that 'the extensive macroeconomic package introduced in 1995 (which included the adoption of a crawling-peg exchange rate regime, an impressive programme of privatization and a substantial fiscal tightening), as well as the deepening of structural reforms implemented earlier, created the conditions for the remarkable progress of the Hungarian economy over the past two years.'

Currency. A decree of 26 July 1946 instituted a new monetary unit, the *forint* (HUF) of 100 *fillér*. The forint was made fully convertible in Jan. 1991, and in June 2001 it was floated. Inflation had been 28% in 1995, but in Nov. 2002 was at an annualized rate of 4·8%, the lowest rate since the political changes of 1989. Foreign exchange reserves were US$9,695m. in June 2002 and gold reserves 101,000 troy oz. Total money supply in April 2002 was 2,662·29bn. forints.

Budget. Government revenue and expenditure (in 1bn. forints), year ending 31 Dec.:

	1995	1996	1997	1998	1999	2000
Revenue	2,268·7	2,712·0	3,194·0	3,686·2	4,402·5	4,790·0
Expenditure	2,773·0	3.024·0	3,747·1	4,523·2	4,939·4	6,069·7

VAT is 25·0%.

Performance. Real GDP growth was 4·2% in 1999, rising in 2000 to an impressive 5·2%. The economy then grew by only 3·8% in 2001, but this was still more than double the EU average. Total GDP was US$52·4bn. in 2001.

Banking and Finance. In 1987 a two-tier system was established. The National Bank (*Director,* Zsigmond Járai) remained the central state financial institution, responsible for the circulation of money and foreign currency exchange, but also became a central clearing bank, with general (but not operational) control over commercial banks and development banks. There are over 40 commercial banks and 20 insurance companies based in Budapest. The largest bank is OTP Bank Rt. (the National Savings and Commercial Bank of Hungary), with assets in 2000 of US$5·8bn. A law of June 1991 sets capital and reserve requirements, and provides for foreign investment in Hungarian banks. Permission is needed for investments of more than 10%. Privatization of the banking system is well under way.

The Hungarian International Trade Bank opened in London in 1973. In 1980 the Central European International Bank was set up in Budapest with seven western banks holding 66% of the shares.

A stock exchange was opened in Budapest in Jan. 1989.

Weights and Measures. The metric system is in use.

ENERGY AND NATURAL RESOURCES

Environment. According to the *World Bank Atlas* Hungary's carbon dioxide emissions in 1998 were the equivalent of 5·8 tonnes per capita. An *Environmental Sustainability Index* compiled for the World Economic Forum meeting in Feb. 2002 ranked Hungary 11th in the world, with 62·7%. The index measured the ability of countries to maintain favourable environmental conditions and examined various factors including pollution levels and the use or abuse of natural resources.

Electricity. Installed capacity in 1997 was 8m. kW, about a quarter of which is nuclear. There is an 880 mW nuclear power station at Paks with four reactors. It produced an estimated 38% of total output in 1999. In 1998, 35·1bn. kWh of electricity were produced (approximately 40% by nuclear power); in 1995, 4,400m. kWh were imported. Consumption per capita in 1998 was 2,888 kWh.

Oil and Gas. Oil and natural gas are found in the Szeged basin and Zala county. Oil production in 1996 was 11m. bbls.; gas production in 1999 was 3·0bn. cu. metres with proven reserves of 80bn. cu. metres.

Minerals. Production in 1997 (in 1,000 tonnes): lignite, 14,684; hard coal, 924; bauxite (1998), 908.

Agriculture. Agricultural land was collectivized in 1950. It was announced in 1990 that land would be restored to its pre-collectivization owners if they wished to cultivate it. A law of April 1994 restricts the area of land that may be bought by individuals to 300 ha, and prohibits the sale of arable land and land in conservation zones to companies and foreign nationals. Today, although 90% of all cultivated land is in private hands, most farms are little more than smallholdings. Under the 1999 budget, funding for agriculture increased by 40%, with subsidies favouring small family farms. In 1998 agricultural exports totalled US$3bn. (an increase of 10% on 1997), including grain exports of more than 4m. tonnes. 20,000 tonnes of sour cherry and 17,000 tonnes of plums were exported in 1998.

In 1996 the agricultural area was (in 1,000 ha) 6,179, of which 4,716 were arable, 1,148 meadows and pastures, 90 market gardens, and 225 orchards and vineyards.

Agricultural production has dropped drastically since 1989. Production figures (2000, in 1,000 tonnes): maize, 4,874 (6,747 in 1989); wheat, 3,709 (6,509 in 1989); sugarbeets, 1,980 (5,277 in 1989); barley, 905; potatoes, 768; apples, 520; grapes, 500; sunflower seeds, 488.

Livestock has also drastically decreased since 1989 from 7·7m. pigs to 5·3m. by 2000, from 1·6m. cattle to 857,000, and from 2·1m. sheep to 934,000. Thus the pig stock, cattle stock and sheep stock have all declined to levels not seen in fifty years.

The north shore of Lake Balaton and the Tokaj area are important wine-producing districts. Wine production in 2000 was 300,000 tonnes.

Forestry. The forest area in 1995 was 1,719,000 ha, or 18·6% of the land area (up from 1,675,000 ha and 18·1% in 1990). Timber production in 1999 was 4·29m. cu. metres.

Fisheries. There are fisheries in the rivers Danube and Tisza and Lake Balaton. In 1993 there were 27,100 ha of commercial fishponds. In 1999 total catch was 7,514 tonnes, exclusively from inland fishing.

INDUSTRY
The leading companies by market capitalization in Hungary, excluding banking and finance, in Jan. 2002 were: Magyar Távközlési Rt. (MATÁV), the telecommunications company (1trn. forints); MOL Magyar Olaj-és Gázipari Rt (Hungarian Oil and Gas Plc), 489bn. forints; and Richter Gedeon Rt. (335bn. forints), a pharmaceuticals company. In 1995 there were 18,921 limited liability companies, 1,475 co-operative societies and 81,433 individual businesses.

Important items include food and beverages, chemicals and chemical products, motor vehicles, refined petroleum products, base metals and computers. Output growth in 1996 saw highly variable trends among the individual sectors of the manufacturing industry. The most dynamic sector continues to be the engineering industry. Its performance was driven by the 35·6% increase in exports. The manufacturing of non-ferrous mineral products went up by 1·2% (exports rose by 11·1%). With the exception of the engineering industry and manufacturing of non-ferrous mineral products the output of each sector of manufacturing industry declined: the textile and clothing industry by 4·2% and chemical industry by 0·6%. Within this, the domestic sales of the textile and clothing industry dropped by 8·5% and that of the chemical industry by 6·7%, while the exports of both sectors rose (by 3·7% and 35·6% respectively).

Labour. In 2001 out of an economically active population of 4,093,000 there were 3,860,000 employed persons, of which 3,296,000 were employees. Among the employed persons, 59·6% worked in services, 34·2% in industry and construction, and 6·2% in agriculture. Average gross monthly wages in 2001: 103,558 forints. Minimum monthly wage, 2001, 40,000 forints. In Jan. 2003 Hungary had an unemployment rate of 5·8%. Retirement age: men, 60; women, 55. Hungary is one of the few industrialized countries in which women put in longer hours than men. In 1996, 83% of women but only 80% of men put in more than 40 hours a week.

Trade Unions. The former official Communist organization (National Council of Trade Unions), renamed the Confederation of Hungarian Trade Unions (MSZOSZ), groups 70 organizations and claimed 1m. members in 1993. A law of 1991 abolished its obligatory levy on pay packets; its assets derived from this period are to be distributed to other unions. Other unions are grouped in six federations (with 1993 membership): the Association of Autonomous Trade Unions (ASZOK, 0·3m.); Coalition of Christian Trade Unions (KESZOSZ, 0·15m.); Co-operation Forum of Trade Unions (SZEF, 0·5m.); Council of Intellectual Trade Unions (ÉSZT, 0·1m.); League of Independent Trade Unions (Liga, 0·25m.); Works Councils (60,000).

INTERNATIONAL TRADE
Hungary is a member of CEFTA, along with the Czech Republic, Poland, Slovakia and Slovenia. Foreign debt was US$29,415m. in 2000. At the end of 1995 foreign investments totalled US$11,500m. An import surcharge imposed in March 1995 was abolished in July 1997.

Imports and Exports. In 2001 the value of exports was US$30,498m. and that of imports US$33,682m. (up from US$28,092m. and US$32,079m. respectively in 2000). Machinery and transport equipment accounted for 57·5% of exports and 51·5% of imports in 2001, and manufactured goods 31·0% of exports and 35·3% of imports. 75% of exports go to European Union member countries, the highest share of any of the central and eastern European countries hoping to join the EU. The share of CIS countries is only around 2%. In 2001, 34·9% of exports went to Germany and 26·4% of imports came from Germany. Italy was the second biggest supplier of imports in 2001 (8·3% of the total) and Austria the second biggest market for exports (8·7%). In 1999, 1·4% of exports went to Russia, down from 13·1% in 1992. An import surcharge which was imposed in March 1995 was abolished in July 1997.

COMMUNICATIONS

Roads. In 1998 there were 188,203 km of roads, including 438 km of motorways and 29,630 km of main roads. Passenger cars numbered (1998) 2,365,100; trucks, vans and special-purpose vehicles, 325,300; buses, 19,400; and motorcycles, 138,000. 40·9m. tonnes of freight and 494·7m. passengers were transported by road in 1994 (excluding intra-urban passengers). In 1998 there were 19,665 road accidents with 1,478 fatalities.

Rail. Route length of public lines in 1998, 7,873 km, of which 2,594 km were electrified. 49·5m. tonnes of freight and 156·6m. passengers were carried. There is a metro in Budapest (30·1 km), and tram/light rail networks in Budapest (161·2 km), Debrecen, Miskolc and Szeged.

Civil Aviation. Budapest airport (Ferihegy) handled 4,683,000 passengers in 2000 (all on international flights) and 40,100 tonnes of freight. The national carrier is Malév, 65% state-owned. It carried 2,019,000 passengers in 1999 (1,826,000 in 1998).

Shipping. Navigable waterways had (1993) a length of 1,622 km. River craft included: passenger ships, 63; tugs, 35; self-propelled barges and other ships, 21; barges, 170. In 1995, 3·52m. tonnes of cargo and 2·38m. passengers were carried. Merchant shipping totalled 15,000 GRT in 1998. The Hungarian Shipping Company (MAHART) has agencies at Amsterdam, Alexandria, Algiers, Beirut, Rijeka and Trieste. It has three sea-going ships.

Telecommunications. There were 3,798,300 main telephone lines in 2000, equivalent to 372·5 per 1,000 population, and 870,000 PCs in use (85·3 per 1,000 persons). Hungary had 1·8m. mobile phone subscribers in March 2000 (18% of the population) and 1·2m. Internet users in April 2001. In 1997 there were 120,000 fax machines.

Postal Services. In 2001 there were 2,581 post offices.

SOCIAL INSTITUTIONS

Justice. The administration of justice is the responsibility of the Procurator-General, elected by Parliament for six years. There are 111 local courts, 20 labour law courts, 20 county courts, 6 district courts and a Supreme Court. Criminal proceedings are dealt with by the regional courts through three-member councils and by the county courts and the Supreme Court in five-member councils. A new Civil Code was adopted in 1978 and a new Criminal Code in 1979.

Regional courts act as courts of first instance; county courts as either courts of first instance or of appeal. The Supreme Court acts normally as an appeal court, but may act as a court of first instance in cases submitted to it by the Public Prosecutor. All courts, when acting as courts of first instance, consist of 1 professional judge and 2 lay assessors, and, as courts of appeal, of 3 professional judges. Local government Executive Committees may try petty offences.

Regional and county judges and assessors are elected by the appropriate local councils; members of the Supreme Court by Parliament.

The Office of Ombudsman was instituted in 1993. He or she is elected by parliament for a six-year term, renewable once.

There are also military courts of the first instance. Military cases of the second instance go before the Supreme Court.

The death penalty was abolished in Oct. 1990.

The population in penal institutions in Dec. 1997 was 13,405 (135 per 100,000 of national population). 88,436 sentences were imposed on adults in 1999, including 29,474 of imprisonment. There were 11,450 juvenile offenders and 2,250 juveniles were in prison in 1999.

Religion. Church-state affairs are regulated by a law of Feb. 1990 which guarantees freedom of conscience and religion and separates church and state by prohibiting state interference in church affairs. Religious matters are the concern of the Department for Church Relations, under the auspices of the Prime Minister's Office. State aid to all churches was 2,800m. forints in 1993.

In 1995, 67·5% of the population aged 14 and over were Roman Catholic, 20% Calvinist and 5% Lutheran.

The Primate of Hungary is Péter Erdő, Archbishop of Esztergom-Budapest, installed in Jan. 2003. There are 11 dioceses, all with bishops or archbishops. There is one Uniate bishopric.

In 1993 there were estimated to be 7m. Roman Catholics, 1·9m. Calvinists and 0·43m. Lutherans. 47 other sects had registered as churches. There were four

Orthodox denominations with 40,000 members in 1979. The Unitarian Church had 10,000 members, 11 ministers and 6 churches. In 1991 there were 100,000 Jews (444,567 in 1937) with 136 synagogues, 26 rabbis and a rabbinical college that enrols ten students a year.

Education. Adult literacy rate in 1999 was 99·5% (male, 99·5%; female, 99·2%). Education is free and compulsory from 6 to 14. Primary schooling ends at 14; thereafter education may be continued at secondary, secondary technical or secondary vocational schools, which offer diplomas entitling students to apply for higher education, or at vocational training schools which offer tradesmen's diplomas. Students at the latter may also take the secondary school diploma examinations after two years of evening or correspondence study. Optional religious education was introduced in schools in 1990.

In 1999–2000 there were 4,643 kindergartens with 31,409 teachers and 365,700 pupils; in 1999–2000 there were 3,696 primary schools with 82,829 teachers and 960,600 pupils; 1,054 secondary schools with 32,317 teachers and 386,600 pupils; there were, in 1999–2000, 201 schools for special needs with 45,245 pupils and 7,244 teachers, and 356 trade training schools, with 109,500 apprentices and 5,002 teachers and instructors. In 1994–95 there were 317 vocational training schools with 1,305 teachers and 22,241 trainees. In 1999–2000 there were 89 higher education institutions, including 6 universities (Budapest, Pécs, Szeged, Debrecen, Miskolc and Veszprém). At these there were 21,138 teachers and 171,600 full-time students. The number of students in all forms of higher education doubled between 1994 and 2000, when 311,586 students were enrolled. In 1990 only 11% of 18- to 23-year-olds were enrolled in higher education. By 2000 the proportion had risen to 35% and the target for 2010 is 50%.

Schools for ethnic minorities, 1997–98: kindergartens, 386, with 20,440 pupils and 993 teachers; primary schools, 390, with 53,021 pupils and 1,357 teachers; secondary schools, 27, with 2,310 pupils and 179 teachers.

In 1996 total expenditure on education came to 4·6% of GNP.

Health. In 1999 there were 36,386 doctors and 84,247 hospital beds; in 1995 there were 5,069 dentists, 2,024 pharmacies and 2,414 midwives. While there is an excess supply of doctors, there are too few nurses and wages for both groups are exceptionally low. Reform of the healthcare system is one of the most urgent measures required before Hungary can become a member of the EU. Spending on health, which accounts for 4·5% of GDP, is set to increase to 6·5% by 2006.

Welfare. In 1998 the Hungarian parliament decided to place the financial funds of health and pension insurance under government supervision. The self-governing bodies which had previously been responsible for this were dissolved. Medical treatment is free. Patients bear 15% of the cost of medicines. Sickness benefit is 75% of wages, old age pensions (at 60 for men, 55 for women) 60–70%. In 1995, 582,200m. forints were paid out in pensions to 2·98m. pensioners (including old age, 1·6m.; disabled, 0·75m.; widows, 0·22m.). In 1995, 100,200m. forints in family allowances were paid to 1·4m. families on behalf of 2·36m. children. Monthly allowances (in forints) are: one child, 2,750; two, 3,250; three and more, 3,750 (more for single parents). Of nearly 2·5m. minors (aged 0–18), 40% live in poverty.

CULTURE

Broadcasting. The government network *Magyar Rádió* broadcasts four programmes on medium wave and FM and also regional programmes, including transmissions in German, Romanian and Serbo-Croat. There are four other networks, three of them commercial. *Magyar Televizió* operates two TV channels (colour by PAL). *Duna Televizió* broadcasts to Hungarians abroad. In 1996 there were 31 independent radio and 26 independent TV stations. There were 7·01m. radios in use and 4·45m. TV sets in 1997.

Cinema. There were 595 cinemas in 1995; attendance, 14m.; gross box office receipts came to 2,311m. forints; 12 full-length feature films were made.

Press. In 1996 there were 40 daily newspapers with a combined circulation of 1,895,000, at a rate of 186 per 1,000 inhabitants. The most widely read newspaper is *Népszabadság*, the one-time Communist Party newspaper. In 1995 there were

28 weeklies and in 2001 a total of 8,837 book titles were published in 32·62m. copies.

Tourism. In 1999 there were 12·93m. foreign tourists. 11·1m. Hungarians travelled abroad in 2001. Revenue from foreign tourists in 1999 was US$3·39bn. 8% of GDP is produced by tourism.

Festivals. The Budapest Spring Festival, comprising music, theatre, dance etc., takes place in March. The Balaton Festival is in May and the Szeged Open-Air Theatre Festival is in July–Aug.

Libraries. In 2001 there were 3,429 public libraries and three National libraries. They held a combined 45,630,000 volumes for 1,416,000 registered users.

Theatre and Opera. Hungary had 47 theatres in 1997.

Museums and Galleries. There were 776 museums and galleries in 1997.

DIPLOMATIC REPRESENTATIVES
Of Hungary in the United Kingdom (35 Eaton Pl., London, SW1X 8BY)
Ambassador: Béla Szombati.

Of the United Kingdom in Hungary (Harmincad Utca 6, Budapest 1051)
Ambassador: Nigel Thorpe, CVO.

Of Hungary in the USA (3910 Shoemaker St., NW, Washington, D.C., 20008)
Ambassador: András Simonyi.

Of the USA in Hungary (Szabadság Tér 12, Budapest V)
Ambassador: Nancy Goodman Brinker.

Of Hungary to the United Nations
Ambassador: László Molnár.

Of Hungary to the European Union
Ambassador: Endre Juhász.

FURTHER READING
Central Statistical Office. *Statisztikai Évkönyv.* Annual since 1871.—*Magyar Statisztikai Zsebkönyv.* Annual.—*Statistical Yearbook,—Statistical Handbook of Hungary.—Monthly Bulletin of Statistics.*
Bozóki, A., *et al.*, (eds.) *Post-Communist Transition: Emerging Pluralism in Hungary.* London, 1992
Burawoy, M. and Lukács, J., *The Radiant Past: Ideology and Reality in Hungary's Road to Capitalism.* Chicago Univ. Press, 1992
Cox, T. and Furlong, A. (eds.) *Hungary: the Politics of Transition.* London, 1995
Geró, A., *Modern Hungarian Society in the Making: the Unfinished Experience*; translated from Hungarian. Budapest, 1995
Mitchell, K. D. (ed.) *Political Pluralism in Hungary and Poland: Perspectives on the Reforms.* New York, 1992
Molnár, Miklós, *A Concise History of Hungary.* CUP, 2001
Sárközi, Mátyás, *Budapest.* [Bibliography] ABC-Clio, Oxford and Santa Barbara (CA), 1997
Szekely, I. P., *Hungary: an Economy in Transition.* CUP, 1993
Turner, Barry, (ed.) *Central Europe Profiled.* Macmillan, London, 2000

National library: Széchenyi Library, Budapest.
National statistical office: Központi Statisztikai Hivatal/Central Statistical Office, Keleti Károly u. 5/7, H-1024 Budapest. *Director:* Tamás Mellár.
Website: http://www.ksh.hu/

ICELAND

Lyðveldið Ísland
(Republic of Iceland)

Capital: Reykjavík
Population estimate, 2000: 279,000
GDP per capita, 2000: (PPP$) 29,581
HDI/world rank: 0·936/7

KEY HISTORICAL EVENTS

The first settlers came to Iceland in 874. Between 930 and 1262 Iceland was an independent republic, but by the 'Old Treaty' of 1262 the country recognized the King of Norway. In 1380 Iceland, together with Norway, came under the Danish kings, but when Norway was separated from Denmark in 1814, Iceland remained with Denmark. The invention of motorized fishing boats in the late nineteenth century revolutionized the fishing industry and gave impetus to the campaign for self determination. After 1 Dec. 1918 Iceland was acknowledged as a sovereign state. It was united with Denmark only through the common sovereign until it was proclaimed an independent republic on 17 June 1944 following a referendum favouring severance from the Danish crown.

TERRITORY AND POPULATION

Iceland is an island in the North Atlantic, close to the Arctic Circle. Area, 103,000 sq. km (39,758 sq. miles).

There are eight regions:

Region	Inhabited land (sq. km)	Mountain pasture (sq. km)	Waste-land (sq. km)	Total area (sq. km)	Popula-tion (1 Dec. 2001)
Capital area	} 1,266	716	–	1,982	{ 178,000
Southwest Peninsula					{ 16,727
West	5,011	3,415	275	8,711	14,457
Western Peninsula	4,130	3,698	1,652	9,470	8,014
Northland West	4,867	5,278	2,948	13,093	9,310
Northland East	9,890	6,727	5,751	22,368	26,618
East	} 16,921	17,929	12,555	{ 21,991	11,798
South				{ 25,214	21,326
Iceland	42,085	37,553	23,181	102,819	286,250

Of the population of 286,250 in 2001, 18,149 were domiciled in rural districts and 264,588 (92·4%) in towns and villages (of over 200 inhabitants). Population density (2001), 3·0 per sq. km.

The UN gives a projected population for 2010 of 297,000.

The population is almost entirely Icelandic. In 2001 foreigners numbered 9,850 (1,666 Polish, 945 Danish, 601 US, 591 German, 547 Filipino, 501 Yugoslav, 481 Thai, 435 British, 316 Swedish, 314 Norwegian).

The capital, Reykjavík, had on 1 Dec. 2001 a population of 111,517; other towns were: Akranes, 5,520; Akureyri, 15,632; Bolungarvík, 958; Dalvík, 1,455; Eskifjörður, 958; Garðabær, 8,445; Grindavík, 2,336; Hafnarfjörður, 20,223; Húsavík, 2,413; Ísafjörður, 3,026; Keflavík, 7,932; Kópavogur, 24,229; Neskaupstaður, 1,411; Njarðvík, 2,889; Ólafsfjörður, 1,035; Sauðárkrókur, 2,584; Selfoss, 4,814; Seltjarnarnes, 4,662; Seyðisfjörður, 773; Siglufjörður, 1,508; Vestmannaeyjar, 4,458.

The official language is Icelandic.

SOCIAL STATISTICS

Statistics for calendar years:

	Live births	Still-born	Marriages	Divorces	Deaths	Infant deaths	Net immigration
1998	4,178	9	1,529 (12 same sex)	484	1,821	11	880
1999	4,119	19	1,560 (11 same sex)	473	1,901	10	1,122

	Live births	Still-born	Marriages	Divorces	Deaths	Infant deaths	Net immigration
2000	4,329	14	1,777 (12 same sex)	545	1,823	13	1,714
2001	4,091	11	1,484 (13 same sex)	551	1,725	11	968

2001 rates per 1,000 population: births, 14·3; deaths, 6·0. 63% of births are to unmarried mothers, the highest percentage in Europe. Annual population growth rate, 1990–2001, 1·0%. In 2001 the most popular age range for marrying was 25–29 for both males and females. Life expectancy, 2001: males, 78·1 years; females, 82·2. Infant mortality, 2000, 2·7 per 1,000 live births (one of the lowest rates in the world); fertility rate, 2001, 1·9 births per woman.

CLIMATE
The climate is cool temperate oceanic and rather changeable, but mild for its latitude because of the Gulf Stream and prevailing S.W. winds. Precipitation is high in upland areas, mainly in the form of snow. Reykjavík, Jan. 33·8°F (1·0°C), July 51·6°F (10·9°C). Annual rainfall 31·4" (792 mm).

CONSTITUTION AND GOVERNMENT
The President is elected by direct, popular vote for a period of four years.

The *Alþingi* (parliament) was elected by the former electoral law of 1984 but in the next elections a new electoral law will be used.

The new law, from 1999, provides for an *Alþingi* of 63 members. According to the new law the country is divided into a minimum of six and a maximum of seven constituencies. There are currently six constituencies: Northwest (10 seats); Northeast (10 seats); South (10); Southwest (11); Reykjavik north (11); and Reykjavik south (11).

National Anthem. 'Ó Guð vors lands' ('Oh God of Our Country'); words by M. Jochumsson, tune by S. Sveinbjörnsson.

RECENT ELECTIONS
President Ólafur Ragnar Grímsson was reappointed for a second term on 1 Aug. 2000, no opposing candidates having come forward.

In the parliamentary election held on 10 May 2003, the conservative Independence Party (SSF) of Prime Minister Davið Oddsson won 22 of the 63 seats with 33·7% of the votes cast, the Alliance (SF)—consisting of the People's Alliance, the People's Party and the Alliance of the Women's List—20 with 31·0%, the Progressive Party (FSF) 12 with 17·7%, the Left-Green Alliance (VG) 5 with 8·8% and the Liberal Party (FF) 4 with 7·4%. Turn-out was 87·5%.

CURRENT ADMINISTRATION
President: Ólafur Ragnar Grímsson; b. 1943 (People's Alliance; sworn in 1 Aug. 1996 and reappointed 1 Aug. 2000).

In May 2003 the government, formed by the Independence Party (SSF/IP) and the Progressive Party (FSF/PP), comprised:

Prime Minister, Minister for Statistics Iceland: Davíð Oddsson; b. 1948 (IP; sworn in 30 April 1991). He is currently Europe's longest-ruling head of government.

Minister of Foreign Affairs: Halldór Ásgrímsson (PP). *Finance:* Geir H. Haarde (IP). *Social Affairs:* Páll Pétursson (PP). *Fisheries:* Árni Mathiesen (IP). *Justice and Church:* Sólveig Pétursdóttir (IP). *Agriculture:* Guðni Ágústsson (PP). *Environment and Nordic Cooperation:* Siv Friðleifsdóttir (PP). *Health and Social Security:* Jón Kristjánsson (PP). *Education, Science and Culture:* Tomas Ingi Olrich (IP). *Trade and Industry:* Valgerdur Sverrisdóttir (PP). *Communications:* Sturla Böðvarsson (IP).

Government Offices of Iceland Website: http://www.stjr.is

DEFENCE
Iceland possesses no armed forces. Under the North Atlantic Treaty, US forces are stationed in Iceland as the Iceland Defence Force.

Navy. There is a paramilitary coastguard of 125.

INTERNATIONAL RELATIONS

Iceland is a member of the UN, WTO, BIS, NATO, OECD, EFTA, OSCE, the Council of Europe, the Nordic Council and Council of the Baltic Sea States, and is an Associate Member of the WEU. Iceland has acceded to the Schengen Accord, which abolishes border controls between Iceland, Austria, Belgium, Denmark, Finland, France, Germany, Greece, Italy, Luxembourg, the Netherlands, Norway, Portugal, Spain and Sweden.

ECONOMY

Services contributed 62·6% of GDP in 2001, industry 23·5%, and agriculture and fishing 13·9%.

According to the anti-corruption organization *Transparency International,* Iceland ranked 4th in the world in a 2002 survey of the countries with the least corruption in business and government. It received 9·4 out of 10 in the annual index.

Currency. The unit of currency is the *króna* (ISK) of 100 *aurar,* (singular: *eyrir*). Foreign exchange markets were deregulated on 1 Jan. 1992. The krona was devalued 7·5% in June 1993. Inflation was 3·4% in 1999, 5·1% in 2000, 6·6% in 2001 and 4·8% in 2002; the average annual rate during the period 1992–2001 was 3·2%. Foreign exchange reserves were US$366m. and gold reserves 62,000 troy oz in June 2002. Note and coin circulation at 31 Dec. 2001 was 7,406m. kr.

Budget. Total central government revenue and expenditure for calendar years (in 1m. kr.):

	1997	1998	1999	2000	2001[1]	2002[2]
Revenue	151,300	170,500	197,000	209,600	223,100	236,600
Expenditure	148,500	164,300	181,500	193,300	218,100	233,000

[1]Estimated. [2]Budgeted figure.

Central government debt was, on 31 Dec. 2001, 298,300m. kr., of which the foreign debt amounted to 198,289m. kr.

VAT is 24·5%.

Performance. GDP in 2001 totalled US$7·5bn. Real GDP growth was 4·1% in 1999, 5·0% in 2000 and 3·6% in 2001.

Banking and Finance. The Central Bank of Iceland (founded 1961; *Governor,* Birgir Ísleifur Gunnarsson) is responsible for note issue and carries out the central banking functions. There are five commercial banks in Iceland, two of them partly government-owned, and 24 smaller savings banks. The government had by 2002 sold to the public a substantial share of the two banks in which it has held a stake and was in the process of selling off more shares.

On 31 Dec. 2001 the accounts of the Central Bank balanced at 116,144m. kr. Commercial bank deposits were 273,441m. kr., and deposits in the 29 savings banks 82,054m. kr.

There is a stock exchange.

Weights and Measures. The metric system is obligatory.

ENERGY AND NATURAL RESOURCES

Environment. According to the *World Bank Atlas* Iceland's carbon dioxide emissions in 1998 were the equivalent of 7·6 tonnes per capita. An *Environmental Sustainability Index* compiled for the World Economic Forum meeting in Feb. 2002 ranked Iceland eighth in the world, with 63·9%. The index measured the ability of countries to maintain favourable environmental conditions and examined various factors including pollution levels and the use or abuse of natural resources.

Electricity. The installed capacity of public electrical power plants at the end of 2001 totalled 1,427,000 kW; installed capacity of hydro-electric plants was 1,104,500 kW. Total electricity production in public-owned plants in 2001 amounted to 8,028m. kWh; in privately owned plants, 5m. kWh. Consumption per capita was estimated in 2001 to be 28,164 kWh.

Agriculture. Of the total area, about six-sevenths is unproductive, but only about 1·3% is under cultivation, which is largely confined to hay and potatoes. Arable land totalled 7,000 ha in 2001. In 2001 the total hay crop was 2,391,067 cu. metres; the crop of potatoes, 11,366 tonnes; of cucumbers, 1,049 tonnes; and of tomatoes,

964 tonnes. Livestock (end of 2001): horses, 73,809; cattle, 70,168 (milch cows, 26,240); sheep, 473,535; pigs, 4,561; poultry, 128,241. Livestock products (2001, in tonnes): milk, 106,149; butter and dairy margarines, 1,499; cheese, 4,058; lamb, 8,616.

Forestry. In 1995 forests covered 11,000 ha, or approximately 0·1% of the total land area.

Fisheries. Fishing is of vital importance to the economy. Fishing vessels at the end of 2001 numbered 892 with a gross tonnage of 186,573. Total catch in 1998, 1,678,696 tonnes; 1999, 1,732,694; 2000, 1,980,163; 2001, 1,986,584. Virtually all the fish caught is from marine waters. Iceland has received international praise for its management system which aims to avoid the over-fishing that has decimated stocks in other parts of the world. In 2001 fisheries accounted for 12·5% of GDP, down from 16·8% in 1996. The per capita consumption of fish and fishery products is the second highest in the world, after that of the Maldives.

Fishery limits were extended from 12 to 50 nautical miles in 1972 and to 200 nautical miles in 1975.

INDUSTRY
Production, 2000, in 1,000 tonnes: aluminium, 224·4; ferro-silicon, 103·4; fertilizer (1995), 50·6; diatomite, 27·6; sales of cement, 143·7.

Labour. In 2001 the economically active population was 162,700, of which 2·3% were unemployed. In the period 1989–98 Iceland averaged 445 working days lost to strikes per 1,000 employees—the highest number in any western European country. In 1997 public services employed 19·6% of the economically active population, commerce 15·6%, manufacturing 11·9%, fisheries and fish processing 10·6%, finance and insurance companies 9·0% and construction and energy also 9·0%.

Trade Unions. In 2001 trade union membership was 85·1% of the workforce.

INTERNATIONAL TRADE
The economy is heavily trade-dependent.

Imports and Exports. Total value of imports (c.i.f.) and exports (f.o.b.) in 1,000 kr.:

	1997	1998	1999	2000	2001
Imports	143,226,581	176,072,107	182,322,000	203,222,000	220,874,000
Exports	131,213,200	136,591,964	144,928,000	149,273,000	196,582,400

Main exports, 2001 (in 1m. kr.): fish, crustaceans, molluscs and preparations thereof, 106,729; non-ferrous metals, 39,384; fodder for animals (excluding unmilled cereals), 13,127; iron and steel, 5,118. Main imports: petroleum and products, 18,273; electrical machinery and appliances, 14,322; road vehicles, 13,068.

Value of trade with principal countries for three years (in 1,000 kr.):

	1999		2000		2001	
	Imports (c.i.f.)	Exports (f.o.b.)	Imports (c.i.f.)	Exports (f.o.b.)	Imports (c.i.f.)	Exports (f.o.b.)
Australia	4,728,700	88,500	5,343,600	187,900	6,212,200	223,800
Austria	1,206,400	201,300	1,185,700	169,600	1,381,000	266,500
Belgium	3,108,200	2,047,700	3,082,900	2,231,500	4,120,900	2,798,900
Canada	1,539,700	2,243,100	1,867,300	2,346,800	2,271,100	2,115,800
Chile	98,500	181,500	1,560,200	239,300	3,840,700	345,400
China	3,060,600	362,300	3,772,700	878,900	6,352,400	905,200
Denmark	14,723,800	6,678,700	16,152,500	6,311,200	19,077,600	8,282,100
Estonia	913,800	283,000	1,255,800	268,300	3,781,100	388,800
Faroe Islands	382,200	1,283,800	603,800	2,168,400	550,700	2,585,800
Finland	2,868,000	658,200	2,871,900	918,300	3,724,200	1,326,500
France	6,940,000	7,513,600	7,586,000	6,845,300	6,982,600	7,687,900
Germany	21,580,300	18,964,500	24,098,300	24,509,900	26,908,800	29,292,200
Ireland	2,782,000	379,600	2,859,200	315,900	2,487,000	284,100
Italy	6,139,600	2,462,900	6,130,100	2,196,200	6,802,900	2,517,100
Japan	10,091,800	7,296,600	10,039,900	7,814,700	7,297,600	6,838,600
Korea, Rep. of	1,985,700	306,500	1,657,000	344,200	1,369,200	322,500
Netherlands	9,455,300	8,710,600	15,236,700	11,544,900	14,554,400	21,442,100

	1999		2000		2001	
	Imports (c.i.f.)	Exports (f.o.b.)	Imports (c.i.f.)	Exports (f.o.b.)	Imports (c.i.f.)	Exports (f.o.b.)
Nigeria	200	991,900	300	1,211,500	—	2,299,500
Norway	18,957,000	6,929,800	16,512,400	5,940,400	17,234,600	10,384,300
Poland	1,738,200	264,100	2,888,000	409,900	1,820,000	1,035,500
Portugal	1,294,300	6,959,300	1,312,000	8,438,800	1,223,400	10,816,300
Russia	3,548,600	420,700	3,612,200	610,800	3,551,200	715,700
Spain	3,555,700	7,503,800	3,533,600	6,791,600	4,341,800	10,538,600
Suriname	1,543,000	—	1,874,200	—	3,458,000	—
Sweden	11,327,100	1,292,500	13,407,800	1,324,800	12,757,400	2,084,700
Switzerland	2,033,600	5,370,300	2,095,200	3,263,300	3,039,300	6,400,000
Taiwan	1,524,800	1,055,000	1,652,200	1,360,300	1,754,200	1,757,900
UK	16,719,600	28,478,600	18,225,600	28,819,700	16,609,600	35,839,100
USA	19,866,900	21,355,700	22,313,600	18,162,400	24,505,600	20,329,900

COMMUNICATIONS

Roads. On 31 Dec. 2001 the length of the public roads (including roads in towns) was 12,955 km. Of these 8,209 km were main and secondary roads and 4,746 km were provincial roads. Total length of surfaced roads was 3,863 km. A ring road of 1,400 km runs just inland from much of the coast; about 80% of it is smooth-surfaced. Motor vehicles registered at the end of 2001 numbered 181,566, of which 161,575 were passenger cars and 19,990 lorries; there were also 1,752 motorcycles. There were 19 fatal road accidents in 2001 with 24 persons killed.

Civil Aviation. Icelandair is the national carrier. In 1998 it served 12 destinations in western Europe and six in north America as well as operating domestic services. In 1999 it carried 1·3m. passengers. The main international airport is at Keflavík (Leifsstöd), with Reykjavik for flights to the Faroe Islands, Greenland and domestic services. Keflavík handled 1,360,605 passengers in 2001 (of which 331,582 transit passengers) and 41,208 tonnes of freight.

Shipping. Total registered vessels, 1,135 (232,682 gross tonnage) on 31 Dec. 2001; of these, 959 were sea-going fishing vessels.

Telecommunications. In 2001 the number of telephone main lines was 157,528; mobile phone subscribers, 248,031. A survey conducted by EMC World Cellular Database in Sept. 2000 found that Iceland had overtaken Finland as the country with the largest number of mobile phones per capita (75·8 per 100 persons). In 1995 there were 80,000 fax machines; and in 2000, 110,000 PCs (391·5 per 1,000 persons). There were 195,000 Internet users in Dec. 2001, 69·80% of the total population (the highest percentage in the world).

Postal Services. At the end of 2001 the number of post offices was 94.

SOCIAL INSTITUTIONS

Justice. In 1992 jurisdiction in civil and criminal cases was transferred from the provincial magistrates to eight new district courts, separating the judiciary from the prosecution. From the district courts there is an appeal to the Supreme Court in Reykjavík, which has eight judges.

The population in penal institutions in 1995 was 113 (40 per 100,000 of national population).

Religion. The national church, the Evangelical Lutheran, is endowed by the state. There is complete religious liberty. The affairs of the national church are under the superintendence of a bishop. At 1 Dec. 2001, 249,256 (87·1%) of the population were members of it (93·2% in 1980). 11,633 persons (4·1%) belonged to Lutheran free churches. 18,815 persons (6·6%) belonged to other religious organizations and 6,571 persons (2·3%) did not belong to any religious community.

Education. Primary education is compulsory and free from 6–15 years of age. Optional secondary education from 16 to 19 is also free. In 2000–01 there were 44,137 pupils in primary schools, 20,740 in secondary schools (18,291 on day courses) and 11,964 tertiary-level students (10,183 on day courses). Some 15% of tertiary-level students study abroad.

There are eight universities and specialized colleges at the tertiary level in Iceland. The largest is the University of Iceland in Reykjavík (founded 1911). There is also a university in Akureyri (founded 1987). Total enrolment of these two institutions was 6,100 students in 1997–98. In Reykjavík there are a teachers' university, a technical college, business colleges and an agricultural university.

In 2000 public sector spending on education was 5·8% of GNP.

The adult literacy rate in 1998 was at least 99%.

Health. On 31 Dec. 1994 there were 57 hospitals with 3,924 beds. In 2000 there were 968 doctors, 283 dentists, 2,237 nurses and 234 pharmacists. In 2000 there were 3·4 doctors per 1,000 inhabitants. Iceland has one of the lowest alcohol consumption rates in Europe, at 6 litres of alcohol per adult a year (2000), compared to a European Union average of 11 litres.

Iceland has one of the lowest rates of Aids in the EU, with 11·2 cases per 100,000 population.

Welfare. The main body of social welfare legislation is consolidated in six acts:

(i) The social security legislation (a) health insurance, including sickness benefits; *(b)* social security pensions, mainly consisting of old age pension, disablement pension and widows' pension, and also children's pension; *(c)* employment injuries insurance.

(ii) The unemployment insurance legislation, where daily allowances are paid to those who have met certain conditions.

(iii) The subsistence legislation. This is controlled by municipal government, and social assistance is granted under special circumstances, when payments from other sources are not sufficient.

(iv) The tax legislation. Prior to 1988 children's support was included in the tax legislation, according to which a certain amount for each child in a family was subtracted from income taxes or paid out to the family. Since 1988 family allowances are paid directly to all children age 0–15 years. The amount is increased with the second child in the family, and children under the age of seven get additional benefits. Single parents receive additional allowances. The amounts are linked to income.

(v) The rehabilitation legislation.

(vi) Child and juvenile guidance.

Health insurance covers the entire population. Citizenship is not demanded and there is a six-month waiting period. Most hospitals are both municipally and state run, a few solely state run and all offer free medical help. Medical treatment out of hospitals is partly paid by the patient; the same applies to medicines, except medicines of lifelong necessary use, which are paid in full by the health insurance. Dental care is partly paid by the state for children under 17 years old and also for old age and disabled pensioners. Sickness benefits are paid to those who lose income because of periodical illness. The daily amount is fixed and paid from the 11th day of illness.

The pension system is composed of the public social security system and some 90 private pension funds. The social security system pays basic old age and disablement pensions of a fixed amount regardless of past or present income, as well as supplementary pensions to individuals with low present income. The pensions are index-linked, i.e. are changed in line with changes in wage and salary rates in the labour market. The private pension funds pay pensions that depend on past payments of premiums that are a fixed proportion of earnings. The payment of pension fund premiums is compulsory for all wage and salary earners. The pensions paid by the funds differ considerably between the individual funds, but are generally index-linked. In the public social security system, entitlement to old age and disablement pensions at the full rates is subject to the condition that the beneficiary has been resident in Iceland for 40 years at the age period of 16–67. For shorter period of residence, the benefits are reduced proportionally. Entitled to old age pension are all those who are 67 years old, and have been residents in Iceland for three years of the age period of 16–67. Entitled to disablement pension are those who have lost 75% of their working capacity and have been residents in Iceland for three years before application or have had full working capacity at the time when they became residents. Old age and disablement pension are of equally high amount;

in the year 1999 the total sum was 198,645 kr. for an individual. Married pensioners are paid 90% of two individuals' pensions. In addition to the basic amount, supplementary allowances are paid according to social circumstances and income possibilities. Widows' pensions are the same amount as old age and disablement pension, provided the applicant is over 60 when she becomes widowed. Women in the age range 50–60 get a reduced pension. Women under 50 are not entitled to widows' pensions.

The employment injuries insurance covers medical care, daily allowances, disablement pension and survivors' pension and is applicable to practically all employees.

Social assistance is primarily municipal and granted in cases outside the social security legislation. Domestic assistance to old people and disabled is granted within this legislation, besides other services.

Child and juvenile guidance is performed by chosen committees according to special laws, such as home guidance and family assistance. In cases of parents' disablement the committees take over the guidance of the children involved.

CULTURE

Broadcasting. The state-owned public service, The Icelandic State Broadcasting Service, broadcasts 2 national and 3 regional radio programmes and 1 national TV channel. In addition, 23 privately owned radio stations and seven private TV stations were in operation in 2000. At 31 Dec. 2002, 91,418 colour TV sets were licensed (534 black and white).

Cinema. There were 25 cinemas with 51 screens in 2002 of which the capital had nine cinemas and 32 screens. Total admissions numbered 1,529,831 in 2002, with the Reykjavík area accounting for 1,319,760. In 1995 gross box office receipts came to 665m. kr. and seven full-length films were made.

Press. In 2002 there were three daily newspapers and 22 non-daily newspapers (13 paid-for and nine free).

Iceland publishes more books per person than any other country in the world. In 1999, 1,232 volumes of books and 721 volumes of booklets were published.

Tourism. There were 302,913 visitors in 2000. Revenue in 2001 totalled 37,720m. kr. Overnight stays in hotels and guest houses in 2001 numbered 907,029. Tourism accounts for more than 12% of foreign currency earnings. Between 1990 and 2000 the number of visitors increased on average by 7% every year.

Festivals. The Reykjavík Arts Festival is a biennial programme of international artists and performers, and will next be held in 2004.

Libraries. The National and University Library of Iceland is in Reykjavík and contains 860,079 volumes. The eight University libraries contain 190,898 volumes, the 43 special libraries 360,854 volumes.

Theatre and Opera. In 2002 there were nine professional theatres operated on a yearly basis (of which seven were in the capital region) and 18 professional theatre groups (all in the capital region). In the theatrical season 2001–02 there were 276,155 admissions to performances of the professional theatres, 83,296 admissions to the National Theatre and 67,328 admissions to the City Theatre and Idno Theatre. Total audience of the Icelandic Opera was 12,200.

There is one symphonic orchestra operated on a regular basis, the Icelandic Symphony Orchestra. In 2002 the orchestra performed 72 times within the country and abroad, with audiences totalling 34,973.

Museums and Galleries. In 2002 there were 105 museums, botanical gardens, aquariums and zoos in operation, with a total of 957,164 visitors. The National Museum is closed for construction work and so received no visitors in 2002. The National Gallery received 40,464 visitors and 93,500 attended the Reykjavík Municipal Art Museum.

DIPLOMATIC REPRESENTATIVES

Of Iceland in the United Kingdom (2A Hans Street, London, SW1X 0JE)
Ambassador: Sverrir Hakur Gunnlaugsson.

Of the United Kingdom in Iceland (Laufásvegur 31, 101 Reykjavík)
Ambassador and Consul-General: John H. Culver, LVO.

Of Iceland in the USA (1156 15th Street NW, Suite 1200, Washington, D.C., 20005)
Ambassador: Helgi Ágústsson.

Of the USA in Iceland (Laufásvegur 21, 101 Reykjavík)
Ambassador: James I. Gadsen.

Of Iceland to the United Nations
Ambassador: Þorsteinn Ingólfsson.

Of Iceland to the European Union
Ambassador: Gunnar Snorri Gunnarsson.

FURTHER READING

Statistics Iceland, *Landshagir* (Statistical Yearbook of Iceland).—*Hagtíðindi* (Monthly Statistics)

Central Bank of Iceland. *Economic Statistics Quarterly.—The Economy of Iceland.* May 1994

Byock, Jesse, *Viking Age Iceland.* Penguin, London, 2001

Hastrup, K., *A Place Apart: An Anthropological Study of the Icelandic World.* Clarendon Press, Oxford, 1998

Karlsson, G., *The History of Iceland.* Univ. of Minnesota Press, 2000

Lacy, T., *Ring of Seasons: Iceland—Its culture and history.* University of Michigan Press, 1998

McBride F. R., *Iceland.* [Bibliography] 2nd ed. ABC-Clio, Oxford and Santa Barbara (CA), 1996

Smiley, Jane, (ed.) *The Sagas of Icelanders: A Selection.* Penguin, London, 2002

Turner, Barry, (ed.) *Scandinavia Profiled.* Macmillan, London, 2000

National statistical office: Statistics Iceland, Bogartúni 21a, IS-150 Reykjavík.
Website: http://www.hagstofa.is
National library: Landsbókasafn Islands.—Háskólabókasafn, Reykjavík, *Librarian:* Sigrún Klara Hannesdóttir.

INDIA

Bharat

(Republic of India)

Capital: New Delhi
Population estimate, 2000: 1,008·9m.
GDP per capita, 2000: (PPP$) 2,358
HDI/world rank: 0·577/124

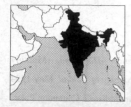

Map. Based upon Survey of India Map with the permission of the Surveyor General of India. The responsibility for the correctness of internal details rests with the pubisher. The territorial waters of India extend into the sea to a distance of 12 nautical miles measured from the appropriate base line. The external boundaries and coastlines of India agree with the Record/Master Copy certified by the Survey of India.

KEY HISTORICAL EVENTS

Approximately 7,000 years ago the valley of the Indus was one of the cradles of civilization. From the Indus Valley, Dravidian peoples spread agriculture and fixed settlements gradually across India, arriving in the far south by about 4,000 years ago. The Indus Valley Harappan civilization, a Bronze Age culture, flourished from around 2300 to 1500 BC and had links with western Asian civilizations in Iran. Writing, fine jewellery and textile production, town planning, metalworking and pottery were the hallmarks of an advanced urban society.

At the same time, another Bronze Age civilization existed in the Ganges Valley. This civilization, whose links were with south-eastern Asia, was based on a rice-growing rural economy. Around 1500 BC a pastoral people, the Aryans, invaded the Indus Valley from Iran and Central Asia. Their arrival completed the destruction of the Harappan civilization and shifted the balance of power in the subcontinent to the Ganges Valley.

The Aryans took over northern and central India, merging their culture with that of the Dravidians. The caste system, still a feature of Indian society, dates back to the Dravidians, but the languages of northern and central India, and the polytheistic religion that is now followed by the majority of the inhabitants of the subcontinent, are both Aryan in origin. From these two cultures, a Hindu civilization emerged.

By 800 BC a series of Hindu kingdoms had developed in the Ganges Valley. This region gave birth to one of the world's great religions: Buddhism. Prince Gautama, the Buddha (c. 563–483 BC), renounced a life of wealth to seek enlightenment. His creed of non-violence was spread throughout India and, later, south-eastern Asia.

Chandragupta Maurya (reigned 321–297 BC) conquered most of northern India before his ascetic death from self-imposed starvation. His grandson, Ashoka, ruled an empire that stretched from the Deccan to Afghanistan from c. 272–c. 231, but he is mainly remembered for his enthusiasm for Buddhist pacifism. Attacked by enemies who did not share this creed, the Mauryan empire collapsed soon after Ashoka's death.

Although no Hindu state managed to unite India, the Hindu religion and culture proved powerful influences throughout the region. By about 500 BC Sri Lanka was within the Hindu sphere of influence. Over the next 800 years Hindu kingdoms were established in Burma, Cambodia, Sumatra, Thailand and Java. From the 4th century BC, Indian merchants spread Buddhism through south-eastern Asia.

While Indian religion and culture spread south and east, an invasion from the west threatened to change the subcontinent. In AD 713 a Muslim army conquered Sind. For the next 300 years, Islamic rulers were largely confined to what is now Pakistan, but in 1000 a raid by the ruler of Ghazni (now in Afghanistan) overran the Punjab. During the 11th and 12th centuries the Hindu states of the Ganges Valley were toppled by Muslim invaders.

In the north, the Delhi Sultanate was replaced by the Mughal Empire. Founded by Babur (reigned 1526–30), it was extended by Akbar the Great (reigned 1556–1605) who conquered Baluchistan, Gujarat, Bengal, Orissa, Rajasthan, Afghanistan and Bihar. In his campaign against Gujarat, Akbar marched his army

800 km (500 miles) in only 11 days. His grandson, Shah Jahan (reigned 1628–58), was a pleasure-seeking ruler, who is remembered for constructing the Taj Mahal as a memorial to his favourite wife.

The decline of the Mughal Empire began under Shah Jahan's son, Aurangzeb I (reigned 1658–1707). Aurangzeb persecuted Hindus with a vengeance. Inter-community violence and wars against Hindu states weakened the empire. Throughout the 18th century, disputed successions and fears of assassination diverted the Mughal emperors. By the close of the 18th century the last emperor was nominal ruler of the environs of Delhi.

By the 16th century, European traders were established along India's coasts. In 1510 the Portuguese took Goa, which remained the centre of the fragmented possessions of Portuguese India until 1962. The creation of the (English) East India Company in 1600 heralded the beginning of what was to become the British Indian Empire. The main threat to British rule in India was France. Although the East India Company controlled parts of Bengal and the Ganges Valley, France was supreme in the Deccan where French forces, and Indian rulers allied to France, held sway over an area twice the size of France itself.

In the 1750s Britain and France fought out their European wars overseas. The defeat of French forces, and France's Indian allies, at the battle of Plassey (1757), by British forces led by Robert Clive (1725–74), confirmed British rule in Bengal and Bihar and ejected France from the Deccan. Henceforth, France was restricted to five small coastal possessions.

Founded by Sivaji (1627–80), the Maratha state was the major power in central and southern India in the 17th and 18th centuries. The Hindu Sivaji came into conflict with the fanatical Muslim Mughal emperor Aurangzeb, who imprisoned Sivaji. After his famous escape from captivity, concealed in a fruit basket, Sivaji made himself emperor of his Maratha state in 1674. This pious monarch ruled competently, establishing an efficient administration, but by the time of his grandson, Shahu (reigned 1707–27), the power of the Maratha emperors had been eclipsed by that of their hereditary chief minister, the Peshwa. In 1727 the Peshwa Baji Rao I (reigned 1720–40) effectively replaced the emperor and established his own dynasty. Baji Rao made the Maratha state the strongest in India. His descendant, Baji Rao II (reigned 1795–1817), raised a weakened state against the British and was crushed. He had been the last important Indian monarch outside British influence.

During the first half of the 19th century, wars against Sind (1843) and the Sikhs in Punjab (1849) extended the borders of British India. By the middle of the 19th century about 60% of the subcontinent was controlled by the East India Company. The remaining 40% was divided between about 620 Indian states, which were, in theory, still sovereign and ruled by their own maharajas, sultans, nawabs and other monarchs, each advised by a British resident. The Indian states ranged from large entities the size of European countries (states such as Hyderabad, Baroda, Mysore and Indore) to tiny states no bigger than an English parish.

Landless peasants and dispossessed princes united in their opposition to British rule. In 1857 a mutiny by soldiers of the East India Company quickly spread into full-scale rebellion. Throughout India those who resented the speed and nature of the changes brought about by British rule made one final attempt to eject the occupiers. The Indian Mutiny took 14 months to put down.

After the Mutiny the British government replaced the East India Company as the ruler of the Indian colonial empire (1858), and the modernization of India began apace. Emphasis was placed on building up an Indian infrastructure, particularly roads and railways. The participation of Indians within the civil administration, the construction of a vast national railway system and the imposition of the English language, through the many new schools, colleges and universities, did much to forge an Indian identity. But industry in India was not modernized, in part through fear of competition. In 1877 the Indian Empire was proclaimed and Queen Victoria became Empress of India (Kaiser-i-Hind).

The divisions fostered by religion proved stronger than any new sense of a national Indian identity. The (Hindu-dominated) Indian National Congress, the forerunner of the Congress Party, first met in 1885, and in 1906 the rival Muslim League was founded. Demands for Home Rule grew in the early years of the 20th century, and nationalist feeling was fuelled when British troops fired without warning on a peaceful nationalist protest meeting—the Amritsar Massacre (1919).

Realizing that change was inevitable, the British government reformed the administration through two Acts of Parliament in 1919 and 1935. These created an Indian federation, effectively removing many of the differences between the Crown territories and the Indian states. These acts granted a new Indian government limited autonomy. The pace of reform was, however, too slow for Indian popular opinion.

In 1920 the Congress party began a campaign of non-violence and non-cooperation with the British colonial authorities, led by the charismatic figure of Mahatma Gandhi (1869–1948). By the start of World War II (1939–45), relations between the Hindu and Muslim communities in India had broken down, and the Muslims were demanding a separate independent Islamic state, later Pakistan.

In 1945 Britain had neither the will nor the resources to maintain the Indian Empire. In 1947 India was divided into India, a predominantly Hindu state led by Jawaharlal (Pandit) Nehru (1889–1964) of the Congress Party, and Pakistan, a Muslim state led by Mohammad Ali Jinnah (1876–1948) of the Muslim League. Partition brought enormous upheaval. More than 70m. Hindus and Muslims became refugees as they trekked across the new boundaries. Many thousands were killed in intercommunal violence. The border remained disputed in many places. Tension increased when Gandhi was assassinated by a Hindu fundamentalist (1948). In 1950 India became a republic.

Tension between India and Pakistan erupted into war in 1947–49 when the two countries fought over Kashmir. The region was divided along a ceasefire line, although neither side recognized this as an international border. India and Pakistan went to war again over Kashmir in 1965, and in 1971 when Bangladesh (formerly East Pakistan) gained its independence as a result of Indian military intervention. Indian forces saw action in 1961 when Indian troops invaded and annexed Portuguese India and in 1962 in a border war with China.

In 1966 Nehru's daughter Indira Gandhi (1917–84) became premier. Under Mrs Gandhi, India continued to assert itself as a regional power and the rival of Pakistan. Although non-aligned, India developed close relations with the Soviet Union. In spite of being the world's largest democracy, India was wracked by local separatism and communal unrest. From 1975 to 1977 Mrs Gandhi imposed a much-criticized state of emergency. Her actions split the Congress Party, allowing Morarji Desai (1896–1995) of the Janata Party to form India's first non-Congress administration. However, his alliance of parties soon shattered and a wing of Congress, led by Mrs Gandhi, was returned to power in 1980.

Violence in Sikh areas, fanned by demands by militant Sikhs for an independent homeland (called Khalistan), increased tensions. In 1984 Mrs Gandhi ordered that the Golden Temple in Amritsar be stormed after it had been turned into a storehouse for weapons by Sikh extremists. Soon afterwards, Mrs Gandhi was assassinated by her Sikh bodyguards.

Mrs Gandhi was succeeded as premier by her son, Ranjiv (1944–91), during whose period of office India became involved in Sri Lanka, supporting the central government against the separatist Tamil Tigers movement. Ranjiv Gandhi was assassinated by a Tamil Tiger suicide bomber during the 1991 election campaign. By 1989 personality clashes had shattered the unity of the once all-powerful Congress Party. Since then coalitions have held office. The right-wing Hindu nationalist Bharatiya Janata Party (BJP) has been part of most these. Support for the BJP increased following violence between Hindus and Muslims over a campaign, which began in 1990, to build a Hindu temple on the site of a mosque in the holy city of Ayodhya.

After the fall of the Soviet Union (1991), India gradually abandoned state ownership and some elements of protectionism. Privatization has been accompanied by an economic revolution that has seen the development of high tech industries. At the same time, India has become a nuclear power, exploding its first nuclear device in 1974. Along with Pakistan, India has yet to sign the Comprehensive Nuclear-Test-Ban Treaty.

There have been 35,000 deaths since the outbreak of the Kashmir insurgency in 1988. Negotiations with Pakistan over the future of the disputed territory of Kashmir began in July 1999. In May 2001 India ended its six-month long ceasefire. It then invited Pakistan's government to enter talks, which ended with hopes of avoiding further violence. In Dec. 2001, in an attack on the Indian parliament by suicide bombers, 13 people died. Although no group claimed responsibility, Kashmiri separatists were blamed. However, Pakistani President Pervez Musharraf's subsequent crackdown on militants helped to bring the two countries back from the brink of war. Tension between India and Pakistan increased following an attack on an Indian army base in Indian-occupied Kashmir on 14 May 2002. The attack, which killed 31 people, was linked to Islamic terrorists infiltrating the Kashmir valley from Pakistan. It drew widespread criticism of President Musharraf for failing to combat terrorism in the disputed region.

TERRITORY AND POPULATION

India is bounded in the northwest by Pakistan, north by China, Tibet, Nepal and Bhutan, east by Myanmar, and southeast, south and southwest by the Indian Ocean. The far eastern states and territories are almost separated from the rest by Bangladesh. The area (excluding the Pakistan and China-occupied parts of Jammu and Kashmir) is 3,166,414 sq. km. A Sino-Indian agreement of 7 Sept. 1993 settled frontier disputes dating from the war of 1962. Population (excluding occupied Jammu and Kashmir), 2001 census (provisional): 1,027,015,247 (495,738,169 females), giving a density of 324 persons per sq. km. There are also 20m. Indians and ethnic Indians living abroad, notably in Malaysia, the USA, Saudi Arabia, the UK and South Africa. 72·2% of the population was rural in 2001 (Goa being the most urban state, at 49·8%; and Himachal Pradesh the most rural, at 90·2%).

The UN gives a projected population for 2010 of 1,164·0m.

By 2050 India is expected to have a population of 1·53bn. and is projected to have overtaken China as the world's most populous country.

Area and population of states and union territories:

	Area in sq. km	Population 2001 census	Density per sq. km (2001)
States			
Andhra Pradesh (And P)	275,069	75,727,541	275
Arunachal Pradesh (Arun P)	83,743	1,091,117	13
Assam (Ass)	78,438	26,638,407	340
Bihar (Bih)	94,163	82,878,796	880
Chhattisgarh	135,191	20,795,956	154
Goa	3,702	1,343,998	363
Gujarat (Guj)	196,022	50,596,992	258
Haryana (Har)	44,212	21,082,989	477
Himachal Pradesh (Him P)	55,673	6,077,248	109
Jammu and Kashmir (J and K)[1]	101,387	10,069,917	99
Jharkhand	79,714	26,909,428	338
Karnataka (Kar)	191,791	52,733,958	275
Kerala (Ker)	38,863	31,838,619	819
Madhya Pradesh (MP)	308,245	60,385,118	196
Maharashtra (Mah)	307,713	96,752,247	314
Manipur (Man)	22,327	2,388,634	107
Meghalaya (Meg)	22,429	2,306,069	103
Mizoram (Miz)	21,081	891,058	42
Nagaland (Nag)	16,579	1,988,636	120
Orissa (Or)	155,707	36,706,920	236
Punjab (Pun)	50,362	24,289,296	482
Rajasthan (Raj)	342,239	56,473,122	165
Sikkim (Sik)	7,096	540,493	76
Tamil Nadu (TN)	130,058	62,110,839	478
Tripura (Tri)	10,486	3,191,168	304
Uttar Pradesh (UP)	240,928	166,052,859	689
Uttaranchal	53,483	8,479,562	159
West Bengal (WB)	88,752	80,221,171	904
Union Territories			
Andaman and Nicobar Islands (ANI)	8,249	356,265	43
Chandigarh (Chan)	114	900,914	7,903
Dadra and Nagar Haveli (DNH)	491	220,451	449
Daman and Diu (D and D)	112	158,059	1,411

	Area in sq. km	Population 2001 census	Density per sq. km (2001)
Union Territories			
Delhi (Del)	1,483	13,782,976	9,294
Lakshadweep (Lak)	32	60,595	1,894
Pondicherry (Pon)	480	973,829	2,029

[1]Excludes the area occupied by Pakistan and China.

Urban agglomerations with populations over 2m., together with their core cities at the 2001 census (provisional):

	State/ Union Territory	Urban Agglomeration	Core City
Bombay (Mumbai)	Maharashtra	16,368,084	11,914,348
Calcutta (Kolkata)	West Bengal	13,216,546	4,580,544
Delhi	Delhi	12,791,458	9,817,439
Madras (Chennai)	Tamil Nadu	6,424,624	4,216,268
Bangalore	Karnataka	5,686,844	4,292,223
Hyderabad	Andhra Pradesh	5,533,640	3,449,878
Ahmedabad	Gujarat	4,519,278	3,515,361
Pune (Poona)	Maharashtra	3,755,525	2,540,069
Surat	Gujarat	2,811,466	2,433,787
Kanpur	Uttar Pradesh	2,690,486	2,532,138
Jaipur	Rajasthan	2,324,319	2,324,319
Lucknow	Uttar Pradesh	2,266,933	2,207,340
Nagpur	Maharashtra	2,122,965	2,051,320

Smaller urban agglomerations and cities with populations over 250,000 (with 1991 census populations, in 1,000):

Agra (UP)	892	Faridabad Complex		Moradabad (UP)	444
Ajmer (Raj)	403	(Har)	618	Mysore (Kar)	481
Akola (Mah)	328	Gaya (Bih)	292	Nanded (Mah)	275
Aligarh (UP)	481	Ghaziabad (UP)	454	Nashik (Mah)	657
Allahabad (UP)	806	Gorakhpur (UP)	506	Nellore (And P)	316
Amravati (Mah)	422	Gulbarga (Kar)	304	New Bombay (Mah)	308
Amritsar (Pun)	709	Guntur (And P)	273	New Delhi (Del)	301
Asansol (WB)	262	Guwahati (Ass)	584	Panihati (WB)	276
Aurangabad (Mah)	573	Gwalior (MP)	691	Patna (Bih)	917
Bareilly (UP)	591	Hubli-Dharwad (Kar)	648	Raipur (Chhattisgarh)	439
Belgaum (Mah)	326	Indore (MP)	1,092	Rajamundry (And P)	325
Bhagalpur (Bih)	253	Jabalpur (MP)	742	Rajkot (Raj)	559
Bhavnagar (Guj)	402	Jalandhar (Pun)	510	Ranchi (Jharkhand)	599
Bhilainagar (MP)	386	Jamnagar (Guj)	342	Saharanpur (UP)	375
Bhiwandi (Mah)	379	Jamshedpur (Bih)	461	Salem (TN)	367
Bhopal (MP)	1,063	Jhansi (UP)	313	Sholapur (Mah)	604
Bhubaneswar (Or)	412	Jodhpur (Raj)	668	Srinagar (J and K)	595
Bikaner (Raj)	416	Kakinada (And P)	280	Thiruvananthapuram	
Bokaro Steel City		Kharagpur (WB)	265	(Ker)	524
(Jharkhand)	334	Kochi (Ker)	565	Tiruchirapalli (TN)	387
Chandigarh (Chan)	511	Kolhapur (Mah)	406	Udaipur (Raj)	309
Coimbatore (TN)	816	Kota (Raj)	537	Ujjain (MP)	362
Cuttack (Or)	403	Kozhikode (Ker)	420	Vadodara (Guj)	1,031
Davangere (Kar)	266	Ludhiana (Pun)	1,043	Varanasi (UP)	932
Dehra Dun		Madurai (TN)	941	Vijayawada (And P)	702
(Uttaranchal)	368	Malegaon (Mah)	342	Visakhapatnam	
Dhanbad (Bih)[1]	815	Mangalore (Kar)	273	(And P)	752
Dhule (Mah)	278	Meerut (UP)	850	Warangal (And P)	448
Durgapur (WB)	426				

[1]Urban agglomeration.

Delhi: Delhi was named after Raj Dhilu of the Mauryan dynasty who reigned in the 1st century BC. It is India's third biggest city. It covers an area of 1,483 sq. km and is located in the northern part of the country. Much of the part of the city known as Old Delhi was built by the Mughals between 1526 and 1712. The capital was moved from Calcutta to Delhi in 1911, and New Delhi was inaugurated as the new capital in 1931. Sir Edwin Lutyens built much of the new city, characterized by its colonial arches, columns and wide tree lined avenues, in the 1920s.

Bombay: Officially renamed Mumbai in 1996, Bombay is India's biggest city and the third largest in the world. Located on the west coast of India, it comprises seven islands joined together by landfills. It became part of the British empire in 1661 and thrived on the cotton industry, quickly becoming one of the world's leading exporters. Now the centre of the country's film industry (Bollywood), Bombay generates around 35% of the country's GNP.

Calcutta: Officially known as Kolkata since 1996, Calcutta was founded in 1690 by the East India Company on the eastern bank of the Houghly river. Between 1772 and 1912 it was the capital of India. In 1947 it became the capital of West Bengal but this was not enough to stem the city's decline and it took government intervention in the 1980s to turn the economy around. Today the city is the second largest in India and the world's largest producer of jute.

SOCIAL STATISTICS

Many births and deaths go unregistered. The Registrar General's data suggests a birth rate for 1995–96 of 28·3 per 1,000 population and a death rate of 9·0, which would indicate in a year approximately 26,500,000 births (equivalent to the population of California in the mid 1980s) and 8,500,000 deaths. The growth rate is, however, slowing, and by the turn of the century had dropped below 1·6%, having been over 2% in 1991. Expectation of life at birth, 1999, 62·4 years for males and 63·3 years for females.

Marriages and divorces are not registered. The minimum age for a civil marriage is 18 for women and 21 for men; for a sacramental marriage, 14 for females and 18 for males. Population growth rate, 1991–2001, 21·35% (the lowest since 1961–71). Infant mortality, 1999, 70 per 1,000 live births; fertility rate, 1999, 3·0 births per woman. Child deaths (under the age of five) were halved between 1980 and 1996, from 172 per 1,000 in 1980 to only 85 per 1,000 in 1996.

CLIMATE

India has a variety of climatic sub-divisions. In general, there are four seasons. The cool one lasts from Dec. to March, the hot season is in April and May, the rainy season is June to Sept., followed by a further dry season until Nov. Rainfall, however, varies considerably, from 4" (100 mm) in the N.W. desert to over 400" (10,000 mm) in parts of Assam.

Range of temperature and rainfall: New Delhi, Jan. 57°F (13·9°C), July 88°F (31·1°C). Annual rainfall 26" (640 mm). Bombay, Jan. 75°F (23·9°C), July 81°F (27·2°C). Annual rainfall 72" (1,809 mm). Calcutta, Jan. 67°F (19·4°C), July 84°F (28·9°C). Annual rainfall 64" (1,600 mm). Cherrapunji, Jan. 53°F (11·7°C), July 68°F (20°C). Annual rainfall 432" (10,798 mm). Darjeeling, Jan. 41°F (5°C), July 62°F (16·7°C). Annual rainfall 121" (3,035 mm). Hyderabad, Jan. 72°F (22·2°C), July 80°F (26·7°C). Annual rainfall 30" (752 mm). Kochi, Jan. 80°F (26·7°C), July 79°F (26·1°C). Annual rainfall 117" (2,929 mm). Madras, Jan. 76°F (24·4°C), July 87°F (30·6°C). Annual rainfall 51" (1,270 mm). Patna, Jan. 63°F (17·2°C), July 90°F (32·2°C). Annual rainfall 46" (1,150 mm).

CONSTITUTION AND GOVERNMENT

The Constitution was passed by the Constituent Assembly on 26 Nov. 1949 and came into force on 26 Jan. 1950. It has since been amended 78 times.

India is a republic and comprises a Union of 28 States and 7 Union Territories. Each State is administered by a Governor appointed by the President for a term of five years while each Union Territory is administered by the President through a Lieut.-Governor or an administrator appointed by him. The head of the Union (head of state) is the *President* in whom all executive power is vested, to be exercised on the advice of ministers responsible to Parliament. The President, who must be an Indian citizen at least 35 years old and eligible for election to the House of the People, is elected by an electoral college of all the elected members of Parliament and of the state legislative assemblies, holds office for five years and is eligible for re-election. There is also a *Vice-President* who is *ex officio* chairman of the Council of States.

There is a *Council of Ministers* to aid and advise the President; this comprises Ministers who are members of the Cabinet and Ministers of State and deputy ministers who are not. A Minister who for any period of six consecutive months is not a member of either House of Parliament ceases to be a Minister at the expiration of that period. The *Prime Minister* is appointed by the President; other Ministers are appointed by the President on the Prime Minister's advice. The salary of each Minister is Rs 12,000 per month.

Parliament consists of the President, the *Council of States* (*Rajya Sabha*) and the *House of the People* (*Lok Sabha*). The Council of States, or the Upper House, consists of not more than 250 members; in Aug. 2002 there were 232 elected members and 12 members nominated by the President. The election to this house is indirect; the representatives of each State are elected by the elected members of the Legislative Assembly of that State. The Council of States is a permanent body not liable to dissolution, but one-third of the members retire every second year. The House of the People, or the Lower House, consists of 545 members, 543 directly elected on the basis of adult suffrage from territorial constituencies in the States, and the Union territories; in Aug. 2002 there were 543 elected members (499 males) and two vacancies. The House of the People unless sooner dissolved continues for a period of five years from the date appointed for its first meeting; in emergency, Parliament can extend the term by one year.

State Legislatures. For every State there is a legislature which consists of the Governor, and (a) two Houses, a Legislative Assembly and a Legislative Council, in the States of Bihar, Jammu and Kashmir, Karnataka, Madhya Pradesh (where it is provided for but not in operation), Maharashtra and Uttar Pradesh, and (b) one House, a Legislative Assembly, in the other States. Every Legislative Assembly, unless sooner dissolved, continues for five years from the date appointed for its first meeting. In emergency the term can be extended by one year. Every State Legislative Council is a permanent body and is not subject to dissolution, but one-third of the members retire every second year. Parliament can, however, abolish an existing Legislative Council or create a new one, if the proposal is supported by a resolution of the Legislative Assembly concerned.

Legislation. The various subjects of legislation are enumerated in three lists in the seventh schedule to the constitution. List I, the Union List, consists of 97 subjects (including defence, foreign affairs, communications, currency and coinage, banking and customs) with respect to which the Union Parliament has exclusive power to make laws. The State legislature has exclusive power to make laws with respect to the 66 subjects in list II, the State List; these include police and public order, agriculture and irrigation, education, public health and local government. The powers to make laws with respect to the 47 subjects (including economic and social planning, legal questions and labour and price control) in list III, the Concurrent List, are held by both Union and State governments, though the former prevails. But Parliament may legislate with respect to any subject in the State List in circumstances when the subject assumes national importance or during emergencies.

Other provisions deal with the administrative relations between the Union and the States, interstate trade and commerce, distribution of revenues between the States and the Union, official language, etc.

Fundamental Rights. Two chapters of the constitution deal with fundamental rights and 'Directive Principles of State Policy'. 'Untouchability' is abolished, and its practice in any form is punishable. The fundamental rights can be enforced through the ordinary courts of law and through the Supreme Court of the Union. The directive principles cannot be enforced through the courts of law; they are nevertheless fundamental in the governance of the country.

Citizenship. Under the Constitution, every person who was on the 26 Jan. 1950 domiciled in India and (a) was born in India or (b) either of whose parents was born in India or (c) who has been ordinarily resident in the territory of India for not less than five years immediately preceding that date became a citizen of India. Special provision is made for migrants from Pakistan and for Indians resident abroad. Under the Citizenship Act, 1955, which supplemented the provisions of the Constitution, Indian citizenship is acquired by birth, by descent, by registration and by naturalization. The Act also provides for loss of citizenship by renunciation, termination and deprivation. The right to vote is granted to every person who is a citizen of India and who is not less than 18 years of age on a fixed date and is not otherwise disqualified.

Parliament. Parliament and the state legislatures are organized according to the following schedule (figures show distribution of seats in Aug. 2001 for the Lok Sabha, the Rajya Sabha and the State Legislatures):

	House of the People (Lok Sabha)	Parliament Council of States (Rajya Sabha)	State Legislatures Legislative Assemblies (Vidhan Sabhas)	Legislative Councils (Vidhan Parishads)
States:				
Andhra Pradesh	42	18	294	–
Arunachal Pradesh	2	1	60	–
Assam	14	7	126	–
Bihar	40	16	243	96
Chhattisgarh	11	5	90	–
Goa	2	1	40	–
Gujarat	26	11	182	–
Haryana	10	5	90	–
Himachal Pradesh	4	3	68	–
Jammu and Kashmir	6	4	87[2]	36[3]
Jharkhand	14	6	81	–
Karnataka	28	12	224	75
Kerala	20	9	140	–
Madhya Pradesh	29	11	230	–
Maharashtra	48	19	288	78
Manipur	2	1	60	–
Meghalaya	2	1	60	–
Mizoram	1	1	40	–
Nagaland	1	1	60	–
Orissa	21	10	147	–
Punjab	13	7	117	–
Rajasthan	25	10	200	–
Sikkim	1	1	32	–
Tamil Nadu	39	18	234	–
Tripura	2	1	60	–
Uttar Pradesh	80	31	403	108
Uttaranchal	5	3	30	–
West Bengal	42	16	295[4]	–
Union Territories:				
Andaman and Nicobar Islands	1	–	–	–
Chandigarh	1	–	–	–
Dadra and Nagar Haveli	1	–	–	–
Delhi	7	3	70	–
Daman and Diu	1	–	–	–
Lakshadweep	1	–	–	–
Pondicherry	1	1	30	–
Nominated by the President under Article 80 (1) (a) of the Constitution	–	12	–	–
Total	545[1]	245	4,081	393[1]

[1]Includes two nominated members to represent Anglo-Indians.
[2]Excludes 24 seats for Pakistan-occupied areas of the State which are in abeyance.
[3]Excludes seats for the Pakistan-occupied areas.
[4]Includes 1 nominated minority community representative.

Language. The Constitution provides that the official language of the Union shall be Hindi in the Devanagari script. Hindi is spoken by over 30% of the population. It was originally provided that English should continue to be used for all official purposes until 1965. But the Official Languages Act 1963 provides that, after the expiry of this period of 15 years from the coming into force of the Constitution, English might continue to be used, in addition to Hindi, for all official purposes of the Union for which it was being used immediately before that day, and for the transaction of business in Parliament. According to the Official Languages (Use for official purposes of the Union) Rules 1976, an employee may record in Hindi or in English without being required to furnish a translation thereof in the other language and no employee possessing a working knowledge of Hindi may ask for an English translation of any document in Hindi except in the case of legal or technical documents.

The 58th amendment to the Constitution (26 Nov. 1987) authorized the preparation of a Constitution text in Hindi.

The following 18 languages are included in the Eighth Schedule to the Constitution (with 1994 estimate of speakers where over 5m.): Assamese (14·8m.), Bengali (68·3m.), Gujarati (44m.), Hindi (350·3m.), Kannada (35·7m.), Kashmiri, Konkani, Malayalam (34·4m.), Manipuri, Marathi (65·8m.), Nepali, Oriya (30·3m.), Punjabi (24·7m.), Sanskrit, Sindhi, Tamil (59·3m.), Telugu (71·9m.), Urdu (46·8m.).

Thakur, R., *The Government and Politics of India*. London, 1995

National Anthem. 'Jana-gana-mana' ('Thou art the ruler of the minds of all people'); words and tune by Rabindranath Tagore.

RECENT ELECTIONS

Presidential elections were held on 18 July 2002. A. P. J. Abdul Kalam was elected by 89·6% of votes cast against one opponent.

Parliamentary elections were held between 5 Sept. and 3 Oct. 1999. Turn-out was 60%. The Bharatiya Janata Party (BJP) gained 182 seats (178 in 1998); the Indian National Congress (INC), 112 (145 in 1998); the Communist Party of India (CPI-M), 32 (32 in 1998); Telugu Desam Party (TDP), 29; Samajwadi Party (SP), 26; Janata Dal-United (JD-U), 20. 35 other parties gained 15 seats or fewer. By securing victory, Atal Behari Vajpayee secured re-election as prime minister, becoming the first Indian prime minister to do so since Indira Gandhi in 1972. In March 2001 the 24-party ruling National Democratic Alliance had 291 seats, Congress and allies 134, left 41 and others 75.

Elections to the Council of States took place on 29 March 2000. The INC won 64 seats, BJP 45, CPI-M 17, TDP 11, SP 9, JD-U 9, Rashtria Janata Dal 9. 22 other parties gained 7 seats or fewer. Non-partisans took 14 seats and 12 went to nominated members.

Singh, V. B., *Elections in India: Data Handbook on Lok Sabha Elections, 1986–91*. Delhi, 1994

CURRENT ADMINISTRATION

President: A. P. J. Abdul Kalam; b. 1931 (sworn in 25 July 2002).

Vice-President: Bhairon Singh Shekhawat.

On 17 April 1999 Prime Minister Atal Behari Vajpayee lost a confidence motion by one vote and the coalition government was removed from power, but he remained in power after the third general election in three years in Sept. and Oct. 1999.

In March 2003 the BJP-led 24-party coalition government was composed as follows:

Prime Minister: Atal Behari Vajpayee; b. 1924 (BJP; sworn in 18 March 1998). *Deputy Prime Minister and Minister of Home Affairs:* Lal Krishna Advani (BJP). *Principal Secretary:* Brajesh Mishra (BJP). *External Affairs:* Yashwant Sinha (BJP). *Defence:* George Fernandes (JD-U). *Civil Aviation:* Syed Shahnawaz Hussain (BJP). *Heavy Industries and Public Enterprises:* Manohar Gajanan Joshi (Shiv Sena). *Human Resources Development, Science, Technology and in charge of Ocean Development:* Murli Manohar Joshi (BJP). *Agriculture:* Ajit Singh (Rashtriya Lok Dal). *Chemicals and Fertilizers:* Sukhdev Singh Dhindsa (Akali Dal). *Information and Broadcasting:* Sushma Swaraj (BJP). *Power:* Anant Geete (Shiv Sena). *Coal and Mines:* Vacant. *Textiles:* Kashi Ram Rana (BJP). *Finance:* Jaswant Singh (BJP). *Labour:* Sharad Yadav (JD-U). *Law, Justice and Company Affairs:* Arun Jaitley (BJP). *Urban Development and Poverty Alleviation:* Ananth Kumar (BJP). *Social Justice and Empowerment:* Satya Narayan Jatiya (BJP). *Communications, Parliamentary Affairs, Information and Technology:* Vacant. *Commerce and Industry:* Murasoli Maran (Dravida Munnetra Kazhagam). *Environment and Forests:* T. R. Baalu (Dravida Munnetra Kazhagam). *Petroleum and Natural Gas:* Ram Naik (BJP). *Tribal Affairs:* Jual Oram (BJP). *Rural Development:* Venkaiah Naidu (BJP). *Disinvestment and Additional Charge of Department of Development of Northeastern Region:* Arun Shourie (BJP). *Consumer Affairs, Food and Public Distribution:* Shanta Kumar (BJP). *Agro and Rural Industries:* Karia Munda (BJP). *Tourism, Programme Implementation and Statistics:* Jagmohan (BJP). *Sport and Youth Affairs:* Vikram Verma (BJP). *Health and Family Welfare:* Chandreshwar Thakur (BJP). *Water Resources:* Arjun Charan Sethi (Biju Janata Dal). *Shipping:* Ved Prakash Goyal (BJP). *Railways:* Nitish Kumar (Janata Dal Samata).

Office of the Prime Minister: http://www.pmindia.nic.in/

DEFENCE

The Supreme Command of the Armed Forces is vested in the President. As well as armed forces of 1,298,000 personnel in 2002, there was an active paramilitary force of 1,090,000, including 174,000 members of the Border Security Force based mainly in the troubled Jammu and Kashmir region. Military service is voluntary but, under the amended constitution, it is regarded as a fundamental duty of every citizen to perform National Service when called upon. Defence expenditure in 2001 was US$14,167m. (US$14 per capita and 2·9% of GDP). Defence accounted for 13% of spending in 1998–99.

Nuclear Weapons. India's first nuclear test was in 1974. Its most recent tests were a series of five carried out in May 1998. According to the Stockholm International Peace Research Institute, India's nuclear arsenal was estimated to consist of between 30 and 35 nuclear warheads in Jan. 2002. India, known to have a nuclear weapons programme, has not signed the Comprehensive Nuclear-Test-Ban-Treaty, which is intended to bring about a ban on any nuclear explosions. According to *Deadly Arsenals*, published by the Carnegie Endowment for International Peace, India has chemical weapons and has a biological weapons research programme.

Army. The Army is organized into five commands each divided into areas, which in turn are subdivided into sub-areas.

The strength of the Army in 2002 was 1·1m. An Aviation Corps operates locally-built helicopters. Army reserves number 300,000 with a further 500,000 personnel available as a second-line reserve force. There is a volunteer Territorial Army of 40,000.

There are numerous paramilitary groups including the Ministry of Defence *Rashtriya Rifles* (numbering 40,000), the Indo-Tibetan Border Police (32,400), the State Armed Police (400,000), the Civil Defence (453,000), the Central Industrial Security Force (95,000) and the Ministry of Home Affairs Assam Rifles (52,500).

Navy. The Navy has three commands; Eastern, Western and Southern, the latter a training and support command. The fleet is divided into two elements, Eastern and Western; and well-trained, all-volunteer personnel operate a mix of Soviet and western vessels.

The principal ship is the light aircraft carrier, *Viraat*, formerly HMS *Hermes*, of 29,000 tonnes, completed in 1959 and transferred to the Indian Navy in 1987 after seeing service in the Falklands War. The fleet includes 12 Soviet-built diesel submarines and 4 new German-designed boats. There are also 8 destroyers and 11 frigates. The Naval Air force, 5,000 strong, operates 35 combat aircraft (including 20 Sea Harriers) and 50 armed helicopters. Main bases are at Bombay (HQ Western Fleet, and main dockyard), Goa, Visakhapatnam (HQ Eastern Fleet) and Calcutta on the sub-continent, Port Blair in the Andaman Islands and Lakshadweep on the Laccadive Islands. HQ Southern Command is at Kochi.

Naval personnel in 2002 numbered 53,000 including 5,000 Naval Air Arm and 1,200 marines.

Air Force. Units of the IAF are organized into five operational commands—Western at Delhi, Central at Allahabad, Eastern at Shillong, Southern at Thiruvananthapuram and South-Western at Gandhinagar.

Equipment includes 701 combat aircraft, in 40 squadrons of aircraft, and 32 armed helicopters. Major combat types include Su-30s, MiG-21s, MiG-23s, MiG-27s, MiG-29s, *Jaguars* and Mirage 2000s. Air Force reserves numbered 140,000 in 2002.

INTERNATIONAL RELATIONS

India is a member of the UN, WTO, BIS, the Commonwealth, Asian Development Bank, Colombo Plan, SAARC and the Antarctic Treaty.

ECONOMY

Agriculture accounted for 29·3% of GDP in 1998, industry 24·8% and services 45·9%.

In the late 1990s there were ever-increasing signs of a divide between the south and west, where a modern economy is booming in cities such as Bangalore, Hyderabad and Madras, and the poorer and politically volatile areas in the north and east.

Overview. In the 1990s India was among the fastest-growing economies and foreign investment rose from almost nothing to over US$2bn. per year. But growth has slowed and poor infrastructure and high interest rates have reduced business confidence. The threat of military conflict with Pakistan has delayed moves towards economic reform. Much of heavy industry is publicly owned and inefficient state-owned enterprises harm growth. The move to privatize state-owned tele-communications companies and Air India is progressing slowly. In 2001 the rupee appreciated and monetary policy was eased. But financial market confidence remains fragile. In 2000 the Fiscal Responsibility and Budget Management Bill was introduced, requiring a deficit reduction of 0·5% of GDP per year to achieve a deficit of 2% of GDP by 2005–06.

Currency. A decimal system of coinage was introduced in 1957. The Indian *rupee* (INR) is divided into 100 *paise*. The paper currency consists of Reserve Bank notes and Government of India currency notes.

Foreign exchange reserves were US$54,703m. in June 2002 and gold reserves 11·50m. troy oz. Inflation was 3·8% in 2001.

The official exchange rate was abolished on 1 March 1993; the rupee now has a single market exchange rate and is convertible. The pound sterling is the currency of intervention. Total money supply in May 2002 was Rs 4,191·12bn.

Budget. Revenue and expenditure (on revenue account) of the central government for years ending 31 March, in Rs 1m.:

	1998–99	1999–2000[1]	2000–01[2]
Revenue	2,015,300	2,336,400	2,825,100
Expenditure	2,610,500	3,069,600	3,547,200

[1]Provisional. [2]Estimate.

Important items of revenue and expenditure on the revenue account of the central government for 1997–98 (estimates), in Rs 1m.:

Revenue		*Expenditure*	
Net tax revenue	1,379,568	General Services	1,167,096
Non-tax revenue	831,188	Defence	276,170
		Major subsidies	182,510

Total capital account receipts (1997–98 budget), Rs 2,774,893m.; capital account disbursements, Rs 2,777,284m. Total (revenue and capital) receipts, Rs 5,085,649m.; disbursements, Rs 5,390,693m.

Under the Constitution (Part XII and 7th Schedule), the power to raise funds has been divided between the central government and the states. Generally, the sources of revenue are mutually exclusive. Certain taxes are levied by the Union for the sake of uniformity and distributed to the states. The Finance Commission (Art. 280 of the Constitution) advises the President on the distribution of the taxes which are distributable between the centre and the states, and on the principles on which grants should be made out of Union revenues to the states. The main sources of central revenue are: customs duties; those excise duties levied by the central government; corporation, income and wealth taxes; estate and succession duties on non-agricultural assets and property, and revenues from the railways and posts and telegraphs.

In March 2002 finance minister Yashwant Sinha imposed a 5% surcharge on income tax to help combat the threat of terrorism in India.

Performance. India has one of the fastest-growing economies in Asia. Real GDP growth for 1998 was 5·8%, indicating that India managed to avoid the worst of the Asian crisis. In 1999 a growth rate of 6·7% was recorded, followed by 5·4% in 2000 and 4·1% in 2001. Critics claim that growth needs to be at least 8% in order to tackle the country's poverty. Total GDP in 2001 was US$477·6bn.

Banking and Finance. The Reserve Bank, the central bank for India, was established in 1934 and started functioning on 1 April 1935 as a shareholder's bank; it became a nationalized institution on 1 Jan. 1949. It has the sole right of issuing currency notes. The *Governor* is Dr Bimal Jalan. The Bank acts as adviser to the government on financial problems and is the banker for central and state governments, commercial banks and some other financial institutions. It manages the rupee public debt of central and state governments and is the custodian of the country's exchange reserve.

The commercial banking system consisted of 300 scheduled banks (*i.e.*, banks which are included in the 2nd schedule to the Reserve Bank Act) and four non-scheduled banks in Jan. 1993; scheduled banks included 196 Regional Rural Banks. Total deposits in commercial banks, March 1997, stood at Rs 5,035,960m. The business of non-scheduled banks forms less than 0·1% of commercial bank business. Of the 300 scheduled banks, 35 were foreign banks which specialize in financing foreign trade but also compete for domestic business. The State Bank of India acts as the agent of the Reserve Bank for transacting government business as well as undertaking commercial functions. The 27 public sector banks (which comprise the State Bank of India and its 7 associate banks and 19 nationalized banks) account for about 80·7% of deposits and about 78% of bank credit of all scheduled commercial banks.

There are stock exchanges in Ahmedabad, Bombay, Calcutta, Delhi, Madras and 18 other centres.

Weights and Measures. Uniform standards of weights and measures, based on the metric system, were established for the first time by the Standards of Weights and Measures Act, 1956.

A second Standards of Weights and Measures Act, 1976, recognizes the International System of Units and is in line with the recommendations of the International Organisation of Legal Metrology. This Act also protects consumers through proper indication of weight, quantity, identity, source, date and price on packaged goods.

While the Standards of Weights and Measures are laid down in the Central Act, enforcement of weights and measures laws is entrusted to the state governments; the central Directorate of Weights and Measures is responsible for co-ordinating activities so as to ensure national uniformity.

Frequent use is made in figures of the terms 'lakh' and 'crore'. 1 lakh = 100,000; 1 crore = 10m.

Calendar. The dates of the Saka era (named after the north Indian dynasty of the first century AD) are used alongside Gregorian dates in issues of the *Gazette* of India, news broadcasts by All-India Radio and government-issued calendars, from 22 March 1957, a date which corresponds with the first day of the year 1879 in the Saka era.

ENERGY AND NATURAL RESOURCES

Environment. According to the *World Bank Atlas* India's carbon dioxide emissions were equivalent to 1·1 tonnes per capita in 1998. An *Environmental Sustainability Index* compiled for the World Economic Forum meeting in Feb. 2002 ranked India 116th in the world out of 142 countries analysed, with 41·6%. The index measured the ability of countries to maintain favourable environmental conditions and examined various factors including pollution levels and the use or abuse of natural resources.

Electricity. Installed capacity in 1997 was 100m. kW. In Nov. 1996, 502,721 villages out of 579,132 had electricity. Production of electricity in 1998–99 (estimated) was 448·6bn. kWh, of which approximately 79% came from thermal stations, 2% from nuclear stations and 19% from hydro-electric stations. In 2001 there were 14 nuclear reactors in use. Electricity consumption per capita in 1998 was 384 kWh.

Oil and Gas. The Oil and Natural Gas Corporation Ltd and Oil India Ltd are the only producers of crude oil. Production 1996–97, 33·43m. tonnes, about 60% of consumption. The main fields are in Assam and Gujarat and offshore in the Gulf of Cambay (the Bombay High field). There were proven reserves of 4·8bn. bbls. in 1999. Natural gas production, 1999, 24·9bn. cu. metres with 650bn. cu. metres of proven reserves.

Water. 89·44m. ha (1995–96) irrigation potential had been created of which 79·89m. ha was utilized. Irrigation projects have formed an important part of all the Five-Year

Plans. The possibilities of diverting rivers into canals being nearly exhausted, the emphasis is now on damming the monsoon surplus flow and diverting that. Ultimate potential of irrigation is assessed at 107m. ha, total cultivated land being 185m. ha.

A Ganges water-sharing accord was signed with Bangladesh in 1997, ending a 25-year dispute which had hindered and dominated relations between the two countries.

Minerals. The coal industry was nationalized in 1973. Production, 1997, 298m. tonnes; recoverable reserves were estimated at 77bn. tonnes (1997). Production of other minerals, 1996–97 (in 1,000 tonnes): iron ore, 66,672; lignite, 23,031 (1997); salt, 9,500 (1998); bauxite, 5,928; chromite, 1,664 (1995–96); copper ore, 3,900; manganese ore, 1,836; gold, 2,712 kg. Other important minerals are lead, zinc, limestone, apatite and phosphorite, dolomite, magnesite, uranium and silver. Value of mineral production, 1996–97, Rs 330,204·3m. of which mineral fuels produced Rs 275,053m., metallic minerals Rs 24,295m. and non-metallic Rs 11,392·4m.

Agriculture. About 70% of the people are dependent on the land for their living. The farming year runs from July to June through three crop seasons: kharif (monsoon); rabi (winter) and summer. In 1998, 161,600,000 ha were used for arable land and 7,900,000 ha for permanent crops. There were 1,550,000 tractors and 4,100 harvester-threshers in 1998.

Agricultural production, 2000 (in 1,000 tonnes): sugarcane, 315,000; rice, 134,150; wheat, 74,251; potatoes, 23,500; mangoes, 15,642; bananas, 13,900; maize, 11,500; coconuts, 11,100; sorghum, 9,500; millet, 9,000; seed cotton, 6,172; rapeseed, 6,120; aubergines, 6,100; groundnuts, 6,100; cassava, 5,800; tomatoes, 5,500; onions, 5,467; soybeans, 5,400; chick-peas, 5,350; cauliflowers, 5,250; dry beans, 4,340; cabbages, 4,250; cottonseed, 4,115; pumpkins and squash, 3,400. Jute is grown in West Bengal (70% of total yield), Bihar and Assam: total yield, 1,740,000 tonnes. The coffee industry is growing: the main cash varieties are Arabica and Robusta (main growing areas Karnataka, Kerala and Tamil Nadu). India is the world's leading producer of a number of agricultural crops, including mangoes, millet, bananas and chick-peas.

The tea industry is important, with production concentrated in Assam, West Bengal, Tamil Nadu and Kerala. India is the world's largest tea producer. The 2000 crop was 749,000 tonnes. Total crop in 1997, 810,600 tonnes; exports in 1997, 203,000 tonnes, valued at US$432m.

Livestock (2000): cattle, 218·8m.; goats, 123·0m.; buffaloes, 93·8m.; sheep, 57·9m.; pigs, 16·5m.; asses, 1·0m.; camels, 1·0m.; horses, 990,000; chickens, 402m. There are more cattle and buffaloes in India than in any other country.

Fertilizer consumption in 1996–97 was 14·31m. tonnes.

Land Tenure. There are three main traditional systems of land tenure: *Ryotwari* tenure, where the individual holders are responsible for the payment of land revenues; *zamindari* tenure, where one or more persons own large estates and are responsible for payment (in this system there may be a number of intermediary holders); and *mahalwari* tenure, where village communities jointly hold an estate and are jointly and severally responsible for payment.

Agrarian reform, initiated in the first Five-Year Plan, being undertaken by the state governments includes: (1) The abolition of intermediaries under *zamindari* tenure. (2) Tenancy legislation designed to scale down rents to ¼–⅕ of the value of the produce, to give permanent rights to tenants (subject to the landlord's right to resume a minimum holding for his personal cultivation), and to enable tenants to acquire ownership of their holdings (subject to the landlord's right of resumption for personal cultivation) on payment of compensation over a number of years. (3) Fixing of ceilings on existing holdings and on future acquisition; the holding of a family is between 4·05 and 7·28 ha if it has assured irrigation to produce two crops a year; 10·93 ha for land with irrigation facilities for only one crop a year; and 21·85 ha for all other categories of land. Tea, coffee, cocoa and cardamom plantations have been exempted. (4) The consolidation of holdings in community project areas and the prevention of fragmentation of holdings by reform of inheritance laws. (5) Promotion of farming by co-operative village management.

The average size of holding for the whole of India in 1991 was 1·57 ha. Of the total 71m. rural households possessing operational holdings, 34% hold on the average less than 0·2 ha of land each.

Opium. By international agreement the poppy is cultivated under licence, and all raw opium is sold to the central government. Opium, other than for wholly medical use, is available only to registered addicts.

Forestry. The lands under the control of the state forest departments are classified as 'reserved forests' (forests intended to be permanently maintained for the supply of timber, etc., or for the protection of water supply, etc.), 'protected forests' and 'unclassed' forest land. In 1995 the total forest area was 650,050 sq. km (21·9% of the land area), up from 649,690 sq. km in 1990. India is one of only two developing countries to have increased its area under forests between 1990 and 1995, the other being Cape Verde. Main types are teak and sal. About 16% of the area is inaccessible, of which about 45% is potentially productive. In 1999, 302·79m. cu. metres of roundwood were produced, making India the third largest producer after China and the USA. Most states have encouraged planting small areas around villages.

Fisheries. Total catch (1999) was 3,316,815 tonnes, of which Kerala, Tamil Nadu, and Maharashtra produced about half. Of the total catch, 2,627,367 tonnes were marine fish. There were 46,918 mechanized boats in 1994–95. There were also 31,726 motorized traditional crafts and 159,481 traditional crafts in 1994–95. There were 11,440 fishermen's co-operatives with 1,250,379 members in 1995–96; total sales, Rs 1,495m. (1994–95).

INDUSTRY

The leading companies by market capitalization in India, excluding banking and finance, in Jan. 2002 were: Hindustan Lever Ltd (HLL), a consumer goods company (Rs 578bn.); Wipro Ltd, an IT solutions and service provider (Rs 380bn.); and the Oil & Natural Gas Corporation Ltd (ONGC), Rs 345bn.

In a number of industries new units are set up only by the state. Industries reserved for the public sector are arms and ammunition and allied items of defence equipment, military aircraft and warships, nuclear energy, coal and lignite, mineral oils and minerals specified in nuclear energy and railway transport. In a further group of industries (road transport, manufacture of chemicals such as drugs, dyestuffs, plastics and fertilizers) the state established new undertakings, but private enterprise may develop either on its own or with state backing.

The information technology industry has become increasingly important, leading Prime Minister Atal Vajpayee to state in 1999 that 'I believe that IT is India's tomorrow'. In 1994–95 the software industry had been valued at just Rs 63,450m., but by 1998–99 it was worth Rs 247,815m., with a forecast for 1999–2000 of a further rapid expansion, making it worth Rs 361,000m. (US$8,390m.).

Oil refinery installed capacity, Dec. 1996, was 60·55m. tonnes. The Indian Oil Corporation was established in 1964 and had (1996) the major portion of the market.

There is expansion in petrochemicals, based on the oil and associated gas of the Bombay High field, and gas from Krishna-Godavari Basin, Rajasthan, Tripura, Assam and Bassein field. Small industries numbering 2·72m. (initial outlay on capital equipment of less than Rs 30m.) are important; they employ about 15·26m. and produced (1995–96) goods worth Rs 3,164,210m.

Industrial production, 1995–96 unless otherwise indicated (in 1,000 tonnes): cement, 67,716; crude steel (1999), 24,300; distillate fuel oil (1997), 23,304; pig iron (1997), 20,027; finished steel, 14,533; sugar (1998), 14,281; residual fuel oil (1997), 10,775; nitrogen fertilizer, 9,768; phosphate fertilizer, 3,792; paper and paperboard (1998), 3,025; jute goods, 1,114; aluminium, 538·8; man-made fibre and yarn, 468; 3·05m. motorcycles, mopeds and scooters (1997); 293,172 commercial vehicles; 1,984,140 diesel engines; electric motors, 6·36m. h.p.; 384,000 passenger cars (1997); 19,044 railway wagons; 83·16bn. cigarettes (1997).

Labour. At the 1991 census there were 285·9m. workers, of whom 110·7m. were cultivators, 74·6m. agricultural labourers, 28·7m. in manufacturing, processing, servicing and repairs, 5·5m. in construction and 8·02m. in transport, communications and storage. Workdays lost by industrial disputes, 1995, 14·29m., through strikes and lockouts.

The unemployment rate was 5·2% of the workforce in 1997.

Companies. The total number of companies limited by shares at work as on 31 March 2002 was 589,246; estimated paid-up capital was Rs 3,870,239m. Of these, 76,279 were public limited companies with an estimated paid-up capital of Rs 2,587,149m., and 512,967 private limited companies (Rs 1,283,090m.).

During 2001–02 there were 21,059 new limited companies registered in the Indian Union under the Companies Act 1956 with a total authorized capital of Rs 53,156m.; 14 were government companies (Rs 5,781m.). There were 479 companies with unlimited liability and 3,007 companies with liability limited by guarantee and association not for profit also registered in 2001–02. During 2001–02, 760 non-government companies with an aggregate paid-up capital of Rs 144·7m. went into liquidation or were struck off the register.

On 31 March 2002 there were 1,261 government companies at work with a total paid-up capital of Rs 1,099,155m.; 658 were public limited companies and 603 were private limited companies. There were 587,985 non-government companies at work on 31 March 2002. Of these 75,621 were public limited companies and 512,364 were private limited companies.

On 31 March 2002, 1,285 companies incorporated elsewhere were reported to have a place of business in India; 241 were of UK and 286 of US origin.

Co-operative Movement. In 1995–96 there were 411,000 co-operative societies with a total membership of 197·8m. These included Primary Co-operative Marketing Societies, State Co-operative Marketing Federations and the National Agricultural Co-operative Marketing Federation of India. There were also State Co-operative Commodity Marketing Federations, and 29 general purpose and 16 Special Commodities Marketing Federations.

There were, in 1995–96, 28 State Co-operative Banks, 362 District Central Co-operative Banks, 90,783 Primary Agricultural Credit Societies, 20 State Land Development Banks, and 2,970 Primary Land Development Banks which provide long-term credits.

Agricultural credit is provided (31 Dec. 1993) through 32,641 rural and semi-rural branches of commercial banks and 14,543 branches of Regional Rural Banks, and (June 1993) 90,783 Primary Agricultural Credit Societies affiliated to 10,775 branches of District Central Co-operative Banks and 2,970 Primary units of Land Development Banks. Total agricultural credit disbursed by Co-operatives in 1995–96 was Rs 26,450m. Value of agricultural produce marketed by Co-operatives in 1994–95 was about Rs 95,000m. Commercial and regional rural banks disbursed agricultural credit of Rs 136,840m. in 1995–96.

In 1994–95 there were 2,601 agro-processing units; 245 sugar factories produced 8·66m. tons; 137 spinning mills (capacity 3·2m. spindles) accounted for 12% of total spindleage in the country in 1995–96; there were 129 oilseed processing units; total storage capacity was 13·55m. tons on 31 March 1996.

In 1994–95 there were 76,500 retail depots distributing 4·12m. tons of fertilizers.

Trade Unions. The Indian National Trade Union Congress (INTUC) had 3,987 affiliated unions with a total membership of 6,726,569 in March 2000.

INTERNATIONAL TRADE

Foreign investment is encouraged by a tax holiday on income up to 6% of capital employed for five years. There are special depreciation allowances, and customs and excise concessions, for export industries. Proposals for investment ventures involving up to 51% foreign equity require only the Reserve Bank's approval under new liberalized policy. In Feb. 1991 India resumed trans-frontier trade with China, which had ceased in 1962.

Foreign debt was US$99,062m. in 2000.

Imports and Exports. The external trade of India (excluding land-borne trade with Tibet and Bhutan) was as follows (in Rs 100,000):

	Imports	Exports and Re-exports
1999–2000	21,552,844	15,956,139
2000–01	23,087,276	20,357,101
2001–02	24,519,972	20,901,797

INDIA

The distribution of commerce by countries was as follows in the year ended 31 March 2000 (in Rs 100,000):

Countries	Exports to	Imports from	Countries	Exports to	Imports from
Afghanistan	14,388	9,121	Nepal	65,529	81,733
Argentina	27,132	150,567	Netherlands	383,592	204,056
Australia	173,737	468,765	New Zealand	27,864	41,817
Austria	32,537	28,855	Nigeria	127,263	1,268,952
Bahrain	26,094	162,807	Norway	22,138	18,638
Bangladesh	275,654	33,865	Pakistan	40,276	29,559
Belgium	578,815	1,595,196	Philippines	62,183	24,371
Brazil	568,482	143,385	Poland	39,718	16,680
Canada	250,446	164,884	Qatar	15,409	90,899
China	233,447	558,028	Romania	5,434	8,706
Czech Republic	14,625	17,093	Russia	410,723	270,043
Denmark	91,451	58,681	Saudi Arabia	321,682	1,307,140
Egypt	102,565	192,339	Senegal	8,691	37,834
France	386,952	311,229	Singapore	289,732	664,901
Germany	759,844	797,995	South Africa	123,426	873,467
Hong Kong	1,078,279	354,418	Spain	237,350	60,616
Hungary	13,737	5,366	Sri Lanka	216,298	19,167
Indonesia	139,810	415,471	Sweden	62,799	103,523
Iran	65,882	542,223	Switzerland	151,335	1,125,656
Israel	215,396	252,169	Taiwan	136,746	179,785
Italy	484,865	318,329	Tanzania	35,522	53,950
Japan	729,408	1,098,830	Thailand	194,718	142,030
Jordan	27,199	113,860	Tunisia	12,178	81,091
North Korea	7,184	29,114	Turkey	82,088	41,841
South Korea	206,196	551,774	UAE	899,208	1,011,494
Kuwait	66,849	828,595	UK	880,123	1,172,929
Malaysia	193,512	877,066	Ukraine	18,355	66,140
Mexico	61,050	41,811	USA	3,632,127	1,544,237
Morocco	11,335	182,040	Vietnam	66,888	4,994
Myanmar	14,772	74,356	Yemen	34,778	113,340

The value (in Rs 100,000) of the leading articles of merchandise was as follows in the year ended 31 March 2000:

Exports	Value
Carpet products (excluding silk)	216,075
Cashew nuts	245,661
Coffee	143,485
Cotton yarn, fabrics and made-up articles	1,338,810
Drugs, pharmaceuticals and fine chemicals	722,108
Dyes, intermediates and coal tar chemicals	254,662
Electronic goods	295,050
Engineering goods	1,900,404
Gems and jewellery	3,248,664
Handicrafts (excluding handmade carpets)	289,737
Inorganic and organic agro-chemicals	275,790
Iron ore	117,532
Leather garments	150,486
Leather goods	163,158
Man-made yarn, fabrics and made-up articles	351,586
Marine products	512,456
Oil meals	163,786
Plastics and linoleum	261,633
Processed minerals	120,079
Ready-made garments, including clothing accessories of all textile materials	2,064,840
Residual chemicals and allied products	139,043
Rice	312,592
Rubber manufactured products (except footwear)	126,409
Spices	176,743
Tea	178,467

Imports	Value
Artificial resins, plastic materials etc.	311,768
Chemical materials and products	156,326
Coal, coke and briquettes, etc.	436,833
Electronic goods	1,211,849
Fertilizers, manufactured	467,556

Imports	Value
Gold	1,799,091
Inorganic chemicals	575,584
Iron and steel	382,555
Machine tools	113,302
Machinery other than electric and electronic	1,189,471
Manufactures of metals	175,517
Medicinal and pharmaceutical products	161,622
Metalliferous ores and metal scrap	378,942
Non-ferrous metal	236,984
Organic chemicals	666,488
Pearls, precious and semi-precious stones	2,355,578
Petroleum, crude oil and related products	5,464,826
Professional instruments other than electronic	365,958
Project goods	427,373
Pulp and waste paper	110,564
Silver	241,195
Textile yarn, fabrics and made-up articles	100,220
Transport equipment	492,507
Vegetable oils (edible)	804,605
Wood and wood products	195,771

Technology industries have become increasingly important in recent years, with software exports having grown more than 50% annually each year during the 1990s. In 1998–99 software exports were worth Rs 109,400m. (US$2,650m.), with 61% going to the USA and Canada, and 23% to Europe. Exports grew by 67·5% in 1998–99 compared to 1997–98.

In 1995–96 the main export markets (percentage of total trade) were: USA, 17·4%; Japan, 6·97%; UK, 6·3%; Germany, 6·22%. Main import suppliers: USA, 10·53%; Germany, 8·66%; Japan, 6·73%; Saudi Arabia, 5·5%; Belgium, 4·64%.

COMMUNICATIONS

Roads. In 1996 there were 3·32m. km of roads, of which 1·46m. km were surfaced. Roads are divided into six main administrative classes, namely: national highways, state highways, other public works department (PWD) roads, *Panchayati Raj* roads, urban roads and project roads. The national highways (34,508 km in 1996) connect capitals of states, major ports and foreign highways. The national highway system is linked with the UN Economic and Social Commission for Asia and the Pacific international highway system. The state highways are the main trunk roads of the states, while the other PWD roads and *Panchayati Raj* roads connect subsidiary areas of production and markets with distribution centres, and form the main link between headquarters and neighbouring districts. A US$12bn. 10-year highway plan is currently under way that aims to have India's main cities, ports and regions linked by more than 13,000 km of highways by 2009.

There were (1996) 4,189,000 private cars, taxis and jeeps, 23,111,000 motorcycles and scooters, 449,000 buses and 1,785,000 goods vehicles.

Rail. The Indian railway system is government-owned (under the control of the Railway Board). Following reconstruction there are 16 zones, 7 of which were created in 2002:

Zone	Headquarters	Year of Creation
Central	Bombay	1951
Southern	Madras	1951
Western	Bombay	1951
Eastern	Calcutta	1952
Northern	Delhi	1952
North Eastern	Gorakhpur	1952
South Eastern	Calcutta	1955
North East Frontier	Guwahati	1958
South Central	Secunderabad	1966
East Central	Hajipur	2002
East Coast	Bhubaneswar	2002
North Central	Allahabad	2002
North Western	Jaipur	2002

Zone	Headquarters	Year of Creation
South East Central	Bilaspur	2002
South Western	Hubli	2002
West Central	Jabalpur	2002

The total length of the Indian railway network is 63,000 km (14,600 electrified), with the Northern zone having the longest network, at 11,040 km.

The Konkan Railway (760 km of 1,676 mm gauge) linking Roha and Mangalore opened in 1996. It is operated as a separate entity.

Principal gauges are 1,676 mm (40,620 km) and 1 metre (18,501 km), with networks also of 762 mm and 610 mm gauge (3,794 km).

Passengers carried in 1998–99 were 4,468m.; freight (1997–98), 423m. tonnes. Revenue (1995–96) from passengers, Rs 61,244·9m.; from goods, Rs 152,904m.

Indian Railways pay to the central government a dividend on capital-at-charge at a rate fixed by the Convention Committee of Parliament. Railway finance in Rs 1m.:

Financial years	Gross traffic receipts	Gross expenditure	Net revenues (receipts)	Net surplus or deficit (after dividend)
1995–96	224,179	185,249	41,351	+23,180
1996–97 revised	244,500	209,650	37,563	+22,410
1997–98 budget	278,550	251,350	30,037	+13,740

There is a metro (16·4 km) in Calcutta. The first section of a metro system in Delhi opened in Dec. 2002.

Civil Aviation. The main international airports are at Bombay, Calcutta, Delhi (Indira Gandhi), Madras and Thiruvananthapuram, with some international flights from Ahmedabad, Amritsar, Bangalore, Calicut, Goa and Hyderabad. Air transport was nationalized in 1953 with the formation of two Air Corporations: Air India for long-distance international air services, and Indian Airlines for air services within India and to adjacent countries. Domestic air transport has been opened to private companies, and by 1996–97, seven private airlines had been given scheduled status, the largest of which is Jet Airways. In 1999 Indian Airlines carried 5,912,100 passengers, Jet Airways 4,647,400 and Air India 3,132,600 passengers.

In 1998 Air India operated routes to Africa (Dar-es-Salaam, Lagos and Nairobi); to Mauritius; to Europe (Copenhagen, Frankfurt, London, Manchester, Moscow, Paris, Rome, Vienna and Zürich); to western Asia (Abu Dhabi, Dhahran, Doha, Dubai, Jeddah, Kuwait, Muscat and Riyadh); to east Asia (Bangkok, Hong Kong, Jakarta, Kuala Lumpur, Osaka, Singapore and Tokyo); and to North America (Chicago, New York and Washington). In addition, freight services are operated to Zürich, Brussels, Dubai, Singapore and Luxembourg.

Indian Airlines operated international flights in 1998 to Bahrain, Bangkok, Colombo, Dhaka, Doha, Fujairah, Karachi, Káthmandu, Kuala Lumpur, Kuwait, Male, Rangoon (Yangon), Ras-al-Khaimah, Sharjah and Singapore.

In 2000 Bombay was the busiest airport, handling 11,538,006 passengers (6,934,116 on domestic flights) and 287,800 tonnes of freight, followed by Delhi, with 8,395,736 passengers (4,900,597 on domestic flights) and 235,425 tonnes of freight.

Shipping. In Oct. 1996, 481 ships totalling 7·02m. GRT were on the Indian Register. In 1998 merchant ships totalled 6·77m. GRT, including oil tankers 2·53m. GRT. Traffic of major ports, 1996–97, was as follows:

Port	Cargo ships cleared	Unloaded (1m. tonnes)	Loaded (1m. tonnes)
Bombay	2,583	18·38	15·35
Cochin	787	8·54	2·09
Haldia	946	} 11·99	5·06
Calcutta	822		
Jawaharlal Nehru	601	4·68	3·39
Kandla	1,527	27·08	4·48
Madras	1,660	21·42	9·40
Mormugao	507	4·77	18·41
New Mangalore	644	4·45	7·97
Paradip	556	3·89	7·72
Tuticorin	905	7·61	1·58
Visakhapatnam	1,437	14·67	13·28

There are about 3,700 km of major rivers navigable by motorized craft, of which 2,000 km are used. Canals, 4,300 km, of which 900 km are navigable by motorized craft.

Telecommunications. The telephone system is in the hands of the Telecommunications Department, except in Delhi and Bombay, which are served by a public corporation. Main telephone lines numbered 32,436,100 in 2000, equivalent to 32·0 for every 1,000 persons; 2·7m. people were still on the waiting list for a line in 1997. There were 1·88m. mobile phone subscribers and 4·6m. PCs in use in 2000, and 150,000 fax machines in 1997. There were still 25,000 telex subscribers in 1997, although telex usage has declined steadily in recent years. India had 7m. Internet users in Dec. 2001.

Postal Services. On 31 March 1995 there were 152,792 post offices and 42,766 telegraph offices. India has twice as many post offices as any other country. In 1995 a total of 13,751m. pieces of mail were processed, or 15 items per person.

SOCIAL INSTITUTIONS

Justice. All courts form a single hierarchy, with the Supreme Court at the head, which constitutes the highest court of appeal. Immediately below it are the High Courts and subordinate courts in each state. Every court in this chain administers the whole law of the country, whether made by Parliament or by the state legislatures.

The states of Andhra Pradesh, Assam (in common with Nagaland, Meghalaya, Manipur, Mizoram, Tripura and Arunachal Pradesh), Bihar, Gujarat, Himachal Pradesh, Jammu and Kashmir, Karnataka, Kerala, Madhya Pradesh, Maharashtra (in common with Goa and the Union Territories of Daman and Diu and Dadra and Nagar Haveli), Orissa, Punjab (in common with the state of Haryana and the Union Territory of Chandigarh), Rajasthan, Tamil Nadu (in common with the Union Territory of Pondicherry), Uttar Pradesh, West Bengal and Sikkim each have a High Court. There is a separate High Court for Delhi. For the Andaman and Nicobar Islands the Calcutta High Court, for Pondicherry the High Court of Madras and for Lakshadweep the High Court of Kerala are the highest judicial authorities. The Allahabad High Court has a Bench at Lucknow, the Bombay High Court has Benches at Nagpur, Aurangabad and Panaji, the Gauhati High Court has Benches at Kohima, Aizwal, Imphal and Agartala, the Madhya Pradesh High Court has Benches at Gwalior and Indore, the Patna High Court has a Bench at Ranchi and the Rajasthan High Court has a Bench at Jaipur. Judges and Division Courts of the Guwahati High Court also sit in Meghalaya. Similarly, judges and Division Courts of the Calcutta High Court also sit in the Andaman and Nicobar Islands. High Courts have also been established in the new states of Chhattisgarh, Jharkhand and Uttaranchal. Below the High Court each state is divided into a number of districts under the jurisdiction of district judges who preside over civil courts and courts of sessions. There are a number of judicial authorities subordinate to the district civil courts. On the criminal side magistrates of various classes act under the overall supervision of the High Court.

The Code of Criminal Procedure came into force with effect from 1 April 1974. It provides for complete separation of the Judiciary from the Executive throughout India.

In Oct. 1991 the Supreme Court upheld capital punishment by hanging.

The population in penal institutions in 1997 was 231,325 (25 per 100,000 of national population).

Police. The states control their own police forces. The Home Affairs Minister of the central government co-ordinates the work of the states. The Indian Police Service provides senior officers for the state police forces. The Central Bureau of Investigation functions under the control of the Cabinet Secretariat.

The cities of Pune, Ahmedabad, Nagpur, Bangalore, Calcutta, Madras, Bombay, Delhi and Hyderabad have separate police commissionerates.

Religion. India is a secular state; any worship is permitted, but the state itself has no religion. The principal religions in 1997 were: Hindus, 777m.; Sunni Muslims, 80m.; Shiah Muslims, 27m.; Sikhs, 19m.; Protestants, 18m.; Roman Catholics, 16m.; Buddhists, 7m.; Jains, 5m.; other, 19m. In Feb. 2001 the Roman Catholic church had four Cardinals.

Education. Adult literacy was 56·5% in 1999 (67·8% among males and 44·5% among females). Of the states and territories, Kerala and Mizoram have the highest rates.

Educational Organization. Education is the concurrent responsibility of state and Union governments. In the Union Territories it is the responsibility of the central government. The Union government is also directly responsible for the central universities and all institutions declared by parliament to be of national importance; the promotion of Hindi as the federal language and co-ordinating and maintaining standards in higher education, research, science and technology. Professional education rests with the Ministry or Department concerned. There is a Central Advisory Board of Education to advise the Union and the State governments on any educational question which may be referred to it.

School Education. The school system has four stages: primary, middle, secondary and senior secondary.

Primary education is imparted either at independent primary (or junior basic) schools or primary classes attached to middle or secondary schools. The period of instruction varies from four to five years and the medium of instruction is in most cases the mother tongue of the child or the regional language. Free primary education is available for all children. Legislation for compulsory education has been passed by some state governments and Union Territories but it is not practicable to enforce compulsion when the reasons for non-attendance are socio-economic. There are residential schools for country children. The period for the middle stage varies from two to three years.

Higher Education. Higher education is given in arts, science or professional colleges, universities and all-India educational or research institutions. In 1995–96 there were 166 universities, 4 institutes established under state legislature act, 11 institutions of national importance and 37 institutions deemed as universities. Of the universities, 13 are central: Aligarh Muslim University; Banaras Hindu University; Delhi University; Hyderabad University; Jamia Millia Islamia, New Delhi; Jawaharlal Nehru University; North Eastern Hill University; Visva Bharati; Pondicherry University; Baba Sahib B. R. Ambedkar University; Assam University; Tezpur University; and Nagaland University. The rest are state universities. Total enrolment at universities, 1995–96, 6,425,624, of which 5,667,400 were undergraduates. Women students numbered 2,191,138.

Grants are paid through the University Grants Commission to the central universities and institutions deemed to be universities for their maintenance and development and to state universities for their development projects only; their maintenance is the concern of state governments. During 1995–96 the University Grants Commission sanctioned grants of Rs 6,245·5m.

Technical Education. The number of institutions awarding degrees in engineering and technology in 1996–97 was 418, and those awarding diplomas, 1,029; the former admitted 328,399 students, the latter 357,891 including 58,454 female students.

Adult Education. The Directorate of Adult Education, established in 1971, is the national resource centre.

There is also a National Literacy Mission.

Educational statistics for 1996–97:

Type of recognized institution	No. of institutions	No. of students on rolls	No. of teachers
Primary/junior basic schools	598,354	110,393,406	1,789,733
Middle/senior basic schools	176,772	41,064,849	1,195,845
High/higher secondary schools[1]	102,183	27,036,856	1,542,360
Training schools and colleges	1,931	237,509	—
Arts, Science and Commerce colleges	6,759	6,425,624	239,488

[1]Including Junior Colleges.

Expenditure. Total budgeted central expenditure on revenue account of education and other departments 1997–98 was estimated at Rs 46,383m. Total public expenditure on education, sport, arts and youth welfare during the Eighth (1992–97) Plan, Rs 212,170·2m.; Seventh Plan spending on adult education, Rs 3,007m. in the central and Rs 6,098m. in the state sectors.

Health. Medical services are primarily the responsibility of the states. The Union government has sponsored major schemes for disease prevention and control which are implemented nationally.

Total central expenditure on health and family welfare in 1997–98 was Rs 14,166·2m. on revenue account. In 1991 there were 15,067 hospitals, and in 1992, 410,875 doctors. In 1993 there were an estimated 1,364 people per hospital bed.

In 1997 approximately 204m. people, representing 22% of the population, were undernourished. In 1979, 38% of the population had been undernourished.

Approximately 3·7m. Indians are HIV-infected, a number only exceeded in South Africa (and equivalent to nearly 9% of all the people believed to be infected worldwide). Some suggestions indicate that there may be as many as 15m. HIV-positive people by 2010.

CULTURE

Broadcasting. In March 1997 there were 187 radio stations and 297 transmitters, 19 channels and 41 programme production centres. Television reached 85·8% of the population, through a network of 834 transmitters (colour by PAL). There were estimated to be 116m. radio sets and 63m. TV sets in 1997. There were 18m. cable TV subscribers in 1997—approximately 29% of households that had TV licences. By 2000 the number of TV sets had increased to 75m. and cable subscribers to 37m.

Cinema. In 1996 there were nearly 13,000 cinemas and 683 feature films were certified. Attendances totalled 90m.–100m. per week. In 1990, 948 full length films were produced.

Press. There were 41,000 registered newspapers in March 1996, with a total circulation of 72·3m. In 1994 there were 369 dailies in 18 languages with a total circulation of 20m. Hindi papers have the highest number and circulation, followed by English, then Urdu, Bengali and Marathi. The newspaper with the highest circulation is *Kerala Kaumudi* (daily average of 1·7m. copies in 1999). In 1996 a total of 11,903 book titles were published.

It was estimated in 1999 that 29% of the electorate of 620m. for the general election had no access to any sort of news media.

Tourism. In 1999 there were 2,482,000 foreign tourists, spending US$3·04bn. Of 2,359,000 foreign tourists in 1998, over 360,000 were from the UK, 229,000 from the USA and 107,000 from Sri Lanka.

DIPLOMATIC REPRESENTATIVES

Of India in the United Kingdom (India House, Aldwych, London, WC2B 4NA)
High Commissioner: Randendra Sen.

Of the United Kingdom in India (Chanakyapuri, New Delhi 110021)
High Commissioner: Sir Rob Young, KCMG.

Of India in the USA (2107 Massachusetts Ave., NW, Washington, D.C., 20008)
Ambassador: Lalit Mansingh.

Of the USA in India (Shanti Path, Chanakyapuri, New Delhi 110021)
Ambassador: Robert Blackwill.

Of India to the United Nations
Ambassador: Vijay K. Nambiar.

Of India to the European Union
Ambassador: Pradeep Kumar Singh.

FURTHER READING
Bhambhri, C. P., *The Political Process in India, 1947–91.* Delhi, 1991
Bose, S. and Jalal, A. (eds.) *Nationalism, Democracy and Development: State and Politics in India.* OUP, 1997
Brown, J., *Modern India: The Origins of an Asian Democracy.* 2nd ed. OUP, 1994
Derbyshire, I., *India.* [Bibliography] 2nd ed. ABC-Clio, Oxford and Santa Barbara (CA), 1995
Gupta, D. C., *Indian Government and Politics.* 3rd ed. London, 1992
Jaffrelot, C. (ed.) *L'Inde Contemporain de 1950 à nos Jours.* Paris, 1996
James, L., *Raj: The Making and Unmaking of British India.* Little, Brown, London, 1997

Joshi, V. and Little, I. M. D., *India's Economic Reforms, 1991–2000*. Oxford, 1996
Keay, John, *India: A History*. HarperCollins, London, 2000
Khilnani, S., *The Idea of India*. London, 1997
King, R., *Nehru and the Language Politics of India*. OUP, 1997
Metcalf, Barbara D. and Metcalf, Thomas R., *A Concise History of India*. CUP, 2001
New Cambridge History of India. 2nd ed. 5 vols. CUP, 1994–96
Robb, Peter, *A History of India*. Palgrave, Basingstoke, 2002
Vohra, R., *The Making of India: A Historical Survey*. Armonk (NY), 1997

National statistical office: Ministry of Statistics and Programme Implementation.
Website: http://mospi.nic.in/
Census India Website: http://www.censusindia.net/
Other more specialized titles are listed under CONSTITUTION AND GOVERNMENT *and* RECENT ELECTIONS, *above.*

STATES AND TERRITORIES

The Republic of India is composed of the following 28 States and 7 centrally administered Union Territories:

States	Capital	States	Capital
Andhra Pradesh	Hyderabad	Maharashtra	Bombay
Arunachal Pradesh	Itanagar	Manipur	Imphal
Assam	Dispur	Meghalaya	Shillong
Bihar	Patna	Mizoram	Aizawl
Chhattisgarh	Raipur	Nagaland	Kohima
Goa	Panaji	Orissa	Bhubaneswar
Gujarat	Gandhinagar	Punjab	Chandigarh
Haryana	Chandigarh	Rajasthan	Jaipur
Himachal Pradesh	Shimla	Sikkim	Gangtok
Jammu and Kashmir	Srinagar	Tamil Nadu	Madras
Jharkhand	Ranchi	Tripura	Agartala
Karnataka	Bangalore	Uttar Pradesh	Lucknow
Kerala	Thiruvananthapuram	Uttaranchal	Dehra Dun (provisional)
Madhya Pradesh	Bhopal	West Bengal	Calcutta

Union Territories. Andaman and Nicobar Islands; Chandigarh; Dadra and Nagar Haveli; Daman and Diu; Delhi; Lakshadweep; Pondicherry.

ANDHRA PRADESH

KEY HISTORICAL EVENTS

Constituted a separate state on 1 Oct. 1953, Andhra Pradesh was the undisputed Telugu-speaking area of Madras. To this region was added, on 1 Nov. 1956, the Telangana area of the former Hyderabad State, comprising the districts of Hyderabad, Medak, Nizamabad, Karimnagar, Warangal, Khammam, Nalgonda and Mahbubnagar, parts of the Adilabad district, some taluks of the Raichur, Gulbarga and Bidar districts and some revenue circles of the Nanded district. On 1 April 1960, 221·4 sq. miles in the Chingleput and Salem districts of Madras were transferred to Andhra Pradesh in exchange for 410 sq. miles from Chittoor district. The district of Prakasam was formed on 2 Feb. 1970. Hyderabad was split into two districts on 15 Aug. 1978 (Ranga Reddy and Hyderabad). A new district, Vizianagaram, was formed in 1979.

TERRITORY AND POPULATION

Andhra Pradesh is in south India and is bounded in the south by Tamil Nadu, west by Karnataka, north and northwest by Maharashtra, northeast by Chhattisgarh and Orissa and east by the Bay of Bengal. The state has an area of 275,069 sq. km and a population (2001 census, provisional) of 75,727,541; density, 275 per sq. km. The principal language is Telugu. Cities with over 250,000 population (1991 census), *see* INDIA: Territory and Population. Other large cities (1991): Nizamabad (241,034); Kurnool (236,800); Ramagundam (214,384); Eluru (212,866); Anantapur (174,924); Tirupati (174,369); Vizianagaram (160,359); Machilipatnam (159,110); Karimnagar (148,583); Tenali (143,726); Adoni (136,182); Proddutur (133,914); Chittoor (133,462); Khammam (127,992); Cuddapah (121,463); Bheemavaram (121,314).

SOCIAL STATISTICS
Growth rate 1991–2001, 13·86%.

CONSTITUTION AND GOVERNMENT
Andhra Pradesh has a unicameral legislature; the Legislative Council was abolished in June 1985. There are 294 seats in the Legislative Assembly. For administrative purposes there are 23 districts in the state. The capital is Hyderabad.

RECENT ELECTIONS
At the State Assembly elections held in Sept. 1999, the Telugu Desam Party gained 180 seats (43% of the vote); the India National Congress party, 91 (40%); the Bharatiya Janata party, 12 (3%); independents, 5 (4%); All India Majlis-E-Ittehadul Muslimeem, 4 (2%); the Communist Party of India (Marxist), 2 (1%).

CURRENT ADMINISTRATION
Governor: Surjit Singh Barnala.
 Chief Minister: N. Chandrababu Naidu.

ECONOMY
Budget. Budget estimate, 1996–97: receipts on revenue account, Rs 114,516·3m.; expenditure, Rs 120,561·8m. Annual plan, 1997–98: Rs 35,330m.

ENERGY AND NATURAL RESOURCES
Electricity. There are 13 hydro-electric plants, 9 thermal stations and 2 gas-based units. Installed capacity, 1996–97, 6,800 MW, power generated 27,865m. kWh. In Nov. 1996 all 27,358 villages were electrified and 1·74m. electric pump sets energized.

Oil and Gas. Crude oil is refined at Visakhapatnam in Andhra Pradesh. Oil/gas structures are found in Krishna-Godavari basin which encompasses an area of 20,000 sq. km on land and 21,000 sq. km up to 200 metres isobath off-shore. Reserves of the land basin are estimated at 760 metric tonnes of oil and oil equivalent of gas.

Water. In 1997, 30 major and 75 medium irrigation projects had created irrigation potential of 5·7m. ha. The Telugu Ganga joint project with Tamil Nadu, now in execution, will irrigate about 233,000 ha, besides supplying drinking water to Madras city (Tamil Nadu).

Minerals. The state is an important producer of asbestos and barytes. Other important minerals are copper ore, coal, iron and limestone, steatite, mica and manganese.

Agriculture. There were (1996) about 13·4m. ha of cropped land, of which 8·2m. ha were under foodgrains. Irrigated area, 1996, 5·30m. ha. Production in 1996 (in tonnes): foodgrains, 11·66m. (rice, 9·01m.); pulses, 0·77m.; sugarcane, 15·16m.; oil seeds, 3·03m.
 Livestock (1993): cattle, 10·95m.; buffaloes, 9·13m.; goats, 4·32m.; sheep, 7·77m.

Forestry. In 1996–97 it was estimated that forests occupy 23·2% of the total area of the state, or 63,813 sq. km; main forest products are teak, eucalyptus, cashew, casuarina, softwoods and bamboo.

Fisheries. Production 1996–97, 152,047 tonnes of marine fish and 207,312 tonnes of inland water fish. The state has a coastline of 974 km.

INDUSTRY
The main industries are textile manufacture, sugar-milling, machine tools, pharmaceuticals, electronic equipment, heavy electrical machinery, aircraft parts and paper-making. There is an oil refinery at Visakhapatnam, where India's major shipbuilding yards are situated. A major steel plant at Visakhapatnam and a railway repair shop at Tirupati are functioning. At 31 March 1997 there were 1,536 large and medium industries employing 644,480 persons, and 124,209 small-scale industries employing 1m. There are cottage industries and sericulture. District

Industries Centres have been set up to promote small-scale industry. Tourism is growing; the main centres are Hyderabad, Nagarjunasagar, Warangal, Arakuvalley, Horsley Hills and Tirupati.

COMMUNICATIONS

Roads. In 1996–97 there were 2,949 km of national highways, 43,763 km of state highways and 103,971 km of major district roads. Number of vehicles as of 31 March 1997 was 2,783,220, including 2,287,029 motorcycles and scooters, 177,516 cars and jeeps and 187,863 goods vehicles.

Rail. There are 5,073 route-km of railway.

Civil Aviation. There are airports at Hyderabad, Tirupati, Vijayawada and Visakhapatnam, with regular scheduled services to Bombay, Delhi, Calcutta, Bangalore and Madras. International flights are operated from Hyderabad to Kuwait, Muscat, Sharjah and Jeddah.

Shipping. The chief port is Visakhapatnam. There are minor ports at Kakinada, Machilipatnam, Bheemunipatnam, Narsapur, Krishnapatnam, Nizampatnam, Vadarevu and Kalingapatnam.

SOCIAL INSTITUTIONS

Justice. The high court of Judicature at Hyderabad has a Chief Justice and 28 puisne judges.

Religion. At the 1991 census Hindus numbered 59,281,950; Muslims, 5,923,954; Christians, 1,216,348; Jains, 26,564; Sikhs, 21,910; Buddhists, 22,153.

Education. In 2001, 61·11% of the population were literate (70·85% of men and 51·17% of women). There were, in 1996–97, 48,899 primary schools (7,898,481 students); 7,733 upper primary (2·30m.); 8,178 high schools (1,055,390). Education is free for children up to 14.

In 1995–96 there were 1,818 junior colleges (676,455 students). In 1996–97 there were 805 degree colleges (427,652 students); 46 oriented colleges and 13 universities: Osmania University, Hyderabad; Andhra University, Waltair; Sri Venkateswara University, Tirupati; Kakatiya University, Warangal; Nagarjuna University, Guntur; Sri Jawaharlal Nehru Technological University, Hyderabad; Hyderabad University, Hyderabad; N. G. Ranga Agricultural University, Hyderabad; Sri Krishnadevaraya University, Anantapur; Smt. Padmavathi Mahila Vishwavidyalayam (University for Women), Tirupati; Dr B. R. Ambedkar Open University, Hyderabad; Patti Sriramulu Telugu University, Hyderabad; and N. T. R. University of Health Science, Vijayawada.

Health. There were (1996) 1,947 allopathic hospitals and dispensaries, 550 Ayurvedic hospitals and dispensaries, 193 Unani and 283 homoeopathy hospitals and dispensaries. There were also 181 nature cure hospitals and (in 1996–97) 1,335 primary health centres. Number of beds in hospitals was 32,116.

ARUNACHAL PRADESH

KEY HISTORICAL EVENTS

Before independence the North East Frontier Agency of Assam was administered for the viceroy by a political agent working through tribal groups. After independence it became the North East Frontier Tract, administered for the central government by the Governor of Assam. In 1972 the area became the Union Territory of Arunachal Pradesh; statehood was achieved in Dec. 1986.

TERRITORY AND POPULATION

The state is in the extreme northeast of India and is bounded in the north by China, east by Myanmar, west by Bhutan and south by Assam and Nagaland. It has 13 districts and comprises the former frontier divisions of Kameng, Tirap, Subansiri,

Siang and Lohit; it has an area of 83,743 sq. km and a population (2001 census, provisional) of 1,091,117; density, 13 per sq. km.

The state is mainly tribal; there are 106 tribes using about 50 tribal dialects.

SOCIAL STATISTICS
Growth rate 1991–2001, 26·21%.

CONSTITUTION AND GOVERNMENT
There is a Legislative Assembly of 60 members. The capital is Itanagar (population, 1991, 16,545).

RECENT ELECTIONS
At the State Assembly elections in Oct. 1999 the India National Congress Party obtained 62% of the vote, winning 53 seats. The Nationalist Congress Party won 4 seats, independents 2 and the Arunachal Party 1.

CURRENT ADMINISTRATION
Governor: Arvind Dave.
Chief Minister: Mukut Mithi.

ECONOMY
Budget. Total estimated receipts, 1997–98, Rs 10,581m.; total estimated expenditure, Rs 10,302m. Plan outlay, 1997–98, Rs 6,000m.

ENERGY AND NATURAL RESOURCES
Electricity. Total installed capacity (1995–96), 43·85 MW. Power generated (1995–96): 70·8m. units. 2,188 out of 3,257 villages have electricity.

Oil and Gas. Production, 1995–96, 28,000 tonnes of crude oil and 32m. cu. metres of gas. Crude oil reserves are estimated at 30m. tonnes.

Minerals. Coal reserves are estimated at 90·23m. tonnes; dolomite, 154·13m. tonnes; limestone, 409·35m. tonnes.

Agriculture. Production of foodgrains, 1995–96, 230,200 tonnes.

Forestry. Area under forest, 51,540 sq. km; revenue from forestry (1995–96) Rs 402m.

INDUSTRY
In 1996 there were 18 medium and 3,306 small industries, 80 craft or weaving centres and 225 sericulture centres. Most of the medium industries are forest-based.

COMMUNICATIONS
Total length of roads in the state, 12,250 km of which 9,855 km are surfaced. There were 14,821 vehicles in 1995–96. The state has 330 km of national highway. Four towns are linked by air services.

SOCIAL INSTITUTIONS
Religion. At the 1991 census Hindus numbered 320,212; Muslims, 11,922; Christians, 89,013; Buddhists, 111,372.

Education. In 2001, 54·74% of the population were literate (64·07% of men and 44·24% of women). There were (1996–97) 1,256 primary schools with 147,676 students, 301 middle schools with 42,197 students, 157 high and higher secondary schools with 24,951 students, 6 colleges and 2 technical schools. Arunachal University, established in 1985, had 4 colleges and 3,240 students in 1994–95.

Health. There are (1996) 13 hospitals, 10 community health centres, 42 primary health centres and 260 sub-centres. There are 2 TB hospitals and 11 leprosy and other hospitals. Total number of beds, 2,539.

FURTHER READING
Bose, M. L., *History of Arunachal Pradesh.* Concept Publications, New Delhi, 1997

ASSAM

KEY HISTORICAL EVENTS

Assam first became a British Protectorate at the close of the first Burmese War in 1826. In 1832 Cachar was annexed; in 1835 the Jaintia Hills were included in the East India Company's dominions, and in 1839 Assam was annexed to Bengal. In 1874 Assam was detached from Bengal and made a separate chief commissionership. On the partition of Bengal in 1905, it was united to the Eastern Districts of Bengal under a Lieut.-Governor. From 1912 the chief commissionership of Assam was revived, and in 1921 a governorship was created. On the partition of India almost the whole of the predominantly Muslim district of Sylhet was merged with East Bengal (Pakistan). Dewangiri in North Kamrup was ceded to Bhutan in 1951. The Naga Hill district, administered by the Union government since 1957, became part of Nagaland in 1962. The autonomous state of Meghalaya within Assam, comprising the districts of Garo Hills and Khasi and Jaintia Hills, came into existence on 2 April 1970, and achieved full independent statehood in Jan. 1972, when it was also decided to form a Union Territory, Mizoram (now a state), from the Mizo Hills district.

TERRITORY AND POPULATION

Assam is in northeast India, almost separated from central India by Bangladesh. It is bounded in the west by West Bengal, north by Bhutan and Arunachal Pradesh, east by Nagaland, Manipur and Myanmar, south by Meghalaya, Bangladesh, Mizoram and Tripura. The area of the state is now 78,438 sq. km. Population (2001 census, provisional) 26,638,407; density, 340 per sq. km. Principal towns with population (1991) are; Guwahati, 584,342; Dibrugarh, 125,667; Silchar, 115,483; Nagaon, 93,350; Tinsukia, 73,918; Dhubri, 66,216; Jorhat, 58,358; Tezpur, 55,084. The principal language is Assamese.

The central government is surveying the line of a proposed boundary fence to prevent illegal entry from Bangladesh.

SOCIAL STATISTICS

Growth rate 1991–2001, 18·85%.

CONSTITUTION AND GOVERNMENT

Assam has a unicameral legislature of 126 members. The capital is Dispur. The state has 23 districts.

RECENT ELECTIONS

In the elections of 10 May 2001 the Indian National Congress (INC) took 70 seats, Asom Gana Parishad 20 and Bharatiya Janata Party (BJP) 8.

CURRENT ADMINISTRATION

Governor: Lieut.-Gen. (retd) S. K. Sinha.
   Chief Minister: Tarun Gogoi.

ECONOMY

Budget. The budget estimates for 1997–98 showed receipts of Rs 72,312m. and expenditure of Rs 75,064·5m. Plan allocation, 1997–98, Rs 15,000m.

ENERGY AND NATURAL RESOURCES

Electricity. In 1996–97 there was an installed capacity of 597 MW. In March 1996, 21,887 villages (out of 21,995) had electricity. New power stations are under construction at Lakwa, and Karbi-Langpi hydro-electricity project.

Oil and Gas. Assam contains important oilfields and produces about 15% of India's crude oil. Production (1995–96): crude oil, 5·04m. tonnes (including Nagaland); gas, 1,881m. cu. metres.

Minerals. Coal production (1991), 982,000 tonnes. The state also has limestone, refractory clay, dolomite and corundum.

Agriculture. There are 848 tea plantations, and growing tea is the principal industry. Production in 1990–91, 380m. kg, over 50% of Indian tea. Over 72% of the cultivated area is under food crops, of which the most important is rice. Total foodgrains, 1995–96, 3·56m. tonnes. Main cash crops: jute, tea, cotton, oilseeds, sugarcane, fruit and potatoes. Wheat production, 95,100 tonnes in 1995–96; rice, 3·39m. tonnes; pulses, 57,100 tonnes. Cattle are important.

Forestry. In 1996 there were 18,242 sq. km of reserved forests under the administration of the Forest Department and 8,530 sq. km of unclassed forests, altogether about 39% of the total area of the state. Revenue from forests, 1993–94, Rs 213·1m.

INDUSTRY
Sericulture and hand-loom weaving, both silk and cotton, are important home industries together with the manufacture of brass, cane and bamboo articles. The main heavy industry is petro-chemicals; there are four oil refineries in the region. Other industries include manufacturing paper, nylon, electronic goods, cement, fertilizers, sugar, jute and plywood products, rice and oil milling.

There were 17,103 small-scale industries in 1994. The state in 1991 ran 480,622 enterprises employing 1·3m. persons.

COMMUNICATIONS
Roads. In March 1992 there were 65,605 km of road maintained by the Public Works Department. There were 2,033 km of national highway in 1990. There were 358,664 motor vehicles in the state in 1995–96.

Rail. The route-km of railways in 1995–96 was 2,441 km.

Civil Aviation. Daily scheduled flights connect the principal towns with the rest of India. There are airports at Guwahati, Tezpur, Jorhat, North Lakhimpur, Silchar and Dibrugarh.

Shipping. Water transport is important in Lower Assam; the main waterway is the Brahmaputra River. Cargo carried in 1988–89 was 109,051 tonnes.

SOCIAL INSTITUTIONS
Justice. The seat of the High Court is Guwahati. It has a Chief Justice and six puisne judges.

Religion. At the 1991 census Hindus numbered 15,047,293; Muslims, 6,373,204; Christians, 744,367; Buddhists, 64,008; Jains, 20,645; Sikhs, 21,910.

Education. In 2001, 64·28% of the population were literate (71·93% of men and 56·03% of women). In 1996–97 there were 30,140 primary/junior basic schools with 3,816,603 students; 7,237 middle/senior basic schools with 1,304,504 students; 4,345 high/higher secondary schools with 664,422 students. There were 247 colleges for general education, 7 medical colleges, 3 engineering and 1 agricultural, 22 teacher-training colleges, and a fisheries college at Raha. There were 5 universities: Assam Agricultural University, Jorhat; Dibrugarh University, Dibrugarh with 86 colleges and 55,982 students (1992–93); Gauhati University, Guwahati with 128 colleges and 80,363 students (1992–93); and 2 central universities, at Silchar and Tezpur.

Health. In 1995–96 there were 161 hospitals (12,873 beds), 581 primary health centres and 316 dispensaries.

BIHAR
KEY HISTORICAL EVENTS
Bihar was part of Bengal under British rule until 1912 when it was separated together with Orissa. The two were joined until 1936 when Bihar became a separate province. As a state of the Indian Union it was enlarged in 1956 by the addition of land from West Bengal.

The state contains the ethnic areas of North Bihar, Santhal Pargana and Chota Nagpur. In 1956 certain areas of Purnea and Manbhum districts were transferred to West Bengal. In 2000 the state of Jharkhand was carved from the mineral-rich southern region of Bihar, substantially reducing the state's revenue-earning power.

TERRITORY AND POPULATION

Bihar is in north India and is bounded north by Nepal, east by West Bengal, south by the new state of Jharkhand, southwest and west by Uttar Pradesh. After the formation of Jharkhand the area of Bihar is 94,163 sq. km (previously 173,877 sq. km). Population (2001 census, provisional), 82,878,796, with a density of 880 per sq. km. Population of principal towns, *see* INDIA: Territory and Population. Other large towns (1991): Muzaffarpur, 241,107; Darbhanga, 218,391; Biharsharif, 201,323; Arrah, 157,082; Munger, 150,112; Chapra, 136,877; Katihar, 154,367; Purnea, 114,912.

The state is divided into 37 districts. The capital is Patna.

The official language is Hindi (55·8m. speakers at the 1981 census), the second, Urdu (6·9m.), and the third, Bengali (2m.).

SOCIAL STATISTICS

Growth rate 1991–2001, 28·43%.

CONSTITUTION AND GOVERNMENT

Bihar has a bicameral legislature. The Legislative Assembly consists of 243 elected members, and the Council 96.

RECENT ELECTIONS

After the elections of 12, 17 and 22 Feb. 2000 the Rashtriya Janata Dal retained power, fighting off the challenge of Prime Minister Vajpayee's alliance. The distribution of seats was: RJD, 124; Bharatiya Janata Party, 67; Samata Party, 34; Indian National Congress, 23; Janata Dal (United), 21; independents, 20; others, 35.

CURRENT ADMINISTRATION

Governor: Vinod Chandra Pande.

  Chief Minister: Rabri Devi.

ECONOMY

Budget. The budget estimates for 1997–98 showed total receipts of Rs 126,770m. and expenditure of Rs 121,216m. Plan allocation, 1997–98, Rs 22,000m. However, projections suggest that the creation of Jharkhand in 2000 could remove up to two-thirds of Bihar's revenue.

ENERGY AND NATURAL RESOURCES

Electricity. Installed capacity (1996–97) 4,470 MW. Power generated (1994–95), 2,700m. kWh; there were (March 1996) 47,805 villages with electricity. Hydro-electric projects in hand will add about 149·2 MW capacity.

Minerals. The new state of Jharkhand contains the majority of mineral reserves that were previously Bihar's. There are deposits of bauxite, dolomite, glass sand, mica, and salt. Revenue received from minerals (1994–95) Rs 7,039·3m.

Agriculture. The irrigated area was 4·13m. ha in 1993–94. Cultivable land, 11·6m. ha, of a total area of 17·4m. ha. Total cropped area, 1991–92, 9·79m. ha. Production (1995–96): rice, 6·91m. tonnes; wheat, 4·18m.; total foodgrains, 13·07m. Other food crops are maize, rabi and pulses. Main cash crops are jute, sugarcane, oilseeds, tobacco and potatoes.

Forests in 1995 covered 26,561 sq. km. There are 12 protected forests.

INDUSTRY

Iron, steel and aluminium are produced and there is an oil refinery. Other important industries are heavy engineering, machine tools, fertilizers, electrical engineering, manufacturing drugs, and fruit processing. There were 500 large and medium industries and 163,000 small and handicraft units in 1996–97.

COMMUNICATIONS

Roads. In March 1997 the state had 87,836 km of roads, including 2,118 km of national highway and 4,192 km of state highway, and 15,526 km of district roads. Passenger transport has been nationalized. There were 1,329,709 motor vehicles registered in March 1996.

Rail. The North Eastern, South Eastern and Eastern railways traverse the state; route-km, 1995–96, 5,283 km.

Civil Aviation. There are airports at Patna and Gaya with regular scheduled services to Calcutta and Delhi.

Shipping. The length of waterways open for navigation is 1,300 km.

SOCIAL INSTITUTIONS

Justice. There is a High Court (constituted in 1916) at Patna with a Chief Justice, 25 puisne judges and 4 additional judges.

Police. The police force is under a Director General of Police; in 1990 there were 1,097 police stations.

Religion. At the 1991 census Hindus numbered 71,193,417; Muslims, 12,787,985; Christians, 843,717; Sikhs, 78,212; Jains, 23,049; Buddhists, 3,518.

Education. At the census of 2001, 47·53% of the population were literate (60·32% of males and 33·57% of females). There were, 1996–97, 4,149 high and higher secondary schools with 1,080,321 pupils, 13,834 middle schools with 2·42m. pupils and 53,652 primary schools with 9,626,855 pupils. Education is free for children aged 6–11.

There were 14 universities in 1996–97: Patna University (founded 1917) with 14,699 students (1994–95); Bihar University, Muzaffarpur (1952) with 95 colleges, and 84,873 students (1989–90); Bhagalpur University (1960) with 140,718 students (1990–91); Kameswar Singh Darbhanga Sanskrit University (1961); Magadh University, Gaya (1962) with 186 colleges and 122,019 students (1994–95); Lalit Narayan Mithila University (1972), Darbhanga; Rajendra Agricultural University, Samastipur (1970); Nalanda Open University, Nalanda; and 4 others. There were 742 degree colleges, 11 engineering colleges, 31 medical colleges and 15 teacher training colleges. Ranchi University, Bisra Agricultural College and Sidhu Kanhu University are now part of Jharkhand.

Health. In 1986 there were 1,289 hospitals and dispensaries with 28,997 beds in 1992.

CULTURE

Tourism. The main tourist centres are Bodh Gaya, Patna, Nalanda, Sasaram, Rajgir and Vaishali.

CHHATTISGARH

KEY HISTORICAL EVENTS

The state was carved from sixteen mainly tribal districts of Madhya Pradesh and became the twenty-sixth state of India on 1 Nov. 2000. Chhattisgarh has been under the administrative control of many different rulers during its history, which can be traced back to the 4th century. Originally known as South Kosala, archaeological excavations made in recent times indicate that the region was a hive of artistic and cultural experimentation in ancient times. During the Sarabhapuriyas, Nalas, Pandavamsis and Kalchuris dynasties between the 6th and 8th centuries vast numbers of brick temples were built in the area. The British took control of the area from the Mahrattas in the early 19th century. Despite possessing its own cultural identity Chhattisgarh was constantly swallowed up by other regions and in 1956, as a direct result of the Indian Union of 1949, it was made part of the new region of Madhya Pradesh. For several years locals in Chhattisgarh voiced the grievance that their region was effectively a 'colony' of Madhya Pradesh, maintaining that the revenue generated by their region, which was termed the 'rice bowl of Madhya Pradesh' and was also rich in minerals, was insufficiently re-invested in the area itself. In 2000 the National Democratic Alliance successfully negotiated the passage of a bill through both houses of the Indian parliament which carved out three new Indian states, Chhattisgarh among them.

TERRITORY AND POPULATION

Chhattisgarh is in central eastern India and is bounded by the new state of Jharkhand to the east, Orissa to the southeast, Andhra Pradesh to the south and Maharashtra and Madhya Pradesh to the west. Chhattisgarh has an area of 135,191 sq. km. Population (2001 census, provisional) 20,795,956; density, 154 per sq. km. The principal languages are Hindi and Chhattisgarhi.

Cities with over 250,000 population, see INDIA: Territory and population. Other large cities (1991): Bilaspur, 192,396; Durg, 150,645; Rajnandgaon, 125,371; Korba, 124,501.

SOCIAL STATISTICS

Growth rate 1991–2001, 18·06%.

CONSTITUTION AND GOVERNMENT

Chhattisgarh is the twenty-sixth state of India. In creating Chhattisgarh it was decided that the 90 members of the Madhya Pradesh Legislative Assembly from Chhattisgarhi districts would become the members of the new state's legislative assembly. For administrative purposes the region is divided into 16 districts. The council of ministers consists of 15 cabinet ministers and eight ministers of state.

The capital and seat of government is at Raipur.

RECENT ELECTIONS

On the basis of elections in Nov. 1998, the Congress (I) Party had 48 of the MLA seats and the Bharatiya Janata party had 36. The Congress (I) Party formed an administration with former AICC general secretary Ajit Jogi becoming the state's first chief minister.

CURRENT ADMINISTRATION

Governor: Dinesh Nandan Sahaya.
  Chief Minister: Ajit Jogi.

ENERGY AND NATURAL RESOURCES

Electricity. Of the 19,720 villages in Chhattisgarh, 18,070 have electricity.

Water. 1·1m. ha. of land is under irrigation. 44,750 residential areas have sufficient drinking water supplies while 7,315 residential areas only have partial supplies and 2,751 areas have insufficient supplies. In total there were 102,063 hand pumps in the state and 701 water fulfilment plans in place in 1999.

Minerals. The state has extensive mineral resources including (1999 estimates): over 27,000m. tonnes of tin ore, 2,000m. tonnes of iron ore, 525m. tonnes of dolomite (accounting for 24% of India's entire share), and 73m. tonnes of bauxite. There are also significant deposits of limestone, copper ore, rock phosphate, coal and manganese ore. Deobogh in the Raipur district contains deposits of diamonds.

Agriculture. Agriculture is the occupation for 1·7m. of the population (around 80%). 5·8m. ha. of land is agricultural and the area provides food grain for over 600 rice mills. The great plains of Chhattisgarh produce 10,000 varieties of rice.

COMMUNICATIONS

Roads. Total length of roads (1999) was 33,182 km. State highways connect Raipur to neighbouring states and to Jagdalpur and Kondagaon in the south of Chhattisgarh and Durg and Rajnandgaon in the west.

Rail. Raipur is at the centre of the state's railway network, linking Chhattisgarh to the states of Orissa and Madhya Pradesh.

SOCIAL INSTITUTIONS

Education. In 2001, 65·18% of the population were literate (77·86% of men and 52·40% of women). There are three universities in Chhattisgarh. Ravishankar University (founded 1964), at Raipur, had 89 affiliated colleges (1992–93); Indira Gandhi Krishi Vishwavidyalaya, Raipur, a music and fine arts institution (founded in 1956); and Guru Ghasidas University, Bilaspur which had 58 colleges and 34,717 students (1992–93).

GOA

KEY HISTORICAL EVENTS

The coastal area was captured by the Portuguese in 1510 and the inland area was added in the 18th century. In Dec. 1961 Portuguese rule was ended and Goa incorporated into the Indian Union as a Territory together with Daman and Diu. Goa was granted statehood as a separate unit on 30 May 1987. Daman and Diu remained Union Territories.

TERRITORY AND POPULATION

Goa, bounded on the north by Maharashtra and on the east and south by Karnataka, has a coastline of 105 km. The area is 3,702 sq. km. Population (2001 census, provisional) 1,343,998; density, 363 per sq. km. Marmagao is the largest town; population (urban agglomeration, 1991) 90,429. The capital is Panaji; population (urban agglomeration 1991) 85,515. The state has two districts. There are 183 village Panchayats. The languages spoken are Konkani (official language), Marathi, Hindi and English.

SOCIAL STATISTICS

Growth rate 1991–2001, 14·89%.

CONSTITUTION AND GOVERNMENT

The Indian Parliament passed legislation in March 1962 by which Goa became a Union Territory with retrospective effect from 20 Dec. 1961. On 30 May 1987 Goa attained statehood. There is a Legislative Assembly of 40 members.

RECENT ELECTIONS

Of the 40 seats available at the elections for the State Assembly on 4 June 1999, the Indian National Congress Party won 21; Bharatiya Janata Party, 10; Maharashtrawadi Gomantak party, 4; United Goans Democratic Party, 2; Goa Rajiv Congress Party, 2; independent, 1. There was a turn-out of 64%.

CURRENT ADMINISTRATION

Governor: Kedar Nath Sahani.
    Chief Minister: Manohar Parrikar.

ECONOMY

Budget. The total budget for 1996–97 was Rs 11,756·8m. Annual plan 1997–98, Rs 2,300m.

ENERGY AND NATURAL RESOURCES

Electricity. In 1996 installed capacity was 0·16m. MW, but Goa receives most of its power supply from the states of Maharashtra and Karnataka. In March 1996, 377 out of 386 villages had electricity.

Minerals. Resources include bauxite, ferro-manganese ore and iron ore, all of which are exported. Iron ore production (1992–93) 12,435,334 tonnes. There are also reserves of limestone and clay.

Agriculture. Agriculture is the main occupation, important crops being rice, pulses, ragi, mango, cashew and coconuts. Area under rice (1995–96) 53,500 ha;

production, 128,100 tonnes. Area under pulses 9,800 ha, sugarcane 1,400 ha, groundnut 1,200 ha. Total production of foodgrains, 1995–96, 136,600 tonnes.

Government poultry and dairy farming schemes produced 94m. eggs and 29,000m. litres of milk in 1992–93.

Forestry. Forests covered 1,250 sq. km in 1995.

Fisheries. Fish is the state's staple food. In 1995–96 the catch of seafish was 84,210 tonnes. There is a coastline of about 104 km and about 2,850 (1994–95) active fishing vessels.

INDUSTRY
In 1992–93 there were 52 large and medium industrial projects and 5,242 small units registered. Production included: nylon fishing nets, ready made clothing, electronic goods, pesticides, pharmaceuticals, tyres, footwear, fertilizers, automotive components and shipbuilding.

In 1992–93 the 5,242 small-scale industry units employed 32,597 persons.

COMMUNICATIONS
Roads. There were 7,419 km of roads in 1993–94 (National Highway, 224 km). Motor vehicles numbered 211,756 in March 1996.

Rail. In 1995–96 there were 79 km of route.

Civil Aviation. An airport at Dabolim is connected with Bombay, Delhi and Bangalore.

Shipping. There are seaports at Panaji, Marmagao and Margao.

SOCIAL INSTITUTIONS
Justice. There is a bench of the Bombay High Court at Panaji.

Religion. At the 1991 census Hindus numbered 756,651; Christians, 349,225; Muslims, 61,455; Sikhs, 1,087.

Education. In 2001, 82·32% of the population were literate (88·88% of men and 75·51% of women). In 1996–97 there were 1,031 primary schools (126,425 students), 97 middle schools (77,275 students) and 445 high and higher secondary schools (73,216 students). There were also 2 engineering colleges, 4 medical colleges, 2 teacher-training colleges, 21 other colleges and 6 polytechnic institutes. Goa University, Taleigao (1985) had 33 colleges and 16,977 students in 1994–95.

Health. There were (1992–93) 129 hospitals (4,232 beds), 256 rural medical dispensaries, health and sub-health centres and 268 family planning units.

FURTHER READING
Hutt, A., *Goa: A Traveller's Historical and Architectural Guide.* Buckhurst Hill, 1988

GUJARAT
KEY HISTORICAL EVENTS
The Gujarati-speaking areas of India were part of the Moghul empire, coming under Mahratta domination in the late 18th century. In 1818 areas of present Gujarat around the Gulf of Cambay were annexed by the British East India Company. The remainder consisted of a group of small principalities, notably Baroda, Rajkot, Bhavnagar and Nawanagar. British areas became part of the Bombay Presidency.

At independence all the area now forming Gujarat became part of Bombay State except for Rajkot and Bhavnagar which formed the state of Saurashtra until incorporated in Bombay in 1956. In 1960 Bombay State was divided and the Gujarati-speaking areas became Gujarat.

In early 2002 as many as 1,000 people, mostly Muslims, were killed in Gujarat in ethnic violence involving Hindus and the Muslim minority.

TERRITORY AND POPULATION

Gujarat is in western India and is bounded in the north by Pakistan and Rajasthan, east by Madhya Pradesh, southeast by Maharashtra, south and west by the Indian ocean and Arabian sea. The area of the state is 196,024 sq. km and the population (2001 census, provisional) 50,656,038; density, 258 per sq. km. The chief cities, *see* INDIA: Territory and Population. Other important towns (2001 census, provisional) are: Junagadh (253,138), Navsari (232,420), Surendranagar (219,828), Anand (218,064), Porbandar (197,414), Nadiad (196,679), Gandhinagar (195,891), Morbi (178,148), Bharuch (176,531), Gandhidham (151,475), Mehsana (141,367), Bhuj (136,327) and Godhra (131,144). Gujarati and Hindi in the Devanagari script are the official languages.

SOCIAL STATISTICS

Growth rate 1991–2001, 22·48%.

CLIMATE

Summers are intensely hot: 33–45°C. Winters: 7–13°C. Monsoon season: 22–36°C. Annual rainfall varies from 35 cm to 189 cm.

CONSTITUTION AND GOVERNMENT

Gujarat has a unicameral legislature, the *Legislative Assembly*, which has 182 elected members.

The capital is Gandhinagar. There are 25 districts.

RECENT ELECTIONS

In elections held in Dec. 2002 the Bharatiya Janata Party retained power with an increased majority, winning 126 seats against 51 for Congress, with ind. and others winning four seats.

CURRENT ADMINISTRATION

Governor: Sunder Singh Bhandari.

Chief Minister: Shri Narendrabhai Modi.

ECONOMY

Budget. The budget estimates for 2002–03 showed revenue receipts of Rs 186,950m. and revenue expenditure of Rs 241,651m. Plan outlay for 2002–03, Rs 76,000m.

Banking and Finance. At June 2002 there were 3,657 branches of commercial banks in the State with combined deposits of Rs 635,990m. Total credit advanced was Rs 279,530m.

ENERGY AND NATURAL RESOURCES

Electricity. In March 2002 total installed capacity was 8,651 MW and 17,940 villages had electricity.

Oil and Gas. There are large crude oil and gas reserves. Production, 2001–02: crude oil, 6·0m. tonnes; gas, 2,797m. cu. metres.

Water. Water resources are limited. In 2002 irrigation potential was 6·49m. ha.

Minerals. Chief minerals produced in 2001–02 (in tonnes) included limestone (15m.), lignite (5·8m.), bauxite (1·5m.), quartz and silica (621,000), dolomite (197,000), crude china clay (71,000), calcareous and sea sand (4,000 in 1999–2000) and agate stone (41). Value of production (2001–02) Rs 48,524m. Reserves of coal lie under the Kalol and Mehsana oil and gas fields. The deposit, mixed with crude petroleum, is estimated at 100,000m. tonnes.

Agriculture. 3·5m. ha of the cropped area was irrigated in June 2002.

Production of principal crops, 2001–02: rice, 1·03m. tonnes from 664,000 ha; foodgrains, 4·9m. tonnes (wheat, 1·15m. tonnes); pulses, 380,000 tonnes; cotton, 1·70m. bales of 170 kg. Tobacco and groundnuts are important cash crops.

Livestock (1997): buffaloes, 6·29m.; other cattle, 6·75m.; sheep and goats, 6·54m.; horses and ponies, 14,381.

Forestry. Forests covered 18,999 sq. km in 2002 (9·69% of total area). The State has four National Parks and 21 sanctuaries.

Fisheries. There were (1997) 158,000 people engaged in fisheries. In 2001–02 there were 29,506 fishing vessels and the catch was 701,603 tonnes.

INDUSTRY

Gujarat ranks among India's most industrialized states. In 2001 there were 256,000 small-scale units and (2000) 20,050 factories including 2,480 textile factories, 3,400 chemical and chemical products factories, 1,875 non-metallic mineral products factories, 1,850 machinery and equipment factories and 975 rubber and plastic products factories. There were 257 industrial estates in 2001. Principal industries are textiles, general and electrical engineering, oil-refining, fertilizers, petrochemicals, machine tools, automobiles, heavy chemicals, pharmaceuticals, dyes, sugar, soda ash, cement, man-made fibres, salt, sulphuric acid, paper and paperboard.

In 2001 state production of soda-ash was 239,000 tonnes (provisional), salt production was 9·65m. tonnes, and cement production 6·73m. tonnes.

COMMUNICATIONS

Roads. At March 2002 there were 74,031 km of roads. Gujarat State Transport Corporation operated 16,052 routes. Number of vehicles, Oct. 2002, 6,292,629.

Rail. In 2001–02 the state had 5,310 route-km of railway line.

Civil Aviation. Ahmedabad is the main airport. There are regular services between Ahmedabad and Bombay, Jaipur and Delhi. There are nine other airports: Bhavnagar, Bhuj, Jamnagar, Kandla, Keshod, Porbandar, Rajkot, Surat and Vadodara.

Shipping. The largest port is Kandla. There are 40 other ports. Cargo handled at the ports in 2001–02 totalled 120·3m. tonnes (37·7m. tonnes at Kandla).

Telecommunications. There were 2,833,880 telephone connections and 467,448 mobile phone connections in the state in 2001–02.

Postal Services. There were (2001–02) 9,056 post offices and 1,775 telegraph offices.

SOCIAL INSTITUTIONS

Justice. The High Court of Judicature at Ahmedabad has a Chief Justice and 30 puisne judges.

Religion. At the 1991 census Hindus numbered 36,964,228; Muslims, 3,606,920; Jains, 491,331; Christians, 181,753; Sikhs, 33,044; Buddhists, 11,615.

Education. In 2001, 69·97% of the population were literate (80·50% of males and 58·60% of females). Primary and secondary education up to Standard XII are free. Education above Standard XII is free for girls. In 2000–01 there were 39,514 primary schools with 8·34m. students and 6,341 secondary schools with 2·19m. students.

There are ten universities in the state. Gujarat University, Ahmedabad, founded in 1950, is teaching and affiliating; it has 154 affiliated colleges and 143,692 students (all student figures for 1998–99). The Maharaja Sayajirao University of Vadodara (1949) is residential and teaching; it has 12 colleges and 26,511 students. The Sardar Patel University, Vallabh-Vidyanagar (1955), has 20 constituent and affiliated colleges and 17,913 students. Saurashtra University at Rajkot (1968) has 113 affiliated colleges and 72,234 students. South Gujarat University at Surat (1967) has 58 colleges and 59,600 students. Bhavnagar University (1978) is residential and teaching with 15 affiliated colleges and 11,195 students. North Gujarat University was established at Patan in 1986 and has 73 colleges and 54,720 students. Gujarat Vidyapith at Ahmedabad is deemed a university under the University Grants Commission Act. There are also Gujarat Agricultural University, Banaskantha and Gujarat Ayurved University, Jamnagar.

There are 25 engineering and technical colleges, 35 polytechnics, 45 medical colleges and 9 agricultural colleges. There are also 339 arts, science and commerce colleges, 42 teacher-training colleges and 31 law colleges. There were 0·4m. students enrolled in 1998–99 in all colleges.

Health. At March 2002 there were 253 community health centres, 1,044 primary health centres and 7,274 sub-centres. There were 25 general hospitals, 23 cottage hospitals (2000) and 22 Taluka-level hospitals. In 2000–01, 32·1m. patients were treated.

CULTURE

Press. At March 2002 there were 2,323 newspapers and periodicals of which 2,170 were published in Gujarati, 78 in English and 47 in Hindu.

Tourism. There are many sights of religious pilgrimage as well as archaeological sights, attractive beaches, the Lion Sanctuary of Gir Forest and the Wild Ass Sanctuary in Kachchh. Mahatma Gandhi's birthplace at Porbandar is also a popular tourist attraction.

Festivals. Tarnetar Fair (Surendranagar district) is held in Aug./Sept.; Madhavraj Fair (Junagadh district) is celebrated in March/April; Ambaji Fair (Banaskantha district) is dedicated to Amba, mother goddess. There are numerous other festivals throughout the region.

FURTHER READING

Desai, I. F., *Untouchability in Rural Gujarat.* Bombay, 1977
Sharma, R. N., *Gujurat Holocaust (Communalism in the Land of Gandhi).* Delhi, 2002

HARYANA

KEY HISTORICAL EVENTS

The state of Haryana, created on 1 Nov. 1966 under the Punjab Reorganization Act, 1966, was formed from the Hindi-speaking parts of the state of Punjab (India). It comprises the districts of Ambala, Bhiwani, Faridabad, Fatehabad, Gurgaon, Hisar, Jhajjar, Jind, Kaithal, Karnal, Kurukshetra, Mahendragarh, Panchkula, Panipat, Rewari, Rohtak, Sirsa, Sonipat and Yamunanagar.

TERRITORY AND POPULATION

Haryana is in north India and is bounded north by Himachal Pradesh, east by Uttar Pradesh, south and west by Rajasthan and northwest by Punjab. Delhi forms an enclave on its eastern boundary. The state has an area of 44,212 sq. km and a population (2001 census, provisional) of 21,082,989; density, 477 per sq. km. Principal cities, *see* INDIA: Territory and Population. Other large towns (1991) are: Rohtak (216,096), Panipat (191,212), Hisar (181,255), Karnal (173,751), Yamunanagar (144,346), Sonipat (143,922), Ambala (139,889), Gurgaon (135,884), Bhiwani (121,629) and Sirsa (112,841). The principal language is Hindi.

SOCIAL STATISTICS

Growth rate 1991–2001, 28·06%.

CONSTITUTION AND GOVERNMENT

The state has a unicameral legislature with 90 members. The capital (shared with Punjab) is Chandigarh. Its transfer to Punjab, intended for 1986, has been postponed. There are 19 districts.

RECENT ELECTIONS

In the elections of 17 and 22 Feb. 2000 Prime Minister Atal Bihari Vajpayee's alliance defeated the main opposition Congress Party, although his Bharatiya Janata Party came second to its regional partner, Indian National Lok Dal. The distribution of seats was: INLD, 47; Indian National Congress, 21; independents, 11; others, 11.

CURRENT ADMINISTRATION

Governor: Babu Parmanand.
   Chief Minister: Om Prakash Chautala.

ECONOMY

Budget. Budget estimates for 1997–98 show revenue income of Rs 74,426m. and revenue expenditure of Rs 81,560m. Annual plan 1997–98, Rs 15,750m.

ENERGY AND NATURAL RESOURCES

Electricity. Approximately 1,000 MW are supplied to Haryana, mainly from the Bhakra Nangal system. In 1996–97 installed capacity was 2,382 MW and all the villages had electric power.

Minerals. Minerals include placer gold, barytes and rare earths. Value of production, 1987–88, Rs 40m.

Agriculture. Haryana has sandy soil and erratic rainfall, but the state shares the benefit of the Sutlej-Beas scheme. Agriculture employs over 82% of the working population; in 1981 there were about 0·9m. holdings (average 3·7 ha), and the gross irrigated area was 2·05m. ha in 1993–94. Area under foodgrains, 1995–96, 4·02m. ha. Foodgrain production, 1995–96, 10·21m. tonnes (rice 1·86m. tonnes, wheat 7·35m. tonnes); pulses, 416,400 tonnes; cotton, 1·5m. bales of 170 kg; sugar (gur) and oilseeds are important.

Forestry. Forests covered 603 sq. km in 1995.

INDUSTRY

Haryana has a large market for consumer goods in neighbouring Delhi. In 1996–97 there were 916 large and medium scale industries and 138,759 small units providing employment to about 1m. persons, and 56,012 rural industrial units. The main industries are cotton textiles, agricultural machinery and tractors, woollen textiles, scientific instruments, glass, cement, paper and sugar milling, cars, tyres and tubes, motorcycles, bicycles, steel tubes, engineering goods, electrical and electronic goods. An oil refinery is being set up at Panipat.

COMMUNICATIONS

Roads. There were (1996–97) 22,757 km of metalled roads, linking all villages. Road transport is nationalized. There were 954,563 motor vehicles in 1995–96. Road transport carried 1·65m. passengers daily in 1996–97 with a fleet of 3,818 buses.

Rail. The state is crossed by lines from Delhi to Agra, Ajmer, Ferozepur and Chandigarh. Route km, 1995–96, 1,452 km. The main stations are at Ambala and Kurukshetra.

Civil Aviation. There is no airport within the state but Delhi is on its eastern boundary.

SOCIAL INSTITUTIONS

Justice. Haryana shares the High Court of Punjab and Haryana at Chandigarh.

Religion. At the 1991 census Hindus numbered 14,686,512; Muslims, 763,775; Sikhs, 956,836; Christians, 15,699; Jains, 35,296.

Education. In 2001, 68·59% of the population were literate (79·25% of men and 56·31% of women). In 1996–97 there were 5,651 primary schools with 1,981,993 students, 3,233 high and higher secondary schools with 511,377 students, 1,631 middle schools with 832,886 students and 129 colleges of arts, science and commerce, 9 engineering and technical colleges and 10 medical colleges. There are three universities: Haryana Agricultural University, Hisar; Kurukshetra University, Kurukshetra with 70 colleges and 70,000 students (1993–94); and Maharshi Dayanand University, Rohtak.

Health. There were (1996–97) 111 hospitals (11,061 beds) and community health centres, 399 primary health centres and 2,416 sub-centres, and 442 Ayurvedic and Unani institutions.

HIMACHAL PRADESH

KEY HISTORICAL EVENTS
Thirty small hill states were merged to form the Territory of Himachal Pradesh in 1948; the state of Bilaspur was added in 1954 and parts of the Punjab in 1966. The whole territory became a state in Jan. 1971. The state is a Himalayan area of hill-tribes, rivers and forests. Its main component areas are Chamba, a former princely state, dominated in turn by Moghuls and Sikhs before coming under British influence in 1848; Bilaspur, an independent Punjab state until it was invaded by Gurkhas in 1814 (the British East India Company forces drove out the Gurkhas in 1815); Simla district around the town built by the Company near Bilaspur on land reclaimed from Gurkha troops (the summer capital of India from 1865 until 1948); Mandi, a princely state until 1948; Kangra and Kullu districts, originally Rajput areas which had become part of the British-ruled Punjab. They were incorporated into Himachal Pradesh in 1966 when the Punjab was reorganized.

TERRITORY AND POPULATION
Himachal Pradesh is in north India and is bounded north by Kashmir, east by Tibet, southeast by Uttaranchal, south by Haryana, southwest and west by Punjab. The area of the state is 55,673 sq. km and a population (2001 census, provisional) of 6,077,248; density, 109 per sq. km. Principal languages are Hindi and Pahari. The capital is Shimla, population (1991 census) of the urban agglomeration, 110,360.

SOCIAL STATISTICS
Growth rate 1991–2001, 17·53%.

CONSTITUTION AND GOVERNMENT
Full statehood was attained, as the 18th State of the Union, on 25 Jan. 1971. On 1 Sept. 1972 districts were reorganized and three new districts created, Solan, Hamirpur and Una, making a total of 12.

There is a unicameral *Legislative Assembly*.

RECENT ELECTIONS
Elections were held in Feb. 2003 in 65 of the 68 constituencies. Congress won 40 seats; Bharatiya Janata Party (BJP), 16; ind. 6; other parties, 3.

CURRENT ADMINISTRATION
Governor: Suraj Bhan.
Chief Minister: Virbhadra Singh.

ECONOMY
Budget. Budget estimates for 1997–98 showed receipts of Rs 27,064·2m. and expenditure of Rs 28,905·4m. Annual plan, 1999–2000, Rs 16,000m.

ENERGY AND NATURAL RESOURCES
Electricity. All 16,807 villages have electricity. Installed capacity (1995–96), 288·7 MW. Electricity generated (1995–96), 1,286m. kWh.

Water. An artificial confluence of the Sutlej and Beas rivers has been made, directing their united flow into Govind Sagar Lake. Other major rivers are Ravi, Chenab and Yamuna.

Minerals. The state has rock salt, slate, gypsum, limestone, barytes, dolomite and pyrites.

Agriculture. Farming employs 71% of the people. Irrigated area is 17% of the area sown. There are about 2,000 tea planters cultivating 2,063 ha. Main crops are seed potatoes, off season vegetables, wheat, maize, rice and fruits such as apples, peaches, apricots, hops, kiwi fruit, strawberries and flowers; 436,000 tonnes of fruits were produced in 1999.

Production (1994–95): rice, 112,200 tonnes; wheat, 412,800 tonnes; pulses, 10,300 tonnes. Total foodgrains (1999), 1·45m. tonnes. Total vegetables (1999), 500,000 tonnes.

Livestock (1992 census): buffaloes, 701,000; other cattle, 2,152,000; goats and sheep, 2·19m.

Forestry. Himachal Pradesh forests cover 63·8% of the state and supply the largest quantities of coniferous timber in northern India. The forests also ensure the safety of the catchment areas of the Yamuna, Sutlej, Beas, Ravi and Chenab rivers. Commercial felling of green trees has been totally halted and forest working nationalized. Area under forests in 1999, 37,591 sq. km.

INDUSTRY

The main sources of employment are the forests and their related industries; there are factories making turpentine and rosin. The state also makes fertilizers, cement, electronic items and TV sets. There is a foundry and a brewery. Other industries include salt production and handicrafts, including weaving. The state has 173 large and medium units, 27,000 small scale units (providing employment for 140,000 people), 7 industrial estates and 21 industrial areas. 300 mineral based industries have also been established.

COMMUNICATIONS

Roads. The national highway from Chandigarh runs through Shimla; other main highways from Shimla serve Kullu, Manali, Kangra, Chamba and Pathankot. The rest are minor roads. Pathankot is also on national highways from Punjab to Kashmir. Length of roads (1999), 25,773 km; number of vehicles (1995–96), 119,037; number of transport buses (1995–96), 1,692.

Rail. There is a line from Chandigarh to Shimla, and the Jammu-Delhi line runs through Pathankot. A Nangal-Talwara rail link has been approved by the central government. There are two narrow gauge lines, from Shimla to Kalka (96 km) and Jogindernagar to Pathankot (113 km), and a broad gauge line from Una to Nangal (16 km). Route-km in 1995–96, 266 km.

Civil Aviation. The state has airports at Bhuntar near Kullu, at Jubbarhatti near Shimla and at Gaggal in Kangra district. There are also 12 state-run helipads across the state.

SOCIAL INSTITUTIONS

Justice. The state has its own High Court at Shimla.

Religion. At the 1991 census Hindus numbered 4,958,560; Muslims, 89,134; Sikhs, 52,050; Buddhists, 64,081; Christians, 4,435.

Education. In 2001, 77·13% of the population were literate (86·02% of men and 68·08% of women). There were (1996–97) 7,732 primary schools with 728,870 students, 1,037 middle schools with 371,622 students, 1,228 high and higher secondary schools with 271,596 students, 62 (including 18 private) arts, science and commerce colleges, 1 engineering college, 2 medical colleges, 1 teacher training college and 3 universities. The universities are Himachal Pradesh University, Shimla (1970) with 48 affiliated colleges and 32,773 students (1992–93), Himachal Pradesh Agricultural University, Palampur (1978) and Dr Y. S. Parmar University of Horticulture and Forestry, Solan (1985).

Health. There were (Dec. 1996) 80 hospitals (9,525 beds), 286 primary and community health centres and 1,831 sub-health centres, and 838 allopathic and Ayurvedic dispensaries.

FURTHER READING

Verma, Vishwashwar, *The Emergence of Himachal Pradesh: A Survey of Constitutional Development*. Indus Publishing Company, New Delhi, 1995

JAMMU AND KASHMIR

KEY HISTORICAL EVENTS

The state of Jammu and Kashmir was brought into being in 1846 at the close of the First Sikh War. By the Treaty of Amritsar, Gulab Singh, de facto ruler of Jammu and Ladakh, added Kashmir to his existing territories, in consideration of his agreeing to pay the indemnity imposed by the British on the defeated Sikh empire. Of the state's three component parts, Ladakh and Kashmir were ancient polities, Ladakh having been an independent kingdom since the tenth century AD till its conquest by Gulab Singh's armies in 1834–42. Kashmir lost its independence to the Mughal empire in 1586, and was conquered in turn by the Afghans (1756) and the Sikhs (1819). Jammu was a collection of small principalities, until these were consolidated by Gulab Singh and his brothers in the early nineteenth century.

British supremacy was recognized until the Indian Independence Act, 1947, when all states decided on accession to India or Pakistan. Kashmir asked for standstill agreements with both. Pakistan agreed, but India desired further discussion with the government of Jammu and Kashmir State. In the meantime the state became subject to armed attack from the territory of Pakistan and the Maharajah acceded to India on 26 Oct. 1947 by signing the Instrument of Accession. India approached the UN in Jan. 1948, and the conflict ended by ceasefire in Jan. 1949, the major part of the state remaining with India, but a significant amount of territory in the north and west going to Pakistan. Hostilities between the two countries broke out in 1965 and again in 1971, but notwithstanding bilateral agreements at the highest level—the Tashkent Declaration (Jan. 1966) and the Simla Agreement (July 1972)—the issue remained and remains unresolved. With Muslims a majority of its population, both India and Pakistan regard the state as a touchstone of their divergent political raisons d'être—Pakistan as a Muslim nation, and India a secular one—and hence their position as non-negotiable. Intermittent violence between nationalistic factions has led to further negotiations between India and Pakistan with both sides pledging a peaceful solution. In Dec. 2002 the new provincial government promised to open talks with separatist groups.

TERRITORY AND POPULATION

The state is in the extreme north and is bounded north by China, east by Tibet, south by Himachal Pradesh and Punjab and west by Pakistan. The area is 222,236 sq. km, of which about 84,100 sq. km is occupied by Pakistan and 36,749 sq. km by China; the population of the territory on the Indian side of the line in the 2001 census (provisional), was 10,069,917. Srinagar (population, 1991, 892,506) is the summer and Jammu (1,207,996) the winter capital. The official language is Urdu; other commonly spoken languages are Kashmiri (3·1m. speakers at 1981 census), Hindi (1m.), Dogri, Gujri, Pahari, Ladakhi and Punjabi.

SOCIAL STATISTICS

Growth rate 1991–2001, 29·04%.

CONSTITUTION AND GOVERNMENT

The Maharajah's son, Yuvraj Karan Singh, took over as Regent in 1950 and, on the ending of hereditary rule (17 Oct. 1952), was sworn in as Sadar-i-Riyasat. On his father's death (26 April 1961) Yuvraj Karan Singh was recognized as Maharajah by the Indian government. The permanent Constitution of the state came into force in part on 17 Nov. 1956 and fully on 26 Jan. 1957. There is a bicameral legislature; the Legislative Council has 36 members and the Legislative Assembly has 87. Since the 1967 elections the 6 representatives of Jammu and Kashmir in the central House of the People are directly elected; there are 4 representatives in the Council of States. After a period of President's rule, a National Conference–Indira Congress coalition government was formed in March 1987. The government was dismissed and the state was brought under President's rule on 18 July 1990.

The state has 14 districts.

RECENT ELECTIONS

Elections to the State Assembly were held in four rounds between 16 Sept. and 8 Oct. 2002. The ruling pro-India National Conference won 28 of the 87 seats (57 in 1996); the Indian Congress Party won 20 (7 in 1996); the People's Democratic Party, 16; and the Bharatiya Janata Party, 1 (8 in 1996). Despite ongoing violence and voter intimidation throughout the elections, turn-out was estimated at 46%. Following the elections, a coalition government was formed by the Indian Congress Party, the People's Democratic Party and other smaller parties.

CURRENT ADMINISTRATION

Governor: Girish Chander Saxena.
  Chief Minister: Mufti Mohammad Sayeed.

ECONOMY

Budget. Budget estimates for 1997–98 show total receipts of Rs 53,628·9m. and total expenditure of Rs 52,748·1m. Annual Plan (1997–98) Rs 15,500m.

ENERGY AND NATURAL RESOURCES

Electricity. Installed capacity (1996–97) 365·8 MW; 6,252 villages had electricity in 1995–96.

Minerals. Minerals include coal, bauxite and gypsum.

Agriculture. About 80% of the population are supported by agriculture. Rice, wheat and maize are the major cereals. The total area under foodgrains (1995–96) was estimated at 887,000 ha. Total foodgrains produced, 1995–96, 1·37m. tonnes (rice, 0·51m. tonnes; wheat, 0·35m. tonnes); pulses, 22,900 tonnes. Fruit is important: production, 1994–95, 0·9m. tonnes; exports, 0·76m. tonnes.
  Irrigated area, 1993–94, 442,000 ha.
  Livestock (1982): cattle, 2,325,200; buffaloes, 5,631,000; goats, 1,003,900; sheep, 1,908,700; horses, 973,000; and poultry, 2,406,760.

Forestry. Forests cover about 20,443 sq. km (1995), forming an important source of revenue, besides providing employment to a large section of the population.

INDUSTRY

There are two central public sector industries and 30 medium-scale. There are 35,576 small units (1994–95) employing over 125,000. There are industries based on horticulture; traditional handicrafts are silk spinning, wood-carving, papier mâché and carpet-weaving. 750 tonnes of silk cocoons were produced in 1994–95.
  The handicraft sector employed 0·26m. persons and had a production turnover of Rs 2,500m. in 1995–96.

COMMUNICATIONS

Roads. Kashmir is linked with the rest of India by the motorable Jammu–Pathankot road. The Jawahar Tunnel, through the Banihal mountain, connects Srinagar and Jammu, and maintains road communication with the Kashmir Valley during the winter months. In 1994–95 there were 12,252 km of roads.
  There were 195,125 motor vehicles in 1995–96.

Rail. Kashmir is linked with the Indian railway system by the line between Jammu and Pathankot; route-km of railways in the state, 1995–96, 88 km.

Civil Aviation. Major airports, with daily service from Delhi, are at Srinagar and Jammu. There is a third airport at Leh.

Telecommunications. There were 202 telephone exchanges and 54,644 telephones in 1994–95.

Postal Services. There were 1,583 post offices in 1994.

SOCIAL INSTITUTIONS

Justice. The High Court, at Srinagar and Jammu, has a Chief Justice and four puisne judges.

Religion. The majority of the population, except in Jammu, are Muslims (making it the only Indian state to have a Muslim majority). At the 1981 census Muslims numbered 3,843,451; Hindus, 1,930,448; Sikhs, 133,675; Buddhists, 69,706; Christians, 8,481; Jains, 1,576.

Education. The proportion of literate people was 54·46% in 2001 (65·75% of men and 41·82% of women). Education is free. There were (1996–97) 1,351 high and higher secondary schools with 227,699 students, 3,104 middle schools with 405,598 students and 10,483 primary schools with 893,005 students. Jammu University (1969) has 5 constituent and 13 affiliated colleges, with 15,278 students (1992–93); Kashmir University (1948) has 18 colleges (17,000 students, 1992–93); the third university is Sher-E-Kashmir University of Agricultural Sciences and Technology. There are 4 medical colleges, 2 engineering and technology colleges, 4 polytechnics, 8 oriental colleges and an Ayurvedic college, 34 arts, science and commerce colleges and 4 teacher training colleges.

Health. In 1993–94 there were 43 hospitals with 9,256 beds, 264 primary health centres and 1,740 sub-centres, and 35 community health centres. There is a National Institute of Medical Sciences.

FURTHER READING
Lamb, A., *Kashmir: a Disputed Legacy, 1846–1990.* Hertingfordbury, 1991.
Wirsing, R. G., *India, Pakistan and the Kashmir Dispute: on Regional Conflict and its Resolution.* London, 1995

JHARKHAND

KEY HISTORICAL EVENTS
The state was carved from Bihar and became the twenty-eighth state of India on 15 Nov. 2000. Located in the plateau regions of eastern India, Jharkhand (literally meaning land of forests) is mentioned in ancient Indian texts as an area inaccessible to the rest of India owing to its unforgiving terrain and the warring nature of the tribes living in its forests. The Mughals attacked the region in 1385 and again in 1616, arresting the King of Jharkhand and imprisoning him while they collected money from local chieftains. During the 17th century Jharkhand was a part of the Mughal empire and spread over areas of present-day Madhya Pradesh and Bihar. The East India Company was granted revenue-collecting power of the area in 1765 and the permanent settlement of 1796 increased the company's grip on the area. In 1858 sovereignty was transferred to the English crown. From 1793 until 1915 there were periodic tribal rebellions throughout Jharkhand against the British. In 1912 Jharkhand was constituted as part of the province of Bihar and Orissa after the former was separated from West Bengal. The Jharkhand Party submitted a request for Jharkhand to become a separate state to the State Reorganisation Committee in 1955. In 2000 a separate Jharkhand state was finally formed after legislation initiated by the National Democratic Alliance passed through parliament. The new state comprised a large area of southern Bihar but not any parts of West Bengal or Orissa as had been originally proposed.

TERRITORY AND POPULATION
Jharkhand is in central eastern India and is bounded by Bihar to the north, West Bengal to the east, Orissa to the south and the new state of Chhattisgarh to the west. Jharkhand has an area of 79,714 sq. km. Population (2001 census, provisional) 26,909,428; density: 338 per sq. km. Cities with over 250,000 population, see INDIA: Territory and population. Other large cities (1991): Dhanbad, 151,789.

SOCIAL STATISTICS
Growth rate 1991–2001, 23·19%.

CONSTITUTION AND GOVERNMENT
Jharkhand is the twenty-eighth state of India. After the region was carved from Bihar it was decided that the 81 Members of the Legislative Assembly (MLAs) from

Jharkhandi districts would become the members of the new state's legislative assembly. For administrative purposes the region is divided into 18 districts.

The capital and seat of government is at Ranchi.

RECENT ELECTIONS

On the basis of elections held in Feb. 2000, the Bharatiya Janata Party was the single largest party with 32 seats. On the formation of the new state they formed a coalition government with Babu Lal Marandi as the state's first chief minister.

CURRENT ADMINISTRATION

Governor: M. Rama Jois.

Chief Minister: Babu Lal Marandi.

ECONOMY

Budget. Budget estimates for Bihar in 1998–99 showed that areas in Jharkhand accounted for almost two-thirds of Bihar's total collected revenues.

ENERGY AND NATURAL RESOURCES

Minerals. Jharkhand is very rich in minerals, with about 40% of national production, including 90% of the country's cooking coal deposits, 40% of its copper, 37% of known coal reserves and 2% of iron ore. Other important minerals: bauxite, quartz, building stones and ceramics, graphite, limestone, kyanite, manganese, lead and silver.

INDUSTRY

There is a major engineering corporation in Jharkhand as well as India's largest steel plant at Bokaro. Other important industries are aluminium and copper plants, forging, explosives, refractories and glass production.

COMMUNICATIONS

Roads. National highways connect Ranchi to the neighbouring states of Bihar in the north, West Bengal to the east and Orissa to the south. State highways connect to the new state of Chhattisgarh in the west.

Rail. Ranchi and the steel city of Bokaro are at the hub of the state's railway network linking Jharkhand to its neighbouring states as well as to Calcutta.

SOCIAL INSTITUTIONS

Education. In 2001, 54·13% of the population were literate (87·94% of men and 39·38% of women). There were three universities in 1999: Ranchi University (founded 1960), with 106 colleges and 55,731 students (1994-95); Bisra Agricultural University in Ranchi (1980); and Sidhu Kanhu University. There were 17 technical institutes, including the Indian School of Mines, the Xavier Labour Relations Institute, the Birla Institute of Technology and the Central Mining Research Institute.

CULTURE

Tourism. The main tourist centre is Ranchi.

KARNATAKA

KEY HISTORICAL EVENTS

The state of Karnataka, constituted as Mysore under the States Reorganization Act, 1956, brought together the Kannada-speaking people distributed in five states, and consisted of the territories of the old states of Mysore and Coorg, the Bijapur, Kanara and Dharwar districts and the Belgaum district (except one taluk) in former Bombay, the major portions of the Gulbarga, Raichur and Bidar districts in former Hyderabad, the South Kanara district (apart from the Kasaragod taluk) and the Kollegal taluk of the Coimbatore district in Madras. The state was renamed Karnataka in 1973.

TERRITORY AND POPULATION
The state is in south India and is bounded north by Maharashtra, east by Andhra Pradesh, south by Tamil Nadu and Kerala, west by the Indian ocean and northeast by Goa. The area of the state is 191,791 sq. km, and its population (2001 census, provisional), 44,977,201; density, 235 per sq. km. Principal cities, *see* INDIA: Territory and Population. The capital is Bangalore. Other large towns (1991) are: Bellary (245,391), Bijapur (186,939), Shimoga (178,882), Raichur (157,551), Tumkur (138,903), Gadag-Betigeri (134,051), Mandya (120,265), Hospet (114,154) and Bidar (108,016).

Kannada is the language of administration and is spoken by about 66% of the people. Other languages include Urdu (9%), Telugu (8·2%), Marathi (4·5%), Tamil (3·6%), Tulu and Konkani.

SOCIAL STATISTICS
Growth rate 1991–2001, 17·25%.

CONSTITUTION AND GOVERNMENT
Karnataka has a bicameral legislature. The Legislative Council has 75 members. The Legislative Assembly consists of 224 elected members.

The state has 27 districts grouped in four divisions: Bangalore, Belgaum, Gulbarga and Mysore.

RECENT ELECTIONS
At the elections in 1999 the Indian National Congress party won 132 seats, the Bharatiya Janata Party, 44; independents, 19; Janata Dal (United), 18; Janata Dal (Secular), 10; All India Anna Dravida Munetra Kazhagam, 1.

CURRENT ADMINISTRATION
Governor: T. N. Chaturvedi.
   Chief Minister: Somanahalli Mallaiah Krishna.

ECONOMY
Budget. Budget estimates, 1997–98: revenue receipts, Rs 117,664·5m.; revenue expenditure, Rs 119,654·5m. Plan allocation 1997–98, Rs 41,300m.

ENERGY AND NATURAL RESOURCES
Electricity. In 1995–96 the state's installed capacity was 3,377·5 MW. Electricity generated, 1994–95, 16,830m. kWh. 26,483 villages had electricity in March 1996.

Minerals. Karnataka is an important source of gold and silver. The estimated reserves of high grade iron ore are 8,798m. tonnes. These reserves are found mainly in the Chitradurga belt. The National Mineral Development Corporation of India has indicated total reserves of nearly 332m. tonnes of magnesite and iron ore (with an iron content ranging from 25 to 40) which have been found in Kudremukh Ganga-Mula region in Chickmagalur District. Value of production (1992–93) Rs 2,590m. The estimated reserves of manganese are over 320m. tonnes.

Limestone is found in many regions; deposits (1992–93) are about 5,892m. tonnes.

Karnataka is the largest producer of chromite. It is one of the only two states of India producing magnesite. The other minerals of industrial importance are corundum and garnet.

Agriculture. Agriculture forms the main occupation of more than three-quarters of the population. Physically, Karnataka divides into four regions—the coastal region, the southern and northern plains, comprising roughly the districts of Bangalore, Tumkur, Chitradurga, Kolar, Bellary, Mandya and Mysore, and the hill country, comprising the districts of Chickmagalur, Hassan and Shimoga. Rainfall is heavy in the hill country, and there is dense forest. The greater part of the plains are cultivated. Coorg district is essentially agricultural.

The main food crops are rice paddy and jowar, and ragi which is also about 30% of the national crop. Total foodgrains production (1995–96), 8·77m. tonnes (rice 3·02m. tonnes, wheat 150,200 tonnes); pulses 0·72m. tonnes. Sugar, groundnut, castor-seed, safflower, mulberry silk and cotton are important cash crops. The state grows about 70% of the national coffee crop.

Production, 1995–96: sugarcane, 24·92m. tonnes; cotton (1993–94), 773,279 bales (each 170 kg).

Livestock (1992–93): buffaloes, 4·07m.; other cattle, 10·18m.; sheep, 4·73m.; goats, 3·89m.

Forestry. Total forest in the state (1995) is 30,382 sq. km, producing sandalwood, bamboo and other timbers.

Fisheries. Production, 1995–96, 304,870 tonnes.

INDUSTRY

There were 7,765 factories, 125 industrial estates and 5,176 industrial sheds employing 818,000 in March 1994. In 1994–95, 163,524 small industries employed 1,076,312 persons. The Vishveshwaraiah Iron and Steel Works is situated at Bhadravati, while at Bangalore are national undertakings for the manufacture of aircraft, machine tools, telephones, light engineering and electronics goods. The Kudremukh iron ore project is of national importance. An oil refinery is in operation at Mangalore. Other industries include textiles, vehicle manufacture, cement, chemicals, sugar, paper, porcelain and soap. In addition, much of the world's sandalwood is processed, the oil being one of the most valuable productions of the state. Sericulture is a more important cottage industry giving employment, directly or indirectly, to about 2·7m. persons; production of raw silk, 1992–93, 7,147 tonnes, over two-thirds of national production.

COMMUNICATIONS

Roads. In 1993–94 the state had 134,832 km of roads, including 1,997 km of national highway. There were (31 March 1996) 2,249,890 motor vehicles.

Rail. In 1995–96 there were 3,124 km of railway (including 149 km of narrow gauge) in the state.

Civil Aviation. There are airports at Bangalore, Hubli, Mysore, Mangalore, Bellary and Belgaum, with regular scheduled services to Bombay, Calcutta, Delhi and Madras.

Shipping. Mangalore is a deep-water port for the export of mineral ores. Karwar is being developed as an intermediate port.

SOCIAL INSTITUTIONS

Justice. The seat of the High Court is at Bangalore. It has a Chief Justice and 21 puisne judges.

Religion. At the 1991 census there were 38,432,027 Hindus; 5,234,023 Muslims; 859,478 Christians; 326,114 Jains; 73,012 Buddhists; 10,101 Sikhs.

Education. In 2001, 67·04% of the population were literate (76·29% of men and 57·50% of women). In 1996–97 the state had 22,870 primary schools with 6,507,805 students, 18,485 middle schools with 2,158,487 students, 7,644 high and higher secondary schools with 1,270,794 students, 172 polytechnic and 125 medical colleges, 49 engineering and technology colleges, 761 arts, science and commerce colleges and 12 universities. Education is free up to pre-university level.

Universities: Mysore (1916); Karnataka (1949) at Dharwar; University of Agricultural Sciences (1964) at Hebbal, Bangalore; Gulbarga; Mangalore; University of Agricultural Sciences, Dharwad; Kuvempu University, Shimoga; Kannada University and National Law School of India. Mysore has 6 university and 125 affiliated colleges; Karnataka, 5 and 240; Bangalore, 204 affiliated; Hebbal, 8 constituent colleges.

The Indian Institute of Science, Bangalore, has the status of a university.

Health. There were in 1993–94, 306 hospitals, 208 dispensaries, 1,459 primary health centres and 459 family welfare centres. Total number of beds in 1993–94, 43,308.

KERALA

KEY HISTORICAL EVENTS

The state of Kerala was created in 1956, bringing together the Malayalam-speaking areas. It includes most of the former state of Travancore-Cochin and small areas from the state of Madras. Cochin, an exceptionally safe harbour, was an early site of European trading in India. In 1795 the British took it from the Dutch and British influence remained dominant. Travancore was a Hindu state which became a British protectorate in 1795, having been an ally of the British East India Company for some years. Cochin and Travancore were combined as one state in 1947, reorganized and renamed Kerala in 1956.

TERRITORY AND POPULATION

Kerala is in south India and is bounded north by Karnataka, east and southeast by Tamil Nadu, southwest and west by the Indian ocean. The state has an area of 38,863 sq. km. The 2001 census showed a population of 31,838,619; density, 819 per sq. km. Chief cities, *see* INDIA: Territory and Population. Other principal towns (1991): Alappuzha (174,666), Kollam (139,852), Palakkad (123,289) and Thalassery (103,577).

Languages spoken in the state are Malayalam, Tamil and Kannada.

SOCIAL STATISTICS

The growth rate during the period 1991–2001, at 9·42%, was the lowest of any Indian state.

CONSTITUTION AND GOVERNMENT

The state has a unicameral legislature of 140 elected (and one nominated) members including the Speaker.

The state has 14 districts. The capital is Thiruvananthapuram.

RECENT ELECTIONS

At the elections of 10 May 2001 the Indian National Congress party won 62 seats, the Communist Party of India (Marxist) (CPM) 23 and the Muslim League Kerala State Committee 16.

CURRENT ADMINISTRATION

Governor: Sikander Bakht.
Chief Minister: A. K. Antony.

ECONOMY

Budget. Budget estimates for 1997–98 showed revenue receipts of Rs 75,534m.; expenditure Rs 87,957m. Annual Plan expenditure, 1997–98, Rs 28,500m.

ENERGY AND NATURAL RESOURCES

Electricity. Installed capacity (1995–96), 1,505 MW; energy generated in 1995–96 was 6,662m. kWh. The Idukki hydro-electric plant produced 3,064m. kWh and the Sabarigiri scheme 1,674m. kWh. All villages have electricity.

Minerals. The beach sands of Kerala contain monazite, ilmenite, rutile, zircon, sillimanite, etc. There are extensive white clay deposits; other minerals of commercial importance include magnesite, china clay, limestone, quartz sand and lignite. Iron ore has been found at Kozhikode (Calicut).

Agriculture. Area under irrigation in 1995–96 was 644,000 ha; 6 irrigation projects were under execution in 1996–97. The chief agricultural products are rice, tapioca, coconut, arecanut, cashew nut, oilseeds, pepper, sugarcane, rubber, tea, coffee and cardamom. About 98% of Indian black pepper and about 95% of Indian rubber is produced in Kerala. Production of principal crops, 1994–95: total foodgrains, 1·1m. tonnes (of which rice 953,026 tonnes from 471,000 ha); pulses, 16,800 tonnes; sugarcane, 464,000 tonnes; rubber, 475,000 tonnes; tea, 64,794 tonnes; coffee, 42,600 tonnes; cashew nuts, 96,780 tonnes.

Livestock (1987): buffaloes, 329,000; other cattle, 3·4m.; goats, 1·6m. In 1995–96 milk production was 2·24m. tonnes; egg production, 1,991m.

Forestry. Forest occupied 10,336 sq. km in 1995, including teak, sandalwood, ebony and blackwood and varieties of softwood. Net forest revenue, 1995–96, Rs 1,607·7m.

Fisheries. Fishing is a flourishing industry; the total catch in 1995–96 was 582,000 tonnes (of which marine, 532,000 tonnes). Fish exports, 78,896 tonnes in 1995–96.

INDUSTRY
There are numerous cashew and coir factories. Important industries are rubber, tea, coffee, tiles, automotive tyres, watches, electronics, oil, textiles, ceramics, fertilizers and chemicals, pharmaceuticals, zinc-smelting, sugar, cement, rayon, glass, matches, pencils, monazite, ilmenite, titanium oxide, rare earths, aluminium, electrical goods, paper, shark-liver oil, etc. The state has a refinery and a shipyard at Kochi (Cochin).

The number of factories registered under the Factories Act 1948 on 31 Dec. 1995 was 15,965, with daily average employment of 0·41m. There were 143,23 small-scale units employing 0·78m. persons on 31 March 1996.

COMMUNICATIONS

Roads. In 1995–96 there were 144,636 km of roads in the state; national highways, 1,011 km. There were 1·17m. motor vehicles at 31 March 1996.

Rail. There is a coastal line from Mangalore in Karnataka which connects with Tamil Nadu. In 1995–96 there were 1,053 route-km of track.

Civil Aviation. There are airports at Kozhikode, Kochi and Thiruvananthapuram with regular scheduled services to Delhi, Bombay and Madras.

Shipping. Port Kochi, administered by the central government, is one of India's major ports; in 1983 it became the out-port for the Inland Container Depot at Coimbatore in Tamil Nadu. There are 12 other ports and harbours.

SOCIAL INSTITUTIONS
Justice. The High Court at Ernakulam has a Chief Justice and 21 puisne judges.

Religion. At the 1991 census there were 16,668,587 Hindus; 6,788,364 Muslims; 5,621,510 Christians; 3,641 Jains; 2,224 Sikhs.

Education. Kerala is the most literate Indian state, with 25·63m. literate people at the 2001 census (90·92%; 94·20% of men and 87·86% of women). Education is free up to the age of 14.

In 1996–97 there were 6,725 primary schools with 2·79m. students, 2,998 middle schools with 1·84m. students and 3,125 high and higher secondary schools with 1·07m. students. There were also 169 junior colleges with 210,074 pupils.

Kerala University (established 1937) at Thiruvananthapuram is affiliating and teaching; in 1995–96 it had 52 affiliated colleges with 113,569 students. The University of Kochi is federal, and for post-graduate studies only. The University of Calicut (established 1968) is teaching and affiliating and has 95 affiliated colleges with 122,343 students (1995–96). Kerala Agricultural University (established 1971) has 7 constituent colleges. Mahatma Gandhi University at Kottayam was established in 1983 and has 64 affiliated colleges with 112,992 students (1995–96). There are two other universities, Sree Sankaracharya University and Malabar University. There were also (1995–96) 6 medical colleges, 15 engineering and technology colleges, 19 teacher training colleges and 211 arts and science colleges.

Health. There were 149 allopathic hospitals, 961 primary health centres, 60 community health centres, 53 dispensaries, 21 TB centres/clinics and 15 leprosy control units, with 42,569 beds in 1995–96. There were also 108 Ayurvedic hospitals with 2,529 beds and 31 homeopathy hospitals with 394 beds.

FURTHER READING
Jeffrey, R., *Politics, Women and Well-Being: How Kerala Became a Model.* London, 1992

MADHYA PRADESH

KEY HISTORICAL EVENTS

The state was formed in 1956 to bring together the Hindi-speaking districts of the area including the 17 Hindi districts of the old Madhya Pradesh, most of the former state of Madhya Bharat, the former states of Bhopal and Vindhya Pradesh and a former Rajput enclave, Sironj. This was an area which the Mahrattas took from the Moghuls between 1712 and 1760. The British overcame Mahratta power in 1818 and established their own Central Provinces. Nagpur became the Province's capital and was also the capital of Madhya Pradesh until in 1956 boundary changes transferred it to Maharashtra. The present capital, Bhopal, was the centre of a Muslim princely state from 1723. An ally of the British against the Mahrattas, Bhopal (with neighbouring small states) became a British-protected agency in 1818. After independence Bhopal acceded to the Indian Union in 1949. The states of Madhya Bharat and Vindhya Pradesh were then formed as neighbours, and in 1956 were combined with Bhopal and Sironj and renamed Madhya Pradesh. In 2000 sixteen mainly tribal districts were carved from Madhya Pradesh to form the new state of Chhattisgarh.

TERRITORY AND POPULATION

The state is in central India and is bounded north by Uttar Pradesh, east by the new state of Chhattisgarh, south by Maharashtra, and west by Gujarat and Rajasthan. Owing to the creation of Chhattisgarh, Madhya Pradesh is no longer the largest Indian state in size. Its revised area is 308,245 sq. km (previously 443,446 sq. km), making it the second largest state in the country. Population (using 2001 census figures), 60,385,118 (31,456,873 males); density, 196 per sq. km.

Cities with over 250,000 population, *see* INDIA: Territory and Population. Other large cities (1991): Ratlam, 195,776; Sagar, 195,346; Burhanpur, 172,710; Dewas, 164,364; Murwara, 163,431; Satna, 160,500; Morena, 147,124; Khandwa, 145,133; Rewa, 128,981; Bhind, 109,755; Shivpuri, 108,271; Guna, 100,490.

Hindi, Marathi, Urdu and Gujarati are spoken. In April 1990 Hindi, which predominates in the state, became the sole official language.

CONSTITUTION AND GOVERNMENT

Madhya Pradesh is one of the nine states for which the Constitution provides a bicameral legislature, but the Vidhan Parishad or Upper House (to consist of 90 members) has yet to be formed. The Vidhan Sabha or Lower House has 230 elected members.

For administrative purposes the state has been split into nine revenue divisions with a Commissioner at the head of each; the headquarters of these are located at Bhopal, Gwalior, Hoshangabad, Indore, Jabalpur, Morena, Rewa, Sagar and Ujjain. There are 22,029 *gram* (village) panchayats, 313 *janpad* (intermediate) panchayats and 45 *zila* (district) panchayats, following the creation of 16 new districts in administrative reforms of 1999 and the creation of Chhattisgarh in 2000.

The seat of government is at Bhopal.

RECENT ELECTIONS

Following the election in Nov. 1998, the Congress (I) Party retained power. Congress (I) won 170 seats, Bharatiya Janata Party (BJP) 117, Pragatisheel Bahujan Samaj Party (BSP) 7, Janata Dal 1, independents and others 18. The remaining seats were vacant. The present Assembly, after the creation of Chhattisgarh, has 128 members from Congress, 83 from the BJP, 4 from each of the BSP and SP, one each from the JD, ABP, RPJ and JP, and seven are independent.

CURRENT ADMINISTRATION

Governor: Bhai Mahavir.
   Chief Minister: Digvijay Singh.

ECONOMY

Budget. Budget estimates for 2001–02 showed revenue receipts of Rs 125,184m. and expenditure of Rs 162,770m. Annual plan, 2002–03, Rs 48,209m.

ENERGY AND NATURAL RESOURCES

Electricity. Madhya Pradesh is rich in low-grade coal suitable for power generation, and also has immense potential for hydro-electric energy. Total installed capacity, 2000–01, 2,941 MW. Power generated, 14,009m. kWh in 2000–01. There are eight hydro-electric power stations of 747·5 MW installed capacity. 50,306 out of 51,806 villages had electricity by 2000–01.

Water. Major irrigation projects include the Chambal Valley scheme (started in 1952 with Rajasthan), the Tawa project in Hoshangabad district, the Barna and Hasdeo schemes, the Mahanadi canal system and schemes in the Narmada valley at Bargi and Narmadasagar. Area under irrigation, 1999–2000, 4·28m. ha.

Minerals. Much of the state's extensive mineral deposits were in the area that has now become the new state of Chhattisgarh. In 2000–01 (1996 figures in brackets) there were 25·04m. tonnes (8,001m.) of limestone, 0·25m. tonnes (126·8m.) of bauxite, 4·04m. tonnes (26,853m.) of coal, and 0·92m. tonnes (2,186·2m.) of iron ore. In 2001–02 the output of diamonds was 73,981 carats and manganese ore 0·43m. tonnes. In 2001–02 revenue from minerals was Rs 5·39m. (Rs 8,500m. in 1997–98) and coal output was 4·4m. tonnes (43·0m. in 1999–2000).

Agriculture. The creation of the new state of Chhattisgarh, previously known as the 'rice bowl' of Madhya Pradesh, in 2000 had serious implications for the state. Agriculture is the mainstay of the state's economy and 76·8% of the people are rural. 43·7% of the land area is cultivable, of which 16·6% is irrigated. Production of principal crops, 2001–02 (in tonnes): foodgrains, 8·93m.; pulses, 3·96m.; cotton, 0·23m. bales of 170 kg.

Livestock (1997): buffaloes, 6·64m.; other cattle, 34·88m.; sheep, 6·56m.; goats, 6·47m.

Forestry. The forested area totals 95,200 sq. km, or about 30·9% of the state. The forests are chiefly of sal, saja and teak species. They are the chief source in India of best-quality teak; they also provide firewood for about 60% of domestic fuel needs, and form valuable watershed protection. Forest revenue, 2001–02, Rs 32·5m.

INDUSTRY

The major industries are steel, aluminium, paper, cement, motor vehicles, ordnance, textiles and heavy electrical equipment. Other industries include electronics, telecommunications, sugar, fertilizers, straw board, vegetable oil, refractories, potteries, textile machinery, steel casting and re-rolling, industrial gases, synthetic fibres, drugs, biscuit manufacturing, engineering, optical fibres, plastics, tools, rayon and art silk. The number of heavy and medium industries in the state is 805; the number of small-scale establishments in production is 497,000.

There are 23 'growth centres' in operation, and five under development. The Government of India has proposed setting up a Special Economic Zone at Indore.

COMMUNICATIONS

Roads. Total length of roads is 68,100 km. The length of national highways is 4,720 km and state highway 6,500 km. In March 2002 there were 3,173,000 motor vehicles.

Rail. The main rail route linking northern and southern India passes through Madhya Pradesh. Bhopal, Bina, Gwalior, Indore, Itarsi, Jabalpur, Katni, Khandwa, Ratlam and Ujjain are important junctions for the central, south, eastern and western networks. Route length (1998–99), 5,764·8 km.

Civil Aviation. There are domestic airports at Bhopal, Gwalior, Indore and Khajuraho with regular scheduled services to Bombay, Delhi, Agra and Varanasi.

SOCIAL INSTITUTIONS

Justice. The High Court of Judicature at Jabalpur has a Chief Justice and 21 puisne judges. Its benches are located at Gwalior and Indore. A National Institute of Law and a National Judicial Academy have been set up at Bhopal.

Religion. At the 1991 census Hindus numbered 61,412,898; Muslims, 3,282,800; Jains, 490,324; Christians, 426,598; Buddhists, 216,667; Sikhs, 161,111.

Education. In 2001, 64·11% of the population were literate (76·80% of men and 50·28% of women). Education is free for children aged up to 14.

In 1998 there were 81,000 primary schools (63,712 in 2001) with 10·33m. students, 20,000 middle schools with 3·46m. students and 7,000 high and higher secondary schools (8,471 in 2001) with 2·03m. students.

There are 11 universities in Madhya Pradesh: Dr Hari Singh Gour University (established 1946), at Sagar, had 97 affiliated colleges and 74,386 students in 1992–93; Rani Durgavati University at Jabalpur (1957) had 46 affiliated colleges and 45,315 students; Vikram University (1957), at Ujjain, had 83 affiliated colleges and 39,723 students; Devi Ahilya University at Indore (1964) had 32 affiliated colleges and 28,196 students; Jiwaji University (1963), at Gwalior, had 60 affiliated colleges and (1991–92) 58,825 students; Jawaharlal Nehru Agricultural University (1964), at Jabalpur, had 10 constituent colleges and 2,053 students; A. P. Singh University, Rewa had 81 colleges and 24,960 students; Barkatullah Vishwavidyalaya, Bhopal had 44 colleges and 18,817 students; Makhanlal Chaturvedi Rashtriya Patrakarita Vishwavidhyalaya Bhopal; Chitrakoot Gramodoya Vishwavidhayalaya, Chitrakoot; and Rajiv Gandhi Technology University, Bhopal. There are also the Bhoj Open University, Bhopal, the Centre for Excellence in Higher Education, Bhopal, and the Maharshi Mahesh Yogi Vedic Vishwavidyalaya, Jabalpur. In 1999 there were 413 government colleges (15 of which were lost to Chhattisgarh in 2000), 252 private colleges (14 of which were lost to Chhattisgarh in 2000), 30 engineering colleges (all to be affiliated to the Rajiv Ghandi Technology University), 7 medical colleges, 44 polytechnics, 5 institutions of architecture and 30 management institutes.

Health. In 2001–02 there were 45 district hospitals, 57 urban civil hospitals, 1,194 primary health centres, 8,835 sub-health centres, 229 community health centres, seven TB hospitals and two TB sanatoriums.

MAHARASHTRA

KEY HISTORICAL EVENTS

The Bombay Presidency of the East India Company began with a trading factory, made over to the Company in 1668. The Presidency expanded, overcoming the surrounding Mahratta chiefs until Mahratta power was finally conquered in 1818. After independence Bombay State succeeded the Presidency; its area was altered in 1956 by adding Kutch and Saurashtra and the Marathi-speaking areas of Hyderabad and Madhya Pradesh, and taking away Kannada-speaking areas (which were added to Mysore). In 1960 the Bombay Reorganization Act divided Bombay State between Gujarati and Marathi areas, the latter becoming Maharashtra. The state of Maharashtra consists of the following districts of the former Bombay State: Ahmednagar, Akola, Amravati, Aurangabad, Bhandara, Bhir, Buldana, Chanda, Dhulia (West Khandesh), Greater Bombay, Jalgaon (East Khandesh), Kolaba, Kolhapur, Nagpur, Nanded, Nashik, Osmanabad, Parbhani, Pune, Ratnagiri, Sangli, Satara, Sholapur, Thane, Wardha, Yeotmal; certain portions of Thane and Dhulia districts have become part of Gujarat.

TERRITORY AND POPULATION

Maharashtra is in central India and is bounded north by Madhya Pradesh, east by Chhattisgarh, south by Andhra Pradesh, Karnataka and Goa, west by the Indian ocean and northwest by Daman and Gujarat. The state has an area of 307,713 sq. km. The population in 2001 (census, provisional) was 96,752,247; density, 314 per sq. km. In 1991 the area of Greater Bombay was 603 sq. km and its population 9·93m. For other principal cities, *see* INDIA: Territory and Population. Other large towns (1991): Jalgaon (242,193), Chandrapur (226,105), Ichalkaranji (214,950), Latur (197,408), Sangli (193,197), Parbhani (190,255), Ahmadnagar (181,339), Jalna (174,958), Bhusawal (145,143), Miraj (125,407), Bid (112,434), Gondiya (109,470), Yavatmul (108,578) and Wardha (102,985).

The official language is Marathi.

SOCIAL STATISTICS
Growth rate 1991–2001, 22·57%.

CONSTITUTION AND GOVERNMENT
Maharashtra has a bicameral legislature. The Legislative Council has 78 members. The Legislative Assembly has 288 elected members and one member nominated by the Governor to represent the Anglo-Indian community.

The Council of Ministers consists of the Chief Minister, 16 other Ministers, and 19 Ministers of State.

The capital is Bombay. The state has 35 districts.

RECENT ELECTIONS
At the elections held between 5–11 Sept. 1999 the Indian National Congress party won 75 seats; Shivsena, 69; Nationalist Congress Party, 58; Bharatiya Janata Party, 56; independents and others with 12 seats or less, 30.

CURRENT ADMINISTRATION
Governor: Mohammad Fazal.
    Chief Minister: Sushil Kumar Shinde.

ECONOMY
Budget. Budget estimates, 1995–96: revenue receipts, Rs 151,802m.; revenue expenditure, Rs 167,657m. Plan outlay, 1997–98, Rs 83,250m.

ENERGY AND NATURAL RESOURCES
Electricity. Installed capacity, 1995–96, 10,039 MW (7,155 MW thermal, 1,602 MW hydro-electric, 1,092 MW gas and 190 MW nuclear). All villages have electricity. Output, 1996–97, 39,599m. kWh.

Oil and Gas. Bombay High (offshore) produced 22·7m. tonnes of crude oil and 16,579,000 cu. metres of natural gas in 1995–96.

Minerals. The state has coal, silica sand, dolomite, kyanite, chromite, limestone, iron ore, manganese and bauxite. Value of mineral production, 1995, Rs 11,590m.

Agriculture. 3·3m. ha of the cropped area of 21·4m. ha are irrigated. In normal seasons the main food crops are rice, wheat, jowar, bajra and pulses. Main cash crops: cotton, sugarcane, groundnuts. Production, 1994–95 (in tonnes): foodgrains, 11·5m. (rice, 2·4m., wheat, 1·11m.); pulses, 1·7m.; cotton, 401,300; sugarcane, 42·68m.; groundnuts, 0·63m.

Livestock (1992 census, in 1,000): buffaloes, 5,447; other cattle, 17,441; sheep and goats, 13,015; poultry, 32,189.

Forestry. Forests occupied 64,300 sq. km in 1995–96. Value of forest products in 1996–97, Rs 2,820m.

Fisheries. In 1995–96 the marine fish catch was estimated at 424,000 tonnes and the inland fish catch at 84,000 tonnes; 18,038 boats, including 8,552 mechanized, were used for marine fishing.

INDUSTRY
Industry is concentrated mainly in Bombay, Nashik, Pune and Thane. The main groups are chemicals and products, textiles, electrical and non-electrical machinery, petroleum and products, aircraft, rubber and plastic products, transport equipment, automobiles, paper, electronic items, engineering goods, pharmaceuticals and food products. The state industrial development corporation invested Rs 77,020m. in 21,452 industrial units in 1994–95. In June 1995 there were 26,642 working factories employing 1·2m. people. In Dec. 1996 there were 203,882 small scale industries employing 1·63m. people.

COMMUNICATIONS
Roads. On 31 March 1996 there were 223,000 km of roads, of which 187,090 km were surfaced. There were 4,359,029 motor vehicles on 1 Jan. 1997, of which 17% were in Greater Bombay. Passenger and freight transport has been nationalized.

Rail. The total length of railway on 31 March 1996 was 5,462 km; 66% was broad gauge, 14% metre gauge and 20% narrow gauge. The main junctions and termini are Bombay, Dadar, Manmad, Akola, Nagpur, Pune and Sholapur.

Civil Aviation. The main airport is Bombay, which has national and international flights. Nagpur airport is on the route from Bombay to Calcutta and there are also airports at Pune and Aurangabad.

Shipping. Maharashtra has a coastline of 720 km. Bombay is the major port, and there are 48 minor ports.

SOCIAL INSTITUTIONS

Justice. The High Court has a Chief Justice and 45 judges. The seat of the High Court is Bombay, but it has benches at Nagpur, Aurangabad and Panaji (Goa).

Religion. At the 1991 census Hindus numbered 64,033,213; Muslims, 7,628,755; Buddhists, 5,040,785; Jains, 965,840; Christians, 885,030; Sikhs, 161,184. Other religions, 99,768; religion not stated, 106,560.

Education. The number of literate people, according to the 2001 census, was 64·57m. (77·27%; 86·27% of men and 67·51% of women). In 1996–97 there were 13,225 high and higher secondary schools with 2,795,567 pupils; 21,969 middle schools with 4,753,257 pupils; and 41,005 primary schools with 11,685,598 pupils. There are 111 engineering and technology colleges, 156 medical colleges (including dental and Ayurvedic colleges), 244 teacher training colleges, 152 polytechnics and 820 arts, science and commerce colleges.

Bombay University, founded in 1857, is mainly an affiliating university. It has 276 colleges with a total (1993–94) of 234,469 students. Nagpur University (1923) is both teaching and affiliating. It has 258 colleges with 95,664 students. Poona University, founded in 1948, is teaching and affiliating; it has 167 colleges and 151,990 students. The SNDT Women's University had 33 colleges with a total of 33,343 students. Dr B. R. Ambedkar Marathwada University, Aurangabad was founded in 1958 as a teaching and affiliating body to control colleges in the Marathwada or Marathi-speaking area, previously under Osmania University; it has 190 colleges and 195,806 students. Shivaji University, Kolhapur, was established in 1963 to control affiliated colleges previously under Poona University. It has 205 colleges and 115,553 students. Amravati University has 130 colleges and 74,484 students. Other universities are: Marathwada Krishi Vidyapeeth, Parbhani; Y. Chavan Maharashtra Open University, Nashik; North Maharashtra University, Jalgaon, with 101 colleges and 66,092 students; Mahatma Phule Krishi University, Rahuri; Punjabrao Krishi University, Akola; Konkan Krishi University, Dapoli; Dr Babasaheb Ambedkar Technological University; North Maharashtra University; and Swami Ramanand Teerth Marathwad University.

Health. In 1995 there were 736 hospitals (124,701 beds), 1,418 dispensaries and 1,695 primary health centres, 161 primary health units and 2,154 TB hospitals and clinics.

MANIPUR

KEY HISTORICAL EVENTS

Formerly a state under the political control of the government of India, Manipur entered into interim arrangements with the Indian Union on 15 Aug. 1947 and the political agency was abolished. The administration was taken over by the government of India on 15 Oct. 1949 under a merger agreement, and it was centrally administered by the government of India through a Chief Commissioner. In 1950–51 an Advisory form of government was introduced. In 1957 this was replaced by a Territorial Council of 30 elected and two nominated members. Later, in 1963, a Legislative Assembly of 30 elected and three nominated members was established under the government of Union Territories Act 1963. Because of the unstable party position in the Assembly, it had to be dissolved on 16 Oct. 1969 and President's Rule introduced. The status of the administrator was raised from Chief

Commissioner to Lieut.-Governor with effect from 19 Dec. 1969. On 21 Jan. 1972 Manipur became a state and the status of the administrator was changed from Lieut.-Governor to Governor. In June 2001 Manipur was placed under central rule.

TERRITORY AND POPULATION
The state is in northeast India and is bounded north by Nagaland, east by Myanmar, south by Myanmar and Mizoram, and west by Assam. Manipur has an area of 22,327 sq. km and a population (2001 census, provisional) of 2,388,634; density, 107 per sq. km. The valley, which is about 1,813 sq. km, is 800 metres above sea-level. The hills rise in places to 3,000 metres, but are mostly about 1,500–1,800 metres. The average annual rainfall is 165 cm. The hill areas are inhabited by various hill tribes who constitute about one-third of the total population of the state. There are about 30 tribes and sub-tribes falling into two main groups of Nagas and Kukis. Manipuri and English are the official languages. A large number of dialects are spoken.

SOCIAL STATISTICS
Growth rate 1991–2001, 30·02%.

CONSTITUTION AND GOVERNMENT
Manipur has a Legislative Assembly of 60 members, of which 19 are from reserved tribal constituencies. There are nine districts. The capital is Imphal.

RECENT ELECTIONS
Elections were held in Feb. 2002. The Indian National Congress party (INC) won 19 seats; the Federal Party of Manipur (FPM), 13; the Manipur State Congress Party (MSCP), 6; the Bharatiya Janata Party (BJP), 4; Samata Party, 3; others, 15. Following the elections a Secular Progressive Front (SPF) was installed in government, comprising the INC, the MSCP, the Nationalist Congress Party and the Communist Party of India.

CURRENT ADMINISTRATION
Governor: Ved Prakash Marwah.
    Chief Minister: Okram Ibobi Singh.

ECONOMY
Budget. Budget estimates for 1995–96 show revenue of Rs 6,437·6m. and expenditure of Rs 7,542·4m. Plan allocation 1997–98, Rs 4,100m.

ENERGY AND NATURAL RESOURCES
Electricity. Installed capacity (1995–96) is 12 MW from diesel and hydro-electric generators. This has been augmented since 1981 by the North Eastern Regional Grid. In March 1996 there were 2,015 villages with electricity.

Water. The main power, irrigation and flood-control schemes are the Loktak Lift Irrigation scheme (irrigation potential, 40,000 ha); the Singda scheme (potential 4,000 ha, and improved water supply for Imphal); the Thoubal scheme (potential 34,000 ha), and four other large projects. By 1994–95, 59,100 ha had been irrigated.

Agriculture. Rice is the principal crop; with wheat, maize and pulses. Total foodgrains, 1995–96, 0·48m. tonnes (rice, 338,100 tonnes).
    Agricultural workforce, 453,040. Only 0·21m. ha are cultivable, of which 134,900 ha are under paddy. Fruit and vegetables are important in the valley, including pineapples, oranges, bananas, mangoes, pears, peaches and plums. Soil erosion, produced by shifting cultivation, is being halted by terracing. Fruit production in 1993–94, 0·11m. tonnes.

Forestry. Forests occupied about 17,588 sq. km in 1995. The main products are teak, jurjan, pine; there are also large areas of bamboo and cane, especially in the Jiri and Barak river drainage areas, yielding about 0·3m. tonnes annually. Total revenue from forests, 1990–91, Rs 9·95m.

Fisheries. Landings in 1995–96, 12,500 tonnes.

INDUSTRY

Handloom weaving is a cottage industry. Larger-scale industries include the manufacture of bicycles and TV sets, sugar, cement, starch, vegetable oil and glucose. Sericulture produces about 45 tonnes of raw silk annually. Estimated non-agricultural workforce, 229,408.

COMMUNICATIONS

Roads. Length of road (1995), 7,003 km; number of vehicles (1996–97) 65,223. A national highway from Kaziranga (Assam) runs through Imphal to the border with Myanmar.

Rail. A railway link was opened in 1990.

Civil Aviation. There is an airport at Imphal with regular scheduled services to Delhi and Calcutta.

SOCIAL INSTITUTIONS

Religion. At the 1991 census Hindus numbered 1,059,470; Christians, 626,669; Muslims, 133,535.

Education. In 2001, 68·87% of the population were literate (77·87% of men and 59·70% of women). In 1996–97 there were 2,548 primary schools with 230,230 students, 555 middle schools with 106,200 students, 553 high and higher secondary schools with 66,160 students, 50 colleges, 1 medical college, 2 teacher training colleges, 3 polytechnics, Manipur University with 62 colleges and 52,352 students (1997–98), and an agricultural university.

Health. In 1996–97 there were 93 hospitals and public health centres, 52 dispensaries, 16 community health centres, 420 sub-centres and 58 other facilities.

MEGHALAYA

KEY HISTORICAL EVENTS

The state was created under the Assam Reorganization (Meghalaya) Act 1969 and inaugurated on 2 April 1970. Its status was that of a state within the State of Assam until 21 Jan. 1972 when it became a fully-fledged state of the Union. It consists of the former Garo Hills district and United Khasi and Jaintia Hills district of Assam.

TERRITORY AND POPULATION

Meghalaya is bounded in the north and east by Assam, south and west by Bangladesh. In 2001 the area was 22,429 sq. km and the population (census, provisional) 2,306,069; density, 103 per sq. km. The people are mainly of the Khasi, Jaintia and Garo tribes. The main languages of the state are Khasi, Jaintia, Garo and English.

SOCIAL STATISTICS

Growth rate 1991–2001, 29·94%.

CONSTITUTION AND GOVERNMENT

Meghalaya has a unicameral legislature. The Legislative Assembly has 60 seats. There are seven districts. The capital is Shillong (population, 1991, 131,719).

RECENT ELECTIONS

In elections held in Feb. 2003 the Indian National Congress won 22 seats; Nationalist Congress Party, 14; United Democratic Party, 9; ind., 5; other parties, 10.

CURRENT ADMINISTRATION

Governor: Mundakkal Matthew Jacob.
Chief Minister: D. D. Lapang.

ECONOMY

Budget. Budget estimates for 1996–97 showed revenue receipts of Rs 7,758m. and expenditure of Rs 6,502m. Annual plan outlay, 1997–98, Rs 3,820m.

ENERGY AND NATURAL RESOURCES

Electricity. Total installed capacity (1995–96) was 186·71 MW. 2,408 villages out of 4,902 had electricity in March 1996.

Minerals. The Khasi Hills, Jaintia Hills and Garo Hills districts produce coal, sillimanite (95% of India's total output), limestone, fire clay, dolomite, feldspar, quartz and glass sand. The state also has deposits of coal (estimated reserves 600m. tonnes), limestone (3,000m.), fire clay (6m.) and sandstone which are so far virtually untapped.

Agriculture. About 83% of the people depend on agriculture. Principal crops are rice, maize, potatoes, cotton, oranges, ginger, tezpata, areca nuts, jute, mesta, bananas and pineapples. Production 1995–96 (in tonnes) of principal crops: rice, 118,900; wheat, 6,400; pulses, 2,400; potatoes, 146,941; maize, 20,800; jute, 43,444; cotton, 5,432; rape and mustard, 4,200.

Forestry. Forests covered 9,496 sq. km in 1995–96. Forest products are the state's chief resources.

INDUSTRY

Apart from agriculture the main source of employment is the extraction and processing of minerals; there are also important timber processing mills and cement factories. Other industries include electronics, tantalum capacitors, beverages and watches. The state has 5 industrial estates, 2 industrial areas and 1 growth centre. In 1995–96 there were 58 registered factories and 2,533 small-scale industries. There were also, in 1994–95, 1,812 sericultural villages, 6 sericultural farms and 8 silk units and, in 1995–96, 5,400 *khadi* and village industrial units.

COMMUNICATIONS

Roads. Three national highways run through the state for a distance of 460 km. In 1995–96 there were 6,572 km of surfaced and unsurfaced roads. Total number of motor vehicles, 1995–96, 44,715.

Rail. The state has only 1 km of railways.

Civil Aviation. Umroi airport (25 km from Shillong) connects the state with main air services.

SOCIAL INSTITUTIONS

Justice. The Guwahati High Court is common to Assam, Meghalaya, Nagaland, Manipur, Mizoram, Tripura and Arunachal Pradesh. There is a bench of the Guwahati High Court at Shillong.

Religion. At the 1991 census Christians numbered 1,146,092; Hindus, 260,306; Muslims, 61,462; Buddhists, 2,934; Sikhs, 2,612.

Education. In 2001, 63·31% of the population were literate (66·14% of men and 60·41% of women). In 1996–97 the state had 4,235 primary schools with 299,961 students, 851 middle schools with 78,858 students, 431 high and higher secondary schools with 44,221 students, 10 teacher training schools and 1 college, 1 polytechnic and 28 colleges. The North Eastern Hill University started functioning at Shillong in 1973; in 1993–94 it had 41 colleges and 54,803 students.

Health. In 1995–96 there were 9 government hospitals, 77 primary health centres, 20 government dispensaries and 325 sub-centres. Total beds (hospitals and health centres), 2,352.

MIZORAM

KEY HISTORICAL EVENTS

On 21 Jan. 1972 the former Mizo Hills District of Assam was created a Union Territory. A long dispute between the Mizo National Front (originally Separatist) and the central government was resolved in 1986. Mizoram became a state by the Constitution (53rd Amendment) and the State of Mizoram Acts, July 1986.

TERRITORY AND POPULATION

Mizoram is one of the easternmost Indian states, lying between Bangladesh and Myanmar, and having on its northern boundaries Tripura, Assam and Manipur. The area is 21,081 sq. km and the population (2001 census, provisional) 891,058; density, 42 per sq. km. The main languages spoken are Mizo and English.

SOCIAL STATISTICS

Growth rate 1991–2001, 29·18%.

CONSTITUTION AND GOVERNMENT

Mizoram has a unicameral Legislative Assembly with 40 seats. The capital is Aizawl (population, 1991, 155,240).

RECENT ELECTIONS

In the elections of Nov. 1998, Congress (I) lost to 2 regional parties and won only 6 of a possible 40 seats. As a result the distribution of seats was: Mizo National Front, 21; Mizoram People's Conference, 12; Indian National Congress, 6; independent, 1.

CURRENT ADMINISTRATION

Governor: Amolak Rattan Kohli.
 Chief Minister: Zoramthanga.

ECONOMY

Budget. Budget estimates for 1997–98 show revenue receipts of Rs 6,769·7m. and expenditure of Rs 5,865·9m. Annual plan outlay, 1997–98, Rs 2,900m.

ENERGY AND NATURAL RESOURCES

Electricity. Installed capacity (1993–94), 24·45 MW. 617 out of 721 villages had electricity in March 1996.

Agriculture. About 60% of the people are engaged in agriculture, either on terraced holdings or in shifting cultivation. Total production of foodgrains, 1995–96, 122,700 tonnes (rice, 101,500 tonnes).
 Total forest area, 1995, 18,576 sq. km.

INDUSTRY

Handloom weaving and other cottage industries are important. The state had (1992) 2,300 small scale industrial units, including furniture industries, steel fabrication, TV manufacturing, truck and bus body building.

COMMUNICATIONS

Roads. Aizawl is connected by road with Silchar in Assam. Total length of roads, 31 March 1992, 5,095 km. There were 18,238 motor vehicles in 1995–96.

Civil Aviation. Aizawl is connected by air with Silchar in Assam and with Calcutta.

SOCIAL INSTITUTIONS

Religion. At the 1991 census Christians numbered 591,342; Buddhists, 54,024; Hindus, 34,788; Muslims, 4,538.

Education. In 2001, 88·49% of the population were literate (90·69% of men and 86·13% of women). In 1996–97 there were 1,263 primary schools with 129,662 students, 702 middle schools with 44,186 students and 346 high and higher secondary schools with 23,140 students; there were 29 colleges, 1 teacher training college, 3 teacher training schools, 1 polytechnic and 29 junior colleges.

Health. In 1993–94 there were 11 hospitals, 38 primary and 22 subsidiary health centres, and 314 health sub-centres. Total beds, 1,444.

NAGALAND

KEY HISTORICAL EVENTS
The state was created in 1961, effective 1963. It consisted of the Naga Hills district of Assam and the Tuensang Frontier Agency. The agency was a British-supervised tribal area on the borders of Myanmar. Its supervision passed to the government of India at independence, and in 1957 Tuensang and the Naga Hills became a Centrally Administered Area, governed by the central government through the Governor of Assam.

A number of Naga leaders fought for independence until a settlement was reached with the Indian government at the Shillong Peace Agreement of 1975. However, calls for a greater Naga state, potentially incorporating parts of neighbouring Manipur, Arunachal Pradesh and Assam, continued to be voiced, notably through the National Socialist Council of Nagaland (NSCN), which had been active since 1954. The national government and NSCN met in Delhi in early Jan. 2003 to hold their first joint talks in 37 years, after which the NSCN declared 'the war is over'.

TERRITORY AND POPULATION
The state is in the northeast of India and is bounded in the north by Arunachal Pradesh, west by Assam, east by Myanmar and south by Manipur. Nagaland has an area of 16,579 sq. km and a population (2001 census, provisional) of 1,988,636; density, 120 per sq. km. The major towns are the capital, Kohima (1991 population, 51,418) and Dimapur (57,182). Other towns include Wokha, Mon, Zunheboto, Mokokchung and Tuensang. The chief tribes in numerical order are: Angami, Ao, Sumi, Konyak, Chakhesang, Lotha, Phom, Khiamngan, Chang, Yimchunger, Zeliang-Kuki, Rengma, Sangtam and Pochury. The main languages of the state are English, Hindi and Nagamese.

SOCIAL STATISTICS
Growth rate 1991–2001, 64·41% (the highest rate of any Indian state).

CONSTITUTION AND GOVERNMENT
An Interim Body (Legislative Assembly) of 42 members elected by the Naga people and an Executive Council (Council of Ministers) of five members were formed in 1961, and continued until the State Assembly was elected in Jan. 1964. The Assembly has 60 members. The Governor has extraordinary powers, which include special responsibility for law and order.

The state has eight districts (Dimapur, Kohima, Mon, Zunheboto, Wokha, Phek, Mokokchung and Tuensang). The capital is Kohima.

RECENT ELECTIONS
At the elections to the State Assembly in Feb. 2003 the Indian National Congress party won 20 seats (53 in 1998); Nagaland People's Front, 19; BJP, 6; Nagaland Democratic Movement, 5; ind.; 4; other parties, 4. Results for two seats were not available.

CURRENT ADMINISTRATION
Governor: Shyamal Datta.
Chief Minister: Neiphiu Rio.

ECONOMY
Budget. Budget estimates for 1996–97 showed total receipts of Rs 9,604·4m. and expenditure of Rs 9,937·8m. Annual plan, 1997–98, Rs 3,500m.

ENERGY AND NATURAL RESOURCES

Electricity. Installed capacity (1995–96) 6·82 MW; all towns and villages have electricity. In 1995–96, seven electricity generation schemes were under implementation.

Oil and Gas. Oil has been located in three districts.

Minerals. In addition to oil, other minerals include: coal, limestone, chromite, magnesite, iron ore, copper ore, clay, glass sand and slate.

Agriculture. 90% of the people derive their livelihood from agriculture. The Angamis, in Kohima district, practise a fixed agriculture in the shape of terraced slopes, and wet paddy cultivation in the lowlands. In the other two districts a traditional form of shifting cultivation (*jhumming*) still predominates, but some farmers have begun tea and coffee plantations and horticulture. About 61,000 ha were under terrace cultivation and 74,040 ha under *jhumming* in 1994–95. Production of rice (1995–96) was 0·185m. tonnes, total foodgrains 238,300 tonnes and pulses 12,300 tonnes. Forests covered 8,625 sq. km in 1995–96.

INDUSTRY

There is a forest products factory at Tijit; a paper-mill (100 tonnes daily capacity) at Tuli, a distillery unit and a sugar-mill (1,000 tonnes daily capacity) at Dimapur, and a cement factory (50 tonnes daily capacity) at Wazeho. Bricks and TV sets are also made, and there are 1,850 small units. There is a ceramics plant and sericulture is also important.

COMMUNICATIONS

Roads. There is a national highway from Kaziranga (Assam) to Kohima and on to Manipur. There are state highways connecting Kohima with the district headquarters. Total length of roads in 1992, 14,933 km. There were 95,020 motor vehicles registered in 1994–95.

Rail. Dimapur has a rail-head. Railway route-km in 1995–96, 13 km.

Civil Aviation. Dimapur has a daily air service to Calcutta.

SOCIAL INSTITUTIONS

Justice. A permanent bench of the Guwahati High Court has been established in Kohima.

Religion. At the 1991 census there were 1,057,940 Christians; 122,473 Hindus; 20,642 Muslims; 1,202 Jains; 732 Sikhs.

Education. In 2001, 67·11% of the population were literate (71·77% of men and 61·92% of women). In 1996–97 there were 1,414 primary schools with 271,932 students, 416 middle schools with 63,437 students, 244 high and higher secondary schools with 24,547 students, 36 colleges, 2 teacher training colleges and 2 polytechnics. The North Eastern Hill University opened at Kohima in 1978. Nagaland University was established in 1994.

Health. In 1995–96 there were 32 hospitals (1,051 beds), 27 primary and 5 community health centres, 65 dispensaries, 243 sub-centres, 5 TB centres and 30 leprosy centres.

FURTHER READING

Aram, M., *Peace in Nagaland,* New Delhi, 1974

ORISSA

KEY HISTORICAL EVENTS

Orissa was divided between Mahratta and Bengal rulers when conquered by the British East India Company, the Bengal area in 1757 and the Mahratta in 1803. The area which now forms the state then consisted of directly controlled British districts and a large number of small princely states with tributary rulers. The British districts were administered as part of Bengal until 1912 when, together with Bihar, they were separated from Bengal to form a single province. Bihar and Orissa were separated from each other in 1936. In 1948 a new state government took control of the whole state, including the former princely states (except Saraikella and Kharswan which were transferred to Bihar, and Mayurbhanj which was not incorporated until 1949).

In Oct. 1999 Orissa was hit by a devastating cyclone which resulted in more than 10,000 deaths.

TERRITORY AND POPULATION

Orissa is in eastern India and is bounded north by Jharkhand, northeast by West Bengal, east by the Bay of Bengal, south by Andhra Pradesh and west by Chhattisgarh. The area of the state is 155,707 sq. km, and its population (2001 census, provisional), 36,706,920; density 236 per sq. km. Cities with over 250,000 population at 1991 census, see INDIA: Territory and Population. Other large cities (1991): Rourkela (urban agglomeration), 398,864; Brahmapur, 210,418; Sambalpur, 131,138; Puri, 125,199. The principal and official language is Oriya.

SOCIAL STATISTICS

Growth rate 1991–2001, 15·94%.

CONSTITUTION AND GOVERNMENT

The Legislative Assembly has 147 members.
The state consists of 30 districts.
The capital is Bhubaneswar (18 miles south of Cuttack).

RECENT ELECTIONS

At the elections of 17 and 22 Feb. 2000 Prime Minister Atal Bihari Vajpayee's alliance defeated the main opposition Congress Party, the distribution of seats being: Biju Janata Dal, 68; Bharatiya Janata Party, 38; Indian National Congress Party, 26; independents, 8; others, 7.

CURRENT ADMINISTRATION

Governor: M. M. Rajendran.
Chief Minister: Naveen Patnaik.

ECONOMY

Budget. Budget estimates, 1996–97, showed total receipts of Rs 79,812m. and total expenditure of Rs 84,683m. Annual plan outlay, 1997–98, Rs 25,000m.

ENERGY AND NATURAL RESOURCES

Electricity. The Hirakud Dam Project on the river Mahanadi irrigates 628,000 acres and has an installed capacity of 307·5 MW. There are other projects under construction; hydro-electric power is now serving a large part of the state. Other hydro-power projects are Balimela (360 MW), Upper Kolab (320 MW) and Rengali (250 MW). Total installed capacity (1995–96) 2,152 MW. In March 1996, 32,068 villages had electricity.

Minerals. Orissa is India's leading producer of chromite (95% of national output), dolomite (50%), manganese ore (25%), graphite (80%), iron ore (16%), fire-clay (34%), limestone (20%), and quartz-quartzite (18%). Production in 1995–96 (1,000 tonnes): coal, 32,660; iron ore, 9,330; bauxite, 2,420; limestone, 2,380; chromite, 1,650; dolomite, 1,350; manganese ore, 630. Value of production in 1995–96 was Rs 16,340m.

Agriculture. The cultivation of rice is the principal occupation of about 80% of the workforce, and only a very small amount of other cereals is grown. Production of foodgrains (1994–95) totalled 7·2m. tonnes from 7·9m. ha (rice 6·4m. tonnes, wheat 58,000 tonnes); pulses, 0·58m. tonnes; oilseeds, 0·27m. tonnes; sugarcane, 781,000 tonnes. Turmeric is cultivated in the uplands of the districts of Ganjam, Phulbani and Koraput, and is exported.

Livestock (1993): buffaloes, 1·04m.; other cattle, 9·2m.; sheep, 1·87m.; goats, 5·4m.; 15·91m. poultry including ducks (1995).

Forestry. Forests occupied 56,059 sq. km in 1995–96. The most important species are sal, teak, kendu, sandal, sisu, bija, kusum, kongada and bamboo.

Fisheries. There were, in March 1996, 603 fishery co-operative societies. Fish production in 1995–96 was 258,040 tonnes. The state has four fishing harbours.

INDUSTRY

289 large and medium industries are in operation (1995–96), mostly based on minerals: steel, pig-iron, ferrochrome, ferromanganese, ferrosilicon, aluminium, cement, automotive tyres and synthetic fibres.

Other industries of importance are sugar, glass, paper, fertilizers, caustic soda, salt, industrial explosives, heavy machine tools, a coach-repair factory, a re-rolling mill, textile mills and electronics. An oil refinery is under implementation. Also, there were 49,611 small-scale industries in 1995–96 employing 349,800 persons, and 1,342,561 artisan units providing employment to 2·33m. persons. Handloom weaving and the manufacture of baskets, wooden articles, hats and nets, silver filigree work and hand-woven fabrics are specially well known.

COMMUNICATIONS

Roads. On 31 March 1996 length of roads was: state highway, 4,360 km; national highway, 1,625 km; other roads, 212,490 km. There were 658,401 motor vehicles in 1995–96. A 144-km expressway, part national highway, connects the Daitari mining area with Paradip Port.

Rail. The route-km of railway in 1995–96 was 2,191 km, of which 143 km was narrow gauge.

Civil Aviation. There is an airport at Bhubaneswar with regular scheduled services to New Delhi, Calcutta, Visakhapatnam and Hyderabad.

Shipping. Paradip was declared a 'major' port in 1966; it handled 11·2m. tonnes of traffic in 1995–96. There are minor ports at Bahabalpur and Gopalpur.

SOCIAL INSTITUTIONS

Justice. The High Court of Judicature at Cuttack has a Chief Justice and 13 puisne judges.

Religion. At the 1991 census Hindus numbered 29,971,257; Christians, 666,220; Muslims, 577,775; Sikhs, 17,296; Buddhists, 9,153; Jains, 6,302.

Education. The percentage of literate people in the population in 2001 was 63·61% (males, 75·95%; females, 50·97%).

In 1996–97 there were 42,104 primary schools with 3·95m. students, 12,096 middle schools with 1·3m. students and 6,198 high and higher secondary schools with 945,000 students. There are 10 engineering and technology colleges, 20 medical colleges, 13 teacher training colleges, 15 engineering schools/polytechnics, 497 arts, science and commerce colleges and 440 junior colleges.

Utkal University was established in 1943 at Cuttack and moved to Bhubaneswar in 1962; it is both teaching and affiliating. It has 368 affiliated colleges and 14,000 students (1993–94). Berhampur University has 33 affiliated colleges with 33,755 students, and Orissa University of Agriculture and Technology has 8 constituent colleges with 641 students. Sambalpur University has 97 affiliated colleges and 43,982 students. Sri Jagannath Sanskrit Viswavidyalaya at Puri was established in 1981 for oriental studies.

Health. There were (1995–96) 180 hospitals, 150 dispensaries, 885 primary health centres and 402 health centres/units. There were also 478 homeopathic and 537 Ayurvedic dispensaries.

CULTURE

Tourism. Tourist traffic is concentrated mainly on the 'Golden Triangle' of Konark, Puri, and Bhubaneswar and its temples. Tourists also visit Gopalpur, the Similipal National Park, Nandankanan and Chilka Lake, Bhiar-Kanika and Ushakothi Wildlife Sanctuary.

PUNJAB (INDIA)

KEY HISTORICAL EVENTS

The Punjab was constituted an autonomous province of India in 1937. In 1947 the province was partitioned between India and Pakistan into East and West Punjab respectively. The name of East Punjab was changed to Punjab (India) under the Constitution of India. On 1 Nov. 1956 the erstwhile states of Punjab and Patiala and East Punjab States Union (PEPSU) were integrated to form the state of Punjab. On 1 Nov. 1966, under the Punjab Reorganization Act, 1966, the state was reconstituted as a Punjabi-speaking state comprising the districts of Gurdaspur (excluding Dalhousie), Amritsar, Kapurthala, Jullundur, Ferozepore, Bhatinda, Patiala and Ludhiana; parts of Sangrur, Hoshiarpur and Ambala districts; and part of Kharar tehsil. The remaining area comprising 47,000 sq. km and an estimated (1967) population of 8·5m. was shared between the new state of Haryana and the Union Territory of Himachal Pradesh. The existing capital of Chandigarh was made joint capital of Punjab and Haryana; its transfer to Punjab alone (scheduled for 1986) has been delayed while the two states seek agreement as to which Hindi-speaking districts shall be transferred to Haryana in exchange.

TERRITORY AND POPULATION

The Punjab is in north India and is bounded at its northernmost point by Kashmir, northeast by Himachal Pradesh, southeast by Haryana, south by Rajasthan, west and northwest by Pakistan. The area of the state is 50,362 sq. km, with a population (2001 census, provisional) of 24,289,296; density, 482 per sq. km. Cities with over 250,000 population at 1991 census, see INDIA: Territory and Population. Other principal towns (1991): Bathinda (159,042), Pathankot (123,930), Moga (108,304), Abohar (107,163). The official language is Punjabi.

SOCIAL STATISTICS

Growth rate 1991–2001, 19·76%.

CONSTITUTION AND GOVERNMENT

Punjab (India) has a unicameral legislature, the Legislative Assembly, of 117 members. Presidential rule was imposed in May 1987 after outbreaks of communal violence. In March 1988 the Assembly was officially dissolved.

There are 17 districts. The capital is Chandigarh.

RECENT ELECTIONS

Legislative Assembly elections were held on 13 Feb. 2002. The Congress Party (INC) won 62 seats, the Shiromani Akali Dal (SAD) 41, the Bharatiya Janata Party (BJP) 3, independents 9 and the Communist Party of India (CPI) 1.

CURRENT ADMINISTRATION

Governor: Lieut.-Gen. J. F. R. Jacob.

Chief Minister: Amarinder Singh.

ECONOMY

Budget. Budget estimates, 1995–96, showed revenue receipts of Rs 72,634·7m. and revenue expenditure of Rs 75,076·4m. Plan outlay, 1997–98, Rs 21,000m.

ENERGY AND NATURAL RESOURCES

Electricity. Installed capacity, 1996–97, was 3,511 MW; all villages had electricity.

Agriculture. About 75% of the population depends on agriculture which is technically advanced. The irrigated area rose from 2·21m. ha in 1950–51 to 4·2m. ha in 1996–97. In 1994–95 wheat production was 13·6m. tonnes; rice, 7·7m.; 1992–93: maize, 333,000; oilseeds, 90,000; cotton, 2·3m. bales of 170 kg.

Livestock (1977 census): buffaloes, 4,110,000; other cattle, 3·31m.; sheep and goats, 1,219,600; horses and ponies, 75,900; poultry, 5·5m.

Forestry. In 1995 there were 1,342 sq. km of forest land.

INDUSTRY

In March 1997 the number of registered industrial units was 194,208, employing about 1·04m. people. In 1996–97 there were 586 large and medium industries. On 31 March 1997 there were 0·19m. small industrial units, investment Rs 25,050m. The chief manufactures are textiles (especially hosiery), sewing machines, sports goods, sugar, bicycles, electronic goods, machine tools, hand tools, automobiles and vehicle parts, surgical goods, vegetable oils, tractors, chemicals and pharmaceuticals, fertilizers, food processing, electronics, railway coaches, paper and newsprint, cement, engineering goods and telecommunications items. An oil refinery is under construction.

COMMUNICATIONS

Roads. The total length of roads on 31 March 1997 was 47,000 km. State transport services cover 1·9m. effective km daily with a fleet of 3,426 buses carrying a daily average of over 1·2m. passengers. Coverage by private operators is estimated at 40%. There were 1,915,059 vehicles in 1995–96.

Rail. The Punjab possesses an extensive system of railway communications, served by the Northern Railway. Route-km (1995–96), 2,121 km.

Civil Aviation. There is an airport at Amritsar, and Chandigarh airport is on the northeastern boundary; both have regular scheduled services to Delhi, Jammu, Srinagar and Leh. There are also Vayudoot services to Ludhiana.

SOCIAL INSTITUTIONS

Justice. The Punjab and Haryana High Court exercises jurisdiction over the states of Punjab and Haryana and the territory of Chandigarh. It is located in Chandigarh. In 1988 it consisted of a Chief Justice and 21 puisne judges.

Religion. At the 1991 census Hindus numbered 6,989,226; Sikhs, 12,767,697; Muslims, 239,401; Christians, 225,163; Jains, 20,763.

Education. Compulsory education was introduced in April 1961; at the same time free education was introduced up to 8th class for boys and 9th class for girls as well as fee concessions. The aim is education for all children of 6–11. In 2001, 69·95% of the population were literate (75·63% of men and 63·55% of women).

In 1996–97 there were 12,590 primary schools with 2,081,965 students, 2,545 middle schools with 968,762 students, 2,159 high schools with 490,888 students and 1,134 higher secondary schools with 259,718 students.

Punjab University was established in 1947 at Chandigarh as an examining, teaching and affiliating body (in 1993–94 it had 94 colleges and 77,868 students). In 1962 Punjabi University was established at Patiala (it had 66 colleges with 40,712 students) and Punjab Agricultural University at Ludhiana. Guru Nanak Dev University was established at Amritsar to mark the 500th anniversary celebrations for Guru Nanak Dev, first Guru of the Sikhs (it had 85 colleges and 80,330 students, 1992–93). Altogether there are 237 affiliated colleges, 190 for arts, science and commerce, 18 for teacher training, 6 medical and 11 engineering, and 30 polytechnic institutes.

Health. There were (1992–93) 219 hospitals, 2,151 allopathic, homeopathic, Ayurvedic and Unani dispensaries, 446 primary health centres and 38 community health centres. Total number of beds (1991–92), 24,742.

FURTHER READING

Singh, Khushwant, *A History of the Sikhs.* 2 vols. OUP, 1999
Singh Tatla, Darshan and Talbot, Ian, *Punjab.* [Bibliography] ABC-Clio, Oxford and Santa Barbara (CA), 1995

RAJASTHAN

KEY HISTORICAL EVENTS

The state is in the largely desert area formerly known as Rajputana. The Rajput princes were tributary to the Moghul emperors when they were conquered by the

Mahrattas' leader, Mahadaji Sindhia, in the 1780s. In 1818 Rajputana became a British protectorate and was recognized during British rule as a group of princely states including Jaipur, Jodhpur and Udaipur. After independence the Rajput princes surrendered their powers and in 1950 were replaced by a single state government. In 1956 the state boundaries were altered; small areas of the former Bombay and Madhya Bharat states were added, together with the neighbouring state of Ajmer. Ajmer had been a Moghul power base; it was taken by the Mahrattas in 1770 and annexed by the British in 1818. In 1878 it became Ajmer-Merwara, a British province, and survived as a separate state until 1956.

TERRITORY AND POPULATION
Rajasthan is in northwest India and is bounded north by Punjab, northeast by Haryana and Uttar Pradesh, east by Madhya Pradesh, south by Gujarat and west by Pakistan. Since the area of Madhya Pradesh was reduced by the creation of Chhattisgarh in 2000, Rajasthan has become the largest Indian state in size, with an area of 342,239 sq. km. Population (2001 census, provisional), 56,473,122; density 165 per sq. km. For chief cities, see INDIA: Territory and Population. Other major towns (1991): Alwar (205,086), Bhilwara (183,965), Ganganagar (161,482), Bharatpur (148,519), Sikar (148,272), Pali (136,842), Beawar (105,363). The main languages spoken are Rajasthani and Hindi.

SOCIAL STATISTICS
Growth rate 1991–2001, 28·33%.

CONSTITUTION AND GOVERNMENT
There is a unicameral legislature, the Legislative Assembly, having 200 members. The capital is Jaipur. There are 32 districts.

RECENT ELECTIONS
After the election in Nov. 1998 the Congress Party came to power. Congress (I), 150; Bharatiya Janata Party, 33.

CURRENT ADMINISTRATION
Governor: Anshuman Singh.
   Chief Minister: Ashok Gehlot.

ECONOMY
Budget. Estimates for 1997–98 show total revenue receipts of Rs 89,894·1m., and expenditure of Rs 91,469·2m. Annual plan, 1997–98, Rs 35,000m.

ENERGY AND NATURAL RESOURCES
Electricity. Installed capacity in 1995–96, 1,981 MW; 30,620 villages (March 1996) and 514,758 wells had electric power.

Minerals. The state is rich in minerals, including silver, tungsten, granite, marble, dolomite, lignite, lead, zinc, emeralds, soapstone, asbestos, feldspar, copper, limestone and salt. Total revenue from minerals in 1995–96, Rs 2,145·2m. Four blocs are being explored for mineral oils and gas.

Agriculture. The state has suffered drought and encroaching desert for several years. The cultivable area is (1995–96) about 25·6m. ha, of which 4·65m. ha is irrigated. Production of principal crops (in tonnes), 1995–96: pulses, 1·46m.; total foodgrains, 9·57m. (wheat, 5·49m.; rice, 117,600); cotton, 1m. bales of 170 kg.
   Livestock (1992): buffaloes, 7·75m.; other cattle, 11·6m.; sheep, 12·17m.; goats, 15·06m.; horses and ponies, 28,000; camels, 731,000.

Forestry. Forests covered 12,320 sq. km in 1995.

INDUSTRY
In 1993–94 there were 167,400 small industrial units with an investment of Rs 13,163·1m. and employment of 0·64m. There were 212 industrial estates. Total capital investment (1993–94) Rs 13,160m. Chief manufactures are textiles, cement, glass, sugar, sodium, oxygen and acetylene units, pesticides, insecticides, dyes,

caustic soda, calcium, carbide, synthetic fibres, fertilizers, shaving equipment, automobiles and automobile components, tyres, watches, nylon tyre cords and refined copper. In 1993–94 there were 583 large and medium industries.

COMMUNICATIONS

Roads. In 1995–96 there were 116,667 km of roads including 61,520 km of good and surfaced roads in Rajasthan; there were 2,846 km of national highway. Motor vehicles numbered 1,768,709 in 1995–96.

Rail. Jodhpur, Marwar, Udaipur, Ajmer, Jaipur, Kota, Bikaner and Sawai Madhopur are important junctions of the northwestern network. Route km (1995–96) 5,924.

Civil Aviation. There are airports at Jaipur, Jodhpur, Kota and Udaipur with regular scheduled services by Indian Airlines.

SOCIAL INSTITUTIONS

Justice. The seat of the High Court is at Jodhpur. There is a Chief Justice and 11 puisne judges. There is also a bench of High Court judges at Jaipur.

Religion. At the 1991 census Hindus numbered 39,201,099; Muslims, 3,525,339; Sikhs, 649,174; Jains, 562,806; Christians, 47,989; Buddhists, 4,467.

Education. The proportion of literate people to the total population was 61·03% at the 2001 census; 76·46% of men and 44·34% of women.

In 1996–97 there were 33,801 primary schools with 6,665,000 students, 12,642 middle schools with 2,091,000 students, 3,439 high schools with 682,600 students and 1,404 higher secondary schools with 500,000 students. Elementary education is free but not compulsory.

In 1996–97 there were 206 colleges. Rajasthan University, established at Jaipur in 1947, is teaching and affiliating; in 1993–94 it had 135 colleges and 160,000 students. There are five other universities: Rajasthan Agricultural University, Bikaner; Mohanlal Sukhadia University, Udaipur; Maharishi Dayanand Saraswati University, Ajmer; Jai Narayan Vyas University, Jodhpur; Kota Open University, Kota. There are also 22 medical colleges, 7 engineering colleges, 21,436 adult and other education centres, 32 sanskrit institutions, 39 teacher-training colleges and 27 polytechnics.

Health. In 1995–96 there were 266 hospitals, 283 dispensaries, 1,453 primary health centres, 384 family welfare centres, 1,104 upgraded sub-centres and 118 maternity centres. There were 34,066 beds in hospitals.

FURTHER READING
Sharma, S. K. and Sharma, Usha, (eds.) *History and Geography of Rajasthan.* New Delhi, 2000

SIKKIM

KEY HISTORICAL EVENTS
A small Himalayan kingdom between Nepal and Bhutan, Sikkim was independent in the 1830s although in continual conflict with larger neighbours. In 1839 the British took the Darjeeling district. British political influence increased during the 19th century, as Sikkim was the smallest buffer between India and Tibet. However, Sikkim remained an independent kingdom ruled by the 14th-century Namgyal dynasty. In 1950 a treaty was signed with the government of India, declaring Sikkim an Indian Protectorate. Indian influence increased from then on. Internal political unrest came to a head in 1973, and led to the granting of constitutional reforms in 1974. Agitation continued until Sikkim became a 'state associated with the Indian Union' later that year. In 1975 the king was deposed and Sikkim became an Indian state, a change approved by referendum.

TERRITORY AND POPULATION
Sikkim is in the Eastern Himalayas and is bounded north by Tibet, east by Tibet and Bhutan, south by West Bengal and west Nepal. Area, 7,096 sq. km. It is

inhabited chiefly by the Lepchas, a tribe indigenous to Sikkim, the Bhutias, who originally came from Tibet, and the Nepalis, who entered from Nepal in large numbers in the late 19th and early 20th century. Population (2001 census, provisional), 540,493; density, 76 per sq km. The capital is Gangtok.

English is the principal language. Lepcha, Bhutia, Nepali and Limboo also have official status.

SOCIAL STATISTICS
Growth rate 1991–2001, 32·98%.

CONSTITUTION AND GOVERNMENT
The Assembly has 32 members.

The official language of the government is English. Lepcha, Bhutia, Nepali and Limboo have also been declared official languages.

Sikkim is divided into four districts for administration purposes, Gangtok, Mangan, Namchi and Gyalshing being the headquarters for the Eastern, Northern, Southern and Western districts respectively.

RECENT ELECTIONS
At the State Assembly election of Oct. 1999 the Sikkim Democratic Front won 24 seats; Sikkim Sangram Parishad, 7; and independents, 1.

CURRENT ADMINISTRATION
Governor: V. Rama Rao.

Chief Minister: Pawan Kumar Chamling.

ECONOMY
Budget. Budget estimates for 1996–97 showed a budget of Rs 61,800m. Annual plan outlay for 1997–98 was Rs 2,200m.

ENERGY AND NATURAL RESOURCES
Electricity. Installed capacity (1995–96) 33·6 MW. There are four hydro-electric power stations. All villages had electricity in 1991.

Minerals. Copper, zinc and lead are mined.

Agriculture. The economy is mainly agricultural; main food crops are rice, maize, millet, wheat and barley; cash crops are cardamom (a spice), mandarin oranges, apples, potatoes, and buckwheat. Foodgrain production, 1995–96, 104,200 tonnes (rice, 21,900 tonnes; wheat, 15,300 tonnes); pulses, 5,700 tonnes. Tea is grown. Medicinal herbs are exported.

Forestry. Forests occupied about 3,127 sq. km. in 1995 and the potential for a timber and wood-pulp industry is being explored.

INDUSTRY
Small-scale industries include cigarettes, distilling, tanning, fruit preservation, carpets and watchmaking. Local crafts include carpet weaving, making handmade paper, wood carving and silverwork. The State Trading Corporation of Sikkim stimulates trade in indigenous products.

COMMUNICATIONS
Roads. There are 1,615 km of roads, all on mountainous terrain, and 18 major bridges under the Public Works Department. Public transport and road haulage is nationalized. There were 8,997 motor vehicles in 1995–96.

Rail. The nearest railhead is at Siliguri (115 km from Gangtok).

Civil Aviation. The nearest airport is at Bagdogra (128 km from Gangtok), linked to Gangtok by helicopter service.

Telecommunications. There are 1,445 telephones (1987) and 37 wireless stations.

SOCIAL INSTITUTIONS

Religion. At the 1991 census there were 277,881 Hindus; 110,371 Buddhists; 13,413 Christians; 3,849 Muslims; 375 Sikhs; 40 Jains.

Education. In 2001, 69·68% of the population were literate (76·73% of men and 61·46% of women). Sikkim had (1996–97) 723 pre-primary schools with 19,946 students, 341 primary schools with 83,410 students, 117 middle schools with 21,955 students, 72 high schools with 8,295 students and 27 higher secondary schools with 3,368 students. Education is free up to class XII; text books are free up to class V. There are 500 adult education centres. There is also a training institute for primary teachers, two degree colleges and a teacher training college.

CULTURE

Broadcasting. A radio broadcasting station, Akashvani Gangtok, was built in 1982, and a permanent station in 1983. Gangtok also has a low-power TV transmitter.

Tourism. There is great potential for the tourist industry, which has been stimulated by the opening of new roads.

TAMIL NADU

KEY HISTORICAL EVENTS

The first trading establishment made by the British in the Madras State was at Peddapali (now Nizampatnam) in 1611 and then at Masulipatnam. In 1639 the English were permitted to make a settlement at the place which is now Madras, and Fort St George was founded. By 1801 the whole of the country from the Northern Circars to Cape Comorin (with the exception of certain French and Danish settlements) had been brought under British rule.

Under the provisions of the States Reorganization Act, 1956, the Malabar district (excluding the islands of Laccadive and Minicoy) and the Kasaragod district taluk of South Kanara were transferred to the new state of Kerala; the South Kanara district (excluding Kasaragod taluk and the Amindivi Islands) and the Kollegal taluk of the Coimbatore district were transferred to the new state of Mysore; and the Laccadive, Amindivi and Minicoy Islands were constituted a separate Territory. Four taluks of the Trivandrum district and the Shencottah taluk of Quilon district were transferred from Travancore-Cochin to the new Madras State. On 1 April 1960, 1,049 sq. km from the Chittoor district of Andhra Pradesh were transferred to Madras in exchange for 844 sq. km from the Chingleput and Salem districts. In Aug. 1968 the state was renamed Tamil Nadu.

TERRITORY AND POPULATION

Tamil Nadu is in south India and is bounded north by Karnataka and Andhra Pradesh, east and south by the Indian Ocean and west by Kerala. Area, 130,058 sq. km. Population (2001 census, provisional), 62,110,839; density 478 per sq. km. Tamil is the principal language and has been adopted as the state language with effect from 14 Jan. 1958. For the principal towns, *see* INDIA: Territory and Population. Other large towns (1991): Ambattur (215,424), Thanjavur City (202,013), Tuticorin (199,854), Nagercoil City (190,084), Avadi (183,215), Dindigul City (182,477), Vellore (175,061), Thiruvottir (168,642), Erode (159,232), Kanchipuram (144,955), Cuddalore City (144,561), Tirunelveli (135,825), Alandur (125,244), Neyveli (118,080), Rajapalaiyam City (114,202), Pallavaram (111,866), Tambaran (107,187). The capital is Madras.

SOCIAL STATISTICS

Growth rate 1991–2001, 15·39%.

CONSTITUTION AND GOVERNMENT

There is a unicameral legislature; the Legislative Assembly has 234 members. There are 30 districts.

RECENT ELECTIONS
In elections held on 10 May 2001 the All India Anna Dravida Munnetra Kazagam gained 132 seats, Dravida Munnetra Kazagam 31, the Tamil Maanila Congress (Moopanar) 23 and the Pattali Makkal Katchi 20.

CURRENT ADMINISTRATION
Governor: P. S. Ramamohan Rao.
Chief Minister: Jayaram Jayalalitha.

ECONOMY
Budget. Budget estimates for 1997–98, revenue receipts, Rs 126,410·5m., revenue expenditure, Rs 143,776·2m. Annual plan, 1997–98, Rs 40,000m.

ENERGY AND NATURAL RESOURCES
Electricity. Installed capacity in 1995–96 was 5,067 MW, of which 1,948 MW was hydro-electricity and 2,970 MW thermal. All villages were supplied with electricity. The Kalpakkam nuclear power plant became operational in 1983; capacity, 330 MW.

Minerals. The state has magnesite, salt, coal, lignite, chromite, bauxite, limestone, manganese, mica, quartz, gypsum and feldspar.

Agriculture. The land is a fertile plain watered by rivers flowing east from the Western Ghats, particularly the Cauvery and the Tambaraparani. Temperature ranges between 6°C and 40°C, rainfall between 442 mm and 934 mm. Of the total land area (13m. ha), 7,158,464 ha were cropped and 298,659 ha of waste were cultivable in 1996. The staple food crops grown are paddy, maize, jawar, bajra, pulses and millets. Important commercial crops are sugarcane, oilseeds, cashew nuts, cotton, tobacco, coffee, tea, rubber and pepper. Production, 1995–96 (in tonnes): total foodgrains, 9·16m. (rice, 7·56m.); pulses, 359,700.

Livestock (1993): buffaloes, 3,116,647; other cattle, 9,318,666; sheep, 5,865,989; goats, 5,938,475; poultry, 21,454,890.

Forestry. Forest area, 1993–94, 2·14m. ha, of which 1,948,627 ha were reserved forest. Forests cover about 17·21% of land area. Main products are teak, soft wood, wattle, sandalwood, pulp wood, cashew and cinchona bark.

Fisheries. In 1995–96, 448,000 tonnes of fish were produced; marine, 340,000 tonnes.

INDUSTRY
The number of working factories was 18,480 in 1994, employing 1m. workers. In 1993–94 there were 178,114 small industries employing over 1·6m. persons. The biggest central sector project is Salem steel plant. Cotton textiles is one of the major industries. There were 449 cotton textile mills in 1991–92 and many spinning mills supplying yarn to the decentralized handloom industry. Other important industries are cement, sugar, manufacture of textile machinery, power-driven pumps, bicycles, electrical machinery, tractors, cars, rubber tyres and tubes, bricks and tiles, and silk.

Main exports: cotton goods, tea, coffee, spices, engineering goods, car ancillaries, leather and granite.

Trade Unions. In 1994 there were 5,981 registered trade unions. Work-days lost by strikes and lockouts in 1994, 1,668,484.

COMMUNICATIONS
Roads. On 31 March 1992 the state had 172,936 km of national and state highways, major and other district roads. In 1995–96 there were 2,771,845 registered motor vehicles.

Rail. On 31 March 1996 there were 4,005 route-km. Madras and Madurai are the main centres.

Civil Aviation. There are airports at Madras, Tiruchirapalli and Madurai, with regular scheduled services to Bombay, Calcutta and Delhi. Madras is an international airport and the main centre of airline routes in south India. In 2000 Madras handled 3,887,993 passengers (2,153,532 on domestic flights) and 104,972 tonnes of freight.

Shipping. Madras and Tuticorin are the chief ports. Important minor ports are Cuddalore and Nagapattinam. Madras handled 26·5m. tonnes of cargo in 1993–94, Tuticorin, 6·7m. The Inland Container Depot at Coimbatore has a capacity of 50,000 tonnes of export traffic; it is linked to Cochin (Kerala).

SOCIAL INSTITUTIONS

Justice. There is a High Court at Madras with a Chief Justice and 26 judges.

Police. Strength of police force, 1 Jan. 1995, 76,447.

Religion. At the 1991 census Hindus numbered 49,532,052 (88·67%), Christians, 3,179,410 (5·69%); Muslims, 3,052,717 (5·47%).

Education. At the 2001 census 73·47% of the population were literate (82·33% of men and 64·55% of women).

Education is free up to pre-university level. In 1996–97 there were 30,619 primary schools with 6·8m. students, 5,503 middle schools with 3·51m. students, 3,574 high schools with 1,465,631 students and 2,734 higher secondary schools with 0·69m. students. There are also 78 medical colleges, 74 engineering and technology colleges, 22 teacher training colleges and 280 general education colleges.

There are 13 universities. Madras University (founded in 1857) is affiliating and teaching (it had 119 colleges and 125,082 students in 1993–94); Annamalai University, Annamalainagar (founded 1929) is residential; Madurai Kamaraj University (founded 1966) is an affiliating and teaching university; ten others include one agricultural university, Mother Theresa Women's University, and Tamil University, Thanjavur. There are four institutions which are deemed to be universities.

Health. There were (1993–94) 427 hospitals, 484 dispensaries (of which 56 were Indian medicine and homoeopathy), 1,683 primary health centres and 8,681 health sub-centres; total number of beds, 48,128.

CULTURE

Tourism. In 1992, 203,985 foreign tourists visited the state.

FURTHER READING

Statistical Information: The Department of Statistics (Fort St George, Madras) was established in 1948 and reorganized in 1953. Main publications: *Annual Statistical Abstract; Decennial Statistical Atlas; Season and Crop Report; Quinquennial Wages Census; Quarterly Abstract of Statistics.*

TRIPURA

KEY HISTORICAL EVENTS

Tripura is a Hindu state of great antiquity having been ruled by the Maharajahs for 1,300 years before its accession to the Indian Union on 15 Oct. 1949. With the reorganization of states on 1 Sept. 1956 Tripura became a Union Territory, and was so declared on 1 Nov. 1957. The Territory was made a State on 21 Jan. 1972.

TERRITORY AND POPULATION

Tripura is bounded by Bangladesh, except in the northeast where it joins Assam and Mizoram. The major portion of the state is hilly and mainly jungle. It has an area of 10,486 sq. km and a population of 3,191,168 (2001 census, provisional); density, 304 per sq. km.

The official languages are Bengali and Kokbarak. Manipuri is also spoken.

SOCIAL STATISTICS

Growth rate 1991–2001, 15·74%.

CONSTITUTION AND GOVERNMENT

The territory has four districts, namely Dhalai, North Tripura, South Tripura and West Tripura. The capital is Agartala (population, 1991, 157,358).

RECENT ELECTIONS

The Communist Party of India (Marxist) won the Legislative Assembly elections in Feb. 2003 with 38 seats; Congress won 13; Indigenous National Party of Tripura (INPT), 6; others, 3.

CURRENT ADMINISTRATION

Governor: Lieut.-Gen. (retd) K. M. Seth.
  Chief Minister: Manik Sarkar.

ECONOMY

Budget. Budget estimates, 1994–95, showed expenditure of Rs 3,605m. Annual plan outlay for 1997–98 was Rs 4,370m.

ENERGY AND NATURAL RESOURCES

Electricity. Installed capacity (1995–96), 69·36 MW; there were (March 1996) 3,640 villages with electricity out of a total of 4,856.

Agriculture. About 24% of the land area is cultivable. The tribes practise shifting cultivation, but this is being replaced by modern methods. The main crops are rice, wheat, jute, mesta, potatoes, oilseeds and sugarcane. Foodgrain production (1995–96), 477,100 tonnes. There are 55 registered tea gardens producing 5,432,000 kg per year, and employing 14,170 in 1994–95.

Forestry. Forests covered 5,538 sq. km in 1995, about 53% of the land area. They have been much depleted by clearance for shifting cultivation and, recently, for refugee settlements of Bangladeshis. About 8% of the forest area still consists of dense natural forest; losses elsewhere are being replaced by plantation. Commercial rubber plantation has also been encouraged. In 1994–95, 30,328 ha were under new rubber plantations.

INDUSTRY

Tea is the main industry. There is also a jute mill producing about 15 tonnes per day and employing about 2,000. Main small industries: aluminium utensils, rubber, saw-milling, soap, piping, fruit canning, handloom weaving and sericulture. There were 1,174 registered factories which employed 31,912 persons, and 700 notified factories with 3,000 workers in 1995–96. 330,980 persons were employed in handloom, handicrafts and sericulture industries in 1995–96.

COMMUNICATIONS

Roads. Total length of roads (1995–96) 5,760 km, of which 2,258 km were surfaced. On 31 March 1996 vehicles registered totalled 34,683, of which 4,701 were trucks.

Rail. There is a railway between Kumarghat and Kalkalighat (Assam). Route-km in 1995–96, 45 km.

Civil Aviation. There is one airport and three airstrips. The airport (Agartala) has regular scheduled services to Calcutta.

SOCIAL INSTITUTIONS

Religion. At the 1991 census Hindus numbered 2,384,934; Muslims, 196,495; Buddhists, 128,260; Christians, 46,472; Sikhs, 740; Jains, 301.

Education. In 2001, 73·66% of the population were literate (81·47% of men and 65·41% of women). In 1996–97 there were 2,045 primary schools (434,143 pupils); 411 middle schools (126,129); 558 high and higher secondary schools (82,273). There were 14 colleges of general education, 1 engineering college, 1 teacher training college and 1 polytechnic. Tripura University, established in 1987, has 20 affiliated colleges with 20,000 students.

Health. There were (1995–96) 27 hospitals, with 2,171 beds, 548 dispensaries, 818 doctors and 729 nurses. There were 53 primary health centres and 67 family planning centres.

UTTAR PRADESH

KEY HISTORICAL EVENTS

In 1833 the then Bengal Presidency was divided into two parts, one of which became the Presidency of Agra. In 1836 the Agra area was styled the North-West Province and placed under a Lieut.-Governor. In 1877 the two provinces of Agra and Oudh were placed under one administrator, styled Lieut.-Governor of the North-West Province and Chief Commissioner of Oudh. In 1902 the name was changed to 'United Provinces of Agra and Oudh', under a Lieut.-Governor, and the Lieut.-Governorship was altered to a Governorship in 1921. In 1935 the name was shortened to 'United Provinces'. On independence, the states of Rampur, Banaras and Tehri-Garwhal were merged with United Provinces. In 1950 the name of the United Provinces was changed to Uttar Pradesh. In 2000 the new state of Uttaranchal was carved from the northern, mainly mountainous, region of Uttar Pradesh.

TERRITORY AND POPULATION

Uttar Pradesh is in north India and is bounded north by the new state of Uttaranchal and Nepal, east by Bihar and Jharkhand, south by Madhya Pradesh and Chhattisgarh and west by Rajasthan, Haryana and Delhi. After the formation of Uttaranchal the area of Uttar Pradesh is 240,928 sq. km (previously 294,411 sq. km). Population (2001 census, provisional), 166,052,859; density, 689 per sq. km. Despite the drop in population caused by the creation of Uttaranchal, Uttar Pradesh still has the highest population of any of the Indian states. If Uttar Pradesh were a separate country it would have the sixth highest population. Cities with more than 250,000 population, *see* INDIA: Territory and Population. Other important towns (1991): Rampur (243,742), Muzaffarnagar (240,609), Shahjahanpur (237,717), Mathura (226,691), Firozabad (215,128), Farrukhabad-Cum-Fatehgarh (194,567), Mirzapur-Cum-Vindhyachal (169,336), Sambhal (150,819), Noida (146,514), Hapur (146,262), Amroha (137,061), Maunath Bhanjan (136,697), Jaunpur (136,062), Bahraich (135,400), Rae Bareli (129,904), Bulandshahr (127,201), Faizabad (124,437), Etawah (124,072), Sitapur (121,842), Fatehpur (117,675), Budaun (116,695), Hathras (113,285), Unnao (107,425), Pilibhit (106,605), Haldwani-Cum-Kathgodam (104,195), Modinagar (101,660). The sole official language has been Hindi since April 1990.

SOCIAL STATISTICS

Growth rate 1991–2001, 25·80%.

CONSTITUTION AND GOVERNMENT

Uttar Pradesh has had an autonomous system of government since 1937. There is a bicameral legislature. The Legislative Council has 108 members; the Legislative Assembly has 403.

There are 14 administrative divisions, each under a Commissioner, and 70 districts.

The capital is Lucknow.

RECENT ELECTIONS

Elections were held in Feb. 2002. The Samajwadi Party (SP) won 145 seats; the Bharatiya Janata Party (BJP), 107; the Bahujan Samaj Party (BSP), 98; the Indian National Congress (INC), 25; ind. and others, 26. Presidential rule was imposed as no party gained the 202 seats needed to form a majority.

CURRENT ADMINISTRATION

Governor: Vishnu Kant Shastri.

Chief Minister: Mayawati.

ECONOMY

Budget. Budget estimates for 1996–97 showed revenue receipts of Rs 155,963·2m.; expenditure, Rs 194,039·9m. Annual plan outlay, 1997–98, Rs 70,800m.

ENERGY AND NATURAL RESOURCES

Electricity. The state had, 1995–96, an installed capacity of 6,049 MW. There were 85,657 villages with electricity in March 1996, out of a total of 112,804.

Minerals. The state has magnesite, china-clay, coal, granite, sandstone, copper-lead-zinc, dolomite, limestone, soapstone, bauxite, diaspore, ochre, phosphorite, pyrophyllite, silica sand and steatite reserves among others. In 1995–96 about 13m. tonnes of minerals were produced.

Agriculture. Agriculture occupies 78% of the workforce. 10·13m. ha are irrigated. The state is India's largest producer of foodgrains; production (1995–96), 38·94m. tonnes (rice 10·4m. tonnes, wheat 22·2m. tonnes); pulses, 2·25m. tonnes. The state is one of India's main producers of sugar; production of sugarcane (1995–96), 119·9m. tonnes. There were (1995–96) 1,965 veterinary centres for cattle.

Forestry. In 1995 forests covered about 51,663 sq. km. However, much of this area is now in the new state of Uttaranchal.

INDUSTRY

Sugar production is important; other industries include oil refining, aluminium smelting, edible oils, textiles, distilleries, brewing, leather working, agricultural engineering, paper, automobile tyres, fertilizers, cement, jute, glass, heavy electricals, chemicals, automobiles and synthetic fibres. Large public-sector enterprises have been set up in electrical engineering, pharmaceuticals, locomotive building, general engineering, electronics and aeronautics. Village and small-scale industries are important; there were 0·64m. small units in 1995–96 providing employment to 1·19m. people. The state had 1,661 large and medium industries with an investment of Rs 223,002m. and employing 0·57m. persons in 1995–96.

COMMUNICATIONS

Roads. There were, 31 March 1995, 185,575 km of roads. In 1995–96 there were 2,977,275 motor vehicles of which 2,057,408 were two-wheelers.

Rail. Lucknow is the main junction of the northern network; other important junctions are Agra, Kanpur, Allahabad, Mughal Sarai and Varanasi. Route-km in 1995–96, 8,934 km.

Civil Aviation. There are airports at Lucknow, Kanpur, Varanasi, Allahabad, Agra, Gorakhpur and five other places.

SOCIAL INSTITUTIONS

Justice. The High Court of Judicature at Allahabad (with a bench at Lucknow) has a Chief Justice and 63 puisne judges including additional judges. There are 63 sessions divisions in the state.

Religion. At the 1991 census Hindus numbered 113,712,829; Muslims, 24,109,684; Sikhs, 675,775; Christians, 383,477; Jains, 176,259; Buddhists, 221,443.

Education. At the 2001 census 77·77m. people were literate (57·36%; 70·23% of men and 42·98% of women). In 1996–97 there were 91,093 primary schools with 16·26m. students, 19,917 middle schools with 5·63m. students, 2,628 high schools with 2,329,904 students and 4,375 higher secondary schools with 1,167,552 students.

Uttar Pradesh has 17 universities including: Allahabad University (founded 1887); Agra University (1927); the Banaras Hindu University, Varanasi (1916); Lucknow University (1921); Aligarh Muslim University (1920) with four colleges and 13,437 students in 1993–94; Roorkee University (1949), formerly Thomason College of Civil Engineering (established in 1847); Gorakhpur University (1957) with 33 colleges and 96,504 students; Sampurnanand Sanskrit Vishwavidyalaya, Varanasi (1958); Kanpur University (1966); Ch. Charan Singh University (1966), with 82 colleges and 96,004 students in 1993–94; H. N. Bahuguna Garhwal University, Srinagar, (1973). C. S. Azad University of Agriculture and Technology, Kanpur, Narendra Deva University of Agriculture and Technology, Faizabad, and Dr Ram Manohar Lohia Awadh (32 colleges and 64,142 students), Kumaon, Rohilkhand (32 colleges and 86,996 students) and Bundelkhand Universities were founded in 1975. Jaunpur University (Purvanchal Vishwavidyalaya) was founded in 1987.

There are also six institutions with university status: Gurukul Kangri Vishwavidyalaya, Hardwar; Indian Veterinary Research Institute; Central Institute of Higher Tibetan Studies; Sanjay Gandhi Post-Graduate Institute of Medical Sciences; and Dayal Bagh Educational Institute. There are 35 medical colleges, 18 engineering colleges, 62 teacher training colleges and 550 arts, science and commerce colleges.

Health. In 1994–95 there were 5,011 allopathic, 2,690 Ayurvedic and Unani and 1,149 homoeopathic hospitals and dispensaries. There were also 3,766 primary health centres and 20,153 sub-centres, and TB hospitals and clinics.

FURTHER READING
Hasan, Z., *Quest for Power: Oppositional Movements and Post-Congress Politics in Uttar Pradesh.* OUP, 1998
Lieten, G. K. and Srivastava, R., *Unequal Partners: Power Relations, Devolution and Development in Uttar Pradesh.* Sage Publications, New Delhi, 1999
Misra, S., *A Narrative of Communal Politics, Uttar Pradesh, 1937–39.* Sage Publications, New Delhi, 2001

UTTARANCHAL

KEY HISTORICAL EVENTS
The state was carved from Uttar Pradesh and became the twenty-seventh state of India on 9 Nov. 2000. It is located in the hilly and mountainous region of the northern border of the Indian subcontinent. The regions of Kumaon and Garhwal contained in the new state were referred to as Uttarakhand in ancient Hindu scriptures. The Chinese suppression of revolt in Tibet in 1959 saw a rapid influx of Tibetan exiles to the region and the Indo-Chinese conflict of 1962 persuaded the Indian government to initiate a modernization programme throughout the Indian Himalayas that resulted in the development of roads and communication networks in the previously backward region. From the 1970s the hill people began to agitate for their districts to be separated from Uttar Pradesh, which had been established in 1950. On 1 Aug. 2000 the Uttar Pradesh Reorganisation bill was passed, allowing for a separate state, called Uttaranchal, to incorporate 12 hill districts and, controversially, the lowland area of Udham Singh Nagar.

TERRITORY AND POPULATION
Uttaranchal is located in northern India and is bounded in the northeast by China and in the east by Nepal. The state of Uttar Pradesh is to the southwest, Haryana to the west and Himachal Pradesh to the northwest. Uttaranchal has an area of 53,483 sq. km. Population (2001 census, provisional), 8,479,562; density, 159 per sq. km. The principal languages are the Hindi dialects of Garhwali and Kumaoni. Cities with over 250,000 population, see INDIA: Territory and population. Other large cities (1991): Hardwar (147,305).

SOCIAL STATISTICS
Growth rate 1991–2001, 19·20%.

CONSTITUTION AND GOVERNMENT
Uttaranchal is the twenty-seventh state of India. After the region was carved from Uttar Pradesh it was decided that the 22 Members of the Legislative Assembly (MLAs) from Uttaranchali districts would become the members of the new state's Legislative Assembly. Subsequently this was increased to 30 when the provisional assembly was established, and ultimately it is scheduled to have 70 members. For administrative purposes the region is divided into 13 districts.

The interim capital and seat of government is at Dehra Dun.

RECENT ELECTIONS

On the formation of the new state the Bharatiya Janata Party (BJP) was the single largest party with 17 seats, enabling them to form a majority administration in the 23-seat assembly with Nityanand Swamy becoming the state's first chief minister.

State assembly elections were held in Feb. 2002. The Indian National Congress party (INC) won 36 seats; the Bharatiya Janata Party (BJP), 19; the Bahujan Samaj Party (BSP), 7; the Uttarakhand Kranti Dal (UKKD), 4; the Nationalist Congress Party (NCP), 1; independents and others, 3.

CURRENT ADMINISTRATION

Governor: Sudarshan Agarwal.

Chief Minister: Narain Dutt Tiwari.

ENERGY AND NATURAL RESOURCES

Electricity. The state has a potential hydroelectric capacity of 40,000 MW. Government figures claim that more than 75% of the state's 17,000 villages have electricity.

Water. Uttaranchal suffers from an acute shortage of water for drinking and irrigation. Only 10% of the water potential is currently utilized.

Minerals. There are deposits of limestone, gypsum, iron ore, graphite and copper.

Agriculture. Agriculture is the occupation for approximately 50% of the population. Subsistence farming is the norm, as only 9% of the land in the state is cultivable.

Forestry. Approximately 65%–70% of the state's area is covered in forest.

INDUSTRY

Tourism is by far the most important industry. The state can offer ski resorts, adventure tourism, mountaineering, hiking and several areas of religious interest. Other industries include: horticulture, floriculture, fruit-processing and medicine production. In the Terai region there are around 350 industrial units and 130 in the Doon Valley.

COMMUNICATIONS

Roads. There are 23 km of roads for every 100 sq. km of land in the state. State highways link Uttaranchal to the neighbouring states of Himachal Pradesh, Haryana and Uttar Pradesh. The state remains very inaccessible in parts.

Rail. Four main railway lines in the south of the state link several districts to Uttar Pradesh and Himachal Pradesh. Railways along the foothills connect Dehra Dun, Hardwar, Rishikesh, Roorkee, Kotdwaar, Ram Nagar, Kathgodam and Tanakpur. The rest of the state is not connected to the rail network.

Civil Aviation. There are airports at Dehra Dun and Udham Singh Nagar.

SOCIAL INSTITUTIONS

Education. In 2001, 77·28% of the population were literate (84·01% of men and 60·26% of women).

WEST BENGAL

KEY HISTORICAL EVENTS

Bengal was under the overlordship of the Moghul emperor and ruled by a Moghul governor (*nawab*) who declared himself independent in 1740. The British East India Company based at Calcutta was in conflict with the *nawab* from 1756 until 1757 when British forces defeated him at Plassey and installed their own *nawab* in 1760. The French were also in Bengal; the British captured their trading settlement at Chandernagore in 1757 and in 1794, restoring it to France in 1815.

The area of British Bengal included modern Orissa and Bihar, Bangladesh and (until 1833) Uttar Pradesh. Calcutta was the capital of British India from 1772 until 1912.

The first division into East and West took place in 1905–11 and was not popular. However, at Partition in 1947 the East (Muslim) chose to join what was then East Pakistan (now Bangladesh), leaving West Bengal as an Indian frontier state and promoting a steady flow of non-Muslim Bengali immigrants from the East. In 1950 West Bengal received the former princely state of Cooch Behar and, in 1954, Chandernagore. Small areas were transferred from Bihar in 1956.

TERRITORY AND POPULATION

West Bengal is in northeast India and is bounded north by Sikkim and Bhutan, east by Assam and Bangladesh, south by the Bay of Bengal, southwest by Orissa, west by Jharkhand and Bihar and northwest by Nepal. The total area of West Bengal is 88,752 sq. km. Its population (2001 census, provisional) was 80,221,171; density, 904 per sq. km. The capital is Calcutta. Population of chief cities, *see* INDIA: Territory and Population. Other major towns (1991): Barddhaman (245,079), South Dum Dum (232,811), Baranagar (224,821), Siliguri (216,950), Bally (181,978), Burnpur (174,933), Uluberia (155,172), Hugli-Chinsura (151,806), Raiganj (151,045), North Dum Dum (149,965), Dabgram (147,217), English Bazar (139,204), Serampur (137,028), Barrackpur (133,265), Naihati (132,701), Medinipur (125,498), Nabadwip (125,037), Krishnanagar (121,110), Chandannagar (120,378), Balurghat (119,796), Baharampur (115,144), Bankura (114,876), Titagarh (114,085), Halisahar (114,028), Santipur (109,956), Kulti-Barakar (108,518), Basirhat (101,409), Haldia (100,347), Habra (100,223), Kanchrapara (100,194). The principal language is Bengali.

SOCIAL STATISTICS

Growth rate 1991–2001, 17·84%.

CONSTITUTION AND GOVERNMENT

The state of West Bengal came into existence as a result of the Indian Independence Act, 1947. The territory of Cooch-Behar State was merged with West Bengal on 1 Jan. 1950, and the former French possession of Chandernagore became part of the state on 2 Oct. 1954. Under the States Reorganization Act, 1956, certain portions of Bihar State (an area of 3,157 sq. miles with a population of 1,446,385) were transferred to West Bengal.

The Legislative Assembly has 295 seats (294 elected and 1 nominated).

For administrative purposes there are three divisions (Jalpaiguri, Burdwan and Presidency), under which there are 18 districts, including Calcutta. The Calcutta Metropolitan Development Authority has been set up to co-ordinate development in the metropolitan area (1,350 sq. km). For the purposes of local self-government there are 16 *zilla parishads* (district boards) excluding Darjeeling, 328 *panchayat samities* (regional boards), 1 *siliguri mahakuma parishad* and 3,247 *gram* (village) *panchayats*. There are 113 municipalities, 6 Corporations and 11 Notified Areas. The Calcutta Municipal Corporation is headed by a mayor in council.

RECENT ELECTIONS

In elections held on 10 May 2001, 143 seats went to the Communist Party of India (Marxist), 60 went to the All India Trinamool Congress, 26 to the Indian National Congress, 25 to the All India Forward Bloc and 17 to the Revolutionary Socialist Party. In winning the election the Communists retained power for a sixth consecutive term.

CURRENT ADMINISTRATION

Governor: Viren J. Shah.
Chief Minister: Buddhadeb Bhattacharjee.

ECONOMY

Budget. Budget estimates for 1998–99, revenue receipts Rs 115,827m. and expenditure Rs 132,740·9m. Plan outlay for 1998–99 was Rs 48,061·2m.

ENERGY AND NATURAL RESOURCES

Electricity. Installed capacity, 1997–98, 6,293 MW; 29,341 villages had electricity in Nov. 1998.

Water. The largest irrigation and power scheme under construction is the Teesta Barrage (irrigation potential, 533,520 ha). Other major irrigation schemes are the Mayurakshi Reservoir, Kangsabati Reservoir, Mahananda Barrage and Aqueduct and Damodar Valley. In 1997–98 there were 11,030 tubewells, 7,170 open dugwells and 3,353 riverlift irrigation schemes.

Minerals. Value of production, 1998, Rs 13,244m. The state has coal (the Raniganj field is one of the three biggest in India) including coking coal. Coal production (1998) 16·54m. tonnes.

Agriculture. About 5·90m. ha were under rice-paddy in 1997–98. Total foodgrain production, 1997–98 (provisional), 14·35m. tonnes (rice 13·24m. tonnes, wheat 810,000 tonnes); pulses, 125,700 tonnes; oilseeds, 386,600 tonnes; jute, 7·5m. bales of 180 kg; tea (1995), 170·3m. kg. The state produces 76·3% of the national output of jute and *mesta* (1997–98).

Livestock (1998 census): 17,832,000 cattle; 998,000 buffaloes; 1,462,000 sheep; 15,648,000 goats; and 46,219,000 poultry.

Forestry. The recorded forest area (1997–98) was 13,451 sq. km.

Fisheries. Landings, 1997–98, 950,000 tonnes, of which inland 786,000 tonnes. During 1997–98 Rs 318·6m. was invested in fishery schemes. The state is the largest inland fish producer in the country.

INDUSTRY

The total number of registered factories, 1997 (provisional), was 11,213 (excluding defence factories); average daily employment, 1997, 905,088. The coalmining industry, 1996, had 105 units with average daily employment of 95,864.

There is a large automobile factory at Uttarpara, and an aluminium rolling-mill at Belur. There is a steel plant at Burnpur (Asansol) and a spun pipe factory at Kulti. Durgapur has a large steel plant and other industries under the state sector—a thermal power plant, coke oven plant, fertilizer factory, alloy steel plant and ophthalmic glass plant. There is a locomotive factory at Chittaranjan and a cable factory at Rupnarayanpur. A refinery and fertilizer factory are operating at Haldia. Other industries include chemicals, engineering goods, electronics, textiles, automobile tyres, paper, cigarettes, distillery, aluminium foil, tea, pharmaceuticals, carbon black, graphite, iron foundry, silk and explosives.

Small industries are important; 490,158 units were registered at 31 March 1998, employing 3m. persons. The silk industry is also important; 667,000 persons were employed in the handloom industry in the organized sector in 1997–98.

COMMUNICATIONS

Roads. In 1996 the total length of roads was 74,459 km. On 31 March 1996 the state had 1,198,733 motor vehicles.

Rail. The route-km of railways within the state (1997–98) is 3,784·96 km. The main centres are Asansol, New Jalpaiguri and Kharagpur. There is a metro in Calcutta (16·4 km).

Civil Aviation. The main airport is Calcutta which has national and international flights. In 2000 it handled 2,622,484 passengers (2,048,766 on domestic flights) and 53,755 tonnes of freight The second airport is at Bagdogra in the extreme north, which has regular scheduled services to Calcutta and Delhi.

Shipping. Calcutta is the chief port: a barrage has been built at Farakka to control the flow of the Ganges and to provide a rail and road link between North and South Bengal. A second port has been developed at Haldia, between the present port and the sea, which is intended mainly for bulk cargoes. West Bengal possesses 779 km of navigable canals.

SOCIAL INSTITUTIONS

Justice. The High Court of Judicature at Calcutta has a Chief Justice and 45 puisne judges. The Andaman and Nicobar Islands come under its jurisdiction.

Police. In March 1995 the police force numbered about 56,550, under a director-general and an inspector-general. Calcutta has a separate force under a commissioner directly responsible to the government; its strength was about 22,000 in March 1995.

Religion. At the 1991 census Hindus numbered 50,866,624; Muslims, 16,075,836; Christians, 383,477; Buddhists, 203,578; Sikhs, 55,392; Jains, 34,355.

Education. In 2001, 69·22% of the total population were literate (men, 77·58%; women, 60·22%). In 1998–99 (provisional) there were 52,123 primary schools, 2,648 junior high schools and 8,077 high and higher secondary schools with 1,881,226 students. Education is free up to higher secondary stage. There are ten universities.

The University of Calcutta (founded 1857) is affiliating and teaching; in 1993–94 it had 212 colleges and 150,000 students. Visva Bharati, Santiniketan, was established in 1951 and is residential and teaching; it had 5,226 students in 1993–94. The University of Jadavpur, Calcutta (1955), had 7,087 students in 1992–93. Burdwan University was established in 1960; in 1992–93 there were 91,379 students. Kalyani University was established in 1960 (2,520 students in 1993–94). The University of North Bengal (1962) had 34,000 students in 1993–94. Rabindra Bharati University had 8,309 students in 1992–93. Bidhan Chandra Krishi Viswavidyalaya (1974) had 389 students in 1992–93. There is also Vidyasagar University, Medinipur. Bengal Engineering College has university status. There are 12 engineering and technology colleges, 19 medical colleges, 24 teacher training colleges, 41 polytechnics and 308 arts, science and commerce colleges.

Health. As at 31 March 1998 (provisional) there were 405 hospitals, 2,651 clinics, 1,266 health centres and 8,126 sub-centres with a total of 69,371 beds, and 571 dispensaries.

FURTHER READING
Chatterjee, P., *The Present History of West Bengal: Essays in Political Criticism.* OUP, 1997

UNION TERRITORIES

ANDAMAN AND NICOBAR ISLANDS

The Andaman and Nicobar Islands are administered by the President of the Republic of India acting through a Lieut.-Governor. There is a 30-member Pradesh Council, five members of which are selected by the Administrator as advisory counsellors. The seat of administration is at Port Blair, which is connected with Calcutta (1,255 km away) and Madras (1,190 km) by steamer service which calls about every ten days; there are air services from Calcutta and Madras. Roads in the islands, 733 km black-topped and 48 km others. There are two districts.

The population (2001 census, provisional) was 356,265. The area is 8,249 sq. km and the density 43 per sq. km. Growth rate 1991–2001, 26·94%. Port Blair (1991), 74,955.

The climate is tropical, with little variation in temperature. Heavy rain (125" annually) is mainly brought by the southwest monsoon. Humidity is high.

Budget figures for 1997–98 show total revenue receipts of Rs 819m., and total expenditure on revenue account of Rs 3,027m. Plan outlay, 1997–98, Rs 2,550m.

In 1996–97 there were 188 primary schools with 41,976 students, 45 middle schools with 22,862 students, 38 high schools with 11,151 students and 42 higher secondary schools with 3,858 students. There is a teachers' training college, 2 polytechnics and 2 colleges. Literacy (2001 census), 81·18% (86·07% of men and 75·29% of women).

Lieut.-Governor. N. N. Jha.

The **Andaman Islands** lie in the Bay of Bengal, 193 km from Cape Negrais in Myanmar, 1,255 from Calcutta and 1,190 from Madras. Five large islands grouped together are called the Great Andamans, and to the south is the island of Little Andaman. There are some 204 islets, the two principal groups being the Ritchie Archipelago and the Labyrinth Islands. The Great Andaman group is about 467 km long and, at the widest, 51 km broad.

The original inhabitants live in the forests by hunting and fishing. The total population of the Andaman Islands (including about 430 aboriginals) was 240,089 in 1991. Main aboriginal tribes: Andamanese, Onges, Jarawas and Sentinelese.

The Great Andaman group, densely wooded (forests covered 7,615 sq. km in 1995), contains hardwood and softwood and supplies the match and plywood industries. Annually the Forest Department export about 25,000 tonnes of timber to the mainland. Coconut, coffee and rubber are cultivated. The islands are slowly being made self-sufficient in paddy and rice, and now grow approximately half their annual requirements. Livestock (1982): 27,400 cattle, 9,720 buffaloes, 17,600 goats and 21,220 pigs. Fishing is important. There is a sawmill at Port Blair and a coconut-oil mill. Little Andaman has a palm-oil mill.

The islands possess a number of harbours and safe anchorages, notably Port Blair in the south, Port Cornwallis in the north and Elphinstone and Mayabandar in the middle.

The **Nicobar Islands** are situated to the south of the Andamans, 121 km from Little Andaman. The British were in possession 1869–1947. There are 19 islands, 7 uninhabited; total area, 1,841 sq. km. The islands are usually divided into three sub-groups (southern, central and northern), the chief islands in each being respectively Great Nicobar, Camotra with Nancowrie and Car Nicobar. There is a harbour between the islands of Camotra and Nancowrie, Nancowrie Harbour.

The population numbered, in 1991, 39,208, including about 22,200 of Nicobarese and Shompen tribes. The coconut and areca nut are the main items of trade, and coconuts are a major item in the people's diet.

CHANDIGARH

On 1 Nov. 1966 the city of Chandigarh and the area surrounding it was constituted a Union Territory. Population (2001), 900,914; density, 7,903 per sq. km; growth rate 1991–2001, 40·33%. Area, 114 sq. km. It serves as the joint capital of both Punjab (India) and the state of Haryana, and is the seat of a High Court. The city will ultimately be the capital of just the Punjab; joint status is to last while a new capital is built for Haryana.

Budget for 1997–98 showed revenue of Rs 3,412m. and expenditure of Rs 3,989m.

There is some cultivated land and some forest (27·5% of the territory).

In 1992 there were 15 large and medium scale industries and about 2,800 small scale industries.

In 1996–97 there were 44 primary schools (60,012 students), 33 middle schools (34,095 students), 50 high schools (18,510 students) and 47 higher secondary schools (16,710 students). There were also 2 engineering and technology colleges, 12 arts, science and commerce colleges, 2 polytechnic institutes and a university.

In 2001, 81·76% of the population were literate (85·65% of men and 78·65% of women).

Administrator. Lieut.-Gen. J. F. R. Jacob.

DADRA AND NAGAR HAVELI

GENERAL DETAILS

Formerly Portuguese, the territories of Dadra and Nagar Haveli were occupied in July 1954 by nationalists, and a pro-India administration was formed; this body made a request for incorporation into the Union on 1 June 1961. By the 10th amendment to the constitution the territories became a centrally administered Union Territory with effect from 11 Aug. 1961, forming an enclave at the southernmost point of the border between Gujarat and Maharashtra, approximately 30 km from the west coast. Area 491 sq. km; population (census 2001, provisional), 220,451; density 449 per sq. km; growth rate 1991–2001, 59·20%. There is an Administrator appointed by the government of India. The day-to-day business is done by various departments, co-ordinated by the Secretaries, Assistant Secretary, Collector and Resident Deputy Collector. Headquarters are at Silvassa. 78·82% of the population is tribal and organized in 72 villages. Languages used are dialects classified under Bhilodi (91·1%), Bhilli, Gujarati, Marathi and Hindi.

CURRENT ADMINISTRATION
Administrator: Mr Arun Mathur, IAS.
  Development Commissioner: Mr A. K. Paitandy, IAS.
  Finance Secretary/Commissioner: Mr R. K. Srivastava, IAS.
  Collector: S. K. Malhotra, IAS.

ECONOMY
Budget. The budget for 2001–02 shows revenue receipts of Rs 1,178·3m. and revenue expenditure of Rs 507m. (plan) and Rs 3,076·2m. (non-plan). For 2002–03 revenue receipt target is Rs 1,212·2m.; budget estimate is Rs 552·8m. under Plan Sector and Rs 3,688·4m. under Non-Plan Sector.

ENERGY AND NATURAL RESOURCES
Electricity. Electricity is supplied from Central Grid, and all villages have been electrified. A major sub-station at Kharadpada village has been completed.

Water. As a result of a joint project with the governments of Gujarat, Goa and Daman and Diu there is a reservoir at Damanganga with irrigation potential of 5,900 ha. Drinking water is made available through wells and piped water supply schemes. The Water and Power Consultancy (India) Ltd. (WAPCO) has prepared plans for 66 Water Harvesting Structures to provide drinking water in remote hilly areas.

Minerals. There are few natural mineral resources although there is some ordinary sand and quarry stone.

Agriculture. Farming is the chief occupation, and 22,352 ha were under net crop in 2001–02. Much of the land is terraced and there is a 100% subsidy for soil conservation. The major food crops are rice and ragi; wheat, small millets and pulses are also grown. There is a coverage of lift irrigation over 6,736 ha. There are nine veterinary aid centres, a veterinary hospital, an agricultural research centre and breeding centres to improve strains of cattle and poultry. During 2001–02 the administration distributed 152 tonnes of high-yielding paddy and wheat seed and 1,574 tonnes of manures and fertilizers.

Forestry. 20,359 ha or 40·8% of the total area is forest, mainly of teak, sadad and khair. In 1985 a moratorium was imposed on commercial felling to preserve the environmental function of the forests and ensure local supplies of firewood, timber and fodder. The moratorium still continued in 2002. The tribals have been given exclusive right to collect minor forest produce from the reserved forest area for domestic use. 92 sq. km of reserved forest was declared a wildlife sanctuary in 2000.

Fisheries. There is some inland fishing in water reservoir project areas and individual ponds. During 2001–02 the total catch was 55 tonnes.

INDUSTRY
There is no heavy industry, and the Territory is a 'No Polluting Industry District'. Industrial estates for small and medium scales have been set up at Pipariya, Masat and Khadoli. In March 2002 there were 1,317 small scale and 383 medium scale units employing 37,297 people.

Labour. The Labour Enforcement Office ensures the application of the Monitoring of Minimum Wages Act (1948), the Industrial Disputes Act (1947), the Contract Labour (Regulation and Abolition) Act (1970) and the Workmen's Compensation

Act (1923). During 2001–02, 81 cases under the Industrial Disputes Act were settled. Under the Contract Labour (Regulation and Abolition) Act (1970), 53 certificates of registration and 56 licences were issued to the industrial establishment. 19 cases under the Workman's Compensation Act (1923) were settled.

Trade Unions. There is one trade union registered under the Trade Union Act.

COMMUNICATIONS

Roads. In 2002 there were 580 km of road of which 545·45 km were surfaced. Out of 72 villages, 68 are connected by all-weather road. There were 27,300 motor vehicles in 2001–02. The National Highway no. 8 passes through Vapi, 18 km from Silvassa.

Rail. Although there are no railways in the territory the line from Bombay to Ahmedabad runs through Vapi, 18 km from Silvassa.

Civil Aviation. The nearest airport is at Bombay, 180 km from Silvassa.

Telecommunications. There are 6 telephone exchanges, 1 telex exchange and 1 wireless station. The Telephone Department has provided over 6,000 telephone connections.

Postal Services. There is currently one post and telegraph office with three sub-post offices and 41 branch post offices covering 66 villages.

SOCIAL INSTITUTIONS

Justice. The territory is under the jurisdiction of the Bombay (Maharashtra) High Court. There is a District and Sessions Court and one Junior Division Civil Court at Silvassa.

Religion. Numbers of religious followers (1991 census): Hindu, 132,213 (95·48% of the population); Muslims, 3,341 (2·41%); Christians, 2,092 (1·51%); Jains, 529 (0·38%); Buddhists, 200 (0·14%). There are also, amongst others, Sikhs and Zoroastrians.

Education. Literacy was 60·03% of the population at the 2001 census (73·32% of men and 42·99% of women). In 2001–02 there were 195 primary and middle schools (35,637 students) and 17 high and higher secondary schools (8,887 students).

Health. The territory had (2001–02) a civil hospital, 6 primary health centres, 36 sub-centres, 3 dispensaries and a mobile dispensary. A Community Health Centre has been established at Khanvel, 20 km from Silvassa. The Pulse Polio Immunisation programme was organized in 1999 and 54,128 polio doses were provided to children below five years of age. There has been a sharp fall in the incidence of malaria, especially cerebral malaria, owing to the sustained efforts of the administration. Hepatitis B vaccination of all inmates in the social welfare hostels was completed with the co-operation of voluntary organizations. A blood testing centre has been established for HIV testing.

Welfare. The Social Welfare Department implements the welfare schemes for poor Scheduled castes, Scheduled tribes, women and physically disabled persons, etc.

CULTURE

Broadcasting. There is a low power Government of India TV transmission centre.

Cinema. There is one cinema at Silvassa.

Press. One daily newspaper and two fortnightly news magazines are published.

Tourism. The territory is a rural area between the industrial centres of Bombay and Surat-Vapi. The Tourism Department is developing areas of natural beauty to promote eco-friendly tourism. Several gardens and the Madhuban Dam are among the tourist sites. A lion safari park has been set up at Vasona over 20 ha. About 380,000 visitors came to Dadra and Nagar Haveli during 2000. The government completed a tourist accommodation complex at Silvassa in 1999.

'Tarpa Utsav' in Nov./Dec. and 'Kite Festival' in Jan. are organized with the assistance of the Government of India's Ministry of Tourism.

Festivals. Normally all Hindu, Muslim and Christian festivals are celebrated in the territory while tribals celebrate their own festivals. Diwaso is celebrated by Dhodia and Varli tribes and Rakhsabandhan is celebrated by Dhodias. The Varli and Koli tribes celebrate Bhavada, and Gramdevi and Khali pooja are celebrated by all tribes before and after the harvesting of the crops.

Libraries. There are ten libraries, one in each of ten Gram Panchayat HQs and one central library in Silvassa.

Museums and Galleries. There is a tribal museum at Silvassa with presentations of the lifestyle and culture of tribals.

DAMAN AND DIU

GENERAL DETAILS

Daman (Damão) on the Gujarat coast, 100 miles (160 km) north of Bombay, was seized by the Portuguese in 1531 and ceded to them (1539) by the Shar of Gujarat. The island of Diu, captured in 1534, lies off the southeast coast of Kathiawar (Gujarat); there is a small coastal area. Former Portuguese forts on either side of the entrance to the Gulf of Cambay, in Dec. 1961 the territories were occupied by India and incorporated into the Indian Union; they were administered as one unit together with Goa, to which they were attached until 30 May 1987, when Goa was separated from them and became a state.

TERRITORY AND POPULATION

Daman, 72 sq. km, population (2001) 113,949; Diu, 40 sq. km, population 44,110. Density, 1,411 per sq. km. The main language spoken is Gujarati.

The chief towns are Daman (population, 1991, 26,905) and Diu (20,643).

Daman and Diu have been governed as parts of a Union Territory since Dec. 1961, becoming the whole of that Territory on 30 May 1987.

The main activities are tourism, fishing and tapping the toddy palm (preparing palm tree sap for consumption). In Daman there is rice-growing, some wheat and dairying. Diu has fine tourist beaches, grows coconuts and pearl millet, and processes salt.

SOCIAL STATISTICS

Growth rate 1991–2001, 55·59%.

CURRENT ADMINISTRATION

Administrator: O. P. Nelkar.

ECONOMY

Budget. The budget for 1997–98 shows revenue receipts of Rs 397·7m. and revenue expenditure of Rs 312·2m. Plan outlay, 1995–96, Rs 230m.

SOCIAL INSTITUTIONS

Education. In 2001, 81·09% of the population were literate (88·40% of men and 70·37% of women). In 1996–97 there were 53 primary schools with 14,531 students, 20 middle schools with 6,834 students, 20 high schools with 3,220 students and 3 higher secondary schools with 1,202 students. There is a degree college and a polytechnic.

DELHI

GENERAL DETAILS

Delhi became a Union Territory on 1 Nov. 1956 and was designated the National Capital Territory in 1995.

TERRITORY AND POPULATION

The territory forms an enclave near the eastern frontier of Haryana and the western frontier of Uttar Pradesh in north India. Delhi has an area of 1,483 sq. km. Its population (2001 census, provisional) is 13,782,976 (density per sq. km, 9,294). Growth rate 1991–2001, 46·31%. In the rural area of Delhi there are 231 villages and 27 census towns. They are distributed in five community development blocks.

CONSTITUTION AND GOVERNMENT
The Lieut.-Governor is the Administrator. Under the New Delhi Municipal Act 1994 New Delhi Municipal Council is nominated by central government and replaces the former New Delhi Municipal Committee.

RECENT ELECTIONS
Elections for the 70-member Legislative Assembly were held in Nov. 1998 and the Congress Party formed the government. The Indian National Congress won 52 seats; Bharatiya Janata Party, 15; others, 3.

CURRENT ADMINISTRATION
Lieut.-Governor: Vijay Kumar Kapoor.
Chief Minister: Sheila Dikshit.

ECONOMY
Budget. Estimates for 1996–97 show revenue receipts of Rs 25,911·2m. and expenditure of Rs 37,624·7m. Plan outlay (1997–98) Rs 23,250m.

ENERGY AND NATURAL RESOURCES
Agriculture. The contribution to the economy is not significant. In 1995–96 about 53,900 ha were cropped (of which 36,000 ha were irrigated). Animal husbandry is increasing and mixed farms are common. Chief crops are wheat, bajra, paddy, sugarcane and vegetables.

INDUSTRY
The modern city is the largest commercial centre in northern India and an important industrial centre. Since 1947 a large number of industrial units have been established; these include factories for the manufacture of razor blades, sports goods, electronic goods, bicycles and parts, plastic and PVC goods including footwear, textiles, chemicals, fertilizers, medicines, hosiery, leather goods, soft drinks and hand tools. There are also metal forging, casting, galvanizing, electro-plating and printing enterprises. The number of industrial units functioning was about 126,000 in 1996–97; average number of workers employed was 1·14m. Production was worth Rs 63,100m. and investment was about Rs 25,240m. in 1996–97.

Some traditional handicrafts, for which Delhi was formerly famous, still flourish; among them are ivory carving, miniature painting, gold and silver jewellery and papier mâché work. The handwoven textiles of Delhi are particularly fine; this craft is being successfully revived.

COMMUNICATIONS
Roads. Five national highways pass through the city. There were (1995–96) 2,629,545 registered motor vehicles. The Transport Corporation had 3,206 buses in 1995–96.

Rail. Delhi is an important rail junction with three main stations. There is an electric ring railway for commuters (route-km in 1995–96, 214).

Civil Aviation. Indira Gandhi International Airport operates international flights; Palam airport operates internal flights.

SOCIAL INSTITUTIONS
Religion. At the 1991 census Hindus numbered 7,882,164; Muslims, 889,641; Sikhs, 455,657; Jains, 94,672; Christians, 83,152; Buddhists, 13,906; others, 1,452.

Education. The proportion of literate people to the total population was 81·82% at the 2001 census (87·37% of males and 75·00% of females). In 1996–97 there were 2,184 primary schools with 1,146,691 students, 559 middle schools with 535,511 students, 324 high schools with 676,209 students and 994 higher secondary schools with 460,334 students. There are 9 engineering and technology colleges, 9 medical colleges and 25 polytechnics.

The University of Delhi was founded in 1922; it had 66 affiliated colleges and 189,332 students in 1994–95. There are also Jawaharlal Nehru University, Indira Gandhi National Open University and the Jamia Millia Islamia University; the Indian Institute of Technology at Hauz Khas; the Indian Agricultural Research Institute at Pusa; the All India Institute of Medical Science at Ansari Nagar and the Indian Institute of Public Administration are the other important institutions.

Health. In 1992 there were 82 hospitals including 46 general, 27 special, 6 Ayurvedic, 1 Unani, 2 Homoeopathic. There were 656 dispensaries.

CULTURE

Press. Delhi publishes major daily newspapers, including the *Times of India, Hindustan Times, The Hindu, Indian Express, National Herald, Patriot, Economic Times, The Pioneer, The Observer of Business and Politics, Financial Express, Statesman, Asian Age* and *Business Standard* (all in English); *Nav Bharat Times, Rashtriya Sahara, Jansatta* and *Hindustan* (in Hindi); and three Urdu dailies.

LAKSHADWEEP

The territory consists of an archipelago of 36 islands (10 inhabited), about 300 km off the west coast of Kerala. It was constituted a Union Territory in 1956 as the Laccadive, Minicoy and Amindivi Islands, and renamed in Nov. 1973. The total area of the islands is 32 sq. km. The northern portion is called the Amindivis. The remaining islands are called the Laccadives (except Minicoy Island). The inhabited islands are: Androth (the largest), Amini, Agatti, Bitra, Chetlat, Kadmat, Kalpeni, Kavaratti, Kiltan and Minicoy. Androth is 4·8 sq. km, and is nearest to Kerala. An Advisory Committee associated with the Union Home Minister and an Advisory Council to the Administrator assist in the administration of the islands; these are constituted annually. Population (2001 census), 60,595, nearly all Muslims. Density, 1,894 per sq. km; growth rate 1991–2001, 17·19%. The language is Malayalam, but the language in Minicoy is Mahl. Budget for 1997–98 showed revenue of Rs 73·1m. and expenditure of Rs 1,255·7m. In 2001, 87·52% of the population were literate (93·15% of men and 81·56% of women). There were, in 1996–97, 9 high schools (2,043 students) and 9 nursery schools (1,197 students), 19 junior basic schools (9,015 students), 4 senior basic schools (4,797 students) and 2 junior colleges. There are two hospitals and seven primary health centres. The staple products are copra and fish; coconut is the only major crop. There is a tourist resort at Bangarem, an uninhabited island with an extensive lagoon. Headquarters of administration, Kavaratti Island. An airport, with Vayudoot services, opened on Agatti island in April 1988. The islands are also served by ship from the mainland and have helicopter inter-island services.

Administrator. K. S. Mehra.

PONDICHERRY

GENERAL DETAILS

Formerly the chief French settlement in India, Pondicherry was founded by the French in 1673, taken by the Dutch in 1693 and restored to the French in 1699. The English took it in 1761, restored it in 1765, re-took it in 1778, restored it a second time in 1785, re-took it a third time in 1793 and finally restored it to the French in 1816. Administration was transferred to India on 1 Nov. 1954. A Treaty of Cession (together with Karaikal, Mahé and Yanam) was signed on 28 May 1956; instruments of ratification were signed on 16 Aug. 1962 from which date (by the 14th amendment to the Indian Constitution) Pondicherry, comprising the four territories, became a Union Territory.

TERRITORY AND POPULATION

The territory is composed of enclaves on the Coromandel Coast of Tamil Nadu and Andhra Pradesh, with Mahé forming an enclave on the coast of Kerala. The total area of Pondicherry is 480 sq. km, divided into four Districts. On Tamil Nadu coast: Pondicherry (290 sq. km; population, 2001 census, 735,004), Karaikal (161; 170,640). On Kerala coast: Mahé (9; 36,823). On Andhra Pradesh coast: Yanam (20; 31,362). Total population (2001 census, provisional), 973,829; density, 1,979 per sq. km. Pondicherry Municipality had (1991) 203,065 inhabitants. The principal languages spoken are Tamil, Telugu, Malayalam, French and English.

SOCIAL STATISTICS
Growth rate 1991–2001, 20·56%. In 1990 family schemes had reduced the birth rate to 19·9 per 1,000 and the infant mortality rate to 34·79 per 1,000 live births.

CONSTITUTION AND GOVERNMENT
By the government of Union Territories Act 1963 Pondicherry is governed by a Lieut.-Governor, appointed by the President, and a Council of Ministers responsible to a Legislative Assembly.

RECENT ELECTIONS
In the elections of 10 May 2001 the Indian National Congress–Tamil Maanila Congress (Moopanar) gained 13 seats, Dravida Munnetra Kazhagam plus allies 12, All India Anna Dravida Munnetra Kazhagam plus allies 3, and others 2.

CURRENT ADMINISTRATION
Governor: K. R. Malkani.
  Chief Minister: N. Rangaswamy.

ECONOMY
Budget. Budget estimates for 1996–97 showed expenditure of Rs 5,354·8m. Plan outlay, 1996–97, Rs 2,000m.

ENERGY AND NATURAL RESOURCES
Electricity. Power is bought from neighbouring states. All 292 villages have electricity. Consumption, 1991–92, 747 units per head. Peak demand, 130 MW; total consumption, 607·73m. units.

Agriculture. Nearly 45% of the population is engaged in agriculture and allied pursuits; 90% of the cultivated area is irrigated. The main food crop is rice. Foodgrain production, 71,600 tonnes in 1995–96. Rice production, 67,100 tonnes from 26,600 ha in 1995–96; principal cash crops are cotton (10,934 bales of 180 kg), sugarcane (258,400 tonnes) and groundnuts; minor food crops include ragi, bajra and pulses.

INDUSTRY
There were, 1994–95, 23 large and 73 medium-scale enterprises manufacturing items such as textiles, sugar, cotton yarn, spirits and beer, potassium chlorate, rice bran oil, vehicle parts, soap, amino acids, paper, plastics, steel ingots, washing machines, glass and tin containers and bio polymers. There were also 5,197 small industrial units engaged in varied manufacturing.

COMMUNICATIONS
Roads. There were (1992–93) 3,282 km of roads of which 1,248 km were surfaced. Motor vehicles (March 1996) 119,290.

Rail. Pondicherry is connected to Villupuram Junction. Route-km in 1995–96, 11 km.

Civil Aviation. The nearest main airport is Madras.

SOCIAL INSTITUTIONS
Education. In 2001, 81·49% of the population were literate (88·89% of men and 74·13% of women). There were, in 1996–97, 178 pre-primary schools (15,107 pupils), 350 primary schools (103,201), 120 middle schools (64,617), 89 high schools (28,731) and 52 higher secondary schools (11,168). There were (1996–97) 7 general education colleges, 2 medical colleges, a law college, an engineering college, an agricultural college and a dental college, and 4 polytechnics. Pondicherry University had, in 1994–95, 19 colleges and 9,910 students.

Health. In 1995–96 there were 9 hospitals, 55 health centres and dispensaries and 79 sub-centres.

INDONESIA

Republik Indonesia

Capital: Jakarta
Population estimate, 2000: 212·09m.
GDP per capita, 2000: (PPP$) 3,043
HDI/world rank: 0·684/110

KEY HISTORICAL EVENTS

In the 16th century Portuguese traders settled in some of the islands which now comprise Indonesia but were ejected by the British who in turn were ousted by the Dutch in 1595. From 1602 the Netherlands East India Company controlled the area until the dissolution of the Company in 1798. The Netherlands government then ruled the colony from 1816 until 1941 when it was occupied by the Japanese until 1945. On 17 Aug. 1945 nationalist leaders proclaimed an independent republic. On 27 Dec. 1949 the Netherlands conceded unconditional sovereignty.

In 1960 President Sukarno assumed power to control and dissolve political parties. He also set up a mass organization, the National Front, and a supreme state body called the Provisional People's Consultative Assembly. On 11–12 March 1966 the military commanders under the leadership of Lieut.-Gen. Suharto took over executive power while leaving President Sukarno as the head of state. The Communist party, which had twice attempted to overthrow the government, was outlawed. On 22 Feb. 1967 Sukarno handed over all his powers to Gen. Suharto. Re-elected president at five-year intervals, on the final occasion on 10 March 1998, Suharto presided over a booming economy but one which was characterized by corruption and croneyism. The weaknesses became apparent when, in 1997, a failure of economic confidence spread from Japan across Asia. By May 1998 Indonesia had regressed to the verge of civil war. As food prices doubled, then trebled, riots broke out in Jakarta destroying homes and shops. The risk of society fragmenting along ethnic and religious lines was emphasized by the particular sufferings of the Chinese community. President Suharto was forced to stand down on 21 May 1998 and was succeeded by his Vice-President, Bacharuddin Jusuf Habibie, who promised political and economic reforms. Continuing protest centred on the Suharto family which until recently exercised control over large parts of the Indonesian economy. Several of the country's discontented regions are wanting to break free.

In Aug. 1999 East Timor, the former Portuguese colony which Indonesia invaded in 1975, voted for independence, a move that was eventually approved by the Indonesian parliament after violent clashes between independence supporters and pro-Indonesian militia groups. It gained independence from Indonesia on 20 May 2002.

In Nov. 1999 up to 1m. people took to the streets in the province of Aceh, in the far west of the country, seeking a referendum on independence. One of the founder provinces of the Republic of Indonesia, there were fears that Aceh's possible secession would threaten the breakup of the country. More than 5,000 people were killed there during the 1990s, and rebellions in a number of other Indonesian provinces were suppressed with heavy loss of life. In Dec. 2002 the government and the separatist Free Aceh Movement signed a peace deal to end the violence. In exchange for disarmament, Aceh was granted autonomy and self-government from 2004.

In Oct. 2002 around 200 people, mainly foreign nationals, died in a car bomb explosion outside a nightclub in Bali. A second bomb exploded near a US consulate. No organization claimed responsibility for the attack, but the Indonesian and Australian governments blamed al-Qaeda.

TERRITORY AND POPULATION

Indonesia, with a land area of 740,356 sq. miles (1,917,525 sq. km), consists of 17,507 islands (6,000 of which are inhabited) extending about 3,200 miles east to west through three time-zones (East, Central and West Indonesian Standard time) and 1,250 miles north to south. The largest islands are Sumatra, Java, Kalimantan (Indonesian Borneo), Sulawesi (Celebes) and West Papua, formerly Irian Jaya (the western part of New Guinea). Most of the smaller islands except Madura and Bali are grouped together. The two largest groups of islands are Maluku (the Moluccas) and Nusa Tenggara (the Lesser Sundas). On the island of Timor Indonesia is bounded in the east by the newly-created independent country of East Timor.

Population at the 1990 census was 179,378,946. Estimate, 1995, 194·75m. (60·2% rural in 1999); density, 102 per sq. km. Indonesia has the fourth largest population in the world, after China, India and the USA.

The UN gives a projected population for 2010 of 237·71m.

Area, population and chief towns of the provinces, autonomous districts and major islands:

	Area (in sq. km)	Population (1999 estimate)	Chief town	Population (1990 census)
Aceh[1]	55,390	4,144,500	Banda Aceh	143,409
Bengkulu	19,789	1,557,000	Bengkulu	146,439
Jambi	53,436	2,589,800	Jambi[2]	301,359
Lampung	35,385	7,080,800	Tanjungkarang	284,275[3]
Riau	94,561	4,290,600	Pakanbaru	341,328
Sumatera Barat	42,898	4,594,800	Padang	477,344
Sumatera Selatan	109,254	7,734,200	Palembang	1,084,483
Sumatera Utara	71,680	11,955,400	Medan	1,685,972
Sumatra	482,393	43,947,100		
DKI Jakarta[1]	664	9,604,900	Jakarta	8,259,266
Jawa Barat	43,177	42,332,200	Bandung	2,026,893
Jawa Tengah	32,549	31,043,700	Semarang	1,005,316
Jawa Timur	47,923	35,160,100	Surabaya	2,421,016
Yogyakarta[1]	3,186	3,052,100	Yogyakarta	412,392
Java and Madura	127,499	121,193,000		
Kalimantan Barat	146,807	3,943,200	Pontianak	387,112
Kalimantan Selatan	36,535	3,102,500	Banjarmasin	443,738
Kalimantan Tengah	153,564	1,771,000	Palangkaraya	60,447[3]
Kalimantan Timur	210,985	2,579,400	Samarinda	335,016
Kalimantan	547,891	11,396,100		
Sulawesi Selatan	72,781	8,090,100	Ujung Padang	913,196
Sulawesi Tengah	69,726	2,129,000	Palu	298,584[3]
Sulawesi Tenggara	27,686	1,744,900	Kendari	41,021[3]
Sulawesi Utara	19,023	2,804,400	Menado	275,374
Sulawesi	189,216	14,768,400		
Bali	5,633	3,052,700	Denpasar	261,263[3]
Maluku	77,871	2,223,000	Amboina	206,260
Nusa Tenggara Barat	20,153	3,921,300	Mataram	141,387[3]
Nusa Tenggara Timur	44,888	3,850,100	Kupang	403,110[3]
West Papua (formerly Irian Jaya)	421,981	2,165,300	Jayapura	149,618[3]
Pulau—Pulau Lain	570,526	15,212,400		

[1]Autonomous District. [2]Formerly Telanaipura. [3]1980 census.

The capital, Jakarta, had a population of 10·62m. in 1999. Other major cities (1997 estimates in 1m.): Bandung, 5·92; Bogor, 5·00; Malang, 3·17; Surabaya, 2·80; Semarang, 2·22.

The principal ethnic groups are the Acehnese, Bataks and Minangkabaus in Sumatra, the Javanese and Sundanese in Java, the Madurese in Madura, the Balinese in Bali, the Sasaks in Lombok, the Menadonese, Minahasans, Torajas and Buginese in Sulawesi, the Dayaks in Kalimantan, Irianese in West Papua (formerly Irian Jaya) and the Ambonese in the Moluccas. There were some 6m. Chinese resident in 1991.

Bahasa Indonesia is the official language; Dutch is spoken as a colonial inheritance.

Jakarta: Indonesia's capital is the country's largest city. It lies on the western tip of the island of Java and covers an area of 590 sq. km. It was captured by the Dutch in 1619 and named Batavia until Indonesia gained full independence in 1949 when it was renamed Jakarta. Since then, Jakarta has undergone huge growth in population and industry and is now one of the most important urban agglomerations in Asia.

SOCIAL STATISTICS
Births, 1995, 4,719,000; deaths, 1,580,000. 1995 birth rate, 23·9 per 1,000 population; death rate, 8·0. Life expectancy in 1999 was 63·9 years for men and 67·7 for women. Annual population growth rate, 1990–99, 1·5%. Infant mortality, 1999, 38 per 1,000 live births; fertility rate, 1999, 2·5 births per woman.

In the Human Development Index, or HDI (measuring progress in countries in longevity, knowledge and standard of living), Indonesia's index improved the most of any country during the last quarter of the 20th century, rising from 0·456 in 1975 to 0·677 in 1999.

CLIMATE
Conditions vary greatly over this spread of islands, but generally the climate is tropical monsoon, with a dry season from June to Sept. and a wet one from Oct. to April. Temperatures are high all the year and rainfall varies according to situation on lee or windward shores. Jakarta, Jan. 78°F (25·6°C), July 78°F (25·6°C). Annual rainfall 71" (1,775 mm). Padang, Jan. 79°F (26·1°C), July 79°F (26·1°C). Annual rainfall 177" (4,427 mm). Surabaya, Jan. 79°F (26·1°C), July 78°F (25·6°C). Annual rainfall 51" (1,285 mm).

CONSTITUTION AND GOVERNMENT
The constitution originally dates from Aug. 1945 and was in force until 1949; it was restored on 5 July 1959.

The political system is based on *pancasila*, in which deliberations lead to a consensus. There is a 700-member *People's Consultative Assembly,* which formerly chose the president, but the constitution was changed on 10 Aug. 2002 to allow for direct elections for the president and the vice-president. The Assembly comprises 500 members of the *House of People's Representatives* and an additional 200 appointed members representing the provinces and so-called 'functional' organizations. There are 38 unelected seats in the *House of People's Representatives* reserved for the security forces, but the constitutional amendments of Aug. 2002 will result in these seats being abolished in 2004.

There is no limit to the number of presidential terms. Although predominantly a Muslim country, the constitution protects the religious beliefs of non-Muslims.

National Anthem. 'Indonesia, tanah jang mulia' ('Indonesia, our native land'); words and tune by W. R. Supratman.

RECENT ELECTIONS
The first free elections in 44 years were held on 7 June 1999 for the 462 elected seats in the House of Representatives. The reformist Indonesian Democratic Party of Struggle (PDIP) won 154 seats with 37·4% of the vote; the Party of the Functional Groups (Golkar) won 120 seats with 20·9%; United Development Party (PPP) 58 with 10·7%; National Awakening Party (PKB) 51 with 17·4%; National Mandate Party (PAN) 35 with 7·3%; Crescent Star Party (PBB) 14 with 1·8%. The Justice Party (PK) and the Justice and Unity Party (PKP) both won 6 seats; the Love the Nation Democratic Party (PDKB), the Nahdlatul Ummat Party (PNU) and the Democratic Party of Indonesia (PDI) each won 3; the People's Sovereignty Party (PDR) won 2; and a number of parties each won a single seat.

On 20 Oct. 1999 the People's Consultative Assembly elected Abdurrahman Wahid president with 373 votes. Megawati Sukarnoputri came second with 313 votes and on 21 Oct. became vice-president. Wahid was summarily dismissed on 23 Sept. 2001 to be replaced by vice-president Megawati Sukarnoputri, following a unanimous parliamentary vote to remove Wahid on grounds of incompetence.

CURRENT ADMINISTRATION
President: Megawati Sukarnoputri; b. 1947 (PDIP; sworn in 23 July 2001).
Vice-President: Hamzah Haz.

In March 2003 the cabinet was composed as follows:

Co-ordinating Ministers: (Political and Security Affairs) Susilo Bambang Yudhoyono; *(Economic Affairs)* Dorodjatun Kuntjoro-Jakti; *(People's Welfare)* Yusuf Kalla.

Minister of Home Affairs: Hari Sabarno. *Foreign Affairs:* Hassan Wirajuda. *Justice and Human Rights:* Yusril Ihza Mahendra. *Defence:* Matori Abdul Jalil. *Religious Affairs:* Said Agiel Munawar. *Education:* Abdul Malik Fajar. *Health:* Dr Ahmad Sujudi. *Finance:* Boediono. *Trade and Industry:* Rini Suwandi. *Manpower and Transmigration:* Jacob Nuwa Wea. *Agriculture:* Bunngaran Saragih. *Forestry:* Mohamad Prakosa. *Transportation and Communications:* Lieut.-Gen. Agum Gumelar. *Maritime Affairs and Fisheries:* Dahuri Rokhmin. *Resettlement and Regional Infrastructure:* Soenarno. *Social Affairs:* Bachtiar Chamsyah. *Culture and Tourism:* I Gede Ardika. *Energy and Mineral Resources:* Yusgiantoro Purnomo.

Government Website: http://www.indonesia.go.id/

DEFENCE

There is selective conscription for two years. Defence expenditure in 2000 totalled US$1,493m. (US$7 per capita), representing 1·0% of GDP.

Army. Army strength in 1999 was estimated at 230,000 with a strategic reserve (KOSTRAD) of 30,000 and further potential mobilizable reserves of 400,000.

There is a paramilitary police some 194,000 strong, and two part-time local auxiliary forces: KAMRA (People's Security), numbering around 1·5m., and WANRA (People's Resistance).

Navy. The Navy in 1999 numbered about 47,000, including 12,000 in the Commando Corps, and 1,000 in the Naval Air Arm. Combatant strength includes 2 diesel submarines and 17 frigates. The Naval Air Arm operates 49 combat aircraft and 21 armed helicopters.

The Navy's principal command is split between the Western Fleet, at Teluk Ratai (Jakarta) and the Eastern Fleet, at Surabaya.

Air Force. Personnel (1999) approximately 21,000. There were 91 combat aircraft, including F-16s, F-5s and British Aerospace *Hawks.*

INTERNATIONAL RELATIONS

Indonesia is in dispute with Malaysia over sovereignty of two islands in the Celebes Sea. Both countries have agreed to accept the Judgment of the International Court of Justice.

Indonesia is a member of the UN, WTO, OPEC, Asian Development Bank, Colombo Plan, APEC, ASEAN, Mekong Group and OIC.

ECONOMY

Agriculture accounted for 19·5% of GDP in 1998, industry 45·3% and services 35·2%.

Overview. The government's plan for growth has been hit by financial instability in the Asian money markets and international concern about corruption, a shaky banking system and the slow pace of deregulation and privatization; but this is not to deny the economic successes that were achieved in the Suharto era. Since 1970 the economy has grown, on average, by more than 6% a year.

Currency. The monetary unit is the *rupiah* (IDR) notionally of 100 *sen*. Annual inflation was running at 58·0% in 1998 but had fallen to 3·8% by 2000 before rising to 11·5% in 2001. Foreign exchange reserves were US$28,127m. and gold reserves 3·10m. troy oz in June 2002. Total money supply in Dec. 2001 was 170,509·0bn. rupiahs.

Budget. By law the budget must balance. The fiscal year starts 1 April. Revenue and expenditure for 1999–2000 were 218,204bn. rupiahs. Routine revenue (in 1bn. rupiahs), 1999–2000, 140,804; routine expenditure, 134,556; development revenue, 77,400; development expenditure, 83,648.

Performance. Economic growth was 8·0% in 1996 and 4·5% in 1997 but declined dramatically in 1998 to −13·1%. There was a slight recovery in 1999, with growth of 0·8%, followed by growth of 4·8% in 2000 and 3·3% in 2001. The Asian economic crisis of 1997 affected Indonesia more than any other country. In 2001 total GDP was US$145·3bn.

Banking and Finance. The Bank Indonesia, successor to De Javasche Bank established by the Dutch in 1828, was made the central bank of Indonesia on 1 July 1953. Its *Governor* is Dr Syahril Sabirin. It had an original capital of 25m. rupiahs; a reserve fund of 18m. rupiahs and a special reserve of 84m. rupiahs. In Jan. 2000 independent auditors declared that the bank was technically bankrupt. In response the IMF stated that future loans would probably depend on recapitalization and an internal reorganization.

There are 117 commercial banks, 28 development banks and other financial institutions, 8 development finance companies and 9 joint venture merchant banks. Commercial banking is dominated by seven state-owned banks: Bank Rakyat Indonesia provides services to smallholder agriculture and rural development; Bank Bumi Daya, estate agriculture and forestry; Bank Negara Indonesia 1946, industry; Bank Dagang Negara, mining; and Bank Expor-Impor Indonesia, export commodity sector. All state banks are authorized to deal in foreign exchange.

There are 70 private commercial banks owned and operated by Indonesians. The 11 foreign banks specialize in foreign exchange transactions and direct lending operations to foreign joint ventures. The government owns one Savings Bank, Bank Tabungan Negara, and 1,000 Post Office Savings Banks. There are also over 3,500 rural and village savings banks and credit co-operatives. At least 16 banks closed in the wake of the 1997 financial crisis.

The World Bank board agreed to resume lending in Indonesia in June 1998 by approving a US$225m. loan to reduce poverty. Also in June 1998 Indonesia reached agreement with foreign banks on a comprehensive private-sector debt restructuring programme, involving the rescheduling of some US$60bn. of Indonesian corporate debt over eight years and the extension by up to four years of Indonesian bank liabilities totalling US$9·2bn. The most important element of the deal was the creation of the Indonesian Debt Restructuring Agency (INDRA) which provided protection against foreign exchange risk covering up to US$60bn. in corporate debt. The Indonesian Bank Restructuring Agency (IBRA) was also established in 1998 by the Indonesian government and is the primary agency responsible for overseeing the rehabilitation of the financial sector. IBRA is authorized to take over and control banks facing financial difficulties.

There is a stock exchange in Jakarta.

Weights and Measures. The metric system is in use.

The following are the old weights and measures: *Pikol* = 136·16 lb avoirdupois; *Katti* = 1·36 lb avoirdupois; *Bau* = 1·7536 acres; *Square Pal* = 227 hectares = 561·16 acres; *Jengkal* = 4 yd; *Pal* (Java) = 1,506 metres; *Pal* (Sumatra) = 1,852 metres.

ENERGY AND NATURAL RESOURCES

Environment. According to the *World Bank Atlas* Indonesia's carbon dioxide emissions in 1998 were the equivalent of 1·1 tonnes per capita.

Electricity. Installed capacity in 1998 was 18·37m. kW. Production was 82·10bn. kWh in 1999. Consumption per capita was 320 kWh in 1998. There were seven hydro-electric plants in 1989. 68,045 villages were supplied with electricity in 1999.

Oil and Gas. The importance of oil in the economy is declining. The 1996 output of crude oil was 553m. bbls. Proven reserves in 1999 totalled 5·0bn. bbls. Natural gas production, 1999, was 67,677m. cu. metres with 2,050bn. cu. metres of proven reserves. In Jan. 2001 a 640-km gas pipeline linking Indonesia's West Natuna field with Singapore came on stream. It is expected to provide Singapore with US$8bn. worth of natural gas over a 20-year period.

Minerals. The high cost of extraction means that little of the large mineral resources outside Java is exploited; however, there is copper mining in West Papua, nickel mining and processing on Sulawesi, and aluminium smelting in northern Sumatra. Open-cast coal mining has been conducted since the 1890s, but since the 1970s coal production has been developed as an alternative to oil. Reserves are estimated at 28,000m. tonnes. Coal production (1997), 54·4m. tonnes. Other minerals: salt (1998 estimate), 650,000 tonnes; bauxite (1998), 513,000 tonnes; iron ore (1994), 334,900 tonnes; copper concentrate (1998), 2·9m. tonnes; silver (1998), 348,730 kg; gold (2000), 139 tonnes; nickel ore (1998), 2·7m. tonnes; tin (1998), 50,833 tonnes.

Agriculture. There were 17·94m. ha of arable land in 1998 and 13·05m. ha of permanent crops. Production (2000, in 1,000 tonnes): rice, 51,000; sugarcane, 21,400; cassava, 16,347; coconuts, 16,235; maize, 9,169; palm oil, 6,900; bananas, 3,377; cabbages, 1,750; sweet potatoes, 1,627; palm kernels, 1,600; natural rubber, 1,488; copra, 1,380; soybeans, 1,198; groundnuts, 1,000; potatoes, 924; dry beans, 900; mangoes, 827; onions, 805; oranges, 645; cucumbers and gherkins, 580; chillies and green peppers, 497; papayas, 450; coffee, 430; cocoa beans, 362; aubergines, 340. Annual nutmeg production is 6,000 tonnes, more than two-thirds of the world total. Indonesia is the world's largest producer of coconuts.

Livestock (2000): goats, 14·12m.; cattle, 12·10m.; pigs, 9·35m.; sheep, 7·50m.; buffaloes, 2·86m.; horses, 579,000; chickens, 800m.; ducks, 26m.

Forestry. In 1995 the area under forests was 109·79m. ha, or 60·6% of the total land area (115·21m. ha and 63·6% in 1990). Approximately 46% of the forested area is scheduled for selective logging, 33% for preservation for national parks and watersheds and 21% for removal for agriculture, industry and settlement. The loss of 5·42m. ha between 1990 and 1995 was exceeded during the same period only in Brazil. In 1999, 190·6m. cu. metres of roundwood were cut, most of it fuelwood and charcoal.

Fisheries. In 1999 total catch was 4,149,420 tonnes, of which 3,855,310 tonnes were sea fish. In 1997 there were 191,270 motorized and 371,007 other fishing vessels.

INDUSTRY

There are shipyards at Jakarta Raya, Surabaya, Semarang and Amboina. There are textile factories, large paper factories, match factories, automobile and bicycle assembly works, large construction works, tyre factories, glass factories, a caustic soda and other chemical factories. Production (1997, in 1,000 tonnes): distillate fuel oil, 14,200; residual fuel oil, 12,000; petrol, 7,950; kerosene, 6,159; cement 23,136 (1995); fertilizers (1993), 3,459; sugar (1995), 1,493; paper and paperboard (1999), 6,978; plywood (1999), 4·4m. cu. metres; 19,000 passengers cars; 1,001,000 TV sets (1993). Indonesia is the third largest producer of plywood after the USA and China.

Labour. Reforms announced in Nov. 1994 included an annual review of regional minimum wages, enhanced enforcement of salary, safety and health regulations, and an improved dispute resolution process. In 1998 the labour force was 92,700,000. In 1997, 41·2% of employed persons worked in agriculture, 19·8% in trade, 14·5% in services, public administration and defence, and 12·9% in manufacturing. National daily average wage, 1996, 4,073 rupiahs. Unemployment in 1998 reached around 17%.

Trade Unions. Workers have a constitutional right to organize and under a law passed in Feb. 2003 have a right to be paid during lawful strikes. Until the fall of Suharto in 1998 unions were expected to affiliate to the All Indonesia Trade Union (SPSI), which enjoyed government approval and was affiliated to the ruling party. Between 1994 and 1996 there were more than 2,000 strikes involving 1m. workers. In Feb. 2003 the Indonesian Trade Union Congress (KSPI), supported by the International Confederation of Free Trade Unions, was inaugurated. It represents 3·1m. members and encompasses 12 industrial federations.

INTERNATIONAL TRADE

Since 1992 foreigners have been permitted to hold 100% of the equity of new companies in Indonesia with more than US$50m. part capital, or situated in remote provinces. Foreign investment in 1994 totalled US$23,724·3m. (including from Hong Kong, US$6,041·7m.; UK, US$2,957·1m.; Taiwan, US$2,487·5m.). Foreign debt was US$141,803m. in 2000 (the sixth highest in the world).

Pressure on Indonesia's currency and stock market led to an appeal to the IMF and World Bank for long-term support funds in Oct. 1997. A bail-out package worth US$38,000m. was eventually agreed on condition that Indonesia tightened financial controls and instituted reforms, including the establishment of an independent privatization board, liberalizing foreign investment, cutting import tariffs and phasing out export levies.

Imports and Exports. In June 1994 import duties were cut on 739 commodities, surcharges on 108 imports were removed and non-tariff barriers on 27 items abolished. Imports and exports in US$1m.:

	1996	1997	1998	1999	2000
Imports f.o.b.	44,240	46,223	31,942	30,598	40,366
Exports f.o.b.	50,188	56,298	50,371	51,242	65,406

Main export items: gas and oil, forestry products, manufactured goods, rubber, coffee, fishery products, coal, copper, tin, pepper, palm products and tea. Main export markets, 1999: Japan, 20·53%; USA, 14·59%; Singapore, 10·03%. Main import suppliers, 1999: USA, 12·34%; Japan, 11·24%; Singapore, 9·76%; Germany, 6·63%.

COMMUNICATIONS

Roads. In 1998 there were 346,863 km of roads (27,357 km of highways or main roads in 1997), of which 195,712 km were surfaced. Motor vehicles, 1998: passenger cars, 2,772,500; buses and coaches, 628,000; trucks and vans, 1,592,600; motorcycles, 12,651,800. There were 272 fatalities in road accidents in 1996.

Rail. In 1997 the national railways totalled 6,458 km of 1,067 mm gauge, comprising 4,967 km on Java (of which 125 km electrified) and 1,491 km on Sumatra. Passenger-km travelled in 1998 came to 16·14bn. and freight tonne-km to 4·96bn.

Civil Aviation. Garuda Indonesia is the state-owned national flag carrier. Merpati Nusantara Airlines is their domestic subsidiary. Domestic services are also provided by Bouraq Indonesia. There are international airports at Jakarta (Sukarno-Hatta), Denpasar (on Bali), Medan (Sumatra), Pekanbaru (Sumatra), Ujung Pandang (Sulawesi), Manado (Sulawesi), Solo (Java) and Surabaya Juanda (Java). Jakarta is the busiest airport, in 2000 handling 9,950,000 passengers (5,387,000 on domestic flights) and 292,300 tonnes of freight. Denpasar handled 3,970,000 and Surabaya Juanda 2,444,000 passengers in 2000. In 1999 scheduled airline traffic of Indonesia-based carriers flew 121·8m. km, carrying 8,047,000 passengers (1,927,000 on international flights).

Shipping. There are 16 ports for ocean-going ships, the largest of which is Tanjung Priok, which serves the Jakarta area and has a container terminal. The national shipping company Pelajaran Nasional Indonesia (PELNI) maintains inter-island communications. Jakarta Lloyd maintains regular services between Jakarta, Amsterdam, Hamburg and London. In 1995 the merchant marine comprised 535 ocean-going ships totalling 4·13m. DWT. 95 vessels (36·22% of total tonnage) were registered under foreign flags. In 1998 total tonnage registered came to 3·35m. GRT, including oil tankers 841,000 GRT. In 1995 vessels totalling 155,869,000 net registered tons entered ports and vessels totalling 48,857,000 NRT cleared.

Telecommunications. In 2000 there were 6,662,600 main telephone lines (31·4 per 1,000 population) and 2·1m. PCs in use (9·9 for every 1,000 persons). There were 2·2m. mobile phone subscribers in 1999 and 185,000 fax machines in 1997. Indonesia had 4·4m. Internet users in Jan. 2002, up from 400,000 in July 2000.

The telephone utility Telekomunikasi Indonesia (Telkom) is the largest of a number of companies up for sale, but an unresolved dispute with foreign tele-communication companies has led to a delay in its privatization.

Postal Services. In 1998 there were 4,572 post offices.

SOCIAL INSTITUTIONS

Justice. There are courts of first instance, high courts of appeal in every provincial capital and a Supreme Court of Justice for the whole of Indonesia in Jakarta.

In civil law the population is divided into three main groups: Indonesians, Europeans and foreign Orientals, to whom different law systems are applicable.

When, however, people from different groups are involved, a system of so-called 'inter-gentile' law is applied.

The present criminal law, which has been in force since 1918, is codified and is based on European penal law. This law is equally applicable to all groups of the population. The death penalty is still in use.

The population in penal institutions in 1997 was 41,699.

Religion. Religious liberty is granted to all denominations. In 1999 there were 179·8m. Muslims (making Indonesia the world's biggest Muslim country), 12·4m. Protestants and 7·8m. Roman Catholics. There were also 3·8m. Hindus, of whom approximately 70% were on Bali, and 2·1m. Buddhists, probably for the greater part Chinese.

Education. Adult literacy in 1999 was 86·3% (91·5% among males and 81·3% among females). In 1997 there were 25,689,693 pupils and 1,158,616 teachers at 151,064 primary schools, and 10,821,139 pupils and 654,505 teachers at 29,398 secondary schools. Number of students in higher education (1997) 2,051,000. In 1994–95 in the state sector there were 31 universities and 1 open university, and 13 institutes of higher education, including 10 teacher training colleges. In the private sector there were 66 universities and the following specialized universities: Adventist, 1; Christian, 7; Islamic, 10; Methodist, 1; Roman Catholic, 5; Veterans', 1. There were 19 institutes of higher education in the private sector, including 12 teacher training colleges.

In 1996 total expenditure on education came to 1·4% of GNP and 7·9% of total government spending.

Health. In 1996 there were 31,887 doctors, 155,911 nurses and midwives and (1994) 3,988 pharmacies. There were 1,090 hospitals in 1997, with a provision in 1994 of six beds per 10,000 population.

CULTURE

Broadcasting. Radio Republik Indonesia, under the Department of Information, operates 49 stations. There were 13·75m. television receivers (colour by PAL) and 31·5m. radio sets in 1997.

Cinema. There were 2,173 cinemas in 1990.

Press. In 1996 there were 69 daily newspapers (combined circulation of 4,665,000 at a rate of 23 per 1,000 inhabitants). In 1996 a total of 4,018 book titles were published in 8·1m. copies.

Tourism. In 1998 there were 4,337,000 foreign tourists, spending US$4·36bn.

DIPLOMATIC REPRESENTATIVES

Of Indonesia in the United Kingdom (38 Grosvenor Sq., London, W1X 9AD)
Ambassador: Vacant.
Chargé d'Affaires a.i.: Nicholas Tandi Dammen.

Of the United Kingdom in Indonesia (Jalan M.H. Thamrin 75, Jakarta 10310)
Ambassador: Richard H. T. Gozney, CMG.

Of Indonesia in the USA (2020 Massachusetts Ave., NW, Washington, D.C., 20036)
Ambassador: Soemadi Djoko M. Brotodiningrat.

Of the USA in Indonesia (Medan Merdeka Selatan 5, Jakarta)
Ambassador: Ralph Leo Boyce.

Of Indonesia to the United Nations
Ambassador: Vacant.
Deputy Permanent Representative: Mochamed Slamet Hidyat.

Of Indonesia to the European Union
Ambassador: Nasrudin Sumintapura.

FURTHER READING
Central Bureau of Statistics. *Statistical Yearbook of Indonesia.—Monthly Statistical Bulletin: Economic Indicator.*
Cribb, R., *Historical Dictionary of Indonesia.* Metuchen (NJ), 1993.—and Brown, C., *Modern Indonesia: a History since 1945.* Harlow, 1995

Forrester, Geoff, (ed.) *Post-Soeharto Indonesia: Renewal or Chaos?* St Martin's Press, New York, 1999

Forrester, Geoff and May, R. J. (eds.) *The Fall of Soeharto.* Hurst, London, 1999

Kingsbury, Damien, *The Politics of Indonesia.* 2nd ed. OUP, 2002

Krausse, G. H. and Krausse, S. C. E., *Indonesia.* [Bibliography] ABC-Clio, Oxford and Santa Barbara (CA), 1994

Ricklefs, M. C., *A History of Modern Indonesia since c. 1200.* 3rd ed. Palgrave, Basingstoke, 2001

Schwarz, Adam, *A Nation in Waiting: Indonesia's Search for Stability.* Revised ed. Westview Press, Boulder (CO), 1999

Schwarz, Adam and Paris, Jonathan, (eds.) *The Politics of Post-Suharto Indonesia.* New York, 1999

Vatikiotis, M. R. J., *Indonesian Politics under Suharto: Order, Development and Pressure for Change.* 2nd ed. London, 1994

National statistical office: Central Bureau of Statistics, POB 1003, Jakarta, 10010.
Website: http://www.bps.go.id

IRAN

Jomhuri-e-Eslami-e-Iran
(Islamic Republic of Iran)

Capital: Tehran
Population estimate, 2000: 63·66m.
GDP per capita, 2000: (PPP$) 5,884
HDI/world rank: 0·721/98

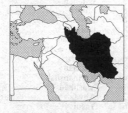

KEY HISTORICAL EVENTS

Persia was ruled by the Shahs as an absolute monarchy from the 16th century until 1906, when the first constitution was granted and a national assembly established. After a coup in 1921, Reza Khan began his rise to power. He was declared Shah on 12 Dec. 1925 and as closer relations with Europe were developed in the mid-1930s so the name Iran began to be used in the west instead of Persia. When in the Second World War Iran supported Germany, the Allies occupied the country and forced Reza Shah to abdicate in favour of his son. Iran's oil industry was nationalized in March 1951 in line with the policy of the National Front Party whose leader, Dr Muhammad Mussadeq, became prime minister in April 1951. He was opposed by the Shah who fled the country until Aug. 1953 when the monarchists staged a coup which led to Mussadeq being deposed. The Shah's policy, which included the redistribution of land to small farmers and the enfranchisement of women, was opposed by the Shia religious scholars who considered it to be contrary to Islamic teaching. Despite economic growth, unrest was caused by the Shah's repressive measures and his extensive use of the Savak, the secret police. The opposition led by Ayatollah Ruhollah Khomeini, the Shia Muslim spiritual leader who had been exiled in 1965, was particularly successful. Following intense civil unrest in Tehran, the Shah left Iran with his family on 17 Jan. 1979 (and died in Egypt on 27 July 1980). The Ayatollah Khomeini returned from exile on 1 Feb. 1979, the Shah's government resigned and parliament dissolved itself on 11 Feb. Following a referendum in March, an Islamic Republic was proclaimed. The constitution gave supreme authority to a religious leader (*wali faqih*), a position held by Ayatollah Khomeini for the rest of his life. In Sept. 1980 border fighting with Iraq escalated into full-scale war. A UN-arranged ceasefire took place on 20 Aug. 1988, and in Aug. 1990, following Iraq's invasion of Kuwait, Iraq offered peace terms and began the withdrawal of troops from Iranian soil. Approximately 30,000 political opponents of the regime are believed to have been executed shortly after the end of the war.

In 1997 the election of Mohammad Khatami as president signalled a shift away from Islamic extremism. A clampdown on Islamic vigilantes who wage a violent campaign against western 'decadence' is the latest sign of a cautiously liberal integration of the constitution. But the conservative faction led by the spiritual leader Ayatollah Ali Khamenei retains huge power including the final say on defence and foreign policy.

In July 1999 riot police fought pitched battles with pro-democracy students in Tehran in the worst unrest since the revolution in 1979. Since then there have been further cautious moves towards a more liberal society, though the Islamic leaders remain bitterly divided on the degree of overlap between politics and religion.

TERRITORY AND POPULATION

Iran is bounded in the north by Armenia, Azerbaijan, the Caspian Sea and Turkmenistan, east by Afghanistan and Pakistan, south by the Gulf of Oman and the Persian Gulf, and west by Iraq and Turkey. It has an area of 1,629,918 sq. km (634,293 sq. miles), but a vast portion is desert. Population (1996 census): 60,055,488 (1999, 61·1% urban). Population density: 36 per sq. km.

The UN gives a projected population for 2010 of 80·81m.

In 2001 Iran had 1·9m. refugees, mostly from Afghanistan. Only Pakistan has more refugees.

The areas, populations and capitals of the 28 provinces *(ostan)* were:

Province	Area *(sq. km)*	Census 1996	Capital
Ardebil	17,881	1,168,011	Ardebil
Azarbayejan, East	45,481	3,325,540	Tabriz
Azarbayejan, West	37,463	2,496,320	Orumiyeh
Bushehr	23,168	743,675	Bushehr
Chahar Mahal and Bakhtyari	16,201	761,168	Shahr-e-Kord
Esfahan	107,027	3,923,255	Esfahan
Fars	121,825	3,817,036	Shiraz
Gilan	13,952	2,241,896	Rasht
Golestan	20,893	1,426,288	Gorgan
Hamadan	19,547	1,677,957	Hamadan
Hormozgan	71,193	1,062,155	Bandar-e-Abbas
Ilam	20,150	487,886	Ilam
Kerman	181,714	2,004,328	Kerman
Kermanshah	24,641	1,778,596	Kermanshah
Khorasan	302,966	6,047,661	Mashhad
Khuzestan	63,213	3,746,772	Ahvaz
Kohgiluyeh and Boyer Ahmad	15,491	544,356	Yasuj
Kordestan	28,817	1,346,383	Sanandaj
Lorestan	28,392	1,584,434	Khorramabad
Markazi	29,406	1,228,812	Arak
Mazandaran	23,833	2,602,008	Sari
Qazvin	15,502	968,257	Qazvin
Qom	11,237	853,044	Qom
Semnan	96,816	501,447	Semnan
Sistan and Baluchestan	178,431	1,722,579	Zahedan
Tehran	19,196	10,343,965	Tehran
Yazd	73,467	750,769	Yazd
Zanjan	21,841	900,890	Zanjan

At the 1996 census the populations of the principal cities were:

	Population		Population
Tehran	6,758,845[1]	Arak	380,755
Mashhad	1,887,405	Ardabil	340,386
Esfahan	1,266,072	Yazd	326,776
Tabriz	1,191,043	Qazvin	291,117
Shiraz	1,053,025	Zanjan	286,295
Karaj	940,968	Sanandaj	277,808
Ahvaz	804,980	Bandar-e-Abbas	273,578
Qom	777,677	Khorramabad	272,815
Kermanshah	692,986	Eslamshahr	265,450
Orumiyeh	435,200	Borujerd	217,804
Zahedan	419,518	Abadan	206,073
Rasht	417,748	Dezful	202,639
Hamadan	401,281	Khorramshahr	105,636
Kerman	384,991		

[1]1999 population, 6,934,750.

The national language is Farsi or Persian, spoken by 45% of the population in 1986. 28% spoke related languages, including Kurdish (9%) and Luri in the west, Gilaki and Mazandarami in the north, and Baluchi in the southeast; 22% speak Turkic languages, primarily in the northwest. Iranians, who are Persians, not Arabs, are less emotionally connected to the plight of the Arab Palestinians than people in other parts of the Middle East. The majority of Iranians are not instinctively anti-American.

Tehran: Situated in northern Iran near Mt Damavand and 100 km from the Caspian sea, Tehran has been the capital since Agha Mohammad Khan, the founder of the Qajar dynasty (1779–1925), gave it the title in 1788. Despite economic and political difficulties arising from the establishment of the Islamic Republic in Iran, Tehran is today the country's administrative, commercial and industrial centre.

SOCIAL STATISTICS

1995 births, 1,179,260; deaths, 378,797. Birth rate (1995, per 1,000 population), 19·2; death rate, 6·2. Iran has one of the youngest populations in the world, with about 55% of the current population being under the age of 25. Abortion is illegal, but a family planning scheme was inaugurated in 1988. Expectation of life at birth,

1999, 70·3 years for females and 67·5 years for males. Infant mortality, 1999, 30·3 per 1,000 live births. Annual population growth rate, 1990–99, 1·47%; fertility rate, 1999, 2·7 births per woman. Iran has had one of the largest reductions in its fertility rate of any country in the world over the past 25 years, having had a rate of 6·4 births per woman in 1975. The suicide rate is 25 for every 100,000 people—more than twice the world average.

CLIMATE
Mainly a desert climate, but with more temperate conditions on the shores of the Caspian Sea. Seasonal range of temperature is considerable, as is rain (ranging from 2" in the southeast to 78" in the Caspian region). Winter is normally the rainy season for the whole country. Abadan, Jan. 54°F (12·2°C), July 97°F (36·1°C). Annual rainfall 8" (204 mm). Tehran, Jan. 36°F (2·2°C), July 85°F (29·4°C). Annual rainfall 10" (246 mm).

CONSTITUTION AND GOVERNMENT
The Constitution of the Islamic Republic was approved by a national referendum in Dec. 1979. It gives supreme authority to the *Spiritual Leader* (*wali faqih*), which position was held by Ayatollah Khomeini until his death on 3 June 1989. Ayatollah Seyed Ali Khamenei was elected to succeed him on 4 June 1989. Following the death of the previous incumbent, Ayatollah Ali Khamenei was proclaimed the *Source of Knowledge (Marja e Taghlid)* at the head of all Shia Muslims in Dec. 1994.

The 86-member *Assembly of Experts* was established in 1982. It is popularly elected every eight years. Its mandate is to interpret the constitution and select the Spiritual Leader. Candidates for election are examined by the *Council of Guardians*.

The *Islamic Consultative Assembly* has 290 members, elected for a four-year term in single-seat constituencies. All candidates have to be approved by the 12-member *Council of Guardians*.

The *President* of the Republic is popularly elected for not more than two four-year terms and is head of the executive; he appoints Ministers subject to approval by the *Islamic Consultative Assembly (Majlis)*.

Legislative power is held by the Islamic Consultative Assembly, directly elected on a non-party basis for a four-year term by all citizens aged 17 or over. A new law passed in Oct. 1999 raised the voting age from 16 to 17, thus depriving an estimated 1·5m. young people from voting. Two-thirds of the electorate is under 30. Voting is secret but ballot papers are not printed; electors must write the name of their preferred candidate themselves. Five seats are reserved for religious minorities. All legislation is subject to approval by the *Council of Guardians* who ensure it is in accordance with the Islamic code and with the Constitution. The Spiritual Leader appoints six members, as does the judiciary.

National Anthem. 'Sar zad az ofogh mehr-e khavaran' ('Rose from the horizon the affectionate sun of the East'); words by a group of poets, tune by Dr Riahi.

RECENT ELECTIONS
Presidential elections held on 8 June 2001 produced a second landslide victory for incumbent Mohammad Khatami. He promised to continue fighting for democratic reforms which were blocked during his preceding tenure by the hardline clerical establishment. There were ten candidates. Mohammad Khatami was elected with 78·3% of votes cast (up from 69% at the 1997 election), against 15·9% for Ahmad Tavakoli and 2·7% for defence minister Ali Shamkhani. Turn-out was 67%.

Elections to the Islamic Consultative Assembly were held on 18 Feb. and 5 May 2000. The electorate was 38·7m. and turn-out was 83%. The Reformists (2nd of Khordad) gained 189 of the 290 available seats, Radical Islamists 54, ind. 42 and religious minorities 5.

Elections to the Assembly of Experts were held on 23 Oct. 1998; turn-out was 46%. Conservative candidates won 54 seats, 13 went to moderates and the remaining 21 went to conservative-allied independents.

CURRENT ADMINISTRATION
In March 2003 the cabinet was composed as follows:

President: Ali Mohammad Khatami-Ardakani; b. 1943 (sworn in 3 Aug. 1997 and re-elected in 2001).

First Vice President: Mohammad Reza Aref-Yazdi.
Vice President for Atomic Energy: Gholamreza Aghazadeh-Khoi. *Vice President for Environmental Protection:* Dr Masoomeh Ebtekar. *Vice President for Legal and Parliamentary Affairs:* Mohammad Ali Abtahi. *Vice President for Physical Training:* Mohsen Mehr-Alizadeh. *Vice President for Planning and Management:* Mohammad Satari-Far. *Government Spokesperson:* Dr Abdullah Ramezanzadeh. *Minister of Foreign Affairs:* Dr Kamal Kharrazi. *Oil:* Bijan Namdar-Zanganeh. *Interior:* Abdol Vahed Musavi-Lari. *Economic Affairs and Finance:* Tahmasb Mazaheri. *Agriculture Jihad:* Muhammad Hojjati. *Commerce:* Mohammad Shariatmadar. *Energy:* Habibollah Bitaraf. *Roads and Transport:* Ahmad Khorram. *Industry and Mines:* Eshaq Jahangiri. *Housing and Urban Development:* Dr Ali Abdolalizadeh. *Labour and Social Affairs:* Safdar Husseini. *Health, Treatment and Medical Education:* Masud Pezekhsian. *Education and Training:* Morteza Haji-Qaem. *Science, Research and Technology:* Dr Mostafa Moin-Najafabadi. *Justice:* Mohammad Esmael Shoushtari. *Defence and Armed Forces Logistics:* V. Adm. Ali Shamkhani. *Islamic Culture and Guidance:* Ahmad Masjed-Jamei. *Co-operatives:* Ali Sufi. *Intelligence and Security:* Mohammad Ali Yunesi. *Information and Communications Technology:* Dr Seyed Ahmad Motamedi.

Speaker of the Islamic Consultative Assembly (Maljes): Mehdi Mahdavi-Karubi.

Presidency Website: http://www.president.ir/

DEFENCE
Two years' military service is compulsory. Military expenditure totalled US$7,329m. in 2000 (equivalent to US$108 per capita), representing 7·5% of GDP, compared to 18·0% in 1985.

Nuclear Weapons. Although Iran is a member of the Non-Proliferation Treaty (NPT), it may be developing weapons using its nuclear power programme. Iran has successfully tested Shahab-3 medium-range ballistic missiles with a range of 1,300 km. According to *Deadly Arsenals*, published by the Carnegie Endowment for International Peace, Iran has a chemical and biological weapons programme.

Army. Strength (2002), 325,000 (about 220,000 conscripts). Reserves are estimated to be around 350,000, made up of ex-service volunteers.

Revolutionary Guard (*Pasdaran Inqilab*). Numbering some 125,000, the Guard is divided between ground forces (100,000), naval forces (some 20,000) and marines (5,000). It controls the Basij, a volunteer 'popular mobilization army' of about 300,000, which can number 1m. strong in wartime.

Navy. The fleet includes six submarines (including three ex-Soviet *Kilo* class) and three ex-UK frigates. Personnel numbered 18,000 in 2002 including 2,000 in Naval Aviation and 2,600 marines.

The Naval Aviation wing operated 5 combat aircraft and 19 armed helicopters.
The main naval bases are at Bandar-e-Abbas, Bushehr and Chah Bahar.

Air Force. In 2002 there were 306 combat aircraft including US F-14 Tomcat, F-5E Tiger II and F-4D/E Phantom II fighter-bombers, and a number of MiG-29 interceptors and Su-24 strike aircraft. The serviceability of the aircraft varies with only 60–80% operational.

Strength (2002) estimated at 52,000 personnel (about 15,000 air defence).

INTERNATIONAL RELATIONS
Iran's foreign policy has been much less doctrinaire since the election to the presidency in May 1997 of Mohammad Khatami. In April 2001 Iran and Saudi Arabia signed a security pact to fight drug trafficking and terrorism, 13 years after the two countries had broken off relations.

Iran is a member of the UN, OPEC, ECO, IOM, OIC and the Colombo Plan.

ECONOMY
Overview. The Third Five-Year Development Plan has been running since 2000. At the beginning of 1991 about 70% of industry was state-owned, much of it nationalized after the 1979 revolution, but the government is now committed to partial privatization. Strategic heavy industry will remain in the public sector.

Currency. The unit of currency is the *rial* (IRR) of which 10 = 1 *toman*. The value of the rial has fallen from IRR 70 to the US$ in 1979 to a low of IRR 8,112 in March 2003. Gold reserves were 5·42m. troy oz in March 1996. Inflation in 2001 was running at 11·4%. Total money supply in Feb 2002 was 130,015bn. rials.

Budget. Total revenue and expenditure for 1998–99 was put at 230,440bn. rials, an increase of 22·2% over the 1997–98 budget. The estimated total revenue and expenditure for 1999–2000 was 276,215bn. rials. The accuracy of budget figures is questionable given the policy of dividing the budget into two parts: the first covering ministerial expenditure, the second dealing with state banks and industries, which receive allocations by the expediency of printing money.

Performance. Real GDP growth was 4·8% in 2001. Total GDP in 2001 was US$118·9bn.

Banking and Finance. The Central Bank is the note issuing authority and government bank. Its *Governor* is Moshen Nurbakhach. All other banks and insurance companies were nationalized in 1979, and re-organized into new state banking corporations, of which there were five in 1994. In April 2000 the government announced that it would permit the establishment of private banks for the first time since the revolution in 1979, ending the state monopoly on banking. The first private bank since the revolution came into existence in Aug. 2001 with the creation of Bank-e-Eqtesadi Novin (Modern Economic Bank).

A stock exchange re-opened in Tehran in 1992.

Weights and Measures. The metric system is in force.

Calendar. The Iranian year is a solar year starting on varying dates between 19 and 22 March. The current solar year is 1382 (21 March 2003 to 20 March 2004). The Islamic *hegira* (622 AD, when Mohammed left Mecca for Medina) year 1424 corresponds to 5 March 2003–21 Feb. 2004, and is the current lunar year.

ENERGY AND NATURAL RESOURCES

Environment. According to the *World Bank Atlas* Iran's carbon dioxide emissions were the equivalent of 4·7 tonnes per capita in 1998.

Electricity. Total installed capacity in 1997 was 29·45m. kW; production (1998), 103·41bn. kWh (approximately 62·76% from steam, 26·97% from gas and combined, 6·78% from hydro-electricity and 3·48% from diesel). Consumption per capita in 1998 was 1,599 kWh. Iran's first nuclear reactor is being built by Russia at Bushehr and is scheduled to be commissioned in late 2003.

Oil and Gas. Iran has 8·9% of proven global oil reserves. Oil is its chief source of revenue. The main oilfields are in the Zagros Mountains where oil was first discovered in 1908. Oil companies were nationalized in 1979 and operations of crude oil and natural gas exploitation are now run by the National Iranian Oil Company. Refining operations of crude oil are run by the National Company for Refining and Distribution of Oil Products. Iran produced 5·1% of the world total oil output in 1999; in 2001 it had reserves amounting to 89·7bn. bbls. In 1999 the most important discovery in more than 30 years was made, with the Azadegan oilfield in the southwest of the country being found to have reserves of approximately 26bn. bbls. In 2001 revenue from oil exports amounted to US$14bn. (US$19bn. in 2000). Iran depends on oil for some 86% of its exports, but domestic consumption has been increasing to such an extent that it is now as high as exports.

Crude petroleum production (1998): 1,341m. bbls. (3,664,000 bbls. a day). Refining capacity (1997): 1,242,000 bbls. a day.

Iran has nearly one fifth of proven global gas reserves. A deal reached in Nov. 1997 between Gazprom, the Russian gas company, and Total, the French energy group, involved the investment of US$2,000m. into the development of a gas field.

In Dec. 1997 the first natural gas pipeline linking Iran with the Caspian Sea via Turkmenistan was opened. The 200-km line links gas fields in western Turkmenistan to industrial markets in northern Iran. Natural gas production (1999): 54,815m. cu. metres. Natural gas reserves in 2000 were 23,000bn. cu. metres, the second largest behind Russia.

Minerals. Production, after dressing (1996, in tonnes): iron ore, 5,236,259; coal, 1,211,403; copper, 370,234; chromite, 322,367; zinc and lead, 321,766; bauxite, 230,420; manganese, 82,694; salt, 1,410,644; decorative stone, 6,120,071. It was announced in Feb. 2003 that uranium deposits had been discovered in central Iran.

Agriculture. Agriculture accounted for approximately 12·7% of GDP in 2000. Cultivable land in 2000 totalled 17,121,500 ha: 10,267,582 ha were under annual crops (of which 5,541,068 ha were irrigated). In 2000 there were 1,977,294 ha and 112,999 ha of productive and non-productive orchards and nurseries respectively.

Crop production (2000, in 1,000 tonnes): wheat, 8,088; sugarbeet, 4,332; potatoes, 3,658; tomatoes, 3,191; grapes, 2,505; sugarcane, 2,367; rice (paddy), 1,971; barley, 1,686; watermelons, 1,650; onions, 1,344; cucumbers and gherkins, 1,343; maize, 1,036; dates, 870; pistachios, 304. Iran's annual production of dates and pistachios is the highest in the world.

Livestock (2000): 55·0m. sheep; 26·0m. goats; 8·1m. cattle; 500,000 buffaloes; 1·6m. asses; 386m. chickens.

Forestry. Approximately 7·4% of Iran is forested, much of it in the Caspian region. Timber production in 2000 was 684,000 cu. metres.

Fisheries. In 2000 total catch was 424,500 tonnes (358,500 tonnes from sea fishing).

INDUSTRY

Major industries: petrochemical, automotive, food, beverages and tobacco, textiles, clothing and leather, wood and fibre, paper and cardboard, chemical products, non-metal mining products, basic materials, machinery and equipment, copper, steel and aluminium. The textile industry uses local cotton and silk; carpet manufacture is an important industry. The country's steel industry is the largest in the Middle East.

Production of selected commodities in large-scale manufacturing establishments with 50 workers and more (1996): sugar, 831,888 tonnes; stockings, 9·7m. pairs; machine-made bricks, 1,792m.; cement, 16,441,701 tonnes.

Labour. The economically active population numbered 20m. in 2002, of which 17·6m. were employed. Approximately 12·2% of the workforce are unemployed and 800,000 Iranians enter the workforce every year.

INTERNATIONAL TRADE

There had been a limit on foreign investment, but legislation of 1995 permits foreign nationals to hold more than 50% of the equity of joint ventures with the consent of the Foreign Investment Board. Foreign debt was US$7,953m. in 2000.

Imports and Exports. Imports and exports for calendar years in US$1m.:

	1996	1997	1998	1999	2000
Imports f.o.b.	14,989	14,123	14,286	13,433	15,207
Exports f.o.b.	22,391	18,381	13,118	21,030	28,345

Main imports: machinery and motor vehicles, iron and steel, chemicals, pharmaceuticals, food. Main exports: oil, carpets, pistachios, leather and caviar. Petroleum and crude oil exports (1996): 2,620,000 bbls. a day. Crude oil exports account for 85% of hard currency earnings. Carpet exports are the second largest hard currency earner. Iran's main trading partners (US$1m, 1996) were Germany (2,100·0), Belgium (926·3), Japan (844·0) for imports; and the UK (3,907·6), Japan (3,816·0), and Italy (1,821·9) for exports.

COMMUNICATIONS

Roads. In 1998 the total length of roads was 167,157 km, of which 890 km were freeways, 24,940 km main roads, 38,043 km (asphalted) by-roads, 15,370 km (gravelled) by-roads, 30,195 km asphalted rural roads and 57,719 km other rural roads. In 1996 there were 1,793,000 passenger cars; 692,000 vans and lorries; 2,565,585 motorcycles and mopeds.

Rail. The State Railways totalled 6,264 km of main lines in 1998, of which 148 km were electrified. In 1998–99 the railways carried 9·56m. passengers and 21·6m. tonnes of freight. An isolated 1,676 mm gauge line (94 km) in the southeast provides a link with Pakistan Railways. A rail link to Turkmenistan was opened in May 1996.

Civil Aviation. There are international airports at Tehran (Mehrabad), Shiraz and Bandar-e-Abbas. Tehran is the busiest airport, in 2000 handling 8,474,000 passengers (6,473,000 on domestic flights). The Imam Khomeini International Airport, construction of which began in 1977 before being halted in 1979, was scheduled to be fully operational by June 2002 but only the first phase has been completed. The completed airport will be able to handle up to 40m. passengers and 450,000 tonnes of freight a year. The state-owned Iran Air carried 5·8m. passengers and 38,343 tonnes of freight in 1998–99.

Shipping. In 1998 the merchant fleet totalled 3·35m. GRT, including oil tankers totalling 1·59m. GRT. In 1998–99, 4,447 ships loaded and unloaded 31·0m. and 41·1m. tonnes of goods respectively (including oil products). In 1997–98 vessels totalling 27,756,000 NRT entered ports.

Telecommunications. In 2000 there were 9,486,160 telephone main lines, equivalent to 149·0 per 1,000 population, and 4·0m. PCs in use (62·8 for every 1,000 persons). Mobile phone subscribers numbered 490,478 in 1999 and there were 30,000 fax machines in 1995. Iran had 250,000 Internet users in Dec. 2000.

Postal Services. In 1998 there were 13,699 post offices. 274m. pieces of mail were processed during the year, or 4·2 items per person.

SOCIAL INSTITUTIONS

Justice. A legal system based on Islamic law (*Sharia*) was introduced by the 1979 constitution. A new criminal code on similar principles was introduced in Nov. 1995. The President of the Supreme Court and the public Prosecutor-General are appointed by the Spiritual Leader. The Supreme Court has 16 branches and 109 offences carry the death penalty. To these were added economic crimes in 1990. There were 71 confirmed executions in 2002.

Religion. The official religion is the Shi'a branch of Islam. Adherents number approximately 89% of the population; 10% are Sunni Muslims. However, less than 2% of the population now attend Friday prayers.

Education. Adult literacy in 1999 was 75·7% (82·7% among males and 68·7% among females). Most primary and secondary schools are state schools. Elementary education in state schools and university education is free; small fees are charged for state-run secondary schools. In 2001–02 there were 7,513,015 pupils and 309,260 teachers at 68,836 primary schools, 9,416,272 pupils and 344,042 teachers at secondary schools, and 1,566,509 pupils and 79,235 academic staff at institutions of higher education.

In 1994–95 there were 30 universities, 30 medical universities, 12 specialized universities (1 agriculture, 1 art, 1 oil engineering, 4 teacher training, 5 technology) and 2 open (distance-learning) universities. There were 289,392 students and 10,745 academic staff.

In 1995 total expenditure on education came to 4·0% of GNP and represented 17·8% of total government expenditure.

Health. There were 717 hospitals in 2001, with 109,152 beds. In 2001 medical personnel totalled 295,325 of which 152,396 were paramedics. There were 25,988 nurses and 8,105 midwives.

CULTURE

Broadcasting. Broadcasting is controlled by the government agency, Islamic Republic of Iran Broadcasting (IRIB). Both television and radio operate under a single organization, the National Iranian Radio and Television Organization (NIRT), established by an Act of Parliament in 1967, which in 1990 employed some 11,620 people. There are two national radio stations (Radio One and Radio Two) and 27 regional radio stations, including a Koran service and an external service (Voice of the Islamic Republic of Iran, which broadcasts in 20 languages). There are no commercial radio stations; radio broadcasting is a state monopoly. There were (1997) 138 radio transmitters in operation. There are four television networks (colour by SECAM H). A ban on TV satellite receiver dishes was imposed in April 1994. There were 17m. radio receivers and 4·6m. television receivers in 1997.

Cinema. There were 312 cinemas with an attendance in 2001 of 33m.

Press. In 2000 there were 117 daily and 259 weekly newspapers. Approximately 80% of the Iranian press is printed in Farsi; much of the remaining 20% is in English or Arabic. As the power struggle continues between the conservative religious establishment and the Khatami government more than 70 reform-minded newspapers have been closed down since 1999.

In 1996 a total of 15,073 book titles were published in 87·86m. copies.

Tourism. There were 1,402,160 foreign tourists in 2001, spending US$441m.

Libraries. In 2001 there were 1,502 libraries affiliated to the Ministry of Culture and Islamic Guidance.

DIPLOMATIC REPRESENTATIVES

Of Iran in the United Kingdom (16 Prince's Gate, London, SW7 1PT)
Ambassador: Morteza Sarmadi.

Of the United Kingdom in Iran (143 Ferdowsi Ave., Tehran 11344)
Ambassador: Richard Dalton, CMG.

The USA does not have diplomatic relations with Iran, but Iran has an Interests Section in the Pakistani Embassy in Washington, D.C., and the USA has an Interests Section in the Swiss Embassy in Tehran.

Of Iran to the United Nations
Ambassador: M. Jarad Zarif.

Of Iran to the European Union
Ambassador: Abolghasem Delfi.

FURTHER READING

Abdelkhah, Fariba, *Being Modern in Iran.* Columbia Univ. Press, 1999
Abrahamian, E., *Khomeinism: Essays on the Islamic Republic.* Univ. of California Press, 1993
Amuzegar, J., *Iran's Economy Under the Islamic Republic.* London, 1992
Daneshvar, P., *Revolution in Iran.* London, 1996
Ehtesami, A., *After Khomeini: the Iranian Second Republic.* London, 1994
Foran, J., *Fragile Resistance: Social Transformation in Iran from 1500 to the Revolution.* Boulder (Colo.), 1993
Fuller, G. E., *Centre of the Universe: Geopolitics of Iran.* Boulder (Colo.), 1992
Hunter, S. T., *Iran after Khomeini.* New York, 1992
Kamrava, M., *Political History of Modern Iran: from Tribalism to Theocracy.* London, 1993
Lahsaelzadeh, A., *Contemporary Rural Iran.* London, 1993
Mir-Hosseini, Ziba, *Islam and Gender: The Religious Debate in Contemporary Iran.* Princeton Univ. Press, 1999
Modaddel, M., *Class, Politics and Ideology in the Iranian Revolution.* Columbia Univ. Press, 1992
Moin, Baqer, *Khomeini: Life of the Ayatollah.* I. B. Tauris, London, 1999
Omid, H., *Islam and the Post-Revolutionary State in Iran.* London, 1994
Rahnema, A. and Behdad, S. (eds.) *Iran After the Revolution: the Crisis of an Islamic State.* London, 1995

National statistical office. Statistical Centre of Iran, Dr Fatemi Avenue, Tehran 14144, Iran. *Website:* http://www.sci.or.ir/

IRAQ

Jumhouriya al 'Iraqia
(Republic of Iraq)

Capital: Baghdad
Population estimate, 2000: 22·95m.
GDP per capita, 2000: (PPP$) 3,197

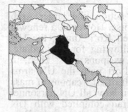

KEY HISTORICAL EVENTS

Iraq, formerly Mesopotamia, was part of the Ottoman Empire from 1534 until it was captured by British forces in 1916. Under a League of Nations mandate, administered by Britain, Amir Faisal Ibn Hussain was crowned king in 1921. On 3 Oct. 1932 Britain's mandate expired, and Iraq became an independent country. The ruling Hashemite dynasty was overthrown by a military coup on 14 July 1958. King Faisal II and Nuri al Said, the prime minister, were killed. A republic was established, controlled by a military-led Council of Sovereignty under Gen. Qassim. In 1963 Qassim was overthrown, and Gen. Abdul Salam Aref became president, with a partial return to a civilian government, but on 17 July 1968 a successful coup was mounted by the Ba'ath Party. Gen. Ahmed Al Bakr became president, prime minister, and chairman of a newly established ruling nine-member Revolutionary Command Council. In July 1979 Saddam Hussein, the vice-president and a Sunni Muslim, became president in a peaceful transfer of power.

In Sept. 1980 Iraq invaded Iran in a dispute over territorial rights in the Shatt-al-Arab waterway which developed into a full-scale war. A UN-arranged ceasefire took place on 20 Aug. 1988 and UN-sponsored peace talks continued in 1989. On 15 Aug. 1990 Iraq offered peace terms and began the withdrawal of troops from Iranian soil.

Early on 2 Aug. 1990 Iraqi forces invaded and rapidly overran Kuwait, meeting little resistance. On 6 Aug. the UN Security Council voted to impose economic sanctions on Iraq until it withdrew from Kuwait. On 7 Aug. the USA announced it was sending a large military force to Saudi Arabia. Further Security Council resolutions included authorization for the use of military force if Iraq did not withdraw by 15 Jan. 1991. On the night of 16–17 Jan. coalition forces began an air attack on strategic targets in Iraq. A land offensive followed on 24 Feb. The Iraqi army was routed. Kuwait City was liberated on 27 Feb. and on 28 Feb. Iraq agreed to the conditions of a provisional ceasefire, including withdrawal from Kuwait.

In June UNSCOM, the United Nations Special Commission, conducted its first chemical weapons inspection in Iraq in accordance with UN Resolution 687. In Sept. a UN Security Council resolution permitted Iraq to sell oil worth US$1,600m. to pay for food and medical supplies. In Oct. the Security Council voted unanimously to prohibit Iraq from all nuclear activities. Imports of materials used in the manufacture of nuclear, biological or chemical weapons were banned, and UN weapons inspectors received wide powers to examine and retain data throughout Iraq.

In Aug. 1992 the USA, UK and France began to enforce an air exclusion zone over southern Iraq in response to the government's persecution of Shi'ite Muslims. Following Iraqi violations of this zone, and incursions over the Kuwaiti border, US, British and French forces made air and missile attacks on Iraqi military targets in Jan. 1993. On 27 June 1993 US forces made a missile attack on an intelligence centre in Baghdad in retaliation for an attempt on former US President Bush's life while he was visiting Kuwait in April. On 10 Nov. 1994 Iraq recognized the independence and boundaries of Kuwait. In the first half of 1995 UN weapons inspectors secured information on an extensive biological weapons programme. At the beginning of Sept. 1996 Iraqi troops occupied the town of Arbol in a Kurdish safe haven in support of the Kurdish Democratic Party faction which was at odds with another Kurdish faction, the Patriotic Union of Kurdistan. On 3 Sept. 1996 US forces fired missiles at targets in southern Iraq and extended the no-fly area northwards to the southern suburbs of Baghdad.

Relations with the USA deteriorated still further in 1997 when Iraq refused co-operation with UN weapons inspectors. On 29 Oct. the Iraqi Revolutionary Command Council announced that it had 'postponed' a decision to stop working with UNSCOM, the UN commission responsible for the destruction of Iraq's ballistic, chemical and biological weapons programmes, but it went on to demand that there should be no American nationals among the UN inspectors. The UN team suspended its operations in Iraq and the Security Council warned Saddam Hussein of 'serious consequences' if he carried out his threat to expel the Americans.

While the USA and the UK threatened retaliatory action, the larger Arab countries with Russia, China and France urged compromise. However, a renewal of hostilities looked probable until late Feb. 1998 when Kofi Annan, the UN Secretary General, forged an agreement in Baghdad allowing for 'immediate, unconditional and unrestricted access' to all suspected weapons sites. Then, in Aug. 1998, Saddam Hussein engineered another stand-off with the UN arms inspectors, demanding a declaration that Iraq had rid itself of all weapons of mass destruction. This the UN chief inspector refused to do. In Nov. all UN personnel left Iraq as the USA threatened air strikes unless Iraq complied with UN resolutions. Russia and France urged further diplomatic efforts, but on 16 Dec. the USA and Britain launched air and missile attacks aimed at destroying Saddam Hussein's arsenal of nuclear, chemical and biological weapons. In all, 97 targets were destroyed. In the aftermath, the USA and Britain continued attacks on selected military and communication targets while encouraging the Iraqi opposition and tightening the trade embargo.

In Feb. 2000 the UN Security Council nominated Sweden's Hans Blix to head the new arms inspectorate to Iraq, but Iraq refused him entry into the country. An oil-for-food scheme, which came into force in 1996 in an effort to alleviate suffering, was administered by the UN. In Feb. 2001 the USA and Britain launched a further series of air attacks on military targets in and around Baghdad. A new UN Security Council resolution was passed in May 2002. Constituting the biggest change since the introduction of the Oil-for-Food scheme in 1996, the new resolution limited import restrictions to a number of specific sensitive goods. The UN and Iraq held a series of talks in early 2002 on the possible resumption of weapons inspections, but without reaching any agreement. In Sept. 2002, as the threat of a US attack on Iraq increased, provisional agreement was given to the return of weapons inspectors but shortly afterwards conditions were imposed which made it unlikely that inspections would resume. In Nov. 2002 the UN Security Council adopted Resolution 1441, holding Iraq in 'material breach' of disarmament obligations. Weapons inspectors under the leadership of Hans Blix returned to Iraq four years after their last inspections, but US and British suspicion that the Iraq regime was failing to comply led to increasing tension, resulting in the USA, the UK and Spain reserving the right to disarm Iraq without the need for a further Security Council resolution. Other Security Council members, notably China, France, Germany and Russia, opposed the proposed action, resulting in a major split in the Security Council.

On 20 March 2003 US forces, supported by the UK, launched attacks on Iraq, initiating a war aimed at 'liberating Iraq'. UK troops entered Iraq's second city, Al-Basrah, on 6 April. On 9 April 2003 American forces took control of central Baghdad, effectively bringing an end to Saddam Hussein's rule. Widespread looting and disorder followed the fall of the capital. The bloodless capture of Tikrit, Saddam Hussein's hometown, on 14 April marked the end of Iraqi resistance. Jay Garner, a retired US general, arrived in Baghdad on 21 April to head the Office of Reconstruction and Humanitarian Assistance for Iraq and to oversee the transition to an interim Iraqi administration. Ole Wøhlers Olsen, a Muslim Danish diplomat, was appointed on 1 May to head the administration of the Al-Basrah region. Garner was replaced as civil administrator on 12 May by Paul Bremer. An interim government was planned until democratic elections could be held. On 22 May the UN Security Council voted to lift economic sanctions against Iraq and to support the US and UK occupation 'until an internationally recognized, representative government is established by the people of Iraq'. Only Syria opposed the resolution by boycotting the session.

TERRITORY AND POPULATION

Iraq is bounded in the north by Turkey, east by Iran, southeast by the Persian (Arabian) Gulf, south by Kuwait and Saudi Arabia, and west by Jordan and Syria. In April 1992 the UN Boundary Commission redefined Iraq's border with Kuwait, moving it slightly northwards in line with an agreement of 1932. Area, 438,317 sq. km. Population, 1997 census, 22,017,983; density, 50·2 per sq. km. In 1998, 75·9% of the population lived in urban areas.

The UN gives a projected population for 2010 of 29·92m.

The areas, populations and capitals of the governorates:

Governorate	Area in sq. km	1991 population estimate	Capital
Al-Anbar	138,501	865,500	Ar-Ramadi
Babil (Babylon)	6,468	1,221,100	Al-Hillah
Baghdad	734	3,910,900	Baghdad
Al-Basrah	19,070	1,168,800	Al-Basrah
Dahuk	6,553	309,300	Dahuk
Dhi Qar	12,900	1,030,900	An-Nasiriyah
Diyala	19,076	1,037,600	Ba'qubah
Irbil	14,471	928,400	Irbil
Karbala	5,034	567,600	Karbala
Maysan	16,072	524,200	Al-Amarah
Al-Muthanna	51,740	350,000	As-Samawah
An-Najaf	28,824	666,400	An-Najaf
Ninawa (Nineveh)	37,323	1,618,700	Mosul
Al-Qadisiyah	8,153	595,600	Ad-Diwaniyah
Salah ad-Din	24,751	772,200	Samarra
As-Sulaymaniyah	17,023	1,124,200	As-Sulaymaniyah
Ta'mim	10,282	605,900	Kirkuk
Wasit	17,153	605,700	Al-Kut

The most populous cities are Baghdad (the capital), population of 4,689,000 in 1999; Irbil, 1,743,000 in 1995; Mosul, 879,000 in 1995. Other large cities included Kirkuk, Al-Basrah, As-Sulaymaniyah and An-Najaf.

The population is approximately 76% Arab, 19% Kurdish (mainly in the north of the country) and 5% Turkmen, Assyrian, Chaldean or other. Shias (predominantly in the south of the country) constitute approximately 60% of the total population and Sunnis (principally in the centre) 20%.

The national language is Arabic. Other languages spoken are Kurdish (official in Kurdish regions), Assyrian and Armenian.

SOCIAL STATISTICS

Births, 1997, 944,000; deaths, 140,000. 1997 rates (per 1,000 population): births, 42·5; deaths, 6·3. Expectation of life in 1998 was 62·3 years for males and 65·3 for females. Annual population growth rate, 1990–99, 2·4%. Infant mortality, 1998, 103 per 1,000 live births, up from 90 per 1,000 live births as far back as 1970, the largest increase anywhere in the world over the same period. Fertility rate, 1999, 5·1 births per woman.

CLIMATE

The climate is mainly arid, with small and unreliable rainfall and a large annual range of temperature. Summers are very hot and winters cold. Al-Basrah, Jan. 55°F (12·8°C), July 92°F (33·3°C). Annual rainfall 7" (175 mm). Baghdad, Jan. 50°F (10°C), July 95°F (35°C). Annual rainfall 6" (140 mm). Mosul, Jan. 44°F (6·7°C), July 90°F (32·2°C). Annual rainfall 15" (384 mm).

CONSTITUTION AND GOVERNMENT

Until the fall of Saddam Hussein, the highest state authority was the Revolutionary Command Council (RCC) but some legislative power was given to the 220-member *National Assembly*.

The only legal political grouping was the National Progressive Front (founded 1973) comprising the Arab Socialist Renaissance (Ba'ath) Party and various Kurdish groups, but a law of Aug. 1991 legalized political parties provided they were not based on religion, racism or ethnicity.

The President and Vice-President were elected by the RCC; the President appointed and led a Council of Ministers responsible for administration.

National Anthem. 'Watanum Mede, al alufqi janalia' ('A homeland which extended its wings over the horizon'); words by S. Jabar Al Kamali, tune by W. G. Gholmieh.

RECENT ELECTIONS

On 15 Oct. 2002 a referendum was held to determine whether President Saddam Hussein should remain in office for a further seven years. The electorate was 11·4m. It was announced that turn-out was 100% and that 100% of votes cast were in favour. In a previous referendum in 1995, 99·96% of votes were declared in favour.

Elections to the National Assembly were held on 27 March 2000. The only candidates permitted to stand were members of the National Progressive Front and non-partisans supporting the Ba'ath government.

CURRENT ADMINISTRATION

Following the war in March–April 2003 there is currently no functioning national government. In May the *de facto* authorities were:

Supreme Commander of Occupation Forces: Gen. Tommy Franks, C.-in-C., US Central Command (b. 1945).

Civil Administrator: Paul Bremer (US presidential envoy, appointed 12 May 2003; b. 1941)

Kurdish-controlled areas:

Secretary-General of the Patriotic Union of Kurdistan: Jalal Talabani (b. 1933).

President of the Kurdish Democratic Party: Massoud Barzani (b. 1966).

INTERNATIONAL RELATIONS

Iraq is a member of the UN, the League of Arab States, OPEC and OIC.

ECONOMY

Currency. The monetary unit is the *Iraqi dinar* (IQD) of 1,000 *fils*. In both 1997 and 1998 inflation was estimated to be 45%.

Budget. Before UN sanctions were applied, oil revenues accounted for nearly 50% and customs and excise for about 26% of the total revenue.

Banking and Finance. All banks were nationalized on 14 July 1964. The Central Bank of Iraq is the sole bank of issue. In 1941 the Rafidain Bank, financed by the Iraqi government, was instituted to carry out normal banking transactions. Its head office is in Baghdad and it has 239 branches, 11 abroad, including London. Its assets were US$47,000m. in Sept. 1990. In addition, there are four government banks which are authorized to issue loans to companies and individuals: the Industrial Bank, the Agricultural Bank, the Estate Bank, and the Mortgage Bank.

There is a stock exchange in Baghdad.

Weights and Measures. The metric system is in general use.

ENERGY AND NATURAL RESOURCES

Environment. According to the *World Bank Atlas* Iraq's carbon dioxide emissions were the equivalent of 3·7 tonnes per capita in 1998. An *Environmental Sustainability Index* compiled for the World Economic Forum meeting in Feb. 2002 ranked Iraq 139th in the world out of 142 countries analysed, with 33·2%. The index measured the ability of countries to maintain favourable environmental conditions and examined various factors including pollution levels and the use or abuse of natural resources.

Electricity. Installed capacity was 10m. kW in 1997. Production in 1998 was 2·84bn. kWh, with consumption per capita in 1997 being 1,414 kWh.

Oil and Gas. Proven oil reserves in 2001 totalled 112·5bn. bbls. Only Saudi Arabia has more reserves. Crude oil production in 1999, at 125m. tonnes, was the highest since before the Gulf War. Since 1991 sanctions against Iraq have held back oil sales of some US$100,000m.

Natural gas production, 1996, 136 petajoules. In 2000 Iraq had natural gas reserves of 3,100bn. cu. metres.

Minerals. The principal minerals extracted are sulphur (475,000 tonnes in 1995) and phosphate rock (440,000 tonnes in 1995).

Agriculture. There were 5·2m. ha of arable land in 1998 and 0·34m. ha of permanent crops. Production (2000 estimates, in 1,000 tonnes): melons and watermelons, 575; tomatoes, 500; dates, 400; wheat, 384; oranges, 270; grapes, 265; barley, 226; cucumbers and gherkins, 215; potatoes, 150; rice, 130.

Livestock (2000): cattle, 1·35m.; sheep, 6·78m.; goats, 1·60m.; asses, 380,000; chickens, 23m.

Forestry. In 1995 forests covered 83,000 ha, representing 0·2% of the land area. Timber production in 1999 was 177,000 cu. metres.

Fisheries. Catches in 1999 totalled 24,606 tonnes, of which almost half were freshwater fish.

INDUSTRY

Iraq is still relatively under-developed industrially but work has begun on new industrial plants. Production figures (1997, in 1,000 tonnes): residual fuel oil, 9,200; distillate fuel oil, 7,000; petrol, 3,010; kerosene, 1,150; jet fuel, 1,140; cement (1992), 2,453; cigarettes (1992), 5,794m. units.

Labour. In 1996 the labour force was 5,573,000 (75% males).

INTERNATIONAL TRADE

Imports and Exports. Imports and exports (in US$1m.):

	1988	1989	1990	1991
Imports	9,311	10,170	6,605	International embargo
Exports	9,613	12,408	10,353	International embargo

Crude oil is the main export commodity, with Jordan and Turkey being significant export partners in 1996. Manufactures and food are the main import commodities, with major partners in 1996 being France, Turkey, Jordan, Vietnam and Australia.

COMMUNICATIONS

Roads. In 1997 there were 11,032 km of main roads and 28,837 km of regional roads. Vehicles in use in 1996 included 773,000 passenger cars and 272,500 lorries and vans.

Rail. In 1993 railways comprised 2,032 km of 1,435 mm gauge route. Passenger-km travelled in 1995 came to 2·2bn. and freight tonne-km to 1·12bn.

Civil Aviation. In 2000 there were international flights for the first time since the 1991 Gulf War, with air links being established between Iraq and Egypt, Jordan and Syria.

Shipping. The merchant fleet in 1998 had a total tonnage of 511,000 GRT, including oil tankers 361,000 GRT. A 565-km canal was opened in 1992 between Baghdad and the Persian (Arabian) Gulf for shipping, irrigation, the drainage of saline water and the reclamation of marsh land.

Telecommunications. In 2000 there were 675,000 main telephone lines (29·4 per 1,000 population). Internet users in Dec. 2000 numbered 12,500.

SOCIAL INSTITUTIONS

Justice. Up until the war in March–April 2003, for civil matters: the court of cassation in Baghdad; six courts of appeal at Al-Basrah, Baghdad (2), Babil (Babylon), Mosul and Kirkuk; 18 courts of first instance with unlimited powers and 150 courts of first instance with limited powers, all being courts of single judges. In addition, six peace courts had peace court jurisdiction only. 'Revolutionary courts' dealt with cases affecting state security.

For religious matters: the Sharia courts at all places where there were civil courts, constituted in some places of specially appointed Qadhis (religious judges) and in other places of the judges of the civil courts. For criminal matters: the court of cassation; six sessions courts (two being presided over by the judge of the local court of first instance and four being identical with the courts of appeal). Magistrates' courts at all places where there were civil courts, constituted of civil judges exercising magisterial powers of the first and second class. There were also a number of third-class magistrates' courts, powers for this purpose being granted to municipal councils and a number of administrative officials.

The death penalty was introduced for serious theft in 1992; amputation of a hand for theft in 1994. It is believed that there are hundreds of executions annually.

Religion. The constitution proclaims Islam the state religion, but also stipulates freedom of religious belief and expression. In 1993 there were 11·9m. Shia Muslims and 6·6m. Sunni Muslims (including 3·5m. Kurds). There were 0·72m. Christians in 14 sects, including: 0·48m. Chaldean (Eastern rite Roman Catholic) Church, with some 100 priests in 9 dioceses; 0·15m. Apostolic Assyrian (Nestorian) Church, with 29 priests in 3 dioceses and 80,000 Syriac Orthodox in 2 dioceses. There were some 10,000 in various Protestant sects.

Education. Primary and secondary education is free; primary education became compulsory in 1976. Primary school age is 6–12. Secondary education is for six years, of which the first three are termed intermediate. The medium of instruction is Arabic; Kurdish is used in primary schools in northern districts.

There were, in 1995, 576 pre-primary schools with 4,972 teachers for 93,028 pupils. In 1995–96 there were 8,145 primary schools with 145,455 teachers for 2,903,923 pupils and 62,296 secondary level teachers for 1·16m. pupils. Adult literacy rate was 53·7% in 1998 (male, 63·9%; female, 43·2%). In 1994–95 there were 10 universities and 1 technological university, 1 institute of administration, 1 institute of applied arts, 1 technical teacher training institute and 22 technical institutes.

Health. In 1993 there were 8,787 doctors, 1,656 dentists, 1,561 pharmacists and 13,206 nurses (1991). There were 185 hospitals in 1993, with a provision of 14 beds per 10,000 population. In 2000 annual health expenditure was US$573 per capita and public health expenditure as a percentage of GDP was 3·7%.

CULTURE

Broadcasting. In 1997 there were 4·8m. radio and 1·75m. TV receivers (colour by SECAM H).

Press. In 1996 there were four main daily newspapers (one of which is in English) with a combined circulation of 407,000.

Tourism. In 1998 there were 51,000 foreign tourists, bringing revenue of US$13m.

DIPLOMATIC REPRESENTATIVES

On 6 Feb. 1991 Iraq broke off diplomatic relations with the United Kingdom and the USA. Jordan looks after Iraqi interest in the UK.

British Office in Iraq (Shariah Salah ud-Din, Kharkh, Baghdad)
Head: Christopher Segar.

Of Iraq to the United Nations
Ambassador: Vacant.

Of Iraq to the European Union
Ambassador: Vacant.

FURTHER READING
Aburish, S. K., *Saddam Hussein: The Politics of Revenge.* Bloomsbury, London, 2000
Butler, R., *Saddam Defiant: The Threat of Weapons of Mass Destruction and the Crisis of Global Security.* Weidenfeld & Nicolson, London, 2000
Mackey, Sandra, *The Reckoning: Iraq and the Legacy of Saddam Hussein.* W. W. Norton, New York, 2002
Sluglett, Marion Farouk and Sluglett, Peter, *Iraq Since 1958: From Revolution to Dictatorship.* 3rd ed. I. B. Tauris, London, 2001
Tripp, Charles, *A History of Iraq.* 2nd ed. CUP, 2002

IRELAND

Éire

Capital: Dublin
Population estimate, 2000: 3·71m.
GDP per capita, 2000: (PPP$) 29,866
HDI/world rank: 0·925/18

KEY HISTORICAL EVENTS

With the collapse of the Roman empire, Ireland developed its own Gaelic culture and language. But from the 12th century, the English dominated. Vast tracts of land were granted to English settlers and English law was introduced. In 1541 Henry VIII was recognized as King of Ireland. Most Irish remained Roman Catholic and in the reign of Elizabeth insurrection broke out against the Protestant overlords. In the early 17th century Scottish settlers in the north of Ireland established a strong Protestant enclave which led to rebellion in 1640. After 1649 Cromwell restored English domination. Irish resistance was brought to a bloody conclusion by the Battle of the Boyne (1690).

For over a century, the Roman Catholic majority had no share in government. The 1801 Act of Union gave Ireland representation at Westminster but opposition to British rule was reinforced in 1846 when the failure of the potato harvest and the apparent unwillingness of Britain to provide aid led to widespread famine. The subsequent mass emigration, chiefly to the United States, further damaged the Irish economy and intensified demands for Home Rule. In the north, however, Home Rule was bitterly opposed by the Protestant interest. In 1898 the Ulster Unionist party was set up to campaign for the right to remain part of the UK.

In April 1916 an insurrection against British rule took place and a republic was proclaimed. The armed struggle was renewed in 1919 and continued until 1921. In 1920 an Act was passed by the British Parliament, under which separate Parliaments were set up for 'Southern Ireland' (26 counties) and 'Northern Ireland' (six counties). The Unionists of the six counties accepted this scheme, and a Northern Parliament was duly elected on 24 May 1921. The rest of Ireland, however, ignored the Act. On 6 Dec. 1921 a treaty was signed between Great Britain and Ireland by which Ireland accepted dominion status subject to the right of Northern Ireland to opt out. This right was exercised, and the border between the Irish Free State (26 counties) and Northern Ireland (six counties) was fixed in Dec. 1925 as the outcome of an agreement between Great Britain, Ireland and Northern Ireland. Subsequently the constitutional links between Ireland and the UK were gradually removed by the *Dáil*. The remaining formal association with the British Commonwealth by virtue of the External Relations Act, 1936 was severed when the Republic of Ireland Act, 1948 came into operation on 18 April 1949.

In the mid-1950s the Irish Republican Army, which had led a violent campaign for Irish unity in the 1920s, re-emerged as a fighting force with a bombing campaign in Northern Ireland. Differences between the two religious communities intensified to the point, in 1969, when British troops had to be deployed to keep the peace. In 1972 the Unionist government in Belfast resigned and direct rule from London was imposed. Between July 1969 and Dec. 1998, around 1,800 civilians, 1,100 security forces personnel and 500 paramilitaries were killed in the troubles.

On 22 Feb. 1995 the Irish and British Prime Ministers (John Bruton and John Major) announced joint proposals for a settlement in Northern Ireland. Under the chairmanship of former US Senator George Mitchell, a marathon negotiating struggle on 9–10 April 1998 led to a framework for sharing power designed to satisfy Protestant demands for a reaffirmation of their national identity as British, Catholic desires for a closer relationship with the predominantly Catholic Republic of Ireland and Britain's wish to return to Northern Ireland the powers London assumed in 1972. In the referendum on 22 May 1998, 94·4% of votes in the Republic and 71·12% in Northern Ireland were cast in favour of the Good Friday peace agreement. On 2 Dec. 1999 the Irish constitution was amended to remove the articles laying claim to Northern Ireland. However, in Oct. 2002 the Northern Irish assembly was suspended for the fourth time in its history over allegations of IRA spying at the Northern Ireland Office. Direct rule from London was subsequently re-imposed.

For details of recent peace negotiations turn to the section on Northern Ireland on page 1700.

TERRITORY AND POPULATION

The Republic of Ireland lies in the Atlantic Ocean, separated from Great Britain by the Irish Sea to the east, and bounded in the northeast by Northern Ireland (UK). The population at the 1996 census was 3,626,087 (1,825,855 females), giving a density of 51·6 persons per sq. km. In 1999, 58·8% of the population lived in urban areas. The population at the 2002 census (preliminary) was 3,917,336 (1,972,149 females).

The UN gives a projected population for 2010 of 4·20m.

The capital is Dublin (Baile Átha Cliath). Town populations, 1996: Greater Dublin, 952,692 (977,000 by 1999); Cork, 179,954; Limerick, 75,729; Galway, 57,363; Waterford, 44,155.

Counties and Cities[1]	Area in ha[2]	Population, 2002[3] Males	Females	Totals
Province of Leinster				
Carlow	89,655	23,302	22,543	45,845
Dublin City	11,758	237,320	257,781	495,101
Dun Laoghaire-Rathdown	12,638	91,126	100,263	191,389
Fingal	45,467	97,365	98,858	196,223
Kildare	169,540	82,764	81,231	163,995
Kilkenny	207,289	40,528	39,893	80,421
Laoighis	171,990	30,112	28,620	58,732
Longford	109,116	15,776	15,351	31,127
Louth	82,613	50,438	51,364	101,802
Meath	234,207	67,662	66,274	133,936
Offaly	200,117	32,185	31,517	63,702
South Dublin	22,364	117,945	121,942	239,887
Westmeath	183,965	35,996	36,031	72,027
Wexford	236,685	58,225	58,318	116,543
Wicklow	202,662	56,782	57,937	114,719
Total of Leinster	1,980,066	1,037,526	1,067,923	2,105,449
Province of Munster				
Clare	345,004	52,049	51,284	103,333
Cork City	3,953	59,356	63,982	123,338
Cork	746,042	163,002	161,841	324,843
Kerry	480,689	66,524	65,900	132,424
Limerick City	2,087	26,094	27,964	54,058
Limerick	273,504	61,576	59,895	121,471
Tipperary, N. R.	204,627	30,905	30,163	61,068
Tipperary, S. R.	225,845	40,033	39,180	79,213
Waterford City	4,103	21,752	22,812	44,564
Waterford	181,556	28,895	28,059	56,954
Total of Munster	2,467,410	550,186	551,080	1,101,266
Province of Connacht				
Galway City	5,057	30,935	34,839	65,774
Galway	609,820	73,157	69,895	143,052
Leitrim	159,003	13,307	12,508	25,815
Mayo	558,605	59,057	58,371	117,428
Roscommon	254,819	27,555	26,248	53,803
Sligo	183,752	28,746	29,432	58,178
Total of Connacht	1,771,056	232,757	231,293	464,050
Province of Ulster (part of)				
Cavan	193,177	28,940	27,476	56,416
Donegal	486,091	68,932	68,451	137,383
Monaghan	129,508	26,846	25,926	52,772
Total of Ulster (part of)	808,776	124,718	121,853	246,571
Total	7,027,308	1,945,187	1,972,149	3,917,336

[1]Cities were previously known as County Boroughs.
[2]Area details provided by Ordnance Survey.
[3]Preliminary figures, based on 2002 Census of Population.

Dublin: An east-coast city with a population of nearly 1m. and once the second largest city in the British Empire, Dublin underwent, after a period of decline, a renaissance in the second half of the 20th century. Not only the Republic of Ireland's capital city but the focal point for Ireland's commercial and cultural life, Dublin is the manufacturing centre of the country and possesses the biggest brewery in the world.

The official languages are Irish (the national language) and English; according to the National Survey of Languages of 1994, Irish is spoken as a mother tongue only by 2% of the population, in certain western areas (Gaeltacht), and is no longer a compulsory subject at school.

SOCIAL STATISTICS
Statistics for six calendar years:

	Births	Marriages	Deaths		Births	Marriages	Deaths
1995	48,787	15,604	32,259	1998	53,969	16,783	31,563
1996	50,655	16,174	31,723	1999	53,924	18,526	32,608
1997	52,775	15,631	31,581	2000[1]	57,882	19,246	29,812

[1]Provisional figures—based on year of registration.

2001 rates (provisional): birth, 15·1; death, 7·8; marriage, 5·0. Annual population growth rate, 1991–2001, 0·9%. Expectation of life at birth, 1999, 73·8 years for males and 79·1 years for females.

In 2001 the suicide rate per 100,000 population (provisional) was 11·7 (men, 18·7; women, 4·8). Infant mortality in 2001, 5·8 per 1,000 live births; fertility rate (2001), 2·0 births per woman.

At a referendum on 24 Nov. 1995 on the legalization of civil divorce the electorate was 1,628,580; 818,852 votes were in favour, 809,728 against. In 2000 Ireland received 10,938 asylum applications, compared to 4,600 in 1998.

In 1999 for the first time Irish citizens were returning to Ireland to live and work, rather than emigrating. In the 12 months to April 2001 immigration to Ireland was estimated to total 46,200. In the same period emigration was 19,900 leaving a net migration figure of 26,300. In 1999 the UK was the destination for 35% of emigrants and the origin of 45% of immigrants (although only 17% were of UK nationality). In 2000 Ireland received 14,800 asylum applications, equivalent to 3·97 per 1,000 inhabitants.

A UNICEF report published in 2000 showed that 16·8% of children in Ireland live in poverty (in households with income below 50% of the national median), compared to 2·6% in Sweden. The report also showed that the poverty rate of children in lone-parent families was 46·4%, compared to 14·2% in two-parent families.

CLIMATE
Influenced by the Gulf Stream, there is an equable climate with mild southwest winds, making temperatures almost uniform over the whole country. The coldest months are Jan. and Feb. (39–45°F, 4–7°C) and the warmest July and Aug. (57–61°F, 14–16°C). May and June are the sunniest months, averaging 5·5 to 6·5 hours each day, but over 7 hours in the extreme southeast. Rainfall is lowest along the eastern coastal strip. The central parts vary between 30–44" (750–1,125 mm), and up to 60" (1,500 mm) may be experienced in low-lying areas in the west. Dublin, Jan. 40°F (4°C), July 59°F (15°C). Annual rainfall 30" (750 mm). Cork, Jan. 42°F (5°C), July 61°F (16°C). Annual rainfall 41" (1,025 mm).

CONSTITUTION AND GOVERNMENT
Ireland is a sovereign independent, democratic republic. Its parliament exercises jurisdiction in 26 of the 32 counties of the island of Ireland. The first Constitution of the Irish Free State came into operation on 6 Dec. 1922. Certain provisions which were regarded as contrary to the national sentiments were gradually removed by successive amendments, with the result that at the end of 1936 the text differed considerably from the original document. On 14 June 1937 a new Constitution was approved by Parliament and enacted by a plebiscite on 1 July 1937. This Constitution came into operation on 29 Dec. 1937. Under it the name Ireland (Éire) was restored. It states that the whole island of Ireland is the national territory, but

that, pending its reintegration, laws enacted by Parliament have the same area and extent of application as those of the former Irish Free State.

The head of state is the *President*, whose role is largely ceremonial, but who has the power to refer proposed legislation which might infringe the Constitution to the Supreme Court.

The *Oireachtas* or National Parliament consists of the President, a House of Representatives (*Dáil Éireann*) and a Senate (*Seanad Éireann*). The *Dáil*, consisting of 166 members, is elected by adult suffrage on the Single Transferable Vote system in constituencies of 3, 4 or 5 members. Of the 60 members of the Senate, 11 are nominated by the *Taoiseach* (Prime Minister), six are elected by the universities and the remaining 43 are elected from five panels of candidates established on a vocational basis, representing the following public services and interests: (1) national language and culture, literature, art, education and such professional interests as may be defined by law for the purpose of this panel; (2) agricultural and allied interests, and fisheries; (3) labour, whether organized or unorganized; (4) industry and commerce, including banking, finance, accountancy, engineering and architecture; (5) public administration and social services, including voluntary social activities. The electing body comprises members of the *Dáil*, Senate, county boroughs and county councils.

A maximum period of 90 days is afforded to the Senate for the consideration or amendment of Bills sent to that House by the *Dáil*, but the Senate has no power to veto legislative proposals.

No amendment of the Constitution can be effected except with the approval of the people given at a referendum.

National Anthem. 'Amhrán na bhFiann' ('The Soldier's Song'); words by P. Kearney, tune by P. Heeney.

RECENT ELECTIONS

A general election was held on 17 May 2002: Fianna Fáil (FF) gained 81 seats with 41·5% of votes cast (in 1997, 77 seats); Fine Gael (FG), 31 with 22·5% (54); Labour Party (L), 21 with 10·8% (17); Progressive Democrats (PD), 8; Green Party (G), 6; Sinn Féin, 5; Socialist Party, 1; ind., 13.

Following elections to the Senate on 16 and 17 July 2002, FF held 30 of the 60 seats, FG had 15, L had 5, PD had 4 and non-partisans and others held 6 seats.

Presidential elections took place on 30 Oct. 1997. There were five candidates in the first round, of whom Mary Patricia McAleese (FF) and Mary Banotti (FG) went on to a run-off. McAleese won with 58·7% of the vote.

European Parliament. Ireland has 15 representatives. At the June 1999 elections turn-out was 50·21%. Fianna Fáil gained 6 seats with 38·64 % of votes cast (group in European Parliament: Union for Europe); Fine Gael, 4 with 24·59% (European People's Party); Greens, 2 with 6·69% (Greens); Labour, 1 with 8·73% (Party of European Socialists); ind., 2 with 13·05% (European Liberal, Democrat and Reform Party; European People's Party).

CURRENT ADMINISTRATION

President: Mary McAleese (b. 1951; FF), elected out of five candidates on 30 Oct. 1997 and inaugurated 11 Nov. 1997.

Following the 2002 election the coalition government that had held office since 1997 between Fianna Fáil (FF) and the Progressive Democrats (PD) was renewed. In March 2003 it was composed as follows:

Taoiseach (Prime Minister): Bertie Ahern; b. 1951 (FF; sworn in 26 June 1997 and re-elected in 2002).

Tánaiste (Deputy Prime Minister), Minister for Enterprise, Trade and Employment: Mary Harney (b. 1953; PD). *Defence:* Michael Smith (b. 1940; FF). *Agriculture and Food:* Joe Walsh (b. 1943; FF). *Finance:* Charlie McCreevy (b. 1949; FF). *Foreign Affairs:* Brian Cowen (b. 1960; FF). *Education and Science:* Noel Dempsey (b. 1953; FF). *Communications, Marine and Natural Resources:* Dermot Ahern (b. 1955; FF). *Community, Rural and Gaeltacht Affairs:* Eamon Ó Cuív (b. 1952; FF). *Health and Children:* Micheál Martin (b. 1960; FF). *Transport:* Séamus Brennan (b. 1948; FF). *Justice, Equality and Law Reform:* Michael McDowell (b. 1949; PD). *Environment and Local Government:* Martin Cullen (b.

1954; FF). *Arts, Sport and Tourism:* John O'Donoghue (b. 1956; FF). *Social and Family Affairs:* Mary Coughlan (b. 1965; FF).

There are 17 Ministers of State.

Attorney-General: Rory Brady.

Speaker of Dail Éireann: Rory O'Hanlon.

Government Website: http://www.irlgov.ie/

DEFENCE

Supreme command of the Defence Forces is vested in the President. Exercise of the supreme command is regulated by law (Defence Act 1954). Military Command is exercised by the government through the Minister for Defence who is the overall commander of the Defence Forces.

The Defence Forces comprise the Permanent Defence Force (the regular Army, the Air Corps and the Naval Service) and the Reserve Defence Force (comprising a First Line Reserve of members who have served in the Permanent Defence Force, a second-line Territorial Army Reserve and a second-line Naval Reserve).

A review of the Reserve Forces is almost complete. The total strength of the Permanent Defence Force in Dec. 2002 was 10,559 (including 472 women). The total strength of the Reserve was 13,743. The Defence Forces had some 483 personnel involved with 19 different peace-support missions throughout the world in Dec. 2002.

Defence expenditure in 2002 totalled €891m. (approximately €240 per capita), representing 0·72% of GDP.

Army. The army strength in Dec. 2002 was 8,620 personnel with 13,249 reservists. There is a Training Centre at the Curragh, Co. Kildare and a Logistics Base, with elements located at the Curragh and Dublin for force level logistical support.

Navy. The Naval Service is based at Haulbowline in Co. Cork. The strength in Dec. 2002 was 1,034 with 422 reserves. It operates eight patrol craft.

Air Corps. The Air Corps has its headquarters at Casement Aerodrome, Baldonnel, Co. Dublin. The Air Corps is a stand-alone Corps which does not form an intrinsic part of the new Army Brigade structure. The Air Corps strength in Dec. 2002 was 905 personnel with 72 reservists. It operates 17 fixed-wing aircraft and 13 helicopters.

INTERNATIONAL RELATIONS

Ireland is a member of the UN, WTO, BIS, OECD, EU, the Council of Europe, the OSCE and IOM.

ECONOMY

Agriculture accounted for 3·5% of GDP in 2001, industry 42·0% and services 54·5%.

Overview. Ireland receives around one-third of US investment in the EU. Multinationals are attracted by access to the singe European market, low corporate taxes and an educated workforce. The tax rate for manufacturing firms is 10% compared to the standard corporate rate of 20%. The European Commission has urged Ireland to commit itself to a uniform corporate tax rate of 12·5%. In 2001 a pension fund was introduced, receiving 1% of GNP each year until 2025 and amounting to 6% of GDP. Inflation differentials between Ireland and the rest of the euro zone remain a concern.

Currency. On 1 Jan. 1999 the euro (EUR) became the legal currency in Ireland; irrevocable conversion rate 0·787564 Irish pounds to 1 euro. The euro, which consists of 100 cents, has been in circulation since 1 Jan. 2002. There are seven euro notes in different colours and sizes denominated in 500, 200, 100, 50, 20, 10 and 5 euros, and eight coins denominated in 2 and 1 euros, then 50, 20, 10, 5, 2 and 1 cents. On the introduction of the euro there was a 'dual circulation' period before the Irish pound ceased to be legal tender on 9 Feb. 2002. Euro banknotes in circulation on 1 Jan. 2002 had a total value of €6·8bn.

Inflation, at 4·9% in 2001, is more than twice the EU average. The Central Bank has the sole right of issuing legal tender notes; token coinage is issued by the

Minister for Finance through the Bank. Gold reserves were 176,000 troy oz in June 2002 and foreign exchange reserves US$4,648m. Total money supply was €3,616m. in June 2002.

Budget. Current revenue and expenditure (in IR£1m.):

Current Revenue	1999	2000[1]
Customs duties	136	164
Excise duties	3,198	3,357
Capital taxes	509	786
Stamp duties	719	872
Income tax	6,323	7,177
Corporation tax	2,710	3,061
Value-added tax	4,878	5,883
Agricultural levies (EU)	10	10
Employment and training levy	77	11
Non-Tax Revenue	434	420
Total	18,993	21,741
Current expenditure		
Debt service	2,198	2,028
Industry and Labour	658	758
Agriculture	637	772
Fisheries, Forestry, Tourism	113	140
Health	3,598	4,037
Education	2,648	2,871
Social Welfare	4,963	5,384
Other (excl. Balances)	2,9446	3,307
Less: Receipts, e.g. social security	(−)3,462	4,142
Total (including other items)	14,246	15,155

[1]Provisional outturn.

VAT as at 1 Jan. 2002 was 20% (reduced rate 12·5%).

Total Public Capital Programme Expenditure amounted to IR£5,534m. in 2000, with provision for IR£6,066m. in 2001. The general government debt at the end of 1999 was IR£34·6bn., 50% of GDP (compared to 120% in 1986). Ireland is one of the largest recipients of EU aid per head of population. It is also one of the largest recipients of US direct investment.

Performance. Until late 2001 Ireland had the fastest-growing economy in the European Union, with real GDP growth in 2000 of 11·5% following growth averaging 9% over the previous six years. In 2001 real GDP growth declined to 6·7% and by the end of 2001 Ireland had gone into a recession. From a GDP per head of only 61% of the EU average in 1986, it was estimated to have risen to 117% of the EU average by 2000. GNP in Ireland is much lower than GDP owing to profit repatriations by the multi-nationals and foreign debt servicing. Ireland's GNP per head is about 97% of the EU average. Total GDP in 2001 was US$101·2bn.

Banking and Finance. The Central Bank (founded in 1943) replaced the Currency Commission as the note-issuing authority. The Central Bank has the power of receiving deposits from banks and public authorities, of rediscounting Exchequer bills and bills of exchange, of making advances to banks against such bills or against government securities, of fixing and publishing rates of interest for rediscounting bills, or buying and selling certain government securities and securities of any international bank or financial institution formed wholly or mainly by governments. The Bank also collects and publishes information relating to monetary and credit matters. The Central Bank Acts, 1971, 1989 and 1997, together with the Building Societies Act, 1989, the Investment Intermediaries Act, 1995 and the Stock Exchange Act, 1995, give further powers to the Central Bank in the regulation and supervision of financial institutions and payment systems.

The Board of Directors of the Central Bank consists of a Governor, appointed for a seven-year term by the President on the advice of the government, and nine directors, all appointed by the Minister for Finance. The *Governor* is John Hurley. The Bank's net profit in 1998 was IR£177·022m., of which IR£152·351m. was paid to the Exchequer.

At 31 Dec. 1996 there were 42 credit institutions authorized to carry on banking business in the State; 5 building societies; and 3 State banks, ICC Bank, ACC Bank and the Trustee Savings Bank. In addition there were 13 credit institutions authorized in another Member State of the European Union operating in Ireland.

At 31 Dec. 1996 total assets of within-the-State offices of all credit institutions amounted to IR£67bn.

The Dublin stock exchange has been affiliated to the London exchange since 1973.

Weights and Measures. Conversion to the metric system is in progress; with some exceptions which are confined to the domestic market, all imperial units of measurement ceased to be legal, for general use, after 31 Dec. 1994.

ENERGY AND NATURAL RESOURCES

Environment. According to the *World Bank Atlas* Ireland's carbon dioxide emissions in 1998 were the equivalent of 10·3 tonnes per capita.

Electricity. The total generating capacity was (1998) 4,297 MW. In 1998 the total sales of electricity amounted to 17,440m. units supplied to 1,528,359 customers. Production in 1998 totalled 20·55bn. kWh; consumption per capita was 11·4 MWh.

Oil and Gas. Over 0·6m. sq. km of the Irish continental shelf has been designated an exploration area for oil and gas; at the furthest point the limit of jurisdiction is 520 nautical miles from the coast. It has been established that there is potential for discoveries both offshore and onshore. In the offshore there is a vast Continental Shelf in which 13 major basins and troughs have been identified. Much of the shelf remains unexplored but from 1971 to date 129 exploration wells have been drilled, and since 1965 a total of 348 separate surveys have been carried out from which approximately 316,000 line km of seismic data has been produced since 1985.

A number of encouraging oil and gas flows have been recorded, including the Corrib North Prospect in the Slyne/Erris Trough and 'Seven Heads' and 'Helvick' fields which are located in the Celtic Sea. In Nov. 1992 revised licensing terms were issued which allowed for a range of generous allowances against tax. In 1994 a Frontier Licensing Round in the Erris and Slyne Troughs resulted in the award of five licences over 28 blocks. A further eight licences over 32 blocks were awarded under the Porcupine Basin Frontier Licensing Round in 1995.

Eleven licences were awarded over 58 full and part blocks under the Petroleum Exploration Licensing Round in the Rockall Trough in June 1997. The area in the Round covered 615 full and 35 part blocks in an area of almost 150,000 sq. km. The Rockall Trough lies some 100 to 650 km west of Ireland with water depths ranging from 500 metres to 2,500 metres.

Comprehensive work programmes will be undertaken that will ensure licensed areas are fully explored. Up to 18,000 km of new 2D seismic, and up to 2,000 sq. km of 3D seismic data will be acquired and assessed by the end of the first four years of the licences.

An invitation was issued to interested petroleum companies to apply for a Lease Undertaking over the 'Seven Heads' oil and gas accumulation in the Celtic Sea. The area which covers almost 520 sq. km has been closed to the granting of authorizations since March 1997.

At the same time details of a Petroleum Licensing Round in the South Porcupine Basin were also announced. The acreage on offer covers 156 blocks in the Irish offshore—an area of over 5,000 sq. km. Owing to the special difficulties created by the physical environment of the area, it has been designated as a Frontier Area. Long term licences for a period of 15 years will be granted.

The South Porcupine Basin lies off the southwest coast of Ireland. Water depths vary from 200 metres in the east to over 2,500 metres in the southwest.

An Onshore Petroleum Prospecting Licence was issued for a three-year period from 1 Dec. 1997 covering 1,960 km of the Northwest Carboniferous Basin in counties Sligo, Leitrim, Roscommon, Cavan and Monaghan.

These steps in conjunction with the maintenance of Ireland's 'open door' approach to licensing, its favourable environment and existing tax regime achieves a risk/reward balance which reflects Ireland's circumstances and acknowledges the realities of competition for internationally mobile exploration and production investment.

Natural gas reserves in 1997 totalled 11,000m. cu. metres. In 1997 consumption of natural gas was 3,400m. cu. metres, of which 70% came from the Kinsale Head gas field, 50 km off the south coast, and the smaller Ballycotton field about 16 km northwest of Kinsale Head field, which was discovered in 1989 and which went into production in July 1991. These gas reserves are expected to be exhausted by the end of 2003. Gas transmission and distribution is carried out by Bord Gais Éireann (Irish Gas Board). A gas pipeline from County Dublin to southwest Scotland was completed in 1994. 30% of gas used in 1997 was imported via the Interconnector. At Dec. 1997 there were 290,000 gas consumers in Ireland.

Peat. The country has very little indigenous coal, but possesses large reserves of peat, the development of which is handled largely by Bord na Móna (Peat Board). To date, the Board has acquired and developed 85,000 ha of bog and has 27 locations around the country. In the year ending 31 March 2001 the Board sold 2·8m. tonnes of milled peat for use in five milled peat electricity generating stations. 301,000 tonnes of briquettes were produced for sale to the domestic heating market. Bord na Móna also sold 136m. cu. metres of horticultural peat, mainly for export. It is estimated that some 1m. tonnes of privately-produced peat was consumed in the same period.

Minerals. Lead and zinc concentrates are important. In 1997 mineable resources stood at over 6m. tonnes of zinc and over 1m. tonnes of lead. Metal content of concentrates production, 2001: zinc, 287,000 tonnes; lead, 50,100 tonnes. Gypsum, limestone and aggregates are important, and there is some production of silver (contained in lead) and dolomite. About 50 companies are involved in exploration, which is centred on base metals, but with interest also in gold, gem minerals, industrial minerals and coal. There is a thriving sand, gravel and aggregate extraction industry, employing some 7,500 people.

Agriculture. The CSO's Quarterly National Household Survey showed in the quarter of March–May 2002 that there were 120,700 people whose primary source of income was from agriculture. A total of 279,000 people worked on farms on a regular basis, working the equivalent of 191,700 full-time jobs. There were 143,000 farm holdings in Ireland, almost all of which were family farms. Average farm size was 29·3 ha. 47% of farms were under 20 ha. 11% of farmers were under 35 and 45% were over 55.

Agriculture, fisheries and forestry represented 3·5% of GDP in 2001. The total area used for agricultural and forestry purposes is 4·4m. ha, and 90% of the agricultural area was devoted to grass in 2002. In 2001 beef and milk production accounted for 58% of gross agricultural output.

Provisional figures at June 2000: barley accounted (in ha) for 182,000; wheat, 83,800; oats, 17,800; other cereals, 9,500 (1999); potatoes, 13,700. Production figures (2000, in 1,000 tonnes): sugarbeets, 1,700; barley, 1,129; wheat, 706; potatoes, 500; oats, 128; cabbages, 51; carrots, 22.

Goods output at producer prices including changes in stock (formerly gross agricultural output) for 2002 was estimated at €4·4bn.; operating surplus (aggregate income) was €2·4bn. Direct income payments, financed or co-financed by the EU, amounted to €1·6bn. or 54% of aggregate income. Livestock (June 2002 provisional): cattle, 7,185,000; sheep, 7,399,800; pigs, 1,769,500; poultry, 13,960,800.

Forestry. Total forest area by the end of 2000 was 649,812 ha (9% of total land area). Timber production in 2000 was 2·95m. cu. metres.

Fisheries. In 1999 approximately 17,600 people were engaged full- or part-time in the sea fishing industry; the fishing fleet consisted of 1,177 vessels. The quantities and values of fish landed during 1999 were: wetfish, 253,245·8 tonnes, value IR£105,870,387·16; shellfish, 53,801·0 tonnes, value IR£59,822,930·48. Total quantity: 307,046·8 tonnes; total value, IR£165,693,317·64. The main types of fish caught were mackerel (58,201·2 tonnes), horse mackerel (59,609·0 tonnes), herring (45,334·2 tonnes) and blue whiting (35,880·0 tonnes). More than 98% of fish caught is from sea fishing.

INDUSTRY
The leading companies by market capitalization in Ireland, excluding banking and finance, in Jan. 2002 were: CRH plc (€11bn.), a building materials company; Elan

Corporation Plc (€7bn.), a drugs and drug-delivery systems company; and Ryanair Holdings Plc (€6bn.).

Enterprise Ireland. Enterprise Ireland was established in 1998 to provide an integrated development package specifically for indigenous firms. Its mission is 'to help client companies develop a sustainable competitive advantage leading to profitable sales, exports and employment'. Enterprise Ireland brings together the key marketing, technology, enterprise development, business training and science and innovation initiatives through which the Government supports the growth of Irish manufacturing and internationally traded sectors.

County Enterprise Boards. The 35 City and County Enterprise Boards (CEB's), which were established in Oct. 1993, are locally controlled enterprise development companies established in each county and local urban authority area in Ireland. The function of the Boards is to develop indigenous enterprise potential and to stimulate economic activity at a local level. This is primarily achieved through the provision of financial support for the development of micro enterprise (ten employees or fewer).

IDA Ireland. The IDA was established by the Irish government in 1969 but its remit was altered in 1993 when responsibility for development of indigenous industry was moved to Enterprise Ireland. The objective of IDA Ireland is to stimulate and support regional and economic development in Ireland by attracting and expanding foreign investment in key business sectors.

Today, Ireland is recognized as a base for a wide range of activities, from software development, business and information technology to international services and pharmaceuticals. Over 1,300 foreign-owned enterprises have established businesses in Ireland.

Shannon Development. Shannon Development, which was established in 1959, is the regional economic development company responsible for industrial, tourism and rural development in the Shannon region. Its regional mandate covers Counties Clare, Limerick, North Tipperary, South Offaly and North Kerry.

Forfás. Forfás is the policy advisory and co-ordination board for industrial development and science and technology. It is the statutory agency through which powers are delegated to Enterprise Ireland for the promotion of indigenous enterprise and to IDA Ireland for the promotion of inward investment,

The main functions of Forfás are to advise the Minister on matters relating to industrial policy, to advise on the development and co-ordination of policy for Enterprise Ireland, and IDA Ireland, and encourage the development of industry, technology, marketing and human resources.

The Chairman of Forfás is Peter Cassells and its Chief Executive is Martin Cronin.

The census of industrial production for 2000 gives the following details of the values (in €1m.) of gross and net output for the principal manufacturing industries.

	Gross output	Net output
Mining and quarrying	913·5	506·9
Manufacture of food products, beverages and tobacco	15,888·0	7,811·3
Manufacture of textiles and textile products	771·9	413·6
Manufacture of leather and leather products	76·3	25·7
Manufacture of wood and wood products	816·7	297·4
Manufacture of pulp, paper and paper products; publishing and printing	9,959·3	8,438·7
Manufacture of chemicals, chemical products and man-made fibres	24,281·9	19,154·6
Manufacture of rubber and plastic products	1,261·5	586·1
Manufacture of other non-metallic mineral products	1,467·6	792·3
Manufacture of basic metals and fabricated metal products	2,037·1	893·1
Manufacture of machinery and equipment n.e.c.	1,699·0	842·6
Manufacture of electrical and optical equipment	31,183·8	13,539·9
Manufacture of transport equipment	1,137·0	518·0
Manufacturing n.e.c.	1,781·0	824·9
Electricity, gas and water supply	2,656·6	1,461·7
Total (all industries)	95,931·3	56,106·7

In 1999 gross output was €77,803·5m. and net output €44,416·7m. In 1999 foreign companies in Ireland generated 90% of the country's manufacturing exports, 76% of manufacturing output and 49% of manufacturing employment.

Labour. The total labour force for 2002 was estimated to be 1,827,000, of which 77,200 were out of work. With the birth rate having peaked around 1980 there is currently a marked increase in the numbers entering the workforce. The unemployment rate in Jan. 2003 was 4·5%, down from nearly 16% in 1993. Of those at work, 1,145,200 were employed in the services sector in 2002, 483,900 in the industrial sector and 120,700 in the agricultural sector. By the end of the 1990s a labour shortage in many fields meant that workers from abroad were being sought to fill vacancies and many Irish who had emigrated in search of work in the past began to return home. FÁS, the training agency, is aiming to attract 200,000 workers to Ireland between 2000 and 2005—more than a tenth of the present workforce. Employment rose by approximately 51% between 1991 and 2001—more than twice as much as in any other industrialized country. In 1999 alone 100,000 new jobs were created. The retirement age is 65 years.

Trade Unions. The number of trade unions in Dec. 2002 was 46; total membership, 532,076. The six largest unions accounted for 68% of total membership. A series of three-year social pacts, which, in addition to covering a range of economic and social policy measures, include provision for pay increases, have been negotiated between the government, trade unions and employees' organizations since 1987. The fifth such agreement concluded in Feb. 2000, the Programme for Prosperity and Fairness (PPF), provided pay increases of 15% of basic pay in the public and private sectors of the economy over the period of the agreement, 2000–02. Owing to escalating inflation a further compensatory 1% lump sum payment was negotiated, for payment in March 2001. The third phase increase (4%) in the public service was not to be paid earlier than Oct. 2002 and was dependent on the establishment of performance indicators by April 2001 and the achievement of sectoral targets by April 2002.

The PPF agreement expired for some workers in the private sector in Dec. 2002; depending on start dates, for others the agreement continues into 2003. The PPF pay element expires in Oct. 2003 for the public service. Talks to negotiate a successor to the PPF collapsed in Dec. 2002.

INTERNATIONAL TRADE

Imports and Exports. Value of imports and exports of merchandise for calendar years (in €1m.):

	1998	1999	2000	2001
Imports	39,715	44,327	55,909	57,178
Exports	57,322	66,956	83,889	92,523

The values of the chief imports and total exports are shown in the following table (in €1m.):

	Imports		Exports	
	2000	2001	2000	2001
Live animals and food	2,826	3,060	5,948	5,726
Raw materials	820	796	942	924
Mineral fuels and lubricants	2,300	2,207	286	286
Animal and vegetable oils and waxes	122	124	27	23
Chemicals	6,105	6,371	27,361	32,275
Manufactured goods	4,351	4,400	1,973	1,966
Machinery and transport equipment	29,740	30,177	34,012	37,923
Manufactured articles	5,893	6,189	8,864	8,782
Beverages and tobacco	522	656	958	958

Ireland is one of the most trade-dependent countries in the world. Exports constitute an increasing share of the economy's output of goods and services. In 2001 the total value of merchandise exports amounted to just over €92·5bn. (the highest ever level) and generated a trade surplus of €35·3bn. In employment terms, taking the economy as a whole, one job in four is directly dependent on exports. When indirect influences are taken into account, almost one job in two depends on exports. Exports of goods and services in 2001 as a percentage of GDP totalled over 96%. In 2001, 61·9% of exports went to other European Union countries and 59·2%

of imports were from within the EU. Information technology has become increasingly important, and by 1999 Ireland had become the largest exporter of software products in the world. Ireland accounts for a third of all personal computers sold across Europe.

Import and export totals for Ireland's top ten export markets in 2001 (€1m.):

	Imports		Exports	
	2000	2001	2000	2001
United Kingdom	17,613	20,226	18,870	22,161
United States of America	9,149	8,712	14,228	15,696
Germany	3,336	3,526	9,415	11,719
France	2,577	2,811	6,343	5,615
Netherlands	1,778	1,925	4,687	4,277
Belgium	913	851	4,152	4,520
Italy	1,253	1,161	3,317	3,313
Japan	2,536	2,004	3,123	3,266
Switzerland	381	481	2,033	2,812
Spain	758	652	2,124	2,277

COMMUNICATIONS

Roads. At 31 May 2000 there were 95,729 km of public roads, consisting of 2,732 km of National Primary Roads (including 103 km of motorway), 2,697 km of National Secondary Roads, 11,690 km of Regional Roads and 78,610 km of Local Roads.

Number of licensed motor vehicles at 31 Dec. 1999: private cars, 1,269,245; public-service vehicles, 19,640; goods vehicles, 188,814; agricultural vehicles, 71,121; motorcycles, 26,677; other vehicles, 26,130. In 2000 a total of 415 people were killed in 362 fatal accidents.

Rail. The total length of railway open for traffic at 31 Dec. 1999 was 1,872 km (38 km electrified), all 1,600 mm gauge. A massive investment in public transport infrastructure is taking place in Ireland. Over the period 2000–06 IR£185m. is being invested in Dublin suburban rail alone. IR£350m. is being invested in a railway safety programme over the period 2000–03.

Railway statistics for years ending 31 Dec.	1998	1999
Passengers (journeys)	32,146,000	32,561,000
Km run by passenger train	11,289,000	11,132,000
Freight (tonne-km)	465,941,000	528,568,000
Km run by freight trains	4,177,000	4,067,000
Receipts (IR£)	102,556,000	105,145,000
Expenditure (IR£)	195,086,000	...

Civil Aviation. Aer Lingus and Ryanair are the two major airlines operating in Ireland.

Aer Lingus was founded in 1936 as a State-owned enterprise. Its principal business is the provision of passenger and cargo services to a range of points in the UK, Europe and the USA. In addition, the airline's membership of the oneworld global alliance allows customers greater access to global route networks.

The impact of the terror attacks in the US on 11 Sept. 2001 changed the nature of the airline industry forever. Aer Lingus had to change urgently and radically. A Survival Plan was prepared by the Board and management, and implemented with great speed. During 2002 Aer Lingus began to move beyond survival to continue to reduce its cost base, significantly cut business and leisure fares and open a series of popular, direct routes out of Ireland. The airline's objective for 2003 is to build on the progress of the past year and continue with the strategy of lower costs and lower fares.

Ryanair began operations in 1985 and now operates to a range of destinations in the UK and Europe.

In addition to Aer Lingus and Ryanair, there are 16 other independent air transport operators. The main operators in this group are Aer Arann Express and Cityjet.

The principal airports (Dublin, Shannon and Cork) are operated by the state-owned Aer Rianta cpt. In 2000 Dublin handled 13,691,000 passengers (13,030,000 on international flights) and 109,400 tonnes of freight. Shannon handled 1,893,210 (1,730,822 on international flights) and 42,217 tonnes of freight. Cork was the third busiest, with 1,657,000 passengers.

There are six privately owned regional airports. The government part funds the scheduled services from Dublin to five of these airports and to the City of Derry airport in Northern Ireland to ensure efficient and speedy access to the more isolated regions of the state for both business and tourist travellers. In 2002 Ireland's three state airports catered for 19·3m. passengers, up 4% on 2001. The principal focus of growth during 2002 was the European market with the Dublin–London air route amongst the busiest in Europe.

Shipping. The merchant fleet totalled 168,081 GRT in 2000. Total cargo traffic passing through the country's ports amounted to 45,795,000 tonnes in 2001.

Inland Waterways. The principal inland waterways open to navigation are the Shannon Navigation (270 km), which includes the Shannon-Erne Waterway (Ballinamore/Ballyconnell Canal), and the Grand Canal and Barrow Navigation (249 km). The Waterways Service of the Department of Arts, Culture and the Gaeltacht is responsible for the waterways system as a public amenity. Merchandise traffic has now ceased and navigation is confined to pleasure craft operated either privately or commercially. The Royal Canal (146 km) from Dublin to Mullingar (53 km) was reopened for navigation in 1995.

Telecommunications. The Minister for Public Enterprise, a member of the government, has overall policy responsibility for the development of the sector. Among the key elements of the government's policy is the objective of creating a fully open and competitive telecommunications market that will stimulate investment in advanced information infrastructure and services in Ireland and develop Ireland as a global leader in the growth of Internet-based industries and electronic commerce.

The Director of Telecommunications Regulation, established by legislation as an independent officer with a separate office and staff in June 1997, is responsible for licensing of operators, allocation of numbers and radio frequency spectrum, supervision of network interconnection arrangements and other regulatory functions.

Ireland's telecommunications sector has been fully liberalized with effect from 1 Dec. 1998 when the last remaining elements of Telecom Éireann's (now called Eircom) exclusive privilege were removed. All elements of the market are now open to competition from other licensed operators and, as of 28 Nov. 2000, 47 general, 29 basic and 3 mobile licences had been issued by the Director of Telecommunications Regulation. The three licensed mobile telephone operators are Eircell (a subsidiary of Telecom Éireann) with both TACS and GSM networks, Esat Digifone, operating a GSM network, and Meteor Mobile Communications Ltd who were awarded a combined GSM and DCS 1800 licence in June 2000.

The Government has also sold the state's entire remaining stake of 50·1% in Eircom by way of an initial public offering of shares in the company. The sale took place in July 1999 and was the 2nd largest European privatization in that year.

eircom plc—Operational Information. The dominant operator in the telecommunications sector is eircom plc (previously Telecom Éireann). Telecom Éireann was a statutory body set up under the Postal and Telecommunications Services Act, 1983. In 1996, 20% of the State's holding was sold to KPN/Telia, a Dutch–Swedish consortium, who had an option of a further 15%, which was taken up in July 1999. In 1998 the government concluded an Employee Share Ownership Scheme under which 14·9% of the company was to be made available to employees and also held an Initial Public Offer (IPO) of shares in the company in July 1999. In Oct. 1999 the newly-privatized Telecom Éireann became eircom plc.

In Jan. 2000 the level of network digitalization was 100%. In Sept. 2000 there were around 1·7m. phone lines (477·7 per 1,000 persons), 1·7m. data lines, 12,000 public payphones and 2·1m. mobile phone customers (Nov. 2000). The number of Internet users in Sept. 2002 was 1·31m. In 2000 there were 1·4m. PCs in use (359·1 per 1,000 persons).

Postal Services. Postal services are provided by An Post, a statutory body established under the Postal and Telecommunications Services Act, 1983. In 1998 there were 1,912 post offices. A total of 748m. pieces of mail were handled during 1998, equivalent to 70 per person. An Post also offers a range of services to the business community through a dedicated unit, Special Delivery Services, and subsidiaries PostGEM, PrintPost and Precision Marketing Information. A range of services are provided through the Post Office network including Savings and Investments, passport applications, bill payments, National Lottery products and the payment of Social Welfare benefits on an agency basis for the State.

SOCIAL INSTITUTIONS

Justice. The Constitution provides that justice shall be administered in public in Courts established by law by Judges appointed by the President on the advice of the government. The jurisdiction and organization of the Courts are dealt with in the Courts (Establishment and Constitution) Act, 1961, the Courts (Supplemental Provisions) Acts, 1961–91, and the Courts and Court Officers Acts, 1995–2002. These Courts consist of Courts of First Instance and a Court of Final Appeal, called the Supreme Court. The Courts of First Instance are the High Court with full original jurisdiction and the Circuit and the District Courts with local and limited jurisdictions. A judge may not be removed from office except for stated misbehaviour or incapacity and then only on resolutions passed by both Houses of the Oireachtas. Judges of the Supreme Court are appointed from among practising barristers or serving Circuit Court judges. High Court judges are appointed from among practising barristers or solicitors of not less than 12 years' standing or serving High Court judges or serving eligible Circuit Court judges. Judges of the Circuit Court are appointed from among practising barristers or solicitors of not less than ten years' standing, or a county registrar who has practised as a barrister or solicitor for not less than ten years before he or she was appointed to that post or serving District Court judges. Judges of the District Court are appointed from among practising barristers or solicitors of not less than ten years standing.

The Supreme Court, which consists of the Chief Justice (who is *ex officio* an additional judge of the High Court) and seven ordinary judges, may sit in two Divisions and has appellate jurisdiction from all decisions of the High Court. The President may, after consultation with the Council of State, refer a Bill, which has been passed by both Houses of the Oireachtas (other than a money bill and certain other bills), to the Supreme Court for a decision on the question as to whether such Bill or any provision thereof is repugnant to the Constitution.

The High Court, which consists of a President (who is *ex officio* an additional Judge of the Supreme Court) and 26 ordinary judges (or 27 when a High Court Judge is appointed as a Commissioner of the Law Reform Commission, as is currently the case), has full original jurisdiction in and power to determine all matters and questions, whether of law or fact, civil or criminal. In all cases in which questions arise concerning the validity of any law having regard to the provisions of the Constitution, the High Court alone exercises original jurisdiction. The High Court on Circuit acts as an appeal court from the Circuit Court.

The Court of Criminal Appeal consists of the Chief Justice or an ordinary Judge of the Supreme Court, together with either two ordinary judges of the High Court or the President and one ordinary judge of the High Court. It deals with appeals by persons convicted on indictment where the appellant obtains a certificate from the trial judge that the case is a fit one for appeal, or, in case such certificate is refused, where the court itself, on appeal from such refusal, grants leave to appeal. The decision of the Court of Criminal Appeal is final, unless that court, the Attorney-General or the Director of Public Prosecutions certifies that the decision involves a point of law of exceptional public importance, in which case an appeal is taken to the Supreme Court.

The Offences against the State Act, 1939 provides in Part V for the establishment of Special Criminal Courts. A Special Criminal Court sits without a jury. The rules of evidence that apply in proceedings before a Special Criminal Court are the same as those applicable in trials in the Central Criminal Court. A Special Criminal Court is authorized by the 1939 Act to make rules governing its own practice and procedure. An appeal against conviction or sentence by a Special Criminal Court may be taken to the Court of Criminal Appeal. On 30 May 1972 Orders were made establishing a Special Criminal Court and declaring that offences of a particular class or kind (as set out) were to be scheduled offences for the purposes of Part V of the Act, the effect of which was to give the Special Criminal Court jurisdiction to try persons charged with those offences.

The High Court exercising criminal jurisdiction is known as the Central Criminal Court. It consists of a judge or judges of the High Court, nominated by the President of the High Court. The Court sits in Dublin and tries criminal cases which are outside the jurisdiction of the Circuit Court.

The Circuit Court consists of a President (who is *ex officio* an additional judge of the High Court) and 30 ordinary judges. The country is divided into eight circuits. The jurisdiction of the court in civil proceedings is subject to a financial ceiling, save by consent of the parties, in which event the jurisdiction is unlimited. In criminal matters it has jurisdiction in all cases except murder, treason, piracy, rape, serious and aggravated sexual assault and allied offences. The Circuit Court acts as an appeal court from the District Court.

The District Court, which consists of a President and 52 ordinary judges, has summary jurisdiction in a large number of criminal cases where the offence is not of a serious nature. In civil matters the Court has jurisdiction in contract and tort (except slander, libel, seduction, slander of title and false imprisonment) where the claim does not exceed €6,348·69; in proceedings founded on hire-purchase and credit-sale agreements, the jurisdiction is also €6,348·69.

All criminal cases, except those of a minor nature, and those tried in the Special Criminal Court, are tried by a judge and a jury of 12. Generally, a verdict need not be unanimous in a case where there are not fewer than 11 jurors if 10 of them agree on the verdict.

The Courts Service Act, 1998, provided for the transfer of responsibility for the day to day management of the Courts from the Minister for Justice, Equality and Law Reform to a new body known as the Courts Service. The Board of the Courts Service consists of 17 members including members of the judiciary, the legal profession, staff and trade union representatives, a representative of court users, a person with commercial/financial experience and a Chief Executive Officer. The Courts Service was formally established on 9 Nov. 1999. While the Minister retains political responsibility to the Oireachtas, the courts are now administered independently by the Board and CEO.

At 31 Dec. 2001 the police force, the Garda Síochána, had a total staff of 11,815. There were 86,633 headline offences recorded in 2001, of which 35,911 were detected, and 326,527 non-headline offences resulted in proceedings. 187,250 persons were convicted in total. There were 1·43 murders per 100,000 population and 8,832 juvenile offenders were cautioned. The population in penal institutions in Sept. 2001 was 3,019 (83 per 100,000 of national population).

Religion. In 1997 there were an estimated 3·34m. Roman Catholics and 300,000 members of other religions. According to the census of population taken in 1991 the principal religious professions were as follows:

	Leinster	Munster	Connacht	Ulster (part of)	Total
Roman Catholics	1,685,334	941,675	397,848	203,470	3,228,327
Church of Ireland (Anglican)	50,912	15,758	5,321	10,849	82,840
Protestants	3,391	1,385	516	1,055	6,347
Presbyterians	3,799	548	333	8,519	13,199
Methodists	2,815	1,185	286	751	5,037
Jewish	1,439	111	21	10	1,581
Other religious denominations	24,829	9,192	3,208	1,514	38,743
Not stated or no religion	88,430	39,679	15,498	6,038	149,645

Seán Brady (b. 1939) is the Roman Catholic Cardinal of Armagh and Primate of All Ireland.

In May 1990 the General Synod of the Church of Ireland voted to ordain women.

Education. In 1999 net total expenditure on education came to 4·7% of GNP. The adult literacy rate in 1998 was at least 99%.

Elementary. Elementary education is free and was given in about 3,293 national schools (including 121 special schools) in 1999–2000. The total number of pupils on rolls in 1999–2000 was 444,310, including pupils in special schools and classes; the number of teachers of all classes was about 21,500 in 1999–2000, including remedial teachers and teachers of special classes. The total expenditure for first level education during the financial year ended 31 Dec. 1999 was IR£897,000,000. The total salaries for teachers for 1998, including superannuation etc., was IR£724,000,000.

Special. Special provision is made for children with disabilities in special schools which are recognized on the same basis as primary schools, in special classes attached to ordinary schools and in certain voluntary centres where educational services appropriate to the needs of the children are provided. Integration of children with disabilities in ordinary schools and classes is encouraged wherever possible, if necessary with special additional support. There are also part-time teaching facilities in hospitals, child guidance clinics, rehabilitation workshops, special 'Saturday-morning' centres and home teaching schemes. Special schools (1999–2000) numbered 121 with approximately 7,200 pupils. There were also some 8,743 pupils enrolled in about 824 special classes, and 2,115 remedial, resource and home/school liaison teachers were employed for pupils in ordinary national schools in 1999–2000. There is a National Education Officer for travelling children.

Secondary. Voluntary secondary schools are under private control and are conducted in most cases by religious orders. These schools receive grants from the State and are open to inspection by the Department of Education. The number of recognized secondary schools during the school year 1999–2000 was 424, and the number of pupils in attendance was 211,369. There were 12,180 teachers in 1998–99.

Vocational Education Committee schools provide courses of general and technical education. Pupils are prepared for State examinations and for entrance to universities and institutes of further education. The number of vocational schools during the school year 1999–2000 was 245, the number of full-time students in attendance was 97,998 and the number of teachers 5,497. These schools are controlled by the local Vocational Education Committees; they are financed mainly by State grants and also by contributions from local rating authorities and Vocational Education Committee receipts. These schools also provide adult education facilities for their own areas.

Comprehensive and Community Schools. Comprehensive schools which are financed by the State combine academic and technical subjects in one broad curriculum so that pupils may be offered educational options suited to their needs, abilities and interests. Pupils are prepared for State examinations and for entrance to universities and institutes of further education. The number of comprehensive and community schools during the school year 1999–2000 was 83 and the number of students in attendance was 51,991. These schools also provide adult education facilities for their own areas and make facilities available to voluntary organizations and to the adult community generally.

The total current expenditure from public funds for second level and further education for 1999 was IR£1,053,700,000.

Education Third-Level. Traditionally, the third-level education system in Ireland has comprised the university sector, the technical and technological colleges and the colleges of education, all of which are substantially funded by the State and are autonomous. In the mid- and late 1990s a number of independent private colleges came into existence, offering a range of mainly business-related courses conferring professional qualifications and, in some instances, recognized diplomas and certificates. Numbers in third-level education have expanded dramatically over the last 25 years, from 21,000 full-time students in 1965 to over 103,000 in 1997–98.

University education is provided by the National University of Ireland, founded in Dublin in 1908, by the University of Dublin (Trinity College), founded in 1592, and by the Dublin City University and the University of Limerick established in 1989. The National University comprises four constituent universities—NUI Dublin, NUI Cork, NUI Galway and NUI Maynooth.

St Patrick's College, Maynooth, Co. Kildare is a national seminary for Catholic priests and a pontifical university with the power to confer degrees up to doctoral level in philosophy, theology and canon law.

Besides the University medical schools, the Royal College of Surgeons in Ireland (a long-established independent medical school) provides medical qualifications which are internationally recognized. Courses to degree level are available at the National College of Art and Design, Dublin.

There are five Colleges of Education for training primary school teachers. For degree awarding purposes, three of these colleges are associated with Trinity College, one with Dublin City University and one with the University of Limerick. There are also two Home Economics Colleges for teacher training, one associated with Trinity College and the other with the National University of Ireland, Galway.

Institutes of Technology in 12 centres (Athlone, Carlow, Cork, Dundalk, Dun Laoghaire, Limerick, Tallaght, Galway, Letterkenny, Sligo, Tralee and Waterford) provide vocational and technical education and training for trade and industry from craft to professional level through certificate, diploma and some degree courses. These colleges (with the exception of Dun Laoghaire) were established on a statutory basis on 1 Jan. 1993. Prior to this they operated under the aegis of the Vocational Education Committees (VECs) for their areas. Dun Laoghaire College of Art and Design was designated under the RTC Act 1992, from 1 April 1997. The Dublin Institute of Technology (DIT) was also established on a statutory basis on 1 Jan. 1993. Prior to this it operated under the aegis of City of Dublin VEC. The DIT provides certificate, degree and diploma level courses in engineering, architecture, business studies, catering, music, etc. The Hotel and Catering College in Killybegs continues to operate under the aegis of Co. Donegal VEC.

Total full-time enrolments in the Institutes of Technology/Other Technological Colleges in the 1998–99 academic year were approximately 43,476. The National Council for Educational Awards, established on a statutory basis in 1979, is the validating and awarding authority for courses in the third-level sector outside the universities.

The total full-time enrolment at third-level in institutions aided by the Department of Education and Science in 1998–99 was 108,509. Whereas in the late 1970s only one in five school leavers went on to university, now one out of two is doing so.

The total current expenditure from public funds on third-level education during the financial year ended 31 Dec. 1999 was approximately IR£673,000,000.

Agricultural. Teagasc, the Agriculture and Food Development Authority, is the State agency responsible for providing advisory, training, research and development services for the agriculture and food industries. Full-time instruction in agriculture is provided for all sections of the farming community. There are four agricultural colleges, administered by Teagasc, and seven private Teagasc-aided agricultural colleges. Courses in commercial horticulture are also offered, and short courses for adults already farming.

Health. Everybody ordinarily resident in Ireland has either full or limited eligibility for the public health services.

A person who satisfies the criteria of a means test receives a medical card, which confers Category 1 or full eligibility on them and their dependants. This entitles the holder to the full range of public health and hospital services, free of charge, i.e. family doctor, drugs and medicines, hospital and specialist services as well as dental, aural and optical services. Maternity care and infant welfare services are also provided.

The remainder of the population has Category 2 or limited eligibility. Category 2 patients receive public consultant and public hospital services subject to certain charges. Persons in Category 2 are liable for a hospital in-patient charge of €40 per night up to a maximum of €400 in any 12 consecutive months (with effect from 1 Jan. 2003). There is no charge for out-patient services. However, persons in Category 2 are liable for a charge of €40 if they attend the Accident and Emergency Department of a hospital without a letter from a General Practitioner.

The Long Term Illness Scheme entitles persons to free drugs and medicines, which are prescribed in respect of 15 specific illnesses. The needs of individuals with significant or ongoing medical expenses are met by a range of other schemes, which provide assistance towards the cost of prescribed drugs and medicines. The *Drug Payment Scheme* was introduced on 1 July 1999 and replaced the Drug Cost Subsidisation Scheme (DCSS) and the Drug Refund Scheme (DRS). Under this scheme no individual or family will have to pay more than €70 from 1 Jan. 2003 in any calendar month for approved prescribed drugs, medicines and appliances for use by the person or his/her family in that month.

Where an individual or a family is subjected to a significant level of ongoing expenditure on medical expenses, such as general practitioner fees or prescribed drugs owing to a long term medical condition, these expenses may be reckoned in determining eligibility for a medical card. Eligibility for a medical card is solely a matter for the Chief Officer of the relevant health board/regional authority to decide.

Services for Children: The health boards and the Eastern Regional Health Authority provide, with the co-operation of a wide range of voluntary organizations, comprehensive child welfare and protection services including adoption, fostering, residential care, day care, social work and family support services.

Welfare Services: There are various services provided for older people and families in stress, such as social support services, day care services for children, home helps, home nursing, meals-on-wheels, day centres, cheap fuel, etc.

Services for People with Disabilities: The Department of Health and Children provides, through the health boards and the Eastern Regional Health Authority, a wide range of services for people with disabilities. These include day care, home support (including personal assistance services), therapy services, training, employment, sheltered work and residential respite care. Transport may also be provided to and from these services. The following allowances and grants for eligible people with disabilities come under the aegis of the Department of Health and Children and are administered by the health boards and the Eastern Regional Health Authority:

Blind Welfare Allowance—provides supplementary financial support to unemployed blind persons who are not maintained in an institution and who are in receipt of a Department of Social, Community and Family Affairs payment, such as Disability Allowance, Blind Pension or Old Age Pension.

Rehabilitative Training Bonus—payable to persons who are attending approved rehabilitative training programmes. The payment of €31·80 replaced the Disabled Persons Rehabilitation Allowance (DPRA) from 1 Aug. 2001.

Domiciliary Care Allowance (DCA)—provides home care for severely disabled or mentally handicapped children up to the age of 16. The maximum rate of DCA in Jan. 2002 was €179·80 per month.

Infectious Diseases Maintenance Allowance (IDMA)—payable to a person who is unable to make reasonable and proper provision for their own maintenance or the maintenance of their dependants because they are undergoing treatment for one of the infectious diseases specified in the IDMA regulations. The personal adult rate in Jan. 2002 was €118·80 per week.

Mobility Allowance—provides financial assistance to severely disabled persons who are unable to walk or use public transport in order to finance the occasional taxi journey. At Jan. 2002 the monthly higher rate, payable only to those who do not claim the 'Disabled Drivers and Passengers Tax Relief', was €126. The lower rate was €63.

Motorized Transport Grant– provides financial assistance to disabled persons who require a car to obtain or retain employment or who have transport needs because they live in very isolated areas. The maximum grant in Jan. 2002 was €4,370.

Respite Care Grant (RCG)—an annual payment of €635 to help carers obtain respite care (June 2002).

Spending Allowance for Persons in Long-Stay Institutions—provides basic spending money for people with disabilities and other eligible people in long stay institutions (e.g. residential accommodation) who have no other source of income to help them meet the cost of basic necessities. The maximum rate in Jan. 2003 was €21 per week.

Health Contributions—A health contribution of 2% of income is payable by those with Category 2 eligibility. Employers meet the levy in respect of those employees who have a medical card.

In 2001 there were 60 publicly funded acute hospitals in operation with an 85% occupancy rate. The average number of in-patient beds available for use over the year was 12,019. There were 92,996 wholetime equivalent numbers employed in health board/regional authority and voluntary/joint board hospitals and homes for the mentally handicapped at 31 Dec. 2001. Of these 6,285 were medical/dental staff, 9,228 were health and social care professionals and 31,429 were nursing staff.

Welfare. Social Welfare Services (SWS) is the executive arm of the Department of Social and Family Affairs and is responsible for the day-to-day administration and delivery of social welfare schemes and services through a network of local, regional and decentralized offices. The Department's local delivery of services is structured on a regional basis. There are a total of ten regions, with offices in Waterford, Cork, Limerick, Galway, Longford, Sligo, Dundalk and three in Dublin.

Social Welfare Schemes. The social welfare supports can be divided into three categories:

—*Social Insurance (Contributory)* payments made on the basis of a Pay Related Social Insurance (PRSI) record. Such payments are funded by employers, employees and the self-employed. Any deficit in the fund is met by Exchequer subvention.

—*Social Assistance (Non Contributory)* payments made on the basis of satisfying a means test. These payments are financed entirely by the Exchequer.

—*Universal services* such as Child Benefit or Free Travel which do not depend on PRSI or a means test.

The Social Welfare Appeals Office (SWAO) is an independent office responsible for determining appeals against decisions on social welfare entitlements.

There are, in addition, four statutory agencies under the aegis of the Department:

—*the Combat Poverty Agency* which has responsibilities in the areas of advice to the Minister, research, action programmes and public information in relation to poverty. It also initiates and evaluates pilot schemes aimed at overcoming poverty and examines the nature, causes and extent of poverty in the state.

—*the Pensions Board* which has the function of promoting the security of occupational pensions, their development and the general issue of pensions coverage.

—*Comhairle* which has the function of ensuring that all citizens have easy access to the highest quality of information, advice and advocacy on social services.

—*Family Support Agency* which aims to support families, promote the continuity of stability in family life, prevent marital breakdown and foster a supportive community environment for families at a local level. It does so by providing a family mediation service, by developing marriage and relationship counselling, undertaking research and by advising the Minister on its functions and family issues.

In 2001 social welfare expenditure accounted for 8·2% of GNP.

CULTURE

Broadcasting. Public service broadcasting is provided by Radio Telefis Éireann (RTÉ), a statutory body established under the Broadcasting Authority Acts 1960–93. RTÉ is financed principally by TV licence and advertising. In 1996 a total of 972,069 TV licences were issued. Legislation enacted in 1988 provided for the establishment of the Independent Radio and Television Commission to arrange provision of independent commercial radio stations and an independent TV service. There were (1996) 21 local commercial radio stations, 10 community radio stations, 2 special interest Irish language radio stations, 1 independent national radio station and 4 hospital radio stations. There were 2·55m. radio receivers and 1·65m. TV receivers (colour by PAL) in 1997. An Irish-language TV channel, TG4, broadcasts for 19 hours a day.

Cinema. In 2001 Ireland made 66 films and there were 314 cinema screens.

Press. In 2001 there were six weekday newspapers and five Sunday newspapers (all in English) with a combined circulation of 1,392,040 for Jan. to June 2001.

Tourism. Total number of overseas tourists in 2001 was 5,990,000 compared to 6,311,000 in 2000 (a 5·1% decrease). Earnings from all visits to Ireland, including cross-border visitors, were €3,922m. In 2001, 58% of visitors were from Great Britain. In 2001 Irish residents made 4,216,000 visits abroad (an 11·4% increase on 2000).

Festivals. Ireland's national holiday, St. Patrick's Day (17 March), is celebrated annually.

Libraries. In 1997 there were 351 public libraries, 2 National libraries and 30 Higher Education libraries; they held a combined 17,128,000 volumes. There were 848,000 registered public library users in 1996.

DIPLOMATIC REPRESENTATIVES

Of Ireland in the United Kingdom (17 Grosvenor Pl., London, SW1X 7HR)
Ambassador: Dáithí O'Ceallaigh.

Of the United Kingdom in Ireland (29 Merrion Rd, Ballsbridge, Dublin, 4)
Ambassador: Sir Ivor Anthony Roberts, KCMG.

Of Ireland in the USA (2234 Massachusetts Ave., NW, Washington, D.C., 20008)
Ambassador: Noel Fahey.

Of the USA in Ireland (42 Elgin Rd, Ballsbridge, Dublin)
Ambassador: Richard J. Egan.

Of Ireland to the United Nations
Ambassador: Richard Ryan.

FURTHER READING

Central Statistics Office. *National Income and Expenditure* (annual), *Statistical Abstract* (annual), *Census of Population Reports* (quinquennial), *Census of Industrial Production Reports* (annual), *Trade and Shipping Statistics* (annual and monthly), *Trend of Employment and Unemployment, Reports on Vital Statistics* (annual and quarterly), *Statistical Bulletin* (quarterly), *Labour Force Surveys* (annual), *Trade Statistics* (monthly), *Economic Series* (monthly).

Ardagh, J., *Ireland and the Irish: a Portrait of a Changing Society.* London, 1994
Chubb, B., *Government and Politics in Ireland.* 3rd ed. London, 1992
Collins, N. (ed.) *Political Issues in Ireland Today.* Manchester Univ. Press, 1994
Cronin, Mike, *A History of Ireland.* Palgrave, Basingstoke, 2001
Delanty, G. and O'Mahony, P., *Rethinking Irish History: Nationalism, Identity and Ideology.* London, 1997
Foster, R. F., *The Oxford Illustrated History of Ireland.* OUP, 1991
Garvin, T., *1922 The Birth of Irish Democracy.* Dublin, 1997
Harkness, D., *Ireland in the Twentieth Century: a Divided Island.* London, 1995
Hussey, G., *Ireland Today: Anatomy of a Changing State.* Dublin, 1993
Institute of Public Administration, *Ireland: a Directory.* Dublin, annual
Kostick, C., *Revolution in Ireland – Popular Militancy 1917–1923.* London, 1997
Munck, R., *The Irish Economy: Results and Prospects.* London, 1993
O'Beirne Ranelagh, J., *A Short History of Ireland.* 2nd ed. CUP, 1999
O'Hagan, J. W. (ed.) *The Economy of Ireland: Policy and Performance of a Small European Country.* London, 1995
Vaughan, W. E. (ed.) *A New History of Ireland,* 6 vols. Oxford, 1996
Wiles, J. L. and Finnegan, R. B., *Aspirations and Realities: a Documentary History of Economic Development Policy in Ireland since 1922.* London, 1992.

National statistical office: Central Statistics Office, Skehard Road, Cork. *Director-General:* Donal Garvey, M.Sc., M.Sc. (Mgt).
Website: http://www.cso.ie/

ISRAEL

Medinat Israel
(State of Israel)

Capital: Jerusalem
Population estimate, 2000: 6·04m.
GDP per capita, 2000: (PPP$) 20,131
HDI/world rank: 0·896/22

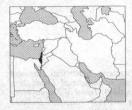

KEY HISTORICAL EVENTS

The area once designated as Palestine, of which Israel forms part, was formerly part of the Ottoman Empire. During the First World War the Arabs under Ottoman rule rebelled and Palestine was occupied by British forces. In 1917 the British Government issued the Balfour Declaration, stating that it viewed 'with favour the establishment in Palestine of a national home for the Jewish people'. In 1922 the League of Nations recognized 'the historical connection of the Jewish people with Palestine' and 'the grounds for reconstituting their national home in that country', and Britain assumed a mandate over Palestine, pending the establishment there of such a national home. In Nov. 1947 the UN General Assembly passed a resolution calling for the establishment of a Jewish and an Arab state in Palestine. On 14 May 1948 the British Government terminated its mandate and the Jewish leaders proclaimed the State of Israel. No independent Arab state was established in Palestine. Instead the neighbouring Arab states invaded Israel on 15 May 1948. The Jewish state defended itself successfully, and the ceasefire in Jan. 1949 left Israel with one-third more land than had been originally assigned by the UN.

In 1967, following some years of uneasy peace, local clashes on the Israeli–Syrian border were followed by Egyptian mass concentration of forces on the borders of Israel. Israel struck out at Egypt on land and in the air on 5–9 June 1967. Jordan joined in the conflict which spread to the Syrian borders. By 11 June the Israelis had occupied the Gaza Strip and the Sinai peninsula as far as the Suez Canal in Egypt, West Jordan as far as the Jordan valley and the heights east of the Sea of Galilee, including Quneitra in Syria.

A further war broke out on 6 Oct. 1973 when Egyptian and Syrian offensives were launched. Following UN Security Council resolutions a ceasefire finally came into being on 24 Oct. In Sept. 1978 Egypt and Israel agreed on frameworks for peace in the Middle East. A treaty was signed in Washington on 26 March 1979 whereby Israel withdrew from the Sinai Desert in two phases; part was achieved on 26 Jan. 1980 and the final withdrawal by 26 April 1982.

In June 1982 Israeli forces invaded the Lebanon. On 16 Feb. 1985 the Israeli forces started a withdrawal, leaving behind an Israeli trained and equipped Christian Lebanese force to act as a control over and buffer against Muslim Shi'a or Palestinian guerrilla attacks.

In 1993 following declarations by the Prime Minister, Yitzhak Rabin, recognizing the Palestine Liberation Organization (PLO) as representative of the Palestinian people, and by Yasser Arafat, leader of the PLO, renouncing terrorism and recognizing the State of Israel, an agreement was signed in Washington providing for limited Palestinian self-rule in the Gaza Strip and Jericho. Negotiations on the permanent status of the West Bank and Gaza began in 1996. On 4 Nov. 1995 Yitzhak Rabin was assassinated by a Jewish religious extremist. In the subsequent election, a right-wing coalition led by Binyamin Netanyahu took office. Peace talks with the Palestinians then stalled. In Oct. 1998 Israel accepted partial withdrawal from the West Bank on condition that the Palestinians cracked down on terrorism. The following month, 2% of the West Bank was handed over to Palestinian control. Further moves were put on hold after the collapse of the Netanyahu coalition and the announcement of early elections.

In Sept. 1999 Ehud Barak provided the first evidence that the Middle East peace process was back on track by releasing nearly 200 Palestinian prisoners and by handing over 430 sq. km of land on the West Bank. In May 2000 Israel completed its withdrawal from south Lebanon, 22 years after the first invasion. By Oct. 2000

934

violence had broken out again between Israelis and Palestinians, fuelled by the conflict over control of Jerusalem, with terrorist acts a daily occurrence, leading to heavy casualties on both sides. With peace talks stalled once again, Barak called for a nationwide vote of confidence by putting himself up for re-election as prime minister. Defeated by the right-wing Ariel Sharon in Feb. 2001, he retired from politics. As violence escalated, in Dec. 2001 Israel ended all direct contact with Yasser Arafat, besieging his compound and putting him under virtual house arrest. Israeli incursions into Palestinian-controlled areas of the West Bank and the Gaza Strip, and suicide attacks by Palestinians, continued unabated in early 2002 with heavy loss of life. In June 2002 Israel began constructing a barrier to cut off the West Bank, with the aim of shielding the country from suicide bombers.

TERRITORY AND POPULATION
The area of Israel, including the Golan Heights (1,150 sq. km) and East Jerusalem (70 sq. km), is 21,946 sq. km (8,473 sq. miles), with a population estimated in 1997 to be 5·53m., including East Jerusalem, the Golan Heights and Israeli settlers in the occupied territories. Population density, 252 per sq. km.

The UN gives a projected population for 2010 of 7·25m.

In 1999, 91·1% of the population lived in urban areas.

Population by place of origin as of 1995: Europe and America, 1·8m.; former USSR, 0·66m.; Morocco, 0·5m.; Poland, 0·25m.; Romania, 0·25m.; Iraq, 0·25m.; Yemen, 0·15m.; Iran, 0·13m.; Algeria and Tunisia, 0·12m.

The Jewish Agency, which, in accordance with Article IV of the Palestine Mandate, played a leading role in establishing the State of Israel, continues to organize immigration.

Israel is administratively divided into six districts:

District	Area (sq. km)	Population[1]	Chief town
Northern	4,501	1,001,900	Nazareth
Haifa	854	774,900	Haifa
Central	1,242	1,307,900	Ramla
Tel Aviv	170	1,140,000	Tel Aviv
Jerusalem[2]	627	701,700	Jerusalem
Southern	14,107	813,500	Beersheba

[1]1997. [2]Includes East Jerusalem.

On 23 Jan. 1950 the Knesset proclaimed Jerusalem the capital of the State and on 14 Dec. 1981 extended Israeli law into the Golan Heights. Population of the main towns (1997): Jerusalem, 622,100; Tel Aviv/Jaffa, 348,600; Haifa, 264,300; Rishon le-Ziyyon, 178,100; Holon, 162,900; Beersheba, 160,300; Petach Tikva, 155,200; Netanya, 152,200; Ashdod, 146,900; Bat Yam, 137,400; Bene Berak, 133,900; Ramat Gan, 127,400.

The official languages are Hebrew and Arabic.

SOCIAL STATISTICS
1999 births, 131,936; deaths, 37,242; marriages, 38,008; divorces, 10,196. 1999 crude birth rate per 1,000 population of Jewish population, 18·5; Non-Jewish: Muslims, 37·7; Christians, 20·7; Druzes, 25·8. Crude death rate (1999), Jewish, 6·9; other religions, 3·1. Infant mortality rate per 1,000 live births (1999), Jewish, 4·5; other religions, 8·4. Life expectancy, 1999, 76·6 years for males and 80·4 for females. Average annual population growth rate, 1995–99, 2·5%. Fertility rate, 1999, 2·6 births per woman.

Immigration. The following table shows the numbers of Jewish immigrants entering Palestine/Israel.

| 1990 | 199,516 | 1992 | 77,057 | 1994 | 79,844 |
| 1991 | 176,100 | 1993 | 76,805 | 1995 | 76,361 |

CLIMATE
From April to Oct., the summers are long and hot, and almost rainless. From Nov. to March, the weather is generally mild, though colder in hilly areas, and this is the wet season. Jerusalem, Jan. 12·8°C, July 28·9°C. Annual rainfall, 657 mm. Tel Aviv, Jan. 17·2°C, July 30·2°C. Annual rainfall, 803 mm.

CONSTITUTION AND GOVERNMENT

Israel is an independent sovereign republic, established by proclamation on 14 May 1948.

In 1950 the Knesset (*Parliament*), which in 1949 had passed the Transition Law dealing in general terms with the powers of the Knesset, President and Cabinet, resolved to enact from time to time fundamental laws, which eventually, taken together, would form the Constitution. The nine fundamental laws that have been passed: the Knesset (1958), Israel Lands (1960), the President (1964), the Government (1968), the State Economy (1975), the Army (1976), Jerusalem, capital of Israel (1980), the Judicature (1984) and the Electoral System (1996).

The *President* (head of state) is elected by the Knesset by secret ballot by a simple majority; his term of office is five years. He may be re-elected once.

The Knesset, a one-chamber Parliament, consists of 120 members. It is elected for a four-year term by secret ballot and universal direct suffrage. Under the system of election introduced in 1996, electors vote once for a party and once for a candidate for Prime Minister. To be elected Prime Minister, a candidate must gain more than half the votes cast, and be elected to the Knesset. If there are more than two candidates and none gain half the vote, a second round is held 15 days later. The Prime Minister forms a cabinet (no fewer than eight members and no more than 18) with the approval of the Knesset.

National Anthem. 'Hatikvah' ('The Hope'); words by N. H. Imber.

RECENT ELECTIONS

Ariel Sharon of Likud (conservative) won the election for *Prime Minister* on 6 Feb. 2001 with 62·4% of the vote, against 37·6% for the incumbent Prime Minister Ehud Barak of Avoda. In the parliamentary (Knesset) elections on 28 Jan. 2003, Prime Minister Ariel Sharon's Likud party (conservative) won 37 of 120 seats, Avoda (social democratic) 19, Shinui-Mifleget Merkaz (liberal) 15, Shas 11, National Union 7, Meretz 6, National Religious Party 5, United Torah Judaism 5 and smaller parties 15. Turn-out was 68·5%.

In a parliamentary vote for the presidency on 31 July 2000, Moshe Katzav defeated Shimon Peres in the second round. He claimed 63 votes against 57 for Peres.

CURRENT ADMINISTRATION

President: Moshe Katzav; b. 1945 (Likud; sworn in 1 Aug. 2000).

Following the election of 6 Feb. 2001 Ariel Sharon formed an eight-party coalition. In Oct. 2002 Labour Party ministers resigned from the cabinet following a dispute over the funding of Jewish settlements in the West Bank. Unable to maintain the coalition without support from the Labour Party, Ariel Sharon was forced to call early elections which were held on 28 Jan. 2003. He subsequently formed a new coalition government which in March 2003 was composed as follows:

Prime Minister: Ariel Sharon; b. 1928 (Likud; sworn in 7 March 2001).

Acting Prime Minister and Minister of Industry and Commerce: Ehud Olmert (Likud). *Deputy Prime Minister and Minister of Foreign Affairs:* Silvan Shalom (Likud). *Deputy Prime Minister and Minister of Justice:* Yosef Lapid (Shinui).

Minister of Agriculture and Rural Development: Yisrael Katz (Likud). *Construction and Housing:* Efraim Eitam (National Religious Party). *Defence:* Shaul Mofaz (Likud). *Education, Culture and Sport:* Limor Livnat (Likud). *Environment:* Yehudit Naot (Shinui). *Finance:* Binyamin Netanyahu (Likud). *Health:* Dani Naveh (Likud). *Immigrant Absorption:* Tzipi Livni (Likud). *Interior and Communications:* Avraham Poraz (Shinui). *Labour and Social Affairs:* Zvulun Orlev (National Religious Party). *National Infrastructure:* Yosef Paritzky (Shinui). *Public Security:* Tzahi Hanegbi (Likud). *Science and Technology:* Eliezer Sandberg (Shinui). *Tourism:* Benny Elon (National Union). *Transportation:* Avigdor Lieberman (Likud). *Minister without Portfolio, responsible for Jerusalem Affairs, Society and the Diaspora:* Natan Scheransky (Likud-Israel Baaliyah). *Ministers without Portfolio:* Uzi Landau (Likud); Gideon Ezra (Likud); Meir Shitrit (Likud).

Office of the Prime Minister: http://www.pmo.gov.il

DEFENCE

Conscription (for Jews and Druze only) is three years (usually four years for officers; two years for women). The Israel Defence Force is a unified force, in which army, navy and air force are subordinate to a single chief-of-staff. The Minister of Defence is *de facto* C.-in-C.

Defence expenditure in 2001 totalled US$10,375m., representing 9·5% of GDP. Expenditure per capita in 2001 was US$1,673, a figure exceeded only by Kuwait and Qatar.

Nuclear Weapons. Israel has an undeclared nuclear weapons capability. Although known to have a nuclear bomb, it pledges not to introduce nuclear testing to the Middle East. According to the Stockholm International Peace Research Institute, the nuclear arsenal was estimated to have approximately 200 warheads in Jan. 2002. Israel has never admitted possessing biological or chemical weapons, but according to *Deadly Arsenals*, published by the Carnegie Endowment for International Peace, it does have a chemical and biological weapons programme.

Army. Strength (2002) 120,000 (conscripts 85,000). There are also 530,000 reservists available on mobilization. In addition there is a paramilitary border police of 8,500.

Navy. The Navy, tasked primarily for coastal protection and based at Haifa, Ashdod and Eilat, includes three small diesel submarines and three corvettes.

Naval personnel in 2002 totalled 6,500 (including a Naval Commando of 300) of whom 2,500 are conscripts. There are also 11,500 naval reservists available on mobilization.

Air Force. The Air Force (including air defence) has a personnel strength (2002) of 35,000 (20,000 conscripts), with 454 (250 stored) first-line aircraft, all jets, of Israeli and US manufacture including F-4E *Phantoms*, F-15s and F-16s, and 135 armed helicopters. There are 20,000 Air Force reservists.

INTERNATIONAL RELATIONS

Israel is a member of the UN, WTO, Inter-American Development Bank and IOM. It is one of the largest recipients of foreign aid, in 1996 receiving US$2·2bn, representing around US$400 per person—the highest amount per person of any country.

ECONOMY

Agriculture accounted for an estimated 2% of GDP in 1997, industry 17% and services 81%.

According to the anti-corruption organization *Transparency International*, Israel ranked equal 18th in the world in a 2002 survey of the countries with the least corruption in business and government. It received 7·3 out of 10 in the annual index.

Overview. Israel is facing its worst recession in 50 years owing to high security costs and a sharp decline in tourism. The tense situation hampers foreign investment, exports and economic reforms. Businesses depending on foreign financial markets are suffering from the US economic slowdown, and in 2000 the government opened the telecommunications sector to foreign competition. In 2002 the government introduced emergency measures, including an increase in the budget deficit to 3·9% from the targeted 3%. State expenditures have been cut through a freeze in social benefits and the minimum wage. Taxes have risen. In early 2002 the Bank of Israel cut interest rates by 2 percentage points and the currency dropped to 4·60 shekel to the US dollar, an all-time low.

Currency The unit of currency is the *shekel* (ILS) of 100 *agorot*. Foreign exchange reserves were US$24,782m. in June 2002. Gold reserves have been negligible since 1998. There was zero inflation in 2000, the lowest rate on record. Total money supply in May 2002 was 37,702m. shekels.

Budget. Budget revenue and expenditure (in 1m. shekels), year ending 31 Dec.:

	1995	1996	1997	1998	1999	2000
Revenue	108,032	123,796	145,110	159,911	173,187	194,736
Expenditure	125,369	149,571	165,250	183,046	197,954	208,603

Performance. There was real GDP growth of 7·4% in 2000, but Israel then experienced a recession in 2001, with the economy shrinking by 0·9%. Total GDP was US$110·4bn. in 2000.

Banking and Finance. The Bank of Israel was established by law in 1954 as Israel's central bank. Its Governor is appointed by the President on the recommendation of the Cabinet for a five-year term. He acts as economic adviser to the government and has ministerial status. The *Governor* is Dr David Klein. There are 26 commercial banks headed by Bank Leumi Le Israel, Bank Hapoalim and Israel Discount Bank, 2 merchant banks, 1 foreign bank, 15 mortgage banks and 9 lending institutions specifically set up to aid industry and agriculture.

There is a stock exchange in Tel Aviv.

Israel was one of 15 countries and territories named in a report in June 2000 as failing to co-operate in the fight against international money laundering. The Financial Action Task Force on Money Laundering was set up by the G7 group of major industrialized nations.

Weights and Measures. The metric system is in general use. The (metrical) *dunam* = 1,000 sq. metres (about 0·25 acre).

Jewish Year. The Jewish year 5763 corresponds to 7 Sept. 2002 to 26 Sept. 2003; 5764 from 27 Sept. 2003 to 15 Sept. 2004.

ENERGY AND NATURAL RESOURCES

Environment. According to the *World Bank Atlas* carbon dioxide emissions in 1998 were the equivalent of 10·1 tonnes per capita.

Electricity. Installed capacity in 1997 was an estimated 7·81m. kW. Electric power production amounted to 35·34bn. kWh in 1998; consumption per capita was 5,475 kWh.

Oil and Gas. The only significant hydrocarbon is oil shale. Crude petroleum reserves in 1997 were 4m. bbls.

Water. In the northern Negev farming has been aided by the Yarkon–Negev water pipeline. This has become part of the overall project of the 'National Water Carrier', which is to take water from the Sea of Galilee (Lake Kinnereth) to the south. The plan includes a number of regional projects such as the Lake Kinnereth–Negev pipeline which came into operation in 1964; it has an annual capacity of 320m. cu. metres. Total water production in 1997 amounted to 2,188m. cu. metres, of which 1,959m. cu. metres was consumed.

Minerals. The most valuable natural resources are the potash, bromine and other salt deposits of the Dead Sea. Potash production in 1996 was 2,500,000 tonnes; phosphate rock production was 2,450,000 tonnes. Annual salt production averages 800,000 tonnes.

Agriculture. In the coastal plain mixed farming, poultry raising, citriculture and vineyards are the main agricultural activities. The Emek (the Valley of Jezreel) is the main agricultural centre of Israel. Mixed farming is to be found throughout the valleys; the sub-tropical Beisan and Jordan plainlands are also centres of banana plantations and fish breeding. In Galilee mixed farming, olive and tobacco plantations prevail. The Hills of Ephraim are a vineyard centre; many parts of the hill country are under afforestation.

There were 351,000 ha of arable land in 1998 and 86,000 ha of permanent crops. Production, 2000 (in 1,000 tonnes): tomatoes, 550; melons and watermelons, 447; grapefruit and pomelos, 370; potatoes, 349; oranges, 300; tangerines and mandarins, 140; bananas, 130; cucumbers and gherkins, 108; chillies and green peppers, 97; onions, 90.

Livestock (2000), 388,000 cattle, 350,000 sheep, 163,000 pigs, 70,000 goats, 28m. poultry.

Types of rural settlement: (1) the *Kibbutz* and *Kvutza* (communal collective settlement), where all property and earnings are collectively owned and work is collectively organized. (115,700 people lived in 268 *Kibbutzim* in 1999.) (2) The *Moshav* (workers' co-operative smallholders' settlement) which is founded on the principles of mutual aid and equality of opportunity between the members, all farms being equal in size (184,500 in 411). (3) The *Moshav Shitufi* (co-operative settlement), which is based on collective ownership and economy as in the *Kibbutz*, but with each family having its own house and being responsible for its own domestic services (18,200 in 43). (4) Other rural settlements in which land and property are privately owned and every resident is responsible for his own well-being. In 1999 there were a total of 259 non-cooperative villages with a population of 314,900.

Forestry. In 1995 forests covered 102,000 ha or 4·9% of the total land area. Timber production was 89,000 cu. metres in 1999.

Fisheries. Catches in 1999 totalled 5,884 tonnes, of which 3,739 tonnes were from marine waters.

INDUSTRY
The leading companies by market capitalization in Israel, excluding banking and finance, in Jan. 2002 were: Teva Pharmaceutical Industries Ltd (40bn. shekels); Check Point Software Technologies Ltd (20bn. shekels); and BEZEQ—The Israel Telecommunications Corporation Ltd (12bn. shekels).

Products include chemicals, metal products, textiles, tyres, diamonds, paper, plastics, leather goods, glass and ceramics, building materials, precision instruments, tobacco, foodstuffs, electrical and electronic equipment.

Labour. The workforce was 2,040,200 in 1997 (884,800 females). Of the total labour force 29·0% worked in education, health, social and personal services, 18·0% in manufacturing and mining, and 15·3% in trade. A 'social-economic pact' between government, employers and trade unions in May 1991 aimed to create some 32,000 new jobs to lessen the impact of increased immigration. Unemployment was 9·3% in May 1998, up from 6·4% in 1996.

Trade Unions. The General Federation of Labour (Histadrut) founded in 1920, had, in 1987, 1·6m. members (including 0·17m. Arab and Druze members); including workers' families, this membership represents 71·5% of the population covering 87% of all wage-earners. Several trades unions also exist representing other political and religious groups.

INTERNATIONAL TRADE
Total foreign debt amounted to US$34,000m. in July 1996.

Imports and Exports. External trade, in US$1m., for calendar years:

	1996	1997	1998	1999	2000
Imports f.o.b.	28,515	27,937	26,315	30,091	34,187
Exports f.o.b.	21,333	22,698	22,974	25,577	30,837

The main exportable commodities are citrus fruit and by-products, fruit juices, flowers, wines and liquor, sweets, polished diamonds, chemicals, tyres, textiles, metal products, machinery, electronic and transportation equipment. The main exports were, in 1995 (US$1m.): diamonds, 4,921·6; chemicals and chemical products, 2,369·7; machinery and equipment, 958·9; agricultural products including citrus fruit, 740·5. Of exports in 1995, US$6,529·8m. went to EU and EFTA countries and US$5,735·9m. to USA. In 1995 the main export markets were: USA, 30·1%; UK, 6·1%; Germany, 5·5%; Belgium, 5·4%. Main import suppliers: USA, 18·6%; Belgium, 12·1%; Germany, 9·7%; UK, 8·3%.

COMMUNICATIONS

Roads. There were 15,965 km of paved roads in 1998 including 56 km of motorway. Registered motor vehicles in 1998 totalled 1,297,965 passenger cars, 14,986 buses and coaches and 282,904 lorries and vans. There were 548 fatalities as a result of road accidents in 1998.

Rail. There were 609 km of standard gauge line in 1997. In 1997, 5,919,000 passengers and 8,639,000 tonnes of freight were carried.

Civil Aviation. There are international airports at Tel Aviv (Ben Gurion), Eilat (J. Hozman), Haifa and Ovda. Tel Aviv is the busiest airport, in 2000 handling 9,815,015 passengers (9,283,287 on international flights) and 336,188 tonnes of

ISRAEL

freight. El Al is the state-owned airline. In 1999 it flew 79·5m. km and carried
2,972,400 passengers (all on international flights). In 1999 services (mainly
domestic) were also provided by another Israeli airline, Arkia, and by over 40
international carriers.

Shipping. Israel has three commercial ports—Haifa, Ashdod and Eilat. In 1997,
6,230 ships departed from Israeli ports; 41,490,000 tonnes of freight and 1,082,000
passengers were handled. The merchant fleet totalled 752,000 GRT in 1998.

Telecommunications. A public company responsible to the Ministry of
Communications administers the telecommunications service. In 2000 there were
3,021,000 main telephone lines (equivalent to 481·8 per 1,000 population) and 1·6m.
PCs (253·6 for every 1,000 persons). Israel had 2·8m. mobile phone subscribers in
1999 and 140,000 fax machines in 1995. There were approximately 1·94m. Internet
users in July 2001.

Postal Services. The Ministry of Communications supervises the postal service. In
1995 there were 662 post offices and postal agencies, and 48 mobile post offices.

SOCIAL INSTITUTIONS

Justice. *Law.* Under the Law and Administration Ordinance, 5708/1948, the first
law passed by the Provisional Council of State, the law of Israel is the law which
was obtaining in Palestine on 14 May 1948 in so far as it is not in conflict with
that Ordinance or any other law passed by the Israel legislature and with such
modifications as result from the establishment of the State and its authorities.

Capital punishment was abolished in 1954, except for support given to the Nazis
and for high treason.

The law of Palestine was derived from Ottoman law, English law (Common Law
and Equity) and the law enacted by the Palestine legislature, which to a great extent
was modelled on English law.

Civil Courts. Municipal courts, established in certain municipal areas, have criminal
jurisdiction over offences against municipal regulations and bylaws and certain
specified offences committed within a municipal area. Magistrates courts,
established in each district and sub-district, have limited jurisdiction in both civil
and criminal matters. District courts, sitting at Jerusalem, Tel Aviv and Haifa, have
jurisdiction, as courts of first instance, in all civil matters not within the jurisdiction
of magistrates courts, and in all criminal matters, and as appellate courts from
magistrates courts and municipal courts. The 14-member Supreme Court has
jurisdiction as a court of first instance (sitting as a High Court of Justice dealing
mainly with administrative matters) and as an appellate court from the district courts
(sitting as a Court of Civil or of Criminal Appeal).

In addition, there are various tribunals for special classes of cases. Settlement
Officers deal with disputes with regard to the ownership or possession of land in
settlement areas constituted under the Land (Settlement of Title) Ordinance.

Religious Courts. The rabbinical courts of the Jewish community have exclusive
jurisdiction in matters of marriage and divorce, alimony and confirmation of wills
of members of their community and concurrent jurisdiction with the civil courts in
all other matters of personal status of all members of their community with the
consent of all parties to the action.

The courts of the several recognized Christian communities have a similar
jurisdiction over members of their respective communities.

The Muslim religious courts have exclusive jurisdiction in all matters of personal
status over Muslims who are not foreigners, and over Muslims who are foreigners,
if under the law of their nationality they are subject in such matters to the jurisdiction
of Muslim religious courts.

Where any action of personal status involves persons of different religious
communities, the President of the Supreme Court will decide which court shall
have jurisdiction, and whenever a question arises as to whether or not a case is
one of personal status within the exclusive jurisdiction of a religious court, the
matter must be referred to a special tribunal composed of two judges of the
Supreme Court and the president of the highest court of the religious community
concerned in Israel.

In 1996 government expenditure on public order and safety totalled 4,481m. shekels.

Religion. Religious affairs are under the supervision of a special Ministry, with departments for the Christian and Muslim communities. The religious affairs of each community remain under the full control of the ecclesiastical authorities concerned: in the case of the Jews, the Sephardi and Ashkenazi Chief Rabbis, in the case of the Christians, the heads of the various communities, and in the case of the Muslims, the Qadis. The Druze were officially recognized in 1957 as an autonomous religious community.

In 1997 there were: Jews, 4,701,600; Muslims, 867,900; Christians, 126,100; Druze, 96,700.

The Chief Rabbi is Israel Meir Lau.

Education. The adult literacy rate in 1999 was 95·8% (male, 97·8%; female, 93·9%). There is free and compulsory education from 5 to 16 years and optional free education until 18. There is a unified state-controlled elementary school system with a provision for special religious schools. The standard curriculum for all elementary schools is issued by the Ministry with a possibility of adding supplementary subjects comprising not more than 25% of the total syllabus. Most schools in towns are maintained by municipalities, a number are private and some are administered by teachers' co-operatives or trustees.

Statistics relating to schools under government supervision, 1995–96:

Type of School[1]	School	Teachers	Pupils
Hebrew Education			
Primary schools	1,365	42,946	528,429
Schools for children with disabilities	203	5,276	12,392
Schools of intermediate division	371	19,945	150,804
Secondary schools	621 ⎫		240,990
Vocational schools	313 ⎬	31,803	102,716
Agricultural schools	23 ⎭		6,513
Arab Education			
Primary schools	326	8,802	150,083
Schools for children with disabilities	43	549	2,461
Schools of intermediate division	104	3,828	44,984
Secondary schools	101 ⎫		43,510
Vocational schools	62 ⎬	3,543	12,765
Agricultural schools	2 ⎭		621

[1]Schools providing more than one type of education are included more than once.

There are also a number of private schools maintained by religious foundations—Jewish, Christian and Muslim—and also by private societies.

The Hebrew University of Jerusalem, founded in 1925, comprises faculties of the humanities, social sciences, law, science, medicine and agriculture. In 1995–96 it had 20,290 students. The Technion in Haifa had 10,370 students. The Weizmann Institute of Science in Rehovoth, founded in 1949, had 760 students.

Tel Aviv University had 26,100 students. The religious Bar-Ilan University at Ramat Gan, opened in 1965, had 19,110 students. The Haifa University had 12,820 students. The Ben Gurion University had 12,250 students.

In 1996 government expenditure on education totalled 20,630m. shekels.

Health. In 1995 there were 259 hospitals with 33,159 beds and (1993) 24,344 doctors (provision of one for every 214 persons). In 1996 government expenditure on health totalled 15,052m. shekels.

Welfare. The National Insurance Law of 1954 provides for old-age pensions, survivors' insurance, work-injury insurance, maternity insurance, family allowances and unemployment benefits. In 1996 government expenditure on social security and welfare totalled 38,082m. shekels.

CULTURE

Broadcasting. Television and the state radio station, Kol Israel (Voice of Israel), are controlled by the Israel Broadcasting Authority. There is a national programme, two commercial programmes, a music programme and a service in Arabic. There were 1·70m. TV sets (colour by PAL) and 3·07m. radio receivers in 1997.

Cinema. There were 266 screens in 1994; attendances totalled 10·0m.

Press. In 1996 there were 34 daily newspapers. Combined circulation was 1,650,000, at a rate of 291 per 1,000 inhabitants.

Tourism. In 1999 there were 2,275,000 foreign tourists, bringing revenue of US$3·05bn.

Libraries. In 1995 there was one National Library with 3m. volumes and 2,176 registered users. In 1993 there were 1,180 public libraries with 11,242,000 volumes and 737,565 registered users.

DIPLOMATIC REPRESENTATIVES
Of Israel in the United Kingdom (2 Palace Green, Kensington, London, W8 4QB)
Ambassador: Zvi Shtauber.

Of the United Kingdom in Israel (192 Hayarkon St., Tel Aviv 63405)
Ambassador: Sherard Cowper-Coles, CMG, LVO.

Of Israel in the USA (3514 International Dr., NW, Washington, D.C., 20008)
Ambassador: Daniel Ayalon.

Of the USA in Israel (71 Hayarkon St., Tel Aviv)
Ambassador: Daniel C. Kurtzer.

Of Israel to the United Nations
Ambassador: Dan Gillerman.

Of Israel to the European Union
Ambassador: Harry Kney-Tal.

FURTHER READING
Central Bureau of Statistics. *Statistical Abstract of Israel.* (Annual)—*Statistical Bulletin of Israel.* (Monthly)
Beitlin, Y., *Israel: a Concise History.* London, 1992
Bleaney, C. H., *Israel.* [Bibliography] 2nd ed. ABC-Clio, Oxford and Santa Barbara (CA), 1994
Freedman, R. (ed.) *Israel Under Rabin.* Boulder (CO), 1995
Garfinkle, A., *Politics and Society in Modern Israel: Myths and Realities.* Armonk (NY), 1997
Gilbert, Martin, *Israel: A History.* New York, 1998
Sachar, H. M., *A History of Israel.* 2 vols. OUP, 1976–87
Schlör, Joachim, *Tel Aviv: From Dream to City.* Reaktion, London, 1999
Segev, T., *1949: The First Israelis.* New York, 1986
Thomas, Baylis, *How Israel Was Won: A Concise History of the Arab–Israeli Conflict (1900–1999).* Lexington Books, Pennsylvania, 2000

Other more specialized titles are entered under PALESTINIAN-ADMINISTERED TERRITORIES.

National statistical office: Central Bureau of Statistics, Prime Minister's Office, POB 13015, Jerusalem 91130.
Website: http://www.cbs.gov.il/
National library: The Jewish National and University Library, Jerusalem

PALESTINIAN-ADMINISTERED TERRITORIES

KEY HISTORICAL EVENTS
Under the Israeli-Palestinian agreement of 28 Sept. 1995 the Israeli army re-deployed from six of the seven largest Palestinian towns in the West Bank and from 460 smaller towns and villages. Following this in April 1996 an 82-member *Palestinian Council* was elected and also a head (*Rais*) of the executive authority of the Council. The rest of the West Bank stayed under Israeli army control with some progressive redeployments at six-month intervals, although Palestinian civil affairs here too were administered by the Palestinian Council. Negotiations on the

permanent status of the West Bank and Gaza began in May 1996. Issues to be resolved include the position of 0·17m. Israelis in the West Bank and 0·18m. in East Jerusalem, the status of Jerusalem, military locations and water supplies.

Following the opening of an archaeological tunnel in Jerusalem, armed clashes broke out at the end of Sept. 1996 between demonstrators and Palestinian police on the one hand and Israeli troops. On 18 Nov. 1996 the Israeli Minister of Defence approved plans for an expansion of Jewish settlement in the West Bank. Under an agreement brokered by King Hussein of Jordan and signed by the Prime Minister of Israel and the President of the Palestinian Authority on 15 Jan. 1997 Israeli troop withdrawals from 80% of Hebron and all rural areas of the West Bank were scheduled to take place in three phases between 28 Feb. 1996 and 31 Aug. 1998.

The Israeli decision in Feb. 1997 to continue to promote Jewish settlement in the Jerusalem suburb of Har Homa was perceived by the Palestinian authorities as a hostile move and caused a setback to peace negotiations. In 1998 an American proposal that Israel should withdraw from 13·1% of the West Bank was not agreed on, but at a meeting in the USA in Oct. Israel accepted partial withdrawal on condition that the Palestinians cracked down on terrorism.

President Netanyahu's defeat by Ehud Barak in Israel's 1999 elections led to improved relations with the Palestinian Liberation Organization. Israel and the PLO signed the Sharm el-Shakh Memorandum in Sept. 1999 which established a time-frame for the implementation of outstanding commitments from earlier Palestinian-Israeli agreements. Israel conducted two more phases of redeployment from the West Bank in Sept. 1999 and Jan. 2000. The permanent status negotiations, having commenced in May 1996, began in earnest in Nov. 1999. In March 2000 Yasser Arafat accepted Israel's plan for a further expansion of self-rule in the West Bank, involving the transfer of another 6·1% of the West Bank to the control of the Palestinian Authority. As a result, 39·8% of the West Bank is under full or partial Palestinian control. But violence escalated, and in Dec. 2001 Israel ended all direct contact with Yasser Arafat, besieging his compound and putting him under virtual house arrest. In March 2002 the UN Security Council endorsed a Palestinian state for the first time. Israeli incursions into Palestinian-controlled areas of the West Bank and the Gaza Strip, and suicide attacks by Palestinians, continued unabated in early 2002 with heavy loss of life. In March 2003 the Palestinian parliament approved the creation of the post of prime minister. Mahmoud Abbas was nominated the Palestinian Authority's first premier, resulting in Yasser Arafat losing many of his powers.

TERRITORY AND POPULATION

The 1997 census population of the Palestinian territory was 2,895,683; 2000 estimate 3,150,000.

The **West Bank** (preferred Palestinian term, Northern District) has an area of 5,651 sq. km; 1997 census population was 1,873,476. The projected population for 2000 was 2,012,000, including 180,000 Jewish settlers and 10,000 troops deployed there. 97% of the population in 1988 were Palestinian Arabs of whom some 85% were Muslims, 7·4% Jewish and 8% Christian. In 1995 there was a Palestinian diaspora of 3·3m. The birth rate in 1999 was estimated at 39·5 per 1,000 population and the death rate 4·6 per 1,000. In 1995 the infant mortality rate was 25·5 per 1,000 live births. The fertility rate in 1997 was 5·61 births per woman. In 1994 there were 77,604 private cars and 21,714 commercial vehicles and trucks registered. There were (1998–99) 447,369 pupils in basic stage education and 38,121 in secondary stage, plus 36,224 students in institutions of higher education. In 1998 there were 43 hospitals.

The **Gaza Strip** (preferred Palestinian term, Gaza District) has an area of 370 sq. km; 1997 census population was 1,022,207. The population doubled between 1975 and 1995. The UN gives a projected population for 2010 of 1·44m. Crude birth rate in 1999 was 44·73 per 1,000 population. The death rate was estimated at 4·39 per 1,000 population. The fertility rate in 1997 was 6·91 births per woman. Infant mortality, 1995, 30·2 per 1,000 live births. Agricultural production, 1998 estimates, in 1,000 tonnes: oranges, 105; tomatoes, 48; potatoes, 35; cucumbers and gherkins, 18; grapefruit and pomelos, 10. In 1998–99 there were 299,545 students in basic stage education, 27,687 in secondary stage and 30,058 students in higher education. In 1998 there were 11 hospitals.

The chief town is Gaza itself. In 1984, over 98% of the population were Arabic-speaking Muslims. In 1995 an estimated 94·2% of the population lived in urban areas. Citrus fruits, wheat and olives are grown, with farm land covering 193 sq. km (1980) and occupying most of the active workforce. In 1993 there were 20,434 private cars and 4,518 commercial vehicles and trucks registered. Gaza International Airport, at the southern edge of the Gaza Strip, opened in Nov. 1998. Telecommunications development has been rapid, the number of fixed line telephone subscribers more than trebling between 1997 and 2000. In March 2000 there were 230,000 subscribers. In 1998 life expectancy at birth was 71·8 years.

CONSTITUTION AND GOVERNMENT

In April 1996 the Palestinian Council removed from its Charter all clauses contrary to its recognition by Israel, including references to armed struggle as the only means of liberating Palestine, and the elimination of Zionism from Palestine. The *President* is directly elected and heads the executive organ, the Palestinian National Authority, one fifth of whose members he appoints, while four fifths are elected by the *National Council*. The latter comprises 88 members and is directly elected by the first-past-the-post system from 16 electoral districts. The Palestinian Authority was created by agreement of the PLO and Israel as an interim instrument of self-rule for Palestinians living on the West Bank and Gaza Strip. The failure of the PLO and Israel to strike a permanent status agreement has resulted in the Authority retaining its powers. It is entitled to establish ministries and subordinate bodies, as required to fulfil its obligations and responsibilities. It possesses legislative and executive powers within the functional areas transferred to it in the 1995 Interim Agreement. Its territorial jurisdiction is restricted to Areas A and B in the West Bank and approximately two-thirds of the Gaza Strip.

Following an Israeli-Palestinian agreement on customs duties and VAT in Aug. 1994 the Palestinians set up their own customs and immigration points into Gaza and Jericho. Israel collects customs dues on Palestinian imports through Israeli entry points and transfers these to the Palestinian treasury.

A special committee is working on drafting a new Palestinian constitution. In March 2003 parliament approved the creation of the position of prime minister. Yasser Arafat nominated Mahmoud Abbas, the PLO Secretary General, to be the first premier.

There is a Palestinian *Council for Reconstruction and Development.*

RECENT ELECTIONS

Elections for *President* and *National Council* were held on 20 Jan. 1996. The electorate was 1,013,200; turn-out was 84%. 672 candidates stood for the Council. Yasser Arafat was elected *President* against 1 opponent by 88·1% of votes cast, and was sworn in on 12 Feb. 1996. In the *National Council* elections, 55 seats went to the Liberation Movement of Palestine, 15 to independents, 7 to Independent Fatah, 4 to Independent Islamists, 3 to Independent Christians, 1 to Samaritans and 1 other, with 2 vacant.

CURRENT ADMINISTRATION

President: Yasser Arafat.
  Prime Minister and Interior Minister: Mahmoud Abbas.
  Minister of External Affairs: Nabeel Shaath. *Finance:* Salam Fayyad.

Palestinian National Authority Website: http://www.pna.net/

ECONOMY

Currency. Israeli currency is in use.

Banking and Finance. Banking is regulated by the Palestinian Monetary Authority. Palestine's leading bank is Arab Bank. A securities exchange, the Palestine Securities Exchange, opened in Nablus in Feb. 1997.

COMMUNICATIONS

Telecommunications. In 1999 there were 270,000 main line telephones, or 84·6 per 1,000 inhabitants. In March 2001 there were 60,000 Internet users.

SOCIAL INSTITUTIONS

Justice. The Palestinian police consists of some 15,000; they are not empowered to arrest Israelis, but may detain them and hand them over to the Israeli authorities.

FURTHER READING

Kimmerling, B. and Migdal J. S., *Palestinians: the Making of a People.* Harvard Univ. Press, 1994

Robinson, G. E., *Building a Palestinian State: the Incomplete Revolution.* Indiana Univ. Press, 1997

Rubin, B., *Revolution until Victory? The Politics and History of the PLO.* Harvard Univ. Press, 1994

Segev, T., *One Palestine, Complete.* Metropolitan Books, New York, 2000

Stendel, O., *The Arabs in Israel.* Brighton, 1996

Tessler, M., *A History of the Israeli-Palestinian Conflict.* Indiana Univ. Press, 1994

Statistical office: Palestinian Central Bureau of Statistics. *Website:* http://www.pcbs.org/

ITALY

Repubblica Italiana

Capital: Rome
Population estimate, 2000: 57·68m.
GDP per capita, 2000: (PPP$) 23,626
HDI/world rank: 0·913/20

KEY HISTORICAL EVENTS

A part of the Roman Empire and the Holy Roman Empire that succeeded it, Italy was divided into several states including a number of city states such as Venice, Florence and Genoa. Much of the territory was under the rule of the Pope while France, Spain and Austria had possessions at various times. From 1815 a strong movement grew throughout the Italian states for *risorgimento* (unification) and for freedom from Austrian control. Victor Emmanuel II, King of Sardinia-Piedmont from 1849, his prime minister from 1852, Count Cavour, and Giuseppe Garibaldi, an Italian soldier, together achieved success for the movement. The first Italian parliament assembled in Feb. 1861, and on 17 March declared Victor Emmanuel King of Italy.

Fascism spread rapidly after 1918 and in 1922 Benito Mussolini, leader of the Fascist Party, was appointed prime minister. In 1924 he established himself as dictator with the title *Duce*. His internal policy, with a programme of public works, greater efficiency and better law and order, was successful. In 1929 the Lateran Treaties with the Papacy ended over a century of tension between Church and State. However, his aggressive foreign policy as evinced by the invasion of Ethiopia in 1935 and his alliance with Nazi Germany in 1936 was eventually to lead to his downfall. During the Second World War (1939–45) British forces captured much of Italy's colonial empire and in 1942 occupied Libya. The allies conquered Sicily and Mussolini was compelled to resign in July 1943. In 1945 he was captured and killed by Italian partisans. On 10 June 1946 Italy became a republic.

In the post war years the ruling Christian Democrat Party resisted the challenge of the Communists and pursued a strongly pro-West and European policy. But no single government was able to reform an ailing economy or face up to lawlessness and corruption. Changes of administration were frequent. From 1947 to the early 1990s, Italy had no fewer than 57 governments. In 1992, in the wake of Italy's humiliating exit from Europe's Exchange Rate Mechanism (ERM), the old political establishment was driven out of office. Several prominent politicians were accused of links to organized crime and some went to prison. A new era for Italian politics opened the way for a radical modernization of the country's economic and social structure.

TERRITORY AND POPULATION

Italy is bounded in the north by Switzerland and Austria, east by Slovenia and the Adriatic Sea, southeast by the Ionian Sea, south by the Mediterranean Sea, southwest by the Tyrrhenian Sea and Ligurian Sea and west by France.

The area is 301,338 sq. km. Populations at successive censuses were as follows:

10 Feb. 1901	33,778	15 Oct. 1961	50,624
10 June 1911	36,921	24 Oct. 1971	54,137
1 Dec. 1921	37,856	25 Oct. 1981	56,557
21 April 1931	41,043	20 Oct. 1991	56,778
21 April 1936	42,399	21 Oct. 2001	56,996
4 Nov. 1951	47,516		

Population estimate, 1 Jan. 2001, 57,844,017 (29,749,160 females). Density: 192 per sq. km.

The UN gives a projected population for 2010 of 56·39m.

In 1999, 66·9% of the population lived in urban areas.

The following table gives area and population of the Autonomous Regions (census 1991 and estimate 2000):

Regions	Area in sq. km (1996)	Resident pop. census, 1991	Resident pop. Dec. 2000	Density per sq. km
Piedmont	25,399	4,302,565	4,289,731	169
Valle d'Aosta[1]	3,263	115,938	120,589	37
Lombardy	23,861	8,856,074	9,121,714	382

946

Regions	Area in sq. km (1996)	Resident pop. census, 1991	Resident pop. Dec. 2000	Density per sq. km
Trentino-Alto Adige[1]	13,607	890,360	943,123	69
Bolzano-Bozen	7,400	440,508	465,264	63
Trento	6,207	449,852	477,859	77
Veneto	18,390	4,380,797	4,540,853	247
Friuli-Venezia Giulia[1]	7,855	1,197,666	1,188,594	151
Liguria	5,421	1,676,282	1,621,016	299
Emilia Romagna	22,124	3,909,512	4,008,663	181
Tuscany	22,997	3,529,946	3,547,604	152
Umbria	8,456	811,831	840,482	99
Marche	9,694	1,429,205	1,469,195	152
Lazio	17,207	5,140,371	5,302,302	308
Abruzzi	10,798	1,249,054	1,281,283	119
Molise	4,438	330,900	327,177	74
Campania	13,595	5,630,280	5,782,244	425
Puglia	19,362	4,031,885	4,086,608	211
Basilicata	9,992	610,528	604,807	61
Calabria	15,080	2,070,203	2,043,288	135
Sicily[1]	25,708	4,966,386	5,076,700	197
Sardinia[1]	24,090	1,648,248	1,648,044	70

[1]With special statute.

Communes of more than 100,000 inhabitants, with population resident at the census of 20 Oct. 1991 and on 31 Dec. 2000:

	1991	2000		1991	2000
Rome	2,775,250	2,655,970	Foggia	156,268	154,760
Milan	1,369,231	1,301,551	Salerno	148,932	141,724
Naples	1,067,365	1,000,470	Perugia	144,732	158,282
Turin	962,507	900,987	Ferrara	138,015	131,713
Palermo	698,556	679,290	Ravenna	135,844	139,771
Genoa	678,771	632,366	Reggio nell'Emilia	132,030	146,092
Bologna	404,376	379,964	Rimini	127,960	131,705
Florence	403,294	374,501	Syracuse	125,941	125,673
Bari	342,309	332,143	Sassari	122,339	120,874
Catania	333,075	336,222	Pescara	122,236	115,448
Venice	309,422	275,368	Monza	120,651	120,900
Verona	255,824	257,477	Bergamo	114,936	117,415
Taranto	232,334	207,199	Forli	109,541	107,827
Messina	231,693	257,302	Terni	108,248	107,739
Trieste	213,100	215,096	Vicenza	107,454	110,454
Padua	215,137	209,641	Latina	106,203	115,019
Cagliari	204,237	162,993	Piacenza	102,268	98,407
Brescia	194,502	194,697	Trento	101,545	105,942
Reggio di Calabria	177,580	179,509	La Spezia	101,442	95,091
Modena	176,990	176,965	Torre del Greco	101,361	92,994
Parma	170,520	170,031	Ancona	101,285	98,404
Livorno	167,512	161,288	Novara	101,112	102,243
Prato	165,707	174,513	Lecce	100,884	97,458

Rome: Built among seven hills, Rome is situated in the central area of Italy. Founded in 753 BC, according to legend Rome gets its name from the twins Romulus and Remus who were suckled by a she-wolf after being abandoned on the banks of the River Tiber. Known as the Eternal City, its wealth of ancient monuments and churches and its rich artistic heritage make it one of the most visited cities in Europe.

The official language is Italian, spoken by 94·1% of the population in 1991. There are 0·3m. German-speakers in Bolzano and 30,000 French-speakers in Valle d'Aosta.

In addition to Sicily and Sardinia, there are a number of other Italian islands, the largest being Elba (363 sq. km), and the most distant Lampedusa, which is 205 km from Sicily but only 113 km from Tunisia.

SOCIAL STATISTICS

Vital statistics (and rates per 1,000 population), 2000: births, 538,999 (9·3); deaths, 559,956 (9·7); marriages, 280,488 (4·9); natural increase, −20,957 (−0·4); infant deaths (up to one year of age), 2,820 (6 per 1,000 live births in 1999). Expectation of life, 1999: females, 81·6 years; males, 75·2. In 2000, 24% of the population was over 60, the highest percentage of any country in the world.

Annual population growth rate, 1990–99, 0·1%; fertility rate, 1999, 1·2 births per woman (one of the lowest rates in the world). With only 8% of births being to unmarried mothers, Italy has one of the lowest rates of births out of wedlock in Europe.

In 2000 there were 3,093 suicides; 75·1% were men.

In Jan. 2000 there were 1,270,553 legal immigrants living in Italy, plus an estimated 250,000 illegal immigrants. In 1998, 56,707 people emigrated from Italy and there were 165,696 immigrants into the country. Italy received 33,000 asylum applications in 1999, equivalent to 0·06 per 1,000 inhabitants. New legislation was introduced in 2002 to tighten up immigration rules.

CLIMATE

The climate varies considerably with latitude. In the south, it is warm temperate, with little rain in the summer months, but the north is cool temperate with rainfall more evenly distributed over the year. Florence, Jan. 47·7°F (8·7°C), July 79·5°F (26·4°C). Annual rainfall 33" (842 mm). Milan, Jan. 38·7°F (3·7°C), July 73·4°F (23·0°C). Annual rainfall 38" (984 mm). Naples, Jan. 50·2°F (10·1°C), July 77·4°F (25·2°C). Annual rainfall 36" (935 mm). Palermo, Jan. 52·5°F (11·4°C), July 78·4°F (25·8°C). Annual rainfall 35" (897 mm). Rome, Jan. 53·4°F (11·9°C), July 76·3°F (24·6°C). Annual rainfall 31" (793 mm). Venice, Jan. 43·3°F (6·3°C), July 70·9°F (21·6°C). Annual rainfall 32" (830 mm).

CONSTITUTION AND GOVERNMENT

The Constitution dates from 1948. Italy is 'a democratic republic founded on work'. Parliament consists of the *Chamber of Deputies* and the *Senate*. The Chamber is elected for five years by universal and direct suffrage and consists of 630 deputies. The Senate is elected for five years on a regional basis by electors over the age of 25, each Region having at least seven senators. The total number of senators is 315. The Valle d'Aosta is represented by one senator only, the Molise by two. The President of the Republic can nominate 11 senators for life from eminent persons in the social, scientific, artistic and literary spheres. The President may become a senator for life. The *President* is elected in a joint session of Chamber and Senate, to which are added three delegates from each Regional Council (one from the Valle d'Aosta). A two-thirds majority is required for the election, but after a third indecisive scrutiny the absolute majority of votes is sufficient. The President must be 50 years or over; term of office, seven years. The Speaker of the Senate acts as the deputy President. The President can dissolve the chambers of parliament, except during the last six months of the presidential term. An attempt to create a new constitution, which had been under consideration for 18 months, collapsed in June 1998.

A *Constitutional Court*, consisting of 15 judges who are appointed, five each by the President, Parliament (in joint session) and the highest law and administrative courts, can decide on the constitutionality of laws and decrees, define the powers of the State and Regions, judge conflicts between the State and Regions and between the Regions, and try the President and Ministers.

The revival of the Fascist Party is forbidden. Direct male descendants of King Victor Emmanuel are excluded from all public offices and have no right to vote or to be elected; their estates are forfeit to the State. For 56 years they were also banned from Italian territory until the constitution was changed in 2002 to allow them to return from exile. Titles of nobility are no longer recognized, but those existing before 28 Oct. 1922 are retained as part of the name.

A referendum was held in June 1991 to decide whether the system of preferential voting by indicating four candidates by their listed number should be changed to a simpler system, less open to abuse, of indicating a single candidate by name. The electorate was 46m. Turn-out was 62·5% (there was a 50% quorum). 95·6% of votes cast were in favour of the change. As a result, an electoral reform of 1993 provides for the replacement of proportional representation by a system in which 475 seats in the Chamber of Deputies are elected by a first-past-the-post single-round vote and 155 seats by proportional representation in a separate single-round vote on the same day. There are 27 electoral regions. There is a 4% threshold for entry to the Chamber of Deputies.

At a further referendum in April 1993, turn-out was 77%. Voters favoured the eight reforms proposed, including a new system of election to the Senate and the abolition of some ministries. 75% of the Senate is now elected by a first-past-the-post system, the remainder by proportional representation; no party may present more than one candidate in each constituency. In July 1997 an all-party parliamentary commission on constitutional reform proposed a directly elected president with responsibility for defence and foreign policy, the devolving of powers to the regions, a reduction in the number of seats in the Senate and in the lower house and the creation of a third chamber to speak on behalf of the regions.

National Anthem. 'Fratelli d'Italia' ('Brothers of Italy'); words by G. Mameli, tune by M. Novaro, 1847.

RECENT ELECTIONS
Parliamentary elections were held on 13 May 2001. The turn-out was 81·2%. The House of Freedoms Alliance (comprised of Forza Italia, the National Alliance and the Northern League) won 368 seats in the Chamber of Deputies and 177 in the Senate, the Olive Tree Alliance (comprised of the Democrats of the Left, the Daisy coalition and the Sunflower coalition) 242 and 125, the Refounded Communists 11 and 3. Minor parties won nine seats in the Chamber of Deputies and ten in the Senate. Forza Italia—the leading party of the House of Freedoms Alliance—received the highest percentage of votes of any of the parties contesting the election, with 30%.

European Parliament. Italy has 87 representatives. At the June 1999 elections turn-out was 70·6%. Forza Italia gained 22 seats with 25·2% of votes cast (group in European Parliament: European People's Party); the Party of the Democrats of the Left (former Communists), 15 with 17·4% (Party of European Socialists); the National Alliance, 9 with 10·3% (Union for Europe); L. Bonina (Radicals), 7 with 8·5% (Non-attached); I. Demo (Prodi Party), 7 with 7·7% (European Liberal, Democrat and Reform Party); the Northern League, 4 with 4·5% (non-affiliated); the Italian People's Party (former Christian Democrats), 4 with 4·3% (European People's Party); the Reformed Communists, 4 with 4·3% (Confederal Group of the European United Left). In addition 10 parties gained either 1 or 2 seats.

CURRENT ADMINISTRATION
President: Carlo Azeglio Ciampi; b. 1920 (sworn in on 18 May 1999).

In March 2003 the government comprised (FI = Forza Italia; AN = National Alliance; LN = The Northern League; CCD CDU = Christian Democratic Centre and United Christian Democrats):

Prime Minister: Silvio Berlusconi; b. 1936 (FI; sworn in on 11 June 2001 having previously held office from 11 May 1994–17 Jan. 1995).

Deputy Prime Minister: Gianfranco Fini (AN). *Defence:* Antonio Martino (FI). *European Affairs:* Rocco Buttiglione (CCD CDU). *Foreign Affairs:* Franco Frattini (FI). *Finance and Economic Affairs:* Giulio Tremonti (FI). *Interior:* Giuseppe Pisanu (FI). *Agriculture:* Giovanni Alemanno (AN). *Environment:* Altero Matteoli (AN). *Health:* Gerolamo Sirchia (ind.). *Justice:* Roberto Castelli (LN). *Labour and Social Affairs:* Roberto Maroni (LN). *Communications:* Maurizio Gasparri (AN). *Public Administration and Security:* Luigi Mazzella (ind.). *Industry and Commerce:* Antonio Marzano (FI). *Transport:* Pietro Lunardi (ind.). *Equal Opportunities:* Stefania Prestigiacomo (FI). *Regional Affairs:* Enrico La Loggia (FI). *Education, University and Scientific Research:* Letizia Moratti (ind.). *Relations with Parliament:* Carlo Giovanardi (CCD CDU). *Culture:* Giuliano Urbani (FI). *Innovation and Technology:* Lucio Stanca (ind.). *Institutional Reform and Devolution:* Umberto Bossi (LN). *Italians Abroad:* Mirko Tremaglia (AN).

Government Website: http://www.governo.it

DEFENCE
Head of the armed forces is the Defence Chief of Staff. There is conscription for ten months, but the military draft is to be phased out by 2006. In Aug. 1998 the government voted to allow women into the armed forces.

In 2001 defence expenditure totalled US$20,966m. (US$365 per capita), representing 2·0% of GDP.

Army. Strength (2002) 128,600 (57,000 conscripts). Equipment includes 440 *Leopard,* 378 *Centauro* and 200 *Ariete* tanks. First line Army reserves number 11,900 with a further 500,000 personnel available for mobilization.

The paramilitary Carabinieri number 111,800. In addition there were 79,000 public security guards run by the Ministry of the Interior and 63,500 Finance Guards run by the Treasury.

Navy. The principal ships of the Navy are the light aircraft carrier *Giuseppe Garibaldi* and the helicopter-carrying cruiser *Vittorio Veneto*. The combatant forces also include 6 diesel submarines, 4 destroyers and 14 frigates. The Naval Air Arm, 2,500 strong, operates 18 combat aircraft and 79 armed helicopters. In addition there is a Special Forces commando of some 600 assault swimmers.

Main naval bases are at La Spezia, Brindisi, Taranto and Augusta. The personnel of the Navy in 2002 numbered 38,000 (5,000 conscripts), including the naval air arm and the marine battalion. There were 23,000 naval reservists.

Air Force. Control is exercised through two regional headquarters near Taranto and Milan.

Air Force strength in 2002 was about 50,800 (8,200 conscripts). There were 261 combat aircraft in operation in 2000 including Tornados and F-104 Starfighters. There were 30,300 Air Force reservists in 2002.

INTERNATIONAL RELATIONS

Italy is a member of the UN, WTO, NATO, BIS, OECD, EU, Council of Europe, WEU, OSCE, CERN, CEI, Inter-American Development Bank, Asian Development Bank, IOM and the Antarctic Treaty. Italy is a signatory to the Schengen Accord of June 1990 which abolishes border controls between Italy, Austria, Belgium, Denmark, Finland, France, Germany, Greece, Iceland, Luxembourg, the Netherlands, Norway, Portugal, Spain and Sweden.

Italy has played an important role in bringing Iran back into the international community, with President Mohammad Khatami visiting Rome in March 1999, in the process becoming the first Iranian leader to visit the west since the 1979 revolution. Foreign minister Lamberto Dini was also quick to re-establish relations with Col. Qadhafi of Libya following the transfer of the Lockerbie suspects for trial in the Netherlands.

ECONOMY

Services account for 68·9% of GDP, industry 28·4% and agriculture 2·8% in 2000.

Overview. The centre-left governments led by Romano Prodi, Massimo D'Alema and Giuliano Amato lowered national debt from 120% of GDP to 110% and the budget deficit from 6·5% of GDP in 1996 to 1·5% in 2000. However, there are still uncertainties about the state of public finances and progress is needed to meet targets agreed under the Stability and Growth Pact. In 2000 Italy's largest state holding company, Istituto per Ricostruzione Industriale (IRI), was liquidated. Major privatizations include the 26,000bn. lire flotation of Telecom Italia in 1997, ENI (energy company) and Banca di Roma.

Currency. On 1 Jan. 1999 the euro (EUR) became the legal currency in Italy; irrevocable conversion rate 1,936·27 lire to 1 euro. The euro, which consists of 100 cents, has been in circulation since 1 Jan. 2002. There are seven euro notes in different colours and sizes denominated in 500, 200, 100, 50, 20, 10 and 5 euros, and eight coins denominated in 2 and 1 euros, then 50, 20, 10, 5, 2 and 1 cents. On the introduction of the euro there was a 'dual circulation' period before the lira ceased to be legal tender on 28 Feb. 2002. Italy is the only country to use euri as the plural of euro—all the other countries have decided to use euros as the plural. Euro banknotes in circulation on 1 Jan. 2002 had a total value of €97·4bn.

Inflation was 1·7% in 1999, 2·6% in 2000 and 2·7% in 2001. In June 2002 gold reserves were 78·83m. troy oz (66·67m. troy oz in 1997) and foreign exchange reserves US$20,533m. (US$45,307m. in Dec. 1999). Total money supply in June 2002 was €54,958m.

Budget. Total revenue and expenditure for calendar years, in 1,000bn. lire:

	Revenue	Expenditure		Revenue	Expenditure
1994	664,920	818,824	1997	879,382	941,079
1995	736,061	860,181	1998	840,722	905,614
1996	801,855	927,504	1999	867,788	899,709

Budgets for 1998 (and 1997) in 1,000,000m. lire: revenue, 581,188 (591,161) of which tax 546,188 (554,194); expenditure, 673,182 (690,737) of which capital expenditure 68,598 (67,070) and interest payments 181,121 (193,002).

The 1998 budget provided for an increase in value-added tax. Some reforms due to take place in 1998 were meant to reallocate the existing tax burden in a more business-friendly way. The rate of corporation tax was to come down from 53·2% to 37%. Other measures include reducing social security contributions, and a new two-tier income tax, brought in to encourage entrepreneurs to reinvest in profits and issue equity. Accompanying the tax reform was the devolution of substantial taxing powers from the central government to the regions. The budget deficit in both 1997 and 1998 was 2·7% of GDP.

The current account balance in 1998 was US$20·4bn.

VAT is 20% (reduced rate, 10%).

The public debt at 31 Dec. 2000 totalled 2,221,000bn. of lire. Between 1992 and 2000 the public deficit came down from more than 10% to 1%, or possibly less, of gross domestic product. Interest rates have also declined significantly.

Performance. Total GDP was US$1,091bn. in 2001. There was real GDP growth of 2·9% in 2000, followed by 1·8% in 2001.

Banking and Finance. The bank of issue is the Bank of Italy (founded 1893). It is owned by public-sector banks. Its *Governor* (Antonio Fazio) is selected without fixed term by the 13 directors of the Bank's non-executive board. In 1991 it received increased responsibility for the supervision of banking and stock exchange affairs, and in 1993 greater independence from the government. Its gold reserve amounted to 40,929bn. lire in Dec. 1998; the foreign credit reserves of the Exchange Bureau (*Ufficio Italiano Cambi*) amounted to 88,611bn. lire.

The number of banks has gradually been declining in recent years, from 1,176 in 1990 to 862 in 2000. Of the 921 banks in 1998, 562 were co-operative banks. Italy's largest bank is Banca Intesa, following its merger with Banca Commerciale Italiana in 1999. In June 2000 it had assets of 643,000bn. lire. Other major banks are San Paolo-IMI and UniCredito Italiano.

The 'Amato' law of July 1990 gave public sector banks the right to become joint stock companies and permitted the placing of up to 49% of their equity with private shareholders.

On 31 Dec. 2000 the post office savings banks had deposits of 270,011bn. lire. In the same year credit institutions had deposits of 1,005,484bn. lire.

Legislation reforming stock markets came into effect in Dec. 1990. In 1996 local stock exchanges, relics of pre-unification Italy, were closed, and stock exchange activities concentrated in Milan.

Weights and Measures. The metric system is in use. 1 quintal = 100 kg.

ENERGY AND NATURAL RESOURCES

Environment. According to the *World Bank Atlas* Italy's carbon dioxide emissions in 1998 were the equivalent of 7·2 tonnes per capita.

Electricity. Installed capacity was 64m. kW in 1997 and the total power generated in 1999 was 252·7bn. kWh (20% hydro-electric). Consumption in 1999 was 267,284m. kWh, of which 60,717m. kWh was for domestic use. Consumption per capita was 4,407 kWh in 1997. Italy has four nuclear reactors in permanent shutdown, the last having closed in 1990.

Oil and Gas. Oil production, 2000, 4,499,420 tonnes. Proven oil reserves in 1999 were 0·6bn. bbls. In 2000 natural gas production was 16·4bn. cu. metres with proven reserves of 230bn. cu. metres.

Minerals. Fuel and mineral resources fail to meet needs. Only sulphur and mercury yield a substantial surplus for exports.

Production of metals and minerals (in tonnes) was as follows:

	1996	1997	1998	1999	2000
Sulphur	3,528,120	3,594,549	3,413,522	3,338,162	3,339,761
Feldspar	2,287,086	2,118,117	2,503,541	2,493,846	2,851,289
Bentonite	471,535	511,760	580,209	562,674	636,589
Lead	20,260	17,630	10,102	9,734	5,961
Zinc	20,137	15,416	5,242	—	—

Agriculture. In 2000, 1,120,000 persons were employed in agriculture, of whom 451,000 were dependent (148,000 female); independently employed were 669,000 (203,000 female). In 1999 there were 18,645 sq. km of agricultural and forest lands, distributed as follows (in 1,000 ha): forage and pasture, 3,727; woods, 3,648; cereals, 4,166; olive trees, 1,156; vines, 837; leguminous plants, 68.

At the 1991 census agricultural holdings numbered 3,023,344 and covered 22,702,356 ha. 2,893,145 owners (95·7%) farmed directly 15,961,093 ha (70·3%); 118,020 owners (3·9%) worked with hired labour on 6,603,522 ha (29·1%); 95,045 share-croppers (3·1%) tilled 1,208,337 ha (5·3%); the remaining 12,179 holdings (0·4%) of 137,740 ha (0·6%) were operated in other ways. By 1999 agricultural and forest lands covered 20,163,776 ha, of which 14,996,531 sq. km was in active agricultural use. There were 2,269,574 farms in 1999. Agriculture accounted for 7·1% of exports and 15·3% of imports in 1998. Figures compiled by the Soil Association, a British organization, show that in 1999 Italy set aside 900,000 ha (5·3% of its agricultural land) for the growth of organic crops.

In 1998, 1,475,000 tractors were in use.

The production of the principal crops (in 1,000 tonnes) in 2000: sugarbeets, 12,788; maize, 10,128; grapes, 8,870; tomatoes, 7,538; wheat, 7,465; olives, 2,819; apples, 2,232; potatoes, 2,050; oranges, 1,700; peaches and nectarines, 1,655; barley, 1,262; rice, 1,186; soybeans, 904; pears, 890; lemons, 615. Italy's annual grape crop is the highest in the world.

Wine production in 2000 totalled 5,390,000 tonnes. Italy and France are by far the largest wine producers in the world. Italy was the leading producer in 1998, but France produced more in 1999. Wine consumption in Italy has declined dramatically in recent times, from more than 110 litres per person in 1966 to 56·6 litres per person in 1999.

Livestock, 2000: cattle, 7,184,000; sheep, 10,970,000; pigs, 8,403,000; goats, 1,364,000; horses, 280,000; buffaloes, 173,000; chickens, 100m.; turkeys, 23m. Livestock products, 2000 (in 1,000 tonnes): cow milk, 11,741; sheep milk, 850; buffalo milk, 158; goat milk, 140; pork, bacon and ham, 1,475; beef and veal, 1,160; poultry meat, 1,140; cheese, 1,011; eggs, 768. Italy is the second largest producer of sheep milk, after China.

Forestry. In 1999 forests covered 6·85m. ha or 22·5% of the total land area. Timber production was 9·91m. cu. metres in 1999.

Fisheries. The fishing fleet comprised, in 1994, 15,798 motor boats of 245,637 gross tonnes. The catch in 1999 was 294,155 tonnes, of which more than 98% were from marine waters.

INDUSTRY

The leading companies by market capitalization in Italy, excluding banking and finance, in Jan. 2002 were: Telecom Italia SpA (€65bn.); Ente Nazionale Idrocarburi (ENI), an integrated oil company (€60bn.); and Telecom Italia Mobile, TIM SpA (€44bn.).

The main branches of industry are (% of industrial value added at factor cost in 1998): metal products except machines and means of transport (13·2%), food, beverages and tobacco (12·0%), machines and mechanical apparatus (10·5%), textiles and clothing (9·3%), electric plants and equipment (7·8%), chemicals and synthetic fibres (7·4%), means of transport (6·9%), energy distribution (5·6%), paper and paper products, printing and publishing (5·6%), mineral and non-metallic mineral products (4·4%), rubber and plastic products (3·7%), leather products (3·2%), oil refining and coke manufacture (2·5%), timber and wooden furniture (2·2%).

Production, 2000: motor vehicles, 1,739,000 units; artificial and synthetic fibres (including staple fibre and waste), 658,436 tonnes; cement, 38,302,256 tonnes; polyethylene resins, 1,230,059 tonnes; crude steel, 26,623,000 tonnes (1999).

Labour. In 2000 the workforce was 23,575,000 (9,080,000 females) of whom 21,080,000 were employed. 2,495,000 (1,316,000 females) were unemployed and looking for work. In Oct. 2002 the unemployment rate was 8·9%, its lowest level for eight years. In 2000, 62·6% of the workforce were in services, 32·1% in industry and 5·3% in agriculture. There are strong indications of labour markets having become less rigid, especially in the north. In the north unemployment was 4·7%; in the centre 8·3%; in the south it was 21%. In 1996 the difference in the unemployment rates in the north and in the south was 12%, compared to a difference of just 2% in the 1960s. Over 60% of Italy's jobless have been out of work for more than a year. Pensionable retirement age was 60 for men and 55 for women in 1991, but this is being progressively raised to 65 for both sexes. In 1998 the rate of employment among people aged 55–64 was just 27%.

In 1997 parliament approved the so-called 'Treu Package', which involves a large number of institutional changes regarding working hours and apprenticeships, mainly for young people from the south, and the introduction of employment agencies. As a consequence, the share of temporary workers over total employees had grown from 6·2% in 1993 to 8·6% in 1998.

Trade Unions. There are three main groups: the Confederazione Generale Italiana del Lavoro (CGIL; formerly Communist-dominated), the Confederazione Italiana Sindacati Lavoratori (CISL; Catholic), and the Unione Italiana del Lavoro (UIL). Membership: CGIL (1996), 5·2m. (2·9m. retired); CISL (1999), 4·0m. (2·0m. retired); UIL (1996), 1·6m. (0·4m. retired). In referendums held in June 1995 the electorate voted to remove some restrictions on trade union representation, end government involvement in public sector trade unions and end the automatic deduction of trade union dues from wage packets.

INTERNATIONAL TRADE
Foreign debt in Dec. 1996 was 68,013bn. lire.

Imports and Exports. The territory covered by foreign trade statistics includes Italy and the Municipality of Livigno; Campione; San Marino and the Vatican City are excluded.

The following table shows the value of Italy's foreign trade (in 1,000m. lire):

	1996	1997	1998	1999	2000
Imports	321,286	357,787	378,783	400,837	495,499
Exports	388,885	409,182	426,183	427,994	498,201

Percentage of trade with EU countries in 1999: imports, 60·6%; exports, 57·2%. Principal import suppliers, 1999 (% of total trade): Germany, 19·2%; France, 12·6%; UK, 6·1%; USA, 5·0%. Principal export markets: Germany, 16·7%; France, 13·0%; USA, 9·5%; UK, 7·1%.

Imports/exports by category, 2000 (% volume):

	Imports	Exports
Chemicals and artificial fibres	12·9	9·3
Electric and precision instruments	14·8	10·1
Food, beverages and tobacco	6·6	5·0
Leather and leather products	2·1	5·1
Machinery and mechanical equipment	7·8	19·5
Metals and metal products	10·2	8·1
Minerals	11·6	0·2
Textiles and clothing	4·9	10·3
Transport equipment	13·6	11·6
Other products	15·5	20·8

COMMUNICATIONS
Roads. Roads totalled 654,676 km in 1997, of which 6,957 km were motorway, 46,043 km were highways and main roads, 113,924 km were secondary roads and 487,752 km other roads. In 2000 there were 40,743,777 motor vehicles, made up of: passenger cars, 32,583,815 (563 per 1,000 inhabitants); buses and coaches, 87,956; vans and trucks, 3,377,573. There were 6,676 fatalities in traffic accidents in 1996; 6,712 in 1997; 6,314 in 1998; 6,633 in 1999; 6,410 in 2000.

Rail. Total length of railways (1995), 19,485 km. The length of state-run railway (*Ferrovie dello Stato*) was 15,955 km (10,202 km electrified). In 1999 the state railways carried 431,503,000 passengers and 82,193,000 tonnes of freight. There are metros in Milan (68 km) and Rome (33·5 km), and tram/light rail networks in Genoa (2·3 km), Milan (240 km), Naples (23 km), Trieste and Turin (119 km).

Civil Aviation. There are major international airports at Bologna (G. Marconi), Genoa (Cristoforo Colombo), Milan (Linate and Malpensa), Naples (Capodichino),

Pisa (Galileo Galilei), Rome (Leonardo da Vinci/Fiumicino), Turin (Caselle) and Venice (Marco Polo). A number of other airports have a small selection of international flights. The national carrier, Alitalia, is 89·3% owned by the state. In 1997 it flew 297·2m. km and carried 24,551,600 passengers. There are a number of other Italian airlines, most notably Meridiana, which flew 24·4m. km and carried 2,935,400 passengers in 1998. The busiest airport for passenger traffic is Rome (Fiumicino), which in 2000 handled 25,879,000 passengers (13,440,000 on international flights) and 201,400 tonnes of freight. Milan Malpensa was the second busiest for passengers, handling 20,532,000 (15,090,000 on international flights), but the busiest for freight, with 300,200 tonnes. Linate, which handled 5,986,000 passengers in 2000 (4,149,000 on domestic flights), had been the principal Milan airport and for many years Italy's second busiest for passenger traffic, but in 1998 a new terminal was opened at Malpensa with many foreign operators subsequently using it instead of Linate.

Shipping. The mercantile marine in 1998 totalled 6·82m. GRT, including oil tankers 1,547,000 GRT. In 1995, 234,115,000 tonnes of cargo were unloaded, and 48,254,000 were loaded. 2,039,697 passengers embarked and 2,185,645 departed in 1995.

Telecommunications. There were 27,153,000 main telephone lines in 2000, or 473·9 per 1,000 persons. In May 1999 Olivetti bought a controlling stake in the telephone operator Telecom Italia, and in July 2001 Pirelli, backed by the Benetton clothing empire, in turn paid 7bn. euros (US$6·1bn.) to take over control of Telecom Italia. In Nov. 2001 mobile phone subscribers numbered 47·09m. TIM (Telecom Italia Mobile) had 21·24m. subscribers, making it Europe's third largest mobile phone operator. Italy's second largest mobile phone operator is Vodafone Omnitel, with 16·3m. subscribers in Nov. 2001. There were 10·3m. PCs in use (179·8 per 1,000 persons) in 2000 and 1·8m. fax machines in 1997. There were still 23,000 telex subscribers in 1995, although telex usage has declined considerably in recent years. There were 19·25m. Internet users in Aug. 2001.

Postal Services. In 1995 there were 14,142 post offices, or one for every 4,050 persons.

SOCIAL INSTITUTIONS

Justice. Italy has one court of cassation, in Rome, and is divided for the administration of justice into 29 appeal court districts, subdivided into 164 tribunal *circondari* (districts). There are also 93 first degree assize courts and 29 assize courts of appeal. For civil business, besides the magistracy above mentioned, *Giudici di pace* have jurisdiction in petty plaints.

3,384,156 crimes were reported in 1999; 524,551 persons were indicted. On 31 Dec. 2000 there were 54,039 persons in prison (2,316 females). The death penalty was abolished for all crimes in 1994.

Religion. The treaty between the Holy See and Italy of 11 Feb. 1929, confirmed by article 7 of the Constitution of the republic, lays down that the Catholic Apostolic Roman Religion is the only religion of the State. Other creeds are permitted, provided they do not profess principles, or follow rites, contrary to public order or moral behaviour.

The appointment of archbishops and of bishops is made by the Holy See; but the Holy See submits to the Italian government the name of the person to be appointed in order to obtain an assurance that the latter will not raise objections of a political nature. In Feb. 2002 there were 37 Cardinals.

Catholic religious teaching is given in elementary and intermediate schools. Marriages celebrated before a Catholic priest are automatically transferred to the civil register. Marriages celebrated by clergy of other denominations must be made valid before a registrar.

There were 47,000,000 Roman Catholics in 1997, 700,000 Muslims and 9,800,000 other (mostly non-religious and atheist).

Education. Five years of primary and three years of secondary education are compulsory from the age of six. In 1999–2000 there were 25,208 pre-school institutions with 1,582,527 pupils (state and non-state schools); 19,068 primary schools with 2,821,085 pupils (state and non-state schools); 8,496 compulsory secondary schools (*scuole medie*) with 1,774,720 pupils (state and non-state schools); and 7,166 higher secondary schools with 2,552,148 pupils (state and non-state schools). Numbers of teachers, 1999–2000: pre-primary institutions, 125,745; primary schools, 283,512; compulsory secondary schools, 205,921; higher secondary schools, 296,664.

Higher secondary education is subdivided into classical (*ginnasio* and classical *liceo*), scientific (scientific *liceo*), language lyceum, professional institutes and technical education: agricultural, industrial, commercial, technical, nautical institutes, institutes for surveyors, institutes for girls (five-year course) and teacher-training institutes (four-year course).

In 1995–96 there were 47 universities, 2 universities of Italian studies for foreigners and 3 specialized universities (commerce; education; Roman Catholic), 3 polytechnical university institutes and 7 other specialized university institutes (architecture; bio-medicine; modern languages; naval studies; oriental studies; social studies; teacher training). In 1999–2000 there were 1,570,230 university students and 62,027 academic staff.

Adult literacy rate, 1999, 98·4% (male 98·8%; female 98·0%).

In 1998–99 total expenditure on education came to 5·0% of GNP.

Health. The provision of health services is a regional responsibility, but they are funded by central government. Medical consultations are free, but a portion of prescription costs are payable. In 1998 there were 846 public hospitals with 247,041 beds and 643 private hospitals with 68,807 beds. In 1998 there were 98,828 doctors in public hospitals and 257,993 auxiliary medical personnel. A survey published by the World Health Organization in June 2000 to measure health systems in all of the sovereign countries and find which country has the best overall health care ranked Italy in second place, behind France.

Italy has the second highest AIDS rate in the EU, after Spain, with 92·6 cases per 100,000 population.

Welfare. Social expenditure is made up of transfers which the central public departments, local departments and social security departments make to families. Payment is principally for pensions, family allowances and health services. Expenditure on subsidies, public assistance to various classes of people and people injured by political events or national disasters are also included.

In 2000 Italians received a state pension at 56 or after 35 years of work, whichever comes first. However, this is gradually being scaled up, to 62 years of age or 37 years in work by 2006. Public pensions are indexed to prices; 21,628,910 pensions were paid in 2000 (18,425,350 private sector, 3,203,580 public sector). Current social security expenditure in 1999 was 359,683,000m. lire, of which 338,499,000m. lire were paid out in benefits. Social contributions totalled 264,359,000m. lire. In 1997 pension expenditure, which was 15% of GDP, was one of the highest in Europe.

CULTURE

Genoa, along with Lille in France, will be one of the European Capitals of Culture for 2004. The title attracts large European Union grants.

Broadcasting. Broadcasting is regulated by the Public Radio-Television Administration Council.

Questions have been raised over the impartiality of state-owned *Radiotelevisione Italiana* (RAI) but all attempts at privatization have been rejected. RAI, the public television company, broadcasts three public channels, RAI 1, RAI 2 and RAI 3. Mediaset, a private company controlled by Fininvest, produces three commercial channels: Canale 5, Italia 1 and Rete 4. RAI 1 has the highest viewing figures, followed by Canale 5, RAI 2 and Italia 1. There are 15 national and about 820 local private TV networks. There were 50·5m. radio receivers and 30·3m. TV sets (colour by PAL) in 1997. In 2000, 16,018,423 television licences were bought.

Cinema. In 1998 there were 4,509 screens and 115,243,003 admissions. In 1998 gross box office receipts came to 1,114bn. lire and 95 full-length films were made.

Press. There were (1998) 126 dailies and 543 weeklies. The combined annual circulation of the dailies (including unsold copies) is 2,206,249,000, and of the weeklies 821,064,000. Several of the papers are owned or supported by political parties. The church and various economic groups exert strong right of centre influence on editorial opinion. Most newspapers are regional but *La Repubblica*, *Corriere della Sera*, *La Stampa* and *Il Giorno* are the most important of those papers that are nationally circulated. In 1999 a total of 35,685 book titles were published in 267m. copies.

Tourism. In 1999, 36,097,000 foreigners visited Italy bringing in receipts of US$28·36bn.

Festivals. One of the most traditional festivals in Italy is the Carnival di Ivrea which lasts for a week in late Feb. or early March. Among the famous arts festivals is the Venice Film Festival in Sept. Venice also plays host, in the ten days before Ash Wednesday, to a large carnival. Major music festivals are the Maggio Musicale Fiorentino in Florence (May–June), the Ravenna Festival (June–July), the Spoleto Festival (June–July), the Rossini Opera Festival at Pesaro (Aug.) and the Verona Summer Opera Festival (July–Sept.).

Libraries. In 1997 there were 2,155 public libraries, 4 National libraries and 1,924 Higher Education libraries; they held a combined 93,629,000 volumes. There were 274,425,000 visits to the public libraries in 1997.

Museums and Galleries. In 2000 there were 30,175,000 visitors to museums, up from 27,296,000 in 1999.

DIPLOMATIC REPRESENTATIVES

Of Italy in the United Kingdom (14 Three Kings Yard, Davies Street, London, W1Y 2EH)
Ambassador: Luigi Amaduzzi, GCVO.

Of the United Kingdom in Italy (Via XX Settembre 80A, 00187, Rome)
Ambassador: Sir John Shepherd, KCVO, CMG.

Of Italy in the USA (3000 Whitehaven Street, NW, Washington, D.C., 20008)
Ambassador: Ferdinando Salleo.

Of the USA in Italy (Via Veneto 119/A, Rome)
Ambassador: Melvin F. Sembler.

Of Italy to the United Nations
Ambassador: Sergio Vento.

FURTHER READING

Istituto Nazionale di Statistica. *Annuario Statistico Italiano.—Compendio Statistico Italiano* (Annual).—*Italian Statistical Abstract* (Annual).—*Bollettino Mensile di Statistica* (Monthly).

Absalom, R., *Italy since 1880: a Nation in the Balance?* Harlow, 1995
Baldassarri, M. (ed.) *The Italian Economy: Heaven or Hell?* London, 1993
Bufacchi, Vittorio and Burgess, Simon, *Italy since 1989.* Macmillan, London, 1999
Burnett, Stanton H. and Mantovani, Luca, *The Italian Guillotine: Operation 'Clean Hands' and the Overthrow of Italy's First Republic.* Rowman and Littlefield, Oxford, 1999
Di Scala, S. M., *Italy from Revolution to Republic: 1700 to the Present.* Boulder (CO), 1995
Duggan, Christopher, *A Concise History of Italy.* CUP, 1994
Frei, M., *Italy: the Unfinished Revolution.* London, 1996
Furlong, P., *Modern Italy: Representation and Reform.* London, 1994
Gilbert, M., *Italian Revolution: the Ignominious End of Politics, Italian Style.* Boulder (CO), 1995
Ginsborg, Paul, *Italy and its Discontents, 1980–2001.* Penguin, London, 2002
Gundie, S. and Parker, S. (eds.) *The New Italian Republic: from the Fall of the Berlin Wall to Berlusconi.* London, 1995
McCarthy, P., *The Crisis of the Italian State: from the Origins of the Cold War to the Fall of Berlusconi.* London, 1996
OECD, *OECD Economic Surveys 1998–99: Italy.* Paris, 1998
Putnam, R., *et al.*, *Making Democracy Work: Civic Traditions in Modern Italy.* Princeton Univ. Press, 1993
Richards, C., *The New Italians.* London, 1994
Smith, D. M., *Modern Italy: A Political History.* Yale Univ. Press, 1997

Sponza, L. and Zancani, D., *Italy.* [Bibliography] ABC-Clio, Oxford and Santa Barbara (CA), 1995

Turner, Barry, (ed.) *Italy Profiled.* Macmillan, London, 1999

Volcanasek, Mary L., *Constitutional Politics in Italy.* Macmillan, London, 1999

National statistical office: Istituto Nazionale di Statistica (ISTAT), 16 Via Cesare Balbo, 00184 Rome.

Website: http://www.istat.it

National library: Biblioteca Nazionale Centrale, Vittorio Emanuele II, Viale Castro Pretorio, Rome.

JAMAICA

Capital: Kingston
Population estimate, 2000: 2·58m.
GDP per capita, 2000: (PPP$) 3,639
HDI/world rank: 0·742/86

KEY HISTORICAL EVENTS
Jamaica was discovered by Columbus in 1494 and was occupied by the Spaniards from 1509 until 1655 when the island was captured by the English. In 1661 a representative constitution was established consisting of a governor, privy council, legislative council and legislative assembly. The slavery introduced by the Spanish was augmented as sugar production increased in value and extent in the 18th century. The plantation economy collapsed with the abolition of the slave trade in the late 1830s. The 1866 Crown Colony government was introduced with a legislative council. In 1884 a partially elective legislative council was instituted. Women were enfranchised in 1919. By the late 1930s, demands for self-government increased and the constitution of Nov. 1944 stated that the governor was to be assisted by a freely-elected house of representatives of 32 members, a legislative council (the upper house) of 15 members, and an executive council. In 1958 Jamaica joined with Trinidad, Barbados, the Leeward Islands and the Windward Islands to create the West Indies Federation; but Jamaica withdrew in 1961. In 1959 internal self-government was achieved and in 1962 Jamaica became an independent state within the British Commonwealth.

TERRITORY AND POPULATION
Jamaica is an island which lies in the Caribbean Sea about 150 km south of Cuba. The area is 4,411 sq. miles (11,425 sq. km). The population at the census of 7 April 1991 was 2,374,193. Estimated population in 1995 was 2,500,025, distributed on the basis of the 13 parishes of the island as follows: Kingston and St Andrew, 683,700; St Thomas, 88,600; Portland, 78,300; St Mary, 111,200; St Ann, 155,800; Trelawny, 72,100; St James, 167,100; Hanover, 67,600; Westmoreland, 133,800; St Elizabeth, 148,200; Manchester, 173,500; St Catherine, 398,600; Clarendon, 221,500. 1995 density; 219 per sq. km.

The UN gives a projected population for 2010 of 2·82m.

Chief towns: Kingston, 655,000 (in 1999), metropolitan area; (1995 figures) Spanish Town, 110,400; Portmore, 93,800; Montego Bay, 82,000; May Pen, 45,900; Mandeville, 39,900.

In 1999, 55·6% of the population were urban. The population is about 75% of African ethnic origin.

SOCIAL STATISTICS
Vital statistics (1999): births, 56,911 (22·0 per 1,000 population); deaths, 17,353 (6·7); marriages, 26,671 (10·3); divorces (1998), 1,420 (0·6). There were 17,669 emigrants in 1995, mainly to the USA. Expectation of life at birth, 1999, 73·1 years for males and 77·1 years for females. Annual population growth rate, 1990–99, 0·9%; infant mortality, 1999, 10 per 1,000 live births; fertility rate, 1999, 2·4 births per woman.

CLIMATE
A tropical climate but with considerable variation. High temperatures on the coast are usually mitigated by sea breezes, while upland areas enjoy cooler and less humid conditions. Rainfall is plentiful over most of Jamaica, being heaviest in May and from Aug. to Nov. The island lies in the hurricane zone. Kingston, Jan. 76°F (24·4°C), July 81°F (27·2°C). Annual rainfall 32" (800 mm).

CONSTITUTION AND GOVERNMENT
Under the Constitution of Aug. 1962 the Crown is represented by a Governor-General appointed by the Crown on the advice of the Prime Minister. The Governor-General

is assisted by a Privy Council of six appointed members. The Legislature comprises the *House of Representatives* and the *Senate*. The Senate consists of 21 senators appointed by the Governor-General, 13 on the advice of the Prime Minister, 8 on the advice of the Leader of the Opposition. The House of Representatives (60 members) is elected by universal adult suffrage for a period not exceeding five years. Electors and elected must be Jamaican or Commonwealth citizens resident in Jamaica for at least 12 months before registration. It is likely that Jamaica will become a republic in the early part of the 21st century, with Queen Elizabeth II being replaced as head of state by a ceremonial president.

National Anthem. 'Eternal Father, bless our land'; words by H. Sherlock, tune by R. Lightbourne.

RECENT ELECTIONS
In parliamentary elections held on 16 Oct. 2002 Prime Minister Percival J. Patterson's People's National Party (PNP) won a fourth consecutive term with 34 seats (down from 50 in 1997) and 52·2% of votes cast, while the Jamaica Labour Party (JLP) took 26 (up from 10 in 1997), with 47·2% of the vote. Turn-out was 56·3%.

CURRENT ADMINISTRATION
Governor-General: Sir Howard Felix Cooke.
　In March 2003 the cabinet comprised:
　Prime Minister and Minister of Defence: Percival J. Patterson, QC; b. 1935 (PNP; elected on 30 March 1992 and re-elected 1997 and 2002).
　Minister of Agriculture: Roger Clarke. *Commerce, Science and Technology:* Phillip Paulwell. *Development:* Paul Robertson. *Education, Youth and Culture:* Maxine Henry-Wilson. *Finance and Planning:* Omar Davies. *Foreign Affairs and Foreign Trade:* Keith Desmond Knight. *Health:* John Junor. *Industry and Tourism:* Aloun N'dombet Assamba. *Information:* Burchell Whiteman. *Justice and Attorney General:* A. J. Nicholson. *Labour and Social Security:* Horace Dalley. *Land and the Environment:* Dean Peart. *Local Government, Community Development and Sport:* Portia Simpson-Miller. *National Security:* Peter Phillips. *Transportation and Works:* Robert Pickersgill. *Water and Housing:* Donald Buchanan.

Cabinet Website: http://www.cabinet.gov.jm/

DEFENCE
In 2000 defence expenditure totalled US$49m. (US$19 per capita), representing 0·7% of GDP.

Army. The Jamaica Defence Force consists of a Regular and a Reserve Force. Total strength (army, 1999), 2,500. Reserves, 950.

Navy. The Coast Guard, numbering 190 in 1999, operates seven inshore patrol craft based at Port Royal.

Air Force. The Air Wing of the Jamaica Defence Force was formed in July 1963 and has since been expanded and trained successively by the British Army Air Corps and Canadian Air Force personnel. There are no combat aircraft. Personnel (1999), 140.

INTERNATIONAL RELATIONS
Jamaica is a member of the UN, WTO, the Commonwealth, OAS, Inter-American Development Bank, ACS, CARICOM and is an ACP member state of the ACP-EU relationship.

ECONOMY
Agriculture accounted for 8% of GDP in 1998, industry 33·7% and services 58·3%.

Currency. The unit of currency is the *Jamaican dollar* (JMD) of 100 *cents*. The Jamaican dollar was floated in Sept. 1990. Inflation in 2001 was 5·0%. Foreign exchange reserves were US$1,839m. in June 2002 and total money supply was J$52,360m.

JAMAICA

Budget. Revenue and expenditure for fiscal years ending 31 March (in J$1m.):

	1997	1998	1999	2000	2001[1]
Revenue	77,505	83,067	93,352	109,510	126,823
Expenditure	106,916	101,270	112,448	122,389	148,316

[1]Estimate.

The chief items of current revenue are income tax; consumption, customs and stamp duties. The other major share of current resources is generated by the Bauxite Production Levy. The chief items of current expenditure are public debt, education and health.

Performance. Jamaica has been experiencing major economic difficulties in recent years, with negative growth in 1996, 1997, 1998 and 1999. The economy then recovered slightly, with growth of 1·1% in 2000, rising to 3·0% in 2001. Total GDP in 2001 was US$7·8bn.

Banking and Finance. The central bank and bank of issue is the Bank of Jamaica. The *Governor* is Derick Milton Latibeaudiere, OJ.

In 1997 there were nine commercial banks with 208 branches and agencies in operation. Five of these banks are subsidiaries of major British and North American banks, of which four are incorporated locally. Total assets of commercial banks in 1995 were J$121,324·9m.; deposits were J$89,135·4m.

There is a stock exchange in Kingston, which participates in the regional Caribbean exchange.

ENERGY AND NATURAL RESOURCES

Environment. In 1998 carbon dioxide emissions were the equivalent of 4·3 tonnes per capita according to the *World Bank Atlas*.

Electricity. The Jamaica Public Service Co. is the public supplier. Total installed capacity, 1995, 624·9 MW. Production in 1998 was 6·39bn. kWh; consumption per capita was 2,252 kWh.

Oil and Gas. There is an oil refinery in Kingston.

Minerals. Jamaica is the third largest producer of bauxite, behind Australia and Guinea. Ceramic clays, marble, silica sand and gypsum are also commercially viable. Production in 1996 (in tonnes): bauxite ore, 10·8m. (12·1m. in 1997); gypsum, 208,017; marble, 2,800; sand and gravel, 1·8m.; industrial lime, 3·4m.

Agriculture. 2000 production (in 1,000 tonnes): sugarcane, 2,600; yams, 196; bananas, 130; coconuts, 115; oranges, 72; grapefruit and pomelos, 42; pumpkins and squash, 42; plantains, 34.

Livestock (2000): cattle, 400,000; goats, 440,000; pigs, 180,000; poultry, 11m. Livestock products, 2000 (in 1,000 tonnes): beef and veal, 15; pork, bacon and ham, 7; poultry meat, 73.

Forestry. Forests covered 175,000 ha in 1995 or 16·2% of the total land area (down from 254,000 ha and 23·5% in 1990). Jamaica's annual deforestation rate in the years from 1990–95 was 7·2%, the second highest in the world over the same period behind Lebanon. Timber production was 343,000 cu. metres in 1999.

Fisheries. Catches in 1999 totalled 8,508 tonnes, of which 95% were sea fish.

INDUSTRY

Alumina production, 1995, 3m. tonnes. Output of other products, 1995 (in tonnes): cement (1997), 591,000; sugar (1998), 183,000; flour, 146,000; molasses, 95,900; fertilizer, 57,500; condensed milk, 15,800; cornmeal, 13,400; edible oils, 6m. litres; petrol, 852·8m. litres; glass bottles, 20,588; cigarettes, 989·8m. units. In 1995 manufacturing contributed J$28,775m. to the total GDP at current prices.

Labour. Average total labour force (1995), 1·15m., of whom 963,300 were employed. 551,400 were employed in services (including 201,400 in trade and catering, 51,600 in business), 223,200 in agriculture, forestry and fisheries, 104,700 in manufacturing, 76,000 in building and 7,000 in mining.

INTERNATIONAL TRADE

Foreign debt was US$4,287m. in 2000.

Imports and Exports. Value of imports and domestic exports for calendar years (in US$1m.):

	1996	1997	1998	1999	2000
Imports f.o.b.	2,715·2	2,832·6	2,743·9	2,685·6	2,908·1
Exports f.o.b.	1,721·0	1,700·3	1,613·4	1,499·1	1,554·6

Principal imports in 1995 (in US$1m.): consumer goods, 686 (24·7%), of which food including beverages, 197 (7·1%); raw materials, 1,548 (55·8%); capital goods, 539 (19·4%), of which machinery and equipment, 284 (10·3%) and construction materials, 144 (5·2%).

Principal domestic exports in 1995 (in US$1m.): traditional exports 916 (64%), of which alumina 632 (44·2%), sugar 96 (6·7%), bauxite 72 (5·0%), bananas 48 (3·4%) and gypsum 1 (0·1%); non-traditional exports 464 (32·5%), of which food 77 (5·4%), chemicals 36 (2·5%), beverages and tobacco 22 (1·5%), manufactured goods 16 (1·1%), mineral fuels, lubricants and related materials 7 (0·5%), crude materials 7 (0·5%), machinery and transport equipment 4 (0·3%) and miscellaneous manufactures 294 (20·5%).

Main import suppliers, 1996: USA, 52·3%; Trinidad and Tobago, 8·3%; Japan, 5·6%; UK, 4·0%. Main export markets, 1996: USA, 37·1%; UK, 13·2%; Canada, 11·8%; Netherlands, 8·9%.

COMMUNICATIONS

Roads. In 1996 the island had 19,000 km of roads (13,400 km surfaced). In 1996 there were 104,000 passenger cars and 22,000 lorries and vans. There were 7,379 traffic accidents in 1995 with 367 fatalities.

Civil Aviation. International airlines operate through the Norman Manley and Sangster airports at Palisadoes and Montego Bay. In 2000 Sangster International was the busiest for passenger traffic, handling 2,739,000 passengers and 6,400 tonnes of freight. Norman Manley airport is busier for freight, handling 20,680 tonnes of freight but only 1,415,862 passengers. Air Jamaica, originally set up in conjunction with BOAC and BWIA in 1966, became a new company, Air Jamaica (1968) Ltd. In 1969 it began operations as Jamaica's national airline. In 1999 scheduled airline traffic of Jamaica-based carriers flew 35·1m. km and carried 1,670,000 passengers.

Shipping. In 1998 the merchant marine totalled 4,000 GRT, including oil tankers 2,000 GRT. In 1995 there were 3,275 visits to all ports; 13·9m. tonnes of cargo were handled. Kingston had 2,120 visits and handled 4·4m. tonnes. In 1997 vessels totalling 12,815,000 NRT entered ports and vessels totalling 6,457,000 NRT cleared.

Telecommunications. In 2000 there were 511,700 main telephone lines (198·6 per 1,000 population). Mobile phone subscribers numbered 144,400 in 2000 and there were 120,000 PCs in use (46·6 for every 1,000 persons). In 1995 there were 600 fax machines and in Dec. 1999 there were 60,000 Internet users.

Postal Services. In 1995 there were 316 post offices and 477 postal agencies.

SOCIAL INSTITUTIONS

Justice. The Judicature comprises a Supreme Court, a court of appeal, resident magistrates' courts, petty sessional courts, coroners' courts, a traffic court and a family court which was instituted in 1975. The Chief Justice is head of the judiciary. Jamaica was one of ten countries to sign an agreement in Feb. 2001 establishing a Caribbean Court of Justice to replace the British Privy Council as the highest civil and criminal court. The Court of Justice is expected to sit for the first time in the second half of 2003.

In 1995, 54,595 crimes were reported, of which 33,889 were cleared up. The daily average prison population, 1995, was 3,289. In 2001 there were 1,138 murders. The rate of 43·6 per 100,000 persons is more than seven times that of the USA.

The population in penal institutions in Jan. 1998 was 3,629 (145 per 100,000 of national population).

Police. The Constabulary Force in 1995 stood at approximately 5,861 officers, sub-officers and constables (men and women).

Religion. Freedom of worship is guaranteed under the Constitution. The main Christian denominations are Anglican, Baptist, Roman Catholic, Methodist, Church of God, United Church of Jamaica and Grand Cayman (Presbyterian-Congregational-Disciples of Christ), Moravian, Seventh-Day Adventist, Pentecostal, Salvation Army and Quaker. Pocomania is a mixture of Christianity and African survivals. Non-Christians include Hindus, Jews, Muslims, Bahai followers and Rastafarians.

Education. Adult literacy was 86·4% in 1999 (90·3% among females but only 82·4% among males).

Education is free in government-operated schools. Schools and colleges in 1994–95 (government-operated and grant-aided): basic, 1,694; infant, 29; primary, 792; primary with infant department, 83; all-age, 430; primary and junior high, 20; new secondary, 47; secondary high, 56; comprehensive high, 23; technical high, 12; agricultural/vocational, 6; special, 11; (independent): kindergarten/preparatory, 126; secondary high with preparatory department, 28; high/vocational, 5; business education, 29; (tertiary): teacher-training, 13.

Numbers of pupils and students, 1994–95: basic schools, 116,390; infant, 9,710; infant departments in primary schools, 6,737; primary, 172,510; all-age and primary and junior high (grades one to six), 132,728; all-age and primary and junior high (grades seven to nine), 54,371; new secondary, 30,797; secondary high, 70,613; technical high, 14,199; comprehensive high, 45,332; agricultural/vocational, 1,699. Numbers of teachers, 1994–95: infant schools, 299; primary, 5,399; all-age and primary and junior high (grades 1 to 9), 6,424; new secondary, 1,852; secondary high, 4,132; technical high, 831; comprehensive high, 2,393; agricultural/vocational, 119.

The University of the West Indies is at Kingston. In 1994–95 it had 12,630 students, 800 external students and about 900 academic staff. The University of Technology in Kingston had 6,374 students, and the College of Agriculture, Science and Education in Portland, 533 students.

In 1996 expenditure on education came to 7·5% of GNP and 12·9% of total government spending.

Health. In 1995 the public health service had 4,058 staff in medicine, nursing and pharmacology; 326 in dentistry; 260 public health inspectors; 70 in nutrition. In 1995 there were 371 primary health centres, 5,021 public hospital beds and 305 private beds.

CULTURE

Broadcasting. There were (1995) seven commercial and one publicly owned broadcasting stations; the latter also operates a television service (colour by NTSC), and there was one commercial television station. In 1997 there were 1·2m. radio and 460,000 TV sets.

Cinema. In 1993 there were 35 cinemas and two drive-in cinemas.

Press. In 1996 there were three daily newspapers with a combined circulation of 158,000, at a rate of 63 per 1,000 inhabitants.

Tourism. In 1999 there were 1,248,000 foreign tourists and (in 1998) 674,000 cruise ship arrivals. Tourism receipts in 1999 totalled US$1,233m.

DIPLOMATIC REPRESENTATIVES

Of Jamaica in the United Kingdom (1–2 Prince Consort Rd., London, SW7 2BZ)
High Commissioner: David Muirhead.

Of the United Kingdom in Jamaica (Trafalgar Rd., Kingston 10)
High Commissioner: Peter Mathers, LVO.

Of Jamaica in the USA (1520 New Hampshire Ave., NW, Washington, D.C., 20036)
Ambassador: Seymour Edwards Mullings.

Of the USA in Jamaica (2 Oxford Rd., Kingston 5)
Ambassador: Sue McCourt Cobb.

Of Jamaica to the United Nations
Ambassador: Stafford O. Neil.

Of Jamaica to the European Union
Ambassador: Douglas A. C. Saunders.

FURTHER READING

Planning Institute of Jamaica. *Economic and Social Survey, Jamaica.* Annual.—*Survey of Living Conditions.* Annual
Statistical Institute of Jamaica. *Statistical Abstract.* Annual.—*Demographic Statistics.* Annual.—*Production Statistics.* Annual

Boyd, D., *Economic Management, Income Distribution, and Poverty in Jamaica.* Praeger Publishers, Westport (CT), 1988
Hart, R., *Towards Decolonisation: Political, Labour and Economic Developments in Jamaica 1938–1945.* Univ. of the West Indies Press, Kingston, 1999
Henke, H. W. and Mills, D., *Between Self-Determination and Dependency: Jamaica's Foreign Relations 1972–1989.* Univ. of the West Indies Press, Kingston, 2000
Ingram, K. E., *Jamaica.* [Bibliography] 2nd ed. ABC-Clio, Oxford and Santa Barbara (CA), 1997

National library: National Library of Jamaica, Kingston.
National statistical office: Statistical Institute of Jamaica (STATIN), POB 643, Kingston 5. *Director General,* Sonia Jackson.
Website: http://www.statinja.com

JAPAN

Nihon (or Nippon[1]) Koku
(Land of the Rising Sun)

Capital: Tokyo
Population estimate, 2000: 126·92m
GDP per capita, 2000: (PPP$) 26,775
HDI/world rank: 0·933/9

KEY HISTORICAL EVENTS

The present imperial family are the direct descendants of the house of Yamato which united the nation in about AD 200. From 1186 until 1867 successive families of the military Shoguns exercised temporal power. For centuries Japan followed a policy of national isolation. The 16th century marked the beginning of foreign trade but in the 17th century all exchange with Europeans and all trade, except with the Dutch, was proscribed. Not until 1859 was the country opened to foreign trade and residence. In 1867 the Emperor Meiji recovered the imperial power after the abdication on 14 Oct. 1867 of the fifteenth and last Tokugawa Shogun Keiko. In 1871 the feudal system (*Hôken Seido*) was abolished and in the early 1890s constitutional government was introduced by the Emperor. Japan's victory over Russia in the war of 1904 prevented Russian expansion into Korea and consolidated Japan's position as the strongest military power in Asia. Japan used the pretext of the Anglo-Japanese alliance to attack Chinese territory during the First World War. Bad feelings over the terms of the subsequent peace treaty led to continuing hostility between the two countries.

Economic distress, population growth (from 30m. in 1868 to 65m. in 1930) and a sense of dissatisfaction with the 'unjapanese' system of constitutional government led to the emergence between the wars of extremist nationalist and militarist movements. Plots among the young army officers, a revolt in Manchuria and the assassination of two prime ministers highlighted the weaknesses of central government. In 1936 a military revolt in Tokyo gave the premiership to Konoe Fumimaro, a popular but ineffective figure, who failed to prevent further militarization of the country. In 1938 a national mobilization law was passed and in 1940 all political parties merged into the Imperial Rule Assistance Association. On 27 Sept. 1940 Germany, Italy and Japan signed a ten-year pact to assure their mutual co-operation in the establishment of a 'new world order', with Japanese leadership recognized in Asia. In 1940 Japan invaded North Indochina and on 7 Dec. 1941 attacked the United States (principally at Pearl Harbour) and British bases in the Pacific, and then declared war on these two countries. Japanese forces eventually surrendered in Aug. 1945 after the dropping of atomic bombs on Hiroshima and Nagasaki. The country was placed under US military occupation and in a new constitution in 1947 the Japanese people renounced the war and pledged themselves to uphold democracy and peace. The Emperor became a constitutional monarch instead of a divine ruler.

At San Francisco on 8 Sept. 1951 a Treaty of Peace was signed by Japan and representatives of 48 countries. A security treaty with the USA provided for the stationing of American troops in Japan until the latter was able to undertake its own defence. The peace treaty came into force on 28 April 1952, when Japan regained her sovereignty. Confidence in what had become a world-beating economy fell drastically after 1997 causing the government to cut taxes, provide financial support for small companies and begin the reform of the heavily indebted banking system.

TERRITORY AND POPULATION

Japan consists of four major islands, Honshu, Hokkaido, Kyushu and Shikoku, and many small islands, with an area of 377,802 sq. km. Census population (1 Oct. 2000) 126,925,843 (males 62,110,764, females 64,815,079); density, 336 per sq. km.

The UN gives a projected population for 2010 of 128·2m.

[1]Both forms are valid, and derive from different pronunciations of a Chinese character.

In 1999, 78·6% of the population lived in urban areas. Foreigners registered on 31 Dec. 2001 were 1,778,642 of whom 632,405 were Koreans, 381,225 were Chinese, 265,962 were Brazilians, 156,667 were Filipinos, 50,052 were Peruvians, 46,244 were Americans, 31,685 were Thais, 20,831 were Indonesians, 19,140 were Vietnamese, 17,527 were British, 11,719 were Indians, 11,032 were Canadians, 10,550 were Australians, 9,150 were Malaysians and 1,941 were stateless persons. In 2001 Japan accepted 26 asylum seekers.

Japanese overseas, Oct. 2001, 833,744; of these 312,936 lived in the USA, 73,492 in Brazil, 53,357 in China (24,356 in Hong Kong), 51,896 in the UK, 41,309 in Australia, 34,446 in Canada, 26,402 in Germany, 23,174 in Singapore, 22,731 in Thailand and 21,785 in France.

The official language is Japanese.

A law of May 1997 'on the promotion of Ainu culture' marked the first official recognition of the existence of an ethnic minority in Japan.

The areas, populations and chief cities of the principal islands (and regions) are:

Island/Region	Sq. km	Pop. census 2000	Chief cities
Hokkaido	83,452	5,683,000	Sapporo
Honshu/Tohoku	66,888	9,817,000	Sendai
Honshu/Kanto	32,422	40,429,000	Tokyo
Honshu/Chubu	66,787	21,627,000	Nagoya
Honshu/Kinki	33,107	22,713,000	Osaka
Honshu/Chugoku	31,913	7,732,000	Hiroshima
Shikoku	18,801	4,154,000	Matsuyama
Kyushu	42,163	13,446,000	Fukuoka
Okinawa	2,269	1,318,000	Naha

The leading cities, with population at the 2000 census (in 1,000), are:

Akashi	293	Kashiwa	328	Okayama	627
Akita	318	Kasugai	288	Okazaki	337
Amagasaki	466	Kawagoe	331	Omiya	456
Aomori	298	Kawaguchi	460	Osaka	2,599
Asahikawa	360	Kawasaki	1,250	Otsu	288
Chiba	887	Kitakyushu	1,011	Sagamihara	606
Fujisawa	379	Kobe	1,494	Sakai	792
Fukui	252	Kochi	331	Sapporo	1,822
Fukuoka	1,341	Koriyama	335	Sendai	1,008
Fukushima	291	Koshigaya	308	Shimonoseki	252
Fukuyama	379	Kumamoto	662	Shizuoka	470
Funabashi	550	Kurashiki	430	Suita	348
Gifu	403	Kyoto	1,468	Takamatsu	333
Hachioji	536	Machida	378	Takatsuki	357
Hakodate	288	Maebashi	284	Tokorozawa	330
Hamamatsu	582	Matsudo	465	Tokushima	268
Higashiosaka	515	Matsuyama	473	Tokyo	8,134
Himeji	478	Miyazaki	306	Toyama	326
Hirakata	403	Morioka	289	Toyohashi	365
Hiroshima	1,126	Nagano	360	Toyonaka	392
Ibaraki	261	Nagasaki	423	Toyota	351
Ichihara	278	Nagoya	2,171	Urawa	485
Ichinomiya	274	Naha	301	Utsunomiya	444
Ichikawa	449	Nara	366	Wakayama	387
Iwaki	360	Neyagawa	251	Yao	275
Kagoshima	552	Niigata	501	Yokkaichi	291
Kakogawa	266	Nishinomiya	438	Yokohama	3,427
Kanazawa	456	Oita	436	Yokosuka	429

The Tokyo conurbation, with a population in 1999 of 26·36m., is the largest in the world, having overtaken New York around 1970. It is projected to relinquish its status to Mumbai (Bombay) in around 2015.

Tokyo: Situated in Tokyo Bay in east central Honshu on the Pacific coast, Tokyo is the largest city in Japan and its capital. It was founded in the 12th century as Edo and its name was changed to Tokyo in 1868. It is the administrative, financial and cultural centre of Japan. Tokyo State covers an area of 2,166 sq. km. The Tokyo Tower, offering views of the city, was modelled on the Eiffel Tower in Paris and was completed in 1958.

SOCIAL STATISTICS

Statistics (in 1,000) for calendar years:

	1995	1996	1997	1998	1999	2000	2001
Births	1,221	1,203	1,209	1,215	1,197	1,194	1,185
Deaths	924	896	921	933	985	968	966

Crude birth rate of Japanese nationals in present area, 2000, was 9·5 per 1,000 population (1947: 34·3); crude death rate, 7·7; marriage rate per 1,000 persons, 6·4 (2000); divorce rate per 1,000 persons (2000), 2·1. In 2000 the most popular age for marrying was 30·4 for males and 28·2 for females. The infant mortality rate per 1,000 live births, 3·2 in 2000, is one of the lowest in the world. Expectation of life was 77·7 years for men and 84·6 years for women in 2000. A World Health Organization report published in June 2000 put the Japanese in first place in a 'healthy life expectancy' list, with an expected 74·5 years of healthy life for babies born in 1999. Japan has over 13,000 centenarians. Japan has a very fast ageing population, stemming from a sharply declined fertility rate and one of the highest life expectancies in the world. Annual population growth rate, 1990–99, 0·3%.

In 2000 the average number of children a Japanese woman bears in her life reached a record low of 1·36.

There were 31,042 suicides in 2001 (down from a record 33,048 in 1999), of which 22,144 were men and 8,898 women.

CLIMATE

The islands of Japan lie in the temperate zone, northeast of the main monsoon region of South-East Asia. The climate is temperate with warm, humid summers and relatively mild winters except in the island of Hokkaido and northern parts of Honshu facing the Japan Sea. There is a month's rainy season in June–July, but the best seasons are spring and autumn, although Sept. may bring typhoons. There is a summer rainfall maximum. Tokyo, Jan. 5·2°C, July 25·2°C. Annual rainfall 1,405 mm. Hiroshima, Jan. 4°C, July 25·7°C. Annual rainfall 1,555 mm. Nagasaki, Jan. 6·4°C, July 26·6°C. Annual rainfall 1,945 mm. Osaka, Jan. 5·5°C, July 27°C. Annual rainfall 1,318 mm. Sapporo, Jan. –4·6°C, July 20·2°C. Annual rainfall 1,130 mm.

CONSTITUTION AND GOVERNMENT

The Emperor is Akihito (b. 23 Dec. 1933), who succeeded his father, Hirohito on 7 Jan. 1989 (enthroned, 12 Nov. 1990); married 10 April 1959, to Michiko Shoda (b. 20 Oct. 1934). *Offspring:* Crown Prince Naruhito (Hironomiya; b. 23 Feb. 1960); Prince Fumihito (Akishinomiya; b. 30 Nov. 1965); Princess Sayako (Norinomiya; b. 18 April 1969). Prince Naruhito married Masako Owada (b. 9 Dec. 1963) 9 June 1993. *Offspring:* Princess Aiko (b. 1 Dec. 2001). The succession to the throne is fixed upon the male descendants. The 1947 constitution supersedes the Meiji constitution of 1889. In it the Japanese people pledge themselves to uphold the ideas of democracy and peace. The Emperor is the symbol of the States and of the unity of the people. Sovereign power rests with the people. The Emperor has no powers related to government. Fundamental human rights are guaranteed.

Legislative power rests with the *Diet*, which consists of the *House of Deputies*, elected by men and women over 20 years of age for a four-year term, and an upper house, the *House of Councillors* of 252 members (100 elected by party list system with proportional representation according to the d'Hondt method and 152 from prefectural districts), one-half of its members being elected every three years.

The number of members in the House of Deputies was reduced from 500 to 480 for the election of June 2000, of whom 300 were to be elected from single-seat constituencies, and 180 by proportional representation on a base of 11 regions. There is a 2% threshold to gain one of the latter seats. Donations to individual politicians are to be supplanted over five years by state subsidies to parties.

A new electoral law passed in Oct. 2000 gives voters a choice between individual candidates and parties when casting ballots for the proportional representation seats in the *House of Councillors*. The bill also reduced the number of upper house seats by ten, from 252 to 242, the first time that the number of seats in the upper chamber had been reduced. In the upper house elections, which were held in July 2001, 121 seats were contested instead of 126, comprising 48 seats under proportional representation and 73 under the constituency system. The number of seats elected under the proportional representation system was reduced from 100 to 96.

On becoming prime minister in April 2001 Junichiro Koizumi established a panel to consider introducing the direct election of prime ministers by popular vote.

National Anthem. 'Kimigayo' ('The Reign of Our Emperor'); words 9th century, tune by Hiromori Hayashi. On 9 Aug. 1999 a law on the national flag and the national anthem was enacted. The law designates the Hinomaru and 'Kimigayo' as the national flag and national anthem of Japan. The 'Kimi' in 'Kimigayo' indicates the Emperor who is the symbol of the State and of the unity of the people, deriving his position from the will of the people with whom resides sovereign power; 'Kimigayo' depicts the state of being of the country as a whole.

RECENT ELECTIONS
Elections to the House of Deputies (lower house) were held on 25 June 2000. Turn-out was 62·5%. The Liberal Democratic Party (LDP) gained 233 seats; Democratic Party, 127; Clean Government Party (Komeito), 31; Liberal Party (LP), 22; Communist Party of Japan, 20; Social Democratic Party (SDP), 19; Conservative Party, 7; Independents' Party, 5; Liberal League, 1. Non-partisans took 15 seats. By May 2002 the LDP had gained eight seats, giving them 241, while the Democratic Party had lost two, giving them 125. The ruling LDP relies on its support primarily from rural areas, with only a tenth of urban voters actively supporting it. Fewer than 4% of seats in the House of Deputies are held by women, compared to nearly 15% in the world as a whole.

Elections to 121 seats of the House of Councillors (upper house) were held on 29 July 2001; turn-out was 56·4%. The Liberal Democratic Party gained 64 seats, Democratic Party 26, Komeito 13, Social Democratic Party 6, Communist Party of Japan 5, Liberal Party 3, Conservative Party 1, and independents 3.

CURRENT ADMINISTRATION
On 6 Jan. 2001 administrative organs were reorganized from one Office and 22 Ministries into one Cabinet Office and 12 Ministries.

Following the election of June 2000 a coalition was formed between the LDP, Komeito and the Conservative Party, but Prime Minister Yoshiro Mori resigned on 24 April 2001 in the wake of a series of scandals.

In March 2003 the government comprised:

Prime Minister: Junichiro Koizumi; b. 1942 (LDP; appointed 26 April 2001).

Minister of Justice: Mayumi Moriyama. *Foreign Affairs:* Yoriko Kawaguchi. *Finance:* Masajuro Shiokawa. *Education, Culture, Sports, Science and Technology:* Atsuko Toyama. *Health, Labour and Welfare:* Chikara Sakaguchi. *Agriculture, Forestry and Fisheries:* Yoshiyuki Kamei. *Economy, Trade and Industry:* Takeo Hiranuma. *Land, Infrastructure and Transport:* Chikage Ogi. *Public Management, Home Affairs, Post and Telecommunications:* Toranosuke Katayama. *Environment:* Shunichi Suzuki. *Director General, Defence Agency:* Shigeru Ishiba. *Chief Cabinet Secretary and Minister of State for Gender Affairs:* Yasuo Fukuda. *Chairman of the National Public Safety Commission:* Sadakazu Tanigaki. *Minister of State for Okinawa and Northern Territories Affairs, Science and Technology, and Information Technology:* Hiroyuki Hosoda. *Minister of State for Financial Services and Economic and Fiscal Policy:* Heizou Takenaka. *Minister of State for Administrative Reform and Regulatory Reform:* Nobuteru Ishihara. *Minister of State for Disaster Management and Special Zones for Structural Reform:* Yoshitada Kounoike.

Office of the Prime Minister: http://www.kantei.go.jp

DEFENCE
Japan has renounced war as a sovereign right and the threat or the use of force as a means of settling disputes with other nations. Its troops had not previously been able to serve abroad, but in 1992 the House of Representatives voted to allow up to 2,000 troops to take part in UN peacekeeping missions. A law of Nov. 1994 authorizes the Self-Defence Force to send aircraft abroad in rescue operations where Japanese citizens are involved. Following the terror attacks on New York and Washington of 11 Sept. 2001, legislation was passed allowing Japan's armed forces to take part in operations in the form of logistical support assisting the US-led war

on terror. The legislation permits troops to take part in limited overseas operations but not to engage in combat.

In Jan. 1991 Japan and the USA signed a renewal agreement under which Japan pays 40% of the costs of stationing US forces and 100% of the associated labour costs. US forces in Japan totalled 38,450 in 2002, nearly half of them on Okinawa. A US-Japanese agreement of Dec. 1996 stipulates that one fifth of the territory on Okinawa occupied by the US military is to be returned to local landowners by 2008.

Total armed forces in 2002 numbered 239,900, including 10,400 women.

Defence expenditure in 2001 totalled US$39,513m. (US$310 per capita), representing 1·0% of GDP.

Army. The 'Ground Self-Defence Force' is organized in five regional commands and in 2002 had a strength of 148,200 and a reserve of 47,000. The USA maintains an army force of 1,800.

Navy. The 'Maritime Self-Defence Force' is tasked with coastal protection and defence of the sea lanes to 1,000 nautical miles range from Japan. Personnel in 2002 numbered 44,400 including the Naval Air Arm.

The combatant fleet, all home-built, includes 16 diesel submarines, 44 destroyers and 10 frigates.

The Air Arm operated 80 combat aircraft and 91 armed helicopters in 2002. Air Arm personnel was estimated at 9,800 in 2002.

The main elements of the fleet are organized into four escort flotillas based at Yokosuka, Kure, Sasebo and Maizuru. The submarines are based at Yokosuka and Kure.

Air Force. An 'Air Self-Defence Force' was inaugurated on 1 July 1954. Its equipment includes (2002) F-15 *Eagles,* F-4E *Phantoms* and Mitsubishi F-1 fighters.

Strength (2002) 45,600 operating 280 combat aircraft.

INTERNATIONAL RELATIONS

In terms of total aid given, Japan was the second most generous country in the world in 2001 after the USA, donating US$9·7bn. in international aid in the course of the year. This represented 0·2% of its GNI.

Japan is a member of the UN, BIS, OECD, Inter-American Development Bank, Asian Development Bank, Colombo Plan, APEC, IOM and the Antarctic Treaty.

ECONOMY

In 1997 agriculture accounted for 1·7% of GDP, industry 37·2% and services 61·1%.

According to the anti-corruption organization *Transparency International*, Japan ranked equal 20th in the world in a 2002 survey of the countries with the least corruption in business and government. It received 7·1 out of 10 in the annual index.

Overview. Japan is experiencing its third recession within a decade caused by a failure to address structural problems which have worsened since the attacks on the USA of 11 Sept. 2001. Owing to deficit spending, Japan's budget is the largest in the industrialized world. From 1992 to 2000, 120trn. yen was spent on fiscal packages. The economy is suffering from spiralling deflation. The economy consists of two tiers, large multinational companies and small enterprises. The government is prioritizing structural reforms and budgetary discipline and has announced tax cuts. In 2000 the Bank of Japan adopted an inflation guideline which will be kept until the inflation rate is stable at around zero or increasing.

Currency. The unit of currency is the *yen* (JPY). Inflation in 1997 was 1·7% slowing to 0·6% in 1998. There was then deflation of 0·3% in 1999, 0·8% in 2000 and 0·7% in 2001. Japan's foreign exchange reserves totalled US$428,850m. in June 2002 (US$172,443m. in 1995)—the highest in the world. Gold reserves in June 2002 were 24·60m. troy oz. In Dec. 2001 the currency in circulation consisted of 69,004,000m. yen Bank of Japan notes and 4,223,000m. yen subsidiary coins.

Budget. Ordinary revenue and expenditure for fiscal year ending 31 March 2003 balanced at 81,230,000m. yen.

Of the proposed revenue (in yen) in 2002, 46,816,000m. was to come from taxes and stamps, 30,000,000m. from public bonds. Main items of expenditure: social security, 18,279,500m.; local government, 16,080,000m.; public works, 8,423,900m.; education, 6,699,800m.; defence, 4,956,000m.

The outstanding national debt incurred by public bonds was estimated in March 2001 to be 380,655,000m. yen.

The estimated 2002 budgets of the prefectures and other local authorities forecast a total revenue of 87,567,000m. yen, to be made up partly by local taxes and partly by government grants and local loans.

Performance. The real GDP growth rate for 2002 was 0·9%. In the first quarter of 2002 the economy expanded for the first time since the first quarter of 2001. Yet, for all the financial blues, Japan remains one of the world's strongest economies with a highly trained workforce and the talent to exploit profitable export markets. In 2001 Japan's total GDP was US$4,245·2bn., the second highest in the world after the USA.

Banking and Finance. The Nippon Ginko (Bank of Japan), founded 1882, finances the government and the banks, its function being similar to that of a central bank in other countries. The Bank undertakes the management of Treasury funds and foreign exchange control. Its *Governor* is Toshihiko Fukui (appointed March 2003 for a five-year term). Its gold bullion and cash holdings at 31 Dec. 2001 stood at 663,000m. yen.

There were in Dec. 2002, 7 city banks, 64 regional banks, 28 trust banks, 2 long-term credit banks, 56 member banks of the second association of regional banks, 342 Shinkin banks (credit associations), 194 credit co-operatives and 73 foreign banks. There are also various governmental financial institutions, including postal savings which amounted to 236,477,600m. yen in Sept. 2002. Total savings by individuals, including insurance and securities, stood at 1,270,873,600m. yen on 30 Sept. 2002, and about 57% of these savings were deposited in banks and the post office. During 1999 a number of important mergers were announced in the banking sector, most notably the proposed merger of the Industrial Bank of Japan, Dai-Ichi Kangyo and Fuji Bank, which in Sept. 2000 created Mizuho Financial Group, the world's biggest bank in terms of assets, at over 140,000bn. yen (US$1,259bn.). Sumitomo and Sakura Bank also merged, in April 2001, to create Sumitomo Mitsui Banking Corporation. Their joint assets are over 113,000bn. yen (US$895bn.), making the new bank the second largest in the world behind Mizuho Financial Group.

Japan's banks are in a situation where many of them would be insolvent if they admitted the market value of the loans, shares and property they hold. At 31 March 2002 it was estimated that the banking system's bad loans amounted to 26,781bn. yen.

There are eight stock exchanges, the largest being in Tokyo, Osaka and Nagoya.

Weights and Measures. The metric system is obligatory.

ENERGY AND NATURAL RESOURCES

Environment. Japan's carbon dioxide emissions in 1998 accounted for 4·8% of the world total and according to the *World Bank Atlas* were equivalent to 9·0 tonnes per capita. According to an *Environmental Sustainability Index* compiled for the World Economic Forum meeting in Feb. 2002 Japan ranked 78th in the world out of 142 countries analysed, with 48·6%. The index measured the ability of countries to maintain favourable environmental conditions and examined various factors including pollution levels and the use or abuse of natural resources.

Electricity. Japan is poor in energy resources, and nuclear power generation is important in reducing dependence on foreign supplies. In 1998 Japan had a nuclear generating capacity of 43,691 MW. Electricity produced in 2000 was 1,091,500m. kWh. In 2001 there were 54 nuclear reactors, producing approximately 34% of electricity. In 2000, ten regional publicly-held supply companies produced 73·1% of output. There are plans to construct a further five nuclear power plants. Consumption per capita in 2000 was an estimated 7,707 kWh.

Oil and Gas. Output of crude petroleum, 2000, was 740,000 kilolitres, almost entirely from oilfields on the island of Honshu, but 250·6m. kilolitres of crude oil had to be imported. Output of natural gas, 2000, 2,453m. cu. metres.

Minerals. Ore production in tonnes, 2000, of coal, 2,964,000; zinc, 63,601; lead, 8,835; copper, 1,211; iron, 523; silver, 103,781 kg; gold, 8,400 kg. Salt production, 2000, 1,374,000 tonnes.

Agriculture. Agricultural workers in 2001 on farms with 0·3 ha or more of cultivated land or 0·5m. yen annual sales were 3·8m. (including 0·26m. subsidiary and seasonal workers), representing 4·6% (1999) of the labour force as opposed to 24·7% in 1962. Land under cultivation in 2001 was 4·8m. ha, down from 6·1m. ha in 1961. Rice is the staple food, but its consumption is declining. Rice cultivation accounted for 1,770,000 ha in 2000.

Average farm size was 1·6 ha in 2001.

In 1998 there were 2,210,000 tractors and 1,208,000 harvester-threshers.

Output of rice (in 1,000 tonnes) was 10,748 in 1995, 9,490 in 2000 and 9,057 in 2001.

Production in 2000 (in 1,000 tonnes) of sugarbeets was 3,673; potatoes, 2,898; cabbages, 1,449; sugarcane, 1,395; onions, 1,247; tomatoes, 806; cucumbers and gherkins, 767; wheat, 688; carrots, 682; aubergines, 477; pumpkins and squash, 254; soybeans, 235; taro, 231; yams, 201. Sweet potatoes, which in the past mitigated the effects of rice famines, have, in view of rice over-production, decreased from 4,955,000 tonnes in 1965 to 1,073,000 tonnes in 2000. Domestic sugar production accounted for only 27% of requirement in 2000. In 2001, 1·53m. tonnes were imported, 43·7% of this being imported from Thailand, 38·5% from Australia, 13·0% from South Africa.

Fruit production, 2000 (in 1,000 tonnes): mandarins, tangerines and satsumas, 1,143; melons and watermelons, 895; apples, 800; pears, 424; persimmons, 279; grapes, 238.

Livestock (2001): 4·53m. cattle (including about 1·73m. milch cows), 9·79m. pigs, 29,000 goats, 27,000 horses, 16,000 sheep, 293m. chickens. Livestock products in 2000 (in 1,000 tonnes): milk, 8,500; meat, 3,015; eggs, 2,508.

Forestry. Forests covered 25·11m. ha in 1999, or 66·4% of the land area. There was an estimated timber stand of 3,709m. cu. metres in 2000. Timber production was 18·12m. cu. metres in 2000.

Fisheries. The catch in 1999 was 5,176,460 tonnes, excluding whaling. More than 98% of fish caught are from marine waters. Japan's annual catch is the third largest in the world after those of China and Peru. It is also the leading importer of fishery commodities, with imports in 1999 totalling US$14·75bn.

INDUSTRY
The leading companies by market capitalization in Japan, excluding banking and finance, in Jan. 2002 were: NTT DoCoMo ('anywhere') Incorporated (14trn. yen), a wireless voice and data communications company; the Toyota Motor Corporation (13trn. yen); and the Nippon Telegraph and Telephone Corporation (NTT), 6trn. yen.

The industrial structure is dominated by corporate groups (*keiretsu*) either linking companies in different branches or linking individual companies with their suppliers and distributors.

Japan's industrial equipment, 1999, numbered 596,863,468 plants of all sizes, employing 9·90m. production workers.

Output in 2000 included: television sets, 3·38m.; radio sets, 2·3m.; watches, 554·1m.; cameras, 9·74m.; computers, 12·4m. The chemical industry ranks fourth in shipment value after machinery, metals and food products. Production, 2000, included (in tonnes): sulphuric acid, 7·1m.; caustic soda, 4·47m.; ammonium sulphate, 1·75m.; calcium superphosphate, 0·26m. A total of 10,145,000 motor vehicles were manufactured in Japan in 2000, making it the second largest producer after the USA. It is the largest producer of passenger cars.

Output (2000), in 1,000 tonnes, of crude steel was 106,444; cement, 81,097; pig iron, 81,071; ordinary rolled steel, 83,044.

In 2000 paper production was 19·04m. tonnes; paperboard, 12·79m. tonnes.

Output of cotton yarn, 2000, 159,000 tonnes, and of cotton cloth, 664m. sq. metres. Output, 2000, 34,000 tonnes of woollen yarns and 98m. sq. metres of woollen fabrics. Output, 2000, of rayon woven fabrics, 241m. sq. metres; synthetic woven fabrics, 1,573m. sq. metres; silk fabrics, 33m. sq. metres.

5,464m. litres of beer were produced in 2000.

Shipbuilding orders in 2001 totalled 14,551,000 GRT. In 2000, 11,646,000 GRT were launched, of which 4,640,000 GRT were tankers.

Labour. Total labour force, 2001, was 64·1m., of which 17·13m. were in commerce and finance, 17·68m. in services (including the professions), 12·84m. in manufacturing, 6·32m. in construction, 4·41m. in transport and other public utilities, 2·9m. in agriculture and forestry, 2·11m. in government work, 0·27m. in fishing and 50,000 in mining. Retirement age is being raised progressively from 60 years to reach 65 by 2013. However, in 1995 the average actual retirement age among males was 66.

In Jan. 2003 unemployment stood at 5·5%, the highest rate on record. It had also been 5·5% in Aug. and Oct. 2002. Almost 1m. people lost their jobs between March and July 2001. In 2000, 35,000 working days were lost in industrial stoppages. In 2001 the average working week was 38·50 hours.

Trade Unions. In 2001 there were 11,212,000 workers organized in 67,706 unions. In Nov. 1989 the 'Japanese Private Sector Trade Union Confederation' (Rengo), which was organized in 1987, was reorganized into the 'Japan Trade Union Confederation' (Rengo) with the former 'General Council of Japanese Trade Unions' (Sohyo) and other unions, and was the largest federation with 7,001,000 members in 2001. The 'National Confederation of Trade Unions' (Zenroren) had 780,000 members in 2001 and the 'National Trade Union Council' (Zenrokyo) 247,000 members in 2001.

INTERNATIONAL TRADE

Imports and Exports. Trade (in US$1m.):

	1996	1997	1998	1999	2000	2001
Imports	333,832	338,705	280,505	311,246	379,718	349,190
Exports	393,035	420,896	387,958	419,358	479,284	403,227

In 1998 Japanese imports accounted for 6·7% of the world total imports and exports 9·7% of the world total exports.

Distribution of trade by countries (customs clearance basis) (US$1m.):

	Exports		Imports	
	2000	2001	2000	2001
Africa	5,033	4,432	4,960	4,543
Australia	8,580	7,683	14,806	14,451
Canada	7,480	6,563	8,704	7,751
China	30,338	30,941	55,116	57,786
Germany	19,998	15,639	12,732	12,395
Hong Kong	27,174	23,248	1,668	1,457
Latin America	21,047	17,855	10,991	9,700
ASEAN	68,488	54,270	59,568	54,382
Korea, Republic of	30,699	25,285	20,452	17,210
Taiwan	35,955	24,214	17,908	14,195
UK	14,337	12,145	6,580	6,003
USA	142,475	121,146	72,169	63,171

Principal items in 2001, with value in 1m. yen were:

Imports, c.i.f.		Exports, f.o.b.	
Machinery and transport		Machinery and transport	
equipment	13,216,000	equipment	35,524,000
Mineral fuels	8,524,000	Chemicals	3,739,000
Foodstuffs	5,251,000	Metals and metal products	2,889,000
Metal ores and scrap	937,000	Textile products	916,000

The importation of rice used to be prohibited, but in 1993–94 there was an emergency importation of 1m. tonnes from Australia, China, Thailand and the USA to offset a poor domestic harvest. The prohibition was lifted in line with WTO agreements. Until 2000 rice imports had limited access; the market is now fully open.

COMMUNICATIONS

Roads. The total length of roads (including urban and other local roads) was 1,166,340 km at 1 April 2000. There were 53,777 km of national roads of which 53,177 km were paved. In 2000, 76·6% of all roads were paved. Motor vehicles, at 31 Dec. 2001, numbered 71,642,000, including 53,541,000 passenger cars and 17,866,000 commercial vehicles. In 1999 there were 4,154,100 new car registrations (4,116,700 in 1998). In 2000 there were 9,066 road deaths (10,679 in 1995).

The world's longest undersea road tunnel, spanning Tokyo Bay, was opened in Dec. 1997. The Tokyo Bay Aqualine, built at a cost of 1·44trn. yen (US$11·3bn.), consists of a 4·4 km (2·7 mile) bridge and a 9·4 km tunnel that allows commuters to cross the bay in about 15 minutes.

Rail. The first railway was completed in 1872, between Tokyo and Yokohama (29 km). Most railways are of 1,067 mm gauge, but the high-speed 'Shinkansen' lines are standard 1,435 mm gauge. In April 1987 the Japanese National Railways was reorganized into seven private companies, the Japanese Railways (JR) Group—six passenger companies and one freight company. Total length of railways in March 2001 was 27,501 km, of which the JR had 20,057 km and other private railways 7,444 km. In 2000 the JR carried 8,671m. passengers (other private, 12,976m.) and 40m. tonnes of freight (other private, 20m.). An undersea tunnel linking Honshu with Hokkaido was opened to rail services in 1988.

There are metros in Tokyo (two systems, total 273 km in 2000), Fukuoka (18 km), Kobe (two systems, total 23 km), Kyoto (26 km), Nagoya (78 km), Osaka (116 km), Sapporo (48 km), Sendai (15 km) and Yokohama (40 km), and tram/light rail networks in 19 cities.

Civil Aviation. There are international airports at Fukuoka, Kagoshima, Nagoya, Osaka (Kansai International), Sapporo and two serving Tokyo—at Narita (New Tokyo International) and Haneda (Tokyo International). The principal airlines are Japan Airlines (JAL), Japan Air System and All Nippon Airways. In the financial year 1999 Japanese companies carried 91·59m. passengers on domestic services and 17·83m. passengers on international services. JAL flew 364·2m. km in 2001 and carried 32,471,532 passengers, All Nippon Airways flew 259·3m. km and carried 43,044,792 passengers, and Japan Air System flew 106·5m. km and carried 21,756,339 passengers.

In 2000 Narita handled 24,813,053 passengers (24,022,075 on international flights) and 1,885,691 tonnes of freight. Osaka (Kansai International) handled 19,499,000 passengers (11,657,000 on international flights) and 966,800 tonnes of freight in 2000. Built on a reclaimed offshore island, it was only opened in Sept. 1994 but in 2000 was the 18th busiest airport in the world for freight, with Narita ranked 3rd. Tokyo Haneda is mainly used for domestic flights, but handled 56,379,000 passengers in 2000 (55,476,000 on domestic flights), making it the 6th busiest airport in the world for overall traffic volume.

Shipping. On 1 July 2000 the merchant fleet consisted of 5,880 vessels of 100 GRT and over; total tonnage 15m. GRT; there were 174 ships for passenger transport (243,000 GRT), 1,752 cargo ships (965,000 GRT) and 815 oil tankers (4,507,000 GRT). In 1997 vessels totalling 438,111,000 net registered tons entered ports.

Coastguard. The 'Japan Coast Guard' consists of 1 headquarters, 11 regional headquarters, 66 offices, 1 maritime guard and rescue office, 53 stations, 5 information and communications control centres, 6 traffic advisory service centres, 14 air stations, 1 transnational organized crime strike force station, 1 special security station, 1 special rescue station, 1 national strike team station, 6 district communications centres, 4 hydrographic observatories, 1 Loran navigation system centre, and 53 aids-to-navigation offices (with 5,597 aids-to-navigation facilities); and controlled 52 large patrol vessels, 44 medium patrol vessels, 23 small patrol vessels, 230 patrol craft, 13 hydrographic service vessels, 5 large firefighting boats, 7 medium firefighting boats, 86 special guard and rescue boats, 1 aids-to-navigation evaluation vessel, 4 buoy tenders and 53 aids-to-navigation tenders in the financial year 2002. Personnel numbered 12,255.

The 'Japan Coast Guard' aviation service includes 29 fixed-wing aircraft and 46 helicopters.

Telecommunications. Telephone services have been operated by private companies (NTT and others) since 1985. There were 74,343,600 main telephone lines (equivalent to 585·8 per 1,000 population) in 2000. In April 2000 Japan had 57·95m. mobile phone subscribers. There were 40·0m. PCs (315·2 per 1,000 persons) in 2000 and 16m. fax machines in 1997. There were 51·34m. Internet users in April 2002. Approximately 70% of Internet users are men. Internet commerce, or e-commerce, amounted to US$1·2bn. in 1998 and was forecast to total US$16bn. in 2001.

Postal Services. There were 24,778 post offices in 2000, handling a total of 26,114m. items of domestic mail, and foreign items of mail numbering 96m. out of and 290m. into Japan.

SOCIAL INSTITUTIONS

Justice. The Supreme Court is composed of the Chief Justice and 14 other judges. The Chief Justice is appointed by the Emperor, the other judges by the Cabinet. Every ten years a justice must submit himself to the electorate. All justices and judges of the lower courts serve until they are 70 years of age.

Below the Supreme Court are eight regional higher courts, district courts in each prefecture (four in Hokkaido) and the local courts.

The Supreme Court is authorized to declare unconstitutional any act of the Legislature or the Executive which violates the Constitution.

In 2000, 3,256,109 penal code offences were reported, including 1,391 homicides. The death penalty is authorized; there were two executions in 2002. The average daily population in penal institutions in 2000 was 58,747 (46 per 100,000 population).

Religion. State subsidies have ceased for all religions, and all religious teachings are forbidden in public schools. In Dec. 2000 Shintoism claimed 107·95m. adherents, Buddhism 95·42m.; these figures obviously overlap. Christians numbered 1·77m.

Education. Education is compulsory and free between the ages of 6 and 15. Almost all national and municipal institutions are co-educational. In May 2001 there were 14,314 kindergartens with 106,703 teachers and 1,753,422 pupils; 23,450 elementary schools with 407,829 teachers and 7,296,920 pupils; 11,118 junior high schools with 255,494 teachers and 3,991,911 pupils; 5,345 senior high schools with 266,548 teachers and 4,061,756 pupils; 559 junior colleges with 15,638 teachers and 289,198 pupils.

There were also 914 special schools for children with physical disabilities (58,617 teachers, 92,072 pupils).

Japan has seven main state universities: Tokyo University (1877); Kyoto University (1897); Tohoku University, Sendai (1907); Kyushu University, Fukuoka (1910); Hokkaido University, Sapporo (1918); Osaka University (1931); and Nagoya University (1939). In addition, there are various other state and municipal as well as private universities. There are 669 colleges and universities altogether with (May 2001) 2,765,705 students and 152,572 teachers.

In 1999–2000 total expenditure on education came to 3·5% of GNI.

The adult literacy rate in 1998 was at least 99%.

Health. Hospitals on 1 Oct. 2000 numbered 9,266 with 1,647,253 beds. The hospital bed provision of 130 per 10,000 population was one of the highest in the world. Physicians at the end of 2000 numbered 255,792 (provision of one for every 496 persons); dentists, 90,857.

Welfare. There are in force various types of social security schemes, such as health insurance, unemployment insurance and age pensions. Citizens over 60 receive pensions of 70% of the average wage. In 1995 the basic retirement pension was 214,300 yen per month, funded by contributions of 17·35% of salary. There were a total of 39m. pensioners in 1999.

In 1999, 12,053,666 persons and 8,448,659 households received some form of regular public assistance, the total of which came to 1,860,272m. yen.

14 weeks maternity leave is statutory.

CULTURE

Broadcasting.. Broadcasting is under the aegis of the public Japan Broadcasting Corporation (Nippon Hoso Kyokai) and the National Association of Commercial Broadcasters (Minporen). The former transmits two national networks and an external service, Radio Japan (22 languages). In 1999 there were 127 commercial television companies operating on terrestrial broadcasting waves. There were 86·5m. TV sets (colour by NTSC) and 120·5m. radio receivers in 1997. In 2000 there were 18·71m. cable TV subscribers, and in 1998 more than 68,000 cable TV stations.

Cinema. In 2001 cinemas numbered 2,585 with an annual attendance of 163m. (1960: 1,014m.). Of 630 new films shown in 2001, 281 were Japanese.

Press. In 2000 daily newspapers numbered 122 with aggregate circulation of 71·90m. (the highest circulation of daily newspapers in the world) including four major English-language newspapers. The newspapers with the highest circulation are *Yomiuri Shimbun* (daily average of 10·3m. copies in 2001) and *Asahi Shimbun* (daily average of 8·3m. copies in 2001). They are also the two most widely read newspapers in the world.

In 2001, 69,003 book titles were published.

Tourism. In 2001, 5,286,310 foreigners visited Japan, 715,036 of whom came from the USA and 390,664 from the UK. Japanese travelling abroad totalled 16,215,657. Tourism receipts in 1999 totalled US$3·43bn.

Festivals. Japan has a huge number of annual festivals, among the largest of which are the Sapporo Snow Festival (Feb.); Hakata Dontaku, Fukuoka City (May); the Sanja Festival of Asakusa Shrine, Tokyo (May); the Tanabata Festival in Hiratsuka City (July) and Sendai City (Aug.); the Nebuta Festival in Aomori City (Aug.); and Jidai Matsuri, Kyoto (Oct.).

The next World Expo is scheduled to be held in Nagoya from March–Sept. 2005.

Libraries. In 1999 public libraries numbered 2,593 including 1 National Diet Library, holding 284m. books.

Theatre and Opera. In 2000 there were four National Theatres: National Theatre (traditional Japanese performances); Nogakudo (Noh Theatre); Bunraku Theatre (Japanese puppet show); and the New National Theatre (Opera House).

Museums and Galleries. In 1999 there were 1,045 museums, including 26 nationals. These included 355 historical, 353 fine arts and 126 general museums.

DIPLOMATIC REPRESENTATIVES

Of Japan in the United Kingdom (101–104 Piccadilly, London, W1J 7JT)
Ambassador: Masaki Orita.

Of the United Kingdom in Japan (1 Ichiban-cho, Chiyoda-ku, Tokyo 102-8381)
Ambassador: Sir Stephen J. Gomersall, KCMG.

Of Japan in the USA (2520 Massachusetts Ave., NW, Washington, D.C., 20008)
Ambassador: Ryozo Kato.

Of the USA in Japan (10–5, Akasaka 1-chome, Minato-ku, Tokyo)
Ambassador: Howard H. Baker.

Of Japan to the United Nations
Ambassador: Koichi Haraguchi.

Of Japan to the European Union
Ambassador: Takayuki Kimura.

FURTHER READING

Statistics Bureau of the Prime Minister's Office: *Statistical Year-Book* (from 1949).—*Statistical Abstract* (from 1950).—*Monthly Bulletin* (from April 1950)
Economic Planning Agency: *Economic Survey* (annual), *Economic Statistics* (monthly), *Economic Indicators* (monthly)
Ministry of International Trade: *Foreign Trade of Japan* (annual)

Allinson, G. D., *Japan's Postwar History.* London, 1997
Argy, V. and Stein, L., *The Japanese Economy.* London, 1996
Bailey, P. J., *Post-war Japan: 1945 to the Present.* Oxford, 1996

Beasley, W. G., *The Rise of Modern Japan: Political, Economic and Social Change Since 1850.* 2nd ed. London, 1995

The Cambridge Encyclopedia of Japan. CUP, 1993

Cambridge History of Japan. vols. 1–5. CUP, 1990–93

Campbell, A. (ed.) *Japan: an Illustrated Encyclopedia.* Tokyo, 1994

Clesse, A., *et al.,* (eds.) *The Vitality of Japan: Sources of National Strength and Weakness.* London, 1997

Eades, J. S., *Tokyo.* [Bibliography] ABC-Clio, Oxford and Santa Barbara (CA), 1998

Gordon, A., *Postwar Japan as History.* Univ. of California Press, 1993

Henshall, K. G., *A History of Japan, From Stone Age to Superpower.* Palgrave, Basingstoke, 2001

Ito, T., *The Japanese Economy.* Boston (Mass.), 1992

Jain, P. and Inoguchi, T., *Japanese Politics Today.* London, 1997

Japan: an Illustrated Encyclopedia. London, 1993

Johnson, C., *Japan: Who Governs? The Rise of the Developmental State.* New York, 1995

McCargo, D., *Contemporary Japan.* Macmillan, London, 2000

McClain, James, *Japan: A Modern History.* W. W. Norton, New York, 2001

Nakano, M., *The Policy-making Process in Contemporary Japan.* London, 1996

Okabe, M. (ed.) *The Structure of the Japanese Economy: Changes on the Domestic and International Fronts.* London, 1994

Perren, R., *Japanese Studies From Pre-History to 1990.* Manchester Univ. Press, 1992

Schirokauer, C., *Brief History of Japanese Civilization.* New York, 1993

Woronoff, J., *The Japanese Economic Crisis.* 2nd ed. London, 1996

National statistical office: Statistics Bureau, Prime Minister's Office, Tokyo.
Website: http://www.stat.go.jp/

JORDAN

Al-Mamlaka Al-Urduniya
Al-Hashemiyah
(Hashemite[1] Kingdom
of Jordan)

Capital: Amman
Population estimate
(Jordanian), 2000: 5·23m.
GDP per capita, 2000: (PPP$) 3,966
HDI/world rank: 0·717/99

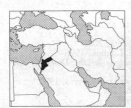

KEY HISTORICAL EVENTS

During the first World War (1914–18) the Arabs of Transjordan and Palestine rebelled against the suzerainty of Turkey, which had become an ally of Germany. Britain supported the rebellion, occupied the areas and in 1920 was given a League of Nations mandate for Transjordan and Palestine. In April 1921 the Amir Abdullah Ibn Hussein (brother of King Feisal of Iraq) became the ruler of Transjordan, which was officially separated from Palestine in 1923. By a treaty signed in London on 22 March 1946 Britain recognized Transjordan as a sovereign independent state. On 25 May 1946 the Amir Abdullah assumed the title of king and the name of the territory was changed to that of the Hashemite Kingdom of Jordan. The part of Palestine remaining to the Arabs under the armistice with Israel on 3 April 1949, with the exception of the Gaza Strip on the Mediterranean coast, was placed under Jordanian rule and formally incorporated in Jordan on 24 April 1950. In June 1967 this territory ('the West Bank') was occupied by Israel. On 31 July 1988 King Hussein announced the dissolution of Jordan's legal and administrative ties with the West Bank. King Hussein, who became king in 1953 at the age of 17 after his father was declared mentally unfit to rule, remained in executive control in the face of attempted assassinations and frequent changes of prime ministers for 35 years until his death on 7 Feb. 1999.

TERRITORY AND POPULATION

Jordan is bounded in the north by Syria, east by Iraq, southeast and south by Saudi Arabia and west by Israel. It has an outlet to an arm of the Red Sea at Aqaba. Its area is 91,860 sq. km. The 1994 census population was 4,095,579; density 44·6 per sq. km. 1997 population estimate, 4,600,000.

The UN gives a projected population for 2010 of 6·42m. (including immigrant workers).

In 1999, 73·6% of the population lived in urban areas. Population of the 12 governorates:

Governorate	1997	Governorate	1997
Ajloun	104,900	Karak	188,600
Amman	1,751,700	Ma'an	88,300
Aqaba	88,800	Madaba	119,100
Balqa	306,800	Mafraq	198,700
Irbid	835,400	Tafilah	69,900
Jerash	137,100	Zarqa	710,700

The largest towns with suburbs, with estimated population, 1994: Amman, the capital, 1,378,000 (1999 estimate); Zarqa, 608,626; Irbid, 379,844.

The official language is Arabic.

SOCIAL STATISTICS

Births, 1999, 130,039; deaths, 37,093. Rates, 1999 per 1,000 population: birth, 21·2; death rate, 6·1. Annual population growth rate, 1990–99, 3·8%. Life expectancy at birth in 1999, 68·9 years for men, 71·5 for women. Jordan has a young population: 1997 estimates showed 44% aged under 15, 53% aged 15–64 and 3% aged 65 and over. Infant mortality, 1999, 29 per 1,000 live births; fertility rate, 1999, 4·7 births per woman.

---

[1]'Hashemite' denotes a descendant of the prophet Mohammed.

CLIMATE

Predominantly a Mediterranean climate, with hot dry summers and cool wet winters, but in hilly parts summers are cooler and winters colder. Those areas below sea-level are very hot in summer and warm in winter. Eastern parts have a desert climate. Amman, Jan. 46°F (7·5°C), July 77°F (24·9°C). Annual rainfall 13·4" (340·6 mm). Aqaba, Jan. 61°F (16°C), July 89°F (31·5°C). Annual rainfall 1·4" (36·7 mm).

CONSTITUTION AND GOVERNMENT

The Kingdom is a constitutional monarchy headed by H. M. King **Abdullah Bin Al Hussein** II, born 30 Jan. 1962, married to H. M. Queen Rania. *Son:* Hussein, b. 28 June 1994; *daughters:* Iman, b. 27 Sept. 1996; Salma, b. 26 Sept. 2000. *Crown Prince:* Prince Hamzah (younger brother of the King). In Jan. 1999 the late King Hussein had confirmed by royal decree that his eldest son, Prince Abdullah, was his heir in place of the King's brother Prince Hassan Bin Talal who had held the position of Crown Prince for 34 years. King Hussein died on 7 Feb. 1999.

The Constitution ratified on 8 Dec. 1952 provides that the Cabinet is responsible to Parliament. The legislature consists of a *Senate* of 40 members appointed by the King and a *Chamber of Deputies* of 104 members (80 until 2001) elected by universal suffrage. Nine seats are reserved for Christians, six for Bedouin and three for Circassians. A law of 1993 restricts each elector to a single vote, replacing a system in which electors had several votes depending on the number of seats in the constituency.

The lower house was dissolved in 1976 and elections postponed because no elections could be held in the West Bank under Israeli occupation. Parliament was reconvened on 9 Jan. 1984. By-elections were held in March 1984 and six members were nominated for the West Bank, bringing Parliament to 60 members. Women voted for the first time in 1984. On 9 June 1991 the King and the main political movements endorsed a national charter which legalized political parties in return for the acceptance of the constitution and monarchy. Movements linked to, or financed by, non-Jordanian bodies are not allowed.

National Anthem. 'Asha al Malik' ('Long Live the King'); words by A. Al Rifai, tune by A. Al Tanir.

RECENT ELECTIONS

Elections were held on 4 Nov. 1997. Of the 80 seats, 76 went to non-partisans of various orientations, 3 to the National Constitutional Party and 1 to the Ba'ath Party.

CURRENT ADMINISTRATION

In March 2003 the government consisted of:

Prime Minister, Minister of Defence: Ali Abu al-Ragheb; b. 1946 (in office since 19 June 2000).

Minister for Foreign Affairs: Marwan Muasher. *Finance:* Michel Marto. *Public Works and Housing:* Hosni Abu Gheida. *Municipal and Rural Affairs, and the Environment:* Abdul Razzaq Tubayshat. *Tourism and Antiquities:* Taleb Rifai. *Education:* Khalid Touqan. *Social Development:* Tamam al-Ghul. *Post and Telecommunications:* Fawwaz Zu'bi. *Awqaf and Islamic Affairs:* Ahmad Hilayel. *Energy and Mineral Resources:* Mohammad Batayineh. *Water and Irrigation:* Hazem al-Nasser. *Health:* Faleh al-Nasser. *Transport:* Nader Dhahabi. *Agriculture:* Mahmoud Duwayri. *Planning:* Bassem Awadallah. *Labour:* Muzahim Muhaisin. *Trade, Industry and Commerce:* Salaleddin al-Bashir. *Interior:* Qaftan al-Majali. *Higher Education and Scientific Research:* Walid Maani. *Culture:* Haidar Mahmoud. *Minister of Justice and Minister of State for Legal Affairs:* Faris Nabulsi. *National Economy and Minister of State:* Mohammad Halaiqa. *Minister of State for Prime Ministry Affairs:* Mustafa al-Qaisi. *Minister of Information and Minister of State for Political Affairs:* Mohammad Affash al-Adwan. *Minister of State for Administrative Development:* Mohammad al-Zunaybat.

DEFENCE

Defence expenditure in 2000 totalled US$510m. (US$76 per capita), representing 6·9% of GDP.

Army. Total strength (1999) 90,000. In addition there were 30,000 army reservists, a paramilitary Public Security Directorate of approximately 10,000 and a civil militia 'People's Army' of approximately 20,000.

Navy. The Royal Jordanian Naval Force numbered 480 in 1999 and operates a handful of patrol boats, all based at Aqaba.

Air Force. Strength (1999) 13,500 personnel (including 3,400 Air defence), 93 combat aircraft (including F-5Es, F16As and Mirage F1s) and 16 armed helicopters.

INTERNATIONAL RELATIONS

A 46-year-old formal state of hostilities with Israel was brought to an end by a peace agreement on 26 Oct. 1994.

Jordan is a member of the UN, WTO, IOM, OIC and the League of Arab States.

ECONOMY

Agriculture accounted for 3·0% of GDP in 1998, industry 25·7% and services 71·3%.

Overview. The public sector has dominated the economy, but privatization has proceeded at a faster pace since 1998.

Currency. The unit of currency is the *Jordan dinar* (JD.) of 1,000 *fils*. Inflation in 2001 was 1·8%. Foreign exchange controls were abolished in July 1997. Foreign exchange reserves were US$3,650m. and gold reserves 408,000 troy oz in June 2002. Total money supply in March 2002 was JD.2,095m.

Budget. Revenue and expenditure over a six-year period (in 1m. dinar):

	1995	1996	1997	1998	1999	2000
Revenue	1,332·6	1,366·9	1,312·6	1,422·4	1,530·5	1,506·6
Expenditure	1,471·5	1,666·9	1,681·9	1,876·8	1,804·1	1,868·6

Performance. Total GDP was US$8·8bn. in 2001. Real GDP growth in 2001 was 4·2%.

Banking and Finance. The Central Bank of Jordan was established in 1964 (*Governor*, Dr Umayya Toukan). In 1995 there were 21 licensed banks with a total of 430 branches. Assets and liabilities of the banking system (including the Central Bank, commercial banks, the Housing Bank and investment banks) totalled JD.8,430·4m. in 1995.

There is a stock exchange in Amman (Amman Financial Market).

Weights and Measures. The metric system is in force. Land area is measured in *dunums* (1 dunum = 0·1 ha).

ENERGY AND NATURAL RESOURCES

Environment. According to the *World Bank Atlas* carbon dioxide emissions in 1998 were the equivalent of 3·0 tonnes per capita.

Electricity. Installed capacity was 1m. kW in 1997. Production (1998) 6·08bn. kWh; consumption per capita was 1,205 kWh.

Oil and Gas. Natural gas reserves in 1997 totalled 6bn. cu. metres, with production (1995) 294m. cu. metres.

Water. 99% of the total population and 100% of the urban population has access to safe drinking water.

Minerals. Phosphate ore production in 1996 was 5·37m. tonnes; potash, 1·8m. tonnes.

Agriculture. The country east of the Hejaz Railway line is largely desert; northwestern Jordan is potentially of agricultural value and an integrated Jordan Valley project began in 1973. In 1993 about 15% of land was given over to agricultural use (including 9% permanent pasture and 4% arable crops). In 1998 there were 75,000 ha of irrigated land. The agricultural cropping pattern for irrigated vegetable cultivation was introduced in 1984 to regulate production and diversify the crops being cultivated. In 1986 the government began to lease state-owned land in the semi-arid southern regions for agricultural development by private investors, mostly for wheat and barley.

Production in 2000 (in 1,000 tonnes): tomatoes, 306; olives, 166; watermelons, 105; potatoes, 93; cucumbers and gherkins, 72; cabbages, 40; lemons and limes, 37; bananas, 36; cauliflowers, 35; apples, 34; pumpkins and squash, 34.

Livestock (2000): 1·6m. sheep; 630,000 goats; 57,000 cattle; 18,000 asses; 18,000 camels; 25m. chickens. Total meat production was 132,000 tonnes in 2000; milk, 145,000 tonnes.

There were 4,800 tractors in 1998.

Forestry. Forests covered 45,000 ha in 1995, or 0·5% of the land area. In 1999, 11,000 cu. metres of roundwood was cut.

Fisheries. Fish landings in 1999 totalled 510 tonnes, mainly from inland waters.

INDUSTRY
According to the Financial Times Survey (FT 500), the largest company by market capitalization in Jordan on 4 Jan. 2001 was Arab Bank (US$1,970·7m.).

The number of industrial units in 1994 was 18,980, employing more than 100,000 persons. The principal industrial concerns are the production or processing of phosphates, potash, fertilizers, cement and oil.

Production (1997, in 1,000 tonnes): cement, 3,251; residual fuel oil, 1,084; distillate fuel oil, 913; chemical acids, 846 (1994); fertilizers, 470 (1994).

Labour. The workforce in 1996 was 935,000. In 1993, 434,806 persons worked in social and public administration, 129,754 in commerce, 91,087 in mining and manufacturing, 57,573 in transport and communications and 54,995 in agriculture. Unemployment was officially 12% in Oct. 2000 but was estimated by economists to be more than 20%. In 2000 Jordan had more than 600,000 foreign workers, many of them Iraqis.

INTERNATIONAL TRADE
Foreign debt was US$8,226m. in 2000. Legislation of 1995 eases restrictions on foreign investment and makes some reductions in taxes and customs duties.

Imports and Exports. Imports (f.o.b.) in 1999 totalled US$3,292·0m. and exports (f.o.b.) US$1,831·9m. Major exports are phosphate, potash, fertilizers, foodstuffs, pharmaceuticals, fruit and vegetables, textiles, cement, plastics, detergent and soap.

Exports in 1999 were mainly to Saudi Arabia, 15·9%; India, 12·6%; and Japan, 5·2%. Principal import sources were from Germany, 9·9%; USA, 8·6%; and Italy, 6·1%.

COMMUNICATIONS
Roads. Total length of roads, 1996 estimate, 6,640 km, of which 2,940 km were main roads. In 1996 there were 213,900 passenger cars (48 per 1,000 inhabitants), 369 motorcycles and mopeds, 10,300 coaches and buses, and 68,850 trucks and vans. There were 552 deaths in road accidents in 1996 (388 in 1992).

Rail. The 1,050 mm gauge Hejaz Jordan and Aqaba Railway runs from the Syrian border at Nassib to Ma'an and Naqb Ishtar and Aqaba Port (total, 618 km). The state railway is only minimally operational. Passenger-km travelled in 1998 came to 2m. and freight tonne-km to 596m.

Civil Aviation. The Queen Alia International airport is at Zizya, 30 km south of Amman. There are also international airports at Amman and Aqaba. Queen Alia International handled 2,384,860 passengers in 2000 (2,350,346 on international flights) and 82,185 tonnes of freight. The national carrier is the Royal Jordanian, which flew 36·2m. km and carried 1,252,200 passengers (all on international flights) in 1999. Royal Jordanian is currently state-owned, but in Oct. 1999 the government announced its intention to sell a 49% stake in the airline.

Shipping. In 1998 sea-going shipping totalled 42,000 GRT. In 1998 vessels totalling 2,608,000 NRT entered ports.

Telecommunications. There were 620,000 main telephone lines in 2000, or 82·9 per 1,000 persons. In Jan. 2000 the government sold a 40% stake in Jordan Telecommunications Company to France Telecom for US$508m. There were 150,000 PCs (22·5 for every 1,000 persons) in 2000 and 35,000 fax machines in

1996. Jordan had 115,000 mobile phone subscribers in early 2000. The number of Internet users in March 2001 was 210,000.

Postal Services. In 1996 there were 836 post offices and agencies.

SOCIAL INSTITUTIONS

Justice. The legal system is based on Islamic law (Shari'a) and civil law, and administers justice in cases of civil, criminal or administrative disputes. The constitution guarantees the independence of the judiciary. Courts are divided into three tiers: regular courts (courts of first instance, magistrate courts, courts of appeal, Court of Cassation/High Court of Justice); religious courts (Shari'a courts and Council of Religious Communities); special courts (e.g. police court, military councils, customs court, state security court).

The death penalty is authorized; there were 13 confirmed executions in 2002. The murder rate in 2000 stood at two per 100,000 population.

Religion. About 96% of the population are Sunni Muslims.

Education. Adult literacy in 1999 was 89·2% (male, 94·5%; female, 83·4%). Basic primary and secondary education is free and compulsory. In 1998–99 there were 1,050 kindergartens (1,048 private) with 3,645 teachers and 80,101 pupils; 2,678 basic schools (497 private) with 46,864 teachers and 1,135,146 pupils; 948 secondary schools (117 private) with 13,377 teachers and 165,475 pupils; and 53 vocational schools with 2,213 teachers and 31,961 pupils. In 1996–97 there were 6 state and 11 private universities. 22,500 Jordanians were studying abroad in 1994.

In 1996 total expenditure on education came to 7·9% of GNP and 19·8% of total government spending.

Health. In 1996 there were 7,322 doctors, 2,180 dentists and 4,304 nurses (1994). In 1995 there were a total of 6,800 hospital beds in 63 hospitals.

Welfare. There are numerous government organizations involved in social welfare projects. The General Union of Voluntary Societies finances and supports the Governorate Unions, voluntary societies, and needy individuals through financial and in-kind aid. There are also 240 day care centres run by non-governmental organizations.

CULTURE

Broadcasting. Broadcasting is the responsibility of the Jordan Radio and Television Corporation, which transmits two national radio services (one in English), a Koran service and an external service, Radio Jordan. There are two television services (colour by PAL). There were 1·66m. radio receivers in use and 500,000 TV sets in 1997.

Press. In 1996 there were four daily (including one in English) and 22 weekly papers. Newspapers were denationalized in 1990, although government institutions still hold majority ownership.

Tourism. Tourism accounts for 11% of GDP. In 1999 there were 1,358,000 foreign tourists, bringing revenue of US$795m.

DIPLOMATIC REPRESENTATIVES

Of Jordan in the United Kingdom (6 Upper Phillimore Gdns., Kensington, London, W8 7HA)
Ambassador: Timoor Daghistani.

Of the United Kingdom in Jordan (PO Box 87, Abdoun, Amman)
Ambassador: Christopher Prentice.

Of Jordan in the USA (3504 International Dr., NW, Washington, D.C., 20008)
Ambassador: Karim Kawar.

Of the USA in Jordan (Abdoun, Amman)
Ambassador: Edward William Gnehm, Jr.

Of Jordan to the United Nations
Ambassador: Prince Zied Ra'ad Zeid Al-Hussein.

Of Jordan to the European Union
Ambassador: Alia Hatough Bouran.

FURTHER READING
Department of Statistics. *Statistical Yearbook*
Central Bank of Jordan. *Monthly Statistical Bulletin*
Dallas, R., *King Hussein, The Great Survivor.* Profile Books, London, 1998
Rogan, E. and Tell, T. (eds.) *Village, Steppe and State: the Social Origins of Modern Jordan.*
    London, 1994
Salibi, Kamal, *The Modern History of Jordan.* I. B. Tauris, London, 1998
Satloff, R. B., *From Abdullah to Hussein: Jordan in Transition.* OUP, 1994
Wilson, M. C., *King Abdullah, Britain and the making of Jordan.* CUP, 1987

National statistical office: National Information Centre, P. O. Box 259 Jubeiha, 11941 Amman
Website: http://www.nic.gov.jo

KAZAKHSTAN

Qazaqstan Respūblīkasy

Capital: Astana
Population estimate, 2000: 16·17m.
GDP per capita, 2000: (PPP$) 5,871
HDI/world rank: 0·750/79

KEY HISTORICAL EVENTS

Turkestan (part of the territory now known as Kazakhstan) was conquered by the Russians in the 1860s. In 1866 Tashkent was occupied, followed in 1868 by Samarkand. Subsequently further territory was conquered and united with Russian Turkestan. In the 1870s Bokhara was subjugated, with the emir, by an agreement of 1873, recognizing Russian suzerainty. In the same year Khiva became a vassal state to Russia. Until 1917 Russian Central Asia was divided politically into the Khanate of Khiva, the Emirate of Bokhara and the Governor-Generalship of Turkestan. In the summer of 1919 the authority of the Soviet Government extended to these regions. The Khan of Khiva was deposed in Feb. 1920, and a People's Soviet Republic was set up, the medieval name of Khorezm being revived. In Aug. 1920 the Emir of Bokhara suffered the same fate and a similar regime was set up in Bokhara. The former Governor-Generalship of Turkestan was constituted an Autonomous Soviet Socialist Republic within the RSFSR on 11 April 1921.

In the autumn of 1924 the Soviets of the Turkestan, Bokhara and Khiva Republics decided to redistribute their territories on a nationality basis; at the same time Bokhara and Khiva became Socialist Republics. The redistribution was completed in May 1925, when the new states of Uzbekistan, Turkmenistan and Tajikistan were accepted into the USSR as Union Republics. The remaining districts of Turkestan populated by Kazakhs were united with Kazakhstan which was established as an Autonomous Soviet Republic in 1925 and became a constituent republic in 1936. Independence was declared on 16 Dec. 1991 when Kazakhstan joined the CIS. Nursultan Nazarbaev became president, and legislation has been introduced to award him privileges for life. Over a million of the country's ethnic Russians and Germans have returned to their homelands in the last ten years. Kazakhstan has been focusing on border disputes with China and Uzbekistan and fighting fundamentalism along with other Central Asian governments.

TERRITORY AND POPULATION

Kazakhstan is bounded in the west by the Caspian Sea and Russia, in the north by Russia, in the east by China and in the south by Uzbekistan, Kyrgyzstan and Turkmenistan. The area is 2,724,900 sq. km (1,052,100 sq. miles). The 1999 census population was 14,953,000 (density of 5·5 per sq. km), of whom Kazakhs accounted for 53·4% and Russians 30·0%. There are also Ukrainians, Uzbeks, Germans, Tatars, Uigurs and smaller minorities. In 1997 the population was 51·4% female; it was 56·4% urban in 1999. During the 1990s some 1·5m. people left Kazakhstan—mostly Russians and Germans returning to their homelands. Approximately 10·8m. Kazakhs live abroad.

The UN gives a projected population for 2010 of 15·8m.

Kazakhstan consists of 14 provinces as follows, with area and population:

	Area (sq. km)	*Population* (1996)		*Area* (sq. km)	*Population* (1996)
Almaty[1]	224,200	2,141,100	Pavlodar	124,800	921,000
Aqmola[2]	92,000	808,600	Qaraghandy	428,000	1,234,100
Aqtöbe	300,600	750,400	Qostanay	225,700	1,328,700
Atyraū[3]	118,600	463,200	Qyzylorda	226,000	679,000
Batys Qazaqstan	151,300	668,500	Shyghys Qazaqstan	283,300	918,800
Mangghystaū	165,600	340,100	Soltüstik Qazaqstan	123,200	575,600
Ongtüstik Qazaqstan	117,300	2,029,100	Zhambyl[4]	144,300	1,037,000

[1]Formerly Alma-Ata. [2]Formerly Tselinograd and then Akmola. [3]Formerly Gurev. [4]Formerly Dzhambul.

In Dec. 1997 the capital was moved from Almaty to Aqmola, which was renamed Astana in May 1998 (the name of the province remained as Aqmola). Astana has a population of 313,000 (2000). Other major cities, with 2000 populations: Almaty (1,129,000); Qaraghandy (437,000); Shymkent (360,000).

The official language is Kazakh.

SOCIAL STATISTICS

1999: births, 209,039; deaths, 144,450. Rates, 1999 (per 1,000 population): births, 14·0; deaths, 9·7. Suicides in 1996 numbered 4,796 (rate of 30·1 per 100,000 population). Expectation of life at birth, 1999, 58·9 years for males and 70·2 years for females. Annual population growth rate, 1990–99, –0·3%; infant mortality, 1999, 20·8 per 1,000 live births; fertility rate, 1999, 2·2 births per woman.

CLIMATE

The climate is generally fairly dry. Winters are cold but spring comes earlier in the south than in the far north. Almaty, Jan. –4°C, July 24°C. Annual rainfall 598 mm.

CONSTITUTION AND GOVERNMENT

Relying on a judgement of the Constitutional Court that the 1994 parliamentary elections were invalid, President Nazarbaev dissolved parliament on 11 March 1995 and began to rule by decree. A referendum on the adoption of a new constitution was held on 30 Aug. 1995. The electorate was 8·8m.; turn-out was 80%. 89% of votes cast were in favour. The Constitution thus adopted allows the President to rule by decree and to dissolve parliament if it holds a no-confidence vote or twice rejects his nominee for Prime Minister. It establishes a parliament consisting of a 39-member Senate (two selected by each of the elected assemblies of Kazakhstan's 16 principal administrative divisions plus seven appointed by the president); and a lower house of 77 (67 popularly elected by single mandate districts, with 10 members elected by party-list vote). The constitution was amended in Oct. 1998 to provide for a seven-year presidential term.

A Constitutional Court was set up in Dec. 1991 and a new Constitution adopted on 28 Jan. 1993, but President Nazarbaev abolished the Constitutional Court in 1995. In June 2000 a bill to provide President Nazarbaev with life-long powers and privileges was passed into law.

National Anthem. 'Zharalghan namystan qaharman khalyqpyz' ('We are brave people, children of honesty'); words by M. Alimbaev, tune by M. Tulebayev and Y. Brusilovsky.

RECENT ELECTIONS

At the presidential elections of 10 Jan. 1999 Nursultan Nazarbaev was re-elected with 79·8% of votes cast against three other candidates.

At the elections of 10 and 24 Oct. 1999 for the National Assembly, Republican Party Otan won 23 seats, the Civil Party 13 seats, the Communist Party 3, the Agrarian Party 3, National Co-operative Party 1 and non-partisans 34. Three seats were vacant.

CURRENT ADMINISTRATION

President: Nursultan Nazarbaev; b. 1940 (elected in 1991 and re-elected in 1999).

In March 2003 the government comprised:

Prime Minister: Imangali Tasmagambetov; b. 1956 (sworn in 28 Jan. 2002).

First Deputy Prime Minister: Alexander Pavlov. *Deputy Prime Ministers:* Karim Masimov; Baurzhan Mukhametzhanov; Akhmetzhan Yesimov (also *Minister of Agriculture*).

Minister of Defence: Col. Gen. Mukhtar Altynbayev. *Economy and Budget Planning:* Kairat Kelimbetov. *Education and Science:* Shamsha Berkimbayeva. *Foreign Affairs:* Kasymzhomart Tokayev. *Internal Affairs:* Kariybek Suleymenov. *Industry and Trade:* Mahzit Yesenbayev. *Energy and Mineral Resources:* Vladimir Shkolnik. *Justice:* Georgiy Kim. *Health:* Zhaksylyk Doskaliyev. *Labour and Social Security:* Gulzhana Karagusova. *Transport and Communications:* Kazhmurat Nagmanov. *Environmental Protection:* Aitkul Samakova. *Culture and Information:* Mukhtar Qul-Muhammed. *Finance:* Zianulla Kakimzhanov.

Chairman, Senate (Upper House): Oralbai Abdukarimov.

Chairman, Majlis (Lower House): Zharmakan Tuyakbayev.

Office of the President: http://www.president.kz/

DEFENCE

In 1991 the former Soviet Union transferred extensive equipment to storage bases in Kazakhstan. However, it is deteriorating. A US funded programme for nuclear dismantlement and demilitarization continues.

Defence expenditure in 2000 totalled US$357m. (US$22 per capita), representing 2·0% of GDP.

Army. Personnel, 1999, 46,800. Paramilitary units: Republican Guard (2,500), Ministry of the Interior Security Troops (20,000), Frontier Guards (12,000).

Navy. Formally constituted in Aug. 1996, a force of 250 personnel (1999) operates on the Caspian Sea.

Air Force. In 1999 there was an Air Force division with about 19,000 personnel with some 131 combat aircraft, including MiG-29 and Su-27 interceptors and MiG-27 and Su-24 strike aircraft.

INTERNATIONAL RELATIONS

In Jan. 1995 agreements were reached for closer integration with Russia, including the combining of military forces, currency convertibility and a customs union.

Kazakhstan is a member of the UN, CIS, OSCE, Asian Development Bank, ECO, IOM, OIC and the NATO Partnership for Peace. Sandwiched between Russia and China, in 1998 President Nazarbaev signed major treaties with both countries in the hope of improving relations with both. Kazakhstan hopes to become a member of the WTO before the end of 2003.

ECONOMY

Agriculture accounted for 9·2% of GDP in 1998, industry 31·2% and services 59·6%.

Overview. A National Council for Economic Reform was instituted in Jan. 1993. A privatization programme for 1993–95 envisaged the sale of most state enterprises with more than 200 employees by a combination of cash and vouchers. Enterprises of national importance remain controlled by the government through holding companies. Economic reform embraces wholesale privatization, the reform of financial and credit systems, the liberalization of prices for goods and services, the adoption of a system of free trade and the attraction of foreign investment.

Currency. The unit of currency is the *tenge* of 100 *tiyn*, which was introduced on 15 Nov. 1993 at 1 tenge = 500 roubles. It became the sole legal tender on 25 Nov. 1993. Inflation was running at nearly 1,880% in 1994, but dropped dramatically and was only 8·3% in 2001. In June 2002 foreign exchange reserves were US$2,280m. and gold reserves amounted to 1·74m. troy oz. Total money supply in May 2002 was 258,470m. tenge.

Budget. Government revenue and expenditure (in 1m. tenge), year ending 31 Dec.:

	1997	1998	1999	2000
Revenue	292,567	262,916	207,765	317,747
Expenditure	332,507	318,253	304,150	372,612

Performance. The break-up of the Soviet Union triggered an economic collapse as orders from Russian factories for Kazakhstan's metals and phosphates, two mainstays of the economy, dried up. Low oil and commodity prices cut revenues by a third in 1998. Real GDP growth was –1·9% in 1998 but there was a slight recovery in 1999, with growth of 2·7%. In 2000 growth was an impressive 9·8% and in 2001 an even more spectacular 13·2%. Total GDP in 2001 was US$22·6bn.

Banking and Finance. The central bank and bank of issue is the National Bank (*Governor,* Grigory Aleksandrovich Marchenko). In 2001 there were 44 domestic banks, with assets totalling US$5·3bn. Foreign direct investment amounted to US$2·8bn. in 2001, more than double the 2000 total.

ENERGY AND NATURAL RESOURCES

Environment. According to the *World Bank Atlas* carbon dioxide emissions in 1998 were the equivalent of 8·2 tonnes per capita.

Electricity. Installed capacity is 17m. kW. Output in 1998 was 49·3bn. kWh. There is one nuclear power station. Consumption per capita was 2,399 kWh in 1998.

Oil and Gas. Proven oil reserves in 1999 were 8bn. bbls. The onshore Tengiz field has estimated oil reserves between 6bn. and 9bn. bbls.; the onshore Karachaganak field has oil reserves of 2bn. bbls., and gas reserves of 600,000m. cu. metres. Output of crude oil (including gas concentrates), 1996, 22·9m. tonnes (1997 estimate, 26·2m. tonnes); natural gas, 1999, 9·2bn. cu. metres with proven reserves of 1,840bn. cu. metres. The first major pipeline for the export of oil from the Tengiz field was opened in March 2001, linking the Caspian port of Atyraū with the Russian Black Sea port of Novorossiisk. In Sept. 1997 Kazakhstan signed oil agreements with China worth US$9·5bn.; these include a 3,000 km pipeline to Xinjiang province in western China. Oil and gas investment by foreign companies is now driving the economy. In 1997 oil production sharing deals were concluded with two international consortia to explore the North Caspian basin and to develop the Karachaganak gas field. A huge new offshore oilfield in the far north of the Caspian Sea, known as East Kashagan, was discovered in early 2000. The field could prove to be the largest find in the last 30 years, and estimates suggest that it may contain 50bn. bbls. of oil. However, tangible results are unlikely to be achieved until 2005 at the earliest. The various recent discoveries have meant that by 2010 Kazakhstan aims to have become the world's sixth largest oil producer.

It is hoped that exploitation of the oil reserves of the Caspian shelf will start during 2003. Initially production is expected to amount to 100,000 bbls. per day, possibly rising to as much as 1·2m. bbls. per day by 2013. It is believed that there may be as much as 14bn. tonnes of oil and gas reserves under Kazakhstan's portion of the Caspian Sea.

Minerals. Kazakhstan is extremely rich in mineral resources, including coal, bauxite, cobalt, vanadium, iron ores, chromium, phosphates, borates and other salts, copper, lead, manganese, molybdenum, nickel, tin, gold, silver, tungsten and zinc. Coal production (1997 estimate, in tonnes), 72·6m.; iron ore (1998), 9m.; lignite (1997), 2·47m.; bauxite (1998), 3·44m.; steel (1996), 3·22m.; copper (1998), 337,000; uranium (1998), 1,250 gold (1997), 12.

Agriculture. Kazakh agriculture has changed from primarily nomad cattle breeding to production of grain, cotton and other industrial crops. In 1997 agriculture accounted for 12% of GDP and there were 30m. ha of arable land and 0·13m. ha of permanent crops. In 1993, 181·3m. ha were under cultivation, of which private subsidiary agriculture accounted for 0·3m. ha and commercial farming 6·3m. ha in 16,300 farms. Around 60,000 private farms have emerged since independence.

Tobacco, rubber plants and mustard are also cultivated. Kazakhstan has rich orchards and vineyards, which accounted for 95,000 ha of cultivated land in 1985. Kazakhstan is noted for its livestock, particularly its sheep, from which excellent quality wool is obtained. Livestock (2000): 4·00m. cattle (down from 9·57m. in 1993), 9·78m. sheep (down from 33·63m. in 1993), 1·03m. pigs, 942,000 horses, 705,000 goats and 18m. chickens.

Output of main agricultural products (in 1,000 tonnes) in 2000: wheat, 9,091; potatoes, 1,694; barley, 1,663; watermelons, 902; onions, 300; tomatoes, 280; sugarbeets, 269; seed cotton, 258; maize, 247; rice, 213; cabbages, 200. Livestock products, 2000 (in 1,000 tonnes): milk, 3,605; meat, 644; eggs, 86. Kazakhstan is a major exporter of grain to Russia, but in recent years there has been a significant reduction in the quantity exported as a result of low crop yields coupled with the need to meet domestic demand.

Forestry. Forests covered 10·50m. ha in 1995, or 3·9% of the land area (up from 9·54m. ha and 3·6% in 1990). Only the USA and Uzbekistan exceeded the 0·96m. ha afforested in Kazakhstan between 1990 and 1995. In 1999, 315,000 cu. metres of timber were cut.

Fisheries. Catches in 1999 totalled 25,758 tonnes, exclusively freshwater fish.

INDUSTRY

Kazakhstan was heavily industrialized in the Soviet period, with non-ferrous metallurgy, heavy engineering and the chemical industries prominent. Output was valued at 30,000m. tenge in current prices in 1996 and 35,000m. tenge in 1997. Production (1997 estimate, in tonnes) included ferroalloy, 680,000; cement, 661,000; mineral fertilizer, 200,000; chemical fibre, 1,900 (1993); cardboard, 7,400

(1996); lead, 85,000; fabrics, 24·6m. sq. metres; leather footwear, 0·8m. pairs; tractors, 3,100 units; radio sets, 600 units; refrigerators and freezers, 12,900 units (1993); washing machines, 23,200 units.

Labour. In 1996 the population of working age was estimated as 7·4m. In 2000 the unemployment rate was 3·7%.

INTERNATIONAL TRADE

In Jan. 1994 an agreement to create a single economic zone was signed with Kyrgyzstan and Uzbekistan. Since Jan. 1992 individuals and enterprises have been able to engage in foreign trade without needing government permission, except for goods 'of national interest' (fuel, minerals, mineral fertilizers, grain, cotton, wool, caviar and pharmaceutical products) which may be exported only by state organizations. Foreign debt was US$6,664m. in 2000.

Imports and Exports. In 2000 imports (f.o.b.) were valued at US$6,849·8m. and exports (f.o.b.) at US$9,615·4m. In 1999, 36·7% of imports came from Russia, 25·3% from the EU (Germany being the largest source) and 9·5% from the USA. Main export markets in 1999 were the EU (22·9% of all exports), Russia (19·8%) and China (8·5%). Main imports: machinery and parts, and industrial materials. Main exports: oil, ferrous and non-ferrous metals, and cotton.

COMMUNICATIONS

Roads. In 1998 there were estimated to be 119,390 km of motor roads, of which 18,884 were national roads. In 1997 an estimated 1bn. passengers used public transport and 1bn. tonnes of freight were carried. Passenger cars in use in 1998 numbered 971,170 (62 per 1,000 inhabitants), and there were also 270,198 trucks and vans and 44,295 buses and coaches. There were 2,026 fatalities as a result of road accidents in 1997.

Rail. In 1997 there were estimated to be 14,400 km of 1,520 mm gauge railways (3,528 km electrified 1994). Passenger-km travelled in 1998 came to 10·7bn. and freight tonne-km to 99·4bn.

Civil Aviation. The national carrier is Air Kazakhstan. There is an international airport at Almaty, which in 1996 handled 1,745,000 passengers and 20,800 tonnes of freight. In 1999 scheduled airline traffic of Kazakhstan-based carriers flew 33·2m. km, carrying 667,000 passengers (318,000 on international flights).

Shipping. There is one large port, Aktau. In 1993, 1·2m. passengers and 4m. tonnes of freight were carried on inland waterways. Merchant shipping totalled 12,000 GRT in 1995.

Telecommunications. Main telephone lines numbered 1,834,200 in 2000, or 113·1 per 1,000 persons. There were 49,500 mobile phone subscribers in 1998 and 1,600 fax machines in 1997. Kazakhstan had 70,000 Internet users in Dec. 1999.

Postal Services. In 1995 there were 4,355 post offices.

SOCIAL INSTITUTIONS

Justice. In 1994, 201,796 crimes were reported; in 1996 there were 2,986 murders. The population in penal institutions in 1997 was 82,945 (495 per 100,000 of national population). The death penalty is in force.

Religion. There were some 4,000 mosques in 1996 (63 in 1990). An Islamic Institute opened in 1991 to train imams. A Roman Catholic diocese was established in 1991. In 1995 the Union of Evangelical Baptist Churches had 140 communities, the Russian Orthodox Church 177, and the Evangelical Lutheran Church 112.

Education. In Jan. 1994, 0·7m. children (39% of those eligible) were attending pre-school institutions. In 1996–97 there were 1,342,035 pupils at primary schools, 1,921,302 pupils at secondary schools and, in 1995–96, 419,460 students at higher education institutions. Adult literacy rate is more than 99%.

Health. In 1995 there were 62,290 doctors, and in Jan. 1994, 187,000 junior medical personnel and 1,899 hospitals with 225,000 beds.

Welfare. In Jan. 1994 there were 2·1m. age and 0·9m. other pensioners. Pension contributions are 20% of salary and are payable to the State Pension Fund.

CULTURE

Broadcasting. Broadcasting is the responsibility of the Kazakh State Radio and Television Co. There are three national and 13 regional radio programmes, a Radio Moscow relay and a foreign service, Radio Alma-Ata (Kazakh, English). There is one TV channel (colour by SECAM). There were 6·47m. radio receivers and 3·88m. television receivers in 1997.

Cinema. In 1995 there were 1,580 cinemas with an annual attendance of 6·2m.; gross box office receipts came to 39m. tenge. Ten full-length films were made.

Press. In 1995 there were 472 periodicals in Kazakh, 511 in Russian and 60 in both languages. There is frequent harassment of independent journalists.

Tourism. Foreign tourists brought in revenue of US$289m. in 1998.

DIPLOMATIC REPRESENTATIVES

Of Kazakhstan in the United Kingdom (33 Thurlowe Sq., London, SW7 2DS)
Ambassador: Erlan Idrissov.

Of the United Kingdom in Kazakhstan (Ul. Furmanova 173, Almaty 480091)
Ambassador: James Lyall Sharp.

Of Kazakhstan in the USA (1401 16th Street, NW, Washington, D.C., 20036)
Ambassador: Kanat B. Saudabayev.

Of the USA in Kazakhstan (Ul. Furmanova 99/97a, Almaty 480091)
Ambassador: Larry C. Napper.

Of Kazakhstan to the United Nations
Ambassador: Madina B. Jarbussynova.

Of Kazakhstan to the European Union
Ambassador: Tuletai Suleimenov.

FURTHER READING

Alexandrov, M., *Uneasy Alliance: Relations Between Russia and Kazakhstan in the Post-Soviet Era, 1992–1997.* Greenwood Publishing Group, Westport (CT), 1999

Nazpary, J., *Post-Soviet Chaos: Violence and Dispossession in Kazakhstan.* Pluto Press, London, 2001

Olcott, Marta Brill, *The Kazakhs.* Stanford, 1987.—*Kazakhstan; Unfilled Promise.* Carnegie Endowment for International Peace, Washington, D. C., 2001

National statistical office: Agency of Kazakhstan on Statistics, 125 Abay Ave., 480008 Almaty, Kazakhstan.
Website: http://www.stat.kz

KENYA

Jamhuri ya Kenya
(Republic of Kenya)

Capital: Nairobi
Population estimate, 2000: 30·67m.
GDP per capita, 2000: (PPP$) 1,022
HDI/world rank: 0·513/134

KEY HISTORICAL EVENTS

Prior to colonialism, the area comprised African farming communities, notably the Kikuyu and the Masai. From the 16th century through to the 19th, they were loosely controlled by the Arabic rulers of Oman. In 1895 the British declared part of the region the East Africa Protectorate, which from 1920 was known as the Colony of Kenya. The influx of European settlers was resented by Africans not only for the whites' land holdings but also for their exclusive political representation in the colonial Legislative Council. A state of emergency existed between Oct. 1952 and Jan. 1960 during the period of the Mau Mau uprising. Over 13,000 Africans and 100 Europeans were killed. The Kenya African Union was banned and its president, Jomo Kenyatta, imprisoned. The state of emergency ended in 1960. Full internal self-government was achieved in 1962 and in Dec. 1963 Kenya became an independent member of the Commonwealth. In 1982 Kenya became a one-party state and in 1986 party preliminary elections were instituted to reduce the number of parliamentary candidates at general elections. Only those candidates obtaining over 30% of the preliminary vote were eligible to stand. On the death of Kenyatta in Aug. 1978 Daniel T. arap Moi, the vice-president, became acting president and was elected in 1979, and then re-elected in 1983, 1988, 1992 and 1997. An attempted coup in 1982 was unsuccessful. A multi-party election was permitted in 1992 and again in 1997, the first genuinely competitive elections since 1963.

TERRITORY AND POPULATION

Kenya is bounded by Sudan and Ethiopia in the north, Uganda in the west, Tanzania in the south and Somalia and the Indian Ocean in the east. The total area is 582,646 sq. km, of which 571,416 sq. km is land area. In the 1989 census the population was 21,443,636 (19% urban; up to 32·1% by 1999). The 1999 census gave a population of 28,686,607 (14,481,018 females).

The UN gives a projected population for 2010 of 36·941m.

The land areas, populations and capitals of the provinces are:

Province	Sq. km	Census 1999	Capital	Census 1989
Rift Valley	182,413	6,987,036	Nakuru	163,927
Eastern	154,354	4,631,779	Embu	26,525
Nyanza	12,507	4,392,196	Kisumu	192,733
Central	13,236	3,724,159	Nyeri	91,258
Western	8,285	3,358,776	Kakamega	58,862
Coast	84,113	2,487,264	Mombasa	461,753
Nairobi	693	2,143,254		
North-Eastern	126,186	962,143	Garissa	31,319

In 1999 Nairobi had a population of 2,205,000. Other towns (1989): Machakos (116,293), Eldoret (111,882), Meru (94,947), Thika (57,603).

Most of Kenya's 26·44m. people belong to 13 tribes, the main ones including Kikuyu (about 22% of the population), Luhya (14%), Luo (13%), Kalenjin (12%), Kamba (11%), Gusii (6%), Meru (5%) and Mijikenda (5%).

Swahili is the official language, but people belonging to the different tribes have their own language as their mother tongue. English is spoken in commercial centres.

SOCIAL STATISTICS

1995 births, 1,013,000; deaths, 312,000. Birth rate (per 1,000 population), 1995, 37·3; death rate, 11·5. Annual population growth rate, 1990–99, 2·6%. Expectation of life at birth in 1999 was 50·4 years for males and 52·2 years for females. Infant mortality, 1999, 76 per 1,000 live births. Fertility rate, 1999, 4·2 births per woman, down from 6·1 in 1990. In 2000 more than half of Kenyans lived below the poverty line, up by over 10% in the space of 10 years.

CLIMATE

The climate is tropical, with wet and dry seasons, but considerable differences in altitude make for varied conditions between the hot, coastal lowlands and the plateau, where temperatures are very much cooler. Heaviest rains occur in April and May, but in some parts there is a second wet season in Nov. and Dec. Nairobi, Jan. 65°F (18·3°C), July 60°F (15·6°C). Annual rainfall 39" (958 mm). Mombasa, Jan. 81°F (27·2°C), July 76°F (24·4°C). Annual rainfall 47" (1,201 mm).

CONSTITUTION AND GOVERNMENT

There is a unicameral *National Assembly*, which until the Dec. 1997 elections had 200 members, comprising 188 elected by universal suffrage for a five-year term, ten members appointed by the President, and the Speaker and Attorney-General *ex officio*. Following a review of constituency boundaries, the National Assembly now has 210 elected members, 12 members appointed and the two *ex officio* members, making 224 in total. The President is also directly elected for five years; he appoints a Vice-President and other Ministers to a Cabinet over which he presides. A constitutional amendment of Aug. 1992 stipulates that the winning presidential candidate must receive a nationwide majority and also the vote of 25% of electors in at least five of the eight provinces. The sole legal political party had been the Kenya African National Union (KANU), but after demonstrations by the pro-reform lobby which led to extreme violence, KANU agreed to legalize opposition parties. A Constitutional Review Commission was established in 1997 to amend the Constitution before elections that were scheduled for 2002. In Sept. 2002 the Commission recommended changes to Kenya's system of government, including the curbing of presidential powers and the introduction of an executive prime ministerial position. However, in Oct. 2002 President Daniel arap Moi announced the dissolution of parliament before the Commission had completed its task, preventing a new constitution from being in place in time for the elections.

National Anthem. 'Ee Mungu nguvu yetu' ('Oh God of all creation'); words by a collective, tune traditional.

RECENT ELECTIONS

Presidential elections held on 27 Dec. 2002 were won by Mwai Kibaki of the opposition National Rainbow Coalition (NARC) with 62·2% of the vote, against 31·3% for Uhuru Kenyatta, candidate of the ruling Kenya African National Union (KANU), and 5·9% for Simeon Nyachae of the Forum for the Restoration of Democracy-People (FORD-People). Turn-out was 56·1%. Mwai Kibaki's victory ended nearly 40 years of KANU rule since Kenya became independent in 1963.

In parliamentary elections also held on 27 Dec. 2002 NARC won 125 of 210 seats, KANU 64, FORD-People 14, Sisi Kwa Sisi 2, Safina 2, Forum for the Restoration of Democracy-Asili 2 and Shirikisho Party of Kenya 1.

CURRENT ADMINISTRATION

President: Mwai Kibaki; b. 1931 (NARC; sworn in 30 Dec. 2002).

Following the elections of 27 Dec. 2002 a new cabinet was formed, composed in March 2003 as follows:

Vice President: Michael Kijana Wamalwa.

Minister of Agriculture and Livestock Development: Kipruto Kirwa. *Co-operative Development:* Peter Njeru Ndwiga. *Education, Science and Technology:* George Saitoti. *Energy:* Ochilo Ayacko. *Environment, Natural Resources and Wildlife:* Dr Newton Kulundu. *Finance:* David Mwiraria. *Foreign Affairs:* Kalonzo Musyoka. *Gender, Sports, Culture and Social Services:* Najib Balala. *Health:* Charity Ngilu. *Home Affairs and National Heritage:* Moody Awori. *Justice and Constitutional Affairs:* Kiraitu Murungi. *Labour and Manpower Development:* Vacant. *Lands and Settlement:* Amos Kimunya. *Local Government:* Emmanuel Karisa Maitha. *Planning and National Development:* Peter Anyang Nyongo. *Roads, Public Works and Housing:* Raila Odinga. *Tourism and Information:* Raphael Tuju. *Trade and*

Industry: Dr Mukhisa Kituyi. *Transportation and Communication:* John Michuki. *Water Resources:* Martha Karua. *Attorney-General:* Amos Wako.

DEFENCE
In 2000 defence expenditure totalled US$307m. (US$10 per capita), representing 2·9% of GDP.

Army. Total strength (1999) 20,500. In addition there is a paramilitary Police General Service Unit of 5,000.

Navy. The Navy, based in Mombasa, consisted in 1999 of 1,200 personnel.

Air Force. An air force, formed on 1 June 1964, was built up with RAF assistance. Equipment includes F-5E/F-5F attack jets. Personnel (1999) 2,500, with 30 combat aircraft and 34 armed helicopters.

INTERNATIONAL RELATIONS
Kenya is a member of the UN, WTO, the Commonwealth, the African Union, African Development Bank, COMESA, EAC, the Intergovernmental Authority on Development, IOM and is an ACP member state of the ACP-EU relationship.

In Nov. 1999 a treaty was signed between Kenya, Tanzania and Uganda to create a new East African Community as a means of developing East African trade, tourism and industry and laying the foundations for a future common market and political federation.

ECONOMY
Services contributed 57·7% of GDP in 1998, agriculture 26·1% and industry 16·2%.

Kenya used to have one of the strongest economies in Africa but years of mismanagement and corruption have had a detrimental effect, made worse in 2000 by one of the longest droughts in living memory. Up to US$1bn. in international aid was frozen during the Moi era because Kenya failed to pass anti-corruption legislation.

Overview. Since a privatization programme was launched in 1992, the government has completed the sale of the majority of the 207 enterprises originally targeted. In 1996 a Presidential Economic Commission was set up to implement reforms to public companies over 1996–98. A US$215m. IMF loan agreement signed in April 1995 was suspended in 1997 while the government considered measures against corruption. However, in July 2000 the IMF decided to release US$198m. and the World Bank announced in Aug. 2000 that it would lend a further US$150m.

Currency. The monetary unit is the *Kenya shilling* (KES) of 100 *cents*. The currency became convertible in May 1994. The shilling was devalued by 23% in April 1993. The annual rate of inflation was 5·8% in 2001. Foreign exchange reserves were US$1,120m. in June 2002. Gold reserves have been negligible since 1998. In May 2002 total money supply was 133,063m. shillings.

Budget. In 1998 total government revenue was 178,181m. shillings (145,545m. in 1997) and expenditure was 179,525m. shillings (152,888m. in 1997). The fiscal year ends on 30 June.

Performance. Real GDP growth was negative in 2000, at –0·1%, but 2001 then saw a slight recovery, with growth of 1·2%. Total GDP in 2001 was US$10·4bn.

Banking and Finance. The central bank and bank of issue is the Central Bank of Kenya (*Governor*, Dr Andrew Mulei, appointed March 2003). There are 50 banks, 40 non-banking financial institutions and a couple of building societies. In March 1995 their combined assets totalled £268,811m. shillings. In 1998 the government offloaded 25% of its stake in the Kenya Commercial Bank, which lowered its shareholding to 35%. The remaining 35% will be sold off before the end of the financial year 2002–03.

There is a stock exchange in Nairobi.

ENERGY AND NATURAL RESOURCES
Environment. According to the *World Bank Atlas* Kenya's carbon dioxide emissions in 1998 were the equivalent of 0·3 tonnes per capita.

Electricity. Installed generating capacity was 1m. kW in 1997; mostly provided by hydropower from power stations on the Tana river, with some from oil-fired power stations and by geothermal power. Production in 1998 was 4·23bn. kWh, with consumption per capita 129 kWh. In 1999 it was decided to encourage the private sector to take part in electricity generation alongside the state-owned Kenya Electricity Generating Company as a means of bringing to an end the shortage of power and the frequent blackouts. In June 2000 a rationing scheme was introduced in much of the country restricting the power supply to 12 hours a day, and sometimes less.

Oil and Gas. Kenya signed an oil and gas exploration deal in 1997 with Canada's Tornado Resources Ltd, who pledged to commit a minimum of US$7m. over a three-year period.

Minerals. Production, 1995 (in 1,000 tonnes): soda ash, 218; fluorite, 80; salt, 71. Other minerals included gold, raw soda, lime and limestone, diatomite, garnets and vermiculite.

Agriculture. As agriculture is possible from sea-level to altitudes of over 2,500 metres, tropical, sub-tropical and temperate crops can be grown and mixed farming is pursued. In 1998 there were 4m. ha of arable land and 520,000 ha of permanent crop land. Four-fifths of the country is range-land which produces mainly livestock products and the wild game which is a major tourist attraction.

Tea and coffee are two of the big foreign exchange earners, along with tourism. Horticultural products, particularly flowers, are in fourth position.

Kenya has about 113,000 ha under tea production, and is the world's fourth largest producer and largest exporter of tea. The production is high quality tea, raised in near-perfect agronomic conditions. It is plucked the whole year round, and almost exclusively by hand. In 2000 production was 239,000 tonnes; in 1996 exports were worth US$350m.

Coffee output in 2000 was 67,000 tonnes; 165,000 ha is under coffee production. Some 70% of the total hectarage under coffee is cultivated by 335,000 smallholders, although their production has been in decline in recent years.

Other major agricultural products (2000, in 1,000 tonnes): sugarcane, 4,750; maize, 1,800; cassava, 950; sweet potatoes, 535; plantains, 370; potatoes, 360; pineapples, 280; bananas, 210; sorghum, 133; wheat, 105.

Maize is Kenya's most important food crop with about 1·3m. ha under cultivation and annual production of nearly 2m. tonnes. Sisal, pyrethrum, maize and wheat are crops of major importance in the Highlands, while coconuts, cashew nuts, cotton, sugar, sisal and maize are the principal crops grown at the lower altitudes.

Livestock (2000): cattle, 13·79m.; sheep, 7·0m.; goats, 9·6m.; camels, 850,000; chickens, 27m.

More than half the agricultural labour force is employed in the livestock sector, accounting for 10% of GDP.

Forestry. Forests covered 1·29m. ha in 1995 (2·3% of the land area), mainly between 1,800 and 3,300 metres above sea-level. There are coniferous, broad-leaved, hardwood and bamboo forests. Timber production was 29·91m. cu. metres in 1999.

Fisheries. Catches in 1999 totalled 205,287 tonnes, of which 198,653 tonnes were freshwater fish. While the aggregate landings from Kenya's inland waters (more than 90% from Lake Victoria) have grown over the past 20 years, marine fishing has not reached its full potential, despite a coastline of 680 km. Fish landed from the sea totals between 5,000 and 7,000 tonnes annually, but there is an estimated potential of 200,000 tonnes in tuna and similar species.

INDUSTRY
In 1994 there were 648 manufacturing firms employing more than 50 persons. The main products are textiles, chemicals, vehicle assembly and transport equipment, leather and footwear, printing and publishing, food and tobacco processing and oil refining. Production included (in tonnes): cement (1997), 1,506,000; sugar (1998), 488,187; maize meal (1994), 233,200; wheat flour (1994), 191,400; animal feed (1988), 184,266; cotton (1996), 28m. sq. metres.

Labour. The labour force in 1996 was 13,953,000 (54% males). In 1997 the unemployment level was close to 3m. The average Kenyan earns US$350 a year.

INTERNATIONAL TRADE

Foreign debt was US$6,295m. in 2000. Foreign investment on the stock exchange has been permitted since 1 Jan. 1995. Export Processing Zones were introduced in 1990, offering foreign companies exemption from taxes and duties for ten years.

Imports and Exports. Imports and exports for calendar years in US$1m.:

	1996	1997	1998	1999	2000
Imports f.o.b.	2,598·2	2,948·4	3,028·7	2,731·8	3,044·0
Exports f.o.b.	2,083·3	2,062·6	2,017·0	1,748·6	1,773·4

Principal exports (in 1,000m. shillings) 1994: tea, 16·9; coffee, 13; horticultural produce, 8·3. Imports: petroleum, 18·6; machinery and transport equipment, 31·8; chemicals (1993), 19·9; manufactures, 14·7.

Main import suppliers, 1996: UK, 13·2%; United Arab Emirates, 8·2%; Japan, 7·4%; Germany, 6·1%. Main export markets, 1996: Uganda, 15·4%; Tanzania, 12·0%; UK, 10·8%; Germany, 7·7%.

The UK is the largest foreign investor in Kenya with over US$1,500m. in more than 60 enterprises.

COMMUNICATIONS

Roads. Of some 63,800 km of roads in 1996, only about 8,900 km, or 14%, have been surfaced. More than 80,000 km of roads are unclassified. The network has seriously deteriorated since the mid 1980s through poor maintenance. Urban roads comprise around 7,000 km, or about 5% of the total road network, but less than half of them are classified as 'good' or in 'fair' condition. Yet more than 70% of all vehicles in the country use urban roads because of the heavy concentration of economic activities in urban areas. Overall, more than 80% of passengers and freight are carried on the roads. There were, in 1996, 278,000 passenger cars, 32,000 motorcycles, 62,000 vans and trucks and 19,200 buses and coaches. There were 11,785 road accidents in 1994 (2,424 fatal).

Rail. In 1994 route length was 2,506 km of metre-gauge. Passenger-km travelled in 1998 came to 432m. and freight tonne-km to 1,111m. Kenya Railways Corporation (KRC) is restructuring in preparation for privatization. In 2003 the Kenyan and Ugandan governments agreed to sell KRC and Uganda Railways Corporation to a single investor.

Civil Aviation. There are international airports at Nairobi (Jomo Kenyatta International) and Mombasa (Moi International). The national carrier is the now privatized Kenya Airways. KLM has a 26% share of Kenya Airways. In 1999 Kenya Airways flew 22·5m. km and carried 1,246,000 passengers (807,600 on international flights). In 2000 Jomo Kenyatta International handled 2,734,108 passengers and 135,619 tonnes of freight, and Moi International 853,944 passengers and 2,716 tonnes of freight.

Shipping. The main port is Mombasa, which handled 8·5m. tonnes of cargo in 1998. Container traffic has nearly doubled since 1990 to 217,028 TEUs (twenty-foot equivalent units) in 1996. The merchant marine totalled 21,000 GRT in 1998, including oil tankers 5,000 GRT. In 1998 vessels totalling 8,413,000 NRT entered ports.

Telecommunications. Kenya had 321,500 main telephone lines in 2000, or 10·5 per 1,000 persons. The government aims to improve telephone availability in rural areas from 0·16 lines per 100 persons in 1997 to 1 line per 100 by 2015, and in urban areas from 4 lines to 20 lines per 100 persons. There were 150,000 PCs in 2000 (4·9 per 1,000 persons) and 3,800 fax machines in 1995. In Dec. 2000 there were 200,000 Internet users, and in Nov. 1999 mobile phone subscribers numbered 9,000.

Postal Services. In 1995 there were 1,061 post offices, or one for every 26,000 persons.

SOCIAL INSTITUTIONS

Justice. The courts of Justice comprises the court of Appeal, the High Court and a large number of subsidiary courts. The court of Appeal is the final Apellant court in the country and is based in Nairobi. It comprises seven Judges of Appeal. In the course of its Appellate duties the court of Appeal visits Mombasa, Kisumu, Nakuru and Nyeri. The High court with full jurisdiction in both civil and criminal matters comprises a total of 28 puisne Judges. Puisne Judges sit in Nairobi (16), Mombasa (two), Nakuru, Kisumu, Nyeri, Eldoret, Meru and Kisii (one each).

The Magistracy consists of approximately 300 magistrates of various cadres based in all provincial, district and some divisional centres. In addition to the above there are the Kadhi courts established in areas of concentrated Muslim populations: Mombasa, Nairobi, Malindi, Lamu, Garissa, Kisumu and Marsabit. They exercise limited jurisdiction in matters governed by Islamic Law.

There were 17,589 criminal convictions in 1993; the prison population was 41,064 in 1996 (140 per 100,000 of national population).

Religion. In 1992 there were 7·12m. Roman Catholics, 1·94m. Protestants and 1·62m. Muslims. Traditional beliefs persist.

Education. The adult literacy rate in 1999 was 81·5% (88·3% among males and 74·8% among females). In 1994 there were 19,083 pre-primary schools with 27,829 teachers and 951,997 pupils. 5,544,998 pupils were in primary schools in 1995 with 181,975 teachers. In 1995 there were also 632,388 pupils and 41,484 teachers in secondary schools; 20 teacher training schools with 16,461 students; 20 technical training institutes with 8,148 students. There were three polytechnics with 10,836 students, and five universities (Nairobi, Moi, Kenyatta, Egerton and Jomo Kenyatta University College of Agriculture and Technology) with 39,340 students.

Health. In 1994 there were 4,558 doctors and 630 dentists. There were 324 hospitals (with 37,271 beds), 522 health centres and 2,868 sub-centres and dispensaries. Free medical service for all children and adult out-patients was launched in 1965.

CULTURE

Broadcasting. Broadcasting is the responsibility of KBC, which transmits the following services: National (in Swahili), General (English), Central (four languages), Western (six languages), North-Eastern and Coastal (four languages). KBC also provides television programmes, mainly in English and Swahili (colour by PAL). There are several private broadcasting stations, including Kenya Television Network (which broadcasts CNN), Stellavision (which broadcasts Sky News), Capital Radio and Metro FM. The BBC has been awarded a licence to broadcast on the FM frequency. Number of sets in 1997: TV, 730,000; radio, 3·07m.

Press. In 1996 there were four daily papers with a total circulation of 263,000. In May 2002 the Kenyan parliament passed a law making it illegal to sell books, newspapers or magazines that had not been submitted to the government for review.

Tourism. In 1999 there were 943,000 holiday visitors. Once Kenya's fastest growing source of foreign exchange, receipts from tourism had dropped from US$500m. a year to US$256m. a year by 1999. A European Union grant is helping to revive the industry. In 1998 tourism employed approximately 200,000 people and contributed 11% of GDP.

DIPLOMATIC REPRESENTATIVES

Of Kenya in the United Kingdom (45 Portland Pl., London, W1N 4AS)
High Commissioner: Nancy Kirui.

Of the United Kingdom in Kenya (Upper Hill Road, Nairobi)
High Commissioner: Edward Clay, CMG.

Of Kenya in the USA (2249 R. St., NW, Washington, D.C., 20008)
Ambassador: Yusef A. Nzibo.

Of the USA in Kenya (Moi/Haile Selassie Ave., Nairobi)
Ambassador: Johnnie Carson.

Of Kenya to the United Nations
Ambassador: Bob Jalang'o.

Of Kenya to the European Union
Ambassador: Peter Nkuraiya.

FURTHER READING

Coger, D., *Kenya.* [Bibliography] 2nd ed. ABC-Clio, Oxford and Santa Barbara (CA), 1996

Haugerud, A., *The Culture of Politics in Modern Kenya.* CUP, 1995

Kyle, Keith, *The Politics of the Independence of Kenya.* Macmillan, London, 1999

Miller, N. N., *Kenya: the Quest for Prosperity.* 2nd ed. Boulder (CO), 1994

Ogot, B. A. and Ochieng, W. R. (eds.) *Decolonization and Independence in Kenya, 1940–93.* London, 1995

Throup, David and Hornsby, Charles, *Multiparty Politics in Kenya.* James Currey, Oxford, 1999

Widner, J. A., *The Rise of a Party State in Kenya: from 'Harambee' to 'Nayayo'.* Univ. of California Press, 1993

National statistical office: Central Bureau of Statistics, Ministry of Planning and National Development, POB 30266, Nairobi

KIRIBATI

Ribaberikin Kiribati
(Republic of Kiribati)

Capital: Bairiki (Tarawa)
Population estimate, 2000: 87,000
GDP per capita: not available
GNP per capita: $910

KEY HISTORICAL EVENTS
The islands that now constitute Kiribati were first settled by early Austronesian-speaking peoples long before the 1st century AD. Fijians and Tongans arrived about the 14th century and subsequently merged with the older groups to form the traditional I-Kiribati Micronesian society and culture. The Gilbert and Ellice Islands were proclaimed a British protectorate in 1892 and annexed at the request of the native governments as the Gilbert and Ellice Islands Colony on 10 Nov. 1915. On 1 Oct. 1975 the Ellice Islands severed constitutional links with the Gilbert Islands and took on a new name, Tuvalu. The Gilberts achieved full independence as Kiribati in 1979. Internal self-government was obtained on 1 Nov. 1976 and independence on 12 July 1979 as the Republic of Kiribati.

TERRITORY AND POPULATION
Kiribati (pronounced Kiribahss) consists of three groups of coral atolls and one isolated volcanic island, spread over a large expanse of the Central Pacific with a total land area of 717·1 sq. km (276·9 sq. miles). It comprises **Banaba** or Ocean Island (5 sq. km), the 16 **Gilbert Islands** (295 sq. km), the 8 **Phoenix Islands** (55 sq. km), and 8 of the 11 **Line Islands** (329 sq. km), the other 3 Line Islands (Jarvis, Palmyra Atoll and Kingman Reef) being uninhabited dependencies of the USA. The capital is the island of Bairiki in Tarawa. The gradual rise in sea levels in recent years is slowly reducing the area of the islands.

Population, 2000 census (provisional), 84,678 (42,851 females); density, 118·1 per sq. km.

In 1995 an estimated 64·3% of the population lived in rural areas. Between 1995 and 2000 the number of people living in urban areas increased by 6·4%. Between 1988 and 1993, 4,700 people were resettled on Teraina and Tabuaeran atolls because the main island group was overcrowded. Since then the government's programme has been suspended owing to the need to improve the physical infrastructure and housing.

The population distribution at the 2000 census was 49·4% in the Outer Islands, 42·9% in South Tarawa (urban area) and 7·7% in the Line and Phoenix Islands. Banaba, all 16 Gilbert Islands, Kanton (or Abariringa) in the Phoenix Islands and 3 atolls in the Line Islands (Teraina, Tabuaeran and Kiritimati—formerly Washington, Fanning and Christmas Islands respectively) are inhabited; their populations in 1995 (census) were as follows:

Banaba (Ocean Is.)	339	Abemama	3,442	Nikunau		2,009
Makin	1,830	Kuria	971	Onotoa		1,918
Butaritari	3,909	Aranuka	1,015	Tamana		1,181
Marakei	2,724	Nonouti	3,042	Arorae		1,248
Abaiang	6,020	Tabiteuea	4,787	Kanton		83
Tarawa	32,354	North Tabiteuea	3,383	Teraina		978
North Tarawa	4,004	South Tabiteuea	1,404	Tabuaeran		1,615
South Tarawa	28,350	Beru	2,784	Kiritimati		3,225
Maiana	2,184					

The remaining 12 atolls have no permanent population; the seven Phoenix Islands comprise Birnie, Rawaki (formerly Phoenix), Enderbury, Manra (formerly Sydney), Orona (formerly Hull), McKean and Nikumaroro (formerly Gardner), while the others are Malden and Starbuck in the Central Line Islands, and Millennium Island (formerly Caroline), Flint and Vostok in the Southern Line Islands. The population is almost entirely Micronesian.

English is the official language; I-Kiribati (Gilbertese) is also spoken.

SOCIAL STATISTICS

1997 births (estimate), 2,200; deaths, 600. 1997 estimated birth rate, 26·8 per 1,000 population; death rate, 7·7 per 1,000; infant mortality rate, 51·5 per 1,000 live births; life expectancy, 62·3 years. Annual population growth rate, 1990–99, 1·4%; fertility rate, 1999, 4·2 births per woman.

CLIMATE

The Line Islands, Phoenix Islands and Banaba have a maritime equatorial climate, but the islands further north and south are tropical. Annual and daily ranges of temperature are small; mean annual rainfall ranges from 50" (1,250 mm) near the equator to 120" (3,000 mm) in the north. Typhoons are prevalent (Nov.–March) and there are occasional tornadoes. Tarawa, Jan. 83°F (28·3°C), July 82°F (27·8°C). Annual rainfall 79" (1,977 mm).

CONSTITUTION AND GOVERNMENT

Under the constitution founded on 12 July 1979 the republic has a unicameral legislature, the *House of Assembly* (Maneaba ni Maungatabu), comprising 41 members, 39 of whom are elected by popular vote, and two (the Attorney-General *ex officio* and a representative from the Banaban community) appointed for a four-year term. The *President* is directly elected and is both Head of State and government.

National Anthem. 'Teirake kain Kiribati' ('Stand up, Kiribatians'); words and tune by U. Ioteba.

RECENT ELECTIONS

The last House of Assembly elections were held on 29 Nov. and 6 Dec. 2002. As a result Boutokanto Koaava (Pillars of Truth) now dominates parliament, having defeated the ruling Mwaneaaban te Mauri Party (MTM). At the presidential election of 25 Feb. 2003 Teburoro Tito (MTM) was re-elected with 50·4% of votes cast, ahead of Taberannang Timeon (Boutokanto Koaava) with 48·4% and Bakeua Bakeua Tekita with 1·2%.

CURRENT ADMINISTRATION

On 28 March 2003 President Teburoro Tito was defeated in a no-confidence motion, the opposition winning 21 out of 40 votes. A caretaker government led by the Speaker of Parliament, Taomati Iuta, was installed. New elections were to take place within three months.

INTERNATIONAL RELATIONS

Kiribati is a member of the UN, Commonwealth, Asian Development Bank, the Pacific Islands Forum and the Pacific Community (formerly the South Pacific Commission), and is an ACP member state of the ACP-EU relationship.

ECONOMY

Agriculture accounted for an estimated 14% of GDP in 1996, industry 7% and services 79%.

Currency. The currency in use is the Australian *dollar*. In 2001 the inflation rate was 7·7%, up from 0·4% in 1999.

Budget. Foreign financial aid, mainly from the UK and Japan, has amounted to 25–50% of GDP in recent years. Budget estimates for 1996 showed revenue at US$33·3m.; expenditure at US$47·7m.

Performance. Real GDP growth was negative in 2000, at –1·7%, but 2001 then saw a slight recovery, with growth of 1·5%.

ENERGY AND NATURAL RESOURCES

Environment. According to the *World Bank Atlas* carbon dioxide emissions were the equivalent of 0·3 tonnes per capita in 1998.

Electricity. Capacity (1994), 5,000 kW; production (1998), 7m. kWh.

Agriculture. Copra and fish represent the bulk of production and exports. The principal tree is the coconut; other food-bearing trees are the pandanus palm and the breadfruit. The only vegetable which grows in any quantity is a coarse calladium (alocasia) with the local name 'bwabwai', which is cultivated in pits; taro and sweet potatoes are also grown. Coconut production (2000), 77,000 tonnes; copra, 12,000 tonnes; bananas, 5,000 tonnes; taro, 2,000 tonnes. Principal livestock: pigs (12,000 in 2000).

Fisheries. Tuna fishing is an important industry; licenses are held by the USA, Japan and the Republic of Korea. Catches in 1999 totalled 48,205 tonnes, exclusively from sea fishing.

INDUSTRY
Industry is concentrated on fishing and handicrafts.

Labour. The economically active population in paid employment (not including subsistence farmers) totalled 11,167 in 1990. In 1994, 11% were employed in agriculture, 4% in industry and 85% in services. Some 70% of the labour force are underemployed; 2% unemployed.

INTERNATIONAL TRADE

Imports and Exports. Total exports (1995 est.), US$6·3m.; imports, US$38·6m. Main trading partners: the Fiji Islands, USA, Australia, Japan and New Zealand. Principal exports: copra, seaweed, fish; imports: foodstuffs, machinery and equipment, manufactured goods and fuel.

COMMUNICATIONS

Roads. There were (1996) 670 km of roads.

Civil Aviation. There were 20 airports in 1996 (nine paved). In 1998 there were scheduled services from Tarawa (Bonriki) to Tuvalu, the Marshall Islands and to the Fiji Islands.

Shipping. The main port is at Betio (Tarawa). Other ports of entry are Banaba, English Harbor and Kanton. There is also a small network of canals in the Line Islands. The merchant marine fleet totalled 4,000 GRT in 1998.

Telecommunications. Main telephone lines numbered 3,400 in 2000, or 40·3 per 1,000 population. There were 200 fax machines in 1995 and 2,000 PCs in use in 2000 (18·0 per 1,000 persons). Kiribati had 1,000 Internet users in July 2000.

SOCIAL INSTITUTIONS

Justice. In 1989 Kiribati had a police force of 232 under the command of a Commissioner of Police. The Commissioner of Police is also responsible for prisons, immigration, fire service (both domestic and airport) and firearms licensing. There is a Court of Appeal and High Court, with judges at all levels appointed by the President.

The population in penal institutions in 1995 was 91 (equivalent to 130 per 100,000 of national population).

Religion. In 1990, 53% of the population were Roman Catholic, 39% Protestant (Congregational); there are also small numbers of Seventh-Day Adventists, Latter-day Saints (Mormons) (6%), Baha'i and Church of God.

Education. In 1997 there were 17,594 pupils and 624 teachers at 86 primary schools and 4,403 pupils in general secondary education with (1996) 260 teachers. There is also a teachers' training college with 110 students (1995) and a marine training centre offering training for about 100 merchant seamen a year. The Tarawa Technical Institute at Betio (389 students in 1986) offers part-time technical and commercial courses.

Health. In 1993 there were 10 doctors and 147 nurses. There was one hospital in 1990.

Welfare. The government maintains free medical and other services. In 1990 there were 16 doctors and 1 hospital on Tarawa with 283 beds, and dispensaries on other islands.

CULTURE

Broadcasting. *Radio Kiribati*, a division of the Broadcasting and Publications Authority, transmits daily in English and I-Kiribati from Tarawa. A satellite link to Australia was established in 1985. There were 17,000 radio receivers and 1,000 TV receivers in 1997.

Cinema. There are no cinemas. There is a private-owned projector with film shows once a week in every village on South Tarawa.

Press. There was (1991) one bilingual weekly newspaper. There is one independent newspaper, the weekly *Kiribati Newstar.*

Tourism. Tourism is in the early stages of development. In 1998 there were 5,000 foreign tourists bringing in revenue of US$1m.

DIPLOMATIC REPRESENTATIVES
Of Kiribati in the United Kingdom
Acting High Commissioner: David Yeeting (resides in Kiribati).
Honorary Consul: Michael Walsh (The Great House, Llanddewi Rydderch, Monmouthshire, NP7 9UY).

Of the United Kingdom in Kiribati
High Commissioner: Charles Mochan (resides at Suva, Fiji Islands).

Of the USA in Kiribati (assigned from Majuro in the Marshall Islands)
Ambassador: Michael J. Senko.

FURTHER READING
Tearo, T., *Coming of Age*. Tarawa, 1989

KOREA

Daehan Minguk
(Republic of Korea)

Capital: Seoul
Population estimate, 2000: 46·13m.
GDP per capita, 2000: (PPP$) 17,380
HDI/world rank: 0·882/27

KEY HISTORICAL EVENTS

Korea was united in a single kingdom under the Silla dynasty from 668. China, which claimed a vague suzerainty over Korea, recognized the latter's independence in 1895. After the Russo-Japanese war of 1904–05, Korea was virtually a Japanese protectorate. It was formally annexed on 29 Aug. 1910. Following the collapse of Japan in 1945, American and Soviet forces entered Korea dividing the country into portions separated by the 38th parallel of latitude. Negotiations between the Americans and the Russians regarding the future of Korea broke down in May 1946. In 1948 two separate states were proclaimed. In the south, Syngman Rhee, former president of the Korean government in exile, was elected president of the Republic of Korea, while in the north, Kim Il-sung, a major in the Red Army who had marched back into Korea with the Soviet forces, was proclaimed premier of the Democratic People's Republic of Korea. The US occupation forces withdrew from South Korea in June 1949. Military equipment promised by the USA as part of their aid programme was still on its way to Korea when the North Koreans launched, in June 1950, a full-scale invasion across the 38th parallel. The war, in which North Korea received support from the Chinese army and South Korea from the UN forces and the USA, lasted for three years, killed some 5m. people and destroyed an estimated 43% of Korea's industrial plants and 33% of her homes. It was concluded by an armistice signed on 27 July 1953 which implicitly recognized the 38th parallel and the *de facto* boundary between North and South Korea.

Syngman Rhee's authoritarian rule collapsed after student demonstrations brought the country to the brink of civil war in April 1960. A military coup in May 1961 led to the dissolution of the National Assembly, the introduction of martial law and the establishment of Gen. Park Chung Hee as president for the next 17 years. Park's assassination in Oct. 1979 threw the country into a state of crisis. A new, more democratic, constitution, approved by both ruling and opposition parties, came into force in 1988. Since then, Korea has created a lively free market economy which has largely avoided East Asia's recent financial troubles.

On 13 June 2000 South Korea's President Kim Dae-jung flew to North Korea to meet the North Korean leader, Kim Jong Il, in the first ever meeting between the heads of state of the two countries. During the three-day summit South Korea agreed to help to rebuild the economy of North Korea in exchange for an end to the threat of war, the opportunity for families to be reunited and the reconnection of the railway link severed since the division of the Korean peninsula in 1945. Co-operation between the two Koreas is increasing, particularly on the economic front through joint business and infrastructure ventures. In Sept. 2002 as relations between the Koreas improved troops began to clear minefields on either side of the border in preparation for the construction of new transport links. In spite of increasing tension between the USA and North Korea, in Feb. 2003 the land border between the two Koreas was opened for the first time in half a century when a group of South Korean tourism officials visited a tourist resort in the North.

TERRITORY AND POPULATION

South Korea is bounded in the north by the demilitarized zone (separating it from North Korea), east by the East Sea, south by the Korea Strait (separating it from Japan) and west by the Yellow Sea. The area is 99,538 sq. km. The population (census, 1 Nov. 2000) was 46,136,101 (22,977,519 females); density, 463·5 per sq. km (one of the highest in the world). In 2000 the urban population was 46·3%. The population estimate for July 2002 was 47·64m.

The UN gives a projected population for 2010 of 49·62m.

The official language is Korean. In July 2000 the Korean government introduced a new Romanization System for the Korean Language to romanize Korean words into English.

There are nine provinces (*do*) and seven metropolitan cities with provincial status. Area and population in 2000:

Province	Area (in sq. km)	Population (in 1,000)	Province	Area (in sq. km)	Population (in 1,000)
Gyeonggi	10,135	8,984	Jeju	1,846	513
Gyeongsangnam	10,516	2,909	Seoul (city)	606	9,895
Gyeongsangbuk	19,024	2,725	Busan (city)	760	3,663
Jeollanam	11,987	1,996	Daegu (city)	886	2,481
Jeollabuk	8,050	1,891	Incheon (city)	965	2,475
Chungcheongnam	8,586	1,845	Daejeon (city)	540	1,368
Gangwon	16,502	1,487	Gwangju (city)	501	1,353
Chungcheongbuk	7,432	1,467	Ulsan (city)	1,056	1,014

Cities with over 500,000 inhabitants (census 2000):

Seoul	9,895,217	Ulsan	1,014,428	Cheongju	586,700
Busan	3,662,884	Suwon	946,704	Anyang	580,544
Daegu	2,480,578	Seongnam	914,590	Ansan	562,920
Incheon	2,475,139	Goyang	763,971	Changwon	517,410
Daejeon	1,368,207	Bucheon	761,389	Pohang	515,714
Gwangju	1,352,797	Jeonju	616,468		

Seoul: Located in the northwest of the country on the Han River, Seoul has been the capital of Korea since 1394. After Korea was annexed by Japan in 1910, Seoul became the centre for Japanese rule until 1945. The Korean War proved devastating for the city but since then it has expanded rapidly and is now a modern metropolis with one of the highest population densities in the world.

SOCIAL STATISTICS
2001: births, 557,228; deaths, 242,730; marriages, 320,063; divorces, 135,014. Rates per 1,000 population in 2001: birth, 11·6; death, 5·1; marriage, 6·9; divorce, 2·8. Expectation of life at birth, 1999, 79·2 years for females and 71·7 for males. In 1955 life expectancy had been 47 and 62 in 1971. Infant mortality, 2001, 5·1 per 1,000 live births; fertility rate, 1·3 births per woman. Annual population growth rate in 2002 was 0·6%. In 2001 the average age of first marriage was 29·6 for men and 26·8 for women, with 28·0 years being the average age that women had their first child. South Korea has one of the most rapidly ageing populations in the world. In 2002, 7·9% of the population were over 65, up from 2·9% in 1960. There were 14·31m. households in 2000, with on average 3·1 members per household. 11,584 South Koreans emigrated in 2001, down from 15,307 in 2000. Between 1962 and 1998 a total of 847,714 Koreans emigrated, 77·8% of them to the USA. 5·65m. Koreans lived abroad in 2001, including 2·1m. in the USA, 1·9m. in China and 640,000 in Japan.

CLIMATE
The country experiences continental temperate conditions. Rainfall is concentrated in the period April to Sept. and ranges from 40" (1,020 mm) to 60" (1,520 mm). Busan, Jan. 36°F (2·2°C), July 76°F (24·4°C). Annual rainfall 56" (1,407 mm). Seoul, Jan. 23°F (–5°C), July 77°F (25°C). Annual rainfall 50" (1,250 mm).

CONSTITUTION AND GOVERNMENT
The 1988 Constitution provides for a *President*, directly elected for a single five-year term, who appoints the members of the *State Council* and heads it, and for a *National Assembly* (*Gukhoe*), currently of 273 members, directly elected for four years (227 from constituencies and 46 from party lists in proportion to the overall vote).

The minimum voting age is 20.

National Anthem. 'Aegukga' ('A Song of Love for the Country'); words anonymous, tune by Ahn Eaktay.

RECENT ELECTIONS

Presidential elections were held on 19 Dec. 2002. Roh Moo-hyun of the ruling Millennium Democratic Party won with 48·9% of votes cast, against 46·6% for Lee Hoi Chang of the Grand National Party. Turn-out was 70·2%.

Elections to the National Assembly were held on 13 April 2000. 1,179 candidates stood. The electorate was 33,482,387. Turn-out was 57·2%. The Grand National Party (GNP) won 133 seats with 39·0% of votes cast; the Millennium Democratic Party (MDP) 115 (35·9%); the United Liberal Democrats (ULD) 17 (9·8%); the Democratic People's Party (DPP) 2 (3·7%); the New Korea Party of Hope 1 (0·4%). The Democratic Labour Party and the Youth Progress Party both polled a higher percentage than the Party of Hope but failed to claim any seats. Non-partisans took five seats. Only 16 seats were held by women in the National Assembly.

CURRENT ADMINISTRATION

President: Roh Moo-hyun (Millennium Democratic Party; sworn in on 25 Feb. 2003).

In March 2003 the cabinet comprised:

Prime Minister: Goh Kun (sworn in on 26 Feb. 2003).

Deputy Prime Minister and Minister of Finance and Economy: Kim Jin-pyo. *Deputy Prime Minister and Minister of Education and Human Resources Development:* Yoon Deok-hong. *Agriculture and Forestry:* Kim Young-jin. *Commerce, Industry and Energy:* Yoon Jin-shik. *Construction and Transportation:* Choi Jong-chan. *Culture and Tourism:* Lee Chang-dong. *Environment:* Han Myung-sook. *Foreign Affairs and Trade:* Yoon Young-kwan. *Health and Welfare:* Kim Hwa-joong. *Information and Communication:* Chin Dae-je. *Justice:* Kang Kum-shil. *Planning and Budget:* Park Bong-heum. *Labour:* Kwon Ki-hong. *Maritime Affairs and Fisheries:* Heo Sung-kwan. *National Defence:* Cho Young-kil. *Gender Equality:* Jie Wun-hee. *Science and Technology:* Park Ho-gun. *Unification:* Jeong Se-hyun. *Government Policy Co-ordination:* Lee Young-tak. *Government Administration and Home Affairs:* Kim Doo-kwan.

National Assembly Speaker: Park Kwan-yong.

Office of the Prime Minister: http://www.opm.go.kr

DEFENCE

Peacetime operational control, which had been transferred to the United Nations Command (UNC) under a US general in July 1950 after the outbreak of the Korean War, was restored to South Korea on 1 Dec. 1994. In the event of a new crisis, operational control over the Korean armed forces will revert to the Combined Forces Command (CFC). Conscription is 26 months in the Army, 28 months in the Navy and 30 months in the Air Force. Conscripts may choose or be required to exchange military service for civilian work. There were 37,140 US personnel based in South Korea in 2002.

Defence expenditure in 2001 totalled US$15,388m. (US$259 per capita), representing 2·8% of GDP.

Army. Strength (31 Dec. 2000) 560,000 (140,000 conscripts). Paramilitary Civilian Defence Corps, 6·28m. The armed forces reserves numbered 3·04m.

Navy. In 2000 the navy had a substantial force of 67,000 (19,000 conscripts), including 25,000 marine corps troops; it continued its steady modernization programme. Current strength includes 160 surface vessels, 20 support vessels, 10 submarines/submersibles and 70 aircraft.

The main bases are at Jinhae, Incheon and Busan.

Air Force. In 2000 the Air Force had a strength of 63,000 men and 540 combat aircraft including 560 fighters, 40 special aircraft and 210 support aircraft.

INTERNATIONAL RELATIONS

Defections to South Korea from North Korea totalled 1,141 in 2002 (583 in 2001, 312 in 2000, 41 in 1995 and 8 in 1993).

South Korea is a member of the UN, WTO, BIS, OECD, Asian Development Bank, Colombo Plan, APEC, IOM and the Antarctic Treaty.

The aim of Korea's foreign policy is to secure international support for peace and stability in Northeast Asia, including a means to reunify the Korean Peninsula without confrontation.

ECONOMY

Agriculture, forestry and fishing accounted for 4·4% of GDP in 2001, industry (including mining, construction and power and water supply) 41·4% and services 54·1%.

Overview. South Korea aims to match competition from China and to achieve a peaceful reunification with North Korea. Inflationary pressures are muted following lower world oil prices and subdued domestic demand. The economy is dependent on international trade. Demand for chips used in mobile phones and computers did boost the economy, but demand has fallen. The *chaebol* (conglomerates), controlled by their founding families, are dominant in the economy. The most troubled *chaebols* are disappearing, having been allowed to borrow too heavily against inadequate returns. During 1997 and 1998 more than a dozen of the 64 *chaebol* went bankrupt and Hyundai was broken up into independent businesses. In Dec. 1997 Korea's international debts were estimated at US$200,000m. An IMF and World Bank rescue was tied to undertakings to transform the economy into one based on market principles instead of state directives. Korea's lack of foreign reserves was also identified as a major problem. Assistance from the IMF and other global financial institutions totalled US$58·3bn.

Reforms so far approved by the National Assembly include greater freedom for the central bank to set monetary policy and the lifting of the 50% ceiling on foreign ownership of listed Korean companies. The Bank of Korea has moved from targeting monetary aggregates to an interest-based policy with a floating exchange rate. The tax system has been reformed, although the ten-year plan to increase competition in the electricity sector (introduced in 1999) has fallen behind.

Currency. The unit of currency is the *won* (KRW). There was inflation in 2001 of 4·3%. Foreign exchange reserves were US$111,934m. in June 2002 (US$31,928m. in 1995) and gold reserves 442,000 troy oz. Total money supply in May 2002 was 53,335bn. won.

Budget. Revenue and expenditure (in 1,000,000m. won), including bond issuances, at the 2002 budget: 105·8 and 105·8. Sources of revenue: national tax, 93·8; non-tax, 12·0. Expenditure includes: economic development, 27·4; education, 18·5; defence, 17·1; infrastructure, 13·9; general administration, 10·0; contingency, 2·5.

External liabilities in Dec. 2002 were 154,114m. won.

Performance. Total GDP in 2001 was US$422·2bn. GDP growth rate was 5·0% in 1997 (6·8% in 1996 and 8·9% in 1995), but fell to −6·7% for 1998. It was 10·9% in 1999, the highest rate of any of the southeast Asian economies, 9·3% in 2000 and 3·0% in 2001. The 1998 economic performance was the worst since the 1960s.

Banking and Finance. The central bank and bank of issue is the Bank of Korea (*Governor*, Park Seung). In Oct. 2002 bank deposits totalled 498,886bn. won, of which 447,329bn. won were savings and time deposits.

In Dec. 2001 there were 20 national and provincial commercial banks. The largest bank is Kookmin Bank, with assets in Sept. 2002 of 204,337bn. won (US$171·47bn.). Other major banks are the National Agricultural Cooperative Federation (NACF), Woori (formerly Hanvit) Bank and Chohung Bank. There were 40 foreign banks in Dec. 2002. In Dec. 2001 non-bank financial institutions included 44 insurance companies, 45 securities companies and three merchant banks. The use of real names in financial dealings has been required since 1994.

South Korea has started to open up once protected industries to foreign ownership, and in 2002 attracted US$9·1bn. in foreign direct investment.

There is a stock exchange in Seoul.

Weights and Measures. The metric system is in use alongside traditional measures. 1 *gwan* = 3·75 kg. 1 *pyeong* = 3·3 sq. metres.

ENERGY AND NATURAL RESOURCES

Environment. According to the World Bank, South Korea's carbon dioxide emissions in 1998 were the equivalent of 7·8 tonnes per capita. An *Environmental Sustainability Index* compiled for the World Economic Forum meeting in Feb. 2002 ranked South Korea 135th in the world out of 142 countries analysed, with 35·9%. The index measured the ability of countries to maintain favourable environmental conditions and examined various factors including pollution levels and the use or abuse of natural resources.

Electricity. Installed capacity in 2001 was 51m. kW. Electricity generated (2001) was 285,224m. kWh. Sources of power in 2001: nuclear, 39·3%; oil, 9·8%; coal, 38·7%; liquefied natural gas, 10·7%; hydro-electric, 1·5%. There were 17 nuclear reactors in use in 2001. Consumption per capita in 2001 was estimated to be 5,444 kWh.

Oil and Gas. In 2001 the imports of petroleum products amounted to 1,099m. bbls., of which crude oil was 859·4m. bbls. The output of petroleum products was 892·8m. bbls., consumption 743·6m. bbls. and the volume of exports 295·0m. bbls. In 2001, 873·4m. bbls. of crude oil were imported. In Sept. 1999 a massive crude oil terminal was opened at Yeosu, Jeollanam-do. It has a capacity to store more than 30m. bbls.

In 2001 imports of natural gas totalled 16·1m. tonnes, consumption 16·0m. tonnes. The total output of city gas in 2001 was 12,657m. cu. metres as was consumption, of which 8,964m. cu. metres was used for household purposes, 3,376m. cu. metres for industrial use and 1,761m. cu. metres for commercial use. In April 1999 a large underwater gas deposit was discovered off the southeastern coast of the country, which was estimated to contain up to 60bn. cu. metres of natural gas.

Water. Water consumption in 2000 was 33,100m. cu. metres, of which 15,800m. cu. metres was for agricultural purposes, 7,300m. cu. metres was supplied to households and 2,900m. cu. metres was for industrial use. Of the total population, 87·8% had tap water in 2001 and per capita supply was 374 litres per day. As of 2001 there were 1,206 dams with walls higher than 15 metres and containing a total of 17·96bn. cu. metres of water.

Minerals. In 2001, 599 mining companies employed 12,103 people. Output, 2001, included (in tonnes): limestone, 82m.; anthracite coal, 3·82m.; iron ore, 0·2m.; zinc ore, 10,259; lead ore, 1,975; gold, 28,595 kg. The largest gold deposits in South Korea were discovered in Suryun Mine near Daegu in June 1999. The mine contained an estimated 9·9 tonnes of gold, worth approximately US$81m. Salt production averages 500,000 tonnes a year.

Agriculture. Cultivated land was 1·88m. ha in 2001, of which 1·15m. ha were rice paddies. In 2001 the farming population was 3·93m. and there were 1·35m. farms. The agricultural workforce was 2·1m. in 2001. There were 201,089 tractors in 2001.

In 2001, 1·08m. ha were sown to rice. Production (2001, in 1,000 tonnes): rice, 5,515; cabbages, 3,450; onions, 1,078; melons and watermelons, 972; tangerines and mandarins, 645; potatoes, 604; barley, 593; grapes, 454; cucumbers and gherkins, 451; pears, 419; chillies and green peppers, 411; garlic, 406; sweet potatoes, 273.

Livestock in 2001 (in 1,000): cows, 1,954; pigs, 8,720; sheep, 441; chickens, 102,393.

Forestry. Forest area was 6·42m. ha in 2001 (64% of the land area). Total stock was 428·3m. cu. metres. In 1997, 70% of the total forest area was privately owned. Timber production was 1·5m. cu. metres in 2001.

Fisheries. In 2001 there were a total of 94,835 boats (864,853 gross tonnes). 482 deep-sea fishing vessels were operating overseas as of Dec. 2002. The fish catch was 1,907,925 tonnes in 2001, mainly from marine waters.

INDUSTRY

The leading companies by market capitalization in South Korea, excluding banking and finance, in Jan. 2002 were: Samsung Electronics Company Ltd (53trn. won); SK Telecom Company Ltd (24trn. won); and Korea Telecom Corporation (18trn. won).

Manufacturing industry is concentrated primarily on oil, petro-chemicals, chemical fibres, construction, iron and steel, mobile phones, cement, machinery, chips, shipbuilding, automobiles and electronics. Tobacco manufacture is a semi-government monopoly. Industry is dominated by giant conglomerates (*chaebol*). There were 3·01m. businesses in 2000, of which 261,119 were incorporated. 916,688 businesses were in wholesale and retail trades, 607,718 in dining and accommodation, 329,488 in services, 313,246 in manufacturing and 265,598 in transport and communications. The leading *chaebol* are Samsung, with assets in early 2001 of 69,873bn. won, Hyundai, with assets of 53,632bn. won, and LG, with assets of 51,965bn. won.

Production in 2001: petroleum products, 857·5m. bbls.; cars (2002), 3·15m.; mobile phones, 90m. Production in 1,000 tonnes: cement, 52,046; crude steel, 43,852; pig iron, 25,898; artificial fertilizers, 3,500.

Shipbuilding orders totalled 6·41m. GT in 2001.

Labour. At Dec. 2001 the population of working age (15 to 59 years) was 36·48m. The economically-active population was 22·18m.; 0·82m. (2001) were registered unemployed. At Nov. 2002, 13·92m. persons were employed in services, 4·2m. in manufacturing, 2·17m. in agriculture, fisheries and forestry, 1·81m. in construction and 19,000 in mining. 6·34m. persons were self-employed in Nov. 2002; unemployment was 2·7%. An annual legal minimum wage is set by the *Minimum Wage Act* (enforced from 1988), which applies to all industries. From Sept. 2002 to Aug. 2003 it is 18,200 won per day and 514,500 won per month. In Dec. 2001 the average monthly wage was 1·75m. won. In 2001 the working week averaged 47 hours. In 2001 the government announced that a five-day working week would be introduced by 2003. It was implemented in the financial sector in July 2002. Workers in South Korea put in the longest hours of any OECD country.

Trade Unions. At Dec. 2001 there were 6,150 unions with a total membership of 1,568,723. 877,827 workers belong to the government-recognized Federation of Korean Trade Unions. Since 1997 unions have been permitted to engage in political activities, and the ban on more than one union in a work place has been extended up to 2006. The Korean Confederation of Trade Unions (*President*, Kwon Young-kil), with 643,506 members, is applying pressure on the government to reduce working hours to 40 a week with a five-day week.

INTERNATIONAL TRADE

Total external foreign debt was US$134,417m. in 2000 (the seventh highest in the world). In May 1998 the government removed restrictions on foreign investment in the Korean stock market. It also began to allow foreign businesses to engage in mergers and acquisitions. From July 1998 foreigners were allowed to buy plots of land for both business and non-business purposes. Since Aug. 1990 South Korean businesses and individuals have been permitted to make investments and set up branch offices in North Korea, on an approval basis. According to the Unification Ministry, the overall volume of inter-Korean trade was US$641m. in 2002 (US$342m. in business transactions and US$298m. in non-profit transactions), a 59·3% increase on 2001.

Imports and Exports. Exports in 2002 (provisional figures) were US$162·8bn.; imports, US$152·0bn. Main import suppliers (in US$1bn.): Japan, 28·83; USA, 22·29; China, 16·86. Main export markets: USA, 31·4; China, 22·77; EU, 20·73; Japan, 16·51 (2001).

Major exports in 2002 included (in US$1bn.): semi-conductor chips, 16·6; continuous woven man-made fibres, 15·6; automobiles, 14·8; codeless communication apparatus, 13·6; computers, 12·9; electrical appliances, 10·7; machinery, 9·2; petro-chemicals, 9·1. Major imports (as of 20 Dec. 2002) included: crude oil, 18·6; semi-conductor chips, 17·0; computers, 5·5; petroleum products, 4·9; liquefied natural gas, 4·0. Rice imports were prohibited until 1994, but following the GATT Uruguay Round the rice market opened to foreign imports in 1995.

Trade Fairs. In 2001 there were about 100 trade fairs hosted by COEX and 30 hosted by BEXCO (Busan). 3,187 Korean companies participated in 145 trade fairs held in other countries supported by KOTRA, the Korea Trade-Investment Agency.

COMMUNICATIONS

Roads. In 2001 there were 91,396 km of roads, of which 77% (70,146 km) were paved. 10·7m. passengers (2000) and 535·76m. tonnes of freight were carried in 2001. In Dec. 2001 motor vehicles registered totalled 12,914,115, including 8,889,327 passenger cars. There were 991,590 new car registrations in 2002 (by Nov.). In 2001 there were 8,097 fatalities as a result of road accidents (9,353 in 2000). At 16·9 deaths per 100,000 people, South Korea has among the highest death rates in road accidents of any industrialized country.

The first of two planned cross-border roads between the two Koreas opened in Feb. 2003.

Rail. In 2001 the National Railroad totalled 3,127 km of 1,435 mm gauge (667·5 km electrified) and 20 km of 762 mm gauge. In 2001 railways carried 912m. passengers and 45m. tonnes of freight. In June 2000 it was agreed to start consultations to restore the railway from Seoul to Sinuiju, on the North Korean/Chinese border, by rebuilding a 12 km long stretch from Munsan, in South Korea, to Jangdan, on the South Korean/North Korean border, and an 8 km long stretch in North Korea. Work on the restoration began in Sept. 2000 but was delayed in part because of the diplomatic crisis between North Korea and the USA, which escalated in Oct. 2002.

There are metros in Seoul (287 km), and smaller ones in Busan (70·5 km), Daegu (25·7 km) and Incheon (24·6 km).

Civil Aviation. There are six international airports in South Korea: at Seoul (Incheon), Busan (Gimhae), Daegu, Jeju, Yangyang and Cheongju. The new Incheon airport, 50 km to the west of Seoul, built on reclaimed land made up of four small islands, opened in March 2001 and is the largest airport in Asia. It has replaced Gimpo Airport as Seoul's International Airport. The national carrier is Korean Air. Another Korean carrier, Asiana Airlines, also provides services, as did in 2002 around 57 foreign airlines. In 2001, 28·5m. passengers and 423,692 tonnes of cargo were carried on domestic routes and 19·7m. passengers and 1·8m. tonnes of cargo on international routes.

In 2000 Seoul's Gimpo airport handled 36,639,067 passengers (18,738,579 on domestic flights), making it the 13th busiest airport in the world for passenger traffic. It handled 1,846,896 tonnes of freight, making it the fourth busiest for freight. Busan handled 9,358,152 passengers (8,015,414 on domestic flights) and 182,402 tonnes of freight. Jeju handled 9,125,939 passengers (8,793,142 on domestic flights) and 280,031 tonnes of freight.

Shipping. In 2002 there were 51 ports (28 for international trade), including Busan, Incheon, Gunsan, Mokpo, Yeosu, Pohang, Donghae, Jeju, Masan, Ulsan and Daesan. In 1997 the merchant marine comprised 562 vessels totalling 25·15m. DWT, representing 3·4% of the world's tonnage. 298 vessels (66·87% of gross tonnage) were registered under foreign flags. Total GRT, 7·42m., including oil tankers 0·38m. GRT and container ships 1·42m. GRT. In 1997 vessels totalling 578,373,000 NRT entered ports and vessels totalling 584,164,000 NRT cleared. The busiest port is Busan, which in 1999 was visited by 69,429 vessels of 450,033,000 GRT. It is the world's third busiest container port, after Hong Kong and Singapore.

In 2001, 9,340,000 domestic passengers and 1,075,000 international passengers took ferries and other ocean-going vessels. There were 6,586 registered vessels accounting for a tonnage of 6,592,758.

Telecommunications. There were 22,725,000 main telephone lines in 2001 (480 per 1,000 persons). In 2001 public telephones totalled 516,000. By the end of 2001 the number of mobile phone subscribers had risen to 29·0m. (62% of the population). The largest operator, SK Telecom, has 39·5% of the market share, ahead of KTF, with 33·7%. 60·1% of households had PCs in 2002. There were approximately 25·6m. Internet users in July 2002.

Postal Services. As of 2001 there were 3,688 post offices operating, with each *myon* (administrative unit comprising several villages) having one or more post offices. In 2002 the mail volume totalled 4,498m. items.

SOCIAL INSTITUTIONS

Justice. Judicial power is vested in the Supreme Court, High Courts, District Courts and Family Court, as well as the Administrative Court and Patent Court. The single six-year term Chief Justice is appointed by the President with the consent of the National Assembly. The other 13 Justices of the Supreme Court are appointed by the President with the consent of the National Assembly, upon the recommendation of the Chief Justice, for renewable six-year terms; the Chief Justice appoints other judges. The death penalty is authorized. In Jan. 2002 there were 1,508 judges, 1,134 prosecutors and about 3,800 private practising lawyers.

The population in penal institutions in June 1998 was 70,303 (155 per 100,000 of national population).

Religion. Traditionally, Koreans have lived under the influence of shamanism, Buddhism (introduced AD 372) and Confucianism, which was the official faith from 1392 to 1910. Catholic converts from China introduced Christianity in the 18th century, but a ban on Roman Catholicism was not lifted until 1882. The Anglican Church was introduced in 1890 and became an independent jurisdiction in 1993 under the Archbishop of Korea. In 1998 it had 110 churches, 175 priests and some 65,000 faithful. There were also 69,000 Latter-day Saints (Mormons) in 1998. Religious affiliations of the population in 1995 (and 1985): Buddhism, 23·2% (27·7%); Protestantism, 19·7% (18·6%); Roman Catholicism, 6·6% (5·7%); Confucianism, 0·5% (1%); others, 0·7% (1%); no religion, 49·3% (46%).

Education. The Korean education system consists of a six-year elementary school, a three-year middle school, a three-year high school and college and university (two to four years). Elementary education for 6–11 year olds is compulsory. Mandatory middle school education began in 2002.

The total number of schools has increased sixfold from 3,000 in 1945 to 19,124 in 2002, with 11,957,388 enrolled students. In 2002 there were 8,343 kindergartens with 550,256 pupils and 29,673 teachers; 5,384 elementary schools with 4,138,366 pupils and 147,497 teachers; 1,841,030 pupils and 95,283 teachers at 2,809 middle schools; and 1,995 high schools with 1,795,509 pupils and 44,177 teachers. In 2002 there were 163 colleges and universities with 1,771,738 students and 44,177 teachers; 11 teacher training colleges with 23,259 students and 721 teachers; 945 graduate schools with 262,867 students; and 19 industrial universities with 187,040 students and 2,543 teachers. In 1996, 5·6% of the population was enrolled in tertiary education, up from just 0·6% in 1970.

In 1995 total expenditure on education came to 3·1% of GNP and 22·8% of total government spending.

The adult literacy was 98% in 2000 (99% among males and 96% among females).

Around 150,000 South Koreans were studying abroad in 2001.

Health. In 2000 there were 285 general hospitals (with 113,518 beds), 20,053 other hospitals and clinics (130,162 beds), 7,412 oriental medical hospitals and clinics (8,436 beds) and 10,527 dental hospitals and clinics. In 2000 there were 72,503 physicians (648 people per doctor), 10,108 oriental medical doctors, 18,039 dentists, 8,728 midwives (1992), 160,295 nurses and 50,623 pharmacists.

In 1998, 67·6% of all adult men smoked (the highest proportion in any country in the world), but only 6·7% of women were smokers.

Welfare. In Dec. 2001, 16·3m. persons were covered by the National Pension System introduced in 1988. Employers and employees make equal contributions; persons joining by choice or in rural areas pay their own contributions. The System covers age pensions, disability pensions and survivors' pensions.

Under a system of unemployment insurance introduced in July 1995, workers laid off after working at least six months for a member employer are entitled to benefits averaging 50% of their previous wage for a period of 90 up to 240 days.

CULTURE

Broadcasting. The Korean Broadcasting System (KBS) is a public corporation which broadcasts 7 radio channels, 2 terrestrial TV channels and 2 satellite TV channels. KBS maintains a nationwide network that connects the key station in Seoul with 25 local stations. It also maintains ten bureaux overseas. In addition to KBS, there is a semi-public TV broadcaster, Munhwa Broadcasting Corporation

(MBC), and one commercial TV network, Education Broadcasting System (EBS). Cable TV was inaugurated in March 1995. It had 3·5m. paying subscribers in 2000 and provided 44 channels. In 2000 there were 950 radio receivers for every 1,000 people and 90 television sets for every 100 people.

Cinema. In 2000 there were 376 cinemas with a seating capacity of 193,775. 48 full-length films were produced in 1999.

Press. There were 123 dailies in 2001 and 6,913 periodicals. The main dailies are *Chosun Ilbo* (average circulation of 2·4m. per issue), *JoongAng Ilbo* (average circulation of 2·1m. per issue) and *Dong-A Ilbo* (average circulation of 2·0m. per issue).

A total of 36,185 book titles and 118m. books were published in 2002.

Tourism. In 2001, 6,084,476 Koreans travelled abroad and 5,147,204 foreign nationals visited South Korea. In 2001 tourist revenues from foreign visitors totalled US$6·4bn.; overseas travel expenditure by Koreans going abroad totalled US$6·5bn. On 18 Nov. 1998 the first South Korean tourists to visit North Korea set sail on a cruise and tour organized by the South Korean firm Hyundai.

Libraries. There were 9,337 libraries in 2001, including 1 national library, 1 congressional, 420 public, 420 university and 7,918 libraries at primary, middle and high schools. There were also 578 specialized and professional libraries.

Theatre and Opera. There are 316 theatres nationwide. 47 have 1,200 seats that can accommodate large-scale dramas, operas, dances and musicals. The Seoul Arts Centre has an opera house.

Museums and Galleries. In 2001 there were 249 museums, including 25 national museums, 36 public museums, 107 private museums and 81 university museums. There were an estimated 500 art galleries in 2001.

DIPLOMATIC REPRESENTATIVES

Of the Republic of Korea in the United Kingdom (60 Buckingham Gate, London, SW1E 6AJ)
Ambassador: Vacant.
Chargé d'Affaires a.i.: Kim Il-soo.

Of the United Kingdom in the Republic of Korea (4 Jeong-dong, Jung-gu, Seoul 100–120)
Ambassador: Charles T. W. Humfrey, CMG.

Of the Republic of Korea in the USA (2450 Massachusetts Ave., NW, Washington, D.C., 20008)
Ambassador: Yang Sung-chul.

Of the USA in the Republic of Korea (82 Sejongno, Jongno-gu, Seoul)
Ambassador: Thomas Hubbard.

Of the Republic of Korea to the United Nations
Ambassador: Sun Joun-yung.

Of the Republic of Korea to the European Union
Ambassador: Park Yang-chun.

FURTHER READING
National Bureau of Statistics. *Korea Statistical Yearbook*
Bank of Korea. *Economic Statistics Yearbook*
Castley, R., *Korea's Economic Miracle.* London, 1997
Cumings, B., *Korea's Place in the Sun: A Modern History.* New York, 1997
Hoare, James E., *Korea.* [Bibliography] ABC-Clio, Oxford and Santa Barbara (CA), 1997
Kang, M.-H., *The Korean Business Conglomerate: Chaebol Then and Now.* Univ. of California Press, 1996
Kim, D.-H. and Tat, Y.-K. (eds.) *The Korean Peninsula in Transition.* London, 1997
Simons, G., *Korea: the Search for Sovereignty.* London, 1995
Smith, H., *Industry Policy in Taiwan and Korea in the 1980s.* Edward Elgar, 2000
Song, P.-N., *The Rise of the Korean Economy.* 2nd ed. OUP, 1994
Tennant, R., *A History of Korea.* London, 1996

National statistical office: National Bureau of Statistics, Ministry of Finance and Economy, Seoul.
Website: http://www.nso.go.kr/

NORTH KOREA

Chosun Minchu-chui
Inmin Konghwa-guk
(Democratic People's Republic
of Korea)

Capital: Pyongyang
Population estimate, 2000: 22·17m.
GDP per capita: not available

KEY HISTORICAL EVENTS

Following the collapse of Japan in 1945 Soviet forces arrived in North Korea, one month ahead of the Americans, and established a Communist-led provisional government. A Democratic People's Republic was proclaimed on 9 Sept. 1948 and Kim Il-sung became premier, purging all rivals. On 25 June 1950 North Korea invaded the south; its advance was stopped with the aid of UN forces. Chinese Communist 'volunteers' joined the war in Oct. 1950. Truce negotiations were begun in 1951 and concluded on 27 July 1953. A demilitarized zone was set up along the final battle line between North and South Korea. On 13 Dec. 1991 the prime ministers of North and South Korea signed a declaration of non-aggression, agreeing not to interfere in each other's internal affairs. Three agreements were reached between the North and South Korean prime ministers in 1992 on proposals for military, economic, political and social co-operation. Kim Il-sung, head of state, Communist Party and the military since 1948, died on 8 July 1994, and was succeeded by his son, Kim Jong Il. On 21 Oct. 1994 an agreement to restrict nuclear power to peaceful purposes in Korea was signed by North Korea and the USA. Since then, negotiations have foundered on evidence of continuing nuclear activity, and in Oct. 2002 North Korea admitted that it had a secret nuclear weapons programme. As the last refuge of Stalinism, North Korea needs a radical economic shake-up to survive but fears the consequences of reform.

Although food aid has been stepped up, the UN World Food Programme estimated in 1997 that 2m. North Koreans face starvation. Good Friends, a Buddhist aid group in Seoul, claims that up to 3·5m. North Koreans have died of starvation since 1995.

On 13 June 2000 South Korea's President Kim Dae-jung flew to North Korea to meet the North Korean leader, Kim Jong Il, in the first ever meeting between the heads of state of the two countries. During the three-day summit South Korea agreed to help to rebuild the economy of North Korea in exchange for an end to the threat of war, the opportunity for families to be reunited and the reconnection of the railway link severed since the division of the Korean peninsula in 1945. In Sept. 2002 as relations between the Koreas improved troops began to clear minefields on either side of the border in preparation for the construction of new transport links. But US suspicion of North Korea as a terrorist haven may slow north–south co-operation. In Oct. 2002 the USA claimed that North Korea acknowledged the existence of a secret nuclear programme, and tension increased in Dec. 2002 when North Korea removed monitoring devices at Yongbyon nuclear plant, a move that the international community feared might represent the restarting of its nuclear-weapons programme. In Jan. 2003 North Korea pulled out of the Nuclear Nonproliferation Treaty. In spite of increasing tension between North Korea and the USA, in Feb. 2003 the land border between the two Koreas was opened for the first time in half a century when a group of tourism officials from the South visited a tourist resort in North Korea.

Since 1995 hunger has been widespread and 300,000 North Koreans have fled to China. Around a third of the population are fed through outside aid.

TERRITORY AND POPULATION

North Korea is bounded in the north by China, east by the sea of Japan, west by the Yellow Sea and south by South Korea, from which it is separated by a demilitarized zone of 1,262 sq. km. Its area is 122,762 sq. km.

The UN gives a projected population for 2010 of 23·69m.

The census population in 1993 was 21,213,378; density 172·8 per sq. km. In the elections to the Supreme People's Assembly held on 26 July 1998, 687 deputies were elected, as was the case in 1990. The South Korean weekly NEWSREVIEW stated that North Korea has made it a rule that there should be one deputy per 30,000 people, suggesting that the population has remained stable since 1990. 30,000 multiplied by 687 would give a population of 20·61m., more than 1·5m. less than official estimates. In 1999, 81·1% of the population were urban.

The area, 1987 population (in 1,000) and chief towns of the provinces and cities with provincial status:

	Area in sq. km	Population	Chief Town
Chagang	16,968	1,156	Kanggye
North Hamgyong	17,570	2,003	Chongjin
South Hamgyong	18,970	2,547	Hamhung
North Hwanghae	8,007	1,409	Sariwon
South Hwanghae	8,002	1,914	Haeju
Kaesong (city)	1,255	331	
Kangwon	11,152	1,227	Wonsan
Nampo (city)	753	715	
North Pyongan	12,191	2,408	Sinuiju
South Pyongan	11,577	2,653	Pyongsan
Pyongyang (city)	2,000	2,355	
Yanggang	14,317	628	Hyesan

Pyongyang, the capital, had a 1999 population of 3,136,000. Other large towns (estimate, 1987): Hamhung (701,000); Chongjin (520,000); Nampo (370,000); Sunchon (356,000).

The official language is Korean.

SOCIAL STATISTICS
1995 births, 477,000; deaths, 122,000. 1995 birth rate, 21·6 per 1,000 population; death rate, 5·5. Annual population growth rate, 1990–99, 1·6%. Marriage is discouraged before the age of 32 for men and 29 for women. Life expectancy at birth, 1997, was 59·8 years for males and 64·5 years for females. Infant mortality, 1990–95, 24 per 1,000 live births; fertility rate, 1999, 2·0 births per woman. It was estimated in 1999 that up to 300,000 North Korean food-seeking refugees had gone to China to escape the famine. 27% of the population is classified as 'hostile' by the regime and 45% as 'unstable'.

CLIMATE
There is a warm temperate climate, though winters can be very cold in the north. Rainfall is concentrated in the summer months. Pyongyang, Jan. 18°F (–7·8°C), July 75°F (23·9°C). Annual rainfall 37" (916 mm).

CONSTITUTION AND GOVERNMENT
The political structure is based upon the Constitution of 27 Dec. 1972. Constitutional amendments of April 1992 delete references to Marxism-Leninism but retain the Communist Party's monopoly of rule. The Constitution provides for a *Supreme People's Assembly* elected every five years by universal suffrage. Citizens of 17 years and over can vote and be elected. The government consists of the *Administration Council* directed by the Central People's Committee.

The head of state is the *President*, elected for four-year terms. On the death of Kim Il-sung on 8 July 1994 his son and designated successor, Kim Jong Il (b. 1942), assumed all his father's posts. On 5 Sept. 1998 he took over as President and 'Supreme Leader'.

Party membership was 2m. in 1995. There are also the puppet religious Chongu and Korean Social Democratic Parties and various organizations combined in a Fatherland Front.

National Anthem. 'A chi mun bin na ra i gang san' ('Shine bright, o dawn, on this land so fair'); words by Pak Se Yong, tune by Kim Won Gyun.

RECENT ELECTIONS

Elections to the Supreme People's Assembly were held on 26 July 1998, the first ones since 1990. Only the list of the Democratic Front for the Reunification of the Fatherland was allowed to participate. 687 deputies were elected. 443 out of the 687, or 64%, were elected to the Assembly for the first time. In 1990 only 31·4% of the deputies were elected for the first time.

CURRENT ADMINISTRATION

President: Kim Jong Il. He also holds the posts of *Supreme Commander of the Korean People's Army* and *Chairman of the National Defence Commission.*

In Feb. 1997 Hong Song Nam (b. 1923) became *Prime Minister.* In March 2003 the government also included:

Vice Prime Ministers: Cho Ch'ang-tok, Kwak Pom-ki, Sin Il-nam. *Agriculture:* Kim Ch'ang-sik. *Chemical Industry:* Pak Pong-chu. *City Management:* Ch'oe Chong-kon. *Commerce:* Yi Yong-son. *Construction and Building Materials Industry:* Cho Yun-hui. *Culture:* Kang Nung-su. *Education:* Pyon Yong-rip. *Electronic Industry:* O Su-yong. *Extractive Industries:* Son Chong-ho. *Finance:* Mun Il-Pong. *Fisheries:* Yi Song-un. *Foreign Affairs:* Paek Nam-sun. *Foreign Trade:* Yi Kwang-kun. *Forestry:* Yi Sang-mu. *Labour:* Yi Won-il. *Land and Environment Protection:* Il-Son Chang. *Land and Marine Transport:* Kim Yong-il. *Light Industry:* Yi Chu-su. *Metal and Machine-Building Industries:* Chong Sunghun. *People's Armed Forces:* V. Mar. Kim Il-ch'ol. *Post and Telecommunications:* Yi Kum-pom. *Power and Coal Industries:* Sin T'ae-nok. *Procurement and Food Administration:* Nam-Kyun Choe. *Public Health:* Kim Su-hak. *Public Security:* V. Mar. Paek Hak-nim. *Railways:* Kim Yong-sam. *State Construction Control:* Pae Talchun. *State Inspection:* Kim Ui-sun.

President, Supreme People's Assembly Praesidium: Kim Yong-nam. *Vice Presidents:* Yang Hyong-sop, Kim Yong-t'ae.

In practice the country is ruled by the Korean Workers' (*i.e.*, Communist) Party which elects a Central Committee which in turn appoints a Politburo.

DEFENCE

The Supreme Commander of the Armed Forces is Kim Jong Il. Military service is compulsory at the age of 16 for periods of 5–8 years in the Army, 5–10 years in the Navy and 3–4 years in the Air Force, followed by obligatory part-time service in the Pacification Corps to age 40. Total armed forces troops were estimated to number 1,082,000 in 2002, up from 840,000 in 1986 although down from 1,160,000 in 1997.

Defence expenditure in 2001 totalled US$2,049m. (US$91 per capita), and represented 11·6% of GDP.

In 1998 North Korea tested a medium-range nuclear-capable Taepo Dong-1 missile. It has also developed a shorter-range No-Dong ballistic missile in addition to Scud B and Scud C missiles, and is known to be developing a longer-range intercontinental ballistic missile, the two-stage Taepo Dong-2, which experts believe could reach Alaska and the westernmost Hawaiian islands.

Nuclear Weapons. North Korea was for many years suspected of having a secret nuclear-weapons programme, and perhaps enough material to build two warheads. In Oct. 2002 it revealed that it had developed a nuclear bomb in violation of an arms control pact agreed with the USA in 1994. North Korea, known to have a nuclear weapons programme, has not signed the Comprehensive Nuclear-Test-Ban-Treaty, which is intended to bring about a ban on any nuclear explosions. North Korea is widely suspected of having biological and chemical weapons.

Army. One of the world's biggest, the Army was estimated at 950,000 personnel in 2002 with around 600,000 reserves. There is also a paramilitary worker-peasant Red Guard of some 3·5m. and a Ministry of Public Security force of 189,000 including border guards.

Equipment includes some 3,500 T-34, T-54/55, T-62 and Type-59 main battle tanks.

Navy. The Navy, principally tasked to coastal patrol and defence, comprises 26 diesel submarines, 3 small frigates and 6 corvettes. Personnel in 2002 totalled about 46,000 with 65,000 reserves.

Air Force. The Air Force had a total of 621 combat aircraft and 86,000 personnel in 2002. Combat aircraft include J-5/6/7s (Chinese built versions of MiG-17/19/23s), MiG-29s, Su-7s and Su-25s.

INTERNATIONAL RELATIONS

In Sept. 1999 following negotiations between Pyongyang and Washington in Berlin, Pyongyang agreed to put off its plan to test-fire an advanced long-range missile whilst the USA agreed gradually to lift economic sanctions imposed in 1950. The gesture on the part of the USA was the most significant since the end of the Korean War.

In 2000 North Korea received US$220m. in foreign aid, of which US$114m. came from South Korea.

North Korea is a member of the UN and the Antarctic Treaty.

ECONOMY

Agriculture is estimated to account for approximately 25% of GDP, industry 60% and services 15%.

Overview. In Dec. 1993 it was officially admitted that the third seven-year plan had failed to achieve its industrial targets owing to the disappearance of Communist markets and aid. Policy now concentrates on the development of agriculture, light industry and foreign trade, but progress is impeded by an all-powerful bureaucracy and a reluctance to depart from the Marxist-Stalinist line. However, in July 2002 signs emerged of changes in the economy, as the authorities revoked the rationing system for rice and began to sell it on the free market. New measures centred on large wage increases and even larger increases in prices for food, electricity and housing.

Currency. The monetary unit is the *won* (KPW) of 100 *chon*. Banknotes were replaced by a new issue in July 1992. Exchanges of new for old notes were limited to 500 won. Inflation was an estimated 5% in 1998.

Budget. Estimated revenue, 1994, 41,525·2m. won; expenditure, 41,525·2m. won.

Performance. The real GDP growth rate was 6·2% in 1999 following a decade of negative growth. This was followed in 2000 by growth of 1·3%, rising in 2001 to 3·7%. GDP per head was put at US$741 in 1997, or about a thirteenth of that of South Korea.

Banking and Finance. The bank of issue is the Central Bank of Korea (*Governor*, Kim Wan-su).

Weights and Measures. While the metric system is in force traditional measures are in frequent use. The *jungbo* = 1 ha; the *ri* = 3,927 metres. A new yearly calendar was announced on 9 July 1997 based on Kim Il-sung's birthday on 15 April 1912. Thus 15 April 2003–14 April 2004 is Year 92.

ENERGY AND NATURAL RESOURCES

Environment. According to the *World Bank Atlas* carbon dioxide emissions in 1997 were the equivalent of 11·4 tonnes per capita. An *Environmental Sustainability Index* compiled for the World Economic Forum meeting in Feb. 2002 ranked North Korea 140th in the world out of 142 countries analysed, with 32·3%. The index measured the ability of countries to maintain favourable environmental conditions and examined various factors including pollution levels and the use or abuse of natural resources.

Electricity. There are three thermal power stations and four hydro-electric plants. Installed capacity was 10m. kW in 1997. Production in 2000 was 19·4bn. kWh. Consumption per capita was an estimated 1,394 kWh in 1995. Hydro-electric potential exceeds 8m. kW. A hydro-electric plant and dam under construction on the Pukhan River near Mount Kumgang has been denounced as a flood threat by the South Koreans, who constructed a defensive 'Peace Dam' in retaliation. American aid to increase energy supply slowed after evidence that North Korea had broken its promise to freeze its nuclear weapons programme. But in Oct. 1998 Japan agreed to contribute US$1bn. towards building two nuclear power stations and the

NORTH KOREA

US Congress agreed to funds to supply fuel oil on condition that North Korea abandons its nuclear ambitions. In Aug. 2002 work began on the construction of the two western-designed light-water nuclear reactors. In Feb. 2003 North Korea reactivated its nuclear reactor at Yongbyon that had been dormant since 1994.

Oil and Gas. Oil wells went into production in 1957. An oil pipeline from China came on stream in 1976. Crude oil refining capacity was 70,000 bbls. a day in 1990.

Minerals. North Korea is rich in minerals. Estimated reserves in tonnes: coal, 11,990m.; manganese, 6,500m.; iron ore, 3,300m.; uranium, 26m.; zinc, 12m.; lead, 6m.; copper, 2·15m. 62m. tonnes of coal were mined in 1997, 11m. tonnes of iron ore in 1996 and 16,000 tonnes of copper ore in 1995. 1997 production of gold was 5,000 kg; silver, 50 tonnes; salt (1997 estimate), 590,000 tonnes.

Agriculture. In 1997 there were 1·7m. ha of arable land and 300,000 ha of permanent crop land. In 1995 there were 0·65m. ha of paddy fields. In 1995, 4·09m. persons were economically active in agriculture.

Collectivization took place between 1954 and 1958. 90% of the cultivated land is farmed by co-operatives. Land belongs either to the State or to co-operatives, and it is intended gradually to transform the latter into the former, but small individually-tended plots producing for 'farmers' markets' are tolerated as a 'transition measure'.

There is a large-scale tideland reclamation project. In 1997, 1·46m. ha were under irrigation, making possible two rice harvests a year. There were 75,000 tractors in 1998. The technical revolution in agriculture (nearly 95% of ploughing, etc., is mechanized) has considerably increased the yield of wheat (sown on 103,000 ha). Production (2000, in 1,000 tonnes): rice, 1,690; potatoes, 1,402; maize, 1,041; apples, 650; cabbages, 630; sweet potatoes, 468; soybeans, 350; dry beans, 280; melons and watermelons, 214.

Livestock, 2000: pigs, 2·97m.; goats, 2·10m.; cattle, 600,000; sheep, 190,000; 10m. chickens.

A chronic food shortage has led to repeated efforts by UN agencies to stave off famine. In Jan. 1998 the UN launched an appeal for US$378m. for food for North Korea, the largest ever relief effort mounted by its World Fund Programme.

Forestry. Forest area in 1995 was 6·17m. ha (51·2% of the land area). Timber production was 7m. cu. metres in 1999.

Fisheries. In 1999 total catch was approximately 210,000 tonnes, of which 90% were sea fish.

INDUSTRY
Industries were intensively developed by the Japanese occupiers, notably cotton spinning, hydro-electric power, cotton, silk and rayon weaving, and chemical fertilizers. Production in 1995: cement, 17m. tonnes; pig iron (1997), 6·6m. tonnes; crude steel (2000), 1·11m. tonnes; textile fabrics (1994), 350m. metres; motor cars (2000), 6,600 units; TV sets, 240,000 units; ships, 50,000 GRT. Annual steel production capacity was 4·3m. tonnes in 1987. Industrial production is estimated to have halved between 1990 and 2000.

Labour. The labour force totalled 11,881,000 (55% males) in 1996. Nearly 35% of the economically active population in 1995 were engaged in agriculture, fisheries and forestry.

INTERNATIONAL TRADE
Joint ventures with foreign firms have been permitted since 1984. A law of Oct. 1992 revised the 1984 rules: foreign investors may now set up wholly-owned facilities in special economic zones, repatriate part of profits and enjoy tax concessions. Economic zones have been set up at the ports of Sonbong and Najin. In 1996 foreign debt was estimated at US$11,830m. The USA imposed sanctions in Jan. 1988 for alleged terrorist activities. Since June 1995 South Korean businesses and individuals have been permitted to make investments and set up branch offices in North Korea.

Imports and Exports. Exports in 2000 were US$560m.; imports, US$1,410m. In 1995 China was the biggest import supplier (33%), followed by Japan (17%) and Russia (5%); Japan was the main export destination (28%), ahead of South Korea

1012

(21%) and China (5%). The chief exports are metal ores and products, the chief imports machinery and petroleum products.

COMMUNICATIONS

Roads. There were around 31,200 km of road in 1996, of which 2,000 km were paved. There were 262,000 passenger cars in 2000. The first of two planned cross-border roads between the two Koreas opened in Feb. 2003.

Rail. The railway network totalled 8,533 km in 1990, of which 3,250 km were electrified. In 1990, 38·5m. tonnes of freight and 35m. passengers were carried. In June 2000 it was agreed to start consultations to restore the railway from Sinuiju, on the North Korean/Chinese border, to Seoul by rebuilding an 8 km long stretch from Pongdong-ni to Changdan, on the North Korean/South Korean border, and a 12 km long stretch in South Korea. The first two rail links between the two Koreas are currently under construction.

There is a metro and tramway in Pyongyang.

Civil Aviation. There is an international airport at Pyongyang (Sunan). There were flights in 1998 to Bangkok, Beijing, Berlin, Dalian, Macao, Moscow, Sofia and Vladivostok. The national carrier is Air Koryo.

Shipping. The leading ports are Chongjin, Wonsan and Hungnam. Pyongyang is connected to the port of Nampo by railway and river. In 1998 the ocean-going merchant fleet totalled 631,000 GRT, including oil tankers 6,000 GRT.

The biggest navigable river is the Yalu, 698 km up to the Hyesan district.

Telecommunications. An agreement to share in Japan's telecommunications satellites was reached in Sept. 1990. There were 1,100,000 main telephone lines in 2000, or 45·8 per 1,000 population. In 1995 there were 3,000 fax machines. North Korea's first Internet cafe opened in May 2002.

SOCIAL INSTITUTIONS

Justice. The judiciary consists of the Supreme Court, whose judges are elected by the Assembly for three years; provincial courts; and city or county people's courts. The procurator-general, appointed by the Assembly, has supervisory powers over the judiciary and the administration; the Supreme Court controls the judicial administration.

In Jan. 1999 approximately 200,000 political prisoners were being held at ten detention camps in the country.

Religion. The Constitution provides for 'freedom of religion as well as the freedom of anti-religious propaganda'. In 1986 there were 3m. Chondoists, 400,000 Buddhists and 200,000 Christians. Another 3m. followed traditional beliefs.

Education. Free compulsory universal technical education lasts 11 years: 1 pre-school year, 4 years primary education starting at the age of 6, followed by 6 years secondary. In 1994–95 there were 37 universities, 31 specialized universities and 108 specialized colleges.

The adult literacy rate is 95%.

Health. Medical treatment is free. In 1993 there were 61,200 doctors, giving a doctor/inhabitant ratio of 1:370. The hospital bed provision in 1989 of 135 per 10,000 population was one of the highest in the world.

North Korea has been one of the least successful countries in the battle against undernourishment in the past 20 years. Between 1980 and 1996 the proportion of undernourished people rose from 16% of the population to 48%. Many people have had to resort to eating twigs, bark and leaves.

CULTURE

Broadcasting. The government-controlled Korean Central Broadcasting Station and Korean Central Television Station are responsible for radio and TV broadcasting. In 1991 there were 34 radio and 11 TV stations (colour by PAL). There were 3·36m. radio and 1·2m. TV sets in 1997. All radio and television stations being government-run, North Koreans know very little of the outside world. They have been told that the food shortages of recent years were a global catastrophe and that they are comparatively well-off.

Cinema. There were 1,778 cinemas in 1985 and 3,515 mobile cinemas.

Press. There were three daily newspapers in 1996. The party newspaper is *Nodong* (or *Rodong*) *Sinmun* (Workers' Daily News). Circulation is about 600,000.

Tourism. A 40-year ban on non-Communist tourists was lifted in 1986. In 1999 there were 130,000 foreign tourists. On 19 Nov. 1998 North Korea received its first tourists from South Korea, on a cruise and tour organized by the South Korean firm Hyundai.

DIPLOMATIC REPRESENTATIVES
Of North Korea in the United Kingdom
Chargé d'Affaires: Ri Tae Gun (resides in Switzerland).

Of the United Kingdom in North Korea (Munsu Dong Diplomatic Compound, Pyongyang)
Ambassador: David Slinn.

Of North Korea to the United Nations
Ambassador: Li Hyong Chol.

FURTHER READING
Harrison, S., *Korean Endgame: A Strategy for Reunification and US Disengagement.* Princeton Univ. Press, 2002
Hunter, H., *Kim Il-Song's North Korea.* Praeger Publishers, Westport (CT), 1999
Kleiner, J., *Korea: a Century of Change.* World Scientific Publishing Co., Singapore, 2001
Oh, K. and Hassig, R. C., *North Korea Through the Looking Glass.* Brookings Institution Press, Washington (D. C.), 2000
Sigal, L. V., *Disarming Strangers: Nuclear Diplomacy with North Korea.* Princeton Univ. Press, 1999
Smith, H., *et al.*, (eds.) *North Korea in the New World Order.* London, 1996

National statistical office: Central Statistics Bureau, Pyongyang.

KUWAIT

Dowlat al Kuwait
(State of Kuwait)

Capital: Kuwait
Population estimate, 2000: 2·19m.
GDP per capita, 2000: (PPP$) 15,799
HDI/world rank: 0·813/45

KEY HISTORICAL EVENTS

The ruling dynasty was founded by Shaikh Sabah al-Awwal, who ruled from 1756 to 1772. In 1899 Shaikh Mubarak concluded a treaty with Great Britain wherein, in return for the assurance of British protection, he undertook to support British interests. In 1914 the British Government recognized Kuwait as an independent government under British protection. On 19 June 1961 an agreement reaffirmed the independence and sovereignty of Kuwait and recognized the Government of Kuwait's responsibility for the conduct of internal and external affairs. On 2 Aug. 1990 Iraqi forces invaded the country. Following the expiry of the date set by the UN for the withdrawal of Iraqi forces, an air offensive was launched by coalition forces, followed by a land attack on 24 Feb. 1991. Iraqi forces were routed and Kuwait City was liberated on 26 Feb. On 10 Nov. 1994 Iraq recognized the independence and boundaries of Kuwait.

TERRITORY AND POPULATION

Kuwait is bounded in the east by the Arabian (Persian) Gulf, north and west by Iraq and south and southwest by Saudi Arabia, with an area of 17,818 sq. km. In 1992–93 the UN Boundary Commission redefined Kuwait's border with Iraq, moving it slightly northwards in conformity with an agreement of 1932. The population at the census of 1995 was 1,575,570 (97·4% urban in 1999), of whom about 58% were non-Kuwaitis. Population density, 88 per sq. km.

The UN gives a projected population for 2010 of 2·47m.

The country is divided into six governorates: the capital (comprising Kuwait City, Kuwait's nine islands and territorial and shared territorial waters) (population 385,675, 1999 estimate); Hawalli (624,962); Ahmadi (368,190); Jahra (287,566), Farwaniya (586,751) and Mubarak Al-Kabir (created in 2000). The capital city is Kuwait, with a population in 1995 of 28,559. Other major cities are (1995 populations): as-Salimiya (130,215), Jahra (111,222), Qalib ash-Shuyukh (102,178), Hawalli (82,238), Hitan-al-Janubiyah (63,628).

The Neutral Zone (Kuwait's share, 2,590 sq. km), jointly owned and administered by Kuwait and Saudi Arabia from 1922 to 1966, was partitioned between the two countries in May 1966, but the exploitation of the oil and other natural resources continues to be shared.

Over 78% speak Arabic, the official language. English is also used as a second language.

SOCIAL STATISTICS

Births, 1999, 41,135; deaths, 4,187. In 1997 the birth rate was 19·5 per 1,000 population. Kuwait's 1999 death rate, at 2·0 per 1,000 population, was the second lowest in the world (only Qatar's was lower). Expectation of life at birth, 1999, 74·3 years for males and 78·4 years for females. Infant mortality, 1999, 9·4 per 1,000 live births. Annual population growth rate, 1990–99, –1·3%; fertility rate, 1999, 2·8 births per woman. Kuwait has had one of the largest reductions in its fertility rate of any country in the world over the past 25 years, having had a rate of 6·3 births per woman in 1975. Kuwait has a young population, with 60% of the population being under 16.

CLIMATE

Kuwait has a dry, desert climate which is cool in winter but very hot and humid in summer. Rainfall is extremely light. Kuwait, Jan. 56°F (13·5°C), July 99°F (36·6°C). Annual rainfall 5" (125 mm).

CONSTITUTION AND GOVERNMENT

The ruler is HH Shaikh Jaber al-Ahmed al-Jaber al-Sabah, the 13th Amir of Kuwait, who succeeded on 31 Dec. 1977.

In 1990 the *National Council* was established, consisting of 50 elected members and 25 appointed by the Amir. It was replaced by a *National Assembly* or *Majlis al-Umma* in 1992, consisting of 50 elected members. The franchise is limited to men over 21 whose families have been of Kuwaiti nationality since before 1920 and the sons of persons naturalized since 1992. In May 1999 the cabinet approved a draft law giving women the right to vote and run for parliament. However, in Dec. 1999 parliament rejected the bill allowing women to vote by a margin of 32 to 20.

National Anthem. 'Watanil Kuwait salemta lilmajdi, wa ala jabeenoka tali ossaadi,' ('Kuwait, my fatherland! May you be safe and glorious! May you always enjoy good fortune!'); words by Moshari al-Adwani, tune by Ibrahim Nassar al-Soula.

RECENT ELECTIONS

At the all-male National Assembly elections on 3 July 1999 Islamist candidates won 20 seats, Liberals 14 (up from 4 at the previous election), the government camp 12 and independents 4. As a result the likelihood of the legislature supporting voting rights for women in the near future increased.

CURRENT ADMINISTRATION

Executive authority is vested in the *Council of Ministers.*

The prime minister and the whole government resigned in Jan. 2001 but the Amir asked the prime minister to form a new cabinet.

In March 2003 the government comprised:

Prime Minister: HRH Crown Prince Shaikh Saad al-Abdullah al-Salim al-Sabah; b. 1930 (appointed 8 Feb. 1978).

First Deputy Prime Minister and Foreign Minister: Shaikh Sabah al-Ahmed al-Jaber al-Sabah. *Deputy Prime Minister and Defence Minister:* Shaikh Jabar Mubarak al-Hamad al-Sabah. *Deputy Prime Minister and State Minister for Cabinet Affairs and National Assembly Affairs:* Muhammad Dayfallah al-Sharar. *Deputy Prime Minister and Interior Minister:* Shaikh Mohammed al-Khalid al-Hamad al-Sabah.

Minister of Social Affairs, Labour, Electricity and Water: Talal Mubarak al-Ayyer. *Commerce and Industry:* Salah Abdurreda Khorsheed. *Communications:* Ahmad Abdallah al-Ahmad al-Sabah. *Justice, Religious Endowments (Awqaf) and Islamic Affairs:* Ahmad Yaqoob Baqer al-Abdullah. *Information, and Oil (acting):* Sheikh Ahmad al-Fahd al-Sabah. *Public Works and Minister of State for Housing Affairs:* Fahad Dheisan al-Mee. *Education and Higher Education:* Musaed al-Haroun. *Finance and Planning (acting):* Muhammad Sabah al-Salim al-Sabah. *Health:* Dr Muhammad Ahmad Jarallah. *Minister of State for Foreign Affairs:* Sheikh Mohammad Sabah al-Salem al-Sabah.

Speaker: Jasim al-Khurafi.

Council of Ministers: http://www.fatwa.gov.kw/

DEFENCE

In Sept. 1991 the USA signed a ten-year agreement with Kuwait to store equipment, use ports and carry out joint training exercises. Conscription is for two years. There were over 5,000 US and UN personnel based in Kuwait in 1999 as well as a UK RAF *Tornado* squadron.

Defence expenditure in 2001 totalled US$5,029m. (US$2,514 per capita), representing 12·1% of GDP. The expenditure per capita in 2001 was the highest in the world.

Army. Strength (1999) about 11,000 including 1,600 foreign personnel. In addition there is a National Guard of 5,000.

Navy. Personnel in 1999 numbered 1,800, including 400 Coast Guard personnel.

Air Force. From a small initial combat force the Air Force has grown rapidly, although it suffered heavy losses after the Iraqi invasion of 1990–91. Equipment includes F/A-18 Hornet strike aircraft and Mirage F-1s. Personnel strength was estimated (1999) at 2,500, with 76 Combat aircraft and 20 armed helicopters.

INTERNATIONAL RELATIONS

Kuwait is a member of the UN, WTO, the League of Arab States, Gulf Co-operation Council, OPEC and OIC.

Kuwait claims that 605 prisoners of war have been held by the former Iraqi regime since the last few days of the Iraqi occupation in Feb. 1991.

ECONOMY

Industry accounted for 55% of GDP in 1996 and services 45%.

Overview. Kuwait's Planning Ministry released a five-year plan in 2001 calling for the development of information technology and modern education to create a suitable environment for a free economy.

Currency. The unit of currency is the *Kuwaiti dinar* (KD) of 1,000 *fils*. Inflation in 2001 was 2·5%. Foreign exchange reserves were US$10,260m. in June 2002, gold reserves were 2·54m. troy oz and total money supply was KD 2,156m.

In 2001 the six Gulf Arab states—Kuwait, along with Bahrain, Oman, Qatar, Saudi Arabia and the United Arab Emirates—signed an agreement to establish a single currency by 2010.

Budget. The fiscal year begins on 1 July. Revenue and expenditure over a five-year span (in KD 1m.):

	1995	1996	1997	1998	1999
Revenue	2,987	3,306	4,271	3,461	3,064
Expenditure	3,790	3,845	3,827	3,902	3,930

Expenditure by function (in 1996): defence, 1,163; social security and welfare, 656; education, 476; public order and safety, 331; health, 247.

Performance. Real GDP growth in negative in 2001, at –1·0%. Total GDP in 2000 was US$37·8bn. In 1997 there was a current account surplus of US$7,816m.

Banking and Finance. The *Governor* of the Central Bank is Sheikh Salem AbdulAziz Al-Sabah. There is also the Kuwait Finance House. In 2001 there were six commercial banks and one Islamic banking firm. The combined assets of banks operating in Kuwait totalled KD 14,133m. in Feb. 2001. Foreign banks are banned.

There is a stock exchange, linked with those of Bahrain and Oman.

Weights and Measures. The metric system is in force.

ENERGY AND NATURAL RESOURCES

Environment. According to the *World Bank Atlas* Kuwait's carbon dioxide emissions were the equivalent of 26·3 tonnes per capita in 1998. An *Environmental Sustainability Index* compiled for the World Economic Forum meeting in Feb. 2002 ranked Kuwait 142nd in the world out of the 142 countries analysed, with 23·9%. The index measured the ability of countries to maintain favourable environmental conditions and examined various factors including pollution levels and the use or abuse of natural resources.

Electricity. There are four power stations with a total installed capacity of 7m. kW in 1997. Production in 1999 was 31·6bn. kWh; consumption per capita in 1998 was 13,800 kWh.

Oil and Gas. Crude oil production in 1999, 683·5m. bbls. Kuwait produced 3·2% of the world total oil output in 1996, and had reserves amounting to 96·5bn. bbls. at the end of 2001. Only Saudi Arabia and Iraq have greater reserves. Most of the oil is in the Great Burgan area (reserves of approximately 70bn. bbls.), comprising the Burgan, Maqwa and Ahmadi fields located south of Kuwait City. Natural gas production was 7·0bn. cu. metres in 1999 with 1,490bn. cu metres of proven reserves.

Water. The country depends upon desalination plants. In 1993 there were four plants with a daily total capacity of 216m. gallons. Fresh mineral water is pumped and bottled at Rawdhatain. Underground brackish water is used for irrigation, street cleaning and livestock. Production, 1996, 89,684m. gallons (67,674m. gallons fresh, 22,010m. gallons brackish). Consumption, 1996, 80,298m. gallons (62,423m. gallons fresh, 17,875m. gallons brackish).

Agriculture. There were 6,000 ha of arable land in 1998 and 1,000 ha of permanent crops. Production of main crops, 2000 (in 1,000 tonnes): cucumbers and gherkins, 33; tomatoes, 32; potatoes, 29; aubergines, 12; dates, 9; chillies and green peppers, 5; pumpkins and squash, 5; cauliflowers, 4.

Livestock (2000): cattle, 20,000; sheep, 450,000; goats, 150,000; camels, 9,000; poultry, 33m. Milk production (2000), 46,000 tonnes.

Forestry. Forests covered 5,000 ha in 1995, or 0·3% of the land area.

Fisheries. The total catch in 1999 was 6,271 tonnes, exclusively from sea fishing. In the space of a month in 2001 more than 2,000 tonnes of dead fish were washed ashore. Some experts claimed the cause was the alleged pumping of raw sewage into the Gulf while others attributed it to waste from the oil industry. Shrimp fishing was important, but has declined since the 1990–91 war through oil pollution of coastal waters. Before the discovery of oil, pearls were at the centre of Kuwait's economy, but today pearl fishing is only on a small scale.

INDUSTRY
According to the Financial Times Survey (FT 500), the largest companies by market capitalization in Kuwait on 4 Jan. 2001 were: The National Bank of Kuwait (US$3,579·8m.); Mobile Telephone (US$2,466·7m.); and Kuwait Finance House (US$1,489·6m.).

Industries, apart from oil, include boat building, fishing, food production, petrochemicals, gases and construction. Production figures in 1997 (in 1,000 tonnes): distillate fuel oil, 13,116; residual fuel oil, 11,623; jet fuel oil, 8,156; liquefied petroleum gas, 3,650; petrol, 1,830; kerosene, 1,496.

Labour. In 1999 the labour force totalled 1,226,000 (82% non-Kuwaitis). Of the total labour force, 50·1% worked in social, community and personal services, 16·0% in trade, hotels and restaurants, 9·6% in construction and 6·4% in manufacturing. Approximately 93% of the workforce are civil servants. Registered unemployment was 1·4% in 1996.

Trade Unions. In 1986 there were 16 trade unions and 17 labour federations.

INTERNATIONAL TRADE
In 2001 Kuwait, along with Bahrain, Oman, Qatar, Saudi Arabia and the United Arab Emirates agreed to the complete implementation of a customs union by 2003.

Imports and Exports. Imports (f.o.b.) were valued at US$6,846m. in 2000 (US$6,705m. in 1999) and exports (f.o.b.) at US$19,576m. (US$12,276m. in 1999). Oil accounts for 93% of revenue from exports, and oil exports account for approximately 40% of GDP. The main non-oil export is chemical fertilizer.

Main export markets, 1999: Japan, 22·8%; USA, 11·5%; Singapore, 8·2%. Main import suppliers, 1999: USA, 15·4%; Japan, 10·2%; Germany, 7·3%.

COMMUNICATIONS
Roads. There were 4,450 km of roads in 1996, 80·6% of which was paved. Number of vehicles in 1996 was 693,000 (538,000 passenger cars, or 359 per 1,000 inhabitants, and 155,000 trucks and vans). There were 15,921 road accidents in 1993 with 290 fatalities.

Civil Aviation. There is an international airport (Kuwait International). The national carrier is the state-owned Kuwait Airways. In 1999 it flew 36·5m. km and carried 2,130,000 passengers (all on international flights). Kuwait International airport handled 3,747,374 passengers in 2000 and 112,478 tonnes of freight.

Shipping. The port of Kuwait formerly served mainly as an entrepôt, but this function is declining in importance with the development of the oil industry. The largest oil terminal is at Mina Ahmadi. Three small oil ports lie to the south of Mina Ahmadi: Mina Shuaiba, Mina Abdullah and Mina Al-Zor. The merchant fleet totalled 2,459,000 GRT in 1998, of which 1,662,000 GRT were tankers. In 1998 vessels totalling 9,357,000 NRT entered ports and vessels totalling 1,178,000 NRT cleared.

Telecommunications. Kuwait had 467,100 main telephone lines in 2000, or 244·0 per 1,000 population, and there were 250,000 PCs (130·6 for every 1,000 persons).

In 1999 mobile phone subscribers numbered 300,000 and in 1997 there were 42,000 fax machines. The number of Internet users in March 2001 was 165,000.

Postal Services. In 1999 there were 94,402 post office boxes. There were 124,820 outgoing telegrams and 75,322 incoming.

SOCIAL INSTITUTIONS

Justice. In 1960 Kuwait adopted a unified judicial system covering all levels of courts. These are: Courts of Summary Justice, Courts of the First Instance, Supreme Court of Appeal, Court of Cassation and a Constitutional Court. Islamic Sharia is a major source of legislation. The death penalty is still in use.

The population in penal institutions in 1997 was 1,735 (100 per 100,000 of national population).

Religion. In 1996, 810,000 people were Sunni Muslims, 540,000 Shia Muslims, 180,000 other Muslims, and 270,000 other (mostly Christian and Hindu).

Education. Education is free and compulsory from 6 to 14 years. In 1999–2000 there were 222 pre-primary schools with 3,800 teachers for 59,666 pupils, 269 primary schools with 10,176 teachers for 140,182 pupils, 244 intermediate schools with 10,749 teachers for 132,904 pupils, and 10,708 teachers in 197 secondary schools for 100,804 pupils. There were 15,808 students at Kuwait University in 1998–99. A pan-Arab Open University based in Kuwait and with branches in several other Middle Eastern countries was opened in Nov. 2002 with an initial enrolment of 3,000 students. Adult literacy rate in 1999 was 81·9% (84·0% among men and 79·4% among women). Total expenditure on education in 1995: KD 490,000,000 or 5·7% of GDP.

Health. Medical services are free to all residents. In 1999 there were 15 hospitals and sanatoria, with a provision of 4,433 beds (21 per 10,000 population); there were 3,178 doctors (15 per 10,000 population), 492 dentists, and (1995) 8,337 nurses and 19 midwives. There were 70 clinics and other health centres and 1,295,132 people were admitted to public hospitals during the year.

CULTURE

Broadcasting. The government-controlled Radio Kuwait and Kuwait Television broadcast a main and a second radio programme, a Koran programme and a service in English and two TV programmes (colour by PAL). In 1997 there were 875,000 TV receivers and 1,175,000 radios.

Cinema. In 1996 there were six cinemas, with a total annual attendance of 800,000.

Press. In 1996 there were eight daily newspapers, with a combined circulation of about 535,000. Formal press censorship was lifted in Jan. 1992.

Tourism. There were 79,000 foreign tourists in 1998, bringing revenue of US$207m. There were 20 hotels providing 3,222 beds in 1999.

Libraries. In 1992 there were 11 non-specialized and 18 public libraries, stocking 407,000 books for 12,500 registered users.

Museums and Galleries. There were six museums attracting 36,000 visitors in 1995.

DIPLOMATIC REPRESENTATIVES
Of Kuwait in the United Kingdom (2 Albert Gate, London, SW1X 7JU)
Ambassador: Khaled al-Duwaisan, GCVO.

Of the United Kingdom in Kuwait (Arabian Gulf St., Kuwait)
Ambassador: Christopher Wilton.

Of Kuwait in the USA (2940 Tilden St., NW, Washington, D.C., 20008)
Ambassador: Salem Abdulla Al-Jaber Al-Sabah.

Of the USA in Kuwait (PO Box 77, Safat, Kuwait)
Ambassador: Richard Henry Jones.

Of Kuwait to the United Nations
Ambassador: Mohammad A. Abulhasan.

Of Kuwait to the European Union
Ambassador: Abdulazeez A. Al-Sharikh.

FURTHER READING

Al-Yahya, M.A., *Kuwait: Fall and Rebirth.* London, 1993

Clements, F. A., *Kuwait.* [Bibliography] ABC-Clio, 2nd ed. Oxford and Santa Barbara (CA), 1996

Crystal, J., *Kuwait: the Transformation of an Oil State.* Boulder (Colo.), 1992

Finnie, D. H., *Shifting Lines in the Sand: Kuwait's Elusive Frontier with Iraq.* London, 1992

National statistical office: Statistics and Information Sector, Ministry of Planning
Website: http://www.mop.gov.kw

KYRGYZSTAN

Kyrgyz Respublikasy

Capital: Bishkek
Population estimate, 2000: 4·92m.
GDP per capita, 2000: (PPP$) 2,711
HDI/world rank: 0·712/102

KEY HISTORICAL EVENTS

After the establishment of the Soviet regime, Kyrgyzstan became part of Soviet Turkestan, which itself became a Soviet Socialist Republic within the Russian Soviet Federal Socialist Republic (RSFSR) in April 1921. In 1924, when Central Asia was reorganized territorially on a national basis, Kyrgyzstan was separated from Turkestan. In Dec. 1936 Kyrgyzstan was proclaimed one of the constituent Soviet Socialist Republics of the USSR. With the collapse of the Soviet Empire, the republic asserted its claim to sovereignty in 1990 and declared independence in Sept. 1991. Askar Akaev became president in 1990 and has since expanded presidential powers substantially. Kyrgyzstan became a member of the CIS in Dec. 1991.

Incursions into Kyrgyz territory by Islamic rebels and border skirmishes in the Fergana Valley are a cause for concern for all Central Asian governments. Kyrgyzstan tripled its defence budget for 2001 to combat terrorism.

TERRITORY AND POPULATION

Kyrgyzstan is situated on the Tien-Shan mountains and bordered in the east by China, west by Kazakhstan and Uzbekistan, north by Kazakhstan and south by Tajikistan. Area, 199,900 sq. km (77,180 sq. miles). Population (census 1999), 4,822,938; density, 24 per sq. km. In 1999, 66·4% of the population lived in rural areas.

The UN gives a projected population for 2010 of 5·51m.

The republic comprises seven provinces: Batken, Djalal-Abad, Issyk-Kul, Naryn, Osh, Talas and Chu. Its capital is Bishkek (formerly Frunze; 1999 population estimate, 619,000). Other large towns are Osh (238,200), Djalal-Abad (74,200), Tokmak (71,200), Przhevalsk (64,300) and Kyzyl-Kiya.

The Kyrgyz are of Turkic origin and formed 64·9% of the population in 1999; the rest included Uzbeks (13·8%), Russians (12·5%), Dungans (1·1%) and Ukrainians (1·0%).

The official languages are Kyrgyz and Russian. After the breakup of the Soviet Union, Russian was only the official language in provinces where Russians are in a majority. However, in May 2000 parliament voted to make it an official language nationwide, mainly in an attempt to stem the ever-increasing exodus of skilled ethnic Russians. The Roman alphabet (in use 1928–40) was re-introduced in 1992.

SOCIAL STATISTICS

1998 births, 104,183; deaths, 34,596; marriages, 25,726. Rates, 1998 (per 1,000 population): birth, 21·7; death, 7·2; infant mortality (per 1,000 live births), 55 (1999). Life expectancy, 1999, 63·4 years for males and 71·4 for females. In 1998 the most popular age range for marrying was 20–24 for both males and females. Annual population growth rate, 1990–99, 0·7%; fertility rate, 1999, 3·1 births per woman.

CLIMATE

The climate varies from dry continental to polar in the high Tien-Shan, to sub-tropical in the southwest (Fergana Valley) and temperate in the northern foothills. Bishkek, Jan. 9°F (–13°C), July 70°F (21°C). Annual rainfall 14·8" (375 mm).

CONSTITUTION AND GOVERNMENT

A new Constitution was adopted on 5 May 1993. The Presidency is executive, and directly elected for renewable five-year terms. At a referendum on 30 Jan. 1994, 96% of votes cast favoured President Akaev's serving out the rest of his term of office; turn-out was 95%. At a referendum on 22–23 Oct. 1994 turn-out was 87%. 75% of votes cast were in favour of instituting referendums as a constitutional mechanism, and 73% were in favour of establishing a new bicameral parliament (*Jogorku Kenesh*), with a 35-member directly-elected legislature, and a 70-member upper house elected on a regional basis and meeting twice a year. 94·5% of votes cast at a referendum on 10 Feb. 1996 were in favour of giving the President the right to appoint all ministers except the Prime Minister without reference to parliament.

National Anthem. 'Ak möngülüü aska yoolor, talaalar' ('High mountains, valleys and fields'); words by Z. Sadikova and S. Kulueva, tune by N. Davlyesova and K. Moldovasanova.

RECENT ELECTIONS

Elections for the Legislative Assembly were held on 20 Feb. and 12 March 2000. Turn-out was 64·4%. The Communists (PKK) won 27·7% of the vote and 15 of the available 60 seats, the Union of Democratic Forces (SDS) 18·6% (4), the Women's Democratic Party (DPZK) 12·7% (2), the Party of War Veterans in Afghanistan (PPVVAA) 8·0% (2), Socialist Party Ata Meken (AM) 6·5% (1) and My Country Party (MS) 5·0% (1). Five other parties received 5% of the vote or less. The remaining seats were taken by non-partisans. Elections to the People's Representative Assembly were held on 20 Feb. 2000 and all 45 seats were taken by non-partisans.

Presidential elections were held on 29 Oct. 2000. President Akaev was re-elected for a third term in office by 74·4% of votes cast against two opponents. Independent monitors said the election did not comply with democratic standards. In June 2000 a special commission had been created to test the knowledge of the Kyrgyz language of the candidates for the presidency. Several potential candidates failed the test, and the strongest rival to President Akaev declined to take the test and was barred from standing.

CURRENT ADMINISTRATION

President: Askar Akaev; b. 1945 (sworn in 28 Oct. 1990 and re-elected in 1995 and 2000).

In March 2003 the government comprised:

Prime Minister: Nikolai Tanayev; b. 1945 (sworn in 30 May 2002).

First Deputy Prime Minister: Kurmanbek Osmanov. *Deputy Prime Minister:* Joomart Otorbayev. *Deputy Prime Minister and Minister of Transport and Communications:* Kubanychbek Jumaliyev. *Chief of Staff:* Bekbolot Talgarbekov. *Defence:* Col. Gen. Esen Topoyev. *Finance:* Bolot Abildayev. *Foreign Affairs:* Askar Aitmatov. *Foreign Trade and Industry:* Sadridin Djiyenbekov. *Health:* Mitalip Mamytov. *Internal Affairs:* Bakirdin Subanbekov. *Justice:* Daniyar Narymbayev. *Labour and Social Welfare:* Roza Aknazarova. *Agriculture and Water Resources:* Alexander Kostyuk. *Ecology and Emergencies:* Satyvaldy Chyrmashev. *Education, Science and Culture:* Ishenkul Boldzhurova.

Chairman, Assembly of People's Representatives: Altay Borubayev. *Chairman, Legislative Assembly:* Abdygany Erkebayev.

President's Website: http://www.president.kg/

DEFENCE

Conscription is for 18 months. Defence expenditure in 2000 totalled US$31m. (US$7 per capita), representing 2·4% of GDP.

Army. Personnel, 1999, 6,800. In addition there is a combined forces reserve of 57,000 and 3,000 border guards.

Air Force. There is an aviation element with MiG-21 fighters and a variety of other ex-Soviet equipment. Personnel, 1999, 2,400.

INTERNATIONAL RELATIONS

Kyrgyzstan is a member of the UN, WTO, CIS, OSCE, Asian Development Bank, ECO, IOM, OIC and the NATO Partnership for Peace.

ECONOMY

Agriculture accounted for 46·0% of GDP in 1998, industry 23·6% and services 30·4%.

Currency. On 10 May 1993 Kyrgyzstan introduced its own currency unit, the *som* (KGS), of 100 *tyiyn*, at a rate of 1 som = 200 roubles. Inflation was 7·0% in 2001. Gold reserves totalled 83,000 troy oz in June 2002 and foreign exchange reserves US$237m. Total money supply in June 2002 was 6,247m. soms.

Budget. Government revenue and expenditure (in 1m. soms), year ending 31 Dec.:

	1995	1996	1997	1998	1999	2000
Revenue	2,691·1	3,747·6	4,840·5	6,090·7	7,873·7	9,280·1
Expenditure	4,482·2	5,227·2	6,869·6	7,531·6	9,611·5	11,761·3

Performance. Real GDP growth was 3·7% in 1999, 5·1% in 2000 and 5·3% in 2001. Total GDP in 2001 was US$1·5bn.

Banking and Finance. The central bank and bank of issue is the National Bank (*Chairman,* Ulan Sarbanov). There were 13 commercial banks and one German-Kyrgyz industrial bank in 1996.

ENERGY AND NATURAL RESOURCES

Environment. According to the *World Bank Atlas* Kyrgyzstan's carbon dioxide emissions were the equivalent of 1·3 tonnes per capita in 1998.

Electricity. Installed capacity was 4m. kW in 1997. Production in 1998 was 12·21bn. kWh, around 90% hydro-electric; consumption per capita in 1998 was 1,431 kWh.

Oil and Gas. Output of oil, 1996, 700,000 bbls.; natural gas, 1996, 1 petajoule.

Water. Kyrgyzstan's most valuable natural resource is water.

Minerals. Coal production totalled 137,000 tonnes in 1996 and lignite production 280,000 tonnes in 1997. Some gold is mined.

Agriculture. Kyrgyzstan is famed for its livestock breeding. In 2000 there were 3,264,000 sheep, 932,000 cattle, 328,000 horses, 234,000 goats and 2m. chickens. Yaks are bred as meat and dairy cattle, and graze on high altitudes unsuitable for other cattle. Crossed with domestic cattle, hybrids give twice the yield of milk. The small Kyrgyz horse is famed.

There were 1·35m. ha of arable land in 1998 and 75,000 ha of permanent crops. Number of farms (1993), 12,800. Private and commercial agriculture accounted for 46% of output by value in 1993. Total output was valued at 2,400m. roubles (in constant 1983 prices) in 1993.

Principal crops include wheat, barley, corn and vegetables. Kyrgyzstan raises wheat sufficient for its own use and other grains and fodder, particularly lucerne; also sugarbeets, hemp, kenaf, kendyr, tobacco, medicinal plants and rice. Sericulture, fruit, grapes and vegetables are major branches.

Output of main agricultural products (in 1,000 tonnes) in 2000: wheat, 1,039; potatoes, 1,033; sugarbeets, 450; maize, 338; tomatoes, 156; barley, 150; onions, 147; carrots, 109; cabbages, 101; cucumbers and gherkins, 90; seed cotton, 88; apples, 86; watermelons, 65. Livestock products, 2000, in 1,000 tonnes: beef and veal, 98; mutton and lamb, 40; milk, 1,090; eggs, 12.

Forestry. In 1995 forests covered 730,000 ha, or 3·8% of the land area. Timber production in 1999 was 42,000 cu. metres.

Fisheries. The catch in 1999 was 48 tonnes, entirely from freshwater fishing.

INDUSTRY

Industrial enterprises include sugar refineries, tanneries, cotton and wool-cleansing works, flour-mills, a tobacco factory, food, timber, textile, engineering, metallurgical, oil and mining enterprises. Output was valued at 3,300m. som in current prices in 1993, 75·8% of the 1992 figure.

Production, 1997: cement, 658,000 tonnes; cotton, 20m. sq. metres; carpets (1995), 0·98m. sq. metres; footwear (1995), 728,000 pairs; 2,000 washing machines.

Labour. Out of 1,641,000 people in employment in 1995, 689,000 were engaged in agriculture and forestry, 240,000 in industry, 170,000 in education and 112,000 in trade and catering. In 2000 the unemployment rate was 3·1%.

INTERNATIONAL TRADE

In Jan. 1994 an agreement to create a single economic zone was signed with Kazakhstan and Uzbekistan. In March 1996 Kyrgyzstan joined a customs union with Russia, Kazakhstan and Belarus. Total external debt was US$1,829m. in 2000.

Imports and Exports. Imports (f.o.b.) were valued at US$502·1m. in 2000 (US$546·9m. in 1999) and exports (f.o.b.) at US$510·9m. (US$462·6m. in 1999). Principal imports in 1995 (in US$1m.): petroleum and gas, 162·4; machinery and metalworking, 103·6; food and beverages, 96·7. Principal exports: food and beverages, 82·8; light industry, 82·6; non-ferrous metallurgy, 62·7.

Main import suppliers in 1995 (in US$1m.): Russia, 114·3; Kazakhstan, 112·5; Uzbekistan, 88·9; Turkey, 38·3; Cuba, 22·7. Main export markets: Russia, 104·8; Uzbekistan, 70·0; People's Republic of China, 68·5; Kazakhstan, 66·8; UK, 27·4.

COMMUNICATIONS

Roads. There were 18,560 km of roads (16,890 km paved) in 1997. Passenger cars in use in 1998 numbered 187,734 (40 per 1,000 inhabitants). There were 585 road accident fatalities in 1998.

Rail. In the north a railway runs from Lugovaya through Bishkek to Rybachi on Lake Issyk-Kul. Towns in the southern valleys are linked by short lines with the Ursatyevskaya–Andizhan railway in Uzbekistan. Total length of railway, 1994, 318 km. Passenger-km travelled in 1998 came to 59m. and freight tonne-km to 471m.

Civil Aviation. There is an international airport at Bishkek (Manas). The national carrier is Kyrgyzstan Airlines. In 2000 Bishkek handled 373,163 passengers (199,441 on international flights) and 7,854 tonnes of freight. In 1999 scheduled airline traffic of Kyrgyzstan-based carriers flew 8·6m. km, carrying 312,000 passengers (136,000 on international flights).

Shipping. The total length of inland waterways was 600 km in 1990. In 1993, 0·1m. tonnes of freight were carried.

Telecommunications. There were 376,100 telephone main lines in 2000, equivalent to 77·1 for every 1,000 persons, and 2,600 mobile phone subscribers in 1999. Internet users numbered 51,600 in Dec. 2000

Postal Services. In 1995 there were 918 post offices.

SOCIAL INSTITUTIONS

Justice. In 1994, 41,155 crimes were reported; in 1996 there were 500 murders. The population in penal institutions in May 1997 was 19,857 (440 per 100,000 of national population). The death penalty is in force.

Religion. In 1996, 70% of the population was Sunni Muslim. There were some 1,000 mosques, 30 Russian Orthodox, 17 Evangelical, 9 Seventh Day Adventist and 8 Lutheran churches.

Education. In 1996 there were 453 pre-primary schools with 4,013 teachers for 35,254 pupils; 1,885 primary schools with 24,086 teachers for 473,077 pupils; 42,286 secondary teachers for 530,854 pupils; and 3,691 university level teachers for 49,744 students. There are 21 higher educational institutions and 51 technical and teachers' training colleges, as well as music and art schools. Kyrgyz University had 7,300 students in 1994–95. Adult literacy was 97% in 1998.

In 1996 total expenditure on education came to 5·3% of GNP and represented 23·5% of total government expenditure.

Health. In 1995 there were 15,000 doctors, 42,300 nurses and 1,100 dentists; in 1994 there were 348 hospitals with 48,900 beds.

Welfare. In Jan. 1994 there were 443,000 age and 196,000 other pensioners.

CULTURE

Broadcasting. Kyrgyz Radio and Kyrgyz Television are state-controlled. There are two national radio programmes, with some broadcasting in English and German. There is one commercial radio station. In 1993 there were three hours of TV broadcasting a day (colour by SECAM). In 1997 there were 520,000 radio and 210,000 television receivers.

Cinema. In 1995 there were 385 cinemas with an annual attendance of 0·6m.; gross box office receipts came to 2·0m. som.

Press. There were three daily newspapers in 1996, with a combined circulation of 67,000.

Tourism. In 1998 there were 59,000 foreign tourists, bringing revenue of US$7m.

DIPLOMATIC REPRESENTATIVES
Of Kyrgyzstan in the United Kingdom (Ascot House, 119 Crawford St., London, W1H 1AF)
Ambassador: Vacant.
Chargé d'Affaires a.i.: Kanat Tursunkulov.

Of the United Kingdom in Kyrgyzstan
Ambassador: James Lyall Sharp (resides at Almaty, Kazakhstan).

Of Kyrgyzstan in the USA (1732 Wisconsin Ave., NW, Washington, D.C., 20007)
Ambassador: Baktybek Abdrissaev.

Of the USA in Kyrgyzstan (66 Erkindik Prospekt, Bishkek 720002)
Ambassador: John Martin O'Keefe.

Of Kyrgyzstan to the United Nations
Ambassador: Kamil Baialinov.

Of Kyrgyzstan to the European Union
Ambassador: Tchinguiz Aitmatov.

FURTHER READING
Anderson, J., *Kyrgyzstan: Central Asia's Island of Democracy?* Routledge, London, 1999

LAOS

Sathalanalath Pasathipatai
Pasasonlao
(Lao People's Democratic
Republic)

Capital: Vientiane
Population estimate, 2000: 5·28m.
GDP per capita, 2000: (PPP$) 1,575
HDI/world rank: 0·485/143

KEY HISTORICAL EVENTS

The Kingdom of Laos, once called Lanxang (the Land of a Million Elephants), was founded in the 14th century. In 1893 Laos became a French protectorate and in 1907 acquired its present frontiers. In 1945, after French authority had been suppressed by the Japanese, an independence movement known as Lao Issara (Free Laos) set up a government which collapsed with the return of the French in 1946. Under a new constitution of 1947 Laos became a constitutional monarchy under the Luang Prabang dynasty and in 1949 became an independent sovereign state within the French Union. An almost continuous state of war began in 1953 between the Royal Lao Government, supported by American bombing and Thai mercenaries, and the Patriotic Front Pathet Lao, supported by North Vietnamese troops. Peace talks resulted in an agreement on 21 Feb. 1973 providing for the formation of a provisional government of national union and the withdrawal of foreign troops. A provisional coalition government was duly formed in 1974. However, after the Communist victories in neighbouring Vietnam and Cambodia in April 1975, the Pathet Lao took over the running of the whole country, maintaining only a façade of a coalition. On 29 Nov. 1975 HM King Savang Vatthana abdicated and the People's Congress proclaimed a People's Democratic Republic of Laos on 2 Dec. 1975. Since then the country has been run by a regime with zero tolerance for dissent and a fierce distrust of foreigners.

TERRITORY AND POPULATION

Laos is a landlocked country of about 91,400 sq. miles (236,800 sq. km) bordered on the north by China, the east by Vietnam, the south by Cambodia and the west by Thailand and Myanmar. Apart from the Mekong River plains along the border of Thailand, the country is mountainous, particularly in the north, and in places densely forested.

The population (1995 census) was 4,581,258 (2,315,931 females); density, 19 per sq. km. Population, 1997 estimate; 5,117,000. In 1999, 77·1% of the population lived in rural areas.

The UN gives a projected population for 2010 of 6·61m.

There are 16 provinces and 1 prefecture divided into 133 districts and one special region (*khetphiset*). Area, population and administrative centres in 1996:

Province	Sq. km	Population (in 1,000)	Administrative centre
Attopeu	10,320	87·7	Samakhi Xai
Bokeo	4,970	114·9	Ban Houei Xai
Bolikhamxai	16,470	164·9	Paksan
Champassak	15,415	503·3	Pakse
Houa Phan	16,500	247·3	Xam Neua
Khammouane	16,315	275·4	Thakhek
Luang Namtha	9,325	115·2	Luang Namtha
Luang Prabang	16,875	367·2	Luang Prabang
Oudomxai	21,190	211·3	Muang Xai
Phongsali	16,270	153·4	Phongsali
Salavan	10,385	258·3	Salavan
Savannakhet	22,080	674·9	Shanthabouli
Sayabouri	11,795	293·3	Sayabouri
Sekong	7,665	64·2	Sekong

Province	Sq. km	Population (in 1,000)	Administrative centre
Vientiane	19,990	286·8	Phonghong
Vientiane[1]	3,920	531·8	Vientiane
Xaisomboun[2]	7,105	54·2	Ban Muang Cha
Xieng Khouang	17,315	201·2	Phonsavanh

[1]Prefecture. [2]Special Region (1995 population).

The capital and largest town is Vientiane, with a population of (1999 estimate) 640,000. Other important towns are (census 1985): Savannakhet, 96,652; Luang Prabang, 68,399; Pakse, 47,323.

The population is divided into three groups: about 67% Lao-Lum (Valley-Lao); 17% Lao-Theung (Lao of the mountain sides); and 7·4% Lao-Sung (Lao of the mountain tops), who comprise the Hmong and Yao (or Mien). Lao is the official language. French and English are spoken.

SOCIAL STATISTICS
Estimated 1997 births, 211,000; deaths, 69,000. 1997 rates per 1,000 population, estimate: birth, 41·2 per 1,000 population; death, 13·4; infant mortality, 93 per 1,000 live births (1999). Life expectancy, 1999: 51·9 years for men and 54·4 for women. Annual population growth rate, 2001, 2·4%. Fertility rate, 1999, 5·6 births per woman.

CLIMATE
A tropical monsoon climate, with high temperatures throughout the year and very heavy rains from May to Oct. Vientiane, Jan. 70°F (21·1°C), July 81°F (27·2°C). Annual rainfall 69" (1,715 mm).

CONSTITUTION AND GOVERNMENT
On 15 Aug. 1991 the National Assembly adopted a new constitution. The head of state is the President, elected by the National Assembly, which consists of 109 members (99 prior to the elections of Feb. 2002).

Under the constitution the Lao People's Revolutionary Party (LPRP) remains the 'central nucleus' of the 'people's democracy'; other parties are not permitted. The LPRP's Politburo comprises 11 members, including Khamtay Siphandone (LPRP, *President*).

National Anthem. 'Xatlao tangtae dayma lao thookthuana xeutxoo sootchay' ('For the whole of time the Lao people have glorified their Fatherland'); words by Sisana Sisane, tune by Thongdy Sounthonevichit.

RECENT ELECTIONS
The National Assembly (Fourth Legislature) elected Khamtay Siphandone as President at the first session of the Fourth National Assembly held on 23–26 Feb. 1998.

There were parliamentary elections on 24 Feb. 2002 in which the Revolutionary People's Party of Laos (PPPL) won 108 seats. Only one (approved) non-partisan candidate won a seat.

CURRENT ADMINISTRATION
President: Gen. Khamtay Siphandone; b. 1924 (PPPL; elected 24 Feb. 1998 and re-elected March 2001).

Vice President: Lt. Gen. Choummali Saignason.

In March 2003 the government consisted of:

Prime Minister: Boungnang Volachit (PPPL; in office since 27 March 2001).

Deputy Prime Ministers: Maj. Gen. Asang Laoli; Thongloun Sisoolit (also *Chairman of State Planning Committee*); Somsavat Lengsavad (also *Minister for Foreign Affairs*).

Minister of Agriculture and Forestry: Sian Saphangthong. *Commerce and Tourism:* Soulivong Daravong. *Communications, Transport, Posts and Construction:* Bouathong Vonglokham. *Defence:* Douangchai Phichit. *Education:* Phimmasone Leuangkhamma. *Finance:* Chansy Phosikham. *Industry and Handicrafts:* Onneua Phommachanh. *Information and Culture:* Phandouangchit

Vongsa. *Security:* Maj. Gen. Soutchay Thammasith. *Justice:* Kham Ouane Boupha. *Labour and Social Welfare:* Somphanh Phengkhammi. *Public Health:* Ponemek Daraloy.

DEFENCE
Military service is compulsory for a minimum of 18 months. Defence expenditure in 2000 totalled US$19m. (US$4 per capita), representing 1·1% of GDP.

Army. There are four military regions. Strength (1999) about 25,000. In addition there are local defence forces totalling over 1m.

Navy. There is a riverine force of about 600 personnel (1999).

Air Force. The Air Force has about 26 combat aircraft, including MiG-21 fighters. Personnel strength, about 3,500 in 1999.

INTERNATIONAL RELATIONS
Laos is a member of the UN, Asian Development Bank, Colombo Plan, ASEAN, Mekong Group and the International Organization of the Francophonie.

ECONOMY
In 2002 agriculture accounted for 50·3% of GDP, industry 23·5% and services 26·2%.

Overview. The fifth five-year plan (2001–05) aims at an annual growth of 7–7·5%.

Currency. The unit of currency is the *kip* (LAK). Inflation was 128% in 1999 but fell to 8·0% in 2001. From Oct. 2001 to Aug. 2002 it was 8·4%. Foreign exchange reserves were US$135m. in May 2002 and total money supply 539,490m. kip. Gold reserves were 66,000 troy oz in June 2002.

Budget. Revenues in 2001–02 met 90% of the targeted 2,335·5bn. kip and expenditure was 3,769bn. kip (93·4% of target).

Performance. Real GDP growth was 5·8% in 2000 and 5·2% in 2001. Total GDP in 2001 was US$1·7bn.

Banking and Finance. The central bank and bank of issue is the State Bank (*Governor*, Phoumy Thipphavone). There were 17 commercial banks in 2002 (7 foreign; branches only permitted). Total savings and time deposits in 1991 amounted to 4,075m. kip.

Weights and Measures. The metric system is in force.

ENERGY AND NATURAL RESOURCES

Environment. In 1998 carbon dioxide emissions were the equivalent of 0·1 tonnes per capita according to the *World Bank Atlas*.

Electricity. Total installed capacity in 2001–02 was 644 MW, of which 627 MW was hydro-electric. In 2001 production was 3,590 GWh, almost exclusively hydro-electric. Consumption was 710 GWh; 2,823 GWh were exported and 182 GWh were repurchased. In 1996, 16% of households had electricity, mainly in Vientiane.

Minerals. 2002 output (in tonnes): coal, 355,000 (330,000 in 2001); gypsum, 160,000 (150,000); tin, 510 (600).

Agriculture. There were 746,775 ha of arable land in 2001 and 52,000 ha of permanent crop land in 1998. The chief products (2001 output in tonnes) are: rice, 2,334,500; sugarcane, 320,000; maize, 111,869; cassava, 71,000 (2000); sweet potatoes, 52,000 (2000); tobacco, 36,000; potatoes, 35,000 (2000); pineapples, 34,000 (2000); soybeans, 33,200; melons, 33,000 (2000); coffee, 25,200; cotton, 12,000. Opium is produced but its manufacture is controlled by the state.

Livestock (2001): cattle, 1·21m.; pigs, 1·36m.; buffaloes, 1·05m.; goats, 123,800; poultry, 13·87m.

Forestry. Forests covered 12·44m. ha in 2002, or 47% of the land area, down from 13·18m. ha in 1990. They produce valuable woods such as teak. Timber production, 1999, 4·87m. cu. metres.

Fisheries. The catch in 1999 was 30,041 tonnes, entirely from inland waters.

INDUSTRY

Production in 2002: cement, 201,000 tonnes; salt, 22,100 tonnes; iron bars, 13,000 tonnes; detergent, 650 tonnes; nails, 650 tonnes; corrugated iron, 2·8m. sheets; plywood, 2·1m. sheets; mineral water, 235m. litres; beer, 60·49m. litres; soft drinks, 13·15m. litres; oxygen, 21,500 cylinders; cigarettes, 38·3m. packets; lumber, 155,000 cu. metres.

Labour. The working age is 16–55 for females and 16–60 for males. At the 1995 census there were 1,086,172 females and 1,051,112 males within those age groups. Over 75% of the economically active population in 1995 were engaged in agriculture, fishing and forestry.

INTERNATIONAL TRADE

Since 1988 foreign companies have been permitted to participate in Lao enterprises. From Dec. 1988 to Feb. 2002 total foreign investments (project costs) were US$7,257,081,090. Total foreign debt was US$2,499m. in 2000.

Imports and Exports. Imports were estimated at US$534·60m. in 2002 (US$528·27m. in 2001) and exports at US$319·60m. (US$324·89m. in 2001). The main imports in 1995 were: electricity, 43·1m. kWh; lorries, 105; motor cars, 1,390; motorcycles, 4,288; bicycles, 17,501; (in tonnes) fuel, 43,200; iron, 4,900; cement, 4,400; medicines, 3,621; sugar, 2,433; fabrics, 2,098; rice, 1,172; paper, 617. Main exports: electricity, 705·2m. kWh; timber, 86,100 cu. metres; lumber, 88,200 cu. metres; plywood, 1,512,000 sheets; gypsum, 110,000 tonnes; coffee, 2,830 tonnes; tin, 653 tonnes. Main import suppliers, 1996: Thailand, 45·0%; Japan, 7·6%; Vietnam, 3·7%, China, 3·4%. Main export markets, 1996: Vietnam, 49·1%; Thailand, 30·2%; France, 2·6%; UK, 2·1%.

COMMUNICATIONS

Roads. In 1996 there were 22,231 km of roads. Classified as: national highways, 4,459 km; provincial roads, 7,650 km. 955,000 tonnes of freight were transported by road in 1995. In 1996 there were 16,320 passenger cars (3·4 per 1,000 inhabitants), 4,200 trucks and vans and 231,000 motorcycles. There were 1,820 traffic accidents with 600 fatalities in 1992. A bridge over the River Mekong, providing an important north-south link, was opened in 1994.

Rail. The Thai railway system extends to Nongkhai, on the Thai bank of the Mekong River.

Civil Aviation. There are two international airports at Vientiane (Wattay) and Luang Prabang. The national carrier is Lao Aviation, which in 2002 operated domestic services and international flights to Bangkok, Chiang Mai, Hanoi, Ho Chi Minh City, Kunming, Phnom Penh and Siem Reap (Cambodia). In 1999 scheduled airline traffic of Laos-based carriers flew 2·0m. km, carrying 197,000 passengers (54,000 on international flights).

Shipping. The River Mekong and its tributaries are an important means of transport. 898,000 tonnes of freight were carried on inland waterways in 1995. Merchant shipping totalled 3,000 GRT in 1995.

Telecommunications. In 2000 there were 40,900 main telephone lines (7·5 per 1,000 persons) and 14,000 PCs in use (2·6 for every 1,000 persons). Laos had 6,000 Internet users in Dec. 2000. There were 6,500 mobile phone subscribers in 1998 and 500 fax machines in 1995.

Postal Services. There were 417 post offices in 1995.

SOCIAL INSTITUTIONS

Justice. Criminal legislation of 1990 established a system of courts and a prosecutor's office. Polygamy became an offence.

Religion. In 1999 some 3·13m. were Buddhists (Hinayana), but about a third of the population follow tribal religions.

Education. In 2000 there were 723 kindergartens with 38,000 pupils and 2,000 teachers, 9,737 primary schools with 891,000 pupils and 27,000 teachers, and 248,000 pupils and 11,400 teachers at general secondary level.

There are eight teacher training institutes (four teacher training colleges and four teacher training schools) and one college of Pali. In June 1995 the National University of Laos (NUOL) was established by merging nine existing higher education institutes and a centre of agriculture. NUOL comprises faculties in agriculture, pedagogy, political science, economics and management, forestry, engineering and architecture, medical science, humanities and social science, science, and literature.

Adult literacy in 1999 was 47·3% (male, 63·0%; female, 31·7%). Laos has only a small educated elite.

Health. In 1995 there were 25 hospitals, 131 health centres, 542 dispensaries and 3,100 doctors.

CULTURE

Broadcasting. The government-controlled National Radio of Laos broadcasts a national and six regional programmes and an external service (six languages). Lao National TV transmits for three hours daily. There were 730,000 radio sets and 52,000 television receivers in 1997 (colour by PAL).

Press. In 1996 there were three dailies (one in English).

Tourism. There were 673,823 foreign visitors in 2001 (270,000 in 1999) and revenue from tourism amounted to US$103·8m.

DIPLOMATIC REPRESENTATIVES
Of Laos in the United Kingdom
Ambassador: Vacant (resides at Paris).

Of the United Kingdom in Laos
Ambassador: Lloyd Barnaby Smith, CMG (resides at Bangkok).

Of Laos in the USA (2222 S. St., NW, Washington, D.C., 20008)
Ambassador: Phanethong Phommahaxay.

Of the USA in Laos (Rue Bartholonie, Vientiane)
Ambassador: Douglas Alan Hartwick.

Of Laos to the United Nations
Ambassador: Alounkèo Kittikhoun.

Of Laos to the European Union
Ambassador: Thongphachanh Sonnasinh.

FURTHER READING
National Statistical Centre. *Basic Statistics about the Socio-Economic Development in the Lao P.D.R.* Annual.

Stuart-Fox, M., *Laos: Politics, Economics and Society.* London, 1986—*History of Laos.* Cambridge Univ. Press, 1997

National statistical office: National Statistical Centre, Vientiane.

LATVIA

Latvijas Republika

Capital: Riga
Population estimate, 2000: 2·42m.
GDP per capita, 2000: (PPP$) 7,045
HDI/world rank: 0·800/53

KEY HISTORICAL EVENTS

The territory that is now Latvia was controlled by crusaders, primarily the German Order of Livonian Knights, until 1561 when Latvia fell into Polish and Swedish hands. Between 1721 and 1795 Latvia was absorbed into the Russian empire. Soviet rule was proclaimed in Dec. 1917, but was overthrown when the Germans occupied all Latvia (Feb. 1918). Restored when the Germans withdrew (Dec. 1918), the Soviets were again overthrown, this time by combined British naval and German military forces (May–Dec. 1919), when a democratic government was set up. This regime was in turn replaced by a coup which took place in May 1934. The secret protocol of the Soviet–German agreement of 23 Aug. 1939 assigned Latvia to the Soviet sphere of interest. On 4 May 1990 the Latvian Supreme Soviet declared, by 138 votes to nil with 58 abstentions, that the Soviet occupation of Latvia on 17 June 1940 was illegal, and resolved to re-establish the 1922 Constitution. In a referendum in March 1991 the principle of independence was supported by 73·6%. A fully independent status was conceded by the USSR State Council in Sept. 1991. The large Russian minority was initially disadvantaged by the introduction of citizenship and language laws which have since been repealed. President Vike-Freiberga was elected as the former Communist bloc's first female president in June 1999. In 2002, as part of a proposed EU expansion plan, Latvia was chosen as one of ten countries nominated for membership in 2004, and one of seven invited to join NATO in the same year.

TERRITORY AND POPULATION

Latvia is situated in northeastern Europe. It is bordered by Estonia on the north and by Lithuania on the southwest, while on the east there is a frontier with the Russian Federation and to the southeast with Belarus. Territory, 64,600 sq. km (larger than Denmark, the Netherlands, Belgium and Switzerland). Population (1996), 2,479,870; density, 38 per sq. km.

The UN gives a projected population for 2010 of 2·29m.

In 1999, 69·0% of the population were urban. Nationalities: Latvians 55·3%, Russians 32·5%, Belarussians 4%, Ukrainians 2·9%, Poles 2·2%, Lithuanians 1·3%, Jews 0·4%, Roma 0·3%, Estonians 0·1%, Germans 0·1%.

There was a population of over 700,000 ethnic Russians in 1998.

There are 26 districts, 56 towns and 37 urban settlements. The capital is Riga (805,9977 in Jan. 1998); other principal towns, with Jan. 1998 populations, are Daugavpils (116,530), Liepāja (96,268), Jelgava (71,004), Jurmala (58,975) and Ventspils (46,600).

The official language is Latvian.

SOCIAL STATISTICS

1999: births, 19,530 (rate of 8·0 per 1,000 population); deaths, 32,850 (13·5 per 1,000 population). 1998: marriages, 9,641 (3·9 per 1,000 population); divorce, 6,211 (2·5 per 1,000 population); infant mortality, 11·4 per 1,000 live births (1999). In 1999 life expectancy was 64·3 years for males but 75·6 years for females. In 1998 the most popular age range for marrying was 20–24 for both males and females. Annual population growth rate, 1990–99, –1·3%; fertility rate, 1999, 1·3 births per woman. In 1995 there were 2,799 immigrants and 13,346 emigrants.

CLIMATE

Owing to the influence of maritime factors, the climate is relatively temperate but changeable. Average temperatures in Jan. range from –2·8°C in the western coastal town of Liepāja to –6·6°C in the inland town of Daugavpils. The average summer temperature is 20°C.

CONSTITUTION AND GOVERNMENT

The Declaration of the Renewal of the Independence of the Republic of Latvia dated 4 May 1990, and the 21 Aug. 1991 declaration re-establishing *de facto* independence, proclaimed the authority of the Constitution *(Satversme)*. The Constitution was fully re-instituted as of 6 July 1993, when the 5th Parliament *(Saeima)* was elected.

The head of state in Latvia is the *President*, elected by parliament for a period of four years.

The highest legislative body is the one-chamber parliament comprised of 100 deputies and elected in direct, proportional elections by citizens 18 years of age and over. Deputies serve for four years and parties must receive at least 5% of the national vote to gain seats in parliament.

In a referendum on 3 Oct. 1998, 53% of votes cast were in favour of liberalizing laws on citizenship, which would simplify the naturalization of the Russian-speakers who make up nearly a third of the total population and who were not granted automatic citizenship when Latvia regained its independence from the former Soviet Union in 1991.

Executive power is held by the *Cabinet of Ministers*.

National Anthem. 'Dievs, svēti Latviju' ('God bless Latvia'); words and tune by Kārlis Baumanis.

RECENT ELECTIONS

Vaira Vike-Freiberga, a Canadian professor who had fled Latvia as a seven-year-old, was elected President of the Republic of Latvia on 17 June 1999.

Parliamentary elections were held on 5 Oct. 2002. Former central bank governor Einars Repše's newly-formed liberal 'New Era' (Jaunais laiks; JL) party won 26 seats with 23·9% of votes cast; For Human Rights in a United Latvia (Par cilvēka tiesībām vienotā Latvijā; PCTVL) won 24 with 18·9%; the People's Party (Tautas partija; TP), 21 with 16·7%; Latvia's First Party (Latvijas Pirmā Partija; LPP), 10 with 9·6%; the Green and Farmer's Union (Zaļo un Zemnieku savienība; ZZS), 12 with 9·5%; and Fatherland and Freedom Alliance/LNNK (Apvienība 'Tēvzemei un Brīvībai'; TB/LNNK), 7 with 5·4%. Prime Minister Andris Berzins Latvia's Way party (Savienība 'Latvijas ceļš'; LC) failed to secure a single seat. Turn-out was 55%.

A seven-member *Constitutional Court* was established in 1996 with powers to invalidate legislation not in conformity with the constitution. Its members are appointed by parliament for ten-year terms.

CURRENT ADMINISTRATION

President: Vaira Vike-Freiberga; b. 1937 (sworn in on 8 July 1999).

In March 2003 the government comprised:

Prime Minister: Einars Repše; b. 1961 (JL; sworn in on 7 Nov. 2002).

Deputy Prime Minister: Ainārs Šlesers (LPP).

Minister of Transport: Roberts Zīle (TB/LNNK). *Education and Science:* Kārlis Šadurskis (JL). *Defence:* Ģirts Valdis Kristovskis (TB/LNNK). *Agriculture:* Mārtiņš Roze (ZZS). *Environmental Protection and Regional Development:* Raimonds Vējonis (ZZS). *Interior:* Māris Gulbis (JL). *Foreign Affairs:* Sandra Kalniete (ind.). *Economics:* Juris Lujāns (LPP). *Finance:* Valdis Dombrovskis (JL). *Welfare:* Dagnija Staķe (ZZS). *Justice:* Aivars Aksenoks (JL). *Culture:* Inguna Rībena (JL). *Special Assignments for Children and Family Affairs:* Ainars Baštiks (LPP). *Special Assignments for Health Affairs:* Āris Auders (JL). *Special Assignments for Regional Development and Local Governments:* Ivars Gaters (JL). *Special Assignments for Society Integration Affairs:* Nils Muižnieks (ind.).

Office of the President: http://www.president.lv

DEFENCE

Since Latvia gained its independence in Aug. 1991, a renewal process for Latvia's armed forces, including the National Armed forces, the Home Guard and Border Guard, has been under way. Military service is compulsory for male citizens from the age of 19 (women and men 18 years and older can join the national defence forces voluntarily) and the duration of military service is 18 months. Conscientious objectors have the option of serving in non-military service. Latvia has signed a defence co-operation treaty with Lithuania and Estonia to co-ordinate Baltic States' defence and security activities. A sub-unit of Latvia's National Armed Forces is participating in the NATO led IFOR operations in the former Yugoslavia as a part of a joint Latvian-Danish military battalion.

In 2000 military expenditure totalled US$70m. (US$30 per capita), representing 1·0% of GDP.

Army. The Army was 2,550 strong in 1999. There is a National Guard reserve of five brigades, and a paramilitary Frontier Guard of 3,500.

Navy. A small coastal protection force, based at Riga and Liepāja, numbered 840 in 1999.

Air Force. Personnel numbered 210 in 1999. There are no combat aircraft.

INTERNATIONAL RELATIONS

Latvia is a member of the UN, WTO, BIS, OSCE, Council of Europe, Council of the Baltic Sea States, IOM and the NATO Partnership for Peace (and is seeking full NATO membership), an Associate Partner in WEU, and an Associate Member of the EU. At the European Union's Helsinki Summit in Dec. 1999 Latvia, along with five other countries, was invited to begin full negotiations for membership in Feb. 2000, and is scheduled to become a member on 1 May 2004.

ECONOMY

Services accounted for 70·5% of GDP in 2000, industry 25% and agriculture 4·5%.

The Latvian Privatization Agency, established in 1994 to oversee the privatization process, has adopted a case-by-case approach. 97% of all state enterprises have been assigned for privatization. The private sector constitutes 66% of GDP and 70% of employment.

Overview. By 1994, 70% of industrial capacity was still state-owned, and a Privatization Agency was set up to accelerate the transfer to private hands. By Jan. 1995, 86·9% of residents had taken out privatization vouchers. 230 state enterprises were privatized in 1995, realising 37·3m. lats, of which 21·8m. lats were provided by vouchers. There have been successful privatizations in banking, transport and gas.

Currency. The unit of currency is the *lats* (LVL) of 100 *santims*. The lats has been pegged to the SDR basket. In 2001 inflation was 2·5%, down from 35·8% in 1994. Gold reserves were 249,000 troy oz in June 2002 and foreign exchange reserves US$1,145m. Total money supply in June 2002 was 924m. lats.

Budget. The financial year is the calendar year. The fiscal deficit in 2000, according to the law 'On State Budget', was projected to be 2% of GDP, declining in 2001 to 1·7% of GDP. In 1999 the fiscal deficit was 4·0% of GDP, mostly as a consequence of the Russian financial crisis.

Government revenue and expenditure (in 1m. lats), year ending 31 Dec.:

	1997	1998	1999	2000
Revenue	1,088·5	1,245·6	1,232·8	1,238·9
Expenditure	1,028·4	1,246·5	1,379·9	1,371·1

Performance. GDP growth of 6·6% was recorded in 2000, rising to 7·6% in 2001. Total GDP was US$7·5bn. in 2001.

Banking and Finance. The Bank of Latvia both legally and practically is a completely independent institution. Governor of the Bank and Council members are appointed by Parliament for office for six years (present *Governor*, Ilmars Rimševičs). In 1999 there were 24 banks in Latvia, including the Riga branches of Société Générale and Vereinsbank. 19 banks out of 24 ended 1999 with a profit. In 1999 the transitional period which had been given for banks to ensure they have capital of 5m. euros ended with 14 banks fulfilling the requirement. Latvia's largest bank is Parex Bank, with assets in July 1998 of US$531·5m.

There is a stock exchange in Riga.

ENERGY AND NATURAL RESOURCES

Environment. According to the *World Bank Atlas* Latvia's carbon dioxide emissions in 1998 were the equivalent of 3·2 tonnes per capita. An *Environmental*

Sustainability Index compiled for the World Economic Forum meeting in Feb. 2002 ranked Latvia tenth in the world, with 63·0%. The index measured the ability of countries to maintain favourable environmental conditions and examined various factors including pollution levels and the use or abuse of natural resources.

Electricity. Electricity production in 1998 totalled 4·77bn. kWh, with consumption per capita 1,879 kWh. 75% of electrical power produced in Latvia is generated in hydro-electric power stations. The largest consumers are industry (34%) and private users (23%).

Oil and Gas. Nearly 29% of the Latvian energy resources come from gas. 60% of gas is used for heat generation, 25% in industry and the remaining 15% by other consumers.

The market share of oil products is about 38%, including heavy fuel oil. 70% of oil is used for heat generation, 20% in industry and the remaining 10% in transport.

Minerals. Peat deposits extend over 645,000 ha or about 10% of the total area, and it is estimated that total deposits are 3bn.–4bn. tons. The average annual output of peat at the moment reaches 450,000–550,000 tonnes.

Resources:

	Deposits (in 1m.)	Production (in 1,000) 1995	1996
Dolomite (metres³)	661·3	379·7	429·4
Clay for bricks (metres³)	218·5	70·5	72·9
Clay for cement (tonnes)	416·6	85·8	120·0
Sand and gravel mix (metres³)	413·2	534·5	775·4
Sand (metres³)	72·8	184·3	153·5
Limestone for cement (tonnes)	477·5	324·0	367·0

Agriculture. In 1998 there were 1·8m. ha of arable land and 30,000 ha of permanent crops. Cattle and dairy farming are the chief agricultural occupations. Oats, barley, rye, potatoes and flax are the main crops.

On 1 Jan. 1989 there were 248 state farms and 331 (including 11 fishery) collective farms. There were 47,429 tractors in 1999 and 5,639 harvester-threshers in 1998. Large state and collective farms have been converted into shareholding enterprises; the remainder have been divided into small private holdings for collective farm workers or former owners. In 1999 there were 101,167 peasant farms, 147,366 household plots, 644 specialized state-owned farms and 17,186 allotments for auxiliary farming.

Persons employed in agriculture, 2000, 15·7%.

In 1996 there were 41% household plots and private subsidiary farms, 35% peasant farms and 24% state farms, collective farms and statutory companies.

Output of crops (in 1,000 tonnes) 2000: grain 927 (made up of: wheat, 385; barley, 322; oats, 115; rye, 105); potatoes, 747; sugarbeets, 408; cabbages, 66; apples, 24; carrots, 21.

Livestock, 2000: cattle, 378,000; pigs, 405,000; sheep, 27,000; poultry, 3m. Livestock products (2000, in 1,000 tonnes): meat, 61; milk, 825; eggs, 26.

Forestry. Latvia's total forest area is 2·9m. ha, or 45% of the land area. The overall resources of wood amount to 502m. cu. metres (an increase of 118m. cu. metres since 1984), including 304m. cu. metres of softwood. Private forests account for 44·2% or 1·27m. ha and comprise about 153,000 holdings. Timber production in 1999 was 14·01m. cu. metres.

The share of the forest sector in gross industrial output is between 13 and 15%. Timber and timber products exports account for 37–38% of Latvia's total exports.

To provide the protection of forests there are three forest categories: commercial forests, 70·4%; restricted management forests, 18·6%; protected forests, 11·0%.

Fisheries. There are seven fishing ports in Latvia. In 1999 the total catch (in tonnes) was 125,389, of which marine fish 124,779. Fish catch in 1996 by fishing ground (1,000 tonnes): inland waters, 0·9; northwest Atlantic, 1; northeast Atlantic 71 of which Baltic Sea, 69·7; East central Atlantic, 63·7; southwest Atlantic, 4·1.

INDUSTRY

In 1996 the decline of production in manufacturing was stopped for the first time since the beginning of economic reforms. Structure of sectors of industry by output in 1999: food products, 33·5%; wood and wood articles, 16·6%; light industry, 13·2%; metal and metal products, 10·2%; manufacture of machinery and equipment, 6·7%; chemical industry, 4·9%.

Labour. In May 1999 there were 1,160,800 economically active persons in Latvia, constituting 58·4% of the total population over the age of 15. Of those in employment, 57% worked in services, 26% in industry and construction, and 17% in agriculture, hunting, forestry and fisheries. In 1999 women constituted 50% of the workforce, a higher percentage than in any other European country. In Jan. 1999 there was a monthly minimum wage of 50 lats. Average monthly salary was 139 lats in 1999. The official unemployment rate in June 2002 was 12·7%. The average monthly salary in the public sector in early 2000 was 168·39 lats.

Trade Unions. The Free Trade Union Federation of Latvia, LBAS (*President:* Pēteris Krīgers) was established in 1990. In 2003 there were 28 branch trade unions and professional employee unions representing more than 250,000 members.

INTERNATIONAL TRADE
External debt of Latvia decreased from 9·6% of GDP in 1998 to 9·5% in 1999. Total central government debt at the end of 1999 was US$850m., or 13·3% of GDP. Total external debt was US$3,379m. in 2000. Foreign direct investment inflow in 1999 was 5·9% of GDP (335m. euros). The accumulated FDI in Jan. 2000 reached 1,099m. lats, representing 453 lats per capita.

A liberal foreign trade regime is a very important precondition for a successful restructuring of the economy.

Imports and Exports. Imports (f.o.b.) were valued at US$3,116m. in 2000 (US$2,916m. in 1999) and exports (f.o.b.) at US$2,058m. (US$1,889m. in 1999). The main exports are wood and wood products (38·8%), textiles and textile articles (13·8%), base metals and articles of base metals (13·3%). The leading imports are machinery and mechanical appliances (20·6%), mineral products (12·4%), products of chemical and allied industries (11·1%), metals and products thereof (8·3%). Main export markets (Jan.–Aug. 2000): UK, 17·9%; Germany, 17·2%; Sweden, 11·1%, Lithuania, 7·6%; Denmark, 5·8%. Main import suppliers (Jan.–Aug. 2000): Germany, 16·0%; Russia, 12·0%; Finland, 8·8%; Lithuania, 7·3%; Sweden, 6·8%. In 1997, 48·9% of exports went to the EU and 53·2% of imports were from the EU. Since 1997 trade with the EU has continued to grow and trade with Russia and other former Soviet republics has declined, with trade between Latvia and Russia halving between 1997 and 2001.

COMMUNICATIONS
Roads. In 1998 there were 59,178 km of roads. In the first nine months of 1999 cargo carried by road transport totalled 26·4m. tonnes. In 1998 there were 4,540 traffic accidents with 627 fatalities. With 21·3 deaths per 100,000 population in 1997 Latvia has one of the highest death rates in road accidents of any industrialized country. In 1996, 213·5 km of road was repaired and 13·1 km of new road built. Passenger cars in 1998 numbered 482,670 (198 per 1,000 inhabitants), in addition to which there were 19,400 motorcycles and mopeds and 11,500 buses and coaches.

Rail. In 1996 there were 2,413 km of 1,520 mm gauge route (271 km electrified). In the first nine months of 1999, 24·9m. tonnes of cargo and 19·9m. passengers were carried by rail. The main groups of freight transported are oil and oil products, mineral fertilizers, ferrous metals and ferrous alloys.

Civil Aviation. There is an international airport at Riga. A new national carrier, Air Baltic, assumed control of Latavio and Baltic International Airlines in 1995 and began flying in Oct. 1995. In 1998 it flew 4·7m. km, carrying 175,000 passengers, on scheduled services to Copenhagen, Frankfurt, Hamburg, Helsinki, Kyiv, London, Minsk, Munich, Stockholm, Tallinn, Vilnius, Warsaw and Zürich. It is 51% state-owned, with SAS owning the remainder. In 2000 Riga handled 574,356 passengers and 3,618 tonnes of freight.

Shipping. There are three large ports (with 54m. tonnes of cargo handled, 1998): Ventspils (35m.), Riga (12m.) and Liepāja (7m.). 4,600 ships in all docked at Riga and Ventspils in 1997. In 1996, 10·06m. tonnes of cargo were transported. In 1998 the merchant marine totalled 118,000 GRT, including oil tankers 9,000 GRT (oil tankers 279,000 GRT in 1996 out of a total of 723,000 GRT).

Ventspils can handle up to 100,000 containers a year and it is estimated that it will be able to handle 250,000 a year when the second stage of a US$70m. development project is completed. This project will change Ventspils from a port principally designed for the export of oil and other products from Russia to one which is also a major import centre.

Telecommunications. Telecommunications are conducted by companies in which the government has a 51% stake, under the aegis of the state-controlled Lattelekom. In 2000 main telephone lines numbered 734,700 (303·1 per 1,000 inhabitants) and 340,000 PCs were in use (140·3 per 1,000 persons). There were 274,300 mobile phone subscribers in 1999 and 900 fax machines in 1995. The number of Internet users in Oct. 2001 was 312,000.

Postal Services. In 1997 there were 993 post offices.

SOCIAL INSTITUTIONS

Justice. A new criminal code came into force in 1998. Judges are appointed for life. There are a Supreme Court, regional and district courts and administrative courts. The death penalty is retained but has been subject to a moratorium since Oct. 1996; it was abolished for peacetime offences in 1999. 36,865 crimes were reported in 1997 (38,205 in 1996), 51·4% of which were solved. There were 382 murders in 1996. The murder rate, at 15·3 per 100,000 population in 1996, is one of the highest in Europe. In Dec. 1997 there were 10,070 people in penal institutions, giving a prison population rate of 410 per 100,000 population.

Religion. In order to practise in public, religious organizations must be licensed by the Department of Religious Affairs attached to the Ministry of Justice. New sects are required to demonstrate loyalty to the state and its traditional religions over a three-year period. Traditionally Lutherans constitute the largest church, with 304,000 members in 1997. Congregations in Jan. 1997: Lutherans, 304; Roman Catholics, 231; Russian Orthodox, 112; Baptists, 78; Old Believers, 62; Adventists, 44; Jews, 5; others, 43.

Education. Adult literacy rate in 1998 was over 99%. The Soviet education system has been restructured on the UNESCO model. Education may begin in kindergarten. From the age of six or seven education is compulsory for nine years in comprehensive schools. This may be followed by three years in special secondary school or one to six years in art, technical or vocational schools. In 1995–96 there were 716 comprehensive schools with 0·35m. pupils and 52 special secondary schools with 17,200 pupils, with a combined total of 34,700 teachers. 188,700 pupils were attending Latvian-language schools, 108,000 Russian and 41,300 mixed. 25,000 pupils were attending vocational schools. Schools for ethnic minorities were established in 1990: there were eight in 1994–95.

In 1997 in the whole field of higher education there were 33 institutions with 64,900 students.

Total expenditure on education in 1996 came to 6·3% of GNP and represented 14·1% of total government expenditure.

Health. In 1995 there were 8,400 doctors, 18,300 paramedics and 166 hospitals with 27,800 beds.

The rate of cigarette smoking among males is one of the highest in the world, at 67% in 1993. However, only 12% of women smoked in 1993.

Welfare. Benefits are paid from the State Social Insurance Fund and the government Budget. It is a statutory requirement that the rate of pensions be reviewed twice a year, taking inflation into account. A compulsory contributory health insurance scheme was inaugurated on 1 Jan. 1997. In 1995 there were 666,000 pensioners, including retirement, 497,000; disability, 103,400; survivors, 38,400; social, 19,600. The average monthly pension was 36 lats in 1996. Legislation of 1995 provides for the phasing in of a new retirement pension scheme which links benefits to contributions made during working years and average life expectancy.

CULTURE

Broadcasting. Broadcasting is overseen by the nine-member National Radio and Television Council appointed by parliament for four-year terms. There are 26 TV broadcasting companies and 23 radio broadcasting companies. Latvijas Radio broadcasts three programmes and an external service (English, German, Swedish). Latvijas Televizija transmits on two networks (colour by PAL). There were 1·76m. radio receivers and 1·22m. television receivers in 1997.

Cinema. In 1997 there were 35 cinemas; attendances totalled 1·27m. In 1995 gross box office receipts came to 700,000 lats and two full-length films were made.

Press. Latvia had 229 newspapers and periodicals in 1997, including 22 dailies, 38 published two–four times a week and one English-language weekly. 2,320 book titles were published in 1997.

Tourism. In 1999 there were 489,000 foreign tourists who brought in revenue of US$111m. 98,002 Latvian nationals travelled abroad in 1997. At the end of 1997 there were 220 hotels and other accommodation facilities.

Festivals. There is an annual Riga Opera Festival in June. The National Song Festival (held every five years) will next be held in 2006.

Libraries. In 1997 there were 998 public libraries with 15·1m. volumes and 514,000 members.

Theatre and Opera. There are a National Opera and Ballet and nine professional theatres.

Museums and Galleries. There are 96 museums.

DIPLOMATIC REPRESENTATIVES

Of Latvia in the United Kingdom (45 Nottingham Place, London, W1M 3FE)
Ambassador: Jānis Dripe.

Of the United Kingdom in Latvia (5 Alunana ielā, Riga, LV 1010)
Ambassador: Andrew Tesoriere.

Of Latvia in the USA (4325 17th St., NW, Washington, D.C., 20011)
Ambassador: Aivis Ronis.

Of the USA in Latvia (7 Raina Boulevard, Riga, LV 1510)
Ambassador: Brian E. Carlson.

Of Latvia to the United Nations
Ambassador: Gints Jegermanis.

Of Latvia to the European Union
Ambassador: Andris Piebalgs.

FURTHER READING

Central Statistical Bureau. *Statistical Yearbook of Latvia.—Latvia in Figures.* Annual.
Dreifeld, J., *Latvia in Transition.* Riga, 1997
Lieven, A., *The Baltic Revolution: Estonia, Latvia, Lithuania and the Path to Independence.* 2nd ed. Yale Univ. Press, 1994
Misiunas, R. J. and Taagepera, R., *The Baltic States: the Years of Dependence, 1940–91.* 2nd ed. Farnborough, 1993
Smith, I. A. and Grunts, M. V., *The Baltic States.* [Bibliography] ABC-Clio, Oxford and Santa Barbara (CA), 1993
Who is Who in Latvia. Riga, 1996

National statistical office: Central Statistical Bureau, Lācplēša ielā 1, 1301 Riga.
Website: http://www.csb.lv/

LEBANON

Jumhouriya al-Lubnaniya
(Republic of Lebanon)

Capital: Beirut
Population estimate, 2000: 3·50m.
GDP per capita, 2000: (PPP$) 4,308
HDI/world rank: 0·755/75

KEY HISTORICAL EVENTS

The Ottomans invaded Lebanon, then part of Syria, in 1516–17 and held nominal control until 1918. After 20 years' French mandatory regime, Lebanon was proclaimed independent on 26 Nov. 1941. In early May 1958 the Muslim opposition to President Chamoun rose in insurrection and for five months the Muslim quarters of Beirut, Tripoli, Sidon and the northern Bekaa were in insurgent hands. On 15 July the US Government landed army and marines who re-established Government authority. Internal problems were exacerbated by the Palestinian problem. An attempt to regulate the activities of Palestinian fighters through the secret Cairo agreement of 1969 was frustrated both by the inability of the Government to enforce its provisions and by an influx of battle-hardened fighters expelled from Jordan in Sept. 1970. From March 1975 Lebanon was beset by civil disorder by which the economy was brought to a virtual standstill.

By Nov. 1976 large-scale fighting had been brought to an end by the intervention of the Syrian-dominated Arab Deterrent Force. Large areas of the country, however, remained outside governmental control, including West Beirut, which was the scene of frequent conflict between opposing militia groups. In March 1978 there was an Israeli invasion following a Palestinian attack inside Israel. Israeli troops eventually withdrew in June, but instead of handing over all their positions to UN Peacekeeping Forces, they installed Israeli-controlled Christian Lebanese militia forces in border areas. In June 1982 Israeli forces once again invaded, this time in massive strength, and swept through the country, eventually laying siege to and bombing Beirut. In Sept. Palestinian forces, together with the PLO leadership, evacuated Beirut. Israeli forces started a withdrawal on 16 Feb. 1985 but it was not until the end of 1990 that the various militias which had held sway in Beirut withdrew. A new Government of National Reconciliation was announced on 24 Dec. 1990. The dissolution of all militias was decreed by the National Assembly in April 1991, but the Shia Muslim militia Hizbollah was allowed to remain active. Following a 17-day Israeli bombardment of Hizbollah positions in April 1996, a US-brokered unsigned 'understanding' of 26 April 1996 guaranteed that Hizbollah guerrillas and Palestinian radical groups would cease attacks on civilians in northern Israel and granted Israel the right to self-defence. Hizbollah maintained the right to resist Israel's occupation of Lebanese soil. In May 2000 Israel completed its withdrawal from south Lebanon, 22 years after the first invasion.

TERRITORY AND POPULATION

Lebanon is mountainous, bounded on the north and east by Syria, on the west by the Mediterranean and on the south by Israel. The area is 10,452 sq. km (4,036 sq. miles). Population (1991 estimate), 2·84m.; density, 265 per sq. km. In 1999, 89·3% of the population were urban.

The UN gives a projected population for 2010 of 4·02m.

The principal towns, with estimated population (1998), are: Beirut (the capital), 1·5m.; Tripoli, 160,000; Zahlé, 45,000; Saida (Sidon), 38,000.

The official language is Arabic. French and, increasingly, English are widely spoken in official and commercial circles. Armenian is spoken by a minority group.

SOCIAL STATISTICS

1995 births, 77,000; deaths, 20,000. Birth rate per 1,000 population, 1995, 25·6; death rate, 6·8. Infant mortality was 29 per 1,000 live births in 1999; expectation of life, 71·3 years for males and 74·4 for females. Annual population growth rate, 1990–99, 2·7%; fertility rate, 1999, 2·6 births per woman.

CLIMATE

A Mediterranean climate with short, warm winters and long, hot and rainless summers, with high humidity in coastal areas. Rainfall is largely confined to the winter months and can be torrential, with snow on high ground. Beirut, Jan. 55°F (13°C), July 81°F (27°C). Annual rainfall 35·7" (893 mm).

CONSTITUTION AND GOVERNMENT

The first Constitution was established under the French Mandate on 23 May 1926. It has since been amended in 1927, 1929, 1943 (twice), 1947 and 1990. It is based on a separation of powers, with a President, a single-chamber *National Assembly* elected by universal suffrage at age 21 in 12 electoral constituencies, and an independent judiciary. In Oct. 1995 the National Assembly extended the President's term of office from six to nine years. The executive consists of the President and a Prime Minister and Cabinet appointed after consultation between the President and the National Assembly. The system is adapted to the communal balance on which Lebanese political life depends by an electoral law which allocates deputies according to the religious distribution of the population, and by a series of constitutional conventions whereby, *e.g.,* the President is always a Maronite Christian, the Prime Minister a Sunni Muslim and the Speaker of the Assembly a Shia Muslim. There is no party system. In Aug. 1990, and again in July 1992, the National Assembly voted to increase its membership, and now has 128 deputies with equal numbers of Christians and Muslims.

On 21 Sept. 1990 President Hrawi established the Second Republic by signing constitutional amendments which had been negotiated at Taif (Saudi Arabia) in Oct. 1989. These institute an executive collegium between the President, Prime Minister and Speaker, and remove from the President the right to recall the Prime Minister, dissolve the Assembly and vote in the Council of Ministers.

National Anthem. 'Kulluna lil watan lil 'ula lil 'alam' ('All of us for our country, flag and glory'); words by Rashid Nachleh, tune by W. Sabra.

RECENT ELECTIONS

Elections were held on 27 Aug. and 3 Sept. 2000. Resistance and Development (Amal–Hizbollah alliance) won 23 seats; al-Karamah (Dignity) won 18; Baalbeck–Hermel al Ii'tilafiah (Baalbeck–Hermel Coalition) 9; al-Jabhar al-Nidal al-Watani (National Defence Front) 8; Wahdal al-Jabal (Mountain Union) 7. Non-partisans won 20 seats. A number of smaller parties won 43 seats between them.

CURRENT ADMINISTRATION

President: Emile Lahoud; b. 1936 (sworn in 24 Nov. 1998).

In March 2003 the government comprised:

Prime Minister: Rafiq al-Hariri; b. 1944 (took office for a second time on 23 Oct. 2000, having previously been prime minister from 1992 to 1998).

Deputy Prime Minister: Issam Fares. *Minister of Foreign Affairs:* Mahmoud Hammoud. *Interior and Municipalities:* Elias Murr. *Agriculture:* Ali Abdallah. *Education and Higher Education:* Abed Al-Rahim Murad. *Youth and Sports:* Sebouh Hovnanian. *Culture:* Ghassan Salameh. *Displaced Persons:* Marwan Hamadeh. *Environment:* Michel Moussa. *Tourism:* Karam Karam. *Finance:* Fouad Siniora. *Industry:* George Frem. *Information:* Ghazi Aridi. *Justice:* Samir Al-Jisr. *Social Affairs:* Asad Diab. *Labour:* Ali Qanso. *National Defence:* Khalil Hrawi. *National Economy and Trade:* Basil Flayhan. *Telecommunications:* Jean Louis Cordahi. *Health:* Sulayman Franjiyah. *Energy and Water:* Mohammad Abed Al-Hamid Baydun. *Public Works and Transportation:* Najib Mikati. *Minister of State for Administrative Reform Affairs:* Fuad Saad.

President's Website: http://www.presidency.gov.lb/

DEFENCE

There were 22,000 Syrian troops in the country in 1999. In the Israeli-occupied southern strip the pro-Israeli South Lebanese Army is estimated to number 2,500. Conscription is for 12 months.

Defence expenditure in 2000 totalled US$553m. (US$168 per capita), representing 3·5% of GDP.

Army. The strength of the Army was 65,000 in 1999 and includes a Presidential Guard and three special forces regiments. There is an internal security force, run by the Ministry of the Interior, some 13,000 strong.

Navy. A force of 1,200 personnel (1999) operate a handful of small craft.

Air Force. The Air Force had (1999) about 1,700 personnel. No combat aircraft were operated.

INTERNATIONAL RELATIONS
A Treaty of Brotherhood, Co-operation and Co-ordination with Syria of May 1991 provides for close relations in the fields of foreign policy, the economy, military affairs and security. The treaty stipulates that Lebanese government decisions are subject to review by six joint Syrian-Lebanese bodies.

Lebanon is a member of the UN, the League of Arab States, OIC and the International Organization of the Francophonie.

ECONOMY
Agriculture accounted for 12·4% of GDP in 1998, industry 26·5% and services 61·1%.

Overview. The semi-autonomous Council of Development and Reconstruction, originally set up in 1977, was revived in 1991 to oversee a post-civil war rehabilitation programme 'Horizon 2000'. In 1995 this programme was revised and extended up to 2007.

Currency. The unit of currency is the *Lebanese pound* (LBP) of 100 *piastres.* There was deflation of 0·4% in both 2000 and 2001. In June 2002 foreign exchange reserves totalled US$4,604m., gold reserves were 9·22m. troy oz and total money supply was £Leb.2,231·10bn. There is a fluctuating official rate of exchange, fixed monthly; in practice it is used only for the calculation of *ad-valorem* customs duties on Lebanese imports and for import statistics. For other purposes the free market is used.

Budget. The fiscal year is the calendar year.

Government revenue and expenditure (in £Leb.1m.):

	1995	1996	1997	1998	1999
Revenue	3,003	3,534	3,753	4,449	4,868
Expenditure	6,342	7,732	9,728	8,385	8,910

Performance. Total GDP was US$16·7bn. in 2001. In 2000 the economy contracted by 0·5%, but there was a slight recovery in 2001, with growth of 2·0% recorded.

Banking and Finance. The Bank of Lebanon (*Governor*, Riad Salameh) is the bank of issue. In 1994 there were 52 domestic banks, 14 subsidiaries and 12 foreign banks, with 590 branches in all. Commercial bank deposits in June 1998 totalled £Leb.41,836,800m. There is a stock exchange in Beirut (closed 1983–95).

Lebanon was one of 15 countries and territories named in a report in June 2000 as failing to co-operate in the fight against international money laundering. The Financial Action Task Force on Money Laundering was set up by the G7 group of major industrialized nations.

Weights and Measures. The use of the metric system is legal.

ENERGY AND NATURAL RESOURCES

Environment. According to the *World Bank Atlas* Lebanon's carbon dioxide emissions in 1998 were the equivalent of 3·9 tonnes per capita.

Electricity. Installed capacity in 1997 was 1m. kW. Production in 1998 was 9·7bn. kWh and consumption per capita 1,820 kWh.

Minerals. There are no commercially viable deposits.

Agriculture. In 1998 there were 180,000 ha of arable land and 128,000 ha of permanent crop land. Crop production (in 1,000 tonnes), 2000: tomatoes, 335; sugarbeets, 330; potatoes, 270; grapes, 245; cucumbers and gherkins, 190; oranges,

165; watermelons, 135; apples, 120; lemons and limes, 111; bananas, 110; olives, 105; onions, 85; cabbages, 83.

Livestock (2000): goats, 485,000; sheep, 380,000; cattle, 77,000; pigs, 64,000; chickens, 32m.

Forestry. The forests of the past have been denuded by exploitation and in 1995 covered 52,000 ha (78,000 ha in 1990). The annual deforestation rate during the years from 1990 to 1995, at 7·8%, was the highest anywhere in the world over the same period. Timber production was 412,000 cu. metres in 1999.

Fisheries. The catch in 1999 was 3,560 tonnes, of which 3,540 tonnes were sea fish.

INDUSTRY

According to the Financial Times Survey (FT 500), the largest company by market capitalization in Lebanon on 4 Jan. 2001 was SOLIDERE (US$1,051·9m.), a Beirut development and reconstruction company.

In 1994 there were 23,518 factories operating. Industrial production (in 1,000 tonnes): cement, 2,703 (1997); residual fuel oil, 156 (1992); distillate fuel oil, 85 (1993).

Labour. The workforce was some 650,000 in 1995, of whom 72,000 worked in agriculture. Following considerable labour unrest, an agreement on wage increases and social benefits was concluded between the government and the GCLW in Dec. 1993.

Trade Unions. The main unions are the General Confederation of Lebanese Workers (GCLW) and the General Confederation of Sectoral Unions.

INTERNATIONAL TRADE

Foreign and domestic trade is the principal source of income. Foreign debt was US$10,311m. in 2000.

Imports and Exports. Imports, 1997: US$7,456m.; exports, US$642m. Major imports are machinery and transport equipment, metals and metal products, and mineral products. Major exports are re-exports, paper products, and food and live animals.

In 1997 the main export markets (in % of total trade) were: Saudi Arabia, 15·1; UAE, 9·1; USA, 6·1; France, 5·0. Main import suppliers: Italy, 13·2; France, 9·5; USA, 9·2.

COMMUNICATIONS

Roads. There were 7,370 km of roads in 1997, of which 6,265 km were paved. Passenger cars in 1997 numbered 1,299,400, and there were also 85,240 trucks and vans, 61,470 motorcycles and mopeds and 6,830 buses and coaches.

Rail. Railways are state-owned. There is 222 km of standard gauge track.

Civil Aviation. Beirut International Airport was served in 1998 by nearly 30 airlines. It handled 2,244,788 passengers (all on international flights) in 2000 and 59,243 tonnes of freight. The national airline is the state-owned Middle East Airlines, which in 1999 flew 17·7m. km, carrying 719,400 passengers (all on international flights).

Shipping. Beirut is the largest port, followed by Tripoli, Jounieh and Saida (Sidon). Total GRT in 1998 was 263,000, including oil tankers 1,000 GRT. There are 58 ships in total (1,000 GRT or over).

Telecommunications. In 2000 telephone main lines numbered 681,500, or 194·9 per 1,000 persons. Two companies were operating a mobile phone network with 425,000 subscribers in 1997. There were 175,000 PCs in use (50·1 for every 1,000 persons) in 2000 and 3,000 fax machines in 1995. The number of Internet users in Dec. 2000 was 300,000.

SOCIAL INSTITUTIONS

Justice. The population in penal institutions in 1997 was 5,000 (160 per 100,000 of national population). The death penalty is in force and was last used in 1998.

Religion. In 1994 it was estimated that the population was 55·3% Muslim (34·0% Shia and 21·3% Sunni), 37·6% Christian (mainly Maronite) and 7·1% Druze. In 1996 there were 119 Roman Catholic bishops.

Education. There are state and private primary and secondary schools. In 1996–97 there were 382,309 pupils at primary schools and 292,002 in general secondary education plus 55,848 in vocational education. There are 13 universities, including two American and one French, and ten other institutions of higher education. In 1995–96 there were 81,588 students in higher education and 10,444 academic staff. Adult literacy was 85·6% in 1999 (91·8% among males and 79·8% among females). In 1996 total expenditure on education came to 2·5% of GNP and 8·2% of total government spending.

There is an Academy of Fine Arts.

Health. There were 153 hospitals in 1995 (provision of 22 beds per 10,000 population), and 6,987 doctors, 3,100 dentists, 3,500 nurses and 2,369 pharmacists.

CULTURE

Broadcasting. The government-controlled Radio Lebanon transmits in Arabic, French, English and Armenian. Télé-Liban, which is government-owned, transmits programmes from 13 stations. Colour is by SECAM H. There were 1·18m. TV sets and 2·85m. radio receivers in 1997.

Press. In 1996 there were 15 daily newspapers with a combined circulation of 435,000, at a rate of 141 per 1,000 inhabitants.

Tourism. In 1999 there were 673,000 foreign tourists, spending US$807m. Lebanon has experienced a tourism boom since the attacks on the USA of 11 Sept. 2001, boosted by large numbers of visitors from Arab Gulf countries wary of travelling to Europe and North America.

DIPLOMATIC REPRESENTATIVES
Of Lebanon in the United Kingdom (15–21 Kensington Palace Gdns., London, W8 4QN)
Ambassador: Jihad Mortada.

Of the United Kingdom in Lebanon (8th St., Rabieh, Beirut)
Ambassador: Richard Kinchen.

Of Lebanon in the USA (2560 28th St., NW, Washington, D.C., 20008)
Ambassador: Dr Farid Abboud.

Of the USA in Lebanon (POB 70–840, Antelias, Beirut)
Ambassador: Vincent Martin Battle.

Of Lebanon to the United Nations
Ambassador: Vacant.
Deputy Permanent Representative: Houssam Asaad Diab.

Of Lebanon to the European Union
Ambassador: Fawzi Fawaz.

FURTHER READING
Choueiri, Y. M., *State and Society in Syria and Lebanon.* Exeter Univ. Press, 1994
Fisk, R., *Pity the Nation: Lebanon at War.* 2nd ed. OUP, 1992
Gemayel, A., *Rebuilding Lebanon.* New York, 1992
Hiro, D., *Lebanon Fire and Embers: a History of the Lebanese Civil War.* New York, 1993

National library: Dar el Kutub, Parliament Sq., Beirut.
National statistical office: Service de Statistique Générale, Beirut.
Website: http://www.cas.gov.lb

LESOTHO

Kingdom of Lesotho

Capital: Maseru
Population estimate, 2000: 2·04m.
GDP per capita, 2000: (PPP$) 2,031
HDI/world rank: 0·535/132

KEY HISTORICAL EVENTS

The Basotho nation was constituted in the 19th century under the leadership of Moshoeshoe I, bringing together refugees from disparate tribes scattered by Zulu expansionism in southern Africa. After war with land-hungry Boer settlers in 1856 (and again in 1886), Moshoeshoe appealed for British protection. This was granted in 1868, and in 1871 the territory was annexed to the Cape Colony (now Republic of South Africa), but in 1883 it was restored to the direct control of the British government through the High Commissioner for South Africa. In 1965 full internal self-government was achieved under King Moshoeshoe II. On 4 Oct. 1966 Basutoland became an independent and sovereign member of the British Commonwealth as the Kingdom of Lesotho. Chief Leabua Jonathan, leader of the Basotho National Party and prime minister from 1965, suspended the constitution when the elections of 1970 were declared invalid. On 20 Jan. 1986, after a border blockade by the Republic of South Africa, Chief Jonathan was deposed in a bloodless military coup led by Maj.-Gen. Justin Lekhanya who granted significant powers to the king. King Moeshoeshoe II was deposed in Nov. 1990 and replaced by King Letsie III. Maj.-Gen. Lekhanya was deposed in May 1991. A democratic constitution was promulgated in April 1993. The elections in May 1998 were won by the ruling Lesotho Congress for Democracy. In Sept. 1998 an army mutiny prompted intervention from South Africa to support the government.

TERRITORY AND POPULATION

Lesotho is an enclave within South Africa. The area is 11,720 sq. miles (30,355 sq. km).

The census in 1996 showed a total population of 1,968,000 persons; density, 64·8 per sq. km. In 1999 the population was 72·9% rural.

The UN gives a projected population for 2010 of 2·18m.

There are ten districts, all named after their chief towns, except Berea (chief town, Teyateyaneng). Area and population:

Region	Area (in sq. km.)	Population (1986 census, in 1,000)	Population (1995 estimate, in 1,000)
Berea	2,222	194·6	206·2
Butha-Buthe	1,767	100·6	135·4
Leribe	2,828	258·0	349·5
Mafeteng	2,119	195·6	259·0
Maseru	4,279	311·1	400·2
Mohale's Hoek	3,530	164·4	231·3
Mokhotlong	4,075	74·7	100·3
Qacha's Nek	2,349	64·0	86·8
Quthing	2,916	110·4	151·9
Thaba-Tseka	4,270	104·1	136·2

In 1999 the capital, Maseru, had an estimated population of 373,000. Other major towns (with 1986 census population) are: Teyateyaneng, 14,251; Mafeteng, 12,667; Qacha's Nek, 10,000 (1992 estimate); Hlotse, 9,595.

The official languages are Sesotho and English.

The population is more than 98% Basotho. The rest is made up of Xhosas, approximately 3,000 expatriate Europeans and several hundred Asians.

SOCIAL STATISTICS

1995 births, 76,000; deaths, 21,000. Rates, 1995: birth (per 1,000 population), 37; death, 10. Annual population growth rate, 1990–99, 2·3%. Life expectancy at birth in 1999 was 47·8 years for males and 48·0 years for females. Approximately 24% of all adults are infected with HIV. Infant mortality, 1999, 93 per 1,000 live births; fertility rate, 1999, 4·7 births per woman.

LESOTHO

CLIMATE
A healthy and pleasant climate, with variable rainfall, but averaging 29" (725 mm) a year over most of the country. The rain falls mainly in the summer months of Oct. to April, while the winters are dry and may produce heavy frosts in lowland areas and frequent snow in the highlands. Temperatures in the lowlands range from a maximum of 90°F (32·2°C) in summer to a minimum of 20°F (–6·7°C) in winter.

CONSTITUTION AND GOVERNMENT
Lesotho is a constitutional monarchy with the King as Head of State. Following the death of his father, Moshoeshoe II, **Letsie III** succeeded to the throne in Jan. 1996.

The 1993 constitution provided for a *National Assembly* comprising an elected 80-member lower house and a *Senate* of 22 principal chiefs and 11 members nominated by the King. For the elections of May 2002 a new voting system was introduced, increasing the number of seats in the National Assembly to 120, elected for a five-year term as before, but with 80 members in single-seat constituencies and 40 elected by proportional representation.

National Anthem. 'Lesotho fatsela bontat'a rona' ('Lesotho, land of our fathers'); words by F. Coillard, tune by L. Laur.

RECENT ELECTIONS
Following the elections of May 1998 the King swore allegiance to a new constitution and the Military Council was dissolved.

Parliamentary elections were held on 25 May 2002. The ruling Lesotho Congress for Democracy (LCD) won 77 seats with 54·9% of votes cast, the Basotho National Party (BNP) 21 with 22·4%, the Lesotho People's Congress (LPC) 5 with 5·8% and the National Independent Party (NIP) 5 with 5·5%. The remaining seats went to smaller parties with less than 5% of votes cast. Turn-out was 68·1%.

CURRENT ADMINISTRATION
In March 2003 the Council of Ministers comprised:

Prime Minister, Minister of Defence: Bethuel Pakalitha Mosisili; b. 1945 (LCD; sworn in 29 May 1998).

Deputy Prime Minister and Minister for Education: Archibald Lesao Lehola. *Minister for Justice, Human Rights and Rehabilitation, and for Law and Constitutional Affairs:* Refiloe Masemene. *Foreign Affairs:* Mohlabi Tsekoa. *Finance and Development Planning:* Timothy Thahane. *Employment and Labour:* Clement Machakela. *Local Government:* Dr Ponts'o Suzan 'Matumelo Sekatle. *Home Affairs:* Motsoahae Thomas Thabane. *Gender, Youth and Sports:* Mathabiso Lepono. *Industry, Trade and Marketing:* Mpho Meli Malie. *Health and Social Welfare:* Dr Motloheloa Phooko. *Tourism and Culture:* Lebohang Ntsinyi. *Communication Information, Broadcasting, Posts and Telecommunications:* Mamphono Khaketla. *Natural Resources:* Monyane Moleleki. *Public Works and Transport:* Mofelehetsi Moerane. *Agriculture, Co-operatives and Land Reclamation:* Vova Bulane. *To the Prime Minister:* Sephiri Enoch Motanyane.

The *College of Chiefs* settles the recognition and succession of Chiefs and adjudicates cases of inefficiency, criminality and absenteeism among them.

Government Website: http://www.lesotho.gov.ls/

DEFENCE
The Royal Lesotho Defence Force has 2,000 personnel. Defence expenditure totalled US$29m. in 2000 (US$13 per capita), representing 4·0% of GDP.

INTERNATIONAL RELATIONS
Lesotho is a member of the UN, WTO, the Commonwealth, the African Union, African Development Bank, SADC and is an ACP member state of the ACP-EU relationship.

ECONOMY
In 1998 agriculture accounted for 11·5% of GDP, industry 42·0% and services 46·5%.

Overview. The Lesotho National Development Corporation promotes industrial and tourist trade development.

Currency. The unit of currency is the *loti* (plural *maloti*) (LSL) of 100 *lisente*, at par with the South African rand, which is legal tender. Total money supply in June 2002 was 1,471m. maloti. Inflation was 6·9% in 2001. Foreign exchange reserves were US$388m. in June 2002.

Budget. Revenue and expenditure (in 1m. maloti):

	1993–94	1994–95	1995–96	1996–97	1997–98[1]
Revenue	1,438·5	1,685·3	2,034·6	2,247·7	2,168·0
Expenditure	1,356·0	1,675·9	2,041·7	2,333·0	2,443·3

[1]Estimate.

Performance. Real GDP growth was 3·5% in 2000 and 4·0% in 2001. Total GDP in 2001 was US$0·8bn.

Banking and Finance. The Central Bank of Lesotho (*Governor,* E. M. Matekane) is the bank of issue, founded in 1982 to succeed the Lesotho Monetary Authority. There are three commercial banks. Savings deposits totalled 342·8m. maloti in 1993.

Weights and Measures. The metric system is in use.

ENERGY AND NATURAL RESOURCES

Electricity. Capacity (1993) 13,400 kW (98% supplied by South Africa). Consumption in 1996 was 335m. kWh.

Minerals. Diamonds are the main product; 1998 output was 2,398 carats. Sandstone production, 16,000 sq. metres (1996).

Agriculture. Agriculture employs two-thirds of the workforce. The chief crops were (2000 production in 1,000 tonnes): maize, 102; sorghum, 25; wheat, 21; dry beans, 9. Peas and other vegetables are also grown. Soil conservation and the improvement of crops and pasture are matters of vital importance. There were 325,000 ha of arable land and permanent crops in 1998.

Livestock (2000): cattle, 520,000; sheep, 750,000; goats, 580,000; asses, 154,000; horses, 100,000; chickens, 2m.

Forestry. Timber production was 1·59m. cu. metres in 1999.

Fisheries. The catch in 1999 was approximately 30 tonnes, exclusively from inland waters.

INDUSTRY

Important industries are food products, beverages, textiles and chemical products.

Labour. The labour force in 1996 was 847,000 (63% males). In 1998, 76,100 were working in mines in South Africa.

INTERNATIONAL TRADE

Lesotho is a member of the Southern African Customs Union (SACU) with Botswana, Namibia, South Africa and Swaziland. Foreign debt was US$716m. in 2000.

Imports and Exports. In 2000 imports (f.o.b.) were valued at US$727·6m. (US$779·2m. in 1999) and exports (f.o.b.) at US$211·1m. (US$172·5m. in 1999).

Principal exports in 1993 (in 1,000 maloti): machinery and transport equipment, 25,540; wool, 16,853; manufactures, 13,426; cattle, 8,409; mohair, 5,131; canned vegetables, 2,275; wheat flour, 1,717.

The bulk of international trade is with South Africa.

COMMUNICATIONS

Roads. The road network in 1996 totalled 4,955 km, of which 887 km were paved. In 1996 there were 12,610 passenger cars (5·7 per 1,000 inhabitants) plus 25,000 trucks and vans. In 1993 there were 1,650 traffic accidents with 286 fatalities.

Rail. A branch line built by the South African Railways, 1 mile long, connects Maseru with the Bloemfontein–Natal line at Marseilles for transport of cargo.

Civil Aviation. There are direct flights from Maseru to Johannesburg. In 2000 Maseru handled 28,613 passengers (28,503 on international flights).

Telecommunications. Lesotho had 22,100 main telephone lines in 2000, or 10·3 for every 1,000 persons. There were 600 fax machines in 1995. In Dec. 2000 there were 1,000 Internet users. Mobile phones have been available since 1996, and in 1998 there were 9,800 subscribers.

Postal Services. In 1995 there were 155 post offices.

SOCIAL INSTITUTIONS

Justice. The legal system is based on Roman-Dutch law. The Lesotho High Court and the Court of Appeal are situated in Maseru, and there are Magistrates' Courts in the districts. 5,888 criminal offences were reported in 1993.

Religion. In 1995 there were 0·88m. Roman Catholics, 0·6m. Evangelical Protestants, 0·44m. other Christians and 0·14m. of other faiths.

Education. Education levels: pre-school, 3 to 5 years; first level (elementary), 6 to 12; second level (secondary or teacher training or technical training), 7 to 13; third level (university or teacher training college). Lesotho has the highest proportion of female pupils at primary schools in Africa, with 53% in 1994, and the highest proportion of female teachers at primary schools in mainland Africa, with 79% in 1994. It also has the highest proportion of female pupils in Africa at secondary level education, with 60% in 1994. In 1996 there were 374,628 pupils in 1,249 primary schools with 7,898 teachers and 68,132 pupils in secondary schools with 2,878 teachers; in 1993–94 there were 751 students in the National Teacher-Training College with 117 teachers and 1,575 students in 8 technical schools with 108 teachers. The National University of Lesotho was established in 1975 at Roma; enrolment in 1992–93, 1,612 students and 190 teaching staff. The adult literacy rate in 1999 was 82·9% (71·7% among males but 93·3% among females). Lesotho has the biggest difference in literacy rates between the sexes in favour of females of any country in the world.

Health. There were 136 doctors in 1993, equivalent to one for every 14,306 persons. In 1990 there were 874 nurses and 60 pharmacists.

CULTURE

Broadcasting. Radio Lesotho transmits daily in English and Sesotho. The broadcasting authority is the Lesotho National Broadcasting Service. In 1997 there were 104,000 radio and 54,000 TV sets (colour by PAL).

Press. There were seven non-daily newspapers and periodicals in 1996. Combined circulation of the two daily papers was 15,000, at a rate of 7·6 per 1,000 inhabitants.

Tourism. In 1999 there were 186,000 foreign tourists, spending US$19m.

DIPLOMATIC REPRESENTATIVES

Of Lesotho in the United Kingdom (7 Chesham Pl., Belgravia, London, SW1 8HN)
High Commissioner: Lebohang Ramohlanka.

Of the United Kingdom in Lesotho (PO Box Ms 521, Maseru 100)
High Commissioner: Frank Martin.

Of Lesotho in the USA (2511 Massachusetts Ave., NW, Washington, D.C., 20008)
Ambassador: Molelekeng Ernestina Rapolaki.

Of the USA in Lesotho (PO Box 333, Maseru 100)
Ambassador: Robert Geers Loftis.

Of Lesotho to the United Nations
Ambassador: Percy M. Mangoaela.

Of Lesotho to the European Union
Ambassador: Retselisitsoe Victor Lechesa.

FURTHER READING
Bureau of Statistics. *Statistical Reports.* [Various years]

Haliburton, G. M., *A Historical Dictionary of Lesotho.* Scarecrow Press, Metuchen (NJ), 1977
Johnston, D., *Lesotho.* [Bibliography] 2nd ed. ABC-Clio, Oxford and Santa Barbara (CA), 1996
Machobane, L. B. B. J., *Government and Change in Lesotho, 1880–1966: A Study of Political Institutions.* Macmillan, Basingstoke, 1990

National statistical office: Bureau of Statistics, PO Box 455, Maseru.

LIBERIA

Republic of Liberia

Capital: Monrovia
Population estimate, 2000: 2·91m.
GDP per capita: not available

KEY HISTORICAL EVENTS

The Republic of Liberia had its origin in efforts to establish freed American slaves in a colony on the West African coast. In 1822 a settlement was formed near the spot where Monrovia now stands. On 26 July 1847 the State was constituted as the Free and Independent Republic of Liberia.

On 12 April 1980 President Tolbert was assassinated and his government overthrown in a coup led by Master-Sergeant Samuel Doe, who was later installed as Head of State. At the beginning of 1990 rebel forces entered Liberia from the north and fought their way successfully southwards to confront President Doe's forces in Monrovia. The rebels comprised the National Patriotic Front of Liberia (NPFL) led by Charles Taylor, and the hostile breakaway Independent National Patriotic Front led by Prince Johnson. A peacekeeping force dispatched by the Economic Community of West African States (ECOWAS) disembarked at Monrovia on 25 Aug. 1990, and attempts to form a new provisional government were made. On 9 Sept. 1990 President Doe was assassinated by Prince Johnson's rebels. ECOWAS installed a provisional government led by Amos Sawyer. Charles Taylor also declared himself president, as did the former vice-president, Harry Moniba. A succession of ceasefires was negotiated and broken. A peace agreement was signed on 17 Aug. 1996 under the auspices of ECOWAS in Abuja which provided for the disarmament of all factions by the end of Jan. 1997 and the election of a president on 31 May 1997. By the end of Jan. 1997 some 20,000 out of perhaps 60,000 insurgents had surrendered their arms. Possession of arms after that date became a criminal offence. The civil war is reckoned to have killed up to 200,000 people and made 1m. homeless. A presidential election was held in July 1997. Charles Taylor was elected by an overwhelming majority. In Feb. 2002 President Taylor declared a state of emergency after an attack by a group of rebels on the town of Kley, the site of refugee camps for thousands of refugees from Sierra Leone.

TERRITORY AND POPULATION

Liberia is bounded in the northwest by Sierra Leone, north by Guinea, east by Côte d'Ivoire and southwest by the Atlantic ocean. The total area is 99,067 sq. km. At the census (1984) the population was 2,101,628. Estimate (1997) 2,602,100, of whom some 25% were refugees abroad. Density, 26 per sq. km.

The UN gives a projected population for 2010 of 4·68m.

In 1995 an estimated 55% of the population were rural. English is the official language spoken by 15% of the population. The rest belong in the main to three linguistic groups: Mande, West Atlantic, and the Kwa. These are in turn subdivided into 16 ethnic groups: Bassa, Bella, Gbandi, Mende, Gio, Dey, Mano, Gola, Kpelle, Kissi, Krahn, Kru, Lorma, Mandingo, Vai and Grebo.

Monrovia, the capital, had (1999) a population of 479,000.

There are 13 counties, whose areas, populations (1986 estimate) and capitals were as follows:

County	Sq. km	1986 population	Chief town
Bomi	1,955	67,300	Tubmanburg
Bong	8,099	268,100	Gbarnga
Grand Bassa	8,759	166,900	Buchanan
Grand Cape Mount	5,827	83,900	Robertsport
Grand Gedeh	17,029	109,000	Zwedru
Lofa	19,360	261,000	Voinjama
Margibi	3,263	104,000	Kakata
Maryland	5,351	137,700	Harper
Montserrado	2,740	582,400	Bensonville

County	Sq. km	1986 population	Chief town
Nimba	12,043	325,700	Saniquillie
Rivercess	4,385	39,900	Rivercess
Sinoe	10,254	65,400	Greenville

The county of Grand Kru (chief town, Barclayville) was created in 1985 from the former territories of Kru Coast and Sasstown.

SOCIAL STATISTICS

1997 births, estimate, 110,000; deaths, 30,000. 1997 rates (per 1,000 population), estimate: birth, 42·3; death, 11·5. Annual population growth rate, 1990–99, 1·4%. Life expectancy at birth (1997 estimate): male, 56·4 years; female, 61·7 years. Infant mortality in the period 1990–95 was the highest in the world, at 200 per 1,000 live births, up from 153 per 1,000 live births over the period 1980–85. Fertility rate, 1999, 6·2 births per woman.

CLIMATE

An equatorial climate, with constant high temperatures and plentiful rainfall, although Jan. to May is drier than the rest of the year. Monrovia, Jan. 79°F (26·1°C), July 76°F (24·4°C). Annual rainfall 206" (5,138 mm).

CONSTITUTION AND GOVERNMENT

A Constitution was approved by referendum in July 1984 and came into force on 6 Jan. 1986. Under it the National Assembly consisted of a 26-member Senate and a 64-member House of Representatives.

National Anthem. 'All hail, Liberia, hail!'; words by President Daniel Warner, tune by O. Lucas.

RECENT ELECTIONS

Presidential and parliamentary elections were held on 20 July 1997. The electorate was 700,000; turn-out was 85%. Charles Taylor (National Patriotic Party) was elected President with 75·3% of the vote. His closest rival, Ellen Johnson-Sirleaf (Unity Party), won 9·6% of the vote. There were two other candidates.

In the elections to the House of Representatives on the same day the National Patriotic Party (NPP) won 49 of the 64 seats, and 21 of the 26 Senate seats. The Unity Party (UP) won 7 seats (and 3 in the Senate) and the All Liberia Coalition Party (ALCOP) won 3 seats (and 2 in the Senate).

CURRENT ADMINISTRATION

President: Charles Taylor; b. 1948 (NPP; sworn in 2 Aug. 1997).

Vice President: Moses Zeh Blah.

In March 2003 the Liberian government comprised:

Minister of Agriculture: Othello Brandy. *Commerce and Industry:* Cora Peabody. *Defence:* Daniel Chea. *Education:* Evelyne Kandakai. *Finance:* Charles Bright. *Foreign Affairs:* Monie Captan. *Health and Social Welfare:* Peter Coleman. *Information, Culture and Tourism:* Reginald Goodridge. *Internal Affairs:* Richard Flomo. *Justice:* Laveli Korboi Johnson. *Labour:* Christian Herbert. *Land, Mines and Energy:* Jenkins Dunbar. *National Security:* Philip Kammah. *Planning and Economic Affairs:* Roland Massaquoi. *Posts and Telecommunications:* Melvin Sogbandi. *Public Works:* Emmett Taylor. *Rural Development:* Hezekiah Bowen. *Transport:* Joe Mulbah. *Gender Development:* Dorothy Musuleng Cooper. *Youth and Sports:* Max Dennis. *Minister of State for Presidential Affairs and Chief of Office Staff:* Jonathan Taylor. *Minister of State for Planning and Economic Affairs:* Wisseh McClain. *Minister of State without Portfolio:* Augustine Zayzay.

DEFENCE

The Armed Forces of Liberia are confined to the capital, Monrovia, and number about 2,000. ULIMO, NPFL and CPL forces control most of the country with combat strengths of 7,000, 12,000 and 2,000 respectively.

An ECOWAS peacekeeping force (ECOMOG, with forces from Ghana, Guinea, Nigeria and Sierra Leone) of some 8,600 is deployed. There is also a 70-strong UN Observer Mission (UNOMIL).

Defence expenditure totalled US$25m. in 2000 (US$8 per capita), representing 5·6% of GDP.

Army. Plans for the new unified armed forces provide for an army of 4,000.

Navy. A new 1,000 strong navy is planned.

Air Force. An Air Force of 300 personnel is planned.

INTERNATIONAL RELATIONS
Liberia is a member of the UN, the African Union, African Development Bank, ECOWAS, IOM and is an ACP member state of the ACP-EU relationship.

ECONOMY
Agriculture accounts for approximately 30% of GDP, industry 36% and services 34%.

Currency. US currency is legal tender. There is a *Liberian dollar* (LRD), in theory at parity with the US dollar. Between 1993 and March 2000 different notes were in use in government-held Monrovia and the rebel-held country areas, but on 27 March 2000 a set of new notes went into circulation to end the years of trading in dual banknotes. Inflation was an estimated 11% in 1998. Total money supply was L$1,859m. in May 2002.

Budget. Revenue in 1993 was L$249·8m.; expenditure was L$273·9m.

Performance. The economy is estimated to have contracted by 4% in 1998, but there followed a recovery, with growth in 1999 estimated at 15%.

Banking and Finance. The National Bank of Liberia opened on 22 July 1974 to act as a central bank. The *Governor* of the bank is Elias Saleeby.

Weights and Measures. Weights and measures are the same as in UK and the USA.

ENERGY AND NATURAL RESOURCES
Environment. According to the *World Bank Atlas* Liberia's carbon dioxide emissions were the equivalent of 0·1 tonnes per capita in 1998.

Electricity. Installed capacity in 1991 was 430,000 kW. Production, 1998, 490m. kWh. Consumption per capita in 1994 was 179 kWh.

Minerals. Iron ore production was 1·1m. tonnes in 1992. Gold production (1997) 500 kg and diamond production (1998) 150,000 carats.

Agriculture. In 1995 more than 70% of the labour force were engaged in agriculture. There were 190,000 ha of arable land in 1998 and 200,000 ha of permanent crops. The soil is productive, but owing to excessive rainfall there are large swamp areas. Principal crops (2000) in 1,000 tonnes: cassava, 380; sugarcane, 250; rice, 200; bananas, 95; palm oil, 42. Coffee, cocoa and palm kernels are produced mainly by the traditional agricultural sector. Livestock (2000): cattle, 36,000; pigs, 120,000; sheep, 210,000; goats, 220,000; chickens, 4m.

Forestry. Forest area was 4·51m. ha (46·8% of the land area) in 1995, down from 4·64m. ha and 48·2% in 1990. In 1999, 3·04m. cu. metres of roundwood were cut. There are rubber plantations.

Fisheries. Fish landings in 1999 were 15,472 tonnes, of which approximately 74% from sea fishing.

INDUSTRY
There are a number of small factories. Production of cement, cigarettes, soft drinks, palm oil and beer are the main industries.

Labour. In 1996 the labour force was 977,000 (61% males). In 1995 around 70% of the population were engaged in agriculture, fisheries and forestry.

INTERNATIONAL TRADE
Foreign debt was US$2,032m. in 2000.

Imports and Exports. Imports in 1996 were US$3·85bn. and exports US$1·14bn. Main import sources in 1996 were South Korea, 25%; Japan, 24%; France, 9%; Singapore, 9%. Major export destinations in 1996 were Belgium-Luxembourg, 48%; Singapore, 12%; Ukraine, 11%; Norway, 6%.

In 1989 iron ore accounted for about 51% of total export earnings, rubber 26% and logs and timber 20%.

COMMUNICATIONS

Roads. There were around 10,600 km of roads in 1996 (660 km paved). In 1996 there were 9,400 cars and 32,000 goods vehicles.

Rail. There is a total of 490 km single track. A 148-km freight line connects iron mines to Monrovia. There is a line from Bong to Monrovia (78 km). All railways have been out of use since 1997 because of the civil war.

Civil Aviation. There are two international airports (Roberts International and Sprigg Payne), both near Monrovia. In 1998 there were services to Abidjan, Accra, Banjul, Conakry, Dakar and Freetown.

Shipping. There are ports at Buchanan, Greenville, Harper and Monrovia. Over 2,000 vessels enter Monrovia each year. The Liberian government requires only a modest registration fee and an almost nominal annual charge and maintains no control over the operation of ships flying the Liberian flag. In 1998 shipping registered totalled 60·49m. GRT, including oil tankers 26·36m. GRT. In 1996 the fleet consisted of 60,492 vessels of 100 GRT or over, including 31,761 tankers. Only Panama has a larger fleet.

Telecommunications. Telephone main lines numbered 6,700 in 2000, or 2·1 per 1,000 persons. In July 2000 there were 300 Internet users.

SOCIAL INSTITUTIONS

Religion. There were (1999) about 1·98m. Christians and 400,000 Sunni Muslims, plus 540,000 followers of traditional beliefs.

Education. Schools are classified as: (1) Public schools, maintained and run by the government; (2) Mission schools, supported by foreign Missions and subsidized by the government, and operated by qualified Missionaries and Liberian teachers; (3) Private schools, maintained by endowments and sometimes subsidized by the government. Adult literacy in 1995 was 38·3%; 53·9% among males, 22·4% among females.

Health. There were 257 physicians in 1992 and 82 hospitals in 1988.

CULTURE

Broadcasting. In 1996 there were 715,000 radio and 60,000 television receivers (colour by PAL).

Press. There were six daily newspapers in 1996 with a combined circulation of 35,000.

DIPLOMATIC REPRESENTATIVES

Of Liberia in the United Kingdom (2 Pembridge Pl., London, W2 4XB)
Ambassador: Vacant.
Chargé d'Affaires a.i.: Jeff Gongoer Dowana, Sr.

Of the United Kingdom in Liberia
Ambassador: Jean François Gordon, CMG (resides at Abidjan, Côte d'Ivoire).

Of Liberia in the USA (5201 16th St., NW, Washington, D.C., 20011)
Ambassador: Vacant.
Chargé d'Affaires a.i.: Aaron B. Kollie.

Of the USA in Liberia (111 United Nations Drive, Mamba Point, Monrovia)
Ambassador: John W. Blaney.

Of Liberia to the United Nations
Ambassador: Lami Kawah.

Of Liberia to the European Union
Ambassador: Dr Othello C. Brandy.

FURTHER READING

Daniels, A., *Monrovia Mon Amour: a Visit to Liberia.* London, 1992
Elwood Dunn, D., *Liberia.* [Bibliography] ABC-Clio, Oxford and Santa Barbara (CA), 1995
Sawyer, A., *The Emergence of Autocracy in Liberia: Tragedy and Challenge.* San Francisco, 1992

LIBYA

Jamahiriya Al-Arabiya
Al-Libiya Al-Shabiya
Al-Ishtirakiya Al-Uzma
(Great Socialist People's
Libyan Arab Republic)

Capital: Tripoli
Population estimate, 2000: 5·29m.
GDP per capita, 2000: (PPP$) 7,570
HDI/world rank: 0·773/64

KEY HISTORICAL EVENTS

Tripoli fell under Ottoman domination in the 16th century and although in 1711 the Arab population secured some measure of independence, the country came under the direct rule of Turkey in 1835. In 1911 Italy occupied Tripoli and in 1912, by the Treaty of Ouchy, Turkey recognized the sovereignty of Italy in Tripoli. During the Second World War, the British army expelled the Italians and their German allies, and Tripolitania and Cyrenaica were placed under British, and Fezzan under French, military administration. This continued until 1950 under a UN directive. Libya became an independent, sovereign kingdom with the former Amir of Cyrenaica, Muhammad Idris al Senussi, as king on 24 Dec. 1951. King Idris was deposed in Sept. 1969 by a group of army officers, 12 of whom formed the Revolutionary Command Council which, chaired by Col. Muammar Qadhafi, proclaimed the Libyan Arab Republic. In 1977 the Revolutionary Command Council was superseded by a more democratic People's Congress. Qadhafi remained head of state. Throughout the 1980s Libya had constant disagreements with its neighbours and its relations with the USA and other Western countries deteriorated, culminating in the US bombing of the capital in April 1987 to punish Qadhafi for his alleged support of international terrorism. A US trade embargo was enforced in 1986. In 1992 the UN imposed sanctions after Libya refused to surrender suspects in the 1988 bombing of a Pan Am flight over Lockerbie in Scotland. In April 1999 Libya handed over the two suspects to be tried in the Netherlands but under Scottish law. In Jan. 2001 Abdelbaset Ali Mohmed al Megrahi was sentenced to life imprisonment after being found guilty of murder. The UN has responded to Libya's disavowal of terrorism with a promise to lift sanctions but a US trade embargo remains in place.

TERRITORY AND POPULATION

Libya is bounded in the north by the Mediterranean Sea, east by Egypt and Sudan, south by Chad and Niger and west by Algeria and Tunisia. The area is estimated at 1,775,500 sq. km. The population at the census on 31 July 1984 was 3,637,488. Estimate (2000), 5·29m. (47·9% female); density, 3·0 per sq. km. In 1999, 87·2% of the population lived in urban areas. Ethnic composition, 1995: Libyan Arab and Berber, 79%; other (mainly Egyptians, Sudanese and Chadians), 21%.

The UN gives a projected population for 2010 of 6·53m.

The country was formerly divided into 13 administrative regions, but following reforms in 1998 there are now 26 administrative regions (*Shabiyat*). They are Shabiya Al-Batan, Shabiya Jabal Al-Akhdar, Shabiya Al-Wahad, Shabiya Al-Jofra, Shabiya Wadi Al-Hait, Shabiya Al-Morqib, Shabiya Tripoli, Shabiya Sabrata/Sorman, Shabiya Yefrin, Shabiya Derna, Shabiya Al-Marj, Shabiya Al-Kofra, Shabiya Murzaq, Shabiya Wadi Al-Shaati, Shabiya Ben Walid, Shabiya Al-Jafarah, Shabiya Nikat Al-Khams, Shabiya Nalout, Shabiya Al-Qoba, Shabiya Benghazi, Shabiya Sirte, Shabiya Sabah, Shabiya Musrata, Shabiya Tarhouna/Msallata, Shabiya Zawiyah and Shabiya Gharyan.

The two largest cities are Tripoli, the capital (population of 1,773,000 in 1999); Benghazi (804,000 in 1995).

The official language is Arabic.

SOCIAL STATISTICS
1997 births, 255,000; deaths, 43,000. Birth rate, 1997 (per 1,000 population), 43·9; death rate, 7·5. Life expectancy (1999), 68·6 years for men and 66·9 for women. Annual population growth rate, 1990–99, 2·64%; infant mortality, 1999, 19 per 1,000 live births; fertility rate, 1999, 3·7 births per woman.

CLIMATE
The coastal region has a warm temperate climate, with mild wet winters and hot dry summers, although most of the country suffers from aridity. Tripoli, Jan. 52°F (11·1°C), July 81°F (27·2°C). Annual rainfall 16" (400 mm). Benghazi, Jan. 56°F (13·3°C), July 77°F (25°C). Annual rainfall 11" (267 mm).

CONSTITUTION AND GOVERNMENT
In 1977 a new form of direct democracy, the state of the masses, was promulgated and the name of the country was changed to Great Socialist People's Libyan Arab Jamahiriya. Under this system, every adult is supposed to be able to share in policy making through the Basic People's Congresses of which there are some 2,000. These Congresses appoint People's Committees to execute policy. Provincial and urban affairs are handled by People's Committees responsible to Municipality People's Congresses, of which there are 26, now called *Shabiyat*. Officials of these Congresses and Committees form at national level the 3,000-member General People's Congress which normally meets for about a week early each year (usually in March). This is the highest policy-making body in the country. The General People's Congress appoints its own General Secretariat and the General People's Committee, whose members (the equivalents of ministers elsewhere) head the government departments which execute policy at national level.

Until 1977 Libya was ruled by a Revolutionary Command Council (RCC) headed by Col. Muammar Qadhafi. Upon its abolition in that year the five surviving members of the RCC became the General Secretariat of the General People's Congress, still under Qadhafi's direction. In 1979 they stood down to be replaced by officials elected by the Congress. Since then, Col. Qadhafi has retained his position as Leader of the Revolution. Neither he nor his former RCC colleagues have any formal posts in the present administration, although they continue to wield considerable authority.

National Anthem. 'Allah Akbar' ('God is Great'); words by Abdullah Al-Din, tune by Mahmoud Al-Sharif.

CURRENT ADMINISTRATION
Leader: Col. Muammar Abu Minyar al-Qadhafi; b. 1942 (came to power 1 Sept. 1969).

In March 2003 the General People's Congress comprised:
Secretary: Muhammad al-Zanati. *Assistant:* Ahmad Mohamed Ibrahim.
In March 2003 the General People's Committee comprised:
Secretary: Mubarak Abdullah Al-Shamikh. *Secretary for African Unity:* Ali Abd Al-Salam Al-Turayki. *Finance:* Al-Ujayli Abd Al-Salam Al-Burayni. *Economy and Trade:* Shukri Mohamed Ghanim. *Foreign Liaison and International Co-operation:* Abd Al-Rahman Mohamed Shalgam. *Justice and Public Security:* Mohamed Ali Al-Masirati. *Human Resources:* Boghdadi Ali Mahmoudi. *Infrastructure, Urban Planning and Environment:* Salem Ahmed Bouig. *Social Affairs:* Selma Chabane Abduljabbar.

DEFENCE
There is selective conscription for one–two years. Defence expenditure in 2000 totalled US$1,176m. (US$210 per capita), representing 3·2% of GDP.

Nuclear Weapons. It is still thought that Libya is interested in acquiring nuclear weapons, but a UN embargo has hampered progress. According to *Deadly Arsenals*, published by the Carnegie Endowment for International Peace, Libya has both biological and chemical weapons research programmes.

Army. There are seven military districts. Strength (1999) 35,000 (25,000 conscripts). In addition there is a People's Militia of 40,000 which acts as a reserve force.

Navy. The fleet, a mixture of Soviet and West European-built ships, includes 4 diesel submarines, 2 frigates and 4 corvettes. There is a small Naval Aviation wing operating 32 armed helicopters.

Personnel in 1999 totalled 8,000, including coastguard. The forces are based at Tripoli, Benghazi, Derna, Tobruk, Sidi Bilal and Al Khums.

Air Force. The Air Force has over 420 combat aircraft, including MiG-21s, MiG-23s, MiG-25s and Mirage 5Ds, but most are in storage. Personnel total (1999) about 22,000, with some of the combat aircraft operated by Syrian aircrew.

INTERNATIONAL RELATIONS
Libya is a member of the UN, the African Union, OPEC, Arab Maghreb Union, African Development Bank and OIC.

ECONOMY
Agriculture accounted for an estimated 5% of GDP in 1996, industry 55% and services 40%.

Overview. An enactment of the People's General Congress in Sept. 1992 authorizes the privatization of enterprises.

Currency. The unit of currency is the *Libyan dinar* (LYD) of 1,000 *millemes*. The dinar was devalued 15% in Nov. 1994, and alongside the official exchange rate a new rate was applied to private sector imports. Foreign exchange reserves were US$13,146m. in June 2002 and total money supply was 7,249m. dinars. Inflation was negative in 2001, at −8·5%.

Budget. In 1995 revenues were estimated to be US$10·4bn. and expenditures US$10·3bn.

Performance. GDP growth was 0·6% in 2001. Total GDP in 2000 was an estimated US$38bn.

Banking and Finance. A National Bank of Libya was established in 1955; it was renamed the Central Bank of Libya in 1972. All foreign banks were nationalized by Dec. 1970. In 1972 the government set up the Libyan Arab Foreign Bank whose function is overseas investment and to participate in multinational banking corporations. The National Agricultural Bank has been set up to give loans and subsidies to farmers to develop their land and to assist them in marketing their crops.

Weights and Measures. Although the metric system has been officially adopted and is obligatory for all contracts, the following weights and measures are still used: *oke* = 1·282 kg; *kantar* = 51·28 kg; *draa* = 46 cm; *handaza* = 68 om.

ENERGY AND NATURAL RESOURCES

Environment. According to the *World Bank Atlas* Libya's carbon dioxide emissions in 1998 were the equivalent of 7·2 tonnes per capita.

Electricity. Installed capacity in 1997 was 5m. kW. Production was 16·92bn. kWh in 1998 and consumption per capita 3,677 kWh.

Oil and Gas. Out of a total GDP of US$32,280·8m. in 1996, the oil sector accounted for US$7,731·5m. Crude oil production (1998) 511m. bbls. (1·4m. bbls. a day). Reserves (2001) 29·5bn. bbls. The Libyan National Oil Corporation (NOC) is the state's organization for the exploitation of oil resources. Since US oil companies withdrew owing to sanctions, European rivals have been quick to move in.

Proven natural gas reserves totalled 1,310bn. cu. metres in 1999. Agip, the Italian oil company, is investing US$3bn. in a project to export natural gas to Europe. Production (1999) 5·9bn. cu. metres.

Water. Since 1984 a US$20bn. project has been under way to bring water from aquifers underlying the Sahara to the inhabited coastal areas of Libya. This scheme, called the 'Great Man-Made River', is intended, on completion, to bring 6,000 cu. metres of water a day along some 4,000 km of pipes. Phase I was completed in Aug. 1991; Phase II of the project (covering the west of Libya) was announced in Sept. 1989. The river is providing Libya's main centres of population with clean water for the first time in their history as well as making possible the improvement and expansion of agriculture. The whole project is more than three-quarters complete.

Minerals. Iron ore deposits have been found in the south.

Agriculture. Only the coastal zone, which covers an area of about 17,000 sq. miles, is really suitable for agriculture. Of some 25m. acres of productive land, nearly 20m. are used for grazing and about 1m. for static farming. The sub-desert zone produces the alfalfa plant. The desert zone and the Fezzan contain some fertile oases. In 1998 there were 1·82m. ha of arable land and 0·3m. ha of permanent crops.

Cyrenaica has about 10m. acres of potentially productive land and is suitable for grazing. Certain areas are suitable for dry farming; in addition, grapes, olives and dates are grown. About 143,000 acres are used for settled farming; about 272,000 acres are covered by natural forests. The Agricultural Development Authority plans to reclaim 6,000 ha each year for agriculture. In the Fezzan there are about 6,700 acres of irrigated gardens and about 297,000 acres are planted with date palms.

Production (2000, in 1,000 tonnes): tomatoes, 250; watermelons, 215; potatoes, 210; olives, 190; onions, 180; wheat, 160; dates, 133; barley, 70; oranges, 43.

Livestock (2000): 5·1m. sheep, 1·9m. goats, 143,000 cattle, 71,000 camels, 25m. chickens.

Forestry. Forest area in 1995 was 6,000 ha (0·2% of the land area). In 1999, 652,000 cu. metres of roundwood were cut.

Fisheries. The catch in 1999 was approximately 32,450 tonnes, entirely from marine waters.

INDUSTRY
Industry is nationalized. Small scale private sector industrialization in the form of partnerships is permitted. Output (1997, in 1,000 tonnes): residual fuel oil, 5,240; distillate fuel oil, 4,272; cement, 2,524; petrol, 1,970.

Labour. The labour force in 1996 was 1,601,000 (79% males).

INTERNATIONAL TRADE
Since 1986 the USA has applied a trade embargo on the grounds of Libya's alleged complicity in terrorism. In 1992 UN sanctions were imposed for Libya's refusal to deliver suspected terrorists for trial in the UK or USA. In Feb. 1989 Libya signed a treaty of economic co-operation with the four other Maghreb countries; Algeria, Mauritania, Morocco and Tunisia.

Imports and Exports. In 1999 imports (f.o.b.) were valued at US$3,996m. (US$5,857m. in 1998) and exports (f.o.b.) at US$6,758m. (US$6,328m. in 1998). Some 80% of GDP derives from trade. Oil accounts for over 95% of exports, worth 3,578·8m. dinars in 1996. Main export markets in 1996 were Italy (41%), Germany (18%), Spain (10%), France (4%) and Turkey (4%); main import suppliers were Italy (21·7%), Germany (13·9%), UK (8·4%), France (6·8%) and Turkey (5·8%).

COMMUNICATIONS

Roads. There were 6,798 km of national roads in 1996, 10,186 km of secondary roads and 7,500 km of other roads. Passenger cars numbered 809,500 in 1996 (154·1 per 1,000 inhabitants), in addition to which there were 356,000 trucks and vans. There were 1,080 deaths as a result of road accidents in 1996.

Civil Aviation. The UN ban on air traffic to and from Libya enforced since April 1992 was lifted in April 1999 following the handing over for trial of two suspected Lockerbie bombers. Libyan Arab Airlines provides both international and domestic services. In 1999 scheduled airline traffic of Libya-based carriers flew 3·8m. km, carrying 571,000 passengers.

Shipping. Sea-going vessels totalled 567,000 GRT in 1998, including oil tankers 395,000 GRT.

Telecommunications. In 2000 main telephone lines numbered 605,000 (107·9 per 1,000 population) and in 1998 there were 20,000 mobile phone subscribers. Internet users numbered 20,000 in March 2001.

Postal Services. In 1994 there were 383 post offices, or one for every 13,700 persons.

SOCIAL INSTITUTIONS

Justice. The Civil, Commercial and Criminal codes are based mainly on the Egyptian model. Matters of personal status of family or succession matters affecting Muslims are dealt with in special courts according to the Muslim law. All other matters, civil, commercial and criminal, are tried in the ordinary courts, which have jurisdiction over everyone.

There are civil and penal courts in Tripoli and Benghazi, with subsidiary courts at Misurata and Derna; courts of assize in Tripoli and Benghazi, and courts of appeal also in Tripoli and Benghazi.

Religion. Islam is declared the State religion, but the right of others to practise their religions is provided for. In 1990, 97% were Sunni Muslims.

Education. In 1995–96 there were 1,460,433 primary and preparatory (called basic education) school pupils, and in 1992–93 there were 310,556 secondary level pupils. In 1994–95 there were 3 universities and 1 medical and 1 technological university. There were 3 other institutes of higher education. In 1994–95 there were 31,140 university students and 1,710 academic staff. Adult literacy in 1999 was 79·1% (male, 90·2%; female, 66·9%).

Health. In 1990 there were 4,749 physicians, 686 dentists and 13,849 nurses. Provision of hospital beds in 1990 was 41 per 10,000 population.

CULTURE

Broadcasting. Broadcasting is controlled by the government Libyan Jamihiriya Broadcasting and People's Revolution Broadcasting-Television. Radio has a home service, external services in English, French and Arabic and a Holy Koran programme. In 1997 there were estimated to be 1·35m. radio and 730,000 TV receivers (colour by SECAM H).

Press. In 1996 there were four daily newspapers with a combined circulation of 71,000.

Tourism. In 1999 there were 40,000 foreign tourists, spending US$28m.

DIPLOMATIC REPRESENTATIVES
Of Libya in the United Kingdom (61–62 Ennismore Gdns., London SW7 1NH)
Ambassador: Mohammed Abdul Qasim Al-Zwai.

Of the United Kingdom in Libya (P. O. Box 4206, Tripoli)
Ambassador: Anthony Layden.
USA suspended all embassy activities in Tripoli on 2 May 1980.

Of Libya to the United Nations
Ambassador: Abuzed Omar Dorda.

Of Libya to the European Union
Ambassador: Hamed Ahmed Elhouderi.

FURTHER READING
Pazzanita, A. G., *The Maghreb.* [Bibliography] ABC-Clio, Oxford and Santa Barbara (CA), 1998
Simons, G., *Libya: the Struggle for Survival.* London, 1993
Vandewalle, D. (ed.) *Qadhafi's Libya, 1969–1994.* London, 1995

LIECHTENSTEIN

Fürstentum Liechtenstein
(Principality of Liechtenstein)

Capital: Vaduz
Population estimate, 2000: 33,000
GDP per capita: not available

KEY HISTORICAL EVENTS

Liechtenstein is a sovereign state with a history dating back to 1342 when Count Hartmann III became ruler of the county of Vaduz. Additions were later made to the count's domains and by 1434 the territory reached its present boundaries. On 23 Jan. 1719 the Emperor Charles VI constituted the two counties as the Principality of Liechtenstein. In 1862 the constitution established an elected diet. After the First World War, Liechtenstein was represented abroad by Switzerland. Swiss currency was adopted in 1921. On 5 Oct. 1921 a new constitution based on that of Switzerland extended democratic rights, but in March 2003 the people of Liechtenstein voted in a referendum to give their prince the power to govern without reference to elected representatives.

TERRITORY AND POPULATION

Liechtenstein is bounded on the east by Austria and the west by Switzerland. Total area 160 sq. km (61·8 sq. miles). The population (census 1997) was 31,320 (16,113 females), including 10,730 resident foreigners, giving a density of 195 per sq. km.

The population of Liechtenstein is predominantly rural. Population of Vaduz (1997) 4,975. The language is German.

SOCIAL STATISTICS

In 1997 there were 435 births and 230 deaths (rates of 13·9 per 1,000 population and 7·3 respectively). The annual population growth rate was 1·0% over the period 1995–99.

CLIMATE

There is a distinct difference in climate between the higher mountains and the valleys. In summer the peaks can often be foggy while the valleys remain sunny and warm, while in winter the valleys can often be foggy and cold whilst the peaks remain sunny and comparatively warm. Vaduz, Jan. 0°C, July 20°C. Annual rainfall 1,090 mm.

CONSTITUTION AND GOVERNMENT

Liechtenstein is a constitutional monarchy ruled by the princes of the House of Liechtenstein.

The reigning Prince is **Hans-Adam II,** b. 14 Feb. 1945; he succeeded his father Prince Francis-Joseph, 13 Nov. 1989 (he exercised the prerogatives to which the Sovereign is entitled from 26 Aug. 1984); married on 30 July 1967 to Countess Marie Kinsky von Wchinitz und Tettau. *Offspring:* Hereditary Prince Alois (b. 11 June 1968), married Duchess Sophie of Bavaria on 3 July 1993. (*Offspring:* Prince Joseph Wenzel, b. 24 May 1995; Marie Caroline, b. 17 Oct. 1996; Georg Antonius, b. 20 April 1999; Nikolaus Sebastian, b. 6 Dec. 2000); Prince Maximilian (b. 16 May 1969), married Angela Brown on 29 Jan. 2000 (*offspring:* Alfons, b. 18 May 2001); Prince Constantin (b. 15 March 1972), married Countess Marie Kálnoky de Köröspatak on 17 July 1999; Princess Tatjana (b. 10 April 1973), married Philipp von Lattorff on 5 June 1999 (*offspring:* Lukas, b. 13 May 2000; Elisabeth, b. 25 Jan. 2002). The monarchy is hereditary in the male line.

The present constitution of 5 Oct. 1921 provided for a unicameral parliament (*Landtag*) of 15 members elected for four years, but this was amended to 25 members in 1988. Election is on the basis of proportional representation. The prince can call and dismiss the parliament, and following a referendum held on 16 March

2003, dismiss the government and veto bills. On parliamentary recommendation, he appoints the prime minister and the four councillors for a four-year term. Any group of 1,000 persons or any three communes may propose legislation (initiative). Bills passed by the parliament may be submitted to popular referendum. A law is valid when it receives a majority approval by the parliament and the prince's signed concurrence. The capital is Vaduz.

National Anthem. 'Oben am jungen Rhein' ('Up above the young Rhine'); words by H. H. Jauch; tune, 'God save the Queen'.

RECENT ELECTIONS

At the elections on 9 and 11 Feb. 2001 the Progressive Citizens' Party (FBPL) gained 13 seats (49·90% of votes cast); the Patriotic Union (VU), 11 (41·34% of votes); Free List (FL), 1 (8·76% of votes).

CURRENT ADMINISTRATION

Head of Government, Minister for Finance and Construction, Family Affairs and Equal Rights: Otmar Hasler; b. 1953 (FBPL; sworn in 5 April 2001).

In March 2003 the cabinet comprised:

Deputy Head of Government, Minister for Education, Transport and Communication, and Justice: Rita Kieber-Beck. *Health, Social Services, Economy:* Hansjörg Frick. *Interior, Culture, Sport, Environment, Agriculture and Forestry:* Alois Ospelt. *Foreign Relations:* Ernst Walch.

Princely House Website: http://www.fuerstenhaus.li/

INTERNATIONAL RELATIONS

Liechtenstein is a member of the UN, WTO, OSCE, EFTA, EEA and the Council of Europe.

ECONOMY

Liechtenstein is one of the world's richest countries with a well diversified economy. Low taxes and strict bank secrecy laws have made Liechtenstein a successful offshore financial centre.

Currency. Swiss currency has been in use since 1921.

Budget. Budget (in Swiss francs), 1998: revenue, 591,317,000; expenditure, 557,492,000. There is no public debt.

Performance. Real GDP growth was 2·1% in 2001.

Banking and Finance. There were eight banks in 1998. Combined total assets were 29,076m. Swiss francs in 1997.

Liechtenstein was one of 15 countries and territories named in a report in June 2000 as failing to co-operate in the fight against international money laundering. The Financial Action Task Force on Money Laundering was set up by the G7 group of major industrialized nations.

Weights and Measures. The metric system is in force.

ENERGY AND NATURAL RESOURCES

Electricity. In 1997 imported capacity was 1,171,569 MW; electricity produced was 77,816 MWh.

Agriculture. In 1996 there were 4,000 ha of cultivated land. In 2000 approximately 660 ha (17% of all agricultural land—the highest proportion of any country) was set aside for organic farming. The rearing of cattle on the Alpine pastures is highly developed. In 1997 there were 5,489 cattle (including 2,614 milch cows), 342 horses, 3,608 sheep, 287 goats, 2,056 pigs. Total production of dairy produce in 1997 was 13,079 tonnes.

Forestry. In 1995 there were 5,560 ha of forest (34·7% of the land area). Timber production in 1999 was 13,000 cu. metres.

INDUSTRY

The country is highly industrialized, and has a great variety of light industries (textiles, ceramics, steel screws, precision instruments, canned food, pharmaceutical products, heating appliances, etc.).

Labour. The farming population went down from 70% in 1930 to 1·3% in 1997. The rapid change-over has led to the immigration of foreign workers (Austrians, Germans, Italians, Spaniards). The workforce was 15,922 in 1997, excluding employees commuting from abroad (8,743 in 1997). Industrial undertakings affiliated to the Liechtenstein Chamber of Commerce in 1996 employed 6,825 workers earning 469·83m. Swiss francs.

INTERNATIONAL TRADE

Liechtenstein has been in a customs union with Switzerland since 1923.

Imports and Exports. Exports of home produce in 1996 (in Swiss francs), for member companies affiliated to the Chamber of Industry and Commerce, amounted to 3,510m. Swiss francs: 458m. (13%) went to Switzerland, 1,584m. (45·2%) went to EEA countries and 1,468m. (41·8%) went to other countries. Imports in 1997 amounted to 1,179m. Swiss francs.

COMMUNICATIONS

Roads. There are 250 km of roads. Postal buses are the chief means of public transportation within the country and to Austria and Switzerland. There were 19,926 cars in 1997. There were 367 road accidents in 1997 (6 fatal).

Rail. The 18·5 km of main railway passing through the country is operated by Austrian Federal Railways.

Telecommunications. In 1996 there were 19,916 telephones and 129 telex machines.

Postal Services. Post and telegraphs are administered by Switzerland.

SOCIAL INSTITUTIONS

Justice. The principality has its own civil and penal codes. The lowest court is the county court, *Landgericht*, presided over by one judge, which decides minor civil cases and summary criminal offences. The criminal court, *Kriminalgericht*, with a bench of five judges is for major crimes. Another court of mixed jurisdiction is the court of assizes (with three judges) for misdemeanours. Juvenile cases are treated in the Juvenile Court (with a bench of three judges). The superior court, *Obergericht*, and Supreme Court, *Oberster Gerichtshof*, are courts of appeal for civil and criminal cases (both with benches of five judges). An administrative court of appeal from government actions and the State Court determines the constitutionality of laws.

The death penalty was abolished in 1989.

Police. The principality has no army. 1998: police force 62, auxiliary police 14.

Religion. In 1997 there were 24,962 Roman Catholics and 2,279 Protestants.

Education. In 1997 there were 14 primary, 3 upper, 5 secondary and 1 grammar schools, with 3,955 pupils and 367 teachers. There is also an evening technical school, a music school and a children's pedagogic-welfare day school.

Health. There is an obligatory sickness insurance scheme. In 1989 there was one hospital, but Liechtenstein has an agreement with the Swiss cantons of St Gallen and Graubünden and the Austrian Federal State of Vorarlberg that her citizens may use certain hospitals. In 1995 there were 32 doctors, 12 dentists and 2 pharmacists.

CULTURE

Broadcasting. In 1997 there were 21,000 radios and 12,000 TV sets.

Cinema. There were two cinemas in 1998.

Press. In 1998 there were two daily newspapers with a total circulation of 17,900, and one weekly with a circulation of 13,900.

Tourism. In 1999, 60,000 tourists visited Liechtenstein.

DIPLOMATIC REPRESENTATIVES

In 1919 Switzerland agreed to represent the interests of Liechtenstein in countries where it has diplomatic missions and where Liechtenstein is not represented in its own right. In so doing Switzerland always acts only on the basis of mandates of a general or specific nature, which it may either accept or refuse, while Liechtenstein is free to enter into direct relations with foreign states or to set up its own additional diplomatic missions.

Of the United Kingdom in Liechtenstein
Ambassador: Basil Eastwood, CMG (resides at Berne).

Of Liechtenstein to the USA (633 Third Avenue, 27th Floor, New York, NY, 10017)
Ambassador: Claudia Fritsche.

Of Liechtenstein to the United Nations
Ambassador: Claudia Fritsche.

Of Liechtenstein to the European Union
Ambassador: Prince Nicolas of Liechtenstein.

FURTHER READING

Amt für Volkswirtschaft. *Statistisches Jahrbuch.* Vaduz

Rechenschaftsbericht der Fürstlichen Regierung. Vaduz. Annual, from 1922
Jahrbuch des Historischen Vereins. Vaduz. Annual since 1901
National library: Landesbibliothek, Vaduz
Meier, Regula A., *Liechtenstein.* [Bibliography] ABC-Clio, Oxford and Santa Barbara (CA), 1993

National statistical office: Amt für Volkswirtschaft, Vaduz

LITHUANIA

Lietuvos Respublika

Capital: Vilnius
Population estimate, 2000: 3·70m.
GDP per capita, 2000: (PPP$) 7,106
HDI/world rank: 0·808/49

KEY HISTORICAL EVENTS

At the time of Tatar-Mongol domination of Russia, Lithuania annexed Russian lands until by the middle of the 15th century Belorussia, along with those parts of Russia and Ukraine as far as the Black Sea, were under its rule. Lithuania united with Poland dynastically in 1385 and politically in 1569. During the partitions of the Polish-Lithuanian Commonwealth by Russia, Prussia and Austria in the 18th century, Lithuania yielded its Russian territories and was absorbed into the Russian empire in 1795. Following the German occupation during the First World War and the Russian revolution on 16 Feb. 1918, heavy fighting occurred between the Soviet, German, Polish and Lithuanian forces. In April 1919 the Soviets withdrew and the re-formed Lithuanian government established a democratic republic. Lithuanian independence was recognized by the Treaty of Versailles. In Dec. 1926 the democratic regime was overthrown by a coup. The secret protocol of the Soviet-German frontier treaty of 23 Sept. 1939 assigned the greater part of Lithuania to the Soviet sphere of influence. Lithuania became a Soviet Socialist Republic of the USSR on 3 Aug. 1940.

On 11 March 1990 the newly-elected Lithuanian Supreme Soviet proclaimed independence, a decision unacceptable to the USSR government. Initially dispatched to Vilnius to enforce conscription, Soviet army units occupied key buildings in the face of mounting popular unrest. On 13 Jan. 1991 the army fired on demonstrators and there were fatal casualties. A referendum on independence was held in Feb. 1991 at which 90·5% voted in favour. A fully independent status was conceded by the USSR on 6 Sept. 1991. The first presidential elections were held in 1993 and won by Algirdas Brazauskas, who was subsequently elected to be the current prime minister. In Oct. 2002 Lithuania was invited to join both the EU and NATO in 2004.

TERRITORY AND POPULATION

Lithuania is bounded in the north by Latvia, east and south by Belarus, and west by Poland, the Russian enclave of Kaliningrad and the Baltic Sea. The total area is 65,300 sq. km (25,170 sq. miles) and the population (2001 census) 3,483,972 (1,854,824 females; 2,332,098, or 66·9%, urban); density, 53·4 per sq. km. Of the 2001 census, Lithuanians accounted for 83·5%, Poles 6·7%, Russians 6·3% (9·4% in 1989), Belorussians 1·2%, Ukrainians 0·7%, and Jews 0·1%.

The UN gives a projected population for 2010 of 3·60m.

There are 10 counties (with capitals of the same name): Alytus; Kaunas; Klaipėda; Marijampolė; Panevėžys; Šiauliai; Tauragė; Telšiai; Utena; Vilnius.

The capital is Vilnius (Jan. 2002 population, 553,373). Other large towns are Kaunas (376,575), Klaipėda (192,498), Šiauliai (133,528) and Panevėžys (119,417).

The official language is Lithuanian, but ethnic minorities have the right to official use of their language where they form a substantial part of the population. All residents who applied by 3 Nov. 1991 received Lithuanian citizenship, requirements for which now are ten years' residence and competence in Lithuanian.

SOCIAL STATISTICS

2001: births, 31,546; deaths, 40,399; marriages, 15,764; divorces, 11,024; infant deaths, 250. Rates (per 1,000 population): birth, 9·1; death, 11·6; marriage, 4·5; divorce, 3·2. The population started to decline in 1994, a trend which is set to continue. Annual population growth rate, 1990–2002, –0·6%. In 2001, 8,006 births were registered to unmarried mothers and there were 20,513 legally induced abortions. Life expectancy at birth in 2001 was 65·88 years for males and 77·41 years for females. In 2001 the most popular age range for marrying was 20–24 for both males and females. Infant mortality, 2001, 7·8 per 1,000 live births; fertility rate, 1·29 births per woman. In 2001 there were 7,253 emigrants and 24,694 immigrants.

Lithuania has the world's highest suicide rate, at 44·1 per 100,000 inhabitants in 2001 (a rate of 77·2 among males but only 15 among women).

CLIMATE
1999: Vilnius, Jan. −2·8°C, July 20·5°C. Annual rainfall 520 mm. Klaipėda, Jan. −0·6°C, July 19·4°C. Annual rainfall 770 mm.

CONSTITUTION AND GOVERNMENT
A referendum to approve a new constitution was held on 25 Oct. 1992. Parliament is the 141-member *Seimas*. Under a new electoral law passed in July 2000, 71 of the parliament's 141 members will defeat rivals for their seats if they receive the most votes in a single round of balloting. Previously they had to win 50% of the votes or face a run-off against the nearest competitor. The parliament's 70 other seats are distributed according to the proportional popularity of the political parties at the ballot box.

The *Constitutional Court* is empowered to rule on whether proposed laws conflict with the constitution or existing legislation. It comprises nine judges who serve nine-year terms, one third rotating every three years.

National Anthem. 'Lietuva, tėvyne mūsų' ('Lithuania, our fatherland'); words and tune by V. Kurdirka.

RECENT ELECTIONS
Presidential elections were held in two rounds on 22 Dec. 2002 and 5 Jan. 2003. In the first round incumbent Valdas Adamkus won 35·3% of the vote, Rolandas Paksas 19·7% and Artūras Paulauskas 8·3%. Turn-out was 53·9%. In the run-off between the two leading candidates from the first round, former prime minister Rolandas Paksas of the Liberal Democratic Party won 54·9% of the vote against 45·1% for Valdas Adamkus.

Parliamentary elections were held on 8 Oct. 2000. Turn-out was 55·9%. The A. Brazauskas Social Democratic Coalition won 51 seats with 31·1% of the vote; New Union (social liberals) won 29 with 19·6%; the Lithuanian Liberal Union, 34 with 17·3%; the Homeland Union–Conservatives of Lithuania, 9 with 8·6%. Other parties and non-partisans won four seats or fewer.

CURRENT ADMINISTRATION
President: Rolandas Paksas; b. 1956 (Liberal Democratic Party; sworn in on 26 Feb. 2003).

Prime Minister: Algirdas Brazauskas; b. 1932 (A. Brazauskas Social Democratic Coalition; in office since 3 July 2001).

In March 2003 the cabinet comprised:

Minister of Foreign Affairs: Antanas Valionis. *Defence:* Linas Linkevičius. *Finance:* Dalia Grybauskaitė. *Economy:* Petras Čėsna. *Social Security and Labour:* Vilija Blinkevičiūtė. *Interior:* Juozas Bernatonis. *Health:* Juozas Olekas. *Justice:* Vytautas Markevičius. *Agriculture and Forestry:* Jeronimas Kraujelis. *Environment:* Arūnas Kundrotas. *Transport:* Zigmantas Balčytis. *Culture:* Roma Dovydėnienė. *Education and Science:* Algirdas Monkevičius.

The *Speaker* is Artūras Paulauskas (New Union).

Government of the Republic of Lithuania: http://www.lrvk.lt/

DEFENCE
Conscription is for 12 months. In 2002 military expenditure totalled US$304·2m. (US$85 per capita), representing 2% of GDP. In 2002 logistic forces numbered 1,044 and Training and Doctrine Command (TRADOC) numbered 3,353.

Army. The Army numbered 7,700 in 2002 and included one motorized infantry brigade ('Iron Wolf'). There are also the National Defence Volunteer Forces, which are around 12,000 strong.

Navy. In 2002 Naval Forces numbered 670 personnel and operated several vessels including two frigates.

Air Force. The Air Force consisted of 1,081 personnel in 2002, divided into three functional categories: military aviation; airspace surveillance; and air defence.

INTERNATIONAL RELATIONS

Lithuania is a member of the UN, WTO, BIS, the NATO Partnership for Peace, EBRD, IMF, UNESCO, FAO, IMO, Council of Europe, OSCE, Council of the Baltic Sea States, IOM and EAPC, is an Associate Member of the EU and Associate Partner of the WEU. In Dec. 1995 Lithuania applied to join the EU. At the European Union's Helsinki Summit in Dec. 1999 Lithuania, along with five other countries, was invited to begin full negotiations for membership in Feb. 2000, and is scheduled to become a member on 1 May 2004. It also received an invitation on 21 Nov. 2002 to start accession negotiations towards NATO membership.

ECONOMY

Agriculture accounted for 7% of GDP in 2001, industry 24% and services 60%.

Overview. Privatization in Lithuania is close to completion. Currently as much as 80% of GDP in Lithuania is generated by the private sector. The restructuring of priority sectors of the Lithuanian economy is facilitated by the second stage of privatization, which gives equal rights to local and foreign investors. The State Property Fund co-ordinates the privatization process and organizes the privatization of the largest state-controlled entities in industry and infrastructure.

Currency. The unit of currency is the *litas* (plural: *litai*) of 100 *cents*, which was introduced on 25 June 1993 and became the sole legal tender on 1 Aug. The litas was pegged to the US dollar on 1 April 1994 at US$1 = 4 litai, but since 2 Feb. 2002 it has been pegged to the euro at 3·4528 litai = one euro. Inflation, which reached a high of 1,161% in the early 1990s, was 1·3% in 2001. Total money supply was 6,678m. litai in May 2002. Gold reserves were 186,000 troy oz in June 2002 and foreign exchange reserves US$2,230m.

Budget. Total revenue in 2002 amounted to 10,330m. litai and and expenditure to 11,466m. litai. Revenue in 2002 included: VAT, 37%; personal income tax, 24%. Expenditure in 2002 included (in 1m. litai): education, 3,073; social welfare, 1,149; public order, 1,009; general public services, 903; defence, 857; transport and communications, 844; health, 613.

VAT is 18%.

Performance. Among the wealthiest provinces of the former Soviet Union, Lithuania has weathered the economic crisis overspilling from Russia. 47·8% of exports in 2001 went to the EU compared to just 11% to Russia. The GDP growth rate for 1998 was 5·1% but in 1999 was negative, at –3·9%. There was then a recovery in 2000, with growth of 3·9%, rising to 5·7% in 2001. Total GDP in 2001 was US$11·8bn.

Banking and Finance. The central bank and bank of issue is the Bank of Lithuania (*Governor*, Reinoldijas Šarkinas). There are two state banks—the Savings Bank and the Agricultural Bank. A programme to restructure and privatize the state banks was started in 1996. There were ten commercial banks and four foreign bank branches in 2002. The largest private bank in Lithuania is JSC Vilniaus Bankas, which controls approximately 37% of the total banking assets in the country.

A stock exchange opened in Vilnius in 1993. In Oct. 1999 its capitalization was US$3·5bn. The trading volume in 1999 was US$575m.

ENERGY AND NATURAL RESOURCES

Environment. According to Lithuania's Ministry of Environment, carbon dioxide emissions were the equivalent of 4·4 tonnes per capita in 2000.

Electricity. Installed capacity was 6·57m. kW in 2001; production was 14·7bn. kWh. A nuclear power station (with two reactors) in Ignalina was responsible for 77·1% of total output in 2001, and there are also two hydro-electric, five public and six autoproducer thermal plants. No other country has such a high percentage of its electricity generated through nuclear power. However, at the EU's insistence the government is committed to closing down Ignalina, with the first reactor being closed in 2005. Electricity consumption per capita in 2001 was 1,852 kWh.

Oil and Gas. Oil production started from a small field at Kretinga in 1990. In Jan. 2002 remaining recoverable reserves were estimated at 3·7m. tonnes; potential recoverable resources, 80m. tonnes. Production in 2001 was 471,000 tonnes.

LITHUANIA

Minerals. Peat reserves totalled 173·7m. tonnes in Jan. 2002. Output, 1991, 259,000 tonnes.

Agriculture. In 2001 agriculture employed about 16·1% of the workforce. As of 1 Jan. 2002 the average farm size was 17·2 ha, one of the lowest in eastern Europe; the agricultural land area was 3,956,200 ha. In 2001, 260,700 persons were employed in agriculture and forestry.

Output of main agricultural products (in 1,000 tonnes) in 2001: wheat, 1,076; potatoes, 1,054; sugarbeets, 880; barley, 776; rye, 231; cabbages, 121; oats, 84; rapeseed, 65. Value of agricultural production, 2001 (in 1m. litai), was 4,501·7, of which from agricultural partnerships and enterprises, 944·7; and from individual farm holdings, 3,557·0.

Livestock, Jan. 2002 (in 1,000): cattle, 751·7 (of which milch cows, 441·8); pigs, 1,010·8; sheep and goats, 36·0; horses, 64·5; poultry, 6,576·1. There were 102,227 tractors in use in 2002. Animal products, 2001 (in 1,000 tonnes): meat, 150·5; milk, 1,729·8; and 742,300 eggs.

Forestry. In 2002 forests covered 2·0m. ha, or 30·6% of Lithuania's territory, and consist of conifers, mostly pine. Timber production in 2001, 3·1m. cu. metres.

Fisheries. In Jan. 2001 the fishing fleet comprised 86 vessels averaging 650 GRT. Total catch in 2001 amounted to 153,931 tonnes (mainly from sea fishing), compared to 57,477 tonnes in 1995.

INDUSTRY

Industrial output included, in 1998 (in 1,000 tonnes): petrol, 6,433; mineral and chemical fertilizers, 783; cement, 714 (1997); sulphuric acid, 504; extraction of peat, 202; sugar, 137; quarrying of stone, clay and sand, 1·47m. cu. metres; television picture tubes, 1,794,000 units; silk, 7·8m. sq. metres; linen, 15·9m. sq. metres; woollen fabrics,14·3m. sq. metres; cotton fabrics, 63·8m. cu. metres; TV sets, 84,100 units; bicycles, 150,000 units; refrigerators, 238,900 units.

Labour. In 2001 the workforce was 1·74m. (70·1% in private enterprises and 29·9% in the public sector). Employed population by activity (as a percentage): manufacturing, 17·9; wholesale and retail trade, 15·4; education, 10·7; health and social work, 7·0; construction, 6·2; transport and communications, 6·0; real estate, 3·7. Employment skills, 72·7% with tertiary education, 55·9% with upper secondary education, 20·8% with lower secondary, primary education. In 2001 the average monthly wage was 991·2 litai; legal minimum wage was 430 litai.

In 2001 old age pension for men started at 61·5 years and for women at 57·5. Average number of persons entitled to pensions in 2001 was 636,900. The unemployment rate in June 2002 was 13·0%.

Trade Unions. On 1 Jan. 2001 there were 655 registered unions (339 in operation) affiliated with four federations: the Lithuanian Trade Union Centre (LPSC); the Lithuanian Trade Union Unification (LPSS); the Lithuanian Workers Union (LDS); the Lithuanian Labour Federation (LDF). A merger is planned between LPSC and LPSS.

INTERNATIONAL TRADE

In order to foster export growth, Lithuania maintains a fairly liberal foreign trade regime. There is no quantitative import restriction and the import duties are one of the lowest in central Europe. By the end of 1998 free trade agreements with the European Union, EFTA, neighbouring Latvia and Estonia, as well as with Central European Free Trade Agreement countries (CEFTA) and Ukraine were signed. Meanwhile, most favoured-nation status is applied to trade with Russia.

Foreign investors may purchase up to 100% of the equity companies in Lithuania. By mid-1999, US$2·1bn. of foreign capital had been invested.

Total foreign debt was US$4,855m. in 2000.

Individual laws on three free economic zones (namely the laws on Šiauliai, Klaipėda and Kaunas) have been cleared by Lithuania's Parliament, the Seimas.

Imports and Exports. In 2001 imports were valued at €7·1bn. and exports at €5·1bn. Main export markets, 2001: UK, 13·8%; Latvia, 12·6%; Germany, 12·6%, Russia, 11·0%; Poland, 6·3%. Main import suppliers: Russia, 25·3%; Germany, 17·2%; Poland, 4·9%; Italy, 4·2%. Main exports are mineral products, textiles and textile articles, electrical equipment, TV sets, chemical products and prepared foodstuffs.

COMMUNICATIONS

Roads. In 2002 there were 76,573 km of roads, of which 91·3% were paved. The Via Baltica, a US$180m. project, will upgrade a 1,000 km (620 mile) international highway linking Finland, Estonia, Latvia, Lithuania and Poland, and there are plans to continue the link to western and southern Europe.

In 2001 there were 1,133,477 passenger cars, 15,171 buses, 470 trolley buses, 100,389 goods vehicles and 20,244 motorcycles. In 2001 public transport carried 346·4m. passengers. There were 5,972 traffic accidents in 2001, with 706 fatalities.

Rail. There are 1,696 km of railway track in operation in Lithuania. The majority of rail traffic is diesel propelled, although 122 km of track are electrified. In 2001, 7·7m. passengers and 29,200 tonnes of freight were carried.

Civil Aviation. The main international airport is based in the capital, Vilnius. Other international airports are at Kaunas, Palanga and Šiauliai. The largest airline, a state-owned joint stock company, Lithuanian Airlines (on the list of privatization), has regular scheduled flights to most of Europe's main transit hubs, and in 2002 a number of other international airlines ran regular scheduled flights. In 1999 Lithuanian Airlines flew 7·7m. km, carrying 201,500 passengers (201,300 on international flights). In 2002 Vilnius was the busiest airport for passenger traffic, handling 634,991 passengers, but Kaunas (which handles approximately 8,500 tonnes per annum) was the busiest for freight.

Shipping. The ice-free port of Klaipėda plays a dominant role in the national economy and Baltic maritime traffic. It has the second largest tonnage in the Baltic region and a cargo capacity of 30m. tonnes per annum. A 205 ha site at the port is dedicated a *Free Economic Zone,* which offers attractive conditions to foreign investors.

In 2002 the merchant fleet numbered 95 ships totalling 377,942 GRT, including 10 bulkers, 54 general cargo ships, 5 tankers and 20 reefers. The turnover of the port in 1999 was 15·7m. tonnes (up from under 13m. in 1995).

In 1999 there were 788 km of navigable inland waterways. The inland fleet comprised 89 vessels.

Telecommunications. A majority stake in Lithuanian Telecom (the only fixed telephone service provider) was sold to the Finnish and Swedish consortium SONERA in 1998 and by Jan. 2003 the telecommunications market was fully liberalized. Lithuanian Telecom had 994,000 subscribers in Jan. 2003. In 1999 there were 332,000 mobile phone subscribers. In 2000 there were 240,000 PCs in use (64·9 per 1,000 persons) and in 1995 there were 6,200 fax machines. The number of Internet users in Oct. 2001 was 297,000.

Postal Services. In 2002 there were 944 post offices.

SOCIAL INSTITUTIONS

Justice. The general jurisdiction court system consists of the Supreme Court, the Court of Appeal, 5 county courts and 54 district courts. Specialized administrative courts were established in 1999. In Jan. 2003 there were 669 judges: 421 in district courts; 139 in county courts; 22 in the Court of Appeal; 33 in the Supreme Court; 41 in the administrative county courts; and 13 in the High Administrative Court.

77,108 crimes were reported in 1999, of which 41·0% were solved. In 1999 there were 343 murders and attempted murders. 2,240 persons were convicted of offences. In Jan. 2003 there were 11,070 prisoners, 8,520 of whom had been convicted. The death penalty was abolished for all crimes in 1998.

Religion. Under the Constitution, the state supports religious groups which have been active in Lithuania for 400 years, i.e., the Roman Catholic, Evangelical Lutheran, Evangelical Reformats and Orthodox Churches. 60–80% of the population are Roman Catholic. As of 1 Jan. 2000 there were 693 Roman Catholic churches with 732 priests, and 43 Orthodox churches with 41 priests. There is an archbishopric of Vilnius and 13 bishops. In 1999 the Lutheran Church had 41 churches, 54 parishes and 23 pastors headed by a bishop.

Education. Education is compulsory from 7 to 16. In 2001–02 there were 699 pre-school establishments with 89,841 pupils and 2,270 general schools with 50,900 teachers and 602,400 pupils, in the following categories:

Type of School	No. of Schools	No. of Pupils
Nursery	157	13,195
Primary	765	39,019
Junior	25	2,379
Basic	645	109,734
Special	65	7,619
Secondary	585	413,973
Adult	25	16,098

106,913 students (63,465 females) attended 16 institutions of higher education and 31,964 (20,198 females) attended vocational colleges in 2001–02. The adult literacy rate in 2001 was 99·7%.

In 2001 total expenditure on education represented 29·4% of total government expenditure.

Health. In 2001 there were 14,031 physicians, 2,490 dentists and 27,787 nurses. There were 197 hospitals with 32,104 beds in 2001, and 2,266 pharmacists.

Welfare. The social security system is financed by the State Social Insurance Fund. In 2001, 637,000 persons were eligible for retirement pensions, 644,600 for disability provisions and 211,800 for widow's/widower's pensions. In 2001 the average state social insurance old age pension was 306 litai (monthly).

CULTURE

Broadcasting. In 2002 there were 2 national and 8 commercial radio networks and 51 local commercial radio stations; 2 national and 3 commercial TV networks and 23 local TV stations (colour by PAL). There were 1·1m. radio receivers and 1·4m. television receivers in 1996.

Cinema. There were 71 cinemas in 2001; attendance, 2,366,853; gross box office receipts came to 14m. litai.

Press. In 2001 there were 368 newspapers (329 in Lithuanian, 25 in Russian, 5 in Polish, 4 in English, 3 in German, 1 in Yiddish and 1 in Belarussian) and 370 magazines. 4,402 book titles were published.

Tourism. There were 4,195,200 foreign tourists in 2001; tourism receipts amounted to US$550m. in 1999.

DIPLOMATIC REPRESENTATIVES

Of Lithuania in the United Kingdom (84 Gloucester Place, London, W1U 6AU)
Ambassador: Aurimas Taurantas.

Of the United Kingdom in Lithuania (Antakalnio g. 2, 2055 Vilnius)
Ambassador: Jeremy Hill.

Of Lithuania in the USA (2622 16th St., NW, Washington, D.C., 20009)
Ambassador: Vygaudas Usackas.

Of the USA in Lithuania (Akmenu g. 6, 2600 Vilnius)
Ambassador: John F. Tefft.

Of Lithuania to the United Nations
Ambassador: Gediminas Šerkšnys.

Of Lithuania to the European Union
Ambassador: Oskaras Jusys.

FURTHER READING
Department of Statistics to the Government. *Statistical Yearbook of Lithuania – Economic and Social Development in Lithuania.* Monthly.
Hood, N., *et al.*, (eds.) *Transition in the Baltic States.* 1997
Lieven, A., *The Baltic Revolution: Estonia, Latvia, Lithuania and the Path to Independence.* 2nd ed. Yale Univ. Press, 1994
Misiunas, R. J. and Taagepera, R., *The Baltic States: the Years of Dependence, 1940–91.* 2nd ed. Farnborough, 1993
Vardys, V. S. and Sedaitis, J. B., *Lithuania: the Rebel Nation.* Boulder (CO), 1997

National statistical office: Department of Statistics to the Government, Gedimino Pr. 29, LT 2600 Vilnius. *Director General:* Algirdas Gediminas Semeta.
Website: http://www.std.lt/

LUXEMBOURG

Grand-Duché de
Luxembourg

Capital: Luxembourg
Population estimate, 2000: 435,700
GDP per capita, 2000: (PPP$) 50,061
HDI/world rank: 0·925/16

KEY HISTORICAL EVENTS

Lying at the heart of Western Europe between Belgium, France and Germany, the Grand-Duchy of Luxembourg has been an independent State ever since the Treaty of London of 19 April 1839. The origins of Luxembourg stretch back to AD 963 when Count Sigfried founded the castle of Lutzilinburhurch. The House of Luxembourg was most prominent on the European scene during the 14th and 15th centuries, when four Counts of the House of Luxembourg became Emperors of the Holy Roman Empire and Kings of Bohemia. The House of Luxembourg subsequently went into decline and was successively occupied by Burgundy, Spain, Austria and finally by revolutionary France. In 1815 the Vienna Treaty decided that the Grand Duchy of Luxembourg would come under the Netherlands ruling house of Orange-Nassau. In 1839 the Walloon-speaking area was joined to Belgium. The union with the Netherlands ended in 1890. In both world wars (1914–18 and 1939–45) Luxembourg, a neutral country, was invaded and occupied by German forces. In June 1942 Luxembourg became the only Nazi-occupied country to stage a general strike against the occupation. In 1948 a Benelux customs union formed by Belgium, the Netherlands and Luxembourg allowed for standardization of prices, taxes and wages and the free movement of labour among the three countries. Luxembourg was a founder member of the European Union.

TERRITORY AND POPULATION

Luxembourg has an area of 2,586 sq. km (999 sq. miles) and is bounded on the west by Belgium, south by France, east by Germany. A census took place on 15 Feb. 2001; the population was 439,539 (including 162,285 foreigners); density, 170 per sq. km. The percentage of foreigners living in Luxembourg has increased dramatically in recent years, from 26% in 1986 to 36·9% in 2001. The main countries of origin of foreigners living in Luxembourg are Portugal (58,657 in Feb. 2001), France (19,979) and Italy (18,996).

In 1999, 91·0% of the population were urban. The capital, Luxembourg, has (Feb. 2001) 76,688 inhabitants; Esch-sur-Alzette, the centre of the mining district, 27,146; Dudelange, 17,230; Differdange, 10,284; Diekirch, 6,068; and Echternach, 4,610.

The UN gives a projected population for 2010 of 490,000.

Lëtzebuergesch is spoken by most of the population, and since 1984 has been an official language with French and German.

SOCIAL STATISTICS

Statistics (figures in parentheses indicate births and deaths of resident foreigners):

	Births	Deaths	Marriages	Divorces
1998	5,386 (2,439)	3,901 (469)	2,040	1,017
1999	5,582 (2,707)	3,793 (521)	2,090	1,043
2000	5,723 (2,806)	3,754 (547)	2,148	1,030
2001	5,459 (2,736)	3,719 (531)	1,983	1,029

2001 rates per 1,000 population; birth, 12·9; death, 8·4; marriage, 4·5; divorce, 2·3. In 2001 the most popular age range for marrying was 25–29 for both males and females. Life expectancy at birth in 1999 was 73·9 years for males and 80·4 years for females. Annual population growth rate, 1990–2001, 1·4%. Infant mortality, 2001, 5·7 per 1,000 live births; fertility rate, 7·6 births per 1000 women. In 2001 Luxembourg received 686 asylum applications.

A UNICEF report published in 2000 showed that only 1·2% of children in Luxembourg live in poverty (in households with incomes below the US official poverty line converted into national currencies), the lowest percentage of any country.

CLIMATE
In general the country resembles Belgium in its climate, with rain evenly distributed throughout the year. Average temperatures are Jan. 0·8°C, July 17·5°C. Annual rainfall 30·8" (782·2 mm).

CONSTITUTION AND GOVERNMENT
The Grand Duchy of Luxembourg is a constitutional monarchy.

The reigning Grand Duke is **Henri**, b. 16 April 1955, son of the former Grand Duke Jean and Princess Joséphine-Charlotte of Belgium; succeeded 7 Oct. 2000 on the abdication of his father; married Maria Teresa Mestre 14 Feb. 1981. (*Offspring:* Prince Guillaume, b. 11 Nov. 1981; Prince Felix, b. 3 June 1984; Prince Louis, b. 3 Aug. 1986; Princess Alexandra, b. 16 Feb. 1991; Prince Sebastian, b. 16 April 1992).

The constitution of 17 Oct. 1868 was revised in 1919, 1948, 1956, 1972, 1983, 1988, 1989, 1994, 1996 and 1998.

The separation of powers between the legislature and the executive is not very strong, resulting in much interaction between the two bodies. Only the judiciary is completely independent.

The 12 cantons are divided into four electoral districts: the South, the East, the Centre and the North. Voters choose between party lists of candidates in multi-member constituencies. The parliament is the *Chamber of Deputies*, which consists of a maximum of 60 members elected for five years. Voting is compulsory and there is universal suffrage. Seats are allocated according to the rules of proportional representation and the principle of the smallest electoral quote. There is a *Council of State* of 21 members appointed by the Sovereign. Membership is for a maximum period of 15 years, with retirement compulsory at the age of 72. It advises on proposed laws and any other question referred to it.

The head of state takes part in the legislative power, exercises executive power and has a part in the judicial power. The constitution leaves to the sovereign the right to organize the government, which consists of a Minister of State, who is Prime Minister, and of at least three Ministers. Direct consultation by referendum is provided for in the Constitution.

National Anthem. 'Ons Hemecht' ('Our Homeland'); words by M. Lentz, tune by J. A. Zinnen.

RECENT ELECTIONS
Elections took place on 13 June 1999. The Christian Social Party (CSV) gained 19 seats, the Democratic Party (DP) 15, the Socialist Workers' Party (LSAP) 13, the Action Committee for Democracy and Pensions Justice (ADR) 7, the Greens (Déi Gréng) 5, and the Left (DL) 1. The Christian Social Party and the Democratic Party subsequently formed a coalition government.

European Parliament. Luxembourg has six representatives. At the June 1999 elections turn-out was 90%. CSV won 2 seats with 31·9% of votes cast (group in European Parliament: European People's Party); LSAP, 2 with 23·2% (Party of European Socialists); the Democratic Party, 1 with 20·8% (Liberal, Democrat and Reform Party); the Greens, 1 with 10·7% (Greens).

CURRENT ADMINISTRATION
In March 2003 the Christian Social Party–Democratic Party coalition comprised:

Prime Minister, Minister of State, Finance and the Exchequer: Jean-Claude Juncker; b. 1954 (CSV; sworn in 20 Jan. 1995).

Deputy Prime Minister, Minister of Foreign Affairs and External Commerce, Civil Service and Administrative Reform: Lydie Polfer (DP). *Agriculture, Viticulture, Rural Development, Middle Classes, Housing and Tourism:* Fernand Boden (CSV). *Treasury and Budget, Justice:* Luc Frieden (CSV). *The Family, Social Solidarity and Youth, Promotion of Women:* Marie-Josée Jacobs (CSV). *Culture, Higher Education, Vocational Training and Research, Public Works:* Erna Hennicot-Schoepges (CSV).

Interior: Michel Wolter (CSV). *Economy and Transport:* Henri Grethen (DP). *Health and Social Security:* Carlo Wagner (DP). *Environment, Co-operation, Humanitarian Action, Defence:* Charles Goerens (DP). *Religious Affairs, Relations with Parliament, Employment and Labour, and Communications:* François Biltgen (CSV). *National Education, Professional Training and Sports:* Anne Brasseur (DP).
The *Speaker* is Jean Spautz.

Government Website: http://www.gouvernement.lu/

DEFENCE
There is a volunteer light infantry battalion of (2001) 842, of which only the career officers are professionals. In recent years Luxembourg soldiers and officers have been actively participating in peacekeeping missions, mainly in the former Yugoslavia. There is also a Gendarmerie of 612. In 2000 the Gendarmerie and the police force merged to form the Police grand-ducale. NATO maintains a squadron of E-3A *Sentries*.

In 2000 military expenditure totalled US$126m. (US$291 per capita), representing 0·8% of GDP.

INTERNATIONAL RELATIONS
Luxembourg is a member of the UN, WTO, NATO, Benelux, the EU, OECD, the Council of Europe, WEU, OSCE, IOM and the International Organization of the Francophonie. The Schengen Accord of June 1990 abolished border controls between Luxembourg, Austria, Belgium, Denmark, Finland, France, Germany, Greece, Iceland, Italy, the Netherlands, Norway, Portugal, Spain and Sweden.

ECONOMY
Services accounted for 81·5% of GDP in 2001, industry 17·9% and agriculture 0·6%.

According to the anti-corruption organization *Transparency International*, Luxembourg ranked equal 7th in the world in a 2002 survey of the countries with the least corruption in business and government. It received 9·0 out of 10 in the annual index.

Overview. The world economic crisis of 1973–74 hit the then monolithic Luxembourg economy very hard. The previously strong steel sector had to be thoroughly restructured and this, along with industrial diversification and the emergence of the new service sector, helped recovery. The financial sector is the country's biggest employer. Other buoyant sectors of the Luxembourg economy include telecommunications, audio-visual and multimedia, industrial plastics, float glass and air transports.

Currency. On 1 Jan. 1999 the euro (EUR) became the legal currency in Luxembourg; irrevocable conversion rate 40·3399 Luxembourg francs to 1 euro. The euro, which consists of 100 cents, has been in circulation since 1 Jan. 2002. There are seven euro notes in different colours and sizes denominated in 500, 200, 100, 50, 20, 10 and 5 euros, and eight coins denominated in 2 and 1 euros, then 50, 20, 10, 5, 2 and 1 cents. On the introduction of the euro there was a 'dual circulation' period before the Luxembourg franc ceased to be legal tender on 28 Feb. 2002. Euro banknotes in circulation on 1 Jan. 2002 had a total value of €5·6bn.

Inflation in 2001 was 2·7%. Foreign exchange reserves were US$24m. in 1997. Gold reserves were 76,000 troy oz in June 2002 and total money supply €505m.

Budget. Revenue and expenditure for calendar years in €1m.:

	1999	2000	2001	2002
Revenue	4,976	5,687	5,709	5,977
Expenditure	4,855	5,595	5,148	5,999

Public debt in 2002 was €640·11m.

VAT is 15%, with reduced rates of 6% and 3% (for books). According to government projections, the general government surplus was expected to be €14,930,500 in 2001. Income taxes and business taxes have been reduced to preserve competitiveness in the international environment. The normal tax rate for companies came down to 37·45% in 1998, compared with 40·3% in 1996.

Performance. In terms of GDP per head, Luxembourg is the richest country in the world, with a per capita PPP (purchasing power parity) GDP of €48,700 in 2001.

Real GDP growth was 6·0% in 1999, 8·9% in 2000 but only 1·0% in 2001. Total GDP in 2001 was US$19·8bn.

The OECD Economic Survey of 2001 reported: 'Luxembourg continues to build on a remarkable economic performance, maintaining high growth rates and low unemployment. Nevertheless, multi-factor productivity growth has slowed and labour market institutions expose the country to the risk of a large increase in structural unemployment if the leading industries were to be hit by an adverse shock.'

Banking and Finance. Luxembourg's Central Bank (formerly the Monetary Institute) was established in July 1998 (*Director-General*, Yves Mersch). In Nov. 2002 there were 179 banks. German banks make up nearly a third of all the banks. Total deposits in 1998 were €8,262·9m.; net assets in unit trusts, €482·1bn. (2001); net assets in investment companies, €441·5bn. (2001). There is a stock exchange.

In 2001 the financial sector accounted for 21·5% of gross added value at basic prices and the banks showed a net profit of €3·6bn. The total number of approved insurance companies in 2001 was 93, with reinsurance companies numbering 264; the amount of premiums due was €6,333·9m.

According to the OECD Economic Survey of 1999: 'Tax advantages in comparison with neighbouring countries, strict bank secrecy rules, a liberal regulatory environment and the rapid implementation of EU directives in Luxembourg law, combined with a favourable geographical location at the heart of Europe and a qualified and multilingual labour force, have been central in creating competitive advantages in financial services.'

Weights and Measures. The metric system is in force.

ENERGY AND NATURAL RESOURCES

Environment. According to the *World Bank Atlas* carbon dioxide emissions in 1998 were the equivalent of 18·0 tonnes per capita.

Electricity. Apart from hydro-electricity and electricity generated from fossil fuels, Luxembourg has no national energy resources. Installed capacity in 2001 was 1·6m. kW. Net electricity production was 1,592m. kWh in 2001 and consumption per capita was 13·4 kWh.

Minerals. The national steel industry mainly relies on imported ore. In 2001 production (in tonnes) of steel, 2,724,679; of pig-iron (1997), 438,030.

Agriculture. The contribution of agriculture, viticulture and forestry to the economy has been gradually declining over the years, accounting for only 0·6% of gross added value at basic prices in 2001. However, the actual output of this sector has nearly tripled during the past 30 years, a trend common to many EU countries. There were 5,289 workers engaged in agricultural work (including wine-growing and forestry) in 2001 (726 wage-earners), and 638 farms with an average area of 55·2 ha; 127,942 ha were under cultivation in 2001.

Production, 2001 (in tonnes) of main crops: grassland and pasturage, 450,761; forage crops, 247,858; maize, 129,272; bread crops, 58,825; potatoes, 22,770; colza (rape), 8,780. Production, 2001 (in 1,000 tonnes) of meat, 27·1; milk, 269·7. In 2001, 134,826 hectolitres of wine were produced. In 2001 there were 7,534 tractors, 706 harvester-threshers, 1,553 manure spreaders and 1,721 gatherer-presses.

Livestock (15 May 2001): 3,126 horses, 205,193 cattle, 78,540 pigs, 8,476 sheep.

Forestry. In 1999 there were 88,620 ha of forests, which in 2000 produced 191,716 cu. metres of broadleaved and 163,504 cu. metres of coniferous wood.

INDUSTRY

According to the Financial Times Survey (FT 500), the largest company by market capitalization in Luxembourg on 4 Jan. 2001 was SES (US$4,557·7m.), the global satellite communications company.

In 2001 there were 2,920 industrial enterprises, of which 1,888 were in the building industry. Production, 2001 (in tonnes): steel, 2,724,679; rolled steel products, 4,518,537. The world's largest steel producer, Arcelor, has its headquarters in Luxembourg. Created in Feb. 2002 through the merger of Arbed of Luxembourg, Aceralia of Spain and Usinor of France, it expects to produce in excess of 40m. tonnes of steel annually and to account for approximately 5% of world steel output.

Labour. In 2001 the estimated total workforce was 277,000. The government fixes a legal minimum wage. Retirement is at 65. Employment creation averaged 3·5% every year between 1985 and 2001, with a total increase in jobs of 58·1% over the period. In Jan. 2003 the standardized unemployment rate was 2·7%. Luxembourg has the lowest rate of unemployment of any EU member country. The OECD Economic Survey of 2001 reported: 'Buoyed by the strength in economic activity, domestic employment growth rose to record 5% in 1999. As usual, cross-border workers took most of the new jobs. Unemployment continued to edge down to less than 3%. Economic activity appears to have strengthened further this year. Again, growth has been very strong in the private services sectors, notably finance.'

Between 1989 and 1998 strikes cost Luxembourg an average of just six days per 1,000 employees a year (the second lowest in the European Union, with Austria having 4 per 1,000), compared to the EU average of 85 per 1,000.

There was a 5·8% increase in employment in 2001. Of the new jobs created, around two-thirds went to so-called *frontaliers,* workers living in surrounding countries who commute into Luxembourg to work. More than 100,000 people cross into Luxembourg every day from neighbouring France, Germany and Belgium to work, principally in the financial services industry.

Trade Unions. The main trade unions are the OGB-L (Socialist) and the LCGB (Christian-Social). Other sectorial unions include ALEBA (the banking sector), FNCTTFEL (railworkers), and FEP (private employers). In Oct. 1998 union representatives were elected in both the private and public sectors.

INTERNATIONAL TRADE
Luxembourg is in the process of turning itself into a centre for electronic commerce, the world's fastest-growing industry.

Imports and Exports. Exports in 2001 (provisional figures) totalled €9,081·9m. and imports €12,335·0m. In 2000, 84·2% of exports went to other EU member countries and 83·1% of imports were from other EU member countries.

Principal imports and exports by standard international trade classification (provisional figures) in €1m.:

	Exports		Imports	
	2000	2001	2000	2001
Food and live animals	318·6	382·0	735·2	826·0
Beverages and tobacco	262·1	230·0	420·0	398·6
Crude materials, oils, fats and waxes	100·1	101·8	599·1	665·9
Mineral fuels and lubricants	9·5	9·9	1,064·7	932·3
Chemicals and related products	558·9	576·7	1,110·0	1,244·5
Manufactured goods in metals	2,544·0	2,548·3	1,451·8	1,396·1
Other manufactured goods classified chiefly by material	1,354·7	1,440·1	802·6	934·2
Machinery	2,004·3	2,183·5	2,514·9	2,657·8
Transport equipment	349·6	390·1	1,760·2	1,876·6
Other manufactured goods	1,093·4	1,219·5	1,289·8	1,403·0
Total	8,595·2	9,081·9	11,748·3	12,335·0

Trade with selected countries (provisional figures) in €1m.:

	Exports		Imports	
	2000	2001	2000	2001
Austria	120·2	111·0	104·5	121·6
Belgium	1,103·2	1,114·9	4,193·2	4,232·8
France	1,766·2	1,781·4	1,458·4	1,574·8
Germany	2,060·9	2,233·1	2,870·6	3,099·5
Italy	470·8	565·6	224·1	210·3
Netherlands	461·3	407·4	559·0	630·4
Spain	249·5	273·7	92·3	117·1
UK	651·3	744·5	363·5	516·5
Total EU	7,249·8	7,688·4	10,042·5	10,698·9
Non-EU Europe	857·2	875·5	1,251·1	1,256·2
Japan	57·6	55·4	128·7	133·2

	Exports		Imports	
	2000	*2001*	*2000*	*2001*
NIEA[1]	199·4	188·3	235·3	252·2
USA	347·5	319·0	769·0	711·5
Total	8,595·2	9,081·9	11,748·3	12,335·0

[1]New industrialized economies of Asia (Singapore, South Korea, Taiwan, Indonesia, Malaysia and China).

Trade Fairs. The *Foires Internationales de Luxembourg* occurs twice a year, and there are a growing number of specialized fairs.

COMMUNICATIONS

Roads. On 1 Jan. 2002 there were 2,875 km of roads of which 126 km were motorways. Motor vehicles registered at 1 Jan. 2002 included 341,272 passenger cars, 21,730 trucks, 1,122 coaches and 11,945 motorcycles. In 2001 there were 774 road accidents with 70 fatalities.

Rail. In 2001 there were 274 km of railway (standard gauge) of which 261 km were electrified; 13·6m. passengers were carried.

Civil Aviation. Findel is the airport for Luxembourg. 1,625,323 passengers and 510,965 tonnes of freight were handled in 2001. The national carrier is Luxair, 23·1% state-owned. Cargolux has developed into one of the major international freight carriers. In 1999 scheduled airline traffic of Luxembourg-based carriers flew 57·1m. km, carrying 843,000 passengers (all on international flights).

Shipping. A shipping register was set up in 1990. In 2001 merchant shipping totalled 1,591,281 tonnes. 159 vessels were registered at 25 June 2002.

Telecommunications. Luxembourg had 346,763 main telephone lines in 2001, or 785 for every 1,000 population. There were 200,000 PCs in use in 2000 (453·2 per 1,000 persons), 209,000 mobile phones in 1999 and 25,000 fax machines in 2001. In Dec. 2000 Luxembourg had 100,000 Internet users.

Postal Services. In 2001 there were 108 post offices. In 2001 a total of 153·2m. items of mail were processed.

SOCIAL INSTITUTIONS

Justice. The Constitution makes the Courts of Law independent in performing their functions, restricting their sphere of activity, defining their limit of jurisdiction and providing a number of procedural guarantees. The Constitution has additionally laid down a number of provisions designed to ensure judges remain independent of persons under their jurisdiction, and to ensure no interference from the executive and legislative organs. All judges are appointed by Grand-Ducal order and are irremovable.

The judicial organization comprises three Justices of the Peace (conciliation and police courts). The country is, in addition, divided into two judicial districts—Luxembourg and Diekirch. District courts deal with matters such as civic and commercial cases. Offences which are punishable under the Penal Code or by specific laws with imprisonment or hard labour fall within the jurisdiction of the criminal chambers of District Courts, as the Assize Court was repealed by law in 1987. The High Court of Justice consists of a Supreme Court of Appeal and a Court of Appeal.

The judicial organization of the Grand-Duchy does not include the jury system. A division of votes between the judges on the issue of guilt/innocence may lead to acquittal. Society before the Courts of Law is represented by the Public Prosecutor Department, composed of members of the judiciary directly answerable to the government.

In 1999 a new Administrative Tribunal, Administrative Court and Constitutional Court were established.

The population in penal institutions in 2001 was 341.

Religion. The population is mostly Roman Catholic. There are small Protestant, Jewish, Greek, Russian Orthodox and Muslim communities as well.

Education. The adult literacy rate in 1998 was at least 99%. Education is compulsory for all children between the ages of 6 and 15. In 2000–01 there were

10,706 children in pre-primary school with 751 teachers; 31,218 pupils in primary schools; 31,278 pupils in secondary schools. In higher education (2001–02) the Higher Institute of Technology (IST) had 360 students and there were 394 students in teacher training. In 2001–02 the University Centre of Luxembourg had 1,778 students. Luxembourg does not have a full-time university, so many students have to go abroad, predominantly to France, Germany and Belgium. In 2000–01, 5,017 students pursued university studies abroad.

Health. In 2001 there were 1,140 doctors (389 GPs and 751 specialists) and 289 dentists. There were 19 hospitals and 3,035 hospital beds in 2000.

Welfare. In Luxembourg the social security system was built in several stages. It has been extended with regard to both the socio-professional categories and the risk groups covered. The law of 26 July 1986 introduced the minimum wage, a mechanism to guarantee private means. It consists of a supplementary benefit paid up to a set threshold determined according to the composition of the household. This benefit is awarded irrespective of the causes of the need.

Public contributions play a growing role in financing the system. In 1995 they accounted for 40% of the resources, with employees' and employers' contributions forming just over half. Around 50% of social security benefits goes towards pension schemes, and around 25% goes to health insurance. Nearly half the ordinary budget is absorbed by social security.

CULTURE

Broadcasting. The major broadcaster of TV and radio programmes is RTL Group, formerly CLT (*Compagnie Luxembourgeoise de Télédiffusion*), along with local and regional radio stations that have emerged since the 1991 Law on Electronic Media. CLT was set up in 1929 and started broadcasting in 1932. In the same year Radio Luxembourg started broadcasting its multilingual programmes. In 1954 CLT received an exclusive licence for broadcasting radio and TV in the Grand-Duchy, which was extended until the end of 2010 in 1995.

With 24 television and 14 radio stations in eight countries, RTL Group is Europe's largest TV, radio and production company. Listed on the London Stock Exchange, the Luxembourg-based media group operates TV channels and radio stations in Germany, France, Belgium, the Netherlands, UK, Luxembourg, Spain and Hungary. CLT-UFA S.A. also broadcast four TV channels and three radio stations via the ASTRA satellite system. The 1991 Law on Electronic Media allowed the creation of four new radio networks and 15 local radio stations, and thus ended the CLT monopoly.

The commercial *Radio-Télé-Luxembourg* broadcasts one programme in Lëtzebuergesch on FM. There are commercial and religious programmes in French, German, English, Italian, Portuguese and Spanish. More than 40 international TV programmes are broadcast by cable. The country's cable penetration is 90%, while satellite amounts to 15·5% and terrestrial to 2·5%. Luxembourg has over 150 local, independent cable networks and counts four major cable operators.

In 1997 there were 163,000 TV sets in use and 285,000 radio receivers. Satellite and cable TV is widespread (colour by SECAM V).

Cinema. In 2000 there were 25 cinema screens throughout the country. Cinema attendances in 2000 totalled 1,362,006.

Press. There were six daily newspapers in 2001 with a circulation of 162,934, equivalent to 369 per 1,000 inhabitants. There are a number of weekly titles with a circulation of 124,166.

Tourism. In 2001 there were 858,686 tourists, and 7,568 hotel rooms and 1,221,852 overnight stays. Tourists spent US$297m. in 1997. Camping is widespread, and weekend and short-stay tourism accounts for many tourists. There were 1,015,300 overnight stays at campsites in 2001.

Festivals. The Festival International Echternach (May–June) and the Festival of Wiltz (June–July) are annual events. Both feature a variety of classical music, jazz, theatre and recitals.

Libraries. In 1998 there were 33 libraries (excluding higher education libraries). There were 298,197 library loans in 1997.

Theatre and Opera. There are several theatres in Luxembourg City, including the *Grand Théâtre de la Ville*, *Théâtre des Capucins* and *Théâtre du Centaure*. There are also a number of smaller theatres elsewhere, notably in Esch/Alzette and Echternach.

Museums and Galleries. The main museums in Luxembourg City are the *Musée d'Histoire de la Ville*, the *Villa Vauban*, the *Musée National d'Histoire Naturelle* and the *Musée National d'Histoire et d'Art*. There are smaller museums in the rest of the country. In 2000 there were two national museums, 11 public museums and three private museums, which had 189,403 visitors.

DIPLOMATIC REPRESENTATIVES
Of Luxembourg in the United Kingdom (27 Wilton Crescent, London, SWIX 8SD)
Ambassador: Jean-Louis Wolzfeld.

Of the United Kingdom in Luxembourg (14 Blvd Roosevelt, L-2450 Luxembourg)
Ambassador: Gordon G. Wetherell.

Of Luxembourg in the USA (2200 Massachusetts Ave., NW, Washington, D.C., 20008)
Ambassador: Arlette Conzemius.

Of the USA in Luxembourg (22 Blvd. Emmanuel Servais, L-2535 Luxembourg)
Ambassador: Peter Terpeluk Jr.

Of Luxembourg to the United Nations
Ambassador: Hubert Wurth.

FURTHER READING
STATEC. *Annuaire Statistique 2002.*

Christophory, J. and Thoma, E., *Luxembourg.* [Bibliography] 2nd ed. ABC-Clio, Oxford and Santa Barbara (CA), 1997
Newcomer, J., *The Grand Duchy of Luxembourg: The Evolution of Nationhood, 963 AD to 1983.* 2nd ed. Editions Emile Borschette, Luxembourg, 1995

National Library: 37 Boulevard Roosevelt, Luxembourg City.
National statistical office: Service Central de la Statistique et des Etudes Economiques (STATEC), CP 304, Luxembourg City, L-2013 Luxembourg. *Director:* Serge Allegrezza. *Website:* http://www.statec.lu

MACEDONIA

Republika Makedonija
The Republic of Macedonia
(Former Yugoslav Republic of
Macedonia)

Capital: Skopje
Population estimate, 2000: 2·03m.
GDP per capita, 2000: (PPP$) 5,086
HDI/world rank: 0·772/65

KEY HISTORICAL EVENTS

The history of Macedonia can be traced to the reign of King Karan (808–778 BC), but the country was at its most powerful at the time of Philip II (359–336 BC) and Alexander the Great (336–323 BC). At the end of the 6th century AD Slavs began to settle in Macedonia. There followed a long period of internal fighting but the spread of Christianity led to consolidation and the creation of the first Macedonian Slav state, the Kingdom of Samuel, 976–1018. In the 14th century it fell to Serbia, and in 1355 to the Turks. After the Balkan wars of 1912–13 Turkey was ousted and Serbia received part of the territory, the rest going to Bulgaria and Greece. In 1918 Yugoslav Macedonia was incorporated into Serbia as South Serbia, becoming a republic in the Socialist Federal Republic of Yugoslavia. Claims to the historical Macedonian territory have long been a source of contention with Bulgaria and Greece. Macedonia declared its independence on 18 Sept. 1991. In April 1999 the Kosovo crisis which led to NATO air attacks on Yugoslavian military targets set off a flood of refugees into Macedonia, although most returned home after the end of the crisis.

In March 2001 there were a series of clashes between government forces and ethnic Albanian separatists near the border between Macedonia and Kosovo. As violence escalated Macedonia found itself on the brink of civil war. In May 2001 the new national unity government gave ethnic Albanian rebels a 'final warning' to end their uprising. As the crisis worsened, a stand-off within the government between the Macedonian and the ethnic Albanian parties was only resolved after the intervention of Javier Solana, the EU's foreign and security policy chief. A number of Macedonian soldiers were killed in clashes with the rebels, and following reverses in the military campaign the commander of the Macedonian army, Jovan Andrevski, resigned in June 2001. In Aug. 2001 a peace accord was negotiated.

TERRITORY AND POPULATION

Macedonia is bounded in the north by Serbia and Montenegro, in the east by Bulgaria, in the south by Greece and in the west by Albania. Its area is 25,713 sq. km. According to the 1994 census final results, the population on 20 June 1994 was 1,945,932. The ethnic groups were Macedonians (1,295,964), Albanians (441,104), Turks (78,019), Rhomas (43,707), Serbs (40,228), Vlachs (8,601). There were 36,427 others and 1,882 not stated. Ethnic Albanians predominate on the western side of Macedonia. Minorities are represented in the Council for Inter-Ethnic Relations. In Dec. 2000 the population estimate was 2·03m.; density, 79 per sq. km. In 1999, 61·6% of the population lived in urban areas.

The UN gives a projected population for 2010 of 2·07m.

The major cities (with 1994 census population) are: Skopje, the capital, 485,000 (in 1999); Bitola, 77,464; Kumanovo, 71,853; Prilep, 68,148; Tetovo, 50,344.

The official languages are Macedonian, which uses the Cyrillic alphabet, and Albanian.

SOCIAL STATISTICS

In 2000: births, 29,308; deaths, 17,253; marriages, 14,255; divorces, 1,325; infant deaths, 346. Rates (per 1,000 population): birth, 14·5; death, 8·5; marriage, 7·0; divorce, 0·6. Infant mortality, 2000 (per 1,000 live births), 11·8. Expectation of life at birth in 1998–2000 was 70·5 years for males and 74·8 years for females. Annual population growth rate, 1990–99, 0·6%. In 1998 the most popular age range for marrying was 20–24 for both males and females. Fertility rate, 2000, 1·9 births per woman.

Migration within the Republic of Macedonia, 2000: 12,419. International (external) migration: emigrated persons, 172; immigrated persons 1,199. Net migration in 2000 was 1,027.

CLIMATE
Macedonia has a mixed Mediterranean-continental type climate, with cold moist winters and hot dry summers. Skopje, Jan. –0·4°C, July 23·1°C.

CONSTITUTION AND GOVERNMENT
At a referendum held on 8 Sept. 1991 turn-out was 74%; 99% of votes cast were in favour of a sovereign Macedonia. On 17 Nov. 1991 parliament promulgated a new constitution which officially proclaimed Macedonia's independence. This was replaced by a constitution adopted on 16 Nov. 2001 which for the first time included the recognition of Albanian as an official language. It also increased access for ethnic Albanians to public-sector jobs.

The *President* is directly elected for five-year terms. Candidates must be citizens aged at least 40 years. The parliament is a 120-member single-chamber *Assembly* (*Sobranie*), elected by universal suffrage for four-year terms. There is a *Constitutional Court* whose members are elected by the assembly for non-renewable eight-year terms, and a *National Security Council* chaired by the President. Laws passed by the Assembly must be countersigned by the President, who may return them for reconsideration, but cannot veto them if they gain a two-thirds majority.

Political Parties. The Law on Political Parties makes a distinction between a political party and an association of citizens. The signatures of 500 citizens with the right to vote must be produced for a party to be legally registered. Presently the country has 34 legally registered parties.

National Anthem. 'Denes nad Makedonija se radja novo sonce na slobodata' ('Today a new sun of liberty appears over Macedonia'); words by V. Maleski, tune by T. Škalovski.

RECENT ELECTIONS
In the presidential election held between 31 Oct. and 5 Dec. 1999 Boris Trajkovski (Internal Macedonian Revolutionary Organization-Democratic Party for Macedonian National Unity) gained 52·9% of votes cast in the final run-off, against 45·9% for Tito Petkovski (Social Democratic League of Macedonia). This was despite having been behind after the previous round. Turn-out was 69·6%.

Parliamentary elections were held on 5 Sept. 2002. The Together for Macedonia coalition, comprising the Social Democratic League of Macedonia (SDSM) and the Liberal-Democratic Party (LDP), won 59 seats with 40·5% of votes cast, defeating Prime Minister Ljubčo Georgievski's Internal Macedonian Revolutionary Organization-Democratic Party for Macedonian National Unity (VMRO-DMPNE-LPM) with 34 seats and 24·4%. The Democratic Union for Integration (DUI) won 16 seats with 11·9%; the Democratic Party of Albanians (PDS), 7 with 5·2%; the Democratic Prosperity Party (PDP), 2 with 2·3%; the National-Democratic Party (NDP), 1 with 2·1%; and the Socialist Party of Macedonia (SPM), 1 with 2·1%. Turn-out was 73·5%.

CURRENT ADMINISTRATION
President: Boris Trajkovski; b. 1956 (VMRO-DPMNE; sworn in 15 Dec. 1999).

Prime Minister: Branko Crvenkovski; b. 1962 (SDSM; sworn in 1 Nov. 2002, having previously served as prime minister between 1992–98).

Following elections in Sept. 2002, a SDSM-LDP-DUI coalition government was formed, which in March 2003 was composed as follows:

Deputy Prime Minister and Minister of Finance: Petar Gosev (LDP). *Deputy Prime Ministers and Ministers Without Portfolio:* Radmila Sekerinska (SDSM); Musa Xhaferi (DUI).

Minister of Agriculture, Forestry and Water Supply: Slavko Petrov (LDP). *Culture:* Blagoja Stefanovski (SDSM). *Defence:* Vlado Buckovski (SDSM). *Economy:* Ilija

Filipovski (SDSM). *Education and Science:* Azis Polozani (DUI). *Environment and Urban Planning:* Ljubomir Janev (SDSM). *Foreign Affairs:* Ilinka Mitreva (SDSM). *Health:* Rexhep Selmani (DUI). *Interior:* Hari Kostov (SDSM). *Justice:* Ismail Dardhishta (DUI). *Labour and Social Policy:* Jovan Manasievski (LDP). *Local Self-Government:* Aleksandar Gestakovski (SDSM). *Transport and Communications:* Milaim Ajdini (DUI). *Minister Without Portfolio:* Vlado Popovski (LDP).

Government Website: http://www.gov.mk

DEFENCE

The President is the C.-in-C. of the armed forces. There is conscription for nine months. Army strength was estimated at 15,000 (8,000 conscripts) in 1999 with potential reserves of 102,000. The Air Force numbered under 700 (1999). There is a paramilitary police force of 7,500.

Defence expenditure in 2000 totalled US$76m. (US$37 per capita), representing 2·1% of GDP.

The European Union's first ever peacekeeping force (EUFOR) officially started work in Macedonia on 1 April 2003, replacing the NATO-led force that had been in the country since 2001.

INTERNATIONAL RELATIONS

On 13 Sept. 1995 under the auspices of the UN, Macedonia and Greece agreed to normalize their relations.

Macedonia is a member of the UN, BIS, the Council of Europe, OSCE, the Central European Initiative, the NATO Partnership for Peace and the International Organization of the Francophonie.

ECONOMY

Agriculture accounted for 11·4% of GDP in 1998, industry 28·3% and services 60·3%.

Overview. According to the Privatization Agency, 1,476 firms had been privatized by the end of June 1999. At the same time, 25 firms which had been experiencing heavy losses were obliged by law to embark on a re-structuring programme.

88·2% of companies are privately owned, 8·5% are publicly owned, 1·6% have mixed ownership, 1·5% are co-operatives and 0·2% are state owned.

By the end of Nov. 1998, 116,705 legal commercial entities were registered in the Institute of Statistics.

Currency. The national currency of Macedonia is the *denar* (MKD), of 100 *deni*.

Gold reserves were 196,000 troy oz in May 2002 and foreign exchange reserves US$825m. Inflation was 5·3% in 2001. Total money supply was 25,725m. denars in June 2002.

Budget. In 1997 revenue and expenditure balanced at 41,564m. denars.

Performance. In 2000 real GDP growth was 4·5%, but in 2001 the political turmoil in the country resulted in the economy contracting by 4·5%. Total GDP in 2001 was US$3·4bn.

Banking and Finance. The central bank and bank of issue is the National Bank of Macedonia. Its Governor is Dr Ljube Trpeski. As of 31 Dec. 1998 commercial banks' total non-government deposits were 23,136m. denars, and non-government savings deposits were 15,095m. denars. The largest banks are Stopanska Banka, followed by Komercijalna Banka; between them they control more than half the total assets of all banks in Macedonia.

A stock exchange opened in Skopje in 1996.

Weights and Measures. The metric system is in use.

ENERGY AND NATURAL RESOURCES

Environment. According to the *World Bank Atlas* Macedonia's carbon dioxide emissions were the equivalent of 6·1 tonnes per capita in 1998.

Electricity. Installed capacity in 1996 was 1·38m. kW. Output in 1998: 7,048,108 MWh, of which 1,082,944 MWh were from hydro-electric plants. Consumption per capita was an estimated 3,372 kWh in 1997.

Oil and Gas. A 230-km long pipeline is under construction at a cost of over US$100m. to bring crude oil to Macedonia from Thessaloniki in Greece. When completed it will have the capacity to provide Macedonia with 2·5m. tonnes of crude oil annually.

Minerals. Macedonia is relatively rich in minerals, including lead, zinc, copper, iron, chromium, nickel, antimony, manganese, silver and gold. Output in 2001 (in tonnes): lignite, 8,056,661; copper ore 2,650,000; lead-zinc ore 571,802; lead-zinc concentrates 53,981; copper concentrate 25,012; chromium concentrate 1,535 (1997); refined silver 23.

Agriculture. At the 1994 census the active agricultural population was 91,354. In 2001 there were 611,982 ha of arable land and 629,825 ha of pasture. 152,887 ha of arable land were owned by agricultural organizations, and 459,095 ha by individual farmers.

Crop production, 2001 (in 1,000 tonnes): wheat, 246; grapes, 230; potatoes, 176; watermelons, 130; tomatoes, 126; wine, 119; maize, 117; peppers, 112; lucerne, 104; barley, 92; cabbages, 75; apples, 38; sugarbeets, 38; onions, 31; cucumbers and gherkins, 29; tobacco, 23; plums, 13.

Livestock, 2001 (in 1,000): cattle, 265; sheep, 1,285; pigs, 189; horses, 46; chickens, 2,750. Livestock products, 2001 (in 1,000 tonnes): pork, bacon and ham, 8; beef, 6; mutton, 6; poultry, 5; cow's milk, 248m. litres; sheep's milk, 47m. litres; eggs (total), 395m.

There were 63,280 tractors in use in 2001.

Forestry. Forests covered 997,374 ha in 2001, chiefly oak and beech. 792,000 cu. metres of timber were cut in 2001.

Fisheries. Total catch in 2001 was 1,135 tonnes, entirely from inland waters.

INDUSTRY

In 1999 there were 94,404 enterprises (90,426 private, 1,112 public, 1,257 co-operative, 1,577 mixed and 32 state-owned). 2001 production (in tonnes): sulphuric acid, 101,058; ferro-alloys, 27,287; detergents, 19,248; cotton yarn, 2,389; medicines, 965. 1997: 4,582 refrigerators.

Labour. At the 1994 census the population of working age was 1,247,481. In 1995, 22·9% of the labour force worked in mining and manufacturing, 11·6% in services, 9·0% in agriculture and 5·7% in trade, with 36·2% unemployed. The economically active population in 2002 was 824,824 and the number of unemployed persons 263,483.

INTERNATIONAL TRADE

The foreign debt of Macedonia, including debt taken over from the former Yugoslavia, was US$1,465m. in 2000.

Imports and Exports. In 2000 imports (f.o.b.) were valued at US$1,875·2m. (US$1,602·2m. in 1999) and exports (f.o.b.) at US$1,317·1m. (US$1,192·1m. in 1999).

Main export markets, 2000: Yugoslavia (25·3%), Germany (19·4%), USA (12·6%), Italy (6·6%), Greece (6·4%). Main import suppliers, 2000: Germany (12·1%), Ukraine (9·9%), Greece (9·6%), Russia (9·2%) and Yugoslavia (9·1%).

COMMUNICATIONS

Roads. In 2001 there were 937 km of main roads, 3,643 km of regional roads and 8,347 km of local roads: 1,176 km of roads were paved and 6,710 km asphalted. 13·7m. passengers and 6·7m. tonnes of freight were transported. There were 309,562 cars, 2,620 buses and 21,727 lorries in 2001.

Rail. In 2001 there were 697 km of railways (233 km electrified). 1·3m. passengers and 2·8m. tonnes of freight were transported.

Civil Aviation. There are international airports at Skopje and Ohrid. There are two Macedonia-based carriers—Interimpex-Avioimpex, which flew 3·3m. km and carried 215,400 passengers in 1999, and the smaller Macedonian Airlines. In 2000 Skopje handled 864,155 passengers (all on international flights) and 3,046 tonnes of freight. Ohrid handled 63,255 passengers (all on international flights) and 65 tonnes of freight.

Telecommunications. In 2001 there were 539,000 main telephone lines (264·9 per 1,000 inhabitants), 138,000 mobile phone subscribers and, in 1999, 3,000 fax machines. In Dec. 2000 there were 100,000 Internet users. In Dec. 2000 the Hungarian firm Matav acquired a 51% stake in MakTel, the state monopoly telecommunications provider, in the most significant economic development in the country's history. The deal, worth €618·2m. (US$568·4m.) over two years, is the biggest foreign investment to date.

Postal Services. In 2001 there were 312 post offices.

SOCIAL INSTITUTIONS

Justice. Courts are autonomous and independent. Judges are tenured and elected for life on the proposal of the *Judicial Council*, whose members are themselves elected for renewable six-year terms. The highest court is the Supreme Court. There are 27 courts of first instance and three higher courts.

The population in penal institutions in Sept. 1997 was 965 (50 per 100,000 of national population).

Religion. Macedonia is traditionally Orthodox but the church is not established and there is freedom of religion. At the 1994 census 66·3% of the population were Orthodox, 30·0% Muslim and 0·4% Roman Catholic. In 1967 an autocephalous Orthodox church split off from the Serbian. Its head is the Archbishop of Ohrid and Macedonia whose seat is at Skopje. It has five bishoprics in Macedonia and representatives in USA, Canada and Australia. It has some 300 priests.

The Muslim Religious Union has a superiorate at Skopje. The Roman Catholic Church has a seat at Skopje.

Education. Adult literacy was 94·6% in 1998. Education is free and compulsory for eight years. In 2001, 36,502 children attended 52 pre-school institutions and 438 infant schools of elementary education. In 2001–02 there were 244,740 pupils enrolled in 1,007 primary, 92,554 in 95 secondary and 1,123 in higher schools, and 343,587 students in higher education. There are universities at Skopje (Cyril and Methodius, founded in 1949; 35,812 students and 1,350 academic staff in 2001–02) and Bitola (founded 1979; 8,898 students and 211 academic staff in 2001–02).

In 1996 total expenditure on education came to 5·6% of GNP and represented 20·0% of total government expenditure.

Health. In 1998 there were 4,501 doctors, 1,144 dentists, 329 pharmacologists, and 58 hospitals with 10,311 beds. In the villages there were 330 medical units.

Welfare. In 2001 social assistance was paid to 80,334 households. Child care and special supplements went to 63,205 children, and 15,909 underage and 78,298 adults received social benefits. There were 241,221 pensioners in 1998.

CULTURE

Broadcasting. The national Macedonian Radio and Television (colour by PAL) is government-funded. It broadcasts on three TV and six radio channels. In 2001 there were also 28 local public broadcasting enterprises (state-owned), 18 of which transmitted only radio programmes while the other 10 transmitted radio and TV programmes. In 2001 there were 50 private radio and 42 private TV stations. In 1997 there were 510,000 TV subscribers and 410,000 radio receivers.

Cinema. There were 26 cinemas and 426,666 admissions in 2001; gross box office receipts came to 29m. denars. Two full-length films were made in 1995.

Press. There were eight daily newspapers and 11 weeklies in 2001, and 117 other newspapers and periodicals published in Macedonian, Albanian, Turkish, English and other languages.

There are two news agencies in Macedonia, the Macedonian Information Agency (national) and Makfax (privately owned).

Tourism. In 2000 tourists numbered 632,523 spending 2·43m. nights in Macedonia.

DIPLOMATIC REPRESENTATIVES

Of Macedonia in the United Kingdom (5th floor, 25 James Street, London, W1U 1DU).
Ambassador: Stevo Crvenkovski.

Of the United Kingdom in Macedonia (Dimitrija Chupovski 26, 1000 Skopje)
Ambassador: George Edgar.

Of Macedonia in the USA (1101 30th Street, NW, Suite 302, Washington, D.C., 20007)
Ambassador: Nikola Dimitrov.

Of the USA in Macedonia (Bd. Ilinden, 1000 Skopje)
Ambassador: Lawrence E. Butler.

Of Macedonia to the United Nations
Ambassador: Srgjan Kerim.

Of Macedonia to the European Union
Ambassador: Sasko Stefkov.

FURTHER READING

Danforth, L. M., *The Macedonian Conflict: Ethnic Nationalism in a Transnational World.* Princeton Univ. Press, 1996
Poulton, H., *Who Are the Macedonians?* Farnborough, 1996

National statistical office: State Statistical Office, Dame Gruev 4, Skopje. *Director:* Blagica Novkovska.
Website: http://www.stat.gov.mk

MADAGASCAR

Repoblikan'i
Madagasikara

Capital: Antananarivo
Population estimate, 2000: 15·97m.
GDP per capita, 2000: (PPP$) 840
HDI/world rank: 0·469/147

KEY HISTORICAL EVENTS

The island was settled by people of African and Indonesian origin when it was visited by the Portuguese explorer, Diego Diaz, in 1500. The island was unified under the Imérina monarchy between 1797 and 1861, but a French protectorate was established in 1895. Madagascar became a French colony on 6 Aug. 1896 and achieved independence on 26 June 1960.

In Feb. 1975 Col. Richard Ratsimandrava, Head of State, was assassinated. The 1975 Constitution instituted a 'Democratic Republic' in which only a single political party was permitted.

After six months of anti-government unrest an 18-month transitional administration was agreed. A new Constitution instituted the Third Republic in Sept. 1992.

Following the presidential election of Dec. 2001 the opposition candidate Marc Ravalomanana claimed victory, although the High Constitutional Court ruled that a run-off was needed. On 22 Feb. 2002 Ravalomanana declared himself president and imposed a state of emergency. However, incumbent Didier Ratsiraka and his government set up a rival capital in Toamasina. In April 2002 both men agreed to a recount of votes to solve the dispute. Ravalomanana was declared president following the recount.

TERRITORY AND POPULATION

Madagascar is situated 400 km (250 miles) off the southeast coast of Africa, from which it is separated by the Mozambique channel. Its area is 587,041 sq. km (226,658 sq. miles). At the 1993 census the population was 12,092,157 (50·45% female); density, 20·6 per sq. km. Estimate (1997), 14,062,000 (71·0% rural, 1999). Population density, 24·0 per sq. km.

The UN gives a projected population for 2010 of 21·10m.

Province	Area in Sq. km	Population (1993 census)	Chief town	Population (1993 census)
Antananarivo	58,283	3,483,236	Antananarivo	1,432,000[1]
Antsiranana	43,046	942,410	Antsiranana	54,418[2]
Fianarantsoa	102,373	2,671,150	Fianarantsoa	99,005
Mahajanga	150,023	1,330,612	Mahajanga	100,807
Toamasina	71,911	1,935,330	Toamasina	127,441
Toliary	161,405	1,729,419	Toliary	61,460[2]

[1]1999 figure. [2]1990 estimate.

The indigenous population is of Malayo-Polynesian stock, divided into 18 ethnic groups of which the principal are Merina (26%) of the central plateau, the Betsimisaraka (15%) of the east coast, and the Betsileo (12%) of the southern plateau. Foreign communities include Europeans, mainly French (30,000), Indians (15,000), Chinese (9,000), Comorians and Arabs.

The official language is Malagasy. French is the language of international communication.

SOCIAL STATISTICS

1997 estimated births, 595,000; deaths, 198,000. Rates, 1997 estimates (per 1,000 population): births, 42·3; deaths, 14·1. Infant mortality, 1999 (per 1,000 live births), 95. Expectation of life in 1999 was 51·1 years for males and 53·4 for females. Annual population growth rate, 1990–99, 3·2%. Fertility rate, 1999, 5·3 births per woman.

CLIMATE

A tropical climate, but the mountains cause big variations in rainfall, which is very heavy in the east and very light in the west. Antananarivo, Jan. 70°F (21·1°C), July

59°F (15°C). Annual rainfall 54" (1,350 mm). Toamasina, Jan. 80°F (26·7°C), July 70°F (21·1°C). Annual rainfall 128" (3,256 mm).

CONSTITUTION AND GOVERNMENT
Following a referendum, a Constitution came into force on 30 Dec. 1975 establishing a Democratic Republic. It provided for a National People's Assembly elected by universal suffrage from the single list of the *Front National pour la Défense de la Révolution Socialiste Malgache*. Executive power was vested in the President with the guidance of a Supreme Revolutionary Council.

Under a convention of 31 Oct. 1991 the powers of the National People's Assembly and the Supreme Revolutionary Council were delegated to a High State Authority for a Provisional government. Following a referendum on 19 Aug. 1992 at which turn-out was 77·68% and 75·44% of votes cast were in favour, a new Constitution was adopted on 21 Sept. 1992 establishing the Third Republic. Under this the *National Assembly* has 160 seats (increased from 150 for the 2002 election). There is also a *Senate* of 90 members.

A referendum on 17 Sept. 1995 was in favour of the President appointing and dismissing the Prime Minister, hitherto elected by parliament. The electorate was 6m.; turn-out was 50%.

National Anthem. 'Ry tanindrazanay malala ô!' ('O our beloved Fatherland'); words by Pastor Rahajason, tune by N. Raharisoa.

RECENT ELECTIONS
At the first round of presidential elections on 16 Dec. 2001 there were six candidates. Turn-out was 66·7%. Official results gave Marc Ravalomanana 46·2% of votes cast against 40·9% for Didier Ratsiraka, forcing the two men into a run-off, but Marc Ravalomanana himself claimed to have won the election outright. Ravalomanana declared himself president on 24 Feb. 2002 but with Ratsiraka refusing to accept defeat there were effectively two presidents. On 18 April 2002 the two men signed a deal designed to end the bitter power struggle. Following the announcement by the Supreme Court of a recount of the votes cast in the presidential election, the two candidates agreed that in the event of neither obtaining a majority, a referendum would be held to settle the issue. In the recount the High Constitutional Court declared Marc Ravalomanana the winner with 51·5% of votes against 35·9% for Didier Ratsiraka, with others obtaining 12·6% between them, although the result was not recognized by Ratsiraka. On 6 May 2002 Marc Ravalomanana was sworn in as president. In protest, four of Madagascar's six provinces declared independence. In June 2002 US President George W. Bush gave formal recognition of Ravalomanana's claim to the presidency. On 5 July 2002 Ratsiraka left Madagascar for the Seychelles amidst warnings of arrest from Ravalomanana's government.

In parliamentary elections held on 15 Dec. 2002 President Marc Ravalomanana's I Love Madagascar party won 103 of the 160 seats, his allies within the National Unity coalition 22, ind. also 22 and minor parties 13. Turn-out was 67·6%.

CURRENT ADMINISTRATION
President: Marc Ravalomanana; b. 1949 (ind., sworn in 6 May 2002).

In March 2003 the cabinet was composed as follows:

Prime Minister: Jacques Sylla; b. 1946 (ind.).

Minister of Foreign Affairs: Gen. Marcel Ranjeva. *Interior:* Jean Seth Rambeloarijaona. *Defence:* Jules Mamizara. *Agriculture:* Yvan Andriasandratriniony. *Civil Service, Labour and Social Laws:* Dr Vola Dieudonne. *Commerce and Consumer Affairs:* Alphonse Ralison. *Communications:* Mamy Rakotoarivelo. *Culture:* Odette Rahaingosoa. *Economy, Planning, Finance and Budget:* Andriamparany Radavidson. *Energy and Mines:* Elise Alitera Razaka. *Environment:* Gen. Charles Sylvain Rabotoarison. *Health:* Andry Rasamindrakotroka. *Higher Education:* Jean Theodore Ranjivason. *Industry and Handicrafts:* David Rajaona. *Justice:* Alice Rajaonah. *Labour and Social Affairs:* Maharavo Rodelys. *Population:* Jacob Felicien Andriampanjava. *Posts and Telecommunications:* Haja Nirina Razafinjatovo. *Primary and Secondary Education:* Michel Razafindrandriatsimaniry. *Public Works:* Jean Lahiniriko. *Public*

Security: Gen. Amady Augustin. *Scientific Research:* Alidina Edouard. *Technical and Vocational Training:* Zoana Blaise. *Tourism:* Ntsay Christian. *Transport and Meteorology:* Olivier Rakotovazaha. *Urban and Regional Planning:* Julien Reboza. *Waters and Forests:* Alibay Jonshon Oneste. *Youth and Sports:* Ndalana Rene.

Government Website (French only): http://www.madagascar.gov.mg/

DEFENCE
There is conscription (including civilian labour service) for 18 months. Defence expenditure totalled US$41m. in 2000 (US$3 per capita), representing 0·8% of GDP.

Army. Strength (1999) 20,000 and gendarmerie 7,500.

Navy. In 1999 the maritime force had a strength of 500 (including 100 marines).

Air Force. Personnel (1999) 500. The 12 combat aircraft are grounded.

INTERNATIONAL RELATIONS
Madagascar is a member of the UN, WTO, the African Union, African Development Bank, COMESA, IOM, the International Organization of the Francophonie and is an ACP member state of the ACP-EU relationship.

ECONOMY
In 1998 services contributed 55·8% of GDP, agriculture 30·6% and industry 13·8%.

Currency. The unit of currency is the *Malagasy franc* (MGFr). 1 *ariary* = MGFr5. In June 2002 foreign exchange reserves were US$393m. Inflation in 2001 was 5·0%. Total money supply in May 2002 was MGFr5,265·55bn.

Budget. Budget revenue and expenditure (in MGFr1bn.), year ending 31 Dec.:

	1997	1998	1999	2000
Revenue	1,746·8	2,077·0	2,666·8	3,067·8
Expenditure	2,879·4	3,477·5	4,068·8	4,477·7

Performance. Total GDP in 2001 was US$4·6bn. Real GDP growth was 6·7% in 2001 (4·8% in 2000).

Banking and Finance. A Central Bank, the *Banque Centrale de Madagascar*, was formed in 1973, replacing the former *Institut d'Emission Malgache* as the central bank of issue. The *Governor* is Gaston Ravelojaona. All commercial banking and insurance was nationalized in 1975 and privatized in 1988. Of the six other banks, the largest are the *Bankin'ny Tantsaha Mpamokatra* and the *BNI—Crédit Lyonnais de Madagascar.*

Weights and Measures. The metric system is in use.

ENERGY AND NATURAL RESOURCES
Environment. According to the *World Bank Atlas* Madagascar's carbon dioxide emissions in 1998 were the equivalent of 0·1 tonnes per capita.

Electricity. Installed capacity was 208,000 kW in 1991. Production in 1998 was 750m. kWh, with consumption per capita in 1997 being 44 kWh.

Oil and Gas. Annual crude oil production is 37,000 tonnes. Natural gas production is 2,500 tonnes per annum; reserves (1997), 2bn. cu. metres.

Minerals. Mining production in 1995 included: salt, 80,000 tonnes; chromite, 74,000 tonnes; graphite, 13,900 tonnes. There have also been discoveries of precious and semi-precious stones in various parts of the country, in particular sapphires, topaz and garnets.

Agriculture. 75–80% of the workforce is employed in agriculture. There were 2·57m. ha of arable land in 1998 and 0·54m. ha of permanent crops. The principal agricultural products in 2000 were (in 1,000 tonnes): rice, 2,300; cassava, 2,228; sugarcane, 2,200; sweet potatoes, 476; potatoes, 293; bananas, 260; mangoes, 204; taro, 155; maize, 150; coconuts, 84; dry beans, 84; oranges, 83. Rice is produced on some 40% of cultivated land.

Cattle breeding and agriculture are the chief occupations. There were, in 2000, 10·36m. cattle, 1·37m. goats, 900,000 pigs, 800,000 sheep and 20m. chickens.

Forestry. In 1995 the area under forests was 15·11m. ha, or 26% of the total land area (27·1% in 1990). The forests contain many valuable woods, while gum, resins and plants for tanning, dyeing and medicinal purposes abound. Timber production was 10·36m. cu. metres in 1999.

Fisheries. In 1989 the fishing fleet numbered 44 vessels over 100 GRT totalling 6,852 GRT. The catch of fish in 1999 was 131,571 tonnes (77% from marine waters).

INDUSTRY

Industry, hitherto confined mainly to the processing of agricultural products, is now extending to cover other fields.

Labour. In 1996 the workforce was 7,199,000 (55% males). In 1995 approximately 75% of the economically active population were engaged in agriculture, fisheries and forestry.

INTERNATIONAL TRADE

Foreign debt was US$4,701m. in 2000.

Imports and Exports. In 2000 imports (f.o.b.) were valued at US$997m. (US$742m. in 1999) and exports (f.o.b.) at US$824m. (US$584m. in 1999). The principal exports in 1995 were coffee (45%), vanilla (20%), plus cloves, shellfish (especially prawns), sugar and petroleum products. Principal imports in 1995 were intermediate manufactures (30%), capital goods (28%), plus petroleum products, consumer goods and foodstuffs. Main import suppliers, 1995: France, 29·7%; Germany, 10·1%; Iran, 10·1%; Southern African Customs Union, 6·3%. Main export markets, 1995: France, 28·4%; Germany, 8·3%; USA, 6·6%; Japan, 6·2%.

COMMUNICATIONS

Roads. In 1998 there were 30,623 km of roads, including 8,528 km of national highways. There were 60,480 passenger cars in 1996, 37,972 trucks and vans and 4,850 buses and coaches. 25 people died in road accidents in 1995.

Rail. In 1994 there were 883 km of railways, all metre gauge. In 1994, 0·6m. passengers and 0·3m. tonnes of freight were transported.

Civil Aviation. There are international airports at Antananarivo (Ivato) and Mahajanga (Amborovy). The national carrier is Air Madagascar, which is 89·5% state-owned. In 1999 it flew 8·7m. km, carrying 317,600 passengers (144,800 on international flights). In 2000 Antananarivo handled 689,210 passengers (350,030 on domestic flights) and 14,914 tonnes of freight. In 1997 scheduled airline traffic of Madagascar-based carriers flew 8·9m. km, carrying 575,000 passengers (131,000 on international flights).

Shipping. In 1989, 760,100 tonnes were loaded and 1,062,900 tonnes unloaded at Toamasina, Mahajanga, Antsiranana and Nosy-Be. In 1998 the merchant marine totalled 42,000 GRT, including oil tankers 11,000 GRT.

Telecommunications. Madagascar had 55,000 main telephone lines in 2000, equivalent to 3·4 per 1,000 persons. In 1997 there were 4,000 mobile phone subscribers and 35,000 PCs were in use in 2000 (2·2 per 1,000 persons). In Dec. 2000 there were 30,000 Internet users.

Postal Services. There are 724 post offices and agencies.

SOCIAL INSTITUTIONS

Justice. The Supreme Court and the Court of Appeal are in Antananarivo. In most towns there are Courts of First Instance for civil and commercial cases. For criminal cases there are ordinary criminal courts in most towns. In 1996 government expenditure on public order and safety totalled MGFr59,200m.

The population in penal institutions in 1997 was 19,743 (125 per 100,000 of national population).

Religion. About 50% of the population practise the traditional religion, 43% are Christians (of whom approximately half are Roman Catholic and half are Protestant, mainly belonging to the Fiangonan'i Jesosy Kristy eto Madagasikara) and 7% Muslim.

Education. Education is compulsory from 6 to 14 years of age. In 1995–96 there were 13,325 primary schools with 44,145 teachers for 1·6m. pupils, 302,035 pupils at secondary level with 16,795 teachers and (1993) 42,681 students at university level. In 1994–95 there were six universities. In 1996 government expenditure on education totalled MGFr255,500m. Adult literacy rate in 1999 was 65·7% (male, 72·8%; female, 58·8%).

Health. In 1990 there were 1,392 doctors, 89 dentists, 3,124 nurses, 19 pharmacists and 1,703 midwives; provision of hospital beds was 9 per 10,000 population. In 1996 government expenditure on health totalled MGFr191,300m.

Welfare. In 1996 government expenditure on social security and welfare totalled MGFr26,000m.

CULTURE

Broadcasting. The government-controlled Radio-Television Malagasy is responsible for broadcasting. There are radio programmes in Malagasy and French, and three–four hours TV transmission a day (colour by PAL). In 1997 there were 3·05m. radio and 325,000 TV sets.

Press. In 1996 there were five daily newspapers with a total circulation of 66,000.

Tourism. There were an estimated 138,000 tourists in 1999. Receipts totalled US$100m.

DIPLOMATIC REPRESENTATIVES
Of Madagascar in the United Kingdom
Ambassador: Vacant.
Chargé d'Affaires a.i.: Maxime Eloi Dovo (resides at Paris).
Honorary Consul: Stephen Hobbs (16 Lanark Mansions, Pennard Rd, London, W12 8DT).

Of the United Kingdom in Madagascar (First Floor, Immeuble 'Ny Havana', Cite de 67 Ha, BP167, Antananarivo)
Ambassador: Brian Donaldson.

Of Madagascar in the USA (2374 Massachusetts Ave., NW, Washington, D.C., 20008)
Ambassador: Vacant.

Of the USA in Madagascar (14–16 rue Rainitovo, Antsahavola, Antananarivo)
Ambassador: Wanda L. Nesbitt.

Of Madagascar to the United Nations
Ambassador: Zina Andrianarivelo.

Of Madagascar to the European Union
Ambassador: Jean Beriziky.

FURTHER READING
Banque des Données de l'Etat. *Bulletin Mensuel de Statistique*
Allen, P. M., *Madagascar.* Boulder (CO), 1995
Brandt, H. and Brown, M., *Madagascar.* [Bibliography] ABC-Clio, Oxford and Santa Barbara (CA), 1993

National statistical office: Banque des Données de l'Etat, Antananarivo.

MALAŴI

Dziko la Malaŵi
(Republic of Malaŵi)

Capital: Lilongwe
Population estimate, 2000: 11·31m.
GDP per capita, 2000: (PPP$) 615
HDI/world rank: 0·400/163

KEY HISTORICAL EVENTS

The explorer David Livingstone reached Lake Nyasa, now Lake Malaŵi, in 1859 and it was the land along the lake's western shore that became, in 1891, the British Protectorate of Nyasaland. In 1884 the British South Africa Company applied for a charter to trade. Pressure on land, the colour bar and other grievances generated Malaŵian resistance. In 1953 Nyasaland was joined with Southern Rhodesia (Zimbabwe) and Northern Rhodesia (Zambia) to form the Federation of Rhodesia and Nyasaland, under British control. This union was dissolved in 1963 when Nyasaland was for a year self-governing, until on 6 July 1964 it became independent, adopting the name of Malaŵi. In 1966 Malaŵi was declared a republic and Dr Hastings Banda became the first president, establishing a one party dictatorship which lasted for 30 years. In 1994 Malaŵi returned to multi-party democracy.

TERRITORY AND POPULATION

Malaŵi lies along the southern and western shores of Lake Malaŵi (the third largest lake in Africa), and is otherwise bounded in the north by Tanzania, south by Mozambique and west by Zambia. Area (including the inland water areas of Lake Malombe, Chilwa, Chiuta and the Malaŵi portion of Lake Malaŵi, which total 24,208 sq. km), 118,484 sq. km (45,747 sq. miles).

Population at census 1998, 9,933,868; density, 83·8 per sq. km. In 1999, 76·5% of the population was rural.

The UN gives a projected population for 2010 of 14·02m.

Population of main towns (estimated 1998): Blantyre, 2m.; Lilongwe, 1m.; Mzuzu, 100,000; Zomba, 70,000. Population of the regions (1998 census): Northern, 1,233,560; Central, 4,066,340; Southern, 4,633,968.

The official languages are Chichewa, spoken by over 50% of the population, and English.

SOCIAL STATISTICS

1998 births, 537,000; deaths, 243,000. The birth rate in 1998 was 50·2 per 1,000 population and the death rate 22·7. Annual population growth rate, 1990–99, 1·5%. Expectation of life at birth in 2000 was 46 years. Infant mortality, 1999, 132 per 1,000 live births; fertility rate, 1999, 6·6 births per woman.

CLIMATE

The tropical climate is marked by a dry season from May to Oct. and a wet season for the remaining months. Rainfall amounts are variable, within the range of 29–100" (725–2,500 mm), and maximum temperatures average 75–89°F (24–32°C), and minimum temperatures 58–67°F (14·4–19·4°C). Lilongwe, Jan. 73°F (22·8°C), July 60°F (15·6°C). Annual rainfall 36" (900 mm). Blantyre, Jan. 75°F (23·9°C), July 63°F (17·2°C). Annual rainfall 45" (1,125 mm). Zomba, Jan. 73°F (22·8°C), July 63°F (17·2°C). Annual rainfall 54" (1,344 mm).

CONSTITUTION AND GOVERNMENT

The *President* is also head of government. Malaŵi was a one-party state, but following a referendum on 14 June 1993, in which 63% of votes cast were in favour of reform, a new Constitution was adopted on 17 May 1994 which ended Hastings Banda's life presidency and provided for the holding of multi-party elections. At these Bakili Muluzi was elected President by 47·16% of votes cast against President Banda and two other opponents.

National Anthem. 'O God Bless our Land of Malaŵi'; words and tune by M.-F. Sauka.

RECENT ELECTIONS

Parliament is composed of 193 members. At the elections of 15 June 1999 the United Democratic Front (UDF) won 93 seats (47·3% of the vote); the Malaŵi Congress Party (MCP—the former single party), 66 (33·8%); and the Alliance for Democracy (AFORD), 29 (10·6%). Independents took 4 seats.

At the presidential elections of 15 June 1999 Bakili Muluzi (UDF) won with 52·4% of the vote, ahead of Gwanda Chakuamba (MCP/AFORD) with 45·2% and Kampelo Kalua (Malaŵi Democratic Party) with 1·4%.

CURRENT ADMINISTRATION

President: Dr Bakili Muluzi; b. 1943 (UDF; sworn in 21 May 1994 and re-elected in 1999).

In Nov. 2000 the President dismissed the entire cabinet after it was revealed that aid money had been used to buy Mercedes-Benz limousines for government officials. In April 2003 he again dismissed the entire cabinet, two days after naming a little-known politician as his successor. He subsequently appointed a new cabinet consisting of members of the ruling United Democratic Front and the opposition Alliance for Democracy. The cabinet comprised:

Vice President and Minister of Privatization: Justin Malewezi. *Second Vice President and Minister of Agriculture, Irrigation and Water Safety:* Chakufwa Chihana.

Minister of Commerce and Industry: Sam Mpasu. *Defence:* Rodwell Munyenyembe. *Economic Planning and Development:* Bingu Wa Mutharika. *Education, Science and Technology:* Dr George Mtafu. *Finance:* Friday Jumbe. *Foreign Affairs and International Co-operation:* Lilian Patel. *Gender and Community Services:* Alice Sumani. *Health and Population:* Yusuf Mwawa. *Housing:* Kaliyoma Phumisa. *Information:* Bernard Chisale. *Internal Affairs and Security:* Monjeza Maluza. *Justice:* Paul Maulidi. *Labour and Vocational Training:* Lee Mlanga. *Lands, Physical Planning and Surveys:* Thengo Maloya. *Natural Resources and Environmental Affairs:* Uladi Mussa. *Sports, Youth and Culture:* Henderson Mabeti. *Tourism, Parks and Wildlife:* Wallace Chiume. *Transport and Public Works:* Clement Stambuli. *Water Development:* Dumbo 'Cowboy' Lemani. *Minister Without Portfolio:* Chipimpha Mughogho. Dumbo Lemani, who entered the cabinet in Nov. 2001, is nicknamed 'Cowboy' for drawing a gun in parliament to threaten opposition MPs.

Government Website (French only): http://www.malawi.gov.mw/

DEFENCE

All services form part of the Army. Defence expenditure totalled US$26m. in 2000 (US$2 per capita), representing 1·8% of GDP.

Army. Personnel (1999) 5,000. In addition there is a paramilitary mobile police force totalling 1,000.

Navy. The Navy, based at Monkey Bay on Lake Nyasa, numbered 220 personnel in 1999.

Air Wing. The Air Wing acts as infantry support and numbered 80 in 1999 with no combat aircraft.

INTERNATIONAL RELATIONS

Malaŵi is a member of the UN, WTO, the Commonwealth, African Development Bank, COMESA (the Common Market for Eastern and Southern Africa), the African Union and SADC and is an ACP member state of the ACP-EU relationship.

ECONOMY

Agriculture accounted for 35·9% of GDP in 1998, industry 17·8% and services 46·4%.

Overview. The government operates a three-year 'rolling' public-sector investment programme, revised annually to take into account changing needs and the expected level of resources available. The greatest part of the development programme is financed from external aid. Some 200 state enterprises are marked down for privatization.

Currency. The unit of currency is the *kwacha* (MWK) of 100 *tambala*. Foreign exchange reserves were US$178m. and gold reserves 10,000 troy oz in May 2002. Foreign exchange controls were abolished in Feb. 1994. Inflation has fallen from 83·1% in 1995 to 27·2% in 2001. Total money supply in Dec. 2001 was K.9,829m.

Budget. Budget (in K.1bn.):

	1998	1999	2000	2001
Revenue	10·84	14·63	20·44	22·60
Expenditure	16·41	23·19	35·82	16·05

Performance. Real GDP growth was 1·7% in 2000, but the economy contracted by 1·5% in 2001. Total GDP was US$1·8bn. in 2001.

Banking and Finance. The central bank and bank of issue is the Reserve Bank of Malaŵi (founded 1964). The *Governor* is Dr Elias Ngalande. There are six commercial banks and an Investment Development Bank of Malaŵi.

Weights and Measures. The metric system is in use.

ENERGY AND NATURAL RESOURCES

Environment. Carbon dioxide emissions in 1998 were the equivalent of 0·1 tonnes per capita according to the *World Bank Atlas*.

Electricity. The Electricity Supply Commission of Malaŵi is the sole supplier. Capacity is 220 MW with demand at 180 MW. Production was 922m. kWh in 1998; consumption per capita in 1997 was 87 kWh. Only 4% of the population has access to electricity.

Oil and Gas. In 1997 Malaŵi and Mozambique came to an agreement on the construction of an oil pipeline between the two countries.

Minerals. Mining operations have been limited to small-scale production of coal, limestone, rubies and sapphires, but companies are now moving in to start exploration programmes. Bauxite reserves are estimated at 29m. tonnes and there are proven reserves of clays, diamonds, glass and silica sands, graphite, limestone, mercurate, phosphates, tanzanite, titanium and uranium. Output, 1995: limestone, 173,800 tonnes; rubies, sapphires and aquamarines, 550 kg (1994).

Agriculture. Malaŵi is predominantly an agricultural country. Agricultural produce contributes 90% of export earnings. There were 1·88m. ha of arable land in 1998 and 125,000 ha of permanent crops. Maize is the main subsistence crop and is grown by over 95% of all smallholders. Tobacco is the chief cash crop, employing 80% of the workforce, generating 35% of GDP and providing 70% of export earnings. Also important are groundnuts, cassava, millet and rice. There are large plantations which produce sugar, tea and coffee. Production (2000, in 1,000 tonnes): maize, 2,300; sugarcane, 2,000; potatoes, 1,700; cassava, 900; plantains, 200; tobacco, 120; groundnuts, 110; bananas, 93; rice, 87; dry beans, 84; sorghum, 55; tea, 50.

Livestock in 2000: cattle, 760,000; goats, 1,270,000; pigs, 240,000; sheep, 115,000; chickens, 15m.

Forestry. In 1995 the area under forests was 3·34m. ha, or 35·5% of the total land area (down from 38·4% in 1990). Timber production in 1999 was 9·96m. cu. metres.

Fisheries. Landings in 1999 were 45,392 tonnes, entirely from inland waters.

INDUSTRY

Index of industrial production in 2001 (1984 = 100): total general industrial production, 101·9; of this goods for the domestic market were at 73·2 and export goods were at 101·5. Electricity and water were at 231·7.

Labour. The labour force in 1996 was 4,807,000 (51% males). Approximately 85% of the economically active population in 1995 were engaged in agriculture, fisheries and forestry.

INTERNATIONAL TRADE

External debt was US$1·31bn. in 2001 (US$3·63bn. in 2000).

MALAŴI

Imports and Exports. In 2001 exports amounted to K.36·22bn. (K.23·63bn. in 2000) and imports K.39·48bn. (K.32·25bn. in 2000). Major exports 2001 (in K.1bn.): tobacco, 18·36; and sugar, 7·85. Major imports: fuel oils, 5·32.

Principal destinations for exports in 1995 were South Africa (16·2%), Germany (14·7%), Japan (11·1%), USA (10·9%). Main sources of imports were South Africa (44·4%), Germany (4·5%), UK (4·3%), USA (3·7%).

Trade Fairs. The annual Malaŵi International Trade Fair takes place in Blantyre, the commercial capital.

COMMUNICATIONS

Roads. The road network consisted of 16,451 km in 1997, of which 4,520 km were highways and main roads, 2,768 km were secondary roads and 9,163 km were other roads. Approximately 5,250 km of roads are paved. A major repair programme is under way. There were 27,000 passenger cars and 29,700 trucks and vans in 1996. 1,090 people died in road accidents in 1996.

Rail. Malaŵi Railways operate 797 km on 1,067 mm gauge, providing links to the Mozambican ports of Beira and Nacala. In 1995 railways carried 0·4m. passengers and 0·3m. tonnes of freight.

Civil Aviation. The national carrier is Air Malaŵi. It flies to a number of regional centres in Mozambique, Zambia, Zimbabwe, South Africa, Tanzania and Kenya and in 1998 operated a service to London. In 1999 scheduled airline traffic of Malaŵi-based carriers flew 2·4m. km, carrying 112,000 passengers (63,000 on international flights). There are international airports at Lilongwe (Lilongwe International Airport) and Blantyre (Chileka). In 2000 Lilongwe handled 175,915 passengers (120,575 on international flights) and 4,182 tonnes of freight, and Blantyre had 101,809 passengers (53,426 on international flights) and 680 tonnes of freight.

Shipping. In 1995 lake ships carried 169,000 passengers and 6,000 tonnes of freight.

Telecommunications. Malaŵi had 45,000 main telephone lines in 2000, or 4·4 for every 1,000 population, and 12,000 PCs were in use (1·2 per 1,000 persons). Mobile phone subscribers numbered 20,000 in Dec. 1999, and there were Internet users 10,000 in July 2000. There were 1,200 fax machines in 1997.

Postal Services. In 1995 there were 307 post offices.

SOCIAL INSTITUTIONS

Justice. Justice is administered in the High Court and in the magistrates' courts. Traditional courts were abolished in 1994. Appeals from magistrates' courts lie to the High Court, and appeals from the High Court to Malaŵi's Supreme Court of Appeal.

The population in penal institutions in 1998 was 6,505 (65 per 100,000 of national population).

Religion. 1997 estimates: 1,970,000 Protestant (mostly Presbyterian); 1,920,000 Muslim; 1,730,000 Roman Catholic; 960,000 traditional beliefs; 950,000 African Christian; 2,080,000 other.

Education. The adult literacy rate in 1999 was 59·2% (73·8% among males and 45·3% among females). Fees for primary education were abolished in 1994. In 1995–96 the number of pupils in primary schools was 3m. The primary school course is of eight years' duration, followed by a four-year secondary course. In 1995–96 there were 141,911 pupils in secondary schools. English is taught from the 1st year and becomes the general medium of instruction from the 4th year.

The University of Malaŵi had 3,657 students and 366 academic staff in 1994–95. A new university at Mzuzu opened in 1998 and provides courses for secondary school teachers. There were also four colleges and one polytechnic.

Health. In 1989 there were 186 doctors, giving a provision of one doctor for every 49,118 persons—the lowest ratio in the world. There are 3 central hospitals, 1 mental hospital, 2 leprosaria and 45 hospitals of which 21 are government district hospitals.

CULTURE
The dances of the Malaŵi are a strong part of their culture. The National Dance Troupe (formerly the Kwacha Cultural Troupe) formed in Nov. 1987 as a part of the Department of Arts and Crafts of the Ministry of Education.

Broadcasting. The Malaŵi Broadcasting Corporation, a statutory body, broadcasts in English, Chichewa, Yao, Tumbuka, Lomwe Sena and Tonga. There were 3·2m. radio sets in 1998, up from 260,000 in 1980. No other country had such a large percentage increase in the number of radio receivers in use over the same period. There is a national radio station in Blantyre providing two channels and five private radio stations have been operating since 1997.

A national television station opened in 1999. There were 23,000 sets in use in 1996.

Press. There are more than 16 newspapers in circulation, the main four being: *The Daily Times* (English, Monday to Friday), 17,000 copies daily; *The Nation* (English, Monday to Friday), 16,000 copies daily; *Malaŵi News* (English and Chichewa, Saturdays), 23,000 copies weekly; and *Weekend Nation* (English and Chichewa, Saturdays), 16,000 copies weekly. In addition there is *Odini* (English and Chichewa), 8,500 copies fortnightly; *Boma Lathu* (Chichewa), 150,000 copies monthly; *Za Alimi* (English and Chichewa), 10,000 copies monthly.

Tourism. There were 150,000 tourists in 1999 bringing in revenue of US$20m.

Museums and Galleries. The main attraction is the Museum of Malaŵi.

DIPLOMATIC REPRESENTATIVES
Of Malaŵi in the United Kingdom (33 Grosvenor St., London, W1X 0DE)
High Commissioner: Bright McBin Msaka.

Of the United Kingdom in Malaŵi (PO Box 30042, Lilongwe 3)
High Commissioner: Norman Ling.

Of Malaŵi in the USA (2408 Massachusetts Ave., NW, Washington, D.C., 20008)
Ambassador: Tony Kandiero.

Of the USA in Malaŵi (PO Box 30016, Lilongwe 3)
Ambassador: Roger Meece.

Of Malaŵi to the United Nations
Ambassador: Isaac Lamba.

Of Malaŵi to the European Union
Ambassador: Dr Jerry Aleksander Alikopaga Jana.

FURTHER READING
National Statistical Office. *Monthly Statistical Bulletin*
Ministry of Economic Planning and Development. *Economic Report*. Annual

Decalo, S., *Malawi.* [Bibliography] 2nd ed. ABC-Clio, Oxford and Santa Barbara (CA), 1995
Kalinga, O. J. M. and Crosby, C. A., *Historical Dictionary of Malawi*. Scarecrow Press, Lanham, Maryland, 1993

National statistical office: National Statistical Office, POB 333, Zomba.
Website: http://www.nso.malawi.net/

MALAYSIA

Persekutuan Tanah Malaysia
(Federation of Malaysia)

Capital: Putrajaya (Administrative),
Kuala Lumpur (Financial)
Population estimate, 2000: 22·22m.
GDP per capita, 2000: (PPP$) 9,068
HDI/world rank: 0·782/59

KEY HISTORICAL EVENTS

Malaysia is a federation consisting of the eleven States of Peninsular Malaysia and the two states of Sabah and Sarawak. The Portuguese were the first Europeans to settle in the area and Malacca became a Portuguese possession in 1541. The Dutch took Malacca in 1641 and held it until 1794 when it was occupied by the British. Although Malacca was returned to the Dutch in 1814, it was finally ceded to Britain in 1824. At the same time (1814–24) Stamford Raffles established a settlement and Singapore became British territory.

Singapore and what is now Malaysia were occupied by the Japanese from 1941 to 1945. Soon thereafter, in Jan. 1946, plans were published to create a Malaysian Union excluding Singapore. The Union came into being in April 1946 but was soon abandoned in the face of opposition. However, in Jan. 1948 the Union was reconstituted as the Federation of Malaya. From 1948 to 1960 a State of Emergency existed to counter a revolt by Malayan Communists. Following lengthy negotiations independence was granted to the Federation of Malaya on 31 Aug. 1957. On 31 Aug. 1963 Malaysia was created from the Federation of Malaya, Singapore, North Borneo (renamed Sabah) and Sarawak. Malaysia became a member of the Commonwealth. Singapore left Malaysia on 9 Aug. 1965 to become an independent sovereign state. Under the leadership of Mahathir Mohamad, southeast Asia's longest-serving leader, Malaysia entered on a period of economic prosperity, broken eventually by the 1997–98 recession. Economic turbulence caused political dissent within the government. In Sept. 1998 Anwar Ibrahim was sacked from his job as finance minister and deputy prime minister and was subsequently jailed for six years.

TERRITORY AND POPULATION

The federal state of Malaysia comprises the 13 states and 3 federal territories of Peninsular Malaysia, bounded in the north by Thailand, and with the island of Singapore as an enclave on its southern tip; and, on the island of Borneo to the east, the state of Sabah (which includes the federal territory of the island of Labuan), and the state of Sarawak, with Brunei as an enclave, both bounded in the south by Indonesia and in the northwest and northeast by the South China and Sulu Seas.

The area of Malaysia is 329,758 sq. km (127,317 sq. miles) and the population (2000 census) is 23·27m.; density, 70·6 per sq. km. Malaysia's national waters cover 515,256 sq. km. In 1999, 56·7% of the population lived in urban areas.

The UN gives a projected population for 2010 of 26·15m.

The growth of the population has been:

Year	Peninsular Malaysia	Sarawak	Sabah/Labuan	Total Malaysia
1980	11,426,613	1,307,582	1,011,046	13,745,241
1990	14,127,556	1,648,217	1,791,209	17,566,982
1997	17,047,400	1,954,300	2,663,800	21,665,500

The areas, populations and chief towns of the states and federal territories are:

Peninsular States	Area (in sq. km)	Population (2000 estimate)	Chief Town	Population (1991 census)
Johor	18,986	2,731,500	Johor Bharu	328,436
Kedah	9,426	1,605,200	Alor Setar	124,412
Kelantan	14,920	1,561,500	Kota Bharu	219,582
Kuala Lumpur[1]	243	1,407,200	Kuala Lumpur	1,145,342[1]
Melaka	1,651	598,900	Melaka	75,909
Negeri Sembilan	6,643	849,800	Seremban	182,869
Pahang	35,965	1,319,100	Kuantan	199,484
Perak	21,005	2,130,000	Ipoh	382,853

Peninsular States	Area (in sq. km)	Population (2000 estimate)	Chief Town	Population (1991 census)
Perlis	795	230,700	Kangar	14,247
Pulau Pinang	1,031	1,259,400	Penang (Georgetown)	219,603
Putrajaya[1]	40	7,000	Putrajaya	. . .
Selangor	7,915	3,287,800	Shah Alam	102,019
Terengganu	12,955	1,064,000	Kuala Terengganu	228,119
Other states				
Labuan[1]	91	75,500	Victoria	. . .
Sabah	73,619	2,894,900	Kota Kinabalu	76,120
Sarawak	124,449	2,027,900	Kuching	148,059

[1]Federal territory.

Other large cities (1997 estimate): Petaling Jaya (254,350), Kelang (243,355), Taiping (183,261), Sibu (126,381), Sandakan (125,841) and Miri (87,167).

Putrajaya, a planned new city described as an 'intelligent garden city', became the administrative capital of Malaysia in 1999 and was created a federal territory on 1 Feb. 2001.

Malay is the national language of the country—60% of the population are Malays. The government promotes the use of the national language to foster national unity. However, the people are free to use their mother tongue and other languages. English as the second language is widely used in business. In Peninsular Malaysia Chinese dialects and Tamil are also spoken. In Sabah there are numerous tribal dialects and Chinese (Mandarin and Hakka dialects predominate). In Sarawak Mandarin and numerous tribal languages are spoken.

SOCIAL STATISTICS

1999 births, 554,200; deaths, 100,900. 1999 rates (per 1,000 population): birth, 24·4; death, 4·4. Life expectancy, 1999: males, 69·9 years; females, 74·8 years. Annual population growth rate, 1991–2000, 2·6%. Infant mortality, 1999, 8 per 1,000 live births; fertility rate, 1999, 3·2 births per woman. Today only 8% of Malaysians live below the poverty line, compared to 50% in the early 1970s.

CLIMATE

Malaysia lies near the equator between latitudes 1° and 7° North and longitudes 100° and 119° East. Malaysia is subject to maritime influence and the interplay of wind systems which originate in the Indian Ocean and the South China Sea. The year is generally divided into the South-East and the North-East Monsoon seasons. The average daily temperature throughout Malaysia varies from 21°C to 32°C. Humidity is high.

CONSTITUTION AND GOVERNMENT

The Constitution of Malaysia is based on the Constitution of the former Federation of Malaya, but includes safeguards for the special interests of Sabah and Sarawak. It was amended in 1983.

The Constitution provides for one of the Rulers of the Malay States to be elected from among themselves to be the *Yang di-Pertuan Agong* (Supreme Head of the Federation). He holds office for a period of five years. The Rulers also elect from among themselves a Deputy Supreme Head of State, also for a period of five years.

In Feb. 1993 the Rulers accepted constitutional amendments abolishing their legal immunity.

Supreme Head of State (Yang di-Pertuan Agong). HRH Syed Sirajuddin ibni al-Marhum Syed Putra Jamalullail, b. 1943, acceded 13 Dec. 2001.

Raja of Perlis. HRH Syed Sirajuddin ibni al-Marhum Syed Putra Jamalullail, b. 1943, acceded 17 April 2000.

Sultan of Kedah. HRH Tuanku Haji Abdul Halim Mu'adzam Shah ibni Al-Marhum Sultan Badlishah, b. 1927, acceded 14 July 1958.

Sultan of Johor. HRH Sultan Mahmood Iskandar ibni Al-Marhum Sultan Ismail, b. 1932, acceded 11 May 1981 (Supreme Head of State from 26 April 1984 to 25 April 1989), returned as Sultan of Johor 26 April 1989.

Sultan of Perak. HRH Sultan Azlan Shah Muhibbuddin Shah ibni Al-Marhum Sultan Yussuf Izzuddin Ghafarullahu-luhu Shah, b. 1928, acceded 3 Feb. 1984.

Yang Di-Pertuan Besar Negeri Sembilan. HRH Tuanku Jaafar ibni Al-Marhum Tuanku Abdul Rahman, b. 1922, acceded 18 April 1967.

Sultan of Kelantan. HRH Sultan Ismail Petra ibni Al-Marhum Sultan Yahya Petra, b. 1949, appointed 29 March 1979.

Sultan of Terengganu. HRH Sultan Mizan Zainal Abidin ibni al-Mahrum Sultan Mahmud Al-Muktafi Billah Shah, b. 1962, acceded 15 May 1998.

Sultan of Pahang. Sultan Haji Ahmad Shah Al-Musta'in Billah ibni Al-Marhum Sultan Abu Bakar Ri'Ayatuddin Al-Mu'Adzam Shah, b. 1930, acceded 8 May 1975.

Sultan of Selangor. HRH Sharafuddin Idris Shah ibni al-Marhum Sultan Salehuddin Abdul Aziz Shah, b. 1945, appointed 22 Nov. 2001.

Yang di-Pertua Negeri Pulau Pinang. HE Datuk Abdul Rahman Haji Abbas, b. 1938, appointed 1 May 2001.

Yang di Pertua Negeri Melaka. HE Tun Datuk Seri Utama Syed Ahmad Al-Haj bin Syed Shahabudin, b. 1925, appointed 4 Dec. 1984.

Yang di-Pertua Negeri Sarawak. HE Tun Datuk Patinggi Abang Mohamad Salaheddin, b. 1921, acceded 4 Dec. 2000.

Yang di-Pertua Negeri Sabah. HE Datuk Ahmad Shah Abdullah, b. 1946, acceded 1 Jan. 2003.

The federal parliament consists of the *Yang di-Pertuan Agong* and two *Majlis* (Houses of Parliament) known as the *Dewan Negara* (Senate) of 69 members (26 elected, 2 by each state legislature; and 43 appointed by the *Yang di-Pertuan Agong*) and *Dewan Rakyat* (House of Representatives) of 193 members. Appointment to the Senate is for three years. The maximum life of the House of Representatives is five years, subject to its dissolution at any time by the *Yang di-Pertuan Agong* on the advice of his Ministers.

National Anthem. 'Negaraku' ('My Country'); words collective, tune by Pierre de Béranger.

RECENT ELECTIONS

Parliamentary and 11 state assembly elections were held on 28–29 Nov. 1999. The 14-party National Front Coalition (BN), in which the United Malays National Organization (UMNO) was the predominant partner, gained 148 of the available 193 seats, obtaining 56% of the votes cast. The three-party Alternative Front (BA), dominated by the Islamic Party of Malaysia (PAS), gained 42 seats and the Bersatu Sabah Party (PBS) won 3. In gaining 45 seats, the opposition almost doubled the number of seats which it won in the 1995 election. The National Front Coalition also gained a majority in every state assembly except Kelantan and Terengganu which were gained by the Islamic Party of Malaysia (PAS).

CURRENT ADMINISTRATION

In March 2003 the government comprised:

Prime Minister and Minister of Finance: Dato' Seri Dr Mahathir Mohamad; b. 1926 (UMNO; in office since July 1981, making him Asia's longest-serving elected leader).

Deputy Prime Minister and Minister for Home Affairs: Dato' Seri Abdullah Ahmad Badawi. *Transport:* Dato' Seri Ling Liong Sik. *Energy, Communications and Multimedia:* Datuk Seri Leo Moggie Anak Irok. *Entrepreneur Development:* Dato' Nazri Abdullah Aziz. *Primary Industries:* Dato' Seri Lim Keng Yaik. *Works:* Dato' Seri S. Samy Vellu. *International Trade and Industry:* Dato' Seri Rafidah Aziz. *Education:* Tan Sri Musa Mohamad. *Rural Development:* Dato' Azmi Khalid. *Agriculture:* Dato' Effendi Norwawi. *Domestic Trade and Consumer Affairs:* Tan Sri Muhyddin Yassin. *Health:* Dato' Chua Jui Meng. *Foreign Affairs:* Dato' Seri Syed Hamid Syed Jaafar Albar. *Defence:* Dato' Seri Mohd Najib Tun Abdul Razak. *Information:* Tan Sri Khalil Yaacob. *Culture, Arts and Tourism:* Dato' Abdul Kadir Sheik Fadzir. *National Unity and Social Development:* Dato' Seri Siti Zahara Sulaiman. *Human Resources:* Dato' Fong Chan Onn. *Science, Technology and Environment:* Dato' Law Hieng Ding. *Housing and Local Government:* Dato' Ong Ka Ting. *Land and Co-operative Development:* Tan Sri Kasitah Gadam. *Women's Affairs:* Shahrizat Abdul Jalil. *Youth and Sports:* Dato' Hishammuddin Tun Hussein.

Office of the Prime Minister: http://www.smpke.jpm.my/

DEFENCE

The Constitution provides for the Head of State to be the Supreme Commander of the Armed Forces who exercises his powers in accordance with the advice of the Cabinet. Under their authority, the Armed Forces Council is responsible for all matters relating to the Armed Forces other than those relating to their operational use. The Ministry of Defence has established bilateral defence relations with countries within as well as outside the region. Malaysia is a member of the Five Powers Defence Arrangement with Australia, New Zealand, Singapore and the UK.

The Malaysian Armed Forces (MAF) are currently undergoing restructuring (1999). The MAF has participated in 16 UN peacekeeping missions in Africa, the Middle East, Indo-China and Europe. Five of the operations are military contingents, the remainder are Observer Groups.

In 2000 defence expenditure totalled US$2,708m. (US$122 per capita), representing 3·1% of GDP.

Army. Strength (1999) about 85,000. There is a paramilitary Police Field Force of 11,000 and a People's Volunteer Corps of 240,000 of which 17,500 are armed.

Navy. The Royal Malaysian Navy is commanded by the Chief of the Navy from the integrated Ministry of Defence in Kuala Lumpur. There are four operational areas: No. 1, Kuantan Naval Base, covering the eastern peninsular coast; No. 2, Labuan naval Base, covering the East Malaysia coast; No. 3, Lumut Naval Base, covering the western peninsular coast; and No. 4, Kuching Naval Base, covering Sarawak's coast. The peacetime tasks include fishery protection and anti-piracy patrols. The fleet includes four frigates. A Naval aviation squadron operates 12 armed helicopters.

Navy personnel in 1999 totalled 12,500 including 160 Naval Air personnel. There were 2,200 naval reserves.

Air Force. Formed on 1 June 1958, the Royal Malaysian Air Force is equipped primarily to provide air defence and air support for the Army, Navy and Police. Its secondary role is to render assistance to government departments and civilian organizations.

Personnel (1999) totalled about 12,500, with 120 combat aircraft including F-5Es, MiG-29s and Bae *Hawks*. There were 600 Air Force reserves.

INTERNATIONAL RELATIONS

Malaysia is in dispute with Indonesia over sovereignty of two islands in the Celebes Sea. Both countries have agreed to accept the Judgment of the International Court of Justice.

Malaysia is a member of the UN, WTO, BIS, the Commonwealth, Asian Development Bank, Colombo Plan, APEC, ASEAN, Mekong Group and the Organization of Islamic Conference.

ECONOMY

In 1998 agriculture accounted for 13·2% of GDP, industry 43·5% and services 43·3%.

Overview. Malaysia's response to the economic crisis that swept Asia in 1997–98 was to put much of the blame on foreign speculators. After a fall in the value of the *ringgit* by 48% between July 1997 and July 1998, Prime Minister Dr Mahathir announced tough restrictions on currency transactions. In 1998 the economy shrank by over 5% and bank debt remains one of the highest in southeast Asia.

Currency. The unit of currency is the Malaysian *ringgit* (RM) of 100 *sen*, which is pegged to the US dollar at 3·8 ringgit = 1 US$. Foreign exchange reserves were US$32,287m. and gold reserves 1·17m. troy oz in June 2002. In 2001 there was inflation of 1·4%. Total money supply in June 2002 was RM85,913m.

Budget. 1998 budget: revenue, RM65·7bn.; expenditure, RM59·1bn. Revenue and expenditure for calendar years, in RM1bn.:

	1995	1996	1997	1998	1999
Revenue	50·9	58·2	65·7	56·7	59·9
Operating expenditure	36·6	43·3	44·7	44·6	48·9

Sources of revenue in 1996: direct taxes, 45·6% (47·5%—1999 est.); indirect taxes, 36% (30·8%—1999 est.); non-tax revenue, 18·4 % (21·7%—1999 est.).

Federal government net development (in addition to operating) expenditure in 1996: RM11,156m. (RM 21,508m. 1999), of which economic services 49·9% (50·9%—1999 est.), social services, 25·3% (27·0%—1999 est.), security, 19·0% (14·3%—1999 est.) and general administration, 5·8% (6·9%—1999 est.).

Performance. Between 1990 and 1996 the average annual real growth in GNP per capita was 6·1%. Malaysia was badly affected by the Asian financial crisis, with the economy contracting by 7·4% in 1998. However, there was a recovery in 1999, with growth of 5·6%, rising to 8·5% in 2000. There was a recession in the second half of 2001 although the economy still expanded by 0·4% in the year as a whole. Total GDP in 2001 was US$87·5bn.

Banking and Finance. The central bank and bank of issue is the Bank Negara Malaysia (*Governor*, Dr Zeti Akhtar Aziz). 37 commercial banks were operating at 31 Dec. 1996 (including 16 foreign) with a total of 1,433 branches. Number of employees 69,154. Total deposits with commercial banks at 31 Dec. 1996 were RM194,974m. There were 12 merchant banks at 31 Dec. 1996. Number of employees 2,592. The Islamic Bank of Malaysia began operations in July 1983. There were 40 finance companies in 1996 with 1,096 offices. Number of employees 26,728.

There is a stock exchange at Kuala Lumpur, known as BSKL, running about RM2bn. daily (Jan. 2000).

Weights and Measures. The metric system is standard, but British imperial units are still in residual use.

ENERGY AND NATURAL RESOURCES

Environment. According to the *World Bank Atlas* Malaysia's carbon dioxide emissions in 1998 were the equivalent of 5·4 tonnes per capita.

Electricity. Installed capacity in 1997, 14m. kW. In 1999, 62,546m. kWh were generated. Electricity consumption in 1999 was 54,433,400 kWh.

Oil and Gas. Crude petroleum reserves, 1999, 3·9bn. bbls. Estimated oil production (1996) 718,600 bbls. a day; 1997, 713,900 bbls.; 1998 (estimate), 726,100 bbls. Natural gas reserves, 2000, 2,300bn. cu. metres. Production of natural gas in 1999 was 43·0bn. cu. metres. In April 1998 Malaysia and Thailand agreed to share equally the natural gas jointly produced in an offshore area which both countries claim as their own territory. It was expected that from 2001 around 18m. cu. metres of natural gas would be produced in the area every day.

Minerals. In 1998 mining contributed 6·9% of GDP. Bauxite production in 1997 was 279,066 tonnes; iron ore, 269,087 tonnes; copper concentrates, 80,675 tonnes; tin, 5,756 tonnes (1998); coal, 83,000 tonnes (1996).

Agriculture. In 1998 agriculture contributed 6·9% of GDP. There were 1·82m. ha of arable land in 1998 and 5·79m. ha of permanent crops. In 1998 approximately 365,000 ha were irrigated. Production in 2000 (in 1,000 tonnes): palm kernels, 3,175; rice, 2,037; sugarcane, 1,600; rubber, 749; coconuts, 683; bananas, 545; cassava, 380. Livestock (2000): pigs, 1·83m.; cattle, 723,000; goats 232,000; sheep, 175,000; buffaloes, 155,000; chickens, 120m. Malaysia's output of palm kernels is the highest of any country. Only Thailand and Indonesia produce more rubber.

Forestry. In 1998 there were 187,612 sq. km of forests, down from 187,752 sq. km in 1997. Timber production in 1999 was 29·46m. cu. metres.

Fisheries. Total catch in 1999 amounted to 1,251,768 tonnes, almost entirely from sea fishing.

INDUSTRY

In 1998 manufacturing contributed 82·9% of gross exports led by electronics products (39·8%). Production figures for 1997 (in 1,000 tonnes): palm oil, 14,870 (1999); cement, 10,104; refined sugar, 1,266; wheat flour, 768; plywood, 3,706,803 cu. metres; radio sets, 33m. units; cigarettes, 20·2bn. units; pneumatic tyres, 13,518,000 units.

Labour. In 1999 the workforce was 8·8m. (44·2% female), of whom 8,741,000 were employed (27·1% in manufacturing, 16·0% in agriculture and 9·2% in construction). Unemployment was 3·4%. It is estimated that Malaysia has some 500,000 illegal workers.

Trade Unions. Membership was 737,484 at 30 Sept. 1997, of which the Malaysian Trades Union Congress, an umbrella organization of 158 unions, accounted for 0·4m. Number of unions was 536.

INTERNATIONAL TRADE
Privatization policy permits foreign investment of 25–30% generally; total foreign ownership is permitted of export-oriented projects. External debt was US$41,797m. in 2000.

Imports and Exports. In 1998 exports reached over 115% of GDP, with exports to the USA worth around 25% of GDP.

In 2000 exports totalled RM373·3bn. and imports RM312·4bn., up from RM321·6bn. and RM248·5bn. respectively in 1999.

In 1999 imports of consumer goods totalled RM13,970m.; intermediate goods, RM175,832m.; capital goods, RM32,317m.

Chief exports, 1998 (in RM1m.): electronics and electrical products, 185,314; palm oil, 13,792; chemicals and chemical products, 10,364; crude oil, 8,734; textiles, clothing and footwear, 8,562; manufactures of metal, 7,535; liquefied natural gas, 5,981; saw logs and sawn timber, 4,787; wood products, 4,772; rubber, 2,195.

In 1999 major imports (in RM1m.) came from Japan (54,803), USA (43,318) and Singapore (34,817). Principal exports went to USA (70,391), Singapore (53,106), Japan (37,288), EU (50,522), ASEAN countries (76,362). Malaysia exports 23% of its GDP to the USA.

COMMUNICATIONS
Roads. Total road length in 1999 was 69,699 km, of which 49,816 km were paved and 16,883 km were unpaved. In 1999 there were 9,929,951 registered motor vehicles. There were 6,035 deaths as a result of road accidents in 2000, which at 29 per 100,000 people ranks among the highest rates in the world.

Rail. In 1999 there were 2,265 km of railway tracks. Passenger-km travelled in 1998 came to 1,397m. and freight tonne-km to 992m.

Civil Aviation. There are a total of 19 airports of which 5 are international airports and 14 are domestic airports at which regular public air transport is operated. *International airports;* Kuala Lumpur, Penang, Kota Kinabalu, Kuching and Langkawi. *Domestic airports;* Johor Bharu, Alor Setar, Ipoh, Kota Bharu, Kuala Terengganu, Kuantan, Melaka, Sandakan, Lahad Datu, Tawau, Labuan, Bintulu, Sibu and Miri. There are 39 Malaysian airstrips of which 10 are in Sabah, 15 in Sarawak and 14 in peninsular Malaysia.

33 international airlines operate through Kuala Lumpur (KLIA-Sepang). Malaysia Airlines, the national airline, is 39% state-owned, and operates domestic flights within Malaysia and international flights to nearly 40 different countries. In 1999 it flew 206·9m. km, carrying 14,984,600 passengers (6,770,550 on international flights). In 2000 Kuala Lumpur handled 14,353,000 passengers (10,249,000 on international flights) and 510,600 tonnes of freight. Kota Kinabalu handled 2,970,000 passengers in 2000 and Penang 2,682,000.

Shipping. The major ports are Port Kelang, Pulau Pinang, Johor Pasir Gudang, Tanjung Beruas, Miri, Rajang, Pelabuhan Sabah, Port Dickson, Kemaman, Teluk Ewa, Kuantan, Kuching and Bintulu. In 1996 there were 2,429 marine vessels including 118 oil tankers (0·73m. GRT), 198 passenger carriers (0·03m. GRT) and 426 general cargo ships (0·76m. GRT), with a total GRT of 4·27m. In 1996, 167·9m. tonnes of cargo were loaded and unloaded. In 1998 merchant shipping totalled 5,209,000, including oil tankers 854,000 GRT.

Telecommunications. In 2000 there were 4,634,300 telephones, or 199·2 per 1,000 inhabitants, and 2·4m. PCs were in use (103·1 for every 1,000 persons). There were 3,092 telex subscribers in 1999 and 150,000 fax machines in 1997. Malaysia had 3·7m. Internet users in Dec. 2000 and 3·5m. mobile phone subscribers in March 2001.

Postal Services. Postal services are the responsibility of the Ministry of Energy, Communications and Multimedia. In 1998 there were 6,036 postal services networks established in Malaysia, including 626 post offices.

SOCIAL INSTITUTIONS

Justice. The judicial power is vested in the Federal Court, the High Court of Malaya, the High Court of Borneo and subordinate courts: Sessions Courts, Magistrates' Courts and *Mukim* chiefs' Courts.

The Federal Court comprises the Lord President—who is also the head of the Judiciary—the Chief Justice of the High Courts and the Judge of the Federal Court. It has jurisdiction to determine the validity of any law made by Parliament or by a State legislature and disputes between States or between the Federation and any State. It also has jurisdiction to hear and determine appeals from the High Courts.

The death penalty is authorized and was used in 2002. The population in penal institutions in Dec. 1997 was 24,400 (115 per 100,000 of national population).

Religion. Malaysia has a multi-racial population divided between Islam, Buddhism, Taoism, Hinduism and Christianity. Under the Federal constitution, Islam is the official religion of Malaysia but there is freedom of worship. In 2000 there were an estimated 12·30m. Muslims, 4·02m. Buddhists, 2·70m. adherents of Chinese traditional religions, 1·63m. Hindus and 1·49m. Christians.

Education. School education is free; tertiary education is provided at a nominal fee. There are 6 years of primary schooling starting at age 7, 3 years of universal lower secondary, 2 years of selective upper secondary and 2 years of pre-university education. During the Seventh Plan period (1996–2000), a number of major changes were introduced to the education and training system with a view to strengthening and improving the system. These efforts are expected to improve the quality of output to meet the manpower needs of the nation, particularly in the fields of science and technology. In addition, continued emphasis will be given to expand educational opportunities for those in the rural and remote areas. Under the Seventh Plan, the Education Ministry allocated RM8,437,200 on this education programme and RM1,661,600 for training purposes.

In 1999 there were 2,897,927 pupils at 7,192 primary schools with 157,415 teachers, 1,957,483 pupils at secondary schools and, in 1997, 229,814 students and 16,175 teachers at higher education institutions.

Adult literacy was 87·0% in 1999 (91·1% among males and 82·8% among females).

In 1998 total expenditure on education was RM9,866,300 (20·9% from the total budget).

Health. In 1998 there were 15,016 doctors, 2,058 dentists and 18,134 nurses. In 1995 there were 42,878 allied health professionals. These were divided into dental, paramedics and auxiliary (2,720), medical assistants and laboratory technologists (5,392), nurses (32,401), occupational therapists and physiotherapists (410), public health inspectors (1,418) and radiographers (537). At the end of 1995 the Ministry of Health ran a total of 1,375 dental clinics. In the same year there were 39,738 beds in hospitals, clinics and other medical institutions.

Welfare. The Employment Injury Insurance Scheme (SOCSO) provides medical and cash benefits and the Invalidity Pension Scheme provides protection to employees against invalidity as a result of disease or injury from any cause. Other supplementary measures are the Employees' Provident Fund, the pension scheme for all government employees, free medical benefits for all who are unable to pay and the provision of medical benefits particularly for workers under the Labour Code. In 1998 there were 49 welfare service institutions with capacity for 7,170.

CULTURE

Broadcasting. There are five TV Stations (colour by PAL). The government-controlled Radio Television Malaysia broadcasts radio and TV programmes nationally. The Voice of Malaysia (broadcasting in eight languages) is beamed internationally. System TV Malaysia Berhad transmits from Kuala Lumpur and is also beamed throughout the country. There were 9·1m. radio receivers and 3·6m. television receivers in 1997.

Cinema. In 1996 there were 233 cinemas with a gross value output of RM115,087m. English, Malay, Chinese, Hindi and Indonesian films are shown.

Press. The Malaysian Media Agencies are comprised of the press, magazine and press agencies/local media, which are further divided into home and foreign news. In 1996 a total of 5,843 book titles were published in 29·04m. copies.

Tourism. In 1999 there were 7,931,000 foreign tourists, spending US$2,822m.

Festivals. National Day (31 Aug.) is celebrated in Kuala Lumpur at the Dataran Merdeka and marks Malaysia's independence.

Libraries. The National Library of Malaysia is strong on information technology. The 14 state public libraries and 31 ministry and government department libraries are linked in a Common User Scheme called *Jaringan Ilmu* (Knowledge Network).

Theatre and Opera. Performances by the National Budaya Group include premiere theatre staging, dance drama, national choir concerts, national symphony orchestra, chamber music, and traditional and folk music. Local theatre groups regularly stage contemporary Asian and western dramas, dance dramas and the *bangsawan* (traditional Malay opera).

Museums and Galleries. There is a National Museum for preserving, restoring and imparting knowledge on the historical and cultural heritage of Malaysia. The National Art Gallery promotes Malaysian visual arts through exhibitions, competitions and support programmes which are held locally and abroad.

DIPLOMATIC REPRESENTATIVES

Of Malaysia in the United Kingdom (45 Belgrave Sq., London, SW1X 8QT)
High Commissioner: Dato' Haji Salim Hashim.

Of the United Kingdom in Malaysia (185 Jalan Ampang, 50450 Kuala Lumpur)
High Commissioner: Bruce Cleghorn, CMG.

Of Malaysia in the USA (2401 Massachusetts Ave., NW, Washington, D.C., 20008)
Ambassador: Dato' Sheikh Abdul Khalid Ghazzali.

Of the USA in Malaysia (376 Jalan Tun Razak, Kuala Lumpur)
Ambassador: Marie T. Huhtala.

Of Malaysia to the United Nations
Ambassador: Datuk Hasmy Agam.

Of Malaysia to the European Union
Ambassador: Dato' Mohamed Ridzam Deva bin Abdullah.

FURTHER READING

Department of Statistics: Kuala Lumpur. *Yearbook of Statistics* (1999)

Prime Minister's Department: Economic Planning Unit. *Malaysian Economy in Figures.* Annual, 1999.
Andaya, B. W. and Andaya, L. Y., *A History of Malaysia.* 2nd ed. Palgrave, Basingstoke, 2001
Drabble, J., *An Economic History of Malaysia, c. 1800–1990.* Palgrave, Basingstoke, 2001
Information Services Department: Kuala Lumpur. *Malaysia Yearbook,* 1995
Kahn, J. S. and Wah, F. L. K., *Fragmented Vision: Culture and Politics in Contemporary Malaysia.* Sydney, 1992
BNM: Kuala Lumpur. *Bank Negara Malaysia, Annual Report.* 1998
Department of Statistics: Kuala Lumpur. *State/District Data Bank of Malaysia.* 1999
Department of Statistics: Kuala Lumpur. *Social Statistics Bulletin of Malaysia.* 1998

National statistical office: Department of Statistics, Wisma Statistik, Jalan Cenderasari, 50514 Kuala Lumpur.
Website: http://www.statistics.gov.my/

MALDIVES

Divehi Raajjeyge
Jumhooriyyaa
(Republic of the Maldives)

Capital: Malé
Population estimate, 2000: 270,000
GDP per capita, 2000: (PPP$) 4,485
HDI/world rank: 0·743/84

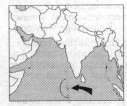

KEY HISTORICAL EVENTS
The islands were under British protection from 1887 until complete independence was achieved on 26 July 1965. The Maldives became a republic on 11 Nov. 1968.

TERRITORY AND POPULATION
The republic, some 400 miles to the southwest of Sri Lanka, consists of 1,200 low-lying (the highest point is 1·8 metres above sea-level) coral islands, grouped into 26 atolls. 199 are inhabited. Area 115 sq. miles (298 sq. km). At the 2000 census the population was 270,101 (137,200 males); density, 906·4 per sq. km.

The UN gives a projected population for 2010 of 393,000.

In 1999, 73·9% of the population lived in rural areas. Capital, Malé (1999 population, 72,000).

The official and spoken language is Divehi.

SOCIAL STATISTICS
1995 births, 10,500; deaths, 2,000. Birth rate, 1995, per 1,000 population, 41·7; death rate, 8·0. Annual population growth rate, 1990–99, 2·9%. Life expectancy at birth in 1999 was 65·3 years for females but 66·9 years for males. With a difference of 1·6 years, no other country has a life expectancy for males so high compared to that for females. Infant mortality, 1999, 60 per 1,000 live births; fertility rate, 1999, 5·2 births per woman.

CLIMATE
The islands are hot and humid, and affected by monsoons. Malé: average temperature 81°F (27°C), annual rainfall 59" (1,500 mm).

CONSTITUTION AND GOVERNMENT
There is a Citizens' *Majlis* (Parliament) which consists of 48 members, 8 of whom are nominated by the President and 40 directly elected (2 each from Malé and the 19 administrative districts) for a term of five years. There are no political parties. The President of the Republic is elected by the Citizens' Majlis.

National Anthem. 'Gavmii mi ekuverikan matii tibegen kuriime salaam' ('In national unity we salute our nation'); words by M. J. Didi, tune by W. Amaradeva.

RECENT ELECTIONS
President Maumoon Abdul Gayoom was re-elected in a referendum held on 16 Oct. 1998. As sole candidate, he won 91% of the 95,168 votes cast. Turn-out was 75%. At the last elections to the Majlis on 19 Nov. 1999 only non-partisans were elected.

CURRENT ADMINISTRATION
In March 2003 the government consisted of:

President, Minister of Defence and National Security, Minister of Finance and Treasury: Maumoon Abdul Gayoom; b. 1937 (in office since 1978; re-elected unopposed for a fifth 5-year term in Oct. 1998).

Minister of Atolls Administration: Abdulla Hameed. *Agriculture, Fisheries and Marine Resources:* Abdul Rasheed Hussain. *Foreign Affairs:* Fathullah Jameel. *Women's Affairs and Social Security:* Rashida Yoosuf. *Home Affairs, Housing and Environment:* Ismail Shafeeu. *Construction and Public Works:* Umar Zahir. *Justice:* Ahmed Zahir. *Transport and Civil Aviation:* Alyas Ibrahim. *Planning and National Development:* Ibrahim Hussain Zaki. *Human Resources, Employment and Labour:*

Abdulla Kamaluddeen. *Tourism:* Hassan Sobir. *Education:* Dr Mohamed Latheef. *Information, Arts and Culture:* Ibrahim Manik. *Trade and Industries:* Abdullah Yameen. *Health:* Ahmed Abdullah. *Science, Technology and Communications:* Midhat Hilmy. *Youth and Sports:* Mohammed Zahir Hussain. *Minister of the President's Office:* Abdullah Jameel. *Attorney General:* Dr Mohamed Mumawar.
Speaker of Citizens' Majlis: Abdulla Hameed.

Office of the President: http://www.presidencymaldives.gov.mv

DEFENCE
In 2000 military expenditure totalled US$44m. (US$176 per capita), representing 9·5% of GDP.

INTERNATIONAL RELATIONS
The Maldives is a member of the UN, WTO, the Commonwealth, Asian Development Bank, Colombo Plan, SAARC and OIC.

ECONOMY
Agriculture accounts for approximately 22% of GDP, industry 15% and services 63%.

Currency. The unit of currency is the *rufiyaa* (MVR) of 100 *laari*. There was inflation in 2001 of 3·7%. Gold reserves were 2,000 troy oz in June 2002 and foreign exchange reserves US$104m. Total money supply in June 2002 was 1,940m. rufiyaa.

Budget. In 1999 (years ending 31 Dec.) government total revenue was 2,062·6m. rufiyaa (2,273·1m. estimated for 2000); expenditure 2,494·9m. rufiyaa (2,819·9m. estimated for 2000).

Performance. Real GDP growth was 5·6% in 2000 and 4·9% in 2001. Total GDP in 2001 was US$0·6bn.

Banking and Finance. The Maldives Monetary Authority (*Governor*, Maumoon Abdul Gayoom), established in 1981, is endowed with the regular powers of a central bank and bank of issue.

ENERGY AND NATURAL RESOURCES

Environment. According to the *World Bank Atlas* carbon dioxide emissions were the equivalent of 1·3 tonnes per capita in 1998.

Electricity. Installed capacity was 18,000 kW in 1994. Production in 1998 was 85m. kWh; consumption per capita in 1997 was 251 kWh.

Minerals. Inshore coral mining has been banned as a measure against the encroachment of the sea.

Agriculture. There were 1,000 ha of arable land in 1998 and 2,000 ha of permanent crops. Principal crops in 2000 (in 1,000 tonnes): coconuts, 16; copra, 3; tree nuts, 2; bananas, 1.

Fisheries. The total catch in 1999 was 133,547 tonnes. The Maldives has the highest per capita consumption of fish and fishery products of any country in the world. In the period 1995–97 the average person consumed nearly 170 kg (375 lb) a year, or more than ten times the average for the world as a whole.

INDUSTRY
The main industries are fishing, tourism, shipping, lacquerwork and garment manufacturing.

Labour. In 1996 the workforce was 107,000 (58% males).

INTERNATIONAL TRADE
Total foreign debt amounted to US$207m. in 2000.

Imports and Exports. In 2000 imports (f.o.b.) were valued at US$342·0m. (US$353·9m. in 1999) and exports (f.o.b.) at US$108·7m. (US$91·4m. in 1999). The Bonito ('Maldive fish') is the main export commodity. It is exported principally to Thailand, Singapore, Sri Lanka, Japan and some European markets. Main import suppliers in 1996 were Singapore (32·0%), India (12·0%), Malaysia (8·5%), Sri Lanka (7·6%). Leading export destinations were UK (21·7%), Sri Lanka (18·3%), Germany (10·8%), USA (10·2%).

COMMUNICATIONS

Roads. In 1996 there were 787 cars, 5,319 motorbikes/autocycles, 377 lorries, trucks and tractors, 209 vans and buses, 658 jeeps, land rovers and pickups, 271 taxis and 274 other vehicles.

Civil Aviation. The former national carrier Air Maldives collapsed in April 2000 with final losses in excess of US$50m. In 2000 there were 1,649,103 passengers (1,073,788 international) and 23,811 tonnes of freight handled at Hulule Airport. There are four domestic airports. In 1999 scheduled airline traffic of Maldives-based carriers flew 5·1m. km, carrying 344,000 passengers (273,000 on international flights).

Shipping. The Maldives Shipping Line operated (1992) ten vessels. In 1998 merchant shipping totalled 101,000 GRT.

Telecommunications. Telephone main lines numbered 24,400 in 2000, equivalent to 90·8 per 1,000 inhabitants. There were 6,000 PCs in 2000 (20·4 for every 1,000 persons), 2,700 mobile phone subscribers in 1999 and 3,500 fax machines in 1995. Internet users numbered 6,000 in Dec. 2000.

Postal Services. In 1995 there were 362 post offices, or one for every 700 persons.

SOCIAL INSTITUTIONS

Justice. Justice is based on the Islamic Shari'ah.

Religion. The State religion is Islam.

Education. Adult literacy in 1999 was 96·2% (male, 96·3%; female, 96·2%) among both males and females. Education is not compulsory. In 1996 there were 60 government schools (40,935 pupils), 32 private schools (40,153 pupils) and 171 community schools (9,509 pupils) with a total of 3,278 teachers.

Health. In 1996 there were 193 beds at the Indira Gandhi Memorial Hospital in Malé, 4 regional hospitals (125 beds) and 27 health centres. In 1996 there were 99 doctors and 303 nurses.

CULTURE

Broadcasting. Voice of Maldives and Television Maldives are government-controlled. In 1997 there were 34,000 radio receivers and 7,000 television sets (colour by PAL).

Press. In 1996 there were 3 daily newspapers, 2 weekly, 2 fortnightly and a number of monthly periodicals.

Tourism. Tourism is the major foreign currency earner. There were 430,000 visitors in 1999, spending US$334m.

DIPLOMATIC REPRESENTATIVES

Of the Maldives in the United Kingdom (22 Nottingham Pl., London W1M 3FB)
High Commissioner (acting): Adam Hassan.

Of the United Kingdom in the Maldives
High Commissioner: Stephen Evans, CMG, OBE (resides at Colombo, Sri Lanka).

Of the USA in the Maldives
Ambassador: E. Ashley Wills (resides at Colombo).

Permanent Representative of the Maldives to the United Nations
Ambassador: Dr Mohamed Latheef.

Of the Maldives to the European Union
Ambassador: Vacant.

FURTHER READING

Gayoom, M. A., *The Maldives: A Nation in Peril*. Ministry of Planning, Human Resources and Environment, Republic of Maldives, 1998
Reynolds, Christopher H. B., *Maldives*. [Bibliography] ABC-Clio, Oxford and Santa Barbara (CA), 1993

National Statistics Office: Statistics Section, Ministry of Planning and National Development.
Website: http://www.planning.gov.mv

MALI

République du Mali

Capital: Bamako
Population estimate, 2000: 11·35m.
GDP per capita, 2000: (PPP$) 797
HDI/world rank: 0·386/164

KEY HISTORICAL EVENTS

Mali's power reached its peak between the 11th and 13th centuries when its gold-based empire controlled much of the surrounding area. The country was annexed by France in 1904. The region became the territory of French Sudan as part of French West Africa. The country became an autonomous state within the French Community on 24 Nov. 1958, and on 4 April 1959 joined with Senegal to form the Federation of Mali. The Federation achieved independence on 20 June 1960, but Senegal seceded on 22 Aug. and Mali proclaimed itself an independent republic on 22 Sept. There was an army coup on 19 Nov. 1968, which brought Moussa Traoré to power. Ruling the country for over 22 years, he wrecked the economy. A further coup followed in March 1991.

In Jan. 1991 a ceasefire was signed with Tuareg insurgents in the north and in April 1992 a national pact was concluded providing for a special administration for the Tuareg north.

Under President Alpha Oumar Konaré, two elections for the National Assembly were held. The first (April 1997) was cancelled by the Constitutional Court and the second, in July 1997, was boycotted by opposition parties. Amadou Toumani Touré, a former military ruler, won presidential elections held in April and May 2002.

TERRITORY AND POPULATION

Mali is bounded in the west by Senegal, northwest by Mauritania, northeast by Algeria, east by Niger and south by Burkina Faso, Côte d'Ivoire and Guinea. Its area is 1,248,574 sq. km (482,077 sq. miles) and it had a population of 9,790,492 (4,943,056 females) at the 1998 census (70·6% rural). Density, 7·8 per sq. km.

The UN gives a projected population for 2010 of 12·23m.

The areas, populations and chief towns of the regions are:

Region	Sq. km	1995 population	Chief town
Gao	170,572	408,000[1]	Gao
Kayes	119,743	1,245,000	Kayes
Kidal	151,430	...[1]	Kidal
Koulikoro	95,848	1,462,000	Koulikoro
Mopti	79,017	1,423,000	Mopti
Ségou	64,821	1,579,000	Ségou
Sikasso	70,280	1,521,000	Sikasso
Tombouctou	496,611	462,000	Tombouctou
Capital District	252	913,000	Bamako

[1]Kidal was created from the northern half of Gao in 1991.
No separate population figure available.

In 1999 the capital, Bamako, had an estimated population of 1,083,000.

In 1996 the principal ethnic groups numbered (in 1,000): Bambara, 2,930; Fulani, 1,290; Senufo, 1,100; Soninke, 800; Tuareg, 675; Songhai, 660; Malinke, 610; Dogon, 370. The official language is French; Bambara is spoken by about 60% of the population.

SOCIAL STATISTICS

1997 estimates: births, 492,000; deaths, 191,000. Vital statistics rates, 1997 estimates (per 1,000 population): births, 50·3; deaths, 19·5. Infant mortality, 1999 (per 1,000 live births), 143. Expectation of life in 1999 was 50·2 years for males and 52·2 for females. Annual population growth rate, 1990–99, 2·4% per annum; fertility rate, 1999, 6·4 children per woman.

1101

CLIMATE

A tropical climate, with adequate rain in the south and west, but conditions become increasingly arid towards the north and east. Bamako, Jan. 76°F (24·4°C), July 80°F (26·7°C). Annual rainfall 45" (1,120 mm). Kayes, Jan. 76°F (24·4°C), July 93°F (33·9°C). Annual rainfall 29" (725 mm). Tombouctou, Jan. 71°F (21·7°C), July 90°F (32·2°C). Annual rainfall 9" (231 mm).

CONSTITUTION AND GOVERNMENT

A constitution was approved by a national referendum in 1974; it was amended by the National Assembly on 2 Sept. 1981. The sole legal party was the *Union démocratique du peuple malien* (UDPM).

A national conference of 1,800 delegates agreed a draft constitution enshrining multi-party democracy in Aug. 1991, and this was approved by 99·76% of votes cast at a referendum in Jan. 1992. Turn-out was 43%.

The *President* is elected for not more than two terms of five years.

There is a *National Assembly*, consisting of 147 deputies (formerly 116) plus 13 Malinese living abroad.

A *Constitutional Court* was established in 1994.

National Anthem. 'A ton appel, Mali' ('At your call, Mali'); words by S. Kouyate, tune by B. Sissoko.

RECENT ELECTIONS

Presidential elections were held in two rounds on 28 April and 12 May 2002. In the first round Amadou Toumani Touré won 28·0% of votes cast, against 22·7% for Soumaïla Cissé and 20·7% for Ibrahim Boubacar Keita. Turn-out was 38·6%. In the run-off between Touré and Cissé on 12 May, Touré won with 64·4% of the vote against 35·7% for Cissé.

Parliamentary elections were held in two rounds on 14 and 28 July 2002. Initial results indicated victory for the Alliance for Democracy in Mali (ADEMA) with 67 seats (down from 128 in 1997) and 47 seats for the Hope 2002 coalition. On 10 Aug. 2002 the Constitutional Court ruled these results invalid and released new results giving 66 seats to the Hope Coalition 2002 against 51 for the Alliance for Democracy in Mali. Turn-out was 25·7%.

CURRENT ADMINISTRATION

President: Amadou Toumani Touré; b. 1948 (sworn in 8 June 2002, having previously been president from March 1991–June 1992 following a coup).

In March 2003 the government comprised:

Prime Minister: Ahmed Mohamed Ag Hamani; b. 1941 (sworn in 9 June 2002). *Minister of Health:* Kéita Rokiatou N'Diaye. *Economy and Finance:* Bassari Touré. *Handicrafts and Tourism:* Bah N'Diaye. *State Territories, Civil Affairs and Housing:* Boubacar Sidiki Touré. *Industry and Commerce:* Choguel Kokala Maïga. *Agriculture, Livestock and Fisheries:* Seydou Traoré. *Education:* Mamadou Lamine Traoré. *Equipment and Transport:* Ousmane Issoufi Maïga. *Foreign Affairs and International Co-operation:* Lassana Traoré. *Defence and Veteran's Affairs:* Mahamane Kalil Maïga. *Territorial Administration and Local Collectivities:* Gen. Kafougouna Koné. *Mines, Energy and Water Resources:* Hamed Diane Semega. *Environment:* Nancouma Kéita. *Internal Security and Civil Protection:* Col. Souleymane Sidibé. *Communications and Information Technology:* Gaoussou Drabo. *Social Development, Solidarity and the Aged:* Diaye Fatoumata Coulibaly. *Labour and Public Works:* Modibo Diakité. *Children's Affairs, Family Affairs and the Promotion of Women:* Berthé Aissata Bengaly. *Culture:* Cheick Oumar Sissoko. *Justice and Guardian of the Seals:* Abdoulaye Garba Tapo. *Youth and Sports:* Djibril Tangara.

DEFENCE

There is a selective system of two years' conscription, for civilian or military service. Defence expenditure totalled US$29m. in 2000 (US$3 per capita), representing 1·0% of GDP.

Army. Strength (1999) 7,350. There are also paramilitary forces of 4,800.

Navy. There is a Navy of 50 operating three patrol craft.

Air Force. Personnel (1999) total about 400. There were around 16 combat aircraft.

INTERNATIONAL RELATIONS

Mali is a member of the UN, WTO, the African Union, African Development Bank, ECOWAS, IOM, OIC, the International Organization of the Francophonie and is an ACP member state of the ACP-EU relationship.

ECONOMY

Agriculture accounted for 46·9% of GDP in 1998, industry 17·5% and services 35·6%.

Currency. The unit of currency is the *franc CFA* (XOF), which replaced the Mali franc in 1984. It has a parity rate of 655·957 francs CFA to one euro. Total money supply in May 2002 was 460,722m. francs CFA and foreign exchange reserves were US$508m. Gold reserves were 19,000 troy oz in June 2000. Inflation was 5·2% in 2001.

Budget. Revenues for 1997 were estimated to be US$730m. and expenditures US$770m.

Performance. Real GDP growth was 3·7% in 2000 and 1·5% in 2001; total GDP in 2001 was US$2·6bn.

Banking and Finance. The bank of issue and the central bank is the regional Central Bank of West African States (BCEAO). The *Governor* is Charles Konan Banny. There are four domestic and two French-owned banks.

ENERGY AND NATURAL RESOURCES

Electricity. Installed capacity in 1990 was 84,100 kW. Production in 1998 totalled 310m. kWh, approximately 78% of it hydro-electric. Consumption per capita was 37 kWh in 1997.

Minerals. There are deposits of iron ore, uranium, diamonds, bauxite, manganese, copper and lithium. Production, 1995: limestone, 20,000 tonnes; phosphate, 3,000 tonnes; gold, 7·5 tonnes.

Agriculture. About 80% of the population depends on agriculture, mainly carried on by small peasant holdings. Mali is second only to Egypt among African cotton producers. In 1998 there were 4·61m. ha of arable land and 44,000 ha of permanent cropland. Production in 2000 included (estimates, in 1,000 tonnes): millet, 953; rice, 810; sorghum, 714; seed cotton, 480; maize, 438; sugarcane, 300; cottonseed, 220; cotton lint, 200; groundnuts, 140.

Livestock, 2000: cattle, 6·20m.; sheep, 6·00m.; goats, 8·55m.; asses, 652,000; camels, 292,000; chickens, 25m.

86,000 ha were irrigated in 1997.

Forestry. In 1995 forests covered 11·58m. ha, or 9·5% of the total land area (down from 12·15m. ha in 1990). Timber production in 1999 was 6·6m. cu. metres.

Fisheries. In 1999, 98,536 tonnes of fish were caught, exclusively from inland waters.

INDUSTRY

The main industries are food processing, followed by cotton processing, textiles and clothes. Cement and pharmaceuticals are also produced.

Labour. In 1996 the workforce was estimated to be 5,472,000 (54% males). In 1995 over 80% of the economically active population were engaged in agriculture, fisheries and forestry. Large numbers of Malians emigrate temporarily to work abroad, principally in Côte d'Ivoire.

INTERNATIONAL TRADE

Foreign debt was US$2,956m. in 2000.

Imports and Exports. In 1997 imports (f.o.b.) were valued at US$551·9m. (US$551·5m. in 1996) and exports (f.o.b.) at US$561·6m. (US$433·5m. in 1996).

Principal export commodities are cotton, livestock and gold. The main export markets are the franc zone, western Europe and the People's Republic of China. Principal import commodities are machinery and equipment, foodstuffs, construction materials, petroleum and textiles. Main import suppliers are also the franc zone (in particular Côte d'Ivoire and France), western Europe and the People's Republic of China.

COMMUNICATIONS

Roads. There were (1996 estimate) 15,100 km of classified roads, of which 1,827 km were paved. In 1996 there were 26,190 passenger cars (three per 1,000 inhabitants) and 18,240 trucks and vans. There were 72 road accident deaths in 1994.

Rail. Mali has a railway from Kayes to Koulikoro by way of Bamako, a continuation of the Dakar–Kayes line in Senegal; total length 642 km (metre-gauge). In 1990 it carried 184m. passenger-km and 273m. tonne-km of freight.

Civil Aviation. There is an international airport at Bamako (Senou), which handled 315,000 passengers (306,000 on international flights) and 5,400 tonnes of freight in 2000. Air Mali operates domestic services to eight other airports. Mali is also a member of Air Afrique. In 1998 there were international flights to Abidjan, Accra, Addis Ababa, Algiers, Banjul, Bobo-Dioulasso, Bouaké, Brazzaville, Brussels, Casablanca, Conakry, Cotonou, Dakar, Douala, Johannesburg, Libreville, N'Djaména, Néma, Niamey, Nouakchott, Ouagadougou, Paris and Zürich. In 1999 scheduled airline traffic of Mali-based carriers flew 3·0m. km, carrying 84,000 passengers (all on international flights).

Shipping. For about seven months in the year small steamboats operate a service from Koulikoro to Tombouctou and Gao, and from Bamako to Kouroussa.

Telecommunications. Mali had 39,200 main telephone lines in 2000, or 3·5 per 1,000 population. In 1998 there were 4,500 mobile phone subscribers and in 2000 there were 13,000 PCs in use (1·2 per 1,000 persons). In July 2000 there were 10,000 Internet users, up from 1,500 in May 1999.

Postal Services. In 1995 there were 124 post offices.

SOCIAL INSTITUTIONS

Justice. The Supreme Court was established at Bamako in 1969 with both judicial and administrative powers. The Court of Appeal is also at Bamako, at the apex of a system of regional tribunals and local *juges de paix*.

The population in penal institutions in 1995 was 4,384 (40 per 100,000 of national population).

Religion. The state is secular, but predominantly Sunni Muslim. About 15% of the population follow traditional animist beliefs and there is a small Christian minority.

Education. The adult literacy rate in 1999 was 39·8% (47·3% among males and 32·7% among females). In 1997–98 there were 197 pre-primary schools with 675 teachers for 23,548 pupils; 2,511 primary schools with 10,853 teachers for 862,875 pupils. During the period 1990–95 only 19% of females of primary school age were enrolled in school. In 1997–98 there were 188,109 secondary level pupils, and in 1990 there were 6,703 students at university level.

Health. In 1993 there were 483 doctors and 1,674 nurses.

CULTURE

Broadcasting. Broadcasting is the responsibility of the autonomous Radiodiffusion Télévision du Mali. Number of sets in 1997: radio, 570,000; TV, 45,000 (colour by SECAM).

Press. In 1996 there were three daily newspapers with a combined circulation of 12,000.

Tourism. There were 83,000 foreign tourists in 1998, bringing in revenue of US$50m.

DIPLOMATIC REPRESENTATIVES
Of Mali in the United Kingdom (resides at Brussels)
Ambassador: Ahmed Mohamed Ag Hamani.

Of the United Kingdom in Mali (Rue 132, Porte 902, Badalabougou-Ouest, BP 2069, Bamako)
Ambassador: Graeme Loten.

Of Mali in the USA (2130 R. St., NW, Washington, D.C., 20008)
Ambassador: Vacant.
Chargé d'Affaires a.i.: Mahamane E. Bania Toure.

Of the USA in Mali (Rue Rochester NY and Rue Mohamed V, Bamako)
Ambassador: Vicki Huddleston.

Of Mali to the United Nations
Ambassador: Moctar Ouane.

Of Mali to the European Union
Ambassador: Ahmed Mohamed Ag Hamani.

MALTA

Repubblika ta' Malta

Capital: Valletta
Population estimate, 2000: 390,000
GDP per capita, 2000: (PPP$) 17,273
HDI/world rank: 0·875/30

KEY HISTORICAL EVENTS
Malta was held in turn by Phoenicians, Carthaginians and Romans, and was conquered by Arabs in 870. From 1090 to 1530 it was subject to the same rulers as Sicily. Subsequently, the Knights of St John ruled until dispersed by Napoleon in 1798. The Maltese rose in rebellion against the French and the island was blockaded by the British aided by the Maltese from 1798 to 1800. The Maltese people requested the protection of the British Crown in 1802 on condition that their rights and privileges be preserved. The islands were finally annexed to the British Crown by the Treaty of Paris in 1814. Malta became independent on 21 Sept. 1964 and a republic within the Commonwealth on 13 Dec. 1974. On 16 July 1990 Malta applied for full membership of the European Union. In 2002 Malta was one of ten countries nominated for membership in 2004. At a referendum in March 2003, EU entry won 53·6% support.

TERRITORY AND POPULATION
The three Maltese islands and minor islets lie in the Mediterranean 93 km (at the nearest point) south of Sicily and 288 km east of Tunisia. The area of Malta is 246 sq. km (94·9 sq. miles); Gozo, 67 sq. km (25·9 sq. miles) and the virtually uninhabited Comino, 3 sq. km (1·1 sq. miles); total area, 316 sq. km (121·9 sq. miles). The census population in 1995 was 376,335. Population, 31 Dec. 2000, 382,525; Malta island, 352,835; Gozo and Comino, 29,690. Density 1,203 per sq. km.

The UN gives a projected population for 2010 of 405,000.

In 1999, 90·3% of the population were urban. Chief town and port, Valletta, population 7,048 (2000) but the southern harbour district, 83,405. Other towns: Birkirkara, 21,566; Qormi, 17,982; Mosta, 17,314; Zabbar, 14,566; Sliema, 12,173.

The constitution provides that the national language and language of the courts is Maltese, but both Maltese and English are official languages.

SOCIAL STATISTICS
2000: births, 4,255; deaths, 2,957; marriages, 2,545; emigrants, 67; returned emigrants, 450. 2000 rates per 1,000 population: birth, 11·2; death, 7·8; marriage, 6·7. Divorce and abortion are illegal. In 2000 the most popular age range for marrying was 25–29 for males and 20–24 for females. Life expectancy at birth in 2000: 74·3 years for males and 80·2 years for females. Annual growth, 2000, 0·6%. Infant mortality in 2000: 6·1 per 1,000 live births; fertility rate, 2000, 1·8 births per woman.

CLIMATE
The climate is Mediterranean, with hot, dry and sunny conditions in summer and very little rain from May to Aug. Rainfall is not excessive and falls mainly between Oct. and March. Average daily sunshine in winter is six hours and in summer over ten hours. Valletta, Jan. 12·8°C (55°F), July 25·6°C (78°F). Annual rainfall 578 mm (23").

CONSTITUTION AND GOVERNMENT
Malta is a parliamentary democracy. The Constitution of 1964 provides for a *President*, a *House of Representatives* of members elected by universal suffrage and a Cabinet consisting of the Prime Minister and such number of Ministers as may be appointed. The Constitution makes provision for the protection of fundamental rights and freedom of the individual, and for freedom of conscience and religious worship, and guarantees the separation of executive, judicial and

legislative powers. In 2000 the House of Representatives had 65 members directly elected on a plurality basis.

National Anthem. 'Lil din l'art helwa, l'omm li tatna isimha' ('Guard her, O Lord, as ever Thou hast guarded'); words by Dun Karm Psaila, tune by Dr Robert Samut.

RECENT ELECTIONS
At the elections of 12 April 2003 turn-out was 96·2%. The Nationalist Party (NP) gained 34 seats with 51·7% of votes cast; the Labour Party (MLP), 31 with 47·6%.

CURRENT ADMINISTRATION
President: Guido de Marco; b. 1931 (NP; sworn in 4 April 1999).

In April 2003 the government comprised:

Prime Minister: Edward Fenech Adami; b. 1934 (NP; sworn in on 6 Sept. 1998 and re-elected in April 2003, having previously held office May 1987–Oct. 1996).

Deputy Prime Minister, Minister for Social Policy and Leader of the House of Representatives: Lawrence Gonzi. *Minister for Foreign Affairs:* Joseph Borg. *Education:* Louis Galea. *Finance:* John Dalli. *Environment:* Francis Zammit-Dimech. *Tourism:* Michael Refalo. *Economic Services:* Josef Bonnici. *Home Affairs:* Tonio Borg. *Transport and Communications:* Censu Galea. *Health:* Louis Deguara. *Agriculture and Fisheries:* Ninu Zammit. *Justice and Local Government:* Austin Gatt. *For Gozo:* Giovanna Debono.

Speaker: Anton Tabone.

Government Website: http://www.gov.mt/

DEFENCE
On 1 Jan. 2000 the Armed Forces of Malta (AFM) had a strength of about 1,777 (including 119 reserves) and consisted of Headquarters and three Regiments. An Emergency Volunteer Reserve Force was introduced in 1998; initial intake, 60. In addition to infantry and low level air defence artillery weapons, the AFM are equipped with helicopters, fixed wing and trainer aircraft. There is no conscription.

Apart from normal military duties, AFM are also responsible for Search and Rescue, airport security, surveillance of Malta's territorial and fishing zones, harbour traffic control and anti-pollution duties.

In 2000 military expenditure totalled US$26m. (US$67 per capita), representing 0·7% of GDP.

Navy. There is a maritime squadron numbering 204 personnel.

Air Force. Italy has an Air Force presence on the island of 17 personnel.

INTERNATIONAL RELATIONS
Malta is a member of the UN, WTO, the Commonwealth, the Council of Europe, the Organization for Security and Co-operation in Europe, the International Atomic Energy Agency, the Organization for the Prohibition of Chemical Weapons, the Comprehensive Test-Ban Treaty Organization and the Inter-Parliamentary Union.

Accession negotiations for Malta to join the EU were formally opened in Feb. 2000. The report on Malta's progress towards accession issued by the Commission in Nov. 2001 and endorsed by the European Council in Laeken in Dec. 2001 confirmed that Malta fulfils all the political and economic criteria for membership. Malta held a referendum on EU membership on 9 March 2003, in which 53·6% of votes cast were in favour of accession, with 46·4% against. Malta is scheduled to become a member of the EU on 1 May 2004.

ECONOMY
Agriculture accounted for an estimated 3% of GDP in 1997, industry 26% and services 71%.

Overview. The prime objectives of economic strategy are the achievement of a sustainable rate of economic growth, high employment and low stable inflation. To compete internationally, the private sector must be the prime mover of the economy. In the 1999 budget, the government committed itself to reducing the budget deficit to 4% of GDP by 2004. To maximize the benefits from privatization, the government aims at strategic partnerships with international enterprises.

An Institute for the Promotion of Small Enterprises (IPSE) has been established and a number of supporting incentive schemes are being implemented. A Business Promotion Act (BPA) has been enacted to update the Industrial Development Act (IDA) of 1988. The aim is to promote industries that demonstrate growth and employment potential. To maintain Malta's competitive position as a tourist attraction, the Malta Tourism Authority launched its first Strategic Plan for the period 2000–02. The Malta Financial Services Centre regulates and supervises credit and financial institutions with effect from 1 Jan. 2002. In preparation for EU membership, the government has embarked on a three-year capital account liberalization.

Currency. The unit of currency is the *Maltese lira* (formerly *pound*) (MTL) of 100 *cents*. Total money supply was Lm644m. in March 2002. Inflation was 2·4% in 2000 and 2·9% in 2001. Gold reserves were 4,000 troy oz in June 2002 and foreign exchange reserves US$1,769m.

Budget. Revenue and expenditure (in Lm1m.):

	1996	1997	1998	1999	2000
Revenue	541·5	684·8	659·1	721·6	642·9
Expenditure	578·7	641·7	666·0	691·0	719·5

The most important sources of revenue are VAT, customs and excise duties, income tax, social security and receipts from the Central Bank of Malta. Also significant in certain years are proceeds from the sale of Government shares, foreign grants and foreign and local loans.

Performance. The average annual GDP growth in 1994–98 was 5·5%, with growth in 1998 itself of 3·4%. Total GDP in 2000 was US$3·6bn. In 2001 real GDP growth was negative, at –0·8%.

Banking and Finance. The Central Bank of Malta (*Governor*, Michael C. Bonello) was founded in 1968. In Dec. 2001 there were five domestic credit institutions undertaking business in the local market. 13 local financial institutions, licensed in terms of the Financial Institutions Act 1994, also provided services that ranged from exchange bureau-related business to merchant banking. There are also 13 international credit institutions that are licensed to undertake business in foreign currency and with non-residents.

Weights and Measures. The metric system is used.

ENERGY AND NATURAL RESOURCES

Environment. According to the *World Bank Atlas* Malta's carbon dioxide emissions in 1998 were the equivalent of 4·7 tonnes per capita.

Electricity. Electricity is generated at two interconnected thermal power stations located at Marsa (272 MW) and Delimara (305 MW). The primary transmission voltages are 132,000, 33,000 and 11,000 volts while the low-voltage system is 400/230V, 50Hz with neutral point earthed. Installed capacity was 577,000 kW in 2000. Production in 2001 was 1·94bn. kWh; consumption per capita was 4,757 kWh.

Oil and Gas. Malta covers a large offshore area, representing the extensions of southeast Sicily, east Tunisia and northwest Libya where significant hydrocarbon reserves and production exist. Active exploration is at present being undertaken by AGIP and Hardman Resources NL in areas to the northwest, southwest and east of Malta. Discussions are also under way with other oil companies. Eni, an Italian distributor, drilled a well during 2002 in search of a hydrocarbon play similar to the one found in Sicily. An extensive seismic survey was carried out in 2001 to evaluate the hydrocarbon potential of the Maltese offshore and subsequently provide a framework for future exploration. Malta intends to intensify exploration by offering companies competitive terms and returns that are commensurate with the risk undertaken.

Water. The demand for water during 2000–01 was 33·7m. cu. metres, a reduction of 9% over the previous year, mainly as a result of improved leakage control. Seawater desalination (Reverse Osmosis Plants) provided 49% of the total potable water requirements.

Agriculture. Malta is self-sufficient in fresh vegetables, pig-meat, poultry, eggs and fresh milk. The main crops are potatoes (the spring crop being the country's primary agricultural export), vegetables and fruits, with some items such as tomatoes serving as the main input in the local canning industry. In 2000 there were about 2,375 full-time farmers and 15,519 part-time. There were around 11,513 agricultural holdings and 950 intensive livestock farm units.

Agriculture contributes around Lm30·8m. annually towards GDP, or 2·6%. 2000 production figures (in 1,000 tonnes): potatoes, 35; tomatoes, 21; melons, 14; wheat, 10; cauliflowers, 6; onions, 6.

Livestock in 2000: cattle, 19,000; pigs, 80,000; sheep, 16,000; chickens, 1m. Livestock produce accounted for 68·5% of the total value of agricultural production during 1998.

Fisheries. In 2001 the fishing industry employed 1,747 power-propelled fishing boats, engaging around 365 full time and 1,598 part-time fisherman. The catch for 2001 was 841 tonnes, valued at Lm1,587,044. It is estimated that during 2001 the local aqua-culture industry produced a total of about 1,235 tonnes of sea bass and bream. 95% of the local production was exported to EU countries in 2000, especially to Italy.

INDUSTRY

Besides manufacturing (food, clothing, chemicals, electrical machinery parts and electronic components and products), the mainstays of the economy are ship repair and shipbuilding, agriculture, small crafts units, tourism and the provision of other services such as the freeport facilities. The majority of state-aided manufacturing enterprises operating in Malta are foreign-owned or with foreign interests. The Malta Development Corporation is the government agency responsible for promoting investment, while the Malta Export Trade Corporation serves as a catalyst to the export of local products.

Labour. The labour supply in Sept. 2001 was 144,692 (females, 41,163), including 37,882 in private direct production (agriculture and fisheries, 2,198; manufacturing, 29,263; oil drilling, construction and quarrying, 6,421), 50,182 in private market services, 48,641 in the public sector (including government departments, armed forces, revenue security corps, independent statutory bodies and companies with public sector majority shareholding), and 1,003 in temporary employment. There were 6,984 registered unemployed (4·8% of labour supply).

Trade Unions. At the end of June 2001 there were 33 Trade Unions with a total membership of 87,158 and 24 employers' associations with a total membership of 8,547. In 1999–2000 the largest union was the General Workers' Union representing 57% of workers in industry and services.

INTERNATIONAL TRADE

Imports are being liberalized. Marsaxlokk is an all-weather freeport zone for transhipment activities. The Malta Export Trade Corporation promotes local exports. External debt was US$10,600m. in 1999.

Imports and Exports. In 2000 imports (f.o.b.) were valued at US$3,097·0m. (US$2,588·4m. in 1999) and exports (f.o.b.) at US$2,476·2m. (US$2,016·9m. in 1999). In 2000 the principal items of imports were: machinery and transport equipment, Lm852·6m.; manufactures, Lm146·8m.; semi-manufactures, Lm145·0m.; fuels, Lm106·5m; foodstuffs, Lm103·6m.; chemicals, Lm92·5m. Of domestic exports: machinery and transport equipment, Lm736·1m.; manufactures, Lm151·3m.; semi-manufactures, Lm53·9m.; foodstuffs, Lm17·1m.; chemicals, Lm13·0m.; beverages and tobacco, Lm3·5m.

In 2000 imports valued at Lm281·9m. came from France; Lm249·7m. from Italy; Lm158·5m. from USA; Lm122·1m. from Germany; Lm119·7m. from UK. Main export markets: USA, Lm286·5m.; Singapore, Lm164·7m.; Germany, Lm96·7m.; France, Lm84·1m.; UK, Lm70·0m.; Italy, Lm33·1m.

Trade Fairs. The Malta Trade Fairs Corporation organizes the International Fair of Malta (1–15 July).

COMMUNICATIONS

Roads. In 2002 there were 2,254 km of roads, including 185 km of motorways. About 94% of roads are paved. Motor vehicles licensed up to 31 Dec. 2001 totalled 254,405 including: private cars, 188,495; commercial vehicles, 44,016; motorcycles, 15,257; buses and minibuses, 1,132. There were 16 deaths as a result of road accidents in 1998.

Civil Aviation. The national carrier is Air Malta, which is 96·4% state-owned. There were scheduled services in 2000 to around 30 different countries. In 2000 there were 36,489 commercial aircraft movements at Malta International Airport. 3,004,714 passengers, 13,699 tonnes of freight and 835 tonnes of mail were handled. In 1999 Air Malta flew 24·0m. km and carried 1,421,300 passengers.

Shipping. There is a car ferry between Malta and Gozo. The number of vessels registered on 31 Dec. 2001 was 3,031 totalling 27,042,430 GT, a total only exceeded by Panama, Liberia and the Bahamas. Ships entering harbour, excluding yachts and fishing vessels, during 2001, 5,565. 357 cruise vessels put in during 2000.

The Malta Freeport plays an important role in the economy as it is effectively positioned to act as a distribution centre in the Mediterranean. Apart from providing efficient transhipment operations to the major shipping lines, the Freeport offers warehouse facilities and the storage and blending of oil products.

Telecommunications. The Maltacom plc group is Malta's leading tele-communications and ancillary services provider. Malta's national network consist of 12 AXE10 Ericsson Digital Exchanges and 1 Siemens EWSD Exchange. Maltacom provides various data services including packet switching, frame relay and high-speed leased lines. The company has an optical fibre-based SDH backbone and large companies are connected to the Network. Maltacom's International Network includes two fully digital gateways, two satellite Standard B Earth Stations (one transmitting to the Atlantic Ocean Region and the other to the Indian Ocean Region) and an optic fibre submarine cable linking Malta to Sicily (Italy) and terrestrially extending to Palermo which is the hub of international submarine cables passing through the Mediterranean.

In 2000 main telephone lines in use numbered 204,200 (521·7 per 1,000 inhabitants) and there were 200,000 PCs (453·2 per 1,000 persons). Mobile phone subscribers numbered 37,500 in 1999 and there were 6,000 fax machines in 1996. In Dec. 2001 there were 59,000 Internet users.

Postal Services. In 1994 there were 50 post offices operated by Maltapost plc. Airmail dispatches are forwarded once daily to the UK, Canada, Australia, USA and Italy. Airmails from most countries are received daily or every other day. There are branch post offices and sub post offices in most towns and villages in Malta and Gozo.

SOCIAL INSTITUTIONS

Justice. The number of persons arrested between 1 Jan. 2001 and 31 Oct. 2001 was 5,451; those found guilty numbered 2,180. 184 persons were committed to prison.

In Jan. 2002 police strength numbered 103 officers (15 women) and 1,451 other ranks (183 women).

Malta abolished the death penalty for all crimes in 2000.

Religion. 98% of the population belong to the Roman Catholic Church, which is established by law as the religion of the country, although full liberty of conscience and freedom of worship are guaranteed.

Education. Adult literacy rate, 1999, 91·8% (male, 91·1%; female, 92·4%).

Education is compulsory between the ages of 5 and 16 and free in government schools from kindergarten to university. Kindergarten education is provided for three- and four-year old children. The primary school course lasts six years. In Oct. 2000 there were 5,300 children in state kindergartens and 21,300 in 79 state primary schools. There are education centres for children with special needs, but they are taught in ordinary schools if possible.

Secondary schools, trade schools and junior lyceums provide secondary education in the state sector. At the end of their primary education, pupils sit the 11+

examination to start a secondary education course. Pupils who qualify are admitted in the junior lyceum, while the others attend secondary schools. In 2001, 11 junior lyceums had a total of 9,200 students (5,600 girls and 3,600 boys). About 8,300 pupils attend secondary schools (3,960 girls, 4,340 boys), and in 1998 there were five centres catering for 1,300 children (400 girls and 900 boys) at secondary level whose cultural capital was low. Secondary schools and junior lyceums offer a five-year course leading to the Secondary Education Certificate and the General Certificate of Education, Ordinary Level.

At the end of the five-year secondary course, students may opt to follow a higher academic or technical or vocational course of from one to four years. The academic courses generally lead to Intermediate and Advanced Level examinations set by the British universities. The junior college, administered by the University, prepares students specifically for a university course. The Matriculation Certificate, which qualifies students for admission to university, is a broad-based holistic qualification covering—among others—the humanities and the sciences, together with systems of knowledge.

About 30% of the student population attend non-state schools, from kindergarten to higher secondary level. In Oct. 2000 there were about 25,900 pupils attending non-state schools, 800 of whom were at post-compulsory secondary level, 17,500 were in schools run by the Roman Catholic Church, while 8,300 students were attending private schools. Under an agreement between the government and the Church, the government subsidizes Church schools and students attending these schools do not pay any fees. During 2001 the government introduced tax rebates for parents whose children attended independent schools.

Nearly 8,500 students (including 550 from overseas) were following courses at the University in 2000, University students receive a stipend.

In Oct. 2000 about 7,600 students were attending adult or evening courses covering a very wide spectrum of studies at different levels. Many of these courses lead to a recognized certification.

In 1996 total expenditure on education came to 5·1% of GNP and represented 10·8% of total government expenditure.

Health. In 2000 there were 2,220 doctors, 157 dentists, 690 pharmacists, 230 midwives and 4,050 nursing personnel. There were eight hospitals (three private) with 2,122 beds. There are also nine health centres.

Welfare. Legislation provides a national contributory insurance scheme and also for the payment of non-contributory allowances, assistances and pensions. It covers the payment of marriage grants, maternity benefits, child allowances, parental allowances, handicapped child allowance, family bonus, sickness benefit, injury benefits, disablement benefits, unemployment benefit, contributory pensions in respect of retirement, invalidity and widowhood, and non-contributory medical assistance, free medical aids, social assistance, a carers' pension and pensions for the handicapped, the blind and the aged.

CULTURE

Broadcasting. Radio and TV services are under the control of the Broadcasting Authority, an independent statutory body. The government-owned Public Broadcasting Services Ltd was set up in 1991 and operates three radio stations and a TV station (colour by PAL). Legislation of 1991 introduced private commercial broadcasting. In 2001 there were 13 radio and 5 TV services and a cable TV network. In 1997 there were 280,000 television sets and 255,000 radio receivers.

Cinema. In 2000 there were five cinemas.

Press. In 2000 there were 2 English and 2 Maltese dailies, 5 Maltese and 3 English weeklies and 2 financial weeklies in English.

Tourism. Tourism is the major foreign currency earner, and accounts for more than 25% of Malta's GDP.

In 2000 an estimated 1·2m. tourists (34·7% from the UK) visited Malta, generating earnings of Lm268·5m. Cruise passenger visits totalled 170,782. In 2000 there were 9,321 persons directly employed by the tourism industry.

Festivals. Major festivals include the Malta Song Festival; Carnival Festivals at Valletta (Feb.); History and Elegance Festival at Valletta and Mdina (April); National Folk Singing (May); Malta International Arts Festival, Malta Jazz Festival, International Food and Beer Festival (June/July); Festa Season (June–Sept.); Malta International Choir Festival, Amateur Film and Video Festival (Nov.).

Libraries. The National Library, housed in one of Valletta's 18th century buildings, is Malta's foremost research Library, founded in 1763. There is a Central Public Library in Floriana, Branch Libraries in government schools in most towns and villages, and the University of Malta Library. *Specialized libraries:* Central Bank of Malta, Central Office of Statistics, Foundation for International Studies, Franco-Maltese Documentation and Research Centre, Malta External Trade Corporation.

Theatre and Opera. The Manoel Theatre (built 1731) is Malta's National Theatre. There is also the Mediterranean Conference Centre in Valletta, and the Astra Theatre in Victoria, Gozo.

Museums and Galleries. In Valletta: National Museum of Archaeology, National Museum of Fine Arts, Palace Armoury, War Museum (Fort St. Elmo). Mdina and Rabat: National Museum of Natural History, Museum of Roman Antiquities, St Paul's Catacombs, the Cathedral Museum. Paula: Hal Saflieni Hypoguem. Qrendi: Hagar Qim and Mnajra Megalithic Temples. Birzebbuga: Ghar Dalam Cave and Museum. Vittoriosa: Maritime Museum. Gozo (Victoria): Museum of Archaeology, Natural Science Museum, Folklore Museum. Xaghra: Ggantija Megalithic Temples.

DIPLOMATIC REPRESENTATIVES

Of Malta in the United Kingdom (36–38 Piccadilly, London, W1V 0PQ)
High Commissioner: George Bonello Du Puis.

Of the United Kingdom in Malta (Whitehall Mansions, Ta'Xbiex Seafront, Msida MSD 11)
High Commissioner: Vincent Fean.

Of Malta in the USA (2017 Connecticut Ave., NW, Washington, D.C., 20008)
Ambassador: John Lowell.

Of the USA in Malta (Development Hse., St Anne St., Floriana)
Ambassador: Anthony Horace Gioia.

Of Malta to the United Nations
Ambassador: Walter Bazan.

Of Malta to the European Union
Ambassador: Victor Camilleri.

FURTHER READING

Central Office of Statistics (Lascaris, Valletta). *Statistical Abstracts of the Maltese Islands*, a quarterly digest of statistics, quarterly and annual trade returns, annual vital statistics and annual publications on shipping and aviation, education, agriculture, industry, National Accounts and Balance of Payments.

Department of Information (3 Castille Place, Valletta). *The Malta Government Gazette, Malta Information, Economic Survey [year], Reports on the Working of Government Departments, The Maltese Economy in Figures, 1986–1995, Business Opportunities on Malta, Acts of Parliament and Subsidiary Legislation, Laws of Malta, Constitution of Malta 1992.*

Central Bank of Malta. *Annual Reports.*
Chamber of Commerce (annual). *Trade Directory.*
Berg, W. G., *Historical Dictionary of Malta.* Metuchen (NJ), 1995
Boswell, D. and Beeley, B., *Malta.* [Bibliography] 2nd ed. ABC-Clio, Oxford and Santa Barbara (CA), 1998.
The Malta Yearbook. Valletta

National statistical office: Central Office of Statistics, Auberge d'Italie, Valletta.
Website: http://www.nso.gov.mt

MARSHALL ISLANDS

Capital: Majuro Atoll
Population estimate, 2000: 652,000
GDP per capita: not available
GNP per capita: $1,950

Republic of the
Marshall Islands

KEY HISTORICAL EVENTS
A German protectorate was formed in 1886 which was occupied at the beginning of the First World War by Japan. Japan was awarded a mandate by the League of Nations in 1919. During the Second World War the Islands were occupied by Allied forces in 1944, and became part of the UN Trust Territory of the Pacific Islands created on 18 July 1947 and administered by the USA. On 21 Oct. 1986 the islands gained independence and a Compact of Free Association with the USA came into force.

TERRITORY AND POPULATION
The Marshall Islands lie in the North Pacific Ocean north of Kiribati and east of Micronesia, and consist of an archipelago of 31 coral atolls, 5 single islands and 1,152 islets strung out in two chains, eastern and western. The land area is 181 sq. km (70 sq. miles). The capital is Majuro Atoll in the eastern chain (population, 1999 estimate, 33,000). The principal atoll in the western chain is Kwajalein, containing the only other town, Ebeye (population estimate, 1997, 15,000). The two archipelagic island chains of Bikini and Enewetak are former US nuclear test sites; Kwajalein is now used as a US missile test range. The islands lay claim to the US territory of Wake Island. At the census of 1999 the population was 50,840; density, 281 per sq. km.

In 1995 some 69% of the population lived in urban areas. About 97% of the population are Marshallese, a Micronesian people.

English is universally spoken and is the official language. Two major Marshallese dialects from the Malayo-Polynesian family, and Japanese, are also spoken.

SOCIAL STATISTICS
1997 births, estimate, 1,607; deaths, 243. 1997 rates per 1,000 population, estimates: birth, 26·4; death, 4·0; infant mortality rate, 31 per 1,000 live births; life expectancy, 64·1 years. Annual population growth rate, 1990–99, 3·4%; fertility rate, 1999, 5·4 births per woman.

CLIMATE
Hot and humid, with wet season from May to Nov. The islands border the typhoon belt. Jaluit, Jan. 81°F (27·2°C), July 82°F (27·8°C). Annual rainfall 161" (4,034 mm).

CONSTITUTION AND GOVERNMENT
Under the constitution which came into force on 1 May 1979, the Marshall Islands form a republic with a *President* as head of state and government, who is elected for four-year terms by the parliament. The parliament consists of a 33-member *House of Assembly* (Nitijela), directly elected by popular vote for four-year terms. There is also a 12-member appointed *Council of Chiefs* (Iroij) which has a consultative and advisory capacity on matters affecting customary law and practice.

RECENT ELECTIONS
The last presidential election was held on 14 Jan. 1997. At the House of Assembly elections on 22 Nov. 1999 only non-partisans were elected.

CURRENT ADMINISTRATION
President: Kessai Note (elected on 3 Jan. 2000; sworn in 10 Jan. 2000).
In March 2003 the government comprised:

Minister of Assistance to the President: Tadashi Lometo. *Education:* Wilfred Kendall. *Finance:* Michael Konelios. *Foreign Affairs and Trade:* Gerald Zackios. *Health and Environment:* Alvin Jacklick. *Internal Affairs and Social Welfare:* Nidal Lorak. *Public Works:* Rien Morris. *Resources, Development and Works:* John Silk. *Transportation and Communications:* Brenson Wase.

DEFENCE
The Compact of Free Association gave the USA responsibility for defence in return for US assistance. There is a police force.

INTERNATIONAL RELATIONS
The Marshall Islands are a member of the UN, Asian Development Bank, Pacific Community (formerly the South Pacific Commission) and the Pacific Islands Forum.

ECONOMY
Agriculture accounts for approximately 15% of GDP, industry 13% and services 72%.

Overview. Fisheries and tourism offer the best potential for economic growth and the government plans to devote increased resources to these activities.

Currency. US currency is used. The average annual inflation rate during the period 1990–96 was 6·4%.

Budget. 1995–96 estimate: revenue, US$80·1m.; expenditure: US$77·4m. Under the terms of the Compact of Free Association, the USA provides approximately US$65m. a year in aid.

Performance. Real GDP growth was 0·6% in 2001 (0·7% in 2000).

Banking and Finance. There are three Banks: the Bank of Marshall Islands, the Bank of Hawaii and the Bank of Guam.

The Marshall Islands were one of 15 countries and territories named in a report in June 2000 as failing to co-operate in the fight against international money laundering. The Financial Action Task Force on Money Laundering was set up by the G7 group of major industrialized nations.

ENERGY AND NATURAL RESOURCES
Electricity. Total installed capacity (1997), 20,200 kW. Production (1994), 57m. kWh.

Minerals. High-grade phosphate deposits are mined on Ailinglaplap Atoll. Deep-seabed minerals are an important natural resource.

Agriculture. A small amount of agricultural produce is exported: coconuts, tomatoes, melons and breadfruit. Other important crops include copra, taro, cassava and sweet potatoes. Pigs and chicken constitute the main livestock.

Fisheries. Total catch in 1999 amounted to approximately 400 tonnes. There is a commercial tuna-fishing industry with a canning factory on Majuro. Seaweed is cultivated.

INDUSTRY
The main industries are copra, fish, tourism, handicrafts (items made from shell, wood and pearl), mining, manufacturing, construction and power.

Labour. The total labour force numbered 11,488 in 1988. An estimated 16% were unemployed in 1991. In 1994 agriculture accounted for 16% of the working population; industry, 14%; services, 70%.

INTERNATIONAL TRADE
The Compact of Free Association with the USA is the major source of income for the Marshall Islands, and accounts for about 70% of total GDP.

Imports and Exports. Imports (mainly oil) were estimated at US$69·9m. in 1995; exports, US$21·3m. Main trading partners: USA and Japan. There is also increasing trade with Australia, New Zealand, the Fiji Islands and Taiwan, and in 1998 trade agreements were initiated with China and Indonesia. Main exports: coconut oil, copra cake, chilled and frozen fish, pet fish, shells and handicrafts.

COMMUNICATIONS

Roads. There are paved roads on major islands (Majuro, Kwajalein); roads are otherwise stone-, coral- or laterite-surfaced. In 1994 there were 1,418 passenger cars and 193 trucks and buses.

Civil Aviation. There were nine paved and seven unpaved airports in 1996. The main airport is Majuro International. In 1998 there were flights to the Fiji Islands, Guam, Honolulu, Johnston Island, Kiribati, Micronesia and Tuvalu as well as domestic services. The national carrier is Air Marshall Islands.

Shipping. Majuro is the main port. In 1998 merchant shipping totalled 6,442,000 GRT, including oil tankers 3,561,000 GRT.

Telecommunications. In 2000 there were 4,000 telephone main lines in use (58·7 per 1,000 persons). There is a US satellite communications system on Kwajalein and two Intelsat satellite earth stations (Pacific Ocean). The National Tele-communications Authority provides domestic and international services. Mobile phone subscribers numbered 300 in 1998 and there were 3,000 PCs in use in 2000 (47·0 per 1,000 persons). There were 500 Internet users in Dec. 1999.

Postal Services. Postal services are available on the main island of Majuro and also in Ebeye.

SOCIAL INSTITUTIONS

Justice. The Supreme Court is situated on Majuro. There is also a High Court, a District Court and 23 Community Courts. A Traditional Court deals with disputes involving land properties and customs.

Religion. The population is mainly Protestant, with Roman Catholics next. Other Churches and denominations include Latter-day Saints (Mormons), Jehovah's Witnesses, Baptists, Baha'i, Seventh Day Adventists and Assembly of God.

Education. In 1994 there were 13,565 pupils in 104 primary schools, and 2,483 pupils in 11 secondary schools. There is a College of the Marshall Islands, and a subsidiary of the University of the South Pacific, on Majuro.

Health. There were two hospitals in 1997, with a total of 129 beds. There are 34 doctors, 141 nurses and health assistants, and 4 dentists.

CULTURE

Broadcasting. There are one TV and three radio stations.

Press. There is a publication called Micronitor (The Marshall Islands Journal).

Tourism. In 1998 there were 6,000 foreign tourists, spending US$3m.

Festivals. Custom Day and the Annual Canoe Race are the main festivals.

Libraries. There is one public library.

DIPLOMATIC REPRESENTATIVES

Of the United Kingdom in the Marshall Islands
Ambassador: Ian Powell (resides at Suva, Fiji Islands).

Of the Marshall Islands in the USA (2433 Massachusetts Ave., NW, Washington, D.C., 20008)
Ambassador: Banny de Brum.

Of the USA in the Marshall Islands (Oceanside Mejen Weto, Long Island, Majuro)
Ambassador: Michael J. Senko.

Of the Marshall Islands to the United Nations
Ambassador: Jackeo A. Relang.

Of the Marshall Islands to the European Union
Ambassador: Laurence N. Edwards.

MAURITANIA

République Islamique Arabe
et Africaine de Mauritanie

Capital: Nouakchott
Population estimate, 2000: 2·67m.
GDP per capita, 2000: (PPP$) 1,677
HDI/world rank: 0·438/152

KEY HISTORICAL EVENTS
Mauritania became a French protectorate in 1903 and a colony in 1920. It achieved full independence on 28 Nov. 1960. Mauritania became a one-party state in 1964.

The 1980s were characterized by territorial disputes with Morocco and Senegal. Seizing power in 1984, Lieut.-Col. Maaouiya Ould Sidi Ahmed Taya prepared the way for a new constitution allowing for a multi-party political system, but which also gave extensive powers to the president.

TERRITORY AND POPULATION
Mauritania is bounded west by the Atlantic Ocean, north by Western Sahara, northeast by Algeria, east and southeast by Mali, and south by Senegal. The total area is 1,030,700 sq. km (398,000 sq. miles) of which 47% is desert, and the population at the census of 2000 was 2,548,157; density, 2·47 per sq. km. In 1999, 56·4% of the population was urban.

The UN gives a projected population for 2010 of 3·58m.

Area, population and chief towns of the Nouakchott Capital District and 12 regions at the 1988 census:

Region	Area (sq. km)	Population (1992 estimate)	Chief town
Açâba	36,600	185,574	Kiffa
Adrar	215,300	62,906	Atâr
Brakna	37,100	207,590	Aleg
Dakhlet Nouâdhibou	22,300	83,246	Nouâdhibou
Gorgol	13,600	201,301	Kaédi
Guidimaka	10,300	129,797	Sélibaby
Hodh ech-Chargui	182,700	234,011	Néma
Hodh el-Gharbi	53,400	175,089	Aïoun el Atrouss
Inchiri	46,800	13,630	Akjoujt
Nouakchott District	1,000	324,037	Nouakchott
Tagant	95,200	67,939	Tidjikdja
Tiris Zemmour	252,900	37,534	Zouérate
Trarza	67,800	217,867	Rosso

Principal towns (1999 population): Nouakchott, 881,000 including the suburbs of Nouâdhibou and Kaédi.

In 1987 there were also 0·43m. nomads.

The major ethnic groups are (with numbers in 1993): Moors (of mixed Arab, Berber and African origin), 1,513,400; Wolof, 147,000; Tukulor, 114,600; Soninke, 60,000.

Arabic is the official language. French no longer has official status. Pulaar, Soninke and Wolof are national languages.

SOCIAL STATISTICS
2000 estimates: births, 109,000; deaths, 34,000. 2000 rates, estimate (per 1,000 population): births, 42·9; deaths, 13·4. Expectation of life at birth in 1999 was 49·5 years for males and 52·7 for females. Annual population growth rate, 1990–99, 2·8%. Infant mortality, 1999, 120 per 1,000 live births; fertility rate, 1999, 5·4 births per woman.

CLIMATE
A tropical climate, but conditions are generally arid, even near the coast, where the only appreciable rains come in July to Sept. Nouakchott, Jan. 71°F (21·7°C), July 82°F (27·8°C). Annual rainfall 6" (158 mm).

CONSTITUTION AND GOVERNMENT
A referendum was held in July 1991 to approve a new constitution instituting multi-party politics. Turn-out was 85·34%; 97·94% of votes cast were in favour.

The new constitution envisages that the President is elected by universal suffrage for renewable six-year terms. There is a 56-member *Senate* and an 81-member *National Assembly.* Parties specifically Islamic are not permitted.

National Anthem. No words, tune by T. Nikiprowetzky.

RECENT ELECTIONS
Presidential elections were held on 12 Dec. 1997. There were five candidates. Col. Maaouiya Ould Sidi Ahmed Taya was re-elected with 90·2% of votes cast, compared to 62·8% in the elections of 24 Jan. 1992.

Elections for the National Assembly were held on 19 and 26 Oct. 2001. The Democratic and Socialist Republican Party (PRDS) gained 64 seats with 51·0% of votes cast. Turn-out was 54·5%. In the Senate elections of 7 and 14 April 2000 the PRDS obtained 52 of the 56 seats.

CURRENT ADMINISTRATION
President: Maaouiya Ould Sidi Ahmed Taya; b. 1943 (PRDS; assumed office 12 Dec. 1984 and re-elected 1992 and 1997).

In March 2003 the government comprised:

Prime Minister: Cheikel Afia Ould Mohamed Khouna (PRDS; in office since Nov. 1998, having previously been prime minister from Jan. 1996 to Dec. 1997).

Minister of National Defence: Kaba Ould Elewa. *Interior, Posts and Tele-communications:* Sidi Mahmoud Ould Chekih Ahmed Lemrabott. *Foreign Affairs and Co-operation:* Mohamed Ould Tolba. *Justice:* Sgheyer Ould M'barek. *Finance:* Bodiel Ould Houmeid. *Economic and Development Affairs:* Mohamed Ould Nani. *Fisheries and Maritime Economy:* Ahmedou Ould Ahmedou. *Trade, Handicrafts and Tourism:* Isselmou Ould Abdel Kader. *Mines and Industry:* Zeidane Ould H'Meyda. *Health and Social Affairs:* Diop Abdoul Hamet. *Culture and Islamic Orientation:* Isselmou Ould Sidi El Moustaph. *Civil Service, Labour, Youth and Sports:* Baba Ould Sidi. *Equipment and Transportation:* Diabira Bakary. *National Education:* Aboubekrine Ould Ahmed. *Rural Development and the Environment:* Moustapha Ould Maouloud. *Hydraulics and Energy:* Kane Moustapha. *Communications and Relations with Parliament:* Cheyakh Ould Ely.

Government Website: http://www.mauritania.mr/

DEFENCE
Conscription is authorized for two years. Defence expenditure in 2000 totalled US$23m. (US$9 per capita), representing 2·8% of GDP.

Army. There are six military regions. Army strength was approximately 15,000 in 1999. In addition there was a Gendarmerie of 3,000 and a National Guard of 2,000.

Navy. The Navy, some 500 strong in 1999, is based at Nouâdhibou.

Air Force. Personnel (1999), 150 with seven combat aircraft.

INTERNATIONAL RELATIONS
Mauritania is a member of the UN, WTO, the African Union, the League of Arab States, Arab Maghreb Union, African Development Bank, OIC, International Organization of the Francophonie and is an ACP member state of the ACP-EU relationship.

ECONOMY
In 1998 agriculture accounted for 24·8% of GDP, industry 29·5% and services 45·7%.

Currency. The monetary unit is the *ouguiya* (MRO) which is divided into 5 *khoums*. In Oct. 1992 the ouguiya was devalued 28%. Foreign exchange reserves were US$284m. in Sept. 2000. Gold reserves were 12,000 troy oz in Jan. 2001. Inflation was 4·7% in 2001. Total money supply in May 2002 was 29,078m. ouguiya.

Budget. Revenues were an estimated US$329m. in 1996 and expenditures US$265m.

Performance. A once highly centralized economy has gone though ten years of structural change to produce economic growth of 5·0% for 2000 and 4·6% in 2001, and an average of 4% between 1994 and 1998. Mauritania's total GDP in 2001 was US$1·0bn.

Banking and Finance. The Central Bank (created 1973) is the bank of issue (*Governor,* Sid'El Mokhtar Ould Naji), and there are four commercial banks. Bank deposits totalled 12,304m. ouguiya in 1992.

Weights and Measures. The metric system is in use.

ENERGY AND NATURAL RESOURCES

Environment. In 1998 carbon dioxide emissions were the equivalent of 1·2 tonnes per capita according to the World Bank Atlas.

Electricity. Installed capacity was 105,000 kW in 1991. Production in 1998 was 152m. kWh; consumption per capita was 62 kWh in 1997.

Minerals. There are reserves of copper, gold, phosphate and gypsum. Iron ore, 11m. tonnes of which were mined in 1998, accounts for about 11% of GNP and 40% of exports. Gold, 1995, 57,900 troy oz. Prospecting licences have also been issued for diamonds.

Agriculture. Only 1% of the country receives enough rain to grow crops, so agriculture is mainly confined to the south, in the Senegal river valley. There were 488,000 ha of arable land in 1998 and 12,000 ha of permanent crops. Production (2000, in 1,000 tonnes): sorghum, 134; rice, 103; dates, 22; millet, 13; maize, 11; watermelons, 8; yams, 3; groundnuts, 2; sweet potatoes, 2.

Herding is the main occupation of the rural population and accounted for 16% of GDP in 1992. In 2000 there were 6·20m. sheep; 4·14m. goats; 1·43m. cattle; 1·21m. camels (1999); 4m. chickens.

Forestry. There were 556,000 ha of forests in 1995 covering 0·5% of the land area, chiefly in the southern regions, where wild acacias yield the main product, gum arabic. In 1999, 16,000 cu. metres of roundwood were cut.

Fisheries. Total catch in 1999 was approximately 47,811 tonnes, of which 90% came from marine waters.

INDUSTRY

Output, 1992 (in tonnes): frozen and chilled fish, 8,300; hides and skins (1994), 4,318.

Labour. In 1996 the workforce was 1,072,000 (56% males). In 1994, 430,000 people worked in agriculture, forestry and fishing, 177,000 in services and 80,000 in industry.

INTERNATIONAL TRADE

Total foreign debt was US$2,500m. in 2000. In Feb. 1989 Mauritania signed a treaty of economic co-operation with the four other Maghreb countries—Algeria, Libya, Morocco and Tunisia.

Imports and Exports. In 1998 imports (f.o.b.) were valued at US$318·7m. (US$316·5m. in 1997) and exports (f.o.b.) at US$358·6m. (US$423·6m. in 1997). Main exports are fish and fish products (57% of total exports) and iron ore (40%). Main imports are foodstuffs, consumer goods, petroleum products and capital goods. Principal export markets in 1997 were Japan (23·3%), followed by Italy and France. Main import suppliers were France (25·5%), followed by Spain and Germany.

COMMUNICATIONS

Roads. There were about 7,660 km of roads in 1996, of which 866 km were asphalted. In 1996 there were 18,810 passenger cars and 10,450 commercial vehicles.

Rail. A 704-km railway links Zouérate with the port of Point-Central, 10 km south of Nouâdhibou, and is used primarily for iron ore exports. In 1995 it carried 11·3m. tonnes of freight.

Civil Aviation. There are international airports at Nouakchott, Nouâdhibou and Néma. Air Mauritanie provides domestic services, and in 1998 operated international services to Banjul, Bissau, Casablanca, Dakar, Las Palmas and Niamey. In 1998 there were also international flights to Algiers, Bamako, Paris and Tunis. Mauritania is a member of Air Afrique. In 1997 scheduled airline traffic of Mauritania-based carriers flew 4·3m. km, carrying 245,000 passengers (110,000 on international flights).

Shipping. In 1998 the merchant fleet totalled 48,000 GRT. The major ports are at Point-Central (for mineral exports), Nouakchott and Nouâdhibou.

Telecommunications. In 2000 Mauritania had 19,000 main telephone lines (7·2 per 1,000 persons) and there were 25,000 PCs in use (9·4 per 1,000 persons). There were 4,000 fax machines in 1996. In July 2000 there were 2,000 Internet users.

Postal Services. In 1995 there were 60 post offices.

SOCIAL INSTITUTIONS

Justice. There are courts of first instance at Nouakchott, Atâr, Kaédi, Aïoun el Atrouss and Kiffa. The Appeal Court and Supreme Court are situated in Nouakchott. Islamic jurisprudence was adopted in 1980.

The population in penal institutions in 1997 was 1,400 (60 per 100,000 of national population).

Religion. Over 99% of Mauritanians are Sunni Muslim, mainly of the Qadiriyah sect.

Education. In 1992–93 there were 36 pre-primary schools with 108 teachers for 800 pupils; in 1996–97 there were 2,392 primary schools with 6,225 teachers for 312,671 pupils. In 1995–96 there were 51,765 secondary level pupils with 2,067 teachers, and 7,501 students at university level (1994). The University of Nouakchott had 2,850 students and 70 academic staff in 1994–95. Adult literacy rate in 1999 was 41·6% (male, 52·2%; female, 31·4%).

Health. There were about 200 doctors in 1994.

In the period 1990–98 only 37% of the population had access to safe drinking water.

CULTURE

Broadcasting. The government-controlled Office de Radiodiffusion-Télévision de Mauritanie is responsible for broadcasting. There are two radio and one TV networks. There were 62,000 TV sets (colour by SECAM) and 360,000 radio sets in 1997.

Press. In 1996 there were two daily newspapers with a circulation of 1,000.

Tourism. In 1998 revenue from foreign tourists totalled US$21m.

DIPLOMATIC REPRESENTATIVES

Of Mauritania in the United Kingdom (1 Chessington Avenue, London, N3 3DS)
Ambassador: Youssouf Diagana.

Of the United Kingdom in Mauritania
Ambassador: Haydon Warren-Gash (resides at Rabat, Morocco).

Of Mauritania in the USA (2129 Leroy Pl., NW, Washington, D.C., 20008)
Ambassador: Mohamedou Ould Michel.

Of the USA in Mauritania (PO Box 222, Nouakchott)
Ambassador: John Limbert.

Of Mauritania to the United Nations
Ambassador: Mahfoudh Ould Deddach.

Of Mauritania to the European Union
Ambassador: Mohamed Salem Ould Lekhal.

FURTHER READING
Belvaud, C., *La Mauritanie*. Paris, 1992
Calderini, S., *et al.*, *Mauritania*. [Bibliography] ABC-Clio, Oxford and Santa Barbara (CA), 1992
Pazzanita, A. G., *The Maghreb*. [Bibliography] ABC-Clio, Oxford and Santa Barbara (CA), 1998

National statistical office: Office National de la Statistique, BP240, Nouakchott.
Website: http://www.ons.mr/

MAURITIUS

Republic of Mauritius

Capital: Port Louis
Population estimate, 2000: 1·18m.
GDP per capita, 2000: (PPP$) 10,017
HDI/world rank: 0·772/67

KEY HISTORICAL EVENTS

Mauritius was discovered by the Portuguese between 1507 and 1512. But the Dutch were the first settlers who named it after their stadtholder, Count Maurice. The British occupied the island in 1810 and it was formally ceded to Great Britain by the Treaty of Paris, 1814. Independence was attained within the Commonwealth on 12 March 1968. Mauritius became a republic on 12 March 1992.

TERRITORY AND POPULATION

Mauritius, the main island, lies 500 miles (800 km) east of Madagascar. Rodrigues is 350 miles (560 km) east. The outer islands are Agalega and the St Brandon Group. Area and population:

Island	Area in sq. km	Census 2000
Mauritius	1,865	1,143,069
Rodrigues	104	35,779
Outer Islands	71	289
Total	2,040	1,179,137

Port Louis is the capital (172,000 inhabitants in 1999). Other towns: Beau Bassin-Rose Hill, 99,069; Vacoas-Phoenix, 96,928; Curepipe, 78,516; and Quatre Bornes, 75,554. In 1999, 58·9% of the population were rural.

The UN gives a projected population for 2010 of 1·26m.

Ethnic composition, 1996: Hindus, 52%; 'General Population' (i.e. European, African, Creole), 33%; Muslims, 10%; Chinese, 5%.

The official language is English, although French is widely used. Creole and Bhojpuri are vernacular languages.

SOCIAL STATISTICS

1999: births, 20,313 (rate of 17·3 per 1,000 population); deaths, 7,943 (6·8 per 1,000); marriages, 11,291 (9·6 per 1,000). In 1996 the suicide rate was 20·6 per 100,000 population among men and 6·4 per 100,000 among women. Annual population growth rate, 1990–99, 1·9%. In 1998 the most popular age range for marrying was 25–29 for males and 20–24 for females. Life expectancy at birth in 1999 was 67·3 years for males and 75·1 for females. Infant mortality, 1999, 19·4 per 1,000 live births; fertility rate, 1999, 1·9 births per woman.

CLIMATE

The sub-tropical climate is humid. Most rain falls in the summer. Rainfall varies between 40" (1,000 mm) on the coast to 200" (5,000 mm) on the central plateau, though the west coast only has 35" (875 mm). Mauritius lies in the cyclone belt, whose season runs from Nov. to April, but is seldom affected by intense storms. Port Louis, Jan. 73°F (22·8°C), July 81°F (27·2°C). Annual rainfall 40" (1,000 mm).

CONSTITUTION AND GOVERNMENT

The head of state is the *President*, elected by a simple majority of members of the National Assembly.

The *National Assembly* consists of 62 elected members (three each for the 20 constituencies of Mauritius and two for Rodrigues) and eight additional seats in order to ensure a fair and adequate representation of each community within the Assembly. Elections are held every five years on the basis of universal adult suffrage.

National Anthem. 'Glory to thee, Motherland'; words by J. G. Prosper, tune by P. Gentille.

RECENT ELECTIONS
Parliamentary elections were held on 11 Sept. 2000. The coalition of the Mauritian Socialist Movement (MSM) and the Mauritian Militant Movement (MMM) won 54 seats with 51·7% of votes cast. The coalition of the Mauritius Labour Party and the Mauritian Party of Xavier Duval won 6 with 36·5% and the remaining 2 seats were won by the Rodrigues People's Organization.

CURRENT ADMINISTRATION
President: Karl Auguste Offmann; b. 1940 (MSM; in office since 25 Feb. 2002).
   Vice President: Raouf Bundhun.
   In March 2003 the cabinet was composed as follows:
   Prime Minister, Minister of Defence and Home Affairs: Sir Anerood Jugnauth; b. 1930 (MSM; sworn in 17 Sept. 2000 for the second time, having previously been prime minister from June 1982 to Dec. 1995).
   Deputy Prime Minister and Minister of Finance: Paul Berenger. *Foreign Affairs:* Anyl Kumarsingh Gayan. *Housing and Land Development:* Mukeshwar Choonee. *Justice, Human Rights and Attorney-General:* Emmanuel Leung Shing. *Labour and Industrial Relations:* Showkatally Soodhun. *Civil Service Affairs and Administrative Reforms:* Jeewah Ahmad. *Co-operatives and Handicrafts:* Prem Koonjoo. *Environment:* Rajesh Bhagwan. *Economic Development, Financial Services and Corporate Affairs:* Khushhal Chand Khushiram. *Education and Scientific Research:* Steve Obeegadoo. *Agriculture, Food Technology and Natural Resources:* Pravind Kumar Jugnauth. *Fisheries:* Sylvio Michel. *Regional Administration, Rodrigues, and Urban and Rural Development:* Georges Pierre Lesjongard. *Arts and Culture:* Motee Ramdass. *Public Infrastructure, Internal Transport and Shipping:* Anyl Kumar Bachoo. *Public Utilities:* Alan Ganoo. *Women's Rights, Child Development and Family Welfare:* Arianne Navarre-Marie. *Youth and Sports:* Ravi Yerrigadoo. *Training, Skills Development and Productivity:* Sangeet Fowdar. *Tourism:* Nandcoomar Bodha. *Health:* Ashock Jugnauth. *Industry, Commerce and International Trade:* Jayen Cuttaree. *Telecommunications and Information Technology:* Deelchand Jeeha. *Social Security, Solidarity, Senior Citizen Welfare and Institutional Reform:* Samioulah Lauthan.
   Government Website: http://ncb.intnet.mu/govt/house.htm

DEFENCE
The Police Department is responsible for defence. Its strength was (1999) 8,500. In addition there is a special mobile paramilitary force of approximately 1,000.
   Defence expenditure totalled US$87m. in 2000 (US$75 per capita), representing 1·8% of GDP.

INTERNATIONAL RELATIONS
Mauritius is a member of the UN, WTO, the Commonwealth, the African Union, African Development Bank, COMESA, International Organization of the Francophonie, SADC and is an ACP member state of the ACP-EU relationship. Mauritius is also a founder member of the Indian Ocean Rim Association for Regional Co-operation.

ECONOMY
Services accounted for 58·3% of GDP in 1998, industry 33·1% and agriculture 8·6%.
   Currency. The unit of currency is the *Mauritius rupee* (MUR) of 100 *cents.* There are Bank of Mauritius notes, cupro-nickel coins, nickel-plated steel coins and copper-plated steel coins. Inflation was 4·4% in 2001. In June 2002 foreign exchange reserves were US$964m., gold reserves totalled 62,000 troy oz and total money supply was Rs 15,131m.
   Budget. For years ending 30 June: total government revenue in 2000 was Rs 25,587m. (Rs 23,082m. in 1999) and total expenditure in 2000 was Rs 27,032m. (Rs 25,479m. in 1999). Principal sources of revenue, 1997–98 (estimate): direct taxes, Rs 3,662m.; indirect taxes, Rs 12,453m.; receipts from public utilities, Rs 277m.; receipts from public services, Rs 516·8m.; rental of government property, Rs 44m.; interest and royalties, Rs 248·7m.; reimbursement, Rs 173·6m. On 30 June 1997 the public debt of Mauritius was Rs 4,505m.

Performance. Real GDP growth was 2·6% in 2000 and 7·2% in 2001. Total GDP in 2001 was US$4·5bn.

Banking and Finance. The Bank of Mauritius (founded 1967) is the central bank. The *Governor* is Rameswurlall Basant Roi. There are ten commercial banks. Non-bank financial intermediaries are the Post Office Savings Bank, the State Investment Corporation Ltd, the Mauritius Leasing Company, the National Mutual Fund, the National Investment Trust and the National Pension Fund. Other financial institutions are the Mauritius Housing Company and the Development Bank of Mauritius. There is also a stock exchange.

ENERGY AND NATURAL RESOURCES

Environment. According to the *World Bank Atlas* carbon dioxide emissions were the equivalent of 1·5 tonnes per capita in 1998.

Electricity. Installed capacity was 235,000 kW in 1991. Production (1998) was 1·22bn. kWh. Consumption per capita in 1997 was 1,128 kWh.

Agriculture. 74,000 ha were planted with sugarcane in 2000; production in 2000 was 5,500,000 tonnes. Main secondary crops (2000, in 1,000 tonnes): potatoes, 17; pumpkins and squash, 13; tomatoes, 10; cabbages, 9; cucumbers and gherkins, 9; onions, 9; bananas, 7. In 1998 there were 100,000 ha of arable land and 6,000 ha of permanent cropland.

Livestock, 2000: cattle, 29,000; goats, 94,000; pigs, 20,000.

Livestock products (2000) in tonnes: beef and veal, 3,000; pork, bacon and ham, 1,000; milk, 5,000; eggs, 5,000.

Forestry. The total forest area was 12,000 ha in 1995 (5·9% of the land area). In 1999 timber production totalled 25,000 cu. metres.

Fisheries. The catch in 1999 totalled 12,004 tonnes, exclusively sea fish.

INDUSTRY
Manufacturing includes: sugar, textile products, footwear and other leather products, diamond cutting, jewellery, furniture, watches and watchstraps, sunglasses, plastic ware, chemical products, electronic products, pharmaceutical products, electrical appliances, ship models and canned food. There were 16 sugar mills in 1998; sugar production in 1998 was 640,000 tonnes. 1995 figures: beer, 30·9m. litres; molasses (1993), 162,000 tonnes; rum (1994), 5·6m. litres.

Labour. In 1996 the labour force was estimated at 492,800. Manufacturing employed the largest proportion, with 27·9% of total employment; community, social and personal services, 26%; trade, restaurants and hotels, 15·6%; agriculture and fishing, 13·6%. The unemployment rate was estimated at 5·5%.

Trade Unions. In 1996 there were 330 registered trade unions with a total membership of about 110,000.

INTERNATIONAL TRADE
External debt was US$2,374m. in 2000.

Imports and Exports. In 2000 imports (f.o.b.) were valued at US$1,953·3m. (US$2,107·9m. in 1999) and exports (f.o.b.) at US$1,559·4m. (US$1,589·2m. in 1999). In 1996 Rs 4,893m. of the imports came from the Republic of South Africa, Rs 4,554m. from France, Rs 2,648m. from the UK and Rs 1,811m. from Australia. In 1996 Rs 10,799m. of the exports went to the UK, Rs 6,109m. to France, Rs 4,092m. to the USA and Rs 1,748m. to Germany.

Sugar exports in 1996 were 612,000 tonnes, worth Rs 8,024m. Other major exports (1996) included articles of apparel and clothing, Rs 270m.; chemicals and related products, Rs 159m.; cut flowers and foliage, Rs 126m. Major imports included (1996) manufactured goods (paper, textiles, iron and steel), Rs 13,715m.; machinery and transport equipment, Rs 8,917m.; food and live animals, Rs 5,922m.

COMMUNICATIONS

Roads. In 1998 there were 36 km of motorway, 902 km of main roads, 972 km of secondary and other roads. In 1998 there were 80,578 cars, 3,312 buses and coaches,

109,143 motorcycles and 24,258 trucks and vans. In 1998 there were 162 deaths as a result of road accidents.

Civil Aviation. In 2000, 1,783,848 passengers and 41,269 tonnes of freight were handled at Sir Seewoosagur Ramgoolam International Airport. The national carrier is Air Mauritius, which is partly state-owned. In 1999 it flew 23·4m. km, carrying 801,700 passengers (743,100 on international flights).

Shipping. A free port was established at Port Louis in Sept. 1991. In 1998 merchant shipping totalled 206,000 GRT. In 1997 vessels totalling 5,485,000 NRT entered ports and vessels totalling 5,263,000 NRT cleared.

Telecommunications. In 2000 there were 280,900 main telephone lines, equivalent to 235·3 per 1,000 population. Mauritius Telecom, formed in 1992, provided telephone services to 183,902 subscribers in 1996 through 58 exchanges. In 1997 there were 37,000 mobile phone subscribers and 28,000 fax machines. Communication with other parts of the world is by satellite and microwave links. In 2000 there were 120,000 PCs in use (100·5 per 1,000 persons). Mauritius had 87,000 Internet users in Dec. 2000.

Postal Services. In 1995 there were 103 post offices.

SOCIAL INSTITUTIONS

Justice. There is an Ombudsman. The death penalty was abolished for all crimes in 1995.

The population in penal institutions in 1997 was 3,239 (295 per 100,000 of national population).

Religion. At the 1990 census (excluding Rodrigues) there were 287,726 Roman Catholics, 4,399 Protestants, 530,456 Hindus and 172,047 Muslims.

Education. The adult literacy rate in 1999 was 84·2% (87·6% among males and 80·8% among females). Primary and secondary education is free, primary education being compulsory. About 91% of children aged 5–11 years attend schools. In 1997 there were 127,109 pupils in 283 primary schools and 93,839 pupils in secondary schools in the island of Mauritius, and 4,934 pupils in 12 primary schools and 2,917 in three secondary schools in Rodrigues. In 1996, 3,061 teachers were enrolled for training at the Mauritius Institute of Education.

In 1997–98 there were 3,462 students and 193 academic staff at the University of Mauritius.

Health. In 1996 (provisional) there were 1,008 doctors, 15 hospitals with 3,420 beds, 156 health centres and 12 private clinics with about 300 beds.

CULTURE

Broadcasting. Broadcasting is run by the commercial Mauritius Broadcasting Corporation. There were 260,000 television sets (colour by SECAM V) and 420,000 radio sets in 1997.

Cinema. In 1997 there were 25 cinemas, with a seating capacity of about 25,000.

Press. There were seven daily papers in French in 1997 (with occasional articles in English), with a combined circulation of about 100,000.

Tourism. In 1999 there were 578,000 visitors, who contributed 5% of GDP bringing in US$545m. in tourist revenue.

DIPLOMATIC REPRESENTATIVES
Of Mauritius in the United Kingdom (32–33 Elvaston Pl., London, SW7 5NW)
High Commissioner: Mohunlall Goburdhun.

Of the United Kingdom in Mauritius (Les Cascades Bldg., Edith Cavell St, Port Louis)
High Commissioner: David Snoxell.

Of Mauritius in the USA (4301 Connecticut Ave., NW, Washington, D.C., 20008)
Ambassador: Dr Usha Jeetah.

Of the USA in Mauritius (Rogers Hse., John Kennedy St., Port Louis)
Ambassador: John Price.

Of Mauritius to the United Nations
Ambassador: Jagdish Dharamchang Koonjul.

Of Mauritius to the European Union
Ambassador: Sutiawan Gunessee.

FURTHER READING
Central Statistical Information Office. *Bi-annual Digest of Statistics*.
Bennett, Pamela R., *Mauritius*. [Bibliography] ABC-Clio, Oxford and Santa Barbara (CA), 1992
Bowman, L. W., *Mauritius: Democracy and Development in the Indian Ocean*. Aldershot, 1991

National statistical office: Central Statistics Office, LIC Building, President John Kennedy Street, Port Louis.
Website: http://ncb.intnet.mu/cso.htm

MEXICO

Estados Unidos Mexicanos
(United States of Mexico)

Capital: Mexico City
Population estimate, 2000: 97·36m.
GDP per capita, 2000: (PPP$) 9,023
HDI/world rank: 0·796/54

KEY HISTORICAL EVENTS
Mexico's history falls into four epochs: the era of the Indian empires (before 1521), the Spanish colonial phase (1521–1810), the period of national formation (1810–1910), which includes the war of independence (1810–21) and the long dictatorship of Porfirio Díaz (1876–80, 1884–1911), and the present period which began with the social revolution of 1910–21. Mexico was conquered for Spain by Cortés in 1521 and became part of the viceroyalty of New Spain. A substantial part of Mexico's territory (including the present state of California) was lost to the USA by the Mexican War of 1846–48. In the 1860s France, Britain and the USA declared war on Mexico; France invaded the country and declared Maximilian, Archduke of Austria, to be Emperor. When the French withdrew in 1867 Maximilian was executed. The constitution of 1917 established a representative, democratic and federal republic, comprising 31 states and a federal district. The PRI (Partido Revolucionario Institucional) remained in power for 71 years until it was defeated by the conservative National Action party in the elections of July 2000. An uprising by the Zapatista National Liberation Army (EZLN) in 1994 sparked off a cycle of violence that has continued to this day despite a supposed ceasefire in Jan. 2002.

TERRITORY AND POPULATION
Mexico is bounded in the north by the USA, west and south by the Pacific Ocean, southeast by Guatemala, Belize and the Caribbean Sea, and northeast by the Gulf of Mexico. It comprises 1,967,375 sq. km (759,603 sq. miles), including uninhabited islands (5,127 sq. km) offshore.

Population at recent censuses: 1970, 48,225,238; 1980, 66,846,833; 1990, 81,249,645; 2000, 97,361,711 (50,007,325 females). Population density, 49·5 per sq. km (2000). 74·2% of the population were urban in 1999.

The UN gives a projected population for 2010 of 112·89m.

Area, population and capitals of the Federal District and 31 states:

	Area (Sq. km)	Population (1995 counting)	Population (2000 census)	Capital
Federal District	1,525	8,489,007	8,591,309	Mexico City
Aguascalientes	5,272	862,720	943,506	Aguascalientes
Baja California Norte	71,505	2,112,140	2,487,700	Mexicali
Baja California Sur	73,948	375,494	423,516	La Paz
Campeche	57,033	642,516	689,656	Campeche
Coahuila de Zaragoza	150,615	2,173,775	2,295,808	Saltillo
Colima	5,466	488,028	540,679	Colima
Chiapas	73,628	3,584,786	3,920,515	Tuxtla Gutiérrez
Chihuahua	245,962	2,793,537	3,047,867	Chihuahua
Durango	122,792	1,431,748	1,445,922	Victoria de Durango
Guanajuato	31,032	4,406,568	4,656,761	Guanajuato
Guerrero	64,791	2,916,567	3,075,083	Chilpancingo de los Bravo
Hidalgo	20,664	2,112,473	2,231,392	Pachuca de Soto
Jalisco	79,085	5,991,176	6,321,278	Guadalajara
México	21,419	11,707,964	13,083,359	Toluca de Lerdo
Michoacán de Ocampo	58,585	3,870,604	3,979,177	Morelia
Morelos	4,961	1,442,662	1,552,878	Cuernavaca
Nayarit	27,103	896,702	919,739	Tepic
Nuevo Léon	64,742	3,550,114	3,826,240	Monterrey
Oaxaca	93,147	3,228,895	3,432,180	Oaxaca de Juárez
Puebla	34,155	4,624,365	5,070,346	Heroica Puebla de Zaragoza
Querétaro de Arteaga	12,114	1,250,476	1,402,010	Santiago de Querétaro
Quintana Roo	39,201	703,536	873,804	Chetumal

	Area (Sq. km)	Population (1995 counting)	Population (2000 census)	Capital
San Luis Potosí	63,778	2,200,763	2,296,363	San Luis Potosí
Sinaloa	58,359	2,425,675	2,534,835	Culiacán Rosales
Sonora	180,605	2,085,536	2,213,370	Hermosillo
Tabasco	24,612	1,748,769	1,889,367	Villahermosa
Tamaulipas	79,686	2,527,328	2,747,114	Ciudad Victoria
Tlaxcala	4,052	883,924	961,912	Tlaxcala de Xicohténcatl
Veracruz-Llave	72,005	6,737,324	6,901,111	Xalapa-Enríquez
Yucatán	43,577	1,556,622	1,655,707	Mérida
Zacatecas	73,829	1,336,496	1,351,207	Zacatecas
Total	1,967,183	91,158,290	97,361,711	

The official language is Spanish, the mother tongue of over 93% of the population (2000), but there are some indigenous language groups (of which Náhuatl, Maya, Zapotec, Otomi and Mixtec are the most important) spoken by 6,044,547 persons over five years of age (census 2000).

The populations (2000 census) of the largest cities (250,000 and more) were:

Mexico City	8,591,309	Saltillo	562,587	Veracruz	411,582
Guadalajara	1,646,183	Morelia	549,996	Reynosa	403,718
Ecatepcec		Mexicali	549,873	Cancún	397,191
de Morelos	1,621,827	Hermosillo	545,928	Heroica	
Heroica Puebla		Culiacán		Matamoros	376,279
de Zaragoza	1,271,673	Rosales	540,823	Xalapa-Enríquez	373,076
Ciudad		Santiago		Villahermosa	330,846
Nezahualcoyotl	1,225,083	de Querétaro	536,463	Mazatlán	327,989
Juárez	1,187,275	Torreón	502,964	Cuernavaca	327,162
Tijuana	1,148,681	San Nicolás		Xico	322,784
Monterrey	1,110,909	de los Garza	496,878	Irapuato	319,148
León de los Aldama	1,020,818	Chimalhuacan	482,530	Tonalá	315,278
Zapopan	910,690	Ciudad López		Nuevo Laredo	308,828
Naucalpan de Juárez	835,053	Mateos	467,544	Tampico	295,442
Tlalnepantla	714,735	Tlaquepaque	458,674	Celaya	277,750
Guadalupe	669,842	Toluca de Lerdo	435,125	Apodaca	270,369
Mérida	662,530	Cuautitlan		Tepic	265,817
Chihuahua	657,876	Izcalli	433,830	San Francisco	
San Luis Potosí	629,208	Victoria		Coalco	252,291
Acapulco de Juárez	620,656	de Durango	427,135	Oaxaca de Juárez	251,846
Aguascalientes	594,092	Tuxtla Gutiérrez	424,579	Ciudad Obregón	250,790

Mexico City: Located on a plateau more than 2,400 metres above sea level, Mexico City was built on the site of the Aztec City of Tenochtitlán which was destroyed in 1521 by Cortés. One of the most highly populated cities in the world, Mexico City suffers from pollution and atmospheric problems. However, that has not prevented it from hosting the Olympic Games and two series of football World Cup Finals.

SOCIAL STATISTICS

Statistics for calendar years:

	Births	Deaths	Marriages	Divorces
1995	2,750,444	430,278	658,114	37,455
1996	2,707,718	436,321	670,523	38,545
1997	2,698,425	440,437	707,840	40,792
1998	2,668,429	444,665	704,456	45,889
1999	2,769,089	443,950	743,856	49,721

Rates per 1,000 population, 1999: births, 28·8; deaths, 4·6. In 1998 the most popular age range for marrying was 20–24 for both males and females. Infant mortality was 27 per 1,000 live births in 1999. Life expectancy at birth in 1999 was 69·8 years for males and 75·8 years for females. Annual population growth rate, 1990–99, 1·8%. Fertility rate, 1999, 2·7 births per woman. Much of the population still lives in poverty, with the gap between the modern north and the backward south constantly growing.

CLIMATE

Latitude and relief produce a variety of climates. Arid and semi-arid conditions are found in the north, with extreme temperatures, whereas in the south there is a humid tropical climate, with temperatures varying with altitude. Conditions on the shores of the Gulf of Mexico are very warm and humid. In general, the rainy season lasts from May to Nov. Mexico City, Jan. 55°F (12·9°C), July 61°F (16·2°C). Annual rainfall 31" (787·6 mm). Guadalajara, Jan. 63°F (17·0°C), July 72°F (22·1°C). Annual rainfall 39" (987·6 mm). La Paz, Jan. 62°F (16·8°C), July 86°F (29·9°C). Annual rainfall 7" (178·3 mm). Mazatlán, Jan. 68°F (20·0°C), July 84°F (29·0°C). Annual rainfall 32" (822·1 mm). Mérida, Jan. 73°F (23·0°C), July 81°F (27·4°C). Annual rainfall 39" (990·0 mm). Monterrey, Jan. 58°F (14·3°C), July 83°F (28·1°C). Annual rainfall 23" (585·4 mm). Puebla de Zaragoza, Jan. 52°F (11·4°C), July 62°F (16·9°C). Annual rainfall 36" (900·8 mm).

CONSTITUTION AND GOVERNMENT

A new Constitution was promulgated on 5 Feb. 1917 and has been amended from time to time. Mexico is a representative, democratic and federal republic, comprising 31 states and a federal district, each state being free and sovereign in all internal affairs, but united in a federation established according to the principles of the Fundamental Law. The head of state and supreme executive authority is the *President*, directly elected for a non-renewable six-year term. The constitution was amended in April 2001, granting autonomy to 10m. indigenous peoples. The amendment was opposed both by the National Congress of Indigenous Peoples and Zapatista rebels who claimed it would leave many indigenous people worse off.

There is complete separation of legislative, executive and judicial powers (Art. 49). Legislative power is vested in a General Congress of two chambers, a *Chamber of Deputies* and a *Senate*. The Chamber of Deputies consists of 500 members directly elected for three years, 300 of them from single-member constituencies and 200 chosen under a system of proportional representation. In 1990 Congress voted a new Electoral Code. This establishes a body to organize elections (IFE), an electoral court (TFE) to resolve disputes, new electoral rolls and introduce a voter's registration card. Priests were enfranchised in 1991.

The Senate comprises 128 members, four from each state and four from the federal district, directly elected for six years. Members of both chambers are not immediately re-eligible for election. Congress sits from 1 Sept. to 31 Dec. each year; during the recess there is a permanent committee of 15 deputies and 14 senators appointed by the respective chambers.

National Anthem. 'Mexicanos, al grito de guerra' ('Mexicans, at the war-cry'); words by F. González Bocanegra, tune by Jaime Nunó.

RECENT ELECTIONS

At the presidential elections of 2 July 2000, Vicente Fox of the Partido Acción Nacional (National Action Party/Alliance for Change) won approximately 42·5% of the vote, defeating Francisco Labastida of the Partido Revolucionario Institucional (Institutional Revolutionary Party/PRI) who gained 36·1%. There were four other candidates. It was the first time in 71 years that the PRI had lost power.

Elections were also held on 2 July 2000 for the Chamber of Deputies and for the Chamber of Senators. In the Chamber of Deputies, Alianza por el Cambio (Alliance for Change, consisting of the National Action Party and the Ecologist Green Party of Mexico) claimed 224 of the 500 seats (44·8%), PRI took 208 (41·6%) and Alianza por México (Alliance for Mexico/AM) 68 (13·6%). Following the election the composition of the Senate was: PRI, 58 of the 128 seats (45·3%); Alliance for Change, 53 (41·4%); AM, 17 (13·3%).

Parliamentary and senate elections were scheduled to take place on 6 July 2003.

CURRENT ADMINISTRATION

President: Vicente Fox Quesada; b. 1942 (Alliance for Change; sworn in 1 Dec. 2000).

In March 2003 the government comprised:

Minister of Government: Santiago Creel Miranda. *Foreign Affairs:* Luis Ernesto Derbéz Bautista. *Defence:* Gen. Gerardo Clemente Ricardo Vega García. *Naval Affairs:* Adm. Marco Antonio Peyrot González. *Finance and Public Credit:* Francisco Gil Díaz. *Social Development:* Josefina Vázquez Mota. *Comptroller-General:* Francisco Barrio Terrazas. *Energy:* Ernesto Martens Rebolledo. *Economy:*

Fernando Canales Clariond. *Agriculture, Livestock, Rural Development, Fisheries and Food:* Javier Usabiaga Arroyo. *Communication and Transport:* Pedro Cerisola y Weber. *Education:* Reyes Támez Guerra. *Health:* Julio Frenk Mora. *Public Security and Justice Services:* Alejandro Gertz Manero. *Labour and Social Welfare:* Carlos Abascal Carranza. *Agrarian Reform:* Maria Teresa Herrera Tello. *Tourism:* Leticia Navarro. *Environment and Natural Resources:* Victor Lichtinger. *Attorney-General:* Gen. Rafael Macedo de la Concha.

Presidency Website: http://www.presidencia.gob.mx

DEFENCE
In 2000 defence expenditure totalled US$5,229m. (US$53 per capita), representing 1·0% of GDP.

Army. Enlistment into the regular army is voluntary, but there is also one year of conscription (four hours per week) by lottery. Strength of the regular army (1999) 130,000 (60,000 conscripts). There are combined reserve forces of 300,000. In addition there is a rural defence militia of 14,000.

Navy. The Navy is primarily equipped and organized for offshore and coastal patrol duties. It includes three destroyers and six frigates. The naval air force, 1,100 strong, operates nine combat aircraft.

Naval personnel in 1999 totalled 37,000, including the naval air force and 10,000 marines.

Air Force. The Air Force had (1999) a strength of about 11,770 with over 125 combat aircraft, including F-5Es, and 95 armed helicopters.

INTERNATIONAL RELATIONS
Mexico is a member of the UN (and most UN System organizations), WTO, BIS, OECD, OAS, Inter-American Development Bank (IADB), LAIA, ACS, APEC, NAFTA and IOM. A free trade agreement was signed with the European Union in 1999.

ECONOMY
Agriculture accounted for 4·9% of GDP in 1998, industry 26·6% and services 68·4%.

Overview. An economic programme for 1995 aimed to reduce inflation and to stimulate investment. After the peso was devalued in Dec. 1994 an emergency economic plan included an agreement between labour and employers to contain inflation, a fiscal adjustment to reduce the current account deficit, further privatization of infrastructural enterprises and the establishment of an international assistance fund. Between 1988 and 1997, 25 companies were privatized. An economic programme to attack 'the roots of poverty' was announced. Since the mid-1980s the economy has become one of the most open in Latin America.

Currency. The unit of currency is the *Mexican peso* (MXP) of 100 *centavos*. A new peso was introduced on 1 Jan. 1993: 1 new peso = 1,000 old pesos. The peso was devalued by 13·94% in Dec. 1994. Foreign exchange reserves were US$45,147m. and gold reserves 191,000 troy oz in June 2002. The annual inflation rate, which in 1995 was 35%, fell to 6·4% in 2001. Total money supply in June 2002 was 507,075m. new pesos.

Budget. Government revenue and expenditure (in 1m. new pesos), year ending 31 Dec.:

	1994	1995	1996	1997	1998	1999
Revenue	212,387	281,138	384,466	468,187	501,231	634,449
Expenditure	212,417	292,479	387,810	516,230	563,990	712,137

Performance. Real GDP grew by 6·9% in 2000, but in 2001 the economy contracted by 0·3%. In 2001 total GDP was US$617·8bn.

Banking and Finance. The Bank of Mexico, established 1 Sept. 1925, is the central bank of issue (*Governor*, Guillermo Ortíz Martínez). It gained autonomy over monetary policy in 1993. Exchange rate policy is determined jointly by the bank and the Finance Ministry. Banks were nationalized in 1982, but in May 1990 the government approved their reprivatization. The state continues to have a majority holding in foreign trade and rural development banks. Foreign holdings are limited to 49%. Mexico's largest bank is Banamex. In 2001 the American financial services company Citigroup bought Mexico's largest financial group, Banacci, and its second largest bank, Banamex, for US$12·5bn., but retained the name Banamex. Most of Mexico's leading banks are now foreign-owned.

There is a stock exchange in Mexico City.

Weights and Measures. The metric system is legal.

ENERGY AND NATURAL RESOURCES

Environment. According to the *World Bank Atlas* Mexico's carbon dioxide emissions in 1998 were the equivalent of 3·9 tonnes per capita.

Electricity. Installed capacity, 1998, 35,256 MW. Output in 1998 was 180·5bn. kWh and consumption per capita 1,513 kWh. In 2001 there were two nuclear reactors in operation.

Oil and Gas. Crude petroleum production was 163m. tonnes in 1999. Mexico produced 4·7% of the world total oil output in 1999, and had reserves amounting to 26·9bn. bbls in 2001. Revenues from oil exports provide about a third of all government revenues. Natural gas production was 37·4bn. cu. metres in 1999 with 850bn. cu. metres in proven reserves.

Minerals. Output (in 1,000 tonnes), 1998: salt, 8,400; iron, 6,341; gypsum, 4,033; silica, 1,732; sulphur, 912·8; fluorite, 620·5; zinc, 370; copper, 344·9; manganese, 202·7; lead, 176·5; barite, 161·5; graphite, 41·9; silver, 2·9; gold, 26,111 kg; coal, 9,100; feldspar, 197·9. Mexico is the biggest producer of silver in the world.

Agriculture. In 1998 Mexico had 25·2m. ha of arable land and 2·10m. ha of permanent cropland. There were 6·5m. ha of irrigated land. There were 172,000 tractors and 19,500 harvester-threshers in 1998. In 1998 agriculture contributed 5·8% of GDP (6·0% in 1997). Some 60% of agricultural land belongs to about 30,000 *ejidos* (with 15m. members), communal lands with each member farming his plot independently. *Ejidos* can now be inherited, sold or rented. A land-titling programme (PROCEDE) is establishing the boundaries of 4·6m. plots of land totalling 102m. ha. Other private farmers may not own more than 100 ha of irrigated land or an equivalent in unirrigated land. There is a theoretical legal minimum of 10 ha for holdings, but some 60% of private farms were less than 5 ha in 1990. Laws abolishing the *ejido* system were passed in 1992.

Sown areas, 2000 (in 1,000 ha) included: maize, 8,661; beans, 2,252; sorghum, 2,170; coffee beans, 757; wheat, 749; sugarcane, 659; barley, 312; chick-peas, 210; chillies and green peppers, 142; safflower seeds, 103; rice, 98.

Production in 2000 (in 1,000 tonnes): sugarcane, 49,275; maize, 18,761; sorghum, 6,400; oranges, 3,390; wheat, 3,300; tomatoes, 2,401; chillies and green peppers, 1,813; bananas, 1,802; potatoes, 1,593; mangoes, 1,529; coconuts, 1,313; lemons and limes, 1,297; beans, 1,219; watermelons, 993; avocados, 939; papayas, 636; barley, 532; melons (excluding watermelons), 500.

Livestock (2000): cattle, 30·29m.; sheep, 5·90m.; pigs, 13·69m.; goats, 9·60m.; horses, 6·25m.; mules, 3·27m.; asses, 3·25m.; chickens, 476m. Meat production, 2000 (in 1,000 tonnes): beef and veal, 1,415; pork, bacon and ham, 1,035; horse, 79; goat, 39; lamb and mutton, 32; poultry meat, 1,896. Dairy production, 2000 (in 1,000 tonnes): cow milk, 9,474; goat milk, 134; eggs, 1,666; cheese, 148; honey, 57.

Forestry. Forests extended over 55·39m. ha in 1995, representing 29% of the land area (down from 57·93m. ha in 1990), containing pine, spruce, cedar, mahogany, logwood and rosewood. There are 14 forest reserves (nearly 0·8m. ha) and 47 national park forests of 0·75m. ha. Timber production was 24·12m. cu. metres in 1999.

Fisheries. The total catch in 1999 was 1,202,178 tonnes, of which 1,110,716 tonnes came from sea fishing.

INDUSTRY

The leading companies by market capitalization in Mexico, excluding banking and finance, in Jan. 2002 were: Teléfonos de México SA de CV (Telemex), 241bn. new pesos; Wal-Mart de México SA de CV (general retailers, formerly Cifra), 133bn. new pesos; and América Móvil SA de CV (a mobile phone company), 122bn. new pesos.

In 1998 the manufacturing industry provided 19·7% of GDP. Output in 1997 (in 1,000 tonnes): cement, 27,548; residual fuel oil, 24,760; petrol, 15,525; distillate fuel oil, 13,506; crude steel (1999), 15,300; crude iron (1996), 6,109; sugar (1998), 5,287; wheat flour (1996), 1,835; zinc (1996), 348·3; copper (1996), 328; lead (1996), 167·1; aluminium (1996), 95·8; butter (1996), 34; beer (1998), 5,456·9m. litres; soft drinks, 10,175·2m. litres; cigarettes, 57·6bn. units; passenger cars, 858,000 units; lorries, 468,931 units. Car production in particular has benefited from membership of NAFTA. Production has increased from 600,000 in 1993 to approaching 1·5bn. in 1999.

Labour. In 1996 the workforce was 24,063,283 (5,644,588 female). In 1997, 23·5% of the workforce were engaged in agriculture, 23·2% in services, public administration and defence, 20·5% in trade and 16·4% in manufacturing. 800,000 new jobs were created in 1997. Registered unemployment rate, 1998, 3·2% (1997, 3·7%). The daily minimum wage at the end of 1999 was 32 pesos.

Trade Unions. The Mexican Labour Congress (CTM) is incorporated into the Institutional Revolutionary Party, and is an umbrella organization numbering some 5m. An agreement, 'Alliance for Economic Recovery', was reached in Nov. 1995 between the government, trade unions and business, providing for an increase in the minimum wage of 10·1%, increased unemployment benefits, tax incentives, the staggering of price increases, and a commitment to reduce public spending. A breakaway from CTM took place in 1997 when rebel labour leaders set up the National Union of Workers (UNT) to combat what they saw as a sharp drop in real wages.

INTERNATIONAL TRADE

In Sept. 1991 Mexico signed the free trade Treaty of Santiago with Chile, envisaging an annual 10% tariffs reduction from Jan. 1992. The North American Free Trade Agreement (NAFTA), between Canada, Mexico and the USA, was signed on 7 Oct. 1992 and came into effect on 1 Jan. 1994. A free trade agreement was signed with Costa Rica in March 1994. Some 8,300 products were free from tariffs, with others to follow over 10 years. The Group of Three (G3) free trade pact with Colombia and Venezuela came into effect on 1 Jan. 1995. Total foreign debt was US$150,288m. in 2000, a figure exceeded only by Brazil and Russia.

Imports and Exports. Trade for calendar years in US$1m.:

	1996	1997	1998	1999	2000
Imports f.o.b.	89,469	109,808	125,374	141,973	174,458
Exports f.o.b.	96,000	110,431	117,459	136,392	166,455

Of total imports in 1999, 74·3% came from USA, 3·5% from Germany, 3·3% from Japan, 1·9% from South Korea and 1·9% from Canada. Of total exports in 1999, 88·4% went to USA, 1·7% to Canada, 1·5% to Germany, 0·7% to Spain and 0·6% to Japan. In 1998 exports to the USA accounted for 21% of GDP.

The in-bond (*maquiladora*) assembly plants generate the largest flow of foreign exchange. Although originally located along the US border when the programme was introduced in the 1960s, they are now to be found in almost every state. In 2000 there were over 3,000 'foreign to Mexico' manufacturing companies, employing more than 1m. people. Manufactured goods account for 90% of trade revenues.

COMMUNICATIONS

Roads. Total length, 1997, was estimated at 323,977 km, of which 48,737 km were main roads, 61,375 km were secondary roads and 213,860 km by-roads. In 1998 there were 9,378,590 motor vehicles, 4,403,950 trucks and 108,690 buses and coaches.

Rail. The National Railway, *Ferrocarriles Nacionales de Mexico*, was split into five companies in 1996 as a preliminary to privatization. It comprises 26,623 km of 1,435 mm gauge (246 km electrified). In 1998 it carried 75·9m. tonnes of freight and 1·58m. passengers. There is a 178 km metro in Mexico City with ten lines. There are light rail lines in Guadalajara (48 km) and Monterrey (23 km).

MEXICO

Civil Aviation. There is an international airport at Mexico City (Benito Juárez) and 55 other international and 29 national airports. Each of the larger states has a local airline which links it with main airports. The national carriers are Aeromexico, Mexicana, Aeromar, Taesa, Aerocalifornia and Aerolíneas Internacionales; Aeromexico and Mexicana, both privatized in the late 1980s, are the main ones. In 1999 Aeromexico carried 8,672,000 passengers (1,959,300 on international flights) and Mexicana 7,359,700 passengers (2,901,500 international). In 2000 Mexico City handled 21,042,610 passengers (13,878,558 on domestic flights). Cancún was the second busiest airport for passengers in 2000, with 7,572,246 (5,915,439 on international flights). Guadalajara handled 5,021,004 passengers (3,279,602 on domestic flights).

Shipping. Mexico had 90 ocean ports in 1998, of which, on the Gulf coast, the most important include Tampico, Coatzacoalcos, Altamira, Progreso, Tuxpan, Morelos and Cozumel. Those on the Pacific Coast include Lazaro Cardenas, Manzanillo, Guaymas, La Paz-Pichilingue, Ensenada, Topolobampo, Mazatlán and Salina Cruz. The privatization of port operations has been taking place since the early 1990s.

Merchant shipping loaded 139·5m. tonnes and unloaded 62m. tonnes of cargo in 1996. In 1998 the merchant marine had a total tonnage of 1,085,000 GRT, including oil tankers 409,000 GRT. In 1997 vessels totalling 33,458,000 NRT entered ports and vessels totalling 125,671,000 NRT cleared.

Telecommunications. Telmex, previously a state-controlled company, was privatized in 1991. It controls about 98% of all the telephone service. There were 12,331,700 telephone main lines in 2000, or 124·7 for every 1,000 persons, and there were 5m. PCs in use (50·6 per 1,000 population). Mexico had 6·13m. mobile phone subscribers in Sept. 1999 and 3·5m. Internet users in Dec. 2001. There were 180,000 fax machines in 1995.

Postal Services. There were 9,149 post offices in 1998 (local administration, offices, agencies), equivalent to one for every 9,950 persons.

SOCIAL INSTITUTIONS

Justice. Magistrates of the Supreme Court are appointed for six years by the President and confirmed by the Senate; they can be removed only on impeachment. The courts include the Supreme Court with 21 magistrates, 12 collegiate circuit courts with 3 judges each and 9 unitary circuit courts with 1 judge each, and 68 district courts with 1 judge each.

The penal code of 1 Jan. 1930 abolished the death penalty, except for the armed forces.

There were 15,596 murders in 1995 (a rate of 17·2 per 100,000 population). The population in penal institutions in Dec. 1996 was 103,262 (110 per 100,000 of national population).

Religion. In 1998 an estimated 89·6% of the population was Roman Catholic, down from 98% in 1950. In Feb. 2001 there were four Cardinals. The Church is separated from the State, and the constitution of 1917 provided strict regulation of this and all other religions. In Nov. 1991 Congress approved an amendment to the 1917 constitution permitting the recognition of churches by the state, the possession of property by churches and the enfranchisement of priests. Church buildings remain state property. In 1998 there were estimated to be 3·67m. Protestants, plus followers of various other religions. There were 811,000 Latter-day Saints (Mormons) in 1998.

Education. Adult literacy was 91·1% in 1999 (male, 93·1%; female, 89·1%). Primary and secondary education is free and compulsory, and secular, although religious instruction is permitted in private schools. By 2000 Mexicans were attending school for an average of 7·6 years, almost a year more than in 1994.

In 1999–2000 there were:

	Establishments	Teachers	Students (in 1,000)
Pre-school	69,916	170,559	3,394
Primary	98,286	596,164	14,766
Secondary	27,512	299,999	5,209
Baccalaureate	7,831	170,642	2,518
Vocational training	1,711	33,249	375

	Establishments	Teachers	Students (in 1,000)
Medium/Professional	607	17,481	216
Higher education	2,172	167,049	1,629
Postgraduate education	1,036	17,004	118

In 2000 total expenditure on education came to 6·1% of GDP, including 1,374m. new pesos on the *Programa de Apoyo Federal a Entidades Federativas* (Federal Support Program to the States).

Health. In 1997 there were 4,506 hospitals (1,539 public), with a total provision of 103,530 beds. In 1997 there were 147,618 doctors, 8,564 dentists and 182,171 nurses.

Welfare. In 1997, 51·43m. persons benefited from the National Health System (of which 39·46m. were beneficiaries of the Mexican Institute of Social Security).

CULTURE

Broadcasting. In 1997 there were 1,342 radio stations and 580 television stations licensed by the *Dirección General de Concesiones y Permisos de Tele-comunicaciones*. Most radio stations carry the 'National Hour' programme. Television services are provided by the Televisa, Televisión Azteca and Multivision. There were 31m. radio receivers and 25·6m. TV sets (colour by NTSC) in 1997.

Cinema. In 1995 there were 1,495 cinemas and 63m. admissions; gross box office receipts came to 888m. new pesos. 14 full-length films were made.

Press. In 1996 there were 295 daily newspapers with a circulation of 9,030,000, equivalent to 97 per 1,000 inhabitants.

Tourism. There were 20·64m. tourists in 2000, putting Mexico 8th in the world list; gross revenue, including border visitors, amounted to US$7,223m. in 1999.

DIPLOMATIC REPRESENTATIVES

Of Mexico in the United Kingdom (42 Hertford Street, London W1J 7JR)
Ambassador: Alma Rosa Moreno Razo.

Of the United Kingdom in Mexico (Rio Lerma 71, Col. Cuauhtémoc, 06500 México, D.F.)
Ambassador: Denise Holt.

Of Mexico in the USA (1911 Pennsylvania Ave., NW, Washington, D.C., 20006)
Ambassador: Juan José Bremer Martino.

Of the USA in Mexico (Paseo de la Reforma 305, 06500 México, D.F.)
Ambassador: Jeffrey Davidow.

Of Mexico to the United Nations
Ambassador: Adolfo Aguilar Zínser.

Of Mexico to the European Union
Ambassador: Porfirio Muñoz Ledo y Lazo de la Vega.

FURTHER READING

Instituto Nacional de Estadística, Geografía e Informática. *Anuario Estadístico de los Estados Unidos Mexicanos. Mexican Bulletin of Statistical Information.* Quarterly.

Aspe, P., *Economic Transformation: the Mexican Way.* Cambridge (MA), 1993
Bartra, R., *Agrarian Structure and Political Power in Mexico.* Johns Hopkins Univ. Press, 1993
Bethell, L. (ed.) *Mexico since Independence.* CUP, 1992
Camp, R. A., *Politics in Mexico.* 2nd ed. OUP, 1996
Hamnett, Brian R., *A Concise History of Mexico.* CUP, 1999
Krauze, E., *Mexico, Biography of Power: A History of Modern Mexico, 1810–1996.* London, 1997
Philip, G. (ed.) *The Presidency in Mexican Politics.* London, 1991.—*Mexico.* [Bibliography] 2nd ed. ABC-Clio, Oxford and Santa Barbara (CA), 1993
Rodríguez, J. E., *The Evolution of the Mexican Political System.* New York, 1993
Ruíz, R. E., *Triumphs and Tragedy: a History of the Mexican People.* New York, 1992
Turner, Barry, (ed.) *Latin America Profiled.* Macmillan, London, 2000
Whiting, V. R., *The Political Economy of Foreign Investment in Mexico: Nationalism, Liberalism, Constraints on Choice.* Johns Hopkins Univ. Press, 1992

National statistical office: Instituto Nacional de Estadística, Geografía e Informática (INEGI), Aguascalientes.
Website: http://www.inegi.gob.mx

MICRONESIA

Federated States of Micronesia

Capital: Palikir
Population estimate, 2000: 133,000
GDP per capita: not available
GNP per capita: $1,830

KEY HISTORICAL EVENTS

Spain acquired sovereignty over the Caroline Islands in 1886 but sold the archipelago to Germany in 1899. Japan occupied the Islands at the beginning of the First World War and in 1921 they were mandated to Japan by the League of Nations. Captured by Allied Forces in the Second World War, the Islands became part of the UN Trust Territory of the Pacific Islands created on 18 July 1947 and administered by the USA. The Federated States of Micronesia came into being on 10 May 1979. American trusteeship was terminated on 3 Nov. 1986 by the UN Security Council and on the same day Micronesia entered into a 15-year Free Association with the USA.

TERRITORY AND POPULATION

The Federated States lie in the North Pacific Ocean between 137° and 163° E, comprising 607 islands with a total land area of 702 sq. km (271 sq. miles). The population (1994 census) was 104,724; 1997 estimate, 127,600; density, 181 per sq. km.

In 1995 an estimated 72·3% of the population lived in rural areas.

The areas and populations of the four major groups of island states (east to west) are as follows:

State	Area (sq. km)	Population (1994 census)	Headquarters
Kosrae	109	7,354	Tofol
Pohnpei	344	33,372	Kolonia
Chuuk	127	52,870	Weno
Yap	119	11,128	Colonia

Kosrae consists of a single island. Its main town is Lelu (2,422 inhabitants in 1989). Pohnpei comprises a single island (covering 334 sq. km with 30,000 inhabitants in 1994) and eight scattered coral atolls. Kolonia (6,169 inhabitants in 1989) was the national capital of the Federated States. The new capital, Palikir, lies approximately 10 km southwest in the Palikir valley. Chuuk consists of a group of 14 islands within a large reef-fringed lagoon (44,000 inhabitants in 1994); the state also includes 12 coral atolls (8,000 inhabitants), the most important being the Mortlock Islands. The chief town is Weno (15,253 inhabitants in 1989). Yap comprises a main group of four islands (covering 100 sq. km with 7,000 inhabitants in 1994) and 13 coral atolls (4,000 inhabitants), the main ones being Ulithi and Woleai. Colonia is its chief town (3,456 inhabitants in 1989).

English is used in schools and is the official language. Trukese, Pohnpeian, Yapese and Kosrean are also spoken.

SOCIAL STATISTICS

1997 births, estimate, 3,500; deaths, 800. 1997 rates, estimate: birth rate, 27·7 per 1,000 population; death rate, 6·1 per 1,000; infant mortality rate, 35·1 per 1,000 live births. 1997 life expectancy, 68·2 years. Annual population growth rate, 1990–99, 2·1%; fertility rate, 1999, 4·6 births per woman.

CLIMATE

Tropical, with heavy year-round rainfall, especially in the eastern islands, and occasional typhoons (June–Dec.). Kolonia, Jan. 80°F (26·7°C), July 79°F (26·1°C). Annual rainfall 194" (4,859 mm).

CONSTITUTION AND GOVERNMENT

Under the Constitution founded on 10 May 1979, there is an executive presidency and a 14-member National Congress, comprising ten members elected for two-year terms from single-member constituencies of similar electorates, and four members elected one from each State for a four-year term by proportional representation. The Federal President and Vice-President first run for the Congress before they are elected by members of Congress for a four-year term.

RECENT ELECTIONS
The last election for Congress was held on 4 March 2003. Only non-partisans were elected. Joseph Urusemal was elected President and Redley Killion was confirmed as Vice-President (elected on 11 May 1999) by Congress on 11 May 2003.

CURRENT ADMINISTRATION
President: Joseph J. Urusemal; b. 1952 (took office 11 May 2003).
  Vice-President: Redley Killion.
  In May 2003 the government comprised:
  Minister of Foreign Affairs: Ieske K. Iehsi. *Finance and Administration:* John Ehsa. *Health, Education and Social Affairs:* Dr Eliuel K. Pretrick. *Economic Affairs:* Sebastian Anefal. *Justice:* Paul McIlrath. *Transportation, Communication and Infrastructure:* Akalino Susaia. *Public Defender:* Beautean Carl Worswick. *Postmaster-General:* Bethwel Henry.
  Speaker of the Congress: Peter Christian.

Government Website: http://www.fsmgov.org/

INTERNATIONAL RELATIONS
Micronesia is a member of the UN, Asian Development Bank, Pacific Community (formerly the South Pacific Commission) and the Pacific Islands Forum.

ECONOMY
Overview. There is a small, modern private sector supported by public services. The traditional sector is based on subsistence farming and fishing.

Currency. US currency is used. Foreign exchange reserves were US$83m. and total money supply was US$19m. in May 2002.

Budget. US compact funds are an annual US$100m. Revenue (1995–96 estimate), US$58m.; expenditure, US$52m.

Performance. Real GDP growth was 2·5% in 2000 and 0·9% in 2001. In 2001 total GDP was US$0·2bn.

Banking and Finance. There are three commercial banks: Bank of Guam, Bank of Hawaii and Bank of the Federated States of Micronesia. There is also a Federated States of Micronesia Development Bank.

ENERGY AND NATURAL RESOURCES
Electricity. Capacity (1995), 38,500 kW.

Minerals. The islands have few mineral deposits except for high-grade phosphates.

Agriculture. Agriculture consists mainly of subsistence farming: coconuts, breadfruit, bananas, sweet potatoes and cassava. A small amount of crops are produced for export, including copra, tropical fruits, peppers and taro. Production (2000, in 1,000 tonnes): coconuts, 140; copra, 18; cassava, 12; sweet potatoes, 3; bananas, 2. Livestock (2000): pigs, 32,000; cattle, 14,000; goats, 4,000.

Fisheries. In 1999 the catch amounted to approximately 11,886 tonnes, almost entirely from marine waters. Fishing licence fees were US$20m. in 1993 and are a primary revenue source.

INDUSTRY
The chief industries are construction, fish processing, tourism and handicrafts (items from shell, wood and pearl).

Labour. Two-thirds of the labour force are government employees. In 1994, 8,092 people worked in public administration and 7,375 in agriculture, fisheries and farming out of a total labour force of 27,573. The unemployment rate was 15·2%.

INTERNATIONAL TRADE

Imports and Exports. Total exports (1994 est.), US$29·1m.; imports, US$141·1m. Main import suppliers, 1994: USA, 32·9%; Japan, 32·0%; Guam, 23·2%. Main export markets, 1994: Japan, 72·7%; Guam, 5·1%; USA, 3·5%. The main exports are copra, bananas, black pepper, fish and garments. Main imports: foodstuffs and beverages, manufactured goods, machinery and equipment.

COMMUNICATIONS

Roads. In 1996 there were 240 km of roads (42 km paved).

Civil Aviation. There are international airports on Pohnpei, Chuuk, Yap and Kosrae. Services are provided by Air Nauru and Continental Airlines. In 1998 there were international flights to Guam, Honolulu, Johnston Island, Manila and the Marshall Islands in addition to domestic services. There were five airports in 1996 (four paved).

Shipping. The main ports are Kolonia (Pohnpei), Colonia (Yap), Lepukos (Chuuk), Okat and Lelu (Kosrae). In 1998 merchant shipping totalled 10,000 GRT.

Telecommunications. Micronesia had 9,600 main telephone lines in 2000, or 81·5 per 1,000 population. There were 470 fax machines in 1996. The islands are interconnected by shortwave radiotelephone. There are four earth stations linked to the Intelsat satellite system. There were 2,000 Internet users in Dec. 1999.

Postal Services. All four states have postal services.

SOCIAL INSTITUTIONS

Justice. There is a Supreme Court headed by the Chief Justice with two other judges, and a State Court in each of the four states with 13 judges in total.

Religion. The population is predominantly Christian. Yap is mainly Roman Catholic; Protestantism is prevalent elsewhere.

Education. In 1987 there were 25,139 pupils in 177 primary schools, with 1,051 teachers; 5,385 pupils in 17 high schools, with 314 teachers; and 799 students (1999) at the College of Micronesia in Pohnpei. The Micronesia Maritime and Fisheries Academy in Yap (est. 1990) provides education and training in fisheries technology at secondary and tertiary levels.

Health. In 1994 there were 45 doctors, and in 1993, 7 dentists, 7 pharmacists, 230 nurses and 4 hospitals with 325 beds.

In the period 1990–98 only 22% of the population had access to safe drinking water.

CULTURE

Broadcasting. There were five radio and six TV stations, and 22,000 radio and 19,800 TV sets in 1996 (colour by NTSC).

Tourism. In 1990 there were 20,475 visitors.

DIPLOMATIC REPRESENTATIVES

Of the United Kingdom in Micronesia
Ambassador: Ian Powell (resides at Suva, Fiji Islands).

Of Micronesia in the USA (1725 N St., NW, Washington, D.C., 20036)
Ambassador: Jesse B. Marehalau.

Of the USA in Micronesia (POB 1286, Kolonia, Pohnpei)
Ambassador: Larry Miles Dinger.

Of Micronesia to the United Nations
Ambassador: Masao Nakayama.

FURTHER READING
Wuerch, W. L. and Ballendorf, D. A., *Historical Dictionary of Guam and Micronesia.* Metuchen (NJ), 1995

MOLDOVA

Republica Moldova

Capital: Chişinău
Population estimate, 2000: 4·30m.
GDP per capita, 2000: (PPP$) 2,109
HDI/world rank: 0·701/105

KEY HISTORICAL EVENTS
In Dec. 1991 Moldova became a member of the CIS, a decision ratified by parliament in April 1994. Fighting took place in 1992 between government forces and separatists in the (largely Russian and Ukrainian) area east of the River Nistru (Transnistria). An agreement signed by the presidents of Moldova and Russia on 21 July 1992 brought to an end the armed conflict and established a 'security zone' controlled by peacekeeping forces from Russia, Moldova and Transnistria. On 21 Oct. 1994 a Moldo-Russian agreement obliged Russian troops to withdraw from the territory of Moldova over three years but the agreement was not ratified by the Russian Duma. On 8 May 1997 an agreement between Transnistria and the Moldovan government to end the separatist conflict stipulated that Transnistria would remain part of Moldova as it was territorially constituted in Jan. 1990. In 1997 some 7,000 Russian troops were stationed in Transnistria. In the autumn of 1999 Ion Sturza's centre-right coalition collapsed, along with privatization plans for the wine and tobacco industries. Communist President Vladimir Voronin, who was elected in 2001, has proposed giving the Russian language official status and joining the Russia–Belarus union.

TERRITORY AND POPULATION
Moldova is bounded in the east and south by Ukraine and on the west by Romania. The area is 33,700 sq. km (13,000 sq. miles). In Jan. 1994 the population was 4,353,000 (52·3% female).

The UN gives a projected population for 2010 of 4·19m.

In 1999, 53·8% of the population lived in rural areas. The 1989 census population was 4,335,360, of whom Moldovans accounted for 64·5%, Ukrainians 13·9%, Russians 13%, Gagauzi 3·5%, Bulgarians 2% and Jews 1·5%.

Apart from Chişinău, the capital (population of 655,000 in 1999), major towns are Tiraspol (185,000 in 1993), Beltsy (156,000 in 1993) and Bender (133,000 in 1992). The official Moldovan language (i.e. Romanian) was written in Cyrillic prior to the restoration of the Roman alphabet in 1989. It is spoken by 75% of the population; the use of other languages (Russian, Gagauz) is safeguarded by the Constitution.

SOCIAL STATISTICS
1999: births, 38,501; deaths, 41,314. Rates, 1999 (per 1,000 population): births, 8·8; deaths, 9·4. In 1998 the most popular age range for marrying was 20–24 for both males and females. Life expectancy at birth in 1999 was 62·8 years for males and 70·3 years for females. Infant mortality, 1998, 17·9 per 1,000 live births; fertility rate, 1999, 1·7 births per woman. By the end of 1998 more than 46% of the population were classified as living in absolute poverty.

CLIMATE
The climate is temperate, with warm summers, crisp, sunny autumns and cold winters with snow. Chişinău, Jan. –7°C, Jul. 20°C. Annual rainfall 677 mm.

CONSTITUTION AND GOVERNMENT
A declaration of republican sovereignty was adopted in June 1990 and in Aug. 1991 the republic declared itself independent. A new Constitution came into effect on 27 Aug. 1994, which defines Moldova as an 'independent, democratic and unitary state'. At a referendum on 6 March 1994 turn-out was 75·1%; 95·4% of votes cast favoured 'an independent Moldova within its 1990 borders'. The referendum (and the Feb. parliamentary elections) were not held by the authorities in Transnistria. In a further referendum on 4 June 1999, on whether to switch from a parliamentary system to a presidential one, turn-out was 58% with the majority of the votes cast being in favour of the change.

Parliament has 104 seats and is elected for four-year terms. There is a 4% threshold for election; votes falling below this are re-distributed to successful parties. The *President* is now elected for four-year terms by parliament, after the constitution had been amended to abolish direct presidential elections.

The 1994 Constitution makes provision for the autonomy of Transnistria and the Gagauz (Gagauzi Yeri) region.

Transnistria. In the predominantly Russian-speaking areas of Transnistria a self-styled 'Dniester Republic' was established in Sept. 1991, and approved by a local referendum in Dec. 1991. A Russo-Moldovan agreement of 21 July 1992 provided for a special statute for Transnistria and a guarantee of self-determination should Moldova unite with Romania. The population in 1998 was 670,000. Romanian here is still written in the Cyrillic alphabet. At a referendum on 24 Dec. 1995, 81% of votes cast were in favour of adopting a new constitution proclaiming independence.

On 17 June 1996 the Moldovan government granted Transnistria a special status as 'a state-territorial formation in the form of a republic within Moldova's internationally recognized border'.

Elections for chief regional executive were held on 9 Dec. 2001. Turn-out was 64%. Igor Smirnov (b. 1941) was re-elected for a third five-year term against two opponents winning nearly 82% of votes cast.

Gagauz Yeri. This was created an autonomous territorial unit by Moldovan legislation of 13 Jan. 1995. In 1995 the population was 153,000. There is a 35-member *Popular Assembly* directly elected for four-year terms and headed by a *Governor*, who is a member of the Moldovan cabinet. At the elections of 28 May and 11 June 1995 turn-out was 68%.

Governor. Gheorghe Tabunscic.

National Anthem. The Romanian anthem was replaced in 1994 by a traditional tune, 'Limbă noastră' ('Our Tongue'); words by Alexei Mateevici, tune by Alexandru Cristi.

RECENT ELECTIONS

At the parliamentary elections held on 25 Feb. 2001 the PCRM (communists) won 71 seats with 49·9% of the votes and the BEAB (centrists) 19 with 13·4%. The PPCD (conservative) won 11 seats with 8·3% of votes cast. Turn-out was 69%.

Following the parliamentary elections of Feb. 2001 parliament elected Vladimir Voronin, the Communist leader, as the new president on 4 April 2001. In so doing Moldova became the first former Soviet republic to choose a Communist as its head of state. Voronin received 71 votes against 15 for the prime minister, Dumitru Braghis, and 3 for another communist candidate, Valerian Cristea.

CURRENT ADMINISTRATION

President: Vladimir Voronin; b. 1941 (PCRM; sworn in 7 April 2001).

In March 2003 the government comprised:

Prime Minister: Vasile Tarlev; b. 1963 (PCRM; sworn in 19 April 2001).

First Deputy Prime Minister: Vasile Iovv. *Deputy Prime Ministers:* Valerian Cristea, Dmitrii Todoroglo (also *Agriculture and Food Industries*), Stefan Odagiu (also *Minister of Economy and Reform*).

Minister of Culture: Veaceslav Madan. *Defence:* Victor Gaiciuc. *Education:* Gheorghe Sima. *Finance:* Zinaida Greceanâi. *Foreign Affairs:* Nicolae Dudău. *Health:* Andrei Gherman. *Industry:* Mihail Garştea. *Energy:* Iacob Timciuc. *Internal Affairs:* George Papuc. *Justice:* Ion Morei. *Labour and Social Protection:* Valerian Revenco. *Reintegration:* Vasile Sova. *Territory Development, Construction and Ecology:* Gheorghe Duca. *Transportation and Communications:* Vasile Zgardan.

Government Website: http://www.moldova.md/

DEFENCE

Conscription is up to 18 months. In 2000 military expenditure totalled US$21m., (US$5 per capita), representing 1·7% of GDP.

Russian troops have remained in Transnistria since Moldova gained independence, but in Nov. 1999 the Organization for Security and Co-operation in Europe (OSCE) passed a resolution at its summit requiring Russia to withdraw its troops to Russia by Dec. 2002, unconditionally and under international observation. This deadline has been extended to Dec. 2003.

Army. Personnel, 1999, 9,600 (5,200 conscripts). There is also a paramilitary Interior Ministry force of 2,500, riot police numbering 900 and combined forces reserves of some 66,000.

Air Force. The Air Force has a small number of MiG-29 fighters. Personnel (including air defence), 1999, 1,050.

INTERNATIONAL RELATIONS
Moldova is a member of the UN, WTO, OSCE, CIS, the Council of Europe, CEI, Danube Commission, BSEC, International Organization of the Francophonie and the NATO Partnership for Peace.

ECONOMY
Agriculture accounted for 28·9% of GDP in 1998, industry 31·3% and services 39·8%.

Overview. Since a privatization programme stared in 1993 more than 1,500 companies have been sold, ranging from small and medium-sized enterprises through to a few large concerns.

Currency. A new unit of currency, the *leu* (MDL), replaced the rouble in Nov. 1993. Inflation was 9·8% in 2001, down from a peak of 2,198% in the early 1990s. Foreign exchange reserves were US$219m. in June 2002 and total money supply 2,607m. lei.

Budget. Total revenue and total expenditure (in 1m. lei), years ending 31 Dec.:

	1996	1997	1998	1999	2000
Revenue	1,976·2	2,843·9	2,808·8	3,064·0	4,033·5
Expenditure	2,217·2	3,709·5	3,271·6	3,660·2	4,738·6

Performance. Moldova's economy has been in dire straits. Economic growth was negative in 1998 at –6·5% and again in 1999, at –3·4%. A limited recovery followed in 2000 with growth of 2·1%, and in 2001 the economy expanded 6·1%.

Between 1990 and 1996 the average annual real growth in GNP per capita was –16·8%. Of all the former Soviet republics Moldova's economy has suffered the most since 1989 when political and economic reforms took place across central and eastern Europe. In 1998 the level of GDP was estimated to be only 32% of that in 1989. Total GDP was US$1·5bn. in 2001. The private sector accounts for over 50% of official GDP.

Banking and Finance. The central bank and bank of issue is the National Bank (*Governor*, Leonid Talmaci). In 1996 there were 26 commercial banks and 1 foreign branch office (Romanian).

ENERGY AND NATURAL RESOURCES
Environment. According to the *World Bank Atlas* Moldova's carbon dioxide emissions in 1998 were the equivalent of 2·2 tonnes per capita.

Electricity. Installed capacity in 1995 was 3·22m. kW. Production was 5·66bn. kWh in 1998; consumption per capita was 689 kWh.

Minerals. There are deposits of lignite, phosphorites, gypsum and building materials.

Agriculture. Agriculture employs about 700,000 people. Land under cultivation in 1997 was 2·5m. ha, of which 0·3m. ha was accounted for by private subsidiary agriculture and 6,700 ha (in 1993) by commercial agriculture in 3,100 farms. Agriculture is Moldova's biggest exporter, accounting for 75% of total exports.

Output of main agricultural products (in 1,000 tonnes) in 2000: sugarbeets, 1,800; maize, 1,091; wheat, 770; grapes, 450; potatoes, 342; sunflower seeds, 280; wine, 240; tomatoes, 189; barley, 152. Livestock (2000): 416,000 cattle, 974,000 sheep, 705,000 pigs, 14m. chickens. Livestock products, 2000 (in 1,000 tonnes): milk, 571; meat, 88, eggs, 32.

Forestry. In 1995 forests covered 357,000 ha, or 10·8% of the total land area. Timber production in 1999 was 49,000 cu. metres.

Fisheries. The south is rich in sturgeon, mackerel and brill. The catch in 1999 was estimated at 500 tonnes and came entirely from inland waters.

INDUSTRY
There are canning plants, wine-making plants, woodworking and metallurgical factories, a factory of ferro-concrete building materials, footwear, dairy products

and textile plants. Output was valued at 1,200m. lei in 1993. Production (in tonnes): rolled ferrous metals (1992), 0·5m.; flour (1995), 282,800; raw sugar (1998), 185,600; cement (1997), 122,000; processed meat (1993), 56,100; fabrics (1993), 31·1m. sq. metres; footwear (1995), 1·5m. pairs; 1,000 tractors (1995); 19,000 TV sets (1997); 94,000 radio receivers (1997); 2,000 refrigerators (1997); 46,000 washing machines (1997); 7·1bn. cigarettes (1995).

Labour. In 1996 the labour force totalled 2,181,000 (51% males). Approximately 45% of the economically active population in 1994 were engaged in agriculture, fisheries and forestry. In 2000 the unemployment rate was 1·8%. Average monthly salaries in 1993 were 21,582 roubles.

INTERNATIONAL TRADE
Foreign debt was US$1,233m. in 2000.

Imports and Exports. In 2000 imports (f.o.b.) were valued at US$783·2m. (US$1,031·7m. in 1998) and exports (f.o.b.) at US$476·6m. (US$643·6m. in 1998). Chief export markets in 1997 were CIS countries—68·1% (of which Russia took 53·7%, Ukraine 6·0%, Belarus 4·3% and Kazakhstan 1·0%). Central and eastern European countries took 16·5% (of which Romania 9·3%, Lithuania 1·9%, Latvia 1·8%, Bulgaria 1·6% and Hungary 0·4%).

Trade with the EU amounted to 9·8% in 1997 (of which Germany 3·7%, Italy 2·6%, Netherlands 1·1%, Austria 0·5%). 61·5% of imports came from CIS countries with central and eastern Europe's share at 16·6% and that of EU countries at 15·1%.

Moldova's main export commodity is wine, ahead of tobacco. Fruit and vegetables, textiles and footwear, and machinery are also significant exports. Leading imports are mineral products and fuel, machinery and equipment, chemicals and textiles.

COMMUNICATIONS
Roads. There were 12,300 km of roads (10,700 km paved) in 1996. Passenger cars in use in 1996 numbered 166,757 (46 per 1,000 inhabitants), and there were also 109,822 motorcycles and mopeds, 58,418 trucks and vans and 9,220 buses and coaches.

Rail. Total length in 1996 was 1,318 km of 1,520 mm gauge. Passenger-km travelled in 1998 came to 656m. and freight tonne-km to 2,575m.

Civil Aviation. The national carriers are Air Moldova, Air Moldova International and Moldavian Airlines. Air Moldova had flights in 1998 to Athens, Bucharest, Ekaterinburg, Istanbul, Larnaca, London, Moscow, Paris, St Petersburg, Varna and Vienna. In 1998 Air Moldova International flew to Amsterdam, Berlin, Chernovtsy, Dnipropetrovsk, Donetsk, Frankfurt, Iasi, Kharkiv, Kyiv, Mineralnye Vody, Munich, Odesa, Volgograd and Warsaw. Moldavian Airlines flew to Bologna, Budapest, Moscow, Prague, Rostov and Verona. In 2000 the airport at Chişinau handled 254,234 passengers (all on international flights) and 2,159 tonnes of freight. In 1999 scheduled airline traffic of Moldovan-based carriers flew 2·3m. km, carrying 43,000 passengers (all on international flights).

Shipping. In 1993, 0·3m. passengers and 0·3m. tonnes of freight were carried on inland waterways.

Telecommunications. In 2000 there were 583,800 telephone main lines (133·3 per 1,000 persons) and 64,000 PCs in use (14·5 per 1,000 persons). There were 18,000 mobile phone subscribers in 1999 and 600 fax machines in 1997. In Dec. 1999 there were 15,000 Internet users. Privatization of the state-owned telecommunications company, Moldtelecom, is a priority for the government. A majority stake offer from MGTS, Moscow's main telephone company, failed in Nov. 2002.

Postal Services. In 1995 there were 1,307 post offices.

SOCIAL INSTITUTIONS
Justice. 47,515 crimes were reported in 1994. The population in penal institutions in 1996 was 9,812 (260 per 100,000 of national population). The death penalty was abolished for all crimes in 1995.

Religion. Religious affiliation in 1999: Romanian Orthodox, 1·5m.; Russian (Moldovan) Orthodox, 410,000.

Education. In 1996–97 there were 133,426 pupils in pre-schools, 320,725 pupils in primary schools and 445,501 pupils in secondary schools, 43,000 students in 97 vocational secondary schools and 54 technical colleges and 47,000 students in nine higher educational institutions including the state university. In Jan. 1994, 0·2m. children (52% of those eligible) attended pre-school institutions. Adult literacy rate in 1999 was 98·7% (male, 99·5%; female, 98·1%).

In 1996 total expenditure on education came to 10·6% of GNP and represented 28·1% of total government expenditure.

Health. In Jan. 1996 there were 17,400 doctors, 48,400 junior medical personnel and 312 hospitals with 54,300 beds.

Welfare. There were 649,000 age pensioners and 267,000 other pensioners in Jan. 1994.

CULTURE

Broadcasting. The government authority Radioteleviziunea Nationala is responsible for broadcasting. There are two national radio programmes, a Radio Moscow relay, and a foreign service, Radio Moldova International. There is a national state TV service and a private TV network. Romanian and Russian channels are also broadcast. There were 1·3m. television receivers and 3·22m. radio receivers in 1997.

Cinema. There were 49 cinemas in 1995, with a total attendance for the year of 1·4m. Gross box office receipts came to 1·8m. lei.

Press. Moldova has 567 newspapers and magazines. Of these 323 are published in Moldovan, four in English and the rest in Russian.

Tourism. In 1998 there were 20,000 foreign tourists, spending US$4m.

Libraries. There is a National Library and around 1,775 public libraries.

Museums and Galleries. There are 83 museums in Moldova.

DIPLOMATIC REPRESENTATIVES
Of Moldova in the United Kingdom (resides in Brussels)
Ambassador: Vacant.
Chargé d'Affaires a.i.: Alexie Cracan.

Of the United Kingdom in Moldova (ASITO Building, Office 320, 57/1 Banulescu-Bodoni Str, Chişinau 2005)
Ambassador: Bernard Whiteside, MBE.

Of Moldova in the USA (2101 S St., NW, Washington, D.C., 20008)
Ambassador: Mihail Manoli.

Of the USA in Moldova (103 Strada Alexei Matveevici, Chişinau)
Ambassador: Pamela Hyde Smith.

Of Moldova to the United Nations
Ambassador: Dr Ion Botnaru.

Of Moldova to the European Union
Ambassador: Ion Capatina.

FURTHER READING
Gribincea, M., *Agricultural Collectivization in Moldavia.* East European Monographs, Columbia Univ. Press, 1996
King, C., *Post-Soviet Moldova: A Borderland in Transition.* International Specialized Book Service, Portland, Oregon, 1997.—*The Moldovans: Romania, Russia, and the Politics of Culture.* Hoover Institution Press, Stanford, 2000
Mitrasca, M., *Moldova: A Romanian Province Under Russian Rule: Diplomatic History from the Archives of the Great Powers.* Algora Publishing, New York, 2002

National Statistical Office: Department for Statistics and Sociology, MD-2028, Hîncesti 53, Chişinau.
Website: http://www.statistica.md

MONACO

Principauté de Monaco

Capital: Monaco
Population estimate, 2000: 32,000
GDP per capita: not available

KEY HISTORICAL EVENTS

From 1297 Monaco belonged to the house of Grimaldi. In 1731 it passed to the female line, Louise Hippolyte, daughter of Antoine I, heiress of Monaco, marrying Jacques de Goyon Matignon, Count of Torigni, who took the name and arms of Grimaldi. The Principality was placed under the protection of the Kingdom of Sardinia by the Treaty of Vienna, 1815, and under that of France in 1861.

TERRITORY AND POPULATION

Monaco is bounded in the south by the Mediterranean and elsewhere by France (Department of Alpes Maritimes). The area is 197 ha (1·97 sq. km). The Principality is divided into four districts: Monaco-Ville, la Condamine, Monte-Carlo and Fontvieille. Population (2000 census), 32,020; there were 6,089 Monegasques (19%), 10,229 French (32%) and 6,410 Italian (20%).

The official language is French.

SOCIAL STATISTICS

2001: births, 748; deaths, 636; marriages, 175; divorces, 77. Rates per 1,000 population, 1998: birth, 26·3; death, 17·8; marriage, 6·0; divorce, 2·5. Annual population growth rate, 1990–99, was 1·2%; fertility rate, 1999, 1·7 births per woman.

CLIMATE

A Mediterranean climate, with mild moist winters and hot dry summers. Monaco, Jan. 50°F (10°C), July 74°F (23·3°C). Annual rainfall 30" (758 mm).

CONSTITUTION AND GOVERNMENT

On 17 Dec. 1962 a new constitution was promulgated which maintains the hereditary monarchy.

The reigning Prince is **Rainier III**, b. 31 May 1923, son of Princess Charlotte, Duchess of Valentinois, daughter of Prince Louis II, 1898–1977 (married 19 March 1920 to Prince Pierre, Comte de Polignac, who had taken the name Grimaldi, from whom she was divorced 18 Feb. 1933). Prince Rainier succeeded his grandfather Louis II, who died on 9 May 1949. He married on 19 April 1956 Miss Grace Kelly, a citizen of the USA (died 14 Sept. 1982). *Offspring:* Princess Caroline Louise Marguerite, b. 23 Jan. 1957; married Philippe Junot on 28 June 1978, divorced 9 Oct. 1980; married Stefano Casiraghi on 29 Dec. 1983 (died 3 Oct. 1990); married Prince Ernst of Hanover on 23 Jan 1999. *Offspring:* Andrea, b. 8 June 1984; Charlotte, b. 3 Aug. 1986; Pierre, b. 7 Sept. 1987; Alexandra, b. 20 July 1999. Prince Albert Alexandre Louis Pierre, b. 14 March 1958 *(heir apparent)*. Princess Stéphanie Marie Elisabeth, b. 1 Feb. 1965, married Daniel Ducruet on 1 July 1995, divorced 4 Oct. 1996. *Offspring:* Louis, b. 27 Nov. 1992; Pauline, b. 4 May 1994; Camille, b. 15 July 1998.

Prince Rainier renounces the principle of divine right. Executive power is exercised jointly by the Prince and a four-member *Council of government*, headed by a Minister of State (a French citizen). A 24-member *National Council* is elected for five-year terms.

The constitution can be modified only with the approval of the National Council. A law of 1992 permits Monegasque women to give their nationality to their children.

National Anthem. 'Principauté Monaco ma patrie' ('Principality of Monaco my fatherland'); words by T. Bellando de Castro, tune by C. Albrecht.

RECENT ELECTIONS
In parliamentary elections held on 9 Feb. 2003 the opposition Union for Monaco won 21 of 24 seats against 3 for the ruling National Democratic Union. Turn-out was about 80%.

CURRENT ADMINISTRATION
Chief of State: Prince Rainier III.
In March 2003 the cabinet comprised:
Minister of State: Patrick Leclercq; b. 1938 (sworn in 5 Feb. 2000).
Minister of Finance and Economics: Franck Biancheri. *Public Works and Social Affairs:* José Badia. *Interior:* Philippe Deslandes. *President of the National Council:* Stéphane Valeri.

Government Website: http://www.monaco.gouv.mc/

INTERNATIONAL RELATIONS
Monegasque relations with France are based on conventions of 1963. French citizens are treated as if in France. Monaco is a member of the UN, OSCE and the International Organization of the Francophonie.

ECONOMY

Overview. A 22-ha site reclaimed from the sea at Fontvieille has been earmarked for office and residential development. The present industrial zone is to be reorganized and developed with a view to attracting light industry.

Currency. On 1 Jan. 1999 the euro (EUR) replaced the French franc as the legal currency in Monaco; irrevocable conversion rate 6·55957 French francs to one euro. The euro, which consists of 100 cents, has been in circulation since 1 Jan. 2002. There are seven euro notes in different colours and sizes denominated in 500, 200, 100, 50, 20, 10 and 5 euros, and eight coins denominated in 2 and 1 euros, then 50, 20, 10, 5, 2 and 1 cents. On the introduction of the euro there was a 'dual circulation' period before the franc ceased to be legal tender on 17 Feb. 2002.

Budget. Revenues in 2001 totalled 4,094·84m. francs (€624·25m.) and expenditures 4,073·77m. francs (€621·04m.).

Performance. Monaco does not publish annual income information, but its economy is estimated to have grown by 1·6% in 2001.

Banking and Finance. There were 44 banks in 2001 of which 22 were Monegasque banks.

Weights and Measures. The metric system is in use.

ENERGY AND NATURAL RESOURCES

Electricity. Electricity is imported from France. 475 GWh were supplied to 24,074 customers in 2001; output capacity, 83 MW.

Oil and Gas. In 2001, 58 GWh of gas were supplied to 4,269 customers; output capacity was 19 MW.

Water. Total consumption (2001), 5·71m. cu. metres.

INDUSTRY
Light industry made up 9·9% of economic activity in 1995. There were some 700 small businesses, including chemicals, plastics, electronics, engineering and paper in 1993.

Labour. There were 39,543 persons employed in Jan. 2001. 36,072 worked in the private sector; 3,471 in the public sector. Some 25,000 French citizens work in Monaco.

Trade Unions. Membership of trade unions was estimated at 2,000 out of a workforce of 25,600 in 1989.

INTERNATIONAL TRADE

Imports and Exports. There is a customs union with France. Exports for 2001 totalled €394m.; imports, €403m. Main imports: pharmaceuticals, perfumes, clothing, paper, synthetic and non-metallic products, and building materials.

COMMUNICATIONS

Roads. There were estimated to be 50 km of roads in 2001 and 32,800 vehicles. Monaco has the densest network of roads of any country in the world. In 2001, 4,065,632 people travelled by bus.

Rail. The 1·7 km of main line passing through the country are operated by the French National Railways (SNCF). In 2001, 3,307,146 people arrived at or departed from Monaco railway station.

Civil Aviation. There are helicopter flights to Nice with Heli Air Monaco and Heli Inter. Helicopter movements (2001) at the Heliport of Monaco (Fontvieille), 49,245; the number of passengers carried was 142,074. The nearest airport is at Nice in France.

Shipping. In 2001 there were 1,052 vessels registered, of which 12 were over 100 tonnes. 1,787 yachts put in to the port of Monaco and 1,029 at Fontvieille in 2001. 119 liners put in to port in Monaco; 2,285 people embarked, 1,692 disembarked and 67,539 were in transit.

Telecommunications. In 2001 there were 34,153 land-based telephone lines and 14,302 mobile phone subscribers.

Postal Services. 20m. items were posted and 26m. items were delivered by the Post Office in 2001.

SOCIAL INSTITUTIONS

Justice. There are the following courts: *Tribunal Suprême, Cour de Révision, Cour d'Appel*, a Correctional Tribunal, a Work Tribunal, a Tribunal of the First Instance, 2 Arbitration Commissions for Rents (1 commercial, 1 domestic), courts for Work-related Accidents and Supervision, a *Juge de Paix*, and a Police Tribunal. There is no death penalty.

Police. In 1993 the police force (Sûreté Publique) comprised 500 personnel. Monaco has one of the highest number of police per head of population of any country in the world.

Religion. 90% of the resident population are Roman Catholic. There is a Roman Catholic archbishop.

Education. In 2002–03, in the public sector, there were 7 pre-school institutions (*écoles maternelles*) with 713 pupils; 4 elementary schools with 1,374 pupils; 3 secondary schools with 2,430 pupils. There were 142 primary teachers and 286 secondary school teachers in total in 2002–03. In the private sector there were 2 pre-school and 3 primary schools with 222 and 525 pupils respectively; and 1 secondary school with 710 pupils. In 2000–01 education amounted to 6·7% of total government expenditure.

The University of Southern Europe in Monaco had 112 students in 1996–97.

Health. In 2000, 18·5% of total government expenditure was spent on public health. In 2002 there were 156 doctors, 21 dentists and 19 childcare nurses. Monaco has the highest provision of hospital beds of any country, with 162 per 10,000 population in 2002.

CULTURE

Broadcasting. Radio Monte Carlo broadcasts FM commercial programmes in French (long- and medium-waves). Radio Monte Carlo owns 55% of *Radio Monte Carlo* Relay Station on Cyprus. The foreign service is dedicated exclusively to religious broadcasts and is maintained by voluntary contributions. It operates in 36 languages under the name 'Trans World Radio' and has relay facilities on Bonaire, West Indies; it is planning to build relay facilities in the southern parts of Africa. *Télé Monte-Carlo* broadcasts TV programmes in French, Italian and English (colour by SECAM H). There is a 30-channel cable service. In 1997 there were 34,000 radio receivers and 25,000 television receivers.

Cinema. In 1996 there were two cinemas.

Press. Monaco had one newspaper in 1995 with a circulation of 8,000, equivalent to 250 per 1,000 inhabitants.

Tourism. In 2001, 296,925 foreign visitors spent a total of 797,842 nights in Monaco. The main visitors are Italians, followed by French and Americans. 82,241 people attended 674 congresses in 2001. There are three casinos run by the state, including the one at Monte Carlo attracting 0·4m. visitors a year.

DIPLOMATIC REPRESENTATIVES
British Consul-General (resident in France)*:* I. Davies.
British Honorary Consul: Eric J. F. Blair.

Consul-General for Monaco in London: Ivan Bozidar Ivanovic.

Of Monaco to the United Nations
Ambassador: Jacques Louis Boisson.

Of Monaco to the European Union
Ambassador: Jean Gréther.

FURTHER READING
Journal de Monaco. Bulletin Officiel. 1858 ff.

Hudson, Grace L., *Monaco.* [Bibliography] ABC-Clio, Oxford and Santa Barbara (CA), 1991

MONGOLIA

Mongol Uls

Capital: Ulan Bator
Population estimate, 2000: 2·37m.
GDP per capita, 2000: (PPP$) 1,783
HDI/world rank: 00·655/113

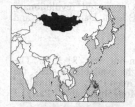

KEY HISTORICAL EVENTS

Temujin became khan of Hamag Mongolia in 1190. Having united by conquest various Tatar and Mongolian tribes he was confirmed as 'Universal' ('Genghis', 'Chingiz') khan in 1206. The expansionist impulse of his nomadic empire (Beijing captured in 1215; Samarkand in 1220) continued after his death in 1227. Tamurlaine (died 1405) was the last of the conquering khans. In 1368 the Chinese drove the Mongols from Beijing, and for the next two centuries Sino-Mongolian relations alternated between war and trade. In 1691 Outer Mongolia accepted Manchu rule. The head of the Lamaist faith became the symbol of national identity, and his seat ('Urga', now Ulan Bator) was made the Mongolian capital. When the Manchu dynasty was overthrown in 1911 Outer Mongolia declared its independence under its spiritual ruler and turned to Russia for support against China. Soviet and Mongolian revolutionary forces set up a provisional government in March 1921. On the death of the spiritual ruler a people's republic and new constitution were proclaimed in May 1924. With Soviet help Japanese invaders were fended off during the Second World War. The Mongols then took part in the successful Soviet campaign against Inner Mongolia and Manchuria. On 5 Jan. 1946 China recognized the independence of Outer Mongolia. Until 1990 sole power was in the hands of the Mongolian People's Revolutionary (Communist) Party (MPRP), but an opposition Mongolian Democratic Party, founded in Dec. 1989, achieved tacit recognition and held its first congress in Feb. 1990. Following demonstrations and hunger-strikes, on 12 March the entire MPRP Politburo resigned and political opposition was legalized.

TERRITORY AND POPULATION

Mongolia is bounded in the north by the Russian Federation, and in the east and south and west by China. Area, 1,565,008 sq. km (604,250 sq. miles). Population (2000 census), 2,373,493 (1,195,512 females). Density, 2000, 1·5 per sq. km. In 2000, 57·0% of the population were urban.

The UN gives a projected population for 2010 of 2·87m.

The population is predominantly made up of Mongolian peoples (81·5% Khalkh). There is a Turkic Kazakh minority (4·3% of the population) and 20 Mongol minorities. The official language is Khalkh Mongol.

The republic is administratively divided into three cities: Ulan Bator, the capital (2000 population, 760,077), Erdenet (68,000 in 2000) and Darhan (66,000 in 2000), and 18 provinces *(aimag)*. The provinces are sub-divided into 334 districts or counties *(suums)*.

SOCIAL STATISTICS

Births, 1996, 51,100; deaths, 15,300. Birth rate (1996), 22·0 per 1,000 population; death rate, 6·6 per 1,000; marriage rate (1995), 12 per 1,000; divorce rate (1995), 0·7 per 1,000. Annual population growth rate, 1989–2000, 1·4%. Infant mortality rate, 1998, 34·1 per 1,000 live births. Expectation of life in 1999 was 60·5 years for males and 64·5 for females. Fertility rate, 1999, 2·5 births per woman.

CLIMATE

A very extreme climate, with six months of mean temperatures below freezing, but much higher temperatures occur for a month or two in summer. Rainfall is very low and limited to the months mid-May to mid-Sept. Ulan Bator, Jan. −14°F (−25·6°C), July 61°F (16·1°C). Annual rainfall 8" (208 mm).

CONSTITUTION AND GOVERNMENT

The Constitution of 12 Feb. 1992 abolished the 'People's Democracy', introduced democratic institutions and a market economy and guarantees freedom of speech. The *President* is directly elected for renewable four-year terms.

Since June 1992 the legislature has consisted of a single-chamber 76-seat parliament, *the Great Hural*, which elects the Prime Minister.

National Anthem. 'Darkhan manai khuvsgalt uls' ('Our sacred revolutionary republic'); words by Tsendiyn Damdinsüren, tune by Bilegin Damdinsüren and Luvsanjamts Murjorj.

RECENT ELECTIONS

At the parliamentary elections of 2 July 2000 turn-out was 81·35%. The Revolutionary People's Party of Mongolia gained 72 of the available 76 seats, the Mongolian National Democratic Party 1, the Civil Will/Green Party 1, Motherland Alliance (Mongol Democratic New Socialist Party and Mongolian Labour Party) 1 and 1 seat went to a non-partisan.

In presidential elections on 20 May 2001, incumbent Natsagiin Bagabandi won with 57·9% of the vote, followed by Radnaasumbereliyn Gonchigdorj with 36·6% and Luvsandamba Dashnyam with 3·6%. Turn-out was 82%.

CURRENT ADMINISTRATION

President: Natsagiin Bagabandi; b. 1940 (Revolutionary People's Party of Mongolia; elected May 1997).

In March 2003 the government comprised:

Prime Minister: Nambaryn Enkhbayar; b. 1958 (Revolutionary People's Party of Mongolia; sworn in 26 July 2000).

Minister of Defence: Jugderdemidiin Gurragchaa. *Finance and Economics:* Chultemin Ulaan. *Foreign Affairs:* Luvsangiin Erdenechuluun. *Health:* Pagvajavyn Nyamdavaa. *Industry and Commerce:* Chimidzorigiin Ganzorig. *Infrastructure:* Byambyn Jigjid. *Education, Science and Culture:* Ayurzanyn Tsanjid. *Environment and Natural Resources:* Ulambayaryn Barsbold. *Food and Agriculture:* Darjaagiin Nasanjargal. *Justice and Internal Affairs:* Tsendiin Nyamdorj. *Social Welfare and Labour:* Shiilegiin Batbayar. *Government Affairs:* Ulziisaikhany Enkhtuvshin.

Government Website: http://www.pmis.gov.mn

DEFENCE

Conscription is for one year for males aged 18–28 years. Defence expenditure in 2000 totalled US$19m. (US$7 per capita), representing 2·0% of GDP.

Army. Strength (1999) 7,500 (4,000 conscripts). There is a border guard of 6,000, 1,200 internal security troops and 500 Civil Defence Troops.

Air Force. The Air Force had a strength of 800 in 1999 with nine combat aircraft, including MiG-21s, and 12 armed helicopters.

INTERNATIONAL RELATIONS

Mongolia is a member of the UN, WTO, the Asian Development Bank and the Colombo Plan.

ECONOMY

In 1998 agriculture accounted for 32·8% of GDP, industry 27·6% and services 39·6%.

Overview. Mongolia has for centuries had a traditional nomadic pastoral economy which the government aims to transform into a market economy. An Agency for National Development, headed by a minister of cabinet rank, co-ordinates economic policy. A law of May 1991 introduced privatization by the distribution of vouchers worth 10,000 tugriks to 2m. citizens to acquire holdings or to buy small businesses or livestock. About 45% of state-owned assets had been privatized by 2001.

Currency. The unit of currency is the *tugrik* (MNT) of 100 *möngö*. The tugrik was made convertible in 1993. In June 2002 foreign exchange reserves were US$210m., gold reserves totalled 41,000 troy oz and total money supply was 187,680m. tugriks. Inflation, which stood at 268% in 1993, had been brought down to below 10% by 1998 and in 2001 was 8·0%.

Budget. Total revenue and expenditure (in 1m. tugriks):

	1997	1998	1999	2000
Revenue	171,744	183,552	196,561	303,215
Expenditure	176,436	201,279	232,795	306,037

Sources of revenue, 1995 (in 1m. tugriks): taxes, 109,269·5 (comprising: income, profits and capital gains tax, 49,999·4; social security contributions, 18,906·1; payroll taxes, 43·5; taxes on goods and services, 27,364·7; taxes on foreign trade, 9,630·5; other, 3,325·3); non-tax revenue, 18,243·2; capital revenue, 3,751·2; grants, 5,010·5. Items of expenditure: current, 105,536·2 (comprising: goods and services, 75,083·5; wages, 25,542·5; employer contributions, 7,161·1; other purchases, 42,379·9); interest payments, 1,794·4; subsidies, 28,658·5; capital, 22,559·3; foreign amortization, 16,836.

Performance. Real GDP growth was 1·1% in both 2000 and 2001. Total GDP in 2001 was US$1·0bn.

Banking and Finance. The Mongolian Bank (established 1924) is the bank of issue, being also a commercial, savings and development bank: the *Governor* is Chook O. Chuluunbat. It has 21 main branches. There are 12 banks in total, the largest being the state-owned Trade and Development Bank.

A stock exchange opened in Ulan Bator in 1992.

Weights and Measures. The metric system is in use.

ENERGY AND NATURAL RESOURCES

Environment. In 1998 carbon dioxide emissions in Mongolia were the equivalent of 3·3 tonnes per capita according to the *World Bank Atlas*.

Electricity. Installed capacity was 900,000 kW in 1995. There are six thermal electric power stations. Production, 1998, 2·66bn. kWh. Consumption per capita was 1,220 kWh in 1997.

Minerals. There are large deposits of copper, nickel, zinc, molybdenum, phosphorites, tin, wolfram and fluorspar; production of the latter in 1996, 565,100 tonnes. There are major coalmines near Ulan Bator and Darhan. In 1997 lignite production was 3·75m. tonnes and coal production 1·17m. tonnes. Copper production, 1996, 351,500 tonnes; gold production, 1997, 8,008 kg.

Agriculture. The prevailing Mongolian style of life is pastoral nomadism. 73% of agricultural production derives from cattle-raising. In 2000 there were 14·0m. sheep, 3·50m. cattle, 3·08m. horses and 360,000 camels. The number of goats rose from 5·5m. to 10m. between 1992 and 2000 as production of cashmere has increased along with the market economy. In late 1999 and early 2000 approximately 3m. animals died as a result of extreme weather and overgrazing, and in late 2000 and early 2001 more than 1·3m. animals died.

The total agricultural area in 1995 was 118·5m. ha. 96% was sown to cereals, 1·6% to fodder and 0·9% to vegetables. In 1998 there were 1·32m. ha of arable land and 1,000 ha of permanent crop land. In 2000 output of major crops was 186,000 tonnes of wheat (down from 607,000 in the period 1989–91); 70,000 tonnes of potatoes (down from 128,000 in 1989–91); 4,000 tonnes of barley (down from 83,000 in 1989–91). Livestock products, 2000 (in 1,000 tonnes): meat, 230; cow's milk, 285; goat's milk, 34; sheep's milk, 22. In 1998 there were 7,000 tractors and 1,550 harvester-threshers.

Collectivized farms, set up in the 1950s under Stalin, have been broken up and the land redistributed.

Forestry. Forests, chiefly larch, cedar, fir and birch, occupied 9·41m. ha in 1995 (6% of the land area). Timber production was 631,000 cu. metres in 1999.

Fisheries. The catch in 1999 was 524 tonnes, entirely from inland waters.

INDUSTRY

Industry is still small in scale and local in character. The food industry accounts for 25% of industrial production. The main industrial centre is Ulan Bator; others are at Erdenet and Baga-Nur, and a northern territorial industrial complex is being developed based on Darhan and Erdenet to produce copper and molybdenum concentrates, lime, cement, machinery and wood- and metal-worked products. Production figures (1996): woollen cloth, 45,200 sq. metres; carpets, 666,300 sq. metres; cement, 112,000 tonnes (1997); lime, 54,600 tonnes; bread, 30,049 tonnes; leather footwear, 141,300 pairs; meat, 11,300 tonnes; soap, 600 tonnes.

Labour. The labour force was 1,103,100 in 1995, including 354,300 in agriculture, 108,100 in industry, 64,800 in trade, 31,600 in transport and communications, and 29,500 in building. Average wage was 16,000 tugriks per month in 1995. In 2000, 17·5% of the labour force was unemployed..

Trade Unions. The Confederation of Mongolian Trade Unions had 450,000 members in 1994.

INTERNATIONAL TRADE
Mongolia is dependent on foreign aid. The largest donor in 1992 was Japan. Foreign debt was US$859m. in 2000.

Joint ventures with foreign firms are permitted. Foreign investors may acquire up to 49% of the equity in Mongolian companies. Foreign companies (except in precious metal mining) have a five-year tax holiday and a further five years at 50% of the tax rate.

Imports and Exports. In 1999 imports (f.o.b.) were valued at US$510·7m. (US$524·2m. in 1998) and exports (f.o.b.) at US$454·3m. (US$462·4m. in 1998). Main exports, 1996 (in tonnes): copper concentrate, 435,000; molybdenum concentrate, 3,438; wheat, 8,300; sawn wood, 37,200 cu. metres; 62,000 horse skins; 1,818,500 sheepskins; 314,600 goatskins; 20,600 woollen blankets.

Main export markets, 1996 (trade in US$1m.): Switzerland, 107·4; Russia, 87·2; China, 75·0; Japan, 36·0; South Korea, 33·9; UK, 18·6; USA, 18·5. Main import suppliers: Russia, 150·1; Japan, 76·9; China, 64·0; Germany, 20·5; South Korea, 17·7; Singapore, 12·8; USA, 10·9.

COMMUNICATIONS
Roads. The total road network covered 49,250 km in 1998 including 11,063 km of highway. There are 1,185 km of surfaced roads running around Ulan Bator, from Ulan Bator to Darhan, at points on the frontier with the Russian Federation and towards the south. Truck services run where there are no surfaced roads. Vehicles in use in 1998 included 29,116 trucks and vans and 37,795 passenger cars. 1·98m. tonnes of freight were carried in 1996 and 108·5m. passengers. There were 271 road accident fatalities in 1998.

Rail. The Trans-Mongolian Railway (1,928 km of 1,524 mm gauge in 1992) connects Ulan Bator with the Russian Federation and China. There are spur lines to Erdenet and to the coalmines at Nalayh and Sharyn Gol. A separate line connects Choybalsan in the east with Borzaya on the Trans-Siberian Railway. Passenger-km travelled in 1998 came to 981m. and freight tonne-km to 2,815m.

Civil Aviation. MIAT-Mongolian Airlines operates internal services, and in 1998 flew from Ulan Bator to Beijing, Berlin, Frankfurt, Hohhot, Irkutsk, Istanbul, Moscow, Osaka and Seoul. In 1999 it flew 6·3m. km, carrying 224,700 passengers (98,300 on international flights). In 1999 Ulan Bator handled 244,939 passengers and 2,556 tonnes of freight.

Shipping. There is a steamer service on the Selenge River and a tug and barge service on Hövsgöl Lake. 70,000 tonnes of freight were carried in 1990.

Telecommunications. Mongolia had 132,200 main telephone lines in 2000, or 55·7 for every 1,000 persons. In 1999 there were 40,000 mobile phone subscribers, up from 5,300 in 1998. This represented an increase of 654·7% over the year—the second largest in the world after Cape Verde. There were 30,000 PCs in use (12·6 for every 1,000 persons) in 2000 and 6,400 fax machines in 1997. There were 30,000 Internet users in Dec. 2000.

Postal Services. There were, in 1995, 391 post offices.

SOCIAL INSTITUTIONS

Justice. The Procurator-General is appointed, and the Supreme Court elected, by parliament for five years. There are also courts at province, town and district level. Lay assessors sit with professional judges. The death penalty is in force.

Religion. Tibetan Buddhist Lamaism is the prevalent religion; the Dalai Lama is its spiritual head. In 1995 there were about 100 monasteries and 2,500 monks.

Education. Adult literacy was 62·3% in 1999 (male, 72·6%; female, 52·1%). In 1995 there were 711 nurseries with 68,100 children. Schooling begins at the age of 7. In 1995 there were 664 general education schools with 403,800 pupils and 19,400 teachers. In 1990–91 there were 31 specialized secondary schools with 18,500 students and 1,300 teachers and 44 vocational technical schools with 29,100 pupils.

In 1994–95 there were 1 university and 4 specialized universities (agricultural; medical; pedagogical; technical). There were also colleges of commerce and business, economics, and railway engineering, and an institute of culture and art.

In 1997 total expenditure on education came to 5·7% of GNP and 15·1% of total government spending.

Health. In 1995 there were 250 doctors and 96 hospital beds per 10,000 population. Annual average per capita consumption (in kg) of foodstuffs in 1995: milk and products, 126; meat, 97; flour, 94; potatoes, 11; sugar, 9; fresh vegetables, 8.

Welfare. In 1995, 102·8m. tugriks were spent on maternity benefits.

CULTURE

Broadcasting. The government-controlled Ulan Bator Radio broadcasts two national programmes and an external service (English, Chinese, Japanese, Russian). Mongol Televiz transmits a daily programme and a Moscow relay (colour by SECAM V). Number of sets: TV (1997), 118,000; radio (1997), 360,000.

Cinema. In 1990 there were 30 cinemas, 522 mobile cinemas and 30 theatres.

Press. In 1996 there were four daily newspapers with a combined circulation of 68,000. In 1995 about 300 other titles were registered, but few were actually publishing. 717 book titles were published in 1990 in 6·4m. copies.

Tourism. In 1999 there were 159,000 foreign tourists, spending US$28m.

DIPLOMATIC REPRESENTATIVES

Of Mongolia in the United Kingdom (7 Kensington Ct., London, W8 5DL)
Ambassador: Davaasambuu Dalrain.

Of the United Kingdom in Mongolia (30 Enkh Taivny Gudamzh, Ulan Bator 13)
Ambassador: Philip Rouse, MBE.

Of Mongolia in the USA (2833 M Street, NW, Washington, D.C., 20007)
Ambassador: Vacant.
Chargé d'Affaires a.i.: Tserendorj Jambaldorj.

Of the USA in Mongolia (Micro Region 11, Big Ring Road, Ulan Bator)
Ambassador: John R. Dinger.

Of Mongolia to the United Nations
Ambassador: Ch. Baatar.

Of Mongolia to the European Union
Ambassador: Sodoviin Onon.

FURTHER READING

State Statistical Office: *Mongolian Economy and Society in [year]: Statistical Yearbook.— National Economy of the MPR, 1924–1984: Anniversary Statistical Collection.* Ulan Bator, 1984

Akiner, S. (ed.) *Mongolia Today.* London, 1992
Becker, J., *The Lost Country.* London, 1992
Bruun, O. and Odgaard, O. (eds.) *Mongolia in Transition.* Richmond, 1996
Griffin, K. (ed.) *Poverty and the Transition to a Market Economy in Mongolia.* London, 1995
Nordby, Judith, *Mongolia in the Twentieth Century.* Farnborough, 1993.—*Mongolia.* [Bibliography] ABC-Clio, Oxford and Santa Barbara (CA), 1993

National statistical office: Government Building 3, Ulan Bator-20A.
Website: http://nso.mn

MOROCCO

Mamlaka al-Maghrebia
(Kingdom of Morocco)

Capital: Rabat
Population estimate, 2000: 29·88m.
GDP per capita, 2000: (PPP$) 3,546
HDI/world rank: 0·602/123

KEY HISTORICAL EVENTS
The native people of Morocco are the Berbers, an ancient race who have suffered the attention of a succession of invaders. When the city of Carthage fell to Rome in the second century BC, the African Mediterranean coast was under Roman dominance for almost six hundred years. When the Roman Empire in turn fell into decline, the area was invaded first by the Vandals in AD 429 and later by Byzantium in AD 533.

An Arab invasion of Morocco in AD 682 marked the end of Byzantium dominance and the first Arab rulers, the Idrisid dynasty, ruled for 150 years. Arab and Berber dynasties succeeded the Idrisids until the 13th century when the country was plunged into bitter civil war between Arab and Berber factions. The reign of Ahmed I al-Man-sur in the first Sharifian dynasty stabilized and unified the country between 1579 and 1603. Moors and Jews expelled from Spain settled in Morocco during this time and the country flourished. In 1415 the Moroccan port of Ceuta was captured by Portugal. Moroccan forces defeated the Portuguese in 1578 and by 1700 had regained control of many coastal towns which had previously been in Portuguese hands. During the 18th and early 19th centuries the Barbary Coast became the scene of widespread piracy.

By the beginning of the 20th century Britain had recognized Morocco as a French sphere of influence and in 1904 Morocco was divided between France and Spain, with the former receiving the larger area. From 1912 to 1956 Morocco was divided into a French protectorate, a Spanish protectorate, and the international zone of Tangier which was established by France, Great Britain and Spain in 1923. On 29 Oct. 1956 the international status of the Tangier Zone was abolished and Morocco became a kingdom on 18 Aug. 1957, with the Sultan taking the title Mohammed V. Succeeding his father on 3 March 1961, King Hassan tried to combine the various parties in government and established an elected House of Representatives but political unrest led him to discard any attempt at a parliamentary government and to rule autocratically from 1965 to 1977. In 1977 a new Chamber of Representatives was elected and under the constitution Morocco became a constitutional monarchy with a single elected chamber.

TERRITORY AND POPULATION
Morocco is bounded by Algeria to the east and southeast, Mauritania to the south, the Atlantic Ocean to the northwest and the Mediterranean to the north. Excluding the Western Saharan territory claimed and retrieved since 1976 by Morocco, the area is 458,730 sq. km and population at the 1994 census was 25,671,403. At the 1984 census Western Sahara had an area of 252,120 sq. km and 163,868 population. The Moroccan superficie is 710,850 sq. km. Population estimate, 1995, 28·3m. (55·3% urban in 1999); density, 61·7 per sq. km.

The UN gives a projected population for 2010 of 35·32m.

There was a census in Sept. 1994. The 49 provinces and 22 prefectures are grouped into seven economic regions (in parentheses). Area and population in 1994:

Province	Area in sq. km	Population in 1,000	Province	Area in sq. km	Population in 1,000
(South)			Oued Eddahab	50,880	37
El-Aaiún	39,360	154	Es-Semara	61,760	40
Agadir	5,910	921	Tan-Tan	17,295	58
Boujdour	100,120	22	Taroudannt	16,460	694
Guelmim	28,750	147	Tata	25,925	119
Ouarzazate	41,550	695	Tiznit	6,960	348

Province	Area in sq. km	Population in 1,000	Province	Area in sq. km	Population in 1,000
(Tensift)			Rabat	⎫	623
Essaouira	6,335	434	Salé	⎬ 1,275	632
El Kelâa Srahna	10,070	682	Skhirate-Témara	⎭	245
Marrakesh	14,755	1,608	Sidi Kacem	4,060	646
Safi	7,285	823	Tangiers	1,195	628
			Tétouan	⎱	
(Centre)			Larache	⎰ 6,025	537
Azilal	10,050	455			
Béni Mellal	7,075	870	(Centre-North)		
Ben Slimane	2,760	213	Boulemane	14,395	162
Aïn Chok-Hay Hassani	⎫	516	Fès (Fez)	5,400	1,161
Aïn Sebaâ-Hay	⎮		Al Hoceima	3,550	383
Mohammadi	⎮	521	Taounate	5,585	629
Ben Msik-Sidi Othmane	⎬ 1,615	704	Taza	15,020	708
Casablanca-Anfa	⎮	523			
Mohammadia-Znata	⎭	170	(Eastern)		
El Jadida	6,000	971	Figuig	55,990	117
Khouribga	4,250	481	Nador	6,130	684
Settat	9,750	847	Oujda	20,700	968
(North-West)			(Centre-South)		
Chefchaouen	4,350	439	Errachidia	59,585	522
Kénitra	4,745	979	Ifrane	3,310	128
Khémisset	8,305	486	Khenifra	12,320	465
			Meknès	3,995	789

The chief cities (with populations in 1,000, 1994) are as follows:

Casablanca	3,448[1]	Agadir	550	Béni Mellal	387
Rabat	1,293[2,3]	Meknès	530	Safi	376
Fès (Fez)	775	Tangiers	526	Tétouan	367
Marrakesh	746	Kénitra	449	Khouribga	295
Oujda	679				

[1]1999 estimate. [2]1995 estimate. [3]Includes Salé.

The official language is Arabic, spoken by 75% of the population; the remainder speak Berber. French and Spanish are considered subsidiary languages and, more recently, English.

SOCIAL STATISTICS

1995 births, 719,000; deaths, 191,000. Rates, 1995 (per 1,000 population): birth, 27·1; death, 7·2. Annual population growth rate, 1990–99, 1·7%. Life expectancy at birth in 1999 was 65·4 years for males and 69·1 years for females. Infant mortality, 1998, 16·8 per 1,000 live births; fertility rate, 1999, 2·9 births per woman.

CLIMATE

Morocco is dominated by the Mediterranean climate which is made temperate by the influence of the Atlantic Ocean in the northern and southern parts of the country. Central Morocco is continental while the south is desert. Rabat, Jan. 55°F (12·9°C), July 72°F (22·2°C). Annual rainfall 23" (564 mm). Agadir, Jan. 57°F (13·9°C), July 72°F (22·2°C). Annual rainfall 9" (224 mm). Casablanca, Jan. 54°F (12·2°C), July 72°F (22·2°C). Annual rainfall 16" (404 mm). Marrakesh, Jan. 52°F (11·1°C), July 84°F (28·9°C). Annual rainfall 10" (239 mm). Tangiers, Jan. 53°F (11·7°C), July 72°F (22·2°C). Annual rainfall 36" (897 mm).

CONSTITUTION AND GOVERNMENT

The ruling King is **Mohammed VI**, born on 21 Aug. 1963, married to Salma Bennani on 21 March 2002; succeeded on 23 July 1999, on the death of his father Hassan II, who reigned 1961–99. The King holds supreme civil and religious authority, the latter in his capacity of Emir-el-Muminin or Commander of the Faithful. He resides usually at Rabat, but occasionally in one of the other traditional capitals, Fès (founded in 808), Marrakesh (founded in 1062), or at Skhirat.

A new Constitution was approved by referendum in March 1972 and amendments were approved by referendum in May 1980 and Sept. 1992. The Kingdom of Morocco is a constitutional monarchy. Parliament consists of a *Chamber of*

Representatives composed of 325 deputies directly elected for five-year terms. For the Sept. 2002 elections a series of measures were introduced, including a new proportional representation voting system and a national list reserved for women candidates to ensure that at least 10% of new MPs are females.

A referendum on 13 Sept. 1996 established a second *Chamber of Counsellors,* composed of 270 members serving nine-year terms, of whom 162 are elected by local councils, 81 by chambers of commerce and 27 by trade unions. The Chamber of Counsellors has power to initiate legislation, issue warnings of censure to the government and ultimately to force the government's resignation by a two-thirds majority vote. The electorate was 12·3m. and turn-out was 82·95%. The King, as sovereign head of State, appoints the Prime Minister and other Ministers, has the right to dissolve Parliament and approves legislation.

A new electoral code of March 1997 fixed voting at 20 and made enrolment on the electoral roll compulsory. In Dec. 2002 King Mohammed VI announced that the voting age was to be lowered from 20 to 18.

National Anthem. 'Manbit al Ahrah, mashriq al anwar' ('Fountain of freedom, source of light'); words by Ali Squalli Houssaini, tune by Leo Morgan.

RECENT ELECTIONS
Elections to the Chamber of Representatives took place on 27 Sept. 2002. The USFP (Union Socialiste des Forces Populaires) won 50 seats, down from 57 seats in 1997; the PI (Istiqlal/Parti d'Indépendence) gained 48 seats, up from 32 in 1997; and the PJD (Parti de la Justice et du Développement), the only Islamic party taking part in the elections, trebled its representation from 14 to 42 seats. The Rassemblement National des Indépendents won 41 seats, the Mouvement Populaire 27, the Mouvement Nationale Populaire 18, the Union Constitutionnelle 16, the Parti National-Démocrate 12, the Front des Forces Démocratiques also 12, the Parti du Progrès et du Socialisme 11, and the Union Democratique 10. A further 11 parties obtained fewer than ten seats each. Turn-out was 51·6%.

In elections to the Chamber of Counsellors on 5 Dec. 1997 the centre Rassemblement National des Indépendents gained 42 seats, ahead of a second centre party, the Mouvement Démocratique et Social, with 33 seats.

CURRENT ADMINISTRATION
In March 2003 the government comprised:

Prime Minister: Driss Jettou; b. 1945 (USFP; in office since 9 Oct. 2002).

Minister for Foreign Affairs and Co-operation: Mohamed Benaissa. *Interior:* Al Mustapha Sahel. *Justice:* Mohamed Bouzoubaa. *Finance and Privatization:* Fathallah Oualalou. *Secretary General of the Government:* Abdessadek Rabiaa. *'Habous' and Islamic Affairs:* Ahmed Toufiq. *Territorial Development, Water Resources and the Environment:* Mohamed El Yazghi. *Agriculture and Rural Development:* Mohand Laenser. *Employment, Social Affairs and Solidarity:* Mustapha Mansouri. *National Education and Youth Affairs:* Habib El Malki. *Higher Education and Scientific Research:* Khalid Alioua. *Minister in Charge of Modernization and the Public Sector:* Najib Zerouali. *Culture:* Mohammed Achaari. *Human Rights:* Mohamed Aujjar. *Handicrafts and Social Economy:* M'Hamed El Khalifa. *Equipment and Transport:* Karim Ghellab. *Industry, Commerce and Telecommunications:* Rachid Talbi El Alami. *Tourism:* Adil Douiri. *Health:* Mohammed Cheikh Biadillah. *Marine Resources:* Mohammed Taieb Rhafes. *Relations with Parliament:* Mohammed Saad El Alami. *Energy and Mines:* Mohammed Boutaleb. *Communications and Government Spokesperson:* Nabil Benabdallah. *Foreign Trade:* Mustapha Mechahouri. *Minister of State:* Abbas El Fassi.

Office of the Prime Minister: http://www.pm.gov.ma/

DEFENCE
Conscription is authorized for 18 months. Defence expenditure in 2000 totalled US$1,680m. (US$59 per capita), representing 5·1% of GDP.

Army. The Army is deployed in two commands: Northern Zone and Southern Zone. There is also a Royal Guard of 1,500. Strength (1999), 175,000 (100,000 conscripts).

There is also a Royal Gendarmerie of 12,000, an Auxiliary Force of 30,000 and reserves of 150,000.

Navy. The Navy includes one Spanish-built frigate and two corvettes.

Personnel in 1999 numbered 7,800, including a 1,500 strong brigade of Naval Infantry. Bases are located at Casablanca, Agadir, Al-Hoceima and Dakhla.

Air Force. Personnel strength (1999) about 13,500, with 89 combat aircraft, including F-5s and Mirage F-1s, and 24 armed helicopters.

INTERNATIONAL RELATIONS
Morocco is a member of the UN, WTO, the League of Arab States, Arab Maghreb Union, African Development Bank, IOM, OIC and the International Organization of the Francophonie.

ECONOMY
Agriculture accounted for 16·6% of GDP in 1998, industry 32·0% and services 51·4%.

Currency. The unit of currency is the *dirham* (MAD) of 100 *centimes*, introduced in 1959. Foreign exchange reserves were US$9,006m. and gold reserves 708,000 troy oz in June 2002. Since 1993 the dirham has been convertible for current account operations. Inflation was 0·6% in 2001. Total money supply in May 2002 was DH248,359m.

Budget. Budget revenue and expenditure (in DH1m.), year ending 30 June:

	1997	1998	1999
Revenue	95,115	97,327	103,221
Expenditure	97,276	106,877	112,488

VAT is 20%.

Performance. Real GDP growth was 1·0% in 2000, rising to 6·5% in 2001. Total GDP in 2001 was US$33·7bn.

Banking and Finance. The central bank is the Bank Al Maghrib (*Governor*, Mohamed Seqat) which had assets of DH60,968m. on 31 Dec. 1993. There are 14 commercial banks (11 foreign). There are also three development banks, specializing respectively in industry, housing and agriculture.

There is a stock exchange in Casablanca. The global volume in 1996 was DH23·9bn., up from DH672m. in 1989.

Weights and Measures. The metric system is in use.

ENERGY AND NATURAL RESOURCES
Environment. Carbon dioxide emissions in 1998 were the equivalent of 1·2 tonnes per capita according to the *World Bank Atlas*.

Electricity. Installed capacity was 4m. kW in 1997. Production was 13·16bn. kWh (approximately 96% fossil fuel) in 1998 and consumption per capita 443 kWh.

Oil and Gas. Natural gas reserves in 1997 were 1·1bn. cu. metres; output (1996), 1 petajoule.

Minerals. The principal mineral exploited is phosphate (Morocco has the largest reserves in the world), the output of which was 20·68m. tonnes in 1995. Other minerals (in tonnes, 1995) are: coal (1996), 504,000; barytine, 273,809; salt (1996), 168,000; zinc, 150,160; lead, 101,545; copper, 33,685; iron ore, 33,500; manganese, 22,000; silver (1997), 261.

Agriculture. Agricultural production is subject to drought; about 1·29m. ha were irrigated in 1998. 85% of farmland is individually owned. Only 1% of farms are over 50 ha; most are under 3 ha. There were 8·98m. ha of arable land in 1998 and 0·92m. ha of permanent crops. Main land usage, 2000 (in 1,000 ha): wheat, 2,902; barley, 2,251; maize, 238.

Production in 2000 (in 1,000 tonnes): sugarbeets, 2,883; wheat, 1,381; sugarcane, 1,326; potatoes, 1,090; melons and watermelons, 874; oranges, 870; tomatoes, 764; tangerines and mandarins, 514; barley, 467; olives, 400; onions, 348.

Livestock, 2000: cattle, 2·67m.; sheep, 17·30m.; goats, 5·12m.; asses, 980,000; chickens, 100m. Livestock products in 2000 included (in 1,000 tonnes): milk, 1,212; meat, 540.

Forestry. Forests covered 3·84m. ha in 1995, or 8·6% of the total land area (down from 3·89m. ha in 1990). Produce includes firewood, building and industrial timber and some cork and charcoal. Timber production was 1·12m. cu. metres in 1999.

Fisheries. The fishing fleet numbered 2,564 coastal vessels in 1993 and 462 deepsea vessels, the latter totalling 152,417 GRT. Total catch in 1999 was 745,431 tonnes (sea fish, 743,268 tonnes). Morocco's annual catch is the highest of any African country. Total catch value in 1994 was DH3,195m.

INDUSTRY
According to the Financial Times Survey (FT 500), the largest companies in Morocco by market capitalization on 4 Jan. 2001 were: ONA (Omnium Nord Africain), a food and beverages conglomerate, at US$1,805·4m.; and BCM (Banque Commerciale du Maroc), at US$1,100·4m.

In 1992 there were 5,855 industrial firms employing 351,149 persons. Of these, 1,785 employed fewer than 10 persons; 80, more than 500. 1,434 firms were engaged in food production, 789 in clothing, 723 in textiles and 397 in paper- and board-making and printing. Production, 1998 (in 1,000 tonnes): cement, 7,155; distillate fuel oil (1997), 2,394; residual fuel oil (1997), 1,711; sugar, 533; paper and paperboard, 110; olive oil, 66. In 1995 the industrial investment was DH14·2bn. of which 92% came from the private sector.

Labour. In 1996 the labour force totalled 10,448,000 (65% males). Approximately 40% of the economically active population in 1994 were engaged in agriculture, fisheries and forestry. In 1993 the monthly non-agricultural minimum wage was DH1,510. The agricultural minimum was DH37·60 per day in 1994.

Trade Unions. In 1996 there were six trade unions: UMT (Union Marocaine de Travail), CDT (Confédération Démocratique du Travail), UGTM (Union Générale des Travailleurs Marocaine), UNTM (National Union of Moroccan Workers), USP (Union of Popular Workers) and the SNP (National Popular Union).

INTERNATIONAL TRADE
In 1989 Morocco signed a treaty of economic co-operation with the four other Maghreb countries: Algeria, Libya, Mauritania and Tunisia. In 1995 Morocco signed an association agreement with the EU to create a free trade zone in 12 years. Foreign debt was US$17,944m. in 2000.

Imports and Exports. Imports and exports for calendar years in US$1m.:

	1996	1997	1998	1999	2000
Imports f.o.b.	9,080	8,903	9,463	9,957	10,654
Exports f.o.b.	6,886	7,039	7,144	7,509	7,419

Imports in 1994 included (in 1,000 tonnes): crude oil, 6,855; sulphur, 2,653; grain, 1,191; sawn wood, 663; chemicals, 588. Exports included: phosphates, 9,527; other mineral products (1993), 2,063; natural and artificial fertilizers, 1,674; foodstuffs and tobacco, 1,310.

Main export markets in 1997: France, 31·7%; Spain, 8·6%; UK, 7·3%; Germany, 6·9%; India, 5·5%. Main import suppliers, 1997: France, 28·0%; Spain, 10·2%; Germany, 7·1%; UK, 6·8%; Italy, 6·5%.

COMMUNICATIONS

Roads. In 1998 there were 57,847 km of classified roads, including 10,647 km of main roads. A motorway links Rabat to Casablanca. 3·4m. passengers and 16·1m. tonnes of freight were carried in 1993. In 1996 there were 1,018,000 passenger cars, 265,000 trucks and vans and 20,000 motorcycles and mopeds. There were 41,701 road accidents in 1998 (3,242 fatalities).

Rail. In 1995 there were 1,907 km of railways, of which 1,003 km were electrified. Passenger-km travelled in 1998 came to 1,725m. and freight tonne-km to 4,828m.

Civil Aviation. The national carrier is Royal Air Maroc. The major international airport is Mohammed V at Casablanca; there are eight other airports. Casablanca handled 3,547,130 passengers in 2000 (2,623,244 on international flights) and 43,487 tonnes of freight. Marrakesh (Menara) handled 1,411,725 passengers and 2,353 tonnes of freight and Agadir (Al Massira) handled 1,126,938 passengers and 1,787 tonnes of freight in 2000. In July 1997 Morocco launched its first private air company, Regional Air Lines, to serve the major regions of the kingdom, in addition to southern Spain and the Canary Islands. In 1999 scheduled airline traffic of Moroccan-based carriers flew 63·1m. km, carrying 3,392,000 passengers (2,587,000 on international flights).

Shipping. There are 12 ports, the largest being Casablanca, Tangiers and Jorf Lasfar. 1·56m. passengers and 40·6m. tonnes of freight were handled in 1994. In 1998 seagoing shipping totalled 444,000 GRT, including oil tankers 12,000 GRT. In 1998 vessels totalling 28,284,000 NRT entered ports.

Telecommunications. In 2000 there were 1,425,000 main telephone lines (equivalent to 50·3 per 1,000 population) and 350,000 PCs in use (12·3 per 1,000 persons). In 1997 there were 18,000 fax machines. At the end of 2000 there were 2·7m. mobile phone subscribers, making Morocco the fastest growing mobile phone market in the world, with a 629% increase on the end of 1999. The mobile network covers some 85% of the population, compared to just 6% for fixed lines. Morocco had 220,000 Internet users in March 2001.

Postal Services. In 1994 there were 621 main post offices.

SOCIAL INSTITUTIONS

Justice. The legal system is based on French and Islamic law codes. There are a Supreme Court, 21 courts of appeal, 65 courts of first instance, 196 centres with resident judges and 706 communal jurisdictions for petty offences.

The population in penal institutions in 1997 was 48,600 (175 per 100,000 of national population). On ascending to the throne in July 1999, King Mohammed VI pardoned and ordered the release of 7,988 prisoners and reduced the terms of 38,224 others.

Religion. Islam is the established state religion. 98% of the population are Sunni Muslims of the Malekite school and 0·16% are Christians, mainly Roman Catholic, and there is a small Jewish community (0·05%).

Education. The adult literacy rate in 1999 was 48% (61·1% among males and 35·1% among females). Education in Berber languages has been permitted since 1994. Education is compulsory from the age of 7 to 13. In 1993–94 there were 28,335 Koranic schools (33,721 in 1990) with 30,367 teachers and 611,729 pupils; 3,563 modern pre-primary schools (343 in 1990) with 5,836 teachers and 171,727 pupils. In 1996–97 there were 5,806 primary schools with 114,406 teachers and 3,160,907 pupils; 84,202 teachers in secondary school and 1,442,049 pupils (38,692 private). There were 13 universities with 7,566 teachers and 218,516 students (89,223 women), 8,390 students (1,761 women) in teacher training and (1992–93) 8,967 students and 1,145 teachers in other higher education institutions. An English-language university was opened at Ifrane in Jan. 1995, initially with a staff of 35 and 300 students (scheduled to rise to 3,500).

Health. In the public sector in 1994 there were 4,422 doctors and 72 dentists; in the private sector there were 4,416 doctors and 1,132 dentists. In 1994 there were 2,470 pharmacists. In 1993 in the public sector there were 98 hospitals with 24,725 beds, 103 health centres with 1,548 beds and 1,220 dispensaries.

CULTURE

Broadcasting. The government-controlled Radiodiffusion Télévision Marocaine broadcasts 3 national (1 in French, English and Spanish) and 8 regional radio programmes and 1 TV channel (colour by SECAM V). Broadcasting in Berber languages commenced in 1994. There is also a government commercial radio service and an independent TV channel. There were 3·1m. TV sets and 6·6m. radio sets in 1997.

Cinema. There were 185 cinemas in 1995 and a total attendance of 17·3m.; gross box office receipts came to DH103m. Five full-length films were made.

Press. In 1995 the number of newspapers was 475, including dailies, weeklies and periodicals, of which 314 come out in Arabic, 160 in French and 1 in English. In 2000 a number of foreign and local newspapers were banned. Some had been accused of trying to destabilize the country's institutions, including the military.

Tourism. There were 3,824,000 foreign tourists in 1999, spending US$1·96bn. The tourism sector employs some 600,000 people, equivalent to 5·8% of the workforce.

DIPLOMATIC REPRESENTATIVES
Of Morocco in the United Kingdom (49 Queen's Gate Gdns., London, SW7 5NE)
Ambassador: Mohammed Belmahi.

Of the United Kingdom in Morocco (17 Blvd de la Tour Hassan, Rabat)
Ambassador: Haydon Warren-Gash.

Of Morocco in the USA (1601 21st St., NW, Washington, D.C., 20009)
Ambassador: Aziz Mekouar.

Of the USA in Morocco (2 Ave. de Mohamed el Fassi, Rabat)
Ambassador: Margaret DeBardeleben Tutwiler.

Of Morocco to the United Nations
Ambassador: Mohamed Bennouna.

Of Morocco to the European Union
Ambassador: Aïcha Belarbi.

FURTHER READING
Direction de la Statistique. *Annuaire Statistique du Maroc.—Conjoncture Économique.* Quarterly *Bulletin Official.* Rabat.

Bourqia, Rahma and Gilson Miller, Susan, (eds.) *In the Shadow of the Sultan: Culture, Power and Politics in Morocco.* Harvard Univ. Press, 2000

Findlay, Anne M. and Allan M., *Morocco.* [Bibliography] 2nd ed. ABC-Clio, Oxford and Santa Barbara (CA), 1995

Pazzanita, A. G., *The Maghreb.* [Bibliography] ABC-Clio, Oxford and Santa Barbara (CA), 1998

National library: Bibliothèque Générale et Archives, Rabat.

National statistical office: Direction de la Statistique, BP178, Rabat.
Website (French only): http://www.statistic.gov.ma

WESTERN SAHARA

The Western Sahara was designated by The United Nations in 1975, its borders having been marked as a result of agreements made between France, Spain and Morocco in 1900, 1904 and 1912. Sovereignty of the territory is in dispute between Morocco and the Polisario Front (Popular Front for the Liberation of the Saguia el Hamra and Rio de Oro), which formally proclaimed a government-in-exile of the Sahrawi Arab Democratic Republic (SADR) in Feb. 1976. According to a new UN proposal agreed in 2001, Western Sahara should be a part of Morocco for four years but at the same time 'autonomous'. There is then to be a referendum to decide whether it remains part of Morocco or becomes a separate state.

Area 266,769 sq. km (102,680 sq. miles). Around 230,000 inhabitants (estimate July 1997) are within Moroccan jurisdiction. Another estimated 196,000 Saharawis live in refugee camps around Tindouf in southwest Algeria. The main towns are El-Aaiún, the capital (159,000 inhabitants in 1995), Dakhla and Es-Semara.

Life expectancy at birth (1997 est.) male, 46·7 years; female, 50·0 years. Birth rate (1997 est.) per 1,000 population: 46·1; death rate: 17·5. The projected population for 2010 is 365,000.

The population is Arabic-speaking, and almost entirely Sunni Muslim.

President: Mohammed Abdelaziz.
Prime Minister: Bouchraya Hammoudi Bayoune.

Rich phosphate deposits were discovered in 1963 at Bu Craa. Morocco holds 65% of the shares of the former Spanish state-controlled company. Production reached 5·6m. tonnes in 1975, but exploitation has been severely reduced by guerrilla activity. After a nearly complete collapse, production and transportation of phosphate resumed in 1978, ceased again, and then resumed in 1982. Installed electrical capacity was 56,000 kW in 1995, with production of 85m. kWh in 1998. There are about 6,100 km of motorable tracks, but only about 500 km of paved roads. There are airports at El-Aaiún and Dakhla. As most of the land is desert, less than 19% is in agricultural use, with about 2,000 tonnes of grain produced annually. There were 56,000 radio receivers and 6,000 television sets in 1997. In 1989 there were 27 primary schools with 14,794 pupils and 18 secondary schools with 9,218 pupils.

FURTHER READING

Zoubir, Y. H. and Volman, D. (eds.) *The International Dimensions of the Western Sahara Conflict*. New York, 1993

MOZAMBIQUE

República de Moçambique

Capital: Maputo
Population estimate, 2000: 18·29m.
GDP per capita, 2000: (PPP$) 854
HDI/world rank: 0·322/170

KEY HISTORICAL EVENTS
Mozambique was at first ruled as part of Portuguese India but a separate administration was created in 1752. Following a decade of guerrilla activity, independence was achieved on 25 June 1975. A one-party state dominated by the Liberation Front of Mozambique (FRELIMO) was set up but armed insurgency led by the Mozambique National Resistance (RENAMO) continued until 4 Oct. 1992. The peace treaty provided for all weapons to be handed over to the UN and all armed groups to be disbanded within six months. In 1994 the country held its first multi-party elections. In early 2000 some 700 people died in the floods which made thousands homeless.

TERRITORY AND POPULATION
Mozambique is bounded east by the Indian ocean, south by South Africa, southwest by Swaziland, west by South Africa and Zimbabwe and north by Zambia, Malaŵi and Tanzania. It has an area of 799,380 sq. km (308,642 sq. miles) and a population, according to the 1997 census, of 16,099,246, giving a density of 20 per sq. km. Up to 1·5m. refugees abroad and 5m. internally displaced persons during the Civil War have begun to return home.

The UN gives a projected population for 2010 of 21·65m.

In 1999 an estimated 61·1% of the population were rural, but urbanization is increasing rapidly. In the period 1990–95 the annual growth in the urban population was 8·7%, a rate only exceeded by Botswana. The areas, populations and capitals of the provinces are:

Province	Sq. km	1 Jan. 1987	Estimate 1997	Capital
Cabo Delgado	82,625	1,109,921	1,284,000	Pemba
Gaza	75,709	1,138,724	1,034,000	Xai-Xai
Inhambane	68,615	1,167,022	1,112,000	Inhambane
Manica	61,661	756,886	975,000	Chimoio
City of Maputo	602	1,006,765	966,000	
Province of Maputo	25,756	544,692	809,000	Maputo
Nampula	81,606	2,837,856	3,065,000	Nampula
Niassa	129,056	607,670	764,000	Lichinga
Sofala	68,018	1,257,710	1,380,000	Beira
Tete	100,724	981,319	1,149,000	Tete
Zambézia	105,008	2,952,251	3,202,000	Quelimane

The capital is Maputo (estimated population, 1999, 2,867,000). Other large cities are Beira (1991 population, 294,197), Nampula (232,670) and Nacala (125,208).

The main ethnolinguistic groups are the Makua/Lomwe (52% of the population), the Tsonga/Ronga (24%), the Nyanja/Sena (12%) and Shona (6%).

Portuguese remains the official language, but vernaculars are widely spoken throughout the country. English is also widely spoken.

SOCIAL STATISTICS
1995 births, 758,000; deaths, 312,000. Birth rate per 1,000 population, 1995, 43·9; death rate, 18·1. Infant mortality per 1,000 live births, 1999, 127. Life expectancy at birth, 1999, was 38·8 years for males and 40·8 years for females. Annual population growth rate, 1990–99, 3·5%; fertility rate, 1999, 6·1 births per woman.

CLIMATE
A humid tropical climate, with a dry season from June to Sept. In general, temperatures and rainfall decrease from north to south. Maputo, Jan. 78°F (25·6°C), July 65°F (18·3°C). Annual rainfall 30" (760 mm). Beira, Jan. 82°F (27·8°C), July 69°F (20·6°C). Annual rainfall 60" (1,522 mm).

CONSTITUTION AND GOVERNMENT

On 2 Nov. 1990 the People's Assembly unanimously voted a new Constitution, which came into force on 30 Nov. This changed the name of the state to 'Republic of Mozambique', legalized opposition parties, provided for universal secret elections and introduced a bill of rights including the right to strike, press freedoms and habeas corpus. The head of state is the *President*, directly elected for a five-year term. Parliament is a 250-member *National Assembly*.

National Anthem. 'Viva, viva a Frelimo' ('Long live Frelimo'); words and tune by J. Sigaulane Chemane. A parliamentary ad-hoc committee has been established to produce a new national anthem to reflect the multi-party democracy prevailing in the country.

RECENT ELECTIONS

The country's first free presidential and parliamentary elections were held in 1994. In the parliamentary elections of 3–5 Dec. 1999 the Liberation Front of Mozambique (FRELIMO) won 133 of the 250 available seats with 48·5% of the vote. The Mozambican National Resistance (RENAMO) won the remaining 117 seats with 38·8%.

In the presidential election, also held from 3–5 Dec. 1999, FRELIMO's Joaquim A. Chissano won a further term of office claiming 52·3% of the vote against RENAMO's Afonso Marceta Macacho Dhlakama.

CURRENT ADMINISTRATION

President: Joaquim A. Chissano; b. 1939 (FRELIMO; sworn in 6 Nov. 1986).

In March 2003 the government comprised:

Prime Minister: Dr Pascoal M. Moçumbi; b. 1941 (FRELIMO; in office since 16 Dec. 1994).

Minister of Parliamentary Affairs (President's Office): Francisco C. J. Madeira. *Defence and Security Affairs (President's Office) and Minister of the Interior:* Almerinho Manhenje. *Foreign Affairs and Co-operation:* Dr Leonardo S. Simão. *Defence:* Tobias Dai. *Justice:* José Ibraimo Abudo. *Planning and Finance:* Luísa Diogo. *Education:* Alcido Nguenha. *Health:* Franciso Songana. *Culture:* Miguel Mkaima. *Industry and Commerce:* Carlos Morgado. *Mineral Resources and Energy:* Castigo Langa. *Labour:* Mario Sevene. *Environmental Action Co-ordinator:* John Kachamila. *State Administration:* José Chichava. *Agriculture and Rural Development:* Hélder Monteiro. *Public Construction and Housing:* Roberto Costley-White. *Transport and Communications:* Tomás Salomão. *Higher Education, Science and Technology:* Lídia Brito. *Tourism:* Fernando Sumbana. *Veterans:* Antonio Thay. *Women's and Social Affairs:* Virgília Matabele. *Youth and Sport:* Joel Libombo.

Government Website: http://www.mozambique.mz/

DEFENCE

The President of the Republic is C.-in-C. of the armed forces. Defence expenditure totalled US$85m. in 2000 (US$5 per capita), representing 3·6% of GDP.

Army. Personnel numbered 4–5,000 (to become 12–15,000) in 1999.

Navy. There is a small flotilla based principally at Maputo, with subsidiary bases at Beira, Nacala, Pemba and Inhambane. Some boats are based at Metangula on Lake Nyasa. Naval personnel in 1999 were believed to total 100.

Air Force. Personnel (1999) 1,000 (including air defence units). There were four armed helicopters but no combat aircraft.

INTERNATIONAL RELATIONS

Mozambique is a member of the UN, WTO, the Commonwealth, the African Union, African Development Bank, SADC, Non-Aligned Movement, Organization of the Islamic Conference, Indian Ocean Rim, Organization of the Portuguese Language Countries and is an ACP member state of the ACP-EU relationship.

IMF projections to 2005 indicate the halving of aid inflows from US$1bn. a year in the 1990s to US$500m. Mozambique is very heavily dependent on foreign aid. In 1996 official aid made up 72% of GDP.

ECONOMY

Agriculture accounted for 34·3% of GDP in 1998, industry 20·8% and services 44·9%.

The government under prime minister Pascoal Mocumbi has attempted to curb corruption. In 1997 the UK's Crown Agents were hired to operate the customs service for three years. More than 100 officials were dismissed and the volume of tariff revenue increased by nearly 50% in the first two years.

Overview. In 1990 the government abandoned economic planning in favour of a market economy. In Dec. 1993 the National Reconstruction Plan was launched to repair the rural economic and social infrastructure. Its implementation is dependent upon foreign aid. A privatization programme launched in 1989 resulted in a decline of the public sector share of GDP from 70% to less than 20% ten years later.

Currency. The unit of currency is the *metical* (MZM) of 100 *centavos*. Inflation was 9·0% in 2001. Foreign exchange reserves were US$706m. in June 2002. Total money supply in May 2002 was 10,364·30bn. meticais.

Budget. In 1996 revenues were an estimated US$324m. and expenditure US$600m.

Performance. GDP growth has averaged 5·3% since 1990, making Mozambique one of Africa's fastest expanding economies. Mozambique was forecast to be among the fastest growing economies in the world in 2000 but the disastrous floods of early 2000 caused a major setback, resulting in growth for the year of only 1·6%. However, the economy then grew by 13·9% in 2001. Total GDP in 2001 was US$3·6bn.

Banking and Finance. Most banks had been nationalized by 1979. The central bank and bank of issue is the Bank of Mozambique (*Governor,* Adriano Afonso Maleiane) which hived off its commercial functions in 1992 to the newly-founded Commercial Bank of Mozambique. In 1998 the Commercial Bank of Mozambique had 35% of deposits. There are 9 commercial banks, 1 investment bank and a leasing institution. The new Mozambique Stock Exchange opened in Maputo in Oct. 1999. By the late 1990s financial services had become one of the fastest-growing areas of the economy.

Weights and Measures. The metric system is in force.

ENERGY AND NATURAL RESOURCES

Environment. According to the *World Bank Atlas* carbon dioxide emissions in 1998 were the equivalent of 0·1 tonnes per capita.

Electricity. Installed capacity was 2m. kW in 1997. Production in 1998 was 1·2m. kWh. Consumption per capita in 1998 was 54 kWh.

Oil and Gas. Natural gas finds are being explored for potential exploitation, and both onshore and offshore foreign companies are prospecting for oil. In 1997 natural gas reserves were 57bn. cu. metres. Some river basins, especially the Rovuma, Zambezi and Limpopo, are of interest to oil prospectors.

Water. Although the country is rich in water resources, the provision of drinking water to rural areas remains a major concern.

Minerals. There are deposits of pegamite, tantalite, graphite, apatite, tin, iron ore and bauxite. Other known reserves are: nepheline, syenite, magnetite, copper, garnet, kaolin, asbestos, bentonite, limestone, gold, titanium and tin.

Output (in 1,000 tonnes): salt (1997 estimate), 60; coal (1996), 40; bauxite (1998), 6; gold (1995), 6,800 kg.

Agriculture. All land is owned by the state but concessions are given. There were 3·12m. ha of arable land in 1998 and 0·23m. ha of permanent crops. Production in 1,000 tonnes (2000): cassava, 4,643; maize, 1,019; sugarcane, 440; coconuts, 300; sorghum, 252; rice, 158; groundnuts, 100; seed cotton, 80; copra, 73; bananas, 59; cottonseed, 51; potatoes, 50.

Livestock, 2000: 1·32m. cattle, 392,000 goats, 125,000 sheep, 180,000 pigs, 28m. chickens.

A quarter of all crops and a third of cattle were lost during the flooding which devastated the country in the early part of 2000.

Forestry. In 1995 there were 16·86m. ha of forests, or 21·5% of the land area (down from 17·44m. ha in 1990), including eucalyptus, pine and rare hardwoods. In 1999 timber production was 18·04m. cu. metres.

Fisheries. The catch in 1999 was 35,560 tonnes, of which 24,823 tonnes were from sea fishing. Prawns and shrimps are the major export at 10,000 tonnes per year. The potential sustainable annual catch is estimated at 500,000 tonnes of fish (anchovies 300,000 tonnes, the rest mainly mackerel).

INDUSTRY
Although the country is overwhelmingly rural, there is some substantial industry in and around Maputo (steel, engineering, textiles, processing, docks and railways). A huge aluminium smelter, completed in 2000, is scheduled to produce 250,000 tonnes annually and is a focal point in the country's strategy of attracting foreign investment.

Labour. The labour force in 1996 totalled 9,221,000 (52% males). In 1998, 83% of the economically active population were engaged in agriculture, 8% in industry and 9% in services. Women represent 48% of the total labour force.

Trade Unions. The main trade union confederation is the Organização dos Trabalhadores de Moçambique, but several unions have broken away.

INTERNATIONAL TRADE
Foreign debt was US$7,135m. in 2000.

Imports and Exports. In 1998 imports (f.o.b.) were valued at US$735·6m. (US$684·0m. in 1997) and exports (f.o.b.) at US$244·6m. (US$230·0m. in 1997). Principal exports, 1995 (in US$1m.): prawns, 70; cotton, 19; sugar, 11; cashew nuts, 3. Main export markets, 1996: Spain, 17·1%; South Africa, 15·8%; Portugal, 11·7%; USA, 10·4%. Main import suppliers: South Africa, 54·6%; Zimbabwe, 6·6%; Saudi Arabia, 5·4%; Portugal, 3·8%.

In 1996 exports rose 33% to US$226m., whilst imports rose only 10%. Exports are forecast to have increased to over US$900m. by 2004.

Trade Fairs. There is an annual trade fair, FACIM, which takes place in Aug. and Sept.

COMMUNICATIONS
Roads. In 1996 there were 5,700 km of paved and 24,700 km of unpaved roads, but most were in bad condition or mined. Passenger cars numbered 4,900 in 1996 (0·3 per 1,000 inhabitants), down from 60,000 in 1993. There were 4,748 road accidents in 1997, with 805 fatalities. The flooding of early 2000 washed away at least one fifth of the country's main road linking the north and the south.

Rail. The state railway consists of five separate networks, with principal routes on 1,067 mm gauge radiating from the ports of Maputo (950 km), Beira (994 km) and Nacala (914 km). Total length in 1995 was 2,983 km of 1,067 mm gauge and 140 km of 762 mm gauge. In 1995, 5·4m. passengers and 3·1m. tonnes of freight were carried. In early 2000 long sections of the railway line linking Mozambique with Zimbabwe were washed away in the floods.

Civil Aviation. There are international airports at Maputo and Beira. The national carrier is the state-owned Linhas Aéreas de Moçambique (LAM). It provides domestic services and in 1998 operated international routes to Harare, Johannesburg and Lisbon. In 1998 Maputo handled 310,000 passengers (188,000 on international flights) and Beira 63,000 (59,000 on domestic flights). In 1999 scheduled airline traffic of Mozambique-based carriers flew 5·3m. km, carrying 235,000 passengers (87,000 on international flights).

Shipping. The principal ports are Maputo, Beira, Nacala and Quelimane. In 1998 the merchant fleet had a total displacement of 35,000 GRT.

Telecommunications. Main telephone lines numbered 85,700 in 2000 (4·4 per 1,000 persons) and there were 60,000 PCs in use (3·0 per 1,000 persons). There were 12,200 mobile phone subscribers in 1999 and 7,200 fax machines in 1995. In July 2000 there were 15,000 Internet users.

Postal Services. In 1995 there were 425 post offices. Postal services in Mozambique are provided by a public company, Correios de Moçambique, EP (CDM).

SOCIAL INSTITUTIONS

Justice. The 1990 Constitution provides for an independent judiciary, habeas corpus, and an entitlement to legal advice on arrest. The death penalty was abolished in Nov. 1990. The judiciary is riddled with bribery and extortion.

Religion. About 40% of the population follow traditional animist religions. In 1992 there were 4·72m. Christians (mainly Roman Catholic) and 1·95m. Muslims.

Education. The adult literacy rate in 1999 was 43·2% (59·3% among males but only 27·9% among females).

In 1997 there were 1,750,000 pupils in 5,600 primary schools and (1995) 185,181 pupils with 5,615 teachers at 239 secondary schools. Mozambique's school enrolment ratio of 25% is one of the lowest in the world. Private schools and universities were permitted to function in 1990. Eduardo Mondlane University had 3,470 students and 390 academic staff in 1995–96. In the late 1990s a further four institutions of higher education opened, namely: the Higher Institute of International Relations (ISRI), the Pedagogical University (UP), the University and Polytechnic Higher Institute (ISPU) and the Catholic University (UC).

Health. There were (1997) 10 hospitals, 418 health centres and 996 medical posts. There were 2 psychiatric hospitals. In 1990 there were 387 doctors (equivalent to one for every 36,320 persons), 1,139 midwives, 3,533 nursing personnel, 108 dentists and 353 pharmacists. Private health care was introduced alongside the national health service in 1992.

CULTURE

Broadcasting. Radio Moçambique is part state-owned and part commercial. There are three national programmes in Tsonga and Portuguese and an external service in English. Television is at a trial stage (colour by PAL). There were 90,000 TV receivers and 730,000 radio sets in 1997.

TVM is the national television station; RTK (Klint Radio and Television) is privately owned.

Press. There are two well-established daily newspapers (*Noticias* and *Diário* in Maputo and Beira respectively). Five additional newspapers were registered in 1998: *Savana*, *Mediacoop*, *Demos*, *Metical* and *Domingo*.

Tourism. Tourism isa potential growth area for the country. There are 2,500 km of Indian Ocean beaches, coral reefs, diving, deep-sea fishing, wildlife, game parks, highlands and plains.

Festivals. There are annual culture festivals throughout the country.

Libraries. As well as libraries at the higher education institutes, there is an independent public library in Maputo.

Theatre and Opera. In addition to state-owned theatres and opera houses, Avenida and Matchedge are privately owned.

DIPLOMATIC REPRESENTATIVES

Of Mozambique in the United Kingdom (21 Fitzroy Sq., London, W1P 5HJ)
High Commissioner: Antonio Gumende.

Of the United Kingdom in Mozambique (Ave. Vladimir I. Lenine 310, Maputo)
High Commissioner: Robert Dewar.

Of Mozambique in the USA (1990 M. St., NW, Washington, D.C., 20036)
Ambassador: Armando Alexandre Panguene.

Of the USA in Mozambique (Ave Kenneth Kaunda 193, Maputo)
Ambassador: Sharon Wilkinson.

Of Mozambique to the United Nations
Ambassador: Carlos dos Santos.

Of Mozambique to the European Union
Ambassador: Alvaro Manuel Trindade O Da Silva.

FURTHER READING
Andersson, H., *Mozambique: a War against the People.* London, 1993
Finnegan, W., *A Complicated War: the Harrowing of Mozambique.* California Univ. Press, 1992
Newitt, M., *A History of Mozambique.* Farnborough, 1996

National statistical office: Instituto Nacional de Estatística, Av. Ahmed Sekou Touré, No. 21
Website (Portuguese only): http://www.ine.gov.mz/

MYANMAR

Myanmar Naingngandaw
(Union of Myanmar)

Capital: Yangon (Rangoon)
Population estimate, 2000: 47·75m.
GDP per capita, 2000: (PPP$) 1,027
HDI/world rank: 0·552/117

KEY HISTORICAL EVENTS

After Burma's invasion of the kingdom of Assam, the British East India Company retaliated in defence of its Indian interests and in 1826 drove the Burmese out of India. Territory was annexed in south Burma but the kingdom of Upper Burma, ruled from Mandalay, remained independent. A second war with Britain in 1852 ended with the British annexation of the Irrawaddy Delta. In 1885 the British invaded and occupied Upper Burma. In 1886 all Burma became a province of the Indian empire. There were violent uprisings in the 1930s and in 1937 Burma was separated from India and permitted some degree of self-government. Independence was achieved in 1948. In 1958 there was an army coup, and another in 1962 led by Gen. Ne Win, who installed a Revolutionary Council and dissolved parliament.

The Council lasted until March 1974 when the country became a one-party socialist republic. On 18 Sept. 1988 the Armed Forces seized power and set up the State Law and Order Restoration Council (SLORC). Since then civil unrest has cost more than 10,000 lives. On 19 June 1989 the government changed the name of the country in English to the Union of Myanmar. Aung San Suu Kyi, leader of the National League for Democracy, was put under house arrest in July 1989. In spite of her continuing detention, her party won the 1990 election by a landslide, but the military junta refused to accept the results. She was eventually freed in July 1995, only to be placed under house arrest for a second time in Sept. 2000 and again released in May 2002.

TERRITORY AND POPULATION

Myanmar is bounded in the east by China, Laos and Thailand, and west by the Indian Ocean, Bangladesh and India. Three parallel mountain ranges run from north to south; the Western Yama or Rakhine Yama, the Bagu Yama and the Shaun Plateau. The total area of the Union is 261,228 sq. miles (676,577 sq. km). The population in 1983 (census) was 35,313,905. Estimate (1996) 45·92m. (23·05m. female); density, 68 per sq. km. In 1999, 72·7% of the population lived in rural areas.

The UN gives a projected population for 2010 of 53·0m.

The leading towns are: Yangon (Rangoon), the capital (1999 population of 4,101,000); other towns (1983 estimates), Mandalay, 532,985; Moulmein, 219,991; Pegu, 150,447; Bassein, 144,092; Sittwe (Akyab), 107,907; Taunggye, 107,607; Monywa, 106,873.

The population of the seven states and seven administrative divisions (1994 estimates): Irrawaddy Division, 6,107,000; Magwe Division, 4,067,000; Mandalay Division, 5,823,000; Pegu Division, 4,607,000; Sagaing Division, 4,889,000; Tenasserim Division, 1,187,000; Yangon Division, 5,037,000; Chin State, 438,000; Kachin State, 1,135,000; Kayah State, 228,000; Karen State, 1,323,000; Mon State, 2,183,000; Rakhine State, 2,482,000; Shan State, 4,416,000. Myanmar is inhabited by many ethnic nationalities. There are as many as 135 national groups with the Bamars, comprising about 68·96% of the population, forming the largest group.

The official language is Burmese; English is also in use.

SOCIAL STATISTICS

1995 births, 1,263,000; deaths, 465,000. Birth rate (1995), 28·0 per 1,000 population; death rate, 10·3. Annual population growth rate, 1990–99, 1·2%. Life expectancy at birth, 1999, was 53·6 years for males and 58·4 years for females. Infant mortality, 1999, 79 per 1,000 live births; fertility rate, 1999, 2·3 births per woman.

CLIMATE
The climate is equatorial in coastal areas, changing to tropical monsoon over most of the interior, but humid temperate in the extreme north, where there is a more significant range of temperature and a dry season lasting from Nov. to April. In coastal parts, the dry season is shorter. Very heavy rains occur in the monsoon months May to Sept. Rangoon, Jan. 77°F (25°C), July 80°F (26·7°C). Annual rainfall 104" (2,616 mm). Akyab, Jan. 70°F (21·1°C), July 81°F (27·2°C). Annual rainfall 206" (5,154 mm). Mandalay, Jan. 68°F (20°C), July 85°F (29·4°C). Annual rainfall 33" (828 mm).

CONSTITUTION AND GOVERNMENT
Following elections in May 1990, the ruling State Law and Order Restoration Council (SLORC) said it would hand over power after the People's Assembly had agreed on a new constitution, but in July 1990 it stipulated that any such constitution must conform to guidelines which it would itself prescribe.

In May 1991, 48 members of the National League for Democracy (NLD) were given prison sentences on charges of treason. In July 1991 opposition members of the People's Assembly were unseated for alleged offences ranging from treason to illicit foreign exchange dealing. Such members, and unsuccessful candidates in the May 1990 elections, are forbidden to stand in future elections.

On 28 Nov. 1995 the government re-opened a 706-member Constitutional Convention in which the NLD was given 107 places. The NLD withdrew on 29 Nov.

In Nov. 1997 the country's ruling generals changed the name of the government to the State Peace and Development Council (SPDC), and reshuffled the cabinet. In Dec. 1997, following a period when the national currency fell to a record low, there were further changes to the cabinet, while corruption investigations were begun against some former ministers.

National Anthem. 'Gba majay Bma' ('We shall love Burma for ever'); words and tune by Saya Tin.

RECENT ELECTIONS
In elections in May 1990 the opposition National League for Democracy (NLD), led by Aung San Suu Kyi (b. 1945), won 392 of the 485 People's Assembly seats contested with some 60% of the valid vote. Turn-out was 72%, but 12·4% of ballots cast were declared invalid. The military ignored the result and refused to hand over power.

CURRENT ADMINISTRATION
In March 2003 the government comprised:

Prime Minister, Chairman of the State Peace and Development Council and Minister of Defence: Senior Gen. Than Shwe; b. 1933 (in office since 23 April 1992).

Minister of Agriculture and Irrigation: Maj. Gen. Nyunt Tin. *Industry (No. 1):* Col. Aung Thaung. *Industry (No. 2), and Hotels and Tourism:* Maj.-Gen. Saw Lwin. *Foreign Affairs:* Win Aung. *National Planning and Economic Development:* Soe Tha. *Transport:* Maj. Gen. Hla Myint Swe. *Labour and Culture:* U Tin Win. *Co-operatives:* Lieut.-Gen. Tin Ngwe. *Rail Transportation:* Pan Aung. *Energy:* Brig.-Gen. Lun Thi. *Education:* Than Aung. *Health:* Maj.-Gen. Ket Sein. *Commerce:* Brig.-Gen. Pyei Sone. *Communications, Posts and Telegraphs:* Brig.-Gen. Thein Zaw. *Finance and Revenue:* Maj. Gen. Hla Tun. *Religious Affairs:* U Aung Khin. *Construction:* Maj.-Gen. Saw Tun. *Immigration and Population:* Maj.-Gen. Sein Htwa. *Science and Technology:* U Thaung. *Information:* Maj.-Gen. Kyi Aung. *Progress of Border Areas, National Races and Development Affairs:* Col. Thein Nyunt. *Electric Power:* Maj.-Gen. Tin Htut. *Sports:* Brig.-Gen. Thura Aye Myint. *Forestry:* Aung Phone. *Home Affairs:* Lieut.-Gen. Tin Hlaing. *Mines:* Brig.-Gen. Ohn Myint. *Social Welfare, Relief and Resettlement:* Maj.-Gen. Sein Htwa. *Livestock and Fisheries:* Brig.-Gen. Maung Maung Thein. *Military Affairs:* Lieut.-Gen. Tin Hla. *Office of the Chairman of the State Peace and Development Council:* Lieut.-Gen. Min Thein; Brig.-Gen. David Oliver Abel. *Office of the Prime Minister:* Maj.-Gen. Tin Ngwe.

DEFENCE

Military expenditure in 1999 totalled US$1,995m. (US$44 per capita), representing 6·9% of GDP. In 1998 Myanmar was estimated to have 50,000 soldiers and rebels under the age of 18—a number only exceeded in Afghanistan.

Army. The strength of the Army was reported to be about 325,000 in 1999. The Army is organized into ten regional commands. There are two paramilitary units: People's Police Force (50,000) and People's Militia (35,000).

Navy. Personnel in 1999 totalled about 10,000 including 800 naval infantry.

Air Force. The Air Force is intended primarily for internal security duties. Personnel (1999) 9,000 operating 83 combat aircraft, including F-7s, and 29 armed helicopters.

INTERNATIONAL RELATIONS

Myanmar is a member of the UN, WTO, Asian Development Bank, Colombo Plan, ASEAN and the Mekong Group.

In 2001 tension between Myanmar and neighbouring Thailand escalated amid a series of border skirmishes, in part over the cross-border trade in drugs. In May 2002 the border between the two countries was closed following a diplomatic row. It was re-opened in Oct. 2002.

ECONOMY

Agriculture accounted for 53·2% of GDP in 1998, industry 9·0% and services 37·8%.

Overview. A short-term plan ran from 1993 to 1996. Liberalization measures to promote a market economy were introduced in 1990.

Currency. The unit of currency is the *kyat* (MMK) of 100 *pyas*. Total money supply was K.779,984m. in Feb. 2002. Foreign exchange reserves were US$454m. in March 2002 and gold reserves 231,000 troy oz in June 2002. Inflation was 15·0% in 2001. Since 1 June 1996 import duties have been calculated at a rate US$1 = K.100.

Budget. Budget revenue and expenditure (in K.1m.), year beginning 1 April:

	1995	1996	1997	1998	1999
Revenue	39,429	54,726	86,690	116,066	122,895
Expenditure	64,884	80,120	98,426	124,064	153,497

State budget estimates are classified into three parts, *viz.* State Administrative Organizations, State Economic Enterprises and Town and City Development Committees.

Performance. Real GDP growth was 5·5% in 2000 and 4·8% in 2001. In spite of recent impressive growth, Myanmar's per capita GDP fell from US$80 in 1968 to US$70 in 1998.

Banking and Finance. The Central Bank of Myanmar was established in 1990. Its *Governor* is U Kyaw Kyaw Maung. In 1995 there were 15 private domestic banks. Since 1996 foreign banks with representative offices (there were 31 in 1996) have been permitted to set up joint ventures with Burmese banks. The foreign partner must provide at least 35% of the capital. The state insurance company is the Myanmar Insurance Corporation. Deposits in savings banks were K.30,963m. in 1994.

A stock exchange opened in Rangoon in 1996.

Weights and Measures. The British system of weights and measures is generally used. The metric system has also been introduced in many areas. But in the markets the use of Myanmar weights and measures, as outlined below, is common:

viss (peit-tha)	= 3·6 lb	= 1·633 kilograms
tical (kyat-tha)	= 0·576 oz	= 16·33 grams
622·22 *viss*	= 1 long ton (2,240 lb)	= 1·016 metric ton
612·39 *viss*	= 2,204·62 lb	= 1 metric ton

ENERGY AND NATURAL RESOURCES

Environment. Myanmar's carbon dioxide emissions in 1998 were the equivalent of 0·2 tonnes per capita according to the *World Bank Atlas*.

Electricity. In 1995–96 the installed capacity of Myanma Electric Power was 1,000 MW, of which 530 MW was natural gas, 328 MW hydro-electric, 62 MW thermal and 80 MW diesel. Capacity of other networks was 344 MW. Total generated, 1998, 4·31bn. kWh. Consumption per capita in 1998 was 64 kWh.

Oil and Gas. Production (1995–96) of crude oil was 6·9m. bbls.; natural gas (1996), 62 petajoules.

Minerals. Production in 1995–96 (in tonnes): copper concentrates, 42,500; hard coal (1996), 31,000; lignite (1997), 28,000; zinc concentrates, 6,070; refined lead, 4,250; tin, tungsten and scheelite mixed, 1,400; tin concentrates, 492; refined tin metal, 310; antimonial lead, 210; tungsten concentrates, 95; nickel speiss, 60; refined silver, 260,000 fine oz; gold, 22,496 troy oz.

Agriculture. In 1995–96, 4·5m. peasant families cultivated 10·1m. ha.

Liberalization measures of 1990 permit farmers to grow crops of their choice. The total sown area in 1995–96 was 9·1m. ha. 1·59m. ha were irrigated in 1998. Production (2000, in 1,000 tonnes): rice, 20,000; sugarcane, 5,147; dry beans, 1,229; groundnuts, 640; onions, 507; plantains, 354; maize, 349; sesame seeds, 302; sunflower seeds, 270; coconuts, 263; potatoes, 245. Opium output in 2001 was 865 tonnes. Myanmar overtook Afghanistan as the world's largest producer of opium in 2001, but following the fall of the Taliban opium production in Afghanistan increased to such an extent that output in 2002 was higher in Afghanistan than in Myanmar.

Livestock (2000): cattle, 10·96m.; buffaloes, 2·44m.; pigs, 3·91m.; goats, 1·39m.; sheep, 390,000; chickens, 44m. There were 6·8m. draught cattle in 1997 and 8,528 tractors in 1998.

Forestry. Forest area in 1995 was 27·15m. ha, covering 41·3% of the total land area (29·09m. ha in 1990). Teak resources cover about 6m. ha (15m. acres). In 1999, 22·57m. cu. metres of roundwood were cut.

Fisheries. In 1999 the total catch was 851,581 tonnes (721,904 tonnes from sea fishing). Aquacultural fish production was 79,851 tonnes in 1995–96. Cultured pearls and oyster shells are produced.

INDUSTRY

Of the 48,601 industrial enterprises in 1995–96, 1,607 were state-owned, 636 were co-operatives and 46,358 were private. Production (1995–96) in 1,000 tonnes: fertilizers, 300; sugar (1998), 51·1; paper (1998), 18; cement (1997), 16; 1,429 cars; 597 tractors; 35,042 bicycles. (1994–95, in 1,000 tonnes) cotton yarn, 16·8. In 1995–96 manufacturing output was valued at K.6,556m.

Labour. The population of working age (15 to 59) in 1995–96 was 26·34m. Economically active persons in 1997: 17·96m., of whom 11·38m. were employed in agriculture, 1·75m. in trade, 1·68m. in services, and 1·57m. in manufacturing. In 1994 there were 541,500 persons registered as unemployed.

INTERNATIONAL TRADE

In Aug. 1991 the USA imposed trade sanctions in response to alleged civil rights violations. Foreign debt was US$6,046m. in 2000. A law of 1989 permitted joint ventures, with foreign companies or individuals able to hold 100% of the shares.

Imports and Exports. Since 1990 in line with market-oriented measures firms have been able to participate directly in trade.

Imports in 2000 totalled US$2,134·9m. and exports US$1,618·8m. Main imports (in K.1m.), 1994–95: raw materials, 1,854·3; transport equipment, 1,251; machinery, 1,099·9; construction materials, 472; tools and spares, 303·5. Leading import suppliers are Japan, Singapore, China and Thailand. Main exports: rice, 1,165·8; teak, 953·1; pulses and beans, 799·4; rubber, 443·1; hardwood, 107·8. Main export markets, 1994–95: Singapore, 883·5; India, 695·4; Thailand, 542·7; China, 277·5; Hong Kong, 269·1.

COMMUNICATIONS

Roads. There were 28,200 km of roads in 1996, of which 3,440 km were surfaced. An estimated 27,000 passenger cars were in use in 1996 (less than one per 1,000 inhabitants). In 1995–96 the state service ran 951 buses, 197 taxis and 1,969 lorries. There were also 155,107 buses and 29,694 lorries in private co-operative ownership. In 1995–96, 121·28m. passengers and 1·19m. tonnes of freight were carried by road.

Rail. In 1995 there were 3,955 km of route on metre gauge. Passenger-km travelled in 1998 came to 3,948m. and freight tonne-km to 988m.

Civil Aviation. Myanma Airways International operates domestic services and in 1998 had international services to Bangkok, Hong Kong and Singapore. In 1999 it flew 4·0m. km, carrying 392,200 passengers.

Shipping. There are nearly 100 km of navigable canals. The Irrawaddy is navigable up to Myitkyina, 1,450 km from the sea, and its tributary, the Chindwin, is navigable for 630 km. The Irrawaddy delta has approximately 3,000 km of navigable water. The Salween, the Attaran and the G'yne provide about 400 km of navigable waters around Moulmein. In 1998 merchant shipping totalled 492,000 GRT. Vessels totalling 2,338,000 NRT entered ports and vessels totalling 1,624,000 NRT cleared in 1995.

In 1995–96, 24·5m. passengers and 1·03m. tonnes of freight were carried on inland waterways. The ocean-going fleet of the state-owned Myanma Five Star Line in 1995 comprised 11 liners, 4 short-haul vessels and 3 coastal passenger/cargo vessels. In 1995–96, 60,000 passengers and 1,030,000 tonnes of freight were transported coastally and overseas. In 1998 vessels totalling 2,955,000 NRT entered ports and vessels totalling 1,235,000 NRT cleared. The port is Rangoon.

Telecommunications. Myanmar had 266,200 main telephone lines in 2000 (5·6 per 1,000 persons) and there were 52,000 PCs in use (1·1 for every 1,000 persons). Mobile phone subscribers numbered 11,400 in 1999 and there were 1,500 fax machines in 1996. There were 500 Internet users in Dec. 1999.

Postal Services. In 1995–96 there were 1,205 post offices.

SOCIAL INSTITUTIONS

Justice. The highest judicial authority is the Chief Judge, appointed by the government. At the end of 1993 there were 53,195 people held in prisons. Amnesty International reported in 2000 that there were more than 2,000 political prisoners in the country's jails.

Religion. About 89·4% of the population—mainly Bamars, Shans, Mons, Rakhines and some Kayins—are Buddhists, while the rest are Christians, Muslims, Hindus and Animists. The Christian population is composed mainly of Kayins, Kachins and Chins. Islam and Hinduism are practised mainly by people of Indian origin.

Education. Education is free in primary, middle and vocational schools; fees are charged in senior secondary schools and universities. In 1995–96 there were 36,499 primary schools with 187,344 teachers and 5,995,015 pupils; 1,578 monastic primary schools (permitted since 1992) with 80,863 pupils; 2,112 middle schools with 60,759 teachers and 1,417,189 pupils; and 927 high schools with 19,120 teachers and 402,411 pupils.

In higher education in 1995–96 there were 12 teacher training schools with 315 teachers and 2,067 students, 5 teacher training institutes with 304 teachers and 2,170 students, 17 technical high schools with 498 teachers and 7,145 students, 11 technical institutes with 668 teachers and 12,080 students, 10 agricultural high schools with 100 teachers and 1,053 students, 7 agricultural institutes with 162 teachers and 1,844 students, 41 vocational schools with 369 teachers and 6,532 students, 6 universities with 3,050 teachers and 154,680 students, 6 degree colleges with 705 teachers and 53,362 students, and 10 colleges with 629 teachers and 40,327 students.

There was also a University for the Development of the National Races of the Union and institutes of medicine (3), dentistry, paramedical science, pharmacy, nursing, veterinary science, economics, technology (2), agriculture, education (2), foreign languages, computer science and forestry. An institute of remote education maintains a correspondence course at university level.

The adult literacy rate was 84·4% in 1999 (88·8% among males and 80·1% among females).

Expenditure on education in 1994 represented 14·4% of total government expenditure.

Health. In 1995–96 there were 12,950 doctors, 860 dentists, 9,851 nurses, 8,143 midwives and 737 hospitals with 28,372 beds. Public spending on health is less than 0·2% of GDP.

Welfare. In 1995–96 contributions to social security totalled (K.1m.) 117·5 (from employers, 73·2; from employees, 43·9). Benefits paid totalled 82·6, and included: sickness, 12·9; maternity, 3·9; disability, 3·7; survivors' pensions, 1·3.

CULTURE

Broadcasting. The government runs a TV and a radio station. There were 260,000 television receivers (colour by NTSC) and 4·2m. radio sets in 1997.

Press. There were five daily newspapers in 1996, with a combined circulation of 449,000, at a rate of 10 per 1,000 inhabitants.

Tourism. In 1999 there were 198,000 foreign tourists, spending US$35m.

DIPLOMATIC REPRESENTATIVES

Of Myanmar in the United Kingdom (19A Charles St., London W1X 8ER)
Ambassador: Dr Kyaw Win.

Of the United Kingdom in Myanmar (80 Strand Rd., Rangoon)
Ambassador: Victoria Bowman.

Of Myanmar in the USA (2300 S. St., NW, Washington, D.C., 20008)
Ambassador: U Linn Myaing.

Of the USA in Myanmar (581 Merchant St., Rangoon)
Ambassador: Carmen Martinez.

Of Myanmar to the United Nations
Ambassador: U Kyaw Tint Swe.

Of Myanmar to the European Union
Ambassador: U Wunna Maung Lwin.

FURTHER READING

Carey, P. (ed.) *Burma: The Challenge of Change in a Divided Society.* London, 1997
Suu Kyi, Aung San, *Freedom from Fear and Other Writings.* London, 1991
Thant, Myint-U, *The Making of Modern Burma.* CUP, 2001

National statistical office: Ministry of National Planning and Economic Development, Rangoon.

NAMIBIA

Republic of Namibia

Capital: Windhoek
Population estimate, 2000: 1·76m.
GDP per capita, 2000: (PPP$) 6,431
HDI/world rank: 0·610/122

KEY HISTORICAL EVENTS

In 1884 South West Africa was declared a German protectorate. Germany then introduced racial segregation and the exploitation of the diamond mines began. In 1915 the Union of South Africa occupied German South West Africa and on 17 Dec. 1920 the League of Nations entrusted the territory as a Mandate to the Union of South Africa. After World War II South Africa applied for its annexation to the Union and continued to administer the territory in defiance of various UN resolutions. In June 1968 the UN changed the name of the territory to Namibia.

After negotiations between South Africa and the UN, a multi-racial Advisory Council was appointed in 1973 in preparation for independence, but despite several attempts at organizing free elections South Africa remained dominant in the area until the UN Transition Assistance Group supervised elections for the constituent assembly in Nov. 1989. Independence was achieved on 21 March 1990.

TERRITORY AND POPULATION

Namibia is bounded in the north by Angola and Zambia, west by the Atlantic Ocean, south and southeast by South Africa and east by Botswana. The Caprivi Strip (Caprivi Region), about 300 km long, extends eastwards up to the Zambezi river, projecting into Zambia and Botswana and touching Zimbabwe. The area, including the Caprivi Strip and Walvis Bay, is 824,269 sq. km. South Africa transferred Walvis Bay to Namibian jurisdiction on 1 March 1994. Census population, 1991, 1,401,711 (720,784 females; urban, 32·76%). Estimate, 1996, 1,677,200; density, 2 per sq. km. In 1999, 69·6% of the population were rural.

The UN gives a projected population for 2010 of 2·10m.

Population by ethnic group at the censuses of 1970 and 1981 and estimates for 1991:

	1970	1981	1991
Ovambos	342,455	506,114	665,000
Kavangos	49,577	95,055	124,000
Damaras	64,973	76,179	100,000
Hereros	55,670	76,296	100,000
Whites	90,658	76,430	85,000
Namas	32,853	48,541	64,000
Caprivians	25,009	38,594	50,000
Coloureds	28,275	42,254	...
Bushmen	21,909	29,443	...
Basters	16,474	25,181	...
Tswanas	4,407	6,706	...
Other	...	12,403	...
	732,260	1,033,196	1,401,711

Namibia is administratively divided into 13 regions. Area, estimated population and chief towns in 1997:

Region	Area (in sq. km)	Population	Chief town
Caprivi (Liambezi)	19,532	92,000	Katima Mulilo
Erongo	63,719	98,500	Swakopmund
Hardap	109,888	80,000	Mariental
Karas	161,324	73,000	Keetmanshoop
Khomas	36,804	174,000	Windhoek
Kunene	144,254	58,500	Opuwo
Ohangwena	10,582	178,000	Oshikango
Okavango	43,417	136,000	Rundu

Region	Area (in sq. km)	Population	Chief town
Omaheke	84,731	55,600	Gobabis
Omusati	13,637	158,000	Outapi
Oshana	5,290	159,000	Oshakati
Oshikoto	26,607	176,000	Tsumeb
Otjozondjupa	105,327	85,000	Grootfontein

Towns with populations over 5,000 (1997): Windhoek, 202,000 (1999); Walvis Bay, 50,000; Oshakati, 37,000; Ondangwa, 33,000; Rehoboth, 21,000; Rundu, 18,000; Swakopmund, 18,000; Keetmanshoop, 16,000; Otjiwarongo, 16,000; Tsumeb, 15,000; Grootfontein, 11,000; Okahandja, 11,000; Mariental, 8,000; Gobabis, 7,000; Khorixas, 7,000; Lüderitz, 7,000.

English is the official language. Afrikaans and German are also spoken.

SOCIAL STATISTICS

1996 births, estimate, 63,000; deaths, 13,000. Rates (1996 estimate) per 1,000 population: birth, 37·3; death, 8·0. Expectation of life, 1999: males, 44·7 years; females, 44·9. Annual population growth rate, 1990–99, 2·6%; infant mortality, 1999, 56 per 1,000 live births; fertility rate, 1999, 4·8 births per woman.

CLIMATE

The rainfall increases steadily from less than 50 mm in the west and southwest up to 600 mm in the Caprivi Strip. The main rainy season is from Jan. to March, with lesser showers from Sept. to Dec. Namibia is the driest African country south of the Sahara.

CONSTITUTION AND GOVERNMENT

On 9 Feb. 1990 with a unanimous vote the Constituent Assembly approved the Constitution which stipulated a multi-party republic, an independent judiciary and an executive *President* who may serve a maximum of two five-year terms. The constitution was amended in 1999 to allow President Sam Nujoma to stand for a third term in office. The bicameral legislature consists of a 78-seat *National Assembly*, 72 members of which are elected for five-year terms by proportional representation and up to six appointed by the president by virtue of position or special expertise, and a *National Council* consisting of two members from each Regional Council elected for six-year terms.

National Anthem. 'Namibia, land of the brave'; words and tune by Axali Doeseb.

RECENT ELECTIONS

Presidential and parliamentary elections were held on 30 Nov. and 1 Dec. 1999. Incumbent Sam Nujoma (SWAPO) was re-elected President with 76·8% of votes cast followed by Ben Ulenga (Congress of Democrats/CoD) with 10·5%, Katuutire Kaura (Democratic Turnhalle Alliance/DTA) with 9·6% and Chief Justus Garoëb (United Democratic Front/UDF) with 3·0%. In parliamentary elections the South West Africa People's Organization (SWAPO) won 55 of the available 72 seats with 76·1% of the vote; the CoD, 7 with 9·9%; DTA, 7 with 9·5%; UDF, 2 with 2·9%; Monitor Action Group, 1 with 0·7%. Turn-out was 53%. The Congress of Democrats, formed early in 1999 as an opposition party to contest the election, represents the best chance of a credible challenge to the dominance of SWAPO and its autocratic leadership in the future in spite of its small share of the vote at the 1999 elections.

CURRENT ADMINISTRATION

President and Minister of Information and Broadcasting (acting): Sam Nujoma; b. 1929 (SWAPO; elected Feb. 1990, re-elected Dec. 1994 and Dec. 1999).

In March 2003 the government comprised:

Prime Minister: Theo-Ben Gurirab; b. 1939 (SWAPO; sworn in 28 Aug. 2002).

Deputy Prime Minister: Hendrik Witbooi.

Minister of Home Affairs: Jerry Ekandjo. *Foreign Affairs:* Hipido Hamutenya. *Defence:* Erikki Nghimtina. *Finance:* Nangolo Mbumba. *Higher Education, Training and Employment Creation:* Nahas Angula. *Health and Social Services:* Dr Libertine Amathila. *Mines and Energy:* Nicky Iyambo. *Justice:* Ngarikutuke

Tjiriange. *Regional and Local Government and Housing:* Joel Natangwe Kaapanda. *Agriculture, Water and Rural Development:* Helmut Angula. *Trade and Industry:* Jesaya Nyamu. *Environment and Tourism:* Philemon Malima. *Works, Transport and Communications:* Moses Amweelo. *Lands, Resettlement and Rehabilitation:* Hifikepunye Pohamba. *Fisheries and Marine Resources:* Abraham Iyambo. *Prisons and Correctional Services:* Andimba Toivo ya Toivo. *Basic Education, Sport and Culture:* John Mutorwa. *Women's Affairs and Child Welfare:* Netumbo Ndaitwah. *Labour:* Marco Hausiko.

Office of the Prime Minister: http://www.opm.gov.na/

DEFENCE
In 2000 defence expenditure totalled US$103m. (US$60 per capita), representing 3·6% of GDP.

Army. Personnel (1999), 9,000.

Coastguard. A force of 100 (1999) is based at Walvis Bay.

Air Force. The Army has an air wing with no combat aircraft.

INTERNATIONAL RELATIONS
Namibia is a member of the UN, WTO, the Commonwealth, the African Union, African Development Bank, COMESA, SADC and is an ACP member state of the ACP-EU relationship.

ECONOMY
Agriculture accounted for 10·0% of GDP in 1998, industry 34·2% and services 55·8%.

The Namibian economy is heavily dependent on mining and fisheries.

Currency. The unit of currency is the *Namibia dollar* (NAD) of 100 *cents*, introduced on 14 Sept. 1993 and pegged to the South African rand. The rand is also legal tender at parity. In 2001 inflation was 13·4%. In June 2002 foreign exchange reserves were US$230m. Gold reserves are negligible. Total money supply in June 2002 was N$7,063m.

Budget. The financial year runs from 1 April. In 1999–2000 total government revenue was N$7,184·9m. (N$7,765·3m. estimated for 2000–01) and total expenditure was N$7,831·3m. (2000–01 estimate, N$8,610·0m.).

Performance. Real GDP growth was 3·4% in 2000 and 2·5% in 2001; total GDP in 2001 was US$3·2bn.

Banking and Finance. The Bank of Namibia is the central bank. Its *Governor* is Tom Alweendo. Commercial banks include First National Bank of Namibia, Namibia Banking Corporation, Standard Bank Namibia, Commercial Bank of Namibia, Bank Windhoek (the only locally-owned bank) and City Savings and Investment Bank. There is a state-owned Agricultural Bank. Total assets of commercial banks were R2,383·2m. at 31 Dec. 1991.

There are two building societies with total assets (31 March 1990) R424·9m. A Post Office Savings Bank was established in 1916. In March 1991 its total assets were R21·8m. A stock exchange (NSE) is in operation.

ENERGY AND NATURAL RESOURCES

Electricity. In 1999 electricity production was 1·2bn. kWh. Namibia also imports electricity from South Africa (890m. kWh in 1999). Consumption per capita in 1995 was 584 kWh.

Oil and Gas. Natural gas reserves in 1997 totalled 85bn. cu. metres.

Water. The 12 most important dams have a total capacity of 589·2m. cu. metres. The Kunene, the Okavango, the Zambezi, the Kwando or Mashi and the Orange River are the only permanently running rivers but water can generally be obtained by sinking shallow wells. Except for a few springs, mostly hot, there is no surface water.

Minerals. There are diamond deposits both inshore and off the coast, with production equally divided between the two. Some 3bn. carats of diamonds are believed to be lying in waters off Namibia's Atlantic coast. Namibia produced 1,611,000 carats in 1999, with 98% of the diamonds being of gem quality. 1996 output (in tonnes): salt, 493,000 (1997); lead, 67,760; zinc, 64,600; copper, 25,000; silver, 34 (1997); gold, 2,205 kg; diamonds, 1,611,000 carats (1999). Uranium production, 1998, 2,762 tonnes.

Agriculture. Namibia is essentially a stock-raising country, the scarcity of water and poor rainfall rendering crop-farming, except in the northern and northeastern parts, almost impossible. There were 816,000 ha of arable land in 1998 and 4,000 ha of permanent crops. Generally speaking, the southern half is suited for the raising of small stock, while the central and northern parts are more suited for cattle. Guano is harvested from the coast, converted into fertilizer in South Africa and most of it exported to Europe. In 1995, 45% of the active labour force worked in the agricultural sector, and 45% of the population was dependent on agriculture.

Livestock (2000): 2·06m. cattle, 2·10m. sheep, 1·65m. goats, 2m. chickens.

In 2000, 75,000 tonnes of milk and 60,000 tonnes of meat were produced. Principal crops (2000, in tonnes): millet, 79,000; maize, 49,000; sorghum, 7,000; seed cotton, 5,000; wheat, 4,000.

Forestry. Forests covered 12·37m. ha in 1995, or 15% of the land area, down from 12·58m. ha in 1990.

Fisheries. Pilchards, mackerel and hake are the principal fish caught. The catch in 1999 was 299,151 tonnes (21,225 tonnes in 1989), of which more than 99% came from marine waters. The rate of growth in the annual catch between 1989 and 1999 was one of the highest in the world. Conservation policies are in place. The policy aims at ensuring that the country's fisheries resources are utilized on a sustainable basis and also aims to ensure their lasting contribution to the country's economy.

INDUSTRY

Of the estimated total of 400 undertakings, the most important branches are food production (accounting for 29·3% of total output), metals (12·7%) and wooden products (7%). The supply of specialized equipment to the mining industry, the assembly of goods from predominantly imported materials and the manufacture of metal products and construction material play an important part. Small industries (including home industries, textile mills, leather and steel goods) have expanded. Products manufactured locally include chocolates, beer, cement, leather shoes, and delicatessen meats and game meat products.

Labour. In 1996 the labour force totalled 650,000 (59% males). Nearly half the economically active population in 1991 were engaged in agriculture, fisheries and forestry. Around 20% of the workforce was unemployed in 1991. The main employers were government services, agriculture and mining.

INTERNATIONAL TRADE

Total foreign debt was US$140m. in 1996. Export Processing Zones were established in 1995 to grant companies with EPZ status some tax exemptions and other incentives. The Offshore Development Company (ODC) is the flagship of the Export Processing Zone regime. The EPZ regime does not restrict; any investor (local or foreign) enjoys the same or equal advantages in engaging themselves in any choice of business (allowed by law).

Imports and Exports. In 1998 imports (f.o.b.) were valued at US$1,450·9m. (US$1,615·0m. in 1997) and exports (f.o.b.) at US$1,278·3m. (US$1,343·3m. in 1997). Exports in 1996 (in US$1m.) included diamonds (542), fish (289), uranium and other minerals (237), meat products (82), cattle (58), small stock (42). The largest import supplier in 1996 was South Africa with 87%; largest export markets: UK, 34%; South Africa, 27%.

COMMUNICATIONS

Roads. In 1997 the total national road network was 63,258 km, including 5,250 km of tarred roads. In 1996 there were 135,200 registered motor vehicles, including 74,875 passenger cars and 59,350 trucks and vans. There were 127 deaths as a result of road accidents in 1996.

Rail. The Namibia system connects with the main system of the South African railways at Ariamsvlei. The total length of the line inside Namibia was 2,382 km of 1,065 mm gauge in 1996. In 1995–96 railways carried 124,000 passengers and 1·7m. tonnes of freight.

Civil Aviation. The national carrier is the state-owned Air Namibia. In 2000 the major airport, Windhoek's Hosea Kutako International, handled 481,000 passengers (437,000 on international flights). Eros is used mainly for domestic flights. In 1999 scheduled airline traffic of Namibian-based carriers flew 7·1m. km, carrying 201,000 passengers (165,000 on international flights).

Shipping. The main port is Walvis Bay. During 1997–98, 808 ships called and 1,156,143 tonnes of cargo were landed. There is a harbour at Lüderitz which handles mainly fishing vessels. In 1998 merchant shipping totalled 55,000 GRT.

Telecommunications. Telecom Namibia is the responsible corporation. In 2000 main telephone lines numbered 110,200 (62·7 per 1,000 inhabitants) and there were 60,000 PCs in use (34·2 per 1,000 persons). Mobile phone subscribers numbered 30,000 in 1999. In Dec. 2000 there were 30,000 Internet users.

Postal Services. The national postal service is run by Namibia Post. In 1996 there were 76 post offices and 15 postal agencies which served 74,400 private box renters and 961 private bag services distributed by rail or road transport.

SOCIAL INSTITUTIONS

Justice. There is a Supreme Court, a High Court and a number of magistrates' and lower courts. An Ombudsman is appointed. Judges are appointed by the president on the recommendation of the Judicial Service Commission.

The population in penal institutions in Aug. 1998 was 4,397 (260 per 100,000 of national population).

Religion. About 90% of the population is Christian.

Education. Literacy was 81·4% in 1999 (male, 82·4%; female, 80·4%). Primary education is free and compulsory. In 1998 there were 400,325 pupils at primary schools, 115,237 at secondary schools and 11,344 at institutions of higher education (1995). The University of Namibia had 2,240 students and 160 academic staff in 1994–95. Namibia has the highest proportion of female students in higher education of any African country, with 61% in 1994.

In 1997 total expenditure on education came to 9·1% of GNP.

Health. In 1992 there were 47 hospitals (4 private) and 238 clinics and health centres. There were 324 doctors, 51 dentists and 4,471 nursing staff.

CULTURE

Broadcasting. The Namibian Broadcasting Corporation operates a national radio service from three stations and vernacular services. It also operates ten TV stations (colour by PAL). In 1997 there were 60,000 TV sets and 232,000 radios in use. One privately-owned television channel and two privately-owned radio stations operate from Windhoek.

Press. There were four daily and three weekly newspapers in 1997.

Tourism. In 1998 there were 560,000 visitors who spent US$288m. The tourism industry was devastated in 2000 by the Angolan civil war spilling over into the north of Namibia.

DIPLOMATIC REPRESENTATIVES

Of Namibia in the United Kingdom (6 Chandos St., London, W1M 0LQ)
High Commissioner: Monica Ndiliawike Nashandi.

Of the United Kingdom in Namibia (116 Robert Mugabe Ave., 9000 Windhoek)
High Commissioner: Alastair MacDermott.

Of Namibia in the USA (1605 New Hampshire Ave., NW, Washington, D.C., 20009)
Ambassador: Leonard Nangolo Iipumbu.

Of the USA in Namibia (14 Lossen St., Private Bag 12029, Windhoek)
Ambassador: Kevin Joseph McGuire.

Of Namibia to the United Nations
Ambassador: Martin Andjaba.

Of Namibia to the European Union
Ambassador: Zedekia Joseph Ngavirue.

FURTHER READING

Herbstein, D. and Evenston, J., *The Devils are Among Us: the War for Namibia.* London, 1989
Kaela, L. C. W., *The Question of Namibia.* London, 1996
Schoeman, Elna and Stanley, *Namibia.* [Bibliography] 2nd ed. ABC-Clio, Oxford and Santa Barbara (CA), 1997
Sparks, D. L. and Green, D., *Namibia: the Nation after Independence.* Boulder, (CO), 1992

National statistical office: Central Statistics Office, Windhoek.

NAURU

Republic of Nauru

Population estimate, 2000: 11,000
GDP per capita: not available

KEY HISTORICAL EVENTS
The island was discovered by Capt. Fearn in 1798, annexed by Germany in Oct. 1888 and surrendered to Australian forces in 1914. It was administered by the UK under a League of Nations mandate from 1920 until 1947 when the UN approved a trusteeship agreement with Australia, New Zealand and the UK. Independence was gained on 31 Jan. 1968.

TERRITORY AND POPULATION
Nauru is a coral island surrounded by a reef situated 0° 32' S. lat. and 166° 56' E. long. Area, 21·3 sq. km. At the 1992 census the population totalled 9,919, of whom 6,832 were Nauruans. Estimated population in July 1997: 10,390; density, 488 per sq. km.

Nauruan is the official language, although English is widely used for government purposes.

SOCIAL STATISTICS
1995 births, 203; deaths, 49; marriages, 57. Rates, 1995 (per 1,000 population): births, 20·3; deaths, 4·9; marriage, 5·7; infant mortality, 41 (per 1,000 live births). Annual population growth rate, 1990–99, 1·9%; fertility rate, 1999, 4·0 births per woman.

CLIMATE
A tropical climate, tempered by sea breezes, but with a high and irregular rainfall, averaging 82" (2,060 mm). Average temperature, Jan. 81°F (27·2°C), July 82°F (27·8°C). Annual rainfall 75" (1,862 mm).

CONSTITUTION AND GOVERNMENT
A Legislative Council was inaugurated on 31 Jan. 1966. An 18-member Parliament is elected on a three-yearly basis.

National Anthem. 'Nauru bwiema, ngabena ma auwe' ('Nauru our homeland, the country we love'); words by a collective, tune by L. H. Hicks.

RECENT ELECTIONS
At the last elections on 3 May 2003, 15 non-partisans and three members of the Nauru First (Naoero Amo) Party were elected.

Derog Gioura was elected acting *President* by parliament after the death of President Bernard Dowiyogo on 10 March 2003.

CURRENT ADMINISTRATION
Acting President and Minister for Public Service, Foreign and Internal Affairs, Civil Aviation, Fisheries and Marine Resources and Women's Affairs: Derog Gioura (since 10 March 2003).

In March 2003 the government comprised:
Minister for Finance and Economic Development, and Transport: Remy Namaduk. *Health and Medical Services, Justice and Good Governance:* Ludwig Scotty. *Industry and Island Development:* Vassal Gadoengin. *Education and Youth Affairs:* Anthony Audoa. *Works and Community Services, Housing and Sports:* Dogabe Jeremiah.

INTERNATIONAL RELATIONS
Nauru is a member of the UN, Asian Development Bank, the Commonwealth, the Pacific Community and the Pacific Islands Forum.

ECONOMY

Currency. The Australian dollar is in use.

Budget. Revenues in 1995–96 were estimated to be US$23·4m. and expenditure US$64·8m.

Performance. Real GDP growth was 7·0% in 1995 (4·5% in 1994).

Banking and Finance. Nauru was one of 15 countries and territories named in a report in June 2000 as failing to co-operate in the fight against international money laundering. The Financial Action Task Force on Money Laundering was set up by the G7 group of major industrialized nations.

ENERGY AND NATURAL RESOURCES

Electricity. Installed capacity in 1995 was 13,250 kW; production was 30m. kWh in 1998.

Minerals. A central plateau contained high-grade phosphate deposits. The interests in the phosphate deposits were purchased in 1919 from the Pacific Phosphate Company by the UK, Australia and New Zealand. In 1967 the British Phosphate Corporation agreed to hand over the phosphate industry to Nauru for approximately $A20m. over three years. Nauru took over the industry in July 1969; production in 1995 totalled 500,000 tonnes. It is estimated that the deposits will be exhausted by 2008. In May 1989 Nauru filed a claim against Australia for environmental damage caused by the mining. In Aug. 1993 Australia agreed to pay compensation of $A73m. In March 1994 New Zealand and the UK each agreed to pay compensation of $A12m.

Agriculture. Livestock (2000): pigs, 3,000. In 2000 the crop of coconuts was an estimated 2,000 tonnes.

Fisheries. The catch in 1999 was approximately 250 tonnes.

INTERNATIONAL TRADE

Imports and Exports. The export trade consists almost entirely of phosphate shipped to Australia, New Zealand, the Philippines and Japan. Imports: food, building construction materials, machinery for the phosphate industry and medical supplies. Exports, 1991 estimate, US$25m.; imports, US$21m.

COMMUNICATIONS

Roads. In 1996 there were 30 km of roads, 24 km of which were paved.

Civil Aviation. There is an airfield on the island capable of accepting medium size jet aircraft. The national carrier, Air Nauru, is a wholly owned government subsidiary. It has one aircraft. In 1998 it flew to Brisbane, Guam, Manila, Melbourne, Pohnpei and Tarawa. In 1999 scheduled airline traffic of Nauru-based carriers flew 2·5m. km, carrying 143,000 passengers (all on international flights).

Shipping. Deep offshore moorings can accommodate medium-size vessels. Shipping coming to the island consists of vessels under charter to the phosphate industry or general purpose vessels bringing cargo by way of imports.

Telecommunications. There were 2,200 main telephone lines in operation in 1996. International telephone, telex and fax communications are maintained by satellite. A satellite earth station was commissioned in 1990.

Postal Services. In 1995 there were 25 post offices, equivalent to approximately one for every 400 persons (the highest ratio of post offices per person of any country in the world).

SOCIAL INSTITUTIONS

Justice. The highest Court is the Supreme Court of Nauru. It is the Superior Court of record and has the jurisdiction to deal with constitutional matters in addition to its other jurisdiction. There is also a District Court which is presided over by the Resident Magistrate who is also the Chairman of the Family Court and the Registrar of Supreme Court. The laws applicable in Nauru are its own Acts of Parliament. A large number of British statutes and much common law has been adopted insofar as is compatible with Nauruan custom.

Religion. The population is mainly Roman Catholic or Protestant.

Education. Attendance at school is compulsory between the ages of 6 and 17. In 1989 there were ten infant and primary schools and two secondary schools with a total of 165 teachers and 2,707 pupils. There is also a trade school with four instructors and an enrolment of 88 trainees. Scholarships are available for Nauruan children to receive secondary and higher education and vocational training in Australia and New Zealand.

CULTURE

Broadcasting. The government-controlled Nauru Broadcasting Service broadcasts a home service in Nauruan and English for three hours daily. There were 7,000 radio sets in use and 500 television sets in 1997. New Zealand television programmes are received.

DIPLOMATIC REPRESENTATIVES
Of Nauru in the United Kingdom
Honorary Consul: Martin Weston (Romshed Courtyard, Underriver, Nr Sevenoaks, Kent TN15 0SD).

Of the United Kingdom in Nauru
High Commissioner: Charles Mochan (resides at Suva, Fiji Islands).

Of the USA in Nauru
Ambassador: David Lyon (resides at Suva).

Of Nauru to the United Nations
Ambassador: Vinci Clodumar.

FURTHER READING
Weeremantry, C., *Nauru: Environmental Damage under International Trusteeship.* OUP, 1992

NEPAL

Nepal Adhirajya
(Kingdom of Nepal)

Capital: Káthmandu
Population estimate, 2000: 23·04m.
GDP per capita, 2000: (PPP$) 1,327
HDI/world rank: 0·490/142

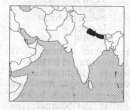

KEY HISTORICAL EVENTS

Nepal is an independent Himalayan Kingdom located between India and the Tibetan region of China. From the 8th to the 11th centuries many Buddhists fled to Nepal from India, which had been invaded by Muslims. In the 18th century Nepal was a collection of small principalities (many of Rajput origin) and the three kingdoms of the Malla dynasty: Káthmandu, Pátan and Bhádgaon. In central Nepal lay the principality of Gurkha (or Gorkha); its ruler after 1742 was Prithvi Náráyan Sháh, who conquered the small neighbouring states. Fearing his ambitions, in 1767 the Mallas brought in forces lent by the British East India Company. In 1769 these forces were withdrawn and Gurkha was then able to conquer the Malla kingdoms and unite Nepal as one state with its capital at Káthmandu. In 1846 the Ráná family became the effective rulers of Nepal, establishing the office of prime minister as hereditary. In 1860 Nepal reached agreement with the British in India whereby Nepali independence was preserved and the recruitment of Gurkhas to the British army was sanctioned.

In 1950 the Sháh royal family allied itself with Nepalis abroad to end the power of the Ránás. The last Ráná prime minister resigned in Nov. 1951, the king having proclaimed a constitutional monarchy in Feb. 1951. A new constitution, approved in 1959, led to confrontation between the king and his ministers; it was replaced by one less liberal in 1962. In Nov. 1990 the king relinquished his absolute power. Nepal remains one of the poorest countries but a five-year plan encompasses economic reform with the hope of ending illiteracy among the young by 2005. The Maoists abandoned parliament in 1996 and launched a 'people's war' in the aim of turning the kingdom into a republic. This has resulted in more than 3,500 deaths.

In June 2001 the king and queen, along with six other members of the royal family, were shot dead by their son and heir to the throne, Crown Prince Dipendra, allegedly following a dispute over his choice of bride. Prince Dipendra then shot himself. The former monarch's younger brother, Gyanendra, was crowned king. In Nov. 2001 King Gyanendra declared a state of emergency and ordered troops to contain a fresh outbreak of Maoist violence. In Jan. 2003 the government and Maoist rebels reached a ceasefire agreement, seen as a first step towards bringing to an end the rebels' seven-year insurgency.

TERRITORY AND POPULATION

Nepal is bounded in the north by China (Tibet) and the east, south and west by India. Area 147,181 sq. km; population census 2001, 23,151,423 of which 11,587,502 were female; density 157·3 per sq. km. In 1999 the rural population was 88·4%.

The UN gives a projected population for 2010 of 28·46m.

The country is divided into five regions and subdivided into 14 zones. Area, population and administrative centres in 1991:

Zone/Region	Sq. km	Population (2001 census)	Administrative centre
Koshi	9,669	2,110,664	Biratnagar
Mechi	8,196	1,307,669	Ilam
Sagarmatha	10,591	1,926,143	Rajbiraj
East Region	28,456	5,344,476	Dhankuta
Bagmati	9,428	3,008,487	Káthmandu
Janakpur	9,669	2,557,004	Jaleswar
Narayani	8,313	2,466,138	Birganj
Central Region	27,410	8,031,629	Káthmandu

Zone/Region	Sq. km	Population (2001 census)	Administrative centre
Dhanlagiri	8,148	556,191	Baglung
Gandaki	12,275	1,487,954	Pokhara
Lumbini	8,975	2,526,868	Butwal
West Region	29,398	4,571,013	Pokhara
Bheri	10,545	1,417,085	Nepalganj
Karuali	21,351	309,084	Jumla
Rapti	10,482	1,286,806	Tulsipur
Mid-West Region	42,378	3,012,975	Surkhet
Mahakali	6,989	860,475	Mahendra Nagar
Seti	12,550	1,330,855	Dhangarhi
Far West Region	19,539	2,191,330	Dipayal

Capital, Káthmandu; population (2001) 671,846. Other towns include (2001 census population): Biratnagar, 166,674; Lalitpur, 162,991; Pokhara, 156,312.

The indigenous people are of Tibetan origin with a considerable Hindu admixture. The Gurkha clan became predominant in 1559 and has given its name to men from all parts of Nepal. There are 18 ethnic groups, the largest being: Newars, Indians, Tibetans, Gurungs, Mogars, Tamangs, Bhotias, Rais, Limbus and Sherpas. The official language is Nepalese but there are 20 new languages divided into numerous dialects.

SOCIAL STATISTICS
Births, 1995, 815,000; deaths, 257,000. 1995 birth rate per 1,000 population, 38·0; death rate, 12·0. Annual population growth rate, 1990–99, 2·5%. Expectation of life was 58·3 years for males and 57·8 years for females in 1999. Infant mortality, 1999, 75 per 1,000 live births; fertility rate, 1999, 4·3 births per woman.

CLIMATE
Varies from cool summers and severe winters in the north to sub-tropical summers and mild winters in the south. The rainfall is high, with maximum amounts from June to Sept., but conditions are very dry from Nov. to Jan. Káthmandu, Jan. 10°C, July, 25°C. Average annual rainfall, 1,424 mm.

CONSTITUTION AND GOVERNMENT
The sovereign is HM Maharajadhiraja **Gyanendra Bir Bikram Shah Dev** (b. 1947), who succeeded Crown Prince Dipendra on 4 June 2001 on the latter's death two days after he had shot and killed his father, the former king Birendra.

Under the constitution of 9 Nov. 1990 Nepal became a constitutional monarchy based on multi-party democracy. *Parliament* has two chambers: a 205-member House of Representatives (*Pratinidhi Sabha*) elected for five-year terms, and a 60-member National Council (*Rastriya Sabha*), of which ten members are nominated by the king. In Oct. 2002 King Gyanendra dismissed the prime minister and his cabinet and assumed full executive powers.

National Anthem. 'Sri man gumbhira nepali prachanda pratapi bhupati' ('May glory crown our illustrious sovereign, the gallant Nepalese'); words by C. Chalise, tune by B. Budhapirthi.

RECENT ELECTIONS
In parliamentary elections held on 3 and 17 May 1999 the Nepali Congress Party (NCP) won an absolute majority, winning 110 of the 205 seats and bringing an end to a succession of weak coalition governments. The Communist Party/Unified Marxist-Leninists won 68 seats, the National Democratic Party 11, Nepalese Goodwill Party 5, National People's Front 5, United People's Front 1, Nepalese Workers' and Farmers' Party 1. Four results were unavailable.

CURRENT ADMINISTRATION
On 4 Oct. 2002 King Gyanendra dismissed Prime Minister Sher Bahadur Deuba's government, following the latter's failure to arrange parliamentary elections for Nov. 2002. On 11 Oct. 2002 King Gyanendra appointed a new cabinet which in March 2003 was composed as follows:

Prime Minister and Minister of Defence and Royal Palace Affairs: Lokendra Bahadur Chand; b. 1939 (sworn in 11 Oct. 2002, having previously served between 1983–86; in 1990; and in 1997).

Deputy Prime Minister, Minister of Agriculture, and Co-operative and Local Development: Badri Prasad Mandal. *Foreign Affairs:* Narendra Bikram Shah. *Finance:* Badri Prasad Shrestha. *Education and Sports:* Devi Prasad Ohji. *Home Affairs, Law, Justice and Parliamentary Affairs:* Dharma Bahadur Thapa. *Women's Affairs, Children's Affairs and Social Welfare:* Gore Bahadur Khapangi. *Health, Science and Technology:* Upendra Devkota. *Labour and Transport Management, Population and Environment:* Kamal Prasad Chaulagai. *Industry, Commerce and Supplies:* Mahesh Lal Pradhan. *Culture, Tourism and Civil Aviation:* Kuber Prasad Sharma. *Land Reforms and Management, Forest and Soil Conservation:* Badri Narayan Basnet. *Information and Communications, General Administration:* Ramesh Nath Pandey. *Physical Planning and Construction:* Narayan Singh Pun. *Water Resources:* Deepak Gyawali.

Office of the Prime Minister: http://www.pmo.gov.np/

DEFENCE
The King is commander-in-chief of the armed forces, but shares supreme military authority with the National Defence Council, of which the Prime Minister is chairman.

Defence expenditure in 2000 totalled US$49m. (US$2 per capita), representing 0·9% of GDP.

Army. Strength (1999) 46,000, and there is also a 40,000-strong paramilitary police force.

Air Force. The Army's air wing has no combat aircraft. Personnel, 1999, 215.

INTERNATIONAL RELATIONS
Nepal is a member of the UN, the Asian Development Bank, the Colombo Plan, the SAARC and is a founding member of Non-aligned Movement (NAM).

ECONOMY
Agriculture accounted for 40·5% of GDP in 1998, industry 22·2% and services 37·3%.

Overview. Since May 1991 the government has been moving forward with economic reforms, particularly those that encourage trade and foreign investment, e.g. by eliminating business licenses and registration requirements to simplify investment. The government has also cut public expenditures by reducing subsidies, privatizing state industries, and laying off civil servants. Prospects for foreign trade and investment, particularly in areas other than power development and tourism, are limited by the small size of the economy, its remoteness and its susceptibility to natural disaster. The international community provides funding for 62% of Nepal's developmental budget and for 34% of total budgetary expenditures. Industrial activity is limited, mainly involving the processing of agricultural produce (jute, sugarcane, tobacco and grain). The production of textiles and carpets accounts for 85% of foreign exchange earnings. Apart from agricultural land and forests, exploitable natural resources are mica, hydropower and tourism. Agricultural production in the late 1980s grew by about 5%, compared to annual population growth of 2·6%.

Currency. The unit of currency is the *Nepalese rupee* (NPR) of 100 *paisas.* 50 *paisas* = 1 *mohur.* Inflation was 2·4% in 2001. Foreign exchange reserves were US$1,034m. in June 2002 and gold reserves totalled 15,000 troy oz (153,000 troy oz in April 2002). Total money supply in Dec. 2001 was NRs 72,161m.

Budget. Revenues and expenditures in NRs 1m. for fiscal years ending 14/15 July:

	1996–97	1997–98	1998–99	1999–2000	2000–01[1]
Revenue	29,344	31,492	34,809	40,484	46,836
Expenditure	47,073	51,964	54,720	60,794	77,285

[1]Provisional.

Performance. Real GDP growth was 6·2% in 2000 and 4·8% in 2001. Nepal's total GDP in 2001 was US$5·5bn.

Banking and Finance. The Central Bank is the bank of issue (*Governor*, Dr Tilak Rawal). There were 438 commercial bank branches in 1994 with total deposits of NRs 52,327·7m.

ENERGY AND NATURAL RESOURCES

Environment. According to the *World Bank Atlas* Nepal's carbon dioxide emissions in 1998 were the equivalent of 0·1 tonnes per capita.

Electricity. Installed capacity is 319,000 kW. Production in 1998 was 1·17bn. kWh, almost entirely hydro-electric. Consumption per capita in 1998 was 54 kWh.

Minerals. Production (in tonnes), 1995: limestone, 350,000; magnesite (1990), 25,000; salt, 7,000; talcum, 1,500; lignite (1994), 290.

Agriculture. Agriculture is the mainstay of the economy, accounting for 43% of income and providing a livelihood for over 80% of the population. Cultivated land accounts for 26·5% of land use; forest and woodland 42·4%. Crop production (2000, in 1,000 tonnes): rice, 4,030; sugarcane, 2,103; maize, 1,445; wheat, 1,184; potatoes, 1,183; millet, 295.

Livestock (2000); cattle, 7·03m.; buffaloes, 3·50m.; sheep, 870,000; goats, 6·50m.; pigs, 900,000; chickens, 18m.

Forestry. In 1995 the area under forests was 4·82m. ha, or 35·2% of the total land area (5·1m. ha and 37·3% in 1990). There are 8 national parks, covering 1m. ha, 5 wildlife reserves (170,490 ha) and 2 conservation areas (349,000 ha). Timber production was 21·96m. cu. metres in 1999, mainly for use as fuelwood and charcoal. Expansion of agricultural land has led to widespread deforestation.

Fisheries. The catch in 1999 was 12,752 tonnes, entirely from inland waters.

INDUSTRY

In 1992 there were 4,271 firms employing ten or more persons in which 223,463 persons were working. Production, 1994: cement (1996–97), 225,000 tonnes; soap, washing powder and detergents (1997), 29,000 tonnes; jute goods, 20,187 tonnes; animal feed, 19,500 tonnes; sugar (1998), 15,000 tonnes; paper (1998), 13,000 tonnes; tea, 2,351 tonnes; synthetic textiles, 14·7m. metres; electrical cable, 9·3m. metres; cotton fabrics, 5·1m. metres; leather, 1,369,750 sq. metres; shoes, 0·69m. pairs; beer (1997), 21·5m. litres. Brewing is one of the successes of Nepal's economy, accounting for some 3% of GDP.

Labour. The labour force in 1996 totalled 10,179,000 (60% males). In 1992, 84% of the economically active population were engaged in agriculture, forestry or fisheries.

INTERNATIONAL TRADE

External debt was an estimated US$2,823m. in 2000.

Imports and Exports. In 2000 imports (f.o.b.) amounted to US$1,578·3m. (US$1,494·2m. in 1999); exports (f.o.b.) US$785·7m. (US$612·3m. in 1999). Principal export commodities are carpets, clothing, leather goods, pulses, raw jute and jute goods, and handicrafts. Hand-knotted woollen carpets are the largest overseas export item constituting almost 32% of foreign exchange earnings. Main partners are India, USA, Germany, UK. Principal import commodities are petroleum products, transport equipment and parts, chemical fertilizer and raw wool. Main partners are India, Singapore, Japan, Germany.

COMMUNICATIONS

Roads. In 1998 there were 11,867 km of roads.

Rail. 101 km (762 mm gauge) connect Jayanagar on the North Eastern Indian Railway with Janakpur and thence with Bizalpura (54 km). 653,000 passengers and 9,151 tonnes of freight were carried in 1994.

Civil Aviation. There is an international airport (Tribhuvan) at Káthmandu. The national carrier is the state-owned Royal Nepal Airlines. It operates domestic services and in 1998 flew to Bangkok, Bombay, Calcutta, Delhi, Dubai, Frankfurt,

Hong Kong, London, Osaka, Paris, Shanghai and Singapore. In 1995 Káthmandu handled 1,357,000 passengers (868,000 on international flights) and 13·9m. tonnes of freight. In 1999 scheduled airline traffic of Nepali-based carriers flew 8·7m. km, carrying 583,000 passengers (452,000 on international flights).

Telecommunications. In 2000 Nepal had 266,900 main telephone lines (11·6 per 1,000 persons) and there were 70,000 PCs in use (3·0 for every 1,000 persons). There were 600 fax machines in 1995. In Dec. 2000 Nepal had 50,000 Internet users. Mobile phones have been introduced in Káthmandu.

Postal Services. In 1996 there were 3,885 post offices.

SOCIAL INSTITUTIONS

Justice. The Supreme Court Act established a uniform judicial system, culminating in a supreme court of a Chief Justice and no more than six judges. Special courts to deal with minor offences may be established at the discretion of the government. The Chief Justice is appointed by the king on recommendation of the Constitutional Council. Other judges are appointed by the king on the recommendation of the Judicial Council.

The death penalty was abolished in 1997.

Religion. Nepal is a Hindu state. Hinduism was the religion of 86·5% of the people in 1998. Buddhists comprise 7·8% and Muslims 3·5%. Christian missions are permitted, but conversion is forbidden.

Education. The adult literacy rate in 1999 was 40·4% (58·0% among males and 22·8% among females). Only Yemen has a bigger difference in literacy rates between the sexes. In 1998 there were 22,994 primary schools; 6,023 lower secondary schools; 3,178 secondary schools; and 310 higher secondary schools. There are five universities; the Tribhuvan University had 93,800 students and 4,300 academic staff in 1995–96.

Health. There were 872 doctors and 4,606 nurses in 1996. There were 82 hospitals with 3,604 beds, 17 health centres and 775 medical posts. More than 40% of the population is undernourished. In 1995 hospital bed provision was just two for every 10,000 persons.

CULTURE

Broadcasting. Radio Nepal is part government-owned and part commercial. It broadcasts in Nepali and English from three stations. The government-owned Nepal Television transmits from one station (colour by PAL). In 1997 there were 840,000 radio and 130,000 TV sets.

Press. In 1998 there were 166 daily newspapers, including the official English-language *Rising Nepal*, 3 bi-weeklies and 814 weeklies. Press censorship was relaxed in June 1991.

Tourism. Foreign tourists visiting Nepal numbered 298,100 in 2001, down from 376,500 in 2000, largely as a consequence of the massacre of the royal family and an upsurge in Maoist rebel violence. Revenue from tourism totalled US$166·8m. in 2000. In 1998, 27,612 hotel beds were available. Tourism accounts for approximately 4% of GDP.

DIPLOMATIC REPRESENTATIVES
Of Nepal in the United Kingdom (12A Kensington Palace Gdns., London, W8 4QU)
Ambassador: Dr Singha B. Basnyat.

Of the United Kingdom in Nepal (Lainchaur, Káthmandu, POB 106)
Ambassador: Keith Bloomfield.

Of Nepal in the USA (2131 Leroy Pl., NW, Washington, D.C., 20008)
Ambassador: Jai Pratap Rana.

Of the USA in Nepal (Pani Pokhari, Káthmandu)
Ambassador: Michael E. Malinowski.

Of Nepal to the United Nations
Ambassador: Murari Raj Sharma.

Of Nepal to the European Union
Ambassador: Narayan Shumshere Thapa.

FURTHER READING
Central Bureau of Statistics. *Statistical Pocket Book.* [Various years]

Borre, O., *et al.*, *Nepalese Political Behaviour.* Aarhus Univ. Press, 1994
Ghimire, K., *Forest or Farm? The Politics of Poverty and Land Hunger in Nepal.* OUP, 1993
Sanwal, D. B., *Social and Political History of Nepal.* London, 1993

National statistical office: Central Bureau of Statistics, National Planning Commission
Secretariat, Káthmandu

THE NETHERLANDS

Koninkrijk der Nederlanden
(Kingdom of the Netherlands)

Capital: Amsterdam
Seat of government: The Hague
Population estimate, 2000: 15·86m.
GDP per capita, 2000: (PPP$) 25,657
HDI/world rank: 0·935/8

KEY HISTORICAL EVENTS

As the German Count of Nassau, William of Orange (1533–84) inherited vast possessions in the Netherlands and the Princedom of Orange in France. The struggle for independence from Spain began in 1568 and by the Union of Utrecht the more easily defensible seven provinces of the North—Holland, Zeeland, Utrecht, Overijssel, Groningen, Drenthe and Friesland—declared themselves independent. At the end of the Thirty Years War, by the Treaty of Westphalia (1648), Spain recognized the Republic of the United Netherlands. In 1689 Willem III acceded to the throne of England, becoming joint sovereign with his wife Mary. Willem III died in 1702 without issue, and there was no stadhouder until a member of the Frisian branch of Orange–Nassau was nominated hereditary stadhouder in 1747. However, his successor, Willem V, had to take refuge in England in 1795 when the French invaded. The country was freed from French domination in Nov. 1813. The Congress of Vienna (1815) joined the Belgian provinces, called the 'Spanish' or the 'Austrian Netherlands' before the French Revolution, to the Northern Netherlands. The union was dissolved by the Belgian revolution of 1830 and in 1839 Belgium and the Netherlands were recognized as two independent kingdoms.

In 1840 Willem I abdicated in favour of his son, Willem II, who moved the Netherlands towards a constitutional monarchy, a process that continued under successive monarchs.

The Netherlands followed a policy of non-participation in the European conflicts of the early 20th century and during the First World War remained neutral. In the Second World War, however, the Netherlands was occupied by Germany from 1940 until 1945. After liberation in 1945, the country abandoned its traditional policy of neutrality. In 1948 the Netherlands joined with Belgium and Luxembourg to form the Benelux economic union; in 1957 it was a founder member of the EEC, and in 1949 joined NATO.

TERRITORY AND POPULATION

The Netherlands is bounded in the north and west by the North Sea, south by Belgium and east by Germany. The area is 41,526 sq. km, of which 33,883 sq. km is land. Projects of sea-flood control and land reclamation (polders) by the construction of dams and drainage schemes have continued since 1920. More than a quarter of the country is below sea level.

The population was 13,060,115 at the census of 1971 and estimated to be 15,987,000 at the end of 2000 (8,077,000 females). Population growth in 2000, 0·65%. On 8 March 2001 the population reached 16m.

The UN gives a projected population for 2010 of 16·31m.

On-going 'rolling' censuses have replaced the former decennial counts.

Area, estimated population and density, and chief towns of the 12 provinces on 1 Jan. 2000:

	Area 1995 (in sq. km)	Population 2000	Density 2000 per sq. km land area	Provincial capital
Groningen	2,967·10	562,600	240	Groningen
Friesland	5,740·75	624,500	186	Leeuwarden
Drenthe	2,680·49	469,800	177	Assen
Overijssel	3,420·06	1,077,600	323	Zwolle
Flevoland	2,412·29	317,200	223	Lelystad
Gelderland	5,143·36	1,919,200	385	Arnhem
Utrecht	1,434·24	1,107,800	813	Utrecht
Noord-Holland	4,059·09	2,518,400	948	Haarlem

	Area 1995 (in sq. km)	Population 2000	Density 2000 per sq. km land area	Provincial capital
Zuid-Holland[1]	3,445·75	3,397,700	1,185	The Hague
Zeeland	2,931·91	371,900	206	Middelburg
Noord-Brabant	5,081·83	2,356,000	478	's-Hertogenbosch
Limburg	2,209·29	1,141,200	527	Maastricht
Total	41,526·16	15,864,000	468	

[1]Since 29 Sept. 1994 includes inhabitants of the municipality of The Hague formerly registered in the abolished Central Population Register.

In 1999, 89·3% of the population lived in urban areas.

Population of municipalities with over 50,000 inhabitants on 1 Jan. 2000:

Alkmaar	92,836	Gouda	71,918	Oosterhout	52,291
Almelo	66,263	Groningen	173,139	Oss	65,763
Almere	142,765	Haarlem	148,484	Purmerend	70,284
Alphen a/d Rijn	69,928	Haarlemmermeer	111,155	Rijswijk	51,922
Amersfoort	126,143	The Hague	441,094	Roosendaal	75,157
Amstelveen	77,623	Heerlen	95,147	Rotterdam	592,673
Amsterdam	731,288	Den Helder	59,441	Schiedam	75,589
Apeldoorn	153,261	Helmond	80,098	Smallingerland	52,437
Arnhem	138,154	Hengelo	79,751	Spijkenisse	71,831
Assen	58,445	's-Hertogenbosch	129,034	Tilburg	193,116
Bergen op Zoom	65,104	Hilversum	82,177	Utrecht	233,667
Breda	160,615	Hoogeveen	52,790	Veenendaal	59,875
Capelle a/d Ijssel	64,251	Hoorn	64,604	Velsen	66,553
Delft	96,095	Kerkrade	51,458	Venlo	64,864
Deventer	83,956	Leeuwarden	88,887	Vlaardingen	73,535
Dordrecht	119,821	Leiden	117,191	Zaanstad	135,762
Ede	101,700	Lelystad	63,098	Zeist	60,020
Eindhoven	201,728	Maastricht	122,070	Zoetermeer	109,941
Emmen	105,972	Nieuwegein	63,118	Zwolle	105,801
Enschede	149,505	Nijmegen	152,200		

Urban agglomerations as at 1 Jan. 2000: Amsterdam, 1,002,868; Rotterdam, 989,956; The Hague, 610,245; Utrecht, 366,186; Eindhoven, 302,274; Leiden, 250,302; Dordrecht, 241,218; Heerlen, 218,078; Tilburg, 215,419; Groningen, 191,722; Haarlem, 191,079; Breda, 160,615; Amersfoort, 154,890; 's-Hertogenbosch, 154,368; Apeldoorn, 153,261; Nijmegen, 152,200; Enschede, 149,505; Arnhem, 139,576; Geleen-Sittard, 127,322; Maastricht, 122,070; Zwolle, 105,801.

The Hague: A coastal city in the south of the Netherlands, The Hague is the home of the Dutch Queen, the national parliament and the International Court of Justice. The Hague's port, Scheveningen, is a popular coastal resort for Dutch holiday-makers as well as an important centre for herring fishing.

Amsterdam: Lying on the rivers Amstel and IJ in the north of the Netherlands, Amsterdam possesses important financial, diamond cutting and polishing trades as well as strong shipbuilding and brewing industries. Since the 1960s the city has also reinvented itself as a centre for radicalism, both in terms of relaxed drugs legislation, strong environmental policies and the decentralization of council power. Amsterdam has a thriving tourist industry and possesses magnificent collections of Dutch, Flemish and modern art.

The first national language is Dutch and the second is Friesian.

SOCIAL STATISTICS

Vital statistics for calendar years:

	Live births		Marriages	Divorces	Deaths
	Total	Outside marriage			
1997	192,443	36,863	85,059	33,740	135,783
1998	199,408	41,439	86,956	32,459	137,482
1999	200,445	45,592	89,428	33,571	140,487
2000	206,619	51,539	88,074	34,650	140,527
2001	201,461	55,080	82,819	37,505	140,729

2001 rates per 1,000 population: birth, 12·5; death, 8·7. Annual population growth rate, 1990–99, 0·6%. Over 1990–95 the suicide rate per 100,000 population was 9·7 (men, 12·3; women, 7·2). In 1997 the average age of marrying was 33·2 years for males and 30·4 for females. Expectation of life, 1999, was 75·3 years for males and 80·7 for females. Infant mortality, 1999, 5·2 per 1,000 live births; fertility rate, 1999, 1·5 births per woman. The annual abortion rate, at under 8 per 1,000 women aged 15–44, is among the lowest in the world. Percentage of population by age in 2000: 0–19 years, 24·4%; 20–39, 30·0%; 40–64, 32·0%; 65 and over, 13·6%. In 2000 the Netherlands received 43,900 asylum applications, equivalent to 2·78 per 1,000 inhabitants.

CLIMATE
A cool temperate maritime climate, marked by mild winters and cool summers, but with occasional continental influences. Coastal temperatures vary from 37°F (3°C) in winter to 61°F (16°C) in summer, but inland the winters are slightly colder and the summers slightly warmer. Rainfall is least in the months Feb. to May, but inland there is a well-defined summer maximum in July and Aug.

The Hague, Jan. 37°F (2·7°C), July 61°F (16·3°C). Annual rainfall 32·8" (820 mm). Amsterdam, Jan. 36°F (2·3°C), July 62°F (16·5°C). Annual rainfall 34" (850 mm). Rotterdam, Jan. 36·5°F (2·6°C), July 62°F (16·6°C). Annual rainfall 32" (800 mm).

CONSTITUTION AND GOVERNMENT
According to the Constitution (promulgated 1814; last revision, 1983), the Kingdom consists of the Netherlands, Aruba and the Netherlands Antilles. Their relations are regulated by the 'Statute' for the Kingdom, which came into force on 29 Dec. 1954. Each part enjoys full autonomy; they are united, on a footing of equality, for mutual assistance and the protection of their common interests.

The Netherlands is a constitutional and hereditary monarchy.

The reigning Queen is **Beatrix Wilhelmina Armgard,** born 31 Jan. 1938, daughter of Queen Juliana and Prince Bernhard; married to Claus von Amsberg on 10 March 1966 (born 6 Sept. 1926, died 6 Oct. 2002); succeeded to the crown on 30 April 1980, on the abdication of her mother. *Offspring:* Prince Willem-Alexander, born 27 April 1967, married to Máxima Zorreguieta on 2 Feb. 2002; Prince Johan Friso, born 25 Sept. 1968; Prince Constantijn, born 11 Oct. 1969, married to Laurentien Brinkhorst on 19 May 2001 (*offspring:* Eloise, born 8 June 2002).

The Queen receives an allowance from the civil list. This was 7·5m. guilders in 1999; and that of Crown Prince Willem-Alexander, 1·8m. guilders. Princess Juliana and Prince Bernhard also receive allowances from the civil list.

Mother of the Queen. Princess Juliana Louise Emma Marie Wilhelmina, born 30 April 1909, daughter of Queen Wilhelmina (born 31 Aug. 1880, died 28 Nov. 1962) and Prince Henry of Mecklenburg-Schwerin (born 19 April 1876, died 3 July 1934); married to Prince Bernhard Leopold Frederik Everhard Julius Coert Karel Godfried Pieter of Lippe-Biesterfeld (born 29 June 1911) on 7 Jan. 1937. Invested as Queen on 6 Sept. 1948 and abdicated in favour of her daughter, the Reigning Queen, on 30 April 1980.

Sisters of the Queen. Princess Irene Emma Elisabeth, born 5 Aug. 1939, married to Prince Charles Hugues de Bourbon-Parma on 29 April 1964, divorced 1981 (*sons:* Prince Carlos Javier Bernardo, born 27 Jan. 1970; Prince Jaime Bernardo, born 13 Oct. 1972; *daughters:* Princess Margarita Maria Beatriz, born 13 Oct. 1972; Princess Maria Carolina Christina, born 23 June 1974); Princess Margriet Francisca, born in Ottawa, 19 Jan. 1943, married to Pieter van Vollenhoven on 10 Jan. 1967 (*sons:* Prince Maurits, born 17 April 1968; Prince Bernhard, born 25 Dec. 1969; Prince Pieter-Christiaan, born 22 March 1972; Prince Floris, born 10 April 1975); Princess Maria Christina, born 18 Feb. 1947, married to Jorge Guillermo on 28 June 1975 (*sons:* Bernardo, born 17 June 1977; Nicolas, born 6 July 1979; *daughter:* Juliana, born 8 Oct. 1981).

The royal succession is in the direct female or male line in order of birth.

The central executive power of the State rests with the Crown, while the central legislative power is vested in the Crown and Parliament (the *States-General*), consisting of two Chambers. The upper *First Chamber* is composed of 75 members, elected by the members of the Provincial States. The 150-member *Second Chamber* is directly elected by proportional representation for four-year terms. Members of the States-General must be Netherlands subjects of 18 years of age or over.

The *Council of State*, appointed by the Crown, is composed of a vice-president and not more than 28 members. The monarch is president, but the day-to-day running of the Council is in the hands of the vice-president. The Council has to be consulted on all legislative matters.

The Hague is the seat of the Court, government and Parliament; Amsterdam is the capital.

The Sovereign has the power to dissolve either Chambers, subject to the condition that new elections take place within 40 days, and the new Chamber be convoked within three months.

Both the government and the Second Chamber may propose Bills; the First Chamber can only approve or reject them without inserting amendments. The meetings of both Chambers are public, although each of them may by a majority vote decide on a secret session. A Minister or Secretary of State cannot be a member of Parliament at the same time.

National Anthem. 'Wilhelmus van Nassaue'; words by Philip Marnix van St Aldegonde, tune anonymous.

RECENT ELECTIONS

Party affiliation in the First Chamber as elected on 2 March 1999: Christian Democrat Appeal (CDA), 20 seats; People's Party for Freedom and Democracy (VVD), 19 Labour Party (PvdA), 15; Green Left, 8; Democrats '66 (D66), 4; Socialist Party (SP), 2; Reformation Political Federation (RFP), 2; Reformed Political League (GPV), 2; Political Reformed Party (SGP), 2; Independent Group in the Senate, 1.

Elections to the Second Chamber were held on 22 Jan. 2003. The CDA won 44 seats with 28·6% of votes cast (42 seats at the 2002 election); the PvdA, 42 seats and 27·3% (23 in 2002); the VVD, 28 seats and 17·9% (24); SP, 9 seats and 6·3% (9); the List Pim Fortuyn party (LPF), 8 seats and 5·7% (26); the Green Left, 8 seats and 5·1% (10); D66, 6 seats and 4·1% (7); the Christian Union party, 3 seats and 2·1% (4); SGP, 2 seats and 1·6% (2). Turn-out was 79·9%.

European Parliament. The Netherlands has 31 representatives. At the June 1999 elections turn-out was 29·9%. The CDA won 9 seats with 26·9% of votes cast (group in European Parliament: European People's Party); the PvdA, 6 with 20·1% (Party of European Socialists); the VVD, 6 with 19·7% (Liberal, Democrat and Reform Party); Greens, 4 with 11·9% (Greens); GPV/RPF/SGP, 3 with 8·7% (Independents for a Europe of Nations); D66, 2 with 5·8% (European Liberal, Democrat and Reform Party); SP, 1 with 5·0% (Confederal Group of the United European Left/Nordic Green Left).

CURRENT ADMINISTRATION

Prime Minister: Jan Peter Balkenende; b. 1956 (CDA).

A coalition government of CDA, VVD and D66 was sworn in on 27 May 2003:
    Deputy Prime Minister and Minister of Finance: Gerrit Zalm (VVD). *Deputy Prime Minister, Minister for Government Reform and Kingdom Relations:* Thom de Graaf (D66). *Foreign Affairs:* Jaap de Hoop Scheffer (CDA). *Justice:* Piet Hein Donner (CDA). *Interior and Kingdom Relations:* Johan Remkes (VVD). *Education, Culture and Science:* Maria van der Hoeven (CDA). *Defence:* Henk Kamp (VVD). *Housing, Spatial Planning and the Environment:* Sybilla Dekker (VVD). *Transport, Public Works and Water Management:* Karla Peijs (CDA). *Economic Affairs:* Laurens Jan Brinkhorst (D66). *Agriculture, Nature Management and Fisheries:* Cees Veerman (CDA). *Health, Welfare and Sport:* Hans Hoogervorst (VVD). *Development Cooperation:* Agnes van Ardenne (CDA). *Immigration and Integration:* Rita Verdonk (VVD).

Office of the Prime Minister: http://www.minaz.nl

DEFENCE

The total strength of the armed forces in 1999 was 56,380, including 1,920 women. In 2000 defence expenditure totalled US$6,392m. (US$405 per capita), representing 1·9% of GDP. Conscription ended on 30 Aug. 1996.

Army. The 1st Netherlands Army Corps is assigned to NATO. It consists of ten brigades and Corps troops.

Personnel in 1999 numbered 27,000. The National Territorial Command forces consist of territorial brigades, security forces, some logistical units and staffs. Some units in the Netherlands may be assigned to the UN as peacekeeping forces. The army is responsible for the training of these units.

There is a paramilitary Royal Military Constabulary, 3,600 strong. In addition there are 60,000 army reservists.

Navy. The principal headquarters and main base of the Royal Netherlands Navy is at Den Helder, with minor bases at Vlissingen (Flushing), Curaçao (Netherlands Antilles) and Oranjestad (Aruba). Command and control in home waters is exercised jointly with the Belgian Navy (submarines excepted).

The combatant fleet includes 4 diesel submarines, 4 destroyers and 12 frigates. In 1999 personnel totalled 13,800 (1,200 women), including 950 in the Naval Air Service and 2,800 in the Royal Netherlands Marine Corps.

Air Force. The Royal Netherlands Air Force (RNLAF) had 11,980 personnel in 1999 (720 women). It has a first-line combat force of 170 combat aircraft (with 11 in store) and 42 armed helicopters. Equipment includes F-16A/Bs. All squadrons are operated by Tactical Air Command.

INTERNATIONAL RELATIONS

The Netherlands is a member of the UN, WTO, NATO, BIS, OECD, EU, Council of Europe, WEU, OSCE, CERN, Inter-American Development Bank, Asian Development Bank, IOM and the Antarctic Treaty. The Netherlands is a signatory of the Schengen Accord which abolishes border controls between the Netherlands and Austria, Belgium, Denmark, Finland, France, Germany, Greece, Iceland, Italy, Luxembourg, Norway, Portugal, Spain and Sweden.

In 1899 the first International Peace Conference was held in The Hague with the aim of developing mechanisms of interventional law to contribute to disarmament, the prevention of war, and the peaceful settlement of disputes. In 1999 The Hague Appeal for Peace 1999 Conference brought together a wide variety of organizations, activists, citizens and world leaders to discuss new projects and initiatives for the promotion of peace in the 21st century from 11–16 May 1999.

The Hague is the seat of several international organizations, including the International Court of Justice.

ECONOMY

Agriculture accounted for an estimated 3·1% of GDP in 1998, industry 26·9% and services 70·0%.

According to the anti-corruption organization *Transparency International*, the Netherlands ranked equal 7th in the world in a 2002 survey of the countries with the least corruption in business and government. It received 9·0 out of 10 in the annual index.

Overview. The economy is characterized by one of the highest levels of average income. The country's geographical position and the small market makes the economy open and outward looking. Multinationals enjoy a favourable tax regime. Government policy is based on free market principles including the introduction of market forces in to the public utilities. The Netherlands is a leader in structural and regulatory reform in Europe, but reforms have slowed down. In 2002 the tax system was reformed. The change shifts the burden from direct taxation to indirect and environmental taxes.

Currency. On 1 Jan. 1999 the euro (EUR) became the legal currency in the Netherlands; irrevocable conversion rate 2·20371 guilders to 1 euro. The euro, which consists of 100 cents, has been in circulation since 1 Jan. 2002. There are seven euro notes in different colours and sizes denominated in 500, 200, 100, 50, 20, 10 and 5 euros, and eight coins denominated in 2 and 1 euros, then 50, 20, 10, 5, 2 and 1 cents. On the introduction of the euro there was a 'dual circulation' period before the guilder ceased to be legal tender on 28 Jan. 2002. Euro banknotes in circulation on 1 Jan. 2002 had a total value of €29·7bn.

Gold reserves were 28·15m. troy oz in June 2002 and foreign exchange reserves US$5,290m. (US$31,060m. in 1995). Inflation was 4·5% in 2001, the highest level for nearly 20 years. Total money supply was €16,206m. in June 2002.

Budget. The revenue and expenditure of the central government were, in 1m. euros, for calendar years:

	1996	1997	1998	1999[1]
Revenue	79,122	82,657	86,082	92,286
Expenditure	81,511	84,851	88,275	91,346

[1]Provisional.

As from Jan. 2001 VAT is 19·0% (reduced rate, 6·0%).

Performance. Real GDP growth in 2001 was 1·4%, having averaged nearly 4% between 1997 and 2000. In 2001 total GDP was US$375·0bn.

Banking and Finance. The central bank and bank of issue is the Netherlands Bank (*President*, Arnout Wellink), founded in 1814 and nationalized in 1948. Its Governor is appointed by the government for seven-year terms. The capital amounts to 75m. guilders.

There is a stock exchange in Amsterdam; it is a component of Euronext, which was created in Sept. 2000 through the merger of the Amsterdam, Brussels and Paris bourses.

Weights and Measures. The metric system is in use.

ENERGY AND NATURAL RESOURCES

Environment. According to the *World Bank Atlas* carbon dioxide emissions in 1998 were the equivalent of 10·4 tonnes per capita.

The Netherlands is one of the world leaders in recycling. In 1998, 46% of all household waste was recycled, including 84% of glass.

Electricity. Installed capacity is 20m. kW in 1997. Production of electrical energy in 1998 was 88·74bn. kWh (approximately 6% nuclear); consumption per capita was 5,908 kWh. 790 windmills were installed in 1994 to produce 238m. kWh. There was one nuclear reactor in operation in 2001.

Oil and Gas. Production of natural gas in 1999, 75,002m. cu. metres. Reserves in 1999 were 1,770bn. cu. metres. In 1996 crude oil production was 22m. bbls., with reserves 88m. bbls. in 1997.

Minerals. In 1998, 5·5m. tonnes of salt were produced.

Agriculture. The Netherlands is one of the world's largest exporters of agricultural produce. There were 120,000 farms in 1998. Agriculture accounted for 22·8% of exports and 15·1% of imports in 1998. The agricultural sector employs 2·7% of the workforce. The total area of cultivated land in 2000 was 1,955,500 ha: grassland, 1,011,900 ha; arable crops, 806,200 ha; horticultural crops, 112,000 ha, of which 101,400 ha was in the open and 10,500 ha was under glass; fallow land, 25,500 ha. In 2000, 282,099 people were employed in agriculture (91,270 women).

The yield of the more important arable crops, in 1,000 tonnes, was as follows:

Crop	1998	1999	2000
Potatoes	5,249·4	8,221·1	8,126·8
Sugarbeets	5,504·5	7,317·4	6,727·5
Wheat	1,072·0	851·4	1,183·3
Sown onions	652·4	755·0	815·0
Barley	214·5	364·5	318·8

Other major fruit and vegetable production in 2000 included (in 1,000 tonnes): tomatoes, 600; apples, 575; cucumbers and gherkins, 465; cabbages, 284; carrots, 274; chillies and green peppers, 250; pears, 125.

Cultivated areas of main flowers (1998) in 1,000 ha: tulips, 10·0; lilies, 3·8; gladioli, 1·9; daffodils, 1·6; hyacinths, 1·2.

Livestock, 2000 (in 1,000) included: 13,118 pigs; 4,070 cattle; 1,308 sheep; 118 horses and ponies; 105,559 turkeys and chickens.

Animal products in 2000 (in 1,000 tonnes) included: pork, bacon and ham, 1,643; beef and veal, 485; poultry, 713; milk, 10,800; cheese, 690; butter, 126; hens' eggs, 660.

Forestry. Forests covered 334,000 ha in 1995, or 9·8% of the land area. In 1999, 1·04m. cu. metres of roundwood were cut.

Fisheries. Marine catch in 1999 totalled 514,611 tonnes (chiefly scad, herring, mackerel and plaice). There were 1,114 fishing vessels in 1999.

INDUSTRY

The leading companies by market capitalization in the Netherlands, excluding banking and finance, in Jan. 2002 were: Royal Dutch Petroleum Company (€119bn.); Unilever NV (€63bn.), a consumer goods firm; and Koninklijke Philips Electronics NV (€37bn.). At 31 Dec. 1999 there were 6,572 enterprises in the manufacturing industry, of which 3,689 had 20–49 employees and 182 had 500 employees or more; total annual sales for 1997 were 151,229m. euros.

The three largest industrial sectors are chemicals, food processing and metal, mechanical and electrical engineering. The food products and beverages industry employed 111,845 people at 30 Sept. 1998 (annual sales for 1998 in €1m., 40,415); electrical machinery and apparatus, 75,291 (12,524); machinery and equipment, 70,949 (10,535); other fabricated metal products, 69,646 (9,688); chemicals and chemical products, 68,436 (26,060); publishing, printing and reproduction of recorded media, 56,130 (8,902); transport equipment, 43,198 (10,401); rubber and plastic products, 27,936 (4,480).

Labour. The total labour force in 1999 was 7,097,000 persons (2,856,000 women) of whom 292,000 (172,000) were unemployed, with 221,000 (106,000) registered unemployed. By education level, the 1999 labour force included (in 1,000): primary education, 564; junior general secondary, 504; pre-vocational secondary, 970; senior general secondary, 395; senior vocational secondary, 2,692; vocational colleges, 1,309; university, 652.

The unemployment rate was 3·1% in Dec. 2002—only Luxembourg among EU member countries had a lower rate.

Although the Netherlands has a very low unemployment rate, for every 100 people below the age of 65 who are active in the labour market, 35 are not. In 1995 the average age for retirement among males was 58.

In 1999 the weekly working hours (excluding overtime) of employees were 35·8 for men and 25·4 for women. In 1999 full-time employees' working hours (excluding overtime) totalled 1,709; part-time 947, and flexible 879. Workers in the Netherlands put in among the shortest hours of any industrialized country. In 1996 only 11% of male workers and 4% of female workers worked more than 40 hours a week. In 2001 part-time work accounted for approximately 33% of all employment in the Netherlands—the highest percentage in any major industrialized country. 76·3% of part-time workers in 2001 were women. Average annual gross earnings of employees in 1999 were 25,500 guilders for men and 14,200 guilders for women. In 1999 gross hourly wage earnings (in euros) by type of employment ranged from €23·86 in mining and quarrying, €19·47 in public utilities and €18·93 in education to €9·42 in hotels and restaurants.

Trade Unions. Trade unions are grouped in three central federations: Christian National Trade Union Confederation (CNV), Trade Union Confederation for Middle and Higher Management (MHP) and General Netherlands Trade Union Confederation (FNV). (A fourth federation, AVC, was merged with the FNV in 1997). Total membership was 1·8m. in 2000, approximately 30% of waged employees. In Nov. 1993 an agreement on wage restraint was concluded between the trade unions and the employers' federations, in return for an enhancement of the roles of works committees and professional training for employees.

INTERNATIONAL TRADE

On 5 Sept. 1944 and 14 March 1947 the Netherlands signed agreements with Belgium and Luxembourg for the establishment of a customs union. On 1 Jan. 1948 this union came into force and the existing customs tariffs of the Belgium–Luxembourg Economic Union and of the Netherlands were superseded by the joint Benelux Customs Union Tariff. It applied to imports into the three countries from outside sources, and exempted from customs duties all imports into each of the three countries from the other two.

Imports and Exports. Imports and exports for calendar years (in US$1m.):

	1996	1997	1998	1999	2000
Imports f.o.b.	172,312	168,051	175,222	179,426	187,107
Exports f.o.b.	195,079	188,988	196,277	197,359	205,653

Value of trade with major partners (in €1m.):

Country	Imports 1999	Exports 1999	Imports (% change on 1998)	Exports (% change on 1998)
Belgium–Luxembourg	17,903	23,029	+1	+2
Denmark	1,932	3,038	+7	0
France	11,565	20,306	−1	+5
Germany	34,426	49,192	+4	+3
Italy	5,652	11,236	0	+7
Japan	7,566	1,985	+5	+22
Spain	3,772	6,542	−4	+7
Sweden	4,787	4,482	+6	+2
Switzerland	2,396	3,314	+14	+7
UK	17,371	20,281	+6	+10
USA	16,963	7,982	+9	+12

The main imports in 1999 (in €1m.) included machines (including electrical machines), 56,365; chemical products, 19,651; food and live animals, 15,364; road vehicles, 14,349; crude petroleum, 7,197; clothing, 5,896; iron and steel, 3,769; oil products, 3,095; non-ferrous metals, 2,947; paper and paperboard, 2,793. Main exports included machines (including electrical machines), 52,489; chemical products, 28,792; food and live animals, 25,225; road vehicles, 10,153; oil products, 7,931; fruit and vegetables, 6,821; beverages and tobacco, 4,760; meat, 3,891; clothing, 3,298; iron and steel, 3,178; natural and manufactured gas, 2,740.

COMMUNICATIONS

Roads. In 1998 the length of the Netherlands road network was 125,575 km, including 2,235 km motorways. 90% of roads are paved. Number of private cars (2000), 6·34m.; trucks and vans, 0·78m.; motorcycles and mopeds (1998), 1·05m. There were 1,082 fatalities as a result of road accidents in 2000.

Rail. All railways are run by the mixed company 'N.V. Nederlandse Spoorwegen'. Route length in 1999 was 2,808 km. Passengers carried (1999), 329m.; goods transported, 23·2m. tonnes. There is a metro (23 km) and tram/light rail network (153 km) in Amsterdam and in Rotterdam (28 km and 141 km). Tram/light rail networks operate in The Hague (122 km) and Utrecht (28 km).

Civil Aviation. There are international airports at Amsterdam (Schiphol), Rotterdam, Maastricht and Eindhoven. The Royal Dutch Airlines (KLM) was founded on 7 Oct. 1919. In 1999 it flew 357·9m. km, carrying 15,568,200 passengers (15,437,400 on international flights). Services were provided in 1998 by around 90 foreign airlines. In 2000 Amsterdam handled 39,271,000 passengers (39,100,000 on international flights) and 1,222,600 tonnes of freight. Rotterdam is the second busiest airport, handling 619,000 passengers in 1999, followed by Maastricht, with 297,000 in 1999.

Sea-going Shipping. Survey of the Netherlands mercantile marine as at 1 Jan. (capacity in 1,000 GRT):

Ships under Netherlands flag	1999 Number	1999 Capacity	2000 Number	2000 Capacity
Passenger ships[1]	12	461	13	522
Freighters (100 GRT and over)	454	2,725	489	2,968
Tankers	58	456	56	481
	524	3,642	558	3,971

[1]With accommodation for 13 or more cabin passengers.

In 1999, 42,433 sea-going ships (including 7,128 Dutch-registered ships) of 549·54m. gross tons entered Netherlands ports.

Total goods traffic by sea-going ships in 1999 (with 1998 figures in brackets), in 1m. tonnes, amounted to 305 (320) unloaded and 92 (85) loaded; total seaborne goods traffic in 1999 (and 1998) at Rotterdam was 299·1 (306·9) and at Amsterdam 36·5 (35·2).

The number of containers (including flats) at Dutch ports in 1999 (and 1998) was: unloaded from ships, 2,035,000 (1,992,000), and 1,971,000 (1,906,000) loaded into ships.

Inland Shipping. The total length of navigable rivers and canals is 5,046 km, of which 2,398 km is for ships with a capacity of 1,000 and more tonnes. On 1 Jan. 2000 the inland fleet used for transport (with carrying capacity in 1,000 tonnes) was composed as follows:

	Number	Capacity
Self-propelled barges	3,746	3,826
Dumb barges	283	222
Pushed barges	542	1,235
	4,571	5,283

In 1999, 234·2m. tonnes of goods were transported on rivers and canals, of which 135·1m. tonnes was by international shipping. Goods transport on the Rhine across the Dutch–German frontier near Lobith amounted to 152·2m. tonnes.

Telecommunications. The Netherlands had 9,879,000 telephone main lines in 2000 (equivalent to 617·9 per 1,000 population), and there were 6·3m. PCs (394·1 per 1,000 persons). In 1997 there were 600,000 fax machines. Mobile phone subscribers numbered 8·65m. in Nov. 2000, and there were 9·73m. Internet users in Sept. 2002.

Postal Services. In 1998 there were 2,387 post offices, equivalent to one for every 6,580 persons.

SOCIAL INSTITUTIONS

Justice. Justice is administered by the High Court (Court of Cassation), by five courts of justice (Courts of Appeal), by 19 district courts and by 61 cantonal courts. The Cantonal Court, which deals with minor offences, comprises a single judge; more serious cases are tried by the district courts, comprising as a rule three judges (in some cases one judge is sufficient); the courts of appeal are constituted of three and the High Court of five judges. All judges are appointed for life by the Sovereign (the judges of the High Court from a list prepared by the Second Chamber of the States-General). They can be removed only by a decision of the High Court.

At the district court the juvenile judge is specially appointed to try children's civil cases and at the same time charged with administration of justice for criminal actions committed by young persons between 12 and 18 years old, unless imprisonment of more than six months ought to be inflicted; such cases are tried by three judges.

The population in penal institutions at 31 Dec. 1999 was 11,872, of which 5,572 were convicted. The total number of inmates during the year was 42,251 (39,376 men). 1,284,300 crimes were reported in 1999.

Police. The police force is divided into 25 regions. There is also a National Police Service which includes the Central Criminal Investigation Office, which deals with serious crimes throughout the country, and the International Criminal Investigation Office, which informs foreign countries of international crimes.

Religion. Entire liberty of conscience is granted to the members of all denominations. The royal family belong to the Dutch Reformed Church.

According to estimates of 1999, the distribution of the population aged 18 years and over was: Roman Catholics, 31%; Dutch Reformed Church, 14%; Calvinist, 7%; other creeds, 8%; no religion, 41%. The government of the Reformed Church is Presbyterian. On 1 July 1992 the Dutch Reformed Church had 1 synod, 9 provincial districts, 75 classes, about 160 districts and about 2,000 parishes. Their clergy numbered 1,735. The Roman Catholic Church had, Jan. 1992, 1 archbishop (of Utrecht), 6 bishops, 4 assistant bishops and about 1,750 parishes and rectorships. The Old Catholics had (1 July 1992) 1 archbishop (Utrecht), 1 bishop and 28 parishes. The Jews had, in 1992, 40 communities. At 1 Jan. 2000 there were an estimated 735,600 Muslims (4·6% of the population) and 86,100 Hindus (0·5%).

Education. Statistics for the scholastic year 1999–2000:

	Schools	Full-time Pupils/Students (in 1,000) Total
Primary education	7,224	1,543
Special education	1,255	125
General secondary education	635	861
Vocational training courses	75	272
Block or day release courses	70	143
Vocational colleges	65	250
University education	13	150

Academic Year 2000–01

	Full-time Students Total	% female
University education:		
Agriculture	3,724	49
Behaviour and Social Sciences	32,133	69
Economics	27,236	29
Education	685	58
Engineering	24,066	18
Health	19,956	62
Language and Culture	21,334	64
Law	24,949	54
Science	12,464	33
Other	401	56
Total	166,948	48

In 1998–99 there were 115,600 participants in adult basic education; and, in 2000–01, 20,100 Open University students.

In 1996 total expenditure on education came to 5·1% of GNP and represented 9·8% of total government expenditure. The adult literacy rate is at least 99%.

Health. On 1 Jan. 2000 there were 7,704 general practitioners; on 1 Jan. 1999, a total of 14,345 specialists, 12,035 physiotherapists and 1,507 midwives; and on 1 Jan. 1998, 7,030 dentists and 1,547 pharmacists. There were 136 hospitals and 57,224 licensed hospital beds (excluding mental hospitals) at 1 Jan. 1999. The 1919 Opium Act (amended in 1928 and 1976) regulates the production and consumption of 'psychoactive' drugs. Personal use of cannabis is effectively decriminalized and the sale of soft drugs through 'coffee shops' is not prosecuted provided certain conditions are met. Euthanasia became legal when the First Chamber (the Senate) gave its formal approval on 10 April 2001 by 46 votes to 28. The Second Chamber had voted to make it legal by 104 votes to 40 in Nov. 2000. The law came into effect on 1 April 2002. During 2000 euthanasia organizations recorded 2,123 instances of doctors helping patients to die. The Netherlands was the first country to legalize euthanasia.

Welfare. The General Old Age Pension Act (AOW) entitles everyone to draw an old age pension from the age of 65. At 31 Dec. 1999 there were 2,305,400 persons entitled to receive an old age pension, and 174,100 a pension under the Surviving Relatives Insurance; 1,826,800 parents were receiving benefits under the General Family Allowances Act. In 1999 there were 918,000 persons claiming labour disablement benefits, and in 1997 there were 382,500 persons claiming benefits under the Unemployment Act.

CULTURE

Broadcasting. Public broadcasting programmes are provided by broadcasting associations representing clearly identifiable social or religious ideals or groupings. The six associations work together in the Netherlands Broadcasting Corporation, *Nederlandse Omroepprogramma Stichting* (NOS). There are three national television channels (colour by PAL) and five radio stations. In addition, there are regional radio stations in every province, a limited number of regional television stations and 400 local radio stations. Commercial broadcasting was introduced in 1992. Dutch-language commercial companies include RTL 4 and 5 which broadcast in Dutch from Luxembourg, Veronica, SBS6, TV10 and the Music Factory. Public broadcasting revenue is obtained from radio and television licences and from advertising.

At 31 Dec. 1997 there were 6,059,000 registered owners of television and radio sets and 121,000 of radio only. There were 5·8m. cable TV subscribers in 1996. Approximately 98% of households with TV licences have cable TV.

Cinema. In 1999 there were 518 cinemas and film houses with a seating capacity of 289,000. Total attendance was 19·0m.

Press. In 1996 there were 38 daily newspapers with a combined circulation of 4·8m., equivalent to 306 per 1,000 inhabitants. The most widely read daily is *De Telegraaf*, with average daily sales of 782,000 copies (1995).

Tourism. Tourism is a major sector of the economy, earning US$7,092m. in revenue in 1999. There were 9,881,000 foreign visitors in that year.

Festivals. Floriade, a world-famous horticultural show, takes place every ten years and is the largest Dutch attraction, being attended by 2·3m. people in 2002. The Maastricht Carnival in April attracts many visitors. The Flower Parade from Noordwijk to Haarlem occurs in late April. Koninginnedag on 30 April is a nationwide celebration of Queen Beatrix's birthday. The Oosterparkfestival, a cultural celebration of that district of Amsterdam, runs for three days in the first week of May. Liberation Day is celebrated every five years on 5 May, with the next occurrence being in 2005. An international music festival, the Holland Festival, is held in Amsterdam throughout June each year and the Early Music Festival is held in Utrecht. The North Sea Jazz Festival, the largest in Europe, takes place in The Hague. Each year the most important Dutch and Flemish theatre productions of the previous season are performed at the Theatre Festival in Amsterdam and Antwerp (Belgium). The Holland Dance Festival is held every other year in The Hague and the Springdance Festival in Utrecht annually. Film festivals include the Rotterdam Film Festival in Feb., the World Wide Video Festival in April, the Dutch Film Festival in Sept. and the International Documentary Film Festival of Amsterdam in Dec.

Libraries. In 1997 there were 1,130 public libraries, 4 National libraries and 856 Higher Education libraries. There were 69,797,000 visits to libraries in 1997.

Theatre and Opera. In 1997–98 there were 56,670 music and theatre performances (including rock and pop concerts) of which 14,530 were plays, 8,240 concerts, 2,390 opera and operetta and 2,900 ballet and dance, with a total attendance of 15,607,000 (excluding rock and pop concerts).

Museums and Galleries. In 1997 there were 942 museums open to the public, to which visits totalled 20,266,000. The Rijksmuseum and Vincent Van Gogh Museums in Amsterdam and the Kröller-Müller Museum in Otterlo attract the most visitors.

DIPLOMATIC REPRESENTATIVES

Of the Netherlands in the United Kingdom (38 Hyde Park Gate, London, SW7 5DP)
Ambassador: Count Jan de Marchant et d'Ansembourg.

Of the United Kingdom in the Netherlands (Lange Voorhout 10, 2514 ED The Hague)
Ambassador: Sir Colin Budd, KCMG.

Of the Netherlands in the USA (4200 Linnean Ave., NW, Washington, D.C., 20008)
Ambassador: Boudewijn van Eenennaam.

Of the USA in the Netherlands (Lange Voorhout 102, The Hague)
Ambassador: Clifford M. Sobel.

Of the Netherlands to the United Nations
Ambassador: Dirk Jan van der Berg.

FURTHER READING

Centraal Bureau voor de Statistiek. *Statistical Yearbook of the Netherlands*. From 1923/24.—*Statistisch Jaarboek*. From 1899/1924.—*CBS Select (Statistical Essays)*. From 1980.—*Statistisch Bulletin*. From 1945; weekly.—*Maandschrift*. From 1944; monthly bulletin.—*90 Jaren Statistiek in Tijdreeksen* (historical series of the Netherlands 1899–1989)

Nationale Rekeningen (National Accounts). From 1948–50.—*Statistische onderzoekingen*. From 1977.—*Regionaal Statistisch Zakboek* (Regional Pocket Yearbook). From 1972
Staatsalmanak voor het Koninkrijk der Nederlanden. Annual. The Hague, from 1814
Staatsblad van het Koninkrijk der Nederlanden. The Hague, from 1814
Staatscourant (State Gazette). The Hague, from 1813
Anderweg, R. B. and Irwin, G. A., *Dutch Government and Politics*. London, 1993
Cox, R. H., *The Development of the Dutch Welfare State: from Workers' Insurance to Universal Entitlement*. Pittsburgh Univ. Press, 1994
Gladdish, K., *Governing from the Centre: Politics and Policy-Making in the Netherlands*. London, 1991
King, P. K. and Wintle, M., *The Netherlands*. [Bibliography] ABC-Clio, Oxford and Santa Barbara (CA), 1988
van Os, Andre, *Amsterdam*. [Bibliography] ABC-Clio, Oxford and Santa Barbara (CA), 1997

National library: De Koninklijke Bibliotheek, Prinz Willem Alexanderhof 5, The Hague.
National statistical office: Centraal Bureau voor de Statistiek, Netherlands Central Bureau of Statistics, POB 959, 2270 AZ Voorburg.
Statistics Netherlands Website: http://www.cbs.nl

ARUBA

KEY HISTORICAL EVENTS

Discovered by Alonzo de Ojeda in 1499, the island of Aruba was claimed for Spain but not settled. It was acquired by the Dutch in 1634, but apart from garrisons, was left to the indigenous Caiquetious (Arawak) Indians until the 19th century. From 1828 it formed part of the Dutch West Indies and, from 1845, part of the Netherlands Antilles with which, on 29 Dec. 1954, it achieved internal self government. Following a referendum in March 1977, the Dutch government announced on 28 Oct. 1981 that Aruba would proceed to independence separately from the other islands. Aruba was constitutionally separated from the Netherlands Antilles from 1 Jan. 1986, and full independence promised by the Netherlands after a ten-year period. However, an agreement with the Netherlands government in June 1990 deletes, at Aruba's request, references to eventual independence.

TERRITORY AND POPULATION

The island, which lies in the southern Caribbean 32 km north of the Venezuelan coast and 68 km west of Curaçao, has an area of 180 sq. km (75 sq. miles) and a population in Dec. 2000 of 91,065; density 506 inhabitants per sq. km. The chief towns are Oranjestad, the capital (1998 population, 29,000) and San Nicolas. Dutch is the official language, but the language usually spoken is Papiamento, a creole language. Over half the population is of Indian stock, with the balance of Dutch, Spanish and mestizo origin.

SOCIAL STATISTICS

Annual growth rate, 1999, 1·1%. Life expectancy in 2000 was 70 years for males and 76 years for females. Birth rate per 1,000 population (1999), 13·9; death rate, 6·3; infant mortality, 7·2.

CLIMATE

Aruba has a tropical marine climate, with a brief rainy season from Oct. to Dec. Oranjestad (1998), Jan. 28°C (82°F), July 29·4°C (85°F). The annual rainfall in 2000 was 551 mm.

CONSTITUTION AND GOVERNMENT

Under the separate constitution inaugurated on 1 Jan. 1986, Aruba is an autonomous part of the Kingdom of the Netherlands with its own legislature, government, judiciary, civil service and police force. The Netherlands is represented by a Governor appointed by the monarch (currently Olindo Koolman). The unicameral legislature *(Staten)* consists of 21 members elected for a four-year term of office.

RECENT ELECTIONS

Elections were held on 28 Sept. 2001. The Movimento Electoral di Pueblo (MEP) won with 12 out of 21 seats (52·4% of the vote), against 6 seats (26·7%) for prime minister Henny Eman's Arubaanse Volkspartij (AVP), 2 seats (9·6%) for the Partido Patriótico Arubiano (PPA) and 1 seat (5·7%) for the Organización Liberal Arubianco (OLA). Turn-out was 86·5%.

CURRENT ADMINISTRATION

Governor General: Olindo Koolman (appointed 1 Jan. 1992).

In March 2003 the government comprised:

Prime Minister and Minister of General Affairs and Equipment: Nelson O. Oduber; b. 1947 (MEP; sworn in for second term in office 30 Oct. 2001, having previously served 1989–1994).

Deputy Prime Minister, Minister of Social Affairs and Infrastructure: Marisol Tromp. *Education:* Fredis Refunjol. *Finance and Economic Affairs:* Nilo Swaen. *Justice:* Hyacintho Croes. *Health:* Candelario Wever. *Sports, Culture, and Labour:* Ramon Lee. *Tourism and Transportation:* Edison Briesen.

Government Website: http://www.aruba.com

ECONOMY

Currency. Since 1 Jan. 1986 the currency has been the *Aruban florin*, at par with the Netherlands Antilles guilder. Total money supply in 2001 was 1,841m. Aflorins. There were 126m. Aflorins in circulation in 2001. Inflation was 4·2% in 2002. Foreign exchange reserves in June 2002 were US$311m.; gold reserves were 100,000 troy oz. Net foreign assets (including gold and revaluation of gold) in 2000 were 556·3m. Aflorins.

Budget. The 2001 budget totalled 731·8m. Aflorins revenue and grants. Tax revenue was 606·3m. Aflorins in 2001.

Performance. There was a recession in 2002, with negative growth of 3·8%. GDP per capita was 35,966 Aflorins in 2002.

Banking and Finance. There were six domestic and Dutch banks, and one foreign bank, in 2000. There is a special tax regime for offshore banks. The *President* of the Central Bank of Aruba is Dr Anthony R. Caram.

ENERGY AND NATURAL RESOURCES

Electricity. In 2001 consumption of electricity was 673,611 MWh.

Water. There is a desalination plant with an annual capacity of 22,000 tonnes. Delivered quantities of water in 2001 totalled 11,352,545 cu. metres.

Fisheries. In 2000 the catch totalled 163 tonnes.

INDUSTRY

The government has established six industrial sites at Oranjestad harbour. An oil refinery, closed in 1985, was re-opened in 1991. The quantity of oil refined in 2001 was 64m. bbls.

Labour. The working age population (15–64 yrs) grew between 1991–2000 from 45,563 to 62,637 persons. The economically active population in 2000 numbered 44,384 persons of which 41,286 are employed and 3,098 unemployed. The employment rate for women grew from 52·8% to 59·2% during the 1990s.

Trade Unions. There are four trade unions: COC, Chambers of Commerce; ATIA, Aruba Trade and Industrial Association; ORMA, Oranjestad Retail and Merchants Association; SNBA, San Nicolas Business Association.

EXTERNAL ECONOMIC RELATIONS

There are two Free Zones at Oranjestad.

Imports and Exports. 2001: exports, 51·7m. Aflorins; imports, 1,318·5m. Aflorins (excluding mineral fuels, storage and transit transactions of the free zone).

COMMUNICATIONS

Roads. In 1984 there were 380 km of surfaced highways. In 2000 there were 39,995 passenger cars and 5,443 commercial vehicles.

Civil Aviation. There is an international airport (Aeropuerto Internacional Reina Beatrix). Air Aruba had flights in 1998 to Amsterdam (jointly with KLM), Bogotá, Bonaire, Caracas, Curaçao, Medellin, Miami, New York and Tampa. In 2002 Aruba handled 13,761 commercial landings and 3,113 non-commercial landings. In total 759,285 passengers arrived by air, 751,106 departed and 153,663 were in transit.

Shipping. Oranjestad has a container terminal and cruise ship port. The port at Barcadera services the offshore and energy sector and a deep-water port at San Nicolas services the oil refinery.

Telecommunications. Aruba had 38,100 main telephone lines in 2000, or 371·6 per 1,000 inhabitants. There were 10,500 mobile phone subscribers in 1999 and 5,736 Internet subscribers.

Postal Services. In 1995 there were four post offices.

SOCIAL INSTITUTIONS

Justice. There is a Common Court of Justice with the Netherlands Antilles. Final Appeal is to the Supreme Court in the Netherlands.

The population in penal institutions in Nov. 1998 was 204 (equivalent to 225 per 100,000 of national population).

Religion. In 2000, 86·2% of the population were Roman Catholic.

Education. In 2000 there were 28 pre-primary, 40 primary, 15 secondary and four middle-level schools, also a teacher training college and law school. Literacy rate (2000 census), 97·3%. The share of education in the 2000 budget was 14·5%.

Health. In 2000 there were 123 doctors, 29 dentists, 18 pharmacists and 1 hospital with 305 beds.

Welfare. All citizens are entitled to an old age pension at the age of 60.

CULTURE

Broadcasting. In 2000 there were 18 radio stations and 3 commercial television stations (colour by NTSC). In 1997 there were 50,000 radio and 20,000 TV sets.

Press. In 1997 there were eight daily newspapers with a combined circulation of 52,000. At more than 700 newspapers per 1,000 inhabitants, Aruba has one of the highest rates of circulation in the world.

Tourism. In 2000 there were 721,224 tourists and 490,148 cruise-ship visitors. In 2000 tourist receipts were 1,498·7m. Aflorins. The majority of tourists are from the USA (63·5%), Venezuela (15·5%), Colombia (4·4%) and the Netherlands (4·2%).

FURTHER READING
Schoenhals, K., *Netherlands Antilles and Aruba.* [Bibliography] ABC-Clio, Oxford and Santa Barbara (CA), 1993
Central Bureau of Statistics Website: http://www.aruba.com/extlinks/govs/cbstats.html

THE NETHERLANDS ANTILLES
De Nederlandse Antillen

KEY HISTORICAL EVENTS
With Aruba, the islands formed part of the Dutch West Indies from 1828, and the Netherlands Antilles from 1845, with internal self-government being granted on 29 Dec. 1954.

TERRITORY AND POPULATION
The Netherlands Antilles comprise two groups of islands, the Leeward group (Curaçao and Bonaire) being situated 100 km north of the Venezuelan coast and the

Windward group (Saba, Sint Eustatius and the southern portion of Sint Maarten) situated 800 km away to the northeast, at the northern end of the Lesser Antilles. The total area is 800 sq. km (308 sq. miles) and the population in 1995 was 207,333. The estimated population for 2000 was 215,000. An estimated 69·2% of the population were urban in 1995. Willemstad is the capital and had a 1999 population of 123,000.

The areas, populations and chief towns of the islands are:

Island	Sq. km	1995 population	Chief town
Bonaire	288	14,218	Kralendijk
Curaçao	444	151,448	Willemstad
Saba	13	1,200	The Bottom
Sint Eustatius	21	1,900	Oranjestad
Sint Maarten[1]	43	38,567	Philipsburg

[1]The northern portion (St Martin) belongs to France.

Dutch is the official language, but the languages usually spoken are Papiamento (derived from Dutch, Spanish and Portuguese) on Curaçao and Bonaire, and English in the Windward Islands.

SOCIAL STATISTICS
1995, live births, 3,753; marriages, 1,056; divorces, 521; deaths, 1,363. Annual growth rate, 1995–99, 1·3%. Expectation of life at birth, 1990–95, was 72·4 years for males and 78·5 for females. Infant mortality, 1990–95, 13 per 1,000 live births; fertility rate, 2·2 births per woman.

CLIMATE
All the islands have a tropical marine climate, with very little difference in temperatures over the year. There is a short rainy season from Oct. to Jan. Willemstad, Feb. 27·7°C, Aug. 29°C. Annual rainfall 499 mm.

CONSTITUTION AND GOVERNMENT
On 29 Dec. 1954 the Netherlands Antilles became an integral part of the Kingdom of the Netherlands but are fully autonomous in internal affairs, and constitutionally equal with the Netherlands and Aruba. The Sovereign of the Kingdom of the Netherlands is Head of State and Government, and is represented by a Governor.

The executive power in internal affairs rests with the Governor and the Council of Ministers, who together form the government. The Ministers are responsible to a unicameral legislature *(States)* consisting of 22 members, elected for a four-year term in three multi-seat constituencies and two single-seat constituencies.

The executive power in external affairs is vested in the Council of Ministers of the Kingdom, in which the Antilles is represented by a Minister Plenipotentiary with full voting powers. On each of the insular communities, local autonomous power is divided between an Island Council (elected by universal suffrage), the Executive Council and the Lieut.-Governor, responsible for law and order.

At a referendum in Curaçao on 19 Nov. 1993, 73% of votes cast favoured maintaining the status quo of Curaçao as part of the Netherlands Antilles. The other options were: autonomy (18%), unification with the Netherlands (8%) or complete independence (1%). At a referendum in Oct. 1994 Sint Maarten, Sint Eustatius and Saba voted to remain part of the Netherlands Antilles.

RECENT ELECTIONS
In elections held on 18 Jan. 2002 the Workers' Liberation Front 30th May (FOL) won 5 seats (with 23·0% of votes cast), the Party for the Restructured Antilles (PAR) 4 (20·6%), the National People's Party 3 (13·4%), the Labour Party People's Crusade 2 (12·1%), the Democratic Party Sint Maarten 2, the Bonaire Patriotic Union 2, the Democratic Party 2, with 1 seat each going to four other parties.

CURRENT ADMINISTRATION
Governor: Frits Goedgedrag.

In March 2003 the cabinet was composed as follows:

Prime Minister and Minister for Foreign Affairs: Etienne Ys (sworn in 3 June 2002).

Deputy Prime Minister, and Minister of Economic Affairs and Labour: Errol Cova. *Éducation, Sport, Culture and Youth Affairs:* Emily de Jongh-Elhage. *Justice:* Norberto Vieira Ribeiro. *Finance:* Ersilla de Lannooy. *Transport and Communications:* Herbert Domacasse. *Health and Social Affairs:* Joan Theodora-Brewster. *Minister Plenipotentiary to the Hague:* Carel de Haseth.

ECONOMY

Currency. The unit of currency is the *Netherlands Antilles guilder, gulden* (ANG) or *florin* (NAfl.) divided into 100 *cents*. The NA guilder has been pegged to the US dollar at US$1 = 1·79 NA guilder since 12 Dec. 1971. Gold reserves were 548,000 troy oz in June 2000 and foreign exchange reserves US$373m. in May 2002. In 2001 inflation was 0·7%. Total money supply in April 2002 was 1,233m. NA guilders.

Budget. The central government budget for 1995 envisaged 470·5m. NA guilders revenue and 565·5m. NA guilders expenditure.

Performance. Real GDP growth was negative in the years 1998–2000, the economy contracting by 2·3% in 2000.

Banking and Finance. At 31 Dec. 1994 the Bank of Netherlands Antilles (*President,* Emsley Tromp) had total assets and liabilities of 514·4m. NA guilders; commercial banks, 3,913m. NA guilders.

ENERGY AND NATURAL RESOURCES

Environment. According to the *World Bank Atlas* carbon dioxide emissions were the equivalent of 36·7 tonnes per capita in 1998.

Electricity. Installed capacity in 1995 was 307,000 kW; production in 1998 totalled 1·02bn. kWh. Consumption per capita in 1994 was estimated at 4,580 kWh.

Oil and Gas. The economy was formerly based largely on oil refining at the Shell refinery on Curaçao, but following an announcement by Shell that closure was imminent, this was sold to the Netherlands Antilles government in Sept. 1985, and leased to Petróleos de Venezuela to operate on a reduced scale. The refinery has a capacity of 470,000 bbls. a day, but output has not reached this for several years.

Minerals. Calcium carbonate (limestone) has been mined since 1980; production (1991), 0·32m. tonnes. Production of limestone, 1990 (estimate), 0·36m. tonnes; salt, 1994, 0·43m. tonnes.

Agriculture. Livestock (1996): cattle, 1,000; goats, 13,000; pigs, 2,000; sheep, 7,000; asses, 3,000.

Fisheries. Total catch estimate (2000), 19,974 tonnes.

INDUSTRY

Curaçao has an oil refinery and a large ship-repair dry docks. Bonaire has a textile factory and a modern equipped salt plant. Sint Maarten's industrial activities are primarily based on a rum factory and a fishing factory.

Labour. In 1997 the economically active population numbered 56,200; of which 18,400 were employed in community and social services, 14,600 in trade, 7,300 in financial services and 5,700 in manufacturing. In 1992 the unemployment rate was 15·3% (Curaçao, 1995: 62,236; unemployment rate 13·1%).

EXTERNAL ECONOMIC RELATIONS

Imports and Exports. Imports and exports for calendar years in US$1m.:

	1991	1992	1993	1994	1995
Imports	1,118	1,168	1,143	1,271	1,318
Exports	211	242	222	245	222

Crude and petroleum products make up approximately 52% of imports and 70% of exports. There is a Free Zone on Curaçao.

COMMUNICATIONS

Roads. In 1989 the Netherlands Antilles had 845 km of surfaced highway distributed as follows: Curaçao, 590; Bonaire, 226; Sint Maarten, 19. Number of motor vehicles registered in 1994, 166,392.

Civil Aviation. There are international airports on Curaçao (Curaçao-Hato Airport), Bonaire (Flamingo Airport) and Sint Maarten (Princess Juliana Airport). The local carrier, AirALM, had seven aircraft in 1998. In addition to operating on domestic routes, in 1998 it also served Amsterdam (jointly with KLM), Aruba, Atlanta, Caracas, Kingston, Miami, Paramaribo, Port au Prince, Port of Spain, Puerto Rico, Santo Domingo and Valencia (Venezuela). In 2000 Sint Maarten handled 1,266,000 passengers and Curaçao 911,000; in 1995 Bonaire handled 286,117, Sint Eustatius 49,369 and Saba (1994) 45,457.

Shipping. 5,152 ships (totalling 31,785,000 GRT) entered the port of Curaçao in 1995; 1,011 ships (15,911,000 GRT) entered the port of Bonaire; 1,400 ships entered the port of Sint Maarten. In 1995 Curaçao handled 171,854 passengers; in 1994 Bonaire handled 12,736 and Sint Maarten 718,550. Merchant shipping in 1998 totalled 971,000 GRT, including oil tankers 135,000 GRT.

Telecommunications. Number of telephone main lines in 2000 was 80,000 (371·6 per 1,000 population). The number of Internet users in Dec. 1999 was 2,000. There were 13,000 mobile phone subscribers in 1996.

SOCIAL INSTITUTIONS

Justice. There is a Court of First Instance, which sits in each island, and a Court of Appeal in Willemstad.

The population in penal institutions in Nov. 1998 was 780 (365 per 100,000 of national population).

Religion. In 1992, 73% of the population were Roman Catholics, 10% were Protestants (Sint Maarten and Sint Eustatius being primarily Protestant).

Education. In 1994–95 there were 23,007 pupils in primary schools, 1,859 pupils in special schools, 8,678 pupils in general secondary schools, 6,685 pupils in junior and senior secondary vocational schools, and 848 students in vocational colleges and universities.

Health. In 1996 there were 314 doctors, 67 dentists, 11 hospitals with 1,466 beds and 1,498 nursing personnel.

CULTURE

Broadcasting. In 1995 there were 32 radio transmitters (8 on Bonaire, 17 on Curaçao, 2 on Saba, 1 on Sint Eustatius and 4 on Sint Maarten) and each island had 1 cable television station. These stations broadcast in Papiamento, Dutch, English and Spanish and are mainly financed by income from advertisements. Broadcasting is administered by Landsradio, Telecommunication Administration and Tele Curaçao. In 1997 there were 217,000 radio and 69,000 TV sets (colour by NTSC) in use. In addition, Radio Nederland and Trans World Radio have powerful relay stations operating on medium- and short-waves from Bonaire.

Press. In 1996 there were six daily newspapers with a combined circulation of 70,000.

Tourism. In 1998, 751,000 tourists visited the islands and there were 1,132,000 cruise passengers.

DIPLOMATIC REPRESENTATIVES
US Consul-General: Deborah A. Bolton (J. B. Gorsiraweg 1, Curaçao).

FURTHER READING
Central Bureau of Statistics. *Statistical Yearbook of the Netherlands Antilles*

Bank of the Netherlands Antilles. *Annual Report.*
Schoenhals, K., *Netherlands Antilles and Aruba.* [Bibliography] ABC-Clio, Oxford and Santa Barbara (CA), 1993

NEW ZEALAND

Capital: Wellington
Population estimate, 2000: 3·8m.
GDP per capita, 2000: (PPP$) 20,070
HDI/world rank: 0·917/19

KEY HISTORICAL EVENTS

New Zealand was first called *Aotearoa* by the Maori who migrated from other northern islands in Polynesia, sometime around AD 1400. The first European to discover New Zealand was Abel Tasman in 1642. He named the south island after the Dutch province of Zeeland. The coast was explored by Capt. Cook in 1769. From about 1800 onwards, New Zealand became a resort for whalers and traders, chiefly from Australia. New Zealand's European constitutional history can be traced back to 1840 when the Maori entered into an agreement with the Crown under the Treaty of Waitangi and New Zealand became a British colony with the Maori retaining full rights of self-governance. However, the effective administration of the country was soon taken over by European settlers although there were movements for Maori self-government. These movements declined in the early 1900s but the struggle for self-determination has re-emerged in recent years which have also seen a relative decline in the number of immigrants from England, Scotland and Ireland. New Zealand had its first elected House of Representatives in 1852 along with a nominated legislative Council and a Governor. Sheep farming came to dominate the economy and in 1882 the first refrigerated meat was sent to Britain.

In the last years of the 19th century, New Zealand adopted a succession of radical social reforms. New Zealand women gained the vote in 1893, the first in the world to be enfranchized.

TERRITORY AND POPULATION

New Zealand lies southeast of Australia in the south Pacific, Wellington being 1,983 km from Sydney. There are two principal islands, the North and South Islands, besides Stewart Island, Chatham Islands and small outlying islands, as well as the territories overseas.

New Zealand (*i.e.*, North, South and Stewart Islands) extends over 1,750 km from north to south. Area, excluding territories overseas, 270,534 sq. km: comprising North Island, 115,777 sq. km; South Island, 151,215 sq. km; Stewart Island, 1,746 sq. km; Chatham Islands, 963 sq. km. The minor islands (total area, 320 sq. miles or 829 sq. km) included within the geographical boundaries of New Zealand (but not within any local government area) are the following: Kermadec Islands (34 sq. km), Three Kings Islands (8 sq. km), Auckland Islands (606 sq. km), Campbell Island (114 sq. km), Antipodes Islands (62 sq. km), Bounty Islands (1 sq. km), Snares Islands (3 sq. km), Solander Island (1 sq. km). With the exception of meteorological station staff on Raoul Island in the Kermadec Group and Campbell Island there are no inhabitants.

The Kermadec Islands were annexed to New Zealand in 1887, have no separate administration and all New Zealand laws apply to them. Situation, 29° 10' to 31° 30' S. lat., 177° 45' to 179° W. long., 1,600 km NNE of New Zealand. The largest of the group is Raoul or Sunday Island, 29 sq. km, smaller islands being Macaulay and Curtis, while Macaulay Island is 5 km in circuit.

Growth in census population, exclusive of territories overseas:

	Total population	Average annual increase (%)		Total population	Average annual increase (%)
1858	115,462	—	1911	1,058,308	2·52
1878	458,007	7·33	1916[1]	1,149,225	1·50
1881	534,030	5·10	1921	1,271,644	2·27
1886	620,451	3·05	1926	1,408,139	2·06
1891	668,632	1·50	1936[2]	1,573,810	1·13
1896	743,207	2·13	1945[1, 2]	1,702,298	0·83
1901[1]	815,853	1·89	1951[1]	1,939,472	2·37
1906	936,304	2·75	1956[1]	2,174,062	2·31

	Total population	Average annual increase (%)		Total population	Average annual increase (%)
1961[1]	2,414,984	2·12	1986[1]	3,307,084	0·82
1966[1]	2,676,919	2·10	1991[1]	3,434,950	0·77
1971[1]	2,862,631	1·34	1996[1]	3,681,546	1·44
1976[1]	3,129,383	1·71	2001[1]	3,820,749	0·76
1981[1]	3,175,737	0·20			

[1]Excluding members of the Armed Forces overseas.

[2]The census of New Zealand is quinquennial, but the census falling in 1931 was abandoned as an act of national economy, and owing to war conditions the census due in 1941 was not taken until 25 Sept. 1945.

The latest census took place on 6 March 2001. Of the 3,820,749 people counted, 3,737,277 were usually resident in the country and 83,472 were overseas visitors.

In 2001, 85·4% of the population lived in urban areas. Density, 14·5 per sq. km (2001).

The usually-resident populations of regional councils (all data conforms with boundaries redrawn after the 1989 re-organization of local government) in 1996 and 2001:

	Total Population		Percentage change
Local Government Region	1996 census	2001 census	1996–2001 (%)
Northland	137,052	140,133	2·2
Auckland	1,068,657	1,158,891	8·4
Waikato	350,112	357,726	2·2
Bay of Plenty	224,364	239,412	6·7
Gisborne	45,786	43,974	−4·0
Hawke's Bay	142,788	142,947	0·1
Taranaki	106,590	102,858	−3·5
Manawatu-Wanganui	228,771	220,089	−3·8
Wellington	414,048	423,765	2·3
Total North Island	2,718,171	2,829,798	4·1
Tasman	37,971	41,352	8·9
Nelson	40,278	41,568	3·2
Marlborough	38,397	39,558	3·0
West Coast	32,514	30,303	−6·8
Canterbury	468,039	481,431	2·9
Otago	185,082	181,542	−1·9
Southland	97,098	91,005	−6·3
Total South Island	899,385	906,753	0·8
Area outside region	747	726	−2·8
Total New Zealand	3,618,303	3,737,277	3·3

The UN gives a projected population for 2010 of 4·04m.

Between 1991 and 2001 the number of people who identified themselves as being of European ethnicity dropped from 83·2% to 80·0%. Pacific Island people made up 6·5% of the population in 2001 (5·0% in 1991); Asian ethnic groups went from 3·0% in 1996 to 6·6% in 2001. Permanent and long-term arrivals in 2001 totalled 81,094, including 16,844 from the UK, 12,186 from Australia, 11,107 from the People's Republic of China, 4,249 from India and 3,920 from Japan. Permanent and long-term departures in 2001 totalled 71,368, including 36,033 to Australia, 14,852 to the UK, 3,151 to the USA and 1,874 to Japan.

Maori population: 1896, 42,113; 1936, 82,326; 1945, 98,744; 1951, 115,676; 1961, 171,553; 1971, 227,414; 1981, 279,255; 1986, 294,201; 1991, 324,000; 1996, 523,374; 2001, 526,281 (13·8% of the total population, up from 9·4% in 1991). In addition, 604,110 people in 2001 said they have Maori ancestry, compared with 434,847 in 1991. There were estimated in 1995 to be 10,123 fully fluent speakers of Maori and a further 12,153 who were at the medium to high fluency level. In the 1996 census, 153,669 New Zealanders said they could hold a conversation about everyday matters in Maori. In 2001, one in four people of Maori ethnicity claimed to speak the language.

From the 1970s organizations were formed to pursue Maori grievances over loss of land and resources. The Waitangi Tribunal was set up in 1975 as a forum for complaints about breaches of the Treaty of Waitangi, and in 1984 empowered to hear claims against Crown actions since 1840. Direct negotiations with the Crown have been offered to claimants and a range of proposals to resolve historical grievances launched for public discussion in Dec. 1994. These proposals specify that all claims are to be met over ten years with treaty rights being converted to economic assets. There have been four recent major treaty settlements: NZ$170m. each for Tainui and Ngai Tahu, the NZ$150m. Sealord fishing agreement and NZ$40m. for Whakatohea in the Bay of Plenty. The Maori Land Court has jurisdiction over Maori freehold land and some general land owned by Maoris under the Te Ture Whenue Maori Act 1993.

Resident populations of main urban areas at the 2001 census were as follows:

North Island		Wanganui	39,423
Auckland	1,074,510	Wellington	339,747
Gisborne	31,719	Whangarei	46,050
Hamilton	166,128		
Hastings and Napier	113,673	South Island	
New Plymouth	47,763	Christchurch	334,107
Palmerston North	72,681	Dunedin	107,088
Rotorua	52,608	Invercargill	46,305
Tauranga	95,697	Nelson	53,688

English and Maori are the official languages.

SOCIAL STATISTICS
Statistics for calendar years:

	Total live births	Single-parent births	Deaths	Marriages	Divorces (decrees absolute)
1993	58,782	22,355	27,100	20,802	9,193
1994	57,321	22,180	26,953	20,587	9,213
1995	57,671	23,499	27,813	20,452	9,574
1996	57,280	23,722	28,255	20,453	10,009
1997	57,604	24,127	27,471	19,953	9,754
1998	57,818	—	26,206	20,135	10,037
1999	57,473	—	28,117	21,085	9,936

Birth rate, 1999, 15·07 per 1,000 population; death rate, 7·37 per 1,000 population; infant mortality, 1999, 6 per 1,000 live births. Annual population growth rate, 1990–99, 1·5%. In 1998 there were 574 suicides (561 in 1997). Expectation of life, 1999: males, 74·8 years; females, 80·1.

In the year ending March 2000 there were 61,089 immigrants (77,563 in 1995) and 70,076 emigrants (49,077 in 1995). Fertility rate, 1999, 2·0 births per woman.

CLIMATE
Lying in the cool temperate zone, New Zealand enjoys very mild winters for its latitude owing to its oceanic situation, and only the extreme south has cold winters. The situation of the mountain chain produces much sharper climatic contrasts between east and west than in a north-south direction. Mean daily maximum temperatures and rainfall figures:

	Jan (°C)	July (°C)	Annual rainfall (mm) in 2000
Auckland	23·3	14·4	1,046
Christchurch	22·5	11·2	706
Dunedin	18·9	9·9	926
Wellington	20·3	11·3	994

The highest extreme temperature recorded in 2000 was 35·0°C, recorded at both Darfield and Culverden on 4 March, and the lowest –12·4°C, at Tekapo on the morning of 24 Aug.

CONSTITUTION AND GOVERNMENT
Definition was given to the status of New Zealand by the (Imperial) Statute of Westminster of Dec. 1931, which had received the antecedent approval of the New Zealand Parliament in July 1931. The Governor-General's assent was given to the Statute of Westminster Adoption Bill on 25 Nov. 1947.

The powers, duties and responsibilities of the Governor-General and the Executive Council are set out in Royal Letters Patent and Instructions thereunder of 11 May 1917. In the execution of the powers vested in him the Governor-General must be guided by the advice of the Executive Council.

At a referendum on 6 Nov. 1993 a change from a first-past-the-post to a proportional representation electoral system was favoured by 53·9% of votes cast.

Parliament is the *House of Representatives*, since 1996 consisting of 120 members: 60 for general seats, 55 for party list seats and 5 for Maori seats, elected by universal adult suffrage on the mixed-member-proportional system (MMP) for three-year terms. The five Maori electoral districts cover the whole country. Maori and people of Maori descent are entitled to register either for a general or a Maori electoral district. As at Sept. 1997 there were 163,310 persons on the Maori electoral roll. There are now six Maori seats at general elections.

Joseph, P. A., *Constitutional Law in New Zealand.* Sydney, 1993.—(ed.) *Essays on the Constitution.* Sydney, 1995

McGee, D. G., *Parliamentary Practice in New Zealand.* 2nd ed. Wellington, 1994

Ringer, J. B., *An Introduction to New Zealand Government.* Christchurch, 1992

Vowles, J. and Aimer, P. (eds.) *Double Decision: the 1993 Election and Referendum in New Zealand.* Victoria (Wellington) Univ. Press, 1994

National Anthem. 'God Defend New Zealand'; words by T. Bracken, tune by J. J. Woods. There is a Maori version, Aotearoa, words by T. H. Smith. The UK national anthem has equal status.

RECENT ELECTIONS

At parliamentary elections on 27 July 2002 turn-out was 75·4%. The Labour Party won 52 seats with 41·3%; the National Party 27 with 20·9%; the right-wing New Zealand First Party 13 with 10·4%; Association of Consumers and Tax Payers 9 with 7·1%; the Green Party 9 with 7·0%; United Future 8 with 6·7%; and Jim Anderton's Progressive Coalition 2 with 1·7%.

CURRENT ADMINISTRATION

Governor-General: Dame Silvia Cartwright, DBE (b. 1943; sworn in 4 April 2001).

The government is formed by a centre-left coalition of the Labour Party and Jim Anderton's Progressive Coalition. In March 2003 the cabinet consisted of:

Prime Minister, Minister of Arts, Culture and Heritage: Helen Clark; b. 1950 (Labour; in office since 10 Dec. 1999).

Deputy Prime Minister, Minister of Finance, and Revenue: Michael Cullen (Labour).

Minister of Economic Development, Industry and Regional Development: James (Jim) Anderton (Progressive Coalition). *Minister of Health, and Food Safety:* Annette King (Labour). *Foreign Affairs and Trade, and Justice:* Phil Goff (Labour). *Agriculture, Biosecurity, Forestry, and Trade Negotiations:* James Sutton (Labour). *Education, State Services, and Sport and Recreation:* Trevor Mallard (Labour). *Environment, and Disarmament and Arms Control:* Marian Hobbs (Labour). *Police, Internal Affairs, Civil Defence, and Veterans' Affairs:* George Hawkins (Labour). *Transport, Communications, and Information Technology:* Paul Swain (Labour). *Conservation, and Local Government:* Chris Carter (Labour). *Energy, Fisheries, Research, Science and Technology, and Crown Research Institutes:* Peter Hodgson (Labour). *Defence, State Owned Enterprises, and Tourism:* Mark Burton (Labour). *Corrections, Housing, Pacific Island Affairs, and Racing:* Mark Gosche (Labour). *Commerce, Immigration, and Senior Citizens:* Lianne Dalziel (Labour). *Attorney General, Courts, Labour, and the Treaty of Waitangi Negotiations:* Margaret Wilson (Labour). *Maori Affairs:* Parekura Horomia (Labour). *Social Services and Employment, and Broadcasting:* Steven Maharey (Labour). *Youth Affairs, Land Information, and Statistics:* John Tamihere (Labour). *Accident Compensation Corporation, and Women's Affairs:* Ruth Dyson (Labour).

Office of the Prime Minister: http://www.govt.nz

DEFENCE

The control and co-ordination of defence activities is obtained through the Ministry of Defence. New Zealand forces serve abroad in Australia and Singapore, and with UN peacekeeping missions.

Defence expenditure in 2000 totalled US$788m. (US$204 per capita), representing 1·5% of GDP.

Rolfe, J., *Defending New Zealand*. Wellington, 1993

Army. Personnel total: regular force 4,400 (520 women), territorial force 3,890 and civilian employees 832.

Navy. The Navy includes three frigates. The main base and Fleet headquarters is at Auckland.

The Royal New Zealand Navy personnel totalled 2,080 uniformed plus 1,350 Reserve personnel.

Air Force. Squadrons are based at RNZAF Base Auckland and RNZAF Base Ohakea. Flying training is conducted at Ohakea and Auckland. Ground training is carried out at RNZAF Base Woodbourne. In May 2001 Prime Minister Helen Clark announced that all 34 of the RNZAF's combat and trainer jet aircraft were to be disbanded.

The uniform strength in 1999 was 3,050 (500 women) with 42 combat aircraft.

INTERNATIONAL RELATIONS

New Zealand is a member of the UN, WTO, the Commonwealth, OECD, Asian Development Bank, the Pacific Community, the Pacific Islands Forum, Colombo Plan, APEC and the Antarctic Treaty.

ECONOMY

Services accounted for 66% of GDP in 1997, industry 25% and agriculture 9%.

According to the anti-corruption organization *Transparency International*, New Zealand ranked equal second in the world behind Finland in a 2002 survey of the countries with the least corruption in business and government. It received 9·5 out of 10 in the annual index.

Currency. The monetary unit is the *New Zealand dollar* (NZD), of 100 *cents*. The total value of notes and coins on issue from the Reserve Bank in Dec. 2000 was NZ$2,069m. Inflation was 1·8% in 2001. In June 2002 foreign exchange reserves were US$1,843m. Gold reserves are negligible. Total money supply in June 2002 was NZ$18,235m.

Budget. The following tables of revenue and expenditure relate to the Consolidated Account, which covers the ordinary revenue and expenditure of the government— *i.e.*, apart from capital items, commercial and special undertakings, advances, etc. Total revenue and expenditure of the Consolidated Account, in NZ$1m., year ended 30 June:

	1995	1996	1997	1998	1999
Revenue	33,648	35,059	34,778	35,581	36,357
Expenditure	30,400	31,743	32,953	34,211	35,825

1999 tax revenue included (in NZ$1m.): income tax, NZ$14,963; company tax, NZ$3,888; withholding taxes, NZ$1,637; domestic goods and services, NZ$8,215. Non-tax revenue was approximately NZ$3,350m.

The gross public debt at June 1999 was NZ$36,712m., of which NZ$29,610m. was held in New Zealand currency and NZ$7,102m. in foreign currency.

New Zealand System of National Accounts. National Accounts aggregates for six years are given in the following table (in NZ$1m.):

Year ended 31 March	Gross domestic product	Gross national income	National income
1994	81,502	76,980	65,453
1995	87,321	81,366	69,433
1996	92,679	86,680	74,273
1997	96,911	89,647	76,782
1998	99,631	93,231	79,748
1999	101,169	96,192	82,063

Performance. GDP at current prices grew to NZ$103,857m. in the year ended March 2000, up from NZ$95,816m. in 1997. The New Zealand economy grew by 3·8% in 2000 and 2·6% in 2001. Total GDP was US$48·3bn. in 2001.

Banking and Finance. The central bank and bank of issue is the Reserve Bank (*Governor*, Dr Alan Bollard).

The financial system comprises a central bank (the Reserve Bank of New Zealand), registered banks, and other financial institutions. Registered banks include banks from abroad, which have to satisfy capital adequacy and managerial quality requirements. Other financial institutions include the regional trustee banks, now grouped under Trust Bank, building societies, finance companies, merchant banks and stock and station agents. The number of registered banks was 18 in 2000 of which only four were operating in New Zealand before 1986. Around 99% of the assets of the New Zealand banking system were under the ownership of a foreign bank parent.

The primary functions of the Reserve Bank are the formulation and implementation of monetary policy to achieve the economic objectives set by the government, and the promotion of the efficiency and soundness of the financial system, through the registration of banks, and supervision of financial institutions. Since 1996 supervision has been conducted on a basis of public disclosure by banks of their activities every quarter.

On 31 Dec. 2000 the funding (financial liabilities including deposits) and claims (financial assets including loans) for all registered banks and other financial institutions were: funding, NZ$179,617m. (in foreign currency, NZ$40,362m.); claims, NZ$142,915m. (foreign currency, NZ$12,398m.).

The stock exchange in Wellington conducts on-screen trading, unifying the three former trading floors in Auckland, Christchurch and Wellington.

Weights and Measures. The metric system of weights and measures operates.

ENERGY AND NATURAL RESOURCES

Environment. According to the *World Bank Atlas* New Zealand's carbon dioxide emissions were the equivalent of 7·9 tonnes per capita in 1998.

Electricity. On 1 April 1987 the former Electricity Division of the Ministry of Energy became a state-owned enterprise, the Electricity Corporation of N.Z. Ltd, which has since been split into two state-owned enterprises causing a competitive wholesale electricity market to be established. Around 75% of the country's electricity is generated by renewable sources. Hydro-electric plants, mainly based in the South Island, account for some 70% with geothermal power, generated in the North Island, accounting for around 5%. The rest comes from natural gas (22%), coal, wind and landfill gas. Electricity generating capacity, 1997, 8m. kW. Consumption per capita was 8,215 kWh in 1998.

Electricity consumption statistics (in GWh) for years ended 31 March are:

	Residential	Commercial	Industrial	Total consumption
1996	10,584	5,595	14,342	30,522
1997	10,959	6,101	14,200	31,260
1998	10,824	6,988	13,577	31,390
1999	10,089	7,195	13,745	32,029

New Zealand also has two wind farms.

Oil and Gas. Crude oil and condensate production was 120·61 petajoules in 1997, all from the Taranaki region. Around two-thirds of production is exported. 168·39 petajoules were imported in 1997.

In 1998 gasfields produced 201 petajoules. Gas reserves are estimated to last until about 2014, with the Maui field possibly running out around 2006.

Minerals. Coal production for the year ended Dec. 1997 was 3·4m. tonnes. Of the 45 mines operating (down from 53 in 1995), 29 were opencast and 16 underground, responsible for about 78% and 22% of total coal production respectively. Only five mines produced over 200,000 tonnes of coal, and 18 operations had an output of less than 10,000 tonnes. Around 60% of New Zealand's exported coal goes to India and Japan.

While New Zealand's best known non-fuel mineral is gold (producing about 12 tonnes annually) there is also production of silver, ironsand, aggregate, limestone, clay, dolomite, pumice, salt, serpentinite, zeolite and bentonite. In addition, there are resources or potential for deposits of titanium (ilmenite beachsands), platinum, sulphur, phosphate, silica and mercury.

Agriculture. Two-thirds of the land area is suitable for agriculture and grazing. The total area of farmland in use at 30 June 1999 was 15,585,027 ha. There were 13,863,279 ha of grazing, arable, fodder and fallow land, 53,692 ha of land for horticulture and 446,954 ha of plantations of exotic timber.

The largest freehold estates are held in the South Island. The number of occupied holdings as at 30 June 1999 were as follows:

Regional Council	No. of farms	Total area of farms (1,000 ha)	Regional Council	No. of farms	Total area of farms (1,000 ha)
Auckland	7,983	318	Canterbury	10,581	3,586
Bay of Plenty	4,020	312	Marlborough	1,419	689
Gisborne	1,092	455	Nelson	111	9
Hawke's Bay	2,988	922	Otago	5,073	2,682
Manawatu-Wanganui	7,560	1,547	Southland	4,791	1,235
Northland	7,554	775	Tasman	1,965	206
Taranaki	5,898	526	West Coast	1,287	260
Waikato	14,478	1,482	*Total South Island*	*25,227*	*8,667*
Wellington	3,540	523			
Total North Island	*55,113*	*6,860*	*Total New Zealand*	*80,340*	*15,527*

Production of main crops (2000, in 1,000 tonnes): potatoes, 500; apples, 482; wheat, 360; barley, 281; maize, 174; pumpkins and squash, 155; tomatoes, 85; carrots, 80; grapes, 80; cauliflower, 63.

Livestock, 2000: sheep, 45·80m.; cattle, 9·46m.; pigs, 344,000; goats, 186,000; deer, 1·7m. (1999); chickens, 13m. Total meat produced in 2000 was 1·33m. tonnes (including 623,000 tonnes of beef and veal, and 525,000 tonnes of lamb and mutton). Meat industry products are New Zealand's second largest export income earner, accounting for about 18% of merchandise exports. New Zealand's main meat exports are lamb, mutton and beef. About 80% of lamb, 80% of mutton and 80% of beef produced in New Zealand in 1997–98 was exported overseas. The domestic market absorbs over 99% of the pigmeat and poultry produced in New Zealand. 54% of the world's exported sheepmeat comes from New Zealand.

Production of wool for the year 1999–2000 was 193,000 tonnes. Milk production for 2000–01 totalled a record 12,322m. litres. In 1998–99 butter production totalled 232,948 tonnes and cheese production 238,535 tonnes.

Forestry. Forests covered 8·1m. ha in 1998 (29% of New Zealand's land area), up from 7·67m. ha in 1990. Of this, about 6·4m. ha are indigenous forest and 1·7m. ha planted productive forest. New planting increased from 15,000 ha in 1991 to 66,000 ha in 1997. Introduced pines form the bulk of the large exotic forest estate and among these radiata pine is the best multi-purpose tree, reaching log size in 25–30 years. Other species planted are Douglas fir and Eucalyptus species. Total roundwood production in 1999–2000 was 18·11m. cu. metres. The table below shows production of rough sawn timber in 1,000 cu. metres for years ending 31 March:

	Indigenous			Exotic			All Species
	Rimu and Miro	Beech	Total	Radiata Pine	Douglas Fir	Total	Total
1995–96	44	4	55	2,631	104	2,849	2,904
1996–97	44	7	56	2,761	122	2,967	3,023
1997–98	28	5	38	2,995	105	3,157	3,195
1998–99	30	4	38	2,996	143	3,188	3,226
1999–2000	21	6	30	3,583	134	3,776	3,806

In 1999–2000 forest industries consisted of 338 sawmills, 6 plywood and 10 veneer plants, 4 particle board mills, 6 wood pulp mills (4 of which also produced paper and paperboard) and 5 fibreboard mills.

The basic products of the pulp and paper mills are mechanical and chemical pulp which are converted into newsprint, kraft and other papers, paperboard and fibreboard. Production of woodpulp in the year ending 31 March 2000 amounted to 1,527,565 tonnes and of paper (including newsprint paper and paperboard) to 829,812 tonnes.

Fisheries. In 1999 the total catch was 594,084 tonnes, almost entirely from sea fishing. The total value of New Zealand fisheries exports during the year ended Dec. 1998 was NZ$1,233m., of which hoki exports constituted NZ$294·6m.

INDUSTRY

The leading companies by market capitalization in New Zealand, excluding banking and finance, in Jan. 2002 were: Telecom Corporation of New Zealand Ltd (TCNZ), NZ$9bn.; Carter Holt Harvey Ltd (NZ$3bn.), a forest products company; and Lion Nathan Ltd (NZ$3bn.), a brewing company.

Statistics of manufacturing industries:

Production year	Hours worked	Salaries and wages paid (NZ$1m.)	Stocks at end of period (NZ$1m.)		Sales and other income (NZ$1m.)	Purchases and other operating expenses
			Materials	Finished goods		
1998–99	460·1m.	8,202	2,365	3,879	50,068	35,985
1999–2000	456·6m.	8,430	2,498	4,096	53,333	37,958

The following is a statement of the value of the products (including repairs) of the principal industries for the year 1999–2000 (in NZ$1m.):

Industry group	Purchases and operating expenses	Stocks at end of period (finished goods)	Sales and other income
Meat and dairy products	9,371	856	11,237
Other food, beverages and tobacco	5,414	778	7,955
Textiles, apparel and leathergoods	1,795	291	2,595
Wood and paper product manufacturing	4,278	468	6,511
Printing, publishing and recorded media	1,325	67	2,500
Chemicals and chemical, petroleum, coal, rubber and plastic products	4,341	536	6,124
Non-metallic mineral products	996	113	1,588
Metal products	4,135	372	6,042
Machinery and equipment	5,164	529	7,036
Other manufacturing industries	1,139	86	1,745
Total	37,958	4,096	53,333

Labour. There were 1,771,000 persons employed in the quarter ending Dec. 1999. Unemployment was 6·3% of the workforce in the same quarter. Unemployment figures for the quarter ending Dec. 1999 were 119,000. By Dec. 2002 the rate had declined to 4·9%.

In Dec. 1999, 52,858 had been unemployed for longer than six months. The weekly average wage in Feb. 2000 was NZ$723·87 for men, NZ$561·84 for women. A minimum wage is set by the government annually. As of March 2003 it was NZ$8·50 an hour; a youth rate of NZ$6·80 per hour applies for 16–17 year-olds. In the year to Dec. 1999 there were 32 industrial stoppages (72 in 1996) with 16,674 working days lost (69,514 in 1996).

Trade Unions. In 2000, 19 industrial unions of workers (representing 80% of all union members) were affiliated to the Council of Trade Unions, NZCTU (*President*, Ross Wilson). Compulsory trade union membership was made illegal in 1991, and the national wage award system was replaced by local wage agreements under the Employment Contracts Act 1991. The NZCTU brings together nearly 300,000 union members in 34 affiliated unions.

INTERNATIONAL TRADE

Total overseas debt was NZ$98,998m. in March 1998. In 1990 New Zealand and Australia completed the Closer Economic Relations Agreement (initiated in 1983), which provides for mutual free trade in goods.

Imports and Exports. Trade in NZ$1m. for recent years:

	Exports, including re-exports (f.o.b.)	Imports (c.i.f.)	Balance of Merchandise Trade
1994–95	20,790	21,261	−471
1995–96	20,546	21,252	−706
1996–97	21,033	21,324	−291
1997–98	21,990	22,589	−599
1998–99	22,600	24,248	−1,648
1999–2000	26,027	29,193	−3,166

The principal imports for the 12 months ended 30 June 2000:

Commodity	Value (NZ$1m. v.f.d.)
Fruit and nuts	157
Sugar and sugar confectionery	123
Beer, wine and spirits	235
Crude petroleum oil	1,403
Inorganic chemicals (excluding aluminium oxide)	186
Aluminium oxide	245
Knitted or crocheted fabrics and articles	526
Glass and glassware	175
Iron and steel	428
Articles of iron and steel	372
Copper and articles of copper	122
Aluminium and articles of aluminium	265
Tools, implements and articles of base metals	267
Machinery and mechanical appliances	3,651
Organic chemicals	318
Pharmaceutical products	703
Plastics and articles of plastic	1,093
Rubber and articles of rubber	309
Paper, paperboard and articles thereof	761
Printed books, newspapers etc.	385
Cotton yarn and fabrics	87
Man-made filaments and fibres	213
Electrical machinery and equipment	2,834
Motor cars, station wagons, utilities	2,301
Trucks, buses and vans	547
Aircraft	1,493
Ships and boats	691
Optical, photographic, technical and surgical equipment	819

The principal exports of New Zealand produce for the 12 months ended 30 June 2000 were:

Commodity	Value (NZ$1m. f.o.b.)	Commodity	Value (NZ$1m. f.o.b.)
Live animals	174	Fish, fresh, chilled or frozen	850
Meat, fresh, chilled or frozen		Vegetables	363
Beef and veal	1,403	Fresh kiwifruit	462
Lamb and mutton	1,697	Fresh apples	404
Dairy products		Forest products	
Milk, cream and yoghurt	1,943	Sawn timber and logs	1,488
Butter	1,004	Paper and paper products	437
Cheese	987	Wood pulp	544
Raw hides, skins and leather	558	Iron and steel and articles thereof	490
Wool	801		
Aluminium and articles thereof	1,114	Machinery and mechanical appliances	944
Casein and caseinates	803	Electrical machinery and equipment	752
Plastic materials and articles thereof	334		
Sausage casings	141		

The leading export destinations in 1998–99 (exports and re-exports f.o.b., in NZ$1m.) were: Australia, 4,841; USA, 3,005; Japan, 2,878; UK, 1,401; Republic of Korea, 883; Germany, 623; China, 619. The principal import suppliers in 1998–99 (imports v.f.d., in NZ$1m.) were: Australia, 5,367; USA, 4,283; Japan, 3,056; China, 1,234; Germany, 1,088; UK, 1,066; Taiwan, 547.

COMMUNICATIONS

Roads. Total length of maintained roads at 1998 was 91,996·4 km (56,338·4 km sealed and 35,628 km gravel) with 15,800 bridges. There were 74 national and provincial state highways comprising 10,453 km of roadway, including the principal arterial traffic routes.

In Feb. 1998 there were 9,110 full-time equivalent persons employed in the provision of road passenger transport and 22,210 persons providing road freight transport.

Total expenditure on roads (including state highways), streets and bridges—by the central government and local authorities combined—amounted to NZ$1·1bn. in 1997.

At 31 March 1999 motor vehicles licensed numbered 2,668,536, of which 1,831,118 were cars. In 1997 there were 16,139 omnibuses/public taxis, and 38,288 motorcycles. Included in the remaining numbers were 8,425 powercycles, 346,489 trucks and 303,371 trailers and caravans.

In 1999 there were 434 deaths in road accidents.

Rail. New Zealand Rail was privatized in 1994 and is now known as Tranz Rail. In 1994 a 24-hour freight link was introduced between Auckland and Christchurch. There were, in 2000, 3,904 km of 1,067 mm gauge railway open for traffic (506 km electrified). In 1998 Tranz Rail carried 11·7m. tonnes of freight and 11·3m. passengers. Total revenue in the financial year 1999–2000 was NZ$594·5m.

At 30 June 2000 Tranz Rail track and rolling stock included 343 diesel, electric and shunting locomotives, 5,948 freight wagons, 321 passenger carriages and commuter units, three rail/road ferries (linking the North and South Islands) and plant and support equipment.

Civil Aviation. There are international airports at Wellington, Auckland and Christchurch, with Auckland International being the main airport. The national carrier is Air New Zealand. Trans-Tasman air travel is subject to agreement between Air New Zealand and Qantas.

New Zealand has one of the highest ratios of aircraft to population in the world with 3,403 aircraft in the year to June 1998. Since 1992 air transport flights have increased by about 9% per year. In 1999 scheduled airline traffic of New Zealand-based carriers flew 172·2m. km, carrying 8,892,000 passengers (2,829,000 on international flights).

Shipping. In 1998 merchant shipping totalled 336,000 GRT, including oil tankers 73,000 GRT.

Telecommunications. The provision of telecommunication services is the responsibility of the Telecom Corporation of New Zealand, formed in 1987 and privatized in 1990; and CLEAR Communications, which began operations in Dec. 1990. In 2000 there were 1,915,000 main lines, or 499·9 for every 1,000 persons, and 1·4m. PCs in use (360·2 per 1,000 persons). Mobile phone subscribers numbered 881,000 (230 per 1,000 persons) in 1999 and there were 65,000 fax machines in 1995. There were 2·06m. Internet users in Aug. 2002. IT spending in 1997, at 8·7% of GDP, is one of the highest in the developed world.

Postal Services. On 1 April 1998 the Postal Services Act removed New Zealand Post's former statutory monopoly on the carriage of letters and opened the postal market to full competition. To carry out a business involving the carriage of letters, a person or company must be registered as a postal operator with the Ministry of Commerce.

In 1997 there were 297 post shops, 705 post centre franchises and 3,663 stamp resellers.

SOCIAL INSTITUTIONS

Justice. The judiciary consists of the Court of Appeal, the High Court and District Courts. All exercise both civil and criminal jurisdiction. Final appeal lies to the Privy Council in London. Special courts include the Maori Land Court, the Maori Appellate Court, Family Courts, the Youth Court, Environment Court and the Employment Court. On 20 Nov. 1997 there were 4,935 sentenced inmates of whom 207 were women. Of the male inmates 44% (some 1,566) identified themselves as Maori only compared to 38% who identified themselves as European only. Some 526,372 offences, including 165 homicides, were reported in the year ending June 1997. The death penalty for murder was replaced by life imprisonment in 1961.

The Criminal Injuries Compensation Act, 1963, which came into force on 1 Jan. 1964, provided for compensation of persons injured by certain criminal acts and the dependants of persons killed by such acts. However, this has now been phased out in favour of the Accident Compensation Act, 1982, except in the residual area of property damage caused by escapees. The Offenders Legal Aid Act 1954 provides that any person charged or convicted of any offence may apply for legal aid which may be granted depending on the person's means and the gravity of the offence etc. Since 1970 legal aid in civil proceedings (except divorce) has been available for persons of small or moderate means. The Legal Services Act 1991 now brings together in one statute the civil and criminal legal aid schemes.

Police. The police are a national body maintained by the central government. Legislation of 1994 permits the private management of prisons and prisoner escort services. For operational purposes New Zealand was divided into four police regions in July 1997, each controlled by an assistant commissioner. In 1991, 1,100 traffic officers merged with the police, who previously did not control traffic. In June 1998 there were 6,760 full-time equivalent sworn officers.

Ombudsmen. The office of Ombudsman was created in 1962. From 1975 additional Ombudsmen have been authorized. There are currently two. Ombudsmen's functions are to investigate complaints under the Ombudsman Act, the Official Information Act and the Local Government Official Information and Meetings Act from members of the public relating to administrative decisions of central, regional and local government.

During the year ended 30 June 2000 a total of 4,798 complaints were received, with files opened on 407 other cases. A total of 34 complaints were sustained during the year and 387 were still under investigation.

Religion. No direct state aid is given to any form of religion. For the Church of England the country is divided into seven dioceses, with a separate bishopric (Aotearoa) for the Maori. The Presbyterian Church is divided into 23 presbyteries and the Maori Synod. The Moderator is elected annually. The Methodist Church is divided into ten districts; the President is elected annually. The Roman Catholic Church is divided into four dioceses, with the Archbishop of Wellington as Metropolitan Archbishop.

Adherents of leading religions at the 2001 census were as follows:

Religious denomination	Adherents	Religious denomination	Adherents
Anglican	584,793	Brethren	20,406
Catholic	486,012	Jehovah's Witnesses	17,826
Presbyterian	417,453	Assemblies of God	16,023
Methodist	120,708	Salvation Army	12,618
Baptist	51,426	Seventh-day Adventist	12,600
Ratana	48,975	All other religious affiliations	398,847
Buddhist	41,664	No religion	1,028,052
Latter-day Saints (Mormons)	39,915	Object to state	239,241
Hindu	39,876	Not specified	211,638
Pentecostal	30,222		
Islam/Muslim	23,637	Total	3,841,932[1]

[1]Where a person reported more than one religious affiliation, they have been counted in each applicable group.

Education. Education is compulsory between the ages of 6 and 15. Children aged three and four years may enrol at the 595 free kindergartens maintained by Free Kindergarten Associations, which receive government assistance. There are also 545 play centres which also receive government subsidy. In 1997 there were 46,756 and 17,058 children on the rolls respectively. There were also 1,288 childcare centres in 1997 with 61,597 children, 705 *te kohanga reo* (providing early childhood education in the Maori language) with 13,505 children, and a number of other smaller providers of early childhood care and education.

In 1997 there were 2,235 state primary schools (including intermediate and state contributing schools), with 432,721 pupils; the number of teachers was 22,289. A correspondence school for children in remote areas and those otherwise unable to attend school had 4,733 primary and secondary pupils. There were 58 registered private primary and intermediate schools with 418 teachers and 13,115 pupils.

In 1997 there were 320 state secondary schools with 14,577 full-time teachers and 212,426 pupils. There were also 58 state composite area schools with 4,831 scholars in the secondary division. In 1997, 3,470 pupils received tuition from the secondary department of the correspondence school. There were 18 registered private secondary schools with 540 teachers and 11,367 pupils.

NEW ZEALAND

New Zealand has seven universities—the University of Auckland, University of Waikato (at Hamilton), Victoria University of Wellington, Massey University (at Palmerston North), the University of Canterbury (at Christchurch), the University of Otago (at Dunedin) and Lincoln University (near Christchurch). The number of equivalent full-time students attending universities in 1999 was 95,120. There were four teachers' training colleges with 8,429 equivalent full-time students in 1999, and 70,338 equivalent full-time students were enrolled in polytechnic courses in 1999.

Total budgeted expenditure estimated in 1998 on education was NZ$5,756m. (16·8% of government expenses). The universities are autonomous bodies. All state-funded primary and secondary schools are controlled by boards of trustees. Education in state schools is free for children under 19 years of age. All educational institutions are reviewed every three years by teams of educational reviewers.

A series of reforms is being implemented by the government following reports of 18 working groups on tertiary education. These include a new funding system, begun in 1991 and based solely on student numbers.

The adult literacy rate in 1998 was at least 99%.

Health. At 31 March 2000 there were 8,615 active medical practitioners. In 1998 there were 109 public hospitals with 14,298 beds and 285 private hospitals with 9,156 beds. Total expenditure on health in 1998–99 was NZ$8,376m. (NZ$6,490 from public sources).

Welfare. Non-contributory old-age pensions were introduced in 1898. Large reductions in welfare expenditure were introduced by the government in Dec. 1990.

From 1 Oct. 1998 anyone receiving unemployment benefit, sickness benefit, a training benefit, a 55 plus benefit, or a young job seekers allowance has received a benefit called the Community Wage. In return for receiving the Community Wage, recipients are expected to search for work, meet with Work and Income New Zealand when asked, take a suitable work offer, and take part in activities that would improve their chances of finding a job. For the year ended 30 June 1998, 154,774 people received Unemployment Benefits (replaced by the Community Wage on 1 Oct. 1998) with total gross expenditure amounting to NZ$1,496,701,000.

In the budget of July 1991 it was announced that current rates of Guaranteed Retirement Income Scheme (GRI) payment would be frozen until 1 April 1993, thereafter to be on the previous year's consumer price index. On 1 April 1992 GRI was replaced by the national superannuation scheme which is income-tested. Eligibility has been gradually increased to 65 years. Universal eligibility is available at 70 years. At 1 April 1999 a married couple received NZ$325·58 per week, a single person living alone NZ$212·69 per week.

Social Welfare Benefits.

Benefits	Number in force at 30 June 1999	Total expenditure 1998–99 (NZ$1,000)
Community Wage—Job Seeker	164,530	1,620,031
Community Wage—Training	4,673	68,035
Community Wage—Sickness	33,022	403,708
Invalids' Benefit	51,284	654,432
Domestic Purposes' Benefit	110,067	1,610,910
Orphans' Benefit/ Unsupported Child's Benefit	5,408	32,152
Widows' Benefit	9,213	93,235
Transitional Retirement Benefit	8,689	105,412
New Zealand Superannuation	440,054	5,221,501
Veterans' Pension	7,159	72,645
Tax on income tested benefits	—	687,133
Other income support	—	487,334
Total Income Support	834,099	11,056,528

Reciprocity with Other Countries. New Zealand has overseas social security agreements with the United Kingdom, the Netherlands, Greece, Ireland, Australia, Jersey and Guernsey, Denmark, Canada and Italy. The main purpose of these agreements is to encourage free movement of labour and to ensure that when a person has lived or worked in more than one country, each of those countries takes a fair share of the responsibility for meeting the costs of that person's social security coverage. New Zealand also pays people eligible for New Zealand Superannuation or veterans' pensions who live in the Cook Islands, Niue or Tokelau.

CULTURE

Broadcasting. Legislation of 1995 split the state-owned Radio New Zealand into a government-owned public radio broadcasting company and some 40 commercial stations.

Television New Zealand operates two channels. Two other channels, TV3 and TV4, are commercial. There are also regional TV networks. Pay television was introduced in May 1990—Sky Entertainment operates on 37 channels. Colour is by PAL. The New Zealand Public Radio Service also includes the Radio New Zealand International, a short-wave which broadcasts to the South Pole. In July 1988 there were 47 AM and 17 FM stations broadcasting in New Zealand, of which 30 were privately owned. There are 21 regional Maori stations for the promotion of Maori culture. In 1997 there 3·75m. radio and 1·9m. television receivers.

Cinema. Attendances at the 315 cinema screens in 1999 totalled 17m., up from 6m. in 1991. Four full-length films were made in 1995 and gross box office receipts came to NZ$82m.

Press. In 1997 there were 29 daily newspapers, of which 21 were evening papers. The *New Zealand Herald,* published in Auckland, had the largest daily circulation of 221,047 in 1998. Other major dailies are *The Press*, *The Dominion* and *The Evening Post*, with circulations of between 50,000–100,000 copies.

There are two Sunday newspapers, *Sunday Star Times* and *Sunday News*, both published by Independent Newspapers Limited and distributed nationwide. The *Sunday Star Times* is a broadsheet and circulates about 190,000 copies while the *Sunday News* is a tabloid and circulates 115,000 copies every Sunday.

Tourism. There were 1,652,000 tourists in the year to March 2000 (in 1998, 1,518,000) of whom 537,775 were from Australia, 186,842 were from the USA, 145,637 were from Japan and 174,838 were from the UK. International tourism generated NZ$3·07bn. in 1998 (3·4% of GDP).

Festivals. The biennial New Zealand Festival takes place in Wellington in Feb./March and will next be held in 2004. The biennial Christchurch Arts Festival takes place in July/Aug. and will next be held in 2003.

DIPLOMATIC REPRESENTATIVES

Of New Zealand in the United Kingdom (New Zealand Hse., Haymarket, London, SW1Y 4TQ)
High Commissioner: Russell Marshall, CNZM.

Of the United Kingdom in New Zealand (44 Hill St., Wellington, 1)
High Commissioner: Richard Fell, CVO.

Of New Zealand in the USA (37 Observatory Cir., NW, Washington, D.C., 20008)
Ambassador: John Wood.

Of the USA in New Zealand (29 Fitzherbert Terr., Wellington)
Ambassador: Charles J. Swindells.

Of New Zealand to the United Nations
Ambassador: Don J. MacKay.

Of New Zealand to the European Union
Ambassador: Dell Clarke Higgie.

FURTHER READING

Statistics New Zealand. *New Zealand Official Yearbook.—Key Statistics: a Monthly Abstract of Statistics.—Profile of New Zealand.*
Belich, James, *Making Peoples: a History of the New Zealanders from Polynesian Settlement to the End of the Nineteenth century.* London, 1997.—*Paradise Reforged: A History of New Zealanders From the 1880s to the Year 2000.* London, 2002
Harland, B., *On Our Own: New Zealand in a Tripolar World.* Victoria Univ. Press, 1992
Harris, P. and Levine, S. (eds.) *The New Zealand Politics Source Book.* 2nd ed. Palmerston North, 1994

Massey, P., *New Zealand: Market Liberalization in a Developed Economy.* London, 1995
Patterson, B. and K., *New Zealand.* [Bibliography] 2nd ed. ABC-Clio, Oxford and Santa Barbara (CA), 1998
Sinclair, K. (ed.) *The Oxford Illustrated History of New Zealand. 2nd ed.* OUP, 1994

For other more specialized titles see under CONSTITUTION AND GOVERNMENT *and* DEFENCE *above.*

National statistical office: Statistics New Zealand, POB 2922, Wellington, 1.
Website: http://www.stats.govt.nz/

TERRITORIES OVERSEAS

Territories Overseas coming within the jurisdiction of New Zealand consist of Tokelau and the Ross Dependency.

Tokelau

Tokelau is situated some 500 km to the north of Samoa and comprises three dispersed atolls—Atafu, Fakaofo and Nukunonu. The land area is 12 sq. km and the population at the 1996 census was 1,507, giving a density of 126 per sq. km.

The British government transferred administrative control of Tokelau to New Zealand in 1925. Formal sovereignty was transferred to New Zealand in 1948 by act of the New Zealand Parliament. New Zealand statute law, however, does not apply to Tokelau unless it is expressly extended to Tokelau. In practice New Zealand legislation is extended to Tokelau only with its consent.

Tokelau's three villages are its foundation, and have remained largely autonomous. There has never been any resident New Zealand administration. At the national level Tokelau's needs remain formally the responsibility of the New Zealand government, and in particular, the Administration of Tokelau.

Under a programme agreed in 1992, the role of Tokelau's political institutions is being better defined and expanded. The process under way enables the base of Tokelau government to be located within Tokelau's national level institutions rather than as before, within a public service located largely in Samoa. In 1994 the Administrator's powers were delegated to the *General Fono* (the national representative body), and when the *General Fono* is not in session, to the *Council of Faipule.* The Tokelau Amendment Act 1996 conferred on the *General Fono* a power to make rules for Tokelau, including the power to impose taxes.

Coconuts (the source of copra) are the only cash crop. Pulaka, breadfruit, papayas, the screw-pine and bananas are cultivated as food crops. Livestock comprises pigs, poultry and goats.

Development prospects are restricted by the small land area and population, geographic isolation, and the relatively high cost of providing education, health and other services including telecommunications and shipping, to three widely separated communities. For these reasons Tokelau relies substantially on external financial support, particularly from New Zealand. Nonetheless the development of government structures at the national level has promoted a wish for Tokelau to be self-reliant to the greatest extent possible.

Tokelau affirmed to the United Nations in 1994 that it had under active consideration both the Constitution of a self-governing Tokelau and an act of self-determination. It also expressed a strong preference for a future status of free association with New Zealand.

Ross Dependency

By Imperial Order in Council, dated 30 July 1923, the territories between 160° E. long. and 150° W. long. and south of 60° S. lat. were brought within the jurisdiction of the New Zealand government. The region was named the Ross Dependency. From time to time laws for the Dependency have been made by regulations promulgated by the Governor-General of New Zealand.

The mainland area is estimated at 400,000–450,000 sq. km and is mostly ice-covered. In Jan. 1957 a New Zealand expedition under Sir Edmund Hillary established a base in the Dependency. In Jan. 1958 Sir Edmund Hillary and four other New Zealanders reached the South Pole.

The main base—Scott Base, at Pram Point, Ross Island—is manned throughout the year, about 12 people being present during winter. Temporary accommodation facilities provide support for specific activities in the Dry Valleys and elsewhere in the Ross Sea Region. The annual activities of 200–300 scientists and support staff are managed by a crown agency, Antarctica New Zealand, based in Christchurch.

SELF-GOVERNING TERRITORIES OVERSEAS

THE COOK ISLANDS

KEY HISTORICAL EVENTS

The Cook Islands, which lie between 8° and 23° S. lat., and 156° and 167° W. long., were made a British protectorate in 1888, and on 11 June 1901 were annexed as part of New Zealand. In 1965 the Cook Islands became a self-governing territory in 'free association' with New Zealand.

TERRITORY AND POPULATION

The islands fall roughly into two groups—the scattered islands towards the north (Northern group) and the islands towards the south (Southern group). The islands with their populations at the census of 1996:

Lower Group—	Area sq. km	Population	Northern Group—	Area sq. km	Population
Aitutaki	18·3	2,389	Manihiki (Humphrey)	5·4	668
Atiu	26·9	956	Nassau	1·3	99
Mangaia	51·8	1,108	Palmerston (Avarua)	2·1	49
Manuae and Te au-o-tu	6·2	—	Penrhyn (Tongareva)	9·8	606
Mauke (Parry Is.)	18·4	652	Pukapuka (Danger)	1·3	779
Mitiaro	22·3	319	Rakahanga (Reirson)	4·1	249
Rarotonga	67·1	11,225	Suwarrow (Anchorage)	0·4	4
			Total	235·4	19,103

Population density in 1996 was 76 per sq. km. In 1996 an estimated 58·8% of the population lived in urban areas. The 2001 total population (17,700) and the estimated resident population (13,400) have fallen since 1996, the latter by approximately 26%.

SOCIAL STATISTICS

Birth rate (1998 estimate, per 1,000 population), 22·5; death rate, 5·2. Life expectancy was estimated (1998) at: males, 62·2 years; females 73·1. Fertility rate, 1999, 3·4 births per woman.

CLIMATE

Oceanic climate where rainfall is moderate to heavy throughout the year, with Nov. to March being particularly wet. Weather can be changeable from day to day and can end in rainfall after an otherwise sunny day. Rarotonga, Jan. 26°C, July 20°C. Annual rainfall 2,060 mm.

CONSTITUTION AND GOVERNMENT

The Cook Islands Constitution of 1965 provides for internal self-government but linked to New Zealand by a common Head of State and a common citizenship, that of New Zealand. It provides for a ministerial system of government with a Cabinet consisting of a Prime Minister and not more than eight nor fewer than six other

Ministers. There is also an advisory council composed of hereditary chiefs, the 15-member House of Ariki, without legislative powers. The New Zealand government is represented by a New Zealand Representative and the Queen, as head of state, by the Queen's Representative. The capital is Avarua on Rarotonga.

The unicameral *Parliament* comprises 25 members elected for a term of five years.

RECENT ELECTIONS

At the elections of 16 June 1999 the centrist Democratic Alliance (DA) won 11 of the 25 seats, the Cook Islands Party (CIP) won 10 seats and the New Alliance (NA) 4 seats.

CURRENT ADMINISTRATION

High Commissioner: Kurt Meyer.
Prime Minister: Robert Woonton (DA).

ECONOMY

Overview. A package of economic reforms including privatization and deregulation was initiated in July 1996 to deal with a national debt of US$141m., 120% of GDP.

Currency. The Cook Island *dollar* was at par with the New Zealand *dollar*, but was replaced in 1995 by New Zealand currency.

Budget. Revenue, 1996–97, NZ$45·8m.; expenditure, NZ$44·8m. Revenue is derived chiefly from customs duties which follow the New Zealand customs tariff, income tax and stamp sales.

Grants from New Zealand, mainly for medical, educational and general administrative purposes, totalled NZ$11·3m. in 1996–97.

Performance. Real GDP growth was 1·3% in 1995 (1·5% in 1994).

Banking and Finance. There are four banks in the Cook Islands. The Cook Islands Savings Bank is state-owned and has deposit services throughout the islands. The Cook Islands Development Bank is a state-owned corporation funded in part by loans from the Asian Development Bank. The two remaining banks are subsidiaries of the Australia and New Zealand Banking Group Limited and the Westpac Bank, which are both Australian-owned and major banks in Australasia.

The Cook Islands were one of 15 countries and territories named in a report in June 2000 as failing to co-operate in the fight against international money laundering. The Financial Action Task Force on Money Laundering was set up by the G7 group of major industrialized nations.

Weights and Measures. The metric system is in operation.

ENERGY AND NATURAL RESOURCES

Electricity. Production in 1998 was 15m. kWh.

Oil and Gas. The Cook Islands has no domestic resources of oil or gas.

Water. There are 12 intakes on the island of Rarotonga. The other inhabited islands obtain their water from either artesian or roof catchment or a combination of the two. The consumption of water in Rarotonga averages 260 litres per person per day. There are periodic water shortages, particularly in the northern group of islands.

Minerals. The islands of the Cook group have no significant mineral resources. However, the seabed, which forms part of the exclusive economic zone, has some of the highest concentrations of manganese nodules in the world. Manganese nodules are rich in cobalt and nickel.

Agriculture. In 1997 there were approximately 4,000 ha of arable land and 3,000 ha of permanent crops. Production estimates (1998, in 1,000 tonnes): coconuts, 5; cassava, 3; mangoes, 3. Livestock (1996): 21,988 pigs, 3,697 goats.

Forestry. Timber production was 5,000 cu. metres in 1999.

Fisheries. In 2000 the total catch was estimated at 500 tonnes, entirely from sea fishing.

INDUSTRY

Labour. In 1996 there were 5,230 persons actively employed in the Cook Islands and 764 unemployed. Of those employed, 3,072 were men and 2,158 were women.

Trade Unions. There are no trade unions although there are a number of worker collectives. These include the Public Service Association, Cook Islands Workers Association, Nurses Association and Teachers Association.

INTERNATIONAL TRADE

Imports and Exports. Exports, mainly to New Zealand, were valued at NZ$6·0m. in 1998. Main items exported were fresh fruit and vegetables and black pearls. Imports totalled NZ$70·7m.

COMMUNICATIONS

Roads. In 1992 there were 320 km of roads and, in 1991, 5,015 vehicles.

Rail. There are no railways in the Cook Islands.

Civil Aviation. New Zealand has financed the construction of an international airport at Rarotonga which became operational for jet services in 1973. There are nine useable airports. Domestic services are provided by Air Rarotonga, and in 1998 there were also services to Auckland, Honolulu, Los Angeles, the Fiji Islands and French Polynesia.

Shipping. A fortnightly cargo shipping service is provided between New Zealand, Niue and Rarotonga. In 1998 merchant shipping totalled 7,000 GRT.

Telecommunications. Eight Satellite Earth Stations are located at eight of the most populated islands with HF Radio provided as backup. In the remaining islands HF radio is the only means of communication. In March 1997 there were 5,141 telephone lines in service. There were 190 mobile phone subscribers in 1997.

Postal Services. A full range of postal services are offered and there are post agents in all inhabited islands.

SOCIAL INSTITUTIONS

Justice. There is a High Court and a Court of Appeal, from which further appeal is to the Privy Council in the UK.
    The population in penal institutions in 1995 was 45 (equivalent to 225 per 100,000 of national population).

Religion. From the census of 1996, 58% of the population belong to the Cook Islands Christian Church; about 17% are Roman Catholics, and the rest are Latter-day Saints and Seventh-Day Adventists and other religions.

Education. In March 1998 there were 28 primary schools with 140 teachers and 2,711 pupils, 23 secondary schools with 129 teachers and 1,779 pupils, and 26 pre-schools with 30 teachers and 460 pupils.

Health. A user pay scheme was introduced in July 1996 where all Cook Islanders pay a fee of NZ$5·00 for any medical or surgical treatment including consultation. Those under the age of 16 years or over the age of 60 years are exempted from payment of this charge. The dental department is privatized except for the school dental health provision. This service continues to be free to all schools.
    The Rarotonga Hospital, which is the referral hospital for the outer islands, consists of 80 beds. The hospital has 8 doctors, 33 registered nurses and 11 hospital aides.

CULTURE

Broadcasting. In 1997 there were approximately 4,000 TV receivers and 14,000 radio receivers.
    There are two radio stations (AM and FM) operating in the Cook Islands

Cinema. There is one cinema, located on the island of Rarotonga.

Press. The *Cook Islands News* (circulation 1,800 in 1996) is the sole daily newspaper. The *Cook Islands Star*, which is published fortnightly, is sold in the Cook Islands and in New Zealand.

Tourism. In 1998 there were 55,552 tourists arrivals.

Libraries. There are three libraries. The Parliamentary Library is available for use by members of the public on written request to the Clerk of the House. The National Library and the Library and Museum Library are both on Rarotonga and are lending libraries open to the public.

Theatre and Opera. All significant cultural events in Rarotonga are held at the Auditorium, also known as the Cultural Centre.

Museums and Galleries. There are two small museums on Rarotonga.

FURTHER READING
Local statistical office: Ministry of Finance and Economic Management, P.O. Box 41, Rarotonga, Cook Islands.

NIUE

KEY HISTORICAL EVENTS
Captain James Cook sighted Niue in 1774 and called it Savage Island. Christian missionaries arrived in 1846. Niue became a British Protectorate in 1900 and was annexed to New Zealand in 1901. Internal self-government was achieved in free association with New Zealand on 19 Oct. 1974, New Zealand taking responsibility for external affairs and defence. Niue is a member of the South Pacific Forum.

TERRITORY AND POPULATION
Niue is the largest uplifted coral island in the world. Distance from Auckland, New Zealand, 2,161 km; from Rarotonga, 933 km. Area, 258 sq. km; height above sea level, 67 metres. The population has been declining steadily, from around 6,000 in the 1960s to 1,812 recorded in the 2001 census, giving a population density of 7 per sq. km. Migration to New Zealand is the main factor in population change. The capital is Alofi.

SOCIAL STATISTICS
Annual growth rate, 1990–99, −2·0%. During 1992 births registered numbered 31, deaths 12.

CLIMATE
Oceanic, warm and humid, tempered by trade winds. May to Oct. are cooler months. Temperatures range from 20°C to 28°C.

CONSTITUTION AND GOVERNMENT
There is a Legislative Assembly (*Fono*) of 20 members, 14 elected from 14 constituencies and 6 elected by all constituencies.

RECENT ELECTIONS
Parliamentary elections were held on 21 April 2002 in which all 20 members of the Legislative Assembly were re-elected. On 1 May 2002 Young Vivian was sworn in as prime minister.

CURRENT ADMINISTRATION
High Commissioner: Sandra Lee.
    Prime Minister: Young Vivian (Niue People's Party).

ECONOMY
Budget. Financial aid from New Zealand, 1995–96, totalled NZ$8·4m.

Banking and Finance. Niue was one of 15 countries and territories named in a report in June 2000 as failing to co-operate in the fight against international money laundering. The Financial Action Task Force on Money Laundering was set up by the G7 group of major industrialized nations.

ENERGY AND NATURAL RESOURCES

Electricity. Production in 1998 was 3m. kWh.

Agriculture. In 1997 there were approximately 5,000 ha of arable land and 2,000 ha of permanent crops. The main commercial crops of the island are coconuts, taro and yams.

In 1996 there were 2,000 pigs.

Fisheries. In 1999 the total catch was 120 tonnes, exclusively from marine waters.

INTERNATIONAL TRADE

Imports and Exports. Exports, 1993, NZ$0·42m.; imports, NZ$3·52m.

COMMUNICATIONS

Civil Aviation. A weekly commercial air service links Niue with New Zealand and there are also flights to Samoa and Tonga.

Telecommunications. There is a wireless station at Alofi, the port of the island. Telephone main lines (1994) 500.

SOCIAL INSTITUTIONS

Justice. There is a High Court under a Chief Justice, with a right of appeal to the New Zealand Supreme Court.

Religion. At the 1991 census, 1,487 people belonged to the Congregational (Ekalesia Niue); Latter-day Saints (213), Roman Catholics (90), Jehovah's Witness (47), Seventh Day Adventists (27), other (63), No religion (34), not stated (1).

Education. In 1991 there was one primary school with 22 teachers and 337 pupils, and one secondary school with 27 teachers and 304 pupils.

Health. In 1992 there were 4 doctors, 1 dentist, 6 midwives and 19 nursing personnel. There is a 24-bed hospital at Alofi.

CULTURE

Broadcasting. There were 1,000 radio receivers in 1997. Cable television is available.

Press. A weekly newspaper is published in English and Niuean; circulation about 400.

Tourism. In 1992 there were 2,329 visitors (1,668 tourists).

NICARAGUA

República de Nicaragua

Capital: Managua
Population estimate, 2000: 5·07m.
GDP per capita, 2000: (PPP$) 2,366
HDI/world rank: 0·635/118

KEY HISTORICAL EVENTS

Colonization of the Nicaraguan Pacific coast was undertaken by Spaniards from Panama, beginning in 1523. France and Britain, however, and later the USA, all tried to play a colonial or semi-colonial role in Nicaragua. Nicaragua became an independent republic in 1838 but its independence was often threatened by US intervention. Between 1910 and 1930 the country was under almost continuous US military occupation.

In 1914 the Bryan-Chamarro Treaty entitled the USA to a permanent option for a canal route through Nicaragua, a 99-year option for a naval base in the Bay of Fonseca on the Pacific coast and occupation of the Corn Islands on the Atlantic coast. The Bryan-Chamarro Treaty was not abrogated until 14 July 1970 when the Corn Islands returned to Nicaragua.

The Somoza family dominated Nicaragua from 1933 to 1979. Through a brutal dictatorship imposed by means of the National Guard, they secured for themselves a large share of the national wealth. In 1962 the radical Sandinista National Liberation Front was formed with the object of overthrowing the Somozas. After 17 years of civil war the Sandinistas triumphed. On 17 July 1979 President Somoza fled into exile. The USA made efforts to unseat the revolutionary government by supporting the Contras (counter-revolutionary forces). It was not until 1988 that the state of emergency was lifted as part of the Central American peace process. Rebel anti-Sandinista activities had ceased by 1990; the last organized insurgent group negotiated an agreement with the government in April 1994.

In Oct. 1998 Hurricane Mitch devastated the country causing 3,800 deaths.

TERRITORY AND POPULATION

Nicaragua is bounded in the north by Honduras, east by the Caribbean, south by Costa Rica and west by the Pacific. Area, 130,671 sq. km (121,428 sq. km dry land). The coastline runs 450 km on the Atlantic and 305 km on the Pacific. The census population in April 1995 was 4,357,099 (density, 33·3 per sq. km). In 1999, 55·8% of the population were urban.

The UN gives a projected population for 2010 of 6·49m.

17 administrative departments are grouped in three zones. Areas (in sq. km), populations at the 1995 census and chief towns:

	Area	Population	Chief town
Pacific Zone	18,429	2,467,742	
Chinandega	4,926	350,212	Chinandega
León	5,107	336,894	León
Managua	3,672	1,093,760	Managua
Masaya	590	241,354	Masaya
Granada	929	155,683	Granada
Carazo	1,050	149,407	Jinotepe
Rivas	2,155	140,432	Rivas
Central-North Zone	35,960	1,354,246	
Chontales	6,378	144,635	Juigalpa
Boaco	4,244	136,949	Boaco
Matagalpa	8,523	383,776	Matagalpa
Jinotega	9,755	257,933	Jinotega
Estelí	2,335	174,894	Estelí
Madriz	1,602	107,567	Somoto
Nueva Segovia	3,123	148,492	Ocotal
Atlantic Zone	67,039	535,111	
Atlántico Norte	32,159	192,716	Puerto Cabezas
Atlántico Sur	27,407	272,252	Bluefields
Río San Juan	7,473	70,143	San Carlos

The capital is Managua with (1999 estimate) 930,000 inhabitants. Other cities (1995 populations): León, 123,865; Chinandega, 97,387; Masaya, 88,971; Granada, 71,783; Estelí, 71,550; Tipitapa, 67,925; Matagalpa, 59,397; Juigalpa, 36,999.

The population is of Spanish and Amerindian origins with an admixture of Afro-Americans on the Caribbean coast. Ethnic groups in 1997: Mestizo (mixed Amerindian and white), 69%; white, 17%; black, 9%; Amerindian, 5%. The official language is Spanish.

SOCIAL STATISTICS

1996 births, estimate, 150,000; deaths, 26,000. Birth rate 35 (per 1,000 population), death rate 6. Annual population growth rate, 1990–99, 2·9%. 1999 life expectancy: male 66·1 years, female 70·9. Infant mortality, 1999, 19·3 per 1,000 live births; fertility rate, 1999, 4·3 births per woman.

CLIMATE

The climate is tropical, with a wet season from May to Jan. Temperatures vary with altitude. Managua, Jan. 81°F (27°C), July 81°F (27°C). Annual rainfall 38" (976 mm).

CONSTITUTION AND GOVERNMENT

A new Constitution was promulgated on 9 Jan. 1987. It provides for a unicameral *National Assembly* comprising 90 members directly elected by proportional representation, together with unsuccessful presidential election candidates obtaining a minimum level of votes.

The *President* and *Vice-President* are directly elected for a five-year term commencing on the 10 Jan. following their date of election. The President may stand for a second term, but not consecutively.

National Anthem. 'Salve a ti Nicaragua' ('Hail to thee, Nicaragua'); words by S. Ibarra Mayorga, tune by L. A. Delgadillo.

RECENT ELECTIONS

Presidential and parliamentary elections took place on 4 Nov. 2001. In the presidential elections Enrique Bolaños Geyer was elected with 56·3% of votes cast, defeating José Daniel Ortega Saavedra (42·3%) and Alberto Saborío (1·4%). At the parliamentary elections the Constitutional Liberal Party gained 47 seats with 53·2% of votes cast; the Sandinista National Liberation Front, 43 (42·1%); and the Conservative Party of Nicaragua, 2 (2·1%).

CURRENT ADMINISTRATION

President: Enrique Bolaños Geyer; b. 1928 (Constitutional Liberal Party; in office since 10 Jan. 2002).

Vice President: José Rizo Castellón.

In March 2003 the government included:

Minister of Agriculture and Forestry: José Augusto Navarro Flores. *Transportation and Infrastructure:* Pedro Solórzano Castillo. *Government:* Arturo Harding Lacayo. *Education, Sports and Culture:* Dr Silvio de Franco Montalbán. *Defence:* Dr José Adán Guerra Pastoras. *Development, Industry and Commerce:* Mario Arana. *Environment and Natural Resources:* Jorge Salazar Cardenal. *Finance and Public Credit:* Eduardo Montealegre Rivas. *Foreign Affairs:* Norman José Caldera Cardenal. *Health:* Lucía Salvo Horvilleur. *Labour:* Virgilio Gurdián Castellón. *Family:* Natalia Barillas Cruz.

DEFENCE

In 2000 defence expenditure totalled US$26m. (US$5 per capita), representing 0·8% of GDP.

Army. The Army is being reorganized. There are five regional commands. Strength (1999) 14,000.

Navy. The Nicaraguan Navy was some 800 strong in 1999.

Air Force. The Air Force has been semi-independent since 1947. Personnel (1999) 1,200, with no combat aircraft and 15 armed helicopters.

INTERNATIONAL RELATIONS

Nicaragua is a member of the UN, WTO, OAS, Inter-American Development Bank, ACS, IOM, SELA and the Central American Common Market.

ECONOMY

In 1998 agriculture accounted for 34·1% of GDP in 1997, industry 21·5% and services 44·4%.

Currency. The monetary unit is the *córdoba* (NIO), of 100 *centavos*, which replaced the córdoba oro in 1991 at par. Inflation was 7·4% in 2001. In May 2002 foreign exchange reserves were US$402m. In March 2002 total money supply was 4,754m. córdobas.

Budget. Total revenue and expenditure (in 1m. córdobas), years ending 31 Dec.:

	1997	1998	1999	2000
Revenue	5,404·8	6,976·5	7,956·2	9,193·4
Expenditure	6,435·3	7,850·5	10,853·5	12,512·1

Expenditure by function, in 1m. córdobas (1994): education 615·86, social security 584·43, health 531·36, public order 316·29, defence 231·56.

Performance. Nicaragua's economy grew at an average annual rate of 5·2% between 1995–2000, with GDP growth of 5·8% in 2000 and 3·0% in 2001. Total GDP in 1998 was US$2·0bn.

Banking and Finance. The Central Bank of Nicaragua came into operation on 1 Jan. 1961 as an autonomous bank of issue, absorbing the issue department of the National Bank. The *President* is Dr Mario Alonso Icabalceta. There were seven private commercial banks in 2000.

Weights and Measures. The metric system is recommended.

ENERGY AND NATURAL RESOURCES

Environment. According to the *World Bank Atlas* Nicaragua's carbon dioxide emissions in 1998 were the equivalent of 0·7 tonnes per capita.

Electricity. Installed capacity in 1995 was 417,700 kW. In 1998, 2·71bn. kWh were produced; consumption per capita was 281 kWh.

Minerals. Production of gold in 1997 was 1,200 kg; silver (1993), 71,900 troy oz; limestone (1993), 12,000 cu. metres.

Agriculture. In 1998 there were 2·5m. ha arable land and 289,000 ha permanent cropland. 88,000 ha were irrigated in 1997. Production (in 1,000 tonnes) in 2000: sugarcane, 4,000; maize, 364; rice, 285; dry beans, 114; sorghum, 102; bananas, 92; coffee, 82; oranges, 71; groundnuts, 67; cassava, 52; pineapples, 47; plantains, 40; soybeans, 23.

In 2000 there were 1·66m. cattle, 400,000 pigs, 245,000 horses and 10m. chickens. Animal products (in 1,000 tonnes), 2000: beef and veal, 49; pork, bacon and ham, 6; poultry, 39; milk, 231; eggs, 30.

Forestry. The forest area in 1995 was 5·56m. ha, or 45·8% of the land area, compared to 6·31m. ha and 52% in 1990. Timber production was 4·31m. cu. metres in 1999.

Fisheries. In 1999 the catch was approximately 20,569 tonnes (19,449 tonnes from sea fishing), up from 4,582 tonnes in 1989.

INDUSTRY

Production in 1993 (in 1,000 tonnes): metallic products, 2,483; raw sugar (1998), 370; cement (1997), 310; residual fuel oil (1997), 355; distillate fuel oil (1997), 220; wheat flour, 48; vegetable oil, 27; main chemical products, 13; rum, 9,868 litres; processed leather, 258 sq. metres.

Labour. The workforce in 1996 was 1,642,000 (64% males). In 1994, 37% of the economically active population were engaged in agriculture, fisheries and forestry, and 17% in trade, restaurants and hotels. There were 0·32m. unemployed in 1993.

INTERNATIONAL TRADE
Foreign debt was US$7,019m. in 2000.

Imports and Exports. Imports and exports in US$1m.:

	1996	1997	1998	1999	2000
Imports f.o.b.	1,044·3	1,371·2	1,397·1	1,698·2	1,647·3
Exports f.o.b.	470·2	581·6	580·1	552·4	652·8

The principal exports are cotton, coffee, chemical products, meat and sugar.
Main import suppliers, 1996: USA, 33·9%; Costa Rica, 8·4%; Guatemala, 8·4%; Japan, 7·7%. Main export markets, 1996: USA, 44·9%; Spain, 11·1%; Germany, 9·2%; El Salvador, 8·8%.

COMMUNICATIONS

Roads. Road length in 1996 was estimated at 18,000 km, of which 1,820 km were asphalted. In 1996 there were 73,000 passenger cars (18·1 per 1,000 inhabitants), 5,200 buses and coaches, 56,430 trucks and vans and 22,770 motorcycles and mopeds.

Civil Aviation. The national carrier is Nicaraguense de Aviación. In 1999 scheduled airline traffic of Nicaragua-based carriers flew 0·8m. km, carrying 59,000 passengers (all on international flights). The Augusto Sandino international airport at Managua handled 758,000 passengers in 2000 (612,000 on international flights) and 19,900 tonnes of freight.

Shipping. The merchant marine totalled 4,000 GRT in 1998. The Pacific ports are Corinto (the largest), San Juan del Sur and Puerto Sandino through which pass most of the external trade. The chief eastern ports are El Bluff (for Bluefields) and Puerto Cabezas. In 1993, 0·2m. tonnes of cargo were loaded, and 1·07m. tonnes discharged.

Telecommunications. In 2000 there were 158,600 main telephone lines, or 31·2 per 1,000 population, and 45,000 PCs in use (8·9 for every 1,000 persons). Mobile phone subscribers numbered 69,000 in 1999. Nicaragua had 20,000 Internet users in Dec. 1999.

Postal Services. In 1994 there were 202 post offices.

SOCIAL INSTITUTIONS

Justice. The judicial power is vested in a Supreme Court of Justice at Managua, 5 chambers of second instance and 153 judges of lower courts.
The population in penal institutions in Dec. 1996 was 3,692 (80 per 100,000 of national population).

Religion. The prevailing form of religion is Roman Catholic (3·75m. adherents in 1992), but religious liberty is guaranteed by the Constitution. There is 1 arch-bishopric, 7 bishoprics and 1 cardinal.

Education. Adult literacy rate in 1999 was 68·2% (male, 66·6%; female, 69·8%). In 1998 there were 7,224 primary schools with 783,002 pupils, 287,246 secondary school pupils and (1993) 32,464 students at university level.
In 1994–95 there were two universities and three specialized universities (agriculture; engineering; polytechnic) with 1,260 academic staff.
In 1997 total expenditure on education came to 3·9% of GNP and represented 8·8% of total government expenditure. A 15-year National Plan for Education is under way which aims to transform education by means of expanding provision in rural areas, providing greater access to pre-school and adult education, improving the quality of teacher training, modernizing the curriculum and investing in materials and infrastructure.

Health. In 1994 there were 56 hospitals, with a provision of 11 beds per 20,000 population. There were 2,577 doctors, 321 dentists and 2,144 nurses.

CULTURE

Broadcasting. Broadcasting is administered by the Instituto Nicaraguense de Telecomunicaciones y Correos (Telcor). There were 320,000 television sets (colour by NTSC) and 1·24m. radio receivers in 1997.

Press. In 1996 there were four daily newspapers in Managua, with a total circulation of 135,000.

Tourism. In 1999 there were 468,000 foreign tourists, spending US$113m. Tourist numbers grew by nearly 500% between 1990 and 1998.

DIPLOMATIC REPRESENTATIVES
Of Nicaragua in the United Kingdom (Suite 31, Vicarage House, 58–60 Kensington Church St., London, W8 4DP)
Ambassador: Juan B. Sacasa.

Of the United Kingdom in Nicaragua (Plaza Churchill Reparto 'Los Robles', Apartado 1–169, Managua)
Ambassador: Timothy Brownbill.

Of Nicaragua in the USA (1627 New Hampshire Ave., NW, Washington, D.C., 20009)
Ambassador: Carlos Ulvert Sanchez.

Of the USA in Nicaragua (Km. 4½ Carretera Sur, Managua)
Ambassador: Barbara C. Moore.

Of Nicaragua to the United Nations
Ambassador: Eduardo J. Sevilla Somoza.

Of Nicaragua to the European Union
Ambassador: Sergio Mario Blandón.

FURTHER READING
Dijkstra, G., *Industrialization in Sandinista Nicaragua: Policy and Party in a Mixed Economy.* Boulder (CO), 1992
Jones, Adam, *Beyond the Barricades: Nicaragua and the Struggle for the Sandanista Press, 1979–1998.* Ohio Univ. Press, Athens (OH), 2002
Woodward, R. L., *Nicaragua.* [Bibliography] 2nd ed. ABC-Clio, Oxford and Santa Barbara (CA), 1994

National statistical office: Dirección General de Estadística y Censos, Managua

NIGER

République du Niger

Capital: Niamey
Population estimate, 2000: 10·8m.
GDP per capita, 2000: (PPP$) 746
HDI/world rank: 0·277/172

KEY HISTORICAL EVENTS
Niger was occupied by France after 1883. It achieved full independence on 3 Aug. 1960. Guerrilla activity by Tuaregs of the Armed Resistance Organization (ORA) seeking local autonomy in the north continued into 1995. On 27 Jan. 1996 the army chief of staff Gen. (then Col.) Barré Maïnassara deposed President Ousmane Mahamane and dissolved parliament. In April 1999 President Maïnassara was assassinated by bodyguards at Niamey airport, prompting troops and tanks onto the streets of the capital. A week after the President's assassination, Daouda Mallam Wanké, leader of the presidential guard and the officer widely suspected of being behind the killing, was named as Maïnassara's successor.

TERRITORY AND POPULATION
Niger is bounded in the north by Algeria and Libya, east by Chad, south by Nigeria, southwest by Benin and Burkina Faso, and west by Mali. Area, 1,186,408 sq. km, with a population at the 1988 census of 7,250,383. Estimate (1997), 9,388,900; density, 8 per sq. km. In 1999, 79·9% of the population were rural.

The UN gives a projected population for 2010 of 15·55m.

The country is divided into the capital, Niamey, an autonomous district, and seven departments. Area, population and chief towns at the 1988 census:

Department	Sq. km	Population	Chief town	Population
Agadez	634,209	203,959	Agadez	49,361
Diffa	140,216	189,316	Diffa	–
Dosso	31,002	1,019,997	Dosso	–
Maradi	38,581	1,388,999	Maradi	109,386
Niamey	670	398,265	Niamey	392,169
Tahoua	106,677	1,306,652	Tahoua	49,941
Tillabéry	89,623	1,332,398	Tillabéry	–
Zinder	145,430	1,410,797	Zinder	119,838

In 1999 Niamey had an estimated population of 731,000.

The population is composed chiefly of Hausa (53%), Songhai and Djerma (21%), Tuareg (10·5%), Fulani (10%) and Kanuri-Manga (4·5%). The official language is French. Hausa, Djerma and Fulani are national languages.

SOCIAL STATISTICS
1997 estimates: births, 504,000; deaths, 225,000. Rates, 1997 estimates, per 1,000 population: birth rate, 53·7 (the highest birth rate in the world); death rate, 24·0; infant mortality, 162 per 1,000 live births (1999). Annual population growth rate, 1990–99, 3·93%. Expectation of life at birth, 1999: 44·5 years for males and 45·1 for females. Fertility rate, 1999, 6·7 children per woman.

CLIMATE
Precipitation determines the geographical division into a southern zone of agriculture, a central zone of pasturage and a desert-like northern zone. The country lacks water, with the exception of the southwestern districts, which are watered by the Niger and its tributaries, and the southern zone, where there are a number of wells. Niamey, 95°F (35°C). Annual rainfall varies from 22" (560 mm) in the south to 7" (180 mm) in the Sahara zone. The rainy season lasts from May until Sept., but there are periodic droughts.

CONSTITUTION AND GOVERNMENT
Theoretically, Niger is a unitary multi-party democracy. The *President* is directly elected for a five-year term renewable once. There is an 83-member *National Assembly* elected for a five-year term by proportional representation.

At a referendum on 12 May 1996, 90% of votes cast were in favour of a new constitution; turn-out was 33%. The ban on political parties which had been in force since 27 Jan. was lifted on 20 May 1996.

National Anthem. 'Auprès du grand Niger puissant' ('By the banks of the mighty great Niger'); words by M. Thiriet, tune by R. Jacquet and N. Frionnet.

RECENT ELECTIONS
In the presidential runoff of 24 Nov. 1999 turn-out was around 39·4%. Tandja Mamadou won 59·9% of votes compared to the 40·1% of Mahamadou Issoufou. There had been a total of seven candidates in the first round on 17 Oct. 1999.

Parliamentary elections were held in Oct. and Nov. 1999. Of 83 available seats, the National Movement for the Development Society (MNSD) won 38, the Democratic and Social Convention 17, the Nigerian Party for Democracy and Socialism 16, Rally for Democracy and Progress 8 and the Nigerian Alliance for Democracy and Progress 4.

CURRENT ADMINISTRATION
President: Tandja Mamadou; b. 1938 (MNSD; sworn in 22 Dec.1999).

In March 2003 the government comprised:

Prime Minister: Hama Amadou; b. 1950 (MNSD; sworn in 3 Jan. 2000, having previously held office Feb. 1995–Jan. 1996).

Minister of Animal Resources: Koroney Maoudé. *Defence:* Sabiou Dady Gaoh. *Basic Education:* Ari Ibrahim. *Finance and Economy:* Ali Badjo Gamatié. *Foreign Affairs, Co-operation, African Integration:* Aïchatou Mindaoudou. *Health:* Ibrahim Koma. *Secondary and Higher Education, Research and Technology:* Salla Habi Salissou. *Interior and Decentralization:* Laouali Amadou. *Justice and Keeper of the Seals, in Charge of Relations with Parliament:* Matty Elhadji Salissou. *Mines and Energy:* Tampóné Ibrahim. *Privatization and Restructuring of Enterprises:* Trapsida Fatima. *Labour and Civil Service, Government Spokesman:* Moussa Seybou Kasseye. *Transport and Communication:* Mamane Sani Mallam Mahamane. *Agricultural Development:* Wassalké Boukary. *Youth:* Souley Hassane 'Bonto'. *Social Development, Promotion of Women and Protection of Children:* Aichatou Foumakoye. *Supplies, Housing and Territorial Development:* Abdou Labo. *Tourism and Handicrafts:* Rhissa Ag Boula. *Water Resources, Environment and Desertification Control:* Amadou Namata. *Sports and Culture:* Issa Lamine.

Government Website (French only): http://www.niger-gouv.org/

DEFENCE
Selective conscription for two years operates. Defence expenditure totalled US$26m. in 2000 (US$3 per capita), representing 1·5% of GDP.

Army. There are three military districts. Strength (1999) 5,200. There are additional paramilitary forces of some 5,400.

Air Force. In 1999 the Air Force had 100 personnel. There are no combat aircraft.

INTERNATIONAL RELATIONS
Niger is a member of the UN, WTO, the African Union, African Development Bank, ECOWAS, the Lake Chad Basin Commission, OIC, International Organization of the Francophonie, and is an ACP member state of the ACP-EU relationship.

ECONOMY
Agriculture accounted for 41·4% of GDP in 1998, industry 17·0% and services 41·7%.

Currency. The unit of currency is the *franc CFA* (XOF) with a parity of 655·957 francs CFA to one euro. In May 2002 total money supply was 84,319m. francs CFA and foreign exchange reserves were US$85m. Gold reserves were 11,000 troy oz in June 2000. Inflation in 2001 was 4·0%.

Budget. In 1998 revenue (in 1,000m. francs CFA) was 164·4 and expenditure 188·0. Taxes accounted for 59·3% of revenues, and external aids and gifts 34·1%. Current expenditures accounted for 69·2% of expenditure.

Performance. Real GDP growth was negative in 2000, at −1·4%, but was then 7·6% in 2001; total GDP in 2001 was US$1·9bn.

NIGER

Banking and Finance. The regional Central Bank of West African States (BCEAO)—*Governor,* Charles Konan Banny—functions as the bank of issue. There were six commercial banks in 1994.

Weights and Measures. The metric system is legal, but traditional units are still in use.

ENERGY AND NATURAL RESOURCES

Environment. According to the *World Bank Atlas,* in 1998 Niger's carbon dioxide emissions were the equivalent of 0·1 tonnes per capita.

Electricity. Installed capacity was 105,000 kW in 1991. Production in 1998 amounted to 180m. kWh; consumption per capita in 1997 was 38 kWh.

Minerals. Large uranium deposits are mined at Arlit and Akouta. Uranium production (1998), 3,731 tonnes. Niger's uranium production is exceeded only by those of Canada and Australia. Phosphates are mined in the Niger valley, and coal reserves are being exploited by open-cast mining (production of hard coal in 1996 was an estimated 173,000 tonnes). Salt production in 1997 was 3,000 tonnes.

Agriculture. Production is dependent upon adequate rainfall. There were 4·99m. ha of arable land in 1998 and 6,000 ha of permanent crops. 66,000 ha were irrigated in 1998. There were 130 tractors in 1998. Production estimates in 2000 (in 1,000 tonnes): millet, 2,250; sorghum, 400; onions, 180; sugarcane, 140; cassava, 120; groundnuts, 110; rice, 73; tomatoes, 65; sweet potatoes, 35.

Livestock (2000): cattle, 2·22m.; goats, 6·60m.; sheep, 4·30m.; asses, 530,000; camels, 410,000; chickens, 20m. Livestock products (in 1,000 tonnes), 2000: milk, 168; meat, 125; cheese, 14; eggs, 9.

Forestry. There is a government programme of afforestation as a protection from desert encroachment. There were 2·56m. ha of forests in 1995 (2% of the land area). Timber production in 1999 was 6·67m. cu. metres, mainly for fuel.

Fisheries. There are fisheries on the River Niger and along the shores of Lake Chad. In 1999 the catch was 11,000 tonnes, exclusively from inland waters.

INDUSTRY

Some small manufacturing industries, mainly in Niamey, produce textiles, food products, furniture and chemicals. Output of cement in 1997 (estimate), 36,000 tonnes.

Labour. The labour force in 1996 totalled 4,497,000 (56% males). Nearly 90% of the economically active population in 1994 were engaged in agriculture, fisheries and forestry.

Trade Unions. The national confederation is the *Union Syndicale des Travailleurs du Niger,* which has 15,000 members in 31 unions.

INTERNATIONAL TRADE

Foreign debt was US$1,638m. in 2000.

Imports and Exports. In 1998 imports were valued at 196,700m. francs CFA and exports at 175,600m. francs CFA. Consumer goods are the principal imports, and uranium followed by livestock the main exports. Major trading partners are France, Côte d'Ivoire, Germany and Belgium for imports, and the USA, Greece, France and the UK for exports.

COMMUNICATIONS

Roads. In 1996 there were approximately 10,100 km of roads including 797 km of paved roads. Niamey and Zinder are the termini of two trans-Sahara motor routes; the Hoggar–Aïr–Zinder road extends to Kano and the Tanezrouft–Gao–Niamey road to Benin. A 648-km 'uranium road' runs from Arlit to Tahoua. There were, in 1996, 38,220 passenger cars (3·8 per 1,000 inhabitants) and 15,200 trucks and vans.

Civil Aviation. There are international airports at Niamey (Diori Hamani Airport) and Agadez. Niamey handled 83,000 passengers in 2000 (81,000 on international flights). Niger is a member of Air Afrique. In 1998 there were international flights to Abidjan, Abu Dhabi, Addis Adaba, Algiers, Bamako, Casablanca, Cotonou, Dakar, Jeddah, Lagos, N'Djaména, Nouakchott, Ouagadougou, Paris and

1228

Tamanrasset. In 1999 scheduled airline traffic of Niger-based carriers flew 3·0m. km, carrying 84,000 passengers (all on international flights).

Shipping. Sea-going vessels can reach Niamey (300 km inside the country) between Sept. and March.

Telecommunications. Niger had 20,000 main telephone lines in 2000 (1·9 per 1,000 population) and there were 5,000 PCs in use (0·5 per 1,000 persons). There were around 100 mobile phone subscribers in Jan. 1998 and 3,000 Internet users in July 2000.

Postal Services. In 1995 there were 66 post offices, or one for every 134,000 persons.

SOCIAL INSTITUTIONS

Justice. There are Magistrates' and Assize Courts at Niamey, Zinder and Maradi, and justices of the peace in smaller centres. The Court of Appeal is at Niamey.

Religion. In 1997 there were 9·34m. Sunni Muslims. There are some Roman Catholics, and traditional animist beliefs survive.

Education. In 1997–98 there were 123 pre-primary schools with 494 teachers for 11,764 pupils and 3,175 primary schools with 11,545 teachers for 482,065 pupils. During the period 1990–95 only 18% of females of primary school age were enrolled in school. In 1996–97 there were 97,675 pupils in secondary schools. In 1988–89 there were five teacher training colleges with 1,578 students, and in 1989–90 there were two professional training colleges with 859 students (61 women) and 69 teachers. There is a university and an Islamic university, with a total in 1994–95 of 3,980 students and 281 academic staff.

Adult literacy in 1999 was 15·3% (male, 23·0%; female, 7·9%). The overall rate and the rates for both males and females are the lowest in the world.

Health. In 1993 there were 237 doctors and 2,213 nurses, and in 1990, 5 dentists, 29 pharmacists and 457 midwives.

CULTURE

Broadcasting. La Voix du Sahel and Télé-Sahel under the government's Office de Radiodiffusion Télévision du Niger are responsible for radio and TV broadcasting (colour by PAL). In 1997 there were estimated to be 660,000 radio and 125,000 TV sets.

Press. In 1998 there were two daily newspapers with a combined circulation of 4,000.

Tourism. In 1999 there were 39,000 foreign tourists, bringing revenue of US$21m.

DIPLOMATIC REPRESENTATIVES
Of Niger in the United Kingdom
Ambassador: Mariama Hima (resides at Paris).

Of the United Kingdom in Niger
Ambassador: Jean François Gordon, CMG (resides at Abidjan, Côte d'Ivoire).

Of Niger in the USA (2204 R. St., NW, Washington, D.C., 20008)
Ambassador: Joseph Diatta.

Of the USA in Niger (PO Box 11201, Niamey)
Ambassador: Barbro A. Owens-Kirkpatrick.

Of Niger to the United Nations
Ambassador: Ousmane Moutari.

Of Niger to the European Union
Ambassador: Houseïni Abdou Saleye.

FURTHER READING
Miles, W. F. S., *Hausaland Divided: Colonialism and Independence in Nigeria and Niger.* Cornell University Press, 1994
Zamponi, Lynda F., *Niger.* [Bibliography] ABC-Clio, Oxford and Santa Barbara (CA), 1994

National statistical office: Direction de la Statistique et de l'Informatique, Ministère du Plan, Niamey.

NIGERIA

Federal Republic of Nigeria

Capital: Abuja
Population estimate, 2000: 113·86m.
GDP per capita, 2000: (PPP$) 896
HDI/world rank: 0·462/148

KEY HISTORICAL EVENTS

The territory was at the centre of the slave trade in the 18th century. The port of Lagos was annexed by Britain in Aug. 1861. Growing British involvement in the Lagos hinterland and in the Niger Delta led to the chartering of the Royal Niger Company which established its own political administration over a wide territory. On 1 Jan. 1900 the Royal Niger Company transferred its territory to the British Crown. The 'colony and protectorate of Nigeria' was created in 1914. Africans were excluded from political power until the end of the Second World War. Full independence was achieved by the Federation of Nigeria on 1 Oct. 1960 and it became a republic on 1 Oct. 1963.

The republic was overthrown by a military coup on 15 Jan. 1966. Ethnic and regional conflict ensued with Hausa northerners fearing domination by the Igbo people from the east of the country. The Eastern Region decided to secede as the Republic of Biafra in May 1967. This set off a bloody civil war, prolonged by international involvement, and a severe famine. Subsequent attempts to re-establish civilian rule were thwarted by the military. Following the execution of Ogoni separatist Ken Saro-wiwa and eight other civil rights activists in Nov. 1995, Nigeria was suspended from the Commonwealth. Gen. Abacha promised to restore constitutional government by Oct. 1998 but died on 8 June 1998, reportedly of a heart attack. He was replaced as president by Gen. Abdulsalam Abubakar who scrapped election plans designed to retain power for Abacha and released political detainees. Chief Moshood Abiola, the imprisoned undeclared winner of the 1993 presidential election, died on 7 July 1998 the day before his expected release from prison.

Gen. Abubakar launched a corruption probe, announced a cabinet with civilians occupying most of the key posts and promised to give up power in May 1999 to allow for a return to civilian rule. Presidential elections were held on 27 Feb. 1999. The victor was Olusegun Obasanjo, a 62-year-old retired general who once led his country as part of a military junta. In Oct. 2000 a state of emergency was declared following violence which had claimed more than 100 lives in Lagos. Violent unrest, mainly between Christians and Muslims, has claimed more than 7,000 lives since 1999.

TERRITORY AND POPULATION

Nigeria is bounded in the north by Niger, east by Chad and Cameroon, south by the Gulf of Guinea and west by Benin. It has an area of 356,669 sq. miles (923,773 sq. km). For sovereignty over the Bakassi Peninsula *see* CAMEROON: Territory and Population. Census population, 1991, 88,244,581 (43,969,970 females, urban, 36%); population density, 95·8 per sq. km. Official estimate, 1997, 107,115,000; density, 116 per sq. km. In 1999, 56·9% of the population were rural.

The UN gives a projected population for 2010 of 146·94m.

There were 30 states and a Federal Capital Territory (Abuja) in 1991.

Area, population and capitals of these states:

State	Area (in sq. km)	Population (1991 census)	Capital
Adamawa	36,917	2,124,049	Yola
Bauchi	64,605	4,294,413	Bauchi
Benue	34,059	2,780,398	Makurdi
Borno	70,898	2,596,589	Maiduguri
Jigawa	23,154	2,829,929	Dutse
Kaduna	46,053	3,969,252	Kaduna
Kano	20,131	5,362,040	Kano
Katsina	24,192	3,878,344	Katsina

NIGERIA

State	Area (in sq. km)	Population (1991 census)	Capital
Kebbi	36,800	2,062,226	Birnin-Kebbi
Kogi	29,833	2,099,046	Lokoja
Kwara	36,825	1,566,469	Ilorin
Niger	76,363	2,482,367	Minna
Plateau	58,030	3,283,784	Jos
Sokoto	65,735	4,392,391	Sokoto
Taraba	54,473	1,480,590	Jalingo
Yobe	45,502	1,411,481	Damaturu
Federal Capital Territory	7,315	378,671	Abuja
Total North	**730,885**	**46,992,039**	

State	Area (in sq. km)	Population (1991 census)	Capital
Abia	6,320	2,297,978	Umuahia
Akwa Ibom	7,081	2,359,736	Uyo
Anambra	4,844	2,767,903	Awka
Cross River	20,156	1,865,604	Calabar
Delta	17,698	2,570,181	Asaba
Edo	17,802	2,159,848	Benin City
Enugu	12,831	3,161,295	Enugu
Imo	5,530	2,485,499	Owerri
Lagos	3,345	5,685,781	Ikeja
Ogun	16,762	2,338,570	Abeokuta
Ondo	20,959	3,884,485	Akure
Osun	9,251	2,203,016	Oshogbo
Oyo	28,454	3,488,789	Ibadan
Rivers	21,850	3,983,857	Port-Harcourt
Total South	**192,883**	**41,252,542**	

Six new states were created in 1996, three in the north and three in the south. In the north, Zamfara State was created from Sokoto, with its headquarters at Gusau; Nassarawa State was created from Plateau, with its headquarters at Lafia; and Gombe State was created from Bauchi, with its headquarters at Gombe. In the south, Ekiti State was created from Ondo, with its capital at Ado-Ekiti; Bayelsa State was created from Rivers, with its headquarters at Yenagoa; and Ebonyi State was created by merging Abia and Enugu, with its headquarters at Abakaliki.

Abuja replaced Lagos as the federal capital and seat of government in Dec. 1991.

Estimated population of the largest cities, 1995:

Lagos	1,484,000[1]	Ila	257,400	Kumo	144,400
Ibadan	1,365,000	Oyo	250,100	Shomolu	144,100
Ogbomosho	711,900	Ikerre	238,500	Oka	139,600
Kano	657,300	Benin City	223,900	Ikare	137,300
Oshogbo	465,000	Iseyin	211,800	Sapele	135,800
Ilorin	464,000	Katsina	201,500	Deba Habe	135,400
Abeokuta	416,800	Jos	201,200	Minna	133,600
Port Harcourt	399,700	Sokoto	199,900	Warri	122,900
Zaria	369,800	Ilobu	194,400	Bida	122,500
Ilesha	369,000	Offa	192,300	Ikire	120,200
Onitsha	362,700	Ikorodu	180,300	Makurdi	120,100
Iwo	353,000	Ilawe-Ekiti	179,900	Lafia	119,500
Ado-Ekiti	350,500	Owo	178,900	Inisa	116,800
Abuja (capital)	339,100	Ikirun	177,000	Shagamu	114,300
Kaduna	333,600	Calabar	170,000	Awka	108,400
Mushin	324,900	Shaki	169,700	Gombe	105,200
Maiduguri	312,100	Ondo	165,400	Igboho	103,300
Enugu	308,200	Akure	158,200	Ejigbo	103,300
Ede	299,500	Gusau	154,000	Agege	100,300
Aba	291,600	Ijebu-Ode	152,500	Ugep	100,000
Ife	289,500	Effon-Alaiye	149,300		

[1]Greater Lagos had a population of 12,763,000 in 1999.

There are about 250 ethnic groups. The largest linguistic groups are the Hausa (21·4% of the total) and the Yoruba (also 21·4%), followed by Igbo (18·0%), Fulani (11·3%), Ibibio (5·6%), Kanuri (4·1%), Edo (3·4%), Tiv (2·2%), Ijaw (1·8%), Bura

(1·5%) and Nupe (1·3%). The official languages are English and (since 1997) French, but 50% of the population speak Hausa as a *lingua franca*.

SOCIAL STATISTICS
1995 births, estimate, 4,760,000; deaths, 1,360,000. Rates, 1995: birth, 49 (per 1,000 population); death, 14. Infant mortality, 1999, 112 (per 1,000 live births). Annual population growth rate, 1990–99, 2·5%. Life expectancy at birth, 1999, was 51·3 years for males and 51·7 years for females. Fertility rate, 1999, 5·0 children per woman.

CLIMATE
Lying wholly within the tropics, temperatures everywhere are high. Rainfall varies greatly, but decreases from the coast to the interior. The main rains occur from April to Oct. Lagos, Jan. 81°F (27·2°C), July 78°F (25·6°C). Annual rainfall 72" (1,836 mm). Ibadan, Jan. 80°F (26·7°C), July 76°F (24·4°C). Annual rainfall 45" (1,120 mm). Kano, Jan. 70°F (21·1°C), July 79°F (26·1°C). Annual rainfall 35" (869 mm). Port Harcourt, Jan. 79°F (26·1°C), July 77°F (25°C). Annual rainfall 100" (2,497 mm).

CONSTITUTION AND GOVERNMENT
The constitution was promulgated on 5 May 1999, and entered into force on 29 May. Nigeria is a federation, comprising 36 states and a federal capital territory. The constitution includes provisions for the creation of new states and for boundary adjustments of existing states. The legislative powers are vested in a *National Assembly*, comprising a *Senate* and a *House of Representatives*. The 109-member Senate consists of three senators from each state and one from the federal capital territory, who are elected for a term of four years. The House of Representatives comprises 360 members, representing constituencies of nearly equal population as far as possible, who are elected for a four-year term. The president is elected for a term of four years and must receive not less than one-quarter of the votes cast at the federal capital territory.

National Anthem. 'Arise, O compatriots, Nigeria's call obey'; words by a collective, tune by B. Odiase.

RECENT ELECTIONS
The preliminary results of the elections to the House of Representatives on 12 April 2003 were: the People's Democratic Party (PDP) 213 seats with 54·5% of the vote, the All Nigeria People's Party (ANPP) 95 seats (27·4%), the Alliance for Democracy (AD) 31 seats (9·3%), the United Nigeria People's Party (UNPP) 2 seats (2·7%), the All Progressives Grand Alliance (APGA) 2 seats (1·4%), the National Democratic Party (NDP) 1 seat (1·9%) and the People's Redemption Party (PRP) 1 seat (0·8%). Turn-out was 50%.

In the Senate elections (preliminary results) on the same days 73 seats went to the PDP, 28 to the ANPP and 6 to the AD. Turn-out was 49%.

Presidential elections were held on 19 April 2003. President Olusegun Obasanjo (PDP) won against 19 opponents with 61·9% of the votes cast. His main opponent, Muhammadu Buhari (ANPP), received 32·2%, and Chukwuemeka Ojukwu (APGA) 3·3%. Buhari refused to accept the result, claiming serious irregularities. Turn-out was 69%.

CURRENT ADMINISTRATION
President: Olusegun Obasanjo; b. 1937 (PDP; sworn in 29 May 1999, re-elected 19 April 2003).

In April 2003 the government comprised:
Vice President: Atiku Abubakar.
Minister of Agriculture: Adamu Bello. *Aviation:* Dr Kema Chikwe. *Commerce:* Mustapha Bello. *Communications:* Dr Bello Mohammed. *Culture and Tourism:* Boma Bromillow Jack. *Defence:* Lieut.-Gen. Theophilus Y Danjuma. *Education:* Prof. Babalola Borishade. *Environment:* Mohammed Kabir Said. *Federal Capital Territory:* Mohammed Abba-Gana. *Finance:* Malam Adamu Ciroma. *Foreign Affairs:* Sule Lamido. *Health:* Prof. Alphonsus Nwosu. *Industries:* Chief Kolawole

Jamodu. *Information:* Prof. Jerry Gana. *Internal Affairs:* Chief Sunday Afolabi. *Justice:* Kanu Agabi. *Labour and Productivity:* Musa Gwadabe. *Police Affairs (acting):* Grace Achibong. *Power and Steel:* Dr Olusegun Agagu. *Science and Technology:* Prof. Turner Isoun. *Solid Minerals:* Dupe Adelaja. *Special Duties:* Chief Yomi Edu. *Sports and Social Development:* Steven Ibn Akiga. *Transport:* Chief Ojo Maduekwe. *Water Resources:* Muktar Shagaril. *Women and Youth:* Aishatu Ismail. *Works and Housing:* Chief Tony Anenih. *Minister of Presidency (Civil Service):* Bello Alhaji Usman. *Of Presidency (Co-operation and Integration):* Chief Bimbola Ogunkelu. *Of Presidency (Economic Matters):* Vincent Ogbuleafor. *Of Presidency (Inter-Government):* Ibrahim Umar Kida.

Government Website: http://www.nigeria.gov.ng/

DEFENCE
In 2000 defence expenditure totalled US$2,340m. (the highest of any country in sub-Saharan Africa), equivalent to US$20 per capita and representing 4·5% of GDP.

Army. Strength (1999) 79,000.

Navy. The Navy includes one frigate with a helicopter and one corvette. The Navy has a small aviation element. Naval personnel in 1999 totalled 5,500, including Coastguard. The main bases are at Apapa (Lagos) and Calabar.

Air Force. The Air Force has been built up with the aid of a German mission; much first-line equipment was received from the former Soviet Union. Personnel (1999) total about 9,500, with 91 combat aircraft including MiG-21s, Jaguars and Alpha Jets. In addition there were 15 armed helicopters.

INTERNATIONAL RELATIONS
Nigeria is a member of the UN, WTO, the African Union, African Development Bank, ECOWAS, the Lake Chad Basin Commission, OIC, OPEC, IOM and is an ACP member state of the ACP-EU relationship.

ECONOMY
Agriculture accounted for 31·7% of GDP in 1998, industry 41·0% and services 27·3%. Nigeria's 'shadow' (black market or underground) economy constitutes 77% of the country's official GDP—one of the highest percentages of any country in the world.

Overview. With the change of leadership in 1999, the long promised three-phased privatization programme is under way. Money owed to oil companies has been paid. Sanctions, except for the ban on arms sales, have been lifted. A ten-year rift with the IMF ended with an agreement (Jan. 1999) on a Fund-monitored economic reform programme. Promised reforms included abolishing the dual exchange rate, ending the subsidy of local fuel and increasing the pace of privatization. If the government sticks to this programme, expected benefits include a rescheduling of foreign debt and a further IMF agreement on a US$1bn. loan. The new legislation is also committed to implementing the Vision 2010 programme drawn up in the mid 1990s, although many observers doubt whether its goals are realistically attainable. Privatization deals since 1999 have raised approaching ₦50bn.

Currency. The unit of currency is the *naira* (NGN) of 100 *kobo*. Foreign exchange reserves were US$9,226m. in May 2002 (US$1,443m. in 1995). A dual exchange rate, abolished in Oct. 1999, allowed the government to purchase US dollars for 25% of the market price. Gold reserves were 687,000 troy oz in May 2002. Inflation was 18·9% in 2001. In March 2002 total money supply was ₦835,923m.

Budget. The financial year is the calendar year. 1997 revenue, ₦384,603m. (of which petroleum royalties and rents accounted for 36·3%); expenditure, ₦312,322m. (of which capital expenditure accounted for 52·0% and recurrent expenditure 48·0%).

Performance. Real GDP growth was 4·3% in 2000 and 2·8% in 2001. Before the discovery of oil in the early 1970s Nigeria's GDP per head was around US$200. By the early 1980s it had reached around US$800, but has now declined to some US$300. Total GDP in 2001 was US$41·2bn.

Banking and Finance. The Central Bank of Nigeria is the bank of issue (*Governor*, Dr Joseph Sanusi). There were 65 commercial banks (with 2,403 branches) and 51 merchant banks in 1995 (with 144 branches), in 20 of which central or state governments held a controlling interest. There are three main banks—Union Bank, First Bank and UBA. Total assets of commercial banks, 1995, ₦463,671m.; merchant banks, ₦91,803m. Total saving deposits, Dec. 1995, ₦121,026m.

A subsequent banking crisis resulted in a decline in the number of banks to 74 at March 1999. Of these, 17 had missed the deadline for increasing their capital to US$5·75m. by the end of 1998 and faced closure if they did not recapitalize, merge or get taken over by the end of the first quarter of 1999. In banking surveys for 1998, 26 banks were classed as 'distressed' and only 25 as 'acceptable risks or better'. It was predicted that there would be further bank closures as the industry becomes more competitive.

There is a stock exchange.

Weights and Measures. The metric system is in force.

ENERGY AND NATURAL RESOURCES

Environment. According to the *World Bank Atlas* Nigeria's carbon dioxide emissions were the equivalent of 0·6 tonnes per capita in 1998. An *Environmental Sustainability Index* compiled for the World Economic Forum meeting in Feb. 2002 ranked Nigeria 133rd in the world out of 142 countries analysed, with 36·7%. The index measured the ability of countries to maintain favourable environmental conditions and examined various factors including pollution levels and the use or abuse of natural resources.

Electricity. Installed capacity, 1997, 6m. kW. Production, 1998, 14·75bn. kWh (38% kWh hydro-electric); consumption per capita was 85 kWh. The government plans to break up and privatize the state-run electricity company NEPA by the end of 2003.

Oil and Gas. Oil accounts for around 97% of Nigeria's exports. The cumulative income from oil over 25 years exceeds US$220,000m. Nigeria's oil production amounted to 766·5m. bbls. in 1998 (equivalent to 2·1m. bbls. a day, up from 1·5m. bbls. per day in 1986). Reserves in 2001 totalled 24·0bn. bbls., although this figure is expected to reach around 30bn. bbls. by 2004. There are four refineries. Oil income in 1998 was around US$1bn. a month, representing more than 75% of government revenue, but unrest which threatened to escalate into civil war caused production to be cut by around a third.

Natural gas reserves, 2000 estimate, were 3,483bn. cu. metres; production, 1999, 5·7bn. cu. metres. Nigeria has signed an agreement for a US$430m., 600-km pipeline to supply natural gas to Benin, Ghana and Togo. It is expected to come into operation in 2005 moving around 1,415,000 cu. metres per day in the first instance. In Dec. 2002 the African Development Bank, six Nigerian banks and 19 international banks announced plans to invest US$1bn. in the Nigeria Liquefied Natural Gas company (NLNG) to exploit exports to the USA and Europe. Ownership of the NLNG is shared between the Nigerian National Petroleum Corporation, Total Fina Elf, Royal Dutch/Shell and AGIP.

Water. 11 River Basin Development Authorities have been established for water resources development.

Minerals. Production, 1998 (in tonnes): limestone, 3·66m.; coal (1996), 50,000; marble, 22,460. There are large deposits of iron ore, coal (reserves estimate 245m. tonnes), lead and zinc. There are small quantities of gold and uranium. Lead production was 3,000 tonnes in 1990; tin, 149 tonnes in 1992.

Agriculture. Of the total land mass, 75% is suitable for agriculture, including arable farming, forestry, livestock husbandry and fisheries. In 1998, 28·2m. ha were arable and 2·54m. ha permanent cropland. 0·23m. ha were irrigated in 1998. 90% of production was by smallholders with less than 3 ha in 1998, and less than 1% of farmers had access to mechanized tractors. Main food crops are millet and sorghum in the north, plantains and oil palms in the south, and maize, yams, cassava and rice in much of the country. The north is, however, the main food producing area. Cocoa is the crop that contributes most to foreign exchange earnings. Output, 2000 (in 1,000 tonnes): cassava, 32,697; yams, 25,873; sorghum, 7,520; millet, 5,960; maize, 5,476; taro, 3,835; rice, 3,277; groundnuts, 2,783; plantains, 1,902; sweet potatoes, 1,662; palm oil, 896; pineapples, 881; tomatoes, 879. Nigeria is the biggest producer of yams, accounting for more than two-thirds of the annual world output. It is also the leading cassava and taro producer and the second largest millet producer.

Livestock, 2000: cattle, 19·83m.; sheep, 20·50m.; goats, 24·30m.; pigs, 4·86m.; chickens, 126m. Products (in 1,000 tonnes), 2000: beef and veal, 298; goat meat, 154; mutton and lamb, 91; pork, bacon and ham, 78; poultry meat, 172; milk, 386; eggs, 435.

Forestry. There were 13·78m. ha of forests in 1995, or 15·1% of the land area (14·39m. ha and 15·8% in 1990). The most important timber species include mahogany, iroko, obeche, abwa, ebony and camwood. Nigeria is Africa's leading roundwood producer, with removals totalling 100·64m. cu. metres in 1999.

Fisheries. The total catch in 1999 was 455,628 tonnes, of which 139,393 tonnes came from inland fishing.

INDUSTRY
Manufacturing contributes about 9% of GDP. 1998 production (in 1,000 tonnes) included: palm oil, 810; paper and products, 57; sugar, 15; cement (1997), 2,520; cigarettes (1994), 9,228. Also plywood (1994), 72,000 cu. metres.

Labour. The labour force in 1996 totalled 45,565,000 (64% males). There were 196 work stoppages in 1995 with 235·1m. working days lost. Unemployment in 1999 was approximately 40%.

Trade Unions. All trade unions are affiliated to the Nigerian Labour Congress.

INTERNATIONAL TRADE
Nigeria's external debt was US$34,134m. in 2000. President Obasanjo failed to settle with the IMF in March 2002, preventing rescheduling and debt relief.

Imports and Exports. Exports in 2000 totalled an estimated US$20·4bn.; imports US$13·7bn. Principal exports, 1992 (in N1m.): oil, 201,349; cocoa, 1,345; rubber, 766; urea and ammonia, 447; fish, 400. Principal imports: machinery and transport equipment, 61,841; other manufactures, 35,072; chemicals, 22,904; foodstuffs, 12,597.

In 1999 the main export markets were: USA, 37·5%; India, 8·9%; Spain, 6·1%; France, 4·9%. Main import suppliers: USA, 11·2%; Germany, 10·1%; UK, 9·7%; France, 8·6%.

COMMUNICATIONS
Roads. The road network covered 194,394 km in 1997, including 1,194 km of motorways. Nigeria has the second longest network of motorways in Africa. In 1996 there were 885,080 motor cars and 912,579 trucks and vans. There were 12,212 road accidents with 4,908 fatalities in 1995.

Rail. In 1995 there were 3,505 route-km of track (1,067 mm gauge). Passenger-km travelled in 1997 came to 179m. and freight tonne-km to 120m.

Civil Aviation. Lagos (Murtala Muhammed) is the major airport, and there are also international airports at Port Harcourt and Kano (Mallam Aminu Kano Airport). The national carrier is Nigeria Airways. It has been the subject of mismanagement investigations after more than US$400m. disappeared between 1983 and 1999. It began European operations again in late 1999, and to London in 2001, having been out of service for some time in the region because of the huge debts. The government sold a 49% stake to a UK leasing company Airwing Aerospace in 2002. In 2000 Lagos handled 2,489,000 passengers (1,435,000 on domestic flights) and, in 1998, 15,100 tonnes of freight. Nigeria Airways flew 2·7m. km in 1999, carrying 109,200 passengers (30,300 on international flights).

Shipping. In 1998 the merchant marine totalled 452,000 GRT, including oil tankers 252,000 GRT. In 1997 vessels totalling 2,464,000 NRT entered ports and vessels totalling 2,510,000 NRT cleared. The principal ports are Lagos, Port Harcourt, Warri and Calabar. There is an extensive network of inland waterways.

Telecommunications. In 2000 there were 492,000 main telephone lines (4·3 per 1,000 persons) and 750,000 PCs in use (6·6 per 1,000 persons). A 51% stake in the state-run telecommunications company NITEL was sold for more than US$1bn. to a consortium of Nigerian investors, European fund managers and Portugal Telecommunications in Nov. 2001 in what was described as Africa's biggest privatization. Mobile phone subscribers numbered 330,000 in 2001. Nigeria had around 100,000 Internet users in July 2000, up from 9,000 in May 1999.

Postal Services. In 1995 there were 3,651 post offices. A total of 812m. pieces of mail were processed in 1995.

SOCIAL INSTITUTIONS

Justice. The highest court is the Federal Supreme Court, which consists of the Chief Justice of the Republic, and up to 15 Justices appointed by the government. It has original jurisdiction in any dispute between the Federal Republic and any State or between States; and to hear and determine appeals from the Federal Court of Appeal, which acts as an intermediate appellate Court to consider appeals from the High Court.

High Courts, presided over by a Chief Justice, are established in each state. All judges are appointed by the government. Magistrates' courts are established throughout the Republic, and customary law courts in southern Nigeria. In each of the northern States of Nigeria there are the Sharia Court of Appeal and the Court of Resolution. Muslim Law has been codified in a Penal Code and is applied through Alkali courts. In Oct. 1999 *sharia*, or Islamic law, was introduced in the northern province of Zamfara. The death penalty is in force and was last used in Jan. 2002.

The population in penal institutions in 1996 was approximately 70,000 (60 per 100,000 of national population).

Religion. Muslims, 48%; Christians, 34% (17% Protestants and 17% Roman Catholic); others, 18%. Northern Nigeria is mainly Muslim; southern Nigeria is predominantly Christian and western Nigeria is evenly divided between Christians, Muslims and animists.

Education. The adult literacy rate was 62·6% in 1999 (71·3% among males and 54·2% among females). Under the new Universal Basic Education scheme it was hoped that this would rise to 70% by 2003. Free, compulsory education is to be provided for all children aged between 6 and 15 under the terms of the scheme. In 1994 there were 38,649 primary schools with 16·19m. pupils and 435,210 teachers, and 6,987 secondary and tertiary schools with 4·64m. students and 162,242 teachers.

In 1995 there were 13 universities, 2 agricultural and 5 technological universities, 21 polytechnics, 7 colleges and 2 institutes. There were 150,072 university students and 10,742 academic staff.

Health. Health provision, 1995: one doctor per 3,707 people; one nurse per 605; one hospital bed per 1,477.

Nigeria has made significant progress in the reduction of undernourishment in the past 20 years. Between 1980 and 1997 the proportion of undernourished people declined from 45% of the population to 8%; but only 50% of Nigerians have access to clean drinking water.

CULTURE

Broadcasting. The Federal Radio Corporation of Nigeria, a statutory body, broadcasts three national radio programmes in English, Yoruba, Hausa and Igbo, and an international service, Voice of Nigeria (five languages). The government Nigerian Television Authority transmits a national service (colour by PAL), and ten states have services. In 1997 there were an estimated 23·5m. radio and 7m. TV sets.

Press. In 1996 there were 25 daily newspapers with a combined circulation of 2,740,000.

Tourism. In 1998 there were 739,000 foreign visitors bringing in revenue of US$142m.

DIPLOMATIC REPRESENTATIVES
Of Nigeria in the United Kingdom (Nigeria Hse., 9 Northumberland Ave., London, WC2N 5BX)
High Commissioner: Dr Christopher Kolade.

Of the United Kingdom in Nigeria (Shehu Shangari Way North, Maitama, Abuja).
High Commissioner: Philip Thomas, CMG.

Of Nigeria in the USA (1333 16th St., NW, Washington, D.C., 20036)
Ambassador: Jibril Muhammed Aminu.

Of the USA in Nigeria (2 Eleke Cres., Lagos)
Ambassador: Howard F. Jeter.

Of Nigeria to the United Nations
Ambassador: Arthur C. I. Mbanefo.

Of Nigeria to the European Union
Ambassador: Gabriel Sam Akunwafor.

FURTHER READING
Forrest, T., *Politics and Economic Development in Nigeria.* Boulder (CO), 1993
Maier, K., *This House Has Fallen: Midnight in Nigeria.* Penguin Press, London and PublicAffairs, New York, 2000
Miles, W. F. S., *Hausaland Divided: Colonialism and Independence in Nigeria and Niger.* Cornell Univ. Press, 1994

NORWAY

Kongeriket Norge
(Kingdom of Norway)

Capital: Oslo
Population estimate, 2000: 4·48m.
GDP per capita, 2000: (PPP$) 29,918
HDI/world rank: 0·942/1

KEY HISTORICAL EVENTS

Norway was under Danish domination from the 14th century. By a Treaty of 14 Jan. 1814, the King of Denmark ceded Norway to the King of Sweden and on 14 Aug. a convention proclaimed the independence of Norway in a personal union with Sweden. This was followed on 4 Nov. by the election of Karl XIII (II) as King of Norway. Norway declared this union dissolved on 7 June 1905 and Sweden agreed to the repeal of the union on 26 Oct. 1905. After a plebiscite, Prince Carl of Denmark was formally elected King on 18 Nov. 1905, taking the name of Haakon VII. He reigned for 52 years, after which he was succeeded by his son. From 1940 to 1944, during the Second World War, Norway was occupied by the Germans who set up a widely resented pro-German government under Vidkun Quisling. Apart from this wartime episode, the Labour Party held office, and the majority in the Storting (parliament), from 1935 to 1965. From 1965 coalitions or minority governments have held power with Labour remaining the largest single party. The discovery of extensive off shore oil reserves in the 1960s transformed the Norwegian economy, making it one of the world's richest.

TERRITORY AND POPULATION

Norway is bounded in the north by the Arctic Ocean, east by Russia, Finland and Sweden, south by the Skagerrak Straits and west by the North Sea. The total area of mainland Norway is 323,758 sq. km, including 17,506 sq. km of fresh water. Total coastline, including fjords, 21,340 km. There are more than 50,000 islands along the coastline. Exposed mountain (either bare rock or thin vegetation) makes up over 70% of the country. 25% of the land area is woodland and 4% tilled land.

Population (1990 census) was 4,247,546 (2,099,881 males; 2,147,655 females); population density per sq. km, 13·8. Estimated population, 1 Jan. 2001, 4,503,436; population density, 13·9. With the exception of Iceland, Norway is the most sparsely populated country in Europe.

The UN gives a projected population for 2010 of 4·61m.

There are 19 counties (*fylke*). Land area, population and densities:

	Land area (sq. km)	Population (1990 census)	Population (2001 estimate)	Density per sq. km 2001
Østfold	3,889	238,296	251,032	65
Akershus	4,587	417,653	471,988	103
Oslo (City)	427	461,190	508,726	1,191
Hedmark	26,120	187,276	187,999	7
Oppland	23,827	182,578	183,419	8
Buskerud	13,856	225,172	238,833	17
Vestfold	2,140	198,399	215,030	100
Telemark	14,186	162,907	165,595	12
Aust-Agder	8,485	97,333	102,714	12
Vest-Agder	6,817	144,917	156,878	23
Rogaland	8,553	337,504	375,225	44
Hordaland	14,962	410,567	438,312	29
Sogn og Fjordane	17,864	106,659	107,590	6
Møre og Romsdal	14,596	238,409	243,810	17
Sør-Trøndelag	17,839	250,978	264,865	15
Nord-Trøndelag	20,777	127,157	127,261	6
Nordland	36,302	239,311	238,295	7
Troms	25,147	146,716	151,777	6
Finnmark	45,879	74,524	74,087	2
Mainland total	306,253¹	4,247,546	4,503,346	15

¹118,244 sq. miles.

The Arctic territories of Svalbard and Jan Mayen have an area of 61,606 sq. km. Persons staying on Svalbard and Jan Mayen are registered as residents of their home Norwegian municipality.

In 1999, 75·1% of the population lived in urban areas.

Population of the principal urban settlements on 1 Jan. 2000:

Oslo	773,498	Kristiansand	61,400	Moss	33,081
Bergen	205,759	Tromsø	49,372	Bodø	32,343
Stavanger/Sandnes	162,083	Tønsberg	43,346	Arendal	30,153
Trondheim	140,631	Haugesund	39,112	Hamar	27,514
Frederikstad/Sarpsborg	93,273	Sandefjord	37,229	Larvik	22,193
Drammen	86,732	Ålesund/Spjelkavik	35,832	Halden	21,294
Porsgrunn/Skien	83,409				

The official language is Norwegian, which has two versions: Bokmål (or Riksmål) and Nynorsk (or Landsmål).

The Sami, the indigenous people of the far north, number some 40,000 and form a distinct ethnic minority with their own culture and language.

SOCIAL STATISTICS
Statistics for calendar years:

	Marriages	Divorces	Births	Still-born	Outside marriage[1]	Deaths
1996	22,478	9,836	60,927	276	29,435	43,860
1997	22,933	9,813	59,801	230	29,133	44,595
1998	22,349	9,213	58,352	247	28,573	44,112
1999	23,456	9,124	59,298	241	30,198	45,170
2000	...	...	59,234	225	29,368	44,002

[1]Excluding still-born.

Rates per 1,000 population, 2000, birth, 13·2; death, 9·8; marriage, 5·3 (1999); divorce, 2·1 (1999). Average annual population growth rate, 1990–2000, 0·57% (2000, 0·56%). In 1998 there were 548 suicides, giving a rate of 12·3 per 100,000 population (men, 18·2 per 100,000; women, 6·7).

Expectation of life at birth, 1999, was 75·62 years for males and 81·13 years for females. Infant mortality, 1999, 4 per 1,000 live births; fertility rate, 2000, 1·85 births per woman. 49% of births are to unmarried mothers. In 1999 the average age at marriage was 34·8 years for males and 31·6 years for females (31·6 years and 28·9 years respectively for first marriages).

At 1 Jan. 2000 the immigrant population totalled 282,487, including 23,240 from Sweden, 22,831 from Pakistan, 18,863 from Denmark and 15,466 from Yugoslavia. In 2000 Norway received 10,842 asylum applications. Most were from Yugoslavia (4,188), Somalia (910), Iraq (766) and Romania (712).

A UNICEF report published in 2000 showed that 3·9% of children in Norway live in poverty (in households with income below 50% of the national median), the second lowest percentage of any country behind Sweden.

In the Human Development Index, or HDI (measuring progress in countries in longevity, knowledge and standard of living), Norway ranked first in the world in the list published in the Human Development Report for both 2001 and 2002, having been second behind Canada for the previous two years.

CLIMATE
There is considerable variation in the climate because of the extent of latitude, the topography and the varying effectiveness of prevailing westerly winds and the Gulf Stream. Winters along the whole west coast are exceptionally mild but precipitation is considerable. Oslo, Jan. 24·3°F (−4·3°C), July 61·5°F (16·4°C). Annual rainfall 30·0" (763 mm). Bergen, Jan. 34·7°F (1·5°C), July 58·1°F (14·5°C). Annual rainfall 88·6" (2,250 mm). Trondheim, Jan. 26°F (−3·5°C), July 57°F (14°C). Annual rainfall 32·1" (870 mm). Bergen has one of the highest rainfall figures of any European city. The sun never fully sets in the northern area of the country in the summer and even in the south, the sun rises at around 3 a.m. and sets at around 11 p.m.

CONSTITUTION AND GOVERNMENT
Norway is a constitutional and hereditary monarchy.

The reigning King is **Harald V**, born 21 Feb. 1937, married on 29 Aug. 1968 to Sonja Haraldsen. He succeeded on the death of his father, King Olav V, on 21 Jan.

1991. *Offspring:* Princess Märtha Louise, born 22 Sept. 1971 (married Ari Behn, b. 30 Sept. 1972, on 24 May 2002); Crown Prince Haakon Magnus, born 20 July 1973 (married Mette-Marit Tjessem Høiby, b. 19 Aug. 1973, on 25 Aug. 2001; *offspring* from previous relationship, Marius, b. Jan. 1997). The king and queen together receive an annual personal allowance of 7·0m. kroner from the civil list, and the Crown Prince and Crown Princess together 4·7m. kroner. Princess Märtha Louise relinquished her allowance in 2002. Women have been eligible to succeed to the throne since 1990. There is no coronation ceremony. The royal succession is in direct male line in the order of primogeniture. In default of male heirs the King may propose a successor to the Storting, but this assembly has the right to nominate another, if it does not agree with the proposal.

The Constitution, voted by a constituent assembly on 17 May 1814 and modified at various times, vests the legislative power of the realm in the *Storting* (Parliament). The royal veto may be exercised; but if the same Bill passes two Stortings formed by separate and subsequent elections it becomes the law of the land without the assent of the sovereign. The King has the command of the land, sea and air forces, and makes all appointments.

The 165-member Storting is directly elected by proportional representation. The country is divided into 19 districts, each electing from 4 to 15 representatives.

The Storting, when assembled, divides itself by election into the *Lagting* and the *Odelsting.* The former is composed of one-fourth of the members of the Storting, and the other of the remaining three-fourths. Each Ting (the Storting, the Odelsting and the Lagting) nominates its own president. Most questions are decided by the Storting, but questions relating to legislation must be considered and decided by the Odelsting and the Lagting separately. Only when the Odelsting and the Lagting disagree, the Bill has to be considered by the Storting in plenary sitting, and a new law can then only be decided by a majority of two-thirds of the voters. The same majority is required for alterations of the Constitution, which can only be decided by the Storting in plenary sitting. The Storting elects five delegates, whose duty it is to revise the public accounts. The Lagting and the ordinary members of the Supreme Court of Justice (the *Høyesterett*) form a High Court of the Realm (the *Riksrett*) for the trial of ministers, members of the *Høyesterett* and members of the Storting. The impeachment before the *Riksrett* can only be decided by the Odelsting.

The executive is represented by the King, who exercises his authority through the Cabinet. Cabinet ministers are entitled to be present in the Storting and to take part in the discussions, but without a vote.

National Anthem. 'Ja, vi elsker dette landet' ('Yes, we love this land'); words by B. Bjørnson, tune by R. Nordraak.

RECENT ELECTIONS

At the elections for the Storting held on 10 Sept. 2001 the following parties were elected: Labour Party (DNA), winning 43 out of 165 seats (with 24·3% of the vote); Conservative Party (H), 38 (21·2%); Progress Party (FrP), 26 (14·7%); Socialist Left Party (SV), 23 (12·4%); Christian People's Party (KrF), 22 (12·5%); Centre Party (Sp), 10 (5·6%); Liberal Party (V), 2 (3·9%); Coastal Party (KYST), 1 (1·7%). Turnout was 74·5%. The governing Labour Party suffered its worst election result in nearly a century and was unable to form a government. The new government comprised the Christian People's Party, the Conservative Party and the Liberal Party.

CURRENT ADMINISTRATION

In March 2003 the minority coalition government comprised:

Prime Minister: Kjell Magne Bondevik; b. 1947 (Christian People's Party; sworn in 19 Oct. 2001, having previously held office from Oct. 1997 to March 2000).

Minister of Local Government and Regional Development: Erna Solberg (H). *Church Affairs and Culture:* Valgerd Svarstad Gaugland (KrF). *Children and Family Affairs:* Laila Dåvøy (KrF). *Industry and Trade:* Ansgar Gabrielsen (H). *Foreign Affairs:* Jan Petersen (H). *Fisheries:* Svein Ludvigsen (H). *Finance:* Per-Kristian Foss (H). *International Development:* Hilde Frafjord Johnson (KrF). *Labour and Government Administration:* Victor Danielsen Norman (H). *Agriculture:* Lars Sponheim (V). *Justice and Police:* Odd Einar Dørum (V). *National Defence:* Kristin Krohn Devold (H). *Transport and Communication:* Torild Skogsholm (V).

Education and Research: Kristin Clemet (H). *Social Affairs:* Ingjerd Schou (H). *Health:* Dagfinn Høbråten (KrF). *Oil and Energy:* Einar Steensnæs (KrF). *Environment:* Børge Brende (H).

Office of the Prime Minister: http://odin.dep.no

DEFENCE

Conscription is for 12 months, with four to five refresher training periods.

In 2000 defence spending totalled US$2,856m. (US$640 per capita), representing 1·8% of GDP. Expenditure per capita was the highest of any European country in 2000.

Army. There are a Northern and a Southern command, and within these the Army is organized in 4 district commands, 1 divisional headquarters and 14 territorial commands.

Strength (1999) 15,200 (including 10,000 conscripts). The fast mobilization reserve numbers 184,000.

Navy. The Royal Norwegian Navy has three components: the Navy, Coast Guard and Coastal Artillery. Main Naval combatants include 12 coastal submarines (including 6 new German-built Ula class) and 4 frigates.

The personnel of the navy totalled 8,200 in 1999, of whom 3,300 were conscripts. 1,000 served in Coastal Artillery and 700 in the Coast Guard. The main naval base is at Bergen (Håkonsvern), with subsidiary bases at Horten, Ramsund and Tromsø.

The naval elements of the Home Guard on mobilization can muster some 5,000 personnel.

Air Force. The Royal Norwegian Air Force comprises the Air Force and the Anti-air Artillery,

Total strength (1999) is about 6,700 personnel, including 3,200 conscripts. There were 79 combat aircraft in operation including F-5A/Bs and F-16A/Bs.

Home Guard. The Home Guard is organized in small units equipped and trained for special tasks. Service after basic training is one week a year. The Home Guard consists of the Land Home Guard (strength, 1999, 77,000), Sea Home Guard and Anti-Air Home Guard organized in 18 districts. *See also under* Navy *above.*

INTERNATIONAL RELATIONS

Norway is a member of the UN, WTO, BIS, NATO, EFTA, OECD, Council of Europe, OSCE, CERN, Council of the Baltic Sea States, Nordic Council, Inter-American Development Bank, Asian Development Bank, IOM and the Antarctic Treaty, and an Associate Member of the WEU. Norway has acceded to the Schengen Accord abolishing border controls between Norway, Austria, Belgium, Denmark, Finland, France, Germany, Greece, Iceland, Italy, Luxembourg, the Netherlands, Portugal, Spain and Sweden.

In a referendum on 27–28 Nov. 1994, 52·2% of votes cast were against joining the EU. The electorate was 3,266,182; turn-out was 88·88%.

ECONOMY

Agriculture accounted for 2·0% of GDP in 1997, industry 32·1% and services 65·9%.

According to the anti-corruption organization *Transparency International*, in 2002 Norway ranked equal 12th in the world in a survey of the countries with the least corruption in business and government. It received 8·5 out of 10 in the annual index.

Overview. Although a small economy, in terms of GDP per capita Norway is one of the world's wealthiest nations. As the central government budget represents a large share of the economy, fiscal policy is a vital component of economic stability. Labour market tensions and high oil revenues have meant that fiscal policies have not met their objectives, which places a heavy burden on monetary policy. In 2002 passenger tax on air travel was abolished, property taxes reduced and duties on alcohol were lowered. Monetary policy aims at a stable exchange rate.

Currency. The unit of currency is the *Norwegian krone* (NOK) of 100 *øre.* After Oct. 1990 the krone was fixed to the ecu in the EMS of the EU in the narrow band of 2·25%, but it was freed in Dec. 1992. Annualized inflation was 3·0% in 2001.

Foreign exchange reserves were US$16,048m. and gold reserves 1·18m. troy oz in June 2002. In May 2002 total money supply was 658,812m. kroner.

Budget. Central government current revenue and expenditure (in 1m. kroner) for years ending 31 Dec.:

	1997	1998	1999[1]	2000[1]
Revenue	466,950	463,066	493,350	640,782
Expenditure	375,747	399,331	424,565	456,677

[1]Provisional.

The standard rate of VAT is 24·0%.

Performance. The strong performance of the Norwegian economy in 1993–98 lifted mainland GDP by 20%, but there was a significant slowdown in 1998 when the oil price collapsed at a time when the labour market was overheated. Real GDP growth, which averaged 5·1% between 1994–97, was 2·4% in 2000 but only 1·4% in 2001. Norway's total GDP in 2001 was US$165·5bn.

Banking and Finance. Norges Bank is the central bank and bank of issue. Supreme authority is vested in the Executive Board consisting of seven members appointed by the King and the Supervisory Council consisting of 15 members elected by the Storting. The *Governor* is Svein Gjedrem. Total assets and liabilities at 31 Dec. 1999 were 506,710m. kroner. This was estimated to have risen to 809,684m. kroner by 31 Dec. 2000.

There are three major commercial banks: Nordea Bank Norge ASA, DNB Holding ASA and Fokus. Total assets and liabilities of the 21 commercial banks at 31 Dec. 1999 were 709,280m. kroner.

The number of savings banks at 31 Dec. 1999 was 130; total assets and liabilities on 31 Dec. 1999 were 488,411m. kroner.

There is a stock exchange in Oslo.

Weights and Measures. The metric system is obligatory.

ENERGY AND NATURAL RESOURCES

Environment. According to the *World Bank Atlas* Norway's carbon dioxide emissions in 1998 were the equivalent of 7·6 tonnes per capita. An *Environmental Sustainability Index* compiled for the World Economic Forum meeting in Feb. 2002 ranked Norway second in the world behind Finland, with 73·0%. The index measured the ability of countries to maintain favourable environmental conditions and examined various factors including pollution levels and the use or abuse of natural resources.

In 2000 there were 18 national parks (total area, 1,386,840 ha), 1,441 nature reserves (279,590 ha), 97 landscape protected areas (779,825 ha) and 75 other areas with protected flora and fauna (9,325 ha).

Norway is one of the world leaders in recycling. In 1999, 38% of all household waste was recycled, including 81% of glass.

Electricity. Norway is the sixth largest producer of hydropower in the world and the largest in Europe. The potential total hydro-electric power was estimated at 180,199m. kWh in 1999. Installed electrical capacity in 1997 was 27m. kW, more than 95% of it hydro-electric. Production, 2000 estimate, was 142,984m. kWh (over 99% hydro-electric). Consumption per capita in 1998 was 24,607 kWh. In 1991 Norway became the first country in Europe to deregulate its energy market. Norway is a net importer of electricity.

Oil and Gas. There are enormous oil reserves in the Norwegian continental shelf. In 1966 the first exploration well was drilled. Production of crude oil, 2000, 158,625,000 tonnes. Norway is the world's third biggest oil exporter after Saudi Arabia and Russia, producing around 3·1m. bbls. a day in 2000. It had proven reserves of 9·4bn. bbls. in 2000. In March 1998 Norway announced that it would reduce its output for the year by 100,000 bbls. per day as part of a plan to cut global crude production. In June 2001 the Norwegian government sold a 17·5% stake in Statoil, the last major state-owned oil company in western Europe. The privatization was the largest in Norway's history.

Output of natural gas, 2000, 53,018m. cu. metres with proven reserves of 1,250bn. cu. metres.

Minerals. Production, 1996 (in tonnes): iron ore, 1,554,599; aluminium (1998), 996,000; ferrotitanium ore, 758,711; coal (1998), 328,000; copper concentrates, 31,736; zinc ore, 8,619; lead ore (1995), 3,721.

Agriculture. Norway is barren and mountainous. The arable area is in strips in valleys and around fjords and lakes.

In 1999 the agricultural area[1] was 1,038,200 ha, of which 638,800 ha were meadow and pasture, 182,600 ha were sown to barley, 91,300 ha to oats, 51,600 ha to wheat and 14,900 ha to potatoes. Production (in 1,000 tonnes) in 1999: hay, 2,671; barley, 624; potatoes, 380; oats, 356; wheat, 230.

Livestock, 1999[1], 1,033,070 cattle (312,948 milch cows), 2,324,789 sheep, 68,714 goats, 738,720 pigs, 3,181,174 hens, 110,000 silver and platinum fox, 350,000 blue fox, 350,000 mink, 183,100 reindeer.

[1]Holdings with at least 50 ha agricultural area in use.

Forestry. In 1995 the total area under forests was 8·07m. ha, or 26·3% of the total land area (7·94m. ha and 25·9% in 1990). Productive forest area, 1997, approximately 67,375 sq. km. About 80% of the productive forest area consists of conifers and 20% of broadleaves. In 1999, 8·42m. cu. metres of roundwood were cut.

Fisheries. The total number of fishermen in 2000 was 20,242, of whom 5,887 had another chief occupation. In 2000 the number of registered fishing vessels (all with motor) was 8,430, and of these 4,585 were open boats.

The catch in 2000 (provisional) totalled 2,701,852 tonnes, almost entirely from sea fishing. The catch of herring totalled 799,732 tonnes, capelin 374,580 tonnes and cod 220,117 tonnes. 20,549 seals were caught in 2000 (of which 18,678 harp and 1,871 hooded seals). Commercial whaling was prohibited in 1988, but recommenced in 1993: 487 whales were caught in 2000. Norway is the second largest exporter of fishery commodities, after Thailand. In 1999 exports were valued at US$3·77bn.

INDUSTRY

The leading companies by market capitalization in Norway, excluding banking and finance, in Jan. 2002 were: Den Norske Stats Oljeselskap AS (Statoil), 143bn. kroner; Norsk Hydro ASA (97bn. kroner), an oil, metals and chemicals producer; and Telenor ASA (67bn. kroner), a telecommunications company.

Industry is chiefly based on raw materials. Paper and paper products, industrial chemicals and basic metals are important export manufactures. In the following table figures are given for industrial establishments in 1998. The values are given in 1m. kroner.

Industries	Establish-ments	Number of employees	Gross value of production	Value added
Coal and peat	11	248	153	49
Metal ores	8	547	537	176
Other mining and quarrying	348	3,209	5,167	1,827
Food products	1,607	47,297	93,449	16,558
Beverages and tobacco	48	5,863	13,779	9,862
Textiles	331	5,301	4,247	1,645
Clothing, etc.	165	2,026	1,371	520
Leather and leather products	46	633	466	148
Wood and wood products	1,051	15,531	17,309	5,001
Pulp, paper and paper products	108	9,830	19,713	5,705
Printing and publishing	2,062	38,168	33,038	13,245
Basic chemicals	82	7,935	23,035	6,568
Other chemical products	115	5,815	12,088	3,730
Coal and refined petroleum products	6	1,189	14,930	1,418
Rubber and plastic products	354	7,034	7,809	2,721
Other non-metallic mineral products	615	9,983	13,447	4,683
Basic metals	121	14,658	40,141	9,938
Metal products, except machinery/equipment	1,344	21,035	20,490	8,095
Machinery and equipment	1,295	24,603	32,155	10,902
Office machinery and computers	18	814	2,053	425
Electrical machinery and apparatus	351	10,426	13,859	5,102
Radio, television, communication equipment	85	4,530	5,985	2,301
Medical, precision and optical instruments	331	6,069	8,803	2,966

Industries	Establish-ments	Number of employees	Gross value of production	Value added
Oil platforms	103	20,999	37,749	9,103
Motor vehicles and trailers	108	4,739	5,263	1,833
Other transport equipment	514	16,378	24,515	6,375
Other manufacturing industries	878	15,409	14,141	4,772
Total (all industries)	12,105	300,269	465,720	135,669

Labour. Norway has a tradition of centralized wage bargaining. Since the early 1960s the contract period has been for two years with intermediate bargaining after 12 months, to take into consideration such changes as the rate of inflation.

The labour force averaged 2,350,000 in 2000 (1,092,000 females). The total number of employed persons in 2000 averaged 2,269,000 (1,057,000 females), of whom 2,099,000 were salaried employees and wage earners, 158,000 self-employed and 8,000 family workers. Distribution of employed persons by occupation in 2000 showed 419,000 in trade; 402,000 in health and social work; 295,000 in manufacturing and mining; 256,000 in finance; 168,000 in transport and communications; 157,000 in public administration, services and defence; 147,000 in construction; 93,000 in agriculture; 28,000 in oil and gas extraction; 20,000 in public utilities.

There were 81,000 registered unemployed in 2000, giving an unemployment rate of 3·4%. By Dec. 2002 the rate had gone up to 4·1%.

There were 29 work stoppages in 2000: 496,568 working days were lost.

Trade Unions. There were 1,485,065 union members at the end of 1999.

INTERNATIONAL TRADE

Imports and Exports. Total imports and exports in calendar years (in 1m. kroner):

	1997	1998	1999	2000	2001
Imports	252,232	282,638	266,677	302,852	291,785
Exports	342,421	304,653	355,172	528,439	521,455

Major import suppliers in 2000 (value in 1m. kroner): Sweden, 44,488·3; Germany, 35,964·5; USA, 24,714·6; UK, 24,569·2; Denmark, 19,298·1; Japan, 15,635·5; France, 12,106·0; Netherlands, 11,807·5; Finland, 10,760·1; Italy, 9,528·7. Imports from economic areas: EU, 189,386·3; Nordic countries, 75,448·9; OECD, 257,672·3.

Major export markets in 2000 (value in 1m. kroner): UK, 109,161·0; Netherlands, 60,497·4; Germany, 54,443·4; France, 52,919·5; Sweden, 44,478·4; USA, 40,164·3; Canada, 29,923·5; Denmark, 20,231·9; Belgium, 18,291·7; Finland, 11,456·9. Exports to economic areas: EU, 405,964·0; Nordic countries, 79,109·9; OECD, 502,095·1.

Principal imports in 2000 (in 1m. kroner): transport equipment except motor vehicles, 38,343·5; motor vehicles, 25,125·7; ships over 100 tonnes, 16,170·1; electrical machinery, 15,299·1; office machines and computers, 15,077·2; passenger cars including station wagons, 13,526·5; general industrial machinery and equipment, 12,785·3; telecommunications and sound apparatus and equipment, 12,564·6; metalliferous ores and metal scrap, 12,478·1; clothing and accessories, 11,341·5; specialized machinery for particular industries, 10,222·1; petroleum and petroleum products, 9,208·2; automatic data processing machines, 9,119·1; manufactures of metals, 9,027·2; iron and steel, 7,245·3. Principal exports in 2000 (in 1m. kroner): petroleum, petroleum products and related materials, 283,578·4 (including crude petroleum, 258,835·7); natural and manufactured gas, 52,052·4 (including natural gas, 47,789·5); non-ferrous metals, 30,558·5 (including aluminium, 20,649·4); fish, crustaceans and molluscs, and preparations thereof, 30,340·5; transport equipment excluding road vehicles, 11,103·2; paper, paperboard and products, 10,235·2; iron and steel, 8,674·8.

COMMUNICATIONS

Roads. In 2001 the length of public roads (including roads in towns) totalled 91,479 km. Total road length in 2001 included: national roads, 26,781 km; provincial roads, 27,216 km; local roads, 37,482 km. Number of registered motor vehicles, 2000, included: 1,851,929 passenger cars (including station wagons and ambulances), 229,204 tractors and special purpose vehicles, 233,248 vans, 115,892 mopeds, 104,868 combined vehicles, 76,224 goods vehicles (including lorries), 85,672 motorcycles and 36,686 buses. In 2000 there were 8,440 road accidents with 301 fatalities.

Rail. The length of state railways in 1999 was 4,021 km (2,456 km electrified). Operating receipts of the state railways in 1998 were 3,958m. kroner; operating expenses, 4,180m. kroner. The state railways carried 8,299,000 tonnes of freight and 50,019,000 passengers in 1999. As recently as 1995, 20,909,000 tonnes of freight had been carried in the year.

There is a metro (98 km) and tram/light rail line (54 km) in Oslo.

Civil Aviation. The main international airports are at Oslo (Gardermoen), Bergen (Flesland), Trondheim (Værnes) and Stavanger (Sola). Kristiansand (Kjevik) and Torp also have a few international flights. Denmark and Norway each hold two-sevenths and Sweden three-sevenths of the capital of SAS (Scandinavian Airlines System), but they have joint responsibility towards third parties. 20,606,700 passengers were carried on all domestic and international flights in 1997. Braathens is the major airline after SAS, carrying 5,936,600 passengers in 1999 (648,700 on international flights).

In 2000 Oslo (Gardermoen) handled 14,194,334 passengers (7,480,800 on domestic flights) and 56,686 tonnes of freight. Bergen is the second busiest airport for passenger traffic, with 3,725,633 in 2000 (3,017,449 on domestic flights), and Trondheim second busiest for freight, with 7,784 tonnes (and 2,829,448 passengers) in 2000. Oslo Fornebu, which had for many years been the busiest airport, closed down in 1998 to be replaced by Gardermoen as the country's main international airport.

Shipping. The Norwegian International Ship Register was set up in 1987. At 31 Dec. 1999, 705 ships were registered (476 Norwegian) totalling 19,109,000 GRT. 177 tankers accounted for 8,450,000 GRT. There were also 954 ships totalling 2,985,000 GRT on the Norwegian Ordinary Register. These figures do not include fishing boats, tugs, salvage vessels, icebreakers and similar special types of vessels. Norway's merchant fleet represents 4·3% of total world tonnage.

In 1999, 46,037,000 passengers were carried by coastwise shipping on long distance, local and ferry services.

The warm Gulf Stream ensures ice-free harbours throughout the year.

Telecommunications. There were 2,386,400 telephone main lines in 2000 (532·1 per 1,000 inhabitants) and 2·2m. PCs (490·5 for every 1,000 persons). In 1997 there were 220,000 fax machines. Norway had 3·23m. mobile phone subscribers in Nov. 2000 and 2·68m. Internet users in July 2002, approximately 59% of the population. In Dec. 2000 the government sold off a 21% stake in Telenor, the country's largest telecommunications operator.

Postal Services. In 2001 post offices began to be converted to Post in Shops. 452 post offices were replaced by 519 Post in Shops. In addition, 29 post offices were upgraded to Post Shops and 5 Business Centres and 5 Call Centres were established. The final target is a minimum of 1,150 Post in Shops, 300 Post Shops and 20 Business Centres. In 1997 a total of 2,524m. items of mail were processed, or 555 per person.

SOCIAL INSTITUTIONS

Justice. The judicature is common to civil and criminal cases; the same professional judges preside over both. These judges are state officials. The participation of lay judges and jurors, both summoned for the individual case, varies according to the kind of court and kind of case.

The 96 city or district courts of first instance are in criminal cases composed of one professional judge and two lay judges, chosen by ballot from a panel elected by the local authority. In civil cases two lay judges may participate. These courts are competent in all cases except criminal cases where the maximum penalty exceeds six years imprisonment. In every community there is a Conciliation Board composed of three lay persons elected by the district council. A civil lawsuit usually begins with mediation by the Board which can pronounce judgement in certain cases.

The five high courts, or courts of second instance, are composed of three professional judges. Additionally, in civil cases two or four lay judges may be summoned. In serious criminal cases, which are brought before high courts in the first instance, a jury of ten lay persons is summoned to determine whether the defendant is guilty according to the charge. In less serious criminal cases the court is composed of two professional and three lay judges. In civil cases, the court of second instance is an ordinary court of appeal. In criminal cases in which the lower court does not have judicial authority, it is itself the court of first instance. In other criminal cases it is an appeal court as far as the appeal is based on an attack against the lower court's assessment of the facts when determining the guilt of the defendant. An appeal based on any other alleged mistakes is brought directly before the Supreme Court.

The Supreme Court *(Høyesterett)* is the court of last resort. There are 18 Supreme Court judges. Each individual case is heard by five judges. Some major cases are determined in plenary session. The Supreme Court may in general examine every aspect of the case and the handling of it by the lower courts. However, in criminal cases the Court may not overrule the lower court's assessment of the facts as far as the guilt of the defendant is concerned.

The Court of Impeachment *(Riksretten)* is composed of five judges of the Supreme Court and ten members of Parliament.

The population in penal institutions in 1998 was 2,466 (55 per 100,000 of national population).

Religion. There is freedom of religion, the Church of Norway (Evangelical Lutheran), however, being the national church, endowed by the State. Its clergy are nominated by the King. Ecclesiastically Norway is divided into 11 bishoprics, 96 archdeaconries and 626 clerical districts. There were 286,000 members of registered and unregistered religious communities outside the Evangelical Lutheran Church, subsidized by central government and local authorities in 2000. There were also 67 Muslim congregations with 56,458 members. The Roman Catholics are under a Bishop at Oslo, a Vicar Apostolic at Trondheim and a Vicar Apostolic at Tromsø.

Education. Free compulsory schooling in primary and lower secondary schools was extended to 10 years from 9, and the starting age lowered to 6 from 7, in July 1997. All young people between the ages of 16 and 19 have the statutory right to three years of upper secondary education. In 1999 there were 5,942 kindergartens (children up to six years old) with 187,612 children and 52,491 staff. In 1999–2000 there were 3,271 primary and lower secondary schools with 580,261 pupils and 44,740 teachers; 705 upper secondary schools with 191,669 pupils and 20,852 teachers; and 60 colleges, with 112,677 students and 5,348 teachers.

There are four universities: Oslo (founded 1811), with 31,821 students in Oct. 2000; Bergen (1946), with 16,379 students; Tromsø (1968), with 6,073 students; and the Norwegian University of Science and Technology (1996, formerly the University of Trondheim and the Norwegian Institute of Technology), with 19,426 students. There are also six university colleges and 26 state colleges. In 2000–01 the universities and university colleges had 81,561 students, and the state colleges 109,893 students. The University of Tromsø is responsible for Sami language and studies.

In 1996 total expenditure on education came to 7·4% of GNP and 15·8% of total government spending. The adult literacy rate in 1998 was at least 99%.

Health. The health care system, which is predominantly publicly financed (mainly by a national insurance tax), is run on both county and municipal levels. Persons who fall ill are guaranteed medical treatment, and health services are distributed according to need. In 1999 there were the equivalent of 6,909 full-time doctors, 21,336 nurses and 5,152 auxiliary nursing personnel. In 1994 provision of hospital beds was 51 per 10,000 population.

In 2000, 31·4% of men and 32·3% of women smoked. The rate among women is one of the highest in the world.

Norway has the EU's lowest rate of AIDS at 11·1 cases per 100,000 population.

Welfare. In 2000 there were 628,890 old age pensioners who received a total of 65,347·4m. kroner, 279,573 disability pensioners who received 30,399·2m. kroner,

27,087 widows and widowers who received 1,879·0m. kroner and 40,382 single parents who received 2,733·6m. kroner. In 2000, 1,047,618 children received family allowances. Maternity leave is for one year on 80% of previous salary; unused portions may pass to a husband. In 2000 sickness benefits totalling 37,870·8m. kroner were paid: 21,774·5m. kroner in sickness allowances and 16,096·3m. kroner in medical benefits. Expenditure on benefits at childbirth and adoption totalled 7,853·6m. kroner to 97,746 cases in 2000.

CULTURE

Broadcasting. The Norwegian Broadcasting Corporation is a non-commercial enterprise operated by an independent state organization and broadcasts one programme (P1) on long, medium, and short-waves and on FM and one programme (P2) on FM. Local programmes are also broadcast. It broadcasts one TV programme from 2,259 transmitters. Colour programmes are broadcast by the PAL system. Number of television licences, 1999, 1,744,336. In 1997 there were over 4m. radio receivers.

Cinema. There were 398 cinemas in 1999, with a seating capacity of 88,674. Attendances totalled 11·35m. 15 full-length films were made in 1995.

Press. There were 65 daily newspapers with a combined average net circulation of 2·29m. in 1999, and 91 weeklies and semi-weeklies with 671,000. Norway has one of the highest circulation rates of daily newspapers in Europe, at 596 per 1,000 inhabitants in 1995.

In 1996 a total of 6,900 book titles were published.

Tourism. In 1999 there were 4,481,000 foreign tourists. In 2000 there were 1,166 hotels and 920 camping sites. Receipts from foreign tourism totalled US$2·23bn. in 1999.

Libraries. In 1999 there were 1,047 public libraries, 3,116 school libraries, and 362 special and research libraries (two national).

Theatre and Opera. There were 6,800 theatre and opera performances attended by 1,403,068 people at 20 theatres in 1999.

Museums and Galleries. There were 435 museums in 1999 (29 art, 360 social history, 14 natural history and 32 mixed social and natural history), with 8,821,947 visitors.

DIPLOMATIC REPRESENTATIVES

Of Norway in the United Kingdom (25 Belgrave Sq., London, SW1X 8QD)
Ambassador: Tarald Osnes Brautaset.

Of the United Kingdom in Norway (Thomas Heftyesgate 8, 0244 Oslo)
Ambassador: Mariot Leslie.

Of Norway in the USA (2720 34th St., NW, Washington, D.C., 20008)
Ambassador: Knut Vollebaek.

Of the USA in Norway (Drammensveien 18, 0244 Oslo)
Ambassador: John D. Ong.

Of Norway to the United Nations
Ambassador: Ole Peter Kolby.

Of Norway to the European Union
Ambassador: Bjørn T. Grydeland.

FURTHER READING

Statistics Norway (formerly Central Bureau of Statistics). *Statistisk Årbok; Statistical Yearbook of Norway.—Economic survey* (annual, from 1935; with English summary from 1952, now published in *Økonomiske Analyser,* annual).—*Historisk Statistikk; Historical Statistics.— Statistisk Månedshefte* (with English index)
Norges Statskalender. From 1816; annual from 1877
Petersson, O., *The Government and Politics of the Nordic Countries.* Stockholm, 1994
Turner, Barry, (ed.) *Scandinavia Profiled.* Macmillan, London, 2000

National library: The National Library of Norway, Drammensveien 42b, 0255 Oslo.
National statistical office: Statistics Norway, PB 8131 Dep., N-0033 Oslo.
Website: http://www.ssb.no/

SVALBARD

An archipelago situated between 10° and 35° E. long. and between 74° and 81° N. lat. Total area, 61,229 sq. km (23,640 sq. miles). The main islands are Spitsbergen, Nordaustlandet, Edgeøya, Barentsøya, Prins Karls Forland, Bjørnøya, Hopen, Kong Karls Land and Kvitøya. The Arctic climate is tempered by mild winds from the Atlantic.

The archipelago was probably discovered by Norsemen in 1194 and rediscovered by the Dutch navigator Barents in 1596. In the 17th century whale-hunting gave rise to rival Dutch, British and Danish-Norwegian claims to sovereignty; but when in the 18th century the whale-hunting ended, the question of the sovereignty of Svalbard lost its significance. It was again raised in the 20th century, owing to the discovery and exploitation of coalfields. By a treaty, signed on 9 Feb. 1920 in Paris, Norway's sovereignty over the archipelago was recognized. On 14 Aug. 1925 the archipelago was officially incorporated in Norway.

Total population on 1 Jan. 1999 was 2,423, of whom 1,476 were Norwegians, 939 Russians and 8 Poles. Coal is the principal product. There are 2 Norwegian and 2 Russian mining camps. 399,940 tonnes of coal were produced from Norwegian mines in 1999 valued at 72,208,000 kroner.

There were 2,413 motor vehicles and trailers registered at 31 Dec. 1999, including 1,145 snow scooters.

There are research and radio stations, and an airport near Longyearbyen (Svalbard Lufthavn) opened in 1975.

Greve, T., *Svalbard: Norway in the Arctic*. Oslo, 1975
Hisdal, V., *Geography of Svalbard*. Norsk Polarinstitutt, Oslo, rev. ed., 1984

JAN MAYEN

This bleak, desolate and mountainous island of volcanic origin and partly covered by glaciers is situated at 71° N. lat. and 8° 30' W. long., 300 miles north-northeast of Iceland. The total area is 377 sq. km (146 sq. miles). Beerenberg, its highest peak, reaches a height of 2,277 metres. Volcanic activity, which had been dormant, reactivated in Sept. 1970.

The island was possibly discovered by Henry Hudson in 1608, and it was first named Hudson's Tutches (Touches). It was again and again rediscovered and renamed. Its present name derives from the Dutch whaling captain Jan Jacobsz May, who indisputably discovered the island in 1614. It was uninhabited, but occasionally visited by seal hunters and trappers, until 1921 when Norway established a radio and meteorological station. On 8 May 1929 Jan Mayen was officially proclaimed as incorporated into the Kingdom of Norway. Its relation to Norway was finally settled by law of 27 Feb. 1930. A LORAN station (1959) and a CONSOL station (1968) have been established.

BOUVET ISLAND

Bouvetøya

This uninhabited volcanic island, mostly covered by glaciers and situated at 54° 25' S. lat. and 3° 21' E. long., was discovered in 1739 by a French naval officer, Jean Baptiste Loziert Bouvet, but no flag was hoisted till, in 1825, Capt. Norris raised the Union Jack. In 1928 Great Britain waived its claim to the island in favour of

Norway, which in Dec. 1927 had occupied it. A law of 27 Feb. 1930 declared Bouvetøya a Norwegian dependency. The area is 59 sq. km (23 sq. miles). Since 1977 Norway has had an automatic meteorological station on the island.

PETER I ISLAND

Peter I Øy

This uninhabited island, situated at 68° 48' S. lat. and 90° 35' W. long., was sighted in 1821 by the Russian explorer, Admiral von Bellingshausen. The first landing was made in 1929 by a Norwegian expedition which hoisted the Norwegian flag. On 1 May 1931 Peter I Island was placed under Norwegian sovereignty, and on 24 March 1933 it was incorporated into Norway as a dependency. The area is 249 sq. km (96 sq. miles).

QUEEN MAUD LAND

Dronning Maud Land

On 14 Jan. 1939 the Norwegian Cabinet placed that part of the Antarctic Continent from the border of Falkland Islands dependencies in the west to the border of the Australian Antarctic Dependency in the east (between 20° W. and 45° E.) under Norwegian sovereignty. The territory had been explored only by Norwegians and hitherto been ownerless. In 1957 it was given the status of a dependency.

OMAN

Saltanat 'Uman
(Sultanate of Oman)

Capital: Muscat
Population estimate, 2000: 2·54m.
GDP per capita, 2000: (PPP$) 13,356
HDI/world rank: 0·751/78

KEY HISTORICAL EVENTS

The ancestors of present day Oman are believed to have arrived in two waves of migration, the first from the Yemen and the second from northern Arabia. In the 9th century maritime trade flourished and Sohar became the greatest sea port in the Islamic world. In the early 16th century the Portuguese occupied Muscat. The Ya'aruba dynasty introduced a period of renaissance in Omani fortunes both at home and abroad, uniting the country and bringing prosperity; but, on the death in 1718 of Sultan bin Saif II, civil war broke out over the election of his successor. Persian troops occupied Muttrah and Muscat but failed to take Sohar which was defended by Ahmad bin Said who expelled the Persians from Oman after the civil war had ended. In 1744 the Al bu Said family assumed power and has ruled to the present day. Oman remained largely isolated from the rest of the world until 1970 when Said bin Taimur was deposed by his son Qaboos in a bloodless coup.

TERRITORY AND POPULATION

Situated at the southeast corner of the Arabian peninsula, Oman is bounded in the northeast by the Gulf of Oman and southeast by the Arabian Sea, southwest by Yemen and northwest by Saudi Arabia and the United Arab Emirates. There is an enclave at the northern tip of the Musandam Peninsula. An agreement of April 1992 completed the demarcation of the border with Yemen, and an agreement of March 1990 finalized the border with Saudi Arabia.

With a coastline of 1,700 sq. km from the Strait of Hormuz in the north to the borders of the Republic of Yemen, the Sultanate is strategically located overlooking ancient maritime trade routes linking the Far East and Africa with the Mediterranean.

The Sultanate of Oman occupies a total area of 309,500 sq. km and includes different terrains that vary from plain to highlands and mountains. The coastal plain overlooking the Gulf of Oman and the Arabian Sea forms the most important and fertile plain in Oman.

The **Kuria Muria** islands were ceded to the UK in 1854 by the Sultan of Muscat and Oman. On 30 Nov. 1967 the islands were retroceded to the Sultan of Muscat and Oman, in accordance with the wishes of the population. They are now known as the **Halaniyat Islands**.

In 1993 the census population was 2,017,591; density 6·5 per sq. km. Estimated population (1999), 2,325,000, chiefly Arabs, and including 0·6m. foreign workers; density 7·5 per sq. km.

The UN gives a projected population for 2010 of 3·52m.

In 1999, 82·2% of the population lived in urban areas. In the period 1990–95 the annual growth in the urban population was 8·2%, a rate only exceeded by Botswana and Mozambique. The estimated population of the capital, Muscat, in 1999 was 635,279.

The official language is Arabic; English is in commercial use.

SOCIAL STATISTICS

1997 births, estimate, 66,000; deaths, 10,000. Birth rate, 1997 estimate (per 1,000 population), 29·0; death rate, 3·8. Consequently Oman has a very young population, with approximately half the population under the age of 15. Expectation of life at birth, 1999, was 69·5 years for males and 72·4 years for females. Fertility rate, 1999, 4·6 births per woman, down from 7·8 in 1988. Oman has achieved some of the most rapid advances ever recorded. Infant mortality declined from 200 per 1,000 live births in 1960 to 14 per 1,000 live births in 1999, and as recently as 1970 life expectancy was just 40.

OMAN

CLIMATE
Oman has a desert climate, with exceptionally hot and humid months from April to Oct., when temperatures may reach 47°C. Light monsoon rains fall in the south from June to Sept., with highest amounts in the western highland region. Muscat, Jan. 28°C, July 46°C. Annual rainfall 101 mm. Salalah, Jan. 29°C, July 32°C. Annual rainfall 98 mm.

CONSTITUTION AND GOVERNMENT
Oman is a hereditary absolute monarchy. The Sultan legislates by decree and appoints a Cabinet to assist him. The Basic Statute of the State was promulgated on 6 Nov. 1996.

The present Sultan is **Qaboos bin Said Al Said** (b. Nov. 1940).

In 1991 a new consultative assembly, the *Majlis al Shura*, replaced the former State Consultative Chamber. The Majlis consists of 83 elected members. It debates domestic issues, but has no legislative or veto powers. In Dec. 2002 the Sultan of Oman extended voting rights to all citizens over the age of 21.

National Anthem. 'Ya Rabbana elifidh lana jalalat al Saltan' ('O Lord, protect for us his majesty the Sultan'); words and tune anonymous.

RECENT ELECTIONS
The last elections to the *Majlis al Shura* were on 14 Sept. 2000. No parties are allowed. 83 legislators were chosen for three-year terms from among 541 candidates (including 21 women).

CURRENT ADMINISTRATION
The Sultan is nominally Prime Minister and Minister of Foreign Affairs, Defence and Finance.

In March 2003 the other Ministers were:
Special Representative of the Sultan: Thuwayni bin Shihab Al Said.

Deputy Prime Minister for Cabinet Affairs: Fahd bin Mahmud Al Said. *Minister Responsible for Foreign Affairs:* Yusuf bin Alawi bin Abdallah. *Agriculture and Fisheries:* Salim bin Hilal bin Ali al-Khalili. *Civil Service:* Abd al-Aziz bin Matar al-Azizi. *Commerce and Industry:* Maqbul bin Ali bin Sultan. *Defence Affairs:* Badr bin Saud bin Harib Al Busaidi. *Transportation and Communications:* Malik bin Sulayman al-Mamari. *Education:* Yahya bin Saud bin Mansour Al Suleimi. *Housing, Electricity and Water:* Suhail bin Mustahail Shamas. *Regional Municipalities, Environment and Water Resources:* Khamis bin Mubarak bin Isa al-Alawi. *National Economy:* Ahmad bin Abd al-Nabi al-Makki. *Health:* Dr Ali bin Muhammad bin Musa. *Information:* Hamad bin Abdallah Muhsin al-Rashidi. *Interior:* Saud bin Ibrahim bin Saud Al Busaidi. *Justice:* Muhammad bin Abdallah bin Zahir al-Hinai. *National Heritage and Culture:* Faysal bin Ali Al Said. *Oil and Gas:* Muhammad bin Hamad bin Seif al-Rumhi. *Social Development:* Amir bin Shuwayn al-Husni. *Awqaf and Religious Affairs:* Abdallah bin Muhammad bin Abdallah al-Salimi. *Diwan of the Royal Court:* Ali bin Hamad bin Ali al-Busaidi. *Palace Office Affairs:* Gen. Ali bin Majid al-Mamari. *Higher Education:* Yahya bin Mahfudh al-Manthiri. *Legal Affairs:* Muhammad bin Ali bin Nasir al-Alawi. *Manpower:* Jama bin Ali bin Juma. *Minister of State and Governor of the Capital:* Mutasim bin Hamud bin Nasir Al Busaidi. *Minister of State and Governor of Dhofar:* Muhammad bin Ali al-Qutaybi.

Government Website: http://www.omanet.com/

DEFENCE
Military expenditure in 2000 totalled US$1,733m. (US$682 per capita), representing 10·0% of GDP.

Army. Strength (1999) about 25,000. In addition there are 6,500 Royal Household troops and the Musandam Security Force (an independent rifle company). A paramilitary tribal home guard numbers 4,000.

Navy. The Navy is based principally at Seeb (HQ) and Wudam. Naval personnel in 1999 totalled 4,200.

The wholly separate Royal Yacht Squadron consists of a yacht and support ship with helicopter and troop-carrying capability.

Air Force. The Air Force, formed in 1959, has 40 combat aircraft including in 1999 two strike/interceptor squadrons of Jaguars and a ground attack squadron of Hawks. Personnel (1999) about 4,100.

INTERNATIONAL RELATIONS
A 1982 Memorandum of Understanding with the UK provided for regular consultations on international and bilateral issues.

Oman is a member of the UN, WTO, the League of Arab States, the Organization of the Islamic Conference and the Gulf Co-operation Council.

ECONOMY
Overview. The sixth five-year development plan (2001–05) encompasses economic balance and sustainable growth, human resources development, economic diversification and private sector development.

Privatization of water and electricity is under way.

Currency. The unit of currency is the *Rial Omani* (OMR). It is divided into 1,000 *baiza*. The rial is pegged to the US dollar. In June 2002 foreign exchange reserves were US$3,133m., total money supply was RO 813m. and gold reserves totalled 1,000 troy oz (291,000 troy oz in April 2002). Inflation was negative in 2001, at −1·1%.

In 2001 the six Gulf Arab states—Oman, along with Bahrain, Kuwait, Qatar, Saudi Arabia and the United Arab Emirates—signed an agreement to establish a single currency by 2010.

Budget. Budget revenue and expenditure (in RO 1m.):

	1996	1997	1998	1999	2000
Revenue	1,990·2	2,267·2	1,846·3	1,796·1	2,289·9
Expenditure	2,253·7	2,307·3	2,221·6	2,269·0	2,656·2

In 1999 approximately 70% of total revenue came from oil.

Performance. In 2001 GDP growth was 7·3%. Total GDP in 1998 was US$15·0bn. The non-oil sector contributed 71·3% of this figure.

Banking and Finance. The bank of issue is the Central Bank of Oman, which commenced operations in 1975 (*President*, Hamood Sangour Al Zadjali). All banks must comply with BIS capital adequacy ratios and have a minimum capital of RO 10m. In 1999 there were 20 commercial banks. The largest bank is BankMuscat SAOG, with assets of OR 1·3bn. It was created in 2000 following a merger between BankMuscat and the Commercial Bank of Oman.

There is a stock exchange in Muscat, which is linked with those in Bahrain and Kuwait.

Weights and Measures. The metric system is in operation.

ENERGY AND NATURAL RESOURCES
Environment. Oman's carbon dioxide emissions in 1998 were the equivalent of 8·8 tonnes per capita according to the *World Bank Atlas*.

Electricity. Installed capacity was 2m. kW in 1997. Production in 1998 was 7·36bn. kWh, with consumption per capita 2,828 kWh.

Oil and Gas. The economy is dominated by the oil industry. Oil in commercial quantities was discovered in 1964 and production began in 1967. Production in 1999 was 904,000 bbls. a day from 2,470 wells. In 1999 exports of oil stood at 309m. bbls. Total proven reserves were estimated in 1999 to be 5·3bn. bbls. It was announced in Aug. 2000 that two new oilfields in the south of the country had been discovered, with a potential combined daily production capacity of 12,200 bbls. a day. Earlier in 2000 oil began to be pumped from two further recently-discovered oilfields. It is hoped that by 2004 daily oil production will have increased to 1m. bbls. a day.

Gas is likely to become the second major source of income for the country. Oman's proven gas reserves were 824bn. cu. metres, until the discovery in 2000 of two new fields which could yield a daily production of 1·78m. cu. metres. Natural gas production was 5·6bn. cu. metres in 1999.

Water. Oman relies on a combination of aquifers and desalination plants for its water, augmented by a construction programme of some 60 recharge dams. Desalination plants at Ghubriah and Wadi Adai provide most of the water needs of the capital area. In 1999 water production was 20,136m. gallons.

Minerals. Production in 1998 (in 1,000 tonnes): limestone, 1,902; marble, 166; gypsum, 165; chromite, 30; salt, 14; copper (1994), 6·5; silver (1994), 3,300 kg; gold, 569 kg. The mountains of the Sultanate of Oman are rich in mineral deposits; these include copper ore, chromite, coal, asbestos, manganese, gypsum, limestone and marble. The government is studying the exploitation of gold, platinum and sulphide.

Agriculture. Agriculture and fisheries are the traditional occupations of Omanis and remain important to the people and economy of Oman to this day. The country now produces a wide variety of fresh fruit, vegetables and field crops. The country is rapidly moving towards its goal of self-sufficiency in agriculture with the total area under cultivation standing at over 70,000 ha and total output more than 1m. tonnes. This effort has not been achieved without effort. In a country where water is a scarce commodity it has meant educating farmers on efficient methods of irrigation and building recharge dams to make the most of infrequent rainfall. According to a census of 1992–93, about 103,000 people were employed in agriculture of whom a third were women.

The coastal plain (Batinah) northwest of Muscat is fertile, as are the Dhofar highlands in the south. In the valleys of the interior, as well as on the Batinah coastal plain, date cultivation has reached a high level, and there are possibilities of agricultural development. Agricultural products, 2000 estimates (in 1,000 tonnes): dates, 135; tomatoes, 34; watermelons, 32; lemons and limes, 31; bananas, 28. Vegetable and fruit production are also important, and livestock are raised in the south where there are monsoon rains. Camels (98,000 in 2000) are bred by the inland tribes. Other livestock, 2000: sheep, 180,000; cattle, 213,000; goats, 729,000; chickens, 3m. Live animals and meat constitute more than 25% of the country's non-oil exports.

Fisheries. The catch was 108,808 tonnes in 1999, exclusively sea fish. More than 80% is taken by some 85,000 self-employed fishermen.

INDUSTRY

Apart from oil production, copper mining and smelting and cement production, there are light industries, mainly food processing and chemical products. The government gives priority to import substitute industries.

Labour. Males constituted 84% of the labour force in 1999. In 1995 there were 619,351 employees in the private sector and 110,529 persons in government service. The employment of foreign labour is being discouraged following 'Omanization' regulations of 1994.

INTERNATIONAL TRADE

Total foreign debt was US$6,267m. in 2000. A royal decree of 1994 permits up to 65% foreign ownership of Omani companies with a five-year tax and customs duties exemption.

In 2001 Oman, along with Kuwait, Bahrain, Qatar, Saudi Arabia and the United Arab Emirates agreed to the complete implementation of a customs union by 2003.

Imports and Exports. Imports and exports in US$1m.:

	1996	1997	1998	1999	2000
Imports f.o.b.	4,231	4,645	5,215	4,300	4,593
Exports f.o.b.	7,373	7,657	5,521	7,239	11,319

In 2000 oil exports made up approximately 79% of total exports. Principal non-oil exports are metal, metal goods, animals and animal products, and textiles. Main export markets (% of total trade; non-oil exports), 1996: United Arab Emirates, 41·6; Iran, 9·3; Hong Kong, 7·8; USA, 5·1. Main import suppliers: United Arab Emirates, 23·7; Japan, 17·2; UK, 8·8; USA, 7·5.

In 2000 the value of Oman's exports rose 56·4% compared to 1999. Over the same period oil exports rose by 61·1%.

COMMUNICATIONS

Roads. A network of adequate graded roads links all the main sectors of population, and only a few mountain villages are not accessible by motor vehicles. In 1996 there were 32,800 km of roads including 550 km of motorways and 2,160 km of main roads. In 1996 there were 211,000 passenger cars and 97,000 vans and lorries. The estimated average distance travelled by a passenger car in the year 1996 was 36,200 km. In 1999 there were 8,947 road accidents and 473 deaths.

Civil Aviation. Oman has a 25% share in Gulf Air with Bahrain, Qatar and the UAE. For details *see* BAHRAIN: Civil Aviation. In 1998 Gulf Air ran services in and out of Seeb international airport (20 miles from Muscat) to Abu Dhabi, Al Ain, Amman, Amsterdam, Athens, Bahrain, Bangkok, Beirut, Bombay, Cairo, Casablanca, Colombo, Dar es Salaam, Delhi, Dhaka, Doha, Dubai, Entebbe, Hong Kong, Jeddah, Karachi, Khartoum, Kuwait, London, Madras, Manila, Nairobi, Ras Al Khaima, Riyadh, Sharjah, Thiruvananthapuram and Zanzibar. Oman Air also flies on some international routes. In 2000 Seeb International Airport (Muscat) handled 2,622,000 passengers and 68,600 tonnes of freight.

Oman's two major airports, Seeb International and Salalah (mainly domestic flights), have been privatized as part of a project to develop Seeb as a regional hub. It will be rebuilt by a consortium (British Airports Authority, Oman's Bahwan Trading Company and ABB Equity Ventures) that was awarded a 25-year concession to operate the airports in Jan. 2002.

Shipping. In Mutrah a deep-water port (named Mina Qaboos) was completed in 1974. The annual handling capacity is 1·5m. tonnes. Mina Salalah, the port of Salalah, has a capacity of 1m. tonnes per year. Sea-going shipping totalled 15,000 GRT in 1998.

Telecommunications. The General Telecommunications Organization maintains a telegraph office at Muscat and an automatic telephone exchange. In 2000 there were 225,400 main telephone lines (88·8 per 1,000 persons) and 80,000 PCs in use (31·5 for every 1,000 persons). The 1999 capacity of the mobile phone network was 220,000 lines, and in 1997 there were 6,300 fax machines. Oman joined the Internet at the end of 1996 and in Dec. 2000 there were 90,000 users.

Postal Services. In 1999 there were 94 post offices. 16m. items of mail were exchanged between Oman and the rest of the world in 1999.

SOCIAL INSTITUTIONS

Religion. In 1995, 87·7% of the population were Muslim.

Education. Adult literacy was 70·3% in 1999 (male, 79·1%; female, 59·6%). In 1999 there were 983 schools. The total number of students in state education in 1999 was 542,580 with 24,973 teachers. Oman's first university, the Sultan Qaboos University, opened in 1986 and in 1998 there were 6,605 students.

In 1997 total expenditure on education represented 16·4% of total government expenditure.

Health. In 1998 there were 47 hospitals (13 of which are considered referral hospitals) with 4,443 beds. There were also 117 health centres. In 1999 there were 3,143 doctors, 237 dentists, 395 pharmacists and 7,525 nursing staff.

CULTURE

Broadcasting. The government-owned Radio Oman broadcasts in Arabic and English. A colour (PAL) television service, the government-owned Oman Television, covering Muscat and the surrounding area, started transmission in 1974. A television service for Dhofar opened in 1975. In 1991 there were seven television stations. Total number of radios (1997), 1·4m.; and televisions (1997), 1·6m. (694 per 1,000 inhabitants). Television usage has increased dramatically since 1980, when there were just 35,000 TV receivers in Oman (31 per 1,000 inhabitants). Oman had both the greatest percentage increase in the number of TV receivers of any country in the world between 1980 and 1997 and the greatest numerical increase in the number of receivers per 1,000 inhabitants.

Cinema. Oman has five cinemas.

Press. In 1996 there were four daily newspapers with a combined circulation of 63,000.

Tourism. Foreign visitors numbered 502,000 in 1999. Expenditure totalled US$104m. In 1999 there were 102 hotels with a total of over 5,138 rooms. Tourism accounts for 1% of GDP.

Festivals. National Day (18 Nov.); Spring Festival in Salalah (July–Aug.); Ramadan (Dec.).

Libraries. Three public libraries are run by the Royal Court of Diwan, the Islamic Institute and the Ministry of National Heritage.

Theatre and Opera. There is one national theatre.

Museums and Galleries. The main attractions are the Omani Museum (est. 1974) at Medinat al-Alam; the Omani-French Museum, Children's Museum and Bait al-Zubair (a historic house) at Muscat; the Natural History Museum at the Ministry of National Heritage and Culture; the National Museum; Salalah Museum; the Sultan's Armed Forces museum at Bait al-Falaj; the Oil & Gas Exhibition at Mina al-Fahal. There is also a museum in the historic fort at Sohar.

In 1998 total museum attendance was 96,000.

DIPLOMATIC REPRESENTATIVES

Of Oman in the United Kingdom (167 Queen's Gate, London, SW7 5HE)
Ambassador: Hussain bin Ali bin Abdullatif.

Of the United Kingdom in Oman (PO Box 300, Muscat)
Ambassador: Stuart Laing.

Of Oman in the USA (2535 Belmont Rd., NW, Washington, D.C., 20008)
Ambassador: Mohamed Ali Al-Khusaiby.

Of the USA in Oman (PO Box 202, Medinat Qaboos, Muscat)
Ambassador: Richard L. Baltimore.

Of Oman to the United Nations
Ambassador: Fuad Mubarak Al-Hinai.

Of Oman to the European Union
Ambassador: Khadija bint Hassan Salman Al-Lawati.

FURTHER READING

Clements, F. A., *Oman.* [Bibliography] 2nd ed. ABC-Clio, Oxford and Santa Barbara (CA), 1994

Owtram, Francis, *A Modern History of Oman: Formation of the State since 1920.* I. B. Tauris, London, 2002

Skeet, I., *Oman: Politics and Development.* London, 1992

National statistical office: Directorate General of National Statistics, POB 881, Muscat 113.

PAKISTAN

Islami Jamhuriya e Pakistan
(Islamic Republic of
Pakistan)

Capital: Islamabad
Population estimate, 2000: 141·26m.
GDP per capita, 2000: (PPP$) 1,928
HDI/world rank: 0·499/138

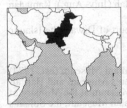

KEY HISTORICAL EVENTS

The State of Pakistan was created on 14 Aug. 1947 to provide Indian Muslims with their own state. Pakistan's status was that of a Dominion within the Commonwealth; it became a republic in 1956 and left the Commonwealth in 1972. Efforts to rejoin were opposed by India until 1989 when Pakistan once more became a full member of the Commonwealth.

The first of several periods of martial law began in 1958, followed by the rule of Field Marshal Mohammad Ayub Khan (until 1969) and Gen. Agha Mohammad Yahya Khan (until 1971). During the latter's term, differences between East and West Pakistan came to a head. Civil war broke out in March 1971 and ended in Dec. 1971 with the creation of Bangladesh. A new constitution came into force on 14 Aug. 1973, providing a federal parliamentary government with a president as head of state and a prime minister as head of the government. Zulfiquar Ali Bhutto became prime minister. His government was thought by traditionalists to be not sufficiently Islamic. There was an army coup led by Gen. Mohammad Zia ul-Haq in July 1977. Zulfiquar Ali Bhutto was hanged for conspiring to murder. His daughter, Benazir, held power twice in the 1990s but was eventually overthrown in 1996 when the President, Farooq Leghari, dismissed the government for corruption and mismanaging the economy.

Relations between Pakistan and India have foundered on the issue of Kashmir, a disputed territory divided by a ceasefire line negotiated by the UN in 1949. On 28 May 1998 Pakistan carried out five nuclear tests in the deserts of Balochistan in response to India's tests earlier in the month. US President Bill Clinton invoked sanctions but Pakistan subsequently carried out a sixth test. With first steps towards a nuclear agreement, the USA lifted most sanctions. On 11 June, following India's example, Pakistan announced a unilateral moratorium on nuclear tests. On 12 Oct. 1999 the military chief, Gen. Pervez Musharraf, seized power in a coup, overthrowing the democratically-elected government of prime minister Nawaz Sharif. The coup, which lasted less than three hours, was launched after the prime minister had tried to dismiss Gen. Musharraf from his position as army chief of staff. The former prime minister and his senior allies were placed under house arrest and subsequently put on trial. Nawaz Sharif was found guilty of corruption and sentenced to life imprisonment. The coup marked the first time in history that a military regime had taken over an affirmed nuclear power.

There have been some 35,000 deaths since the outbreak of the Kashmir insurgency in 1988. Negotiations with India over the future of the disputed territory of Kashmir began in July 1999. In May 2001 India ended its six-month long ceasefire. It then invited Pakistan's government to enter talks about the dispute, which ended with hopes of avoiding further violence. Following the terror attacks on New York and Washington of 11 Sept. 2001 Pakistan found itself in a central role in the war against terrorism. With neighbouring Afghanistan believed to be sheltering Osama bin Laden, the USA persuaded President Musharraf to allow American forces access to Pakistani air bases. In return the USA lifted sanctions imposed on Pakistan after it carried out a series of nuclear tests in 1998. In Dec. 2001 an attack was made on the Indian parliament by suicide bombers. Although no group claimed responsibility, the Indian authorities suspected Kashmiri separatists, leading to increasing tension between Pakistan and India. However, President Musharraf's subsequent crackdown on militants helped to bring the two countries back from the brink of war. Tension between Pakistan and India increased following an attack on an Indian army base in Indian-occupied Kashmir on 14 May 2002. The attack, which killed 31 people, was linked to Islamic terrorists infiltrating into the Kashmir valley from Pakistan. It drew widespread criticism of Pakistani President Pervez Musharraf for failing to combat terrorism in the disputed region. Between 25 and 28 May Pakistan carried out three tests of short-range ballistic missiles.

TERRITORY AND POPULATION

Pakistan is bounded in the west by Iran, northwest by Afghanistan, north by China, east by India and south by the Arabian Sea. The area (excluding the disputed area of Kashmir) is 307,374 sq. miles (796,095 sq. km); population (1998 census, excluding Azad, Kashmir, Baltistan, Diamir and Gilgit), 130,579,571 (females, 62,739,434). In 1999, 63·5% lived in rural areas. There were 2·2m. refugees in 2001, mostly from Afghanistan, the highest number in any country in the world.

The UN gives a projected population for 2010 of 181·39m.

The population of the principal cities is as follows:

1998 census

Karachi	9,269,265	Rawalpindi	1,406,214	Peshawar	988,005
Lahore	5,063,499	Hyderabad	1,151,274	Islamabad	791,085
Faisalabad	1,977,246	Gujranwala	1,124,799	Quetta	560,307

Population of the provinces (census of 1998):

	Area (sq. km)	1998 census population (in 1,000) Total	Male	Female	Urban	1998 density per sq. km
North-West Frontier Province	74,521	17,555	8,963	8,592	2,973	236
Federally administered Tribal Areas	27,219	3,138	1,635	1,503	83	115
Federal Capital Territory Islamabad	907	799	430	369	524	881
Punjab	205,344	72,585	37,509	35,076	22,699	353
Sind	140,914	29,991	15,823	14,168	14,662	213
Balochistan	347,190	6,511	3,481	3,030	1,516	19

Urdu is the national language and the *lingua franca*, although only spoken by about 10% of the population; English is used in business, higher education and in central government. Around 60% of the population speak Punjabi.

Karachi: The capital of Pakistan from the partition in 1947 until 1959 when it was removed to Islamabad, Karachi is situated on the Arabian Sea, northwest of the Indus Delta. It began as a small fishing village in the 18th century and quickly expanded when the British annexed it in 1842. It is now the country's busiest sea port and handles all marine imports for Pakistan and Afghanistan.

SOCIAL STATISTICS

1997 estimates: births, 4,950,000; deaths, 1,240,000. Rates, 1997 (per 1,000 population): birth, 36; death, 9; infant mortality (per 1,000 live births), 84 (1999). Formal registration of marriages and divorces has not been required since 1992. Expectation of life in 1999 was 59·8 years for men and 59·5 years for women. Annual population growth rate, 1990–99, 2·8%. Fertility rate, 1999, 4·9 births per woman.

CLIMATE

A weak form of tropical monsoon climate occurs over much of the country, with arid conditions in the north and west, where the wet season is only from Dec. to March. Elsewhere, rain comes mainly in the summer. Summer temperatures are high everywhere, but winters can be cold in the mountainous north. Islamabad, Jan. 50°F (10°C), July 90°F (32·2°C). Annual rainfall 36" (900 mm). Karachi, Jan. 61°F (16·1°C), July 86°F (30°C). Annual rainfall 8" (196 mm). Lahore, Jan. 53°F (11·7°C), July 89°F (31·7°C). Annual rainfall 18" (452 mm). Multan, Jan. 51°F (10·6°C), July 93°F (33·9°C). Annual rainfall 7" (170 mm). Quetta, Jan. 38°F (3·3°C), July 80°F (26·7°C). Annual rainfall 10" (239 mm).

CONSTITUTION AND GOVERNMENT

Under the 1973 Constitution, the *President* is elected for a five-year term by a college of parliamentary deputies, senators and members of the Provincial Assemblies.

Parliament is bicameral, comprising a *Senate* of 87 members and a *National Assembly* of 217. The four Provincial Assemblies each elect 19 senators, the tribal areas are represented by eight senators elected by the National Assembly and the Federal Capital has three representatives. About half the senators are elected for six-year terms every three years. The National Assembly is directly elected with 10 religious minority representatives. However, since the 1999 coup all legislative bodies (national parliament and the four provincial assemblies) and their members have been suspended. Following the coup Gen. Musharraf announced that the Constitution was to be held 'in abeyance' and issued a 'Provisional Constitution Order No. 1' in its place. In Aug. 2002 he unilaterally amended the constitution to grant himself the right to dissolve parliament.

During the period of martial law from 1977–85 the Constitution was also in abeyance, but not abrogated. In 1985 it was amended to extend the powers of the President, including those of appointing and dismissing ministers and vetoing new legislation until 1990. Legislation of 1 April 1997 abolished the President's right to dissolve parliament, appoint provincial governors and nominate the heads of the armed services.

Gen. Pervez Musharraf, Chief of the Army Staff, assumed the responsibilities of the chief executive of the country following the removal of Prime Minister Nawaz Sharif on 12 Oct. 1999. He formed a National Security Council consisting of six members belonging to the armed forces and a number of civilians with expertise in various fields. A Federal Cabinet of Ministers was also installed working under the guidance of the National Security Council. Also formed was the National Reconstruction Bureau, a think tank providing institutional advice and input on economic, social and institutional matters. The administration declared that it intended to first restore economic order before holding general elections to install a civilian government. The Supreme Court of Pakistan allowed the administration a three-year period, which expired on 12 Oct. 2002, to accomplish this task. Elections were held on 10 Oct. 2002. On 30 April 2002 a referendum was held in which 97·7% voted in favour of extending Musharraf's rule by a further five years. Turn-out was around 50%. He amended the constitution in Aug. 2002 to formally extend his mandate by five years.

The Constitution obliges the government to enable the people to order their lives in accordance with Islam.

National Anthem. 'Pak sarzamin shadbad' ('Blessed be the sacred land'); words by Abul Asr Hafeez Jaulandhari, tune by Ahmad G. Chaagla.

RECENT ELECTIONS

Pakistan's first general elections since the military coup in 1999 took place on 10 Oct. 2002. The pro-Musharraf Pakistan Muslim League (Quaid-e-Azam) took 77 of 272 seats with 24·8% of votes cast; former prime minister Benazir Bhutto's Pakistan People's Party won 62 with 25·0%, while a coalition of six hardline Islamic parties, Muttahida Majlis-e-Amal, won 52 with 11·1%. Despite winning 11·2% of the vote, the Pakistan Muslim League (Nawaz Sharif) of exiled former prime minister Nawaz Sharif took only 14 seats. Three seats were left undeclared. Turn-out was 41%.

CURRENT ADMINISTRATION

President: Gen. Pervez Musharraf; b. 1943 (since 20 June 2001).

Following the overthrow of prime minister Nawaz Sharif in Oct. 1999, Gen. Pervez Musharraf assumed power. He appointed a National Security Council to function as the country's supreme governing body and subsequently a full cabinet of ministers. In June 2001 he declared himself president. Following the elections of Oct. 2002 a coalition government was formed. In March 2003 it comprised:

Prime Minister: Mir Zafarullah Khan Jamali; b. 1944 (Pakistan Muslim League; sworn in 23 Nov. 2002).

Minister for Commerce: Humayoon Akhtar Khan. *Defence:* Rao Sikandar Iqbal. *Education:* Zubeda Jalal. *Food, Agriculture and Livestock:* Sardar Yar Mohammad Rind. *Foreign Affairs, and Law, Justice and Human Rights:* Mian Khursheed Mehmood Kasuri. *Health:* Mohammad Nasir Khan. *Industries and Production:* Liaqat Ali Jatoi. *Information and Media Development:* Sheikh Rashid Ahmad. *Information Technology and Telecommunications:* Awais Ahmad Khan Leghari.

Interior and Narcotics Control: Makhdoom Syed Faisal Saleh Hayat. *Labour, Manpower and Overseas Pakistanis:* Abdul Sattar Laleka. *Petroleum and Natural Resources:* Chaudhry Nauriz Shakoor Khan. *Railways:* Ghaus Bakhsh Khan Mahr. *Water and Power:* Aftab Ahmad Khan Sherpao.

Government Website: http://www.pakistan.gov.pk/

DEFENCE

A *Council for Defence and National Security* was set up in Jan. 1997, comprising the President, the Prime Minister, the Ministers of Defence, Foreign Affairs, Interior, Finance and the military chiefs of staff. The Council advised the government on the determination of national strategy and security priorities, but was disbanded in Feb. 1997. The Council was revived in Oct. 1999 following the change of government but was to have a wider scope and not restrict itself to defence matters.

Defence expenditure in 2001 totalled US$2,395m. (US$17 per capita), representing 4·4% of GDP.

Nuclear Weapons. Pakistan began a secret weapons programme in 1972 to reach parity with India, but was restricted for some years by US sanctions. According to the Stockholm International Peace Research Institute, the nuclear arsenal was estimated to have between 15 and 20 nuclear weapon components in Jan. 2001. In May 1998 Pakistan carried out six nuclear tests in response to India's tests earlier in the month. Pakistan, known to have a nuclear weapons programme, has not signed the Comprehensive Nuclear-Test-Ban-Treaty, which is intended to bring about a ban on any nuclear explosions. According to *Deadly Arsenals*, published by the Carnegie Endowment for International Peace, Pakistan has both chemical and biological weapon research programmes.

Army. Strength (2002) 520,000. There were also 292,000 personnel in paramilitary units: National Guard, Frontier Corps and Pakistan Rangers. Army reserves number around 500,000.

Most armoured equipment is of Chinese origin including over 2,350 main battle tanks. There is an air wing with fixed-wing aircraft and 20 attack helicopters.

Navy. The combatant fleet includes seven French-built diesel submarines, three midget submarines for swimmer delivery and eight ex-British frigates. The Naval Air wing operates six combat aircraft and nine armed helicopters.

The principal naval base and dockyard are at Karachi. Naval personnel in 2002 totalled 25,000. There is a marine force estimated at 1,200 personnel and naval reserves of 5,000.

Air Force. The Pakistan Air Force came into being on 14 Aug. 1947. It has its headquarters at Peshawar and is organized within three air defence sectors, in the northern, central and southern areas of the country. There is a flying college at Risalpur and an aeronautical engineering college at Korangi Creek.

Total strength in 2002 was 366 combat aircraft and 45,000 personnel. Equipment included Mirage IIIs, Mirage 5s, F-16s, Q-5s and J-7s. There were 8,000 Air Force reservists.

INTERNATIONAL RELATIONS

Pakistan is a member of the UN, WTO, the Commonwealth (not 1972–89), Asian Development Bank, Economic Co-operation Organisation (ECO), South Asian Association for Regional Co-operation (SAARC), IOM, Organisation of Islamic Conference (OIC), Non-Aligned Movement (NAM), Inter-Parliamentary Union (IPU), IMCO, International Atomic Energy Agency (IAEA), D-8, Conference on Disarmament, United Nations Commission on Human Rights, International Narcotics Control Board, United Nations Environment Programme and the Colombo Plan.

ECONOMY

Agriculture accounted for 26·4% of GDP in 1997, industry 24·7% and services 48·9%. In Jan. 1999 the IMF approved a loan of US$575m. to Pakistan.

Currency. The monetary unit is the *Pakistan rupee* (PKR) of 100 *paisas.* Gold reserves in June 2002 were 2·09m. troy oz; foreign exchange reserves, US$4,822m.

Inflation was 4·4% in 2000, falling to 3·1% in 2001. The rupee was devalued by 3·65% in Sept. 1996 and 8% in Oct. 1997, and by 4·2% in June 1998 in response to the financial problems in Asia. In May 2002 total money supply was Rs978,848m.

Budget. The financial year ends on 30 June. The consolidated federal and provincial revenue collection for 1999–2000 was Rs570,900m. (Rs443,000m. from taxes and Rs128,000m. from non-taxes) and expenditure was Rs694,000m. (current expenditure, Rs578,000m.; development, Rs116,000m.). Total revenue in 2000 was Rs531,300m. and total expenditure was Rs725,642m.

Performance. Real GDP growth was 4·3% in 2000 and 3·6% in 2001. Pakistan's total GDP in 2001 was US$59·6bn.

Banking and Finance. The State Bank of Pakistan is the central bank (*Governor*, Dr Ishrat Hussain); it came into operation as the Central Bank on 1 July 1948 and was nationalized in 1974 with other banks.

The State Bank of Pakistan is the issuing authority of domestic currency, custodian of foreign exchange reserves and bankers for the federal and provincial governments and for scheduled banks. It also manages the rupee public debt of the federal and provincial governments. The National Bank of Pakistan acts as an agent of the State Bank where the State Bank has no offices of its own.

The State Bank of Pakistan was granted more autonomy in Feb. 1994 to regulate the monetary sector of the economy.

In Dec. 1999 the Supreme Court ruled that Islamic banking methods, whereby interest is not permitted, had to be used from 1 July 2001.

In June 1998 total assets of the issue department of the State Bank of Pakistan amounted to Rs238,999m. and those of the banking department Rs254,670m.; total deposits, Rs170,769m.

In June 1998 there were 56 banks (21 foreign) with total assets of Rs1,654,094m.

There are stock exchanges in Islamabad, Karachi and Lahore.

Weights and Measures. The metric system is in general use.

ENERGY AND NATURAL RESOURCES

Environment. According to the *World Bank Atlas* Pakistan's carbon dioxide emissions were the equivalent of 0·7 tonnes per capita in 1998.

Electricity. Installed capacity of the State Power System in 1998–99 was 19·4m. kW, of which 4·83m. kW was hydro-electric, 10·76m. kW was thermal and 0·14 kW was nuclear. In 2001 there were two nuclear reactors in use. Production in 1998–99 was 43·47bn. kWh, of which 65% was hydro-electric and 35% was thermal. Around 3,771 MW was from private power generation. Consumption per capita in 1998 was 337 kWh. By 1999, 10·55m. consumers had access to electric power including 66,949 villages (of a total of 125,083).

Oil and Gas. Oil production in 1998–99 was 55,703 bbls. Exploitation is mainly through government incentives and concessions to foreign private sector companies. Natural gas production in 1999 was 17·8bn. cu. metres with 61bn. cu. metres of proven reserves.

Water. Pakistan's Indus Basin irrigation system is the largest and oldest in the world. It includes a network of 43 independent canal systems and two storage reservoirs. Total length of main canals is 58,000 km which serve 35m. acres of cultivatable land.

Currently three major surface water projects are under way, as are flood control schemes and programmes to check the problems of waterlogging and salinity.

Minerals. Production (tonnes, 1998–99): limestone, 8·72m.; coal, 2·31m.; rock salt, 870,000; gypsum, 160,000; dolomite, 102,859; china clay, 66,000; fire clay, 61,000; chromite, 22,000; barytes, 20,000; fullers earth, 11,000; bauxite, 5,000. Other minerals of which useful deposits have been found are magnesite, sulphur, marble, antimony ore, bentonite, celestite, fluorite, phosphate rock, silica sand and soapstone.

Agriculture. The north and west are covered by mountain ranges. The rest of the country consists of a fertile plain watered by five big rivers and their tributaries. Agriculture is dependent almost entirely on the irrigation system based on these rivers. Area irrigated, 1998–99, 18m. ha. Agriculture employs around half of the workforce. In 1998–99 it provided 24·5% of GDP.

Pakistan is self-sufficient in wheat, rice and sugar. Areas harvested, 2000: wheat, 8·46m. ha; seed cotton, 2·95m. ha; rice, 2·31m. ha; sugarcane, 1·01m. ha; chick-peas, 0·97m. ha; maize, 0·89m. ha. Production, 2000 (1,000 tonnes): sugarcane, 46,333; wheat, 21,079; rice, 7,000; seed cotton, 5,735; cottonseed, 3,824; cotton lint, 1,912; potatoes, 1,868; onions, 1,648; maize, 1,351; oranges, 1,310; mangoes, 938; apples, 600; dates, 580; chick-peas, 565.

A Land Reforms Act of 1977 reduced the upper limit of land holding to 100 irrigated or 200 non-irrigated acres. A new agricultural income tax was introduced in 1995, from which holders of up to 25 irrigated or 50 unirrigated acres are exempt. Of about 5m. farms, 12% are of less than 10 ha. In 1998–99, 21·92m. ha were arable land; 23·04m. ha were cropland; 4·20m. ha were forest.

Livestock, 2000 (in 1m.): goats, 47·4; sheep, 24·1; buffaloes, 22·7; cattle, 22·0; asses, 4·5; camels, 1·2; poultry, 148·0.

Livestock products, 2000 (in 1,000 tonnes): beef and veal, 357; poultry, 327; goat, 323; mutton and lamb, 190; buffalo milk, 16,910; cow milk, 8,039; goat milk, 586; eggs, 331; wool, 62.

Forestry. The area under forests in 1998–99 was 4·2m. ha, some 4·8% of the total land area. The government considers a 20–25% coverage desirable for economic growth and environmental stability. Timber production in 1999 totalled 33·08m. cu. metres.

Fisheries. In 1999 the catch totalled 654,530 tonnes, approximately 73% from marine waters and the rest from inland waters.

INDUSTRY
Industry is based largely on agricultural processing, with engineering and electronics. Government policy is to encourage private industry, particularly small businesses. The public sector, however, is still dominant in large industries. Steel, cement, fertilizer and vegetable ghee are the most valuable public sector industries.

Production in tonnes in 1998–99: cement, 6,822,000; sugar, 3,081,000; cotton yarn, 895,000; pig iron, 735,000; vegetable ghee, 615,000; coke, 443,000; paper and board, 256,000; steel billets, 212,000; soda ash, 186,000; caustic soda, 82,000; jute textiles, 63,000; sulphuric acid, 20,000; cotton cloth, 443m. sq. metres; jeeps and cars, 28,815 items; bicycles, 409,000 items.

Labour. Out of 33·05m. people in employment in 1995, 4·81m. were females. In 1999, 44·1% of the economically active workforce were engaged in agriculture, forestry and fishing, 10·3% in manufacturing; the textile industry was the largest single manufacturing employer. Trade employed 14·6%; construction, 6·8%; transport, storage and communication, 5·7%. 2·36m. were unemployed in 1999.

In 1994 there were 25 industrial disputes and 341,196 working days were lost.

Trade Unions. In 1997 there were 7,355 trade unions with a membership of 1,022,275.

INTERNATIONAL TRADE
Foreign debt was US$32,091m. in 2000. Most foreign exchange controls were removed in Feb. 1991. Foreign investors may repatriate both capital and profits, and tax exemptions are available for companies set up before 30 June 1995. Foreign investment was US$600m. in 1997–98, but fell under the government of Nawaz Sharif to US$499m. in 1998–99.

Imports and Exports. Trade in US$1m.:

	1996	1997	1998	1999	2000
Imports f.o.b.	12,164	10,750	9,834	9,520	9,898
Exports f.o.b.	8,507	8,351	7,850	7,673	8,739

Major exports in 1998–99 (in Rs1m.): cotton cloth, 40,295; cotton yarns, 33,928; rice, 19,439; carpets, 6,723; leather, 6,346. Major imports in 1998–99 (in Rs1m.): machinery, 52,759; petroleum and petroleum products, 44,867; chemicals, 40,329; edible oils, 31,892; transport equipment, 18,247; grains, pulses and flour, 14,948; dyes and colours, 4,770.

Major export markets in 1998–99 (in Rs1m.): USA, 60,890; Hong Kong, 20,654; Germany, 18,929; UK, 18,537; UAE, 14,421; Japan, 9,696. Major import suppliers in 1998–99 (in Rs1m.): USA, 26,737; Japan, 26,597; Saudi Arabia, 21,825; Kuwait, 17,478; UK, 14,395; Germany, 13,413.

COMMUNICATIONS

Roads. In 1998 there were 247,811 km of roads, of which 339 km were motorway and 6,587 km highways or national roads. In 1999 there were 131,000 trucks, 120,000 buses, 63,000 taxis, 1,084,000 cars, jeeps and station wagons, 2,051,000 motorcycles (two wheels) and 80,000 motorcycles (three wheels), and 714,000 other vehicles. There were 12,336 road accidents in 1997, with 5,127 fatalities.

A US$1bn. 333-km motorway linking Islamabad and Lahore was opened in 1998, and a new Karachi to Peshawar highway is under construction. Work is also in progress on Islamabad-Peshawar, Karachi-Hyderabad and Pindi Bhattian-Faisalabad links.

All traffic in Pakistan drives on the left. All cars must be insured and registered. Minimum age for driving: 18 years.

Rail. Pakistan Railways had (1998–99) a route length of 8,774 km (of which 293 km electrified) mainly on 1,676 mm gauge, with some metre gauge line. In 1997–98, 64·9m. passengers were carried; and in 1998–99, 48·0m. tonnes of freight were carried.

Civil Aviation. There are international airports at Karachi, Islamabad, Peshawar and Quetta.

The national carrier is Pakistan International Airlines, or PIA (founded 1955; 56% of shares are held by the government). It covers 55 international and 37 domestic stations. During 1998–99, 59,097,000 revenue km were flown, compared with 78,796,000 during 1996–97. The revenue passengers carried totalled 3·86m. during 1998–99 and revenue tonne km came to 1,001m. Operating revenues of the corporation stood at Rs16,745bn. and operating expenditure at Rs19,603bn. during 1997–98.

Shipping. In 1998 ocean-going shipping totalled 401,000 GRT, including oil tankers 50,000 GRT. There are ports at Karachi and Port Qasim. Cargo handled at Karachi in 1998–99 (in tonnes): imports, 13,302,000; exports, 4,224,000. Port Qasim: imports, 7,529,000; exports, 484,000. In 1998–99, 1,262 international vessels were handled at the port of Karachi.

Telecommunications. The telegraph and telephone system is government-owned. Main telephone lines numbered 3,053,500 in 2000, or 21·6 per 1,000 inhabitants, and there were 590,000 PCs in use (4·2 for every 1,000 persons). In March 1999 there were 401 telegraph offices and 155 customer service centres working in the country. There were 265,600 mobile phone subscribers in 1999 and 159,000 fax machines in 1995. Pakistan had 1·2m. Internet users in May 2000.

Postal Services. In 1998–99 there were 13,294 post offices.

SOCIAL INSTITUTIONS

Justice. The Federal Judiciary consists of the Supreme Court of Pakistan, which is a court of record and has three-fold jurisdiction; original, appellate and advisory. There are four High Courts in Lahore, Peshawar, Quetta and Karachi. Under the Constitution, each has power to issue directions of writs of *Habeas Corpus, Mandamus, Certiorari* and others. Under them are district and sessions courts of first instance in each district; they have also some appellate jurisdiction. Criminal cases not being sessions cases are tried by judicial magistrates. There are subordinate civil courts also.

The Constitution provides for an independent judiciary, as the greatest safeguard of citizens' rights. There is an Attorney-General, appointed by the President, who has right of audience in all courts and the Parliament, and a Federal Ombudsman.

A Federal Shariat Court at the High Court level has been established to decide whether any law is wholly or partially un-Islamic. In Aug. 1990 a presidential ordinance decreed that the criminal code must conform to Islamic law (Shariah), and in May 1991 parliament passed a law incorporating it into the legal system.

320,807 crimes were reported in 1994. Execution of the death penalty for murder, in abeyance since 1986, was resumed in 1992. In 2002 there were four reported executions. There were 8,303 murders in 1994. The population in penal institutions in 1996 was 72,700 (50 per 100,000 of national population).

Religion. Pakistan was created as a Muslim state. The Muslims are mainly Sunni, with an admixture of 15–20% Shia. Religious groups: Muslims, 97%; Christians, 2%; Hindus, Parsees, Buddhists, Qadianis and others. There is a Minorities Wing at the Religious Affairs Ministry to safeguard the constitutional rights of religious minorities.

Education. The National Education Policy (1998–2010) was launched in March 1998. The major aim was the eradication of illiteracy and the spread of a basic education. The policy stresses vocational and technical education, disseminating a common culture based on Islamic ideology. The principle of free and compulsory primary education has been accepted as the responsibility of the state; duration has been fixed provisionally at five years. The adult literacy rate in 1999 was 45·0% (58·9% among males and 30·0% among females). Adult literacy programmes are being strengthened.

About 77% of children aged 5–9 are enrolled at school. Figures for 1998–99:

	Students (in 1,000)	Teachers (in 1,000)	Institutions
Primary	17,298	374·5	163,746
Middle	3,984	100·8	17,007
Secondary	1,680	162·0	10,519
Secondary vocational	85	7·0	498
Arts and Science Colleges	760	24·9	735
Professional Colleges	136	7·7	265
Universities	93	7·0	26

There are also more than 4,000 seminary schools. In 1997 total expenditure on education came to 2·7% of GNP and 7·1% of total government spending.

Health. In 1998 there were 872 hospitals and 4,551 dispensaries (with a total of 90,659 beds) and 852 maternity and child welfare centres. There were 82,682 doctors, 32,938 nurses, 22,103 midwives and 3,444 dentists.

CULTURE

There is a Pakistan National Council of the Arts, a cultural organization to promote art and culture in Pakistan and abroad.

Broadcasting. The Pakistan Broadcasting Corporation is an autonomous body operating 24 stations for 19 regional languages and 16 foreign languages. Five of its major stations have three channels (two AM and one FM). The second AM is generally reserved for sports, educational and entertainment broadcasting whilst FM channels cater mostly for music lovers. There is a school channel broadcasting on FM.

The network of PBC transmitters consists of 28 medium wave transmitters with a radiating power of 2,261 kW, 13 short wave transmitters of 1,131 kW and 5 FM transmitters of 12 kW. It covers 95% of the population and 80% of the total area of the country. A separate government authority, Azad Kashmir Radio, broadcasts in Kashmir.

The commercial Pakistan Television Corporation transmits on 13 VHF/UHF channels (colour by PAL). PTV's signal is also uplinked through Asiasat Transponder. There are six PTV centres in the major cities—Islamabad, Lahore, Karachi, Peshawar and Quetta—and 36 rebroadcast centres. Its headquarters is in

Islamabad. Its transmissions reach 88% of the population. Number of sets in use: TV (1997), 3·1m.; radio (1997), 13·5m.

Cinema. There were 600 screens in 1999. 49 full-length films were made in 1999 in Urdu, Punjabi, Pushto and Sindhi. There were seven film studios.

Press. In 1995 there were 370 dailies, 506 weeklies, 62 fortnightlies and 373 periodicals of lesser frequencies. Average circulation of all dailies in 1995 was 3,580,934.

Tourism. In 1998 there were 429,000 foreign tourists, of whom 21·5% came from the UK. More than half of foreign tourist arrivals in 1997 were for the purpose of visiting friends and relatives, followed by business (18·3%), holidays and recreation (13·4%) and religion (2·5%). Tourist revenue in 1999 was US$76m.

Festivals. Pakistan is rich in culture. Famous festivals include the Eid Festival, Eid-e-Milad un Nabi (Birthday of Prophet Muhammad P.B.U.H.), the Basnat Festival, Shab-e-Baraat Festival, and the Independence Day Festival.

Libraries. The Liaqat National Library is in Karachi, and the library of the National Archives is in Islamabad. Baitul Quran at Lahore is exclusively devoted to the manuscripts of the Holy Quran. The libraries of the Punjab University, Karachi University and the Quaid-i-Azam library in Lahore hold a combined 700,000 volumes. The Islamic Research Institute Library at Islamabad has an important collection on Islam.

Theatre and Opera. There are regular theatrical productions in the major cities. There are 15 fully equipped theatre halls in Rawalpindi, Lahore, Karachi and Peshawar, and traditional street theatre is still prominent.

Museums and Galleries. There are dozens of galleries and museums in Islamabad, Lahore, Karachi, Peshawar and Quetta. Amongst the most famous are the National Art Gallery, Shakir Ali Museum, Choukandi Art Gallery, Karachi Art Council, Tasneen Art Gallery, the Lahore Art Museum, the National Heritage Museum and the National Archives. There are also dozens of archaeological sites in Pakistan dating back to 3,000 BC including Moen jo Daro, Harppa, Taxilla, Kot Diji and Dir.

DIPLOMATIC REPRESENTATIVES

Of Pakistan in the United Kingdom (35–36 Lowndes Sq., London, SW1X 9JN)
High Commissioner: Abdul Kader Jaffer.

Of the United Kingdom in Pakistan (Diplomatic Enclave, Ramna 5, Islamabad)
High Commissioner: Mark J. Lyall Grant, CMG.

Of Pakistan in the USA (2315 Massachusetts Ave., NW, Washington, D.C., 20008)
Ambassador: Ashraf Jehangir Qazi.

Of the USA in Pakistan (Diplomatic Enclave, Ramna, 5, Islamabad)
Ambassador: Nancy J. Powell.

Of Pakistan to the United Nations
Ambassador: Munir Akram.

Of Pakistan to the European Union
Ambassador: Shaukat Umer.

FURTHER READING

Government Planning Commission. *Eighth Five Year Plan, 1993–1998.* Karachi, 1994
Federal Bureau of Statistics.—*Pakistan Statistical Yearbook.—Statistical Pocket Book of Pakistan.* (annual)
Ahmed, A. S., *Jinnah, Pakistan and Islamic Identity: The Search for Saladin.* London, 1997
Ahsan, A., *The Indus Saga and the Making of Pakistan.* Oxford, 1997
Akhtar, R., *Pakistan Year Book.* Karachi/Lahore
Bhutto, B., *Daughter of the East.* London, 1988
Burki, S. J., *Pakistan: the Continuing Search for Nationhood.* 2nd ed. Boulder (Colo.), 1992

PAKISTAN

James, W. E. and Roy, S. (eds.) *The Foundations of Pakistan's Political Economy: Towards an Agenda for the 1990s.* London, 1992

Joshi, V. T., *Pakistan: Zia to Benazir.* Delhi, 1995

Malik, I. H., *State and Civil Society in Pakistan: the Politics of Authority, Ideology and Ethnicity.* London, 1996

National library: National Library of Pakistan, Islamabad.

National statistical office: Federal Bureau of Statistics, Statistics Division, Islamabad.
Website: http://www.statpak.gov.pk/

1265

PALAU

Republic of Palau

Capital: Koror
Population estimate, 2000: 19,000
GDP per capita: not available

KEY HISTORICAL EVENTS

Spain acquired sovereignty over the Palau Islands in 1886 but sold the archipelago to Germany in 1899. Japan occupied the islands in 1914 and in 1921 they were mandated to Japan by the League of Nations. Captured by Allied Forces in 1944, the islands became part of the UN Trust Territory of the Pacific Islands created on 18 July 1947 and administered by the USA. Following a referendum in July 1978 in which Palauans voted against joining the new Federated States of Micronesia, the islands became autonomous from 1 Jan. 1981. A referendum in Nov. 1993 favoured a Compact of Free Association with the USA. Palau became an independent republic on 1 Oct. 1994.

TERRITORY AND POPULATION

The archipelago lies in the western Pacific and has a total area of 1,632 sq. km (630 sq. miles); water covers 1,124 sq. km (434 sq. miles). It comprises 26 islands and over 300 islets. Only eight of the islands are inhabited, the largest being Babelthuap (368 sq. km), but most inhabitants live on the small island of Koror (8 sq. km) to the south, containing the present headquarters (a new capital is being built in eastern Babelthuap). The total population of Palau at the time of the 2000 census was 19,129, giving a density of 37·7 per sq. km. Koror's population according to the 2000 census was 13,303. In 1995 approximately 73% of the population were Palauans.

In 1995 an estimated 71·2% of the population lived in urban areas. Some 6,000 Palauans live abroad. The local language is Palauan; both Palauan and English are official.

SOCIAL STATISTICS

1996 births (approx.), 370; deaths, 110. Rates, 1996 (per 1,000 population): births, 21·6; deaths, 6·6; infant mortality (per 1,000 live births), 25·1. Annual population growth rate, 1990–99, 2·5%. Expectation of life: males, 69 years; females, 73. Fertility rate, 1999, 2·5 births per woman.

CLIMATE

Palau has a pleasantly warm climate throughout the year with temperatures averaging 81°F (27°C). The heaviest rainfall is between July and Oct.

CONSTITUTION AND GOVERNMENT

The Constitution was adopted on 2 April 1979 and took effect from 1 Jan. 1981. The Republic has a bicameral legislature, the *Olbiil era Kelulau* (National Congress), comprising a 16-member *Senate* (one from each of the Republic's 16 component states) and an 18-member *House of Delegates*, both elected for a term of four years as are the *President* and *Vice-President*. Customary social roles and land and sea rights are allocated by a matriarchal 16-clan system.

RECENT ELECTIONS

At the elections on 7 Nov. 2000 Tommy Remengesau Jr was elected president with 52·0% of votes cast against Peter Sugiyama's 46·2%. At the National Congress elections which were also held on 7 Nov. 2000 only non-partisans were elected.

CURRENT ADMINISTRATION

President: Tommy Remengesau Jr; b. 1956 (in office since 1 Jan. 2001).
  Vice-President and Minister of Health: Sandra Pierantozzi.
  In March 2003 the cabinet consisted of:
  Minister of Administration: Elbuchel Sadang. *Commerce and Trade:* Otoichi Besebes. *Community and Cultural Affairs:* Alexander Merep. *Education:* Mario

Katosang. *Justice:* Michael Rosenthal. *Resources and Development:* Fritz Koshiba. *State:* Temmy Shmull.

INTERNATIONAL RELATIONS

Palau is a member of the UN, IMF, the Pacific Islands Forum and the Pacific Community.

ECONOMY

Currency. US currency is used.

Budget. Revenues for 1997 are estimated at US$52·9m. and expenditures at US$59·9m.

Performance. Real GDP growth was 1·1% in 2001, following negative growth in 2000, of –0·7%.

Banking and Finance. The National Development Bank of Palau is situated in Koror.

ENERGY AND NATURAL RESOURCES

Environment. According to the *World Bank Atlas* Palau's carbon dioxide emissions in 1996 were the equivalent of 13·9 tonnes per capita.

Electricity. Electricity production was 200m. kWh in 1996.

Agriculture. The main agricultural products are bananas, coconuts, copra, cassava and sweet potatoes. In 1997 agriculture contributed 7% of GDP.

Fisheries. In 1999 the catch totalled approximately 1,800 tonnes, mainly tuna.

INDUSTRY

There is little industry, but the principal activities are food-processing and boat-building.

Labour. The economically active population totalled 10,686 in 1995, of whom 2,630 worked in government services, 1,896 in agriculture and 1,005 in tourism.

INTERNATIONAL TRADE

Imports and Exports. Imports (1999–2000) US$126m. Exports (1996) US$14m. The main trading partners are the USA and Japan for exports and the USA for imports.

COMMUNICATIONS

Roads. There were 61 km of roads in 1996 of which 36 km are paved.

Civil Aviation. The main airport is on Koror (Airai). In 1998 there were scheduled flights to Guam, Manila, Yap (Micronesia) and Kaohsiung (Taiwan).

Shipping. In 1985, 56,000 tonnes of cargo were discharged and 2,000 tonnes were loaded.

Telecommunications. In 1994 there were 2,615 telephone main lines.

SOCIAL INSTITUTIONS

Justice. There is a Supreme Court and various subsidiary courts.

Religion. The majority of the population is Roman Catholic.

Education. In 1993 there were 2,635 pupils at primary schools and 1,021 at secondary schools. In 1987 there were 26 primary schools and 6 secondary schools. There were 509 students at Palau Community College in 1993. The adult literacy rate is 92%.

Health. In 1990 there were 10 doctors and 84 nurses, and in 1986, 1 hospital with 70 beds.

CULTURE

Broadcasting. There is a radio station (WSZB) which broadcasts daily on AM and FM, and ICTV Cable TV presents 12 channels with CNN. In 1997 there were an estimated 11,000 televisions and 12,000 radios.

Press. The local newspaper *Tia Belau* is published bi-weekly.

Tourism. Tourism is a major industry, particularly marine-based. There were 55,000 foreign tourists in 1999.

DIPLOMATIC REPRESENTATIVES

Of the United Kingdom in Palau
Ambassador: Ian Powell (resides at Suva, Fiji Islands).

Of Palau in the USA (1150 18th Street, NW, Suite 750, Washington D.C., 20036)
Ambassador: Hersey Kyota.

Of the USA in Palau
Ambassador: Francis Joseph Ricciardone, Jr (resides at Manila).

Of Palau to the United Nations
Ambassador: Vacant.

PANAMA

República de Panamá

Capital: Panama City
Population estimate, 2000: 2·84m.
GDP per capita, 2000: (PPP$) 6,000
HDI/world rank: 0·787/57

KEY HISTORICAL EVENTS

A revolution, inspired by the USA, led to the separation of Panama from the United States of Colombia and the declaration of its independence on 3 Nov. 1903. This was followed by an agreement making it possible for the USA to build and operate a canal connecting the Atlantic and Pacific oceans through the Isthmus of Panama. The treaty granted the USA in perpetuity the use, occupation and control of a Canal Zone, in which the USA would possess full sovereign rights. In return the USA guaranteed the independence of the republic. The Canal was opened on 15 Aug. 1914.

The US domination of Panama has provoked frequent anti-American protests. In 1968 Col. Omar Torrijos Herrera took power in a coup and attempted to negotiate a more advantageous treaty with the USA. Two new treaties between Panama and the USA were agreed on 10 Aug. and signed on 7 Sept. 1977. One dealt with the operation and defence of the Canal until the end of 1999 and the other guarantees permanent neutrality.

Torrijos vacated the presidency in 1978 but maintained his power as head of the National Guard until his death in an air crash in 1981. Subsequently Gen. Manuel Noriega, Torrijos' successor as head of the National Guard, became the strong man of the regime. His position was threatened by some internal political opposition and economic pressure applied by the USA but in Oct. 1989 a US-backed coup attempt failed. On 15 Dec. Gen. Noriega declared a 'state of war' with the USA. On 20 Dec. the USA invaded. Gen. Noriega surrendered on 3 Jan. 1990. Accused of drug dealing he was convicted by a court in Miami and is now serving a 40-year jail sentence. All remaining US troops left the country when the Panama Canal was handed back to Panama at the end of 1999.

TERRITORY AND POPULATION

Panama is bounded in the north by the Caribbean Sea, east by Colombia, south by the Pacific Ocean and west by Costa Rica. The area is 75,517 sq. km. Population at the census of 1990 was 2,329,329 (49% urban; 56·0% in 1999). 2000 census population, 2,839,177); density, 37·6 per sq. km.

The UN gives a projected population for 2010 of 3·27m.

The largest towns (1995) are Panama City, the capital, on the Pacific coast (658,102); its suburb San Miguelito (290,919); Colón, the port on the Atlantic coast (156,289); and David (113,527).

The areas and populations of the nine provinces and the Special Territory were:

Province	Sq. km	Census 1980	1995 (est.)	Capital
Bocas del Toro	9,506	53,579	119,336	Bocas del Toro
Chiriquí	8,924	287,801	407,849	David
Coclé	4,981	140,320	189,579	Penonomé
Colón	7,205 }	166,439	226,139	Colón
San Blas (Special Territory)	3,206 }			El Porvenir
Darién	15,458	26,497	55,538	La Palma
Herrera	2,185	81,866	101,198	Chitré
Los Santos	4,587	70,200	79,935	Las Tablas
Panama	11,400	830,278	1,232,390	Panama City
Veraguas	11,226	173,195	219,049	Santiago

The population is a mix of African, American, Arab, Chinese, European and Indian immigrants. The official language is Spanish.

SOCIAL STATISTICS

1997 births, 68,009; deaths, 12,179; marriages, 10,357. Birth rate, 1997 (per 1,000 population): 25·0; death rate: 4·5. Annual population growth rate, 1990–99, 1·8%.

1269

Expectation of life at birth, 1999, was 72·0 years for males and 76·6 years for females. In 1997 the most popular age range for marrying was 25–29 for both males and females. Infant mortality, 1999, 21 per 1,000 live births; fertility rate, 1999, 2·6 births per woman.

CLIMATE
Panama has a tropical climate, unvaryingly with high temperatures and only a short dry season from Jan. to April. Rainfall amounts are much higher on the north side of the isthmus. Panama City, Jan. 79°F (26·1°C), July 81°F (27·2°C). Annual rainfall 70" (1,770 mm). Colón, Jan. 80°F (26·7°C), July 80°F (26·7°C). Annual rainfall 127" (3,175 mm). Balboa Heights, Jan. 80°F (26·7°C), July 81°F (27·2°C). Annual rainfall 70" (1,759 mm). Cristóbal, Jan. 80°F (26·7°C), July 81°F (27·2°C). Annual rainfall 130" (3,255 mm).

CONSTITUTION AND GOVERNMENT
The 1972 Constitution, as amended in 1978 and 1983, provides for a *President*, elected for five years, two *Vice-Presidents* and a 72-seat *Legislative Assembly* to be elected for five-year terms by a direct vote. To remain registered, parties must have attained at least 50,000 votes at the last election. A referendum held on 15 Nov. 1992 rejected constitutional reforms by 64% of votes cast. Turn-out was 40%. In a referendum on 30 Aug. 1998 voters rejected proposed changes to the constitution which would allow for a President to serve a second consecutive term.

National Anthem. 'Alcanzamos por fin la victoria' ('We achieve victory in the end'); words by J. de la Ossa, tune by Santos Jorge.

RECENT ELECTIONS
In the presidential election on 2 May 1999, Mireya Elisa Moscoso of the conservative Arnulfist Party won, obtaining 44·9% of votes cast against two other candidates. She thus became Panama's first woman president. Turn-out was 75%, up from 74% in 1994 and 64% in 1989. In the Legislative Assembly elections, also held on 2 May 1999, the New Nation Alliance won 41 seats (Revolutionary Democratic Party, 34; Solidarity Party, 4; National Liberal Party, 3) with a combined 57·7% of the vote. The Union for Panama Alliance won 24 seats (Arnulfist Party, 18; Liberal Republican Nationalist Movement, 5; National Renewal Movement, 1) with a combined 33·8%. The remaining six seats went to Opposition Action (Christian Democrat Party, 5; Civil Renewal Party, 1) with 8·5%.

CURRENT ADMINISTRATION
President: Mireya Elisa Moscoso; b. 1946 (Arnulfist Party; sworn in 1 Sept. 1999).
    First Vice-President: Arturo Ulises Vallarino. *Second Vice-President:* Dominador 'Kaiser' Baldonero Bazan.
    In March 2003 the government comprised:
    Minister of Government and Justice: Arnulfo Escalona Avila. *Foreign Relations:* Harmodio Arias Cerjack. *Canal Affairs:* Jerry Salazar. *Public Works:* Eduardo Antonio Quirós. *Economy and Finance:* Norberto Duran Delgado. *Agricultural Development:* Lynette María Stanziola Apolayo. *Commerce and Industry:* Joaquín Jacome Díaz. *Health:* Fernando Gracia García. *Labour:* Jaime Moreno Díaz. *Education:* Doris Rosas de Mata. *Housing:* Miguel Cardenas. *Women, Youth, Family and Childhood:* Rosabel Vergara. *Minister of the Presidency:* Ivonne Young Valdes.

Office of the President: http://www.presidencia.gob.pa

DEFENCE
The armed forces were disbanded in 1990 and constitutionally abolished in 1994. Divided between both coasts, the National Maritime Service, a coast guard rather than a navy, numbered around 400 personnel in 1999. In addition there is a paramilitary police force of 11,000 and a paramilitary air force of 400 with no combat aircraft. In 2000 defence expenditure totalled US$127m. (US$45 per capita), representing 1·3% of GDP. For Police *see* JUSTICE *below*.

INTERNATIONAL RELATIONS

Panama is a member of the UN, WTO, OAS, Inter-American Development Bank, CACM, Andean Community, ACS, IOM, Non-aligned Movement and WTO.

ECONOMY

Agriculture accounted for an estimated 7·8% of GDP in 1998, industry 18·4% and services 73·8%.

Overview. A five-year programme of trade liberalization aims to attract foreign investment. Hopes of diversifying an economy heavily dependent on the Canal rest largely on shipping services, mining and tourism.

Currency. The monetary unit is the *balboa* (PAB) of 100 *centésimos*, at parity with the US dollar. The only paper currency used is that of the USA. US coinage is also legal tender. Inflation in 2000 was 0·7%. In June 2002 foreign exchange reserves were US$1,055m. In March 2002 total money supply was 1,121m. balboas.

Budget. Budget revenue and expenditure (in 1m. balboas), year ending 31 Dec.:

	1995	1996	1997	1998	1999
Revenue	2,065·1	2,140·3	2,202·8	2,331·2	2,664·5
Expenditure	1,953·3	2,255·3	2,341·3	2,606·8	2,650·9

Performance. Real GDP growth was 2·5% in 2000, but only 0·3% in 2001. Total GDP in 2001 was US$10·2bn.

Banking and Finance. There is no statutory central bank. Banking is supervised and promoted by the Superintendency of Banks (formerly the National Banking Commission); the *Superintendente* is Delia Cárdenas. Government accounts are handled through the state-owned *Banco Nacional de Panama*. There are two other state banks. The number of commercial banks was 108 in 1996. Total assets, June 1996, US$33,400m., total deposits, US$25,000m. (including offshore, US$15,900m.).

Panama was one of 15 countries and territories named in a report in June 2000 as failing to co-operate in the fight against international money laundering. The Financial Action Task Force on Money Laundering was set up by the G7 group of major industrialized nations.

Weights and Measures. US Customary weights and measures are in general use; the metric system is the official system.

ENERGY AND NATURAL RESOURCES

Environment. According to the *World Bank Atlas* Panama's carbon dioxide emissions in 1998 were the equivalent of 2·1 tonnes per capita.

Electricity. In 1995 capacity was 921 MW. Production was 4·52bn. kWh in 1998, with consumption per capita 1,211 kWh.

Minerals. Limestone, clay and salt are produced. There are known to be copper deposits.

Agriculture. In 1998 there were 500,000 ha of arable land and 155,000 ha of permanent crops. Production in 2000 (in 1,000 tonnes): sugarcane, 2,000; bananas, 807; rice, 319; plantains, 111; melons and watermelons, 102; oranges, 85; maize, 80; cassava, 32; pineapples, 29; potatoes, 22; yams, 20. Livestock (2000): 1,360,000 cattle, 280,000 pigs, 166,000 horses and 12m. chickens.

Forestry. Forests covered 2·8m. ha in 1995 (37·6% of the land area), compared to 3·12m. ha in 1990. There are great timber resources, notably mahogany. Production in 1999 totalled 1·05m. cu. metres.

Fisheries. In 1999 the catch totalled 120,498 tonnes, almost entirely from sea fishing. Shrimps are the principal species caught.

INDUSTRY

The main industry is agricultural produce processing. Other areas include oil refining, chemicals and paper-making. Cement production, 1997, 700,000 tonnes; sugar production, 1998, 142,000 tonnes.

Labour. In 1996 the workforce (persons 15 years and over) numbered 1,001,439, of whom 870,622 were employed.

Trade Unions. 77,500 workers belonged to trade unions in 1994, of whom 27,000 were members of the *Confederación de Trabajadores de la República de Panamá*.

INTERNATIONAL TRADE

The Colón Free Zone is an autonomous institution set up in 1953. 1,556 companies were operating there in 1997. Factories in export zones are granted tax exemption on profits for 10–20 years and exemption from the provisions of the labour code. Foreign debt was US$7,056m. in 2000.

Imports and Exports. Imports and exports in US$1m.:

	1996	1997	1998	1999	2000
Imports f.o.b.	6,467·0	7,355·7	7,711·2	6,714·5	7,039·7
Exports f.o.b.	5,822·9	6,655·4	6,349·7	5,299·5	5,748·8

Main exports: bananas, shellfish, sugar. Chief export markets, 1996: USA, 37·5%; Germany, 12·2%; Sweden, 9·0%; Costa Rica, 7·1%; Belgium, 7·0%. Chief import suppliers, 1996: USA, 38%; Japan, 7%; Ecuador, 4%; Costa Rica, 3%.

COMMUNICATIONS

Roads. In 1998 there were 11,384 km of roads, about one-third paved or tarred. The road from Panama City westward to the cities of David and Concepción and to the Costa Rican frontier, with several branches, is part of the Pan-American Highway. The Trans-Isthmian Highway connects Panama City and Colón. In 1997 there were 214,890 passenger cars, 62,060 lorries and vans and 16,180 buses and coaches. There were 534 road accident fatalities in 1998.

Rail. The 1,524 mm gauge *Ferrocarril de Panama*, which connects Ancón on the Pacific with Cristóbal on the Atlantic along the bank of the Panama Canal, is the principal railway. Passenger-km travelled in 1997 came to 5,684m. The United Brands Company runs 376 km of railway, and the Chiriquí National Railroad 171 km.

Civil Aviation. There is an international airport at Panama City (Tocumén International). The national carrier is COPA, which flew to 22 destinations in 16 countries in 1996. In 1999 it flew 23·9m. km and carried 932,500 passengers. In 1999 Tocumén International handled 1,233,316 passengers and 70,690 tonnes of freight.

Shipping. Panama, a nation with a transcendental maritime career and a strategic geographic position, is the shipping world's preferred flag for ship registry. The Ship Registry System equally accepts vessels of local or international ownership, as long as they comply with all legal parameters. Ship owners also favour Panamanian registry because fees are low. Today, the Panamanian fleet is the largest in the world with 6,222 ships registered and 103,581,459 net tons in 2001.

All the international maritime traffic for Colón and Panama runs through the Canal ports of Cristóbal, Balboa and Manzanillo International.

Panama Canal. The Panama Canal Commission is concerned primarily with the operation of the Canal. In Oct. 2002 a new toll structure was adopted based on ship size and type. The Canal's tolls revenue in financial year 2001 was 579·5m. balboas.

At present some 90% of the world's shipping fleet can use the Canal, but this is set to drop as many new ships are too wide for the Canal. Feasibility studies for an additional set of locks that could take today's largest ships are under way.

Administrator of the Panama Canal Authority. Alberto Alemán Zubieta.

Particulars of the ocean-going commercial traffic through the Canal are given as follows:

Fiscal year ending 30 Sept.	No. of vessels transiting	Cargo in long tons	Tolls revenue (in US$1)
1999	14,337	195,900,000	568,800,000
2000	13,653	193,700,000	574,200,000

In the fiscal year ending 30 Sept. 1999, 14,337 ships of all sizes passed through the Canal. Most numerous transits by flag: Panama, 2,905; Liberia, 1,737; Bahamas, 1,074; Cyprus, 747; USA, 675; Norway, 503.

Statistical Information: The Panama Canal Authority Corporate Communications Division
Annual Reports on the Panama Canal, by the Administrator of the Panama Canal
Rules and Regulations Governing Navigation of the Panama Canal. The Panama Canal
Authority
    Major, J., *Prize Possession: the United States and the Panama Canal, 1903–1979.* CUP,
1994

Telecommunications. Panama had 429,100 main telephone lines in 2000, or 151·2
per 1,000 persons, and there were 105,000 PCs in use (37·0 for every 1,000 persons).
In 1999 there were 242,000 mobile phone subscribers. There were 45,000 Internet
users in Dec. 1999.

Postal Services. In 1995 there were 343 post offices.

SOCIAL INSTITUTIONS

Justice. The Supreme Court consists of nine justices appointed by the executive.
There is no death penalty. The police force numbered 13,000 in 1999, and includes
a Presidential Guard.
    The population in penal institutions in Dec. 1996 was 7,322 (270 per 100,000 of
national population).

Religion. 85% of the population is Roman Catholic, 5% Protestant, 4·5% Muslim.
There is freedom of religious worship and separation of Church and State.
Clergymen may teach in the schools but may not hold public office.

Education. Adult literacy was 91·7% in 1999 (male, 93·1%; female, 91·0%).
Elementary education is compulsory for all children from 7 to 15 years of age. In
1996 there were 371,250 pupils at 2,849 primary schools and 221,022 pupils with
12,239 teachers at secondary schools. There were 3 universities and 1 technological
university with a total of 75,951 students and 4,106 academic staff. There were also
a nautical school, a business school and institutes of teacher training and tourism.
    In 1997 expenditure on education came to 5·1% of GNP and 16·3% of total
government spending.

Health. In 1995 there were 3,074 doctors, 656 dentists and 2,823 nursing personnel.
There were 59 hospitals, 174 health centres and 443 health sub-centres with a total
of 7,138 beds.

CULTURE

Broadcasting. There are about 60 broadcasting stations, mostly commercial,
grouped in the Asociación Panameña de Radiodifusión. There are four television
channels (colour by NTSC) and an educational channel. In 1997 there were 815,000
radio and 510,000 TV sets in use.

Press. In 1996 there were seven dailies with a combined circulation of 166,000,
equivalent to 62 per 1,000 inhabitants.

Tourism. In 1998 there were 431,000 foreign tourists, bringing revenue of
US$379m.

DIPLOMATIC REPRESENTATIVES
Of Panama in the United Kingdom (40 Hertford Street, London, W1J 7SH)
Ambassador: Ariadne Singares Robinson.

Of the United Kingdom in Panama (Torre Swiss Bank, Calle 53, Apartado 889,
Panama City 1)
Ambassador: Jim Malcolm, OBE.

Of Panama in the USA (2862 McGill Terr., NW, Washington, D.C., 20008)
Ambassador: Vacant.
Chargé d'Affaires a.i.: Mylene Mayuly Marrone.

Of the USA in Panama (Apartado 6959, Panama City 5)
Ambassador: Vacant.
Chargé d'Affaires a.i.: Christopher McMullen.

Of Panama to the United Nations
Ambassador: Ramón A. Morales.

Of Panama to the European Union
Ambassador: Rolando A. Guevara Alvarado.

FURTHER READING
Statistical Information: The Controller-General of the Republic (Contraloria General de la República, Calle 35 y Avenida 6, Panama City) publishes an annual report and other statistical publications.

McCullough, D. G., *The Path Between the Seas: The Creation of the Panama Canal, 1870–1914.* Simon and Schuster, New York, 1999
Sahota, G. S., *Poverty Theory and Policy: a Study of Panama.* Johns Hopkins Univ. Press, 1990

Other titles are listed under PANAMA CANAL, *above.*

National library: Biblioteca Nacional, Departamento de Información, Calle 22, Panama.
Website (Spanish only): http://www.contraloria.gob.pa

PAPUA NEW GUINEA

Capital: Port Moresby
Population estimate, 2000: 4·81m.
GDP per capita, 2000: (PPP$) 2,280
HDI/world rank: 0·535/133

KEY HISTORICAL EVENTS

The Spanish first claimed the island in 1545 but the first attempt at colonization was made in 1793 by the British. The Dutch, however, claimed the west half of the island as part of the Dutch East Indies in 1828. On 6 Nov. 1884 a British Protectorate was proclaimed over the southern portion of the eastern half of New Guinea and in 1888 the territory was annexed. On 1 Sept. 1906 the Governor-General of Australia declared that British New Guinea was to be known henceforth as the Territory of Papua. The northern portion of New Guinea was a German colony until 1914 when Australian armed forces occupied it and it remained under their administration until becoming a League of Nations mandated territory in 1921, administered by Australia, and later a UN Trust Territory (of New Guinea). Australia granted Papua New Guinea self-government on 1 Dec. 1973, and on 16 Sept. 1975 Papua New Guinea became a fully independent state.

What began in 1988 as an armed campaign by tribes claiming traditional land rights against the Australian owner of the massive Panguna copper field soon escalated into a civil war for the secession of the island of Bougainville. Fighting between the government and the Bougainville Revolutionary Army (BRA) continued until 3 Sept. 1994 when a peace agreement set up a provisional Bougainville government. The ceasefire was broken by the rebels in mid-1995. In April 1998 the government of Papua New Guinea signed a 'permanent' truce with the secessionists. The nine-year rebellion claimed 20,000 lives. In Jan. 2001 the government and Bougainville signed a peace agreement that sets Bougainville on course to an autonomous government and a referendum on independence.

TERRITORY AND POPULATION

Papua New Guinea extends from the equator to Cape Baganowa in the Louisiade Archipelago to 11° 40' S. lat. and from the border of West Irian to 160° E. long. with a total area of 462,840 sq. km. According to the 1990 census the population was 3,529,538 (excluding North Solomons, estimated 1990 population 159,500). Estimate, 1994, 4·07m.; density, 9 per sq. km. The most recent census took place in 2000.

The UN gives a projected population for 2010 of 5·99m.

In 1999, 82·9% of the population lived in rural areas. In 1999 population of Port Moresby (National Capital District) was 293,000. Population of other main towns (1990 census): Lae, 80,655; Madang, 27,057; Wewak, 23,224; Goroka, 17,855; Mount Hagen, 17,392; Rabaul, 17,022. Area and population of the provinces:

Provinces	Sq. km	Census 1980	Census 1990	Capital
Central	29,500	116,964	140,584	Port Moresby
Chimbu	6,100	178,290	183,801	Kundiawa
Eastern Highlands	11,200	276,726	299,619	Goroka
East New Britain	15,500	133,197	184,408	Rabaul
East Sepik	42,800	221,890	248,308	Wewak
Enga	12,800	164,534	238,357	Wabag
Gulf	34,500	64,120	68,060	Kerema
Madang	29,000	211,069	270,299	Madang
Manus	2,100	26,036	32,830	Lorengau
Milne Bay	14,000	127,975	157,288	Alotau
Morobe	34,500	310,622	363,535	Lae
National Capital District	240	123,624	193,242	—
New Ireland	9,600	66,028	87,194	Kavieng
Northern	22,800	77,442	96,762	Popondetta
North Solomons	9,300	128,794	⋯	Arawa
Southern Highlands	23,800	236,052	302,724	Mendi

Provinces	Sq. km	Census 1980	Census 1990	Capital
Western	99,300	78,575	108,705[1]	Daru
Western Highlands	8,500	265,656	291,090	Mount Hagen
West New Britain	21,000	88,941	127,547	Kimbe
West Sepik	36,300	114,192	135,185[2]	Vanimo

[1]Excludes three census divisions, estimated total 1,500.
[2]Excludes two census divisions, estimated total 3,000.

The principal local languages are Neo-Melanesian (or Pidgin, a creole of English) and Hiri Motu. English is in official use.

SOCIAL STATISTICS

1995 births, 142,000; deaths, 44,000. 1995 birth rate, 32·9 per 1,000 population; death rate, 10·3. Expectation of life at birth in 1999 was 55·4 years for males and 57·3 years for females. Annual population growth rate, 1990–99, 2·3%. Infant mortality, 1999, 79 per 1,000 live births; fertility rate, 1999, 4·5 births per woman.

CLIMATE

There is a monsoon climate, with high temperatures and humidity the year round. Port Moresby is in a rain shadow and is not typical of the rest of Papua New Guinea, Jan. 82°F (27·8°C), July 78°F (25·6°C). Annual rainfall 40" (1,011 mm).

CONSTITUTION AND GOVERNMENT

The head of state is the British sovereign, who is represented by a Governor-General, nominated by parliament for six-year terms. A single legislative house, known as the *National Parliament*, is made up of 109 members from all parts of the country. The members are elected by universal suffrage; elections are held every five years. All citizens over the age of 18 are eligible to vote and stand for election. Voting is by secret ballot and follows the preferential system.

National Anthem. 'Arise, all you sons of this land'; words and tune by T. Shacklady.

RECENT ELECTIONS

Parliamentary elections were scheduled to take place between 15 June and 29 July 2002 but a troubled electoral process meant that results in some areas were left undeclared. Sir Michael Somare's National Alliance Party won 19 out of 109 seats; Sir Mekere Morautu's People's Democratic Movement, 12 seats; the People's Progress Party, 8; the Papua and Niugini Union Pati, 6; the People's Action Party, 5; the People's Labour Party, 4; ind., 17.

CURRENT ADMINISTRATION

Governor-General: Sir Silas Atopare.

In March 2003 the government included:

Prime Minister: Sir Michael Somare; b. 1936 (National Alliance Party; sworn in on 5 Aug. 2002 for the third time, having previously been prime minister from 1975 to 1980 and from 1982 to 1985).

Deputy Prime Minister and Minister of Trade and Industry: Alan Marat.

Finance and Treasury: Bart Philemon. *Agriculture and Livestock:* Moses Maladina. *Communications and Information:* Ben Semri. *Correctional Institutional Services (CIS):* Peter Oresi. *Culture and Tourism:* Alois King. *Defence:* Yarka Kappa. *Education:* Michael Laimo. *Environment and Conservation:* Sasa Zibe. *Fisheries:* Andrew Baing. *Foreign Affairs and Immigration:* Sir Rabbie Namaliu. *Forestry:* Patrick Pruaitch. *Health:* Melchior Pep. *Housing:* Yuntuvi Bao. *Inter-Governmental Relations:* Sir Peter Barter. *Internal Security:* Yawa Silupa. *Justice:* Mark Maipakai. *Labour and Industrial Relations:* Peter O'Neill. *Lands and Physical Planning:* Robert Koopaol. *Mining:* Sam Akoitai. *National Planning and Monitoring:* Sinai Brown. *Oil and Energy:* Sir Moi Avei. *Public Service:* Puka Temu. *Science and Technology:* Alphonse Morial Willie. *Transport and Civil Aviation:* Don Poyle. *Welfare and Social Development:* Lady Carol Kidu. *Works:* Gabriel Karpis.

Government Website: http://www.pngonline.gov.pg/

DEFENCE

The Papua New Guinea Defence Force had a total strength of 3,800 in 1999 consisting of land, maritime and air elements. The Navy is based at Port Moresby and Manus. Personnel numbered 400 in 1999. The Defence Force has an Air Transport Squadron, grounded through shortage of funds in 1996.

Defence expenditure in 2000 totalled US$55m. (US$11 per capita), representing 1·2% of GDP.

INTERNATIONAL RELATIONS

Papua New Guinea is a member of the UN, WTO, the Commonwealth, Asian Development Bank, Colombo Plan, APEC, Antarctic Treaty, the South Pacific Commission and the Pacific Community and is an observer at ASEAN and an ACP member state of the ACP-EU relationship.

ECONOMY

Industry accounted for 42·3% of GDP in 1998, agriculture 24·4% and services 33·3%.

Currency. The unit of currency is the *kina* (PGK) of 100 *toea*. The kina was floated in Oct. 1994. Foreign exchange reserves were US$457m. and gold reserves 63,000 troy oz in April 2002. Inflation was 10·2% in 2001. In March 2002 total money supply was K1,663m.

Budget. Budget revenue and expenditure (in K1m.):

	1995	1996	1997	1998	1999
Revenue	1,499·8	1,730·7	1,711·9	1,686·5	1,750·6
Expenditure	1,721·9	1,857·3	2,003·7	2,127·3	2,457·8

In 1999, 97% of total revenue came from taxation.

Performance. Papua New Guinea has been experiencing a recession, with the economy shrinking by 0·8% in 2000 and 3·4% in 2001. Total GDP in 2001 was US$3·0bn.

Banking and Finance. The Bank of Papua New Guinea (*Governor*, L. Wilson Kamit, CBE) assumed the central banking functions formerly undertaken by the Reserve Bank of Australia on 1 Nov. 1973. A national banking institution, the Papua New Guinea Banking Corporation, has been established. This bank has assumed the Papua New Guinea business of the Commonwealth Trading Bank of Australia.

There are five commercial banks, three Australian and two with 51% Papuan ownership. Total deposits, 1992, K1,318·2m. Total savings account deposits, 1992, K226·8m.

In addition, the Agriculture Bank of Papua New Guinea had assets of K82·6m. in 1992, and finance companies and merchant banks had total assets of K198·4m.

Weights and Measures. The metric system is in force.

ENERGY AND NATURAL RESOURCES

Environment. According to the *World Bank Atlas* carbon dioxide emissions in 1998 were the equivalent of 0·5 tonnes per capita.

Electricity. Installed capacity was 252,000 kW in 1992. Production in 1998 was 1·74bn. kWh, around 30% of it hydro-electric. Consumption per capita in 1997 was 399 kWh.

Oil and Gas. Natural gas reserves in 1997 were 15bn. cu. metres; output in 1996 was 3 petajoules. Crude oil production (1996), 39m. bbls. Oil predominantly comes from the Iagifu field in the Southern Highlands. There were 0·3bn. bbls. of proven oil reserves in 1999.

Minerals. In 1991 mining produced 15% of GDP. Copper is the main mineral product. Gold, copper and silver are the only minerals produced in quantity. The Misima open-pit gold mine was opened in 1989 but its resources were depleted by the end of 2001. The Porgera gold mine opened in 1990 with an expected life of 20 years. Major copper deposits in Bougainville have proven reserves of about 800m. tonnes; mining was halted by secessionist rebel activity. Copper and gold deposits in the Star Mountains of the Western Province are being developed by Ok Tedi Mining Ltd at the M. Fubilan mine. Production of gold commenced in 1984 and of copper concentrates in 1987. In 1996 Ok Tedi Mining Ltd produced 47 tonnes of gold, 127,700 tonnes of copper and 39m. barrels of crude oil. Gold mining also began at Lihir in 1997. In 2000 total gold production was 86 tonnes.

Agriculture. In 1995 it employed nearly 78% of the workforce. In 1998 there were 60,000 ha of arable land and 610,000 ha of permanent cropland. Minor commercial crops include pyrethrum, tea, peanuts and spices. Locally consumed food crops include sweet potatoes, maize, taro, bananas, rice and sago. Tropical fruits grow abundantly. There is extensive grassland. The sugar industry has made the country self-sufficient in this commodity while a beef-cattle industry is being developed.

Production (2000, in 1,000 tonnes): coconuts, 826; bananas, 700; sweet potatoes, 480; sugarcane, 430; palm oil, 299; yams, 220; copra, 170; taro, 170; cassava, 120; coffee, 83.

Livestock (2000): pigs, 1·55m.; cattle, 87,000; chickens, 4m.

Forestry. The forest area totalled 36·94m. ha in 1995 (81·6% of the land area), of which about 15m. ha of high quality tropical hardwoods are considered suitable for development. In 1990 the area under forests had been 37·6m. ha (83% of the land area). Timber production is important for both local consumption and export. Timber production was 8·6m. cu. metres in 1999.

Fisheries. Tuna is the major resource. In 1999 the fish catch was an estimated 53,746 tonnes (75% sea fish).

INDUSTRY
Secondary and service industries are expanding for the local market. The main industries are food processing, beverages, tobacco, timber products, wood and fabricated metal products. In 1988 there were 692 factories employing 30,503 persons. Value of output K768m. Copra oil production for export, 1996, 49,600 tonnes.

Labour. The labour force in 1996 totalled 2,160,000 (58% males). In 1996 formal employment in the building and construction industries rose by 27·5%, but around 85% of the population is dependent on non-monetarized agriculture.

INTERNATIONAL TRADE
Australian aid amounts to an annual $A300m. The 'Pactra II' agreement of 1991 establishes a free trade zone with Australia and protects Australian investments. Foreign debt was US$2,604m. in 2000.

Imports and Exports. Exports in 1999 were US$1,927·4m. (US$1,773·3m. in 1998); imports, US$1,071·4m. (US$1,078·3m. in 1998). The main imports in terms of value are machinery and transport equipment, manufactured goods, and food and live animals; and the main exports crude petroleum, gold and logs.

Of exports in 1995, Australia took 30·0%, Japan 24·3% and Germany 10·0%; of imports, Australia furnished 52·2%, the USA 14·8% and Singapore 7·4%.

COMMUNICATIONS
Roads. In 1996 there were 19,600 km of roads, only about 700 km of which were paved. Motor vehicles numbered 116,000 in 1996 (31,000 passenger cars and 85,000 trucks and vans).

Civil Aviation. Jacksons International Airport is at Port Moresby. The state-owned national carrier is Air Niugini. In 1998 there were scheduled international flights to Brisbane, Cairns, Honiara, Manila, Singapore, Sydney and Townsville. There are a total of 177 airports and airstrips with scheduled services.

Shipping. There are 12 entry and four other main ports served by five major shipping lines; the Papua New Guinea Shipping Corporation is state-owned. Sea-going shipping totalled 61,000 GRT in 1998, including oil tankers 3,000 GRT.

Telecommunications. In 2000 there were 64,800 main telephone lines, or 13·5 for every 1,000 inhabitants. There were 3,000 mobile phone subscribers in 1996 and 800 fax machines in 1995. There were 2,000 Internet users in Dec. 1999.

SOCIAL INSTITUTIONS
Justice. In 1983 over 1,500 criminal and civil cases were heard in the National Court and an estimated 120,000 cases in district and local courts. The discretionary use of the death penalty for murder and rape was introduced in 1991.

The population in penal institutions in 1996 was 3,728 (100 per 100,000 of national population).

Religion. In 1999 there were 2·83m. Protestants and 1·33m. Roman Catholics.

Education. Obligatory universal primary education is a government objective. In 1990 about two-thirds of eligible children were attending school. In 1995 there were 2,790 primary schools with 525,995 pupils and 13,652 teachers, 78,759 pupils in secondary schools and 13,663 students in institutes of higher education. There are two universities (the University of Papua New Guinea and the Papua New Guinea University of Technology). Adult literacy rate was 63·9% in 1999 (71·4% among males and 56% among females).

Health. In 1993 there were 736 doctors and 2,614 nurses. Provision of hospital beds in 1993 was 34 per 10,000 persons.

CULTURE

Broadcasting. The National Broadcasting Commission operates three networks: national, provincial and commercial. A national service is relayed throughout the country. Each province has a broadcasting service, while the larger urban centres are also covered by a commercial network relayed from Port Moresby. Two commercial television stations broadcast from Port Moresby (colour by PAL). In 1997 there were 42,000 television and 410,000 radio receivers.

Press. In 1996 there were two daily newspapers with a combined circulation of 65,000, equivalent to 15 per 1,000 inhabitants, and a number of weeklies and monthlies.

Tourism. In 1999 there were 70,000 foreign tourists, bringing revenue of US$104m.

DIPLOMATIC REPRESENTATIVES

Of Papua New Guinea in the United Kingdom (3rd Floor, 14 Waterloo Pl., London, SW1R 4AR)
High Commissioner: Jean Kekedo, OBE.

Of the United Kingdom in Papua New Guinea (PO Box 212, Waigani NCD 131)
High Commissioner: Simon Scaddan.

Of Papua New Guinea in the USA (1779 Massachusetts Ave., NW, Washington D.C., 20036)
Ambassador: Vacant.
Chargé d'Affaires a.i.: Graham Michael.

Of the USA in Papua New Guinea (Douglas St., Port Moresby)
Ambassador: Susan S. Jacobs.

Of Papua New Guinea to the United Nations
Ambassador: Peter Dickson Donigi.

Of Papua New Guinea to the European Union
Ambassador: Gabriel Pepson.

FURTHER READING

National Statistical Office. *Summary of Statistics.* Annual.—*Abstract of Statistics.* Quarterly.—*Economic Indicators.*
Monthly Bank of Papua New Guinea. *Quarterly Economic Bulletin.*
Turner, A., *Historical Dictionary of Papua New Guinea.* Metuchen (NJ), 1995
Waiko, J. D., *Short History of Papua New Guinea.* OUP, 1993

National statistical office: National Statistical Office, PO Wards Strip.
Website: http://www.nso.gov.pg

PARAGUAY

República del Paraguay

Capital: Asunción
Population estimate, 2000: 5·5m.
GDP per capita, 2000: (PPP$) 4,426
HDI/world rank: 0·740/90

KEY HISTORICAL EVENTS

Paraguay was occupied by the Spanish in 1537 and became a Spanish colony as part of the viceroyalty of Peru. The area gained its independence, as the Republic of Paraguay, on 14 May 1811. Paraguay was then ruled by a succession of dictators. During a devastating war fought from 1865 to 1870 between Paraguay and a coalition of Argentina, Brazil and Uruguay, Paraguay's population was reduced from about 600,000 to 233,000. Further severe losses were incurred during the war with Bolivia (1932–35) over territorial claims in the Chaco inspired by the unfounded belief that minerals existed in the territory. A peace treaty by which Paraguay obtained most of the area her troops had conquered was signed in July 1938.

A new constitution took effect in Feb. 1968 under which executive power is discharged by an executive president. Gen. Alfredo Stroessner Mattiauda was re-elected 7 times between 1958 and 1988. Since then, Paraguay has been under more or less democratic government. On 23 March 1999 Paraguay's vice-president Luis Maria Argaña was assassinated. The following day, Congress voted to impeach President Cubas who was said to be implicated in the murder. He then resigned.

TERRITORY AND POPULATION

Paraguay is bounded in the northwest by Bolivia, northeast and east by Brazil and southeast, south and southwest by Argentina. The area is 406,752 sq. km (157,042 sq. miles).

The 1992 census population was 4,123,550; estimate (2002) 5·88m., giving a density of 14·5 per sq. km. In 1999, 55·3% lived in urban areas.

The UN gives a projected population for 2010 of 6·98m.

In 1999 the capital, Asunción (and metropolitan area), had an estimated population of 1,224,000. Other major cities (1992 census populations) are: Ciudad del Este, 133,893; San Lorenzo, 133,311; Lambaré, 99,681.

There are 17 departments and the capital city. Area and population at the 1992 census:

Department	Area in sq. km	Population	Department	Area in sq. km	Population
Asunción (city)	117	502,426	Caazapá	9,496	128,550
Central	2,465	864,540	Amambay	12,933	97,158
Alto Paraná	14,895	403,858	Canendiyú	14,667	96,826
Caaguazú	11,474	383,319	Misiones	9,556	88,624
Itapúa	16,525	375,748	Neembucú	12,147	69,884
San Pedro	20,002	277,110	*Oriental*	*159,827*	*4,026,342*
Cordillera	4,948	206,097	Presidente Hayes	72,907	59,100
Paraguari	8,705	203,012	Boquerón[1]	91,669	26,292
Concepción	18,051	166,946	Alto Paraguay[2]	83,349	11,816
Guairá	3,846	162,244	*Occidental*	*246,925*	*97,208*

[1]Incorporates former department of Nueva Asunción.
[2]Incorporates former department of Chaco.

The population is mixed Spanish and Guaraní Indian. There are some 46,700 unassimilated Indians of other tribal origin, in the Chaco and the forests of eastern Paraguay. 40·1% of the population speak only Guaraní; 48·2% are bilingual (Spanish/Guaraní); and 6·4% speak only Spanish.

Mennonites, who arrived in three groups (1927, 1930 and 1947), are settled in the Chaco and eastern Paraguay. There are also Korean and Japanese settlers.

SOCIAL STATISTICS

1997 births, estimate, 172,000; deaths, 24,000. Rates, 1997 estimates (per 1,000 population): birth, 30·5; death, 4·2. Annual population growth rate, 1990–99, 2·7%.

Expectation of life, 1999: 67·8 years for men and 72·3 for women. Infant mortality, 1999, 27 per 1,000 live births; fertility rate, 1999, 4·1 births per woman.

CLIMATE
A tropical climate, with abundant rainfall and only a short dry season from July to Sept., when temperatures are lowest. Asunción, Jan. 81°F (27°C), July 64°F (17·8°C). Annual rainfall 53" (1,316 mm).

CONSTITUTION AND GOVERNMENT
On 18 June 1992 a Constituent Assembly approved a new constitution. The head of state is the *President*, elected for a non-renewable five-year term. Parliament consists of an 80-member *Chamber of Deputies*, elected from departmental constituencies, and a 45-member *Senate*, elected from a single national constituency.

National Anthem. 'Paraguayos, república o muerte!' ('Paraguayans, republic or death!'); words by F. Acuña de Figueroa, tune by F. Dupuy.

RECENT ELECTIONS
Parliamentary and presidential elections were held on 27 April 2003. Nicanor Duarte Frutos of the ruling Asociación Nacional Republicana–Partido Colorado (Republican National Alliance–Colorado Party/ANR) was elected President with 37·1% of votes cast. Julio César Franco Gómez of the Partido Liberal Radical Auténtico (PLRA) won 24·0%, Pedro Fadul Niella of the Movimiento Patria Querida (MPQ) 21·3% and Guillermo Sánchez Guffanti of the Unión Nacional de Ciudadanos Éticos (UNACE) 13·5%. Turn-out was 64·2%. Duarte is scheduled to take office on 15 Aug.

In the Chamber of Deputies the ANR won 37 seats with 35·3% of votes cast, the PLRA won 21 seats (25·7%), the MPQ won 10 seats (15·3%), the UNACE won 10 seats (14·7%) and the Partido País Solidario (PPS) won 2 seats (3·3%). Turn-out was 64%. In the Senate the ANR won 16 seats, the PLRA won 12, the MPQ won 8, the UNACE won 7 and the PPS won 2. Turn-out was 58·8%.

CURRENT ADMINISTRATION
President: Luis González Macchi; b. 1947 (ANR; sworn in 28 March 1999).
Vice-President: Vacant.
In March 2003 the cabinet comprised:
Minister of Agriculture and Livestock: Dario Baumgarten. *Finance and Economy:* Alcides Jiménez. *National Defence:* Miguel Angel Candia. *Education and Culture:* Blanca Ovelar de Duarte. *Foreign Relations:* José Antonio Moreno Ruffinelli. *Industry and Commerce:* Roberto Fernandez. *Interior:* Osvaldo Ruben Benítez. *Justice and Labour:* José Angel Burro. *Public Health and Social Welfare:* José Antonio Mayans. *Public Works and Communications:* Antonio Adam Nill. *Secretary General for the Presidency:* Stella Samaniego.

Paraguayan Parliament: http://www.camdip.gov.py

DEFENCE
The army, navy and air forces are separate services under a single command. The President of the Republic is the active C.-in-C. Conscription is for 12 months (two years in the navy).

In 2000 defence expenditure totalled US$121m. (US$22 per capita), representing 1·3% of GDP.

Army. Strength (1999) 14,900 (10,400 conscripts). In addition there is a paramilitary Special Police Force numbering 14,800.

Navy. Personnel in 1999 totalled 3,600 including 900 marines, 800 naval aviation and 1,900 conscripts.

Air Force. The Air Force has three combat units. Personnel (1999) 1,700 (600 conscripts). There are 28 combat aircraft including F-5E/Fs.

INTERNATIONAL RELATIONS

Paraguay is a member of the UN, WTO, OAS, Inter-American Development Bank, Mercosur, LAIA and IOM.

ECONOMY

In 1998 services accounted for 48·9% of GDP, agriculture 24·9% and industry 26·2%.

Overview. There is a privatization programme for large state enterprises.

Currency. The unit of currency is the *guaraní* (PYG), notionally divided into 100 *céntimos*. In May 2002 total money supply was 2,373·85bn. guaranís. Foreign exchange reserves were US$450m. in June 2002 and gold reserves 35,000 troy oz. Inflation was 7·7% in 2001.

Budget. In 1996 (in 1m. guaranís) revenue was 2,937,992 and expenditure 3,335,481.

Revenue items, 1995 (in 1m. guaranís): domestic taxes, 587,572; import duties, 369,650; income tax, 308,584. Items of expenditure: education, 579,754; public works, 445,570; public debt service, 293,632; defence, 267,373; agriculture, 283,794; health, 192,151.

Performance. In 2001 real GDP growth was just 0·8%. GDP per capita has fallen from US$1,930 in 1996 to approximately US$1,125 in 2000. Total GDP in 2001 was US$6·9bn.

Banking and Finance. The Central Bank is a state-owned autonomous agency with the sole right of note issue, control over foreign exchange and the supervision of commercial banks (*Governor*, Juan Ortiz Vely). In 1994 there were 28 commercial banks (mostly foreign), 2 other banking institutions, 1 investment bank, 1 development bank and 6 building societies.

There is a stock exchange in Asunción.

Weights and Measures. The metric system was officially adopted in 1901, but some traditional measures continue in use.

ENERGY AND NATURAL RESOURCES

Environment. According to the *World Bank Atlas* Paraguay's carbon dioxide emissions were the equivalent of 0·9 tonnes per capita in 1998.

Electricity. There is a vast hydro-electric potential; only 2% of output is thermal. Installed capacity was 7m. kW in 1997. Output (1998), 50·32bn. kWh; consumption per capita was 756 kWh.

Minerals. The country is poor in minerals. Limestone, gypsum, kaolin and salt are extracted. Deposits of bauxite, iron ore, copper, manganese and uranium exist. 1995 output: limestone, 600,000 tonnes; kaolin, 74,000 tonnes; gypsum, 4,500 tonnes.

Agriculture. In 1999 agriculture employed 35% of the workforce and produced 90% of the country's exports. In 1998 there were approximately 2·2m. ha of arable land and 85,000 ha of permanent crops.

At the agrarian census of 1991 there were 307,221 farms working 23,799,737 ha. 122,750 farms had fewer than 5 ha; 884 had over 5,000 ha.

Output (in 1,000 tonnes), 2000: cassava, 3,500; sugarcane, 2,850; soybeans, 2,750; maize, 900; wheat, 250; oranges, 209; seed cotton, 205; cottonseed, 123; watermelons, 110; rice, 93; sunflower seeds, 80; sweet potatoes, 80. *Yerba maté*, or strongly flavoured Paraguayan tea, continues to be produced but is declining in importance.

Livestock (2000); 9·91m. cattle, 2·70m. pigs, 413,000 sheep, 400,000 horses and 25m. chickens.

Forestry. The area under forests in 1995 was 11·53m. ha, or 29% of the total land area (13·16m. ha and 33·1% in 1990). Palm and tung oil are produced. Timber production was 8·1m. cu. metres in 1999.

Fisheries. In 1999 the catch totalled approximately 25,000 tonnes, exclusively from inland waters.

INDUSTRY
Production, 1994 (1,000 tonnes): cement, 528·8; soybean, peanut and coconut flour, 468·0; cotton fibre, 136·8; sugar (1998), 114·3; rice, 81·9; edible oil, 78·9; wheat flour, 47·8; frozen meat, 45·8; industrial oil, 10·0; tung oil, 6·8; cigarettes (1988) (1m. packets), 46,598; matches (1,000 boxes), 8,979.

Labour. The labour force in 1996 totalled 1,831,000 (71% males). Over 40% of the economically active population in 1993 were engaged in agriculture, fisheries and forestry.

Trade Unions. Trade unionists number about 30,000 (*Confederación Paraguaya de Trabajadores* and *Confederación Cristiana de Trabajadores*).

INTERNATIONAL TRADE
Foreign debt was US$3,091m. in 2000. In 1992 direct foreign investment totalled US$117m. (40% from Brazil, 19% from France, 12% from USA).

Imports and Exports. Trade in US$1m.:

	1996	1997	1998	1999	2000
Imports f.o.b.	4,383·4	4,192·4	3,941·5	3,041·5	2,905·6
Exports f.o.b.	3,796·9	3,327·5	3,548·6	2,681·3	2,373·3

Main exports in 1994 (in US$1m.): soya, 222·3; cotton fibre, 170·9; timber, 78·6; hides, 63·0; meat, 55·4. Main imports: machinery, 476·2; vehicles, 276·8; beverages and tobacco, 179·0; fuel and lubricants, 159·4; chemicals, 145·0; foodstuffs, 99·1.

Main export markets in 1996: Brazil, 49·9%; Netherlands, 16·5%; Argentina, 9·2%; Uruguay, 4·2%; USA, 3·5%. Main import suppliers, 1996: Brazil, 32·7%; Argentina, 19·5%; USA, 10·7%; Japan, 6·2%; South Korea, 3·4%.

COMMUNICATIONS

Roads. In 1996 there were around 29,500 km of roads, of which 9·2% were paved. Passenger cars numbered 71,000 in 1996 (14·3 per 1,000 inhabitants), and there were 50,000 trucks and vans.

Rail. The President Carlos Antonio López (formerly Paraguay Central) Railway runs from Asunción to Encarnación, on the Río Alto Paraná, with a length of 441 km (1,435 mm gauge), and connects with Argentine Railways over the Encarnación-Posadas bridge opened in 1989. In 1994 traffic amounted to 182,000 tonnes and 24,000 passengers.

Civil Aviation. There is an international airport at Asunción (Silvio Pettirossi). The main Paraguay-based carrier is Transportes Aereos del Mercosur, which flew 4·3m. km and carried 195,000 passengers (all on international flights) in 1999. In 2000 Asunción handled 466,000 passengers (422,000 on international flights) and 6,600 tonnes of freight.

Shipping. Asunción, the chief port, is 950 miles from the sea. In 1998 ocean-going shipping totalled 45,000 GRT, including oil tankers 4,000 GRT.

Telecommunications. In 1999 telephone main lines numbered 268,100 (50·0 per 1,000 population) and there were 435,600 mobile phone subscribers. There were 70,000 PCs in use in 2000 (12·7 for every 1,000 persons) and 1,700 fax machines in 1995. Paraguay had approximately 20,000 Internet users in Dec. 1999.

Postal Services. In 1995 there were 321 post offices.

SOCIAL INSTITUTIONS

Justice. The 1992 constitution confers a large measure of judicial autonomy. The highest court is the Supreme Court with nine members. Nominations for membership must be backed by six of the eight members of the Magistracy Council, which appoints all judges, magistrates and the electoral tribunal. The Council comprises elected representatives of the Presidency, Congress and the bar. There are special Chambers of Appeal for civil and commercial cases, and criminal cases. Judges of first instance deal with civil, commercial and criminal cases in six departments. Minor cases are dealt with by Justices of the Peace.

The Attorney-General represents the State in all jurisdictions, with representatives in each judicial department and in every jurisdiction.

The population in penal institutions in Dec. 1996 was 3,097 (60 per 100,000 of national population). The death penalty was abolished for all crimes in 1992.

Religion. Religious liberty was guaranteed by the 1967 constitution. Article 6 recognized Roman Catholicism as the official religion of the country. It had 4·5m. adherents in 1997. There are Mennonite, Anglican and other communities as well. In 1997 followers of other religions (mostly Protestants) totalled 590,000.

Education. Adult literacy was 93·0% in 1999 (male, 94·2%; female, 91·9%). Education is free and nominally compulsory. In 1997 there were 905,813 pupils at primary schools and 327,775 at secondary level. In 1994 there were 11 universities (1 Roman Catholic) in 1994–95 and 1 institute of education catering for 43,000 students.

In 1997 total expenditure on education came to 4·0% of GNP and 19·8% of total government spending.

Health. In 1993 there were 3,341 doctors, and in 1992, 1,160 dentists and 4,558 nurses. Provision of hospital beds in 1993 was 12 per 10,000 population.

CULTURE

Broadcasting. In 1993 there were 30 commercial radio stations and in 1999 there were 4 TV stations (colour by PAL M) and 2 cable TV stations. In 1997 there were 515,000 television and 925,000 radio receivers.

Cinema. There are 15 cinemas in Asunción.

Press. In 1996 there were five daily newspapers with a combined circulation of 213,000, at a rate of 43 per 1,000 inhabitants.

Tourism. In 1998 there were 350,000 foreign tourists, bringing revenue of US$710m.

DIPLOMATIC REPRESENTATIVES

Of Paraguay in the United Kingdom (Braemar Lodge, Cornwall Gdns, London, SW7 4AQ)
Ambassador: Vacant.
Chargé d'Affaires a.i.: Maria Cristina Acosta Alvarez.

Of the United Kingdom in Paraguay (Avda. Boggiani 5848, C/R16 Boqueron, Asunción)
Ambassador: Anthony Cantor.

Of Paraguay in the USA (2400 Massachusetts Ave., NW, Washington, D.C., 20008)
Ambassador: Leila Teresa Rachid Cowles.

Of the USA in Paraguay (1776 Mariscal López Ave., Asunción)
Ambassador: David N. Greenlee.

Of Paraguay to the United Nations
Ambassador: Eladio Loizaga.

Of Paraguay to the European Union
Ambassador: Manuel María Cáceres Cardozo.

FURTHER READING

Gaceta Official, published by Imprenta Nacional, Estrella y Estero Bellaco, Asunción
Anuario Daumas. Asunción
Anuario Estadístico de la República del Paraguay. Asunción. Annual
Nickson, R. A. and Lambert, P. (eds.) *The Transition to Democracy in Paraguay.* Macmillan, London and St Martin's Press, New York, 1997

National library: Biblioteca Nacional, Calle de la Residenta, 820 c/ Perú, Asunción.
National statistical office: Dirección General de Estadísticas, Enuestas y Censos.
Website (Spanish only): http://www.dgeec.gov.py

PERU

República del Perú

Capital: Lima
Population estimate, 2000: 25·66m.
GDP per capita, 2000: (PPP$) 4,799
HDI/world rank: 0·747/82

KEY HISTORICAL EVENTS

The Incas of Peru were conquered by the Spanish in the 16th century and subsequent Spanish colonial settlement made Peru the most important of the Spanish viceroyalties in South America. On 28 July 1821 Peru declared its independence, but it was not until after a war which ended in 1824 that the country gained its freedom. In a war with Chile (1879–83) Peru's capital, Lima, was captured and she lost some of her southern territory. Tacna, in the far south of the country, remained in Chilean control from 1880 until 1929. In 1924 Dr Victor Raúl Haya de la Torre founded the *Alianza Popular Revolucionaria Americana* to oppose the dictatorial government then in power. The party was banned between 1931 and 1945 and between 1948 and 1956 its leader failed regularly in the presidential elections but it was at times the largest party in Congress. The closeness of the 1962 elections led Gen. Ricardo Pérez Godoy, Chairman of the Joint Chiefs-of-Staff, to seize power. A coup led by Gen. Nicolás Lindley López deposed him in 1963. There followed, after elections, a period of civilian rule but the military staged yet another coup in 1968. In 1978–79 a constituent assembly drew up a new constitution, after which a civilian government was installed. However, Peru was plagued by political violence for some 15 years between the early 1980s and the mid-1990s with 30,000 people killed by Maoist insurgents and government forces. On 6 April 1992 President Alberto Fujimori suspended the constitution and dissolved the parliament. A new constitution was promulgated on 29 Dec. 1993. But while Peru has enjoyed stability and economic growth, there was still rule by autocracy which put some politicians above the law. Embroiled in a bribery and corruption scandal, President Fujimori's discredited administration came to an end in Nov. 2000 with his resignation while out of the country.

TERRITORY AND POPULATION

Peru is bounded in the north by Ecuador and Colombia, east by Brazil and Bolivia, south by Chile and west by the Pacific Ocean. Area, 1,285,216 sq. km.

For an account of the border dispute with Ecuador, *see* ECUADOR: Territory and Population.

Census population, 1993, 22,639,443. 1998 estimate, 24,801,000 (72·4% urban, 1999); density, 19 per sq. km.

The UN gives a projected population for 2010 of 29·89m.

Area and 1998 population estimate of the 24 departments and the constitutional province of Callao, together with their capitals:

Department	Area (in sq. km)	Population	Capital	Population
Amazonas	39,249	391,078	Chachapoyas	17,527
Ancash	35,826	1,045,921	Huaraz	79,012
Apurímac	15,666	418,775	Abancay	49,513
Arequipa	63,345	1,035,773	Arequipa	710,103
Ayacucho	43,814	525,601	Ayacucho	118,960
Cajamarca	33,247	1,377,297	Cajamarca	108,009
Callao[1]	147	736,243	Callao	424,294
Cusco	71,892	1,131,061	Cusco	278,590
Huancavelica	22,131	423,041	Huancavelica	35,123
Huánuco	36,938	747,263	Huánuco	129,688
Ica	21,328	628,684	Ica	194,820
Junín	44,410	1,161,581	Huancayo	305,039
La Libertad	25,570	1,415,512	Trujillo	603,657
Lambayeque	14,231	1,050,280	Chiclayo	375,058
Lima	34,802	7,194,816	Lima	6,464,693
Loreto	368,852	839,748	Iquitos	334,013

Madre de Dios	85,183	79,172	Puerto Maldonado	27,407
Moquegua	15,734	142,475	Moquegua	44,824
Pasco	25,320	245,651	Cerro de Pasco	70,058
Piura	35,892	1,506,716	Piura	308,155
Puno	71,999	1,171,838	Puno	101,578
San Martín	51,253	692,408	Moyobamba	31,256
Tacna	16,076	261,336	Tacna	215,683
Tumbes	4,669	183,609	Tumbes	87,557
Ucayali	102,411	394,889	Pucallpa	220,866

¹Constitutional province.

In 1991 there were some 100,000 Peruvians of Japanese origin.

The official languages are Spanish (spoken by 80·3% of the population in 1993), Quechua (16·5%) and Aymara (3%).

Lima: Founded by the Spanish conquistador, Pizarro, in 1535, Lima quickly became an important centre of justice and religion, being the headquarters of the Inquisition and the High Court in Peru. Situated on the Rio Rimac, 8 miles from the Pacific ocean, it covers an area of 70 sq. km. Despite being devastated by an earthquake in 1746, Lima expanded massively and today its citizens account for around a third of the total population of Peru.

SOCIAL STATISTICS
1999 estimates: births, 609,800; deaths, 159,000; infant deaths (under 1 year), 42,500. Rates per 1,000 population (1999 estimate): birth, 24·2; death, 6·3. Annual population growth rate, 1990–99, 1·8%; infant mortality, 1999, 69·7 per 1,000 live births. Life expectancy, 1999: males, 66·3 years; females, 71·3. Fertility rate, 1999, 2·9 births per woman.

CLIMATE
There is a very wide variety of climate, ranging from equatorial to desert (or perpetual snow on the high mountains). In coastal areas, temperatures vary very little, either daily or annually, though humidity and cloudiness show considerable variation, with highest humidity from May to Sept. Little rain is experienced in that period. In the Sierra, temperatures remain fairly constant over the year, but the daily range is considerable. There the dry season is from April to Nov. Desert conditions occur in the extreme south, where the climate is uniformly dry, with a few heavy showers falling between Jan. and March. Lima, Jan. 74°F (23·3°C), July 62°F (16·7°C). Annual rainfall 2" (48 mm). Cusco, Jan. 56°F (13·3°C), July 50°F (10°C). Annual rainfall 32" (804 mm). El Niño is the annual warm Pacific current which moves to the coasts of Peru and Ecuador. El Niño in 1982–83 resulted in agricultural production down by 8·5% and fishing output down by 40%. El Niño in 1991–94 was unusually long. El Niño in 1997–98 resulted in a sudden rise in the surface temperature of the Pacific by 9°F (5°C) and caused widespread damage and loss of life.

CONSTITUTION AND GOVERNMENT
The 1980 Constitution provided for a legislative *Congress* consisting of a *Senate* (60 members) and a *Chamber of Deputies* (180 members) and an Executive formed of the President and a Council of Ministers appointed by him. Elections were to be every five years with the President and Congress elected, at the same time, by separate ballots.

On 5 April 1992 President Fujimori suspended the 1980 constitution and dissolved Congress.

A referendum was held on 31 Oct. 1993 to approve the twelfth constitution, including a provision for the president to serve a consecutive second term. 52·24% of votes cast were in favour. The constitution was promulgated on 29 Dec. 1993. In Aug. 1996 Congress voted for the eligibility of the President to serve a third consecutive term of office. All citizens over the age of 18 are eligible to vote. Voting is compulsory.

In 1998 President Fujimori estimated that El Niño caused US$12m. worth of infrastructure damage, killed over 100 people and resulted in tens of thousands becoming homeless. The government declared a state of emergency in nine out of the country's 24 regions. A programme to rebuild the infrastructure, namely communication lines (bridges, roads, railway lines and canals) and healthcare facilities, to prevent the spread of epidemics, was initiated.

National Anthem. 'Somos libres, seámoslo siempre' ('We are free, let us always be so'); words by J. De La Torre Ugarte, tune by J. B. Alcedo.

RECENT ELECTIONS

Elections were held on 8 April and 3 June 2001 for president and 8 April for the 120-member, single-chamber congress. There were eight presidential candidates in the first round of voting. Alejandro Toledo Manrique of the personalist Peru Possible Party (36·5%) and Alan Gabriel Ludwig García Pérez of the American Revolutionary People's Alliance (25·8%) met in a run-off, which Toledo won with 53·1%. Toledo had withdrawn from presidential elections in 2000 amidst complaints made against the electoral process. He is Peru's first democratically-elected president of indigenous descent.

In the congressional elections of 8 April 2001 the Peru Possible party gained 45 seats with 26·3% of votes cast. The American Revolutionary People's Alliance gained 26 seats (19·7%), the National Unity Party 17 (13·8%), the Moralizing Independent Front 11 (11·0%), Union for Peru 6 (4·1%) and We Are Peru 4 (5·8%). Other parties received less than 5% of votes and won three seats or fewer.

CURRENT ADMINISTRATION

President: Alejandro Toledo Manrique; b. 1946 (Peru Possible; sworn in 28 July 2001).

In March 2003 the government comprised:

President of the Council of Ministers (Prime Minister): Luis Solari de la Fuente; b. 1948 (Peru Possible; sworn in 12 July 2002).

Minister of Foreign Affairs: Allan Wagner Tizón. *Defence:* Aurelio Loret de Mola. *Economy and Finance:* Javier Silva Ruete. *Interior:* Alberto Sanabria Ortiz. *Justice:* Fausto Alvarado Humberto Dodero. *Education:* Gerardo Ayzanoa del Carpio. *Health:* Fernando Carbone. *Agriculture:* Alvaro Enrique Quijandria Salmón. *Labour and Promotion of Employment:* Fernando Villaran. *Foreign Trade and Tourism:* Raul Diez Canseco. *Energy and Mines:* Jaime Quijandria Salmón. *Transport and Communications:* Javier Reátegui Roselló. *Women's Affairs and Social Development:* Ana María Romero Lauezzari. *Production:* Eduardo Iriarte Jiménez. *Housing, Construction and Sanitation:* Carlos Bruce Montes de Oca.

DEFENCE

There is selective conscription for two years. In 2000 defence expenditure totalled US$861m. (US$34 per capita), representing 1·3% of GDP.

Army. There are six military regions. In 1999 the Army comprised approximately 75,000 personnel (52,000 conscripts) and 188,000 reserves. In addition there is a paramilitary national police force of 77,000 personnel.

Navy. The principal ships of the Navy are the former Netherlands cruisers *Almirante Grau* and *Aguirre* built in 1953. Other combatants include 6 diesel submarines, 1 modernized former British destroyer and 4 Italian-built frigates.

The Naval Aviation branch operates 31 combat aircraft, including 6 Super Etendards, and 8 armed helicopters.

Callao is the main base, where the dockyard is located and most training takes place. Smaller ocean bases exist at Paita and Talara.

Naval personnel in 1999 totalled 25,000 (12,500 conscripts) including 800 Naval Air Arm and 3,000 Marines.

Air Force. The operational force consists of five combat groups. There are military airfields at Talara, Chiclayo, Piura, Pisco, Lima (2), Iquitos and La Joya, and a floatplane base at Iquitos.

In 1999 there were some 15,000 personnel (2,000 conscripts) and 114 combat aircraft (including Su-22s, Su-25s, Mirage 2000s, Mirage 5s and MiG-29s) and 23 armed helicopters.

INTERNATIONAL RELATIONS

Peru is a member of the UN, WTO, OAS, Inter-American Development Bank, the Andean Group, LAIA, APEC, IOM and Antarctic Treaty.

PERU

ECONOMY
Agriculture produced 7·1% of GDP in 1998, industry 36·8% and services 56·1%.

Overview. Privatization began in 1991 under the aegis of the Privatization Commission (COPRI). By early 1995, 95 state companies had been sold bringing in revenue of US$4,400m. In 1996, 31 state companies were sold, bringing in US$871m. In 1994 a 'citizen participation' scheme was initiated to increase the extent of private shareholding in state enterprises; retirement pensions may also be taken as shares.

Currency. The monetary unit is the *nuevo sol* (PES), of 100 *céntimos*, which replaced the inti in 1990 at a rate of 1m. intis = 1 nuevo sol. Inflation, which had been over 7,000% in 1990, was down to 2·0% in 2001, the lowest rate in more than 40 years. Foreign exchange reserves were US$8,053m. in June 2002, gold reserves totalled 1·10m. troy oz and total money supply was 21,506m. sols.

Budget. Budget revenue and expenditure (in 1m. sols), year ending 31 Dec:

	1996	1997	1998	1999	2000
Revenue	24,023	27,705	29,380	28,747	30,543
Expenditure	24,686	27,232	30,104	34,168	36,052

At US$10·2bn., the 1998 budget was 10% higher in real terms than in 1997. There was a trade deficit of US$1·7bn. in 1997. In 1997 the World Bank approved a US$150m. loan to help Peru overcome expected problems associated with El Niño.

Performance. Real GDP growth 3·1% in 2000, but just 0·2% in 2001. Total GDP in 2001 was US$54·0bn.

Banking and Finance. The bank of issue is the Banco Central de Reserva (*President of the Directorate*, Richard Webb Duarte), which was established in 1922. The government's fiscal agent is the Banco de la Nación. In 1995 there were additionally 17 domestic commercial, 1 foreign and 4 multinational banks. Legislation of April 1991 permitted financial institutions to fix their own interest rates and reopened the country to foreign banks. The Central Reserve Bank sets the upper limit.

There are stock exchanges in Lima and Arequipa.

Weights and Measures. The metric system is in use.

ENERGY AND NATURAL RESOURCES
Peru lays claim to 84 of the world's 114 ecosystems; 28 of its climate types; 19% of all bird species; 20% of all plant species; and 25 conservation areas (7 national parks, 8 national reserves, 7 national sanctuaries and 3 historic sanctuaries).

Environment. According to the *World Bank Atlas* Peru's carbon dioxide emissions in 1998 were the equivalent of 1·1 tonnes per capita.

Electricity. In 1998 output was 18·28bn. kWh (75% hydro-electric). Total generating capacity was 5m. kW in 1997. 66·1% of the population were supplied with electricity in 1996. Consumption per capita in 1998 was 642 kWh. Peru's reliance on hydro-generated electricity means that electricity production was affected by the drought brought on by the 1997–98 El Niño.

Oil and Gas. Proven oil reserves in 1999 amounted to 400m. bbls. Output, 1996, 43·91m. bbls. Development of the huge Camisea gas field, Peru's largest commercial project, is on hold while negotiations continue with the Shell-Mobil consortium.

Natural gas reserves in 1997 were 200bn. cu. metres; output in 1997 was 40 petajoules.

Minerals. Mining accounted for some 8·4% of GDP in 1996. Lead, copper, iron, silver, zinc and petroleum are the chief minerals exploited. Mineral production, 1996 (in 1,000 tonnes): iron, 2,875·6; zinc (1998), 869; copper (1998), 522; lead, 248·8; silver (1998), 1·93; gold (2000), 133 tonnes. Early in 1998 Southern Peru Copper, the country's largest mining company, estimated that 3,000 tonnes of copper production had been lost as a result of flooding caused by El Niño.

Agriculture. There are four natural zones: the Coast strip, with an average width of 80 km; the Sierra or Uplands, formed by the coast range of mountains and the Andes proper; the Montaña or high wooded region which lies on the eastern slopes of the Andes; and the jungle in the Amazon Basin, known as the Selva. Legislation of 1991 permits the unrestricted sale of agricultural land. Workers in co-operatives may elect to form limited liability companies and become shareholders.

Production in 2000 (in 1,000 tonnes): sugarcane, 7,750; potatoes, 3,187; rice, 1,665; plantains, 1,415; maize, 1,271; cassava, 986; onions, 367; oranges, 318; lemons and limes, 310; sweet potatoes, 230; tomatoes, 197; mangoes, 180; barley, 175; seed cotton, 175.

Livestock, 2000: sheep, 14·4m.; cattle, 4·9m.; pigs, 2·8m.; alpacas, 2·6m. (1996); poultry, 81m. Livestock products (in 1,000 tonnes), 2000: poultry meat, 580; beef and veal, 136; pork, bacon and ham, 95; mutton and lamb, 31; milk, 1,048.

Arable land (in 1,000 ha), 1996: 35,381·8, of which 5,477 was given over to agricultural production: 4,314·4 was cultivated, 892·3 was permanent crops and 270·3 was permanent pasture. 29,904·8 ha of arable land was not used for agricultural production, with 16,906·4 natural pasture, 9,053·7 left wild and 3,944·7 was other types of earth. In Nov. 1997 more than 3,000 ha of farmlands were washed away in floods caused by El Niño.

Coca was cultivated in 2000 on approximately 34,000 ha, down from 115,000 ha in 1995.

Forestry. In 1995 the area covered by forests was 67·56m. ha, or 52·8% of the total land area (68·65m. ha and 53·6% in 1990). The forests contain valuable hardwoods; oak and cedar account for about 40%. In 1999 roundwood removals totalled 9·16m. cu. metres.

Fisheries. Sardines and anchovies are caught offshore to be processed into fishmeal, of which Peru is a major producer. Fishing in deeper waters is being developed, subject to government conservation by the imposition of quotas and fishing bans. Total catch in 1999 was 8,429,290 tonnes, almost entirely from sea fishing. In 1995 the catch had a value of US$936·7m. Peru's annual catch is the second largest in the world after that of China. In the first nine months of 1997, 1·3m tonnes of fishmeal was produced, up 3·4% over the same period for 1996.

INDUSTRY

About 70% of industries are located in the Lima/Callao metropolitan area. Production, 1997 (in 1,000 tonnes): cement, 4,300; residual fuel oil, 2,561; distillate fuel oil, 1,869; petrol, 1,175; kerosene, 1,001; prepared animal feeds (1994), 853; sugar (1998), 570; crude steel, 510; beer, 742·8m. litres; cigarettes, 2·8bn. units.

Labour. The labour force in 1996 totalled 8,652,000 (71% males). In 1993, 1,852,800 people worked in agriculture, 1,167,000 in commerce, 783,900 in manufacturing, 599,700 in services, 347,500 in transport, 255,000 in building, 72,200 in mining and 18,700 in electricity production. In 1999 an estimated 7·9% of the workforce was unemployed, up from 5·9% in 1991.

Trade Unions. Trade unions have about 2m. members (approximately 1·5m. in peasant organizations and 500,000 in industrial). The major trade union organization is the *Confederación de Trabajadores del Perú*, which was reconstituted in 1959 after being in abeyance for some years. The other labour organizations recognized by the government are the *Confederación General de Trabajadores del Perú*, the *Confederación Nacional de Trabajadores* and the *Central de Trabajadores de la Revolución Peruana*.

INTERNATIONAL TRADE

An agreement of 1992 gives Bolivia duty-free transit for imports and exports through a corridor leading to the Peruvian Pacific port of Ilo from the Bolivian frontier town of Desaguadero, in return for Peruvian access to the Atlantic via Bolivia's roads and railways. Foreign debt was US$28,560m. in 2000.

Imports and Exports. Trade in US$1m.:

	1996	1997	1998	1999	2000
Imports f.o.b.	7,884	8,554	8,219	6,749	7,349
Exports f.o.b.	5,898	6,831	5,757	6,116	7,026

In 1996 the main export markets (in US$1m.) were: USA, 1,154·4; UK, 424·2; China, 419·4; Japan, 388·0; Germany, 300·7. Main import suppliers: USA, 1,858·4; Colombia, 633·2; Venezuela, 528·7; Brazil, 328·6; Japan, 317·8. Main exports, 1996 (in US$1m): fishmeal, 834·9; refined copper, 715·6; gold, 579·3; zinc, 273·3. By 1999 gold had become the leading export, shipping 128 tonnes worth US$1·19bn.

COMMUNICATIONS

Roads. In 1998 there were 78,034 km of roads, of which about 13% were paved. By the end of March 1998, 700 km of road had been affected by El Niño. In 1998 there were 1,032,465 registered motor vehicles, including 645,935 cars, 343,195 lorries and vans and 43,370 buses and coaches. There were 80,961 road accidents in 1997 with 3,216 fatalities.

Rail. Total length (1996), 1,992 km on 1,435- and 914-mm gauges. Passenger-km travelled in 1997 came to 206m. and freight tonne-km to 829m.

Civil Aviation. There is an international airport at Lima (Jorge Chávez International). The national carrier is Aeroperú. In 1996 there were 32 airports. 180 civil aircraft were registered in 1996, of which 87 were in commercial use, 13 were in tourist use and 80 were for private use. In 1998 services were also provided by the domestic airlines Aero Continente and Trans Perú, and by more than 20 international carriers. In 1999 scheduled airline traffic of Peruvian-based carriers flew 27·2m. km, carrying 1,900,000 passengers (150,000 on international flights). In 2000 Jorge Chávez International handled 4,506,000 passengers (2,258,000 on international flights) and 105,400 tonnes of freight.

Shipping. In 1994 there were 30 sea-going vessels and 519 lake and river craft. In 1998 sea-going shipping totalled 0·27m. GRT (including oil tankers 31,000 GRT). In 1997 vessels totalling 6,693,000 net registered tons entered ports and vessels totalling 5,961,000 NRT cleared.

Telecommunications. Peru had 1,635,900 main telephone lines in 2000, or 63·7 per 1,000 population, and there were 1,050,000 PCs in use (40·9 for every 1,000 persons). There were 990,000 mobile phone subscribers in 1999 and 15,000 fax machines in 1995. In Feb. 2000 there were 400,000 Internet users.

Postal Services. In 1994 there were 836 post offices.

SOCIAL INSTITUTIONS

Justice. The judicial system is a pyramid at the base of which are the justices of the peace who decide minor criminal cases and civil cases involving small sums of money. The apex is the Supreme Court with a president and 12 members; in between are the judges of first instance, who usually sit in the provincial capitals, and the superior courts.

The police had some 85,000 personnel in 1991. The population in penal institutions in 1995 was 20,899 (90 per 100,000 of national population).

Religion. Religious liberty exists, but the Roman Catholic religion is protected by the State, and since 1929 only Roman Catholic religious instruction is permitted in schools, state or private. There were 21·65m. Catholics in 1997 as well as 1,620,000 Protestants and 1,100,000 with other beliefs (mostly non-religious).

Education. Adult literacy was 89·6% in 1999 (male, 94·4%; female, 84·9%). Elementary education is compulsory and free between the ages of 7 and 16; secondary education is also free. In 1997 there were 688,425 children in pre-school education, 4,185,489 pupils in primary (1998) and 1,969,501 in secondary schools. In 1993 the number of students at the 28 state and 23 private universities was 727,200. There were 251,700 students in other forms of further education.

Health. There were 455 hospitals and 1,083 health centres, 23,771 doctors, 7,945 dentists, 15,026 nurses, 5,940 pharmacists and 3,520 midwives in 1992.

Peru made the greatest progress of any country in the reduction of undernourishment during the 1990s. Between 1990–92 and 1997–99 the proportion of undernourished people declined from 41% of the population to 13%.

Welfare. An option to transfer from state social security (IPSS) to privately-managed funds was introduced in 1993.

CULTURE

Broadcasting. Radio broadcasting is conducted by hundreds of national, provincial and local stations grouped in the Asociación de Radiodifusores del Perú and the Unión de Radioemisores de Provincias del Perú. There are 59 TV companies (colour by NTSC). There were 3·06m. TV sets in use and 6·65m. radio receivers in 1997.

Press. There were 74 dailies in 1996 with a combined circulation of 2m.

Tourism. There were 833,000 foreign visitors in 1998 (485,000 in 1995), bringing foreign exchange earnings of US$878m.

DIPLOMATIC REPRESENTATIVES

Of Peru in the United Kingdom (52 Sloane St., London, SW1X 9SP)
Ambassador: Armando Lecaros-de-Cossio.

Of the United Kingdom in Peru (Torre Parque Mar, Piso 22, Avenida Jose Larco 1301, Miraflores, Lima)
Ambassador: Roger D. Hart, CMG.

Of Peru in the USA (1700 Massachusetts Ave., NW, Washington, D.C., 20036)
Ambassador: Roberto Danino.

Of the USA in Peru (PO Box 1995, Lima)
Ambassador: John R. Hamilton.

Of Peru to the United Nations
Ambassador: Oswaldo de Rivero Barreto.

Of Peru to the European Union
Ambassador: José Urrutia Ceruti.

FURTHER READING

Instituto Nacional de Estadística e Informática.—*Anuario Estadistico del Perú.—Perú: Compendio Estadístico*. Annual.—*Boletin de Estadistica Peruana.* Quarterly
Banco Central de Reserva. Monthly Bulletin.—*Renta Nacional del Perú.* Annual, Lima

Cameron, M. A., *Democracy and Authoritarianism in Peru: Political Coalitions and Social Change.* London, 1995
Daeschner, J., *The War of the End of Democracy: Mario Vargas Llosa vs. Alberto Fujimori.* Lima, 1993
Gorriti, Gustavo, (trans. Robin Kirk) *The Shining Path: A History of the Millenarian War in Peru.* Univ. of North Carolina Press, 1999
Stokes, S. C., *Cultures in Conflict: Social Movements and the State in Peru.* California Univ. Press, 1995
Strong, S., *Shining Path.* London, 1993
Vargas Llosa, A., *The Madness of Things Peruvian: Democracy under Siege.* Brunswick (NJ), 1994

National statistical office: Instituto Nacional de Estadística e Informática, Avenida 28 de Julio, 1056 Lima
Website (Spanish only): http://www.inei.gob.pe

PHILIPPINES

Republika ng Pilipinas

Capital: Manila
Population estimate, 2000: 75·65m.
GDP per capita, 2000: (PPP$) 3,971
HDI/world rank: 0·754/77

KEY HISTORICAL EVENTS

Discovered by Magellan in 1521, the Philippine islands were conquered by Spain in 1565 and named after the Spanish king, Philip. In Dec. 1898, following the Spanish-American War, the Philippines were ceded to the USA. The Philippines acquired self-government as a Commonwealth of the USA in March 1934. The islands were occupied by the Japanese from 1942 to 1945. Independence was achieved in July 1946. From independence until 1972 the Philippines were governed under a constitution based largely on the US pattern. In Sept. 1972 President Ferdinand Marcos declared martial law. In May 1980 Benigno Aquino, Jr, the leading opponent of Marcos, was released from prison to go to the USA for medical treatment. He was killed when he returned to the Philippines after three years in exile. At the presidential elections of Feb. 1986 Ferdinand Marcos was opposed by Aquino's widow, Corazón. Aquino became president, Marcos fled the country and a new constitution limiting the president to a single, six-year term in office was ratified in Feb. 1987. Insurgent activities carried out since 1972 by the Moro National Liberation Front (Muslims) were ended by a peace agreement of 2 Sept. 1996 which provides for a Muslim autonomous region in an area of Mindanao island in southern Philippines. The rebellion left more than 120,000 people dead. In Oct. 2000 impeachment proceedings began against President Estrada who was alleged to have received more than US$10·8m. from gambling kickbacks. His impeachment trial collapsed in Jan. 2001 when he was forced from office by mass protests. Subsequently Estrada's supporters tried to force his successor, Gloria Macapagal Arroyo, from office. In Nov. 2001 the fragile peace between the government and Islamic militants was shattered.

TERRITORY AND POPULATION

The Philippines is situated between 21° 25' and 4° 23' N. lat. and between 116° and 127° E. long. It is composed of 7,107 islands and islets, 2,773 of which are named. Approximate land area, 300,000 sq. km (115,830 sq. miles). The largest islands (in sq. km) are Luzon (104,688), Mindanao (94,630), Samar (13,080), Negros (12,710), Palawan (11,785), Panay (11,515), Mindoro (9,735), Leyte (7,214), Cebu (4,422), Bohol (3,865), Masbate (3,269).

The census population in May 2000 was 76,498,735; density, 255·0 per sq. km. In 1999, 57·7% of the population lived in urban areas.

The UN gives a projected population for 2010 of 89·89m.

The area (in 1,000) and population of the 16 regions (from north to south):

Region	Sq. km	2000	Region	Sq. km	2000
Ilocos	12,840	4,200,478	Central Visayas	14,952	5,701,064
Cordillera[1]	18,294	1,365,220	Eastern Visayas	21,432	3,610,355
Cagayan Valley	26,838	2,813,159	Northern Mindanao	14,033	2,747,585
Central Luzon	18,231	8,030,945	Southern Mindanao	27,141	5,189,335
National Capital	636	9,932,560	Central Mindanao	14,373	2,598,210
Southern Tagalog	46,924	11,793,655	Western Mindanao	16,042	3,091,208
Bicol	17,633	4,674,855	Muslim Mindanao[2]	11,638	2,412,159
Western Visayas	20,223	6,208,733	Caraga	18,847	2,095,367

[1]Administrative region. [2]Autonomous region.

City populations (2000 census, in 1,000) are as follows; all on Luzon unless indicated in parenthesis.

Quezon City[1]	2,160	Zamboanga (Mindanao)	600
Manila (the capital)[1]	1,673	Pasig[1]	582
Caloocan[1]	1,233	Makati[1]	524
Davao (Mindanao)	1,147	Valenzuela[2]	521
Cebu (Cebu)	662	Taguig[2]	510

Las Piñas[2]	499	Butuan (Mindanao)	267
Parañaque[2]	489	Mandaue (Cebu)	256
Cagayan de Oro (Mindanao)	462	Navotas[2]	254
Marikina[2]	437	Baguio[1]	250
Bacolod (Negros)	429	Batangas	245
General Santos (Mindanao)	412	Angeles	243
Muntilupa[1]	393	Lipa City	219
Iloilo (Panay)	366	Cabanatuan	218
Pasay[1]	363	San Pablo	205
Malabon[2]	356	Lapu-Lapu (Cebu)	200
Mandaluyong[1]	304	Lucena City	196
Iligan (Mindanao)	285	Olongapo	194

[1]City within Metropolitan Manila. Population of Metro Manila in 1999, 10,546,000.
[2]Municipality within Metropolitan Manila.

Filipino (based on Tagalog) is spoken by 55% of the population, but as a mother tongue by only 27·9%; among the 76 other indigenous languages spoken, Cebuano is spoken as a mother tongue by 24·3% and Ilocano by 9·8%. English is widely spoken. In 2000 some 5·5m. Filipinos were living and working abroad, including 2m. in the USA, 850,000 in Saudi Arabia and 620,000 in Malaysia.

Manila: Metro Manila is a single region composed of four cities and 13 municipalities on the island of Luzon. Though destroyed during World War II, the city has grown to become a huge industrial and commercial centre with a stock exchange, major banks, and large-scale production of textiles and pharmaceuticals.

SOCIAL STATISTICS
Births, 1998, 1,595,257; deaths, 1996, 344,363. Birth rate per 1,000 population (1998), 21·4; death rate (1996), 4·8. Expectation of life at birth, 2000, was 66·3 years for males and 71·6 years for females. Annual population growth rate, 1990–2000, 2·3%. Infant mortality, 1999, 31 per 1,000 live births; fertility rate, 1999, 3·5 births per woman.

CLIMATE
Some areas have an equatorial climate while others experience tropical monsoon conditions, with a wet season extending from June to Nov. Mean temperatures are high all year, with very little variation. Manila. Jan. 77°F (25°C), July 82°F (27·8°C). Annual rainfall 83·3" (2,115·9 mm).

CONSTITUTION AND GOVERNMENT
A new Constitution was ratified by referendum in 1987 with the approval of 78·5% of voters. The head of state is the executive *President*, directly elected for a non-renewable six-year term. Congress consists of a 24-member upper house, the *Senate* (elected for a six-year term by proportional representation, half of them renewed every three years), and a *House of Representatives* of 250 members.

A campaign led by the president at the time, Fidel Ramos, to amend the constitution to allow him to stand for a second term was voted down by the Senate by 23 to one in Dec. 1996.

National Anthem. 'Land of the Morning', lyric in English by M. A. Sane and C. Osias, tune by Julian Felipe; 'Lupang Hinirang', Tagalog lyric by the Institute of National Language.

RECENT ELECTIONS
At the presidential elections on 11 May 1998 Joseph Estrada, a former movie actor, received 46·4% of the votes cast against seven opponents. The electorate was 32,674,959. Elections to the House of Representatives were also held on 11 May 1998. 110 out of a total of 221 seats went to Laban ng Masang Pilipino (Party of the Philippine Masses), 50 to Lakas ng Edsa (National Union of Christian Democrats and United Muslim Democratic Party alliance), 15 to the Nationalist People's Coalition, 14 to the Partido Liberal and 7 to Laban ng Demokratikong Pilipino (Philippine Democratic Party). The other 26 seats were shared among party list representatives, non-partisans and others or were vacant. Senate elections were also most recently held on 11 May 1998, following which Laban ng Masang Pilipino had 10 seats, Lakas ng Edsa 7, non-partisans and others 6 with 1 vacant.

CURRENT ADMINISTRATION

President: Gloria Macapagal-Arroyo; b. 1947 (sworn in 20 Jan. 2001). Her father, Diosdado Macapagal, had been president from 1961 to 1965.

In March 2003 the government comprised:

Vice-President: Teofisto Guingona.

Minister of Justice: Simeon Datumanong. *National Defence:* Angelo Reyes. *Trade and Industry:* Manuel Roxas. *Finance:* Jose Camacho. *Agriculture:* Luis Lorenzo. *Foreign Affairs:* Blas Ople. *Public Works and Highways:* Bayani Fernando. *Energy:* Vicente Perez. *Education, Culture and Sports:* Edilberto de Jesus. *Labour and Employment:* Patricia Santo Thomas. *Health:* Manuel Dayrit. *Agrarian Reform:* Roberto Pagdanganan. *Tourism:* Richard Gordon. *Budget and Management:* Emilia Boncodin. *Transport and Communications:* Leandro Mendoza. *Science and Technology:* Estrella Alabastro. *Environment and Natural Resources:* Elisea Gozun. *Social Welfare and Development:* Corazon Soliman. *Socio-Economic Planning:* Romulo Neri. *Interior and Local Government:* Jose Lina.

Executive Secretary: Alberto Romulo.

Government Website: http://www.gov.ph/

DEFENCE

An extension of the 1947 agreement granting the USA the use of several army, navy and air force bases was rejected by the Senate in Sept. 1991. An agreement of Dec. 1994 authorizes US naval vessels to be repaired in Philippine ports. The Philippines is a signatory of the South-East Asia Collective Defence Treaty.

Defence expenditure in 2000 totalled US$1,497m. (US$20 per capita), representing 1·9% of GDP.

Army. The Army is organized into five area joint-service commands.

Strength (1999) 73,000, with reserves totalling 100,000. The paramilitary Philippines National Police numbered 40,500 in 1999 with a further 62,000 auxiliaries.

Navy. The Navy consists principally of ex-US ships completed in 1944 and 1945, and serviceability and spares are a problem. The modernization programme in progress has been revised and delayed, but the first 30 inshore patrol craft of US and Korean design have been delivered. The present fleet includes one ex-US frigate.

Navy personnel in 1999 was estimated at 20,500 including 8,500 marines.

Air Force. The Air Force had a strength of 16,500 in 1999, with 42 combat aircraft and 97 armed helicopters. Its fighter-bomber wing is equipped with one squadron of F-5As (only three or four operational).

INTERNATIONAL RELATIONS

The Philippines is a member of the UN, WTO, Asian Development Bank, ASEAN, APEC, the Colombo Plan and IOM.

ECONOMY

Agriculture accounted for 16·9% of GDP in 1998, industry 31·6% and services 51·5%.

Overview. In 1992–95 most state industrial assets were privatized. In 1996 a 'third wave' of privatization was initiated involving state pensions and social security funds. Monopolies have been dismantled in the telecommunication, oil, civil aviation, shipping, water and power industries. In Dec. 1997 a comprehensive tax reform was approved, setting an exemption level of 98,400 pesos for a family of six.

Currency. The unit of currency is the *peso* (PHP) of 100 *centavos.* Inflation was 6·1% in 2001. Foreign exchange reserves were US$14,163m. in June 2002 and gold reserves 8·22m. troy oz (3·58m. troy oz in 1995). Total money supply in April 2002 was 410,581m. pesos.

Budget. Total government revenue and expenditure (in 1m. pesos), year ending 31 Dec.:

	1995	1996	1997	1998	1999	2000
Revenue	360,232	409,880	470,105	462,119	478,210	513,386
Expenditure	341,726	401,017	467,319	511,398	585,435	645,804

Expenditure (1998) included (in 1,000m. pesos): social services, 178·4; economic services, 141·5; general public administration, 97·6; defence, 42·7.

Total internal public debt was 809,900m. pesos in 1998.

Performance. Total GDP in 2001 was US$71·4bn. Real GDP growth was 4·4% in 2000 and 3·2% in 2001, and an estimated 4·6% in 2002.

Banking and Finance. The Central Bank (*Chairman*, Rafael Buenaventura) issues the currency, manages foreign exchange reserves and supervises the banking system. At 30 June 1999 there were 41 commercial banks, 12 foreign banks, 36 building societies, 41 private development banks, 43 stock savings and loan associations and 819 rural banks. In June 1995 the total number of banking institutions was 5,269, with total assets of 1,509,600m. pesos and total deposits of 860,900m. pesos.

There is a stock exchange in Manila.

The financial crisis that struck southeast Asia in 1997 led to the floating of the peso in July. It subsequently lost 36% of its value against the dollar.

The Philippines was 1 of 15 countries and territories named in a report in June 2000 as failing to co-operate in the fight against international money laundering. The Financial Action Task Force on Money Laundering was set up by the G7 group of major industrialized nations.

Weights and Measures. The metric system was established by law in 1869 and since 1916 has come into general use, but there are local units including the picul (63·25 kg) for sugar and fibres, and the cavan (16·5 gallons) for cereals.

ENERGY AND NATURAL RESOURCES

Environment. According to the *World Bank Atlas* carbon dioxide emissions in 1998 were the equivalent of 1·0 tonnes per capita.

Electricity. Total installed capacity was 11,636 MW in 1997. Production was 39·62bn. kWh in 1998. Consumption per capita was 563 kWh in 1999.

Oil and Gas. The discovery in 1997 of a gas field off the island of Palawan is expected to yield up to 73·6bn. cu. metres of natural gas. It is estimated that reserves of approximately 960bn. cu. metres are waiting to be discovered. Natural gas reserves in 1997 were 109bn. cu. metres.

Crude petroleum reserves were 213m. bbls. in 1997.

Water. Water production in 1997 was 997m. cu. metres and water consumption 230m. cu. metres. Breakdown of water consumption: industrial, 89m. cu. metres; residential, 82m. cu. metres; and commercial, 59m. cu. metres.

Minerals. Mineral production in 1998 (in tonnes): silica sand, 1,550,000; coal, 1,157,000; salt, 728,000; nickel ore (1997), 567,616; copper, 177,800; chromite refractory ore, 19,700; gold, 34,000 kg; silver, 18,200 kg. Other minerals include rock asphalt, sand and gravel. Total value of mineral production, 1998, 36,829m. pesos.

Agriculture. Agriculture is a mainstay of the economy, contributing up to 30% of national output. In 1998 there were approximately 5·5m. ha of arable land and 4·4m. ha of permanent crops. In Oct. 1995, 12,465,340 persons were employed in agriculture (44·5% of the working population). In the period 1990–97 agriculture grew on average by 1·9% a year, but in 1998 contracted by 6·6%.

Output (in 1,000 tonnes) in 2000: sugarcane, 33,732; rice, 12,415; coconuts, 5,761; maize, 4,486; bananas, 4,156; copra, 2,000; cassava, 1,771; pineapples, 1,524. The output of copra is the highest of any country in the world. Minor crops are fruits, nuts, vegetables, coffee, cacao, peanuts, ramie, rubber, maguey, kapok, abaca and tobacco.

Livestock, 2000: buffaloes, 3·02m.; cattle, 2·55m.; pigs, 10·40m.; goats, 6·78m.; poultry, 142m.

Forestry. Forests covered 6·7m. ha (22·7% of the land area) in 1995, compared to 8·08m. ha and 27·1% in 1990. Approximately two-thirds of the total forest area is timberland. Timber production was 43·4m. cu. metres in 1999.

Fisheries. The catch in 1999 was 1,870,450 tonnes (83% from marine waters).

INDUSTRY
Leading sectors are foodstuffs, oil refining and chemicals. Production, 1997 (in 1,000 tonnes): cement, 14,671; residual fuel oil, 6,849; distillate fuel oil, 5,385; sugar (1998), 1,549; paper and paperboard (1998), 613; plywood, 367.

Labour. In 2000 the total workforce was 30,911,000, of whom 27,453,000 were employed (17,271,000 in non-agricultural work). Employees by sector, 2000: 12·8m. in services, 10·2m. in agriculture, forestry and fisheries, 2·7m. in manufacturing, 2·0m. in transport and communications and 1·5m. in construction. 3·5m. persons were registered unemployed in 2000. 669,188 persons worked overseas as of Sept. 2000.

The unemployment rate in 2000 was 11·2%.

Trade Unions. In the third quarter of 2000 there were 10,217 unions with a total membership of 3,778,000.

INTERNATIONAL TRADE
Foreign debt totalled US$50,063m. in 2000. A law of June 1991 gave foreign nationals the right to full ownership of export and other firms, considered strategic for the economy.

Imports and Exports. Values of imports and exports in US$1m.:

	1996	1997	1998	1999	2000
Imports f.o.b.	31,885	36,355	29,524	29,252	30,381
Exports f.o.b.	20,543	25,228	29,496	34,210	37,298

Principal exports: electronics, garments, coconut oil, woodcraft and furniture, ignition wiring sets. In 1999 electronics exports were worth US$20bn.; in 1998 they constituted 68% of all exports. In 1992 they had been worth just US$3bn.

Main imports: electronics and components, mineral fuels, lubricants and related materials, industrial machinery and equipment, telecommunications equipment, transport equipment.

Main export markets, 1998: USA, 34·9%; Japan, 16·6%; Singapore, 6·4%. Main sources of import: Japan, 20·6%; USA, 19·9%; Singapore, 6·0%.

COMMUNICATIONS
Roads. In 1998 roads totalled 199,950 km; of these, 28,162 km were national roads and 50,086 km were regional roads. In 1999, 3,533,700 motor vehicles were registered, including 773,800 passenger cars, 243,400 trucks, 33,200 buses and 1,144,700 motorcycles. In 1997 there were 2,049 fatalities in road accidents (645 in 1996).

Rail. In 1995 the National Railways totalled 429 km (1,067 mm gauge). In 1997 passenger-km totalled 171·6m. There is a light railway in Manila.

Civil Aviation. There are international airports at Manila (Ninoy Aquino) and Cebu (Mactan International). In Sept. 1998 the Asian economic crisis forced the closure of the national carrier, Philippine Airlines, after it had suffered huge losses. However, it has in the meantime resumed its operations both internally and externally. In 1999 scheduled airline traffic of Philippine-based carriers flew 53·0m. km, carrying 5,004,000 passengers (1,922,000 on international flights). In 2000 Manila handled 12,668,000 passengers (7,130,000 on international flights) and 399,500 tonnes of freight.

Shipping. In 1998 there were 407 ports; the main ones are Manila, Cebu, Iloilo and Zamboanga. In 1998 merchant shipping totalled 8,508,000 GRT, including oil tankers 162,000 GRT. North Harbour, in Manila, handled more than half of all cargo entering or leaving the Philippines in 1998 and 44% of container traffic. The former president, Joseph Estrada, made the privatization of the country's ports a major priority.

Telecommunications. Main telephone lines numbered 3,061,400 in 2000, or 40·0 per 1,000 inhabitants, and there were 1·5m. PCs in use (equivalent to 19·3 for every 1,000 persons). In March 2001 there were 4·1m. mobile phone subscribers and in Dec. 2000 approximately 2m. Internet users. In 1995 there were 35,000 fax machines.

Postal Services. In 1995 there were 1,948 post offices.

SOCIAL INSTITUTIONS

Justice. There is a Supreme Court which is composed of a chief justice and 14 associate justices; it can declare a law or treaty unconstitutional by the concurrent votes of the majority sitting. There is a Court of Appeals, which consists of a presiding justice and 50 associate justices. There are 15 regional trial courts, one for each judicial region, with a presiding regional trial judge in its 720 branches. There is a metropolitan trial court in the Metropolitan Manila Area, a municipal trial court in each of the other cities or municipalities and a municipal circuit trial court in each area defined as a municipal circuit comprising one or more cities and/or one or more municipalities.

The Supreme Court may designate certain branches of the regional trial courts to handle exclusively criminal cases, juvenile and domestic relations cases, agrarian cases, urban land reform cases which do not fall under the jurisdiction of quasijudicial bodies and agencies and/or such other special cases as the Supreme Court may determine. The death penalty, abolished in 1987, was restored in 1993 for 13 offences. No-one can be executed until a year after final appeal. In Feb. 1999 a rapist was executed, ending the *de facto* ban on capital punishment which had been in place since 1976.

In 1994 there were 96,365 police. Local police forces are supplemented by the Philippine Constabulary, which is part of the armed forces.

In 1997 the prison population was 19,541 (30 per 100,000 of national population).

Constabulary. Since 1990 public order has been maintained completely by the Philippine National Police. Qualified Philippine Constabulary personnel were absorbed by the PNP or were transferred to branches or services of the Armed Forces of the Philippines.

Religion. In 1990 there were 50,217,801 Roman Catholics, 3,287,355 Protestants, 2,769,643 Muslims, 1,590,208 Aglipayans, 1,414,393 Iglesia ni Kristo, 323,789 Born Again Christians and 736,239 members of other religions. There were 398,000 Latter-day Saints (Mormons) in 1998.

The Roman Catholics are organized with 3 cardinals, 23 archbishoprics, 91 bishoprics, 79 diocese, 2,328 parishes and some 20,873 chapels or missions.

Education. Public elementary education is free and schools are established almost everywhere. The majority of secondary and post-secondary schools are private. Formal education consists of an optional one to two years of pre-school education; six years of elementary education; four years of secondary education; and four to five years of tertiary or college education leading to academic degrees. Three-year post-secondary non-degree technical/vocational education is also considered formal education. In 1998–99 there were 8,647 pre-school institutions (3,183 private) with, in 1990–91, 9,644 teachers. In 1998–99 there were 39,011 elementary schools (3,394 private) with 328,517 teachers; 7,021 secondary schools (1,330 private) with 108,981 teachers; and 1,383 tertiary schools (1,118 private). In 1998–99 there were 525,000 pupils in pre-school, 12,474,000 pupils in elementary schools, 5,066,000 in secondary schools; and in 2000, 2,347,204 students in tertiary education.

Non-formal education consists of adult literacy classes, agricultural and farming training programmes, occupation skills training, youth clubs, and community programmes of instructions in health, nutrition, family planning and co-operatives.

In 1994–95 in the public sector there were 20 universities, 1 technological university, 1 polytechnic and 1 technological institute, and 123 other institutions of higher education. In the private sector there were 49 universities, 4 specialized universities (1 Christian; 1 Roman Catholic; 1 medical; 1 for women) and 405 other institutions of higher education.

The adult literacy rate in 1999 was 95·1% (95·3% among males and 94·9% among females).

In 1997 total expenditure on education came to 3·4% of GNP and 15·7% of total government spending.

Health. In 1998 there were 1,713 hospitals (1,097 private) with 81,200 beds (1·1 beds per 1,000 inhabitants). In 1997 there were 1,370 dentists, 4,096 nurses and 13,275 midwives. In 1993 there were 76,913 doctors.

Welfare. The Social Security System (SSS) is a contributory scheme for employees. Disbursements in 1994 (in 1m. pesos): SSS (sickness, maternity, disability, survivors'; benefits), 14,861; medicare (hospitalization), 1,754; employees' compensation (occupational accidents or sickness), 596.

CULTURE

Broadcasting. In 1998 there were 539 AM and FM radio stations and 137 television stations (colour by NTSC). There were 3·7m. TV sets in use and 11·5m. radio receivers in 1997.

Cinema. In 1998 there were 1,046 cinemas with a seating capacity of 611,214. 456 full-length films were made in 1995.

Press. There were 47 daily newspapers in 1996, with a combined circulation of 5,700,000, equivalent to 82 per 1,000 inhabitants. In 1996 a total of 1,507 book titles were published.

Tourism. In 1999, 2,170,514 foreign visitors brought foreign exchange receipts of US$2,413m. (US$2,831m. in 1997).

DIPLOMATIC REPRESENTATIVES

Of the Philippines in the United Kingdom (9A Palace Green, London, W8 4QE)
Ambassador: César Bautista.

Of the United Kingdom in the Philippines (Floors 15–17, LV Locsin Building, 6752 Ayala Ave., Makati, Metro Manila)
Ambassador: Paul Dimond.

Of the Philippines in the USA (1600 Massachusetts Ave., NW, Washington, D.C., 20036)
Ambassador: Albert F. del Rosario.

Of the USA in the Philippines (1201 Roxas Blvd., Manila)
Ambassador: Francis Joseph Ricciardone, Jr.

Of the Philippines to the United Nations
Ambassador: Enrique A. Manalo.

Of the Philippines to the European Union
Ambassador: Clemencio Montesa.

FURTHER READING

National Statistics Office. *Philippine Statistical Yearbook.*
Boyce, J. K., *The Political Economy of Growth and Impoverishment in the Marcos Era.* London, 1993
Hamilton-Paterson, J., *America's Boy: The Marcoses and the Philippines.* Granta, London, 1998
Kerkvliet, B. J. and Mojares, R. B. (eds.) *From Marcos to Aquino: Local Perspectives on Political Transition in the Philippines.* Hawaii Univ. Press, 1992
Larkin, J. A., *Sugar and the Origins of Modern Philippine Society.* California Univ. Press, 1993
Vob, R. and Yap, J. T., *The Philippine Economy: East Asia's Stray Cat? Structure, Finance and Adjustment.* London and The Hague, 1996

National statistical office: National Statistics Office, POB 779, Manila
Website: http://www.census.gov.ph

POLAND

Rzeczpospolita Polska

Capital: Warsaw
Population estimate, 2000: 38·64m
GDP per capita, 2000: (PPP$) 9,051
HDI/world rank: 0·833/37

KEY HISTORICAL EVENTS

Poland takes its name from the Polanie ('plain dwellers'), whose ruler Mieszko I had achieved a federation by 966, a date taken as that of the foundation of the Polish state. He placed Poland under the Roman Holy See around 990. His son Bolesław I (992–1025) continued his father's territorial expansionism until by the time of his coronation in 1024 Poland's boundaries were much as they are today. The tendency of this state to fragment under German pressure was formalized by Bolesław III (1102–38), whose sons divided the kingdom into three duchies. In the 13th century Poland was laid waste by pagan proto-Russians and Mongols. In 1320 Władysław of Kraków was crowned king of Poland. The work of unification was consolidated by his son, Kazimierz III (1333–70). A descendant of his married the pagan duke of Lithuania, Jagiełło, who was converted to Catholicism and became king of Poland in 1386, uniting Poland and Lithuania in a vast multi-ethnic empire. The Jagiełłonian period to 1572 is regarded as an economic and cultural 'golden age'.

In 1648 a Cossack revolt in Ukraine resulted in a Russian victory and soon afterwards Sweden occupied and devastated the whole country. Poland's involvement in the Russo-Swedish wars of 1700–09 brought further economic ruin and political dependence on the might of Peter the Great. In the 'First Partition' of 1772 Russia and Prussia in conjunction with Austria took over a third of Poland's territory. Poland was wiped off the map by the Second and Third partitions (1793, 1795), except for a brief independent interlude under Napoleon.

Risings in 1830, 1846, 1848 and 1863 were unsuccessful. Thereafter nationalist efforts were channelled more into cultural and economic development. After the First World War, Poland was promised independence and access to the sea. A constitution was voted in March 1921. Poland's frontiers were not established until 1923 after plebiscites in Silesia and East Prussia and a war with Soviet Russia in 1920 which Poland nearly lost. In foreign affairs Poland attempted to maintain a balance between Germany and the USSR, but after Munich it accepted a British guarantee of its independence. In Aug. 1939 Hitler signed a non-aggression pact with Stalin which provided for a partition of Poland; this took place a few days after the outbreak of war.

Poland was rapidly overrun but Polish forces were able to reform on Allied soil under a government-in-exile. Subsequently, Moscow recognized the Polish Committee of National Liberation (the 'Lublin committee') which proclaimed itself the sole legal government when Lublin was liberated in July 1944. In Aug. and Sept. the Soviet army stopped short of the city while the resistance forces were destroyed in the Warsaw uprising. Elections held on 19 Jan. 1947 led to victory for the Communist-dominated 'Democratic Bloc'.

After riots in Poznań in June 1956 nationalist anti-Stalinist elements gained control of the Communist Party under the leadership of Władysław Gomułka. The raising of meat prices on 1 July 1980 resulted in a wave of strikes which broadened into generalized wage demands. Workers in Gdańsk, Gdynia and Sopot elected a joint strike committee, led by Lech Wałęsa, to demand the right to strike and to form independent trade unions, the abolition of censorship, access to the media and the release of political prisoners. On 17 Sept. various trade unions decided to form a national confederation ('Solidarity'). On 13 Dec. 1981 the Government imposed martial law and set up a Military Council of National Salvation. Solidarity was proscribed. Following strikes and demands for the reinstatement of Solidarity, the government resigned in Sept. 1988. Free parliamentary elections were instituted in Oct. 1991.

Poland joined NATO in 1999. In Oct. 2002 Poland was one of ten countries included in plans for EU enlargement scheduled for 2004.

TERRITORY AND POPULATION

Poland is bounded in the north by the Baltic Sea and Russia, east by Lithuania, Belarus and Ukraine, south by the Czech Republic and Slovakia and west by Germany. Poland comprises an area of 312,685 sq. km (120,628 sq. miles).

At the census of 7 Dec. 1988 the population was 37,879,000 (18·47m. males; 63·7% urban). Population in 2001, 38,632,000 (51·4% female and 65·2% urban in 1999), density, 123·5 per sq. km.

The UN gives a projected population for 2010 of 38·25m.

The country is divided into 16 regions or voivodships (*wojewodztwo*), created from the previous 49 on 1 Jan. 1999 following administrative reform. Area (in sq. km) and population (in 1,000) in 2001 (density per sq. km in brackets).

Voivodship	Area	Population	
Dolnośląskie	19,948	2,970	(149)
Kujawsko-Pomorskie	17,970	2,102	(117)
Lubelskie	25,114	2,228	(89)
Lubuskie	13,984	1,024	(73)
Łódzkie	18,219	2,633	(145)
Małopolskie	15,144	3,241	(214)
Mazowieckie	35,598	5,079	(143)
Opolskie	9,412	1,080	(115)
Podkarpackie	17,926	2,131	(119)
Podlaskie	20,180	1,220	(60)
Pomorskie	18,293	2,204	(120)
Śląskie	12,294	4,830	(393)
Świętokrzyskie	11,672	1,320	(113)
Warmińsko-Mazurskie	24,203	1,469	(61)
Wielkopolskie	29,826	3,366	(113)
Zachodniopomorskie	22,902	1,734	(76)

Population (in 1,000) of the largest towns and cities (1999):

Warsaw	1,618·4	Lublin	356·3	Gliwice	212·1
Łódź	810·6	Katowice	345·9	Toruń	206·2
Kraków (Cracow)	740·7	Białystok	283·9	Bytom	205·6
Wrocław (Breslau)	637·9	Częstochowa	257·8	Zabrze	200·2
Poznań	578·2	Gdynia	253·5	Bielsko-Biała	180·3
Gdańsk	459·0	Sosnowiec	244·1	Olsztyn	170·9
Szczecin (Stettin)	417·0	Radom	232·2	Rzeszów	162·0
Bydgoszcz	386·9	Kielce	212·3	Ruda Śląska	159·7

Warsaw: Lying in the east on the River Vistula, Warsaw became the capital city of Poland when fire destroyed the King's Kraków residence in 1596. It has had a mercurial history, suffering from partition in 1795, Nazi occupation from 1939–45 and the overbearing influence of the Soviet Union. Since the fall of the Iron Curtain in 1989, however, Warsaw has grown as a communications centre and has a burgeoning tourist industry.

Ethnic minorities are not identified. There were estimated to be 1·2m. Germans in 1984, and there are Ukrainians, Belorussians and Lithuanians. A movement for Silesian autonomy has attracted sufficient support to suggest that further moves towards decentralization may soon be considered. A Council of National Minorities was set up in March 1991. There is a large Polish diaspora, some 65% in the USA.

The national language is Polish.

SOCIAL STATISTICS

2001 (in 1,000): births, 368·2; deaths, 363·2; marriages, 195·1; divorces, 45·3; infant deaths, 2·8. Rates (per 1,000 population): birth, 9·5; death, 9·4; marriage (per 1,000 population), 5·0; divorce, 1·2; infant mortality (per 1,000 live births), 7·7. A law prohibiting abortion was passed in 1993, but an amendment of Aug. 1996 permits it in cases of hardship or difficult personal situation. The average age for first marrying in 1998 was 23·4 years for females and 24·8 years for males. Expectation of life at birth, 1999, was 69·0 years for males and 77·3 years for females. In 1998 there were 22,200 emigrants (including 16,100 to Germany) and 8,900 immigrants. 71% of Polish emigrants between 1990 and 1998 settled in Germany. Number of suicides, 1997, 4,936; in 1996 the suicide rate per 100,000 population was 24·1 among males and 4·6 among females. Annual population growth rate, 1990–99, 0·2%; fertility rate, 1999, 1·5 births per woman.

CLIMATE
Climate is continental, marked by long and severe winters. Rainfall amounts are moderate, with a marked summer maximum. Warsaw, Jan. 24°F (−4·3°C), July 64°F (17·9°C). Annual rainfall 18·3" (465 mm). Gdańsk, Jan. 29°F (−1·7°C), July 63°F (17·2°C). Annual rainfall 22·0" (559 mm). Kraków, Jan. 27°F (−2·8°C), July 67°F (19·4°C). Annual rainfall 28·7" (729 mm). Poznań, Jan. 26°F (−3·3°C), July 64°F (17·9°C). Annual rainfall 21·0" (534 mm). Szczecin, Jan. 27°F (−3·0°C), July 64°F (17·7°C). Annual rainfall 18·4" (467 mm). Wrocław, Jan. 24°F (−4·3°C), July 64°F (17·9°C). Annual rainfall 20·7" (525 mm).

CONSTITUTION AND GOVERNMENT
The present Constitution was adopted on 2 April 1997. The head of state is the *President*, who is directly elected for a five-year term (renewable once). The President may appoint, but may not dismiss, cabinets.

The authority of the republic is vested in the *Sejm* (Parliament of 460 members), elected by proportional representation for four years by all citizens over 18. There is a 5% threshold for parties and 8% for coalitions, but seats are reserved for representatives of ethnic minorities even if their vote falls below 5%. 69 of the Sejm seats are awarded from the national lists of parties polling more than 7% of the vote. The Sejm elects a *Council of State* and a *Council of Ministers*. There is also an elected 100-member upper house, the *Senate*. The President and the Senate each has a power of veto which only a two-thirds majority of the Sejm can override. The President does not, however, have a veto over the annual budget. The Prime Minister is chosen by the President with the approval of the Sejm.

A Political Council consultative to the presidency consisting of representatives of all the major political tendencies was set up in Jan. 1991.

National Anthem, 'Jeszcze Polska nie zginęła' ('Poland has not yet perished'); words by J. Wybicki, tune by M. Ogiński.

RECENT ELECTIONS
At the presidential elections on 8 Oct. 2000, 12 candidates stood; the electorate was 29,122,304 and turn-out was 61·0%. President Aleksander Kwaśniewski of the former communist Democratic Left Alliance (SLD) gained 53·9% of votes cast, Andrzej Olechowski (independent) 17·3% and Marian Krzaklewski of Solidarity Electoral Action (AWS) 15·6%. Other candidates obtained 6% or less.

Parliamentary elections were held on 23 Sept. 2001. The coalition of the Democratic Left Alliance (SLD) and the Union of Labour (UP) won 216 out of 460 seats with 41·0% of the votes. Other parties winning seats were: Citizen's Platform (PO), with 65 seats (12·7%); Self-Defense of the Polish Republic (S), 53 (10·2%); Law and Justice Party (PiS), 44 (9·5%); Polish People's Party (PSL), 42 (9·0%); League of Polish Families (LPR), 38 (7·9%); German Minority (MN), 2 (0·4%). In the Senate, the coalition of the Democratic Left Alliance and the Union of Labour won 75 seats, with the Blok Senat 2001 winning 15. The remaining eight seats were taken by other parties. Turn-out was 46·3%

CURRENT ADMINISTRATION
President: Aleksander Kwaśniewski; b. 1954 (SLD; elected Nov. 1995 and re-elected Oct. 2000).

In March 2003 the government, which was formed by the SLD, UP and PSL, collapsed when Prime Minister Leszek Miller ejected the Polish People's Party after it voted in parliament against a government measure to levy a tax to improve the country's roads. As a result the coalition of SLD and UP consisted of:
Prime Minister: Leszek Miller; b. 1946 (SLD; sworn in 19 Oct. 2001).

Deputy Prime Minister and Minister of Infrastructure: Marek Pol (UP). *Deputy Prime Minister and Minister of Finance:* Grzegorz Kolodko (ind.). *Agriculture and Rural Development:* Adam Tański (ind.). *Culture and National Heritage:* Waldemar Dąbrowski (ind.). *Economy, Labour and Social Policy:* Jerzy Hausner (SLD). *Education:* Krystyna Łybacka (SLD). *Environment:* Czesław Śleziak (SLD). *Foreign Affairs:* Włodzimierz Cimoszewicz (SLD). *Health:* Marek Balicki (SLD). *Internal Affairs and Administration:* Krzysztof Janik (SLD). *Justice:* Grzegorz Kurczuk (SLD). *National Defence:* Jerzy Szmajdziński (SLD). *Science:* Michał

Kleiber (ind.). *Treasury:* Sławomir Cytrycki (ind.). *Office of the Prime Minister:* Marek Wagner (SLD). *Spokesman for the Government:* Michał Tober (SLD). *Minister Without Portfolio:* Lech Nikolski (SLD).
Speaker of the Sejm: Marek Borowski (SLD).

Office of the Prime Minister: http://www.kprm.gov.pl

DEFENCE
Poland is divided into four military districts: Warsaw, Pomerania, Kraków and Silesia. In 2000 military expenditure totalled US$3,191m. (US$82 per capita), representing 2·0% of GDP.

Three-year civilian duty as a conscientious alternative to conscription of 12 months was introduced in 1988.

Army. Strength (1999) 142,500 (including 101,670 conscripts). In accordance with a programme of modernization of the armed forces, the land component of the Army is expected to reach a final number of around 108,000 soldiers. In addition there were 343,000 Army reservists in 1999 and 13,500 border guards.

Navy. The fleet comprises 3 ex-Soviet diesel submarines, 1 ex-Soviet destroyer, 1 small frigate and 4 corvettes. Naval Aviation operated 23 combat aircraft (including MiG-21s) and 11 armed helicopters.

Personnel in 1999 totalled 17,100 including 9,500 conscripts and 2,460 in Naval Aviation. Bases are at Gdynia, Hel, Świnoujście and Kolobrzeg.

Air Force. The Air Force had a strength (1999) of 55,300 (30,430 conscripts). There are 7 air defence regiments (16 squadrons) with 297 combat aircraft (including MiG-21/23/29s and Su-22s) and 32 attack helicopters.

INTERNATIONAL RELATIONS
A treaty of friendship with Germany signed on 17 June 1991 renounced the use of force, recognized Poland's western border as laid down at the Potsdam conference of 1945 (the 'Oder-Neisse line') and guaranteed minority rights in both countries.

Poland is a member of the UN, WTO, BIS, the Council of Europe, NATO, OECD, OSCE, CEFTA, CERN, CEI, Council of the Baltic Sea States, IOM, the Antarctic Treaty, an associate partner of the WEU and an associate member of the EU. Poland became a member of NATO on 12 March 1999. A European Commission report endorsed in Dec. 1999 named Poland (along with Hungary) as the country from central and eastern Europe most likely to be the first to join the EU. There is expected to be a referendum on EU membership in late 2003, with Poland scheduled to become a member on 1 May 2004.

ECONOMY
Poland is fast becoming two nations, one of relatively well-off city dwellers and one of poor villagers, many of whom work on family farms. An east–west divide has also been emerging, with the west benefiting from its close ties to Germany while the east suffers from its proximity to the much poorer Belarus and Ukraine.

Overview. The Central Planning Office was absorbed by the newly created Economies Ministry in Jan. 1997. An economic plan ran from 1994 to 1997. In 1995, 15 National Investment Funds were set up to oversee the privatization of 444 state enterprises. All citizens may buy shares in the enterprises. As of Dec. 1997, 9,143 enterprises had been privatized, with revenues from privatization totalling US$5·5bn.

Currency. The currency unit is the *złoty* (PLN) of 100 *groszy*. A new złoty was introduced on 1 Jan. 1995 at 1 new złoty = 10,000 old złotys. Inflation dropped from 249% in 1990 to 14·9% in 1997, and further to 5·5% in 2001. The złoty became convertible on 1 Jan. 1990. In 1995 the złoty was subject to a creeping devaluation of 1·2% per month; it was allowed to float in a 14% (+/–7%) band from 16 May 1995. In April 2000 Poland introduced a floating exchange rate. Foreign exchange reserves were US$26,557m. and gold reserves 3·31m. troy oz in June 2002 (0·47m. troy oz in 1996). In Feb. 2002 total money supply was 88,109m. złotys.

Budget. Budget revenue and expenditure (in 1m. złotys):

	1996	1997	1998	1999	2000
Revenue	144,454	172,507	196,952	201,131	213,865
Expenditure	153,047	185,431	207,370	216,685	236,711

Performance. Real GDP growth was 4·1% in 1999 and 4·0% in 2000, although only 1·1% in 2001. Total GDP in 2001 was US$174·6bn. Poland's economy is one of the fastest growing of the ex-communist countries in Europe. Real GDP in 1998 was 17% higher than in 1989. No other ex-communist country has seen such consistent progress. In almost all the other former communist economies, GDP was lower in 1998 than it had been in 1989 at the time of the changes which swept through central and eastern Europe. The private sector accounts for more than 70% of GDP.

Banking and Finance. The National Bank of Poland (established 1945) is the central bank and bank of issue. Its Governor is nominated by the President and approved by the Sejm (*Governor*, Dr Leszek Balcerowicz). There were 73 banks operating at the end of 2000, of which only 7 were controlled—directly or indirectly—by the Polish government through its state treasury. The two largest banks are PKO BP and Pekao, which had assets in 2000 of US$12·2bn. and US$12·0bn. respectively. Other leading banks are Bank Przemysłowo-Handlowy PBK and Bank Handlowy (a member of Citigroup). The General Savings Bank (Powszechna Kasa Oszczędności) exercises central control over savings activities.

In 2000 Poland received US$10,600m. of foreign direct investment, up from just US$89m. in 1990. It receives the most foreign direct investment of any of the former socialist countries of central and eastern Europe. The total stock of FDI at the end of 2000 was US$49·4bn.

There is a stock exchange in Warsaw.

Weights and Measures. The metric system is in general use.

ENERGY AND NATURAL RESOURCES

Environment. Poland's carbon dioxide emissions in 1998 were the equivalent of 8·3 tonnes per capita according to the *World Bank Atlas*.

Electricity. Installed capacity was 33·3m. kW in 2000. Production (2001) 142·76bn. kWh; consumption per capita was 2,458 kWh in 1998.

Oil and Gas. Total oil reserves amount to some 100m. tonnes. Crude oil production was 289,000 tonnes in 1997; natural gas (2001), 5·2m. cu. metres. The largest oil distributor is Polski Koncern Naftowy ORLEN SA, created by the merger of Petrochemia Płock and Centrala Produktów Naftowych, both former state monopolies.

Minerals. Poland is a major producer of coal (reserves of some 120,000m. tonnes), copper (56m. tonnes) and sulphur. Production in 2001 (in tonnes): coal, 103·9m.; brown coal, 59·5m.; copper ore (1999), 523,000 tonnes.

Agriculture. Poland's agriculture sector employed 18·8% of the working population in 2000. In 1997 there were 18·66m. ha of agricultural land, comprising: arable, 14·29m. ha; meadows, 2·42m. ha; pasture, 1·63m. ha; orchards, 0·29m. ha. In 1997, 15·17m. ha were owned by private farmers, 1·37m. ha by state farms and 0·54m. ha by co-operatives. 6·68m. ha were irrigated in 1997. There were 2m. farms in 2000. In 1997 agriculture contributed 6% of GDP.

Some government subsidies and guaranteed prices were restored in 1992.

Output in 2000 (in 1,000 tonnes): potatoes, 24,232; sugarbeets, 13,134; wheat, 8,503; rye, 4,003; barley, 2,783; cabbages, 1,899; apples, 1,450; oats, 1,070.

Livestock, 2001 (in 1m.): cattle, 5·73 (including cows, 3·01); pigs, 17·11. 1997 (in 1m.): sheep, 0·39; horses, 0·54; chickens, 45·18. Milk production (2001) was 7,025m. litres; meat (2000), 2·85m. tonnes; eggs (2000), 425,000 tonnes.

Tractors in use in 1998: 1,310,500 (in 15-h.p. units).

Forestry. In 1997 forest area was 8·80m. ha (predominantly coniferous), or 28·1% of the land area. The area under forests in 1990 had been 8·67m. ha. In 1997, 7·3m. ha were in the public domain and 1·5m. in the private. In 1995, 77,800 ha were afforested. Timber production in 1999 was 23·3m. cu. metres.

Fisheries. The catch was 235,111 tonnes in 1999, of which 221,236 tonnes were sea fish.

INDUSTRY

The leading companies by market capitalization in Poland, excluding banking and finance, in Jan. 2002 were: Telekomunikacja Polska SA (TPSA), 21bn. złotys; Polski Koncern Naftowy Orlen SA (PKN), an oil company (9bn. złotys); and Agora SA, a media company (3bn. złotys).

In March 1996 there were 4,197 state firms, 101,687 limited liability companies, 220,234 other companies and 19,834 co-operatives. Production in 2001 (in 1,000 tonnes): cement, 11,918; steel, 8,814; fertilizers (1997), 7,893; distillate fuel oils (1997), 5,099; residual fuel oil (1997), 4,283; petrol, 4,281; paper and paperboard (1998), 1,640; sugar, 1,543; sulphur, 1,066; plastics (1997), 860; cellulose (1997), 707; vodka, 575; refined copper, 498; cleaning agents (1997), 319; beer, 2,488·6m. litres; mineral water (1996), 1,218·2m. litres; television receivers, 7,481,000 units; tractors, 5,667,000 units; washing machines, 685,000 units; refrigerators and freezers, 589,000 units; telephone sets, 496,000 units; cars, 364,000 units; metalworking machines (1997), 17,200 units; buses, 1,643 units; bricks (1997), 1,156m. units.

Output of light industry in 1997: cotton fabrics, 229m. cu. metres; woollen fabrics, 31·8m. metres; synthetic fibres, 46·2m. metres; silk fabrics, 75,400 tonnes; shoes, 71·8m. pairs.

Restructuring plans were announced in June 1998 aimed at halving within five years the 330,000 workforce employed in the coal and steel industries, with 24 out of 65 coal-mines due to be closed. There has been some privatization in the steel industry.

Labour. In Dec. 1998 the population of working age was 28·38m. (14·92m. females). In 1997 the economically active population was 17,052,000 (7,788,000 females). In Dec. 2001, 3,008,000 persons worked in industry (27·8% of the working population), 2,096,000 in trade and repairs, 916,000 in education, 865,000 in health and social services, 841,000 in property, renting and business activities, 772,000 in construction, and 734,000 in transport, storage and communications. The unemployment rate has been steadily rising in the past few years and was 20·2% in Jan. 2003, compared to the EU average of 7·9%. Workers made redundant are entitled to one month's wages after one year's service, two months after two years' service and three months after three or more years' service. A five-day working week was introduced in May 2001. The number of hours worked—42 until 2000—was reduced to 40 in 2003. Retirement age is 60 for women and 65 for men.

Trade Unions. In 1980 under Lech Wałęsa, Solidarity was an engine of political reform. Dissolved in 1982 it was re-legalized in 1989 and successfully contested the parliamentary elections, but was defeated in 1993. It had 2·3m. members in 1991 and 1·2m. in 1998. The official union in the 1980s, OPZZ, had 5m. members in 1990; there were also about 4,000 small unions not affiliated to it. In 1998 OPZZ had 3m. members, and there were some 340 registered unions nationwide. As 22% of members of parliament belong to the two leading unions, they constitute a significant political influence.

INTERNATIONAL TRADE

Since Jan. 1989 foreign investors have been allowed to own 100% of companies on Polish soil. There were over 30,000 joint ventures in Dec. 1998. Legislation of 1991 removed limits on the repatriation of profits, reduced the number of cases needing licences and ended a 10% ceiling on share purchases. Licenses are required for investment in ports, airports, arms manufacture, estate agency and legal services. In Dec. 1998 foreign investments totalled US$29bn.

Foreign debt was US$63,561m. in 2000.

An agreement of Dec. 1992 with the Czech Republic, Hungary and Slovakia abolished tariffs on raw materials and goods where exports do not compete directly with locally-produced items, and envisaged tariff reductions on agricultural and industrial goods in 1995–97.

POLAND

Imports and Exports. Trade in US$1m.:

	1996	1997	1998	1999	2000
Imports f.o.b.	34,844	40,553	45,303	45,132	48,210
Exports f.o.b.	27,557	30,731	32,467	30,060	35,902

The main commodity exports in 2000 were machines and equipment, electrical and electrotechnical equipment (20·3%); transport equipment (14·3%); non-precious metals and articles (12·8%); and textile fabrics and articles (8·7%). Leading imports were machines and equipment, electrical and electrotechnical equipment (26·7%); mineral products (12·0%); transport equipment (10·4%); and chemical industry products (10·3%).

Main export markets, 2000: Germany, 34·9%; Italy, 6·3%; France, 5·2%; Netherlands, 5·0%; United Kingdom, 4·5%. Main import suppliers, 2000: Germany, 23·9%; Russia, 9·4%; Italy, 8·3%; France, 6·4%; UK, 4·4%. In 2000 trade with the European Union accounted for 70·0% of Polish exports and 61·2% of Polish imports.

Trade Fairs. Over 400 trade fairs took place in Poland in 1998. The majority of firms organizing fairs are associated in *Polska Korporacja Targowa*. The leader of fair organizers is the International Poznań Fairs with 454,353 sq. metres of exhibition area.

COMMUNICATIONS

Roads. In 1998 there were 381,046 km of roads, including 268 km of motorways. In 1999 there were 9,283,000 passenger cars, 1,663,000 lorries and truck-tractors and 79,000 buses; and, in 1998, 1·56m. motorcycles and mopeds. Public road transport carried 1,065m. passengers and 1,110·76m. tonnes of freight in 1997. There were 7,080 road accident fatalities in 1998.

Rail. In 1999 Poland had 22,891 km of railways in use (11,614 km electrified). Over 95% is standard 1,435 mm gauge with the rest narrow gauge. By 2000 PKP, the country's train operator, was 6bn. złotys (US$1·3bn.) in debt. In 2001 railways carried 332·2m. passengers and 166·9m. tonnes of freight. In 1998 revenues totalled 9·6bn. złotys. Some regional railways are operated by local authorities. A 12 km metro opened in Warsaw in 1995, and there are tram/light rail networks in 13 cities.

Civil Aviation. The main international airport is at Warsaw (Okęcie), with some international flights from Kraków (John Paul II Balice International), Gdańsk, Katowice, Poznań, Szczecin and Wrocław. The national carrier is LOT-Polish Airlines (52% state-owned). It flew 49·0m. km in 1999, carrying 2,140,700 passengers (1,791,100 on international flights). In 2000 Warsaw handled 4,325,815 passengers (3,820,330 on international flights) and 39,600 tonnes of freight.

Shipping. The principal ports are Gdańsk, Szczecin, Świnoujście and Gdynia. 47·75m. tonnes of cargo were handled in 2001. Ocean-going services are grouped into Polish Ocean Lines based on Gdynia and operating regular liner services, and the Polish Shipping Company based on Szczecin and operating cargo services. Poland also has a share in the Gdynia America Line. In 1997, 25·48m. tonnes of freight and 583,000 passengers were carried. In 1998 the merchant marine totalled 1,424,000 GRT. 524,000 GRT of shipping completed building in 1995. In 1998 vessels totalling 25,549,000 NRT entered ports and vessels totalling 30,065,000 NRT cleared.

In 1999 there were 3,813 km of navigable inland waterways. 9·34m. tonnes of freight were carried in 1997 (including coastal traffic).

Telecommunications. There were 10,945,600 telephone subscribers in 2000, or 282·4 per 1,000 persons. There were 6·7m. mobile phone subscribers by the end of 2000, compared to 82,000 in 1995. The privatization of *Telekomunikacja Polska* (TP SA), the former state telecom operator, was inaugurated in Nov. 1998 and was completed in 2001.

In 2000 there were 2·7m. PCs (68·9 per 1,000 persons), and in 1995, 55,000 fax machines. The number of Internet users in Oct. 2001 was 6·4m.

Postal Services. In 1999 there were 7,888 post offices. A total of 1,217m. pieces of mail were handled in 1995, or 32 items per person.

SOCIAL INSTITUTIONS

Justice. The penal code was adopted in 1969. Espionage and treason carry the severest penalties. For minor crimes there is provision for probation sentences and fines. In 1995 the death penalty was suspended for five years; it had not been applied since 1988. A new penal code abolishing the death penalty was adopted in June 1997.

There exist the following courts: 1 Supreme Court, 1 high administrative court, 10 appeal courts, 44 voivodship courts, 288 district courts, 66 family consultative centres and 34 juvenile courts. Judges and lay assessors are appointed. Judges for higher courts are appointed by the President of the Republic from candidatures proposed by the National Council of the Judiciary. Assessors are nominated by the Minister of Justice. Judges have life tenure. An ombudsman's office was established in 1987.

Family consultative centres were established in 1977 for cases involving divorce and domestic relations, but divorce suits were transferred to ordinary courts in 1990. 238,391 criminal sentences were passed in 1997. There were 1,093 convictions for murder in 1997. The population in penal institutions in Oct. 1998 was 56,596 (145 per 100,000 of national population).

Religion. Church-State relations are regulated by laws of 1989 which guarantee religious freedom, grant the Church radio and TV programmes and permit it to run schools, hospitals and old age homes. The Church has a university (Lublin), an Academy of Catholic Theology and seminaries. On 28 July 1993 the government signed a Concordat with the Vatican regulating mutual relations. The archbishop of Warsaw is the primate of Poland (since 1981, Cardinal Józef Glemp; b. 1929). The religious capital is Gniezno, whose archbishop will be the future primate. In Oct. 1978 Cardinal Karol Wojtyła, archbishop of Cracow, was elected Pope as John Paul II. In Feb. 2001 there were six Cardinals.

Statistics of major churches as at Dec. 1997:

Church	Congregations	Places of Worship[1]	Clergy	Adherents
Roman Catholic	9,941	17,188	26,911	34,841,893
Uniate	63	101	72	110,380
Old Catholics	149	148	145	50,918
Polish Orthodox	249	3250	292	555,765
Protestant (30 sects)	1,189	865	1,882	159,906
Muslim	10	12	10	5,227
Jewish	24	17	3	1,402
Jehovah's Witnesses	1,692	–	–	122,982

[1]Dec. 1994.

Education. Basic education from 7 to 16 is free and compulsory. Free secondary education is then optional in general or vocational schools. Primary schools are organized in complexes based on wards under one director ('ward collective schools'). In 1997–98 there were: nursery schools, 20,576 with 979,500 pupils and 74,400 teachers; primary schools, 19,299 with 4,896,400 pupils and 308,400 teachers; secondary schools, 1,847 with 757,700 pupils and 38,100 teachers; vocational schools, 7,455 with 1,568,258 pupils and 83,918 teachers; 1,831 tertiary (post-lycée) schools with 190,800 students; and 246 institutions of higher education (including 13 universities, 30 polytechnics, 10 agricultural schools, 93 schools of economics, 19 teachers' training colleges, 16 theological colleges and 11 medical schools) with 1,091,800 students and 73,041 teaching staff. In the 15 years from 1980 to 1995 the number of university students in Poland more than trebled. During the 1990s there was a boom in private higher education—by 1998 a quarter of all students in higher education were at private colleges.

The adult literacy rate in 1999 was 99·7%.

Religious (Catholic) instruction was introduced in all schools in 1990; for children of dissenting parents there are classes in ethics.

In 1997 total expenditure on education came to 5·2% of total government expenditure.

Health. Medical treatment is free and funded from the state budget. Medical care is also available in private clinics. In Dec. 1997 there were 717 hospitals and 48 psychiatric hospitals with 209,961 beds. In 1997 there were 91,121 doctors, 17,869 dentists, 20,139 pharmacists and 215,295 nurses. In Jan. 1999 reform of the health care system was inaugurated. All citizens can now choose their own doctor, who is paid by one of the health-maintenance organizations which are financed directly from the state budget. The share of income tax paid by employers, equalling 7·5% of the amount earned by them, is assigned for the financing of the health care system.

Welfare. Social security benefits are administered by the State Insurance Office and funded 45% by a payroll tax and 55% from the state budget. Pensions, disability payments, child allowances, survivor benefits, maternity benefits, funeral subsidies, sickness compensation and alimony supplements are provided. In 2000 social benefits totalling 108,597·7m. złotys were paid (including 92,680·0m. złotys in retirement pay and pensions). There were a total of 9,412,000 pensioners in 2000. Unemployment benefits are paid from a fund financed by a 3% payroll tax. It is indexed in various categories to the average wage and payable for 12 months. Social assistance is administered and partly-funded by local government. It provides last-resort benefits in cash and kind. A special social security system for independent farmers is administered by the Agricultural Social Security Fund.

CULTURE

Broadcasting. The public *Polskie Radio i Telewizja* broadcasts three radio programmes and two TV programmes. There are also four commercial TV channels, *Polsat, TVN, RTL7* and *Nasza TV*. Colour programmes are transmitted by the PAL system. A direct-to-home satellite pay television service was launched in 1998. A digital TV platform *Wizja TV* started broadcasting in Sept. 1998, followed by *Canal Plus'* digital platform. Links with the West are provided through the Eutelstat satellite. Some cable programmes are broadcast in Polish from abroad. In 1992 independent radio and TV broadcasting were introduced under the aegis of a nine-member National Council of Broadcasting and Television. Radio sets in use in 1997, 20·2m.; TV sets in 1997, 16m.

Cinema. In Dec. 1997 there were 686 cinemas; admissions, 24·33m. 20 full-length films were made in 1997.

Press. In 1996 there were 87 newspapers with an overall daily circulation of 3·87m. and 5,260 periodicals. 14,104 book titles were published in 1996. The most popular newspapers are *Gazeta Wyborcza, Rzeczpospolita* and the tabloid *Super Express*. In 1996 a total of 14,104 book titles were published in 80·31m. copies.

Tourism. There were 17·95m. foreign visitors in 1999 bringing in revenue of US$6·1bn.

Festivals. The most significant festivals are the International Chopin Festival at Duszniki Zdrój, held in Aug., and the Warsaw Autumn Festival, held in Sept. The Kraków 2000 Festival had four main themes—Images of God, Sounds of Eternity, Places of Mystery and Magical Words.

Libraries. In 1997, 9,230 libraries housed 135·87m. books.

Theatre and Opera. The audience in 127 theatres in 1997 was 5·63m. and the 21 opera houses had a total audience for the year of 1·49m.

Museums and Galleries. There were 608 museums and 218 art galleries in 1998, with 17·69m. and 2·26m. visitors respectively.

DIPLOMATIC REPRESENTATIVES
Of Poland in the United Kingdom (47 Portland Pl., London, W1B 1JH)
Ambassador: Stanisław Komorowski.

Of the United Kingdom in Poland (Emilii Plater 28, 00-688 Warsaw)
Ambassador: Michael Pakenham, CMG.

Of Poland in the USA (2640 16th St., NW, Washington, D.C., 20009)
Ambassador: Przemysław Grudziński.

Of the USA in Poland (Aleje Ujazdowskie 29/31, 00-540 Warsaw)
Ambassador: Christopher Robert Hill.

Of Poland to the United Nations
Ambassador: Janusz Stańczyk.

Of Poland to the European Union
Ambassador: Marek Grela.

FURTHER READING

Central Statistical Office, *Rocznik Statystyczny.* Annual.—*Concise Statistical Yearbook of Poland.—Statistical Bulletin.* Monthly.

Lukowski, Jerzy and Zawadzki, Hubert, *A Concise History of Poland.* CUP, 2001

Mitchell, K. D. (ed.) *Political Pluralism in Hungary and Poland: Perspectives on the Reforms.* New York, 1992

Sanford, G. and Gozdecka-Sanford, A., *Poland.* [Bibliography] 2nd ed. ABC-Clio, Oxford and Santa Barbara (CA), 1993

Sikorski, R., *The Polish House: An Intimate History of Poland.* London, 1997; US title: *Full Circle.* New York, 1997

Slay, B., *The Polish Economy: Crisis, Reform and Transformation.* Princeton Univ. Press, 1994

Staar, R. F. (ed.) *Transition to Democracy in Poland.* New York, 1993

Turner, Barry, (ed.) *Central Europe Profiled.* Macmillan, London, 2000

Wedel, J., *The Unplanned Society: Poland During and After Communism.* Columbia Univ. Press, 1992

National library: Biblioteka Narodowa, Rakowiecka 6, Warsaw.
National statistical office: Central Statistical Office, Aleje Niepodległości 208, 00-925 Warsaw.
Website: http://www.stat.gov.pl

PORTUGAL

República Portuguesa

Capital: Lisbon
Population estimate, 2000: 10·01m.
GDP per capita, 2000: (PPP$) 17,290
HDI/world rank: 0·880/28

KEY HISTORICAL EVENTS

Portugal has been an independent state since the 12th century apart from one period of Spanish rule (1580–1640). It became a kingdom in 1139 under Alfonso I. During the 15th century Portugal played a leading role in oceanic exploration, opening up new trade routes and establishing colonies. Portuguese influence extended to Guinea, Brazil, the Indies and the African coast. In 1807, during the Napoleonic wars, the Spaniards again invaded Portugal, but were driven out by the Duke of Wellington and Portuguese guerrillas during the peninsula war. Nationalistic republicans deposed King Manual II on 5 Oct. 1910. Another coup on 28 May 1926 replaced the unstable parliamentary republic with a military government which in turn was succeeded by civil dictatorship. In the 1960s Portugal faced economic stagnation at home and rebellion in her colonies. Goa was seized by India in 1961. War raged in the African colonies. There was a coup on 25 April 1974, establishing a junta of National Salvation. During 1974–75 most of the Portuguese overseas possessions, notably the African colonies, gained independence.

Following an attempted revolt on 11 March 1975, the junta was dissolved and a Supreme Revolutionary Council formed which ruled until 25 April 1976 when constitutional government was resumed. The transit to full civilian government was completed in 1982 when the constitution was revised to reduce the powers of the president.

Macao, Portugal's colony on the coast of China, was handed back to China on 20 Dec. 1999.

TERRITORY AND POPULATION

Mainland Portugal is bounded in the north and east by Spain and south and west by the Atlantic Ocean. The Atlantic archipelagoes of the Azores and of Madeira form autonomous but integral parts of the republic, which has a total area of 91,905 sq. km. Population (2001 census, provisional), 10,318,304 (5,330,024 females).

Mainland Portugal is divided into five regions, with estimated 1999 populations: North (3,585,400); Central (1,709,800); Lisbon and Tagus Valley (3,329,700); Alentejo (508,000); Algarve (349,200). Population of the Azores (245,500); Madeira, 261,000. Density (1999), 107 per sq. km (North, 169; Central, 72; Lisbon and Tagus Valley, 279; Alentejo, 19; Algarve, 70; Azores, 105; Madeira, 335).

The UN gives a projected population for 2010 of 10·08m.

In 1999, 62·7% of the population lived in urban areas. Portugal has a higher percentage of its population living in rural areas than any other European country. The populations of the districts and Autonomous Regions (2001 census, provisional):

Areas	Population	Areas	Population
North	*3,680,379*	Pinhal Interior Norte	138,652
Alto Trás os Montes	223,037	Pinhal Interior Sul	44,833
Ave	508,674	Pinhal Litoral	248,931
Cávado	392,672	Serra da Estrela	49,902
Douro	221,568	*Lisbon and Tagus Valley*	*3,447,173*
Entre Douro e Vouga	276,682	Grande Lisboa	1,878,006
Grande Porto	1,256,633	Lezíria do Tejo	240,322
Minho-Lima	249,848	Médio Tejo	226,009
Tâmega	551,265	Oeste	393,032
Central	*1,779,672*	Península de Setúbal	709,804
Baixo Mondego	339,666	*Alentejo*	*534,365*
Baixo Vouga	385,434	Alentejo Central	173,403
Beira Interior Norte	114,872	Alentejo Litoral	99,567
Beira Interior Sul	78,248	Alto Alentejo	126,841
Cova da Beira	93,454	Baixo Alentejo	134,914
Dão Lafões	285,680	*Algarve*	*391,819*

In 1999, 190,896 foreigners were legally registered: 89,516 African; 20,887 Brazilian; 13,344 British; 11,152 Spanish; 7,975 USA. 200,000 immigrants have come to Portugal from eastern Europe since 1999.

The chief cities are Lisbon (the capital; 1999 population, 3,754,000), Oporto (1,615,000 in 1995), Amadora, Setúbal and Coimbra.

Lisbon: Located 17 km from the Atlantic coast, Lisbon lies on the North Bank of the River Tagus. It covers an area of 226 sq. km and is Portugal's largest city. It has been the capital since its integration into the kingdom of Portugal in 1147. In 1755 it suffered a devastating earthquake. Some traces of mediaeval architecture can still be seen in the older districts of which Alfalma, near St George's Castle, is the oldest. Its name derives from the Arab word Alhama, meaning 'good water' or 'hot fountain'.

The national language is Portuguese.

The Azores islands lie in the mid-Atlantic Ocean, between 1,200 and 1,600 km west of Lisbon. They are divided into three widely separated groups with clear channels between, São Miguel (759 sq. km) together with Santa Maria (97 sq. km) being the most easterly; about 160 km northwest of them lies the central cluster of Terceira (382 sq. km), Graciosa (62 sq. km), São Jorge (246 sq. km), Pico (446 sq. km) and Faial (173 sq. km); still another 240 km to the northwest are Flores (143 sq. km) and Corvo (17 sq. km), the latter being the most isolated and undeveloped of the islands. São Miguel contains over half the total population of the archipelago.

Madeira comprises the island of Madeira (745 sq. km), containing the capital, Funchal; the smaller island of Porto Santo (40 sq. km), lying 46 km to the northeast of Madeira; and two groups of uninhabited islets, Ilhas Desertas (15 sq. km), being 20 km southeast of Funchal and Ilhas Selvagens (4 sq. km), near the Canaries.

SOCIAL STATISTICS
Statistics for calendar years:

	Marriages	Live births	Still births	Deaths	Divorces
1995	65,776	107,184	747	103,939	12,322
1996	63,672	110,363	759	107,259	13,429
1997	65,770	113,047	692	105,157	14,078
1998	66,598	113,510	687	106,382	15,278
1999	68,710	116,038	671	108,268	17,881

Vital statistics rates, 1999 (per 1,000 population): birth, 11·6; death, 10·8. Annual population growth rate, 1990–99, 0·0%. In 1997 the most popular age range for marrying was 25–29 for males and 20–24 for females. Expectation of life at birth, 1999, was 71·9 years for males and 79·1 years for females. Infant mortality in 1999 was 5·6 per 1,000 live births, down from 77 per 1,000 live births in 1960, representing the greatest reduction in infant mortality rates in Europe over the past 40 years. Fertility rate, 1999, 1·4 births per woman.

In 1998 the births comprised 58,589 boys and 54,921 girls; deaths, 55,904 males and 50,670 females. Around one in five babies are born outside marriage, up from one in 14 in 1970. In 1998 Portugal received 330 asylum applications, equivalent to 0·03 per 1,000 inhabitants.

CLIMATE
Because of westerly winds and the effect of the Gulf Stream, the climate ranges from the cool, damp Atlantic type in the north to a warmer and drier Mediterranean type in the south. July and Aug. are virtually rainless everywhere. Inland areas in the north have greater temperature variation, with continental winds blowing from the interior. Lisbon, Jan. 52°F (11°C), July 72°F (22°C). Annual rainfall 27·4" (686 mm). Oporto, Jan. 48°F (8·9°C), July 67°F (19·4°C). Annual rainfall 46" (1,151 mm).

CONSTITUTION AND GOVERNMENT
A new Constitution, replacing that of 1976, was approved by the Assembly of the Republic (by 197 votes to 40) on 12 Aug. 1982 and promulgated in Sept. It abolished the (military) Council of the Revolution and reduced the role of the President under it. Portugal is a sovereign, unitary republic. Executive power is vested in the *President*, directly elected for a five-year term (for a maximum of two consecutive

terms). The President appoints a Prime Minister and, upon the latter's nomination, other members of the Council of Ministers.

The 230-member *National Assembly* is a unicameral legislature elected for four-year terms by universal adult suffrage under a system of proportional representation. Women did not have the vote until 1976.

Portugal's first referendum, on whether to ease abortion restrictions, was held on 28 June 1998. Turn-out was just 32%, but the result would have had legal force only if more than half the electorate had voted. 51% of voters favoured keeping most abortions a crime, against 49%in favour of permitting the procedure on demand.

National Anthem. 'Herois do mar, nobre povo' ('Heroes of the sea, noble breed'); words by Lopes de Mendonça, tune by Alfredo Keil.

RECENT ELECTIONS

At the presidential elections of 14 Jan. 2001, Jorge Fernando Branco de Sampãio was re-elected President by 55·8% of votes cast against Joaquim Ferreira do Amaral (Social Democrat) who gained 34·5%.

At the parliamentary elections of 17 March 2002 the Social Democratic Party (PSD) won 102 seats (40·1% of votes cast); the Socialist Party (PS), 95 (37·8%); the Popular Party, 14 (8·7%); the Communist Party/Green Party coalition, 12 (6·9%); and the Left Bloc, 3 (2·7%).

European Parliament. Portugal has 25 representatives. At the June 1999 elections turn-out was 40·4%. The Socialist Party won 12 seats with 43·1% of votes cast (group in European Parliament: Party of European Socialists); the Social Democratic Party, 9 with 31·1% (European People's Party); the Social Democratic Centre, 2 with 8·2% (Union for Europe); the United Democratic Coalition, 2 with 10·3% (Confederal Group of the European United Left).

CURRENT ADMINISTRATION

President: Jorge Sampãio; b. 1939 (PS; first sworn in 9 March 1996 and re-elected Jan. 2001).

In March 2003 the government was composed as follows:

Prime Minister: José Manuel Durão Barroso; b. 1956 (PSD; sworn in 6 April 2002).

Minister of Finance: Maria Manuela Disa Ferreira Leite. *Defence:* Paulo Sacadura Cabral Portas. *Foreign Affairs and Portuguese Communities:* António Manuel de Mendonça Martins da Cruz. *Internal Affairs:* António Jorge de Figueiredo Lopes. *Justice:* Maria Celeste Ferreira Lopes Cardona. *Parliamentary Affairs:* Luís Manuel Gonçalves Marques Mendes. *Economy:* Carlos Manuel Tavares da Silva. *Agriculture, Rural Development and Fisheries:* Armando José Cordeiro Sevinate Pinto. *Education:* José David Gomes Justino. *Science and Higher Education:* Pedro Augusto Lynce de Faria. *Culture:* Pedro Manuel da Cruz Roseta. *Health:* Luís Filipe da Conceição Pereira. *Social Security and Labour:* António José de Castro Bagão Félix. *Public Works, Transportation and Housing:* Luís Francisco Valente de Oliveira. *Urban Affairs and the Environment:* Isaltino Afonso de Morais. *Minister of the Presidency:* Nuno Albuquerque Morais Sarmento. *Minister Assisting the Prime Minister:* José Luís Fazenda Arnaut Duarte.

Government Website: http://www.portugal.gov.pt

DEFENCE

A new Military Service law passed in 1999 abolished conscription. Portugal aimed to have a purely professional army by 2003.

In 2000 defence expenditure totalled US$2,197m. (US$222 per capita), representing 2·2% of GDP.

Army. Strength (1999) 25,650 (5,500 conscripts). There are Army reserves totalling 210,000. Paramilitary forces include the National Republican Guard (20,900) and the Public Security Police (20,000).

Navy. The combatant fleet comprises three French-built diesel submarines and six frigates. Naval personnel in 1999 totalled 16,600 (970 conscripts) including 1,540 marines. There were 930 naval reserves.

Air Force. The Air Force in 1999 had a strength of about 7,445. There were 60 combat aircraft including one interceptor unit with F16s.

INTERNATIONAL RELATIONS

Portugal is a member of the UN, WTO, BIS, EU, OECD, NATO, WEU, the Council of Europe, OSCE, CERN, Inter-American Development Bank and IOM. Portugal is a signatory to the Schengen Accord abolishing border controls between Portugal, Austria, Belgium, Denmark, Finland, France, Germany, Greece, Iceland, Italy, Luxembourg, the Netherlands, Norway, Spain and Sweden.

The Community of Portuguese-speaking Countries (CPLP, comprising Angola, Brazil, Cape Verde, Guinea-Bissau, Mozambique, Portugal and São Tomé e Príncipe) was founded in July 1996 with headquarters in Lisbon, primarily as a cultural and linguistic organization.

ECONOMY

Agriculture accounted for an estimated 3·9% of GDP in 1998, industry 35·2% and services 60·9%.

Overview. A reform of the tax system is a priority. Tax evasion is high but there are low and lightly enforced penalties. Portugal needs more public investment to close its development gap with the rest of the EU, but also needs to cut its budget deficit. This will require increased tax revenues. In 2001 the trade balance worsened. Low interest rates have encouraged domestic companies to invest abroad. Foreign investment has slowed and with low-cost manufacturing locations in central and eastern Europe, Portugal can no longer rely on low wages to attract foreign investment. The privatization programme has been ambitious, although no major enterprises have been privatized since 1999.

Currency. On 1 Jan. 1999 the euro (EUR) became the legal currency in Portugal; irrevocable conversion rate 200·482 escudos to 1 euro. The euro, which consists of 100 cents, has been in circulation since 1 Jan. 2002. There are seven euro notes in different colours and sizes denominated in 500, 200, 100, 50, 20, 10 and 5 euros, and eight coins denominated in 2 and 1 euros, then 50, 20, 10, 5, 2 and 1 cents. On the introduction of the euro there was a 'dual circulation' period before the escudo ceased to be legal tender on 28 Feb. 2002. Euro banknotes in circulation on 1 Jan. 2002 had a total value of €10·6bn.

Inflation in 2001 was 4·4%. Gold reserves were 19·51m. troy oz in June 2002 and foreign exchange reserves US$10,125m. Total money supply was €7,091m. in June 2002.

Budget. Budget revenue and expenditure (in 1bn. escudos):

	1994	1995	1996	1997	1998
Revenue	5,016·5	5,456·7	5,759·9	6,391·8	6,984·7
Expenditure	6,137·9	6,613·6	6,974·5	7,242·2	7,795·1

Under the previous socialist government the budget deficit was 4·1% of GDP in 2001, above the EU growth and stability pact's 3% limit.

The standard rate of VAT is 19·0%.

Performance. In both 1999 and 2000 real GDP growth was 3·4%, falling to 1·9% in 2001. In the years since Portugal joined the European Union its GDP per head has risen from being 53% of the EU average to being 75% in 2000. Portugal's total GDP in 2001 was US$108·5bn.

Banking and Finance. The central bank and bank of issue is the Bank of Portugal, founded in 1846 and nationalized in 1974. Its *Governor* is Vítor Manuel Ribeiro Constâncio.

On 31 Dec. 1998 there were 81 banks, 6 savings institutions and 160 mutual agricultural credit institutions. The largest Portuguese bank is the state-owned Caixa Geral de Depósitos, which held 21% of all deposits at the end of 1998. There were 19 branches of foreign credit institutions operating in Portugal in 1998.

There are stock exchanges in Lisbon and Oporto.

Weights and Measures. The metric system is the legal standard.

ENERGY AND NATURAL RESOURCES

Environment. According to the *World Bank Atlas* Portugal's carbon dioxide emissions in 1998 were the equivalent of 5·5 tonnes per capita.

Electricity. Installed capacity was 9m. kW in 1997. Production in 1998 was 38·58bn. kWh; consumption per capita was 3,396 kWh.

Minerals. Portugal possesses considerable mineral wealth. Production in tonnes (1997): salt 597,772; copper, 111,017; tin, 6,459; tungsten, 1,790; marble and similar rocks (1995), 940,756; non-crystalline limestone (1993), 32,176,852; granite (1993), 17,771,910; kaolin (1987), 66,736; wolframite (1987), 2,011; uranium (1987), 167; tin ore (1987), 90.

Agriculture. There were 489,000 farms in 1998. Agriculture accounted for 8·3% of exports and 16·5% of imports in 1998. It accounts for 13% of GDP, down from 24% in 1960. The agricultural sector employs 11·5% of the workforce. In 1997 there were 2·15m. ha of arable land and 747,000 ha of permanent crops.

The following figures show the production (in 1,000 tonnes) of the chief crops:

Crop	1997	1998	1999	Crop	1997	1998	1999
Cabbages[1]	140	140	140	Olive oil[2]	424	361	512
Carrots	116	145	174	Olives	278	286	262
Fruits				Onions	105	101	121
oranges	204	262	204	Potatoes	1,049	1,225	947
apples	283	162	292	Rice	164	162	152
grapes	843	500	1,041	Sugarbeets	150	183	507
pears	173	19	131	Tomatoes	793	1,089	1,010
Maize	913	1,024	935	Wheat	329	151	352
Oats	44	29	100	Wine[2]	5,914	3,580	7,602

[1]Estimates. [2]In hectolitres.

Livestock (1,000 head):

	1997	1998	1999
Cattle	1,386	1,409	1,421
Pigs	2,394	2,385	2,350
Sheep	3,432	3,590	3,584
Goats	673	676	630
Poultry[1]	28,000	28,000	28,000

[1]Estimates.

Animal products (mainland) in 1999 (1,000 tonnes): meat, 763·5; milk, 1,636·6; eggs, 90·2; cheese, 51·1. Net income from family agricultural activity, 1998: 246,304m. escudos (1997, 298,855m. escudos).

Forestry. Forests covered 2·87m. ha (31·3% of the land area) in 1995, compared to 2·75m. ha and 30% in 1990. Portugal is a major producer of cork. Estimated production, 1998, 193,000 tonnes, production of resin (1999), 20,000 tonnes. Timber production was 8·98m. cu. metres in 1999.

Fisheries. The fishing industry is important, and the Portuguese eat more fish per person than in any other European Union member country (more than twice the EU average). In 1999 there were 10,933 registered fishing vessels (8,556 with motors) and 26,638 registered fishermen. The catch was 188,022 tonnes in 1999 (almost exclusively from marine waters), down from 410,000 tonnes in 1986.

The 1999 fishing catch consisted of:

Species	Tonnes	Escudos (1m.)
Sardine	69,448	7,835
Mackerel	30,200	4,623
Shellfish	23,570	18,258
Other	64,804	33,314
Total	188,022	64,030

INDUSTRY

The leading companies by market capitalization in Portugal, excluding banking and finance, in Jan. 2002 were: Modelo Continente SGPS SA (€11bn.), a retail company; Portugal Telecom SGPS SA (€11bn.); and EDP—Electricidade de Portugal (€7bn.).

Output of major industrial products (in tonnes unless otherwise specified):

Product	1998	1999
Ready-mix concrete	16,358,158	21,025,065
Portland cement	9,784,058	10,078,694
Refined sugar	381,200	359,662
Preparation of animal food feeds	3,883,029	3,737,917
Beer (hectolitres)	7,072,383	6,944,028
Discontinuous synthetic fibre fabric[1]	71,706	66,453
Footwear with leather uppers (1,000 pairs)	61,813	69,900
Wood pulp	1,688,263	1,741,803
Paper and cardboard	1,122,417	1,142,804
Petrol	2,792,796	2,651,908
Diesel fuel	4,339,836	4,278,908
Glass bottles (1,000)	2,943,432	3,366,832

[1]In 1,000 sq. metres.

Labour. The maximum working week was reduced to 40 hours in 1997. A minimum wage is fixed by the government. Retirement is at 65 years for men and 62 for women. In 2000, out of a working population of 5,113,100 (2,782,700 male), 4,908,500 (2,694,800 male) were employed. Unemployment was 6·1% in Jan. 2003, up from 5·0% in July 2002. Employment (in 1,000) by sector, 2000 (males in parentheses): services, 2,572·5 (1,187·1); industry, construction, energy and water, 1,719·6 (1,205·3); agriculture, forestry and fishing, 616·3 (302·3). The immigrant population makes up 10% of the labour force.

Trade Unions. In 1999 there were 380 unions. An agreement between trade unions, employers and the government for 1997 involved employment, social security, investment, tax reform and education.

INTERNATIONAL TRADE
In 1998 the foreign debt was 2,906,099m. escudos and the domestic debt was 8,955,726m. escudos.

Imports and Exports. Trade in US$1m.:

	1996	1997	1998	1999	2000
Imports f.o.b.	35,345	35,721	37,829	39,207	38,891
Exports f.o.b.	25,623	25,379	25,618	25,440	24,750

Imports, in 1999, included (in 1m. escudos): machinery and transport equipment, 2,942,518; manufactured goods, 1,351,769; miscellaneous manufactured articles, 823,650; food and live animals, 771,469; chemicals and related products, 722,776; mineral fuels, lubricants and related materials, 508,212.

Exports, 1999 included (in 1m. escudos): machinery and transport equipment, 1,577,108; miscellaneous manufactured articles, 1,142,552; manufactured goods, 1,069,529; chemicals and related products, 229,965; inedible crude materials, except fuels, 190,372; food and live animals, 177,450.

Imports and exports to main EU trading partners, 1998 and 1999 (in 1m. escudos):

From or to	Imports		Exports	
	1998	1999	1998	1999
EU	5,402,273	5,874,028	3,658,120	3,841,390
Belgium/Luxembourg	235,203	235,404[1]	212,838	217,812[1]
France	778,115	858,559	632,360	643,642
Germany	1,052,289	1,107,000	906,741	911,752
Italy	546,498	582,218	180,750	192,504
Netherlands	338,724	359,268	213,579	203,549
Spain	1,687,817	1,898,985	707,934	834,087
UK	471,187	511,892	536,550	555,939
Others	292,440	320,702	267,368	282,105

[1]1999 figure is for Belgium only.

In 1999 fellow European Union members accounted for 78·1% of Portugal's imports and 83·2% of exports. In 1999 Portuguese imports from the USA totalled (in 1m. escudos) 212,308 and exports to the USA totalled 228,588; imports from Japan in 1999 (in 1m. escudos) totalled 202,984 and exports to Japan totalled 20,056.

COMMUNICATIONS

Roads. In 1999 there were 11,991 km of national roads on the mainland, including 1,441 km of motorways. In 1997 the number of vehicles registered included 766,252 motorcycles and mopeds, 3,080,412 passenger cars, 363,483 vans and lorries and 12,700 buses and coaches. In 1999 there were 1,699 deaths in road accidents. With 17 deaths per 100,000 population in 1999, Portugal has among the highest death rates in road accidents of any industrialized country.

The 17-km Vasco da Gama bridge across the River Tagus north of Lisbon is the longest in Europe. It opened in March 1998.

Rail. In 1999 total railway length was 3,579 km. Passenger-km travelled in 1999 came to 4·38bn. and freight tonne-km to 2·56bn. There is a metro (19 km) and tramway (94 km) in Lisbon.

Civil Aviation. There are international airports at Portela (Lisbon), Pedras Rubras (Oporto), Faro (Algarve) and Funchal (Madeira). The national carrier is the state-owned TAP-Air Portugal, with some domestic and international flights being provided by Portugália. In 1998 TAP flew 77·7m. km, carrying 4,680,900 passengers; Portugália flew 18·4m. km, carrying 841,600 passengers (472,300 international). In 2000 Lisbon handled 9,213,724 passengers (7,040,503 on international flights) and 104,254 tonnes of freight. Faro was the second busiest in terms of passenger traffic, with 4,571,022 passengers, and Oporto was the second busiest for freight, with 40,755 tonnes.

Shipping. In 1999, 21,296 vessels of 229·06m. tonnes entered the mainland ports. 213,402 passengers embarked and 210,315 disembarked at all Portuguese ports during 1999; 13·88m. tonnes of cargo were loaded and 47·08m. tonnes unloaded. In 1998 merchant ships totalled 1,130,000 GRT, including oil tankers 416,000 GRT.

Telecommunications. Portugal Telecom (PT) was formed from a merger of three state-owned utilities in 1994. It is now fully privatized. Main telephone lines numbered 4,313,600 in 2000 (430·3 per 1,000 population) and there were 3·0m. PCs in use (299·3 per 1,000 persons). Portugal had 5·7m. mobile phone subscribers in Nov. 2000 and 4·4m. Internet users in June 2002. In 1997 there were 70,000 fax machines.

Postal Services. The number of post offices was 1,060 in 1999; a total of 1,221m. pieces of mail were processed during 1999.

SOCIAL INSTITUTIONS

Justice. There are four judicial districts (Lisbon, Oporto, Coimbra and Evora) divided into 47 circuits. In 1999 there were 353 common courts, including 319 of the first instance. There are also 29 administration and fiscal courts.

There are four courts of appeal in each district, and a Supreme Court in Lisbon. Capital punishment was abolished completely in the Constitution of 1976.

In 1999 there were 53 prisons with an inmate capacity of 11,185. The prison population in Jan. 1999 was 14,929 including 13,510 men and 742 inmates aged under 21 years. The prison population rate in 1999 (149 per 100,000 population) was the highest in the European Union.

Religion. There is freedom of worship, both in public and private, with the exception of creeds incompatible with morals and the life and physical integrity of the people. There were 9·21m. Roman Catholics in 1999.

Education. Adult literacy rate, which was 80% in 1990, was 91·9% in 1999 (male 94·5%; female 89·5%). Portugal has the lowest literacy rate in the European Union. Compulsory education has been in force since 1911, but only 9·8% of the population goes on to further education, compared to the EU average of 21·2%.

In 1997–98 there were 5,552 pre-school establishments (3–6 years) with 200,797 pupils, and 10,480 compulsory basic school establishments (6–10 years) with 1,287,707 pupils. There were 435,757 pupils in secondary schools in 1997–98. There were 35,285 teachers on the mainland in the 1st cycle of basic school, and 109,043 in the 2nd and 3rd cycles of basic school and in secondary schools.

The state university system consists of 14 universities in the public sector and one institute, the Higher Institute of Employment and Business Sciences. There are also ten universities in the private sector and a Roman Catholic university. In 1997–98 there were a total of 204 higher education institutes altogether with a total of 351,784 students. Females account for 64% of Portugal's university graduates. In 1996 total expenditure on education came to 5·8% of GNP.

Health. In 1998 there were 215 hospitals (with four hospital beds per 1,000 inhabitants); and in 1999, 39 clinics and 512 medical centres. In 1999 there were 31,758 doctors, 2,676 dentists, 7,114 pharmacists and 32,984 nurses. Portugal has one of the highest alcohol consumption rates in Europe. Among EU countries only the French drink more. The average Portuguese adult drinks 13·6 litres of alcohol a year, compared to the EU average of 11·1 litres. In 1994 the Portuguese smoked an average 1,777 cigarettes per person.

Behind Spain and Italy, Portugal has the third highest occurrence of AIDS in the EU, with 91 cases per 100,000 population.

Welfare. In 1999, 4,278,479m. escudos were paid in social security benefits. Cash payments in escudos (and types) were: 1,560,983m. (old age), 1,433,485m. (sickness), 517,389m. (disability), 309,051m. (survivors), 223,117m. (family), 159,571m. (unemployment), 74,281m. (social exclusion), 602m. (housing).

CULTURE

Broadcasting. *Radiodifusão Portuguesa* broadcasts three programmes on medium wave and on FM as well as three regional services and an external service, Radio Portugal (English, French, Italian). There are two state-owned TV channels (Canal 1 and Radiotelevisão Portuguesa 2) and two independent channels, including one religious (colour by PAL). Radio Trans Europe is a high-powered short-wave station, retransmitting programmes of different broadcasting organizations. Number of receivers: TV (1997), 5·2m.; radio (1996), 3m. In 1999 there were 760,000 cable TV subscribers.

Cinema. In 1999 there were 211 cinemas (387 screens) with a seating capacity of 100,247; admissions totalled 20·1m.

Press. In 1999 there were 35 daily newspapers (morning and evening editions) including seven in the Azores and two on Madeira, with a combined annual circulation of 545,092,479. In addition there were 845 periodicals in 1999 with a combined circulation of 219,376,189. In 1996 a total of 7,868 book titles were published in 26·94m. copies.

Tourism. In 1999 tourist revenue increased to US$5,169m. In 1999 there were (in 1,000) 27,016 foreign visitors (26,560 in 1998), including from Spain, 20,507; UK, 1,970; Germany, 980; France, 763; the Netherlands, 483; Italy, 307. There were 1,722 hotel establishments with 216,828 accommodation capacity in 1999.

Libraries. There were, in 1999, 1,917 libraries with 9,261,924 registered users.

Theatre and Opera. In 1998 there were 49 theatres with a seating capacity of 16,668; in 1999 admissions totalled 407,000.

Museums and Galleries. In 1998, 5,083,441 persons visited the 321 museums and 2,660,136 persons visited 16 monuments and sites.

DIPLOMATIC REPRESENTATIVES
Of Portugal in the United Kingdom (11 Belgrave Sq., London, SW1X 8PP)
Ambassador: José Gregorio Faria.

Of the United Kingdom in Portugal (Rua de São Bernardo 33, 1200 Lisbon)
Ambassador: Dame Glynne Evans, DBE, CMG.

Of Portugal in the USA (2125 Kalorama Rd., NW, Washington, D.C., 20008)
Ambassador: Pedro Manuel Dos Reis Alves Catarino.

Of the USA in Portugal (Ave. das Forcas Armadas, 1600 Lisbon)
Ambassador: John N. Palmer.

Of Portugal to the United Nations
Ambassador: Gonçalo Aires de Santa Clara Gomes.

FURTHER READING

Instituto Nacional de Estatística. *Anuário Estatístico de Portugal/Statistics Year-Book.—Estatísticas do Comércio Externo*. 2 vols. Annual from 1967

Birmingham, David, *A Concise History of Portugal*. CUP, 1993
Corkill, D., *The Portuguese Economy since 1974*. Edinburgh Univ. Press, 1993
Laidlar, John, *Lisbon*. [Bibliography] ABC-Clio, Oxford and Santa Barbara (CA), 1997
Maxwell, K., *The Making of Portuguese Democracy*. CUP, 1995
Page, Martin, *The First Global Village: How Portugal Changed the World*. Editorial Notícias, Lisbon, 2002
Saraiva, J. H., *Portugal: A Companion History*. Manchester, 1997
Wheeler, D. L., *Historical Dictionary of Portugal*. Metuchen (NJ), 1994

National library: Biblioteca Nacional de Lisboa, Campo Grande, Lisbon.
National statistical office: Instituto Nacional de Estatística (INE), Avenida António José de Almeida, 1000 Lisbon.
Website: http://www.ine.pt

QATAR

Dawlat Qatar
(State of Qatar)

Capital: Doha
Population estimate, 2000: 565,000
GDP per capita, 2000: (PPP$) 18,789
HDI/world rank: 0·803/51

KEY HISTORICAL EVENTS

Qatar embraced Islam in the 7th century AD, and since then it has been noted regularly in the accounts of Arab historians and writers. Like all countries in the area, it came under Turkish rule for several centuries. Ottoman power was nominal, with real power being in the hands of local sheikhs and tribal leaders. In 1915 the Turks withdrew, and on 3 Nov. 1916 Qatar signed a protection treaty with Britain. The dominant economic activity had traditionally been pearl diving, but around 1930 the pearl market collapsed. In 1939 oil was discovered. Although the Second World War delayed progress, exporting began in 1949. This was to change Qatar dramatically. Qatar declared its independence from Britain on 3 Sept. 1971, ending the Treaty of 1916 which was replaced by a treaty of friendship between the two countries.

TERRITORY AND POPULATION

Qatar is a peninsula running north into the Arabian Gulf. It is bounded in the south by the United Arab Emirates. The territory includes a number of islands in the coastal waters of the peninsula, the most important of which is Halul, the storage and export terminal for the offshore oilfields. Area, 11,437 sq. km; population census (1997) 522,023 (342,459 males); density 45·6 per sq. km. In 1999, 92·3% of the population lived in urban areas.

The UN gives a projected population for 2010 of 653,000.

Area and estimated population of municipalities, 1993:

Municipality	(in sq. km)	Population	Municipality	(in sq. km)	Population
Doha	131·8	339,471	Al Jumayliyah	2,564·8	8,674
Al Rayyan	889·2	143,046	Al Shamal	901·3	5,347
Al Wakra	1,114·0	30,976	Jarian Al Batnah	3,714·7	2,518
Umm Salal	492·6	16,785	Al Ghwayriyah	622·3	2,517
Al Khour	996·3	10,234			

The capital is Doha, which is the main port, and had an estimated population in 1999 of 391,000. Other towns are Dukhan (the centre of oil production), Umm Said (the oil-terminal of Qatar), Ruwais, Wakra, Al-Khour, Umm Salal Mohammad and Umm-Bab.

About 40% of the population are Arabs, 18% Indian, 18% Pakistani and 10% Iranian. Other nationalities make up the remaining 14%.

The official language is Arabic.

SOCIAL STATISTICS

Births, 1997, 10,447; deaths, 1,060. 1997 rates per 1,000 population: births, 18·4; deaths, 1·9 (the lowest in the world). Infant mortality, 1999 (per 1,000 live births), 12. Expectation of life in 1999 was 68·5 years for males and 71·0 for females. Annual population growth rate, 1990–99, 2·2%. Fertility rate, 1999, 3·6 births per woman.

CLIMATE

The climate is hot and humid. Doha, Jan. 62°F (16·7°C), July 98°F (36·7°C). Annual rainfall 2·5" (62 mm).

CONSTITUTION AND GOVERNMENT

Qatar is ruled by an *Amir.* HH Sheikh Hamad bin Khalifa Al Thani, KCMG (b. 1950) assumed power after deposing his father on 27 June 1995. The heir apparent is Sheikh Hamad's son, Jasim bin Hamad Al Thani (b. 1978).

There is no Parliament, but a *Council of Ministers* is assisted by a 30-member nominated Advisory Council.

RECENT ELECTIONS
It was decided in 1998 that the Central Municipal Council should be an elected Assembly. A commission is currently working on a draft constitution allowing for the elected parliament.

CURRENT ADMINISTRATION
In March 2003 the government comprised:

Amir, Minister of Defence and C.-in-C. of the Armed Forces: HH Sheikh Hamad bin Khalifa Al Thani; b. 1952.

Prime Minister, Minister of the Interior: Sheikh Abdallah bin Khalifa Al Thani; b. 1959 (in office since 29 Oct. 1996).

Deputy Prime Minister: Muhammad bin Khalifa Al Thani. *Economy and Commerce:* Sheikh Hamad bin Faisal Al Thani. *Finance:* Yusif Husayn al-Kamal. *Foreign Affairs:* Sheikh Hamad bin Jasim bin Jabir Al Thani. *Education:* Ahmad bin Khalifa Bushbarak al-Mansouri. *Justice:* Hasan bin Abdallah al-Ghanim. *Endowments and Islamic Affairs:* Ahmad Abdallah al-Marri. *Municipal Affairs and Agriculture:* Ali bin Muhammad al-Khatir. *Communications and Transport:* Sheikh Ahmad bin Nasir Al Thani. *Public Health:* Dr Hajar bin Ahmad al-Hajar. *Housing and Civil Service Affairs:* Sheikh Falah bin Jasim bin Jabir Al Thani. *Energy and Industry, Electricity and Water:* Abdallah bin Hamad al-Attiyah.

DEFENCE
Defence expenditure in 2001 totalled US$1,243m. (US$2,072 per capita), representing 7·1% of GDP. The expenditure per capita in 2001 was the second highest in the world after that of Kuwait.

Army. Personnel (1999) 8,500.

Navy. Personnel in 1999 totalled 1,800; the base is at Doha.

Air Force. The Air Force operates 18 combat aircraft including Mirage 2000 fighters. Personnel (1999) 1,500 with 18 combat aircraft and 18 armed helicopters.

INTERNATIONAL RELATIONS
Qatar is a member of the UN, WTO, the League of Arab States, OPEC, the Gulf Co-operation Council and OIC.

In March 2001 the International Court of Justice ruled on a long-standing dispute between Bahrain and Qatar over the boundary between the two countries and ownership of certain islands. Both countries accepted the decision.

ECONOMY
Agriculture accounted for an estimated 1% of GDP in 1996, industry 49% and services 50%.

Currency. The unit of currency is the *Qatari riyal* (QAR) of 100 *dirhams*, introduced in 1973. Foreign exchange reserves were US$1,184m. in April 2002 and gold reserves 169,000 troy oz. Total money supply in April 2002 was 5,685m. riyals. There was deflation of 0·7% in 2001.

In 2001 the six Gulf Arab states—Qatar, along with Bahrain, Kuwait, Oman, Saudi Arabia and the United Arab Emirates—signed an agreement to establish a single currency by 2010.

Budget. Revenue (1995–96) US$2·5bn.; expenditure US$3·5bn.

Performance. Real GDP growth was 11·6% in 2000, one of the highest rates in the world, and 7·2% in 2001. Qatar's total GDP in 2000 was US$14·5bn.

Banking and Finance. The Qatar Monetary Agency, which functioned as a bank of issue, became the Central Bank in 1995 (*Governor*, Abdullah Atiyya). In 1993 there were six domestic and eight foreign banks with total deposits of 18,870·7bn. riyals.

A stock exchange was established in Doha by the Amir's decree in 1995, initially to trade only in Qatari stocks.

Heavy investment in energy development increased foreign debt from US$1,300bn. in 1991 to US$10,400bn. in 1997.

Weights and Measures. The metric system is in general use.

ENERGY AND NATURAL RESOURCES

Environment. According to the *World Bank Atlas* Qatar's carbon dioxide emissions in 1998 were the equivalent of 85·7 tonnes per capita, the highest of any sovereign country.

Electricity. Installed capacity was 1m. kW in 1997. Production was 6·71bn. kWh in 1998; consumption per capita was 13,912 kWh.

Oil and Gas. Proven reserves of oil (1999) 3,700m. bbls. Output, 2000, 795,000 bbls. a day.

The North Field, the world's biggest single reservoir of gas and containing 12% of the known world gas reserves, is half the size of Qatar itself. Development cost is estimated at US$25bn. In 2000 natural gas reserves were 8,500bn. cu. metres (the third largest after Russia and Iran); output in 1999 was 24·0bn. cu. metres.

Water. Two main desalination stations have a daily capacity of 167·6m. gallons of drinkable water. A third station is planned, with a capacity of 40m. gallons a day.

Agriculture. 10% of the working population is engaged in agriculture. Percentage of total agricultural area under various crops in 1993: vegetables, 28%; green fodder, 23%; cereals, 22%; palm dates, 20%; and fruits, 7%. Government policy aims at ensuring self-sufficiency in agricultural products. In 1998, 13,000 ha were irrigated. Production (2000) in 1,000 tonnes: dates, 17; tomatoes, 11; pumpkins and squash, 9; aubergines, 5; barley, 5; cucumbers and gherkins, 5; melons and watermelons, 5; onions, 4.

Livestock (2000): sheep, 215,000; goats, 179,000; camels, 50,000; cattle, 14,000; chickens, 4m. Livestock products, 2000 (in 1,000 tonnes): meat, 13; milk, 11; eggs, 4.

Fisheries. The catch in 1999 totalled 4,207 tonnes, entirely from sea fishing. The state-owned Qatar National Fishing Company has three trawlers and its refrigeration unit processes 10 tonnes of shrimps a day.

INDUSTRY

According to the Financial Times Survey (FT 500), the largest companies in Qatar by market capitalization on 4 Jan. 2001 were Qatar Telecom Company (US$1,642·7m.) and Qatar National Bank (US$1,283·4m.).

1993 output (in 1,000 tonnes): urea, 825·0; ammonia, 763·0; cement (1997), 692·0; propane, 646·1; reinforcing steel bars, 608·6; butane, 454·7; ethylene, 351·6; polyethylene, 181·5; sulphur, 68·2; flour, 33·0; bran, 11·5. There is an industrial zone at Umm Said.

Labour. In 1998 the labour force totalled 293,000. In 1999 males constituted 85% of the labour force—only the United Arab Emirates had a lower percentage of females in its workforce.

INTERNATIONAL TRADE

In 2001 Qatar, along with Bahrain, Kuwait, Oman, Saudi Arabia and the United Arab Emirates agreed to the complete implementation of a customs union by 2003.

Imports and Exports. Imports in 1997 were an estimated US$4·4bn. and exports an estimated US$5·6bn. The main exports are petroleum products (75%), steel and fertilizers. Main imports are machinery and equipment, consumer goods, food and chemicals. The principal partners for exports in 1994 were Japan (61%), Australia (5%), and the United Arab Emirates and Singapore; and for imports, Germany (14%), Japan (12%), UK (11%), USA (9%) and Italy (5%).

COMMUNICATIONS

Roads. In 1996 there were about 1,230 km of roads, of which 1,100 km were paved. Passenger cars in 1996 numbered 126,000 (219 per 1,000 inhabitants) and there were 64,000 trucks and vans. In 1993 there were 76 fatal accidents with 84 deaths.

Civil Aviation. Gulf Air is owned equally by Qatar, Bahrain, Oman and the UAE. For details *see* BAHRAIN: Civil Aviation. In 1998 it operated services from Doha International to Abu Dhabi, Al Ain, Amsterdam, Bahrain, Beirut, Bombay, Cairo, Damascus, Delhi, Dhahran, Dhaka, Dubai, Frankfurt, Fujairah, Jeddah, Karachi,

Khartoum, Kuwait, London, Madras, Manila, Muscat, Paris, Riyadh, Sana'a, Sharjah, Shiraz, Tehran and Thiruvananthapuram. A Qatari airline, Qatar Airways, operates on some of the same routes, and in 1998 additionally flew to Colombo, Káthmandu and Peshawar. Doha handled 2,642,000 passengers (all on international flights) and 67,600 tonnes of freight in 2000.

Shipping. In 1998 sea-going vessels totalled 744,000 GRT, including oil tankers 263,000 GRT. In 1993, 1,383 vessels with a total tonnage of 66,255,841 GRT and 2,697,629 tonnage of cargo was discharged.

Telecommunications. Qatar had 160,200 main telephone lines in 2000, or 267·7 per 1,000 persons, and there were 90,000 PCs in use. There were 84,000 mobile phone subscribers in 1999 and 10,000 fax machines in 1996. In March 2001 there were approximately 75,000 Internet users.

Postal Services. There were 30 post offices in 1995.

SOCIAL INSTITUTIONS

Justice. The Judiciary System is administered by the Ministry of Justice which comprises three main departments: legal affairs, courts of justice and land and real estate register. There are five Courts of Justice proclaiming sentences in the name of H. H. the Amir: the Court of Appeal, the Labour Court, the Higher Criminal Court, the Civil Court and the Lower Criminal Court. The death penalty is in force.

All issues related to personal affairs of Muslims under Islamic Law embodied in the Holy Quran and Sunna are decided by Sharia Courts.

Religion. The population is almost entirely Muslim.

Education. Adult literacy rate was 80·8% in 1999 (80·1% among males and 82·6% among females). There were, in 1994–95, 52,130 pupils and 5,853 teachers at 169 primary schools, 37,635 pupils and 3,858 teachers at secondary schools and, in 1995–96, 8,271 students and 645 teachers at higher education institutions. There were 48 Arab and foreign private schools with 27,895 pupils and 1,692 teachers in 1992–93. The University of Qatar had 7,294 students and 881 academic staff in 1993–94.

Students abroad (1993–94) numbered 1,262. In 1992–93, 3,567 men and 2,639 women attended night schools and literacy centres.

Health. There were four hospitals in 1995, with a provision of 18 beds for every 10,000 persons. In 1995 there were 715 government-employed doctors, 88 government-employed dentists, 187 government-employed pharmacists and 1,834 government-employed nurses.

CULTURE

Broadcasting. The government ministry of information operates the Qatar Broadcasting Service and the Qatar Television Service. The Qatar Television Service transmits in Arabic (Qatar Television One, on channels 9 and 11) and in English (Qatar Television Two, on channel 37). Transmissions are received from Bahrain, the United Arab Emirates or Saudi Arabia. There are also satellite and cable broadcasters (Al-Jazeera Satellite Channel and Qatar Cable Vision). Al-Jazeera has a reputation for outspoken, independent reporting and has become increasingly high-profile since the attacks on the USA on 11 Sept. 2001. There were 230,000 television receivers in use (colour by PAL) and 256,000 radios in 1997.

Press. In 1996 there were five daily newspapers, with a combined circulation of 90,000.

Tourism. In 1998 there were 451,000 foreign tourists.

DIPLOMATIC REPRESENTATIVES
Of Qatar in the United Kingdom (1 South Audley St., London, WIY 5DQ)
Ambassador: Nasser Bin Hamid M. Al-Khalifa.

Of the United Kingdom in Qatar (PO Box 3, Doha, Qatar)
Ambassador: David MacLennan.

Of Qatar in the USA (4200 Wisconsin Ave., New Hampshire Ave., NW, Washington, D.C., 20016)
Ambassador: Bader Omar Al Dafa.

Of the USA in Qatar (149 Ahmed bin Ali St., Fariq Bin Omran, Doha)
Ambassador: Maureen Quinn.

Of Qatar to the United Nations
Ambassador: Nassir Abdulaziz Al-Nasser.

Of Qatar to the European Union
Ambassador: Vacant.

FURTHER READING
Central Statistical Organization. *Annual Statistical Abstract.*
El-Nawawy, Mohammed and Iskandar, Adel, *Al-Jazeera: How the Free Arab News Network Scooped the World and Changed the Middle East.* Westview Press, Boulder (CO), 2002
Unwin, P. T. H., *Qatar.* [Bibliography] ABC-Clio, Oxford and Santa Barbara (CA), 1982

National statistical office: Central Statistical Organization, Presidency of the Council of Ministers, Doha.

ROMANIA

Romania

Capital: Bucharest
Population estimate, 2000: 22·4m.
GDP per capita, 2000: (PPP$) 6,423
HDI/world rank: 0·775/63

KEY HISTORICAL EVENTS

The foundation of the feudal 'Danubian Principalities' of Wallachia and Moldavia in the late 13th and early 14th centuries marks the beginning of modern Romania. The nobility acted as the Turks' agents until 1711 when, suspected of pro-Russian sentiments, they were replaced by Greek merchant adventurers, the Phanariots. The Phanariot period of ruthless extortion and corruption was ameliorated by Russian influence. Between 1829 and 1834 the foundations of the modern state were laid but Russian interference soon became repressive. The Moldavian and Wallachian assemblies were fused in 1862. In 1866 Carol of Hohenzollern came to the throne and a constitution adopted based on that of Belgium of 1831. Romania was formally declared independent by the Treaty of Berlin of 1878.

This was a period of expansion for an economy controlled by land-owners and nascent industrialists. The condition of the peasantry remained miserable and the rebellion of 1907 was an expression of their discontent. Romania joined the First World War on the allied side in 1916. The spoils of victory brought Transylvania (with large Hungarian and German populations), Bessarabia, Bukovina and Dobrudja into the union with the 'Old Kingdom'. Hit by the world recession, Romania was drawn into Germany's economic orbit. Against this background the fascist Iron Guard assassinated the Liberal leader in 1934. Carol II adopted an increasingly totalitarian rule. Following Nazi and Soviet annexations of Romanian territory in 1940, he abdicated in favour of his son Michael. The government of the fascist Ion Antonescu declared war on the USSR on 22 June 1941. On 23 Aug. 1944 Michael, with the backing of a bloc of opposition parties, deposed Antonescu and switched sides.

The armistice of Sept. 1944 gave the Soviet army control of Romania's territory. This, and the 'spheres of influence' diplomacy of the Allies, predetermined the establishment of communism in Romania. Transylvania was restored to Romania (although it lost Bessarabia and Southern Dobrudja), and large estates were broken up for the benefit of the peasantry. Elections in Nov. 1946 were held in an atmosphere of intimidation and fraudulence. Michael was forced to abdicate and a people's republic was proclaimed. The communist leader, Gheorghe Gheorghiu-Dej, purged himself of his fellow leaders in the early 1950s. Under his successor, Nicolae Ceauşescu, Romania took a relatively independent stand in foreign affairs while becoming increasingly repressive and impoverished domestically.

An attempt by the authorities on 16 Dec. 1989 to evict a Protestant pastor, László Tökés, from his home in Timişoara, provoked a popular protest which escalated into a mass demonstration against the government. A state of emergency was declared but the Army went over to the rebels and Nicolae and Elena Ceauşescu fled the capital. A dissident group which had been active before the uprising, the National Salvation Front (NSF), proclaimed itself the provisional government. The Ceauşescus were captured and after a secret two hour trial by military tribunal, summarily executed on 25 Dec. The following day Ion Iliescu, leader of the National Salvation Front, was sworn in as President. But the Iliescu-led administration, while committed to reform, was inhibited by its communist origins. The economy stalled and the debts piled up. Iliescu was voted out of office and his government replaced by a four-party coalition led by President Emil Constantinescu. Iliescu returned as president in 2000. The economy continued to struggle but in 2002 Romania was invited to join NATO in 2004 and was given a target date of 2007 for EU membership.

TERRITORY AND POPULATION

Romania is bounded in the north by Ukraine, in the east by Moldova, Ukraine and the Black Sea, south by Bulgaria, southwest by Serbia and Montenegro and

1323

northwest by Hungary. The area is 238,391 sq. km. Population (2002 census), 21,698,181; density, 91·0 per sq. km. In 1999, 55·9% of the population lived in urban areas.

The UN gives a projected population for 2010 of 21·82m.

Romania is divided into 41 counties (*judeţ*) and the municipality of Bucharest (Bucuresti).

County	Area in sq. km	Population (2002 census)	Capital	Population (in 1,000) (2002)
Bucharest[1]	238	1,921,751		
Alba	6,242	382,999	Alba Iulia	66
Arad	7,754	461,730	Arad	173
Argeş	6,826	653,903	Piteşti	169
Bacău	6,621	708,751	Bacău	176
Bihor	7,544	600,223	Oradea	206
Bistriţa-Năsăud	5,355	312,325	Bistriţa	81
Botoşani	4,986	454,023	Botoşani	115
Brăila	4,766	373,897	Brăila	217
Braşov	5,363	588,366	Braşov	284
Buzău	6,103	494,982	Buzău	133
Călăraşi	5,088	324,629	Călărasi	70
Caraş-Severin	8,520	333,396	Reşita	84
Cluj	6,674	703,269	Cluj-Napoca	318
Constanţa	7,071	715,172	Constanţa	310
Covasna	3,710	222,274	Sf. Gheorghe	61
Dîmboviţa	4,054	541,326	Tîrgovişte	89
Dolj	7,414	734,823	Craiova	303
Galaţi	4,466	619,522	Galaţi	299
Giurgiu	3,526	298,022	Giurgiu	70
Gorj	5,602	387,409	Tîrgu Jiu	97
Harghita	6,639	326,020	Miercurea-Ciuc	42
Hunedoara	7,063	487,115	Deva	69
Ialomiţa	4,453	296,486	Slobozia	53
Iaşi	5,476	819,044	Iaşi	322
Ilfov[1]	1,583	300,109	—	
Maramureş	6,304	510,688	Baia Mare	138
Mehedinţi	4,933	306,118	Drobeta-Turnu Severin	104
Mureş	6,714	579,862	Tîrgu Mureş	150
Neamţ	5,896	557,084	Piatra-Neamţ	105
Olt	5,498	490,276	Slatina	79
Prahova	4,716	829,224	Ploieşti	232
Sălaj	3,864	248,407	Zalău	63
Satu Mare	4,418	369,096	Satu Mare	116
Sibiu	5,432	422,224	Sibiu	155
Suceava	8,553	690,941	Suceava	106
Teleorman	5,790	436,926	Alexandria	51
Timiş	8,697	677,744	Timişoara	318
Tulcea	8,499	258,639	Tulcea	93
Vâlcea	5,765	413,570	Râmnicu Vâlcea	108
Vaslui	5,318	455,550	Vaslui	70
Vrancea	4,867	390,268	Focşani	103

[1]Bucharest municipality and surrounding localities of Ilfov cover 1,821 sq. km.

At the 1992 census the following ethnic minorities numbered over 100,000: Hungarians, 1,624,959 (mainly in Transylvania); Roma (Gypsies), 401,087; Germans, 119,462. By 1998 the number of Germans had declined to 17,000. A *Council of National Minorities* made up of representatives of the government and ethnic groups was set up in 1993. The actual number of Roma is estimated to be nearer 2m. Romania has the largest Roma population of any country.

The official language is Romanian.

SOCIAL STATISTICS

1998: births, 237,297; deaths, 269,166; infant deaths, 4,868; marriages, 145,303; divorces, 39,985. Rates, 1998 (per 1,000 population): live births, 10·5; deaths, 12·0; marriages, 6·5; divorces, 1·8. Infant mortality, 1999 (per 1,000 live births), 21. Expectation of life at birth, 1999, was 66·5 years for males and 73·3 years for females. In 1998 the most popular age range for marrying was 20–24 for both males and females. Measures designed to raise the birth rate were abolished in 1990, and abortion and contraception legalized. The annual abortion rate, at nearly 80 per 1,000 women aged 15–44, ranks among the highest in the world. Annual population growth rate, 1990–99, –0·4%; fertility rate, 1999, 1·2 births per woman.

CLIMATE
A continental climate with an annual average temperature varying between 8°C in the north and 11°C in the south. Bucharest, Jan. 27°F (–2·7°C), July 74°F (23·5°C). Annual rainfall 23·1" (579 mm). Constanța, Jan. 31°F (–0·6°C), July 71°F (21·7°C). Annual rainfall 15" (371 mm).

CONSTITUTION AND GOVERNMENT
A new Constitution was approved by a referendum on 8 Dec. 1991. Turn-out was 66%, and 77·3% of votes cast were in favour. The Constitution defines Romania as a republic where the rule of law prevails in a social and democratic state. Private property rights and a market economy are guaranteed.

The head of state is the *President*, who must not be a member of a political party, elected by direct vote for a maximum of two four-year terms. The President is empowered to veto legislation unless it is upheld by a two-thirds parliamentary majority. The National Assembly consists of a 343-member *Chamber of Deputies* and a 143-member *Senate*; both are elected for four-year terms from 41 constituencies by modified proportional representation, the number of seats won in each constituency being determined by the proportion of the total vote. 15 seats in the Chamber of Deputies are reserved for ethnic minorities. There is a 3% threshold for admission to either house. Votes for parties not reaching this threshold are redistributed.

There is a *Constitutional Court*.

National Anthem. 'Deşteaptăte, Române, din somnul cel de moarte' ('Wake up, Romanians, from your deadly slumber'); words by A. Muresianu, tune by A. Pann.

RECENT ELECTIONS
The first rounds of the presidential and parliamentary elections were held on 26 Nov. 2000. Turn-out was 56·5%. There were nine presidential candidates. Ion Iliescu won with 36·4% of votes cast. At the second run-off round of the presidential elections on 10 Dec. turn-out was 50·4%. Iliescu was elected with 66·8% of votes cast, against 33·2% for the far-right nationalist Corneliu Vadim Tudor.

At the parliamentary elections, the Democratic Social Pole of Romania (PDSR) bloc won 36·6% of votes cast; the Party of Great Romania (PRM), 19·5%; the Democratic Party (PD), 7·0%; the National Liberal Party (PNL), 6·9%; the Hungarian Democratic Union of Romania (UDMR), 6·8%. Seats gained:

Party	Chamber of Deputies seats	Senate seats
Democratic Social Pole of Romania	155	65
Democratic Social Party of Romania (PDSR)	*142*	*60*
Romanian Social Democratic Party (PSDR)	*7*	*1*
Humanist Party of Romania (PUR)	*6*	*4*
Party of Great Romania (PRM)	84	37
Democratic Party (PD)	31	13
National Liberal Party (PNL)	30	13
Hungarian Democratic Union of Romania (UDMR)	27	12

CURRENT ADMINISTRATION
President: Ion Iliescu; b. 1930 (PDSR; sworn in 20 Dec. 2000).

In March 2003 the government comprised:

Prime Minister: Adrian Năstase; b. 1950 (PDSR; sworn in 28 Dec. 2000).

Minister of Defence: Ioan Mircea Paşcu. *Interior:* Ioan Rus. *Foreign Affairs:* Dan Mircea Geoană. *Finance:* Mihai Nicolae Tănăsescu. *Development and Strategy:* Gheorghe Leonard Cazan. *Justice:* Rodica Mihaela Stănoiu. *Industry and Resources:* Dan Ioan Popescu. *Labour and Social Protection:* Marian Sârbu. *Food and Agriculture:* Ilie Sârbu. *Public Works, Transport and Housing:* Miron Tudor Mitrea. *Water and Environmental Protection:* Aurel Constantin Ilie. *Education:* Ecaterina Andronescu. *European Integration:* Carola Hildergard Puwak. *Health:* Daniela Bartoş. *Culture:* Răzvan Theodorescu. *Youth and Sports:* Giorgiu Gingăraş.

ROMANIA

Public Administration: Octav Cozmâncă. *Tourism:* Dan Matei Agathon. *Communication and Information Technology:* Dan Nica. *Minister-Delegate for Ethnic Minorities:* Peter Eckstein-Kovacs.

Government Website: http://www.gov.ro

DEFENCE
Military service is compulsory for 12 months in the Army and Air Force and 18 months in the Navy.

In 2000 military expenditure totalled US$809m. (US$36 per capita), representing 2·2% of GDP.

Army. Strength (1999) 106,000 (71,000 conscripts) and 470,000 reservists. The Ministry of the Interior operates a paramilitary Frontier Guard (22,900 strong) and a Gendarmerie (53,000).

Navy. The fleet includes 1 ex-Soviet diesel submarine, 1 destroyer and 6 frigates. There was a naval infantry force some 10,200 strong in 1999.

The headquarters of the Navy is at Mangalia with the main base at Constanţa. The Danube flotilla is based at Brăila. Personnel in 1999 totalled 20,800 (12,600 conscripts). There were 30,000 naval reserves.

Air Force. The Air Force numbered some 43,500, with 367 combat aircraft and 16 armed helicopters, in 1999. These included MiG-21, MiG-23 and MiG-29 fighters, and IAR-93 fighter-bombers. There were 40,000 Air Force reserves.

INTERNATIONAL RELATIONS
Romania is a member of the UN, WTO, BIS, the NATO Partnership for Peace, the Council of Europe, the Central European Initiative, OSCE, BSEC, Danube Commission, IOM, Antarctic Treaty, the International Organization of the Francophonie and is an Associate Partner of the WEU and an Associate Member of the EU. At the European Union's Helsinki Summit in Dec. 1999 Romania, along with five other countries, was invited to begin full negotiations for membership in Feb. 2000, but entry into the EU is unlikely before 2007. Romania also hopes to become a member of NATO.

ECONOMY
Agriculture accounted for 16·4% of GDP in 1998, industry 40·1% and services 43·4%.

Overview. With the change of government, the pace of reform has accelerated. There have been privatizations in a number of sectors of the economy, from telecommunications to the motor industry, steel to banking. Future privatizations are expected in oil and electricity, and the national airline Tarom is also set to be sold off.

Legislation of Nov. 1995 compensates former owners of 0·2m. nationalized properties. Compensation is limited to the ownership of one home if lived in or 50m. lei.

Currency. The monetary unit is the *leu*, pl. *lei* (ROL) notionally of 100 *bani*. Foreign exchange reserves were US$6,352m. and gold reserves 3·38m. troy oz in May 2002. Inflation was 154·8% in 1997, but was brought down to 34·5% in 2001. Total money supply was 57,213·9bn. lei in May 2002.

Budget. Total revenue and expenditure (in 1bn. lei) for calendar years:

	1995	1996	1997	1998	1999
Revenue	21,327	30,194	68,394	107,051	171,135
Expenditure	22,927	34,033	79,734	124,595	191,341

VAT, introduced in July 1993, is 19%.

Performance. Romania experienced a recession from 1997 to 1999. However, this was followed in 2000 by growth of 1·8% and 2001 of 5·3%. Total GDP in 2001 was US$39·7bn.

Banking and Finance. The National Bank of Romania (founded 1880; nationalized 1946) is the central bank and bank of issue under the Minister of Finance. Its

Governor is Dr Mugur Isărescu. The number of commercial banks increased from five in 1990 to 45 in 2000, of which 37 were Romanian entities and eight branches of foreign banks. Only three banks remain state-owned. The largest bank is Romanian Commercial Bank (Banca Comerciala Romana), with assets in 2000 of US$2·4bn.

A stock exchange re-opened in Bucharest in 1995.

Weights and Measures. The Gregorian calendar was adopted in 1919. The metric system is in use.

ENERGY AND NATURAL RESOURCES

Environment. According to the *World Bank Atlas* Romania's carbon dioxide emissions were the equivalent of 4·1 tonnes per capita in 1998.

Electricity. Installed electric power 1998: 19,400,000 kW; output, 1998, 52·5bn. kWh (32% hydro-electric). Consumption per capita was 1,626 kWh in 1998. A nuclear power plant at Cernavoda began working in April 1996.

Oil and Gas. Oil production in 1998 was 6·3m. tonnes, but with annual consumption of 11m. tonnes a large amount has to be imported. There were 1·4bn. bbls. of proven oil reserves in 1999. In the late 1850s Romania was the world's leading oil producer, with an output of 200 tonnes a year. Natural gas production in 1999 totalled 13·8bn. cu. metres with 370bn. cu. metres in proven reserves.

Minerals. The principal minerals are oil and natural gas, salt, lignite, iron and copper ores, bauxite, chromium, manganese and uranium. Output, 1997 (in 1,000 tonnes): coal and lignite, 37,000; salt, 2,689; iron ore (1995), 184; bauxite, 127; zinc (1995), 35; methane gas (1991), 17,252m. cu. metres.

Agriculture. Romania has the biggest agricultural area in eastern Europe after Poland. In 2000, 42·8% of the workforce was employed in agriculture. There were 14,797,500 ha of agricultural land in 1994. There were 2,880,000 ha of irrigated land in 1998. In 1997 there were 9·3m. ha of arable land and 600,000 ha of permanent crops. In 1997 private households had on average 2·53 ha per family. There were 165,000 tractors in 1998.

Production (2000, in 1,000 tonnes): wheat, 4,320; maize, 4,200; potatoes, 3,650; sugarbeets, 1,500; cabbages, 1,000; grapes, 981; sunflower seeds, 900; melons and watermelons, 900; tomatoes, 758; barley, 750.

Livestock, 2000 (in 1,000): cattle, 3,155; sheep, 7,972; pigs, 5,951; horses, 842; goats, 554; chickens, 72,000.

A law of Feb. 1991 provided for the restitution of collectivized land to its former owners or their heirs up to a limit of 10 ha. Land may be resold, but there is a limit of 100 ha on total holdings. By 1997, 72% of farmed land was in private hands. The government has pledged an end to state ownership of farms.

Forestry. Total forest area was 6·25m. ha in 1995 (27·1% of the land area) including 1·91m. ha coniferous, 1·90m. ha beech and 1·14m. ha oak. 14,744 ha were afforested in 1994. Timber production in 1999 was 11·65m. cu. metres.

Fisheries. The catch in 1999 totalled 7,843 tonnes (216,938 tonnes in 1988), of which 5,336 tonnes were from inland waters.

INDUSTRY

In 1994 there were 33,824 industrial enterprises, of which 2,182 were state-controlled, 374 local government-controlled and 554 co-operatives. 50 enterprises employed more than 5,000 persons; 31,043 fewer than 100.

Output of main products in 1997 (in 1,000 tonnes): cement, 7,298; crude steel (1994), 6,790; pig iron, 4,557; rolled steel (1994), 4,510; chemical fertilizers (1994), 1,163; steel tubes (1994), 472; sulphuric acid, 329; paper and paperboard (1998), 324; plastics (1994), 304; caustic soda (1994), 291; edible oils (1994), 194; sugar (1998), 189; chemical fibres (1994), 83. In 1,000 units (1997): TV sets, 89; washing machines, 82; tractors (1994), 14.

Labour. The labour force in 1996 totalled 10·67m. The employed population in 1994 was 10·01m., of whom 3·6m. worked in agriculture and 3·4m. in industry and building. In 1994, 46% of the total workforce, and 39·4% of the industrial workforce, were women. The average retirement ages of 50 for women and 54 for men are among the lowest in the world. A minimum monthly wage was set in 1993; it was 45,000 lei in 1994. The average monthly wage was 250,000 lei in 1997. Unemployment was 10·5% in 2000 (11·5% in 1999).

Trade Unions. In 1994 the National Confederation of Free Trade Unions-Fratia had 65 branch federations and 3·7m. members. The other major confederations were Alfa Cartel and the National Trade Union Bloc.

INTERNATIONAL TRADE
Foreign debt was US$10,224m. in 2000. In Nov. 1993 the USA granted Romania most-favoured-nation status.

Foreign investors may establish joint ventures or 100%-owned domestic companies in all but a few strategic industries. After an initial two-year exemption, profits are taxed at 30%, dividends at 10%. The 1991 constitution prohibits foreign nationals from owning real estate.

Imports and Exports. Trade in US$1m.:

	1996	1997	1998	1999	2000
Imports f.o.b.	10,555	10,411	10,927	9,595	12,050
Exports f.o.b.	8,085	8,431	8,302	8,503	10,366

Main export commodities are textiles, mineral products and chemicals; principal imports are mineral fuels, machinery and transport equipment, and textiles.

In 1997 Romania's main export markets were: Italy (19·5%); Germany (16·8%); France (5·5%); Turkey (4·2%); USA (3·8%). Romania's main import sources in 1997 were: Germany (16·4%); Italy (15·8%); Russia (12·0%); France (5·7%); South Korea (5·1%). The EU accounts for approximately 65% of Romanian exports and 59% of imports.

COMMUNICATIONS

Roads. There were 78,492 km of roads in 2001: 113 km of motorways, 14,822 km of national roads, 35,853 km of country roads and 27,817 km of communal roads. In addition there were 119,988 km of urban roads in 2000. At least two-thirds of the main roads are in urgent need of repair. Passenger cars in 2001 numbered 3,225,512 (144 per 1,000 inhabitants).

Rail. Length of standard-gauge route in 2001 was 10,958 km, of which 3,950 km were electrified; there were 378 km of narrow-gauge lines and 57 km of 1,524 mm gauge. Freight carried in 2001, 72·6m. tonnes; passengers, 113·7m. There is a metro (76·5 km) and tram/light rail network (353 km) in Bucharest, and tramways in 13 other cities.

Civil Aviation. Tarom (*Transporturi Aeriene Române*) is the 95%-state-owned airline. Its sale is a top priority for the government in the privatization process. In 2002 it provided domestic services and international flights to Amman, Amsterdam, Ancona, Athens, Beijing, Beirut, Berlin, Bologna, Brussels, Budapest, Cairo, Copenhagen, Damascus, Dubai, Düsseldorf, Frankfurt, Istanbul, Kishinev, Larnaca, London, Luxembourg, Madrid, Milan, Moscow, Munich, New York, Paris, Prague, Rome, Sofia, Stuttgart, Tel Aviv, Thessaloniki, Treviso, Verona, Vienna, Warsaw and Zürich. In 1999 it flew 23·7m. km, carrying 978,600 passengers (842,700 on international flights). Other Romanian airlines which operated international flights in 2001 were Romavia, Jaro International, Grivco Air, Acvila Air, Carpat Air and Tiriac Air.

Bucharest's airports are at Baneasa (mainly domestic flights) and Otopeni (international flights). Constanţa, Cluj-Napoca, Oradea, Arad, Sibiu and Timişoara also have some international flights. Otopeni handled 1,981,000 passengers in 2001 (all on international flights) and 11,475 tonnes of freight in 2000; Timişoara handled 173,000 passengers in 2001 and Banaesa 73,000.

Shipping. In 2001 the merchant marine comprised 163 vessels totalling 1·45m. DWT. The total GRT was 403,974, including oil tankers and container ships, in

2000. In 2001 vessels totalling 12·65 NRT entered ports and vessels totalling 13·82 NRT cleared. The main ports are Constanţa and Constanţa South Agigea on the Black Sea and Galaţi, Brăila and Tulcea on the Danube. In 2001 sea-going transport carried 0·38m. tonnes of freight. In 2001 the length of navigable inland waterways was 1,779 km including: Danube River, 1,075 km; Black Sea Canal, 64 km; Poarta Alba–Midia Navodari Canal, 28 km. The Romanian inland waterway fleet comprised 169 tugs and pushers and 1,695 dumb and pushed vessels with a carrying capacity of 2·23m. tonnes. The freight carried by Romanian vessels was 383,700 tonnes. The traffic of goods in the Romanian inland ports amounted to 18·7m. tonnes.

Telecommunications. Main telephone lines numbered 3,899,200 in 2000, or 174·6 per 1,000 population, and there were 713,000 PCs in use (31·9 per 1,000 persons). Romania had 1·4m. mobile phone subscribers in 1999 and 21,000 fax machines in 1995. The number of Internet users in Dec. 2001 was 1·0m.

Postal Services. There were 5,243 post offices in 1995.

SOCIAL INSTITUTIONS

Justice. Justice is administered by the Supreme Court, the 41 county courts, 81 courts of first instance and 15 courts of appeal. Lay assessors (elected for four years) participate in most court trials, collaborating with the judges. In 1994 there were 2,471 judges.

The *Procurator-General* exercises 'supreme supervisory power to ensure the observance of the law'. The Procurator's Office and its organs are independent of any organs of justice or administration, and only responsible to the Grand National Assembly, which appoints the Procurator-General for four years.

The death penalty was abolished in Jan. 1990 and is forbidden by the 1991 constitution. The population in penal institutions in Dec. 1997 was 45,121 (200 per 100,000 of national population).

Religion. The State Secretariat for Religious Denominations oversees religious affairs. Churches' expenses and salaries are paid by the State. There are 14 Churches, the largest being the Romanian Orthodox Church. It is autocephalous, but retains dogmatic unity with the Eastern Orthodox Church. It is organized into 12 dioceses grouped into five metropolitan bishoprics and headed by Patriarch Teoctist Arapasu. There are some 11,800 churches, 2 theological colleges and 6 'schools of cantors', as well as seminaries. The Uniate (Greek Catholic) Church (which severed its connection with the Vatican in 1698) was suppressed in 1948 but in 1990 was re-legalized. Property seized by the state in 1948 was restored to it, but not property which had passed to the Orthodox Church.

Religious affiliation at the 1992 census: Romanian Orthodox, 19,762,135; Roman Catholic, 1,144,820; Protestant, 801,577; Uniate, 228,377; Pentecostal, 220,051; Baptist, 109,677; Seventh Day Adventist, 78,658; Unitarian, 76,333; Muslim, 55,988.

Education. Education is free and compulsory from 7 to 16, consisting of eight years of primary school and one year of lower secondary school. Further secondary education is available at *lycées*, professional schools or advanced technical schools. From 2003, primary school is being extended from eight years to nine years, and the secondary system will also be comprehensively reformed.

In 1999–2000 there were 12,795 kindergartens with 36,000 teachers and 616,000 children; 13,314 primary and secondary schools with 166,000 teachers and 2,498,000 pupils; 1,307 *lycées* (upper secondary schools) with 71,000 teachers and 916,000 pupils; in post-secondary vocational schools there were 4,000 teachers and 95,000 pupils. In 1999–2000 primary and secondary education in Hungarian was given to 124,427 pupils, in German to 9,495 pupils and in other national minority languages to 1,429 pupils.

In 1999–2000 there were 57 higher education institutions with 361 faculties, 23,000 teaching staff and 277,666 students (254,294 for long-term studies and 23,372 for short-term studies). The distribution of pupils and subjects studied was as follows: technical subjects, 35·2%; economics, 17·6%; medicine and pharmacy, 10·6%; agriculture, 4·3%; law, 4·0%; arts, 2·3%. There are about 68 private higher institutions with 130,000 students.

Adult literacy rate in 1999 was 98·0% (male 99·0%; female 97·1%).

In 2000 total expenditure on education came to 3·6% of GNP and represented 12·2% of total government expenditure.

Health. In 2000 there were 439 hospitals, 166,817 hospital beds and 47,354 doctors (including 4,983 dentists).

Welfare. In Dec. 2002 pensioners comprised 3,096,000 old age and retirement, 1,620,000 retired farmers, 719,900 disability, 650,300 survivor allowance and 5,800 social assistance. These drew average monthly pensions ranging from 565,631 lei to 2,060,203 lei. The social security spending in 2002 was 10·4% of GDP.

CULTURE

Broadcasting. A National Audiovisual Council was established in 1992, and is the only authority which is permitted to grant broadcasting audiovisual licences to private stations. Between 1992 and Nov. 1999 it granted 2,046 cable licences, 217 television broadcasting licences, 341 radio broadcasting licences, 14 licences for satellite television stations and nine licences for satellite radio stations. The public radio and TV stations have broadcasts in Romanian, and in Hungarian and German as well as other minority languages in Romania. The public television station also broadcasts by satellite in its programme *TVR International*. The public radio stations broadcast three radio programmes on medium wave and FM. Radio receivers, 1997, 7·2m.; TV (colour by SECAM H), 5·25m.

Cinema. In 1999 there were 306 cinemas (excluding private ones), with 109,000 seats. Nine full-length films were made in 1995.

Press. There were, in 1999, 100 daily papers and 2,200 periodicals, including 200 periodicals in minority languages.

8,000 book titles were published in 1999.

Tourism. In 1999 there were 3,209,000 foreign tourists, bringing revenue of US$254m.

Libraries. In 1997 there were 3,246 public libraries, 48 National libraries and 339 Higher Education libraries; they held a combined 92,382,000 volumes. There were 1,994,000 registered public library users in 1997.

DIPLOMATIC REPRESENTATIVES

Of Romania in the United Kingdom (Arundel House, 4 Palace Green, London, W8 4QD)
Ambassador: Dan Ghibernea.

Of the United Kingdom in Romania (24 Strada Jules Michelet, 70154 Bucharest)
Ambassador: Quinton Quayle.

Of Romania in the USA (1607 23rd St., NW, Washington, D.C., 20008)
Ambassador: Sorin Dumitru Ducaru.

Of the USA in Romania (7–9 Strada Tudor Arghezi, Bucharest)
Ambassador: Michael E. Guest.

Of Romania to the United Nations
Ambassador: Alexandru Niculescu.

Of Romania to the European Union
Ambassador: Lazar Comanescu.

FURTHER READING

Comisia Nationala pentru Statistica. *Anuarul Statistic al României/Romanian Statistical Yearbook.* Bucharest, annual.—*Revista de Statistica.* Monthly

Gallagher, T., *Romania after Ceauşescu; the Politics of Intolerance*. Edinburgh Univ. Press, 1995

Rady, M., *Romania in Turmoil: a Contemporary History*. London, 1992

Siani-Davies, M. and P., *Romania*. [Bibliography] 2nd ed. ABC-Clio, Oxford and Santa Barbara (CA), (rev. ed.) 1998

National statistical office: Comisia Nationala pentru Statistica, 16 Libertatii Ave., sector 5, Bucharest.

Website: http://www.insse.ro

1331

RUSSIA

Rossiiskaya Federatsiya

Capital: Moscow
Population estimate, 2000: 145·49m.
GDP per capita, 2000: (PPP$) 8,377
HDI/world rank: 0·781/60

KEY HISTORICAL EVENTS

Archaeological evidence points to the influence of Arabic and Turkish cultures prior to the 4th century AD. Avar, Goth, Hun and Magyar occupations punctuated the development of the East Slavs over the next five centuries, while trade with Germanic, Scandinavian and Middle Eastern regions began in the 8th century.

In 882 the Varangian prince Oleg of Novgorod made Kyiv the capital of Kievan Rus, the first unified state of the East Slavs. During the 10th century, trade was extended between the Baltic and Black Seas forming Kyiv's main economy. Successful campaigns against the Varangians, the Khazars and the Bulgars consolidated the East Slav State. The political structure was developed by Vladimir the Great, religion and culture by his successor Yaroslav, but inter-tribal struggles led to Kyiv's demise at the end of the 11th century.

In 1223 Genghis Khan's grandson, Batu Khan, conquered Kievian Rus beginning the Mongols' rule of the 'Golden Horde' area. Trade and cities flourished until internal struggles forced the break-up of the empire in the 15th century. Moscow was then consolidated under Ivan III, the empire strengthened and expanded by Vasily III and reformed by Vasily's successor Ivan 'the Terrible' (1547–84). He led a bloody and suppressive rule although the empire was further expanded. In a fit of pique Ivan murdered his son in 1581 leaving a hereditary gap. The following chaotic period brought various contenders for the throne, dividing Russia and its foreign supporters (such as Poland and Sweden) in their fight for control of the realm. Eventually some stability was restored under Tsar Mikhail Fyodorovich Romanov (the first in a dynasty that would rule until 1917).

Peter the Great's rule (1689–1725) signalled a new era for Russia and established the empire as the leading Baltic power. Administrative reforms and military and industrial expansion were introduced, although peasants' rights were abolished and serfdom began. The capital was transferred from Moscow to the newly built St Petersburg (1712). His daughter Elizabeth I's reign (1741–62) consolidated Peter's reforms and Western culture and literature flourished. The politically ambitious wife of Elizabeth's successor, Catherine the Great, claimed the throne in 1762. She led an aggressive expansion plan that fortified Russia's status as the leading European power.

Russia's position declined over the 19th century with military defeats to France, Turkey and Britain. Some modernization included the partial emancipation of the serfs in 1861, although harsh labour reforms and neglect of agricultural policy under Alexander III resulted in widespread famine in 1891. At the turn of the 20th century, industrial growth and appalling working conditions fuelled revolutionary feelings among the working class while Socialism grew among the middle classes. An unpopular war with Japan (1904) exacerbated public discontent. The massacre of protesting factory workers by Tsar Nicholas II's troops in 1905 caused a countrywide strike, violence and rebellion. World War I temporarily unified Russians in the war effort, but depleting military resources and social hardship led to a succession of anti-tsar demonstrations.

The revolution of 8 March 1917 led to the abdication of Tsar Nicholas II and the proclamation of a republic. However, a political struggle went on between the supporters of the Provisional Government—the Mensheviks and the Socialist Revolutionaries—and the Bolsheviks. When they had won majorities in the Soviets of the principal cities and of the armed forces on several fronts, the Bolsheviks organized an insurrection through a Military-Revolutionary Committee of the

Petrograd Soviet. On 7 Nov. 1917 the Committee arrested the Provisional Government and transferred power to the second All-Russian Congress of Soviets. This elected a new government, the Council of People's Commissars, headed by Lenin. From about 1929 Joseph Stalin's authority was supreme. Resistance to agricultural collectivization was ruthlessly suppressed. A series of Five-Year Plans (1928, 1933, 1937, 1946 and 1951) transformed the USSR into a powerful industrial state. Opposition in party and government was crushed by the purges of 1933 and 1936–38. In Sept. 1939 (under a secret clause of the ten-year non-aggression signed with Nazi Germany on 23 Aug. 1939) Soviet troops occupied eastern Poland. After Hitler invaded Russia, Stalin allied himself with the USA and Britain while extending his power in Central and Eastern Europe. Following the death of Stalin in 1953, Nikita Khrushchev condemned his regime. This encouraged a liberalizing of the Russian-backed communist regimes of Hungary and Poland, and later Czechoslovakia (1968) which the USSR crushed.

A policy of 'peaceful co-existence' with the West, especially after the war scare with the USA in 1962 over Cuban missiles, led to years of strained relations with China. After 1985, with Mikhail Gorbachev as Secretary-General of the Communist Party, a new period of *glasnost* (openness) and *perestroika* (reconstruction) was inaugurated. On 19 Aug 1991 hardliners in the Kremlin attempted to overthrow President Gorbachev, and tanks were sent on to the streets as it was announced that Gorbachev had in effect been deposed. Russian President Boris Yeltsin orchestrated the opposition to the coup, and after three days it ended in failure. This was followed by declarations of independence by the various constituent republics which made up the Soviet Union.

After the dissolution of the USSR in Dec. 1991, Russia became one of the founding members of the Commonwealth of Independent States. Boris Yeltsin was elected Russian President in June 1991. A period of confrontation in 1992–93 between President Yeltsin and parliament climaxed when thousands of armed anti-Yeltsin demonstrators assembled on 3 Oct. and were urged to seize the Kremlin and television centre. On 4 Oct. troops took the parliament building by storm after a 10-hour assault in which 140 people died. Vice-President Rutskoi and Speaker Khasbulatov were arrested.

Russian troops were sent to the breakaway region of Chechnya in 1994, the war lasting for two years. Boris Yeltsin was re-elected president in 1996. Many took this as a signal of confidence in the new, democratic Russia. But the reality was a state in which democratic institutions were weakened to the point of impotence by racketeering and bureaucratic dead-weight. Russia defaulted on its debt, the rouble halved in value, imports fell by 45% and oil revenues slumped. On 17 Aug. 1998 the government freed the rouble, in effect devaluing it, imposed currency controls and froze the domestic debt market.

In Aug. 1999 Boris Yeltsin appointed as prime minister Vladimir Putin, who had been a KGB colonel and director of the KGB's successor organization, the FSB. A series of bomb blasts hit Moscow and one of Putin's first tasks was to send in troops to Chechnya once more, receiving much popular support from Russians despite criticism abroad. On 31 Dec. 1999 Yeltsin resigned the presidency, nominating Putin as his *ad interim* successor, a job he retained after a clear-cut victory in the presidential election of March 2000.

As president, Putin has achieved a certain level of political stability and reform. One of his primary aims has been to reduce the power of the oligarchs behind Yeltsin's success and fight corruption. Tax cuts have been introduced, and in 2000 his programme of regional reform divided Russia's 89 regions into seven new districts run by Kremlin representatives.

Putin has proposed a sweeping reform of Russia's justice system. Headway has also been made in defence policy, with America and Russia agreeing on the Anti-Ballistic Missile treaty. The war in Chechnya remains a cause for humanitarian concern, with reports of atrocities and thousands of refugees.

Following the terror attacks on New York and Washington of 11 Sept. 2001 President Putin made clear his support for the war on terrorism. In Oct. 2002 a group of Chechen rebels took control of a Moscow theatre and held hostage 800 people for three days, before Russian troops stormed the building. An anaesthetic gas, used to combat the rebels, also killed many of the hostages. The rebels had been demanding that Russia end the war in Chechnya. The new relationship with the USA has faltered as a result of the war with Iraq which Russia has opposed.

TERRITORY AND POPULATION

Russia is bounded in the north by various seas (Barents, Kara, Laptev, East Siberian) which join the Arctic Ocean, and in which is a fringe of islands, some of them large. In the east Russia is separated from the USA (Alaska) by the Bering Strait; the Kamchatka peninsula separates the coastal Bering and Okhotsk Seas. Sakhalin Island, north of Japan, is Russian territory. Russia is bounded in the south by North Korea, China, Mongolia, Kazakhstan, the Caspian Sea, Azerbaijan, Georgia, the Black Sea and Ukraine, and in the west by Belarus, Latvia, Estonia, the Baltic Sea and Finland. Kaliningrad (the former East Prussia) is an exclave on the Baltic Sea between Lithuania and Poland in the west. Russia's area is 17,075,400 sq. km and it has 11 time zones. Its 1989 census population was 147,021,869 (53·3% female), of whom 81·5% were Russians, 3·8% Tatars, 3% Ukrainians, 1·2% Chuvash, 0·9% Bashkir, 0·8% Belorussians, and 0·7% Mordovians. Chechens, Germans, Udmurts, Mari, Kazakhs, Avars, Jews and Armenians all numbered 0·5m. or more. Population estimate, 1998, 147,100,000 (female, 53%); density, 9 per sq. km.

In 1999, 77·3% of the population lived in urban areas.

The UN gives a projected population for 2010 of 136·98m.

The two principal cities are Moscow, the capital, with a 1999 population of 8·30m. and St Petersburg (formerly Leningrad), with 4·66m. (also 1999). Other major cities (with 1999 populations) are: Novosibirsk (1·40m.), Nizhny Novgorod (1·35m.), Yekaterinburg (1·26m.), Samara (1·16m.) and Omsk (1·15m.). In May 2000 President Putin signed a decree dividing Russia into seven federal districts, replacing the previous structure of 89 regions. The new districts, with their administrative centres in brackets, are: Central (Moscow), North-Western (St Petersburg), North Caucasus (Rostov-on-Don), Volga (Nizhny Novgorod), Ural (Yekaterinburg), Siberian (Novosibirsk) and Far-Eastern (Khaborovsk).

Moscow: A settlement area since pre-historic times, Moscow is Russia's political, economic and transport centre. Having developed radially from its historic centre it is a city that has preserved its traditional structure. Moscow has a significant cultural framework and a lucrative tourist industry that has thrived since the end of the Cold War.

The national language is Russian.

SOCIAL STATISTICS

1999 births, 1,214,689; deaths, 2,144,316; marriages, 911,162; divorces, 532,533. Rates, 1999 (per 1,000 population): birth, 8·3; death, 14·7: marriage, 6·3; divorce, 3·7. At the beginning of the 1970s the death rate had been just 9·4 per 1,000 population. The annual abortion rate, at approximately 70 per 1,000 women aged 15–44, ranks among the highest in the world. Infant mortality, 1999 (per 1,000 live births), 17·1. The divorce rate, which rose to 5·3 per 1,000 population in 2001, is also among the highest in the world. The most popular age range for marrying in 1995 was 20–24 for both males and females. Expectation of life at birth, 1999, was 60·1 years for males and 72·5 years for females. With a difference of 12·4 years, no other country has a life expectancy for females so high compared to that for males. The low life expectancy (down from 64·6 years for males and 74 years for females in the USSR as a whole in 1989) and the low birth rate (down from 17·6 per 1,000 population in the USSR in 1989) is causing a demographic crisis, with the population declining by approximately 750,000 a year. If current trends continue, the population could fall by nearly 40m. in the first half of the 21st century. Disease, pollution, poor health care and alcoholism are all contributing to the dramatic decline in the population. In 2000, 35% of Russians were living below the poverty line, up from 21% in 1997. Annual population growth rate, 1990–99, −0·1%; fertility rate, 1999, 1·4 births per woman. The suicide rate, at 35·3 per 100,000 population in 1998, is one of the highest in the world. Among males it was 62·6 per 100,000 population in 1998.

CLIMATE
Moscow, Jan. –9·4°C, July 18·3°C. Annual rainfall 630 mm. Arkhangelsk, Jan. –15°C, July 13·9°C. Annual rainfall 503 mm. St Petersburg, Jan. –8·3°C, July 17·8°C. Annual rainfall 488 mm. Vladivostok, Jan. –14·4°C, July 18·3°C. Annual rainfall 599 mm.

CONSTITUTION AND GOVERNMENT
The Russian Soviet Federative Socialist Republic (RSFSR) adopted a constitution in April 1978. In June 1990, pending the promulgation of a new constitution, it adopted a declaration of republican sovereignty by 544 votes to 271. It became a founding member of the CIS in Dec. 1991, and adopted the name 'Russian Federation'. A law of Nov. 1991 extended citizenship to all who lived in Russia at the time of its adoption and to those in other Soviet republics who requested it.

There is a 19-member *Constitutional Court*, whose functions under the 1993 Constitution include making decisions on the constitutionality of federal laws, presidential and government decrees, and the constitutions and laws of the subjects of the Federation. It is governed by a Law on the Constitutional Court, adopted in July 1994. Judges are elected for non-renewable 12-year terms.

At a referendum on 25 April 1993 the electorate was 107·3m.; turn-out was 69·2m. Four questions were put: confidence in President Yeltsin (58·7% of votes cast); approval of economic reforms (53% of votes cast); early presidential elections (31·7% of the electorate); early parliamentary elections (43·1% of the electorate). This referendum had no constitutional effect, however.

Voting was held on 12 Dec. 1993 on the adoption of a new constitution and the election of a new parliament for a two-year term. The electorate was 106,170,335; turn-out was 54·8%. The constitution was approved by 58·4% of votes cast, and came into effect on 24 Dec. 1993.

According to the 1993 Constitution the Russian Federation is a 'democratic federal legally-based state with a republican form of government'. The state is a secular one, and religious organizations are independent of state control. Individuals have freedom of movement within or across the boundaries of the Federation; there is freedom of assembly and association, and freedom to engage in any entrepreneurial activity not forbidden by law. All citizens have a right to housing, to free medical care, and to a free education. The state itself is based upon a separation of powers and upon federal principles, including a Constitutional Court. The most important matters of state are reserved for the federal government, including socio-economic policy, the budget, taxation, energy, foreign affairs and defence. Other matters, including the use of land and water, education and culture, health and social security, are for the joint management of the federal and local governments, which also have the right to legislate within their spheres of competence. A central role is accorded to the *President*, who defines the 'basic directions of domestic and foreign policy' and represents the state internationally. The President is directly elected for a four-year term, and for not more than two consecutive terms; he or she must be at least 35 years old, a Russian citizen, and a resident in Russia for at least the previous ten years. 1m. signatures are needed to validate a presidential candidate, no more than 7% of which may come from any one region or republic. The President has the right to appoint the prime minister, and (on his nomination) to appoint and dismiss deputy prime ministers and ministers, and may dismiss the government as a whole. In the event of the death or incapacity of the President, the Prime Minister becomes head of state.

Parliament is known as the *Federal Assembly*. The 'representative and legislative organ of the Russian Federation', it consists of two chambers: the *Council of the Federation* and the *State Duma*. The Council of the Federation, or upper house, consists of 178 deputies. The Federation is made up of 21 republics, 1 autonomous region, 10 autonomous areas, 6 territories, 49 regions and 2 federal cities. The State Duma, or lower house, consists of 450 deputies chosen for a four-year term. 225 of these are elected from single-member constituencies on the first-past-the-post system, the remainder from party lists by proportional representation. To qualify for candidacy an individual must obtain signatures from at least 1% of voters in the constituency; a party or electoral alliance must obtain a minimum of 100,000 supporting signatures from at least seven regions, but not more than 15% from any one region. There is a 5% threshold for the party-list seats. Parties which gain at least 35 seats may register as a faction, which gives them the right to join the Duma Council and chair committees. Any citizen aged over 21 may be elected to the State Duma, but may not at the same time be a member of the upper house or of other representative bodies, and all deputies work on a 'permanent professional basis'. Both houses elect a chair, committees and commissions. The Council of the Federation considers all matters that apply to the Federation as a whole, including state boundaries, martial law, and the deployment of Russian forces elsewhere. The Duma approves nominations for Prime Minister, and adopts federal laws (they are also considered by the Council of the Federation, but any objection may be overridden by a two-thirds majority; objections on the part of the President may be overridden by both houses on the same basis). The Duma for its part can reject nominations for Prime Minister, but after the third such rejection it is automatically dissolved. It is also dissolved if it twice votes a lack of confidence in the government as a whole, or if it refuses to express confidence in the government when the matter is raised by the Prime Minister.

National Anthem. In Dec. 2000 the Russian parliament, on President Putin's initiative, decided that the tune of the anthem of the former Soviet Union should be reintroduced as the Russian national anthem. Written by Alexander Alexandrov in 1943, the anthem was composed for Stalin. New words were written by Sergei Mikhalkov, who had written the original words for the Soviet anthem in 1943. The new anthem is 'Rossiya—svyashennaya nasha derzhava, Rossiya—lyubimaya nasha strana' ('Russia—our holy country, Russia—our beloved country'). Boris Yeltsin had introduced a new anthem during his presidency—'Patriotic Song', from an opera by Mikhail Glinka and arranged by Andrei Petrov.

RECENT ELECTIONS

Vladimir Putin became President for a four-year term at the elections of 26 March 2000, gaining 52·6% of the votes cast against ten opponents and thus avoiding a second round. His nearest opponent was Gennadiy Zyuganov, the Communist Party candidate, who won 29·3% of the vote. Turn-out was around 70%.

Elections for the State Duma were held on 19 Dec. 1999. The Communist Party gained 113 seats with 24·3% of the vote; Inter-Regional Unity Movement, 72 (23·3%); Fatherland All Russia, 66 (13·3%); Union of Right Forces, 29 (8·5%); Yabloko (Apple), 21 (5·9%); Zhironovsky Blok (Liberal Democrat Party of Russia), 17 (6·0%); Our Home is Russia, 7 (1·2%); All Russian Political Movement in Support of the Army, 2 (0·6%); Pensioners' Party, 1 (2·0%); Congress of Russian Communities and Movement of Y. Boldurev, 1 (0·6%); Russian Socialist Party, 1 (0·2%). Non-partisans claimed 106 seats.

Parliamentary elections are scheduled to take place on 14 Dec. 2003.

CURRENT ADMINISTRATION

President: Vladimir Putin; b. 1952 (sworn in 7 May 2000 having been acting President since 31 Dec. 1999).

In March 2003 the government comprised:

Prime Minister: Mikhail Kasyanov; b. 1957 (sworn in 17 May 2000).

Deputy Prime Ministers: Viktor Khristenko; Aleksey Kudrin (also *Minister of Finance*); Aleksey Gordeyev (also *Minister of Agriculture and Food*).

Minister of Anti-Monopoly Policy and Enterprise Support: Ilya Yuzhanov. *Atomic Energy:* Alexander Rumyantsev. *Civil Defence, Emergencies and Natural Disasters:* Sergey Shoygu. *Culture:* Mikhail Shvydkoy. *Defence:* Sergey Ivanov. *Economic Development and Trade:* German Gref. *Industry, Science and Technology:* Ilya Klebanov. *Foreign Affairs:* Igor Ivanov. *Energy:* Igor Khanukovich Yusufov. *Education:* Vladimir Filippov. *Health:* Yuriy Shevchenko. *Internal Affairs (MVD):* Boris Gryzlov. *Property Relations:* Farit Gazizullin. *Justice:* Yuriy Chayka. *Labour and Social Development:* Aleksandr Pochinok. *Press, Television and Radio Broadcasting, and Mass Communications:* Mikhail Lesin. *Natural Resources:* Vitaliy Grigoryevich Artyukhov. *Railways:* Gennadii Fadeev. *Socioeconomic Development in Chechnya:* Stanislav Ilyasov. *Taxes and Levies:* Gennadiy Bukayev.

Telecommunications and Information: Leonid Reyman. *Transportation:* Sergey Frank. *Nationalities:* Vladimir Yuryevich Zorin.
Chairman of the State Duma: Guennadi N. Seleznev.

Government Website: http://www.gov.ru/

DEFENCE

The President of the Republic is C.-in-C. of the armed forces. Conscription was raised from 18 months to two years in April 1995. There are plans to end conscription by 2005.

The START 2 nuclear arms cutting treaty was ratified by the Duma in April 2000, seven years after it had been signed. This obliged both Russia and the USA to reduce their stocks of strategic weapons from some 6,000 nuclear warheads to 3,500. At the height of the Cold War each side had possessed over 10,000.

A presidential decree of Feb. 1997 ordered a cut in the armed forces of 200,000 men, reducing them to an authorized strength of 1,004,100 in 1999. This figure included 200,000 staff at the Ministry of Defence and 478,000 paramilitary troops (including 196,000 border troops).

Military expenditure totalled US$63,684m. in 2001 (US$440 per capita), representing 4·3% of GDP. Only the USA spent more on defence in 2001.

Nuclear Weapons. Russia's warhead count is now shrinking and stood at 4,951 in Jan. 2002 according to the Stockholm International Peace Research Institute. Shortfalls in planned investments to replace current systems as they reach the end of their service lives means the number of strategic warheads will decline rapidly over the next decade. Current plans are to cut stockpiles to between 2,000 and 2,500, but President Putin has proposed that the target for both Russia and the USA should be 1,500, with even further reductions to follow. On 24 May 2002 the USA and Russia signed an arms control treaty to reduce the number of US and Russian warheads, from between 6,000 and 7,000 each to between 1,700 and 2,200 each, over the next ten years. Russia has pledged to dismantling its biological and chemical weapons programme and to destroy its stockpiles of such weapons, believed to be the largest in the world.

Army. A Russian Army was created by presidential decree in March 1992. In 2002 forces numbered 321,000 (190,000 conscripts). There were estimated to be around 20,000,000 reserves (all armed forces) of whom 2,400,000 had seen service within the previous five years. There were around 17,000 Russian troops stationed outside Russia (including 7,800 in Tajikistan and 4,000 in Georgia) in 2002, the majority in various states of the former USSR.

The Army is deployed in six military districts and one Operational Strategic Group. Equipment includes some 13,870 main battle tanks (including T-55, T-62, T-64A/-B, T-72L/-M, T-80/-U/UD/UM and T-90s) plus 150 light tanks (PT-76). In addition 8,000 main battle tanks were in store.

The Army air element has some 2,300 attack helicopters in the inventory (of which 600 in store) including Mi-24s and Ka-50s. Funding shortages have reduced serviceability drastically.

Strategic Nuclear Ground Forces. In 2002 there were four rocket armies, each with launcher groups, 10 silos and one control centre. Inter-continental ballistic missiles numbered 735. Personnel, 100,000 (50,000 conscripts).

Navy. The Russian Navy continues to reduce steadily and levels of sea-going activity remain very low with activity concentrated on a few operational units in each fleet. The safe deployment and protection of the reduced force of strategic missile-firing submarines remains its first priority; and the defence of the Russian homeland its second. The strategic missile submarine force operates under command of the Strategic Nuclear Force commander whilst the remainder come under the Main Naval Staff in Moscow, through the Commanders of the fleets.

The Northern and Pacific fleets count the entirety of the ballistic missile submarine force, all nuclear-powered submarines, the sole operational aircraft carrier and most major surface warships. The Baltic Fleet organization is based in the St Petersburg area and in the Kaliningrad exclave. Some minor war vessels have been ceded to the Baltic republics. The Black Sea Fleet was for some years the object of wrangling between Russia and Ukraine. Russia eventually received four-fifths of the Black Sea Fleet's warships, with Ukraine receiving about half of the facilities. It was agreed that Russia would rent three harbours for warships and two airfields for a period of 20 years, for a payment of approximately US$100m. annually. The small Caspian Sea flotilla, formerly a sub-unit of the Black Sea Fleet, has been divided between Azerbaijan (25%), and Russia, Kazakhstan and Turkmenistan, the littoral republics (75%).

The material state of all the fleets is suffering from continued inactivity and lack of spares and fuel. The nuclear submarine refitting and refuelling operations in the Northern and Pacific Fleets remain in disarray, given the large numbers of nuclear submarines awaiting defuelling and disposal. The strength of the submarine force has now essentially stabilized, but there are still large numbers of decommissioned vessels awaiting their turn for scrapping in a steadily deteriorating state. In Jan. 2003 it was announced that up to a fifth of the fleet was to be scrapped.

The aircraft carrier *Admiral Kuznetsov* is now operational, albeit with a limited aviation capability, and she deployed to the Mediterranean in Dec. 1995.

In 2002 there were 13 operational nuclear-fuelled ballistic-missile submarines, constituted as follows:

Class	No.	Missiles	Total no. of missiles
Delta-IV	6	16 SS-N-23	96
Delta-III	5	16 SS-N-18	80
Typhoon	2	20 SS-N-20	40
			216

The attack submarine fleet comprises a wide range of classes, from the enormous 16,250 tonne 'Oscar' nuclear-powered missile submarine to diesel boats of around 2,000 tonnes. The inventory of tactical nuclear-fuelled submarines comprises 6 'Oscar II', 1 former strategic 'Yankee'-class, 9 'Akula'-class, 1 'Sierra'-class and 5 'Victor III'-class submarines.

The diesel-powered 'Kilo' class, of which the Navy operates nine, is still building at a reduced rate mostly for export. There are a further four diesel submarines on the active list.

Cruisers are divided into two categories; those optimized for anti-submarine warfare (ASW) are classified as 'Large Anti-Submarine Ships' and those primarily configured for anti-surface ship operations are classified 'Rocket Cruisers'. The principal surface ships of the Russian Navy include the following classes:

Aircraft Carrier. The *Admiral Kuznetsov* of 67,500 tonnes was completed in 1989. It is capable of embarking 20 aircraft and 15–17 helicopters. All other aircraft carriers have been decommissioned or scrapped.

Cruisers. The ships of this classification are headed by the two ships of the Kirov-class, the largest combatant warships, apart from aircraft carriers, to be built since the Second World War. There are, in addition, 3 Slava-class, 1 of the Nikolaev ('Kara') class and 1 Kynda class ship in operation.

Destroyers. There are 7 Udaloy-class, the first of which entered service in 1981, 1 Udaloy II-class and 4 Sovremenny-class guided missile destroyers in operation. In addition there is a single remaining 'modified Kashin'-class ship and a further one unmodified 'Kashin' also in operation.

Frigates. There are 10 frigates in operation including the first of a new class, the 'Neustrashimy', 7 Krivak I-class and 2 Krivak II-class ships.

The Russian Naval Air Force operates some 217 combat aircraft including 45 Tu-22M bombers and 52 Su-24, 10 Su-25 and 52 Su-27 fighters. There were an additional 102 armed helicopters in operation.

Total Naval personnel in 2002 numbered 171,500, of whom an estimated 16,000 were conscripts. Some 11,000 serve in the strategic submarine force, 35,000 in naval aviation, 9,500 naval infantry/coastal defence troops.

Air Force. The Air Force (VVS) and Air Defence Troops (PVO) amalgamated in March 1998 under one Air Force command. Personnel is estimated at 185,000 and comprises some 1,736 combat aircraft but no aircraft.

The Air Force is organized into three main Commands: Long-Range Aviation, Tactical Aviation and Military Transport Aviation.

Long-Range Aviation comprised in 2002 (numbers in brackets) Tu-160 (15), Tu-22M (117) and Tu-95 (63) bombers, some equipped to carry nuclear weapons.

Tactical Aviation comprised in 2002 (numbers in brackets) Su-24 (371) and Su-25 (235) fighter-bombers and MiG-29 (255), MiG-31 (256) and Su-27 (392) fighters. In addition MiG-25 and Su-24s are used for reconnaissance missions.

INTERNATIONAL RELATIONS

Russia is a member of the UN (Security Council), BIS, the NATO Partnership for Peace, CIS, the Council of Europe, OSCE, Council of the Baltic Sea States, BSEC, Danube Commission, APEC and the Antarctic Treaty. On 16 May 1997 NATO ratified a 'Fundamental Act on Relations, Co-operation and Mutual Security' with Russia. Although not a member of the World Trade Organization, President Putin has made it a stated goal. Russian officials think that the country could join the WTO by the end of 2003.

ECONOMY

Agriculture accounted for 7·3% of GDP in 1998, industry 35·3% and services 57·4%.

In Oct. 1991 a programme was launched to create a 'healthy mixed economy with a powerful private sector'. The prices of most commodities were freed on 2 Jan. 1992.

Privatization, overseen by the State Committee on the Management of State Property, began with small and medium-sized enterprises. A state programme of privatization of state and municipal enterprises was approved by parliament in June 1992, and vouchers worth 10,000 roubles each began to be distributed to all citizens in Oct. 1992. These could be sold or exchanged for shares. Employees were the right to purchase 51% of the equity of their enterprises. 25 categories of industry (including raw materials and arms) remain in state ownership. The voucher phase of privatization ended on 30 June 1994. A post-voucher stage authorized by presidential decree of 22 July 1994 provides for firms to be auctioned for cash following the completion of the sale of up to 70% of manufacturing industry for vouchers. By Dec. 1997 a total of 127,000 enterprises had been privatized; 59% of these were in trade, public catering and personal services, 33% in manufacturing, construction, transport and communications and 2·4% in agriculture. While there is still widespread corruption and a reluctance in some sectors to loosen state control, there are encouraging signs of an economy pulling into shape.

Overview. In the late 1990s the Asian crisis, the weakening of capital flows to emerging markets and the collapse of oil prices all hurt the economy. It has since benefited from improved oil revenues and tighter fiscal management. The transition from the centrally planned system to one based mainly on markets disrupted the economy and the collection of data. Much of the private sector goes unrecorded owing to tax avoidance. Goskomstat (the State Statistic Committee) adjusts figures upward on the basis that an estimated 25% of production is informal. The 1999 Tax Code limits the number and type of taxes employed at various levels of government.

Currency. The unit of currency is the *rouble* (RUR), of 100 *kopeks*. In Jan. 1998 the rouble was redenominated by a factor of a thousand. Foreign exchange reserves were US$39,838m. and gold reserves 12·44m. troy oz in June 2002. In 1997 the rouble was tied to the US dollar on a sliding scale ranging from US$1 = 5,500–6,100 roubles on 1 Jan. 1997 to 6 roubles on 31 Jan. 1998. Inflation, which was 879% in 1993, stood at 20·7% in 2001. In 1995 the total external debt was US$120,461m., most of it inherited from the Soviet Union. Total money supply in June 2002 was 1,254·51bn. roubles. In Nov. 2000 President Putin and President Lukashenka of Belarus agreed the introduction of a single currency, with the Russian rouble to be introduced in Belarus by 2005 and a single currency in 2008. The draft agreement has to be ratified by the parliaments of the two countries.

Budget. In 2000 revenue totalled 1,843,958m. roubles (of which tax 1,522,364m. roubles) and expenditure 1,672,353m. roubles. In 1997 the budget deficit was 6·1% of GDP. The current account surplus was US$3,336m.

Performance. GDP grew by 0·9% in 1997, the first expansion since the Soviet Union's collapse in 1991; but many economists believe that the booming informal economy adds over 25% to the value of GDP. With oil revenues well down and a collapse of the rouble in 1998, Russia defaulted on its debt. In 1998 real GDP growth was −4·9%. There was then a highly impressive turnaround, with growth of 5·4% in 1999 and a record 9·0% in 2000. In 2001 there was growth of 5·0%, in spite of the world economic slowdown and the effects of the attacks on New York and Washington of 11 Sept. 2001. GDP declined by 17% between 1992 and 1997 and GDP per person by 25% over the same period. Total GDP was US$310·0bn. in 2001.

Banking and Finance. The central bank and bank of issue is the State Bank of Russia (*Governor*, Sergey Mikhailovich Ignatiev). The Russian Bank for Reconstruction and Development and the State Investment Company were created in 1993 to channel foreign and domestic investment. Foreign bank branches have been operating since Nov. 1992.

By 1995 the number of registered commercial banks had increased to around 5,000 but following the Aug. 1997 liquidity crisis, owing to the ensuing bankruptcies, mergers and the Central Bank's revoking of licences, the number fell to 2,500. Approximately 80% of the commercial banks were state-owned through ministries or state enterprises. At the end of 2000 the leading banks were Sberbank (assets of 551·8bn. roubles), Vneshtorgbank (111·5bn. roubles) and Gazprombank (82·3bn. roubles).

In the wake of one of the worst financial crises which Russia's market economy had experienced, the central bank tripled interest rates to 150% in May 1998 in an effort to restore stability to the financial system. In 2002 the banking sector in Russia was healthier than at any time since the collapse of the former Soviet Union.

There are stock exchanges in St Petersburg and Vladivostok.

Russia was one of 15 countries and territories named in a report in June 2000 as failing to co-operate in the fight against international money laundering. The Financial Action Task Force on Money Laundering was set up by the G7 group of major industrialized nations.

Weights and Measures. The metric system is in use. The Gregorian Calendar was adopted as from 14 Feb. 1918.

ENERGY AND NATURAL RESOURCES

Environment. Russia's carbon dioxide emissions in 1998 accounted for 6·3% of the world total (the third highest after the USA and China), and according to the *World Bank Atlas* were equivalent to 9·8 tonnes per capita. An *Environmental Sustainability Index* compiled for the World Economic Forum meeting in Feb. 2002 ranked Russia 72nd in the world, with 49·1%. The index measured the ability of countries to maintain favourable environmental conditions and examined various factors including pollution levels and the use or abuse of natural resources.

Electricity. Installed capacity was 206m. kW in 1997. Production in 1998 was 771·95bn. kWh and consumption per capita 3,937 kWh. The dominant electricity company is United Energy Systems (52% state-owned), which controls 80% of Russia's generating capacity. There were 30 nuclear plants in use in 2001.

Oil and Gas. Oil and gas companies account for around a quarter of the Russian economy. In Feb. 2003 British Petroleum (BP) announced a US$6·75bn. investment in the Russian oil industry. The programme aims to create a new company producing 1·2m. bbls. of crude oil per day.

In 2001 there were proven crude petroleum reserves of 48·6bn. bbls., enough to last until 2021. In 1999 production of crude petroleum was 303m. tonnes. Russia is one of the world's leading oil producers and a major exporter. In 1996 there were 63,000 km of pipeline for crude petroleum. In 2002 a deal to supply oil from the Ural region to the US West Coast was agreed. A deepwater port at Murmansk is being planned. Russia is also looking to secure American investment in its oil industry. Work on a new 3,700-km long oil pipeline stretching to Nakhodka, on Russia's eastern coast, is set to commence during 2003.

Output of natural gas in 1999 was 589,484m. cu. metres, making Russia the world's largest producer. Russia also has the largest reserves of natural gas—in 2000 it had proven reserves of 48,100bn. cu. metres.

Minerals. Russia contains great mineral resources: iron ore, coal, gold, platinum, copper, zinc, lead, tin and rare metals. Output, 1997 (in tonnes): coal, 261m.; nickel,

260m.; chrome ore, 151m.; lignite (1997), 88·6m.; iron ore, 70·8m.; molybdenum, 8·5m.; tin, 7·5m.; bauxite, 3·3m.; gold (2000), 155. Salt production, 1997 estimate: 2·1m. tonnes. Diamond production, 2000: 20·5m. carats. Only Australia and Botswana produce more diamonds. Annual uranium production is 2,000 tonnes.

Agriculture. A presidential decree of Dec. 1991 authorized the private ownership of land on a general basis; a further decree of March 1996 authorized its free sale. Collective and state farms which wish to start private farming are required to re-register as co-operatives or share companies. Members of collectives may withdraw with a certificate of land ownership and a share of the collective's equipment or compensation in lieu; members may also elect to remain in co-operatives voluntarily. The decree permits foreign nationals to own land through joint ventures.

In Jan. 1995 there were 26,900 agricultural enterprises including 6,000 collective farms, 3,600 state farms and 17,300 commercial farms; 6·4m. were employed in agriculture, and output was valued at 38,491,000m. roubles. In 1995, 220·8m. ha were in cultivation, of which 105·1m. ha were in the hands of companies and co-operatives, 32·2m. ha in collective farms, 18·5m. ha in state farms, 10·1m. ha in commercial farms and 5·7m. ha in individual private plots. By 1997 there were 126·0m. ha of arable land and 1·94m. ha of permanent crops. In 2001 nearly 90% of Russia's agricultural land was privately owned.

Output in 2000 (in 1,000 tonnes) included: wheat, 36,000; potatoes, 35,297; sugarbeets, 14,041; barley, 13,266; oats, 5,500; rye, 5,300; cabbages, 4,500; sunflower seeds, 3,900; tomatoes, 1,985; maize, 1,800; carrots, 1,605; onions, 1,320; apples, 1,200. Russia is the world's largest producer of oats and the second largest producer of potatoes and sunflower seeds.

Livestock, 2000: cattle, 27·5m.; pigs, 18·3m; sheep, 14·0m.; poultry, 342m. Livestock products in 2000 (in tonnes): meat, 4·3m.; milk, 31·8m.; eggs, 1·9m.; cheese, 364,000.

Forestry. Russia has the largest area covered by forests of any country in the world, with 7,635,000 sq. km in 1995 (45·2% of the land area). In 1999 timber production was 111m. cu. metres, down from 228·52m. in 1992. In 1999 Russia was the world's largest exporter of roundwood with 27% of the world total.

Fisheries. Total catch in 1999 was 4,141,157 tonnes (up from 3,705,081 tonnes in 1994, but down from 8,211,516 tonnes in 1989). Approximately 93% of the fish caught are from marine waters.

INDUSTRY

The leading companies by market capitalization in Russia, excluding banking and finance, in Jan. 2002 were: NK Yukos OAO (438bn. roubles), an oil and gas company; Gazprom OAO (428bn. roubles), a gas company; and Surgutneftegas OAO (357bn. roubles), an oil and gas field construction company.

Output in 1994 (in tonnes) included: crude steel (1999), 51·5m.; cast iron, 36·5m.; rolled iron, 35·9m.; cement (1997), 26·7m.; cellulose (1995), 4·1m.; steel pipe, 3·6m.; paper and paperboard (1998), 3·3m.; confectionery, 1·5m.; sugar, 1·37m.; caustic soda, 1·1m.; soap, washing powder and detergents (1997), 435,000; synthetic fibre, 198,000; (in sq. metres) glass, 58·6m.; (in units) bricks, 14,700m.; tractors, 28,700; combine harvesters, 12,100; bulldozers, 2,200; tins of food, 2,817m.; personal computers, 82,100; watches, 25·9m.; televisions (1997), 327,000; refrigerators (1997), 1·11m.; motor vehicles (1997), 1,264,000; cigarettes (1997), 140·1bn.; mineral water (1997), 411m. litres; vodka and liquors (1995), 1,220m. litres; and beer (1997), 2,610m. litres. Total output in physical terms in 1994 was 79% of the 1993 total, and 51% of 1990.

Labour. In 1997 the subsistence minimum was estimated at 393,600 roubles; 22% of the population fell below it. In Jan. 1997 the official monthly minimum wage was 83,490 roubles; the average monthly wage was 870,000 roubles. The state Federal Employment Service was set up in 1992. Unemployment benefits are paid for 15 months: three months at full salary, three months at 75% and a final nine months at a progressively reducing rate. Annual paid leave is 24 working days. The workforce was 72·52m. in 1998, of which 16·76m. worked in services, 14·15m. in mining, manufacturing and public utilities, 8·90m. in trade, 8·28m. in agriculture, 5·41m. in construction, 5·04m. in transport and communications, and 2·57m., in public administration and defence. Unemployment in June 2001 stood at 8%. In 1996, 4,007 man-days were lost through strikes. In 1996, 84·3m. people were of working age and 30·5m. people were above working age. Retirement age is 55 years for women, 60 for men.

Trade Unions. The Federation of Independent Trade Unions (founded 1990) is the successor to the former Communist official union organization. In 1993 it comprised 77 regional and 46 sectoral trade unions, with a total membership of 60m. There are also free trade unions.

INTERNATIONAL TRADE

Foreign debt was US$160,300m. in 2000, a figure exceeded only by Brazil. Most CIS republics have given up claims on Soviet assets in return for Russia assuming their portion of foreign debt. A Foreign Investment Agency was set up in Dec. 1992. In Jan. 1994 there were 6,359 joint enterprises in operation, employing 304,000 and accounting for 8% of foreign trade. Following an agreement to supply oil to the US West Coast in 2002, Russia is looking to secure American investment in its oil industry.

Imports and Exports. Trade in US$1m.:

	1996	1997	1998	1999	2000
Imports f.o.b.	68,093	71,982	58,014	39,537	44,862
Exports f.o.b.	90,564	89,008	74,883	75,666	105,565

In 2000 Germany accounted for 9·0% of exports, USA 7·7%, Italy 7·0%, Belarus 5·4% and China 5·1%. Germany provided 11·5% of imports in 2000, Belarus 11·1%, Ukraine 10·8%, the USA 8·0% and Kazakhstan 6·5%. In 1998, of exports, 36·4% by value were fuels and lubricants, 19·3% metals, and 9·2% machinery and transport equipment. Of imports, 23·9% by value was machinery and transport equipment, 17·5% foodstuffs and 10·3% chemical products.

COMMUNICATIONS

Roads. In 1997 there were 570,719 km of roads, of which 80% were hard surfaced; in 1995, 22,817m. passengers were carried by bus services, 8,547m. by trolley buses and 7,564m. by trams. 40% of villages cannot be reached by road. There were 17,631,600 passenger cars in 1997 (119·8 per 1,000 inhabitants) and 4,905,900 trucks and vans. There were 29,021 road deaths in 1998 (1,286 deaths per 1m. vehicles).

Rail. Length of railways in 1996 was 87,000 km of 1,520 mm gauge (of which 44% were electrified). Passenger-km travelled in 1996 came to 168·7bn. and freight tonne-km to 1,131·0bn. There are metro services in six cities. It is estimated that 10% of all railways are in some way defective.

Civil Aviation. The main international airports are at Moscow (Sheremetevo) and St Petersburg (Pulkovo). The national carrier is Aeroflot International Russian Airlines, which is 51% state- and 49% employee-owned. Pulkovo, Siberia, Trasaero and Vnukovo Airlines also operate internationally.

In 1999 Aeroflot carried 4,438,900 passengers (3,275,800 on international flights) and flew 164·2m. km; Pulkovo Airlines carried 1,337,800 passengers (464,900 on international flights) and flew 29·1m. km. Moscow Sheremetevo handled 10,764,000 passengers in 2000 (7,825,000 on international flights) and 102,100 tonnes of freight. Moscow Vnukovo is mainly used for internal flights and was the second busiest airport in 2000, handling 3,451,000 passengers (2,802,000 on domestic flights) and 44,000 tonnes of freight. St Petersburg was the third busiest in 2000 for passengers (2,568,304) and for freight (19,101 tonnes).

Shipping. In 1998 the merchant fleet comprised 4,723 vessels (including 340 tankers) totalling 11,090,000 GRT. In 1995, 236 vessels (24% of tonnage) were registered under foreign flags. In 1994, 155m. tonnes of freight (about two-thirds was building materials) and 40m. passengers were carried on the 94,000 km of inland waterways. Kaliningrad was opened to shipping in May 1991. In 1996, 14,120,000 tonnes of freight were loaded and 1,423,000 tonnes were unloaded at Russian docks.

Telecommunications. Russia had 32,070,000 main telephone lines in 2000, or 218·3 for every 1,000 persons, but 7·8m. people were on the waiting list for a line in 1998—the highest number anywhere in the world. There were 6·3m. PCs in use in 2000 (42·9 per 1,000 persons) and 106,000 fax machines in 1997. Russia had 18·0m. Internet users in Dec. 2001 and 16·6m. mobile phone subscribers in Dec. 2002.

Postal Services. In mid-1995 there were 51,800 post offices (35,400 in rural areas).

SOCIAL INSTITUTIONS

Justice. The Supreme Court is the highest judicial body on civil, criminal and administrative law. The Supreme Arbitration Court deals with economic cases. The KGB, and the Federal Security Bureau which succeeded it, were replaced in Dec. 1992 by the Federal Counter-Intelligence Service. The legal system is, however, crippled by incompetence and corruption.

A new civil code was introduced in 1993 to replace the former Soviet code. It guarantees the inviolability of private property and includes provisions for the freedom of movement of capital and goods.

12-member juries were introduced in a number of courts after Nov. 1993, but in the years that followed jury trials were not widely used. However, on 1 Jan. 2003 jury trials began to be phased in nationwide. A new criminal code came into force on 1 Jan. 1997, based on respect for the rights and freedoms of the individual and the sanctity of private property. A further new code that entered force on 1 July 2002 introduced new levels of protection for defendants and restrictions on law enforcement officials. The death penalty is retained for five crimes against the person. It is not applied to minors, women or men over 65.

In 1998 there were 33,553 murders, giving a rate of 22·9 per 100,000 population. In 1994, 924,600 sentences were passed, of which 36% involved imprisonment. In 1996 there were 140 executions (86 in 1995; 1 in 1992). President Yeltsin placed a moratorium on capital punishment in 1996 when Russia joined the Council of Europe, but parliament has refused to abolish the death penalty. Organized crime groups control up to 40,000 commercial organizations. In 1998 there were 1,007,000 prisoners, or 685 prisoners per 100,000 population, among the highest rates in the world.

Religion. The Russian Orthodox Church, represented by the Patriarchate of Moscow, had, in 1997, an estimated 24m. adherents. In 1996 there were over 14,000 parishes, 136 monasteries, and 26 secondary and higher educational institutions. There are still many Old Believers, whose schism from the Orthodox Church dates from the 17th century. The Russian Church is headed by the Patriarch of Moscow and All Russia (Metropolitan Aleksi II of St Petersburg and Novgorod, b. 1929; elected June 1990), assisted by the Holy Synod, which has seven members—the Patriarch himself and the Metropolitans of Krutitsy and Kolomna (Moscow), St Petersburg and Kiev *ex officio*, and three bishops alternating for six months in order of seniority from the three regions forming the Moscow Patriarchate. The Patriarchate of Moscow maintains jurisdiction over 119 eparchies, of which 59 are in Russia; there are parishes of Russian Orthodox abroad, in Belarus, Ukraine, Kazakhstan, Moldova, Uzbekistan, the Baltic states, and in Damascus, Geneva, Prague, New York and Japan. There is a spiritual mission in Jerusalem, and a monastery at Mt Athos in Greece. There are Jewish communities, primarily in Moscow and St Petersburg, that numbered 590,000 in 2001; there were also 10,980,000 Muslims and 1,320,000 Protestants. The *Grand Mufti* is Talgat Tadschuddin.

Education. Adult literacy rate in 1999 was 99·5% (male, 99·7%; female, 99·4%). In 1998 there were 23·97m. pupils in 72,169 primary and secondary day schools; 3·60m. students in 914 higher educational establishments (including correspondence students); and in 1995, 3·6m. students in 6,800 technical colleges of all kinds (including correspondence students); and 5·6m. children in 68,600 pre-school institutions. In 1994–95 there were 822 grammar schools and 505 *lycées* with a combined total of 1m. students. In addition there were 447 private schools with 40,000 pupils.

In 1957 a Siberian branch of the Academy of Sciences was organized. Pre-dating the foundation of a Russian Academy of Sciences, St Petersburg and Urals branches were founded in 1990 and 1991 respectively. The Soviet became the Russian Academy of Sciences in Dec. 1991. There were 3,968 scientific institutes, of which 2,166 are independent research institutes.

In 1995 total expenditure on education came to 3·5% of GNP.

A survey for the 1999 *World Competitiveness Yearbook* showed that well-educated people in Russia are the most likely of any country in the world to emigrate—87 out of every 100 well-educated Russians go abroad to live and work.

Health. Doctors in 1998 numbered 682,000, and hospital beds 1·73m. In 1995 the doctor/inhabitant ratio was 1:235 and in 1994 hospital bed provision was 119 for every 10,000 persons. There were 12,300 hospitals. At the end of 1999 there were 130,000 people living with HIV/AIDS. In 1999 and 2000 Russia experienced the highest rate of growth of HIV cases in the world. In 1998, 48% of Russians aged 15 and over smoked—the highest percentage of any country. An estimated 280,000 people died in 1995 from tobacco use. This represented 18% of all deaths.

Welfare. Vouchers are issued to cover basic health care and pensions contributions. These may be topped up to buy better services. A transition from state-financed to insurance-based health care is taking place.

There were 37·1m. pensioners in 1996. A lump sum of 2,700 roubles was payable in 1992 to parents on the birth of a child. From Dec. 1996 the minimum pension was 75,900 roubles a month. The average monthly pension in June 1995 was 201,874 roubles.

Personal pensions conferred by the former Communist regime conferring special benefits on party or state personnel or awarded for services rendered were abolished in 1992.

Over 80m. Russians live in areas where concentrations of air pollutants are well in excess of permissible levels. 30–40% of children's diseases are caused by air pollution; respiratory diseases such as asthma have increased sixfold since the early 1990s.

CULTURE

Broadcasting. In 1997 there were 57·3m. television receivers. Television broadcasting is still largely state-controlled. In Nov. 2001 a court ordered that the parent company of TV6, the last independent station, be liquidated. It was closed down in Jan. 2002. There are two major channels, ORT (Russian Public Television) and RTR (Russian Television). Colour is by SECAM H. In 1994, 98·8% of the population could receive TV broadcasts. There are also local city channels. Access to cable TV varies with locality; satellite TV reached about 5% of the population in 1993. As well as state radio, 24% of the population in 1995 could receive commercial broadcasts. In 1997 there were 61·5m. radio receivers.

Cinema. There were 2,016 cinemas in 1995; attendances in the year totalled 140·1m. 46 long films were made.

Press. In 1996 there were 285 daily newspapers with a combined circulation of 15,517,000 (105 per 1,000 population). In the same year there were 4,596 non-daily newspapers with a combined circulation of 98,558,000 (665 per 1,000 population). A presidential decree of 22 Dec. 1993 brought the press agencies ITAR-TASS and RIA-Novosti under state control. In 1996, 30,200 titles (books and brochures) were published. Russia's media is becoming relatively independent, but press freedom has suffered setbacks since Vladimir Putin became president.

Tourism. There were 18,496,000 foreign visitors in 1999 bringing in revenue of US$7·77bn.

Libraries. In 1995 there were two National Libraries and 96,177 public libraries, which held 983,356,000 volumes for 54,201,300 registered users.

Theatre and Opera. In 1995 there were 470,000 theatres.

Museums and Galleries. Russia had 1,725 museums in 1995.

DIPLOMATIC REPRESENTATIVES

Of Russia in the United Kingdom (13 Kensington Palace Gdns., London, W8 4QX)
Ambassador: Grigory B. Karasin.

Of the United Kingdom in Russia (Smolenskaya Naberezhnaya 10, 121099 Moscow)
Ambassador: Sir Roderic Lyne, KBE, CMG.

Of Russia in the USA (2650 Wisconsin Ave., NW, Washington, D.C., 20007)
Ambassador: Yury Ushakov.

Of the USA in Russia (Novinski Bul'var 19/23, Moscow)
Ambassador: Alexander R. Vershbow.

Of Russia to the United Nations
Ambassador: Sergey V. Lavrov.

Of Russia to the European Union
Ambassador: Vasiliy Likhachev.

FURTHER READING

Rossiiskii Statisticheskii Ezhegodnik. Moscow, annual (title varies)
Acton, E., *et al., Critical Companion to the Russian Revolution.* Indiana Univ. Press, 1997
Aron, Leon, *Boris Yeltsin: A Revolutionary Life.* HarperCollins, London, 2000
Aslund, Anders, (ed.) *Economic Transformation in Russia.* New York, 1994.—*Building Capitalism: the Transformation of the Former Soviet Bloc.* CUP, 2002
Brady, Rose, *Kapitalizm: Russia's Struggle to Free its Economy.* Yale Univ. Press, 2000
Cambridge Encyclopedia of Russia and the Former Soviet Union. CUP, 1995
Dunlop, J., *Russia Confronts Chechnya: Roots of a Separatist Conflict, Vol. 1.* CUP, 1998
Fowkes, B. (ed.) *Russia and Chechnia: The Permanent Crisis, Essays on Russo-Chechen Relations.* St Martin's Press, New York, 1998
Freeze, G. (ed.) *Russia: A History.* OUP, 1997
Gall, C. and de Waal, T., *Chechnya: Calamity in the Caucasus.* New York, 1998
Gorbachev, Mikhail, *On My Country and the World;* translated from Russian. Columbia Univ. Press, New York, 2000
Granville, Brigitte and Oppenheimer, Peter, (eds.) *Russia's Post-Community Economy.* OUP, 2001
Gustafson, Thane, *Capitalism Russian-Style.* Cambridge Univ. Press, 2000
Hollander, Paul, *Political Will and Personal Belief: The Decline and Fall of Soviet Communism.* Yale Univ. Press, 2000
Hosking, Geoffrey, *Russia and the Russians, A History from Rus to the Russian Federation.* Allen Lane/The Penguin Press, London, 2001
Kochan, L., *The Making of Modern Russia.* 2nd ed., revised by R. Abraham. London, 1994
Kotkin, Stephen, *Armageddon Averted: the Soviet Collapse 1970–2000.* OUP, 2001
Lieven, A., *Chechnya: Tombstone of Russian Power.* Yale Univ. Press, 1998
Lloyd, J., *Rebirth of a Nation.* London, 1998
Marks, Steven, *How Russia Shaped the Modern World: From Art to Anti-Semitism, Ballet to Bolshevism.* Princeton Univ. Press, 2002
Paxton, J., *Encyclopedia of Russian History.* Denver (CO), 1993
Pitman, L., *Russia/USSR.* [Bibliography] 2nd ed. ABC-Clio, Oxford and Santa Barbara (CA), 1994
Putin, Vladimir, *First Person;* interviews, translated from Russian. Hutchinson, London, 2000
Remnick, D., *Resurrection: The Struggle for a New Russia.* Picador, London, 1998
Riasanovsky, N. V., *A History of Russia.* 5th ed. OUP, 1993
Sakwa, R., *Russian Politics and Society.* 2nd ed. London, 1996
Service, Robert, *A History of Twentieth-Century Russia.* Harvard Univ. Press, 1997.—*Lenin: A Biography.* Macmillan, London, 2000.—*Russia: Experiment with a People.* Pan Macmillan, London, 2002
Shriver, G. (ed. and transl.) *Post-Soviet Russia, A Journey Through the Yeltsin Era.* Columbia Univ. Press, 2000
Westwood, J. N., *Endurance and Endeavour: Russian History, 1812–1992.* 4th ed. OUP, 1993
White, Stephen, *et al., How Russia Votes.* Chatham House (NJ), 1997
White, Stephen, Pravda, Alex and Gitelman, Zvi, (eds.) *Developments in Russian Politics.* Palgrave, Basingstoke, 2001
Woodruff, David, *Money Unmade: Barter and the Fate of Russian Capitalism.* Cornell Univ. Press, 2000
Yeltsin, B., *The View from the Kremlin* (in USA *The Struggle for Russia*). London and New York, 1994

National statistical office: Gosudarstvennyi Komitet po Statistike (*Goskomstat*), Moscow.
Website: http://www.gks.ru

THE REPUBLICS

Status

The 21 republics that with Russia itself constitute the Russian Federation were part of the RSFSR in the Soviet period. On 31 March 1992 the federal government concluded treaties with the then 20 republics, except Checheno-Ingushetia and Tatarstan, defining their mutual responsibilities. The *Council of the Heads of the Republics* is chaired by the Russian President and includes the Russian Prime Minister. Its function is to provide an interaction between the federal government and the republican authorities.

ADYGEYA

Part of Krasnodar Territory. Area, 7,600 sq. km (2,934 sq. miles); population (1996), 450,000. Capital, Maikop (1996 population, 165,500). Established 27 July 1922; granted republican status in 1991.

President: Hazret Sovmen.

Chief industries are timber, woodworking, food processing and there is some engineering and gas production. Agriculture consists primarily of crops (beets, wheat, maize), on partly irrigated land. Industrial output was valued in 1993 at 112,000m. roubles, agricultural output at 68,000m. roubles.

In 1994–95 there were 174 schools with 67,000 pupils, 3 technical colleges with 5,200 students and 2 higher educational institutions with 6,200 students.

In 1995 the rates of doctors and hospital beds per 10,000 population were 32·7 and 113 respectively.

ALTAI

Part of Altai Territory. Area, 92,600 sq. km (35,740 sq. miles); population (1996), 202,000. Capital, Gorno-Altaisk (1996 population, 48,300). Established 1 June 1922 as Oirot Autonomous Region; renamed 7 Jan. 1948; granted republican status in 1991 and renamed in 1992.

Chairman of the Government: Mikhail Lapshin.

Chief industries are clothing and footwear, foodstuffs, gold mining, timber, chemicals and dairying. Cattle breeding predominates; pasturages and hay meadows cover over 1m. ha, but 142,000 ha are under crops. Industrial output was valued at 19,900m. roubles in 1993, agricultural output at 43,000m. roubles.

In 1994–95 there were 39,000 pupils in 194 schools; 4 technical colleges had 3,100 students and 3,700 students were attending a pedagogical institute.

The rates of doctors and hospital beds per 10,000 population in 1995 were 32·7 and 153 respectively.

BASHKORTOSTAN

Area 143,600 sq. km (55,430 sq. miles), population (1998), 4,096,000. Capital, Ufa (1996 population, 1,096,400). Bashkiria was annexed to Russia in 1557. It was constituted as an Autonomous Soviet Republic on 23 March 1919. A declaration of republican sovereignty was adopted in 1990, and a declaration of independence on 28 March 1992. A treaty of Aug. 1994 with Russia preserves the common legislative framework of the Russian Federation while defining mutual areas of competence. The population, census 1989, was 39·3% Russian, 28·4% Tatar, 21·9% Bashkir, 3·0% Chuvash and 2·7% Mari.

A constitution was adopted on 24 Dec. 1993. It states that Bashkiria conducts its own domestic and foreign policy, that its laws take precedence in Bashkiria, and that it forms part of the Russian Federation on a voluntary and equal basis.

President: Murtaza Gubaidullovich Rakhimov. *Prime Minister:* Rafael Baidavletov.

Industrial production was valued at 4,188,000m. roubles in 1993, agricultural output at 617,000m. roubles. The most important industries are oil and oil products; there are also engineering, glass and building materials enterprises. Agriculture specializes in wheat, barley, oats and livestock.

In 1994–95 there were 658,000 pupils in 3,317 schools. There is a state university and a branch of the Academy of Sciences with eight learned institutions (511 research workers). There were 59,800 students in 75 technical colleges and 49,800 in 11 higher educational establishments.

In 1995 the rates of doctors and hospital beds per 10,000 population were 40·1 and 131 respectively.

BURYATIA

Area is 351,300 sq. km (135,650 sq. miles). The Buryat Republic, situated to the south of Sakha, adopted the Soviet system on 1 March 1920. This area was penetrated by the Russians in the 17th century and finally annexed from China by the treaties of Nerchinsk (1689) and Kyakhta (1727). The population (1996) was 1,050,000. Capital, Ulan-Ude (1996 population, 368,100). The population (1989 census) was 69·9% Russian, 24·0% Buryat, 2·2% Ukrainian, 1·0% Tatar and 0·5% Belorussian.

There is a 65-member parliament, the *People's Hural.*

President: Leonid Potapov.

The main industries are engineering, brown coal and graphite, timber, building materials, sheep and cattle farming. Industrial production was valued at 384,000m. roubles in 1993, agricultural output at 181,000m. roubles.

In 1994–95 there were 615 schools with 196,000 pupils, 20 technical colleges with 13,400 students and four higher educational institutions with 19,300 students. A branch of the Siberian Department of the Academy of Sciences had four institutions with 281 research workers.

In 1995 the rates of doctors and hospital beds per 10,000 population were 37·4 and 114 respectively.

CHECHNYA

The area of the former Checheno-Ingush Republic was 19,300 sq. km (7,350 sq. miles); population (1997), around 500,000. Capital, Dzhohar (since March 1998; previously known as Grozny). The Chechens and Ingushes were conquered by Russia in the late 1850s. In 1918 each nationality separately established its 'National Soviet' within the Terek Autonomous Republic, and in 1920 (after the Civil War) were constituted areas within the Mountain Republic. The Chechens separated out as an Autonomous Region on 30 Nov. 1922 and the Ingushes on 7 July 1924. In Jan. 1934 the two regions were united, and on 5 Dec. 1936 constituted as an Autonomous Republic. This was dissolved in 1944 and the population was deported en masse, allegedly for collaboration with the German occupation forces. It was reconstituted on 9 Jan. 1957: 232,000 Chechens and Ingushes returned to their homes in the next two years. The population (1989 census) included 70·7% Chechens and Ingushes, 23·1% Russians, 1·2% Armenians and 1% Ukrainians.

In 1991 rebel leader Jokhar Dudayev seized control of Chechnya and called elections for Oct. 1991, which he won. In Nov. 1991 he declared an independent Chechen Republic. (A separate Ingush Republic was declared in June 1993).

In April 1993 President Dudaev dissolved parliament. Hostilities continued throughout 1994 between the government and forces loosely grouped under the 'Provisional Chechen Council'. The Russian government, which had never recognized the Chechen declaration of independence of Nov. 1991, moved troops and armour into Chechnya on 11 Dec. 1994 'to re-establish constitutional order'. Grozny was bombed and attacked by Russian ground forces at the end of Dec. 1994 and the presidential palace was captured on 19 Jan. 1995, but fighting continued. On 30 July 1995 the Russian and Chechen authorities signed a ceasefire. On 8 Dec. 1995 an agreement between the Russian and Chechen prime ministers amnestied insurgents who laid down their arms. However, hostilities, raids and hostage-taking continued. The Chechen President was killed during fighting in April 1996. A further ceasefire was concluded on 30 Aug. 1996. On 23 Nov. 1996 the Russian President decreed the withdrawal of all Russian troops by the end of 1996. Fighting broke out again, however, in Sept. 1999 as Russian forces launched attacks on what it described as 'rebel bases'. The Russian defence ministry said that the attacks would continue until all Islamic militants in the breakaway republic were 'wiped out'. In the months that followed fighting intensified, with civilian casualties through bombing raids. More than 200,000 civilians were forced to flee their homes, most of them heading for neighbouring Ingushetia. After Russia seized Gudermes, the second largest town, in Nov. 1999 the Kremlin announced that it would henceforth be the new capital. By Feb. 2000 much of Grozny had been reduced to a heap of rubble. Wary of a possible counterstrike by rebels, the Russians closed the city. In June 2000 Vladimir Putin declared direct rule, postponing elections indefinitely. In April 2001 Grozny was restored as the capital. The war continues, with estimates of the number of deaths varying from 6,500 to 15,000. Over 4,000 Russian soldiers have been killed. However, in Oct. 2001 the Russian envoy to Chechnya, Viktor Kazantsev, announced that talks to end the war would begin imminently, and on 18 Nov. 2001 the first official meeting between negotiators for the Russian government and Chechen separatists took place. In Oct. 2002 a group of Chechen rebels took control of a Moscow theatre and held hostage 800 people for three days, before Russian troops stormed the building. An anaesthetic gas, used to combat the rebels, also killed many of the hostages. The rebels had been demanding that Russia end the war in Chechnya. On 23 March 2003 a referendum was held on a new constitution that would keep Chechnya within Russia but give it greater autonomy, and provide a new president and parliament for the republic. Although 96% of votes cast were in favour of the new constitution there was criticism of the conduct of the referendum, with human rights organizations questioning the legitimacy of holding a vote in conditions of war.

Presidential and a first round of parliamentary elections were held on 27 Jan. 1997. The electorate was 513,000. There were 14 presidential candidates. There were some 150 foreign observers, including 72 from OSCE. The second round of parliamentary elections was declared invalid because turn-out failed to reach the necessary 50%. A third round was held in May 1997.

President: Aslan Maskhadov. *Prime Minister:* Anatoly Popov.

Ingush desire to separate from Chechnya led to fighting along the Chechen-Ingush border and a deployment of Russian troops. An agreement to withdraw was reached between Russia and Chechnya on 15 Nov. 1992. The separation of Chechnya and Ingushetia was formalized by an amendment of Dec. 1992 to the Russian Constitution.

In 1992 it was decided to revert to the Roman alphabet (which had replaced Arabic script in 1927 and been itself replaced by Cyrillic in 1938).

Checheno-Ingushetia had a major oilfield, and a number of engineering works, chemical factories, building materials works and food canneries. There was a timber, woodworking and furniture industry. Industrial output in the two republics was valued at 213,000m. roubles in 1993, agricultural output at 79,000m. roubles.

There were, in the Chechen and Ingush republics in 1993–94, 548 schools with 251,000 pupils, 12 technical colleges with 8,700 students and three places of higher education with 13,100 students.

In 1995 the rates of doctors and hospital beds in the Chechen and Ingush republics per 10,000 population were 21·1 and 91 respectively.

FURTHER READING
Lieven, A. and Bradner, H., *Chechnya: Tombstone of Russian Power.* Yale Univ. Press, 1999

CHUVASHIA

Area, 18,300 sq. km (7,064 sq. miles); population (1996), 1,360,800. Capital, Cheboksary (1996 population, 461,600). The territory was annexed by Russia in the middle of the 16th century. On 24 June 1920 it was constituted as an Autonomous Region, and on 21 April 1925 as an Autonomous Republic. The population (1989 census) was 67·8% Chuvash, 26·7% Russian, 2·7% Tatar and 1·4% Mordovian. Republican sovereignty was declared in Sept. 1990.

President: Nikolai Fedorov.

The timber industry antedates the Soviet period. Other industries include railway repair works, electrical and other engineering industries, building materials, chemicals, textiles and food industries. Grain crops account for nearly two-thirds of all sowings and fodder crops for nearly a quarter. Industrial output was valued at 641,000m. roubles in 1993, agricultural output at 224,000m. roubles.

In 1994–95 there were 218,000 pupils at 719 schools, 20,000 students at 27 technical colleges and 18,900 students at three higher educational establishments.

In 1995 the rates of doctors and hospital beds per 10,000 population were 37·9 and 124 respectively.

DAGESTAN

Area, 50,300 sq. km (19,416 sq. miles); population (1998), 2,060,000. Capital, Makhachkala (1995 population, 340,200). Over 30 nationalities inhabit this republic apart from Russians (9·2% at 1989 census); the most numerous are Dagestani nationalities (80·2%), Azerbaijanis (4·2%), Chechens (3·2%) and Jews (0·5%). Annexed from Persia in 1723, Dagestan was constituted an Autonomous Republic on 20 Jan. 1921. In 1991 the Supreme Soviet declared the area of republican, rather than autonomous republican, status. Many of the nationalities who live in Dagestan have organized armed militias, and in May 1998 rebels stormed the government building in Makhachkala. In Aug. 1999 Dagestan faced attacks from Islamic militants who invaded from Chechnya. Although Russian troops tried to restore order and discipline, the guerrilla campaign continued.

Chairman of the State Council, Head of the Republic: Magomedali Magomedovich Magomedov. *Prime Minister:* Khizri Shikhsaidov.

There are engineering, oil, chemical, woodworking, textile, food and other light industries. Agriculture is varied, ranging from wheat to grapes, with sheep farming and cattle breeding. Industrial output was valued at 136,000m. roubles in 1993, agricultural output at 155,000m. roubles.

In 1994–95 there were 1,609 schools with 413,000 pupils, 17,700 students at 27 technical colleges and six higher education establishments with 28,400 students.

In 1995 the rates of doctors and hospital beds per 10,000 population were 36·5 and 88 respectively.

INGUSHETIA

The history of Ingushetia is interwoven with that of Chechnya (*see above*). Ingush desire to separate from Chechnya led to fighting along the Chechen-Ingush border and a deployment of Russian troops. The separation of Ingushetia from Chechnya was formalized by an amendment of Dec. 1992 to the Russian Constitution. On 15 May 1993 an extraordinary congress of the peoples of Ingushetia adopted a declaration of state sovereignty within the Russian Federation. Skirmishes between Ingush refugees and local police broke out in Aug. 1999 and tensions remained high with the danger of further outbreaks of fighting. The Russian attacks on neighbouring Chechnya in Sept. 1999 led to thousands of Chechen refugees fleeing to Ingushetia.

The capital is Magas (since 1999; formerly Nazran).

Area, 3,600 sq. km (1,390 sq. miles) (to be confirmed); estimated population, 1997, 301,900.

There is a 27-member parliament. On 27 Feb. 1994 presidential elections and a constitutional referendum were held. Turn-out was 70%. At the referendum 97% of votes cast approved a new constitution stating that Ingushetia is a democratic law-based secular republic forming part of the Russian Federation on a treaty basis.

President: Murat Zyazikov. *Prime Minister:* Viktor Aleksentsev.

A special economic zone for Russian residents was set up in 1994, and an 'offshore' banking tax haven in 1996.

In 1995 the rates of doctors and hospital beds per 10,000 population were 19·6 and 59 respectively.

KABARDINO-BALKARIA

Area, 12,500 sq. km (4,825 sq. miles); population (1997), 800,000. Capital, Nalchik (1996 population, 237,100). Kabarda was annexed to Russia in 1557. The republic was constituted on 5 Dec. 1936. Population (1989 census) included Kabardinians (48·2%), Balkars (9·4%), Russians (31·9%), Ukrainians (1·7%), Ossetians (1·3%) and Germans (1·1%).

A treaty with Russia of 1 July 1994 defines their mutual areas of competence within the legislative framework of the Russian Federation.

President: Valeri Kokov.

Main industries are ore-mining, timber, engineering, coal, food processing, timber and light industries, building materials. Grain, livestock breeding, dairy farming and wine-growing are the principal branches of agriculture. Industrial output was valued at 176,000m. roubles in 1993, agricultural output at 113,000m. roubles.

In 1994–95 there were 252 schools with 139,000 pupils, 6,900 students in 8 technical colleges and 12,900 students at 3 higher educational establishments.

In 1995 the rates of doctors and hospital beds per 10,000 population were 44·8 and 120 respectively.

KALMYKIA

Area, 76,100 sq. km (29,382 sq. miles); population (1997), 320,000. Capital, Elista (1996 population, 96,200). The population (1989 census) was 45·4% Kalmyk, 37·7% Russian, 2·6% Chechen, 1·9% Kazakh and 1·7% German.

The Kalmyks migrated from western China to Russia (Nogai Steppe) in the early 17th century. The territory was constituted an Autonomous Region on 4 Nov. 1920, and an Autonomous Republic on 22 Oct. 1935; this was dissolved in 1943. On 9 Jan. 1957 it was reconstituted as an Autonomous Region and on 29 July

1958 as an Autonomous Republic once more. In Oct. 1990 the republic was renamed the Kalmyk Soviet Socialist Republic; it was given its present name in Feb. 1992.

President: Kirsan Nikolaevich Ilyumzhinov.

In April 1993 the Supreme Soviet was dissolved and replaced by a professional parliament consisting of 25 of the former deputies. On 5 April 1994 a specially-constituted 300-member constituent assembly adopted a 'Steppe Code' as Kalmykia's basic law. This is not a constitution and renounces the declaration of republican sovereignty of 18 Oct. 1990. It provides for a *President* elected for five-year terms with the power to dissolve parliament, and a 27-member parliament, the *People's Hural,* elected every four years. It stipulates that Kalmykia is an equal member and integral part of the Russian Federation, functioning in accordance with the Russian constitution.

Main industries are fishing, canning and building materials. Cattle breeding and irrigated farming (mainly fodder crops) are the principal branches of agriculture. Industrial output was valued at 35,600m. roubles in 1993, agricultural output at 89,000m. roubles.

In 1994–95 there were 59,000 pupils in 252 schools, 4,200 students in 6 technical colleges and 5,100 in higher education.

In 1995 the rates of doctors and hospital beds per 10,000 population were 48·8 and 151 respectively.

KARACHAI-CHERKESSIA

Area, 14,300 sq. km (5,521 sq. miles); population (1997), 440,000. Capital, Cherkessk (1996 population, 119,900). A Karachai Autonomous Region was established on 26 April 1926 (out of a previously united Karachaevo-Cherkess Autonomous Region created in 1922), and dissolved in 1943. A Cherkess Autonomous Region was established on 30 April 1928. The present Autonomous Region was re-established on 9 Jan. 1957. The Region declared itself a Soviet Socialist Republic in Dec. 1990. Tension between the two ethnic groups increased after the first free presidential election in April 1999 was won by Vladimir Semyonov, an ethnic Karchayev. Despite numerous allegations of fraud the result was upheld by the Supreme Court. There were subsequently fears that the ethnic Cherkess opposition would attempt to set up breakaway government bodies.

President: Vladimir Semyonov.

There are ore-mining, engineering, chemical and woodworking industries. The Kuban-Kalaussi irrigation scheme irrigates 200,000 ha. Livestock breeding and grain growing predominate in agriculture. Industrial output was valued at 114,000m. roubles in 1993, agricultural output at 92,000m. roubles.

In 1994–95 there were 74,000 pupils in 188 secondary schools, 6 technical colleges with 4,800 students and two institutes with 6,200 students.

In 1995 the rates of doctors and hospital beds per 10,000 population were 29 and 102 respectively.

KARELIA

The Karelian Republic, capital Petrozavodsk (1996 population, 282,200), covers an area of 172,400 sq. km, with a population of 800,000 (1997). Karelians represent 10% of the population, Russians 73·6%, Belorussians 7% and Ukrainians 3·6% (1989 census).

Karelia (formerly Olonets Province) became part of the RSFSR after 1917. In June 1920 a Karelian Labour Commune was formed and in July 1923 this was transformed into the Karelian Autonomous Soviet Socialist Republic (one of the autonomous republics of the RSFSR). On 31 March 1940, after the Soviet-Finnish war, practically all the territory (with the exception of a small section in the neighbourhood of the Leningrad area) which had been ceded by Finland to the USSR was added to Karelia, and the Karelian Autonomous Republic was transformed into the Karelo-Finnish Soviet Socialist Republic as the 12th republic of the USSR. In 1946, however, the southern part of the republic, including its whole seaboard and the towns of Viipuri (Vyborg) and Keksholm, was attached to the RSFSR, reverting in 1956 to autonomous republican status within the RSFSR. In Nov. 1991 it declared itself the 'Republic of Karelia'.

Head of the Republic: Sergei Leonidovich Katanandov.

Karelia has a wealth of timber, some 70% of its territory being forest land. It is also rich in other natural resources, having large deposits of mica, diabase, spar, quartz, marble, granite, zinc, lead, silver, copper, molybdenum, tin, baryta and iron ore. Its lakes and rivers are rich in fish.

There are timber mills, paper-cellulose works, mica, chemical plants, power stations and furniture factories. Industrial output was valued at 520,000m. roubles in 1993, agricultural output at 97,000m. roubles.

In 1994–95 there were 0·12m. pupils in 341 schools. There were 9,700 students in three institutions of higher education and 11,300 in 16 technical colleges.

In 1995 the rates of doctors and hospital beds per 10,000 population were 47·2 and 135 respectively.

KHAKASSIA

Area, 61,900 sq. km (23,855 sq. miles); population (1997), 585,000. Capital, Abakan (1996 population, 163,100). Established 20 Oct. 1930; granted republican status in 1991.

Chairman of the Government: Aleksei Lebed.

There are coal- and ore-mining, timber and woodworking industries. The region is linked by rail with the Trans-Siberian line. Industrial output was valued at 545,000m. roubles in 1993, agricultural output at 83,000m. roubles.

In 1994–95 there were 97,000 pupils in 282 secondary schools, 6,200 students in seven technical colleges and 5,600 students at a higher education institution.

In 1995 the rates of doctors and hospital beds per 10,000 population were 36 and 132 respectively.

KOMI

Area, 415,900 sq. km (160,540 sq. miles); population (1997), 1,200,000. Capital, Syktyvkar (1995 population, 228,800). Annexed by the princes of Moscow in the 14th century, the territory was constituted as an Autonomous Region on 22 Aug. 1921 and as an Autonomous Republic on 5 Dec. 1936. The population (1989 census) was 57·7% Russian, 23·3% Komi, 8·3% Ukrainian and 2·1% Belorussian.

A declaration of sovereignty was adopted by the republican parliament in Sept. 1990, and the designation 'Autonomous' dropped from the republic's official name.

Head of the Republic, Chairman of the Government: Vladimir Alexandrovich Torlopov.

There are coal, oil, timber, gas, asphalt and building materials industries, and light industry is expanding. Livestock breeding (including dairy farming) is the main branch of agriculture. Crop area, 92,000 ha. Industrial output was valued at 1,038,000m. roubles in 1993, agricultural output at 134,000m. roubles.

In 1994–95 there were 196,000 pupils in 595 schools, 11,300 students in three higher educational establishments, 14,200 students in 20 technical colleges;

and a branch of the Academy of Sciences with four institutions (297 research workers).

In 1995 the rates of doctors and hospital beds per 10,000 population were 39·6 and 134 respectively.

MARI-EL

Area, 23,200 sq. km (8,955 sq. miles); population (1998), 760,000. Capital, Yoshkar-Ola (1996 population, 250,900). The Mari people were annexed to Russia, with other peoples of the Kazan Tatar Khanate, when the latter was overthrown in 1552. On 4 Nov. 1920 the territory was constituted as an Autonomous Region, and on 5 Dec. 1936 as an Autonomous Republic. The republic renamed itself the Mari Soviet Socialist Republic in Oct. 1990, and adopted a new constitution in June 1995. In Dec. 1991 Vladislav Zotin was elected the first president. The population (1989 census) was 47·5% Russian, 43·3% Mari and 5·9% Tatar.

President, Head of the Government: Leonid Markelov.

Coal is mined. The main industries are metalworking, timber, paper, woodworking and food processing. Crops include grain, flax, potatoes, fruit and vegetables. Industrial output was valued at 257,000m. roubles in 1993, agricultural output at 153,000m. roubles.

In 1994–95 there were 432 schools with 128,000 pupils; 14 technical colleges and 3 higher education establishments had 8,900 and 13,100 students respectively.

In 1995 the rates of doctors and hospital beds per 10,000 population were 38 and 126 respectively.

MORDOVIA

Area, 26,200 sq. km (10,110 sq. miles); population (1997), 956,000. Capital, Saransk (1996 population, 319,700). By the 13th century the Mordovian tribes had been subjugated by Russian princes. In 1928 the territory was constituted as a Mordovian Area within the Middle-Volga Territory, on 10 Jan. 1930 as an Autonomous Region and on 20 Dec. 1934 as an Autonomous Republic. The population (1989 census) was 60·8% Russian, 32·5% Mordovian and 4·9% Tatar.

President: Nikolai Merkushkin. *Chairman of the Government of the Republic:* Vladimir Dmitrievich Volkov.

Industries include wood-processing and the production of building materials, furniture, textiles and leather goods. Agriculture is devoted chiefly to grain, sugarbeet, sheep and dairy farming. Industrial output was valued at 457,000m. roubles in 1993, agricultural output at 185,000m. roubles.

In 1994–95 there were 139,000 pupils in 828 schools, 12,600 students in 21 technical colleges and 22,900 attending 2 higher educational institutions.

In 1995 the rates of doctors and hospital beds per 10,000 population were 45·2 and 155 respectively.

NORTH OSSETIA (ALANIA)

Area, 8,000 sq. km (3,088 sq. miles); population (1997), around 700,000. Capital, Vladikavkaz (1996 population, 313,300). North Ossetia was annexed by Russia from Turkey and named the Terek region in 1861. On 4 March 1918 it was proclaimed an Autonomous Soviet Republic, and on 20 Jan. 1921 set up with others as the Mountain Autonomous Republic, with North Ossetia as the Ossetian (Vladikavkaz)

Area within it. On 7 July 1924 the latter was constituted as an Autonomous Region and on 5 Dec. 1936 as an Autonomous Republic. In the early 1990s there was a conflict with neighbouring Ingushetia to the east, and to the south the decision of the Georgian government to disband the republic of South Ossetia led to ethnic war, with North Ossetia supporting the South Ossetians. Pressure for Ossetian reunification continues.

A new Constitution was adopted on 12 Nov. 1994 under which the republic reverted to its former name, Alania. The population (1989 census) was 53% Ossetian, 29% Russian, 5·2% Chechen, 1·9% Armenian and 1·6% Ukrainian.

President: Aleksandr Dzasokhov.

The main industries are non-ferrous metals (mining and metallurgy), maize processing, timber and woodworking, textiles, building materials, distilleries and food processing. There is also a varied agriculture. Industrial output was valued at 167,000m. roubles in 1993, agricultural output at 175,000m. roubles.

There were, in 1994–95, 104,000 children in 214 schools, 10,800 students in 14 technical colleges and 18,100 students in 5 higher educational establishments.

In 1995 the rates of doctors and hospital beds per 10,000 population were 68·3 and 127 respectively.

SAKHA

The area is 3,103,200 sq. km (1,197,760 sq. miles), making Sakha the largest republic in the Russian Federation; population (1997), 1,028,400. Capital, Yakutsk (1996 population, 196,400). The Yakuts were subjugated by the Russians in the 17th century. The territory was constituted an Autonomous Republic on 27 April 1922. The population (1989 census) was 50·3% Russian, 33·4% Yakut, 7% Ukrainian and 1·6% Tatar.

President: Vyacheslav Shtyrov.

The principal industries are mining (gold, tin, mica, coal) and livestock-breeding. Silver- and lead-bearing ores and coal are worked. Large diamond fields have been opened up; Sakha produces most of the Russian Federation's output. Timber and food industries are developing. Trapping and breeding of fur-bearing animals (sable, squirrel, silver fox) are an important source of income. Industrial production was valued at 1,771,000m. roubles in 1993, agricultural output at 373,000m. roubles.

In 1994–95 there were 193,000 pupils in 715 secondary schools, 10,400 students at 19 technical colleges and 9,700 attending three higher education institutions.

In 1995 the rates of doctors and hospital beds per 10,000 population were 41·3 and 156 respectively.

TATARSTAN

Area, 68,000 sq. km (26,250 sq. miles); population (1997), 3,766,500. Capital, Kazan (1999 population, 1,101,500). From the 10th to the 13th centuries this was the territory of the Volga-Kama Bulgar State; conquered by the Mongols, it became the seat of the Kazan (Tatar) Khans when the Mongol Empire broke up in the 15th century, and in 1552 was conquered again by Russia. On 27 May 1920 it was constituted as an Autonomous Republic. The population (1989 census) was 48·5% Tatar, 43·3% Russian, 3·7% Chuvash, 0·9% Ukrainian and 0·8% Mordovian.

In Oct. 1991 the Supreme Soviet adopted a declaration of independence. At a referendum in March 1992, 61·4% of votes cast were in favour of increased autonomy. A Constitution was adopted in April 1992, which proclaims Tatarstan a sovereign state which conducts its relations with the Russian Federation on an equal basis. On 15 Feb. 1994 the Russian and Tatar presidents signed a treaty defining Tatarstan as a state united with Russia on the basis of the constitutions of both, but the Russian parliament has not ratified it.

President: Mintimer Sharipovich Shaimiyev. *Prime Minister:* Rustam Minnikhanov.

The republic has engineering, oil and chemical, timber, building materials, textiles, clothing and food industries. Industrial production was valued at 2,955,000m. roubles in 1993, agricultural output at 532,000m. roubles.

In 1994–95 there were 2,463 schools with 0·56m. pupils, 65 technical colleges with 52,500 students and 16 higher educational establishments with 63,000 students (including a state university). There is a branch of the USSR Academy of Sciences with five institutions (512 research workers).

In 1995 the rates of doctors and hospital beds per 10,000 population were 42·3 and 124 respectively.

TUVA

Area, 170,500 sq. km (65,810 sq. miles); population (1998), 310,000. Capital, Kyzyl (1996 population, 95,400). Tuva was incorporated in the USSR as an autonomous region on 11 Oct. 1944 and elevated to an Autonomous Republic on 10 Oct. 1961. The population (1989 census) was 64·3% Tuvans and 32% Russian. Tuva renamed itself the 'Republic of Tuva' in Oct. 1991.

A new constitution was promulgated on 22 Oct. 1993 which adopts the name 'Tyva' for the republic. This constitution provides for a 32-member parliament (*Supreme Hural*), and a *Grand Hural* alone empowered to change the constitution, asserts the precedence of Tuvan law and adopts powers to conduct foreign policy. It was approved by 62·2% of votes cast at a referendum on 12 Dec. 1993.

Chairman of the Government: Sherig-ool Dizizhikovich Oorzhak.

Tuva is well-watered and hydro-electric resources are important. The Tuvans are mainly herdsmen and cattle farmers and there is much good pastoral land. There are deposits of gold, cobalt and asbestos. The main exports are hair, hides and wool. There are mining, woodworking, garment, leather, food and other industries. Industrial production was valued at 25,800m. roubles in 1993, agricultural output at 44,000m. roubles.

In 1994–95 there were 167 schools with 62,000 pupils; 6 technical colleges with 3,800 students, and one higher education institution with 2,800 students.

In 1995 the rates of doctors and hospital beds per 10,000 population were 36·7 and 187 respectively.

UDMURTIA

Area, 42,100 sq. km (16,250 sq. miles); population (1998), 1,639,000. Capital, Izhevsk (1995 population, 654,400). The Udmurts (formerly known as 'Votyaks') were annexed by the Russians in the 15th and 16th centuries. On 4 Nov. 1920 the Votyak Autonomous Region was constituted (the name was changed to Udmurt in 1932), and on 28 Dec. 1934 was raised to the status of an Autonomous Republic. The population (1989 census) was 58·9% Russian, 30·9% Udmurt, 6·9% Tatar, 0·9% Ukrainian and 0·6% Mari. A declaration of sovereignty and the present state title were adopted in Sept. 1990.

A new parliament was established in Dec. 1993 consisting of a 50-member upper house, the *Council of Representatives,* and a full-time 35-member lower house.

Chairman of the State Council: Alexander Alexandrovich Volkov. *Chairman of the Council of Ministers:* Yury Pitkevich.

Heavy industry includes the manufacture of locomotives, machine tools and other engineering products, most of them for the defence industries, as well as timber and building materials. There are also light industries: clothing, leather, furniture and food. Industrial production was valued at 958,000m. roubles in 1993, agricultural output at 368,000m. roubles.

In 1994–95 there were 902 schools with 263,000 pupils; there were 19,900 students at 30 technical colleges and 24,800 at five higher educational institutions.

In 1995 the rates of doctors and hospital beds per 10,000 population were 48·1 and 129 respectively.

JEWISH AUTONOMOUS REGION (BIROBIJAN)

Part of Khabarovsk Territory. Area, 36,000 sq. km (13,895 sq. miles); population (1997), 208,000 (1989 census, Russians, 83·2%; Ukrainians, 7·4%; Jews, 4·2%). Capital, Birobijan (1994 population, 86,000). Established as Jewish National District in 1928, became an Autonomous Region 7 May 1934. In Oct. 1991 the region declared itself an Autonomous Republic.

Governor, Chairman of the Government: Nikolai Volkov.

The chief industries are non-ferrous metallurgy, building materials, timber, engineering, textiles, paper and food processing. There were 161,000 ha under cultivation in 1983; main crops are wheat, soya, oats, barley. Industrial production was valued at 74,500m. roubles in 1993, agricultural output at 73,000m. roubles.

In 1991–92 there were 35,000 pupils in 111 schools; students in 6 technical colleges numbered 4,900. There are a Yiddish national theatre, newspaper and broadcasting service.

In 1995 the rates of doctors and hospital beds per 10,000 population were 38·3 and 175 respectively.

AUTONOMOUS AREAS

Agin-Buryat

Situated in Chita region (Eastern Siberia); area, 19,000 sq. km, population (1997), 78,400. Capital, Aginskoe. Formed 1937, its economy is basically pastoral.

Chukot

Situated in Magadan region (Far East); area, 737,700 sq. km. Population (1997), 90,000. Capital, Anadyr. Formed 1930. Population chiefly Russian, also Chukchi, Koryak, Yakut, Even. Minerals are extracted in the north, including gold, tin, mercury and tungsten.

Evenki

Situated in Krasnoyarsk territory (Eastern Siberia); area, 767,600 sq. km, population, (1997) 20,000, chiefly Evenks. Capital, Tura. Formed 1930.

Khanty-Mansi

Situated in Tyumen region (western Siberia); area, 523,100 sq. km, population (1997), 1,336,000, chiefly Russians but also Khants and Mansi. Capital, Khanty-Mansiisk. Formed 1930.

Komi-Permyak

Situated in Perm region (Northern Russia); area, 32,900 sq. km, population (1997), 160,000, chiefly Komi-Permyaks. Formed 1925. Capital, Kudymkar. Forestry is the main occupation.

Koryak

Situated in Kamchatka; area, 301,500 sq. km, population (1997), 32,000. Capital, Palana. Formed 1930.

Nenets

Situated in Archangel region (Northern Russia); area, 176,700 sq. km, population (1997), 46,600. Capital, Naryan-Mar. Formed 1929.

Taimyr

Situated in Krasnoyarsk territory, this most northerly part of Siberia comprises the Taimyr peninsula and the Arctic islands of Severnaya Zemlya. Area, 862,100 sq. km, population (1997), 46,300, excluding the mining city of Norilsk which is separately administered. Capital, Dudinka. Formed 1930.

Ust-Ordyn-Buryat

Situated in Irkutsk region (Eastern Siberia); area, 22,400 sq. km, population (1996), 145,000. Capital, Ust-Ordynsk. Formed 1937.

Yamalo-Nenets

Situated in Tyumen region (western Siberia); area, 750,300 sq. km, population (1997), 600,000. Capital, Salekhard. Formed 1930.

RWANDA

Republika y'u Rwanda

Capital: Kigali
Population estimate, 2000: 7·61m.
GDP per capita, 2000: (PPP$) 943
HDI/world rank: 0·403/162

KEY HISTORICAL EVENTS

In 1959 an uprising of the Hutu destroyed the Tutsi feudal hierarchy and overthrew the monarchy. Elections and a referendum under the auspices of the UN in Sept. 1961 resulted in an overwhelming majority for the republican party. The republic proclaimed by the Parmehutu on 28 Jan. 1961 was recognized by the Belgian administration in Oct. 1961. The Republic of Rwanda became independent on 1 July 1962.

Conflict between the Hutu and Tutsi was renewed with much bloodshed in 1972–73. A coup on 5 July 1973 led to a military government. There was gradual return to civilian rule and in 1978 a new constitution was accepted by a national referendum. In Oct. 1990 rebel Tutsi forces of the Rwandan Patriotic Front (RPF) invaded from Uganda. A peace agreement was signed on 4 Aug. 1993 at Arusha (Tanzania). On 5 Oct. the UN Security Council decided to send a peacekeeping force but rebel Tutsi forces of the RPF began an attack from the north of the country. Most UN forces were withdrawn during the fighting and massacres of April 1994 but following a UN Security Council resolution of 17 May 1994 a new force of 5,500 was sent in. On 22 June 1994 the UN Security Council approved France's dispatch of 2,000 troops on a humanitarian mission. The French forces maintained a 'safe zone' for refugees in the southwest of Rwanda until their withdrawal on 21 Aug. 1994. It is estimated that more than 1m. Rwandans were killed in 1994 through genocide and the civil war, and that more than 2m. were forced to flee to neighbouring countries. UN forces left Rwanda on 8 March 1996, and although progress has been made since then, the civil strife between the two factions continues, particularly in the northwest of the country. In Sept. 1998 Jean Kambanda, the former Prime Minister, was sentenced to life imprisonment for his part in the 1994 genocide.

TERRITORY AND POPULATION

Rwanda is bounded south by Burundi, west by the Democratic Republic of the Congo, north by Uganda and east by Tanzania. A mountainous state of 26,338 sq. km (10,169 sq. miles), its western third drains to Lake Kivu on the border with the Democratic Republic of the Congo and thence to the Congo river, while the rest is drained by the Kagera river into the Nile system.

The population was 7,164,994 at the 1991 census, of whom over 90% were Hutu, 9% Tutsi and 1% Twa (pygmy). Estimate (1996) 5,100,000; density, 193·6 per sq. km.

The UN gives a projected population for 2010 of 9·43m.

In 1998 the percentage of the population considered as urban was the lowest of any country in the world, at 6·1% (93·9% rural).

The areas and populations of the ten prefectures are:

Prefecture	Area (in sq. km)	Population (1991 census)	Prefecture	Area (in sq. km)	Population (1991 census)
Butare	1,837	766,839	Gitarama	2,189	851,516
Byumba	4,761	783,350	Kibungo	4,046	655,368
Cyangugu	1,845	515,129	Kibuye	1,705	470,747
Gikongoro	2,057	464,585	Kigali	3,118	1,156,651
Gisenyi	2,050	734,697	Ruhengeri	1,663	766,112

Kigali, the capital, had 369,000 inhabitants in 1999; other towns are Butare, Ruhengeri and Gisenyi.

Kinyarwanda, the language of the entire population, French and English (since 1996) are the official languages. Swahili is spoken in the commercial centres.

SOCIAL STATISTICS

1998 estimates: births, 260,000; deaths, 127,000. Estimated birth rate (per 1,000 population, 1998), 39; estimated death rate (per 1,000 population, 1998), 19. Annual population growth rate, 1990–99, 0·4%.

Life expectancy at birth in 1999 was 40·6 years for females and 39·1 for males, up from 23·1 years for females and 22·1 years for males during the period 1990–95 (at the height of the civil war). Infant mortality, 1999, 110 per 1,000 live births; fertility rate, 1999, 6·0 births per woman.

CLIMATE

Despite the equatorial situation, there is a highland tropical climate. The wet seasons are from Oct. to Dec. and March to May. Highest rainfall occurs in the west, at around 70" (1,770 mm), decreasing to 40–55" (1,020–1,400 mm) in the central uplands and to 30" (760 mm) in the north and east. Kigali, Jan. 67°F (19·4°C), July 70°F (21·1°C). Annual rainfall 40" (1,000 mm).

CONSTITUTION AND GOVERNMENT

Under the 1978 Constitution the MRND was the sole political organization.

A new Constitution was promulgated in June 1991 which permits multi-party democracy.

The Arusha Agreement of Aug. 1994 provided for a transitional 70-member National Assembly, which began functioning in Nov. 1994. The seats won by the MRNDD (formerly MRND) were taken over by other parties on the grounds that the MRNDD was culpable of genocide.

National Anthem. 'Rwanda Nziza' ('Beautiful Rwanda'); words by F. Murigo, tune by Capt. J.-B. Hashakaimana.

RECENT ELECTIONS

In a vote for the presidency held by government ministers and parliamentarians on 17 April 2000, incumbent Paul Kagame won 81 votes against the 5 of Charles Muligande.

CURRENT ADMINISTRATION

President: Paul Kagame; b. 1957 (RPF—Tutsis; sworn in 22 April 2000 having been acting president since 24 March 2000).

In March 2003 the government comprised:

Prime Minister: Bernard Makuza; b. 1961 (MDR/Republican Democratic Movement—Hutus; sworn in 8 March 2000).

Minister of Agriculture, Livestock and Forestry: Dr Ephrem Kabayija. *Defence and National Security:* Maj. Gen. Marcel Gatsinzi. *Land Resettlement and Environment:* Laurent Nkusi. *Commerce, Industry and Tourism:* Alexandre Lyambabaje. *Education, Science, Technology and Research:* Romain Murenzi. *Gender and Women's Development:* Marie Mukantabana. *Finance and Planning:* Donat Kaberuka. *Foreign Affairs and Regional Co-operation:* Charles Murigande. *Health:* Abel Dushimiyimana. *Justice:* Jean de Dieu Mucyo. *Internal Affairs:* Jean de Dieu Ntiruhungwa. *Youth, Culture and Sports:* Robert Bayigamba. *Local Government, Information and Social History:* Christophe Bazivamo. *Infrastructure:* Jean Ntawukuriryayo Damascene. *Public Service, Skills Development, Vocational Training and Labour:* Andre Habib Bumaya. *Minister to the President's Office:* Solina Nyirahabimana.

Government Website: http://www.rwanda1.com/government/

DEFENCE

In 2000 defence expenditure totalled US$109m. (US$13 per capita), representing 4·7% of GDP.

Army. Strength (1999) about 30,000–40,000. There was a paramilitary gendarmerie of some 7,000.

INTERNATIONAL RELATIONS
Rwanda is a member of the UN, WTO, the African Union, African Development Bank, COMESA, IOM, the International Organization of the Francophonie and is an ACP member state of the ACP-EU relationship.

ECONOMY
Agriculture accounted for 47·4% of GDP in 1998, industry 21·2% and services 31·4%.

Currency. The unit of currency is the *Rwanda franc* (RWF) notionally of 100 *centimes*. On 3 Jan. 1995, 500-, 1,000- and 5,000-Rwanda franc notes were replaced by new issues, demonetarizing the currency taken abroad by exiles. The currency is not convertible. Foreign exchange reserves were US$180m. in June 2002. Gold reserves are negligible. Inflation was 3·4% in 2001. Total money supply in Dec. 2001 was 63,606m. Rwanda francs.

Budget. In 1996 revenues were estimated to be US$231m. and expenditures US$319m.

Performance. Real GDP growth was 35·2% in 1995, following five years of negative growth peaking in a rate of −50·2% in 1994 at the height of the civil war. By 2000 the growth had slowed, but was still 6·0%. In 2001 it rose again to 6·7%. Total GDP in 2001 was US$1·7bn.

Banking and Finance. The central bank is the National Bank of Rwanda (founded 1960; *Governor*, François Kanimba) which became the bank of issue in 1964. There are five commercial banks (Banque de Kigali, Banque de Commerce et de Développement Industriel, Banque Continentale Africaine au Rwanda, Banque à la Confiance d'Or and Compagnie Générale de Banque), one development bank (Rwandan Development Bank) and one credit union system (Rwandan Union of Popular Banks).

ENERGY AND NATURAL RESOURCES

Environment. According to the *World Bank Atlas* carbon dioxide emissions in 1998 were the equivalent of 0·1 tonnes per capita.

Electricity. Installed capacity is 60,000 kW. Production was 159m. kWh in 1998 and consumption per capita in 1997 was 29 kWh.

Minerals. Production (1993): cassiterite, 400 tonnes; wolfram (1994), 30 tonnes. About 1m. cu. metres of natural gas are obtained from under Lake Kivu each year.

Agriculture. There were 800,000 ha of arable land in 1998 and 250,000 ha of permanent crops. Production (2000 estimates, in 1,000 tonnes): plantains, 2,212; sweet potatoes 1,033; cassava, 821; dry beans, 215; pumpkins and squash, 206; potatoes, 175; sorghum, 155; taro, 91; maize, 63; sugarcane, 40; coffee, 15; dry peas, 15; tea, 14; rice, 12.

Long-horned Ankole cattle play an important traditional role. Efforts are being made to improve their present negligible economic value. There were, in 2000, 725,000 cattle, 700,000 goats, 320,000 sheep, 160,000 pigs and 1m. chickens.

Forestry. Forests covered 250,000 ha (10·1% of the land area) in 1995. Timber production in 1999 was 7·84m. cu. metres.

Fisheries. The catch in 1999 totalled 6,433 tonnes, entirely from inland waters.

INDUSTRY
There are about 100 small-sized modern manufacturing enterprises in the country. Food manufacturing is the dominant industrial activity (64%) followed by construction (15·3%) and mining (9%). There is a large modern brewery.

Labour. The labour force in 1996 totalled 3,021,000 (51% males). Over 90% of the economically active population in 1995 were engaged in agriculture, fisheries and forestry.

INTERNATIONAL TRADE

With Burundi and the Democratic Republic of the Congo, Rwanda forms part of the Economic Community of the Great Lakes. Foreign debt was US$1,271m. in 2000.

Imports and Exports. In 2000 imports (f.o.b.) amounted to US$222·3m. (US$249·7m. in 1999); exports (f.o.b.) US$69·1m. (US$62·3m. in 1999). Major exports are coffee, tea and tin. Main export markets, 1991: Germany, 21·3%; Netherlands, 18·8%; Belgium, 11·8%; UK, 6·4%. Main import suppliers: Belgium, 17·1%; Kenya, 13·4%; South Africa, 10·4%; France, 6·8%.

COMMUNICATIONS

Roads. There were an estimated 14,900 km of roads in 1996, of which 1,350 km were surfaced. There are road links with Burundi, Uganda, Tanzania and the Democratic Republic of the Congo. In 1996 there were 13,000 passenger cars and 17,100 trucks and vans.

Civil Aviation. There is an international airport at Kigali (Gregoire Kayibanda), which handled 101,000 passengers (96,000 on international flights) in 2000. In 1998 there were flights to Addis Ababa, Brussels, Dar es Salaam, Douala, Entebbe, Johannesburg, Luanda, Mwanza and Nairobi. Rwanda does not have a national airline.

Telecommunications. Rwanda had 17,600 telephone main lines in 2000 (equivalent to 2·3 per 1,000 persons) and 11,000 mobile phone subscribers in 1999. Internet users numbered 5,000 in Dec. 2000. In 1995 there were 500 fax machines.

Postal Services. In 1994 there was just one post office serving the entire population.

SOCIAL INSTITUTIONS

Justice. A system of Courts of First Instance and provincial courts refer appeals to Courts of Appeal and a Court of Cassation situated in Kigali.

In 1998 a number of people were executed who had been found guilty of genocide during the civil war in 1994, including 22 at five different locations throughout the country on 24 April 1998.

Religion. In 1997 approximately 65% of the population were Roman Catholics, 9% Protestants and 1% Muslims. Some of the population follow traditional animist religions. Before the civil war there were nine Roman Catholic bishops and 370 priests. By the end of 1994, three bishops had been killed and three reached retiring age; 106 priests had been killed and 130 had sought refuge abroad.

Education. In 1992 there were 1,710 primary schools with 18,937 teachers for 1·1m. pupils; 94,586 secondary pupils with 3,413 teachers; and 3,389 students at university level. Adult literacy rate in 1999 was 65·8% (male, 71·9%; female, 59·1%).

Health. In 1992 there were 150 doctors, and in 1989, 7 dentists, 25 pharmacists and 835 nursing personnel. Hospital bed provision in 1990 was 1 per 588 people.

There were 10,706 reported cases of AIDS by Dec. 1996, and 1·38m. reported of malaria in 1992.

CULTURE

Broadcasting. The state-controlled *Radiodiffusion de la République Rwandaise* is responsible for broadcasting. Colour transmission is on the SECAM V system. There were about 601,000 radio sets and 600 television sets in 1997.

Press. In 1996 there was one daily newspaper with a circulation of 500, equivalent to a rate of one per 10,000 population.

Tourism. In 1998, 2,000 foreign tourists brought in revenue of US$19m.

DIPLOMATIC REPRESENTATIVES

Of Rwanda in the United Kingdom (Uganda Hse., 58–59 Trafalgar Sq., London, WC2N 5DX)
Ambassador: Rosemary K. Museminali.

Of the United Kingdom in Rwanda (Parcelle No. 1131, Blvd. de l'Umuganda, Kacyira-Sud, POB 576, Kigali)
Ambassador: Sue Hogwood, MBE.

Of Rwanda in the USA (1714 New Hampshire Ave., NW, Washington, D.C., 20009)
Ambassador: Dr Richard Sezibera.

Of the USA in Rwanda (Blvd. de la Révolution, Kigali, POB 28)
Ambassador: Margaret K. McMillion.

Of Rwanda to the United Nations
Ambassador: Anastase Gasana.

Of Rwanda to the European Union
Ambassador: Vacant.
Chargé d'Affaires a.i.: Augustin Habimana.

FURTHER READING

Braeckman, C., *Rwanda: Histoire d'un Génocide*. Paris, 1994
Dorsey, L., *Historical Dictionary of Rwanda*. Metuchen (NJ), 1995
Fegley, Randall, *Rwanda*. [Bibliography] ABC-Clio, Oxford and Santa Barbara (CA), 1993
Gourevitch, P., *We Wish to Inform You That Tomorrow We Will Be Killed With Our Families*. Picador, London, 1998
Prunier, G., *The Rwanda Crisis: History of a Genocide*. Farnborough, 1995

ST KITTS AND NEVIS

Federation of St Kitts and Nevis

Capital: Basseterre
Population estimate, 2000: 45,000
GDP per capita, 2000: (PPP$) 12,510
HDI/world rank: 0·814/44

KEY HISTORICAL EVENTS
The islands of St Kitts (formerly St Christopher) and Nevis were discovered and named by Columbus in 1493. They were settled by Britain in 1623 and 1628 respectively, but ownership was disputed with France until 1783. In Feb. 1967 the colonial status was replaced by an 'association' with Britain, giving the islands full internal self-government. St Kitts and Nevis became fully independent on 19 Sept. 1983. In Oct. 1997 the five-person Nevis legislature voted to end the federation with St Kitts. However, in a referendum held on 10 Aug. 1998 voters rejected independence, only 62% voting for secession when a two-thirds vote in favour was needed. In Sept. 1998 Hurricane Georges caused devastation, leaving 25,000 people homeless, with some 80% of the houses in the islands damaged.

TERRITORY AND POPULATION
The two islands of St Kitts and Nevis are situated at the northern end of the Leeward Islands in the eastern Caribbean. Nevis lies 3 km to the southeast of St Kitts. Population, census (1991) 40,618. Estimate, 1997, 44,000 (9,000 on Nevis). In 1998, 66·0% of the population were rural.

	Sq. km	Census 1991	Estimate 1999	Chief town	1991 census
St Kitts	176·1	31,824	33,040	Basseterre	12,605
Nevis	93·3	8,794	7,580	Charlestown	1,411
	269·4	40,618	40,620		

In 1991, 94·9% of the population were Black. English is the official and spoken language.

SOCIAL STATISTICS
Births, 1999, 864; deaths, 418. Rates, 1999 (per 1,000 population): births, 21·3; deaths, 10·3. Infant mortality, 1999 (per 1,000 live births), 12·7. Expectation of life in 1999 was 68·0 years for males and 71·8 for females. Annual population growth rate, 1990–99, –0·9%; fertility rate, 1999, 2·64 births per woman.

CLIMATE
Temperature varies between 21·4–30·7°C, with a sea breeze throughout the year and low humidity. Rainfall in 1999 was 1,706·9 mm.

CONSTITUTION AND GOVERNMENT
The British sovereign is the head of state, represented by a Governor-General. The 1983 Constitution described the country as 'a sovereign democratic federal state'. It allowed for a unicameral Parliament consisting of 11 elected Members (eight from St Kitts and three from Nevis) and three appointed Senators. Nevis was given its own Island Assembly and the right to secession from St Kitts.

National Anthem. 'O Land of beauty! Our country where peace abounds'; words and tune by K. A. Georges.

RECENT ELECTIONS
At the National Assembly elections on 6 March 2000 the Labour Party gained 8 seats, the Concerned Citizens Movement 2 and the Nevis Reformation Party 1. Turn-out was just over 67%.

CURRENT ADMINISTRATION

Governor-General: Sir Cuthbert Montraville Sebastian, GCMG, OBE; b. 1921 (appointed 1 Jan. 1996).

In March 2003 the government comprised:

Prime Minister, Minister of Finance, Development and Planning, National Security: Dr Denzil L. Douglas; b. 1936 (Labour Party; sworn in 7 July 1995).

Deputy Prime Minister, Minister of International Trade, Labour, Social Security, Telecommunications and Technology, and CARICOM Affairs: Sam Condor.

Minister of Agriculture, Fisheries, Co-operatives, Lands and Housing: Cedric Liburd. *Community, Social Development and Gender Affairs:* Rupert Herbert. *Foreign Affairs and Education:* Timothy Harris. *Justice and Legal Affairs:* Bart Delano. *Public Works, Utilities, Transport and Posts:* Halva Hendrickson. *Tourism, Commerce and Consumer Affairs:* G. A. Dwyer Astaphan. *Information, Youth, Sports and Culture:* Jacinth Lorna Henry-Martin. *Health and Environment:* Dr Earl Asim Martin.

The *Nevis Island* legislature comprises an Assembly of three nominated members and elected members from each electoral district on the Island, and an Administration consisting of the Premier and two other persons appointed by the Deputy Governor-General.

The Premier of *Nevis* is Vance Amory.

Government Website: http://www.stkittsnevis.net

INTERNATIONAL RELATIONS

St Kitts and Nevis is a member of the UN, WTO, the Commonwealth, OAS, ACS, CARICOM, OECS and is an ACP member state of the ACP-EU relationship.

ECONOMY

Agriculture accounted for 5·25% of GDP in 1999, industry 11·9% and services 70%.

Currency. The East Caribbean *dollar* (XCD) (of 100 *cents*) is in use. Inflation was 2·1% in 2001. In May 2002 foreign exchange reserves were US$65m. Total money supply was XC$106m. in May 2002.

Budget. In 1999 recurrent revenues were XC$191·4m. (US$70·9m.) and recurrent expenditures XC$236·8m. (US$87·7m.). In 2000 revenues were estimated to be XC$237·8m. (US$88·1m.) and expenditures XC$243·7m. (US$90·3m.). Estimates for 2001 were: revenues, XC$231·4m. (US$85·7m.); expenditure, XC$268·8m. (US$99·6m.).

Performance. Real GDP growth was 7·5% in 2000, but only 1·8% in 2001. Total GDP was US$0·3bn. in 2001.

Banking and Finance. The East Caribbean Central Bank (*Governor*, Sir Dwight Venner) is located in St Kitts. It is a regional bank that serves the OECS countries. There are six commercial banks, including four foreign. Nevis has some 9,000 offshore businesses registered.

St Kitts and Nevis was one of 15 countries and territories named in a report in June 2000 as failing to co-operate in the fight against international money laundering. The Financial Action Task Force on Money Laundering was set up by the G7 group of major industrialized nations.

ENERGY AND NATURAL RESOURCES

Environment. According to the *World Bank Atlas* carbon dioxide emissions in 1998 were the equivalent of 2·5 tonnes per capita.

Electricity. Installed capacity was 16,280 kW in 1999. Production in 1999 was 96·7m. kWh.

Agriculture. The main crops are sugar, coconut, copra and cotton. In 1995, 3,327 ha were sown to sugarcane. Most of the farms are small-holdings and there are a number of coconut estates amounting to some 400 ha under public and private ownership. Production, 2000 (in 1,000 tonnes): sugarcane, 188; coconuts, 1.

Livestock (2000): goats, 15,000; sheep, 7,000; cattle, 4,000; pigs, 3,000.

Forestry. The area under forests in 1995 was 11,000 ha, or 30·6% of the total land area.

Fisheries. The catch in 1999 was 352 tonnes.

INDUSTRY
There are three industrial estates on St Kitts and one on Nevis. Export products include electronics and data processing equipment, and garments for the US market. Other small enterprises include food and drink processing, particularly sugar and cane spirit, and construction. Production of raw sugar (1999), 23,000 tonnes; molasses (1994), 6,000 tonnes.

Labour. In 1994 the economically active population numbered 16,608, of which 22·3% worked in services, finance and real estate, 20·3% in trade and restaurants, 16·5% in public administration and defence, and 10·5% in construction.

INTERNATIONAL TRADE
Foreign debt in 2000 amounted to US$140m.

Imports and Exports. Exports, 1999, XC$75·9m.; imports, XC$414·6m. Main trading partners are the USA, the UK and other CARICOM members. The chief export is sugar. Other significant exports are machinery, food, electronics, beverages and tobacco. Main imports include machinery, manufactures, food and fuels.

COMMUNICATIONS
Roads. There were (1999) about 250 km of roads, of which 200 km were surfaced (124 km paved), and (1999) 5,326 passenger cars and 3,742 commercial vehicles.

Rail. There are 58 km of railway operated by the sugar industry.

Civil Aviation. The main airport is the Robert Llewelyn Bradshaw International Airport (just over 3 km from Basseterre). In 1999 there were flights to Anguilla, Antigua, Barbados, British Virgin Islands, Netherlands Antilles, Nevis (Newcastle), Puerto Rico and the US Virgin Islands, with weekly flights to the UK.

Shipping. There is a deep-water port at Bird Rock (Basseterre). 202,000 tons of cargo were unloaded in 1999 and 24,000 tons loaded. The government maintains a commercial motor boat service between the islands.

Telecommunications. In 2000 there were 21,900 telephone subscribers, or 568·8 per 1,000 inhabitants, and 7,000 PCs in use (181·7 for every 1,000 persons). In Dec. 1999 there were 2,000 Internet users. Mobile phone subscribers numbered 700 in 1999.

Postal Services. There are two post offices with seven branches.

SOCIAL INSTITUTIONS
Justice. Justice is administered by the Supreme Court and by Magistrates' Courts. They have both civil and criminal jurisdiction. St Kitts and Nevis was one of ten countries to sign an agreement in Feb. 2001 establishing a Caribbean Court of Justice to replace the British Privy Council as the highest civil and criminal court. The Court of Justice is expected to sit for the first time in the second half of 2003.

The population in penal institutions in Jan. 1998 was 109 (equivalent to 250 per 100,000 of national population).

Religion. In 1991, 27·5% of the population were Anglican, 25·3% Methodist, 6·9% Roman Catholic, 5·5% Pentecostal, 3·9% Baptist and 3·9% Church of God.

Education. Adult literacy was 98% in 1998–99. Education is compulsory between the ages of 5 and 17. In 1998–99 there were 2,490 pupils in 71 pre-primary schools and 28 nurseries with 196 pre-primary teachers. In 1998–99 there were 5,947 pupils (3,556 male) and 293 teachers (57 male) in 23 primary schools, 4,528 pupils and 345 teachers in 7 secondary schools, and 1,153 pupils (555 male) and 70 teachers (13 male) in 9 private schools. There is an Extra-Mural Department of the University of the West Indies, a Non-formal Youth Skills Training Centre (with 55 students) and a Teachers' Training College. Clarence Fitzroy Bryant College has a Sixth Form Division (with 234 students), a Nursing Division (34 students), a Teaching

Education Division (61 students), a Division of Technical and Vocational Studies (145 students) and an Adult Education Division (500 students).

Health. In 1999 there were 46 doctors, 14 dentists, 184 nurses and 17 pharmacists; and 4 hospitals, with a provision of 49 beds per 10,000 population.

CULTURE

Broadcasting. There are three AM radio stations and two TV stations. Cable television is also available. In 1997 there were 10,000 television (colour by NTSC) and 28,000 radio receivers.

Press. In 2000 there were two weekly and one twice weekly newspapers.

Tourism. In 1999 an estimated 84,000 tourists visited out of a total of 224,397 arrivals including 137,389 by yacht. In 1999, 40·9% of visitors came from the USA and 15·5% from the UK. There were 30 hotels in 1999 (20 on St Kitts and 10 on Nevis) with 1,508 rooms. Receipts from tourism in 1999 totalled US$66m.

DIPLOMATIC REPRESENTATIVES

Of St Kitts and Nevis in the United Kingdom (2nd Floor, 10 Kensington Ct., London, W8 5DL)
High Commissioner: James Williams.

Of the United Kingdom in St Kitts and Nevis
High Commissioner: John White (resides at Bridgetown, Barbados).

Of St Kitts and Nevis in the USA (OECS Building, 3216 New Mexico Ave., NW, 3rd Floor, Washington, D.C., 20016)
Ambassador: Izben Cordinal Williams.

Of the USA in St Kitts and Nevis
Ambassador: Earl Norfleet Phillips, Jr (resides at Bridgetown).

Of St Kitts and Nevis to the United Nations
Ambassador: Joseph Christmas.

Of St Kitts and Nevis to the European Union
Ambassador: Edwin Laurent.

FURTHER READING

Statistics Division. *National Accounts.* Annual.—*St Kitts and Nevis Quarterly.*
Moll, Verna Penn, *St Kitts and Nevis.* [Bibliography] ABC-Clio, Oxford and Santa Barbara (CA), 1995

National library: Public Library, Burdon St., Basseterre.
National statistical office: Statistics Division, Ministry of Development, Church St., Basseterre.

ST LUCIA

Capital: Castries
Population estimate, 2000: 156,000
GDP per capita, 2000: (PPP$) 5,703
HDI/world rank: 0·772/66

KEY HISTORICAL EVENTS
The island was probably discovered by Columbus in 1502. An unsuccessful attempt to colonize by the British took place in 1605 and again in 1638 when settlers were soon murdered by the Caribs who inhabited the island. France claimed the right of sovereignty and ceded it to the French West India Company in 1642. St Lucia regularly and constantly changed hands between Britain and France, until it was finally ceded to Britain in 1814 by the Treaty of Paris. Since 1924 the island has had representative government. In March 1967 St Lucia gained full control of its internal affairs while Britain remained responsible for foreign affairs and defence. On 22 Feb. 1979 St Lucia achieved independence, opting to remain in the British Commonwealth.

TERRITORY AND POPULATION
St Lucia is an island of the Lesser Antilles in the eastern Caribbean between Martinique and St Vincent, with an area of 238 sq. miles (617 sq. km). Population (census, 1991) 133,308; density, 216·1 per sq. km. In 1998 the population was 37·4% urban.

Area and estimated population of the ten administrative districts in 1992 were:

Districts	Sq. km	Population estimate	Districts	Sq. km	Population estimate
Ane-la-Raye	47	{ 5,218	Gros Inlet	101	13,996
Canaries		{ 1,864	Laborie	38	7,763
Castries	79	53,883	Micoud	78	15,636
Choiseul	31	6,638	Soufrière	51	7,962
Dennery	70	11,574	Vieux Fort	44	13,617

The official language is English, but 80% of the population speak a French Creole. In 1990 over 90% of the population was Black, 6% were of mixed race and 3% of south Asian ethnic origin.

The capital is Castries (population, 1999, 57,000).

SOCIAL STATISTICS
1998 births, 2,860; deaths, 973. Rates, 1998 (per 1,000 population): births, 18·8; deaths, 6·4. Infant mortality, 1998 (per 1,000 live births), 18. Expectation of life in 1997 was 71·3 years (67·7 for males and 75·2 for females). Annual population growth rate, 1990–99, 1·4% per annum; fertility rate, 1999, 2·3 births per woman.

CLIMATE
The climate is tropical, with a dry season from Jan. to April. Most rain falls in Nov.–Dec.; annual amount varies from 60" (1,500 mm) to 138" (3,450 mm). The average annual temperature is about 80°F (26·7°C).

CONSTITUTION AND GOVERNMENT
The head of state is the British sovereign, represented by an appointed Governor-General. There is a 17-seat *House of Assembly* elected for five years and an 11-seat *Senate* appointed by the Governor-General.

National Anthem. 'Sons and daughters of St Lucia'; words by C. Jesse, tune by L. F. Thomas.

RECENT ELECTIONS
At the elections of 3 Dec. 2001 the St Lucia Labour Party gained 14 seats and the United Workers' Party 3.

CURRENT ADMINISTRATION

Governor-General: Dr Perlette Louisy; b. 1946 (appointed 17 Sept. 1997).

In March 2003 the government comprised:

Prime Minister and Minister of Finance, Economic Affairs, International Financial Services and Information: Dr Kenny Davis Anthony; b. 1951 (appointed 24 May 1997).

Deputy Prime Minister and Minister of Education, Human Resource Development, Youth and Sports: Mario Michel.

Minister of Agriculture, Forestry and Fisheries: Callixte George. *Commerce, Tourism, Investment and Consumer Affairs:* Philip Pierre. *Communications, Works, Transport and Public Utilities:* Felix Finisterre. *Foreign Affairs, International Trade and Civil Aviation:* Julian Hunte. *Health, Human Services and Family Affairs:* Damian Greaves. *Development, Planning, Environment and Housing:* Ignatius Jean. *Labour Relations, Public Service and Co-operatives:* Velon John. *Home Affairs and Gender Relations:* Sarah Flood-Beaubrun. *Justice:* Petrus Compton. *Social Transformation, Culture and Local Government:* Menissa Rambally.

Government Website: http://www.stlucia.gov.lc/

INTERNATIONAL RELATIONS

St Lucia is a member of the UN, WTO, OAS, ACS, CARICOM, OECS, the Commonwealth, the International Organization of the Francophonie and is an ACP member state of the ACP-EU relationship.

ECONOMY

In 1998 services contributed 72·9% of GDP, industry 18·9% and agriculture 8·2%.

Currency. The East Caribbean *dollar* (XCD) (of 100 *cents*) is in use. US dollars are also normally accepted. Inflation was 2·5% in 2001. Foreign exchange reserves were US$90m. in May 2002. Total money supply was EC$320m. in May 2002.

Budget. Revenues were an estimated US$155m. in the fiscal year 1996–97, and expenditures US$169m.

Performance. Real GDP growth was 0·7% in 2000 and 0·5% in 2001. Total GDP in 2001 was US$0·7bn.

Banking and Finance. The East Caribbean Central Bank based in St Kitts and Nevis functions as a central bank. The *Governor* is Sir Dwight Venner. There are three domestic and four foreign banks. Inflation in 1996 was 3%.

ENERGY AND NATURAL RESOURCES

Environment. According to the *World Bank Atlas* carbon dioxide emissions in 1998 were the equivalent of 1·3 tonnes per capita.

Electricity. Installed capacity in 1995 was 34,000 kW. Production in 1998 was 110m. kWh; consumption per capita in 1997 was 777 kWh.

Agriculture. Bananas, cocoa, breadfruit and mango are the principal crops, but changes in the world's trading rules and changes in taste are combining to depress the banana trade. Farmers are experimenting with okra, tomatoes and avocados to help make up for the loss. Production, 2000 (in 1,000 tonnes): bananas, 92; mangoes, 28; coconuts, 12; yams, 5; copra, 2.

Livestock (2000): pigs, 15,000; sheep, 13,000; cattle, 12,000; goats, 10,000.

Forestry. In 1995 the area under forests was 5,000 ha (8·2% of the total land area).

Fisheries. In 1999 the total catch was 1,718 tonnes.

INDUSTRY

The main areas of activity are clothing, assembly of electronic components, beverages, corrugated cardboard boxes, tourism, lime processing and coconut processing.

Labour. In 1993 the economically active population totalled 81,000, around a quarter of whom were engaged in agriculture, fisheries and forestry.

INTERNATIONAL TRADE

Foreign debt in 2000 amounted to US$237m.

Imports and Exports. Imports and exports for calendar years in US$1m.:

	1992	1993	1994	1995	1996
Imports	270·8	264·0	265·5	269·3	270·6
Exports	122·8	119·7	94·8	108·9	79·5

Bananas accounted for 60% of exports in 1995. The main export markets in 1991 were the UK (56%), followed by the USA (22%) and CARICOM countries (19%). In 1995 manufactured goods accounted for 21% of imports, as did machinery and transportation equipment. Main import suppliers, 1995: USA, 38·1%; Trinidad and Tobago, 12·4%; UK, 11·1%; Japan, 4·6%. Main export markets, 1995: UK, 53·1%; USA, 26·0%; Dominica, 5·4%; Trinidad and Tobago, 3·0%.

COMMUNICATIONS

Roads. The island had 1,210 km of roads in 1996, of which 150 km were main roads and a further 150 km secondary roads. Passenger cars numbered 14,550 in 1996.

Civil Aviation. There are international airports at Hewanorra (near Vieux-Fort) and Vigie (near Castries). In 2000 Vigie handled 376,000 (370,000 on international flights) and Hewanorra 350,000 passengers (343,000 on international flights).

Shipping. There are two ports, Castries and Vieux Fort. Merchant shipping in 1995 totalled 1,000 GRT. In 1997 vessels totalling 6,803,000 net registered tons entered the ports.

Telecommunications. Main telephone lines numbered 48,900 in 2000 (313·5 per 1,000 persons), and there were 22,000 PCs (141 for every 1,000 persons). In 1994 there were 68 telex and 560 fax machines. There were 1,900 mobile phone subscribers in 1999, and Internet users numbered 5,000 in April 2000.

SOCIAL INSTITUTIONS

Justice. The island is divided into two judicial districts, and there are nine magistrates' courts. Appeals lie to the Eastern Caribbean Supreme Court of Appeal. St Lucia was one of ten countries to sign an agreement in Feb. 2001 establishing a Caribbean Court of Justice to replace the British Privy Council as the highest civil and criminal court. The Court of Justice is expected to sit for the first time in the second half of 2003.

The population in penal institutions in Jan. 1998 was 325 (225 per 100,000 of national population).

Religion. In 1997 over 80% of the population was Roman Catholic.

Education. Primary education is free and compulsory. In 1996–97 there were 89 primary schools with 1,214 teachers for 31,615 pupils, and 11,753 pupils and 682 teachers at secondary level. There is a community college. Adult literacy rate is 82%.

Health. In 1992 there were 64 doctors, 6 dentists and 256 nursing personnel employed by the government, 4 hospitals with 435 beds and 34 health centres.

CULTURE

Broadcasting. There were 32,000 TV (colour by PAL) and 111,000 radio receivers in 1997.

Press. In 1993 there were three newspapers with a nationwide circulation.

Tourism. The total number of visitors during 1998 was 252,000, plus 372,000 cruise ship arrivals. Receipts in 1998 totalled US$290m.

DIPLOMATIC REPRESENTATIVES

Of St Lucia in the United Kingdom (1 Collingham Gdns, Earls Court, London, SW5 0HW)

High Commissioner: Emmanuel H. Cotter, MBE.

Of the United Kingdom in St Lucia (NIS Waterfront Building, 2nd Floor, Castries)
High Commissioner: John White (resides at Bridgetown, Barbados).

Of St Lucia in the USA (3216 New Mexico Ave., NW, Washington, D.C., 20016)
Ambassador: Sonia Merlyn Johnny.

Of the USA in St Lucia
Ambassador: Earl Norfleet Phillips, Jr (resides at Bridgetown).

Of St Lucia to the United Nations
Ambassador: Earl S. Huntley.

Of St Lucia to the European Union
Ambassador: Edwin Laurent.

FURTHER READING
Momsen, Janet Henshall, *St Lucia*. [Bibliography] ABC-Clio, Oxford and Santa Barbara (CA),
1996

National statistical office: Central Statistical Office, Chreiki Building, Micoud street, Castries
Website: http://www.stats.gov.lc/

ST VINCENT AND THE GRENADINES

Capital: Kingstown
Population estimate, 2000: 118,000
GDP per capita, 2000: (PPP$) 5,555
HDI/world rank: 0·733/91

KEY HISTORICAL EVENTS

St Vincent was discovered by Columbus on 22 Jan. (St Vincent's Day) 1498. British and French settlers occupied parts of the islands after 1627. In 1773 the Caribs recognized British sovereignty and agreed to a division of territory between themselves and the British. Resentful of British rule, the Caribs rebelled in 1795, aided by the French, but the revolt was subdued within a year. On 27 Oct. 1969 St Vincent became an Associated State with the UK responsible only for foreign policy and defence, while the islands were given full internal self-government. On 27 Oct. 1979 the colony gained full independence as St Vincent and the Grenadines.

TERRITORY AND POPULATION

St Vincent is an island of the Lesser Antilles, situated in the eastern Caribbean between St Lucia and Grenada, from which latter it is separated by a chain of small islands known as the Grenadines. The total area of 389 sq. km (150 sq. miles) comprises the island of St Vincent itself (345 sq. km) and those of the Grenadines attached to it, of which the largest are Bequia, Mustique, Canouan, Mayreau and Union.

The population at the 1991 census was 106,499, of whom 8,367 lived in the St Vincent Grenadines. 1996 estimate, 115,000 (52·2% urban in 1998); density 296 per sq. km.

The capital, Kingstown, had 28,000 inhabitants in 1999 (including suburbs). The population is mainly of black (82%) and mixed (13·9%) origin, with small white, Asian and American minorities.

English and French patois are spoken.

SOCIAL STATISTICS

Births, 1999, 2,106; deaths, 796. 1999 birth rate, 18·8 per 1,000 population; death rate, 7·1. Infant mortality, 1999, 20 per 1,000 live births; life expectancy, 73 years. Annual population growth rate, 1990–99, 0·8%; fertility rate, 1999, 1·9 births per woman.

CLIMATE

The climate is tropical marine, with northeast Trades predominating and rainfall ranging from 150" (3,750 mm) a year in the mountains to 60" (1,500 mm) on the southeast coast. The rainy season is from June to Dec., and temperatures are equable throughout the year.

CONSTITUTION AND GOVERNMENT

The head of state is Queen Elizabeth II, represented by a Governor-General. Parliament is unicameral and consists of a 21-member *House of Assembly,* 15 of which are directly elected for a five-year term from single-member constituencies. The remaining six are senators appointed by the Governor-General (four on the advice of the Prime Minister and two on the advice of the Leader of the Opposition).

National Anthem. 'St Vincent, land so beautiful'; words by Phyllis Punnett, tune by J. B. Miguel.

RECENT ELECTIONS

At the elections to the House of Assembly on 28 March 2001 the opposition Unity Labour Party (ULP, social-democratic) won 12 of the 15 elected seats, against 3 for the ruling New Democratic Party (NDP, conservative).

CURRENT ADMINISTRATION

Governor-General: Sir Frederick Ballantyne (since 2 Sept. 2002).

In March 2003 the government comprised:

Prime Minister, Minister for Finance, Planning, Economic Development, Labour, Information, Grenadine Affairs and Legal Affairs: Dr Ralph E. Gonsalves; b. 1946 (ULP; sworn in 29 March 2001).

Deputy Prime Minister and Minister of Foreign Affairs, Commerce and Trade: Louis Straker. *Minister of National Security, the Public Service and Airport Development:* Vincent Beache. *Education, Youth and Sports:* Mike Browne. *Social Development, Co-operatives, the Family, Gender and Ecclesiastical Affairs:* Selmon Walters. *Agriculture, Lands and Fisheries:* Girlyn Miguel. *Tourism and Culture:* Rene Baptiste. *Telecommunications, Science, Technology and Industry:* Dr Jerrol Thompson. *Health and Environment:* Dr Douglas Slater. *Transport, Works and Housing:* Julian Francis.

INTERNATIONAL RELATIONS

St Vincent and the Grenadines is a member of UN, WTO, OAS, ACS, CARICOM, OECS, the Commonwealth and is an ACP member state of the ACP-EU relationship.

ECONOMY

Agriculture accounted for 10·9% of GDP in 1997, industry 26·9% and services 62·2%.

Currency. The currency in use is the *East Caribbean dollar* (XCD). In 2001 inflation was 0·8%. Foreign exchange reserves were US$60m. in May 2002, and total money supply was EC$272m.

Budget. Total revenue and expenditure in XC$1m. for calendar years:

	1996	1997	1998	1999	2000[1]
Revenue	220·1	240·5	260·3	276·1	286·0
Expenditure	236·9	337·0	320·9	315·1	327·6

[1]Provisional.

Performance. Real GDP growth was 1·7% in 2001 (1·8% in 2000). In 2001 total GDP was US$0·3bn.

Banking and Finance. The East Caribbean Central Bank is the bank of issue. The *Governor* is Sir Dwight Venner. There are branches of Barclays Bank PLC, the Caribbean Banking Corporation, the Canadian Imperial Bank of Commerce and the Bank of Nova Scotia. Locally-owned banks: First St Vincent Bank, the National Commercial Bank and St Vincent Co-operative Bank.

St Vincent and the Grenadines was one of 15 countries and territories named in a report in June 2000 as failing to co-operate in the fight against international money laundering. The Financial Action Task Force on Money Laundering was set up by the G7 group of major industrialized nations.

ENERGY AND NATURAL RESOURCES

Environment. According to the *World Bank Atlas* carbon dioxide emissions were the equivalent of 1·4 tonnes per capita in 1998.

Electricity. Installed capacity was 20,000 kW in 1993. Production in 1998 was 64m. kWh; consumption per capita in 1997 was 714 kWh.

Agriculture. According to the 1985–86 census of agriculture, 29,649 acres of the total acreage of 85,120 were classified as agricultural lands; 5,500 acres were under forest and woodland and all other lands accounted for 1,030 acres. The total arable land was about 8,932 acres, of which 4,016 acres were under temporary crops, 2,256 acres under temporary pasture, 2,289 acres under temporary fallow and other arable land covering 371 acres. 16,062 acres were under permanent crops, of which approximately 5,500 acres were under coconuts and 7,224 acres under bananas; the remainder produce cocoa, citrus, mangoes, avocado pears, guavas and miscellaneous crops. In 1997 there were an estimated 4,000 acres of arable land and 7,000 acres of permanent cropland. The sugar industry was closed down in 1985 although some sugarcane is grown for rum production. Production (2000, in 1,000 tonnes): bananas, 43; coconuts, 24; sugarcane, 20; copra, 2; maize, 2; sweet potatoes, 2.

Livestock (2000, in 1,000): sheep, 13; pigs, 10; cattle, 6; goats, 6.

Forestry. Forests covered 11,000 ha in 1995, or 28·2% of the land area.

Fisheries. Total catch, 1999, 15,573 tonnes (all from sea fishing).

INDUSTRY
Industries include assembly of electronic equipment, manufacture of garments, electrical products, animal feeds and flour, corrugated galvanized sheets, exhaust systems, industrial gases, concrete blocks, plastics, soft drinks, beer and rum, wood products and furniture, and processing of milk, fruit juices and food items. Rum production, 1994, 0·4m. litres.

Labour. The Department of Labour is charged with looking after the interest and welfare of all categories of workers, including providing advice and guidance to employers and employees and their organizations and enforcing the labour laws. In 1991 the total labour force was 41,682, of whom 33,355 (11,699 females) were employed.

INTERNATIONAL TRADE
Foreign debt was US$192m. in 2000.

Imports and Exports. Imports and exports for calendar years in US$1m.:

	1992	1993	1994	1995	1996
Imports	116·2	117·3	114·4	118·4	126·3
Exports	78·9	57·1	46·2	59·4	49·4

Principal exports, 1995 (in US$1m., preliminary): manufactured goods, 232 (flour, 87; rice, 64); bananas, 219; dasheen, 15. Principal imports: manufactured goods, 448; chemicals, 165; food, 24; machinery and transport equipment, 21.

Main export markets, 1995 (in US$1m., preliminary): St Lucia, 71; USA, 54; UK, 9; Trinidad and Tobago, 5. Main import suppliers: USA, 436; Trinidad and Tobago, 203; UK, 154.

COMMUNICATIONS
Roads. In 1996 there were 1,040 km of roads, of which just over 30% were paved. Vehicles in use (1995): 5,300 passenger cars; 3,700 commercial vehicles.

Civil Aviation. There is an airport (E. T. Joshua) on mainland St Vincent at Arnos Vale. An airport on Union also has regular scheduled services. In 1995 E. T. Joshua handled 185,000 passengers and 1,200 tonnes of freight.

Shipping. In 1994 there were some 200 ships in the Vincentian open register. Merchant shipping in 1998 totalled 7,875,000 GRT, including oil tankers 913,000 GRT. In 1998 vessels totalling 1,274,000 net registered tons entered.

Telecommunications. There is a fully digital automatic telephone system with 24,900 main telephone lines in 2000, equivalent to 219·6 for every 1,000 inhabitants; 17,500 stations and digital radio provide links to Bequia, Mustique, Union, Petit St Vincent and Palm Island. The telephone network has almost 100% geographical coverage. There were 800 mobile phone subscribers in 1999 and 12,000 PCs in use (105·8 for every 1,000 persons) in 2000. In Dec. 2000 there were 3,500 Internet users.

Postal Services. There is a General Post Office at Kingstown and 56 district post offices.

SOCIAL INSTITUTIONS
Justice. Law is based on UK common law as exercised by the Eastern Caribbean Supreme Court on St Lucia. Final appeal lies to the UK Privy Council. In 1995 there were 4,700 criminal matters disposed of in the three magisterial districts which comprise 11 courts. 62 cases were dealt with in the Criminal Assizes in the High Court. Strength of police force (1995), 663 (including 19 gazetted officers).

The population in penal institutions in Jan. 1998 was 420 (380 per 100,000 of national population).

Religion. In 1997 there were estimated to be 47,000 Anglicans, 23,000 Methodists, 13,000 Roman Catholics and 29,000 followers of other religions.

Education. In 1994 there were 97 pre-primary schools with 175 teachers for 2,500 pupils and 65 primary schools with 1,080 teachers for 21,386 pupils. In 1991 there were 10,719 secondary pupils with 431 teachers and, in 1989, 677 students at university level. Adult literacy in 1998 was 82%.

Health. In 1992 there was a general hospital in Kingstown with 207 beds, 6 rural hospitals, 2 private hospitals and 38 clinics. There were 40 doctors, 6 dentists, 224 registered nurses, 144 nursing assistants and 39 community health aides.

CULTURE

Broadcasting. The National Broadcasting Corporation is part government-owned and part commercial. In 1997 there were 77,000 radio and 18,000 TV sets (colour by NTSC).

Press. In 1996 there was one daily newspaper with a circulation of 1,000, at a rate of 9 per 1,000 inhabitants.

Tourism. There were 68,000 visitors in 1999, and 35,000 cruise ship arrivals in 1998. Tourism receipts in 1999 totalled US$77m.

Libraries. There is a St Vincent Public Library at Kingstown.

DIPLOMATIC REPRESENTATIVES

Of St Vincent and the Grenadines in the United Kingdom (10 Kensington Ct, London, W8 5DL)
High Commissioner: Cenio Elwin Lewis.

Of the United Kingdom in St Vincent and the Grenadines (POB 132, Granby St., Kingstown)
High Commissioner: John White (resides at Bridgetown, Barbados).

Of St Vincent and the Grenadines in the USA (3216 New Mexico Ave., NW, Washington, D.C., 20016)
Ambassador: Ellsworth I. A. John.

Of the USA in St Vincent and the Grenadines
Ambassador: Earl Norfleet Phillips, Jr (resides at Bridgetown).

Of St Vincent and the Grenadines to the United Nations
Ambassador: Margaret Hughes Ferrari.

Of St Vincent and the Grenadines to the European Union
Ambassador: Edwin Laurent.

FURTHER READING

Potter, Robert B., *St Vincent and the Grenadines*. [Bibliography] ABC-Clio, Oxford and Santa Barbara (CA), 1992
Sutty, L., *St Vincent and the Grenadines*. London, 1993

SAMOA

O le Malo Tutoatasi o Samoa
(Independent State of Samoa)

Capital: Apia
Population estimate, 2000: 159,000
GDP per capita, 2000: (PPP$) 5,041
HDI/world rank: 0·715/101

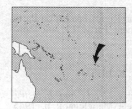

KEY HISTORICAL EVENTS
Polynesians settled in the Samoan group of islands in the southern Pacific from about 1000 BC. Although probably sighted by the Dutch in 1722, the first European visitor was French in 1768. Treaties were signed between the Chiefs and European nations in 1838–39. Continuing strife among the chiefs was compounded by British, German and US rivalry for influence. In the Treaty of Berlin 1889 the three powers agreed to Western Samoa's independence and neutrality. When unrest continued, the treaty was annulled and Western Samoa became a German protectorate until in 1914 it was occupied by a New Zealand expeditionary force. The island was administered by New Zealand from 1920 to 1961. On 1 Jan. 1962 Western Samoa became an independent sovereign state. In July 1997 the country renamed itself the Independent State of Samoa.

TERRITORY AND POPULATION
Samoa lies between 13° and 15° S. lat. and 171° and 173° W. long. It comprises the two large islands of Savai'i and Upolu, the small islands of Manono and Apolima, and several uninhabited islets lying off the coast. The total land area is 1,093 sq. miles (2,830·8 sq. km), of which 659·4 sq. miles (1,707·8 sq. km) are in Savai'i, and 431·5 sq. miles (1,117·6 sq. km) in Upolu; other islands, 2·1 sq. miles (5·4 sq. km). The islands are of volcanic origin, and the coasts are surrounded by coral reefs. Rugged mountain ranges form the core of both main islands. The large area laid waste by lava-flows in Savai'i is a primary cause of that island supporting less than one-third of the population of the islands despite its greater size than Upolu.

Population at the 1991 census, 161,298. The population at the 1991 census was 116,248 in Upolu (including Manono and Apolima) and 45,040 in Savai'i. The capital and chief port is Apia in Upolu (population 38,000 in 1999). In 1999, 78·5% of the population lived in rural areas.

The UN gives a projected population for 2010 of 168,000.

The official languages are Samoan and English.

SOCIAL STATISTICS
Births, 1995, 4,400; deaths, 1,000. 1995 birth rate per 1,000 population, 25·8; death rate, 6·1. Expectation of life in 1999 was 65·9 years for males and 72·5 for females. Annual population growth rate, 1990–99, was 1·1%. Infant mortality, 1999, 21 per 1,000 live births; fertility rate, 1999, 4·4 births per woman.

CLIMATE
A tropical marine climate, with cooler conditions from May to Nov. and a rainy season from Dec. to April. The rainfall is unevenly distributed, with south and east coasts having the greater quantities. Average annual rainfall is about 100" (2,500 mm) in the drier areas. Apia, Jan. 80°F (26·7°C), July 78°F (25·6°C). Annual rainfall 112" (2,800 mm).

CONSTITUTION AND GOVERNMENT
HH Malietoa Tanumafili II is the sole Head of State for life. Future Heads of State will be elected by the Legislative Assembly and hold office for five-year terms.

The executive power is vested in the *Head of State*, who swears in the *Prime Minister* (who is elected by the Legislative Assembly) and, on the Prime Minister's advice, the Ministers to form the Cabinet. The Constitution also provides for a *Council of Deputies* of three members, of whom the chairman is the Deputy Head of State.

Before 1991 the 49-member *Legislative Assembly* was elected exclusively by *matai* (customary family heads). At the elections of April 1991 the suffrage was universal, but only the approximately 20,000 *matai* could stand as candidates. The electorate was 56,000.

National Anthem. 'Samoa, tula'i ma sisi ia laufu'a ('Samoa, Arise and Raise your Banner'); words and tune by S. I. Kuresa.

RECENT ELECTIONS
At the most recent elections, on 4 March 2001, the Human Rights Protection Party (HRPP) won 23 seats; the Samoan National Development Party, 13; and non-partisans, 13.

CURRENT ADMINISTRATION
Head of State: HH Malietoa Tanumafili II, GCMG, CBE; b. 1913.
  In March 2003 the cabinet was composed as follows:
  Prime Minister, Minister of Foreign Affairs, Commerce, Trade and Industry, Treasury, Inland Revenue and Customs: Tuila'epa Sailele Malielegaoi; b. 1945 (HRPP; sworn in 23 Nov. 1998 and re-elected in 2001).
  Minister of Agriculture, Forestry, Fisheries and Meteorological Services: Molio'o Teofilo. *Education:* Fiame Naomi Mata'afa. *Finance:* Misa Telefoni Retzlaff. *Health:* Vacant. *Immigration, Internal Affairs, Police and Prisons, and Public Service:* Tofilau Eti Alesana. *Lands, Survey and Environment:* Tuala Sale Tagaloa Kerslake. *Justice:* Solia Papu Vaai. *Women's Affairs:* Leniu Tofaeono Avamagalo. *Labour:* Polataivao Fosi. *Transportation and Civil Aviation:* Hans Joachim Keil. *Public Works:* Vacant.

Government Website: http://www.samoa.net.ws/govtsamoapress/

INTERNATIONAL RELATIONS
Samoa, as an independent state, deals directly with other governments and international organizations. It has diplomatic relations with a number of countries.
  Samoa is a member of the UN, the Commonwealth, Asian Development Bank, the Pacific Community, the Pacific Islands Forum and is an ACP member state of the ACP-EU relationship.

ECONOMY
Agriculture accounts for approximately 40% of GDP, industry 25% and services 35%.

Currency. The unit of currency is the *tala* (WST) of 100 *sene*. In 2001 there was inflation of 4·0%. Foreign exchange reserves were US$61m. in June 2002. Total money supply was 92m. tala in June 2002.

Budget. For 1996–97 revenue was WS$288·4m.; expenditure, WS$312·7m. For 1997–98 budgeted revenue was WS$292·6m. and expenditure WS$306·6m.

Performance. Real GDP growth was 6·5% in 2001 (6·9% in 2000). In 2001 total GDP was US$0·3bn.

Banking and Finance. The Central Bank of Samoa (founded 1984) is the bank of issue. The *Governor* is Papali'i Tommy Scanlan.

ENERGY AND NATURAL RESOURCES
Environment. According to the *World Bank Atlas* Samoa's carbon dioxide emissions in 1998 were the equivalent of 0·8 tonnes per capita.

Electricity. Installed capacity in 1990 was 29,000 kW. Production was 65m. kWh. in 1998; consumption per capita in 1997 was estimated at 378 kWh.

Agriculture. In 1998 there were 55,000 ha of arable land and 67,000 ha of permanent cropland. The main products (2000 estimates, in 1,000 tonnes) are coconuts (130), taro (37), copra (11), bananas (10), papayas (10), pineapples (6) and mangoes (5).
  Livestock (2000): cattle, 26,000; pigs, 179,000; asses, 7,000.

Forestry. Forests covered 136,000 ha (48·1% of the land area) in 1995, compared to 144,000 ha and 50·9% in 1990. Timber production was 131,000 cu. metres in 1999.

Fisheries. Fish landings in 1999 totalled 9,750 tonnes.

INDUSTRY
Some industrial activity is being developed associated with agricultural products and forestry.

Labour. In 1991 the total labour force numbered 57,142 (39,839 males).

INTERNATIONAL TRADE
Total external debt was US$197m. in 2000.

Imports and Exports. In 1999 exports (f.o.b.) were valued at US$18·15m. (US$20·40m. in 1998) and imports (f.o.b.) at US$115·66m. (US$96·91m. in 1998). Principal exports are coconuts, palm oil, taro and taamu, coffee and beer. Main imports are machinery and transport equipment, foodstuffs and basic manufactures. New Zealand is the principal trading partner, in 1995 accounting for 44·2% of exports and 36·6% of imports. Australia is the second biggest supplier of imports and the second biggest export market.

COMMUNICATIONS
Roads. In 1996 the road network covered 790 km, of which 240 km were highways and main roads. In 1993 there were 1,269 private cars, 1,936 pick-up trucks, 472 trucks, 334 buses, 936 taxis and 67 motorcycles.

Civil Aviation. There is an international airport at Apia (Faleolo), which handled 153,000 passengers (152,000 on international flights) in 2000. The national carrier is Polynesian Airlines. In 2002 it operated domestic services and international flights to American Samoa, Auckland, Brisbane, the Fiji Islands, Honolulu, Los Angeles, Melbourne, Niue, Sydney, Tonga and Wellington. Samoa Aviation provides international services between Samoa and American Samoa (a US Trust Territory).

Shipping. Sea-going shipping totalled 3,000 GRT in 1998. Samoa is linked to Japan, USA, Europe, the Fiji Islands, Australia and New Zealand by regular shipping services.

Telecommunications. There are three radio communication stations at Apia. Radio telephone service connects Samoa with American Samoa, the Fiji Islands, New Zealand, Australia, Canada, USA and UK. Main telephone lines numbered 8,500 in 2000 (47·3 per 1,000 population) and there were 1,000 PCs in use (6·1 per 1,000 persons). There were 3,000 mobile phone subscribers in 1999 and 490 fax machines in 1997. Samoa had 500 Internet users in Dec. 1999.

Postal Services. In 1995 there were 38 post offices.

SOCIAL INSTITUTIONS
Justice. The population in penal institutions in 1995 was 255 (155 per 100,000 of national population).

Religion. In 1997 there were 44,000 Latter-day Saints (Mormons), 42,000 Congregationalists, 36,000 Roman Catholics, 21,000 Methodists, and 26,000 of other beliefs.

Education. In 1995 there were 35,811 pupils at 155 primary schools with 1,475 teachers, and 13,241 pupils and 715 teachers at secondary schools. The University of the South Pacific has a School of Agriculture in Samoa, at Apia. A National University was established in 1984. In 1994–95 it had 614 students and 30 academic staff. There is also a Polytechnic Institute which provides mainly vocational and training courses.

The adult literacy in 1999 was 80·2% (81·4% among males and 78·8% among females).

Health. In 1994 there were 2 national hospitals, 14 district hospitals, 9 health centres and 22 subcentres. There were 60 doctors in 1992.

CULTURE

Broadcasting. Samoa has a state-run commercial TV station, *Televise Samoa* and, since 2001, *Pro-Com Sky Cable TV*. There are four radio stations, three on FM and one on AM. In 1997 there were 12,000 television sets (colour by NTSC) and 178,000 radio receivers.

Cinema. In 1995 there were three cinemas.

Press. There are two dailies, plus a weekly, a fortnightly and a monthly. The most widely read newspaper is the independent *Samoa Observer*.

Tourism. In 1999 there were 85,000 foreign tourists, bringing revenue of US$42m.

DIPLOMATIC REPRESENTATIVES

Of Samoa in the United Kingdom and to the European Union
High Commissioner: Tauiliili Uili Meredith (resides at Brussels).
Honorary Consul: Prunella Scarlett, LVO (18 Northumberland Ave., London WC2N 5BJ).

Of the United Kingdom in Samoa
High Commissioner: Richard Fell, CVO (resides at Wellington).
Honorary Consul: c/o Kruse Enari and Barlow, 2nd Floor, NPF Building, Beach Road, PO Box 2029, Apia).

Of the USA in Samoa
Ambassador: Charles J. Swindells (resides at Wellington).

Of Samoa in the USA and to the United Nations (800 Second Ave., Suite 400D, New York, NY, 10017)
Ambassador: Tuiloma Neroni Slade.

FURTHER READING

Hughes, H. G. A., *American Samoa, Western Samoa, Samoans Abroad.* [Bibliography] ABC-Clio, Oxford and Santa Barbara (CA), 1997

SAN MARINO

Repubblica di San Marino

Capital: San Marino
Population estimate, 2000: 27,000
GDP per capita: not available

KEY HISTORICAL EVENTS

San Marino is a small republic situated on the Adriatic side of central Italy. According to tradition, St Marinus and a group of Christians settled there to escape persecution. By the 12th century San Marino had developed into a commune ruled by its own statutes and consul. Unsuccessful attempts were made to annex the republic to the papal states in the 18th century and when Napoleon invaded Italy in 1797 he respected the rights of the republic and even offered to extend its territories. In 1815 the Congress of Vienna recognized the independence of the republic. On 22 March 1862 San Marino concluded a treaty of friendship and co-operation, including a *de facto* customs union, with the Kingdom of Italy, thus preserving its independence although completely surrounded by Italian territory.

TERRITORY AND POPULATION

San Marino is a land-locked state in central Italy, 20 km from the Adriatic. Area is 61·19 sq. km (23·6 sq. miles) and the population (2000), 26,841; at Dec. 1999 some 13,104 citizens lived abroad.

In 1998 an estimated 90% of the population were urban. Population density, 440·5 per sq. km. The capital, San Marino, has 4,429 inhabitants (2000); the largest town is Serravalle (8,547 in 2000), an industrial centre in the north.

SOCIAL STATISTICS

Births, 1999, 303; deaths, 198; marriages, 231; divorces, 42 (1996). Birth rate, 1995–99 (per 1,000 population), 10·8; death rate, 7·0. Annual population growth rate, 1990–99, 1·0%; fertility rate, 1999, 1·5 births per woman.

CLIMATE

Temperate climate with cold, dry winters and warm summers.

CONSTITUTION AND GOVERNMENT

The legislative power is vested in the *Great and General Council* of 60 members elected every five years by popular vote, two of whom are appointed every six months to act as *Captains Regent,* who are the heads of state.

Executive power is exercised by the ten-member *Congress of State,* presided over by the Captains Regent. The *Council of Twelve,* also presided over by the Captains Regent, is appointed by the Great and General Council to perform administrative functions and is a court of third instance.

National Anthem. No words, tune monastic, transcribed by F. Consolo.

RECENT ELECTIONS

In parliamentary elections on 10 June 2001 the Christian Democratic Party won 25 of 60 seats, with 41·4% of the vote; the Socialist Party 15 with 24·2%; the Progressive Democratic Party 12 with 20·8%; the Popular Democratic Alliance 5 with 8·2%; the Communist Refoundation 2 with 3·4%; and the National Alliance 1 with 1·9%.

CURRENT ADMINISTRATION

In March 2003 the Congress of State comprised:
Minister of Foreign and Political Affairs, Economic Planning and Co-operation: Fiorenzo Stolfi. *Internal Affairs and Civil Protection:* Loris Francini. *Finance, Budget, and Post and Telecommunications:* Pier Marino Mularoni. *Industry and Craftmanship:* Maurizio Rattini. *Public Education, Universities, Cultural Institutions and Social Affairs:* Pasquale Valentini. *Territory, Agriculture and*

Environment: Fabio Berardi. *Tourism, Trade, Transport and Sports:* Paride Andreoli. *Health and Social Security:* Rosa Zafferani. *Labour and Co-operation:* Gian Carlo Venturini. *Justice, Relations with Local Governments, and Information:* Alberto Cecchetti.

Government Website (Italian only): http://www.interni.segreteria.sm/

DEFENCE
Military service is not obligatory, but all citizens between the ages of 16 and 55 can be called upon to defend the State. They may also serve as volunteers in the Military Corps. There is a military Gendarmerie.

INTERNATIONAL RELATIONS
San Marino maintains a traditional neutrality, and remained so in the First and Second World Wars. It has diplomatic and consular relations with over 70 countries.

San Marino is a member of the UN, the Council of Europe, the OSCE and various UN specialized agencies.

ECONOMY
Currency. Since 1 Jan. 2002 San Marino has been using the euro. Italy has agreed that San Marino may mint a small part of the total Italian euro coin contingent with their own motifs.

Budget. The budget (ordinary and extraordinary) for the financial year ending 31 Dec. 2000 balanced at 452m. euri.

Performance. Real GDP growth was 9·0% in 1999.

Banking and Finance. The Instituto di Credito Sammarinese (*President*, Valentini Antonio), the central bank and bank of issue, was set up in 1986 with public and private resources.

ENERGY AND NATURAL RESOURCES
Electricity. Electricity is supplied by Italy.

Agriculture. There were 1,000 ha of arable land in 2000. Wheat, barley, maize and vines are grown.

INDUSTRY
Labour. Out of 18,077 people in employment in 2000, 5,867 worked in manufacturing and 3,509 in wholesale and retail trade. In Dec. 2000 there were 428 registered unemployed persons.

Trade Unions. There are two Confederations of Trade Unions: the Democratic Confederation of Sammarinese Workers and the Sammarinese Confederation of Labour.

INTERNATIONAL TRADE
Imports and Exports. Export commodities are building stone, lime, wine, baked goods, textiles, varnishes and ceramics. Import commodities are a wide range of consumer manufactures and foodstuffs. San Marino maintains a customs union with Italy.

COMMUNICATIONS
Roads. A bus service connects San Marino with Rimini. There are 252 km of public roads and 40 km of private roads, and (1999) 26,320 passenger cars and 2,763 commercial vehicles.

Civil Aviation. The nearest airport is Rimini, 10 km to the east, which had flights in 1998 to Baku, London, Moscow and Rome.

Telecommunications. San Marino had 19,970 telephones in 1999. In 1997 there were 2,300 mobile phone subscribers.

Postal Services. In 1999 there were ten post offices.

SOCIAL INSTITUTIONS

Justice. Judges are appointed permanently by the Great and General Council; they may not be San Marino citizens. Petty civil cases are dealt with by a justice of the peace; legal commissioners deal with more serious civil cases, and all criminal cases and appeals lie to them from the justice of the peace. Appeals against the legal commissioners lie to an appeals judge, and the Council of the Twelve functions as a court of third instance.

Religion. The great majority of the population are Roman Catholic.

Education. Education is compulsory up to 16 years of age. In 2000 there were 15 nursery schools with 991 pupils and 119 teachers, 14 elementary schools with 1,894 pupils and 240 teachers, 3 junior high schools with 729 pupils and 140 teachers, and 1 high school with 1,348 pupils and 87 teachers. The University of San Marino began operating in 1988.

Health. In 2000 there were 141 hospital beds and 117 doctors. A survey published by the World Health Organization in June 2000 to measure health systems in all of the sovereign countries and find which country has the best overall health care ranked San Marino in third place.

CULTURE

Broadcasting. San Marino RTV (colour by PAL) is the state broadcasting company. In 1999 there were 8,932 television receivers. There were 15,000 radio receivers in 1998.

Cinema. In 1998 there were four cinemas with a seating capacity of 1,800. In 1995 gross box office receipts came to 253m. lira.

Press. San Marino had three daily newspapers in 1999.

Tourism. By the end of Nov. 2000, 3·07m. tourists had visited San Marino during the year.

DIPLOMATIC REPRESENTATIVES
Of the United Kingdom to San Marino
Ambassador: Sir John Shepherd, KCVO, CMG (resides at Rome).

Of San Marino to the United Nations
Ambassador: Vacant.

Of San Marino to the European Union
Ambassador: Savina Zafferani.

FURTHER READING
Edwards, Adrian and Michaelides, Chris, *San Marino.* [Bibliography] ABC-Clio, Oxford and Santa Barbara (CA), 1996

Information: Office of Cultural Affairs and Information of the Department of Foreign Affairs.

SÃO TOMÉ E PRÍNCIPE

República Democrática de São
Tomé e Príncipe

Capital: São Tomé
Population estimate, 2000: 149,000
GDP per capita, 2000: (PPP$) 1,792
HDI/world rank: 0·632/119

KEY HISTORICAL EVENTS

The islands of São Tomé and Príncipe off the west coast of Africa were colonized by Portugal in the fifteenth century. There may have been a few African inhabitants or visitors earlier but most of the population arrived during the centuries when the islands served as an important slave-trading depot for South America. In the 19th century the islands became the first parts of Africa to grow cocoa. Although in 1876 Portugal abolished slavery in name, in practice it continued thereafter with many Angolans, Mozambicans and Cape Verdians being transported to work on the cocoa plantations. Because the slave-descended population was cut off from African culture, São Tomé had a higher proportion than other Portuguese colonies of *assimilados* (Africans acquiring full Portuguese culture and certain rights). São Tomé saw serious riots against Portuguese rule in 1953. From 1960 a Movement for the Liberation of São Tomé e Príncipe operated from neighbouring African territories. In 1970 Portugal formed a 16-member legislative council and a provincial consultative council. Following the Portuguese revolution of 1974 a transitional government was formed. Independence came on 12 July 1975. Independent São Tomé e Príncipe officially proclaimed Marxist-Leninist policies but maintained a non-aligned foreign policy and has received aid from Portugal.

TERRITORY AND POPULATION

The republic, which lies about 200 km off the west coast of Gabon, in the Gulf of Guinea, comprises the main islands of São Tomé (845 sq. km) and Príncipe and several smaller islets including Pedras Tinhosas and Rolas. It has a total area of 1,001 sq. km (387 sq. miles). Population (census, 1991) 120,146. Estimate (1997), 147,900; density, 148 per sq. km. In 1998, 54·8% of the population were rural.

Areas and populations of the two provinces:

Province	Sq. km	Census 1991	Estimate 1995	Chief town	Census 1991
São Tomé	859	114,507	125,200	São Tomé	43,420
Príncipe	142	5,639	5,900	São António	1,000

The official language is Portuguese. Lungwa São Tomé, a Portuguese Creole, and Fang, a Bantu language, are the spoken languages.

SOCIAL STATISTICS

1997 births 5,000 (estimate); deaths, 1,200. Rates (1997 estimate): birth rate per 1,000 population, 33·8; death rate, 8·4; infant mortality (per 1,000 live births), 60 (1998). Expectation of life, 64·1 years. Annual population growth rate, 1990–99, 2·2%; fertility rate, 1999, 6·1 births per woman.

CLIMATE

The tropical climate is modified by altitude and the effect of the cool Benguela current. The wet season is generally from Oct. to May, but rainfall varies considerably, from 40" (1,000 mm) in the hot and humid northeast to 150–200" (3,800–5,000 mm) on the plateau. São Tomé, Jan. 79°F (26·1°C), July 75°F (23·9°C). Annual rainfall 38" (951 mm).

CONSTITUTION AND GOVERNMENT

The 1990 constitution was approved by 72% of votes at a referendum of Aug. 1990. It abolished the monopoly of the Movement for the Liberation of São Tomé e Príncipe (MLSTP). The *President* must be over 34 years old, and is elected by universal suffrage for one or two (only) five-year terms. He or she is also head of government and appoints a Council of Ministers. The 55-member *National Assembly* is elected for four years.

Since April 1995 **Príncipe** has enjoyed internal self-government, with a five-member regional government and an elected assembly.

National Anthem. 'Independência total, glorioso canto do povo' ('Total independence, glorious song of the people'); words by A. N. do Espírito Santo, tune by M. de Sousa e Almeida.

RECENT ELECTIONS

At the presidential election on 29 July 2001 Fradique de Menezes (Independent Democratic Action) was elected by 56·3% of votes cast against Manuel Pinto da Costa (Liberation Movement of São Tomé e Príncipe) with 38·4% and three other opponents. Turn-out was 62·4%.

At the National Assembly elections on 3 March 2002 the Liberation Movement of São Tomé e Príncipe (MLSTP) won 24 seats with 39·6% of votes cast, the coalition of the Force for Change Democratic Movement (MDFM) and the Democratic Convergence Party (PCD) 23 (39·4%), and the Uê Kédadji (UK) 8 (16·2%).

CURRENT ADMINISTRATION

President, C.-in-C: Fradique Bandeira Melo de Menezes; b. 1942 (IDA; sworn in 3 Sept. 2001).

In March 2003 the government comprised:

Prime Minister: Maria das Neves; b. 1958 (MLSTP; in office since 7 Oct. 2002).

Minister of Agriculture, Fisheries and Rural Development: Júlio Lopes Lima da Silva. *Defence:* Fernando da Trindade Danquá. *Education and Culture:* Maria Fernanda Pontifice de Jesus Bonfim. *Foreign Affairs and Co-operation:* Mateus Meira Rita. *Health:* Dr Claudina Augusto Cruz. *Industry, Commerce and Tourism:* Arzemiro Dos Prazeres. *Justice:* Justino Tavares Viegas. *Labour and Solidarity:* Damião Vaz de Almeida. *Planning and Finance:* Maria dos Santos Tebús Torres. *Public Construction, Infrastructure and Natural Resources:* Joaquim Rafael Branco. *Youth, Sport and Professional Training:* José Viegas Santiago. *Secretary of State for Public Administration and State Reform:* Elsa Teixeira Pinto. *Secretary of State for Environment:* Arlindo de Carvalho.

INTERNATIONAL RELATIONS

São Tomé e Príncipe is a member of the UN, the African Union, African Development Bank, the International Organization of the Francophonie and is an ACP member state of the ACP-EU relationship.

ECONOMY

In 1998 agriculture accounted for 21·3% of GDP, industry 16·7% and services 62·0%.

Overview. Most branches of the economy were nationalized after independence, but economic liberalization began in 1985 and was increased in 1991.

Currency. The unit of currency is the *dobra* (STD) of 100 *centimos*. From a rate of 69·0% in 1997 inflation had fallen to 9·5% by 2001. In Dec. 1997 foreign exchange reserves were US$12m. Total money supply in April 2002 was 98,789m. dobras (up from 23,683m. dobras in Dec. 1996).

Budget. The 1995 budget set revenue at 11,000m. dobras and expenditure at 50,000m. dobras.

Performance. Real GDP growth was 3·0% in 2000, rising to 4·0% in 2001.

Banking and Finance. In 1991 the Banco Central de São Tomé e Príncipe (*Governor*, Maria do Carmo Silveira) replaced the Banco Nacional as the central bank and bank of issue. A private commercial bank, the Banco Internacional de São Tomé e Príncipe, began operations in 1993.

Weights and Measures. The metric system is in use.

ENERGY AND NATURAL RESOURCES

Environment. In 1998, according to the *World Bank Atlas,* carbon dioxide emissions were the equivalent of 0·5 tonnes per capita.

Electricity. Installed capacity, 1992, 7,200 kW. Production was 15m. kWh in 1998, with consumption per capita in 1997 being 109 kWh.

Oil and Gas. There are large oil reserves around São Tomé e Príncipe that could greatly add to the country's wealth.

Agriculture. After independence all landholdings over 200 ha were nationalized into 15 state farms. These were partially privatized in 1985 by granting management contracts to foreign companies, and distributing some state land as small private plots. There were 2,000 ha of arable land in 1998 and 39,000 ha of permanent crops. Production (2000 in 1,000 tonnes): coconuts, 29; bananas, 19; cassava, 5; palm kernels, 4; cocoa beans, 3; maize, 2. There were 4,000 cattle, 3,000 sheep, 2,000 pigs and 5,000 goats in 2000.

Forestry. In 1995 forests covered 56,000 ha, or 76% of the land area. In 1999, 9,000 cu. metres of timber were cut.

Fisheries. There are rich tuna shoals. The total catch in 1999 came to 3,756 tonnes.

INDUSTRY

Manufacturing contributes less than 10% of GDP. There are a few small factories in agricultural processing (including beer and palm oil production), timber processing, bricks, ceramics, printing, textiles and soap-making.

Labour. In 1994 the economically active population was 54,000. There were 15,000 registered unemployed.

INTERNATIONAL TRADE

Foreign debt was US$316m. in 2000. In 1999 São Tomé e Príncipe was the most heavily indebted country in the world in relation to the GNP, owing 615% of its GNP.

Imports and Exports. Trade figures for 1996 (estimates): imports, US$26m.; exports, US$8m. The main exports are cocoa (92% in 1995), copra, coffee, bananas and palm-oil.

Main export markets, 1996: Netherlands (63·9%); Germany (20·9%); Portugal (2·0%). Main import suppliers, 1996: Portugal (29·0%); Angola (13·3%); Belgium (10·1%); Japan (10·1%).

COMMUNICATIONS

Roads. There were 320 km of roads in 1996, 218 km of which were asphalted. Approximately 4,000 passenger cars were in use in 1996 (30 per 1,000 inhabitants), plus 1,540 trucks and vans.

Civil Aviation. São Tomé airport had flights in 1998 to Abidjan, Cabinda, Libreville, Lisbon, Luanda, Malabo and Port Gentil. In 1999 São Tomé handled 32,298 passengers and 1,877 tonnes of freight. There is a light aircraft service to Príncipe.

Shipping. São Tomé is the main port, but it lacks a deep water harbour. Neves handles oil imports and is the main fishing port. Portuguese shipping lines run routes to Lisbon, Oporto, Rotterdam and Antwerp. In 1998 merchant shipping totalled 10,000 GRT.

Telecommunications. There were 4,600 main telephone lines in 2000, or 31·0 per 1,000 population. Internet users numbered 6,500 in Dec. 2000. In 1995 there were 200 fax machines.

Postal Services. In 1994 there were ten post offices.

SOCIAL INSTITUTIONS

Justice. Members of the Supreme Court are appointed by the National Assembly. There is no death penalty.

Religion. About 90% of the population are Roman Catholic. There is a small Protestant church and a Seventh Day Adventist school.

Education. Adult literacy was 57·0% in 1998. Education is free and compulsory. In 1995 there were 64 primary schools and 21,760 pupils, and 9 secondary schools and 12,047 pupils; more than 90% of primary age children were attending school. There is a vocational centre, a school of agriculture and a pre-university *lycée*.

Health. In 1989 there were 61 doctors, 5 dentists, 223 nurses, 1 pharmacist and 54 midwives.

CULTURE

Broadcasting. Radio broadcasting is conducted by the government-controlled Rádio Nacional. There is a Voice of America radio station, a religious station and a private German station. There were 38,000 radio receivers and 23,000 TV receivers in 1997.

Press. There are four weekly newspapers.

Tourism. In 1998 there were 2,000 foreign tourists, bringing revenue of US$2m.

DIPLOMATIC REPRESENTATIVES
Of São Tomé e Príncipe in the United Kingdom (resides at Brussels)
Ambassador: Vacant.
Chargé d'Affaires a.i.: Armindo de Brito Fernandes.

Of the United Kingdom in São Tomé e Príncipe
Ambassador: John Thompson, MBE (resides at Luanda, Angola).

Of São Tomé e Príncipe in the USA
Ambassador: Vacant.

Of the USA in São Tomé e Príncipe
Ambassador: Kenneth P. Moorefield (resides at Libreville, Gabon).

Of São Tomé e Príncipe to the United Nations
Ambassador: Vacant.
Chargé d'Affaires a.i.: Domingos Augusto Ferreira.

Of São Tomé e Príncipe to the European Union
Ambassador: Vacant.
Chargé d'Affaires a.i.: António de Lima Viegas.

FURTHER READING
Shaw, Caroline S., *São Tomé e Príncipe*. [Bibliography] ABC-Clio, Oxford and Santa Barbara (CA), 1994

SAUDI ARABIA

Al-Mamlaka al-Arabiya
as-Saudiya
(Kingdom of Saudi Arabia)

Capital: Riyadh
Population estimate, 2000: 20·35m.
GDP per capita, 2000: (PPP$) 11,367
HDI/world rank: 0·759/71

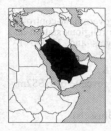

KEY HISTORICAL EVENTS

The Kingdom of Saudi Arabia is a union of two regions, Nejd and Hejaz. In the 18th century, Nejd was an autonomous region governed from Diriya, the stronghold of the Wahhabis, a puritanical Islamic sect. It subsequently fell under Turkish rule but in 1913 Abdulaziz Ibn Abdul Rahman Al-Saud defeated the Turks and also captured the Turkish province of al Hasa. In 1920 he captured the Asir and in 1921 he added the Jebel Shammar territory of the Rashid family. In 1925 he completed the conquest of the Hejaz. Great Britain recognized Abdulaziz as an independent ruler by the Treaty of Jeddah on 20 May 1927. The name was changed to the Kingdom of Saudi Arabia in Sept. 1932. Although commencing before the Second World War, oil exploitation developed strongly with the support of the USA after 1945.

TERRITORY AND POPULATION

Saudi Arabia, which occupies nearly 80% of the Arabian peninsula, is bounded in the west by the Red Sea, east by the Arabian/Persian Gulf and the United Arab Emirates, north by Jordan, Iraq and Kuwait and south by Yemen and Oman. For the border dispute with Yemen *see* YEMEN: Territory and Population. The total area is estimated to be 849,400 sq. miles (2·2m. sq. km). Riyadh is the political, and Mecca the religious, capital.

The total population at the 1992 census was 16,948,388. 1995 estimate, 17·88m.; density, 8·1 per sq. km. Approximately 76% of the population are Saudi nationals. In 1999, 85·1% of the population lived in urban areas.

The UN gives a projected population for 2010 of 27·59m.

Principal cities with 1995 population estimates (in 1m.): Riyadh, 3·18 (in 1999); Jeddah, 1·49; Mecca, 0·77; Taif, 0·41 (1991); Madinah, 0·40 (1991); Dammam, 0·35 (1991).

The Neutral Zone (3,560 sq. miles, 5,700 sq. km), jointly owned and administered by Kuwait and Saudi Arabia from 1922 to 1966, was partitioned between the two countries in 1966, but the exploitation of the oil and other natural resources continues to be shared.

The official language is Arabic.

SOCIAL STATISTICS

Births, 1995, 633,000; deaths, 80,000. Birth rate (1995) was 34·7 per 1,000 population; death rate, 4·4. 75% of the population is under the age of 30. Expectation of life at birth, 1999, was 70·3 years for males and 72·7 years for females, up from 61·4 for males and 64·1 for females over the period 1980–85. No other country had such a large increase in its life expectancy over the same period. Annual population growth rate, 1990–99, 3·0%. Infant mortality, 1999, was 19·5 per 1,000 live births, down from 58 in the years 1980–85. Fertility rate, 1999, 5·6 births per woman.

CLIMATE

A desert climate, with very little rain and none at all from June to Dec. The months May to Sept. are very hot and humid, but winter temperatures are quite pleasant. Riyadh, Jan. 58°F (14·4°C), July 108°F (42°C). Annual rainfall 4" (100 mm). Jeddah, Jan. 73°F (22·8°C), July 87°F (30·6°C). Annual rainfall 3" (81 mm).

CONSTITUTION AND GOVERNMENT

The reigning King, **Fahd Ibn Abdulaziz Al-Saud** (b. 1923), Custodian of the two Holy Mosques, succeeded in May 1982, after King Khalid's death. In 1995 King Fahd suffered a stroke, since when he has been incapacitated. *Crown Prince:* Prince Abdullah Ibn Abdulaziz Al-Saud, half-brother of the King, is the *de facto* leader.

Constitutional practice derives from Sharia law. There is no formal Constitution, but three royal decrees of 1 March 1992 established a Basic Law which defines the systems of central and municipal government, and set up a 60-man Consultative Council (*Majlis Al-Shura*) of royal nominees in Aug. 1993. The *Chairman* is Dr Salih bin Abdullah bin Hemaid. In July 1997 the King decreed an increase of the Consultative Council to a chairman plus 90 members, selected from men of science and experience; and in May 2001 it was increased again to a chairman plus 120 members.

Saudi Arabia is an absolute monarchy; executive power is discharged through a *Council of Ministers,* consisting of the King, Deputy Prime Minister, Second Deputy Prime Minister and Cabinet Ministers.

The King has the post of *Prime Minister* and can veto any decision of the Council of Ministers within 30 days.

National Anthem. 'Sarei lil majd walaya' ('Onward towards the glory and the heights'); words by Ibrahim Khafaji, tune by Abdul Rahman al Katib.

CURRENT ADMINISTRATION

In March 2003 the Council of Ministers comprised:

Prime Minister: Fahd Ibn Abdulaziz Al-Saud.

First Deputy Prime Minister and Commander of the National Guard: Crown Prince Abdullah Ibn Abdulaziz Al-Saud. *Second Deputy Prime Minister and Minister of Defence and Aviation:* Prince Sultan Ibn Abdulaziz Al-Saud.

Minister of Housing and Public Works: Prince Met'eb Ibn Abdulaziz Al-Saud. *Interior:* Prince Naif Ibn Abdulaziz Al-Saud. *Foreign Affairs:* Prince Saud Al-Faisal Ibn Abdulaziz Al-Saud. *Labour and Social Affairs:* Ali Ibn Ibrahim Namla. *Communications:* Dr Nasir Ibn Mohammed Al-Salloum. *Civil Service:* Muhammad Ibn Ali Fayiz. *Finance and National Economy:* Dr Ibrahim Ibn Abdulaziz Al-Assaf. *Information:* Dr Fouad Ibn Abdul Salaam Farsi. *Industry and Electricity:* Dr Hashim Ibn Abdullah Ibn Hashim Al-Yamani. *Commerce:* Osama Ibn Jafar Faqih. *Justice:* Dr Abdullah Ibn Mohammed Ibn Ibrahim Al-Shaik. *Education:* Dr Mohammed Ibn Ahmed Al-Rasheed. *Higher Education:* Dr Khalid Ibn Mohammed Al-Angary. *Petroleum and Mineral Resources:* Ali Ibn Ibrahim Al-Naimi. *Islamic Guidance:* Salih Ibn Abdulaziz Ibn Muhammad Ibn Ibrahim Shaykh. *Pilgrimage Affairs and Religious Trusts:* Iyyad Ibn Amin Madani. *Municipal and Rural Affairs:* Dr Mohammed Ibn Ibrahim Al-Jarallah. *Planning and Post, Telephone and Telegraph:* Khalid Ibn Muhammad Ghusaybi. *Agriculture:* Dr Abdullah Ibn Abdulaziz Ibn Mu'amar. *Water:* Dr Ghazi bin Abdulrahman Al-Qusaibi. *Health:* Dr Osama Ibn Abdul Majeed Shobokshi.

Majlis Website: http://www.shura.gov.sa

DEFENCE

In the period 1997–2001 Saudi Arabia spent US$6·7bn. on defence imports, mainly from the USA and the UK, making it the world's third largest buyer of arms, although expenditure in 2000 and 2001 was greatly reduced. Defence expenditure in 2001 totalled US$24,266m. (US$1,156 per capita), representing 14·1% of GDP.

The USA has Air Force units based in Saudi Arabia but co-operation between the two countries has been less close since the war in Afghanistan. The Peninsular Shield Force of about 7,000 comprises units from all Gulf Co-operation Council countries.

Army. Strength (1999) was approximately 70,000. There is a paramilitary Frontier Force (approximately 10,500) and a National Guard (see below).

Navy. The Royal Saudi Naval Forces fleet includes eight frigates. Naval Aviation forces operate 31 armed helicopters, both ship and shore based.

The main naval bases are at Jeddah (Red Sea) and Jubail (The Gulf). Naval personnel in 1998 totalled 13,500, including 3,000 marines.

Air Force. Current combat units include F-15 Eagle interceptors, F-5E Tiger II supersonic fighter-bombers, Tornado strike aircraft and Tornado interceptors. The Air Force operates 432 combat aircraft in all and numbered about 18,000 personnel in 1999.

Air Defence Force. This separate Command was formerly part of the Army. In 1998 it operated surface-to-air missile batteries and had a strength of 4,000.

National Guard. The total strength of the National Guard amounted to approximately 77,000 (57,000 active, 20,000 tribal levies) in 1999. The National Guard's primary role is the protection of the Royal Family and vital points in the Kingdom. It is directly under royal command. The UK provides small advisory teams to the National Guard in the fields of general training and communications.

INTERNATIONAL RELATIONS

Saudi Arabia is a member of the UN, BIS, the League of Arab States, the Gulf Co-operation Council, OPEC and the OIC.

In April 2001 Saudi Arabia and Iran signed a security pact to fight drug trafficking and terrorism, 13 years after the two countries had broken off relations.

ECONOMY

Agriculture accounted for 6·7% of GDP in 1999 and industry 9·8%.

Overview. The seventh five-year development plan (2000–04) offers foreign investors an opportunity to tap into sectors of the economy that have recently undergone privatization: healthcare, electrical power generation and water desalination. The Planning Ministry expects economic growth to create 817,000 new jobs for Saudi citizens.

Currency. The unit of currency is the *rial* (SAR) of 100 *halalah*. Foreign exchange reserves totalled US$14,859m. in June 2002 and gold reserves were 4·60m. troy oz. Inflation was negative in 2001, at –0·8%. Total money supply in June 2002 was SAR193,002m.

In 2001 the six Gulf Arab states—Saudi Arabia, along with Bahrain, Kuwait, Oman, Qatar and the United Arab Emirates—signed an agreement to establish a single currency by 2010.

Budget. In 1986 the financial year became the calendar year. 1998 budget: revenue, SAR178bn.; expenditure, SAR196bn.

Oil sales account for 80% of state income. Expenditure in 1998: defence and security, 39·9%; human resource development, 23·2%; public administration, municipal transfers and subsidies, 20·1%; health and social development, 8·4%.

Performance. Real GDP growth was 1·2% in 2001. Total GDP in 2000 was US$173·3bn. The current account surplus stood at US$254m. in 1997.

Banking and Finance. The Saudi Arabian Monetary Agency (*Governor*, Hamad Saud Al-Sayari, appointed 1983), established in 1953, functions as the central bank and the government's fiscal agent. There were ten commercial banks with 1,196 branches in 1999. The leading banks are National Commercial Bank (assets in 1999 of US$22,895m.), Saudi-American (US$20,520m.) and Riyad Bank (US$17,167m.). Sharia (the religious law of Islam) forbids the charging of interest; Islamic banking is based on sharing clients' profits and losses and imposing service charges. In 1999 total assets of commercial banks were 415,227m. rials.

A number of industry sectors are closed to foreign investors, including petroleum exploration, defence-related activities and financial services.

There is a stock exchange.

Calendar. Saudi Arabia follows the Islamic *hegira* (AD 622, when Mohammed left Mecca for Medina), which is based upon the lunar year of 354 days. The Islamic year 1424 corresponds to 5 March 2003–21 Feb. 2004, and is the current lunar year.

ENERGY AND NATURAL RESOURCES

Environment. According to the *World Bank Atlas* Saudi Arabia's carbon dioxide emissions in 1998 were the equivalent of 14·4 tonnes per capita. An *Environmental Sustainability Index* compiled for the World Economic Forum meeting in Feb. 2002 ranked Saudi Arabia 138th in the world out of the 142 countries analysed, with 34·2%. The index measured the ability of countries to maintain favourable environmental conditions and examined various factors including pollution levels and the use or abuse of natural resources.

Electricity. By 1995 over 100 electricity producers had been amalgamated into four companies. Installed capacity was 20·2m. kW in 1999. All electricity is thermally generated. Production was 105·6bn. kWh in 1999; consumption per capita was 4,692 kWh in 1998.

Oil and Gas. Proven oil reserves (2001) 261·8bn. bbls. (the highest of any country and around 25% of world resources). Oil production began in 1938 by Aramco, which is now 100% state-owned and accounts for about 99% of total crude oil production. Saudi crude output in 1999 totalled 426m. tonnes and accounted for 12·4% of the world total oil output.

Production comes from 14 major oilfields, mostly in the Eastern Province and offshore, and including production from the Neutral Zone. The Ghawar oilfield, located between Riyadh and the Persian gulf, is the largest in the world, with estimated reserves of 70bn. bbls.

Saudi Arabia is dependent on oil earnings for over 70% of budget revenues. In 1998 oil export revenues were US$33bn., rising to US$41bn. in 1999 and US$70bn. in 2000, before falling to US$56bn. in 2001. Oil reserves are expected to run out in approximately 2085.

In 2000 natural gas reserves were 5,800bn. cu. metres; output in 1999 was 46·2bn. cu. metres. The gas sector has been opened up to foreign investment.

Water. Efforts are under way to provide adequate supplies of water for urban, industrial, rural and agricultural use. Most investment has gone into sea-water desalination. In 1996, 33 plants produced 1·9m. cu. metres a day, meeting 70% of drinking water needs. Total annual consumption was 18,200m. cu. metres in 1995. Irrigation for agriculture consumes the largest amount, from fossil reserves (the country's principal water source), and from surface water collected during seasonal floods. In 1996 there were 183 dams with a holding capacity of 450m. cu. metres. Treated urban waste water is an increasing resource for domestic purposes; in 1996 there were two recycling plants in operation.

Minerals. Production began in 1988 at Mahd Al-Dahab gold mine, the largest in the country, which produces 170,000 oz of gold a year. In 1997 production totalled 7,530 kg. Deposits of iron, phosphate, bauxite, uranium, silver, tin, tungsten, nickel, chrome, zinc, lead, potassium ore and copper have also been found.

Agriculture. Since 1970 the government has spent substantially on desert reclamation, irrigation schemes, drainage and control of surface water and of moving sands. Undeveloped land has been distributed to farmers and there are research and extension programmes. Large scale private investment has concentrated on wheat, poultry and dairy production.

In 1998 there were 3·7m. ha of arable land and 130,000 ha of permanent cropland. In 1995, 13·9% of the economically active population were engaged in agriculture.

About 200,000 tonnes of barley are produced annually as animal fodder. Production of other crops, 2000 (in 1,000 tonnes): wheat, 2,046; dates, 712; melons and watermelons, 426; potatoes, 394; tomatoes, 277; sorghum, 204; cucumbers and gherkins, 125; grapes, 116; onions, 95.

Livestock (2000): 297,000 cattle, 7,576,000 sheep, 4,305,000 goats, 400,000 camels and 130m. chickens. Livestock products (2000, in 1,000 tonnes): milk, 747; meat, 579; eggs, 136.

Forestry. The area under forests was 222,000 ha (0·1% of the land area) in 1995.

Fisheries. In 1999 the total catch was 46,897 tonnes, entirely from sea fishing.

INDUSTRY

According to the Financial Times Survey (FT 500), the largest companies in Saudi Arabia by market capitalization on 28 March 2002 were SABIC (Saudi Basic Industries), at US$12,139·4m., and the Saudi American Bank (US$10,132·8m.).

The government encourages the establishment of manufacturing industries. Its policy focuses on establishing industries that use petroleum products, petrochemicals and minerals. Petrochemical and oil-based industries have been concentrated at eight new industrial cities, with the two principal cities at Jubail and Yanbu. In 1996 there were 15 major plants and other industrial facilities, a dedicated desalination plant, a vocational training institute and a college at Jubail, and three major refineries, a petrochemical complex and many manufacturing and support enterprises at Yanbu. Products include chemical, plastics, industrial gases, steel and other metals. In 1995 there were 2,234 factories employing 196,000 workers.

Labour. The labour force in 1997 totalled 6,187,000. In 1999 females constituted 15% of the labour force—only the United Arab Emirates had a lower percentage of females in its workforce. In 1995, 32·3% of the economically active population were engaged in community and personal services, 15·5% in construction and 15·1% in trade. Less than 1% worked in the oil sector. There are 6m. foreign workers, including over 1m. Egyptians and over 1m. Indians. Unemployment, which was less than 8% in 1999, reached 12% in 2002.

INTERNATIONAL TRADE
In 1999 foreign debt totalled US$9bn.

In 2001 Saudi Arabia, along with Bahrain, Kuwait, Oman, Qatar and the United Arab Emirates agreed to the complete implementation of a customs union by 2003.

Imports and Exports. Trade in US$1m.:

	1996	1997	1998	1999	2000
Imports f.o.b.	25,358	26,370	27,535	25,717	27,797
Exports f.o.b.	60,729	60,731	38,822	50,757	78,973

The principal export is crude oil; refined oil, petro-chemicals, fertilizers, plastic products and wheat are other major exports. Saudi Arabia is the world's largest exporter of oil, accounting for over 92% of all the country's exports in 2000. Main export destinations, 1999: USA, 18·8%; Japan, 17·5%; South Korea, 9·2%; Singapore, 5·9%. Imports, 1999: USA, 20·8%; Japan, 9·1%; UK, 7·4%; South Korea, 3·5%.

COMMUNICATIONS

Roads. In 1999 there were 15,251 km of main roads. The total length of all asphalted roads was 45,518 km. A causeway links Saudi Arabia with Bahrain. Passenger cars in use in 1996 numbered 1,744,000 (100 per 1,000 inhabitants) and there were 1,169,000 trucks and vans. The average distance travelled by a passenger car in 1994 was 30,794 km. Women are not allowed to drive.

Rail. 1,435 mm gauge lines of 1,392 km link Riyadh and Dammam with stops at Hofuf and Abqaiq. The network is to be extended by 2,000 km at an estimated cost of US$2·6bn., in four phases, consisting of links to Jeddah, the Jordanian border, Jubail, and Mecca and Madinah. In 1999 railways carried 770,400 passengers and 1·8m. tonnes of freight.

Civil Aviation. The national carrier is the state-owned Saudia. In 1999 Saudia carried 12·7m. passengers, 260,300 tonnes of air cargo and operated 115,300 flights. At the end of 1999 Saudia owned 125 aircraft. There are four major international airports, at Jeddah (King Abdulaziz), Dhahran, Riyadh (King Khaled), and the newly constructed King Fahd International Airport at Dammam. There are also 22 domestic airports. In 2000 Jeddah handled 10,465,147 passengers (5,747,916 on international flights) and 204,581 tonnes of freight. Riyadh was the second busiest airport in 2000, handling 8,379,573 passengers (5,194,469 on domestic flights) and 165,879 tonnes of freight. In 1999, 26·1m. passengers travelled through the country's airports. The volume of air cargo carried was 463,000 tonnes.

Shipping. The ports of Dammam and Jubail are on the Arabian/Persian Gulf and Jeddah, Yanbu and Jizan on the Red Sea. There is a deepwater oil terminal at Ras Tanura, and 16 minor ports. In 1999 the ports handled 88·5m. tonnes of cargo. In 1995 the merchant marine comprised 110 vessels totalling 8·2m. DWT, representing 1·24% of the world's total fleet tonnage. 49 vessels (89·13% of tonnage) were registered under foreign flags. In 1998 shipping totalled 1·28m. GRT, including oil tankers 220,000 GRT.

Telecommunications. Saudi Arabia had 2,964,700 main telephone lines in 2000 or 137·2 per 1,000 inhabitants, and there were 1·3m. PCs in use (60·2 per 1,000 population). There were 5m. mobile phone subscribers in 2002, and 75,000 fax machines and 10,100 telex machines in 1995. The number of Internet users in March 2001 was 570,000. The government sold a 30% stake in Saudi Telecom Company in Dec. 2002.

Postal Services. In 1999 there were 461 main post offices, 185 branch offices, 85 express mail centres and 69 private sector postal agencies.

SOCIAL INSTITUTIONS

Justice. The religious law of Islam (Sharia) is the common law of the land, and is administered by religious courts, at the head of which is a chief judge, who is responsible for the Department of Sharia Affairs. Sharia courts are concerned primarily with family inheritance and property matters. The Committee for the Settlement of Commercial Disputes is the commercial court. Other specialized courts or committees include one dealing exclusively with labour and employment matters; the Negotiable Instruments Committee, which deals with cases relating to cheques, bills of exchange and promissory notes; and the Board of Grievances, whose preserve is disputes with the government or its agencies and which also has jurisdiction in trademark-infringement cases and is the authority for enforcing foreign court judgements.

The death penalty is in force for murder, rape, sodomy, armed robbery, sabotage, drug trafficking, adultery and apostasy; executions may be held in public. There were 49 confirmed executions in 2002.

Religion. In 1997, 18,210,000 persons were Sunni Muslims and 640,000 Shias. There were 230,000 with other beliefs. The *Grand Mufti*, Sheikh Abdul Aziz bin Abdullah bin Mohammed Al-Sheikh, has cabinet rank. A special police force, the Mutaween, exists to enforce religious norms.

The annual *Hajj*, the pilgrimage to Mecca, takes place from the 8th to the 13th day of Dhu al Hijjah, the last month of the Islamic year. It attracts more than 1·8m. pilgrims annually. In the current Islamic year, 1424, the *Hajj* will begin on 31 Jan. 2004 in the Gregorian calendar.

Education. The educational system provides students with free education, books and health services. General education consists of kindergarten, six years of primary school and three years each of intermediate and high school. In 1996–97 there were 893 pre-primary schools with 7,703 teachers and 85,484 pupils. In 1998–99 there were 12,234 primary schools with 189,008 teachers and 2,259,849 pupils; 5,901 intermediate schools with 86,630 teachers and 1,035,363 pupils; 3,117 secondary schools with 53,618 teachers and 704,566 pupils. At teacher training colleges there were 1,438 teachers and 21,366 students and at vocational schools 2,536 teachers and 21,551 students. Students can attend either high schools offering programmes in arts and sciences, or vocational schools. Girls' education is administered separately. In 1996 there were more than 30 special schools for the handicapped with about 4,550 students. The adult literacy rate in 1999 was 76·1% (83·5% among males and 65·9% among females).

Saudi Arabia's rapidly-growing population has meant that some 3,000 new schools are to be built between 2000 and 2005.

In 1996 there were 2,343 adult education centres. In 1997–98 there were 7 universities, 2 Islamic universities and 1 university of petroleum and minerals. In 1999 there were 120,666 students in higher education institutions with 18,925 teachers. In 1997 total expenditure on education came to 7·5% of GNP and 22·8% of total government spending.

Health. In 1999 there were 1,756 health care centres and clinics, 706 private dispensaries and 313 hospitals with 45,508 beds. 30,601 doctors, 67,241 nursing and 37,077 technical staff were employed at these facilities. At Jeddah there is a quarantine centre for pilgrims.

CULTURE

Broadcasting. The government-controlled Broadcasting Service of the Kingdom of Saudi Arabia and Saudi Arabian Television are responsible for broadcasting. Radio programmes include two home services, two religious services, services in English and French and an external service. Aramco Oil has a private station. There are TV programmes in Arabic and English; Channel 3 TV is a non-commercial independent. Colour is by SECAM H. In 1997 there were estimated to be 6·25m. radio and 5·1m. TV sets.

Press. In 1996 there were 13 daily newspapers with a combined circulation of 1,105,000, equivalent to 59 per 1,000 inhabitants. In 1995 there were 168 non-daily newspapers with a combined circulation of 2,150,000 or 117 per 1,000. The most widely read newspaper is *Asharq Al-Awsat* ('Middle East'), with an average daily circulation of 248,482 in Jan.–June 1998. In 1996 a total of 3,900 book titles were published.

Tourism. There were 3,700,000 foreign tourists in 1998, bringing revenue of US$1·46bn.

Libraries. There was 1 National library in 1995 and in 1993 there were 21 higher education libraries, holding a combined 4,904,000 volumes for 490,111 registered users.

DIPLOMATIC REPRESENTATIVES
Of Saudi Arabia in the United Kingdom (30 Charles St., London, W1X 7PM)
Ambassador: HRH Prince Turki Al-Faisal.

Of the United Kingdom in Saudi Arabia (PO Box 94351, Riyadh 11693)
Ambassador: Sir Derek Plumbly, KCMG.

Of Saudi Arabia in the USA (601 New Hampshire Ave., NW, Washington, D.C., 20037)
Ambassador: HRH Prince Bandar Bin Sultan.

Of the USA in Saudi Arabia (PO Box 94309, Riyadh)
Ambassador: Robert W. Jordan.

Of Saudi Arabia to the United Nations
Ambassador: Fawzi Bin Abdul Majeed Shobokshi.

Of Saudi Arabia to the European Union
Ambassador: Nassir Alassaf.

FURTHER READING
Al-Rasheed, Madawi, *A History of Saudi Arabia.* CUP, 2002
Azzam, H., *Saudi Arabia: Economic Trends, Business Environment and Investment Opportunities.* London, 1993
Kostiner, J., *The Making of Saudi Arabia: from Chieftaincy to Monarchical State.* OUP, 1994
Mackey, Sandra, *The Saudis: Inside the Desert Kingdom.* Revised ed. W. W. Norton, New York, 2003
Peterson, J. E., *Historical Dictionary of Saudi Arabia.* Metuchen (NJ), 1994
Wright, J. W. (ed.) *Business and Economic Development in Saudi Arabia: Essays with Saudi Scholars.* London, 1996

National statistical office: Ministry of Finance and National Economy, Department of Statistics, Riyadh.
Website: http://www.saudinf.com/

SENEGAL

République du Sénégal

Capital: Dakar
Population estimate, 2000: 9·42m.
GDP per capita, 2000: (PPP$) 1,510
HDI/world rank: 0·431/154

KEY HISTORICAL EVENTS

While in the mid-1400s the Portuguese were the first Europeans to reach the area around the Senegal river estuary, in succeeding centuries the French became the dominant Europeans on the coast in that area, except for The Gambia, where the British were installed. The French founded Saint-Louis in 1659 and also occupied the island of Goree, an important slave-trading depot. In the 19th century French rule, interrupted earlier by occasional British occupation, was confirmed over Saint-Louis and Goree. Free Africans received the vote in 1833 and the franchise was further extended in 1848 when slavery was abolished in all French colonies. The Africans in Saint-Louis and Goree, and also in Dakar and Rufisque, were called the *originaires* and had the rights of French citizens. They elected a deputy to the French national Assembly and voted for local *communes*.

From the late 1870s France began a sustained push up the river and into the interior. Here, groundnuts were already being grown for export to France but African monarchs still ruled and there was strong resistance. French rule was established by the mid-1890s, while the British consolidated their rule inland in The Gambia. On 4 April 1959 Senegal joined with French Sudan to form the Federation of Mali, which achieved independence on 20 June 1960. On 22 Aug. Senegal withdrew from the Federation and became a separate independent republic. Senegal was a one-Party state from 1966 until 1974, when a pluralist system was re-established.

TERRITORY AND POPULATION

Senegal is bounded by Mauritania to the north and northeast, Mali to the east, Guinea and Guinea-Bissau to the south and the Atlantic to the west with The Gambia forming an enclave along that shore. Area, 196,190 sq. km; population (census, 1988), 6,982,084; estimate, 1996: 9·09m. (53·3% urban in 1999). Population density, 40·5 per sq. km. Age structure: 1–14 years, 48%; 15–64, 49%; 65 and over, 3%.

The UN gives a projected population for 2010 of 12·05m.

The areas, populations and capitals of the ten regions:

Region	Area (in sq. km)	1994 estimate	Capital
Dakar	550	1,869,000	Dakar
Diourbel	4,359	750,000	Diourbel
Fatick	7,935	569,000	Fatick
Kaolack	16,010	948,000	Kaolack
Kolda	21,011	689,000	Kolda
Louga	29,188	525,000	Louga
Saint-Louis	44,127	749,000	Saint-Louis
Tambacounda	57,602	449,000	Tambacounda
Thiès	6,601	1,115,000	Thiès
Ziguinchor	7,339	467,000	Ziguinchor

Dakar, the capital, had an estimated population in 1995 of 1,999,000. Other large cities (with 1994 estimated population) are: Thiès (216,000), Kaolack (193,000), Ziguinchor (162,000) and Saint-Louis (132,000).

Ethnic groups are the Wolof (36% of the population), Serer (16%), Fulani (16%), Tukulor (9%), Diola (9%), Malinké (6%), Bambara (6%) and Sarakole (2%).

The official language is French; Wolof is widely spoken.

SOCIAL STATISTICS

Births, 1995, 349,000; deaths, 126,000. Birth rate (1995) per 1,000 population, 42; death rate (1997), 18. Annual population growth rate, 1990–99, 2·6%; infant mortality (1999), 68 per 1,000 live births. Life expectancy in 1999 was 51·1 years for men and 54·8 for women. Fertility rate, 1999, 5·4 births per woman.

CLIMATE

A tropical climate with wet and dry seasons. The rains fall almost exclusively in the hot season, from June to Oct., with high humidity. Dakar, Jan. 72°F (22·2°C), July 82°F (27·8°C). Annual rainfall 22" (541 mm).

CONSTITUTION AND GOVERNMENT

A new constitution was approved by a referendum held on 7 Jan. 2001. The head of state is the *President*, elected by universal suffrage for not more than two five-year terms (previously two seven-year terms). The *President* has the power to dissolve the National Assembly, without the agreement, as had been the case, of a two-thirds majority. The new constitution also abolished the upper house (the Senate), confirmed the status of the prime minister and for the first time gave women the right to own land. For the unicameral, 140-member National Assembly, 70 members are elected in multi-seat and single-seat constituencies and 70 by proportional representation, all for a five-year term.

National Anthem. 'Pincez tous vos koras, frappez les balafos' ('All pluck the koras, strike the balafos'); words by Léopold Sédar Senghor, tune by Herbert Pepper.

RECENT ELECTIONS

Presidential elections took place on 27 Feb. and 19 March 2000. In the first round of voting, incumbent Abdou Diouf won 41·3% of the vote, Abdoulaye Wade of the Senegalese Democratic Party received 31·0%, Moustapha Niasse 16·8% and Djibo Ka 7·1%. In the run-off between Diouf and Wade, Wade won, in his 5th attempt to become President, with 58·5% of the vote, ending 40 years of uninterrupted rule by the Socialist Party. 'Some commentators seized upon the peaceful transition as evidence of Africa's maturing democratic tradition. But while Senegal's success story is worth celebrating it remains an exception'. (*Time*, 10 July 2000).

Parliamentary elections were held on 27 April 2001. Turn-out was 67·4%. Coalition 'Sopi', a coalition led by President Abdoulaye Wade's Senegalese Democratic Party, took 89 seats with 49·6% of votes cast, the Alliance of Progressive Forces 11 with 16·1%, the Socialists 10 with 17·4% and the Union for Democratic Renewal 3 with 3·7%. Six other parties claimed two seats or fewer.

CURRENT ADMINISTRATION

President: Abdoulaye Wade; b. 1926 (PDS; sworn in 1 April 2000).

In March 2003 the government was composed as follows:

Prime Minister: Idrissa Seck; b. 1959 (PDS; sworn in 4 Nov. 2002).

Minister of State for Foreign Affairs, the African Union and Senegalese Abroad: Cheikh Tidiane Gadio. *Minister of State for Mines, Energy and Water Resources:* Macky Sall. *Minister of State for Industry and Handicrafts:* Landing Savane. *Minister of State for Sports:* Youssoupha Ndiaye.

Minister for Justice and Guardian of the Seals: Serigne Diop. *Interior:* Mamadou Niang. *Defence:* Bécaye Diop. *Economy and Finance:* Abdoulaye Diop. *Infrastructure, Equipment and Transport:* Mamadou Seck. *Education:* Moustapha Sourang. *Environment:* Modou Fada Diagne. *Health:* Awa Marie Coll Seck. *Agriculture:* Habib Sy. *Family Affairs and National Solidarity:* Awa Gueye Kebe. *Fisheries:* Pape Diouf. *Tourism:* Ousmane Masseck Ndiaye. *Housing:* Madické Niang. *Civil Service, Labour and Employment:* Yéro De. *Social Development:* Maïmouna Sourang Ndir. *Culture and Communications:* Abdou Fall. *Relations with National and Regional Governments, and the African Union:* Mamadou Diop. *Decentralization and Regional Planning:* Soukeyna Ndiaye Ba. *Scientific and Technological Research:* Christian Sina Diatta. *Commerce and Small- and Medium-Sized Enterprises:* Aïcha Agne Pouye. *Planning and Territorial Development:* Seydou Sy Sall. *Women's Enterprises and Micro-Credit:* Saoudatou Ndiaye Seck. *Youth Affairs:* Aliou Sow.

Government Website (French only): http://www.primature.sn/

DEFENCE

There is selective conscription for two years. Defence expenditure totalled US$68m. in 2000 (US$7 per capita), representing 1·2% of GDP.

Army. There are four military zones. The Army had a strength of 10,000 (3,500 conscripts) in 1999. There is also a paramilitary force of gendarmerie and customs of about 5,800.

Navy. Personnel (1999) totalled 600, and bases are at Dakar and Casamance.

Air Force. The Air Force, formed with French assistance, has eight combat aircraft but serviceability is low. Personnel (1999) 400.

INTERNATIONAL RELATIONS
Senegal is a member of the UN, WTO, the African Union, African Development Bank, ECOWAS, OIC, IOM, International Organization of the Francophonie and is an ACP member state of the ACP-EU relationship.

A short section of the boundary with The Gambia is indefinite.

ECONOMY
Agriculture accounted for 17·4% of GDP in 1998, industry 24·1% and services 58·5%.

Overview. Privatization began in 1987. An austerity programme was adopted in 1993 and the currency devalued by 50%. A start has been made on liberalizing labour laws, closing tax loopholes and ending monopolies. With IMF targets met, the second part of a loan facility was approved in 1995.

Currency. Senegal is a member of the Union Economique et Monétaire Ouest-Africaine (UEMOA). The unit of currency is the *franc CFA* (XOF) with a parity of 655·957 francs CFA to one euro. In May 2002 total money supply was 567,374m. francs CFA. and foreign exchange reserves totalled US$507m. In June 2000 gold reserves were 29,000 troy oz. Inflation was 3·0% in 2001.

Budget. In 1999 the government's total revenue was 506·8bn. francs CFA (562·3bn. estimated for 2000) and total expenditure was 604·6bn. francs CFA (639·9bn. estimated for 2000).

Performance. Real GDP growth was 5·6% in both 2000 and 2001. Senegal's total GDP in 2001 was US$4·6bn.

Banking and Finance. The Banque Centrale des États de l'Afrique de l'Ouest is the bank of issue of the franc CFA for all the countries of the West African Economic and Monetary Union (Benin, Burkina Faso, Côte d'Ivoire, Mali, Niger, Senegal and Togo) but has had its headquarters in Dakar, the Senegalese capital, since 1973. Its *Governor* is Charles Konan Banny. There are few major banks, the largest including the Banque Internationale pour le Commerce et l'Industrie and Banque de l'Habitat (9% state-owned).

ENERGY AND NATURAL RESOURCES

Environment. According to the *World Bank Atlas* Senegal's carbon dioxide emissions in 1998 were the equivalent of 0·4 tonnes per capita.

Electricity. In 1996 installed capacity was 230 MW. Production in 1998 was estimated to be 1·2bn. kWh and consumption per capita 111 kWh.

Minerals. 1,128,000 tonnes of calcium phosphate were produced in 1992 and 93,000 tonnes of aluminium phosphate in 1989. In 1995 the Sabodala mine in eastern Senegal had proven gold ore reserves of 2·6m. tonnes; annual gold production is approximately 600 kg. Exploration of further gold reserves increased greatly throughout the 1990s. While only three research permits were issued in 1994 this figure had risen to 35 by 1998, with South African, British, American, Canadian and Australian companies all active in the country.

Agriculture. Because of erratic rainfall 25% of agricultural land needs irrigation. Most land is owned under customary rights and holdings tend to be small. In 1998, 2·23m. ha were used as arable land and 36,000 ha for permanent crops. Production, 2000 (in 1,000 tonnes): sugarcane, 889; groundnuts, 828; millet, 506; watermelons, 260; rice, 240; sorghum, 147; mangoes, 75; maize, 66; onions, 65.

Livestock (2000): 4·30m. sheep, 3·59m. goats, 2·96m. cattle, 510,000 horses, 384,000 asses, 330,000 pigs. Animal products (2000, in 1,000 tonnes): meat, 162; milk, 135.

Forestry. Forests covered 7·63m. ha in 1990 and 7·38m. ha (38·3% of the land area) in 1995. Roundwood production in 1999 amounted to 5·04m. cu. metres.

Fisheries. The fishing fleet comprises 167 vessels totalling 40,600 GRT. In 1999 the total catch was 418,125 tonnes (378,125 tonnes from sea fishing).

INDUSTRY
Predominantly agricultural and fish processing, phosphate mining, petroleum refining and construction materials.

Labour. The workforce (10 years and over) in 1996 was 2,509,000, of whom 77% were engaged in subsistence farming; 60% of the workforce is in the public sector.

Trade Unions. There are two major unions, the *Union Nationale des Travailleurs Sénégalais* (government-controlled) and the *Confédération Nationale des Travailleurs Sénégalais* (independent) which broke away from the former in 1969 and in 1994 comprised 75% of salaried workers.

INTERNATIONAL TRADE
Foreign debt was US$3,372m. in 2000.

Imports and Exports. In 1999 imports (f.o.b.) totalled US$1,372·8m. (US$1,280·6m. in 1998) and exports (f.o.b.) US$1,027·1m. (US$967·7m. in 1998). Chief exports: fish, groundnuts, petroleum products, phosphates and cotton. Chief imports: food and beverages, capital goods. Main import suppliers, 1995: France, 31·6%; Nigeria, 6·4%; USA, 5·7%; Japan, 3·7%. Main export markets, 1995: India, 25·7%; France, 11·1%; Mali, 8·5%; Italy, 7·2%.

COMMUNICATIONS
Roads. The length of roads in 1996 was 14,576 km, of which 4,270 km were bitumenized. There were 85,500 passenger cars (10 per 1,000 inhabitants), 24,000 trucks and vans and 10,350 buses and coaches in 1996. There were 791 deaths as a result of road accidents in 1995.

Rail. There are four railway lines: Dakar-Kidira (continuing in Mali), Thiès-Saint-Louis (193 km), Diourbel-Touba (46 km), and Guinguinéo-Kaolack (22 km). Total length (1996), 905 km (metre gauge). In 1996 railways carried 6·38m. passengers and 429,332 tonnes of freight, of which 331,850 were for export.

Civil Aviation. The international airport is at Dakar/Yoff (Léopold Sédar Senghor), which handled 1,074,000 passengers (1,042,000 on international flights) and 27,800 tonnes of freight in 2000. Air Sénégal is 50% state-owned, and in 1998 flew to Banjul, Nouakchott and Praia in addition to operating on domestic routes. Senegal is also a member of the multinational Air Afrique. In 1999 scheduled airline traffic of Senegal-based carriers flew 3·3m. km, carrying 103,000 passengers (84,000 on international flights).

Shipping. In 1998 the merchant marine totalled 51,000 GRT. 5·5m. tonnes of freight were handled in the port of Dakar in 1995. There is a river service on the Senegal from Saint-Louis to Podor (363 km) open throughout the year, and to Kayes (924 km) open from July to Oct. The Senegal River is closed to foreign flags. The Saloum River is navigable as far as Kaolack, the Casamance River as far as Ziguinchor.

Telecommunications. In 2000 main telephone lines numbered 205,900 (21·6 for every 1,000 persons) and there were 160,000 PCs in use (16·8 per 1,000 persons). Senegal had 73,500 mobile phone subscribers in 1999. Internet users numbered 40,000 in Dec. 2000.

Postal Services. There were, in 1995, 131 post offices.

SOCIAL INSTITUTIONS

Justice. There are *juges de paix* in each *département* and a court of first instance in each region. Assize courts are situated in Dakar, Kaolack, Saint-Louis and Ziguinchor, while the Court of Appeal resides in Dakar. The death penalty is authorized.

The population in penal institutions in 1997 was 4,653 (55 per 100,000 of national population).

Religion. The population is 90% Sunni Muslim, the remainder being Christian (mainly Roman Catholic) or animist.

Education. The adult literacy rate in 1999 was 36·4% (46·4% among males and 26·7% among females). In 1997–98 there were 1,026,570 pupils and 18,373 teachers in 3,884 primary schools; 215,988 pupils in secondary schools; and (1996–97), 26,616 students at 3 universities (Cheikh Anta Diop, Gaston Berger and Dakar Bourguiba). In 1995–96 there were a further 19 institutions of higher education.

Health. In 1996 there were 17 government hospitals, 646 maternity homes, 53 health centres and 768 clinics. There were 649 doctors (266 in government service), 93 dentists, 588 midwives (547 government) and 1,876 other medical personnel (1,630 government). There were 322 pharmacists (16 in government service). Senegal has been one of the most successful countries in Africa in the prevention of AIDS. Levels of infection have remained low, with the anti-AIDS programme having started as far back as 1986. The infection rate has been kept below 2%.

CULTURE

Broadcasting. The government-owned *Office de Radio-Télévision du Sénégal* broadcasts a national and an international radio service from ten main transmitters. There are also regional services. There is also a TV service (colour by SECAM V). In 1997 there were 1·24m. radio receivers (141 per 1,000 inhabitants) and 361,000 TV receivers (41 per 1,000 inhabitants). As recently as 1980 there had been just 8,000 TV receivers, or only 1·4 per 1,000. The percentage rise in the proportion of the population having TV receivers, at more than 2,800%, was the highest anywhere in the world over the same period.

Press. In 1996 there was one daily newspaper with a circulation of 45,000, equivalent to 5·3 per 1,000 inhabitants.

Tourism. 369,000 foreign tourists visited in 1999. Revenue in 1999 amounted to US$166m.

DIPLOMATIC REPRESENTATIVES
Of Senegal in the United Kingdom (39 Marloes Rd, London, W8 6LA)
Ambassador: El Hadj Amadou Niang.

Of the United Kingdom in Senegal (20 Rue du Docteur Guillet, Dakar)
Ambassador: Alan Burner.

Of Senegal in the USA (2112 Wyoming Ave., NW, Washington, D.C., 20008)
Ambassador: Amadou Lamine Ba.

Of the USA in Senegal (Ave. Jean XXIII, Dakar)
Ambassador: Harriet L. Elam-Thomas.

Of Senegal to the United Nations
Ambassador: Papa Louis Fall.

Of Senegal to the European Union
Ambassador: Vacant.
Chargé d'Affaires a.i.: Mahmoudou Cheikh Kane.

FURTHER READING

Centre Français du Commerce Extérieur. *Sénégal: un Marché*. Paris, 1993

Adams, A. and So, J., *A Claim in Senegal, 1720–1994*. Paris, 1996

Dilley, Roy M. and Eades, Jerry S., *Senegal*. [Bibliography] ABC-Clio, Oxford and Santa Barbara (CA), 1994

Phillips, L. C., *Historical Dictionary of Senegal*. 2nd ed, revised by A. F. Clark. Metuchen (NJ), 1995

National statistical office: Direction de la Statistique, BP 116, Dakar.

SERBIA AND MONTENEGRO

Capital: Belgrade
Population estimate, 2000: 10·63m.
GDP per capita: not available

Državna Zajednica Srbija i
Crna Gora
(State Community of Serbia
and Montenegro)

KEY HISTORICAL EVENTS

The assassination of Archduke Franz Ferdinand of Austria in Sarajevo on 28 June 1914 precipitated the First World War. In the winter of 1915–16 the Serbian army was forced to retreat to Corfu, where the government aimed at a centralized, Serb-run state. But exiles from Croatia and Slovenia wanted a South Slav federation. This was accepted by the victorious Allies as the basis for the new state. The Croats were forced by the pressure of events to join Serbia and Montenegro on 1 Dec. 1918. From 1918–29 the country was known as the Kingdom of the Serbs, Croats and Slovenes.

A constitution of 1921 established an assembly but the trappings of parliamentarianism could not bridge the gulf between Serbs and Croats. The Croat peasant leader Radić was assassinated in 1928; his successor, Vlatko Maček, set up a separatist assembly in Zagreb. On 6 Jan. 1929 the king suspended the constitution and established a royal dictatorship, redrawing provincial boundaries without regard for ethnicity. In Oct. 1934 he was murdered by a Croat extremist while on an official visit to France.

During the regency of Prince Paul, the government pursued a pro-fascist line. On 25 March 1941 Paul was induced to adhere to the Axis Tripartite Pact. On 27 March he was overthrown by military officers in favour of the boy king Peter. Germany invaded on 6 April. Within ten days Yugoslavia surrendered; king and government fled to London. Resistance was led by a royalist group and the communist-dominated partisans of Josip Broz, nicknamed Tito. Having succeeded in liberating Yugoslavia, Tito instituted a Soviet-type constitution. He was too independent for Stalin, who sought to topple him. But Tito made a *rapprochement* with the west and it was the Soviet Union under Khrushchev which had to extend the olive branch in 1956. Yugoslavia evolved its 'own road to socialism'. Collectivization of agriculture was abandoned; and Yugoslavia became a champion of international 'non-alignment'. A collective presidency came into being with the death of Tito in 1980.

Dissensions in Kosovo between Albanians and Serbs, and in parts of Croatia between Serbs and Croats, reached crisis point after 1988. On 25 June 1991 Croatia and Slovenia declared independence. Fighting began in Croatia between Croatian forces and Serb irregulars from Serb-majority areas of Croatia. On 25 Sept. the UN Security Council imposed a mandatory arms embargo on Yugoslavia. Slovenia and Croatia declared their independence from the Yugoslav federation on 8 Oct, after a three-month moratorium agreed at EU peace talks on 30 June had expired. After 13 ceasefires had failed, a fourteenth was signed on 23 Nov. under UN auspices. Fighting, however, continued. On 15 Jan. 1992 the EU recognized Croatia and Slovenia as independent states. Bosnia-Herzegovina was recognized on 7 April 1992 and the former Yugoslav Republic of Macedonia on 8 April 1993. A UN delegation began monitoring the ceasefire on 17 Jan. and the UN Security Council on 21 Feb. voted to send a 14,000-strong peace-keeping force to Croatia and Yugoslavia. On 27 April 1992 Serbia and Montenegro created a new federal republic of Yugoslavia. On 30 May, responding to further Serbian military activities in Bosnia and Croatia, the UN Security Council voted to impose sanctions. In mid-1992 NATO committed air, sea and eventually land forces to enforce sanctions and protect humanitarian relief operations in Bosnia. Following the Bosnian-Croatian-Yugoslav (Dayton) agreement all UN sanctions were lifted in Nov. 1995.

In 1998 unrest in Kosovo, with its largely Albanian population, led to a bid for outright independence. Violence flared resulting in what a US official described as 'horrendous human rights violations', including massive shelling of civilians and destruction of villages. A US-mediated agreement, accepted in principle by President Slobodan Milošević, allowed negotiations to proceed and lifted the immediate threat of NATO air strikes. The sticking point on the Serbian side was the international insistence on having 28,000 NATO-led peacemakers in Kosovo to keep apart the warring factions. Meanwhile, the scale of Serbian repression in Kosovo persuaded the NATO allies to take direct action. On the night of 24 March 1999 NATO aircraft began a bombing campaign against Yugoslavian military targets. Further Serbian provocation in Kosovo caused hundreds of thousands of ethnic Albanians to seek refuge in neighbouring countries. On 9 June after 78 days of air attacks NATO and Yugoslavia signed an accord on the Serb withdrawal from Kosovo, and on 11 June NATO's peacekeeping force, KFOR, entered Kosovo.

The general election held on 24 Sept. 2000 resulted in a victory for the opposition democratic leader Vojislav Koštunica, but President Milošević demanded a second round of voting. A strike by miners at the Kolubara coal mine on 29 Sept. led to a relatively peaceful revolution centred on Belgrade on 5 Oct. On 6 Oct. Slobodan Milošević accepted defeat. He was arrested on 1 April 2001 and on 28 June he was handed over to the United Nations War Crimes Tribunal in The Hague.

On 14 March 2002 Serbia and Montenegro agreed to remain part of a single entity called Serbia and Montenegro, thus relegating the name Yugoslavia to history. The agreement was ratified in principle by the federal parliament and the republican parliaments of Serbia and Montenegro on 9 April 2002. The new union came into force on 4 Feb. 2003. Most powers in this loose confederation are divided between the two republics. After 4 Feb. 2006 Serbia and Montenegro will have the right to vote for independence. The final status of Kosovo, which is legally part of Serbia, remains unresolved.

TERRITORY AND POPULATION

Serbia and Montenegro is bounded in the north by Hungary, northeast by Romania, east by Bulgaria, south by Macedonia and Albania, and west by the Adriatic Sea, Bosnia-Herzegovina and Croatia. Area, 102,173 sq. km. Population (mid-2001), 10,651,690 (5,370,754 females). Population density (2001), 104·2 per sq. km. In 2001 an estimated 51·6% of the population lived in urban areas.

The UN gives a projected population for 2010 of 10·40m.

In Feb. 2003 the new confederation of Serbia and Montenegro came into being: this comprised the two republics of Montenegro and Serbia, and the two provinces of Kosovo and Metohija, and Vojvodina within Serbia. The confederal capital is Belgrade (Beograd); some capital functions, including the Supreme Court, will be sited in Podgorica. Populations (2001 estimates) of principal towns:

Belgrade	1,581,129	Subotica	142,166
Novi Sad	266,176	Zrenjanin	130,070
Niš	248,561	Pančevo	122,435
Kragujevac	180,192	Smederevo	116,592
Podgorica	168,069	Čačak	114,794

The 1991 census was not carried out in Kosovo and Metohija. 1991 estimated population: Priština, 155,499; Prizren 92,303; Peć 68,163; Kosovska Mitrovica, 64,323.

Ethnic groups at the 1991 census: Serbs, 6,504,048; Albanians, 1,714,768; Montenegrins, 519,766; Hungarians, 344,147; Muslims, 336,025; Gypsies, 143,519; Croats, 111,650; Slovaks, 66,863; Macedonians, 47,118; Romanians, 42,364; Bulgarians, 26,922; Valachians, 17,810; Turks, 11,263. At the 1991 census, 361,452 nationals worked abroad.

Refugees and internally displaced persons are estimated at about 600,000.

The official language is Serbian, the eastern variant (Croatian is the western) of Serbo-Croat. Serbian is written in the Cyrillic alphabet.

SOCIAL STATISTICS

2001 (including Kosovo and Metohija): live births, 130,194; deaths, 113,063; marriages, 57,165; divorces, 8,723. 2001 rates (per 1,000 population): births, 12·2; death, 10·6; marriage, 5·4; infant mortality, 13·1 (per 1,000 live births). In 2001 the most popular age for marrying was 24 for males and 20 for females. Expectation of life in 2001: males, 70·1 years; females, 75·2. Annual population growth rate, 1991–2001, 0·25%. Fertility rate, 2001, 1·71 births per woman.

CLIMATE

Most parts have a central European type of climate, with cold winters and hot summers. 2000, Belgrade, Jan. −1·0°C, July 23·5°C. Annual rainfall 367·7 mm. Podgorica, Jan. 2·8°C, July 26·5°C. Annual rainfall 1,499 mm.

CONSTITUTION AND GOVERNMENT

The head of state is the *President*, elected by the members of the federal parliament for a non-renewable four-year term.

The union parliament, the *Assembly of Serbia and Montenegro*, has 126 members, 91 elected from the assembly of Serbia and 35 elected from the assembly of Montenegro for a term of four years. Its assent is necessary to all legislation. The Assembly elects the President and the five-member Cabinet, which has responsibility for foreign affairs, defence, human and minority rights, international economic relations and internal economic affairs.

National Anthem. 'Hej, Slaveni, jošte živi rečnaših dedova' ('O Slavs, our ancestors' words will live'), with words by S. Tomašik and tune anonymous, is the provisional anthem of Serbia and Montenegro. The union parliament is expected to vote upon a new anthem (and other national symbols including a new flag) before the end of 2003.

RECENT ELECTIONS

Svetozar Marović, a Montenegrin and deputy leader of the Democratic Party of Socialists, was elected president by the members of the Union Assembly on 7 March 2003, receiving 65 votes, with 47 against.

On 25 Feb. 2003 the assemblies of Serbia and Montenegro elected deputies from their own number to serve concurrently as members of the Union Assembly. In these elections the Democratic Opposition of Serbia (DOS) gained 37 seats, the Democratic List for European Montenegro (DLECG) (including the Democratic Party of Socialists/DPS) 19, the Democratic Party of Serbia (DSS) 17, (Montenegrin) Together for Changes (ZP) 14, the Serb Socialist Party (SPS) 12, the Serb Radical Party (SRS) 8, the Social Democratic Party (SDP) 5, the Party of Serb Unity (SSJ) 5, the Christian Democratic Party of Serbia (DHSS) 2, the (Serb) Democratic Alternative (DA) 2, others 5.

CURRENT ADMINISTRATION

In March 2003 the multi-party coalition of, among others, the Democratic Opposition of Serbia (DOS) and the Democratic List for European Montenegro/ Democratic Party of Socialists (DLECG/DPS), comprised the following:

Union President: Svetozar Marović; b. 1955 (Democratic Party of Socialists/DPS; sworn in 7 March 2003).

Minister for Foreign Affairs: Goran Svilanović. *Defence:* Boris Tadić. *Human and Minority Rights:* Rasim Ljajić. *International Economic Relations:* Branko Lukovac. *Internal Economic Affairs:* Amir Nurković.

Government Website: http://www.ssinf.sv.gov.yu

DEFENCE

Military service for 12 to 15 months is compulsory. Military expenditure totalled US$1,654m. in 1999 (US$149 per capita), representing 12·4% of GDP. In 1985 expenditure had been US$4,951m.

Army. Personnel (1999) were about 85,000 (37,000 conscripts). In addition there are Ministry of Interior troops whose strength is unknown.

Navy. The Navy comprises five diesel submarines and four frigates. A Marine force of 900 is divided into two 'brigades'.

Personnel in 1999 totalled 7,000 including Coastal Defence and Marines. The force is based at Kotor.

Air Force. Personnel (1999) 16,700 (3,000 conscripts), with 238 combat aircraft and 52 armed helicopters.

INTERNATIONAL RELATIONS

The former Yugoslavia (SFRY) was a member of the UN and its self-proclaimed successor state (Federal Republic of Yugoslavia) was excluded during the Milošević era from the General Assembly and related bodies such as the IMF and World Bank. However, after Vojislav Koštunica became president in Oct. 2000 Yugoslavia was admitted both to the UN and the IMF. Serbia and Montenegro has succeeded the former Yugoslavia in membership of the UN. It is also a member of the Danube Commission, BIS and IOM.

ECONOMY

Currency. The unit of currency of Serbia is the *dinar* (YUD) of 100 *paras*. On 1 Jan. 2001 Yugoslavia adopted a managed float regime. The National Bank of Yugoslavia began setting the exchange rate of the dinar daily in the foreign exchange market on the previous day. Montenegro adopted the euro as its sole legal currency on 1 Jan. 2002, having made the Deutsche Mark legal tender alongside the dinar on 2 Nov. 1999. In the new Serbia and Montenegro there is a National Bank of Serbia and a Central Bank of Montenegro. In Kosovo both the dinar and the euro are legal tender. Headline inflation declined to 39% in 2001, compared with 113% in Dec. 2000. Foreign exchange reserves were US$5,706m. in Feb. 1998. Total money supply in Feb. 1998 was 227,479bn. dinars.

Budget. The federal budget for 2001 was set at US$4·3bn.

Performance. In 2001 there was real GDP growth of 5%. Ten years of conflict and economic mismanagement have had severe effects. Economic activity is recovering from a very low base. Total GDP in 2001 was US$10·9bn.

Banking and Finance. The banking system of Serbia and Montenegro consists of the central bank, commercial banks and other financial organizations, such as the Post Office Savings Bank, savings and credit organizations and savings and loan associations. The National Bank is the bank of issue responsible for the monetary policy, stability of the currency of Serbia, the dinar, control of the money supply and prescribing the method of maintaining internal and external liquidity. The dinar became fully convertible in May 2002. The present *Governor* of the National Bank of Serbia is Mladjan Dinkić. In Dec. 2000 total foreign exchange reserves were US$890m. and in Dec. 2001 foreign exchange reserves reached US$1,808m. Total money supply was 101·7bn. dinars in Nov. 2001.

There is a stock exchange in Belgrade.

Weights and Measures. The metric weights and measures have been in use since 1883. The Gregorian calendar was adopted in 1919.

ENERGY AND NATURAL RESOURCES

Environment. According to the *World Bank Atlas* Serbia and Montenegro's carbon dioxide emissions were the equivalent of 4·7 tonnes per capita in 1997.

Electricity. Installed capacity in 1999 was 10·08m. kW. Output in 2000 (without Kosovo and Metohija), was 34,360m. kWh, of which 22,330m. kWh were thermal and 12,030m. kWh hydro-electric. Consumption per capita was 1,942 kWh in 2000 (without Kosovo and Metohija).

Oil and Gas. Crude oil production (2001, without Kosovo and Metohija), 805,000 tonnes; natural gas, 160m. cu. metres.

Minerals. Lignite production (2000, without Kosovo and Metohija), 33,638,000 tonnes; copper ore, 12,896,000 tonnes; brown coal, 398,000 tonnes.

Agriculture. In 2001 (without Kosovo and Metohija) there were 5,629,000 ha of agricultural land, of which 3,402,000 ha were arable (2,128,000 ha cereals; 323,000 ha industrial crops), 717,000 ha meadow and 1,147,000 ha pasture. 4,403,000 ha were in private farms and 1,226,000 ha in agricultural organizations. The economically active agricultural population was 1,061,488 in 1991.

Crop production, 2001 (without Kosovo and Metohija, in 1,000 tonnes): maize, 5,921; wheat, 2,534; sugarbeets, 1,806; potatoes, 1,097; grapes, 416; plums, 338; soybeans, 207.

Livestock, 2001 (without Kosovo and Metohija, in 1,000): cattle, 1,366; pigs, 3,634; sheep, 1,783; horses, 41; poultry, 20,081.

Livestock products, 2001 (without Kosovo and Metohija): meat, 474,000 tonnes; milk, 1,789,000 litres; eggs, 1,419m. In 2001, 130,327,000 litres of wine were produced.

Forestry. The forest area is 2,858,000 ha, of which 1,341,000 ha are in private hands. Timber production in 2001 (without Kosovo and Metohija) was 2·62m. cu. metres.

Fisheries. In 2000 the landings of fish were (in tonnes): freshwater, 672; salt-water, 431; crustacea and shell, 15.

INDUSTRY

In Dec. 2000 there were 211,195 enterprises and institutions, including 122,789 private enterprises, 439 public enterprises, 166 co-operatives and 1,983 social enterprises. In 2000 industrial production was only 39% of the 1989 total.

Industrial output (in 1,000 tonnes) in 2001 (without data for Kosovo and Metohija): cement, 2,418; crude steel, 598; pig iron, 461; artificial fertilizers, 368; sugar, 209; plastics, 157; sulphuric acid, 68; steel castings, 13; refrigerators, 19,967 units; passenger cars, 7,197 units; TV sets, 5,256 units; tractors, 1,757 units; lorries, 590 units.

Labour. In 2001 there were 2,242,788 workers in the social sector, including 744,016 in industry, 230,231 in trade, 141,844 in transport and communications, 128,899 in education and culture; and, in 2000, 92,000 in communities and organizations, 90,000 in commercial services, 85,000 in catering and tourism and 79,000 in agriculture. In Oct. 2001 in the private sector there were 360,772 self-employed and employed people Average monthly wage in 2001 (without Kosovo and Metohija) was 5,458 dinars. Unemployment in 2001 was officially 30%.

INTERNATIONAL TRADE

According to the law on foreign investments that was in force in 2000, foreign investors were allowed to make investments in all activities except those in the field of production and turnover of armaments, public information and communications systems, and restricted zones, where they could own up to 49% of capital. In 2000 there were 373 contracts on foreign investments registered. UN sanctions against Yugoslavia were lifted in Nov. 1995 following the Bosnian-Croatian-Yugoslav (Dayton) agreement on Bosnia. External debt was US$11,960m. in 2000.

Imports and Exports. Foreign trade, in US$1m., for calendar year:

	1998	1999	2000	2001
Imports	4,849	3,296	3,711	4,837
Exports	2,858	1,498	1,723	1,903

Breakdown by Standard International Trade Classification categories (value in US$1m.):

	Imports		Exports	
	2000	2001	2000	2001
0. Food and live animals	279	441	255	275
1. Beverages and tobacco	53	99	15	17
2. Crude materials	221	188	123	101
3. Fuels and lubricants	745	1,001	4	50
4. Animal and vegetable oils	9	10	17	18
5. Chemicals	556	698	145	132
6. Manufactured goods	772	948	632	652
7. Machinery and transport equipment	820	1,029	215	243
8. Miscellaneous manufactured items	237	355	270	363
9. Other	19	68	47	50

Main trading partners, 2001 (imports and exports in US$1m.): Russia, 685 and 797; Germany, 589 and 231; Italy, 500 and 312; Bosnia-Herzegovina, 135 and 249; Bulgaria, 324 and 23; Macedonia, 130 and 176.

COMMUNICATIONS

Roads. In 2001 (without data for Kosovo and Metohija) there were 44,993 km of roads comprising 5,422 km of main roads, 11,351 km of regional roads and 28,220 km of other roads. In 2000 there were 1,406,949 passenger cars, 123,135 trucks and vans, and 9,760 buses and coaches. Passenger-km in 2001, without Kosovo and Metohija, were 5,769m. (public transport); tonne-km of freight carried, 553m. There were 1,048 deaths in road accidents in 2000.

Rail. In 2001 there were 4,058 km of railway, of which 1,385 km were electrified. 10,985,000 passengers and 3,376,000 tonnes of freight were carried.

Civil Aviation. There are five airports, the chief ones being at Belgrade and Tivat. The national carrier is JAT (Jugoslovenski Aero Transport) which operates internal flights and in 2001 flew to most major centres in Europe and the Middle East. In March 2003 the airline stated it would retain its name despite the change of name of the country.

Shipping. In 2000 Serbia and Montenegro possessed one sea-going passenger vessel and five cargo vessels totalling 205,000 GRT.

Length of navigable waterways (2001), 1,419 km. In 2001 there were 437 cargo vessels and 3,609,000 tonnes of freight were transported.

Telecommunications. Main telephone lines numbered 2,406,200 in 2000 (226·1 for every 1,000 persons) and there were 240,000 PCs in use (22·6 per 1,000 persons). There were 2,200,000 mobile phone subscribers in 2001 (Serbia) and 14,700 fax machines in 1997. In Dec. 2000 there were 400,000 Internet users.

Postal Services. There were 1,646 post offices in 2001.

SOCIAL INSTITUTIONS

Justice. In 2000 there were 2 supreme courts, 32 district courts and 153 communal courts, with 2,607 judges and 8,196 lay assessors (without data for Montenegro). There were also 19 economic courts with 287 judges.

In 2000, 34,379 criminal sentences were passed.

The death penalty was abolished for all crimes in 2001.

Religion. Religious communities are separate from the State and are free to perform religious affairs. All religious communities recognized by law enjoy the same rights. Religious breakdown, 1999: Serbian Orthodox, 6·7m.; Muslims, 2·0m.; Roman Catholics, 0·6m.

Serbia has been traditionally Orthodox. Muslims are found in the south as a result of the Turkish occupation. The Serbian Orthodox Church with its seat in Belgrade has 27 bishoprics within the boundaries of former Yugoslavia and 12 abroad (5 in the USA and Canada, 5 in Europe and 2 in Australia). The Serbian Orthodox Church numbers about 2,000 priests. Its *Patriarch* is Pavle (enthroned 22 May 1994).

As well as in Serbia, the Serbian Orthodox Church is the official church in Montenegro. The Montenegrin church was banned in 1922, but in Oct. 1993 a breakaway Montenegrin church was set up under its own patriarch.

Relations with the Vatican are regulated by a 'Protocol' of 1966.

The Jewish religion has nine communities making up a common league of Jewish Communities with its seat in Belgrade.

Education. Compulsory primary education lasts eight years, secondary 3–4 years. In 2001 (without data for Kosovo and Metohija) there were 1,798 nursery schools with 180,662 pupils and 18,211 employees of which 9,082 were teachers. In 2000–01 there were 4,087 primary schools with 782,559 pupils and 48,770 teachers, and 519 secondary schools with 345,939 pupils and 26,891 teachers. There were 52 institutions of tertiary education with 49,350 students and 1,577 teachers, and 90 institutions of higher education with 141,469 full-time students and 10,356 academic staff.

Adult literacy rate, 1995, 97·9% (male, 98·6%; female, 97·3%).

Health. In 2000 there were 23,141 doctors, 4,107 dentists, 1,383 pharmacists and 56,933 hospital beds.

Welfare. In 2000 there were 1,349,252 pensioners, of whom 557,754 were old age, 431,527 disability and 339,971 survivors' pensioners. 7,229,004 working days were lost through sickness. In 1999 pensions and disability insurance totalled 25,534,514,000 dinars; old age pension, 8,511,079,000 dinars; and disability, 4,866,896,000 dinars. In 1999, 1,353m. dinars were paid in child allowances.

CULTURE

Broadcasting. In 2001 (without data for Kosovo and Metohija) there were 70 TV centres (24 private) with 291,324 hours of programme, of which information and documentary 66,990 hours; and 184 broadcasting radio stations (80 private) with 1,004,000 hours of programme, of which 150,000 information and documentary. There were 2,282,000 TV (colour by PAL) and 1,143,000 radio receivers in use in 2001.

Cinema. In 2001 (without data for Kosovo and Metohija) there were 167 cinemas. Cinema attendances were 4,017,000; in 2000, three full-length films were made in 1999.

Press. In 2001 there were 27 dailies, 580 other newspapers and 491 periodicals. 4,643 book titles (840 by foreign authors) were published in 2001 in a total of 6,189,000 copies.

Tourism. There were 1,281,029 foreign tourists in 2001 (without data for Kosovo and Metohija). Tourist receipts totalled US$39·9m.

Libraries. In 1998 (without data for Kosovo and Metohija) there were 3 National, 689 public, 143 Higher Education and 11 non-specialized libraries with a combined 33,681,000 volumes and 8,332,811 registered users.

Museums and Galleries. In 2000 (without data for Kosovo and Metohija) there were 32 art galleries with 1,055 exhibitions and 142 museums with 1,361,000 visitors.

DIPLOMATIC REPRESENTATIVES

Of Serbia and Montenegro in the United Kingdom (5–7 Lexham Gdns., London, W8 5JJ)
Ambassador: Vladeta Janković.

Of the United Kingdom in Serbia and Montenegro (Generala Zdanova 46, 11000 Belgrade)
Ambassador: Charles Graham Crawford, CMG.

Of Serbia and Montenegro in the USA (2410 California St., NW, Washington, D.C., 20008)
Ambassador: Ivan Vujacic.

Of the USA in Serbia and Montenegro (Kneza Miloša, 50, 11000 Belgrade)
Ambassador: William Montgomery.

Of Serbia and Montenegro to the United Nations
Ambassador: Dejan Šahović.

Of Serbia and Montenegro to the European Union
Ambassador: Pavle Jevremović.

FURTHER READING
Federal Statistical Office. *Statistical Yearbook of Yugoslavia.*

Allcock, J. B., *Explaining Yugoslavia.* Columbia Univ. Press, 2000
Anzulovic, Branimir, *Heavenly Serbia: From Myth to Genocide.* Hurst, London, 1999
Bennett, C., *Yugoslavia's Bloody Collapse: Causes, Course and Consequences.* Farnborough, 1995
Bokovoy, M. K., *et al.*, (eds.) *State-Society Relations in Yugoslavia 1945–1992.* London, 1997
Carpenter, Ted Galen, (ed.) *Nato's Empty Victory.* Cato Institute, Washington, D.C., 2000
Cohen, L. J., *Broken Bonds: the Disintegration of Yugoslavia.* Boulder (CO), 1993

Dyker, D. and Vejvoda, I. (eds.) *Yugoslavia and After: a Study in Fragmentation, Despair and Rebirth.* Harlow, 1996

Friedman, F. (ed.) *Yugoslavia: a Comprehensive English-Language Bibliography.* London, 1993

Glenny, M., *The Fall of Yugoslavia.* London, 1992

Gow, J., *Triumph of the Lack of Will: International Diplomacy and the Yugoslav War.* London and Columbia Univ. Press, 1997

Judah, Tim, *The Serbs: History, Myth and the Destruction of Yugoslavia.* Yale Univ. Press, 1997.—*Kosovo: War and Revenge.* Yale Univ. Press, 2000

Magaš, B., *The Destruction of Yugoslavia: Tracking the Break-up, 1980–92.* London, 1993

Thomas, Robert, *Serbia Under Milosevic: Politics in the 1990s.* Hurst, London, 1999

Udovicki, J., and Ridgeway, J. (eds.) *Burn This House: The Making and Unmaking of Yugoslavia.* Duke, 1997

Woodward, S. L., *Balkan Tragedy: Chaos and Dissolution after the Cold War.* Brookings Institution (Washington), 1995

National statistical office: Federal Statistical Office, Kneza Miloša 20, Belgrade. *Director (acting):* Ranko Nedeljković.

Website: http://www.szs.sv.gov.yu

REPUBLICS AND PROVINCES

In Feb. 2003 the new Union of Serbia and Montenegro comprised the two republics of Montenegro and Serbia, and the two provinces of Kosovo and Metohija, and Vojvodina within Serbia.

MONTENEGRO

KEY HISTORICAL EVENTS

Montenegro emerged as a separate entity on the break-up of the Serbian Empire in 1355. Owing to its mountainous terrain, it was never effectively subdued by Turkey. It was ruled by Bishop Princes until 1851, when a royal house was founded. The Treaty of Berlin (1828) recognized the independence of Montenegro and doubled the size of the territory. The remains of King Nicholas I, who was deposed in 1918, were returned to Montenegro for reburial in Oct. 1989. As part of the Yugoslav federation, Montenegro holds jealously to its independence and tries to keep its political distance from Serbia.

On 14 March 2002 Montenegro and Serbia agreed to a new structure for the Yugoslav federation. Following European Union-brokered talks it was agreed that they would remain part of a single entity called Serbia and Montenegro, thus relegating the name Yugoslavia to history. The parliaments of both Montenegro and Serbia ratified the agreement on 9 April 2002. The new entity came into being on 4 Feb. 2003.

TERRITORY AND POPULATION

Montenegro is a mountainous region which opens to the Adriatic in the southwest. It is bounded in the west by Croatia, northwest by Bosnia-Herzegovina, in the northeast by Serbia and in the southeast by Albania. The capital is Podgorica (population, 1997 estimate, 162,172). Some capital functions are to be transferred to Cetinje, the historic capital of the former kingdom of Montenegro. Its area is 13,812 sq. km. Population at the 1991 census was 615,035, of which the predominating ethnic groups were Montenegrins (380,467), Muslims (89,614), Serbs (57,453) and Albanians (40,415). Population density per sq. km, 44·5. Estimate, 1998, 650,000; density, 47·1 per sq. km.

SOCIAL STATISTICS
Statistics for calendar years:

	Live births	Marriages	Deaths	Growth rate per 1,000
1994	8,887	3,753	4,660	6·7
1995	9,477	3,791	4,921	7·2
1996	9,193	3,869	5,029	6·5
1997	8,758	3,993	5,153	5·6

CONSTITUTION AND GOVERNMENT
There is an 75-member single-chamber National Assembly.

A referendum was held on 29 Feb.–1 March 1992 to determine whether Montenegro should remain within a common state, Yugoslavia, as a sovereign republic. The electorate was 412,000, of whom 66% were in favour. President Milo Djukanović had pledged a referendum on independence in May 2002, but this was postponed with the announcement of the creation of the new entity of Serbia and Montenegro, which came into being on 4 Feb. 2003. After 4 Feb. 2006 Montenegro will be empowered to hold a referendum on independence.

RECENT ELECTIONS
Parliamentary elections were held on 20–21 Oct. 2002. President Milo Djukanović's pro-independence Democratic List for a European Montenegro (including the Democratic Socialist Party) won 39 out of 75 seats with 44·8% of votes cast; the 'Together for Changes' coalition won 30 with 35·9%; the Liberal Alliance, 4 with 5·4%; and the 'Albanians Together' Democratic Coalition, 2 with 2·3%. Turn-out was 77·5%.

In presidential elections held on 22 Dec. 2002 acting president Filip Vujanović won 83·9% of the vote but the result was not valid because the turn-out was less than the required 50%. A follow-up election on 9 Feb. 2003 also failed with a turn-out of 47·7%. Parliament's subsequent amendment of the law on turn-out allowed Vujanović to claim victory on 11 May 2003 with 63·3% against Miodrag ZivkovIć with 30·8% and Dragan Hajduković with 3·9%. Turn-out was 48·5%.

CURRENT ADMINISTRATION
President (acting): Filip Vujanović; b. 1954 (sworn in on 25 Nov. 2002).
Prime Minister: Milo Djukanović; b. 1962 (sworn in on 8 Jan. 2003).

Government Website: http://www.montenegro.yu/

ECONOMY
Currency. On 2 Nov. 1999 the pro-Western government decided to make the Deutsche Mark legal tender alongside the dinar. Subsequently it was made the sole official currency, and consequently the euro became the currency of Montenegro on 1 Jan. 2002.

Budget. In 1997 the budget was set at 1,999,000,000 dinars.

Banking and Finance. The Central Bank of Montenegro (*President of the Council,* Ljubisa Krgović) was established in Nov. 2000. Montenegro has 11 commercial banks.

ENERGY AND NATURAL RESOURCES
Electricity. Electricity production in 1997 was 2·27m. kWh.

Minerals. Bauxite production in 1998 totalled 900,000 tonnes.

Agriculture. In 1998 the cultivated area was 189,000 ha. Yields (in 1,000 tonnes): wheat, 5; maize, 9; potatoes, 51. Livestock (1,000 head): cattle, 180; sheep, 439; pigs, 22.

Forestry. Timber cut in 1997: 232,000 cu. metres.

INDUSTRY
Production (1997): lignite, 1,282,194 tonnes; bauxite, 470,000 tonnes; heavy semi-manufactures, 24,807 tonnes; cotton carded yarn, 166 tonnes.

Labour. In 1997 there were 123,011 workers in the public sector, including 37,491 in industry, 18,589 in trade, catering and tourism, 13,827 in education and culture, 12,003 in transport and communications, 9,020 in communities and organizations and 3,400 in commercial services. In Oct. 1997 in the private sector there were 41,941 self-employed and employed, including 15,150 in trade, 5,774 in catering and tourism and 3,466 in transport and communications. Average monthly salary in Dec. 1998 was 1,556 dinars. Unemployment was running at 33%.

SOCIAL INSTITUTIONS

Justice. In 1997 there were 2 District Courts, 15 Communal Courts and 2 Economic courts of law with 222 judges.

Education. In 1997 there were: 69 nurseries with 10,269 pupils; 485 primary schools with 9,129 pupils; 43 secondary schools with 27,747 pupils; 1 high school with 79 students; 12 higher schools with 7,266 students.

FURTHER READING

Treadway, J. D., *The Falcon and the Eagle: Montenegro and Austria-Hungary, 1908–1914.* Purdue University Press, 1998

SERBIA

KEY HISTORICAL EVENTS

The Serbs received Orthodox Christianity from the Byzantines in 891, but shook off the latter's suzerainty to form a prosperous state, firmly established under Stevan Nemanja (1167–96). A Serbian Patriarchate was established at Peć during the reign of Stevan Dušan (1331–55). Dušan planned the conquest of Constantinople, but he was forestalled by incursions of Turks. After he died many Serbian nobles accepted Turkish vassalage; the reduced Serbian state under Prince Lazar received the coup de grace at Kosovo on St Vitus day, 1389. Turkish preoccupations with a Mongol invasion and wars with Hungary, however, postponed the total incorporation of Serbia into the Ottoman Empire until 1459.

The Turks permitted the Orthodox church to practise, though the Patriarchate was abolished in 1776. The native aristocracy was eliminated and replaced by a system of fiefdoms held in return for military or civil service. Local self-government based on rural extended family units (*zadruga*) continued. In its heyday the Ottoman system probably bore no harder on the peasantry than the Christian feudalism it had replaced, but with the gradual decline of Ottoman power, corruption, oppression and reprisals led to economic deterioration and social unrest.

In 1804 murders carried out by mutinous Turkish infantry provoked a Serbian rising under Djordje Karadjordje. The Sultan's army disciplined the mutineers, but was then defeated by the intransigent Serbs. By the Treaty of Bucharest (1812), however, Russia agreed that Serbia, known as Servia until 1918, should remain Turkish. The Turks reoccupied Serbia with ferocious reprisals. A new rebellion broke out in 1815 under Miloš Obrenović which, this time with Russian support, won autonomy for Serbia within the Ottoman empire. Obrenović had Karadjordje murdered in 1817. In 1838 he was forced to grant a constitution establishing an appointed state council, and abdicated in 1839. In 1842 a coup overthrew the Obrenovićs and Alexander Karadjordjević was elected as ruler. He was deposed in 1858.

During the reign of the western-educated Michael Obrenović (1860 until his assassination in 1868) the foundations of a modern centralized and militarized state were laid, and the idea of a 'Great Serbia', first enunciated in Prime Minister Garašanin's *Draft Programme* of 1844, took root. Milan Obrenović, adopting the title of king, proclaimed formal independence in 1882. He suffered defeats against Turkey (1876) and Bulgaria (1885) and abdicated in 1889. Alexander Obrenović was assassinated in 1903, and replaced by Peter Karadjordjević, who brought in a period of stable constitutional rule.

In its foreign policy, Serbia's striving for an outlet to the sea was consistently thwarted by Austria. Annexing Bosnia in 1908, Austria forced the Serbs to withdraw from the Adriatic after the first Balkan war (1912).

Following the break-up of Yugoslavia, in March 1998 a coalition government was formed between the Socialist Party of Slobodan Milošević and the ultra-nationalist Radical Party.

On 14 March 2002 Serbia and Montenegro agreed to a new structure for the Yugoslav federation. Following European Union-brokered talks it was agreed that they would remain part of a single entity called Serbia and Montenegro, thus relegating the name Yugoslavia to history. The parliaments of both Serbia and Montenegro ratified the agreement on 9 April 2002. The new entity came into being on 4 Feb. 2003. On 12 March 2003 Serb prime minister Zoran Djindjić was assassinated.

TERRITORY AND POPULATION

Serbia is bounded in the northwest by Croatia, in the north by Hungary, in the northeast by Romania, in the east by Bulgaria, in the south by Macedonia and in the west by Albania, Montenegro and Bosnia-Herzegovina. It includes the two provinces (formerly autonomous) of Kosovo and Metohija in the south and Vojvodina in the north. With these Serbia's area is 88,361 sq. km; without, 55,968 sq. km. The capital is Belgrade (population estimate, 1997, 1,597,599). Population at the 1991 census was (with Kosovo and Vojvodina) 9,778,991, of which the predominating ethnic group was Serbs (6,446,595). Population density per sq. km, 110·7; (without Kosovo and Vojvodina), population estimate 5,808,906, of which the predominating ethnic group was Serbs (5,108,682). Population density per sq. km, 103·8. 1997 estimate (with Kosovo and Vojvodina), 9,956,662; density, 112·7 per sq. km; (without) 5,791,643; density, 103·5 per sq. km.

SOCIAL STATISTICS

Statistics for calendar years (without Kosovo and Vojvodina):

	Live births	Marriages	Deaths	Growth rate per 1,000
1995	63,737	32,295	66,756	−0·5
1996	60,924	29,703	69,218	−1·4
1997	59,071	29,638	69,422	−1·8

CONSTITUTION AND GOVERNMENT

In Sept. 1990 a new constitution was adopted by the National Assembly. It defined Serbia as a 'democratic' instead of a 'socialist' republic, laid down a framework for multi-party elections, and described Serbia as 'united and sovereign on all its territory', thus stripping Kosovo and Vojvodina of the attributes of autonomy granted by the 1974 federal constitution.

There is a 250-member single-chamber National Assembly. The *President* is elected by universal suffrage for not more than two five-year terms.

RECENT ELECTIONS

In the first round of presidential elections held on 29 Sept. 2002 Yugoslav President Vojislav Koštunica won 30·9% of votes cast, with 27·4% of the vote going to Miroljub Labus and 23·2% for Vojislav Seselj, the favoured candidate of former premier Slobodan Milošević. Turn-out was 55·5%. A run-off between Koštunica and Labus took place on 13 Oct. 2002 but was declared invalid owing to a turn-out of 45·5%—less than the legally-required 50%. A further attempt to hold a new election on 8 Dec. 2002 again failed when fewer than 50% of the electorate voted.

Elections to the Serbian Parliament were held on 3 Dec. 2000. Reformers of the Democratic Opposition of Serbia (DOS) alliance won 64·1% of the vote and 176 of 250 seats, the Socialist Party of Serbia (SPS) 13·8% and 37 seats, and the Radical Party 8·5% and 23 seats. Turn-out was 57·7%.

CURRENT ADMINISTRATION

President (acting): Nataša Micić; b. 1965 (in office since 30 Dec. 2002).

Prime Minister: Zoran Živković; b. 1960 (Democratic Party; in office since 18 March 2003).

Government Website: http://www.serbia.sr.gov.yu/

ECONOMY

Budget. In 1997 the budget was set at 13,820,000,000 dinars.

ENERGY AND NATURAL RESOURCES

Electricity. Electricity production in 1997 was 32·77m. kWh.

Agriculture. (Excluding Kosovo and Vojvodina). In 1997 the cultivated area was an estimated 2,614,000 ha. Yields in 1997 (in 1,000 tonnes): maize, 6,855; wheat, 2,920; sugarbeet, 2,037; potatoes, 918; plums, 489; grapes, 397. Livestock estimates (in 1,000): cattle, 402; sheep, 369; pigs, 74; poultry, 2,577.

Forestry. Timber cut in 1997: 1,614,000 cu. metres.

INDUSTRY

(Excluding Kosovo and Vojvodina). 1997: lignite, 32,608,711 tonnes; steel, 862,944 tonnes; copper ore, 20,507,148 tonnes; lorries, 1,269 units; cars, 9,512 units; sulphuric acid, 150,371 tonnes; plastics, 27,220 tonnes; cement, 924,308 tonnes; sugar, 14,682 tonnes; cotton fabrics, 17,228,000 sq. metres; woollen fabrics, 10,097,000 sq. metres. By late 2000 industry had virtually come to a standstill.

Labour. In 1997 there were 1,921,763 workers in the public sector, including 782,676 in industry, 196,149 in trade, catering and tourism, 165,585 in education and culture, 128,458 in transport and communications, 84,035 in communities and organizations, 71,225 in commercial services. In Oct. 1997 in the private sector there were 486,183 self-employed and employed, including 136,443 in trade, 51,553 in arts and crafts, 36,771 in catering and tourism, 18,468 in transport and communications. Average monthly salary in Dec. 1998 was 1,313 dinars. Unemployment was running at 25%, but by late 2000 had increased to around 50%.

SOCIAL INSTITUTIONS

Justice. In 1997 there were 30 District Courts, 138 Communal Courts and 16 Economic Courts of Law with 1,997 judges.

Education. In 1997 there were: 1,730 nurseries with 174,621 pupils; 3,975 primary schools with 816,059 pupils; 523 secondary schools with 323,781 pupils; 53 high schools with 37,366 students; 83 higher schools with 144,330 students.

FURTHER READING

Judah, T., *The Serbs: History, Myth and the Destruction of Yugoslavia.* Yale Univ. Press, 1997

KOSOVO AND METOHIJA

KEY HISTORICAL EVENTS

Kosovo has a large ethnic Albanian majority. Following Albanian-Serb conflicts, the Kosovo and Serbian parliaments adopted constitutional amendments in March 1989 surrendering much of Kosovo's autonomy to Serbia. Renewed Albanian rioting broke out in 1990. The Prime Minister and six other ministers resigned in April 1990 over ethnic conflicts. In July 1990, 114 of the 130 Albanian members of the National Assembly voted for full republican status for Kosovo but the Serbian National Assembly declared this vote invalid and unanimously voted to dissolve the Kosovo Assembly. Direct Serbian rule was imposed causing widespread violence. Western demands for negotiations in granting Kosovo some kind of special status were rejected. Ibrahim Rugova, the leader of the main Albanian party, the Democratic League of Kosovo (LDK), declared himself 'president' demanding talks on independence. In 1998 armed conflict between Yugoslavia and the Kosovo Liberation Army led to 200,000 people, or a tenth of the population of the whole province, fleeing the fighting. Further repression by Serbian forces led to the threat of NATO direct action. Air strikes against Yugoslavian military targets began on 24 March 1999. Retaliation against Albanian Kosovars led to a massive exodus of refugees. On 9 June after 78 days of air attacks NATO and Yugoslavia signed an accord on the Serb withdrawal from Kosovo, and on 11 June NATO's peacekeeping force, KFOR, entered Kosovo. In Nov. 2001 the Organization for Security and Co-operation in Europe mounted elections for a provincial assembly that were deemed fair and democratic.

TERRITORY AND POPULATION

Area: 10,887 sq. km. The capital is Priština. The 1991 census was not taken. Population estimate of Kosovo and Metohija, 1991, 1,956,196 (1,596,072 Albanians, 194,190 Serbs); density, 179·7 per sq. km. The population in 1998 was 2,190,000 (84% Albanians, 9% Serbs and 7% others). By Sept. 1999 the population had declined to 1,506,000. Although the number of Albanians had dropped by over 430,000, the breakdown of the population had changed to 93% Albanians, 5% Serbs and 2% others. Population estimate of Priština, 1997, 242,000.

SOCIAL STATISTICS

Statistics for calendar years:

	Live births	Marriages	Deaths	Growth rate per 1,000
1994	43,450	11,959	7,667	17·2
1995	44,776	12,979	8,671	17·1
1996	45,343	12,309	8,142	17·3
1997	42,920	11,866	8,624	15·7

CONSTITUTION AND GOVERNMENT

There is a 120-member multi-ethnic parliamentary assembly, which first convened on 10 Dec. 2001. The new assembly brought together representatives of Kosovo's ethnic Albanian majority and its Serbian minority for the first time in more than a decade.

RECENT ELECTIONS

Municipal elections organized by the United Nations Interim Administration Mission in Kosovo took place on 28 Oct. 2000. The Democratic League of Kosovo, led by the moderate pacifist Ibrahim Rugova (the former leader of the now-dissolved 'Republic of Kosovo') won with 58·0% of votes cast. The authorities in Belgrade did not recognize the election as Kosovo's 100,000-strong Serb population had not participated.

Further elections were held on 17 Nov. 2001 with a turn-out of 63·2%. The Democratic League of Kosovo won 47 seats with 46·3% of votes cast, against the Democratic Party of Kosovo, 26 (25·5%); the Coalition Returning (Serbian minority), 22 (11·0%); and the Alliance for the Future of Kosovo, 8 (7·8%). Other parties won less than 2% of the vote.

Ibrahim Rugova was elected president by the 120-member parliamentary assembly on 4 March 2002. He received 88 votes after three failed attempts in the previous three months to gain the required majority.

CURRENT ADMINISTRATION

President: Ibrahim Rugova; b. 1944 (Democratic League of Kosovo; sworn in 4 March 2002).

Prime Minister: Bajram Rexhepi; b. 1954 (Democratic Party of Kosovo; sworn in 4 March 2002).

Special Representative and Head of the United Nations Interim Administration in Kosovo (UNMIK): Michael Steiner (Germany); b. 1949 (took office on 14 Feb. 2002).

ECONOMY

Budget. In 1997 the budget was set at 13,000,000 dinars.

Banking and Finance. In Aug. 1999 the Deutsche Mark became legal tender alongside the Yugoslav dinar, and on 1 Jan. 2002 the euro became the official currency of Kosovo. The Serb dinar is also legal tender in Kosovo but is used only by ethnic Serbs.

ENERGY AND NATURAL RESOURCES

Electricity. Electricity production in 1997 was 4·87m. kWh.

Agriculture. The cultivated area in 1997 was an estimated 398,000 ha. Yields in 1997 (in 1,000 tonnes): maize, 296; wheat, 272; potatoes, 92; grapes, 69; plums, 15. Livestock (in 1,000): cattle, 402; sheep, 369; pigs, 74; poultry, 2,577.

Forestry. Timber cut in 1997: 130,000 cu. metres.

INDUSTRY

Production (1997): lignite, 8,421,991 tonnes; sulphuric acid, 26,900 tonnes; cement, 89,528 tonnes.

Labour. In 1997 there were 120,763 workers in the public sector, including 54,223 in industry, 10,471 in education and culture, 9,245 in trade, catering and tourism, 8,933 in transport and communications, 7,880 in communities and organizations, 1,526 in commercial services. In Oct. 1997 in the private sector there were 35,869 self-employed and employed, including 15,113 in trade, 5,023 in catering and tourism, 4,364 in arts and crafts, and 2,006 in transport and communications. Average monthly salary in Dec. 1998 was 1,066 dinars.

SOCIAL INSTITUTIONS

Education. In 1997 there were: 111 nurseries with 8,179 pupils; 335 primary schools with 42,114 pupils; 55 secondary schools with 14,092 pupils; 4 high schools with 1,621 students; 15 higher schools with 12,725 students.

FURTHER READING

Malcolm, N., *Kosovo: a Short History*. New York Univ. Press, 1998
Vickers, M., *Between Serb and Albanian: A History of Kosovo*. Hurst, London, 1998

VOJVODINA

KEY HISTORICAL EVENTS

After the Battle of Kosovo in 1389 Turkish attacks on the Balkans led to mass migrations of Serbian people to Vojvodina. Turkish rule ended after their 1716–18 war with Austria and the Požarevac peace agreement. In exchange for acting as frontier protectors, the Austrians granted the people of Vojvodina freedom of confession and religious autonomy. However, by 1848 discontent had brewed and a short-lived revolution occurred, in which the Serbs formed an alliance with the Croats, and Vojvodina was briefly declared as an independent dukedom. After the First World War Vojvodina became part of the first Yugoslav state. In 1974 President Tito granted autonomy to Vojvodina, but this status was brought into question after Vojvodina's largely anti-Milošević provincial assembly resigned their positions in 1988. In 1989 the Serbian government, led by Slobodan Milošević, stripped Vojvodina of most of its autonomous rights and secured Serbian control. Politicians and citizens made frequent demands for autonomy to be reinstated during the Milošević era, and since his fall in Oct. 2000 there have again been movements for increased autonomy. However, the Assembly of Vojvodina has now only very limited powers.

TERRITORY AND POPULATION

Area: 21,506 sq. km. The capital is Novi Sad. Population of Vojvodina at the 1991 census, 2,013,889 (1,143,723 Serbs, 339,491 Hungarians). Estimate, 1997, 1,976,936; density, 91·9 per sq. km. Population of Novi Sad, 1997, 266,808.

SOCIAL STATISTICS
Statistics for calendar years:

	Live births	Marriages	Deaths	Growth rate per 1,000
1994	21,595	11,048	27,518	−3·0
1995	22,499	11,260	27,177	−2·4
1996	20,483	11,112	28,832	−4·2
1997	20,645	10,706	28,646	−4·0

CONSTITUTION AND GOVERNMENT
The 1990 Serbian constitution deprived Vojvodina of its autonomy. Serbo-Croat was declared the only official language in 1991.

RECENT ELECTIONS
In March 2003 the Assembly of Vojvodina comprised 120 deputies, of which the Democratic Opposition of Serbia had 117 seats and the coalition of the Socialist Party of Serbia and Yugoslav Left 2.

CURRENT ADMINISTRATION
President of the Assembly: Nenad Čanak; b. 1959 (in office since 23 Oct. 2000).
Chairman of the Executive Council: Djordje Djukić; b. 1948 (in office since 23 Oct. 2000).

ECONOMY
Budget. In 1997 the budget was set at 68,000,000 dinars.

ENERGY AND NATURAL RESOURCES
Electricity. Electricity production in 1997 was 387m. kWh.

Agriculture. The cultivated area in 1997 was an estimated 1,649,000 ha. Yields (in 1,000 tonnes): maize, 3,847; wheat, 1,423; sugarbeet, 1,805; potatoes, 255. Livestock estimates (in 1,000): cattle, 231; sheep, 267; pigs, 1,691; poultry, 7,863.

Forestry. Timber cut in 1997: 548,000 cu. metres.

INDUSTRY
Production (1997): crude petroleum, 965,655 tonnes; plastics, 212,352 tonnes; cement, 997,491 tonnes.

Labour. In 1997 there were 452,005 workers in the public sector, including 181,672 in industry, 38,382 in trade, catering and tourism, 38,000 in education and culture, 26,876 in transport and communications, 18,543 in communities and organizations, and 16,901 in commercial services. In Oct. 1997 in the private sector there were 86,320 self-employed and employed including 39,612 in trade, 13,053 in arts and crafts, 5,436 in catering and tourism, and 3,985 in transport and communications. Average monthly salary in Dec. 1998 was 1,493 dinars.

SOCIAL INSTITUTIONS
Education. In 1997 there were: 604 nurseries with 48,024 pupils; 535 primary schools with 212,453 pupils; 122 secondary schools with 81,893 pupils; 9 high schools with 7,790 students; and 15 higher schools with 25,505 students.

SEYCHELLES

Republic of Seychelles

Capital: Victoria
Population estimate, 2000: 82,000
GDP per capita, 2000: (PPP$) 12,508
HDI/world rank: 0·811/47

KEY HISTORICAL EVENTS

The Seychelles were colonized by the French in 1756 to establish spice plantations to compete with the Dutch monopoly. The islands were captured by the English in 1794. Subsequently, Britain offered to return Mauritius and its dependencies which included the Seychelles to France if that country would renounce all claims to her possessions in India. France refused and the Seychelles were formally ceded to Britain as a dependency of Mauritius. In Nov. 1903 the Seychelles archipelago became a separate British Crown Colony. Internal self-government was achieved on 1 Oct. 1975 and independence as a republic within the British Commonwealth on 29 June 1976.

The first president, James Mancham, was deposed in a coup on 5 June 1977. Under the new constitution, the Seychelles People's Progressive Front became the sole legal party. There were several attempts to overthrow the regime, but in 1979 and 1984 Albert René was the only candidate in the presidential elections. Under the new constitution approved in June 1993, President René was re-elected against two opponents.

TERRITORY AND POPULATION

The Seychelles consists of 115 islands in the Indian Ocean, north of Madagascar, with a combined area of 175 sq. miles (455 sq. km) in two distinct groups. The Granitic group of 40 islands cover 92 sq. miles (239 sq. km); the principal island is Mahé, with 59 sq. miles (153 sq. km) and 75,876 inhabitants at the 1997 census, the other inhabited islands of the group being Praslin, La Digue, Silhouette, Fregate and North, which together had 7,100 inhabitants.

The Outer or Coralline group comprises 75 islands spread over a wide area of ocean between the Mahé group and Madagascar, with a total land area of 83 sq. miles (214 sq. km) and a population of about 450 at the 1997 census. The main islands are the Amirante Isles (including Desroches, Poivre, Daros and Alphonse), Coetivy Island and Platte Island, all lying south of the Mahé group; the Farquhar, St Pierre and Providence Islands, north of Madagascar; and Aldabra, Astove, Assumption and the Cosmoledo Islands, about 1,000 km southwest of the Mahé group. Aldabra (whose lagoon covers 55 sq. miles), Farquhar and Desroches were transferred to the new British Indian Ocean Territory in 1965, but were returned by Britain to the Seychelles on the latter's independence in 1976. Population, 76,400 (1996); 56·9% urban (1998). Victoria, the chief town, had an estimated population of 28,000 in 1999.

The official languages are Creole, English and French but 95% of the population speak Creole.

SOCIAL STATISTICS

(1999) births, 1,460; deaths, 560. 1999 rates per 1,000 population, birth, 18·2; death, 7·0; infant mortality, 10 per 1,000 births. Annual population growth rate, 1990–99, 1·1%. Life expectancy at birth in 1997 was estimated to be 70 years (65 for males and 74 for females). Fertility rate, 1999, 2·0 births per woman.

CLIMATE

Though close to the equator, the climate is tropical. The hot, wet season is from Dec. to May, when conditions are humid, but southeast trades bring cooler conditions from June to Nov. Temperatures are high throughout the year, but the islands lie outside the cyclone belt. Victoria, Jan. 80°F (26·7°C), July 78°F (25·6°C). Annual rainfall 95" (2,287 mm).

CONSTITUTION AND GOVERNMENT

Under the 1979 Constitution the Seychelles People's Progressive Front (SPPF) was the sole legal Party. There is a unicameral People's Assembly consisting of 33 seats, of which 25 are directly elected and eight are allocated on a proportional basis, and an executive president directly elected for a five-year term. A constitutional amendment of Dec. 1991 legalized other parties. A commission was elected in July 1992 to draft a new constitution. The electorate was some 50,000; turn-out was 90%. The SPPF gained 14 seats on the commission, the Democratic Party, 8; the latter, however, eventually withdrew. At a referendum in Nov. 1992 the new draft constitution failed to obtain the necessary 60% approval votes. The commission was reconvened in Jan. 1993. At a further referendum on 18 June 1993 the constitution was approved by 73·6% of votes cast.

National Anthem. 'Koste Seselwa' ('Seychelles, Unite').

RECENT ELECTIONS

In parliamentary elections held on 4–6 Dec. 2002 President France-Albert René's Seychelles People's Progressive Front won 23 of the 34 seats with 54·3% of the vote, against 11 for the Seychelles National Party (42·6%). Turn-out was 87%. In presidential elections held between 31 Aug.–2 Sept. 2001 France Albert René was re-elected for a 6th term, obtaining 54·2% of the votes, with his nearest rival, Wavel Ramkalawan of the Seychelles National Party, polling 44·9%.

CURRENT ADMINISTRATION

President: France Albert René; b. 1935 (SPPF; president since 1977 and re-elected for a 6th term in 2001). The President is *Minister of Internal Affairs, Defence and Legal Affairs.*

Vice-President, Minister of Finance, Environment and Transport: James Alix Michel.

In March 2003 the government comprised:

Minister of Administration: Noellie Alexander. *Agriculture and Marine Resources:* Dolor Ernesta. *Culture and Information:* Ronny Jumeau. *Education:* Danny Faure. *Foreign Affairs:* Jeremie Bonnelame. *Health:* Jacqueline Dugasse. *Industry and International Business:* Patrick Pillay. *Land Use and Habitat:* Joseph Belmont. *Local Government, Youth and Sports:* Sylvette Frichot. *Social Affairs and Manpower Development:* William Herminie. *Tourism and Civil Aviation:* Simone de Comarmond.

DEFENCE

The Defence Force comprises all services. Personnel (1999) Army, 200; Paramilitary, 250; Coastguard-naval, 200; Air Wing, 20.

Defence expenditure totalled US$10m. in 2000 (US$133 per capita), representing 1·8% of GDP.

Coastguard. There is no longer a navy or air force in the Seychelles. Instead, the Seychelles Coast Guard has superseded these former forces. Based at Port Victoria it includes a small air wing with no combat aircraft.

INTERNATIONAL RELATIONS

Seychelles is a member of the UN, the Commonwealth, the African Union, African Development Bank, COMESA and the International Organization of the Francophonie and is an ACP member state of the ACP-EU relationship.

ECONOMY

Agriculture accounted for 4·1% of GDP in 1998, industry 23·5% and services 72·4%.

Overview. Since the early 1990s the government has attempted to create a free market economy. Tourism forms the backbone of the economy followed by the fisheries sector. In recent years the Seychelles has undertaken efforts to develop an offshore sector as the third pillar of the economy and to position itself as a provider of business and financial services.

Currency. The unit of currency is the *Seychelles rupee* (SCR) divided into 100 *cents*. In June 2002 foreign exchange reserves were US$39m. In April 2002 total money supply was 1,384m. rupees. In both 2000 and 2001 there was deflation of 0·1%.

Budget. Fiscal budget in 1m. rupees, for calendar years:

	1996	1997	1998	1999	2000
Total revenue	1,151·1	1,273·5	1,372·9	1,491·9	1,377·1
Total expenditure	1,495·2	1,680·9	1,879·7	1,905·0	1,969·8

Performance. Total GDP was US$0·6bn. in 2000. Seychelles has been in recession since 1999, with the economy contracting by 5·4% in 2000 and 8·1% in 2001.

Banking and Finance. The Central Bank of Seychelles (established in 1983; *Governor*, Francis Chang Leng), which is the bank of issue, and the Development Bank of Seychelles provide long-term lending for development purposes. There are also six commercial banks, including two local banks (the Seychelles Savings Bank and the Seychelles International Mercantile Banking Co-operation or NOUVOBANQ), and four branches of foreign banks (Barclays Bank, Banque Française Commerciale, Habib Bank and Bank of Baroda).

Weights and Measures. The metric system is employed.

ENERGY AND NATURAL RESOURCES

Environment. According to the *World Bank Atlas* carbon dioxide emissions were the equivalent of 2·5 tonnes per capita in 1998.

Electricity. Installed capacity on Mahé and Praslin combined was 42,000 kW in 1998. Production in 1998 was 159m. kWh. Consumption was 135m. kWh. Consumption per capita in 1998 was 1,775 kWh.

Water. There are two raw water reservoirs, the Rochon Dam and La Gogue Dam, which have a combined holding capacity of 1·05bn. litres.

Treated water consumption in 1998 was 5·5bn. litres.

Agriculture. The main cash crop in 1998 was cinnamon bark, of which 289 tonnes were exported, followed by tea production with exports of 250 tonnes (green leaf). Crops grown for local consumption include bananas, cassava, sweet potatoes, yams, oranges, paw-paw and vegetables. The staple food crop, rice, is imported from Asia. Livestock, 2000: 18,000 pigs, 5,000 goats, 1,000 cattle and 1m. chickens. In 2000 there were 1,000 ha of arable land and 6,000 ha of permanent crop land.

Forestry. In 1995 forests covered 4,000 ha, or 8·9% of the total land area. The Ministry of Environment has a number of ongoing forestry projects which aim at preserving and upgrading the local system. There are also a number of terrestrial nature reserves including three national parks, four special reserves and an area of outstanding natural beauty.

Fisheries. The fisheries sector is the Seychelles' second largest foreign exchange earner. In 1998 it accounted for at least 93% of export revenue. Total 1998 fisheries exports amounted to 457·7m. rupees, of which: canned tuna, 412·2m.; fresh/frozen fish, 11·9m.; frozen prawns, 33·6m. Total 1998 fish production (in tonnes) was as follows: canned tuna, 18,939; fresh/frozen fish, 3,334; frozen prawns, 642.

INDUSTRY

Local industry is expanding, the largest development during 1998 and 1999 being tuna canning, with an increase in output of 3,806 tonnes. This is followed by drinks brewing, which had an increase in output of 2,033,000 litres from 1997 to 1998. Other main activities include production of cigarettes (62m. in 1996), dairy production, prawn production, paints and processing of cinnamon barks.

Labour. Some 71% of the workforce is employed in services. In 1999, 3,791 people worked in hotels and restaurants and 1,217 in other tourism related jobs. 15,700 are formally employed in the private sector, 6,800 in the public sector and 4,200 in the parastatal sector.

Trade Unions. There are two major trade unions, the National Workers' Union and the Forum for Progress.

INTERNATIONAL TRADE
Foreign debt totalled US$163m. in 2000.

Imports and Exports. Total trade, in 1m. rupees, for calendar years:

	1994	1995	1996	1997	1998
Imports (less re-exports)	1,042·4	1,109·2	1,881·9	1,711·1	1,129·0[1]
Domestic exports	114·3	113·7	205·0	349·6	474·2

[1]Provisional figure.

Principal imports (1998): manufactured goods, 583·7m. rupees; food, beverages and tobacco, 485·2m. rupees; mineral fuel, 189·5m. rupees; chemicals, 131·8m. rupees; machinery and transport equipment, 603·3m. rupees. Principal origins of imports (1996): USA (26·5%), UK (11·3%), Yemen (10·6%) and South Africa (10·4%). Principal exports (1998, provisional): canned tuna, 412·1m. rupees; fresh and frozen fish, 11·9m. rupees; frozen prawns, 33·6m. rupees; cinnamon bark, 2·7m. rupees. Main export markets, 1995, China (15·0%), UK (12·4%), Thailand (11·5%) and India (3·5%).

COMMUNICATIONS

Roads. In 1998 there were 343 km of surfaced roads and 54 km of unsurfaced roads. There were 9,068 vehicles registered in 1998.

Rail. There are no railways in the Seychelles.

Civil Aviation. Seychelles International airport is on Mahé. In 1998 Air Seychelles flew on domestic routes and to Bombay, Dubai, Frankfurt, Johannesburg, London, Mauritius, Paris, Rome, Singapore and Zürich. In 1999 it flew 8·8m. km, carrying 347,200 passengers (109,500 on international flights). In 2000 Seychelles International handled 604,415 passengers (315,024 on international flights) and 6,259 tonnes of freight.

Shipping. The main port is Victoria, which is also a tuna-fishing and fuel and services supply centre. In 1998 merchant shipping totalled 18,000 GRT. In 1994 vessels totalling 764,000 net registered tons entered. Sea freight (1998) included: imports, 636,000 tonnes; exports, 47,000 tonnes; transhipments (fish), 39,000 tonnes.

Telecommunications. There were 19,000 main telephone lines in 2000, or 234·5 per 1,000 population, and 11,000 PCs were in use (135·6 per 1,000 persons). In 1996 there were approximately 1,100 mobile phone subscribers and 640 fax machines. Internet users numbered 6,000 in Dec. 2000.

Postal Services. In 1995 there were five post offices. The central post office is in Victoria.

SOCIAL INSTITUTIONS

Justice. In 1998, 3,951 criminal and other offences were recorded by the police. The death penalty was abolished for all crimes in 1993.

Religion. 90% of the inhabitants are Roman Catholic, 8% Anglican and 2% other religions (mainly 7th Day Adventists, Bahai, Muslim, Hindu, Pentecostal, Jehovah's Witnesses, Buddhist or followers of the Grace and Peace church).

Education. Adult literacy was 84% in 1998. Education is free from 5 to 12 years in primary schools, and 13 to 17 in secondary schools. There are three private schools providing primary and secondary education and one dealing only with secondary learning. Education beyond 18 years of age is funded jointly by the government and parents. In 1999 there were 9,912 pupils and 642 teachers in primary schools, 7,787 pupils and 551 teachers in secondary schools and 1,847 students and 199 teachers at polytechnic level.

In 1996 expenditure on education came to 7·9% of GNP and 24·1% of total government spending.

Health. In 1999 there were 108 doctors, 15 dentists and 406 nurses. In 1998 there were 426 hospital beds. The health service is free.

Welfare. Social security is provided for people of 63 years and over, for the disabled and for families needing financial assistance. There is also assistance via means testing for those medically unfit to work and for mothers who remain out of work for longer than their designated maternity leave. Orphanages are also subsidized by the government.

CULTURE

Broadcasting. Broadcasting is under the auspices of the Seychelles Broadcasting Corporation (SBC), an independent body. The SBC owns two radio stations; the AM station which hosts most programmes in Creole with frequent use of English and French; and Paradise FM which broadcasts mainly in English. There is also a religious station, FEBA. The RFI and BBC also transmit programmes locally.

There is only one local TV station directed by the SBC. International TV channels can be reached through Cable TV. TV colour is by PAL. In 1997 there were 42,000 radio receivers and in 1999 there were 18,429 TV sets.

Cinema. There is one cinema, based in Victoria.

Press. There are 1 daily and 2 weekly newspapers, as well as 2 monthly magazines.

Tourism. Tourism is the main foreign exchange earner. Visitor numbers were 125,000 in 1999. Receipts in 1998 totalled US$111m.

Festivals. There are numerous religious festivals including Kavadi, an annual procession organized by the Hindu Association of Seychelles. Secular festivals include the annual Youth Festival, Jazz Festival, Creole Festival, Kite Festival and the Subios Festival, a celebration of the underwater world.

Libraries. There is a national library in Victoria with branches on Praslin and La Digue Islands. It also provides a mobile service, and there are libraries in all educational institutions.

Theatre and Opera. There are three national theatres, all located on Mahé. The Mont Fleuri Theatre and the International Conference Centre serve central Mahé while the Anse Royale Theatre caters for the southern region of the island.

Museums and Galleries. There are four museums: the Historical Museum, the Natural History Museum, the National Heritage Museum and the Eco Musée, a museum of the country's economic activities. There is also a National Art Gallery, located in the National Library, and a number of smaller galleries exhibiting mostly local artists.

DIPLOMATIC REPRESENTATIVES
Of Seychelles in the United Kingdom (Box 4PE, 2nd Floor, Eros House, 111 Baker Street, London, W1M 1FE)
High Commissioner: Bertrand Rassool.

Of the United Kingdom in Seychelles (Victoria Hse., 3rd Floor, PO Box 161, Victoria, Mahé)
High Commissioner: Fraser Wilson, MBE.

Of Seychelles in the USA (800 2nd Avenue, Suite 400C, New York, NY 10017)
Ambassador: Claude Morel.

Of the USA in Seychelles
Ambassador: John Price (resides at Port Louis, Mauritius).

Of Seychelles to the United Nations
Ambassador: Claude Morel.

Of Seychelles to the European Union
Ambassador: Callixte d'Offay.

FURTHER READING
Bennett, G. and Bennett, P. R., *Seychelles*. [Bibliography] ABC-Clio, Oxford and Santa Barbara (CA), 1993
Scarr, D., *Seychelles Since 1970: History of a Slave and Post-Slavery Society*. Africa World Press, Lawrenceville (NJ), 2000

National statistical office: Statistics and Database Administration Section (MISD), P. O. Box 206, Victoria, Mahé. *Seychelles in Figures*
Website: http://www.seychelles.net/misdstat/

SIERRA LEONE

Republic of Sierra Leone

Capital: Freetown
Population estimate, 2000: 4·41m.
GDP per capita, 2000: (PPP$) 490
HDI/world rank: 0·275/173

KEY HISTORICAL EVENTS

The Colony of Sierra Leone originated in 1787 when English settlers bought a piece of land intended as a home for natives of Africa who were waifs in London. The land was later used as a settlement for Africans rescued from slave-ships. The hinterland was declared a British protectorate on 21 Aug. 1896. Sierra Leone became independent as a member state of the British Commonwealth on 27 April 1961. In a general election in March 1967, Dr Siaka Stevens' All People's Congress came to power and was installed despite a military coup to prevent his taking office. Sierra Leone became a republic on 19 April 1971 with Dr Siaka Stevens as executive president. Following a referendum in June 1978, a new constitution was instituted under which the ruling All People's Congress became the sole legal party.

A military coup on 29 April 1992 deposed the president and set up a National Provisional Ruling Council whose chairman was in turn deposed in a military coup on 16 Jan. 1996. Presidential and parliamentary elections in Feb.–March 1996 resulted in a new government led by President Ahmed Tejan Kabbah. He was ousted in May 1997 by a group of junior officers. In Feb. 1998 a Nigerian-led intervention force launched an air and artillery offensive against the military junta. For the first time a group of African states joined together to restore a democratically-elected president. On 10 March President Kabbah returned from exile in Guinea, promising a 'new beginning'. But in Jan. 1999 the country again erupted into civil war. Nigeria sent troops to support President Kabbah but having lost control of the diamond fields and with no other resources, the government was powerless. The war, which continued for nearly ten years, has reduced Sierra Leone to one of the poorest countries in the world.

The government reached an agreement with the rebel movement in July 1999 to bring the civil war to an end. Under the terms of the accord the Revolutionary United Front (RUF) was to gain four key government posts along with effective control of the country's mineral resources. In return the RUF was to surrender its weapons. However, civil war broke out again in early 2000. Responding to a government appeal British forces were sent to back up the UN peacekeeping force (UNMASIL). Foday Sankoh, rebel leader of the RUF, was captured and handed over to UN forces in May 2000. In July 2001 the RUF announced that it was formally recognizing the civil government under President Ahmed Tejan Kabbah. By Sept. 2001 there were signs that the civil war might be at an end, and in Jan. 2002 President Kabbah declared the war over. He was re-elected in a presidential election in May 2002 and has been at the forefront of the fight against corruption. Both the UN and the International Monetary Fund have praised the 'remarkable progress' made in Sierra Leone.

TERRITORY AND POPULATION

Sierra Leone is bounded on the northwest, north and northeast by Guinea, on the southeast by Liberia and on the southwest by the Atlantic Ocean. The area is 27,925 sq. miles (73,326 sq. km). Population (census 1985), 3,517,530, of whom about 2,000 were Europeans, 3,500 Asiatics and 30,000 non-native Africans. Estimate (1995), 4,509,000; density, 61·5 per sq. km. In 1999, 64·1% of the population were rural.

The UN gives a projected population for 2010 of 6·28m.

The capital is Freetown, with 822,000 inhabitants in 1999.

Sierra Leone is divided into four provinces:

	Sq. km	Census 1985	Capital	Estimate 1988
Eastern Province	15,553	960,551	Kenema	13,000
Northern Province	35,936	1,262,226	Makeni	12,000

	Sq. km	Census 1985	Capital	Estimate 1988
Southern Province	19,694	740,510	Bo	26,000
Western Province	557	554,243	Freetown	469,776

The provinces are divided into districts as follows: Bo, Bonthe, Moyamba, Pujehun (Southern Province); Kailahun, Kenema, Kono (Eastern Province); Bombali, Kambia, Koinaduga, Port Loko, Toukolili (Northern Province).

The principal peoples are the Mendes (34% of the total) in the south, the Temnes (31%) in the north and centre, the Konos, Fulanis, Bulloms, Korankos, Limbas and Kissis. English is the official language; a Creole (Krio) is spoken.

SOCIAL STATISTICS

Births, 1995, 201,000; deaths, 116,000. Rates (1995, per 1,000 population): birth, 47·8; death, 27·7. Annual population growth rate, 1990–99, 1·9%. Expectation of life at birth in 1999 was 37·0 years for males and 39·6 years for females, the lowest life expectancy of any country in the world. A World Health Organization report published in June 2000 ranked Sierra Leone in last place of all 191 sovereign countries in a 'healthy life expectancy' list, with an expected 25·9 years of healthy life for babies born in 1999. Infant mortality was 182 per 1,000 live births in 1999. Fertility rate, 1999, 5·9 births per woman.

CLIMATE

A tropical climate, with marked wet and dry seasons and high temperatures throughout the year. The rainy season lasts from about April to Nov., when humidity can be very high. Thunderstorms are common from April to June and in Sept. and Oct. Rainfall is particularly heavy in Freetown because of the effect of neighbouring relief. Freetown, Jan. 80°F (26·7°C), July 78°F (25·6°C). Annual rainfall 135" (3,434 mm).

CONSTITUTION AND GOVERNMENT

In a referendum in Sept. 1991 some 60% of the 2·5m. electorate voted for the introduction of a new constitution instituting multi-party democracy. There is a 68-member *National Assembly*.

There is a *Supreme Council of State (SCS)*, and a *Council of State Secretaries*.

National Anthem. 'High We Exalt Thee, Realm of the Free'; words by C. Nelson Fyle, tune by J. J. Akar.

RECENT ELECTIONS

Presidential and parliamentary elections were held on 14 May 2002. In the presidential election, incumbent Ahmad Tejan Kabbah won with 70·6% of the vote ahead of Ernest Koroma with 22·4% and Alimany Paolo Bangura with 1·7%. There were six other candidates. In parliamentary elections, Kabbah's Sierra Leone People's Party (SLPP) won 83 of the 112 seats with Koroma's All People's Congress taking 27 seats.

CURRENT ADMINISTRATION

President and Minister of Defence: Ahmed Tejan Kabbah; b. 1931 (SLPP; elected 17 March 1996 and re-elected in May 2002).

Vice-President: Solomon Berewa.

In March 2003 the government comprised:

Minister of Agriculture and Food Security: Sama Sahr Mondeh. *Country Planning, Forestry, Environment and Social Welfare:* Alfred Bobson Sesay. *Development and Economic Planning:* Mohamed Daramy. *Education, Science and Technology:* Alpha Wurie. *Energy and Power:* Emmanuel Grant. *Finance:* Joseph Dauda. *Foreign Affairs and International Co-operation:* Momodu Koroma. *Health and Sanitation:* Agnes Taylor-Lewis. *Information and Broadcasting:* Septimus Kaikai. *Internal Affairs:* Sam Hinga Norman. *Justice:* Eke Ahmed Halloway. *Labour, Industrial Relations and Social Security:* Alpha Timbo. *Local Government and Community Development:* Sidikie Brima. *Marine Resources:* Okere Adams. *Mineral Resources:* Mohamed Swarray Alhaji Deen. *Political and Parliamentary Affairs:* George Banda Thomas. *Social Welfare, Gender and Children's Affairs:* Shirley Yema

Gbujama. *Trade and Industry:* Kadi Sesay. *Transport and Communications:* Prince Harding. *Works, Housing and Technical Maintenance:* Caiser Boima. *Youth and Sport:* Dennis Bright.

DEFENCE
In 2000 military expenditure totalled US$9m. (US$2 per capita), representing 1·2% of GDP.

The UN peacekeeping force numbered 17,275 personnel in May 2002, making it the largest peacekeeping operation in the world at the time.

Army. Following the civil war, the army has disbanded and a new National Army is expected to form with a strength of some 5,000.

Navy. Based in Freetown there is a small naval force of 200 operating three patrol craft.

INTERNATIONAL RELATIONS
Sierra Leone is a member of the UN, WTO, the African Union, African Development Bank, ECOWAS, IOM, OIC and the Commonwealth and is an ACP member state of the ACP-EU relationship.

ECONOMY
Agriculture accounted for 44·2% of GDP in 1998, industry 23·8% and services 32·0%.

Currency. The unit of currency is the *leone* (SLL) of 100 *cents*. Foreign exchange reserves were US$28m. in June 2002. Inflation was 2·2% in 2001, down from 36·0% in 1998. Exchange controls were liberalized in 1993. Total money supply in June 2002 was 191,105m. leones.

Budget. In 1999 (year ending 31 Dec.) the government's total revenue was 85,819m. leones (77,199m. in 1998) and total expenditure was 252,884m. leones (147,052m. in 1998).

Performance. GNP per capita was US$200 in 1996 compared to US$390 in 1982. Real GDP growth was −0·8% in 1998, but the civil war resulted in the economy shrinking by 8·1% in 1999. There was positive growth in 2000 for the first time since 1994, with a rate of 3·8%, rising to 5·4% in 2001. Total GDP in 2001 was US$0·3bn. Sierra Leone is among the world's bottom five countries in income and life expectancy.

Banking and Finance. The bank of issue is the Bank of Sierra Leone which was established 1964 (*Governor*, James Koroma). There are four commercial banks (two foreign).

Weights and Measures. The metric system is in use.

ENERGY AND NATURAL RESOURCES
Environment. According to the *World Bank Atlas* carbon dioxide emissions in 1998 were the equivalent of 0·1 tonnes per capita. An *Environmental Sustainability Index* compiled for the World Economic Forum meeting in Feb. 2002 ranked Sierra Leone 134th in the world out of 142 countries analysed, with 36·5%. The index measured the ability of countries to maintain favourable environmental conditions and examined various factors including pollution levels and the use or abuse of natural resources.

Electricity. Installed capacity was 126 MW in 1991. Production in 1998 was 235m. kWh; consumption per capita in 1997 was 55 kWh.

Minerals. The chief minerals mined are gold (16 kg in 1996), diamonds (80,000 carats in 1998), and rutile (203,000 tonnes in 1994–95). There are also deposits of iron ore and bauxite. The presence of rich diamond deposits partly explains the close interest of neighbouring countries in the politics of Sierra Leone.

Agriculture. Agriculture engaged nearly 67% of the workforce in 1995, mainly in small-scale peasant production. Cattle production is important in the north. Production (2000 estimates, in 1,000 tonnes): cassava, 241; rice, 199; palm oil, 36;

plantains, 28; sweet potatoes, 28; sugarcane, 21. In 1998 there were 0·48m. ha of arable land and 0·06m. ha of permanent crops.

Livestock (2000): cattle, 420,000; goats, 200,000; sheep, 365,000; pigs, 52,000; chickens, 6m.

Forestry. In 1995 forests covered 1,309,000 ha, or 18·3% of the total land area (down from 1,522,000 ha in 1990). Timber production in 1999 was 3·42m. cu. metres.

Fisheries. In 1999, 59,407 tonnes of fish were caught (44,927 tonnes from marine waters).

INDUSTRY

There are palm oil and rice mills; sawn timber, joinery products and furniture are produced.

Labour. The workforce was 1,610,000 in 1996 (64% males). In 1995 around two-thirds of the economically active population were engaged in agriculture, fisheries and forestry. 14,800 persons were registered unemployed in 1992.

INTERNATIONAL TRADE

Foreign debt was US$1,273m. in 2000.

Imports and Exports. Total trade for 1996: imports, US$212m.; exports, US$47m.

Main exports are bauxite, diamonds, gold, coffee and cocoa. A UN-mandated diamond export certification scheme is in force. The Security Council has commended Sierra Leone's government for its efforts in monitoring trade to prevent diamonds from becoming a future source of conflict.

The main import suppliers in 1994–95 were USA (42·7%), Netherlands (14·2%), UK (5·7%) and Indonesia (3·7%). Principal export markets in 1994–95 were USA (44·8%), UK (17·3%), Belgium (16·8%) and Netherlands (4·1%).

COMMUNICATIONS

Roads. There were 11,300 km of roads in 1997, of which 900 km were surfaced. In 1996 there were 20,670 passenger cars and 3,890 commercial vehicles.

Civil Aviation. Freetown Airport (Lungi) is the international airport. In 1998 Sierra National Airlines flew to Accra and Lagos. In 1999 scheduled airline traffic of Sierra Leone-based carriers flew 0·3m. km, carrying 19,000 passengers (all on international flights).

Shipping. The port of Freetown has a very large natural harbour. Iron ore is exported through Pepel, and there is a small port at Bonthe. In 1998 the merchant fleet totalled 19,000 GRT; including oil tankers 1,000 GRT. 2·31m. tonnes of cargo were loaded in 1993 and 0·59m. tonnes discharged.

Telecommunications. In 2000 telephone provision was 19,000 main lines (3·9 per 1,000 population) and in 1996 there were around 1,700 fax machines. The country's telecommunications network was virtually destroyed during the civil war, and reconstruction and modernization is regarded as a matter of extreme urgency. In Dec. 2000 Sierra Leone had 20,000 Internet users. By mid-2002 there were 35,000 mobile phone subscribers.

Postal Services. In 1995 there were 54 post offices.

SOCIAL INSTITUTIONS

Justice. The High Court has jurisdiction in civil and criminal matters. Subordinate courts are held by magistrates in the various districts. Native Courts, headed by court Chairmen, apply native law and custom under a criminal and civil jurisdiction. Appeals from the decisions of magistrates' courts are heard by the High Court. Appeals from the decisions of the High Court are heard by the Sierra Leone Court of Appeal. Appeal lies from the Sierra Leone Court of Appeal to the Supreme Court which is the highest court.

The death penalty is in force, and 24 soldiers were executed on 19 Oct. 1998 for their part in the May 1997 coup.

Religion. There were 1·72m. Muslims in 1992. Traditional animist beliefs persist.

Education. The adult literacy rate in 1998 was 31·0%. Primary education is partially free but not compulsory. In 1992–93 there were 1,643 primary schools with 267,425 pupils and 10,595 teachers, 167 secondary schools with 70,900 pupils and 4,313 teachers, and 44 vocational training colleges and teacher training schools with 7,756 students and 709 staff. There were five institutes of higher education with 4,742 students and 600 teachers. Fourah Bay College and Njala University College are the two constituent colleges of the University of Sierra Leone. They had 2,571 students and 257 academic staff in 1990–91.

Health. In 1992 there were 404 doctors, and in 1998, 4,025 hospital beds. In the period 1990–98 only 34% of the population had access to safe drinking water.

CULTURE

Broadcasting. Broadcasting is under the auspices of the government-controlled Sierra Leone Broadcasting Service and Sierra Leone Television, which is part commercial. There were 53,000 TV sets (colour by PAL) and 1·12m. radio sets in 1997.

Press. In 1996 there was one daily newspaper with a circulation of 20,000. A second daily has been launched in the meantime.

Tourism. In 1998 there were 50,000 foreign tourists, bringing revenue of US$57m.

DIPLOMATIC REPRESENTATIVES

Of Sierra Leone in the United Kingdom (Oxford Circus House, 245 Oxford Street, London, W1R 1LF)
High Commissioner: Sulaiman Tejan-Jalloh.

Of the United Kingdom in Sierra Leone (Spur Rd., Freetown)
High Commissioner: David Alan Jones.

Of Sierra Leone in the USA (1701 19th St., NW, Washington, D.C., 20009)
Ambassador: Vacant.
Chargé d'Affaires a.i.: Hassan Mohamed Conteh.

Of the USA in Sierra Leone (Corner Walpole and Siaka Stevens St., Freetown)
Ambassador: Peter R. Chaveas.

Of Sierra Leone to the United Nations
Ambassador: Vacant.

Of Sierra Leone to the European Union
Ambassador: Peter J. Kuyembeh.

FURTHER READING
Binns, Margaret and J. Anthony, *Sierra Leone.* [Bibliography] ABC-Clio, Oxford and Santa Barbara (CA), 1992
Conteh-Morgan, E. and Dixon-Fyle, M., *Sierra Leone at the End of the Twentieth Century: History, Politics, and Society.* Peter Lang Publishing, Berne, 1999
Ferme, M., *The Underneath of Things: Violence, History, and the Everyday in Sierra Leone.* Univ. of California Press, 2001

SINGAPORE

Republic of Singapore

Population (Singaporean), 2000: 4·01m.

GDP per capita, 2000: (PPP$) 23,356
HDI/world rank: 0·885/25

KEY HISTORICAL EVENTS

Singapore Island became part of the Javanese Majapahit Empire in the 14th century. The Portuguese took control of the area in the 16th century, followed by the Dutch a hundred years later. In 1819 Sir Thomas Stamford Raffles, the British East India Administrator, established a trading settlement. The lease to the British East India Company by the Sultan of Johore was followed by the treaty of 2 Aug. 1824 ceding the entire island in perpetuity to the company. In 1826 Penang, Malacca and Singapore were combined as the Straits Settlements. With the opening of the Suez Canal in 1869 and the advent of the steamship, an era of prosperity began for Singapore. Growth continued with the export of tin and rubber from the Malay peninsula.

Singapore fell to the Japanese in 1942 whose occupation continued until the end of the Second World War. In 1945 Singapore became a Crown Colony, being separated from Penang and Malacca. In June 1959 the state was granted internal self-government. When the Federation of Malaysia was formed in Sept. 1963, Singapore became one of the 14 states of the newly created country. On 7 Aug. 1965, by agreement with the Malaysian government, Singapore left the Federation of Malaysia and became an independent sovereign state.

TERRITORY AND POPULATION

The Republic of Singapore consists of Singapore Island and some 63 smaller islands. Singapore Island is situated off the southern extremity of the Malay peninsula, to which it is joined by a 1·1 km causeway carrying a road, railway and water pipeline across the Strait of Johor and by a 1·9 km bridge at Tuas, opened on 2 Jan. 1998. The Straits of Johor between the island and the mainland are 914 metres wide. The island is 682·3 sq. km in area, including the offshore islands.

Census of population (2000): Chinese residents 2,505,379 (76·8%), Malays 453,633 (13·9%), Indians 257,791 (7·9%) and others 46,406 (1·45%); resident population, 3,263,209. Total population in June 2001 was 4,131,200. The population is 100% urban. Population density, 6,055 per sq. km.

The UN gives a projected resident population for 2010 of 4·60m.

Malay, Chinese (Mandarin), Tamil and English are the official languages; Malay is the national language and English is the language of administration.

SOCIAL STATISTICS

1999 births, 43,316; deaths, 15,516. Birth rate per 1,000 population, 1999, 12·8; death rate, 4·5. Annual population growth rate, 1995–99, 1·7%; infant mortality, 2000, 3·3 per 1,000 live births (one of the lowest in the world); life expectancy, 1999, 75·6 years for males and 79·6 years for females. Fertility rate, 1999, 1·5 births per woman. In 1998 the most popular age for marrying was 25–29 for both men and women.

CLIMATE

The climate is equatorial, with relatively uniform temperature, abundant rainfall and high humidity. Rain falls throughout the year but tends to be heaviest from Nov. to Jan. Average daily temperature is 26·8°C with a maximum daily average of 30·9°C and a minimum daily average of 23·9°C. Mean annual rainfall is 2,345 mm.

CONSTITUTION AND GOVERNMENT

Singapore is a republic with a parliamentary system of government. The organs of state—the executive, the legislature and the judiciary—are provided for by a written constitution. The Constitution is the supreme law of Singapore and any law enacted after the date of its commencement, which is inconsistent with its provisions, is void.

The Head of State is the President. The administration of the government is vested in the Cabinet headed by the Prime Minister. The Prime Minister and the other Cabinet Members are appointed by the President from among the Members of Parliament (MPs). The Cabinet is collectively responsible to Parliament.

Parliament is unicameral consisting of 83 elected members and 1 Non-Constituency MP (NCMP), elected by secret ballot from single-member and group representation constituencies as well as nine Nominated Members of Parliament (NMPs) who are appointed for a two-year term on the recommendation of a Special Select Committee of Parliament. With the customary exception of those serving criminal sentences, all citizens over 21 are eligible to vote. Voting in an election is compulsory. Group representation constituencies may return up to six Members of Parliament (four before 1996), one of whom must be from the Malay community, the Indian or other minority communities. To ensure representation of parties not in the government, provision is made for the appointment of three (or up to a maximum of six) NCMPs. The number of NCMPs is reduced by one for each opposition candidate returned. There is a common roll without communal electorates.

A Presidential Council to consider and report on minorities' rights was established in 1970. The particular function of this council is to draw attention to any Bill or to any subsidiary legislation which, in its opinion, discriminates against any racial or religious community.

National Anthem. 'Majulah Singapura' ('Onward Singapore'); words and tune by Zubir Said.

RECENT ELECTIONS

A parliamentary election was scheduled to take place on 3 Nov. 2001, but the ruling People's Action Party (PAP) won by default as it was unopposed in 55 of the 84 seats when nominations for the election closed. Nevertheless, voting did take place as a formality, and following the election and the appointment of members by the president the PAP held 82 of the 90 seats.

Presidential elections were scheduled for 24 Aug. 1999. However, these were cancelled after S. R. Nathan emerged as the only candidate who satisfied the requirements of the certificate of eligibility. He thus gained the presidency unopposed.

CURRENT ADMINISTRATION

President: S. R. Nathan; b. 1924 (sworn in 1 Sept. 1999).

In March 2003 the cabinet comprised:

Prime Minister: Goh Chok Tong; b. 1941 (PAP; sworn in 28 Nov. 1990).

Senior Minister, Prime Minister's Office: Lee Kuan Yew, GCMG, CH. *Deputy Prime Ministers:* Lee Hsien Loong (*Minister of Finance*); Dr Tony Tan Keng Yam (*Minister of Defence*).

Minister of Health: Lim Hng Kiang (*also Second Minister of Finance*). *Environment:* Lim Swee Say. *Information, Communications and the Arts (acting):* David Lim. *Education:* RAdm (NS) Teo Chee Hean (*also Second Minister for Defence*). *Law and Foreign Affairs:* Prof. Shunmugam Jayakumar. *Manpower:* Dr Lee Boon Yang. *Home Affairs:* Wong Kan Seng. *Community Development and Sports (acting):* Assoc. Prof. Yaacob Ibrahim (*also in charge of Muslim Affairs*). *Transport:* Yeo Cheow Tong. *National Development:* Mah Bow Tan. *Trade and Industry:* BG (NS) George Yong-Boon Yeo. *Ministers in Prime Minister's Office:* Lim Boon Heng; Lee Yock Suan.

Government Website: http://www.gov.sg

DEFENCE

Compulsory military service in peacetime for all male citizens and permanent residents was introduced in 1967. The period of service for officers and non-commissioned officers is 30 months, other ranks 24 months. Reserve liability continues to age 50 for officers, 40 for other ranks. In 2000 the SAF (Singapore Armed Forces) comprised 350,000 Operationally Ready National Servicemen and an estimated 60,000 regulars and full-time National Servicemen.

An agreement with the USA in Nov. 1990 provided for an increase in US use of naval and air force facilities.

Singapore is a member of the Five Powers Defence Arrangement, with Australia, New Zealand, Malaysia and the UK.

In 2000 defence expenditure totalled US$4,707m. (US$1,320 per capita), representing 4·9% of GDP.

Army. Strength (2000) 50,000 (including 35,000 conscripts) plus 260,000 reserves. In addition there is a Civil Defence Force totalling over 87,000 including 3,720 conscripts, 23,000 Operationally Ready National Servicemen and 55,146 civil defence volunteers.

Navy. The Republic of Singapore Navy comprises four commands: Fleet, Coastal Command (COSCOM), Naval Logistics Command and Training Command. The fleet includes four diesel submarines. The Navy numbers an estimated 9,600 personnel including approximately 6,000 conscripts and 3,600 regulars. There are two naval bases: Tuas Naval Base and Changi Naval Base, the first phase of which was completed in 2000 and replaces Brani Naval Base.

Air Force. The Republic of Singapore Air Force (RSAF) has fighter squadrons comprising the F16 Falcon and the F5S/F Tiger.

Personnel strength (2000) about 13,500 (3,000 conscripts), with 165 combat aircraft and 20 armed helicopters.

INTERNATIONAL RELATIONS

Singapore is a member of the UN, BIS, WTO, the Commonwealth, Asian Development Bank, Colombo Plan and ASEAN and has ratified the Convention on the Prohibition of the Development, Production, Stockpiling and Use of Chemical Weapons and on their Destruction (CWC), and the UN Framework Convention on Climate Change (UNFCCC).

ECONOMY

Manufacturing (14%), transport and communications (7%), and wholesale and trade (7%) were the main engines for growth in 1999. Services accounted for 64% of GDP in 2000, goods producing industries 33% and owner-occupied dwellings 3·2%.

According to the anti-corruption organization *Transparency International*, Singapore ranked equal 5th in the world in a 2002 survey of the countries with the least corruption in business and government. It received 9·3 out of 10 in the annual index.

Overview. The central objective is to build up a strong science and technology base to support high-tech industries and to exploit new products and processes, with special emphasis on the life sciences. The government recognizes the need for Singapore to adopt information technology (IT) to remain competitive.

The Economic Development Board (EDB) is the leading government agency responsible for the implementation of economic and industrial development strategies. Its purpose is to develop Singapore into a global city with total business capabilities by attracting foreign investments and developing local enterprise as well as promoting outward investments into the region. Under its Industry 21 plan, EDB's focus will be on developing Singapore into a global hub of knowledge-driven industries.

Currency. The unit of currency is the *Singapore dollar* (SGD) of 100 *cents*. Total money supply in June 2002 was S$34,888m. There was inflation in 2001 of 1·0%. Total foreign reserves at June 2002 were S$79,668m.

Budget. The fiscal year begins on 1 April. Budgetary central government revenue and expenditure for financial years (in S$1m.):

	1998	1999	2000	2001
Revenue	28,212·5	28,619·2	33,526·6	30,885·1
Expenditure	24,793·4	24,946·7	28,014·5	27,844·1

Singapore has the largest current account surplus of any country in relation to the size of its economy, standing at S$36·4bn. in 1999, representing 24% of GNP.

Performance. Real GDP growth was only 1·5% in 1998 but increased to 5·4% in 1999 following the recovery from the Asian financial crisis. It then rose by 9·9% in 2000, but there followed a recession, with the economy contracting by 2·0% in 2001. Total GDP was US$92·3bn. in 2000. Singapore was placed fourth in the world in the Growth Competitiveness Index Ranking in the World Economic Forum's *Global Competitiveness Report 2002–03*. It had been first in 1999. In the 2002 *World Competitiveness Yearbook*, compiled by the International Institute for Management Development, Singapore came fifth in the world ranking, down from second in 2001.

Banking and Finance. The Monetary Authority of Singapore (*Governor*, Lee Hsien Loong) performs the functions of a central bank, except the issuing of currency which is the responsibility of the Board of the Commissioners of Currency.

The Development Bank of Singapore and the Post Office Savings Bank were merged in 1998 to become the largest bank in South-East Asia and one of the leading banks in Asia, with a customer base of more that 3·3m. and a total deposit base of about S$71bn. Together, their total asset value is approximately S$106·5bn.

At the end of 2001 there were 128 commercial banks in Singapore, of which eight were local. The total assets/liabilities amounted to S$384,600m. in Dec. 2001. Total deposits of non-bank customers in Dec. 1999 amounted to S$174,454·1m. and advances including bills financing totalled S$147,185·5m. in 1999. There were 66 merchant banks as at 31 Dec. 1999.

The Singapore Exchange (SGX), a merger of the Stock Exchange of Singapore and the Singapore International Monetary Exchange, was officially launched on 1 Dec. 1999. By the end of 1999, SGX had 335 mainboard companies with a market capitalization of S$462·5bn., 81 SESDAQ (Stock Exchange of Dealing and Automated Quotation) companies with a market capitalization of S$8·42bn., 12 futures contracts and 7 options contracts listed for derivatives trading. Total trading volume on SGX Derivatives Trading for 1999 amounted to 25·86m. lots. The average daily turnover was 101,502 lots.

Weights and Measures. The metric system is in use.

ENERGY AND NATURAL RESOURCES

Environment. Singapore's carbon dioxide emissions in 1998 were the equivalent of 21·0 tonnes per capita according to the *World Bank Atlas*.

Electricity. In 1995 Singapore Power Pte. Ltd. took over from the Public Utilities Board the responsibility for the provision of electricity and gas. Electrical power is generated by five gas and oil-fired power stations, with a total generating capacity of 7,657m. kW (2001). Production (2001) 33,061m. kWh. Consumption per capita (2000) 8,800 kWh.

Oil and Gas. Replacing the Kallang Gasworks, the Senoko Gasworks started operations in Oct. 1996. It had a total gas production capacity of 1·6m. cu. metres per day. In Jan. 2001 a 640-km gas pipeline linking Indonesia's West Natuna field with Singapore came on stream. It is expected to provide Singapore with US$8bn. worth of natural gas over a 20-year period.

Water. Singapore uses an average of 1·25m. cu. metres of water per day. Singapore's water supply comes from local sources and sources in Johor, Malaysia. The total water supply system comprises 19 raw water reservoirs, 9 treatment works, 15 storage or service reservoirs and 5,150 km of pipelines.

Agriculture. Only about 1·49% of the total area is used for farming. Local farms provide only about 35% of hen eggs, 1·6% of chickens and 2·4% of ducks. 18,928 tonnes of vegetables and fruits were produced for domestic consumption in 1999. In 2001 alone Singapore imported 44·1m. chickens, 7m. ducks, 722m. hen eggs, 210,077 tonnes of meat and meat products, 226,126 tonnes of fish and fish products, 352,919 tonnes of vegetables and 358,595 tonnes of fruits for local consumption.

Agro-technology parks house large-scale intensive farms to improve production of fresh food. As of the end of 2000, a total of 1,465 ha of land in Murai, Sungei Tengah, Nee Soon, Loyang, Mandai and Lim Chu Kang had been developed into

Agro-technology Parks. Through open tenders, auctions and direct allocations, 247 farms have been allocated 777 ha of land for the production of livestock, eggs, milk, aquarium fish, food fish (fish for consumption), fruits, vegetables, orchids and ornamental and aquatic plants, as well as for the breeding of birds and dogs. When the Agro-technology Parks are fully developed, their output is expected to reach S$450m.

Forestry. In 1999 forests covered 2,860 ha, or 4·3% of the total land area.

Fisheries. The total local supply of fish in 1999 was 9,477 tonnes. Singapore imported 241,000 tonnes of fish and fish products. There are 93 fish processing establishments supplying products for the domestic market, 9 establishments for the EU export market and 88 licensed marine farms.

INDUSTRY
According to the Financial Times Survey (FT 500), the largest companies in Singapore by market capitalization on 28 March 2002 were Singapore Tele-communications (US$15,371·3m.), the United Overseas Bank (US$12,953·8m.) and the DBS Group (US$11,615·8m.).

The largest industrial area is at Jurong, with 35 modern industrial estates housing over 4,036 establishments (engaging ten people or more) in 1999, and 340,907 workers.

Production, 1999 (in S$1m.), totalled 134,533: including electronic products, 70,140·4; chemicals and chemical products, 13,684·1; petroleum, 13,621·6; fabricated metal products, 6,253·9; transport equipment, 5,772·8; food, beverages and tobacco, 3,407·2; publishing, printing and reproduction of recorded media, 2,997·0.

Labour. In 2001 Singapore's labour force comprised 2,119,700 people, of whom 72,900 were unemployed. The majority were employed in community, social and personal services, (436,300 in 1999); manufacturing, 395,600; wholesale and retail trade, 278,900; transport, storage and communications, 203,700; business and real estate, 196,800. In 1998, 25% of the active workforce were foreign workers, up from 12% in 1992. The economic crisis, which started in late 1997, saw a net job loss of approximately 23,400 in 1998. However, in 1999 total employment registered a positive gain of 41,900, which occurred in all major sectors, including the service industries (55,400) and manufacturing (4,600), except for the construction sector which lost 18,300. The unemployment rate averaged 3·3% throughout 2001, compared to the 9-year steady of 2% from 1988–97.

Legislation regulates the principal terms and conditions of employment such as hours of work, sick leave and other fringe benefits. Young people of 14–16 years may work in industrial establishments, and children of 12–14 years may be employed in approved apprenticeship schemes. A trade dispute may be referred to the Industrial Arbitration Court.

The Ministry of Manpower operates an employment service and provides the handicapped with specialized on-the-job training. The Central Provident Fund was established in 1955 to make provision for employees in their old age. At the end of 1999 there were 2,828,000 members with S$88,397m. standing to their credit in the fund. The legal retirement age is 62.

Trade Unions. In 2001 there were 71 registered employee trade unions, 3 employer unions and 1 federation of trade unions—the National Trades Union Congress (NTUC). The total membership of the trade unions increased from 272,769 in 1998 to 338,311 in 2001. The vast majority (99%) of the total union membership belonged to the 69 NTUC-affiliated unions. The largest union, the United Workers of Electronic Industries (UWEEI), had 39,508 members in 2000.

INTERNATIONAL TRADE
Foreign investment of up to 40% of the equity of domestic banks is permitted. Total external trade in 2001 was S$425·7bn.

Imports and Exports. In 2000 exports reached over 150% of GDP, with exports to Malaysia worth around 27% of GDP.

Imports and exports (in S$1m.), by country, 1999:

	Imports (c.i.f.)	Exports (f.o.b.)
Australia	2,464	5,373
China	9,649	6,643
France	4,397	3,709
Germany	6,111	5,522
Hong Kong	5,400	14,915
Italy	2,026	734
Japan	31,325	14,421
Korea (South)	7,063	6,027
Malaysia	29,283	32,164
Saudi Arabia	5,536	547
Taiwan	7,540	9,477
Thailand	8,889	8,536
UK	4,623	7,247
USA	32,044	37,215

The major export markets for 2000 were Malaysia (18%), USA (17%), European Union (13%), Hong Kong (8%) and Japan (7%). Total imports declined from S$232,175m. in 2000 to S$207,692m. in 2001. Exports also declined, from S$237,826m. in 2000 to S$218,026m. in 2001.

Exports (1999, in S$1m.): machinery and transport equipment, 128,807; mineral fuels, 15,335; chemicals and chemical products, 15,326; manufactured goods, 8,445; food, beverages and tobacco, 4,934; crude materials, 1,562; animal and vegetable oils, 483; miscellaneous manufactured articles, 16,414; miscellaneous transactions necessary, 2,984.

Imports (1999, in S$1m.): machinery and transport equipment, 113,365; mineral fuels, 17,075; manufactured goods, 14,973; chemicals and chemical products, 11,212; food, beverages and tobacco, 6,948; crude materials, 1,471; animal and vegetable oils, 504; miscellaneous manufactured articles, 19,575; miscellaneous transactions necessary, 3,019.

Trade Fairs. Singapore ranked as the world's 5th most important convention city in 2001, and the leading convention city in Asia, according to the Union des Associations Internationales (UAI). In 1999 Singapore hosted 140 meetings recognized by UAI, 2,314 incentive groups, 880 conventions and CommunicAsia, Asia Pacific's largest communications and IT event. The number of conferences with more than 1,000 delegates had doubled in 2000 over the previous year to ten.

COMMUNICATIONS

Roads. In 2000 there were 3,122 km of public roads, of which 3,090 km are asphalt-paved. Singapore has one of the densest road networks in the world. In 2001 there were 405,354 private cars, 12,624 buses, 130,910 motorcycles and scooters, 18,798 taxis and 127,273 goods and other vehicles.

Rail. A 25·8-km main line runs through Singapore, connecting with the States of Malaysia and as far as Bangkok. Branch lines serve the port of Singapore and the industrial estates at Jurong. The total rail length of Mass Rapid Transit metro is 85 km. Work began on the 20 km North-East Line in 1998, which was expected to become operational in the first half of 2003. In late 1999 the light Rapid Transit System (LRT) began operations, linking the Bukit Panjang Estate with Choa Chu Kang in the North West region.

Civil Aviation. As of Dec. 2001 Singapore Changi Airport was served by 61 airlines with more than 3,200 weekly flights to and from 138 cities in 50 countries. The national airline is Singapore Airlines, which in 1999 carried 14,527,200 passengers and flew 313·6m. km. Its subsidiary, Silk Air, serves Asian destinations. A total of 28,093,759 passengers were handled in 2001, and 1,507,062 tonnes of freight.

Shipping. Singapore has a large container port, the world's busiest in terms of shipping tonnage in 2001 and second only to Hong Kong in terms of containers handled. The economy is dependent on shipping and entrepôt trade. A total of 146,265 vessels of 960m. gross tonnes (GT) entered Singapore during 2001. In 2001, 3,353 vessels with a total of 23·2m. GT were registered in Singapore. The Singapore merchant fleet ranked 7th among the principal merchant fleets of the world in 2001. Total cargo handled in 2000 was 326·11m. tonnes, and total container throughput in 2001 was 15,570,000 TEUs (twenty-foot equivalent units), ranking Singapore second behind Hong Kong on container traffic.

Telecommunications. In Dec. 2001 there were 1,948,500 telephone lines (penetration rate of 485 per 1,000 population), 2,858,800 mobile phone subscribers and 481,600 pager subscribers. In 1997 Singapore Telecom, one of the largest companies in Asia, lost its monopoly with the entry of a new mobile phone operator and three new paging operators. Singapore had three mobile phone operators, six Internet service providers, and three paging operators as of Feb. 2001. In April 2002 there were 2·31m. Internet users, or 51·84% of the population. In Aug. 2000, 42% of households were Internet subscribers. The Telecommunication Authority of Singapore (TAS) is the national regulator and promoter of the telecommunication and postal industries. As of Nov. 1999 PC penetration in homes had reached 59% of the population. In 2000 there were 1·9m. PCs or 483·1 per 1,000 inhabitants.

Postal Services. In 1999 there were various postal outlets in operation, comprising 62 main branches and 90 smaller branches. Various services included stamp vendors, postage label vending machines and Self-Service Automated Machines (SAM). A total of 1,487m. postal articles were handled in 1999. During the late 1990s mail volume increased by about 30m. items per year.

SOCIAL INSTITUTIONS

Justice. There is a Supreme Court in Singapore which consists of the High Court and the Court of Appeal. The Supreme Court is composed of a Chief Justice and 11 Judges. The High Court has unlimited original jurisdiction in both civil and criminal cases. The Court of Appeal is the final appellate court. It hears appeals from any judgement or order of the High Court in any civil matter. The Subordinate Courts consist of a total of 47 District and Magistrates' Courts, the Civil, the Family and Crime Registries, the Primary Dispute Resolution Centre, and the Small Claims Tribunal. The right of appeal to the UK Privy Council was abolished in 1994.

Penalties for drug trafficking and abuse are severe, including a mandatory death penalty. In 1994 there were 76 executions, although since then the average annual number has been declining—there were 30 in 1999 and 7 in 2002.

The Technology Court was introduced in 1995 where documents were filed electronically. This process was implemented in Aug. 1998 in the Magistrates appeal and the Court of Appeal.

The population in penal institutions in 1997 was 15,746 (465 per 100,000 of national population).

Religion. In 2000, 51% of the population aged 15 years and above were Buddhists and Taoists, 14·9% Muslims, 14·6% Christians and 4·0% Hindus; 0·6% belonged to other religions.

Education. The general literacy rate rose from 84% in 1980 to 93% in 2000. Kindergartens are private and fee-paying. Compulsory primary state education starts at 6 years and culminates at 11 or 12 years with an examination which influences choice of secondary schooling. There are 17 autonomous and 8 private fee-paying secondary schools. Tertiary education at 16 years is divided into 3 branches: junior colleges leading to university; 4 polytechnics; and 10 technical institutes.

Statistics of schools in 2001.

	Schools	Pupils	Teachers
Primary schools	194	302,733	12,011
Secondary schools	162	187,858	9,491
Junior colleges and Centralized institutes	17	24,582	1,869

There are three universities: the National University of Singapore (established 1905) with 32,028 students in 2001–02, the Nanyang Technological University (established 1991) with 23,025 in 2001–02, and the Singapore Management University (established in 2000).

In 2000 total expenditure on education came to 4% of the GNP and accounted for 20·5% of total government expenditure.

Health. There are 27 hospitals (5 general hospitals, 1 community hospital, 7 specialist hospitals/centres and 14 private) with 11,897 beds in 2001. In 2000 there were 5,577 doctors, 1,028 dentists, 16,611 registered nurses and midwives and 1,098 pharmacists.

The leading causes of death are cancer (4,238 deaths in 2000), heart disease (3,940) and pneumonia (1,794).

Welfare. The Central Provident Fund (CPF) was set up in 1955 to provide financial security for workers upon retirement or when they are no longer able to work. In 2001 there were 2,922,673 members with S$92,221m. standing to their credit in the Fund.

CULTURE

The National Arts Council (NAC) was established in 1991 to spearhead the development of the arts.

Broadcasting. The Television Corporation of Singapore broadcasts mainly English and Chinese programmes. Malay and Tamil programmes are offered on Suria and Central, two channels launched in Jan. 2000. A sports only channel, Sportscity, was also launched in Jan. 2000. Colour is by PAL. There were 816,000 TV licences in 2001 and 2·55m. radio receivers in 1997. Cable subscribers numbered 302,000 in 2001.

Cinema. In 2001 there were 131 cinemas with a total seating capacity of 39,000. The total number of admissions was 13·6m.

Press. In 2001 there were 10 daily newspapers, in four languages, with a total daily circulation of about 1·59m. copies. In 2001 a new newspaper, *Project Eyeball*, and two free commuter tabloids, *Streats* and *Today,* were launched.

Tourism. There were 7,522,200 visitors in 2001. Most came from Indonesia, Japan, Malaysia, Australia, the UK, China, the USA and Taiwan. The total tourism receipts for 2001 came to S$9·16bn. The total number of gazetted hotels increased from 94 in 1997 to 101 in 2000, providing 30,700 rooms.

Festivals. Every Jan. or Feb. the Lunar New Year is celebrated. Other Chinese festivals include Qing Ming (a time for the remembrance of ancestors), Yu Lan Jie (Feast of the Hungry Ghosts) and the Mid-Autumn Festival (Mooncake or Lantern festival).

Muslims in Singapore celebrate Hari Raya Puasa (to celebrate the end of a month-long fast) and Hari Raya Haji (a day of prayer and commemoration of the annual Mecca pilgrimage). There are also Muharram (a New Year celebration) and Maulud (Prophet Muhammad's birthday).

Hindus celebrate the Tamil New Year in mid-April. Thaipusam is a penitential Hindu festival popular with Tamils; and Deepavali, the Festival of Lights, is celebrated by Hindus and Sikhs. Other festivals include Thimithi (a fire-walking ceremony) and Navarathiri (nine nights' prayer).

Buddhists observe Vesak Day, which commemorates the birth, enlightenment and Nirvana of the Buddha, and falls on the full moon day in May.

Christmas, Good Friday and Easter Sunday are also recognized.

Libraries. The National Library Board (NLB) was inaugurated on 3 July 1996, having become a statutory board in Sept. 1995. The Board's main aim is to implement the recommendations set down in the Library 2000 Report on how libraries can meet the needs of the 21st century.

The NLB has 2 regional libraries, 18 community libraries and 45 community children's libraries. In 1999 NLB's membership numbered 1,759,996 and its service outlets held 6,087,097 books, 515,846 serials and 255,051 audio-visual and other special materials in four languages. In 2001 library loans numbered 25m.

Theatre and Opera. Some of the main theatre companies in Singapore, performing mainly in English, include TheatreWorks, The Necessary Stage and the Singapore Repertory Theatre. Other language companies include Teater Kami (Malay), The Theatre Practice (Chinese) and Ravindran Drama Group (Tamil).

Museums and Galleries. The National Heritage Board was formed on 1 Aug. 1993 through the amalgamation of the National Archives, the National Museum and the Oral History Department. The Board's National Museum arm comprises the

Singapore History Museum, the Singapore Art Museum, the Asian Civilisations Museum and the Singapore Philatelic Museum.

DIPLOMATIC REPRESENTATIVES

Of Singapore in the United Kingdom (9 Wilton Crescent, London SW1X 8SP)
High Commissioner: Michael Eng Cheng Teo.

Of the United Kingdom in Singapore (100 Tanglin Rd, Singapore 247919)
High Commissioner: Alan Collins, CMG.

Of Singapore in the USA (3501 International Pl., NW, Washington, D.C., 20008)
Ambassador: Chan Heng Chee.

Of the USA in Singapore (27 Napier Rd, Singapore 258508)
Ambassador: Franklin L. Lavin.

Of Singapore to the United Nations
Ambassador: Kishore Mahbubani.

Of Singapore to the European Union
Ambassador: Ampalavanar Selverajah.

FURTHER READING
Department of Statistics. *Monthly Digest of Statistics.—Yearbook of Statistics.*
The Constitution of Singapore. Singapore, 1992
Information Division, Ministry of Information and the Arts. *Singapore [year]: a Review of [the previous year].*
Ministry of Trade and Industry, *Economic Survey of Singapore.* (Quarterly and Annual)

Chew, E. C. T., *A History of Singapore.* Singapore, 1992
Huff, W. G., *Economic Growth of Singapore: Trade and Development in the Twentieth Century.* CUP, 1994
Myint, S., *The Principles of Singapore Law.* 2nd ed. Singapore, 1992
Tan, C. H., *Financial Markets and Institutions in Singapore.* 7th ed. Singapore, 1992
Vasil, R. K., *Governing Singapore.* Singapore, 1992

National library: National Library, Stamford Rd, Singapore 178896.
National statistical office: Department of Statistics, Minister of Trade and Industry, Singapore 068811.
Website: http://www.singstat.gov.sg/

SLOVAKIA

Slovenská Republika

Capital: Bratislava
Population estimate, 2000: 5·40m.
GDP per capita, 2000: (PPP$) 11,243
HDI/world rank: 0·835/36

KEY HISTORICAL EVENTS

The Czechoslovak State came into existence on 28 Oct. 1918 after the dissolution of Austria-Hungary. Two days later the Slovak National Council declared its wish to unite with the Czechs. The Treaty of St Germain-en-Laye (1919) recognized the Czechoslovak Republic, consisting of the Czech lands (Bohemia, Moravia, part of Silesia) and Slovakia. In March 1939 the German-sponsored Slovak government proclaimed Slovakia independent and Germany incorporated the Czech lands into the Reich as the 'Protectorate of Bohemia and Moravia'. A government-in-exile, headed by Dr Edvard Beneš, was set up in London. Liberation by the Soviet Army and US Forces was completed by May 1945. Territories taken by the Germans, Poles and Hungarians were restored to Czechoslovak sovereignty. Elections were held in May 1946 following which a coalition government under a Communist Prime Minister, Klement Gottwald, remained in power until 20 Feb. 1948, when 12 of the non-Communist ministers resigned in protest against infiltration of Communists into the police. In Feb. a predominantly Communist government was formed by Gottwald. In May 1948 elections resulted in an 89% majority for the government and President Beneš resigned.

In 1968 pressure for liberalization culminated in the overthrow of the Stalinist leader, Antonín Novotný, and his associates. Under Alexander Dubček's leadership the 'Prague Spring' began to take shape and the outlines of a new political system described as 'socialism with a human face' began to appear as the Communist Party introduced an 'Action Programme' of far-reaching reforms. Soviet pressure to abandon this programme was exerted between May and Aug. 1968 and finally Warsaw Pact forces occupied Czechoslovakia on 21 Aug. The Czechoslovak government was compelled to accept a policy of 'normalization' (*i.e.*, abandonment of most reforms) and the stationing of Soviet forces.

Mass demonstrations demanding political reform began in Nov. 1989. After the authorities' use of violence to break up a demonstration on 17 Nov., the Communist leader resigned. On 30 Nov. the Federal Assembly abolished the Communist Party's sole right to govern, and a new Government was formed on 3 Dec. The protest movement continued to grow and on 10 Dec. another Government was formed. Gustáv Husák resigned as President and was replaced by Václav Havel on the unanimous vote of 323 members of the Federal Assembly on 29 Dec.

At the June 1992 elections the Movement for Democratic Slovakia led by Vladimír Mečiar campaigned on the issue of Slovak independence, and on 17 July the Slovak National Council adopted a declaration of sovereignty by 113 to 24 votes. President Havel resigned as Federal president on 20 July. On 1 Sept. 1992 the Slovak National Council adopted, by 114 votes to 16 with 4 abstentions (and a boycott by the Hungarian deputies), a Constitution for an independent Slovakia to come into being on 1 Jan. 1993. Economic property was divided between Slovakia and the Czech Republic in accordance with a Czechoslovakian law of 13 Nov. 1992. Government real estate became the property of the republic in which it was located. Other property was divided by specially-constituted commissions in the proportion of two (Czech Republic) to one (Slovakia) on the basis of population size. Military material was divided on the two:one principle. Regular military personnel were invited to choose which armed force they would serve in.

In Oct. 2002 Slovakia was one of ten countries included in plans for EU enlargement scheduled for 2004, and one of seven invited to join NATO in the same year.

TERRITORY AND POPULATION

Slovakia is bounded in the northwest by the Czech Republic, north by Poland, east by Ukraine, south by Hungary and southwest by Austria. Its area is 49,039 sq. km.

Census population in 2001 was 5,379,455 (2,612,515 male, 2,766,940 female); density, 109·7 per sq. km.

The UN gives a projected population for 2010 of 5·43m.

In 1999, 57·3% of the population lived in urban areas. There are eight administrative regions *(Kraj)*, one of which is the capital, Bratislava. They have the same name as the main city of the region.

Region	Area in sq. km	2001 population
Banská Bystrica	9,455	662,121
Bratislava	2,053	599,015
Košice	6,753	766,012
Nitra	6,343	713,422
Prešov	8,993	789,968
Trenčin	4,501	605,582
Trnava	4,148	551,003
Žilina	6,788	692,332

The capital, Bratislava, had a population in 1999 of 460,000. The population of other principal towns (1997, in 1,000): Košice, 242; Prešov, 93; Nitra, 88; Žilina, 87; Banská Bystrica, 85; Trnava, 70; Trenčin, 61; Martin, 59.

The population is 85·8% Slovak, 9·7% Hungarian, 1·6% Roma and 0·8% Czech, with some Ruthenians, Ukrainians, Germans and Poles.

A law of Nov. 1995 makes Slovak the sole official language.

SOCIAL STATISTICS

Births, 2000, 55,151; deaths, 52,724; marriages, 25,903; divorces, 9,273. Rates (per 1,000 population), 2000: birth, 10·2; death, 9·8; marriage, 4·8; divorce, 1·7. Expectation of life, 2000, was 68 years for males and 77 for females. In 1995 the most popular age range for marrying was 20–24 for both males and females. Annual population growth rate, 1990–99, 0·3%. Infant mortality, 1999 (per 1,000 live births), 9. Fertility rate, 1999, 1·4 births per woman.

CLIMATE

A humid continental climate, with warm summers and cold winters. Precipitation is generally greater in summer, with thunderstorms. Autumn, with dry, clear weather and spring, which is damp, are each of short duration. Bratislava, Jan. –0·7°C. June 19·1°C. Annual rainfall 649 mm.

CONSTITUTION AND GOVERNMENT

Parliament is the *National Council*. It has 150 members elected by proportional representation.

There is a *Constitutional Court* whose judges are normally nominated by the President.

Citizenship belongs to all citizens of the former federal Slovak Republic; other residents of five years standing may apply for citizenship. Slovakia grants dual citizenship.

National Anthem. 'Nad Tatrou sa blýska' ('Over the Tatras lightning flashes'); words by J. Matuška, tune anonymous.

RECENT ELECTIONS

Elections to the National Council were held on 20 and 21 Sept. 2002. Former prime minister Vladimír Mečiar's Movement for a Democratic Slovakia (HZDS) won 36 seats with 19·5% of votes cast against the Slovak Democratic and Christian Union (SDKU) who won 28 seats with 15·1%; the Direction Party (Smer), 25 with 13·5%; the Party of the Hungarian Coalition (SMK), 20 with 11·2%; the Christian Democratic Movement (KDH), 15 with 8·3%; the New Civic Alliance (ANO), 15 with 8·0%; and the Slovak Communist Party (KSS), 11 with 6·3%. Turn-out was 70·0%.

In the first round of presidential elections, the government's candidate Rudolf Schuster won 47·4% of the votes cast on 15 May 1999 against former prime minister Vladimír Mečiar, who received 37·2%, and four other candidates. Turn-out was 73·9%. In the run-off held on 29 May Schuster gained 57·2% of the votes, compared to 42·8% for Mečiar. In becoming the country's first president to be directly elected by the people, his victory brought to an end a period of 15 months during which there was not a head of state.

CURRENT ADMINISTRATION
President: Rudolf Schuster; b. 1934 (ind.; sworn in on 15 June 1999).

A coalition government was appointed on 15 Oct. 2002 composed of members of the Slovak Democratic and Christian Union (SDKU), the Party of the Hungarian Coalition (SMK), the Christian Democratic Movement (KDH) and the New Civic Alliance (ANO). In March 2003 the cabinet was composed as follows:

Prime Minister: Mikuláš Dzurinda; b. 1955 (SDKU; sworn in 30 Oct. 1998; re-appointed 15 Oct. 2002).

Deputy Prime Ministers: Daniel Lipšic (KDH; also *Minister of Justice*); Ivan Mikloš (SDKU; also *Minister of Finance*); Pál Csáky (SMK; also *Minister of European Integration, Human Rights and Minorities*); Robert Nemcsics (ANO; also *Minister of Economy and the Administration and Privatization of State Property*).

Minister of Foreign Affairs: Eduard Kukan (SDKU). *Interior:* Vladimír Palko (KDH). *Defence:* Ivan Šimko (SDKU). *Culture:* Rudolf Chmel (ANO). *Health Care:* Rudolf Zajac (ANO). *Education:* Martin Fronc (KDH). *Labour, Social Affairs and Family Affairs:* Ludovít Kaník (SDKU). *Environment:* László Miklós (SMK). *Agriculture:* Zsolt Simon (SMK). *Transport, Post and Telecommunications:* Pavol Prokopovič (SDKU). *Construction and Public Works:* László Gyurovszky (SMK).

The *Speaker* is Jozef Migas.

Office of the Prime Minister: http://www.government.gov.sk/

DEFENCE
Conscription is for 12 months. In 2000 military expenditure totalled US$340m. (US$63 per capita), representing 1·8% of GDP.

Army. Personnel (1999), 23,800 (including 13,600 conscripts). In addition there are an internal security force of 1,400 and 1,200 civil defence troops.

Air Force. There are 102 combat aircraft, including Su-22, Su-25, MiG-21 and MiG-29 fighters and 19 attack helicopters. Personnel (1999), 12,000.

INTERNATIONAL RELATIONS
Slovakia is a member of the UN, WTO, BIS, NATO Partnership for Peace, Council of Europe, OSCE, OECD, CEFTA, CERN, CEI, Danube Commission, IOM and an associate partner of the WEU. An application to join the EU was made in June 1995. A referendum on whether Slovakia should apply to join NATO took place on 23–24 May 1997. Turn-out was 9·8% and the results were declared invalid. 55% of votes cast were against participation. Following the Sept. 1998 general election interest in joining NATO increased and Slovakia was added to the list of aspirant members. At the European Union's Helsinki Summit in Dec. 1999 Slovakia, along with five other countries, was invited to begin full negotiations for membership in Feb. 2000, and is scheduled to become a member on 1 May 2004.

Slovakia has had a long-standing dispute with Hungary over the Gabčíkovo-Nagymaros Project, involving the building of dam structures in both countries for the production of electric power, flood control and improvement of navigation on the Danube as agreed in a treaty signed in 1977 between Czechoslovakia and Hungary. In late 1998 Slovakia and Hungary signed a protocol easing tensions between the two nations and settling differences over the dam.

ECONOMY
Agriculture accounted for 4·4% of GDP in 1998, industry 31·6% and services 64·0%.

Overview. New economic policy in 1998 had the key aims of the substantial reduction of the fiscal deficit, an increase in regulated prices towards international levels and the acceleration of the restructuring of state-owned banks and enterprises. Following Rudolf Schuster's victory in the presidential election in May 1999 hopes were high that Slovakia would begin accession negotiations with the European Union. By mid-1999 approximately 85% of the economy was in private hands, but although 1,000 sell-offs of state assets had been approved over the previous four years, only three had been bought by foreign investors.

Legislation of July 1995 ended privatization by vouchers, which became exchangeable instead against state securities. At the end of 1995 the private sector share of total GDP reached 64·9%.

Currency. The unit of currency is the *Slovak koruna* or crown (SKK) of 100 *haliers*, introduced on 8 Feb. 1993. The koruna was revalued 4% in May 1995. Foreign exchange reserves were US$4,420m. and gold reserves 1·13m. troy oz in June 2002. Inflation was 6·5% in 2001. Total money supply in Dec. 2001 was 225,566m. koruny.

Budget. Government revenue and expenditure (in 1m. koruny):

	1996	1997	1998	1999	2000
Revenue	239,659	252,953	261,492	301,349	307,596
Expenditure	251,963	277,834	293,421	303,360	350,601

VAT, personal and company income tax, real estate taxes and inheritance taxes came into force in Jan. 1993. VAT is 23%, with a reduced rate of 10%.

Performance. In 1998 real GDP growth was 4·1%, but then just 1·9% in 1999. In 2000 the rate was 2·2%, rising to 3·3% in 2001. Slovakia's total GDP in 2001 was US$20·5bn.

Banking and Finance. The central bank and bank of issue is the Slovak National Bank, founded in 1993 (*Governor*, Marian Jusko). It has an autonomous statute modelled on the German Bundesbank, with the duties of maintaining control over monetary policy and inflation, ensuring the stability of the currency, and supervising commercial banks. However, it is now proposed to amend the central bank law to allow the government to appoint half the members of the board and force the bank to increase its financing of the budget deficit.

In Oct. 1998 the Slovak National Bank abandoned its fixed exchange rate system, whereby the crown's value was fixed within a fluctuation band against a number of currencies, and chose to float the currency.

Decentralization of the banking system began in 1991, and private banks began to operate. The two largest Slovak banks were both privatized in 2001. Erste BankÖsterreich bought an 87·18% stake in Slovenská Sporiteľňa (Slovak Savings Bank) and the Italian bank IntesaBci bought a 94·47% stake in Všeobecná úverová banka (General Credit Bank). In 2000 Slovenská Sporiteľňa had assets of US$3·3bn. and Všeobecná úverová banka US$2·8bn.

Foreign direct investment in Slovakia in 2000 totalled US$1,986·9m., more than the total amount in the previous seven years of the country's existence.

There is a stock exchange in Bratislava.

Weights and Measures. The metric system is in force.

ENERGY AND NATURAL RESOURCES

Environment. According to the *World Bank Atlas* Slovakia's carbon dioxide emissions in 1998 were the equivalent of 7·1 tonnes per capita.

Electricity. Installed capacity in 2002 was 7·4m. kW, of which 2·3m. kW is hydro-electric and 2·2m. kW nuclear. Production in 1998 was 20·04bn. kWh, with consumption per capita 3,899 kWh. There were six nuclear reactors in use in 2001. In 2001 about 53% of electricity was nuclear-generated.

Oil and Gas. In 1998 natural gas reserves were 15bn. cu. metres and oil reserves 9·0m. bbls. The government plans to sell a 49% stake in Slovensky Plynárensky Priemysel (SPP), the monopoly state enterprise in the Slovak gas industry. Slovakia is a net energy importer, relying heavily on Russia for its oil and gas.

Minerals. In 1997, 3·92m. tonnes of lignite were produced; and in 1994, 1·04m. tonnes of hard coal. 820,000 tonnes of iron ore were extracted in 1995. There are also reserves of copper, lead, zinc, limestone, dolomite, rock salt and others.

Agriculture. In 1998 there were 1·48m. ha of arable land and 127,000 ha of permanent crops. In 1998 agriculture employed 6·4% of the workforce.

A federal law of May 1991 returned land seized by the Communist regime to its original owners, to a maximum of 150 ha of arable to a single owner.

Production, 2000 (in 1,000 tonnes): wheat, 1,254; sugarbeets, 961; maize, 440; potatoes, 419; barley, 397; rapeseed, 134; sunflower seeds, 117; cabbages, 99; apples, 81; tomatoes, 73; rye, 64; grapes, 61.

Livestock, 2000: cattle, 665,000; pigs, 1·56m.; sheep, 340,000; chickens, 12m. Livestock products, 2000 (in 1,000 tonnes): meat, 303; milk, 1,116; eggs, 65; cheese, 54.

Forestry. The area under forests in 1995 was 1·99m. ha, or 41·4% of the total land area. In 1999 timber production was 5·78m. cu. metres.

Fisheries. In 1999 the total catch was 1,391 tonnes, exclusively freshwater fish.

INDUSTRY
In Czechoslovakia Slovakia was less industrialized than the Czech Republic, though there are concentrations of heavy engineering and munitions plants. Consumer industries include textiles and footwear. 1997 output included (in 1m. tonnes): crude steel, 3·87; pig iron, 3·07; cement (1995), 2·98; coke (1995), 1·85; plastic materials (1995), 0·45.

Labour. Out of 2,147,000 people in employment in 1995, 575,000 were in manufacturing, 222,000 in wholesale and retail trade and 197,000 in agriculture, fishing and forestry. The average monthly salary in 2001 was 12,365 koruny. In Oct. 2002 the monthly minimum wage was increased to 5,570 koruny. Unemployment was 18·6% in 2002.

INTERNATIONAL TRADE
A memorandum envisaging a customs union and close economic co-operation was signed with the Czech Republic in Oct. 1992. An agreement of Dec. 1992 with the Czech Republic, Hungary and Poland abolishes tariffs on raw materials and goods where exports do not compete directly with locally-produced items, and envisaged tariff reductions on agricultural and industrial goods in 1995–97.

Tax holidays of up to seven years are available to foreign investors.

Foreign debt was US$9,462m. in 2000.

Imports and Exports. Imports and exports in US$1bn.:

	1997	1998	1999	2000	2001
Imports f.o.b.	11·7	13·1	11·3	12·8	14·8
Exports f.o.b.	8·8	10·7	10·2	11·9	12·6

In 2000 the leading export markets were: Germany, 27%; Czech Republic, 15%; Italy, 9%; Austria, 8%; Poland, 6%; France, 5%; Hungary, 5%; and Netherlands 3%. Principal import sources in 2000 were: Germany, 27%; Russia, 18%; Czech Republic, 15%; Italy, 6%; Austria, 4%; Poland, 4%; and France, 3%.

COMMUNICATIONS

Roads. In 2000 there were 17,520 km of roads. In 1998 there were 1,196,109 passenger cars, 154,771 trucks and lorries, 11,293 buses and coaches and 100,891 motorcycles and mopeds.

Rail. In 2000 the length of railway routes was 3,665 km. In 1995 approximately 40% of the railways were electrified. Most of the network is 1,435 mm gauge with short sections on three other gauges. Passenger-km travelled in 1998 came to 3,092m. and freight tonne-km to 11,754m. There are tram/light rail networks in Bratislava and Košice.

Civil Aviation. The main international airport is at Bratislava (M. R. Stefánik), with some international flights from Košice. There are three Slovakia-based airlines. In 1998 Air Slovakia had flights to Kuwait and Tel Aviv, Slovak Airlines operated domestic services and flew to Moscow, and Tatra Air operated domestic services and had flights to Zürich. In 2000 Bratislava handled 278,654 passengers (264,470 on international flights) and 2,608 tonnes of freight.

Shipping. Merchant shipping in 1998 totalled 15,000 GRT and vessels totalling 381,000 NRT entered ports.

Telecommunications. There were 1,698,000 telephone main lines in 2000, or 314·2 per 1,000 persons, and 740,000 PCs in use (136·9 per 1,000 persons). In 2000 Deutsche Telekom bought a 51% stake in the state-owned Slovakia Telecom. There were 918,000 mobile phone subscribers in 1999 and 56,000 fax machines in 1997. Slovakia had around 700,000 Internet users in Dec. 1999.

Postal Services. In 1995 there were 1,617 post offices.

SOCIAL INSTITUTIONS

Justice. The post-Communist judicial system was established by a federal law of July 1991. This provided for a unified system of four types of court: civil, criminal, commercial and administrative. Commercial courts arbitrate in disputes arising from business activities. Administrative courts examine the legality of the decisions of state institutions when appealed by citizens. In addition, there are military courts which operate under the jurisdiction of the Ministry of Defence. There is a Supreme Court, and a hierarchy of courts under the Ministry of Justice at republic, region and district level. District courts are courts of first instance. Cases are usually decided by senates comprising a judge and two associate judges, although occasionally by a single judge. (Associate judges are citizens in good standing over the age of 25 who are elected for four-year terms). Regional courts are courts of first instance in more serious cases and also courts of appeal for district courts. Cases are usually decided by a senate of two judges and three associate judges, although again occasionally by a single judge. The Supreme Court interprets law as a guide to other courts and functions also as a court of appeal. Decisions are made by senates of three judges. The judges of the Supreme Court are nominated by the President; other judges are appointed by the National Council.

The population in penal institutions in Jan. 1998 was 7,511 (140 per 100,000 of national population).

Religion. A federal Czechoslovakian law of July 1991 provides the basis for church-state relations and guarantees the religious and civic rights of citizens and churches. Churches must register to become legal entities but operate independently of the state. A law of 1993 restored confiscated property to churches and religious communities unless it had passed into private hands, co-operative farms or trading companies. An estimated 68·9% of the population are Roman Catholic, 6·9% members of the Evangelical Church of the Augsburg Confession, 4·1% Greek Catholic and 2·0% Calvinist.

Education. In 1996–97 there were 3,396 pre-school institutions with 170,138 children and 15,633 teachers. In 1995–96 there were 2,485 primary schools with 661,082 pupils and 39,224 teachers, 190 grammar schools with 76,380 students and 5,457 teachers, and 364 vocational schools with 119,853 pupils and 9,558 teachers. There were 357 secondary vocational apprentice training centres with 139,688 pupils and 6,056 teachers; and 400 special schools with 29,914 children and 3,862 teachers. There were 14 universities or university-type institutions with 74,322 students.

In 1996 total expenditure on education came to 5·0% of GNP. The adult literacy rate in 1999 was at least 99%.

Health. In 1995 there were 14,447 doctors. Population per doctor: 371. There were 62,634 beds in health establishments in total, of which 41,727 were in hospitals.

CULTURE

Broadcasting. Broadcasting is the responsibility of the government-controlled Slovak Broadcasting Council. The state-run Slovak Radio broadcasts on four wavelengths, and there are 12 private regional stations. Slovak Television is a public corporation. It transmits on two channels (colour by PAL), the second being shared with a commercial station. There are several independent local TV stations, and two cable networks. Number of sets: TV (1997), 2·16m.; radio (1997), 3·12m.

Cinema. There were 472 cinemas in 1995. 57 films were completed in 1995, of which four were full-length feature films. Gross box office receipts came to Sk152m.

Press. Slovakia had 20 daily newspapers in 1996 with 989,000 readers. In 1996 a total of 3,800 book titles were published in 6·14m. copies.

Tourism. In 1999 there were 975,000 foreign tourists, spending US$461m. Tourism is not highly developed, and only contributes some 2% towards Slovakia's GDP.

Festivals. The Bratislava Rock Festival takes place in June and the Bratislava Music Festival and Interpodium is in Oct. The Myjava Folklore Festival is held each June, the Zvolen Castle Games in June–July, Theatrical Nitra is in Sept., and there is an annual Spring Music Festival in Košice.

Libraries. In 1997 there were 2,630 public libraries, 1 National library and 524 Higher Education libraries; they held a combined 29,944,000 volumes. There were 923,000 registered library users in 1997.

Museums and Galleries. The Slovak National Museum and the Slovak National Gallery are both in Bratislava. The Slovak National Uprising Museum is in Banská Bystrica and the Museum of Eastern Slovakia in Košice.

DIPLOMATIC REPRESENTATIVES

Of Slovakia in the United Kingdom (25 Kensington Palace Gdns., London, W8 4QY)
Ambassador: František Dlhopolček.

Of the United Kingdom in Slovakia (Panska 16, 81101 Bratislava)
Ambassador: Ric Todd.

Of Slovakia in the USA (3523 International Court, NW, Washington, D.C., 20008)
Ambassador: Martin Butora.

Of the USA in Slovakia (4 Hviezdoslavovo Namestie, 81102 Bratislava)
Ambassador: Ronald Weiser.

Of Slovakia to the United Nations
Ambassador: Dr Peter Tomka.

Of Slovakia to the European Union
Ambassador: Juraj Migas.

FURTHER READING

Kirschbaum, S. J., *A History of Slovakia: the Struggle for Survival.* London and New York, 1995
Krejcí, Jaroslav and Machonin, Pavel, *Czechoslovakia 1918–1992: A Laboratory for Social Change.* Macmillan, London, 1996
Wheaton, B. and Kavan, Z., *Velvet Revolution: Czechoslovakia 1988–91.* Boulder (CO), 1992

National statistical office: Statistical Office of the Slovak Republic, Miletičova 3, 82467 Bratislava.
Website: http://www.statistics.sk/

SLOVENIA

Republika Slovenija

Capital: Ljubljana
Population estimate, 2000: 1·99m.
GDP per capita, 2000: (PPP$) 17,367
HDI/world rank: 0·879/29

KEY HISTORICAL EVENTS

The lands originally settled by Slovenes in the 6th century were steadily encroached upon by Germans. Slovenia developed as part of Austria-Hungary, after the defeat of the latter in the First World War becoming part of the Kingdom of the Serbs, Croats and Slovenes (Yugoslavia) on 1 Dec. 1918.

In Oct. 1989 the Slovene Assembly voted a constitutional amendment giving it the right to secede from Yugoslavia. On 2 July 1990 the Assembly adopted a 'declaration of sovereignty' and a referendum was held on 23 Dec. 1990 in which 88·5% of participants voted for independence. On 25 June 1991 Slovenia declared independence but agreed to suspend this for three months at peace talks sponsored by the EU. Federal troops moved into Slovenia on 27 June to secure Yugoslavia's external borders, but after some fighting withdrew by the end of July. After the agreed three-month moratorium Slovenia (and Croatia) declared their independence from the Yugoslav Federation on 8 Oct. 1991. In 2002 Slovenia was nominated as one of ten countries eligible for EU membership in 2004. In the same year it was invited to join NATO. At a referendum in March 2003, EU entry won 89·6% support.

TERRITORY AND POPULATION

Slovenia is bounded in the north by Austria, in the northeast by Hungary, in the southeast and south by Croatia and in the west by Italy. The length of coastline is 47 km. Its area is 20,273 sq. km. The capital is Ljubljana: June 2002 population, 253,785. Maribor (population of 95,875 in 2002) is the other major city. In 2002 the census population was 1,948,250 (provisional). Population (30 June 2002), 1,995,718 (females, 1,019,607); density per sq. km, 98·4. In 1999, 50·3% of the population lived in urban areas.

The UN gives a projected population for 2010 of 1·95m.

The official language is Slovene.

SOCIAL STATISTICS

Statistics for calendar years:

	Live births	Deaths	Growth rate per 1,000	Marriages	Divorces
1997	18,165	18,928	−0·4	7,500	1,996
1998	17,856	19,039	−0·6	7,528	2,074
1999	17,533	18,885	−0·7	7,716	2,074
2000	18,180	18,588	−0·2	7,201	2,125
2001	17,477	18,508	−0·5	6,935	2,274

Rates, 2001 (per 1,000 population): birth, 8·8; death, 9·3. Infant mortality, 2001: 4·2 (per 1,000 live births). There were 581 suicides in 2001 (31 suicides per 1,000 deaths).

In 2001 the most popular age range for marrying was 25–29 years for both males and females. Expectation of life, 2000–01, was 72·1 years for males and 79·6 for females. Annual population growth rate, 1990–2001, −0·1%. Fertility rate, 2001, 1·2 births per woman.

CLIMATE

Summers are warm, winters are cold with frequent snow. Ljubljana, Jan. −4°C, July 22°C. Annual rainfall 1,383 mm.

CONSTITUTION AND GOVERNMENT

There is a bicameral parliament consisting of a 90-member *National Assembly*, elected for four-year terms by proportional representation with a 4% threshold; and a 40-member *State Council*, elected for five-year terms by interest groups and regions. It has veto powers over the National Assembly.

National Anthem. 'Zdravljica' ('A Toast'); words by Dr France Prešeren, tune by Stanko Premrl.

RECENT ELECTIONS

Elections were held for the National Assembly on 15 Oct. 2000; turn-out was 70·3%. The Liberal Democracy of Slovenia (LDS) won 34 seats with 36·2% of votes cast; Social Democratic Party of Slovenia, 14 with 15·8%; United List of Social Democrats of Slovenia (former Communists), 11 with 12·1%; Slovene People's Party (SLS), 9 with 9·5%; New Slovenia Christian People's Party, 8 with 8·8%. Other parties gained four seats or fewer.

Presidential elections were held on 10 Nov. 2002. The turn-out was 70·8%. Prime Minister Janez Drnovšek (LDS) received 44·4% of votes cast against 30·8% for Barbara Brezigar, his nearest rival. In the run-off held on 1 Dec. 2002 Janez Drnovšek received 56·6% of votes cast against 43·4% for Barbara Brezigar.

CURRENT ADMINISTRATION

President: Janez Drnovšek; b. 1950 (LDS; sworn in 22 Dec. 2002).

In March 2003 the coalition government of LDS, United List of Social Democrats (ZLSD), Slovene People's Party (SLS) and Democratic Party of Pensioners of Slovenia (DeSUS) comprised:

Prime Minister: Anton Rop; b. 1960 (LDS; sworn in on 11 Dec. 2002).

Minister of Agriculture, Food and Forestry: Franc But (SLS). *Culture:* Andreja Rihter (ZLSD). *Defence:* Anton Grizold (LDS). *Economic Affairs:* Tea Petrin (LDS). *Education and Sport:* Slavko Gaber (LDS). *Environment and Physical Planning:* Janez Kopač (LDS). *Finance:* Dušan Mramor (ind.). *Foreign Affairs:* Dimitrij Rupel (LDS). *Health:* Dušan Keber (LDS). *Information Society:* Pavel Gantar (LDS). *Interior:* Rado Bohinc (ZLSD). *Justice:* Ivan Bizjak (SLS). *Labour, Family and Social Affairs:* Vlado Dimovski (ZLSD). *Transport and Communications:* Jakob Presečnik (SLS). *Without Portfolio Responsible for European Affairs:* Janez Potočnik (ind.). *Without Portfolio Responsible for Regional Development:* Zdenka Kovač (ind.).

Office of the Prime Minister: http://www.sigov.si/

DEFENCE

There is military service for seven months with between 10,000–12,000 conscripts annually.

In 2000 military expenditure totalled US$223m. (US$112 per capita), representing 1·2% of GDP.

Army. There are six military districts. Personnel (1999), 9,500 (4,200 conscripts) and an army reserve of 61,000. There is a paramilitary police force of 4,500 with 5,000 reserves.

Navy. There is an Army Maritime element numbering 100 personnel.

Air Force. The Army Air element numbers 120 with eight armed helicopters.

INTERNATIONAL RELATIONS

Slovenia is a member of the UN, WTO, BIS, NATO Partnership for Peace, Council of Europe, OSCE, CEFTA, CEI, the Inter-American Development Bank and IOM, and is an Associate Partner of the WEU and an Associate Member of the EU. Intensive negotiations regarding Slovenia's accession to full membership of the EU began in April 1998. Slovenia is scheduled to become a member on 1 May 2004. Slovenia held a referendum on EU membership on 23 March 2003, in which 89·6% of votes cast were in favour of accession.

ECONOMY

Agriculture, hunting and forestry accounted for 3·1% of GDP in 2001, industry 31·0% and service activities 60·1%.

Overview. Privatization is being carried out in two stages, beginning with small businesses, by transferring the capital to an investment fund to act as intermediary. 20% of the capital is to be transferred to savings banks, 10–20% to commercial banks, 20% to wage-earners and 10% to former owners. In 2001 plans for the sale of larger companies were under way.

Currency. The unit of currency is the *tolar* (SLT) of 100 *stotinas*, which replaced the Yugoslav dinar. It is based on the euro according to a floating exchange rate, and became convertible on 1 Sept. 1995. Inflation was 8·4% in 2001 and 7·5% in 2002. Foreign exchange reserves were US$5,268m. and gold reserves 243,000 troy oz in June 2002. Total money supply in June 2002 was 495,309m. tolars.

Budget. The 2000 budget was adopted by the Parliament in Jan. 2000. It set public expenditure at 1,059·7bn. tolars, or 44·35% of GDP. Revenue in 1999 was 1,590bn. tolars; expenditure, 1,613bn. tolars. Tax revenues in 1999 totalled 1,499bn. tolars, including domestic taxes on goods and services, 601bn. tolars; social security contributions, 496bn. tolars; general sales taxes and value-added taxes, 473bn. tolars; and employees' contributions, 306bn. tolars. In 1998 items of expenditure included (in 1m. tolars): central government, 483,575; local government, 137,964; pensions, 387,447; health care, 195,583; privatization expenditure, 14,800.

Performance. The GDP growth rate was 4·6% in 2000, with growth of 3·0% in 2001. Between 1997 and 2001 the growth rate averaged 4·2%. Of all the central and eastern European countries hoping to join the European Union, Slovenia has the highest per capita GDP. Real GDP in 1998 was 4% higher than in 1989. Only Poland among the ex-socialist countries has seen greater progress since 1989—in almost all of the other former communist states GDP was lower in 1998 than it had been in 1989 at the time of the changes which swept through central and eastern Europe. Total GDP in 2001 was US$18·8bn.

Banking and Finance. A central bank and bank of issue, the Bank of Slovenia, was founded in June 1991. Its *Governor* is Mitja Gaspari. In 1996 there were 31 commercial banks (three foreign) and seven savings banks. The largest bank is Nova Ljubljanska banka (NLB), with assets in 2000 of US$3·1bn. Other large banks are Nova Kreditna Banka Maribor (NKBM) and SKB banka.

There is a stock exchange in Ljubljana (LSE).

ENERGY AND NATURAL RESOURCES

Environment. According to the *World Bank Atlas* Slovenia's carbon dioxide emissions were the equivalent of 7·4 tonnes per capita in 1998.

Electricity. Installed capacity was 2·62m. kW in 1999. There was one nuclear power station in operation in 2002. In 2001, 5,257m. kWh were nuclear-produced, 5,413m. kWh thermal and 3,796m. kWh hydro-electric. The total amount of electricity produced in 2001 was 14,466m. kWh. Consumption per capita in 2001 was 5,568 kWh.

Minerals. Brown coal production was 685,000 tonnes in 2001.

Agriculture. Only around 11% of the population work in agriculture. Output (in 1,000 tonnes) in 2001: maize, 258; sugarbeets, 186; wheat, 180; potatoes, 148; grapes, 107.

Livestock in 2001: pigs, 599,895; cattle, 477,075; sheep, 94,068; poultry, 5,217,000 (2000). Livestock products, 2000: meat, 170,000 tonnes; milk (2001), 633,820 tonnes.

Forestry. In 2001 the area under forests was 1·14m. ha, or 56·5% of the total land area. Timber production in 1999 was 2·13m. cu. metres.

Fisheries. Total marine fish catch in 2001 was 1,774 tonnes. Freshwater catch was 1,314 tonnes.

INDUSTRY

Industry contributed 31·0% of GDP in 2001. Traditional industries are metallurgy, furniture-making and textiles. The manufacture of electric goods and transport equipment is being developed.

Production (in 1,000 tonnes): cement, 1,224 (1999); paper and paperboard, 582 (2000); crude steel, 368 (1997); passenger cars, 124,843 units (2000); refrigerators for household use, 692,000 units (1997); washing machines, 405,000 units (1997).

Labour. Registered labour force was 880,897 in 2001. In 2001, 427,553 people worked in services, 309,629 in industry, and 41,860 in agriculture and forestry. There were 101,856 registered unemployed in 2001. Unemployment was 11·6% in 2001, down from 12·2% in 2000. In 2001 the average monthly gross wage per employee was 214,561 tolars.

INTERNATIONAL TRADE

Foreign debt amounted to US$5,491m. in 1999. In 1997 Slovenia accepted 18% of the US$4,400m. commercial bank debt of the former Yugoslavia.

Imports and Exports. Exports (f.o.b.) in 2000 were worth US$8,805·9m. (US$8,622·7m. in 1999) and imports (f.o.b.) US$9,887·3m. (US$9,867·9m. in 1999). Major exports are road vehicles and parts, electrical machinery, apparatus, appliances and furniture. Major imports are road vehicles, electrical machinery, industrial machinery, petroleum and petroleum products, industrial machinery, iron and steel. Share of exports to principal markets in 1999: Germany, 30·7%; Italy, 13·8%; Croatia, 7·8%; Austria, 7·3%; France, 5·7%. Imports: Germany, 20·1%; Italy, 16·8%; France, 11·0%; Austria, 8·0%; Croatia, 4·5%. More than 65% of trade is with EU countries.

COMMUNICATIONS

Roads. In 2001 there were 20,236 km of road including 435 km of motorways. There were in 2001: 862,648 passenger cars; 2,212 buses; 45,811 trucks; and 11,723 motorcycles. 72·5m. passengers and 4·6m. tonnes of freight were carried by road in 2001. There were 9,199 traffic accidents in 2001 in which 278 persons were killed.

Rail. In 2001 there were 1,229 km of 1,435 mm gauge, of which 504 km were electrified. In 2001, 14·5m. passengers and 15·0m. tonnes of freight were carried.

Civil Aviation. There is an international airport at Ljubljana (Brnik), which handled 986,000 passengers (all on international flights) and 5,800 tonnes of freight in 2000. The national carrier, Adria Airways, has flights to most major European cities and Tel Aviv. In 2000 Ljubljana handled 986,000 passengers (all on international flights) and 5,800 tonnes of freight. In 1999 scheduled airline traffic of Slovenia-based carriers flew 9·1m. km, carrying 556,000 passengers.

Shipping. The biggest port at Koper. Sea-going shipping totalled 9,146 GRT in 2001. In 1999 vessels totalling 9,273,000 NRT entered ports and vessels totalling 9,318,000 NRT cleared.

Telecommunications. In 2001 Slovenia had 945,295 fixed-line telephone subscribers (473·8 per 1,000 inhabitants), 662,619 mobile phone subscribers and 11,072 fax machines. The number of Internet users in Dec. 2000 was 600,000. There were 548,000 PCs in use (275·9 per 1,000 persons) in 2000.

Postal Services. In 2001 there were 545 post offices.

SOCIAL INSTITUTIONS

Justice. There are eight courts of first instance, four higher courts and a supreme court. The population in penal institutions in Dec. 1997 was 752 (40 per 100,000 of national population).

Religion. 71% of the population were Roman Catholic according to the 1991 census.

Education. Adult literacy rate in 1999 was 99·6% (99·7% male; 99·6% female). In 2000–01 there were 816 primary schools with 181,390 pupils and 15,287 teachers; and 149 secondary schools with 104,845 pupils and 9,351 teachers. In 2001–02 there were 46 institutions of higher education with 72,320 students and 6,894 teaching staff. There are two universities, at Ljubljana and Maribor.

In 1995 total expenditure on education came to 5·7% of GNP and represented 12·6% of total government expenditure.

Health. In 2000 there were 4,483 doctors and 10,745 hospital beds.

Welfare. There were 485,895 people receiving pensions in 2001, of which 296,160 were old-age pensioners. Disability and pension insurance expenses were 655,233m. tolars in 2001.

CULTURE

Broadcasting. The government-controlled Radiotelevizija Slovenija broadcasts three national radio programmes, and also programmes in Hungarian and Italian. There are six nationwide radio networks as well as regional and local stations. Public television transmission is carried out by the two stations of Televizija Slovenija (colour by PAL). There are also national independent TV networks, a network serving Ljubljana and district and several local stations. There were 710,000 TV receivers and 805,000 radio sets in 1997.

Cinema. There were 78 cinemas with a total of 22,400 seats in 2000, and an annual attendance of 2·2m. Nine full-length films were made in 2000.

Press. In 2001 there were 7 national daily newspapers, 57 weeklies and 3 published twice a week. In 2001 a total of 3,598 book titles were published.

Tourism. 1,090,000 foreign tourists came to Slovenia in 2000; receipts from tourism in 2000 totalled US$957m.

Libraries. In 2000 there were 1 national library, 54 higher education libraries, 138 special libraries, 60 public libraries and 648 school libraries; they held a combined 25,554,000 volumes.

Theatre and Opera. In 2000 there were nine professional theatres.

Museums and Galleries. Museums totalled 85 in 1996, with 2·0m. visitors that year.

DIPLOMATIC REPRESENTATIVES

Of Slovenia in the United Kingdom (Cavendish Crt, 11–15 Wigmore St., London, W1H 9LA)
Ambassador: Marjan Šetinc.

Of the United Kingdom in Slovenia (4th Floor, 3 Trg Republike, 1000 Ljubljana)
Ambassador: Hugh Mortimer, LVO.

Of Slovenia in the USA (1525 New Hampshire Ave., NW, Washington, D.C., 20036)
Ambassador: Davorin Kračun.

Of the USA in Slovenia (4 Prazakova, 1000 Ljubljana)
Ambassador: Johnny Young.

Of Slovenia to the United Nations
Ambassador: Ernest Petrič.

Of Slovenia to the European Union
Ambassador: Ciril Stokelj.

FURTHER READING

Benderly, J. and Kraft, E. (eds.) *Independent Slovenia: Origins, Movements, Prospects.* London, 1995
Carmichael, Cathie, *Slovenia.* [Bibliography] ABC-Clio, Oxford and Santa Barbara (CA), 1996

National statistical office: National Statistical Office, Vožarski Pot 12, 1000 Ljubljana.
Website: http://www.sigov.si/zrs/

SOLOMON ISLANDS

Capital: Honiara
Population estimate, 2000: 447,000
GDP per capita, 2000: (PPP$) 1,648
HDI/world rank: 0·622/121

KEY HISTORICAL EVENTS

The Solomon Islands were discovered by Europeans in 1568 but 200 years passed before contact was made again. The southern Solomon Islands were placed under British protection in 1893; the eastern and southern outliers were added in 1898 and 1899. Santa Isabel and the other islands to the north were ceded by Germany in 1900. Full internal self-government was achieved on 2 Jan. 1976 and independence on 7 July 1978.

In June 2000 there was a coup by rebels from the island of Malaita. Prime Minister Bartholomew Ulufa'alu was held at gunpoint for two days. The conflict between the so-called Malaita Eagles and the Isatabu Freedom Movement threatens civil war.

TERRITORY AND POPULATION

The Solomon Islands lie within the area 5° to 12° 30' S. lat. and 155° 30' to 169° 45' E. long. The group includes the main islands of Guadalcanal, Malaita, New Georgia, San Cristobal (now Makira), Santa Isabel and Choiseul; the smaller Florida and Russell groups; the Shortland, Mono (or Treasury), Vella La Vella, Kolombangara, Ranongga, Gizo and Rendova Islands; to the east, Santa Cruz, Tikopia, the Reef and Duff groups; Rennell and Bellona in the south; Ontong Java or Lord Howe to the north; and many smaller islands. The land area is estimated at 10,954 sq. miles (28,370 sq. km). The larger islands are mountainous and forest clad, with flood-prone rivers of considerable energy potential. Guadalcanal has the largest land area and the greatest amount of flat coastal plain. Population (1997 estimate), 426,900; density per sq. km, 15·0. In 1998, 81·4% of the population lived in rural areas.

The UN gives a projected population for 2010 of 619,000.

The islands are administratively divided into a Capital Territory and nine provinces. Area and population:

Province	Sq. km	Census 1986	Estimate 1997	Capital
Central Islands	615 ⎫	18,457	30,07 ⎧	Tulagi
Rennell and Bellona	671 ⎭			Tigoa
Guadalcanal	5,336	49,831	61,243	Honiara
Isabel	4,136	14,616	22,653	Buala
Makira and Ulawa	3,188	21,796	29,110	Kirakira
Malaita	4,225	80,032	105,882	Auki
Temotu	895	14,781	21,159	Lata (Santa Cruz)
Western	5,475 ⎫	55,250	95,193 ⎧	Gizo
Choiseul	3,837 ⎭			Taro
Capital Territory	22	30,413	45,610	...

The capital, Honiara, on Guadalcanal, is the largest urban area, with an estimated population in 1999 of 68,000. 93% of the population are Melanesian; other ethnic groups include Polynesian, Micronesian, European and Chinese.

English is the official language, and is spoken by 1–2% of the population. In all 120 indigenous languages are spoken; Melanesian languages are spoken by 85% of the population.

SOCIAL STATISTICS

Births, 1997, 15,900; deaths, 1,800. 1997 birth rate (per 1,000 population), 37·3; death rate, 4·3. Life expectancy, 1998, 74·1 years for women and 69·9 for men. Annual population growth rate, 1990–99, 3·3%. Infant mortality, 1998, 22 per 1,000 live births; fertility rate, 1999, 4·7 births per woman.

CLIMATE

An equatorial climate with only small seasonal variations. Southeast winds cause cooler conditions from April to Nov., but northwest winds for the rest of the year bring higher temperatures and greater rainfall, with annual totals ranging between 80" (2,000 mm) and 120" (3,000 mm).

CONSTITUTION AND GOVERNMENT
The Solomon Islands is a constitutional monarchy with the British Sovereign (represented locally by a Governor-General, who must be a Solomon Island citizen) as Head of State. Legislative power is vested in the single-chamber *National Parliament* composed of 50 members, elected by universal adult suffrage for five years. Parliamentary democracy is based on a multi-party system. Executive authority is effectively held by the Cabinet, led by the Prime Minister.

The Governor-General is appointed for up to five years, on the advice of Parliament, and acts in almost all matters on the advice of the Cabinet. The Prime Minister is elected by and from members of Parliament. Other Ministers are appointed by the Governor-General on the Prime Minister's recommendation, from members of Parliament. The Cabinet is responsible to Parliament. Emphasis is laid on the devolution of power to provincial governments, and traditional chiefs and leaders have a special role within the arrangement.

National Anthem. 'God save our Solomon Islands from shore to shore'; words and tune by P. Balekana.

RECENT ELECTIONS
National elections were held on 5 Dec. 2001. The People's Action Party won 20 seats, the Association of Independent Members 13, the Solomon Islands Alliance for Change 12, the People's Progressive Party 3 and the Labour Party 1.

A run-off vote for the premiership was held on 17 Dec. 2001. The former deputy prime minister, Sir Allan Kemakeza, who had been dismissed two months prior to the national elections, defeated Mannasseh Sogavare and Bartholomew Ulafu'alu, both former prime ministers.

CURRENT ADMINISTRATION
Governor-General: Sir John Lapli (since 7 July 1999).

In March 2003 the government comprised:

Prime Minister: Sir Allan Kemakeza, b. 1951 (sworn in 17 Dec. 2001).

Deputy Prime Minister, Minister of National Planning and Human Resource Development, and Finance: Snyder Rini.

Minister of Agriculture and Livestock: Edward Huniehu. *Trade and Commerce:* Trevor Olavae. *Tourism and Aviation:* Alex Bartlett. *Education and Training:* Mathias Taro. *Economic Reform and Structural Adjustment:* Daniel Fa'afuna. *Fisheries and Marine Resources:* Nelson Kile. *Foreign Affairs:* Laurie Chan. *Forests, Environment and Conservation:* David Holosivi. *Health and Medical Services:* Benjamin Una. *Home Affairs:* Clement Rojumana. *Lands and Surveys:* Siriako Usa. *Mines and Energy:* Stephen Paeni. *National Unity, Reconciliation and Peace:* Nathaniel Waena. *Police, National Security and Justice:* Augustine Taneko. *Provincial Government and Rural Development:* Walton Naezon. *Transport, Works and Communications:* David Giro. *Youth, Sports and Women:* Vacant.

DEFENCE
The marine wing of the Royal Solomon Islands Police operates three patrol boats and a number of fast crafts for surveillance of fisheries and maritime boundaries. There is also an RSI Police Field Force stationed at the border with Papua New Guinea.

INTERNATIONAL RELATIONS
The Solomon Islands is a member of the UN, WTO, the Commonwealth, the Asian Development Bank, the Pacific Community, the Pacific Islands Forum and is an ACP member state of the ACP-EU relationship. The Solomon Islands is also a member of the World Trade Organization and other organizations for regional technical co-operation. It maintains bilateral relations with 46 countries in the international community.

ECONOMY

Overview. When the Solomon Islands Alliance for Change (SIAC) coalition assumed office in Aug. 1997, the government had SI$200m. in debts despite a 6% growth rate the previous year. The debt was reduced to SI$147m. by Sept. 1998 in a debt-servicing programme established jointly with the Central Bank of the Solomon Islands. The SIAC coalition embarked on a reform programme to encourage private enterprise which included a reduction of the civil service and a tightening of government revenue collection. The 1998 and 1999 government estimates were based on a balanced budgeting. In Dec. 1997 the Solomon Islands dollar was devalued by 20%.

Currency. The *Solomon Island dollar* (SBD) of 100 *cents* was introduced in 1977. It was devalued by 20% in Dec. 1997 and 25% in March 2002. Inflation in 2001 was 7·0%. In Jan. 2002 foreign exchange reserves were US$28m. Total money supply was SI$243m. in Sept. 2000.

Budget. The budget estimate for 1998 was for expenditure of SI$631·8m.; total revenue forecast, SI$482m. plus SI$149m. to be secured through concessionary loans.

Performance. Real GDP growth was negative in both 2000 and 2001, at −14·0% and −3·0% respectively. Total GDP in 2001 was US$0·3bn.

Banking and Finance. The Central Bank of Solomon Islands is the bank of issue; its *Governor* is Rick N. Houenipwela ('Hou'). There are three commercial banks.

Weights and Measures. The metric system is in force.

ENERGY AND NATURAL RESOURCES

Environment. According to the *World Bank Atlas* carbon dioxide emissions in 1998 were the equivalent of 0·4 tonnes per capita.

Electricity. Installed capacity in 1994 was 20,000 kW. Production in 1998 was 30m. kWh and consumption per capita in 1997 was an estimated 79 kWh. The Solomon Islands Electricity Authority is undertaking projects to increase power generation capacity including the construction of a major hydro-electricity power plant.

Oil and Gas. The potential for oil, petroleum and gas production has yet to be tapped.

Water. Supply of clean drinking water is abundant in most of the large islands, though smaller and outlying islands have to rely on underground table water.

Minerals. Gold earned SI$1·3m. in 1991, decreasing to SI$0·3m. for 8 kg in 1994. The three Gold Ridge mines opened in July/Aug. 1998, one of them owned by an Australian firm, Ross Mining. There is the prospect of nickel mining on San George Island and other mineral deposits are known to exist.

Agriculture. Land is held either as customary land (88% of holdings) or registered land. Customary land rights depend on clan membership or kinship. Only Solomon Islanders own customary land; only Islanders or government members may hold perpetual estates of registered land. Coconuts, cocoa, rice and other minor crops are grown. Production, 2000 (in 1,000 tonnes): coconuts, 318; sweet potatoes, 75; taro, 32; palm oil, 28; yams, 25; copra, 23; palm kernels, 7. Agricultural produce earned SI$104·7m. in exports in 1997.

Livestock (2000): pigs, 59,000; cattle, 12,000.

Forestry. Forests covered 2·39m. ha in 1995 (85·4% of the land area). Earnings from forest resources increased from SI$266·6m. in 1994 to SI$309·9m. in 1995 and SI$349·3m. in 1996 but then slumped in 1997 to SI$309·4m. owing to a fall in prices and a government moratorium on the issue of new logging licences. Timber production was 872,000 cu. metres in 1999.

Fisheries. Solomon Islands' waters are among the richest in tuna. Catches have remained well below the maximum sustainable catch limits. Previously closed areas within its territorial waters have been opened to American fishing interests but sustainable harvest rates will not be at risk. The total catch in 1999 was an estimated 82,334 tonnes.

INDUSTRY
Industries include processed fish production (34,700 tonnes in 1993), palm oil manufacture (29,000 tonnes in 1998), rice milling, fish canning, fish freezing, saw milling, food, tobacco and soft drinks. Other products include wood and rattan furniture, fibreglass articles, boats, clothing and spices.

Labour. The Labour Division of the Ministry of Commerce, Employment and Tourism monitors and regulates the domestic labour market. The labour force in 1996 totalled 202,000 (54% males). Around 38% of the economically active population in 1993 were engaged in community, social and personal services and 27% in agriculture, fisheries and forestry.

Trade Unions. Trade Unions exist by virtue of the Trade Unions Act of 1976. The Solomon Islands Council of Trade Unions (SICTU) is the central body. Affiliated members of the SICTU are Solomon Islands National Union of Workers and the Solomon Islands Public Employees Union (SIPEU). SIPEU, which represents employees of the public sector, is the largest single trade union.

INTERNATIONAL TRADE
The Solomon Islands is a member of the World Trade Organization. The government recognizes the private sector as an engine for growth. Through encouraging the private sector the government hopes that the base for a broad diversification of tradeable goods and services can be established.

Total foreign debt in 2000 was US$155m.

Imports and Exports. Imports 1999 (1998), US$110·04m. (US$159·90m.); exports, US$164·57m. (US$141·83m.). Value of main imports, 1996: machinery and transport equipment, SI$162·8m.; manufactured goods, SI$119·1m.; food, SI$81·3m.; fuels and lubricants, SI$60·8m.; chemicals, SI$23·8m.; drinks and tobacco, SI$12·0m.; and others, SI$77·0m. Main exports: timber, SI$309·4m.; fish, SI$182·4m.; palm products, SI$57·4m.; cocoa, SI$44·5m.; coconut products, SI$17·7m.; and others, SI$37·3m. In 1997 the principal suppliers were Australia (37·2%), Japan (17·1%), New Zealand (9·6%) and Singapore (8·4%); the principal export markets were Japan (41·1%), South Korea (14·1%) and UK (13·1%).

Trade Fairs. An annual National Cultural and Trade Show/Fair is held in July to coincide with the anniversary of independence.

COMMUNICATIONS

Roads. In 1996 there was estimated to be a total of 1,360 km of roads, of which 34 km were paved. The unpaved roads included 800 km of private plantation roads.

Civil Aviation. A new terminal has been opened at Henderson International Airport in Honiara. The national carrier is Solomon Airlines. In 1999 scheduled airline traffic of Solomon Islands-based carriers flew 4·1m. km, carrying 98,000 passengers (23,000 on international flights).

Shipping. There are international ports at Honiara, Yandina in the Russell Islands and Noro in New Georgia, Western Province. In 1998 the merchant marine totalled 10,000 GRT.

Telecommunications. Telecommunications are operated by Solomon Telekom, a joint venture between the government of Solomon Islands and Cable & Wireless (UK). Telecommunications between Honiara and provincial centres are facilitated by modern satellite communication systems. Main telephone lines numbered 7,700 in 2000 (17·6 per 1,000 inhabitants) and there were 20,000 PCs in use (45·7 per 1,000 inhabitants). There were approximately 700 mobile phone subscribers in 1998 and 900 fax machines in 1997. Internet users numbered 3,000 in Dec. 1999.

Postal Services. The Solomon Islands Postal Corporation, a statutory company established in 1996, administers postal services. In 1995 there were 140 post offices.

SOCIAL INSTITUTIONS

Justice. Civil and criminal jurisdiction is exercised by the High Court of Solomon Islands, constituted 1975. A Solomon Islands Court of Appeal was established in 1982. Jurisdiction is based on the principles of English law (as applying on 1 Jan.

1981). Magistrates' courts can try civil cases on claims not exceeding SI$2,000, and criminal cases with penalties not exceeding 14 years' imprisonment. Certain crimes, such as burglary and arson, where the maximum sentence is for life, may also be tried by magistrates. There are also local courts, which decide matters concerning customary titles to land; decisions may be put to the Customary Land Appeal Court. There is no capital punishment.

The population in penal institutions in 1997 was 147 (40 per 100,000 of national population).

Religion. 95% of the population are Christians.

Education. In 1994 there were 12,627 pre-primary pupils, and 60,493 primary pupils with 2,514 teachers. There were 7,981 pupils at secondary level in 1995. The adult literacy rate in 1998 was 62·0%.

Training of teachers and trade and vocational training is carried out at the college of Higher Education. The University of the South Pacific Centre is at Honiara. Other rural training centres run by churches are also involved in vocational training.

Health. A free medical service is supplemented by the private sector. An international standard immunization programme is conducted in conjunction with the WHO for infants. Tuberculosis has been eradicated but malaria remains a problem. In 1997 there were 11 hospitals, 31 doctors and 464 registered nurses and 283 nursing aides.

CULTURE

Broadcasting. The Solomon Islands Broadcasting Corporation (SIBC) operates a national service and an FM service for Honiara. The other FM station—FM100— is privately operated and broadcasts news and entertainment on a 24-hour basis. There were 4,000 TV receivers and 57,000 radio receivers in 1997.

Cinema. Private interests operate three cinemas in the capital. There are small cinemas in the provincial centres.

Press. There are two main newspapers in circulation. *The Solomon Star* is daily and the *Solomon Voice* is weekly. The Government Information Service publishes a monthly issue of the *Solomon Nius* which exclusively disseminates news of government activities. Non-government organizations such as the Solomon Islands Development Trust (SIDT) also publish monthly papers on environmental issues.

Tourism. Tourism in the Solomon Islands is still in a development stage. The emphasis is on establishing major hotels in the capital and provincial centres, to be supplemented by satellite Eco-tourism projects in the rural areas. The Solomon Islands Visitors Bureau is the statutory institution for domestic co-ordination and international marketing. In 1998 there were 13,000 foreign tourists, bringing revenue of US$13m.

Festivals. Festivities and parades in the capital and provincial centres normally mark the National Day of Independence. The highlight is the annual National Trade and Cultural Show.

Libraries. There is a National Library operated by the government in Honiara. The other library facilities are those of the Solomon Islands College of Higher Education and the University of the South Pacific (SI) Centre.

Museums and Galleries. There is a National Museum which has a display of traditional artefacts. Early government and public records are kept at the National Archives and a National Art Gallery displays a number of fine arts and works by Solomon Islands artists.

DIPLOMATIC REPRESENTATIVES

Of the Solomon Islands in the United Kingdom (resides at Brussels).
High Commissioner: Robert Sisilo.

Of the United Kingdom in the Solomon Islands (Telekom House, Mendana Ave., Honiara)
High Commissioner: Brian Baldwin.

SOLOMON ISLANDS

Of the USA in the Solomon Islands
Ambassador: Susan S. Jacobs (resides at Port Moresby, Papua New Guinea).

Of the Solomon Islands in the USA and to the United Nations (800 2nd Ave, Suite 400L, New York, NY 10017)
Ambassador: Vacant.
Chargé d'Affaires a.i.: Jeremiah Manele.

Of the Solomon Islands to the European Union
Ambassador: Robert Sisilo.

FURTHER READING
Bennett, J. A., *Wealth of the Solomons: A History of a Pacific Archipelago, 1800–1978.* Univ. of Hawaii Press, 1987

SOMALIA

Jamhuriyadda Dimugradiga
ee Soomaaliya
(Somali Democratic Republic)

Capital: Mogadishu
Population estimate, 2000: 8·78m.
GDP per capita: not available

KEY HISTORICAL EVENTS

The origins of the Somali people can be traced back 2,000 years when they displaced an earlier Arabic people. They converted to Islam in the 10th century and were organized in loose Islamic states by the 19th century. The northern part of Somaliland was created a British protectorate in 1884. The southern part belonged to two local rulers who, in 1889, accepted Italian protection for their lands. The Italian invasion of Ethiopia in 1935 was launched from Somaliland and in 1936 Somaliland was incorporated with Eritrea and Ethiopia to become Italian East Africa. In 1940 Italian forces invaded British Somaliland but in 1941 the British, with South African and Indian troops, recaptured this territory as well as occupying Italian Somaliland. After the Second World War British Somaliland reverted to its colonial status and ex-Italian Somaliland became the UN Trust Territory of Somaliland, administered by Italy.

The independent Somali Republic came into being on 1 July 1960 as a result of the merger of the British Somaliland Protectorate, which first became independent on 26 June 1960, and the Italian Trusteeship Territory of Somaliland. On 21 Oct. 1969 Maj.-Gen. Mohammed Siyad Barre took power in a coup. Various insurgent forces combined to oppose the Barre regime in a bloody civil war. Barre fled on 27 Jan. 1991 but interfactional fighting continued. In Aug. 1992 a new coalition government agreed a UN military presence to back up relief efforts to help the estimated 1·5–2m. victims of famine. On 11 Dec. 1992 the leaders of the two most prominent of the warring factions, Ali Mahdi Muhammad and Muhammad Farah Aidid, agreed to a peace plan under the aegis of the UN and a pact was signed on 15 Jan. 1993. At the end of March, the warring factions agreed to disarm and form a 74-member National Transitional Council. On 4 Nov. 1994 the UN Security Council unanimously decided to withdraw UN forces; the last of these left on 2 March 1995.

The principal insurgent group in the north of the country, the Somali National Movement, declared the secession of an independent **'Somaliland Republic'** on 17 May 1991, based on the territory of the former British protectorate, with a capital at Hargeysa and a port at Berbera. The Somalian government rejected the secession and Muhammad Aidid's forces launched a campaign to reoccupy the 'Republic' in Jan. 1996. Muhammad Farah Aidid was assassinated in July 1996 and succeeded by his son Hussein Aidid. In July 1998 leaders in the northeast of Somalia proclaimed an 'autonomous state' named **Puntland.** Neither Somaliland nor Puntland has received international recognition.

Peace efforts in neighbouring Djibouti culminated in July 2000 in the establishment of a power-sharing agreement and a national constitution to see Somalia through a three-year transitional period. The election of members of parliament and a civilian government followed in Aug. 2000, and in Oct. the new government moved from Djibouti back to Somalia.

TERRITORY AND POPULATION

Somalia is bounded north by the Gulf of Aden, east and south by the Indian ocean, and west by Kenya, Ethiopia and Djibouti. Total area 637,657 sq. km (246,201 sq. miles). In 1987 the census population was 7,114,431. Estimated population (1998): 8,206,000; density, 12·9 per sq. km. Population counting is complicated owing to large numbers of nomads and refugee movements as a result of famine and clan warfare.

The UN gives a projected population for 2010 of 13·07m.

In 1995 an estimated 74·4% of the population were rural.

The country is administratively divided into 18 regions (with chief cities): Awdal (Saylac), Bakol (Xuddur), Bay (Baydhabo), Benadir (Mogadishu), Bari (Boosaso), Galgudug (Duusa Marreeb), Gedo (Garbahaarrey), Hiran (Beledweyne), Jubbada Dexe (Jilib), Jubbada Hoose (Kismayo), Mudug (Gaalkacyo), Nogal (Gaarowe), Woqooyi Galbeed (Hargeysa), Sanaag (Ceerigabo), Shabeellaha Dhexe (Jawhar), Shabeellaha Hoose (Marka), Sol (Las Anod), Togder (Burao). Somaliland comprises the regions of Awdal, Woqooyi Galbeed, Togder, Sanaag and Sol. Puntland consists of Bari, Nogal and northern Mudug.

The capital is Mogadishu (1999 population, 1,162,000). Other large towns are (with 1990 estimates) Hargeysa (90,000), Kismayo (90,000), Berbera (70,000) and Marka (62,000).

The national language is Somali. Arabic is also an official language and English and Italian are spoken extensively.

SOCIAL STATISTICS

Births, 1997 estimate, 300,000; deaths, 121,000. Rates, 1997 estimate (per 1,000 population): birth, 45·5; death, 18·3. Infant mortality, 1997, 126 per 1,000 live births. Annual population growth rate, 1990–99, 2·5%. Life expectancy in 1997, 46·2 years. Fertility rate, 1999, 7·2 births per woman.

CLIMATE

Much of the country is arid, although rainfall is more adequate towards the south. Temperatures are very high on the northern coasts. Mogadishu, Jan. 79°F (26·1°C), July 78°F (25·6°C). Annual rainfall 17" (429 mm). Berbera, Jan. 76°F (24·4°C), July 97°F (36·1°C). Annual rainfall 2" (51 mm).

CONSTITUTION AND GOVERNMENT

The Constitution of 1984 authorized a sole legal party, the Somali Revolutionary Socialist Party. There was an elected President and People's Assembly.

A conference of national reconciliation in July 1991 and again in March 1993 allowed for the setting up of a transitional government charged with reorganizing free elections, but inter-factional fighting and anarchy have replaced settled government.

In Aug. 2000 the country's first parliament for nine years was inaugurated in neighbouring Djibouti. Under an agreed charter the transitional assembly was to elect a president who in turn was to form a government. However, ongoing wrangling between Somalia's rival factions continues. In Nov. 2002 leaders of the Somali factions met in order to begin the process of drawing up a new federal constitution.

National Anthem. No words, tune by G. Blanc.

RECENT ELECTIONS

For nearly ten years Somalia had no functioning government as such, but on 25 Aug. 2000 Abdiqassim Salad Hassan was elected president by the interim government. He defeated Abdillahi Ahmed Adow in a third ballot by 145 votes to 92.

On 28 Oct. 2001, after only 13 months rule, Prime Minister Ali Khalif Galaid's government was defeated by a no-confidence motion. Out of 174 votes cast, 141 voted against Galaid. He was replaced on 12 Nov. 2001 by Hassan Abshir Farah.

CURRENT ADMINISTRATION

President: Abdiqassim Salad Hassan; b. 1942 (sworn in 27 Aug. 2000).

In March 2003 the government comprised:

Prime Minister: Hassan Abshir Farah; b. 1945 (sworn in 12 Nov. 2001).

Minister of Defence: Gen. Abdulwahab Mohamed Hussein. *Education:* Mohammed Osman Hussein. *Finance:* Mahmud Sheikh Hussein Hussein. *Foreign Affairs:* Yousuf Hassan Ibrahim Dheeg. *Higher Education:* Mohamud Haji Abdi Zakaria. *Industry:* Ma'alin Amin Yussuf. *Information:* Adan Ibrahim Ibbi Abdirahman. *Interior and Rural Development:* Sheikh Muhammad Dahir. *Justice and Religious Affairs:* Umar Farah Mahmud. *Culture and Heritage:* Mohammed Ali Mursale. *Energy:* Warsame Abokor Sayid. *Environment:* Abdik Usman Abubakar. *Livestock and Animal Husbandry:* Ahmad Sheikh Dahir Savid. *International Co-operation:* Elabe Fahiye Hussein. *Constitution and Federalism:* Hirsi Ali Abdirahman. *Health:* Nurani Bakar Mohammed. *Labour:* Mohammed Shirwa Abdullahi. *Local Government:* Nur Jiley Mohammed. *Minerals and Water Resources:* Mohammed Danulle Ahmad. *Reconciliation and Conflict Resolution:* Meydane Burale Mohammed. *Tourism and Wildlife:* Farah Hujale Hassan. *Women's Affairs:* Aweys Hussein Saynab. *Monetary Affairs:* Hashi Adan Umar. *Diaspora and Refugee Affairs:* Abdullahi Jama Ahmad. *Disabled and Rehabilitation:* Mohammed Abdulle Abdiqadir. *Ports and Marine Transport:* Jama Warsame Abdiwali. *Public Works:* Warsame Ali Mohammed. *Reconstruction and Resettlement:* Yussuf Mohammed Abdiqadir. *Science and Technology:* Sheikh Mukhtar Abdi'aziz. *Sports and Youth Affairs:* Mukhtar Qaridi Abdulasis. *Transport:* Mohamed Abdi Gouled.

DEFENCE
With the breakdown of government following the 1991 revolution armed forces broke up into clan groupings, four of them in the north and six in the south.

Defence expenditure totalled US$39m. in 2000 (US$6 per capita), representing 4·5% of GDP.

Army. Following the 1991 revolution there are no national armed forces. In Northern Somalia the Somali National Movement controls an armed clan of 5–6,000 out of a total of 12,900 armed forces in the area. In the rest of the country several local groups control forces of which the Ali Mahdi Faction controls the largest, an armed clan of 10,000.

INTERNATIONAL RELATIONS
Somalia is a member of the UN, the African Union, African Development Bank, OIC, the League of Arab States and the Intergovernmental Authority on Development and is an ACP member state of the ACP-EU relationship.

ECONOMY
Agriculture accounts for approximately 59% of GDP, industry 10% and services 31%.

Currency. The unit of currency is the *Somali shilling* (SOS) of 100 *cents.*

Budget. Budget for 1991: revenue, Som.Sh. 151,453m.; expenditure, Som.Sh. 141,141m.

Performance. Real GDP growth was 0·0% in both 1997 and 1998.

Banking and Finance. The bank of issue is the Central Bank of Somalia (founded in 1960 as the Somali National Bank); the *Governor* is Mahamud Mohamed Ulusow. All banks were nationalized in 1970. The Somali Development Bank (founded 1983) and the Commercial Bank of Somalia are the only banks.

Weights and Measures. The metric system is in use.

ENERGY AND NATURAL RESOURCES

Electricity. Capacity: 144,000 kW prior to the civil war, now largely shut down; some localities operate their own generating plants. Production (1998): 265m. kWh.

Oil and Gas. Natural gas reserves were 6bn. cu. metres in 1997.

Minerals. There are deposits of chromium, coal, copper, gold, gypsum, lead, limestone, manganese, nickel, silver, titanium, tungsten, uranium and zinc.

Agriculture. Somalia is essentially a pastoral country, and about 80% of the inhabitants depend on livestock-rearing (cattle, sheep, goats and camels). Half the population is nomadic. In 1998 there were 1·39m. ha of arable land and 22,000 ha of permanent cropland. Estimated production, 2000 (in 1,000 tonnes): sugarcane, 220; maize, 210; sorghum, 100; cassava, 70; bananas, 55; watermelons, 26; sesame seed, 23.

Livestock (2000): 13·1m. sheep; 12·3m. goats; 6·1m. camels; 5·1m. cattle. Somalia has the greatest number of camels of any country in the world.

Forestry. In 1995 the area under forests was 754,000 ha, or 1·2% of the total land area. In 1999, 8·33m. cu. metres of roundwood were cut. Wood and charcoal are the main energy sources. Frankincense and myrrh are produced.

Fisheries. Approximately 20,250 tonnes of fish were caught in 1999, almost entirely from marine waters.

INDUSTRY
A few small industries exist including sugar refining (production was 18,600 tonnes in 1998), food processing, textiles and petroleum refining.

Labour. The labour force totalled 4,291,000 in 1996 (57% males). Approximately 74% of the economically active population in 1995 were engaged in agriculture, fisheries and forestry.

INTERNATIONAL TRADE
Foreign debt was US$2,562m. in 2000.

Imports and Exports. Exports in 1995 were estimated at US$145m. and imports at US$193m.
Principal exports: livestock, hides and skins, bananas. Main export markets in 1996: Saudi Arabia, 55%; Yemen, 19%; Italy, 11%; United Arab Emirates, 9%. Main import suppliers: Kenya, 28%, Djibouti, 21%; Brazil, 6%; Saudi Arabia, 6%.

COMMUNICATIONS
Roads. In 1996 there were an estimated 22,100 km of roads, of which 2,600 km were paved. Passenger cars numbered 1,020 in 1996, and there were 6,440 trucks and vans.

Civil Aviation. There are international airports at Mogadishu, Berbera and Erigavo. In 1998 there were flights to Djibouti in addition to internal services.

Shipping. There are deep-water harbours at Kismayo, Berbera, Marka and Mogadishu. The merchant fleet (1998) totalled 11,000 GRT.

Telecommunications. Somalia had 15,000 main telephone lines in 2000, equivalent to 1·5 for every 1,000 persons. There were just 200 Internet users in July 2000.

SOCIAL INSTITUTIONS
Justice. There are 84 district courts, each with a civil and a criminal section. There are eight regional courts and two Courts of Appeal (at Mogadishu and Hargeysa), each with a general section and an assize section. The Supreme Court is in Mogadishu. The death penalty is in force and was used in 2000.

Religion. The population is almost entirely Sunni Muslims.

Education. The nomadic life of a large percentage of the population inhibits education progress. In 1990 adult literacy was estimated at 24%. In 1985 there were 194,335 pupils and 9,676 teachers in primary schools, there were 37,181 pupils and 2,320 teachers in secondary schools, and in 1984, 613 students with 30 teachers at teacher-training establishments. The National University of Somalia in Mogadishu (founded 1959) had 4,650 students and 550 academic staff in 1994–95.

Health. In 1986 there were 88 hospitals, 358 doctors, 113 pharmacists, 2 dentists, 556 midwives and 1,834 nursing personnel.
Somalia has the highest percentage of undernourished people of any country in the world—73% in 1996, up from fewer than 60% in the early 1980s. In the period 1990–98 only 31% of the population had access to safe drinking water.

CULTURE
Broadcasting. The state radio stations transmit in Somali, Arabic, English and Italian from Mogadishu and Hargeysa. The television station was destroyed in fighting in 1991; in 1997 there were estimated to be 470,000 radio and 135,000 TV receivers (colour by PAL).

Press. In 1996 there were two daily newspapers, with a combined circulation of 10,000.

Tourism. In 1998 there were 10,000 foreign tourists.

DIPLOMATIC REPRESENTATIVES
The Embassy of Somalia in the United Kingdom closed on 2 Jan. 1992.

Of the United Kingdom in Somalia (Waddada Xasan Geedd Abtoow 7–8, Mogadishu)
Staff temporarily withdrawn.

The Embassy of Somalia in the USA closed on 8 May 1991. A liaison office opened in March 1994, and withdrew to Nairobi in Sept. 1994.

Of Somalia to the United Nations
Ambassador: Ahmed Abdo Hashi.

Of Somalia to the European Union
Ambassador: Vacant.

FURTHER READING
Abdisalam, M. I.-S., *The Collapse of the Somali State*. London, 1995
Ghalib, J. M., *The Cost of Dictatorship: the Somali Experience*. New York, 1995
Lewis, I. M., *Blood and Bone: the Call of Kinship in Somali Society*. Lawrenceville (NJ), 1995.—*Understanding Somalia: a Guide to Culture, History and Social Institutions*. 2nd ed. London 1995
Omar, M. O., *The Road to Zero: Somalia's Self-Destruction*. London, 1995
Samatar, A. I. (ed.) *The Somali Challenge: from Catastrophe to Renewal?* Boulder (CO), 1994

National statistical office: Central Statistical Department, State Planning Commission, Mogadishu.

SOUTH AFRICA

Republic of South Africa

Capital: Pretoria (Administrative),
Cape Town (Legislative),
Bloemfontein (Judicial)
Seat of Parliament: Cape Town
Seats of Government: Cape Town,
Pretoria
Population estimate, 2000: 43·7m.
GDP per capita, 2000: (PPP$) 9,401
HDI/world rank: 0·695/107

KEY HISTORICAL EVENTS

The Dutch first established a trading post at the Cape in 1652. The hinterland was then inhabited by the Khoisan peoples and, further east and north, by Bantu-speaking peoples. There was some white settlement over the next century. During the Napoleonic Wars, Britain took possession of the Cape and later many Boer (Dutch) settlers migrated northeast in the Great Trek. In the mid-19th century Britain ruled the Cape Colony and Natal along the coast of southern Africa, while in the interior the Afrikaners or Boers, descendants of Dutch settlers, established their own independent republics in the Transvaal and the Orange Free State. Some Bantu African peoples remained unconquered, notably the Xhosas east of the Cape Colony and, north of Natal, the Zulus. Meanwhile, British settlers emigrated to Cape Colony and Natal in the 19th century, and from the 1860s many Indians were brought to Natal as indentured labourers on the sugar plantations. The population of the Cape Colony included many Afrikaners as well as the 'Coloured' community, descendants of Dutch settlers and indigenous Khoisan women and of Malay slaves. Most coloureds spoke Afrikaans, the offshoot of Dutch spoken by the Boers.

Britain annexed the Transvaal in 1877, and fought in 1879 with the Zulus who, under King Ketshwayo, won a victory at Isandhlwana but were then defeated at Ulundi. Britain restored independence to the Transvaal (South African Republic) in 1884 and annexed Zululand in 1887. Both the British and the Boers fought African resistance for many years, the last major rising being in Natal in 1906. However, the British and Boers were also rivals for supremacy, especially after the discovery of diamonds at Kimberley in 1867 and of gold in the Transvaal in 1884. This led to an economic boom and wealth for many, of whom Cecil Rhodes, for a time prime minister of the Cape, was the dominant entrepreneurial figure.

In the South African War of 1899–1902 the British defeated and annexed the Boer republics. The Boer republics were given self-government again in 1907 and on 31 May 1910 Cape Colony, Natal, the Transvaal and the Orange Free State combined to form the Union of South Africa, a self-governing dominion under the British Crown. The Union's economy was based on gold and diamond mining, for which there was organized recruitment of migrant African labourers from Union territory and other parts of Africa. Pass Laws were in operation, controlling Africans' movements in the towns and industrial areas, where they were regarded officially as temporary residents and segregated in 'townships'. By an Act of 1913, 87% of the land was reserved for white ownership only, much of it being owned by white farmers, while Africans farmed as tenants or squatters. African protests at segregation and lack of political rights were led by the African National Congress (ANC).

African rights were further suppressed after the coming to power in 1924 of the Afrikaner Nationalist Party, led by J. B. Hertzog. Hertzog's government secured recognition of full independence for South Africa by the Statute of Westminster on 11 Dec. 1931. It also promoted the status of the Afrikaans language and introduced new segregation measures. From 1948 the National Party government reinforced the segregation system, developing it into the system of Apartheid. The shooting by police of protesters against the Pass Laws at Sharpeville on 21 March 1960 led to a major crisis from which, however, the government emerged only stronger. The ANC and the Pan African Congress were banned, and the leaders forced to operate from exile after internal ANC leaders, including Nelson Mandela, were jailed in 1964. On 31 May 1961 South Africa became a Republic outside the Commonwealth.

On 16 June 1976 thousands of students demonstrated in Soweto, an African township outside Johannesburg, against mandatory schooling in Afrikaans. Many died when police broke up the demonstration and rioting spread throughout the country. When P. W. Botha became prime minister in 1978, elements of the Apartheid system were modified. Africans were allowed to form legal trade unions and the Acts banning marriage and sexual relations between people of different races were repealed.

A new constitution, approved in a referendum of white voters on 2 Nov. 1983 and in force from 3 Sept. 1984, created a new three-part parliament, with a House of Assembly for the Whites, a House of Representatives for the Coloureds and a House of Delegates for the Indians; Africans remained without representation. From late 1984 Blacks in the cities and industrial areas staged large-scale protests. In June 1986 a state of emergency was imposed. Foreign condemnation of this led to the first economic sanctions against South Africa, imposed by a number of countries including the USA.

By 1989 a start had been made on dismantling Apartheid, and the government announced its willingness to consider the extension of Black South Africans' political rights. In Feb. 1990 a 30-year ban on the African National Congress (ANC) was lifted; its leader, Nelson Mandela, was released from prison on 11 Feb. 1990. At the Whites-only referendum on 17 March 1992, on the granting of constitutional equality to all races, 1,924,186 (68·7%) votes were in favour; 875,619 against.

On 22 Dec. 1993 parliament approved (by 237 votes to 45) a Transitional Constitution paving the way for a new multi-racial parliament which was elected on 26–29 April 1994, and South Africa rejoined the Commonwealth. On 9 May 1994 Nelson Mandela was elected President. He was succeeded by Thabo Mbeki on 16 June 1999.

TERRITORY AND POPULATION

South Africa is bounded in the north by Namibia, Botswana and Zimbabwe, northeast by Mozambique and Swaziland, east by the Indian Ocean, and south and west by the South Atlantic, with Lesotho forming an enclave. Area: 1,219,090 sq. km. This area includes the uninhabited Prince Edward Island (41 sq. km) and Marion Island (388 sq. km), lying 1,900 km southeast of Cape Town and taken possession of in Dec. 1947 after the British Government had decided to give them to South Africa in order to prevent their falling into hostile hands. In 1994 Walvis Bay was ceded to Namibia, and Transkei, Bophuthatswana, Venda and Ciskei were re-integrated into South Africa.

At the census of 1996 the population was 40,583,573 (21,062,685 females), consisting of: African/Black, 31,127,631 (76·7% of total population); White, 4,434,697 (10·9%); Coloured, 3,600,446 (8·9%); Indian/Asian, 1,045,596 (2·6%). Estimated population at 30 June 2001 was 44,560,644 (23,121,651 females).

The UN gives a projected population for 2010 of 45·14m.

55·2% of the population was urban in 2000. In 1999 cities with the largest populations were (estimate in 1,000): Johannesburg (Gauteng), 4,074·6; Durban (KwaZulu-Natal), 2,554·4; Cape Town (Western Cape), 2,522·5; Port Elizabeth (Eastern Cape), 1,327·7; Pretoria (Gauteng), 1,411·9; Bloemfontein (Free State), 583,903; East London (Eastern Cape), 332,102.

Pretoria: Named after Andries Pretorius whose Voortrekkers had started moving into the area some 18 years earlier, Pretoria was established on 16 Nov. 1855. It was declared a city in 1931 and became the administrative capital of the Republic of South Africa in 1961. Often called the Jacaranda City owing to the number of Jacaranda trees, it is also known as Tshwane. The Union Buildings are the home of the South African Government and was the site of the swearing in of President Nelson Mandela on 10 May 1994 and President Thabo Mbeki on 16 June 1999.

Cape Town: Situated on the southwest coast of Africa, Cape Town is home to South Africa's Parliament. The city is dominated by Table Mountain, over 1,000 metres high. Table Mountain was declared a National Monument in 1998 and is a World Heritage site. Robben Island (Seal Island), a former asylum and leper colony before becoming a prison, is also a National Monument.

There were 3,053 immigrants in 2000 and 10,262 emigrants (8,402 in 1999). An estimated 20% of skilled South Africans have left the country and up to 70% of those who remain consider emigrating.

Population by province, according to the 1996 census:

Province	Total (including unspecified)	African	White	Coloured	Indian/ Asian
Eastern Cape	6,302,525	5,448,495	330,294	468,532	19,356
Free State	2,633,504	1,223,940	316,459	79,038	2,805
Gauteng	7,348,423	5,147,444	1,702,343	278,692	161,289
KwaZulu-Natal	8,417,021	6,880,652	558,182	117,951	790,813
Mpumalanga	2,800,711	2,497,834	253,392	20,283	13,083
Northern Cape	840,321	278,633	111,844	435,368	2,268
Northern Province (now Limpopo)	4,929,368	4,765,255	117,878	7,821	5,510
NorthWest	3,354,825	3,058,686	222,755	46,652	10,097
Western Cape	3,956,875	826,691	821,551	2,146,109	40,376

There are 11 official languages. Numbers of home speakers at the 1996 census: IsiZulu, 9,200,144 (22·9% of population); IsiXhosa, 7,196,118 (17·9%); Afrikaans, 5,811,547 (14·4%); Sepedi, 3,695,846 (9·2%); English, 3,457,467 (8·6%); Setswana, 3,301,774 (8·2%); Sesotho, 3,104,197 (7·7%); Xitsonga, 1,756,105 (4·4%); Siswati, 1,013,193 (2·5%); Tshivenda, 876,409 (2·2%); IsiNdebele, 586,961 (1·5%). The use of any of these is a constitutional right 'wherever practicable'. Each province may adopt any of these as its official language. English is the sole language of command and instruction in the armed forces.

SOCIAL STATISTICS

Births: the number of recorded births has decreased from 720,988 in 1991 to 409,359 in 2001.

Officially recorded marriages: the following statistics reflect marriages contracted and divorces granted during 1999, as registered by the civil registration system. (From 1998, under a new bill, customary and traditional marriages are recognized in law.) The total number of marriages officially recorded in 1999 was 155,807. The crude marriage rate was 355 per 100,000 of the population. Western Cape had the highest rate (596 per 100,000), Gauteng the second highest (523 per 100,000) followed by Free State (481 per 100,000). KwaZulu-Natal had the lowest rate (166 per 100,000), in part owing to unregistered customary and traditional marriages occurring mostly in this largely rural province. Of the total marriages officially recorded in 1999, 70,544 (45·3%) were solemnized in magistrates' courts and 52,630 in religious ceremonies. 32,633 were classed under 'unspecified'. In 1999 the median age for marrying was 33·7 years for men and 29·5 years for women. Divorces granted in 1999 totalled 37,098; the modified divorce rate was 660 per 100,000 of the population. Gauteng had the highest rate (1,253 per 100,000); Western Cape (1,140); and Northern Cape (797).

Deaths: the recorded number of deaths increased from 260,373 in 1997 to 362,450 in 2000. According to the State of SA's Population Report 2000 the annual population growth rate 1996–2001 was 2·2% and the fertility rate 2·9 births per woman. Life expectancy at birth, 1999, was 51·6 years for males and 56·2 for females. Deaths from AIDS, at 5,000 a week, are likely to result in life expectancy being just 38 by 2010. Infant mortality, 1999, 54 per 1,000 live births.

CLIMATE

There is abundant sunshine and relatively low rainfall. The southwest has a Mediterranean climate, with rain mainly in winter, but most of the country has a summer maximum, although quantities show a decrease from east to west. Pretoria, Jan. 73·4°F (23·0°C), July 53·6°F (12·0°C). Annual rainfall 26·5" (674 mm). Bloemfontein, Jan. 73·4°F (23·0°C), July 45·9°F (7·7°C). Annual rainfall 22" (559 mm). Cape Town, Jan. 69·6°F (20·9°C), July 54·0°F (12·2°C). Annual rainfall 20·3" (515 mm). Johannesburg, Jan. 68·2°F (20·1°C), July 50·7°F (10·4°C). Annual rainfall 28·1" (713 mm).

CONSTITUTION AND GOVERNMENT

An Interim *Constitution* came into effect on 27 April 1994 and was in force until 3 Feb. 1997. Under it, the National Assembly and Senate formed a Constitutional Assembly which had the task of drafting a definitive Constitution. This was signed into law in Dec. 1996 and took effect on 4 Feb. 1997. The 1996 Constitution defines the powers of the President, Parliament (consisting of the National Assembly and the new National Council of Provinces—NCOP), the national executive, the judiciary, public administration, the security services and the relationship between the three spheres of government. It incorporates a Bill of Rights pertaining to, *inter alia*, education, housing, food and water supply, and security, in addition to political rights. All legislation must conform to the Constitution and the Bill of Rights. The Constitution was amended in 2001 to provide that Constitutional Court judges are appointed for a non-renewable 12-year term of office, or until they reach the age of 70 years, except where an Act of Parliament extends the term of office of a Constitutional Court judge. This Constitution Amendment Act also made the head of the Constitutional Court the Chief Justice. The head of the Supreme Court of Appeal is now the President of that Court.

A *Constitutional Court*, consisting of a president, a deputy president and nine other judges, was inaugurated in Feb. 1995. The Court's judges are appointed by the President of the Republic from a list provided by the Judicial Service Commission, after consulting the President of the Constitutional Court (now the Chief Justice) and the leaders of parties represented in the National Assembly.

Parliament is the legislative authority and has the power to make laws for the country in accordance with the Constitution. It consists of the National Assembly and the NCOP. Parliamentary sittings are open to the public.

The *National Assembly* consists of no fewer than 350 and no more than 400 members directly elected for five years, 200 from a national list and 200 from provincial lists in the following proportions: Eastern Cape, 28; Free State, 14; Gauteng, 44; KwaZulu-Natal, 42; Limpopo, 25; Mpumalanga, 11; Northern Cape, 4; North-West, 12; Western Cape, 20. In terms of the 1993 Constitution, which still regulated the 1999 elections, the nine provincial legislatures are elected at the same time and candidates may stand for both. If elected to both, they have to choose between sitting in the national or provincial assembly. In the former case, the runner-up is elected to the Provincial Assembly.

The *National Council of Provinces* (NCOP) consists of 54 permanent members and 36 special delegates and aims to represent provincial interests in the national sphere of government. Delegations from each province consist of ten representatives. Bills (except finance bills) may be introduced in either house but must be passed by both. A finance bill may only be introduced in the National Assembly. If a bill is rejected by one house it is referred back to both after consideration by a joint National Assembly-NCOP committee called the Mediation Committee. Bills relating to the provinces must be passed by the NCOP. By Aug. 2002, 703 bills had been passed since 1994.

The Constitution mandates the establishment of *Traditional Leaders* by means of either provincial or national legislation. The National House of Traditional Leaders was established in April 1997. Each provincial House of Traditional Leaders nominated three members to be represented in the National House. The National House advises national government on the role of traditional leaders and on customary law. During 2001 all appointed traditional leaders were granted powers to become commissioners of oaths, bringing justice services closer to communities, particularly in rural areas.

National Anthem. A combination of shortened forms of 'Die Stem van Suid-Afrika'/'The Call of South Africa' (words by C. J. Langenhoven; tune by M. L. de Villiers) and the ANC anthem 'Nkosi sikelel' iAfrika'/'God bless Africa' (words and tune by Enos Santonga).

RECENT ELECTIONS

Parliamentary elections were held on 2 June 1999. The electorate was 22·7m.; turn-out, 89%. Of the 19 parties which took part in the elections, 13 are represented in Parliament, based on the election results. The African National Congress (ANC) won 266 seats in Parliament's National Assembly with 66·35% of votes cast, the

Democratic Party (DP) 38 with 9·56%, the Inkatha Freedom Party (IFP) 34 with 8·58%, the New National Party (NNP) 28 with 6·87%, the United Democratic Movement (UDM) 14 with 3·42%, the African Christian Democratic Party (ACDP) 6 with 1·43%, the Freedom Front (FF) 3 with 0·8%, the United Christian Democratic Party (UCDP) 3 with 0·78%, the Pan-Africanist Congress (PAC) 3 with 0·71%, the Freedom Alliance (FA) 2 with 0·54%, the Minority Front (MF) 1 with 0·3%, the Afrikaner Eenheidsbeweging (AEB) 1 with 0·29% and the Azanian People's Organization (AZAPO) 1 with 0·17%.

CURRENT ADMINISTRATION
President: Thabo M. Mbeki; b. 1942 (ANC; sworn in 16 June 1999).

In March 2003 the government comprised:

Executive Deputy President: Jacob G. Zuma. *Minister of Agriculture and Land Affairs:* A. Thoko Didiza. *Arts, Culture, Science and Technology:* Dr Ben S. Ngubane. *Communications:* Dr Ivy F. Matsepe-Cassaburri. *Correctional Services:* Ben M. Skosana. *Defence:* M. G. Patrick Lekota. *Education:* Prof. A. Kader Asmal. *Environmental Affairs and Tourism:* M. Valli Moosa. *Finance:* Trevor A. Manuel. *Foreign Affairs:* Dr Nkosazana C. Dlamini-Zuma. *Health:* Dr Manto E. Tshabalala-Msimang. *Home Affairs:* Dr Mangosuthu G. Buthelezi. *Housing:* Sankie D. Mthembi-Mahanyele. *Intelligence:* Dr Lindiwe N. Sisulu. *Justice and Constitutional Development:* Penuell M. Maduna. *Labour:* Membathisi M. S. Mdladlana. *Minerals and Energy:* Phumzile Mlambo-Ngcuka. *Provincial and Local Government:* F. Sydney Mufamadi. *Public Enterprises:* Jeff T. Radebe. *Public Service and Administration:* Geraldine J. Fraser-Moleketi. *Public Works:* Stella N. Sigcau. *Safety and Security:* Charles Nqakula. *Social Development and Welfare:* Zola S. T. Skweyiya. *Sport and Recreation:* B. M. Ngconde Balfour. *Trade and Industry:* Alec Erwin. *Transport:* Dullah Omar. *Water Affairs and Forestry:* Ronnie Kasrils. *Minister in the Presidency:* Essop G. Pahad.

Government Website: http://www.gov.za/

DEFENCE
There are four Services constituting the South African National Defence Force (SANDF), namely the SA Army, the SA Air Force, the SA Navy and the SA Military Health Service (SAMHS). SAMHS personnel at the end of 2000 totalled 7,328 (3,900 women) and 725 reserves. The final strength of the SANDF is still under discussion although reduction in total force strength is envisaged.

Defence expenditure totalled US$1,912m. in 2000 (equivalent to US$47 per capita), and represented 1·6% of GDP. Defence expenditure in 1985 was US$4,256m. (US$127 per capita and 2·7% of GDP).

Army. Personnel of the SA Army Regular Force in 2000 totalled 38,942 (including 6,032 civilian personnel); Reserve Force personnel totalled 85,074.

Navy. Navy personnel in 2000 totalled 5,000 uniformed, 2,500 civilian and 1,000 active reserve members. The fleet is based at the naval bases at Simon's Town on the west coast and Durban on the east and includes six *Warrior* class fast attack craft (missile) and two *Daphne* class submarines (to be supplemented from 2005 with three submarines on order from the German Submarine Consortium).

Air Force. Personnel in 2000 totalled 11,574. 12 attack and reconnaissance helicopters are scheduled to be based at Air Force Base Bloemspruit.

INTERNATIONAL RELATIONS
South Africa is a member of the UN, BIS, the Commonwealth (except during 1961–94), the African Union, the Southern African Development Community, the Non-Aligned Movement, the African Development Bank, the Antarctic Treaty and is an ACP member state of the ACP-EU relationship. South Africa played an active role in negotiating and drafting the Lusaka Ceasefire Agreement, signed on 10 July 1999. On 1 Dec. 1999 the eighth Regional Summit appointed Nelson Mandela facilitator of the Arusha peace process.

ECONOMY

Overview. To control inflation the central bank has adopted tight macro-economic policies. Strong public finances sustain a competitive exchange rate and low interest rates, while monetary policy contains inflationary pressures. However, economic and employment growths remain slow. In Aug. 2001 the rand fell to its weakest level ever, a rate of 8·43 to the US dollar. Since the apartheid era the government has focused on controlling the deficit while increasing spending on social programmes to combat inequality. The government's Medium Term Expenditure Framework focuses on education, health, welfare, police and justice. Foreign debt relative to GDP declined in 2001. HIV/AIDS, in addition to human costs, hampers economic and social progress.

Currency. The unit of currency is the *rand* (ZAR) of 100 *cents*. A single free-floating exchange rate replaced the former two-tier system on 13 March 1995. The year-on-year rate of increase in the CPIX—the new measure of consumer price inflation for inflation targeting purposes, which excludes home mortgage rates from the overall consumer price index for metropolitan and other urban areas—was 8·2% in Aug. 2000, 5·9% in Oct. 2001 and 12·5% in Oct. 2002. The inflation target is 3 to 6% for the annual average of CPIX inflation for the years 2002 and 2003. The official inflation rate or the 12-month rate of change in the consumer price index (CPI) fell from 7·8% in Feb. 2001 to 4·0% in Oct. 2001.

Foreign exchange reserves were US$5,673m. and gold reserves 5·72m. troy oz in June 2002. Total money supply was R339,233m. in June 2002.

Budget. The central government's State Revenue Account in R1bn.:

	1998–99	1999–2000	2000–01	2001–02	2002–03
Revenue	184·0	198·2	215·6	248·1	265·2
Expenditure	201·4	214·8	233·9	262·6	287·9

The 2002 budget provided for expenditure of 26·6% of GDP; revenue, 24·5% of GDP. South Africa's deficit is revised to 2·1% in 2002–03 and is projected to decline to 1·7% by 2004–05. About R47·5bn. or 4·4% of GDP is spent on debt servicing.

VAT has remained at 14% since 1993. Corporate taxes were reduced to 30% in 1999. A tiered corporate tax was introduced in 2000 with taxes for small businesses reduced by half. R9·9bn. was returned to taxpayers in reduced personal income tax for all income groups but particularly for lower and middle income groups. The marginal tax rate for high-income earners was cut to 42% from 45%. A capital gains tax was introduced from 1 April 2001 and became effective on 1 Oct. 2001.

Performance. Economic growth averaged 2·7% annually between 1994–2000. The emerging market financial crisis led to a slowdown in growth in 1998 and a marked depreciation of the rand. Uncertainty in emerging markets combined with the Zimbabwean land seizures contributed to the heightened depreciation of the rand.

In the late 1990s the budget deficit was steadily reduced to less than 3% of GDP. In 2001–02 a deficit of 1·4% was achieved. The government's Medium Term Expenditure Framework prioritizes spending on education, health and welfare, while also providing for stronger police and justice expenditure. The high prevalence of HIV/AIDS is another threat to the resources of the South African economy.

Total GDP in 2001 was US$113bn. while the growth in real GDP for 2000 was 3·1%. For the first nine months of 2002 it was 3·1% year-on-year. Gross international reserves were about US$7·9bn. in Dec. 2002.

Banking and Finance. The central bank and bank of issue is the South African Reserve Bank (established 1920), which functions independently. Its *Governor* is Tito Mboweni. The Banks Act, 1990 governs the operations and prudential requirements of banks. As at 31 Oct. 2001 the minimum capital adequacy requirement was 10%.

As at 31 Dec. 2001, 53 banks, including 14 branches of foreign banks and 2 mutual banks, were registered with the Office of the Registrar of Banks. 55 foreign banks have authorized representative offices in South Africa. The registered banking institutions collectively had 120,527 employees at 10,437 branches and agencies; their combined assets amounted to R970·9bn. (31 Oct. 2001).

The stock exchange, the JSE Securities Exchange, is based in Johannesburg. Foreign nationals have been eligible for membership since Nov. 1995.

Weights and Measures. The metric system is in use.

ENERGY AND NATURAL RESOURCES

Environment. According to the *World Bank Atlas* South Africa's carbon dioxide emissions in 1998 were the equivalent of 8·3 tonnes per capita.

Electricity. South African households use over 25% of the country's energy. Coal supplies 75% of primary energy requirements, followed by oil (20·7%), nuclear (3·0%) and natural gas (1·3%). There is 1 nuclear power station (Koeberg) with 2 reactors, 2 gas turbine generators, 2 conventional hydroelectric plants and 2 pumped storage stations. Nuclear energy is being investigated as a future potential energy source and alternative to coal. The government has announced it is to sell off Eskom, the *parastatal* or government-related organization. Eskom generates 95% of the country's electricity (as well as two-thirds of the electricity for the African continent) and owns and operates the national transmission system.

The energy sector contributes about 15% to GDP and employs about 250,000 people. Because of South Africa's large coal deposits, the country is one of the four cheapest electricity suppliers in the world. Residential use is characterized by poor access to facilities and inefficient or hazardous energy sources, such as fuel wood and paraffin being used. An estimated 7·12m. (66%) of South Africa's 10·77m. households had electricity at the end of 2001; 2·17m. rural and 1·48m. urban households remain without electrical power.

Oil and Gas. South Africa has no significant oil reserves and relies on coal for most of its oil production. It has a highly developed synthetic fuels industry, as well as small deposits of oil and natural gas. Sasol Oil and Petro SA are the two major players in the synthetic fuel market. Synfuels meet approximately 40% of local demand. The prospects for natural gas production have increased by the discovery of offshore reserves close to the Namibian border in 2000. Production will commence in 2004 and will be channelled to regulate electricity production. Petro SA is responsible for exploration of both offshore natural gas and onshore coal-bed methane. South Africa is one of the major oil refining nations in Africa with a crude refining capacity of 543,000 bbls. per day.

Water. Rivers are the main source of water in South Africa. Ninety per cent of all water used in the country is abstracted from surface water and 10% from ground water. Average annual rainfall is a little less than 500 mm compared to the world average of about 860 mm. On average, only some 9% of rainfall reaches the rivers. 65% of the country receives less than 500 mm, which is generally accepted as the minimum required for successful dryland farming. 21% of the country, mainly in the arid west, receives less than 200 mm annually. On average only some 8% of rainfall reaches the rivers. The resultant surface water run-off is estimated to be about 50,000m. cu. metres, including that flowing out of Lesotho.

Irrigation and stock watering accounts for about 61% of the water used; 2% for stock watering, 2% for rural domestic, 15% for urban domestic, 7% for municipal, 8% for industry, 3% for mining and 2·3% for power generation. During 2000–01 over 1m. people were provided with basic water, reaching a total of 7m. since 1994.

On 1 July 2001 the Free Basic Water Policy was implemented, allowing every household to receive 6,000 litres of free water every month.

In 1998 a new National Water Act came into effect with the nation's water resources becoming a national resource belonging to the nation as a whole. Water availability is distributed poorly in relation to regions of economic growth and, as a result, major inter-basin water transfer schemes are a feature of the South African infrastructure. The latest such scheme, the first phase of which has been completed, is the Lesotho Highlands Water Project. This diverts the Orange River headwaters within Lesotho through tunnels into the Vaal River System, which serves an area where about 60% of the GDP of the country is generated. Lesotho receives royalties in exchange.

Minerals. Total value of all minerals sold, 1999: R76,387·1m.

Mineral production (in tonnes), 2001: coal, 223·5m.; silver, 109·6; iron ore, 34·8m.; limestone, 18·8m.; chrome ore, 5·5m.; manganese, 3·3m.; aluminium, 662,000; copper, 141,000; nickel, 36,400; platinum-group metals, 28,747; diamonds, 11,162,630 carats. South African gold production continued to slide in 1999, with output falling 4·5% to 443 tonnes, while total revenue increased by 3·5% to R25·1bn. Owing to the accelerated weakening of the rand, the average rand price of gold improved by 21% from R1,932·50 per oz in 2000 to R2,338·20 per oz in 2001. In 2001, 749 mines and quarries employed 407,154 people.

Agriculture. Much of the land suitable for mechanized farming has unreliable rainfall. Of the total farming area, natural pasture occupies 81% (69·6m. ha) and planted pasture 2·3% (2m. ha). About 13% of South Africa's surface area can be used for crop production. High potential arable land comprises only 22% of the total arable land. Annual crops and orchards are cultivated on 9·9m. ha of dry land and 1·4m. ha under irrigation. Primary agriculture contributes about 2·9% to GDP and almost 9% of formal employment.

Production (2001, in 1,000 tonnes): sugarcane, 21,156; maize, 7,772; wheat, 2,467; potatoes, 1,655; oranges, 1,268; sunflower seeds, 690; apples, 567; table grapes, 239; groundnuts, 222; sorghum, 206.

Livestock, in 1,000 (2002): 13,437 cattle, 29,034 sheep, 6,692 goats, 1,570 pigs; chickens, 61,000 (2000).

The 2002 production of red meat was 807,000 tonnes; poultry meat, 949,000 tonnes; wool (2001), 43,101 tonnes; eggs, 330,000 tonnes; milk, 2·4m. tonnes.

The value of agricultural imports increased by 13·9% and the value of exports increased by 37·6% for 2001 compared to 2000. Based on 2001 export values, sugar (R2,703m.), wine (R1,963m.), citrus fruit (R1,799m.), grapes (R1,327m.), and preserved fruit and nuts (R990m.) were the most important export products. Rice (R954m.), oil-cake (R762m.), undenatured ethyl alcohol (R602m.), tobacco (R456m.) and palm oil (R455m.) were the most important import products. During 2001 the UK, the Netherlands, Japan and Mozambique were the largest export destinations.

In 1999 the gross value of agricultural production was R43,647m. (field crops, R14,302m.; livestock products, R17,669m.; horticulture, R11,676m.). Primary agriculture contributes about 3·2% to GDP and almost 9% of formal employment. South Africa is one of the largest exporters in the world of avocados, grapes, citrus and deciduous fruit and, for the past five years, agricultural exports have contributed on average approximately 8% (7% in 2000) of total exports.

Forestry. South Africa has developed one of the largest man-made forestry resources in the world. Production from these plantations approached 16m. cu. metres valued at R2·3bn. in 1998–99. Together with the products processed from it, the total industry turnover in 2000–01 was around R11·8bn. (R19bn. in 1998–99). Collectively, the industry employs more than 135,000 people both in primary production and primary wood processing operations. The forest products industry exported R8·7bn. worth of products in 2000 making it a net exporter to the value of more than R5bn. in that year. Raw material exports (e.g. logs) made up only 1·6% of these exports. The forestry industry currently ranks among the top exporting industries in the country, contributing some 9% to the overall export of manufactured goods in 2000.

Indigenous high forest covers only about 534,000 ha or 0·4% of the country's surface. The private sector owns 971,098 ha of exotic plantations (especially pine, eucalyptus and wattle) or 66% of the total plantation area, as well as virtually all the processing plants in the country. In 2000–01 there were 1,280 registered private timber growers and more than 14,000 unregistered growers, the latter being small emergent black timber growers.

Fisheries. The commercial marine fishing industry is valued at more than R3bn. annually and employs 28,000 people directly. It is an important employer because it pays a relatively high average individual income (approximately R36,000) to its employees, of whom the majority are semi-skilled. In 2000 the commercial fishing fleet consisted of 4,477 vessels licensed by the Department of Environmental Affairs and Tourism. Line-fishing vessel permits numbered 2,731 and 480 tuna permits were issued to 5,150 fishers. The total catch in 1999 was 588,001 tonnes, 99% of which came from marine fishing. Deep sea hake amounts to over half of the total catch and an estimated 35% of fish is exported.

INDUSTRY
The leading companies by market capitalization in South Africa, excluding banking and finance, in Jan. 2002 were: Anglo Amercian Platinum Corp. Ltd (R108bn.), the world's primary platinum group metals producer; Sasol Ltd (R73bn.), a coal, oil and gas producer; and AngloGold Ltd (R63bn.), the world's leading gold producer.

Net value of sales of the principal groups of industries (in R1m.) in 1999: food and food products, 57,136; chemicals and products, 45,353; vehicles and vehicle parts, 42,719; basic iron and steel products, 25,867; fabricated metal products except machinery, 23,536; beverages, 20,653; petroleum products, 20,464; paper and products, 20,400. Total net value including other groups, R397,320m. Manufacturing contributed R108,470m. towards GDP of R544,654m. in 1999, and thus accounted for 20% of the total.

Labour. The Employment Equity Act, 1998 signalled the beginning of the final phase of transformation in the job market, which began with the implementation of the Labour Relations Act. It aims to avoid all discrimination in employment. The Basic Conditions of Employment Act, 1997 applies to all workers except for the South African National Defence Force (SANDF), the South African Secret Service (SASS) and the National Intelligence Agency (NIA). The new provisions include a reduction in the maximum hours of work from 46 to 45 hours per week (however, the Act includes a process for the progressive reduction of working hours to 40 per week).

The number of those who are economically active—both the employed and the unemployed—was 16·1m. in Feb. 2002. The number of unemployed rose from 1·8m. in 1995 to 3·2m. in 1999. In Feb. 2001 the unemployment rate was 26·4% (26·7% in Feb. 2000).

Trade Unions. At the end of 2000 there were 464 registered trade unions with 3·6m. members. The most important trade union groups or federations are Federation of Trade Unions of South Africa (FEDUSA), National Council of Trade Unions (NACTU) and Congress of South African Trade Unions (COSATU). The three largest trade unions are the National Union of Mineworkers (NUM), the National Union of Metalworkers of South Africa (NUMSA), both COSATU affiliates, and the Public Servants Association, an affiliate of FEDUSA. Employers also have the right to associate with employer organizations and register their organizations with the Department of Labour. In Jan. 2000 there were 242 registered employer organizations and 10 federations of employer organizations. The Labour Court has been operating since Nov. 1996.

INTERNATIONAL TRADE
Since 1994 the (rand) value of both exports and imports in manufactured goods has more than doubled. South Africa's four main trading partners in 1999 were the UK, US, Germany and Japan. In regional terms Europe is the leading trading partner, taking more than one third of exports, followed by Asia (18·5%), Africa (13·6%) and North America (13·2%). In 1999 approximately 30% of exports were destined for Africa. Trade with the Southern African Development Community (SADC) has increased significantly from R16bn. in 1998 to R22bn. in 2000. In 1999 merchandise exports represented 86% (R148·9bn.) of total exports (merchandise plus net gold exports and excluding receipts for services).

A Trade, Co-operation and Development Agreement with the European Union was signed by the EU and South Africa in 1999 which will result in the abolition of tariffs on more than 90% of trade, currently worth in excess of R10bn. annually, between the 15 EU countries and South Africa within 12 years. Trade and development co-operation agreements worth R635m. were signed by South Africa and the EU in April 1999. EU grants made between 1995 and 1998 exceeded R3bn.

Total foreign debt in 2000 was US$24,861m. Total net gold exports in 1999 amounted to R24·2bn. During 1999 the value of merchandise imports was R150·3bn.

Imports and Exports. Trade in US$1m.:

	1996	1997	1998	1999	2000
Imports f.o.b.	27,568	28,848	27,208	24,474	27,202
Exports f.o.b.	30,263	31,171	29,264	28,624	31,434

Main imports (in R1bn.):

	1997	1998	1999
Machinery and mechanical appliances	40,555	52,057	45,629
Mineral products	16,782	12,943	15,507
Chemicals or allied industries	13,836	15,667	16,959
Vehicles, aircraft, vessels and associated transport equipment	7,116	8,914	10,689
Plastics and articles thereof	5,349	5,871	6,100

Main exports (in R1bn.):

	1997	1998	1999
Natural or cultured pearls	32,345	33,538	35,173
Base metals and articles thereof	20,859	22,461	24,619
Mineral products	18,418	19,037	21,512
Products of chemicals or allied industries	8,908	9,218	9,987
Vehicles, aircraft, vessels and associated transport equipment	6,604	7,933	12,217
Machinery and mechanical appliances	8,278	9,916	12,008

In Oct. 1998 a transshipment facility for containers opened at Kidatu, southwest of Dar es Salaam, Tanzania, providing a link between the 1,067 mm gauge railways of the southern part of Africa and the 1,000 mm gauge lines of the north. With the opening up of new markets for South Africa elsewhere in the continent, it will help to boost trade and facilitate the shipment of cargo to countries to the north.

COMMUNICATIONS

The public company Transnet Limited was established on 1 April 1990. Annually, Transnet handles 180m. tonnes of rail freight, 2·1m. tonnes of road freight, 2·5m. passengers by road, 194m. tonnes through the harbours; and 15,400m. litres are pumped through its petrol pipelines. The company flies 6·1m. domestic, international and regional passengers per year. In total, Transnet is worth R58·5bn. in fixed assets and has a workforce of some 80,000 employees.

Transnet consists of eight divisions—Spoornet, Port Authority, Port Operations, Freight Dynamics, Petronet, Metrorail, Propnet and Transtel, as well as South African Airways and a number of related and support businesses. For the financial year ended 31 March 2001 Transnet reported a profit of R3,287m. (compared to a net loss of R779m. for 2000).

Roads. The total length of the road network is 754,200 km, which includes 7,200 km of national roads, 357,333 km of provincial roads, 221,000 km of un-proclaimed roads and 168,000 km of metro, municipal and other roads. Toll-roads cover about 1,900 km. The network includes 1,400 km of dual-carriage freeways, 440 km of single-carriage freeways and 5,436 km of single-carriage main roads with restricted access. South Africa has the longest motorway network of any country in Africa. As at 31 Dec. 2002 there were 6·99m. registered motor vehicles, more than 4m. of which were motor cars. In 1999 there were 452,915 road accidents with 10,523 fatalities.

Rail. The South African Rail Commuter Corporation Limited (SARCC), an agency of the Department of Transport, is responsible for the provision of commuter rail services. It owns all commuter rail assets and property worth R5bn. SARCC contracts Metrorail (a division of Transnet) to provide services on its behalf. Metrorail carries more than 2·2m. passengers daily, serves 470 stations and operates one of the longest tracks in the world, covering 2,400 km through five metropolitan areas. Spoornet provides cargo transport and some long-distance passenger transport, including the luxurious Blue Train.

Civil Aviation. Responsibility for civil aviation safety and security lies with the South African Civil Aviation Authority (SACAA). The Airports Company South Africa (ACSA) owns and operates South Africa's principal airports—Johannesburg, Cape Town and Durban international airports, and the airports at Kimberley, Port Elizabeth, Bloemfontein, George, East London and Upington. Together, the nine airports handle more than 196,000 aircraft landings and 10m. departing passengers annually. Johannesburg is expected to deal with 13·5m. passengers a year by 2005. ACSA also has a 35-year concession to operate Pilanesberg International Airport near Sun City in North-West Province.

South African Airways (SAA), Comair, SA Express and SA Airlink operate scheduled international air services. 13 independent operators provide internal flights which link up with the internal network of SAA, Comair and SA Express.

In 2000 Johannesburg handled 11,187,948 passengers (5,981,562 on domestic flights) and 439,994 tonnes of freight. Cape Town handled 4,654,000 passengers (3,645,000 on domestic flights). Durban handled 2,501,999 passengers (2,440,929 on domestic flights) and 14,737 tonnes of freight.

Shipping. The South African Maritime Safety Authority (SAMSA) was established on 1 April 1998 as the authority responsible for ensuring the safety of life at sea and the prevention of sea pollution from ships. The National Ports Authority supervises 16 of South Africa's ports. The largest ports include the deep water ports of Richards Bay, with its multi-product dry bulk handling facilities, multi-purpose terminal and the world's largest bulk coal terminal, and Saldanah featuring a bulk ore terminal adjacent to a bulk oil jetty with extensive storage facilities. Durban, Cape Town and Port Elizabeth provide large container terminals for deep-sea and coastal container traffic. East London, the only river port, has a multi-purpose terminal and dry dock facilities. Mossel Bay is a specialized port serving the south coast fishing industry and offshore gas fields.

In 1998 the merchant fleet totalled 631,059,096 GRT. During 1998 the major ports handled a total of 187,008,889 tonnes of cargo, and a total of 13,559 ships' calls were registered.

Telecommunications. In July 2000 there were 1·8m. PC and Internet users (42 per 1,000 population) and 150,000 fax machines. South Africa has approximately 5·3m. installed telephones and 4·3m. installed exchange lines, representing 39% of total lines installed in Africa.

Telkom SA, the national operator, was awarded a five-year licence in May 1997 giving the company the exclusive right to provide telecommunications services. It was required to install 2·8m. new lines, including 120,000 payphones in the five years to March 2002. Over the same period it was required to provide first-time telephone services for over 3,000 villages, install more than 20,000 new lines for priority customers such as schools and hospitals and replace around 1,200m. analogue lines with digital technology. The transmission network is almost wholly digital.

South Africa, with the operators Vodacom and MTN, is the fourth fastest-growing GSM (Global Systems for Mobile Communications) market in the world. It is currently worth R13bn. and will grow to around R20bn. by 2004. The third operator, Cell C, started operating in Nov. 2001. There were 11·2m. mobile phone users in Jan. 2002; there are forecast to be 21m. by 2006.

Postal Services. By March 2001 the Post Office had 2,680 postal outlets and 26 mail processing centres throughout the country and delivered 8m. letters daily. Public Information Terminals (PiTs) offer government information and an e-mail service, Internet browsing, business sections and educational services. By Sept. 2001, 100 kiosks had been installed in post offices.

SOCIAL INSTITUTIONS

Justice. All law must be consistent with the Constitution and its Bill of Rights. Judgments of courts declaring legislation, executive action, or conduct to be invalid are binding on all organs of state and all persons. The common law of the Republic was based on Roman-Dutch law—that is the uncodified law of Holland as it was at the date of the cession of the Cape to the United Kingdom in 1806. South African law has, however, developed its own unique characteristics since then. All courts so as to promote the spirit, purport and objects of the Bill of Rights must now develop it.

The Judicial authority of the Republic is vested in the courts. The higher courts are presided over by Judges. Judges hold office until they attain the age of 70 years, or if they have not served for 15 years, until they have completed 15 years of service or have reached the age of 75, when they are discharged from active service. A judge discharged from active service has to be available to perform service for an aggregate of three months a year until the age of 75. The Chief Justice of South Africa, the Deputy Chief Justice, the President of the Supreme Court of Appeal and the Deputy President of the Supreme Court of Appeal are appointed by the President after consulting the Judicial Service Commission. In the case of the Chief Justice and Deputy Chief Justice, the President must also consult the leaders of parties represented in the National Assembly. The President on the advice of the Judicial Service Commission (JSC) appoints all other judges. No judge may be removed from office unless the JSC finds that the judge suffers from incapacity, is grossly incompetent or is guilty of gross misconduct, and the National Assembly calls for that judge to be removed by a resolution supported by at least two thirds of its members.

The higher courts include the following: 1) *The Constitutional Court* (CC), which consists of the Chief Justice of South Africa, the Deputy Chief Justice of South Africa and nine other judges. It is the highest court in all matters in which the interpretation of the Constitution or its application to any law, including the common law, is relevant; 2) *The Supreme Court of Appeal*, consisting of a President, a Deputy President and the number of judges of appeal determined by an Act of Parliament. It is the highest court of appeal in all other matters; 3) *The High Courts*, which may decide constitutional matters other than those which are within the exclusive jurisdiction of the Constitutional Court, and any other matter other than one assigned by Parliament to a court of a status similar to that of a High Court. Each High Court is presided over by a Judge President who may divide the area under his jurisdiction into circuit districts. In each such district there shall be held at least twice in every year and at such times and places determined by the Judge President, a court which shall be presided over by a judge of the High Court. Such a court is known as the circuit court for the district in question; 4) *The Land Claims Court*, established under the Restitution of Land Rights Act of 1994 deals with claims for restitution of rights in land to persons or communities dispossessed of such rights after 1913 as a result of past racially discriminatory laws or practices. It has jurisdiction throughout the Republic and the power to determine such claims and related matters such as compensation and rights of occupation; 5) *The Labour Court*, established under the Labour Relations Act, 1995 deals with labour disputes. It is a superior court that has authority, inherent powers and standing in relation to matters under its jurisdiction, equal to that the High Court has in relation to matters under its jurisdiction. Appeals from decisions of the Labour Court lie to the Labour Appeal Court which has authority in labour matters equivalent to that of the Supreme Court of Appeal in other matters.

The lower courts are called Magistrates' Courts. The nine provinces are divided into 370 magisterial districts each with a magistrates court having a prescribed civil and criminal jurisdiction. There are 746 magistrates court offices. From the magistrates court there is an appeal to the High Court having jurisdiction in that area, and then to the Supreme Court of Appeal. In cases involving constitutional matters there is a further appeal to the Constitutional Court. Sentences imposed by district magistrates above a prescribed limit are in most cases subject to automatic review by a judge.

All criminal and civil cases are dealt with by judges (in the high courts) and magistrates (in the lower courts). A limited civil and criminal jurisdiction is also conferred upon courts of traditional leaders. In addition to civil jurisdiction at magisterial and high court level, there are currently 140 small claims courts, which have been introduced since 1984. These courts (where Commissioners preside) have jurisdiction only, limited by the quantum of damages and the nature of the claim. The current limit for claims in the Small Claims Courts is R3,000.

The death penalty was abolished in June 1995 and no executions have taken place since 1989.

In 1999 there were 24,210 murders, a rate of 56·2 per 100,000 persons (1994: 26,832 murders, representing a rate of 69·5 per 100,000 persons). South Africa has one of the highest murder rates in the world. Spending on police, prisons and justice services amounted to R23·5bn. in 1999.

Religion. Almost 80% of the population in South Africa professes the Christian faith. Other major religious groups are the Hindus, Muslims and Jews. A sizeable minority of the population does not belong to any of the major religions but regard themselves as traditionalists or of no specific religious affiliation. Freedom of worship is guaranteed by the Constitution and official policy is one of non-interference in religious practices. In 1992 the Anglican Church of Southern Africa voted by 79% of votes cast for the ordination of women.

Education. The South African Schools Act, 1996 became effective on 1 Jan. 1997 and provides for: compulsory education for students between the ages of 7 and 15 years of age, or students reaching the ninth grade, whichever occurs first. Curriculum 2005, the brand name of the new national curriculum framework for schools, is based on the concept of outcomes-based education (OBE), the focus being on what students should know and do. The new learning programmes are being introduced in phases.

In 2002–03 education was allocated a budget of R59,669m., with R7,469m. allocated to universities and technikons, and R50,865m. to college and school education. During 2000 around 76,100 students benefited from the Government's National Student Financial Aid Scheme for universities and technikons (R443·5m.); R500m. was earmarked for 2002–03.

There are more than 11·6m. school pupils, 26,789 primary and secondary schools with 348,362 educators. There were 22 universities in 2002 (407,401 students enrolled in 2002), two of which are mainly non-residential institutions offering distance tuition; and 15 technikons (202,730 students enrolled, 2002). During 1999 provincial education departments reached 300,000 Adult Basic Education and Training (ABET) students. Expenditure on ABET increased from R160m. in the 1995–96 financial year to R343m. in 1998–99.

The University of South Africa (UNISA) is the oldest and largest university in South Africa and one the largest distance education institutions in the world. There were 130,347 students and 1,168 teaching and research staff in 2001.

According to the *State of South Africa's Population Report 2000,* 18·3% of the population over 20 years of age has had no schooling. The adult literacy rate in 1999 was 84·9% (85·7% for males and 84·2%, females). The female literacy rate is the highest in Africa.

Health. Some 40% of South Africans live in poverty and 75% of these live in rural areas where they are deprived of access to health services. An estimated 29,927 doctors, including doctors working for the State, doctors in private practice and specialists, were registered with the Health Profession Council of South Africa (HPCSA) in Dec. 2001. Doctors train at the medical schools of eight universities. The majority of doctors practise privately.

In Dec. 2001 a total of 4,503 dentists, 381 dental and oral specialists (2000), 849 oral hygienists and 347 dental therapists were registered with the HPSCA. In Dec. 2001, 10,782 pharmacists were registered with the South African Pharmacy Council; there were 172,338 registered and enrolled nurses and enrolled nursing auxiliaries.

A network of mobile clinics run by the Government form the main role of primary and preventive health care. Clinics are being built or expanded throughout the country. By April 1999, 168 private medical schemes had been registered in terms of the provisions of the Medical Schemes Act, 1967.

In Oct. 1998 the first traditional hospital was opened in Mpumalanga—the Samuel Traditional Hospital. There are about 350,000 traditional healers in South Africa providing services to between 60% and 80% of their communities.

Approximately 4·7m. South Africans are HIV-infected, the highest number in the world (equivalent to nearly 11% of the population of South Africa and nearly 12% of all the people believed to be infected worldwide).

Welfare. As of Dec. 2002 the Department of Social Development was disbursing grants through its provincial offices to more than 4·8m. beneficiaries at a monthly cost of R2·5bn. Recipients are means-tested to determine their eligibility. The primary beneficiaries are 2m. older persons (women aged 60 and above, men aged 65 and above, who receive an Old Age Grant of R640 per month. A further 1·8m. children aged less than seven receive a R140 Child Support Grant (CSG) per month. The number of children in payment has increased steadily since the introduction of the CSG in March 1998. Other benefits paid are the Disability, Foster Child, Care Dependency and War Veteran's Grants as well as Institutional Grants and Grants in Aid.

The total budget allocation for the payment of social assistance by the provincial departments of social development was R18,798bn. in 2000–01.

CULTURE

Broadcasting. The South African Broadcasting Corporation (SABC), the country's public broadcaster, provides six television channels in 11 languages. Four are free-to-air, namely SABC1, SABC2, SABC3 and Bop-TV, while Africa2Africa and SABC Africa are pay-television channels, broadcast by satellite.

There are more than 4m. licensed television households. About 50% of all programmes transmitted are produced in South Africa.

M-Net, the country's first private subscription television service, was launched in 1986 and today has over 1·23m. subscribers in 41 countries across Africa. On 15 Nov. 1999 a new Afrikaans television channel—KykNET—was launched on M-Net's digital satellite television (DStv) service.

SABC has 19 radio stations, attracting 20m. listeners daily. Its external service, launched in 1966 as Radio South Africa and now known as Channel Africa, broadcasts to Africa and the Indian Ocean Islands. It offers an all-African radio service providing programmes with a specifically African content. Channel Africa is in the process of commercialization and expansion, turning it into a commercial enterprise, with R28m. budgeted for this purpose. The UK's BBC World Service and the SABC announced details of a new working agreement between the two corporations in Oct. 1999. In June 2000 the IBA licensed XK-FM, the first SABC community radio station.

The following private radio stations have been granted licences by the ICASA: Classic FM in Gauteng; Punt Geselsradio, operating in Gauteng and the Western Cape; Cape Talk MW in the Western Cape; P4 in Cape Town and Durban; Kaya FM, in Gauteng; Y-FM, broadcasting in Johannesburg in IsiZulu, Sesotho and English; Radio KFM; Radio Algoa; Radio Oranje; Highveld Stereo; Radio 702 in Gauteng; East Coast Radio; and Radio Jacaranda. More than 80 community radio stations have been licensed since 1995.

In Sept. 1999, 85% of the population was able to receive a television signal (colour by PAL).

Press. The major press groups are Independent Newspapers, Nasionale Media, Perskor and Times Media (TML). Other important media players are Primedia, Nail (New Africa Investments Limited) and Kagiso Media. The flagship publication of New Africa Media is the biggest English daily in South Africa, *Sowetan* (circulation Jan.–June 2000, 209,855).

The only truly national newspapers are the three Sundays: *Sunday Times* (circulation, Jan.–June 2000, 504,845), *Rapport* (340,023) and *The Sunday Independent* (42,653), and the weekly newspaper *City Press*. *Die Burger Saterdag* (Cape Town) is the largest Afrikaans daily (109,728 in 2000). There are 16 dailies and 11 weekly newspapers.

Tourism. South Africa has one of the fastest-growing tourist industries in the world, contributing R25bn. to the economy in 2000 (about 4·9% of GDP). It has gone from a world ranking of fifty-fifth in 1990 to twenty-fifth in 1998, attracting more tourists than any other country in Africa. The number of foreign tourists is growing by around 12% a year. In 2001 arrivals from outside the continent continued to grow by 2·7% despite the global slowdown. Tourism employs an estimated 7% of the country's workforce and it is projected that more than 1·2m. people will be employed (directly and indirectly) in tourism by 2010. Tourism is the fourth-largest industry in South Africa, supporting some 700 hotels, 2,800 guest houses and bed-and-breakfast establishments and 10,000 restaurants.

Festivals. Best-known arts festivals: the Klein Karoo Festival (Oudtshoorn, Western Cape), which has a strong Afrikaans component, is held in April; the Grahamstown Arts Festival in Eastern Cape province is held in June/July; the Manguang African Cultural Festival (Macufe) is held in Sept. in Bloemfontein; and the Potchefstroom Arts Festival, in North-West province, is held in Oct.

Libraries. There are two national libraries (in Cape Town and Pretoria) and hundreds of public (municipal) libraries, special libraries, government libraries, and university and college libraries.

The Legal Deposit Act, 1997 came into effect in July 1998. There are now five places of legal deposit—the National Library of South Africa (Cape Town as well as Pretoria), the Library of Parliament, the Bloemfontein Public Library, the Natal Society Library and the National Film, Video and Sound Archives.

Theatre and Opera. The four regional performing arts councils are obliged to ensure that they become representative of the full diversity of South African culture. A national arts council (NAC), which is broadly representative of all South Africans, has been established to address the promotion and development of all South African art forms on a national level. The main theatres are the Artscape in Cape Town, the Playhouse Company in Durban, the Performing Arts Centre in Bloemfontein and the State Theatre in Pretoria.

Museums and Galleries. More than 300 of the approximately 1,000 museums in Africa are situated in South Africa. The newest national museum is the Robben Island Museum which includes the cell in which former President Nelson Mandela was imprisoned. The largest museums are situated in Johannesburg, Pretoria, Cape Town, Durban, Pietermaritzburg and Bloemfontein. Art galleries include: South African National Gallery, Cape Town; Johannesburg Art Gallery; Pretoria Art Museum; William Humphreys Art Gallery, Kimberley.

There are several open-air museums which show the black cultures of the country including Tsongakraal near Letsitele, Limpopo; the Ndebele Museum at Middelburg, Mpumalanga; the Bakhoni (Northern Sotho) Museum at Pietersburg, Limpopo; and the South Sotho Museum at Witsieshoek, Free State.

DIPLOMATIC REPRESENTATIVES
Of South Africa in the United Kingdom (South Africa Hse., Trafalgar Sq., London, WC2N 5DP)
High Commissioner: Lindiwe Mabuza.

Of the United Kingdom in South Africa (255 Hill St., Arcadia, Pretoria 0001)
High Commissioner: Ann Grant.

Of South Africa in the USA (3051 Massachusetts Ave., NW, Washington, D.C., 20008)
Ambassador: Makate Sheila Sisulu.

Of the USA in South Africa (877 Pretorius St., Arcadia, Pretoria 0083)
Ambassador: Cameron R. Hume.

Of South Africa to the United Nations
Ambassador: Dumisana Shadrack Kumalo.

Of South Africa to the European Union
Ambassador: Jeremy Matthews Matjila.

FURTHER READING
Government Communication and Information System (GCIS), including extracts from the *South Africa Yearbook 2000/01*, compiled and published by GCIS.

Beinart, W., *Twentieth Century South Africa.* OUP, 1994
Brewer, J. (ed.) *Restructuring South Africa.* London, 1994
Davenport, T. R. H., *South Africa: a Modern History.* 5th ed. Macmillan, Basingstoke, 2000
Davis, G. V., *South Africa.* [Bibliography] 2nd ed. ABC-Clio, Oxford and Santa Barbara (CA), 1994
De Klerk, F. W., *The Last Trek—A New Beginning,* Macmillan, London, 1999
Fine, B and Rustomjee Z., *The Political Economy of South Africa,* 1997
Hough, M. and Du Plessis, A. (eds.) *Selected Documents and Commentaries on Negotiations and Constitutional Development in the RSA, 1989–1994.* Pretoria Univ., 1994
Johnson, R. W. and Schlemmer, L. (eds.) *Launching Democracy in South Africa: the First Open Election, 1994.* Yale Univ. Press, 1996
Mandela, N., *Long Walk to Freedom: the Autobiography of Nelson Mandela.* Abacus, London, 1994
Meredith, M., *South Africa's New Era: the 1994 Election.* London, 1994
Mostert, N., *Frontiers: the Epic of South Africa's Creation and the Tragedy of the Xhosa People.* London, 1992

Nattrass, N. and Ardington, E. (eds.) *The Political Economy of South Africa*. Cape Town and OUP, 1990
Thompson, L., *A History of South Africa*. 2nd ed. Yale Univ. Press, 1996
The Truth and Reconciliation Commission of South Africa Report, 5 vols. Macmillan, London, 1999
Turner, Barry, (ed.) *Southern Africa Profiled*. Macmillan, London, 2000
Waldmeir, P., *Anatomy of a Miracle: the End of Apartheid and the Birth of the New South Africa*, London, 1997
Who's Who in South African Politics. 5th ed. London, 1995

National statistical office: Statistics South Africa, Private Bag X44, Pretoria 0001.
Website: http://www.statssa.gov.za/

SOUTH AFRICAN PROVINCES

In 1994 the former provinces of the Cape of Good Hope, Natal, the Orange Free State and the Transvaal, together with the former 'homelands' or 'TBVC countries' of Transkei, Bophuthatswana, Venda and Ciskei, were replaced by nine new provinces. Transkei and Ciskei were integrated into Eastern Cape, Venda into Northern Province (now Limpopo), and Bophuthatswana into Free State, Mpumalanga and North-West.

The administrative powers of the provincial governments in relation to the central government are set out in the 1999 Constitution after a revision of the original text demanded by the Constitutional Court in 1996.

EASTERN CAPE

TERRITORY AND POPULATION

The area is 169,580 sq. km and the population at the Oct. 1996 census was 6,302,525, the third largest population in South Africa. Of that number: female, 3,394,469; African/Black, 5,448,495 (86% of the population); White, 330,294 (5%); Coloured, 468,532 (7%); Indian/Asian, 19,356 (0·3%). 37% of the population lived in urban areas. Estimated population at 30 June 2000 was 6,847,010 (3,668,844 females); density, 40 per sq. km. Life expectancy at birth, 1996, was 60·4 years. At the 1996 census 83·8% spoke IsiXhosa as their home language, 9·6% Afrikaans, 3·7% English and 2·2% Sesotho.

Eastern Cape comprises 77 administrative districts (including Umzimkulu district, an enclave within KwaZulu-Natal).

CONSTITUTION AND GOVERNMENT

The provincial capital is Bisho. There is a 63-seat provincial legislature.

RECENT ELECTIONS

At the provincial elections held on 2 June 1999, 47 seats were won by the ANC, 9 by UDM, 4 by DP, 2 by NNP and 1 by PAC.

CURRENT ADMINISTRATION

In March 2003 the ANC Executive Council comprised:
Premier: Rev. Makhenkesi Arnold Stofile; b. 1944 (ANC).
Minister of Agriculture: Max M. Mamase. *Education and Training:* Nomsa Lizzie Jajula. *Finance, Economic Affairs, Environment and Tourism:* Enoch Godongwana. *Health:* M. Bevan Goqwana. *Housing, Local Government and Traditional Affairs:* Gugile E. Nkwinti. *Provincial Safety, Liaison and Transport:* Dennis Neer. *Roads and Public Works:* Gloria Barry. *Social Development:* Neo Moerane. *Sports, Recreation, Arts and Culture:* Nosimo Balindlela.
Speaker: M. M. Matomela. *Director-General:* Dr M. E. Tom (ANC).

ENERGY AND NATURAL RESOURCES

Electricity. In 1998, 6,818 GWh of electricity were consumed. Approximately 42% of households have electricity.

Water. An estimated 48% of the population do not have access to basic supplies.

Minerals. Total output of mining and quarrying in 1999 was valued at R57m. with 7,154 persons employed.

Agriculture. There are around 6,000 commercial farms with an average area of 1,500 ha. Of this area only 7% is arable land with 45% not farmed at present owing to land ownership disputes in the former homelands (Transkei and Ciskei). Livestock accounts for 77% of commercial agricultural production; 18% comprises horticulture. Total value of agriculture, forestry and fishing output for 1999 was R2,063m.

Forestry. Forestry activities are found in the northeast area of the former Transkei, in Stutterheim and in the northwest of the province. In 1999 there were 169,484 ha of plantation forests.

Fisheries. There is a relatively small sea-fishing industry based on squid, sardines, hake, kinglip and crayfish. Aquaculture produces abalone for export to the Far East.

INDUSTRY

Manufacturing is based mainly in Port Elizabeth and East London with motor manufacturing as the prime industry. Wool, mohair and hides are an important area of the province's agro-industry. Value of manufacturing output in 1999 totalled R14,783m. with 97,035 persons employed.

Labour. As at Oct. 1999 the economically active population numbered 1,419,000, of whom 423,000 were unemployed (29·8%).

COMMUNICATIONS

Roads. Total road network at Dec. 2000 was 38,000 km. Between Dec. 1999 and April 2000 the province's roads were severely damaged by floods. A R40m. reconstruction programme commenced in Oct. 2000. In 1995 there were 31,750 road accidents with 724 fatalities.

Civil Aviation. The province has four airports (Port Elizabeth, East London, Umtata and Bulembu).

Shipping. There are two deep-water ports—Port Elizabeth and East London—with a third planned at Coega.

Telecommunications. Large areas of the province have fewer than four telephones per 1,000 people. A total of R400m. was invested in a new telecommunications infrastructure for the Eastern Cape during the 1997–98 financial year.

SOCIAL INSTITUTIONS

Education. In 1998 there were 2,301,930 enrolled in schools and a total of 68,033 teaching staff. In that year a total of 37,349 students attended the Province's four universities and three technikons. At Oct. 1999 more than 20·9% of people aged 20 years and above had no schooling at all, while 4·7% had completed higher education.

Health. In 1998 there were 108 hospitals (including 42 private hospitals) and 20,538 hospital beds. In the 1997–98 financial year a total of R112m. was allocated to the Primary School Nutrition Programme.

Welfare. The budget allocated for welfare in 2000–01 was R3,950,911, an increase of 7·5% on 1999–2000.

CULTURE

Broadcasting. In 1996 there were 243,662 TV licence holders.

Museums and Galleries. The East London Museum and Port Elizabeth Museum are two of South Africa's best-known natural history museums.

FREE STATE

TERRITORY AND POPULATION

The Free State lies in the centre of South Africa and is situated between the Vaal River in the north and the Orange River in the south. It borders on the Northern Cape, Eastern Cape, North-West, Mpumalanga, KwaZulu-Natal and Gauteng Province and shares a border with Lesotho. The area is 129,480 sq. km, 10·62% of South Africa's total surface area. The province is the third largest in South Africa but has the second smallest population and the second lowest population density (22 persons per sq. km). The population at the Oct. 1996 census was 2,633,504. Of that number: female, 1,335,156; African/Black, 2,223,940 (84% of the population); White, 316,459 (12%); Coloured, 79,038 (3%); Indian/Asian, 2,805 (0·1%). 63% of the population are between 15 and 64. At least 69% of the population lived in urban areas (in 1911, 80% lived in rural areas). Annual population growth rate: 1–2%. Estimated population at 30 June 2000 was 2,826,076; density, 22 per sq. km. Life expectancy at birth, 1996, was 52·8 years. At the 1996 census, 62·1% of the population spoke Sesotho as their home language, 14·5% Afrikaans, 9·4% IsiXhosa, 6·5% Setswana, 4·8% IsiZulu and 1·3% English.

Free State comprises 52 administrative districts. The provincial capital is Bloemfontein (meaning 'fountain of flowers'). Bloemfontein's indigenous name is Mangaung, which means 'place of the big cats'.

CLIMATE

Temperatures are mild with averages ranging from 19·5°C in the west to 15°C in the east. Maximum temperatures in the west can reach 36°C in summer. Winter temperatures in the high-lying areas of the eastern Free State can drop as low as −15°C. The western and southern areas are semi-desert.

CONSTITUTION AND GOVERNMENT

There is a 30-seat provincial legislature. The Free State Executive Council, headed by the *Premier*, administers the province through ten Departments.

The Free State House of Traditional Leaders advises the Legislature on matters pertaining to traditional authorities and tribal matters.

RECENT ELECTIONS

In the election held on 2 June 1999, the ANC retained its majority and won 25 of the 30 seats; DP, 2; NNP, 2; and Freedom Front, 1.

CURRENT ADMINISTRATION

In March 2003 the ANC Executive Council comprised:

Premier: Isabella Winkie Direko; b. 1929.

Minister of Finance and Expenditure: Zingili Dingani. *Education:* D. A. 'Papi' Kgnare. *Public Works and Transport:* Sekhopi Malebo. *Health Services:* Ouma Tsopo. *Agriculture:* Mann Oelrich. *Tourism, Environmental and Tourism:* Sakhiwe Belot. *Local Government and Housing:* Lechesa Tsenoli. *Social Welfare:* Beatrice Marshoff. *Safety and Security:* Benny Kotsoane. *Sport, Arts, Culture, Science and Technology:* Webster Mfebe.

Speaker: Mkhangeli Matomela. *Director-General:* Khotso de Wee.

ECONOMY

Overview. Economic policy for the province is in line with the South African government's Macro-Economic Policy. It is aimed at obtaining higher levels of growth, development and employment through accelerated growth of non-gold exports, a brisk expansion in private-sector capital formation, growth of public-sector investment, an improvement in the employment intensity of investment and output growth and an increase in infrastructural development and service delivery making intensive use of labour-based techniques. The central thrust of trade and industry development is the expansion of the manufacturing industry and the promotion of value-added exports.

ENERGY AND NATURAL RESOURCES

Electricity. In the Free State, Eskom distributes electricity through 3,000 km of distribution lines, 9,000 km of reticulation (network) lines; and has an installed capacity of 1,200,740 MVA. Mining (60% of sales) and local governments (30% of sales) are Eskom's biggest Free State's customers.

In 1998, 9,110 GWh of electricity were consumed.

Water. The largest sources of water are the Vaal and Orange Rivers and their tributaries, particularly the Modder, Riet and Caledon rivers. The largest storage dams are the Gariep and Vanderkloof dams, both of which have hydro-electric stations. There are a number of large irrigation schemes in the province.

According to the 1996 census, piped water was available in the homes of 41% of the population while a further 19% was supplied by communal village standpipes.

Minerals. The province contributes about 16·5% of South Africa's total mineral output. Apart from rich gold and diamond deposits, the Free State is the source of numerous other minerals and is the founding home of South Africa's famous oil-from-coal industry centred on Sasolburg. Bentonite clays, gypsum, salt and phosphates are to be found while large concentrates of thorium-ilminite-zircon also occur. In 1999, 69,547 people were employed in mining.

Agriculture. Good agricultural conditions allow for a wide variety of farming industries. Of the total 12·7m. ha, 90% (11·5m. ha) is utilized as farmland. Of this, 63·9% is natural grazing; 2·1% is for nature conservation; and 1·1% is used for other purposes. Dryland cultivation is practised on 97% of the arable land, while the remaining 3% is under irrigation.

In 1998 there was a total of 11,647 commercial farmers working 48,420 farming units in the province. The eastern region is the major producer of small grains; the northern region, maize and beef; and the southern region, mutton and wool. The province produces about 40% of total maize and 50% of total wheat production in South Africa.

INDUSTRY

Labour. As at Oct. 1999 the economically active population numbered 965,000, of whom 225,000 were unemployed (23·3%).

COMMUNICATIONS

Roads. The Free State Department of Public Works, Roads and Transport is responsible for maintenance of a rural network, which consists of 20,452 km tertiary gravel roads, 21,470 km secondary gravel roads, 6,965 km primary paved roads, and 910 km national roads, of which 25 km are not tarred. In 1995 there were 26,163 road accidents with 997 fatalities.

Rail. Spoornet is one of the biggest companies in the Free State with 4,217 employees. Spoornet transports most of the province's maize, wheat, gold ore, petroleum and fertilizer. The Spoornet infrastructure consists of approximately 4,000 km of tracks, of which 1,300 km are electrified.

Postal Services. In 1998 there were 330 post offices, 29 part-time post offices, 7 Postpoints (situated in locations such as chainstores, etc.) and 144 retail postal agencies.

SOCIAL INSTITUTIONS

Justice. Small claims courts operate in 11 centres, providing informal forums where citizens appear in person before a commissioner. The decision of the commissioner is final and the parties cannot appeal to a higher court. Civil claims can be instituted in the magistrates' court, there being 67 magistrate's offices in the province. The Free State provincial division of the Supreme Court is in Bloemfontein. The Circuit Court is a local division of the provincial division of the Supreme Court which visits certain areas. The Circuit Court tries criminal cases only. In 1998, 523 attorneys and 42 advocates practised in the province.

Education. In 1998 there were 810,000 pupils and 24,078 teachers. More than 2,000 farm schools cater for 95,000 pupils. Nine technical colleges provide vocational training for school leavers. Technikon Free State has 8,000 students on the main campus in Bloemfontein and four campuses for distance education situated in Welkom, Kimberley, Kroonstad and Qwaqwa. There are eight teacher training colleges with 4,600 students. The University of the Orange Free State is the only fully fledged residential university and, in 1998, had a student population of 9,787. 1998 literacy rate: 84·42%. According to the 1996 census, 16% of those aged 20 and over had no schooling; 33% had some secondary education.

Health. In 1999 there were 33 public hospitals, 26 private hospitals and 234 clinics. Total hospital beds (1999), 2,277.

CULTURE

Broadcasting. Apart from the national broadcaster, SABC, several private and community radio stations exist, catering for the three primary language groups in the province. In 1996 there were 164,092 TV licence holders.

Press. There is one daily newspaper, *Di Volksblad*, which is published in Afrikaans. Several 'knockanddrop'-type weekly newspapers are produced on a regional basis.

Festivals. A Water and Wine Festival is held annually in Feb./March at Jacobsdal; the Witblitz Festival in Philippolis is held annually at the end of March/beginning of April; the Ficksburg Cherry Festival is held annually during the cherry season in Nov.; and the Bloemfontein Show, the largest agricultural show in the country, is held each March.

Libraries. There are 128 community and public libraries and 15 library depots.

Theatre and Opera. The Performing Arts Council of the Free State (PACOFS) operates from the Sand du Plessis Theatre complex in Bloemfontein, one of the most modern theatre complexes in South Africa. The Andre Huguenet Theatre is housed in the same complex. The Observatory Theatre is based in a former observatory in Bloemfontein.

Museums and Galleries. There are over 30 museums in the province, including the National Museum and the War Museum in Bloemfontein.

FURTHER READING
Free State: The Winning Province. Chris van Rensburg Publications, Johannesburg, 1997
South African Yearbook 1998. Government Communication and Information System, ABC, Cape Town, 1997

GAUTENG

TERRITORY AND POPULATION
Gauteng is the smallest province in South Africa, covering an area of 18,810 sq. km (approximately 1·4% of the total land surface of South Africa). The population at the Oct. 1996 census was 7,348,423. Of that number: female, 3,597,578; African/Black, 5,147,444 (70%); White, 1,702,343 (23%); Coloured, 278,692 (3·8%); Indian/Asian, 161,289 (2·2%). 97% of the population lived in urban areas. Population estimate at 30 June 2000 was 7,873,205 (3,878,231 females); density, 474 per sq. km. Life expectancy at birth, 1996, was 59·6 years. At the 1996 census, 21·5% spoke IsiZulu as their home language, 16·7% Afrikaans, 13·1% Sesotho, 13·0% English, 9·5% Sepedi, 7·9% Setswana, 7·5% IsiXhosa, 5·3% Xitsonga, 1·6% IsiNdebele, 1·4% Tshivenda and 1·3% SiSwati.

The province of Gauteng, at first called Pretoria-Witwatersrand-Vereeniging (PWV), comprises 23 administrative districts. The provincial capital is Johannesburg. In the Sesotho language, Gauteng means 'Place of Gold'.

CONSTITUTION AND GOVERNMENT
There is a 73-seat provincial legislature.

RECENT ELECTIONS

At the provincial elections held on 2 June 1999, 50 seats were won by the ANC, 13 by DP, 3 by IFP, 3 by NNP, and 1 each by ACDP, FA, UDM and FF.

CURRENT ADMINISTRATION

In Feb. 2003 the ANC Executive Council comprised:

Premier: Mbhazima Sam Shilowa.

Minister of Agriculture, Conservation, Environment and Land Affairs: Mary E. Metcalfe. *Development Planning and Local Government and Leader of the House:* Trevor G. Fowler. *Education:* Ignatius P. Jacobs. *Finance and Economic Affairs:* P. Jabu Moleketi. *Health:* Gwendoline M. Ramokgopa. *Housing:* S. Paul Mashatile. *Provincial Safety and Liaison:* Nomvula P. Mokonyane. *Sport, Recreation, Arts and Culture:* Mondli Gungubele. *Transport, Roads and Public Works:* Elias Gabisi Mosunkutu. *Social Services and Population Development:* Angelina Matsie Motshekga.

Speaker: Firoz Cachalia. *Director-General:* Mogopodi Mokoena.

ENERGY AND NATURAL RESOURCES

Electricity. In 1998, 56,548 GWh of electricity were consumed (30% of South Africa's total consumption).

Water. The largest source of water is the Vaal River which is the most highly regulated and overworked river in South Africa. Significant water transfers are made by means of the Thukela Vaal transfer from KwaZulu-Natal, the Lesotho Highlands project from Katse Dam and the Usutu Vaal Scheme in Mpumalanga to augment water supplies which all enter the Upper Vaal Water Management Area (WMA). The largest storage dam on the southern edge of the province is the Vaal Dam. In 1996 piped water was available in the homes of about 68% of the population while 15% was supplied by communal village standpipes.

Minerals. In 1999, 104,017 people were employed in mining.

Agriculture. In 1996 there were 2,342 farms with 339,295 agricultural workers; gross farming income amounted to R2,283·3m.

INDUSTRY

Labour. As at Oct. 1999 the economically active population numbered 3,416,000, of whom 705,000 were unemployed (20·6%).

COMMUNICATIONS

Roads. In 1995 there were 202,583 road accidents with 2,318 fatalities.

Civil Aviation. Johannesburg International Airport is the main airport in the province.

Telecommunications. In 1996 at least 45% of the population had telephones or mobile phones; 4% had no access at all to a telephone.

SOCIAL INSTITUTIONS

Education. In 1998 there were 1·6m. children enrolled in schools with a total of 44,324 teaching staff. In that year a total of 336,004 students attended the Province's six universities and five technikons. According to the 1996 census, 40% of the population had some secondary education—the highest rate in any of South Africa's provinces.

Health. In 1998 there were 137 hospitals (including 108 private hospitals) and 32,852 hospital beds.

CULTURE

Broadcasting. There were 978,762 TV licence holders in 1996.

Museums and Galleries. There are over 60 museums in the province, the most notable being the MuseumAfrica in Johannesburg which opened in 1994.

KWAZULU-NATAL

TERRITORY AND POPULATION

The area is 92,180 sq. km and the population at the Oct. 1996 census was 8,417,021. Of that number: female, 4,466,493; African/Black, 6,880,652 (82·0% of the population); Indian/Asian, 790,813 (9·4%); White, 558,182 (6·6%); Coloured, 117,951 (1·4%). 43% lived in urban areas. Estimated population at 30 June 2000 was 8,986,857 (4,768,109 females); density, 99 per sq. km. Life expectancy at birth, 1996, was 53·0 years. At the 1996 census, 79·8% spoke IsiZulu as their home language, 15·8% English, 1·6% Afrikaans and 1·6% IsiXhosa.

KwaZulu-Natal comprises 66 administrative districts. The provincial capital is Pietermaritzburg, chosen by referendum in 1995.

CONSTITUTION AND GOVERNMENT

There is an 80-seat provincial legislature.

RECENT ELECTIONS

At the provincial elections held on 2 June 1999, 34 seats were won by the Inkatha Freedom Party (IFP), 32 by the ANC, 7 by DP, 3 by NNP, 2 by MF and 1 each by ACDP and UDM.

CURRENT ADMINISTRATION

In March 2003 the IFP/ANC coalition government comprised:

Premier: Lionel P. H. M. Mtshali (IFP).

Minister of Agriculture and Environmental Affairs: Narend Singh (IFP). *Economic Development and Tourism:* Michael Mabuyakhulu (ANC). *Education and Culture:* Prof. L. B. Gabriel Ndabandaba (IFP). *Finance:* Peter Miller (IFP). *Health:* Dr Zweli Mkhize (ANC). *Housing:* Dumisani Makhaye (ANC). *Public Works:* Rev. Celani Mtetwa (IFP). *Traditional and Local Government Affairs, Safety and Security:* Inkosi Nyanga Ngubane (IFP). *Transport:* J. S'Bu Ndebele (ANC). *Social Welfare and Population Development:* Prince Gideon Zulu (IFP).

Speaker: Chief Bonga Mdletshe (IFP). *Director-General:* Adv. R. K. Sizani.

ENERGY AND NATURAL RESOURCES

Electricity. 37,344 GWh of electricity were consumed in 1999.

Water. The main sources of water are the Thukela, Mgeni, Mkomazi, Phongolo, Mfolozi, Mzimkulu and Mhlatuze rivers. The large storage dams include the Pongolapoort, Woodstock, Spioenkop, Chelmsford, Midmar, Albert Falls, Inanda and Zaaihoek dams. In 1996 piped water was available in the homes of 39% of the population.

Minerals. Coal is mined in the north of the province. In 1999, 6,888 people were employed in mining.

Agriculture. In 1996 there were 5,037 farms with 115,496 agricultural workers; gross farming income amounted to R4,490·3m. Sugarcane production is the main agricultural activity.

INDUSTRY

Labour. As at Oct. 1999 the economically active population numbered 2,635,000, of whom 682,000 were unemployed (25·9%).

COMMUNICATIONS

Roads. In 2000 the road network totalled 42,000 km. There were 1,575 fatalities as a result of road traffic accidents in 1997.

Civil Aviation. Durban International Airport is the main airport in the province.

Shipping. Durban harbour is the busiest in South Africa and one of the ten largest harbours in the world. Coal is exported from Richards Bay.

SOCIAL INSTITUTIONS

Education. Since 1995 education has been provided by a unified KwaZulu-Natal Education Department (KZNED). In 1998 there were 2,725,371 children enrolled in schools with a total of 74,834 teaching staff. In that year a total of 30,684 students attended the Province's three universities and three technikons. According to the 1996 census, 23% of the population aged 20 and above had no schooling; 32% had some secondary education.

Health. In 1998 there were 114 hospitals (including 48 private hospitals) and 31,673 hospital beds.

CULTURE

Broadcasting. There were 392,573 TV licence holders in 1996.

Museums and Galleries. The Natal Museum is in Pietermaritzburg.

LIMPOPO

TERRITORY AND POPULATION

The area is 123,280 sq. km and the population at the Oct. 1996 census was 4,929,368. Of that number: female, 2,676,296; African/Black, 4,765,255 (96% of the population); White, 117,878 (2·4%); Coloured, 7,821 (0·2%); Indian/Asian, 5,510 (0·1%). 11·9% lived in urban areas. Estimated population at 30 June 2000 was 5,400,868; density, 44 per sq. km. Life expectancy at birth, 1996, was 60·1 years. At the 1996 census 52·7% spoke Sepedi as their home language, 22·6% Xitsonga, 15·5% Tshivenda, 2·2% Afrikaans and 1·5% IsiNdebele.

Limpopo (Northern Province until March 2003) comprises 32 administrative districts. The provincial capital is Pietersburg.

CONSTITUTION AND GOVERNMENT

There is a 49-seat provincial legislature.

RECENT ELECTIONS

At the provincial elections held on 2 June 1999, 44 seats were won by the ANC, and 1 each by ACDP, DP, NNP, PAC and UDM.

CURRENT ADMINISTRATION

In March 2003 the ANC Executive Council comprised:
Premier: Ngoako A. Ramathlodi.
Minister of Agriculture: Dr P. Aaron Motsoaledi. *Education:* Joyce Mashamba. *Finance, Economic Affairs, Tourism and Environment:* Thaba Mufamadi. *Health and Welfare:* Sello Moloto. *Local Government and Housing:* Ms Joe Maswanganyi. *Minister in the Office of the Premier:* Catherine Mabuza. *Public Works:* Collins Chabane. *Safety, Security and Liaison:* Dikeledi Magadzi. *Sports, Arts and Culture:* Rosina Semenya. *Transport:* Dean Tshenuwani Farisani.
Speaker: P. Robert Malavi. *Director-General:* Ms M. B. Monama.

ENERGY AND NATURAL RESOURCES

Electricity. In 1998, 7,234 GWh of electricity were consumed.

Water. Susceptible to drought, the province's main sources of water are the Mogol, Phalala, Luvhuvu, Letaba, Mogalakwena, Sand and Oliphant rivers. The larger storage dams include the Mokolo, Ebenezer, Tzaneen and Middle Letaba dams. In 1996 piped water was available in the homes of 17% of the population, with 40% relying on public taps.

Minerals. In 1999, 39,805 people were employed in mining.

Agriculture. In 1996 (excluding the former Venda now within the province) there were 7,273 farms with 121,757 agricultural workers; gross farming income amounted to R3,934·5m.

INDUSTRY

Labour. As at Oct. 1999 the economically active population numbered 1,050,000, of whom 357,000 were unemployed (34·0%).

COMMUNICATIONS

Roads. In 1995 there were 15,841 road accidents with 693 fatalities.

SOCIAL INSTITUTIONS

Education. In 1998 there were 1,810,603 children enrolled in schools with a total of 57,155 teaching staff. 17,933 students attended the Province's two universities in the same year. According to the 1996 census, almost 37% of the population aged 20 years and over had no schooling.

Health. In 1998 there were 49 hospitals (including two private hospitals) and 13,342 hospital beds.

CULTURE

Broadcasting. There were 99,362 TV licence holders in 1996.

Museums and Galleries. An open-air museum, the Bakhoni (Northern Sotho) Museum in Pietersburg, shows the black cultures of the province with traditional architecture, lifestyles and crafts.

MPUMALANGA

TERRITORY AND POPULATION

The area is 78,370 sq. km and the population at the Oct. 1996 census was 2,800,711. Of that number: female, 1,438,683; African/Black, 2,497,834 (89% of the population); White, 253,392 (9%); Coloured, 20,283 (0·7%); Indian/Asian, 13,083 (0·5%). 39·1% lived in urban areas. Estimated population at 30 June 2000 was 3,042,637 (1,563,534 females); density, 39 per sq. km. Life expectancy at birth, 1996, was 53·5 years. At the 1996 census, 30·0% spoke SiSwati as their home language, 25·4% IsiZulu, 12·5% IsiNdebele, 10·5% Sepedi, 8·3% Afrikaans, 3·5% Xitsonga, 3·2% Sesotho, 2·7% Setswana, 2·0% English and 1·4% IsiXhosa.

Mpumalanga comprises 28 administrative districts. The provincial capital is Nelspruit.

CONSTITUTION AND GOVERNMENT

There is a 30-seat provincial legislature.

RECENT ELECTIONS

At the provincial elections held on 2 June 1999, 26 seats were won by the ANC and 1 each by DP, NNP, UDM and FF.

CURRENT ADMINISTRATION

In Feb. 2003 the ANC government comprised:

Premier: Ndaweni J. Mahlangu, b. 1948.

Minister of Agriculture, Conservation and Environment: K. Candith Mashego-Diamini. *Finance and Economic Affairs:* Jacob I. Mabena. *Education:* Craig N. M. Padayachee. *Health:* Sibongile Manana. *Housing and Land Administration:* Mabhuza Simeon Ginindza. *Local Government and Traffic:* Mohammed Bhabha. *Public Works, Roads and Transport:* Jabulani Stephen Mabona. *Social Services and Population Development:* M. E. Coleman. *Sports, Recreation, Arts and Culture:* Siphosezwe Masango. *Safety and Security:* Thabang Makwetla.

Speaker: Sipho William Lubisi. *Director-General:* Adv. M. S. Soko.

ENERGY AND NATURAL RESOURCES

Electricity. In 1998, 24,200 GWh of electricity were consumed.

Water. The province has the second-highest mean annual rainfall in South Africa (736 mm per annum). The largest sources of water are the Komati, Crocodile, Sabie, Sand, Usutu, upper Vaal and Olifants rivers. The larger storage dams include the Nooitgedacht, Grootdraai, Loskop, Westoe, Jericho and Heyshope dams. Currently about 65% of the population receive water from house connections, with 20% relying on communal taps.

Minerals. In 1999, 61,826 people were employed in mining.

Agriculture. In 1996 (excluding that part of the former Bophuthatswana now within the province) there were 4,675 farms with 101,051 agricultural workers; gross farming income amounted to R3,972·8m.

INDUSTRY

Labour. As at Oct. 1999 the economically active population numbered 916,000, of whom 224,000 were unemployed (24·4%).

COMMUNICATIONS

Roads. In 1995 there were 22,744 road accidents with 1,191 fatalities.

SOCIAL INSTITUTIONS

Education. In 1998 there were 935,528 children enrolled in schools with a total of 1,967 teaching staff. According to the 1996 census, 28% of those aged 20 years and over had no schooling; 38% had some secondary education.

Health. In 1998 there were 36 hospitals (including 11 private hospitals) and 5,506 hospital beds. In Oct. 1998 the first traditional hospital was opened in Mpumalanga—the Samuel Traditional Hospital.

CULTURE

Broadcasting. There were 138,085 TV licence holders in 1996.

Museums and Galleries. There is a mining museum at Pilgrim's Rest where the first economically viable gold field was discovered. An open-air folk museum, the Ndebele Museum at Middelburg, reflects the black culture of the province.

NORTHERN CAPE

TERRITORY AND POPULATION

The area is 361,800 sq. km and the population at the Oct. 1996 census was 840,321. Of that number: female, 427,639; Coloured, 435,368 (52% of the population); African/Black, 278,633 (33%); White, 111,878 (13%); Indian/Asian, 2,268 (0·3%). At least 70% lived in urban areas. Estimated population at 30 June 2000 was 874,788; density, 2 per sq. km. Life expectancy at birth, 1996, was 55·6 years. At the 1996 census, 69·3% spoke Afrikaans as their home language, 19·9% Setswana, 6·3% IsiXhosa and 2·4% English.

Northern Cape comprises six administrative districts: Diamond Fields with Kimberley as the provincial and economic capital; Kalahari, which is the second richest and densely populated area in the province and includes the magisterial districts of Kuruman and Postmasburg; Hantam (North-West) with the towns of Calvinia, Sutherland, Williston, Fraserburg and Carnavon; Benede-Orange with Upington as the agricultural, economic and cultural capital of the region; Bo-Karoo with De Aar as the capital of the area; and Namaqualand which is strong in mining.

CONSTITUTION AND GOVERNMENT

There is a 30-seat provincial legislature.

RECENT ELECTIONS
At the provincial elections held on 2 June 1999, 20 seats were won by the ANC, 8 by NNP and 1 each by DP and FF.

CURRENT ADMINISTRATION
In March 2003 the ANC Executive Council comprised:
Premier: Manne E. Dipico.
Minister of Agriculture, Conservation and Environment Affairs: Dawid Rooi. *Economic Affairs and Tourism:* Thabo Makweya. *Education:* Tina M. Joemat-Petterson. *Finance:* Goolam H. Akharawaray. *Health:* Elizabeth Dipuo Peters. *Local Government and Housing:* Ouneas P. Dikgetsi. *Safety and Liaison:* Connie Seoposengwe. *Social Services and Population Development:* Fred Wyngaard. *Sport, Arts and Culture:* Sebastian Bonokwane. *Transport, Roads and Public Works:* John F. Block.
Speaker: C. A. T. Smith. *Director-General:* M. van Zyl (ANC).

ENERGY AND NATURAL RESOURCES

Electricity. In 1998, 3,034 GWh of electricity were consumed.

Water. The province's largest source of water is the Orange River. Significant transfers are made by means of the Boegoeberg Dam Irrigation Scheme, the Kalahari Rural Water Supply Scheme, the Pelladrift and Springbok Water Supply Schemes and a transfer scheme from Sendelingsdrift. The larger storage dams include the Boegoeberg and Smart Syndicate Dams. In 1996 piped water was available in the homes of almost 49% of the population with 21% supplied by communal stand pipes.

Minerals. The province is well endowed with a variety of mineral deposits. Diamonds are found in shallow water at Port Nolloth, Hondeklipbaai and Lamberts Bay, and also mined inland along the entire coastal strip from the Orange river mouth in the north to Lamberts Bay in the south. Copper is mined in Namaqualand. Iron and manganese occur in two parallel north-south belts from Postmasburg in the south to Sishen/Kathu/Hotazel in the north. Limestone, asbestos and gypsum salt are also mined. In 1999, 19,235 people were employed in mining.

Agriculture. Intensive irrigation takes place along the Orange River which supports vineyards and agribusiness. Stock farming predominates in the Bo-Karoo and Hantam areas. In 1996 there were 6,730 farms with 58,198 agricultural workers; gross farming income amounted to R1,418·9m.

INDUSTRY

Labour. As at Oct. 1999 the economically active population numbered 298,000, of whom 54,000 were unemployed (18·1%).

COMMUNICATIONS

Roads. In 1995 there were 7,273 road accidents with 326 fatalities.

Rail. The main rail link is between Cape Town and Johannesburg, via Kimberley. Other main lines link the Northern Cape with Port Elizabeth via De Aar while another links Upington with Namibia.

Civil Aviation. Five airports are used for scheduled flights—Kimberley, Upington, Aggeneys, Springbok and Alexander Bay.

SOCIAL INSTITUTIONS

Education. In 1998 there were 206,597 children enrolled in schools with a total of 7,142 teaching staff. According to the 1996 census, almost 21% of those aged 20 years and over had no schooling; 31% had some secondary education.

Health. In 1998 there were 48 hospitals (including 29 private hospitals) and 2,966 hospital beds.

CULTURE

Broadcasting. There were 85,140 TV licence holders in 1996.

Tourism. Parks are a major tourism asset with the total area under protection being 1,080,200 ha. Provincial nature reserves occupy 50,240 ha. Hunting is a growing activity in the province.

Museums and Galleries. The De Beers Museum at the Big Hole (the biggest hole ever made by man with pick and shovel) in Kimberley includes an open-air museum featuring buildings dating back to the era of the diamond diggings.

NORTH-WEST

TERRITORY AND POPULATION

The area is 116,190 sq. km and the population at the Oct. 1996 census was 3,354,825. Of that number: female, 1,704,990; African/Black, 3,058,686 (91·0% of the total population); White, 222,755 (6·6%); Coloured, 46,652 (1·4%); Indian/Asian, 10,097 (0·3%). Estimated population at 30 June 2000 was 3,629,947; density, 31 per sq. km. Life expectancy at birth, 1996, was 53·3 years. At the 1996 census (including the former Bophuthatswana) 67·2% spoke Setswana as their home language, 7·5% Afrikaans, 5·4% IsiXhosa, 5·1% Sesotho, 4·7% Xitsonga, 4·0% Sepedi, 2·5% IsiZulu, 1·3% IsiNdebele, 1·0% English and 0·5% SiSwati.

North-West Province comprises 32 administrative districts. The provincial capital is Mmabatho.

CONSTITUTION AND GOVERNMENT

There is a 33-seat provincial legislature.

RECENT ELECTIONS

At the provincial elections held on 2 June 1999 the ANC won 27 seats, UCDP 3, with 1 seat each going to DP, NNP and FF.

CURRENT ADMINISTRATION

In March 2003 the ANC Executive Council comprised:
Premier: Dr Popo S. Molefe.
Minister of Agriculture, Conservation and the Environment: B. E. E. Molewa. *Developmental Local Government and Housing:* D. E. Africa. *Economic Development and Tourism:* M. I. Modiselle. *Education:* Z. P. Tolo. *Finance:* Martin J. Kuscus. *Health:* Dr Molefi Sefularo. *Safety and Liaison:* R. N. Rasmeni. *Social Services, Arts, Culture and Sport:* Mandlenkosi Eliot Mayisela. *Transport:* Frans P. Vilakazi. *Roads and Public Works:* J. D. Thibedi.
Speaker: Rev. O. J. Tselapedi. *Director-General:* M. M. Bakane-Tuoane.

ENERGY AND NATURAL RESOURCES

Electricity. In 1998, 27,920 GWh of electricity were consumed.

Water. The main sources are the Crocodile, Marico, Molopo, Harts and Vaal rivers. The larger storage dams include the Vaalkop, Roodekopjes, Klipvoor Dams in the Crocodile catchment area, Molatedi Dam in the Marico catchment and Bloemhof and Spitskop Dams on the border with the Vaal catchment. Groundwater is an important source for mines and rural users. In 1996 piped water was available in the homes of almost 30% of the population. The most-used source of water was the public tap, used by more than 31% of the population.

Minerals. In 1999, 132,499 people were employed in mining.

Agriculture. In 1996 (excluding the TBVC countries of Transkei, Bophuthatswana, Venda and Ciskei now within the province) there were 7,512 farms with 98,349 agricultural workers; gross farming income amounted to R3,038·3m.

INDUSTRY

Labour. As at Oct. 1999 the economically active population numbered 1,018,000, of whom 240,000 were unemployed (23·5%).

COMMUNICATIONS

Roads. In 1995 there were 13,453 road accidents with 624 fatalities.

Telecommunications. Around 17% of the population had telephones or mobile phones in 1996; 19% had no access at all to a telephone.

SOCIAL INSTITUTIONS

Education. In 1998 there were 953,737 children enrolled in schools with a total of 31,962 teaching staff. In the same year, 24,296 students attended the Province's two universities and one technikon. According to the 1996 census, almost 22% of those aged 20 or over had no schooling.

Health. In 1998 there were 49 hospitals (including 17 private hospitals) and 10,012 hospital beds.

CULTURE

Broadcasting. In 1996 there were 116,680 TV licence holders.

Tourism. In 1999 there was a total of 343,915 international visitors (5·5% of total international visitors to South Africa) with 114,639 jobs created as a result.

WESTERN CAPE

TERRITORY AND POPULATION

The area is 129,386 sq. km. Population, 1996 census, 3,956,875. Of that number: females, 2,021,381; urban, 3·5m. (85% of total population); Coloured, 2,146,109 (54·2%); African/Black, 826,691 (20·9%); White, 821,551 (20·8%); Indian/Asian, 40,376 (1·0%). Estimated population at 30 June 2000 was 4,267,952; density, 33 per sq. km. Life expectancy at birth, 1996, was 60·8 years. At the 1996 census, 50% spoke Afrikaans as their home language, 22% English and Afrikaans, 25% IsiXhosa.

There are 41 administrative districts. The capital is Cape Town.

CONSTITUTION AND GOVERNMENT

There is a 42-seat provincial parliament.

RECENT ELECTIONS

At the provincial elections held on 2 June 1999, 18 seats were won by the ANC, 17 by the New National Party (NNP), 5 by DP, and 1 each by ACDP and UDM.

CURRENT ADMINISTRATION

In March 2003 the provincial cabinet comprised:
Premier: Marthinus van Schalkwyk (NNP).
Minister of Agriculture, Tourism and Gambling: Johan Gelderblom (NNP). *Community Safety:* Leonard Ramatlakane (ANC). *Education:* Adv. André Gaum (NNP). *Environmental Affairs and Development Planning:* Johan Gelderblom (acting). *Finance and Economic Development:* Ebrahim Rasool (ANC). *Health:* Piet Meyer (NNP). *Housing:* Nomatyala Hangana (NNP). *Local Government:* Cobus Dowry (NNP). *Social Services and Poverty Alleviation:* Marius Fransman (ANC). *Cultural Affairs, Sport and Recreation:* Patrick McKenzie (NNP). *Transport, Public Works and Property Management:* Tasneem Essop (ANC).
Speaker: Lynne Brown. *Director-General:* Dr Gilbert Lawrence.

ENERGY AND NATURAL RESOURCES

Electricity. In 1998, 15,305 GWh of electricity were consumed.

Water. Water requirements in the Greater Cape Town Metropolitan Area have long since outstripped the available local resources. Water is transferred from the Berg and Breede Basins and the Palmiet and Steenbras Rivers to Cape Town. Many small rural towns and farming communities rely on groundwater for domestic water supplies. In comparison with the rest of the country relatively few people in the province do not have access to adequate water supplies.

Minerals. In 1999, 2,561 people were employed in mining.

Agriculture. There were 9,759 farms with 198,378 agricultural workers in 1996; gross farming income amounted to R7,533·6m.

INDUSTRY

Labour. As at Oct. 1999 the economically active population numbered 1,811,000, of whom 248,000 were unemployed (13·7%).

COMMUNICATIONS

Roads. Motor vehicles registered (1996) totalled 1,102,226, including 679,977 passenger cars, 238,087 light commercial vehicles, 35,478 heavy commercial vehicles and 28,153 motorcycles. In 1995 there were 87,117 road accidents with 1,286 fatalities.

Civil Aviation. Cape Town International Airport is the main airport in the province.

Telecommunications. In 1996, 55·2% of the population had a telephone or mobile phone; 3% had no access at all to a telephone.

SOCIAL INSTITUTIONS

Education. In 1998 there were 902,879 children enrolled in schools with a total of 25,393 teaching staff. In that year, 60,330 students attended the Province's three universities and two technikons. According to the 1996 census, 10·6% of people aged 20 years and over had higher education qualifications.

Health. In 1998 there were 114 hospitals (including 69 private hospitals) and 18,533 hospital beds.

CULTURE

Broadcasting. There were 681,644 TV licence holders in 1996.

Tourism. Domestic visitors to the province in 2001 totalled 4,326,000; overseas visitors, 805,636 (excluding Africa).

Museums and Galleries. The South Africa Museum and National Gallery are in Cape Town and an agricultural museum, Kleinplasie, is at Worcester.

SPAIN

Reino de España
(Kingdom of Spain)

Capital: Madrid
Population estimate, 2000: 39·5m.
GDP per capita, 2000: (PPP$) 19,472
HDI/world rank: 0·913/21

KEY HISTORICAL EVENTS

The modern Spanish state was founded in 1469 with the marriage of Isabel and Fernando to the crowns of Castile and Aragón. Under their joint reign Spain recovered Granada, the last Islamic territory in the Iberian peninsula and sponsored the modern discovery of America, both events in 1492. After 1700 the French Bourbon dynasty was enthroned, with Felipe V as its first king; the present monarch, Juan Carlos I, installed in 1975, is his direct descendant.

Queen Isabel II, who came to the throne in 1833, was deposed in 1868. The Cortes (Parliament) approved a new constitution and the deputies chose as the new king Amadeo I of the then reigning Italian dynasty of Savoy. Unable to adapt to Spanish politics, he abdicated on 11 Feb. 1873. The Cortes immediately proclaimed a republic. The first brief republican experience saw great instability. On 29 Dec. 1874 a coup restored the Bourbon monarchy, with Alfonso XII, the son of the exiled Queen Isabel II, as king. A general election took place early in 1876 and the new Cortes approved a constitution which was effective until 1923. During this period, known as the Restoration, Spain still had a backward economy and low standards of living. At the same time Spain was embroiled in external conflicts, with wars in northern Morocco and in the remaining colonies of Cuba and the Philippines. US intervention led to the cession of Philippines, Puerto Rico and Guam, and also of Cuba which formally became independent in 1901.

Spain was neutral in the First World War, leading to a boom in industry and trade. A new industrial working class was then emerging, amidst a climate of industrial unrest which also showed itself in opposition to conscription for the war in Morocco. In Sept. 1923 Gen. Primo de Rivera led a coup and abolished the 1876 constitution, closed down the Cortes and governed by decree until his resignation in Jan. 1930. An interim period followed until the municipal elections of 12 April 1931, which were won by a republican-socialist coalition in Madrid, provincial capitals and other urban areas. Two days later Alfonso XIII exiled himself and the republic was proclaimed a second time. An election in Feb. 1936 gave power to the Popular Front, a coalition of all left parties, including the then tiny Communist party. On 18 July 1936 the colonial army in northern Morocco, led by Gen. Francisco Franco, rebelled against the government. The rebellion was crushed in Madrid, Barcelona and Valencia but the rural regions were easily controlled by the rebels who received substantial help from Germany, Italy and Portugal. Franco's forces overcame all resistance and the war ended on 1 April 1939. As chief of state till his death on 20 Nov. 1975, Franco modelled his regime on those of the Axis countries. Nevertheless, Spain did not take part in the Second World War.

A nominal monarchy existed from 1947 but with a vacant throne until 1969 when the francoist state accepted the future succession in favour of Juan Carlos de Borbón, grandson of Alfonso XIII. Franco recognized the independence of Morocco in 1956. On 22 Nov. 1975, following Gen. Franco's death, Juan Carlos was proclaimed king. A referendum held in Dec. 1976 endorsed some key reforms making possible a free election on 15 June 1977. The elected bicameral Cortes drafted a new constitution which came into force on 29 Dec. 1978. On 23 Feb. 1981 there was an attempted fascist coup, when for 18 hours the deputies of the lower house of Parliament and the Cabinet were held hostage. This was the last attempt to put the clock back. A vigorous democracy has been matched by a thriving economy.

In the Basque region terrorist activity by the separatist organization ETA has brought a reaction from the local population in the form of a strong peace movement. ETA announced an indefinite ceasefire in Sept. 1998. However, in Dec. 1999 the ceasefire was called off and ETA announced that it would restart its campaign of terror. In Aug. 2002 Batasuna, the political wing of ETA, was accused of providing logistical support for terrorist attacks in Spain and was banned by the Spanish parliament.

TERRITORY AND POPULATION

Spain is bounded in the north by the Bay of Biscay, France and Andorra, east and south by the Mediterranean and the Straits of Gibraltar, southwest by the Atlantic and west by Portugal and the Atlantic. Continental Spain has an area of 492,592 sq. km, and including the Balearic and Canary Islands and the towns of Ceuta and Melilla on the northern coast of Africa, 504,750 sq. km (194,884 sq. miles). Population (census, 2001), 40,847,371 (20,825,521 females). In 1999, 77·4% of the population lived in urban areas; population density in 1995 was 80 per sq. km. In Dec. 2001 foreigners resident in Spain numbered 1,109,060, including 234,937 from Morocco, 84,699 from Ecuador, 80,183 from the UK, 62,506 from Germany and 48,710 from Colombia.

The UN gives a projected population for 2010 of 39·57m.

The growth of the population has been as follows:

Census year	Population	Rate of annual increase	Census year	Population	Rate of annual increase
1860	15,655,467	0·34	1960	30,903,137	1·05
1910	19,927,150	0·72	1970	33,823,918	0·95
1920	21,303,162	0·69	1981	37,746,260	1·05
1930	23,563,867	1·06	1991	38,872,268	0·30
1940	25,877,971	0·98	2001	40,847,371	0·51
1950	27,976,755	0·81			

Area and population of the autonomous communities (in italics) and provinces at the 2001 census:

Autonomous community/ Province	Area (sq. km)	Population	Per sq. km	Autonomous community/ Province	Area (sq. km)	Population	Per sq. km
Andalusia	*87,595*	*7,357,558*	*84*	Burgos	14,292	348,934	24
Almería	8,775	536,731	61	León	15,581	488,751	31
Cádiz	7,436	1,116,491	150	Palencia	8,052	174,143	22
Córdoba	13,771	761,657	55	Salamanca	12,350	345,609	28
Granada	12,647	821,660	65	Segovia	6,921	147,694	21
Huelva	10,128	462,579	45	Soria	10,306	90,717	9
Jaén	13,496	643,820	46	Valladolid	8,111	498,094	61
Málaga	7,306	1,287,017	176	Zamora	10,561	199,090	19
Sevilla	14,036	1,727,603	123	*Catalonia*	*32,113*	*6,343,110*	*198*
Aragón	*47,720*	*1,204,215*	*25*	Barcelona	7,728	4,805,927	622
Huesca	15,636	206,502	13	Gerona	5,910	565,304	96
Teruel	14,810	135,858	9	Lérida	12,172	362,206	30
Zaragoza	17,274	861,855	50	Tarragona	6,303	609,673	97
Asturias	*10,604*	*1,062,998*	*100*	*Extremadura*	*41,634*	*1,058,503*	*25*
Baleares	*4,992*	*841,669*	*169*	Badajoz	21,766	654,882	30
Basque				Cáceres	19,868	403,621	20
Country	*7,234*	*2,082,587*	*288*	*Galicia*	*29,575*	*2,695,880*	*91*
Álava	3,037	286,387	94	Coruña, La	7,951	1,096,027	138
Guipúzcoa	1,980	673,563	340	Lugo	9,856	357,648	36
Vizcaya	2,217	1,122,637	506	Orense	7,273	338,446	47
Canary Islands	*7,492*	*1,694,477*	*226*	Pontevedra	4,495	903,759	201
Palmas, Las	4,111	887,676	216	*Madrid*	*8,028*	*5,423,384*	*676*
Santa Cruz				*Murcia*	*11,314*	*1,197,646*	*106*
de Tenerife	3,381	806,801	239	*Navarra*	*10,391*	*555,829*	*53*
Cantabria	*5,321*	*535,131*	*101*	*Rioja, La*	*5,045*	*276,702*	*55*
Castilla-La				*Valencian*			
Mancha	*79,461*	*1,760,516*	*22*	*Community*	*23,255*	*4,162,776*	*175*
Albacete	14,924	364,835	24	Alicante	5,817	1,461,925	251
Ciudad Real	19,813	478,957	24	Castellón	6,632	484,566	73
Cuenca	17,140	200,346	12	Valencia	10,806	2,216,285	205
Guadalajara	12,214	174,999	14	*Ceuta*[1]	*20*	*71,505*	*3,575*
Toledo	15,370	541,379	35	*Melilla*[1]	*12*	*66,411*	*5,534*
Castilla y León	*94,224*	*2,456,474*	*26*				
Ávila	8,050	163,442	20	*Total*	*506,030*	*40,847,371*	*81*

[1]Ceuta and Melilla gained limited autonomous status in 1994.

The capitals of the autonomous communities are: *Andalusia*: Seville; *Aragón*: Zaragoza (Saragossa); *Asturias*: Oviedo; *Baleares*: Palma de Mallorca; *Basque Country*: Vitoria; *Canary Islands*, dual capitals, Las Palmas and Santa Cruz de Tenerife; *Cantabria*: Santander; *Castilla-La Mancha*: Toledo; *Castilla y León*: Valladolid; *Catalonia*: Barcelona; *Extremadura:* Mérida; *Galicia*: Santiago de Compostela; *Madrid*: Madrid; *Murcia*: Murcia (but regional parliament in Cartagena); *Navarra*: Pamplona; *La Rioja*: Logroño; *Valencian Community*: Valencia.

The capitals of the provinces are the towns from which they take the name, except in the cases of Álava (capital, Vitoria), Guipúzcoa (San Sebastián) and Vizcaya (Bilbao).

The islands which form the Balearics include Majorca, Minorca, Ibiza and Formentera. Those which form the Canary Archipelago are divided into two provinces, under the name of their respective capitals: Santa Cruz de Tenerife and Las Palmas de Gran Canaria. The province of Santa Cruz de Tenerife is constituted by the islands of Tenerife, La Palma, Gomera and Hierro; that of Las Palmas by Gran Canaria, Lanzarote and Fuerteventura, with the small barren islands of Alegranza, Roque del Este, Roque del Oeste, Graciosa, Montaña Clara and Lobos.

Places under Spanish sovereignty in Africa (Alhucemas, Ceuta, Chafarinas, Melilla and Peñón de Vélez) constitute the two provinces of Ceuta and Melilla.

Populations of principal towns in 2001:

Town	Population	Town	Population	Town	Population
Albacete	152,155	Getafe	153,868	Pamplona	189,364
Alcalá de Henares	179,602	Gijón	270,211	Parla	80,545
Alcobendas	95,104	Granada	240,522	Reus	91,616
Alcorcón	149,594	Guecho	84,024	Sabadell	187,201
Algeciras	106,710	Hermanas, Dos	103,282	Salamanca	156,006
Alicante	293,629	Hospitalet	244,323	San Baudilio del	
Almería	173,338	Huelva	140,862	Llobregat	80,041
Avilés	83,511	Jaén	112,921	San Fernando	84,014
Badajoz	136,851	Jerez de la Frontera	187,087	San Sebastián	181,700
Badalona	210,370	Laguna, La	135,004	Santa Coloma de	
Baracaldo	95,515	Leganés	173,163	Grammanet	115,568
Barcelona	1,527,190	León	135,794	Santa Cruz de	
Bilbao	353,950	Lérida	115,000	Tenerife	217,415
Burgos	167,962	Logroño	136,841	Santander	184,661
Cáceres	84,439	Lorca	79,481	Santiago de	
Cádiz	136,236	Lugo	89,509	Compostela	93,273
Cartagena	188,003	Madrid	3,016,788	Sevilla	704,114
Castellón de		Málaga	535,686	Tarragona	117,184
la Plana	153,225	Marbella	115,871	Tarrasa	179,300
Córdoba	314,805	Mataró	109,298	Telde	91,160
Cornellá de		Móstoles	198,819	Torrejón de Ardoz	101,056
Llobregat	81,881	Murcia	377,888	Valencia	761,871
Coruña, La	242,458	Orense	109,011	Valladolid	318,576
Coslada	79,862	Oviedo	202,938	Vigo	288,324
Elche	201,731	Palencia	80,801	Vitoria	221,270
Ferrol, El	79,520	Palma de Mallorca	358,462	Zaragoza	620,419
Fuenlabrada	179,735	Palmas, Las	370,649		

Madrid: The capital city of Spain, Madrid is located on a plateau in the centre of the country on the River Manzanares. The hub of the country's transport network and financial dealings, Madrid cedes status as Spain's cultural centre to Barcelona despite possessing a proliferation of 17th and 18th century baroque and neo-classical buildings, famed art galleries and the national library.

Languages. The Constitution states that 'Castilian is the Spanish official language of the State', but also that 'All other Spanish languages will also be official in the corresponding Autonomous Communities'. At the last census (1991) Catalan (an official EU language since 1990) was spoken in Catalonia by 68% of people, Baleares (66·9%), Valencian Community (51%, where it is frequently called Valencian), and in Aragón, a narrow strip close to the Catalonian and Valencian Community boundaries. Galician, a language very close to Portuguese, was spoken by a majority of people in Galicia (91%); Basque by a significant and increasing minority in the Basque Country (26·3%), and by a small minority in northwest

Navarra (12%). It is estimated that one-third of all Spaniards speaks one of the other three official languages as well as standard Castilian. In bilingual communities, both Castilian and the regional language are taught in schools and universities.

SOCIAL STATISTICS
Statistics for calendar years:

	Marriages	Births	Deaths
1997	196,499	369,035	349,521
1998	207,041	365,193	360,511
1999	208,129	380,130	371,102
2000[1]	209,854	395,756	359,148
2001[1]	206,254	403,859	358,856

[1]Provisional.

Rate per 1,000 population, 2001: births, 10·0; deaths, 8·9; marriages, 5·1. In 1997 the most popular age for marrying was 30·4 for males and 28·1 for females. Annual population growth rate, 1990–99, 0·1%. Suicide rate (per 100,000 population), 1998: 6·6. Expectation of life, 1999, was 74·8 years for males and 81·9 for females. Infant mortality, 1999, 6·0 per 1,000 live births; fertility rate, 1999, 1·2 births per woman (one of the lowest rates in the world). In 2001 Spain received 9,219 asylum applications, equivalent to 0·2 per 1,000 inhabitants.

CLIMATE
Most of Spain has a form of Mediterranean climate with mild, moist winters and hot, dry summers, but the northern coastal region has a moist, equable climate, with rainfall well distributed throughout the year, mild winters and warm summers, and less sunshine than the rest of Spain. The south, in particular Andalusia, is dry and prone to drought.

Madrid, Jan. 41°F (5°C), July 77°F (25°C). Annual rainfall 16·8" (419 mm). Barcelona, Jan. 46°F (8°C), July 74°F (23·5°C), Annual rainfall 21" (525 mm). Cartagena, Jan. 51°F (10·5°C), July 75°F (24°C). Annual rainfall 14·9" (373 mm). La Coruña, Jan. 51°F (10·5°C), July 66°F (19°C). Annual rainfall 32" (800 mm). Sevilla, Jan. 51°F (10·5°C), July 85°F (29·5°C). Annual rainfall 19·5" (486 mm). Palma de Mallorca, Jan. 51°F (11°C), July 77°F (25°C). Annual rainfall 13·6" (347 mm). Santa Cruz de Tenerife, Jan. 64°F (17·9°C), July 76°F (24·4°C). Annual rainfall 7·72" (196 mm).

CONSTITUTION AND GOVERNMENT
Following the death of General Franco in 1975 and the transition to a democracy, the first democratic elections were held on 15 June 1977. A new Constitution was approved by referendum on 6 Dec. 1978, and came into force 29 Dec. 1978. It established a parliamentary monarchy.

The reigning king is **Juan Carlos I**, born 5 Jan. 1938. The eldest son of Don Juan, Conde de Barcelona, Juan Carlos was given precedence over his father as pretender to the Spanish throne in an agreement in 1954 between Don Juan and General Franco. Don Juan, who resigned his claims to the throne in May 1977, died on 1 April 1993. King (then Prince) Juan Carlos married, in 1962, Princess Sophia of Greece, daughter of the late King Paul of the Hellenes and Queen Frederika. *Offspring:* Elena, born 20 Dec. 1963, married 18 March 1995 Jaime de Marichalar (*Offspring:* Froilán, b. 17 July 1998; Victoria, b. 9 Sept. 2000); Cristina, born 13 June 1965, married 4 Oct. 1997 Iñaki Urdangarín (*Offspring:* Juan, b. 29 Sept. 1999; Pablo, b. 6 Dec. 2000); Felipe, Prince of Asturias, heir to the throne, born 30 Jan. 1968.

The King receives an allowance, part of which is taxable, approved by parliament each year. In 1997 it was 990m. pesetas. There is no formal court; the (private) *Diputación de la Grandeza* represents the interests of the aristocracy.

Legislative power is vested in the *Cortes Generales*, a bicameral parliament composed of the Congress of Deputies (lower house) and the Senate (upper house). The *Congress of Deputies* has not less than 300 nor more than 400 members (350 in the general election of 2000) elected in a proportional system under which electors choose between party lists of candidates in multi-member constituencies.

The *Senate* has 259 members of whom 208 are elected by a majority system: the 47 mainland provinces elect four senators each, regardless of population; the larger islands (Gran Canaria, Mallorca and Tenerife) elect three senators and each of the smaller islands or groups of islands (Ibiza-Formentera, Menorca, Fuerteventura, Gomera, Hierro, Lanzarote and La Palma) elect one senator. To these each self-governing community appoints one senator, and an additional senator for every million inhabitants in their respective territories. Currently 51 senators are appointed by the self-governing communities. Deputies and senators are elected by universal secret suffrage for four-year terms. The Prime Minister is elected by the Congress of Deputies.

The *Constitutional Court* is empowered to solve conflicts between the State and the Autonomous Communities; to determine if legislation passed by the Cortes is contrary to the Constitution; and to protect the constitutional rights of individuals violated by any authority. Its 12 members are appointed by the monarch. It has a nine-year term, with a third of the membership being renewed every three years.

National Anthem. 'Marcha Real' ('Royal March'); no words, tune anonymous.

RECENT ELECTIONS

A general election took place on 12 March 2000. Turn-out was around 70%. In the *Congress of Deputies* the Popular Party (PP) won 183 seats with 44·6% of votes cast; the Spanish Workers' Socialist Party (PSOE), 125 with 34·1%; Convergence and Union (CiU; Catalan nationalists), 15 with 4·2%; the Communist-led United Left Coalition (IU), 8 with 5·5%; Basque Nationalist Party (PNV), 7 with 1·5%; Canarian Coalition (CC), 4 with 1·1%; Galician Nationalist Bloc (BNG), 3 with 1·3%; the regionalist Andalusian Party (PA), 1 with 0·9%; the Catalan separatist Republican Left of Catalunya (ERC), 1 with 0·8%; the regionalist/green Initiative for Catalonia-Greens (IC-V), 1 with 0·5%; the non-radical Basque separatist Basque Solidarity Party (EA), 1 with 0·4%; the regionalist Aragonese Junta, 1 with 0·3%. In the *Senate*, the Popular Party won 126 seats; PSOE, 62; CiU, 8; PNV, 6; CC, 5; the Party of Independents from Lanzarote, 1.

European Parliament. Spain has 64 representatives. At the June 1999 elections turn-out was 64·3%. The PP won 27 seats with 39·8% of votes cast (political affiliation in European Parliament: European People's Party); the PSOE, 24 with 35·3% (Party of European Socialists); the IU, 4 with 5·8% (Confederal Group of the European United Left); the CiU, 3 with 4·4% (European People's Party; European Liberal, Democrat and Reform Party); the Nationalist Coalition, 2 with 3·2% (European Radical Alliance); PNV/EA, 2 with 2·9% (Greens/European Free Alliance); EH (regional party), 1 with 1·5% (Non-attached); BNG (regional party), 1 with 1·6% (Greens/European Free Alliance).

CURRENT ADMINISTRATION

In March 2003 the government comprised:

President of the Council and Prime Minister: José María Aznar López; b. 1953 (PP; elected 3 March 1996 and sworn in 5 May 1996; re-elected 12 March 2000).

First Deputy Prime Minister and Minister of the Presidency, Government Spokesman: Mariano Rajoy Brey (PP). *Second Deputy Prime Minister and Minister of Economy:* Rodrigo Rato Figaredo (PP). *Finance:* Cristóbal Montoro (PP). *Foreign Affairs:* Ana Palacio (PP). *Justice:* Jose María Michavila (PP). *Interior:* Ángel Acebes (PP). *Defence:* Federico Trillo-Figueroa (PP). *Education, Culture and Sport:* Pilar del Castillo (ind.). *Labour and Social Affairs:* Eduardo Zaplana (PP). *Agriculture, Fisheries and Food:* Miguel Arias Cañete (PP). *Public Administration:* Javier Arenas (PP). *Health and Consumer Affairs:* Ana María Pastor (PP). *Environment:* Elvira Rodriguez Herrer (PP). *Science and Technology:* Josep Piqué (PP). *Development:* Francisco Alvárez-Cascos (PP).

Government Website: http://www.la-moncloa.es

DEFENCE

Conscription was abolished in 2001. The government had begun the phased abolition of conscription in 1996. In 2002 the armed forces became fully professional. However, a shortfall in recruitment in Spain has meant that descendants of Spanish migrants, many of whom have never been to Europe, are now joining. Since 1989 women have been accepted in all sections of the armed forces.

In 2001 defence expenditure totalled US$6,938m. (US$174 per capita), representing 1·2% of GDP.

Army. A Rapid Reaction Force is formed from the Spanish Legion and the airborne and air-portable brigades. There is also an Army Aviation Brigade consisting of 153 helicopters (28 attack).

Strength (2002) 118,000 (including 6,600 women). Of these 4,450 are stationed on the Balearic Islands, 8,600 on the Canary Islands and 8,100 in Ceuta and Melilla. There were 265,000 army reservists in 2002.

Guardia Civil. The paramilitary *Guardia Civil* numbers 72,600.

Navy. The principal ship of the Navy is the *Príncipe de Asturias*, a light vertical/short take-off and landing aircraft carrier. Her air group includes AV-8S Matador (Harrier) combat aircraft. There are also 8 French-designed submarines and 15 frigates.

The Naval Air Service operates 17 combat aircraft and 37 armed helicopters. Personnel numbered 700 in 2002. There are 5,600 marines.

Main naval bases are at Ferrol, Rota, Cádiz, Cartagena, Palma de Mallorca, Mahón and Las Palmas (Canary Islands).

In 2002 personnel totalled 26,950 (1,600 women) including the marines and naval air arm. There were 18,500 naval reservists in 2002.

Air Force. The Air Force is organized as an independent service, dating from 1939. It is administered through four operational commands. These are geographically oriented following a reorganization in 1991 and comprise Central Air Command, Strait Air Command, Eastern Air Command and Air Command of the Canaries.

There were 198 combat aircraft in 2002 including 91 EF/A-18s, 23 F-5Bs and 65 Mirage F-1s.

Strength (2002) 22,750 (including 1,200 women). There were 45,000 Air Force reservists in 2002.

INTERNATIONAL RELATIONS
Spain is a member of the UN, WTO, BIS, the Council of Europe, NATO, OECD, WEU, the EU, OSCE, CERN, Inter-American Development Bank, Asian Development Bank and the Antarctic Treaty, and is a signatory to the Schengen Accord, which abolishes border controls between Spain, Austria, Belgium, Denmark, Finland, France, Germany, Greece, Iceland, Italy, Luxembourg, the Netherlands, Norway, Portugal and Sweden.

Spain is the largest net recipient of EU development aid, receiving €5·1bn. in 2000.

ECONOMY
Agriculture accounted for an estimated 3% of GDP in 1997, industry 33% and services 63%.

According to the anti-corruption organization *Transparency International*, Spain ranked equal 20th in the world in a 2002 survey of the countries with the least corruption in business and government. It received 7·1 out of 10 in the annual index.

Overview. The core factor determining Spain's economic growth has been EU membership. In 2002 downturn in GDP growth was blamed on the economic slowdown in the euro area, the main destination of exports. Interest rates are low and credit growth has remained rapid owing to higher inflation than in most euro-area countries. Fiscal policies are focused on raising the medium-term efficiency in the use of public and private resources. A stability bill has been introduced to establish fiscal discipline in a country that is among the most decentralized in the OECD. Corporate income tax reforms aim to boost investment.

Currency. On 1 Jan. 1999 the euro (EUR) became the legal currency in Spain; irrevocable conversion rate 166·386 pesetas to 1 euro. The euro, which consists of 100 cents, has been in circulation since 1 Jan. 2002. There are seven euro notes in different colours and sizes denominated in 500, 200, 100, 50, 20, 10 and 5 euros, and eight coins denominated in 2 and 1 euros, then 50, 20, 10, 5, 2 and 1 cents. On the introduction of the euro there was a 'dual circulation' period before the peseta ceased to be legal tender on 28 Feb. 2002. Euro banknotes in circulation on 1 Jan. 2002 had a total value of €68·6bn.

Foreign exchange reserves were US$28,939m. in June 2002 (US$65,773m. in Feb. 1998) and gold reserves 16·83m. troy oz. Inflation in 2000 was 3·4%, rising to 3·6% in 2001. Total money supply was €34,255m. in June 2002.

Budget. A Convergence Plan covering 1997–2000 envisaged an annual GDP growth of 3·2%, a reduction of public debt to 1·6% of GDP, the limitation of inflation to below 2·5%, and the creation of 1m. jobs by deregulating and increasing the flexibility of the economy and redistributing taxes. Spain's current account balance in 1998 was US$–1·1bn (US$2·5bn. in 1997).

Revenue and expenditure in 1m. pesetas:

	1995	1996	1997	1998
Revenue	19,402,252	18,448,253	16,209,545	17,351,000
Expenditure	19,402,252	19,448,253	23,882,592	24,111,000

The budget for 1998 was made up as follows (in 1m. pesetas):

Revenue		Expenditure	
Direct taxes	7,950,000	Staff costs	3,071,000
Indirect taxes	6,901,000	Current goods	
Levies and various revenues	355,000	and services	316,000
Current transfers	742,000	Financial costs	3,190,000
Income on assets	979,000	Current transfers	10,369,000
Sale on real investments	23,000	Real investment	873,000
Capital transfers	293,000	Capital transfers	911,000
Financial assets	109,000	Financial investments	1,048,000

VAT is normally 16%, with a rate of 7% on certain services (catering and hospitality), and 4% on basic foodstuffs.

Performance. The *OECD Economic Survey* of Jan. 2000 reports: 'Spain is enjoying the third year of strong growth... Interest rates eased considerably prior to entry into EMU, boosting economic activity in 1998 and 1999, while moderate wage claims and progress in reforming the labour market have bolstered job creation. Inflation has slowed to historically low levels, though it has remained above the euro average. The good performance has also been underpinned by important progress in critical areas of structural reform... The privatization process, one of the most ambitious in the OECD, has been further stepped up... As a result of sustained growth, Spain's per capita GDP has come closer to the EU average. However, despite a sharp decline, the unemployment rate still remains the highest in the OECD.'

Real GDP growth was 4·1% in 2000 and 2·8% in 2001. Total GDP (2001): US$577·5bn.

Banking and Finance. The central bank is the Bank of Spain (*Governor*, Jaime Caruana) whichgained autonomy under an ordinance of 1994. Its Governor is appointed for a six-year term. The Banking Corporation of Spain, *Argentaria*, groups together the shares of all state-owned banks, and competes in the financial market with private banks. In 1993 the government sold 49·9% of the capital of Argentaria; the remainder in two flotations ending on 13 Feb. 1998.

Spanish banking is dominated by two main banks—BSCH (Banco Santander Central Hispano) and BBVA (Banco Bilbao Vizcaya Argentaria). In Sept. 1999 BSCH had assets of 40·7trn. pesetas (US$260·7bn.) and BBVA 37·7trn. pesetas (US$241·4bn.).

There are stock exchanges in Madrid, Barcelona, Bilbao and Valencia.

Weights and Measures. The metric system was introduced in 1859.

ENERGY AND NATURAL RESOURCES

Environment. In 1998 Spain's carbon dioxide emissions were the equivalent of 6·3 tonnes per capita according to the *World Bank Atlas*.

Electricity. Installed capacity was 43m. kW in 1997. The total electricity output in 1998 amounted to 179·47bn. kWh, of which 19% was hydro-electric, 31% nuclear, and 50% other (carbon, natural gas, petroleum). Consumption per capita in 1998 was 4,195 kWh.

In Oct. 2000 Endesa SA and Iberdrola SA, the country's two largest electricity companies, announced merger plans. The new company would have been in charge of 80% of Spain's electricity output. However, in Feb. 2001 the two companies shelved the proposed merger. In 2001 there were nine nuclear reactors in operation.

Oil and Gas. Spain is heavily dependent on imported oil; Mexico is its largest supplier. Crude oil production (1996), 554,000 tonnes.

The government sold its remaining stake in the oil, gas and chemicals group Repsol in 1997. Natural gas production (2001) totalled 509m. cu. metres. Ever increasing consumption means that Spain has to import large quantities of natural gas, primarily from Algeria.

Wind. Spain is one of the world's largest wind-power producers, with an installed capacity of 4,830 MW at the end of 2002.

Minerals. Spain has a relatively wide range of minerals; the mining sector accounted for 1% of GDP in 1994. Coal production (1996), 13·61m. tonnes; other principal minerals (1992, in 1,000 tonnes): anthracite, 6,177; lignite (1997), 12,587; salt (1995), 4,776; iron ore (1993), 1,166; potassium salts, 594; pyrites, 406; zinc, 205; fluorspar (1997), 120; lead, 30; (1992, in tonnes) uranium, 862; tin, 7. In 1995 a large mercury deposit was found in southern Spain which could raise mercury levels to within a quarter of proven world reserves. Gold production, 1997, 1,824 kg.

Agriculture. There were 1,384,000 farms in Spain in 1998. Agriculture employed about 9·3% of the workforce in 1998. It accounts for 15·8% of exports and 15·6% of imports.

There were 14·29m. ha of arable land in 1998 and 4·77m. ha of permanent crops. In 1998 there were 841,932 tractors, 49,729 harvesters and in 1992, 280,989 motor ploughs in use.

Principal crops	Area (in 1,000 ha)			Yield (in 1,000 tonnes)		
	1998	1999	2000	1998	1999	2000
Barley	3,535	3,107	3,307	10,895	7,434	11,283
Sugarbeets	149	135	136	8,866	8,162	8,344
Wheat	1,913	2,422	2,370	5,436	5,084	7,333
Maize	459	398	425	4,349	3,769	3,867
Potatoes	136	136	123	3,129	3,367	3,138
Oats	413	410	427	726	531	952
Sunflower seeds	1,048	850	841	1,190	579	849
Rice	113	112	115	796	845	798

Spain has more land dedicated to the grape than any other country in the world and is ranked third among wine producers (behind Italy and France). Wine exports increased in value by nearly 600% from 1991–97. A large part of Spain's output goes to Italy for bottling. Production of wine (2000), 3,413,000 tonnes; of grapes, 5,646,000 tonnes.

The area planted with tomatoes in 2000 was 63,000 ha, yielding 3,597,000 tonnes; with onions, 23,000 ha, yielding 1,014,000 tonnes; chillies and green peppers, 23,000 ha, yielding 936,000 tonnes.

In fruit, Spain contributes a fifth of EU total harvest, and more than half of all citrus fruits. Fruit production (2000, in tonnes): oranges, 2,706,000; mandarins and satsumas, 1,798,000; melons and watermelons, 1,760,000; tangerines, peaches and nectarines, 1,096,000; lemons and limes, 927,000; apples, 675,000; pears, 587,000.

Production of olives, 2000, 4,183,000 tonnes; olive oil (2000), 905,000 tonnes. Spain is the world's leading producer both of olives and olive oil.

Livestock (2000): cattle, 6·20m.; sheep, 23·70m.; goats, 2·87m.; pigs, 23·68m.; chickens, 128·0m.; asses and mules, 0·26m.; horses, 0·25m. Livestock products (2000, in 1,000 tonnes): pork, bacon and ham, 2,962; beef and veal, 697; mutton and lamb, 222; poultry meat, 891; milk, 6,526; cheese, 175; eggs, 522.

Forestry. In 1995 the area under forests was 8·39m. ha, or 16·8% of the total land area. In 1999 timber production was 15·11m. cu. metres.

Fisheries. Spain is the second largest fishing country in the EU after Denmark; it is also the EU's leading importer of fishery commodities. Fishing vessels had a total tonnage of 524,602 tonnes in 1995 (596,441 GRT in 1994); fleets have been gradually reduced from 20,558 boats in 1991 to 18,091 in 1996. Total catch in 1999 amounted to approximately 1,167,242 tonnes, almost exclusively sea fish.

INDUSTRY

The leading companies by market capitalization in Spain, excluding banking and finance, in Jan. 2002 were: Telefónica SA (€62bn.); Telefónica Móviles SA (€32bn.); and Amadeus Global Travel Distribution SA (€27bn.), a reservation and ticketing systems company.

Industrial products (1998, in tonnes): cement, 31·08m.; steel (1999), 14·9m.; paper and paperboard, 4m.; sulphuric acid (1997), 2·82m.; plastics (1993), 2·7m.; nitrogenous fertilizers (1993), 642,000.

The number of vehicles manufactured in 1997 was 2,531,000. In 1997, 1·96m. refrigerators, 2·6m. cookers, hotplates and microwaves, and 1·53m. washing machines, dishwashers and clothes driers were manufactured; number of TV sets (1995), 5·39m. 2,278·3m. litres of mineral water were produced in 1997; and 2,478·6m. litres of beer. There are also important toy and shoe industries.

Labour. The economically active population numbered 16·84m. in 2000. The monthly minimum wage for adults (2002) was €442·20, 35% of the average Spanish wage. The average working week in 1996 was 40·6 hours. The retirement age is 65 years. In 1999 part-time work accounted for less than 8% of all employment in Spain—the lowest percentage in any major industrialized country.

Spain has the highest unemployment rate among EU member countries, although after reaching a peak of nearly 25% in 1994 the rate was down to 11·2% in May 2002 before rising again to 12·1% in Jan. 2003. The unemployment rate among women is double that among men. Between 1996 and early 2000 Spain created as many new jobs as were created in the rest of the EU put together—the number of people in employment has risen by 15% since José María Aznar became Prime Minister in 1996. In spite of the high unemployment rate, by 2000 there were labour shortages in agriculture and construction, as a result of which the government reached an agreement with Morocco to import temporary contract labour.

Between 1989 and 1998 strikes cost Spain an average of 346 days per 1,000 employees a year, compared to the EU average of 85 per 1,000. Spain's figure was the highest in the EU.

Trade Unions. The Constitution guarantees the establishment and activities of trade unions provided they have a democratic structure. The most important trade unions are *Comisiones Obreras* (CO), with 790,000 members in 1997, and *Unión General de Trabajadores* (UGT), which had 775,000 members in 1997.

INTERNATIONAL TRADE

Imports and Exports. Trade in US$1m.:

	1996	1997	1998	1999	2000
Imports f.o.b.	119,017	120,333	132,744	143,002	147,836
Exports f.o.b.	102,735	106,926	111,986	112,664	115,081

Breakdown of exports in 2000 (in €1m.): intermediate goods, 57,505 (including intermediate industrial products, 51,788); consumer goods, 49,179 (including cars, 18,805; food, beverages and tobacco, 14,052); capital goods, 16,416 (including machinery and other equipment goods, 9,778; transport material, 5,238).

Breakdown of imports in 2000 (in €1m.): intermediate goods, 95,144 (including intermediate industrial products, 71,756; intermediate energy products, 19,893); consumer goods, 41,061 (including cars, 12,331; food, beverages and tobacco, 9,905); capital goods, 29,934 (including machinery and other equipment goods, 20,702; transport material, 6,375).

Leading export markets in 1998 were: France (18·4%), Germany (11·1%), Italy (9·2%), Portugal (9·2%); leading import sources in 1998 were France (18·1%), Germany (15·4%), Italy (9·6%), United Kingdom (7·3%). In 2000 the EU accounted for 63·1% of Spain's imports and 69·6% of exports.

COMMUNICATIONS

Roads. In 1997 the total length of highways and roads was 346,858 km; the main network comprised 9,063 km of motorways, 23,397 km of highways/national roads and 139,398 km of secondary roads. 99% of all roads in Spain were paved in 1997. Travel by road accounted for 90·6% of internal passenger traffic in 1995; and for 77·24% of freight. Number of cars (1998), 16,050,100; trucks and vans, 3,393,400;

buses, 51,800; motorcycles and mopeds, 1,361,200. In 2000, 5,776 persons were killed in road accidents.

Rail. The total length of the state railways in 1995 was 13,060 km, mostly broad (1,668-mm) gauge (6,736 km electrified). State railways are run by the National Spanish Railway Network (RENFE). There is a high-speed standard-gauge (1,435-mm) railway from Madrid to Seville. Passenger-km travelled in 2000 came to 19·9bn. and freight tonne-km to 12·1bn. There are metros in Madrid (121 km), Barcelona (81 km) and Bilbao (28 km), and a light railway in Valencia.

Civil Aviation. There are international airports at Madrid (Barajas), Barcelona (Prat del Llobregat), Alicante, Almería, Bilbao, Gerona, Las Palmas de Gran Canaria, Ibiza, Lanzarote, Málaga, Palma de Mallorca, Santiago de Compostela, Seville, Tenerife (Los Rodeos and Reina Sofia), Valencia, Valladolid and Zaragoza. There are 43 airports open to civil traffic. A small airport in Seo de Urgel operates in Andorra. The national carrier is Iberia Airlines. Iberia Airlines, which was 99·8% state-owned, went through the first stage of privatization in 1999 before the 2nd phase was indefinitely postponed in Nov. 1999. Of other airlines, the largest are Air Europa and Spanair. Services are also provided by about 70 foreign airlines. In 1999 Iberia flew 258·8m. km, carrying 22,203,700 passengers (8,447,600 on international flights). Madrid was the busiest airport in 2000, handling 32,566,066 passengers (16,517,059 on domestic flights) and 305,499 tonnes of freight. Barcelona was the second busiest in 2000, with 19,375,338 (9,988,206 on domestic flights) and 87,300 tonnes of freight. Palma de Mallorca was the third busiest for passengers, with 19,296,722 (14,460,592 on international flights). Las Palmas was the third busiest for freight, with 43,568 tonnes in 2000.

Shipping. The merchant navy in 1998 had 1,570 vessels with a gross tonnage of 1,838,000; shipyards launched 219,673 GRT in 1996. In 1997 vessels totalling 152,915,000 NRT entered ports and vessels totalling 54,243,000 NRT cleared.

Telecommunications. In 2000 there were 17,101,700 main telephone lines (421·2 per 1,000 persons) and 5·8m. PCs in use (142·9 per 1,000 persons). The government disposed of its remaining 21% stake in Telefónica in Feb. 1997, bringing 1·4m. shareholders into the company's equity base. A second operator, Rétévision, accounts for 3% of the domestic market, which was wholly deregulated in 1998. The mobile phone business was deregulated in 1995; the market is shared by Telefónica, Airtel and Amena (Rétévision).

Spain had 21·43m. mobile phone subscribers in Nov. 2000 (582 for every 1,000 persons) and 7·89m. Internet users in May 2002. In 1996 fax machines numbered 700,000.

Postal Services. In 1998 there were 4,093 post offices; a total of 4,574m. pieces of mail were processed during the year, or 115 items per person.

SOCIAL INSTITUTIONS

Justice. Justice is administered by Tribunals and Courts, which jointly form the Judicial Power. Judges and magistrates cannot be removed, suspended or transferred except as set forth by law. The Constitution of 1978 established the *General Council of the Judicial Power*, consisting of a President and 20 magistrates, judges, attorneys and lawyers, governing the Judicial Power in full independence from the state's legislative and executive organs. Its members are appointed by the *Cortes Generales*. Its President is that of the Supreme Court (*Tribunal Supremo*), who is appointed by the monarch on the proposal of the General Council of the Judicial.

The Judicature is composed of the Supreme Court; 17 Higher Courts of Justice, 1 for each autonomous community; 52 Provincial High Courts; Courts of First Instance; Courts of Judicial Proceedings, not passing sentences; and Penal Courts, passing sentences.

The Supreme Court consists of a President, and various judges distributed among 7 chambers: 1 for civil matters, 3 for administrative purposes, 1 for criminal trials, 1 for social matters and 1 for military cases. The Supreme Court has disciplinary faculties; is court of appeal in all criminal trials; for administrative purposes decides in first and second instance disputes arising between private individuals and the State; and in social matters makes final decisions.

A new penal code came into force in May 1996, replacing the code of 1848. It provides for a maximum of 30 years imprisonment in specified exceptional cases, with a normal maximum of 20 years. Sanctions with a rehabilitative intent include fines adjusted to means, community service and weekend imprisonment. The death penalty was abolished by the 1978 Constitution. The prison population in 1997 was 42,827 (110 per 100,000 of national population); 110,844 criminal sentences were passed in 1996. A jury system commenced operating in Nov. 1995 in criminal cases (first trials in May 1996). Juries consist of nine members.

A juvenile criminal law of 1995 lays emphasis on rehabilitation. It raised the age of responsibility from 12 to 14 years. Criminal conduct on the part of children under 14 is a matter for legal protection and custody. 14- and 15-year-olds are classified as 'minors'; 16- and 17-year-olds as 'young persons'; and the legal majority for criminal offences is set at 18 years. Persons up to the age of 21 may, at the courts' discretion, be dealt with as juveniles.

The *Audiencia Nacional* deals with terrorism, monetary offences and drug-trafficking where more than one province is involved. Its president is appointed by the General Council of the Judicial Power.

There is an Ombudsman (*Defensor del Pueblo*), who is elected for a five-year term (currently Enrique Múgica Herzog; b. 1932).

Religion. There is no official religion. Roman Catholicism is the religion of the majority. In Feb. 2001 there were seven Cardinals. There are 11 metropolitan sees and 52 suffragan sees, the chief being Toledo, where the Primate resides. The archdioceses of Madrid-Alcalá and Barcelona depend directly from the Vatican. There are about 0·25m. other Christians, including several Protestant denominations, about 60,000 Jehovah's Witnesses and 29,000 Latter-day Saints (Mormons), and 0·45m. Muslims, including Spanish Muslims in Ceuta and Melilla. The first synagogue since the expulsion of the Jews in 1492 was opened in Madrid on 2 Oct. 1959. The number of people of Judaist faith is estimated at about 15,000.

Education. In 1991 the General Regulation of the Educational System Act came into force. This Act gradually extends the school-leaving age to 16 years and determines the following levels of education: infants (3–5 years of age), primary (6–11), secondary (12–15) and baccalaureate or vocational and technical (16–17). Primary and secondary levels of education are now compulsory and free. Religious instruction is optional.

In Sept. 1997 a joint declaration with trade unions, parents' and schools' associations was signed in support of a new finance law guaranteeing that spending on education will reach 6% of GDP within five years, thus protecting it from changes in the political sphere. In 1996 expenditure on education came to 5·0% of GNP and 11·0% of total government spending.

A new compulsory secondary education programme has replaced the Basic General Education programme which was in force since 1970. In addition, university entrance exams underwent reform in 1997, resulting in greater emphasis now being placed on the teaching of Humanities at secondary level.

In 2000–01 pre-primary education (under 6 years) was undertaken by 1,164,156 pupils; primary or basic education (6–14 years): 2,494,067 pupils. In 1997–98 there were 215,584 teachers in pre-primary and primary schools. Secondary education (14–17 years), including high schools and technical schools, was conducted at 5,449 schools, with 3,492,726 pupils and 150,220 teachers.

In 1997–98 there were 60 universities: 40 public state universities, 3 polytechnic universities, 13 private universities (including 3 Catholic); plus 4 Open universities. In 2000–01 there were 1,425,209 students at state universities; 115,387 at private universities.

Adult literacy rate, 1999, 97·6% (male 98·5%; female 96·7%).

Health. In 1998 there were 171,494 doctors (4·3 per 1,000 inhabitants), 16,133 dentists, 46,761 pharmacists and 203,504 nurses (including 6,699 midwives). Number of hospitals (1995), 782, with 154,644 beds.

Spain has the highest AIDS rate in the EU, with 167·7 cases per 100,000 people.

Welfare. The social security budget was 12,134,637m. pesetas in 1997. The budget for 1998 was: for pensions, 8,356,100m. pesetas; health, 3,822,000m.; social benefits and incapacity, 1,554,000m.; unemployment, 1,495,400m. The minimum pension in 2001 was 839,860 pesetas per year, made in 14 payments.

In 1997 the system of contributions to the social security and employment scheme was: for pensions, sickness, invalidity, maternity and children, a contribution of 28·3% of the basic wage (23·6% paid by the employer, 4·7% by the employee); for unemployment benefit, a contribution of 7·8% (6·2% paid by the employer, 1·6% by the employee). There are also minor contributions for a Fund of Guaranteed Salaries, working accidents and professional sicknesses, and for vocational training.

CULTURE

Broadcasting. *Radio Nacional de España* broadcasts five programmes on medium-wave and FM, as well as many regional programmes; it has one commercial programme. The most successful domestic network is that of an independent, Cadena SER (*Sociedad Española de Radiodifusión*); *Cadena de Ondas Populares Españolas* (COPE) is owned by the Roman Catholic church. Two independent radio networks cover the whole of Spain. They are *Antena 3* and *Radio 80* (taken over by SER in 1992). *Radio Exterior* broadcasts abroad, and *Antena 3* has been broadcasting to 400,000 subscribers in Miami since Sept. 1997.

Televisión Española broadcasts two channels (TVE1 and TVE2) and also has an international channel. There are three nationwide commercial TV networks: *Antena 3*, *Tele 5* and the pay-TV channel *Canal Plus*, which had 1·4m. subscribers in 1997. There were in 1999 the following regional TV networks: *TV3* (launched in 1983) and *Canal 33* (1989), both broadcasting in Catalan; *ETB1* (1983) and *ETB2* (1987), both broadcasting in Basque—*ETB1* exclusively so and *ETB2* partly so, but additionally with much output in Castilian; *Televisión de Galicia* (1985), in Galician; *TM3* (1989), in Castilian, for the area of Madrid; *Canal 9* (1989), mostly in Valencian (Catalan); and *Tele-Sur* (1989), in Castilian, for Andalusia. There are two digital TV channels, *Vía Digital* and *Canal Satélite Digital*, both launched in 1997. Colour transmissions are carried by PAL.

Number of receivers: radios (1997), 13·1m. (331 per 1,000 population); TV (1997), 19·9m. (501 per 1,000 population).

Cinema. There were, in 2000, 3,377 cinemas with an audience of 137·7m. (13·6m. for Spanish films and 124·0m. for foreign films). In Nov. 1997 the Madrid School of Cinema was established. It is backed by the Spanish Academy and Ministry of Education and Culture. In 1995 gross box office receipts came to 48,229m. pesetas.

Press. In 1996 there were about 90 daily newspapers with a total daily circulation of 3·93m. copies. Eight publishing groups controlled around 80% of the daily press, with another 100 or so independents accounting for the other 20%. Prisa, the biggest conglomerate, had a daily readership of 541,691 in 1996 (13·7% of the sector). The main titles are: *El País, ABC* and *El Mundo,* along with the dedicated sports paper, *Marca*.

In 2000, 62,011 book titles were published. Approximately 80% were in Castilian and 10% in Catalan.

Tourism. In 1999 Spain was behind only France in the number of foreign visitor arrivals, and behind only the USA for tourism receipts. In 1997 tourism accounted for 10·4% of GDP; receipts for 1999 amounted to US$32,913m. In 1999, 51·77m. tourists visited Spain. Overnight stays in hotels in 1998 totalled 178,355,712, of which 111,803,276 were by foreigners.

Festivals. Religious Festivals: Epiphany (6 Jan.), the Feast of the Assumption (15 Aug.), All Saints Day (1 Nov.) and Immaculate Conception (8 Dec.) are all public holidays. Cultural Festivals: Day of Andalucia (28 Feb.), the Feast of San José in Valencia (19 March) is the culmination of a 13-day festival; the Festival of the Sardine in Murcia is an end of Easter parade in which a huge papier mâché sardine is burned; Feria de Abril is a huge festival in Seville at the end of April which features flamenco dancing and bull-fighting; the San Fermines Festival, which takes place in mid-July, is most famous for the running of the bulls in the streets of Pamplona; La Tomatina, a battle of revellers armed with 50 tonnes of tomatoes, takes place on the last Wednesday in Aug. and is the highlight of the annual fiesta in Buñol, Valencia; National Day of Catalonia (11 Sept.); Spanish National Day (12 Oct.).

Libraries. In 1997 there were 3,600 public libraries, 2 National libraries and 947 Higher Education libraries; they held a combined 53,430,000 volumes. There were 207,523,000 visits to libraries in 1997.

Museums and Galleries. Spain had 1,438 museums in 2000 with 3·7m. visitors. The Museu del Prado in Madrid received 1·8m. visitors in 2000.

DIPLOMATIC REPRESENTATIVES

Of Spain in the United Kingdom (39 Chesham Pl., London, SW1X 8SB)
Ambassador: The Marqués de Tamarón.

Of the United Kingdom in Spain (Calle de Fernando el Santo, 16, 28010 Madrid)
Ambassador: Stephen J. L. Wright, CMG.

Of Spain in the USA (2375 Pennsylvania Ave., NW, Washington, D.C., 20037)
Ambassador: Javier Rupérez.

Of the USA in Spain (Serrano 75, 28006 Madrid)
Ambassador: George L. Argyros.

Of Spain to the United Nations
Ambassador: Inocencio F. Arias Llamas.

FURTHER READING

Carr, Raymond, (ed.) *Spain: A History.* OUP, 2000
Conversi, D., *The Basques, The Catalans and Spain.* Hurst, London, 1997
Heywood, P., *The Government and Politics of Spain.* London, 1995
Hooper, J., *The New Spaniards.* 2nd ed. [of *The Spaniards*] London, 1995
Péréz-Díaz, V. M., *The Return of Civil Society: the Emergence of Democratic Spain.* Harvard Univ. Press, 1993
Powell, C., *Juan Carlos of Spain: Self-Made Monarch.* London and New York, 1996
Shields, Graham J., *Spain.* [Bibliography] 2nd ed. ABC-Clio, Oxford and Santa Barbara (CA), 1994.—*Madrid.* [Bibliography] ABC-Clio, Oxford and Santa Barbara (CA), 1996

National library: Biblioteca Nacional, Madrid.
National statistical office: Instituto Nacional de Estadística (INE), Paseo de la Castellana, 183, Madrid.
Website: http://www.ine.es

SRI LANKA

Sri Lanka Prajathanthrika
Samajavadi Janarajaya
(Democratic Socialist
Republic of Sri Lanka)

Capital: Sri Jayewardenepura Kotte
(Administrative and Legislative),
Colombo (Commercial)
Population estimate, 2000: 18·92m.
GDP per capita, 2000: (PPP$) 3,530
HDI/world rank: 0·741/89

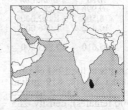

KEY HISTORICAL EVENTS
In the 18th century the central kingdom, Kandy, was the only surviving independent state on the island of Ceylon. The Dutch, who had obtained their first coastal possessions in 1636, had driven out the Portuguese to become the dominant power in the island. In 1796 the British East India Company sent a naval force to Ceylon (as the British then called it). The Dutch surrendered their possessions, which left the British in control of the maritime areas surrounding Kandy. These areas were at first attached to the Madras Presidency of India but in 1802 they were constituted a separate colony under the Crown. Once the British began to develop their new territory they came to see Kandy as a threat. The Kandyan Convention of 1815 annexed Kandy to British Ceylon while recognizing most of the traditional rights of the chiefs. However, in 1817 the chiefs rebelled. The rebellion was suppressed and the rights established by the Convention were abolished.

Ceylon was then united for the first time since the 12th century. The British built up a plantation economy. Coffee was dominant until an outbreak of *Hoemilia vastatrix* fungus destroyed the plants in 1870. Spices, cocoa and rice all followed but tea became the main cash crop after successful experiments in the 1880s. Foreign rule served to subdue the traditional hostility between northern Tamils and southern Sinhalese. The Ceylon National Congress, formed in 1919, contained both Sinhalese and Ceylon Tamil groups. (The Indian Tamils brought in as a labour force for the tea estates were a separate community.) Tamil national feeling, however, was expressed over the issue of the use of Tamil languages in schools. As early as 1931 a general election took place under universal suffrage, just two years after the first one in the UK. On 4 Feb. 1948 Ceylon became a Dominion of the Commonwealth. In 1956 Solomon Bandaranaike became prime minister at the head of the People's United Front, advocating neutral foreign policy and the promotion of Sinhalese national culture at home. In Sept. 1959 he was murdered; his widow Sirimavo Bandaranaike succeeded him in July 1960 at the head of an increasingly socialist government. In May 1972 Ceylon became a republic and adopted the name Sri Lanka. In July 1977 the United National Party (dominant until 1956) returned to power and in 1978 a new constitution set up a presidential system. The problem of communal unrest remained unsolved and Tamil separatists were active. In 1983 the Tamil United Liberation Front members of parliament were asked to renounce their objective for a separate Tamil state in the north and the east of the country. They refused and withdrew from parliament. Militant Tamils then began armed action which developed into civil war. A state of emergency ended on 11 Jan. 1989, but violence continued.

President Ranasinghe Premadasa was assassinated on 1 May 1993. A ceasefire was signed on 3 Jan. 1995, but fighting broke out again in April. The 'Liberation Tigers of the Tamil Eelam' stronghold of Jaffna in the far north of the country was captured by government forces in Dec. 1995 and by mid-1997 was under government control. In April 2000 the Tamil Tigers captured a military garrison at Elephant Pass, the isthmus that links Jaffna to the rest of Sri Lanka, increasing the possibility that they might re-take the Jaffna peninsula. A month-long ceasefire began in Dec. 2001 amid signs that the Tigers might be willing to engage in peace talks, and on 22 Feb. 2002 the government and Tamil Tiger leaders agreed to an internationally-monitored ceasefire, paving the way to the first full-scale peace talks for seven years. An estimated 61,000 people died during the 19-year long conflict. In Sept. 2002 the ban on the Tamil Tigers was formally lifted and they subsequently abandoned their ambitions for a separate state, settling instead for regional autonomy.

TERRITORY AND POPULATION

Sri Lanka is an island in the Indian Ocean, south of the Indian peninsula from which it is separated by the Palk Strait. On 28 June 1974 the frontier between India and Sri Lanka in the Palk Strait was redefined, giving to Sri Lanka the island of Kachchativu.

Area (in sq. km) and population (1994 estimates):

Provinces	Area	Population	Provinces	Area	Population
Western	3,684	4,599,000	Eastern	9,996	1,282,000
Southern	5,544	2,330,000	Uva	8,500	1,102,000
Central	5,674	2,261,000	North-Central	10,472	1,086,000
North-Western	7,888	2,107,000			
Sabaragamuwa	4,968	1,735,000	Total	65,610	17,865,000
Northern	8,884	1,363,000			

Population (in 1,000) according to ethnic group and nationality at the 1981 census: 10,980 Sinhalese, 1,887 Sri Lanka Tamils, 1,047 Sri Lanka Moors, 819 Indian Tamils, 47 Malays, 39 Burghers, 28 others. Non-nationals of Sri Lanka totalled 635,150. Population, 1997 (estimate), 18,721,200 (9,437,500 females); density, 285 per sq. km. In 1999, 76·7% of the population lived in rural areas. Ethnic mix, 74% Sinhalese, 18% Tamil.

The UN gives a projected population for 2010 of 20·7m.

By 1997 approximately 0·3m. Tamils had left the country since the mid-1980s, one-third as refugees to India and two-thirds to seek political asylum in the West.

Colombo (the largest city) had 690,000 inhabitants in 1999. Other major towns and their populations (1990 estimates) are: Dehiwela-Mt. Lavinia, 196,000; Moratuwa, 170,000; Jaffna, 129,000; Sri Jayewardenepura Kotte (now the administrative and legislative capital), 109,000; Kandy, 104,000; Galle, 84,000.

Sinhala and Tamil are the official languages; English is in use.

SOCIAL STATISTICS

Births, 1998, 329,148; deaths, 112,657. 1998 birth rate (per 1,000 population), 17·5; death rate, 6·0; infant mortality rate, 1999 (per 1,000 live births), 17. Life expectancy, 1999, 75·0 years for females and 69·3 for males. Annual population growth rate, 1990–99, 1·0%. Infant mortality, 1998, 17 per 1,000 live births; fertility rate, 1999, 2·1 births per woman. Sri Lanka has the third oldest population in Asia, after Japan and Singapore, thanks largely to relatively good health and a low fertility rate.

CLIMATE

Sri Lanka, which has an equatorial climate, is affected by the North-east Monsoon (Dec. to Feb.), the South-west Monsoon (May to July) and two inter-monsoons (March to April and Aug. to Nov.). Rainfall is heaviest in the southwest highlands while the northwest and southeast are relatively dry. Colombo, Jan. 79·9°F (26·6°C), July 81·7°F (27·6°C). Annual rainfall 95·4" (2,424 mm). Trincomalee, Jan. 78·8°F (26°C), July 86·2°F (30·1°C). Annual rainfall 62·2" (1,580 mm). Kandy, Jan. 73·9°F (23·3°C), July 76·1°F (24·5°C). Annual rainfall 72·4" (1,840 mm). Nuwara Eliya, Jan. 58·5°F (14·7°C), July 60·3°F (15·7°C). Annual rainfall 75" (1,905 mm).

CONSTITUTION AND GOVERNMENT

A new constitution for the Democratic Socialist Republic of Sri Lanka was promulgated in Sept. 1978.

The Executive *President* is directly elected for a seven-year term renewable once.

Parliament consists of one chamber, composed of 225 members (196 elected and 29 from the National List). Election is by proportional representation by universal suffrage at 18 years. The term of Parliament is six years. The Prime Minister and other Ministers, who must be members of Parliament, are appointed by the President.

National Anthem. 'Sri Lanka Matha, Apa Sri Lanka' ('Mother Sri Lanka, thee Sri Lanka'); words and tune by A. Samarakone. There is a Tamil version, 'Sri Lanka thaaya, nam Sri Lanka'; words anonymous.

SRI LANKA

RECENT ELECTIONS
Presidential elections were held on 21 Dec. 1999. Incumbent Chandrika Kumaratunga was re-elected against two opponents by 51·1% of votes cast. Turn-out was around 73%.

Parliamentary elections were held on 5 Dec. 2001. The United National Party gained 109 seats with 45·6% of the vote; the People's Alliance (a coalition of five parties) 77 with 37·3%; the People's United Liberation Front 16 with 9·1%; the Tamil United Liberation Front 15 with 3·9%; and the Sri Lanka Muslim Congress 5 with 1·2%. Other parties won less than 1% of votes cast. Turn-out was 75·8%.

Following the Dec. 2001 election Sri Lanka had a prime minister from one party and a president from a rival party for the first time in seven years.

CURRENT ADMINISTRATION
In March 2003 the government comprised:

President: Chandrika Bandaranaike Kumaratunga; b. 1945 (Sri Lanka Freedom Party; sworn in 12 Nov. 1994, re-elected 21 Dec. 1999).

Prime Minister, Minister of Policy Development, Implementation, and Poverty Alleviation: Ranil Wickremasinghe; b. 1949 (United National Party; sworn in 9 Dec. 2001).

Minister of Agriculture and Livestock: S. B. Dissanayake. *Constitutional Affairs, Enterprise Development, Industrial Policy, and Investment Promotion:* G. L. Peiris. *Co-operatives:* Abdul Rahim Mohideen Abdul Cader. *Defence and Transport, Highways and Aviation:* Thilak Marapone. *Environment and Natural Resources:* Rukman Senanayake. *Foreign Affairs:* Tyronne Fernando. *Finance:* K. N. Choksy. *Fisheries:* Mahinda Wijeyesekera. *Health, Nutrition, and Welfare:* P. Dayaratne. *Home Affairs, Provincial Councils, and Local Government:* Alick Aluvihara. *Housing and Plantation Infrastructure:* Arumugam Thondaman. *Interior:* John Anthony Amaratunge. *Irrigation and Water Management:* Gamini Jayawickrema Perera. *Justice, Law Reform, National Reconciliation, and Minister of Buddha Sasana:* W. J. M. Lokubandara. *Plantation Industries:* Lakshman Bandara Kiriella. *Power and Energy:* Karu Jayasuriya. *Rural Economy:* Bandula Gunawardena. *Science and Technology, and Economic Reform:* Milinda Moragoda. *Tourism:* Gamini Kulawansa Lokuge. *Women's Affairs:* Amara Piyasiri Ratnayake. *Central Region Development:* Tissa Attanayake. *Port Development and Shipping, Eastern Development and Muslim Religious Affairs:* Rauf Hakeem. *Southern Region Development:* Ananda Kularatne. *Western Region Development:* Mohamad Hanifa Mohamed.

Government Website: http://www.priu.gov.lk

DEFENCE
Defence expenditure in 2000 totalled US$862m. (US$46 per capita), representing 5·3% of GDP.

Army. Strength (1999), 90–95,000. In addition there were 1,100 reserves. Paramilitary forces consist of the Ministry of Defence Police (70,100, including 1,000 women and a 3,000-strong anti-guerrilla force), the Home Guard (15,200) and the National Guard (some 15,000).

Navy. The main naval base is at Trincomalee. Personnel in 1999 numbered 10,000, including a reserve of about 1,100.

Air Force. Air Force bases are at Anuradhapura, Katunayake, Ratmalana, Vavuniya and China Bay, Trincomalee. Total strength (1999) about 10,000 with 22 combat aircraft and 15 armed helicopters. Main attack aircraft types included F-7s and FT-5s.

INTERNATIONAL RELATIONS
Sri Lanka is a member of the UN, WTO, the Commonwealth, the Asian Development Bank, the Colombo Plan, SAARC and IOM.

ECONOMY
Agriculture accounted for 21·1% of GDP in 1998, industry 27·5% and services 71·1%.

The conflict with the minority separatists, the Tamil Tigers, is estimated to have cost the country between 1 and 1·5% in growth per year.

Overview. President Kumaratunga is embarking on a radical programme of privatization. In 2001 she hoped to raise between 10bn. and 15bn. rupees (between US$120m. and US$180m.).

Currency. The unit of currency is the *Sri Lankan rupee* (LKR) of 100 *cents*. Foreign exchange reserves were US$884m. and gold reserves 626,000 troy oz in Dec. 2001. Inflation was 6·2% in 2000, rising to 14·2% in 2001. Total money supply in March 2002 was Rs 125,695m.

Budget. Revenue and expenditure of central government in Rs 1m. for financial years ending 31 Dec.:

	1995	1996	1997	1998	1999	2000[1]
Revenue	136,257	146,280	165,036	175,032	195,905	211,282
Expenditure	195,880	212,787	228,732	253,808	267,611	322,048

[1]Provisional.

The principal sources of revenue in 2001 were: general sales tax, 21%; excise taxes, 19%; national security levy, 18%; import duties, 13%; income tax, 13%; non-tax revenue, 11%; stamp duties, 4%; motor vehicle levy and others, 1%.

The principal items of recurrent expenditure in 2001 were: public debt interest, 32%; defence, 22%; public service, 15%; provincial councils, 10%; pensions, 9%; welfare, 8%; corporations and institutions, 3%; contingency and others, 1%.

Performance. GDP growth in 2000 was 6·0%, but in 2001 the economy contracted by 1·4%. Total GDP in 2001 was US$16·3bn.

Banking and Finance. The Central Bank of Sri Lanka is the bank of issue (*Governor*, A. S. Jayawardena). Two state-owned commercial banks, the Bank of Ceylon and the People's Bank, account for about 70% of bank lending. There are also 21 private banks (17 foreign). Total assets of commercial banks at 31 Dec. 1994, Rs 286,933m. Assets of the Sri Lanka National Savings Bank at 31 Dec. 1999 were Rs 100,813m. There are five main long-term credit institutions. In the five years to Sept. 2000 Sri Lanka attracted US$715m. in foreign direct investment, including more than US$200m. in 1999.

There is a stock exchange in Colombo.

Weights and Measures. The metric system has been established.

ENERGY AND NATURAL RESOURCES

Environment. According to the *World Bank Atlas* carbon dioxide emissions in 1998 were the equivalent of 0·4 tonnes per capita.

Electricity. Installed capacity (1997), 2m. kW. Production, 1998, 5·51bn. kWh; the main source was hydro-electric (approximately 95%). An 80 MW hydro-electricity station on the Kukule Ganga river (70 km southeast of Colombo) is to be constructed by a Swiss-German consortium. Consumption per capita in 1998 was 244 kWh.

Oil and Gas. Construction of a US$1·6bn. oil refinery at Hambantota in the south of the island began in 1999.

Water. The Mahaweli Authority scheme, which began in 1978, had led to the irrigation of 354,000 ha of land by 2001.

Minerals. Gems are among the chief minerals mined and exported. Graphite is also important; production in 1994 was 5,000 tonnes. Production of ilmenite, 1994, 60,400 tonnes. Some rutile is also produced (2,741 tonnes in 1992). Salt extraction is the oldest industry. The method is solar evaporation of sea-water. Estimated production, 1997, 65,000 tonnes.

Agriculture. There were 868,000 ha of arable land in 1998 and 1,020,000 ha of permanent crops. Agriculture engages 47·5% of the labour force. Main crops in 2000 (in 1,000 tonnes): rice, 2,767; coconuts, 1,950; sugarcane, 1,114; plantains, 600; tea, 285; cassava, 260; rubber, 99; mangoes, 86. Tea plantations are being returned to the private sector after nationalization in 1975.

Livestock in 2000: 1,617,000 cattle; 728,000 buffaloes; 514,000 goats; 10m. chickens.

Forestry. The area under forests in 1995 was 1,796,000 ha, or 27·8% of the land area (1,897,000 and 29·4% in 1990). In 1999, 10·34m. cu. metres of roundwood were cut.

Fisheries. Total catch in 1999 was approximately 271,595 tonnes (90% from sea fishing). In 1992 there were 27,435 fishing craft, of which 15,637 were not motorized.

INDUSTRY
The main industries are the processing of rubber, tea, coconuts and other agricultural commodities, tobacco, textiles, clothing and leather goods, chemicals, plastics, cement, and petroleum refining. Industrial production grew by 7% in 1997.

Labour. The labour force in 1996 totalled 5,586,900 (68% males), of which 1,962,700 worked in agriculture, 1,083,000 in community and social services, 838,100 in manufacturing industries and 705,100 in trade, hotels and restaurants. In 1995 the unemployment rate was 12·5%. In 1994, 42% of the economically active population were engaged in agriculture, 40% in services and 18% in industry.

Trade Unions. In 1994 there were 1,304 registered trade unions.

INTERNATIONAL TRADE
Foreign debt in 2000 was US$9,066m. A free trade pact with India, signed in Dec. 1998, is expected to create growth in exports.

Imports and Exports. Trade in US$1m.:

	1996	1997	1998	1999	2000
Imports f.o.b.	4,895·0	5,278·3	5,313·4	5,365·5	6,483·6
Exports f.o.b.	4,095·2	4,638·7	4,808·0	4,596·2	5,439·6

Principal exports in 1994 (in Rs 1m.): tea, 20,964; precious stones, 12,159; rubber, 3,582; copra, coconut oil and desiccated coconut, 2,696; textiles and garments (1992), 52,588.

In 1996 the main export markets were the USA (34·1%), the UK (9·5%), Japan (6·2%), Germany (5·8%) and Belgium-Luxembourg (5·3%). The main import suppliers were India (11·2%), Japan (9·9%), Hong Kong (7%), South Korea (7%) and Singapore (7%).

COMMUNICATIONS

Roads. There were (1998 estimate) 11,285 km of national roads. Number of motor vehicles, 1998, 1,388,685, comprising 284,259 passenger cars, 60,097 buses and coaches, 292,391 trucks and vans and 751,938 motorcycles and mopeds. There were 1,921 fatalities in road accidents in 1998.

Rail. In 1996 there were 1,463 km of railway (1,676 mm gauge). Passenger-km travelled in 1997 came to 3,343m. and freight tonne-km to 105m.

Civil Aviation. There is an international airport at Colombo (Bandaranaike). The national carrier is SriLankan Airlines (formerly Air Lanka), which has been part-owned and managed by Emirates since 1998. In 1999 SriLankan Airlines flew 28·1m. km and carried 1,421,500 passengers (all on international flights). Colombo handled 2,880,387 passengers and 127,116 tonnes of freight in 2000.

Shipping. In 1998 the merchant marine totalled 189,000 GRT, including oil tankers 5,000 GRT. Colombo is a modern container port; Trincomalee and Galle are natural harbours. In 1994, 3,568 merchant vessels totalling 55m. GRT entered the ports: 9,588,000 tonnes of goods were unloaded and 5,892,000 tonnes loaded. In 1997 vessels totalling 33,188,000 NRT entered ports.

Telecommunications. Sri Lanka had 767,400 telephone main lines in 2000 (40·6 per 1,000 population) and there were 135,000 PCs in use (7·1 for every 1,000 persons). In 1999 there were 174,200 mobile phone subscribers and, in 1995, 11,000 fax machines. There were approximately 121,500 Internet users in Dec. 2000.

Postal Services. In 1994 there were 557 post offices, 3,375 sub-post offices and 173 agency post offices.

SOCIAL INSTITUTIONS

Justice. The systems of law which are valid are Roman-Dutch, English, Tesawalamai, Islamic and Kandyan.

Kandyan law applies in matters relating to inheritance, matrimonial rights and donations; Tesawalamai law applies in Jaffna as above and in sales of land. Islamic law is applied to all Muslims in respect of succession, donations, marriage, divorce and maintenance. These customary and religious laws have been modified by local enactments.

The courts of original jurisdiction are the High Court, Provincial Courts, District Courts, Magistrates' Courts and Primary Courts. District Courts have unlimited civil jurisdiction. The Magistrates' Courts exercise criminal jurisdiction. The Primary Courts exercise civil jurisdiction in petty disputes and criminal jurisdiction in respect of certain offences.

The Constitution of 1978 provided for the establishment of two superior courts, the Supreme Court and the Court of Appeal.

The Supreme Court is the highest and final superior court of record and exercises jurisdiction in respect of constitutional matters, jurisdiction for the protection of fundamental rights, final appellate jurisdiction in election petitions and jurisdiction in respect of any breach of the privileges of Parliament. The Court of Appeal has appellate jurisdiction to correct all errors in fact or law committed by any court, tribunal or institution.

Police. The strength of the police service in 1994 was 30,236. The population in penal institutions in 1997 was 14,090 (75 per 100,000 of national population).

Religion. In 1994 the population was 73% Buddhist, 15% Hinduist, 7% Muslim and 5% Christian.

Education. Education is free and is compulsory from age 5 to 14 years. The literacy rate in 1999 was 91·4% (male, 94·3%; female, 88·6%). Sri Lanka's rate compares very favourably with the rates of 56·5% in India and 45·0% in Pakistan.

In 1995 there were 9,657 primary schools with 70,537 teachers for 1·9m. pupils. There were 2·3m. secondary pupils with 103,572 teachers and 63,660 students in higher education with 2,636 staff. There are 9 universities, 1 open (distance) university and 1 Buddhist and Pali university.

In 1996 total expenditure on education came to 3·4% of GNP and represented 8·9% of total government expenditure.

Health. In 1993 there were 426 hospitals, including 84 maternity homes, and 350 central dispensaries. The hospitals had 48,948 beds. There were 3,713 Department of Health doctors. Total state budget expenditure on health, 1993, Rs 7,160m.

Welfare. The activities of the Department of Social Services include: payment of public assistance, monthly allowance, financial assistance to needy tuberculosis, leprosy and cancer patients and their dependents; relief of those affected by widespread distress, such as floods, drought, cyclone; custodial care and welfare services to the elderly and infirm; vocational training, aids and appliances for the physically and mentally handicapped; custodial care, vocational training and rehabilitation for socially handicapped persons; community-based rehabilitation of treated drug addicts; registration of and financial assistance to voluntary organizations which engage in social welfare activities.

The government's Poverty Alleviation ('Janasaviya') Programme targets 0·35m. of the neediest families, who received a monthly Rs 1,458 (in 1992) in return for 20 days' community service. Total budget was Rs 4,900m. in 1992.

CULTURE

Broadcasting. Broadcasting is provided by the Sri Lanka Broadcasting Corporation. There were 1·53m. TV sets (colour by PAL) and 3·85m. radio receivers in 1997.

Cinema. In 1995 there were 259 cinemas and 27·2m. admissions.

Press. In 1996 there were six daily newspapers with a combined circulation of 530,000, at a rate of 29 per 1,000 inhabitants.

Tourism. In 1999 there were 436,000 foreign tourists, bringing revenue of US$275m.

DIPLOMATIC REPRESENTATIVES

Of Sri Lanka in the United Kingdom (13 Hyde Park Gdns, London, W2 2LU)
High Commissioner: Faisz Musthapha.

Of the United Kingdom in Sri Lanka (190 Galle Rd., Kollupitiya, Colombo 3)
High Commissioner: Stephen Evans, CMG, OBE.

Of Sri Lanka in the USA (2148 Wyoming Ave., NW, Washington, D.C., 20008)
Ambassador: Devinda Rohan Subasinghe.

Of the USA in Sri Lanka (210 Galle Rd., Kollupitiya, Colombo 3)
Ambassador: E. Ashley Wills.

Of Sri Lanka to the United Nations
Ambassador: John de Saram.

Of Sri Lanka to the European Union
Ambassador: Chrysantha Romesh Jayasinghe.

FURTHER READING

De Silva, C. R., *Sri Lanka: a History.* Delhi, 1991
McGowan, W., *Only Man is Vile: the Tragedy of Sri Lanka.* New York, 1992

National statistical office: Department of Census and Statistics, POB 563, Colombo 7
Website: http://www.statistics.gov.lk/

SUDAN

Jamhuryat es-Sudan
(The Republic of The Sudan)

Capital: Khartoum
Population estimate, 2000: 29·9m.
GDP per capita, 2000: (PPP\$) 1,797
HDI/world rank: 0·499/139

KEY HISTORICAL EVENTS

In 1821 the area that is now Sudan was conquered by the Egyptians. In 1881 Muhammad Ahmad, proclaiming himself the Mahdi, led an uprising and gained control until, in 1899, an Anglo-Egyptian army defeated the Mahdi and established an Anglo-Egyptian condominium.

On 1 Jan. 1956 Sudan was proclaimed a sovereign independent republic. In 1958 a coup led to a military government until the end of 1964 when a civilian government was re-established. The government was faced with constant difficulties from the southern provinces which considered themselves dominated by the north. Rebellions began in 1965. On 25 May 1969 the government was taken over by a ten-man Revolutionary Council. The Council was dissolved in 1972, legislative power was placed with a National Assembly, an elected body, and some measure of self-government was granted to the southern provinces. However, discontent continued and in April 1985 a Military Council was set up prior to the promised re-establishment of civilian rule. Elections were held, although they were suspended in parts of the southern provinces, in April 1986. On 30 June 1989 Brig.-Gen. (later Lieut.-Gen.) Omar Hassan Ahmad al-Bashir overthrew the civilian government in a military coup.

The rebel Sudan People's Liberation Army (SPLA), consisting of non-Muslim southerners, maintains guerrilla activities in the south while the National Democratic Alliance (NDA), northern Muslims opposed to the ruling National Islamic Front, and non-Muslim southerners of the SPLA fight on in the north. Fighting also erupted in Jan. 1997 along the border with Ethiopia. On 9 July 1997 at a meeting attended by representatives of Djibouti, Eritrea, Ethiopia, Kenya and Uganda the Sudanese government accepted a 'Declaration of Principles' as a framework for negotiations to end the civil war, including the separation of state and religion and self-determination for the Christian and animist south of Sudan. After 18 years Sudan's civil war has killed nearly 2m. people and reduced the south to a level barely above subsistence. It is among the most devastating wars in African history. In Dec. 1999 President al-Bashir dissolved the National Assembly, declaring a state of national emergency. In July 2002 peace talks were held between the government and the SPLA, leading to a framework deal on ending the civil war. Although fighting continues there are hopes that a peace agreement may soon be signed.

TERRITORY AND POPULATION

Sudan is bounded in the north by Egypt, northeast by the Red Sea, east by Eritrea and Ethiopia, south by Kenya, Uganda and the Democratic Republic of the Congo, west by the Central African Republic and Chad, and northwest by Libya. Its area is 967,500 sq. miles (2,505,815 sq. km). In 1993 the census population was 25·6m. Population estimate (2000), 29·82m., giving a density of 11·9 per sq. km. In 1999, 64·9% of the population were rural.

The UN gives a projected population for 2010 of 38·67m.

In Feb. 1994 the former nine regions were subdivided to form 26 federal states as follows:

Former region	New states
Khartoum	Khartoum
Bahr al-Ghazal	Western Bahr al-Ghazal; Northern Bahr al-Ghazal; Warab
Central	Gezira; White Nile; Sinnar; Blue Nile
Darfur	Northern Darfur; Southern Darfur; Western Darfur
Eastern	Red Sea; Gedaref; Kassala
Equatoria	Eastern Equatoria; Western Equatoria; Bahr al-Jabal
Kurdufan	Northern Kurdufan; Southern Kurdufan; Western Kurdufan
Northern	Nile; Northern State
Upper Nile	Upper Nile; Unity State; Jonglei; Buheyrat

The capital, Khartoum, had a population of 2,628,000 in 1999. Other major cities, with 1993 populations, are Port Sudan (305,385), Kassala (234,270), Nyala (228,778), al-Obeid (228,096), Wadi Medani (218,714), al-Qadarif (189,384).

The northern and central thirds of the country are populated by Arab and Nubian peoples, while the southern third is inhabited by Nilotic and Bantu peoples. Sudan has more internally displaced people (4m. in 2000) than any other country.

Arabic, the official language, is spoken by 60% of inhabitants. English is the second language.

SOCIAL STATISTICS
1997 births, 1,323,000; deaths, 365,000. Rates, 1997 estimates (per 1,000 population); births, 40·6; deaths, 11·2. Infant mortality, 1999 (per 1,000 live births), 67. Expectation of life in 1999 was 57·0 years for females and 54·2 for males. Annual population growth rate, 1990–99, 2·0% per annum. Fertility rate, 1999, 4·5 births per woman.

CLIMATE
Lying wholly within the tropics, the country has a continental climate and only the Red Sea coast experiences maritime influences. Temperatures are generally high for most of the year, with May and June the hottest months. Winters are virtually cloudless and night temperatures are consequently cool. Summer is the rainy season inland, with amounts increasing from north to south, but the northern areas are virtually a desert region. On the Red Sea coast, most rain falls in winter. Khartoum, Jan. 64°F (18·0°C), July 89°F (31·7°C). Annual rainfall 6" (157 mm). Juba, Jan. 83°F (28·3°C), July 78°F (25·6°C). Annual rainfall 39" (968 mm). Port Sudan, Jan. 74°F (23·3°C), July 94°F (34·4°C). Annual rainfall 4" (94 mm). Wadi Halfa, Jan. 50°F (10·0°C), July 90°F (32·2°C). Annual rainfall 0·1" (2·5 mm).

CONSTITUTION AND GOVERNMENT
The constitution was suspended after the 1989 coup and a 12-member Revolutionary Council then ruled. A 300-member Provisional National Assembly was appointed in Feb. 1992 as a transitional legislature pending elections. These were held in March 1996. The President is elected for a five-year term by the people. The National Assembly (*Majlis Watani*), currently suspended, normally has 400 members, 275 of whom are directly elected for four years in single-seat constituencies, 125 indirectly elected by national conference.

On 26 May 1998 President Omar Hassan Ahmad al-Bashir approved a new constitution. Notably this lifted the ban on opposition political parties, although the government continued to monitor and control criticism until the constitution legally came into effect.

National Anthem. 'Nahnu Jundullah, Jundu Al-Watlan' ('We are the defenders of our homeland, blessed by Allah'); words by A. M. Salih, tune by A. Murjan.

RECENT ELECTIONS
Presidential elections were held from 13–22 Dec. 2000. President Omar Hassan Ahmed al-Bashir was re-elected by 86·5% of votes cast, with his nearest rival, former president Gaafar Nimeiry, gaining 9·6%. The main opposition groups and most of the electorate boycotted the polls. At the National Assembly elections held at the same time the ruling National Congress Party (NCP) won 355 of the 360 seats.

CURRENT ADMINISTRATION
President: Lieut.-Gen. Omar Hassan Ahmad al-Bashir; b. 1944 (NCP; appointed 1989, re-elected March 1996 and Dec. 2000).

First Vice-President: Ali Osman Mohammed Taha. *Second Vice-President:* Moses Machar.

In March 2003 the government comprised:

Assistant to the President: Mubarak al-Fadil al-Mahdi. *Minister of the Interior:* Abdulraheem Mohammed Hussein. *Presidential Affairs:* Salah Ahmad Mohammed Salih. *Foreign Affairs:* Mustafa Osman Ismail. *Defence:* Maj. Gen. Bakri Hassan Salih. *Justice and Attorney General:* Ali Muhammad Osman Yasin. *Finance and*

Planning: al-Zubeir Ahmed al-Hassan. *Culture:* Abdulbasit Abdulmajid. *National Heritage and Tourism:* Abdel Jalil al-Basha Mohamed Ahmed. *Agriculture and Forestry:* Majzoub el Khalifa Ahmed. *Irrigation:* Kamal Mohamed Ali. *Energy and Mining:* Awad Ahmed al-Jaz. *Industry and Investment:* Jalal Yousif el Degair. *External Trade:* Abdulhameed Musa Kasha. *Welfare and Social Planning:* Samya Ahmed Mohammed. *Higher Education:* Mubarak Mohammed Al Maghzoub. *Urban Development and Environment:* Tigani Adam Tahir. *Education:* Ahmed Babikir Nahar. *Electricity:* Ali Tameem Fartak. *Civil Aviation:* Joseph Malwal. *Roads and Bridges:* Mohamed Tahir Aela. *Federal Rule:* Nafie Ali Nafie. *Federal Relations:* Ibrahim Suleiman. *Health:* Dr Ahmed Ballal Osman. *Information and Communication:* Al-Zahawi Ibrahim Malik. *Labour:* Alison Manani Magaya. *Cabinet Affairs:* Martin Malwal Arop. *Animal Resources:* Riek Gai. *Science and Technology:* El Zubair Taha. *Youth and Sports:* Hassan Osman Rizig. *Parliamentary Affairs:* Abdulbasit Sabdarat. *Religious Guidance and Endowments:* Isam Ahmed el Bashir. *International Co-operation:* Yusuf Suleiman Takana.

DEFENCE
There is conscription for three years. Defence expenditure totalled US$568m. in 2000 (US$19 per capita), representing 6·1% of GDP. According to *Deadly Arsenals*, published by the Carnegie Endowment for International Peace, Sudan has both biological and chemical weapons research programmes.

Army. Strength (2000) 100,000 (20,000 conscripts). There is a paramilitary People's Defence Force of about 15,000 and additional army reserves of 85,000.

Navy. The navy operates in the Red Sea and also on the River Nile. The flotilla suffers from lack of maintenance and spares. Personnel in 2000 were believed to number 1,500. Major bases are at Port Sudan (HQ), Flamingo Bay and Khartoum.

Air Force. Personnel totalled (2000) about 3,000, with over 30 combat aircraft including F-5s, J-5/6s and F-7s (Chinese-built versions of MiG-17/19/21s), and MiG-23s.

INTERNATIONAL RELATIONS
Sudan is a member of the UN, the African Union, African Development Bank, COMESA, the Intergovernmental Authority on Development, IOM, OIC, the League of Arab States, Lake Chad Basin Commission and is an ACP member state of the ACP-EU relationship.
    Following the attacks on New York and Washington on 11 Sept. 2001 Sudan sought to distance itself from fundamentalism and international terrorism.

ECONOMY
Agriculture accounts for approximately 39·2% of GDP, industry 18·2% and services 42·6%.

Currency. Until 1992 the monetary unit was the *Sudanese pound* (SDP) of 100 *piastres* and 1,000 *milliemes*. This was replaced in May 1992 by the *dinar* at a rate of 1 dinar = £S10. Sudanese pounds remain legal tender. Inflation was 5·0% in 2001. Foreign exchange reserves were US$224m. in June 2002 and total money supply was 307,763m. dinars.

Budget. In 1999 total revenues were 215,562m. dinars (162,143m. in 1998) and total expenditure 227,265m. dinars (171,129m. in 1998).

Performance. Real GDP growth was 9·7% in 2000 and 5·3% in 2001. Sudan's total GDP in 2001 was US$12·6bn.

Banking and Finance. The Bank of Sudan (*Governor:* Sabir Mohammed Hassan) opened in Feb. 1960 with an authorized capital of £S1·5m. as the central bank and bank of issue. Banks were nationalized in 1970 but in 1974 foreign banks were allowed to open branches. The application of Islamic law from 1 Jan. 1991 put an end to the charging of interest in official banking transactions, and seven banks are run on Islamic principles. Mergers of seven local banks in 1993 resulted in the formation of the Khartoum Bank, the Industrial Development Bank and the Savings Bank. In 1994 there were 27 commercial and private banks.

A stock exchange opened in Khartoum in 1995.

Weights and Measures. The metric system is in use.

ENERGY AND NATURAL RESOURCES

Environment. According to the *World Bank Atlas* Sudan's carbon dioxide emissions in 1998 were the equivalent of 0·1 tonnes per capita.

Electricity. Installed capacity was 1m. kW in 1997. Production in 1998 was 1·82bn. kWh, with consumption per capita 47 kWh.

Oil and Gas. In 1997 oil reserves totalled 300m. bbls. In June 1998 Sudan began exploiting its reserves and on 31 Aug. 1999 it officially became an oil producing country, producing 180,000 bbls. of crude oil per day. An oil refinery with a capacity of 2·5m. tonnes is under construction at Al-Jayli. Natural gas reserves in 1997 were 85bn. cu. metres.

Minerals. Mineral deposits include graphite, sulphur, chromium, iron, manganese, copper, zinc, fluorspar, natron, gypsum and anhydrite, magnesite, asbestos, talc, halite, kaolin, white mica, coal, diatomite (kieselguhr), limestone and dolomite, pumice, lead, wollastonite, black sands and vermiculite pyrites. Chromite and gold are mined. Production of salt, 1997 estimate: 50,000 tonnes; gold, 1996: 96,000 troy oz; chromium ore (metal content), 1994: 3,000 tonnes.

Agriculture. 80% of the population depends on agriculture. Land tenure is based on customary rights; land is ultimately owned by the government. There were 16·7m. ha of arable land in 1998 and 0·2m. ha of permanent crops.

Production (2000 estimates) in 1,000 tonnes: sugarcane, 4,982; sorghum, 2,521; groundnuts, 990; millet, 496; sesame seed, 305; seed cotton, 245; tomatoes, 242; wheat, 214; mangoes, 192; dates, 176; melons and watermelons, 169; cottonseed, 157.

Livestock (2000): cattle, 37·09m.; sheep, 42·80m.; goats, 37·80m.; chickens, 42m.; camels, 3·8m.

Forestry. Forests covered 41·61m. ha in 1995, or 17·5% of the total land area (43·38m. ha and 18·3% of the land area in 1990). The loss of 1·77m. ha of forests between 1990 and 1995 was exceeded among African nations only in the Democratic Republic of the Congo. In 1999, 9·68m. cu. metres of roundwood were cut.

Fisheries. In 1999 the total catch was 49,500 tonnes, of which 44,000 tonnes were freshwater fish.

INDUSTRY

Production figures for 1995 (in 1,000 tonnes): sugar (1998), 610; wheat flour, 350; distillate fuel oil (1997), 330; residual fuel oil (1997), 320; cement, 199; vegetable oils, 70. In Oct. 2000 an industrial complex assembling 12,000 vehicles a year was opened.

Labour. The total workforce in 1996 was 10,652,000 (71% males). There was a monthly minimum wage of 15,000 dinars in 1996. Approximately 68% of the economically active population in 1995 were engaged in agriculture, fisheries and forestry.

INTERNATIONAL TRADE

Foreign debt was US$15,741m. in 2000.

Imports and Exports. In 2000 imports (f.o.b.) amounted to US$1,366·3m. (US$1,256·0m. in 1999); exports (f.o.b.) US$1,806·7m. (US$780·1m. in 1999). The main exports are cotton, gum arabic, oil seeds, sorghum, livestock, sesame, gold and sugar. Main imports are petroleum products, machinery and equipment, foodstuffs, manufactured goods, medicines and chemicals. The main import sources in 1996 were Saudi Arabia (11·3%), UK (6·9%), France (5·5%) and Germany (4·7%). Principal export markets in 1996 were Saudi Arabia (18·9%), UK (12·6%), Italy (7·7%) and Thailand (7·6%).

COMMUNICATIONS

Roads. In 1996 there were 11,900 km of roads, of which 4,320 km were paved, and 45,000 km of tracks. There were an estimated 285,000 passenger cars and 53,000 trucks and vans in 1996.

Rail. The total length of the railways is 7,484 km. In 1994 the railways carried 0·6m. passengers and 1·9m. tonnes of freight.

Civil Aviation. There is an international airport at Khartoum. The national carrier is the government-owned Sudan Airways, which operates domestic and international services. In 1999 scheduled airline traffic of Sudan-based carriers flew 6·7m. km, carrying 390,000 passengers (245,000 on international flights).

Shipping. Supplementing the railways are regular steamer services of the Sudan Railways. Port Sudan is the major seaport; another port at Suakin was opened in 1991. Traffic on the River Nile has ceased owing to the civil war. Sea-going shipping totalled 43,000 GRT in 1998, including oil tankers 1,000 GRT.

Telecommunications. In 2000 Sudan had 386,800 main telephone lines (12·4 per 1,000 persons) and 100,000 PCs were in use (3·2 per 1,000 persons). In 1997 there were 12,000 fax machines and 3,800 mobile phone subscribers. The number of Internet users in March 2001 was 28,000.

Postal Services. In 1995 there were 411 post offices.

SOCIAL INSTITUTIONS

Justice. The judiciary is a separate independent department of state, directly and solely responsible to the President of the Republic. The general administrative supervision and control of the judiciary is vested in the High Judicial Council.

Civil Justice is administered by the courts constituted under the Civil Justice Ordinance, namely the High Court of Justice—consisting of the Court of Appeal and Judges of the High Court, sitting as courts of original jurisdiction—and Province Courts—consisting of the Courts of Province and District Judges. The law administered is 'justice, equity and good conscience' in all cases where there is no special enactment. Procedure is governed by the Civil Justice Ordinance.

Justice for the Muslim population has always been administered by the Islamic law courts, which form the Sharia Divisions of the Court of Appeal, High Courts and Kadis Courts; President of the Sharia Division is the Grand Kadi. In Dec. 1990 the government announced that Sharia would be applied in the non-Muslim southern parts of the country as well.

Criminal Justice is administered by the courts constituted under the Code of Criminal Procedure, namely major courts, minor courts and magistrates' courts. Serious crimes are tried by major courts, which are composed of a President and two members and have the power to pass the death sentence. Major Courts are, as a rule, presided over by a Judge of the High Court appointed to a Provincial Circuit or a Province Judge. There is a right of appeal to the Chief Justice against any decision or order of a Major Court, and all its findings and sentences are subject to confirmation by him.

Lesser crimes are tried by Minor Courts consisting of three Magistrates and presided over by a Second Class Magistrate, and by Magistrates' Courts.

The population in penal institutions in 1997 was 32,000 (115 per 100,000 of national population).

Religion. Islam is the state religion. In 1992 there were 21·9m. Sunni Muslims, concentrated in the north, and 2·4m. Christians and some 5m. traditionalist animists in the south.

Education. In 1996–97 there were 7,541 pre-primary schools with 8,897 teachers for 343,767 pupils; 11,158 primary schools with 102,987 teachers for 3·0m. pupils; and 15,504 secondary school teachers for 405,583 pupils. In 1996 there were 17 universities, 2 Islamic universities, 1 university of science and technology, and an institute of advanced banking. There were also 14 colleges or other institutions of higher education. Adult literacy rate in 1999 was 56·9% (male, 68·9%; female, 44·9%).

Health. In 1994 there were 2,600 doctors, equivalent to one for every 11,300 persons. Hospital bed provision in 1986 was eight per 10,000 population.

CULTURE

Broadcasting. Broadcasting is controlled by the Sudan National Broadcasting Corporation and Sudan Television (colour by PAL). There are also two regional TV stations, in the centre and in the north of the country. There were 2·4m. TV sets and 7·55m. radio receivers in 1997.

Press. In 1999 there were around 20 daily newspapers. Opposition newspapers are permitted although they are vetted by an official censor.

Tourism. In 1998 there were 39,000 foreign tourists, bringing revenue of US$8m. In 2000 there were seven National Parks and ten protected areas.

DIPLOMATIC REPRESENTATIVES
Of Sudan in the United Kingdom (3 Cleveland Row, London, SW1A 1DD)
Ambassador: Dr Hassan Abdin Mohammad Osman.

Of United Kingdom in Sudan (off Sharia Al Baladia, Khartoum East)
Ambassador: William Patey.

Of Sudan in the USA (2210 Massachusetts Ave., NW, Washington, D.C., 20008)
Ambassador: Vacant.
Chargé d'Affaires a.i.: Khidir Haroun Ahmed.

Of the USA in Sudan (Sharia Ali Abdul Latif, POB 699, Khartoum)
Ambassador: Vacant.

Of Sudan to the United Nations
Ambassador: Elfatih Mohamed Ahmed Erwa.

Of Sudan to the European Union
Ambassador: Ali Youssif Ahmed.

FURTHER READING
Daly, M. W., *Sudan.* [Bibliography] 2nd ed. ABC-Clio, Oxford and Santa Barbara (CA), 1992
Daly, M. W. and Sikainga, A. A. (eds.) *Civil War in the Sudan.* I. B. Tauris, London, 1993
Deng, F. M., *War of Visions: Conflict of Identities in the Sudan.* The Brookings Institution, Washington (D.C.), 1995

SURINAME

Republic of Suriname

Capital: Paramaribo
Population estimate, 2000: 436,000
GDP per capita, 2000: (PPP$) 3,799
HDI/world rank: 0·756/74

KEY HISTORICAL EVENTS

The first Europeans to reach the area were the Spanish in 1499 but it was the British who established a colony in 1650. At the peace of Breda (1667), Suriname was assigned to the Netherlands in exchange for the colony of New Netherland in North America. Suriname was twice in British possession during the Napoleonic Wars, in 1799–1802 and 1804–16, when it was returned to the Netherlands.

On 25 Nov. 1975 Suriname gained full independence. On 25 Feb. 1980 the government was ousted in a coup and a National Military Council (NMC) established. A further coup on 13 Aug. replaced several members of the NMC and the State President. Other attempted coups took place in 1981 and 1982, with the NMC retaining control. In Oct. 1987 a new constitution was approved by referendum. Following elections in Nov. Suriname returned to democracy in Jan. 1988 but on 24 Dec. 1990 a further military coup deposed the government. There was a peace agreement with rebel groups in Aug. 1992 and elections were held in May 1996.

TERRITORY AND POPULATION

Suriname is located on the northern coast of South America between 2–6° North latitude and 54–59° West longitude. It is bounded in the north by the Atlantic Ocean, east by French Guiana, west by Guyana, and south by Brazil. Area, 163,820 sq. km. Census population (1995), 407,000. Estimate, Jan. 1997, 417,000; density, 3 per sq. km.

The UN gives a projected population for 2010 of 433,000.

The capital, Paramaribo, had (2000 estimate) 294,000 inhabitants.

Suriname is divided into ten districts. They are (with 2000 population estimate and chief town): Brokopondo, population 7,663 (Brokopondo); Commewijne, 22,134 (Nieuw Amsterdam); Coronie, 3,092 (Totness); Marowijne, 13,351 (Albina); Nickerie, 35,577 (Nieuw Nickerie); Para, 15,190 (Onverwacht); Paramaribo, 225,218—representing 52% of Suriname's total population (Paramaribo); Saramacca, 13,250 (Groningen); Sipaliwini, 24,823 (local authority in Paramaribo); Wanica, 73,219 (Lelydorp).

Major ethnic groups in percentages of the population in 1991: Creole, 35%; Indian, 33%; Javanese, 16%; Bushnegroes (Blacks), 10%; Amerindian, 3%. 73·5% of the population lived in urban areas in 1999.

The official language is Dutch. English is widely spoken next to Hindi, Javanese and Chinese as inter-group communication. A vernacular, called 'Sranan' or 'Surinamese', is used as a *lingua franca*. In 1976 it was decided that Spanish was to become the nation's principal working language.

SOCIAL STATISTICS

Births, 1999, 10,144; deaths, 2,992. 1999 rates per 1,000 population: birth rate, 23·6; death rate, 7·0. The population growth rate in 1999 was 1·5%. Expectation of life, 1999, was 67·8 years for males and 73·0 for females. Infant mortality, 1999, 27 per 1,000 live births; fertility rate, 1999, 2·2 births per woman.

CLIMATE

The climate is equatorial, with uniformly high temperatures and rainfall. The temperature is an average of 27°C throughout the year; there are two rainy seasons (May–July and Nov.–Jan.) and two dry seasons (Aug.–Oct. and Feb.–April). Paramaribo, Jan. 21°C, July 32·4°C. Average rainfall 182·3 mm.

CONSTITUTION AND GOVERNMENT

Parliament is a 51-member *National Assembly*. The head of state is the *President*, elected for a five-year term by a two-thirds majority by the National Assembly, or, failing that, by an electoral college, the United People's Conference (UPC) enlarged by the inclusion of regional and local councillors, by a simple majority.

National Anthem. 'God zij met ons Suriname' ('God be with our Suriname'); words by C. A. Hoekstra, tune by J. C. de Puy. There is a Sranan version, 'Opo kondreman oen opo'; words by H. de Ziel.

RECENT ELECTIONS
Parliamentary elections were held on 25 May 2000. The New Front for Democracy (NF) won 32 of the available 51 seats (47·3% of the vote). The NF alliance comprises the National Party of Suriname (14 seats), the Progressive Reform Party (9), Pertjajah Luhur (7) and the Suriname Labour Party (2). The Millennium Combination alliance won 10 seats (15·1%), Democratic National Platform 2000 alliance won 3 seats (10%), Democratic Alternative '91 alliance won 2 seats (6·1%) and the Political Wing of the FAL won 2 seats (4·1%). Nine other groupings won 3·2% of the vote or less, with the Progressive Workers' and Farmers' Union claiming 1 seat with 0·7%.

On 4 Aug. 2000 Ronald Venetiaan was elected *President* by the National Assembly, claiming 37 out of 51 votes. Jules Ajodhia was elected *Vice-President* and *Prime Minister*.

CURRENT ADMINISTRATION
President: Runaldo Ronald Venetiaan; b. 1936 (National Party of Suriname; sworn in 12 Aug. 2000 for a second time, having previously held office from Sept. 1991 to Sept. 1996).

Vice-President and Prime Minister: Jules Ajodhia (Progressive Reform Party; sworn in 12 Aug. 2000 for a second time, also having previously held office from Sept. 1991 to Sept. 1996).

In March 2003 the government comprised:

Minister of Foreign Affairs: Marie Levens. *Defence:* Ronald Assen. *Finance:* Humphrey Hildenberg. *Natural Resources:* Franco Rudy Demon. *Justice and Police:* Siegfried Gilds. *Regional Development:* Romeo van Russel. *Education and Human Development:* Walter Sandriman. *Transport, Communication and Tourism:* Guno Castelen. *Planning and Development Co-operation:* Keremchand Raghoebarsingh. *Public Works:* Dewanand Balesar. *Health:* Mohamed Rakieb Khudabux. *Social Affairs:* Vacant. *Labour:* Clifford Marica. *Agriculture and Fisheries:* Geetapersad Gangaram Panday. *Interior:* Urmila Joella-Sewnundum. *Trade and Industry:* Vacant.

DEFENCE
In 2000 defence expenditure totalled US$11m. (US$26 per capita), representing 2·7% of GDP.

Army. Total strength was estimated at 1,400 in 1999.

Navy. In 1999 personnel, based at Paramaribo, totalled 240.

Air Force. Personnel (1999): 160. There were four combat aircraft.

INTERNATIONAL RELATIONS
In June 2000 a maritime dispute arose between Suriname and Guyana over offshore oil exploration.

Suriname is a member of the UN, WTO, OAS, Inter-American Development Bank, ACS, CARICOM, OIC and is an ACP member state of the ACP-EU relationship.

ECONOMY
In 1996 agriculture contributed 10% of GDP, industry 32% and services 58%.

Currency. The unit of currency is the *Suriname guilder* (SRG; written as Sf[lorin]) of 100 *cents.* Foreign exchange reserves totalled US$114m. and gold reserves were 263,000 troy oz in June 2002. Total money supply in April 2002 was 417,896m. Sf. Inflation in 2001 was 42·3%.

Budget. 1999 revenue (in 1m. Sf) was 301,495·5, made up of: direct taxes, 84,360·0; indirect taxes, 117,902·0; bauxite levy and other revenues, 31,641·5; aid, 67,592·0.

Total expenditure in 1999 (in 1m. Sf) was 139,071·1, made up of: wages and salaries, 72,116·2; grants and contributions, 16,701·8; other current expenditures, 32,979·0; and capital expenditure, 17,274·1.

Performance. Real GDP growth was negative in 2000, at –5·7%, but there was then a slight recovery in 2001, with growth of 1·3%. In 2001 total GDP was US$0·8bn.

Banking and Finance. The Central Bank of Suriname (*Governor,* Andre Telting) is a bankers' bank and also the bank of issue. There are three commercial banks; the Suriname People's Credit Bank operates under the auspices of the government. There is a post office savings bank, a mortgage bank, an investment bank, a long-term investments agency, a National Development Bank and an Agrarian Bank.

Weights and Measures. The metric system is in use.

ENERGY AND NATURAL RESOURCES

Environment. Suriname's carbon dioxide emissions in 1998 were the equivalent of 5·2 tonnes per capita according to the *World Bank Atlas.*

Electricity. Installed capacity in 1995 was 425,000 kW. Production (1998) 2·01bn. kWh; consumption per capita in 1997 was 3,947 kWh.

Oil and Gas. Crude petroleum production (1996), 3m. bbls. Reserves in 1997 were 74m. bbls.

Minerals. Bauxite is the most important mineral. Production (1998), 3,931,000 tonnes.

Agriculture. Agriculture is restricted to the alluvial coastal zone; in 1998 there were 65,000 ha of arable land, 11,000 ha of permanent cropland and 30,000 ha of pasture. The staple food crop is rice. Production (in 1,000 tonnes), 180 in 1999; 164 in 2000. Other crops (2000 in 1,000 tonnes): sugarcane, 90; bananas, 49; plantains, 11; oranges, 10; coconuts, 9; groundnuts, 9; cassava, 3. Livestock in 2000: cattle, 128,727; sheep, 7,360; goats, 6,930; pigs, 22,280; poultry, 2·0m.

Forestry. Forests covered 14·72m. ha in 1998, or 94·8% of the land area (14·78m. ha in 1990). In terms of percentage coverage, Suriname and Guyana were the world's most heavily forested countries in 1995. Production of roundwood in 2000 was 54,325 cu. metres.

Fisheries. The catch in 1999 amounted to an estimated 12,960 tonnes, of which 12,760 were from marine waters.

INDUSTRY
There is no longer any aluminium smelting, but there are food-processing and wood-using industries. Production, 1994: cement, 24,665 tonnes (estimate); palm oil, 1,051,000 litres (estimate); beer (1996) 7·2m. litres; alumina, 1,498,000 tonnes; aluminium (1997), 32,000 tonnes; cigarettes (1996), 483m.; shoes, 99,000 pairs (estimate); plywood, 6,864 cu. metres.

Labour. Out of 82,900 people in employment in 1997, 30,300 were in community, social and personal services, 16,300 in trade, restaurants and hotels and 6,200 in manufacturing. There were 9,000 unemployed persons, or 10% of the workforce.

INTERNATIONAL TRADE

Imports and Exports. In 2000 imports (f.o.b.) amounted to US$246·1m. (US$297·9m. in 1999); exports (f.o.b.) US$399·1m. (US$342·0m. in 1999).

Principal imports, 1995 (in 1m. Sf): raw materials and semi-manufactured goods, 94,254·3; investment goods, 65,128·7; fuels and lubricants, 28,629·4; foodstuffs, 24,987·6; cars and motorcycles, 9,244·8; textiles, 3,986·0. Principal exports, 1994 (in 1m. Sf): alumina, 42,358·2; aluminium, 5,278·2; shrimps, 5,257·4; rice, 3,402·3; bananas and plantains, 1,274·3; wood and wood products, 261·4.

In 1998 exports (in US$1m.) were mainly to Netherlands (97·97), Norway (90·49), USA (84·50), Canada (44·82) and France (35·92); imports were mainly from the USA (231·9), Netherlands (141·4), Trinidad and Tobago (57·4), Netherlands Antilles (32·3) and Japan (30·69).

COMMUNICATIONS

Roads. The road network covered 4,470 km in 1996, of which 1,160 km were paved. In 1998 there were 55,400 passenger cars, 18,700 goods vehicles, 2,100 buses, 780 motorcycles and 30,000 mopeds.

Rail. There are two single-track railways.

Civil Aviation. There is an international airport at Paramaribo (Johan Adolf Pengel). The national carrier is Surinam Airways, which in 1998 had flights to Amsterdam, Aruba, Barbados, Belem, Cayenne, Curaçao, Georgetown, Macapa, Miami and Port of Spain. In 1999 scheduled airline traffic of Suriname-based carriers flew 5·6m. km, carrying 194,000 passengers (190,000 on international flights). In 1998 there were 131,014 passenger arrivals and 131,012 departures.

Shipping. The Royal Netherlands Steamship Co. operates services to the Netherlands, the USA, and regionally. The Suriname Navigation Co. maintains services from Paramaribo to Georgetown, Cayenne and the Caribbean area. Merchant shipping in 1998 totalled 6,000 GRT. In 1998 vessels totalling 1,411,000 net registered tons entered ports and vessels totalling 2,206,000 NRT cleared.

Telecommunications. Main telephone lines numbered 75,300 in 2000, equivalent to 173·5 for every 1,000 persons. There were 17,500 mobile phone subscribers in 1999 and 800 fax machines in 1996. In Dec. 2000 there were 11,700 Internet users.

SOCIAL INSTITUTIONS

Justice. Members of the court of justice are nominated by the President. There are three cantonal courts. Suriname was one of ten countries to sign an agreement in Feb. 2001 establishing a Caribbean Court of Justice to replace the British Privy Council as the highest civil and criminal court. The Court of Justice is expected to sit for the first time in the second half of 2003.

The population in penal institutions in Jan. 1998 was 560 (125 per 100,000 of national population).

Religion. In 1998 in the districts of Paramaribo and Wanica there were estimated to be 92,000 Hindus, 125,000 Christians of varying denominations and 47,000 Muslims.

Education. Adult literacy was 93·0% in 1998. In 1999–2000, 269 primary schools out of a total of 306 had 2,845 teachers and 61,418 pupils. 107 secondary schools had 1,744 teachers and 27,930 pupils. In 2000–01 the university had 2,745 students. There is a teacher training college with (2000–01) 1,942 students.

Health. In 2000 there were 1,683 general hospital beds and 224 physicians.

CULTURE

Broadcasting. The government controls the partly commercial Stichting Radio Omroep Suriname and Radio Suriname Internationaal, and Surinaamse Televisie Stichting. There were 63,000 TV sets (colour by NTSC) and 300,000 radio receivers in 1997. There were 41 radio and 9 television stations in 1999.

Cinema. There were two cinemas in Paramaribo in 1999.

Press. There were three daily newspapers in 1998. In 1995 their combined circulation was 43,000, equivalent to 101 per 1,000 inhabitants.

Tourism. In 1999 there were 130,686 foreign tourist arrivals; in 1998 receipts totalled US$45m.

Festivals. The people of Suriname celebrate Chinese New Year (Jan.); Phagwa, a Hindu celebration (March–April); Id-Ul-Fitre, the sugar feast at the end of Ramadan (May); Avondvierdaagse, a carnival (during the Easter holidays); Suriflora, a celebration of plants and flowers (April–May); Keti koti, an Afro-Surinamese holiday to commemorate the abolition of slavery (1 July); Suri-pop, a popular music festival (July); Nationale Kunstbeurs, arts and crafts (Oct.–Nov.); Divali, the Hindu ceremony of light (Nov.); Djaran Kepang, a Javanese dance held on feast days; Winti-prey, a ceremony for the Winti gods.

Museums and Galleries. The main museums (1998) were: Surinaams Museum and Fort Zeelandia in Paramaribo; the Open Air Museum at Nieuw Amsterdam. Art Galleries include: Suriname Art 2000; the Academy for Higher Arts and Cultural Education; and the Ready Tex Art Boutique, all in Paramaribo; and Nola Hatterman Instituut at Fort Zeelandia.

DIPLOMATIC REPRESENTATIVES
Of Suriname in the United Kingdom
Ambassador: Vacant.
Chargé d'Affaires a.i.: Nell J. Stadwisk-Kappel (resides at The Hague).

Of the United Kingdom in Suriname
Ambassador: Stephen Hiscock (resides at Georgetown, Guyana).

Of Suriname in the USA (4301 Connecticut Ave., NW, Washington, D.C., 20008)
Ambassador: Henry Lothar Illes.

Of the USA in Suriname (Dr Sophie Redmondstraat 129, Paramaribo)
Ambassador: Daniel A. Johnson.

Of Suriname to the United Nations
Ambassador: Vacant.
Chargé d'Affaires a.i.: Dr Irma Loemban Tobing-Klein.

Of Suriname to the European Union
Ambassador: Gerhard Otmar Hiwat.

FURTHER READING
Dew, E. M., *Trouble in Suriname, 1975–1993*. New York, 1995

National statistical office: Algemeen Bureau voor de Statistiek, POB 244, Paramaribo.

SWAZILAND

Umbuso weSwatini
(Kingdom of Swaziland)

Capital: Mbabane (Administrative),
Lobamba (Legislative)
Population estimate, 2000: 925,000
GDP per capita, 2000: (PPP$) 4,492
HDI/world rank: 0·577/125

KEY HISTORICAL EVENTS

The Swazi migrated into the country to which they have given their name in the last half of the 18th century. The independence of the Swazis was guaranteed in the conventions of 1881 and 1884 between the British Government and the Government of the South African Republic. In 1894 the South African Republic was given powers of protection and administration. In 1902, after the conclusion of the Boer War, a special commissioner took charge, and under an order-in-council in 1903 the Governor of the Transvaal administered the territory. Swaziland became independent on 6 Sept. 1968. A state of emergency imposed in 1973 is still in force. On 25 April 1986 King Mswati III was installed as King of Swaziland.

TERRITORY AND POPULATION

Swaziland is bounded in the north, west and south by South Africa, and in the east by Mozambique. The area is 6,705 sq. miles (17,400 sq. km). Resident population (census 1997), 912,876; density, 52·5 per sq. km. In 1993, 53·3% of the population were females. More than 50% of the population is under 18 years of age.

The UN gives a projected population for 2010 of 987,000.

In 1999, 73·9% of the population were rural. Main urban areas: Mbabane, the administrative capital (73,000 inhabitants in 1999); Manzini; Big Bend; Mhlume; Havelock Mine; Nhlangano.

The population is 84% Swazi and 10% Zulu. The official languages are Swazi and English.

SOCIAL STATISTICS

1996 births, 33,000; deaths, 9,000. Birth rate, 1996 (per 1,000 population), 35·4; death rate, 9·8. As a result of the impact of AIDS, expectation of life has gradually been declining. It was 58 years in 1995, but by 1999 was down to 46 years for males and 48 years for females. Approximately 25% of all adults are infected with HIV. In Sept. 2001 King Mswati III told the teenage girls of the country to stop having sex for five years as part of the country's drive to reduce the spread of HIV. Annual population growth rate, 1990–99, 3·0%. Infant mortality, 1999, 62 per 1,000 live births; fertility rate, 1999, 4·6 births per woman.

CLIMATE

A temperate climate with two seasons. Nov. to March is the wet season, when temperatures range from mild to hot, with frequent thunderstorms. The cool, dry season from May to Sept. is characterized by clear, bright sunny days. Mbabane, Jan. 68°F (20°C), July 54°F (12·2°C). Annual rainfall 56" (1,402 mm).

CONSTITUTION AND GOVERNMENT

The reigning King is **Mswati III** (b. 1968; crowned 25 April 1986), who succeeded his father, King Sobhuza II (reigned 1921–82). The King rules in conjunction with the Queen Mother (his mother, or a senior wife). Critics of the king or his mother run the risk of arrest.

There is a *House of Assembly* of 65 members, 55 of whom are elected each from one constituency (*inkhundla*), and 10 appointed by the King; and a *House of Senators* of 30 members, 10 of whom are elected by the House of Assembly and 20 appointed by the King. Elections are held in two rounds, the second being a run-off between the five candidates who come first in each constituency.

There is also a traditional *Swazi National Council* headed by the King and Queen Mother at which all Swazi men are entitled to be heard.

A commission has been established to review the constitution.

National Anthem. 'Nkulunkulu mnikati wetibusiso temaSwati' ('O Lord our God bestower of blessings upon the Swazi'); words by A. E. Simelane, tune by D. K. Rycroft.

RECENT ELECTIONS
At the elections of 19 Sept. and 24 Oct. 1998 the electorate was approximately 200,000. Only non-partisans were elected. Political parties are illegal, and advocates of multi-party politics are considered to be troublemakers.

CURRENT ADMINISTRATION
In March 2003 the cabinet was composed as follows:

Prime Minister: Dr Barnabas Sibusiso Dlamini; b. 1942 (sworn in 26 July 1996). *Deputy Prime Minister:* Arthur R. V. Khoza. *Foreign Affairs, Defence and Trade:* Rev. Abednego Ntshangase. *Enterprise and Employment:* Lutfo E. Dlamini. *Agriculture and Co-operatives:* Roy Fanourakis. *Education:* John P. Carmichael. *Health and Social Welfare:* Dr Phetsile Dlamini. *Justice and Constitutional Affairs:* Chief Maweni Simelane. *Home Affairs:* Prince Sobandla. *Tourism, Environment and Communications:* Stella Lukhele. *Public Service and Information:* Magwagwa Mdluli. *Economic Planning and Development, and Natural Resources and Energy:* Prince Guduza. *Finance:* Majozi Sithole. *Housing and Urban Development:* Albert H. N. Shabangu. *Public Works and Transport:* Titus Mlangeni.

Government Website: http://www.swazi.com/government/

DEFENCE
Army Air Wing. There are two Israeli-built Arava transports with weapon attachments for light attack duties.

INTERNATIONAL RELATIONS
Swaziland is a member of the UN, WTO, the African Union, African Development Bank, COMESA, SADC, the Commonwealth and is an ACP member state of the ACP-EU relationship.

ECONOMY
Industry accounted for 38·7% of GDP in 1998, services 45·3% and agriculture 16·0%.

At the core of Swazi society is Tibiyo Taka Ngwane. Created in 1968 by Royal Charter, Tibiyo is a national development fund which operates outside the government and falls directly under the King, who holds it in trust for the nation. Its money derives from its stake in virtually every sector of Swazi commerce and industry.

Currency. The unit of currency is the *lilangeni* (plural *emalangeni*) (SZL) of 100 cents but Swaziland remains in the Common (formerly Rand) Monetary Area and the South African rand is legal tender. In 2001 inflation was 7·5%. In June 2002 foreign exchange reserves were US$253m. and total money supply was 832m. emalangeni.

Budget. The fiscal year begins on 1 April. Total revenue in financial year 2000 totalled 2,708·2m. emalangeni and total expenditure 2,899·7m. emalangeni.

Performance. Real GDP growth was 2·2% in 2000 and 1·6% in 2001. Total GDP in 2001 was US$1·3bn.

Banking and Finance. The central bank and bank of issue is the Central Bank of Swaziland (*Governor,* Martin Dlamini), established in 1974. There were 24 commercial banks in 1992. Foreign banks include Nedbank, Standard Chartered, Stanbic and First National. The Swaziland Development and Savings Bank concentrates on agricultural and housing loans.

In 1990 Swaziland Stock Brokers was established to trade in stocks and shares for institutional and private clients.

ENERGY AND NATURAL RESOURCES

Environment. According to the *World Bank Atlas* Swaziland's carbon dioxide emissions were the equivalent of 0·4 tonnes per capita in 1998.

Electricity. Installed capacity was 50,000 kW in 1993. Production was 420m. kWh in 1998; consumption per capita was 612 kWh in 1993. Swaziland imports about 60% of its electricity from South Africa.

Minerals. Output (in tonnes) in 1995: coal (1996), 126,000; asbestos, 28,591; quarry stone, 117,175 cu. metres. Diamond production was 64,000 carats in 1994. The diamond mine closed down in 1998 and in 1999 it was decided that the asbestos mine would close within five years.

The oldest known mine (iron ore) in the world, dating back to 41,000 BC, was located at the Lion Cavern Site on Ngwenya Mountain.

Agriculture. In 1998 there were 168,000 ha of arable land and 12,000 ha of permanent cropland. Production (2000, in 1,000 tonnes): sugarcane, 4,436; maize, 72; grapefruit and pomelos, 47; oranges, 36; seed cotton, 23; cottonseed, 15; pineapples, 11; groundnuts, 8; cotton lint, 7.

Livestock (2000): cattle, 610,000; goats, 440,000; pigs, 33,000; chickens, 3m.

Forestry. Forests covered 146,000 ha in 1995, or 8·5% of the land area. In 1999 timber production was 890,000 cu. metres.

Fisheries. Estimated total catch, 1999, 70 tonnes, exclusively from inland waters.

INDUSTRY

Most industries are based on processing agricultural products and timber. Footwear and textiles are also manufactured, and some engineering products.

Labour. The formal labour force numbered 88,290 in 1994; 15,892 Swazis worked in gold mines in South Africa. Unemployment rose to 30% in 1999.

Trade Unions. In 1998 there were 21 affiliated trade unions grouped in the Swaziland Federation of Trade Unions with a combined membership of 83,000, and four unions grouped in the Swaziland Federation of Labour.

INTERNATIONAL TRADE

Swaziland has a customs union with South Africa and receives a pro rata share of the dues collected. External debt was US$262m. in 2000.

Imports and Exports. In 2000 imports (f.o.b.) amounted to US$921·3m. (US$1,018·6m. in 1999); exports (f.o.b.) US$810·8m. (US$896·9m. in 1999). Main export commodities are soft drink concentrates, sugar, wood pulp and cotton yarn; main import products are motor vehicles, machinery, transport equipment, foodstuffs, petroleum products and chemicals. By far the most significant trading partner is South Africa, followed by the UK.

COMMUNICATIONS

Roads. Total length of roads (1997), 2,896 km, of which 1,363 km were highways. There were 31,900 passenger cars in 1997 plus 29,300 trucks and vans. There were 3,534 road accidents in 1997 with 260 fatalities.

Rail. In 1997 the system comprised 301 km of route, and carried 4,129,000 tonnes of freight in 1995–96.

Civil Aviation. There is an international airport at Manzini (Matsapha). The national carrier, Royal Swazi National Airways Corporation, is 50% state-owned. It had flights in 1998 to Dar es Salaam, Harare, Johannesburg, Lusaka, Maputo and Nairobi. In 1999 scheduled airline traffic of Swaziland-based carriers flew 0·6m. km, carrying 12,000 passengers (all on international flights).

Telecommunications. Swaziland had 32,200 telephone main lines in 2000, or 31·9 for every 1,000 persons. In 1996 there were 1,200 fax machines. There were around 3,000 Internet users and 11,000 mobile phone subscribers in 2000.

Postal Services. There were 65 post offices in 1995, or one for every 14,900 persons.

SOCIAL INSTITUTIONS

Justice. The constitutional courts practice Roman-Dutch law. The judiciary is headed by the Chief Justice. There is a High Court and various Magistrates and Courts. A Court of Appeal with a President and three Judges deals with appeals from the High Court. There are 16 courts of first instance. There are also traditional Swazi National Courts.

The population in penal institutions in Sept. 1998 was 2,221 (240 per 100,000 of national population).

Religion. There are about 0·12m. Christians and about 30,000 of other faiths.

Education. In 1998 there were 446 pre-schools with 19,000 children, and 543 primary schools with 212,292 children and 5,347 teachers. The teacher/pupil ratio has decreased from 40/1 in the 1970s to 33/1. About half the children of secondary school age attend school. There are also private schools. In 1998 there were 69,009 children in secondary and high school classes. Many secondary and high schools teach agricultural activities.

The University of Swaziland, at Matsapha, had 2,533 students in 1996–97. There are three teacher training colleges (total enrolment in 1994–95, 857) and eight vocational institutions (1,150 students and 147 teachers in 1991). There is also an institute of management.

Rural education centres offer formal education for children and adult education geared towards vocational training. The adult literacy rate in 1999 was 78·9% (80·0% among males and 77·9% among females).

Health. In 1998 there were 176 hospitals, clinics and health centres.

CULTURE

Broadcasting. The Broadcasting Corporation and Swaziland Television Authority are government-owned. Swaziland Broadcasting Services run on a semi-commercial basis. In 1997 there were 155,000 radio and 21,000 television receivers (colour by PAL).

Press. In 1996 there were three daily newspapers with a combined circulation of 24,000.

Tourism. There were 319,000 foreign tourists in 1998, bringing revenue of US$37m.

Libraries. There is a government-subsidized National Library Service, which comprises two libraries at Mbabane and Manzini with 11 branches throughout the country.

DIPLOMATIC REPRESENTATIVES

Of Swaziland in the United Kingdom (20 Buckingham Gate, London, SW1E 6LB)
High Commissioner: Rev. Percy S. Mngomezulu.

Of the United Kingdom in Swaziland (2nd Floor, Lilunga House, Gifillan Street, Mbabane)
High Commissioner: David Reader.

Of Swaziland in the USA (1712 New Hampshire Ave., NW, Washington, D.C., 20009)
Ambassador: Mary M. Kanya.

Of the USA in Swaziland (PO Box 199, Mbabane)
Ambassador: James David McGee.

Of Swaziland to the United Nations
Ambassador: Clifford Sibusiso Mamba.

Of Swaziland to the European Union
Ambassador: Thembayena Annastasia Dlamini.

FURTHER READING

Matsebula, J. S. M., *A History of Swaziland.* 3rd ed. London, 1992

Nyeko, B., *Swaziland.* [Bibliography] 2nd ed. ABC-Clio, Oxford and Santa Barbara (CA), 1994

National statistical office: Central Statistical Office, POB 456, Mbabane.

SWEDEN

Konungariket Sverige
(Kingdom of Sweden)

Capital: Stockholm
Population estimate, 2000: 8·87m.
GDP per capita, 2000: (PPP$) 24,277
HDI/world rank: 0·941/2

KEY HISTORICAL EVENTS

Sweden was organized as an independent unified state in the 10th century when the Swedes in the north of the country and the Goths in the south were united by Olof. Finland was acquired in the 13th century. In the 14th century Sweden was joined with Norway and Denmark in the Kalmar Union; however, under Gustavus Vasa Sweden regained her independence in 1523. Under Gustavus Adolphus (1611–32) Sweden became a first rank military power and, at the close of the Thirty Years War in 1648, was in possession of Pomerania and of extensive territories on the eastern shores of the Baltic. But war with Russia and her allies in the early 18th century ended disastrously for Sweden. By the treaty of Nystad (1721) Sweden lost her Baltic empire. In 1810 the French marshal, Bernadotte, was made crown prince. With the fall of Napoleon, Norway was taken from Denmark and attached to Sweden. Bernadotte became King in 1818. Sweden became a constitutional monarchy in 1809, in which year she also ceded Finland to Russia. Norway became independent in 1905. Sweden remained neutral during the two world wars of 1914–18 and 1939–45.

From 1932 to 1976 Sweden was governed by the Social Democratic Party which set the model for welfare reform, combined with rapid economic growth. But high taxation brought a reaction in the 1970s when the Centre Party (representing chiefly small farmers and traders) and the Conservatives staged a comeback which brought them to power in coalition with the Liberal Party in 1976. However, in 1981 the Social Democrat leader, Olof Palme, became prime minister with support from the Communist Party. On 28 Feb. 1986 Olof Palme was assassinated in Stockholm by unknown assailants. In 1991 a Conservative-led coalition took over the government at a time of recession. Austerity measures helped in the revival of the Social Democrats who returned to power in 1994 but with a commitment to economic stringency. Although the Social Democrats won the 1998 election, they saw their support fall to its lowest level since the First World War. Sweden joined the EU on 1 Jan. 1995 and is likely soon to hold a referendum on adopting the euro.

TERRITORY AND POPULATION

Sweden is bounded in the west and northwest by Norway, east by Finland and the Gulf of Bothnia, southeast by the Baltic Sea and southwest by the Kattegat. The area is 449,964 sq. km. At the 1990 census the population was 8,587,353. Estimate, Dec. 2000, 8,882,792; density 19·7 per sq. km. In 1999, 83·3% of the population lived in urban areas.

The UN gives a projected population for 2010 of 8·70m.

Area, population and population density of the counties (*län*):

	Land area (in sq. km)	Population (1990 census)	Population (31 Dec. 2000)	Density per sq. km (31 Dec. 2000)
Stockholm	6,490	1,640,389	1,823,210	281
Uppsala	6,989	268,503	294,196	42
Södermanland	6,062	255,546	256,033	42
Östergötland	10,562	402,849	411,345	39
Jönköping	9,944	308,294	327,829	33
Kronoberg	8,458	177,880	176,639	21
Kalmar	11,171	241,149	235,391	21
Gotland	3,140	57,132	57,313	18
Blekinge	2,941	150,615	150,392	51
Skåne	11,027	1,068,587	1,129,424	102
Halland	5,454	254,568	275,004	50

SWEDEN

	Land area (in sq. km)	Population (1990 census)	Population (31 Dec. 2000)	Density per sq. km (31 Dec. 2000)
Västra Götalands	23,942	1,458,166	1,494,641	62
Värmland	17,586	283,148	275,003	16
Örebro	8,517	272,474	273,615	32
Västmanland	6,302	258,544	256,889	41
Dalarna	28,193	288,919	278,259	10
Gävleborg	18,192	289,346	279,262	15
Västernorrland	21,678	261,099	246,903	11
Jämtland	49,443	135,724	129,566	3
Västerbotten	55,401	251,846	255,640	5
Norrbotten	98,911	263,546	256,238	3

There are some 17,000 Sami (Lapps).

On 31 Dec. 2000 aliens in Sweden numbered 394,609. Of these, 117,208 were from Nordic countries; 125,648 from the rest of Europe; 23,080 from Africa; 13,132 from North America; 16,669 from South America; 94,922 from Asian countries; 1,634 from the former USSR; 2,161 from Oceania; and 155 country unknown. The main individual countries of origin of aliens were: Finland, 72,477; Iraq, 30,802; Norway, 23,513.

Immigration: 1998, 49,391; 1999, 49,839; 2000, 58,659. Emigration: 1998, 38,518; 1999, 35,705; 2000, 34,091.

Population of the 50 largest communities, 1 Jan. 2001:

Stockholm	750,348	Huddinge	84,535	Gotland	57,313
Göteborg	466,990	Karlstad	80,323	Solna	56,605
Malmö	259,579	Södertälje	77,882	Mölndal	56,137
Uppsala	189,569	Nacka	74,974	Örnsköldsvik	55,702
Linköping	133,168	Kristianstad	74,161	Falun	54,426
Västerås	126,328	Växjö	73,901	Trollhättan	52,891
Örebro	124,207	Botkyrka	73,097	Varberg	52,648
Norrköping	122,199	Skellefteå	72,476	Norrtälje	52,611
Helsingborg	117,737	Luleå	71,652	Skövde	49,313
Jönköping	117,095	Haninge	69,644	Nyköping	49,063
Umeå	104,512	Kungsbacka	65,113	Uddevalla	48,971
Lund	98,948	Karlskrona	60,564	Hässleholm	48,580
Borås	96,883	Järfälla	60,471	Borlänge	47,208
Sundsvall	93,126	Täby	60,197	Motala	42,175
Gävle	90,742	Kalmar	59,308	Lidingö	40,584
Eskilstuna	88,208	Östersund	58,249	Piteå	40,363
Halmstad	85,200	Sollentuna	58,048		

A 16-km long fixed link with Denmark was opened in July 2000 when the Öresund motorway and railway bridge between Malmö and Copenhagen was completed.

Stockholm: Founded in the 13th century during the rule of Birger Jarl, Stockholm covers an area of 6,490 sq. km and is Sweden's most populous city. It is situated on the islands and shores of Saltsjön Bay and Lake Mälaren. Its first mention as the capital was in the 14th century. The castle was built in the 13th century, remains of which can still be seen as part of the Royal Palace, completed in the 1750s.

The official language is Swedish.

SOCIAL STATISTICS
Statistics for calendar years:

	Total living births	To mothers single, divorced or widowed	Stillborn	Marriages	Divorces	Deaths exclusive of still-born
1996	95,297	51,348	330	33,484	21,377	94,133
1997	90,502	48,945	314	32,313	21,009	93,326
1998	89,028	48,658	306	31,598	20,761	93,271
1999	88,173	48,751	339	35,628	21,000	94,726
2000	90,441	50,037	355	39,895	21,502	93,461

Rates, 2000, per 1,000 population: births, 10·2; deaths, 10·5; marriages, 4·5; divorces, 2·4. Sweden has one of the highest rate of births outside marriage in Europe, at over 55% in 2000. In 2000 the most popular age range for marrying was 25–29 for women and 30–34 for men. Expectation of life in 1999: males, 77·0 years; females, 82·1. Annual population growth rate, 1990–99, 0·4%. Infant mortality,

1999, 3·4 per 1,000 live births (one of the lowest rates in the world). Fertility rate, 2000, 1·5 births per woman. In 2000 Sweden received 16,303 asylum applications, equivalent to 1·84 per 1,000 inhabitants.

A UNICEF report published in 2000 showed that 2·6% of children in Sweden live in poverty (in households with income below 50% of the national median), the lowest percentage of any country. The report also showed that the poverty rate of children in lone-parent families was 6·7%, compared to 1·5% in two-parent families.

CLIMATE
The north has severe winters, with snow lying for 4–7 months. Summers are fine but cool, with long daylight hours. Further south, winters are less cold, summers are warm and rainfall well distributed throughout the year, although slightly higher in the summer. Stockholm, Jan. 0·4°C, July 17·2°C. Annual rainfall 385 mm.

CONSTITUTION AND GOVERNMENT
The reigning King is **Carl XVI Gustaf**, b. 30 April 1946, succeeded on the death of his grandfather Gustaf VI Adolf, 15 Sept. 1973, married 19 June 1976 to Silvia Renate Sommerlath, b. 23 Dec. 1943 (Queen of Sweden). *Daughter* and *Heir Apparent:* Crown Princess Victoria Ingrid Alice Désirée, Duchess of Västergötland, b. 14 July 1977; *son:* Prince Carl Philip Edmund Bertil, Duke of Värmland, b. 13 May 1979; *daughter:* Princess Madeleine Thérèse Amelie Josephine, Duchess of Hälsingland and Gästrikland, b. 10 June 1982. *Sisters of the King.* Princess Margaretha, b. 31 Oct. 1934, married 30 June 1964 to John Ambler; Princess Birgitta (Princess of Sweden), b. 19 Jan. 1937, married 25 May 1961 (civil marriage) and 30 May 1961 (religious ceremony) to Johann Georg, Prince of Hohenzollern; Princess Désirée, b. 2 June 1938, married 5 June 1964 to Baron Niclas Silfverschiöld; Princess Christina, b. 3 Aug. 1943, married 15 June 1974 to Tord Magnuson. *Uncles of the King.* Count Sigvard Bernadotte of Wisborg, b. on 7 June 1907, died on 4 Feb. 2002; Count Carl Johan Bernadotte of Wisborg, b. on 31 Oct. 1916.

Under the 1975 Constitution Sweden is a representative and parliamentary democracy. The King is Head of State, but does not participate in government. Parliament is the single-chamber *Riksdag* of 349 members elected for a period of four years in direct, general elections.

The manner of election to the *Riksdag* is proportional. The country is divided into 29 constituencies. In these constituencies 310 members are elected. The remaining 39 seats constitute a nationwide pool intended to give absolute proportionality to parties that receive at least 4% of the votes. A party receiving less than 4% of the votes in the country is, however, entitled to participate in the distribution of seats in a constituency, if it has obtained at least 12% of the votes cast there.

A parliament, the *Sameting*, was instituted for the Sami (Lapps) in 1993.

National Anthem. 'Du gamla, du fria' ('Thou ancient, thou free'); words by R. Dybeck; folk-tune.

RECENT ELECTIONS
In parliamentary elections held on 15 Sept. 2002 Prime Minister Göran Persson's Swedish Social Democratic Labour Party (SAP) won 144 seats with 39·8% of votes cast (131 with 36·4% in 1998), the Moderate Alliance Party 55 with 15·2% (82 with 22·9%), the Liberal Party 48 with 13·3% (17 with 4·7%), the Christian Democratic Party 33 with 9·1% (42 with 11·8%), the Left Party 30 with 8·3% (43 with 12·0%), the Centre Party 22 with 6·1% (18 with 5·1%) and the Green Party 17 with 4·6% (16 with 4·5%). Turn-out was 80·1%. Prior to the 2002 election, of the 349 Members of Parliament there were 198 men (56·7%) and 151 women (43·3%), the highest percentage of women for any parliament in the world.

European Parliament. Sweden has 22 representatives. At the June 1999 elections turn-out was 38·3%. The Social Democratic Party won 6 seats with 26·1% of votes cast (group in European Parliament: Party of European Socialists); the Moderate Party, 5 with 20·6% (European People's Party); Vänsterpartiet (Far Left), 3 with 15·8% (Confederal Group of the European United Left/Nordic Green Left); the Liberal Party, 3 with 13·8% (Liberal, Democrat and Reform Party); the Green Party,

SWEDEN

2 with 9·4% (Greens); the Christian Democratic Party, 2 with 7·7% (European People's Party); the Centre Party, 1 with 6·0% (Liberal, Democrat and Reform Party).

CURRENT ADMINISTRATION

A minority Social Democratic government was formed in Oct. 1998. Following parliamentary elections in Sept. 2002 a new Social Democratic government was formed. In March 2003 it comprised:

Prime Minister: Göran Persson; b. 1949 (SAP; sworn in 21 March 1996).
Deputy Prime Minister: Margareta Winberg.
Minister of Justice: Thomas Bodström. *Foreign Affairs:* Anna Lindh. *Agriculture, Food and Fisheries:* Ann-Christin Nykvist. *Culture:* Marita Ulvskog. *Education and Science:* Thomas Östros. *Environment:* Lena Sommestad. *Finance:* Bosse Ringholm. *Health and Social Affairs:* Lars Engqvist. *Industry, Employment and Communications:* Leif Pagrotsky. *Defence:* Leni Björklund.

The *Speaker* is Björn von Sydow.

Office of the Prime Minister: http://www.sweden.gov.se

DEFENCE

The Supreme Commander is, under the government, in command of the three services. The Supreme Commander is assisted by the Swedish Armed Forces HQ. There is also a Swedish Armed Forces Logistics Organization.

The conscription system consists of 7½–18 months of military service for males. Females have the possibility to serve on a voluntary basis.

In 2002 military expenditure totalled US$4·8bn. (US$540 per capita), representing an estimated 1·98% of GDP. Sweden's national security policy is currently undergoing a shift in emphasis. Beginning with the decommissioning of obsolete units and structures, the main thrust of policy is the creation of contingency forces adaptable to a variety of situations.

The government stressed that Sweden's membership of the EU (in 1995) did not imply any change in Sweden's traditional policy of non-participation in military alliances, with the option of staying neutral in the event of war in its vicinity.

Sweden has modern air raid shelters with capacity for some 7m. people. Since this falls short of providing protection for the whole population, evacuation and relocation operations would be necessary in the event of war.

The National Board of Psychological Defence, whose main task is to safeguard the free, undisrupted transmission of news, has also made preparations for 'psychological defence' in wartime. This is regarded as the best possible antidote against enemy propaganda, disinformation and rumour-mongering of the kind that can be expected in times of war.

Army. The Army consists of 1 division HQ and divisional units, 6 army brigade command and control elements, and 54 battalions. Army strength, Jan. 2003, 20,000 (10,769 conscripts). The Army can mobilize a reserve of approximately 200,000 of whom 85,000 are Home Guard and 11,100 reservists.

The Home Guard is part of the army. Its main task is to protect important local installations against sabotage.

Navy. The Navy has 2 surface warfare flotillas, 1 mine warfare flotilla, 1 submarine flotilla and 1 amphibious brigade.

The personnel of the Navy in Jan. 2003 totalled 5,600 (active manpower, including 2,600 conscripts). Strength available for mobilization, 20,000 (includes 2,500 reservists).

Air Force. The Air Force consists of 3 fighter control and air surveillance battalions, 8 air-base battalions, 8 fighter squadrons, 2 air transport squadrons (central) and 2 air transport squadrons (regional).

Strength (Jan. 2003) 6,500 (2,000 conscripts), plus 16,000 available for mobilization (including 1,670 reservists).

During peacetime all the helicopters of the Swedish Armed Forces are organized into a detached organization directly under the Swedish Armed Forces Headquarters.

INTERNATIONAL RELATIONS

Sweden is a member of the UN, WTO, BIS, NATO Partnership for Peace, BIS, OECD, EU, Council of Europe, OSCE, CERN, Nordic Council, Council of the Baltic Sea States, Inter-American Development Bank, Asian Development Bank, IOM and the Antarctic Treaty. Sweden is a signatory to the Schengen Accord, which abolishes border controls between Sweden, Austria, Belgium, Denmark, Finland, France, Germany, Greece, Iceland, Italy, Luxembourg, the Netherlands, Norway, Portugal and Spain.

ECONOMY

Services accounted for 73% of GDP in 2001, industry 25% and agriculture 2%.

According to the anti-corruption organization *Transparency International*, in 2002 Sweden ranked equal 5th in the world in a survey of the countries with the least corruption in business and government. It received 9·3 out of 10 in the annual index.

Overview. Sweden combines an extensive welfare state with a market economy. Expenditure ceilings and a target for the cyclically adjusted budget surplus have governed fiscal policy sine 1997. In 2002 an expansionary fiscal policy and competitive exports contributed to sound economic developments. Fiscal stimulus for 2002 has targeted household expenditure. As the fiscal position is expected to deteriorate in 2003, the government could breach its self-imposed ceilings on public expenditure. Monetary policy has targeted a 2% inflation rate since 1993, but in 2001 inflation was 2·7% before dropping to 2% in May 2002. In Sept. 2003 the government will hold a referendum on adopting the euro.

Currency. The unit of currency is the *krona* (SEK), of 100 *öre*. The annual inflation rate was 2·9% in Jan. 2002 (1·7% in Jan. 2001 and 0·8% in Jan. 2000). Foreign exchange reserves were US$14,967m. and gold reserves 5·96m. troy oz in June 2002.

Budget. Revenue of 725·0bn. kr. and expenditure of 716·6bn. kr is estimated for the total budget (Current and Capital) for financial year 2002.

Revenue and expenditure for 2001 (1m. kr.):

Revenue

Taxes on income	134,874	Financial security in the event of	
Tax on income—legal entities	*94,062*	illness and disability	107,316
Social security fees	238,766	Financial security in old age	33,839
Estate tax	23,330	Financial security for families	
Other taxes on property	16,533	and children	48,289
VAT	184,787	The labour market and working life	67,134
Excise duties	86,729	Study support	19,089
Compensation for municipalities and		Education and university research	32,259
county councils	20,874	Culture, the media, religious	
Other revenue	−19,650	organizations and leisure	7,814
Income from government activities	50,813	Community planning, housing	
Income from sale of assets	188	supply and construction	10,434
Loans repaid	2,590	Regional balance and development	3,258
Computed revenue	8,447	General environment and	
Contributions, etc., from the EU	8,485	conservation	2,153
		Energy	1,950
Total revenue	755,126	Communications	24,568
		Agriculture and forestry,	
Expenditure		fisheries, etc.	16,627
The Swedish political system	5,413	Business sector	3,348
Economy and fiscal administration	2,122	General grants to municipalities	100,639
Tax administration and collection	6,432	Interest on Central Government	
Justice	24,149	Debt, etc.	81,260
Foreign policy administration and		Contribution to the European	
international co-operation	3,015	Community	23,271
Total defence	44,895	Other expenditure	0
International development assistance	16,989		
Immigrants and refugees	5,282	Total expenditure	722,036
Health care, medical care,			
social services	29,492		

VAT is 25% (reduced rate, 12% and 6%). In 2001 tax revenues were 54·2% of GDP (the highest percentage of any developed country).

Performance. Real GDP growth was 3·6% in 1998, 4·6% in 1999 and 4·4% in 2000, but only 0·8% in 2001. Sweden's total GDP in 2001 was US$210·1bn.

The OECD reported in 2001 that 'Sweden is now profiting from macroeconomic and structural reforms undertaken in the wake of the severe recession of the early 1990s. Output has been growing at around 4% per year, while inflation has been lower than in almost all other OECD countries.' But even with healthy external and fiscal balances, the economy is still growing faster than can be sustained in the medium term. Higher interest rates are expected to start to relieve the pressure. The OECD report concludes: 'Sweden is well placed to maintain admirable economic outcomes and to achieve an even higher standard of living as long as it continues pursuing macroeconomic policies and satisfactorily addresses its remaining structural weaknesses.'

In 2001 the state debt amounted to 1,154bn. kr.

Banking and Finance. The central bank and bank of issue is the *Sveriges Riksbank*. The bank has 11 trustees, elected by parliament, and is managed by a directorate, including the governor, appointed by the trustees. In Jan. 2003 a new *Governor*, Lars Heikensten, was appointed for a six-year term. On 31 Dec. 2000 there were 48 commercial banks. Their total deposits amounted to 1,104,570m. kr.; advances to the public amounted to 975,212m. kr. In April 2003 there were 77 savings banks and 20 branches of foreign banks. The largest banks are Nordea Bank AB (previously MeritaNorbanken, formed in 1997 when Nordbanken of Sweden merged with Merita of Finland), Svenska Handelsbanken, Skandinavska Enskilda Banken and FöreningsSparbanken. In April 2000 MeritaNordbanken acquired Denmark's Unidanmark, thereby becoming the Nordic region's biggest bank in terms of assets. It became Nordea Bank AB in Dec. 2001. By Oct. 2000 approximately 27% of the Swedish population were using e-banking.

In 1999 Sweden received US$60bn. worth of foreign direct investment, equivalent to 25·1% of its GDP—the highest percentage of any country in the world.

There is a stock exchange in Stockholm.

Weights and Measures. The metric system is obligatory.

ENERGY AND NATURAL RESOURCES

Environment. According to the *World Bank Atlas* Sweden's carbon dioxide emissions in 1998 were the equivalent of 5·5 tonnes per capita. An *Environmental Sustainability Index* compiled for the World Economic Forum meeting in Feb. 2002 ranked Sweden third in the world, with 72·6%. The index measured the ability of countries to maintain favourable environmental conditions and examined various factors including pollution levels and the use or abuse of natural resources.

Electricity. Sweden is rich in hydro-power resources. Installed capacity was 34,080 MW in 1999, of which 16,433 MW was in hydro-electric plants, 10,076 MW in nuclear plants and 7,375 MW in thermal plants. Electricity production in 2000 was 144,966m. kWh; consumption was 160,203 kWh. In 1998 consumption per capita was 13,955 kWh. A referendum of 1980 called for the phasing out of nuclear power by 2010. In Feb. 1997 the government began denuclearization by designating one of the 12 reactors for decommissioning. The state corporation Vattenfall was given the responsibility of financing and overseeing the transition to the use of non-fossil fuel alternatives. In 2001 there were 11 nuclear reactors in operation.

Minerals. Sweden is a leading producer of iron ore with around 2% of the world's total output. It is the largest iron ore exporter in Europe. There are also deposits of copper, lead, zinc and alum shale containing oil and uranium. Iron ore produced, 1998, 20·9m. tonnes; copper ore, 270,000 tonnes; zinc concentrates, 297,000 tonnes.

The mining industry accounts for 1·0% of the market value of Sweden's total industrial production and employs 0·5% of the total industrial labour force.

Agriculture. In 1999 the total area of land given over to farms of 2 ha or more was 7,630,720 ha, of which 2,746,929 ha was arable land; 447,149 was natural pasture; 3,734,193 was forest; and 702,449 other. Of the land used for arable farming, 2–5 ha holdings covered a total area of 43,524 ha; 5·1–10 ha holdings covered 114,858 ha; 10·1–20 ha, 244,007; 20·1–30 ha, 230,210; 30·1–50 ha, 448,199; 50·1–100 ha, 762,368 and holdings larger than 100 ha covered 903,765 ha. There were 80,119 agricultural enterprises in 1999 compared to 150,014 in 1971 and 282,187 in 1951. Around 40% of the enterprises were between 5 and 20 ha. Figures compiled by the Soil Association, a British organization, show that in 1999 Sweden set aside 268,000 ha (11·2% of its agricultural land—one of the highest proportions in the world) for the growth of organic crops.

Agriculture accounts for 5·8% of exports and 7·9% of imports. The agricultural sector employs 3% of the workforce.

	Area (1,000 ha)			Production (1,000 tonnes)		
Chief crops	1998	1999	2000	1998	1999	2000
Ley	742·1	760·2	917·3	. . .	. . .	. . .
Sugarbeet	58·7	59·9	55·5	2,570·8	2,752·6	2,602·7
Barley	445·0	482·0	411·2	1,686·9	1,852·5	1,634·4
Wheat	398·0	275·4	401·6	2,248·7	1,658·9	2,399·9
Oats	311·5	305·7	295·5	1,136·2	1,055·1	1,151·1
Potatoes	33·7	32·8	32·9	792·5	990·8	980·1
Rye	34·6	24·5	34·5	160·5	117·4	187·3

Milk production (in 1,000 tonnes) 2000, 3,348; meat, 475; cheese, 127; butter, 50.

Livestock 2000: cattle, 1,683,767; sheep and lambs (1999), 437,200; pigs, 1,917,917; poultry (1999), 7,849,842. There were 122,124 reindeer in Sami villages in 2000. Harvest of moose during open season 2000: 108,688.

Forestry. Forests form one of the country's greatest natural assets. The growing stock includes 46% Norway spruce, 36% Scots pine, 12% birch and 6% other. In the period 1995–99 forests covered 22,740,000 ha (55% of the land area). The state owns only 5% of productive forest lands. During 1993 most government-owned timberland was transferred to a forest production corporation (AssiDomän) in which the state owns 51% of shares, and the remaining 49% are quoted on the stock exchange. Public ownership accounts for 8% of the forests, limited companies own 37%, the state 5% and the remaining 50% is in private hands. Of the 58·7m. cu. metres of wood felled in 1999, 30·3m. cu. metres were sawlogs, 21·5m. cu. metres pulpwood, 5·9m. cu. metres fuelwood and 1·0 cu. metres other.

Fisheries. In 2000 the total catch was 332,408 tonnes, worth 955·1m. kr.

INDUSTRY

The leading companies by market capitalization in Sweden, excluding banking and finance, in Jan. 2002 were: Telefonaktiebolaget LM Ericsson (385bn. kr); H & M—Hennes & Mauritz AB (157bn. kr), a clothing and cosmetics company; Telia AB (131bn. kr), a telecommunications company. Telia AB has in the meantime merged with the Finnish company Sonera to become TeliaSonera.

Manufacturing is mainly based on metals and forest resources. Chemicals (especially petro-chemicals), building materials and decorative glass and china are also important.

Industry groups	No. of establishments 1996	Average no. wage-earners 1996	Sales value of of production (gross) in 1m. kr. 1999
Manufacturing industry	8,856	411,118	1,169,917
Food products, beverages and tobacco	842	41,518	109,517
Textiles and textile products, leather and leather products	270	8,450	12,206
Wood and wood products	714	23,747	56,286
Pulp, paper and paper products, publishers and printers	1,197	54,253	154,232
Coke, refined petroleum products and nuclear fuel	16	1,228	7,056
Chemicals, chemical products and man-made fibres	317	14,339	82,222
Rubber and plastic products	407	15,656	29,548
Other non-metallic mineral products	357	11,543	19,799
Basic metals	159	23,913	67,449
Fabricated metal products, machinery and equipment	4,018	196,655	589,838
Other manufacturing industries	410	14,488	30,483
Mines and quarries	149	5,328	11,282

Labour. In 2000 there were 4,159,000 persons in the labour force, employed as follows: 799,000 in trade and communication; 796,000 in manufacturing, mining, quarrying, electricity and water services; 770,000 in health and social work; 553,000 in financial services and business activities; 361,000 in education, research and development; 328,000 in personal services and cultural activities, and sanitation; 223,000 in public administration; 98,000 in agriculture, forestry and fishing. The unemployment rate in Jan. 2003 was 5·3%. In 1999, 74·8% of men and 70·9% of women between the ages of 15 and 64 were in employment. No other major industrialized nation has such a small gap between the employment rates of the sexes.

In 2000 a total of 272 working days were lost through strikes, compared to 733,284 in 1995.

Trade Unions. At 31 Dec. 2000 the Swedish Trade Union Confederation (LO) had 18 member unions with a total membership of 2,016,208; the Central Government Organization of Salaried Employees (TCO) had 18, with 1,244,589; the Swedish Confederation of Professional Associations (SACO) had 26, with 492,706; the Central Organization of Swedish Workers (SAC) had 8,203 members.

In March 1997 employers' organizations and trade unions signed an agreement on the conduct of wage negotiations in 1998. The agreement involved 0·8m. workers, and provided for the establishment of an Industrial Committee to promote the development of industry.

INTERNATIONAL TRADE

Imports and Exports. Imports and exports (in 1m. kr.):

	1996	1997	1998	1999	2000[1]
Imports	448,739	501,180	544,984	568,009	666,864
Exports	569,167	632,567	675,209	700,960	796,549

[1]Provisional.

Breakdown by Standard International Trade Classification (SITC, revision 3) categories (value in 1m. kr.; 2000 figures are estimates):

	Imports		Exports	
	1999	2000	1999	2000
0. Food and live animals	33,919	35,172	15,319	16,622
1. Beverages and tobacco	5,381	5,168	2,927	3,251
2. Crude materials	17,715	22,241	38,779	48,067
3. Fuels and lubricants	34,442	60,609	16,514	26,732
4. Animal and vegetable oils	1,312	1,119	946	986
5. Chemicals	62,092	64,086	67,499	75,045
6. Manufactured goods	82,253	92,938	142,934	159,595
7. Machinery and transport equipment	251,953	299,495	354,052	399,734
8. Miscellaneous manufactured items	78,881	85,877	61,132	65,432
9. Other	57	158	857	817

Principal exports in 1999 (in tonnes): iron ore and concentrates, 13,819,603; paper and board, 6,770,764; newsprint, 2,038,087; flat-rolled products of iron, 1,198,177; flat-rolled products of alloy steel, 1,044,157; power-generating non-electrical machinery, 167,867; mechanical handling equipment, 167,842; lumber, sawn and planed, 11,063,000 sq. metres. The engineering industry accounts for some 55% of Swedish exports. This includes mobile telephony, which is the largest product group in the Swedish export market. The telecommunications company Ericsson is now the leading export company, ahead of Volvo.

Imports and exports by countries (in 1m. kr.):

	Imports from		Exports to	
	1999	2000	1999	2000
Belgium	21,363	24,523	30,027	33,684
Denmark	37,264	50,382	39,028	46,348
Finland	29,510	36,939	35,675	44,461
France	33,694	39,295	36,560	41,657
Germany	94,916	117,364	74,566	87,350
Netherlands	43,645	50,669	41,684	39,670
UK	55,208	63,666	65,253	74,847
USA	33,257	44,726	64,262	75,349

In 2000 other EU member countries accounted for 53·6% of exports and 60·3% of imports. Exports were equivalent to 44% of Sweden's GDP in 1999.

COMMUNICATIONS

Roads. In 2001 there were 212,000 km of roads open to the public of which 98,173 km were state-administered roads (main roads, 15,079 km; secondary roads, 83,094 km). A total of 77·2% were surfaced. There were also 1,499 km of motorway. Motor vehicles in 2000 included 3,999,000 passenger cars, 374,000 lorries, 14,000 buses and 310,000 motorcycles and mopeds. There were 993,000 Volvos, 396,000 Volkswagens, 376,000 Saabs and 364,000 Fords registered in 2000. Sweden has one of the lowest death rates in road accidents of any industrialized country, at 6·7 deaths per 100,000 people. 591 people were killed in traffic accidents in 2000.

Rail. Total length of railways at 31 Dec. 2000 was 11,041 km (7,507 km electrified). In 2000, 132m. passengers and 56·7m. tonnes of freight were carried. There is a metro in Stockholm (108 km), and tram/light rail networks in Stockholm, Göteborg (81 km) and Norrköping.

Civil Aviation. The main international airports are at Stockholm (Arlanda), Göteborg (Landvetter) and Malmö (Sturup). The principal carrier is Scandinavian Airlines System (SAS), of which SAS Sverige AB is the Swedish partner (SAS Denmark A/S and SAS Norge ASA being the other two). SAS has a joint paid-up capital of 14,241m. Sw. kr. Capitalization of SAS Sverige AB, 5,560m. Sw. kr., of which 50% is owned by the government and 50% by private enterprises.

In 1997 the total distance flown was 109·0m. km; passenger-km, 8,893·7m.; goods, 294·7m. tonne-km. These figures represent the Swedish share of the SAS traffic (Swedish domestic and three-sevenths of international traffic). Malmö Aviation and Skyways AB, both Sweden-based carriers, operate some international as well as domestic flights.

In 2000 Stockholm (Arlanda) handled 18,263,926 passengers (11,503,799 on international flights) and 120,535 tonnes of freight. Göteborg (Landvetter) was the second busiest airport, handling 4,205,541 passengers (2,841,619 on international flights) and 57,510 tonnes of freight. Malmö handled 2,036,414 passengers (1,250,864 on domestic flights).

Shipping. The mercantile marine consisted on 31 Dec. 2000 of 402 vessels of 2·80m. GRT. Cargo vessels entering Swedish ports in 2000 numbered 27,349 (192·63m. GRT) while passenger ferries numbered 85,861 (772·48m. GRT). The number of cargo vessels leaving Swedish ports in 2000 totalled 27,419 (190·90m. GRT) and the number of passenger ferries leaving was 85,932 (772·81m. GRT).

The busiest port is Göteborg. In 2000 a total of 33·26m. tonnes of goods were loaded and unloaded there (29·8m. tonnes unloaded from and loaded to foreign ports). Other major ports are Brofjorden, Trelleborg, Helsingborg and Luleå.

Telecommunications. There were 6,056,800 main telephone lines in 2000, or 682·0 per 1,000 population. In June 2000 the state sold off a 30% stake in the Swedish telecommunications operator Telia. In Dec. 2002 Telia and the Finnish telecommunications operator Sonera merged to become TeliaSonera. The Swedish state owns 46% and the Finnish state 19%. 5·58m. mobile phones were in use in Nov. 2000. More than 57% of Swedes are mobile phone subscribers—one of the highest penetration rates in the world. There were 4·5m. PCs in 2000 (506·7 per 1,000 population) and 450,000 fax machines in 1996. In Sept. 2002 there were 6·02m. Internet users, or 67·81% of the total population (the second highest percentage in the world, after Iceland).

Sweden has been one of the most active countries in the adoption of information technology. Kista Science Park, in the northwest of Stockholm, was ranked second equal in the world behind Silicon Valley by *Wired Magazine* in 2000 in a listing of the most significant locations for IT research and development.

Postal Services. There were 1,741 post offices at the end of 2000. In the meantime many traditional post offices have closed down and have been replaced by up to 3,000 new postal service outlets in locations such as shops and petrol stations. A total of 5,555m. pieces of mail were processed in 1999, equivalent to 627 per person.

SOCIAL INSTITUTIONS

Justice. Sweden has two parallel types of courts—general courts that deal with criminal and civil cases and general administrative courts that deal with cases related to public administration. The general courts have three instances: 23 county administrative courts, 4 administrative courts of appeal and the Supreme Administrative Court. There are 72 district courts, of which 25 also serve as real estate courts. In addition, a number of special courts and tribunals have been established to hear specific kinds of cases and matters.

Every district court, court of appeal, county administrative court and administrative court of appeal has a number of lay judges. These take part in the adjudication of both specific concrete issues and matter of law; each has the right to vote.

Criminal cases are normally tried by one judge and three lay judges. Civil disputes are normally heard by a single judge or three judges. In the courts of appeal, criminal cases are determined by three judges and two lay judges. Civil cases are tried by three or four judges. In the settlement of family cases, lay judges take part in the proceedings in both the district court and in the court of appeal. Proceedings in the general administrative courts are in writing; i.e. the court determines the case on the basis of correspondences between the parties. Nevertheless, it is also possible to hold a hearing. The cases are determined by a single judge or one judge and three lay judges. In the administrative court of appeal, cases are normally heard by three judges or three judges and two lay judges.

Those who lack the means to take advantage of their rights are entitled to legal aid. Everyone suspected of a serious crime or taken into custody has the right to a public counsel (advocate). The title advocate can only be used by accredited members of the Swedish Bar Association. Qualifying as an advocate requires extensive theoretical and practical training. All advocates in Sweden are employed in the private sector.

The control over the way in which public authorities fulfil their commitments is exercised by the Parliamentary Ombudsmen and the Chancellor of Justice. In 2000–01 the Ombudsmen received 4,664 cases altogether, of which 133 were instituted on their own initiative. Sweden has no constitutional court. However, in each particular case the courts do have a certain right to ascertain whether a statute meets the standards set out by superordinate provisions.

On average, approximately 4,000 people are held in prison every day. There are 55 prisons spread throughout the country.

There were 166 reported murders in 2001 (121 in 1990 and 175 in 2000).

Religion. The Swedish Lutheran Church was disestablished in 2000. It is headed by Archbishop Karl Gustaf Hammar (b. 1943) and has its metropolitan see at Uppsala. In 1996 there were 13 bishoprics and 2,544 parishes. The clergy are chiefly supported from the parishes and the proceeds of the church lands. Around 87% of the population, equivalent to 7·7m. people, belong to the Church of Sweden. Other denominations, in 2000: Pentecostal Movement, 89,670 members; The Mission Covenant Church of Sweden, 66,082; InterAct, 28,964; Salvation Army, 24,109; Örebro Missionary Society (1996), 22,801; Swedish Evangelical Mission, 17,551; The Baptist Union of Sweden, 17,942; Swedish Alliance Missionary Society, 12,833; Holiness Mission (1996), 6,393. There were also 158,000 Roman Catholics (under a Bishop resident at Stockholm). The Orthodox and Oriental churches number around 98,500 members.

There were around 18,000 Jews and 250,000 Muslims in Sweden in 1998.

Education. In 2000–01 there were 728,872 pupils in primary education (grades 1–6 in compulsory comprehensive schools); secondary education at the lower stage (grades 7–9 in compulsory comprehensive schools) comprised 323,057 pupils. In secondary education at the higher stage (the integrated upper secondary school), there were 305,270 pupils in Oct. 2000 (excluding pupils in the fourth year of the technical course regarded as third-level education). The folk high schools, 'people's colleges', had 29,060 pupils on courses of more than 15 weeks in the autumn of 2000.

In municipal adult education there were 227,634 students in 2000.

There are also special schools for pupils with visual and hearing handicaps (807 pupils in 2000) and for those who are intellectually disabled (18,623 pupils).

In 1999–2000 there were in integrated institutions for higher education 319,0911 students enrolled for undergraduate studies. The number of students enrolled for postgraduate studies in 2000 was 18,162.

In 1997 total expenditure on education came to 7·65% of GDP. The adult literacy rate is at least 99%. In an OECD literacy survey carried out between 1994 and 1999, analysing prose literacy, document literacy and quantitative literacy, Sweden led the world, ahead of Denmark and Norway.

Health. In 2000 there were 24,500 doctors, 4,400 dentists, 77,700 nurses and midwives and in 2000 there were 31,765 hospital beds. In 1996 the total cost of healthcare was 128bn. kr., representing 7·6% of GNP.

The Swedes smoked an average of 992 cigarettes per person in 1994.

Welfare. Social insurance benefits are granted mainly according to uniform statutory principles. All persons resident in Sweden are covered, regardless of citizenship. All schemes are compulsory, except for unemployment insurance. Benefits are usually income-related. Most social security schemes are at present undergoing extensive discussion and changes. Recent proposals include the introduction of a new pension scheme.

Type of social insurance scheme	Payments 2000 (in 1m. kr.)
Old-age pension	163,488
Sickness insurance	84,559
Unemployment insurance	27,872
Child allowance	18,878
Parental insurance	16,488
Survivor's pension	13,806
Housing supplement	9,641
Work injury insurance	7,343

In 1996, 34·8% of GNP was spent on social security—the highest percentage of any EU-member country.

Under a Pension Reform Plan Sweden is one of the world's leaders in the shift to private pension systems. In the new system each worker's future pension will be based on the amount of money accumulated in two separate individual accounts. The bulk of retirement income will come from a notional account maintained by the government on behalf of the individual, but a significant portion of retirement income will come from a completely private individual account. There are two types of pension—the income pension and the premium pension. The income pension comes under a pay-as-you-go system, with the premium pension being a scheme where contributions are invested in a fund chosen by the insured person.

CULTURE

Broadcasting. 3,360,000 combined radio and TV reception fees were paid in 2000. There were an estimated 8m. radio receivers in 1997 and 4·7m. television sets in 1997. There were 1·93m. cable TV subscribers in 1997. *Sveriges Radio AB* is a non-commercial semi-governmental corporation, transmitting three national programmes and regional programmes. It also broadcasts two TV programmes (colour by PAL). One channel, TV4, is commercial but semi public service, and there are five fully commercial satellite channels, TV3, Kanal 5, TV6, ZTV and TV8.

Cinema. In 2000 there were 1,131 cinemas. Total attendance was 17m. A total of 185 new foreign films and 38 new Swedish films were shown during 2000. In 1995 gross box office receipts came to 905m. kr.

Press. In 2000 there were 169 daily newspapers with an average weekday net circulation of 4,089,000. More than 80% of people in Sweden read a daily newspaper. The leading papers in terms of circulation are the tabloid Social Democratic *Aftonbladet*, with average daily sales of 412,000 in 1998; the independent *Dagens Nyheter*, with average daily sales of 361,000 in 1998; the liberal tabloid *Expressen*, with average daily sales of 328,000 in 1998; and the liberal *Göteborgs-Posten*, with average daily sales of 258,000 in 1998. In 2000 a total of 10,976 book titles were published.

Tourism. There were 2,595,000 foreign tourists in 1999, bringing revenue of US$3·89bn. In 2000 foreign visitors stayed 4,223,349 nights in hotels and 835,397 in holiday villages and youth hostels. In 2000 there were 2,524 accommodation establishments with 255,163 beds.

Libraries. In 2000 there were 1 national library, 331 public libraries, 36 university libraries and 20 special libraries.

Theatre and Opera. State-subsidized theatres gave 12,453 performances for audiences totalling 2,332,158 during 1999. The National Theatre (Kungliga Dramatiska Teatern) and the National Opera (Operan) are both located in Stockholm.

Museums and Galleries. Sweden had 234 public museums and art galleries in 1999 with a combined total of 16,292,884 visits.

DIPLOMATIC REPRESENTATIVES

Of Sweden in the United Kingdom (11 Montagu Pl., London, W1H 2AL)
Ambassador: Mats Bergquist, CMG.

Of the United Kingdom in Sweden (Skarpögatan 6–8, S-115 93 Stockholm)
Ambassador: John D. K. Grant, CMG.

Of Sweden in the USA (1501 M Street, NW, Suite 900, Washington, D.C., 20005-1702)
Ambassador: Jan Eliasson.

Of the USA in Sweden (Strandvägen 101, S-115 89 Stockholm)
Ambassador: Charles A. Heimbold.

Of Sweden to the United Nations
Ambassador: Pierre Schori.

FURTHER READING

Statistics Sweden. *Statistik Årsbok/Statistical Yearbook of Sweden.—Historisk statistik för Sverige* (Historical Statistics of Sweden). 1955 ff.—*Allmän månadsstatistik* (Monthly Digest of Swedish Statistics).—*Statistiska meddelanden* (Statistical Reports). From 1963

Henrekson, M., *An Economic Analysis of Swedish Government Expenditure.* Aldershot, 1992
Petersson, O., *Swedish Government and Politics.* Stockholm, 1994
Sveriges statskalender. Published by Vetenskapsakademien. Annual, from 1813
Turner, Barry, (ed.) *Scandinavia Profiled.* Macmillan, London, 2000

National library: Kungliga Biblioteket, Stockholm.
National statistical office: Statistics Sweden, S-115 81 Stockholm.
Website: http://www.scb.se/
Swedish Institute Website: http://www.si.se

SWITZERLAND

Schweizerische
Eidtgenossenschaft—
Confédération Suisse—
Confederazione Svizzera[1]

Capital: Berne
Population estimate, 2000: 7·29m.
GDP per capita, 2000: (PPP$) 28,769
HDI/world rank: 0·928/11

KEY HISTORICAL EVENTS

The history of Switzerland can be traced back to Aug. 1291 when the Uri, Schwyz and Unterwalden entered into a defensive league. In 1353 the league included 8 members and in 1515, 13. In 1648 the league became formally independent of the Holy Roman Empire. No addition was made to the number of cantons until 1798 in which year, under the influence of France, the unified Helvetic Republic was formed. This failed to satisfy the Swiss and in 1803 Napoleon granted a new constitution and increased the number of cantons to 19. In 1815 the perpetual neutrality of Switzerland and the inviolability of her territory were guaranteed by Austria, France, Great Britain, Portugal, Prussia, Spain and Sweden, and the Federal Pact, which included three new cantons, was accepted by the Congress of Vienna. In 1848 a new constitution was approved. The 22 cantons set up a federal government (consisting of a federal parliament and a federal council) and a federal tribunal. This constitution, in turn, was on 29 May 1874 superseded by the present constitution, which also combines the federal principle with a national and local use of referendums. Female franchise dates only from Feb. 1971. In a national referendum held in Sept. 1978, 69·9% voted in favour of the establishment of a new canton, Jura, which was established on 1 Jan. 1979.

Switzerland was neutral in both world wars. After the First World War, it joined the League of Nations, which was based in Geneva. But after the Second World War neutrality was thought to conflict with membership of the UN, though Switzerland participates in its agencies, and since 1948 has been a contracting party to the Statute of the International Court of Justice. In March 2001 a referendum on whether to begin immediate talks on joining the European Union was rejected, with 76·7% of voters against. But in a referendum in March 2002 Switzerland did vote to join the UN, with 54·6% of voters in favour of membership.

TERRITORY AND POPULATION

Switzerland is bounded in the west and northwest by France, north by Germany, east by Austria and south by Italy. Area and population by canton (with date of establishment):

Canton	Area (sq. km) (31 Dec. 1997)	Census Population (1 Dec. 1980)	Population Estimate (31 Dec. 2001)
Uri (1291)	1,077	33,883	35,000
Schwyz (1291)	908	97,354	131,400
Obwalden (1291)	491	25,865	32,700
Nidwalden (1291)	276	28,617	38,600
Lucerne (1332)	1,494	296,159	350,600
Zürich (1351)	1,729	1,122,839	1,228,600
Glarus (Glaris) (1352)	685	36,718	38,300
Zug (1352)	239	75,930	100,900
Fribourg (Freiburg) (1481)	1,671	185,246	239,100
Solothurn (Soleure) (1481)	791	218,102	245,500
Basel-Town (Bâle-V.) (1501)	37	203,915	186,700
Basel-Country (Bâle-C.) (1501)	518	219,822	261,400
Schaffhausen (Schaffhouse) (1501)	298	69,413	73,400
Appenzell-Outer Rhoden (1513)	243	47,611	53,200

[1]The Latin 'Confoederatio Helvetica' is also in use.

Canton	Area (sq. km) (31 Dec. 1997)	Census Population (1 Dec. 1980)	Population Estimate (31 Dec. 2001)
Appenzell-Inner Rhoden (1513)	173	12,844	15,000
Berne (1553)	5,959	912,022	947,100
St Gallen (St Gall) (1803)	2,026	391,995	452,600
Graubünden (Grisons) (1803)	7,105	164,641	185,700
Aargau (Argovie) (1803)	1,404	453,442	550,900
Thurgau (Thurgovie) (1803)	991	183,795	228,200
Ticino (Tessin) (1803)	2,812	265,899	311,900
Vaud (Waadt) (1803)	3,212	528,747	626,200
Valais (Wallis) (1815)	5,224	218,707	278,200
Neuchâtel (Neuenburg) (1815)	803	158,368	166,500
Geneva (1815)	282	349,040	414,300
Jura (1979)	838	64,986	69,100
Total	41,284	6,365,960	7,261,200

In 1999 there were 3,663,700 females and 1,406,600 resident foreign nationals. In 2000 foreign nationals made up 19·3% of the population, one of the highest proportions in western Europe. In 1999, 67·7% of the population lived in urban areas. Population density in 1997 was 172 per sq. km. The population at the 2000 census was 7,288,010.

The UN gives a projected population for 2010 of 7·07m.

German, French and Italian are the official languages; Romansch (spoken mostly in Graubünden), hitherto a national language, was upgraded to 'semi-official' in 1996. German is spoken by the majority of inhabitants in 19 of the 26 cantons, French in Fribourg, Vaud, Valais, Neuchâtel, Jura and Geneva, and Italian in Ticino. At the 1990 census 63·6% of the population gave German as their mother tongue, 19·2% French, 7·6% Italian, 0·6% Romansch and 8·9% other languages. 1997 statistics were 65% German, 18·4% French, 9·8% Italian and 0·8% Romansch.

At the end of 2001 the five largest cities were Zürich (340,900); Geneva (176,000); Basle (164,900); Berne (122,500); Lausanne (115,600). At the end of 1999 the population figures of conurbations were: Zürich, 943,400; Geneva, 457,500; Basle, 401,600; Berne, 319,100; Lausanne, 288,100; other towns, 1999 (and their conurbations), Winterthur, 88,000 (119,700); St Gallen, 69,800 (132,500); Lucerne, 57,000 (181,400); Biel, 48,800 (84,200).

SOCIAL STATISTICS
Statistics for calendar years:

	Live births	Marriages	Divorces	Deaths
1996	83,007	40,649	16,172	62,627
1997	80,584	39,102	17,073	62,839
1998	78,949	38,683	17,868	62,569
1999	78,408	40,645	20,809	62,503
2000	78,458	...	10,511	62,528

Rates (1999, per 1,000 population): birth, 11·0; death, 8·7; marriage, 5·7; divorce, 2·9. In 1998 the most popular age range for marrying was 25–29 for both males and females. Expectation of life, 1999: males, 75·6 years; females, 82·0. Over the period 1990–95 the suicide rate per 100,000 population was 22·7 (men, 34·3; women, 11·6). Annual population growth rate, 1990–99, 0·8%. Infant mortality, 1999, 4·6 per 1,000 live births; fertility rate, 1999, 1·5 births per woman. In 1998 Switzerland received 41,200 asylum applications, equivalent to 5·75 per 1,000 inhabitants (the highest rate of any European country). In 1999 the number of applications rose to 46,130.

CLIMATE
The climate is largely dictated by relief and altitude, and includes continental and mountain types. Summers are generally warm, with quite considerable rainfall; winters are fine, with clear, cold air. Berne, Jan. 32°F (0°C), July, 65°F (18·5°C). Annual rainfall 39·4" (986 mm).

CONSTITUTION AND GOVERNMENT
A new Constitution was accepted on 18 April 1999 in a popular vote and came into effect on 1 Jan. 2000, replacing the constitution dating from 1874. Switzerland is a

republic. The highest authority is vested in the electorate, i.e., all Swiss citizens over 18. This electorate, besides electing its representatives to the Parliament, has the voting power on amendments to, or on the revision of, the Constitution as well as on Switzerland joining international organizations for collective security or supranational communities (mandatory referendum). It also takes decisions on laws and certain international treaties if requested by 50,000 voters or eight cantons (facultative referendum), and it has the right of initiating constitutional amendments, the support required for such demands being 100,000 voters (popular initiative). The Swiss vote in more referendums—three or four a year—than any other nation. A mandatory referendum and a Constitutional amendment demanded by popular initiative require a double majority (a majority of the voters and a majority of the cantons voting in favour of the proposal) to be accepted while a facultative referendum is accepted if a majority of the voters vote in favour of the proposal. Between 1971 and 2000, 85 initiatives were put to the vote but only five were adopted. Turn-out had dropped from a peak of 80·5% in 1933 to 43·8% in 2000.

The Federal government is responsible for legislating matters of foreign relations, defence (within the framework of its powers), professional education and technical universities, protection of the environment, water, public works, road traffic, nuclear energy, foreign trade, social security, residence and domicile of foreigners, civil law, banking and insurance, monetary policy and economic development. It is also responsible for formulating policy concerning statistics gathering, sport, forests, fishery and hunting, post and telecommunications, radio and television, private economic activity, competition policy, alcohol and gambling.

The legislative authority is vested in a parliament of two chambers: the Council of States (*Ständerat/Conseil des États*) and the National Council (*Nationalrat/ Conseil National*). The Council of States is composed of 46 members, chosen and paid by the 23 cantons of the Confederation, two for each canton. The mode of their election and the term of membership depend on the canton. Three of the cantons are politically divided—Basle into Town and Country, Appenzell into Outer-Rhoden and Inner-Rhoden, and Unterwalden into Obwalden and Nidwalden. Each of these 'half-cantons' sends one member to the State Council. The Swiss parliament is a militia/semi-professional parliament.

The National Council has 200 members directly elected for four years, in proportion to the population of the cantons, with the proviso that each canton or half-canton is represented by at least one member. The members are paid from federal funds. The parliament sits for at least four ordinary three-week sessions annually. Extraordinary sessions can be held if necessary and if demanded by the Federal Council, 25% of the National Council or five cantons.

The 200 seats are distributed among the cantons according to population size:

Zürich	34	Thurgau (Thurgovie)	6
Berne	27	Graubünden (Grisons)	5
Vaud (Waadt)	17	Neuchâtel (Neuenburg)	5
Aargau (Argovie)	15	Schwyz	3
St Gallen (St Gall)	12	Zug	3
Geneva	11	Schaffhausen (Schaffhouse)	2
Lucerne	10	Appenzell Outer-Rhoden	2
Ticino (Tessin)	8	Jura	2
Solothurn (Soleure)	7	Uri	1
Basel-Country (Bâle-C.)	7	Obwalden	1
Valais (Wallis)	7	Nidwalden	1
Basel-Town (Bâle-V.)	6	Glarus	1
Fribourg (Freiburg)	6	Appenzell Inner-Rhoden	1

A general election takes place by ballot every four years. Every citizen of the republic who has entered on his 18th year is entitled to a vote, and any voter may be elected a deputy. Laws passed by both chambers may be submitted to direct popular vote, when 50,000 citizens or eight cantons demand it; the vote can be only 'Yes' or 'No'. This principle, called the *referendum*, is frequently acted on.

The chief executive authority is deputed to the *Bundesrat*, or Federal Council, consisting of seven members, elected for four years by the *United Federal Assembly*, i.e., joint sessions of both chambers, such as to represent both the different geographical regions and language communities. The members of this council must not hold any other office in the Confederation or cantons, nor engage in any calling or business. In the Federal Parliament legislation may be introduced either by a member, or by either chamber, or by the Federal Council (but not by the people). Every citizen who has a vote for the National Council is eligible to become a member of the executive.

The *President* of the Federal Council (called President of the Confederation) and the Vice-President are the first magistrates of the Confederation. Both are elected by the United Federal Assembly for one calendar year from among the Federal Councillors, and are not immediately re-eligible to the same offices. The Vice-President, however, may be, and usually is, elected to succeed the outgoing President.

The seven members of the Federal Council act as ministers, or chiefs of the seven administrative departments of the republic. The city of Berne is the seat of the Federal Council and the central administrative authorities.

National Anthem. 'Trittst im Morgenrot daher'/'Sur nos monts quand le soleil'/'Quando il ciel' di porpora' ('Step into the rosy dawn'); German words by Leonard Widmer, French by C. Chatelanat, Italian by C. Valsangiacomo, tune by Alberik Zwyssig.

RECENT ELECTIONS
In the parliamentary elections of 24 Oct. 1999 the Social Democratic Party of Switzerland (SPS) won 51 seats (22·5% of the vote), the Swiss People's Party/Democratic Centre Union (SPPDCU) won 44 seats (22·6%), the Radicals (FDP) 43 seats (19·9%), the Christian Democratic People's Party (CDP) 35 (15·8%) and the Greens 9 (5%). There were ten other parties with six seats or fewer. In the Council of States, the Radicals held 18 seats, the Christian Democratic People's Party 15, the Swiss People's Party/Democratic Centre Union 7 and the Social Democratic Party of Switzerland 6.

At the presidential election held in the United Federal Assembly on 4 Dec. 2002 Pascal Couchepin was elected president.

Parliamentary elections are scheduled to take place on 19 Oct. 2003.

CURRENT ADMINISTRATION
President of the Confederation and Chief of the Department of Home Affairs: Pascal Couchepin; b. 1942 (FDP; sworn in 1 Jan. 2003).

Vice President and Chief of the Department of Justice and Police: Ruth Metzler-Arnold (CDP).

In March 2003 the Federal Council comprised:

Minister of Foreign Affairs: Micheline Calmy-Rey (SPS). *Finance:* Kaspar Villiger (FDP). *Defence, Civil Protection and Sports:* Samuel Schmid (SPPDCU). *Transport, Communications and Energy:* Moritz Leuenberger (SPS). *Economic Affairs:* Joseph Deiss (CDP).

Federal Authorities Website: http://www.admin.ch

DEFENCE
There are fortifications in all entrances to the Alps and on the important passes crossing the Alps and the Jura. Large-scale destruction of bridges, tunnels and defiles are prepared for an emergency.

In 2000 military expenditure totalled US$2,900m. (US$393 per capita), representing 1·2% of GDP.

Army. There are about 2,000 regular soldiers, but some 380,000 conscripts undergo training annually (15 weeks recruit training at 20; 10 refresher courses of 19 days every two years between 21 and 42). Proposals ('Army 95') implemented in 1995 envisaged an Armed Forces based on the three areas of promoting peace, defence and general civil affairs support. Troop levels will gradually be cut to 120,000. The Swiss Army Bicycle Brigade is scheduled for abolition before the end of 2003.

The administration of the Swiss Army is partly in the hands of the Cantonal authorities, who can promote officers up to the rank of captain. In peacetime the Army has no general; in time of war the Federal Assembly in joint session of both Houses appoints a general.

In 1999 for the first time a small Swiss contingent was deployed outside the country, in Kosovo, but without arms and under the protection of Austrian troops.

Navy. The Army includes a Marine force with patrol boats.

Air Force. The air force has three flying regiments. The fighter squadrons are equipped with Swiss-built F-5E Tiger IIs and Mirage IIIS/RS. Personnel (1999), 30,200 on mobilization, with 150 combat aircraft.

INTERNATIONAL RELATIONS
Switzerland is a member of the UN, WTO, BIS, OECD, the Council of Europe and the NATO Partnership for Peace, OSCE, EFTA, CERN, Inter-American Development Bank, Asian Development Bank, IOM, Antarctic Treaty and the International Organization of the Francophonie. In a referendum in 1986 the electorate voted against UN membership, but in a further referendum on 4 March 2002, 54·6% of votes cast were in favour of joining. Switzerland officially became a member at the UN's General Assembly in Sept. 2002. An official application for membership of the EU was made in May 1992, but in Dec. 1992 the electorate voted against joining the European Economic Area. At a referendum in March 2001, 76·7% of voters rejected membership talks with the EU, with just 23·3% in favour; turn-out was 55·1%. However, the government reaffirmed plans to begin entry talks by 2007.

ECONOMY
Agriculture accounted for 2% of GDP in 1998, industry 31% and services 67%.

According to the anti-corruption organization *Transparency International*, Switzerland ranked equal 12th in the world in a 2002 survey of the countries with the least corruption in business and government. It received 8·5 out of 10 in the annual index.

Overview. Switzerland is a small but open economy with one of the highest living standards in the world. Owing to a lack of raw materials, prosperity is built on labour skills and technological expertise. Earnings from services include tourism and banking. High labour costs and product market rigidities in the sheltered economy pose problems of competitiveness. In 2000 the National Bank introduced a monetary policy framework, aiming at keeping inflation below 2%. Monetary independence is crucial to Switzerland, as it permits lower interest rates than those prevailing in the euro zone to give Swiss companies a competitive advantage.

Currency. The unit of currency is the *Swiss franc* (CHF) of 100 *centimes* or *Rappen*. Foreign exchange reserves were US$33,309m. and gold reserves 66·24m. troy oz in June 2002 (83·28m. troy oz in March 2000). Inflation was 1·0% in 2001. Total money supply in June 2002 was 171,584m. Swiss francs.

Budget. Government revenue and expenditure in millions of Swiss francs, years ending 31 Dec.:

	1995	1996	1997	1998	1999
Revenue	84,627	87,080	87,946	94,153	93,293
Expenditure	96,791	101,469	103,528	107,454	107,526

VAT is 7·6%, with reduced rates of 3·6% and 2·4%.

Performance. Total GDP was US$247·4bn. in 2001. Real GDP growth in 1999 was 1·5%, but in 2000 growth reached 3·2%, the highest for ten years. For 2001 growth of 0·9% was recorded. In 1999 the current account surplus was 44,996m. Swiss francs. Switzerland's current account surplus is nearly 13% of GDP.

Banking and Finance. The National Bank, with headquarters divided between Berne and Zürich, opened on 20 June 1907. It has the exclusive right to issue banknotes. The *Chairman* is Jean-Pierre Roth.

On 31 Dec. 2000 there were 375 banks with total assets of 2,124,880m. Swiss francs. They included 24 cantonal banks, 3 big banks, 103 regional and saving banks, 1 *Raiffeisen* (consisting of 537 member banks) and 244 other banks. The number of banks has come down from over 495 in 1990. In 2001 the largest banks in order of capitalization were UBS (US$60·4bn.) and Crédit Suisse Groupe (US$52·3bn.), ranked third and sixth in Europe by market capitalization respectively. Banking and finance is one of Switzerland's most successful industries, and contributes 7·1% of the country's GDP and 11·2% of the GDP's added values (1998). Switzerland is the capital of the offshore private banking industry. It is reckoned that a third of the internationally invested private assets worldwide are managed by Swiss banks.

Money laundering was made a criminal offence in Aug. 1990. Complete secrecy about clients' accounts remains intact, but anonymity was abolished in July 1991.

The stock exchange system has been reformed under federal legislation of 1990 on securities trading and capital market services. The four smaller exchanges have been closed and activity concentrated on the major exchanges of Zürich, Basle and Geneva, which harmonized their operations with the introduction of the Swiss Electronic Exchange (EBS) in Dec. 1995. Zürich is a major international insurance centre.

In Aug. 1998 Crédit Suisse and UBS AG agreed a deal to pay US$1·25bn. (£750m.) to Holocaust survivors over a three-year-period in an out-of-court settlement. The deal brought to an end the issue of money left in Holocaust victims' Swiss Bank accounts which were allowed to remain dormant after the war.

Weights and Measures. The metric system is legal.

ENERGY AND NATURAL RESOURCES

Environment. In 1998, according to the *World Bank Atlas,* carbon dioxide emissions were the equivalent of 5·9 tonnes per capita. An *Environmental Sustainability Index* compiled for the World Economic Forum meeting in Feb. 2002 ranked Switzerland fifth in the world, with 66·5%. The index measured the ability of countries to maintain favourable environmental conditions and examined various factors including pollution levels and the use or abuse of natural resources.

Switzerland is the world leader in recycling. In 1998, 52% of all household waste was recycled, including 91% of glass and 89% of aluminium cans (in both cases the highest percentage of any country).

Electricity. The Energy 2000 programme aims to stabilize consumption. Installed capacity was 16·4m. kW in 1999. Production was 166·7bn. kWh in 1999. 35·6% of energy produced was nuclear, 35·9% hydro-electric from storage power stations, 25·6% hydro-electric from turbine power stations and 3·8% from conventional thermal. In Sept. 1990, 54% of citizens voted for a ten-year moratorium on the construction of new nuclear plants. There are currently five nuclear reactors in use. Consumption per capita in 1998 was 7,148 kWh.

Minerals. Approximately 6,000 people work in mining and quarrying. Salt production, 1997: 400,000 tonnes.

Agriculture. The country is self-sufficient in wheat and meat. Agriculture is protected by subsidies, price guarantees and import controls. Farmers are guaranteed an income equal to industrial workers. Agriculture occupied 5·9% of the total workforce in 1996. In 1999 there were 293,949 ha of open arable land, 115,933 ha of cultivated grassland and 608,798 ha of natural grassland and pastures. In 1999 there were 12,921 ha of vineyards. In 1999 there were 73,591 farms (41% in mountain or hill regions), of which 5,258 were under 1 ha, 18,154 over 20 ha, and 23,300 in part-time use (1996). Approximately 7·8% of all agricultural land is used for organic farming—one of the highest proportions in the world.

Area harvested, 1999 (in 1,000 ha): cereals, 182; coarse grains, 89; sugarbeets, 17; potatoes, 14. Production, 2000 (in 1,000 tonnes): sugarbeets, 1,410; potatoes, 584; wheat, 548; barley, 273; maize, 209; carrots, 56; rapeseed, 39. Fruit production (in 1,000 tonnes) in 2000 was: apples, 380; grapes, 165; pears, 130. Wine is produced in 25 of the cantons. In 2000 vineyards produced 128,000 tonnes of wine.

Livestock, 2000: cattle, 1,600,000; pigs, 1,450,000; horses, 45,000; sheep, 450,000; goats, 65,000; chickens, 7m. Livestock products, 2000 (in 1,000 tonnes): meat, 415; milk, 3,910; cheese, 155.

Forestry. The forest area was 1,212,570 ha in 1997 (29·4% of the land area). In 1999, 5·0m. cu. metres of roundwood were cut.

Fisheries. Total catch, 2000, 1,659 tonnes, exclusively freshwater fish.

INDUSTRY

The leading companies by market capitalization in Switzerland, excluding banking and finance, in Jan. 2002 were: Novartis AG (160bn. Swiss francs,), a pharmaceuticals company; Nestlé SA (146bn. Swiss francs,), a world leader in food and beverages; and Roche AG (97bn. Swiss francs,), a healthcare company.

There were 347,500 firms in 1991, of which 84·9% employed fewer than 10 persons. The chief food producing industries, based on Swiss agriculture, are the manufacture of cheese, butter, sugar and meat. Among the other industries, the manufacture of textiles, clothing and footwear, chemicals and pharmaceutical products, the production of machinery (including electrical machinery and scientific and optical instruments) and watch and clock making are the most important.

Labour. In 2002 the total working population was 3,634,000, of whom 690,000 people were in manufacturing, 624,000 in trade, 398,000 in property, renting and business activities, and 397,000 in health and social services. In Feb. 2003 the unemployment rate stood at 3·9%; in the canton of Uri the rate was just 1·3%. Unemployment halved between 1997 and 2001. In 1997, 86% of men and 69% of women between the ages of 15 and 64 were in employment. No other major industrialized nation had such a high percentage of men in employment.

The foreign labour force with permit of temporary residence was 939,000 in Aug. 1995 (326,600 women). Of these 261,400 were Italian, 146,700 Yugoslav, 108,600 French, 103,400 Portuguese and 89,600 German. In 1997 approximately 800,000 EU citizens worked in Switzerland.

Trade Unions. The Swiss Federation of Trade Unions had about 419,000 members in 1996.

INTERNATIONAL TRADE

Legislation of 1991 increased the possibilities of foreign ownership of domestic companies.

Imports and Exports. Imports and exports, excluding gold (bullion and coins) and silver (coins), were (in 1m. Swiss francs):

	1997	1998	1999	2000	2001
Imports	110,087	115,847	120,057	139,402	141,889
Exports	110,417	114,055	120,725	136,015	138,492

In 2001 the EU accounted for 76·2% of imports (108·2bn. Swiss francs) and 60·0% of exports (83·1bn. Swiss francs). Main import suppliers in 2001 (share of total trade): Germany, 30·1%; France, 10·3%; Italy, 9·4%; USA, 5·9%; UK, 5·8%. Main export markets: Germany, 21·7%; USA, 11·3%; France, 8·9%; Italy, 8·0%; UK, 5·5%.

Main imports in 2001 (in 1m. Swiss francs): consumer goods, 51,805; equipment goods, 36,435; raw materials and semi-manufactures, 35,392.

Main exports in 2001 (in 1m. Swiss francs): chemicals, 41,833; machinery and electronics, 36,022; precision instruments, clocks and watches and jewellery, 21,641.

COMMUNICATIONS

Roads. In 1999 there were 71,149 km of roads, including 1,642 km of motorways, 18,110 km of cantonal roads and 51,397 km of local roads. Motor vehicles in 1999 (in 1,000): passenger cars, 3,467; commercial vehicles, 274; buses, 15; motorcycles, 464. Goods transport by road, 1998, totalled 19,504m. tonne-km. There were 75,351 road accidents (23,737 accidents involving personal injury) in 2000 with 592 fatalities. In 1990 there had been 954 fatalities.

Rail. In 1997 the length of the general traffic railways was 5,035 km, of which the Swiss Federal Railways (SBB) 3,007 km. In 1996 the Federal Railway carried 256m. passengers and 44·1m. tonnes of freight. In 2000 work began on what is set to be the world's longest rail tunnel—the 58-km long tunnel under the Gotthard mountain range in the Alps linking Erstfeld and Bodio. The tunnel is scheduled to open in 2006. There are tram/light rail networks in Basle, Berne, Geneva, Lausanne, Neuchâtel and Zürich. There are many other lines, the most important of which are the Berne–Lötschberg–Simplon (114 km) and Rhaetian (377 km) networks.

Civil Aviation. There are international airports at Basle (which also serves Mulhouse in France), Berne (Belp), Geneva (Cointrin), Lugano and Zürich. Swissair, the former national carrier, faced collapse and grounded flights in Oct. 2001. In 1998 it flew 218·8m. km, carrying 12,144,500 passengers (11,163,200 on international flights). In April 2002 a successor airline, swiss, took over as the national carrier. Crossair is the second largest airline, flying 39·1m. km in 1997 and carrying 1,735,900 passengers (1,352,300 on international flights). Services were also provided in 1998 by over 80 foreign airlines. Zürich is the busiest airport, handling 22,446,000 passengers in 2000 (21,192,000 on international flights) and 395,100 tonnes of freight. Geneva handled 7,677,000 passengers (6,604,000 on international flights) and 36,300 tonnes of freight in 2000.

Shipping. In 1997 there were 1,214 km of navigable waterways. 12·3m. tonnes of freight were transported. A merchant marine was created in 1941, the place of registry of its vessels being Basle. In 1998 it totalled 383,000 GRT.

Telecommunications. Switzerland had 5,235,000 main telephone lines in 2000 (726·7 per 1,000 persons) and there were 3·6m. PCs in use, equivalent to 499·7 per 1,000 population—one of the highest rates in the world. Mobile phone subscribers numbered 3·8m. in Nov. 2000 and there were 3·85m. Internet users in June 2002. There were 207,000 fax machines in 1996.

Postal Services. In 1995 there were 3,674 post offices, or one for every 1,920 persons.

SOCIAL INSTITUTIONS

Justice. The Federal Court, which sits at Lausanne, consists of 30 judges and 30 supplementary judges, elected by the Federal Assembly for six years and eligible for re-election; the President and Vice-President serve for two years and re-election is not practised. The Tribunal has original and final jurisdiction in suits between the Confederation and cantons; between different cantons; between the Confederation or cantons and corporations or individuals; between parties who refer their case to it; or in suits which the constitution or legislation of cantons places within its authority. It is a court of appeal against decisions of other federal authorities, and of cantonal authorities applying federal laws. The Tribunal comprises two courts of public law, two civil courts, a chamber of bankruptcy, a chamber of prosecution, a court of criminal appeal, a court of extraordinary appeal and a federal criminal court.

A Federal Insurance Court sits in Lucerne, and comprises nine judges and nine supplementary judges elected for six years by the Federal Assembly.

A federal penal code replaced cantonal codes in 1942. It abolished capital punishment except for offences in wartime; this latter proviso was abolished in 1992.

There were 70,336 adult criminal convictions in 1999 (85·6% males; 47·4% foreign).

Religion. There is liberty of conscience and of creed. At the 1990 census 46·1% of the population were Roman Catholic, 40·0% Protestant and 7·4% without religion. In 1997 the figures were estimated to be: Roman Catholics, 3,280,000; Protestants, 2,850,000; other, 990,000.

Education. Education is administered by the confederation, cantons and communes and is free and compulsory for nine years. Compulsory education consists of four years (Basel-Town and Vaud), five years (Aargau, Basel-Country, Neuchâtel and Ticino) or six years (other cantons) of primary education, and the balance in Stage I secondary education. This is followed by three to five years of Stage II secondary education in general or vocational schools. Tertiary education is at universities, universities of applied science, higher vocational schools and advanced vocational training institutes.

In 1999–2000 there were 157,751 children in pre-primary schools. There were 807,101 pupils in compulsory education (475,044 at primary, 283,317 at lower secondary and 48,740 at special schools), 94,481 in Stage II general secondary education and 208,497 in Stage II vocational education, and 116,511 students in higher education, including 95,657 students at universities and 16,749 at universities of applied sciences.

There are ten universities (date of foundation and students in 1999–2000): Basle (1460, 7,783), Berne (1528, 10,127), Fribourg (1889, 8,900), Geneva (1559, 12,873), Lausanne (1537, 9,762), Lucerne (16th century, 251); Neuchâtel (1866, 3,256), St Gallen (1899, 4,549), Ticino (1996, 1,191), Zürich (1523, 20,360); and three institutions of equivalent status: St Gallen PHS (1867, 312), Federal Institute of Technology Lausanne (1853, 4,841), Federal Institute of Technology Zürich (1854, 11,492). The seven universities of applied sciences were founded in 1997. Enrolment figures for 1999–2000 were: Berne, 2,416; Western Switzerland, 4,236; Northwestern Switzerland, 2,266; Central Switzerland, 1,009; Ticino, 658; Eastern Switzerland, 1,748; Zürich, 4,416.

In 1998 total expenditure on education came to 20,759m. Swiss francs, or 5·5% of GNP, and represented 17·5% of total government expenditure. The adult literacy rate is at least 99%.

Health. In 1998 there were an estimated 23,700 doctors (one for every 301 persons) and there were 1,651 pharmacies. There were 3,470 dentists in 1998. Hospital bed provision in 1998 was 64 for every 10,000 persons.

In 1998 the Swiss smoked an average 2,734 cigarettes per person.

New cases of infectious diseases, 1997: tuberculosis, 747; malaria, 257; AIDS, 310.

In 2000 Switzerland spent 10·7% of its GDP on health—the highest percentage of any European country.

Although active euthanasia is illegal in Switzerland, doctors may help patients die if they have given specific consent.

Welfare. The Federal Insurance Law against accident and illness, of 13 June 1911, entitled all citizens to insurance against illness; foreigners could also be admitted to the benefits. Major reform of the law was ratified in 1994 and came into effect in 1996, making it compulsory for all citizens. Subsidies are paid by the Confederation and the Cantons only for insured persons with low incomes. Also compulsory are the Old-Age and Survivors' Insurance (OASI, since 1948), Invalidity Insurance (II, since 1960) and Accident Insurance (1984/1996). Unemployment Insurance (1984) and Occupational benefit plans (Second Pillar, 1985) are compulsory for employees only.

The following amounts (in 1m. Swiss francs) were paid in social security benefits:

	1996	1997	1998
Federal Old-Age Pensions	24,817	25,803	26,731
Federal Invalidity Insurance	7,313	7,652	7,965
Supplementary Benefits (OASI/II)	1,326	1,376	1,420
Occupational benefit plans	26,110[1]	27,300	28,688[1]
Loss of Earnings Insurance	621	582	558
Unemployment Insurance	6,124	8,028[2]	6,208[2]
Family Allowances	4,100	4,263	4,316
Sickness Insurance	17,192	17,672	18,403
Accident Insurance for employees	5,887	6,060	5,975

[1]Federal Office for Social Insurances estimate. [2]Provisional.

CULTURE

Broadcasting. Schweizerische Radio- und Fernsehgesellschaft/Société Suisse de Radiodiffusion et Télévision/Società Svizzera di Radiotelevisione is a non-profit-making company responsible for radio and television services. There are German, French and Italian radio and TV networks (colour by PAL). The German radio service has three programmes, local programmes and also broadcasts in Romansch; the French service ('Suisse Romande') has three programmes, as does the Italian. There is an external service, Swiss Radio International (Arabic, English, Spanish) and four city-based private stations. The UN and the Red Cross have radio stations. There were 3·8m. TV sets in use in 1997 and 7m. radio receivers in 1996. More than 90% of households have cable TV—in 1999 there were 2·62m. TV licences altogether and 2·39m. cable TV subscribers.

Cinema. There were 482 cinemas in 1999; total attendance for the year was 15·4m. 75 films were produced in 1999.

Press. There were 78 daily newspapers in 2000 with a total circulation of 2,628,600 (365 per 1,000 population). There were 120 non-daily papers with a combined circulation of 1,196,000 in 1999 (168 per 1,000 population). 13,694 book titles were published in 1999.

Tourism. Tourism is an important industry. In 1999 there were 7,167,000 foreign tourists staying in hotels and health establishments, bringing revenue of US$7·7bn. In 1999 overnight stays by tourists totalled 67,772,000. 12·01m. Swiss citizens travelled abroad in 1999.

Festivals. The Lucerne Festival is one of Europe's leading cultural events and since 2001 has been split into three festivals: Ostern during Lent, Sommer in Aug.–Sept. and Piano in Nov. The 2002 festivals were attended by a total of 102,800 people.

Libraries. In 1999 there was one National library with 3,109,000 volumes and 12,466 registered users, and 34 non-specialized libraries with 8,886,000 volumes and 472,217 users. In 1998 there were 9 higher education libraries with 23,090,000 volumes and 186,232 users; and in 1998 approximately 6,000 libraries in total.

Museums and Galleries. In 1999 there were 929 museums.

DIPLOMATIC REPRESENTATIVES

Of Switzerland in the United Kingdom (16–18 Montagu Pl., London, W1H 2BQ)
Ambassador: Bruno Max Spinner.

Of the United Kingdom in Switzerland (Thunstrasse 50, 3005 Berne)
Ambassador: Basil Eastwood, CMG.

Of Switzerland in the USA (2900 Cathedral Ave., NW, Washington, D.C., 20008)
Ambassador: Christian Blickenstorfer.

Of the USA in Switzerland (Jubilaeumstrasse 93, 3005, Berne)
Ambassador: Mercer Reynolds.

Of Switzerland to the United Nations
Ambassador: Jenö C. A. Staehelin.

Of Switzerland to the European Union
Ambassador: Dante Martinelli.

FURTHER READING

Office Fédéral de la Statistique. *Annuaire Statistique de la Suisse.*

New, M., *Switzerland Unwrapped: Exposing the Myths.* London, 1997

National library: Bibliothèque Nationale Suisse, Hallwylstr. 15, 3003 Berne.
National statistical office: Office Fédéral de la Statistique, Schwarztorstr. 96, 3003 Berne.
SFSO Information Service e-mail: *information@bfs.admin.ch*
Website: http://www.statistik.admin.ch/

SYRIA

Jumhuriya al-Arabya
as-Suriya
(Syrian Arab Republic)

Capital: Damascus
Population estimate, 2000: 16·19m.
GDP per capita, 2000: (PPP$) 3,556
HDI/world rank: 0·691/108

KEY HISTORICAL EVENTS

Syria was under Turkish control from the 12th century and part of the Ottoman Empire from the 16th century until the First World War. Following the defeat of the Turks, the League of Nations granted France a mandate for Syria from 1920. On 27 Sept. 1941 Gen. Catroux, the Free French C.-in-C., proclaimed the independence of Syria. The evacuation of all foreign troops in April 1946 marked the complete independence of Syria, but the political situation was unsettled and military coups were staged in Dec. 1949 and in Feb. 1954. Syria merged with Egypt to form the United Arab Republic from 2 Feb. 1958 until 29 Sept. 1961, when Syrian independence was resumed following a coup. Following the fifth coup of the decade, Lieut.-Gen. Hafiz al-Assad became prime minister on 13 Nov. 1970 and assumed the presidency on 22 Feb. 1971. A new constitution, approved by plebiscite on 12 March 1973, confirmed the Arab Socialist Renaissance (Ba'ath) Party as the 'leading party in the state and society'.

TERRITORY AND POPULATION

Syria is bounded by the Mediterranean and Lebanon in the west, by Israel and Jordan in the south, by Iraq in the east and by Turkey in the north. The frontier between Syria and Turkey was settled by the Franco-Turkish agreement of 22 June 1929. The area is 185,180 sq. km (71,498 sq. miles). The census of 1994 gave a population of 13,782,000. Estimate (1997), 14,972,000 (54·0% urban, 1999); density, 81 per sq. km.

The UN gives a projected population for 2010 of 20·78m.

Area and population (1996 estimate, in 1,000) of the 14 districts *(mohafaza)*:

	Sq. km	Population		Sq. km	Population
Aleppo	18,500	3,694	Homs	42,223	1,471
Damascus (City)	105	1,347	Idlib	6,097	1,270
Damascus (District)	18,032	1,237	Lattakia	2,297	936
Dará	3,730	689	Qunaytirah	1,861	330
Deir Ez-Zor	33,060	994	Raqqah	19,616	592
Hama	8,883	1,415	Suwaydá	5,550	380
Hasakah	23,334	1,013	Tartous	1,892	730

The capital is Damascus, with a 1999 population of 2,270,000. Other principal towns (population, 1994 in 1,000): Aleppo, 1,840 (1995); Homs, 558; Lattakia, 303; Hama, 273; Al-Kamishli, 165; Raqqah, 138; Deir Ez-Zor, 133.

Arabic is the official language, spoken by 89% of the population, while 6% speak Kurdish (chiefly Hasakah governorate), 3% Armenian and 2% other languages.

SOCIAL STATISTICS

1997 births, estimate, 625,000; deaths, 92,000. Rates, 1997 estimate (per 1,000 population): birth, 38·7; death, 5·7. Infant mortality, 1999 (per 1,000 live births), 25. Expectation of life, 1999, was 69·8 years for males and 72·1 for females. Annual population growth rate, 1990–99, 2·7%. Fertility rate, 1999, 3·9 births per woman.

CLIMATE

The climate is Mediterranean in type, with mild wet winters and dry, hot summers, though there are variations in temperatures and rainfall between the coastal regions and the interior, which even includes desert conditions. The more mountainous parts are subject to snowfall. Damascus, Jan. 38·1°F (3·4°C), July 77·4°F (25·2°C). Annual

1544

rainfall 8·8" (217 mm). Aleppo, Jan. 36·7°F (2·6°C), July 80·4°F (26·9°C). Annual rainfall 10·2" (258 mm). Homs, Jan. 38·7°F (3·7°C), July 82·4°F (28°C). Annual rainfall 3·4" (86·7 mm).

CONSTITUTION AND GOVERNMENT
A new Constitution was approved by plebiscite on 12 March 1973 and promulgated on 14 March. It confirmed the Arab Socialist Renaissance *(Ba'ath)* Party, in power since 1963, as the 'leading party in the State and society'. Legislative power is held by a 250-member People's Assembly *(Majlis al-Sha'ab)*, renewed every four years in 15 multi-seat constituencies, in which 167 seats are guaranteed for the Al Jabha al Watniyah at Wahdwamiyah (JWW/National Progressive Front) alliance of parties (i.e. the Ba'ath party and partners). The government is formed by the Ba'ath.

The president is appointed by the Parliament and is confirmed for a seven-year term in a referendum. At a referendum on 10 July 2000 Bashar Al-Assad (b. 1965) was confirmed as *President* following the death of his father, who had been president since 1971.

National Anthem. 'Humata al Diyari al aykum salaam' ('Defenders of the Realm, on you be peace'); words by Khalil Mardam Bey, tune by M. S. and A. S. Flayfel.

RECENT ELECTIONS
Elections were held on 5 March 2003. The ruling National Progressive Front (led by the Ba'ath Party) won 167 of 250 seats and non-partisan candidates the remaining 83. Turn-out was 63%.

CURRENT ADMINISTRATION
Following the death of Lieut.-Gen. Hafiz al-Assad on 10 June 2000, a presidential referendum was held on 10 July 2000. The former president's son Bashar Al-Assad won 97·3% of the vote.

President: Bashar Al-Assad; b. 1965 (Ba'ath; sworn in 17 July 2000).

Vice-Presidents: Abd al-Halim ibn Said Khaddam, Mohammad Zuhayr Mashariqa.

In March 2003 the government comprised:

Prime Minister: Mohammed Mustafa Miro; b. 1941 (Ba'ath; sworn in 13 March 2000).

Deputy Prime Minister and Minister of Defence: Lieut.-Gen. Mustafa Talas; *Deputy Prime Minister for Economic Affairs:* Muhammad al-Hussein; *Deputy Prime Minister for Services Affairs:* Mohammad Naji Otri; *Deputy Prime Minister for Foreign Affairs:* Farouq al-Shara.

Minister of Education: Dr Mahmud al-Sayyid. *Higher Education:* Dr Hassan Rishah. *Interior:* Maj.-Gen. Ali Hammoud. *Information:* Adnan Umran. *Local Government:* Hilal al-Atrash. *Supply and Internal Trade:* Bassam Muhammad Rustom. *Transport:* Makram Ubayd. *Labour and Social Welfare:* Ghada al-Jabi. *Economy and Foreign Trade:* Dr Ghassan al-Rifai. *Culture:* Najwa Qassab Hassan. *Tourism:* Dr Saadallah Agha al-Qallaa. *Health:* Dr Mohammad Iyad al-Shatti. *Irrigation:* Muhammad Radwan Martini. *Electricity:* Munib bin Assad Saim al-Dahar. *Oil and Mineral Resources:* Ibrahim Haddad. *Construction:* Husam al-Aswad. *Housing:* Ayman Wanly. *Agriculture and Agrarian Reform:* Nouriddin Mina. *Finance:* Muhammad al-Atrash. *Justice:* Nabil al-Khatib. *Industry:* Dr Issam al-Za'im. *Presidential Affairs:* Haytham Duwayhi. *Awqaf:* Mohammad bin-abd-al-Rauf Ziyadah. *Communications:* Bashir al-Munajed.

The President's Website: http://www.assad.org

DEFENCE
Military service is compulsory for a period of 30 months. Defence expenditure in 2000 totalled US$760m. (US$47 per capita), representing 5·6% of GDP. According to *Deadly Arsenals*, published by the Carnegie Endowment for International Peace, Syria has a chemical weapons programme and a biological weapons research programme.

Army. Strength (1999) about 215,000 (including conscripts) with an additional 300,000 available reservists. In addition there is a gendarmerie of 8,000 and a Workers Militia of approximately 100,000.

Navy. The Navy includes three diesel submarines and two small frigates. A small naval aviation branch of the Air Force operates anti-submarine helicopters. Personnel in 1999 numbered approximately 6,000. The main base is at Tartous.

Air Force. The Air Force, including Air Defence Command, had (1999) about 40,000 personnel, over 589 combat aircraft and 72 armed helicopters, including 170 MiG-21, 134 MiG-23, 30 MiG-25 and 20 MiG-29 supersonic interceptors. In addition there were 90 Su-22 and 20 Su-24 fighter-bombers, as well as some MiG-25 reconnaissance aircraft.

INTERNATIONAL RELATIONS

A Treaty of Brotherhood, Co-operation and Co-ordination with Lebanon of May 1991 provides for close relations in the fields of foreign policy, the economy, military affairs and security. By the treaty the Lebanese government's decisions are subject to review by six joint Syrian-Lebanese bodies.

Syria is a member of the UN, the League of Arab States and the OIC.

ECONOMY

In 1997 agriculture accounted for 26% of GDP, industry 21% and services 53%.

Overview. The relaxation of state control and foreign exchange regulations in response to the 1980s' recession has led to a consumer boom. Since 1991 the proportion of the economy in private hands has risen from 35% to 70%, but further reforms have stalled.

Currency. The monetary unit is the *Syrian pound* (SYP) of 100 *piastres*. Inflation was 1·0% in 2001. Gold reserves were 833,000 troy oz in April 2002. Total money supply in Dec. 2001 was £Syr.419,916m.

Budget. Budget revenue and expenditure (in £Syr. 1m.):

	1994	1995	1996	1997	1998
Revenue	111,892	131,002	152,231	179,202	180,437
Expenditure	132,016	141,957	155,596	181,723	185,973

Performance. There was growth of 2·8% in 2001; total GDP in 2001 was US$17·9bn.

Banking and Finance. The Central Bank is the bank of issue. Commercial banks were nationalized in 1963. The *Governor* of the Central Bank is Mohammed Bashar Kabarra. In Aug. 2000 it was announced that private banks were to be established for the first time in nearly 40 years and that a stock exchange would be set up for the first time ever. In Dec. 2002 the Syrian government licensed five foreign private banks.

Weights and Measures. The metric system is legal, although former weights and measures may still be in use: 1 *okiya* = 0·47 lb; 6 *okiyas* = 1 *oke* = 2·82 lb; 2 *okes* = 1 *rottol* = 5·64 lb; 200 *okes* = 1 *kantar*.

ENERGY AND NATURAL RESOURCES

Environment. According to the *World Bank Atlas* Syria's carbon dioxide emissions in 1998 were the equivalent of 3·3 tonnes per capita.

Electricity. Installed capacity was 4m. kW in 1997. Production in 1998 was 17·5bn. kWh, with consumption per capita 838 kWh.

Oil and Gas. Crude oil production (1996), 220m. bbls. Reserves in 1999 were 2,500m. bbls. Gas reserves (1997), 235,000m. cu. metres. Natural gas production (1996), 192 petajoules.

Water. In 1992 there were 5 main dams and 127 surface dams. Production of drinking water, 1995, 608·86m. cu. metres.

Minerals. Phosphate deposits have been discovered. Production, 1995, 1,598,000 tonnes; other minerals are salt (72,000 tonnes in 1996) and gypsum (336,000 tonnes in 1995). There are indications of lead, copper, antimony, nickel, chrome and other minerals widely distributed. Sodium chloride and bitumen deposits are being worked.

Agriculture. The arable area in 1998 was 4,771,000 ha and there were 750,000 ha of cropland. In 1998 there were 93,327 tractors.

Production of principal crops, 2000 (in 1,000 tonnes): wheat, 3,105; sugarbeets, 1,300; seed cotton, 930; olives, 750; tomatoes, 610; cottonseed, 602; potatoes, 450; grapes, 400; oranges, 400; apples, 320; watermelons, 270; barley, 213; maize, 180.

Production of animal products, 2000 (in 1,000 tonnes): milk, 1,696; meat, 350; eggs, 120; cheese, 89.

Livestock (2000, in 1,000): sheep, 14,500; goats, 1,100; cattle, 920; asses, 198; chickens, 22,000.

Forestry. In 1995 there were 219,000 ha of forest (1·2% of the land area). Timber production in 1999 was 50,000 cu. metres.

Fisheries. The total catch in 1999 was 7,945 tonnes (68% freshwater fish).

INDUSTRY

Public-sector industrial production in 1995 included (in tonnes): cotton yarn, 40,417; cotton and mixed textiles, 16,597; mixed woollen yarn, 1,442; manufactured tobacco, 9,699; iron bars, 36,675; asbestos, 15,623; vegetable oil, 33,435; 77,001 electrical engines; 261,000 refrigerators (1997); 80,010 water meters; woollen carpets, 538,000 sq. metres.

Labour. In 1996 the labour force totalled 4,396,000 (74% males). Unemployment was nearly 20% in 2000.

Trade Unions. In 1995 there were 199 trade unions with 460,967 members.

INTERNATIONAL TRADE

Legislation of 1991 permits foreign investors a ten-year tax-exemption duty-free import of equipment and repatriation of profits. Foreign debt was US$21,657m. in 2000.

Imports and Exports. Trade in US$1m.:

	1996	1997	1998	1999	2000
Imports f.o.b.	4,516	3,603	3,320	3,590	3,723
Exports f.o.b.	4,178	4,057	3,142	3,806	5,146

Main imports, 1995 (in £Syr.1) included: petroleum and products, 318,463; iron and steel bars and rods, 3,269,247; cane sugar, 1,014,390; yarn of continuous synthetic fibres, 1,627,972; alternating current motors and generators, 185,388; passenger transport motor vehicles, 374,583. Main exports included: petroleum and products, 27,862,627; raw cotton, 2,390,774; printed woven cotton fabrics, 34,418; natural phosphate, 251,061.

In 1995 imports came mainly from Germany, Italy, USA, China, Turkey, Japan and Romania. Exports went mainly to Italy, France, Lebanon and Spain.

COMMUNICATIONS

Roads. In 1997 there were 41,451 km of roads, including 887 km of motorways and 29,215 km of primary roads. There were in 1998 a total of 138,620 passenger cars, 40,140 buses and coaches and 278,890 vans and lorries.

Rail. In 1995 the network totalled 2,423 km of 1,435 mm gauge (Syrian Railways) and 327 km of 1,050 mm gauge (Hedjaz-Syrian Railway). Passenger-km travelled in 1997 came to 294m. and freight tonne-km to 1,472m.

Civil Aviation. The main international airport is at Damascus, with some international traffic at Aleppo, Lattakia and Deir Ez-Zor. The national carrier is the state-owned Syrian Arab Airlines. In 1998 it flew 12·8m. km, carrying 665,300 passengers (642,800 on international flights). Damascus handled 1,656,184 passengers in 1999 (1,560,200 on international flights) and 26,296 tonnes of freight. Aleppo was the second busiest airport in 1999, handling 222,674 passengers (156,440 on international flights) and 2,489 tonnes of freight.

Shipping. In 1995 the merchant marine totalled 0·45m. GRT. Vessels totalling 2,901,000 net registered tons entered ports and vessels totalling 2,792,000 NRT cleared in 1996.

Telecommunications. There were 1,675,200 main telephone lines in 2000 (103·5 per 1,000 inhabitants), but in 1997 a total of 2·95m. people had been on the waiting list for a line. There were 250,000 PCs in use (15·4 for every 1,000 persons) in 2000 and 21,000 fax machines in 1996. The number of Internet users in March 2001 was 32,000.

Postal Services. There were 650 post offices in 1995.

SOCIAL INSTITUTIONS

Justice. Syrian law is based on both Islamic and French jurisprudence. There are two courts of first instance in each district, one for civil and one for criminal cases. There is also a Summary Court in each sub-district, under Justices of the Peace. There is a Court of Appeal in the capital of each governorate, with a Court of Cassation in Damascus. The death penalty is in force, and executions may be held in public.

The population in penal institutions in 1997 was 14,000 (95 per 100,000 of national population).

Religion. In 1997 there were an estimated 12·91m. Muslims (namely Sunni with some Shias and Ismailis). There are also Druzes and Alawites. Christians (830,000 in 1997) include Greek Orthodox, Greek Catholics, Armenian Orthodox, Syrian Orthodox, Armenian Catholics, Protestants, Maronites, Syrian Catholics, Latins, Nestorians and Assyrians. There are also Jews and Yezides.

Education. In 1995 there were 1,037 kindergartens with 90,681 children; 10,420 primary schools with 113,384 teachers and 2,651,247 pupils; 2,526 intermediate and secondary schools with 50,779 teachers and 841,964 pupils. In 1995, 14 teacher colleges had 766 teachers and 4,989 students; 292 schools for technical education had 10,105 teachers and 72,859 students. Adult literacy in 1999 was 73·6% (male, 87·7%; female, 59·3%).

In 1995–96 there were four universities and one higher institution of political science, with 161,185 students and 4,806 academic staff.

Health. In 1995 there were 17,623 beds in 294 hospitals, and 795 health centres. In 1995 there were 15,391 doctors, 8,025 dentists, 5,919 pharmacists, 6,063 midwives and 23,151 nursing personnel.

CULTURE

Broadcasting. Broadcasting is controlled by the government-owned Syrian Broadcasting and Television Organization. There are two national radio programmes and an external service and two TV programmes (colour by SECAM H). In 1997 there were 4·15m. radio and 1·05m. TV sets.

Cinema. In 1994 there were 49 cinemas with 25,111 seats.

Press. In 1996 there were eight national daily newspapers with a combined circulation of 287,000.

Tourism. In 1999 there were 1,386,000 foreign tourists, bringing revenue of US$1·36bn. Tourism contributes less than 3% of GDP, but the government aims to increase this. Visitors from other Arab countries account for approximately two-thirds of all tourists.

DIPLOMATIC REPRESENTATIVES

Of Syria in the United Kingdom (8 Belgrave Sq., London, SW1X 8PH)
Ambassador: Mouafak Nassar.

Of the United Kingdom in Syria (Kotob Building, 11 Mohammad Kurd Ali St., Malki, Damascus POB 37)
Ambassador: Henry G. Hogger.

Of Syria in the USA (2215 Wyoming Ave., NW, Washington, D.C., 20008)
Ambassador: Rostom Al Zoubi.

Of the USA in Syria (Abu Rumaneh, Al Mansur St. No. 2, Damascus)
Ambassador: Theodore H. Kattouf.

Of Syria to the United Nations
Ambassador: Mikhail Wehbe.

Of Syria to the European Union
Ambassador: Vacant.
Chargé d'Affaires a.i.: Dr Hani Habeeb.

FURTHER READING
Choueiri, Y., *State and Society in Syria and Lebanon.* Exeter Univ. Press, 1994
Kienle, Eberhard, *Contemporary Syria: Liberalization Between Cold War and Peace.* I. B.
   Tauris, London, 1997

National statistical office: Central Bureau of Statistics, Office of the Prime Minister, Damascus.

TAJIKISTAN

Jumkhurii Tojikiston

Capital: Dushanbe
Population estimate, 2000: 6·13m.
GDP per capita, 2000: (PPP$) 1,152
HDI/world rank: 0·667/112

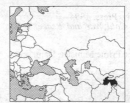

KEY HISTORICAL EVENTS

The Tajik Soviet Socialist Republic was formed from those regions of Bokhara and Turkestan where the population consisted mainly of Tajiks. It was admitted as a constituent republic of the Soviet Union on 5 Dec. 1929. In Aug. 1990 the Tajik Supreme Soviet adopted a declaration of republican sovereignty and in Dec. 1991 the republic became a member of the CIS. After demonstrations and fighting, the Communist government was replaced by a Revolutionary Coalition Council on 7 May 1992. Following further demonstrations, President Nabiev was ousted on 7 Sept. Civil war broke out, and the government resigned on 10 Nov. On 30 Nov. it was announced that a CIS peacekeeping force would be sent to Tajikistan. A state of emergency was imposed in Jan. 1993. On 23 Dec. 1996 a ceasefire was signed. A further agreement on 8 March 1997 provided for the disarmament of the Islamic-led insurgents, the United Tajik Opposition, and their eventual integration into the regular armed forces. A peace agreement brokered by Iran and Russia was signed in Moscow on 27 June 1997 stipulating that the opposition should have 30% of ministerial posts in a Commission of National Reconciliation. The country's first multi-party parliamentary election was held in Feb. 2000, although it was criticized by observers for failing to meet democratic standards. President Rakhmonov, first elected in 1994, won a second term in 1999.

Ethnic conflict and terrorist attacks continue to plague Tajikistan, with Russia offering military support. Fighting in the Fergana Valley, particularly by the Islamist Movement of Uzbekistan, is a cause for concern for all Central Asian governments.

TERRITORY AND POPULATION

Tajikistan is bordered in the north and west by Uzbekistan and Kyrgyzstan, in the east by China and in the south by Afghanistan. Area, 143,100 sq. km (55,240 sq. miles). It includes 2 provinces (Khudzand and Khatlon) and 43 rural districts, 18 towns and 49 urban settlements, together with the Badakhshan Autonomous Republic. 2000 census population, 6,127,000 (3,082,000 males); density, 42·8 per sq. km. 80% of the population in 2000 were Tajiks, 15% Uzbeks and 1% Russians.

The UN gives a projected population for 2010 of 6·62m.

In 2000, 73·5% of the population lived in rural areas, making it the most rural of the former Soviet republics.

The capital is Dushanbe (1999 population estimate, 523,000). Other large towns are Khudzand (formerly Leninabad), Kurgan-Tyube and Kulyab.

The official language is Tajik, written in Arabic script until 1930 and after 1992 (the Roman alphabet was used 1930–40; the Cyrillic, 1940–92).

SOCIAL STATISTICS

1999 births, estimate, 110,300; deaths, 24,900. Rates, 1999 estimate (per 1,000 population): births, 17·7; deaths, 4·0. Life expectancy, 1999, 64·5 years for men and 70·4 for women. Annual growth, 1990–99, 1·6%. Infant mortality, 1999, 19·9 per 1,000 live births; fertility rate, 1999, 4·0 births per woman.

CLIMATE

Considering its altitude, Tajikistan is a comparatively dry country. July to Sept. are particularly dry months. Winters are cold but spring comes earlier than farther north. Dushanbe, Jan. −10°C, July 25°C. Annual rainfall 375 mm.

CONSTITUTION AND GOVERNMENT

In Nov. 1994 a new Constitution was approved by a 90% favourable vote by the electorate, which enhanced the President's powers. The head of state is the *President*, elected by universal suffrage for five years. Parliament is the 181-member National Assembly (*Majlisi Oli*), elected for a five-year term in single-seat constituencies.

RECENT ELECTIONS

At presidential elections on 6 Nov. 1999 President Rakhmonov was re-elected with around 97% of votes cast. His opponent, Davlat Ismonov, received around 2%. Turn-out was 98%.

The country's first multi-party elections to the Assembly of Representatives were held on 27 Feb. and 12 March 2000. Turn-out in the first round was put at 93·2%. The People's Democratic Party of Tajikistan (HDKT) won 64·5% of the vote and 30 of the 63 available seats, the Communist Party (CP) 20·6% and 13, the Islamic Renaissance Party (IRP) 7·5% and 2. Three other parties won 3·5% of the vote or less. 15 seats went to non-partisans and 3 were left vacant or unavailable. Elections to the National Assembly were held on 12 March 2000. 25 of the 33 seats were voted for by local majlisi deputies and 8 were appointed by the president.

CURRENT ADMINISTRATION

President: Emomali Rakhmonov; b. 1952 (HDKT; as Speaker elected by the former Supreme Soviet 19 Nov. 1992, re-elected 6 Nov. 1994).

In March 2003 the government comprised:

Prime Minister: Akil Akilov; b. 1944 (HDKT; sworn in 20 Dec. 1999).

First Deputy Prime Minister: Hajji Akbar Turajonzoda. *Deputy Prime Ministers:* Kozidavlat Koimdodov, Nigina Sharopova, Zokir Vazirov, Maj.-Gen. Saidamir Zuhurov.

Minister of Agriculture: Tursun Rahmatov. *Communications:* Saidmahmad Zubaidov. *Culture:* Karomatullo Olimov. *Defence:* Col.-Gen. Sherali Khairullaev. *Economy and Trade:* Hakim Soliyev. *Education:* Safarali Rajabov. *Emergency Situations:* Mirzo Ziyoyev. *Protection of the Environment:* Usmonqul Shokirov. *Finance:* Safarali Najmuddinov. *Internal Affairs:* Khomiddin Sharipov. *Justice:* Halifabobo Hamidov. *Foreign Affairs:* Talbak Nasarov. *Transport:* Abdujalol Salimov. *Energy:* Abdullo Yorov. *Grain Products:* Bekmurod Urokov. *Health:* Nusratullo Faizulloev. *Labour, Employment and Social Welfare:* Rafiqa Musoyeva. *Land Improvement and Water Resources:* Abduqohir Nazirov. *Security:* Khayriddin Abdurahimov. *Industry:* Zayd Saidov. *State Revenue:* Ghulomjon Babaev.

DEFENCE

In 1999 the Army had a strength of 7,000. There is a paramilitary Border Guard of 1,200. An estimated 12,000 Russian Federal Border Guards, 7,800 Russian Army personnel and some Air Force units are stationed in the country.

Defence expenditure in 2000 totalled US$80m. (US$13 per capita), representing 6·5% of GDP.

Army. Personnel strength approximately 7,000.

INTERNATIONAL RELATIONS

Tajikistan is a member of the UN, the NATO Partnership for Peace, CIS, OSCE, ECO, IOM and OIC.

ECONOMY

Currency. The unit of currency is the *somoni* (TJS) of 100 *dirams*, which replaced the Tajik rouble on 30 Oct. 2000 at 1 somoni = 1,000 Tajik roubles. The introduction of the new currency is intended to strengthen the national banking system. The IMF has voiced their support for the new currency, which it believes will contribute to macroeconomic stability and expedite the transition to a market economy. Inflation in 1993 was 2,195%, declining to 418% in 1996 and still further to 32·9% in 2000, the reduction being helped by a US$22m. IMF loan in 1996 and maintenance of a tighter monetary regime. In 2001 the rate rose to 38·6%.

Budget. Total revenue in 2000 was 189·9m. somoni and total expenditure was 204·3m. somoni.

Performance. Annual real GDP growth was negative for four consecutive years in the mid-1990s. However, the economy slowly recovered and in 2000 growth was 8·3%, rising to 10·2% in 2001. Total GDP in 2001 was US$1·1bn.

Banking and Finance. The central bank and bank of issue is the National Bank (*Chairman*, Murotali Alimardonov). In 1998 there were 27 commercial and private banks.

ENERGY AND NATURAL RESOURCES

Environment. In 1998 Tajikistan's carbon dioxide emissions were the equivalent of 0·8 tonnes per capita according to the *World Bank Atlas*.

Electricity. Installed capacity in 1997 was 4m. kW. Production was 13·27bn. kWh in 1998 and consumption per capita 2,046 kWh.

Oil and Gas. In 1996 oil production was 700,000 bbls.; natural gas output in 1996 was 2 petajoules.

Minerals. There are deposits of brown coal, lead, zinc, iron ore, antimony, mercury, gold, silver, tungsten and uranium. Coal production, 1996, 20,000 tonnes. Aluminium production, 1996, 198,000 tonnes.

Agriculture. Area under cultivation in 1997 was 9·6m. ha, mainly in the hands of state and collective farms. Cotton is the major cash crop, with various fruits, sugarcane, jute, silk, rice and millet also being grown.

Output of main agricultural products (in 1,000 tonnes) in 2000: wheat, 358; seed cotton, 294; potatoes, 250; cottonseed, 210; tomatoes, 185; onions, 128. Livestock, 2000: 1·59m. sheep; 1·04m. cattle; 590,000 goats; 1m. chickens. Livestock products, 2000 (in 1,000 tonnes): meat, 31; milk, 331.

Forestry. Forests covered 410,000 ha in 1995, or 2·9% of the land area.

INDUSTRY

Major industries: aluminium, electro-chemical plants, textile machinery, carpet weaving, silk mills, refrigerators, hydro-electric power. Output, 1993 (in tonnes unless otherwise stated): mineral fertilizer, 20,000; cement (1997), 36,000; fabrics, 114m. cu. metres; footwear, 3·9m. pairs; 1,100 lathes; 2,000 refrigerators (1997).

Labour. The labour force in 1996 totalled 2,238,000 (56% males). In 1993, 55·3% of the economically active population worked in the state sector, 25·1% in the private sector and 18·4% in co-operatives. In 2000 the unemployment rate was 3·0%.

INTERNATIONAL TRADE

Total external debt was US$1,170m. in 2000.

Imports and Exports. In 1996 imports were estimated to be valued at US$657m. and exports at US$768m. Main imports: petroleum products, grain, manufactured consumer goods; main exports: cotton and aluminium. The main trading partners are former Soviet republics, most notably Russia and Uzbekistan.

COMMUNICATIONS

Roads. In 1996 there were estimated to be 13,700 km of roads (11,300 km surfaced). In 1993, 139·9m. passengers and 12·3m. tonnes of freight were carried. There were an estimated 8,820 passenger cars, buses, lorries and vans in 1996.

Rail. Length of railways, 1995, 474 km. Passenger-km travelled in 1996 came to 95m. and freight tonne-km to 1·72bn.

Civil Aviation. There are international airports at Dushanbe and Khujand. The national carrier is Tajikistan Airlines, which in 2002 flew to Istanbul, Moscow, Munich and a variety of Asian cities. In 2002 there were weekly flights to Samara and Novosibirsk with Samara Airlines and Siberia Airlines respectively. In 1999 scheduled airline traffic of Tajikistan-based carriers flew 4·1m. km, carrying 156,000 passengers (79,000 on international flights).

Telecommunications. There were 218,500 main telephone lines in 2000, or 35·7 for every 1,000 persons. In 1998 there were 400 mobile phone subscribers, and in 1997, 1,800 fax machines. There were 2,000 Internet users in Dec. 1999.

Postal Services. In 1995 there were 736 post offices.

SOCIAL INSTITUTIONS

Justice. In 1994, 14,279 crimes were reported, including 636 murders or attempted murders. The population in penal institutions in 1996 was approximately 6,000 (95 per 100,000 of national population). The death penalty is in force.

Religion. The Tajiks are predominantly Sunni Muslims (80%); Shi'a Muslims, 5%.

Education. The adult literacy rate in 1999 was 99·1% (99·5% among males and 98·7% among females). In 1994–95 there were 593,526 pupils and 25,698 teachers at (1993) 625 primary schools, and 724,056 pupils at secondary schools, plus 108,203 students at higher education institutions.

There is one university, which had 7,220 students in 1994–95.

Health. There were 374 hospitals in Jan. 1994 with 60,000 beds, 13,000 doctors and 42,800 junior medical personnel.

Welfare. In Jan. 1994 there were 0·41m. old age pensioners and 0·2m. other pensioners.

CULTURE

Broadcasting. Broadcasting is controlled by the State Teleradio Broadcasting Company. Tajik Radio broadcasts three national programmes, a Radio Moscow relay and a foreign service (Dari, Iranian). In 1997 there were 850,000 radio and 20,000 TV receivers.

Cinema. In 1995 there were 159 cinemas with a seating capacity of 39,000 and an annual attendance of 400,000; gross box office receipts came to 6·0m. roubles.

Press. There were two daily newspapers in 1996 with a combined circulation of 120,000, equivalent to 21 per 1,000 inhabitants.

Tourism. In 1998, 511,000 foreign tourists visited Tajikistan.

DIPLOMATIC REPRESENTATIVES
Of Tajikistan in the United Kingdom
Honorary Consul: Benjamin Brahms (33 Ovington Square, London, SW3 1LJ).

Of the United Kingdom in Tajikistan (Lufti 43, Dushanbe)
Ambassador: Michael Smith.

Of the USA in Tajikistan (Oktyabrskaya Hotel, 105A Prospekt Rudaki, Dushanbe)
Ambassador: Franklin Pierce Huddle.

Of Tajikistan to the United Nations
Ambassador: Rashid Alimov.

Of Tajikistan to the European Union
Ambassador: Sharif Rahimov.

FURTHER READING
Abdullaev, K. and Akbarzadeh, S., *Historical Dictionary of Tajikistan.* Rowman and Littlefield Publishing, Lanham, Maryland, 2002
Akiner, S., *Tajikistan: Disintegration or Reconciliation?* Royal Institute of International Affairs, London, 2001
Djalili, M. R. (ed.) *Tajikistan: The Trials of Independence.* Macmillan, Basingstoke, 1998

BADAKHSHAN AUTONOMOUS REPUBLIC

Comprising the Pamir massif along the borders of Afghanistan and China, the province was set up on 2 Jan. 1925, initially as the Special Pamir Province. Area, 63,700 sq. km (24,590 sq. miles). The population at the 1989 census was 161,000 (89·5% Tajik, 6·7% Kirghiz). Estimate, 1990, 164,300. Capital, Khorog (14,800). The inhabitants are predominantly Ismaili Muslims.

Mining industries are developed (gold, rock-crystal, mica, coal, salt). Wheat, fruit and fodder crops are grown, and cattle and sheep are bred in the western parts. In 1990 there were 74,200 cattle and 329,500 sheep and goats. Total area under cultivation, 18,400 ha.

In 1990–91 there were 47,600 students at all levels of education. There were 140 doctors and 1,400 junior medical personnel in 1991.

TANZANIA

Jamhuri ya Muungano
wa Tanzania
(United Republic of Tanzania)

Capital: Dodoma
Population estimate, 2000: 35·12m.
GDP per capita, 2000: (PPP$) 523
HDI/world rank: 0·440/151

KEY HISTORICAL EVENTS

At the end of the 17th century the inhabitants of Zanzibar drove out the Portuguese with the assistance of the Arabs of Oman. In 1887 the Sultan of Zanzibar handed over the administration of his possessions to the north of Vanga on the African continent to the British East Africa Association. These territories eventually passed to the British government and are now part of Kenya. In 1888 a similar concession was granted to the German East Africa Association of the Sultan's mainland territories between the River Umba and Cape Delgado. German East Africa was conquered by the Allies in the First World War and subsequently divided between the Belgians, the Portuguese and the British. The country was administered as a League of Nations mandate until 1946, and then as a UN trusteeship territory until 9 Dec. 1961.

Tanganyika (Tanzania) achieved responsible government in Sept. 1960 and full self-government on 1 May 1961. On 9 Dec. 1961 Tanganyika became a sovereign independent member state of the Commonwealth of Nations. On 9 Dec 1962 the country adopted a republican form of government (still within the British Commonwealth) and Dr Nyerere was elected as the first president.

On 24 June 1963 Zanzibar became an internal self-governing state which achieved independence on 9 Dec. 1963. On 12 Jan. 1964 her sultanate was overthrown by a revolt of the Afro-Shirazi Party leaders who established the People's Republic of Zanzibar. Also in Jan. 1964 there was an attempted coup against Nyerere who had to seek British military help. On 26 April 1964 Tanganyika, Zanzibar and Pemba combined to form the United Republic of Tanzania. The first multi-party elections were held in 1995.

TERRITORY AND POPULATION

Tanzania is bounded in the northeast by Kenya, north by Lake Victoria and Uganda, northwest by Rwanda and Burundi, west by Lake Tanganyika, southwest by Zambia and Malawi, and south by Mozambique. Total area 945,037 sq. km (364,881 sq. miles), including the offshore islands of Zanzibar (1,660 sq. km) and Pemba (984 sq. km) and inland water surfaces (59,050 sq. km). The total population was estimated in July 1997 to be 29,460,800; density, 31·2 per sq. km.

The UN gives a projected population for 2010 of 44·06m.

In 1999, 68·4% of the population lived in rural areas. 0·5m. Hutu refugees were forcibly repatriated to Rwanda in Dec. 1996. Tanzania has the highest refugee population in Africa, with 650,000 at the end of 2001.

The chief towns (1988 census populations) are Dar es Salaam, the chief port and former capital (2,545,000 in 1999), Tabora (1,600,000 in 1999), Mwanza (783,000 in 1995), Dodoma, the new capital (189,000 in 1995), Tanga (187,634) and Zanzibar Town (157,634). Between 1975 and 1995 Tabora's population grew at a faster rate than that of any other major city in the world, increasing by nearly 2,500%.

The United Republic is divided into 25 administrative regions of which 20 are in mainland Tanzania, 3 in Zanzibar and 2 in Pemba. Areas and 1994 populations of the regions:

Region	Sq. km	Population	Region	Sq. km	Population
Arusha	82,306	1,596,000	Kigoma	37,037	1,015,000
Dar es Salaam	1,393	1,606,000	Kilimanjaro	13,309	1,308,000
Dodoma	41,311	1,461,000	Lindi	66,046	763,000
Iringa	56,864	1,427,000	Mara	19,566	1,146,000
Kagera	28,388	1,607,000	Mbeya	60,350	1,742,000

Region	Sq. km	Population	Region	Sq. km	Population
Morogoro	70,799	1,483,000	Tabora	76,151	1,223,000
Mtwara	16,707	1,050,000	Tanga	26,808	1,546,000
Mwanza	19,592	2,217,000	Zanzibar and Pemba	2,460	758,000
Pwani (Coast)	32,407	753,000	Pemba North	574 }	314,000
Rukwa	68,635	820,000	Pemba South	332 }	
Ruvuma	63,498	924,000	Zanzibar North	470 }	
Shinyanga	50,781	2,092,000	Zanzibar South	854 }	444,000
Singida	49,341	934,000	Zanzibar West	230 }	

The official languages are English and Swahili (spoken as a mother tongue by only 8·8% of the population, but used as a *lingua franca* by 90%).

SOCIAL STATISTICS

1997 births, estimate, 1,208,000; deaths, 583,000. 1997 rates per 1,000 population: birth, 41·0; death, 19·8. Annual population growth rate, 1990–99, 2·8%. Life expectancy in 1999 was 50·0 years for men and 52·2 for women. 45% of the population was below 15 years old in 1997. Infant mortality, 1999, 90 per 1,000 live births; fertility rate, 1999, 5·3 births per woman.

CLIMATE

The climate is very varied and is controlled largely by altitude and distance from the sea. There are three climatic zones: the hot and humid coast, the drier central plateau with seasonal variations of temperature, and the semi-temperate mountains. Dodoma, Jan. 75°F (23·9°C), July 67°F (19·4°C). Annual rainfall 23" (572 mm). Dar es Salaam, Jan. 82°F (27·8°C), July 74°F (23·3°C). Annual rainfall 43" (1,064 mm).

CONSTITUTION AND GOVERNMENT

The *President* is head of state, chairman of the party and commander-in-chief of the armed forces. The second Vice-President is head of the executive in Zanzibar. The Prime Minister and first Vice-President is also the leader of government business in the National Assembly.

The *Bunge (National Assembly)* is composed of 232 Members of Parliament elected from the Constituencies, 5 delegates from the Zanzibar House of Representatives, the Attorney General and 37 women, making 275 in total.

In Dec. 1979 a separate Constitution for Zanzibar was approved. Although at present under the same Constitution as Tanzania, Zanzibar has, in fact, been ruled by decree since 1964.

National Anthem. 'God Bless Africa/Mungu ibariki Afrika'; words collective, tune by M. E. Sontonga and V. E. Webster.

RECENT ELECTIONS

Presidential and parliamentary elections were held on 29 Oct. 2000, in many places postponed or extended because of administrative problems or faults. International observers described the elections in the semi-autonomous island of Zanzibar as chaotic. Benjamin Mkapa was elected President with 71·7% of votes cast. His party, Chama Cha Mapinduzi (Revolutionary State Party), gained 244 seats, the Civic United Front gained 15, Chama Cha Democracia na Maendeleo (Party for Democracy and Progress) 4, the Tanzania Labour Party 3 and the United Democratic Party 2.

CURRENT ADMINISTRATION

President: Benjamin Mkapa; b. 1938 (Chama Cha Mapinduzi/CCM; sworn in 30 Nov. 1995 and re-elected in Oct. 2000).

Vice-President: Dr Ali Mohamed Sheni.

In March 2003 the government consisted of:

Prime Minister: Frederick Sumaye; b. 1950 (CCM; sworn in 28 Nov. 1995).

President of Zanzibar: Amani Abeid Karume.

Minister of Home Affairs: Omar Ramadhani Mapuri. *Finance:* Basil Mramba. *Justice and Constitutional Affairs:* Bakari Mwapachu. *Defence:* Philemon Sarungi. *Industries and Trade:* Juma Ngasongwa. *Communications and Transport:* Mark

Mwandosya. *Agriculture and Food:* Charles Kennja. *Health:* Anna Abdalla. *Foreign Affairs and International Co-operation:* Jakaya Kikwete. *Education:* James Mungai. *Energy and Mineral Resources:* Daniel Yona. *Water and Livestock Development:* Edward Lowassa. *Tourism, Natural Resources and Environment:* Zakhia Meghji. *Lands and Human Settlements:* Gideon Cheyo. *Science, Technology and Higher Education:* Ng'wandu Pius. *Works:* John Magufuli. *Labour, Youth Development and Sports:* Juma Kapuya. *Community Development, Women's Affairs and Children:* Asha Rose Migiro. *Co-operatives and Marketing:* George Kahama. *Regional Affairs and Local Government:* Hassan Nigwilizi.

Government Website: http://www.tanzania.go.tz/

DEFENCE
Conscription is for two years, which may include civilian service. Defence expenditure totalled US$141m. in 2000 (US$4 per capita), representing 1·8% of GDP.

Army. Strength (1999), 30,000. There is also a Citizen's Militia of 80,000 and a paramilitary Police Field Force of 1,400.

Navy. Personnel in 1999 totalled about 1,000. The principal bases are at Dar es Salaam, Zanzibar and Mwanza.

Air Force. The Tanzanian People's Defence Force Air Wing was built up initially with the help of Canada, but combat equipment has been acquired from China. Personnel totalled 3,000 in 1999 (including some 2,000 air defence troops), with F-7 (MiG-21), F-6 (MiG-19) and F-5 (MiG-17) combat aircraft, mostly in store.

INTERNATIONAL RELATIONS
Tanzania is a member of the UN, WTO, the African Union, the Commonwealth, African Development Bank, COMESA, SADC, EAC, IOM, and is an ACP member state of the ACP-EU relationship.

In Nov. 1999 a treaty was signed between Tanzania, Kenya and Uganda to create a new East African Community as a means of developing East African trade, tourism and industry and laying the foundations for a future common market and political federation.

ECONOMY
Agriculture accounted for 45·7% of GDP in 1998, industry 14·9% and services 39·4%.

Overview. Between 1993 and 1999 a total of 295 out of 395 public enterprises were privatized. The Presidential Parastatal Sector Reform Commission aims to complete the privatization programme by the end of 2003.

Currency. The monetary unit is the *Tanzanian shilling* (TZS) of 100 *cents.* Foreign exchange reserves were US$1,199m. in June 2002. Inflation, which was 26·5% in 1995, had fallen to 5·2% in 2001, the lowest rate for more than 20 years. Total money supply in May 2002 was Sh. 792,213m.

Budget. The fiscal year ends 30 June. Total revenues in 1996–97 were an estimated US$959m. and expenditure US$1·1bn. Import duties accounted for 29·7% of revenues, and sales and excise tax 25·0%. Public administration accounted for 27·4% of expenditures, and interest payments on debt 14·8%.

Performance. Real GDP growth was 5·6% in 2001, up from 5·1% in 2000. Total GDP in 2001 was US$9·1bn.

Banking and Finance. The central bank is the Bank of Tanzania (*Governor*, Daudi Ballali).

On 6 Feb. 1967 all commercial banks with the exception of National Co-operative Banks were nationalized, and their interests vested in the National Bank of Commerce on the mainland (fully privatized in March 2000) and the Peoples' Bank in Zanzibar. However, in 1993 private-sector commercial banks were allowed to open. In 1997 the National Commercial Bank, which controls 70% of the country's banking and has 34 branches, was split into a trade bank, a regional rural bank and a micro-finance bank. It is scheduled for privatization, with the South African concern Absa Group Limited purchasing a 70% stake. In 2000 there were 17 banks operating in Tanzania.

A stock exchange opened in Dar es Salaam in 1996.

Weights and Measures. The metric system is in use.

ENERGY AND NATURAL RESOURCES

Environment. According to the *World Bank Atlas* Tanzania's carbon dioxide emissions in 1998 were the equivalent of 0·1 tonnes per capita.

Electricity. Installed capacity was 1m. kW in 1997. Production in 1998 was 1·7bn. kWh, with consumption per capita 54 kWh. In 1998 only 10% of the population had access to electricity. By 2015 the government aims to have increased this to 40% under a new structure principally managed by the private sector.

Oil and Gas. A number of international companies are exploring for both gas and oil. In 1997 natural gas reserves were 21bn. cu. metres.

Minerals. Tanzania's mineral resources include gold, nickel, cobalt and diamonds. International funds injected to improve Tanzania's economy have resulted in notable increases, particularly in gold production. The first commercial gold mine began operating in Mwanza in 1998. By 2000 production revenue had reached US$184m., up from US$3·3m. in 1998. Large deposits of coal and tin exist but mining is on a small scale.

Agriculture. About 80% of the workforce are engaged in agriculture, chiefly in subsistence farming. Agricultural produce contributes around 85% of exports. There were 3·8m. ha of arable land in 1998 and 0·9m. ha of permanent crops. Production of main agricultural crops in 2000 (in 1,000 tonnes) was: cassava, 5,758; maize, 2,551; sugarcane, 1,355; bananas and plantains, 1,304; sweet potatoes, 480; rice, 379; coconuts, 350; sorghum, 335; dry beans, 260; potatoes, 250. Zanzibar is a major producer of cloves.

Livestock (2000): 14·38m. cattle; 4·20m. sheep; 9·95m. goats; 28m. chickens. Livestock products (2000, in 1,000 tonnes): milk, 781; meat, 326; eggs, 58; honey, 25.

Forestry. Forests covered 32·51m. ha in 1995 (36·8% of the total land area), down from 34·12m. ha and 38·6% of the land area in 1990. In 1999, 39·85m. cu. metres of roundwood were cut.

Fisheries. Catch (1999) approximately 310,020 tonnes, of which 260,020 tonnes were from inland waters.

INDUSTRY

Industry is limited, and is mainly textiles, petroleum and chemical products, food processing, tobacco, brewing and paper manufacturing.

INTERNATIONAL TRADE

Foreign debt was US$7,445m. in 2000 (figure refers to mainland Tanzania only).

Imports and Exports. In 2000 imports (f.o.b.) amounted to US$1,339·8m. (US$1,368·3m. in 1999); exports (f.o.b.) US$665·7m. (US$542·9m. in 1999). Principal exports, 1995: coffee, 21·6%; cotton, 18·2%; cashew nuts, 9·7%; tobacco, 4·1%. Principal imports: machinery, 31·3%; consumer goods, 27·1%; chemicals, 4·7%; food, 2·3%. Main export markets, 1998: India, 19·5%; UK, 10·1%; Germany, 8·3%; Japan, 7·7%; and Netherlands, 7·6%. Main import suppliers, 1998: Japan, 8·3%; UK, 7·8%; India, 5·7%; Netherlands, 5·7%; and Germany, 4·9%.

COMMUNICATIONS

Roads. In 1996 there were around 88,200 km of roads, of which 3,700 km were tarred. Passenger cars in use in 1996 numbered 23,760; and there were 86,000 buses and coaches, and 29,700 trucks and vans.

Rail. In 1977 the independent Tanzanian Railway Corporation was formed. The network totals 2,600 km (metre-gauge), excluding the joint Tanzanian Zambian (Tazara) railway's 969 km in Tanzania (1,067 mm gauge) operated by a separate administration. In 1994 the state railway carried 1·2m. passengers and 1·2m. tonnes of freight, and the Tazara carried 1·8m. passengers and 0·6m. tonnes of freight.

In Oct. 1998 a transhipment facility for containers opened at Kidatu, southwest of Dar es Salaam, providing a link between the 1,067 mm gauge railways of the southern part of Africa and the 1,000 mm gauge lines of the north.

Civil Aviation. There are three international airports: Dar es Salaam, Zanzibar and Kilimanjaro (Moshi/Arusha). Air Tanzania Corporation, the state-owned national carrier, provides domestic services and in 1998 had flights to the Democratic Republic of the Congo, Kenya, Oman, Rwanda, Saudi Arabia, South Africa, Uganda, Yemen, Zambia and Zimbabwe. Tanzania is a partner with Uganda and South African Airways in Alliance Airlines. In 1999 Air Tanzania Corporation flew 3·1m. km, carrying 190,000 passengers (75,400 on international flights). Dar es Salaam is the busiest airport, handling 556,785 passengers in 2000 (348,558 on international flights) and 11,048 tonnes of freight.

Shipping. In 1998 the merchant marine totalled 36,000 GRT, including oil tankers 4,000 GRT. The main seaports are Dar es Salaam, Mtwara, Tanga and Zanzibar. There are also ports on the lakes. In 1991, 1m. tonnes of freight were loaded, and 2·9m. unloaded.

Telecommunications. Tanzania had 173,600 main telephone lines in 2000 (4·9 per 1,000 inhabitants) and there were 100,000 PCs in use (2·8 per 1,000 inhabitants). There were 37,900 mobile phone subscribers in 1998 and 100 fax machines in 1995. Tanzania had 115,000 Internet users in Dec. 2000, up from 2,500 in Jan. 1999.

Postal Services. In 1995 there were 525 post offices.

SOCIAL INSTITUTIONS

Justice. The Judiciary is independent in both judicial and administrative matters and is composed of a four-tier system of Courts: Primary Courts; District and Resident Magistrates' Courts; the High Court and the Court of Appeal. The Chief Justice is head of the Court of Appeal and the Judiciary Department. The Court's main registry is at Dar es Salaam; its jurisdiction includes Zanzibar. The Principal Judge is head of the High Court, also headquartered at Dar es Salaam, which has resident judges at seven regional centres.

The population in penal institutions in 1998 was 38,135 (120 per 100,000 of national population).

Religion. In 1992 there were 8·4m. Roman Catholics, Anglicans and Lutherans, and 9m. Muslims. Muslims are concentrated in the coastal towns; Zanzibar is 99% Muslim. Some 23% follow traditional religions.

Education. In 1997 there were 11,290 primary schools with 109,936 teachers for 4·06m. pupils. At secondary level there were 234,743 pupils with 12,496 teachers, and at university level in 1995 there were 12,776 students with 1,650 staff. Primary school fees were abolished in Jan. 2002.

Technical and vocational education is provided at several secondary and technical schools, and at the Dar es Salaam Technical College. There are 42 teacher training colleges, including the college at Chang'ombe for secondary-school teachers.

There is one university, one university of agriculture and one open university. There are also nine other institutions of higher education.

Adult literacy rate in 1999 was 74·7% (male, 84·0%; female, 65·7%).

Health. In 1993 there were 1,365 doctors, and in 1991, 173 hospitals with 24,130 beds.

CULTURE

Broadcasting. The government-controlled Radio Tanzania and Sauti ya Tanzania Zanzibar are responsible for radio broadcasting on the mainland and on Zanzibar respectively. On the mainland there is a national service and a commercial programme in Swahili and an external service in English. There is television only on Zanzibar provided by the government-run Television Zanzibar (colour by PAL). There were 103,000 TV sets and 8·8m. radio receivers in 1997.

Cinema. In 1995 there were 27 cinemas with a seating capacity of 10,000 and an annual attendance of 1·8m.

Press. In 1996 there were three dailies (one in English), with a combined circulation of 120,000.

Tourism. Tourism contributes approximately 15% of GDP, but it is hoped that by 2010 the share will exceed 25%. There were, in 2001, 12 national parks in Tanzania. In 1999 there were 627,000 foreign tourists, bringing revenue of US$733m. compared to 153,000 visitors in 1990. Tourism ranks among the country's largest foreign exchange earners.

DIPLOMATIC REPRESENTATIVES

Of Tanzania in the United Kingdom (43 Hertford St., London, W1Y 8DB)
High Commissioner: Hassan Omar Gumbo Kibelloh.

Of the United Kingdom in Tanzania (POB 9200, Social Security Hse., Samora Ave., Dar es Salaam)
High Commissioner: Richard Clarke.

Of Tanzania in the USA (2139 R. St., NW, Washington, D.C., 20008)
Ambassador: Andrew Mhando Daraja.

Of the USA in Tanzania (36 Laibon Rd., Dar es Salaam)
Ambassador: Robert V. Royall.

Of Tanzania to the United Nations
Ambassador: Daudi Ngelautwa Mwakawago.

Of Tanzania to the European Union
Ambassador: Ali Abeid Aman Karume.

FURTHER READING
Darch, C., *Tanzania.* [Bibliography] 2nd ed. ABC-Clio, Oxford and Santa Barbara (CA), 1996

National statistical office: National Bureau of Statistics, Box 796, Dar es Salaam.

THAILAND

Prathet Thai

(Kingdom of Thailand)

Capital: Bangkok

Population estimate, 2000: 60·61m.

GDP per capita, 2000: (PPP$) 6,402

HDI/world rank: 0·762/70

KEY HISTORICAL EVENTS

The Thais migrated to the present territory from Nan Chao in the Yunnan area of China in the 8th and 9th centuries. Thailand's leading general, Chao Phraya Chakkri, assumed the throne in 1782, thus establishing the dynasty which still heads the Thai state. Siam, as Thailand was called until 1939, remained an independent state ruled by an absolute monarchy until 24 June 1932. Discontented with the social, political and economic stagnation of the country, a group of rebels calling themselves the People's Party precipitated a bloodless coup. The rebels seized control of the army and persuaded the king to accept the introduction of constitutional monarchy. When, the following year, the king tried to dissolve the newly appointed General Assembly, the army moved to prevent him, thus becoming the dominant force behind the government, which they have remained ever since. Nationalism dominated political life through the 1930s. In 1939 Field Marshal Pibul Songgram became premier and embarked on a pro-Japanese policy that brought Thailand into the Second World War on Japan's side.

After 1945 political life was characterized by periods of military rule interspersed with short attempts at democratic, civilian government. Democratic government was reintroduced for a short time after 1963 and again from 1969 to 1971 when another successful military coup was staged, aimed at checking the high crime rate and the growth of Communist insurgence. A new, moderately democratic constitution was introduced in 1978.

On 23 Feb. 1991 a military junta seized power in the most recent of 17 coups since 1932. Following the appointment of Gen. Suchinda Kraprayoon as prime minister on 17 April 1992 there were massive anti-government demonstrations over several weeks in the course of which many demonstrators were killed. Gen. Suchinda resigned and in May the legislative assembly voted that future prime ministers should be elected by its members rather than appointed by the military. The 1995 election was fought against a background of political and financial corruption. After the 1996 election a new constitution was drafted allowing for the separation of the executive, legislative and judicial branches of government.

TERRITORY AND POPULATION

Thailand is bounded in the west by Myanmar, north and east by Laos and southeast by Cambodia. In the south it becomes a peninsula bounded in the west by the Indian Ocean, south by Malaysia and east by the Gulf of Thailand. Area is 513,115 sq. km (198,114 sq. miles).

At the 2000 census the population was 60,617,200 (30,767,100 females); density, 118 per sq. km. 20,759,900 lived in the Northeastern region, 11,367,800 in the Northern region, 14,101,500 in the Central region, 8,067,800 in the Southern region and 6,320,200 in Bangkok. In 1999, 78·8% of the population lived in rural areas.

The UN gives a projected population for 2010 of 69·68m.

Thailand is divided into 4 regions, 76 provinces and Bangkok, the capital. Population of Bangkok (1999), 7,133,000. Other towns (1993 estimates): Nonthaburi (261,355), Nakhon Ratchasima (188,171), Chiangmai (170,397), Hat Yai (148,632).

Thai is the official language, spoken by 53% of the population as their mother tongue. 27% speak Lao (mainly in the northeast), 12% Chinese (mainly in urban areas), 3·7% Malay (mainly in the south) and 2·7% Khmer (along the Cambodian border).

Bangkok: Situated on the Chao Phraya river, 40 km from the Gulf of Thailand, Bangkok was established as the capital of Thailand, then called Siam, in 1782 by

King Rama I, the founder of the Chakkri dynasty. The city has since grown, combining traditions such as the building of Wats (temples), with modern industry, to become one of Asia's busiest and most important commercial and industrial centres.

SOCIAL STATISTICS
1995 births, 1,013,000; deaths, 373,000. 1995 birth rate per 1,000 population, 17·4; death rate, 6·4. Annual population growth rate, 1990–99, 1·0%. Of the total population in 1997, 25% were under 15 years, 69% between 15 and 64 years, and 6% aged 65 and over. Expectation of life (1999): 67·0 years for men; 72·9 years for women. Infant mortality, 1999, 26 per 1,000 live births; fertility rate, 1999, 1·7 births per woman.

CLIMATE
The climate is tropical, with high temperatures and humidity. Over most of the country, three seasons may be recognized. The rainy season is June to Oct., the cool season from Nov. to Feb. and the hot season is March to May. Rainfall is generally heaviest in the south and lightest in the northeast. Bangkok, Jan. 78°F (25·6°C), July 83°F (28·3°C). Annual rainfall 56" (1,400 mm).

CONSTITUTION AND GOVERNMENT
The reigning King is **Bhumibol Adulyadej,** born 5 Dec. 1927. King Bhumibol married on 28 April 1950 Princess Sirikit, and was crowned 5 May 1950 (making him currently the world's longest-reigning monarch). *Offspring:* Princess Ubol Ratana (born 5 April 1951, married Aug. 1972 Peter Ladd Jensen); Crown Prince Vajiralongkorn (born 28 July 1952, married 3 Jan. 1977 Soamsawali Kitiyakra); Princess Maha Chakri Sirindhorn (born 2 April 1955); Princess Chulabhorn (born 4 July 1957, married 7 Jan. 1982 Virayudth Didyasarin).

Parliament consists of a 200-member *Senate,* fully elected for the first time in 2000, and a 500-member *House of Representatives,* elected for four-year terms by universal suffrage of citizens over 17 years, with 400 constituency MPs and 100 from party lists. The present constitution dates from 1997. It is Thailand's 16th since 1932 and the first to emerge from public consultation rather than a military coup. It particularly tries to eradicate vote-buying. It introduced proportional representation for some seats, established an independent election commission, and required that votes be counted away from the polling stations. The constitution further required all cabinet members to resign their parliamentary seats.

The *Prime Minister* is elected by the House of Representatives.

National Anthem. 'Prathet Thai ruam nua chat chua Thai' ('Thailand, cradle of Thais wherever they may be'); words by Luang Saranuprapan, tune by Phrachen Duriyang.

RECENT ELECTIONS
At the elections to the House of Representatives of 6 and 29 Jan. 2001, the Thai Rak Thai Party (TRT) gained 248 seats; the Democratic Party (PP), 128; Thai Nation (PCT), 41; New Aspiration (PKWM), 36; National Development (PCP), 29; other parties gained a total of 18 seats. Thai Rak Thai has since merged with both New Aspiration and a second party, giving them a total of 296 seats.

There were elections to the Senate on 4 March, 29 April and 4 June 2000. 200 members were elected in single-seat constituencies. Only non-partisans were allowed to stand. A number of members were disqualified amid allegations of vote fraud.

CURRENT ADMINISTRATION
Following the 2001 election a coalition was formed between the TRT, PCT and PKWM. In March 2003 it comprised:

Prime Minister: Thaksin Shinawatra; b. 1949 (TRT; sworn in 9 Feb. 2001).

Deputy Prime Ministers: Gen. Chavalit Yongchaiyudh; Suwit Khunkitti; Chaturon Chaisang; Korn Dabbaransi; Prommin Lertsuridej; Wissanu Krea-ngam; Somkid Jatusripitak; Purachai Piumsombun.

Minister of Defence: Thamarak Isarangura. *Finance:* Suchart Jaovisidha. *Foreign Affairs:* Surakiart Sathirathai. *Tourism and Sports:* Sontaya Kunplome. *Social Development and Human Services:* Anurak Chureemas. *Agriculture and Co-operatives:* Sora-at Klinpratoom. *Transport:* Suriya Jungrungreangkit. *Natural Resources and Environment:* Prapat Panyachatraksa. *Information and Communications Technology:* Surapong Suebwonglee. *Energy:* Prommin Lertsuridej. *Commerce:* Adisai Bodharamik. *Interior:* Wan Muhamad Noor Matha. *Justice:* Pongthep Thepkanjana. *Labour:* Suwat Liptapanlop. *Culture:* Uraiwan Thienthong. *Education:* Pongpol Adireksarn. *Public Health:* Sudarat Keyuraphan. *Industry:* Somsak Thepsuthin. *Science and Technology:* Pinij Jarusombat.

Office of the Prime Minister: http://www.spokesman.go.th/

DEFENCE
Conscription is for two years. In 2000 defence expenditure totalled US$2,464m. (US$40 per capita), representing 2·0% of GDP.

Army. Strength (1999) 190,000. In addition there were 50,000 National Security Volunteer Corps, 18,500 *Thahan Phran* (a volunteer irregular force), 18,000 Border Police and a 50,000 strong paramilitary provincial police force.

Navy. The Royal Thai Navy is, next to the Chinese, the most significant naval force in the South China Sea. The fleet includes a small Spanish-built vertical/short-take-off-and-land carrier *Chakrinareubet,* which entered service in 1997 and operates eight ex-Spanish AV-8A Harrier aircraft and helicopters, and 15 frigates. Manpower was 73,000 (1999) including 20,000 marines and a naval air wing of 1,700.

The main bases are at Bangkok, Sattahip, Songkla and Phang Nga, with the riverine forces based at Nakhon Phanom.

Air Force. The Royal Thai Air Force had a strength (1999) of 43,000 personnel and 162 combat aircraft, including F-16s and F-5Es. The RTAF is made up of a headquarters and Combat, Logistics Support, Training and Special Services Groups.

INTERNATIONAL RELATIONS
Thailand is a member of the UN, WTO, BIS, Asian Development Bank, ASEAN, the Colombo Plan, APEC, the Mekong Group and IOM.

In 2001 tension between Thailand and neighbouring Myanmar escalated amid a series of border skirmishes, in part over the cross-border trade in drugs. In May 2002 the border between the two countries was closed following a diplomatic row. It was re-opened in Oct. 2002.

ECONOMY
In 1998 agriculture accounted for 11·2% of GDP, industry 41·2% and services 47·6%.

Thailand's 'shadow' (black market) economy is estimated to constitute approximately 70% of the country's official GDP, one of the highest percentages of any country in the world.

Overview. The financial crisis that spread across southeast Asia in 1997 started as a result of the devaluation of the baht (the Thai currency) in July and hit Thailand with particular force. Over 50 finance companies suspended business and the Thai stock exchange lost 82% of its 1995 peak value. An IMF rescue package of US$17·2bn. gained time to put reforms in place, including tighter budgetary control, the merging of banks and the restructuring of the country's outmoded financial system.

In May 1998 the government agreed to adopt a strategy for the eventual privatization of the four commercial banks nationalized earlier in the year.

Currency. The unit of currency is the *baht* (THB) of 100 *satang*. After being pegged to the US dollar, the baht was devalued and allowed to float on 2 July 1997. It was the devaluation of the baht that sparked the financial turmoil that spread throughout the world over the next year. Foreign exchange reserves were US$35,985m. and gold reserves 2·50m. troy oz in June 2002. Inflation was 1·7% in 2001. Total money supply in May 2002 was 598,378m. baht.

Budget. The fiscal year starts on 1 Oct. Total revenues and expenditures (in 1m. baht):

	1995–96	1996–97	1997–98	1998–99	1999–2000
Revenue	872,967	870,421	753,347	739,136	786,719
Expenditure	757,961	957,707	1,051,667	1,160,241	884,432

Principal expenditure in 1996 (in 1m. baht) was on: education (159,035), defence (95,601), health (59,205), public order and safety (46,615), and social security and welfare (28,637).

Performance. Following the financial crisis in the second half of 1997 the economy contracted by 10·5% in 1998. Growth recovered to 4·4% in 1999 and in 2000 was 4·6%, but 2001 saw growth of only 1·8%. Thailand's total GDP in 2001 was US$114·8bn.

Banking and Finance. The Bank of Thailand (founded in 1942) is the central bank and bank of issue, an independent body although its capital is government-owned. Its assets and liabilities in Dec. 1991 were 580,844·5m. baht. Its *Governor* is Pridiyathorn Devakula. In 1997 there were 21 domestic commercial banks, 14 foreign banks with branch licences and 22 foreign banks with representative offices. Total credits of commercial banks, Dec. 1995, 4,144,000m. baht. Deposits, Dec. 1995, 3,141,500m. baht. There is a Government Savings Bank.

There is a stock exchange (SET) in Bangkok.

Weights and Measures. The metric system was made compulsory in 1923. Traditional units are also widely used.

ENERGY AND NATURAL RESOURCES

Environment. According to the *World Bank Atlas* Thailand's carbon dioxide emissions were the equivalent of 3·2 tonnes per capita in 1998.

Electricity. Installed capacity, 1997, was 17m. kW. Output, 1998, 85bn. kWh, with consumption per capita 1,345 kWh. Privatization of the Electricity Generating Authority (EGAT) was set to start during 1999.

Oil and Gas. Proven crude petroleum reserves in 1999 were 300m. bbls. Production of crude petroleum (1996), 22m. bbls. Thailand and Vietnam settled an offshore dispute in 1997 which stretched back to 1973. Demarcation allowed for petroleum exploration in the Gulf of Thailand, with each side required to give the other some revenue if an underground reservoir is discovered which straddles the border.

Production of natural gas (1999) 17·1bn. cu. metres. Estimated reserves, 1999, 350bn. cu. metres. In April 1998 Thailand and Malaysia agreed to share equally the natural gas jointly produced in an offshore area which both countries claim as their own territory.

Minerals. The mineral resources include cassiterite (tin ore), wolfram, scheelite, antimony, coal, copper, gold, iron, lead, manganese, molybdenum, rubies, sapphires, silver, zinc and zircons. Production, 1997 (in tonnes): limestone, 58·80m.; lignite (1997), 23·39m.; gypsum, 8·56m.; salt, 655,000; kaolin clay, 367,000; zinc ore, 91,132; iron ore (1995), 34,500; lead concentrates (1995), 22,800; fluorite, 7,826.

Agriculture. In 1998 there were 16·8m. ha of arable land and 3·58m. ha of permanent cropland; 4·78m. ha were irrigated in 1998. The chief produce is rice, a staple of the national diet. Output of the major crops in 2000 was (in 1,000 tonnes): sugarcane, 51,210; rice, 23,403; cassava, 18,509; maize, 4,571; pineapples, 2,281; natural rubber, 2,236; bananas, 1,720; coconuts, 1,373; mangoes, 1,350; tangerines, mandarins and satsumas, 640; palm oil, 520; watermelons, 400; soybeans, 346; oranges, 320; onions, 300; sorghum, 250. Thailand is the world's leading producer of both natural rubber and pineapples.

Livestock, 2000: cattle, 6,100,000; pigs, 7,682,000; buffaloes, 2,100,000; goats, 130,000; sheep, 42,000; chickens, 172,000,000; ducks, 22,000,000.

Forestry. Forests covered 11·63m. ha in 1995, or 22·8% of the land area (down from 13·28m. ha in 1990). Teak and other hardwoods grow in the deciduous forests of the north; elsewhere tropical evergreen forests are found, with the timber yang the main crop (a source of yang oil). In 1999, 36·63m. cu. metres of roundwood were cut.

Fisheries. In 1999 the total catch came to 3,004,900 tonnes with marine fishing accounting for over 92% of all fish caught. Thailand is the leading exporter of fishery commodities in the world, with exports in 2000 totalling US$4·37bn.

INDUSTRY

Production of manufactured goods in 1995 included 33·4m. tonnes of cement, 14·3m. tonnes of distillate fuel oil (1997), 8·57m. tonnes of residual fuel oil (1997), 4·14m. tonnes of sugar (1998), 540,800 tonnes of synthetic fibre, 756·8m. litres of beer (1997), 48bn. cigarettes, 250,500 tonnes of tin plate, 126,000 automobiles and 324,000 commercial vehicles (1994), 370,000 tonnes of galvanized iron sheets, and 2·1m. tonnes of crude steel (1997).

Labour. In 1997 the total labour force (aged 13 and over) was 33·2m., of which 50% were in agriculture, 14% in commerce, 13% in manufacturing industry, and 13% in community and social services. The unemployment rate was 2·6% in 1996. A minimum wage is set by the National Wages Committee. It varied between 133 baht and 165 baht per day in Jan. 2001.

INTERNATIONAL TRADE

Foreign debt was US$79,675m. in 2000.

Imports and Exports. Trade in US$1m.:

	1996	1997	1998	1999	2000
Imports f.o.b.	63,897	55,084	36,515	42,762	56,192
Exports f.o.b.	54,408	56,656	52,753	56,775	67,949

Main exports by category in 1996: electrical machinery, 18·1%; power-generating equipment, 16·8%; garments, 6·0%; rubber products, 5·8%; live fish, 4·5%; precious jewellery, 4·0%. Imports, 1996: power-generating equipment, 19·4%; electrical machinery, 18·7%; mineral fuels and lubricants, 8·6%; road vehicles, 7·0%; iron and steel, 6·0%; plastics, 3·2%.

The main import sources in 1997 were Japan (25·6%), USA (13·9%), Singapore (5·0%) and Malaysia (4·8%). Principal export destinations were USA (19·6%), Japan (15·0%), Singapore (11·0%) and Hong Kong (5·9%).

COMMUNICATIONS

Roads. In 1996 there were 64,600 km of highways, of which 97·5% was paved. Vehicles in use in 1996 comprised: 1·66m. passenger cars, 2·85m. commercial vehicles and 10·2m. motorcycles.

Rail. The State Railway totals 4,623 km. Passenger-km travelled in 1996 came to 12·2bn. and freight tonne-km to 3·3bn. A metro ('Skytrain') was opened in Bangkok in 1999.

Civil Aviation. There are international airports at Bangkok (Don Muang), Chiangmai, Phuket and Hat Yai. The national carrier, Thai Airways International, is 92·85% state-owned, although the government has stated that it wishes to reduce its stake to less than 50%. In 1999 it flew 163·4m. km, carrying 15,950,500 passengers (10,100,400 on international flights). Bangkok handled 28,323,474 passengers in 2000 (20,965,985 on international flights) and 873,792 tonnes of freight. Phuket is the second busiest airport for passenger traffic, with 3,562,636 passengers in 2000 (2,213,874 on domestic flights), and Chiangmai the second busiest for freight, with 23,804 tonnes in 2000. Work on a new Bangkok airport (Suvarnabhumi) is scheduled for completion in 2004.

Shipping. In 1998 merchant shipping totalled 1,999,000 GRT, including oil tankers 364,000 GRT. In 1995, 2,524 vessels of 21·7m. NRT entered the port of Bangkok.

Telecommunications. In 2000 main telephone lines numbered 5,591,100 (92·3 per 1,000 population), there were 3·4m. mobile phone subscribers and 1·5m. PCs were in use (24·3 for every 1,000 inhabitants). In 1997 there were 150,000 fax machines. Thailand had 1·2m. Internet users in Dec. 2000.

Postal Services. There were 4,264 post offices in 1994, or one for every 13,900 persons.

SOCIAL INSTITUTIONS

Justice. The judicial power is exercised in the name of the King, by *(a)* courts of first instance, *(b)* the court of appeal *(Uthorn)* and *(c)* the Supreme Court *(Dika)*. The King appoints, transfers and dismisses judges, who are independent in conducting trials and giving judgment in accordance with the law.

Courts of first instance are subdivided into 20 magistrates' courts *(Kwaeng)* with limited civil and minor criminal jurisdiction; 85 provincial courts *(Changwad)* with unlimited civil and criminal jurisdiction; the criminal and civil courts with exclusive jurisdiction in Bangkok; the central juvenile courts for persons under 18 years of age in Bangkok.

The court of appeal exercises appellate jurisdiction in civil and criminal cases from all courts of first instance. From it appeals lie to Dika Court on any point of law and, in certain cases, on questions of fact.

The Supreme Court is the supreme tribunal of the land. Besides its normal appellate jurisdiction in civil and criminal matters, it has semi-original jurisdiction over general election petitions. The decisions of Dika Court are final. Every person has the right to present a petition to the government who will deal with all matters of grievance.

The death penalty is still in force and there were six executions in 2002. The population in penal institutions in mid-2001 was 217,697 (357 per 100,000 of national population).

Religion. At the 2000 census 94·6% of the population were Buddhists and 4·6% Muslims.

Education. Education is compulsory for children for nine years and is free in local municipal schools. In 1996 there were 34,001 primary schools with 5·9m. pupils. There were 3·7m. secondary school pupils with (in 1994) 151,008 teachers. In higher education there were 1·2m. students (481,936 at university level). In 1996 there were 13 universities, 2 open (distance) universities, 4 institutes of technology and 1 institute of development administration in the public sector, and 9 universities and 1 institute of technology in the private sector.

The adult literacy rate in 1999 was 95·3% (97·0% among males and 93·5% among females).

In 1996 total expenditure on education came to 4·8% of GNP.

Health. In 1992 there were 1,097 hospitals, with a provision of 17 beds per 10,000 population. In 1996 there were 17,355 doctors and, in 1994, 2,984 dentists, 5,575 pharmacists, 94,103 nurses and 10,342 midwives. Thailand has been one of the most successful countries in the developing world in the fight against AIDS. By the mid-1990s the government was spending US$80m. a year on AIDS education, and the number of sexually transmitted diseases reported from government clinics fell from some 400,000 in 1986 to below 50,000 in 1995. However, since 1996 AIDS expenditure has been declining rapidly. As a result, HIV infections are now increasing among several risk groups after a period of overall decline.

CULTURE

Broadcasting. The Radio and Television Executive Committee controls the administrative, legal, technical and programming aspects of broadcasting, and consists of representatives of various government bodies. All radio stations are operated by, or under the supervision of, government agencies. Radio Thailand broadcasts three national programmes, provincial programmes, an educational service and an external service (nine languages), and the Voice of Free Asia. Television of Thailand is the state service (colour by PAL). There are three commercial channels and an Army service. At the 2000 census 91·5% of households had televisions and 77·2% had radios.

Cinema. In 1993 there were 600 cinemas with a seating capacity of 380,011.

Press. In 1996 there were 30 daily newspapers, with a combined circulation of about 3·8m.

Tourism. In 1999, 8·65m. foreigners visited Thailand. Tourist revenue was US$6·7bn.

DIPLOMATIC REPRESENTATIVES
Of Thailand in the United Kingdom (29–30 Queen's Gate, London, SW7 5JB)
Ambassador: Vacant.
Chargé d'Affaires a.i.: Arbhorn Manasvanich.

Of the United Kingdom in Thailand (Wireless Rd., Bangkok 10330)
Ambassador: Lloyd Barnaby Smith, CMG.

Of Thailand in the USA (1024 Wisconsin Ave., NW, Washington, D.C., 20007)
Ambassador: Sakthip Krairiksh.

Of the USA in Thailand (120 Wireless Rd., Bangkok 10330)
Ambassador: Darryl Norman Johnson.

Of Thailand to the United Nations
Ambassador: Chuchai Kasemsarn.

Of Thailand to the European Union
Ambassador: Surapong Posayanond.

FURTHER READING
National Statistical Office *Thailand Statistical Yearbook.*

Krongkaew, M. (ed.) *Thailand's Industrialization and its Consequences.* London, 1995
Kulick, E. and Wilson, D., *Thailand's Turn: Profile of a New Dragon.* London and New York, 1993 (NY, 1994)
Smyth, David, *Thailand.* [Bibliography] 2nd ed. ABC-Clio, Oxford and Santa Barbara (CA), 1998

National statistical office: National Statistical Office, Thanon Lan Luang, Bangkok 10100.
Website: http://www.nso.go.th

TOGO

République Togolaise

Capital: Lomé
Population estimate, 2000: 4·53m.
GDP per capita, 2000: (PPP$) 1,442
HDI/world rank: 0·493/141

KEY HISTORICAL EVENTS

Europeans, beginning with the Portuguese who first visited the area in 1471–72, traded on the coast for centuries, especially in slaves. In the 19th century palm oil exports flourished at Anecho, Agoue and Porto Seguro, where British, French and German traders operated. Several prominent Togolese families of partly Brazilian or Portuguese origin, still important among the coastal African élite, arose at that time. Despite the important rival influences of Britain and France in the area, it was Germany that established colonial rule on the coast in 1884. German control was then extended inland but encountered strong resistance and only in 1912 was the colony fully subdued.

German Togo was overrun by the Allies in 1914. It was partitioned in 1919 into British and French Mandated Territories under the League of Nations. After the Second World War French Togo and British Togoland became Trust Territories under the United Nations. In British Togoland a referendum was held on 9 May 1956, in which a majority voted for union with Gold Coast, although most people in the south voted for union with French Togo. The whole territory was merged with what soon afterwards became independent Ghana, but many Togolese objected. In French Togo partial self-government was granted in 1956. On 27 April 1960 the country became independent.

On 13 Jan. 1963 President Olympio was murdered by soldiers. His successor was deposed in a bloodless military coup in Jan. 1967 and on 14 April 1967 Gen. (then Col.) Gnassingbé Eyadéma assumed the Presidency. A new constitution was approved in 1992.

TERRITORY AND POPULATION

Togo is bounded in the west by Ghana, north by Burkina Faso, east by Benin and south by the Gulf of Guinea. The area is 56,785 sq. km. The population of Togo in 1981 (census) was 2,700,982; 1997 (estimate) 4·32m.; density, 76 per sq. km.

The UN gives a projected population for 2010 of 5·83m.

In 1999, 67·3% of the population lived in rural areas, and in 1997, 46% were below the age of 15. The capital is Lomé (population in 1999, 790,000), other towns being Sokodé (51,000), Lama-Kara (35,000), Kpalimé (30,000), Atakpamé (30,000), Bassar (22,000), Dapaong (22,000) and Mango (20,000).

Area, population and chief town of the five regions:

Region	Area in sq. km	Population (1981 census)	Population (1989 estimate)	Chief town
Centrale	13,182	269,174	339,000	Sokodé
De La Kara	11,630	432,626	531,500	Lama-Kara
Des Plateaux	16,975	561,656	810,500	Atakpamé
Des Savanes	8,602	326,826	410,500	Dapaong
Maritime	6,396	1,039,700	1,147,800[1]	Lomé

[1]1984 figure.

There are 37 ethnic groups. The south is largely populated by Ewe-speaking peoples (forming 44% of the population) and related groups, while the north is mainly inhabited by Hamitic groups speaking Kabre (27%), Gurma (14%) and Tem (4%). The official language is French but Ewe and Kabre are also taught in schools.

SOCIAL STATISTICS

Births, 1996, 197,000; deaths, 55,000. 1996 birth rate (per 1,000 population), 45·5; death rate, 12·8. Expectation of life (1999) was 50·4 years for males and 52·8 for females. Annual population growth rate, 1990–99, 2·8%. Infant mortality, 1999, 80 per 1,000 live births; fertility rate, 1999, 5·9 births per woman.

CLIMATE
The tropical climate produces wet seasons from March to July and from Oct. to Nov. in the south. The north has one wet season, from April to July. The heaviest rainfall occurs in the mountains of the west, southwest and centre. Lomé, Jan. 81°F (27·2°C), July 76°F (24·4°C). Annual rainfall 35" (875 mm).

CONSTITUTION AND GOVERNMENT
A referendum on 27 Sept. 1992 approved a new constitution by 98·11% of votes cast. Under this the *President* and the *National Assembly* were directly elected for five-year terms. Initially the president was allowed to be re-elected only once. However, on 30 Dec. 2002 parliament approved an amendment to the constitution lifting the restriction on the number of times that the president may be re-elected. The National Assembly has 81 seats and is elected for a five-year term in single-seat constituencies.

National Anthem. 'Terre de nos aïeux' ('Land of our forefathers').

RECENT ELECTIONS
In the presidential elections held on 21 June 1998 it was clear that the chief opposition candidate Gilchrist Olympio, son of the country's first president, was going to win, but the paramilitary police intervened and prevented the count in the capital city, Lomé, from being completed; it was also reported that ballot boxes were seized and burnt. The head of the electoral commission resigned in protest along with four of its members and the EU and American observers declared the election to be fraudulent. The interior minister pronounced Gen. Gnassingbé Eyadéma the winner, enabling him to continue as the country's ruler, having already been in power since 1967.

At the parliamentary elections on 27 Oct. 2002 the main opposition parties to the Togolese People's Assembly (RPT, the former sole party) boycotted the election, protesting a lack of transparency in the voting process. Turn-out was put at around 60% and preliminary results showed the RPT had won 72 of the available 81 seats, down 7 on its 1999 showing.

CURRENT ADMINISTRATION
President: Gen. Gnassingbé Eyadéma; b. 1937 (RPT; since 1967, most recently re-elected on 21 June 1998).

In March 2003 the government comprised:
Prime Minister: Koffi Sama; b. 1944 (RPT; sworn in 29 June 2002).

Minister of Agriculture, Animal Breeding and Fisheries: Komikpiné Bamenante. *Civil Service, Labour and Employment:* Kokou Tozoun. *Communication and Civic Education:* Pitang Tchalla. *Economy, Finance and Privatization:* Ayaovi Demba. *Environment and Forest Resources:* Rodolphe Osseyi. *Foreign Affairs and Co-operation:* Roland Yao Kpotsra. *Industry, Commerce, Transport and the Development of the Franc Zone:* Drama Dramani. *Interior, Security and Decentralization:* Akila Esso Boco. *Justice, Human Rights and Keeper of the Seals, Democracy and Rule of Law Promotion:* Katari Foli-Bazi. *Mines, Energy, Posts and Telecommunications:* Tchamdja Andjo. *National Defence and War Veterans:* Gen. Assani Tidjani. *National Education and Research:* Charles Kondi Agba. *Public Health, Social Welfare, Women's Affairs and Children:* Suzanne Aho Assouma. *Relations with the National Assembly:* Harry Olympio. *Technical Education and Professional Training:* Edo Kodjo Maurille Agbobli. *Tourism, Leisure and Handicrafts:* Takpandja Lalle. *Town Planning and Housing:* Dovi Kavégué. *Youth, Sports and Culture:* Komi Klassou.

Government Website: http://www.republicoftogo.com/

DEFENCE
There is selective conscription which lasts for two years. Defence expenditure totalled US$30m. in 2000 (US$7 per capita), representing 2·0% of GDP.

Army. Strength (1999) 6,500, with a further 750 in a paramilitary gendarmerie.

Navy. In 1999 the Naval wing of the armed forces numbered 150 and was based at Lomé.

Air Force. The Air Force—established with French assistance—numbered (1999) 250, with 16 combat aircraft.

INTERNATIONAL RELATIONS

Togo is a member of the UN, WTO, the African Union, African Development Bank, ECOWAS and the International Organization of the Francophonie, OIC and is an ACP member state of the ACP-EU relationship.

ECONOMY

Agriculture contributed 42·1% of GDP in 1998, industry 21·1% and services 36·8%.

Overview. After civil and economic turmoil in the early 1990s, a structural redevelopment programme, launched in 1994, resulted in positive growth after two years of negative growth and two years of growth at less than 1%. Private-sector development is encouraged and there are plans to privatize some 20 state companies.

Currency. The unit of currency is the *franc CFA* (XOF) with a parity of 655·957 francs CFA to one euro. Foreign exchange reserves were US$201m. in May 2002 and total money supply was 173,247m. francs CFA. Gold reserves were 13,000 troy oz in June 2000. Inflation in 2001 was 6·8%.

Budget. In 1997 revenues were an estimated US$232m. and expenditures US$252m.

Performance. The economy shrank by 1·9% in 2000, but 2001 saw growth of 2·7%. Total GDP in 2001 was US$1·3bn.

Banking and Finance. The bank of issue is the Central Bank of West African States (BCEAO). The *Governor* is Charles Konan Banny. 10 commercial and 2 development banks were based in Lomé in 1997. Bank deposits totalled 168,700m. francs CFA in 1989.

Weights and Measures. The metric system is in use.

ENERGY AND NATURAL RESOURCES

Environment. According to the *World Bank Atlas* Togo's carbon dioxide emissions in 1998 were the equivalent of 0·2 tonnes per capita.

Electricity. Installed capacity in 1995 was 34,000 kW. In 1998 production totalled 90m. kWh. Additional electricity is imported from Ghana. Consumption per capita in 1997 was 97 kWh.

Minerals. Output of phosphate rock (1995) 2,500,000 tonnes. Other minerals are limestone, iron ore (550m. tonnes in 1992) and marble.

Agriculture. Agriculture supports about 80% of the population. Most food production comes from individual holdings under 3 ha. Inland, the country is hilly; dry plains alternate with arable land. There were 2·3m. ha of arable land in 1998 and 0·1m. ha of permanent crops. There are considerable plantations of oil and cocoa palms, coffee, cacao, kola, cassava and cotton. Production, 2000 (in 1,000 tonnes): cassava, 694; yams, 666; maize, 494; seed cotton, 162; sorghum, 142; cottonseed, 91; rice, 81; cotton lint, 65; dry beans, 45; millet, 39; groundnuts, 35.

Livestock (2000, in 1,000): cattle, 215; sheep, 740; pigs, 850; goats, 1,110; chickens, 8,000.

Forestry. Forests covered 1,245,000 ha in 1995, or 22·9% of the land area (compared to 1,338,000 ha in 1990). Teak plantations covered 8,600 ha. In 1999, 1·23m. cu. metres of roundwood were cut.

Fisheries. The catch in 1999 totalled 22,924 tonnes (78% from marine waters).

INDUSTRY

Industry is small-scale. Cement and textiles are produced and food processed.

Labour. In 1996 the workforce was 1,739,000 (60% males). Around 62% of the economically active population in 1995 were engaged in agriculture, fisheries and forestry. In 1994 the statutory minimum wage was 75·60 francs CFA per hour.

Trade Unions. With the abandonment of single-party politics, the former monolithic Togo National Workers Confederation (CNTT) has split into several federations and independent trade unions.

INTERNATIONAL TRADE

A free trade zone was established in 1990. Foreign debt was US$1,435m. in 2000.

Imports and Exports. In 2000 imports (f.o.b.) amounted to US$489·4m. (US$553·5m. in 1999); exports (f.o.b.) US$391·5m. (US$420·3m. in 1999). The main import suppliers in 1994 were France (24·0%), Germany (9·9%) and Côte d'Ivoire (6·3%). Principal export destinations were Canada (17·0%), Bolivia (7·6%) and Indonesia (5·7%).

COMMUNICATIONS

Roads. There were, in 1996, 7,520 km of roads, of which 2,380 km were paved. In 1996 there were 79,200 passenger cars, 59,000 motorcycles and 33,660 commercial vehicles.

Rail. There are four metre-gauge railways connecting Lomé, with Aného (continuing to Cotonou in Benin), Kpalimé, Tabligbo and (via Atakpamé) Blitta; total length 525 km. In 1994 the railways carried 5·7 tonne-km and 0·6m. passengers.

Civil Aviation. Togo is a member of the multinational Air Afrique. In 1998 it had flights from Tokoin airport, near Lomé, to Abidjan, Accra, Bamako, Bangui, Brazzaville, Cotonou, Dakar, Douala, Libreville, N'Djaména, Ouagadougou, Paris and Pointe Noire. Air Burkina also provided an internal service from Lomé to Niamtougou in 1998, and had flights from Niamtougou to Ouagadougou. In 2000 Tokoin handled 166,000 passengers (all on international flights) and 5,400 tonnes of freight. In 1999 scheduled airline traffic of Togo-based carriers flew 3·0m. km, carrying 84,000 passengers (all on international flights).

Shipping. In 1998 merchant shipping totalled 2,000 GRT.

Telecommunications. Togo had 42,800 main telephone lines in 2000 (9·2 per 1,000 population) and there were 100,000 PCs in use (21·6 per 1,000 persons). There were 17,000 fax machines in 1997 and 17,000 mobile phone subscribers in 1999. Togo had approximately 20,000 Internet users in Dec. 2000.

Postal Services. In 1995 there were 50 post offices.

SOCIAL INSTITUTIONS

Justice. The Supreme Court and two Appeal Courts are in Lomé, one for criminal cases and one for civil and commercial cases. Each receives appeal from a series of local tribunals.

The population in penal institutions in 1998 was 2,043 (45 per 100,000 of national population).

Religion. In 1997, 60% of the population followed traditional animist religions; 28·5% were Christian and 12% Muslim.

Education. The adult literacy rate in 1999 was 56·3% (73·6% among males and 39·6% among females). In 1996–97 there were 859,574 pupils and 18,535 teachers in primary schools, and 178,254 pupils in secondary schools; in 1994–95 there were 11,172 students in higher education institutions. In 1990 about 50% of children of school age were attending school. The University of Benin at Lomé (founded in 1970) had 9,139 students and 134 academic staff in 1994–95. An estimated 23,800m. francs CFA was spent on education in 1995.

Health. In 1990 hospital bed provision was 16 per 10,000 population. In 1991 there were 319 doctors, 22 dentists, 65 pharmacists, 222 midwives and 1,187 nursing staff. Government expenditure on health in 1995 was estimated at 5,900m. francs CFA.

CULTURE

Broadcasting. Broadcasting is provided by the government-controlled Radiodiffusion-Télévision Togolaise. There were 73,000 TV receivers (colour by SECAM V) and 940,000 radio sets in 1997.

Press. There is one government-controlled daily newspaper (circulation 15,000).

Tourism. In 1998 there were 94,000 foreign tourists, bringing revenue of US$15m.

DIPLOMATIC REPRESENTATIVES

The Embassy of Togo in the United Kingdom closed on 30 Sept. 1991.
Of the United Kingdom in Togo
Ambassador: Dr Rod Pullen (resides at Accra, Ghana).

Of Togo in the USA (2208 Massachusetts Ave., NW, Washington, D.C., 20008)
Ambassador: Akoussouleou Bodjona.

Of the USA in Togo (Rue Pelletier Caventou and Rue Vauban, Lomé)
Ambassador: Karl Hofmann.

Of Togo to the United Nations
Ambassador: Roland Yao Kpotsra.

Of Togo to the European Union
Ambassador: Ohara Kati Korga.

FURTHER READING

Decalo, Samuel, *Togo*. [Bibliography] ABC-Clio, Oxford and Santa Barbara (CA), 1995

TONGA

Kingdom of Tonga

Capital: Nuku'alofa
Population estimate, 2000: 100,000
GDP per capita: not available
GNP per capita: $1,730

KEY HISTORICAL EVENTS

The Tongatapu group of islands in the south western Pacific Ocean were discovered by Tasman in 1643. The Kingdom of Tonga attained unity under Taufa'ahau Tupou (George I) who became ruler of his native Ha'apai in 1820, of Vava'u in 1833 and of Tongatapu in 1845. By 1860 the kingdom had become converted to Christianity. In 1862 the king granted freedom to the people from arbitrary rule of minor chiefs and gave them the right to the allocation of land for their own needs. These institutional changes, together with the establishment of a parliament of chiefs, paved the way towards a democratic constitution. By the Anglo-German Agreement of 14 Nov. 1899, the Tonga Islands became a British protectorate. The protectorate was dissolved on 4 June 1970 when Tonga, the only ancient kingdom surviving from the pre-European period in Polynesia, achieved independence within the Commonwealth.

TERRITORY AND POPULATION

The Kingdom consists of some 169 islands and islets with a total area of 289 sq. miles (748 sq. km; including inland waters), and lies between 15° and 23° 30' S. lat and 173° and 177° W. long, its western boundary being the eastern boundary of the Fiji Islands. The islands are split up into the following groups (reading from north to south): the Niuas, Vava'u, Ha'apai, Tongatapu and 'Eua. The three main groups, both from historical and administrative significance, are Tongatapu in the south, Ha'apai in the centre and Vava'u in the north. Census population (1996) 97,446; density, 130 per sq. km. In 1995, 59% of the population lived in rural areas.

The capital is Nuku'alofa on Tongatapu, population (1999) 37,000.

There are five divisions comprising 23 districts:

Division	Sq. km	Census 1996	Capital
Niuas	72	2,018	Hihifo
Vava'u	119	15,779	Neiafu
Ha'apai	110	8,148	Pangai
Tongatapu	261	66,577	Nuku'alofa
'Eua	87	4,924	Ohonua

Tongan and English are both spoken.

SOCIAL STATISTICS

Births, 1994, 2,770; deaths, 388; marriages, 748; divorces, 75. Annual population growth rate, 1990–99, 0·3%. Infant mortality, 1999 estimate, 38 per 1,000 live births. Fertility rate, 1999, 4·0 births per woman.

CLIMATE

Generally a healthy climate, although Jan. to March hot and humid, with temperatures of 90°F (32·2°C). Rainfall amounts are comparatively high, being greatest from Dec. to March. Nuku'alofa, Jan. 25·8°C, July 21·3°C. Annual rainfall 1,643 mm. Vava'u, Jan. 27·3°C, July 23·4°C. Annual rainfall 2,034 mm.

CONSTITUTION AND GOVERNMENT

The reigning King is **Taufa'ahau Tupou IV**, GCVO, GCMG, KBE, born 4 July 1918, succeeded on 16 Dec. 1965 on the death of his mother, Queen Salote Tupou III.

The present Constitution is almost identical with that granted in 1875 by King George Tupou I. There is a Privy Council, Cabinet, Legislative Assembly and Judiciary. The 30-member *Legislative Assembly*, which meets annually, is composed of the King, 9 nobles elected by their peers, 9 elected representatives of the people and the Privy Councillors (numbering 11); the King appoints one of the 9 nobles to be the Speaker. The elections are held triennially.

National Anthem. 'E 'Otua, Mafimafi, ko ho mau 'eiki Koe' ('Oh Almighty God above, thou art our Lord and sure defence'); words by Prince Uelingtoni Ngu Tupoumalohi, tune by K. G. Schmitt.

RECENT ELECTIONS
Elections were held on 7 March 2002 for the nine elected seats. Seven seats were won by the Human Rights and Democracy Movement.

CURRENT ADMINISTRATION
In March 2003 the government comprised:

Prime Minister, Minister of Agriculture, Communications, Defence, Fisheries, Foreign Affairs, Civil Aviation, Forestry and Marine Affairs: Prince Lavaka ata Ulukalala (one of the King's sons).

Deputy Prime Minister, Minister of Marines, Environment, Public Works and Disaster Relief Activities: Cecil James Cocker.

Minister of Justice and Attorney General: 'Aisea Taumoepeau. *Education (acting):* Paul Bloomfield. *Labour, Commerce, Industries and Tourism:* Hulioo Tukikolongahau Paunga. *Health:* Dr Vailami Tangi. *Police and Prisons:* Clive Edwards. *Finance:* Siosiua Utoikamanu. *Lands, Surveys and Natural Resources:* Fielakepa.

Government Website: http://www.pmo.gov.to/

DEFENCE
Navy. A naval force, some 125-strong in 1999, was based at Touliki, Nuku'alofa.

Air Force. An Air Force was created in 1996 and operates three Beech 18s for maritime patrol.

INTERNATIONAL RELATIONS
Tonga is a member of the UN, the Commonwealth, the Asian Development Bank, the Pacific Community and the Pacific Islands Forum, and is an ACP member state of the ACP-EU relationship. It became a member of the UN in Sept. 1999.

ECONOMY
In 1997 agriculture accounted for 32% of GDP, industry 10% and services 58%.

Currency. The unit of currency is the *pa'anga* (TOP) of 100 *seniti*. In 2001 there was inflation of 7·0%. In June 2002 foreign exchange reserves were US$22m. Total money supply in June 2002 was T$42m.

Budget. Revenues were estimated to be US$49m. in 1996–97, with expenditures US$120m.

Performance. In 2001 real GDP growth was 3·0%. Total GDP in 2001 was US$142m.

Banking and Finance. The National Reserve Bank of Tonga (*Governor,* S. T. T. Utoikamanu) was established in 1989 as a bank of issue and to manage foreign reserves. The Bank of Tonga and the Tonga Development Bank are both situated in Nuku'alofa with branches in the main islands. Other commercial banks in Nuku'alofa are ANZ Banking Group Ltd and the MBF Bank Ltd.

ENERGY AND NATURAL RESOURCES
Environment. According to the *World Bank Atlas* Tonga's carbon dioxide emissions in 1998 were the equivalent of 1·2 tonnes per capita.

Electricity. Production (1998) 35m. kWh. Installed capacity (1995) 7,000 kW.

Agriculture. Production (2000 estimates, in 1,000 tonnes): yams, 31; cassava, 28; taro, 27; coconuts, 25; sweet potatoes, 5; plantains, 4; lemons and limes, 3; oranges, 3.

Livestock (2000): pigs, 81,000; goats, 14,000; horses, 11,000; cattle, 9,000.

Forestry. Timber production in 1999 was 2,000 cu. metres.

Fisheries. In 1999 the catch totalled 3,903 tonnes.

INTERNATIONAL TRADE
Foreign debt in 2000 amounted to US$58m.

Imports and Exports. In 1997–98 imports were valued at US$78·9m. and exports at US$11·9m. Main exports are coconut oil, vanilla beans, root crops, desiccated coconut and watermelons; main imports are food and live animals, basic manufactures, machinery and transport equipment, and mineral fuels and lubricants. The leading import suppliers in 1995–96 were New Zealand (36·1%), Australia (28·9%), USA (11·5%) and Japan (8·0%). Principal export markets in 1995–96 were Japan (51·8%), USA (27·7%), New Zealand (8·3%) and Australia (4·0%).

COMMUNICATIONS

Roads. In 1996 there were 680 km of roads (184 km paved). Vehicles in use in 1996 numbered approximately 1,140 passenger cars, 740 trucks and vans, and 40 buses and coaches.

Civil Aviation. There is an international airport at Tongatapu (Fua'Amotu International). The national carrier is the state-owned Royal Tongan Airlines, which in 1998 provided domestic services and had flights to Auckland, the Fiji Islands, Honolulu, Los Angeles, Niue, Samoa and Sydney. In 1998 Fua'Amotu International handled 129,000 passengers (88,000 on international flights) and 1,100 tonnes of freight.

Shipping. In 1998 sea-going shipping totalled 22,000 GRT. Two shipping lanes provide monthly services to American Samoa, Australia, the Fiji Islands, Kiribati, New Caledonia, New Zealand, Samoa and Tuvalu.

Telecommunications. The operation and development of the National Telecommunication Network and Services are the responsibilities of the Tonga Telecommunication Commission (TCC). There were 9,700 main telephone lines in 2000, or 98·7 per 1,000 population. In 1996 mobile phone subscribers numbered 300, and there were approximately 200 fax machines in 1995. In Dec. 1999 there were 1,000 Internet users. Ucall mobile GSM digital has been in operation in Tonga since Dec. 2001 with a target of 2,000 to 5,000 connections in the first year.

SOCIAL INSTITUTIONS

Justice. The judiciary is presided over by the Chief Justice. The enforcement of justice is the responsibility of the Attorney-General and the Minister of Police. In 1994 the UK ceased appointing Tongan judges and subsidizing their salaries.

Religion. In 1997 there were 44,000 adherents of the Free Wesleyan Church, 42,000 Latter-day Saints (Mormons) and 16,000 Roman Catholics.

Education. In 1994 there were 115 primary schools, with a total of 16,540 pupils. In 1993 there were 7 government and 32 mission schools, and 1 private school offering secondary education, with a total roll of 15,000. There is an extension centre of the University of the South Pacific at Nuku'alofa, a teacher training college and three technical institutes.

Adult literacy in 1996 was estimated at 98·5%.

Health. There were 4 hospitals in 1993, and 45 doctors, 9 dentists and 292 nurses.

CULTURE

Broadcasting. The Tonga Broadcasting Commission is an independent statutory board which operates two programmes. There is also a religious service. There were 61,000 radio sets in 1997. There are two television channels, and in 1997 an estimated 2,000 TV receivers.

Press. In 1996 there was one daily newspaper with a circulation of 7,000.

Tourism. There were 31,000 visitors in 1999. Receipts totalled US$14m.

DIPLOMATIC REPRESENTATIVES
Of Tonga in the United Kingdom (36 Molyneux St., London, W1H 6AB)
High Commissioner: Colonel Fetu'utolu Tupou.

Of the United Kingdom in Tonga (POB 56 Nuku'alofa)
High Commissioner: Paul Nessling.

Of Tonga in the USA (800 Second Avenue, Suite 400B, New York, NY 10017)
Ambassador: Sonatane Tua Taumoepeau Tupou.

Of the USA in Tonga
Ambassador: David Lyon (resides at Suva, Fiji Islands).

Of Tonga to the United Nations
Ambassador: Sonatane Tua Taumoepeau Tupou.

Of Tonga to the European Union
Ambassador: Fetu'utolu Tupou.

FURTHER READING
Campbell, I. C., *Island Kingdom: Tonga, Ancient and Modern.* Canterbury (NZ) Univ. Press, 1994
Wood-Ellem, E., *Queen Salote of Tonga, The Story of an Era 1900–1965.* Auckland Univ. Press, 2000

TRINIDAD AND TOBAGO

Capital: Port-of-Spain
Population estimate, 2000: 1·29m.
GDP per capita, 2000: (PPP$) 8,964
HDI/world rank: 0·805/50

Republic of Trinidad
and Tobago

KEY HISTORICAL EVENTS

When Columbus visited Trinidad in 1498 the island was inhabited by Arawak Indians. Tobago was occupied by the Caribs. Trinidad remained a neglected Spanish possession for almost 300 years until it was surrendered to a British naval expedition in 1797. The British first attempted to settle Tobago in 1721 but the French captured the island in 1781 and transformed it into a sugar-producing colony. In 1802 the British acquired Tobago and in 1899 it was administratively combined with Trinidad. When slavery was abolished in the late 1830s, the British subsidized immigration from India to replace plantation labourers. Sugar and cocoa declined towards the end of the 19th century. Oil and asphalt became the dominant sources of income. On 31 Aug. 1962 Trinidad and Tobago became an independent member of the Commonwealth. A Republican Constitution was adopted on 1 Aug. 1976.

TERRITORY AND POPULATION

The island of Trinidad is situated in the Caribbean Sea, about 12 km off the northeast coast of Venezuela; several islets, the largest being Chacachacare, Huevos, Monos and Gaspar Grande, lie in the Gulf of Paria which separates Trinidad from Venezuela. The smaller island of Tobago lies 30·7 km further to the northeast. Altogether, the islands cover 5,124 sq. km (1,978 sq. miles), of which Trinidad (including the islets) has 4,828 sq. km (1,864 sq. miles) and Tobago 303 sq. km (116 sq. miles). In 1990 the census population was 1,169,572. The population in 1995 was 1,259,972 (Trinidad, 1,208,625; Tobago, 51,347). Estimate, 1999, 1,285,700; density, 250 per sq. km.

The UN gives a projected population for 2010 of 1·36m.

In 1999, 73·6% of the population were urban. Capital, Port-of-Spain (1995 census, 45,284; 1999 estimate, 53,000); other important towns, San Fernando (55,432), Arima (25,328) and Point Fortin (20,084). The main town on Tobago is Scarborough. Those of African descent are (1990 census) 39·6% of the population, East Indians, 40·3%, mixed races, 18·4%, European, Chinese and others, 1·6%.

English is generally spoken.

SOCIAL STATISTICS

1999 birth rate (per 1,000 population), 14·5; death rate, 7·3; growth rate, 0·6%. Births, 1999, 18,600; deaths, 9,400. Expectation of life, 1999, was 71·8 years for males and 76·5 for females. Annual population growth rate, 1990–99, 0·7%. Infant mortality, 1999, 17 per 1,000 live births; fertility rate, 1999, 1·6 births per woman.

CLIMATE

A tropical climate cooled by the northeast trade winds. The dry season runs from Jan. to June, with a wet season for the rest of the year. Temperatures are uniformly high the year round. Port-of-Spain, Jan. 76·3°F (24·6°C), July 79·2°F (26·2°C). Annual rainfall 1,869·8 mm.

CONSTITUTION AND GOVERNMENT

The 1976 Constitution provides for a bicameral legislature of a *Senate* and a *House of Representatives*, who elect the *President*, who is head of state. The *Senate* consists of 31 members, 16 being appointed by the President on the advice of the Prime

Minister, 6 on the advice of the Leader of the Opposition and 9 at the discretion of the President.

The *House of Representatives* consists of 36 (34 for Trinidad and 2 for Tobago) elected members and a Speaker elected from within or outside the House.

Executive power is vested in the Prime Minister, who is appointed by the President, and the Cabinet.

National Anthem. 'Forged from the love of liberty'; words and music by P. Castagne.

RECENT ELECTIONS

In parliamentary elections held on 7 Oct. 2002 the People's National Movement (PNP) won 20 out of 36 seats with 50·7% of votes cast, against 16 seats with 46·5% for the United National Congress (UNC). Turn-out was 69·8%. As a result Patrick Manning of the People's National Movement was returned to power. The elections ended a year-long deadlock between Manning and opposition leader, Basdeo Panday. Panday, who previously served as the country's first prime minister of East Indian descent between 1995–2001, refused to accept Manning's appointment as prime minister following the election of Dec. 2001, in which both parties had taken 18 seats.

CURRENT ADMINISTRATION

President: Maxwell Richards; b. 1931 (PNM; sworn in 17 March 2003).

In March 2003 the cabinet comprised:

Prime Minister, Minister for Finance: Patrick Manning; b. 1946 (PNM; sworn in 24 Dec. 2001).

Minister for Agriculture: John Rahael. *Culture and Tourism:* Eudine Job-Davis. *Education:* Hazel Manning. *Energy and Energy Industries:* Eric Williams. *Foreign Affairs:* Knowlson Gift. *Health:* Colm Imbert. *Housing:* Danny Montano. *Labour, and Small and Micro Enterprise Development:* Lawrence Achong. *Legal Affairs:* Camille Robinson-Regis. *Local Government:* Jarrette Narine. *National Security:* Howard Chin Lee. *Planning and Development:* Dr Keith Rowley. *Public Administration and Information:* Lenny Saith. *Public Utilities and the Environment:* Martin Joseph. *Social Development:* Penelope Beckles. *Sports and Youth Affairs:* Roger Boynes. *Trade, Industry and Consumer Affairs:* Ken Valley. *Works and Transport:* Arnold Piggot. *Attorney General:* Glenda Morean.

Office of the Prime Minister: http://www.opm.gov.tt

DEFENCE

The Defence Force has 1 infantry battalion, 1 engineer and 1 service battalion. The small air element is under the control of the Coast Guard. Personnel in 2000 totalled 2,400.

The police force has 4,294 personnel.

In 2000 defence expenditure totalled US$35m. (US$27 per capita), representing 0·5% of GDP. In the 1999–2000 budget the Ministry of National Security received a total allocation of $1,154m.

Navy. In 1999 there was a coastguard of 700 including an air wing of 50.

INTERNATIONAL RELATIONS

Trinidad and Tobago is a member of the UN and many of its specialized agencies including WIPO, IMF, the World Bank, IDA, IFC, IOB and ILO; and of WTO, the Commonwealth, OAS, Inter-American Development Bank, CARICOM, Association of Caribbean States (ACS), Caribbean Development Bank, Andean Development Bank, and is an ACP member state of the ACP-EU relationship.

ECONOMY

Agriculture accounted for 3·2% of GDP in 2000, industry 46% and services 52%.

Currency. The unit of currency is the *Trinidad and Tobago dollar* (TTD) of 100 *cents*. Inflation in 2001 was 2·5%. In April 1994 the TT dollar was floated and managed by the Central Bank at TT$6·06 to US$1·00. Foreign exchange reserves in April 2002 were US$1,875m. and gold reserves 61,000 troy oz. Total money supply in March 2002 was TT$6,697m.

Budget. The fiscal year for the Budget is 1 Oct. to 30 Sept. In 1999–2000 total government revenue was TT$12,028·5m. (TT$10,263·6m. in 1998–99) and total expenditure was TT$12,308·5m. (TT$10,526·3m. in 1998–99). The 2000–01 budget envisaged total recurrent revenue of TT$12,539·0m. (TT$9,998·2m. in 1998–99) and total capital expenditure of TT$1,027·0m. (TT$1,033·8m. in 1999–2000).

Performance. Real GDP growth was 4·5% in 2001 (4·8% in 2000). Total GDP in 2001 was US$8·4bn.

Banking and Finance. The Central Bank of Trinidad and Tobago began operations in 1964 (*Governor*, Ewart Williams). Its net reserves were US$1,281·1m. in Aug. 2000. There are six commercial banks. Government savings banks are established in 69 offices, with a head office in Port-of-Spain. The stock exchange in Port-of-Spain participates in the regional Caribbean exchange.

ENERGY AND NATURAL RESOURCES

Environment. According to the *World Bank Atlas* carbon dioxide emissions were the equivalent of 17·4 tonnes per capita in 1998.

Electricity. In 1999 installed capacity was 1·42m. kW, electricity production was 5,279m. kWh and consumption per capita 3,667 kWh.

Oil and Gas. Oil production is one of Trinidad's leading industries. Commercial production began in 1908; production of crude oil in 1999 was 45·5m. bbls. Reserves in Jan. 2001 totalled 686m. bbls. Crude oil is also imported for refining. Oil accounted for 30% of GDP and 75% of revenues in 1996, but dependence on the oil industry is declining.

In 1999 production of natural gas was 10·9bn. cu. metres. Proven reserves of natural gas were 605bn. cu. metres as of Jan. 2001. A major discovery of approximately 50bn. cu. metres was made by BP in 2000, followed by a further discovery of approximately 30bn. cu. metres in 2002.

Agriculture. Production of main crops (2000 estimates, in 1,000 tonnes): sugarcane, 1,500; coconuts, 23; oranges, 20; grapefruit and pomelos, 8; pumpkins and squash, 8; rice, 7; bananas, 6; maize, 5; plantains, 4. In 1999 there were 75,000 ha of arable land and 47,000 ha of permanent cropland, and 11,000 ha of pasture. 22,000 ha were irrigated in 1997.

Livestock (2000): goats, 59,000; pigs, 41,000; cattle, 35,000; sheep, 12,000; chickens, 10m. Livestock products, 2000 estimates: meat, 30,000 tonnes (including poultry, 26,000 tonnes); milk, 10,000 tonnes.

Forestry. Forests covered 161,524 ha in 1998, or 32·8% of the land area (down from 174,000 ha in 1990). Timber production for 1999 was 44,000 cu. metres.

Fisheries. The catch in 1999 was estimated at 15,000 tonnes.

INDUSTRY

In 1997, 2,655,100 tonnes of iron and steel were produced. Other manufacturing includes ammonia and urea (production, 1998, 3,946,700 tonnes), methanol (1999, 2,149,800 tonnes), cement (1999, 688,000 tonnes), rum (1998, 3,916,000 proof gallons), beer (1998, 5·57m. litres), cigarettes (1998, 1,282,000 kg), sugar (1999, 112,000 tonnes), fertilizer (1999, 3,946,700 tonnes). Trinidad and Tobago ranks among the world's largest producers of ammonia and methanol.

Labour. The working population in 1999 was 563,400. In 1999 the number of unemployed was 74,000. In the fourth quarter of 1999, 32,200 people worked in agriculture; 16,400 in petroleum and gas; 51,800 in manufacturing (including other mining and quarrying); 66,000 in construction (including electricity and water); 39,500 in transport storage and communication; other services, 277,700. Total employment: 484,000.

Trade Unions. About 30% of the labour force belong to unions, which are grouped under the National Trade Union Centre.

INTERNATIONAL TRADE

The Foreign Investment Act of 1990 permits foreign investors to acquire land and shares in local companies, and to form companies. External debt was US$2,467m. in 2000.

Imports and Exports. Exports in 1999 were TT$17,661·2m., of which TT$9,553·9m. was mineral fuels and products. Imports totalled TT$17,263·0m. of which TT$5,880·4m. was for machinery and transport equipment. Exports in 1998 were TT$14,258m.; imports were TT$18,965·6m. The principal import sources in 1999 were USA (40·0%), Venezuela (11·9%), Colombia (5·2%) and Canada (5·2%). The main export markets in 1999 were USA (39·8%), Jamaica (8·4%), Barbados (5·2%) and the Netherlands Antilles (3·6%).

COMMUNICATIONS

Roads. In 1996 there were 8,320 km of roads. Just over 51% were paved. Motor vehicles registered in 1997 totalled 237,299.

Civil Aviation. There is an international airport at Port-of-Spain (Piarco) and in Tobago (Crown Point). In 2000 Piarco handled 1,768,932 passengers (1,329,879 on international flights) and 32,057 tonnes of freight. The national carrier is BWIA International Trinidad and Tobago Airways, which was privatized in March 1995 by the Acker group of companies. In 2000 it flew to Antigua, Barbados, Caracas, Georgetown, Grenada, Kingston, London, Miami, New York, St Kitts, St Lucia, Toronto and Washington. In 1999 it carried 1,111,700 passengers (1,045,900 on international flights).

Shipping. Sea-going shipping totalled 12,554·16 GRT in 1999; 3,687,328 tonnes of cargo were handled at Port-of-Spain during the year. There is a deep-water harbour at Scarborough (Tobago). The other main harbour is Point Lisas.

Telecommunications. International and domestic communications are provided by Telecommunications Services of Trinidad and Tobago (TSTT) by means of a satellite earth station and various high-quality radio circuits. The marine radio service is also maintained by TSTT. There were 229,100 telephone main lines in 2000, or 231·1 per 1,000 inhabitants, and 80,000 PCs (61·8 for every 1,000 persons). In 1999 there were 127,300 mobile phone subscribers, and in 1997, 2,400 fax machines. Internet users numbered 42,800 in Dec. 2000.

Postal Services. Number of post offices (1998), 75; postal agencies, 167.

SOCIAL INSTITUTIONS

Justice. The High Court consists of the Chief Justice and 11 puisne judges. In criminal cases a judge of the High Court sits with a jury of 12 in cases of treason and murder, and with nine jurors in other cases. The Court of Appeal consists of the Chief Justice and seven Justices of Appeal. In hearing appeals, the Court is comprised of three judges sitting together except when the appeal is from a Summary Court or from a decision of a High Court judge in chambers. In such cases two judges would comprise the Court. There is a limited right of appeal from it to the Privy Council. There are 3 High Courts and 12 magistrates' courts. There is an *Ombudsman*. Trinidad and Tobago was one of ten countries to sign an agreement in Feb. 2001 establishing a Caribbean Court of Justice to replace the British Privy Council as the highest civil and criminal court. The Court of Justice is expected to sit for the first time in the second half of 2003.

The death penalty is authorized and still used. There were ten executions in 1999.

The population in penal institutions in April 1998 was 4,715 (365 per 100,000 of national population).

Religion. In 1998, 14·4% of the population were Anglicans (under the Bishop of Trinidad and Tobago), 32·2% Roman Catholics (under the Archbishop of Port-of-Spain), 24·3% Hindus and 6% Muslims.

Education. In 1999–2000 there were 162,736 pupils enrolled in 481 primary schools, 17,715 in government secondary schools, 21,068 in assisted secondary schools, 33,053 in junior secondary schools, 21,930 in senior comprehensive schools, 3,057 in senior secondary schools, 8,677 in composite schools and 3,935 in technical and vocational schools. There were 4,121 pupils enrolled in the three Technical and Vocational schools for the period 1998–99. The University of the West Indies campus in St Augustine (1999–2000) had 7,585 students and 477 academic staff. 1,307 of the students were from other countries.

Adult literacy was 93·4% in 1998 (male, 95·3%; female, 91·5%).

In 1998–99 total expenditure on education came to US$1,151m.

Health. In 1999 there were 1,171 physicians, 189 dentists, 500 pharmacists and 71 hospitals and nursing homes with 4,384 beds. There were 1,936 nurses and midwives and 1,486 nursing assistants in government institutions.

CULTURE

Broadcasting. Radio programmes are overseen by the Telecommunications Authority. There are 16 commercial stations. There are three TV stations, as well as community and cable services. There were 425,000 television receivers (colour by NTSC) and 680,000 radio sets in 1997.

Cinema. In 2000 there were 26 cinemas, including 1 drive-in cinema.

Press. As at Dec. 1999 there were 3 daily newspapers with a total daily circulation of 195,692, 3 Sunday newspapers with a total circulation of 165,646, 5 weekly and 1 bi-weekly newspaper.

Tourism. There were 358,836 visitors in 1999, plus 57,230 cruise ship visitors. Revenue from tourism in 1999 was US$1·2m.

Festivals. Religious festivals: the Feast of La Divina Pastora, or Sipari Mai, a Catholic and Hindu celebration of the Holy Mother Mary; Saint Peter's Day Celebration, the Patron Saint of Fishermen; Hosein, or Hosay, a Shia Muslim festival; Phagwah, a Hindu spring festival; Santa Rosa, celebrated on 30 Aug.; Eid-ul-Fitr, a Muslim festival at the end of Ramadan; Divali, the Hindu festival of light; Christmas.

Cultural festivals: Carnival (on 23 and 24 Feb. in 2004); Spiritual Baptist Shouter Liberation Day (30 March), a recognition of the Baptist religion; Indian Arrival Day (30 May), commemorating the arrival of the first East Indian labourers; Sugar and Energy Festival; Pan Ramajay, a music festival of all types; Emancipation (1 Aug.), a recognition of the period of slavery; Tobago Heritage Festival, celebrating Tobago's traditions and customs; Parang Festival, traditional folk music of Christmas; Pan Jazz Festival; Music Festival, predominantly classical music but Indian and Calypso are included.

When a public holiday falls on a Sunday, the holiday is celebrated on the Monday immediately following.

Museums and Galleries. Port-of-Spain has a National Museum and Art Gallery, the Aquarela Galleries, the 101 Art Gallery, and Gallery 1.2.3.4. The Chaguaramas Military History and Aviation Museum is at Chaguaramas; Art Creators is at Saint Ann's; Okazions is in Westmoorings; and On Location is at St James.

DIPLOMATIC REPRESENTATIVES

Of Trinidad and Tobago in the United Kingdom (42 Belgrave Sq., London, SW1X 8NT)
High Commissioner: Vacant.
Acting High Commissioner: Sandra McIntyre-Trotman.

Of the United Kingdom in Trinidad and Tobago (19 St Clair Ave., Port-of-Spain)
High Commissioner: Peter G. Harborne.

Of Trinidad and Tobago in the USA (1708 Massachusetts Ave., NW, Washington, D.C., 20036)
Ambassador: Marina Annette Valere.

Of the USA in Trinidad and Tobago (15 Queen's Park West, Port-of-Spain)
Ambassador: Roy L. Austin.

Of Trinidad and Tobago to the United Nations
Ambassador: Philip Sealy.

Of Trinidad and Tobago to the European Union
Ambassador: Vacant.
Chargé d'Affaires a.i.: Susan Gordon.

FURTHER READING
Chambers, F., *Trinidad and Tobago.* [Bibliography] ABC-Clio, Oxford and Santa Barbara (CA), 1986
Williams, E., *History of the People of Trinidad and Tobago.* Africa World Press, Lawrenceville (NJ), 1993

Central library: The Central Library of Trinidad and Tobago, Queen's Park East, Port-of-Spain.
National statistical office: Central Statistical Office, 2 Edward St., Port-of-Spain.

TUNISIA

Jumhuriya at-Tunisiya
(Republic of Tunisia)

Capital: Tunis
Population estimate, 2000: 9·5m.
GDP per capita, 2000: (PPP$) 6,363
HDI/world rank: 0·722/97

KEY HISTORICAL EVENTS

Settled by the Phoenicians, the area became a powerful state under the dynasty of the Berber Hafsids (1207–1574). Tunisia was nominally a part of the Ottoman Empire from the end of the 17th century and descendants of the original Ottoman ruler remained Beys of Tunis until the modern state of Tunisia was established. A French protectorate since 1883, Tunisia saw considerable anti-French activity in the late 1930s. However, Tunisia supported the Allies in the Second World War and was the scene of heavy fighting. France granted internal self-government in 1955 and Tunisia became fully independent on 20 March 1956. A constitutional assembly was established and Habib Bourguiba became prime minister. A republic was established in 1957, the Bey deposed and the monarchy was abolished; Bourguiba became president. In 1975 the constitution was changed so that Bourguiba could be made President-for-life. Bourguiba was overthrown in a bloodless coup in 1987. His successor as president, Zine El Abidine Ben Ali, introduced democratic reforms but a long running struggle with Islamic fundamentalists has been marked by sporadic violence and the suspension of political rights.

TERRITORY AND POPULATION

Tunisia is bounded in the north and east by the Mediterranean Sea, west by Algeria and south by Libya. The area is 154,530 sq. km. In 1994 the census population was 8,785,364. The 1999 official estimate put the total population at 9,456,700; density, 61 per sq. km. In 1999, 64·8% of the population were urban.

The UN gives a projected population for 2010 of 10·63m.

The areas and populations (1994) of the 23 governorates:

	Area in sq. km	Population		Area in sq. km	Population
Aryanah	1,558	570,500	Qasrayn (Kassérine)	8,066	388,500
Bajah (Béja)	3,558	306,500	Qayrawan (Kairouan)	6,712	532,500
Banzart (Bizerta)	3,685	485,800	Qibili (Kebili)	22,084	132,000
Bin Arus	761	372,900	Safaqis (Sfax)	7,545	753,300
Jundubah (Jendouba)	3,102	405,100	Sidi Bu Zayd		
Kaf (Le Kef)	4,965	273,200	(Sidi Bouzid)	6,994	379,300
Madaniyin (Médénine)	8,588	386,900	Silyanah (Siliana)	4,631	246,500
Mahdiyah (Mahdia)	2,966	335,200	Susah (Sousse)	2,621	436,500
Munastir (Monastir)	1,019	364,600	Tatawin (Tataouine)	38,889	135,600
Nabul (Nabeul)	2,788	581,800	Tawzar (Tozeur)	4,719	89,300
Qabis (Gabès)	7,175	311,300	Tunis	346	893,000
Qafsah (Gafsa)	8,990	308,700	Zaghwan (Zaghouan)	2,768	143,400

Tunis, the capital, had (1999 in 1,000) 1,860·1 inhabitants. Other main cities (1994 census population in 1,000): Sfax, 230·9; Aryanah, 152·7; Ettadhamen, 149·2; Sousse, 125; Kairouan, a holy city of the Muslims, 102·6; Gabès, 98·9; Bizerta, 98·9; Bardo, 72·7; Gafsa, 71·1.

The official language is Arabic but French is the main language in the media, commercial enterprise and government departments. Berber-speaking people form less than 1% of the population.

SOCIAL STATISTICS

Births, 1998, 166,718; deaths, 52,000; marriages (1995), 53,726. Rates (1998): birth, 17·9 per 1,000 population; death, 5·6. Annual population growth rate, 1990–99, 1·7%. In 1996 the most popular age range for marrying was 25–29 for males and

20–24 for females. Expectation of life, 1999, was 68·8 years for males and 71·2 for females. Infant mortality, 1999, 24 per 1,000 live births; fertility rate, 1999, 2·5 births per woman.

CLIMATE
The climate ranges from warm temperate in the north, where winters are mild and wet and the summers hot and dry, to desert in the south. Tunis, Jan. 48°F (8·9°C), July 78°F (25·6°C). Annual rainfall 16" (400 mm). Bizerta, Jan. 52°F (11·1°C), July 77°F (25°C). Annual rainfall 25" (622 mm). Sfax, Jan. 52°F (11·1°C), July 78°F (25·6°C). Annual rainfall 8" (196 mm).

CONSTITUTION AND GOVERNMENT
The Constitution was promulgated on 1 June 1959 and reformed in 1988. The office of President-for-life was abolished and Presidential elections were to be held every five years. The *President* and the *National Assembly* are elected simultaneously by direct universal suffrage for a period of five years. On 27 May 2002 a referendum was held in which 99% of votes cast were in favour of abolishing the three-term limit on the presidency and on raising the age limit for incumbent presidents from 70 to 75 years. The results were viewed with scepticism by human rights groups and opposition figures, who saw the referendum as an attempt by President Zine El Abidine Ben Ali to retain power. Ben Ali was due to retire in 2004 after his third presidential term.

The National Assembly has 163 seats, 144 directly elected by the first-past-the-post system and 19 distributed nationally by proportional representation to parties that fail to win seats under the first-past-the-post system.

National Anthem. 'Humata al Hima' ('Defenders of the Homeland'); words by Mustapha al Rafi, tune by M. A. Wahab.

RECENT ELECTIONS
Presidential and parliamentary elections were held on 24 Oct. 1999; turn-out was 91·4%. President Zine El Abidine Ben Ali was re-elected by 99·4% of votes cast against 2 opponents. In the parliamentary elections the ruling Constitutional Democratic Assembly (CDA) won 148 of 182 available National Assembly seats with 91·6% of votes cast. The Movement of Social Democrats won 13 seats and there were 4 other parties with 7 seats or fewer.

CURRENT ADMINISTRATION
President: Zine El Abidine Ben Ali; b. 1936 (CDA; sworn in 7 Nov. 1987, re-elected March 1994 and Oct. 1999).

In March 2003 the cabinet comprised:
Prime Minister: Mohamed Ghannouchi; b. 1941 (CDA; sworn in 17 Nov. 1999).
Minister of Defence: Dali Jazi. *State Property and Property Affairs:* Ridha Grira. *Justice and Human Rights:* Béchir Tekkari. *Foreign Affairs:* Habib Ben Yahia. *Interior and Local Development:* Hédi M'henni. *Development and International Co-operation:* Mohamed Nouri Jouini. *Social Affairs and Solidarity:* Chadli Neffati. *Finance:* Taoufik Baccar. *Infrastructure, Housing and Urban Planning:* Slaheddine Belaïd. *Tourism, Trade and Handicrafts:* Mondher Zenaidi. *Education and Training:* Moncer Rouissi. *Higher Education, Scientific Research and Technology:* Sadok Chaâbane. *Employment:* Chadli Laroussi. *Public Health:* Habib M'Barek. *Culture, Youth and Leisure:* Abdelbaki Hermassi. *Director of the Presidential Office:* Ahmed Iyadh Ouederni. *Minister of State and Special Adviser to the President:* Abdelaziz Ben Dhia. *Religious Affairs:* Jalloul Jeribi. *Industry and Energy:* Moncef Ben Abdallah. *Family, Children and Women's Affairs:* Néziha Ben Yedder. *Sport:* Abderrahim Zouari. *Agriculture, Environment and Water Resources:* Habib Haddad. *Communications Technology and Transport:* Sadok Rabah.

Government Website: http://www.ministeres.tn/

DEFENCE
Selective conscription is for one year. Defence expenditure in 2000 totalled US$350m. (US$36 per capita), representing 1·7% of GDP.

Army. Strength (1999) 27,000 (22,000 conscripts). There is also a National Guard numbering 12,000.

Navy. In 1999 naval personnel totalled 4,500. Forces are based at Bizerta, Sfax and Kelibia.

Air Force. The Air Force operated 44 combat aircraft including 15 F-5E/F Tiger II fighters. Personnel (1999) about 3,500 (700 conscripts).

INTERNATIONAL RELATIONS

Tunisia is a member of the UN, WTO, the African Union, the Islamic Conference, the League of Arab States, Arab Maghreb Union, African Development Bank, IOM and the International Organization of the Francophonie.

ECONOMY

In 1998 agriculture accounted for 12·4% of GDP, industry 28·4% and services 59·1%.

Currency. The unit of currency is the *Tunisian dinar* (TND) of 1,000 *millimes*. The currency was made convertible on 6 Jan. 1993. Foreign exchange reserves were US$2,195m. and gold reserves 218,000 troy oz in June 2002. Inflation was 1·9% in 2001. Total money supply was 6,687m. dinars in April 2002.

Budget. The fiscal year is the calendar year. Revenue and expenditure in 1m. dinars:

	1997	1998	1999	2000[1]
Revenue	6,012·8	7,058·2	7,180·2	7,775·0
Expenditure	6,677·4	7,160·2	7,864·8	8,544·1

[1]Estimate.

Performance. Real GDP growth was 5·1% in 2001 (5·0% in 2000). Tunisia's total GDP in 2001 was US$20·0bn.

Banking and Finance. The Central Bank of Tunisia (*Governor*, Mohamed Daouas) is the bank of issue. In 1988 there were 9 development banks, 10 deposit banks and 9 off-shore banks.

There is a small stock exchange (16 companies trading in 1993).

Weights and Measures. The metric system is legal. Some traditional weights are still in use: 12 *sa* = 1 *wiba* = 1 bushel; 16 *wiba* = 1 *kfiz*; 1 *ounce* = 31·487 grammes.

ENERGY AND NATURAL RESOURCES

Environment. Tunisia's carbon dioxide emissions in 1998 were the equivalent of 2·4 tonnes per capita according to the *World Bank Atlas*.

Electricity. Installed capacity was estimated to be 2m. kW in 1997. Production in 1998 was 7·94bn. kWh; consumption per capita was 824 kWh.

Oil and Gas. Crude petroleum production (1996) was 32m. bbls with 0·3bn. bbls. in proven reserves. Natural gas production (1996), 33 petajoules.

Water. In 1993 there were 20 large dams, 250 hillside dams and some 1,000 artificial lakes.

Minerals. Mineral production (in 1,000 tonnes) in 1995: calcium phosphate, 6,302; salt (1996), 478; iron ore, 225; zinc ore (concentrated), 80·0; lead ore (concentrated), 11·0.

Agriculture. There are five agricultural regions: the *north*, mountainous with large fertile valleys; the *northeast*, with the peninsula of Cap Bon, suited for the cultivation of oranges, lemons and tangerines; the *Sahel*, where olive trees abound; the *centre*, a region of high tablelands and pastures; and the *desert* of the south, where dates are grown.

Some 23% of the population are employed in agriculture. Large estates predominate; smallholdings are tending to fragment, partly owing to inheritance laws. There were some 0·4m. farms in 1990 (0·32m. in 1960). Of the total area of 15,583,000 ha, about 9m. ha are productive, including 2m. under cereals, 3·6m. used as pasturage, 0·9m. forests and 1·3m. uncultivated. In 1998, 380,000 ha were irrigated. The main crops are cereals, citrus fruits, tomatoes, melons, olives, dates, grapes and olive oil. Production, 2000 (in 1,000 tonnes): olives, 1,000; tomatoes,

905; wheat, 842; melons, including watermelons, 475; potatoes, 290; barley, 242; chillies and green peppers, 190; grapes, 150; onions, 133; oranges, 115; apples, 108; dates, 103; sugarbeets, 76; peaches and nectarines, 73; tree nuts, 61; almonds, 60.

Livestock, 2000 (in 1,000): sheep, 6,600; goats, 1,400; cattle, 790; camels, 231; asses, 230; mules, 81; horses, 56. Livestock products, 2000 (in 1,000 tonnes): meat, 219; milk, 919; eggs, 80.

Forestry. In 1995 there were 555,000 ha of forests (3·6% of the land area). Timber production in 1999 was 2·84m. cu. metres.

Fisheries. In 1999 the catch amounted to 92,075 tonnes, almost exclusively from marine waters.

INDUSTRY

Production, 1996 (in 1,000 tonnes): phosphoric acid, 1,063; cement (1997), 4,431; lime, 464. Vehicle production (1996): 2,010 cars, 1,003 (assembled) lorries (1997), 1,240 vans, 220 buses and coaches, 330 tractors.

Labour. The labour force in 1996 totalled 3,459,000 (69% males). Unemployment was 15·0% in 1996.

Trade Unions. The Union Générale des Travailleurs Tunisiens won 27 seats in the parliamentary elections of 1 Nov. 1981. There are also the Union Tunisienne de l'Industrie, du Commerce et de l'Artisanat (UTICA, the employers' union) and the Union National des Agriculteurs (UNA, farmers' union).

INTERNATIONAL TRADE

In Feb. 1989 Tunisia signed a treaty of economic co-operation with the other countries of Maghreb: Algeria, Libya, Mauritania and Morocco. Foreign debt was US$10,610m. in 2000.

Tunisia was the first country to sign a partnership agreement with the European Union. The agreement aims at creating a non-agricultural free trade zone by 2008.

Imports and Exports. Trade in US$1m.:

	1996	1997	1998	1999	2000
Imports f.o.b.	7,280	7,514	7,875	8,014	8,092
Exports f.o.b.	5,519	5,559	5,724	5,873	5,840

Main exports in 1994: clothing and accessories, 40·1%; chemicals and related products, 11·5%; mineral fuels and lubricants, 9·5%; machinery and transport equipment, 8·6%; olive oil, 6·6%. Main imports in 1994: machinery and transport equipment, 29·2%; textile yarn and fabrics, 16·4%; chemicals and related products, 8·5%; mineral fuels and lubricants, 7·7%; food and live animals, 7·4%.

The main import suppliers in 1995 were France (25·6%), Italy (15·4%) and Germany (12·5%). Main export markets in 1995 were France (28·1%), Italy (18·7%) and Germany (15·7%).

COMMUNICATIONS

Roads. In 1996 there were 23,100 km of roads (18,225 km surfaced). Vehicles in 1996 numbered 581,000 (269,000 passenger cars and 312,000 trucks and vans).

Rail. In 1994 there were 2,152 km of railways (468 km of 1,435 mm gauge and 1,684 km of metre-gauge), of which 110 km were electrified. Passenger-km travelled in 1996 came to 988m. and freight tonne-km to 2,329m. There is a light rail network in Tunis (33 km).

Civil Aviation. The national carrier, Tunis Air, is 84·86% state-owned. It carried 1,922,600 passengers in 1999 (all on international flights) and flew 27·3m. km. There are six international airports. In 2000 Monastir (Habib Bourguiba) handled 3,887,000 passengers (3,878,000 on international flights) and 1,300 tonnes of freight. Tunis-Carthage handled 3,331,000 (3,062,000 on international flights) and 24,000 tonnes of freight. Djerba handled 2,100,000 passengers (1,870,000 on international flights) and 2,412 tonnes of freight.

Shipping. The main port is Tunis, and its outer port is Tunis-Goulette. These two ports, and Sfax, Sousse and Bizerta, are directly accessible to ocean-going vessels. The ports of La Skhirra and Gabès are used for the shipping of Algerian and Tunisian oil. In 1998 sea-going shipping totalled 193,000 GRT, including oil tankers 22,000 GRT. In 1998 vessels totalling 43,546,000 NRT entered ports and vessels totalling 43,513,000 NRT cleared.

Telecommunications. There were 850,400 main telephone lines (89·9 per 1,000 persons) in 1999, and 219,000 PCs in use (22·9 per 1,000 persons) in 2000. Tunisia had 265,000 mobile phone subscribers in Nov. 2001 and 280,000 Internet users in March 2001. In 1997 there were 31,000 fax machines.

Postal Services. In 1995 there were 955 post offices. A total of 117m. pieces of mail were processed in 1995.

SOCIAL INSTITUTIONS

Justice. There are 51 magistrates' courts, 13 courts of first instance, 3 courts of appeal (in Tunis, Sfax and Sousse) and the High Court in Tunis.

A Personal Status Code was promulgated on 13 Aug. 1956 and applied to Tunisians from 1 Jan. 1957. This raised the status of women, made divorce subject to a court decision, abolished polygamy and decreed a minimum marriage age.

The population in penal institutions in Dec. 1996 was 23,165 (250 per 100,000 of national population).

Religion. The constitution recognizes Islam as the state religion. In 1992 there were 8·36m. Sunni Muslims. There are about 20,000 Roman Catholics, under the Prelate of Tunis.

Education. The adult literacy rate in 1999 was 69·9% (80·4% among males and 59·3% among females). All education is free from primary schools to university. In 1997–98 there were 4,417 primary schools with 59,708 teachers and 1,440,479 pupils; and 36,528 teachers and 833,372 pupils in secondary schools.

Higher education includes 6 universities, 3 of them being specialized by faculty, a teacher training college, a school of law, 2 centres of economic studies, 2 schools of engineering, 2 medical schools, a faculty of agriculture, 2 institutes of business administration and 1 school of dentistry.

Health. There were 169 hospitals and specialized institutes and centres in 2000. In 1994 provision of beds was 18 per 10,000 population. In 2000 there were 7,339 doctors, 1,319 dentists, 12,195 nurses (1994) and 1,841 pharmacists.

Welfare. A system of social security was set up in 1950 (amended 1963, 1964 and 1970).

CULTURE

Broadcasting. The government-controlled Radiodiffusion-Télévision Tunisienne provides a national radio programme, an international service—Radio Tunisie Internationale (French and Italian)—and two regional programmes. There are Arabic and French TV networks (colour by SECAM V). Number of sets: TV (1997), 920,000; radio (1996), 2·06m.

Press. In 1996 there were eight daily newspapers with a combined circulation of 280,000, giving a rate of 31 per 1,000 inhabitants. Press freedom is severely limited.

Tourism. In 1999 there were 4,832,000 foreign tourists, bringing revenue of US$1·56bn. Revenues doubled between 1991 (US$685m.) and 1996, and tourism now accounts for 10% of GDP.

DIPLOMATIC REPRESENTATIVES
Of Tunisia in the United Kingdom (29 Prince's Gate, London, SW7 1QG)
Ambassador: Khémaies Jhinaoui.

Of the United Kingdom in Tunisia (5 Place de la Victoire, Tunis)
Ambassador: Robin Kealy, CMG.

Of Tunisia in the USA (1515 Massachusetts Ave., NW, Washington, D.C., 20005)
Ambassador: Hatem Atallah.

Of the USA in Tunisia (144 Ave. de la Liberté, 1002 Tunis-Belvedere)
Ambassador: Rust M. Denning.

Of Tunisia to the United Nations
Ambassador: Nourreddine Mejdoub.

Of Tunisia to the European Union
Ambassador: Slaheddine Ben M'Barek.

FURTHER READING
Pazzanita, A. G., *The Maghreb.* [Bibliography] ABC-Clio, Oxford and Santa Barbara (CA), 1998

National statistical office: Institut National de la Statistique, 27 Rue de Liban, Tunis.
Website (French only): http://www.ins.nat.tn

TURKEY

Türkiye Cumhuriyeti
(Republic of Turkey)

Capital: Ankara
Population estimate, 2000: 66·67m.
GDP per capita, 2000: (PPP$) 6,974
HDI/world rank: 0·742/85

KEY HISTORICAL EVENTS

The area of modern Turkey equates to the ancient region of Anatolia (Asia Minor). There is evidence of human habitation in Anatolia around 7500 BC. Between 1900 and 1600 BC the area came under Hittite rule, vying for power with Egypt and eventually extending into Syria. Anatolia was regularly invaded by forces from the Greek islands and was overrun by invading Persians in the 6th century BC.

Alexander the Great defeated the Persians around 330 BC. After his death there was a long civil war between the Seleucids and the Ptolemies, while the kingdoms of Galatia, Armenia, Pergamum, Cappadocia, Bithynia and Pontus all established footholds in the region. Rome gained dominance around the 2nd century BC and brought stability, prosperity and, eventually, Christianity. In AD 324 the Emperor Constance began construction of what would become Constantinople. Constantinople became the centre of the Byzantine (Eastern Roman) Empire, which reached its pinnacle under Justinian in the mid-6th century.

Islamic troops attacked Constantinople during the 670s and there ensued several centuries of warfare and rivalry between Islamic forces and Byzantium. The Great Seljuk Empire established dominance over an area that encompassed modern Turkey during the 11th century. They came under threat during the Crusades and from the Mongols but fell to the Ottomans (an alliance of Turkish warriors who emerged in the 13th century). The Ottomans, under Mehmet, seized Constantinople in 1453. Under the rule of Suleiman the Magnificent (1494–1566) the empire expanded to its fullest extent (including an area from Morocco to Persia and westwards into the Balkans) and Constantinople developed into a centre of cultural and intellectual excellence.

From the late 16th century, however, the Empire began to decline, its power weakening rapidly in the 19th century. The Kingdom of Greece broke away from Ottoman rule in 1832, with Serbs, Romanians, Armenians, Albanians, Bulgarians and Arabs demanding independence soon afterwards. Attempts by Turkey to re-define itself were further hindered in the 20th century by World War I, during which it sided with Germany. In fighting with Greece over disputed territory from 1920–22, the Turkish National Movement was led by Mustafa Kemal (Atatürk: 'Father of the Turks'), who wanted a republic based on a modern secular society. Turkey became a republic on 29 Oct. 1923. Islam ceased to be the official state religion in 1928 and women were given the franchise.

On 27 May 1960 the Turkish Army overthrew the government and party activities were suspended. A new constitution was approved in a referendum held on 9 July 1961 and general elections held the same year. On 12 Sept. 1980 the Turkish armed forces again drove the government from office. A new constitution was enforced after a national referendum on 7 Nov. 1982. In the face of mounting Islamicization of government policy, the Supreme National Security Council reaffirmed its commitment to the secularity of the state. On 6 March 1997 Prime Minister Neçmettin Erbakan, leader of the pro-Islamist Welfare Party, promised to combat Muslim fundamentalism but in June he was forced to resign by a campaign led by the Army.

There are quarrels with Greece over the division of Cyprus, oil rights under the Aegean and ownership of uninhabited islands close to the Turkish coast. Kurdish rebels have for many years been active in the southeast, occupying a large part of the Turkish army. However, in Feb. 2000 the Kurdish Workers' party (PKK) formally abandoned its 15-year rebellion and adopted the democratic programme urged by its imprisoned leader, Abdullah Öçalan. The conflict has cost nearly 40,000 lives.

TERRITORY AND POPULATION

Turkey is bounded in the west by the Aegean Sea and Greece, north by Bulgaria and the Black Sea, east by Georgia, Armenia and Iran, and south by Iraq, Syria and the Mediterranean. The area (including lakes) is 780,580 sq. km (301,382 sq. miles). At the 1990 census the population was 56,473,035. The most recent census took place in Oct. 2000, by when the population had increased to 67,844,903. In 1999, 74·1% of the population lived in urban areas.

The UN gives a projected population for 2010 of 75·15m.

Turkish is the official language. Kurdish and Arabic are also spoken.

Some 12m. Kurds live in Turkey. In Feb. 1991 limited use of the Kurdish language was sanctioned, and in Aug. 2002 parliament legalized Kurdish radio and television broadcasts.

Area and population of the 81 provinces at the 2000 census:

	Area in sq. km	Population		Area in sq. km	Population
Adana	12,788	1,849,478	İzmir	11,973	3,370,866
Adıyaman	7,614	623,811	Karabük	4,074	225,102
Afyon	14,230	812,416	Karaman	9,163	243,210
Ağri	11,376	528,744	Kars	9,442	325,016
Aksaray	7,626	396,084	Kastamonu	13,108	375,476
Amasya	5,520	365,231	Kayseri	16,917	1,060,432
Ankara	25,706	4,007,860	Kilis	1,338	114,724
Antalya	20,591	1,719,751	Kırıkkale	4,365	383,508
Ardahan	5,576	133,756	Kırklareli	6,550	328,461
Artvin	7,436	191,934	Kırşehir	6,570	253,239
Aydin	8,007	950,757	Kocaeli	3,626	1,206,085
Balıkesir	14,292	1,076,347	Konya	38,157	2,192,166
Bartın	2,140	184,178	Kütahya	11,875	656,903
Batman	4,694	456,734	Malatya	12,313	853,658
Bayburt	3,652	97,358	Manisa	13,810	1,260,169
Bilecik	4,307	194,326	K. Maraş	14,327	1,002,384
Bingöl	8,125	253,739	Mardin	8,891	705,098
Bitlis	6,707	388,678	Muğla	13,338	715,328
Bolu	10,037	270,654	Muş	8,196	453,654
Burdur	6,887	256,803	Nevşehir	5,467	309,914
Bursa	10,963	2,125,140	Niğde	7,312	348,081
Çanakkale	9,737	464,975	Ordu	6,001	887,765
Çankırı	7,388	270,355	Osmaniye	3,320	458,782
Çorum	12,820	597,065	Rize	3,920	365,938
Denizli	11,868	850,029	Sakarya	4,817	756,168
Diyarbakır	15,355	1,362,708	Samsun	9,579	1,209,137
Düzce	1,014	314,266	Siirt	5,406	263,676
Edirne	6,276	402,606	Sinop	5,862	225,574
Elaziğ	9,153	569,616	Şırnak	7,172	353,197
Erzincan	11,903	316,841	Sivas	28,488	755,091
Erzurum	25,066	937,389	Tekirdağ	6,218	623,591
Eskişehir	13,652	706,009	Tokat	9,958	828,027
Gaziantep	6,207	1,285,249	Trabzon	4,685	975,137
Giresun	6,934	523,819	Tunceli	7,774	93,584
Gümüşhane	6,575	186,953	Ş. Urfa	18,584	1,443,422
Hakkâri	7,121	236,581	Uşak	5,341	322,313
Hatay	5,403	1,253,726	Van	19,069	877,524
İçel	15,853	1,651,400	Yalova	674	168,593
Iğdir	3,539	168,634	Yozgat	14,123	682,919
Isparta	8,933	513,681	Zonguldak	3,481	615,599
İstanbul	5,220	10,018,735			

Population of cities of over 200,000 inhabitants in 2000:

İstanbul	8,831,805	Mersin	544,318
Ankara	3,203,362	Kayseri	524,818
İzmir	2,250,149	Eskişehir	482,793
Bursa	1,184,144	Urfa	383,870
Adana	1,133,028	Malatya	381,081
Gaziantep	862,033	Erzurum	366,962
Konya	761,145	Samsun	362,756
Antalya	606,447	Sakarya	294,398
Diyarbakır	551,046	Van	284,464

Denizli	273,515	Balikesir	215,436
Elazığ	269,647	Trabzon	215,058
Sivas	250,307	Manisa	214,345
Batman	248,406	Kırıkkale	205,078
Gebze	237,494[1]		

[1] 1997.

İstanbul: Given the title of New Rome by Constantine the Great, İstanbul has been the capital city of the Byzantine Empire, the Ottoman Empire and the Turkish Republic (until 1923). Situated in European Turkey, İstanbul is a peninsular city surrounded by the Sea of Marmara, the Golden Horn (or Haliç) and the Bosporus, and is now Turkey's largest city and seaport.

SOCIAL STATISTICS

Births, 1999, 1,405,000; deaths, 438,000. 1999 birth rate per 1,000 population, 21·8; death rate, 6·8. 1998 marriages, 485,112 (rate of 7·6 per 1,000 population); divorces (1998), 32,167 (rate of 0·5 per 1,000 population). Annual population growth rate, 1990–99, 1·7%. Expectation of life, 1999, was 67·0 years for males and 72·1 for females. Infant mortality, 1990–95, was 53 per 1,000 live births, down from 102 in 1980–85. The rate dropped more in Turkey than in any other country over the same period. By 1999 it had declined to 40 per 1,000 live births. Fertility rate, 1999, 2·4 births per woman. In 1997 the most popular age for marrying was 20–24 for both men and women.

CLIMATE

Coastal regions have a Mediterranean climate, with mild, moist winters and hot, dry summers. The interior plateau has more extreme conditions, with low and irregular rainfall, cold and snowy winters, and hot, almost rainless summers. Figures for 1999: Ankara, Jan. 31·8°F (−0·1°C), July 73·6°F (23·1°C). Annual rainfall 14·9" (377·7 mm). İstanbul, Jan. 42·1°F (5·6°C), July 73·7°F (23·2°C). Annual rainfall 26·7" (677·2 mm). İzmir, Jan. 47·5°F (8·6°C), July 81·7°F (27·6°C). Annual rainfall 27·2" (691·1 mm).

CONSTITUTION AND GOVERNMENT

On 7 Nov. 1982 a referendum established that 98% of the electorate were in favour of a new Constitution. The *President* is elected for seven-year terms. The Presidency is not an executive position, and the President may not be linked to a political party. There is a 550-member *Grand National Assembly*, elected by universal suffrage (at 18 years and over) for five-year terms by proportional representation. There is a *Constitutional Court* consisting of 15 regular and 5 alternating members.

National Anthem. 'Korkma! Sönmez bu şafaklarda yüzen al sancak' ('Be not afraid! Our flag will never fade'); words by Mehmed Akif Ersoy, tune by Zeki Güngör.

RECENT ELECTIONS

Parliamentary elections were held on 3 Nov. 2002. The Justice and Development Party (AKP)—former Islamists—won 363 of the 550 seats with 34·3% of votes cast, against 178 seats and 19·4% for the Republican People's Party (CHP). Remaining seats went to independents. Parties which failed to secure the 10% of votes needed to gain parliamentary representation included the True Path Party (DYP) with 9·6%; the Nationalist Action Party (MHP), 8·3%; the Youth Party (GP), 7·2%; the Democratic People's Party (DEHAP), 6·2%; the Motherland Party (ANAP), 5·1%; the Saadet Party (SP), 2·5%; the Democratic Left Party (DSP) of outgoing Prime Minister Bülent Ecevit, 1·2%; the Grand Unity Party (BBP), 1·1%; and the New Turkey Party (YTP), 1·0%. Turn-out was 78·9%. An absolute majority was achieved in a Turkish parliamentary election for the first time in 15 years.

Voting for president took place on 1 May 2000 in parliament. Ahmet Necdet Sezer failed to get the required two-thirds majority in the first two rounds. However, in the third round only a simple majority is required, which he received gaining 330 of the 550 available votes.

CURRENT ADMINISTRATION

President: Ahmet Necdet Sezer; b. 1941 (sworn in 16 May 2000).

In March 2003 the government comprised:

Prime Minister: Recep Tayyip Erdoğan; b. 1954 (AKP; sworn in 14 March 2003).

Deputy Prime Ministers: Abdullah Gül (also *Foreign Minister*); Abdüllatif Şener (also *Minister of State*); Mehmet Ali Şahin (also *Minister of State*).

Minister of Defence: Vecdi Gönül. *Development and Public Works:* Zeki Ergezen. *Interior:* Abdülkadir Aksu. *Justice:* Cemil Çiçek. *Finance:* Kemal Unakıtan. *Education:* Hüseyin Çelik. *Health:* Recep Akdağ. *Transport:* Binalı Yıldırım. *Agriculture:* Sami Güçlü. *Labour:* Murat Başesgioğlu. *Trade and Industry:* Ali Coşkun. *Energy:* Hilmi Güler. *Culture:* Erkan Mumcu. *Tourism:* Güldal Akşit. *Forestry:* Osman Pepe. *Environment:* Kürşat Tüzmen. *Ministers of State:* Mehmet Aydın; Beşir Atalay; Ali Babacan.

The *Speaker* is Bülent Arınç.

Office of the Prime Minister: http://www.byegm.gov.tr/

DEFENCE

The *Supreme Council of National Security*, chaired by the Prime Minister and comprising military leaders and the ministers of defence and the economy, also functions as a *de facto* constitutional watchdog.

Conscription is 18 months.

In 2001 defence expenditure totalled US$7,219m., up from US$3,470m. in 1985. Spending per capita in 2001 was US$107, up from US$69 per capita in 1985. The 2001 expenditure represented 5·0% of GDP.

Army. Strength (2002) 402,000 (325,000 conscripts) with a potential reserve of 258,700. There is also a paramilitary gendarmerie-cum-national guard of 150,000. In addition 36,000 Turkish troops are stationed in Northern Cyprus.

Navy. The fleet includes 13 diesel submarines and 19 frigates. The main naval base is at Gölcük in the Gulf of İzmit. There are others at Aksaz-Karaağaç, Eregli, İskenderun, İzmir and Mersin. There are three naval shipyards: Gölcük, İzmir and Taşkizak.

The naval air component operates 16 armed helicopters. There is a Marine Regiment some 3,100-strong.

Personnel in 2002 totalled 52,750 (34,500 conscripts) including marines.

Air Force. The Air Force is organized as two tactical air forces, with headquarters at Eskisehir and Diyarbakır. There were 485 combat aircraft in operation in 2002 including F-5A/Bs, F-4E Phantoms and F-16C/Ds.

Personnel strength (2002), 60,100 (31,500 conscripts).

INTERNATIONAL RELATIONS

In Oct. 1998 Turkish troops mobilized on the border with Syria in protest against Syrian support for Kurdish rebels operating from its territory.

Following the terror attacks on New York and Washington of 11 Sept. 2001 Turkey expressed support for the USA, later becoming the first Muslim country to send soldiers to Afghanistan, to help train anti-Taliban fighters and to administer aid. The decision may have been influenced by Turkey's application to join the European Union.

Turkey is a member of the UN, WTO, BIS, OECD, NATO, Council of Europe, OSCE, BSEC, Asian Development Bank, ECO, OIC and an Associate Member of the WEU, and has applied to join the EU. At the European Union's Helsinki Summit in Dec. 1999 Turkey was awarded candidate status, although talks on membership will not take place for some years.

ECONOMY

Agriculture accounted for 17·6% of GDP in 1998, industry 25·4% and services 57·0%.

Overview. Privatization is co-ordinated by the Public Participation Fund. The pace of economic reform is likely to accelerate as Turkey gets closer to EU membership.

Currency. The unit of currency is the *Turkish lira* (TRL) notionally of 100 *kuruş*. Gold reserves were 3·73m. troy oz in June 2002 and foreign exchange reserves US$22,238m. In 2001 inflation was running at an annualized rate of 65%. Total money supply in Dec. 2001 was TL5,188,070bn.

Budget. The fiscal year is the calendar year. Revenue and expenditure in TL1trn.:

	1997	1998	1999	2000
Revenue	6,327·0	12,657·0	19,798·3	35,425·8
Expenditure	8,616·9	16,762·4	29,467·3	49,134·2

Tax revenues were TL9,232trn. in 1998.

Performance. Real GDP growth was negative in 1999, at −5·0%, but in 2000 there was growth of 7·5%. In 2001, however, the economy shrank again, by 9·4%—the worst performance since the Second World War. Total GDP was US$147·6bn. in 2001.

Banking and Finance. The Central Bank (Merkez Bankası; *Governor*, Süreyya Serdengeçti) is the bank of issue. In 1997 there were 57 commercial banks (7 state-owned, 29 private, 21 foreign), and 12 development and investment banks. The Central Bank's assets were TL11,618,169,900m. in 1998. The assets and liabilities of deposit money banks were TL33,478,370,900m. Turkey's largest bank is the state-owned Ziraat Bankası, with assets in 1999 of TL10,202,000,000m. At the end of 1998 it held nearly 18% of all bank deposits. Foreign investment in 1995 was US$1·1bn. compared to US$150m. in 1985. In Sept. 2000 a Banking Regulation and Audit Board was established to serve as an independent banking regulator. In Dec. 2000 the IMF gave Turkey an emergency loan of US$7·5bn. as the country experienced a financial crisis after ten banks were placed in receivership. The economic crisis continued as the *lira* was floated on the international market and lost 30% of its value against the US dollar in the space of 12 hours in Feb. 2001. Within a week the lira had been devalued by approximately 40%. In April 2001 Turkey secured a further US$10bn. loan from the IMF and the World Bank. This was followed in Feb. 2002 with a three-year US$16bn. loan from the IMF, taking total loans paid or pledged to US$$31bn.

There is a stock exchange in İstanbul (ISE).

Weights and Measures. The metric system is in use. The Gregorian calendar has been in exclusive use since 26 Dec. 1925.

ENERGY AND NATURAL RESOURCES

Environment. In 1998, according to the *World Bank Atlas*, Turkey's carbon dioxide emissions were the equivalent of 3·2 tonnes per capita.

Electricity. In 1998 installed capacity was 23·4m. kW (9·9m. kW hydro-electric in 1995), gross production was 111,022m. kWh and consumption per capita was 1,382 kWh.

Oil and Gas. Crude oil production (1997) was 3,427,814 tonnes; motor oil, 7,406,023 tonnes; fuel oil, 7,209,003 tonnes. Total refining capacity (1997) was 683,000 bbls. per day. In 1997, 23,357,173 tonnes of crude petroleum were imported. Natural gas output was 8 petajoules in 1996.

Accords for the construction of an oil pipeline from Azerbaijan through Georgia to the Mediterranean port of Ceyhan in southern Turkey, and a gas pipeline from Turkmenistan through Azerbaijan and Georgia, to Erzurum in northeastern Turkey, were signed in Nov. 1999. Work on the oil pipeline, which is expected to become operational in 2005, began in Sept. 2002.

Minerals. Turkey is rich in minerals, and is a major producer of chrome. Production of principal minerals (in 1,000 tonnes) was:

	1994	1995	1996	1997
Coal	4,211	3,377	3,582	3,646
Lignite	55,038	56,031	57,532	56,461
Chrome	1,270	2,080	1,279	1,646
Copper	3,346	2,928	3,519	3,795
Magnesite	1,280	1,928	2,342	2,051
Iron	5,773	4,931	6,280	5,987
Boron	2,088	1,769	2,401	2,602
Salt	1,353	1,444	2,068	2,000[1]

[1]Estimate.

Agriculture. At the 1991 census of agriculture there were 4,091,530 households engaged in farming, of which 148,190 were engaged purely in animal farming. Holdings are increasingly fragmented by the custom of dividing land equally amongst sons. Agriculture accounts for 46% of the workforce but only 15% of GDP. There are government price supports to cereal growers. The sown area in 1998 was 18,748,000 ha; 4,890,000 ha was fallow; vineyards, orchards and olive groves occupied 2,530,000 ha.

Production (2000, in 1,000 tonnes) of principal crops: sugarbeets, 16,854; wheat, 16,500; barley, 6,800; tomatoes, 6,800; melons and watermelons, 5,800; potatoes, 5,475; grapes, 3,400; apples, 2,500; maize, 2,500; onions, 2,300; seed cotton, 2,151; cucumbers and gherkins, 1,550; chillies and green peppers, 1,400; cottonseed, 1,360; oranges, 1,100; aubergines, 850; tree nuts, 831; sunflower seeds, 800; cotton lint, 791; cabbages, 732; olives, 600; hazelnuts, 550; lemons and limes, 520; apricots, 500; chick-peas, 500; tangerines and mandarins, 500. Turkey is the largest producer of apricots and hazelnuts.

Livestock, 2000 (in 1,000): sheep, 29,435; cattle, 11,031; goats, 8,057; asses, 603; horses, 330; buffaloes, 176; mules, 133; chickens, 27,000. Livestock products, 2000 (in 1,000 tonnes): milk, 9,876; meat, 1,386; eggs, 660; cheese, 131; honey, 71.

Forestry. There were 8·86m. ha of forests in 1995 (11·5% of the land area). Timber production was 17·62m. cu. metres in 1999.

Fisheries. The catch in 1999 totalled 575,097 tonnes (524,907 tonnes from marine waters and 50,190 tonnes from inland waters). Aquaculture production, 1995, 21,607 tonnes (mainly carp and trout). There were (1996) 1,165 sea fishing boats.

INDUSTRY
Production in 1997 (in 1,000 tonnes unless otherwise stated): cement, 36,035; crude steel, 13,644; crude iron, 5,567; fertilizers, 5,242; coke, 3,186; sugar (1998), 2,784; olive oil (1998), 1,220; cigarettes, 75bn. (units); iron and steel bars, 1,193; paper and paperboard (1998), 951; sulphuric acid, 787; ammonia, 624; pig iron, 577; cotton yarn, 523; ethylene, 380; polyethylene, 293; PVC, 189; cotton textiles, 677·84m. metres; woollen textiles, 47·4m. metres; carpets, 15,971,057 sq. metres; lorries, 73,946 assembled units (1997); motor cars, 196,176 units (1996); tractors, 45,656 units (1996).

Labour. In 1997 there were 20,814,000 people in employment (5,450,000 women): 8,219,000 were engaged in agriculture, forestry and fishing, 3,603,000 in manufacturing, 3,024,000 in services and 2,969,000 in trade, restaurants and hotels. In April 1999 the unemployment rate stood at 6·4%. Workers in Turkey put in among the longest hours of any country in the world. In 1996, 93% of male workers and 80% of female workers worked more than 40 hours a week. The proportion of adults between the ages of 15 and 64 in employment has gradually fallen, from 69% in 1975 to only 50% in 1997. Although the population of working age has been growing at an average of 3% a year, total employment has grown at only 1·5% a year.

Trade Unions. There are four national confederations (including Türk-İş and Disk) and six federations. There are 35 unions affiliated to Türk-İş and 17 employers' federations affiliated to Disk, whose activities were banned on 12 Sept. 1980. In 1996 labour unions totalled 114 and employers' unions 55. Some 2·2m. workers belonged to unions in 1990. Membership is forbidden to civil servants (including schoolteachers). There were 38 strikes in 1995, with 274,322 working days lost, and 3 lock-outs, with 160,368 working days lost.

INTERNATIONAL TRADE
Total foreign debt in 2000 was US$116,209m. (the eighth highest in the world). A customs union with the EU came into force on 1 Jan. 1996.

Imports and Exports. Trade in US$1m.:

	1996	1997	1998	1999	2000
Imports f.o.b.	43,028	48,029	45,440	39,768	54,041
Exports f.o.b.	32,446	32,631	31,220	29,325	31,664

Chief exports (1998) in US$1m.: ready-made garments, 7,074; food products, 4,688; machinery and automotive industry products, 4,092; textile products, 3,557; iron and steel, 1,824. Chief imports: machinery and automotive industry products, 18,232; chemicals, 6,579; minerals and oil, 4,506; food and agricultural raw materials, 4,321; iron and steel, 2,230.

The main export markets in 1998 (in US$1m.) were: Germany, 5,460; USA, 2,233; UK, 1,740; Italy, 1,557; Russia, 1,348; France, 1,305. Main import suppliers: Germany, 7,311; Italy, 4,235; USA, 4,043; France, 3,033; UK, 2,681; Russia, 2,155; Japan, 2,045. By 2001 the EU was accounting for 51·4% of exports and 44·2% of imports.

COMMUNICATIONS

Roads. In 1998 there were 382,059 km of roads, including 1,726 km of motorway. In 1998 the total number of road vehicles was 6,264,084. In 1998 there were 4,050,179 cars, 997,387 trucks and vans, 108,414 buses and coaches and 940,934 motorcycles and mopeds. There were 4,352 fatalities from road accidents in 1998.

Rail. Total length of railway lines in 1998 was 8,607 km (1,435 mm gauge), of which 1,706 km were electrified; 109·8m. passengers and 15·8m. tonnes of freight were carried.

Civil Aviation. There are international airports at İstanbul (Atatürk), Dalaman (Muğla), Ankara (Esenboga), İzmir (Adnan Menderes), Adana and Antalya. The national carrier is Turkish Airlines, which is 98·2% state-owned. In 1998 it flew 123·4m. km and carried 10,131,700 passengers (3,987,800 on international flights).

In 2000 İstanbul handled 14,647,818 passengers (9,465,965 on international flights) and 219,244 tonnes of freight. Antalya was the second busiest airport for passenger traffic, with 7,456,658 passengers (6,779,733 on international flights), and Ankara third with 4,027,928 passengers (2,800,943 on domestic flights).

Shipping. There were 5,711 ships and boats in 1998. In 1998 there were 959 cargo ships totalling 5,916,111 GRT, 269 tankers totalling 967,037 GRT and 687 passenger ships totalling 146,188 GRT. The main ports are: İstanbul, İzmir, Samsun, Mersin, İskenderun and Trabzon.

Coastal shipping, 1998: 15,270 vessels handled; 413,951 passengers entered, and 273,872 cleared; 21·6m. tonnes of goods entered, 17·2m. cleared. International shipping: 24,237 vessels handled; 563,114 passengers entered, 568,693 cleared; 78·2m. tonnes of goods entered, 24·8m. cleared.

Telecommunications. In 2000 main telephone lines numbered 18,395,200 (280·0 for every 1,000 persons) and there were 2·5m. PCs in use (38·1 per 1,000 persons). In 1998 there were 119,000 fax machines. Turkey had 2·5m. Internet users in Dec. 2001 and 9·6m. mobile phone subscribers in Nov. 2000. The long-delayed privatization of Türk Telecom remains high on the government's agenda.

Postal Services. In 1996 there were 24,860 post, telegraph and telephone offices.

SOCIAL INSTITUTIONS

Justice. The unified legal system consists of: (1) justices of the peace (single judges with limited but summary penal and civil jurisdiction); (2) courts of first instance (single judges, dealing with cases outside the jurisdiction of (3) and (4)); (3) central criminal courts (a president and two judges, dealing with cases where the crime is punishable by imprisonment over five years); (4) commercial courts (three judges); (5) state security courts, to prosecute offences against the integrity of the state (a president and four judges, two of the latter being military).

The civil and military High Courts of Appeal sit at Ankara. The Council of State is the highest administrative tribunal; it consists of five chambers. Its 31 judges are nominated from among high-ranking personalities in politics, economy, law, the army, etc. The Military Administrative Court deals with the judicial control of administrative acts and deeds concerning military personnel. The Court of Jurisdictional Disputes is empowered to resolve disputes between civil, administrative and military courts. The Supreme Council of Judges and Public Prosecutors appoints judges and prosecutors to the profession and has disciplinary powers.

The Civil Code and the Code of Obligations have been adapted from the corresponding Swiss codes. The Penal Code is largely based upon the Italian Penal Code, and the Code of Civil Procedure closely resembles that of the Canton of Neuchâtel. The Commercial Code is based on the German.

The population in penal institutions in Sept. 1997 was 59,275 (95 per 100,000 of national population).

The death penalty, not used since 1984, was abolished in peacetime in Aug. 2002.

Religion. Islam ceased to be the official religion in 1928. The Constitution guarantees freedom of religion but forbids its political exploitation or any impairment of the secular character of the republic.

In 1998 there were 64·41m. Muslims, two-thirds Sunni and one-third Shia (Alevis). The administration of the Sunni Muslim religious organizations is the responsibility of the Department of Religious Affairs. The Greek Orthodox, Gregorian Armenian, Armenian Apostolic and Roman Catholic Churches are represented in İstanbul, and there are small Uniate, Protestant and Jewish communities.

Education. Adult literacy in 1999 was 84·6% (male, 93·2%; female, 75·9%). Primary education from 6 to 14 is compulsory and co-educational and, in state schools, free. Religious instruction (Sunni Muslim) in state schools is now compulsory. In Aug. 2002 parliament legalized education in Kurdish. In 1991 there were 5,197 religious secondary schools with 0·29m. pupils up to 14 years.

Statistics for 1996–97	Number	Teachers	Students
Pre-school institutions	6,082	9,971	174,710
Primary schools	47,313	217,131	6,389,060
Junior high schools	8,844	71,808	2,269,620
High schools	2,300	71,514	1,158,095
Vocational and technical junior high schools	986	356	352,974
Vocational and technical high schools	3,060	75,151	980,203
Higher education institutes	863	53,805	1,222,362

In 1995–96 there were 54 universities. In 1996–97 a total of 1,222,000 students enrolled at 863 establishments of higher education (including the universities); teaching staff numbered 53,805. In 1996, 27,452 students were studying abroad.

In 1995 total expenditure on education came to 2·2% of GNP.

Health. There were 70,947 physicians in 1996, equivalent to one physician for 867 persons. In 1997 there were 41,148 general practitioners, 32,511 specialist doctors, 12,737 dentists, 67,265 nurses and 20,557 pharmacists. In 1998 there were 987 hospitals with 148,987 beds (including maternity hospitals) and 151 health centres. In 1998, 39% of the population aged 15 and over smoked—a rate only exceeded in Russia and the Fiji Islands.

Welfare. In 1997, 1,161,645 beneficiaries received TL487,326,585m. from the Government Employees Retirement Fund. Of these, 678,749 persons were retired and 340,459 were widows, widowers or orphans of retired persons. There were 2,731,793 beneficiaries from the Social Insurance Institution in 1997 (2,614,138 through disability, old age and death insurance).

CULTURE

Broadcasting. Broadcasting is regulated by the nine-member Radio and Television Supreme Council. The government monopoly of broadcasting was abolished in 1994 and in 1997 there were 35 national, 109 regional and 990 local radio stations; and 16 national, 15 regional and 304 local TV stations (colour by PAL). The Turkish Radio Television Corporation (TRT) broadcasts tourist radio programmes and a foreign service, Voice of Turkey. Number of receivers in use (1998): TV, 24·3m.; radio, 12·9m.

Cinema. In 1998 there were 358 cinemas; attendances totalled 15,750,946.

Press. In 1996 there were 57 daily newspapers with a combined average daily circulation of 6·85m. and 1,321 non-daily newspapers with a combined circulation per issue of 2m. The most widely read newspapers are *Hürriyet* and *Sabah*, with average daily circulations of 640,000 and 470,000 respectively. In 1998, 9,383 book titles were published.

Tourism. In 1999 there were 6,893,000 foreign visitors; revenue totalled US$5·20bn. Terrorism threats and an earthquake that killed 15,000 people meant that 1999 saw a decline in numbers, to 6·9m. However, 2000 saw record numbers, with some 10m. tourists coming to Turkey. Tourism accounts for 4·7% of the country's GDP.

Libraries. There were 1,185 libraries serving a readership of 20,318,223 in 1998.

Theatre and Opera. In 1997–98 there were 74 theatre halls, at which 331 shows were performed, attended by 1,956,990 spectators. There were also six opera and ballet theatres, where 89 shows (62 foreign) were attended by 220,069 spectators.

Museums and Galleries. Approximately 17·3m. persons visited the 168 museums and ruins maintained by museums in 1998.

DIPLOMATIC REPRESENTATIVES
Of Turkey in the United Kingdom (43 Belgrave Sq., London, SW1X 8PA)
Ambassador: Akin Alptuna.

Of the United Kingdom in Turkey (Sehit Ersan Caddesi 46/A, Cankaya, Ankara)
Ambassador: Peter Westmacott, CMG, LVO.

Of Turkey in the USA (2525 Massachusetts Ave., NW, Washington, D.C., 20008)
Ambassador: Osman Faruk Loğoğlu.

Of the USA in Turkey (110 Atatürk Blvd., Ankara)
Ambassador: W. Robert Pearson.

Of Turkey to the United Nations
Ambassador: Ümit Pamir.

Of Turkey to the European Union
Ambassador: Mustafa Oguz Demiralp.

FURTHER READING
State Institute of Statistics. *Türkiye İstatistik Yilliği/Statistical Yearbook of Turkey.—Diş Ticaret İstatistikleri/Foreign Trade Statistics* (Annual).—*Aylik İstatistik Bülten* (Monthly).

Abramowitz, Morton, (ed.) *Turkey's Transformation and American Policy.* Century Foundation, New York, 2000
Ahmad, F., *The Making of Modern Turkey.* London, 1993
Barkey, Henri J. and Fuller, Graham E., *Turkey's Kurdish Question.* Rowman and Littlefield, Lanham (MD), 1999
Goodwin, Jason, *Lords of the Horizons: a History of the Ottoman Empire.* Henry Holt, New York, USA, 1999
Howe, Marvin, *Turkey Today: A Nation Divided over Islam's Revival.* Westview, Oxford, 2000
Inalcık, H., Faroqhi, S., McGowan, B., Quataert, D. and Pamuk, Ş., *An Economic and Social History of the Ottoman Empire.* Cambridge Univ. Press, 1994
Kedourie, S., *Turkey: Identity, Democracy, Politics.* London, 1996
Mango, Andrew, *Ataturk.* John Murray, London and Overlook, New York, 1999
McDowall, David, *A Modern History of the Kurds.* I. B. Tauris, London, 1996
Pettifer, J., *The Turkish Labyrinth: Atatürk and the New Islam.* London, 1997
Pope, N. and Pope, H., *Turkey Unveiled: Atatürk and After.* London, 1997
Zürcher, E. J., *Turkey: a Modern History.* London and New York, 1993 (NY, 1994)

National statistical office: State Institute of Statistics Prime Ministry, Necatibey Caddesi no. 114, 06100 Ankara.
Website: http://www.die.gov.tr/ENGLISH/index.html

TURKMENISTAN

Capital: Ashgabat
Population estimate, 2000: 4·74m.
GDP per capita, 2000: (PPP$) 3,956
HDI/world rank: 0·741/87

KEY HISTORICAL EVENTS
Until 1917 Russian Central Asia was divided politically into the Khanate of Khiva, the Emirate of Bokhara and the Governor-Generalship of Turkestan. The Khan of Khiva was deposed in Feb. 1920 and a People's Soviet Republic was set up. In Aug. 1920 the Emir of Bokhara suffered the same fate. The former Governor-Generalship of Turkestan was constituted an Autonomous Soviet Socialist Republic within the RSFSR on 11 April 1921. In the autumn of 1924 the Soviets of the Turkestan, Bokhara and Khiva Republics decided to redistribute their territories on a nationality basis. The redistribution was completed in May 1925 when the new states of Uzbekistan, Turkmenistan and Tadzhikistan were accepted into the USSR as Union Republics. Following the break-up of the Soviet Union, Turkmenistan declared independence in Oct. 1991. Saparmurad Niyazov was elected president and founded the Democratic Party of Turkmenistan, the country's only legal party. Also prime minister and Supreme Commander of the armed forces, parliament proclaimed him head of state for life in Dec. 1999. He holds the official title of 'Turkmenbashi', leader of all Turkmen. In July 2000 President Niyazov introduced a law requiring all officials to speak Turkmen.

TERRITORY AND POPULATION
Turkmenistan is bounded in the north by Kazakhstan, in the north and northeast by Uzbekistan, in the southeast by Afghanistan, in the southwest by Iran and in the west by the Caspian Sea. Area, 448,100 sq. km (186,400 sq. miles). The 1995 census population was 4,483,251; density 10·0 per sq. km. In 1999, 85% of the population were Turkmen, 7% Russian, 5% Uzbek, and 3% other. In 1999, 55·3% of the population lived in rural areas.

The UN gives a projected population for 2010 of 5·65m.

There are five administrative regions (*velayaty*): Ahal, Balkan, Dashoguz, Lebap and Mary, comprising 42 rural districts, 15 towns and 74 urban settlements. The capital is Ashgabat (formerly Ashkhabad; 1999 population, 525,000); other large towns are Turkmenabat (formerly Chardzhou), Mary (Merv), Balkanabad (Nebit-Dag) and Dashoguz.

Languages spoken include Turkmen, 72%; Russian, 12%; Uzbek, 9%; other, 7%. There is a dual citizenship agreement with Russia.

SOCIAL STATISTICS
1998 births, 98,461; deaths, 29,628. Rates per 1,000 population, 1998: birth, 20·3; death, 6·1. Annual population growth rate, 1990–99, 2·0%. Life expectancy, 1999: 62·5 years for males and 69·3 for females. Infant mortality, 1999, 52 per 1,000 live births; fertility rate, 1999, 3·5 births per woman.

CLIMATE
The summers are warm to hot but the humidity is relatively low. The winters are cold but generally dry and sunny over most of the country. Ashgabat, Jan. –1°C, July 25°C. Annual rainfall 375 mm.

CONSTITUTION AND GOVERNMENT
A new constitution was adopted on 18 May 1992. It provides for an executive head of state. The 50-member *Majlis* (Assembly) serves as the main legislative body. The 65-member *Khalk Maslakhaty* (People's Council) is the highest representative body. It is composed of the 50 Majlis members, 10 appointees, 50 directly elected

representatives, the Council of Ministers, the Supreme Court chairman, the Procurator General and the heads of local councils. It is charged with constitutional and legislative review and may pass a motion of no-confidence in the president.

At a referendum on 16 Jan. 1994, 99·99% of votes cast were in favour of prolonging President Niyazov's term of office to 2002. In 1999 the *Khalk Maslakhaty* declared him president for life.

National Anthem. 'Turkmenbasyn guran beyik binasy' ('The country which Turkmenbashi has built'); composed by Veli Muhatov.

RECENT ELECTIONS

At the presidential elections of June 1992, the electorate was 1·86m. Saparmurad Niyazov was re-elected unopposed by 99·5% of votes cast.

Majlis elections were held on 12 Dec. 1999. The only party standing was the Democratic Party (DP; former Communists). One candidate stood in each constituency, but to be elected had to receive 51% of the vote. Elections to the *Khalk Maslakhaty* took place on 7 April 2003 under the same system.

CURRENT ADMINISTRATION

In March 2003 the government comprised:

President and Prime Minister: Saparmurad Niyazov (Saparmurad Turkmenbashi since 1993); b. 1940 (DP; sworn in 27 Oct. 1990).

Minister of Agriculture: Rustem Artykov. *Culture:* Orazgeldy Aydogdoiyev. *Communications:* Resulberdi Khozhagurbanov. *Defence:* Rejepbay Arazov. *Economics and Finance:* Geldiyevna Atayeva. *Education:* Mammetdurdy Saryhanov. *Energy and Industry:* Annaguly Jumaguljov. *Environmental Protection:* Matkarim Rajapov. *Foreign Affairs:* Rashid Meredov. *Health and Medical Industry:* Gurganguly Berdimukhamedov. *Industry and Construction Materials:* Mukhammetnazar Hudayguliyev. *Internal Affairs:* Annaberdy Kakabayev. *Justice:* Gurban Mukhammet Kasimov. *National Security:* Batyr Busakov. *Oil and Gas Industries and Mineral Resources:* Gurban Nazarov. *Social Security:* Orazmurat Begmuradov. *Textile Industry:* Dortguly Aydogdiyev. *Trade and Foreign Economic Relations:* Charymammed Gayibov. *Water Resources:* Gurbangeldi Velmuradov.

Chairman, Supreme Council (Majlis): Tagandurdy Hallyev.

DEFENCE

Defence expenditure in 2000 totalled US$173m. (US$35 per capita), representing 4·0% of GDP.

Army. In 1999 the Army was 14–16,000-strong.

Navy. The government has announced its intention to form a Navy/Coast Guard. The Caspian Sea Flotilla is operating as a joint Russian, Kazakhstani and Turkmenistani flotilla under Russian command. It is based at Astrakhan.

Air Force. The Air Force, with 3,000 personnel, had 89 combat aircraft (with an additional 218 in store) including Su-17s and MiG-29s.

INTERNATIONAL RELATIONS

Turkmenistan is a member of the UN, the NATO Partnership for Peace, OSCE, CIS, Asian Development Bank, ECO and OIC.

ECONOMY

In 1998 agriculture accounted for an estimated 24·6% of GDP, industry 41·8% and services 33·6%. In 1999 an estimated 25% of economic output was being produced by the private sector.

Currency. The unit of currency is the *manat* (TMM) of 100 *tenesi*. Foreign exchange reserves were US$300m. in 1993. Inflation was 11·3% in 2001. The manat was devalued in 1994 to an official rate of US$1 = 230 manat.

Budget. Revenues were an estimated US$521m. in 1996 and expenditure US$548m.

Performance. Total GDP in 2001 was US$6·0bn. Annual real GDP growth averaged –10·6% between 1994 and 1997. However, a revival in the economy led to growth of 7·0% in 1998, followed by a spectacular 16·5% in 1999, 18·0% in 2000 (the highest rate in the world) and 20·5% in 2001. The rapid growth of recent years is largely down to large-scale gas exports to Russia.

Banking and Finance. There are two types of bank in Turkmenistan—state commercial banks and joint stock open-end commercial banks. The central bank is the State Central Bank of Turkmenistan (*Acting Chairman*, Shekersoltan Mukhammedova). In 1999 the total number of banks was reduced from 67 to 13.

Calendar. In Aug. 2002 President Saparmurat Niyazov renamed the days of the week and the months, for example with January becoming 'Turkmenbashi' after the president's official name, meaning 'head of all the Turkmen'. April has been renamed in honour of the president's mother. Tuesday is now 'Young Day' and Saturday 'Spiritual Day'.

ENERGY AND NATURAL RESOURCES

Environment. According to the *World Bank Atlas* carbon dioxide emissions in 1998 were the equivalent of 5·7 tonnes per capita.

Electricity. Installed capacity in 1997 was 4m. kW. Production was 8·75m. kWh in 1998, with consumption per capita 859 kWh.

Oil and Gas. Turkmenistan possesses the world's fifth largest reserves of natural gas, and substantial oil resources, but disputes with Russia have held up development. So far, Turkmenistan has been unable to get its gas to world markets. Ownership of offshore oil reserves is disputed by Iran and Azerbaijan.

In 2000 gas reserves were estimated at 2,300bn. cu. metres and oil reserves at 700m. tonnes. In 1996 crude petroleum production was 32m. bbls.; natural gas (1999), 21·3bn. cu. metres.

Turkmenistan's biggest oil development deal was signed in July 1998 when Mobil of the USA and Monument Oil of the UK, in co-operation with the state oil group Turkmeneft, agreed to spend some US$100m. over three years. In 1998 the two companies were producing 14,000 bbls. a day in western Turkmenistan but it was hoped that expansion and development of the Garashsyzlyk area could lead to production of approaching 500,000 bbls. a day by 2007.

Accords for the construction of a gas pipeline from Turkmenbashi on the Caspian Sea coast through Azerbaijan and Georgia, to Ceyhan on the Mediterranean in Turkey, were signed in Nov. 1999. It is scheduled for completion in 2004.

Minerals. There are reserves of coal, sulphur, magnesium, potassium, lead, barite, viterite, bromine, iodine and salt.

Agriculture. Cotton and wheat account for two-thirds of agricultural production. Barley, maize, corn, rice, wool, silk and fruit are also produced. 2000 produced a bumper wheat harvest. Production of main crops (2000, in 1,000 tonnes): wheat, 1,700; seed cotton, 1,040; cottonseed, 625; cotton lint, 187; grapes, 152; tomatoes, 145; watermelons, 65. There were 1·63m. ha of arable land in 1997 and 0·06m. ha of permanent crops.

Livestock, 2000: sheep, 5·60m.; cattle, 850,000; goats, 368,000; pigs, 46,000; chickens, 4m.

Forestry. There were 3·75m. ha of forests (8% of the land area) in 1995.

Fisheries. There are fisheries in the Caspian Sea. The total catch in 1999 was 8,789 tonnes, exclusively freshwater fish.

INDUSTRY

Main industries: oil refining, gas extraction, chemicals, manufacture of machinery, fertilizers, textiles and clothing. Output, 1997 (in tonnes): residual fuel oil, 1,600,000; distillate fuel oil, 1,520,000; cement (1996), 451,000; mineral fertilizer (1993), 130,000; fabrics (1993), 48·3m. sq. metres; footwear (1993), 3·4m. pairs.

Labour. The labour force in 1996 totalled 1,750,000 (55% males). Of the total workforce, 44% were engaged in agriculture, 21% in services and 10% in mining, manufacturing and public utilities. Average monthly wage in 1994 was 1,000 manat.

INTERNATIONAL TRADE

External debt was US$2,259m. in 2000.

Imports and Exports. Exports, 1997, US$774·2m.; imports, US$1,005·1m. Main imports: light manufactured goods, processed food, metalwork, machinery and parts. Main exports: gas, oil and cotton. The main import suppliers in 1995 were USA (25·8%), Ukraine (17·4%), Turkey (13·1%) and Russia (10·1%). The leading export markets in 1995 were Russia (62·5%), Switzerland (6·5%), Hong Kong (6·2%) and Turkey (4·7%).

COMMUNICATIONS

Roads. Length of roads in 1998, 13,597 km (6,463 km highways and national roads). In 1993, 273·1m. passengers and 46·3m. tonnes of freight were carried. In 1998 there were 492 fatalities as a result of road accidents.

Rail. Length of railways in 1995, 2,164 km of 1,520 mm gauge. A rail link to Iran was opened in May 1996, and there are plans to build a further 2,000 km of rail network. In 1995, 5·5m. passengers and 22·2m. tonnes of freight were carried.

Civil Aviation. The national carrier is Turkmenistan Airlines. In 1998 it operated flights from Ashgabat to Abu Dhabi, Almaty, Delhi, Birmingham, Istanbul, Karachi, Kyiv, London, Moscow and Tashkent. In 1999 scheduled airline traffic of Turkmenistan-based carriers flew 8·6m. km, carrying 220,000 passengers (all on international flights).

Shipping. In 1998 sea-going shipping totalled 38,000 GRT (including oil tankers, 2,000 GRT). In 1993, 1·1m. tonnes of freight were carried by inland waterways.

Telecommunications. Main telephone lines numbered 358,900 in 2000 (81·9 per 1,000 population). There were 3,000 mobile phone subscribers in 1998 and 2,000 Internet users in Dec. 1999.

SOCIAL INSTITUTIONS

Justice. In 1994, 14,824 crimes were reported, including 308 murders and attempted murders. The death penalty was abolished in 1999 (there were over 100 executions in 1996). The population in penal institutions in 1998 was approximately 18,000 (400 per 100,000 of national population).

Religion. Around 90% of the population are Sunni Muslims.

Education. There is compulsory education until the age of 14. In 1994–95 there were 1,900 primary and secondary schools with 940,600 pupils; and in 1993–94 there were 11 higher educational institutions with 38,900 students, 41 technical colleges with 29,000 students, and 11 music and art schools.

In Jan. 1994, 0·2m. children (29·5% of those eligible) were attending pre-school institutions. In 1999 adult literacy was over 98%.

Health. There were 13,500 doctors in 1995 and 368 hospitals with 46,000 beds, and 43,000 junior medical personnel in 1994.

Welfare. In Jan. 1994 there were 0·3m. old-age, and 0·16m. other, pensioners.

CULTURE

Broadcasting. Turkmen Radio is government-controlled. It broadcasts two national and one regional programmes, a Moscow Radio relay and a foreign service, Voice of Turkmen. There is one state-run TV station broadcasting on three channels. In 1997 there were 1·2m. radio receivers and 820,000 television sets.

Press. In 1995 there were 130 newspapers and periodicals.

Tourism. In 1998 there were 300,000 foreign tourists. Receipts totalled US$192m.

DIPLOMATIC REPRESENTATIVES

Of Turkmenistan in the United Kingdom (2nd Floor, St George's Hse., 14–17 Wells St, London, W1P 3FP)
Ambassador: Chary Babaev.

Of the United Kingdom in Turkmenistan (3rd Floor, Office Building, Ak Atin Plaza Hotel, Ashgabat)
Ambassador: Paul Brummell.

TURKMENISTAN

Of Turkmenistan in the USA (2207 Massachusetts Ave., NW, Washington, D.C., 20008)
Ambassador: Meret Bairamovich Orazov.

Of the USA in Turkmenistan (9 Puskin St., Ashgabat)
Ambassador: Laura E. Kennedy.

Of Turkmenistan to the United Nations
Ambassador: Aksoltan T. Ataeva.

Of Turkmenistan to the European Union
Ambassador: Niyazklych Nurklychev.

TUVALU

Capital: Fongafale
Population estimate, 2000: 11,000
GDP per capita: not available

KEY HISTORICAL EVENTS
Formerly known as the Ellice Islands, Tuvalu is a group of nine islands in the western central Pacific. Joining the British controlled Gilbert Islands Protectorate in 1916, they became the Gilbert and Ellice Islands colony.

After the Japanese occupied the Gilbert Islands in 1942, US forces occupied the Ellice Islands. A referendum held in 1974 produced a large majority in favour of separation from the Ellice Islands. Independence was achieved on 1 Oct. 1978. Early in 1979 the USA signed a treaty of friendship with Tuvalu and relinquished its claim to the four southern islands in return for the right to veto any other nation's request to use any of Tuvalu's islands for military purposes.

TERRITORY AND POPULATION
Tuvalu lies between 5° 30' and 11° S. lat. and 176° and 180° E. long. and comprises Nanumea, Nanumaga, Niutao, Nui, Vaitupu, Nukufetau, Funafuti (administrative centre; 2000 estimated population, 4,483), Nukulaelae and Niulakita. Population (census 1991) 9,043, excluding an estimated 1,500 who were working abroad, mainly in Nauru and Kiribati. Estimate, 2000, 10,781. Area approximately 10 sq. miles (26 sq. km). Density, 2000, 415 per sq. km.

In 2002 an estimated 52·9% of the population lived in rural areas. The population is of a Polynesian race.

Both Tuvaluan and English are spoken.

SOCIAL STATISTICS
2000 births, 229; deaths, 109; rates, (per 1,000 population): births, 21; deaths, 10; infant mortality (per 1,000 live births), 35. Expectation of life: males, 64 years; females, 71. Annual population growth rate, 1990–99, 2·8%; fertility rate, 2000, 2·9 births per woman.

CLIMATE
A pleasant but monotonous climate with temperatures averaging 86°F (30°C), though trade winds from the east moderate conditions for much of the year. Rainfall ranges from 120" (3,000 mm) to over 160" (4,000 mm). Funafuti, Jan. 84°F (28·9°C), July 81°F (27·2°C). Annual rainfall 160" (4,003 mm). Although the islands are north of the recognized hurricane belt they were badly hit by hurricanes in the 1990s, raising fears for the long-term future of Tuvalu as the sea level continues to rise.

CONSTITUTION AND GOVERNMENT
The Head of State is the British sovereign, represented by an appointed Governor-General. The Constitution provides for a Prime Minister and the cabinet ministers to be elected from among the members of the *House of Parliament.*

National Anthem. 'Tuvalu mote Atua' ('Tuvalu for the Almighty'); words and tune by A. Manoa.

RECENT ELECTIONS
Elections were held on 2 Aug. 2002. Only non-partisans were elected as there are no political parties.

CURRENT ADMINISTRATION
Governor-General: HE Dr Tomasi Puapua; b. 1938 (appointed June 1998).
In March 2003 the cabinet comprised:
Prime Minister: Saufatu Sopoanga (sworn in 2 Aug. 2002).

Deputy Prime Minister and Minister of Works and Energy, Communications and Transport: Maatia Toafa. *Finance, Economic Planning and Industries:* Bikenibeu Paeniu. *Natural Resources and Land:* Samuelu P. Teo. *Home Affairs and Rural Development:* Otinielu T. Tausi. *Health, Education and Sport:* Alesana Seluka.
Speaker: Saloa Tauia.

INTERNATIONAL RELATIONS
Tuvalu is a member of the UN, the Commonwealth, Asian Development Bank, the Pacific Community and the Pacific Islands Forum, and is an ACP member state of the ACP-EU relationship.

ECONOMY
Currency. The unit of currency is the Australian *dollar* although Tuvaluan coins up to $A1 are in local circulation.

Budget. In 2001 the budget envisaged revenue of $A26·7m. and expenditure of $A35·3m.

Performance. Real GDP growth was 5·2% in 2001.

Banking and Finance. The Tuvalu National Bank was established at Funafuti in 1980, and is a joint venture between the Tuvalu government and Wespac International.

ENERGY AND NATURAL RESOURCES
Electricity. Installed capacity was 2·6 MW in 2002; production was 4,355 MWh.

Agriculture. Coconut palms are the main crop. Production of coconuts (2000 estimate), 2,000 tonnes. Fruit and vegetables are grown for local consumption. Livestock, 2000: pigs, 13,000.

Fisheries. Sea fishing is excellent, particularly for tuna. Total catch, 1999, approximately 5,045 tonnes. A seamount was discovered in Tuvaluan waters in 1991 and is an excellent location for deep-sea fish. The sale of fishing licences to American and Japanese fleets provides a significant source of income.

INTERNATIONAL TRADE
Imports and Exports. Commerce is dominated by co-operative societies, the Tuvalu Co-operative Wholesale Society being the main importer. Main sources of income are copra, stamps, handicrafts and remittances from Tuvaluans abroad. 1998 imports, US$7·2m.; 1997 exports, US$276,000. The leading import supplier and export destination is Australia.

COMMUNICATIONS
Roads. In 2002 there were 20 km of roads.

Civil Aviation. In 2002 Air Kiribati operated four flights a week from Funafuti International to Suva.

Shipping. Funafuti is the only port and a deep-water wharf was opened in 1980. In 2002 merchant shipping totalled 49,000 GRT.

Telecommunications. In 2002 there were approximately 700 main telephone lines in operation.

SOCIAL INSTITUTIONS
Justice. There is a High Court presided over by the Chief Justice of the Fiji Islands. A Court of Appeal is constituted if required. There are also eight Island Courts with limited jurisdiction.

Religion. The majority of the population are Christians, mainly Protestant, but with small groups of Roman Catholics, Seventh Day Adventists, Jehovah's Witnesses and Baha'is. There are some Muslims and Latter-day Saints (Mormons).

TUVALU

Education. There were 1,798 pupils at nine primary schools in 2001, and 558 pupils at Motufoua Secondary School in 2001. The Fetuvalu High School reopened in 2002 with Form 3 only. Education is free and compulsory from the ages of 6 to 13. There is a Maritime Training School at Funafuti, and the University of the South Pacific, based in the Fiji Islands, has an extension centre at Funafuti.

Health. In 2002 there was one central hospital situated at Funafuti and clinics and a nurse on each island; there were seven doctors and 34 nurses.

CULTURE

Broadcasting. The Tuvalu Broadcasting Service transmits daily, and all islands have daily radio communication with Funafuti. There were about 4,000 radio receivers in 1997 and 100 TV sets in 1996.

Press. The Government Broadcasting and Information Division produces *Tuvalu Echoes*, a fortnightly publication, and *Te Lama*, a monthly religious publication.

Tourism. There were 1,304 visitor arrivals in 2002 (639 in 1995).

DIPLOMATIC REPRESENTATIVES
Of Tuvalu in the United Kingdom (Tuvalu House, 230 Worple Road, London SW20 8RH).
Honorary Consul: Iftikhar Ayaz.

Of the United Kingdom in Tuvalu
High Commissioner: Charles Mochan (resides at Suva, Fiji Islands).

Of Tuvalu in the USA
Ambassador: Vacant.

Of the USA in Tuvalu
Ambassador: David Lyon (resides at Suva).

Of Tuvalu to the United Nations
Ambassador: Enele S. Sopoaga.

FURTHER READING
Bennetts, P. and Wheeler, T., *Time and Tide: The Islands of Tuvalu*. Lonely Planet Publications, Melbourne, 2001

1605

UGANDA

Republic of Uganda

Capital: Kampala
Population estimate, 2000: 22·21m.
GDP per capita, 2000: (PPP$) 1,208
HDI/world rank: 0·444/150

KEY HISTORICAL EVENTS

The Luo (a Nilotic-speaking people) invaded the territory of present-day Uganda in the late 15th and 16th centuries founding several kingdoms of which the most prominent was Buganda. Uganda became a British Protectorate in 1894, the province of Buganda being recognized as a native kingdom under its Kabaka. In 1961 Uganda was granted internal self-government with federal status for Buganda. Uganda became an independent member of the Commonwealth on 9 Oct. 1962 and a republic on 8 Sept. 1967. President Milton Obote set about returning land given to the Buganda by the British in 1900 to its original Bunyoro owners. He also abolished Buganda's federal status and autonomy in the country. A rebellion by Buganda was quelled but in 1971 Obote was overthrown by troops under Gen. Idi Amin. Amin's rule was characterized by widespread repression and, in 1972, the expulsion of Asian residents. In April 1979 a force of the Tanzanian Army and Ugandan exiles advanced into Uganda, taking Kampala on 11 April. Amin fled into exile. In Dec. 1980, following elections, Dr Obote again became president, but on 27 July 1985 was overthrown.

TERRITORY AND POPULATION

Uganda is bounded in the north by Sudan, in the east by Kenya, in the south by Tanzania and Rwanda, and the west by the Democratic Republic of the Congo. Total area 241,547 sq. km, including inland waters.

The 2002 census population was 24,748,977 (12,124,761 males, 12,624,216 females); density, 102 per sq. km. The largest city is Kampala, the capital (population of 1,208,544 in 2002). Other major towns are Jinja, Mbale, Masaka, Gulu, Entebbe, Soroti and Mbarara.

The projected population for 2010 is 32·59m.

An estimated 86·2% of the population lived in rural areas in 1999.

The country is administratively divided into 56 districts, which are grouped in four geographical regions (which do not have administrative status). Area and estimated population of the regions in 2002:

Region	Area in sq. km	Population in 1,000
Central Region	61,352	6,683·9
Eastern Region	39,524	6,301·7
Western Region	55,278	6,417·4
Northern Region	85,392	5,346·0

The official language is English, but Kiswahili is used as a *lingua franca*. About 70% of the population speak Bantu languages; Nilotic languages are spoken in the north and east.

Uganda is host to around 500,000 refugees from a number of neighbouring countries, and internally displaced people. Probably in excess of 100,000 southern Sudanese fled to Uganda during 1996.

SOCIAL STATISTICS

Births, 1995, 1,004,000; deaths, 421,000. Rates per 1,000 population, 1995: birth, 51·0; death, 21·4. Uganda's life expectancy at birth in 1999 was 42·5 years for males and 43·8 years for females, down from an average of 47 years in 1985. The sharp decline is largely attributed to the huge number of people in the country with HIV. Annual population growth rate, 1990–99, 2·8%. Infant mortality, 1999, 83 per 1,000 live births; fertility rate, 1999, 7·0 births per woman.

CLIMATE

Although in equatorial latitudes, the climate is more tropical, because of its elevation, and is characterized by two distinct rainy seasons, March–May and

Sept.–Nov. June–Aug. and Dec.–Feb. are comparatively dry. Temperatures vary little over the year. Kampala, Jan. 74°F (23·3°C), July 70°F (21·1°C). Annual rainfall 46·5" (1,180 mm). Entebbe, Jan. 72°F (22·2°C), July 69°F (20·6°C). Annual rainfall 63·9" (1,624 mm).

CONSTITUTION AND GOVERNMENT

The *President* is head of state and head of government, and is elected for a five-year term by adult suffrage. The constitution allows the incumbent no more than two consecutive terms.

Having lapsed in 1966, the kabakaship was revived as a ceremonial office in 1993. Ronald Muwenda Mutebi (b. 13 April 1955) was crowned Mutebi II, 36th Kabaka, on 31 July 1993.

Until 1994 the national legislature was the 278-member National Resistance Council, but this was replaced by a 276-member *Constituent Assembly* in March 1994. A new constitution was adopted on 8 Oct. 1995. A referendum on the return of multiparty democracy was held on 29 June 2000, but 88% of voters supported President Museveni's 'no-party' Movement system of government. Turn-out was 51%. In Feb. 2003 President Museveni pledged to lift the ban on political parties.

National Anthem. 'Oh, Uganda, may God uphold thee'; words and tune by G. W. Kakoma.

RECENT ELECTIONS

Presidential elections were held on 12 March 2001. President Museveni was re-elected by 69·3% of votes cast, with his main rival, Kizza Besigye, receiving 27·8% of the vote. Turn-out was 70·3%. Local non-government monitors described the election as flawed.

Parliamentary elections were held on 26 June 2001. 214 non-partisan members were directly elected in single-seat constituencies. 78 other members had been elected earlier in the month from special interest groups (53 District Women Representatives, 10 army representatives, and 5 each to represent the disabled, the trade unions and youth). Turn-out was 70·3%.

CURRENT ADMINISTRATION

President: Yoweri K. Museveni; b. 1945 (NRM; sworn in 27 Jan. 1986; re-elected 1996 and 2001).

In May 2003 the government comprised:

Vice-President designate: Prof. Gilbert Bukenya (nominated 23 May 2003).

Prime Minister: Apollo Nsibambi; b. 1938 (NRM; sworn in 5 April 1999).

First Deputy Prime Minister and Minister of Internal Affairs: Eriya Kategaya. *Second Deputy Prime Minister and Minister of Disaster Preparedness and Refugees:* Brig. Gen. Moses Ali. *Third Deputy Prime Minister and Minister of Foreign Affairs:* Wapakhabulo James Wambogo.

Minister of Defence: Amama Mbabazi. *Education and Sports:* Edward Kiddu Makubuya. *Tourism, Wildlife and Antiquities:* Edward Rugumayo. *Energy and Mineral Development:* Syda Bbumba. *Health:* Jim Katugugu Muhwezi. *Gender, Labour and Social Development:* Zoe Bakoko Bakoru. *Justice and Constitutional Affairs:* Janat Balunzi Mukwaya. *Local Government:* Jaberi Bidandi Ssali. *Public Service:* Henry Muganwa Kajura. *Water, Lands and Environment:* Ruhakana Rugunda. *Public Works, Transport, Housing and Communications:* John Nasasira. *Finance, Planning and Economic Development:* Gerald Sendawula. *Agriculture, Animal Industry and Fisheries:* Wilberforce Kisamba Mugerwa. *Minister without Portfolio:* Crispus Kiyonga. *Attorney General:* Francis Ayume. *In Charge of the Presidency:* Prof. Gilbert Bukenya. *Office of the Prime Minister:* Mondo George Kagonyera.

Government Website: http://www.government.go.ug/

DEFENCE

In 2000 defence expenditure totalled US$247m. (US$11 per capita), representing 3·0% of GDP.

Army. The Uganda People's Defence Forces had a strength estimated at 30–40,000 in 1999. There is a Border Defence Unit about 600-strong and local defence units estimated at 5–10,000.

Navy. There is a Marine unit of the police (400-strong in 1999).

Air Force. The Army's aviation wing operated four combat aircraft and two armed helicopters in 1999.

INTERNATIONAL RELATIONS

Uganda is a member of UN, WTO, the African Union, African Development Bank, COMESA, EAC, IOM, Islamic Conference Organization, the Commonwealth, the Intergovernmental Authority on Development and is an ACP member state of the ACP-EU relationship.

In Nov. 1999 a treaty was signed between Uganda, Tanzania and Kenya to create a new East African Community as a means of developing East African trade, tourism and industry and laying the foundations for a future common market and political federation.

ECONOMY

In 1998 agriculture accounted for 44·6% of GDP, industry 17·6% and services 37·8%.

Overview. A privatization programme, instituted in 1991, is managed by the Public Enterprise Reform and Divestiture Secretariat. The state is to retain ownership of certain utilities, national parks and the development bank. Most enterprises previously in state ownership have been privatized.

Currency. The monetary unit is the *Uganda shilling* (UGS) notionally divided into 100 *cents*. In 1987 the currency was devalued by 77% and a new 'heavy' shilling was introduced worth 100 old shillings. Inflation was 4·6% in 2001. Foreign exchange reserves in May 2002 were US$893m. Total money supply in April 2002 was Shs 966,075m.

Budget. The provisional total expenditure for the financial year 2001 (year ending 30 June) was Shs 1,516bn., compared to actual expenditure of Shs 1,258·3bn. in 1998. In 2000 total revenue (provisional) was Shs 1,104·6bn. (Shs 827·9bn. in 1998). Expenditures (in Shs) in 2000–01 included: education, 401·5bn. (117bn. 1994–95); defence, 212bn.; roads, 138bn. (25·8bn. 1994–95); health, 111bn. (47·4bn. 1994–95); agriculture, 22bn. (15·1bn. 1994–95).

Performance. Real GDP growth was 5·0% in 2000 and 5·6% in 2001. In spite of growth rates which averaged 6·4% over 10 years to 1998, per capita income is only just around the level of 1971, when Gen. Idi Amin came to power. Uganda's total GDP in 2001 was US$5·7bn.

Banking and Finance. The Bank of Uganda (*Governor*, Emmanuel Tumusiime Mutebile) was established in 1966 and is the central bank and bank of issue. The Uganda Credit and Savings Bank, established in 1950, was on 9 Oct. 1965 reconstituted as the Uganda Commercial Bank, with its capital fully owned by the government. In 1992 it had 188 branches. In addition there are 4 foreign, 2 private and 2 development banks and 1 co-operative bank.

ENERGY AND NATURAL RESOURCES

Environment. According to the *World Bank Atlas* Uganda's carbon dioxide emissions were the equivalent of 0·1 tonnes per capita in 1998.

Electricity. Installed capacity in 1995 was 155 MW, about 95% of which was provided by the Owen Falls Extension Project (a hydro-electric scheme). Production (1998) 792m. kWh. Per capita consumption in 1997 was 34 kWh. Only about 5% of the population has access to electricity, and less than 1% of the rural population.

Oil and Gas. Oil was discovered in north-west Uganda in 1999. A Canadian company Heritage Oil Corporation and Energy Africa are expecting to begin commercial exploitation in July/Aug. 2003.

Minerals. In Nov. 1997 extraction started on the first of an estimated US$400m. worth of cobalt from pyrites. Tungsten and tin concentrates are also mined. There are also significant quantities of clay and gypsum.

Agriculture. 80% of the workforce is involved with agriculture. In 1998 the agricultural area included 5·06m. ha of arable land and 1·75m. ha of permanent crops. Agriculture is one of the priority areas for increased production, with many projects funded both locally and externally. In 1996 it recorded 24·2% growth. It contributes 90% of exports. Production (2000 estimates) in 1,000 tonnes: plantains, 9,533; cassava, 4,966; sweet potatoes, 2,398; sugarcane, 1,550; maize, 1,096; bananas, 610; millet, 534; potatoes, 478; dry beans, 420; sorghum, 361; coffee, 205. Coffee is the mainstay of the economy, accounting for more than 50% of the annual commodity export revenue. Uganda is the world's leading producer of plantains.

Livestock (2000): cattle, 5·97m.; goats, 3·70m.; sheep, 1·98m.; pigs, 0·97m.; chickens, 25m. Livestock products, 2000 (in 1,000 tonnes): milk, 511; meat, 234; eggs, 20.

Forestry. In 1995 the area under forests was 6·1m. ha, or 30·6% of the total land area (6·4m. ha and 32·1% in 1990). Exploitable forests consist almost entirely of hardwoods. Timber production in 1999 totalled 17m. cu. metres. Uganda has great potential for timber-processing for export, manufacture of high-quality furniture and wood products, and various packaging materials.

Fisheries. In 1999 fish landings totalled 226,097 tonnes, entirely from inland waters. Fish farming (especially carp and tilapia) is a growing industry. Uganda's fish-processing industry has greatly expanded in recent years, and by 1998 export earnings were in excess of US$100m. per year

INDUSTRY
Production (in 1,000 tonnes) in 1997: cement, 203; sugar (1998), 111; soap, 67; beer, 89·6m. litres. The manufacturing sector is growing by around 14% annually.

Labour. The labour force in 1996 totalled 10,084,000 (52% males). Around 80% of the workforce are involved in the coffee business.

INTERNATIONAL TRADE
Foreign debt was US$3,409m. in 2000. Over the period 1981–96 foreign investment totalled US$850m.

Imports and Exports. In 1999 imports (f.o.b.) amounted to US$1,096·5m. (US$1,166·3m. in 1998); exports (f.o.b.) US$500·1m. (US$510·2m. in 1998). Coffee, cotton, tea and tobacco are the principal exports. Coffee accounts for nearly 70% of exports—in 1998–99 coffee exports were worth US$282·2m. Timber, tea and fish exports are increasingly important. In 1996 the main export markets were Spain (21·1%), France (11·1%) and Germany (8·8%). Main import suppliers in 1996 were Kenya (29·4%), UK (11·8%) and India (6·1%). During the 1990s exports grew by an average of 30% every year.

COMMUNICATIONS
Roads. In 1994 there were 6,727 km of highways and in 1995, 2,276 km of secondary roads. There were 35,360 passenger cars in 1996, 35,500 lorries and vans and 11,900 buses and coaches.

In 1997 the government embarked upon a ten-year road-improvement programme, costing US$1·5bn., funded by international loans.

Rail. The Uganda Railways network totals 1,241 km (metre gauge). In 1996 railways carried 184,000 passengers and 877,000 tonnes of freight.

A US$20m. project is under way to establish a direct rail link between Kampala and Johannesburg, South Africa.

Civil Aviation. There is an international airport at Entebbe, 40 km from Kampala. The national carrier is the state-owned Uganda Airlines, which in 1998 flew to Dar es Salaam, Dubai, Harare, Johannesburg, Kigali, Lusaka and Nairobi. Uganda and Tanzania are partners, with South African Airways, in Alliance Air. In 1999 scheduled airline traffic of Uganda-based carriers flew 4·6m. km, carrying 179,000 passengers (36,000 on international flights). In 2000 Entebbe handled 373,064 passengers (343,746 on international flights) and 26,048 tonnes of freight.

Telecommunications. There were 61,700 telephone main lines in 2000 (2·8 per 1,000 persons); there had been 100,000 in 1971 when Idi Amin seized power. There were 60,000 PCs in use (2·7 per 1,000 persons) in 2000 and 56,400 mobile phone subscribers in 1999. Fax machines numbered 3,000 in 1996. In July 2000 Uganda had 25,000 Internet users.

Postal Services. In 1995 there were 306 post offices.

SOCIAL INSTITUTIONS

Justice. The Supreme Court of Uganda, presided over by the Chief Justice, is the highest court. There is a Court of Appeal and a High Court below that. Subordinate courts, presided over by Chief Magistrates and Magistrates of the first, second and third grade, are established in all areas: jurisdiction varies with the grade of Magistrate. Chief and first-grade Magistrates are professionally qualified; second- and third-grade Magistrates are trained to diploma level at the Law Development Centre, Kampala. Chief Magistrates exercise supervision over and hear appeals from second- and third-grade courts, and village courts.

The population in penal institutions in June 1998 was 21,971 (105 per 100,000 of national population). The death penalty is still in force. In 2002 there were two executions.

Religion. In 1992 there were 8·53m. Roman Catholics, 4·5m. Anglicans and 1·13m. Muslims.

Education. In 1995 there were 2,636,400 pupils in 7,905 primary schools (of which 7,420 were government-aided schools and 485 private schools); 255,158 students in 774 secondary schools; 13,174 students in 94 primary teacher training colleges; 13,360 students in 24 technical institutes and colleges; 22,703 students in 10 national teachers colleges; 1,628 students in 5 colleges of commerce; 504 students in the Uganda Polytechnic, Kyambogo; 800 students in the National College of Business Studies, Nakawa. In 1995–96 there was 1 university and 1 university of science and technology in the public sector, and 2 universities, 1 Christian, 1 Roman Catholic and 1 Islamic university in the private sector, catering for 29,343 students. The adult literacy rate was 66·1% in 1999 (76·8% among males and 55·5% among females).

Primary school attendance has doubled since Yoweri Museveni became president of Uganda in 1986.

Health. In 1988 there were 980 health centres (217 private), and in 1989 there were 81 hospitals and 20,136 hospital beds. In 1993 there were 840 doctors and 2,782 nurses. Uganda has been one of the most successful African countries in the fight against AIDS. A climate of free debate, with President Museveni recognizing the threat as early as 1986 and making every government department take the problem seriously, resulted in HIV prevalence among adults declining from approximately 30% in 1992 to 11% in 2000.

CULTURE

Broadcasting. The government runs Radio Uganda, which has ten stations and transmits three regional programmes, and Uganda Television with nine stations and one programme. Colour is by PAL. There were about 2·6m. radio receivers and about 315,000 television sets in 1997. There are three private television operators.

Press. There were two daily newspapers in 1996 with a combined circulation of 40,000, and four non-daily newspapers and periodicals.

Tourism. In 1998 there were 238,000 foreign tourists, bringing revenue of US$142m.

Festivals. The main festivals are for Islamic holidays (March and June), Martyrs' Day (3 June), Heroes' Day (9 June) and Independence Day (9 Oct.).

Theatre and Opera. There is a National Theatre at Kampala.

Museums and Galleries. The Nommo Gallery houses famous works of art, and is involved in educational and other cultural programmes.

DIPLOMATIC REPRESENTATIVES

Of Uganda in the United Kingdom (Uganda Hse., 58/59 Trafalgar Sq., London, WC2N 5DX)
High Commissioner: George Kirya.

Of the United Kingdom in Uganda (10/12 Parliament Ave., Kampala)
High Commissioner: Adam Wood.

Of Uganda in the USA (5911 16th St., NW, Washington, D.C., 20011)
Ambassador: Edith Ssempala.

Of the USA in Uganda (Parliament Ave., Kampala)
Ambassador: Vacant.

Of Uganda to the United Nations
Ambassador: Vacant.

Of Uganda to the European Union
Ambassador: Vacant.
Chargé d'Affaires a.i.: Lewis Balinda.

FURTHER READING

Museveni, Y., *What is Africa's Problem?* London, 1993.—*The Mustard Seed.* London, 1997
Mutibwa, P., *Uganda since Independence: a Story of Unfulfilled Hopes.* London, 1992
Nyeko, B., *Uganda.* [Bibliography] 2nd ed. ABC-Clio, Oxford and Santa Barbara (CA), 1996

National statistical office: Uganda Bureau of Statistics, P. O. Box 13, Entebbe.
Website: http://www.ubos.org/

UKRAINE

Ukraina

Capital: Kyiv (formerly Kiev)
Population estimate, 2000: 49·57m.
GDP per capita, 2000: (PPP$) 3,816
HDI/world rank: 0·748/80

KEY HISTORICAL EVENTS

Kyiv (formerly Kiev) was the centre of the Rus principality in the 11th and 12th centuries and is still known as the Mother of Russian cities. The western Ukraine principality of Galicia was annexed by Poland in the 14th century. At about the same time, Kyiv and the Ukrainian principality of Volhynia were conquered by Lithuania before being absorbed by Poland. Poland, however, could not subjugate the Ukrainian cossacks, who allied themselves with Russia. Ukraine, except for Galicia (part of the Austrian Empire, 1772–1919), was incorporated into the Russian Empire after the second partition of Poland in 1793.

In 1917, following the Bolshevik revolution, the Ukrainians in Russia established an independent republic. Austrian Ukraine proclaimed itself a republic in 1918 and was federated with its Russian counterpart. The Allies ignored Ukrainian claims to Galicia, however, and in 1918 awarded that area to Poland. From 1922 to 1932, drastic efforts were made by the USSR to suppress Ukrainian nationalism. Ukraine suffered from the forced collectivization of agriculture and the expropriation of foodstuffs; the result was the famine of 1932–33 when more than 7m. people died. Following the Soviet seizure of eastern Poland in Sept. 1939, Polish Galicia was incorporated into the Ukrainian SSR. When the Germans invaded Ukraine in 1941 hopes that an autonomous or independent Ukrainian republic would be set up under German protection were disappointed. Ukraine was re-taken by the USSR in 1944. The Crimean region was joined to Ukraine in 1954.

On 5 Dec. 1991 the Supreme Soviet declared Ukraine's independence. Ukraine was one of the founder members of the CIS in Dec. 1991. After independence Crimea, which was part of Russia until 1954, became a source of contention between Moscow and Kyiv. The Russian Supreme Soviet laid claim to the Crimean port city of Sevastopol, the home port of the 350-ship Black Sea Fleet, despite an agreement to divide the fleet. There was also conflict between Ukraine and Russia over possession and transfer of nuclear weapons, delivery of Russian fuel to Ukraine and military and political integration within the CIS. Leonid Kuchma was elected president in 1994 and re-elected in 1999. Support for him has dimmed after public demonstrations against maladministration including the accusation that he was responsible for the murder of a radical journalist. Conflicts between the presidential administration and government led to the sacking of reform-minded prime minister Viktor Yushchenko in April 2001, who was replaced by Kuchma loyalist Anatolii Kinakh at the end of May. The Pope's historic visit to Ukraine in June 2001 was accompanied by disturbances, particularly in the capital.

TERRITORY AND POPULATION

Ukraine is bounded in the east by the Russian Federation, north by Belarus, west by Poland, Slovakia, Hungary, Romania and Moldova, and south by the Black Sea and Sea of Azov. Area, 603,700 sq. km (233,090 sq. miles). The 1995 census population was 51·7m., of whom 73% were Ukrainians, 22% Russians, 1% Jews and 4% other—Belarusians, Moldovans, Hungarians, Bulgarians, Poles and Crimean Tatars (most of the Tatars were forcibly transported to Central Asia in 1944 for anti-Soviet activities during the Second World War). In 2001 the census population was 48,416,000, of whom 25,941,000 were female (67·0% urban in 2001); density, 80 per sq. km.

The UN gives a projected population for 2010 of 45·24m.

Ukraine is divided into 24 provinces, 2 municipalities (Kyiv and Simferopol) and the Autonomous Republic of Crimea. Area and populations (2001 census):

	Area (sq. km)	Population (in 1,000)		Area (sq. km)	Population (in 1,000)
Cherkaska	20,900	1,402	Lvivska	21,800	2,626
Chernihivska	31,900	1,236	Mykolaïvska	24,600	1,264
Chernivetska	8,100	923	Odeska	33,300	2,468
Crimea	26,100	2,031	Poltavska	28,800	1,630
Dnipropetrovska	31,900	3,560	Rivnenska	20,100	1,173
Donetska	26,500	4,843	Sevastopol	900	378
Ivano-Frankivska	13,900	1,409	Sumska	23,800	1,300
Kharkivska	31,400	2,910	Ternopilska	13,800	1,142
Khersonska	28,500	1,174	Vinnytska	26,500	1,772
Khmelnytska	20,600	1,431	Volynska	20,200	1,061
Kirovohradska	24,600	1,129	Zakarpatska	12,800	1,258
Kyiv	800	2,607	Zaporizhska	27,200	1,926
Kyivska	28,100	1,828	Zhytomyrska	29,900	1,389
Luhanska	26,700	2,546			

The capital is Kyiv (population 2,602,000 in 2001). Other towns with 2001 populations over 0·2m. are:

	Population (in 1,000)		Population (in 1,000)		Population (in 1,000)
Kharkiv	1,470	Vinnytsya	357	Dniprodzerzhynsk	256
Dnipropetrovsk	1,064	Simferopol	343	Khmelnitsky	254
Odesa	1,029	Sevastopol	341	Kirovohrad	253
Donetsk	1,016	Kherson	328	Rivne	249
Zaporizhzhya	814	Poltava	318	Chernivtsi	240
Lviv	732	Chernihiv	301	Kremenchuk	234
Kryvy Rih	667	Cherkasy	295	Ternopil	228
Mykolaïv	514	Sumy	293	Ivano-Frankivsk	218
Mariupol	492	Horlivka	292	Lutsk	209
Luhansk	463	Zhytomyr	284	Bila Tserkva	200
Makiïvka	390				

The 1996 Constitution made Ukrainian the sole official language. Russian (the language of 22% of the population), Romanian, Polish and Hungarian are also spoken. Additionally, the 1996 Constitution abolished dual citizenship, previously available if there was a treaty with the other country (there was no such treaty with Russia). Anyone resident in Ukraine since 1991 may be naturalized.

SOCIAL STATISTICS
1998 births, 419,238; deaths, 719,954; marriages, 310,504; divorces, 179,688. Rates (per 1,000 population), 1998: births, 8·4; deaths, 14·4. Annual population growth rate, 1990–99, –0·3%. Life expectancy, 1999: males, 62·7 years, females, 73·5. In 1998 the most popular age range for marrying was 20–24 for both males and females. Infant mortality, 1999, 17 per 1,000 live births; fertility rate, 1999, 1·4 births per woman.

CLIMATE
Temperate continental with a subtropical Mediterranean climate prevalent on the southern portions of the Crimean Peninsula. The average monthly temperature in winter ranges from 17·6°F to 35·6°F (–8°C to 2°C), while summer temperatures average 62·6°F to 77°F (17°C to 25°C). The Black Sea coast is subject to freezing, and no Ukrainian port is permanently ice-free. Precipitation generally decreases from north to south; it is greatest in the Carpathians where it exceeds more than 58·5" (1,500 mm) per year, and least in the coastal lowlands of the Black Sea where it averages less than 11·7" (300 mm) per year.

CONSTITUTION AND GOVERNMENT
In a referendum on 1 Dec. 1991, 90·3% of votes cast were in favour of independence. Turn-out was 83·7%.

A new Constitution was adopted on 28 June 1996. It defines Ukraine as a sovereign, democratic, unitary state governed by the rule of law and guaranteeing civil rights. The head of state is the *President*. Parliament is the 450-member unicameral *Supreme Council*, elected by universal suffrage for four-year terms. For an election to be valid, turn-out in an electoral district must reach 50%. The Prime

Minister is nominated by the President with the agreement of more than half the Supreme Council. There is an 18-member *Constitutional Court*, six members being appointed by the President, six by parliament and six by a panel of judges. Constitutional amendments may be initiated at the President's request to parliament, or by at least one third of parliamentary deputies. The Communist Party was officially banned in the country in 1991, but was renamed the Socialist Party of Ukraine. Hard-line Communists protested against the ban, which was rescinded by the Supreme Council in May 1993.

National Anthem. 'Shche ne vmerla, Ukraïny i slava, i volya' ('Ukraine's freedom and glory has not yet perished'); words by P. Chubynsky, tune by M. Verbytsky.

RECENT ELECTIONS
Parliamentary elections were held on 30 March 2002. Former Prime Minister Viktor Yushchenko's Our Ukraine Party won 112 of 450 seats with 23·6% of votes cast, For United Ukraine 102 (11·8%), the Communist Party of Ukraine 66 (20·0%), the Socialist Party of Ukraine 24 (6·9%), the United Social-Democratic Party of Ukraine 24 (6·3%) and the Juliya Tymoshenko Election Bloc 21 (7·2%). Other parties and non-partisans accounted for the remainder. There were widespread accusations of vote-rigging.

In the presidential election run-off held on 14 Nov. 1999 incumbent Leonid Kuchma gained 56·3% of votes against the 37·8% of Petro Symonenko. Turn-out was 74%. There were five other candidates in the first round of voting.

CURRENT ADMINISTRATION
President: Leonid Kuchma; b. 1938 (sworn in 19 July 1994).

In March 2003 the government comprised:

Prime Minister: Viktor Yanukovich; b. 1950 (sworn in 21 Nov. 2002).

First Deputy Prime Minister and Minister of Finance: Mykola Azarov. *Deputy Prime Ministers:* Ivan Kyrylenko; Vitaliy Hayduk; Dmytro Tabachnyk.

Minister of Foreign Affairs: Anatoliy Zlenko. *Defence:* Volodymyr Shkidchenko. *Interior:* Yuri Smirnov. *Culture and Arts:* Yuriy Bogutskyy. *Economy:* Valeriy Khoroshkovskyy. *Justice:* Oleksandr Lavrynovych. *Fuel and Energy:* Serhiy Yermilov. *Education and Science:* Vasyl Kremen. *Agriculture:* Serhiy Ryzhuk. *Health:* Andriy Pidayev. *Labour and Social Policy:* Mykhaylo Papiyev. *Transport:* Hryhoriy Kirpa. *Emergency Situations:* Hryhoriy Reva. *Ecology and Natural Resources:* Vasyl Shevchuk. *Industrial Policy:* Anatoliy Myalytsa.

Government Website: http://www.kmu.gov.ua

DEFENCE
The 1996 Constitution bans the stationing of foreign troops on Ukrainian soil, but permits Russia to retain naval bases. Conscription is for 18 months. On 31 May 1997 the presidents of Ukraine and Russia signed a Treaty of Friendship and Co-operation which provided *inter alia* for the division of the former Soviet Black Sea Fleet and shore installations. There were around 1m. armed forces reserves in 1999.

Military expenditure in 2000 totalled US$1,081m. (US$21 per capita), representing 3·4% of GDP.

Army. In 1999 ground forces numbered about 154,900. There were three Operational Commands (North, South and West). Equipment included 4,014 main battle tanks (T-55, T-62, T-64, T-72 and T-80), including 933 in store, and 236 attack helicopters.

In addition there were 42,000 Ministry of Internal Affairs troops, a National Guard (26,600 strong) and 34,000 Border Guards.

Strategic Nuclear Forces. There were 44 ICBMs and 43 nuclear-bombers based in Ukraine in 1999. All nuclear forces based in Ukraine were due to be eliminated under START.

Navy. In 1999 the Ukrainian elements of the former Soviet Black Sea Fleet numbered 13,000, including 2,500 Naval Aviation and an estimated 3,000 naval infantry, with fleet units based at Sevastopol and Odesa. The operational forces include 1 submarine, 7 frigates and 1 cruiser (*Ukraina*).

The aviation forces of the former Soviet Black Sea Fleet under Ukrainian command include anti-submarine and maritime reconnaissance aircraft. The personnel of the Ukrainian Naval Aviation Force numbered (1999) about 2,500.

Air Force. Ukraine is limited to 1,090 combat aircraft and 330 armed helicopters under the Conventional Forces in Europe Agreement, and will have to dispose of some material.

Equipment includes 521 combat aircraft with a further 542 in store. Active aircraft type include MiG-23s, MiG-29s, Su-24s, Su-25s and Su-27s.

Personnel (including Air Defence), 1999, 100,000.

INTERNATIONAL RELATIONS

Ukraine is a member of the UN, CIS, the Council of Europe, OSCE, CEI, BSEC, Danube Commission, the NATO Partnership for Peace and IOM.

Ukraine has received over US$2bn. in US assistance, more than any other former Soviet republic.

ECONOMY

In 1998 services accounted for 51·2% of GDP, industry 34·4% and agriculture 14·4%.

Overview. Ukraine's economy experienced a revival in 2000 and 2001 after eight years of steep decline. This was partly as a result of home market driven growth including expansion of domestic demand, in particular increased household consumption and in-country investment, which was up by more than 20% in 2001, and partly thanks to the rise of export-oriented industries and the expansion of foreign, notably Russian, export markets for Ukrainian products.

Currency. The unit of currency is the *hryvnia* of 100 *kopiykas*, which replaced karbovanets on 2 Sept. 1996 at 100,000 karbovanets = 1 hryvnia. Inflation had been as a high as 4,735% in 1993 but declined to 12·0% in 2001, and in 2002 there was deflation of 0·6%. Foreign exchange reserves in June 2002 were US$3,105m.; gold reserves were 494,000 troy oz (negligible in 1992). 2000 saw the introduction of a floating exchange rate for the hryvnia. Total money supply in June 2002 was 32,530m. hryvnias.

Budget. 2000 budget (in 1m. hryvnias): revenue, 45,591·3; expenditure, 48,074·0.

Sources of revenue in 1997 included: VAT, 8,242·3; profits tax, 5,792·1. Expenditure included: welfare, 15,949·3; population social protection, 5,607·7; administration, 2,974·9; defence, 1,738·9.

Performance. Ukraine's economy has seen some progress in the last two years. Between 1994 and 1998 average annual real GDP growth was –10·0%, and it was still negative in 1999, at –0·2%. In 2000, however, the economy expanded by 5·9% and in 2001 real GDP growth was 9·1%. In 2001 total GDP was US$37·6bn.

Banking and Finance. A National Bank was founded in March 1991. It operates under government control, its Governor being appointed by the President with the approval of parliament. Its *Governor* is Sergiy Tihipko. There were 219 banks in all in 1996.

There is a stock exchange in Kyiv.

ENERGY AND NATURAL RESOURCES

Environment. According to the *World Bank Atlas* carbon dioxide emissions in 1998 were the equivalent of 7·0 tonnes per capita. An *Environmental Sustainability Index* compiled for the World Economic Forum meeting in Feb. 2002 ranked Ukraine 136th in the world out of the 142 countries analysed, with 35·0%. The index measured the ability of countries to maintain favourable environmental conditions and examined various factors including pollution levels and the use or abuse of natural resources.

Electricity. Installed capacity was 53·9m. kW in 1997. In 1998 production was 171bn. kWh; consumption per capita was 2,350 kWh. A Soviet programme to greatly expand nuclear power-generating capacity in the country was abandoned in the wake of the 1986 accident at Chernobyl. Chernobyl was closed down on 15

Dec. 2000. It is planned that two new reactors will be built to replace it. In 2001 there were 13 nuclear reactors in use, supplying 47% of output.

Oil and Gas. In 1997 output of crude oil and gas concentrate was 4·1m. tonnes; in 1999 production of natural gas was 16·8bn. cu. metres with 1,120bn. cu. metres of proven gas reserves.

Water. In 1997 water consumption totalled 15,623m. cu. metres.

Minerals. Ukraine's industrial economy, accounting for more than a quarter of total employment, is based largely on the republic's vast mineral resources. The Donetsk Basin contains huge reserves of coal, and the nearby iron-ore reserves of Kryvy Rih are equally rich. Among Ukraine's other mineral resources are manganese, bauxite, nickel, titanium and salt. Coal accounts for roughly 30% of the country's energy production. Coal production, 1997, 79·0m. tonnes; iron ore production, 1998, 51m. tonnes; manganese production, 1997, 3·2m. tonnes; salt production, 1997 estimate, 2·5m. tonnes.

Agriculture. Ukraine has extremely fertile black-earth soils in the central and southern portions, totalling nearly two-thirds of the territory. The original vegetation of the area formed three broad belts that crossed the territory of Ukraine latitudinally. Mixed forest vegetation occupied the northern third of the country, forest-steppe the middle portion and steppe the southern third of the country. Now, however, much of the original vegetation has been cleared and replaced by cultivated crops. In 1997 there were 33·1m. ha of arable land and 1·0m. ha of permanent crops.

Output (in 1,000 tonnes) in 2000: sugarbeets, 13,185; potatoes, 13,037; wheat, 10,159; barley, 6,873; maize, 3,840; sunflower seeds, 3,460; apples, 1,325; tomatoes, 1,320; pumpkins and squash, 1,100; cabbages, 1,070. Livestock, 2000: 10,627,000 cattle, 10,073,000 pigs, 10,060,000 sheep, 825,000 goats, 698,000 horses, 94m. chickens, 22m. ducks. Livestock products, 2000 (in 1,000 tonnes): meat, 1,720; milk, 12,562; eggs, 477.

Forestry. The area under forest in Ukraine in 1995 was 9·2m. ha. In 1999, 10·05m. cu. metres of timber were produced. In 1997 there were 24 national parks and reservations with a total area of 761,800 ha.

Fisheries. In 1999 the catch totalled 407,856 tonnes, of which 403,318 tonnes were from sea fishing. The total catch in 1988 had been 1,048,157 tonnes.

INDUSTRY

In 1997 there were 9,989 industrial enterprises. Output, 1997 (in tonnes unless otherwise stated): crude steel (1999), 27·5m.; rolled ferrous metals, 21m.; cement, 5·1m.; mineral fertilizer, 3·9m.; sugar (1998), 2·16m.; milk products, 661,000; processed meats, 558,000; paper and paperboard (1998), 261,000; butter, 117,000; synthetic fibre, 10,600; cigarettes, 54·5bn. units; fabrics, 82m. sq. metres; footwear, 10·4m. pairs; TV sets, 5·0m. units; refrigerators, 380,000 units; lathes, 2,300 units; cars, 2,000 units; tractors, 4,600 units.

Labour. At 1 Jan. 1997 the labour force totalled 28·4m. In 1997, 22·6m. were employed in business activity (37·9% in the state sector, 22·9% in the private sector and 39·2% in the collective sector). In April 2001 there were 1,149,200 unemployed and the registered level of unemployment was 4·2%.

Trade Unions. There are 13 trade unions grouped in a Federation of Ukrainian Trade Unions (*Chair*, Oleksandr Stoyan).

INTERNATIONAL TRADE

In 2000 total foreign debt was US$12,166m.

Imports and Exports. Trade in US$1m.:

	1996	1997	1998	1999	2000
Imports f.o.b.	19,843	19,623	16,283	12,945	14,943
Exports f.o.b.	15,547	15,418	13,699	13,189	15,722

In 1997 Ukraine traded with 189 different countries. 40·8% of exports went to CIS countries and 59·2% to the rest of the world. 60% of all imports came from CIS countries. In 1997 Russia accounted for 39·9% of all imports, followed by

Germany with 6·7%. 24·7% of exports in 1997 went to Russia, with China the second biggest export destination, at 7·0%.

Main exports, 1997 (% share of trade): ferrous metals and ferrous alloy products, 31·6%; chemical and associated products, 10·6%; machinery and equipment, 9·6%. Main imports: mineral fuel, oil and its processed products, 45·6%; machinery and equipment, 15·2%.

COMMUNICATIONS

Roads. In 1998 there were 176,310 km of roads. There were 4·87m. passenger cars in 1998 and 2·6m. motorcycles and mopeds. There were 36,299 road accidents in 1998 (5,522 fatalities).

Rail. Total length was 22,701·5 km in 1997, of which 8,711 km were electrified. Passenger-km travelled in 1998 came to 49·9bn. and freight tonne-km to 158·7bn. There are metros in Kyiv, Kharkiv and Dnipropetrovsk.

Civil Aviation. The main international airport is Kyiv (Boryspil), and there are international flights from seven other airports. The largest Ukrainian carrier is Air Ukraine, which in 1998 flew 13·0m. km and carried 313,100 passengers. Air Ukraine operates domestic services and had international flights in 1998 to Beijing, Bratislava, Bucharest, Budapest, Cairo, Damascus, Delhi, Dubai, Istanbul, Moscow, Murmansk, New York, Novosibirsk, Prague, Sharjah, Sofia, Tashkent, Tbilisi, Toronto, Tunis, Tyumen and Warsaw. Ukraine International Airlines also operated on some domestic routes, with international flights in 1998 to Amsterdam, Barcelona, Berlin, Brussels, Frankfurt, London, Omsk, Paris, Rome, Rostov, Vienna and Zürich.

In 2000 Kyiv handled 1,359,303 passengers (1,309,872 on international flights) and 12,015 tonnes of freight. Simferopol was the second busiest airport for passenger traffic in 1999, with 298,235 passengers (230,048 on international flights), and Odesa the second busiest for freight, with 3,839 tonnes.

Shipping. In 1997, 2m. passengers and 9m. tonnes of freight were carried by inland waterways. In 1995 there were 649 ocean-going vessels, totalling 5·83m. DWT. 38 vessels (5·09% of total tonnage) were registered under foreign flags. In 1998 GRT totalled 2,033,000, including oil tankers 62,000 GRT. The main seaports are Mariupol, Odesa, Kherson and Mykolaïv. Odesa is the leading port, and takes 30m. tonnes of cargo annually. In 1998 vessels totalling 4,843,000 NRT entered ports and vessels totalling 36,027,000 NRT cleared.

Telecommunications. In 1999 main telephone lines numbered 10,074,000 (198·9 per 1,000 persons), but in 1997 a total of 2·96m. people had been on the waiting list for a line. There were 150 fax machines in 1997, 115,500 mobile phone subscribers in 1998 and 890,000 PCs in use (17·6 per 1,000 persons) in 2000. In June 2001 there were 750,000 Internet users.

Postal Services. In 1995 there were 16,421 post offices. In 1997, 359m. letters, 17m. telegrams and 2m. packages were handled.

SOCIAL INSTITUTIONS

Justice. The death penalty was abolished in 1999. Over the period 1991–95, 642 death sentences were awarded and 442 carried out; there were 169 executions in 1996. In March 1997 death penalties were still being awarded but not carried out. 589,200 crimes were reported in 1997. A new civil code was voted into law in June 1997.

The population in penal institutions in Jan. 1998 was 211,568 (415 per 100,000 of national population).

Religion. The majority faith is the Orthodox Church, which is split into three factions. The largest is the Ukrainian Orthodox Church, Moscow Patriarchate (the former exarchate of the Russian Orthodox Church), headed by Volodymyr (Sabodan), Metropolitan of Kyiv and All Ukraine, which recognizes Aleksi II (Aleksey Mikhailovich Ridiger) as Patriarch of Moscow and All Russia and insists that all Ukrainian churches should be under Moscow's jurisdiction. The second largest is the Ukrainian Orthodox Church, Kyivan Patriarchate, headed by

Metropolitan Filaret, Patriarch of Kyiv and All Rus-Ukraine, which was created in June 1992. Metropolitan Filaret was excommunicated by the Ukrainian Orthodox Church, Moscow Patriarchate in Feb. 1997. The third faction is the Ukrainian Autocephalous Orthodox Church, headed by Metropolitan Mefodiy (Kudryakov) of Ternopil, which favours the unification of the three bodies. Only the Ukrainian Orthodox Church, Moscow Patriarchate is in communion with world Orthodoxy.

The hierarchy of the Roman Catholic Church (*Primate*, Cardinal Marian Jaworski, Archbishop Metropolitan of Lviv) was restored by the Pope's confirmation of ten bishops in Jan. 1991. The Ukrainian Greek Catholic Church (*Head*, Cardinal Lubomyr Husar, Major Archbishop, Metropolitan of Lviv and Galicia) is a Church of the Byzantine rite, which is in full communion with the Roman Church. Catholicism is strong in the western half of the country.

Education. In 1997 the number of pupils in 22,100 primary and secondary schools was 7m.; 280 further education establishments had 1,110,000 students, and 660 technical colleges, 526,400 students; 1,172,000 children were attending pre-school institutions.

In 1995–96 there were seven universities and an international university of science and technology.

Adult literacy rate in 1999 was 99·6% (male, 99·7%; female 99·5%).

In 1995 total expenditure on education came to 7·3% of GNP.

Health. Doctors and dentists numbered 227,000 in 1997 and junior medical personnel 566,000. There were 503,000 beds in 3,400 hospitals.

Welfare. There were 10·6m. old-age pensioners in 1997 and 3·7m. other pensioners.

CULTURE

Broadcasting. Broadcasting is administered by the government State Teleradio Company of Ukraine. The state-controlled Ukrainian Radio broadcasts three national and various regional programmes, a shared relay with Radio Moscow, and a foreign service (Ukrainian, English, German and Romanian). There were four independent stations in 1993 and 45m. radio receivers in 1997. The state-controlled Ukrainian Television broadcasts on two channels (colour by SECAM H). In 1997 there were 25m. television receivers.

Cinema. In 1997 there were 10,800 cinemas. Six full-length films were made in 1995 and gross box office receipts came to 567,688m. hryvnias.

Press. As at June 1996, 5,325 periodicals were registered, including 3,953 newspapers and 1,025 journals. In 1997, 1,270m. newspapers and magazines were sold. In 1995 a total of 6,225 book titles were published in 68·88m. copies.

Tourism. There were 6,208,000 foreign tourists in 1998 and total receipts came to US$5,407m. 631,000 Ukrainian citizens travelled to foreign countries in 1997.

Libraries. In 1997 there were 21,504 libraries with 355·7m. copies of books and magazines.

DIPLOMATIC REPRESENTATIVES
Of Ukraine in the United Kingdom (60 Holland Park, London, W11 3SJ)
Ambassador: Ihor Mitiukov.

Of the United Kingdom in Ukraine (01025 Kyiv, Desyatinna 9)
Ambassador: Robert Brinkley.

Of Ukraine in the USA (3350 M St., NW, Washington, D.C., 20007)
Ambassador: Kostyantyn Gryshchenko.

Of the USA in Ukraine (01901 Kyiv, Yurii Kotsiubynskyi 10)
Ambassador: Carlos Pascual.

Of Ukraine to the United Nations
Ambassador: Valeriy P. Kuchynsky.

Of Ukraine to the European Union
Ambassador: Roman Vasyliovych Shpek.

FURTHER READING
Encyclopedia of Ukraine, 5 vols. Toronto, 1984–93
D'Anieri, Paul, *Economic Interdependence in Ukrainian–Russian Relations*. State Univ. of New York Press, 2000
Koropeckyj, I. S., *The Ukrainian Economy: Achievements, Problems, Challenges*. Harvard Univ. Press, 1993
Kuzio, Taras, *Ukraine under Kuchma: Political Reform, Economic Transformation and Security Policy in Independent Ukraine*. London, 1997
Kuzio, Taras, Kravchuk, Robert and D'Anieri, Paul, *State and Institution Building in Ukraine*. St Martin's Press, New York, 2000
Kuzio, T. and Wilson, A., *Ukraine: Perestroika to Independence*. London, 1994
Lieven, Anatol, *Ukraine and Russia: A Fraternal Rivalry*. United States Institute of Peace Press, 2000
Magocsi, P. R., *A History of Ukraine*. Toronto Univ. Press, 1997
Motyl, A. J., *Dilemmas of Independence: Ukraine after Totalitarianism*. New York, 1993
Nahaylo, B., *Ukrainian Resurgence*. 2nd ed. Univ. of Toronto Press, 2000
Reid, A., *Borderland: A Journey Through the History of Ukraine*. Weidenfeld, London, 1997
Wilson, Andrew, *The Ukrainians: Unexpected Nation*. Yale University Press, 2000

National statistical office: State Committee of Statistics of Ukraine.
Website (Russian and Ukrainian only): http://www.ukrstat.gov.ua/

CRIMEA

The Crimea is a peninsula extending southwards into the Black Sea with an area of 26,100 sq. km. Population (1991 estimate), 2,549,800 (Ethnic groups, Sept. 1993: Russians, 61·6%; Ukrainians, 23·6%; Tatars, 9·6%). The capital is Simferopol.

It was occupied by Tatars in 1239, conquered by Ottoman Turks in 1475 and retaken by Russia in 1783. In 1921 after the Communist revolution it became an autonomous republic, but was transformed into a province (*oblast*) of the Russian Federation in 1945, after the deportation of the Tatar population in 1944 for alleged collaboration with the German invaders in the Second World War. 46% of the total Tatar population perished during the deportation. Crimea was transferred to Ukraine in 1954 and became an autonomous republic in 1991. About half the surviving Tatar population of 0·4m. had returned from exile by mid-1992.

At elections held in two rounds on 16 and 30 Jan. 1994 Yuri Meshkov was elected *President*. The post of president was abolished by Ukraine after calls for a referendum on Crimean independence.

Parliamentary elections were held on 31 March 2002. Turn-out was around 63%. The Serhii Kunitsyn Block obtained 39 seats, the Leonid Hrach Block 28, Crimean Tatars 5, the Russian Block 5, SDPUo 3 and ind. 20. Serhii Kunitsyn was subsequently appointed *Prime Minister* and Boris Deich *Chairman of Parliament*. The *Speaker* is Leonid Hrach.

On 2 Nov. 1995 parliament adopted a new constitution which defines the Crimea as 'an autonomous republic forming an integral part of Ukraine'. The status of 'autonomous republic' was confirmed by the 1996 Ukrainian Constitution, which provides for Crimea to have its own constitution as approved by its parliament. The Prime Minister is appointed by the Crimean parliament with the approval of the Ukrainian parliament.

The Tatar National Kurultay (Parliament) elects an executive board (*Mejlis*). The *Chairman* is Mustafa Jemilev. In 1993 the Kurultay decided to participate in Ukrainian elections.

UNITED ARAB EMIRATES

(UAE)
Imarat al-Arabiya al-Muttahida

Capital: Abu Dhabi
Population estimate, 2000: 2·61m.
GDP per capita, 2000: (PPP$) 17,935
HDI/world rank: 0·812/46

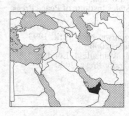

KEY HISTORICAL EVENTS

From Sha'am, 35 miles southwest of Ras Musam dam, for nearly 400 miles to Khor al Odeid at the southeastern end of the peninsula of Qatar, the coast, formerly known as the Trucial Coast, of the Gulf (together with 50 miles of the coast of the Gulf of Oman) belongs to the rulers of the 7 Trucial States. In 1820 these rulers signed a peace treaty with the British Government followed by further agreements under which the sheikhs undertook not to enter into any agreement with any power other than the British Government.

British forces withdrew from the Gulf at the end of 1971 and the treaties whereby the UK had been responsible for the defence and foreign relations were replaced by a treaty of friendship. The United Arab Emirates (formed 2 Dec. 1971) consists of the former Trucial States: Abu Dhabi, Dubai, Sharjah, Ajman, Umm al Qaiwain, Ras al-Khaimah (joined in Feb. 1972) and Fujairah. The small state of Kalba was merged with Sharjah in 1952.

TERRITORY AND POPULATION

The Emirates are bounded in the north by the Persian (Arabian) Gulf, northeast by Oman, east by the Gulf of Oman and Oman, south and west by Saudi Arabia, and northwest by Qatar. Their area is approximately 32,300 sq. miles (83,657 sq. km), excluding over 100 offshore islands. The total population at the 1995 census was 2,377,453 (797,710 females). About one-tenth are nomads. Population density, 28 per sq. km. In 1999, 85·5% of the population lived in urban areas. Approximately 88% of the population are foreigners, the highest percentage in any country in the world.

The UN gives a projected population for 2010 of 3·07m.

Populations of the seven Emirates, 1997 estimates (in 1,000): Abu Dhabi, 1,101; Ajman, 137; Dubai, 757; Fujairah, 83; Ras al-Khaimah, 152; Sharjah, 439; Umm al Qaiwain, 39.

The chief cities are Abu Dhabi, the federal capital (population of 904,000 in 1999), Dubai, Sharjah and Ras al-Khaimah. In addition to being the most populous Emirate, Abu Dhabi is also the wealthiest, ahead of Dubai.

The official language is Arabic; English is widely spoken.

SOCIAL STATISTICS

1997 births, 42,000; deaths, 7,000. 1997 birth rate (per 1,000 population), 18·4; death rate, 3·0; infant mortality rate (per 1,000 live births), 8 (1999). Life expectancy, 1999: 73·5 years for men and 77·8 years for women. Annual population growth rate, 1990–99, 2·5%; fertility rate, 1999, 3·3 births per woman.

CLIMATE

The country experiences desert conditions, with rainfall both limited and erratic. The period May to Sept. is generally rainless. Dubai, Jan. 74°F (23·4°C), July 108°F (42·3°C). Annual rainfall 2·4" (60 mm). Sharjah, Jan. 64°F (17·8°C), July 91°F (32°C). Annual rainfall 4·2" (105 mm).

CONSTITUTION AND GOVERNMENT

The Emirates is a federation, headed by a *Supreme Council of Rulers* which is composed of the seven rulers which elects from among its members a *President* and

Vice-President for five-year terms, and appoints a *Council of Ministers*. The Council of Ministers drafts legislation and a federal budget; its proposals are submitted to a *Federal National Council* of 40 elected members which may propose amendments but has no executive power. There is a *National Consultative Council* made up of citizens.

National Anthem. There are no words, tune by M. A. Wahab.

CURRENT ADMINISTRATION
President: HH Sheikh Zayed bin Sultan al-Nahyan, Ruler of Abu Dhabi.

Members of the Supreme Council of Rulers:

President: HH Sheikh Zayed bin Sultan al-Nahyan; b. 1918 (appointed 2 Dec. 1971).

Vice-President and Prime Minister: HH Sheikh Maktoum bin Rashid al-Maktoum, Ruler of Dubai.

HH Dr Sheikh Sultan bin Mohammed al-Qassimi, Ruler of Sharjah.

HH Sheikh Saqr bin Mohammed al-Qassimi, Ruler of Ras al-Khaimah.

HH Sheikh Hamad bin Mohammed al-Sharqi, Ruler of Fujairah.

HH Sheikh Humaid bin Rashid al-Nuaimi, Ruler of Ajman.

HH Sheikh Rashid bin Ahmed al-Mualla, Ruler of Umm al Qaiwain.

In March 2003 the cabinet comprised:

Prime Minister: HH Sheikh Maktoum bin Rashid al-Maktoum; b. 1946 (sworn in for second time 20 Nov. 1990, having held office from 1971–79).

Deputy Prime Minister: HH Sheikh Sultan bin Zayed al-Nahyan.

Minister of the Interior: Lieut.-Gen. Dr Mohammed Saeed al-Badi. *Finance and Industry:* HH Sheikh Hamdan bin Rashid al-Maktoum. *Defence:* Gen. Sheikh Mohammed bin Rashid al-Maktoum. *Economy and Commerce:* Sheikh Fahim bin Sultan al-Qassimi. *Information and Culture:* Sheikh Abdullah bin Zayed al-Nahyan. *Communications:* Ahmed Humaid al-Tayer. *Public Works and Housing:* Rakad bin Salem al-Rakad. *Education and Youth:* Abdul Aziz al-Sharhan. *Petroleum and Mineral Resources:* Obeid bin Saif al-Nassiri. *Electricity and Water:* Humaid bin Nasser al-Owais. *Labour and Social Affairs:* Mattar Humaid al-Tayer. *Planning:* HH Sheikh Humaid bin Ahmed al-Mualla. *Agriculture and Fisheries:* Saeed Mohammed al-Ragabani. *Justice, Islamic Affairs and Endowments:* Mohammed Mukhaira al-Dhahiri. *Foreign Affairs:* Rashid Abdullah al-Nuaimi. *Higher Education and Scientific Research:* Sheikh Nahyan bin Mubarak al-Nahyan. *Health:* Hamad Abdul Rahman al-Madfa.

Government Website: http://www.uae.gov.ae/

DEFENCE
In 2000 defence expenditure totalled US$3,338m. (US$1,368 per capita), representing 5·9% of GDP.

Army. The strength was (1999) 59,000.

Navy. The combined naval flotilla of the Emirates includes two frigates. Personnel in 1999 numbered 1,500. The main base is at Taweela (Sharjah), with minor bases in the other Emirates.

Air Force. Personnel (1999) 4,000, with 99 combat aircraft (including Mirage 2000s and *Hawks*), and 42 armed helicopters.

The USA maintains 390 Air Force personnel in the UAE.

INTERNATIONAL RELATIONS
The UAE is a member of the UN, WTO, OPEC, the Gulf Co-operation Council and the League of Arab States.

ECONOMY
In 1996 industry accounted for an estimated 52% of GDP, services 45% and agriculture 3%.

Currency. The unit of currency is the *dirham* (AED) of 100 *fils*. Gold reserves were 397,000 troy oz in May 2002 and foreign exchange reserves US$13,428m. Inflation was 0·9% in 2001. Total money supply in May 2002 was DH 44,564m.

In 2001 the six Gulf Arab states—the United Arab Emirates, along with Bahrain, Kuwait, Oman, Qatar and Saudi Arabia—signed an agreement to establish a single currency by 2010.

Budget. The fiscal year is the calendar year. Revenue and expenditure in 1m. dirhams:

	1996	1997	1998	1999[1]
Revenue	5,017	5,609	5,938	6,863
Expenditure	16,952	18,050	19,170	20,050

[1]Provisional.

Revenue is principally derived from oil-concession payments. Revenues in 1998 were DH 19,895m. and expenditure DH 21,393m. Expenditure included: interior and defence, DH 7,936m.; education and health, DH 3,158m.; development, DH 1,222m.; loans and equity, DH 582m.

Performance. In 1998 total GDP was US$47·2bn. In 2001 the GDP growth rate was 5·1%.

Banking and Finance. The UAE Central Bank was established in 1980 (*Governor*, Sultan bin Nasser Al-Suweidi). The largest banks are National Bank of Abu Dhabi, National Bank of Dubai, Emirates Bank International, MashreqBank and Abu Dhabi Commercial Bank. Foreign banks are restricted to 8 branches each.

ENERGY AND NATURAL RESOURCES

Environment. In 1998, according to the *World Bank Atlas,* carbon dioxide emissions were the equivalent of 32·4 tonnes per capita. An *Environmental Sustainability Index* compiled for the World Economic Forum meeting in Feb. 2002 ranked the United Arab Emirates 141st in the world out of 142 countries analysed, with 25·7%. Only Kuwait was ranked lower. The index measured the ability of countries to maintain favourable environmental conditions and examined various factors including pollution levels and the use or abuse of natural resources.

Electricity. Installed capacity was 5m. kW in 1997. Production in 1998 was 20·11bn. kWh, with consumption per capita 9,892 kWh.

Oil and Gas. Oil and gas provided about 33·4% of GDP in 1994. Oil production, 1998, 839·5m. bbls. (2·3m. bbls. per day). The UAE produced 3·5% of the world total oil output in 1996, and had reserves amounting to 97·8bn. bbls. in 2001. Oil production in Abu Dhabi is 85% of the UAE's total.

Abu Dhabi has reserves of natural gas, nationalized in 1976. There is a gas liquefaction plant on Das Island. Gas proven reserves (2000) were 6,000bn. cu. metres. Natural gas production, 1999, 38·0bn. cu. metres.

Water. Production of drinking water by desalination of sea water (1994) was 117,000m. gallons.

Minerals. Sulphur, gypsum, chromite and lime are mined.

Agriculture. The fertile Buraimi Oasis, known as Al Ain, is largely in Abu Dhabi territory. By 1994, 21,194 farms had been set up on land reclaimed from sand dunes. Owing to lack of water and good soil, there are few natural opportunities for agriculture, but there is a programme of fostering agriculture by desalination of water, dam-building and tree-planting; and strawberries, flowers and dates are now cultivated for export. The total area under cultivation in 1994 was 72,370 ha. In 1998 there were 40,000 ha of arable land and 41,000 ha of cropland. Output, 2000 (estimates, in 1,000 tonnes): tomatoes, 780; dates, 318; melons and watermelons, 78; cabbages, 58; pumpkins and squash, 31; aubergines, 28; lemons and limes, 18. Livestock products, 2000 (in 1,000 tonnes): meat, 89; milk, 45; eggs, 13.

Livestock (2000): goats, 1·2m.; sheep, 467,000; camels, 200,000; cattle, 110,000; chickens, 15m.

Forestry. The area under forests in 1995 was 60,000 ha, or 0·7% of the total land area.

Fisheries. In 1994 there were 4,000 fishing boats and (1992) 11,074 fishermen. Catch, 2000, 105,456 tonnes (exclusively marine fish).

UNITED ARAB EMIRATES

INDUSTRY

According to the Financial Times Survey (FT 500), the largest companies in the United Arab Emirates by market capitalization on 4 Jan. 2001 were Etisalat (market capitalization of US$6,164·2m.), National Bank of Dubai (market capitalization of US$1,689·3m.) and Emaar Properties (market capitalization of US$1,594·5m.).

In 1993 there were 904 industrial firms. Products include aluminium, cable, cement, chemicals, fertilizers (Abu Dhabi), rolled steel and plastics (Dubai, Sharjah), and tools and clothing (Dubai). The diamond business is becoming increasingly important in Dubai.

Labour. Males constituted 86% of the labour force in 1999 (the highest percentage of any country in the world). The labour force totalled 1,289,654 in 1995.

INTERNATIONAL TRADE

There are free trade zones at Jebel Ali (administered by Dubai), Sharjah and Fujairah. Foreign companies may set up wholly owned subsidiaries. In 1994 there were 650 companies in the Jebel Ali zone.

In 2001 the United Arab Emirates, along with Bahrain, Kuwait, Oman, Qatar and Saudi Arabia agreed to the complete implementation of a customs union by 2003.

Imports and Exports. Imports in 1997 totalled DH 109·1bn.; exports DH 139·5bn., of which crude petroleum 37·6% and natural gas 7·1%.

Main import suppliers, 1997: USA (9·6%), Japan (9·3%), UK (9·3%), Germany (6·5%) and South Korea (5·4%). Main export markets: Japan (36·3%), South Korea (8·7%), India (5·4%), Singapore (5·2%), Oman (3·8%).

COMMUNICATIONS

Roads. In 1998 there were 1,988 km of roads. In 1996 there were 535,150 motor vehicles (excluding bikes and mopeds).

Civil Aviation. There are international airports at Abu Dhabi, Al Ain, Dubai, Fujairah, Ras al-Khaimah and Sharjah. Dubai is the busiest airport, handling 11,117,000 passengers and 562,700 tonnes of freight in 2000. Abu Dhabi handled 2,894,000 passengers and Sharjah 196,200 tonnes of freight. Gulf Air is owned equally by Abu Dhabi, Bahrain, Oman and Qatar. For details see BAHRAIN: Civil Aviation. Dubai set up its own airline, Emirates, in 1985. It now operates internationally, and in 1997 carried 3,555,700 passengers (all on international flights).

Shipping. There are 15 commercial seaports, of which five major ports are on the Persian (Arabian) Gulf (Zayed in Abu Dhabi, Rashid and Jebel Ali in Dubai, Khalid in Sharjah, and Saqr in Ras al-Khaimah) and two on the Gulf of Oman: Fujairah and Khor Fakkan. Rashid and Fujairah are important container terminals. 45m. tonnes of cargo were handled in 1994. In 1998 the merchant marine totalled 933,000 GRT, including oil tankers 369,000 GRT.

Telecommunications. Main telephone lines numbered 1,020,100 in 2000 (391·4 per 1,000 persons) and there were 400,000 PCs in use (153·4 for every 1,000 persons). There were 832,300 mobile phone subscribers in 1999 and 50,000 fax machines in 1997. There were approximately 735,000 Internet users in Dec. 2000.

Postal Services. In 1995 there were 180 post offices.

SOCIAL INSTITUTIONS

Justice. The basic principles of the law are Islamic. Legislation seeks to promote the harmonious functioning of society's multi-national components while protecting the interests of the indigenous population. Each Emirate has its own penal code. A federal code takes precedence and ensures compatibility. There are federal courts with appellate powers, which function under federal laws. Emirates have the option to merge their courts with the federal judiciary.

The death penalty for drug smuggling was introduced in April 1995.

Religion. Nearly all the inhabitants are Muslim of the Sunni, and a small minority of the Shia, sects.

Education. In 1996 there were 19,290 pre-primary pupils with 1,128 teachers, 152,741 primary pupils with 10,123 teachers, and 121,736 secondary pupils with

1623

9,832 teachers. In 1995 there were 11,576 students at the Emirates University and 2,324 students in three higher colleges of technology. There are some 1,600 students at the four faculties of Zayed University and 1,000 at University City campus in Sharjah. The adult literacy rate in 1999 was 75·1% (73·8% among males and 78·0% among females).

Health. In 1996 there were 36 government hospitals with 4,344 beds. In 1994 there were 14 private hospitals, 128 government health centres, a herbal medicine centre, 752 private clinics, 4,095 doctors, 563 dentists and 8,506 nurses.

CULTURE

Broadcasting. There are several government authorities providing broadcasting nationally (Voice of the United Arab Emirates, Capital Radio, which is partly commercial, and United Arab Emirates Television Service), and regionally (UAE Radio and Television-Dubai, Ras al-Khaimah Broadcasting, Umm al Qaiwain Broadcasting and Sharjah TV). There were 310,000 TV sets (colour by PAL) and 820,000 radio receivers in 1997.

Press. In 1996 there were nine daily newspapers (five Arabic and four English) with a combined circulation of 0·3m.

Tourism. In 1999 there were 2,481,000 foreign tourists bringing in a total revenue of US$607m.

DIPLOMATIC REPRESENTATIVES
Of the UAE in the United Kingdom (30 Prince's Gate, London, SW7 1PT)
Ambassador: Easa Saleh Al Gurg, CBE.

Of the United Kingdom in the UAE (POB 248, Abu Dhabi)
Ambassador: Patrick M. Nixon, CMG, OBE.

Of the UAE in the USA (3522 International Court, NW, Washington, D.C., 20037)
Ambassador: Alasari Saeed Aldhahri.

Of the USA in the UAE (POB 4009, Abu Dhabi)
Ambassador: Marcelle M. Wahba.

Of the UAE to the United Nations
Ambassador: Abdulaziz Nasser Al-Shamsi.

Of the UAE to the European Union
Ambassador: Abdel Hadi Abdel Wahid Al-Khajah.

FURTHER READING
Clements, F. A., *United Arab Emirates.* [Bibliography] ABC-Clio, Oxford and Santa Barbara (CA), (rev. ed.) 1998
Vine, P. and Al Abed, I., *United Arab Emirates: A New Perspective.* Trident Press, Naples, Florida, 2001

UNITED KINGDOM OF GREAT BRITAIN AND NORTHERN IRELAND

Capital: London
Population estimate, 2000: 58·79m
GDP per capita, 2000: (PPP$) 23,509
HDI/world rank: 0·928/13

KEY HISTORICAL EVENTS

After the withdrawal of the Roman legions, 5th century Celtic Britain was invaded by Scandinavian and Teutonic tribes, collectively called the English. In the course of the next 150 years the English conquered the east and centre of the country, pinning down the Celtic Britons on the higher lands to the west. More than 200 years passed before the prevailing tribes recognized one king.

Then came the Danish invasion, their incomplete defeat by Alfred the Great, the consolidation of the kingdom under Alfred's successors and the Norman Conquest led by William, duke of Normandy, who was crowned king in 1066. When William died in 1087, he left Normandy to his eldest son Robert, thus separating it from England. The French dialect known as Anglo Norman was spoken by the ruling class in England for two centuries after the Conquest.

The Norman heritage was preserved also in the overlap between French and English feudal lords. Henry II, the founder of the Plantagenet dynasty, was feudatory lord of half of France. But most of the French possessions were lost by Henry's son John. Thereafter, the Norman baronage came to regard themselves as English.

The ambitions of Edward III began and those of Henry V renewed the Hundred Years War (1338–1453) with France, which ended with the loss of all the remaining French possessions except Calais.

The dynastic struggle between the rival houses of York and Lancaster culminated in the Tudor ascendancy over political and clerical factions. Henry VII was a unifying monarch preparing the way for Henry VIII who forced the Church to submit to lay rule. Tudor power reached its zenith with Elizabeth I when England, allied with other Protestant powers, humbled the Spanish Armada.

Elizabeth's death brought on a great struggle for supremacy between Crown and Parliament. There followed the Civil War, the execution of Charles I, the rule of Protector Cromwell by military dictatorship, and the restoration of the Stuart monarchy on terms which conceded financial authority and thus decision-making power to Parliament.

The attempt of James II to restore the royal prerogative led to the intervention of William of Orange. James fled the country and the crown was taken by William and his wife Mary as Queen. The accession of William involved England in a protracted war against France but before peace was achieved, the 1688 revolution was confirmed by the Hanoverian succession, and the history of England was merged with that of Great Britain by the union with Scotland in 1707.

The United Kingdom may be said to date from 1707 when the parliaments of England and Scotland were united but the name was not adopted until 1801 when the government of Ireland was incorporated into the United Kingdom of Great Britain and Ireland. With the accession of the Hanoverian George I (1714), the system of Parliamentary party government took hold. Relations between Parliament and Crown went through an unsettled period in the reign of George III, who took the blame for the loss of the American colonies. The War of Independence ended with Britain's recognition of American right to self-government in 1783. The humiliation was softened by economic development at home where the Industrial Revolution was in full swing. In 1793 revolutionary France declared war, and was not finally defeated until 1815. The demands of war stimulated the new, steam-powered industries. After 1815 there was frequent unrest as an increasingly urban and industrial society found its interests poorly represented by a parliament composed chiefly of landowners. The Reform Act of 1832 improved representation in Parliament, and further acts (1867, 1884, 1918 and 1928) led gradually to universal adult suffrage. The accession of Victoria in 1837 was the beginning of an era of unprecedented material progress. Early industrial development produced great national wealth but its distribution was uneven and the condition of the poor improved slowly. Whereas early Victorian reforms were responses to obvious distress, governments after 1868 were more inclined towards preventive state action.

Abroad, there was war with Russia in the Crimea (1854–56); most wars, however, were fought to conquer or pacify colonies. The 19th-century empire included India, Canada, Australasia, and vast territories in Africa and Eastern Asia. After 1870 the Suez Canal enabled Britain to control the empire more efficiently; she became a 40% shareholder in 1875 and the controlling power in Egypt in 1882.

The most serious imperial wars were the Boer Wars of 1881 and 1899–1902. Britain negotiated a Union of South Africa, by which South Africa enjoyed the same autonomy agreed for Canada (1867), Australia (1901) and later New Zealand (1907). The 'dominion status' of these countries was clarified by the Statute of Westminster (1931).

On 3 Aug. 1914 Germany invaded Belgium. Britain was obliged by treaty to retaliate by declaring war. At this time, a rebellion was staged in Ireland, born of the failure of successive attempts to agree a formula for Irish Home Rule. The issue was complicated by factional disagreement in southern Ireland and the wish of northern Ireland to remain in the United Kingdom. In 1920 after four years' conflict the Government of Ireland Act partitioned the country. The northern six counties remained British, a parliament was created and a Unionist government took office. The southern 26 counties moved by stages to complete independence as the Republic of Ireland.

Germany revived as a military power in the 1930s, and invaded Poland on 1 Sept. 1939. Britain, bound once more by treaty, declared war. The Second World War ended with German and Japanese defeat in 1945. It was a time of great social upheaval. In the 1945 election a Labour government was returned with a large majority, and a socialist programme which emphasized wealth distribution above wealth creation was implemented. Subsequent governments modified but generally accepted the changes. After 1979, however, Conservative governments reversed much of this legislation before Labour regained power in 1997 on a free-market manifesto which promised better economic management and job creation.

Beginning with the independence and partition of India and Pakistan in 1947, there was rapid progress to independence for all the colonies. The new concept was of a Commonwealth of freely associated states, recognizing the British monarch as symbolic Commonwealth head (some states chose to retain the monarch as head of state).

The Second World War all but bankrupted Britain, but the option of joining other European countries in moves towards unity was resisted in favour of a 'special relationship' with the USA. It was not until 1961 that economic reality persuaded Britain of the need to join the European Economic Community. The application was rebuffed by France but a second application was successful in 1973. Membership of the Community was endorsed by referendum in 1975.

TERRITORY AND POPULATION
Area (in sq. km) and population at the census taken on 29 April 2001:

Divisions	Area	Population
England	130,281	49,138,831
Wales	20,732	2,903,085
Scotland	77,925	5,062,011
Northern Ireland	14,135	1,685,267
	243,073	58,789,194

Population of the United Kingdom (present on census night) at the four previous decennial censuses:

Divisions	1961	1971	1981	1991
England[1]	43,460,525	46,018,371	46,226,100[2]	46,382,050
Wales	2,644,023	2,731,204	2,790,500[2]	2,811,865
Scotland	5,179,344	5,228,963	5,130,700	4,998,567
Northern Ireland	1,425,042	1,536,065	1,532,196[3]	1,577,836
United Kingdom	52,708,934	55,514,603	55,679,496[2]	55,770,318

[1]Areas now included in Wales formed the English county of Monmouthshire until 1974.
[2]The final counts for England and Wales are believed to be over-stated as a result of an error in processing. The preliminary counts presented here rounded to the nearest hundred are thought to be more accurate.
[3]There was a high level of non-enumeration in Northern Ireland during the 1981 census mainly as a result of protests in Catholic areas about the Republican hunger strikes.

UK population estimate, mid-2002, 59,001,000 (30,301,000 females and 28,699,000 males); density, 243 per sq. km. In 1999, 89·4% of the population lived in urban areas.

The projected population for 2010 is 60·35m.

Population of the United Kingdom by sex at census day 2001:

Divisions	Males	Females
England	23,923,390	25,215,441
Wales	1,403,900	1,499,185
Scotland	2,432,494	2,629,517
Northern Ireland	821,449	863,818
United Kingdom	28,581,233	30,207,961

Households in the United Kingdom at the 2001 census: England, 21,262,000; Wales, 1,276,000; Scotland, 2,192,000; Northern Ireland, 627,000.

The age distribution in the United Kingdom at census day in 2001 was as follows (in 1,000):

Age-group	England and Wales	Scotland	Northern Ireland	United Kingdom
Under 5	3,094	277	115	3,486
5 and under 10	3,308	307	123	3,738
10 ,, 15	3,425	323	133	3,881
15 ,, 20	3,217	317	129	3,663
20 ,, 25	3,122	314	109	3,545
25 ,, 35	7,419	699	242	8,360
35 ,, 45	7,749	781	247	8,777
45 ,, 55	6,887	689	199	7,775
55 ,, 65	5,507	550	162	6,219
65 ,, 70	2,292	239	65	2,596
70 ,, 75	2,074	207	58	2,339
75 ,, 85	2,933	271	77	3,281
85 and upwards	1,012	88	23	1,123

In 2001, 18·85% of the population of the UK were under the age of 14, 60·35% between 15 and 59, 13·29% between 60 and 74, and 7·51% aged 75 and over. In 1951 only 3·54% of the population had been 75 and over.

London: Located in the southeast of England on the River Thames, London is the third largest city in Europe, after Paris and Moscow, and is a major banking, insurance and commodities centre. With origins dating back to Roman times, London has a rich historical and cultural fabric, which serves to attract swathes of tourists despite a crumbling transport infrastructure.

England and Wales. The census population (present on census night) of England and Wales 1801 to 2001:

Date of enumeration	Population	Pop. per sq. mile[1]	Date of enumeration	Population	Pop. per sq. mile[1]
1801	8,892,536	152	1881	25,974,439	445
1811	10,164,256	174	1891	29,002,525	497
1821	12,000,236	206	1901	32,527,843	558
1831	13,896,797	238	1911	36,070,492	618
1841	15,914,148	273	1921	37,886,699	649
1851	17,927,609	307	1931	39,952,377	685
1861	20,066,224	344	1951	43,757,888	750
1871	22,712,266	389	1961	46,104,548	791

Date of enumeration	Population	Pop. per sq. mile	Date of enumeration	Population	Pop. per sq. mile[1]
1971	48,749,575	323	1991	49,193,915	330
1981	49,016,600	325	2001	52,041,916	345

[1]Per sq. km from 1971.

Estimated population of England and Wales, mid-2002, 52,251,000 (26,808,000 females and 25,444,000 males).

The birthplaces of the population of Great Britain at census day 2001 were: England, 43,967,372; Wales, 2,815,088; Scotland, 5,229,366; Northern Ireland, 256,503; Ireland, 494,154; other European Union countries, 763,171; elsewhere, 3,578,273.

Ethnic Groups. The 1991 census was the first to include a question on ethnic status.

Percentage figures from the 2001 census relating to ethnicity in England and Wales:

	England and Wales (%)	England (%)	Wales (%)
White			
British	87·5	87·0	96·0
Irish	1·2	1·3	0·6
Other	2·6	2·7	1·3
Mixed			
White and Black Caribbean	0·5	0·5	0·2
White and Black African	0·2	0·2	0·1
White and Asian	0·4	0·4	0·2
Other Mixed	0·3	0·3	0·1
Asian or Asian British			
Indian	2·0	2·1	0·3
Pakistani	1·4	1·4	0·3
Bangladeshi	0·5	0·6	0·2
Other Asian	0·5	0·5	0·1
Black or Black British			
Caribbean	1·1	1·1	0·1
African	0·9	1·0	0·1
Other Black	0·2	0·2	0·0
Chinese	0·4	0·4	0·2
Other ethnic groups	0·4	0·4	0·2

In Scotland about 2% of the population in 2001 were from a minority (non-White) ethnic group, compared with 1·3% in 1991. Pakistanis formed the largest such group, constituting 0·3%.

11 'Standard Regions' (also classified as 'level 1 regions' for EU purposes) are identified in the UK as economic planning regions. They have no administrative significance. They are: Northern Ireland, Scotland, Wales, and eight regions of England (East Anglia, East Midlands, North, North West, South East, South West, West Midlands, Yorkshire and Humberside).

The following table shows the distribution of the urban and rural population of England and Wales (persons present) in 1951, 1961, 1971, and 1981:

	England and Wales	Population Urban districts[1]	Rural districts[1]	Percentage Urban	Rural
1951	43,757,888	35,335,721	8,422,167	80·8	19·2
1961	46,071,604	36,838,442	9,233,162	80·0	20·0
1971	48,755,000	38,151,000	10,598,000	78·2	21·5
1981	49,011,417	37,686,863	11,324,554	76·9	23·1

[1]As existing at each census.

Urban and rural areas were re-defined for the 1981 and 1991 censuses on a land use basis. In Scotland 'localities' correspond to urban areas. The 1981 census gave the usually resident population of England and Wales as 48,521,596, of which 43,599,431 were in urban areas; and of Scotland as 5,035,315, of which 4,486,140 were in localities.

British Citizenship. Under the British Nationality Act 1981 there are three main forms of citizenship: citizenship for persons closely connected with the UK; British Dependent Territories citizenship; British Overseas citizenship. British citizenship is acquired automatically at birth by a child born in the UK if his or her mother or father is a British citizen or is settled in the UK. A child born abroad to a British citizen is a British citizen by descent. British citizenship may be acquired by registration for stateless persons, and for children not automatically acquiring such citizenship or born abroad to parents who are citizens by descent; and, for other adults, by naturalization. Requirements for the latter include five years' residence (three years for applicants married to a British citizen). The Hong Kong (British Nationality) Order 1986 created the status of British National (Overseas) for citizens connected with Hong Kong before 1997, and the British Nationality (Hong Kong) Act 1990 made provision for up to 50,000 selected persons to register as British citizens.

Emigration and Immigration. Immigration is mainly governed by the Immigration Act 1970 and Immigration Rules made under it. British and Commonwealth citizens with the right of abode before 1983 are not subject to immigration control, nor are citizens of European Economic Area countries. Other persons seeking to work or settle in the UK must obtain a visa or entry clearance.

Migration statistics are derived from the government's International Passenger Survey, and exclude the Republic of Ireland.

Immigrants (in 1,000) by sex and occupation:

	Total	Females	Professional	Manual/ Clerical	Non-Employed
1997	285	142	93	44	147
1998	332	165	117	74	142
1999	354	173	131	77	146
2000	364	173	163	64	137

Emigrants (in 1,000) by sex and occupation:

1997	225	103	86	48	91
1998	199	99	79	41	79
1999	245	114	97	70	79
2000	278	124	128	59	90

In 2001 there were 106,820 acceptances for settlement in the UK (125,090 in 2000), including from: Asia, 43,340; Africa, 31,430; Europe, 13,795. Main individual countries were: Pakistan, 11,535; Somalia, 8,290; India, 7,280; Nigeria, 5,040; South Africa, 4,755; USA, 4,385; Bangladesh, 4,050; Sri Lanka, 4,040; Turkey, 3,240; Australia, 3,205.

Asylum. In 2001 there were 71,365 applications for asylum (80,315 applications in 2000 but 29,650 in 1996 and 2,905 in 1984). The main countries of origin were Afghanistan, Iraq, Somalia and Sri Lanka. The 2001 figure was the second highest in Europe, after Germany. Applications, excluding dependants, rose in 2002 to 85,865. While respecting its obligations to political refugees under the UN Convention and Protocol relating to the status of Refugees, the government has powers under the Asylum and Immigration Act 1996 to weed out applicants seeking entry for non-political reasons and to designate certain countries as not giving risk of persecution. 24% of applicants were accepted in 1998 (6% in 1995).

Coleman, D. and Salt, J., *The British Population: Patterns, Trends and Processes.* OUP, 1992

See also ENGLAND, SCOTLAND, WALES *and* NORTHERN IRELAND: Territory and Popoulation.

SOCIAL STATISTICS
UK statistics, 2001: births, 669,000 (268,000 outside marriage); deaths, 602,268; marriages (2000), 305,912; divorces, 156,814. Great Britain statistics, 2001: births, 647,000; deaths, 587,755; marriages (2000), 298,328; divorces, 154,449; abortions, 188,416. The number of births in 2001 was the lowest since 1977. In 1976, uniquely in British history, deaths in the UK (680,800) exceeded births (675,500). In 1999 lung disease, including pneumonia, lung cancer, tuberculosis and asthma, caused 153,000 deaths, making it the biggest killer, ahead of coronary heart disease, at 132,000, and cancers excluding those linked to the respiratory system, at 119,000. UK life expectancy, 1998–2000: males, 75·1 years; females, 80·0. A World Health Organization report published in June 2000 put Britons in 14th place in a 'healthy life expectancy' list, with an expected 71·7 years of healthy life for babies born in 1999. Annual population growth rate, 1999–2000, 0·2%. In 2000 the suicide rate

was 10 per 100,000 population. The average rate in the European Union as a whole in 1998 was 12 per 100,000. Infant mortality, 2001, 5·5 per 1,000 live births. Fertility rate, 1999, 1·7 births per woman. Of the 669,000 live births in the UK in 2001, 40·1% were to unmarried women, up from 6% in 1961 and 23% in 1987. In 1998 the average age of a woman giving birth was 28·9 years, the highest average age since records began in 1964. In 1999 for the first time there were more births to women in the 30–34 age group than in the 25–29 bracket. UK birth rate (per 1,000 population), 2001, 11·4; death rate, 2001, 10·2. The average age of first marriage in 1997 was 27·5 years for brides and 29·6 years for bridegrooms, compared to 24·3 years and 26·4 years respectively in 1987. 40% of marriages in 1999 were religious and 60% civil, compared to 52% religious and 48% civil in 1981.

In 2001, 15·9% of the total population was over 65, up from 11·7% in 1960. As the ageing population continues to grow, it has been estimated that by 2010 there will be 350,000 more people over the age of 80 than there were at the end of the 20th century. The first decade of the new century is also expected to see a rise of 1·4m., or 23%, in the number of people between 55 and 64. By 2000 the number of centenarians had surpassed 8,000.

In 2000 the average household in Great Britain consisted of 2·4 people, down from 3·1 in 1961. The proportion of single-parent families was 25% in 1998, up from 21% in 1996.

England and Wales statistics (in 1,000), 2001 (and 2000): births, 595 (604); deaths, 530 (536). 2000 (1999) marriages (in 1,000), 268 (264); divorces, 144 (141). The 2001 births total of 595,000 was the lowest since 1977.

Britain has one of the highest rates of drug usage in Europe. Figures released in Nov. 1999 showed that approaching 40% of schoolchildren aged 15 and 16 have tried cannabis, and 9% of adults did so in the previous 12 months. Use of ecstasy, amphetamines and LSD in England and Wales was the highest in the European Union. Drug-related deaths increased by 70% between 1992 and 1999.

A UNICEF report published in 2000 showed that 19·8% of children in Great Britain live in poverty (in households with income below 50% of the national median), compared to just 2·6% in Sweden. The report also showed that the poverty rate of children in lone-parent families was 45·6%, compared to 13·3% in two-parent families.

See also NORTHERN IRELAND: Social Statistics.

CLIMATE

The climate is cool temperate oceanic, with mild conditions and rainfall evenly distributed over the year, though the weather is very changeable because of cyclonic influences. In general, temperatures are higher in the west and lower in the east in winter and rather the reverse in summer. Rainfall amounts are greatest in the west, where most of the high ground occurs.

London, Jan. 39°F (3·9°C), July 64°F (17·8°C). Annual rainfall 25" (635 mm).
Aberdeen, Jan. 38°F (3·3°C), July 57°F (13·9°C). Annual rainfall 32" (813 mm).
Belfast, Jan. 40°F (4·5°C), July 59°F (15·0°C). Annual rainfall 37·4" (950 mm).
Birmingham, Jan. 38°F (3·3°C), July 61°F (16·1°C). Annual rainfall 30" (749 mm).
Cardiff, Jan. 40°F (4·4°C), July 61°F (16·1°C). Annual rainfall 42·6" (1,065 mm).
Edinburgh, Jan. 38°F (3·3°C), July 58°F (14·5°C). Annual rainfall 27" (686 mm).
Glasgow, Jan. 39°F (3·9°C), July 59°F (15·0°C). Annual rainfall 38" (965 mm).
Manchester, Jan. 39°F (3·9°C), July 61°F (16·1°C). Annual rainfall 34·5" (876 mm).

CONSTITUTION AND GOVERNMENT

The reigning Queen, Head of the Commonwealth, is **Elizabeth II** Alexandra Mary, b. 21 April 1926, daughter of King George VI and Queen Elizabeth; married on 20 Nov. 1947 Lieut. Philip Mountbatten (formerly Prince Philip of Greece), created Duke of Edinburgh, Earl of Merioneth and Baron Greenwich on the same day and created Prince Philip, Duke of Edinburgh, 22 Feb. 1957; succeeded to the crown on the death of her father, on 6 Feb. 1952.

Offspring. Prince Charles Philip Arthur George, Prince of Wales (Heir Apparent), b. 14 Nov. 1948; married Lady Diana Frances Spencer on 29 July 1981; after divorce, 28 Aug. 1996, Diana, Princess of Wales. She died in Paris in a road accident on 31 Aug. 1997. *Offspring:* William Arthur Philip Louis, b. 21 June 1982; Henry Charles

Albert David, b. 15 Sept. 1984. Princess Anne Elizabeth Alice Louise, the Princess Royal, b. 15 Aug. 1950; married Mark Anthony Peter Phillips on 14 Nov. 1973; divorced, 1992; married Cdr Timothy Laurence on 12 Dec. 1992. *Offspring of first marriage:* Peter Mark Andrew, b. 15 Nov. 1977; Zara Anne Elizabeth, b. 15 May 1981. Prince Andrew Albert Christian Edward, created Duke of York, 23 July 1986, b. 19 Feb. 1960; married Sarah Margaret Ferguson on 23 July 1986; after divorce, 30 May 1996, Sarah, Duchess of York. *Offspring:* Princess Beatrice Mary, b. 8 Aug. 1988; Princess Eugenie Victoria Helena, b. 23 March 1990. Prince Edward Antony Richard Louis, created Earl of Wessex and Viscount Severn, 19 June 1999, b. 10 March 1964; married Sophie Rhys-Jones, Countess of Wessex, on 19 June 1999.

Widow of the Uncle of the Queen. Princess Alice Christabel, Duchess of Gloucester, b. 25 Dec. 1901, married the late Duke of Gloucester 6 Nov. 1935.

Sister of the Queen. Princess Margaret Rose, Countess of Snowdon, b. 12 Aug. 1930; married Antony Armstrong-Jones (created Earl of Snowdon, 3 Oct. 1961) on 6 May 1960; divorced, 1978; died 9 Feb. 2002. *Offspring:* David Albert Charles (Viscount Linley), b. 3 Nov. 1961, married Serena Alleyne Stanhope on 8 Oct. 1993. *Offspring:* Charles Patrick Inigo Armstrong Jones, b. 1 July 1999. Lady Sarah Frances Elizabeth Chatto, b. 1 May 1964; married Daniel Chatto on 14 July 1994. *Offspring:* Samuel David Benedict Chatto, b. 28 July 1996; Arthur Robert Nathaniel Chatto, b. 5 Feb. 1999.

Cousins of the Queen. Richard Alexander Walter George, Duke of Gloucester, b. 26 Aug. 1944; married Birgitte van Deurs on 8 July 1972 (*offspring:* Alexander Patrick Gregers Richard, Earl of Ulster, b. 24 Oct. 1974; Lady Davina Elizabeth Alice Benedikte Windsor, b. 19 Nov. 1977; Lady Rose Victoria Birgitte Louise Windsor, b. 1 March 1980). Edward George Nicholas Paul Patrick, Duke of Kent, b. 9 Oct. 1935; married Katharine Worsley on 8 June 1961 (*offspring:* George Philip Nicholas, Earl of St Andrews, b. 26 June 1962; married Sylvania Tomaselli on 9 Jan. 1988 (*offspring:* Edward Edmund Maximilian George, Baron Downpatrick, b. 2 Dec. 1988; Lady Marina Charlotte Alexandra Katharine Windsor, b. 30 Sept. 1992; Lady Amelia Sophia Theodora Mary Margaret Windsor, b. 24 Aug. 1995); Lady Helen Marina Lucy Windsor, b. 28 April 1964; married 18 July 1992 Timothy Verner Taylor (*offspring:* Columbus George Donald Taylor, b. 6 Aug. 1994; Cassius Edward Taylor, b. 26 Dec. 1996; Eloise Taylor, b. 2 March 2003); Lord Nicholas Charles Edward Jonathan Windsor, b. 25 July 1970). Princess Alexandra Helen Elizabeth Olga Christabel, the Hon. Lady Ogilvy, b. 25 Dec. 1936; married 24 April 1963 Sir Angus Ogilvy (*offspring:* James Robert Bruce, b. 29 Feb. 1964; married 30 July 1988, Julia Rawlinson; Lady Marina Victoria Alexandra, Mrs Mowatt, b. 31 July 1966, married 2 Feb. 1990 Paul Mowatt (*offspring:* Zenouska May Mowatt, b. 26 May 1990; Christian Alexander Mowatt, b. 4 June 1993); separated, 11 April 1996. Prince Michael George Charles Franklin, b. 4 July 1942; married Baroness Marie-Christine von Reibnitz on 30 June 1978 (*offspring:* Lord Frederick Michael George David Louis Windsor, b. 6 April 1979; Lady Gabriella Marina Alexandra Ophelia Windsor, b. 23 April 1981).

The Queen's legal title rests on the statute of 12 and 13 Will. III, ch. 3, by which the succession to the Crown of Great Britain and Ireland was settled on the Princess Sophia of Hanover and the 'heirs of her body being Protestants'. By proclamation of 17 July 1917 the royal family became known as the House and Family of Windsor. On 8 Feb. 1960 the Queen issued a declaration varying her confirmatory declaration of 9 April 1952 to the effect that while the Queen and her children should continue to be known as the House of Windsor, her descendants, other than descendants entitled to the style of Royal Highness and the title of Prince or Princess, and female descendants who marry and their descendants should bear the name of Mountbatten-Windsor.

Lineage to the throne. 1) Prince of Wales. 2) Prince William of Wales. 3) Prince Henry of Wales. 4) Duke of York. 5) Princess Beatrice of York. 6) Princess Eugenie of York.

By letters patent of 30 Nov. 1917 the titles of Royal Highness and Prince or Princess are restricted to the Sovereign's children, the children of the Sovereign's sons and the eldest living son of the eldest son of the Prince of Wales.

Provision is made for the support of the royal household, after the surrender of hereditary revenues, by the settlement of the Civil List soon after the beginning of each reign. The Civil List Act of 1 Jan. 1972 provided for a decennial, and the Civil List (Increase of Financial Provision) Order 1975 for an annual review of the List, but in July 1990 it was again fixed for one decade.

The Civil List of 2001–2010 provides for an annuity of £7,900,000 to the Queen; and £359,000 to Prince Philip. These amounts are the same as for the period 1991–2000. The income of the Prince of Wales derives from the Duchy of Cornwall. The Civil List was exempted from taxation in 1910. The Queen has paid income tax on her private income since April 1993.

The supreme legislative power is vested in Parliament, which consists of the Crown, the House of Lords and the House of Commons, and dates in its present form from the middle of the 14th century. A Bill which is passed by both Houses and receives Royal Assent becomes an Act of Parliament and part of statute law.

Parliament is summoned, and a General Election is called, by the sovereign on the advice of the Prime Minister. A Parliament may last up to five years, normally divided into annual sessions. A session is ended by prorogation, and most Public Bills which have not been passed by both Houses then lapse, unless they are subject to a carry over motion. A Parliament ends by dissolution, either by will of the sovereign or by lapse of the five-year period.

Under the Parliament Acts 1911 and 1949, all Money Bills (so certified by the Speaker of the House of Commons), if not passed by the Lords without amendment, may become law without their concurrence within one month of introduction in the Lords. Public Bills, other than Money Bills or a Bill extending the maximum duration of Parliament, if passed by the Commons in two successive sessions and rejected each time by the Lords, may become law without being passed by the Lords provided that one year has elapsed between Commons second reading in the first session and third reading in the second session, and that the Bill reaches the Lords at least one month before the end of the second session. The Parliament Acts have been used three times since 1949: in 1991 for the War Crimes Act, in 1999 for the European Parliamentary Elections Act and for the Sexual Offences (Amendment) Act in 2000.

Peerages are created by the sovereign, on the advice of the prime minister, with no limits on their number. The following are the main categories of membership: 1) *Lords Spiritual*, comprising two archbishops and the 24 most senior diocesan bishops of the Church of England. They cease to be members when they retire; 2) *Lords Temporal*, comprising *Life Peers*, *Hereditary Peers* and *Lords of Appeal*. Life peers are appointed under the Life Peerages Act 1958 (547 as at 3 Feb. 2003). Most hereditary peers left the House under the terms of the House of Lords Act 1999 on 11 Nov. 1999, except for 92. These consist of 75 elected by their party or Crossbench group, 15 Office holders elected by the whole House and two peers who sit by virtue of holding Royal Office (the Earl Marshal, the Duke of Norfolk; and the Lord Great Chamberlain, the Marquess of Cholmondeley). Lords of Appeal (Law Lords, both active and retired) were granted peerages of life under the Appellate Jurisdiction Act 1876, in order to enable them to hear appeal cases in the House of Lords. As at 3 Feb. 2003 there were 690 members, of whom 113 were women. The average attendance at each sitting of the House for end of session 2001–02 was 370.

The House of Commons consists of members (of both sexes) representing constituencies determined by the Boundary Commissions. Persons under 21 years of age, Clergy of the Church of England and of the Scottish Episcopal Church, Ministers of the Church of Scotland, Roman Catholic clergymen, civil servants, members of the regular armed forces, policemen, most judicial officers and other office-holders named in the House of Commons (Disqualification) Act are disqualified from sitting in the House of Commons. No peer eligible to sit in the House of Lords can be elected to the House of Commons unless he has disclaimed his title, but Irish peers and holders of courtesy titles, who are not members of the House of Lords, are eligible.

The Representation of the People Act 1948 abolished the business premises and University franchises, and the only persons entitled to vote at Parliamentary elections are those registered as residents or as service voters. No person may vote in more than one constituency at a general election. Persons may apply on certain grounds to vote by post or by proxy. Elections are held on the first-past-the-post system, in which the candidate who receives the most votes is elected.

All persons over 18 years old and not subject to any legal incapacity to vote and who are either British subjects or citizens of Ireland are entitled to be included in the register of electors for the constituency containing the address at which they were residing on the qualifying date for the register, and are entitled to vote at elections held during the period for which the register remains in force.

Members of the armed forces, Crown servants employed abroad, and the wives accompanying their husbands, are entitled, if otherwise qualified, to be registered as 'service voters' provided they make a 'service declaration'. To be effective for a particular register, the declaration must be made on or before the qualifying date for that register. In certain circumstances, British subjects living abroad may also vote.

The Parliamentary Constituencies Act 1986, as amended by the Boundary Commissions Act 1992, provided for the setting up of Boundary Commissions for England, Wales, Scotland and Northern Ireland. The Commissions' last reports were made in 1995, and thereafter reports are due at intervals of not less than eight and not more than 12 years; and may be submitted from time to time with respect to the area comprised in any particular constituency or constituencies where some change appears necessary. Any changes giving effect to reports of the Commissions are to be made by Orders in Council laid before Parliament for approval by resolution of each House. The Parliamentary electorate of the United Kingdom and Northern Ireland in the register in 2001–02 numbered 44,403,238, of whom 36,991,780 were in England, 2,236,143 in Wales, 3,984,306 in Scotland and 1,191,009 in Northern Ireland. In 1991 it was officially estimated that 7·1% of eligible voters failed to register on the electoral roll.

At the UK general election held in June 2001, 659 members were returned, 529 from England, 72 from Scotland, 40 from Wales and 18 from Northern Ireland. Every constituency returns a single member.

One of the main aspects of the Labour government's programme of constitutional reform is Scottish and Welsh devolution. In the referendum on Scottish devolution on 11 Sept. 1997, 1,775,045 votes (74·3%) were cast in favour of a Scottish parliament and 614,400 against (25·7%). The turn-out was 60·4%, so around 44·8% of the total electorate voted in favour. For the second question, on the Parliament's tax-raising powers, 1,512,889 votes were cast in favour (63·5%) and 870,263 against (36·5%). This represented 38·4% of the total electorate.

On 18 Sept. 1997 in Wales there were 559,419 votes cast in favour of a Welsh assembly (50·3%) and 552,698 against (49·7%). The turn-out was 51·3%.

In Aug. 1911 provision was first made for the payment of a salary of £400 per annum to members of the Commons, other than those already in receipt of salaries as officers of the House, as Ministers or as officers of Her Majesty's household. For current salaries *see below*. Members of the House of Lords are unsalaried but may recover expenses incurred in attending sittings of the House within maxima for each day's attendance of £61·00 for day subsistence, £122·00 for night subsistence and £51·00 for secretarial and research assistance and office expenses. Additionally, Members of the House who are disabled may recover the extra cost of attending the House incurred by reason of their disablement. In connection with attendance at the House and parliamentary duties within the UK, Lords may also recover the cost of travelling to and from home.

The executive government is vested nominally in the Crown, but practically in a committee of Ministers, called the Cabinet, which is dependent on the support of a majority in the House of Commons. The head of the Cabinet is the *Prime Minister*, a position first constitutionally recognized in 1905. The Prime Minister's colleagues in the Cabinet are appointed on his recommendation.

Governments and Prime Ministers since the Second World War (Con = Conservative Party; Lab = Labour Party):

1945–51	Lab	Clement Attlee	1970–74	Con	Edward Heath
1951–55	Con	Winston Churchill	1974–76	Lab	Harold Wilson
1955–57	Con	Sir Anthony Eden	1976–79	Lab	James Callaghan
1957–63	Con	Harold Macmillan	1979–90	Con	Margaret Thatcher
1963–64	Con	Sir Alec Douglas-Home	1990–97	Con	John Major
1964–70	Lab	Harold Wilson	1997–	Lab	Tony Blair

Salaries. Members of Parliament receive an annual parliamentary salary of £55,118 (2002–03). The salaries of Ministers who are MPs include this as a component in addition to their ministerial salary. Total salaries accepted for 2002–03: Prime Minister, £171,554; Cabinet Ministers, £69,861 or £124,979 if also members of the House of Commons (Cabinet Ministers in the House of Lords, £94,826); Lord Chancellor, £180,045; Ministers of State, £91,358 (in the Lords £74,040); Parliamentary Under-Secretaries, £82,624 (in the Lords, £64,485); Government Chief Whip, £124,979 (in the Lords, £69,861); Leader of the Opposition, £119,159 (in the Lords, £64,485); Speaker, £124,979; Attorney-General, £99,200; Solicitor-General, £115,989; Advocate-General for Scotland, £115,989. In addition to pay, MPs are entitled to Office Costs, Supplementary London, Additional Costs, Mileage, Temporary Assistance and Winding Up Allowances, reimbursement of costs owing to recall during a recess and a Resettlement Grant. Ministers receive a severance payment of three months' salary. The Prime Minister is entitled to a salary of £116,436 in addition to the parliamentary salary of £55,118. Cabinet ministers are entitled to salaries of £69,861 (Commons) and £94,826 (Lords). Cabinet ministers in the Commons also receive the parliamentary salary, but those in the Lords do not.

The Privy Council. Before the development of the Cabinet System, the Privy Council was the chief source of executive power, but now its functions are largely formal. It advises the monarch to approve Orders in Council and on the issue of royal proclamations, and has some independent powers such as the supervision of the registration of the medical profession. It consists of all Cabinet members, the Archbishops of Canterbury and York, the Speaker of the House of Commons and senior British and Commonwealth statesmen. There are a number of advisory Privy Council committees. The Judicial Committee is the final court of appeal from courts of the UK dependencies, the Channel Islands and the Isle of Man, and some Commonwealth countries.

Bogdanor, V., *Devolution in the United Kingdom.* OPUS, 1999
Bruce, A., *et al. The House of Lords: 1,000 Years of British Tradition.* London, 1994
Butler, D. and Butler, G., *British Political Facts, 1900–1994.* London, 1994
Dod's Parliamentary Companion. London [published after elections]
Harrison, B., *The Transformation of British Politics, 1860–1995.* OUP, 1996
Norris, P., *Electoral Change in Britain since 1945.* Oxford, 1996
Shell, D., *The House of Lords.* 2nd ed. Hemel Hempstead, 1992
The Times Guide to the House of Commons. London, [published after elections]
Waller, R., *The Almanac of British Politics.* 4th ed. London, 1991
See also NORTHERN IRELAND.

Local Government. Administration is carried out by four types of bodies: (i) local branches of some central ministries, such as the Departments of Health and Social Security; (ii) local sub-managements of nationalized industries; (iii) specialist authorities such as the National Rivers Authority; and (iv) the system of local government described below. The phrase 'local government' has come to mean that part of the local administration conducted by elected councils. There are separate systems for England, Wales and Scotland.

The Local Government Act 1992 provided for the establishment of new unitary councils (authorities) in England, responsible for all services in their areas, though the two-tier structure of district and county councils remained for much of the country. In 1996 all of Wales and Scotland was given unitary local government systems.

Local authorities have statutory powers and claims on public funds. Relations with central government are maintained through the Department of the Environment, Transport and the Regions in England, and through the Welsh and Scottish Executives. In England the Home Office and the Department of Education and Skills are also concerned with some local government functions. (These are performed by departments within the Welsh and Scottish Offices.) Ministers have powers of intervention to protect individuals' rights and safeguard public health, and the government has power to cap (i.e. limit) local authority budgets.

The chair of the council is one of the councillors elected by the rest. In boroughs and cities his or her title is Mayor. Mayors of cities may have the title of Lord Mayor conferred on them. 53 towns in England and Wales and five in Scotland have the status of city. Brighton and Hove, Wolverhampton and Inverness were awarded city status in 2000. In 2002 Preston, Newport, Stirling, Lisburn and Newry were given city status to mark Queen Elizabeth II's golden jubilee. This status is granted by the personal command of the monarch and confers no special privileges or powers. In Scotland, the chair of city councils is deemed Lord Provost, and is elsewhere known as Convenor or Provost. In Wales, the chair is called Chairman in counties and Mayor in county boroughs. Any parish or community council can by simple resolution adopt the style 'town council' and the status of town for the parish or community. Basic and other allowances are payable to councillors (except Scottish community councillors).

Functions. Legislation in the 1980s initiated a trend for local authorities to provide services by, or in collaboration with, commercial or voluntary bodies rather than provide them directly. Savings are encouraged by compulsory competitive tendering. In England, county councils are responsible for strategic planning, transport planning, non-trunk roads and regulation of traffic, personal social services, consumer protection, disposal of waste, the fire and library services and, partially, for education. District councils are responsible for environmental health, housing, local planning applications (in the first instance) and refuse collection. Unitary authorities combine the functions of both levels.

Finance. Revenue is derived from the Council Tax, which supports about one-fifth of current expenditure, the remainder being funded by central government grants and by the redistribution of revenue from the national non-domestic rate (property tax). Capital expenditure is financed by borrowing within government-set limits and sales of real estate.

Elections. England: The 36 metropolitan districts are divided into wards, each represented by three councillors. One-third of the councillors are elected each year for three years out of four. All metropolitan districts had an election on 1 May 2003. The 238 district councils and the 47 English unitary authorities are divided into wards. Each chooses either to follow the metropolitan district system, or to have all seats contested once every four years, or to elect by halves every two years. 232 district councils had an election on 1 May 2003. The 34 county councils have one councillor for each electoral division, elected every four years, with elections scheduled for 2005.

In London there are 33 councils (including the City of London), the whole of which are elected every four years. London borough elections will next be held in 2006. The Greater London Authority has a 25-member Assembly, elected using AMS (Additional Member System), and a directly elected mayor, elected by the SV (Supplementary Vote) system. For the election of London Assembly members London is divided into 14 constituencies. Each constituency elects one member, in addition to which there are 11 'London Member' seats. Elections take place every four years, the next being in June 2004.

Wales: The 22 unitary authorities are split between single and multi-member wards, elected every four years. The next elections will be in 2004.

Scotland: The 32 unitary authorities hold elections every four years. The last elections were held on 1 May 2003.

Resident citizens of the UK, Ireland, a Commonwealth country or an EU country may (at age 18) vote and (at age 21) stand for election.

Election Results. Local government elections for 340 councils on 1 May 2003 resulted in the Conservative control of 110 councils, Labour 66, the Liberal Democrats 28, ind. 10, Residents' Associations 2 and the Scottish National Party 1, with no overall control in 123. The Conservatives gained 566 seats (bringing their total to 4,423), Labour lost 833 (total 3,001), the Liberal Democrats gained 193 (total 2,624) and the Scottish Nationalists lost 21 (182).

The first election to provide London with an elected Mayor and a 25-member London Assembly took place on 4 May 2000. Ken Livingstone (ind.) won with 57·92% of the vote after counting second preferences. He gained 776,427 first and second votes (667,877 as first votes), beating Steve Norris (Conservative) into second place. Ken Livingstone took office on 3 July 2000.

National Anthem. 'God Save the Queen' (King) (words and tune anonymous; earliest known printed source, 1744).

RECENT ELECTIONS

At the general election of 7 June 2001, 31,286,284 votes were cast, with a turn-out of 59·2% (the lowest since the war). The Labour Party won 413 seats with 42·0% of votes cast (418 seats with 43·2% in 1997); the Conservative Party 166 with 32·7% (165 with 30·7%); the Liberal Democratic Party 52 with 18·8% (46 with 16·8%); ind. 1 (1). Regional parties (Scotland): the Scottish National Party won 5 seats (6 in 1997); (Wales): Plaid Cymru 4 (4); (Northern Ireland): the Ulster Unionist Party 6 (10); the Democratic Unionist Party 5 (2); the Social and Democratic Labour Party 3 (3); Sinn Féin 4 (2).

Labour gained 146 seats and lost 1; the Conservatives gained no seats and lost 178; the Liberal Democrats gained 30 seats and lost 2.

In Feb. 2002, 17·9% of the seats in parliament were held by women; Sweden had the highest proportion of women MPs, with 43·3%.

European Parliament. The United Kingdom has 87 representatives. At the June 1999 elections turn-out was 24·0%—the lowest in any of the EU member countries. The Conservative Party won 36 seats with 35·8% of votes cast (group in European Parliament: European People's Party); the Labour Party, 29 with 28·0% (Party of European Socialists); the Liberal Democratic Party, 10 with 12·7% (European Liberal, Democrat and Reform Party); UK Independence, 3 with 7·0% (Europe of Democracies and Diversities); the Green Party, 2 with 6·2% (Greens); the Scottish National Party, 2 with 2·7% (European Radical Alliance); Plaid Cymru, 2 with 1·8% (Greens/European Free Alliance). Voting for these parties was on a proportional system, used for the first time in Britain. Voting in Northern Ireland was by the transferable vote system: the Democratic Ulster Unionist Party (non-affiliated), the Social Democrat and Labour Party (Party of European Socialists) and the Official Ulster Union Party (Independents for a Europe of Nations) gained 1 seat each.

CURRENT ADMINISTRATION

In March 2003 the government consisted of the following:

(a) 23 MEMBERS OF THE CABINET
Prime Minister, First Lord of the Treasury and Minister for the Civil Service: Tony Blair, b. 1953.
Deputy Prime Minister, responsible for Local Government and the Regions: John Prescott, b. 1938.
Chancellor of the Exchequer: Gordon Brown, b. 1951.
Secretary of State for Foreign and Commonwealth Affairs: Jack Straw, b. 1946.
Lord Chancellor: Lord Irvine of Lairg, QC, b. 1940.
Secretary of State for the Home Department: David Blunkett, b. 1947.
Secretary of State for Education and Skills: Charles Clarke, b. 1950.
President of the Council and Leader of the House of Commons: Dr John Reid, b. 1947.
Secretary of State for the Environment, Food and Rural Affairs: Margaret Beckett, b. 1943.
Secretary of State for Scotland: Helen Liddell, b. 1950.
Parliamentary Secretary to the Treasury and Chief Whip: Hilary Armstrong, b. 1945.
Secretary of State for Culture, Media and Sport: Tessa Jowell, b. 1947.
Secretary of State for International Development: Baroness Amos, b. 1954.
Secretary of State for Work and Pensions: Andrew Smith, b. 1951.
Secretary of State for Trade and Industry, Minister for Women and e-Minister: Patricia Hewitt, b. 1948.
Secretary of State for Transport: Alistair Darling, b. 1953.
Secretary of State for Health: Alan Milburn, b. 1958.
Secretary of State for Wales: Peter Hain, b. 1950.
Secretary of State for Northern Ireland: Paul Murphy, b. 1948.
Secretary of State for Defence: Geoff Hoon, b. 1953.
Minister without Portfolio and Party Chair: Ian McCartney, b. 1951.
Chief Secretary to the Treasury: Paul Boateng, b. 1951.
Lord Privy Seal, Leader of the House of Lords: Lord Williams of Mostyn, QC, b. 1941.

(Non-cabinet members but attend cabinet meetings): Lord Grocott, b. 1940, *Lords Chief Whip and Captain of the Gentlemen at Arms;* Nick Brown, b. 1950, *Minister for Work.*

(b) LAW OFFICERS

Attorney-General: Lord Goldsmith, QC, b. 1950.
Solicitor-General: Harriet Harman, b. 1950.
Advocate-General for Scotland: Dr Lynda Clark, QC, b. 1949.

(c) MINISTERS OF STATE (BY DEPARTMENT)

Cabinet Office: Lord Macdonald of Tradeston, CBE, b. 1940, *Minister for the Cabinet Office and Chancellor of the Duchy of Lancaster;* Douglas Alexander, b. 1967.

Office of the Deputy Prime Minister: Barbara Roche, b. 1954, *Minister for Social Exclusion and Deputy Minister for Women;* Nick Raynsford, b. 1945, *Minister for Local Government and the Regions;* Lord Rooker, b. 1941, *Minister for Housing and Planning.*

Department of Culture, Media and Sport: Richard Caborn, b. 1943, *Minister for Sport;* Baroness Blackstone, b. 1942, *Minister for the Arts.*

Ministry of Defence: Adam Ingram, b. 1947.

Department of Education and Skills: David Miliband, b. 1965, *Minister for Schools;* Margaret Hodge, b. 1944, *Minister for Universities.*

Department of the Environment, Food and Rural Affairs: Michael Meacher, b. 1939, *Minister for the Environment;* Alun Michael, b. 1943, *Minister for Rural Affairs.*

Foreign and Commonwealth Affairs Office: Peter Hain, b. 1950, *Minister for Europe;* Baroness Symons of Vernham Dean, b. 1951, *Minister for Trade and Investment and Deputy Leader of the House of Lords.*

Department of Health: John Hutton, b. 1955; Jacqui Smith, b. 1962.

Home Office: Bev Hughes, b. 1950, *Minister for Asylum and Immigration;* Lord Falconer of Thoroton, QC, b. 1951, *Minister for Criminal Policy.*

Department for International Development: Hilary Benn, b. 1953.

Northern Ireland Office: Jane Kennedy, b. 1958.

Department of Trade and Industry: Stephen Timms, b. 1955, *Minister for e-commerce and Competitiveness;* Baroness Symons of Vernham Dean, b. 1951, *Minister for Trade and Investment and Deputy Leader of the House of Lords;* Brian Wilson, b. 1948, *Minister for Industry and Energy;* Alan Johnson, b. 1950, *Minister for Employment Relations and the Regions.*

Department of Transport: John Spellar, b. 1947.

Treasury: Ruth Kelly, b. 1968, *Financial Secretary;* John Healey, b. 1960, *Economic Secretary;* Dawn Primarolo, b. 1954, *Paymaster-General.*

Department for Work and Pensions: Vacant, *Minister for Pensions.*

(d) PARLIAMENTARY SECRETARIES AND UNDER-SECRETARIES (BY DEPARTMENT)

Office of the Deputy Prime Minister: Christopher Leslie, b. 1972; Tony McNulty, b. 1958.

Department of Culture, Media and Sport: Dr Kim Howells, b. 1946.

Ministry of Defence: the Lord Bach of Lutterworth, b. 1946; Dr Lewis Moonie, b. 1947.

Department for Education and Skills: Baroness Ashton of Upholland, b. 1956; Ivan Lewis, b. 1967; Stephen Twigg, b. 1966.

Department for the Environment, Food and Rural Affairs: Elliot Morley, b. 1952; the Lord Whitty of Camberwell, b. 1943.

Foreign and Commonwealth Office: Dr Denis MacShane, b. 1948; Mike O'Brien, b. 1954.

Department of Health: Hazel Blears, b. 1956; David Lammy, b. 1972.

Home Office: Paul Goggins, b. 1953; Robert Ainsworth, b. 1952; Michael Wills, b. 1952; Lord Filkin, CBE, b. 1944.

Lord Chancelloris Department: Baroness Scotland of Asthal, b. 1965; Rosie Winterton, b. 1958; Yvette Cooper, b. 1969.

Privy Council Office: Ben Bradshaw, b. 1960.

Department of Trade and Industry: Lord Sainsbury of Turville, b. 1940; Melanie Johnson, b. 1955; Nigel Griffiths, b. 1955.

Department for Transport: David Jamieson, b. 1947.
Department for International Development: Sally Keeble, b. 1951.
Northern Ireland Office: Des Browne, b. 1955; Ian Pearson, b. 1959; Angela Smith, b. 1959.
Scotland Office: Anne McGuire, b. 1949.
Wales Office: Don Touhig, b. 1947.
Department for Work and Pensions: Baroness Hollis of Heigham, DL, b. 1941; Malcolm Wicks, b. 1947; Maria Eagle, b. 1961.

(e) OPPOSITION FRONT BENCH
Leader of the Opposition: Iain Duncan Smith, b. 1954.
Shadow leader of the House of Lords: Lord Strathclyde, b. 1960.
The *Speaker* of the House of Commons is Michael Martin (Labour), elected on 23 Oct. 2000.

Government Website: http://www.ukonline.gov.uk

DEFENCE
The Defence Council was established on 1 April 1964 under the chairmanship of the Secretary of State for Defence, who is responsible to the Sovereign and Parliament for the defence of the realm. Vested in the Defence Council are the functions of commanding and administering the Armed Forces. The Secretary of State heads the Department of Defence.

Defence policy decision-making is a collective governmental responsibility. Important matters of policy are considered by the full Cabinet or, more frequently, by the Defence and Overseas Policy Committee under the chairmanship of the Prime Minister.

In 2000 there were 20,610 UK armed forces personnel based in Germany, 1,050 based in Brunei, 3,200 based in Cyprus and 330 in Gibraltar. In addition there were 2,700 serving as part of SFOR II in Bosnia, 300 in Iraq/Kuwait (all RAF) and an estimated 3,500 in Yugoslavia.

The ban on homosexuals serving in the armed forces, which had been upheld by a House of Commons vote in May 1996, was suspended in Sept. 1999 after the European Court of Human Rights ruled that the current ban was unlawful.

Defence Budget. The defence budget for 2003–04 is £24,978m. (US\$38,918m.), up from £24,198m. (US\$37,703m.) in 2002–03 and £23,570m. in 2001–02 (US\$36,724m.). Defence spending in 2001 represented 2·5% of GDP, down from 5·2% in 1985. Per capita defence expenditure in 2001 totalled £402 (US\$583), compared to £593 (US\$852) in 1985. It was announced in July 2002 that the defence budget would rise by £3·5bn. (US\$5·4bn.) over three years, the largest sustained increase in planned defence spending in 20 years.

Nuclear Weapons. Having carried out its first test in 1952, there have been 45 tests in all. The nuclear arsenal consisted of approximately 185 warheads in Jan. 2002 according to the Stockholm International Peace Research Institute.

Arms Trade. The UK is a net-exporter of arms and in 2001 was the world's second largest exporter after the USA (with sales worth US\$4bn., or 18·8% of the world total).

In 2000 BAE SYSTEMS was the 3rd largest arms producing company in the OECD, behind Lockheed Martin and Boeing. It accounted for US\$14·40bn. of arms sales (Lockheed Martin US\$18·61bn., Boeing US\$16·90bn.). Rolls Royce was the 14th largest producer, accounting for US\$2·13bn. of sales.

The UK was the 12th largest recipient of major conventional weapons in the world during the period 1997–2001, spending US\$1,247m. in 2001. Only Chnia spent more in 2001.

Army. The Field Army is run from Headquarters Land Command, based at Wilton. The Ministry of Defence retains direct control of units in Northern Ireland, although day-to-day military responsibility is given to the Chief of the General Staff. The Permanent Joint Headquarters, recently formed at Northwood, is responsible for overseas garrisons, which include the Falkland Islands, Cyprus and Brunei.

The established strength of the Regular Army in 2002 was 114,800 which includes soldiers under training and Gurkhas. In addition there were some 4,500

Royal Irish Home Service soldiers. There were 3,800 Gurkhas and 8,050 women in 2002. The strength of the Regular Reserves was 160,800. There were 7,800 soldiers based in Northern Ireland in 2002 in addition to the 4,500 Royal Irish Home Service soldiers.

The role of the Territorial Army (TA) is to act as a general Reserve for the Army by reinforcing it as required, with individuals, sub-units and other units, either in the UK or overseas; and by providing the framework and basis for regeneration and reconstruction to cater for the unforeseen in times of national emergency. The TA also provides a nationwide link between the military and civil communities. Strength, 2002, 40,350. In addition, men who have completed service in the Regular Army normally have some liability to serve in the Regular Reserve. All members of the TA and Regular Reserve may be called out by a Queen's Order in time of emergency of imminent national danger, and most of the TA and a large proportion of the Regular Reserve may be called out by a Queen's Order when warlike operations are in preparation or in progress. The Home Service Battalions of the Royal Irish Regiment are only liable for service in Northern Ireland.

Equipment includes 205 Challenger, 386 Challenger 2 and 3 Chieftain main battle tanks.

Women serve throughout the Army in the same regiments and corps as men. There are only a few roles in which they are not employed such as the Infantry and Royal Armoured Corps.

The Oxford Illustrated History of the British Army. OUP, 1995

Navy. Control of the Royal Navy is vested in the Defence Council and is exercised through the Admiralty Board, chaired by the Secretary of State for Defence.

Changes in management structure, reductions in strength, base closures and rationalization were initiated in 1994. The Chief of Fleet Support and Controller of the Navy are now located in the Bristol area and their various support agencies rationalized. The naval bases at Rosyth and Portland closed in 1995. Although the dockyards at Rosyth and Devonport remain largely committed to naval refit work, both yards have now been sold to commercial operators.

The C.-in-C. Fleet, headquartered at Northwood, is responsible for the command of the fleet, while command of naval establishments in the UK is exercised by the C.-in-C. Naval Home Command from Portsmouth. Main naval bases are at Devonport, Portsmouth and Faslane, with a minor base overseas at Gibraltar.

The Royal Naval Reserve (RNR) and the Royal Marines Reserve (RMR) are volunteer forces which together in 2002 numbered 4,100. The RNR provides trained personnel in war to supplement regular forces. In addition, men who have completed service in the Royal Navy and the Royal Marines have a commitment to serve in the Royal Fleet Reserve, currently 10,300-strong.

The roles of the Royal Navy are first, to deploy the national strategic nuclear deterrent, second to provide maritime defence of the UK and its dependent territories, third to contribute to the maritime elements of NATO's force structure and fourth to meet national maritime objectives outside the NATO area. Personnel strength has reduced steadily over the past five years and is now stabilizing at about 42,350 (including Royal Marines) in 2002, with operational strength at 12 nuclear attack submarines, 2 aircraft carriers (with an additional 1 in refit) and 32 destroyers and frigates.

The strategic deterrent is now borne principally by the four new Trident submarines—*Vanguard, Victorious, Vigilant* and *Vengeance*. They are each capable of deploying 16 US-built Trident II D5 missiles. The last missile submarine of the Resolution class, *Renown*, deploying Polaris missiles, decommissioned in Aug. 1996.

The strength of the fleet's major units in the respective years:

	1991	1998	1999	2000	2001	2002
Strategic Submarines	4	3	3	4	4	4
Nuclear Submarines	15	12	12	12	12	12
Diesel Submarines	6	nil	nil	nil	nil	nil
Aircraft Carriers	2[1]	2[1]	2[1]	2[1]	2[1]	2[1]
Destroyers	12	11	11	11	11	11
Frigates	33	20	20	20	20	21

[1]Following government policy, of the three Carriers held, only two are kept in operational status.

The nuclear-powered submarine force numbers 12. The four diesel-electric submarines of the Upholder class were decommissioned in 1994.

The principal surface ships are the Light vertical/short take-off and landing Aircraft Carriers of the Invincible class (*Invincible, Illustrious* and *Ark Royal*) completed 1980–85, embarking an air group including Sea Harrier vertical/short take-off and landing fighters. Two of these ships are maintained in the operational fleet, with the third (currently *Illustrious*) either in refit or reserve. A new Helicopter Carrier, specifically designed for amphibious operations, *HMS Ocean*, has now entered service.

The Fleet Air Arm, 6,200-strong in 2002, has 214 aircraft of which 34 combat aircraft (Sea Harrier vertical/short take-off and landing fighter aircraft) and 120 armed helicopters.

The Royal Marines corps, 6,200-strong in 2002, provides a commando brigade comprising three commando groups. The Special Boat Squadron and specialist defence units complete the operational strength.

The total number of trained naval service personnel was (in 1,000) on 1 April: 1996, 45·6; 1997, 41·7; 1998, 40·5; 1999, 39·3; 2000; 38·9; 2001, 38·5; 2002, 37·5.

Jane's Fighting Ships. London, annual
The Oxford Illustrated History of the Royal Navy. OUP, 1996

Air Force. The Royal Flying Corps was established in May 1912, with military and naval wings, of which the latter became the independent Royal Naval Air Service in July 1914. On 2 Jan. 1918 an Air Ministry was formed, and on 1 April 1918 the Royal Flying Corps and the Royal Naval Air Service were amalgamated, under the Air Ministry, as the Royal Air Force (RAF).

In 1937 the units based on aircraft carriers and naval shore stations again passed to the operational and administrative control of the Admiralty, as the Fleet Air Arm. In 1964 control of the RAF became a responsibility of the Ministry of Defence.

The RAF is administered by the Air Force Board, of which the Secretary of State for Defence is Chairman. Following recommendations in the 1998 Strategic Defence Review, which placed increased emphasis on Joint and Expeditionary operations, the RAF has experienced considerable restructuring. The creation of the tri-service Defence Logistics Organisation (DLO) resulted in the closure of Logistics Command on 31 Oct. 1999 with most of the logistics support functions previously carried out by the Command now subsumed into the new organization. However, those former Logistics Command Units responsible for tasks falling to the RAF rather than DLO have now been passed to the two remaining RAF Commands: Strike Command and Personnel and Training Command.

Strike Command's mission is to deliver and develop air power in the most effective manner to meet the UK's foreign and security policy. It is responsible for all of the RAF's frontline forces. It operates 427 combat aircraft (plus 121 in store) including 217 Tornados, 53 Jaguars and 60 Harriers (used for battlefield support).

As an expeditionary force, the RAF, on an increasing basis, exercises and operates overseas. Current and recent basing/deployments include the Falklands, Cyprus, Italy and the Balkans, Scandinavia, North America, the Middle East and the Far East. Headquarters RAF Strike Command is based at RAF High Wycombe.

Personnel and Training Command, which is based at RAF Innsworth in Gloucestershire, was established in 1994, and exercises responsibility for the RAF Personnel Management Agency (RAF PMA) and Training Group Defence Agency (TGDA). RAF PMA handles career management of RAF Regular and Reserve Forces, whilst the TGDA is responsible for recruitment and training. HQ PTC also provides department of state functions, such as defence policy-making and service to ministers and Parliament, and the career management of civilian personnel worldwide.

RAF personnel, 1 Dec. 2002, 53,040 (including 5,844 women); total trained personnel, 48,493. Since Dec. 1991 women have been eligible to fly combat aircraft. There were also 14,000 Air Force reserves in 2002 including 1,900 volunteers. In addition there were 28,000 ex-RAF personnel with a recall liability, having left the RAF with a service pension.

INTERNATIONAL RELATIONS

The UK is a member of the UN, WTO, NATO, BIS, OECD, EU, the Council of Europe, WEU, OSCE, CERN, the Commonwealth, Inter-American Development Bank, Asian Development Bank, the Pacific Community, IOM and the Antarctic Treaty.

In 2000 the UK gave US$4·5bn. in international aid, representing 0·31% of its GDP. In actual terms this made the UK the 4th most generous country in the world, but as a percentage of GDP only the 9th most generous.

ECONOMY

In 1997 services accounted for 67% of GDP, industry 31·5% and agriculture 1·5%.

According to the anti-corruption organization *Transparency International*, in 2002 the United Kingdom ranked 10th in the world in a survey of the countries with the least corruption in business and government. It received 8·7 out of 10 in the annual index.

Overview. In 1997 the conduct of monetary policy was delegated to the Monetary Policy Committee (MPC) of the Bank of England, which was made independent. After autumn 1999, the risk of the economy overheating called for a tighter monetary policy. However, the 11 Sept. 2001 attacks on New York and Washington led to a relaxation with half a percentage point interest rate cut in Nov. 2001. The Code for Fiscal Stability, introduced in 1998, sets out the fiscal framework—transparency, stability, responsibility, fairness and efficiency. Fiscal policy has tightened since 1997.

Currency. The unit of currency is the *pound sterling* (£; GBP) of 100 *pence* (p.). Before decimalization on 15 Feb. 1971 £1 = 20 shillings (*s*) of 12 pence (*d*). A gold standard was adopted in 1816, the sovereign or twenty-shilling piece weighing 7·98805 grammes 0·916⅔ fine. Currency notes for £1 and 10s. were first issued by the Treasury in 1914, replacing the circulation of sovereigns. The issue of £1 and 10s. notes was taken over by the Bank of England in 1928. 10s. notes were withdrawn in 1970 and £1 notes (in England and Wales) in 1988. Sterling was a member of the exchange rate mechanism of the European Monetary System from 8 Oct. 1990 until 16 Sept. 1992 ('Black Wednesday').

Inflation. Underlying inflation was 1·5% in June 2002, the lowest rate since records began in 1975, before rising to 3·0% in Feb. 2003, the highest rate in nearly five years.

Coinage. Coins in circulation at 31 Dec. 2001: £2, 185m.; £1, 1,306m.; 50p, 634m.; 20p, 1,873m.; 10p, 1,454m.; 5p, 3,265m.; 2p, 5,772m.; 1p, 9,495m. Commemorative coin: 2000 Queen Mother's 100th birthday £5 Crowns, 3·1m.

Banknotes. The Bank of England issues notes in denominations of £5, £10, £20 and £50 up to the amount of the fiduciary issue. Under the provisions of the Currency Act 1983 the amount of the fiduciary issue is limited, but can be altered by direction of HM Treasury on the advice of the Bank of England. Since Nov. 1998 the limit has been £34,300m., although this was temporarily raised to £50,000m. over the millennium period.

All current series Bank of England notes are legal tender in England and Wales. Some banks in Scotland (Bank of Scotland, Clydesdale Bank and the Royal Bank of Scotland) and Northern Ireland (Bank of Ireland, First Trust Bank, Northern Bank and Ulster Bank) have note-issuing powers.

The total amount of Bank of England notes issued at 31 Dec. 2002 was £33,900m., of which £33,897m. represented notes with other banks and the public, and £3m. notes in the Banking Department of the Bank of England.

Foreign exchange reserves were US$34,583m. and gold reserves 10·10m. troy oz in June 2002 (22·98m. troy oz in April 1999).

Budget. According to the April 2003 budget, public sector net borrowing is set to rise from £24bn. in 2002–03 to £27bn. in 2003–04, but then fall to £24bn. in 2004–05, £23bn. in 2005–06 and £22bn. in 2006–07. Public sector net debt as a proportion of gross domestic product will rise from 30·9% in 2002–03 to 32·2% in 2003–04 and 33·8% by 2007–08.

Current spending, which excludes investment, will rise from £395bn. in 2002–03 to £422bn. in 2003–04, £447bn. in 2004–05, £475bn. in 2005–06 and £500bn. in 2006–07. Net investment will rise from £12·2bn. in 2002–03 to £27bn. by 2006–07.

'While the the eyes of the world were on Baghdad, Mr Brown used the least substantial budget of his tenure to hold out the promise of better times around the corner, and let borrowing take the strain instead of tax rises.' (*Financial Times*, 10 April 2003).

The 2003 budget was the first delivered during wartime for half a century. A total of £3bn. was set aside for the conflict in Iraq as was £332m. for domestic counter-terrorism measures.

Current Budget (in £1bn.).	2001–02	2002–03	2003–04
	Outturn	Estimate	Projection
Current Receipts	389·9	397·1	428·3
Current Expenditure	366·6	395·0	422·0

Surplus on Current Budget (in £1bn.).	2001–02	2002–03	2003–04
	Outturn	Estimate	Projection
	9·9	–11·7	–8·0

Current Receipts (in £1bn.).	2001–02	2002–03	2003–04
	Outturn	Estimate	Projection
Total Inland Revenue			
(net of tax credits)	216·9	216·5	235·8
Total Customs and Excise	104·9	108·8	113·1
Net Taxes and Social			
Security Contributions	369·7	376·5	402·9
Current Receipts	389·9	397·1	428·3

Departmental Expenditure Limits (Resource Budget, in £1bn.).	2001–02	2002–03	2003–04
	Outturn	Estimate	Planned
Education and Skills	17·0	20·6	22·0
Health	52·1	57·4	63·0
of which: NHS	50·9	55·1	60·8
Transport	4·4	6·0	7·3
Office of the Deputy Prime Minister	2·7	4·1	4·8
Local Government	36·9	37·4	41·0
Home Office	10·3	11·3	11·7
Lord Chancellor's Departments	3·1	3·3	3·1
Attorney General's Departments	0·4	0·5	0·5
Defence	32·3	41·4[1]	30·8
Foreign and Commonwealth Office	1·4	1·6	1·7
International Development	3·2	3·6	3·6
Trade and Industry	5·4	4·6	4·7
Environment, Food and Rural Affairs	2·7	2·7	2·7
Culture, Media and Sport	1·2	1·3	1·4
Work and Pensions	6·2	7·5	8·0
Scotland	16·0	17·3	18·4
Wales	8·2	9·1	9·8
Northern Ireland Executive	5·7	6·2	6·4
Northern Ireland Office	1·0	1·2	1·1
Chancellor's Departments	4·1	4·6	4·6
Cabinet Office	1·5	1·7	1·8

[1]One-off increase in defence non-cash expenditure in line with agreed asset management policy.

VAT, introduced on 1 April 1973, is 17·5% (reduced rate, 5·0%).

Performance. In 2001 total GDP was £969,201m. (US$1,406,310m.), the fourth highest in the world after the USA, Japan and Germany.

Economic growth was 2·3% in 1999, rising to 3·0% in 2000 and was 2·2% in 2001 (the fastest rate of any of the Group of Seven leading industrialized countries during the year). However, there was zero growth in the period Oct.–Dec. 2001, the weakest since the recession of the early 1990s. In 2002 the growth rate of 1·6% was the lowest in a decade. Between 1997 and 2000 annual growth averaged 2·7%.

In the 2003 budget the estimated growth rate for the year was cut by 0·5 percentage points to 2·0–2·5%, but the forecast for 2004 remained unchanged at 3·0–3·5%.

In the World Economic Forum's *Global Competitiveness Report 2002–03* the UK was placed 11th in the world in the Growth Competitiveness Ranking and 3rd in the Microeconomic Competitiveness Ranking

Banking and Finance. The Bank of England, Threadneedle Street, London, is the government's banker and the 'banker's bank'. It has the sole right of note issue in England and Wales. It was founded by Royal Charter in 1694 and nationalized in 1946. The capital stock has, since 1 March 1946, been held by HM Treasury. The *Governor* (appointed for five-year terms) is The Rt. Hon Sir Edward George GBE (b. 1938; took office 1993).

The statutory Bank Return is published weekly. End-Dec. figures are as follows (in £1m.):

	Notes in circulation	Notes and coins in Banking Department	Public deposits (government)	Other deposits[1]
1998	25,722	8	229	8,022
1999	30,282	9	164	12,783
2000	30,690	10	382	10,062
2001	32,895	5	451	11,317
2002	33,897	3	690	14,049

[1]Including Special Deposits.

Major British Banking Groups' statistics at end Dec. 2002: total deposits (sterling and currency), £1,318,734m.; sterling market loans, £263,544m.; market loans (sterling and currency), £420,703m.; advances (sterling and currency), £1,031,825m.; sterling investments, £97,060m.

Britain's largest bank is HSBC, both by assets and market capitalization. It had assets in June 2001 of US$674bn. The Royal Bank of Scotland is the second largest, both by assets and market capitalization.

By Oct. 2000 approximately 5% of the British population were using e-banking.

In May 1997 the power to set base interest rates was transferred from the Treasury to the Bank of England. The government continues to set the inflation target but the Bank has responsibility for setting interest rates to meet the target. Base rates are now set by a nine-member Monetary Policy Committee at the Bank; members include the Governor. Membership of the Court (the governing body) was widened. Responsibility for supervising banks was transferred from the Bank to the Financial Services Authority (FSA). The base rate was lowered from 4·00% to 3·75% on 6 Feb. 2003, the lowest rate since 1955.

National Savings Bank. Statistics for 2001 and 2002:

	Ordinary accounts		Investment accounts	
	2001	2002	2001	2002
Amounts—	in £1,000	in £1,000	in £1,000	in £1,000
Received	668,522	651,513	909,592	927,439
Interest credited	23,007	11,567	374,261	282,162
Paid	(672,908)	(654,082)	(1,605,234)	(1,414,741)
Due to depositors at 31 March	1,368,686	1,377,684	7,638,055	7,432,915

There are stock exchanges in Belfast, Birmingham, Glasgow and Manchester which function mainly as representative offices for the London Stock Exchange (called International Stock Exchange until May 1991). In July 1991 the 91 shareholders voted unanimously for a new memorandum and articles of association which devolves power to a wider range of participants in the securities industry, and replaces the Stock Exchange Council with a 14-member board. The FTSE 100 ended 2002 at 3,940·40, down from 5,217·40 at the end of 2001 (representing a drop of 1,277·0 points on the year, or 24·5%—its worst ever annual performance).

In 2000 the UK received a record total of US$111·67bn. worth of foreign direct investment. Investment from Europe increased from US$57·14bn. in 1999 to US$78·31bn. in 2000 while investment from the Americas dropped from US$24·94bn. to US$23·64bn. in the same period.

Roberts, R. and Kynaston, D. (eds.) *The Bank of England: Money, Power and Influence, 1694–1994.* OUP, 1995

Weights and Measures. Conversion to the metric system, which replaced the imperial system, became obligatory on 1 Oct. 1995. The use of the pint for milk deliveries and bar sales, and use of miles and yards in road signs, is exempt indefinitely, and the use of the pound (weight) in selling greengrocery was exempt until 1999.

ENERGY AND NATURAL RESOURCES

Environment. According to the *World Bank Atlas* the UK's carbon dioxide emissions in 1998 were the equivalent of 9·2 tonnes per capita. The UK's total emission of greenhouse gases is estimated to have fallen from 762m. tonnes in 1990 to 664m. tonnes in 2000. An *Environmental Sustainability Index* compiled for the World Economic Forum meeting in Feb. 2002 ranked the UK 91st in the world out of 142 countries analysed, with 46·1%. The index measured the ability of countries to maintain favourable environmental conditions and examined various factors including pollution levels and the use or abuse of natural resources.

In England and Wales 8% of household waste was recycled in 1998, compared to 52% in Switzerland. The rate in Scotland was under 6%.

Electricity. The Electricity Act of 1989 implemented the restructuring and transfer to the private sector of the electricity supply industry.

(England and Wales)

Generators. Under the 1989 Act, National Power and Powergen took over the fossil fuel and hydro-electric power stations previously owned by the Central Electricity Generating Board, and were privatized in 1991. National Power was split into two companies in 2000, International Power plc and Innogy plc. Nuclear Electric, responsible for operating the 12 nuclear power stations, and Scottish Nuclear were merged as a single holding company in 1996 with two new operating subsidiaries, Magnox Electric and British Energy. Both were privatized in 1996. Under licence, generating companies may also be involved in electricity supply. There were a total of 31 nuclear reactors in use in the UK at 15 nuclear power stations in the UK in Sept. 2002. The UK generation market is now very diverse, with 42 major power producers compared to seven in 1990.

Transmission. The privatized National Grid Transco is responsible for operating the transmission system and for co-ordinating the operation of power stations connected to it. The company also operates the Cross-Channel link with France and the interconnection with the Scottish power system.

Distribution and Supply. The 12 Area Boards were replaced under the 1989 Act by 12 successor companies, which were privatized in 1990. These were: East Midlands Electricity (now Powergen Energy); Eastern Electricity (now part of Powergen); London Electricity (now LE Group); Manweb (now part of ScottishPower); Midlands Electricity (now Aquila Networks Services); Northern Electric (supply business now owned by Innogy); Norweb (now part TXU Europe, part United Utilities); SEEBOARD (now part of LE Group); Southern Electric (now part of Scottish and Southern Energy); SWALEC (renamed Hyder, and now part of Western Power Distribution); South Western Electricity (now part of Western Power Distribution); and Yorkshire Electricity (supply business owned by Innogy, distribution business owned by Northern Electric). The companies are in the main responsible for maintaining their local distribution networks, and have a statutory duty to supply electricity to their tariff customers. However, following a number of mergers and takeovers in the industry, some companies are now responsible only for distribution or supply in their areas. Some of the companies are also involved in the retailing of electrical goods and electrical contracting, and some have diversified into other business activities.

See also SCOTLAND.

The Electricity Association. The Electricity Association is the trade association of the UK electricity companies, providing a forum for members to discuss matters of common interest, a collective voice for the electricity industry when needed, and specialist research and professional services. It publishes an annual *Electricity Industry Review*, which contains detailed information on the development of the industry during the previous year.

Regulation. The Office of Electricity Regulation *('Offer')* was set up under the 1989 Act to protect consumer interests following privatization. In 1999 it was merged with the Office of Gas Supply ('*Ofgas*') to form the Office of Gas and Electricity Markets ('*Ofgem*'), reflecting the opening up of all markets for electricity and gas supply to full competition from May that year, with many suppliers now offering both gas and electricity to customers.

Statistics. The electricity industry contributes about 1·3% of the UK's Gross Domestic Product. The installed capacity of all UK power stations in 2001 was 67,965 MW. In 2000 the fuel generation mix was: coal-fired 34%, nuclear 25%, gas 38%, hydro and renewables 2%, and oil 1%. 314,586 GWh were supplied to 28m. customers, of which domestic users took 29%, industrial users 29% and commercial and other users the remaining 42%. The average domestic consumption per capita in 2000 was 4,256 kWh.

Electricity Association. *Electricity Industry Review.* Annual

Surrey, J. (ed.) *The British Electricity Experience: Privatization—the Record, the Issues, the Lessons.* London, 1996

Oil and Gas. Production in 1,000 tonnes, in 2001: throughput of crude and process oils, 84,503; refinery use, 5,162. Refinery output: gas/diesel oil, 26,794; motor spirit, 21,455; fuel oil, 9,941; aviation turbine fuel, 5,910; naphtha, 3,428; burning oil, 3,088; propane, butane and other petroleum gases, 1,856; bitumen, 1,707; petroleum coke, 765. Total output of petroleum products, 76,931. Crude oil production (2001), 116·7m. tonnes. The UK's oil production is the second highest in Europe after that of Norway, and is the ninth highest in the world, greater than that of either Kuwait or Libya. The UK had proven oil reserves of 4·9bn. bbls. in Dec. 2000, but reserves are expected to be exhausted by 2007.

In 2000 the total income from sales of oil produced was £16,129m., with the value of net exports of oil and oil products in 2000 equal to £6bn., the highest level seen since the mid-1960s.

The first significant offshore gas discovery was made in 1965 in the North Sea, followed in 1967 by the first oil offshore. Offshore production of gas began in 1967 and oil in 1975.

Oil and gas have played an important part in providing the UK's energy needs. In 2000, either through direct use or as a source of energy to produce electricity, oil and gas accounted for some 73% of total UK energy consumption, with UK-based production supplying some 98% of the gas consumed.

Oil products also provide important contributions to other industries, such as feedstocks for the petro-chemical industry and lubricants for various uses. While the importance of oil as a source of energy for electrical generation and use by industry and commercial operations has declined in recent years with the increasing use of gas, oil still makes up 18% of total industrial uses of energy. Its prime importance is in the transport sector, where it provides 99% of the total energy used.

The United Kingdom usually exports around two-thirds of the oil it produces, with the key export markets being the USA and other EU countries.

The reform of the old nationalized gas industry began with the Gas Act of 1986, which paved the way for the privatization later that year of the British Gas Corporation, and established the Director General of Gas Supply (DGSS) as the independent regulator. This had a limited effect on competition, as British Gas retained a monopoly on tariff (domestic) supply. Competition progressively developed in the industrial and commercial (non-tariff) market.

The Gas Act 1995 amended the 1986 Act to prepare the way for full competition, including the domestic market. It created three separate licences—for Public Gas Transporters who operate pipelines, for Shippers (wholesalers) who contract for gas to be transported through the pipelines, and for Suppliers (retailers) who then market gas to consumers. It also placed the DGSS under a statutory duty to secure effective competition.

The domestic market was progressively opened to full competition from 1996 until May 1998.

In 1997 British Gas took a commercial decision to de-merge its trading business. Centrica plc (a new company) was formed to handle the gas sales, gas trading, services and retail businesses of BG, together with the gas production businesses of the North and South Morecambe Field. The remaining parts of the business, including transportation and storage and the international downstream activities, were contained in BG plc. Subsequent de-merging has led to the creation of the

Lattice Group, owner of Transco, who own and operate the UK's National Gas Transmission System.

In 1998 a new Director General of Gas Supply (Callum McCarthy) was appointed for a five-year term. In recognition of the increasing convergence between the gas and electricity markets, he was also appointed as Director General of Electricity Supply from Jan. 1999.

A European Directive introducing rules for the internal market in natural gas entered into force in Aug. 1998 (98/80/EC). Member states had two years to give effects to its provisions. A pipeline (the Interconnector) linking the UK and European gas grids opened in Oct. 1998. It has an export capacity of 20bn. cu. metres a year and an import capacity of 8·5bn. cu. metres a year.

Proven gas reserves are some 740,000m. cu. metres. Production was 1,258,549 GWh in 2000, 34% of which was used by domestic users and 28% by electricity generators.

The *Office of Gas Supply ('Ofgas')* is the regulator charged with protecting gas consumers' interests.

See also NORTHERN IRELAND.

Wind. In 2001 there were 69 wind farms and 941 turbines with a capacity of 473·6 MW for electricity generation.

Water. Annual average water usage in the UK is just under 2,000 cu. metres per person—less than a ninth of usage in the USA.

Minerals. Legislation to privatize the coal industry was introduced in 1994 and a new Coal Authority has taken over from British Coal. The Coal Authority is the owner of coal reserves; it licenses private coal-mining and deals with claims in former mining areas and disposes of unworked assets. In 1995 there were 15 British Coal collieries and 32 large deep mines in the private sector, employing some 13,500 mineworkers.

Total production from deep mines was 17·3m. tonnes in 2001 (83·8m. tonnes in 1988). Output from opencast sites, 2001, 14·2m. tonnes (1988, 17·9m. tonnes). In 2001 inland coal consumption was 54·5m. tonnes (113·3m. tonnes in 1988).

Output of non-fuel minerals in Great Britain, 2001 (in 1,000 tonnes): sand and gravel, 88,210; limestone, 83,492; igneous rock, 45,053; sandstone, 11,897; clay and shale, 10,426; chalk, 8,205; salt (1999), 5,800; industrial sand, 3,848; china clay, 2,804.

Steel and metals. Steel production in recent years (in 1m. tonnes):

1997	18·5
1998	17·3
1999	16·6
2000	15·2
2001	13·5

Deliveries of finished steel products from UK mills in 2001 were worth £6bn. in product sales and comprised 6·7m. tonnes to the UK domestic market and 6·3m. tonnes for export. About three-quarters of UK steel exports went to other EU countries. UK steel imports in 2001 were about 6·8m. tonnes. The UK steel industry's main markets are construction (22%), automotive (17%), mechanical engineering (24%) and metal goods (14%). Corus Group (formerly British Steel) is the UK's largest steel producer (and the third largest steel company in the world) and produces about 85% of UK crude steel. The UK steel industry has improved productivity nearly 5-fold over the past 20 years.

Agriculture. Land use in 1996: agriculture, 77%; urban, 10%; forests, 10%; other, 3%. In 2001 (and 2000) agricultural land in the UK totalled (in 1,000 ha) 18,555 (18,311), comprising agricultural holdings, 17,323 (17,083) and common grazing, 1,232 (1,228). Land use of the former (in 1,000 ha): all grasses 6,789 (6,590); crops, 4,454 (4,665); rough grazing, 4,435 (4,445); bare fallow, 43 (37); other, 1,602 (1,346). Area sown to crops (in 1,000 ha): cereals, 3,014 (3,348); other arable crops, 1,102 (979); horticultural crops, 173 (172); fruit, 37 (38).

Figures compiled by the Soil Association show that in April 2002 the area of fully organic farmland in the UK was 458,600 ha. Including land in conversion, 4·3% of the agricultural land was managed organically. Organic food sales for the UK in 2001–02 totalled £920m., up from £805m. in 2000–01.

Farmers receiving financial support under the EU's Common Agricultural Policy are obliged to 'set-aside' land in order to control production. In 2000 such set-aside totalled 567,000 ha (572,000 ha in 1999). There were 500,000 tractors and 47,000 harvester-threshers in 1998.

The number of workers employed in agriculture was, in 2001, 184,000 (48,500 female) of whom 63,200 were seasonal or casual workers. Of the 120,800 regular workers, 40,900 were part-time. In 1990 the number of workers employed in agriculture had been 273,800. There were some 234,900 farm holdings in 1995, about 66% owner-occupied. Average size of holdings, 72·4 ha.

Total farm incomes dropped from £5·3bn. to £1·5bn. between 1995 and 2000. Food and live animals accounted for 2·9% of exports and 6·4% of imports in 2001, down from 4·5% of exports and 8·6% of imports in 1991.

Area given over to principal crops in the UK:

	Wheat	Sugarbeets	Potatoes	Barley	Oilseed rape	Oats
			Area (1,000 ha)			
1996	1,976	199	177	1,267	356	96
1997	2,036	196	166	1,359	445	100
1998	2,045	189	164	1,255	506	98
1999	1,847	183	178	1,179	417	92
2000	2,086	173	166	1,128	332	109

Production of principal crops in the UK:

	Wheat	Sugarbeets	Potatoes	Barley	Oilseed rape	Oats
			Total product (1,000 tonnes)			
1996	16,100	10,420	7,225	7,790	1,412	590
1997	15,020	11,084	7,125	7,830	1,527	575
1998	15,470	10,002	6,417	6,630	1,566	585
1999	14,870	10,584	7,100	6,580	1,737	540
2000	16,700	9,335	...	6,490	1,129	640

Horticultural crops. 2000 output (in 1,000 tonnes): carrots, 455; onions, 379; cabbage, 251; apples, 201; peas, 181; cauliflowers, 152; lettuce, 138; tomatoes, 113.

Livestock in the UK as at June in each year (in 1,000):

	1997	1998	1999	2000	2001
Cattle	11,637	11,519	11,423	11,135	10,602
(dairy)	(2,478)	(2,439)	(2,440)	(2,336)	(2,251)
(beef)	(1,862)	(1,947)	(1,924)	(1,842)	(1,708)
Sheep	42,823	44,471	44,656	42,264	36,716
Pigs	8,072	8,146	7,284	6,482	5,845
Poultry	—	—	149,867	154,503	—

Livestock products, 2000 (1,000 tonnes): hens' eggs, 827; poultry meat, 1,707; beef and veal, 922; mutton and lamb, 494; pork, 1,001; bacon and ham, 477; milk, 14·46m. tonnes.

In March 1996 the government acknowledged the possibility that bovine spongiform encephalopathy (BSE) might be transmitted to humans as a form of Creutzfeldt-Jakob disease via the food chain. Confirmed cases of BSE in cattle in the UK: 1988, 2,180; 1989, 7,133; 1990, 14,181; 1991, 25,026; 1992, 36,680; 1993, 34,370; 1994, 23,943; 1995, 14,301; 1996, 8,013; 1997, 4,309; 1998, 3,179; 1999, 2,254; 2000, 1,311; 2001, 781; 2002, 443. Confirmed deaths attributed to nvCJD (new variant Creutzfeldt-Jakob Disease, the form of the disease thought to be linked to BSE): 1995, 3; 1996, 10; 1997, 10; 1998, 18; 1999, 15; 2000, 28; 2001, 20; 2002, 17.

British beef was widely banned overseas and in March 1996 the European Commission introduced a ban on the export of bovine animals, semen and embryos, beef and beef products and mammalian meat and bonemeal from the UK. The government introduced a number of preventive measures including bans on sales of older meat and the use of meat in animal feed and fertilizer, and compensation schemes. Following inspections, the European Commission allowed for the export of deboned beef and beef products beginning 1 Aug. 1999.

In Feb. 2001 the UK was hit by a major foot-and-mouth disease epidemic for the first time since 1967–68, with 2,030 confirmed cases and 4,050,000 animals being slaughtered during the months which followed. The last confirmed case was on 30 Sept. 2001. In the 1967–68 epidemic there had been 2,364 cases with approximately 434,000 animals slaughtered.

Forestry. In March 2002 the area of woodland in Britain was 2,716,000 ha, of which the Forestry Commission managed 794,000 ha. There were approximately 29,500 full-time equivalent jobs in the forestry industry and wood-processing industries in 1998–99, of which 11,200 were in wood processing, 5,900 in forest establishment and maintenance, 5,800 in harvesting and haulage, 4,600 in other non-forest activities such as office work research, and 2,000 in other forest activities such as nurseries and road construction. In 2001 a total of 7·23m. cu. metres of roundwood was produced.

New planting (2001–02), 13,194 ha (248 ha, Forestry Commission; 12,946 ha, private woodlands).

Forestry Commission (*Website:* http://www.forestry.gov.uk). *Forestry Facts and Figures.* Annual

Fisheries. Quantity (in 1,000 tonnes) and value (in £1,000) of fish of British taking, landed in Great Britain (excluding salmon and sea-trout):

Quantity	1997	1998	1999	2000	2001
Wet fish	467·2	428·3	389·8	337·6	332·1
Shell fish	126·1	124·2	116·7	127·0	136·2
	593·5	552·5	506·5	464·7	458·3
Value					
Wet fish	314,712	323,297	297,831	268,816	256,364
Shell fish	152,983	160,708	166,299	153,247	167,323
	467,695	484,005	464,131	422,063	423,687

In Dec. 2000 the fishing fleet comprised 7,242 registered vessels. Major fishing ports: (England) Fleetwood, Grimsby, Hull, Lowestoft, North Shields; (Wales) Milford Haven; (Scotland) Aberdeen, Mallaig, Lerwick, Peterhead.

In the period 1995–97 the average person in the UK consumed 20 kg of fish and fishery products a year, compared to the European Union average of just over 23 kg.

INDUSTRY

The largest companies by market capitalization in the UK on 9 March 2003 were: BP, at £88,329m. (US$141,591m.), compared to £141,231m. (US$201,424m.) in March 2002; Vodafone, at £73,666m. (US$118,087m.), compared to £88,093m. (US$125,638m.); and GlaxoSmithKline, at £63,613m. (US$101,972m.), compared to £102,845m. (US$146,678m.).

In 2002 there were 167,970 manufacturing firms, of which 215 employed 1,000 or over persons, and 116,205 employed nine or fewer.

Chemicals and chemical products. Manufacturers' sales, (in £1m.) in 2000: primary plastics and other plastic products, 17,436; pharmaceutical preparations and basic pharmaceutical products, 8,799; organic basic chemicals, 5,412; perfumes and toilet products, 2,656; paints, etc., 2,600; rubber products, 2,563; soap, polish and detergents, 1,961; inorganic basic chemicals, 1,155; dyes, 1,095.

Construction. Total value (in £1m.) of constructional work in Great Britain in 2001 was 74,690, including new work, 39,970 (of which housing, 10,233). Cement production, 2001, 11,854,000 tonnes; brick production, 2001, 2,754m. units.

Electrical Goods. Manufacturers' sales (in £1m.) for 2000: computers, etc., 11,661; telephone and telegraph equipment, 5,467; radio and electronic capital goods, 4,895; electronic valves and tubes and other electronic components, 4,542; television and radio receivers, sound or video recording, 3,457.

Engineering, machinery and instruments. Manufacturers' sales (in £1m.) for 2000: motor vehicles, 19,689; aircraft and spacecraft, 12,794; parts and accessories for motor vehicles and engines, 8,365; appliances for measuring, checking and testing, 5,053; lifting and handling equipment, 2,679; machine tools, 1,792; medical and surgical equipment and orthopaedic appliances, 1,643. Car production, 2001, 1,492,365 units (1,786,623 in 1999).

Foodstuffs, etc. Manufacturers' sales (in £1m.) for 2000: operation of dairies, 5,570; bread, fresh pastry goods and cakes, 4,035; beer, 3,685; cocoa, chocolate and sugar confectionery, 3,414; meat production and preservation, 3,334; biscuits, rusks, preserved pastry goods and cakes, 2,974 (1998); mineral water and soft drinks, 2,776 (1999); grain mill products, 2,615; tobacco products, 2,282; distilled alcoholic beverages, 2,031; fruit and vegetable processing and preservation, 2,009; prepared feeds for farm animals, 2,002; poultry production and preservation, 1,872. Alcoholic beverage production, 2001: beer, 5,680·2m. litres (5,955·2m. litres in 1991); wine, 1,033·6m. litres (658·3m. litres in 1991); spirits, 436·8m. litres (447·6m. litres in 1991).

Metals. Manufacturers' sales (in £1m.) for 2000: metal structures and parts of structures, 4,791; general mechanical engineering, 2,777; forging, pressing, stamping and roll forming of metal, 2,116; treatment and coating of metals, 1,055; steel tubes, 1,053.

Textiles and clothing. Manufacturers' sales (in £1m.) in 2001: women's outerwear and underwear, 1,423; household textiles, 909; carpets and rugs, 904; textile weaving, 836; preparation and spinning of textile fibres, 673; men's outerwear and underwear, 573.

Wood products, furniture, paper and printing. Manufacturers' sales (in £1m.) in 2000: furniture of whatever construction, 7,011; journals and periodicals, 6,985; wood products except furniture, 4,775; newspapers, 3,883; paper and paperboard, 3,339; cartons, boxes and cases, 3,254; publishing of books, 3,240.

Labour. In 2002 the UK's total economically active population (i.e. all persons in employment plus the claimant unemployed) was (in 1,000) 29,183 (13,388 females), of whom 27,659 (12,773 females) were in employment, including 24,339 (11,832 females) as employees and 3,124 (831 females) as self-employed. In 1993 only 25,245,000 people had been in employment, representing an increase of 2,414,000 in nine years. UK employees by form of employment in 2002 (in 1,000): wholesale and retail trade, repair of motor vehicles, motorcycles and household goods, 4,466; real estate renting and business activities, 3,907; manufacturing industry, 3,668; health and social work, 2,796; education, 2,183; hotels and restaurants, 1,696; transport, storage and communications, 1,524; public administration and defence, compulsory social security, 1,443; construction, 1,186; financial intermediation, 1,062; agriculture, hunting, forestry and fishing, 255. Between 1997 and 2002 employment in service industries increased by 1,887,000 while employment in manufacturing declined by 508,000 over the same period. The fastest-growing job creation sector in Britain has been the call centre, with 500,000 operators working from some 5,000 centres across the country by the end of 2000. It is estimated that 2% of the workforce in 2000 were employed in call centres.

Registered unemployed in UK as at spring (in 1,000; figures not seasonally adjusted): 1997, 2,036 (7·2%); 1998, 1,775 (6·3%); 1999, 1,759 (6·1%); 2000, 1,636 (5·7%); 2001, 1,428 (4·9%)—the lowest rate in more than 20 years; 2002, 1,524 (5·2%). Of the 1,524,000 unemployed people, 909,000 were men and 615,000 women. The number of unemployed people on benefits was 928,500 in Jan. 2003 (giving a rate of 3·1%), the lowest since records began in 1975. The unemployment rate on the International Labour Organization (ILO) definition, which includes all those who are looking for work whether or not claiming unemployment benefits, was 5·1% in Oct.–Dec. 2002.

In 2001 there were 3·7m. businesses in the UK of which 1·6m. were registered at Companies House. Approximately 99% of UK businesses have fewer than 50 employees. There were an estimated 342,000 business start-ups in 2001, with business closures numbering 410,000.

Workers (in 1,000) involved in industrial stoppages (and working days lost): 1998, 93 (0·28m.); 1999, 141 (0·24m.); 2000, 183 (0·50m.); 2001, 180 (0·52m.). In 1975, 6m. working days had been lost through stoppages. Between 1989 and 1998 strikes cost Britain an average of 47 working days per 1,000 employees a year, compared to the EU average of 85 per 1,000. The equivalent figure in France was 37 per 1,000.

The Wages Councils set up in 1909 to establish minimum rates of pay (in 1992 of 2·5m. workers) were abolished in 1993. The Labour government, elected in May

1997, was committed to the introduction of a National Minimum Wage and established a Low Pay Commission to advise on its implementation. It is currently £4·20 an hour. In April 2002 the average gross salary in Britain was £24,603 (£34,762 in London). Average hourly pay excluding overtime in April 2002 in Britain was £11·73 (£12·59 for males and £10·22 for females), ranging from averages of £9·93 in the North-East up to £16·23 in London.

Britons work an average of 43·6 hours a week, the second longest working week in the European Union behind Greece. In 1996, 60% of males and 20% of females put in more than 40 hours a week.

Trade Unions. In Jan. 2003 there were 69 unions affiliated to the Trades Union Congress (TUC) with a total membership of 6·7m. (2·7m. of them women), down from a peak of 12·2m. in 1980. The unions affiliated to the TUC in 2001 ranged in size from UNISON with 1·27m. members to the Sheffield Wool Shear Workers' Union with 15 members. The four largest unions, however, account for more than half the total membership. In 1998, 60% of public-sector employees and 19% of private-sector employees were unionized.

The TUC's executive body, the General Council, is elected at the annual Congress. Congress consists of representatives of all unions according to the size of the organization, and is the principal policy-making body.

The General Secretary (Brendan Barber, b. 1951) is elected from nominations submitted by the unions. The TUC draws up policies and promotes and publicizes them. It makes representations to government, employers and international bodies. The TUC also carries out research and campaigns, and provides a range of services to unions including courses for union representatives.

The TUC is affiliated to the International Confederation of Free Trade Unions, the Trade Union Advisory Committee of OECD, the Commonwealth Trade Union Council and the European Trade Union Confederation. The TUC provides a service of trade union education. It provides members to serve, with representatives of employers, on the managing boards of such bodies as the Health and Safety Commission and the Advisory, Conciliation and Arbitration Service.

Clegg, H. A., *A History of British Trade Unions since 1889* [until 1951]. 3 vols. Oxford, 1994

Pelling, H., *A History of British Trade Unionism*. 5th ed. London, 1992.

Taylor, R., *The TUC From the General Strike to New Unionism*. Palgrave, Basingstoke, 2000

Willman, P. *et al.*, *Union Business: Trade Union Organization and Financial Reform in the Thatcher Years*. CUP, 1993

INTERNATIONAL TRADE
Imports and Exports. Value of the imports and exports of merchandise, excluding bullion and specie (in US$1m.):

	Total imports	Total exports
2001	325,044·0	271,134·0
2002	335,769·6	276,961·2

Until 1992 all overseas trade statistics were compiled from Customs declarations. With the inception of the Single Market on 1 Jan. 1993, however, the requirement for Customs declarations in intra-EU trade was removed.

In 2002 the UK's trade with non-EU countries was: imports, US$161,108·4m.; exports, US$117,016·8m. (2001 figures were imports US$162,127·2m. and exports US$116,214·4m.).

In 2002 other European Union members accounted for 54·6% of the UK's foreign trade, compared with 25·2% in 1956. The USA accounted for 13·5%, up from 9·1% in 1956, and the rest of the world 31·9%, down from 65·7% in 1956.

Figures for trade by countries and groups of countries (in US$1m.):

	Imports from		Exports to	
EU countries	*2000*	*2001*	*2000*	*2001*
EU	162,916·8	174,661·2	154,917·6	159,944·4
Austria	2,654·4	3,362·4	1,723·2	1,845·6
Belgium and Luxembourg	16,478·4	17,968·8	13,840·8	15,277·2
Denmark	3,861·6	3,997·2	3,240·0	4,018·8
Finland	4,177·2	4,053·6	2,299·2	2,122·8
France and Monaco	26,906·4	27,408·0	27,034·8	27,229·2

	Imports from		Exports to	
EU countries	2000	2001	2000	2001
Germany	40,702·8	45,043·2	33,186·0	31,983·6
Greece	664·8	837·6	1,581·6	1,770·0
Ireland	13,357·2	13,675·2	20,163·6	22,960·8
Italy	14,278·8	15,691·2	11,817·6	12,331·2
Netherlands	21,322·8	22,249·2	20,491·2	20,228·4
Portugal, Azores and Madeira	2,242·8	2,451·6	2,238·0	2,208·0
Spain	9,698·4	11,598·0	11,364·0	12,369·6
Sweden	6,571·2	6,326·4	5,612·4	5,599·2
Other foreign countries				
Europe—				
Baltic States	1,374·0	1,626·0	439·2	488·4
Czech Republic	1,620·0	1,910·4	1,552·8	1,549·2
Hungary	1,044·0	1,302·0	884·4	1,125·6
Iceland	430·8	468·0	226·8	212·4
Norway	8,502·0	8,346·0	2,732·4	2,728·8
Poland	1,717·2	1,935·6	1,869·6	1,977·6
Romania	660·0	801·6	492·0	648·0
Russia	3,032·4	2,990·4	1,293·6	1,488·0
Slovakia	260·4	324·0	277·2	302·4
Switzerland and Liechtenstein	6,986·4	7,432·8	5,425·2	4,963·2
Turkey	2,556·0	3,488·4	1,734·0	2,076·0
Other in Europe	1,563·6	1,844·4	2,295·6	2,380·8
Africa—				
Algeria	339·6	519·6	170·4	198·0
Egypt	607·2	648·0	655·2	697·2
Morocco	657·6	705·6	532·8	501·6
Nigeria	99·6	144·0	985·2	1,077·6
South Africa and Namibia	4,695·6	4,477·2	2,246·4	2,430·0
Tunisia	172·8	171·6	204·0	202·8
Other in Africa	3,645·6	3,721·2	2,140·8	2,121·6
Asia and Oceania—				
Australia	2,646·0	2,665·2	3,345·6	3,193·2
China	8,589·6	10,512·0	2,476·8	2,250·0
Hong Kong	8,610·0	8,685·6	3,889·2	3,656·4
India	2,713·2	2,808·0	2,563·2	2,647·2
Indonesia	1,716·0	1,620·0	453·6	495·6
Japan	13,498·8	12,730·8	5,344·8	5,403·6
Korea (South)	4,099·2	4,308·0	1,849·2	2,199·6
Malaysia	2,896·8	2,701·2	1,486·8	1,321·2
New Zealand	808·8	820·8	463·2	487·2
Pakistan	630·0	734·4	330·0	366·0
Philippines	1,729·2	1,465·2	565·2	532·8
Singapore	3,093·6	3,054·0	2,308·8	2,187·6
Taiwan	4,166·4	3,715·2	1,269·6	1,284·0
Thailand	2,403·6	2,419·2	856·8	799·2
Other in Asia and Oceania	2,364·0	2,622·0	691·2	660·0
Middle East—				
Iran	42·0	54·0	620·4	601·2
Israel	1,405·2	1,360·8	1,966·8	2,151·6
Kuwait	448·8	435·6	514·8	466·8
Saudi Arabia	1,429·2	1,090·8	2,182·8	2,090·4
United Arab Emirates	750·0	1,036·8	1,788·0	1,716·0
Other Middle East	472·8	606·0	1,707·6	1,706·4
America—				
Argentina	309·6	369·6	382·8	192·0
Brazil	1,910·4	2,126·4	1,171·2	1,332·0
Canada	5,452·8	5,544·0	4,680·0	4,724·4
Chile	693·6	711·6	188·4	175·2
Colombia	462·0	327·6	151·2	126·0
Mexico	1,011·6	784·8	987·6	1,063·2
USA	45,051·6	39,895·2	42,861·6	42,934·8
Venezuela	238·8	286·8	451·2	348·0
Other in America	1,392·0	1,671·6	1,233·6	1,309·2
Total, foreign countries (including some not specified above)	325,044·0	335,769·6	271,134·0	276,961·2

In 2002 machinery and transport equipment accounted for 43·1% of the UK's imports and 45·6% of exports; chemicals, manufactured goods classified chiefly by material and miscellaneous manufactured articles 41·5% of imports and 39·4% of exports; food, live animals, beverages and tobacco 8·3% of imports and 5·4% of exports; mineral fuels, lubricants and related materials 4·3% of imports and 8·1% of exports; and crude materials, inedible, animal and vegetable oil and fats 2·9% of imports and 1·5% of exports. The UK was the second largest exporter of services in 1998 behind the USA. The trade surplus in services was £15·1bn. in 2000, whereas there was a deficit of £30·3bn. in trade in goods.

Trade Fairs. London ranked as the second most popular convention city behind Paris in 2001 according to the Union des Associations Internationales (UAI).

COMMUNICATIONS

Roads. Responsibility for the construction and maintenance of trunk roads belongs to central government. Roads not classified as trunk roads are the responsibility of county or unitary councils.

In 2001 there were 392,408 km of public roads, classified as: motorways, 3,472 km; trunk roads, 11,725 km; other major roads, 34,825 km; minor roads, 342,386 km.

In 2001 journeys by car, vans and taxis totalled 624bn. passenger km (less than 60bn. in the early 1950s). Even in the early 1950s passenger km in cars, vans and taxis exceeded the annual total at the end of the 20th century by rail. Motor vehicles in 2001 included 23,899,000 passenger cars, 882,000 mopeds, scooters and motorcycles, 89,000 public transport vehicles and 2,544,000 other private and light goods vehicles. The average distance travelled by a passenger car in the year 1998 was 16,000 km. In 2001, 74% of households had regular use of a car with 30% of households having use of two or more cars. New vehicle registrations in 2001, 3,137,700. Driving tests, 2001–02 (in 1,000): applications, 1,315; tests held, 1,216; tests passed, 527; pass rate, 43%. The driving test was extended in 1996 to include a written examination.

Road casualties in Great Britain in 2001, 313,309 including 3,450 killed. Britain has the lowest death rates in road accidents of any industrialized country, at 5·9 deaths per 100,000 people.

Inter- and intra-urban bus and coach journeys average 46bn. passenger-km annually. Passenger journeys by local bus services, 2000–01, 4,309m. For London buses *see* Transport for London *under* RAILWAYS, *below.*

Rail. In 1994 the nationalized railway network was restructured to allow for privatization. Ownership of the track, stations and infrastructure was vested in a government-owned company, Railtrack, which was privatized in May 1996.

Passenger operations were reorganized into 25 train-operating companies, which were transferred to the private sector by Feb. 1997. By March 1997 all freight operations were also privatized. On 7 Oct. 2001 Railtrack plc was taken into administration because the company was, or was likely to become, unable to pay its debts. The High Court appointed Ernst & Young as Joint Special Administrators of Railtrack plc. On 3 Oct. 2002 a new private sector not-for-profit company limited by guarantee, Network Rail, took over from Railtrack plc as network owner and operator. The train-operating companies pay Network Rail for access to the rail network, and lease their rolling stock from three private-sector companies.

Eurotunnel PLC holds a concession from the government to operate the Channel Tunnel (49·4 km), through which vehicle-carrying and Eurostar passenger trains are run in conjunction with French and Belgian railways. A new dedicated high-speed line is planned to connect the Channel Tunnel to London St Pancras. This line will be used by both international and domestic trains. Construction is being undertaken in two sections with the first section planned to open before the end of 2003. The entire line should open in 2007.

The rail network comprises around 16,500 route km (a third electrified). Annual passenger km have increased from 32·1bn. in 1996–97 to 39·1bn. in 2000–01, an increase of almost 22%. Passenger journeys have increased by 20% from 801m. in 1996–97 to 960m. in 2001–02. The amount of freight moved declined gradually over many years to 13·0bn. tonne km in 1995–96. Following privatization it rose sharply to 18·1bn. tonne km in 2000–01 and further to 19·4bn. tonne km in 2001–02, its highest level in more than 20 years. In 2001–02, 32 people (excluding trespassers and suicides) were fatally injured on the railways (compared to 3,450 deaths in road accidents in 2001).

Transport *for* London (T/L) is accountable to the Mayor of London and responsible for implementing his Transport Strategy as well as planning and delivering a range of transport facilities. T/L's remit covers London Buses, the Docklands Light Railway and Tramlink, Victoria Coach Station, London River Services, the Public Carriage Office and Street Management. London Underground will become part of T/L once agreement on its management and funding is reached with the Government. T/L also manages a 580 km network of London's main roads and its 4,600 traffic signals and regulates taxis and private hire trade. It helps to co-ordinate schemes for transport users with reduced mobility and plans and works to improve conditions on London's streets for walkers, cyclists and freight, whilst reducing congestion. In 1999–2000 London Underground carried 3m. passengers a day to and from 274 stations on 12 lines. These stations include 12 managed by Silverlink Train Services; 2 by SouthWest Trains; and 22 stations with interchanges managed by national rail service operators. Some 6,500 buses, run under contract to London Transport by independent companies, carried 4·8m. passengers a day on some 700 routes.

The privately franchised Docklands Light Railway is operated in east inner London.

There are metros in Glasgow and Newcastle, and light rail systems in Birmingham/Wolverhampton, Manchester and Sheffield.

Civil Aviation. All UK airports handled a total of 180·0m. passengers during 2000. Of those, 115·8m. were handled by London area airports (Heathrow, Gatwick, London City, Luton and Stansted).

Busiest airports in 2000:

	Passengers	International		Freight (tonnes)
Heathrow	64,279,079	56,875,158	Heathrow	1,306,918
Gatwick	31,948,939	29,036,589	Gatwick	318,962
Manchester	18,352,115	15,485,480	East Midlands	178,765
Stansted	11,860,335	10,443,265	Stansted	167,829
Birmingham	7,493,220	6,281,696	Manchester	117,019

Heathrow is Europe's busiest airport for passenger traffic, ahead of Frankfurt, Paris Charles de Gaulle, Amsterdam, Madrid and Gatwick, the sixth busiest (in 2000). More international passengers use Heathrow than any other airport in the world.

Following the Civil Aviation Act 1971, the Civil Aviation Authority (CAA) was established as an independent public body responsible for the economic and safety regulation of British civil aviation. A CAA wholly owned subsidiary, National Air Traffic Services, operates air traffic control. Highlands and Islands Airports Ltd is owned by the Scottish Office and operates 10 airports.

There were 16,666 civil aircraft registered in the UK at 1 Nov. 2002.

British Airways is the largest UK airline, with a total of 340 aircraft at 31 Dec. 2000. It operates long- and short-haul international services, as well as an extensive domestic network. British Airways also has franchise agreements with other UK operators: British Mediterranean Airways, British Regional Airlines, Brymon Airways, CityFlyer Express, GB Airways, Loganair and Maersk Air. British Airways (European Operations at Gatwick) Limited had 38 aircraft at 31 Dec. 2000. Other major airlines in 2000 (with numbers of aircraft): Air 2000 (27); Airtours International Airways Ltd (31); Britannia Airways (32); British Midland (45); British European (31), formerly Jersey European Airways (UK); KLM UK (38); Manx Airlines/British Regional Airlines (49); Virgin Atlantic (32). According to CAA airline statistics, in 2000–01 British Airways flew 601·4m. km and carried 35,335,602 passengers (26,283,992 on international flights in 1998, out of 31,152,382 passengers carried). Virgin Atlantic ranked second on the basis of aircraft-km flown (115·8m. km) and Britannia Airways second on the basis of passengers carried (8,058,769). British Airways carried more passengers on international flights in 2000 than any other airline. In recent years low-cost airlines such as Ryanair and easyJet have become increasingly popular. Serving only domestic and European destinations, they recovered quickly from the slump of the airline business following the attacks on New York and Washington on 11 Sept. 2001.

The most frequently flown route into and out of the UK in 2001 was Heathrow–New York John F. Kennedy and vice-versa (2,325,539 passengers), followed by Heathrow–Amsterdam and vice-versa (2,136,733) and Heathrow–Paris Charles de Gaulle and vice-versa (2,120,079).

Shipping. The UK-owned merchant fleet (trading vessels over 100 GT) in June 2001 totalled 612 ships of 12·0m. DWT and 9·4m. GT. The UK-owned and registered fleet totalled 369 ships of 3·2m. DWT.

The average age (DWT) of the UK-owned fleet was 10·2 years, while that of the world fleet was 13·3 years. Total gross international revenue in 2000 was £5,122m. The net direct contribution to the UK balance of payments was £1,435m.; there were import savings of £1,830m., giving a total contribution of £3,266m.

The principal ports are (with 1m. tonnes of cargo handled in 2001): Grimsby and Immingham (54·8), Tees and Hartlepool (50·8), London (50·7), Forth (41·6), Southampton (35·4). Total traffic in 2001 was 566·4m. tonnes.

Inland Waterways. There are approximately 3,500 miles (5,630 km) of navigable canals and river navigations in Great Britain. Of these, the publicly-owned British Waterways (BW) is responsible for some 385 miles (620 km) of commercial waterways (maintained for freight traffic) and some 1,160 miles (1,868 km) of cruising waterways (maintained for pleasure cruising, fishing and amenity). BW is also responsible for a further 450 miles (732 km) of canals, some of which are not navigable. BW's direct income for the year to 31 March 2002 was £111·0m. This comprised principally: income for externally funded restoration schemes (£43·0m.), leisure (£19·9m.), the estate (£28·8m.) and commercial uses (£11·8m.). Additionally, British Waterways was in receipt of grants from the Department of the Environment, Food and Rural Affairs of £64·6m.

River navigations and canals managed by other authorities include the Thames, Great Ouse and Nene, Norfolk Broads and Manchester Ship Canal.

The Association of Inland Navigation Authorities (AINA) represents some 30 navigation authorities providing an almost complete UK coverage.

Telecommunications. In 1997 there were 148 licensed telecommunications operators: 125 cable operators, 19 national and regional public telecommunications operators and, in 2003, five mobile phone operators. Fixed-link telephone services were offered by BT, Mercury Communications, Kingston Communications (Hull), most of the cable operators and the public telecommunications operators. BT (then British Telecom) was established in 1981 to take over the management of telecommunications from the Post Office. In 1984 it was privatized as British Telecommunications plc, changing its trading name from British Telecom to BT in 1991.

In 1998 all of the BT system was served by digital exchanges. There are almost 3·5m. km of optical fibre in place. In 2000 there were 35,177,000 main telephone lines (equivalent to 588·6 per 1,000 population). In 1996, 76% of the lines were residential and 24% business. There were 138,000 public payphones and 200,000 private rented payphones in 1996. BT handles a daily average of 103m. telephone calls a day and 22m. calls to emergency fire, police or ambulance services a year.

In 1996 there were 1·99m. fax receivers. There were still 20,000 telex subscribers in 1996, although telex usage has declined considerably in recent years. Electronic services include electronic mail ('email') and a complete corporate global messaging network. BT telephone, television and business services are carried by 15–20 satellites. In 1995 BT had some 20 offices worldwide and employed 137,561 persons.

In Nov. 2001 there were 43·45m. mobile telephone subscribers in the UK. Orange was the largest operator, with 12·12m. customers, followed by BT Cellnet (now O2) with 11·02m., Vodafone with 10·76m. and One2One (now T-Mobile) with 9·52m. At the beginning of 1999 there had been 13m. mobile phone subscribers. Virgin Mobile, launched in Nov. 1999, had 650,000 subscribers by Nov. 2001. 3 was launched by Hutchison on 3 March 2003 and is the UK's first mainland third generation mobile network.

Telecommunications services are regulated by OFTEL in the interests of consumers.

Internet. In Sept. 2002 there were 34·3m. Internet users in the UK (more than in any other country in Europe), just over 57% of the total population. According to a survey published in Dec. 1999, 3·6m. children between the ages of 7 and 16 used the Internet, with 52% of users being boys, compared to 61% in March 1999. In Oct. 1998, 42% of users were at home and 38% at work. In 2000, 45% of households had a home computer; there were 20·2m. PCs in total in 2000 (33·8 per 1,000 inhabitants).

Postal Services. Royal Mail Group plc operates three distinct businesses: Royal Mail (letter delivery), Parcelforce Worldwide (parcel delivery) and Post Office Ltd (retailing and agency services). Every area of the country is served by regional offices for each of the businesses. Royal Mail collects and delivers 82m. letters a day to the 27m. UK addresses. Other services include electronic mail, guaranteed mail deliveries (same-day and overnight to UK addresses), and Swiftair deliveries to 140 other countries and territories. The British Postal Consultancy Service provides advice to administrations abroad.

In 2002 there were almost 17,500 post offices, around 600 operated directly by Post Office Ltd, the remainder (sub-post offices) on a franchise or agency basis, and 120,000 posting points. Staff numbered 200,000 in 2001–02.

SOCIAL INSTITUTIONS

Justice. *England and Wales.* The legal system of England and Wales, divided into civil and criminal courts, has at the head of the superior courts, as the ultimate court of appeal, the House of Lords, which hears each year a number of appeals in civil matters, including a certain number from Scotland and Northern Ireland, as well as some appeals in criminal cases. In order that civil cases may go from the Court of Appeal to the House of Lords, it is necessary to obtain the leave of either the Court of Appeal or the House itself, although in certain cases an appeal may lie direct to the House of Lords from the decision of the High Court. An appeal can be brought from a decision of the Court of Appeal or the Divisional Court of the Queen's Bench Division of the High Court in a criminal case provided that the Court is satisfied that a point of law 'of general public importance' is involved, and either the Court or the House of Lords is of the opinion that it is in the public interest that a further appeal should be brought. As a judicial body, the House of Lords consists of the Lord Chancellor, the Lords of Appeal in Ordinary, commonly called Law Lords, and such other members of the House as hold or have held high judicial office. The final court of appeal for certain of the Commonwealth countries is the Judicial Committee of the Privy Council which, in addition to Privy Counsellors who are or have held high judicial office in the UK, includes others who are or have been Chief Justices or Judges of the Superior Courts of Commonwealth countries.

Civil Law. The main courts of original civil jurisdiction are the High Court and county courts.

The High Court has exclusive jurisdiction to deal with specialist classes of case e.g. judicial review. It has concurrent jurisdiction with county courts in cases involving contract and tort although it will only hear those cases where the issues are complex or important. The High Court also has appellate jurisdiction to hear appeals from lower tribunals.

The judges of the High Court are attached to one of its three divisions: Chancery, Queen's Bench and Family; each with its separate field of jurisdiction. The Heads of the three divisions are the Lord Chief Justice (Queen's Bench), the Vice-Chancellor (Chancery) and the President of the Family Division. In addition there are 99 High Court judges (92 men and 7 women). For the hearing of cases at first instance, High Court judges sit singly. Appellate jurisdiction is usually exercised by Divisional Courts consisting of two (sometimes three) judges, though in certain circumstances a judge sitting alone may hear the appeal. High Court business is dealt with in the Royal Courts of Justice and by over 130 District Registries outside London.

County courts can deal with all contract and tort cases, and recovery of land actions, regardless of value. They have upper financial limits to deal with specialist classes of business such as equity and Admiralty cases. Certain county courts have been designated to deal with family, bankruptcy, patents and discrimination cases.

There are about 230 county courts located throughout the country, each with its own district. A case may be heard by a circuit judge or by a district judge. Defended claims are allocated to one of three tracks—the small claims track, the fast track and the multi-track. The small claims track provides a simple and informal procedure for resolving disputes, mainly in claims for debt, where the value of the claim is no more than £5,000. Parties should be able to do this without the need for a solicitor. Other claims valued between £5,000 and £15,000 will generally be allocated to the fast track, and higher valued claims which could not be dealt with justly in the fast track may be allocated to the multi-track.

The Restrictive Practices Court was set up in 1956 under the Restrictive Trade Practices Act and is responsible for deciding whether a restrictive trade agreement is in the public interest. It is presided over by a High Court judge, but laymen sit on the bench also. Another specialist court is the Employment Appeal Tribunal, with similar composition, which hears appeals in employment cases from lower tribunals.

The Court of Appeal (Civil Division) hears appeals in civil actions from the High Court and county courts, and certain special courts such as the Restrictive Practice Court and Employment Appeal Tribunal. Its President is the Master of the Rolls, aided by up to 35 Lords Justices of Appeal (as at 1 Jan. 2003) sitting in six or seven divisions of two or three judges each.

Civil proceedings are instituted by the aggrieved person, but as they are a private matter, they are frequently settled by the parties through their lawyers before the matter comes to trial. In very limited classes of dispute (e.g. libel and slander), a party may request a jury to sit to decide questions of fact and the award of damages.

Criminal Law. At the base of the system of criminal courts in England and Wales are the magistrates' courts which deal with over 96% of criminal cases. In general, in exercising their summary jurisdiction, they have power to pass a sentence of up to six months imprisonment and to impose a fine of up to £5,000 on any one offence. They also deal with the preliminary hearing of cases triable at the Crown Court. In addition to dealing summarily with over 2·0m. cases, which include thefts, assaults, drug abuse, etc., they also have a limited civil and family jurisdiction.

Magistrates' courts normally sit with a bench of three lay justices. Although unpaid they are entitled to loss of earnings and travel and subsistence allowance. They undergo training after appointment and they are advised by a professional justices' clerk. In central London and in some provincial areas full-time stipendiary magistrates have been appointed. Generally they possess the same powers as the lay bench, but they sit alone. On 1 Jan. 2000 the total strength of the lay magistracy was 30,308 including 14,764 women. Justices are appointed on behalf of the Queen by the Lord Chancellor, except in Greater Manchester, Merseyside and Lancashire, where they are appointed by the Chancellor of the Duchy of Lancaster.

Justices are selected and trained specially to sit in Youth and Family Proceedings Courts. Youth Courts deal with cases involving children and young persons up to the age of 18 charged with criminal offences (other than homicide and other grave offences). These courts normally sit with three justices, including at least one man and one woman, and are accommodated separately from other courts.

Family Proceedings Courts deal with matrimonial applications and Children Act matters, including care, residence and contact and adoption. These courts normally sit with three justices including at least one man and one woman.

Above the magistrates' courts is the Crown Court. This was set up by the Courts Act 1971 to replace quarter sessions and assizes. Unlike quarter sessions and assizes, which were individual courts, the Crown Court is a single court which is capable of sitting anywhere in England and Wales. It has power to deal with all trials on indictment and has inherited the jurisdiction of quarter sessions to hear appeals, proceedings on committal of persons from the magistrates' courts for sentence, and certain original proceedings on civil matters under individual statutes.

The jurisdiction of the Crown Court is exercisable by a High Court judge, a Circuit judge or a Recorder or Assistant Recorder (part-time judges) sitting alone, or, in specified circumstances, with justices of the peace. The Lord Chief Justice has given directions as to the types of case to be allocated to High Court judges (the more serious cases) and to Circuit judges or Recorders respectively.

Appeals from magistrates' courts go either to a Divisional Court of the High Court (when a point of law alone is involved) or to the Crown Court where there is a complete re-hearing on appeals against conviction and/or sentence. Appeals from the Crown Court in cases tried on indictment lie to the Court of Appeal (Criminal Division). Appeals on questions of law go by right, and appeals on other matters by leave. The Lord Chief Justice or a Lord Justice sits with judges of the High Court to constitute this court. Thereafter, appeals in England and Wales can be made to the House of Lords.

There remains as a last resort the invocation of the royal prerogative exercised on the advice of the Home Secretary. In 1965 the death penalty was abolished for murder and abolished for all crimes in 1998.

All contested criminal trials, except those which come before the magistrates' courts, are tried by a judge and a jury consisting of 12 members. The prosecution or defence may challenge any potential juror for cause. The jury decides whether the accused is guilty or not. The judge is responsible for summing up on the facts and explaining the law; he sentences convicted offenders. If, after at least two hours and ten minutes of deliberation, a jury is unable to reach a unanimous verdict it may, on the judge's direction, provided that in a full jury of 12 at least ten of its members are agreed, bring in a majority verdict. The failure of a jury to agree on a unanimous verdict or to bring in a majority verdict may involve the retrial of the case before a new jury.

The Employment Appeal Tribunal. The Employment Appeal Tribunal, which is a superior Court of Record with the like powers, rights, privileges and authority of the High Court, was set up in 1976 to hear appeals on questions of law against decisions of employment tribunals and of the Certification Officer. The appeals are heard by a High Court Judge sitting with two members (in exceptional cases four) appointed for their special knowledge or experience of industrial relations either on the employer or the trade union side, with always an equal number on each side. The great bulk of their work is concerned with the problems which can arise between employees and their employers.

Military Courts. Offences committed by persons subject to service law under the Army Act 1955, the Air Force Act 1955 or the Naval Discipline Act 1957 may be dealt with either summarily or by courts-martial.

The Personnel of the Law. All judicial officers are independent of Parliament and the Executive. They are appointed by the Crown on the advice of the Prime Minister or the Lord Chancellor, and hold office until retiring age. Under the Judicial Pensions and Retirement Act 1993 judges normally retire by age 70 years.

The legal profession is divided; barristers, who advise on legal problems and can conduct cases before all courts, usually act for the public only through solicitors, who deal directly with the legal business brought to them by the public and have rights to present cases before certain courts. The distinction between the two branches of the profession has been weakened since the passing of the Courts and Legal Services Act 1990, which has enabled solicitors to obtain the right to appear as advocates before all courts. Long-standing members of both professions are eligible for appointment to most judicial offices.

For all judicial appointments up to and including the level of Circuit Judge (except for Recordership, which is achieved on promotion from assistant Recordership), it is necessary to apply in writing to be considered for appointment. Vacancies are advertised. A panel consisting of a judge, an official and a lay member decide whom to invite for interview and also interview the shortlisted applicants. They make recommendations to the Lord Chancellor, who retains the right of final recommendation to the Sovereign or appointment, as appropriate.

Legal Services. The system of legal aid in England and Wales was established after the Second World War under the Legal Aid and Advice Act 1949. The Legal Aid Board was then set up under the Legal Aid Act 1988, and took over the administration of legal aid from the Law Society in 1989. The Legal Services Commission (LSC) was set up under the Access to Justice Act 1999 and replaced the Legal Aid Board on 1 April 2000. The LSC is an executive non-departmental public body. It comprises a Chair and ten members, all appointed by the Lord

Chancellor. It is responsible for the development and administration of two schemes in England and Wales: the *Community Legal Service*, which from 1 April 2000 replaced the old civil scheme of legal aid, bringing together networks of funders and suppliers into partnerships to provide the widest possible access to information and advice; and the *Criminal Defence Service*, which from 2 April 2001 replaced the old system of criminal legal aid and provides criminal services to people accused of crimes. Only organizations with a contract with the LSC are able to provide advice or representation funded by the LSC.

Under the Community Legal Service, which improves access to justice for those most in need, the LSC directly funds legal services for eligible clients. Some solicitors are prepared to give a free or low-cost initial interview whether or not the client qualifies for funding. The different levels of service in civil matters are *Legal Help, Help at Court, Approved Family Help, Family Mediation, Legal Representation*, and *Support Funding*. Approved Family Help is available in two forms (*Help with Mediation* and *General Family Help*), as are Legal Representation (*Investigative Help* and *Full Representation*) and Support Funding (*Investigative Support* and *Litigation Support*).

The purpose of the Criminal Defence Service is to ensure that people suspected or accused of a crime have access to advice, assistance and representation, as the interests of justice require. The different levels of service are *Advice and Assistance, Advocacy Assistance* and *Representation*. Advice and Assistance covers help from a solicitor including giving general advice, writing letters, negotiating, getting a barrister's opinion and preparing a written case. Advocacy Assistance covers the cost of a solicitor preparing a client's case and initial representation in certain proceedings in both the magistrates' court and the crown court. Representation covers the cost of a solicitor to prepare a client's defence before a court appearance and to represent the client there, including dealing with issues such as bail.

In 2001–02 the Commission received funding of £1·2bn. with which to fund the provision of services and spent £71·6m. on administration costs. Community Legal Services payments in 2001–02 came to £734·5m. (1,005,000 acts of assistance) and net Criminal Defence Services payments to £508·3m. (1,697,200 acts of assistance), giving net Legal Services Commission payments of £1,242·8m. and a total of 2,702,200 acts of assistance.

Police. In England and Wales there are 43 police forces, each maintained by a police authority typically comprising nine local councillors, three magistrates and five independent members. London is policed by the Metropolitan Police Service (responsible to the 23-member Metropolitan Police Authority, 12 of whom are members of the Greater London Assembly) and the City of London Police (whose police authority is the City of London Corporation). In Scotland the unitary councils are the police authorities.

Figures show that the total strength of the police service in England and Wales at 31 March 2002 was 129,603 (including 23,089 women). In addition there were 11,598 special constables (including 3,584 women). Total provision for policing in England and Wales to be supported by grant in 2003–04 is £9,683m. This is a cash increase of £566m. over 2002–03, or 6·2%, and builds on substantial government investment in the Police Service over the past three years.

See also SCOTLAND.

CIVIL JUDICIAL STATISTICS

ENGLAND AND WALES	1999
Appellate Courts	
Judicial Committee of the Privy Council	64
House of Lords	76
Court of Appeal	1,127
High Court of Justice (appeals and special cases from inferior courts)	5,080
Courts of First Instance (excluding Magistrates'	
Courts and Tribunals)	
High Court of Justice:	
Chancery Division	37,281
Queen's Bench Division	72,161

Courts of First Instance (excluding Magistrates'
  Courts and Tribunals)
County courts: Matrimonial suits   167,775
County courts: Other   2,000,357
Restrictive Practices Court   4

CRIMINAL STATISTICS
ENGLAND AND WALES

	Total number of offenders[1]		Indictable offences[1]	
	2000	2001	2000	2001
Aged 10 and over				
Proceeded against in magistrates' courts	1,904,677	1,837,733	491,822	500,912
Found guilty at magistrates' courts	1,367,304	1,293,308	271,624	270,425
Found guilty at the Crown Court	56,398	56,365	53,890	53,782
Cautioned	238,978	229,858	150,899	143,929
Aged 10 and under 18				
Proceeded against in magistrates' courts	141,689	150,067	81,457	84,485
Found guilty at magistrates' courts	87,719	92,172	45,625	47,061
Found guilty at the Crown Court	3,704	3,358	3,566	3,244
Cautioned	97,541	98,042	64,336	63,505

[1]On the principal offence basis.

In the year to March 2002 crimes recorded by the police in England and Wales totalled 5·5m, an increase of 7% compared to the year to March 2001, although it is thought that most of the increase is owing to changes in recording practices. 82% of all crimes were against property. In the 12 months ending March 2001 a total of 5·2m. offences were recorded by the police in England and Wales. In Nov. 2002 the prison population in England and Wales was 72,272 (68,452 in Nov. 2001). In 2001 the incarceration rate of 127 people per 100,000 inhabitants was the second highest in western Europe after Portugal. The annual average prison population rose 58% between 1992 and 2002, but the recorded crime level went up by only 18%. During this time the female prison population rose by 174%, from 1,560 to 4,280, but the male prison population only rose by 53%. These figures do not include prisoners held in police cells.

See also SCOTLAND *and* NORTHERN IRELAND.

Religion. The Anglican Communion has originated from the Church of England and parallels in its fellowship of autonomous churches the evolution of British influence beyond the seas from colonies to dominions and independent nations. The Archbishop of Canterbury presides as *primus inter pares* at the decennial meetings of the bishops of the Anglican Communion at the Lambeth Conference and at the biennial meetings of the Primates and the Anglican Consultative Council. The last Conference was held in Canterbury in 1998 and was attended by 743 bishops. Anglican membership in Britain in 2000 numbered 1·6m., compared to 3·5m. in 1950.

The Anglican Communion consists of 38 member Churches. These are: The Anglican Church of Aotearoa, New Zealand and Polynesia; The Anglican Church of Australia; The Church of Bangladesh; The Episcopal Anglican Church of Brazil; The Church of the Province of Burundi; The Anglican Church of Canada; The Church of the Province of Central Africa; The Anglican Church of the Central America Region; The Province of the Anglican Church of the Congo; The Church of England; Hong Kong Sheng Kung Hui; The Church of the Province of the Indian Ocean; The Church of Ireland; Nippon Sei Ko Kai; The Episcopal Church in Jerusalem and the Middle East; The Church of the Province of Kenya; The Anglican Church of Korea; The Church of the Province of Melanesia; The Anglican Church of Mexico; The Church of the Province of Myanmar (Burma); The Church of the Province of Nigeria; The Church of North India; The Church of Pakistan; The Anglican Church of Papua New Guinea; The Philippine Episcopal Church; The Province of the Episcopal Church of Rwanda; The Scottish Episcopal Church; The Church of the Province of South East Asia; The Church of the Province of Southern Africa; The Anglican Church of the Southern Cone of America; The Church of South India; The Episcopal Church of the Sudan; The Church of the Province of Tanzania; The Church of the Province of Uganda; The Episcopal Church in the United States of America; The Church in Wales; The Church of the Province of West Africa; and The Church in the Province of the West Indies. There are Extra Provincial Dioceses of Bermuda, Cuba, Portugal, Puerto Rico, Spain, Sri Lanka and

Venezuela, and new provinces are also currently in formation. Churches in Communion include the Mar Thoma Syrian Church, the Philippine Independent Church, and some Lutheran and Old Catholic Churches in Europe. The Church in China is known as a 'post denominational' Church whose formation included Anglicans in the Holy Catholic Church in China.

England and Wales. The established Church of England, which baptizes about 20% of the children born in England (i.e. excluding Wales but including the Isle of Man and the Channel Islands), is Anglican. Civil disabilities on account of religion do not attach to any class of British subject. Under the Welsh Church Acts, 1914 and 1919, the Church in Wales and Monmouthshire was disestablished as from 1 April 1920, and Wales was formed into a separate Province.

The Queen is, under God, the supreme governor of the Church of England, with the right, regulated by statute, to nominate to the vacant archbishoprics and bishoprics. The Queen, on the advice of the First Lord of the Treasury, also appoints to such deaneries, prebendaries and canonries as are in the gift of the Crown, while a large number of livings and also some canonries are in the gift of the Lord Chancellor.

There are two archbishops (at the head of the two Provinces of Canterbury and York), and 42 diocesan bishops including the bishop of the diocese in Europe, which is part of the Province of Canterbury. Dr Rowan Williams was enthroned as *Archbishop of Canterbury* in Feb. 2003. Each archbishop has also his own particular diocese, wherein he exercises episcopal, as in his Province he exercises metropolitan, jurisdiction. In Dec. 2001 there were 64 suffragan and assistant bishops, 36 deans and provosts of cathedrals and 114 archdeacons. The *General Synod*, which replaced the Church Assembly in 1970 in England, consists of a House of Bishops, a House of Clergy and a House of Laity, and has power to frame legislation regarding Church matters. The first two Houses consist of the members of the Convocations of Canterbury and York, each of which consists of the diocesan bishops and elected representatives of the suffragan bishops, six for Canterbury province and three for York (forming an Upper House); deans and archdeacons, and a certain number of proctors elected as the representatives of the priests and deacons in each diocese, together with, in the case of Canterbury Convocation, four representatives of the Universities of Oxford, Cambridge, London and the Southern Universities, and in the case of York two representatives of the Universities of Durham and Newcastle and the other Northern Universities, and three archdeacons to the Armed Forces, the Chaplain General of Prisons and two representatives of the Religious Communities (forming the Lower House). The House of Laity is elected by the lay members of the Deanery Synods but also includes three representatives of the Religious Communities. The Houses of Clergy and Laity also include a small number of *ex officio* members. Every Measure passed by the General Synod must be submitted to the Ecclesiastical Committee, consisting of 15 members of the House of Lords nominated by the Lord Chancellor and 15 members of the House of Commons nominated by the Speaker. This committee reports on each Measure to Parliament, and the Measure receives the Royal Assent and becomes law if each House of Parliament resolves that the Measure be presented to the Queen.

Parochial affairs are managed by annual parochial church meetings and parochial church councils. In 2001 there were 13,000 ecclesiastical parishes, inclusive of the Isle of Man and the Channel Islands. These parishes do not, in many cases, coincide with civil parishes. Although most parishes have their own churches, not every parish nowadays can have its own incumbent or priest. About 2,000 non-stipendiary clergy hold a bishop's licence to officiate at services.

In 2001 there were 5,161 incumbents excluding dignitaries, 1,993 other clergy of incumbent status and 1,498 assistant curates working in the parishes.

Women have been admitted to Holy Orders (but not the Episcopate) as deacons since 1987 and as priests since 1994. At 31 Dec. 2001 there were 1,194 full-time stipendiary women clergy, 1,125 of whom were in the parochial ministry. Between 1993 and 2001, 487 clergymen resigned because they disagreed with the ordination of women. 64 clergymen subsequently re-entered the Church of England ministry and of the 487 who resigned, 258 are known to have joined the Roman Catholic Church and 29 the Orthodox Church.

Private persons possess the right of presentation to over 2,000 benefices; the patronage of the others belongs mainly to the Queen, the bishops and cathedrals, the Lord Chancellor, and the colleges of the universities of Oxford and Cambridge. In addition to the dignitaries and parochial clergy already identified there were, in 2001, 114 cathedral and 330 full-time non-parochial clergy working within the diocesan framework, giving a total of 9,352 full-time stipendiary clergy working within the diocesan framework as at Dec. 2001. In addition there were over 200 part-time stipendiary clergy. Although these figures account for the majority of active clergy in England, there are many others serving in parishes and institutions who cannot be quantified with any certainty. They include some 1,100 full-time hospital, Forces, prison, industrial, and school and college chaplains.

Of the 40,609 buildings registered for the solemnization of marriages at 30 June 2000 (statistics from the Office of National Statistics), 16,481 belonged to the Church of England and the Church in Wales, and 24,128 to other religious denominations (Methodist, 6,641; Roman Catholic, 3,342; Baptist, 3,109; United Reformed, 1,675; Congregational, 1,257; Calvinistic Methodist, 1,084; Jehovah's Witnesses, 817; Brethren, 742; Salvation Army, 751; Unitarians, 165; other Christian, 4,095; Sikhs, 147; Muslims, 127; other non-Christian, 176). Of the 267,961 marriages celebrated in 2000 (331,150 in 1990), 65,536 were in the Established Church and the Church in Wales (115,328 in 1990), 31,625 in other denominations (43,837 in 1990), and 170,800 were civil marriages in Register Offices (156,875 in 1990).

Roman Catholics in England and Wales were estimated at 4,121,004 in 2000. There are 22 dioceses in five provinces and one Bishopric of the Forces (also covers Scotland). Cormac Murphy O'Connor was installed as *Archbishop of Westminster* in March 2000. He was created a Cardinal in Feb. 2001. There are 5 archbishops, 17 other diocesan bishops and 7 auxiliary or assistant bishops. There are 5,429 priests in active ministry and 2,814 parish churches. There are 1,260 convents of female religious, who number 8,656.

Membership of other denominations in the UK in 1991 (and 1975): Presbyterians, 1,291,672 (1·65m.); Methodists, 483,387 (0·61m.); Baptists, 241,842 (0·27m.); other Protestants, 123,677; independent churches, 408,999; Orthodox, 265,258 (0·2m.); Afro-Caribbean churches, 69,658; Latter-day Saints (Mormons) (1998), 173,800; Jehovah's Witnesses, 0·12m.; Spiritualists, 60,000; Muslims, 0·99m. (0·4m.); Sikhs, 0·39m. (0·12m.); Hindus, 0·14m. (0·1m.); Jews, 108,400 (0·11m.).

In 2001 for the first time the census asked an optional question about religion. In England and Wales 37·3m. people described themselves as Christian. In England, 3·1% of the population stated their religion as Muslim, 1·1% Hindu, 0·7% Sikh, 0·5% Jewish and 0·3% Buddhist. In Wales, 0·7% of the population stated their religion as Muslim, 0·2% Hindu, 0·1% Sikh, 0·1% Jewish and 0·2% Buddhist. In England and Wales 7·7m. people said they had no religion (14·6% in England and 18·5% in Wales). Just over 4m. people chose not to answer the religion question.

In Scotland the 2001 census asked two questions on religion—religion of upbringing and current religion. For religion of upbringing, the largest groups were Church of Scotland (47%), no religion (18%) and Roman Catholic (17%). The equivalent percentages for current religion were 42%, 28% and 16%.

Across all denominations, adult church attendance in the UK was less than 8% of the population in 2000.

The Salvation Army is established in 94 countries. In 1991 in the UK and Ireland it had 1,792 ministers, 55,000 members and 837 churches.

There is a 400-member Board of Deputies of British Jews.

There were approximately 2·5m. visits to Westminster Abbey in 1997, 2m. to both St Paul's Cathedral and York Minster, and 1·6m. to Canterbury Cathedral.

See also SCOTLAND *and* NORTHERN IRELAND.

Bradley, I., *Marching to the Promised Land: Has the Church a Future?* London, 1992.
De La Noy, M., *The Church of England: a Portrait.* London, 1993.

Education. 'Around a fifth of working age adults in England have a low level of literacy (capable of reading but with little understanding) or a very low level (struggling with the simplest text). Up to a quarter have very low levels of numeracy (unable to perform the simplest calculations) and a further quarter a low level (unable to handle fractions or percentages with any confidence)'. (*A Fresh Start. Improving Literacy and Numeracy*—Report of the working group chaired by Sir Claus Moser published in 1999). In response to the recommendations in the Moser report, the government established the Adult Basic Skills Strategy Unit to drive forward adult literacy and numeracy.

The Publicly Maintained System of Education. Compulsory schooling begins at the age of 5 (4 in Northern Ireland) and the minimum leaving age for all pupils is 16. No tuition fees are payable in any publicly maintained school (but it is open to parents, if they choose, to pay for their children to attend other schools—completely outside the public sector are independent schools run by individuals, companies or charitable institutions). The post-school or tertiary stage, which is voluntary, includes universities, further education establishments and other higher education establishments (including those which provide courses for the training of teachers), as well as adult education and the youth service. Financial assistance (grants and loans) is generally available to students on higher education courses in the university and non-university sectors, and to some students on other courses in further education.

National Curriculum. The National Curriculum for England was revised in 1999. Statutory subjects at ages 5–11 (Key stages 1 and 2) are English, mathematics, science (core subjects), design and technology, information and communication technology, history, geography, art, music and PE. At 11–14 a modern foreign language and citizenship are added. Statutory subjects at 14–16 are English, mathematics, science, design technology, a foreign language and physical education. Religious education and, at secondary level, sex education, are not prescribed in the curriculum but are requirements; parents may withdraw their children from these lessons. Careers and personal, social and health education are also statutory at secondary level.

Early Years Education. Early years education services encompass a wide range of different providers, including: state nursery schools, nursery classes in primary schools and reception classes; private, voluntary and independent sector nursery schools; and childminder networks. There are 35,000 settings in the state private and voluntary sectors delivering the government's early education curriculum. Since Sept. 1998 there has been a free early education place for all 4-year-olds and by Sept. 2004, every 3-year-old will enjoy this entitlement. At March 2002, 66% of 3-year-olds group were able to enjoy a free early education place.

Primary Schools. These provide compulsory education for pupils from the age of five up to the age of 11 (12 in Scotland). Most public sector primary schools take both boys and girls in mixed classes. Some pre-compulsory age pupils attend nursery classes within primary schools, however, and in England some middle schools cater for pupils at either side of the secondary education transition age. In 2000–01 there were 22 pupils per teacher at primary schools in Great Britain as a whole, and there were 21,978 public sector mainstream primary schools.

Middle Schools. A number of local education authorities in England operate a middle school system. These provide for pupils from the age of 8, 9 or 10 up to the age of 12, 13 or 14, and are deemed either primary or secondary according to the age range of the pupils.

Secondary Schools. These usually provide for pupils from the age of 11 upwards and in 2000–01 there were 4,099 secondary schools in Great Britain. Some local authorities have retained selection at age 11 for entry to grammar schools, of which there were 159 (in England) in 2000–01. There were 145 secondary modern schools in 2000–01 providing a general education up to the minimum school leaving age of 16, although exceptionally some pupils stay on beyond that age. In public sector mainstream secondary schools in Great Britain in 2000–01 there were an average 17 pupils per teacher.

Almost all local education authorities operate a system of comprehensive schools to which pupils are admitted without reference to ability or aptitude. In 2000–01 there were 3,443 such schools in Great Britain with over 3·3m. pupils. With the development of comprehensive education, various patterns of secondary schools have come into operation. Principally these are: 1) All-through schools with pupils aged 11 to 18 or 11 to 16; pupils over 16 being able to transfer to an 11 to 18 school or a sixth form college providing for pupils aged 16 to 19. (Since 1 April 1993, sixth form colleges have been part of the further education sector—there were 105 sixth form colleges in England in 2000–01). 2) Local education authorities operating a three-tier system involving middle schools where transfer to secondary school is at ages 12, 13 or 14. These correspond to 12 to 18, 13 to 18 and 14 to 18 comprehensive schools respectively. 3) In areas where there are no middle schools a two-tier system of junior and senior comprehensive schools for pupils aged 11 to 18, with optional transfer to these schools at age 13 or 14.

Specialist Schools. Business and Enterprise Colleges, Mathematics and Computing Colleges, Science Colleges, Engineering Colleges, Technology Colleges, Language Colleges, Art Colleges and Sports Colleges. A programme to help existing maintained secondary schools to specialize in a particular area of the curriculum, while continuing to cover the full National Curriculum. To be included in the programme, schools must raise sponsorship and then prepare development plans, in competition with other schools, to seek extra government funding. They must demonstrate how they will share their resources and expertise with local schools and the wider community. The first Technology Colleges operated from Sept. 1994. By Sept. 2001 there were 685 Specialist Schools in England. The government's latest target is for 1,500 by Sept. 2005, 46% of secondary schools.

City Technology Colleges. 15 independent all-ability secondary schools established in partnership between government and business sponsors, under the Education Reform Act 1988. They teach the full National Curriculum but give special emphasis to technology, science and mathematics. Government meets all recurrent costs. Sponsors are required to provide a 20% contribution towards the cost of all capital projects.

Assisted Places Scheme. The government is phasing out the assisted places scheme and is using the money saved to reduce infant class sizes in the maintained sector. The Education (Schools) Act 1997, which came into force on 1 Sept. 1997, has the effect of preventing any further intakes to assisted places after the start of the 1997–98 school year. However, the government has made a commitment to provide continued support for existing assisted pupils for the remainder of the current phase of their education. Children receiving secondary education will continue to hold their assisted places until the completion of their secondary education. Children receiving primary education will normally hold their place until the completion of their primary education. There is a discretionary power under the Act to allow some pupils to hold their assisted places for a further period in which they receive secondary education.

Music and Dance Scheme (formerly the Music and Ballet Scheme). The 'Aided Pupil Scheme' for boys and girls with outstanding talent in music or dance (principally ballet) helps parents with the fees and boarding costs at eight specialist private schools in England. This scheme provides a specialist provision not readily available in the maintained sector and will therefore continue to operate and develop further.

Special Education. Under the Education Act 1996 children have special educational needs if they have a learning difficulty which calls for special educational provision to be made for them. It has been estimated that, nationally, some 20% of the school population will have special educational needs at some time during their school career. In a minority of cases, perhaps just over 2% of children, the Local Education Authority will need to make a statutory assessment of special educational needs under the Education Act 1996, which may ultimately lead to a 'statement'. (In Scotland pupils are assessed for a Record of Needs.)

The Education Act 1996 and regulations made thereunder build upon the principles and practices first set out in the 1981 Education Act. They place duties and responsibilities on Local Education Authorities and schools, and all those who help them work with children with special educational needs. Maintained schools must use their best endeavours to make provision for such pupils. The Special Educational Needs Code of Practice, a revised version of which came into force on 1 Jan. 2002, replacing the original published in Sept. 1994, gives practical guidance to these bodies as to how they fulfil their duties. Provision for all children with special educational needs will be made by the most appropriate agency, which in most cases will be the child's mainstream school. The Code of Practice recognizes that there is a continuum of needs and a continuum of provision, which may be made in a variety of different forms. However, even before reaching statutory school age, a child may have special educational needs requiring the intervention of the Local Education as well as the Health Authority.

Some pupils with 'statements' remain in school after the age of 16. Local Education Authorities remain responsible for such pupils until they are 19. Others with statements leave school at 16, moving perhaps to a college within the further education sector, or to social services provision.

Ancillary Services. Local Education Authorities (LEAs) and governing bodies of schools that have a budgetary element for school meals delegated to them may provide registered pupils with meals, milk and other refreshment and make such charges as they think fit. However, they must charge the same price for the same quantity of the same item. It is for LEAs and governing bodies of schools, as described above, to decide on the presentation and content of school meals. They must provide meals free of charge to pupils whose parents receive income support, income-based Jobseekers' Allowance, or support provided under part VI of the Immigration and Asylum Act 1999. Pupils who receive income support or income-based jobseekers allowance in their own right are also entitled to receive free school meals. Where LEAs decide to provide milk, they have a duty to provide it free of charge to these categories of pupils.

Further Education (Non-University). Up to March 2001 further education (FE) courses in FE sector colleges in England and in Wales were largely funded through grants from the respective Further Education Funding Councils. In April 2001, however, the Learning and Skills Council (LSC) took over the responsibility for funding the FE sector in England, and the National Council for Education and Training for Wales (CETW) did so for Wales. The LSC is primarily responsible for funding full- and part-time education and training provision for people aged 16 to 19 in England delivered through the FE sector, including through FE colleges, sixth form colleges, work-based learning providers, and LEA maintained institutions. It also funds some higher education in FE sector colleges and since April 2002 has had responsibility for school sixth form funding. It also has a duty to secure provision for people age 19 and over, including basic skills provision, and adult and community learning.

Further education is the largest sector providing educational opportunities to the over 16s. There are 411 colleges in the further education sector in England, and 3·8m. students were enrolled in 2000–01. Of the students on Council funded provision, 18% were under 19 and 82% were adults.

In Wales, the National Council funds FE provision made by FE institutions via a third party or sponsored arrangements. The Scottish FEFC (SFEFC) funds FE colleges in Scotland, while the Department for Employment and Learning funds FE colleges in Northern Ireland.

The Youth Service. Youth Services provide informal personal and social education for young people. The priority age group for the service is 13–19 year olds, but the target age group may extend to 11–25 year olds in some cases. Provision is usually in the form of youth clubs and centres, or through 'detached' or outreach work aimed at young people at risk from alcohol or drug misuse, or of drifting into crime. There is an increasing emphasis on youth workers working with disaffected, and socially excluded, young people.

The statutory requirement for an LEA to provide a youth service is contained in section 508 of the Education Act, 1996. OFSTED inspect youth work using the *'Inspecting Youth Work: a revised framework for inspection,* June 2001'. Should an OFSTED inspection deem a youth service to be providing less than value for money the Secretary of State could couch in a direction which would achieve the desired result.

The Learning and Skills Act, 2000 gives the Secretary of State a new power to secure the provision of support for all 13–19 year olds for the purpose of encouraging and enabling young people to stay on and participate effectively in education and training.

Local Authority youth services receive Standard Spending Assessment through their Rate Support Grant to provide a local youth service. They are required to provide adequate facilities for further education including social, physical and recreational training and organized leisure time. These provisions cover the Youth Service. It is for individual authorities to decide how they discharge this requirement, taking into account a range of local factors and priorities.

The Youth Service has a key contribution to make to the Connexions Service and will bring expertise and a wide-ranging network to the Connexions Partnerships. Youth Service provision for 13–19 year olds is an integral part of the Connexions Service delivery.

Through its three-year cycle of funding to National Voluntary Youth Organisations (NVYOs), the Department for Education and Skills (DfES) aims to promote the personal and social education of young people. The level of grant for the period from April 1999–March 2002 was £12m. This scheme has been focused on two broad ministerial objectives: tackling social exclusion through targeting priority groups and raising the standard and quality of youth work. DfES' NVYO Grant Scheme is the only source of direct government support for the voluntary youth sector.

The current cycle of grants, to the headquarters of 81 national voluntary youth organisations, supports a total of 84 projects. This includes nine joint projects involving two or more organizations. The Scheme has already involved many thousands of young people in youth service activities for the first time and provides a very wide range of personal and social education programmes for young people.

The two key funding objectives—tackling social exclusion and raising the quality of youth work—are being retained for the Scheme's current three year cycle from 2002 to 2005. A key feature of the Scheme for 2002–05 is the encouragement of NVYOs to become involved with Connexions Partnerships.

The Connexions Service helps schools, colleges and all those involved with young people to make a step change in learning achievement—both formal and informal—for all teenagers, stretching the most gifted, raising aspirations and providing opportunities for all young people to achieve their potential. Connexions brings together all the services—public, voluntary or private sector—that young people need to make a smooth transition to adult life. It identifies and helps those who need additional support, when and where they need it. No young person is outside the scope of the Connexions Service, whatever their needs and regardless of the issues they have to address before they can take advantage of the opportunities available for learning and personal development. The Service began operating in England in April 2001. By the end of 2002–03 some £420m. was expected to have been invested in the Connexions Service across England.

Independent/State School Partnerships Grant Scheme. The aim of this scheme is to promote collaborative working between the independent and state school sectors to raise standards in education. In its first four years, 150 projects worth £3m. were funded. £450,000 of this was provided by the Sutton Trust, an educational charity established to provide educational opportunities for young people from non-privileged backgrounds. A further £200,000 was provided by John Beckwith, Chairman of Youth Sport Trust, and an anonymous donor, for projects focusing on Sport. £800,000 funding was available for 2002–03, and schools in England were invited to apply for funding.

Higher Education (HE) Student Support. Depending on their own, and their families' income, students are expected to make a contribution towards their tuition fees. The maximum that a student was expected to pay towards their tuition in 2002–03 was £1,100. In 2002–03 the annual income threshold at which fees start to be payable was set at £20,480. Consequently, it was expected that about 50% of all students would not have to pay any fees at all. In addition, students on courses of initial teacher training (other than first degrees), in the fifth or later years of medical and dental courses, and on NHS-funded courses in professions allied to medicine, pay no fees, whatever their and their family's income.

Loans are available to help with students' living costs. All students are entitled to 75% of the maximum loan, with the remaining quarter subject to income assessment. The maximum amounts of loan available to new students in 2002–03 were: £4,815 (living away from home and studying in London); £3,815 (living away from home and studying outside London); and £3,090 (living at home). These loans do not have to be repaid until the student has left university or college and is earning over £10,000 a year. They are repaid on what is known as an income contingent basis, set at 9% of gross income over £10,000 a year. This means that repayments rise and fall in line with income.

Help is also available to part-time students. Those on benefits or low incomes can apply to get their fees paid for them and may also be entitled to £500 loans for help with other course costs.

Applications for support in HE are made through Local Education Authorities. Students' loan accounts are managed by the Student Loans Company (SLC). Loan payments are made by the SLC direct to the student's bank account except for the first instalment each year, which is usually paid by cheque via the student's university or college.

Extra, non-repayable, help is targeted at certain students: those with disabilities; those with dependants; and those entering HE from low-income families in inner city areas. Help is also available from universities and colleges for those who get into financial difficulties as students. In 2001–02 the amount available to be distributed by universities and colleges to students in financial difficulties was £93m.

Opportunity Bursaries were introduced by the government in 2001–02 as part of the Excellence Challenge programme. For 2002–03 there were bursaries worth £2,000 each for 8,200 new and 6,580 continuing students from low-income families with little or no background in higher education.

Studentships and research grants are available for postgraduate courses from the Research Councils and the Arts and Humanities Research Board (AHRB). There are six Research Councils, five providing for science and technology and one funding economic and social sciences, who report to the Office of Science and Technology in the Department for Trade and Industry. They offer awards to students studying topics within the broad spectrum of agriculture and food; the biological sciences; man's natural environment; science and engineering and the social sciences. They offer three types of funding: advanced course studentships which are for masters level taught courses, usually of one year's duration, research masters training awards and standard research studentships, which are for PhD or MPhil students on programmes of up to three years full-time or five years part-time.

The AHRB also makes awards for postgraduate study and research. It funds studentships in the humanities for Masters and Doctoral programmes, as well as awards for students undertaking a range of professional or vocational training in a variety of arts and humanities subject areas. Both Research Council and AHRB funding is awarded on a competitive basis and securing a place on a course at a higher education institution does not in any way guarantee support. In 1999–2000 the six Research Councils granted 6,791 awards in total, while in the same year the AHRB made 1,592 awards. The British Academy seeks to complement the work of the AHRB and the Economic and Social Research Council by supporting individual scholars in providing small personal research grants, for amounts up to £5,000; postdoctoral fellowships; research readerships and professorships; grants with international programmes, including overseas exchange schemes; and support for conferences.

Many postgraduate students also look to the public sector for support and obtain loans from banks, seek sponsorship, receive help from educational trusts and charities, or pursue their studies on a part-time basis.

Career Development Loans (CDLs) were introduced in 1988 to provide adults with the opportunity to invest in their learning. CDLs are deferred repayment commercial bank loans specifically designed to help individuals acquire and improve vocational skills, and are aimed at those who would otherwise not have reasonable or adequate access to the funds required to learn. Loans of between £300 and £8,000 can be applied for to support up to two years of education or learning (plus up to one year's practical work experience where it forms part of the course). The Department for Education and Skills operates the programme in partnership with four high street banks (Barclays, The Co-operative, Clydesdale and the Royal Bank of Scotland). The Department for Education and Skills pays the interest on the loan for the period of supported learning and for up to one month afterwards. The individual then repays the loan to the bank in accordance with their loan agreement. Subject to certain conditions it may be possible for individuals to further defer their loan re-payments for up to 17 months.

By Jan. 2002 over £549m. had been advanced to over 160,000 applicants since the programme was launched.

Teachers. In order to teach in a maintained school or a non-maintained special school in England or Wales, it is normally first necessary to achieve qualified teacher status (QTS). This is generally achieved by successfully completing an undergraduate or postgraduate course of initial teacher training. Computerized skills tests in numeracy and literacy now form part of the requirements for QTS. Since May 2002 all trainees seeking QTS have had to pass a further test in information and communication technology (ICT). Newly qualified teachers in England are then required to satisfactorily complete an induction programme during their first year of teaching. There is no statutory induction programme in Wales.

Those who are recognized as qualified teachers in Scotland or Northern Ireland are also entitled to apply to the General Teaching Council for England or the General Teaching Council for Wales for qualified teacher status. Teachers who are nationals of participating member states of the European Economic Area who are recognized as qualified in their own countries may also be entitled to apply for qualified teacher status if they meet the requirements on the mutual recognition of qualifications.

Those who have trained overseas in a country outside of the European Economic Area can also gain qualified teacher status through special employment-based arrangements. Overseas-trained teachers with at least two years' teaching experience may be eligible for assessment against the induction and qualified teacher status standards at the same time without further training. Those who are successful are exempted from serving an induction period.

In addition, from Sept. 2000, a new, flexible, modular postgraduate route was introduced to allow trainees to receive more individualized teacher training that better matches their needs and circumstances. This training takes account of any prior learning and experience, and is broken up into flexible modules which trainees can undertake when convenient to them.

In 2000–01 there were about 50,500 students on initial teacher training courses; this figure includes students on the Open University and school-centred courses.

In 2000–01, 450,100 full-time equivalent teachers were employed in public sector maintained nursery, primary and secondary schools in Great Britain.

Finance. Total managed education and training expenditure by central and local government in the UK for the year ending 1999–2000 was £40·9bn. This equates to 4·5% of GDP. By the end of 2001–02 this was expected to rise to £49·7bn. (approximately 5% of GDP). By 2003–04 it is expected to rise to £58·1bn. (5·3% of GDP).

Independent Schools. All independent schools in England (and Wales) are required to be registered by the Department for Education and Skills (and the National Assembly for Wales). Just over half of all independent schools belong to an association affiliated to the Independent Schools Council (ISC). Independent schools which belong to an association affiliated to the Independent Schools Council are now subject to an inspection regime agreed between the government and the ISC. These arrangements provide for inspections which are broadly comparable with the OFSTED framework for inspections of maintained schools and to the same 6-year cycle. They result in publicly available reports which enable parents and others to have information about the general quality and standards achieved in ISC schools. Independent schools which belong to an association account for approximately 80% of the total independent school pupil population. Non-association schools will continue to be inspected by HM inspectors from OFSTED on a five–six year cycle.

The earliest of the schools were founded by, and attached to, medieval churches. Many were founded as 'grammar' (classical) schools in the 16th century, receiving charters from the reigning sovereign. Reformed mainly in the middle of the 19th century, among the best-known are Eton College, founded in 1440 by Henry VI; Winchester College (1394), founded by William of Wykeham, Bishop of Winchester; Harrow School, founded in 1560 as a grammar school by John Lyon, a yeoman; and Charterhouse (1611). Among the earliest foundations are King's School, Canterbury, founded 600; King's School, Rochester (604) and St Peter's, York (627).

Higher Education. Higher education has been through considerable changes over the last 30 years. In 2000–01 there were almost 2·1m. higher education students in the UK at some 90 universities, 60 higher education colleges or on higher education courses in further education colleges. The number of male and female students is roughly equal, although female students do now outnumber males. 25% of the UK population between the ages of 25 and 64 have been through tertiary education, compared to an OECD average of 22%.

Total revenue for higher education institutions was around £12·8bn. in 1999–2000. Approximately 60% of this comes from UK or European Union governments in the form of grants via the funding councils, public contributions to standard tuition fees and research grants and contracts. Higher education institutions are funded by four UK funding bodies, one each for England, Scotland, Wales and Northern Ireland. They are responsible to Parliament for higher education. Their roles include: allocating funds for teaching and research; promoting high-quality education and research; advising government on the needs of higher education; informing students about the quality of higher education available; and ensuring the proper use of public funds.

The *Open University* received its Royal Charter on 1 June 1969 and is an independent, self-governing institution, awarding its own degrees at undergraduate and postgraduate level. It is financed by the government through the HEFCE for all its students in England, Wales and Northern Ireland and through the Scottish HEFC for the teaching of its students in Scotland, and by the receipt of students' fees. At the heart of most courses is a series of specially produced textbooks or 'course units' (which are also widely used in the rest of the HE sector). They are closely integrated with a varying mix of set books, recommended reading, television programmes, audio and video tapes, home experiment kits, computer-based learning programmes, multimedia resources and network services. There are also 331 local tutorial centres where face-to-face tutorials may be offered. No formal qualifications are required for entry to undergraduate courses. Residents from most countries of Western Europe aged 18 or over may apply (though some courses are not available outside the UK). There are over 200 undergraduate courses; many are available on a one-off basis. In 2000–2001 there were over 134,000 undergraduates, and over 23,500 postgraduate level students. The university has some 4,000 full-time staff working at Milton Keynes and in 13 Regional Centres throughout the country. There are over 7,000 part-time associate lecturers.

One university is independent of the state system, the *University of Buckingham*, which opened in 1976 and received a Royal charter in 1983. It offers two-year courses towards its own honours degrees, the academic year commencing in Jan. or July and consisting of four ten-week terms. There are four areas of study: Business; Humanities; Law; and Sciences. In 1999 there were 583 full-time and 45 part-time undergraduate students and 79 full-time and 14 part-time postgraduate students. There were 75 teachers (3 part-time).

All universities charge fees, but financial help is available to students from several sources, and the majority of students receive some form of financial assistance.

See also SCOTLAND *and* NORTHERN IRELAND.

The British Council. The purpose of the British Council is to win recognition abroad for the UK's values, ideas and achievements, and to nurture lasting, mutually beneficial relationships with other countries. Established in 1934 and incorporated by Royal Charter in 1940, it is the UK's international organization for educational and cultural relations. An independent, non-political organization, it is represented in 109 countries, running a mix of offices, libraries, resource centres and English-teaching operations. Its headquarters are in London and Manchester, with further centres in Belfast, Cardiff and Edinburgh. The British Council's total revenue in 2000–01 was £430m. This was made up of government grants (£142m.), revenues from English-language teaching and client-funded education services (£173m.), and development programmes, principally in education and training, which are managed on behalf of the British government and other clients (£115m.). The British Council teaches English, supports arts events, funds scientific and other research links, manages development projects, and runs libraries and information centres.

Chair. Baroness Helena Kennedy QC.
Director-General. David Green CMG.
Headquarters. 10 Spring Gdns., London, SW1A 2BN.

Website: http://www.britishcouncil.org

Health. The National Health Service (NHS) in England and Wales started on 5 July 1948. There is a separate Act for Scotland.

The NHS is a charge on the national income in the same way, for example, as the armed forces. Every person normally resident in the UK is entitled to use any part of the service, and no insurance qualification is necessary.

Since 1948 a weekly NHS contribution has been payable by employees and the self-employed. In 1957 this contribution was extended to employers. For convenience this contribution is collected with the National Insurance contribution and amounts to 1·05% of the latter for employees and 0·9% for employers. The NHS is funded 12·1% by these contributions, 82% by general taxation and 2·3% by charges for drugs and dental treatment, and the rest from other receipts. Health authorities may raise funds from voluntary sources; hospitals may take private, paying patients.

In 2000–01 the UK spent 5·55% of its GDP on the NHS, with public spending amounting to £53,039m.

Organization. The National Health Service and Community Care Act, 1990, provided for a major restructuring of the NHS. From 1 April 1991 health authorities became the purchasers of healthcare, concentrating on their responsibilities to plan and obtain services for their local residents by the placement of health service contracts with the appropriate units. Day-to-day management tasks became the responsibility of hospitals and other units, with whom the contracts are placed, in their capacity as providers of care.

In April 1996 the Regional Health Authorities were replaced by eight regional offices of the NHS Executive. The District Health Authorities and Family Health Service Authorities were replaced by comprehensive Health Authorities directly financed by central government's Hospital and Community Health Services funds. The budget for 1996–97 was £2,260m.

The key responsibility of Health Authorities is to ensure that the health needs of their local communities are met. They have the purchasing power to commission hospital and community health services for their residents. In doing so they have a duty to ensure that high standards are maintained and that they are securing the best possible value for money.

The Health Authorities manage the Family Doctor (or General Medical) Service and also organize the general dental, pharmaceutical and ophthalmic services for their areas. Any doctor may take part in the Family Doctor Service, and are paid for their NHS work; they may also take private fee-paying patients.

NHS Trusts are established as self-governing units within the NHS. Trusts are responsible for the ownership and management of the hospitals or other establishments or facilities vested in them, and for carrying out the individual functions set out in their establishment orders. In April 1996 there were 520 Trusts, representing most hospitals.

General practitioners (GPs) may apply for fundholding status, responsible for their own NHS budget for a specified range of goods and services. There are two types of fundholder: Standard fundholders for practices with at least 5,000 patients in England and 4,000 in Wales and Scotland, who purchase the full range of in- and out-patient services; and Community fundholders, for smaller practices of at least 3,000 patients, who purchase only community nursing services and diagnostic tests. In 1996 there were some 14,000 fundholding GPs in 3,300 practices, covering 47% of the population.

Services. The NHS broadly consists of hospital and specialist services, general medical, dental and ophthalmic services, pharmaceutical services, community health services and school health services. In general these services are free of charge; the main exceptions are prescriptions, spectacles, dental and optical examination, dentures and dental treatment, amenity beds in hospitals, and some community services, for which contributory charges are made with certain exemptions.

The total cost of the NHS was estimated at £53,039m. for 2000–01.

In 2001 there were 27,843 GPs in England each with an average of 1,841 patients. There were 1,796 in Wales with an average of 1,685 patients each and 3,756 in Scotland with an average of 1,409. There were 16,451 general dental practitioners in England, 931 in Wales and 1,866 in Scotland. In hospitals in Great Britain in 2001 there were 71,107 medical staff and 437,417 nurses and midwives (down from 490,545 in 1989) excluding agency staff. In 1998 provision of beds in the UK was 42 per 10,000 population. In 1998 there were 194,000 hospital beds (108,000 acute-care beds).

In the UK in 1995 there were 193 public and private hospices for the terminally ill with 2,982 beds.

Private. In recent years increasing numbers of people have turned to private medical insurance. This covers the costs of private medical treatment (PMI) for curable short-term medical conditions. PMI includes the costs of surgery, specialists, nursing and accommodation at a private hospital or in a private ward of an NHS hospital. Approximately 11% of the UK population have private medical insurance. The leading companies are BUPA Healthcare, PPP healthcare and Norwich Union Healthcare Ltd.

In 1998, 28% of the population of the UK aged 15 and over smoked. In 1974 the percentage had been 45%, with 51% of males and 41% of females smoking. Over the years the difference between the percentage of men and of women who smoke has been declining, and by the mid-1990s there was a similar rate among men and women. Among schoolchildren 12% of girls but only 9% of boys smoked in 1998. The average British adult smokes 4·2 cigarettes a day, slightly less than the European Union average of 4·5 a day. Alcohol consumption has increased in recent years. Whereas in 1961 the average Briton consumed the equivalent of 4·5 litres of pure alcohol a year, by 1998 this figure had risen to 7·5 litres. By 2000, 21·0% of the population were considered obese (having a body mass index over 30), compared to 14·0% in 1991 and 7·0% in 1980.

The UK's AIDS rate stands at 24·1 cases per 100,000 population.

A survey published by the World Health Organization in June 2000 to measure health systems in all of the sovereign countries and find which country has the best overall health care ranked the UK in 18th place.

See also NORTHERN IRELAND.

Personal Social Services. Under the Local Authority Social Services Act, 1970, and in Scotland the Social Work (Scotland) Act, 1968, the welfare and social work services provided by local authorities were made the responsibility of a new local authority department—the Social Services Department in England and Wales, and Social Work Departments in Scotland headed by a Director of Social Work, responsibility in Scotland passing in 1975 to the local authorities. The social services thus administered include: the fostering, care and adoption of children, welfare services and social workers for people with learning difficulties and the mentally ill, the disabled and the aged, and accommodation for those needing residential care services. Legislation of 1996 permits local authorities to make cash payments as an alternative to community care. In Scotland the Social Work Departments' functions also include the supervision of persons on probation, of adult offenders and of persons released from penal institutions or subject to fine supervision orders.

Personal Social Services staff numbered 212,000 in 2001. The total cost of these services was estimated at £12,226m. for 2000–01. Expenditure is reviewed by the Social Services Inspectorate and the Audit Commission (in Scotland by the Social Work Services Inspectorate and the Accounts Commission).

Welfare. The National Insurance Act 1946 came into operation on 5 July 1948, repealing the existing schemes of health, pensions and unemployment insurance. This Act, along with later legislation, was consolidated as the National Insurance Act 1965. The scheme now operates under the Social Security Contributions and Benefits Act 1992 and the Social Security Administration Act 1992.

Since 1975 Class 1 contributions have been related to the employee's earnings and are collected with PAYE income tax, instead of by affixing stamps to a card.

Class 2 and Class 3 contributions remain flat-rate, but, in addition to Class 2 contributions, those who are self-employed may be liable to pay Class 4 contributions, which for the year 2002–03 were at the rate of 7% on profits or gains between £4,615 and £30,420, which are assessable for income tax under Schedule D. The non-employed and others whose contribution record is not sufficient to give entitlement to benefits were able to pay a Class 3 contribution of £6·85 per week in 2002–03 voluntarily, to qualify for a limited range of benefits. Class 2 weekly contributions for 2002–03 for men and women were £2·00. Class 1A contributions are paid by employers who provide employees with a car and fuel for their private use.

From 6 April 1978 the Social Security Pensions Act 1975 introduced earnings-related retirement, invalidity and widows' pensions. Members of occupational pension schemes may be contracted out of the earnings-related part of the state scheme relating to retirement and widows' benefits. Employee's national insurance contribution liability depends on whether he/she is in contracted-out or not contracted-out employment.

Full-rate contributions for non-contracted-out employment in 2002–03:

Weekly Earnings (in £1)	Employee pays	Employer pays
Nil–75	Nil	Nil
75–89	10%	Nil
89–585	10%	11·8%
Over 585	£49·60	11·8%

For contracted-out employment, the contracted-out rebate for primary contributions (employee's contribution) is 1·6% of earnings between the lower earnings limit and the upper earnings limit for all forms of contracting-out; the contracted-out rebate for secondary contributions (employer's contributions) is 3·5% of earnings between the lower earnings limit and the upper earnings limit. The employees' and employers' rates will both increase by 1·0% in 2003–04, increasing the rate paid by employees to 11% and that paid by employers to 12·8%.

From April 1996 employers who engage a trainee, or a person who has been unemployed for at least two years, are eligible for a year's rebate of contributions.

Contributions together with interest on investments form the income of the *National Insurance Fund* from which benefits are paid. A Treasury grant was instituted in 1993. 27,950,000 persons (12,360,000 women) paid contributions in 2000–01, including 25,360,000 employees at standard rate.

Receipts, 2000–01 (in £1m.), 72,480·2, including: contributions, 55,664·7; investment income, 884·1; compensation from Consolidated Fund for recoveries, 687·7. Disbursements (in £1m.), 52,574·0, including: Retirement Pensions, 42,349·8; administration, 1,197·4; Widow's Pensions, 1,008·0; Jobseekers' Allowance (Contributory), 449·3; transfers to Northern Ireland, 200·0; Redundancy Payments, 195·3; Pensioners' Lump Sums, 123·4; Maternity Allowances, 46·0; Guardian's Allowances, 1·6.

Statutory Sick Pay (SSP). Employers are responsible for paying statutory sick pay (SSP) to their employees who are absent from work through illness or injury for up to 28 weeks in any three-year period. Basically, all employees aged between 16 and 65 (60 for women) with earnings above the Lower Earnings Limit are covered by the scheme whenever they are sick for four or more days consecutively. The weekly rate is £63·25. For most employees SSP completely replaces their entitlement to state incapacity benefit which is not payable as long as any employer's responsibility for SSP remains.

Contributory benefits. Qualification for these depends upon fulfilment of the appropriate contribution conditions, except that persons who are incapable of work as the result of an industrial accident may receive incapacity benefit followed by invalidity benefit without having to satisfy the contributions conditions.

Jobseekers' Allowance. This replaced unemployment benefit on 7 Oct. 1996. Unemployed persons claiming the allowance must sign a 'Jobseekers' Agreement' setting out a plan of action to find work. The allowance is not payable to persons who left their job voluntarily or through misconduct. Claimants with sufficient

National Insurance contributions are entitled to the allowance for six months regardless of their means; otherwise, recipients qualify through a means test and the allowance is fixed according to family circumstances, at a rate corresponding to Income Support for an indefinite period. In May 2002 there were 827,500 people receiving the Jobseekers' Allowance (634,600 males). Payments start at £32·50 per week.

Incapacity benefit. This replaced the former sickness benefit and invalidity benefit on 13 April 1995. Entitlement begins when entitlement to SSP (if any) ends. There are three rates: a lower rate for the first 28 weeks; a higher rate between the 29th and 52nd week; and a long-term rate from the 53rd week of incapacity. It also comprises certain age additions and increases for adult and child dependants. A more objective medical test of incapacity for work was introduced for incapacity benefit as well as for other social security benefits paid on the basis of incapacity for work. This test applies after 28 weeks' incapacity for work and assesses ability to perform a range of work-related activities rather than the ability to perform a specific job. Benefit is taxable after 28 weeks. Some 1,496,900 claims were being made in Feb. 2002.

Statutory Maternity Pay. Pregnant working women may be eligible to receive statutory maternity pay directly from their employer for a maximum of 18 weeks if average gross earnings are £75 a week or more (2002–03). There are two rates: a lower rate of £75·00 for up to 12 weeks, and a higher rate (90% of average earnings for six weeks). For women who do not qualify for Statutory Maternity Pay, including self-employed women, there is a Maternity Allowance.

A payment of £500 from the Social Fund (Sure Start Maternity Grant) may be available if the mother or her partner are receiving income support, income-based Jobseeker's Allowance, Working Families' Tax Credit or Disabled Person's Tax Credit. It is also available if a woman adopts a baby.

Bereavement Benefits. Available to both men and women, Bereavement Benefits were introduced from 9 April 2001 to replace the former widow's benefit scheme. There are three main types of Bereavement Benefits available to men and women widowed on or after that date: bereavement payment, widowed parent's allowance, bereavement allowance. *Bereavement Payment* is a single tax-free lump sum payment of £2,000 payable immediately to help with costs arising on bereavement. A widower/widow may be able to get this benefit if his/her late spouse has paid enough National Insurance Contributions (NIC) and he/she was under 60 when her husband died; or her husband/wife was not getting a Category A State Retirement Pension when he/she died. *Widowed Parent's Allowance* is a weekly benefit payable to widowed parents. A widower/widow may be able to get this benefit if his/her late spouse has paid enough NIC and the widower/widow is receiving Child Benefit or can be treated as entitled to Child Benefit, or the late spouse was receiving Child Benefit, or she is expecting her husband's baby, or in certain cases of artificial insemination. The amount of Widowed Parent's Allowance they will get is based on their late spouse's NIC record. He/she may also get benefit for her eldest dependent child and further higher benefit for each subsequent child and may also include an additional pension based on their late spouse's earnings. If their late spouse was a member of a contracted-out occupational scheme or a personal pension scheme, that scheme is responsible for paying the whole or part of the additional pensions. Widowed Parent's Allowance is taxable. *Bereavement Allowance* is a weekly benefit payable to widows and widowers without dependent children and is payable between age 45 and State Pension age. The amount of Bereavement Allowance payable to a widower/widower between 45 and 54 is related to their age at the date of entitlement. Their weekly rate is reduced by 7% for each year they are aged under 55 so that they get 93% rate at age 54, falling to 30% at age 45. Those aged 55 or over at the date of entitlement will get the full rate of Bereavement Allowance. The amount of Bereavement Allowance they will get is based on their late spouse's NIC record and is payable for a maximum of 52 weeks from the date of bereavement. A widower/widow cannot get a Bereavement Allowance at the same time as a Widowed Parent's Allowance. If Widowed Parent's Allowance ends within 52 weeks of bereavement, Bereavement Allowance is payable up to the 52nd week from the late spouse's death. Bereavement Allowance is taxable.

A widower/widow cannot get bereavement benefits based on their late spouse's NIC if: he/she had been divorced from the man/woman who has died; or he/she was living with the man/woman as if he/she were married to him/her, but without being legally married to him/her; or he/she is living with another man/woman as if he/she is married to him/her; or he/she was in prison or held in legal custody.

Women widowed before 9 April 2001 will continue to receive their widows benefit entitlement on the arrangements that existed before that date so long as they continue to satisfy the qualifying conditions. There were some 255,500 recipients of widows' benefits in Feb. 2001.

Retirement Pension. The state retirement ('old-age') pension scheme has two components: a basic pension and an earnings-related pension (State Earnings Related Pension—SERPS). The amount of the first is subject to National Insurance contributions made; SERPS is 1·25% of average earnings between the lower weekly earnings limit for Class I contribution liability and the upper earnings limit for each year of such earnings, building up to 25% in 20 years. For individuals reaching pensionable age after 6 April 1999, changes in the way pensions are calculated will be phased in over 10 years to include a lifetime's earnings with an accrual rate of 20%. Pensions are payable to women at 60 years of age and men at 65, but the age differential will be progressively phased out starting in April 2010. Women born before 6 April 1950 will be unaffected; women born after 5 March 1955 will receive their pension at 65; pension age for women between these dates will move up gradually from 60 to 65. There are standard rates for single persons and for married couples, the latter being 159% of two single-person rates. Proportionately reduced pensions are payable where contribution records are deficient.

Employees in an occupational scheme may be contracted out of SERPS provided that the occupational scheme provides a pension not less than the 'guaranteed minimum pension'. Self-employed persons, and also employees, may substitute personal pension schemes for SERPS. An independent statutory body, the Occupational Pension Board, is responsible for supervising contracted-out schemes.

Self- and non-employed persons may contribute voluntarily for retirement pension.

Persons who defer claiming their pension during the five years following retirement age are paid an increased amount, as do men and women who had paid graduated contributions. Although no further graduated contributions have been paid after April 1975, pension already earned will be paid along with the basic pension in the normal way. In March 2002 some 11,124,000 persons were receiving National Insurance retirement pensions (6,982,500 women and 4,141,500 men). The basic state pension in 2002–03 was £75·50 per week for a single person and £120·70 per week for a married couple. Since 1 Oct. 1989 the pension for which a person has qualified may be paid in full whether a person continues in work or not irrespective of the amount of earnings. Although for males the official retirement age is 65, in 1995 the average actual retirement age among males was 62.

At the age of 80 a small age addition is payable. In addition non-contributory pensions are now payable, subject to residence conditions, to persons aged 80 and over who do not qualify for a retirement pension or qualify for one at a low rate. These pensions are financed by Exchequer funds.

Pensioners whose pension is insufficient to live on may qualify for Income Support.

Non-Contributory Benefits.

Child Benefit. Child benefit is a tax-free cash allowance for children normally paid to the mother. The weekly rates are highest for the eldest qualifying child and less for each other child. Child benefit is payable for children under 16, for 16- and 17-year-olds registered for work or training, and for those under 19 receiving full-time non-advanced education. Some 7,066,400 families received benefit in 2002 at any one time.

Child Support Agency. The Agency, which started work in April 1993, is gradually replacing the court system for obtaining maintenance for children being brought up by single parents. The Agency is responsible for assessing, collecting and enforcing child maintenance payments and for tracing absent parents. Assessments are made using a formula which takes into account each parent's income and essential outgoings. Changes to the child support arrangements were introduced in Feb. 1994 to take account of concerns raised by members of the public and MPs. These are designed to reduce the amount of child maintenance that many absent parents are required to pay, and to give some families more time to adjust to increased bills. Legislation of 1995 introduced the possibility of fixing maintenance alongside the formula-assessment method. Appeals on points of law may be made to the Child Support Commissioners. The Agency receives over 330,000 applications a year and at Nov. 1999 was handling over 998,900 cases.

Working Families' Tax Credit. This was introduced on 5 Oct. 1999 and replaced Family Credit. It aims to provide a better deal for working families and is administered by the Inland Revenue; it is paid through the pay packet. It is available to families (either couples or lone parents) who work at least 16 hours a week, who have one or more children under 16 (or under 19 if in full-time education up to A-level or equivalent standard), who are resident in and entitled to work in the UK, and who have savings of £8,000 or less. In Dec. 2001 there were 1,293,700 WFTC awards current. The average award in Aug. 2000 was £76·86 per week.

Guardian's Allowance. A person responsible for an orphan child may be entitled to a guardian's allowance in addition to child benefit. Normally, both the child's parents must be dead but when they never married or were divorced, or one is missing, or serving a long sentence of imprisonment, the allowance may be paid on the death of one parent only. In May 2002 there were 2,300 recipients.

Attendance Allowance. This is a tax-free Social Security benefit for disabled people over 65 who need help with personal care. The rates are increased for the terminally ill. There were some 1,291,400 recipients in Feb. 2002.

Invalid Care Allowance. This is a taxable benefit which may be paid to those who forego the opportunity of full-time work to care for a person who is receiving attendance allowance, constant attendance allowance or the highest or middle-core component of Disability Living Allowance. There is a weekly rate, with increases for dependants. In March 2002 there were 387,000 recipients.

Disability Living Allowance. This is a non-taxable benefit available to people disabled before the age of 65, who need help with getting around or with personal care for at least three months. The mobility component has two weekly rates, the care component has three. There were some 2,322,800 recipients in Feb. 2002.

Disabled Person's Tax Credit. This is a tax-free benefit for people with an illness or disability who are already working at least 16 hours a week. The allowance is not payable if assets exceed £16,000. Applicants must be receiving or must have been receiving a qualifying benefit such as disability living allowance or attendance allowance. The maximum weekly rates for single people is £62·10 and for a couple or lone parent £95·30.

Industrial Injuries Disablement and Death Benefits. The Industrial Injuries Act, which also came into operation on 5 July 1948, with its later amending Acts, was consolidated as the National Insurance (Industrial Injuries) Act, 1965. This legislation was incorporated in the Social Security Act, 1975. The scheme provides a system of insurance against 'personal injury by accident arising out of and in the course of employment' and against certain prescribed diseases and injuries owing to the nature of the employment. It takes the place of the Workmen's Compensation Acts and covers persons who are employed earners under the Social Security Act. There are no contribution conditions for the payment of benefit. There were 280,400 recipients in 2001 at any one time. Two types of benefit are provided:

—*Disablement benefit.* This is payable where, as the result of an industrial accident or prescribed disease, there is a loss of physical or mental faculty. The loss of faculty will be assessed as a percentage by comparison with a person of the same age and sex whose condition is normal. If the assessment is between 14–100% benefit will be paid as weekly pension; 14–19% are payable at the 20% rate. The rates vary from 20% disabled to 100% disablement. Assessments of less than 14% do not normally attract basic benefit except for certain progressive chest diseases. Pensions for persons under 18 are at a reduced rate. When injury benefit was abolished for industrial accidents occurring and prescribed diseases commencing on or after 6 April 1983, a common start date was introduced for the payment of disablement benefit 90 days (excluding Sundays) after the date of the relevant accident or onset of the disease. The following increases can be paid with disablement benefit: *Constant attendance allowance* – where the disability for which the claimant is receiving disablement benefit is assessed at 100% and is so severe that they need constant care and attention. There are four rates depending on the amount of attendance needed. *Exceptionally severe disablement allowance* – where the claimant is in receipt of constant attendance allowance at one of the two higher rates and the need for attendance is likely to be permanent. *Reduced earnings allowance* (REA) is a separate benefit. Entitlement exists if the claimant has not retired and cannot go back to their normal job or do another job for the same pay because of the effects of the disability caused by an accident or disease which occurred on or before 30 Sept. 1990. It can be paid whether or not disablement benefit is paid, providing the disablement benefit assessment is 1% or more (e.g. where disablement is assessed at less than 14%) and on top of 100% disablement benefit. From 1 Oct. 1989, if a claimant is of pensionable age (60 for a woman, 65 for a man) they can continue to receive REA if they are in regular employment, or in some cases if they are receiving Sickness Benefit, Invalidity Benefit or Unemployment Benefit. It will not matter whether or not they receive State Retirement Pension. If they are not in regular employment, then entitlement to REA will cease. In most cases it will be replaced by Retirement Allowance.

—*Death Benefit.* This is payable to the widow of a person who died before 11 April 1988 as the result of an industrial accident or a prescribed disease. Deaths which occurred on or after 11 April 1988—a widow is entitled to full widow's benefits even if her late husband did not satisfy the contribution condition, if he died as a result of an industrial accident or prescribed disease. Allowances may be paid to people who are suffering from pneumoconiosis or byssinosis or certain other slowly developing diseases due to employment before 5 July 1948. They must not at any time have been entitled to benefit for the disabled under the Industrial Injuries provision of the Social Security Act, or compensation under Workmen's Compensation Acts, or have received damages through the courts. In certain cases supplementation allowances are payable to people who are getting or are entitled to compensation under the Workmen's Compensation Acts.

War Pensions. Pensions are payable for disablement or death as a result of service in the armed forces. Similar schemes exist for other groups such as merchant seaman injured as a result of war or for civilians injured by enemy action in the Second World War. The amount depends on the degree of disablement. Various supplements may apply. There were some 272,730 recipients in 2001 at any one time.

Severe Disablement Allowance. A severe disablement allowance as well as an age-related addition may be payable to people under pensionable age who have been continuously incapable of work for at least 28 weeks, but who do not qualify for incapacity benefit. Those over 20 who are unable to work and are 80% disabled but do not qualify for the National Insurance invalidity pension because they have not paid sufficient contributions may be entitled to severe disablement allowance. Additions for adult dependants and for children may also be paid. There were some 399,000 beneficiaries in 1998–99.

Housing Benefit. The housing benefit scheme assists persons who need help to pay their rent, using general assessment rules and benefit levels similar to those for the income support scheme. People whose net income is below certain specified levels qualify for housing benefit of up to 100% of their rent. The scheme sets a limit of £16,000 on the amount of capital a person may have and still remain entitled. Restrictions on the granting of benefit to persons under 25 were introduced in 1995. In 2002 some 2,037,600 claims for rent rebate and 1,775,000 for rent allowance were being made at any one time.

Income Support. Income Support is a non-contributory benefit and the full basis for entitlement is set out in regulations. People in Great Britain who are aged 16 or over, not working 16 hours or more a week or with a partner not working more than 24 hours or more per week, and not required to be available for employment are eligible to claim Income Support. These include single parents, long-term sick or disabled persons, and those caring for them who qualify for Invalid Care

Allowance. It is payable to person whose resources are below a certain level. Income Support is not payable if the claimant (or claimant and partner together) has capital assets that total more than £8,000. These include savings, investments or property other than their home. Savings/capital assets worth under £3,000 are ignored. Savings between £3,000 and £8,000 are treated as if each £250 or part of £250 brings in an income of £1 per week. Some groups have capital treated differently. These include Income Support claimants whose partners are of pension age; in these circumstance they are allowed to have up to £12,000 and still be entitled to Income Support. However, only £6,000 will be disregarded. In addition claimants in residential care and nursing homes have their capital treated differently. They are allowed to have up to £16,000 and still be entitled to Income Support. However, only £10,000 of their assets are disregarded. The amount of benefit that a claimant can receive is calculated using an 'applicable amount' and takes account of any resources they have. Receipt of Income Support also automatically entitles the claimant and his dependants to certain other welfare benefits. Applicable amounts are specified by regulations and are used to calculate the maximum amount of benefit that a claimant can receive. These consist of: a personal allowance—which depends upon the age of the claimant and the presence and age of a partner; additions for any dependants; 'premiums'—which provide additional allowances in recognition of special needs such as old age or disability; and certain types of housing costs. In 2002 there were 3,929,800 Income Support claimants at any one time. The average weekly award was £69·94 in May 2002.

Council Tax Benefit. The scheme offers help to those claiming income support and others with low incomes. Subject to rules broadly similar to those governing the provision of income support and housing benefit, people may receive rebates of up to 100% of their council tax. In 2002 some 4,601,700 households received such help at any one time. A person who is liable for the council tax may also claim benefit (called 'second adult rebate') for a second adult who is not liable to pay the council tax and who is living in the home on a non-commercial basis.

The Social Fund. The Fund makes payments and loans to help recipients meet intermittent expenses. The Regulated Social Fund comprises: *Sure Start Maternity Grant* (a payment of up to £500 for each baby expected, born or adopted, payable to persons receiving Income Support, Income-based Jobseekers' Allowance, Disabled Person's Tax Credit or Working Families' Tax Credit); *Funeral Payments* (a payment of fees levied by the burial authorities and crematoria, plus up to £600 for other funeral expenses, to persons receiving Income Support, Income-based Jobseekers' Allowance, Disabled Person's Tax Credit, Working Families' Tax Credit, Housing Benefit or Council Tax Benefit); *Cold Weather Payments* (a payment of £8·50 for any consecutive seven days when the temperature is below freezing to persons receiving income support who are pensioners, disabled or have a child under five); *Winter Fuel Payments* (a payment of £200 to every household with a person aged 60 or over providing they do not live permanently in a hospital, residential care or nursing home). The Discretionary Social Fund comprises: *Community Care Grants* (payments to help persons receiving income support to move into the community or avoid institutional care); *Budgeting Loans* (interest-free loans to persons receiving income support for expenses difficult to budget for); *Crisis Loans* (interest-free loans to anyone without resources in an emergency where there is no other means of preventing serious risk to health or safety). Savings over £500 (£1,000 for persons aged 60 or over) are taken into account before payments are made.

Hill, M., *The Welfare State in Britain: a Political History since 1945.* Aldershot, 1993
Timmins, N., *The Five Giants: a Biography of the Welfare State.* London, 1995

CULTURE

Broadcasting. Radio and television services are provided by the British Broadcasting Corporation (BBC), by licensees of the Radio Authority and the Independent Television Commission (ITC) and by the Welsh-language Sianel Pedwar Cymru (S4C, Channel 4 Wales). The BBC, constituted by Royal Charter until 31 Dec. 1996, has responsibility for providing domestic and external broadcast services, the former financed from the television licence revenue, the latter by government grant. The domestic services provided by the BBC include two national television services, five national radio network services and a network of local radio stations. Government proposals for the future of the BBC after 1996 were published in July 1994.

The ITC is responsible for licensing and regulating all non-BBC TV services (except S4C), provided in and from the UK whether analogue or digital. These include ITV (regional and breakfast-time licensees), Channel 4, Channel 5, cable and satellite and additional services, such as teletext, carried on the spare capacity of TV signals. The Radio Authority is responsible for licensing and regulating independent national and local radio services. S4C is transmitted in Wales, and is funded by the government. It acts as both broadcaster and regulator.

The BBC's domestic radio services are available on Long Wave, Medium Wave and VHF/FM; those of the Radio Authority on Medium Wave and VHF/FM. Television services other than those only on cable and satellite are broadcast at UHF in 625-line definition and in colour (by PAL). The BBC World Service, which started life in 1932 as the Empire Service, broadcast in 43 languages to an audience estimated at 150m. in 2001. As the self-financed BBC Worldwide TV, the BBC is also involved in commercial joint ventures to provide international television services.

The broadcasting authorities, whose governing bodies are appointed (by HM the Queen in the case of the BBC and by the Secretary of State for Culture, Media and Sport in the case of the ITC, the Radio Authority and S4C) as trustees for the public interest in broadcasting, are independent of government and are publicly accountable to Parliament for the discharge of their responsibilities. Their duties and powers are laid down in the BBC Royal Charter and the Broadcasting Act 1990.

All independent (non-BBC) radio and television services other than S4C are financed by the sale of broadcasting advertising time, commercial sponsorship, or, in some cable and satellite services, by subscription.

The Broadcasting Standards Commission (BSC) was established on 1 April 1997 by the Broadcasting Act 1996, through the merger of the Broadcasting Standards Council and Broadcasting Complaints Commission. Combining the functions of the two predecessor bodies, it acts as a forum for public concern about fairness and taste and decency on television and radio. The Commission considers and reaches findings on taste and decency complaints received from the public and adjudicates upon complaints of unfair or unjust treatment in broadcast programmes, and of unwarranted infringement of privacy in programmes or in their preparation. It also undertakes and commissions research and the monitoring of public attitudes, and must draw up a code of practice on both broadcasting standards and fairness which the broadcasters and regulators are required to reflect in their own programming guidelines. The Commission is half-funded by the Department, half by contributions from the BBC, ITC, Radio Authority and S4C.

The number of television receiving licences in force on 31 March 2002 was 23,157,000, of which 23,040,000 were for colour. There were 9·4m. satellite and cable TV subscribers in early 2002 (5·8m. with BSkyB, 2·3m. with NTL and 1·3m. with Telewest). In 1997 there were 84·5m. radio receivers, or 1,443 per 1,000 inhabitants—a figure only exceeded in the USA, with 2,116 per 1,000 inhabitants.

Cinema. In 2001 cinemas had 2,509 screens. Admissions were 141·0m. in 2001. Admissions had totalled 500m. in 1960, but had fallen as low as 54m. in 1984. Gross box office takings in 2001 amounted to £550·1m. 96 full-length films were made in 2001 (128 in 1996). In 1997 British films took 27% of the national market, but in 1998 this dropped to 13%.

Press. In 2003 there were ten national dailies with a combined average daily circulation in Jan. 2003 of 12,427,715, and ten national Sunday newspapers (13,381,334). There were also about 100 morning, evening and Sunday regional newspapers and 2,000 weeklies (about 1,000 of these for free distribution). There were about 6,500 other commercial periodicals and 4,000 professional and business journals. In 1996 an average of 18·3m. newspapers were sold per day, down from over 23m. in 1980. The most widely read daily is the tabloid *The Sun*, with an average daily circulation of 3,578,302 in Jan. 2003. The most widely read Sunday paper is the tabloid *News of the World*, which had an average circulation of 3,971,846 in Jan. 2003.

In Jan. 1991 the Press Complaints Commission replaced the former Press Council. It has 15 members and a chair, including seven editors. It is funded by the newspaper industry.

In 1996, 101,504 book titles were published, including 89,984 non-fiction. 95,064 titles were published in 1995.

Tourism. In 2001 UK residents made 163·1m. trips within the UK, passing 529·6m. nights in accommodation and spending £26,094m. Of these, 101·2m. were holiday-makers spending £17,016m. There were 22·8m. overseas visitors in 2001 staying 189·5m. nights in accommodation and spending £11,306m. UK residents made 58·3m. trips abroad in 2001. The main countries of origin for foreign visitors in 2001 were: USA (3·6m.), France (2·9m.), Germany (2·3m.), Ireland (2m.) and the Netherlands (1·4m.). Between 1997 and 2001, visits by USA residents to the UK increased by 148,000, the largest increase for any single country. Over the same period visits by French residents of the UK fell by the greatest number. The UK is the 5th most popular tourist destination in the world. In 2001 tourism was affected by the foot-and-mouth epidemic which closed parts of the countryside.

The leading attraction in 2001 was Blackpool Pleasure Beach, Lancs, with an estimated 6·5m. visits. The leading tourist attractions charging admission in 2001 were: the British Airways London Eye, with 3,850,000; the Tower of London, with 2,019,210 visits; Eden Project in St Austell, with 1,700,000; Natural History Museum in London, with 1,696,176; and Legoland Windsor, with 1,632,000 visits.

In Sept. 2001 there were 2·1m. (not seasonally adjusted) people working in tourism-related industries.

France is the most popular destination for Britons travelling abroad (12m. British visitors in 2001), followed by Spain (11·7m.) and USA (4m.). There were 58·3m. trips abroad made by British residents in 2001, up from 13·4m. in 1978.

Festivals. Among the most famous music festivals are the Promenade Concerts or 'Proms', which take place at the Royal Albert Hall in London every year from July to Sept; the Glyndebourne season in Sussex (May to Aug.); the Aldeburgh Festival in Suffolk (June); the Glastonbury Festival in Somerset (June); and the Buxton Festival in Derbyshire (July). The annual London Film Festival takes place in Nov. Literary festivals include the Hay Festival in Herefordshire (late May/early June) and Cheltenham Festival of Literature in Gloucestershire (Oct.). The Edinburgh Festival and the Fringe Festival both take place in Aug./early Sept. and are major international festivals of culture. The Brighton Festival in May is England's largest arts festival. The multicultural Notting Hill Carnival in London takes place at the end of Aug. Other major events in the annual calendar are the New Year's Parade in London, the Crufts Dog Show at the Birmingham National Exhibition Centre (March), the Ideal Home Exhibition in London (March–April), the London Marathon (April), the Chelsea Flower Show (May), Royal Ascot (horse racing, in June), Wimbledon (tennis, in June–July), Henley Royal Regatta (July), Cowes (yachting, in Aug.) and the Lord Mayor's Show in London (Nov.).

Libraries. In 1997 there were 5,183 public libraries, 18 National libraries and 781 Higher Education libraries; they held a combined 249,361,000 volumes. There were 61,415,000 registered library users in 1997.

Museums and Galleries. The museums with the highest number of visitors are all in London. In 2001 there were 4,918,985 visits to the National Gallery, 4,800,938 to the British Museum, 3,551,885 to the Tate Modern, 1,696,176 to the Natural History Museum and 1,446,344 to the Victoria and Albert Museum.

DIPLOMATIC REPRESENTATIVES

Of the USA in Great Britain (24/31 Grosvenor Sq., London, W1A 1AE)
Ambassador: William S. Farish.

Of Great Britain in the USA (3100 Massachusetts Ave., NW, Washington, D.C., 20008)
Ambassador: Sir David Manning.

Of Great Britain to the United Nations
Ambassador: Sir Jeremy Greenstock, KCMG.

Great Britain's permanent representative to the European Union
Ambassador: Sir Stephen Wall, KCMG, LVO.

FURTHER READING

Government publications are published by The Stationery Office (TSO).
Office for National Statistics. *UK 20xx.* TSO.—*Annual Abstract of Statistics.* TSO.—*Monthly Digest of Statistics.* TSO.—*Social Trends.* TSO.—*Regional Statistics.* TSO
Central Office of Information. *The Monarchy.* 1992
Directory of British Associations. Beckenham, annual
Beloff, M., *Britain and the European Union: Dialogue of the Deaf.* London, 1997
Black, Jeremy, *A History of the British Isles.* 2nd ed. Palgrave Macmillan, Basingstoke, 2002
Bogdanor, Vernon, *Devolution in the United Kingdom.* OUP, 1999
Cairncross, A., *The British Economy Since 1945: Economic Policy and Performance, 1945–1995.* 2nd ed. London, 1995
Creaton, Heather, *London.* [Bibliography] ABC-Clio, Oxford and Santa Barbara (CA), 1996
Dunleavy, P., Gamble, A., Holliday, I. and Peele, G. (eds.) *Developments in British Politics.* Macmillan, London, 2000
Gascoigne, B. (ed.) *Encyclopedia of Britain.* London, 1994
Harbury, C. D. and Lipsey, R. G., *Introduction to the UK Economy.* 4th ed. Oxford, 1993
Irwin, J. L., *Modern Britain: an Introduction.* 3rd ed. London, 1994
Leventhal, F. M. (ed.) *20th-Century Britain: an Encyclopedia.* New York, 1995
Marr, A., *Ruling Britannia: the Failure and Future of British Democracy.* London, 1995
Oakland, J., *British Civilization: an Introduction.* 3rd ed. London, 1995
Oxford History of the British Empire. 2 vols. OUP, Oxford, 1999
Palmer, A. and Palmer, V., *The Chronology of British History.* London, 1995
Penguin History of Britain. 9 vols. London, 1996
Sked, A. and Cook, C., *Post-War Britain: a Political History.* 4th ed. London, 1993
Speck, W. A., *A Concise History of Britain, 1707–1975.* CUP, 1993
Strong, R., *The Story of Britain.* London, 1996
Turner, Barry, (ed.) *UK Today.* Macmillan, London, 2000

Other more specialized titles are listed under TERRITORY AND POPULATION; CONSTITUTION AND GOVERNMENT; ARMY; NAVY; BANKING AND FINANCE; ELECTRICITY; TRADE UNIONS; RELIGION; *and* WELFARE, *above. See also Further Reading in England, Scotland, Wales and Northern Ireland.*

National Statistical Office: National Statistics, 1 Drummond Gate, London SW1V 2QQ. *Director:* Len Cook.
Website: http://www.statistics.gov.uk/

ENGLAND

KEY HISTORICAL EVENTS

After the withdrawal of the Roman legions, 5th century Celtic Britain was invaded by Scandinavian and Teutonic tribes. In the course of the next 150 years they conquered the east and centre of the country, pinning down the Celtic Britons on the higher lands to the west. More than 200 years passed before the prevailing tribes recognized one king.

For much of the 1st century AD, Viking invaders were dominant in England. An Anglo-Saxon counter-attack was led by King Alfred, whose successors consolidated their hold on the country. After the departure of the Scandinavians, England attracted the interest of France or, more particularly, Normandy. In 1066 William, Duke of Normandy, was victorious against King Harold at the Battle of Hastings. William was crowned king. When William died in 1087, he left Normandy to his eldest son Robert, thus separating it from England. The French dialect known as Anglo Norman was spoken by the ruling class in England for two centuries after the Conquest.

The Norman heritage was preserved also in the overlap between French and English feudal lords. Henry II, the founder of the Plantagenet dynasty, was feudatory lord of half France. But most of the French possessions were lost by Henry's son John. Thereafter, the Norman baronage came to regard themselves as English.

The ambitions of Edward III began and those of Henry V renewed the Hundred Years War (1338–1453) with France, which ended with the loss of all the remaining French possessions except Calais.

The dynastic struggle between the rival houses of York and Lancaster culminated in the Tudor ascendancy over political and clerical factions. Henry VII was a unifying monarch preparing the way for Henry VIII who forced the Church to submit to lay rule. Tudor power reached its zenith with Elizabeth I when England, allied with other Protestant powers, humbled the Spanish Armada.

Elizabeth's death brought on a great struggle for supremacy between Crown and Parliament. There followed the Civil War, the execution of Charles I, the rule by Protector Cromwell by military dictatorship, and the restoration of the Stuart monarchy on terms which conceded financial authority and thus decision-making power to Parliament.

The attempt of James II to restore the royal prerogative led to the intervention of William of Orange. James fled the country and the crown was taken by William and his wife Mary as Queen. The accession of William involved England in a protracted war against France but before peace was achieved, the 1688 revolution was confirmed by the Hanoverian succession, and the history of England was merged with that of Great Britain by the union with Scotland in 1707.

TERRITORY AND POPULATION

At the census taken on 29 April 2001 the area of England was 130,281 sq. km and the population 49,138,831, giving a density of 377 per sq. km. England covers 53·7% of the total area of the United Kingdom. Households at the 2001 census: 21,262,000. Estimated population of England, mid-2002, 49,343,000.

Population (present on census night) at the four previous decennial censuses:

1961	*1971*	*1981*	*1991*
43,460,525[1]	46,018,371[1]	46,226,100[2]	46,382,050

[1]Area now included in Wales formed the English county of Monmouthshire until 1974.
[2]The final count is believed to be over-stated as a result of an error in processing. The preliminary counts presented here rounded to the nearest hundred are thought to be more accurate.

Population at census day 2001:

Males	*Females*	*Total*
23,923,390	25,215,441	49,138,831

For further statistical information, see under Territory and Population, United Kingdom.

Eight 'Standard Regions' (also classified as 'level 1 regions' for EU purposes) are identified in England as economic planning regions. They have no administrative significance. Estimated population of the regions of England (in 1,000), 2001, East Anglia, 2,177; East Midlands, 4,175; West Midlands, 5,267; North, 3,004; North West, 6,244; South East, 18,412 (including Greater London, 7,188); South West, 4,934; Yorkshire and Humberside, 4,967. Although the populations of most of the regions increased during the 1990s, the North, North West, and Yorkshire and Humberside saw their population declines, by 88,000, 148,000 and 16,000 respectively between 1991 and 2001. The population on census day in 2001 in the nine English Government Office regions was as follows: East, 5,388,154; East Midlands, 4,172,179; London, 7,172,036; North East, 2,515,479; North West, 6,730,800; South East, 8,000,550; South West, 4,928,458; West Midlands, 5,267,337; Yorkshire and the Humber, 4,965,838.

Following the local government reorganization in the mid-1990s, there is a mixed pattern to local government in England. Apart from Greater London, England is divided into 34 counties with 2 tiers of administration; a county council and district councils. There are 6 metropolitan county areas containing 36 single-tier metropolitan districts.

In addition, there are 46 single-tier unitary authorities which, with the exception of the Isle of Wight, were formally district councils in the shire counties of England. The Isle of Wight is a unitary county council.

As a consequence of the establishment of the 46 unitary authorities, a number of county areas were abolished. These were Avon, Cleveland and Humberside. Berkshire County Council was also abolished but the county itself is retained for ceremonial purposes. Greater London comprises 32 boroughs and the City of London.

Area in sq. km of English counties and unitary authorities, and population at census day 2001:

Metropolitan counties	Area (sq. km)	Population	Unitary Authorities	Area (sq. km)	Population
Greater Manchester	1,276	2,482,352	Bath and North East		
Merseyside	645	1,362,034	Somerset	346	169,045
South Yorkshire	1,552	1,266,337	Blackburn with		
Tyne and Wear	540	1,075,979	Darwen	137	137,471
West Midlands	902	2,555,596	Blackpool	35	142,284
West Yorkshire	2,029	2,079,217	Bournemouth	46	163,441
			Bracknell Forest	109	109,606
Non-metropolitan counties			Brighton and Hove	83	247,820
Bedfordshire (Beds)	1,192	381,571	Bristol, City of	110	380,615
Buckinghamshire			Darlington	197	97,822
(Bucks)	1,565	479,028	Derby	78	221,716
Cambridgeshire			East Riding of		
(Camb)	3,046	552,655	Yorkshire	2,408	314,076
Cheshire	2,083	673,777	Halton	79	118,215
Cornwall and Isles			Hartlepool	94	88,629
of Scilly	3,563	501,267	Herefordshire,		
Cumbria	6,768	487,607	County of	2,180	174,844
Derbyshire	2,547	734,581	Isle of Wight	380	132,719
Devon	6,564	704,499	Kingston upon Hull,		
Dorset	2,542	390,986	City of	71	243,595
Durham	2,226	493,470	Leicester	73	279,923
East Sussex	1,709	492,324	Luton	43	184,390
Essex	3,465	1,310,922	Medway	192	249,502
Gloucestershire			Middlesbrough	54	134,847
(Gloucs)	2,653	564,559	Milton Keynes	309	207,063
Hampshire (Hants)	3,679	1,240,032	North East		
Hertfordshire			Lincolnshire	192	157,983
(Herts)	1,643	1,033,977	North Lincolnshire	846	152,839
Kent	3,544	1,329,653	North Somerset	374	188,556
Lancashire (Lancs)	2,903	1,134,976	Nottingham	75	266,995
Leicestershire			Peterborough	343	156,060
(Leics)	2,083	609,579	Plymouth	80	240,718
Lincolnshire			Poole	65	138,299
(Lincs)	5,921	646,646	Portsmouth	40	186,704
Norfolk	5,371	796,733	Reading	40	143,214
Northamptonshire			Redcar and Cleveland	245	139,141
(Northants)	2,364	629,676	Rutland	382	34,560
Northumberland	5,013	307,186	Slough	33	119,070
North Yorkshire			Southampton	50	217,478
(N. Yorks)	8,038	569,660	Southend-on-Sea	42	160,256
Nottinghamshire			South		
(Notts)	2,085	748,503	Gloucestershire	497	245,644
Oxfordshire			Stockton-on-Tees	204	178,405
(Oxon)	2,605	605,492	Stoke-on-Trent	93	240,643
Shropshire (Salop)	3,197	283,240	Swindon	230	180,061
Somerset (Som)	3,451	498,093	Telford and Wrekin	290	158,285
Staffordshire			Thurrock	163	143,042
(Staffs)	2,620	806,737	Torbay	63	129,702
Suffolk	3,801	668,548	Warrington	181	191,084
Surrey	1,663	1,059,015	West Berkshire	704	144,445
Warwickshire	1,975	505,885	Windsor and		
West Sussex	1,991	753,612	Maidenhead	197	133,606
Wiltshire (Wilts)	3,255	432,973	Wokingham	179	150,257
Worcestershire	1,741	542,107	York	272	181,131

Source: Office of National Statistics

In 2001 London had a population of 7,172,000. Populations of next largest cities were: Birmingham (2001), 976,000; Leeds (2001), 716,000; Sheffield (2001), 513,000; Bradford (1996), 483,000; Liverpool (2001), 439,000; Bristol (1999), 405,000; Manchester (2001), 393,000.

Greater London Boroughs. Total area 1,572 sq. km. Population at census day 2001: 7,172,036 (inner London, 2,765,975). Population by borough (census day 2001):

Barking and		Bexley	218,307	Camden[1]	198,027
Dagenham	163,944	Brent	263,463	Croydon	330,688
Barnet	314,561	Bromley	295,530	Ealing	300,947

Enfield	273,563	Islington[1]	175,787	Richmond		
Greenwich	214,540	Kensington and		upon Thames	172,327	
Hackney[1]	202,819	Chelsea[1]	158,922	Southwark[1]	244,867	
Hammersmith		Kingston		Sutton	179,667	
and Fulham[1]	165,243	upon Thames	147,295	Tower Hamlets[1]	196,121	
Haringey[1]	216,510	Lambeth[1]	266,170	Waltham Forest	218,277	
Harrow	207,389	Lewisham[1]	248,924	Wandsworth[1]	260,383	
Havering	224,248	Merton	187,908	Westminster,		
Hillingdon	242,435	Newham[1]	243,737	City of[1]	181,279	
Hounslow	212,344	Redbridge	238,628			

[1]Inner London borough.

Source: Office of National Statistics

The City of London (677 acres) is administered by its Corporation which retains some independent powers. Population at census day 2001: 7,186.

CLIMATE
For more detailed information, see under Climate, United Kingdom.

London, Jan. 39°F (3·9°C), July 64°F (17·8°C). Annual rainfall 25" (635 mm). Birmingham, Jan. 38°F (3·3°C), July 61°F (16·1°C). Annual rainfall 30" (749 mm). Manchester, Jan. 39°F (3·9°C), July 61°F (16·1°C). Annual rainfall 34·5" (876 mm).

CONSTITUTION AND GOVERNMENT
The Parliamentary electorate of England in the register numbered 36,991,780 in 2001–02.

RECENT ELECTIONS
At the UK general election held in June 2001, 529 members were returned from England.

See also Constitution and Government, Recent Elections and Current Administration in United Kingdom.

DEFENCE
For information on defence, see United Kingdom.

ECONOMY
For information on the economy, see United Kingdom.

ENERGY AND NATURAL RESOURCES
For information on energy and natural resources, see United Kingdom.

Water. The Water Act of Sept. 1989 privatized the nine water and sewerage authorities in England: Anglian; North West (now United Utilities Water plc); Northumbrian; Severn Trent; South West; Southern; Thames; Wessex; Yorkshire. There are also 16 water only companies in England and Wales. The Act also inaugurated the National Rivers Authority, with environmental and resource management responsibilities, and the 'regulator' *Office of Water Services (Ofwat)*, charged with protecting consumer interests.

INDUSTRY
Labour. The unemployment rate in the spring of 2001 was 4·6%, compared to 4·8% for the UK as a whole. Unemployment was lowest in the southeast (3·0%) and highest in the northeast (7·4%).

INTERNATIONAL TRADE
For information on international trade, see United Kingdom.

COMMUNICATIONS
For information on communications, see United Kingdom.

Shipping. Total cargo handled in 1998 was 367·6m. tonnes.

SOCIAL INSTITUTIONS
Education. For details on the nature and types of school, see under Education, United Kingdom.

In 2001–02 education and skills expenditure by Central and Local government in England is expected to top £42·7bn. In Jan. 2001 there were 506 public-sector nursery and primary schools with nursery classes in England; in addition, there were 1,500 independent schools with provision for children under five (including direct grant nurseries). In 2001 there were 44,990 pupils under five attending nursery schools and pupils under five in nursery and infant classes in primary schools. Some of these children were attending part-time.

In Jan. 2001 there were 4,406,215 pupils at 18,069 primary schools in England, of which 2,070 were infant schools providing for pupils up to the age of about 7, the remainder mainly taking pupils from age 5 through to 11. Nearly all primary schools take both boys and girls. 15% of primary schools had 100 full-time pupils or fewer.

In Jan. 2001 there were 463 middle schools in England deemed either primary or secondary according to the age range of the school concerned.

In Jan. 2001 there were 3,481 secondary schools in England. Some local authorities have retained selection at age 11 for entry to grammar schools, of which there were 159 in 2001. There were a small number of technical schools in 2001 which specialize in technical studies. There were 145 secondary modern schools in 2001, providing a general education up to the minimum school leaving age of 16, although exceptionally some pupils stay on beyond that age.

Almost all local education authorities operate a system of comprehensive schools to which pupils are admitted without reference to ability or aptitude. In Jan. 1997 there were 2,882 such schools in England with over 2·6m. pupils. With the development of comprehensive education, various patterns of secondary schools have come into operation. Principally these are: 1) All-through schools with pupils aged 11 to 18 or 11 to 16; pupils over 16 being able to transfer to an 11 to 18 school or a sixth form college providing for pupils aged 16 to 19. (There are currently 102 sixth form colleges in England). 2) Local education authorities operating a three-tier system involving middle schools where transfer to secondary school is at ages 12, 13 or 14. These correspond to 12 to 18, 13 to 18 and 14 to 18 comprehensive schools respectively; or 3) In areas where there are no middle schools a two-tier system of junior and senior comprehensive schools for pupils aged 11 to 18 with optional transfer to these schools at age 13 or 14.

Under the Education Act 1996 children have special educational needs if they have a learning difficulty which calls for special educational provision to be made for them. In some cases the Local Education Authority will need to make a statutory assessment of special educational needs under the Education Act 1996, which may ultimately lead to a 'statement'. In England the total number of pupils with statements in 2001 was 258,200. In 2001 there were 1,113 maintained special schools and 62 non-maintained special schools.

Outside the state system of education there were in England about 2,188 independent schools in Jan. 2001, ranging from large prestigious schools to small local ones. Some provide boarding facilities but the majority include non-resident day pupils. There are about 569,253 pupils in these schools, which represent about 7% of the total pupil population in England.

Further Education (Non-University). In 2000–01, 3·8m. students were enrolled at FE colleges in England. Those on Learning and Skills Council funded provision were studying for 6·6m. qualifications. Total funding for the FE sector in 2001–02 was £4,029m.

Higher Education. In England in 2002–03 there were 132 institutions of higher education directly funded by the HEFCE (Higher Education Funding Council for England), of which 77 were universities. The HEFCE distributes public money for teaching and research to universities and colleges. It works in partnership with the higher education sector and advises the government on higher education policy. In 2002–03 the HEFCE distributed £5·1bn. in funding, including £3,271m. for teaching and £940m. for research.

a) *Universities*

Name (Location)	No. of students (2000–01)	No. of academic staff (1999–2000)
Anglia Polytechnic Univ. (Chelmsford)	18,180	860
Aston Univ. (Birmingham)	7,060	400

a) *Universities (cont.)*

Name (Location)	No. of students (2000–01)	No. of academic staff (1999–2000)
Univ. of Bath	9,990	870
Univ. of Birmingham	23,830	2,740
Birkbeck College[1]	12,590	630
Bournemouth Univ. (Poole)	12,100	630
Univ. of Bradford	11,040	570
Univ. of Brighton	15,760	790
Univ. of Bristol	17,920	2,300
Brunel Univ. (Uxbridge)	13,580	790
Univ. of Cambridge	20,670	4,230
Univ. of Central England in Birmingham	19,390	930
Univ. of Central Lancashire (Preston)	25,400	880
City Univ. (London)	13,290	670
Coventry Univ.	16,350	900
De Montfort Univ. (Leicester)	26,670	1,370
Univ. of Derby	15,320	720
Univ. of Durham	13,400	1,700
Univ. of East Anglia (Norwich)	12,640	910
Univ. of East London (London)	11,620	630
Univ. of Essex (Colchester)	7,580	590
Univ. of Exeter	12,240	870
Goldsmiths College[1]	7,660	530
Univ. of Greenwich (London)	16,660	1,010
Univ. of Hertfordshire (Hatfield)	19,120	1,070
Univ. of Huddersfield	16,010	700
Univ. of Hull	15,890	830
Imperial College of Science, Technology and Medicine[1]	11,860	3,240
Keele Univ. (Newcastle-under-Lyme)	8,980	570
Univ. of Kent at Canterbury	11,180	660
King's College London[1]	17,750	3,110
Kingston Univ. (Kingston-upon-Thames)	14,610	920
Lancaster Univ.	11,330	820
Univ. of Leeds	27,320	2,740
Leeds Metropolitan Univ.	31,334	1,010
Univ. of Leicester	16,020	1,430
Univ. of Lincolnshire and Humberside (Hull)	12,480	430
Univ. of Liverpool	20,440	1,950
Liverpool John Moores Univ.	19,360	1,110
London Guildhall Univ.	13,600	570
Loughborough Univ. of Technology	13,550	1,250
Univ. of Luton	10,670	670
Univ. of Manchester	23,810	3,290
Univ. of Manchester Institute of Science and Technology	6,900	950
Manchester Metropolitan Univ.	29,520	1,490
Middlesex Univ. (London)	22,420	1,080
Univ. of Newcastle upon Tyne	16,500	2,190
Univ. of North London	14,120	720
Univ. of Northumbria at Newcastle	19,660	1,210
Univ. of Nottingham	23,970	2,240
Nottingham Trent Univ.	21,810	1,340
Open University	151,400	1,230
Univ. of Oxford	20,540	4,170
Oxford Brookes Univ.	14,290	860
Univ. of Plymouth	20,601	1,330
Univ. of Portsmouth	19,080	910
Queen Mary and Westfield College[1]	9,420	1,480
Univ. of Reading	13,210	1,240
Royal Holloway, Univ. of London[1]	5,840	610
Univ. of Salford	21,760	1,010
Univ. of Sheffield	22,670	2,320
Sheffield Hallam Univ.	22,660	1,290
Univ. of Southampton	22,650	2,060
South Bank Univ. (London)	17,210	1,040
Staffordshire Univ. (Stoke-on-Trent)	17,460	740
Univ. of Sunderland	11,960	1,010
Univ. of Surrey (Guildford)	11,430	1,050
Univ. of Sussex (Brighton)	11,230	960

a) *Universities (cont.)*

Name (Location)	No. of students (2000–01)	No. of academic staff (1999–2000)
Univ. of Teesside (Middlesbrough)	13,120	630
Thames Valley Univ. (London)	15,580	460
Univ. College London[1]	20,750	4,460
Univ. of Warwick (Coventry)	19,580	1,560
Univ. of Westminster (London)	21,190	1,280
Univ. of the West of England, Bristol	20,950	1,280
Univ. of Wolverhampton	19,640	1,050
Univ. of York	9,330	1,020

[1]Part of the University of London, which in 2000–01 had 106,100 internal students plus 28,000 external students, and 7,881 teachers, readers and professors.

b) *Other Institutions*

Bath Spa University College; Bishop Grosseteste College (Lincoln); Bolton Institute of Higher Education; Bretton Hall (Wakefield); Buckinghamshire Chilterns University College (High Wycombe); Institute of Cancer Research; Central School of Speech and Drama (London); Centre for Career and Personal Development (Tunbridge Wells); Cheltenham and Gloucester College of Higher Education; Chester College of Higher Education; Univ. College Chichester; Cranfield University; Cumbria College of Art and Design; Dartington College of Arts (Totnes); Edge Hill College of Higher Education (Ormskirk); Institute of Education; Falmouth College of Arts; Harper Adams University College (Newport); Homerton College, Cambridge; Kent Institute of Art and Design (Maidstone); King Alfred's College, Winchester; Liverpool Hope; Univ. of London (Institutes and Activities); London Business School; London School of Economics and Political Science; London School of Hygiene and Tropical Medicine; The London Institute; Newman College (Birmingham); University College Northampton; Northern School of Contemporary Dance; Norwich School of Art and Design; School of Oriental and African Studies; School of Pharmacy (London); Ravensbourne College of Design and Communication (Bromley); RCN Institute (London); College of Ripon and York St. John (York); University of Surrey Roehampton; Rose Bruford College of Speech and Drama (Sidcup); Royal Academy of Music (London); Royal College of Art (London); Royal College of Music (London); Royal Northern College of Music (Manchester); Royal Veterinary College; St George's Hospital Medical School, College of St Mark and St John (Plymouth); St Martin's College (Lancaster); St Mary's College (Twickenham); Southampton Institute; The Surrey Institute of Art and Design, University College (Farnham); Trinity and All Saints (Leeds); Trinity College of Music (London); Wimbledon School of Art; University College, Worcester; Writtle College (Chelmsford).

The Teaching and Higher Education Act 1998 made provision for colleges of higher education with degree-awarding powers to adopt the title 'university college'.

CULTURE

Tourism. The leading attraction in 2001 was Blackpool Pleasure Beach, Lancs, with an estimated 6·5m. visits. The leading tourist attractions charging admission in 2001 were: the British Airways London Eye, with 3,850,000; the Tower of London, with 2,019,210 visits; Eden Project in St Austell, with 1,700,000; Natural History Museum in London, with 1,696,176; and Legoland Windsor, with 1,632,000 visits.

FURTHER READING

Day, Alan, *England*. [Bibliography] ABC-Clio, Oxford and Santa Barbara (CA), 1993
Lloyd, T. O., *Empire, Welfare State, Europe: English History, 1906–1992*. 4th ed. OUP, 1993
Heffer, Simon, *Nor Shall My Sword: The Reinvention of England*. Weidenfeld and Nicolson, London, 1999
Oxford History of England. 16 vols. OUP, 1936–91

SCOTLAND

KEY HISTORICAL EVENTS

Earliest evidence of human settlement in Scotland dates from the Middle Stone Age. Hunters and fishermen on the west coast were succeeded by farming communities who made homes as far north as Shetland. The Romans were active in the first century AD but made so little impact on hostile tribes they built Hadrian's Wall between the Tyne and Solway Firth as their northern frontier. At this time, the Picts with their own language and culture consolidated their strength beyond the Firth of Clyde, but it was the southern Scots, a Celtic people from Ireland, who gave their name to the land.

In 843 Kenneth MacAlpine united the Scots and the Picts to found the kingdom of Scotland. A legal and administrative uniformity was established by David I whose 29-year reign ended in 1153. His successors maintained an understanding with England which allowed for a century of peace, but in 1286 Edward I of England asserted his claim as overlord of Scotland and appointed his son to succeed to the crown.

Resistance to English rule was led by Robert Bruce, who turned back the English at Bannockburn. His son, David II, was less successful in the battlefield, but defended independence by clever diplomacy. He died in 1371 and was succeeded by his nephew Robert, the first king of the Stuart line.

The reigns of five James's occupied the century and a half between the death of Robert III in 1406 and the accession of Mary. This was the time when the alliance between France and Scotland was cemented by common hostility to England.

James IV reinforced a peace agreement with Henry VII by marrying his daughter Margaret in 1503. Religious differences put a strain on the alliance, and when Henry VIII invaded France, James attacked England only to be killed in the Battle of Flodden.

The young James V was assailed by conflicting pressures from pro-French and pro-English factions but having secured his personal rule, he entered into two successive French marriages. His second wife, Mary, was the mother of Mary, Queen of Scots, who married the Dauphin in 1558. Protestant opposition to French influence was bolstered by Elizabeth I of England who sent troops. Mary was then in France. Returning to Scotland after her husband's death in 1561 she was beset by religious enemies and forced to take refuge in England, where she was the nearest heir to Elizabeth. Her son James VI survived the animosity between his own and his mother's followers to make an alliance with England. With the execution of his mother by a nervous Protestant establishment in England, James became heir to the English throne to which he succeeded in 1603.

The crowns of England and Scotland were now worn by the same monarch but for a century more the two countries remained independent. Reflecting the religious and political divisions of the Civil War in England, which led to the execution of Charles I, Scottish armies fought for both sides. The Scots soon united, however, to accept Charles II as their king. Having established dominance in England, Cromwell moved against Scotland forcing Charles II into exile. His restoration in 1660 was welcomed in both kingdoms. His successor James VII of Scotland and James II of Great Britain and Ireland was less astute in managing religious and political differences. The collapse of his regime in 1688 and the arrival of William of Orange confirmed the Protestant ascendancy in Scotland and England.

The union of parliament, which followed in 1707, brought Scotland more directly under English authority but in many respects the country retained its own system of government.

The remaining supporters of James VII, the Jacobites, led two abortive risings on behalf of James's son and grandson (the old and new Pretenders) but were defeated decisively at Culloden in 1746.

TERRITORY AND POPULATION

The total area of Scotland is 77,925 sq. km (2001), including its islands, 186 in number, and inland water 1,580 sq. km. Scotland covers 32·1% of the total area of the United Kingdom.

Population (including military in the barracks and seamen on board vessels in the harbours) at the dates of each census:

Date of enumeration	Population	Pop. per sq. mile[1]	Date of enumeration	Population	Pop. per sq. mile[1]
1801	1,608,420	53	1851	2,888,742	97
1811	1,805,864	60	1861	3,062,294	100
1821	2,091,521	70	1871	3,360,018	113
1831	2,364,386	79	1881	3,735,573	125
1841	2,620,184	88	1891	4,025,647	135

Date of enumeration	Population	Pop. per sq. mile[1]	Date of enumeration	Population	Pop. per sq. mile[1]
1901	4,472,103	150	1961	5,179,344	174
1911	4,760,904	160	1971	5,228,963	67
1921	4,882,497	164	1981	5,130,735	66
1931	4,842,980	163	1991	4,998,567	60
1951	5,096,415	171	2001	5,062,011	65

[1]Per sq. km from 1971.

Population at census day 2001:

Males	Females	Total
2,432,494	2,629,517	5,062,011

In 2001, 58,652 people aged three and over spoke Gaelic (65,978 in 1991). Households at the 2001 census: 2,192,000.

The age distribution in Scotland at census day on 2001 was as follows (in 1,000):

Age-group		
Under	5	277
5 and under	10	307
10 „	15	323
15 „	20	317
20 „	25	314
25 „	35	699
35 „	45	781
45 „	55	689
55 „	65	550
65 „	70	239
70 „	75	207
75 „	85	271
85 and upwards		88

Land area and population by administrative area (census day 2001):

Council Area	Area (sq. km)	Population
Aberdeen City	186	212,125
Aberdeenshire	6,313	226,871
Angus	2,182	108,400
Argyll and Bute	6,909	91,306
Clackmannanshire	159	48,077
Dumfries and Galloway	6,426	147,765
Dundee City	60	145,663
East Ayrshire	1,262	120,235
East Dunbartonshire	175	108,243
East Lothian	679	90,088
East Renfrewshire	174	89,311
Edinburgh, City of	264	448,624
Eilean Siar[1]	3,071	26,502
Falkirk	297	145,191
Fife	1,325	349,429
Glasgow City	175	577,869
Highland	25,659	208,914
Inverclyde	160	84,203
Midlothian	354	80,941
Moray	2,238	86,940
North Ayrshire	885	135,817
North Lanarkshire	470	321,067
Orkney Islands	990	19,245
Perth and Kinross	5,286	134,949
Renfrewshire	261	172,867
Scottish Borders	4,732	106,764
Shetland Islands	1,466	21,988
South Ayrshire	1,222	112,097
South Lanarkshire	1,772	302,216
Stirling	2,187	86,212
West Dunbartonshire	159	93,378
West Lothian	427	158,714
Total	77,925	5,062,011

[1]Formerly Western Isles.

Estimated population of Scotland, mid-2002, 5,056,000.

Glasgow is Scotland's largest city, with a census day population of 577,869 in 2001, followed by Edinburgh, the capital (448,624 on census day 2001), and Aberdeen, with 212,125 on census day 2001.

The birthplaces of the 2001 census day population in Scotland were: Scotland, 4,410,400; England, 408,948; Wales, 16,623; Northern Ireland, 33,528; Ireland 21,774; other European Union countries, 44,432; elsewhere, 126,306.

SOCIAL STATISTICS

	Estimated resident population at 30 June[1]	Total births	Live births outside marriage	Deaths	Marriages	Divorces, annulments and dissolutions
1996	5,128,000	59,296	21,360	60,654	30,242	12,308
1997	5,122,500	59,440	22,388	59,494	29,611	12,222
1998	5,120,000	57,319	22,319	59,164	29,668	12,384
1999	5,119,200	55,147	22,722	60,281	29,940	11,864
2000	5,114,600	53,076	22,625	57,799	30,367	11,143
2001	5,064,200	52,527	22,760	57,382	29,621	10,631

[1]Includes merchant navy at home and forces stationed in Scotland.

Birth rate, 2001, per 1,000 population, 10·4; death rate, 11·3; marriage, 5·8; infant mortality per 1,000 live births, 5·5; sex ratio, 1,041 male births to 1,000 female. Average age of marriage in 2001: males, 34·8, females, 32·3. Expectation of life, 2001: males, 73·4 years, females, 78·8.

CLIMATE

For more detailed information, see under Climate, United Kingdom.

Aberdeen, Jan. 38°F (3·3°C), July 57°F (13·9°C). Annual rainfall 32" (813 mm). Edinburgh, Jan. 38°F (3·3°C), July 58°F (14·5°C). Annual rainfall 27" (686 mm). Glasgow, Jan. 39°F (3·9°C), July 59°F (15°C). Annual rainfall 38" (965 mm).

CONSTITUTION AND GOVERNMENT

One of the main aspects of the British Labour government's programme of constitutional reform is devolution. In the referendum on Scottish devolution on 11 Sept. 1997, 1,775,045 votes (74·3%) were cast in favour of a Scottish parliament and 614,400 against (25·7%). The turn-out was 60·4%, so around 44·8% of the total electorate voted in favour. For the second question, on the Parliament's tax-raising powers, 1,512,889 votes were cast in favour (63·5%) and 870,263 against (36·5%). This represented 38·4% of the total electorate.

The Parliamentary electorate of Scotland in the register numbered 3,984,306 in 2001–02.

RECENT ELECTIONS

At the UK general election held in June 2001, 72 members were returned from Scotland. The Scottish National Party gained 5 seats (6 in 1997). At the June 1999 European Parliament elections Labour won 3 seats, the Scottish National Party 2, the Conservatives 2 and Liberal Democrats 1.

In elections to the Scottish Parliament on 1 May 2003, Labour won 50 seats (4 by regional list), against 27 (18 by regional list) for the Scottish National Party, 18 (15 by regional list) for the Conservatives, 17 (4 by regional list) for the Liberal Democrats, 7 (all by regional list) for the Greens, 6 (all by regional list) for the Scottish Socialist Party (SSP) and 4 independents. Of the 129 seats, 73 were won on a first-past-the-post basis and 56 through proportional representation (regional list). Turn-out was 49%. Donald Dewar was elected as *First Minister* on 13 May 1999. He died on 11 Oct. 2000. Jim Wallace was acting first minister until the election of Henry McLeish on 26 Oct. 2000. McLeish resigned on 8 Nov. 2001 and Wallace again assumed the post temporarily. Jack McConnell was elected first minister on 23 Nov. 2001 and re-elected on 15 May 2003.

See also Constitution and Government, Recent Elections and Current Administration in United Kingdom.

CURRENT ADMINISTRATION

First Minister: Jack McConnell; b. 1960 (Labour).
Presiding Officer: George Reid.

Scottish Executive: http://www.scotland.gov.uk

DEFENCE

For information on defence, see United Kingdom.

ECONOMY

Currency. The Bank of Scotland, Clydesdale Bank and the Royal Bank of Scotland have note-issuing powers. The underlying inflation rate rose to 2·6% in Dec. 1998.

Budget. Government expenditure in Scotland came to £33·1bn. in 1998–99 (including social security £9·2bn., health and personal social services £6·1bn. and education £4·2bn.). Revenues totalled £28·2bn. (including income tax £6·4bn., social security receipts £4·7bn. and VAT £4·3bn.).

Performance. GDP rose by 0·4% in the first quarter of 2001 and 1·1% in the year ending the first quarter of 2001.

Banking and Finance. There is a stock exchange in Glasgow.

ENERGY AND NATURAL RESOURCES

Electricity. The Electricity Act 1989 created three new companies in Scotland. ScottishPower and Scottish Hydro-Electric (now renamed Scottish and Southern Energy) are vertically integrated companies carrying out generation, transmission, distribution and supply of electricity within their areas. They were privatized in 1990. Scottish Nuclear, responsible for operating the two Scottish nuclear power stations, was merged with Nuclear Electric in 1996. ScottishPower now owns Manweb in England, and Scottish Hydro-Electric has merged with Southern Electric under its new group name.

Water. Water supply is the responsibility of the Regional and Island local authorities. Seven river purification boards are responsible for environmental management.

Agriculture. In 1997 total agricultural area was 6,122,000 ha, of which 3,494,000 ha were used for rough grazing and 1,809,000 ha for crops and grass.

Selected crop production, 1997 (1,000 tonnes): barley, 1,813; potatoes, 1,149; wheat, 821; oats, 121.

Livestock, 1997 (in 1,000): cattle, 2,079; sheep, 9,563; pigs, 645; poultry, 14,725.

Forestry. Total forest area in 2002 was 1,324,000 ha, of which 475,000 ha was owned by the Forestry Commission.

Fisheries. The major fishing ports are Aberdeen, Mallaig, Lerwick and Peterhead. In 1997 there were 2,770 fishing vessels that landed 686,400 tonnes of fish worth £278·7m.

INDUSTRY

Labour. In 1999 the economically active population numbered 2,467,000 (1,121,000 females), of whom 182,000 (63,000) were unemployed. This equates to an unemployment rate of 7·4% (8·9% for men and 5·6% for women). By Sept. 2001 employment in Scotland was at its highest in 40 years. In Sept. 1997, 22·7% of the active workforce were in distribution, hotels and catering and repairs, 21·2% in education, social work and health services, 16·4% in manufacturing, and 14·85% in financial and business services.

COMMUNICATIONS

Roads. Responsibility for the construction and maintenance of trunk roads belongs to the Scottish Office. Roads not classified as trunk roads are the responsibility of county or unitary councils. In 1997 there were 53,100 km of public roads, of which 329 km were motorways. There were 1,779,000 licensed private and light goods vehicles.

Rail. Total railway length in 1997 was 2,696 km. There is a metro in Glasgow.

Civil Aviation. There are major airports at Aberdeen, Edinburgh, Glasgow and Prestwick. In 2000 Glasgow was the sixth busiest for passenger traffic in the UK, with 6,924,226 passengers (3,568,148 on domestic flights). Prestwick was the sixth busiest UK airport for freight in 2000, handling 41,458 tonnes. In 1998,

14,382,437 passengers and 68,516 tonnes of freight were carried by Scottish airports.

Shipping. The principal Scottish port is Forth, which handled 44·0m. tonnes of cargo in 1998.

SOCIAL INSTITUTIONS

Justice. The High Court of Justiciary is the supreme criminal court in Scotland and has jurisdiction in all cases of crime committed in any part of Scotland, unless expressly excluded by statute. It consists of the Lord Justice General, the Lord Justice Clerk and 30 other Judges, who are the same Judges who preside in the Court of Session, the Scottish Supreme Civil Court. One Judge is seconded to the Scottish Law Commission. The Court is presided over by the Lord Justice General, whom failing, by the Lord Justice Clerk, and exercises an appellate jurisdiction as well as being a court of first instance. The home of the High Court is Edinburgh, but the court visits other towns and cities in Scotland on circuit and indeed the busiest High Court sitting is in Glasgow. The court sits in Edinburgh both as a Court of Appeal (the *quorum* being two judges if the appeal is against sentence or other disposals, and three in all other cases) and on circuit as a court of first instance. Although the decisions of the High Court are not subject to review by the House of Lords, with the Scotland Act 1998 coming into force on 20 May 1999, there is a limited right of appeal against the termination of a devolution issue to the Judicial Committee of the Privy Council. One Judge sitting with a Jury of 15 persons can, and usually does, try cases, but two or more Judges (with a Jury) may do so in important or complex cases. The court has a privative jurisdiction over cases of treason, murder, rape, breach of duty by Magistrates and certain statutory offences under the Official Secrets Act 1911 and the Geneva Conventions Act 1957. It also tries the most serious crimes against person or property and those cases in which a sentence greater than imprisonment for three years is likely to be imposed.

The appellate jurisdiction of the High Court of Justiciary extends to all cases tried on indictment, whether in the High Court or the Sheriff Court, and persons so convicted may appeal to the court against conviction or sentence, or both, except where the sentence is fixed by law. In such an appeal, a person may bring under review any alleged miscarriage of justice including an alleged miscarriage of justice based on the existence and significance of evidence not heard at the original proceedings provided there is reasonable explanation of why it was not heard and an alleged miscarriage of justice where the Jury returned a verdict which no reasonable Jury, properly directed, could have returned. It is also a court of review from courts of summary jurisdiction, and on the final termination of any summary prosecution the convicted person may appeal to the court by way of stated case on questions of law, but not on questions of fact, except in relation to a miscarriage of justice alleged by the person accused on the basis of the existence and significance of additional evidence not heard at the original proceedings provided that there is a reasonable explanation of why it was not heard. Before cases proceed to a full hearing, leave of appeal must first be granted. Grounds of appeal and any relevant reports are sifted by a Judge sitting alone in chambers, who will decide if there are arguable grounds of appeal. Should leave of appeal be refused, this decision may be appealed to the High Court within 14 days, when the matter will be reviewed by three Judges. The Lord Advocate is entitled to appeal to the High Court against any sentence passed on indictment on the ground that it is unduly lenient, or on a point of law. Both the prosecution and defence, at any time in solemn and summary proceedings, may appeal by way of Bill of Advocation in order to correct irregularities in the preliminary stages of a case. In summary proceedings the accused may appeal by Bill of Suspension, where he desires to bring under review a warrant, conviction or judgement issued by an inferior Judge. In summary proceedings the accused can also appeal against sentence alone by way of Stated Case. In summary proceedings the Crown can appeal against a sentence on the grounds that it is unduly lenient. The court also hears appeals under the Courts-Martial (Appeals) Act 1951.

The Sheriff Court has an inherent universal criminal jurisdiction (as well as an extensive civil one), limited in general to crimes and offences committed within a sheriffdom (a specifically defined region), which has, however, been curtailed by statute or practice under which the High Court of Justiciary has exclusive jurisdiction in relation to the crimes mentioned above. The Sheriff Court is presided over by a Sheriff Principal or a Sheriff, who when trying cases on indictment sits with a Jury of 15 people. His powers of awarding punishment involving imprisonment are restricted to a maximum of three years, but he may under certain statutory powers remit the prisoner to the High Court for sentence if this is felt to be insufficient. The Sheriff also exercises a wide summary criminal jurisdiction and when doing so sits without a Jury; and he has concurrent jurisdiction with every other court within his Sheriff Court district in regard to all offences competent for trial in summary courts. The great majority of offences which come before courts are of a more minor nature and as such are disposed of in the Sheriff Summary Courts or in the District Courts (*see* below). Where a case is to be tried on indictment either in the High Court of Justiciary or in the Sheriff Court, the Judge may, before the trial, hold a preliminary or first diet to decide questions of a preliminary nature, whether relating to the competency or relevancy of proceedings or otherwise. Any decision at a preliminary diet (other than a decision to adjourn the first or preliminary diet or discharge trial diet) can be the subject of an appeal to the High Court of Justiciary prior to the trial. The High Court also has the exclusive power to provide a remedy for all extraordinary occurrences in the course of criminal business where there is no other mode of appeal available. This is known as the Nobile Officium powers of the High Court and all petitions to the High Court as the Nobile Officium must be heard before at least three judges.

In cases to be tried on indictment in the Sheriff Court a first diet is mandatory before the trial diet to decide questions of a preliminary nature and to identify cases which are unlikely to go to trial on the date programmed. Likewise in summary proceedings, an intermediate diet is again mandatory before trial. In High Court cases such matters may be dealt with at a preliminary diet.

District Courts have jurisdiction in more minor offences occurring within a district which before recent local government reorganization corresponded to district council boundaries. These courts are presided over by Lay Magistrates, known as Justices, who have limited powers for fine and imprisonment. In Glasgow District there are also Stipendiary Magistrates, who are legally qualified, and who have the same sentencing powers as Sheriffs.

The Court of Session, presided over by the Lord President (the Lord Justice General in criminal cases), is divided into an inner-house comprising two divisions of five judges each with a mainly appellate function, and an outer-house comprising 22 single Judges sitting individually at first instance; it exercises the highest civil jurisdiction in Scotland, with the House of Lords as a Court of Appeal.

Police. In Scotland, the unitary councils have the role of police authorities. Establishment levels were abolished in Scotland on 1 April 1996. The actual strength at 31 March 2002 was 12,513 men and 2,738 women. There were 1,119 special constables. The total police net expenditure in Scotland for 1999–2000 was £752·9m.

CIVIL JUDICIAL STATISTICS

	2000	2001
House of Lords (Appeals from Court of Session)	14	2
Court of Session—		
General Department	3,912	4,187
Petition Department	1,006	1,119
Sheriff Courts—Ordinary Cause	46,619	49,001
Sheriff Courts—Summary Cause	42,134	40,931
Small Claims	45,786	39,193

CRIMINAL STATISTICS
(Persons proceeded against in Scottish courts)

	1999	2000	2001
All Crimes and Offences			
All persons proceeded against	146,841	137,026	139,956
Persons with a charge proved	127,435	118,009	120,076
Crimes			
All persons proceeded against	53,295	49,248	51,222
Persons with a charge proved	43,449	39,826	41,665
Children (aged 8–15) proceeded against[1]	105	86	105

[1]Except for serious offences which qualify for solemn proceedings, children aged 8–15 are not proceeded against in Scottish courts. Children within this age group that commit crime are generally referred to the reporter of the children's panel or are given a police warning.

UNITED KINGDOM OF GREAT BRITAIN AND NORTHERN IRELAND

In 2000 there were 423,000 crimes reported, of which 23,000 were violent. The average prison population in Scotland in 2000 was 5,869.

Religion. The Church of Scotland, which was reformed in 1560, subsequently developed a presbyterian system of church government which was established in 1690 and has continued to the present day.

The supreme court is the General Assembly, which now consists of some 800 members, ministers and elders in equal numbers, together with members of the diaconate commissioned by presbyteries. It meets annually in May, under the presidency of a Moderator appointed by the Assembly. The Queen is normally represented by a Lord High Commissioner, but has occasionally attended in person. The royal presence in a special throne gallery in the hall but outside the Assembly symbolizes the independence from state control of what is nevertheless recognized as the national Church in Scotland.

There are also 46 presbyteries in Scotland, together with 1 presbytery of England, 1 presbytery of Europe, and 1 presbytery of Jerusalem. At the base of this conciliar structure of Church courts are the kirk sessions, of which there were 1,555 on 31 Dec. 2000. The total communicant membership of the Church at that date was 607,714.

The Episcopal Church of Scotland is a province of the Anglican Church and is one of the historic Scottish churches. It consists of seven dioceses. As at 31 Dec. 2001 it had 304 churches and missions, 349 clergy and 46,237 members, of whom 29,810 were communicants.

There are in Scotland some small outstanding Presbyterian bodies and also Baptists, Congregationalists, Methodists and Unitarians.

The Roman Catholic Church which celebrated the centenary of the restoration of the Hierarchy in 1978, had in Scotland (1998) 1 cardinal archbishop, 1 archbishop, 5 bishops, 20 permanent deacons, 907 clergy, 463 parishes and 705,650 adherents.

The proportion of marriages in Scotland according to the rites of the various Churches in 2001 was: Church of Scotland, 38·5%; Roman Catholic, 6·9%; Baptist Union of Scotland, 1·1%; others, 14·7%; civil, 38·8%.

Education. In Sept. 2001 there were 2,855 publicly funded (local authority, grant-aided and self-governing) primary, secondary and special schools. All teachers employed in these schools require to be qualified.

Pre-school Education. In Jan. 2002 there were 2,597 pre-school centres that were in partnership with their local authority and 98,769 pupils enrolled in these centres.

Primary Education. In Sept. 2001 there were 2,271 publicly funded primary schools with 420,523 pupils and 22,289 full-time equivalent teachers.

Secondary Education. In Sept. 2001 there were 387 publicly funded secondary schools with 316,368 pupils and 1,296 adults. All but 21 schools provided a full range of Scottish Certificate of Education courses and non-certificate courses. Pupils who start their secondary education in schools which do not cater for a full range of courses may be transferred at the end of their second or fourth year to schools where a full range of courses is provided. There were 24,552 full-time equivalent teachers in secondary schools.

Independent schools. There were 155 independent schools in Sept. 2001, with a total of 30,400 pupils. A small number of the Scottish independent schools are of the 'public school' type, but they are not known as 'public schools' since in Scotland this term is used to denote education authority (i.e., state) schools.

Special Education. In Sept. 2001 there were 197 publicly funded special schools with 8,183 pupils.

Further Education. Under the Further and Higher Education (Scotland) Act 1992 funding of the Further Education colleges was transferred to central government in 1993. With effect from 1 July 1999 Scotland's FE colleges are funded by the Scottish Further Education Funding Council, a new executive Non Departmental Public Body established by the Secretary of State for Scotland on 1 Jan. 1999.

There are 42 incorporated FE colleges as well as the FE colleges in Orkney and Shetland, which are run by the local education authorities, and 2 privately managed colleges, Sabhal Mor Ostaig and Newbattle Abbey College. The colleges offer training in a wide range of vocational areas and co-operate with the Scottish Qualifications Authority, the Enterprise and Lifelong Learning Department and the Education Department of the Scottish Executive in the development of new courses. The qualifications offered by colleges aim to improve the skills of the nation's workforce and increase the country's competitiveness. The colleges benefit from co-operation with industry, through involvement with Industry Lead Bodies and National Training Organizations whose responsibility it is to identify education, training and skills needs at sectoral level. Industry is also represented on college boards of management. Colleges and schools in Scotland are directly involved in providing the new national qualifications introduced in 1999 as a result of the Higher Still development programme.

In 2000–01 there were 383,543 students enrolled on vocational courses at Scotland's 46 further education institutions; the full-time equivalent staff number in the colleges was 12,310.

Full-time students resident in Scotland (and EU students) undertaking non-advanced (further education) courses are mainly supported through discretionary further education bursaries which are administered locally by further education colleges within National Policy Guidelines issued by the Scottish Further Education Funding Council. The Colleges have delegated discretionary powers for some aspects of the bursary support award.

In May 2000 the Scottish Executive announced the abolition of tuition fees for all eligible Scottish (and EU) full-time further education students from Autumn 2000. The Executive also made a commitment to take steps to align, from Autumn 2001, the levels of support available on a weekly basis for FE students with those that will apply for HE students and to begin to align the systems of assessment of parental/family contributions.

Higher Education. In Scotland in 2002 there were 21 institutions of higher education funded by the Scottish Higher Education Funding Council (SHEFC), with the exception of the Scottish Agricultural College which is funded by the Scottish Executive Rural Affairs Department. Included in this total is the Open University. SHEFC took over the responsibility for funding the Open University in Scotland at the start of the 2000–01 academic session. University education in Scotland has a long history. Four universities—St Andrews, Glasgow, Aberdeen and Edinburgh, known collectively as the 'four ancient Scottish universities'—were founded in the 15th and 16th centuries. Four further universities—Strathclyde, Heriot-Watt, Stirling and Dundee—were formally established as independent universities between 1964 and 1967, and four others—Napier, Paisley, Robert Gordon and Glasgow Caledonian—were granted the title of university in 1992, with a fifth, the University of Abertay, Dundee, being added in 1994.

Of the remaining higher education institutions, which all offer courses at degree level (although not themselves universities), five were formerly Central Institutions: Edinburgh College of Art, Glasgow School of Art, Queen Margaret University College (Edinburgh), Royal Scottish Academy of Music and Drama (Glasgow) and Scottish Agricultural College (Perth).

Two additional higher education institutions were established in 2001. UHIMI Millennium Institute was designated as a higher education institution on 1 April when it took over from the local colleges of further education and other non-SHEFC funded institutions responsibility for all HE provision and all students on courses of HE in the Academic Partner institutions. Bell College of Technology became a higher education institution on 1 Aug. when its transfer from the further to the higher education sector was completed.

Further education colleges may also provide higher education courses.

University and selected HE student and staff figures:

Name (and Location)	Full-time and sandwich students (2000–01)	Full-time academic staff (2000–01)
Aberdeen Univ.	10,043	1,218
Abertay Dundee Univ.	3,789	254
Dundee Univ.	8,615	1,241
Edinburgh College of Art	1,553	70
Edinburgh Univ.	18,887	2,695
Glasgow School of Art	1,470	67

Name (and Location)	Full-time and sandwich students (2000–01)	Full-time academic staff (2000–01)
Glasgow Caledonian Univ.	10,889	658
Glasgow Univ.	16,337	2,253
Heriot-Watt Univ. (Edinburgh)	5,531	672
Napier Univ. (Edinburgh)	9,315	604
Northern College of Education[1]	1,116	107
Paisley Univ.	6,593	458
Queen Margaret University College	3,148	187
Robert Gordon Univ. (Aberdeen)	7,608	512
St Andrews Univ.	6,578	734
Stirling Univ.	6,636	590
Strathclyde Univ. (Glasgow)	14,534	1,370

[1]Merged with the Univ. of Dundee and the Univ. of Aberdeen in 2001.

In 2000–01 there were 72,855 full-time students in further education colleges (31,362 studying at higher education level and 41,493 studying at further education level) of which 37,537 were female (16,807 HE and 20,730 FE).

All the higher education institutions are independent and self-governing. In addition to funding through the higher education funding councils, they receive tuition fees from the Students Awards Agency for Scotland for students domiciled in Scotland, and through local education authorities for students domiciled in England and Wales. Institutions which carry out research may also receive funding through the five Research Councils administered by the Office of Science and Technology.

Health. In 1999 there were 3,697 GPs with average patient list size of 1,441, and 1,833 dental practitioners with an average list size of (1997) 2,800.

Welfare. In 1997 there were 861,600 recipients of National Insurance retirement pensions, 29,000 recipients of contribution-based Jobseekers' Allowance, and 74,000 families receiving family income supplement/family credit.

CULTURE

Press. Average daily circulation in Feb. 2002 for the daily *Scotsman* was 80,223 and the *Daily Record* 578,778; and for *Scotland on Sunday* 89,651 and the *Sunday Mail* 689,761.

Tourism. There were 1,589,000 overseas visitors to Scotland in 2001, spending £757m. Overall tourism receipts totalled £4·17bn. The tourist attraction receiving the most visitors is Edinburgh Castle, with 1,127,000 visits in 2001. In 2001 around 9% of the workforce was employed in the tourism industry.

Festivals. The Edinburgh Festival and the Fringe Festival both take place in Aug./early Sept. and are major international festivals of culture.

Museums and Galleries. The most visited museum is Kelvingrove Art Gallery and Museum in Glasgow, with 1,031,138 visits in 2001.

FURTHER READING
Scottish Executive. Scottish Economic Report. TSO (twice yearly).—*Scottish Abstract of Statistics.* TSO (annual)

Brown, A., *et al.*, *Politics and Society in Scotland.* London, 1996
Bruce, D., *The Mark of the Scots.* Birch Lane Press, 1997
Dennistoun, R. and Linklater, M. (eds.) *Anatomy of Scotland.* Edinburgh, 1992
Devine, T. M. and Finlay, R. J. (eds.) *Scotland in the 20th Century.* Edinburgh Univ. Press, 1996
Harvie, C., *Scotland and Nationalism: Scottish Society and Politics, 1707–1994.* 2nd ed. London, 1994
Hunter, J., *A Dance Called America.* Edinburgh, 1997
Keay, J. and J., *Collins Encyclopedia of Scotland: The Story of a Nation.* London, 2000
Macleod, J., *Highlanders: A History of the Gaels.* London, 1997
Magnusson, M., *Scotland: The Story of a Nation.* London, 2000
McCaffrey, J. F., *Scotland in the Nineteenth Century.* London, 1998

WALES

KEY HISTORICAL EVENTS

After the Roman evacuation, Wales divided into tribal kingdoms. Cunedda Wledig, a prince from southern Scotland, founded a dynasty in the northwest district of Gwynedd to become the centrepoint for Welsh unity. Offa's Dyke, the defensive earthwork built in the time of King Offa of Mercia, was the dividing line between England and Wales but over the next two centuries a succession of Welsh kings deferred to the English monarchy.

With the accession of Llewelyn (1194–1240) the house of Gwynedd overcame rival claims from Powys and Deneubarth to forge a stable political state under English suzerainty. But when Llywelyn ap Gruffydd (1246–82) intrigued against Edward I, Wales was annexed and Edward's infant son, born at Caernarvon, was made Prince of Wales.

In the Tudor period, Welsh loyalty to Henry VIII, who was of Welsh descent, was fully reciprocated. The Act of Union in 1536 made English law general and admitted Welsh representatives to Parliament.

TERRITORY AND POPULATION

At the census taken on 29 April 2001 the population was 2,903,085. The area of Wales is 20,732 sq. km. Population density, 2001 census: 140 per sq. km. Wales covers 8·5% of the total area of the United Kingdom.

Population at census day 2001:

Males	Females	Total
1,403,900	1,499,185	2,903,085

Population (present on census night) at the four previous decennial censuses:

1961	1971	1981	1991
2,644,023[1]	2,731,204[1]	2,790,500[2]	2,811,865

[1]Areas now recognized as Monmouthshire and small sections of various other counties formed the county of Monmouthshire in England until 1974.

[2]The final count is believed to be over-stated as a result of an error in processing. The preliminary counts presented here rounded to the nearest hundred are thought to be more accurate.

Estimated population, mid-2002, 2,908,000. Cardiff, the capital and largest city, had a population in 2001 of 305,340; Swansea, the second largest city, had a population of 223,293 in 2001.

In 2001, 457,950 people aged three and over were able to speak, read and write Welsh. Households at the 2001 census: 1,276,000.

For further statistical information, see under Territory and Population, United Kingdom.

Wales is divided into 22 unitary authorities (cities and counties, counties and county boroughs).

Designations, areas and populations of the unitary authority areas at census day 2001:

Unitary Authority	Designation	Area (sq. km)	Population
Blaenau Gwent	County Borough	109	70,058
Bridgend	County Borough	251	128,650
Caerphilly	County Borough	278	169,521
Cardiff	City and County	139	305,340
Carmarthenshire	County	2,394	173,635
Ceredigion	County	1,792	75,384
Conwy	County Borough	1,126	109,597
Denbighshire	County	837	93,092
Flintshire	County	438	148,565
Gwynedd	County	2,535	116,838
Isle of Anglesey	County	711	66,828
Merthyr Tydfil	County Borough	111	55,983
Monmouthshire	County	849	84,879
Neath and Port Talbot	County Borough	441	134,471
Newport	County Borough	190	137,017
Pembrokeshire	County	1,589	112,901
Powys	County	5,181	126,344
Rhondda Cynon Taff	County Borough	424	231,952

Unitary Authority	Designation	Area (sq. km)	Population
Swansea	City and County	378	223,293
The Vale of Glamorgan	County Borough	331	119,500
Torfaen	County Borough	126	90,967
Wrexham	County Borough	504	128,477

SOCIAL STATISTICS

2000: births, 31,304 (10·6 per 1,000 population), of which 14,763 outside marriage; deaths, 33,323 (11·3 per 1,000 population); marriages (1999), 14,025 (4·8 per 1,000 population); divorces, 7,704; still births, 145 (5 per 1,000 births); infant mortality, 165 (5 per 1,000 live births).

CLIMATE

For more detailed information, see under Climate, United Kingdom.
Cardiff, Jan. 40°F (4·4°C), July 61°F (16·1°C). Annual rainfall 42·6" (1,065 mm).

CONSTITUTION AND GOVERNMENT

One of the main aspects of the British Labour government's programme of constitutional reform is devolution. On 18 Sept. 1997 in the referendum there were 559,419 votes cast in favour of a Welsh assembly (50·3%) and 552,698 against (49·7%). The turn-out was 51·3%.

The Parliamentary electorate of Wales in the register in 2001–02 numbered 2,236,143.

RECENT ELECTIONS

At the UK general election of 7 June 2001, 40 members were returned from Wales. Labour won 34 seats (34 in 1997), Plaid Cymru, 4 seats (4), Liberal Democrats, 2 seats (2).

At the 1999 European Parliamentary elections, 2 Labour candidates were elected, 2 Plaid Cymru and 1 Conservative.

In the elections to the Welsh Assembly on 1 May 2003, Labour won 30 seats (all constituencies), followed by Plaid Cymru with 12 (7 by regional list), the Conservatives with 11 (10 by regional list), the Liberal Democrats with 6 (3 by regional list) and 1 independent constituency. Of the 60 seats, 40 seats were won on a first-past-the-post basis and 20 through proportional representation (regional list). 30 seats were won by women. Turn-out was 38%.

See also Constitution and Government, Recent Elections and Current Administration in United Kingdom.

CURRENT ADMINISTRATION

First Secretary: Rhodri Morgan; b. 1939 (Labour).
Presiding Officer: Dafydd Elis-Thomas.

National Assembly for Wales: http://www.wales.gov.uk

DEFENCE

For information on defence, see United Kingdom.

ECONOMY

For information on the economy, see United Kingdom.

Budget. General government expenditure in 1996–97 amounted to £4,620m.

Performance. Total GDP in 1999 (provisional) was £30,689m.

ENERGY AND NATURAL RESOURCES

For information on energy and natural resources, see United Kingdom.

Water. The Water Act of Sept. 1989 privatized Welsh Water (Dwr Cymru Cyfyngedig), along with the nine water authorities in England. Daily output, 1997, was 2,305 megalitres.

Agriculture. In 1997 there were 27,973 agricultural holdings. Of these, 916 were under 2 ha, 9,997 were between 2 and 19 ha, 5,671 were between 20 and 39 ha and 9,820 were over 40 ha. 1,569 were rough-grazing holdings.

A total of 74,200 ha were used for crops, 76,000 ha for tillage and 1,900 ha left bare fallow. Major crops, 1997 (1,000 tonnes): barley, 174; wheat, 107; potatoes, 58; oats, 18.

Livestock, 1997: cattle, 1,323,000; sheep and lambs, 10,915,100; pigs, 98,600; poultry, 8,364,000.

Forestry. In 2002 there were 113,000 ha of Forestry Commission woodland and 175,000 ha of non-Forestry Commission woodland.

Fisheries. The major fishing port is Milford Haven. In 1997, in all ports, 19,211 tonnes of fish worth £12,835,600 were landed. There were 513 fishing vessels in all.

INDUSTRY
Selected industrial production, 1996 (£1m.): basic metals and fabricated metal products, 1,656·7; electrical and optical equipment, 1,145·4; food products, beverages and tobacco, 877·6; chemicals, chemical products and man-made fibres, 736·3; transport equipment, 730·9.

Labour. At June 1998 the workforce numbered 1,227,000. There were 67,000 people claiming unemployment benefit and 172,000 people were self-employed. The largest employment sectors were: services, 699,000; production and construction industries, 265,000; manufacturing, 213,000. The unemployment rate in the spring of 2001 was 5·7%, compared to 4·8% for the UK as a whole. In 1994, 13,000 working days were lost due to industrial disputes.

INTERNATIONAL TRADE
For information on international trade, see United Kingdom.

COMMUNICATIONS

Roads. Responsibility for the construction and maintenance of trunk roads belongs to the Welsh Office. Roads not classified as trunk roads are the responsibility of county or unitary councils. In 1998 there were 133 km of motorway, 1,585 km of trunk roads and 2,685 km of principal roads. 1,300,500 vehicles were registered, including 1,112,300 private and light goods vehicles. In 1997 there were 10,251 reported accidents which led to 14,835 casualties and 221 deaths.

Civil Aviation. Cardiff Airport handled 1,499,824 passengers in 2000 (1,405,057 on international flights) and 982 tonnes of freight. A new airline, Air Wales, began services from Cardiff to Cork in 2000 and now flies from Cardiff and Swansea to Dublin and Cork, Swansea to Jersey, and Plymouth to Dublin and Cork.

Shipping. The principal ports are (with 1m. tonnes of cargo handled in 1998): Milford Haven (29·0) and Port Talbot (13·0).

Postal Services. In 1997–98 the Post Office handled 712m. letters and 3·4m. parcels.

SOCIAL INSTITUTIONS

Justice. In 1997 police strength amounted to 6,598. During that year there were 236,937 notable offences, including 17,387 violent and 1,874 sexual offences. The clear-up rate was 40·6%. 17,350 people were found guilty of indictable offences in Magistrates' Courts and 4,040 in Crown Courts. A total of 4,158 people were given custodial sentences.

Religion. Under the Welsh Church Acts, 1914 and 1919, the Church in Wales and Monmouthshire was disestablished as from 1 April 1920, and Wales was formed into a separate Province.

Education. There were 41 maintained nursery schools in Jan. 2001, and 66,324 pupils under five years provided for in nursery schools and in nursery or infants classes in primary schools.

In Jan. 2001 there were 285,786 pupils at 1,631 primary schools. Within these figures, 440 primary schools use Welsh as the sole or main medium of instruction. Such schools are to be found in all parts of Wales but are mainly concentrated in the predominantly Welsh-speaking areas of west and northwest Wales. Generally, children transfer from primary to secondary schools at 11 years of age.

In Jan. 2001 there were 229 secondary schools. All maintained secondary schools are classified as comprehensive; there are no middle schools in Wales. In 2000–01, 53 of the secondary schools were classed as Welsh-speaking as defined in section 354(b) of the Education Act 1996.

Since Sept. 1999, in accordance with the Schools Standards and Framework Act 1998, all maintained schools, including grant maintained schools, in Wales had to change category to one of the following: Community, Community Special, Foundation, Voluntary Controlled, Voluntary Aided. These categories continue to remain in place with the introduction of the Education Act 2002.

Under the Education Act 1996, children have special educational needs if they have a learning difficulty which calls for special educational provision to be made for them. In a minority of cases the local education authority will need to make a statutory assessment of special educational needs under the Education Act 1996, which may ultimately lead to a 'statement of Special Educational Needs'. The total number of pupils with statements in Jan. 2001 was 17,415. From April 2002 Special Educational Needs (SEN) guidance for Wales is set out in the SEN Code of Practice for Wales.

In Jan. 2001, 9,257 full-time pupils attended 54 independent schools.

Post-16 Learning. The National Council for Education and Training Wales (ELWa) was formed from the merger of the four TECs (training and enterprise councils), the Council of Welsh TECs and Further Education Funding Council for Wales (FEFCW) and has been operational since April 2001. It is responsible for the planning and promoting of further, adult and continuing education, work-based training and school sixth forms. Grant in aid allocation for 2002–03 was £489·22m. In 2000–01 the FEFCW supported 42,833 full-time and sandwich students and 192,978 students studying part-time in the further education sector at 27 further education institutions and 9 higher education institutions. In addition, the four TECs supported 30,487 starts in work-based training or with training to return to the workplace. In 2001, 12% of 16- to 18-year-olds did not have a qualification; 5 percentage points lower than in 1996. The percentage of adults with no qualification fell from 23% in 1996 to 21% in 2001; and 40% of adults had an NVQ level three or equivalent, up from 35% in 1996. Between 1996 and 1999 it was estimated that around 7 in 10 adults had functional basis skills in either literacy or numeracy.

Higher Education. In 2000–01 there were 13 institutions of higher education funded directly by the Higher Education Funding Council for Wales (HEFCW), including the University of Glamorgan and the colleges of the University of Wales. In 2002–03 the total budget was £327·44m. There were 110,546 students in the higher education sector in 2000–01, excluding those registered with the Open University, of which 68,491 were full-time and 42,055 part-time students, including those enrolled on higher education provision at further education colleges.

Higher Education Institutes (HEIs)	Full-time/sandwich HE students at HEIs (2000–01)	No. of academic staff (2000–01)[1]
Univ. of Glamorgan (Pontypridd)	9,886	689
Univ. of Wales, Aberystwyth	6,701	621
Univ. of Wales, Bangor	6,987	688
Cardiff University[2]	16,103	1,749
Univ. of Wales, Lampeter	1,001	101
Univ. of Wales, Swansea	8,418	852
Univ. of Wales College of Medicine	2,490	676
Univ. of Wales Institute, Cardiff	6,126	387
Univ. of Wales College, Newport	2,702	183
North East Wales Institute of Higher Education (Wrexham)	2,403	208
Swansea Institute of Higher Education	3,225	196
Trinity College Carmarthen	1,160	81[3]
Welsh College of Music and Drama	540	99

[1]Staff who meet the 25% full-time equivalent threshold.
[2]The public name of the University of Wales, Cardiff.
[3]Excludes part-time staff meeting 25% threshold.

Health. In 1997–98 there were 1,874 GPs, 924 dentists and 23,400 nurses, midwives and health visitors. The average daily number of hospital beds available was 15,200, of which 12,000 were occupied. 521,100 in-patient cases were reported, with stays lasting an average 8·4 days. 69,900 people were on hospital waiting lists.

Welfare. 230,000 people received some form of income support in 1997.

CULTURE

Broadcasting. Radio and television services are provided by the Welsh-language Sianel Pedwar Cymru (S4C, Channel 4 Wales). S4C is funded by the government. It acts as both broadcaster and regulator. In 1997–98 there were 1,260,900 television licences, of which 1,235,000 were colour.

Tourism. In 2001 there were 11·6m. domestic trips (from elsewhere in the UK) into Wales. Visitors stayed 44·6m. nights and spent £1·7bn.

Festivals. Every year there are local and national *eisteddfods* (festivals for musical competitions, etc.). The national *eisteddfod* is held every Aug. in a different location (near Meifod, Montgomeryshire in 2003).

Libraries. In 1996–97 there were 731 libraries with 6,128,000 books. 1,499,000 items were borrowed. The National Library is in Aberystwyth.

Theatre and Opera. There is a Welsh National Opera and the BBC National Orchestra of Wales.

Museums and Galleries. The leading museum is the Museum of Welsh Life in Cardiff, which received 694,899 visits in 2001–02.

FURTHER READING

National Assembly. Digest of Welsh Statistics. National Statistics. Great Britain (annual)
Andrews, Leighton, *Wales Says Yes. The Inside Story of the Yes for Wales Referendum Campaign.* Seren, Bridgend, 1999
Davies, J., *History of Wales.* London, 1993
History of Wales, vols. 3, 4 (1415–1780). 2nd ed. OUP, 1993
Jenkins, G. H., *The Foundations of Modern Wales 1642–1780.* Oxford, 1988.—*The Welsh Language and its Social Domains 1801–1911: A Social History of the Welsh Language.* Univ. of Wales Press, 2000
Jones, G. E., *Modern Wales: a Concise History.* 2nd ed. CUP, 1994
May, J. (ed.) *Reference Wales.* Wales Univ. Press, 1994
Morgan, K. and Mungham, G., *Redesigning Democracy. The Making of the Welsh Assembly.* Seren, Bridgend, 2000

NORTHERN IRELAND

KEY HISTORICAL EVENTS

Northern Ireland is part of the United Kingdom. The Government of Ireland Act 1920 granted Northern Ireland its own bicameral parliament (Stormont), and between 1921 and 1972 it had full responsibility for local affairs except for such matters as defence and the armed forces, foreign and trade policies, and taxation and customs. However, in the late 1960s a Civil Rights campaign and reactions to it escalated into serious rioting and sectarian violence involving the Irish Republican Army (IRA, an illegal organization aiming to unify Northern Ireland with the Republic of Ireland) and loyalist paramilitary organizations. The Northern Ireland government resigned and direct rule by the UK government began in 1972. The Northern Ireland parliament was abolished in 1973. The Northern Ireland Constitution Act 1973 provided for devolved government on a power-sharing basis, but this collapsed in May 1974.

Under the Northern Ireland Act 1974 the UK parliament approves all laws for Northern Ireland and the Northern Ireland departments are under the direction and control of a UK Cabinet Minister, the Secretary of State for Northern Ireland.

Attempts have been made by successive governments to find a means of restoring greater power to Northern Ireland's political representatives on a widely acceptable basis, including a Constitutional Convention (1975–76), a Constitutional Conference (1979–80) and 78-member Northern Ireland Assembly elected by proportional representation in 1982. This was dissolved in 1986, partly in response to Unionist reaction to the Anglo-Irish Agreement signed on 15 Nov. 1985, which established an Intergovernmental Conference of British and Irish ministers to monitor political, security, legal and other issues of concern to the nationalist community.

On 15 Dec. 1993 the Prime Ministers of the UK and the Republic of Ireland (John Major and Albert Reynolds) issued a joint declaration as a basis for all-party talks to achieve a political settlement. They invited Sinn Féin ('Ourselves Alone', pro-Republican nationalist party and the political wing of the IRA) to join the talks in an All-Ireland Forum three months after the cessation of terrorist violence.

The IRA announced 'a complete cessation of military operations' on 31 Aug. 1994. On 13 Oct. 1994 the anti-IRA Combined Loyalist Military Command also announced a ceasefire 'dependent upon the continued cessation of all nationalist republican violence'.

Elections were held on 30 May 1996 to constitute a 110-member forum to take part in talks with the British and Irish governments. Each of the 18 Northern Ireland constituencies returned five delegates. The ten parties receiving the most votes received two extra delegates. The Ulster Unionist Party won 30 seats with 24·2% of votes cast; the Social Democratic and Labour Party, 21 with 21·4%; the Democratic Unionist Party, 24 with 18·8%; and Sinn Féin, 17 with 15·5%.

Opening Plenary talks, excluding Sinn Féin, began under the chairmanship of US Senator George Mitchell on 12 June 1996. A marathon negotiating struggle on 9–10 April 1998 led to agreement on a framework for sharing power designed to satisfy Protestant demands for a reaffirmation of their national identity as British, Catholic desires for a closer relationship with the predominantly Catholic Republic of Ireland and Britain's wish to return to Northern Ireland the powers London assumed in 1972 when the local Stormont legislature was disbanded.

Under the Good Friday Agreement, there was to be a democratically elected legislature in Belfast, a ministerial council giving the governments of Northern Ireland and Ireland joint responsibilities in areas like tourism, transportation and the environment, and a consultative council meeting twice a year to bring together ministers from the British and Irish parliaments, and the three assemblies being created in Northern Ireland and in Scotland and Wales. The Irish government has eliminated from its constitution its territorial claim on Northern Ireland.

The critical issues of police and judicial-system reform, the release of paramilitary prisoners, and the dismantling of the vast underground arsenals of weaponry in the province are the subject of further study and recommendations.

In the referendum on 22 May 1998, 71·12% of votes in Northern Ireland were cast in favour of the Good Friday peace agreement and 94·4% in the Republic of Ireland. As a consequence, in June, Northern Ireland's 1·2m. voters elected the first power-sharing administration since the collapse of the Sunningdale Agreement in 1974. But IRA blockage on the decommissioning of arms continues to hold up the transfer of powers from London to Belfast.

On 15 Aug. 1998 a 200 kg bomb exploded in the centre of Omagh. 29 people died and over 200 were injured, making it the single bloodiest incident of the Troubles. The dissident republican group the 'Real IRA' claimed responsibility.

In Nov. 1999 the Mitchell talks finally produced an agreement between the Ulster Unionists and Sinn Féin which paved the way for the formation of a government with devolved powers. The new Northern Ireland Assembly met for the first time on 29 Nov. 1999, and on 2 Dec. legislative powers were fully devolved from London to Belfast, with the new executive of Unionists, nationalists and republicans meeting for the first time. In the Republic of Ireland on 2 Dec. 1999 the Irish constitution was amended to remove the articles which referred to claims to Northern Ireland. However, on 11 Feb. 2000 the Assembly was suspended following a breakdown in negotiations on the decommissioning of IRA weapons. Direct rule from London was restored while politicians searched for a way forward. Devolved government resumed on 30 May after the IRA agreed to open their arms dumps to independent inspection. First Minister David Trimble resigned on 30 June 2001 to pressure republicans over decommissioning, but on 22 Oct. Sinn Féin president Gerry Adams announced that he had recommended a 'ground-breaking' step on the arms issue. The IRA made a start on decommissioning arms, ammunition and explosives. David Trimble was re-elected First Minister on 6 Nov. 2001.

On 15 Oct. 2002 the Assembly executive was again suspended over allegations of IRA spying at the Northern Ireland Office. Direct rule from London was re-imposed and on 30 Oct. the IRA cut off its links with the weapons de-commissioning body. The Ulster Volunteer Force followed suit on 17 Jan. 2003.

Tony Blair and Bertie Ahern held talks in March 2003 but failed to produce a solution. Clarification of the IRA's intent have so far failed to satisfy the British government or the unionists.

Elections to form a new power-sharing administration, planned for 29 May 2003, have been postponed until late 2003 at the earliest.

TERRITORY AND POPULATION

Area (revised by Ordnance Survey of Northern Ireland) and population were as follows:

District	Population present on census day 2001	Area in ha. (including inland water)
Antrim	48,366	57,686
Ards	73,244	37,619
Armagh	54,263	67,060
Ballymena	58,610	63,202
Ballymoney	26,894	41,820
Banbridge	41,392	45,263
Belfast	277,391	11,488
Carrickfergus	37,659	8,184
Castlereagh	66,488	8,514
Coleraine	56,315	48,551
Cookstown	32,581	62,244
Craigavon	80,671	37,842
Derry (Londonderry)	105,066	38,731
Down	63,828	64,670
Dungannon	47,735	78,360
Fermanagh	57,527	187,582
Larne	30,832	33,567
Limavady	32,422	58,558
Lisburn	108,694	44,684
Magherafelt	39,780	57,280
Moyle	15,933	47,976
Newry and Mourne	87,058	90,243
Newtownabbey	79,995	15,056
North Down	76,323	8,149
Omagh	47,952	113,045
Strabane	38,248	86,165
Northern Ireland	*1,685,267*	*1,413,540*

Northern Ireland's area of 14,135 sq. km represents 5·8% of the total area of the United Kingdom. Chief town (population present on census day 2001): Belfast, 277,391.

Population by gender at the 2001 census was: females, 51·26%; males, 48·74%.

SOCIAL STATISTICS

In 2001 there were 21,962 births and 14,513 deaths, 7,281 marriages and 2,365 divorces.

CLIMATE

For more detailed information, see under Climate, United Kingdom.

Belfast. Jan. 40°F (4·5°C), July 59°F (15·0°C). Annual rainfall 37·4" (950 mm).

CONSTITUTION AND GOVERNMENT

Under the Northern Ireland Act 1998 power that was previously exercised by the NI Departments was devolved to the Northern Ireland Assembly and its Executive Committee of Ministers. The Secretary of State remains responsible for those matters specified in Schedules 2 and 3 of the Act. These broadly equate to policing, security policing, criminal justice, and international relations.

The Parliamentary electorate of Northern Ireland in the register in 2001–02 numbered 1,191,009.

Secretary of State for Northern Ireland. Rt Hon. Paul Murphy, MP.

RECENT ELECTIONS

At the general election of 7 June 2001, 18 members were returned from Northern Ireland. The Ulster Unionist Party gained 6 seats (10 in 1997); the Democratic Unionist Party 5 (2); Sinn Féin 4 (2); the Social and Democratic Labour Party 3 (3).

In the Northern Ireland Assembly elections on 25 June 1998, the Ulster Unionist Party (UUP) won 28 of the 108 seats, the Social Democratic and Labour Party 24, the Democratic Unionist Party 20, Sinn Féin 18, Alliance 6, United Kingdom Unionist Party 5, Independent Unionists 3, Popular Unionist Party 2 and Women's Coalition also 2.

At the June 1999 European Parliament elections, voting was by the single transferable vote system: the Democratic Ulster Unionist Party (28·4%), the Social Democrat and Labour Party (European Socialist Party) (28·1%) and the Ulster Unionist Party (Popular European Party) (17.6%) gained 1 seat each. Turn-out was 57·8%.

CURRENT ADMINISTRATION

David Trimble (Ulster Unionist Party) was elected as the Northern Ireland Assembly's 'First Minister' on 6 Nov. 2001 at a special meeting of the Assembly, having resigned from the post on 30 June 2001. Mark Durkan (Social Democratic and Labour Party) was elected deputy first minister. They are joint leaders of the administration.

Northern Ireland Executive: http://www.nics.gov.uk/

ECONOMY

Overview. The Northern Ireland government department concerned with economic development is the Department of Enterprise, Trade and Investment (DETI). It is responsible for economic policy development, energy, tourism, mineral development, health and safety at work, Companies Registry, Insolvency Service, consumer affairs, and labour market and economic statistics services. It also has a role in ensuring the provision of the infrastructure for a modern economy. DETI has four agencies: Invest Northern Ireland (Invest NI), the Northern Ireland Tourist Board (NITB), the Health and Safety Executive for Northern Ireland (HSENI) and the General Consumer Council for Northern Ireland (GCCNI).

Currency. Banknotes are issued by Allied Irish Banks, Bank of Ireland, First Trust Bank, Northern Bank and Ulster Bank.

Banking and Finance. The Department of Finance and Personnel is responsible for control of the expenditure of Northern Ireland departments, liaison with HM Treasury and the Northern Ireland Office on financial matters, economic and social research and analysis, Citizens Charter Unit, the Valuation and Lands Agency, the Government Purchasing Service (Northern Ireland) and the Legal Services.

Income of the Northern Ireland Consolidated Fund (in £1,000 sterling):

	1999–2000	2000–01	2001–02
Attributed share of UK taxes	3,104,385 }	7,405,400[1]	7,998,998[1]
Grant in Aid from UK government	3,745,000 }		
Regional and district rates	503,500	544,600	568,184
Other receipts	276,850	547,028	404,257
Total	7,629,735	8,497,028	8,971,439

[1]In 2000–01 the funding mechanism was changed to replace the 'Grant in Aid' and 'Attributed share of UK taxation' with a 'Block Grant'.

The public debt at 31 March 2002 was as follows: Ulster Savings Certificates, £21,176,000; Ulster Development Bonds, £12,239,000; borrowing from UK government, £1,473,875,323; borrowing from Northern Ireland government funds, £3,226,732. Excess of public income over public expenditure at 31 March 2002: £334,100,561. Net assets available for debt repayment: £183,075,680.

The above amount of public debt is offset by equal assets in the form of loans from government to public and local bodies, and of cash balances.

ENERGY AND NATURAL RESOURCES

Electricity. There are three power stations with an installed capacity of some 2,100 MW.

A 500 MW interconnector linking the Northern Ireland Electricity (NIE) and Scottish Power networks was officially opened in April 2002. A number of interconnectors also link the NIE network with the Electricity Supply Board (ESB) network in the Republic of Ireland.

Oil and Gas. Natural Gas was brought to Northern Ireland in 1996 via the Scotland to Northern Ireland Gas Pipeline. This allowed Ballylumford Power Station to be converted to gas firing and to make gas available to industrial, commercial and domestic consumers in the Greater Belfast and Larne areas. In Sept. 2001 the Northern Ireland executive approved grant support for the development of the gas network to the North/North West region and for the construction of a South/North pipeline.

Minerals. Output of minerals (in 1,000 tonnes), 2001: sandstone, 8,070; basalt and igneous rock (other than granite), 6,448; sand and gravel, 6,194; limestone, 4,746; other minerals (rocksalt, fireclay, diatomite, granite, chalk, clay and shale), 750. There are lignite deposits of 1,000m. tonnes which have not yet been developed.

Agriculture. Provisional gross output in 2001:

	Quantity	Value (£1m.)		Quantity	Value (£1m.)
Cattle and calves	481,500	331·2	Fruit (1,000 tonnes)	50·5	6·1
Sheep and lambs	1,267,000	82·7	Vegetables (1,000 tonnes)	44·5	15·1
Pigs	935,300	62·0	Mushrooms (1,000 tonnes)	22·2	27·6
Poultry (1,000 tonnes)	159·7	105·2	Other crops	...	21·8
Eggs (m. dozen)	65·8	22·5	Flowers	...	10·4[1]
Milk (1m. litres)	1,798·0	352·5	Capital formation	...	60·8
Other livestock products	...	8·9	Contract work	...	36·7
Cereals (1,000 tonnes)	211·5	23·7	Other items	...	11·2
Potatoes (1,000 tonnes)	252·9	21·5			
			Gross output	...	1,189·5

[1]1999.

Area (in 1,000 ha) on farms:

	2000	2001	2002		2000	2001	2002
Cereals	40·7	39·5	38·1	Grass	829·4	840·1	843·7
Potatoes	6·8	6·7	6·7	Rough grazing	156·5	154·1	151·6
Horticulture	3·3	3·1	3·12	Other land	20·4	20·0	19·3
Other crops	3·3	4·8	4·6				
				Total area	1,060·5	1,068·2	1,067·3

Livestock (in 1,000 heads) on farms at June census:

	2000	2001	2002		2000	2001	2002
Dairy cows	284	295	298	Sows	42	41	39
Beef cows	318	312	307	Laying hens	2,300	2,143	2,099
Other cattle	1,074	1,072	1,080	Broilers	9,655	8,864	11,273
Ewes	1,333	1,232	1,129				

INDUSTRY

Labour. The main sources of employment statistics are the Census of Employment, conducted every two years, and the Quarterly Employment Survey. In Dec. 1999 there were 625,030 employees, of whom 309,010 were males. Employment in manufacturing and construction amounted to 137,340, 22% of the total employees in employment. 19,400 of these jobs were in the food, drink and tobacco industries, 9,360 in the manufacture of wearing apparel, 9,100 in textiles, 30,840 in construction and 68,640 in other sectors of manufacturing. Unemployment in the spring of 2000, at 7·0%, was the lowest in 26 years.

COMMUNICATIONS

Roads. In April 2002 the total length of public roads was 24,788 km, graded for administrative purposes as follows: motorway, 133 km (including 19 km slip roads);

Class '1' dual carriageway, 149 km; Class '1' single carriageway, 2,118 km; Class '2', 2,869 km; Class '3', 4,704 km; unclassified, 14,834 km.

Ulsterbus and Citybus subsidiaries of N.I. Transport Holding Company (NITHC) provide co-ordinated services with N.I. Railways (NIR) Ltd under the service brand name of Translink.

At 31 March 2000 there were 1,963 professional hauliers and 5,322 vehicles licensed to engage in road haulage.

The number of motor vehicles licensed at 31 Dec. 1999 was 720,645, comprising private light goods, 608,316; motorcycles, scooters and mopeds, 13,088; buses, 2,204; goods vehicles, 17,075; agricultural vehicles, 5,505; exempt including crown vehicles, 73,229; and others, 1,228.

Rail. NIR, a subsidiary of NITHC, provides rail services within Northern Ireland and cross-border services to Dublin, jointly with Irish Rail. The number of track-km. operated is 340. In 2000–01 railways carried 5·9m. passengers, generating passenger receipts of £14·1m.

Civil Aviation. There are scheduled air services to three airports in Northern Ireland: Belfast International, Belfast City and City of Derry. Scheduled services are provided by easyJet, bmi British Midland, British Airways' franchise partners and British European (Flybe). Belfast International, the busiest airport, is Northern Ireland's main charter airport with holiday flights operated direct to European destinations by a wide range of local and UK tour operators. In 2001–02 the airports collectively handled 5m. passengers. Belfast International handled 3,602,702 passengers in 2000.

Belfast City Airport offers commuter services to 16 regional airports in Great Britain including services to London Heathrow. The City of Derry Airport is situated 14 km from Londonderry and provides services from the northwest of Ireland to Dublin and to three United Kingdom destinations (Glasgow, London Stansted, Manchester). There are two other licensed airfields at St Angelo and Newtownards. They are used principally by flying clubs, private owners and air taxi businesses.

Shipping. Belfast is the largest port, competing with Larne for the majority of the passenger and Roll-on Roll-off services that operate to and from Northern Ireland. Passenger services are currently available to Liverpool, Stranraer, Cairnryan, Heysham and Troon. In addition, Belfast, Londonderry and Warrenpoint ports offer bulk cargo services mostly for British and European markets. They also occasionally service other international destinations direct.

Total traffic in Northern Ireland in 1999 was 22·8m. tonnes. Belfast handled 12·9m. tonnes of cargo in 1999.

SOCIAL INSTITUTIONS

Justice. The Lord Chancellor has responsibility for the administration of all courts through the Northern Ireland Court Service and for the appointment of judges and magistrates. The court structure has three tiers: the Supreme Court of Judicature of Northern Ireland (comprising the Court of Appeal, the High Court and the Crown Court), the County Courts and the Magistrates' Courts. There are 20 Petty Sessions districts which when grouped together for administration purposes form seven County Court Divisions and four Crown Court Circuits.

The County Court has general civil jurisdiction subject to an upper monetary limit. Appeals from the Magistrates' Courts lie to the County Court, or to the Court of Appeal on a point of law, while appeals from the County Court lie to the High Court or, on a point of law, to the Court of Appeal.

Police. Following legislation introduced in the House of Commons in May 2000, the Royal Ulster Constabulary has now been replaced by the Police Service of Northern Ireland (PSNI). The Police Authority for Northern Ireland has been replaced by the newly formed Northern Ireland Policing Board. The Police Service continues to undergo significant changes arising from the recommendations of the Commission into the future of policing in Northern Ireland published in 1999. In 2002 the PSNI comprised 7,220 regular officers including those student officers undergoing training, 1,786 full-time reserve officers and 955 part-time reserves. The proportion of Catholic regular officers, which was around 8% in Sept. 1999, had increased to 11·6% by Dec. 2002.

Religion. According to the 2001 census there were: Roman Catholics, 678,462; Presbyterians, 348,742; Church of Ireland, 257,788; Methodists, 59,173; other Christian, 102,221; other religions and philosophies, 5,028. There were also 233,853 persons with no religion or religion was not stated.

Education. Public education, other than university education, is presently administered by the Department of Education, the Department of Employment and Learning, and locally by five Education and Library Boards. The Department of Education is concerned with the range of education from nursery education through to secondary, youth services and for the development of community relations within and between schools. The Department of Employment and Learning is responsible for higher education, further education, student support, postgraduate awards, and the funding of teacher training.

Each Education and Library Board is the local education authority for its area. Boards were first appointed in 1973, the year of local government reorganization, and are normally reappointed every four years following the District Council elections. The membership of each Board consists of District councillors, representatives of transferors of schools, representatives of trustees of maintained schools and other persons who are interested in the service for which the Board is responsible. Boards have a duty, amongst other things, to ensure that there are sufficient schools of all kinds to meet the needs of their areas. The Boards are responsible for costs associated with capital works at controlled schools. Voluntary schools, including maintained and voluntary grammar schools, can receive grant-aid from the Department of Education toward capital works of up to 85%, or 100% if they have opted to change their management structures so that no single interest group has a majority of nominees. Most voluntary grammar schools can receive the same rate of grant on the purchase of equipment. The Boards award university and other scholarships; they provide school milk and meals; free books and assisted transport for certain pupils; they enforce school attendance; provide a curriculum advisory and support service to all schools in their area; regulate the employment of children and young people; and secure the provision of youth and recreational facilities. They are also required to develop a comprehensive and efficient library service for their area. Board expenditure is funded at 100% by the Department of Education. Integrated schools receive 100% funding for recurrent costs from the Department of Education, and, where long-term viability has been established, for capital works.

The Education Reform (NI) Order 1989 made provision for the setting up of a Council for Catholic Maintained Schools with effect from April 1990. The Council has responsibility for all maintained schools under Roman Catholic Management which are under the auspices of the diocesan authorities and of religious orders. The main objective of the Council is to promote high standards of education in the schools for which it is responsible. Its functions include providing advice on matters relating to its schools, the employment of teaching staff and administration of appointment procedures, the promotion of effective management, and the promotion and co-ordination of effective planning and rationalization of school provision in the Catholic Maintained sector. The membership of the Council consists of trustee representatives appointed by the Northern Roman Catholic Bishops, parents, teachers, and persons appointed by the Head of the Department of Education in consultation with the Bishops.

There is a Council for the Curriculum, Examinations and Assessment which conducts public examinations and oversees the selection procedure and arrangements for pupil assessment. There is also the Northern Ireland Council for Integrated Education, both of which are grant-aided by the Department of Education.

Integrated Schools. The Department of Education has a statutory duty to encourage and facilitate the development of integrated education. It does not seek to impose integration but responds to parental demand for new integrated schools where this does not involve unreasonable public expenditure. The emphasis for future development of the integrated sector has increasingly been on the transformation of existing schools to integrated status. In Dec. 2002 there were 47 grant-aided integrated schools, with a total enrolment of 14,626 pupils, about 4% of all pupils.

Irish Medium Education. Following a commitment in the Belfast Agreement, the 1998 Education Order placed a statutory duty on the Department to encourage and facilitate the development of Irish-medium education. It also provided for the funding of an Irish-medium promotional body, and funding of Irish-medium schools on the same basis as integrated schools. In Dec. 2002 there were 13 Irish-medium primary schools, one post-primary and nine units, two of which are post-primary catering for over 2,000 pupils.

Pre-school Education is provided in nursery schools or nursery classes in primary schools, reception classes and in funded places in voluntary and private settings. There were 96 nursery schools in 2001–02 with 6,093 pupils, and 7,012 nursery pupils in primary schools. A further 1,474 reception pupils were enrolled in primary schools. In addition there were 5,340 children in funded places in voluntary and private pre-school centres.

Primary Education is from 4 to 11 years. In 2001–02 there were 899 primary schools with 167,883 pupils. There were also 21 preparatory departments of grammar schools with 2,670 pupils. In 2001–02 there were 8,781 FTE primary school teachers and 160 FTE preparatory department teachers.

Secondary Education is from 11 to 18 years. In 2001–02 there were 71 grammar schools with 62,743 pupils and 164 secondary schools with 92,760 pupils. In 2001–02 there were 6,698 FTE secondary school teachers and 4,111 FTE grammar school teachers.

Further Education. There are 17 institutions of further education. In 1999–2000 there were 2,031 full-time and 2,764 part-time teachers, approximately 24,000 full-time enrolments, approximately 33,000 part-time enrolments and approximately 32,000 evening students on vocational courses. There were about 60,000 students on non-vocational (mostly evening) courses.

Special Education. The Education and Library Boards provide for children with special educational needs up to the age of 19. This provision may be made in ordinary classes in primary or secondary schools or in special units attached to those schools, or in special schools. In 1999–2000 there were 53 special schools with 4,861 pupils. This includes three hospital schools.

Universities. There are two universities: the Queen's University of Belfast (founded in 1849 as a college of the Queen's University of Ireland and reconstituted as a separate university in 1908) had 21,021 students, 1,361 full-time and 96 part-time academic staff in 1998–99. The University of Ulster, formed on 1 Oct. 1984, has campuses in Belfast, Coleraine, Jordanstown and Londonderry. In the 1998–99 academic year it had 19,479 students, 1,190 full-time and 67 part-time academic staff.

Full-Time Initial Teacher Education takes place at both universities and at two university colleges of education—Stranmillis, and St. Mary's—the latter mainly for the primary school sector, in respect of which four-year (Hons) BEd courses are available. The training of teachers for secondary schools is provided, in the main, in the education departments of the two universities, but four-year (Hons) BEd courses are also available in the colleges for intending secondary teachers of religious education, business studies and craft, design and technology. There were a total of 1,632 students (1,325 women) in training at the two university colleges and the two universities during 1999–2000.

Health. The Department of Health and Social Services is responsible for the provision of integrated health and personal social services. Four Health and Social Services Boards are responsible for assessing the requirements of their resident populations and for purchasing appropriate services. Since 1 April 1996 services have been delivered exclusively by HSS Trusts (similar to NHS Trusts in the rest of the UK) established under the Health and Personal Social Services (NI) Order 1991.

A total of 19 HSS Trusts are fully operational. Seven HSS Trusts based on acute hospitals and the regional Northern Ireland Ambulance Service are identical in structure and management to NHS Trusts in Great Britain. Of the remaining 12, five provide community-based health and personal social services and six provide both hospital and community-based health and personal social services, reflecting the integrated nature of these services in Northern Ireland. In 2000 there were 1,066 doctors (principals), with an average of 1,662 patients each.

Welfare. The Social Security Agency's remit is now part of the Department for Social Development, and social security schemes are similar to those in Great Britain.

National Insurance. During the year ended 31 March 1999 the expenditure of the National Insurance Fund at £1,251·1m. exceeded contributions by £163·7m. The shortfall in income was made up by a Treasury Grant, investment income and a transfer from the Great Britain Fund. Total benefit expenditure was £1,177·9m., excluding £4·1m. which was subsequently recovered from damages paid to recipients of National Insurance Fund Benefits. Employers received £1m. reimbursement in respect of Statutory Sick Pay paid to their employees. £14·6m. was paid in Jobseekers' Allowance contributions. Widows Benefit amounted to £33·2m. and Retirement Pensions to £802·2m. Incapacity Benefits totalled £323·7m. Maternity Allowance of £1·1m. was paid and employers were reimbursed £17·6m. in respect of Statutory Maternity Pay. £39·3m. was given to personal pension plan providers.

Child Benefit. During the year ended 31 March 1999, £261·4m. was paid. *Income Support:* In 1998–99, £513·6m. was paid. *Family Credit:* In 1998–99, £98·0m. was paid.

CULTURE

Tourism. There were an estimated 1·68m. visits to Northern Ireland in 2001, contributing £282m. to the economy. The Northern Ireland Tourist Board is responsible for encouraging tourism. Nine Areas of Outstanding Natural Beauty and 45 Statutory Nature Reserves have been declared, and there are many country and regional parks.

FURTHER READING

Aughey, A. and Morrow, D. (eds.) *Northern Ireland Politics.* Harlow, 1996
Bardon, Jonathan, *A History of Ulster.* Blackstaff Press, Belfast, 1992
Bloomfield, D., *Peacemaking Strategies in Northern Ireland.* London, 1998
Bow, P. and Gillespie, G., *Northern Ireland: a Chronology of the Troubles, 1968–1993.* Dublin, 1993
Dixon, Paul, *Northern Ireland: The Politics of War and Peace.* Palgrave, Basingstoke, 2001
Fay, Marie-Thérèse, Morrisey, Mike and Smyth, Marie, *Northern Ireland's Troubles.* Pluto Press, London, 1999
Fletcher, Martin, *Silver Linings: Travels Around Northern Ireland.* Little, Brown, London, 2000
Hennessey, T., *A History of Northern Ireland 1920–96.* London, 1998
Kennedy-Pipe, C., *The Origins of the Present Troubles in Northern Ireland.* Harlow, 1997
Keogh, D. and Haltzel, M. (eds.) *Northern Ireland and the Politics of Reconciliation.* CUP, 1994
Loughlin, James, *The Ulster Question Since 1945.* Macmillan, London, 1998
McDonald, Henry, *Trimble.* Bloomsbury, London, 2000
McGarry, J. and O'Leary, B. (eds.) *Explaining Northern Ireland: Broken Images.* Oxford, 1995
Rose, Peter, *How the Troubles Came to Northern Ireland.* Macmillan, London, 1999
Ruane, J. and Todd, J., *The Dynamics of Conflict in Northern Ireland: Power, Conflict and Emancipation.* CUP, 1997

ISLE OF MAN

KEY HISTORICAL EVENTS

The Isle of Man was first inhabited approximately 10,000 years ago and the Island became attached to Norway in the 9th century. In 1266 it was ceded to Scotland, but it came under English control in 1333.

The Isle of Man has been a British Crown dependency since 1765, with the British government responsible for its defence and foreign policy. Otherwise it has extensive right of self-government.

A special relationship exists between the Isle of Man and the European Union providing for free trade, and adoption by the Isle of Man of the EU's external trade policies with third countries. The Island remains free to levy its own system of taxes.

TERRITORY AND POPULATION
Area, 221 sq. miles (572 sq. km); resident population census April 2001, 76,315, giving a density of 134 per sq. km. In 2001 an estimated 73% of the population lived in urban areas. The principal towns are Douglas (population, 25,308), Onchan (adjoining Douglas; 8,706), Ramsey (7,626), Peel (3,779), Castletown (3,082). The Island is divided into six sheadings—Ayre, Garff, Glenfaba, Michael, Middle and Rushen. Garff is further subdivided into two parishes and the others each have three parishes.

SOCIAL STATISTICS
2000: births, 831; deaths, 897; marriages, 417. Annual growth rate, 1996–2000, 1·3%.

CLIMATE
Lying in the Irish Sea, the Island's climate is temperate and lacking in extremes. Thunderstorms, snow and frost are infrequent, although the Island tends to be windy. July and Aug. are the warmest months with an average daily maximum temperature of around 17·6°C (63°F).

CONSTITUTION AND GOVERNMENT
As a result of Revestment in 1765, the Isle of Man became a dependency of the British Crown. The UK government is responsible for the external relations of the Island, including its defence and international affairs, and the Island makes a financial contribution to the cost of these services. The Isle of Man has a special relationship with the European Union. It neither contributes funds to, nor receives money from, the EU. The Isle of Man is not represented in either the UK or European Parliaments.

The Island is administered in accordance with its own laws by the High Court of *Tynwald*, consisting of the President of Tynwald, the *Legislative Council* and the *House of Keys*. The Legislative Council is composed of the Lord Bishop of Sodor and Man, eight members selected by the House of Keys and the Attorney General, who has no vote. The House of Keys is an assembly of 24 members chosen by adult suffrage. The President of Tynwald is chosen by the Legislative Council and the House of Keys, sitting together as Tynwald. An open-air Tynwald ceremony is held in early July each year at St Johns. Until 1990 the Lieut.-Governor, appointed by the UK government, presided over Tynwald.

A Council of Ministers was instituted in 1990, replacing the Executive Council which had acted as an advisory body to the Lieut.-Governor. The Council of Ministers consists of the Chief Minister (elected for a five-year term) and the ministers of the nine major departments, being the Treasury; Agriculture, Fisheries and Forestry; Education; Health and Social Security; Home Affairs; Local Government and the Environment; Tourism and Leisure; Trade and Industry; and Transport.

RECENT ELECTIONS
Elections to the House of Keys were held on 22 Nov. 2001. The Manx Labour Party won 2 seats with 17·3% of the vote; the Alliance for Progressive Government 3 seats (14·6% of the vote) while non-partisans won 17 seats. The Manx Nationalist Party boycotted the elections. Turn-out was 57·6%.

CURRENT ADMINISTRATION
Lieut.-Governor: Ian Macfadyen.
    President: Noel Cringle (elected April 2000).
    In March 2003 the *Chief Minister* was Richard Corkill. *Finance Minister:* Alan Bell.

Website: http://www.gov.im

ECONOMY

Overview. The Isle of Man's economic policy is the pursuit of manageable and sustainable growth based on a diversified economy.

Currency. The Isle of Man government issues its own notes and coins on a par with £ sterling. Various commemorative coins have been minted. Inflation was around 1% at the end of 2001.

Budget. The Isle of Man is statutorily required to budget for a surplus of revenue over expenditure. Revenue is raised from income tax, taxes on expenditure, health and social security contributions, and fees and charges for services.

The standard rate of tax is 12% for personal income, and there is a higher rate of 18%. Companies are liable at 12% on their first £500,000 of taxable income and 28% on the balance.

There is a Customs and Excise Agreement with the UK, and rates of tax on expenditure are the same as those in the UK with very few exceptions. In addition, there is a reciprocal agreement on social security with the UK, and the rates of health and social security (National Insurance) contributions are the same as in the UK.

In 2001–02 the Isle of Man government budgeted for expenditure of £603m. and revenue of £625m.

Performance. In 1999–2000 GNP was £1,032m. and GDP was £973m. Real GDP growth in 1999–2000 was 13·7%. Just over 80% of national income is generated from services with the finance sector being the single largest contributor (41%).

Banking and Finance. The banking sector is regulated by the Financial Supervision Commission which is responsible for the licensing and supervision of banks, deposit-takers and financial intermediaries giving financial advice, and receiving client monies for investment and management. A compensation fund to protect investors was set up in 1991 under the Commission.

In June 2001 the deposit base was £27bn., and there were 60 licensed banks, 80 investment businesses and 3 building societies with Isle of Man licences.

The insurance industry is regulated by the Insurance and Pensions Authority. In Sept. 2001 there were 183 insurance companies.

Weights and Measures. Both metric and avoirdupois are used.

ENERGY AND NATURAL RESOURCES

Electricity. The Manx Electricity Authority generates most of the Island's electricity by oil-fired power stations although there is a small hydro-electric plant. A cable link with the UK power grid came into operation in Nov. 2000. In 2001, 377m. kWh were sold.

Oil and Gas. At present, all oil and gas needs are met from imports, although a link to the Scotland–Eire gas pipeline is under consideration. The Island's gas suppliers and distributors are in the private sector.

Water. The Isle of Man Water Authority is the statutory body for supply of water in the Island.

Minerals. Although lead and tin mining industries were major employers in the past, they have long since shut down and the only mining activity in the Island is now for aggregates. The Lady Isabella, built in 1854 to drain the mines above Laxey, is one of the largest waterwheels in Europe.

Agriculture. The area farmed is about 113,000 acres, being 80% of a total land area of around 141,500 acres. 66,000 acres are grassland with a further 35,000 acres for rough grazing. There are approximately 178,000 sheep, 35,000 cattle, 15,000 poultry and 6,000 pigs on the Island's 766 farms. Agriculture now contributes less than 2% of the Island's GDP.

Forestry. The Department of Agriculture, Fisheries and Forestry has a forestry estate of some 6,800 acres. Commercial forestry is directed towards softwood production. The Manx National Glens and other amenity areas are maintained for public use by the Department, which owns some 18,000 acres of the Island's hills and uplands open for public use.

Fisheries. The Isle of Man is noted for the Manx kipper, a gutted smoked herring. Scallops and the related queen scallops (queenies) are the economic mainstay of the Manx fishing fleet. In 2000 the total catch was 3,431 tonnes.

INDUSTRY

Labour. The economically active population in 1996 was 34,811, of whom 5,695 were self-employed and 1,234 were unemployed. Employment by sector: professional services, 18%; finance, 18%; construction, 10%; manufacturing, 11%; distributive services, 11%.

At the end of 2001 there were fewer than 200 persons on the unemployment register, giving an unemployment rate of 0·5%.

Trade Unions. There were 48 registered trade unions in 2001.

INTERNATIONAL TRADE

The Isle of Man forms part of the customs union of the European Union, although the Island is not part of the EU itself. The relationship with the EU provides for free trade and the adoption of the EU's external trade policies and tariffs with non-EU countries.

Imports and Exports. The Isle of Man is in customs and excise union with the United Kingdom, which is also its main trading partner.

COMMUNICATIONS

Roads. There are 800 km of good roads. At the end of March 2001 there were 56,455 licensed vehicles, with 45,195 of these being private cars. Omnibus services operate to all parts of the Island. The TT (Tourist Trophy) motorcycle races take place annually on the 60·75-km Mountain Circuit.

Rail. Several novel transport systems operate on the Island during the summer season from May to Sept. Horse-drawn trams run along Douglas promenade, and the Manx Electric Railway links Douglas, Laxey, Ramsey and Snaefell Mountain (621 metres) in the north. The Isle of Man Steam Railway also operates between Douglas and Port Erin in the south.

Civil Aviation. Ronaldsway Airport in the south handles scheduled services linking the Island with London, Manchester, Dublin, Belfast, Glasgow, Liverpool, Blackpool, Birmingham, Leeds, Luton, Newcastle, Cardiff and Jersey. Air taxi services also operate.

Shipping. Car ferries run between Douglas and the UK and the Irish Republic. In 2001 there were 2,580 merchant vessels on the Island's shipping register.

Telecommunications. Manx Telecom Limited, a wholly owned subsidiary of British Telecom, holds the telecommunications licence issued by the Communications Commission for the Isle of Man.

Postal Services. The Isle of Man Post Office Authority operates the Island's mail system and issues various commemorative stamps.

SOCIAL INSTITUTIONS

Justice. The First Deemster is the head of the Isle of Man's judiciary. The Isle of Man Constabulary numbered 244 all ranks in 2001.

The population in penal institutions in Dec. 2001 was 68 (equivalent to 89 per 100,000 of national population).

Religion. The Island has a rich heritage of Christian associations, and the Diocese of Sodor and Man, one of the oldest in the British Isles, has existed since 476.

Education. Education is compulsory between the ages of 5 and 16. In 2000 there were 6,609 pupils in the 33 primary schools and 5,166 pupils in the 5 secondary schools operated by the Department of Education. The Department also runs a college of further education and a special school. Government expenditure on education totalled £66m. in 2001–02. The Island has a private primary school and a private secondary school.

Health. The Island has had its own National Health Service since 1948, providing medical, dental and ophthalmic services. In 2001–02 government expenditure on the NHS was £95m. There are two hospitals and a further hospital was under construction in 2001.

Welfare. Numbers receiving certain benefits at March 2001: Retirement Pension, 15,182; Child Benefit, 9,212; Sick and Disablement Benefits, 4,739; Supplementary Benefit, 3,361; Jobseekers' Allowance, 71. Total government expenditure on the social security system in 2001–02 was £142·7m.

CULTURE

Broadcasting. Manx Radio is a commercial broadcaster operated by the government from Douglas.

Cinema. There are two cinemas in Douglas, one of which is owned and operated by the Isle of Man government.

Press. In 2001 there were three weekly newspapers, two bi-weekly newspapers and one monthly newspaper. There are also various magazines concentrating on Manx issues.

Tourism. During the late 19th century through to the middle of the 20th century, tourism was one of the Island's main sources of income and employment. Tourism now contributes around 5% of the Island's GDP. There were 260,000 visitors during 2000.

Festivals. There is a Manx language festival, Feailley Ghaelgagh; and a Manx cultural festival, Yn Chruinnaght.

Libraries. The Manx Museum Library in Douglas has an extensive collection relating to all aspects of the Island's history, culture and folklore. The Central Reference Library in Government Office specializes in the central administration of the Island.

Theatre and Opera. The main theatre is the government-owned Gaiety in Douglas, staging a wide variety of drama, musicals and opera throughout the year. Designed by Frank Matcham and opened in 1900, the theatre has undergone extensive restoration to its Victorian decor. A larger concert hall, the Villa Marina, is owned by central government.

Museums and Galleries. The Manx Museum is the Island's major museum and houses the National Art Gallery. Castle Rushen in Castletown is one of Britain's best-preserved medieval castles and Peel Castle on St Patrick's Isle dates back to the 11th century. There is also the Nautical Museum in Castletown, Cregneash Village Folk Museum and the Grove Rural Life Museum in Ramsey. The House of Mannannan in Peel explores various aspects of the Island's history and culture. Small private museums include the Motor Cycle Museum, the Manx Regiment Museum and the T. E. Leece Museum.

FURTHER READING

Additional information is available from: Economic Affairs Division, 2 Circular Rd, Douglas, Isle of Man IM1 1PQ. *e-mail: economics@gov.im*
Isle of Man Digest of Economic and Social Statistics, Isle of Man Government, annual

Belchem, J. (ed.) *A New History of the Isle of Man, Volume V—The Modern Period 1830–1999,* Liverpool Univ. Press, 2000
Kermode, D. G., *Offshore Island Politics: The Constitutional and Political Development of the Isle of Man in the Twentieth Century,* Liverpool Univ. Press, 2001
Moore, A. W., *A History of the Isle of Man*, London, 1900; reprinted Manx National Heritage, 1992
Solly, M., *Government and Law in the Isle of Man.* London, 1994

Manx National Heritage publishes a series of booklets including *Early Maps of the Isle of Man, The Art of the Manx Crosses, The Ancient & Historic Monuments of the Isle of Man, Prehistoric Sites of the Isle of Man.*

CHANNEL ISLANDS

KEY HISTORICAL EVENTS

The Channel Islands consist of Jersey, Guernsey and the following dependencies of Guernsey: Alderney, Brechou, Great Sark, Little Sark, Herm, Jethou and Lihou. They were an integral part of the Duchy of Normandy at the time of the Norman Conquest of England in 1066. Since then they have belonged to the British Crown and are not part of the UK. The islands have created their own form of self-government, with the British government at Westminster being responsible for defence and foreign policy. The Lieut.-Governors of Jersey and Guernsey, appointed by the Crown, are the personal representatives of the Sovereign as well as being the commanders of the armed forces. The legislature of Jersey is 'The States of Jersey', and that of Guernsey is 'The States of Deliberation'.

From 1940 to 1945 the islands were left undefended and were the only British territory to fall to the Germans.

TERRITORY AND POPULATION

The Channel Islands cover a total of 75 sq. miles (194 sq. km), and in 2001 had a population of approximately 150,000.

The official languages are French and English, but English is now the main language.

CLIMATE

The climate is mild, with an average temperature for the year of 11·5°C. Average yearly rainfall totals: Jersey, 862·9 mm; Guernsey, 858·9 mm. The wettest months are in the winter. Highest temperatures recorded: Jersey, 34·8°C; Guernsey, 31·7°C. Maximum temperatures usually occur in July and Aug. (daily maximum 20·8°C in Jersey, slightly lower in Guernsey). Lowest temperatures recorded: Jersey, −10·3°C; Guernsey, −7·4°C. Jan. and Feb. are the coldest months (mean temperature approximately 6°C).

CONSTITUTION AND GOVERNMENT

The Lieut.-Governors and Cs.-in-C. of Jersey and Guernsey are the personal representatives of the Sovereign, the Commanders of the Armed Forces of the Crown, and the channel of communication between the Crown and the insular governments. They are appointed by the Crown and have a voice but no vote in the islands' legislatures. The Secretaries to the Lieut.-Governors are their staff officers.

EXTERNAL ECONOMIC RELATIONS

The Channel Islands are not members of the EU, but participate in ERM through their monetary union with the UK. Trade with the UK is classed as domestic.

COMMUNICATIONS

Civil Aviation. Scheduled air services are maintained by Aer Lingus, Air Corbière, Air UK, Aurigny Air Services, British Airways, British Midland, Crossair, Delta, Gill Aviation, Jersey European Airways, KLM, Loganair, Lufthansa and Manx Airlines.

Shipping. Passenger and cargo services between Jersey, Guernsey and England (Poole) are maintained by Condor Ltd hydrofoil; between Guernsey, Jersey and England and St Malo by the Commodore Shipping Co. Emeraude Ferries connect Jersey and Guernsey with St Malo; local companies run between Guernsey, Alderney and England, and between Guernsey and Sark. In 1998 the merchant marine totalled 2,000 GRT.

SOCIAL INSTITUTIONS

Justice. Justice is administered by the Royal Courts of Jersey and Guernsey, each of which consists of the Bailiff and 12 Jurats, the latter being elected by an electoral college. There is an appeal from the Royal Courts to the Courts of Appeal of Jersey and of Guernsey. A final appeal lies to the Privy Council in certain cases. A stipendiary magistrate in each, Jersey and Guernsey, deals with minor civil and criminal cases.

Religion. Jersey and Guernsey each constitutes a deanery under the jurisdiction of the Bishop of Winchester. The rectories (12 in Jersey; 10 in Guernsey) are in the gift of the Crown. The Roman Catholic and various Nonconformist Churches are represented.

FURTHER READING

Lemprière, R., *History of the Channel Islands.* Rev. ed. London, 1980

JERSEY

TERRITORY AND POPULATION

The area is 116·2 sq. km (44·9 sq. miles). Resident population (2001 census), 87,186 (44,701 females); density, 750 per sq. km. The chief town is St Helier on the south coast. It had a population of 28,310 in 2001. The official language is English (French until 1960). The island has its own language, known as Jersey French, or Jérriaise. French and Portuguese are also spoken.

SOCIAL STATISTICS

In 2001 there were 973 births and 784 deaths. Infant mortality rate, 1995 (per 1,000 live births), 6·5. In 2001 there were 664 marriages, 324 division petitions for divorce and 273 decree absolutes. Life expectancy, 1999: males, 75 years; females, 81 years.

CONSTITUTION AND GOVERNMENT

The island parliament is the *States of Jersey.* The States comprises the Bailiff, the Lieut.-Governor, the Dean of Jersey, the Attorney-General and the Solicitor-General, and 53 members elected by universal suffrage: 12 Senators (elected for six years, six retiring every third year), the Constables of the 12 parishes (every third year) and 29 Deputies (every third year). They all have the right to speak in the Assembly, but only the 53 elected members have the right to vote; the Bailiff has a casting vote. Except in specific instances, enactments passed by the States require the sanction of The Queen-in-Council. The Lieut.-Governor has the power of veto on certain forms of legislation.

Administration is carried out by Committees of the States.

CURRENT ADMINISTRATION

Lieut.-Governor and C.-in-C. of Jersey: Air Chief Marshal Sir John Cheshire, KBE, CBE.

Secretary and Aide-de-Camp to the Lieut.-Governor: Lieut.-Col. C. Woodrow, OBE, MC, QGM.

Bailiff of Jersey and President of the States: Sir Philip Bailhache.

Government Website: http://www.jersey.gov.uk/

ECONOMY

Currency. The States issue banknotes in denominations of £50, £20, £10, £5 and £1. Coinage from 1p to 50p is struck in the same denominations as the UK. There were £55,215,158 worth of States of Jersey banknotes and £4,997,000 worth of coinage in circulation in 2002. Inflation in Sept. 2002 was 4·2%.

Budget. 2002 forecast: revenue, £421m.; expenditure, £375m. Income from taxation was forecast to be £366m. The standard rate of income tax is 20p in the pound.

Parochial rates are payable by owners and occupiers.

Performance. GDP grew by an estimated 6·3% in 1999.

Banking and Finance. The finance sector accounts for 60% of GDP and employs about a seventh of the population. In 2001 there were 64 banks; combined deposits were £132bn. There were 32,992 live companies in 2001, of which 2,760 were registered in that year.

ENERGY AND NATURAL RESOURCES

Agriculture. 2001 total agricultural exports, £38,632,508. Jersey Royal New Potatoes account for 72% of the agricultural exports to the UK. 49·6% of the island's land area was farmed commercially in 2001. In 2001 there were 352 commercial farms with 7,227 cattle (4,552 milch cows).

Fisheries. There were 213 fishing vessels in 2001. The total catch in 2000 was 1,851 tonnes. The value of the fishing industry in 2001 was estimated at £8,544,230.

INDUSTRY

Principal activities: light industry, mainly electrical goods, textiles and clothing.

Labour. At the 2001 census 46,590 persons were economically active, and 150 persons were registered unemployed. Financial services was the largest employment sector, followed by distributive trades, construction, and then hotels and restaurants. By Oct. 2001 there was full employment and over 3,310 unfilled vacancies.

INTERNATIONAL TRADE

Imports and Exports. Since 1980 the Customs have ceased recording imports and exports. Principal imports: machinery and transport equipment, manufactured goods, food, mineral fuels, and chemicals. Principal exports: machinery and transport equipment, food, and manufactured goods.

COMMUNICATIONS

Roads. In 2001 there were 71,059 private cars, 4,210 hire cars, 7,562 vans, 3,617 lorries, 777 buses and coaches, and 7,886 motorcycles and scooters.

Civil Aviation. Jersey airport is situated at St Peter. It covers approximately 375 acres. In 2001 the airport handled 1,613,469 passengers.

Shipping. All vessels arriving in Jersey from outside Jersey waters report at St Helier or Gorey on first arrival. There is a harbour of minor importance at St Aubin. Number of commercial vessels entering St Helier in 2001, 2,048; number of visiting yachts, 6,527. There were 450,195 passenger arrivals and 451,952 passenger departures in 2001.

Telecommunications. Postal, and overseas telephone and telegraph services, are maintained by the Postal Administration of Jersey. The local telephone service is maintained by the Insular Authority. In 2001 main telephone lines numbered 73,878. There were 61,167 mobile phone subscribers.

Postal Services. In 2001 there were 20 post offices; a total of 74·3m. letters were processed.

SOCIAL INSTITUTIONS

Justice. Justice is administered by the Royal Court, consisting of the Bailiff and 12 Jurats (magistrates). There is a final appeal in certain cases to the Sovereign in Council. There is also a Court of Appeal, consisting of the Bailiff and two judges. Minor civil and criminal cases are dealt with by a stipendiary magistrate.

In 2001 there were 14,851 telephone calls requiring operational response, there were 6,235 crime offences, 1,134 disorder offences and 716 road traffic accidents. In 2001 the daily average prison population was 141.

Education. In 2001 there were seven States secondary schools, one high school and three special needs secondary schools. There were 25 States primary schools. 4,858 pupils attended secondary schools and 5,877 attended primary schools. There were 613 full-time students at the further education college. Expenditure on public education amounted to £81m. in 2001.

Health. Expenditure on public health in 1999 was £79,829,619. In 2000 there were five hospitals with 651 beds. In 2001 there were 94 doctors (general practitioners).

Welfare. A contributory Health Insurance Scheme is administered by the Social Security Department. In 2001 state expenditure for supplementation on the Social Security Fund was £41,197,403. £5,050,614 was paid out in Family Allowance, £5,383,134 on Disability Transport Allowance, £2,749,260 on Non-native Welfare,

£3,749,260 on Attendance Allowance and £1,116,087 on the administration of states funded benefits.

CULTURE

Cinema. Film-making is beginning to emerge as a potential new industry for Jersey.

Tourism. In 2001 there were 896,000 visitors to the island, spending £249m.

FURTHER READING

Balleine, G. R., *A History of the Island of Jersey.* Rev. ed. Chichester, 1981

States of Jersey Library: Halkett Place, St Helier.

GUERNSEY

TERRITORY AND POPULATION

The area is 63·4 sq. km. Census population (2001) 59,807. The main town is St Peter Port.

English and French are spoken, as is a Norman-French dialect in country areas.

SOCIAL STATISTICS

Births during 2001 were 593; deaths, 560.

CONSTITUTION AND GOVERNMENT

The States of Deliberation, the Parliament of Guernsey, is composed of the following members: the Bailiff, who is President *ex officio*; H.M. Procureur and H.M. Comptroller (Law Officers of the Crown), who have a voice but no vote; 45 People's Deputies elected by popular franchise; 10 Douzaine Representatives elected by their Parochial Douzaines; 2 representatives of the States of Alderney.

The States of Election, an electoral college, elects the Jurats. It is composed of the following members: the Bailiff (President *ex officio*); the 12 Jurats or 'Jurés-Justiciers'; H.M. Procureur and H.M. Comptroller; the 45 People's Deputies and 34 representatives from the 10 Parochial Douzaines.

Since Jan. 1949 all legislative powers and functions (with minor exceptions) formerly exercised by the Royal Court have been vested in the States of Deliberation. Projets de Loi (Bills) require the sanction of The Queen-in-Council.

RECENT ELECTIONS

Elections for People's Deputies were held on 12 April 2000.

CURRENT ADMINISTRATION

Lieut.-Governor and C.-in-C. of Guernsey and its Dependencies: Lieut.-Gen. Sir John Foley, KCB, OBE, MC.

Secretary and Aide-de-Camp to the Lieut.-Governor: Colonel R. H. Graham MBE.

Bailiff of Guernsey and President of the States: Sir de Vic Carey.

Deputy Bailiff of Guernsey: G. R. Rowland, QC.

Government Website: http://www.gov.gg/

ECONOMY

Budget. Year ended 31 Dec. 2001: revenue, including Alderney, £280,165,000; expenditure, including Alderney, £222,901,000. The standard rate of income tax is 20p in the pound. States and parochial rates are very moderate. No super-tax or death duties are levied.

Banking and Finance. There were 67 banks in 2002. Financial services account for about 66% of the export economy.

INDUSTRY

Trade Unions. There is a Transport & General Workers' Union.

INTERNATIONAL TRADE

Imports and Exports. Horticulture exports (2001) in £1m.: plant production, 20·28; cut flowers, 11·68; postal flowers, 6·10; food, 3·65; seeds, 0·26. In 2002, 74,066,580 litres of petrol and oils were imported.

Trade Fairs. There are several trade fairs each year.

COMMUNICATIONS

Rail. There is no rail system.

Civil Aviation. The airport is situated at La Villiaze. There are direct flights to Alderney, Amsterdam, Birmingham, Dinard, East Midlands, Exeter, Jersey, London (Gatwick and Stansted), Manchester, Southampton and Zürich. In 2002 passenger movements totalled 837,916.

Shipping. The principal port is St Peter Port. There is also a harbour at St Sampson's (mainly for commercial shipping). In 2002 passenger movements totalled 592,102. Ships registered at 31 Dec. 2002 numbered 2,223 and 250 fishing vessels. In 2002, 9,644 yachts visited Guernsey.

Telecommunications. There were 55,000 main telephone lines in 2002, or 874 per 1,000 population. Mobile phone subscribers numbered 37,000 in 2002 and there were 700 fax machines in 1995.

SOCIAL INSTITUTIONS

Justice. The population in penal institutions in Oct. 1998 was 64 (equivalent to 110 per 100,000 of national population).

Education. There are two public schools, one grammar school, a number of modern secondary and primary schools, and a College of Further Education. The total number of schoolchildren in Sept. 2002 was 8,993. Facilities are available for the study of art, domestic science and many other subjects of a technical nature.

Health. Guernsey is not covered by the UK National Health Service. Public health is overseen by the States of Guernsey Insurance Authority and Board of Health. A private medical insurance scheme to provide specialist cover for all residents was implemented by the States on 1 Jan. 1996.

CULTURE

Broadcasting. Guernsey is served by BBC Radio Guernsey, Island FM and Channel Television.

Cinema. There are two cinemas.

Press. The *Guernsey Evening Press* is published daily except Sundays.

Tourism. There were 405,000 visitors in 2001; tourism contributed 12% of the economy.

Festivals. Liberation Day is on 9 May.

Libraries. The two principal libraries are the Guille-Alles Library and the Priaulx Library.

Museums and Galleries. The island is home to the Guernsey Museum and Art Gallery, Victor Hugo House and several small museums.

FURTHER READING

Marr, L. J., *A History of Guernsey.* Chichester, 1982

Statistical office: Policy and Research Unit, P. O. Box 43, Sir Charles Frossard House, La Charroterie, St. Peter Port, GY1 1FH.
Website: http://www.gov.gg/esu

ALDERNEY

GENERAL DETAILS

Population (2001 estimate, 2,400). The main town is St Anne's. The island has an airport.

The Constitution of the island (reformed 1987) provides for its own popularly elected President and States (12 members), and its own Court. Elections were held for the President and four members of the States in Dec. 1993. Alderney levies its taxes at Guernsey rates and passes the revenue to Guernsey, which charges for the services it provides.

President of the States. Sir Norman Browse.
Clerk of the States. David Jenkins.
Clerk of the Court. Robert Lynton Barnwell.

FURTHER READING

Coysh, V., *Alderney.* Newton Abbot, 1974

SARK

GENERAL DETAILS

2001 population estimate, 580. The Constitution is a mixture of feudal and popular government with its Chief Pleas (parliament), consisting of 40 tenants and 12 popularly elected deputies, presided over by the Seneschal. The head of the island is the Seigneur. Sark has no income tax. Motor vehicles, except tractors, are not allowed.

Seigneur. J. M. Beaumont.
Seneschal. R. J. Guille.

FURTHER READING

Hathaway, S., *Dame of Sark: An Autobiography.* London, 1961

UNITED KINGDOM OVERSEAS TERRITORIES

There are 14 British Overseas Territories: Anguilla, Bermuda, British Antarctic Territory, British Indian Ocean Territory, British Virgin Islands, Cayman Islands, Falkland Islands, Gibraltar, Montserrat, Pitcairn Islands, St Helena and its Dependencies (Ascension Island and Tristan da Cunha), South Georgia and the South Sandwich Islands, the Sovereign Base Areas of Akrotiri and Dhekelia in Cyprus, and the Turks and Caicos Islands. Three (British Antarctic Territory, British Indian Ocean Territory and South Georgia and the South Sandwich Islands) have no resident populations and are administered by a commissioner instead of a governor.

Gibraltar is a peninsula bordering the south coast of Spain; the Sovereign Base Areas are in Cyprus and the remainder are islands in the Caribbean, Pacific, Indian Ocean and South Atlantic. Gibraltar and the Falkland Islands are the subjects of territorial claims by Spain and Argentina respectively.

The Overseas Territories are constitutionally not part of the United Kingdom. They have separate constitutions, and most of them have elected governments with varying degrees of responsibilities for domestic matters. The Governor, who is appointed by, and represents, HM the Queen, retains responsibility for external affairs, internal security, defence, and in most cases the public service.

At the launch of the White Paper 'Partnership for Progress and Prosperity', in March 1999, the Foreign Secretary of the time, Robin Cook, outlined four underlying principles for the relationship between Britain and the Overseas Territories: self-determination for the Territories; mutual obligations and responsibilities; freedom for the Territories to run their own affairs to the greatest degree possible; and Britain's firm commitment to help the territories develop economically and to assist them in emergencies. He also offered British citizenship, with the right of abode in the UK, to those citizens of the Overseas Territories who did not already enjoy it. On 21 May 2002 the citizenship provisions of the British Overseas Territories Act came into force. It granted British citizenship to the citizens of all Britain's Overseas Territories (except those who derived their British nationality by virtue only of a connection with the Sovereign Base Areas of Akrotiri and Dhekelia in Cyprus).

ANGUILLA

KEY HISTORICAL EVENTS

Anguilla was probably given its name by the Spaniards or the French because of its eel-like shape. It was inhabited by Arawaks for several centuries before the arrival of Europeans. Anguilla was colonized in 1650 by English settlers from neighbouring St Kitts. In 1688 the island was attacked by a party of Irishmen who then settled. Anguilla was subsequently administered as part of the Leeward Islands, and from 1825 became even more closely associated with St Kitts. In 1875 a petition sent to London requesting separate status and direct rule from Britain met with a negative response. Again in 1958 the islanders formally petitioned the Governor requesting a dissolution of the political and administrative association with St Kitts, but this too failed. From 1958 to 1962 Anguilla was part of the Federation of the West Indies.

Opposition to rule from St Kitts erupted on 30 May 1967 when St Kitts policemen were evicted from the island and Anguilla refused to recognize the authority of the State government any longer. During 1968–69 the British government maintained a 'Senior British Official' to advise the local Anguilla Council and devise some solution to the problem. In March 1969, following the ejection from the island of a high-ranking British civil servant, British security forces occupied Anguilla. A Commissioner was installed, and in 1969 Anguilla became *de facto* a separate dependency of Britain, a situation rendered *de jure* on 19 Dec. 1980 under the Anguilla Act 1980 when Anguilla formally separated from the state of St Kitts, Anguilla-Nevis. A new constitution came into effect in 1982 providing for a large measure of autonomy under the Crown.

TERRITORY AND POPULATION

Anguilla is the most northerly of the Leeward Islands, some 70 miles (112 km) to the northwest of St Kitts and 5 miles (8 km) to the north of St Martin/Sint Maarten. The territory also comprises the island of Sombrero and several other off-shore islets or cays. The total area of the territory is about 60 sq. miles (155 sq. km). *De jure* census population (2001) was 11,561; density of 74·6 per sq. km. Average annual population increase between 1992 and 2001 was 3·2%. People of African descent make up 90% of the population, mixed origins 5% and white 4%. The capital is The Valley. In 1995 an estimated 89% of the population lived in rural areas.

The official language is English.

SOCIAL STATISTICS

Births, 1999, 176; deaths, 58. In 2001 life expectancy at birth for females was 78·0 years and for males 77·9 years. Households numbered 3,788 in 2001.

CLIMATE

Tropical oceanic climate with rain throughout the year, particularly between May and Dec. Tropical storms and hurricanes may occur between July and Nov.

Generally summers are hotter than winters although there is little variation in temperatures.

CONSTITUTION AND GOVERNMENT
A set of amendments to the constitution came into effect in 1990, providing for a Deputy Governor, a Parliamentary Secretary and an Opposition Leader. The *House of Assembly* consists of a Speaker, Deputy Speaker, seven directly elected members for five-year terms, two nominated members and two *ex officio* members: the Deputy Governor and the Attorney-General. The Governor discharges his executive powers on the advice of an Executive Council comprising a Chief Minister, three Ministers and two *ex officio* members: the Deputy Governor, Attorney-General and the Secretary to the Executive Council.

RECENT ELECTIONS
In parliamentary elections held on 3 March 2000 the United Front (Anguilla National Alliance and Anguilla Democratic Party) won 4 of 7 seats, the Anguilla United Movement 2, and an independent 1. Turn-out was 64%. A coalition of Anguilla National Alliance and Anguilla Democratic Party was formed following the election to serve a second term.

CURRENT ADMINISTRATION
Governor: Peter Johnstone.
  Chief Minister: Osbourne Fleming; b. 1940 (Anguilla National Alliance; sworn in 6 March 2000).

Government Website: http://www.gov.ai/

ECONOMY
Currency. The *Eastern Caribbean dollar* (*see* ANTIGUA AND BARBUDA).

Budget. In 1998 government revenue was EC$72·3m. and expenditure EC$71·0m. The main sources of revenue are custom duties, tourism and bank licence fees. There is little taxation. A 'Policy Plan' with the UK provided for £10·5m. of aid in 1994–97.

Performance. Real GDP growth was –4·3% in 1995 and 7·0% in 1994.

Banking and Finance. The East Caribbean Central Bank based in St Kitts-Nevis functions as a central bank. The *Governor* is Sir Dwight Venner. There is a small offshore banking sector. In 1996 there were two domestic and two foreign commercial banks.

ENERGY AND NATURAL RESOURCES
Electricity. Production (1996) 28·5m. kWh.

Agriculture. Because of low rainfall, agriculture potential is limited. About 1,200 ha are cultivable. Main crops are pigeon peas, maize and sweet potatoes. Livestock consists of sheep, goats, pigs and poultry. The island relies on imports for food.

Fisheries. Fishing is a thriving industry (mainly lobster). The estimated total catch in 2000 was 250 tonnes.

INDUSTRY
Labour. The unemployment rate was 7·0% in 1998.

COMMUNICATIONS
Roads. There are about 40 miles of tarred roads and 25 miles of secondary roads. In 1991 there were 2,450 passenger cars and 733 commercial vehicles.

Civil Aviation. Wallblake is the airport for The Valley. Anguilla is linked to neighbouring islands by services operated by Air Anguilla, LIAT, Tyden Air, WINAIR and American Eagle.

Shipping. The main seaports are Sandy Ground and Blowing Point, the latter serving passenger and cargo traffic to and from St Martin. In 1995 merchant shipping totalled 2,000 GRT.

Telecommunications. There is a modern internal telephone service with (1997) 5,422 main lines in operation; and international telegraph, telex, fax and Internet services. In Dec. 1998 there were 800 mobile phone subscribers.

SOCIAL INSTITUTIONS

Justice. Justice is based on UK common law as exercised by the Eastern Caribbean Supreme Court on St Lucia. Final appeal lies to the UK Privy Council.

Religion. There were in 2001 Anglicans (29%), Methodists (24%), plus Seventh Day Adventists, Pentecostals, Church of God, Baptists and Roman Catholics as significant minorities.

Education. Adult literacy was 80% in 1995. Education is free and compulsory between the ages of 5 and 17 years. There are six government primary schools with (1996) 1,540 pupils and one comprehensive school with (1996) 1,060 pupils. Higher education is provided at regional universities and similar institutions.

Health. In 1996 there was one hospital with a total of 60 beds, four health centres and a government dental clinic. There were five government-employed and three private doctors.

Welfare. A social security system was instituted in 1982 to provide age and disability pensions, and sickness and maternity benefits.

CULTURE

Broadcasting. There is one government (Radio Anguilla) and two other radio broadcasters. TV is privately owned; there are two channels and a cable system. In 1997 there were 3,000 radio and 1,000 television receivers.

Press. In 1995 there were one daily, two weeklies and a quarterly periodical.

Tourism. Tourism accounts for 50% of GDP. In 1998 there were 44,000 visitor arrivals (around two-thirds from the USA). Revenue totalled US$48m. in 1995.

FURTHER READING
Petty, C. L., *Anguilla: Where there's a Will, there's a Way.* Anguilla, 1984.—*A Handbook History of Anguilla.* Anguilla, 1991.

BERMUDA

KEY HISTORICAL EVENTS
The islands were discovered by Juan Bermúdez, probably in 1503, but were uninhabited until British colonists were wrecked there in 1609. A plantation company was formed; in 1684 the Crown took over the government. A referendum in Aug. 1995 rejected independence from the UK.

TERRITORY AND POPULATION
Bermuda consists of a group of 138 islands and islets (about 20 inhabited), situated in the western Atlantic (32° 18' N. lat., 64° 46' W. long.); the nearest point of the mainland, 940 km distant, is Cape Hatteras (North Carolina). The area is 20·59 sq. miles (53·3 sq. km). In June 1995 the USA surrendered its lease on land used since 1941 for naval and air force bases. At the 2000 census the population numbered 62,098; density, 1,165 per sq. km. Capital, Hamilton; population, 2000, 969. Population of St George's, 2000, 1,752.

Ethnic composition, 2000: black, 54·8%; white, 34·0%.

The official language is English. Portuguese is also used.

SOCIAL STATISTICS
In 1998 there were 825 live births, 1,033 marriages and 505 deaths. Annual growth rate, 1996, 1·5%. Life expectancy at birth, 1996: 70 years (male); 78 years (female).

BERMUDA

Bermuda limits cars to one per household and bans hire vehicles. There are heavy fines for breaking the 35 km/h (22 mph) speed limit. Bermuda is the only country in the world where McDonald's restaurants are banned by law.

CLIMATE

A pleasantly warm and humid climate, with up to 60" (1,500 mm) of rain spread evenly throughout the year. Hamilton, Jan. 63°F (17·2°C), July 79°F (26·1°C). Annual rainfall 58" (1,463 mm).

CONSTITUTION AND GOVERNMENT

Under the 1968 constitution the *Governor*, appointed by the Crown, is normally bound to accept the advice of the Cabinet in matters other than external affairs, defence, internal security and the police, for which he retains special responsibility. The legislature consists of a Senate of 11 members, five appointed by the Governor on the recommendation of the Premier, three by the Governor on the recommendation of the Opposition Leader and three by the Governor in his own discretion. The 40 members of the *House of Assembly* are elected, two from each of 20 constituencies by universal suffrage.

At a referendum on 17 Aug. 1995, 16,369 votes were cast against the option of independence, and 5,714 were in favour. The electorate was 38,000; turn-out was 58%.

RECENT ELECTIONS

A general election was held on 10 Nov. 1998. Turn-out was 81%. The Progressive Labour Party (PLP) won 26 of the 40 seats in parliament, with 54·2% of votes cast, throwing out the United Bermuda Party (UBP) government which had dominated politics for 35 years. The PLP is largely representative of the black population, while the UBP membership is mostly white.

CURRENT ADMINISTRATION

Governor: Sir John Vereker; b. 1944 (sworn in 1 April 2002).
Premier: Jennifer Smith; b. 1947 (sworn in 10 Nov. 1998).

Government Website: http://www.gov.bm/

DEFENCE

The Bermuda Regiment numbered 684 in 1996.

ECONOMY

Bermuda is the world's third largest insurance market after London and New York. Reserves of insurance companies total $39bn.

Currency. The unit of currency is the *Bermuda dollar* (BMD) of 100 *cents* at parity with the US dollar. Inflation was 2·9% in 2001, up from 2·7% in 2000.

Budget. The fiscal year ends on 31 March. The 1997–98 budget envisaged revenue of BD$488m. and current expenditure of BD$448m. The estimated chief sources of revenue (in BD$1m.) in 1997–98: customs duties, 144; payroll tax, 133; companies fees, 38; land tax, 24; passenger tax, 20; vehicle licences, 17.

Performance. Real GDP growth was 2·9% in 2000–01. GDP for 1998 was $30,000.

Banking and Finance. Bermuda is an offshore financial centre with tax exemption facilities. At 31 Dec. 1996, 9,252 international companies were registered in Bermuda, with insurers the most important category. There are three commercial banks, with total assets of BD$8,475m. in 1995. At the end of the first quarter of 1997 there were 8,703 exempted companies, 292 exempted partnership companies, 520 non-resident companies and 26 non-resident insurance companies on the Bermuda register. Bermuda is now the world's third largest insurance market after London and New York. The Bermuda Monetary Authority (*General Manager,* D. Munro Sutherland) acts as a central bank. There is a stock exchange, the BSX.

Weights and Measures. Metric, except that US and Imperial (British) measures are used in certain fields.

ENERGY AND NATURAL RESOURCES

Environment. According to the *World Bank Atlas* Bermuda's carbon dioxide emissions in 1996 were the equivalent of 7·4 tonnes per capita.

Electricity. Installed capacity was 145,000 kW in 1996. Production in 1998 was 420m. kWh, with consumption per capita 7,856 kWh.

Minerals. Bermuda is rich in limestone.

Agriculture. The chief products are fresh vegetables, bananas and citrus fruit. In 1995, 839 acres were being used for production of vegetables, fruit and flowers as well as for pasture, forage and fallow. In 1996, 503 persons were employed in agriculture. In 1995 the total value of agricultural products was BD$5,989,000. By 1999 agriculture accounted for less than 1% of GDP. Livestock, 1996: 1,000 cattle, 1,000 horses, 1,000 pigs, 1,000 goats.

Forestry. Approximately 20% of land is woodland.

Fisheries. In 1996 there were 194 fishing vessels and 274 registered fishermen. The total catch in 2000 was 286 tonnes. Fishing is centred on reef-dwelling species such as groupers and lobsters.

INDUSTRY

Bermuda's leading industry is tourism, with annual revenue in excess of US$480m.

Labour. The labour force numbered 34,633 in 1996. Unemployment was 3% of the working population in 2000.

Trade Unions. There are nine trade unions with a total membership (1995) of 8,728.

INTERNATIONAL TRADE

Foreign firms conducting business overseas only are not subject to a 60% Bermuda ownership requirement. In 1996 over 8,200 international companies had a physical presence in Bermuda.

Imports and Exports. The visible adverse balance of trade is more than compensated for by invisible exports, including tourism and off-shore insurance business.

Merchandise imports in 2001 (and 2000) were US$750m. (US$719m.); exports in 2001 (and 2000) were US$45m. (US$51m.). In 1999 the USA accounted for 17·8% of imports and 9·8% of exports, and the UK 15·4% of imports and 6·9% of exports. The EU (excluding the UK) accounted for 77·9% of exports and 35·4% of imports.

Principal imports are food, beverages and tobacco, machinery, chemicals, clothing, fuels and transport equipment. The bulk of exports comprise sales of fuel to aircraft and ships, and re-exports of pharmaceuticals.

COMMUNICATIONS

Roads. There are 225 km of public highway and 222 km of private roads. There are approximately 21,100 private cars, 22,100 motorcycles, scooters and mopeds, 700 buses, taxis and limousines, and 3,600 lorries and tank wagons. The speed limit is 35 km/h (22 mph).

Civil Aviation. The Bermuda International Airport is 19 km from Hamilton. It handled 913,000 passengers and 5,600 tonnes of freight in 2000. Bermuda is served on a regularly scheduled basis by Air Canada, American Airlines, British Airways, Continental Airlines, Delta Airlines, Northwest Airlines and US Air.

Shipping. There are three ports, Hamilton, St George's and Dockyard. There is an open shipping registry. In 1998 ships registered totalled 4·81m. GRT, including oil tankers 2·14m. GRT.

Telecommunications. Main telephone lines numbered 56,100 in 2000, equivalent to 869·8 for every 1,000 inhabitants—the highest penetration rate in the world—and there were 30,000 PCs in use (465·4 per 1,000 inhabitants). In 1998 there were 12,600 mobile phone subscribers. Bermuda had 25,000 Internet users in April 2000.

Postal Services. There were 15 post offices in 1995.

SOCIAL INSTITUTIONS

Justice. There are four magistrates' courts, three Supreme Courts and a Court of Appeal. The police had a strength of about 500 men and women in 1996.

Religion. Many religions are represented, but the larger number of worshippers are attracted to the Anglican, Roman Catholic, Seventh Day Adventist, African Methodist Episcopal, Methodist and Baptist faiths.

Education. Education is compulsory between the ages of 5 and 16, and government assistance is given by the payment of grants and, where necessary, school fees. In 1995–96 there were 6,362 pupils in state schools and 3,179 in independent schools. There were 515 full-time students attending the Bermuda College in 1995. A restructuring of secondary education has resulted in the construction of a new state-of-the-art secondary school, Cedarbridge Academy, which opened in Sept. 1997.

In 1996 the adult literacy rate was 98%.

Health. In 1996 there were 2 hospitals, 100 physicians and surgeons, 49 dentists and dental hygienists, 6 optometrists, 27 pharmacists, 8 dieticians and 553 nurses.

CULTURE

Broadcasting. Radio and television broadcasting are commercial; there are two broadcasting companies which offer a choice of five AM and three FM radio stations, and three TV channels. A cable TV service also offers some 40 channels (colour by NTSC). In 1997 there were 82,000 radio and 66,000 TV receivers, or 1,042 per 1,000 inhabitants—more than anywhere else in the world. The USA ranked second, with 806 per 1,000 inhabitants in 1997.

Press. In 1996 there was one daily newspaper with a circulation of about 17,000 and two weeklies with a combined circulation of about 15,000.

Tourism. In 2000, 543,126 tourists, including 209,727 cruise ship passengers, visited Bermuda. Visitor expenditure in 1998 was US$480m.

FURTHER READING

Government Statistical Department. *Bermuda Facts and Figures.* Annual.
Ministry of Finance. *Bermuda Digest of Statistics.* Annual.

Boultbee, P. and Raine, D., *Bermuda.* [Bibliography] ABC-Clio, Oxford and Santa Barbara (CA), 1998
Zuill, W. S., *The Story of Bermuda and Her People.* 2nd ed. London, 1992

National library: The Bermuda Library, Hamilton.
National statistical office: Government Statistical Department, Hamilton.

BRITISH ANTARCTIC TERRITORY

KEY HISTORICAL EVENTS

The British Antarctic Territory was established on 3 March 1962, as a consequence of the entry into force of the Antarctic Treaty, to separate those areas of the then Falkland Islands Dependencies which lay within the Treaty area from those which did not (i.e. South Georgia and the South Sandwich Islands).

TERRITORY AND POPULATION

The territory encompasses the lands and islands within the area south of 60°S latitude lying between 20°W and 80°W longitude (approximately due south of the Falkland Islands and the Dependencies). It covers an area of some 1,700,000 sq. km, and its principal components are the South Orkney and South Shetland Islands, the Antarctic Peninsula (Palmer Land and Graham Land), the Filchner and Ronne Ice Shelves and Coats Land.

There is no indigenous or permanently resident population. There is, however, an itinerant population of scientists and logistics staff of about 300, manning a number of research stations.

CURRENT ADMINISTRATION
Commissioner: Alan Huckle (non-resident).
Administrator: Dr Michael Richardson.

BRITISH INDIAN OCEAN TERRITORY

KEY HISTORICAL EVENTS
This territory was established to meet UK and US defence requirements by an Order in Council on 8 Nov. 1965, consisting then of the Chagos Archipelago (formerly administered from Mauritius) and the islands of Aldabra, Desroches and Farquhar (all formerly administered from Seychelles). The latter islands became part of Seychelles when that country achieved independence on 29 June 1976. In Nov. 2000 the High Court ruled that the 2,000 Ilois people deported between 1967 and 1973 had been removed unlawfully.

TERRITORY AND POPULATION
The group, with a total land area of 23 sq. miles (60 sq. km), comprises five coral atolls (Diego Garcia, Peros Banhos, Salomon, Eagle and Egmont), of which the largest and southernmost, Diego Garcia, covers 17 sq. miles (44 sq. km) and lies 450 miles (724 km) south of the Maldives. A US Navy support facility has been established on Diego Garcia. There is no permanent population.

CURRENT ADMINISTRATION
Commissioner: Alan Huckle; since 2001 (resident in UK).
Administrator: Charles Hamilton; since 2002 (resident in UK).
Commissioner's Representative: Cdr Adam Peters.

BRITISH VIRGIN ISLANDS

KEY HISTORICAL EVENTS
Discovered by Columbus on his second voyage in 1493, British Virgin Islands were first settled by the Dutch in 1648 and taken over in 1666 by a group of English planters. The islands were annexed to the British Crown in 1672. Constitutional government was granted in 1773, but was later surrendered in 1867. A Legislative Council formed in that year was abolished in 1902. In 1950 a partly nominated and partly elected Legislative Council was restored. A ministerial system of government was introduced in 1967.

TERRITORY AND POPULATION
The Islands form the eastern extremity of the Greater Antilles and number 60, of which 16 are inhabited. The largest, with population (1991 census), are Tortola, 13,568, Virgin Gorda, 2,495, Anegada, 156; and Jost Van Dyke, 141. Other islands had a total population (estimate 1990) of 183; marine population (estimate 1989), 124. Total area 59·3 sq. miles (130 sq. km); total population (1991 census), 16,749. The most recent estimate of the population of the British Virgin Islands was 20,254 in 2000. In 1995 an estimated 56% of the population were urban. The capital, Road Town, on the southeast of Tortola, is a port of entry; population (estimate, 2000), 7,974.

The official language is English. Spanish and Creole are also spoken.

SOCIAL STATISTICS
Birth rate, 2000, was 16·2 per 1,000 population; death rate, 4·5 per 1,000. Life expectancy in 2001 was an estimated 75·5 years. Annual growth rate, 1·96% in 2000.

CLIMATE
A pleasant healthy sub-tropical climate with summer temperatures lowered by sea breezes and cool nights. Road Town (1999), Jan. 21°C, July 27°C; rainfall (1998), 1471 mm.

CONSTITUTION AND GOVERNMENT
The Constitution dates from 1967 but was amended in 1977 and 1994. The Executive Council consists of the Governor, the Chief Minister, the Attorney-General *ex officio* and four ministers. The ministers are appointed by the Governor from among the elected members of the Legislative Council. The *Legislative Council* consists of the five ministers, five directly elected members from constituencies and four members from 'at large' seats covering the territory as a whole. The Speaker is elected from outside the Council.

RECENT ELECTIONS
In parliamentary elections on 17 May 1999 the Virgin Islands Party won seven of the 13 seats with 38·0% of votes cast, ahead of the National Democratic Party with 5 and 36·9% of the votes. The Concerned Citizens' Movement won 2 seats.

CURRENT ADMINISTRATION
Governor: Tom Macan.
 Chief Minister: Ralph T. O'Neal (Virgin Islands Party; sworn in 25 May 1995).
Government Website: http://www.gov.vg/

INTERNATIONAL RELATIONS
The Islands are an associate member of CARICOM, OECS, UNESCO and ECLAC.
 The UK government is responsible for the international relations of the Territory. Through this link, the Territory is party to a large number of treaties and international covenants.

ECONOMY
The economy is based on tourism and international financial services.
Currency. The official unit of currency is the US dollar.
Budget. In 2000 revenue was US$183·1m. and expenditure US$134·6m. (goods and services, US$63·7m.; wages and salaries, US$50·1m.; subsidies and transfers, US$19·7m.; interest payments, US$1·2m.). Outstanding debt, in 2000, US$37·1m.
Performance. Real GDP growth was 8·7% in 2001 following growth of 4·4% in 2000. In 2001 the GDP per capita was US$35,954.
Banking and Finance. In 1999 there were 13 banks and 189 trust companies. As of Sept. 2001 total deposits were US$1,143·8m. Financial Services has surpassed the performance of the tourism industry to become the largest contributor to the GDP. As of 30 June 2001, 448,767 International Business Companies were registered in the British Virgin Islands.

ENERGY AND NATURAL RESOURCES
Electricity. Production, 2000, 260·1m. kWh.
Water. The major part of the water supplied in the public mains is from wells and sea water produced by reverse osmosis desalination plants.
Agriculture. The value of agricultural production in 1997 was US$1·52m. despite three destructive hurricanes in the course of the year. In 1994: total land suitable for agriculture, 5,324 acres; crops, 1,767 acres; and pastures, 3,557 acres. Agricultural production is limited, with the chief products being livestock (including poultry), fish, fruit and vegetables. Production, 1994, in tonnes: fruits, 525; vegetables/ root crop, 153; beef, 172; mutton, 29; pork, 39; and 1,535 cases of eggs.
 Livestock (1996): cattle, 2,000; pigs, 2,000; sheep, 5,000; and goats (1995), 10,000.
Forestry. The area under forests in 1995 was 4,000 ha, or 26·7% of the total land area.
Fisheries. The total catch was 944 tonnes in 1998.

INDUSTRY

The construction industry is a significant employer. There is a rum distillery, ice-making plants and cottage industries producing tourist items.

Labour. In 1997 of the 11,996 strong labour force there were 21·4% employed in the public sector, 0·2% in agriculture, 3·6% in industry and 74·8% employed in other areas. In 1991 the unemployment rate was 3·6%.

EXTERNAL ECONOMIC RELATIONS

Imports and Exports. There is a very small export trade, almost entirely with the Virgin Islands of the USA. In 2000 imports were US$237·6m. and exports US$26·6m.

COMMUNICATIONS

Roads. In 2000 there were 362·09 km of paved roads and 10,631 registered vehicles.

Civil Aviation. Beef Island Airport, about 16 km from Road Town, is capable of receiving 80-seat short-take-off-and-landing jet aircraft. American Eagle, Continental Airlines (Gulf Stream), Liat and Caribbean Star provide scheduled flights to Puerto Rico and the Eastern Caribbean. A new airport is currently under construction.

Shipping. There are two deep-water harbours: Port Purcell and Road Town. There are services to the Netherlands, UK, USA and other Caribbean islands. Merchant shipping totalled 4,000 GRT in 1998.

Telecommunications. In 1996 there were 13,320 main telephone lines, and in 1998, 25,000 mobile phone subscribers. There were 21 telex subscribers and 582 fax machine subscribers in 1995. An external telephone service links Tortola with Bermuda and the rest of the world.

SOCIAL INSTITUTIONS

Justice. Law is based on UK common law. There are courts of first instance. The appeal court is in the UK.

Religion. There are Anglican, Methodist, Seventh-Day Adventist, Roman Catholic, Baptist, Pentecostal and other Christian churches in the Territory. There are also Jehovah's Witness and Hindu congregations.

Education. In 1997 adult literacy was 98·2%. Primary education is provided in 15 government schools, three secondary divisions, 16 private schools and one school for children with special needs. Total number of pupils in primary schools (1997) 2,633.

Secondary education to GCSE level and Caribbean Examination Council level is provided by the BVI High School, and the secondary divisions of the schools on Virgin Gorda and Anegada. Total number of secondary level pupils (1997), 1,424. In 1996 the total number of classroom teachers in all government schools was 116.

In 1986 a branch of the Hull University (England) School of Education was established.

Government expenditure, 1995 (estimate), US$4·3m.

Health. As of 31 Dec. 2000 there were 19 doctors, 74 nurses, 44 public hospital beds and one private hospital with ten beds. Expenditure, 2000 (estimate) was US$7·6m.

CULTURE

Broadcasting. Radio ZBVI transmits 10,000 watts; and British Virgin Islands Cable TV operates a cable system of 43 television channels and one pay-per-view channel (colour by NTSC). In 2000 there were 9,000 radio sets and 6,200 TV receivers.

Press. In 2000 there were three weekly newspapers.

Tourism. Tourism is the most important industry and in 2000 accounted for some 14·1% of economic activity. There were 519,409 foreign tourists in 2000 of which 281,119 were overnight visitors, 188,522 were cruise ship arrivals and 49,768 day-trippers. Total tourist expenditure for 2000 was US$315m. In 1999 the tourism industry employed 12,509 people.

FURTHER READING
Moll, V. P., *Virgin Islands*. [Bibliography] ABC-Clio, Oxford and Santa Barbara (CA), 1991

CAYMAN ISLANDS

KEY HISTORICAL EVENTS
The islands were discovered by Columbus on 10 May 1503 and (with Jamaica) were recognized as British possessions by the Treaty of Madrid in 1670. Grand Cayman was settled in 1734 and the other islands in 1833. They were administered by Jamaica from 1863, but remained under British sovereignty when Jamaica became independent on 6 Aug. 1962.

TERRITORY AND POPULATION
The Islands consist of Grand Cayman, Cayman Brac and Little Cayman. Situated in the Caribbean Sea, about 200 miles (320 km) northwest of Jamaica. Area, 100 sq. miles (260 sq. km). Census population of 1999, 39,410 (52·5% Caymanians by birth). Estimate, 1996, 35,000; density, 135 per sq. km. The estimated population 2001, 41,400. The spoken language is English. The chief town is George Town with a population of 20,626.

The areas and populations of the islands are:

	Sq. km	1979	1989	1999
Grand Cayman	197	15,000	23,881	37,473
Cayman Brac	39	1,607	1,441	1,822
Little Cayman	26	70	33	115

SOCIAL STATISTICS
2001: births, 622; deaths, 133. 2000: resident marriages, 397; Annual growth rate, 1989–99, 4·5%.

CLIMATE
The climate is tropical maritime, with a cool season from Nov. to March. The average yearly temperature is 27°C, and rainfall averages 57" (1,400 mm) a year at George Town. Hurricanes may be experienced between July and Nov.

CONSTITUTION AND GOVERNMENT
The 1972 Constitution provides for a *Legislative Assembly* consisting of the Speaker (who may be an elected member), three official members (the Chief Secretary, the Attorney General, and the Financial Secretary) and 15 elected members. The *Executive Council* consists of the Governor (as Chairman), the three official members and five ministers elected by the elected members of the Legislative Assembly. The Islands are a self-governing overseas territory of the United Kingdom.

RECENT ELECTIONS
At the Legislative Assembly elections on 8 Nov. 2000, no national teams were formed. Eight seats were won by teams formed at district level. The new assembly has eight incumbents, six new legislators and one re-elected member (prior service 1988–96). In Nov. 2001, ten members of the Legislative Assembly formed the United Democratic Party. In 2002 the opposition formed the People's Progressive Movement.

CURRENT ADMINISTRATION
Governor: Bruce Dinwiddy.

Government Website: http://www.gov.ky

ECONOMY

Currency. The unit of currency is the *Cayman Island dollar* (KYD/CI$) of 100 cents.

Budget. 31 Dec. 2001: revenue, CI$273·2m.; expenditure, CI$288·8m. Public debt, CI$92·5m.; total reserves, CI$10·2m.

Performance. Real GDP growth in 2002 was an estimated 1·9%; in 2000 growth slowed to an estimated 3·2%, down from a five-year average of 5%.

Banking and Finance. Financial services, the Island's chief industry, are monitored by the Cayman Islands Monetary Authority (*Chairman,* George McCarthy OBE), inaugurated in Jan. 1997. At Dec. 2001, 545 commercial banks and trust companies held licenses that permit the holders to offer services to the public, 31 domestically. Most of the world's leading banks have branches or subsidiaries in the Cayman Islands. At the end of 2001, 64,495 companies, almost all offshore, were registered as well as 2,937 mutual funds and 542 insurance companies.

ENERGY AND NATURAL RESOURCES

Electricity. Installed capacity was 115 MW in 2000, and an all-time peak demand of 70·18 MW occurred in Oct. 2000. Production in 1998 was 290m. kWh; consumption per capita in 1994 was 8,800 kWh.

Agriculture. Mangoes, bananas, citrus fruits, yams, cassava, breadfruit, tomatoes, honey, beef, pork and goatmeat are produced for local consumption.

Fisheries. In 1999 the total catch was 125 tonnes.

INDUSTRY

Labour. Unemployment rate: 7·5% of workforce in Oct. 2002 (10% Oct. 2001).

EXTERNAL ECONOMIC RELATIONS

Imports and Exports. Exports, 1998, totalled US$1·44m.; imports, US$505·56m.

COMMUNICATIONS

Roads. There were (2000) about 461 miles of road on Grand Cayman; 25 miles on Cayman Brac and on the three islands 25,061 licensed motor vehicles.

Civil Aviation. George Town (O. Roberts) on Grand Cayman and Cayman Brac have international airports. George Town handled 901,000 passengers (834,000 on international flights) and 3,900 tonnes of freight in 2000. Cayman Airways and Island Air provide a regular inter-island service. Cayman Airways also flies to Miami, Houston, Tampa, Cuba and Jamaica. Eight additional international airlines provide services to London, Toronto, Jamaica, the Bahamas, Honduras and five US cities, including New York and Atlanta.

Shipping. Motor vessels ply regularly between the Cayman Islands, Jamaica, Cuba and Florida. In 2001, 192,303 tonnes of cargo were offloaded at the port on Grand Cayman, 13,552 on Cayman Brac and, in 2000, 1,845 at Little Cayman.

Telecommunications. At the end of 2001 there were 31,926 direct telephone lines and over 17,000 mobile customers.

SOCIAL INSTITUTIONS

Justice. There is a Grand Court, sitting six times a year for criminal sessions at George Town under a Chief Justice and two puisne judges. There are three Magistrates presiding over the Summary Court.

The population in penal institutions in 1997 was 210 (equivalent to 575 per 100,000 of national population).

Religion. The residents are primarily Christian (85%) and over 12 denominations meet regularly; Church of God, Presbyterian/United, Roman Catholic, Baptist and Seventh-Day Adventists are the largest. Other religions, including Ba'hai, Buddhism, Hinduism, Islam, and Judaism, have representation in the community.

Education. In 2002 there were ten government primary schools with 2,212 pupils, and 1,913 pupils attended the three government high schools. In 2001 about 2,240 students were enrolled in ten private schools. There are two government facilities for special educational needs: a school for children and a training centre for adults. Four institutions—a private four-year college, a private medical college, the government community college and law school—provide tertiary education.

Health. The government's health services complex in George Town includes a 124-bed hospital, a dental clinic and an eye clinic. On Grand Cayman there are four district health centres. There is a hospital on Cayman Brac (18 beds) and a health centre on Little Cayman. In 2001 there were 38 doctors in government service (including 4 on Cayman Brac) and 37 in private practice.

CULTURE

Broadcasting. There are seven radio stations (one Christian), four broadcast television channels (two Christian) and a 38-channel microwave relay cable system.

Cinema. There is one cinema with two theatres.

Press. There are two newspapers, both printed on weekdays. News and opinion are also available on at least seven Internet sites.

Tourism. Tourism is the chief industry after financial services, and in 2000 there were 3,756 beds in hotels and 2,341 rooms in apartments, guest houses and cottages. There were 334,071 tourist arrivals by air and 1,214,757 cruise ship arrivals. Tourism receipts in 1998 totalled US$510m.

Festivals. Festivals include: Pirates Week, the national festival; Cayfest, an arts festival; Batabano, a carnival; annual Agricultural Show.

Libraries. The main public library (about 27,000 volumes in 2001) is in George Town. There are three branches on Grand Cayman and one on Cayman Brac.

Theatre and Opera. The Harquail Theatre is managed by the Cayman National Cultural Foundation. The foundation generally produces four shows per year; the theatre is also used as a venue for other events. Founded in 1970, the Cayman Drama Society opened the Prospect Playhouse in 1990 and presents about seven productions a year.

Museums and Galleries. The National Museum (founded 1990) in George Town has permanent exhibits on cultural and natural history, undertakes land and marine archaeology and hosts special events and activities. The Brac Museum displays artefacts, documents and photographs chronicling the island's history. The National Gallery (1999), housed in temporary facilities in George Town, is building a collection, hosts local and visiting exhibitions, and runs workshops.

FURTHER READING
Compendium of Statistics of the Cayman Islands, 1994. Cayman Islands Government Statistics Office, 1995
Cayman Islands Annual Report 1996. Cayman Islands Government Information Services, 1996
Boultbee, Paul G., *Cayman Islands.* [Bibliography] ABC-Clio, Oxford and Santa Barbara (CA), 1996

FALKLAND ISLANDS

KEY HISTORICAL EVENTS
France established a settlement in 1764 and Britain a second settlement in 1765. In 1770 Spain bought out the French and drove off the British. This action on the part of Spain brought that country and Britain to the verge of war. The Spanish restored the settlement to the British in 1771, but the settlement was withdrawn on economic grounds in 1774. In 1806 Spanish rule was overthrown in Argentina, and the Argentine claimed to succeed Spain in the French and British settlements in 1820. The British objected and reclaimed their settlement in 1832 as a Crown Colony.

On 2 April 1982 Argentine forces occupied the Falkland Islands. On 3 April the UN Security Council called, by 10 votes to 1, for Argentina's withdrawal. After a military campaign, but without a formal declaration of war, the UK regained possession on 14–15 June when Argentina surrendered.

In April 1990 Argentina's Congress declared the Falkland and other British-held South Atlantic islands part of the new Argentine province of Tierra del Fuego though the threat of hostilities has been lifted.

TERRITORY AND POPULATION

The Territory comprises numerous islands situated in the South Atlantic Ocean about 480 miles northeast of Cape Horn covering 12,200 sq. km. The main East Falkland Island, 6,760 sq. km; the West Falkland, 5,410 sq. km, including the adjacent small islands. The population at the census of 2001 was 2,379. The only town is Stanley, in East Falkland, with a 2001 population of 1,989. The population is nearly all of British descent, with 1,326 born in the Islands (2001 census figures) and 925 in the UK. In 1995, 84·1% lived in urban areas. A British garrison of about 2,000 servicemen, stationed in East Falkland in 1991, is not included in the 2001 census figures, but the 534 civilians employed there are.

The official language is English.

SOCIAL STATISTICS

In 2000 there were 27 births and 11 deaths on the islands.

CLIMATE

A cool temperate climate, much affected by strong winds, particularly in spring. Stanley, Jan. 49°F (9·4°C), July 35°F (1·7°C). Annual rainfall 24" (625 mm).

CONSTITUTION AND GOVERNMENT

A new Constitution came into force in 1997, updating the previous constitution of 1985 which incorporated a chapter protecting fundamental human rights, and in the preamble recalled the provisions on the right of self-determination contained in international covenants.

Executive power is vested in the Governor who must consult the Executive Council except on urgent or trivial matters. He must consult the Commander British Forces on matters relating to defence and internal security (except police).

There is a *Legislative Council* consisting of eight members (five from Stanley and three from Camp, elected every four years) and two *ex officio* members, the Chief Executive and Financial Secretary. Only elected members have a vote. The Commander British Forces has a right to attend and take part in its proceedings but has no vote. The Attorney General also has a similar right to take part in proceedings with the consent of the person presiding. The Governor presides over sittings. He also presides over the monthly sittings of the Executive Council which consists of three elected members (elected by and from the elected members of Legislative Council) and the Chief Executive and Financial Secretary (*ex officio*). The Commander British Forces and Attorney General have a right to attend but may not vote.

British citizenship was withdrawn by the British Nationality Act 1981, but restored after the Argentine invasion of 1982.

RECENT ELECTIONS

Elections to the Legislative Assembly were held on 22 Nov. 2001. Only non-partisans were elected.

CURRENT ADMINISTRATION

Governor: Howard Pearce.
 Chief Executive: Dr Michael Blanch.

Government Website: http://www.falklands.gov.fk/

DEFENCE

Since 1982 the Islands have been defended by a 2,000-strong garrison of British servicemen. In addition there is a local volunteer defence force.

ECONOMY

The GNP of the Islands is estimated to have tripled from 1985–87 as a result of the expansion of the fishing industry. In 1998–99 the GNP was estimated at £53m.

Overview. In 2001 the Falklands Islands government published the Islands Plan, a three-year rolling programme aimed at achieving sustainable economic growth whilst preserving the natural environment and unique culture of the Falkland Islands.

Policy-making is also influenced by the Falkland Islands Development Corporation (FIDC), established in 1984. Activities in 1998–99 included assisting a chemical-free wool project and initiating surveys into deposits of calcified seaweed.

Currency. The unit of currency is the *Falkland Islands pound* (FKP) of 100 *pence*, at parity with £1 sterling.

Budget. Revenue and expenditure (in £ sterling) for fiscal year ending 30 June 2000 was: revenue, 52·3m.; expenditure, 40·4m.

Banking and Finance. The only bank is Standard Chartered Bank, which had assets of £31m. in 1997. Credit cards are, as yet, generally not accepted on the island.

ENERGY AND NATURAL RESOURCES

Electricity. Electricity production in 1998 totalled 12m. kWh.

Oil and Gas. In 1996 the Falkland Islands government awarded production licences to Shell, Amerada Hess, Desire Petroleum and International Petroleum Corporation (Sodra), allowing them to begin oil exploration. The licensed areas are situated 150 km north of the Islands over the North Falkland Basin. Six exploration wells were drilled in 1998 and analysis of the findings suggested that in excess of 60bn. bbls. of oil have been generated in the basin.

Agriculture. The economy was formerly based solely on agriculture, principally sheep farming. Following a programme of sub-division, much of the land is divided into family-size units. There were 100 farms in 1997, averaging 33,600 acres and 8,200 sheep. During 1991 the Falklands Islands Co. sold its agricultural holdings to the Falkland Island government. Less than 5% of the total land area is owned outside the islands. Wool is the principal product; 1,870,000 tonnes worth £2,292,000 was exported to the UK in 1998.

Livestock: in April 2000 there were over 700,000 sheep. 1996: cattle, 4,000; horses, 1,000.

Fisheries. Since the establishment of a 150-mile interim conservation and management zone around the Islands in 1986 and the consequent introduction, on 1 Feb. 1987, of a licensing regime for vessels fishing within the zone, income from the associated fishing activities is now the largest source of revenue. Licences raised £25m. in 1992 but this figure had fallen to £20m. by 1998–99. In 2000 the fish catch (1,000 tonnes) was: illex, 190; loligo, 64; blue whiting, 23; hoki, 20; hake, 3; others, 19. The growth in the annual fish catch since the mid 1980s has been one of the fastest in the world.

On 26 Dec. 1990 the Falklands outer conservation zone was introduced which extends beyond the 150-mile zone out to 200 miles from baselines. In Nov. 1992 commercial fishing in the outer zone was banned, the zone was reopened to fishing in 1994. A UK-Argentine South Atlantic Fisheries Commission was set up in 1990; it meets at least twice a year. In 2001 there were 27 registered fishing vessels.

INDUSTRY

Labour. In 2001 there were 2,025 people employed full-time, including 358 in construction and 326 in agriculture, hunting and fishing. The growth of the fishing industry has ensured practically zero unemployment.

EXTERNAL ECONOMIC RELATIONS

Around 85% of trade is with the UK, the rest with Latin America, mainly Chile. In 1998 imports totalled £23·5m.; exports (mainly wool), £3·5m. (1995).

COMMUNICATIONS

Roads. There are over 50 km of surfaced roads and another 400 km of unsurfaced road. This includes the 80 km between Stanley and Mount Pleasant Airport. Other settlements outside Stanley are linked by tracks. There were about 1,100 private cars in 1996.

Civil Aviation. Air communication is currently via Ascension Island. An airport, completed in 1986, is sited at Mount Pleasant on East Falkland. RAF Tristar aircraft operate a twice-weekly service between the Falklands and the UK. Internal air links are provided by the government-operated air service, which carries passengers, mail, freight and medical patients between the settlements and Stanley on non-scheduled flights in Islander aircraft. A Chilean airline, LanChile, runs a weekly service to Punta Arenas. Aircraft movements at Stanley Airport in 1998 amounted to 4,264 with 7,715 passengers moving through the airport.

Shipping. A charter vessel calls four or five times a year to/from the UK. Vessels of the Royal Fleet Auxiliary run regularly to South Georgia. Sea links with Chile and Uruguay began in 1989. In 1995 merchant shipping totalled 20,000 GRT.

Telecommunications. Number of telephone main lines (March 1998) 1,856—one of the highest penetration rates in the world. International direct dialling is available, as are international telex and facsimile links. In 1996, 257 households had a PC and 213 had a fax machine.

Postal Services. The Post Office and the Philatelic Bureau work in tandem. In 1998 there were two post offices and 740 post boxes. Airmail is generally received and dispatched twice weekly and surface post is airlifted out about once every two weeks. Surface mail is received approximately once every three weeks.

SOCIAL INSTITUTIONS

Justice. There is a Supreme Court, and a Court of Appeal sits in the UK; appeals may go from that court to the judicial committee of the Privy Council. Judges may only be removed for inability or misbehaviour on the advice of the judicial committee of the Privy Council. The senior resident judicial officer is the Senior Magistrate. There is an Attorney General and a Senior Crown Counsel.

Education. Education is compulsory between the ages of 5 and 16 years. In Stanley in 2002 there were 30 pre-school pupils, 190 primary pupils (18 teachers) and 160 pupils in the 11–16 age range (18 teachers). In rural areas students attend small settlement schools or are visited by one of seven travelling teachers. Lessons may also be carried out over the radio or telephone. All teachers are trained in the United Kingdom. Students achieving the required number of GCSE passes at Grades A–C are funded for A Level/GNVQ courses on the British mainland. Estimated recurrent expenditure on education and training from own funds in 1994–95, £2,041,440.

Health. The Government Medical Department is responsible for all medical services to civilians. Primary and secondary health care facilities are based at the King Edward VII Memorial Hospital, the only hospital on the islands. It has 28 beds. It is staffed by five doctors, six sisters (including four midwives), eight staff nurses, a health visitor, counsellor, physiotherapist, social worker and an auxiliary nursing staff. The Royal Army Medical Corps staff the surgical facilities. Regular visits are received from specialists based in the UK. Most services are free to residents and British citizens, though some charges are made. There are two dentists on the island. Estimated expenditure (1994–95), £2,092,490.

Welfare. In 1998 total amount spent on old age pension payments was £504,075. Total amount spent on family allowance payments was £336,365.

CULTURE

Broadcasting. The Falkland Islands Broadcasting Station (FIBS), in conjunction with British Forces Broadcasting Service (BFBS), broadcasts 24 hours a day on FM and MW. Some BBC World Service programmes are also available.

BFBS also provides a single channel TV service (UKPAL) to Stanley, Mount Pleasant and most outlying camp settlements and a cable TV service is also in operation. In 1997 there were 1,000 TV and 1,000 radio sets.

Tourism. In the 1999–2000 season there were estimated to be 30,000 cruise ship visitors, representing a 400% increase over three seasons. There are tourist lodges at Port Howard, San Carlos, Sea Lion Island and Pebble Island. Stanley has two hotels.

FURTHER READING

Day, Alan, *The Falkland Islands, South Georgia and the South Sandwich Islands.* [Bibliography] ABC-Clio, Oxford and Santa Barbara (CA), 1996
Gough, B., *The Falkland Islands/Malvinas: the Contest for Empire in the South Atlantic.* London, 1992

GIBRALTAR

KEY HISTORICAL EVENTS

The Rock of Gibraltar was settled by Moors in 711. In 1462 it was taken by the Spaniards, from Granada. It was captured by Admiral Sir George Rooke on 24 July 1704, and ceded to Great Britain by the Treaty of Utrecht, 1713. The cession was confirmed by the treaties of Paris (1763) and Versailles (1783). In 1830 Gibraltar became a British crown colony.

On 10 Sept. 1967 a UN resolution on the decolonization of Gibraltar led to a referendum to ascertain whether the people of Gibraltar wished to retain their link with the UK. Out of an electorate of 12,762, an overwhelming majority voted to retain the British connection.

The border was closed by Spain in 1969, opened to pedestrians in 1982 and fully opened in 1985. In 1973 Gibraltar joined the European Community as a dependent territory of the United Kingdom. In 2001 talks were held between Britain and Spain over the colony's sovereignty. In a joint statement, the British and Spanish foreign ministers said they would work towards a comprehensive agreement by the summer of 2002. Gibraltar's government held an unofficial referendum on sharing sovereignty with Spain on 7 Nov. 2002 in which 98·97% of votes cast were against joint sovereignty. While Britain sees the principle of shared sovereignty as the definitive solution, Spain maintains its historic claim to outright control.

TERRITORY AND POPULATION

Gibraltar is situated in latitude 36°07' N and longitude 05°21' W. Area, 2½ sq. miles (6·5 sq. km) including port and harbour. Highest point is 426 metres. Total population, (2000), 27,033 (of whom 21,121 were British Gibraltarian, 3,696 Other British and 2,216 Non-British); density, 4,159 per sq. km. The population is mostly of Genoese, Portuguese and Maltese and Spanish descent.

The official language is English. Spanish, Italian and Portuguese are also spoken.

SOCIAL STATISTICS

Statistics (2000): births, 409; deaths, 262; marriages, 721. Rates per 1,000 population: birth, 15·1; death, 9·7; marriage, 26·7 (the highest in Europe and one of the highest in the world).

CLIMATE

The climate is warm temperate, with westerly winds in winter bringing rain. Summers are pleasantly warm and rainfall is low. Mean maximum temperatures: Jan. 16°C, July 28°C. Annual rainfall 722 mm.

CONSTITUTION AND GOVERNMENT

A new Constitution was introduced in 1969. The Legislative and City Councils were merged to produce an enlarged legislature known as the *Gibraltar House of Assembly.* Executive authority is exercised by the Governor, who is also Commander-in-Chief. The Governor retains direct responsibility for matters relating to defence, external affairs and internal security. He has the power to intervene in the conduct of domestic affairs in support of this responsibility and has certain powers of intervention in the interests of maintaining financial and economic stability. However, he is normally required to act in accordance with the advice of the Gibraltar Council, which consists of four *ex officio* members (the Deputy Governor, the Deputy Fortress Commander, the Attorney-General and the Financial and Development Secretary) together with five elected members of the House of Assembly appointed by the Governor after consultation with the Chief Minister. Matters of primarily domestic concern are devolved to elected Ministers. There is a Council of Ministers presided over by the Chief Minister.

The House of Assembly consists of a Speaker appointed by the Governor, 15 elected and two *ex officio* members (the Attorney-General and the Financial and Development Secretary). No more than eight of the elected seats may go to the winning party at elections.

Gibraltarians have full UK citizenship.

A Mayor of Gibraltar is elected by the elected members of the Assembly.

RECENT ELECTIONS

At the elections of 10 Feb. 2000 the electorate was 18,600 and turn-out was 83%. The ruling Gibraltar Social Democratic Party (GSD) gained eight seats with 58·0% of votes cast. The opposition alliance of the Gibraltar Socialist Labour Party and the Liberal Party gained seven with 41·0%. Independent Liberal Forum and Pro-Settlement each received 0·5%. All of the parties advocate self-determination.

CURRENT ADMINISTRATION

Governor and C.-in-C: David Durie.

   Chief Minister: Peter Caruana; b. 1956 (elected in 1996, re-elected in 2000; GSD).

   Deputy Chief Minister and Minister for Trade, Industry and Telecommunications: Keith Azopardi. *Education, Training, Culture and Health:* Dr Bernard Linares. *Government Services and Sport:* Ernest Britto. *Tourism and Transport:* Joe Holliday. *Social Affairs:* Yvette Del Agua. *Employment and Consumer Affairs:* Hubert Corby Netto. *Housing:* Jaime Netto.

   Speaker (House of Assembly): John E. Alcantara.

Government Website: http://www.gibraltar.gov.gi/

DEFENCE

The Ministry of Defence presence consists of a tri-service garrison numbering approximately 900 uniformed personnel. Supporting the garrison are approximately 1,100 locally-employed civilian personnel. In addition to the defence of the Rock, the garrison supports a NATO Headquarters, provides and operates communications and surveillance facilities, operates the airfield and provides berthing facilities for naval vessels in the harbour.

ECONOMY

Overview. The economy is primarily dependent on service industries and port facilities, with income derived from tourism and, perhaps most importantly in terms of growth, the provision of financial services.

Currency. The legal tender currency is UK sterling. Also legal tender are Government of Gibraltar Currency notes and coins for the *Gibraltar pound* (GIP) of 100 *pence*, at parity with the UK £1 sterling. The total of Government of Gibraltar notes in circulation at 31 March 1999 was £12·6m. The annual rate of inflation was 0·8% in 1999.

Budget. Departmental revenue credited to the Consolidated Fund for the year ending 31 March 2000 totalled £140·6m. whilst expenditure amounted to £104·9m. Consolidated Fund charges totalled £21·5m. of which £6·6m. were public debt charges. The main sources of Consolidated Fund revenues were Income Tax (£49·6m.), import duties (£27·6m.) and General Rates (£11·2m.). Main items of expenditure: education, youth culture and consumer affairs (£15·7m.); environment and health (£13·6m.); electricity (£10·5m.); tourism and transport (£6·9m.); police (£6·8m.).

Performance. In 1995–96 Gibraltar's provisional GDP was £327·7m., equivalent to £11,680 per head.

Banking and Finance. In Dec. 2001 there were 20 banks and 2 building societies. The financial sector employs 12% of the working population. In 1989 the Financial Services Commission was established to regulate financial activities. A number of Spanish banks have established offices in Gibraltar, encouraging the territory's growth as an off-shore centre, as has the absence of taxes for non-residents.

ENERGY AND NATURAL RESOURCES

Electricity. Installed capacity was 33,000 kW in 1993. Generation in 2001 amounted to 126m. kWh.

Oil and Gas. Gibraltar is dependent on oil and butane gas imports.

Water. There are no permanent natural water supplies in Gibraltar. The main sources of water supply are the distillation plants which purify sea water.

Minerals. There are no natural mineral resources for this sector and there is total dependence on imports.

Agriculture. Gibraltar lacks agricultural land and natural resources; the territory is dependent on imports of foodstuffs and fuels.

INDUSTRY

The industrial sector (including manufacturing, construction and power) employed around 17% of the working population in 1999.

Labour. The total insured labour force at Oct. 1998 was 12,774. Principal areas of employment (Oct. 1998): community, social and personal services, 5,937; trade, restaurants and hotels, 3,739; manufacturing, 402; electricity and water, 232; other, 1,511. (Figures cover only non-agricultural activities, excluding mining and quarrying). An estimated 5% of the labour force were unemployed in 1999.

Trade Unions. In 1991 there were eight registered trade unions.

EXTERNAL ECONOMIC RELATIONS

Gibraltar has a special status within the EU which exempts it from the latter's fiscal policy.

Imports and Exports. Imports in 2000 totalled £305·6m. and exports £86·8m (excluding petroleum products).

Britain provided 37% of imports in 2001 and is the largest source. Other major trade partners include the Netherlands, Spain and Japan. Foodstuffs accounted for 10% of total imports in 2001 (excluding petroleum products). Value of non-fuel imports, 1995, £276·2m. Mineral fuels comprised about 32% of the value of total imports in 1998. Exports are mainly re-exports of petroleum and petroleum products supplied to shipping, and include manufactured goods, wines, spirits, malt and tobacco. Gibraltar depends largely on tourism, offshore banking and other financial sector activity, the entrepôt trade and the provision of supplies to visiting ships. Exports of local produce are negligible. In 2001 Gibraltar recorded a visible trade deficit of £218·8m. (excluding petroleum products).

COMMUNICATIONS

Roads. There are 56 km of roads including 6·8 km of pedestrian way. In 2001 there were 25,717 private vehicles, 8,873 motorcycles, 15 buses, 2,000 commercial vehicles and 199 omnibuses including taxis.

Civil Aviation. There is an international airport, Gibraltar North Front. Scheduled flights were operated in 2001 by British Airways to London (Gatwick) and London (Heathrow), and by Monarch Airlines to London (Luton). In 2001, 108,800 passengers arrived by air and 110,400 departed; 77 tonnes of freight were loaded and 306 tonnes were unloaded (figures exclude military passengers and freight). The airport was designed to accommodate 1m. passengers a year, but is underutilized owing to Spain's exclusion of Gibraltar as a European regional airport.

Shipping. The Strait of Gibraltar is a principal ocean route between the Mediterranean and Black Sea areas and the rest of the world. Tax concessions are available to ship-owners who register their ships at Gibraltar. A total of 6,303 merchant ships of 133·97m. GRT entered port during 2000, including 4,489 deep-sea ships of 106·9m. GRT. In 2000, 4,643 calls were made by yachts of 279,662 GRT. 175 cruise liners called during 2000 involving 133,059 passengers.

Telecommunications. The telephone service is operated by Gibraltar Nynex Communications, a joint venture company between the government of Gibraltar and Verizon Communications Inc., from the USA. The number of telephone stations (2001) was 29,352. The number of exchange lines stood at 24,512. International direct dialling is available to over 150 countries via the Gibraltar Tele-communications Ltd (Gibtel) Earth Satellite Station and other international circuits. Gibtel began operating a mobile system in 1994. By the end of 2001 there were 9,797 mobile phone customers of whom 5,916 were prepaid. During 2001 GNC's subsidiary company, GNC Networks Limited, continued to develop and expand Internet services and by the end of the year 2,953 customers had been connected.

Postal Services. Airmail is dispatched to London, and via London to destinations worldwide, six times a week in direct flights. Surface letter mail and parcel mail to and from the United Kingdom is dispatched and received via the land frontier five times a week.

SOCIAL INSTITUTIONS

Justice. The judicial system is based on the English system. There is a Court of Appeal, a Supreme Court, presided over by the Chief Justice, a Court of First Instance and a Magistrates' Court.

The population in penal institutions in Oct. 1998 was 34 (equivalent to 125 per 100,000 of national population).

Religion. According to the 1991 census 76·9% of the population were Roman Catholic, 6·9% Muslim, 6·9% Church of England and 2·3% Jewish. In 2000 there were 7 Roman Catholic and 3 Anglican churches (including 1 Catholic and 1 Anglican cathedral), 1 Presbyterian and 1 Methodist church, 4 synagogues and 1 mosque. Annual subsidy to each communion, £500.

Education. Free compulsory education is provided between ages 5 and 15 years. The medium of instruction is English. The comprehensive system was introduced in Sept. 1972. There were (2001) 11 primary and 2 secondary schools. Primary schools are mixed and divided into first schools for children aged 4–8 years and middle schools for children aged 8–12 years. The secondaries are single-sex. In addition, there is one Services primary school, one private primary school and one private Jewish secondary school for girls. A purpose-built Special School for children aged 2–16 years with severe physical disabilities was opened in 1977, and there are four Special Units for children with special educational needs (one attached to a first school, one to a middle school and one at each secondary school), five nurseries for children aged 3–4 years, and an occupational therapy centre for adults. In Sept. 1997 a new observation and assessment unit was opened at the Special School to monitor the progress of pre-school children with special educational needs.

Vocational education and training is available at the Gibraltar College of Further Education, the Construction Training Centre and the Cammel Laird Training Centre; the former two are managed by the Gibraltar government and the latter by Cammel Laird (and part-funded by the Government). In Sept. 2001 there were 3,025 pupils at government primary schools, 249 at government nursery schools, 322 at private and 240 at the Services school; 17 at the special school; 871 at the boys' comprehensive school and 923 at the girls' comprehensive. There were 224 full-time and 953 part-time students in the Gibraltar College of Further Education in Sept. 2001. Scholarships are made available for universities, teacher training and other higher education in the UK. Government expenditure on education in the year ended 31 March 2001 was £16·32m.

Health. The Gibraltar Health Authority is the organization responsible for providing health care in Gibraltar. The Authority operates a Group Practice Medical Scheme which is a contributory scheme and enables registered persons to access free medical treatment. A programme of visits by consultants from the United Kingdom covers certain specialities which are not provided by staff permanently employed in Gibraltar. In 2000 there were two hospitals with 226 beds. Total expenditure on medical and health services during year ended 31 March 2000 was £28,426,048.

Welfare. The social security system consists of three contributory schemes: the Social Security (Employment Injuries Insurance) Scheme which only applies to employed persons and provides cash benefits for those who because of an accident at work or certain industrial diseases are unable to work or are disabled, and for widows and widowers and certain other dependants or industrial casualties; the Social Security (Short-Term Benefits) Scheme which provides for payments of maternity grants, death grants and unemployment benefit; the Social Security (Open Long-Term Benefits) Scheme which provides for pensions on reaching pensionable age, allowances on widowhood and for guardians of orphans.

CULTURE
Gibraltar's main events are organized by the Ministry of Culture.

Broadcasting. Radio Gibraltar broadcasts for 24 hours daily, in English and Spanish; and GBC Television operates for 24 hours daily in English (colour by PAL). In 2001 there were 7,950 TV licences. In 1997 there were 37,000 radios. Radio receivers are not required to be licensed.

Cinema. There is one cinema.

Press. There is one daily and three weekly papers.

Tourism. In 2000 more than 7·3m. tourists visited Gibraltar (including day-visitors) bringing in revenue of £162m. There are around 2,000 hotel beds in Gibraltar. Tourism accounts for an estimated 35% of GDP.

Libraries. There is one public library in Gibraltar.

Museums and Galleries. The Gibraltar Museum documents Gibraltar's history with an audio-visual presentation and several galleries.

FURTHER READING
Gibraltar Year Book. Gibraltar (Annual)

Morris, D. S. and Haigh, R. H., *Britain, Spain and Gibraltar, 1945–90: the Eternal Triangle.* London, 1992

MONTSERRAT

KEY HISTORICAL EVENTS
Montserrat was discovered by Columbus in 1493 and colonized by Britain in 1632, who brought Irish settlers to the island. Montserrat formed part of the federal colony of the Leeward Islands from 1871 until 1958, when it became a separate colony following the dissolution of the Federation.

On 18 July 1995 the Soufriere Hills volcano erupted for the first time in recorded history, which led to over half the inhabitants being evacuated to the north of the island, and the relocation of the chief town, Plymouth. Another major eruption on 25 June 1997 caused a number of deaths and led to further evacuation.

TERRITORY AND POPULATION
Montserrat is situated in the Caribbean Sea, 43 km southwest of Antigua. The area is 39·5 sq. miles (102 sq. km). Census population, 1991, 10,639; estimate, 2002, 4,500. What was previously the capital, Plymouth, is now deserted as a result of the continuing activity of the Soufriere Hills volcano. The safe area is in the north of the island.

The official language is English.

CLIMATE
A tropical climate with an average annual rainfall of 60" (1,500 mm) the wettest months being Sept.–Dec., with a hurricane season June–Nov. Plymouth, Jan. 76°F (24·4°C), July 81°F (27·2°C).

CONSTITUTION AND GOVERNMENT

Montserrat is a British Overseas Territory. The Constitution dates from the 1989 Montserrat Constitutional Order. The head of state is Queen Elizabeth II, represented by a *Governor* who heads an Executive Council, comprising also the Chief Minister, the Financial Secretary, the Attorney-General and three other ministers. The *Legislative Council* consists of seven elected members, two civil service officials (the Attorney-General and Financial Secretary) and two nominated members; it sits for five-year terms.

RECENT ELECTIONS

In elections to the Legislative Council on 2 April 2001 the New People's Liberation Movement won 7 of the 9 seats against 2 for the National Progressive Party.

CURRENT ADMINISTRATION

Governor: Tony Longrigg (since 11 May 2001).

Chief Minister: John Osborne (since 5 April 2001, having previously been in office from 1978 to 1991).

INTERNATIONAL RELATIONS

Montserrat is a member of CARICOM and the OECS.

ECONOMY

Currency. Montserrat's currency is the *Eastern Caribbean dollar* (*see* ANTIGUA AND BARBUDA: Currency).

Budget. In 1998 the estimated expenditure was EC$60·6m. compared with actual expenditure of EC$63·5m. in 1997, a reduction of 5%.

Performance. Real GDP growth was –2·9% in 1995 and 0·8% in 1994.

Banking and Finance. The East Caribbean Central Bank based in St Kitts and Nevis functions as a central bank. The *Governor* is Sir Dwight Venner. In 1996 there were 3 commercial and 21 offshore banks. Responsibility for overseeing offshore banking rests with the Governor. In late 1998 there were two commercial banks on the island.

Weights and Measures. Both metric and imperial weights and measures are in use.

ENERGY AND NATURAL RESOURCES

Electricity. Production (1998) 10m. kWh.

Agriculture. 3,700 ha are normally suitable for agriculture, with about half in use, but only 1,000 ha were available in 1996 because of the volcanic crisis. In 1998 there were 2,000 ha of arable and permanent crop land. Potatoes, tomatoes, onions, mangoes and limes were produced in recent times. Meat production began in 1994 and the island soon became self-sufficient in chicken, mutton and beef.

Livestock (1996); cattle, 10,000; pigs, 1,000; sheep, 5,000; goats, 7,000.

Forestry. The area under forests in 1995 was 3,000 ha, or 30% of the total land area.

Fisheries. The total catch in 1999 was estimated at 50 tonnes.

INDUSTRY

Manufacturing has in recent years contributed about 6% to GDP and accounted for 10% of employment, but has been responsible for about 80% of exports. It has been limited to rice milling and the production of light consumer goods such as electronic components, light fittings, plastic bags and leather goods. The volcanic activity has put a halt to the milling of rice in the exclusion zone and curtailed the production of light consumer goods.

Trade Unions. There is one trade union, the Montserrat Allied Workers Union (MAWU).

EXTERNAL ECONOMIC RELATIONS

Imports and Exports. Imports in 1995 totalled US$80m.; exports, US$5m. The USA was the main trading partner.

COMMUNICATIONS

Roads. In 1995 there were 205 km of paved roads, 25 km of unsurfaced roads and 50 km of tracks. In 1995 there were 2,700 cars and 400 commercial vehicles registered. These figures changed as a result of the volcanic eruptions of 1995 and 1997 but since then the government, through the Ministry of Communications and Works, has been focusing its road developments in the north of the island, and a number of road work projects are under way.

Civil Aviation. At the W. H. Bramble airport LIAT used to provide services to Antigua with onward connections to the rest of the eastern Caribbean, but it was closed in June 1997 as volcanic activity increased.

Shipping. Plymouth is the port of entry, but alternative anchorage was provided at Old Bay Road during the volcanic crisis.

Telecommunications. Number of telephone main lines, 1997, 3,800. With the migration of people to the north and overseas, and the subsequent destruction of the southern part of the island, the number of telephones has since shrunk to 2,100. There were 300 mobile phone subscribers in 1997.

SOCIAL INSTITUTIONS

Justice. Law is based on UK common law as exercised by the Eastern Caribbean Supreme Court. Final appeal lies to the UK Privy Council. Law is administered by the West Indies Associated States Court, a Court of Summary Jurisdiction and Magistrate's Courts.

Religion. In 1997, 25% of the population were Anglican, 20% Methodist, 15% Pentecostal, 10% Roman Catholic and 10% Adventist.

Education. In 1996–97 there were 11 primary schools (only four open), a comprehensive secondary school with three campuses, and a technical college. Schools are run by the government, the churches and the private sector. There is a medical school, the American University of the Caribbean.

Health. In 1996 there were 4 medical officers, 1 surgeon, 1 dentist and 1 hospital with 69 beds.

CULTURE

Broadcasting. There is a government-owned radio station (ZJB) and two commercial stations (Radio Antilles and GEM Radio). There is a commercial cable TV company (colour by NTSC).

Press. In 1996 there was one weekly newspaper.

Tourism. Tourism at one time contributed about 30% of GDP; earnings in 1993 were EC$40m. There were 36,077 visitors including 11,636 cruise ship arrivals in 1994. However, after the volcanic eruptions the tourist industry declined dramatically, although there were still some 6,000 visitors in 1998.

FURTHER READING

Fergus, H. A., *Montserrat: History of a Caribbean Colony.* London, 1994

PITCAIRN ISLAND

KEY HISTORICAL EVENTS

Pitcairn was discovered by Carteret in 1767, but remained uninhabited until 1790, when it was occupied by 9 mutineers of HMS *Bounty*, with 12 women and 6 men from Tahiti. Nothing was known of their existence until the island was visited in 1808.

TERRITORY AND POPULATION

Pitcairn Island (1·75 sq. miles; 4·6 sq. km) is situated in the Pacific Ocean, nearly equidistant from New Zealand and Panama (25° 04' S. lat., 130° 06' W. long.). Adamstown is the only settlement. The population in 2001 was 47. The uninhabited islands of Henderson (31 sq. km), Ducie (3·9 sq. km) and Oeno (5·2 sq. km) were annexed in 1902. Henderson is a World Heritage Site.

CLIMATE

An equable climate, with average annual rainfall of 80" (2,000 mm) spread evenly throughout the year. Mean monthly temperatures range from 75°F (24°C) in Jan. to 66°F (19°C) in July.

CONSTITUTION AND GOVERNMENT

The Local Government Ordinance of 1964 constitutes a *Council* of ten members, of whom six are elected, three are nominated (one by the six elected members and two by the Governor), and the Island Secretary is an *ex officio* member. No political parties exist. The Island Magistrate, who is elected triennially, presides over the Council; other members hold office for only one year. Liaison between Governor and Council is through a Commissioner in the Auckland, New Zealand, office of the British Consulate-General.

CURRENT ADMINISTRATION

Governor: Richard Fell.
  Island Magistrate: Jay Warren (re-elected Dec. 1999).

Government Website: http://www.government.pn/

ECONOMY

Currency. New Zealand currency is used.

Budget. For the year to 31 March 1997 revenue was NZ$604,234 and expenditure NZ$601,665.

ENERGY AND NATURAL RESOURCES

Fisheries. The catch in 1999 was approximately 8 tonnes.

COMMUNICATIONS

Roads. There were (1997) 6 km of roads. In 1997 there were 29 motorcycles.

SOCIAL INSTITUTIONS

Justice. The Island Court consists of the Island Magistrate and two assessors.

Education. In Aug. 1997 there was one teacher and eight pupils.

FURTHER READING

Murray, S., *Pitcairn Island: the First 200 Years.* La Canada (CA), 1992

ST HELENA

KEY HISTORICAL EVENTS

The island was uninhabited when discovered by the Portuguese in 1502. It was administered by the East India Company from 1659 and became a British colony in 1834. Napoleon died there in exile in 1821.

  Public demonstrations took place in April 1997 against government spending cuts and the Governor's imposition of his own head of social services.

TERRITORY AND POPULATION

St Helena, of volcanic origin, is 3,100 km from the west coast of Africa. Area, 47 sq. miles (121·7 sq. km), with a cultivable area of 243 ha. The population at the

1998 census was 5,157. In 1995 an estimated 62·6% of the population were urban. The capital and port is Jamestown, population (1998) 1,300.

The official language is English.

Ascension is a small island of volcanic origin, of 34 sq. miles (88 sq. km), 700 miles northwest of St Helena. There are 120 ha providing fresh meat, vegetables and fruit. The estimated population in 1999 was 1,050.

The island is the resort of sea turtles, rabbits, the sooty tern or 'wideawake', and feral donkeys.

A cable station connects the island with St Helena, Sierra Leone, St Vincent, Rio de Janeiro and Buenos Aires. There is an airstrip (Miracle Mile) near the settlement of Georgetown; the Royal Air Force maintains an air link with the Falkland Islands.

Administrator: Andrew Kettlewell.

Tristan da Cunha is the largest of a small group of islands in the South Atlantic, lying 1,320 miles (2,124 km) southwest of St Helena, of which they became dependencies on 12 Jan. 1938. Tristan da Cunha has an area of 98 sq. km and a population (2002) of 284, all living in the settlement of Edinburgh. Inaccessible Island (10 sq. km) lies 20 miles west, and the three Nightingale Islands (2 sq. km) lie 20 miles south of Tristan da Cunha; they are uninhabited. Gough Island (90 sq. km) is 220 miles south of Tristan and has a meteorological station.

Tristan consists of a volcano rising to a height of 2,060 metres, with a circumference at its base of 34 km. The volcano, believed to be extinct, erupted unexpectedly early in Oct. 1961. The whole population was evacuated without loss and settled temporarily in the UK; in 1963 they returned to Tristan. Potatoes remain the chief crop. Cattle, sheep and pigs are now reared, and fish are plentiful.

Population in 1996, 292. The original inhabitants were shipwrecked sailors and soldiers who remained behind when the garrison from St Helena was withdrawn in 1817.

At the end of April 1942 Tristan da Cunha was commissioned as HMS *Atlantic Isle*, and became an important meteorological and radio station. In Jan. 1949 a South African company commenced crawfishing operations. An Administrator was appointed at the end of 1948 and a body of basic law brought into operation. The Island Council, which was set up in 1932, consists of a Chief Islander, three nominated and eight elected members (including one woman), under the chairmanship of the Administrator.

Administrator: Bill Dickson.

SOCIAL STATISTICS
1998 figures for St Helena: births, 59; deaths, 39; marriages, 29; divorces, 5. Annual growth rate, 1990–95, 0·6%.

CLIMATE
A mild climate, with little variation. Temperatures range from 75–85°F (24–29°C) in summer to 65–75°F (18–24°C) in winter. Rainfall varies between 13" (325 mm) and 37" (925 mm) according to altitude and situation.

CONSTITUTION AND GOVERNMENT
The St Helena Constitution Order of 1988 entered into force on 1 Jan. 1989. The *Legislative Council* consists of the Governor, two *ex officio* members (the Government Secretary and the Treasurer) and 12 elected members. The Governor is assisted by an *Executive Council* consisting of the two *ex officio* members and the chairs of the six Council Committees.

RECENT ELECTIONS
The last Legislative Council elections were on 9 July 1997. Only non-partisans were elected.

CURRENT ADMINISTRATION
Governor and C.-in-C: David Hollamby.
  Chief Secretary: Michael Clancy.

Government Website: http://www.sainthelena.gov.sh/

ENERGY AND NATURAL RESOURCES

Electricity. Production in 1998 totalled 6m. kWh.

Agriculture. In 1998 there were 4,000 ha of arable and permanent crops.

Fisheries. The total catch in 1999 was 572 tonnes.

INDUSTRY

Labour. In 1995 there were 300 registered unemployed persons.

INTERNATIONAL TRADE

The economy is dependent on UK and EU aid of £8·5m. a year.

COMMUNICATIONS

Roads. There were (1988) 94 km of all-weather motor roads. There were 1,301 vehicles in 1987.

Shipping. There is a service from Cardiff (UK) six times a year, and links with South Africa and neighbouring islands. In 1995 vessels entered totalling 55,000 net registered tons.

Telecommunications. In 1997 there were 1,800 main telephone lines in operation.

SOCIAL INSTITUTIONS

Justice. Police force, 32; cases are dealt with by a police magistrate.

Religion. There are 10 Anglican churches, 4 Baptist chapels, 3 Salvation Army halls, 1 Seventh Day Adventist church and 1 Roman Catholic church.

Education. 3 pre-school playgroups, 7 primary and 1 comprehensive school controlled by the government had 1,188 pupils in 1987. The Prince Andrew School (opened in 1989) offers vocational courses leading to British qualifications.

Health. There were 3 doctors, 1 dentist and 1 hospital in 1992.

CULTURE

Broadcasting. The Cable & Wireless Ltd cable connects St Helena with Cape Town and Ascension Island. The government-run Radio St Helena broadcasts daily and relays BBC programmes. Number of radio receivers (1997), approximately 3,000. Television reception was introduced in 1996 from the BBC World Service, South African M-Net and a US Satellite channel. There were some 2,000 TV receivers in 1997.

FURTHER READING

Day, A., *St. Helena, Ascension and Tristan da Cunha.* [Bibliography] ABC-Clio, Oxford and Santa Barbara (CA), 1997

SOUTH GEORGIA AND THE SOUTH SANDWICH ISLANDS

KEY HISTORICAL EVENTS

The first landing and exploration was undertaken by Captain James Cook, who formally took possession in the name of George III on 17 Jan. 1775. British sealers arrived in 1788 and American sealers in 1791. Sealing reached its peak in 1800. A German team was the first to carry out scientific studies there in 1882–83. Whaling began in 1904 and ceased in 1966, and the civil administration was withdrawn. Argentine forces invaded South Georgia on 3 April 1982. A British naval task force recovered the Island on 25 April 1982.

TERRITORY AND POPULATION

South Georgia lies 1,300 km southeast of the Falkland Islands and has an area of 3,760 sq. km. The South Sandwich Islands are 760 km southeast of South Georgia and have an area of 340 sq. km. In 1993 crown sovereignty and jurisdiction were extended from 12 miles (19 km) to 200 miles (322 km) around the islands. There is no permanent population. There is a small military garrison. The British Antarctic Survey have a biological station on Bird Island. The South Sandwich Islands are uninhabited.

CLIMATE

The climate is wet and cold, with strong winds and little seasonal variation. 15°C is occasionally reached on a windless day. Temperatures below −15°C at sea level are unusual.

CONSTITUTION AND GOVERNMENT

Under the new Constitution which came into force on 3 Oct. 1985 the Territories ceased to be dependencies of the Falkland Islands. Executive power is vested in a Commissioner who is the officer for the time being administering the government of the Falkland Islands. The Commissioner is obliged to consult the officer for the time being commanding Her Majesty's British Forces in the South Atlantic on matters relating to defence and internal security (except police). The Commissioner, whenever practicable, consults the Executive Council of the Falkland Islands on the exercise of functions that in his opinion might affect the Falkland Islands. There is no Legislative Council. Laws are made by the Commissioner (Donald Lamont, resident in the Falkland Islands).

ECONOMY

Budget. The total revenue of the Territories (estimate, 1988–89) £268,240, mainly from philatelic sales and investment income. Expenditure (estimate), £194,260.

COMMUNICATIONS

There is occasional communication by sea with the Falkland Islands by means of research and ice patrol ships. Royal Fleet Auxiliary ships, which serve the garrison, run regularly to South Georgia. Mail is dropped from military aircraft.

SOCIAL INSTITUTIONS

Justice. There is a Supreme Court for the Territories and a Court of Appeal in the United Kingdom. Appeals may go from that court to the Judicial Committee of the Privy Council. There is no magistrate permanently in residence. The Officer Commanding the garrison is usually appointed a magistrate.

FURTHER READING

Day, Alan, *The Falkland Islands, South Georgia and the South Sandwich Islands.* [Bibliography] ABC-Clio, Oxford and Santa Barbara (CA), 1996

SOVEREIGN BASE AREAS OF AKROTIRI AND DHEKELIA IN CYPRUS

KEY HISTORICAL EVENTS

The Sovereign Base Areas (SBAs) are those parts of the island of Cyprus that stayed under British jurisdiction and remained British sovereignty territory when the 1960 Treaty of Establishment created the independent Republic of Cyprus. The Akrotiri facility formed a strategic part of the West's nuclear capacity during the Cold War. The SBAs were used for the deployment of troops in the Gulf War in 1991. Military intelligence is now the key role of the SBAs. The construction of massive antennae at the RAF communications base at Akrotiri sparked violent riots in 2001 and 2002, led by a Greek Cypriot MP. In Feb. 2003 the British Government offered to surrender approximately half the area of the SBAs as an incentive for a settlement between the Greek and Turkish administrations in Cyprus.

TERRITORY AND POPULATION
The Sovereign Base Areas (SBAs), with a total land area of 254 sq. km (98 sq. miles), comprise the Western SBA (123 sq. km), including Episkopi Garrison and RAF Akrotiri (opened 1956), and the Eastern SBA (131 sq. km), including Dhekelia Garrison. The SBAs cover 3% of the land area of the island of Cyprus. There are approximately 3,000 military personnel and approximately 5,000 civilians. The British Government has declared that it will not develop the SBAs for other than military purposes. Citizens and residents of the Republic of Cyprus are guaranteed freedom of access and communications to and through the SBAs.

The SBAs are administered as military bases reporting to the Ministry of Defence in London. The Administrator is the Commander, British Forces Cyprus. The joint force headquarters are at Episkopi. Greek and English are spoken.

CURRENT ADMINISTRATION
Administrator: Air Vice-Marshall Bill Rimmer (appointed Sept. 2000).

THE TURKS AND CAICOS ISLANDS

KEY HISTORICAL EVENTS
After a long period of rival French and Spanish claims the islands were eventually secured to the British Crown in 1766, and became a separate colony in 1973 after association at various times with the colonies of the Bahamas and Jamaica.

TERRITORY AND POPULATION
The Islands are situated between 21° and 22°N. lat. and 71° and 72°W. long., about 80 km east of the Bahamas, of which they are geographically an extension. There are over 40 islands, covering an estimated area of 192 sq. miles (497 sq. km). Only eight are inhabited: Grand Caicos, the largest, is 48 km long by 3 to 5 km broad; Grand Turk, the capital and main political and administrative centre, is 11 km long by 2 km broad. Population, 1990 census, 12,350; Grand Turk, 3,761; Providenciales, 5,586; South Caicos, 1,220; Middle Caicos, 275; North Caicos, 1,305; Salt Cay, 213. The estimated population for 2000 was 19,350. An estimated 56·4% of the population were rural in 1995.

The official language is English.

SOCIAL STATISTICS
Vital statistics (1997): births, 160; deaths, 58. Annual growth rate, 1995–99, 3·3%.

CLIMATE
An equable and healthy climate as a result of regular trade winds, though hurricanes are sometimes experienced. Grand Turk, Jan. 76°F (24·4°C), July 83°F (28·3°C). Annual rainfall 21".

CONSTITUTION AND GOVERNMENT
A new Constitution was introduced in 1988 and amended in 1992. The Executive Council comprises two official members: the Chief Secretary and the Attorney-General; a Chief Minister and five other ministers from among the elected members of the Legislative Council; and is presided over by the Governor. The Legislative Council consists of a Speaker, the two official members of the Executive Council, 13 elected members and three appointed members.

RECENT ELECTIONS
At general elections held on 4 March 1999 for the 13 elective seats on the Legislative Council, the People's Democratic Movement gained 9 seats and the People's National Party 4.

CURRENT ADMINISTRATION
Governor: Jim Poston.
  Chief Minister: Derek Taylor.

INTERNATIONAL RELATIONS
The Islands are a member of CARICOM.

ECONOMY
Overview. The economy is based on free-market private sector-led development. The government plays a supplementary role by providing the necessary legislature, infrastructure, and resources to aid development. The government development trust is aimed at promoting orderly development of the islands. The focus is on the service sector, but tourism and finance are still the dominant industries.

Currency. The US dollar is the official currency.

Budget. 1996–97 recurrent revenue was US$41·2m. and expenditure US$38·8m.

Performance. GDP growth was 8·1% in 1996 (16·7% in 1995).

Banking and Finance. There are four commercial banks. Offshore finance is a major industry.

Weights and Measures. The Imperial system is generally in use.

ENERGY AND NATURAL RESOURCES
Electricity. Electrical services are provided to all of the inhabited islands. Total electricity production for 1998 was 5m. kWh. For all US appliances, 110 volts, 60 cycles, are suitable.

Oil and Gas. Both oil and gas are imported.

Water. Fresh water receptacles are commonly used; there is also piped potable supply.

Agriculture. Farming is done on a small scale mainly for subsistence.

Fisheries. In 1999 the total catch was estimated at 1,300 tonnes. Conch and lobster are the traditional catches.

INDUSTRY
Labour. In 1989, out of a total population of 4,885 aged 14 or over, 4,043 were working, 573 unemployed and 269 economically inactive.

EXTERNAL ECONOMIC RELATIONS
Imports and Exports. Exports, 1992–93, US$6·47m.; imports, US$39·83m. The main export is dried, frozen and processed fish.

COMMUNICATIONS
Civil Aviation. The international airports are on Grand Turk and Providenciales. Turks and Caicos Airways had two aircraft in 1995. Services are also provided by American Airlines and Carnival Airlines. An internal air service provides regular daily flights between the inhabited islands.

Shipping. The main ports are at Grand Turk, Cockburn Harbour and Providenciales. There is a service to Miami. In 1998 the merchant fleet totalled 1,000 GRT.

Telecommunications. There are internal and international cable, telephone, telex, telegraph and fax services.

Postal Services. Postal services are provided on all of the inhabited islands by the government. Postal agencies such as UPS and Federal Express also exist.

SOCIAL INSTITUTIONS
Justice. Laws are a mixture of Statute and Common Law. There is a Magistrates Court and a Supreme Court. Appeals lie from the Supreme Court to the Court of

Appeal which sits in Nassau, Bahamas. There is a further appeal in certain cases to the Privy Council in London.

Religion. There are Anglican, Methodist, Baptist and Evangelists groups.

Education. The adult literacy rate is 98%. Education is free between the ages of 5 and 14 in the 10 government primary schools; there are also four private primary schools. In March 1993 the average number of pupils in the four government secondary schools was 1,075.

Health. In 1995 there were 6 doctors, 1 dentist, 56 nurses and midwives, and 36 hospital beds.

CULTURE

Broadcasting. The government operates the semi-commercial Radio Turks and Caicos. There are also two commercial stations and one religious. In 1997 there were about 8,000 radio sets. There is cable and satellite TV.

Press. There is one weekly and one bi-weekly newspaper.

Tourism. Number of visitors, 1998, 106,000. Tourism receipts (US$125m. in 1998) account for some 45% of the country's total revenue.

FURTHER READING

Boultbee, P. G., *Turks & Caicos Islands*. [Bibliography] ABC-Clio, Oxford and Santa Barbara (CA), 1991

UNITED STATES OF AMERICA

Capital: Washington, D.C.
Population estimate, 2000: 281·42m.
GDP per capita, 2000: (PPP$) 34,142
HDI/world rank: 0·939/6

KEY HISTORICAL EVENTS

The earliest inhabitants of the north American continent can be traced back to Palaeolithic times but it was not until the twelfth century that permanent settlements were created, particularly in the east where rich opportunities for cultivation and fishing supported major fortified towns. The first Europeans to make their presence felt were Spaniards who based themselves in Florida before venturing north and west. Santa Fe in New Mexico was founded in 1610. But by the mid-sixteenth century there was competition from the French centred on Quebec who colonized along the St Lawrence River.

Elizabethan adventurers were eager to exploit the New World but it was not until 1607 that a British colony was established. This was at Jamestown in what is now southern Virginia. After a perilous start when disease and malnutrition carried off most of the settlers, Virginia's population grew rapidly to meet the European demand for tobacco. Maryland, originally a refuge for persecuted Catholics, also thrived on the tobacco trade. To make up for the shortage of labour, slaves were imported from Africa.

In 1620 a hundred pilgrims landed at Plymouth Rock to found a Puritan enclave which became the colony of Massachusetts. Other settlements soon followed, accommodating a bewildering variety of Christian radicals who had fled from persecution. Not all were tolerant of beliefs that differed from their own. Pennsylvania, the colony named after the Quaker William Penn, was exceptional in offering freedom of worship to 'all persons who confess and acknowledge the one almighty and eternal God'. In 1664 the British took control of neighbouring Dutch colonies. New Amsterdam became New York. Almost all of the eastern seaboard was now claimed by British settlers who were also venturing inland.

Their main European rivals were the French who claimed a vast area around and to the southwest of the Great Lakes. With Indian tribes allied to both sides, there was heavy fighting in 1744 and 1748. But within a decade British forces had captured most of the French strongholds. After the Treaty of Paris in 1763, Britain commanded the whole of North America east of the Mississippi while Spain, having surrendered Florida, gained Louisiana from France. For a brief period colonization was restricted to the area east of the Appalachians, the rest of the territory being reserved for Indian tribes. This soon became a point of issue between the settlers who were intent on expansion and their masters in London who wanted a settled, self-supporting community benefiting British trade. Having disposed of the French threat, the colonists felt confident enough to defy orders that ignored their interests. In particular, they objected to the Navigation Acts which required goods to be carried in British vessels and to various taxes imposed without consultation. 'No taxation without representation' became a rallying cry for disaffected colonists. The centre of opposition was Boston, scene of the infamous 'tea party' when, in 1763, militants destroyed a cargo of East India tea. In 1775 the arrest of rebel ringleaders served only to provoke the 13 colonies to co-operate in further acts of rebellion, including the setting up of a *de facto* government which appointed George Washington commander of American forces.

The War of Independence was by no means a clear-cut affair. British forces, never more than 50,000 strong, were supported by a powerful body of colonists who remained loyal to the Crown. The war lasted for seven years from 1776 with both sides often getting close to a conclusive victory. The decisive moment came at last with the surrender of General Burgoyne and his 8,000 troops in upper New York state in Oct. 1777, a defeat that persuaded a cautious France to enter the war. Under the peace terms secured in 1783 Britain kept Canada leaving the new United States

1747

with territory stretching from the Atlantic to the Mississippi. A constitution based on democratic principles buttressed by inalienable rights including the ownership of property came into force in 1789. It allowed for a federal government headed by a president and executive, a legislature with a House of Representatives and a Senate, and a judiciary with ultimate authority on constitutional matters exercised by a Supreme Court. The first president was George Washington, who was elected in 1789. In 1800 Washington, D.C. was declared the national capital.

Hostilities with Britain resumed in 1812 amidst accusations that Britain was using the excuse of the Napoleonic wars to harass American shipping and to encourage Indian resistance to expansion into the mid west. Most of the fighting took place on the Canadian border where an attempted invasion was decisively repulsed. But Louisiana, having reverted to French rule and subsequently sold to the US, was secured for the Union. With the exception of Louisiana, other American territories that had once been part of the Spanish empire fell to Mexico. But not for long. In 1836 Texas broke away from Mexico, surviving as an independent republic until 1845 when it was annexed by the US. This provoked war with Mexico which ended in 1848 with the US taking over what are now the states of California, Arizona, Colorado, Utah, Nevada and New Mexico. Any temptation there might have been for European involvement in the struggle was removed by the Monroe Doctrine, a declaration by President Monroe that interference from the Old World in matters concerning the western hemisphere would not be tolerated. It was a measure of the growing military and economic self confidence of the US that such a warning, delivered in 1823, was taken seriously.

The westward expansion began soon after independence but accelerated with the destruction of Indian power and the removal of the native population to designated reservations. In 1846 a long-running dispute with Britain confirming US title to Oregon acted as a spur to migration as did the Californian gold rush of 1848. By the 1850s the railway network was bringing people and economic prosperity to the mid west. Population quadrupled between 1815 to 1860, from 8m. to almost 31m. In 1862 the Homestead Act allocated 160 acres to anyone who was ready to farm it. By 1890 the west was won.

The transition from a rural society to an industrial power of world importance created tensions, not least between the slave-owning southern states and the rest of the Union which favoured the abolition of slavery. Economic as well as humanitarian factors were in play since the North resented the advantage cheap labour gave to the South. The opposing view held that the South, by now the world's largest cotton producer, depended on slavery for its commercial survival. Mutual antagonism came to a head with the secession of the southern states from the Union in 1860–61 and their formation as a Confederacy. Despite sporadic outbreaks of violence, civil war was not in prospect until Confederate troops fired on the US flag at Fort Sumter. Lincoln ordered a blockade of the South. The recruitment of rival armies followed within weeks. The war turned out to be much bloodier than anyone had expected. More American lives were lost in the Civil War than in the two world wars combined. The military balance was maintained until 1863 when the North secured a crushing victory at the Battle of Gettysburg. However, the war continued until April 1865 when Robert E. Lee surrendered to Ulysses S. Grant at Appomattox Courthouse in Virginia. A few days later Lincoln was assassinated, a loss that the southern states had subsequent cause to regret. Contrary to Lincoln's hopes, a generous settlement was now out of the question. Instead of a gradual transition to a new society, the South was rushed into a social revolution. This in turn led to terrorist violence and acts of vengeance against freed slaves. From this carnage emerged the notorious Ku Klux Klan as the standard bearer of lynch law. While the 13th amendment prohibited slavery, political freedom was denied to the black community by state imposed literacy tests and discriminatory property taxes.

That America had interests beyond its own borders was made evident by the Spanish war of 1898 which resulted in the US becoming the dominant power in the Caribbean though the effort to take over in the Philippines came up against Filipino resistance and led to a heavy death toll.

By 1900 the US rivalled Britain and Germany as the world's dominant power. With vast natural resources and a manufacturing capacity that secured 11% of world trade, it was clear that Europe was soon to lose its grip on world affairs. Ironically, though, it was Europe as the chief supplier of labour that gave the US the impetus it needed to fulfil its promise. Between 1881 and 1920, 23m. immigrants entered the US, the largest population movement ever recorded.

Given the nationalistic mix that constituted early twentieth century America it is scarcely surprising that popular opinion was against involvement in the First World War. But events, including German U-boat harassment of American shipping, soon proved that isolationism was not an option. It was not until 1917 that America joined the hostilities but the resurgence of energy created by the arrival of the American Expeditionary Force was critical to the Allied breakthrough.

Post-war America, relatively unscathed by the European conflict, was unquestionably the most powerful nation and as such was able to dictate terms at the Versailles peace conference. But President Wilson's much vaunted 'fourteen points' which set out a plan for collective security policed by a League of Nations failed to win support in the one country that was critical to its success. The Treaty was rejected by the Senate in 1920 and America retreated once again into isolationism.

A resumption of economic growth was accompanied by a struggle to impose a common set of values, chiefly white, Protestant, on an incredibly diverse population. To outsiders the most extraordinary experiment in social engineering was Prohibition, a federal imposed attempt to outlaw all alcoholic drinks. Whatever gain there was to the health of the nation, the chief beneficiaries were the bosses of organized crime.

Dreams of everlasting prosperity were shattered by the 1929 Stock Market Crash. A succession of bank failures was followed by widespread bankruptcies and mass unemployment which sent the economy into a further downward spin. The beginning of the end to the agony came with the election to the presidency of Franklin D. Roosevelt, who pushed through Congress a series of radical measures known collectively as the New Deal aimed at revitalizing the nation. Cheap loans to restart factories and farms and huge investment in public works proved to be the key to recovery though unemployment remained high until production was boosted by the demands of another world war.

Roosevelt was well aware of the dangers to the US if the fascist dictators were allowed to triumph, but as in 1914, there was formidable opposition to direct involvement. Roosevelt compromised by supplying Britain with much needed armaments on favourable terms. But it was events in Asia rather than in Europe that eventually persuaded America of the need for direct action. Opposition to Japanese expansion into China and South East Asia, including an oil embargo and a freezing of Japanese assets in the US, brought a savage retaliation at Pearl Harbour, when much of the US fleet was destroyed. America declared war on Japan while Germany declared war on America. The US military effort focused initially on the Pacific but after 1942 American forces were also committed to the campaign in north Africa and Europe. With the D-Day landings in June 1944, US troops led the attack on Germany before forcing a Japanese surrender by sacrificing Hiroshima and Nagasaki to the atomic bomb.

This time, in the aftermath of war, the US needed no encouragement to assume the leadership of the free world. The threat of a Soviet takeover in Europe was countered by the formation of NATO and the provision of dollar aid under the Marshall Plan to kick start European economic recovery. The risk of a return to isolationism receded still further when China fell to communism. In 1950 American troops went to the aid of South Korea when it was invaded by the communist North. Though technically under the aegis of the UN, the campaign was an almost entirely American affair led by General Douglas MacArthur. When Chinese forces became involved, MacArthur spoke openly of extending the war to the Chinese mainland, a threat countered strongly by President Truman who forced MacArthur's resignation to establish undisputed political control over the military. A ceasefire was negotiated after Dwight Eisenhower was elected President in 1953 and the US took the lead in setting up the South East Asia Treaty Organization on the same lines as NATO.

At home, civil rights were high on the political agenda. The thuggish tactics of Senator Joe McCarthy and the House Committee on Un-American Activities brought into focus basic democratic freedoms guaranteed by the Constitution while growing protests against racial discrimination led to legislation to enforce equality of opportunity in education and employment. The civil rights movement peaked in the early sixties when the imposition of federal law in the South led to acts of violence against liberal protesters. Social tensions were exacerbated by the Cold War confrontation. On acceding to the presidency in 1961, one of the first challenges President Kennedy had to face was the placing of Soviet missiles in Cuba. For a time, the prospect of world war was only too real. But an agreement between the two nations allowed for a withdrawal of the missiles on the condition of a US promise not to invade Cuba. Another optimistic sign was the Nuclear Test Ban Treaty of 1963 which, for the first time, put a brake on the spread of nuclear weapons. Less hopeful was the acceleration of the conflict in Vietnam. Following President Kennedy's assassination in 1963, US military involvement in Vietnam was intensified but opposition at home led to withdrawal of forces in 1973.

In 1974 President Nixon was forced to resign amidst charges of corruption known collectively as Watergate. A revival of Republican fortunes came with the election of Ronald Reagan in the 1980 presidential race. In international affairs, Reagan was resolutely anti-Communist, raising fears of confrontation with the Soviet Union over his Strategic Defense Initiative, otherwise known as his 'Star Wars' system of defence. However, relations between the two superpowers improved in the mid-eighties with successful negotiations on nuclear arms limitations. The collapse of the Soviet empire in 1990 extended US economic aid to Eastern Europe. The Democrats regained control of the White House with the election of Bill Clinton, who combined economic recovery at home with an active foreign policy which underlined America's role as the only superpower.

On 11 Sept. 2001 the heart of New York City was devastated after hijackers flew two jet airliners into the World Trade Center. A plane also crashed into the Pentagon, in Washington, D.C., and a fourth hijacked plane crashed near the town of Shanksville, Pennsylvania. The death toll was 2,800, with 67 countries reporting dead or missing citizens. Osama bin Laden, a Saudi dissident believed to be living in Afghanistan at the invitation of the ruling Taliban, immediately became the chief suspect and military action against Afghanistan followed, with air strikes beginning on 7 Oct. 2001.

On 20 March 2003 US forces, supported by the UK, launched attacks on Iraq, and initiated a war aimed at 'liberating Iraq'. On 9 April 2003 American forces took control of central Baghdad, effectively bringing an end to Saddam Hussein's rule.

TERRITORY AND POPULATION

The United States is bounded in the north by Canada, east by the North Atlantic, south by the Gulf of Mexico and Mexico, and west by the North Pacific Ocean. The area of the USA is 3,794,083 sq. miles (9,826,629 sq. km), of which 3,537,438 sq. miles (9,161,922 sq. km) are land and 256,645 sq. miles (664,707 sq. km) are water (comprising Great Lakes, inland and coastal water).

Population at each census from 1790 to 2000 (including Alaska and Hawaii from 1960). Figures do not include Puerto Rico, Guam, American Samoa or other Pacific islands, or the US population abroad. Residents of Indian reservations not included before 1890.

	White	Black	Other races	Total
1790	3,172,464	757,208	—	3,929,672
1800	4,306,446	1,002,037	—	5,308,483
1810	5,862,073	1,377,808	—	7,239,881
1820	7,866,797	1,771,562	—	9,638,359
1830	10,537,378	2,328,642	—	12,866,020
1840	14,195,805	2,873,648	—	17,069,453
1850	19,553,068	3,638,808	—	23,191,876
1860	26,922,537	4,441,830	78,954	31,443,321
1870	34,337,292	5,392,172	88,985	39,818,449
1880	43,402,970	6,580,793	172,020	50,155,783
1890	55,101,258	7,488,676	357,780	62,947,714
1900	66,868,508	8,834,395	509,265	76,212,168
1910	81,812,405	9,828,667	587,459	92,228,531
1920	94,903,540	10,463,607	654,421	106,021,568
1930	110,395,753	11,891,842	915,065	123,202,660
1940	118,357,831	12,865,914	941,384	132,165,129

	White	Black	Other races	Total
1950	135,149,629	15,044,937	1,131,232	151,325,798
1960	158,831,732	18,871,831	1,619,612	179,323,175
1970	177,748,975	22,580,289	2,882,662	203,211,926
1980	188,371,622	26,495,025	11,679,158	226,545,805
1990	199,686,070	29,986,060	19,037,743	248,709,873
2000	211,460,626	34,658,190	35,303,090	281,421,906

The mid-year population estimate for 2002 was 288,369,000.

The UN gives a projected population for 2010 of 308·56m.

2000 density, 30·7 per sq. km (79·6 per sq. mile). Urban population (persons living in places with at least 2,500 inhabitants) at the 2000 census was 222,360,539 (79·0%); rural, 59,061,367. In 1990 it was 75·2%; in 1980, 73·7%; in 1970, 73·6%.

Sex distribution by race of the population at the 2000 census:

	Males	Females
White	103,773,194	107,687,432
Black or African American	16,465,185	18,193,005
American Indian and Alaska Native	1,233,982	1,241,974
Asian	4,948,741	5,294,257
Native Hawaiian and Other Pacific Islander	202,629	196,206
Other Race	8,009,214	7,349,859
Two or More Races	3,420,618	3,405,610
Total	138,053,563	143,368,343

Alongside these racial groups, and applicable to all of them, a category of 'Hispanic origin' comprised 35,305,818 persons (including 20,640,711 of Mexican ancestry), up 12,927,277 from 22,378,541 in 1990.

Among 10-year age groups the 35–44 age group contained most people according to the 2000 census, with a total of 45,148,527 (16·0% of the population).

At the 2000 census there were 105,480,101 households, up from 91,947,410 in 1990.

At the 2000 census there were an 50,454 people aged 100 or over, compared to 36,000 in 1990. Of the 50,454, 40,397 were female, and of the 36,000 in 1990, 28,000 were female.

The 2000 census showed that 47·0m. persons five years and over spoke a language other than English in the home, including Spanish or Spanish Creole by 28·1m.; French or French Creole by 2·1m.; Chinese by 2·0m.

The following table includes population statistics, the year in which each of the original 13 states (Connecticut, Delaware, Georgia, Maryland, Massachusetts, New Hampshire, New Jersey, New York, North Carolina, Pennsylvania, Rhode Island, South Carolina, Virginia) ratified the constitution, and the year when each of the other states was admitted into the Union. Traditional abbreviations for the names of the states are shown in brackets with postal codes for use in addresses.

The USA is divided into four geographic regions comprised of nine divisions. These are, with their 2000 census populations: Northeast (comprised of the New England and Middle Atlantic divisions), 53,594,378; Midwest (East North Central, West North Central), 64,392,776; South (South Atlantic, East South Central, West South Central), 100,236,820; West (Mountain, Pacific), 63,197,932.

Geographic divisions and states		Land area: sq. miles 2000	Census population 1 April 2000	Pop. per sq. mile, 2000
United States		3,537,438	281,421,906	79·6
New England		62,810	13,922,517	221·7
Connecticut (1788)	(Conn./CT)	4,845	3,405,565	702·9
Maine (1820)	(Me./ME)	30,862	1,274,923	41·3
Massachusetts (1788)	(Mass./MA)	7,840	6,349,097	809·8
New Hampshire (1788)	(N.H./NH)	8,968	1,235,786	137·8

Geographic divisions and states		Land area: sq. miles 2000	Census population 1 April 2000	Pop. per sq. mile, 2000
Rhode Island (1790)	(R.I./RI)	1,045	1,048,319	1,003·2
Vermont (1791)	(Vt./VT)	9,250	608,827	65·8
Middle Atlantic		99,448	39,671,861	398·9
New Jersey (1787)	(N.J./NJ)	7,417	8,414,350	1,134·4
New York (1788)	(N.Y./NY)	47,214	18,976,457	401·9
Pennsylvania (1787)	(Pa./PA)	44,817	12,281,054	274·0
East North Central		243,477	45,155,037	185·5
Illinois (1818)	(Ill./IL)	55,584	12,419,293	223·4
Indiana (1816)	(Ind./IN)	35,867	6,080,485	169·5
Michigan (1837)	(Mich./MI)	56,804	9,938,444	175·0
Ohio (1803)	(Oh./OH)	40,948	11,353,140	277·3
Wisconsin (1848)	(Wis./WI)	54,310	5,363,675	98·8
West North Central		507,913	19,237,739	37·9
Iowa (1846)	(Ia./IA)	55,869	2,926,324	52·4
Kansas (1861)	(Kans./KS)	81,815	2,688,418	32·9
Minnesota (1858)	(Minn./MN)	79,610	4,919,479	61·8
Missouri (1821)	(Mo./MO)	68,886	5,595,211	81·2
Nebraska (1867)	(Nebr./NE)	76,872	1,711,263	22·3
North Dakota (1889)	(N.D./ND)	68,976	642,200	9·3
South Dakota (1889)	(S.D./SD)	75,885	754,844	9·9
South Atlantic		266,115	51,769,160	194·5
Delaware (1787)	(Del./DE)	1,954	783,600	401·0
Dist. of Columbia (1791)	(D.C./DC)	61	572,059	9,378·0
Florida (1845)	(Fla./FL)	53,927	15,982,378	296·4
Georgia (1788)	(Ga./GA)	57,906	8,186,453	141·4
Maryland (1788)	(Md./MD)	9,774	5,296,486	541·9
North Carolina (1789)	(N.C./NC)	48,711	8,049,313	165·2
South Carolina (1788)	(S.C./SC)	30,109	4,012,012	133·2
Virginia (1788)	(Va./VA)	39,594	7,078,515	178·8
West Virginia (1863)	(W. Va./WV)	24,078	1,808,344	75·1
East South Central		178,626	17,022,810	95·3
Alabama (1819)	(Al./AL)	50,774	4,447,100	87·6
Kentucky (1792)	(Ky./KY)	39,728	4,041,769	101·7
Mississippi (1817)	(Miss./MS)	46,907	2,844,658	60·6
Tennessee (1796)	(Tenn./TN)	41,217	5,689,283	138·0
West South Central		426,094	31,444,850	73·8
Arkansas (1836)	(Ark./AR)	52,068	2,673,400	51·3
Louisiana (1812)	(La./LA)	43,562	4,468,976	102·6
Oklahoma (1907)	(Okla./OK)	68,667	3,450,654	50·3
Texas (1845)	(Tex./TX)	261,797	20,851,820	79·7
Mountain		856,078	18,172,295	21·2
Arizona (1912)	(Ariz./AZ)	113,635	5,130,632	45·2
Colorado (1876)	(Colo./CO)	103,718	4,301,261	41·5
Idaho (1890)	(Id./ID)	82,747	1,293,953	15·6
Montana (1889)	(Mont./MT)	145,552	902,195	6·2
Nevada (1864)	(Nev./NV)	109,826	1,998,257	18·2
New Mexico (1912)	(N. Mex./NM)	121,356	1,819,046	15·0
Utah (1896)	(Ut./UT)	82,144	2,233,169	27·2
Wyoming (1890)	(Wyo./WY)	97,100	493,782	5·1
Pacific		896,874	45,025,637	50·2
Alaska (1959)	(Ak./AK)	571,951	626,932	1·1

Geographic divisions and states		Land area: sq. miles 2000	Census population 1 April 2000	Pop. per sq. mile, 2000
California (1850)	(Calif./CA)	155,959	33,871,648	217·2
Hawaii (1960)	(Hi./HI)	6,423	1,211,537	188·6
Oregon (1859)	(Oreg./OR)	95,997	3,421,399	35·6
Washington (1889)	(Wash./WA)	66,544	5,894,121	88·6

Geographic divisions and states	Land area: sq. miles 1990	Census population 1 April 1990	Pop. per sq. mile, 1990
Outlying Territories, total	4,228[2]	3,862,431[2]	823·3[2]
American Samoa (1900)	77	57,291[1]	607
Guam (1898)	209	154,805[1]	637
Johnston Atoll (1858)	1	173	157
Midway Islands (1867)	3	13	5
Northern Marianas (1947)	184	69,221[1]	235
Puerto Rico (1898)	3,425	3,808,610[1]	1,112
Virgin Islands (1917)	134	108,612[1]	761
Wake Island (1898)	3	7	3

[1]2000 census figure. [2]Totals include details for Palau, which gained independence in 1994.

The 2000 census showed 31,107,889 foreign-born persons. The 10 countries contributing the largest numbers who were foreign-born were: Mexico, 9,177,487; Philippines, 1,369,070; India, 1,022,552; China, 988,857; Vietnam, 988,174; Cuba, 872,716; Korea, 864,125; Canada, 820,771; El Salvador, 817,336; Germany, 706,704; Dominican Republic, 687,677. A total of 660,477 immigrants were admitted in 1998 (1,536,483 in 1990).

Population of cities with over 100,000 inhabitants at the censuses of 1990 and 2000:

Cities	Census 1990	Census 2000	Cities	Census 1990	Census 2000
New York, NY	7,322,564	8,008,278	Long Beach, CA	429,433	461,522
Los Angeles, CA	3,485,398	3,694,820	Albuquerque, NM	384,736	448,607
Chicago, IL	2,783,726	2,896,016	Kansas City, MO	435,146	441,545
Houston, TX	1,630,553	1,953,631	Fresno, CA	354,202	427,652
Philadelphia, PA	1,585,577	1,517,550	Virginia Beach, VA	393,069	425,257
Phoenix, AZ	983,403	1,321,045	Atlanta, GA	394,017	416,474
San Diego, CA	1,110,549	1,223,400	Sacramento, CA	369,365	407,018
Dallas, TX	1,006,877	1,188,580	Oakland, CA	372,242	399,484
San Antonio, TX	935,933	1,144,646	Mesa, AZ	288,091	396,375
Detroit, MI	1,027,974	951,270	Tulsa, OK	367,302	393,049
San Jose, CA	782,248	894,943	Omaha, NE	335,795	390,007
Indianapolis, IN	741,952	791,926	Minneapolis, MN	368,383	382,618
San Francisco, CA	723,959	776,733	Honolulu, HI	365,272	371,657
Jacksonville, FL	635,230	735,617	Miami, FL	358,548	362,470
Columbus, OH	632,910	711,470	Colorado Springs,		
Austin, TX	465,622	656,562	CO	281,140	360,890
Baltimore, MD	736,014	651,154	St Louis, MO	396,685	348,189
Memphis, TN	610,337	650,100	Wichita, KS	304,011	344,284
Milwaukee, WI	628,088	596,974	Santa Ana, CA	293,742	337,977
Boston, MA	574,283	589,141	Pittsburgh, PA	369,879	334,563
Washington, DC	606,900	572,059	Arlington, TX	261,721	332,969
Nashville-Davidson,			Cincinnati, OH	364,040	331,285
TN	510,784	569,891	Anaheim, CA	266,406	328,014
El Paso, TX	515,342	563,662	Toledo, OH	332,943	313,619
Seattle, WA	516,259	563,374	Tampa, FL	280,015	303,447
Denver, CO	467,610	554,636	Buffalo, NY	328,123	292,648
Charlotte, NC	395,934	540,828	St Paul, MN	272,235	287,151
Fort Worth, TX	447,619	534,694	Corpus Christi, TX	257,453	277,454
Portland, OR	437,319	529,121	Aurora, CO	222,103	276,393
Oklahoma City, OK	444,719	506,132	Raleigh, NC	207,951	276,093
Tucson, AZ	405,390	486,699	Newark, NJ	275,221	273,546
New Orleans, LA	496,938	484,674	Lexington-Fayette,		
Las Vegas, NV	258,295	478,434	KY	225,366	260,512
Cleveland, OH	505,616	478,403	Anchorage, AK	226,338	260,283

Cities	Census 1990	Census 2000	Cities	Census 1990	Census 2000
Louisville, KY	269,063	256,231	Springfield, MO	140,494	151,580
Riverside, CA	226,505	255,166	Santa Clarita, CA	110,642	151,088
St Petersburg, FL	238,629	248,232	Salinas, CA	108,777	151,060
Bakersfield, CA	174,280	247,057	Tallahassee, FL	124,773	150,624
Stockton, CA	210,943	243,771	Rockford, IL	139,426	150,115
Birmingham, AL	265,968	242,820	Pomona, CA	131,723	149,473
Jersey City, NJ	228,537	240,055	Paterson, NJ	140,891	149,222
Norfolk, VA	261,229	234,403	Overland Park, KS	111,790	149,080
Baton Rouge, LA	219,531	227,818	Santa Rosa, CA	113,313	147,595
Hialeah, FL	188,004	226,419	Syracuse, NY	163,860	147,306
Lincoln, NE	191,972	225,581	Kansas City, KS	149,767	146,866
Greensboro, NC	183,521	223,891	Hampton, VA	133,793	146,437
Plano, TX	128,713	222,030	Lakewood, CO	126,481	144,126
Rochester, NY	231,636	219,773	Vancouver, WA	46,380	143,560
Glendale, AZ	148,134	218,812	Irvine, CA	110,330	143,072
Garland, TX	180,650	215,768	Aurora, IL	99,581	142,990
Madison, WI	191,262	208,054	Moreno Valley, CA	118,779	142,381
Fort Wayne, IN	173,072	205,727	Pasadena, TX	119,363	141,674
Fremont, CA	173,339	203,413	Hayward, CA	111,498	140,030
Scottsdale, AZ	130,069	202,705	Brownsville, TX	98,962	139,722
Montgomery, AL	187,106	201,568	Bridgeport, CT	141,686	139,529
Shreveport, LA	198,525	200,145	Hollywood, FL	121,697	139,357
Augusta-Richmond County, GA	44,639	199,775	Warren, MI	144,864	138,247
Lubbock, TX	186,206	199,564	Torrance, CA	133,107	137,946
Chesapeake, VA	151,976	199,184	Eugene, OR	112,669	137,893
Mobile, AL	196,278	198,915	Pembroke Pines, FL	65,452	137,427
Des Moines, IA	193,187	198,682	Salem, OR	107,786	136,924
Grand Rapids, MI	189,126	197,800	Pasadena, CA	131,591	133,936
Richmond, VA	203,056	197,790	Escondido, CA	108,635	133,559
Yonkers, NY	188,082	196,086	Sunnyvale, CA	117,229	131,760
Spokane, WA	177,196	195,629	Savannah, GA	137,560	131,510
Glendale, CA	180,038	194,973	Fontana, CA	87,535	128,929
Tacoma, WA	176,664	193,556	Orange, CA	110,658	128,821
Irving, TX	155,037	191,615	Naperville, IL	85,351	128,358
Huntington Beach, CA	181,519	189,594	Alexandria, VA	111,183	128,283
Arlington, VA[1]	170,897	189,453	Rancho Cucamonga, CA	101,409	127,743
Modesto, CA	164,730	188,856	Grand Prairie, TX	99,616	127,427
Durham, NC	136,611	187,035	Fullerton, CA	114,144	126,003
Columbus, GA	179,278	186,291	Corona, CA	76,095	124,966
Orlando, FL	164,693	185,951	Flint, MI	140,761	124,943
Boise City, ID	125,738	185,787	Mesquite, TX	101,484	124,523
Winston-Salem, NC	143,485	185,776	Sterling Heights, MI	117,810	124,471
San Bernardino, CA	164,164	185,401	Sioux Falls, SD	100,814	123,975
Jackson, MS	196,637	184,256	New Haven, CT	130,474	123,626
Little Rock, AR	175,795	183,133	Topeka, KS	119,883	122,377
Salt Lake City, UT	159,936	181,743	Concord, CA	111,348	121,780
Reno, NV	133,850	180,480	Evansville, IN	126,272	121,582
Newport News, VA	170,045	180,150	Hartford, CT	139,739	121,578
Chandler, AZ	90,533	176,581	Fayetteville, NC	75,695	121,015
Laredo, TX	122,899	176,576	Cedar Rapids, IA	108,751	120,758
Henderson, NV	64,942	175,381	Elizabeth, NJ	110,002	120,568
Knoxville, TN	165,121	173,890	Lansing, MI	127,321	119,128
Amarillo, TX	157,615	173,627	Lancaster, CA	97,291	118,718
Providence, RI	160,728	173,618	Fort Collins, CO	87,758	118,652
Chula Vista, CA	135,163	173,556	Coral Springs, FL	79,443	117,549
Worcester, MA	169,759	172,648	Stamford, CT	108,056	117,083
Oxnard, CA	142,216	170,358	Thousand Oaks, CA	104,352	117,005
Dayton, OH	182,044	166,179	Vallejo, CA	109,199	116,760
Garden Grove, CA	143,050	165,196	Palmdale, CA	68,842	116,670
Oceanside, CA	128,398	161,029	Columbia, SC	98,052	116,278
Tempe, AZ	141,865	158,625	El Monte, CA	106,209	115,965
Huntsville, AL	159,789	158,216	Abilene, TX	106,654	115,930
Ontario, CA	133,179	158,007	North Las Vegas, NV	47,707	115,488
Chattanooga, TN	152,466	155,554	Beaumont, TX	114,323	113,866
Fort Lauderdale, FL	149,377	152,397	Waco, TX	103,590	113,726
Springfield, MA	156,983	152,082	Independence, MO	112,301	113,288
			Peoria, IL	113,504	112,936

Cities	Census 1990	Census 2000	Cities	Census 1990	Census 2000
Inglewood, CA	109,602	112,580	Wichita Falls, TX	96,259	104,197
Springfield, IL	105,227	111,454	Erie, PA	108,718	103,717
Simi Valley, CA	100,217	111,351	Daly City, CA	92,311	103,621
Lafayette, LA	94,440	110,257	Clarksville, TN	75,494	103,445
Gilbert, AZ	29,188	109,697	Norwalk, CA	94,279	103,298
Carrollton, TX	82,169	109,576	Gary, IN	116,646	102,746
Bellevue, WA	86,874	109,569	Berkeley, CA	102,724	102,743
West Valley City, UT	86,976	108,896	Santa Clara, CA	93,613	102,361
Clearwater, FL	98,784	108,787	Green Bay, WI	96,466	102,313
Costa Mesa, CA	96,357	108,724	Cape Coral, FL	74,991	102,286
Peoria, AZ	50,618	108,364	Arvada, CO	89,235	102,153
South Bend, IN	105,511	107,789	Pueblo, CO	98,640	102,121
Downey, CA	91,444	107,323	Athens-Clarke		
Waterbury, CT	108,961	107,271	County, GA	45,734	101,489
Manchester, NH	99,567	107,006	Cambridge, MA	95,802	101,355
Allentown, PA	105,090	106,632	Westminster, CO	74,625	100,940
McAllen, TX	84,021	106,414	San Buenaventura		
Joliet, IL	76,836	106,221	(Ventura), CA	92,575	100,916
Lowell, MA	103,439	105,167	Portsmouth, VA	103,907	100,565
Provo, UT	86,835	105,166	Livonia, MI	100,850	100,545
West Covina, CA	96,086	105,080	Burbank, CA	93,643	100,316

[1]Arlington CDP (census designated place) is not incorporated as a city.

Washington, D.C.: The capital of the United States, the city is located at the head of the Potomac River, and was carved from Virginia and Maryland in 1790 to form the permanent seat of government for the new nation. The city is home to many of the most important monuments, artifacts and museums in the country. The larger metropolitan city, however, suffers from complex social and economic problems.

New York: Located on the Eastern Atlantic coast of the United States at the mouth of the Hudson River, it became the focus for the first European immigrants in the 17th century. Greater New York was formed in 1898 by the amalgamation of the five boroughs—The Bronx, Brooklyn, Manhattan, Queens and Staten Island. Affectionately known as the 'Big Apple' it covers an area of 301 sq. miles. It was the world's most populous city until overtaken by Tokyo in the late 1960s. New York is one of the world's leading financial centres and is the headquarters of the United Nations.

Los Angeles: Sprawling across some 464 sq. miles (1,202 sq. km), Los Angeles is the second most populous city and metropolitan area in the United States after New York. Developing from an 18th century missionary settlement, the city was opened up by the railroads at the end of the 19th century. The city has become a centre for the US film industry and has the busiest harbour on the West Coast. It is one of the most ethnically diverse and divided cities in the US.

Chicago: Chicago is the third most populous city and metropolitan area in the United States. Owing to its strategic position at the lakeside interior of a rapidly expanding country, Chicago developed in the early 19th century to become a nexus for goods transport via canals and railways. Industry followed and Chicago emerged as the major city of the Midwest. The city is famous for its prohibition-period gangster history and its skyline of skyscrapers including the Sears Tower, the second tallest building in the world.

Immigration and naturalization. The Immigration and Nationality Act, as amended, provides for the numerical limitation of most immigration. The Immigration Act of 1990 established major revisions in the numerical limits and preference system regulating legal immigration. The numerical limits are imposed on visas issued and not admissions. The maximum number of visas allowed to be issued under the preference categories in 1998 was 268,997: 191,480 for family-sponsored immigrants and 77,517 for employment-based immigrants. Within the overall limitations the per-country limit for independent countries is set to 7% of the total family and employment limits, while dependent areas are limited to 2% of the total.

Immigrant aliens admitted to the USA for permanent residence, by country or region of birth, for fiscal years:

Country or region of birth	1995	Immigrants admitted 1996	1997	1998
All countries	720,500	915,900	798,378	660,477
Europe	128,200	147,581	119,871	90,793
Germany	6,200	6,748	5,723	5,472
Greece	1,300	1,452	1,049	863
Italy	2,200	2,501	1,982	1,831
Poland	13,800	15,772	12,038	1,043
Portugal	2,600	2,984	1,665	1,536
Spain	1,300	1,659	1,241	823
UK	12,400	13,624	10,708	9,018
Yugoslavia	8,300	11,854	10,750	8,011
Other Europe	80,100	90,987	74,715[1]	62,196
Asia	267,900	307,807	265,810	219,696
China and Taiwan	44,900	55,129	47,892	43,981
Hong Kong	7,200	7,834	5,577	5,275
India	34,700	44,859	38,071	36,482
Japan	4,800	6,011	5,097	5,138
Korea (North and South)	16,000	18,185	14,239	14,268
Philippines	51,000	55,876	49,117	34,466
Thailand	5,100	4,310	3,094	3,102
Other Asia	104,200	115,603	102,723	76,984
North America	231,500	340,540	307,488	252,996
Canada	12,900	15,825	11,609	10,190
Mexico	89,900	163,572	146,865	131,575
Cuba	17,900	26,466	33,587	17,375
Dominican Republic	38,500	39,604	27,053	20,387
Haiti	14,000	18,386	15,057	13,449
Jamaica	16,400	19,089	17,840	15,146
Trinidad and Tobago	5,400	7,344	6,409	4,852
Other Caribbean	4,100	5,912	5,353	4,312
Central America	31,800	44,289	43,676	35,679
Other North America	60	53	39	31
South America	45,700	61,769	52,877	45,394
Colombia	10,800	14,283	13,004	11,836
Ecuador	6,400	8,321	7,780	6,852
Other South America	28,500	39,165	32,093	26,706
Africa	42,500	52,889	47,791	40,660
Australia and New Zealand	2,478	2,750	2,285	1,775
Other countries	2,219	2,564	2,256	9,163

[1]Immigration from the former USSR in 1997 included 16,600 from Russia and 15,700 from Ukraine. Figures from 1996 were: Russia, 19,700; Ukraine, 15,700; Armenia, 2,400; Azerbaijan, 2,000; Belarus, 4,300; Moldova, 1,800; Uzbekistan, 4,700.

The total number of immigrants admitted from 1820 up to 30 Sept. 1998 was 64,599,082; this included 7,156,257 from Germany, and 5,431,454 from Italy.

The number of immigrants admitted for legal permanent residence in the United States in the fiscal year 1998 was 660,477. Included in this total were 357,037 aliens previously living abroad who obtained immigrant visas through the US Department of State and became legal permanent residents upon entry into the United States. The remaining 303,440 legal immigrants, including former undocumented immigrants, refugees, and asylees, had been living in the United States an average of three years and adjusted status through the Immigration and Naturalization Service (INS). Legal immigration in 1998 was 17% lower than in 1997 (798,378). The decrease was due primarily to an increase in the number of adjustment of status applications pending a decision at INS, not to a decline in the demand to immigrate.

A total of 463,060 persons were naturalized in fiscal year 1998. This number would have been much higher were it not for a backlog of more than 1m. applications pending a decision at the end of 1997.

The refugee admissions ceiling for the fiscal year 1998 was fixed at 83,000, including 54,000 from Eastern Europe and the former Soviet Union and 4,000 from Asia East and South-East Asia.

SOCIAL STATISTICS
Figures include Alaska beginning with 1959 and Hawaii beginning with 1960.

	Live births	Deaths	Marriages	Divorces	Deaths under 1 year
1900	—	343,217	709,000	56,000	—
1910	2,777,000	696,856	948,000	83,000	—
1920	2,950,000	1,118,070	1,274,476	170,505	170,911
1930	2,618,000	1,327,240	1,126,856	195,961	143,201
1940	2,559,000	1,417,269	1,595,879	264,000	110,984
1950	3,632,000	1,452,454	1,667,231	385,144	103,825
1960	4,257,850	1,711,982	1,523,000	393,000	110,873
1970	3,731,386	1,921,031	2,158,802	708,000	74,667
1980	3,612,258	1,989,841	2,390,252	1,189,000	45,526
1990	4,158,212	2,148,463	2,448,000	1,182,000	38,351
1991	4,110,907	2,169,518	2,371,100	1,189,000	36,766
1992	4,065,014	2,175,613	2,362,000	1,215,000	34,628
1993	4,000,240	2,268,553	2,334,000	1,187,000	33,000
1994	3,952,767	2,278,994	2,362,000	1,191,000	31,000
1995	3,899,589	2,312,132	2,336,000	1,169,000	30,000
1996	3,891,494	2,314,690	2,344,000	1,150,000	28,000
1997	3,880,894	2,314,245	2,384,000	1,163,000	28,000
1998	3,941,553	2,337,256	2,244,000	1,135,000	28,000
1999	3,959,417	2,391,399	2,358,000	—	28,000
2000	4,058,814	2,403,351	2,329,000	—	27,000
2001	4,025,933	2,419,000[1]	2,327,000[1]	—	28,000[1]

[1]Preliminary.

Rates (per 1,000 population):

	Birth	Death	Marriage	Divorce
1994	15·2	8·8	9·1	4·6
1995	14·8	8·8	8·9	4·4
1996	14·7	8·7	8·8	4·3
1997	14·5	8·6	8·9	4·3
1998	14·6	8·6	8·3	4·2
1999	14·5	8·8	8·6	4·1
2000	14·7	8·7	8·5	4·2
2001	14·5	8·7[1]	8·4[1]	4·0[1]

[1]Preliminary.

Rate of natural increase per 1,000 population: 7·7 in 1991; 6·0 in 2000. Annual population growth rate, 1990–2000, 1·3%.

Even though the marriage rate shows a gradual decline, it remains much higher than in most other industrial countries. The most popular age range for marrying is 25–29 for males and 20–24 for females. Estimated number of births to unmarried women in 1997 was 1,257,000 (32·4% of all births), compared to 666,000 in 1980. The USA has the highest rate of births to teenage woman in the industrialized world, at 52·1 per 1,000 women in 1998. Between 1970 and 1998 the annual number of births rose by 5·7%. The number of births within marriage declined by 19·2% whereas the number outside of marriage rose by 223·6%. The number of lone-parent families rose by 190·2% over the same period. Whereas in 1970 as many as 83·4% of children lived with both biological parents, by 2000 only 60·4% were living with married biological parents and 2·1% with unmarried biological parents.

Infant mortality rates, per 1,000 live births: 29·2 in 1950; 12·9 in 1980; 7·1 in 1999. Fertility rate, 1999, 2·0 births per woman (3·6 in 1960).

There were 1·31m. abortions in 2000 (1·61m. in 1990), giving a rate of 21·3 for every 1,000 women aged 15–44, compared to a high of 29·3 per 1,000 in 1980 and 1981.

Expectation of life, 1970: males, 67·1 years; females, 74·7 years; 1999: males, 73·9 years; females, 79·7 years.

Numbers of deaths by principal causes, 1998 (and as a percentage of all deaths): heart disease, 724,900 (31·0%); cancer, 541,500 (23·2%); stroke, 158,400 (6·8%); obstructive lung disease, 112,600 (4·8%); accidents, 97,800 (4·2%); pneumonia and influenza, 91,800 (3·9%); diabetes mellitus, 64,800 (2·8%); suicide, 30,600 (1·3%); kidney diseases, 26,200 (1·1%); liver diseases, 25,200 (1·1%); septicemia, 23,700 (1·0%); AIDS, 18,200 (0·8%).

The number of Americans living in poverty in 2000 was 31·1m. or 11·3% of the total population, down from 15·1% in 1993.

A UNICEF report published in 2000 showed that 22·4% of children in the USA live in poverty (in households with income below 50% of the national median), compared to just 2·6% in Sweden. The report also showed that the poverty rate of children in lone-parent families was 55·4%, compared to 15·8% in two-parent families.

CLIMATE

For temperature and rainfall figures, *see* entries on individual states as indicated by regions, below, of mainland USA.

Pacific Coast. The climate varies with latitude, distance from the sea and the effect of relief, ranging from polar conditions in North Alaska through cool to warm temperate climates further south. The extreme south is temperate desert. Rainfall everywhere is moderate. *See* Alaska, California, Oregon, Washington.

Mountain States. Very varied, with relief exerting the main control; very cold in the north in winter, with considerable snowfall. In the south, much higher temperatures and aridity produce desert conditions. Rainfall everywhere is very variable as a result of rain-shadow influences. *See* Arizona, Colorado, Idaho, Montana, Nevada, New Mexico, Utah, Wyoming.

High Plains. A continental climate with a large annual range of temperature and moderate rainfall, mainly in summer, although unreliable. Dust storms are common in summer and blizzards in winter. *See* Nebraska, North Dakota, South Dakota.

Central Plains. A temperate continental climate, with hot summers and cold winters, except in the extreme south. Rainfall is plentiful and comes at all seasons, but there is a summer maximum in western parts. *See* Mississippi, Missouri, Oklahoma, Texas.

Mid-West. Continental, with hot summers and cold winters. Rainfall is moderate, with a summer maximum in most parts. *See* Indiana, Iowa, Kansas.

Great Lakes. Continental, resembling that of the Central Plains, with hot summers but very cold winters because of the freezing of the lakes. Rainfall is moderate with a slight summer maximum. *See* Illinois, Michigan, Minnesota, Ohio, Wisconsin.

Appalachian Mountains. The north is cool temperate with cold winters, the south warm temperate with milder winters. Precipitation is heavy, increasing to the south but evenly distributed over the year. *See* Kentucky, Pennsylvania, Tennessee, West Virginia.

Gulf Coast. Conditions vary from warm temperate to sub-tropical, with plentiful rainfall, decreasing towards the west but evenly distributed over the year. *See* Alabama, Arkansas, Florida, Louisiana.

Atlantic Coast. Temperate maritime climate but with great differences in temperature according to latitude. Rainfall is ample at all seasons; snowfall in the north can be heavy. *See* Delaware, District of Columbia, Georgia, Maryland, New Jersey, New York State, North Carolina, South Carolina, Virginia.

New England. Cool temperate, with severe winters and warm summers. Precipitation is well distributed with a slight winter maximum. Snowfall is heavy in winter. *See* Connecticut, Maine, Massachusetts, New Hampshire, Rhode Island, Vermont. *See also* Hawaii and Outlying Territories.

CONSTITUTION AND GOVERNMENT

The form of government of the USA is based on the constitution adopted on 17 Sept. 1787 and effective from 4 March 1789.

By the constitution the government of the nation is composed of three co-ordinate branches, the executive, the legislative and the judicial.

The Federal government has authority in matters of general taxation, treaties and other dealings with foreign countries, foreign and inter-state commerce, bankruptcy, postal service, coinage, weights and measures, patents and copyright, the armed forces (including, to a certain extent, the militia), and crimes against the USA; it has sole legislative authority over the District of Columbia and the possessions of the USA.

The 5th article of the constitution provides that Congress may, on a two-thirds vote of both houses, propose amendments to the constitution, or, on the application of the legislatures of two-thirds of all the states, call a convention for proposing amendments, which in either case shall be valid as part of the constitution when ratified by the legislatures of three-fourths of the several states, or by conventions in three-fourths thereof, whichever mode of ratification may be proposed by Congress. Ten amendments (called collectively 'the Bill of Rights') to the constitution were added 15 Dec. 1791; two in 1795 and 1804; a 13th amendment, 6 Dec. 1865, abolishing slavery; a 14th in 1868, including the important 'due process' clause; a 15th, 3 Feb. 1870, establishing equal voting rights for white and black; a 16th, 3 Feb. 1913, authorizing the income tax; a 17th, 8 April 1913, providing for popular election of senators; an 18th, 16 Jan. 1919, prohibiting alcoholic liquors; a 19th, 18 Aug. 1920, establishing woman suffrage; a 20th, 23 Jan. 1933, advancing the date of the President's and Vice-President's inauguration and abolishing the 'lameduck' sessions of Congress; a 21st, 5 Dec. 1933, repealing the 18th amendment; a 22nd, 26 Feb. 1951, limiting a President's tenure of office to 2 terms, or to 2 terms plus 2 years in the case of a Vice-President who has succeeded to the office of a President; a 23rd, 30 March 1961, granting citizens of the District of Columbia the right to vote in national elections; a 24th, 4 Feb. 1964, banning the use of the poll-tax in federal elections; a 25th, 10 Feb. 1967, dealing with Presidential disability and succession; a 26th, 22 June 1970, establishing the right of citizens who are 18 years of age and older to vote; a 27th, 7 May 1992, providing that no law varying the compensation of Senators or Representatives shall take effect until an election has taken place.

National motto. 'In God we trust'; formally adopted by Congress 30 July 1956.

Presidency. The executive power is vested in a president, who holds office for four years, and is elected, together with a vice-president chosen for the same term, by electors from each state, equal to the whole number of senators and representatives to which the state may be entitled in the Congress. The President must be a natural-born citizen, resident in the country for 14 years, and at least 35 years old.

The presidential election is held every fourth (leap) year on the Tuesday after the first Monday in Nov. Technically, this is an election of presidential electors, not of a president directly; the electors thus chosen meet and give their votes (for the candidate to whom they are pledged, in some states by law, but in most states by custom and prudent politics) at their respective state capitals on the first Monday after the second Wednesday in Dec. next following their election; and the votes of the electors of all the states are opened and counted in the presence of both Houses of Congress on the sixth day of Jan. The total electorate vote is one for each senator and representative. Electors may not be a member of Congress or hold federal office. If no candidate secures the minimum 270 college votes needed for outright victory, the 12th Amendment to the Constitution applies, and the House of Representatives chooses a president from among the first three finishers in the electoral college. (This last happened in 1824).

If the successful candidate for President dies before taking office the Vice-President-elect becomes President; if no candidate has a majority or if the successful candidate fails to qualify, then, by the 20th amendment, the Vice-President acts as President until a president qualifies. The duties of the Presidency, in absence of the President and Vice-President by reason of death, resignation, removal, inability or failure to qualify, devolve upon the Speaker of the House under legislation enacted on 18 July 1947. In case of absence of a Speaker for like reason, the presidential duties devolve upon the President *pro tem.* of the Senate and successively upon those members of the cabinet in order of precedence, who have the constitutional qualifications for President.

The presidential term, by the 20th amendment to the constitution, begins at noon on 20 Jan. of the inaugural year. This amendment also installs the newly elected Congress in office on 3 Jan. instead of—as formerly—in the following Dec. The President's salary is $400,000 per year (taxable), with in addition $50,000 to assist in defraying expenses resulting from official duties. Also he may spend up to $100,000 non-taxable for travel and $19,000 for official entertainment. In 1999 the presidential salary was increased for the president taking office in Jan. 2001, having remained at $200,000 a year since 1969. The office of Vice-President carries a salary of $192,600 and $10,000 allowance for expenses, all taxable. The Vice-President is *ex officio* President of the Senate, and in the case of 'the removal of the President, or of his death, resignation, or inability to discharge the powers and duties of his office', he becomes the President for the remainder of the term.

PRESIDENTS OF THE USA

Name	From state	Term of service	Born	Died
George Washington	Virginia	1789–97	1732	1799
John Adams	Massachusetts	1797–1801	1735	1826
Thomas Jefferson	Virginia	1801–09	1743	1826
James Madison	Virginia	1809–17	1751	1836
James Monroe	Virginia	1817–25	1759	1831
John Quincy Adams	Massachusetts	1825–29	1767	1848
Andrew Jackson	Tennessee	1829–37	1767	1845
Martin Van Buren	New York	1837–41	1782	1862
William H. Harrison	Ohio	Mar.–Apr. 1841	1773	1841
John Tyler	Virginia	1841–45	1790	1862
James K. Polk	Tennessee	1845–49	1795	1849
Zachary Taylor	Louisiana	1849–July 1850	1784	1850
Millard Fillmore	New York	1850–53	1800	1874
Franklin Pierce	New Hampshire	1853–57	1804	1869
James Buchanan	Pennsylvania	1857–61	1791	1868
Abraham Lincoln	Illinois	1861–Apr. 1865	1809	1865
Andrew Johnson	Tennessee	1865–69	1808	1875
Ulysses S. Grant	Illinois	1869–77	1822	1885
Rutherford B. Hayes	Ohio	1877–81	1822	1893
James A. Garfield	Ohio	Mar.–Sept. 1881	1831	1881
Chester A. Arthur	New York	1881–85	1830	1886
Grover Cleveland	New York	1885–89	1837	1908
Benjamin Harrison	Indiana	1889–93	1833	1901
Grover Cleveland	New York	1893–97	1837	1908
William McKinley	Ohio	1897–Sept. 1901	1843	1901
Theodore Roosevelt	New York	1901–09	1858	1919
William H. Taft	Ohio	1909–13	1857	1930
Woodrow Wilson	New Jersey	1913–21	1856	1924
Warren Gamaliel Harding	Ohio	1921–Aug. 1923	1865	1923
Calvin Coolidge	Massachusetts	1923–29	1872	1933
Herbert C. Hoover	California	1929–33	1874	1964
Franklin D. Roosevelt	New York	1933–Apr. 1945	1882	1945
Harry S Truman	Missouri	1945–53	1884	1972
Dwight D. Eisenhower	New York	1953–61	1890	1969
John F. Kennedy	Massachusetts	1961–Nov. 1963	1917	1963
Lyndon B. Johnson	Texas	1963–69	1908	1973
Richard M. Nixon	California	1969–74	1913	1994
Gerald R. Ford	Michigan	1974–77	1913	—
James Earl Carter	Georgia	1977–81	1924	—
Ronald W. Reagan	California	1981–89	1911	—
George H. Bush	Texas	1989–93	1924	—
Bill (William J.) Clinton	Arkansas	1993–2001	1946	—
George W. Bush	Texas	2001–	1946	—

VICE-PRESIDENTS OF THE USA

Name	From state	Term of service	Born	Died
John Adams	Massachusetts	1789–97	1735	1826
Thomas Jefferson	Virginia	1797–1801	1743	1826
Aaron Burr	New York	1801–05	1756	1836
George Clinton	New York	1805–12[1]	1739	1812
Elbridge Gerry	Massachusetts	1813–14[1]	1744	1814
Daniel D. Tompkins	New York	1817–25	1774	1825
John C. Calhoun	South Carolina	1825–32[1]	1782	1850
Martin Van Buren	New York	1833–37	1782	1862
Richard M. Johnson	Kentucky	1837–41	1780	1850
John Tyler	Virginia	Mar.–Apr.1841[1]	1790	1862
George M. Dallas	Pennsylvania	1845–49	1792	1864
Millard Fillmore	New York	1849–50[1]	1800	1874
William R. King	Alabama	Mar.–Apr. 1853[1]	1786	1853
John C. Breckinridge	Kentucky	1857–61	1821	1875
Hannibal Hamlin	Maine	1861–65	1809	1891
Andrew Johnson	Tennessee	Mar.–Apr. 1865[1]	1808	1875

Name	From state	Term of service	Born	Died
Schuyler Colfax	Indiana	1869–73	1823	1885
Henry Wilson	Massachusetts	1873–75[1]	1812	1875
William A. Wheeler	New York	1877–81	1819	1887
Chester A. Arthur	New York	Mar.–Sept. 1881[1]	1830	1886
Thomas A. Hendricks	Indiana	Mar.–Nov. 1885[1]	1819	1885
Levi P. Morton	New York	1889–93	1824	1920
Adlai Stevenson	Illinois	1893–97	1835	1914
Garret A. Hobart	New Jersey	1897–99[1]	1844	1899
Theodore Roosevelt	New York	Mar.–Sept. 1901[1]	1858	1919
Charles W. Fairbanks	Indiana	1905–09	1855	1920
James S. Sherman	New York	1909–12[1]	1855	1912
Thomas R. Marshall	Indiana	1913–21	1854	1925
Calvin Coolidge	Massachusetts	1921–Aug. 1923[1]	1872	1933
Charles G. Dawes	Illinois	1925–29	1865	1951
Charles Curtis	Kansas	1929–33	1860	1935
John N. Garner	Texas	1933–41	1868	1967
Henry A. Wallace	Iowa	1941–45	1888	1965
Harry S Truman	Missouri	1945–Apr. 1945[1]	1884	1972
Alben W. Barkley	Kentucky	1949–53	1877	1956
Richard M. Nixon	California	1953–61	1913	1994
Lyndon B. Johnson	Texas	1961–Nov. 1963[1]	1908	1973
Hubert H. Humphrey	Minnesota	1965–69	1911	1978
Spiro T. Agnew	Maryland	1969–73	1918	1996
Gerald R. Ford	Michigan	1973–74	1913	—
Nelson Rockefeller	New York	1974–77	1908	1979
Walter Mondale	Minnesota	1977–81	1928	—
George Bush	Texas	1981–89	1924	—
Danforth Quayle	Indiana	1989–93	1947	—
Albert Gore	Tennessee	1993–2001	1948	—
Richard B. Cheney	Wyoming	2001–	1941	—

[1]Position vacant thereafter until commencement of the next presidential term.

Cabinet. The administrative business of the nation has been traditionally vested in several executive departments, the heads of which, unofficially and *ex officio*, formed the President's cabinet. Beginning with the Interstate Commerce Commission in 1887, however, an increasing amount of executive business has been entrusted to some 60 so-called independent agencies, such as the Housing and Home Finance Agency, Tariff Commission, etc.

All heads of departments and of the 60 or more administrative agencies are appointed by the President, but must be confirmed by the Senate.

Congress. The legislative power is vested by the Constitution in a Congress, consisting of a Senate and House of Representatives.

Electorate. By amendments of the constitution, disqualification of voters on the ground of race, colour or sex is forbidden. The electorate consists of all citizens over 18 years of age. Literacy tests have been banned since 1970. In 1972 durational residency requirements were held to violate the constitution. In 1973 US citizens abroad were enfranchised.

With limitations imposed by the constitution, it is the states which determine voter eligibility. In general states exclude from voting: persons who have not established residency in the jurisdiction in which they wish to vote; persons who have been convicted of felonies whose civil rights have not been restored; persons declared mentally incompetent by a court.

Illiterate voters are entitled to receive assistance in marking their ballots. Minority-language voters in jurisdictions with statutorily prescribed minority concentrations are entitled to have elections conducted in the minority language as well as English. Disabled voters are entitled to accessible polling places. Voters absent on election days or unable to go to the polls are generally entitled under state law to vote by absentee ballot.

The Constitution guarantees citizens that their votes will be of equal value under the 'one person, one vote' rule.

Senate. The Senate consists of two members from each state (but not from the District of Columbia), chosen by popular vote for six years, approximately one-third retiring or seeking re-election every two years. Senators must be no less than 30 years of age; must have been citizens of the USA for nine years, and be residents in the states for which they are chosen. The Senate has complete freedom to initiate legislation, except revenue bills (which must originate in the House of Representatives); it may, however, amend or reject any legislation originating in the lower house. The Senate is also entrusted with the power of giving or withholding its 'advice and consent' to the ratification of all treaties initiated by the President with foreign powers, a two-thirds majority of senators present being required for approval. (However, it has no control over 'international executive agreements' made by the President with foreign governments; such 'agreements' cover a wide range and are more numerous than formal treaties.).

The Senate has 21 Standing Committees to which all bills are referred for study, revision or rejection. The House of Representatives has 20 such committees. In both Houses each Standing Committee has a chairman and a majority representing the majority party of the whole House; each has numerous sub-committees. The jurisdictions of these Committees correspond largely to those of the appropriate executive departments and agencies. Both Houses also have a few select or special Committees with limited duration.

House of Representatives. The House of Representatives consists of 435 members elected every second year. The number of each state's representatives is determined by the decennial census, in the absence of specific Congressional legislation affecting the basis. The number of representatives for each state in the 108th congress, which began in Jan. 2003 (based on the 2000 census), is given below:

Alabama	7	Indiana	9	Nebraska	3	South Carolina	6
Alaska	1	Iowa	5	Nevada	3	South Dakota	1
Arizona	8	Kansas	4	New Hampshire	2	Tennessee	9
Arkansas	4	Kentucky	6	New Jersey	13	Texas	32
California	53	Louisiana	7	New Mexico	3	Utah	3
Colorado	7	Maine	2	New York	29	Vermont	1
Connecticut	5	Maryland	8	North Carolina	13	Virginia	11
Delaware	1	Massachusetts	10	North Dakota	1	Washington	9
Florida	25	Michigan	15	Ohio	18	West Virginia	3
Georgia	13	Minnesota	8	Oklahoma	5	Wisconsin	8
Hawaii	2	Mississippi	4	Oregon	5	Wyoming	1
Idaho	2	Missouri	9	Pennsylvania	19		
Illinois	19	Montana	1	Rhode Island	2		

The constitution requires congressional districts within each state to be substantially equal in population. Final decisions on congressional district boundaries are taken by the state legislatures and governors. By custom the representative lives in the district from which he is elected. Representatives must be not less than 25 years of age, citizens of the USA for seven years and residents in the state from which they are chosen.

In addition, five delegates (one each from the District of Columbia, American Samoa, Guam, the US Virgin Islands and Puerto Rico) are also members of Congress. They have a voice but no vote, except in committees. The delegate from Puerto Rico is the resident commissioner. Puerto Ricans vote at primaries, but not at national elections. Each of the two Houses of Congress is sole 'judge of the elections, returns and qualifications of its own members'; and each of the Houses may, with the concurrence of two-thirds, expel a member. The period usually termed 'a Congress' in legislative language continues for two years, terminating at noon on 3 Jan.

The salary of a senator is $150,000 per annum, with tax-free expense allowance and allowances for travelling expenses and for clerical hire. The salary of the Speaker of the House of Representatives is $192,600 per annum, with a taxable allowance. The salary of a Member of the House is $150,000 ($166,700 for the Majority Leader and Minority Leader).

No senator or representative can, during the time for which he is elected, be appointed to any *civil* office under authority of the USA which shall have been created or the emoluments of which shall have been increased during such time; and no person holding *any* office under the USA can be a member of either House during his continuance in office. No religious text may be required as a qualification to any office or public trust under the USA or in any state.

Indians. By an Act passed on 2 June 1924 full citizenship was granted to all Indians born in the USA, though those remaining in tribal units were still under special federal jurisdiction. The Indian Reorganization Act of 1934 gave the tribal Indians, at their own option, substantial opportunities of self-government and the establishment of self-controlled corporate enterprises empowered to borrow money and buy land, machinery and equipment; these corporations are controlled by democratically elected tribal councils. Recently a trend towards releasing Indians from federal supervision has resulted in legislation terminating supervision over specific tribes. In 1988 the federal government recognized that it had a special relationship with, and a trust responsibility for, federally recognized Indian entities in continental USA and tribal entities in Alaska. In 1993 the Bureau of Indian Affairs listed 552 'Indian Entities Recognized and Eligible to Receive Services'. Indian lands (1991) amounted to 52,092,247 acres, of which 41,868,582 was tribally owned and 10,233,665 in trust allotments. Indian lands are held free of taxes. Total Indian population at the 1990 census was 1,959,000, of which Oklahoma, Arizona, California and New Mexico accounted for 832,466.

The **District of Columbia**, ceded by the State of Maryland for the purposes of government in 1791, is the seat of the US government. It includes the city of Washington, and embraces a land area of 61 sq. miles. The Reorganization Plan No. 3 of 1967 instituted a Mayor Council form of government with appointed officers. In 1973 an elected Mayor and elected councillors were introduced; in 1974 they received power to legislate in local matters. Congress retains power to enact legislation and to veto or supersede the Council's acts. Since 1961 citizens have had the right to vote in national elections. On 23 Aug. 1978 the Senate approved a constitutional amendment giving the District full voting representation in Congress. This has still to be ratified.

The Commonwealth of Puerto Rico, American Samoa, Guam and the Virgin Islands each have a local legislature, whose acts may be modified or annulled by Congress, though in practice this has seldom been done. Puerto Rico, since its attainment of commonwealth status on 25 July 1952, enjoys practically complete self-government, including the election of its governor and other officials. The conduct of foreign relations, however, is still a federal function and federal bureaux and agencies still operate in the island.

General supervision of territorial administration is exercised by the Office of Territories in the Department of Interior.

Local Government. The Union comprises 13 original states, 7 states which were admitted without having been previously organized as territories, and 30 states which had been territories—50 states in all. Each state has its own constitution (which the USA guarantees shall be republican in form), deriving its authority, not from Congress, but from the people of the state. Admission of states into the Union has been granted by special Acts of Congress, either (1) in the form of 'enabling Acts' providing for the drafting and ratification of a state constitution by the people, in which case the territory becomes a state as soon as the conditions are fulfilled, or (2) accepting a constitution already framed, and at once granting admission.

Each state is provided with a legislature of two Houses (except Nebraska, which since 1937 has had a single-chamber legislature), a governor and other executive officials, and a judicial system. Both Houses of the legislature are elective, but the senators (having larger electoral districts usually covering two or three counties compared with the single county or, in some states, the town, which sends one representative to the Lower House) are less numerous than the representatives, while in 38 states their terms are four years; in 12 states the term is two years. Of the four-year senates, Illinois, Montana and New Jersey provide for two four-year terms and one two-year term in each decade. Terms of the lower houses are usually shorter; in 45 states, two years. The trend is towards annual sessions of state legislatures; most meet annually now whereas in 1939 only four did.

The Governor is elected by direct vote of the people over the whole state for a term of office ranging in the various states from two to four years, and with a salary ranging from $70,000 (Maine) to $179,000 (New York). His duty is to see to the faithful administration of the law, and he has command of the military forces of the state. He may recommend measures but does not present bills to the legislature. In some states he presents estimates. In all but one of the states (North Carolina) the Governor has a veto upon legislation, which may, however, be overridden by the two Houses, in some states by a simple majority, in others by a three-fifths or two-thirds majority. In some states the Governor, on his death or resignation, is succeeded by a Lieut.-Governor who was elected at the same time and has been presiding over the state Senate. In several states the Speaker of the Lower House succeeds the Governor.

National Anthem. The Star-spangled Banner, 'Oh say, can you see by the dawn's early light'; words by F. S. Key, 1814, tune by J. S. Smith; formally adopted by Congress 3 March 1931.

RECENT ELECTIONS
At the presidential election on 7 Nov. 2000 turn-out was 51·2% (49% in 1996). George W. Bush (R.) received 50,461,080 votes (48·1%), Albert Arnold ('Al') Gore Jr (D.) 50,994,082 (48·3%), Ralph Nader (Green Party) 2,858,843 (2·6%), Pat Buchanan (Reform Party) 438,760 (0·4%), Harry Browne (Libertarian Party) (0·4%). Electoral college votes: Bush, 271; Gore, 267; other candidates, nil. Bush's victory was only confirmed on 13 Dec. 2000 after a recount in Florida gave him a total of 271 electoral colleges, one more than he needed to win the presidency. In becoming president as George Bush had 12 years earlier, George W. Bush became only the second son of a former US president to follow his father into office. John Quincy Adams became president in 1825, 24 years after his father John Adams had left office.

Voting percentages and electoral college votes by state:

a) Majority for Bush

State	Bush (%)	Gore (%)	Nader (%)	Electoral College (votes)
Alabama	57	42	1	9
Alaska	59	28	10	3
Arizona	51	45	3	8
Arkansas	51	45	2	6
Colorado	51	42	5	8
Florida	49	49	2	25
Georgia	55	43	1	13
Idaho	69	28	2[1]	4
Indiana	57	41	1[1]	12
Kansas	58	37	3	6
Kentucky	57	41	2	8
Louisiana	53	45	1	9
Mississippi	57	42	1	7
Missouri	51	47	1	11
Montana	58	34	6	3
Nebraska	63	33	3	5
Nevada	49	46	2	4
New Hampshire	48	47	4	4
North Carolina	56	43	1[2]	14
North Dakota	61	33	3	3
Ohio	50	46	3	21
Oklahoma	60	38	1[1]	8
South Carolina	57	41	2	8
South Dakota	60	38	1[1]	3
Tennessee	51	48	1	11
Texas	59	38	2	32
Utah	67	26	5	5
Virginia	52	45	2	13
West Virginia	52	46	2	5
Wyoming	69	28	1[1]	3

[1]Buchanan. [2]Browne.

b) Majority for Gore

	Gore	Bush	Nader	
California	54	42	4	54
Connecticut	56	39	4	8
Delaware	55	42	3	3
DC	86	9	5	3
Hawaii	56	38	6	4
Illinois	55	43	2	22
Iowa	49	48	2	7

UNITED STATES OF AMERICA

	Gore	Bush	Nader	
Maine	49	44	6	4
Maryland	57	40	3	10
Massachusetts	60	33	6	12
Michigan	51	47	2	18
Minnesota	48	46	5	10
New Jersey	56	41	3	15
New Mexico	48	48	4	5
New York	60	35	4	33
Oregon	47	47	5	7
Pennsylvania	51	47	2	23
Rhode Island	61	32	6	4
Vermont	51	41	7	3
Washington	50	45	4	11
Wisconsin	48	48	4	11

Following the mid-term elections of 5 Nov. 2002 the 108th Congress (2003–04) is constituted as follows: Senate—51 Republicans, 48 Democrats and 1 ind. (50 Democrats, 49 Republicans and 1 ind. for the 107th Congress); House of Representatives—229 Republicans, 205 Democrats and 1 ind. (223 Republicans, 210 Democrats, 1 ind. and 1 vacancy for the 107th Congress). For the first time since the Second World War the party of the president increased its number of seats at the first mid-term elections in both the House of Representatives and the Senate. Never before had the party that controls the White House won back the Senate.

The next presidential elections are scheduled to take place on 2 Nov. 2004.

The Speaker of the House of Representatives is Dennis Hastert (R.). The Majority Leader of the Senate is Bill Frist (R.).

CURRENT ADMINISTRATION

President of the United States: George W. Bush, of Texas; b. 1946. Majored in History at Yale (1968); MA in Business Administration (1975); unsuccessfully ran for congress (1977); became shareholder in Texas Rangers baseball team (1988); governor of Texas (1994–2000).

Vice President: Richard 'Dick' Cheney, of Wyoming, b. 1941. Deputy White House counselor in Nixon administration (1970); assistant to the president and White House chief of staff during the Ford administration (1974); House of Representatives (1979–89); Secretary of Defense (1989–93).

In March 2003 the cabinet consisted of the following:

1. *Secretary of State* (created 1789). Colin Powell, b. New York, 1937. Two tours of duty in Vietnam (1962 and 1968); Military adviser to the South Vietnamese Army (1962); Senior military assistant to Defence Secretary (1983–86); National Security Adviser to President Reagan (1987–88); Commander in Chief, US Forces Command (1989); Chairman of the Joint Chiefs of Staff (1989–93).

2. *Secretary of the Treasury* (1789). John Snow, b. Ohio, 1939. Phd in Economics (1965) and LLB (1967). Entered Department of Transportation in 1972. Deputy Undersecretary of Transportation in Ford administration (1975–76). Joined Chessie System Inc. in 1977. President and CEO (1989) of CSX Corp. and Chairman (1991).

3. *Secretary of Defense* (1947). Donald Rumsfeld, b. Illinois, 1932. Elected to the House of Representatives (1962–69); Ambassador to the North Atlantic Treaty Organisation (1973–74); Secretary of Defence to President Ford (1975–77); Special US negotiator for Middle Eastern problems (1983–84).

4. *Attorney-General* (Department of Justice, 1870). John Ashcroft, b. Illinois, 1942. Law degree from the University of Chicago's Law school; Auditor for Missouri (1973–74); Missouri state Attorney General (1976–85); Governor of Missouri (1985–93); Elected to the US Senate (1994).

5. *Secretary of the Interior* (1849). Gale Norton, b. Kansas, 1954. Assistant to the Deputy Secretary of Agriculture (1984–85); associate solicitor at the Department of the Interior (1985–1990); Colorado attorney general and chair of the Environment Committee for the National Association of Attorneys General (1991–1999); Environment Committee chair for the Republican National Lawyers Association (1999–2001).

6. *Secretary of Agriculture* (1889). Ann Veneman, b. California, 1949. Deputy Undersecretary of Agriculture for International Affairs and Commodity Programmes

(1989–1991); Deputy Secretary of the US Department of Agriculture (USDA) (1991–93); Secretary of the California Department of Food and Agriculture (1995–99).

7. *Secretary of Commerce* (1903). Donald Evans, b. Texas, 1946. BS in mechanical engineering from University of Texas; MBA from University of Texas; oil rig crewman, president and chief executive officer for the energy company, Tom Brown Inc. (1975–2000).

8. *Secretary of Labor* (1913). Elaine Chao, b. Taiwan, 1953. White House Fellow (1983–84); Deputy Secretary of the US Department of Transportation in Washington (1989–91); Director of the Peace Corps (1992); President of United Way of America (1992–96); Chairman of Heritage Foundation's Asian Studies Center Advisory Council (1998).

9. *Secretary of Health and Human Services* (1953). Tommy Thompson, b. Wisconsin, 1941. Tours of Duty in Europe, Asia and Vietnam (1965–66); Governor of Wisconsin (1987–2000); Chairman of the National Governors Association; Chairman of the Republican Governors Association.

10. *Secretary of Housing and Urban Development* (1966). Mel Martinez, b. Cuba, 1947. Chairman, Orlando Housing Authority (1984–86); President, Orlando Utilities Commission (1994–96); Chairman, Orange County Government (1998–2000).

11. *Secretary of Transportation* (1967). Norman Mineta, b. California, 1931. Congressman for Silicon Valley (1974–95); Chairman, US House of Representatives Committee on Public Works and Transportation (1993); Chairman, Federal Aviation Administration's National Civil Aviation Review Commission (1997). He is the only Democrat in the cabinet.

12. *Secretary of Energy* (1977). Spencer Abraham, b. Michigan, 1952. Law degree from Harvard University of Law (1979); assistant law professor, Thomas M. Cooley Law School (1981–83); deputy chief of staff to Vice President Dan Quayle, (1990–92); US Senator for Michigan (1995–2000).

13. *Secretary of Education* (1979). Rod Paige, b. Mississippi, 1933. Dean of the College of Education at Texas Southern University; HISD Board of Education (1989–94); Superintendent, Houston Independent School District (1994–2000).

14. *Secretary of Veterans' Affairs* (1989). Anthony J. Principi, b. New York, 1944. Gained decorations for combat in Vietnam during career in U.S. Navy (1967–80); deputy administrator in Veterans Affairs (1983–84); Republican chief counsel and staff director of Senate Committee on Veterans Affairs (1984–88); first deputy secretary of Veterans Affairs (1989–92); acting secretary of Veterans Affairs (1992–93).

15. *Secretary of Homeland Security* (2002). Tom Ridge, b. Pennsylvania, 1945. Scholarship to Harvard, graduated 1967; gained Bronze Star in Vietnam; law degree from Dickinson School of Law (1972); Assistant District Attorney for Erie County; elected to Congress (1982) six times; Governor of Pennsylvania (1995–2001); Head of new Office of Homeland Security (Sept. 2001).

Each of the above cabinet officers receives an annual salary of $166,700 and holds office during the pleasure of the President.

A number of administrators also have honorary cabinet status.

Key White House Posts: White House Chief of Staff: Andrew Card; National Security Adviser: Condoleezza Rice; White House Counsel: Al Gonzales; Press Secretary: Ari Fleischer; Assistant for Economic Affairs: Stephen Friedman; Office of Management and Budget: Mitchell E. Daniels, Jr; Council of Economic Advisors: R. Glenn Hubbard; Office of the U.S. Trade Representative: Robert Zoellick.

Office of the President: http://www.whitehouse.gov

DEFENCE
The President is C.-in-C. of the Army, Navy and Air Force.

The National Security Act of 1947 provides for the unification of the Army, Navy and Air Forces under a single Secretary of Defense with cabinet rank. The President is also advised by a National Security Council and the Office of Civil and Defense Mobilization.

Defence expenditure in 2001 totalled US$322,365m. (US$1,128 per capita), representing 3·2% of GDP (down from 6·5% of GDP in 1985). The USA spent more on defence in 2001 than the next ten biggest spenders combined. US expenditure was 38% of the world total. In 1997 the Quadrennial Defense Review (QDR) was implemented—a plan to transform US defence strategy and military forces. In Oct. 2002 the US Senate approved the biggest increase in military spending in two decades by agreeing to a defence budget of US$355·1bn. for the fiscal year 2003, an increase of US$37·5bn. on 2002.

The estimated number of active military personnel in 2001 was 1,367,700.

The USA is the world's largest exporter of arms, with sales in 2001 worth $9·7bn., or 45·5% of the world total. In 2000 Lockheed Martin and Boeing were the two largest arms producing companies in the USA and in the world, accounting for $18·61bn. and $16·90bn. worth of sales respectively.

The USA's last nuclear test was in 1993. In accordance with START I—the treaty signed by the US and USSR in 1991 to reduce strategic offensive nuclear capability—the number of nuclear warheads (intercontinental ballistic missiles, submarine-launched ballistic missiles and bombers) in Jan. 2002 was approximately 6,480. In 1990 the number of warheads had been 12,718. Strategic nuclear delivery vehicles were made up as follows:

Intercontinental ballistic missiles: 500 Minuteman III; 50 Peacekeeper (MX).
Submarine-launched ballistic missiles: 168 Trident I (C-4); 264 Trident II (D-5).
Bombers: 93 B-52H; 21 B-2.

The USA had what was believed to be the world's second largest stockpile of chemical weapons, but by federal law is committed to unilateral destruction of the weapons by 2004.

In May 2001 President Bush called for the development of an anti-missile shield to move beyond the constraints of the Anti-Ballistic Missile Treaty. In Dec. 2001 he announced that the USA was unilaterally abandoning the Treaty. As the relationship with Russian president Vladimir Putin strengthened following the events of 11 Sept. 2001 he proposed a reduction of operational nuclear warheads to between 1,700 and 2,200 by 2010. On 24 May 2002 the USA and Russia signed an arms control treaty to reduce the number of US and Russian warheads, from between 6,000 and 7,000 each to between 1,700 and 2,200 each, over the next ten years.

Army. *Secretary of the Army.* Vacant.

The Secretary of the Army is the head of the Department of the Army. Subject to the authority of the President as C.-in-C. and of the Secretary of Defense, he is responsible for all affairs of the Department.

The Army consists of the Active Army, the Army National Guard of the US, the Army Reserve and civilian workforce; and all persons appointed to or enlisted into the Army without component; and all persons serving under call or conscription, including members of the National Guard of the States, etc., when in the service of the US. The strength of the Active Army was (2002) 485,500 (including 71,400 women).

The Army budget for fiscal years 2002–04 is as follows: 2002, $86,099m.; 2003, $90,933m.; 2004, $93,903m.

The US Army Forces Command, with headquarters at Fort McPherson, Georgia, commands the Third US Army; four continental US Armies, and all assigned Active Army and US Army Reserve troop units in the continental US, the Commonwealth of Puerto Rico, and the Virgin Islands of the USA. The headquarters of the continental US Armies are: First US Army, Fort George G. Meade, Maryland; Second US Army, Fort Gillem, Georgia; Fifth US Army, Fort Sam Houston, Texas; Sixth US Army, Presidio of San Francisco, California. The US Army Space Command, with headquarters in Colorado Springs (CO), is the Army component to the US Space Command.

Approximately 32% of the Active Army is deployed outside the continental USA. Several divisions, which are located in the USA, keep equipment in Germany and can be flown there in 48–72 hours. Headquarters of US Seventh and Eighth Armies are in Europe and Korea respectively.

Combat vehicles of the US Army are the tank, armoured personnel carrier, infantry fighting vehicle, and the armoured command vehicle. The first-line tanks are the M1A1 Abrams tank, and the M1 Abrams. The standard armoured infantry personnel carrier is the M2 Bradley Fighting Vehicle (BFV), which is replacing the older M113.

The Army has over 5,000 aircraft, all but about 280 of them helicopters, including AH-1 Cobra and AH-64 Apache attack helicopters.

Over 95% of recruits enlisting in the Army have a high-school education and over 50% of the Army is married. Women serve in both combat support and combat service support units.

The National Guard is a reserve military component with both a state and a federal role. Enlistment is voluntary. The members are recruited by each state, but are equipped and paid by the federal government (except when performing state missions). As the organized militia of the several states, the District of Columbia, Puerto Rico and the Territories of the Virgin Islands and Guam, the Guard may be called into service for local emergencies by the chief executives in those jurisdictions; and may be called into federal service by the President to thwart invasion or rebellion or to enforce federal law. In its role as a reserve component of the Army, the Guard is subject to the order of the President in the event of national emergency. In 2002 it numbered 464,300 (Army, 355,900; Air Force, 108,400).

The Army Reserve is designed to supply qualified and experienced units and individuals in an emergency. Members of units are assigned to the Ready Reserve, which is subject to call by the President in case of national emergency without declaration of war by Congress. The Standby Reserve and the Retired Reserve may be called only after declaration of war or national emergency by Congress. In 2002 the Army Reserve numbered 358,100.

Navy. *Secretary of the Navy (acting).* Hansford T. Johnson.

The Navy's Operating Forces include the Atlantic Fleet, divided between the 2nd fleet (home waters) and 6th fleet (Mediterranean) and the Pacific Fleet, similarly divided between the 3rd fleet (home waters), the 7th fleet (West Pacific) and the 5th fleet (Indian Ocean), which was formally activated in 1995 and maintained by units from both Pacific and Atlantic.

The authorized budget for the Department of the Navy (which includes funding both for the Navy and Marine Corps) for fiscal years 2002–04 is as follows: 2002, \$104,836m.; 2003, \$111,184m.; 2004, \$114,720m.

Personnel and fleet strength declined during the mid-1990s but are now stabilizing. The '600-ship battle force' planned in the late 1980s has reduced to a current figure of 317. The Navy personnel total in 2002 was 385,400.

The operational strength of the Navy in the year indicated:

Category	1992	1997	2002
Strategic Submarines	23	18	18
Nuclear Attack Submarines	87	67	54
Aircraft Carriers	12	11[1]	12[1]
Amphibious Carriers	13	11	11
Cruisers	46	30	27
Destroyers	51	56	55
Frigates	90	31	28

[1]Includes the USS *John F. Kennedy* as 'operational and training reserve carrier' in the Naval Reserve Force.

Ships in the inactive reserve are not included in the table, but those serving as Naval Reserve Force training ships are.

Submarine Forces. A principal part of the US naval task is to deploy the seaborne strategic deterrent from nuclear-powered ballistic missile-carrying submarines (SSBN), of which there were 18 in 2002, all of the Ohio class. The listed total of 54 nuclear-powered attack submarines (SSN) includes two of three new Seawolf class and 51 of the Los Angeles class. There is also one of the Sturgeon class.

Surface Combatant Forces. The surface combatant forces are comprised of modern cruisers, destroyers and frigates. These ships provide multi-mission capabilities to achieve maritime dominance in the crowded and complex littoral warfare environment.

The cruiser force consists of 27 Ticonderoga class ships. There are 33 guided-missile Arleigh Burke Aegis class destroyers, 20 Spruance class destroyers and 35 (28 active and 7 in the reserve force) Oliver Hazard Perry class guided missile frigates.

Aircraft carriers. There are eight nuclear-powered Nimitz class carriers. The USS *Enterprise,* completed in 1961, was the prototype nuclear-powered carrier. The two ships of the Kitty Hawk and one of the John F. Kennedy classes were completed between 1961 and 1968, and represent the last oil-fuelled carriers built by the US Navy. All carriers deploy an air group which comprises on average two squadrons each of F-14 Tomcat fighters and three squadrons each of F/A-18 Hornet fighter/ground attack aircraft.

Naval Aviation. The principal function of the naval aviation organization (currently 12,110 pilots and Naval flight officers) is to train and provide combat ready aviation forces. The main carrier-borne combat aircraft in the current inventory are 232 F-14 fighters and 821 F/A-18 Hornet dual-purpose fighter/attack aircraft.

The Marine Corps. While administratively part of the Department of the Navy, the Corps ranks as a separate armed service, with the Commandant serving in his own right as a member of the Joint Chiefs of Staff, and responsible directly to the Secretary of the Navy. Its strength had stabilized at 173,400 by 2002.

The role of the Marine Corps is to provide specially trained and equipped amphibious expeditionary forces. The Corps includes an autonomous aviation element numbering 35,650 in 2002 with some 442 combat aircraft and 515 helicopters. They include F/A 18 Hornets and AV-8B Harriers.

The US Coast Guard. The Coast Guard operates under the Department of Transportation in time of peace and as part of the Navy in time of war or when directed by the President. The act of establishment stated the Coast Guard 'shall be a military service and branch of the armed forces of the United States at all times'.

The Coast Guard is the country's oldest continuous sea-going service and its missions include maintenance of aids to navigation, icebreaking, environmental response (oil spills), maritime law enforcement, marine licensing, port security, search and rescue and waterways management.

The workforce in 2002 was made up of approximately 34,480 military personnel augmented by 5,840 civilians. On an average Coast Guard day, the service saves 14 lives, conducts 120 law enforcement boardings, seizes 209 pounds of marijuana and 170 pounds of cocaine, boards 90 large vessels for port safety checks, processes 120 seaman's documents, investigates 17 marine accidents, inspects 64 commercial vessels, assists 328 people in distress, saves $2,490,000 in property, services 150 aids to navigation and interdicts 176 illegal immigrants.

Air Force. *Secretary of the Air Force.* James G. Roche.

The Department of the Air Force was activated within the Department of Defense on 18 Sept. 1947, under the terms of the National Security Act of 1947.

The USAF has the mission to defend the USA through control and exploitation of air and space. For operational purposes the service is divided into 8 major commands, 37 field operating agencies and 3 direct-reporting units.

The bulk of the combat forces are grouped under the Air Combat Command, which controls strategic bombing, tactical strike, air defence and reconnaissance assets in the USA.

Air Force bombers include the B-1B Lancer, the B-2A and the B-52G/H Stratofortress, which has been the primary manned strategic bomber for over 35 years. In the fighter category are the F-15 Eagle, the F-16 Fighting Falcon and the F-117A, the world's first operational aircraft to exploit low-observable stealth technology.

The Air Force budget for fiscal years 2002–04 is as follows: 2002, $100,266m.; 2003, $108,451m.; 2004, $113,805m.

In 2002 the Air Force had approximately 369,700 military personnel. 56,400 Air Force members are women. Since 1991 women have been authorized to fly combat aircraft, but not until 1993 were they allowed to fly fighters.

INTERNATIONAL RELATIONS

The USA is a member of the UN, WTO, NATO, BIS, OECD, OSCE, OAS, Inter-American Development Bank, Asian Development Bank, Pacific Community, Colombo Plan, IOM and the Antarctic Treaty.

In 2001 the USA gave US$10·9bn. in international aid, the highest figure of any country. In terms of a percentage of GNI, however, the USA was the least generous major industrialized country, giving just 0·1% (compared to more than 0·6% in the early 1960s).

ECONOMY

Services accounted for approximately 80% of GDP in 1999, industry 18% and agriculture 2%.

According to the anti-corruption organization *Transparency International*, in 2002 the USA ranked 16th in the world in a survey of the countries with the least corruption in business and government. It received 7·7 out of 10 in the annual index.

Per capita income in 2001 was $30,472, up from $19,572 in 1990.

Overview. In March 2001 the US economy entered its first recession in a decade after the longest period of expansion in US history. The economy declined further following the 11 Sept. 2001 attacks. Economic policies have moved from short-term stabilization to strengthening the base for durable growth. In Dec. 2000 monetary policy was eased and in Jan. 2001 interest rates were cut by 50 basis points, the first cut since 1992. The 11 Dec. 2001 rate cut was the eleventh interest fall of 2001. In June 2002 short-term interest rates were at a 40-year low. Worsened economic conditions have led to a smaller federal budget surplus than forecast. In March 2002 there was a budget deficit over 1% of GDP. Spending plans for 2003 include a 14% increase in the defence budget and a 50% increase on homeland security.

Currency. The unit of currency is the *dollar* (USD) of 100 *cents*. Notes are issued by the 12 Federal Reserve Banks, which are denoted by a branch letter (A = Boston, MA; B = New York, NY; C = Philadelphia, PA; D = Cleveland, OH; E = Richmond, VA; F = Atlanta, GA; G = Chicago, IL; H = St Louis, MO; I = Minneapolis, MN; J = Kansas City, MO; K = Dallas, TX; L = San Francisco, CA).

Inflation was 2·2% in 1999, 3·4% in 2000 and 2·8% in 2001. Foreign exchange reserves in June 2002 were US$32,166m. Gold reserves in June 2002 262·0m. troy oz. The USA has the most gold reserves of any country, and more than the combined reserves of the next two (Germany and France). Total money supply in March 2002 was $1,552bn.

Budget. The budget covers virtually all the programmes of federal government, including those financed through trust funds, such as for social security, Medicare and highway construction. Receipts of the government include all income from its sovereign or compulsory powers; income from business-type or market-orientated activities of the government is offset against outlays. The fiscal year ends on 30 Sept. (before 1977 on 30 June). Budget receipts and outlays, including off-budget receipts and outlays (in $1m.):

Fiscal year ending in	Receipts	Outlays	Surplus (+) or deficit (−)
1950	39,443	42,562	−3,119
1960	92,492	92,191	+301
1970	192,807	195,649	−2,842
1980	517,112	590,947	−73,835
1990	1,031,969	1,253,198	−221,229
1995	1,351,830	1,515,837	−164,007
1996	1,453,062	1,560,572	−107,510
1997	1,579,292	1,601,282	−21,990
1998	1,721,798	1,652,619	+69,179
1999	1,827,454	1,701,932	+125,522
2000	2,025,218	1,788,826	+236,392
2001	1,991,030	1,863,926	+127,104
2002[1]	1,946,136	2,052,320	−106,184
2003[1]	2,048,060	2,128,230	−80,170

[1]Estimates.

Budget and off-budget receipts, by source, for fiscal years (in $1m.):

Source	2001	2002[1]	2003[1]
Individual income taxes	994,339	949,239	1,006,354
Corporation income taxes	151,075	201,445	205,489
Social insurance and retirement receipts	693,967	708,035	749,212
Excise taxes	66,068	66,871	69,021
Other	85,581	20,546	17,984
Total	1,991,030	1,946,136	2,048,060

[1]Estimates.

UNITED STATES OF AMERICA

Budget and off-budget outlays, by function, for fiscal years (in $1m.):

Function	2001	2002[1]	2003[1]
National defence	308,533	347,986	379,012
International affairs	16,601	23,520	22,467
General science, space and technology	19,896	21,759	22,168
Energy	89	561	566
Natural resources and environment	26,335	30,238	30,601
Agriculture	26,553	28,830	24,226
Commerce and housing credit	6,030	3,764	3,700
Transportation	55,220	62,130	59,449
Community and regional development	11,977	15,365	17,389
Education, training, employment and social service	57,302	71,697	79,023
Health	172,634	195,237	231,935
Medicare	217,464	226,395	234,361
Income security	269,770	310,733	319,680
Social security	433,129	459,662	475,925
Veterans' benefits and services	45,828	51,527	56,582
Administration of justice	30,443	34,442	40,619
General government	15,153	18,262	17,632
Net interest	206,199	178,385	180,659
Allowances	—	27,000	6,356
Undistributed offsetting receipts	−55,230	−55,173	−74,120
Total	1,863,926	2,052,320	2,128,230

[1]Estimates.

Budget and off-budget outlays, by agency, for fiscal years (in $1m.):

Agency	2001	2002[1]	2003[1]
Legislative branch	3,135	3,625	3,970
The Judiciary	4,519	4,977	5,4978
Executive Office of the President	254	464	334
International assistance programmes	11,792	13,287	12,969
Agriculture	68,599	76,565	74,443
Commerce	5,137	5,495	5,670
Corps of engineers	4,834	4,975	4,347
Defence—Military functions	293,995	330,553	360,989
Defence—Civil	34,167	35,537	40,933
Education	35,748	47,587	53,800
Energy	16,490	19,093	19,784
Health and Human Services	426,767	459,366	488,794
Housing and Urban Development	33,994	30,948	34,600
Interior	8,249	10,290	10,822
Justice	21,296	23,073	29,385
Labor	39,367	58,579	56,554
State	7,524	11,132	9,883
Transportation	54,838	60,788	58,843
Treasury	390,569	382,616	398,188
Veterans Affairs	45,839	51,451	56,513
Environmental Protection Agency	7,490	7,790	8,061
Federal Emergency Management Administration	4,426	5,789	7,550
General Services Administration	−1	586	−52
National Aeronautics and Space Administration	14,199	14,484	14,885
National Science Foundation	3,696	4,564	4,886
Office of Personnel Management	50,919	54,277	67,940
Small Business Administration	−550	1,073	587
Social Security Administration	462,026	492,671	509,655
Other independent agencies	13,952	19,967	17,258
Allowances	—	27,000	6,356
Undistributed offsetting receipts	−199,344	−206,282	−235,214
Total	1,863,926	2,052,320	2,128,230

[1]Estimates.

National Debt. Federal debt held by the public (in $1m.), and per capita debt (in $1) on 30 June to 1976 and on 30 Sept. since then:

	Public debt	Per capita		Public debt	Per capita
1920	24,299	229	1950	219,023	1,447
1930	16,185	132	1960	236,840	1,321
1940	42,772	324	1970	283,198	1,394

	Public debt	Per capita		Public debt	Per capita
1980	711,923	3,143	2001	3,540,427	12,409
1990	2,411,558	9,696	2002	3,878,438	13,450
2000	3,409,804	12,082			

National Income. The Bureau of Economic Analysis of the Department of Commerce prepares detailed estimates on the national income and product. In Oct. 1999 the Bureau revised these accounts back to 1959, and in April 2000 back to 1929. The principal tables are published monthly in *Survey of Current Business;* the complete set of national income and product tables are published in the *Survey* normally each Aug., showing data for recent years. *The National Income and Product Accounts of the United States* (1929–97, 2 vols.) were published in Sept. 2001. The conceptual framework and statistical methods underlying the accounts are described in National Income and Product Account (NIPA) Methodology Papers 1–6. Subsequent limited changes are described in the Aug. 1999, Sept. 1999, Oct. 1999, Dec. 1999, April 2000, Aug. 2000, Aug. 2001 and Aug. 2002 *Surveys.*

Gross Domestic Product
(in $1,000m.)

	1997	1998	1999	2000	2001
Gross Domestic Product	8,318·4	8,781·5	9,274·3	9,824·6	10,082·2
Personal consumption expenditures	5,529·3	5,856·0	6,246·5	6,683·7	6,987·0
Durable goods	642·5	693·2	755·9	803·9	835·9
Nondurable goods	1,641·6	1,708·5	1,830·1	1,972·9	2,041·3
Services	3,245·2	3,454·3	3,660·5	3,906·9	4,109·9
Gross private domestic investment	1,390·5	1,538·7	1,636·7	1,755·4	1,586·0
Fixed investment	1,327·7	1,465·6	1,577·2	1,691·8	1,646·3
Nonresidential	999·4	1,101·2	1,173·5	1,265·8	1,201·6
Structures	255·8	282·4	283·7	314·2	324·5
Equipment and software	743·6	818·9	889·8	951·6	877·1
Residential	328·2	364·4	403·7	426·0	444·8
Change in private inventories	62·9	73·1	59·5	63·6	−60·3
Net exports of goods and services	−89·3	−151·7	−249·9	−365·5	−348·9
Exports	966·4	964·9	989·3	1,101·1	1,034·1
Goods	688·9	681·3	697·3	785·0	733·5
Services	277·5	283·6	292·0	316·1	300·6
Imports	1,055·8	1,116·7	1,239·2	1,466·6	1,383·0
Goods	885·1	930·0	1,045·3	1,243·1	1,167·2
Services	170·7	186·7	193·9	223·5	215·8
Government consumption expenditures and gross investment	1,487·9	1,538·5	1,641·0	1,751·0	1,858·0
Federal	538·2	539·2	565·0	589·2	628·1
National defence	352·6	349·1	364·3	374·9	399·9
Nondefence	185·6	190·1	200·7	214·3	228·2
State and local	949·7	999·3	1,076·0	1,161·8	1,229·9

Relation of Gross Domestic Product, Gross National Product, Net National Product, National Income, and Personal Income
(in $1,000m.)

	1997	1998	1999	2000	2001
Gross domestic product	8,318·4	8,781·5	9,274·6	9,824·6	10,082·2
Plus: Income receipts from the rest of the world	281·3	286·1	316·9	383·4	316·9
Less: Income payments to the rest of the world	274·2	289·6	294·1	360·0	295·0
Equals: Gross national product	8,325·4	8,778·1	9,297·1	9,848·0	10,104·1
Less: Consumption of fixed capital	1,013·3	1,072·0	1,145·2	1,228·9	1,329·3
Private	832·4	884·3	947·3	1,018·0	1,106·8
Capital consumption allowances	844·5	905·6	985·6	1,037·1	1,168·4
Less: Capital consumption adjustment	12·1	21·3	38·3	19·1	61·6
Government	180·9	187·6	197·9	210·9	222·4
General government	154·6	160·1	168·6	179·5	187·7
Government enterprises	26·3	27·6	29·3	31·5	34·8
Equals: Net national product	7,312·1	7,706·1	8,151·9	8,619·1	8,774·8

Relation of Gross Domestic Product, Gross National Product,
Net National Product, National Income, and Personal Income
(in $1,000m.)

	1997	1998	1999	2000	2001
Less: Indirect business tax and non-tax					
liability	646·2	681·3	712·9	753·6	774·8
Business transfer payments	36·8	38·0	41·5	43·7	42·5
Statistical discrepancy	29·7	−31·0	−38·8	−128·5	−117·3
Plus: Subsidies less current surplus of					
government enterprises	19·1	23·5	32·5	34·1	47·3
Equals: National income	**6,618·4**	**7,041·4**	**7,468·7**	**7,984·4**	**8,122·0**
Less: Corporate profits with inventory					
valuation and capital consumption					
adjustments	833·8	777·4	805·8	788·1	731·6
Net interest	423·9	511·9	526·6	611·5	649·8
Contributions for social insurance	587·8	623·3	660·4	701·3	726·1
Wage accruals less disbursements	−2·9	−0·7	5·2	0	0
Plus: Personal interest income	864·0	964·4	969·2	1,077·0	1,091·3
Personal dividend income	334·9	348·3	328·0	375·7	409·2
Government transfer payments to					
persons	934·4	955·0	98702	1,037·3	1,137·0
Business transfer payments to persons	27·9	28·8	31·3	33·0	33·4
Equals: Personal income	**6,937·0**	**7,426·0**	**7,786·5**	**8,406·6**	**8,685·3**
Addenda:					
Gross domestic income	8,288·6	8,812·5	9,313·1	9,953·1	10,199·4
Gross national income	8,295·7	8,809·1	9,335·8	9,976·5	10,221·4
Net domestic product	7,305·0	7,709·5	8,129·1	8,595·7	8,752·9

National Income by Type of Income
(in $1,000m.)

	1997	1998	1999	2000	2001
National income	6,618·4	7,041·4	7,468·7	7,984·4	8,122·0
Compensation of employees	4,651·3	4,989·6	5,308·8	5,723·4	5,874·9
Wage and salary accruals	3,886·0	4,192·1	4,475·6	4,836·3	4,950·6
Government	664·3	692·7	724·2	768·9	810·8
Other	3,221·7	3,499·4	3,751·4	4,067·4	4,139·8
Supplements to wages and salaries	765·3	797·5	833·2	887·1	924·3
Employer contributions for social insurance	289·9	306·9	323·0	342·9	353·9
Other labour income	475·4	490·6	510·2	544·2	570·4
Proprietors' income with inventory valuation					
and capital consumption adjustments	581·2	623·8	678·4	714·8	727·9
Farm	29·7	25·6	27·7	22·6	19·0
Proprietors' income with inventory					
valuation adjustment	37·5	33·1	35·8	30·2	26·7
Capital consumption adjustment	−7·8	−7·5	−8·0	−7·6	−7·7
Nonfarm	551·5	598·2	650·7	692·2	708·8
Proprietors' income	507·2	547·6	589·6	621·2	621·6
Inventory valuation adjustment	0·7	1·2	−0·9	−1·6	0·9
Capital consumption adjustment	43·6	49·4	62·0	72·6	86·3
Rental income of persons with					
capital consumption adjustment	128·3	138·6	149·1	146·6	137·9
Rental income of persons	178·3	190·3	206·8	206·6	204·4
Capital consumption adjustment	−50·0	−51·7	−57·6	−60·0	−66·5
Corporate profits with inventory valuation and					
capital consumption adjustments	833·8	777·4	805·8	788·1	731·6
Corporate profits with inventory					
valuation adjustment	800·8	739·4	757·9	767·3	675·1
Profits before tax	792·4	721·1	762·1	782·3	670·2
Profits tax liability	237·2	238·8	247·8	259·4	199·3
Profits after tax	555·2	482·3	514·3	522·9	470·9
Dividends	335·2	348·7	328·7	376·1	409·6
Undistributed profits	220·0	133·6	185·9	146·8	61·2
Inventory valuation adjustment	8·4	18·3	−4·2	−15·0	5·0
Capital consumption adjustment	32·9	38·0	47·9	20·8	56·5
Net interest	423·9	511·9	526·6	611·5	649·8

UNITED STATES OF AMERICA

National Income by Type of Income
(in $1,000m.)

	1997	1998	1999	2000	2001
Addenda:					
Corporate profits after tax with inventory valuation and capital consumption adjustments	596·6	538·6	558·0	528·7	532·3
Net cash flow with inventory valuation and capital consumption adjustments	842·9	810·0	895·0	873·7	911·8
Undistributed profits with inventory valuation and capital consumption adjustments	261·3	189·9	229·6	152·6	122·7
Consumption of fixed capital	581·5	620·2	665·5	721·1	789·1
Less: Inventory valuation adjustment	8·4	18·3	−4·2	−15·0	5·0
Equals: Net cash flow	834·4	791·7	899·3	888·7	906·8

Real Gross Domestic Product
(in 1,000m. chained [1996] dollars[1])

	1997	1998	1999	2000	2001
Gross domestic product	8,159·5	8,508·9	8,859·0	9,191·4	9,214·5
Personal consumption expenditures	5,423·9	5,683·7	5,964·5	6,223·9	6,377·2
Durable goods	657·3	726·7	812·5	878·9	931·9
Nondurable goods	1,619·9	1,686·4	1,765·1	1,833·8	1,869·8
Services	3,147·0	3,273·4	3,395·4	3,524·5	3,594·9
Gross private domestic investment	1,393·3	1,558·0	1,660·5	1,762·9	1,574·6
Fixed investment	1,328·6	1,480·0	1,595·2	1,691·9	1,627·4
Nonresidential	1,009·3	1,135·9	1,228·4	1,324·2	1,255·1
Structures	245·4	262·2	258·6	275·5	270·9
Equipment and software	764·2	875·4	975·9	1,056·0	988·2
Residential	319·7	345·1	368·3	372·4	373·5
Change in private inventories	63·8	76·7	62·8	65·0	−61·4
Net exports of goods and services	−113·3	−221·1	−320·5	−398·8	−415·9
Exports	981·5	1,002·4	1,036·3	1,137·2	1,076·1
Goods	708·1	722·9	750·0	834·7	785·2
Services	273·6	279·8	286·8	304·1	292·0
Imports	1,094·8	1,223·5	1,356·8	1,536·0	1,492·0
Goods	923·1	1,031·4	1,157·5	1,313·7	1,270·5
Services	171·7	192·2	200·3	223·6	222·4
Government consumption expenditures and gross investment	1,455·4	1,483·3	1,540·6	1,582·5	1,640·4
Federal	529·6	525·4	537·7	544·4	570·6
National defence	347·7	341·6	348·8	348·7	366·0
Non-defence	181·8	183·8	188·8	195·6	204·4
State and local	925·8	957·7	1,002·4	1,037·4	1,069·4
Residual	0·0	0·8	1·4	2·1	22·6

[1]In 1996 the chain-weighted method of estimating GDP replaced that of constant base-year prices. In chain-weighting the weights used to value different sectors of the economy are continually updated to reflect changes in relative prices.

Performance. Total GDP in 2001 was US$10,082·2bn., representing approximately 32% of the world's total GDP. Real GDP growth was 4·3% in 1998, 4·1% in 1999 and 3·8% in 2000. In the first quarter of 2001 the economy contracted for the first time since 1993, shrinking by 0·6%. The recession came to an end in the final quarter of 2001, with growth of 2·7%, giving a growth rate for 2001 as a whole of 0·3%. In the 2002 *World Competitiveness Yearbook*, compiled by the International Institute for Management Development, the USA came top in the world ranking. The USA was top in both the Growth Competitiveness Ranking and the Microeconomic Competitiveness Ranking in the World Economic Forum's *Global Competitiveness Report 2002–03*, up from second in both in 2001–02.

Banking and Finance. The Federal Reserve System, established under The Federal Reserve Act of 1913, comprises the Board of seven Governors, the 12 regional Federal Reserve Banks with their 25 branches, and the Federal Open Market Committee. The seven members of the Board of Governors are appointed by the President with the consent of the Senate. Each Governor is appointed to a full term of 14 years or an unexpired portion of a term, one term expiring every two years.

The Board exercises broad supervisory authority over the operations of the 12 Federal Reserve Banks, including approval of their budgets and of the appointments of their presidents and first vice presidents; it designates three of the nine directors of each Reserve Bank including the Chairman and Deputy Chairman. The Chairman of the Federal Reserve Board is appointed by the President for four-year terms. The *Chairman* for 2000–04 is Alan Greenspan. The Board has supervisory and regulatory responsibilities over banks that are members of the Federal Reserve System, bank holding companies, bank mergers, Edge Act and agreement corporations, foreign activities of member banks, international banking facilities in the USA, and activities of the US branches and agencies of foreign banks. Legislation of 1991 requires foreign banks to prove that they are subject to comprehensive consolidated supervision by a regulator at home, and have the Board's approval to establish branches, agencies and representative offices. The Board also assures the smooth functioning and continued development of the nation's vast payments system. Another area of the Board's responsibilities involves the implementation by regulation of major federal laws governing consumer credit.

In 2001, four of the five largest banks in the world in terms of market capitalization were US banks. Citigroup was the largest ($255·2bn.). The third, fourth and fifth largest were Bank of America ($95·7bn.), JP Morgan Chase ($88·4bn.) and Wells Fargo ($74·7bn.).

The key stock exchanges are the New York Stock Exchange (NYSE), the Nasdaq Stock Exchange (NASDAQ) and the American Stock Exchange (ASE). There are several other stock exchanges, in Philadelphia, Boston, San Francisco (Pacific Stock Exchange) and Chicago, although trading is very limited in them.

In 1999 the USA received $276bn. worth of foreign direct investment—three times as much as any other country.

By Oct. 2000 approximately 18% of the population were using e-banking.

Weights and Measures. The US Customary System derives from the British Imperial System. It differs in respect of the *gallon* (= 0·83268 Imperial gallon); *bushel* (= 0·969 Imperial bushel); *hundredweight* (= 100 lb); and the *short* or *net ton* (= 2,000 lb).

ENERGY AND NATURAL RESOURCES

Environment. The USA's carbon dioxide emissions in 1998 accounted for 24·3% of the world total, higher than any other country, and according to the *World Bank Atlas* were equivalent to 19·8 tonnes per capita. The population of the USA is only 4·6% of the world total. An *Environmental Sustainability Index* compiled for the World Economic Forum meeting in Feb. 2002 ranked the USA 45th in the world, with 53·2%. The index measured the ability of countries to maintain favourable environmental conditions and examined various factors including pollution levels and the use or abuse of natural resources.

In March 2001 President Bush rejected the 1997 Kyoto Protocol, which aims to combat the rise in the earth's temperature through the reduction of industrialized nations' carbon dioxide emissions by an average 5·2% below 1990 levels by 2012. In Feb. 2002 he unveiled an alternative climate-change plan to the Kyoto Protocol, calling for voluntary measures to reduce the rate of increase of US carbon dioxide emissions.

The USA recycled 31·5% of its household waste in 1998, ranking it seventh in the world.

Electricity. Net capacity in 1999 was 639·3m. kW. Fossil fuel accounts for approximately 70% of electricity generation. In 2001, 20% of electricity was produced by 104 nuclear reactors. (The last one to begin commercial operation was in 1996.) The US has more nuclear reactors in use than any other country in the world. In 1999 the USA had a nuclear generating capacity of 97,200 MW. Electricity production in 1999 was the highest in the world, at 3,173,674m. kWh.[1] Consumption per capita in 1998 was 11,832 kWh.

[1]Does not include non-utility production.

Oil and Gas. Crude oil production (2001), 1,830m. bbls. Production has been gradually declining since the mid-1980s, when annual production was 3,274m. bbls.

Only Saudi Arabia produces more oil. Proven reserves were 22·0bn. bbls. in 2001, but they are expected to be exhausted by 2011. Output (1999) was valued at $33·40bn. Imported supplies account for approximately half of US oil consumption, with Saudi Arabia supplying a sixth of US oil imports. In Oct. 2002 the USA took its first delivery of Russian oil for its Strategic Petroleum Reserve as a consequence of an energy dialogue declared by Presidents George W. Bush and Vladimir Putin at their summit in May 2002.

The USA is by far the largest single consumer of natural gas, and the second largest producer after Russia. Natural gas production, 2001, was 19·21trn. cu. ft. Proven gas reserves in 2001 totalled 177trn. cu. ft.

Wind. The USA is one of the largest producers of wind-power. By the end of 2002 total installed capacity amounted to 4,685 MW.

Water. The total area covered by water is 256,645 sq. miles. Americans' average annual water usage is nearly 67,000 cu. ft per person—more than twice the average for an industrialized nation.

Non-Fuel Minerals. The USA is wholly dependent upon imports for columbium, bauxite, mica sheet, manganese, strontium and graphite, and imports over 80% of its requirements of industrial diamonds, fluorspar, platinum, tantalum, tungsten, chromium and tin.

Total value of non-fuel minerals produced in 1999 was $40,100m. ($33,445m. in 1990). Details of some of the main minerals produced are given in the following tables.

Production of metals:

	Unit	Quantity 1999	Value ($1m.) 1997
Copper	1,000 tonnes	1,600	4,580
Gold	tonnes	341	3,850
Iron ore	1m. tonnes	58	1,890
Lead	1,000 tonnes	520	460
Magnesium metal	1,000 tonnes	106[1]	400
Silver	tonnes	1,950	338
Zinc	1,000 tonnes	843	860
Total metals			13,074

[1] 1998.

Precious metals are mined mainly in California and Utah; (gold) and Nevada, Arizona and Idaho (silver).

Production of non-metals:

	Unit	Quantity 1999	Value ($1m.) 1998
Barite	1,000 tonnes	434	15
Boron	1,000 tonnes	1,220	—
Bromine	1,000 tonnes	239	227
Cement	1m. short tons	86	—
Clays	1,000 tonnes	42,200	—
Diatomite	1,000 tonnes	747	182
Feldspar	1,000 tonnes	875	40
Garnet (industrial)	1,000 tonnes	61	—
Gypsum	1m. tonnes	22	137
Lime	1m. short tons	20	—
Phosphate rock	1m. tonnes	41	1,131
Pumice	1,000 tonnes	643	15
Salt	1m. tonnes	45	993
Sand and gravel	1m. tonnes	1,139	4,778
Sodium sulphate	1,000 tonnes	599	—
Stone (crushed)	1m. tonnes	1,540	—

Aluminium production for 1999, 3·8m. tonnes; uranium production for 1997, 2,170 tonnes. The USA is the world's leading producer of both salt and aluminium.

Coal. Demonstrated coal reserves were 507,740m. short tons at 1 Jan. 1997. Output in 1999 (in 1m. short tons): 1,099·1 including bituminous coal, 621·3; sub-bituminous coal, 388·3; lignite, 84·4; anthracite, 5·2. 1998 output from opencast workings, 699,807; underground mines, 417,728. Value of total output, 1998, $19·75bn.

Agriculture. Agriculture in the USA is characterized by its ability to adapt to widely varying conditions, and still produce an abundance and variety of agricultural products. From colonial times to about 1920 the major increases in farm production were brought about by adding to the number of farms and the amount of land under cultivation. During this period nearly 320m. acres of virgin forest were converted to crop land or pasture, and extensive areas of grasslands were ploughed. Improvident use of soil and water resources was evident in many areas.

During the next 20 years the number of farms reached a plateau of about 6·5m., and the acreage planted to crops held relatively stable around 330m. acres. The major source of increase in farm output arose from the substitution of power-driven machines for horses and mules. Greater emphasis was placed on development and improvement of land, and the need for conservation of basic agricultural resources was recognized.

Since the Second World War the uptrend in farm output has been greatly accelerated by increased production per acre and per farm animal. These increases are associated with a higher degree of mechanization; greater use of lime and fertilizer; improved varieties, including hybrid maize and grain sorghums; more effective control of insects and disease; improved strains of livestock and poultry; and wider use of good husbandry practices, such as nutritionally balanced feeds, use of superior sites and better housing.

All land in farms totalled less than 500m. acres in 1870, rose to a peak of over 1,200m. acres in the 1950s and declined to 941m. acres in 2001, even with the addition of the new States of Alaska and Hawaii in 1960. The number of farms declined from 6·35m. in 1940 to 2·16m. in 2001, as the average size of farms doubled. The average size of farms in 2001 was 436 acres, but ranged from a few acres to many thousand acres. In 1997 the total value of land and buildings was $912,344m. The average value of land and buildings per acre in 1998 was $1,000.

At the 1990 census 66,964,000 persons (22·5% of the population) were rural, of whom 4,591,000 (under 2%) lived on farms. In 1997 there were an estimated 1,317,000 farm operators and managers and 2,030,000 persons in other agricultural and related occupations, of which 796,000 were farm workers. There were in 1998 4·8m. tractors and 662,000 harvester-threshers.

Cash receipts from farm marketings and government payments (in $1bn.):

	Crops	Livestock and livestock products	Total
1996	106·2	93·0	199·2
1997	111·1	96·5	207·6
1998	102·5	94·1	196·6
1999	93·1	95·5	188·6

Net farm income was $46·4bn. in 2000.

The harvest area and production of the principal crops for 1998 and 1999 were:

	1999			2000		
	Harvested 1m. acres	Produc- tion 1m.	Yield per acre	Harvested 1m. acres	Produc- tion 1m.	Yield per acre
Corn for grain (bu.)	70·5	9,431	134	72·7	9,968	137
Soybeans (bu.)	72·4	2,654	36·6	72·7	2,770	38·1
Wheat (bu.)	53·8	2,299	42·7	53·0	2,233	41·9
Cotton (bales)[1]	13·4	17·0	607	13·1	17·2	631
Tobacco (lb)	0·6	1,293	1,997	0·5	1,100	2,264
Potatoes (cwt.)	1·3	478	359	1·4	516	382
Hay (sh. tons)	63·2	160	2·53	59·9	152	2·54

[1]Yield in lb.

The USA is the world's leading producer of maize, soybeans, sorghum and tree nuts and the second largest producer of tomatoes, carrots, seed cotton, cottonseed, sugarbeets and apples.

Fruit. Utilized production, in 1,000 tons:

	1998	1999	2000
Apples	5,381	5,223	5,192
Oranges and tangerines	14,030	10,151	13,564
Grapes	5,816	6,235	7,657

The farm value of the above crops in 2000 was: apples, $1,336m.; oranges and tangerines, $1,866m.; and grapes, $3,104m.

Figures compiled by the Soil Association, a British organization, show that in 1999 the USA set aside 2·2m. acres (0·2% of its agricultural land) for the growth of organic crops. The projected figure of organic food sales for the USA in 1999–2000 was US$4bn. (the highest in the world).

Dairy produce. In 2000 production of milk was 168,000m. lb; cheese, 8,255m. lb; butter, 1,274m. lb; ice cream, 970m. gallons; non-fat dry milk, 1,457m. lb; yoghurt, 1,835m. lb. The USA is the world's largest producer of both cheese and milk.

Livestock. In 2000 there were 8,263m. broilers and 270m. turkeys. Eggs produced, 2000, 84·4bn.

Value of production (in $1m.) was:

	1998	1999	2000
Cattle and calves	24,153	26,051	28,388
Hogs and pigs	8,674	7,666	10,791
Broilers	15,145	15,129	13,953
Turkeys	2,679	2,810	2,843
Eggs	4,439	4,287	4,347

Livestock numbered, in 2001 (1m.): cattle and calves (including milch cows), 97·3; sheep and lambs, 6·9; hogs and pigs, 59·3. Approximate value of livestock (in $1bn.), 2001: cattle, 70·6; hogs and pigs, 4·5; sheep and lambs (in $1m.), 661.

Forestry. Forests covered a total area of 525m. acres (212m. ha) in 1995, or 23% of the land area. Between 1990 and 1995 new planting resulted in the total area under forests growing by 7·2m. acres (2·9m. ha), the largest increase in any country in the world over the same period. The national forests had an area of 191,854,000 acres in 1999. In 1996 there were 518m. acres of timberland (124m. acres federally owned or managed, 35m. acres state, county or municipality owned, 357m. acres private). Timber production was 500·75m. cu. metres in 1999. The USA is the world's second largest producer of roundwood after China (15% of the world total in 1999). It is also the second highest consumer of roundwood; timber consumption in 1999 totalled 17·49bn. cu. ft.

There are 624 designated wilderness areas throughout the USA, covering a total of 104m. acres (42m. ha). More than half of the areas are in Alaska (56%), followed by California (13%), Arizona, Washington and Idaho.

Fisheries. In 1999 the domestic catch was 9,339m. lb, valued at $3,467m. (including 1,527m. lb of shellfish valued at $1,908·8m.). Main species landed in terms of value ($1m.): shrimp, 560·5; crab, 521·2; salmon, 359·8; American lobster, 323·0; Alaska pollock, 162·8. Disposition of the domestic catch (1m. lb): fresh or frozen, 6,416; tinned, 712; cured, 133; reduced to meal or oil, 2,078. The USA's imports of fishery commodities in 1999 ($9·41bn.) were exceeded only by those of Japan.

In the period 1995–97 the average American citizen consumed 46·1 lb (20·9 kg) of fish and fishery products a year, compared to an average 34·6 lb (15·7 kg) for the world as a whole.

Tennessee Valley Authority. Established by Act of Congress, 1933, the TVA is a multiple-purpose federal agency which carries out its duties in an area embracing some 41,000 sq. miles in the seven Tennessee River Valley states: Tennessee, Kentucky, Mississippi, Alabama, North Carolina, Georgia and Virginia. In addition, 76 counties outside the Valley are served by TVA power distributors. Its three directors are appointed by the President, with the consent of the Senate; headquarters are in Knoxville (TN). Under a policy announced in Dec. 1994 the TVA is subject to a debt ceiling of $30,000m. Total debt in 1994 was $26,000m.

The primary task of the TVA was the multipurpose development of the Tennessee River for flood control, navigation, and electric power production. In 1994 three nuclear reactors were in operation.

The TVA has also contributed to controlling erosion on the land, introducing better fertilizers and new farming practices, eradicating malaria, demonstrating ways electricity could lighten the burdens in the home and increase production on the farm, and the creation of potential job-producing enterprises.

INDUSTRY

The largest companies in the USA—and the world—by market capitalization in Jan. 2002 were: The General Electric Company (US$372bn.); The Microsoft Corporation (US$327bn.), the world's leading software company; and The Exxon Mobil Corporation (US$300bn.), the world's largest integrated oil company. According to a survey published by the New York-based Interbrand in July 2000, Coca-Cola is the most valuable brand, worth US$72·5bn.

The following table presents industry statistics of manufactures as reported at various censuses from 1909 to 1980 and from the Annual Survey of Manufactures for years in which no census was taken.

The annual Surveys of Manufactures carry forward the key measures of manufacturing activity which are covered in detail by the Census of Manufactures. The large plants in the surveys account for approximately two-thirds of the total employment in operating manufacturing establishments in the USA.

	Number of establish- ments	Production workers (average for year)	Production workers' wages total ($1,000)	Value added by manufacture ($1,000)
1909	264,810	3,261,736	3,205,213	8,160,075
1919	270,231	9,464,916	9,664,009	23,841,624
1929	206,663	8,369,705	10,884,919	30,591,435
1933	139,325	5,787,611	4,940,146	14,007,540
1939	173,802	7,808,205	8,997,515	24,487,304
1950	260,000	11,778,803	34,600,025	89,749,765
1960	...	12,209,514	55,555,452	163,998,531
1970	...	13,528,000	91,609,000	300,227,600
1980	...	13,900,100	198,164,000	773,831,300
1990	...	12,100,000	272,000,000	1,326,000,000
2000	...	11,959,000	363,272,000	2,002,649,000

The total number of employees in the manufacturing industry in 2000 was approximately 16,681,000. In 2000 manufacturing contributed 17% of GDP and provided 14% of jobs, down from 27% of GDP and 31% of jobs in 1960. Industrial production grew far faster during the 1990s than in any other major economy, output expanding by 34% during the period 1990–98. Employees worked an average of 41·5 hours per week in 2000 for an average weekly income of $597.

The leading industries in 1999 in terms of value added by manufacture (in $1m.) were: transportation equipment, 268,511; computer and electronic products, 265,442; chemicals and allied products, 229,284; food, 177,659; fabricated metal products, 142,451. In 1999 a total of 13,022,000 motor vehicles were made in the USA, making it the world's leading vehicle producer.

In 1999 principal commodities produced (by value of shipments, in $1m.) were: transportation equipment, 675,122; computer and electronic products, 458,485; food, 429,053; chemicals and allied products, 419,674; machinery, 277,117.

The USA is the world's largest beer producer, with 6,248m. gallons in 1999.

Net profits (1999) for manufacturing corporations reached a record $356bn. before tax ($261bn. after tax).

Iron and Steel. Output of the iron and steel industries (in 1m. net tons of 2,000 lb), according to figures supplied by the American Iron and Steel Institute, was:

	Pig iron (including ferro- alloys)	Raw steel	Steel by method of production[1] Electric	Basic Oxygen
1994	54·4	100·6	39·6	61·0
1995	56·1	104·9	42·4	62·5
1996	54·5	105·3	44·9	60·4
1997	54·7	108·6	47·5	61·1
1998	53·2	108·8	49·1	59·7
1999	51·0	107·4	49·7	57·7

[1]The sum of these two items should equal the total in the preceding column; any difference is due to rounding.

In 1997 companies comprising 65% of raw steel production employed 83,466 wage-earners who worked an average of 42·7 hours per week and earned an average of $23·90 per hour: total employment costs were $6,465m. and total employment costs for 28,359 salaried employees were $2,378m.

Labour The Bureau of Labor Statistics estimated that in 2002 the civilian labour force was 144,863,000 (66·6% of those 16 years and over), of whom 136,485,000 were employed and 8,378,000 (5·8%) were unemployed. By April 2000 the unemployment rate was down to 3·8%—the lowest rate since 1970. However, it has risen in the meantime, and was 5·7% in Jan. 2003. Total non-farm payroll employment fell by 230,000 in the 12 months ending Dec. 2002. Employment by industry in 2002:

Industry Group	Male	Female	Total	Percentage distribution
Employed (1,000 persons):	72,903	63,582	136,485	100·0
Agriculture, forestry and fisheries	2,585	893	3,479	2·5
Mining	453	63	516	0·4
Construction	8,772	897	9,669	7·1
Manufacturing: Durable goods	8,104	2,836	10,940	8·0
Manufacturing: Non-durable (including not specified)	4,467	2,740	7,207	5·3
Transportation, communication and other public utilities	6,910	2,770	9,680	7·1
Wholesale and retail trade	14,971	13,125	28,096	20·6
Finance, insurance and real estate	3,890	5,235	9,125	6·7
Services	19,365	32,225	51,588	37·8
—Private households	79	765	844	0·6
—Other services	19,285	31,460	50,744	37·2
(Professional services	10,405	24,410	34,815	25·5)
Public administration	3,386	2,798	6,184	4·5

A total of 29 strikes and lockouts of 1,000 workers or more occurred in 2001, involving 99,000 workers and 1·2m. idle days; the number of idle days was less than one out of every 10,000 available workdays. Between 1989 and 1998 strikes cost the USA an average of 54 days per 1,000 employees a year.

On 1 Sept. 1997 the federal hourly minimum wage was raised from $4·75 to $5·15 an hour. On 1 Oct. 1996 it had been raised from $4·25 to $4·75 an hour, the first time it had been raised since 1991. Americans work among the longest hours in the world, averaging 1,996 hours in 1997.

Labour relations are legally regulated by the National Labor Relations Act, amended by the Labor–Management Relations (Taft–Hartley) Act, 1947 as amended by the Labor–Management Reporting and Disclosure Act, 1959, again amended in 1974, and the Railway Labor Act of 1926, as amended in 1934 and 1936.

A survey for the World Economic Forum's *1999 Global Competitiveness Report* showed that the USA was the easiest country in the world in which to set up a business.

Trade Unions. The labour movement comprises 78 national and international labour organizations plus a large number of small independent local or single-firm labour organizations. The American Federation of Labor and the Congress of Industrial Organizations merged into one organization, the AFL–CIO, in 1955, with 13m. members in 2000. Its president is John Sweeney, elected 1995. There were 16,258,200 union members in total in 2000.

Unaffiliated or independent labour organizations, inter-state in scope, had an estimated total membership excluding all foreign members (1993) of about 3m.

Labour organizations represented 14·6% (17·8m.) of wage and salary workers in 2002; a newly developing 'associative unionism' is not based on the workplace, but provides representation for employees which is portable throughout their work history; 13·2% (16·1m.) were actual members of unions. 37·5% of employees in the public sector, and 8·5% in the private sector, were members of unions in 2002. Strongholds of organized labour are, industry-wise, iron and steel, railways, coal mining and car building; region-wise, East coast cities and the mid-West industrial belt.

INTERNATIONAL TRADE
The North American Free Trade Agreement (NAFTA) between the USA, Canada and Mexico was signed on 7 Oct. 1992 and came into effect on 1 Jan. 1994. The UK has had 'most-favoured-nation' status since 1815. In 1998 foreign direct investment totalled $811,756m., the leading investor still being the United Kingdom.

Imports and Exports. Total value of exports and imports (in $1bn.):

	Exports	Imports
1995	584·7	743·4
1996	625·1	795·3
1997	689·2	870·7
1998	682·1	911·9
1999	698·0	1,024·6
2000	781·9	1,218·0

The USA is both the world's leading importer and the leading exporter. In 1998 its trade accounted for 17·0% of the world's exports and 22·5% of imports.

Exports and imports (in $1m.), 2000:

	Exports	Imports
Agricultural commodities		
Animal feeds	3,791	597
Coffee	9	2,350
Corn	4,704	160
Cotton, raw and linters	1,904	28
Hides and skins	1,484	109
Meat and preparations	7,305	3,840
Soybeans	5,270	34
Sugar	4	462
Tobacco, unmanufactured	1,222	568
Vegetables and fruits	7,497	9,283
Wheat	3,379	229
Total, including others	*50,387*	*37,755*
Manufactured goods		
ADP equipment, office machinery	46,661	92,165
Airplanes	24,700	12,393
Airplane parts	15,060	5,550
Alcoholic beverages	427	2,946
Aluminium	3,766	6,955
Artwork/antiques	1,388	5,876
Basketware, etc.	3,291	4,842
Chemicals – cosmetics	5,316	3,541
Chemicals – dyeing	4,106	2,676
Chemicals – fertilizers	2,301	1,689
Chemicals – inorganic	5,370	6,096
Chemicals – medicinal	12,882	14,694
Chemicals – organic	18,034	28,563
Chemicals – plastics	19,630	10,643
Chemicals – other	12,279	5,731
Cigarettes	3,308	258
Clothing	8,173	64,296
Cork, wood, lumber	4,321	8,235
Electrical machinery	89,763	108,813
Footwear	604	14,854
Furniture and parts	4,744	18,927
Gem diamonds	1,289	12,060
General industrial machinery	32,925	34,709
Gold, non-monetary	5,894	2,659
Iron and steel mill products	5,720	15,808
Lighting, plumbing	1,392	5,106
Metal manufactures, misc.	13,272	16,228
Metalworking machinery	6,169	7,731
Optical goods	3,247	4,021
Paper and paperboard	10,775	15,184
Photographic equipment	4,239	6,915
Plastic articles	7,613	8,034
Platinum	897	5,688
Power generating machinery	32,542	33,815
Printed materials	4,778	3,698
Records/magnetic media	5,427	5,166
Rubber articles	1,649	1,963
Rubber tyres and tubes	2,405	4,782
Scientific instruments	30,799	22,014
Ships, boats	1,044	1,178
Silver and bullion	225	775

	Exports	Imports
Spacecraft	158	217
Specialized industrial machinery	30,918	22,733
Television, VCR, etc.	27,898	70,487
Textile yarn, fabric	10,540	15,175
Toys/games/sporting goods	3,605	20,017
Travel goods	351	4,432
Vehicles	56,873	161,682
Watches/clocks/parts	348	3,485
Wood manufactures	1,856	7,222
Total, including others	623,986	1,013,480
Mineral fuel		
Coal	2,173	805
Crude oil	444	89,786
Petroleum preparations	5,748	25,657
Natural gas	411	10,966
Total, including others	13,134	133,590

Imports and exports by selected countries for the calendar years 1999 and 2000 (in $1m.):

Country	General imports		Exports incl. re-exports	
	1999	2000	1999	2000
Belgium	9,196	9,931	12,381	13,960
Brazil	11,314	13,855	13,203	15,360
Canada	198,711	229,209	166,600	178,786
China	81,788	100,063	13,111	16,253
France	25,709	29,782	18,877	20,253
Germany	55,228	59,737	26,800	29,244
Hong Kong	10,528	11,452	12,652	14,625
Ireland	10,994	16,410	6,384	7,727
Italy	22,357	25,050	10,091	11,000
Japan	130,864	146,577	57,466	65,254
South Korea	31,179	40,300	22,958	27,902
Malaysia	21,424	25,568	9,060	10,996
Mexico	109,721	135,911	86,909	111,721
Netherlands	8,475	9,704	19,437	21,974
Philippines	12,353	13,937	7,222	8,790
Singapore	18,191	19,187	16,247	17,816
Taiwan	35,204	40,514	19,131	24,380
Thailand	14,330	16,389	4,985	6,643
UK	39,237	43,459	38,407	41,579
Venezuela	11,335	18,649	5,354	5,552

COMMUNICATIONS

Roads. On 31 Dec. 1999 the total public road mileage was 3,917,240 miles (urban, 846,059; rural, 3,071,181). Of the urban roads, 111,000 were state controlled and 740,000 under local control. 663,000 miles of rural roads were controlled by the states, about 2,299,000 miles of rural roads were under local control, and, in 1996, there were about 169,000 miles of federal park and forest roads. State highway funds were $83,675m. in 1999.

Motor vehicles registered in 1999: 216,309,000, of which 132,432,000 automobiles, 83,148,000 trucks and 729,000 buses. There were 187,170,000 licensed drivers in 1999 and 4,111,000 motorcycle registrations. The average distance travelled by a passenger car in the year 1999 was 11,900 miles. There were 41,717 deaths in road accidents in 1999.

Rail. Freight service is provided by 12 major independent railroad companies and several hundred smaller operators. Long-distance passenger trains are run by the National Railroad Passenger Corporation (Amtrak), which is federally assisted. Amtrak was set up in 1971 to maintain a basic network of long-distance passenger trains, and is responsible for almost all non-commuter services over some 38,000 route-km, of which it owns only 1,256 km (555 km electrified). Outside the major conurbations, there are almost no regular passenger services other than those of Amtrak, which carried 21,544,000 passengers in 1999. Passenger revenue for Amtrak (1999) was $1,067·8m.; revenue passenger miles, 5,289m.

Civil Aviation. The busiest airport in 2001 was Atlanta (Hartsfield International), which handled 37,181,068 passenger enplanements (34,382,731 on domestic flights). The second busiest was Chicago (O'Hare) with 31,529,561 passenger enplanements (27,519,219 on domestic flights), followed by Los Angeles International, with 29,365,436 passenger enplanements (22,134,944 on domestic flights). As well as being the three busiest airports in the USA for passenger traffic in 2001, they are also the three busiest in the world. New York (John F. Kennedy) was the busiest airport in the USA for international passenger enplanements in 2001, with 7,610,411, ahead of Los Angeles International, with 7,230,492. The leading domestic routes for 2000 were Los Angeles to/from New York (3,583,680 passengers), New York to/from Orlando (3,063,930) and Chicago to/from New York (3,057,540).

The leading airports in 2001 on the basis of aircraft departures completed were Chicago, O'Hare (463,948); Atlanta, Hartsfield International (449,450); Dallas/Fort Worth (417,874).

There were 35 airports with more than 100,000 international enplanements in 2001. These were, in descending order: New York (John F. Kennedy); Los Angeles; Miami; Chicago (O'Hare); New York (Newark); San Francisco; Atlanta (Hartsfield); Houston (George Bush); Honolulu; Dallas/Fort Worth; Washington, D.C. (Dulles International); Boston; Guam; Detroit (Metropolitan-Wayne County); Philadelphia; San Juan (Luis Muñoz Marin International); Orlando International; Seattle; Minneapolis/St Paul; Orlando (Sanford); New York (La Guardia); Fort Lauderdale (Hollywood International); Saipan; Phoenix; Denver; Las Vegas (McCarran); Charlotte; Baltimore; Cincinnati (Northern Kentucky International); Pittsburgh; San Jose; St Louis (Lambert); San Diego (Lindbergh Field); Tampa; Memphis.

In 2001 Delta Air Lines carried the most passengers of any airline in the world with 90,520,588 (around 4% on international flights), ahead of Southwest Airlines, with 73,742,202 (all on domestic flights) and American Airlines, with 69,881,469 (around 10% on international flights). American Airlines carried the most international passengers of any US carrier, ahead of United Airlines. American Airlines also flew the furthest of any carrier in the world in 1999, covering 1,550·1m. km (963·2m. miles), ahead of United Airlines, with 1,477·9m. km (918·3m. miles). In Dec. 2002 United Airlines filed for bankruptcy following a record loss of $2·1bn. in 2001 and reported losses of approximately $1·7bn. for the first nine months of 2002.

In 2001 US flag carriers in scheduled service enplaned 621m. revenue passengers (665m. in 2000).

Shipping. In Oct. 2001 the cargo-carrying US flag fleet consisted of 31,387 vessels, of which 3,835 were of 1,000 GRT and over (2,148 liquid carriers, 760 dry bulk carriers, 126 containerships and 801 other freighters). Of 27,552 vessels of less than 1,000 GRT, 1,767 were liquid carriers, 21,705 dry bulk carriers, 4 containerships and 4,076 other freighters. Shipping capacity in Oct. 2001 was 72,816,000 GRT, of which the vessels of 1,000 GRT and over totalled 31,877,000 GRT while those of less than 1,000 GRT totalled 40,939,000 GRT. On 1 Jan. 2002 the US merchant marine included 443 ocean-going self-propelled merchant vessels of 1,000 gross tons or over, with an aggregate 15·0m. DWT. This included 130 tankers of 7·5m. DWT.

In 1999 vessels totalling 440,341,000 NRT entered, and 302,344,000 NRT cleared, all US ports.

Telecommunications. Regional private companies formed from the American Telephone and Telegraph Co. after its dissolution in 1995 ('Baby Bells') operate the telephone, telegraph, telex and electronic transmission services system at the national and local levels. In 2000 main telephone lines numbered 192,518,800 (or 699·7 per 1,000 persons). There were 100·7m. mobile phone subscribers by the end of 2000, with the largest operators being Verizon and Cingular (ranked 3rd and 5th in the world, with 27·5m. and 19·7m. subscribers respectively). There were 161m. PCs in 2000 (585·2 for every 1,000 persons—the highest rate in the world) and in 1997 there were 21m. fax machines. The number of Internet users in April 2002 was estimated to be 165·75m., or 59·1% of the population (among the highest percentages in the world).

Legislation on the media and telecommunications of 1996 coming into force on 31 March 1999 aimed at deregulating the market while preserving safeguards against over-concentration of individual ownership: a single company may not control a network reaching more than 35% of TV viewers, or produce a newspaper and a television service in the same market. Local companies are now permitted to operate long-distance telephone services and also cable TV services.

Postal Services. The US Postal Service superseded the Post Office Department on 1 July 1971.

Postal business for the years ended in Sept. included the following items:

	1997	1998	1999	2000
Number of post offices, stations and branches	38,019	38,159	38,169	38,060
Operating revenue ($1m.)	58,331	60,116	62,755	64,581
Operating expenditures ($1m.)	54,873	57,786	60,642	62,992

SOCIAL INSTITUTIONS

Justice. Legal controversies may be decided in two systems of courts: the federal courts, with jurisdiction confined to certain matters enumerated in Article III of the Constitution, and the state courts, with jurisdiction in all other proceedings. The federal courts have jurisdiction exclusive of the state courts in criminal prosecutions for the violation of federal statutes, in civil cases involving the government, in bankruptcy cases and in admiralty proceedings, and have jurisdiction concurrent with the state courts over suits between parties from different states, and certain suits involving questions of federal law.

The highest court is the Supreme Court of the US, which reviews cases from the lower federal courts and certain cases originating in state courts involving questions of federal law. It is the final arbiter of all questions involving federal statutes and the Constitution; and it has the power to invalidate any federal or state law or executive action which it finds repugnant to the Constitution. This court, consisting of nine justices appointed by the President who receive salaries of $184,400 a year (the Chief Justice, $192,600), meets from Oct. until June every year. For the term ended June 2000 it disposed of 8,445 cases, deciding 81 on their merits. In the remainder of cases it either summarily affirms lower court decisions or declines to review. A few suits, usually brought by state governments, originate in the Supreme Court, but issues of fact are mostly referred to a master.

The US courts of appeals number 13 (in 11 circuits composed of three or more states and one circuit for the District of Columbia and one Court of Appeals for the Federal Circuit); the 179 circuit judges receive salaries of $159,100 a year. Any party to a suit in a lower federal court usually has a right of appeal to one of these courts. In addition, there are direct appeals to these courts from many federal administrative agencies. In the year ending 30 June 1997, 53,742 appeals were filed in the courts of appeals, including 1,417 in the Federal Circuit.

The trial courts in the federal system are the US district courts, of which there are 89 in the 50 states, one in the District of Columbia and one each in the Commonwealth of Puerto Rico and the Territories of the Virgin Islands, Guam and the Northern Marianas. Each state has at least one US district court, and three states have four apiece. Each district court has from one to 28 judgeships. There are 649 US district judges ($150,000 a year), who received 261,162 civil cases from 1 July 1997 to 30 June 1998.

In addition to these courts of general jurisdiction, there are special federal courts of limited jurisdiction. The US Court of Federal Claims (16 judges at $150,000 a year) decides claims for money damages against the federal government in a wide variety of matters; the Court of International Trade (9 judges at $150,000) determines controversies concerning the classification and valuation of imported merchandise.

The judges of all these courts are appointed by the President with the approval of the Senate; to assure their independence, they hold office during good behaviour and cannot have their salaries reduced. This does not apply to judges in the Territories, who hold their offices for a term of ten years or to judges of the US Court of Federal Claims. The judges may retire with full pay at the age of 70 years if they have served a period of ten years, or at 65 if they have 15 years of service, but they are subject to call for such judicial duties as they are willing to undertake.

In 1998–99, of the 251,511 civil cases filed in the district courts, 159,205 arose under various federal statutes (such as labour, social security, tax, patent, securities, antitrust and civil rights laws); 39,785 involved personal injury or property damage claims; 46,721 dealt with contracts; and 5,787 were actions concerning real property.

In 2000 the number of lawyers in the USA passed the 1m. mark, equivalent to 363 per 100,000 people.

Among the 66,055 offenders convicted in 1999 in the district courts, 24,275 persons were charged with alleged infractions of drug laws, 17,097 with public order offences, 12,712 with property offences and 2,781 with violent offences. All other people convicted were charged with miscellaneous general offences.

Persons convicted of federal crimes may be fined, released on probation under the supervision of the probation officers of the federal courts, confined in prison, or confined in prison with a period of supervised release to follow, also under the supervision of probation officers of the federal courts. Federal prisoners are confined in 87 institutions incorporating various security levels that are operated by the Bureau of Prisons. On 31 Dec. 2001 the total number of prisoners under the jurisdiction of Federal or State adult correctional authorities was 1,406,031. A record 1,962,220 inmates were held in Federal or State prisons or local jails at the end of 2001, giving a rate of 686 per 100,000 population.

The state courts have jurisdiction over all civil and criminal cases arising under state laws, but decisions of the state courts of last resort as to the validity of treaties or of laws of the USA, or on other questions arising under the Constitution, are subject to review by the Supreme Court of the US. The state court systems are generally similar to the federal system, to the extent that they generally have a number of trial courts and intermediate appellate courts, and a single court of last resort. The highest court in each state is usually called the Supreme Court or Court of Appeals with a Chief Justice and Associate Justices, usually elected but sometimes appointed by the Governor with the advice and consent of the State Senate or other advisory body; they usually hold office for a term of years, but in some instances for life or during good behaviour. The lowest tribunals are usually those of Justices of the Peace; many towns and cities have municipal and police courts, with power to commit for trial in criminal matters and to determine misdemeanours for violation of the municipal ordinances.

There were no executions from 1968 to 1976. The US Supreme Court had held the death penalty, as applied in general criminal statutes, to contravene the eighth and fourteenth amendments of the US constitution, as a cruel and unusual punishment when used so irregularly and rarely as to destroy its deterrent value. The death penalty was reinstated by the Supreme Court in 1976, but has not been authorized in Alaska, the District of Columbia, Hawaii, Iowa, Kansas, Maine, Massachusetts, Michigan, Minnesota, North Dakota, Rhode Island, Vermont, West Virginia and Wisconsin. There were, in Oct. 2002, 3,697 (including 53 women) prisoners under sentence of death. In 2002 there were 71 executions (66 in 2001 but only 14 in 1991). From 1976–2002 there were 820 executions of which 289 were in Texas and 87 in Virginia. The execution of young offenders under the age of 18 is still permitted and carried out in some states. For the first time since 1963, there were two executions under federal jurisdiction in 2001.

There were 15,517 murders in 2000, the lowest total since 1969. The murder rate in 2000 was 5·5 per 100,000 persons, down from 10·2 per 100,000 in 1980. 67·8% of all murders in 1997 were carried out with guns (53·3% of which were handguns).

Religion. *The Yearbook of American and Canadian Churches*, published by the National Council of the Churches of Christ in the USA, New York, gave the following figures available from official statisticians of church bodies: the principal religions (numerically or historically) or groups of religious bodies (in 1999 unless otherwise stated) are shown below:

Protestant Churches	No. of churches	Membership (in 1,000)
Baptist bodies		
Southern Baptist Convention (1998)	40,870	15,729
National Baptist Convention, USA (1992)	33,000	8,200
National Baptist Convention of America, Inc. (1987)	2,500	3,500
American Baptist Churches in the USA	5,755	1,454
American Baptist Association (1998)	1,760	275

Protestant Churches	No. of churches	Membership (in 1,000)
Baptist bodies (cont.)		
Conservative Baptist Association of America (1998)	1,200	200
Free Will Baptists (1998)	2,297	210
Baptist Missionary Association of America	1,334	235
Christian Church (Disciples of Christ)	3,765	831
Christian Churches and Churches of Christ (1998)	5,579	1,072
Church of the Nazarene (1998)	5,101	627
Churches of Christ	15,000	1,500
Progressive National Baptist Convention, Inc. (1995)	2,000	2,500
The Episcopal Church (1998)	7,390	2,318
Jehovah's Witnesses	11,064	1,040
Latter-day Saints		
Church of Jesus Christ of Latter-day Saints (Mormons) (2001)	11,731	5,210
Reorganized Church of Jesus Christ of Latter-day Saints	1,236	137
Lutheran bodies		
Evangelical Lutheran Church in America	10,851	5,150
The Lutheran Church–Missouri Synod	6,220	2,582
Wisconsin Evangelical Lutheran Synod (1997)	1,239	723
Mennonite churches		
Mennonite Church	935	92
Old Order Amish (1993)	898	81
Methodist bodies		
United Methodist Church	35,609	8,378
African Methodist Episcopal Church	6,200	2,500
African Methodist Episcopal Zion Church	3,125	1,277
Wesleyan Church (USA)	1,594	121
Pentecostal bodies		
The Church of God in Christ (1991)	15,300	5,500
Assemblies of God	12,055	2,575
Church of God (Cleveland, Tenn.)	6,328	870
Pentecostal Assemblies of the World, Inc. (1998)	1,750	1,500
Presbyterian bodies		
Presbyterian Church (USA)	11,216	3,561
Presbyterian Church in America	1,206	299
Reformed Churches		
Reformed Church in America	901	293
Christian Reformed Church in North America	732	198
The Salvation Army	1,410	473
United Church of Christ	5,961	1,402
Seventh-day Adventist Church	4,421	862
Roman Catholic Church[1]	19,627	62,391
Orthodox Churches		
Greek Orthodox Archdiocese of America	523	1,955
Orthodox Church in America	710	1,000
Oriental Orthodox Churches		
Armenian Apostolic Church of America	36	360
Armenian Apostolic Church, Diocese of America (1991)	72	414
Coptic Orthodox Church (1992)	85	180
Non-Christian Religions (1990)		
Hindus	—	227
Islam	—	527
Jews	—	6,041
Buddhist	—	401

[1]In Feb. 2001 there were 13 Cardinals.

Education. The adult literacy rate is at least 99%.

Elementary and secondary education is mainly a state responsibility. Each state and the District of Columbia has a system of free public schools, established by law, with courses covering 12 years plus kindergarten. There are three structural patterns in common use; the K8-4 plan, meaning kindergarten plus eight elementary grades followed by four high school grades; the K6-3-3 plan, or kindergarten plus six elementary grades followed by a three-year junior high school and a three-year senior high school; and the K5-3-4 plan, kindergarten plus five elementary grades followed by a three-year middle school and a four-year high school. All plans lead to high-school graduation, usually at age 17 or 18. Vocational education is an integral part of secondary education. Many states also have two-year colleges in which education is provided at a nominal cost. Each state has delegated a large degree of control of the educational programme to local school districts (numbering 14,891 in school year 1998–99), each with a board of education (usually three to nine members) selected locally and serving mostly without pay. The school policies of the local school districts must be in accord with the laws and the regulations of their state Departments of Education. While regulations differ from one jurisdiction to another, in general it may be said that school attendance is compulsory from age 7 to 16.

'Charter schools' are legal entities outside the school boards administration. They retain the basics of public school education, but may offer unconventional curricula and hours of attendance. Founders may be parents, teachers, public bodies or commercial firms. Organization and conditions depend upon individual states' legislation. The first charter schools were set up in Minnesota in 1991. By Sept. 1999, 1,484 charter schools were operating in 31 states and Washington, D.C.

In 1940 a new category was established—the 'functionally illiterate', meaning those who had completed fewer than five years of elementary schooling; for persons 25 years of age or over this percentage was 1·6 in March 1999 (for the Black population it was 1·9%); it was 0·6% for white and 0·4% for Blacks in the 25–29-year-old group. It was reported in March 1999 that 83·4% of all persons 25 years old and over had completed four years of high school or more, and that 25·2% had completed a bachelor's degree or more. In the age group 25 to 29, 87·8% had completed four years of high school or more, and 28·2% had completed a bachelor's degree or more. However, according to a report published in 2001 nearly a third of American fourth graders (aged 9–10) are unable to read.

In the autumn of 1998, 14,549,000 students (8,582,000 full-time and 8,163,000 women) were enrolled in 3,913 colleges and universities; 2,218,000 were first-time students. 36·6% of the population between the ages of 18 and 24 were enrolled in colleges and universities. It is projected that in 2010 the student population will number 17,490,000.

Public elementary and secondary school revenue is supplied from the county and other local sources (44·8% in 1997–98), state sources (48·4%) and federal sources (6·8%). In 1998–99 expenditure for public elementary and secondary education totalled about $349,200m., including $303,500m. for current operating expenses, $37,700m. for capital outlay and $8,000m. for interest on school debt. The current expenditure per pupil in average daily attendance was about $6,900. The total cost per pupil, also including capital outlay and interest, amounted to about $7,960.

In 1998–99 total expenditure on education came to about 7·1% of GDP. Estimated total expenditures for private elementary and secondary schools in 1998–99 were about $27,700m. In 1998–99 college and university spending totalled about $246,300m., of which about $152,400m. was spent by institutions under public control. The federal government contributed about 12% of total current-fund revenue; state governments, 23%; student tuition and fees, 28%; and all other sources, 37%.

Vocational education below college grade, including the training of teachers to conduct such education, has been federally aided since 1918. Federal support for vocational education in 1998–99 amounted to about $1,128m. Many public high schools offer vocational courses in addition to their usual academic programmes.

Summary of statistics of regular schools (public and private), teachers and pupils for 1998–99 (compiled by the US National Center for Education Statistics):

Schools by level	Number of schools[1]	Teachers (in 1,000)	Enrolment (in 1,000)
Elementary schools:			
Public	67,344	1,701	30,542
Private	24,915[2]	277[3]	4,597[3]
Secondary schools:			
Public	25,873	1,125	15,993
Private	10,779[2]	114[3]	1,327[3]

Schools by level	Number of schools[1]	Teachers (in 1,000)	Enrolment (in 1,000)
Higher education:			
Public	1,688	693[3]	11,176
Private	2,382	301[3]	3,373
Total	132,981	4,211	67,008

[1]Schools with both elementary and secondary grades are counted twice, once with the elementary and once with the secondary schools.
[2]Data from 1997–98.
[3]Estimated.

In the autumn of 1998 there were 18·0 pupils per teacher in public elementary schools in the USA and 14·2 pupils per teacher in public secondary schools.

Most of the private elementary and secondary schools are affiliated with religious denominations. In 1998–99 there were 6,990 Roman Catholic elementary schools with 1,876,000 pupils and 105,900 teachers, and 1,227 secondary schools with 620,000 pupils and 47,100 teachers.

During the school year 1998–99 high-school graduates numbered about 2,740,000 (of whom about 2,456,000 were from public schools). Institutions of higher education conferred about 1,184,000 bachelor's degrees during the year 1998–99, 559,000 associate's degrees; 430,000 master's degrees; 46,000 doctorates; and 78,600 first professional degrees. In 1998–99 the US Department of Education provided $11,685m. in grants, loans, work-study programmes and other financial assistance to post-secondary students. Other agencies of the Federal Government provided about $2,945m. in additional assistance.

During the academic year 1999–2000, 515,000 foreign students were enrolled in American colleges and universities. The countries with the largest numbers of students in American colleges were: China, 54,500; Japan, 46,900; India, 42,300; South Korea, 41,200; Taiwan, 29,200; Canada, 23,500.

In 1998–99, 130,000 US students were enrolled at colleges and universities abroad. The country attracting the most students from the USA was the United Kingdom, with 27,700.

School enrolment, Oct. 1999, embraced 96·0% of the children who were 5 and 6 years old; 98·7% of the children aged 7–13 years; 98·2% of those aged 14–15, 93·6% of those aged 16–17 and 60·6% of those aged 18–19.

The US National Center for Education Statistics estimates the total enrolment in the autumn of 2000 at all of the country's elementary, secondary and higher educational institutions (public and private) at 68·1m. (67·6m. in the autumn of 1999).

The number of teachers in regular public and private elementary and secondary schools in the autumn of 2000 was expected to increase slightly to about 3,250,000. The average annual salary of public school teachers was $40,600 in 1998–99.

A survey for the 1999 *World Competitiveness Yearbook* showed that well-educated people in the USA are the least likely of any country in the world to emigrate.

Health. Admission to the practice of medicine (for both doctors of medicine and doctors of osteopathic medicine) is controlled in each state by examining boards directly representing the profession and acting with authority conferred by state law. Although there are a number of variations, the usual time now required to complete training is eight years beyond the secondary school with up to three or more years of additional graduate training. Certification as a specialist may require between three and five more years of graduate training plus experience in practice. In Jan. 1999 the estimated number of active physicians (MD and DO—in all forms of practice) in the USA, Puerto Rico and outlying US areas was 756,700 (684,400 in 1994 and 552,700 in 1985).

Dental employment in 1998 numbered 202,000.

Number of hospitals listed by the American Hospital Association in 1999 was 5,890, with 994,000 beds (equivalent to 3·6 beds per 1,000 population). Of the total, 264 hospitals with 55,000 beds were operated by the federal government; 1,197 with 136,000 beds by state and local government; 3,012 with 587,000 beds by non-profit organizations (including church groups); 747 with 107,000 beds were investor-owned. The categories of non-federal hospitals were (1999): 4,956 short-term general and special hospitals with 830,000 beds; 129 non-federal long-term general and special hospitals with 20,000 beds; 516 psychiatric hospitals with 87,000 beds; 4 tuberculosis hospitals with fewer than 500 beds.

Patient admissions to community hospitals (1999) was 32,359,000; average daily census was 525,500. There were 495·3m. outpatient visits.

Personal health-care costs projected for 1999 totalled $998,200m., distributed as follows: hospital care, $383,200m.; doctors, $221,400m.; nursing-home care, $87,300m.; drugs, $106,100m.; dentists, $53,700m.; medical durables, $14,300m.; home health care, $33,200m.; other personal health care, $32,400m. Total national health expenditure in 1998 (projected) amounted to $1,146·8bn. In 2000 the USA spent 13·0% of its GDP on health—over 2% more than any other leading industrialized nation. Public spending on health amounted to 44·3% of total health spending in 2000 (the lowest percentage of any major industrialized nation). A survey published by the World Health Organization in June 2000 to measure health systems in all of the sovereign countries and find which country has the best overall health care ranked the USA in 37th place.

In 1999, 22·7% of Americans (24·2% of males and 20·9% of females) were smokers, down from a peak of over 40% in 1964. By 1999, 26% of the population were considered obese (having a body mass index over 30), compared to 14·5% in the late 1970s.

Welfare. Social welfare legislation was chiefly the province of the various states until the adoption of the Social Security Act of 14 Aug. 1935. This as amended provides for a federal system of old-age, survivors and disability insurance; health insurance for the aged and disabled; supplemental security income for the aged, blind and disabled; federal state unemployment insurance; and federal grants to states for public assistance (medical assistance for the aged and aid to families with dependent children generally and for maternal and child health and child welfare services).

Legislation of Aug. 1996 began the transfer of aid administration back to the states, restricted the provision of aid to a maximum period of five years, and abolished benefits to immigrants (both legal and illegal) for the first five years of their residence in the USA. The Social Security Administration (formerly part of the Department of Health and Human Services but an independent agency since March 1995) has responsibility for a number of programmes covering retirement, disability, Medicare, Supplemental Security Income and survivors. The Administration for Children and Families (ACF), an agency of the Department of Health and Human Services, is responsible for federal programmes which promote the economic and social wellbeing of families, children, individuals and communities. ACF has federal responsibility for the following programmes: Temporary Assistance for Needy Families; low income energy assistance; Head Start; child care; child protective services; and a community services block grant. The ACF also has federal responsibility for social service programmes for children, youth, native Americans and persons with developmental disabilities.

The Administration on Aging (AoA), an agency in the US Department of Health and Human Services, is one of the nation's largest providers of home- and community-based care for older persons and their caregivers. Created in 1965 with the passage of the Older Americans Act (OAA), AoA is part of a federal, state, tribal and local partnership called the National Network on Aging. It serves about 7m. older persons and their caregivers, and consists of 56 State Units on Aging, 655 Area Agencies on Aging, 236 Tribal and Native organizations, 2 organizations that serve Native Hawaiians, 29,000 service providers and thousands of volunteers. These organizations provide assistance and services to older individuals and their families in urban, suburban, and rural areas throughout the USA.

The Health Care Financing Administration, an agency of the Health and Human Services Department, has federal responsibility for health insurance for the aged and disabled. Unemployment insurance is the responsibility of the Department of Labor.

In 1999 an average of 2,512,000 families (6,722 recipients) were receiving payments under Temporary Assistance for Needy Families. Total payments under

Temporary Assistance for Needy Families were $22,585m. in 1999. The role of Child Support Enforcement is to ensure that children are supported by their parents. Money collected is for children who live with only one parent because of divorce, separation or out-of-wedlock birth. In 1999 approximately $15,843m. was collected on behalf of these children.

The Social Security Act provides for protection against the cost of medical care through Medicare, a two-part programme of health insurance for people age 65 and over, people of any age with permanent kidney failure, and for certain disabled people under age 65 who receive Social Security disability benefits. In 2000 payments totalling $130,284m. were made under the hospital portion of Medicare. During the same period, $88,991m. was paid under the voluntary medical insurance portion of Medicare. A total of 29·6m. people received Medicare payments in 1998.

In 2000 about 44·3m. beneficiaries were on the rolls; the average paid to a retired worker (not counting any benefits paid to his/her dependants) in 2000 was $845 per month. Full retirement benefits are now payable at age 65, with reduced benefits available as early as age 62. Beginning in 2000, the age for full retirement benefits will gradually increase until it reaches 67 in 2027. In 1995 the average actual retirement age for males was 63.

Medicaid is a jointly-funded, Federal-State health insurance programme for certain low-income and needy people. It covers 36m. individuals including children, the aged, blind, and/or disabled, and people who are eligible to receive federally-assisted income maintenance payments.

In Dec. 1999, 6·56m. persons were receiving Supplementary Security Income payments. 1,308,000 old-age persons received $4,725m. in benefits; 79,000 blind people received $391m.; and 5,169,000 disabled people received $25,772m. Payments, including supplemental amounts from various states, totalled $30,959m. in 1999.

In 1998 a total of $391,733m. was spent on cash and non-cash benefits (such as food stamps) for persons with limited incomes. In 2000 the food stamp programme helped 17,163,000 persons at a cost of $14,985m.; and 27,200,000 persons received help from the national school lunch programme at a cost of $5,489m.

CULTURE

Broadcasting. The licensing agency for broadcasting stations is the Federal Communications Commission, an independent federal body composed of five Commissioners appointed by the President. Its regulatory activities comprise: allocation of spectrum space; consideration of applications to operate individual stations; and regulation of their operations. In 1996 there were 12,313 commercial radio stations, 1,174 commercial TV stations, 352 non-commercial TV stations and 11,119 cable TV systems. Programming is targeted to appeal to a given segment of the population or audience taste. There are five national TV networks (three commercial; colour by NTSC) with 46 national cable networks. All major cities have network affiliates and additional commercial stations.

Legislation on the media and telecommunications of 1996 came into force on 31 March 1999 deregulating the market while preserving safeguards against over-concentration of individual ownership: a single company may not control a network reaching more than 35% of TV viewers, or produce a newspaper and a television service in the same market. Local companies are now permitted to operate long-distance telephone services and also cable TV services.

Broadcasting to countries abroad is conducted by The Voice of America, which functions under a seven-member council nominated by the President and reviewed by Congress. Voice of America has an annual audience of 94m. and broadcasts in over 50 languages.

In 1997 there were 575m. radio receivers in use, equivalent to 2,116 per 1,000 inhabitants. No other country averaged more than 1,500 radios per 1,000. There were 219m. TV receivers in use in 1997, equivalent to 806 per 1,000 inhabitants (a rate exceeded only in Bermuda). In 1999 there were 66·7m. cable TV subscribers.

Cinema. In Jan. 1994 there were 25,737 screens, including 850 drive-ins; gross box office receipts came to US$5·25bn. 628 full-length films were made in 1999. An estimated 66% of adults went to the cinema in 1997.

UNITED STATES OF AMERICA

Press. In 2000 there were 1,480 daily newspapers with a combined daily circulation of 55·8m., the second highest in the world behind Japan. There were 766 morning papers and 727 evening papers, plus 917 Sunday papers (circulation, 59·4m.). Unlike Japan, where circulation is rising, in the USA it has fallen since 1985, when daily circulation was 62·8m. The most widely read newspapers are *USA Today* (average daily circulation in March 2001 of 1·85m.), followed by the *Wall Street Journal* (1·82m.) and the *New York Times* (1·16m.).

Books published in 1998 totalled 120,244, of which 14,645 were sociology and economics, 11,016 fiction, 9,195 juvenile and 9,103 technology.

Tourism. In 1999 the USA received 48,491,000 visitors, of whom 14,110,000 were from Canada and 9,915,000 from Mexico. 23% of all tourists were from Europe. Only France and Spain received more tourists than the USA in 1999.

In 1999 visitors to the USA spent approximately $74,448m. (excluding transportation paid to US international carriers). The USA has the highest annual revenue from tourists of any country (more than twice as much as Spain, which received the second most in 1999). Expenditure by US travellers in foreign countries for 1999 was an estimated $59,331m. (excluding transportation paid to foreign flag international carriers).

Festivals. There are major opera festivals at Glimmerglass, New York (July–Aug.), Santa Fe, New Mexico (June–Aug.) and Seattle, Washington (Aug.). Among the many famous film festivals are the Sundance Film Festival in Jan. and the New York Film Festival in late Sept./early Oct.

Museums and Galleries. Among the most famous museums are the National Gallery in Washington, D.C., the Museum of Fine Arts in Boston, the Metropolitan Museum, the Guggenheim Museum, and the Museum of Modern Art, all in New York, and the Museum of Art in Philadelphia. In 1997, 35% of US adults visited an art museum at least once.

DIPLOMATIC REPRESENTATIVES

Of the USA in the United Kingdom (24 Grosvenor Sq., London, W1A 1AE)
Ambassador: William S. Farish.

Of the United Kingdom in the USA (3100 Massachusetts Ave., NW, Washington, D.C., 20008)
Ambassador: Sir David Manning.

Of the United States to the United Nations
Ambassador: John Negroponte.

Of the United States to the European Union
Ambassador: Rockwell A. Schnabel.

FURTHER READING

OFFICIAL STATISTICAL INFORMATION

The Office of Management and Budget, Washington, D.C., 20503 is part of the Executive Office of the President; it is responsible for co-ordinating all the statistical work of the different Federal government agencies. The Office does not collect or publish data itself. The main statistical agencies are as follows:

(1) Data User Services Division, Bureau of the Census, Department of Commerce, Washington, D.C., 20233. Responsible for decennial censuses of population and housing, quinquennial census of agriculture, manufactures and business; current statistics on population and the labour force, manufacturing activity and commodity production, trade and services, foreign trade, state and local government finances and operations. (*Statistical Abstract of the United States*, annual, and others).

(2) Bureau of Labor Statistics, Department of Labor, 441 G Street NW, Washington, D.C., 20212. (*Monthly Labor Review* and others).

(3) Information Division, Economic Research Service, Department of Agriculture, Washington, D.C., 20250. (*Agricultural Statistics*, annual, and others).

(4) National Center for Health Statistics, Department of Health and Human Services, 3700 East-West Highway, Hyattsville, MD 20782. (*Vital Statistics of the United States*, monthly and annual, and others).

UNITED STATES OF AMERICA

(5) Bureau of Mines Office of Technical Information, Department of the Interior, Washington, D.C., 20241. (*Minerals Yearbook*, annual, and others).

(6) Office of Energy Information Services, Energy Information Administration, Department of Energy, Washington, D.C., 20461.

(7) Statistical Publications, Department of Commerce, Room 5062 Main Commerce, 14th St and Constitution Avenue NW, Washington, D.C., 20230; the Department's Bureau of Economic Analysis and its Office of Industry and Trade Information are the main collectors of data.

(8) Center for Education Statistics, Department of Education, 555 New Jersey Avenue NW, Washington, D.C., 20208.

(9) Public Correspondence Division, Office of the Assistant Secretary of Defense (Public Affairs P.C.), The Pentagon, Washington, D.C., 20301-1400.

(10) Bureau of Justice Statistics, Department of Justice, 633 Indiana Avenue NW, Washington, D.C., 20531.

(11) Public Inquiry, APA 200, Federal Aviation Administration, Department of Transportation, 800 Independence Avenue SW, Washington, D.C., 20591.

(12) Office of Public Affairs, Federal Highway Administration, Department of Transportation, 400 7th St. SW, Washington, D.C., 20590.

(13) Statistics Division, Internal Revenue Service, Department of the Treasury, 1201 E St. NW, Washington, D.C., 20224.

Statistics on the economy are also published by the Division of Research and Statistics, Federal Reserve Board, Washington, D.C., 20551; the Congressional Joint Committee on the Economy, Capitol; the Office of the Secretary, Department of the Treasury, 1500 Pennsylvania Avenue NW, Washington, D.C., 20220.

OTHER OFFICIAL PUBLICATIONS

Economic Report of the President. Annual. Bureau of the Census. *Statistical Abstract of the United States.* Annual. *Historical Statistics of the United States, Colonial Times to 1970.*
United States Government Manual. Washington. Annual.
The official publications of the USA are issued by the US Government Printing Office and are distributed by the Superintendent of Documents, who issued in 1940 a cumulative *Catalogue of Public Documents of the Congress and of All Departments of the Government of the United States.* This *Catalog* is kept up to date by *United States Government Publications, Monthly Catalog* with annual index and supplemented by *Price Lists.* Each *Price List* is devoted to a special subject or type of material.
Treaties and other International Acts of the United States of America (Edited by Hunter Miller), 8 vols. Washington, 1929–48. This edition stops in 1863. It may be supplemented by *Treaties, Conventions, International Acts, Protocols and Agreements Between the US and Other Powers, 1776–1937* (Edited by William M. Malloy and others). 4 vols. 1909–38. A new Treaty Series, *US Treaties and Other International Agreements,* was started in 1950.
Writings on American History. Washington, annual from 1902 (except 1904–5 and 1941–47).

NON-OFFICIAL PUBLICATIONS

The Cambridge Economic History of the United States. vol. 1. CUP, 1996; vol. 2. CUP, 2000; vol. 3. CUP, 2000

Bacevich, Andrew J., *American Empire: The Realities and Consequences of US Diplomacy.* Harvard Univ. Press, 2002

Brogan, H., *The Longman History of the United States of America.* 2nd ed. Longman, London and New York, 1999

Fawcett, E. and Thomas, T., *America and the Americans.* London, 1983

Foner, E. and Garraty, J. A. (eds.) *The Reader's Companion to American History.* New York, 1992

Haass, Richard, *The Reluctant Sheriff: The United States After the Cold War.* New York, 1998

Herstein, S. R. and Robbins, N., *United States of America.* [Bibliography] ABC-Clio, Oxford and Santa Barbara (CA), 1982

Jennings, F., *The Creation of America.* CUP, 2000

Jentleson, B. W. and Paterson, T. G. (eds.) *Encyclopedia of US Foreign Relations.* 4 vols. OUP, 1997

Lord, C. L. and E. H., *Historical Atlas of the US.* Rev. ed. New York, 1969

Merriam, L. A. and Oberly, J. (eds.) *United States History: an Annotated Bibliography.* Manchester Univ. Press, 1995

Morison, S. E. with Commager, H. S., *The Growth of the American Republic.* 2 vols. 5th ed. OUP, 1962–63

Norton, M. B., *People and Nation: the History of the United States.* 4th ed. 2 vols. New York, 1994

Pfucha, F. P., *Handbook for Research in American History: a Guide to Bibliographies and Other Reference Works.* 2nd ed. Nebraska Univ. Press, 1994

Zunz, Oliver, *Why the American Century?* Univ. of Chicago Press, 1999

Who's Who in America. Annual

National library: The Library of Congress, Independence Ave. SE, Washington, D.C., 20540. *Librarian:* James H. Billington.

National statistical office: Bureau of the Census, Washington, D.C., 20233.

Website: http://www.census.gov

STATES AND TERRITORIES

GENERAL DETAILS

Against the names of the Governors, Lieut.-Governors and the Secretaries of State, (D.) stands for Democrat and (R.) for Republican.

Figures for the revenues, expenditures and debt outstanding of the various states are those of the Federal Bureau of the Census, which takes the original state figures and arranges them on a common pattern so that those of one state can be compared with those of any other.

See also Local Government on page 1763.

FURTHER READING

Official publications of the various states and insular possessions are listed in the *Monthly Check-List of State Publications,* issued by the Library of Congress since 1910.

The Book of the States. Biennial. Council of State Governments, Lexington, 1953 ff.

State Government Finances. Annual. Dept. of Commerce, 1966 ff.

Bureau of the Census. *State and Metropolitan Area Data Book.* Irregular.—*County and City Data Book.* Irregular.

Hill, K. Q., *Democracy in the 50 States.* Nebraska Univ. Press, 1995

ALABAMA

KEY HISTORICAL EVENTS

The early European explorers were Spanish, but the first permanent European settlement was French, as part of French Louisiana after 1699. During the 17th and 18th centuries the British, Spanish and French all fought for control of the territory; it passed to Britain in 1763 and thence to the USA in 1783, except for a Spanish enclave on Mobile Bay, which lasted until 1813. Alabama was organized as a Territory in 1817 and was admitted to the Union as a state on 14 Dec. 1819.

The economy was then based on cotton, grown in white-owned plantations by black slave labour imported since 1719. Alabama seceded from the Union at the beginning of the Civil War (1861) and joined the Confederate States of America; its capital Montgomery became the Confederate capital. After the defeat of the Confederacy the state was re-admitted to the Union in 1878. Attempts made during the reconstruction period to find a role for the newly freed black slaves—who made up about 50% of the population—largely failed, and when whites regained political control in the 1870s a strict policy of segregation came into force. At the same time Birmingham began to develop as an important centre of iron- and steel-making. Most of the state was still rural. In 1915 a boll-weevil epidemic attacked the cotton and forced diversification into other farm produce. More industries developed from the power schemes of the Tennessee Valley Authority in the 1930s. The black population remained mainly rural, poor and without political power, until the 1960s when confrontations on the issue of civil rights produced reforms.

TERRITORY AND POPULATION

Alabama is bounded in the north by Tennessee, east by Georgia, south by Florida and the Gulf of Mexico and west by Mississippi. Land area, 50,744 sq. miles (131,426 sq. km). Census population, 1 April 2000, 4,447,100 (55·4% urban), an increase of 10·1% since 1990; July 2002 estimate, 4,486,508.

Population in five census years was:

	White	Black	Indian	Asiatic	Total	Per sq. mile
1930	1,700,844	944,834	465	105	2,646,248	51·3
			All others			
1970	2,533,831	903,467	6,867		3,444,165	66·7
1980	2,872,621	996,335	24,932		3,893,888	74·9
1990	2,975,797	1,020,705	44,085		4,040,587	79·6
2000	3,162,808	1,155,930	128,362		4,447,100	87·6

Of the total population in 2000, 2,300,596 were female, 3,323,678 were 18 years old or older and 2,462,673 were urban. In 2000 the Hispanic population was 75,830, up from 24,629 in 1990 (an increase of 207·9%).

The large cities (2000 census) were: Birmingham, 242,820 (metropolitan area, 921,106); Montgomery (the capital), 201,568 (333,055); Mobile, 198,905 (540,258); Huntsville, 158,216 (342,376); Tuscaloosa, 77,906 (164,875).

SOCIAL STATISTICS

Births, 2000, 63,166 (14·2 per 1,000 population); deaths, 44,967 (10·1); infant deaths (under 1 year), 594 (9·4 per 1,000 live births); marriages, 47,087 (10·6); divorces, 24,630 (5·5).

CLIMATE

Birmingham, Jan. 46°F (7·8°C), July 80°F (26·7°C). Annual rainfall 54" (1,372 mm). Mobile, Jan. 52°F (11·1°C), July 82°F (27·8°C). Annual rainfall 62" (1,575 mm). Montgomery, Jan. 49°F (9·4°C), July 81°F (27·2°C). Annual rainfall 52" (1,321 mm). The growing season ranges from 190 days (north) to 270 days (south). Alabama belongs to the Gulf Coast climate zone (see UNITED STATES: Climate).

CONSTITUTION AND GOVERNMENT

The present constitution dates from 1901; it has had 708 amendments (as at Nov. 2001). The legislature consists of a Senate of 35 members and a House of Representatives of 105 members, all elected for four years. The Governor and Lieut.-Governor are elected for four years.

For the 108th Congress, which convened in Jan. 2003, Alabama sends seven members to the House of Representatives. It is represented in the Senate by Richard Shelby (D. 1987–94; R. 1994–2005) and Jeff Sessions (R. 1997–2009).

Applicants for registration must take an oath of allegiance to the United States and fill out an application showing evidence that they meet State voter registration requirements.

Montgomery is the capital.

RECENT ELECTIONS

In the 2000 presidential election Bush polled 941,173 votes; Gore, 692,611; Nader, 18,323.

CURRENT ADMINISTRATION

Governor: Bob Riley (R.), 2003–07 (salary: $81,151).
  Lieut.-Governor: Lucy Baxley (D.), 2003–07 ($48,620).
  Secretary of State: Nancy Worley (D.), 2003–07 ($70,000).

Government Website: http://www.alabama.gov

ECONOMY

Per capita income (2000) was $23,460.

Budget. In 1999 total state revenue was $15,502m. Total expenditure was $14,702m. (education, $5,752m.; public welfare, $3,195m.; health and hospitals, $1,616m.; highways, $922m.; police protection, $114m.). Outstanding debt, in 1999, $4,467m.

Performance. Gross State Product was $119,921m. in 2000.

ENERGY AND NATURAL RESOURCES

Oil and Gas. In 1997 Alabama produced 15m. bbls. of crude petroleum.

Water. The total area covered by water is approximately 1,486 sq. miles.

Minerals. Principal minerals, 1999–2000 (in net 1,000 tons): limestone, 41,766; coal, 20,317; sand and gravel, 7,846. Value of non-fuel mineral production (1999) was $1,080m.

Agriculture. The number of farms in 2000 was some 47,000, covering 9·0m. acres; the average farm had 210 acres and was valued at $1,262 per acre in 1995.

Cash receipts from farm marketings, 2000: crops, $588m.; livestock and poultry products, $2,684m.; total, $3,272m. Principal sources: broilers, cattle and calves, eggs, hogs, dairy products, greenhouses and nurseries, peanuts, soybeans, cotton and vegetables. In 2000 broilers accounted for the largest percentage of cash receipts from farm marketings; cattle and calves were second, eggs third, cotton fourth.

Forestry. Area of national forest lands, 1999, 665,000 acres. Area of commercial timberland, 1990, 21,931,600 acres, of which 1,161,700 acres were public forests and 20,769,900 acres private forests. Harvest volumes in 1995, 294·12m. cu. ft softwood saw timber, 78·63m. cu. ft hardwood saw timber, 744·47m. cu. ft paper fibre and 11·74m. cu. ft poles. Total harvest, 1994, was 1,128·9m. cu. ft. The estimated delivered timber value of forest products in 1994 was $1,359m.

INDUSTRY

Alabama is both an industrial and service-oriented state. The chief industries are lumber and wood products, food and kindred products, textiles and apparel, non-electrical machinery, transportation equipment and primary metals.

Labour. In 2002, 1,895,200 were employed in non-agricultural sectors, of whom 481,800 were in services; 434,700 in trade; 353,500 in government; 328,800 in manufacturing; 104,300 in construction; 92,600 in transport and public utilities. In 2002 the total labour force numbered 2,153,300, of whom 5·6% (121,700) were unemployed. A seasonally adjusted calculation for Dec. 2002 numbered the labour force at 2,165,300, with 116,800 (5·4%) unemployed. Average weekly earnings were $547·69 in Dec. 2002.

COMMUNICATIONS

Roads. Total road length in 2000 was 94,311 miles, including 73,639 miles of rural road and 20,672 miles of urban road. Registered motor vehicles, 2000, 3,960,149.

Rail. At Sept. 1997 the railways had a length of 5,072 miles including side and yard tracks.

Civil Aviation. In 1997 the state had 98 public-use airports. Eight airports are for commercial service, three are relief airports for Birmingham and the rest general aviation. There were 2,433,432 passenger enplanements in 1999.

Shipping. There are 1,600 miles of navigable inland water and 50 miles of Gulf Coast. The only deep-water port is Mobile, with a large ocean-going trade; total tonnage (1997), 36·3m. tons. The Alabama State Docks also operates a system of ten inland docks; there are several privately run inland docks.

SOCIAL INSTITUTIONS

Justice. In 2000 there were 371 law enforcement agencies and five state agencies employing 10,270 sworn and 5,009 civilian people. There were 191,141 offences reported in 2000 of which 19% were cleared by arrest. Total property value stolen in 2000 was $210,382,447 of which 16% was recovered. In total, for past and present felony and misdemeanour crimes, there were 27,512 people arrested for Part I offences, 173,981 for Part II offences, 14,890 for drug violations and 32,435 for alcohol violations. There were 314 homicides in 2000. As of 30 Sept. 2001 there were 26,728 people in prison or community-based facilities of which 186 were on death row awaiting execution. There were also 36,120 people on probation and/or parole. Following the reinstatement of the death penalty by the US Supreme Court in 1976 death sentences have been awarded since 1983. There were two executions in 2002 but none in 2001.

In 41 counties the sale of alcoholic beverage is permitted, and in 26 counties it is prohibited; but it is permitted in 8 cities within those 26 counties. Draught beverages are permitted in 22 counties.

Religion. Membership in selected religious bodies (in 1993): Southern Baptist Convention (1,049,441), Black Baptist (estimated 315,331), United Methodist Church (264,968), African Methodist Episcopal Zion Church (134,305), Roman Catholic (137,834 adherents), Churches of Christ (91,660), Assemblies of God (38,442).

Education. In the school year 1996–97 the 1,333 public elementary and high schools required 44,942 teachers to teach 717,284 students enrolled in grades K-12. In 1995–96 there were 16 public senior institutions with 127,465 students and 4,887 faculty members. As of autumn 1998–99 the 19 community colleges had 73,432 students and 4,811 faculty members; 2 public junior colleges had 3,465 students and 257 faculty members; 9 public technical colleges had 8,686 students and 652 faculty members.

Health. In 1999 there were 109 community hospitals with 16,300 beds. A total of 670,000 patients were admitted during the year.

Welfare. Medicare enrolment in July 2001 totalled 695,195. In Dec. 2000 there were 825,773 Old-Age, Survivors, and Disability Insurance (OASDI) beneficiaries. A total of 55,168 people were receiving payments under Temporary Assistance for Needy Families (TANF) in June 2000.

CULTURE

Tourism. In 2001 tourists spent approximately $6·1bn. in Alabama, representing an increase of 1% over 2000 spending.

FURTHER READING
Alabama Official and Statistical Register. Montgomery. Quadrennial
Alabama County Data Book. Alabama Dept. of Economic and Community Affairs. Annual
Directory of Health Care Facilities. Alabama State Board of Health
Economic Abstract of Alabama. Center for Business and Economic Research, Univ. of Alabama, 2000

ALASKA

KEY HISTORICAL EVENTS
Discovered in 1741 by Vitus Bering, Alaska's first settlement, on Kodiak Island, was in 1784. The area known as Russian America with its capital (1806) at Sitka was ruled by a Russo-American fur company and vaguely claimed as a Russian colony. Alaska was purchased by the United States from Russia under the treaty of 30 March 1867 for $7·2m. Settlement was boosted by gold workers in the 1880s. In 1884 Alaska became a 'district' governed by the code of the state of Oregon. By Act of Congress approved 24 Aug. 1912 Alaska became an incorporated Territory; its first legislature in 1913 granted votes to women, seven years in advance of the Constitutional Amendment.

During the Second World War the Federal government acquired large areas for defence purposes and for the construction of the strategic Alaska Highway. In the 1950s oil was found. Alaska became the 49th state of the Union on 3 Jan. 1959. In the 1970s new oilfields were discovered and the Trans-Alaska pipeline was opened in 1977. The state obtained most of its income from petroleum by 1985.

Questions of land-use predominate; there are large areas with valuable mineral resources, other large areas held for the native peoples and some still held by the Federal government. The population increased by over 400% between 1940 and 1980.

TERRITORY AND POPULATION
Alaska is bounded north by the Beaufort Sea, west and south by the Pacific and
east by Canada. The total area is 663,267 sq. miles (1,717,854 sq. km), making it
the largest state of the USA; 571,951 sq. miles (1,481,346 sq. km) are land and
91,316 sq. miles (236,507 sq. km) are water. It is also the least densely populated
state. Census population, 1 April 2000, was 626,932, an increase of 14·0% over
1990; July 2002 estimate, 643,786.

Population in five census years was:

	White	Black	All Others	Total	Per sq. mile
1950	92,808	. . .	35,835	128,643	0·23
1970	236,767	8,911	54,704	300,382	0·53
1980	309,728	13,643	78,480	401,851	1·00
1990	415,492	22,451	112,100	550,043	1·00
2000	434,534	21,787	170,611	626,932	1·10

Of the total population in 2000, 324,1212 were male, 436,215 were 18 years old
or older and 411,257 were urban. Alaska's Hispanic population was 24,795 in 2000,
up from 17,803 in 1990.

The largest county equivalent and city is in the borough of Anchorage, which had
a 2000 census population of 260,283. Census populations of the other 14 county
equivalents, 2000: Fairbanks North Star, 82,840; Matanuska-Susitna 59,322; Kenai
Peninsula, 49,691; Juneau, 30,711; Bethel, 16,006; Ketchikan Gateway, 14,070;
Kodiak Island, 13,913; Valdez-Cordova, 10,195; Nome, 9,196; Sitka, 8,835; North
Slope, 7,385; Northwest Arctic, 7,208; Wade Hampton, 7,028; Wrangell-Petersburg,
6,684. Largest incorporate places in 2000 were: Anchorage, 260,683; Juneau,
30,711; Fairbanks, 30,224; Sitka, 8,335; Ketchikan, 7,922; Kenai, 6,942; Kodiak,
6,334; Bethel, 5,471; Wassila, 5,469; Barrow, 4,581.

SOCIAL STATISTICS
Births, 1999, 9,913 (16 per 1,000 population); deaths, 2,614 (4·2). 1998: infant
mortality rate, 5·9 per 1,000 live births; marriages, 5,900; divorces, 3,200.

CLIMATE
Anchorage, Jan. 12°F (−11·1°C), July 57°F (13·9°C). Annual rainfall 15" (371 mm).
Fairbanks, Jan. −11°F (−23·9°C), July 60°F (15·6°C). Annual rainfall 12" (300 mm).
Sitka, Jan. 33°F (0·6°C), July 55°F (12·8°C). Annual rainfall 87" (2,175 mm). Alaska
belongs to the Pacific Coast climate zone (see UNITED STATES: Climate).

CONSTITUTION AND GOVERNMENT
The state has the right to select 103·55m. acres of vacant and unappropriated public
lands in order to establish 'a tax basis'; it can open these lands to prospectors for
minerals, and the state is to derive the principal advantage in all gains resulting
from the discovery of minerals. In addition, certain federally administered lands
reserved for conservation of fisheries and wild life have been transferred to the state.
Special provision is made for federal control of land for defence in areas of high
strategic importance.

The constitution of Alaska was adopted by public vote, 24 April 1956. The state
legislature consists of a Senate of 20 members (elected for four years) and a House
of Representatives of 40 members (elected for two years).

For the 108th Congress, which convened in Jan. 2003, Alaska sends one member
to the House of Representatives. It is represented in the Senate by Ted Stevens (R.
1968–2009) and Lisa Murkowski (R. 2002–05). The franchise may be exercised by
all citizens over 18.

The capital is Juneau.

RECENT ELECTIONS
In the 2000 presidential election Bush polled 167,398 votes; Gore, 79,004; Nader,
28,747.

CURRENT ADMINISTRATION
Governor: Frank Murkowski (R.), 2003–07 (salary: $85,779).
   Lieut.-Governor: Loren Leman (R.), 2003–07 ($80,043).

Government Website: http://www.state.ak.us

ECONOMY

Per capita personal income (2000) was $29,597.

Budget. In 1999 total state revenue was $7,313m. Total expenditure was $6,141m. (education, $1,325m.; public welfare, $790m.; highways, $578m.; health and hospitals, $182m.; police protection, $61m.). Outstanding debt, in 1999, $3,911m.

Performance. 2000 Gross State Product was $27,747m.

ENERGY AND NATURAL RESOURCES

Oil and Gas. Alaska ranks second behind Texas among the leading oil producers in the USA, with 18% of the national total. Commercial production of crude petroleum began in 1959 and by 1961 had become the most important mineral by value. Production: 1997, 473m. bbls. (of US gallons). Proven reserves at 31 Dec. 1997 were 5,161m. bbls. Oil comes mainly from Prudhoe Bay, the Kuparuk River field and several Cook Inlet fields. Revenue to the state from petroleum in 1993 was $2,684·8m. (87% of general fund revenues). General fund unrestricted revenues, 1993: severance taxes, 33%; oil and gas royalties, 25%; investment earnings, 2%; other oil and gas, 27%; non-petroleum, 13%. In 1996, 9,294bn. cu. ft of natural gas was produced. Natural gas (liquid) production, 1997, 35m. bbls. Proven reserves as at 31 Dec. 1997, 631m. bbls.

Oil from the Prudhoe Bay Arctic field is now carried by the Trans-Alaska pipeline to Prince William Sound on the south coast, where a tanker terminal has been built at Valdez.

Water. The total area covered by water is approximately 44,856 sq. miles.

Minerals. Estimated value of production, 1994, in $1,000: gold, 70,291; silver, 10,391; lead, 25,513; zinc, 296,103; industrial minerals (including sand, gravel and building stone), 68,009; coal, 36,750; peat, 439·5. Total 1994 value, $507·5m. Value of non-fuel mineral production (1997), $827m.

Agriculture. In some parts of the state the climate during the brief spring and summer (about 100 days in major areas and 152 days in the southeastern coastal area) is suitable for agricultural operations, thanks to the long hours of sunlight, but Alaska is a food-importing area. In 2000 there were 580 farms covering a total of 920,000 acres. The average farm had 1,586 acres in 2000.

Total value of agricultural products in 1994: $27,766,000 of which $2,828,000 was from feed crops, $2,738,000 from vegetables (including potatoes), $6·1m. from livestock and poultry, $2,465,000 from dairy products and $15,833,000 from greenhouse and nursery industries. Net income from farms in 1996 was $10m.

At 1 Jan. 1995 there were 9,900 cattle and calves and 1,700 sheep and lambs; at 1 Dec. 1994, 2,000 hogs and pigs and 2,000 poultry. There were about 33,000 reindeer in western Alaska in 1994. Sales of reindeer meat and by-products in 1994 were valued at $1,366,000.

Forestry. Of the 129m. forested acres of Alaska, 24m. acres are classified as timberland or commercial forest. The interior forest covers 115m. acres; more than 13m. acres are considered commercial forest, of which 3·4m. acres are in designated parks or wilderness and unavailable for harvest. The coastal rain forests provide the bulk of commercial timber volume; of their 13·6m. acres, 7·6m. acres support commercial stands, of which 1·9m. acres are in parks or wilderness and unavailable for harvest. In 1992, 590m. bd ft of timber were harvested from private land for a total value of $548·9m., and in 1993, 9·38m. bd ft from state land for $342·6m.

There are 624 designated wilderness areas throughout the USA, covering a total of 104m. acres (42m. ha). Nearly 56% of the system is in Alaska (58·18m acres or 23·54m. ha).

Fisheries. The catch for 1993 was 2·7m. lb of fish and shellfish having a value to fishermen of $905m. The most important species are salmon, crab, herring, halibut and pollock.

INDUSTRY

The largest manufacturing sectors are wood processing, seafood products and printing and publishing.

Labour. Total non-agricultural employment, 1999, 278,000. Employees by branch, 1999: government, 74,000; services, 71,000; wholesale and retail trade, 57,000. With a rate of 6·4%, Alaska had among the highest unemployment rates in the USA in 1999.

COMMUNICATIONS

Roads. Alaska's highway and road system, 2000, totalled 12,823 miles. Registered motor vehicles, 2000, 594,399.

The Alaska Highway extends 1,523 miles from Dawson Creek, British Columbia, to Fairbanks, Alaska. It was built by the US Army in 1942, at a cost of $138m. The greater portion of it, because it lies in Canada, is maintained by Canada.

Rail. There is a railway of 111 miles from Skagway to the town of Whitehorse, the White Pass and Yukon route, in the Canadian Yukon region (this service operates seasonally). The government-owned Alaska Railroad runs from Seward to Fairbanks, a distance of 471 miles. This is a freight service with only occasional passenger use. A passenger service operates from Anchorage to Fairbanks via Denali National Park in the tourist season.

Civil Aviation. Alaska's largest international airports are Anchorage and Fairbanks. In 1999 Alaska Airlines flew 209·2m. km, carrying 13,604,000 passengers (1,530,300 on international flights). There were 2,710,848 passenger enplanements statewide in 1999. General aviation aircraft in the state per 1,000 population is about 10 times the US average.

Shipping. Regular shipping services to and from the USA are furnished by two steamship and several barge lines operating out of Seattle and other Pacific coast ports. A Canadian company also furnishes a regular service from Vancouver, BC. Anchorage is the main port.

A 1,435 nautical-mile ferry system for motor cars and passengers (the 'Alaska Marine Highway') operates from Bellingham, Washington and Prince Rupert (British Columbia) to Juneau, Haines (for access to the Alaska Highway) and Skagway. A second system extends throughout the south-central region of Alaska linking the Cook Inlet area with Kodiak Island and Prince William Sound.

SOCIAL INSTITUTIONS

Justice. The death penalty was abolished in Alaska in 1957. In June 2000 the prison population totalled 4,025.

Religion. Many religions are represented, including the Russian Orthodox, Roman Catholic, Episcopalian, Presbyterian, Methodist and other denominations.

Education. Total expenditure on public schools in fiscal year 1994 was $896,307,252. In 1994 there were 7,195 teachers; average salary, fiscal year 1994, $46,263. In 1994 there were 121,396 pupils enrolled at public schools. The University of Alaska (founded in 1922) main campuses had (autumn 1993) 33,087 students. Other colleges had 2,718 students in autumn 1993.

Health. In 1993 there were 27 acute care hospitals with 1,892 beds, of which 7 were federal public health hospitals and 1 mental hospital. Many hospitals offer mental health services and most communities have mental health services and/or centres.

Welfare. Old-age assistance was established under the Federal Social Security Act; in 1993 aid to dependent children covered a monthly average of 11,300 households; payments, an average of $834 per month; aid to the disabled was given to a monthly average of 4,698 persons receiving on average $348 per month. An average of 3,666 aged per month received $351.

CULTURE

Tourism. About 1·05m. tourists visited the state in 1993.

FURTHER READING

Statistical Information: Department of Commerce and Economic Development, Economic Analysis Section, POB 110804, Juneau 99811. Publishes *The Alaska Economy Performance Report.*

Alaska Industry–Occupation Outlook to 1995. Department of Labor, Juneau.
Annual Financial Report. Department of Administration, Juneau.
Falk, Marvin W., *Alaska.* [Bibliography] ABC-Clio, Oxford and Santa Barbara (CA), 1995
Naske, C.-M. and Slotnick, H. E., *Alaska: a History of the 49th State.* 2nd ed. Univ. of Oklahoma Press, 1995

State library: POB 110571, Juneau, Alaska 99811-0571.

ARIZONA

KEY HISTORICAL EVENTS

Spaniards looking for sources of gold or silver entered Arizona in the 16th century, finding there people from several Native American groups, including Tohono O'odham, Navajo, Hopi and Apache. The first Spanish Catholic mission was founded in the early 1690s by Father Eusebio Kino, settlements were made in 1752 and a Spanish army headquarters was set up at Tucson in 1776. The area was governed by Mexico after the collapse of Spanish colonial power. Mexico ceded it to the USA in the Treaty of Guadelupe Hidalgo after the Mexican-American war (1848). Arizona was then part of New Mexico; the Gadsden Purchase (of land south of the Gila River) was added to it in 1853. The whole was organized as the Arizona Territory on 24 Feb. 1863.

Miners and ranchers began settling in the 1850s. Conflicts between Indian and immigrant populations intensified when troops were withdrawn to serve in the Civil War. The Navajo surrendered in 1865, but the Apache continued to fight, under Geronimo and other leaders, until 1886. Arizona was admitted to the Union as the 48th state in 1912.

Large areas of the state have been retained as Indian reservations and as parks to protect the exceptional desert and mountain landscape. In recent years this landscape and the Indian traditions have been used to attract tourist income.

TERRITORY AND POPULATION

Arizona is bounded north by Utah, east by New Mexico, south by Mexico, west by California and Nevada. Land area, 113,634 sq. miles (294,313 sq. km). Of the total area in 1992, 28% was Indian Reservation, 17% was in individual or corporate ownership, 19% was held by the US Bureau of Land Management, 15% by the US Forest Service, 13% by the State and 8% by others. Census population on 1 April 2000 was 5,130,632, an increase of 40·0% over 1990. July 2002 estimate, 5,456,453. The rate of Arizona's population increase during the 1990s was the second fastest in the USA, at 40%. Nevada is the only state to have had faster growth.

Population in six census years:

	White	Black	American Indian	Chinese	Japanese	Total	Per sq. mile
1910	171,468	2,009	29,201	1,305	371	204,354	1·8
1930	378,551	10,749	43,726	1,110	879	435,573	3·8
1960	1,169,517	43,403	83,387	2,937	1,501	1,302,161	11·3
					All others		
1980	2,260,288	74,159	162,854		383,768	2,718,215	23·9
1990	2,963,186	110,524	203,527		387,991	3,665,228	32·3
2000	3,873,611	158,873	255,879		842,269	5,130,632	45·2

Of the total population in 2000, 2,561,057 were female, 3,763,685 were 18 years old or older and 4,523,535 were urban. Arizona's Hispanic population was 1,295,617 in 2000 (25·3%) up from 739,861 in 1990 (an increase of 88·2%).

In 2000 the population of Phoenix was 1,321,045; Tucson, 486,699; Mesa, 396,375; Glendale, 218,812; Scottsdale, 202,705; Chandler, 176,581; Tempe, 158,625; Gilbert, 109,697; Peoria, 108,364; Yuma, 77,515. The Phoenix–Mesa metropolitan area had a 2000 census population of 3,251,876.

SOCIAL STATISTICS

In 2000: births, 84,985 (16·6 per 1,000); deaths, 40,202 (7·8 per 1,000); infant deaths, 568; marriages, 40,630; dissolutions of marriages, 23,440.

CLIMATE
Phoenix, Jan. 53·6°F (12°C), July 93·5°F (34°C). Annual rainfall 7·66" (194 mm). Yuma, Jan. 56·5°F (13·6°C), July 93·7°F (34·3°C). Annual rainfall 3·17" (80 mm). Flagstaff, Jan. 28·7°F (−1·8°C), July 66·3°F (19·1°C). Annual rainfall 22·8" (579 mm). Arizona belongs to the Mountain States climate zone (*see* UNITED STATES: Climate).

CONSTITUTION AND GOVERNMENT
The state constitution (1911, with 129 amendments) placed the government under direct control of the people through the initiative, referendum and the recall provisions. The state Senate consists of 30 members, and the House of Representatives consists of 60, all elected for two years.

For the 108th Congress, which convened in Jan. 2003, Arizona sends eight members to the House of Representatives. It is represented in the Senate by John McCain (R. 1987–2005) and Jon Kyl (R. 1995–2007).

The state capital is Phoenix. The state is divided into 15 counties.

RECENT ELECTIONS
In the 2000 presidential election Bush polled 781,652 votes; Gore, 685,341; Nader, 45,645.

CURRENT ADMINISTRATION
Governor: Janet Napolitano (D.), 2003–07 (salary: $95,000).
  Secretary of State: Janice K. Brewer (R.), 2003–07 ($70,000).

Government Website: http://www.az.gov

ECONOMY
Per capita income in 2000 was $24,991.

Budget. In 1999 total state revenue was $15,122m. Total expenditure was $14,278m. (education, $1,736m.; public welfare, $2,461m.; highways, $1,630m.; health and hospitals, $804m.; police protection, $151m.). Outstanding debt, in 1999, $2,725m.

Performance. Gross State Product was $156,303m. in 2000.

ENERGY AND NATURAL RESOURCES
Primary energy sources are coal (43%), nuclear (41%) and hydropower (13%).

Electricity. As of 1998, 34 power generating plants were located in Arizona, 14 in Maricopa County. The plants are operated by eight public power entities.

Oil and Gas. In 2000 oil production totalled 57,483 bbls. from 21 producing wells. Gas totalled 368m. cu. ft. from nine producing wells.

Water. The total area covered by water is approximately 364 sq. miles.

Minerals. The mining industry historically has been and continues to be a significant part of the economy. By value the most important mineral produced is copper. Production in 1999 was 1,213,000 tons. Most of the state's silver and gold are recovered from copper ore. Other minerals include sand and gravel, molybdenum, coal and gemstones. Total value of minerals mined in 1999 was $2,790m.

Agriculture. Arizona, despite its dry climate, is well suited for agriculture along the water-courses and where irrigation is practised on a large scale from great reservoirs constructed by the USA as well as by the state government and private interests. Irrigated area in 1997 was 1,014,000 acres. The wide pasture lands are favourable for the rearing of cattle and sheep, but numbers are either stationary or declining compared with 1920.

In 2000 Arizona contained 7,500 farms and ranches and the total farm and pastoral area was 26·7m. acres; there were 1,344,091 acres of crop land. In 2000 the average farm was estimated at 3,560 acres. Farming is highly commercialized and mechanized and concentrated largely on cotton picked by machines.

Area under cotton in 2000: upland cotton, 280,000 acres (791,000 bales harvested); American Pima cotton, 5,000 acres (7,200 bales harvested).

In 2000 the cash income from crops was $1,228m., and from livestock and products $1,063m. Most important cereals are wheat, corn and barley; most important crops include cotton, citrus fruit, lettuce, broccoli, grapes, cauliflower, melons, onions, potatoes and carrots. In 2001 there were 850,000 cattle, 132,000 sheep, 90,000 hogs, 34,000 goats.

Forestry. The national forests in the state had an area of 11,255,000 acres in 2000.

INDUSTRY

Labour. In the first quarter of 2001 (preliminary data) the state had 117,318 employers with an average of 2,258,199 employees earning an average quarterly wage of $8,260.

COMMUNICATIONS

Roads. In 2001 there were 55,195 miles of public roads and streets, 67·8% in rural areas and 32·2% in urban areas. There were 4,664,838 registered vehicles.

Civil Aviation. In 2001 there were 6,194 registered aircraft and 318 landing facilities of which 218 were airports (including 87 for public use) and 100 were heliports. There were 17,878,581 passenger enplanements statewide in 1999.

SOCIAL INSTITUTIONS

Justice. A 'right-to-work' amendment to the constitution, adopted 5 Nov. 1946, makes illegal any concessions to trade-union demands for a 'closed shop'.

At 30 Sept. 2001 the Arizona state prison held 25,374 male and 2,077 female prisoners. Chain gangs were reintroduced into prisons in 1995. The minimum age for the death penalty is 16. There were three executions in 2000 but none in 2001 or 2002.

Religion. The leading religious bodies are Roman Catholics and Latter-day Saints (Mormons); others include United Methodists, Presbyterians, Baptists, Lutherans, Episcopalians, Eastern Orthodox, Jews and Muslims.

Education. School attendance is compulsory between the ages of 6 and 16. In 1999–2000, K-12 enrolment numbered 835,404 students. There are 222 school districts containing 1,024 elementary schools and 195 high schools. Charter schools first opened their doors in 1995. There are 261 charter schools providing parents and students with expanded educational choices. In 1999–2000 the total funds appropriated by the state legislature for all education, including the Board of Regents and community colleges, was $3,304,468,400. The state maintains three universities: the University of Arizona (Tucson) with an enrolment of 35,000 in 2001; Arizona State University (three campuses) with 50,000; Northern Arizona University (Flagstaff) with 19,728.

Health. In 2001 there were 78 hospitals; capacity 10,798 beds; 15,258 licensed physicians; 3,062 dentists; 47,213 registered nurses and 9,237 licensed practical nurses.

Welfare. Old-age assistance (maximum depending on the programme) is given to needy citizens 65 years of age or older through the federal supplemental security income (SSI) programme. In Dec. 2000 SSI payments went to 13,196 aged, and 68,297 disabled and blind (average of $387·11 each.). In Sept. 2001, 100,618 individuals received Cash Assistance for an average $110·03 each. Cash Assistance cases numbering 39,059 received an average of $283·45 each.

CULTURE

Tourism. In 1999 Arizona had 28m. visitors and 368,045 tourism-related jobs. The state's tourism industry generates about $30bn. in economic activity each year.

Museums and Galleries. There are many museums and galleries within the state including the Arizona Historical Society, Arizona State Capitol Museum, Arizona State Museum, Grand Canyon National Park Visitor Center and the Phoenix Art Museum.

FURTHER READING

Statistical information: College of Business and Public Administration, Univ. of Arizona, Tucson 85721. Publishes *Arizona Statistical Abstract.*

Alexander, David V., *Arizona Frontier Military Place Names: 1846–1912.* Las Cruces, NM, 1998

Arizona Commission of Indian Affairs. *Resource Directory, 1997/98.* Phoenix, 1998

Arizona Department of Commerce. *Community Profiles.* Phoenix, 1999

Arizona Department of Health Services, Center for Health Statistics. *Arizona Health Status and Vital Statistics, 1998.* Phoenix, 2000

Arizona Historical Society. *1999/2000 Official Directory, Arizona Historical Museums and Related Support Organizations.* Tucson, 1999

August, Jack L., *Vision in the Desert: Carl Hayden and the Hydropolitics in the American Southwest.* Texas Christian Univ. Press, Fort Worth, 1999

Leavengood, Betty, *Lives Shaped by Landscape: Grand Canyon Women.* Pruett Co., Boulder, 1999

Office of the Secretary of State. *Arizona Blue Book, 1997–98.* 1998

Shillingberg, William B., *Tombstone, A. T.: A History of Early Mining, Milling and Mayhem.* Arthur H. Clark Co., Spokane, 1999

State Government Website: http://www.state.az.us

Arizona State Library, Archives & Public Records (ASLAPR) Website: http://www.lib.az.us

ARKANSAS

KEY HISTORICAL EVENTS

In the 16th and 17th centuries French and Spanish explorers entered Arkansas, finding there tribes of Chaddo, Osage and Quapaw. The first European settlement was French, at Arkansas Post in 1686, and the area became part of French Louisiana. The USA bought Arkansas from France as part of the Louisiana Purchase in 1803, it was organized as a Territory in 1819 and entered the Union on 15 June 1836 as the 25th state.

The eastern plains by the Mississippi were settled by white plantation-owners who grew cotton with black slave labour. The rest of the state attracted a scattered population of small farmers. The plantations were the centre of political power. Arkansas seceded from the Union in 1861 and joined the Confederate States of America. At that time the slave population was about 25% of the total.

In 1868 the state was re-admitted to the Union. Attempts to integrate the black population into state life achieved little, and a policy of segregation was rigidly adhered to until the 1950s. In 1957 federal authorities ordered that high school segregation must end. The state governor called on the state militia to prevent desegregation; there was rioting, and federal troops entered Little Rock, the capital, to restore order. It was another ten years before school segregation finally ended.

The main industrial development followed the discovery of large reserves of bauxite.

TERRITORY AND POPULATION

Arkansas is bounded north by Missouri, east by Tennessee and Mississippi, south by Louisiana, southwest by Texas and west by Oklahoma. Land area, 52,068 sq. miles (134,855 sq. km). Census population on 1 April 2000 was 2,673,400, an increase of 13·7% from that of 1990. July 2002 estimate, 2,710,079.

Population in five census years was:

	White	Black	Indian	Asiatic	Total	Per sq. mile
1910	1,131,026	442,891	460	472	1,574,449	30·0
1960	1,395,703	388,787	580	1,202	1,786,272	34·0
			All others			
1980	1,890,332	373,768		22,335	2,286,435	43·9
1990	1,944,744	373,912		32,069	2,350,725	45·1
2000	2,138,598	418,950		115,852	2,673,400	51·3

Of the total population in 2000, 1,368,707 were female, 1,993,031 were 18 years old or older and 1,404,179 were urban. In 2000 the Hispanic population of Arkansas was 86,866, up from 19,876 in 1990. The increase of 337% was the second largest increase in the USA over the same period.

Little Rock (capital) had a population of 183,183 in 2000; Fort Smith, 80,268; North Little Rock, 60,433; Fayetteville, 58,047; Jonesboro, 55,515; Pine Bluff, 55,085; Springdale, 45,798; Conway, 43,167. The population of the largest metropolitan statistical areas in 2000 was: Little Rock–North Little Rock, 583,845; Fayetteville–Springdale–Rogers, 311,121; Fort Smith, 207,290; Texarkana, 129,749; Pine Bluff, 84,278.

SOCIAL STATISTICS

Births, 1999, were 36,882 (14·5 per 1,000); deaths, 27,454 (10·8 per 1,000); (1996) infant mortality rate (per 1,000 live births), 9·3. Marriages (1997), 35,200; divorces 14,000.

CLIMATE

Little Rock, Jan. 39·9°F, July 84°F. Annual rainfall 52·4". Arkansas belongs to the Gulf Coast climate zone (see UNITED STATES: Climate).

CONSTITUTION AND GOVERNMENT

The General Assembly consists of a Senate of 35 members elected for four years, partially renewed every two years, and a House of Representatives of 100 members elected for two years. The sessions are biennial and usually limited to 60 days. The Governor and Lieut.-Governor are elected for four years.

For the 108th Congress, which convened in Jan. 2003, Arkansas sends four members to the House of Representatives. It is represented in the Senate by Blanche Lincoln (D. 1999–2005) and Mark Pryor (D. 2003–09).

The state is divided into 75 counties; the capital is Little Rock.

RECENT ELECTIONS

In the 2000 presidential election Bush polled 472,940 votes; Gore, 422,768; Nader, 13,421.

CURRENT ADMINISTRATION

Governor: Mike Huckabee (R.), 2003–07 (salary: $75,296).
 Lieut.-Governor: Winthrop Rockefeller (R.), 2003–07 ($36,392).
 Secretary of State: Charlie Daniels (D.), 2003–07 ($47,060).

Government Website: http://www.state.ar.us

ECONOMY

Per capita personal income (2000) was $21,945.

Budget. In 1999 total revenue was $10,361m. Total expenditure was $8,943m. (education, $3,667m.; public welfare, $1,895m.; highways, $699m.; health and hospitals, $691m.; police protection, $67m.). Outstanding debt (1999) was $2,448m.

Performance. 2000 Gross State Product was $67,724m.

Banking and Finance. In 1993–94 total bank deposits were $22,107·8m.

ENERGY AND NATURAL RESOURCES

Oil and Gas. Arkansas is the second largest oil producer in the USA after Texas. 1998 production of crude oil was 429m. bbls.; natural gas, 467bn. cu. ft.

Water. The total area covered by water is approximately 1,107 sq. miles.

Minerals. The U.S. Bureau of Mines estimated Arkansas' mineral value in 1992 at $287m. Mining employment totalled 3,600 in Oct. 1992. Crushed stone was the leading mineral commodity produced, in terms of value, followed by bromine. Value of domestic non-fuel mineral production in 1997 was $535m.

Agriculture. In 2000, 48,000 farms had a total area of 14·6m. acres; average farm was 304 acres. 8·2m. acres were harvested cropland (1993). Arkansas ranked first in the production of broilers in 1993 (1,050m. birds) and in the acreage and production of rice (40% of US total production) and third in turkeys (25m. birds). Total farm income, 1996, $5,887m.

Forestry. The national forests had a total area of 3,495,232 acres in 1997.

INDUSTRY

In 1996 total employment averaged 1,234,000 (including 254,000 manufacturing, 247,000 wholesale and retail trade, 179,000 government). The Arkansas Department of Labor estimated that 196,700 factory production workers earned an average $370·77 per week (41·8 hours). In the manufacturing group, food and kindred products employed 52,400, electric and electronic equipment 20,500, and lumber and wood products 21,500. In Aug. 1994 estimated employment was 1,153,700, including 1,025,300 non-agricultural waged and salaried jobs.

Labour. Total non-agricultural employment, 1999, 1,142,000. Employees by branch, 1999 (in 1,000): services, 271; wholesale and retail trade, 262; manufacturing, 253; government, 188.

COMMUNICATIONS

Roads. Total road mileage (2000), 97,600 miles—urban, 10,627; rural, 86,973. In 2000 there were 1,840,193 registered motor vehicles.

Rail. In 1991 there were in the state 3,169 miles of commercial railway. In 1994 rail service was provided by 4 Class I and 23 short-line railways.

Civil Aviation. In Oct. 1994, seven air carriers and two commuter airlines served the state; there were 175 airports (96 public-use and 79 private). There were 1,654,734 passenger enplanements statewide in 1999.

Shipping. There are about 1,000 miles of navigable rivers, including the Mississippi, Arkansas, Red, White and Ouachita Rivers. The Arkansas River/Kerr-McClellan Channel flows diagonally eastward across the state and gives access to the sea via the Mississippi River.

SOCIAL INSTITUTIONS

Justice. In June 2000 there were 11,509 federal and state prisoners. In 1996, 524,000 violent crimes were committed and a total of 4,175,000 property crimes. The minimum age for the death penalty is 16. There was one execution in 2001 but none in 2002.

Religion. Main Protestant churches in 1990: Southern Baptist (617,524), United Methodist (197,402), Church of Christ (86,502), Assembly of God (55,438). Roman Catholics (1990), 72,952.

Education. In the school year 1992–93 public elementary and secondary schools had 440,682 enrolled pupils and 25,771 classroom teachers. Average salary of teachers in elementary schools was $25,771, junior high $27,492 and high $27,760.

Higher education is provided at 34 institutions: 9 state universities, 1 medical college, 12 private or church colleges, 12 community or two-year branch colleges and 12 technical colleges. Total enrolment in institutions of higher education in the autumn of 1993 was 99,344.

In the autumn of 1993 there were two vocational-training schools and nine technical institutes with 28,261 students.

Health. There were 99 licensed hospitals (13,329 beds) in 1994, and 273 nursing facilities (25,888 licensed beds), excluding private facilities.

Welfare. In Dec. 1993, 481,910 persons drew social security payments; 271,510 were retired workers; 53,240 were disabled workers; 68,920 were widows and widowers; 36,050 were spouses. Monthly payments were $251·5m., including $159·6m. to retired workers and their dependants and $31·6m. to disabled workers.

CULTURE

Broadcasting. An educational TV network provides 24-hour a day telecasting; it had five transmitters in 2000.

FURTHER READING
Statistical information: Arkansas Institute for Economic Advancement, Univ. of Arkansas at Little Rock, Little Rock 72204. Publishes *Arkansas State and County Economic Data.*
Agricultural Statistics for Arkansas. Arkansas Agricultural Statistics Service, Little Rock, 1993
Current Employment Developments. Dept. of Labor, Little Rock, 1994
Statistical Summary for the Public Schools of Arkansas. Dept. of Education, Little Rock, 1990–92

CALIFORNIA

KEY HISTORICAL EVENTS

There were many small Indian tribes, but no central power, when the area was discovered in 1542 by the Spanish navigator Juan Cabrillo. The Spaniards did not begin to establish missions until the 18th century, when the Franciscan friar Junipero Serra settled at San Diego in 1769. The missions became farming and ranching villages with large Indian populations. When the Spanish empire collapsed in 1821, the area was governed from newly independent Mexico.

The first wagon-train of American settlers arrived from Missouri in 1841. In 1846, during the war between Mexico and the USA, Americans in California proclaimed it to be part of the USA. The territory was ceded by Mexico on 2 Feb. 1848 and became the 31st state of the Union on 9 Sept. 1850.

Gold was discovered in 1848–49 and there was an immediate influx of population. The state remained isolated, however, until the development of railways in the 1860s. From then on the population doubled on average every 20 years. The sunny climate attracted fruit-growers, market-gardeners and wine producers. In the early 20th century the bright lights and cheap labour attracted film-makers to Hollywood, Los Angeles.

Southern California remained mainly agricultural with an Indian or Spanish-speaking labour force until after the Second World War. Now more than 90% of the population is urban, with the main manufacture being hi-technology equipment, much of it for the aerospace, computer and office equipment industries.

TERRITORY AND POPULATION

Land area, 155,959 sq. miles (403,932 sq. km). Census population, 1 April 2000, 33,871,648, an increase of 4,111,627, or 13·8%, over 1990. July 2002 estimate, 35,116,033, an increase of 1·74% from 2001. The growth rate reflects continued high though somewhat reduced natural increase (excess of births over deaths) as well as substantial net immigration.

Population in five census years was:

	White	Black	Japanese	Chinese	Total (incl. all others)	Per sq. mile
1910	2,259,672	21,645	41,356	36,248	2,377,549	15·2
1930	5,408,260	81,048	97,456	37,361	5,677,251	36·4
1960	14,455,230	883,861	157,317	95,600	15,717,204	100·8
	White	Black	Asian/other	Hispanic	Total	Per sq. mile
1990	20,524,327	2,208,801	7,026,893	7,687,938	29,760,021	190·8
2000	20,170,059	2,263,882	11,437,707	10,966,556	33,871,648	217·2

Of the total population in 2000, 16,996,756 (49·8%) were female, 24,621,819 were 18 years old or older and 31,871,648 were urban (94·44%, the highest of the states).

California has the largest Hispanic population of any state in the USA in terms of numbers and the second largest in terms of percentage of population. In 2000 there were 10,966,556 Hispanics living in California (32·4% of the overall population), representing a rise of 3,278,618 since 1990, the largest numeric rise of any state over the same period. By 2015 Hispanics are projected to form a majority.

The 50 largest cities with 2002 population estimates are:

Los Angeles	3,807,400	San Francisco	793,600	Sacramento	426,000
San Diego	1,255,700	Long Beach	473,100	Oakland	408,800
San Jose	918,000	Fresno	441,900	Santa Ana	343,700

Anaheim	334,700	Santa Clarita	158,300	Orange	132,900
Riverside	269,400	Irvine	157,500	Sunnyvale	132,800
Bakersfield	257,900	Pomona	153,900	Fullerton	129,300
Stockton	253,800	Santa Rosa	152,900	Concord	123,900
Fremont	208,600	Salinas	148,400	Palmdale	123,700
Glendale	200,200	Moreno Valley	146,400	Lancaster	123,100
Modesto	198,600	Hayward	144,300	Thousand Oaks	121,000
Huntington Beach	194,600	Torrance	142,100	El Monte	119,500
Chula Vista	190,900	Fontana	139,100	Vallejo	118,600
San Bernardino	189,800	Pasadena	138,800	Simi Valley	115,500
Oxnard	182,000	Rancho		Inglewood	115,100
Garden Grove	168,600	Cucamonga	137,100	Costa Mesa	110,700
Oceanside	167,200	Escondido	137,000	Downey	110,400
Ontario	162,300	Corona	134,000	West Covina	109,100

Metropolitan areas (2002 census): Los Angeles–Riverside–Orange County, 17,131,700; San Francisco–Oakland–San Jose, 7,215,000; San Diego, 2,935,100; Sacramento–Yolo, 1,912,500; Fresno, 967,200.

SOCIAL STATISTICS
Births in 2001, 531,000 (15·3 per 1,000 population); deaths, 227,000 (6·6 per 1,000 population); infant deaths (1996), approximately 2,815 (5·4 per 1,000 live births). Marriages (1998), 194,100; divorces (1990), 127,967.

CLIMATE
Los Angeles, Jan. 58°F (14·4°C), July 74°F (23·3°C). Annual rainfall 15" (381 mm). Sacramento, Jan. 45°F (7·2°C), July 76°F (24·4°C). Annual rainfall 18" (457 mm). San Diego, Jan. 57°F (13·9°C), July 71°F (21·7°C). Annual rainfall 10" (259 mm). San Francisco, Jan. 51°F (10·6°C), July 59°F (15°C). Annual rainfall 20" (508 mm). Death Valley, Jan. 52°F (11°C), July 100°F (38°C). Annual rainfall 1·6" (40 mm). California belongs to the Pacific Coast climate zone (see UNITED STATES: Climate).

CONSTITUTION AND GOVERNMENT
The present constitution became effective from 4 July 1879; it has had numerous amendments since 1962. The Senate is composed of 40 members elected for four years—half being elected every two years—and the Assembly, of 80 members, elected for two years. Two-year regular sessions convene in Dec. of each even numbered year. The Governor and Lieut.-Governor are elected for four years.

For the 108th Congress, which convened in Jan. 2003, California sends 53 members to the House of Representatives. It is represented in the Senate by Dianne Feinstein (D. 1993–2007) and Barbara Boxer (D. 1993–2005).

The capital is Sacramento. The state is divided into 58 counties.

RECENT ELECTIONS
In the 2000 presidential election Gore polled 5,861,203 votes; Bush, 4,567,429; Nader, 418,707. In the 2002 gubernatorial election Gray Davis polled 3,533,490 votes and Bill Simon polled 3,169,801.

CURRENT ADMINISTRATION
Governor: Gray Davis (D.), 2003–07 (salary: $175,000).
  Lieut.-Governor: Cruz Bustamante (D.), 2003–07 ($131,250).
  Secretary of State: Kevin Shelley (D.), 2003–07 ($131,250).
  Attorney General: Bill Lockyer (D.), 2003–07 ($148,750).

Government Website: http://www.ca.gov

ECONOMY
Per capita personal income (2001) was $32,702.

Budget. For the year ending 30 June 2002, total state revenues were $82·9bn. Total expenditures were $96·2bn. (education, $40·4bn.; health and human services, $26·5bn.; youth and adult corrections, $5·7bn.). Debt outstanding (2002) $25·3bn.

Performance. California's economy, the largest among the 50 states and one of the largest in the world, has major components in high technology, trade, entertainment, agriculture, manufacturing, tourism, construction and services. California experienced an economic recession in 2001 and a sluggish recovery in 2002, with greatest impacts in the high technology sector. The economy improved in the first half of 2002, with employment and total state personal income posting gains. The improvement had faltered by the middle of the year, however, and the economy was sluggish in the second half of 2002, with unemployment varying narrowly between 6·4% and 6·6% and employment faltering by about 28,000. If California were a country in its own right it would be the world's fifth largest economy, after the USA, Japan, Germany and the United Kingdom. 2000 Gross State Product was $1,344,623m., representing more than 13% of the USA's total GDP. Taxable sales in 2001 totalled $441,518m.

Banking and Finance. In 1997 there were 9,796 establishments of depository institutions which included 5,740 commercial banks, 2,626 savings institutions and 1,306 credit unions.

In 2001 savings and loan associations had deposits of $169,637m. Total mortgage loans were $243,326m. On 31 Dec. 2001 all insured commercial banks had demand deposits of $45,428m. and time and savings deposits of $197,217m. Total loans reached $241,927m., of which real-estate loans were $145,732m.

ENERGY AND NATURAL RESOURCES

Electricity. Californians spent $20bn. on electricity in 1999. Total consumption amounted to 260,936m. kWh. 75% of electricity is derived from in-state resources. In Jan. 2001 Governor Gray Davis announced a state of emergency after power shortages led to a series of blackouts.

Oil and Gas. California is the nation's 4th largest oil producing state. Total onshore and offshore production was 261m. bbls. in 2001. California ranks 10th out of US states for the production of natural gas. Net natural gas production in 2001 was 338bn. cu. ft.

Water. The total area covered by water is approximately 2,895 sq. miles. Water quality is judged to be good along 83% of the 960 miles of assessed coastal shoreline.

Minerals. Gold output was 13,972 kg in 2001. Asbestos, boron minerals, diatomite, sand and gravel, lime, salt, magnesium compounds, clays, cement, silver, gypsum and iron ore are also produced.

In 2001 California ranked 1st among the states in non-fuel mineral production, accounting for more than 8% of the US total. The value of non-fuel minerals produced (2001) was $3·27bn.; the mining industry employed around 24,000 persons in 2001 (compared to 48,000 in the early 1980s).

Agriculture. California is the most diversified agricultural economy in the world, producing more than 350 agricultural commodities. In 2001 California led the nation in the production of more than 75 agricultural products. There were some 88,000 farms, comprising 28m. acres; average farm, 315 acres. Agricultural production and gross cash income in 2001 increased to $27·6bn., 1% more than the previous year but fractionally less than the record income set in 1997. Nuts and fruit remained the most significant cash crop (2001), accounting for 41% of the nation's total fruit and nut production and 26% of the state's gross agricultural income. Livestock and poultry accounted for 27%; vegetables, 22%; field crops, 9%; nursery, greenhouse products and floriculture, 11%. The state's leading billion-dollar agricultural products included milk and cream with receipts of $4·63bn.; grapes, $2·65bn.; nursery products, $2·09bn.; lettuce, $1·37bn.; cattle and calves, $1·35bn.; hay, $1·02bn.

Production of cotton lint, 2000, was 578,200 short tons; other field and seed crops included (in 1m. short tons): hay and alfalfa, 9; sugarbeet, 2; rice, 1·9; wheat, 1·1. Principal fruit, nut and vegetable crops in 2001 (in 1,000 short tons): tomatoes, 9,183; wine, table and raisin grapes, 5,962; lettuce, 3,623; oranges, 2,044; lemons, 859; almonds, 415; grapefruit, 211.

In 2001 there were 1·6m. milch cows; 5·2m. all cattle and calves; 0·84m. sheep and lambs; and 0·15m. hogs and pigs.

Forestry. There are about 16·6m. acres of productive forest land, from which about 2,900m. bd ft are harvested annually. Total value of timber harvest, 2000, $909m ($764m. in 1999). Lumber production, 2001, 1,603m. bd ft.

Fisheries. The catch in 2001 was 443m. lb; leading species in landings were squid, sardine, anchovy, mackerel, urchin, tuna, sole, herring, whiting and crab.

INDUSTRY

In 2002 the fastest-growing industries were in public and private education, retail trade, health services, social services, management consulting and engineering. The continuing high technology slump made high technology business services and manufacturing the leading job-losing sectors. The manufacturing sector employed 1,816,008 people in 2002, including 242,025 in the field of electronic equipment, 264,275 in industrial machinery and 184,608 in food and similar products.

Labour. In 2002 the civilian labour force was 17·6m., of whom 16·5m. were employed. A total of 38,408 jobs were lost during 2002, led by electronic equipment manufacturing, computer-related services and computer and office equipment manufacturing. By the end of 2002 unemployment had risen to 6·6% from 6·1% a year earlier.

INTERNATIONAL TRADE

Imports and Exports. Estimated foreign trade through Californian ports totalled $341bn. in 2001. Exports of made-in-California goods slowed in 2001 as the global economy slipped into recession. Exports to all but five of California's top 25 trading partners declined during 2001. High technology goods dominate California's exports, comprising almost three-quarters of all made-in-California exports. Electronic components and computers account for almost half of total exports. Even though exports of other commodities grew almost 4% during 2001 the reduction of high technology exports was great enough to cause a 10·8% overall drop.

Total agricultural exports for 2000 were $6·6bn. California's top markets are Canada, Japan, Mexico, South Korea, UK, Taiwan, Hong Kong, Germany, Netherlands and Spain.

COMMUNICATIONS

Roads. In 2001 California had 71,131 miles of roads inside cities and 97,678 miles outside. There were about 19·7m. registered cars and about 6·4m. commercial vehicles. Motor vehicle collision fatalities in 2001 were 3,926.

Rail. In addition to Amtrak's long-distance trains, local and medium-distance passenger trains run in the San Francisco Bay area sponsored by the California Department of Transportation, and a network of commuter trains around Los Angeles opened in 1992. There are metro and light rail systems in San Francisco and Los Angeles, and light rail lines in Sacramento, San Diego and San Jose.

Civil Aviation. In 1996 there were a total of 933 public and private airports, heliports, stolports and seaplane bases.

A total of 61,606,253 passengers (15,950,228 international; 45,656,025 domestic) embarked/disembarked at Los Angeles airport in 2001. It handled approximately 1,779,065 tonnes of freight (931,092 international; 847,972 domestic). At San Francisco airport, in 2001, 34,632,474 passengers (7,539,723 international; 26,404,659 domestic) embarked/disembarked, and 517,124 tonnes of freight (325,224 tonnes international; 191,900 tonnes domestic) were handled.

Shipping. The chief ports are San Francisco and Los Angeles.

SOCIAL INSTITUTIONS

Justice. A 'three strikes law', making 25-years-to-life sentences mandatory for third felony offences, was adopted in 1994 after an initiative (i.e. referendum) was 72% in favour. However, the state's Supreme Court ruled in June 1996 that judges may disregard previous convictions in awarding sentences. In 2002 there were 33 adult prisons. State prisons, 30 June 2002, had 148,153 male and 9,826 female inmates. In June 2002 there were some 5,954 juveniles in custody. As of 30 June 2002 there were 7,291 adults serving 'three strikes' sentences. The death penalty (minimum age 18) has been authorized following its reinstatement by the US Supreme Court in 1976. Death sentences have been passed since 1980. There was one execution in 2002.

Religion. There is a strong Roman Catholic presence. There were 739,000 Latter-day Saints (Mormons) in 1998.

Education. Full-time attendance at school is compulsory for children from 6 to 18 years of age for a minimum of 175 days per annum. In autumn 2001 there were 6·8m. pupils enrolled in both public and private elementary and secondary schools. Total state expenditure on public education, 1999–2000, was $40·4bn.

Community colleges had 1,640,033 students in autumn 2001.

California has two publicly-supported higher education systems: the University of California (1868) and the California State University and Colleges. In autumn 2001 the University of California, with campuses for resident instruction and research at Berkeley, Los Angeles, San Francisco and six other centres, had 191,920 students. California State University and Colleges with campuses at Sacramento, Long Beach, Los Angeles, San Francisco and 15 other cities had 388,605 students. In addition to the 28 publicly-supported institutions for higher education there are 117 private colleges and universities which had a total estimated enrolment of 293,027 in the autumn of 2001.

Health. In 1999 there were 395 community hospitals; capacity, 73,700 beds. On 30 June 2001 state hospitals for the mentally disabled had 4,814 patients.

Welfare. On 1 Jan. 1974 the federal government (Social Security Administration) assumed responsibility for the Supplemental Security Income/State Supplemental Program which replaced the State Old-Age Security. The SSI/SSP provides financial assistance for needy aged (65 years or older), blind or disabled persons. An individual recipient may own assets up to $2,000; a couple up to $3,000, subject to specific exclusions. In 2000–01 fiscal year an average of 87,935 cases per month were receiving an average of $233·00 in assistance in the general relief programme.

CULTURE

Tourism. The travel and tourism industry provides 5·5% of the state's $1·4trn. economy. Visitors in 2001 spent $75·4bn. generating $4·8bn. in state and local tax revenues. California was the state most visited by overseas travellers in 2001, with 4·9m. overseas visitors—22% of the market share. In 2001 there were 317m. person trips, 308m. from within the United States and 9m. from abroad.

Libraries. The California State Library is in Sacramento.

FURTHER READING
California Government and Politics. Hoeber, T. R., *et al*, (eds.) Sacramento, Annual
California Statistical Abstract. 43rd ed. Dept. of Finance, Sacramento, 2002
Economic Report of the Governor. Dept. of Finance, Sacramento, Annual
Bean, W. and Rawls, J. J., *California: an Interpretive History.* 6th ed. New York, 1993
Gerston, L. N. and Christensen, T., *California Politics and Government: a Practical Approach.* 3rd ed. New York, 1995

State Library: The California State Library, Library-Courts Bldg, Sacramento 95814.

COLORADO

KEY HISTORICAL EVENTS
Spanish explorers claimed the area for Spain in 1706; it was then the territory of the Arapaho, Cheyenne, Ute and other Plains and Great Basin Indians. Eastern Colorado, the hot, dry plains, passed to France in 1802 and then to the USA as part of the Louisiana Purchase in 1803. The rest remained Spanish, becoming Mexican when Spanish power in the Americas ended. In 1848, after war between Mexico and the USA, Mexican Colorado was ceded to the USA. A gold rush in 1859 brought a great influx of population, and in 1861 Colorado was organized as a Territory.

The Territory officially supported the Union in the Civil War of 1861–65, but its settlers were divided and served on both sides.

Colorado became a state in 1876. Mining and ranching were the mainstays of the economy. In the 1920s the first large projects were undertaken to exploit the Colorado River. The Colorado River Compact was agreed in 1922, and the Boulder Dam (now Hoover Dam) was authorized in 1928. Since then irrigated agriculture has overtaken mining as an industry and is as important as ranching. In 1945 the Colorado-Big Thompson project diverted water by tunnel beneath the Rocky Mountains to irrigate 700,000 acres (284,000 ha) of northern Colorado. Now more than 80% of the population is urban, with the majority engaged in telecommunications, aerospace and computer technology.

TERRITORY AND POPULATION

Colorado is bounded north by Wyoming, northeast by Nebraska, east by Kansas, southeast by Oklahoma, south by New Mexico and west by Utah. Land area, 103,718 sq. miles (268,628 sq. km).

Population in five census years was:

	White	Black	Indian	Asiatic	Total	Per sq. mile
1910	783,415	11,453	1,482	2,674	799,024	7·7
1950	1,296,653	20,177	1,567	5,870	1,325,089	12·7
			All others			
1980	2,571,498	101,703	216,763		2,889,964	27·9
1990	2,905,474	133,146	255,774		3,294,394	31·8
2000	3,560,005	165,063	576,193		4,301,261	41·5

In July 2002 the Census Bureau estimate was 4,506,542, an increase of 4·8% since the 2000 census. Colorado is the sixth fastest growing state in the USA.

Of the total population in 2000, 2,165,983 were male, 3,200,466 were 18 years old or older and 3,633,185 were urban. The Hispanic population in 2000 was 735,601, up from 424,302 in 1990 (an increase of 73·4%). Large cities, with 2001 populations: Denver City, 560,365; Colorado Springs, 369,853; Aurora, 283,650; Lakewood, 144,426; Fort Collins, 122,521; Pueblo, 103,030; Westminster, 102,905; Arvada, 102,470.

Main metropolitan areas (2001): Denver–Boulder–Greeley, 2,660,666; Colorado Springs, 533,526; Fort Collins–Loveland, 259,707; Pueblo, 144,383.

SOCIAL STATISTICS

Births, 2000, were 65,429 (15·1 per 1,000 population); deaths, 27,229 (6·5); infant deaths, 402 (6·1 per 1,000 live births); marriages, 36,104 (8·4 per 1,000 population); divorces, 20,063.

CLIMATE

Denver, Jan. 31°F (−0·6°C), July 73°F (22·8°C). Annual rainfall 14" (358 mm). Pueblo, Jan. 30°F (−1·1°C), July 83°F (28·3°C). Annual rainfall 12" (312 mm). Colorado belongs to the Mountain States climate zone (see UNITED STATES: Climate).

CONSTITUTION AND GOVERNMENT

The constitution adopted in 1876 is still in effect with (1989) 115 amendments. The General Assembly consists of a Senate of 35 members elected for four years, one-half retiring every two years, and of a House of Representatives of 65 members elected for two years. Sessions are annual, beginning 1951. Qualified as electors are all citizens, male and female (except convicted, incarcerated criminals), 18 years of age, who have resided in the state and the precinct for 32 days immediately preceding the election. There is a seven-member State Supreme Court.

For the 108th Congress, which convened in Jan. 2003, Colorado sends seven members to the House of Representatives. It is represented in the Senate by Ben Campbell (R. 1993–2005) and Wayne Allard (R. 1997–2009).

The capital is Denver. There are 64 counties.

RECENT ELECTIONS

In the 2000 presidential election Bush polled 883,748 votes; Gore, 738,227; Nader, 91,434.

CURRENT ADMINISTRATION

Governor: Bill Owens (R.), 2003–2007 (salary: $90,000).
Lieut.-Governor: Jane Norton (R.), 2003–2007 ($68,500).
Secretary of State: Donetta Davidson (R.), 2003–2007 ($68,500).

Government Website: http://www.colorado.gov

ECONOMY

Per capita personal income (2001) was $33,470.

Overview. The state constitution limits revenues and expenditures to annual increases of no more than the sum of population growth plus inflation. Economic development programmes include Enterprise Zones to encourage investment and job creation in lagging areas, customized job training assistance, Economic Development Commission, Community Development infrastructure assistance and Revolving Loan Funds.

Budget. In 2001 the total state revenue was $7,200·9m. Total expenditure was $6,976m. Major areas of expenditure are (1999 figures): education, $4,604m.; public welfare, $2,828m.; highways, $1,159m.; health and hospitals, $448m. Debt outstanding, in 1999, was $4,059m.

Performance. 2000 Gross State Product was $167,918m.

Banking and Finance. There are 180 commercial banks insured with the Federal Deposit Insurance Corporation, with $47,631m. in total assets.

ENERGY AND NATURAL RESOURCES

Oil and Gas. In 2001 Colorado produced 803bn. cu. ft of natural gas and 19·2m. bbls. of crude oil. It ranked sixth in the USA for daily gas production, and eleventh in crude oil production. Total production value of all hydrocarbons was $3·05bn.

Water. The Rocky Mountains of Colorado form the headwaters for four major American rivers: the Colorado, Rio Grande, Arkansas and Platte. The total area covered by water is approximately 371 sq. miles.

Minerals. Coal (2001): 33·4m. short tons were produced. In 2001 there were 14,000 people employed in mining, including 8,300 in extracting oil and natural gas. Value of non-fuel minerals $576m.

Agriculture. In 2001 farms and ranches numbered 30,000, with a total of 31·3m. acres of agricultural land. 5,748,610 acres were harvested crop land; average farm, 1,043 acres. Average value of farmland and buildings per acre in 1996 was $558. Farm income 1995: from crops, $1,361m.; from livestock, $2,624m.

Production of principal crops in 2001: corn for grain, 149·8m. bu.; wheat for grain, 69·2m. bu.; barley for grain, 8·6m. bu.; hay, 4,780,000 tons; dry beans, 1,785,000 cwt; oats and sorghum, 11·4m. bu.; sugarbeets, 824,000 tons; potatoes, 23,274,000 cwt; vegetables, 9,523 tons; fruits, 21,900 tons.

In 2001 the number of farm animals was: 3,050,000 cattle, 91,000 milch cows, 780,000 swine and 370,000 sheep.

Forestry. In 1997 there were 15m. acres of national forest.

INDUSTRY

In 2001, 2,233,400 were employed in non-agricultural sectors, of which 527,300 were in trade; 692,400 in services; 346,800 in government; 198,500 in manufacturing; 145,800 in construction; 144,500 in finance and insurance; 144,000 in transportation and communications; 14,000 in mining. In manufacturing in 2002 the biggest sub-sectors were: non-electrical machinery, 28,800; food products, 25,400; printing and publishing, 24,900; instruments, 20,500; and electrical machinery, 16,700.

Labour. In 2002 the total labour force was estimated at 2,369,600 of which 2,243,400 were employed. The unemployment rate stood at 5·3%.

Trade Unions. In 2000, 9% of all wage and salary workers were members of unions, compared to a national average of 13·5%. Among manufacturing workers, only 6·6% belonged to labour unions.

INTERNATIONAL TRADE

Imports and Exports. In 2001 Colorado exported $6·1bn. in goods. The largest trading partners were Canada, Japan, Germany, United Kingdom, China (including Hong Kong), Mexico and France. Largest export categories are electronic integrated circuits and microassemblies, automatic data processing machines, components for office machines, measuring instruments and medical devices.

Trade Fairs. The National Western Stock Show and Rodeo is the largest event of its kind in the USA, drawing over 600,000 visitors.

COMMUNICATIONS

Roads. In 2001 there were 85,272 miles of road, 14,001 urban and 71,271 rural. 9,135 miles are highways, of which 1,152 are interstate or freeway highways. There were 4,224,830 motor vehicle registrations.

Rail. There were 3,439 miles of railway in 1995.

Civil Aviation. In 2000 there were 79 airports open to the public; 17 with commercial service, 62 public non-commercial (general aviation) and 14 private non-commercial. There were 19,333,528 passenger enplanements statewide in 1999.

Telecommunications. Colorado is headquarters to Qwest Communications and AT&T Broadband and Internet Services. Other major communications employers are Level 3 Communications, Avaya and MCIWorldCom.

SOCIAL INSTITUTIONS

Justice. In 2002 there were 18,382 federal and state prisoners. The death penalty is authorized (minimum age 18) but has not been used since 1997.

Religion. In 1984 the Roman Catholic Church had 550,300 members; the ten main Protestant denominations had 350,900 members; the Jewish community had 45,000 members. Buddhism is among other religions represented.

Education. In 2001 the public elementary and secondary schools had 742,145 pupils, 41,104 teachers (1999); teachers' salaries averaged $36,291. Enrolments in four-year state universities and colleges in 2000 were: University of Colorado (Boulder), 25,458 students; University of Colorado (Denver), 11,328; University of Colorado (Colorado Springs), 6,581; University of Colorado Health Sciences Centre, 2,358; Colorado State University (Fort Collins), 22,939; University of Northern Colorado (Greeley), 10,926; Colorado School of Mines (Golden), 3,287; Metropolitan State College (Denver), 16,773; University of Southern Colorado (Pueblo), 4,085; Mesa College (Grand Junction), 4,893; Fort Lewis College (Durango), 4,260; Adams State College (Alamosa), 2,511; Western State College (Gunnison), 2,456.

2000 total enrolments: private four-year universities and colleges, 23,000; two-year colleges, 80,168; all universities and colleges, 221,023.

Health. In 2000 there were 67 community hospitals.

Welfare. In 1999, 2·2% of the population received public assistance. Public welfare programme expenditures were $2,295m. in 1997.

CULTURE

Broadcasting. There are 97 commercial and public radio stations, broadcasting on both AM and FM frequencies. There are also 14 commercial and four public television stations.

Press. There are 27 daily newspapers. In addition there are 41 weekly newspapers including seven regional business journals.

Tourism. Skiing is a major tourist attraction. Colorado is particularly renowned for the Rocky Mountain National Park and the Mesa Verde National Park, a World Heritage Site.

Festivals. Cherry Creek Arts Festival takes place in July. In addition there are annual festivals at Aspen and Boulder and an annual Blue Grass festival at Telluride, plus arts and music festivals in many communities.

Libraries. There are 249 public libraries.

Theatre and Opera. The main venues are the Denver Performing Arts Center, Opera Colorado and Red Rocks Amphitheater.

Museums and Galleries. There are 110 museums statewide and numerous galleries, most notably Denver Art Museum and Denver Museum of Natural History.

FURTHER READING
Statistical information: Business Research Division, Univ. of Colorado, Boulder 80309. Publishes *Statistical Abstract of Colorado.*
Griffiths, M. and Rubright, L., *Colorado: a Geography.* Boulder, 1983

State Government Website: http://www.colorado.gov
State Library: Colorado State Library, 201 E. Colfax, Rm. 314, Denver 80203.

CONNECTICUT

KEY HISTORICAL EVENTS
Formerly territory of Algonquian-speaking Indians, Connecticut was first colonized by Europeans during the 1630s, when English Puritans moved there from Massachusetts Bay. Settlements were founded in the Connecticut River Valley at Hartford, Saybrook, Wethersfield and Windsor in 1635. They formed an organized commonwealth in 1637. A further settlement was made at New Haven in 1638 and was united to the commonwealth under a royal charter in 1662. The charter confirmed the commonwealth constitution, drawn up by mutual agreement in 1639 and called the Fundamental Orders of Connecticut.

The area was agricultural and its population of largely English descent until the early 19th century. After the War of Independence Connecticut was one of the original 13 states of the Union. Its state constitution came into force in 1818 and survived with amendment until 1965 when a new one was adopted.

In the early 1800s a textile industry was established using local water power. By 1850 the state had more employment in industry than in agriculture, and immigration from the continent of Europe (and especially from southern and eastern Europe) grew rapidly throughout the 19th century. Some immigrants worked in whaling and iron-mining, but most sought industrial employment. Settlement was spread over a large number of small towns, with no single dominant culture.

Yale University was founded at New Haven in 1701. The US Coastguard Academy was founded in 1876 at New London, a former whaling port.

TERRITORY AND POPULATION
Connecticut is bounded in the north by Massachusetts, east by Rhode Island, south by the Atlantic and west by New York. Land area, 4,845 sq. miles (12,548 sq. km).

Census population, 1 April 2000, 3,405,565, an increase of 3·6% since 1990. July 2002 estimate, 3,460,503.

Population in five census years was:

	White	Black	Indian	Asian	Total	Per sq. mile
1910	1,098,897	15,174	152	533	1,114,756	231·3
1930	1,576,700	29,354	162	687	1,606,903	328·0
1980	2,799,420	217,433	4,533	18,970	3,107,576	634·3
	White	Black	Indian	Asian	Others	Total	Per sq. mile
1990	2,859,353	274,269	6,654	50,078	96,762	3,287,116	678·6
2000	2,780,355	309,843	9,639	82,313	148,567	3,405,565	702·9

Of the total population in 2000, there were 320,323 persons of Hispanic origin, up from 213,116 in 1990 (an increase of 50·3%). Of the total population in 2000, 1,756,246 were female, 2,563,877 were 18 years old or older and 2,988,057 were urban. There were 183 residents in five Indian Reservations.

The chief cities and towns are (2000 census populations):

Bridgeport	139,529	Hartford	121,578	Waterbury	107,271
New Haven	123,626	Stamford	117,083	Norwalk	82,951

| Danbury | 74,848 | West Hartford | 63,589 | Bristol | 60,062 |
| New Britain | 71,538 | Greenwich | 61,101 | Meriden | 58,244 |

SOCIAL STATISTICS

Births (1999) were 43,499 (13·3 per 1,000 population); deaths, 29,991 (9·1); (1996) infant mortality rate (per 1,000 live births), 6·4. Marriages (1997), 22,600; divorces, 11,200.

CLIMATE

New Haven: Jan. 25°F (−3·8°C), July 74°F (23·4°C). Annual rainfall 45" (1,143 mm). Connecticut belongs to the New England climate zone (*see* UNITED STATES: Climate).

CONSTITUTION AND GOVERNMENT

The 1818 Constitution was revised in 1955. On 30 Dec. 1965 a new constitution went into effect, having been framed by a constitutional convention in the summer of 1965 and approved by the voters in Dec. 1965.

The General Assembly consists of a Senate of 36 members and a House of Representatives of 151 members. Members of each House are elected for the term of two years. Legislative sessions are annual.

For the 108th Congress, which convened in Jan. 2003, Connecticut sends five members to the House of Representatives. It is represented in the Senate by Christopher Dodd (D. 1981–2005) and Joseph Lieberman (D. 1989–2007).

There are eight counties. The state capital is Hartford.

RECENT ELECTIONS

In the 2000 presidential election Gore polled 816,659 votes; Bush, 561,104; Nader, 64,452.

CURRENT ADMINISTRATION

Governor: John G. Rowland (R.), 2003–07 (salary: $150,000).

Lieut.-Governor: M. Jodi Rell (R.), 2003–07 ($110,000).

Secretary of State: Susan Bysiewicz (D.), 2003–07 ($110,000).

Government Website: http://www.ct.gov

ECONOMY

Per capita personal income (2000) was $40,870, the highest in the country.

Budget. In 1999 total state revenue was $16,437m. Total expenditure was $15,213m. (education, $3,286m.; public welfare, $3,023m.; health and hospitals, $1,581m.; highways, $719m.; police protection, $128m.). Outstanding debt, in 1999, $17,505m.

Performance. Gross State Product in 2000 was $159,288m.

ENERGY AND NATURAL RESOURCES

Water. The total area covered by water is approximately 698 sq. miles.

Minerals. The state has some mineral resources: crushed stone, sand, gravel, clay, dimension stone, feldspar and quartz. Total non-fuel mineral production in 1998 was valued at $105m.

Agriculture. In 2000 the state had 3,900 farms with a total area of 360,000 acres; the average farm size was 92 acres, valued at $7,800 per acre in 1998. Farm income (1996): crops $252m., and livestock and products $237m. Principal crops are grains, hay, tobacco, vegetables, maize, melons, fruit, nuts, berries and greenhouse and nursery products.

Livestock (1993): 77,000 all cattle (value $59·3m.), 10,900 sheep ($1·1m.), 6,000 swine ($630,000) and 4·6m. poultry ($11·5m.).

Forestry. The state has 144,464 acres of state forest land.

INDUSTRY

Total non-agricultural employment in Sept. 1997 was 1,629,100. The main employers are manufacturers (275,000 workers mainly in transport equipment, machinery, computer, electronic and electrical equipment and fabricated metals); retail trade (273,000 workers); services (504,700) and government (225,800). There were 79,300 unemployed.

Labour. Total non-agricultural employment, 1999, 1,672,000. Employees by branch, 1999 (in 1,000): services, 527; wholesale and retail trade, 360; manufacturing, 269; government, 236.

COMMUNICATIONS

Roads. The total length of highways in 2000 was 20,845 miles including 11,804 miles of urban road and 9,041 miles of rural road. Motor vehicles registered in 2000 numbered 2,853,449.

Rail. In 1994 there were 570 miles (912 km) of railway route miles.

Civil Aviation. In 1995 there were 61 airports (20 commercial, 6 state-owned and 35 private), 63 heliports and 8 seaplane bases. There were 2,949,991 passenger enplanements statewide in 1999.

SOCIAL INSTITUTIONS

Justice. In June 2000 there were 18,616 federal and state prisoners. The death penalty for murder is authorized (minimum age 18), but has not been used since 1960.

Religion. The leading religious denominations (1990) in the state are the Roman Catholic (1,374,000 members), United Churches of Christ (135,000), Protestant Episcopal (78,000), Jewish (115,000), Methodist (56,000), Black Baptist (64,000), Presbyterian and Greek Orthodox.

Education. Instruction is free for all children and young people between the ages of 4 and 21 years, and compulsory for all children between the ages of 7 and 16 years. In 2000 there were 971 public local schools, 3 academies, 17 state vocational-technical schools, 30 state or state-aided schools, 6 regional educational service centres and 335 non-public schools. In 1999 there were 545,500 public school pupils and in 1998–99 there were 36,012 full-time, professional public teachers. Expenditure of the state on public schools, 1999–2000, $5,300m. Average salary of teachers in public schools, 1999, $51,000 (the highest in the United States). In 1999–2000 expenditure per pupil (public elementary and secondary) was $9,365. There were an estimated 28,200 public high-school graduates in 1999.

In 2000 Connecticut had 42 colleges, of which 1 state university, 1 external degree college, 4 state colleges, 12 community-technical colleges and a US Coast Guard Academy were state funded. The University of Connecticut at Storrs, founded 1881, had 21,398 students in 1998. Yale University, New Haven, founded in 1701, had 11,032 students; Wesleyan University, Middletown, founded 1831, 3,204 students; Trinity College, Hartford, founded 1823, 2,258 students; Connecticut College, New London, founded 1915, 1,800 students; The University of Hartford, founded 1877, 6,892 students. The state colleges had 39,354 students in 1998. The US Coast Guard Academy had 795 students in 1998. There were 19 independent (four-year course) colleges and four independent (two-year course) colleges as well as two seminaries, a College of Hospitality Management and a Learning Collaborative.

Health. Hospitals listed by the American Hospital Association, 1993, numbered 62. The state operated 1 general hospital (252 beds), 7 hospitals for the mentally ill (891 patients), 1 training school for the mentally retarded, and 6 regional centres (5,705 clients in residential settings). In 1996 there were 33 community hospitals with approximately 7,300 beds; 11,015 non-federal physicians; and 33,400 nurses.

Welfare. Disbursements in 1992 amounted to $42m. in aid to the aged and disabled (with an average payment per month of $664·82). In other areas of welfare, there was an average of 57,000 cases for aid to families with dependent children comprising 162,000 recipients. In 1996 there were a total of 596,000 beneficiaries; annual payments amounted to $5,003m.

CULTURE

Broadcasting. In 1994 there were 75 broadcasting stations and 11 television stations.

Press. In 1994 there were 141 daily, Sunday, weekly and monthly newspapers.

FURTHER READING

State Register and Manual. Secretary of State. Hartford (CT). Annual
Halliburton, W. J., *The People of Connecticut.* Norwalk, 1985

State Library: Connecticut State Library, 231 Capitol Avenue, Hartford (CT) 06105.
State Book Store: Dept. of Environmental Protection, 79 Elm St., Hartford (CT) 06106.
Business Incentives: Connecticut Economic Resource Center, 805 Brook St., Rocky Hill (CT) 06067.
Connecticut Tourism: Dept. of Economic and Community Development, 865 Brook St., Rocky Hill (CT) 06067.

DELAWARE

KEY HISTORICAL EVENTS

Delaware was the territory of Algonquian-speaking Indians who were displaced by European settlement in the 17th century. The first settlers were Swedes who came in 1638 to build Fort Christina (now Wilmington), and colonize what they called New Sweden. Their colony was taken by the Dutch from New Amsterdam in 1655. In 1664 the British took the whole New Amsterdam colony, including Delaware, and called it New York.

In 1682 Delaware was granted to William Penn, who wanted access to the coast for his Pennsylvania colony. Union of the two colonies was unpopular, and Delaware gained its own government in 1704, although it continued to share a royal governor with Pennsylvania until the War of Independence. Delaware then became one of the 13 original states of the Union and the first to ratify the federal constitution (on 7 Dec. 1787).

The population was of Swedish, Finnish, British and Irish extraction. The land was low-lying and fertile, and the use of slave labour was legal. There was a significant number of black slaves, but Delaware was a border state during the Civil War (1861–65) and did not leave the Union.

19th-century immigrants were mostly European Jews, Poles, Germans and Italians. The north became industrial and densely populated, more so after the Second World War with the rise of the petrochemical industry. Industry in general profited from the opening of the Chesapeake and Delaware Canal in 1829; it was converted to a toll-free deep channel for ocean-going ships in 1919.

TERRITORY AND POPULATION

Delaware is bounded in the north by Pennsylvania, northeast by New Jersey, east by Delaware Bay, south and west by Maryland. Land area 1,954 sq. miles (5,061 sq. km). Census population, 1 April 2000, was 783,600, an increase of 17·6% since 1990. July 2002 estimate, 807,385.

Population in five census years was:

	White	Black	Indian	Asiatic	Total	Per sq. mile
1910	171,102	31,181	5	34	202,322	103·0
1960	384,327	60,688	597	410	446,292	224·0
			All others			
1980	488,002	96,157	10,179		594,338	290·8
1990	535,094	112,460	18,614		666,168	325·9
2000	584,773	150,666	48,161		783,600	401·0

Of the total population in 2000, 403,059 were female, 589,013 were 18 years old or older and 627,758 were urban. The Hispanic population in 2000 was 37,277, up from 15,824 in 1990 (an increase of 135·6%).

The 2000 census figures show Wilmington with a population of 72,664; Dover, 32,135; Newark, 28,547; Milford City, 6,732; Seaford City, 6,699; Middletown, 6,161.

SOCIAL STATISTICS
Births in 1999, 10,591 (14·0 births per 1,000 population); deaths, 6,677 (8·9 per 1,000 population); (1997) infant deaths, 81 (7·8 per 1,000 live births); marriages, 5,372 (7·3 per 1,000 population); divorces, 3,009 (4·7).

CLIMATE
Wilmington, Jan. 31°F (−0·6°C), July 76°F (24·4°C). Annual rainfall 43" (1,076 mm). Delaware belongs to the Atlantic Coast climate zone (see UNITED STATES: Climate).

CONSTITUTION AND GOVERNMENT
The present constitution (the fourth) dates from 1897, and has had 51 amendments; it was not ratified by the electorate but promulgated by the Constitutional Convention. The General Assembly consists of a Senate of 21 members elected for four years and a House of Representatives of 41 members elected for two years.

For the 108th Congress, which convened in Jan. 2003, Delaware sends one member to the House of Representatives. It is represented in the Senate by Joseph Biden (D. 1973–2009) and Thomas Carper (D. 2001–07).

The state capital is Dover. Delaware is divided into three counties.

RECENT ELECTIONS
In the 2000 presidential election Gore polled 180,068 votes; Bush, 137,288; Nader, 8,307.

CURRENT ADMINISTRATION
Governor: Ruth Ann Minner (D.), 2001–05 (salary: $114,000).
   Lieut.-Governor: John C. Carney Jr (D.), 2001–05 ($62,400).
   Secretary of State: Dr Harriet Smith Windsor (D.), appointed 2001 ($106,000).

Government Website: http://www.delaware.gov

ECONOMY
Per capita personal income (2000) was $31,074.

Budget. In 1999 total revenue was $2,190·7m. Total expenditure was $2,152·5m. (education, $654·2m.; public welfare, health and social services and hospitals, $484·9m.; police protection, $89·2m.). Debt outstanding, in 1999, $3,713m.

Performance. 2000 Gross State Product was $36,336m.

Banking and Finance. Delaware National Bank has branches statewide. Also based in Delaware, MBNA is the world's largest independent credit card issuer, with managed loans of $97·5bn.

ENERGY AND NATURAL RESOURCES

Electricity. Net generation of electric energy, 1995, 8·3bn. kWh.

Water. The total area covered by water is approximately 442 sq. miles.

Minerals. The mineral resources of Delaware are not extensive, consisting chiefly of clay products, stone, sand and gravel and magnesium compounds. Total non-fuel mineral production in 1998 was valued at $11m. (includes production for District of Columbia).

Agriculture. Delaware is mainly an industrial state, with agriculture as its principal industry. There were 580,000 acres in 2,600 farms in 2000. The average farm was valued (land and buildings) at $745,000 in 1997. The major product is broilers, accounting for $529,875m. in cash receipts, out of total farm cash receipts of $748,933m. in 1997.

The chief field crops are soybeans and corn for feed.

INDUSTRY
In 1998 manufacturing establishments employed 59,500 people; main manufactures were chemicals, transport equipment and food.

Labour. Total non-agricultural employment, 1999, 412,000. Employees by branch, 1999 (in 1,000): services, 116; wholesale and retail trade, 90; manufacturing, 60; government, 55; finance, insurance and property, 49.

COMMUNICATIONS

Roads. The state in 1999 maintained 5,049 miles of roads and streets, including 321·04 miles of roads in the National Highway System. There were also 674·7 miles of municipally maintained streets. In 2000 total vehicles registered numbered 630,446.

Rail. In 1999 the state had 271 miles of active rail line, 23 miles of which is part of Amtrak's high-speed Northeast corridor. In 1999 there were 710,245 passenger trips beginning or ending in Delaware—645,808 of which were commuter trips. An important component of Delaware's freight infrastructure is the rail access to the Port of Wilmington.

Civil Aviation. In 1998 Delaware had 11 public use airports and one helistop. There were 204 passenger enplanements statewide in 1999.

SOCIAL INSTITUTIONS

Justice. State prisons had a daily average of 5,795 inmates in 1999. The minimum age for the death penalty is 16. There were two executions in 2001 but none in 2002.

Religion. The leading religious denominations are Roman Catholics, Methodists, Episcopalians and Lutherans.

Education. The state has free public schools and compulsory school attendance. In Sept. 1999 the elementary and secondary public schools had 113,598 enrolled pupils and 7,023 classroom teachers. Another 26,584 children were enrolled in private and parochial schools. State appropriation for public schools (financial year 1998–99) was about $615m. Average salary of classroom teachers (financial year 1998–99), $43,164. The state supports the University of Delaware at Newark (1834) which had 930 full-time faculty members and 21,346 students in Sept. 1998, Delaware State University, Dover (1892), with 177 full-time faculty members and 3,155 students, and the four campuses of Delaware Technical and Community College (Wilmington, Stanton, Dover and Georgetown) with 301 full-time faculty members and 45,535 students.

Health. In 1999 there were seven short-term general hospitals. During the fiscal year 1999 the average daily census in state mental hospitals was 329.

Welfare. In 1974 the federal Supplemental Security Income (SSI) programme lessened state responsibility for the aged, blind and disabled. Total SSI payments in Delaware from Oct. 1996 through Sept. 1997 were $144,969,349. Provisions are also made for the care of dependent children; in the same period there were 2,882 children under the age of 20 receiving SSI payments totalling $39,679,812.

FURTHER READING

Statistical information: Delaware Economic Development Office, Dover, DE 19901. Publishes *Delaware Statistical Overview.*

State Manual, Containing Official List of Officers, Commissions and County Officers. Secretary of State, Dover. Annual

Smeal, L., *Delaware Historical and Biographical Index.* New York, 1984

DISTRICT OF COLUMBIA

KEY HISTORICAL EVENTS

The District of Columbia, organized in 1790, is the seat of the government of the USA, for which the land was ceded by the states of Maryland and Virginia to the USA as a site for the national capital. It was established under Acts of Congress in 1790 and 1791. Congress first met in it in 1800 and federal authority over it became vested in 1801. In 1846 the land ceded by Virginia (about 33 sq. miles) was given back.

TERRITORY AND POPULATION

The District forms an enclave on the Potomac River, where the river forms the southwest boundary of Maryland. The land area of the District of Columbia is 61 sq. miles (159 sq. km).

Census population, 1 April 2000, was 572,059 (100% urban), a decrease of 5·72% from that of 1990. July 2002 estimate, 570,898. Metropolitan area of Washington, D.C.–Baltimore (2000), 7,608,070. The Hispanic population in 2000 was 44,953, up from 32,710 in 1990 (an increase of 37·4%). Of the total population in 2000, 302,693 were female and 457,067 were 18 years old or older.

Population in five census years was:

	White	Black	Indian	Chinese and Japanese	Total	Per sq. mile
1910	236,128	94,446	68	427	331,069	5,517·8
1960	345,263	411,737	587	3,532	763,956	12,523·9
				All others		
1980	171,768	448,906		17,659	638,333	10,464·4
1990	179,667	339,604		87,629	606,900	9,949·2
2000	176,101	343,312		52,646	572,059	9,378·0

SOCIAL STATISTICS

Births, 1999, were 7,668 (14·8 per 1,000 population); deaths, 5,893 (11·4); (1996) infant mortality rate (per 1,000 live births), 14·9. Marriages (1997), 3,800 (7·3 per 1,000 population in 1995); divorces, 1,200 (1997), 2·3. The abortion rate, at 68·1 for every 1,000 women in 2000, is the highest of any US state.

CLIMATE

Washington, Jan. 34°F (1·1°C), July 77°F (25°C). Annual rainfall 43" (1,064 mm). The District of Columbia belongs to the Atlantic Coast climate zone (see UNITED STATES: Climate).

CONSTITUTION AND GOVERNMENT

Local government, from 1 July 1878 until Aug. 1967, was that of a municipal corporation administered by a board of three commissioners, of whom two were appointed from civil life by the President, and confirmed by the Senate, for a term of three years each. The other commissioner was detailed by the President from the Engineer Corps of the Army. The Commission form of government was abolished in 1967 and a new Mayor Council instituted with officers appointed by the President with the advice and consent of the Senate. On 24 Dec. 1973 the appointed officers were replaced by an elected Mayor and councillors, with full legislative powers in local matters as from 1974. Congress retains the right to legislate, to veto or supersede the Council's acts. The 23rd amendment to the federal constitution (1961) conferred the right to vote in national elections. The District has two delegates in Congress who may vote in committees but not on the House floor.

RECENT ELECTIONS

In the 2000 presidential election Gore polled 171,923 votes; Bush, 18,073; Nader, 10,576.

CURRENT ADMINISTRATION

Mayor: Anthony A. Williams (D.), 2003–07 (salary: $133,700).

Government Website: http://www.dc.gov

ECONOMY

Per capita personal income (2000) was $38,374, the second highest in the country.

Budget. The District's revenues are derived from a tax on real and personal property, sales taxes, taxes on corporations and companies, licences for conducting various businesses and from federal payments. The District of Columbia has no bonded debt not covered by its accumulated sinking fund.

Performance. Gross State Product was $59,397m. in 2000.

ENERGY AND NATURAL RESOURCES

Water. The total area covered by water is approximately 7 sq. miles.

Minerals. Non-fuel mineral production is included in figures for Delaware.

INDUSTRY

The main industries are government service, service, wholesale and retail trade, finance, real estate, insurance, communications, transport and utilities.

Labour. Total non-agricultural employment, 1999, 616,000. Employees by branch, 1999 (in 1,000): services, 276; government, 223; wholesale and retail trade, 48.

COMMUNICATIONS

Roads. Within the District are 340 miles of bus routes. There are 1,102 miles of streets maintained by the District; of these, 673 miles are local streets, 262 miles are major arterial roads. In 2000 there were 242,081 registered vehicles.

Rail. There is a metro in Washington extending to 130 km, and two commuter rail networks.

Civil Aviation. The District is served by three general airports; across the Potomac River in Arlington, Va., is National Airport; in Chantilly, Va., is Dulles International Airport; and in Maryland is Baltimore–Washington International Airport.

SOCIAL INSTITUTIONS

Justice. The death penalty was declared unconstitutional in the District of Columbia on 14 Nov. 1973. In June 2000 there were 8,575 federal and state prisoners.

The District's Court system is the Judicial Branch of the District of Columbia. It is the only completely unified court system in the United States, possibly because of the District's unique city-state jurisdiction. Until the District of Columbia Court Reform and Criminal Procedure Act of 1970, the judicial system was almost entirely in the hands of Federal government. Since that time, the system has been similar in most respects to the autonomous systems of the states.

Religion. The largest churches are the Protestant and Roman Catholic Christian churches; there are also Jewish, Eastern Orthodox and Islamic congregations.

Education. In 1996 there were an estimated 105,700 pupils enrolled at elementary and secondary public schools. Average expenditure per pupil in 1997 was $8,167.

Higher education is given through the Consortium of Universities of the Metropolitan Washington Area, which consists of six universities and three colleges: Georgetown University, founded in 1795 by the Jesuit Order; George Washington University, non-sectarian founded in 1821; Howard University, founded in 1867; Catholic University of America, founded in 1887; American University (Methodist), founded in 1893; University of D.C., founded 1976; Gallaudet College, founded 1864; Trinity College, founded 1897. There are 18 institutes of higher education altogether.

Health. The District government provides primary health care for residents, mainly through its Department of Human Services. In 1994 there were 12 community hospitals with 4,000 beds.

Welfare. There were 77,000 beneficiaries of social security in 1996 including 53,000 retired workers and dependants, 15,000 survivors of deceased workers and 9,000 disabled workers and dependants. Total annual payments were $539m.

CULTURE

Tourism. About 17m. visitors stay in the District every year and spend about $1,000m.

FURTHER READING

Statistical Information: The Metropolitan Washington Board of Trade publications.
Reports of the Commissioners of the District of Columbia. Annual. Washington
Bowling, K. R., *The Creation of Washington D.C.: the Idea and the Location of the American Capital.* Washington (D.C.), 1991

FLORIDA

KEY HISTORICAL EVENTS

There were French and Spanish settlements in Florida in the 16th century, of which the Spanish, at St Augustine in 1565, proved permanent. Florida was claimed by Spain until 1763 when it passed to Britain. Although regained by Spain in 1783, the British used it as a base for attacks on American forces during the war of 1812. Gen. Andrew Jackson captured Pensacola for the USA in 1818. In 1819 a treaty was signed which ceded Florida to the USA with effect from 1821 and it became a Territory of the USA in 1822.

Florida had been the home of the Apalachee and Timucua Indians. After 1770 groups of Creek Indians began to arrive as refugees from the European-Indian wars. These 'Seminoles' or runaways attracted other refugees including slaves, the recapture of whom was the motive for the first Seminole War of 1817–18. A second war followed in 1835–42, when the Seminoles retreated to the Everglades swamps. After a third war in 1855–58 most Seminoles were forced or persuaded to move to reserves in Oklahoma.

Florida became a state in 1845. About half of the population were black slaves. At the outbreak of Civil War in 1861 the state seceded from the Union.

During the 20th century Florida continued to grow fruit and vegetables, but real-estate development (often for retirement) and the growth of tourism and the aerospace industry set it apart from other ex-plantation states.

TERRITORY AND POPULATION

Florida is a peninsula bounded in the west by the Gulf of Mexico, south by the Straits of Florida, east by the Atlantic, north by Georgia and northwest by Alabama. Land area, 53,927 sq. miles (139,670 sq. km). Census population, 1 April 2000, 15,982,378, an increase of 23·5% since 1990. July 2002 estimate, 16,713,149.

Population in five federal census years was:

	White	Black	All Others	Total	Per sq. mile
1950	2,166,051	603,101	2,153	2,771,305	51·1
1970	5,719,343	1,041,651	28,449	6,789,443	125·6
1980	8,319,448	1,342,478	84,398	9,746,324	180·1
1990	10,749,285	1,759,534	429,107	12,937,926	238·9
2000	12,465,029	2,335,505	1,181,844	15,982,378	296·4

Of the total population in 2000, 8,184,663 were female, 12,336,038 were 18 years old or older and 14,270,020 were urban. The Hispanic population in 2000 was 2,682,715, up from 1,574,143 in 1990 (a rise 70·4%, the third largest numeric increase of any state in the USA).

The largest cities in the state, 2000 census (and 1990) are: Jacksonville, 735,617 (635,230); Miami, 362,470 (358,548); Tampa, 303,447 (280,015); St Petersburg, 248,232 (238,629); Hialeah, 226,419 (188,004); Orlando, 185,951 (164,693); Fort Lauderdale, 152,397 (149,377); Tallahassee, 150,624 (124,773); Hollywood, 139,357 (121,697); Pembroke Pines, 137,427 (65,452); Coral Springs, 117,549 (79,443); Clearwater, 108,787 (98,784); Cape Coral, 102,286 (74,991); Gainesville, 95,447 (84,770); Port St Lucie, 88,769 (55,759); Miami Beach, 87,933 (92,639); Sunrise, 85,779 (65,683); Plantation, 82,934 (66,814); West Palm Beach, 82,103 (67,764); Palm Bay, 79,413 (62,543); Lakeland, 78,452 (70,576); Pompano Beach, 78,191 (72,411).

Population of the largest metropolitan areas (2000): Miami–Fort Lauderdale, 3,876,380; Tampa-St Petersburg-Clearwater, 2,395,997; Orlando, 1,644,561.

SOCIAL STATISTICS

Births in 1999 were 195,784 (13·0 per 1,000 population); deaths, 159,752 (10·6 per 1,000); in 1996, infant deaths, 7·5 (per 1,000); (1997) marriages, 161,000; divorces and other dissolutions, 83,000.

CLIMATE

Jacksonville, Jan. 55°F (12·8°C), July 81°F (27·2°C). Annual rainfall 54" (1,353 mm). Key West, Jan. 70°F (21·1°C), July 83°F (28·3°C). Annual rainfall 39" (968 mm). Miami, Jan. 67°F (19·4°C), July 82°F (27·8°C). Annual rainfall 60" (1,516 mm). Tampa, Jan. 61°F (16·1°C), July 81°F (27·2°C). Annual rainfall 51" (1,285 mm). Florida belongs to the Gulf Coast climate zone (*see* UNITED STATES: Climate).

CONSTITUTION AND GOVERNMENT
The 1968 Legislature revised the constitution of 1885. The state legislature consists of a Senate of 40 members, elected for four years, and House of Representatives with 120 members elected for two years. Sessions are held annually, and are limited to 60 days.

For the 108th Congress, which convened in Jan. 2003, Florida sends 25 members to the House of Representatives. It is represented in the Senate by Bob Graham (D. 1971–77, 1987–2005) and Bill Nelson (D. 2001–07).

The state capital is Tallahassee. The state is divided into 67 counties.

RECENT ELECTIONS
In the 2000 presidential election, following a recount, Bush polled 2,912,790 votes; Gore, 2,912,253; Nader, 97,488.

CURRENT ADMINISTRATION
Governor: John Ellis 'Jeb' Bush (R.), 2003–07 (salary: $123,175).
    Lieut.-Governor: Toni Jennings (R.), appointed March 2003 ($117,990).
    Secretary of State: Glenda E. Hood (R.), appointed Feb. 2003 ($121,931).

Government Website: http://www.myflorida.com

ECONOMY
Per capita personal income (2000) was $27,836.

Budget. In 1999 total state revenue was $49,209m. Total expenditure was $42,459m. (education, $13,475m.; public welfare, $8,499m.; highways, $3,575m.; health and hospitals, $2,881m.; police protection, $343m.). Outstanding debt, in 1999, $17,825m.

Performance. 2000 Gross State Product was $472,105m.

ENERGY AND NATURAL RESOURCES
Oil and Gas. In 1996, 6bn. bbls. of crude oil was produced; natural gas production was 6bn. cu. ft.

Water. The total area covered by water is approximately 5,991 sq. miles.

Minerals. Chief mineral is phosphate rock, of which marketable production in 1998 was 34·0m. tonnes. This was approximately 75% of US and 25% of the world supply of phosphate in 1998. Total non-fuel mineral production for 1998 was valued at $1,960m.

Agriculture. In 2000 there were 10·3m. acres of farmland; 44,000 farms with an average of 234 acres per farm. The total value of land and buildings was $23,690m. in 1997; average value (1998) of land and buildings per acre, $2,300.

Farm income from crops and livestock (1996) was $6,131m., of which crops provided $4,942m. Major crop contributors were oranges, grapefruit, tomatoes, peppers, other winter vegetables, indoor and landscaping plants and sugarcane. In 1994 poultry farms produced 132·7m. chickens, 2,538m. eggs and (in 1997) 596m. lb of broilers. On 1 Jan. 1995 the state had 2·02m. cattle, including 176,000 milch cows (1994), and about 0·1m. swine.

Forestry. The national forests covered an area of 1·1m. acres in 1997. There were 16,548,922 acres of commercial forest and 33 state forests of 596,137 acres.

Fisheries. Florida has extensive fisheries with shrimp the highest value fishery. Other important catches are spiny lobster, snapper, crabs, hard clams, swordfish and tuna. Total catch (1998) was 128·2m. lb, valued at $210·6m.

INDUSTRY
In 1994 there were 15,831 manufacturers. They employed 483,754 persons. Main industries included: printing and publishing, machinery and computer equipment,

apparel and finished products, fabricated metal products, and lumber and wood products.

Labour. Total non-agricultural employment, 1999, 6,877,000. Employees by branch, 1999 (in 1,000): services, 2,531; wholesale and retail trade, 1,721; government, 967; manufacturing, 488; finance, insurance and property, 449; construction, 365. In 1999 the unemployment rate was 3·9%.

COMMUNICATIONS

Roads. The state (2000) had 116,651 miles of highways, roads and streets (67,424 miles being rural roads); there were 11,781,010 vehicle registrations in 2000.

Rail. In 1993 there were 2,988 miles of railway and 14 rail companies. There is a metro of 20 miles (33 km), a peoplemover and a commuter rail route in Miami.

Civil Aviation. In 1993 Florida had 133 public use airports (12 international) of which 20 have scheduled commercial service, and 28 seaplane bases. There were 48,598,757 passenger enplanements statewide in 1999.

SOCIAL INSTITUTIONS

Justice. The minimum age for the death penalty is 17. There have been 54 executions since 1976, including three in 2002. In June 2000 there were 71,233 federal and state prisoners. Chain gangs were introduced in 1995.

Religion. The main Christian churches are Roman Catholic, Baptist, Methodist, Presbyterian and Episcopalian. There were 107,000 Latter-day Saints (Mormons) in 1998.

Education. Attendance at school is compulsory between 7 and 16. In the 1994–95 school year the public elementary and secondary schools had 2,107,514 pupils enrolled in grades K-12. Total expenditure on public schools (1994) was $17,035m. The state maintains 28 community colleges, with a full-time equivalent enrolment of 192,698 in 1995.

There are nine universities in the state system, with a total of 207,812 students in 1995: the University of Florida at Gainesville (founded 1853) with 39,417 students; the Florida State University (founded at Tallahassee in 1857) with 30,268; the University of South Florida at Tampa (founded 1960) with 36,146; Florida A. & M. University at Tallahassee (founded 1887) with 10,267; Florida Atlantic University (founded 1964) at Boca Raton with 18,240; the University of West Florida at Pensacola with 8,250; the University of Central Florida at Orlando with 26,555; the University of North Florida at Jacksonville with 10,463; Florida International University at Miami with 28,206.

Health. In 1994 there were 218 community hospitals with 51,400 beds.

Welfare. From 1974 aid to the aged, blind and disabled became a federal responsibility. The state continued to give aid to families with dependent children and general assistance. In 1996 there were 3,034,000 beneficiaries, including: 2,269,000 retired workers and dependants; 428,000 widows and widowers; 337,000 disabled workers and dependants. Total annual payments (1996), $24,195m.

CULTURE

Tourism. During 1994, 39·8m. tourists visited Florida. They spent $33,390m., making tourism one of the biggest industries in the state. In 1996 Florida was the second most visited state by overseas travellers (behind California) with 5,710,000 visitors (25·2% of the market). There are 148 state parks, 33 state forests, 3 national parks, 8 national memorials, monuments, seashores and preserves and 3 national forests.

FURTHER READING
Statistical information: Bureau of Economic and Business Research, Univ. of Florida, Gainesville 32611. Publishes *Florida Statistical Abstract.*
Huckshorn, R. J. (ed.) *Government and Politics in Florida.* Florida Univ. Press, 1991
Morris, A., *The Florida Handbook.* Tallahassee. Biennial
Shermyen, A. H. (ed.) *1991 Florida Statistical Abstract.* Florida Univ. Press, 1991

State Library: Gray Building, Tallahassee.

GEORGIA

KEY HISTORICAL EVENTS

Originally the territory of Creek and Cherokee tribes, Georgia was first settled by Europeans in the 18th century. James Oglethorpe founded Savannah in 1733, intending it as a colony which offered a new start to debtors, convicts and the poor. Settlement was slow until 1783, when growth began in the cotton-growing areas west of Augusta. The Indian population was cleared off the rich cotton land and moved beyond the Mississippi. Georgia became one of the original 13 states of the Union.

A plantation economy developed rapidly, using slave labour. In 1861 Georgia seceded from the Union and became an important source of supplies for the Confederate cause, although some northern areas never accepted secession and continued in sympathy with the Union during the Civil War. At the beginning of the war 56% of the population were white, descendants of British, Austrian and New England immigrants; the remaining 44% were black slaves.

The city of Atlanta, which grew as a railway junction, was destroyed during the war but revived to become the centre of southern states during the reconstruction period. Atlanta was confirmed as state capital in 1877. Also in Atlanta were developed successive movements for black freedom in social, economic and political life. The Southern Christian Leadership Conference, led by Martin Luther King (assassinated in 1968), was based in King's native city of Atlanta.

TERRITORY AND POPULATION

Georgia is bounded north by Tennessee and North Carolina, northeast by South Carolina, east by the Atlantic, south by Florida and west by Alabama. Land area, 57,906 sq. miles (149,976 sq. km). Census population, 1 April 2000, was 8,186,453, an increase of 26·4% since 1990. July 2002 estimate, 8,560,310.

Population in five census years was:

	White	Black	Indian	Asiatic	Total	Per sq. mile
1910	1,431,802	1,176,987	95	237	2,609,121	44·4
1930	1,837,021	1,071,125	43	317	2,908,506	49·7
			All others			
1980	3,948,007	1,465,457	50,801		5,464,265	92·7
1990	4,600,148	1,746,565	131,503		6,478,216	110·0
2000	5,327,281	2,349,542	509,630		8,186,453	141·4

Of the total population in 2000, 4,159,340 were female, 6,017,219 were 18 years old or older and 5,864,163 were urban. The estimated Hispanic population was 435,277 in 2000, up from 108,933 in 1990 (an increase of 299·6%).

The largest cities are: Atlanta (capital), with a population (2000 census) of 416,474; Augusta-Richmond County, 199,775; Columbus, 186,291; Savannah, 131,510; Athens-Clarke County, 101,489. The Atlanta metropolitan area had a 2000 census population of 4,112,198.

SOCIAL STATISTICS

Births, 1999, were 122,385 (15·7 per 1,000 population); deaths, 60,930 (7·8); (1995) infant deaths, 1,058 (9·4 per 1,000 live births); 1997 marriages, 61,900 (8·3 per 1,000 population); divorces and annulments, 36,300 (4·8).

CLIMATE

Atlanta, Jan. 43°F (6·1°C), July 78°F (25·6°C). Annual rainfall 49" (1,234 mm). Georgia belongs to the Atlantic Coast climate zone (see UNITED STATES: Climate).

CONSTITUTION AND GOVERNMENT

A new constitution was ratified in the general election of 2 Nov. 1976, proclaimed on 22 Dec. 1976 and became effective on 1 Jan. 1977. The General Assembly consists of a Senate of 56 members and a House of Representatives of 180 members, both elected for two years. Legislative sessions are annual, beginning the 2nd Monday in Jan. and lasting for 40 days.

Georgia was the first state to extend the franchise to all citizens 18 years old and above.

For the 108th Congress, which convened in Jan. 2003, Georgia sends 13 members to the House of Representatives. It is represented in the Senate by Zell Miller (D. 2000–05) and Saxby Chambliss (R. 2003–09).

The state capital is Atlanta. Georgia is divided into 159 counties.

RECENT ELECTIONS

In the 2000 presidential election Bush polled 1,419,720 votes; Gore, 1,116,230; Buchanan, 10,926.

CURRENT ADMINISTRATION

Governor: Sonny Perdue (R.), 2003–07 (salary: $127,303).
  Lieut.-Governor: Mark Taylor (D.), 2003–07 ($83,148).
  Secretary of State: Cathy Cox (D.), 2003–07 ($112,776).

Government Website: http://www.georgia.gov

ECONOMY

Per capita personal income (2000) was $27,790.

Budget. In 1999 total state revenue was $27,639m. Total expenditure was $23,203m. (education, $9,905m.; public welfare, $4,834m.; highways, $1,574m.; health and hospitals, $1,416m.; police protection, $169m.). Outstanding debt, in 1999, $6,269m.

Performance. Gross State Product was $296,142m. in 2000.

ENERGY AND NATURAL RESOURCES

Water. The total area covered by water is approximately 1,058 sq. miles.

Minerals. Georgia is the leading producer of kaolin. The state ranks first in production of crushed and dimensional granite, and second in production of fuller's earth and marble (crushed and dimensional). Total value of non-fuel mineral production for 1998 was $2,140m.

Agriculture. In 2000, 50,000 farms covered 11·1m. acres; the average farm was of 222 acres. In 1995 the average value of farmland and buildings was $1,256 per acre. For 1995 cotton output was 1,941m. bales (of 480 lb). Other major crops include tobacco, corn, wheat, soybeans, peanuts and pecans. Cash income, 1996, $5,687m.: from crops, $2,408m.; from livestock and products, $3,279m.

In 1996 farm animals included 1·56m. all cattle, 0·90m. swine and 1,070m. (1995) poultry.

Forestry. The forested area in 1996 was 23·6m. acres.

INDUSTRY

In 1996 the state's 10,598 manufacturing establishments had 583,314 workers; the main groups were textiles, apparel, food and transport equipment. Trade employed 887,466, services 826,165 and government 558,753.

Labour. Total non-agricultural employment, 1999, 3,890,000. Employees by branch, 1999 (in 1,000): services, 1,066; wholesale and retail trade, 969; manufacturing, 599; government, 589. Georgia's unemployment rate in 1999 was 4·0%.

COMMUNICATIONS

Roads. In 2000 there were 114,726 miles of roads and 7,155,006 motor vehicles registered.

Rail. In 1996 there were 4,962 miles of railways and a metro in Atlanta.

Civil Aviation. In 1997 there were 106 public airports, 9 with scheduled commercial services. There were 38,279,533 passenger enplanements statewide in 1999.

Shipping. There are deepwater ports at Savannah, the principal port, and Brunswick.

SOCIAL INSTITUTIONS

Justice. In June 2000 there were 43,626 federal and state prisoners. The death penalty is authorized for capital offences and its minimum age is 17. There were four executions in 2002.

Under a Local Option Act, the sale of alcoholic beverages is prohibited in some counties.

Religion. An estimated 57·6% of the population are church members. Of the total population, 45·6% are Protestant, 3·2% are Roman Catholic and 1·1% are Jewish.

Education. Since 1945 education has been compulsory; tuition is free for pupils between the ages of 6 and 18 years. In 1996 there were 1,799 public elementary and public secondary schools with 1·3m. pupils and 81,058 teachers. Teachers' salaries averaged $33,869 in 1996. Expenditure on public schools (1995–96), $7,781m. or $1,080 per capita and $4,589 per pupil.

The University of Georgia (Athens) was founded in 1785 and was the first chartered State University in the USA (29,404 students in 1996–97). Other institutions of higher learning include Georgia Institute of Technology, Atlanta (12,985); Emory University, Atlanta (11,308); Georgia State University, Atlanta (23,410); and Georgia Southern University, Statesboro (14,312). The Atlanta University Center, devoted primarily to Black education, includes Clark Atlanta University (5,230) and Morris Brown College (2,169) co-educational; Morehouse (2,884), a liberal arts college for men; Interdenominational Theological Center (419), a co-educational theological school; and Spelman College (1,961), the first liberal arts college for Black women in the USA. Atlanta University serves as the graduate school centre for the complex. Wesleyan College (445) near Macon is the oldest chartered women's college in the world.

Health. In 1995 general hospitals licensed by the Department of Human Resources numbered 158 with 24,756 beds.

Welfare. In Dec. 1995, 43,666 persons were receiving Supplemental Security Income old-age assistance and 126,662 receiving benefits for blind and disabled persons. In 1996 a total of 1,027,000 beneficiaries received $7,677m., of which there were 132,625 families receiving aid to dependant children.

CULTURE

Tourism. In 1996 tourists spent $14,775m. There are 44 state parks.

FURTHER READING

Statistical information: Selig Center for Economic Growth, Univ. of Georgia, Athens 30602. Publishes *Georgia Statistical Abstract.*
Rowland, A. R., *A Bibliography of the Writings on Georgia History.* Hamden, Conn., 1978

State Library: Judicial Building, Capital Sq., Atlanta.

HAWAII

KEY HISTORICAL EVENTS

The islands of Hawaii were settled by Polynesian immigrants, probably from the Marquesas Islands, about AD 400. A second major immigration, from Tahiti, occurred around 800–900. In the late 18th century all the islands of the group were united into one kingdom by Kamehameha I. Western exploration began in 1778, and Christian missions were established after 1820. Europeans called Hawaii the Sandwich Islands. The main foreign states interested were the USA, Britain and France. Because of the threat imposed by their rivalry, Kamehameha III placed Hawaii under US protection in 1851. US sugar-growing companies became dominant in the economy and in 1887 the USA obtained a naval base at Pearl Harbour. A struggle developed between forces for and against annexation by the USA. In 1893 the monarchy was overthrown. The republican government agreed to be annexed to the USA in 1898, and Hawaii became a US Territory in 1900.

The islands and the naval base were of great strategic importance during the Second World War, when the Japanese attack on Pearl Harbour brought the USA into the war.

Hawaii became the 50th state of the Union in 1959. The 19th-century plantation economy encouraged the immigration of workers, especially from China and Japan. Hawaiian laws, religions and culture were gradually adapted to the needs of the immigrant community.

TERRITORY AND POPULATION

The Hawaiian Islands lie in the North Pacific Ocean, between 18° 54' and 28° 15' N. lat. and 154° 40' and 178° 25' W. long., about 2,090 nautical miles southwest of San Francisco. There are 137 named islands and islets in the group, of which 7 major and 5 minor islands are inhabited. Land area, 6,423 sq. miles (16,636 sq. km). Census population, 1 April 2000, 1,211,537, an increase of 9·3% since 1990; density was 188·6 per sq. mile in 1990. July 2002 estimate, 1,244,898. Of the total population in 2000, 608,671 were male, 915,770 were 18 years old or older, and 1,108,225 were urban (91·47%, the fourth most urban state).

The principal islands are Hawaii, 4,028 sq. miles, population 1990, 120,317; Maui, 727 sq. miles, population 91,361; Oahu, 600 sq. miles, population 836,231; Kauai, 552 sq. miles, population 50,947; Molokai, 260 sq. miles, population 6,717; Lanai, 141 sq. miles, population 2,426; Niihau, 70 sq. miles, population 230; Kahoolawe, 45 sq. miles (uninhabited). The capital Honolulu—on the island of Oahu—had a population in 2000 of 371,657, and Hilo—on the island of Hawaii—40,759.

Estimated figures in 1999 for racial groups (excluding persons in institutions or military barracks) were: 252,742 white; 223,193 Hawaiian; 219,855 Japanese; 145,248 Filipinos; 44,787 Chinese; 17,430 black (1998); 13,693 Samoan and Tongan; 11,737 Korean; 95,456 Hispanic; 128,144 all others (1998).

SOCIAL STATISTICS

Births, 1999, were 16,864 (14·2 per 1,000 population); deaths, 8,369 (7·1). Infant deaths, 1998, were at a rate of 6·8 per 1,000 live births. There were 22,873 resident marriages (7·4 per 1,000 population), and divorces and annulments numbered 4,376 (4·1 per 1,000 population) in 1999. Inter-marriage between the races is common. In 1998, 46·3% of marriages were inter-racial. 58·3% were non-resident marriages.

CLIMATE

All the islands have a tropical climate, with an abrupt change in conditions between windward and leeward sides, most marked in rainfall. Temperatures vary little. Average temperatures in Honolulu in 1999: warmest month 81·4°F, coolest month 72·9°F. Annual rainfall in Honolulu (1997) 22·02".

CONSTITUTION AND GOVERNMENT

Hawaii was officially admitted into the United States on 21 Aug. 1959. However, the constitution of the State of Hawaii was created by the 1950 Constitutional Convention, ratified by the voters of the Territory on 7 Nov. 1950, and amended on 27 June 1959. There have been two constitutional conventions since 1950, in 1968 and 1978. In addition to amendments proposed by these conventions the Legislature is able to propose amendments to voters during the general election. This has resulted in numerous amendments.

For the 108th Congress, which convened in Jan. 2003, Hawaii sends two members to the House of Representatives. It is represented in the Senate by Daniel Inouye (D. 1963–2005) and Daniel Akaka (D. 1990–2007).

The state capital is Honolulu. There are five counties.

RECENT ELECTIONS

In the 2000 presidential election Gore polled 205,286 votes; Bush, 137,845; Nader, 21,623.

CURRENT ADMINISTRATION

Governor: Linda Lingle (R.), 2002–06 (salary: $94,780).
  Lieut.-Governor: James R. 'Duke' Aiona Jr (R.), 2002–06 ($90,041).

Government Website: http://www.ehawaiigov.org

ECONOMY

Estimated *per capita* personal income (2000) was $27,819.

Budget. Revenue is derived mainly from taxation of sales and gross receipts, real property, corporate and personal income, and inheritance taxes, licences, public land sales and leases.

In 1999 total state revenue was $6,646m. Total expenditure was $6,266m. (education, $1,778m.; public welfare, $948m.; health and hospitals, $539m.; highways, $282m.; police protection, $6m.). Outstanding debt, in 1999, $5,421m.

Performance. 2000 Gross State Product was $42,364m.

Banking and Finance. In 1999 there were five state-chartered banks with assets of $22,705m., and one federal bank.

ENERGY AND NATURAL RESOURCES

Electricity. Installed capacity in 1999 was 1,669,000 kW; total power consumed was 9,380m. kWh.

Oil and Gas. In 1999, $48m. was generated by gas sales.

Water. The total area covered by water is approximately 36 sq. miles. Water consumption in 1999 amounted to 77,610m. gallons.

Minerals. Total value of non-fuel mineral production, 1999, $89m.; mainly crushed stone (5·7m. tonnes, value $57m.) and cement (300,000 tonnes, value $26m.).

Agriculture. Farming is highly commercialized and highly mechanized. In 1998 there were about 5,500 farms covering an area of 1·44m. acres; average number of acres per farm, 262; paid workforce totalled 7,400.

Sugar and pineapples are the staple crops. Farm income, 1998, from crop sales was $419·8m., and from livestock $72·8m. The sugar crop was valued at $87·4m.; pineapples, $92·7m.; other crops, $239·6m.

Forestry. In 1997 conservation district forest land amounted to 971,876 acres (of which 328,742 was privately owned); there were 46,191 acres of planted forest; and 109,164 acres of natural area.

Fisheries. In 1999 the commercial fish catch was 25·96m. lb with a value of $53·3m. to primary producers. There were 3,798 commercial fishermen.

INDUSTRY

In 1997 manufacturing establishments employed 15,100 workers of which 9,900 were production workers.

Labour. The labour force amounted to 594,800 in 1999; 5·6% (33,350) were unemployed.

Trade Unions. In 1999 there were 115 trade unions with a combined membership of 206,189. In 1998, 19·4% of workers in the private sector belonged to a union: 53·7% in the public sector.

INTERNATIONAL TRADE

Imports and Exports. Sugar exports brought in $168·8m. in 1996; pineapple exports, $147m.

COMMUNICATIONS

Roads. In 2000 there were 4,279 miles of roads. In 1999 there were 929,474 registered motor vehicles (725,142 passenger vehicles; 161,067 trucks; 22,530 tractors; 3,028 buses; and 17,008 motorcycles).

Civil Aviation. There were nine commercial airports in 1999. Passengers arriving from overseas numbered 7·73m., and there were 10·17m. passengers between the islands. In 1999 Hawaiian Airlines flew 34·8m. km, carrying 5,409,700 passengers (19,100 on international flights).

Shipping. Several lines of steamers connect the islands with the mainland USA, Canada, Australia, the Philippines, China and Japan. In 1999, 1,262 overseas and 2,249 inter-island vessels entered the port of Honolulu carrying a total of 45,494 overseas and 47,950 inter-island passengers as well as 5,721,503 tonnes of overseas and 1,730,662 tonnes inter-island cargo.

Telecommunications. There were 737,653 telephone access lines in 1999.

SOCIAL INSTITUTIONS

Justice. There is no capital punishment in Hawaii. In 1999 there were 3,724 prisoners in federal and state prisons and 87 boys and girls in juvenile facilities.

Religion. 1999 estimated membership of leading religious denominations: Roman Catholic Church, 215,000; Buddhism, 100,000; Church of Jesus Christ of Latter-day Saints, 56,000; United Church of Christ, 19,000; Southern Baptists, 17,000; Assembly of God, 11,000; Judaism, 10,000; Episcopal Church, 10,000.

Education. Education is free, and compulsory for children between the ages of 6 and 18. The language in the schools is English. In 1997–98 there were 251 public schools and 126 private schools. In 1999 there were 185,860 pupils in public schools and 36,226 pupils in private schools. In 1997–98 there were 11,400 teachers in public schools and 2,658 teachers in private schools. In 1997–98, $1,636m. was spent on education and the average annual salary for teachers was $36,598. In 1999 the number of students to enrol at college or university was 60,081.

Health. In 1999 there were 77 state-approved hospitals (acute care/long-term/speciality care) with 7,681 beds.

Welfare. Between July 1999 and June 2000 there were 79,517 individuals (29,789 cases) in receipt of state assistance, receiving on average $175 per month.

CULTURE

Broadcasting. There were (1998) 48 radio and television stations. There were, in addition, two cable television companies (colour by NTSC).

Cinema. In 1999 there were 29 cinemas.

Press. A total of 22 newspapers were in circulation in 1999.

Tourism. Tourism is outstanding in Hawaii's economy. Tourist arrivals numbered only 687,000 in 1965, but were 6·7m. in 1999. Tourist expenditure ($380m. in 1967) contributed $10,279·7m. to the state's economy in 1999.

Libraries. There were 50 libraries employing a total of 512 people in 1999.

FURTHER READING
Statistical information: Hawaii State Department of Business, POB 2359, Honolulu 96804. Publishes *The State of Hawaii Data Book.*
Atlas of Hawaii. 3rd ed. Hawaii Univ. Press, 1998
Morris, Nancy J. and Dean, Love, *Hawai'i.* [Bibliography] ABC-Clio, Oxford and Santa Barbara (CA), 1992
Oliver, Anthony M., *Hawaii Facts and Reference Book: Recent Historical Facts and Events in the Fiftieth State.* Honolulu, 1995

IDAHO

KEY HISTORICAL EVENTS
The original people of Idaho were Kutenai, Kalispel, Nez Percé and other tribes, living on the Pacific watershed of the northern Rocky Mountains. European exploration began in 1805, and after 1809 there were trading posts and small

settlements, with fur-trapping as the primary economic activity. The area was disputed between Britain and the USA until 1846 when British claims were dropped. In 1860 gold and silver were found, and there was a rush of immigrant prospectors. The newly enlarged population needed organized government. An area including that which is now Montana was created a Territory in March 1863. Montana was separated from it in 1864. Population growth continued, stimulated by refugees from the Confederate states after the Civil War and by settlements of Mormons from Utah.

Fur-trapping and mining gave way to farming, especially of grains, as the main economic activity. Idaho became a state in 1890, with its capital at Boise. The Territory capital, Idaho City, had been a gold-mining boom town in the 1860s whose population (about 40,000 at its height) was the largest in the Pacific Northwest. The population declined to 1,000 by 1869.

During the 20th century the Indian population shrunk to nearly 1%. The Mormon community has grown to include much of southeastern Idaho and more than half the church-going population of the state.

Industrial history has been influenced by the development of the Snake River of southern Idaho for hydro-electricity and irrigation, especially at the American Falls and reservoir. Processing food, minerals and timber are important to the economy. Much of the state, however, remains sparsely populated and rural. Rapid growth of high technology companies in Idaho's metropolitan areas has prompted economic diversification and rapid population growth.

TERRITORY AND POPULATION

Idaho is within the Rocky Mountains and bounded north by Canada, east by Montana and Wyoming, south by Nevada and Utah, west by Oregon and Washington. Land area, 82,747 sq. miles (214,314 sq. km). Census population, 1 April 2000, 1,293,953, an increase of 28·5% since 1990. July 2002 estimate, 1,341,131.

Population in five census years was:

	White	Black	American Indian	Asiatic	Total	Per sq. mile
1910	319,221	651	3,488	2,234	325,594	3·9
1930	438,840	668	3,638	1,886	445,032	5·4
1980	901,641	2,716	10,521	5,948	943,935	11·3
1990	950,451	3,370	13,780	9,365	1,006,749	12·2
2000	1,177,304	5,456	17,645	13,197	1,293,953	15·6

Of the total population in 2000, 648,660 were male, 924,923 were 18 years old or older and 859,497 were urban. In 2000 Idaho's Hispanic population was 101,690, up from 52,927 in 1990 (an increase of 92·1%).

The largest cities are: Boise City, with 2000 population of 185,787; Pocatello, 51,466; Nampa, 51,867; Idaho Falls, 50,730; Twin Falls, 34,469; Coeur d'Alene, 34,514; Lewiston, 30,904.

SOCIAL STATISTICS

Births (2001), 20,586 (15·7 per 1,000 population); deaths, 9,751 (7·4); marriages, 14,820 (11·2 per 1,000 population); divorces, 7,025 (5·3); infant deaths, 129; infant mortality rate, 6·2 (per 1,000 live births).

CLIMATE

Boise City, Jan. 29°F (−1·7°C), July 74°F (23·3°C). Annual rainfall 12" (303 mm). Idaho belongs to the Mountain States climate zone (see UNITED STATES: Climate).

CONSTITUTION AND GOVERNMENT

The constitution adopted in 1890 is still in force; it has had 105 amendments. The Legislature consists of a Senate of 35 members and a House of Representatives of 70 members, all the legislators being elected for two years. It meets annually.

For the 108th Congress, which convened in Jan. 2003, Idaho sends two members to the House of Representatives. It is represented in the Senate by Larry Craig (R. 1991–2009) and Michael Crapo (R. 1999–2005).

The state is divided into 44 counties. The capital is Boise City.

RECENT ELECTIONS
In the 2000 presidential election Bush polled 336,937 votes; Gore, 138,637; Nader, 12,292.

CURRENT ADMINISTRATION
Governor: Dirk Kempthorne (R.), 2003–07 (salary: $92,500).
    Lieut.-Governor: Jim Risch (R.), 2003–07 ($24,500).
    Secretary of State: Ben Ysursa (R.), 2003–07 ($75,000).

Government Website: http://www.accessidaho.org

ECONOMY
Per capita personal income (2001) was $24,621.

Budget. In fiscal year 2000 total state revenue was $5,576m. Total expenditure was $4,493m. (education, $1,664m.; public welfare, $762m.; highways, $470m.; health and hospitals, $141m.; police protection, $39m.). Outstanding debt, in fiscal year 2000, $2,279m.

Performance. 2000 Gross State Product was $37,031m.

ENERGY AND NATURAL RESOURCES
Electricity. Idaho's rivers provide dependable and low-cost electrical power. Almost two-thirds of Idaho's electrical needs come from this resource, resulting in electricity rates much lower than those found in the East and Midwest.

Water. The total area covered by water is approximately 821 sq. miles. Much of Idaho's surface water flows out of the high mountains and is generally of high quality. High quality groundwater is pumped for agricultural, industrial and residential use. Idaho is second only to California in the amount of water used for irrigating crops.

Minerals. Principal non-fuel minerals are processed phosphate rock, silver, gold, molybdenum and sand and gravel. The estimated value of total mineral output, 2000, was $708m.

Agriculture. Agriculture is the second largest industry, although a great part of the state is naturally arid. Extensive irrigation works have been carried out, bringing an estimated 3·5m. acres under irrigation, and there are over 50 soil conservation districts.

In 2001 there were 24,000 farms with a total area of 11·9m. acres; average value per acre (1997), $1,017. In 2000 the average farm was 496 acres.

Farm income, 1997, from crops, $1,944m., and livestock, $1,408m. The most important crops are potatoes and wheat. Other crops are sugarbeet, alfalfa, barley, field peas and beans, onions and apples. In 1997 there were 1·75m. cattle, 285,000 sheep, 33,000 hogs and 1·19m. poultry. The dairy industry is the fastest growing sector in Idaho agriculture.

Forestry. In 1997 a total of 21,598,522 acres was forest.

Fisheries. 75% of the commercial trout processed in the USA is produced in Idaho.

INDUSTRY
Manufacturing is the leading industry with revenue in 1999 of $7,308·9m. Electronics and computer equipment made up the largest manufacturing component with revenue of $3,215·4m.

Labour. In 2001, 151,033 people were employed in services ,140,928 in trade, 110,192 in government and 75,279 in manufacturing. The workforce totalled 682,228 in 2001; state unemployment was running at 5·0%.

Trade Unions. Idaho has a right-to-work law. In 1997, 43,400 people were union members.

COMMUNICATIONS

Roads. In 2001 there were 49,166 miles of roads (42,115 miles rural, 4,195 urban and 2,856 Native American Reservation) and 1,247,084 registered motor vehicles.

Rail. The state had (2001) approximately 1,700 miles of railways (including 1 Amtrak route).

Civil Aviation. There were 68 municipally-owned airports in 2001. There were 1,478,832 passenger enplanements statewide in 1999.

Shipping. Water transport is provided from the Pacific to the port of Lewiston, by way of the Columbia and Snake rivers, a distance of 464 miles.

Postal Services. Idaho is served by the United States Postal Service. Major private carriers, including UPS, Federal Express, Airborne Express and DHL Worldwide Express, provide Idaho residents with global shipping access. There are numerous local mailing and shipping services available in Idaho's larger cities.

SOCIAL INSTITUTIONS

Justice. The death penalty (minimum age 16) may be imposed for first degree murder or aggravated kidnapping, but the judge must consider mitigating circumstances before imposing a sentence of death. The only execution since 1976 was in 1994. In June 2000 there were 5,465 federal and state prisoners.

Religion. The leading religious denominations are the Church of Jesus Christ of Latter-day Saints (Mormons; 339,000 adherents in 1998), Roman Catholics, Methodists, Presbyterians, Episcopalians and Lutherans.

Education. In 2001–02 public elementary schools (grades K to 6) had 132,406 pupils and 6,981 teachers; secondary schools had 114,009 pupils and 7,550 classroom teachers. Average salary (2001–02) of teachers was $39,314 (elementary) and $39,027 (secondary).

The University of Idaho, founded at Moscow in 1889, had 468 full-time instructional faculty in 2002, and a total enrolment of 12,423. Boise State University had 463 full-time instructional faculty in 2002 and a total enrolment of 17,688. There were eight other higher education institutions, four of them public institutions. College and university enrolment in the autumn of 2002 was 70,354.

Health. In 2001 there were 3,102 hospital beds in 48 licensed facilities.

Welfare. Old-age survivor disability insurance (OASDI) is granted to persons if they meet needs qualifications. 2000: total beneficiaries, 195,695 with annual benefit payments of $146·7m.

CULTURE

Broadcasting. In 2001 there were 77 radio stations and 22 television stations.

Cinema. There were 65 movie theatres in 2002.

Press. Idaho has 13 daily newspapers and 54 weekly papers.

Tourism. Money spent by travellers in 1997 was about $1,700m.

Festivals. Idaho hosts Ballet Idaho, the Idaho Shakespeare Festival, the Lionel Hampton Jazz Festival, the International Folk Dance Festival, the Boise River Festival and the National Old Time Fiddler's Contest.

Libraries. 83% of the population had access to library services in 1997.

Museums and Galleries. Amongst Idaho's many museums and galleries are the Boise Art Museum, the Idaho State Historical Museum and the Nez Percé National Historic Park and Museum.

FURTHER READING

Statistical information: Department of Commerce, 700 West State St., Boise 83720. Publishes *Idaho County Profiles, Idaho Community Profiles* and *Profile of Rural Idaho.*

Schwantes, C. A., *In Mountain Shadows: a History of Idaho.* Nebraska Univ. Press, 1996

Website: http://www.idoc.state.id.us

ILLINOIS

KEY HISTORICAL EVENTS

Territory of a group of Algonquian-speaking tribes, Illinois was explored first by the French in 1673. France claimed the area until 1763 when, after the French and Indian War, it was ceded to Britain along with all the French land east of the Mississippi. In 1783 Britain recognized the US' title to Illinois, which became part of the North West Territory of the USA in 1787, and of Indiana Territory in 1800. Illinois became a Territory in its own right in 1809, and a state in 1818.

Settlers from the eastern states moved on to the fertile farmland, immigration increasing greatly with the opening in 1825 of the Erie Canal from New York along which settlers could move west and their produce back east for sale. Chicago was incorporated as a city in 1837 and quickly became the transport, trading and distribution centre of the middle west. Once industrial growth had begun there, a further wave of immigration took place in the 1840s, mainly of European refugees looking for work. This movement continued with varying force until the 1920s, when it was largely replaced by immigration of black work-seekers from the southern states.

During the 20th century the population became largely urban and heavy industry was established along an intensive network of rail and waterway routes. Chicago recovered from a destructive fire in 1871 to become the hub of this network and at one time the second largest American city.

TERRITORY AND POPULATION

Illinois is bounded north by Wisconsin, northeast by Lake Michigan, east by Indiana, southeast by the Ohio River (forming the boundary with Kentucky), and west by the Mississippi River (forming the boundary with Missouri and Iowa). Land area in 2000: 55,584 sq. miles (143,962 sq. km). Census population, 2000, 12,419,293, an increase of 8·6% since 1990. July 2002 estimate, 12,600,620.

Population in five census years was:

	White	Black	Indian	All others		Total	Per sq. mile
1910	5,526,962	109,049	188	2,392		5,638,591	100·6
1930	7,266,361	328,972	469	35,321		7,630,654	136·4
				All others			
1980	9,233,327	1,675,398		517,793		11,426,518	203·0

	White	Black	American Indian, or Alaska Native	Asian or Pacific Islander	Other	Total	Per sq. mile
1990	8,957,923	1,690,855	24,077	284,944	472,803	11,430,602	205·6
2000	9,125,471	1,876,875	31,006	428,213	957,728	12,419,293	223·4

Of the total population in 2000, 6,338,957 were female, 9,173,842 were 18 years old or older and 10,909,520 were urban. In 2000 the Hispanic population was 1,527,573 (904,449 in 1990).

The most populous cities (2000 census population) are: Chicago, 2,896,016; Rockford, 150,115; Aurora, 142,990; Naperville, 128,358; Peoria, 112,936; Springfield, 111,454; Joliet, 106,221; Elgin, 94,487; Waukegan, 87,901; Cicero, 85,616.

Metropolitan area populations, 2000 census: Chicago–Gary–Kenosha, 9,157,540; Rockford, 371,236; Peoria–Pekin, 347,387; Springfield, 201,437; Champaign–Urbana; 179,669.

SOCIAL STATISTICS

Births in 2001 were 184,022 (14·7 per 1,000); deaths, 104,858 (8·4 per 1,000); infant mortality rate (1998) 8·2 per 1,000 live births; marriages (2000), 89,469; divorces and annulments (2000), 39,429.

CLIMATE

2001 statistics: Jan. 24·6°F (−4·1°C), July 74·6°F (23·6°C) average mean (O'Hare International Airport). Average annual rainfall 35·55". In 2000 total rainfall was 31·43". Illinois belongs to the Great Lakes climate zone (*see* UNITED STATES: Climate).

CONSTITUTION AND GOVERNMENT

The present constitution became effective on 1 July 1971. The General Assembly consists of a House of Representatives of 118 members elected for 2 years, and a Senate of 59 members who are divided into 3 groups; in one, they are elected for terms of 4 years, 4 years, and 2 years; in the next, for terms of 4 years, 2 years, and 4 years; and in the last, for terms of 2 years, 4 years, and 4 years. Sessions are annual. The state is divided into legislative districts, in each of which 1 senator is chosen; each district is divided into 2 representative districts, in each of which 1 representative is chosen.

For the 108th Congress, which convened in Jan. 2003, Illinois sends 19 members to the House of Representatives. It is represented in the Senate by Richard Durbin (D. 1997–2009) and Peter Fitzgerald (R. 1999–2005).

The capital is Springfield.

RECENT ELECTIONS

In the 2000 presidential election Gore polled 2,589,026 votes; Bush, 2,019,421; Nader, 103,759.

CURRENT ADMINISTRATION

Governor: Rod Blagojevich (D.), 2003–07 (salary: $150,691).
　Lieut.-Governor: Pat Quinn (D.), 2003–07 ($115,235).
　Secretary of State: Jesse White (D.), 2003–07 ($123,700).

Government Website: http://www.illinois.gov

ECONOMY

Important industries include financial services, manufacturing, retail and transportation. *Per capita* personal income (2000) was $31,842 in Illinois.

Budget. In 2001 Illinois' appropriations (all funds total) were $64,493m.; total state revenues (projected) $31,864m.; general funds receipts (est.) $20,898m. Debt outstanding, in 1999, $26,582m.

Performance. Gross State Product in 2000 was $467,284m.

Banking and Finance. In 2000 there were 526 state-chartered banks, 32 foreign banks and 245 national banks. The assets of banks in Illinois totalled $435,669,401,000 in 2000.

ENERGY AND NATURAL RESOURCES

Electricity. Electricity production 1999, 149·8bn. kWh. There were 11 nuclear plants, with net production of 81·4bn. kWh.

Oil and Gas. Natural gas consumption in 1999 was 1,035bn. cu. ft; total petroleum consumption was 250,369,000 bbls.

Water. The total area covered by water is approximately 2,531 sq. miles. In 1999 there were 26,443 miles of streams.

Minerals. Chief mineral product is coal; in 2001 there were 19 operative mines; the coal output was 33,793,509 tons. Mineral production also includes sand, gravel and limestone. Value of non-fuel mineral production in 2000 was $907m.

Agriculture. In 2001 there were 76,000 farms in Illinois that contained 27·7m. acres of land. The average size of farms was 364 acres. In 2002 cash receipts from farm marketings in Illinois totalled $7·53bn. Cash receipts: for corn totalled $2·9bn.; for soybeans, $2·1bn.; for livestock and products, $1·8bn.; for hogs, $920m.; for cattle, $528m.; for dairy products, $301m.; for wheat, $111m. In 2000 Illinois was the second largest producer among US states of corn and soybeans. There were 4·85m. hogs and pigs on 1 Dec. 1998. On 1 Jan. 2000 there were 1·51m. cattle including 445,000 beef cows and 125,000 milch cows.

Forestry. In 2000 there were 6 state forests and 27 conservation areas. The gross forest area within unit boundaries in 1997 was 846,000 acres of which 278,000 acres was National Forest Land.

Fisheries. In 2001 four hatcheries in Illinois had 75m. fish.

INDUSTRY
On 12 March 2000 there were 308,067 establishments (5,501,036 employees) with an annual payroll of $201,319,268,000.

Labour. Selected employee sectors, 12 March 2000: manufacturing, 852,646; retail trade, 636,996; healthcare and social assistance, 631,926; accommodation and food services, 406,601; finance and insurance, 344,564; wholesale trade, 344,027; construction, 265,481; transportation and warehousing, 215,439; arts, entertainment and recreation, 72,105; utilities, 31,173; mining, 8,939. The unemployment rate in 1999 was 4·3%.

Trade Unions. Labour union membership in 2000 was 1,046,300. Approximately 18·9% of workers in Illinois were members of unions in 1998.

INTERNATIONAL TRADE

Imports and Exports. In 2001 exports from Illinois totalled approximately $31·8bn. Exports included computer equipment, industrial machinery, chemicals and agricultural products.

Trade Fairs. Through the Illinois Department of Commerce and Community Affairs (Illinois Trade Office), activities are held to promote trade. Between Aug. 2000 and July 2001 approximately 20 major events (catalogue shows and trade missions including Canada, Mexico, South America, the Middle East, Africa and Asia Pacific) were held.

COMMUNICATIONS

Roads. In 2000 there were 137,577 miles of roads, which included 16,298 miles of state highways. There were 7,524,909 passenger cars in 2001, 1,249,505 pickup trucks, 290,299 recreational vehicles, buses and trucks, 222,607 motorcycles and 176,870 Interstate Registration Plan vehicles.

Rail. Union Station, Chicago is the home of Amtrak's national hub. Amtrak trains provide service to cities in Illinois to many destinations in the US. Illinois is also served by a metro (CTA) system, and by seven groups of commuter railways controlled by METRA, which has many stations and serves several Illinois counties. Total passengers using Amtrak stations in 2000 were 3,583,707. State system mileage, Dec. 2001: Federal aid interstate non-toll, 1,890 miles; other marked non-toll, 11,422 miles; state supplementary non-toll, 2,638 miles; total length, 15,950 miles.

Civil Aviation. In 2001 there were 134 public airports, 496 restricted landing areas and 272 heliports. There were 38,634,305 passenger enplanements statewide in 1999.

Shipping. In 2000 total cargo handled by Chicago's ports was 23,929,489 tons.

Telecommunications. In March 2000, 48,395 employees were on a payroll of $3,000·5m.

Postal Services. In 2001 there were more than 1,000 postal stations.

SOCIAL INSTITUTIONS

Justice. In fiscal year 2001 there were 27 adult correctional centers with an adult inmate population of 45,629. The total number of adult admissions in 2000 was 28,045 and the total number of exits 27,636.

Executions began in 1990 following the US Supreme Court's reinstatement of capital punishment in 1976, with the most recent execution being on 17 March 1999. The minimum age for the death penalty is 18. However, on 31 Jan. 2000 the death penalty was suspended.

A Civil Rights Act (1941), as amended, bans all forms of discrimination by places of public accommodation, including inns, restaurants, retail stores, railroads, aeroplanes, buses, etc., against persons on account of 'race, religion, colour, national ancestry or physical or mental handicap'; another section similarly mentions 'race or colour'.

The Fair Employment Practices Act of 1961, as amended, prohibits discrimination in employment based on race, colour, sex, religion, national origin or ancestry, by employers, employment agencies, labour organizations and others. These principles are embodied in the 1971 constitution.

The Illinois Human Rights Act (1979) prevents unlawful discrimination in employment, real property transactions, access to financial credit and public accommodations, by authorizing the creation of a Department of Human Rights to enforce, and a Human Rights Commission to adjudicate, allegations of unlawful discrimination.

Religion. In 1997 there were 6,579,000 Christians and 269,000 Jews in Illinois. Among the larger Christian denominations are: Roman Catholic (3·6m.), Presbyterian Church, USA (0·2m.), Lutheran Church in America (0·2m.), Lutheran Church Missouri Synod (325,000), American Baptist (105,000), Disciples of Christ (75,000), United Methodist (505,000), Southern Baptist (265,000), United Church of Christ (192,000), Assembly of God (63,000) and Church of Nazarene (50,000).

Education. Education is free and compulsory for children between 7 and 16 years of age. In 2000–01 pre K-8 enrolment (public) was 1,471,360; pre K-8 (non-public), 254,817; grades 9–12 enrolment (public), 577,432; grades 9–12 (non-public), 68,559. The total number of elementary teachers (public) was 70,023; elementary teachers (non-public), 11,104; secondary teachers (public), 31,726; secondary teachers (non-public), 4,415. The median salary for all classroom (pre K-12) teachers was $44,977. In autumn 2001 higher education institutions had a total enrolment of 752,753 at 9 public universities, 48 community colleges, 97 not-for-profit and 25 for-profit independent colleges and universities.

Major colleges and universities (autumn 2001):

Founded	Name	Place	Control	Enrolment
1851	Northwestern University	Evanston	Independent	17,000
1857	Illinois State University	Normal	Public	21,240
1867	University of Illinois	Urbana/Champaign	Public	39,291
		Springfield (1969)		4,288
		Chicago (1946)		24,955
1867	Chicago State University	Chicago	Public	7,079
1869	Southern Illinois University	Carbondale	Public	21,598
		Edwardsville (1957)		12,442
1890	Loyola University of Chicago	Chicago	Roman Catholic	13,019
1891	University of Chicago	Chicago	Independent	12,883
1895	Eastern Illinois University	Charleston	Public	10,531
1895	Northern Illinois University	DeKalb	Public	23,783
1897	Bradley University	Peoria	Independent	5,996
1899	Western Illinois University	Macomb	Public	13,206
1940	Illinois Institute of Technology	Chicago	Independent	6,050
1945	Roosevelt University	Chicago	Independent	7,490
1961	Northeastern Illinois University	Chicago	Public	10,999
1969	Governors State University	University Park	Public	5,860

Health. In 2000 there were 196 community hospitals. There were 40,254 beds in 1997. Total admissions in 2000 were 1,530,800.

Welfare. In fiscal year 2002 the estimated amount spent on medical assistance programmes was $7·66bn.; child support enforcement, $233m.; Office of the Inspector General, $22m.; Public Aid Recoveries, $19m.; administration, $113m.

In 1999 there were 42,300 participating providers in the state and 24,540,000 medical claims processed.

CULTURE

Broadcasting. In 1999 there were 219 radio stations, 9 radio networks and 67 television broadcasting establishments. In 1997 there were 184 cable and other pay TV services establishments.

Cinema. In 2000 there were 478 motion picture and video industries establishments in Illinois.

Press. In 1999 there were 983 newspapers, periodicals, book and database publisher establishments.

Tourism. Tourism revenue in 1997 was $19·5bn. The recommended appropriations for tourism for fiscal year 2002 were $69,091,300.

Festivals. In 2002 there were more than 100 festivals, parades and special celebrations.

Libraries. There were, in 2000, 643 public libraries, 188 college and university libraries, 2,440 school libraries and 544 special libraries. In 1999 information services establishments had an annual payroll of $205,048,000.

Theatre and Opera. There were 146 theatre companies and dinner theatre establishments in 2000 and 36 other performing arts company establishments in 1998. Illinois had three opera houses in 2001.

Museums and Galleries. There were 282 museums in 2001.

FURTHER READING
Statistical information: Department of Commerce and Community Affairs, 620 Adams St., Springfield 62701. Publishes *Illinois State and Regional Economic Data Book.* Bureau of Economic and Business Research, Univ. of Illinois, 1206 South 6th St., Champaign 61820. Publishes *Illinois Statistical Abstract.*
Blue Book of the State of Illinois. Edited by Secretary of State. Springfield. Biennial

Miller, D. L., *City of the Century: The Epic of Chicago and the Making of America.* Simon and Schuster, New York, 1996

The Illinois State Library: Springfield, IL 62756.

INDIANA
KEY HISTORICAL EVENTS
The area was inhabited by Algonquian-speaking tribes when the first European explorers (French) laid claim to it in the 17th century. They established some fortified trading posts but there was little settlement. In 1763 the area passed to Britain, with other French-claimed territory east of the Mississippi. In 1783 Indiana became part of the North West Territory of the USA; it became a separate territory in 1800 and a state in 1816. Until 1811 there had been continuing conflict with the Indian inhabitants, who were then defeated at Tippecanoe.

Early farming settlement was by families of British and German descent, including Amish and Mennonite communities. Later industrial development offered an incentive for more immigration from Europe, and, later, from the southern states. In 1906 the town of Gary was laid out by the United States Steel Corporation and named after its chairman, Elbert H. Gary. The industry flourished on navigable water midway between supplies of iron ore and of coal. Trade and distribution in general benefited from Indiana Port on Lake Michigan, especially after the opening of the St Lawrence Seaway in 1959. The Ohio River was also exploited for carrying freight.

Indianapolis was built after 1821 and became the state capital in 1825. Natural gas was discovered in the neighbourhood in the late 19th century. This stimulated the growth of a motor industry, celebrated by the Indianapolis 500 race, held annually since 1911.

TERRITORY AND POPULATION
Indiana is bounded west by Illinois, north by Michigan and Lake Michigan, east by Ohio and south by Kentucky across the Ohio River. Land area, 35,867 sq. miles (92,895 sq. km). Census population, 1 April 2000, was 6,080,485, an increase of 9·7% since 1990. July 2002 estimate, 6,159,068.

Population in five census years was:

	White	Black	Indian	Asiatic	Other	Total	Per sq. mile
1930	3,125,778	111,982	285	458	....	3,238,503	89·4
1960	4,388,554	269,275	948	2,447	....	4,662,498	128·9
1980	5,004,394	414,785	7,836	20,557	42,652	5,490,224	152·8
1990	5,020,700	432,092	12,720	37,617	41,030	5,544,159	154·6
2000	5,320,022	510,034	15,815	61,131	173,483	6,080,485	169·5

Of the total population in 2000, 3,098,011 were female, 4,506,089 were 18 years old or older and 4,304,011 were urban. Indiana's Hispanic population was 214,536 in 2000, a 117·2% increase on the 1990 total of 98,789.

The largest cities with census population, 2000, are: Indianapolis (capital), 761,296; Fort Wayne, 205,727; Evansville, 121,582; South Bend, 107,789; Gary, 102,746; Hammond, 83,048; Bloomington, 69,291; Muncie, 67,430; Anderson, 59,734; Terre Haute, 59,614.

SOCIAL STATISTICS
1999 statistics: births, 86,031 (14·5 per 1,000 population); deaths, 54,761 (9·3); infant mortality rate, 7·8 (per 1,000 live births). Marriages (1998), 47,254.

CLIMATE
Indianapolis, Jan. 29°F (−1·7°C), July 76°F (24·4°C). Annual rainfall 41" (1,034 mm). Indiana belongs to the Mid-West climate zone (see UNITED STATES: Climate).

CONSTITUTION AND GOVERNMENT
The present constitution (the second) dates from 1851; it has had (as of Aug. 1999) 41 amendments. The General Assembly consists of a Senate of 50 members elected for four years, and a House of Representatives of 100 members elected for two years. It meets annually.

For the 108th Congress, which convened in Jan. 2003, Indiana sends nine members to the House of Representatives. It is represented in the Senate by Richard Lugar (R. 1977–2007) and Evan Bayh (D. 1999–2005).

The state capital is Indianapolis. The state is divided into 92 counties and 1,008 townships.

RECENT ELECTIONS
In the 2000 presidential election Bush polled 1,245,836 votes; Gore, 901,980; Nader, 18,531.

CURRENT ADMINISTRATION
Governor: Frank O'Bannon (D.), 2001–05 (salary: $95,000).
  Lieut.-Governor: Joseph Kernan (D.), 2001–05 ($76,000).
  Secretary of State: Todd Rokita (R.), 2003–07 ($66,000).

Government Website: http://www.in.gov

ECONOMY
Per capita personal income (2000) was $26,838.

Budget. In 1999 total state revenue was $19,149m. Total expenditure was $18,614m. (education, $7,161m.; public welfare, $3,728m.; highways, $1,881m.; health and hospitals, $663m.; police protection, $182m.). Outstanding debt, in 1999, $7,056m.

Performance. In 2000 Gross State Product was $192,195m.

ENERGY AND NATURAL RESOURCES

Oil and Gas. Production of crude oil in 1998 was 2,210,000 bbls.; $1m. worth of natural gas was produced in 1996.

Water. The total area covered by water is approximately 550 sq. miles.

Minerals. The state produced 60,800,000 tonnes of crushed stone and 192m. tonnes of dimension stone in 1998. Total reserves of coal (1996), 9,991m. short tons. Value of domestic non-fuel mineral production, in 1998, $700m.

Agriculture. Indiana is largely agricultural, about 75% of its total area being in farms. In 2000, 64,000 farms had 15·5m. acres (average, 242 acres). The average value of land and buildings per acre was $2,230 in 2000. Acreage harvested in 2000 was 12·7m., with a market value of $3,245m. for the top two crops (corn and soybeans).

Farm income 2000, $4·6bn.: crops were $3,041m.; livestock and products, $1,654m. The four most important products were corn, soybeans, hogs and chicken eggs. The livestock on 1 Jan. 2001 included 880,000 all cattle, 151,000 milch cows, 59,000 sheep and lambs, 3·35m. hogs and pigs, 28·7m. chickens, 13·5m. turkeys. In 2000 the wool clip yielded 385,000 lbs of wool from 61,000 sheep and lambs.

Forestry. In 1997 there were 644,000 acres of forest including Hoosier National Forest (192,000 acres).

INDUSTRY

In 1997, 9,724 manufacturing establishments employed 669,701 workers, earning $23,731,760,000. The steel industry is the largest in the country.

Labour. In Sept. 1999, of the 3,088,271 labour force, 95,557 persons (3·1% of the population) were unemployed.

INTERNATIONAL TRADE

Imports and Exports. Exports valued $12,038,738,139 in 1998.

COMMUNICATIONS

Roads. In 2000 there were 93,607 miles of road (73,664 miles rural) and 5,714,791 registered motor vehicles.

Rail. In 1997 there were 4,964 miles of mainline railway of which 3,635 miles were class 1.

Civil Aviation. Of airports in 2000, 117 were for public use and 564 were for private use. There were 4,378,553 passenger enplanements statewide in 1999.

SOCIAL INSTITUTIONS

Justice. Following the US Supreme Court's reinstatement of the death penalty in 1976, death sentences have been awarded since 1980. The minimum age is 16. There were two executions in 2001 but none in 2002. In 2001, 20,125 prisoners were under the jurisdiction of state and federal correctional authorities.

The Civil Rights Act of 1885 forbids places of public accommodation to bar any persons on grounds not applicable to all citizens alike; no citizen may be disqualified for jury service 'on account of race or colour'. An Act of 1947 makes it an offence to spread religious or racial hatred.

A 1961 Act provided 'all of its citizens equal opportunity for education, employment and access to public conveniences and accommodations' and created a Civil Rights Commission.

Religion. Religious denominations include Methodists, Roman Catholic, Disciples of Christ, Baptists, Lutheran, Presbyterian churches, Society of Friends, Episcopal.

Education. School attendance is compulsory from 7 to 16 years. In 2000–01 there were an estimated 551,577 pupils attending elementary schools and 437,114 at secondary schools. The average expenditure per pupil was $7,652. Teachers' salaries averaged $43,311 (2000–01). Total expenditure for public schools, 1998, $6,833m.

Some leading institutions for higher education were (1998):

Founded	Institution	Control	Students (full-time)
1801	Vincennes University	State	8,185
1824	Indiana University, Bloomington	State	35,600
1837	De Pauw University, Greencastle	Methodist	2,250
1842	University of Notre Dame	R.C.	10,301
1850	Butler University, Indianapolis	Independent	4,126
1859	Valparaiso University, Valparaiso	Evangelical Lutheran Church	3,720
1870	Indiana State University, Terre Haute	State	10,970
1874	Purdue University, Lafayette	State	38,757
1898	Ball State University, Muncie	State	18,924
1902	University of Indianapolis, Indianapolis	Methodist	3,764
1963	Ivy Tech State College, Indianapolis	State	5,116
1985	University of Southern Indiana	State	5,415

Health. In 1996 there were 115 community hospitals with 19,500 beds and 6,930 patients admitted. Patients receiving treatment each day: 11·1 per 1,000 (outpatients 12·3 per 1,000).

Welfare. Of the $2,752,037,667 of Federal funds received by Indiana from Public Assistance Programs in 1998–99, 65% was from Medicaid, 9·3% from Food Stamps, 9·1% from Child Support and 3·9% from Child Care. In total $4,143·8m. was spent on public assistance in Indiana in 1999 (including all state, federal and county expenditure).

CULTURE

Broadcasting. In 1999 there were 60 television stations. There were (1992) 208 radio stations: 81 AM; 127 FM.

Press. There were 70 dailies and 21 Sunday newspapers in circulation in 1997.

Tourism. Tourists—60% of whom travelled from outside the state—spent $5·93bn. in 1996.

Festivals. Over 750 festivals were held in Indiana in 1999.

Libraries. In 2000 there were 239 public libraries (with 3,446,904 registered borrowers) and 84 (1998) college and university libraries.

Museums and Galleries. There were 372 museums listed in 1998. The first Cine Dome theatre in the country is attached to the Children's Museum of Indianapolis.

FURTHER READING
Statistical information: Indiana Business Research Center, Indiana Univ., Indianapolis 46202. Publishes *Indiana Factbook.*
Gray, R. D. (ed.) *Indiana History: a Book of Readings.* Indiana Univ. Press, 1994
Martin, J. B., *Indiana: an Interpretation.* Indiana Univ. Press, 1992

State Library: Indiana State Library, 140 North Senate, Indianapolis 46204.

IOWA

KEY HISTORICAL EVENTS
Originally the territory of the Iowa Indians, the area was explored by the Frenchmen Marquette and Joliet in 1673. French trading posts were set up, but there was little other settlement. In 1803 the French sold their claim to Iowa to the USA as part of the Louisiana Purchase. The land was still occupied by Indians but, in the 1830s, the tribes sold their land to the US government and migrated to reservations. Iowa became a US Territory in 1838 and a state in 1846.

The state was settled by immigrants drawn mainly from neighbouring states to the east. Later there was more immigration from Protestant states of northern Europe. The land was extremely fertile and most immigrants came to farm. Not all the Indian population had accepted the cession and there were some violent confrontations, notably the murder of settlers at Spirit Lake in 1857. The capital, Des Moines, was founded in 1843 as a fort to protect Indian rights. It expanded rapidly with the growth of a local coal field after 1910.

TERRITORY AND POPULATION
Iowa is bounded east by the Mississippi River (forming the boundary with Wisconsin and Illinois), south by Missouri, west by the Missouri River (forming the boundary with Nebraska), northwest by the Big Sioux River (forming the boundary with South Dakota) and north by Minnesota. Land area, 55,869 sq. miles (144,700 sq. km). Census population, 1 April 2000, 2,926,324, an increase of 5·4% since 1990. July 2002 estimate, 2,936,760.

Population in five census years was:

	White	Black	Indian	Asiatic	Total	Per sq. mile
1870	1,188,207	5,762	48	3	1,194,020	21·5
1930	2,452,677	17,380	660	222	2,470,939	44·1
				All others		
1980	2,839,225	41,700		32,882	2,913,808	51·7
1990	2,683,090	48,090		45,575	2,776,755	49·7
2000	2,748,640	61,853		115,831	2,926,324	52·4

Of the total population in 2000, 1,490,809 were female, 2,192,686 were 18 years old or older and 1,787,432 were urban. In 2000 the Hispanic population was 82,473, up from 32,647 in 1990 (an increase of 152·6%).

The largest cities in the state, with their population in 2000, are: Des Moines (capital), 198,682; Cedar Rapids, 120,758; Davenport, 98,359; Sioux City, 85,013; Waterloo, 68,747; Iowa City, 62,220; Council Bluffs, 58,268; Dubuque, 57,686; Ames, 50,731; West Des Moines, 46,403; Cedar Falls, 36,145; Bettendorf, 31,275; Mason City, 29,172; Urbandale, 29,072; Clinton, 27,772.

SOCIAL STATISTICS
2001 statistics: births, 37,610 (12·9 per 1,000); deaths, 27,741 (9·5 per 1,000); infant deaths, 211; marriages, 21,127; dissolutions of marriages, 9,542.

CLIMATE
Cedar Rapids, Jan. 17·6°F, July 74·2°F. Annual rainfall 34". Des Moines, Jan. 19·4°F, July 76·6°F. Annual rainfall 33·12". Iowa belongs to the Mid-West climate zone (see UNITED STATES: Climate).

CONSTITUTION AND GOVERNMENT
The constitution of 1857 still exists; it has had 46 amendments. The General Assembly comprises a Senate of 50 and a House of Representatives of 100 members, meeting annually for an unlimited session. Senators are elected for four years, half retiring every second year: Representatives for two years. The Governor and Lieut.-Governor are elected for four years.

For the 108th Congress, which convened in Jan. 2003, Iowa sends five members to the House of Representatives. It is represented in the Senate by Chuck Grassley (R. 1981–2005) and Tom Harkin (D. 1985–2009).

Iowa is divided into 99 counties; the capital is Des Moines.

RECENT ELECTIONS
In the 2000 presidential election Gore polled 638,517 votes; Bush, 634,373; Nader, 29,374.

CURRENT ADMINISTRATION
Governor: Tom Vilsack (D.), 2003–07 (salary: $107,482).
   Lieut.-Governor: Sally Pederson (D.), 2003–07 ($76,698).
   Secretary of State: Chet Culver (D.), 2003–07 ($87,990).

Government Website: http://www.iowaccess.org

ECONOMY
Per capita personal income (2001) was $27,331.

Budget. In the fiscal year 2002 net state general fund revenue was $4,691·4m. Total state general fund expenditure was $4,605·8m. (education, $2,746·2m.; human services, $848·4m.; justice, $438·5m.; administration and regulation, $400·3m.; health and human rights, $84·3m.; agriculture and natural resources, $41·0m.; economic development, $27·5m.; transportation, $14·2m.; oversight, $5·4m.). Debt outstanding in 2000 was $250m.

Performance. Gross State Product was $89,600m. in 2000.

ENERGY AND NATURAL RESOURCES
Water. The total area covered by water is approximately 401 sq. miles.

Minerals. Production in 2000: crushed stone, 43m. tonnes; sand and gravel, 12·1m. tonnes. The value of domestic non-fuel mineral products in 2000 was $570m.

Agriculture. Iowa is the wealthiest of the agricultural states, partly because nearly the whole area (92%) is arable and included in farms. The average farm in 2001 was 350 acres. The average value of buildings and land per acre was, in 2001, $1,926. The number of farms declined in the latter years of the 20th century, from 174,000 in 1960 to 93,500 in 2001.

Farm income (2001), $15,000m.: from livestock, $4,700m., and from crops, $93,500m. Production of corn was 1,664m. bu.[1], value $3,495m. and soybeans, 480m. bu.[1], value $2,066m. In 2001 livestock included: swine, 15·4m.[1]; milch cows, 210,000; all cattle, 3·65m.; sheep and lambs, 270,000. The wool clip yielded 1·42m. lb.

[1]More than any other state.

INDUSTRY

Labour. In Sept. 2002 services employed 395,300 people; trade, 347,000; manufacturing establishments, 246,100. Iowa had an unemployment rate of 3·9% in Sept. 2002.

COMMUNICATIONS

Roads. In 2002 there were 113,226 miles of streets and highways. There were 2,122,000 licensed drivers and 3,872,250 registered vehicles.

Rail. The state, in 2002, had 4,163 miles of track, 3 Class I, 4 Class II and 11 Class III railways.

Civil Aviation. Airports numbered 215 in 2002, consisting of 105 publicly owned, 102 privately owned and 8 commercial facilities. There were 3,770 registered aircraft and 1,461,856 passenger enplanements in Iowa in 2001.

SOCIAL INSTITUTIONS

Justice. The death penalty was abolished in Iowa in 1965. In 2002 the nine state prisons had 8,310 inmates.

Religion. Chief religious bodies in 2002: Roman Catholic, 533,036 members; United Methodists, 199,736; Evangelical Lutheran in America, 269,073 baptized members; USA Presbyterians, 55,442; United Church of Christ, 39,698.

Education. School attendance is compulsory for 24 consecutive weeks annually during school age (7–16). In 2001–02, 489,523 pupils were attending primary and secondary schools; 38,881 pupils attending non-public schools; classroom teachers numbered 33,878 for public schools with an average salary of $38,230. In 2002 the state spent an average of $5,959 on each elementary and secondary school student.

Leading institutions for higher education enrolment figures (autumn 2002) were:

Founded	Institution	Control	Professors	Full-time Students
1843	Clarke College, Dubuque	Independent	77	779
1846	Grinnell College, Grinnell	Independent	141	1,432
1847	University of Iowa, Iowa City	State	1,649	23,552
1851	Coe College, Cedar Rapids	Independent	74	1,190
1852	Wartburg College, Waverly	Evangelical Lutheran	100	1,615
1853	Cornell College, Mount Vernon	Independent	82	992
1854	Upper Iowa University, Fayette	Independent	34	2,606
1858	Iowa State University, Ames	State	1,396	24,342
1859	Luther College, Decorah	Evangelical Lutheran	191	2,501
1876	Univ. of Northern Iowa, Cedar Falls	State	556	11,489
1881	Drake University, Des Moines	Independent	244	3,789
1882	St Ambrose University, Davenport	Roman Catholic	260	2,207
1891	Buena Vista University, Storm Lake	Presbyterian	81	2,377
1894	Morningside College, Sioux City	Methodist	65	744

Health. In 2002 the state had 116 community hospitals (11,542 beds).

Welfare. Iowa has a Civil Rights Act (1939) which makes it a misdemeanour for any place of public accommodation to deprive any person of 'full and equal enjoyment' of the facilities it offers the public.

Supplemental Security Income (SSI) assistance is available for the aged (65 or older), the blind and the disabled. As of June 2002, 4,078 elderly persons were drawing an average of $191·81 per month, 743 blind persons $321·26 per month, and 35,043 disabled persons $352·29 per month. As of July 2002 temporary assistance to needy families (TANF) was received by 19,529 cases representing 57,084 recipients.

CULTURE
There were a total of 80 venues for live performances (2002).

Broadcasting. In 2002 there were 254 radio stations and 23 television stations.

Cinema. There were 135 cinemas in 2002.

Press. In 2002 there were a total of 327 newspapers.

Tourism. In 2001 there were 15,900,000 visitors; value of industry, $4·3bn.

Festivals. There were over 2,000 events in 2002, including music festivals, fairs, concerts, antique shows and art festivals.

Libraries. In 2002 there were 543 public libraries and 73 special libraries.

Museums and Galleries. There were 80 art museums and 173 history museums in 2002.

FURTHER READING
Annual Survey of Manufactures. US Department of Commerce
Government Finance. US Department of Commerce
Official Register. Secretary of State. Des Moines. Biennial
Smeal, L., *Iowa Historical and Biographical Index.* New York, 1984

State Government Website: http://www.iowa.gov
State Library of Iowa: Des Moines 50319.

KANSAS

KEY HISTORICAL EVENTS
The area was explored from Mexico in the 16th century, when Spanish travellers found groups of Kansas, Wichita, Osage and Pawnee tribes. The French claimed Kansas in 1682 and they established a valuable fur trade with local tribes in the 18th century. In 1803 the area passed to the USA as part of the Louisiana Purchase and became a base for pioneering trails further west. After 1830 it was 'Indian Territory' and a number of tribes displaced from eastern states were settled there. In 1854 the Kansas Territory was created and opened for white settlement. The early settlers were farmers from Europe or New England, but the Territory's position brought it into contact with southern ideas also. Until 1861 there were frequent outbreaks of violence over the issue of slavery. Slavery had been excluded from the future Territory by the Missouri Compromise of 1820, but the 1854 Kansas-Nebraska Act had affirmed the principle of 'popular sovereignty' to settle the issue, which was then fought out by opposing factions throughout 'Bleeding Kansas'.

Kansas finally entered the Union (as a non-slavery state) in 1861; the part of Colorado which had formed part of the Kansas Territory was then separated from it.

The economy developed through a combination of cattle-ranching and railways. Herds were driven to the railheads and shipped from vast stockyards, or slaughtered and processed in railhead meat-packing plants. Wheat and sorghum also became important once the plains could be ploughed on a large scale.

TERRITORY AND POPULATION
Kansas is bounded north by Nebraska, east by Missouri, with the Missouri River as boundary in the northeast, south by Oklahoma and west by Colorado. Land area, 81,815 sq. miles (211,900 sq. km). Census population, 1 April 2000, 2,688,418, an increase of 8·5% since 1990. July 2002 estimate, 2,715,884.

Population in five federal census years was:

	White	Black	Indian	Asiatic	Total	Per sq. mile
1870	346,377	17,108	914	—	364,399	4·5
1930	1,811,997	66,344	2,454	204	1,880,999	22·9
				All others		
1980	2,168,221	126,127		69,888	2,364,236	28·8
1990	2,231,986	143,076		102,512	2,477,574	30·3
2000	2,313,944	154,198		220,276	2,688,418	32·9

Of the total population in 2000, 1,359,944 were female, 1,975,425 were 18 years old or older and 1,920,669 were urban. In 1999 the estimated Hispanic population was 188,252, up from 93,671 in 1990 (an increase of 101·0%).

Cities, with 2000 census population: Wichita, 344,284; Overland Park, 149,080; Kansas City, 146,866; Topeka (capital), 122,377; Olathe, 92,962; Lawrence, 80,098.

SOCIAL STATISTICS
Vital statistics 1999: births, 38,463 (14·5 per 1,000 population); deaths, 24,209 (9·1); 1996, infant deaths, 8·3 per 1,000 live births. Marriages (1997), 20,400; divorces, 11,500.

CLIMATE
Dodge City, Jan. 29°F (−1·7°C), July 78°F (25·6°C). Annual rainfall 21" (518 mm). Kansas City, Jan. 30°F (−1·1°C), July 79°F (26·1°C). Annual rainfall 38" (947 mm). Topeka, Jan. 28°F (−2·2°C), July 78°F (25·6°C). Annual rainfall 35" (875 mm). Wichita, Jan. 31°F (−0·6°C), July 81°F (27·2°C). Annual rainfall 31" (777 mm). Kansas belongs to the Mid-West climate zone (*see* UNITED STATES: Climate).

CONSTITUTION AND GOVERNMENT
The year 1861 saw the adoption of the present constitution; it has had 78 amendments. The Legislature includes a Senate of 40 members, elected for four years, and a House of Representatives of 125 members, elected for two years. Sessions are annual.

For the 108th Congress, which convened in Jan. 2003, Kansas sends four members to the House of Representatives. It is represented in the Senate by Pat Roberts (R. 1997–2009) and Sam Brownback (R. 1997–2005).

The capital is Topeka. The state is divided into 105 counties.

RECENT ELECTIONS
In the 2000 presidential election Bush polled 622,332 votes; Gore, 399,276; Nader, 36,086.

CURRENT ADMINISTRATION
Governor: Kathleen Sebelius (D.), 2003–07 (salary: $94,036).
  Lieut.-Governor: John E. Moore (D.), 2003–07 ($26,598).
  Secretary of State: Ron Thornburgh (R.), 2003–07 ($73,052).

Government Website: http://www.accesskansas.org

ECONOMY
Per capita income (2000) was $27,408.

Budget. In 1999 total state revenue was $8,687m. Total expenditure was $8,371m. (education, $3,718m.; public welfare, $1,257m.; highways, $960m.; health and hospitals, $506m.; police protection, $46m.). Outstanding debt, in 1999, $1,482m.

Performance. Gross State Product in 2000 was $85,063m.

ENERGY AND NATURAL RESOURCES
Water. The total area covered by water is approximately 459 sq. miles.

Minerals. Important fuel minerals are coal, petroleum and natural gas. Non-fuel minerals, mainly cement, salt and crushed stone, were worth $535m. in 1998.

Agriculture. Kansas is pre-eminently agricultural, but sometimes suffers from lack of rainfall in the west. In 1999 there were some 65,000 farms with a total acreage of 47·5m. Average number of acres per farm was 731. Average value of farmland and buildings per acre, in 1999, was $590. Farm income, 1999, from livestock and products, $5,009m.; from crops, $2,607m. Chief crops: wheat, sorghum, maize, hay. Wheat production was 432·4m. bu. in 1999. There is an extensive livestock industry, comprising, in 2000, 6·55m. cattle, 100,000 sheep, 1·46m. pigs and 1·75m. poultry.

Forestry. In 1997 Kansas had 108,000 acres of National Forest System Land.

INDUSTRY
Employment distribution (1996): total non-farm workforce 1,228,000, of which 303,000 were in wholesale and retail; 301,000 in services; 235,000 in government; 196,000 in manufacturing; 70,000 in transport and utilities; 59,000 in finance, insurance and real estate; 57,000 in construction. The slaughtering industry, other food processing, aircraft, the manufacture of transport equipment and petroleum refining are also important.

Labour. Total non-agricultural employment, 1999, 1,327,000. Employees by branch, 1999 (in 1,000): services, 343; wholesale and retail trade, 319; government, 240; manufacturing, 213; transportation and public utilities, 78. In 1999 the state unemployment rate was 3·0%.

COMMUNICATIONS
Roads. In 2000 there were 134,583 miles of roads (124,375 miles rural) and 2,296,135 registered motor vehicles.

Rail. There were 7,273 miles of railway in Jan. 1982.

Civil Aviation. There is an international airport at Wichita. There were 551,686 passenger enplanements statewide in 1999.

SOCIAL INSTITUTIONS
Justice. In June 2000 there were 8,780 federal and state prisoners. The death penalty is authorized for capital murder, but has not been used since 1965.

Religion. The most numerous religious bodies are Roman Catholic, Methodists and Disciples of Christ.

Education. In 1995 there were approximately 463,000 public elementary and secondary pupils enrolled and (1994–95) 30,588 teachers.

Kansas has six state-supported institutions of higher education: Kansas State University, Manhattan (1863); The University of Kansas, Lawrence, founded in 1865; Emporia State University, Emporia; Pittsburg State University, Pittsburg; Fort Hays State University, Hays; and Wichita State University, Wichita. The state also supports a two-year technical school, Kansas Technical Institute, at Salina.

Education expenditure by state and local governments in 1997 was $2,874m.

Health. In 1995 Kansas had 132 community hospitals with 10,800 beds.

Welfare. In 1996, 436,000 people received social security benefit totalling $3,545m. Average monthly payment to retired workers was $764.

FURTHER READING
Statistical information: Institute for Public Policy and Business Research, Univ. of Kansas, 607 Blake Hall, Lawrence 66045. Publishes *Kansas Statistical Abstract.*
Annual Economic Report of the Governor. Topeka
Drury, J. W., *The Government of Kansas.* Lawrence, Univ. of Kansas, 1970

State Library: Kansas State Library, Topeka.

KENTUCKY

KEY HISTORICAL EVENTS
Lying west of the Appalachians and south of the Ohio River, the area was the meeting place and battleground for the eastern Iroquois and the southern Cherokees.

Northern Shawnees also penetrated. The first successful white settlement took place in 1769 when Daniel Boone reached the Bluegrass plains from the eastern, trans-Appalachian, colonies. After 1783 immigration from the east was rapid, settlers travelling by river or crossing the mountains by the Cumberland Gap. The area was originally attached to Virginia but became a separate state in 1792.

Large plantations dependent on slave labour were established, as were small farms worked by white owners. The state became divided on the issue of slavery, although plantation interests (mainly producing tobacco) dominated state government. In the event the state did not secede in 1861, and the majority of citizens supported the Union. Public opinion swung round in support of the south during the difficulties of the reconstruction period.

The eastern mountains became an important coal-mining area, tobacco-growing continued and the Bluegrass plains produced livestock, including especially fine thoroughbred horses.

TERRITORY AND POPULATION

Kentucky is bounded in the north by the Ohio River (forming the boundary with Illinois, Indiana and Ohio), northeast by the Big Sandy River (forming the boundary with West Virginia), east by Virginia, south by Tennessee and west by the Mississippi River (forming the boundary with Missouri). Land area, 39,728 sq. miles (102,895 sq. km). Census population, 2000, 4,041,769, an increase of 9·7% since 1990. July 2002 estimate, 4,092,891.

Population in five census years was:

	White	Black	All others	Total	Per sq. mile
1930	2,388,364	226,040	185	2,614,589	65·1
1960	2,820,083	215,949	2,124	3,038,156	76·2
1980	3,379,006	259,477	22,294	3,660,777	92·3
1990	3,391,832	262,907	30,557	3,685,296	92·8
2000	3,640,889	295,994	104,886	4,041,769	101·7

Of the total population in 2000, 2,066,401 were female, 3,046,951 were 18 years old or older and 2,253,800 were urban. Kentucky's Hispanic population was estimated to be 59,939, up 172·4% on the 1990 census figure of 22,005.

The principal cities with census population in 2000 are: Lexington-Fayette, 260,512; Louisville, 256,321; Owensboro, 54,067; Bowling Green, 49,296; Covington, 43,370; Hopkinsville, 30,089; Frankfort (capital), 27,741; Henderson, 27,373; Richmond, 27,152, Jeffersontown 26,633.

SOCIAL STATISTICS

In 2000: births, 56,197 (14·1 per 1,000 population); deaths, 39,175 (9·6); infant deaths, 388 (6·9 per 1,000 live births); marriages, 39,671 (11·4 per 1,000 population); divorces, 21,593 (5·6).

CLIMATE

Kentucky is in the Appalachian Mountains climatic zone (see UNITED STATES: Climate). It has a temperate climate. Temperatures are moderate during both winter and summer, precipitation is ample without a pronounced dry season, and winter snowfall amounts are variable. Mean annual temperatures range from 52°F in the northeast to 58°F in the southwest. Annual rainfall averages at about 45". Snowfall ranges from 5 to 10" in the southwest of the state, to 25" in the northeast, and 40" at higher altitudes in the southeast.

CONSTITUTION AND GOVERNMENT

The constitution dates from 1891; there had been three preceding it. The 1891 constitution was promulgated by convention and provides that amendments be submitted to the electorate for ratification. The General Assembly consists of a Senate of 38 members elected for four years, one half retiring every two years, and a House of Representatives of 100 members elected for two years. It has annual sessions. All citizens of 18 or over are qualified as electors. Registered voters, Nov. 2000, 2,556,815.

For the 108th Congress, which convened in Jan. 2003, Kentucky sends six members to the House of Representatives. It is represented in the Senate by Mitch McConnell (R. 1985–2009) and Jim Bunning (R. 1999–2005).

The capital is Frankfort. The state is divided into 120 counties.

RECENT ELECTIONS

In the 2000 presidential election Bush polled 872,520 votes; Gore, 638,923; Nader, 23,118.

In gubernatorial elections on 2 Nov. 1999 Paul Patton was returned as governor with 59% of the vote. Republican Peppy Martin gained 23% and Reformist Gatewood Gabraith 16%.

CURRENT ADMINISTRATION

Governor: Paul E. Patton (D.), 1999–2003 (salary: $104,619).
  Lieut.-Governor: Stephen L. Henry (D.), 1999–2003 ($88,941).
  Secretary of State: John Y. Brown III (D.), 2000–2004 ($88,941).

Government Website: http://kentucky.gov

ECONOMY

Per capita personal income (2000) was $24,057.

Budget. In 1999 total state revenue was $12,990·1m. Total expenditure was $12,453·3m. (education, $3,728·3m.; human service benefits, $3,426·0m.; transportation, $907·3m.). Debt outstanding, in 1999, $7,422m.

Performance. Gross State Product in 2000 was $118,508m.

ENERGY AND NATURAL RESOURCES

Electricity. In 1999 production was 92,633m. kWh, of which 88,915m. kWh was from coal.

Oil and Gas. Production of crude oil in 2000 was 2·9m. bbls. (of 42 gallons); natural gas, 81,545m. cu. ft.

Water. Kentucky has 12 major river basins that contain nearly 90,000 miles of streams. Virtually all of these streams form part of the larger Ohio River basin. The state's surface water includes more than 2,700 natural and artificial impoundments, of which roughly one-third are larger than 10 acres in size. Wetlands comprise approximately 300,000 acres in the state. Kentucky has two major ground water regions—the alluvial valley along the Ohio River and beach and gravel deposits located west of Kentucky Lake. The total area covered by water is approximately 679 sq. miles.

Minerals. The principal mineral is coal: 139·6m. short tons were mined in 1999, value $3,281m.; crushed stone, 56m. short tons, value $295m.; clay, 0·9m. tonnes, value $3·8m.; sand and gravel, 9·6m. short tons, value $33·0m. Other minerals include fluorspar, ball clay, gemstones, dolomite, cement and lime.

Agriculture. In 2001, 88,000 farms covered an area of 13·6m. acres. The average farm was 155 acres. In 2001 the average value of farmland and buildings per acre was $1,850.

Farm income, 2001, from crops, $1·28bn., and from livestock, $2·27bn. The chief crop is tobacco: production, in 2001, 254·6m. lb. Other principal crops include corn (156·2m. bu.), soybeans, wheat, hay, fruit and vegetables, sorghum grain and barley.

Stock-raising is important in Kentucky, which has long been famous for its horses. The livestock in 2001 included 128,000 milch cows, 2·3m. cattle and calves, 21,000 sheep, 5·6m. chickens and 0·45m. swine.

Forestry. State forest area, 1997, 264,000 acres.

Fisheries. Cash receipts from aquaculture totalled $1·1m. in 2001.

INDUSTRY

In 2000 the state had 4,209 manufacturing plants and in 2001 there were 293,003 manufacturing employees. The value added by manufacture in 2000 was $32,795m. The leading manufacturing industries (by employment) in 2001 were transportation equipment, industrial machinery, food products, fabricated metal products and electronic equipment.

Labour. In Sept. 2002 the civilian labour force numbered 1,990,531. Of the 1,712,366 employed, 549,210 were engaged in services, 375,795 in trade, transportation and utilities, 293,003 in manufacturing, 40,028 in agriculture and 559,694 in other employment. The unemployment rate in 2001 was 5·5%.

Trade Unions. In 2000, 208,000 (13·6%) workers were union members.

INTERNATIONAL TRADE

Imports and Exports. Exports in 2001 totalled $9·04bn. with manufactured goods accounting for 95% of total exports. Transportation equipment, industrial machinery and chemicals were important manufactured exports. Livestock and coal were major non-manufactured goods exported.

COMMUNICATIONS

Roads. In 2000 there were 79,266 miles of roads and 2,826,403 registered motor vehicles.

Rail. In 1997 there were 2,892 miles of railway.

Civil Aviation. There were (1996) 70 publicly used airports and (1992) 2,294 registered aircraft. Commercial airports providing scheduled airline services in Kentucky are located in Erlanger (Covington/Cincinnati area), Louisville, Lexington, Owensboro and Paducah. There were 2,241,655 passenger enplanements statewide in 1999.

Shipping. There is barge traffic on the 1,100 miles of navigable rivers. There are 6 public river ports, over 30 contract terminal facilities and 150 private terminal operations. Kentucky's waterways have access to the junction of the upper and lower Mississippi, Ohio and Tennessee-Tombigbee navigation corridors.

SOCIAL INSTITUTIONS

Justice. There are 12 adult prisons within the Department of Corrections Adult Institutions and 3 privately run adult institutions; average daily population (1998–99), 11,255 in prisons, 943 in jails awaiting incarceration, and 2,755 in local community centres. There were also 17,494 individuals on parole.

The death penalty is authorized for murder and kidnapping; the minimum age is 16. As of Nov. 1999 there were 39 persons under sentence of death. The last execution was in 1999.

Religion. The chief religious denominations in 2000 were: Southern Baptists, with 979,994 members, Roman Catholic (406,021), United Methodists (208,720), Christian Churches and Church of Christ (106,638) and Christian (Disciples of Christ) (67,611).

Education. Attendance at school between the ages of 5 and 16 years (inclusive) is compulsory, the normal term being 175 days. In 2001–02, 40,789 teachers were employed in public elementary and secondary schools. There were 630,436 pupils in public elementary and secondary schools. Public school classroom teachers' salaries (2001–02) averaged $36,688. The average total expenditure per pupil was $6,720.

There were also 4,207 teachers working in private elementary and secondary schools with some 71,812 students in 2001–02.

The state has 28 universities and senior colleges, 1 junior college and 28 community and technical colleges, with a total enrolment of 187,270 students (autumn 2001). Of these universities and colleges, 36 are state-supported and the remainder are supported privately. The largest of the institutions of higher learning are (autumn 2001): University of Kentucky, with 24,791 students; University of Louisville, 20,394; Western Kentucky University, 16,579; Eastern Kentucky University, 14,697; Northern Kentucky University, 12,548; Murray State University, 9,648; Morehead State University, 9,027; Kentucky State University, 2,314. Five of the several privately endowed colleges of standing are Berea College, Berea; Centre

College, Danville; Transylvania University, Lexington; Georgetown College, Georgetown; and Bellarmine College, Louisville.

Health. In 2001 the state had 123 licensed hospitals (18,616 beds). There were 422 licensed long-term care facilities (34,825 beds), 259 family care homes, 126 home health agencies and 1,856 miscellaneous health facilities and laboratories.

Welfare. In the all-state funded Supplementation programme, payments were made in Sept. 1999 to 5,060 persons, of whom 2,320 were senior citizens, 40 blind and 2,700 disabled. The average State Supplementation payment was $284·60 to senior citizens, $160·75 to blind and $282·97 to disabled.

In the Kentucky Transitional Assistance Program (as of Sept. 1999) aid was given to 92,415 persons in 40,118 families. The average payment per person was $92·59, per family $224·80.

In addition to money payments, medical assistance, food stamps and social services are available.

CULTURE

The Kentucky Center for the Arts hosts productions by the Kentucky Opera Association, the Louisville Ballet, the Louisville Orchestra and Broadway touring productions.

Tourism. In 1999 tourist expenditure was $8,191·9m., producing over $888m. in tax revenues and generating 148,781 jobs. The state had (1999) 1,093 hotels and motels, 248 camping grounds and 50 state parks.

Libraries. There were, in 2000, 192 public libraries, 90 academic libraries, 105 institutional and special libraries, 1,261 school libraries and 79 archive collections.

FURTHER READING

Kentucky Deskbook of Economic Statistics, Lackey, Brent, (ed.) Kentucky Cabinet for Economic Development, Frankfort

Miller, P. M., *Kentucky Politics and Government: Do We Stand United?* Nebraska Univ. Press, 1994

Ulack, R. (ed.) *Atlas of Kentucky*. The Univ. Press of Kentucky, 1998

LOUISIANA

KEY HISTORICAL EVENTS

Originally the Territory of Choctaw and Caddo tribes, the whole area was claimed for France in 1682. The French founded New Orleans in 1718 and it became the centre of a crown colony in 1731. During the wars which the European powers fought over their American interests, the French ceded the area west of the Mississippi (most of the present state) to Spain in 1762 and the eastern area, north of New Orleans, to Britain in 1763. The British section passed to the USA in 1783, but France bought back the rest from Spain in 1800, including New Orleans and the mouth of the Mississippi. The USA, fearing to be excluded from a strategically important and commercially promising shipping area, persuaded France to sell Louisiana again in 1803. The present states of Missouri, Arkansas, Iowa, North Dakota, South Dakota, Nebraska and Oklahoma were included in the purchase.

The area became the Territory of New Orleans in 1804 and was admitted to the Union as a state in 1812. The economy at first depended on cotton and sugarcane plantations. The population was of French, Spanish and black descent, with a growing number of American settlers. Plantation interests succeeded in achieving secession in 1861, but New Orleans was occupied by the Union in 1862. Planters re-emerged in the late 19th century and imposed rigid segregation of the black population, denying them their new rights.

The state has become mainly urban industrial, with the Mississippi ports growing rapidly. There is petroleum and natural gas, and a strong tourist industry based on the French culture and Caribbean atmosphere of New Orleans.

TERRITORY AND POPULATION
Louisiana is bounded north by Arkansas, east by Mississippi, south by the Gulf of Mexico and west by Texas. Land area, 43,562 sq. miles (112,825 sq. km). Census population, 1 April 2000, 4,468,976, an increase of 5·9% since 1990. July 2002 estimate, 4,482,646.

Population in five census years was:

	White	Black	Indian	Asiatic	Total	Per sq. mile
1930	1,322,712	776,326	1,536	1,019	2,101,593	46·5
1960	2,211,715	1,039,207	3,587	2,004	3,257,022	72·2
				All others		
1980	2,911,243	1,237,263		55,466	4,205,900	93·5
1990	2,839,138	1,299,281		81,554	4,219,973	96·9
2000	2,856,161	1,451,944		160,871	4,468,976	102·6

Of the total population in 2000, 2,306,073 were female, 3,249,177 were 18 years old or older and 3,245,665 were urban. The Hispanic population was 107,738 in 2000, an increase of 14,671 (15·8%) on the 1990 census figure of 93,067.

The largest cities with their 2000 census population are: New Orleans, 484,674; Baton Rouge, 227,818; Shreveport, 200,145; Lafayette, 100,257; Lake Charles, 71,757; Kenner, 70,517; Bossier City, 56,461; Monroe, 53,107.

SOCIAL STATISTICS
Statistics 2000: live births, 67,843 (15·2 per 1,000 population); deaths, 40,928 (9·2 per 1,000); infant deaths, 2000, 8·9 per 1,000 live births; marriages, 40,561; divorces, 14,923.

CLIMATE
New Orleans, Jan. 54°F (12·2°C), July 83°F (28·3°C). Annual rainfall 58" (1,458 mm). Louisiana belongs to the Gulf Coast climate zone (see UNITED STATES: Climate).

CONSTITUTION AND GOVERNMENT
The present constitution dates from 1974. The Legislature consists of a Senate of 39 members and a House of Representatives of 105 members, both chosen for four years. Sessions are annual; a fiscal session is held in even years.

For the 108th Congress, which convened in Jan. 2003, Louisiana sends seven members to the House of Representatives. It is represented in the Senate by John Breaux (D. 1987–2005) and Mary Landrieu (D. 1997–2009).

Louisiana is divided into 64 parishes (corresponding to the counties of other states). The capital is Baton Rouge.

RECENT ELECTIONS
In the 2000 presidential election Bush polled 927,871 votes; Gore, 792,344; Buchanan, 20,473.

CURRENT ADMINISTRATION
Governor: M. J. 'Mike' Foster (R.), 2000–04 (salary: $95,000).
Lieut.-Governor: Kathleen Blanco (D.), 2000–04 ($85,000).
Secretary of State: W. Fox McKeithen (R.), 2000–04 ($85,000).

Government Website: http://www.state.la.us

ECONOMY
Per capita personal income (2001) was $24,535.

Budget. In fiscal year 2000–01 total revenue was $15,661·5m. Total expenditure was $13,275·3m. (health and welfare, $5,653·2m.; education, $5,522·3m.; highways, $340·6m.; public safety and corrections, $213·9m.) Debt outstanding, in 1999, $7,152m.

Performance. Gross State Product in 2000 was $137,7004m.

ENERGY AND NATURAL RESOURCES
Electricity. 64,649m. kWh of electricity were produced in 1999.

Oil and Gas. Louisiana ranks fourth among states of the USA for oil production and second for natural gas production. Production in 2001 of crude oil was 71m. bbls.; and of natural gas, 1,378·4bn. cu. ft.

Water. The area covered by water is approximately 6,085 sq. miles.

Minerals. Principal non-fuel minerals are sulphur, salt and sand, and gravel. Total non-fuel mineral production in 2000 was $404m.

Agriculture. The state is divided into two parts, the uplands and the alluvial and swamp regions of the coast. A delta occupies about one-third of the total area. Manufacturing is the leading industry, but agriculture is important. The number of farms in 2001 was 29,000 covering 8·1m. acres; the average farm had 278 acres. Average value of non-irrigated cropland per acre in 2001 was $1,180 and the average value for pasture per acre was $1,160.

Principal crops, 2001 production, were: soybeans, 20·13m. bu.; sugarcane, 14·36m. tons; rice, 30·01m. cwt; corn, 45·44m. bu.; cotton, 1·03m. bales; sweet potatoes, 3·19m. cwt.; sorghum, 17·85m. bu.

Forestry. Forestlands cover 48% of the state's area, or 13·8m. acres. Production 2001: sawtimber, 1,155·62m. bd ft; cordwood, 5·81m. standard cords. Value of manufactured products in 1997: $1,882·54m.

Fisheries. In 2001 Louisiana's commercial fisheries catch for all species totalled 1,191,593,336 lb (540,503 tonnes), valued at $345,090,503.

INDUSTRY

Louisiana's leading manufacturing activity is the production of chemicals, followed, in order of importance, by the processing of petroleum and coal products, the production of transportation equipment and production of paper products.

Labour. Non-agricultural employment for Oct. 2002 was 1,941,000, including: service industries, 548,900; wholesale and retail trade, 454,100; government, 381,600; manufacturing, 177,900; construction, 123,100; transportation, communications and public utilities, 116,700; finance, insurance and real estate, 86,100; mining, 52,600.

In 2001 the civilian labour force totalled 2,055,100. There were 115,000 persons unemployed, a rate of 5·6% (5·8% preliminary rate for Oct. 2002).

INTERNATIONAL TRADE

In 2001 exports were valued at $16,588·96m. In 1999 foreign investment amounted to $31·8bn.

COMMUNICATIONS

Roads. In 2001 there were 60,829 miles of public roads (46,890 miles rural) and 3,608,559 registered motor vehicles.

Rail. In 1999 there were approximately 2,747 miles of main-line track in the state. There is a tramway in New Orleans.

Civil Aviation. In 2002 there were 72 public airports. There were 5,751,501 passenger enplanements statewide in 1999.

Shipping. There are ports at New Orleans, Baton Rouge, St Bernard, Plaquemines and Lake Charles. The Mississippi and other waterways provide 7,500 miles of navigable water.

SOCIAL INSTITUTIONS

Justice. In Oct. 2002 there were 36,328 prisoners in correctional institutions and the juvenile offender population totalled 7,079. The minimum age for the death penalty is 16. There was one execution in 2002.

Religion. The Roman Catholic Church is the largest denomination in Louisiana. The leading Protestant Churches are Southern Baptist and Methodist.

Education. School attendance is compulsory between the ages of 7 and 15, both inclusive. In 2001 there were 1,499 public elementary and secondary schools with 741,553 registered pupils, and 49,915 teachers paid an average salary of $33,682.

There are 16 public colleges and universities and 10 non-public institutions of higher learning. There are 42 state trade and vocational technical schools, three law schools, three medical schools and a biomedical research centre affiliated with Louisiana's universities.

In 2001–02 there were 178,990 students enrolled at public two- and four-year colleges and universities. Enrolment, 2001–02, in the University of Louisiana System was 78,371 (Lafayette, 15,489; Southeastern, 14,522; Louisiana Tech., 10,694; Northwestern, 9,415; Monroe, 8,765; McNeese, 7,780; Nicholls, 7,206; Grambling, 4,500); Louisiana State University, 61,421 (with campuses at Alexandria, Baton Rouge, Eunice, New Orleans and Shreveport); Southern University System, 14,281. Major private institutions: Tulane University, 7,863 undergraduates; Loyola University, 5,509; Xavier University, 3,912; Dillard University, 2,137.

Health. In 2002 there were 174 hospitals with 25,895 beds.

Welfare. In fiscal year 2001–02 Family Independence Temporary Assistance Program (FITAP) payments to 604,875 recipients totalled $54,755,699. In the fiscal year 2001–02 Food Stamp benefits totalling $566,569,725 were paid to 6,542,010 recipients.

CULTURE

Broadcasting. In 2002 there were 218 radio stations (80 AM; 138 FM) and 42 television stations.

Press. In 2002 there were 318 newspapers in circulation.

Tourism. Tourism is the second most important industry for state income. In 2000 there were 23·1m. visitors from within the USA and approximately 600,000 from abroad. Tourism was a $8·7bn. industry in 2000; it provided more than 118,000 jobs and generated $571·0m. in federal tax revenues and $365·1m. in state tax revenues.

Libraries. There were 226 libraries in 2001, of which 65 were public, 36 academic, 28 institutional and 97 special libraries.

Museums and Galleries. Museums and galleries include: Louisiana Arts and Sciences Center, Baton Rouge; Rural Life Museum, Baton Rouge; New Orleans Museum of Art; Louisiana State Museum.

FURTHER READING

1997 Statistical Abstract of Louisiana, 10th Edition, New Orleans, LA: Division of Business and Economic Research, College of Business Administration, Univ. of New Orleans, 1997.
Calhoun, Milburn, (ed.) *Louisiana Almanac 2002–2003 Edition.* Pelican Publishing Co., 2002
Wall, Bennett H., *et al.,* (eds.) *Louisiana: a History, Third Edition.* Harlan Davidson, Inc, 1997
Wilds, J., *et al.,* (eds.) *Louisiana Yesterday and Today: a Historical Guide to the State.* Louisiana State Univ. Press, 1996

State Library: The State Library of Louisiana, Baton Rouge, Louisiana.

MAINE

KEY HISTORICAL EVENTS

Originally occupied by Algonquian-speaking tribes, the Territory was disputed between different groups of British settlers, and between the British and French, throughout the 17th and most of the 18th centuries. After 1652 it was governed as part of Massachusetts, and French claims finally failed in 1763. Most of the early settlers were English and Protestant Irish, with many Quebec French.

The Massachusetts settlers had gained control when the original colonist, Sir Ferdinando Gorges, supported the losing royalist side in the English civil war. Their control was questioned during the English-American war of 1812, when Maine residents claimed that the Massachusetts government did not protect them against British raids. Maine was separated from Massachusetts and entered the Union as a state in 1820.

Maine is a mountainous state and even the coastline is rugged, but the coastal belt is where most settlement has developed. In the 19th century there were manufacturing towns making use of cheap water-power, and the rocky shore supported a shell-fish industry. The latter still flourishes, together with intensive horticulture, producing potatoes and fruit. The other main economic development has been in exploiting the forests for timber, pulp and paper.

The capital is Augusta, a river trading post which was fortified against Indian attacks in 1754, incorporated as a town in 1797 and chosen as capital in 1832.

TERRITORY AND POPULATION

Maine is bounded west, north and east by Canada, southeast by the Atlantic, south and southwest by New Hampshire. Land area, 30,862 sq. miles (79,932 sq. km). Census population, 1 April 2000, 1,274,923, an increase of 3·8% since 1990. July 2002 estimate, 1,294,464.

Population for five census years was:

	White	Black	Indian	Asiatic	Total	Per sq. mile
1910	739,995	1,363	992	121	742,371	24·8
1950	910,846	1,221	1,522	185	913,774	29·4
			All others			
1980	1,109,850	3,128	12,049		1,125,027	36·3
1990	1,208,360	5,138	14,430		1,227,928	39·8
2000	1,236,014	6,760	32,149		1,274,923	41·3

Of the total population in 2000, 654,614 were female, 973,685 were 18 years old or older and 762,045 were rural (59·8%). Only Vermont has a more rural population. In 2000 the Hispanic population was 9,360, an increase of 37·1% on the 1990 census figure of 6,829. Only North Dakota and Vermont have fewer persons of Hispanic origin in the USA.

The largest city in the state is Portland, with a census population of 64,249 in 2000. Other cities (with population in 2000) are: Lewiston, 35,690; Bangor, 31,473; South Portland, 23,324; Auburn, 23,203; Brunswick, 21,172; Augusta (capital), 21,819; Biddeford, 20,942; Sanford, 20,806.

SOCIAL STATISTICS

Births, 1999, 13,793 (11·0 per 1,000 population); deaths, 12,164 (9·7); (1996) infant mortality rate, 4·4 (per 1,000 live births). Marriages (1995), 10,800 (8·7 per 1,000 population); divorces 5,500 (4·4).

CLIMATE

Average maximum temperatures range from 56·3°F in Waterville to 48·3°F in Caribou, but record high (since c. 1950) is 103°F. Average minimum ranges from 36·9°F in Rockland to 28·3°F in Greenville, but record low (also in Greenville) is –42°F. Average annual rainfall ranges from 48·85" in Machias to 36·09" in Houlton. Average annual snowfall ranges from 118·7" in Greenville to 59·7" in Rockland. Maine belongs to the New England climate zone (see UNITED STATES: Climate).

CONSTITUTION AND GOVERNMENT

The constitution of 1820 is still in force, but it has been amended 153 times. In 1951, 1965 and 1973 the Legislature approved recodifications of the constitution as arranged by the Chief Justice under special authority.

The Legislature consists of the Senate with 35 members and the House of Representatives with 151 members, both Houses being elected simultaneously for two years. Sessions are annual.

For the 108th Congress, which convened in Jan. 2003, Maine sends two members to the House of Representatives. It is represented in the Senate by Olympia Snowe (R. 1995–2007) and Susan Collins (R. 1997–2009).

The capital is Augusta. The state is divided into 16 counties.

RECENT ELECTIONS

In the 2000 presidential election Gore polled 319,951 votes; Bush, 286,616; Nader, 37,127.

CURRENT ADMINISTRATION
Governor: John Baldacci (D.), 2003–07 ($70,000).
Secretary of State: Dan Gwadosky (D.), appointed in 1997 ($78,000).

Government Website: http://www.state.me.us

ECONOMY
Per capita income (2000) was $25,399.

Budget. In 1999 total state revenue was $5,888m. Total expenditure was $2,865m. (education, $1,221m.; public welfare, $1,407m.; highways, $359m.; health and hospitals, $322m.; police protection, $44m.). Outstanding debt, in 1999, $3,875m.

Performance. Gross State Product was $35,981m. in 2000.

ENERGY AND NATURAL RESOURCES
Water. The total area covered by water is approximately 2,876 sq. miles.

Minerals. Minerals include sand and gravel, stone, lead, clay, copper, peat, silver and zinc. Domestic non-fuel mineral output, 1998, was valued at $76m.

Agriculture. In 2000 some 6,800 farms occupied 1·2m. acres; the average farm was 187 acres. Average value of farmland and buildings per acre in 1998 was $1,320. Farm income, 1996: crops, $224m.; livestock and products, $262m. Principal commodities are potatoes, dairy products, chicken eggs and aquaculture.

Forestry. There are some 17·5m. acres of commercial forest, mainly pine, spruce and fir. Wood products industries are of great economic importance.

Fisheries. In 1998 the commercial catch was 184·1m. lb, valued at $217·0m.

INDUSTRY
Total non-agricultural workforce, 1996, 540,000. Services employed 150,000; wholesale and retail, 136,000; government, 93,000; manufacturing, 88,000; the main manufacture is paper at 47 plants, producing about 34% of manufacturing value added.

Labour. Total non-agricultural employment, 1999, 586,000. Employees by branch, 1999 (in 1,000): services, 174; wholesale and retail trade, 146; government, 96; manufacturing, 86; finance, insurance and property, 31.

COMMUNICATIONS
Roads. In 2000 there were 22,669 miles of roads (20,036 miles rural) and 1,024,096 registered motor vehicles.

Rail. In 1999 there were 1,516 miles of mainline railway tracks.

Civil Aviation. There are international airports at Portland and Bangor. There were 528,964 passenger enplanements statewide in 1999.

SOCIAL INSTITUTIONS
Justice. In June 2000 there were 1,715 federal and state prisoners. Capital punishment was abolished in 1887.

Religion. The largest religious bodies are Roman Catholics, Baptists and Congregationalists.

Education. Education is free for pupils from 5 to 21 years of age, and compulsory from 7 to 17. In 1994–95 there were 212,322 pupils and 15,398 teachers in public elementary and secondary schools. Education expenditure by state and local government in 1997, $1,494m.

The state University of Maine, founded in 1865, has seven locations; Bowdoin College, founded in 1794 at Brunswick; Bates College at Lewiston; Colby College at Waterville; Husson College, Bangor; Westbrook College at Westbrook; Unity College at Unity; and the University of New England (formerly St Francis College) at Biddeford.

Health. In 1995 there were 39 community hospitals with 4,000 beds.

Welfare. Supplemental Security Income (SSI) is administered by the Social Security Administration. It became effective on 1 Jan. 1974 and replaces former aid to the aged, blind and disabled, administered by the state with state and federal funds. SSI is supplemented by Medicaid for nursing home patients or hospital patients. Aid to families with dependent children is granted where one or both parents are disabled or absent and income is insufficient. There is a programme of assistance for catastrophic illness. Child welfare services include basic child protective services, enforcing child support, establishing paternity and finding missing parents, foster home placements, adoptions; services in divorce cases and licensing of foster homes, day care and residential treatment services, and public guardianship. There are also protective services for adults. In 1996, 242,000 persons received a total of $1,777m. in welfare assistance.

FURTHER READING

Statistical information: Maine Department of Economic and Community Development, State House Station 59, Augusta 04333. Publishes *Maine: a Statistical Summary.*
Palmer, K. T., *et al., Maine Politics and Government.* Univ. of Nebraska Press, 1993

MARYLAND

KEY HISTORICAL EVENTS

The first European visitors found groups of Algonquian-speaking tribes, often under attack by Iroquois from further north. The first white settlement was made by the Calvert family, British Roman Catholics, in 1634. The settlers received some legislative rights in 1638. In 1649 their assembly passed the Act of Toleration, granting freedom of worship to all Christians. A peace treaty was signed with the Iroquois in 1652, after which it was possible for farming settlements to expand north and west. The capital (formerly at St Mary's City) was moved to Annapolis in 1694. Baltimore, which became the state's main city, was founded in 1729.

The first industry was tobacco-growing, which was based on slave-worked plantations. There were also many immigrant British small farmers, tradesmen and indentured servants.

At the close of the War of Independence the treaty of Paris was ratified in Annapolis. Maryland became a state of the Union in 1788. In 1791 the state ceded land for the new federal capital, Washington, and its economy has depended on the capital's proximity ever since. Baltimore also grew as a port and industrial city, attracting much European immigration in the 19th century. Although strong sympathy for the south was expressed, Maryland remained within the Union in the Civil War albeit under the imposition of martial law.

TERRITORY AND POPULATION

Maryland is bounded north by Pennsylvania, east by Delaware and the Atlantic, south by Virginia and West Virginia, with the Potomac River forming most of the boundary, and west by West Virginia. Chesapeake Bay almost cuts off the eastern end of the state from the rest. Land area, 9,774 sq. miles (25,315 sq. km). Census population, 1 April 2000, 5,296,486, an increase since 1990 of 10·8%. July 2002 estimate, 5,458,137.

Population for five federal censuses was:

	White	Black	Indian	Asiatic	Total	Per sq. mile
1920	1,204,737	244,479	32	400	1,449,661	145·8
1930	1,354,226	276,379	50	857	1,631,526	165·0
1960	2,573,919	518,410	1,538	5,700	3,100,689	314·0
			All others			
1990	3,393,964	1,189,899	197,605		4,781,468	489·2
2000	3,391,308	1,477,411	427,767		5,296,486	541·9

Of the total population in 2000, 2,738,692 were female, 3,940,314 were 18 years old or older and 4,558,668 were urban. In 2000 Maryland's Hispanic population was 227,916, up from 125,102 in 1990 (an increase of 82·2%).

The largest city in the state (containing 12·3% of the population) is Baltimore, with 651,154 (2000 census); Washington, D.C.–Baltimore metropolitan area, 7,608,070 (2000). Maryland residents in the Washington, D.C., metropolitan area total more than 1·8m. Other main population centres (2000 census) are Columbia (88,254); Silver Spring (76,540); Dundalk (62,306); Wheaton-Glenmont (57,694); Ellicott City (56,397); Germantown (55,419); and Bethesda (55,277). Incorporated places, 2000: Frederick, 52,767; Gaithersburg, 52,613; Bowie, 50,269; Rockville, 47,388; Hagerstown, 36,687; Annapolis, 35,838; College Park, 24,657; Salisbury, 23,743; Cumberland, 21,518; Greenbelt, 21,456.

SOCIAL STATISTICS
In 1999 births were 71,782 (13·9 per 1,000 population); deaths, 42,690 (8·3 per 1,000); infant deaths (1998), 8·6 (per 1,000 live births). Marriages (1997), 42,896; divorces, 16,810.

CLIMATE
Baltimore, Jan. 36°F (2·2°C), July 79°F (26·1°C). Annual rainfall 42" (1,066 mm). Maryland belongs to the Atlantic Coast climate zone (*see* UNITED STATES: Climate).

CONSTITUTION AND GOVERNMENT
The present constitution dates from 1867; it has had 125 amendments. Amendments are proposed and considered annually by the General Assembly and must be ratified by the electorate. The General Assembly consists of a Senate of 47, and a House of Delegates of 141 members, both elected for four years, as are the Governor and Lieut.-Governor. Voters are citizens who have the usual residential qualifications.

For the 108th Congress, which convened in Jan. 2003, Maryland sends eight members to the House of Representatives. It is represented in the Senate by Paul Sarbanes (D. 1977–2007) and Barbara Mikulski (D. 1987–2005).

The state capital is Annapolis. The state is divided into 23 counties and Baltimore City.

RECENT ELECTIONS
In the 2000 presidential election Gore polled 1,143,888 votes; Bush, 813,724; Nader, 53,763. In the 1998 gubernatorial election, Glendening polled 846,972 votes; Sauerbrey, 688,357.

CURRENT ADMINISTRATION
Governor: Robert L. Ehrlich, Jr (R.), 2003–07 (salary: $135,000).
  Lieut.-Governor: Michael S. Steele (R.), 2003–07 ($112,500).
  Secretary of State: R. Karl Aumann (R.) 2003–07 ($74,375).

Government Website: http://www.maryland.gov

ECONOMY
Per capita income (2000) was $33,621.

Budget. In 1999 total state revenue was $19,613m. Total expenditure was $17,593m. (education, $5,163m.; public welfare, $3,600m.; highways, $1,323m.; health and hospitals, $1,267m.; police protection, $289m.). Outstanding debt, in 1999, $11,201m. Outstanding long term obligations in 1999 was $9,115m.

Performance. Gross State Product in 2000 was $186,108m.

ENERGY AND NATURAL RESOURCES
Electricity. The territory is served by 4 investor-owned utilities, 5 municipal systems and 4 rural co-operatives. 75% of electricity comes from fossil fuels and 25% from nuclear power.

Oil and Gas. Natural gas is produced from one field in Garrett County; 63m. cu. ft (1·78m. cu. metres) in 1998. A second gas field is used for natural gas storage. No oil is produced and there are no major reserves located in Maryland.

Water. The total area covered by water is approximately 2,632 sq. miles. Abundant fresh water resources allow water withdrawals for neighbouring states and the District of Columbia. The state straddles the upper portions of the world's largest freshwater estuary, Chesapeake Bay.

Minerals. Value of non-fuel mineral production, 1997, was $230m. Sand and gravel (12·8m. tonnes) and stone (31·5m. tonnes) account for 70% of the total value. Stone is the leading mineral commodity by value followed by coal, Portland cement, and sand and gravel. Output of stone was about 31m. tonnes, valued at $158m.; coal output was 4·16m. short tons, valued at $125m.

Agriculture. In 2000 there were approximately 12,400 farms with an area of 2·1m. acres. The average number of acres per farm was 169. The average value per acre in 1997 was $3,176. In 1997, 350,000 people were employed in agriculture.

Farm animals, Jan. 1999 were: milch cows, 86,000; all cattle, 250,000; swine, 65,000; and sheep, 23,000. As of Dec. 1997, chickens (not broilers), 4·6m. Farm income cash receipts, 1998: $1,554m.; from livestock and livestock products, $999m.; and crops, $587m. Milk (1998 value $210m.) and broilers ($533m.) are important products.

Fisheries. In 1997 the wholesale value of aquafarm-raised products totalled nearly $21·4m. Estimates for 1997 indicated that Maryland aquafarmers produced 285,000 lb of hybrid striped bass; 50,000 lb of catfish; 1,340,000 lb of tilapia; and 20,000 lb of trout. Nearly 11m. individual ornamental fish and 8m. oysters were harvested.

INDUSTRY

In 1998 manufacturers had a workforce of 174,700. Total value added by manufacture in 1996 was $17,454·6m. Chief industries included food processing ($2,728·7m.), instruments ($1,266·6m.), chemicals and products ($2,306·8m.), printing and publishing (2,175·6m.), primary metal industries ($1,465·7m.) and machinery and equipment ($1,429·7m.).

Total non-agricultural employment, 1998: 2,317,500.

Labour. In 1997, 24·1% of the workforce were professional and technical workers, more than any other state in the USA. The workforce is well educated with 32% of the population over age 25 holding a bachelor's or higher degree in 1998; it has the second highest concentration of PhD degrees in the sciences of US states—with 352 per 100,000 of the population.

COMMUNICATIONS

Roads. In 2000 the state highway maintained 5,130 miles of highways. The counties maintained 20,222 miles of highways; municipalities maintained 4,440 miles of streets and alleys. Total mileage of public highways, streets and alleys (2000), 30,497 miles. In 2000 there were 3,847,538 registered vehicles.

Rail. Maryland is served by CSX Transportation, Norfolk Southern Railroad as well as by six short-line railroads. Metro lines also serve Maryland in suburban Washington D.C. Amtrak provides passenger service linking Baltimore and BWI Airport to major cities on the Atlantic Coast. MARC commuter rail serves the Baltimore–Washington metropolitan area.

Civil Aviation. There were (1998) 38 public-use airports, and 45 commercial airlines at Baltimore/Washington International Airport (BWI). The airport served 17m. passengers in 1999. A newly opened passenger pier serves the airport's increasing numbers of international customers. Air cargo throughput has grown rapidly to over 350m. tons per annum, with increases planned.

Shipping. In 1997 Baltimore was the 9th largest US seaport in value of imports, and 12th largest in value of exports; in 1996 it ranked 16th in annual tonnage handled. It is located as much as 200 miles further inland than any other Atlantic seaport.

SOCIAL INSTITUTIONS

Justice. Prisons in Dec. 1999 held 23,200 inmates; 454 per 100,000 population. Maryland's prison system has conducted a work-release programme for selected prisoners since 1963. All institutions have academic and vocational training programmes. The minimum age is 18 for the death penalty, which was last used in 1998.

Religion. Maryland was the first US state to give religious freedom to all who came within its borders. Present religious affiliations of the population are approximately: Protestant, 32%; Roman Catholic, 24%; Jewish, 10%; remaining 34% is non-related and other faiths.

Education. Education is compulsory from 6 to 16 years of age. In 1998–99 public schools (including pre-kindergarten through secondary schools) had 828,477 pupils; teachers numbered 65,486; average salary was $43,081. Expenditure on education, 1998–99, was $5·9bn., of which the state's contribution was $2·4bn. Per pupil cost (1998–99) was $6,821.

There are 54 institutions of higher learning (34 four-year and 20 two-year). The largest is the Maryland University system, with 125,000 students (autumn 1998), consisting of 11 campuses, 2 major research institutions, and over 250 learning centres in Europe and the Far East. Career and technical education is available through a network of community colleges and in some 200 secondary schools.

Health. In Oct. 1999 there were 74 hospitals (with 18,195 beds) licensed by the State Department of Health and Mental Hygiene.

The Maryland State Department of Health, organized in 1874, was in 1969 made part of the Department of Health and Mental Hygiene which performs its functions through its central office, 23 county health departments and the Baltimore City Health Department. For the fiscal year 1998 the department's budget was $3,464m., of which $1,934·2m. were general funds and $118·7m. special funds appropriated by the General Assembly. The balance of the budget, $1,411·1m., is derived from federal funds.

During fiscal year 1998 Maryland's programme of medical care for indigent and medically indigent patients covered 441,448 persons. The programme, which covers in-patient and out-patient hospital services, laboratory services, skilled nursing home care, physician services, pharmacy services, dental services and home health services, cost approximately $2,047·7m.

Welfare. Under the supervision of the Department of Human Resources, local departments of social services administer Temporary Assistance to Needy Families, which amounted to $121,419,676 in 1998; an average monthly amount of $117·85 for the 136,005 beneficiaries. General Public Assistance—called Transitional Emergency Medical and Housing Assistance (TEMHA)—cost the state $14,896,100 (1998), assisting 12,414 persons with an average monthly payment of $100.

CULTURE
Cultural venues include: Frostburg Performing Arts Center, Strathmore Hall Arts Center, and Center Stage. Performing arts institutions include the Baltimore Opera Company, Peabody Music Conservatory and Arena Players.

Broadcasting. There are 15 TV stations, 22 cable television stations, 48 FM radio and 31 AM radio stations.

Cinema. Maryland is a popular filming location. Recent films include *The Blair Witch Project, Washington Square, Enemy of the State, Pecker* and *Runaway Bride*. The economic impact of film making on the state in 1998 was $77m.

Tourism. Tourism is one of the state's leading industries. In 1997 tourists spent over $6,500m. Direct employment in tourism (1997) was 94,100.

Festivals. The Rossborough Festival is hosted in Maryland every four years. The acclaimed annual Renaissance Festival draws visitors and performers from all over the US and around the world. Numerous annual festivals celebrate Maryland cultural traditions including blues music, seafood, history and ethnic heritage.

Theatre and Opera. The main venues are the Lyric Opera House and Meyerhoff Symphony Hall, Mechanic Theatre and Center Stage Theatre.

Museums and Galleries. Galleries include the Walter's Art Gallery, the Baltimore Museum of Art, and the American Visionary Art Museum. Specialized museums cover historical and cultural aspects of life, from the B&O Railroad Museum to the

US Naval Academy Museum, from battlefields to the Goddard Space Flight Center, from colonial life to baseball. Baltimore's Inner Harbor is home to four floating museums, three ships and a submarine.

FURTHER READING
Statistical Information: Maryland Department of Economic and Employment Development, 217 East Redwood St., Baltimore 21202.
DiLisio, J. E., *Maryland.* Boulder, 1982
Rollo, V. F., *Maryland's Constitution and Government.* Maryland Hist. Press, Rev. ed., 1982

State Library: Maryland State Library, Annapolis.

MASSACHUSETTS

KEY HISTORICAL EVENTS
The first European settlement was at Plymouth, when the *Mayflower* landed its company of English religious separatists in 1620. In 1626–30 more colonists arrived, the main body being a large company of English Puritans who founded a Puritan commonwealth. This commonwealth, of about 1,000 colonists led by John Winthrop, became the Massachusetts Bay Colony and was founded under a company charter. Following disagreement between the English government and the colony the charter was withdrawn in 1684, but in 1691 a new charter united a number of settlements under the name of Massachusetts Bay. The colony's government was rigidly theocratic.

Shipbuilding, iron-working and manufacturing were more important than farming from the beginning, the land being poor. The colony was Protestant and of English descent until the War of Independence. The former colony adopted its present constitution in 1780. In the struggle which ended in the separation of the American colonies from the mother country, Massachusetts took the foremost part, and on 6 Feb. 1788 became the 6th state to ratify the US constitution. The state acquired its present boundaries (having previously included Maine) in 1820.

During the 19th century industrialization and immigration from Europe both increased while Catholic Irish and Italian immigrants began to change the population's character. The main inland industry was textile manufacture, the main coastal occupation was whaling; both have now gone. Boston has remained the most important city of New England, attracting a large black population since 1950.

TERRITORY AND POPULATION
Massachusetts is bounded north by Vermont and New Hampshire, east by the Atlantic, south by Connecticut and Rhode Island and west by New York. Land area, 7,840 sq. miles (20,306 sq. km). Census population, 1 April 2000, 6,349,097, an increase of 5·5% since 1990. July 2002 estimate, 6,427,801.

Population at five federal census years was:

	White	Black	Other	Total	Per sq. mile
1950	4,611,503	73,171	5,840	4,690,514	598·4
1970	5,477,624	175,817	35,729	5,689,170	725·8
1980	5,362,836	221,279	152,922	5,737,037	732·0
1990	5,405,374	300,130	310,921	6,016,425	767·6
2000	5,367,286	343,454	638,357	6,349,097	809·8

Of the total population in 2000, 3,290,281 were female, 4,849,003 were 18 years old or older and 5,801,367 were urban (91·37%). In 2000 the Hispanic population was 428,729, up from 287,549 in 1990 (an increase of 49·1%).

Population of the largest cities at the 2000 census: Boston, 589,141; Worcester, 172,648; Springfield, 152,082; Lowell, 105,167; Cambridge, 101,355; Brockton, 94,304; New Bedford, 93,768; Fall River, 91,938; Lynn, 89,050; Quincy, 88,025; Newton, 83,829. The Boston–Worcester–Lawrence metropolitan area had a 2000 census population of 5,819,100.

SOCIAL STATISTICS
1999: births, 81,719 (13·2 per 1,000 population); deaths, 55,894 (9·1); infant deaths (1998), 5·1 per 1,000 live births; marriages (1997), 42,400; divorces, 16,200.

CLIMATE
Boston, Jan. 28°F (−2·2°C), July 71°F (21·7°C). Annual rainfall 41" (1,036 mm). Massachusetts belongs to the New England climate zone (*see* UNITED STATES: Climate).

CONSTITUTION AND GOVERNMENT
The constitution dates from 1780 and has had 116 amendments. The legislative body, styled the General Court of the Commonwealth of Massachusetts, meets annually, and consists of the Senate with 40 members and the House of Representatives of 160 members, both elected for two years.

For the 108th Congress, which convened in Jan. 2003, Massachusetts sends ten members to the House of Representatives. It is represented in the Senate by Edward Kennedy (D. 1962–2007) and John Kerry (D. 1985–2009).

The capital is Boston. The state has 14 counties.

RECENT ELECTIONS
In the 2000 presidential election Gore polled 1,616,487 votes; Bush, 878,502; Nader, 173,564.

CURRENT ADMINISTRATION
Governor: W. Mitt Romney (R.), 2003–07 (salary: $135,000, but not taken).
  Lieut.-Governor: Kerry Healey (R.), 2003–07 ($120,000, but not taken).
  Secretary of the Commonwealth: William F. Galvin (D.), 2003–07 ($120,000).

Government Website: http://www.mass.gov

ECONOMY
Per capita income (2000) was $37,710, the third highest in the country.

Budget. In 1999 total state revenue was $28,120m. Total expenditure was $28,030m. (public welfare, $6,076m.; education, $5,851m.; highways, $2,257m.; health and hospitals, $1,892m.; police protection, $428m.). Outstanding debt, in 1999, $35,798m.

Performance. Gross State Product in 2000 was $284,934m.

ENERGY AND NATURAL RESOURCES
Water. The total area covered by water is approximately 1,403 sq. miles.

Minerals. Total domestic non-fuel mineral output in 1998 was valued at $192m., of which most came from sand, gravel, crushed stone and lime.

Agriculture. In 2000 there were approximately 6,100 farms with an average area of 93 acres and a total area of 570,000 acres. Average value per acre in 1998 was $6,450. Farm income in 1996: crops, $369m.; livestock and products, $109m. Principal crops included cranberries and greenhouse products.

Forestry. About 68% of the state is forest. State forests cover about 256,000 acres. Total forest land covers about 3m. acres. Commercially important hardwoods are sugar maple, northern red oak and white ash; softwoods are white pine and hemlock.

INDUSTRY
Labour. Total non-agricultural employment, 1999, 3,236,000. Employees by branch, 1999 (in 1,000): services, 1,161; wholesale and retail trade, 738; manufacturing, 443; government, 369; manufacturing, 188. The state unemployment rate was 3·2% in 1999.

COMMUNICATIONS
Roads. In 2000 there were 35,312 miles of public roads (12,211 miles rural) and 5,265,399 registered motor vehicles.

Rail. In 1984 there were 1,310 miles of mainline railway. There are metro, light rail, tramway and commuter networks in and around Boston.

Civil Aviation. There is an international airport at Boston. There were 11,084,588 passenger enplanements statewide in 1999.

Shipping. The state has three deep-water harbours, the largest of which is Boston. Other ports are Fall River and New Bedford.

SOCIAL INSTITUTIONS

Justice. There were 11,150 federal and state prisoners in June 2000. The death penalty was abolished in 1984.

Religion. The principal religious bodies are the Roman Catholics, Jewish Congregations, Methodists, Episcopalians and Unitarians.

Education. School attendance is compulsory for ages 6–16. In 1994–95 there were 58,893 classroom teachers and 890,240 pupils.

Some leading higher education institutions are:

Year opened	Name and location of universities and colleges	Students 1998
1636	Harvard University, Cambridge	24,373[1]
1839	Framingham State College	5,697[1]
1839	Westfield State College	4,985[1]
1840	Bridgewater State College	8,955[1]
1852	Tufts University, Medford[2]	8,876
1854	Salem State College	8,081[1]
1861	Mass. Institute of Technology, Cambridge	9,885
1863	University of Massachusetts, Amherst	25,031[1]
1863	Boston College (RC), Chestnut Hill	14,745
1865	Worcester Polytechnic Institute, Worcester	3,821
1869	Boston University, Boston	29,131
1874	Worcester College	5,212[1]
1894	Fitchburg State College	5,557[1]
1894	University of Massachusetts, Lowell	12,038[1]
1895	University of Massachusetts, Dartmouth	6,963[1]
1898	Northeastern University, Boston[3]	24,027
1899	Simmons College, Boston[4]	3,401[1]
1905	Wentworth Institute of Technology	3,076
1906	Suffolk University	6,445
1917	Bentley College	5,775
1919	Western New England College	4,941
1919	Babson College	3,353
1947	Merrimack College	2,693
1948	Brandeis University, Waltham	4,405
1964	University of Massachusetts, Boston	13,778[1]

[1]1999 figure. [2]Includes Jackson College for women. [3]Includes Forsyth Dental Center School. [4]For women only.

Health. In 1995 there were 96 community hospitals with 18,900 beds and 106,000 personnel.

Welfare. In 1996, 1,052,000 persons received welfare totalling $8,548m.: including 746,000 retired workers and dependants who received on average $748 per month; and 154,000 disabled workers and dependants who received on average $697 per month.

FURTHER READING
Levitan, D. with Mariner, E. C., *Your Massachusetts Government.* Newton, Mass., 1984

MICHIGAN

KEY HISTORICAL EVENTS
The French were the first European settlers, establishing a fur trade with the local Algonquian Indians in the late 17th century. They founded Sault Ste Marie in 1668

and Detroit in 1701. In 1763 Michigan passed to Britain, along with other French territory east of the Mississippi, and from Britain it passed to the USA in 1783. Britain, however, kept a force at Detroit until 1796, and recaptured Detroit in 1812. Regular American settlement did not begin until later. The Territory of Michigan (1805) had its boundaries extended after 1818 and 1834. It was admitted to the Union as a state (with its present boundaries) in 1837.

During the 19th century there was rapid industrial growth, especially in mining and metalworking. The largest groups of immigrants were British, German, Irish and Dutch. Other significant groups came from Scandinavia, Poland and Italy. Many groups of immigrants came to settle as miners, farmers and industrial workers. The motor industry became dominant, especially in Detroit. Lake Michigan ports shipped bulk cargo, especially iron ore and grain.

Detroit was the capital until 1847, when that function passed to Lansing. Detroit remained, however, an important centre of flour-milling and shipping and, after the First World War, of the motor industry.

TERRITORY AND POPULATION
Michigan is divided into two by Lake Michigan. The northern part is bounded south by the lake and by Wisconsin, west and north by Lake Superior, east by the North Channel of Lake Huron; between the two latter lakes the Canadian border runs through straits at Sault Ste Marie. The southern part is bounded in the west and north by Lake Michigan, east by Lake Huron, Ontario and Lake Erie, south by Ohio and Indiana. Total area is 96,716 sq. miles (250,493 sq. km) of which 56,804 sq. miles (147,122 sq. km) are land and 39,912 sq. miles (103,372 sq. km) water. Census population, 1 April 2000, 9,938,444, an increase of 6·9% since 1990. July 2002 estimate, 10,050,446.

Population of five federal census years was:

	White	Black	Indian	Asiatic	Total	Per sq. mile
1910	2,785,247	17,115	7,519	292	2,810,173	48·9
1930	4,663,507	69,453	7,080	2,285	4,842,325	84·9
			All others			
1980	7,872,241	1,199,023	190,814		9,262,078	162·6
1990	7,756,086	1,291,706	247,505		9,295,297	160·0
2000	7,966,053	1,412,742	559,649		9,938,444	175·0

Of the total population in 2000, 5,065,349 were female, 7,342,677 were 18 years old or older and 7,419,457 were urban. In 2000 the Hispanic population was 323,877, up from 201,596 in 1990 (an increase of 60·7%).

Populations of the chief cities in 2000 were: Detroit, 951,270; Grand Rapids, 197,800; Warren, 138,247; Flint, 124,943; Sterling Heights, 124,471; Lansing, 119,128; Ann Arbor, 114,024; Livonia, 100,545. The Detroit–Ann Arbor–Flint metropolitan area had a 2000 census population of 5,456,428.

SOCIAL STATISTICS
In 2000 live births were 136,084 (13·8 per 1,000), an increase of 2% from 1999; deaths were 86,998 (8·8 per 1,000); infant deaths were 1,112 (8·2 per 1,000 live births); marriages were 66,326 and divorces were 38,932.

CLIMATE
Detroit, Jan. 23·5°F (−5·0°C), July 72°F (22·5°C). Annual rainfall 32" (810 mm). Grand Rapids, Jan. 22°F (−5·5°C), July 71·5°F (22·0°C). Annual rainfall 34" (860 mm). Lansing, Jan. 22°F (−5·5°C), July 70·5°F (21·5°C). Annual rainfall 29" (740 mm). Michigan belongs to the Great Lakes climate zone (*see* UNITED STATES: Climate).

CONSTITUTION AND GOVERNMENT
The present constitution became effective on 1 Jan. 1964. The Senate consists of 38 members, elected for four years, and the House of Representatives of 110 members, elected for two years. Sessions are biennial.

For the 108th Congress, which convened in Jan. 2003, Michigan sends 15 members to the House of Representatives. It is represented in the Senate by Carl Levin (D. 1979–2009) and Debbie Stabenow (D. 2001–07).

The capital is Lansing. The state is organized in 83 counties.

RECENT ELECTIONS
In the 2000 presidential election Gore polled 2,170,418 votes; Bush, 1,953,139; Nader, 84,165.

CURRENT ADMINISTRATION
Governor: Jennifer Granholm (D.), 2003–07 (salary: $177,000).
Lieut.-Governor: John D. Cherry (D.), 2003–07 ($123,900).
Secretary of State: Terry Land (R.), 2003–07 ($124,900).

Government Website: http://www.michigan.gov

ECONOMY
Per capita income (2001) was $29,788.

Budget. In the fiscal year ending 2002, total state revenue was $39,476·8m. Total expenditure was $38,720·1m. (community health, $8,525·72m.; family independence, $3,805·68m.; transportation, $3,076·07m.; corrections, $1,682·25m., education, $995·10m.). Total budget deficit for 2002 was $1·4bn. Total debt outstanding was $13,418m. in 2000.

Performance. New for-profit business incorporations and new limited liability companies for 2001–02 totalled 50,954. In 2001 Michigan's real income per person declined 1·7% compared with a 0·5% national decline. Gross State Product in 2000 was $325,384m.

ENERGY AND NATURAL RESOURCES
Electricity. Electricity sales for 2001 were 102,935m. kWh.

Oil and Gas. Natural gas production in 2001 was 231·8bn. cu. ft; demand was 863·1bn. cu. ft; and production of crude oil averaged 20,000 bbls. per day.

Water. The total area covered by water is approximately 39,895 sq. miles. Total freshwater withdrawn (1995) was 667m. gallons per day; 1,260 gallons per capita.

Minerals. Domestic non-fuel mineral output in 2000 was at an estimated value of $1·67bn. according to the U.S. Geological Survey. Output was mainly iron ore, cement, crushed stone, sand and gravel.

Agriculture. The state, formerly agricultural, is now chiefly industrial. It contained 52,000 farms in 2001, with a total area of 10·4m. acres; the average farm was 200 acres. In 2000, 6,898,000 acres were harvested. Average value per acre in 2000 was $2,300. Principal crops are wheat, corn, oats, sugarbeets, soybeans, hay and dry beans. Total crop cash receipts for 2001, $1,979·80m. Principal fruit crops include apples, cherries (tart and sweet), plums and peaches. In 2002 there were 297,000 milch cows, 73,000 beef cows, 3·66m. chickens and 960,000 pigs. 77,000 lb of blueberries, 20,160 pots of geraniums and 335,000 cwt of black beans. Farm income in 2001: total $3·47bn.; crops, $1·98bn.; livestock and products, $1·49bn. Net farm income in 2001 fell by 39% to $191m.

Forestry. The forests in 1993 covered 19·3m. acres. About 18·6m. acres of this total is timberland acreage. Three-quarters of the timber volume is hardwoods, principally hard and soft maples, aspen, oak and birch. Christmas trees are another important forest crop. Net annual growth of growing stock and saw timber was 830m. cu. ft and 3·1bn. board feet respectively in 1993.

Fisheries. In 1997 recreational fishing licences were purchased by 1·4m. residents and 129,000 non-residents. Recreational fishing revenue (1997) was approximately $1·5bn.

INDUSTRY
Manufacturing is important; among principal products are motor vehicles and trucks, machinery, fabricated metals, primary metals, cement, chemicals, furniture, paper, foodstuffs, rubber, plastics and pharmaceuticals.

Labour. Total non-agricultural labour force in 2002 was 4,439,500, of which 906,500 were in manufacturing.

COMMUNICATIONS

Roads. In 2000 there were 119,877 miles of roads (9,711 miles of state highways, 89,499 miles of county roads and 20,667 miles of municipal). In 2001 there were 9,757,968 registered motor vehicles.

Rail. In 2000 there were 3,950 miles of railway in Michigan.

Civil Aviation. There are international airports at Detroit, Flint, Grand Rapids, Kalamazoo, Port Huron, Saginaw and Sault Ste Marie. In 2000 there were 4,359,931 aircraft operations at Michigan's 235 public-use airports and 26 carriers provided passenger service at 19 airports. There were 20,255,728 passenger enplanements statewide in 2000.

Shipping. There are over 100 commercial and recreational ports spanning the state's 3,200 miles of shoreline. In 2000, 39 of these ports served commercial cargoes. The 20 ferry services carried 848,998 passengers and 529,809 vehicles in 68,571 crossings in 2000. Stone, sand, iron ore and coal accounted for 89% of approximately 96m. tonnes of traffic in 1999.

SOCIAL INSTITUTIONS

Justice. A Civil Rights Commission was established, and its powers and duties were implemented by legislation in the extra session of 1963. Statutory enactments guaranteeing civil rights in specific areas date from 1885. The legislature has a unique one-person grand jury system. The Michigan Supreme Court consists of seven non-partisan elected justices. In 2001 there were 2,291 cases filed at the Supreme Court; it disposed of 2,359 cases during the year. In 2001 there were 47,563 prisoners in state correctional institutions. Capital punishment was officially abolished in 1964 but there has never been an execution in Michigan.

Religion. Roman Catholics make up the largest body and the largest Protestant denominations are: Lutherans, United Methodists, United Presbyterians and Episcopalians.

Education. Education is compulsory for children from 6 to 16 years of age. Education expenditure by state and local governments in 2000–01 was $215,490,700. In 2000–01 there were 1,720,335 pupils and 76,920 teachers in public elementary and secondary schools.

In 1998 there were 96 institutes of higher education with (autumn 1998) 551,683 students.

Universities and students (autumn 2002):

Founded	Name	Students
1817	University of Michigan, Ann Arbor	38,972
1959	University of Michigan, Dearborn	10,379
1956	University of Michigan, Flint	6,524
1849	Eastern Michigan University	23,710
1855	Michigan State University	41,114
1884	Ferris State University	11,074
1885	Michigan Technological University	6,625
1868	Wayne State University	28,161
1892	Central Michigan University	19,380
1899	Northern Michigan University	8,577
1903	Western Michigan University	28,931
1946	Lake Superior State University	3,077
1957	Oakland University	16,059
1960	Grand Valley State College	19,762
1963	Saginaw Valley College	8,938

Health. There were, in 2000, 178 Medicare and Medicaid certified hospitals (31,895 beds); 12 psychiatric hospitals (2,547 beds) and 5 rehabilitation hospitals (315 beds).

In the fiscal year 1998 the Medicaid programme disbursed (with federal support) $4,345m. in medical assistance payments to 1,363,000 people. In 1998 the Medicare programme disbursed $6,716m. in medical assistance payments to 1,384,000 people.

Welfare. Old-age assistance is provided for persons 65 years of age or older who have resided in Michigan for one year before application; assets must not exceed various limits. In 1974 federal Supplementary Security Income (SSI) replaced the adults' programme. A monthly average of 69,786 families received $400·09 per month in 2002 through the Family Independence Agency.

CULTURE

Tourism. In 1998, 379,000 overseas visitors (1·6% of the market share), excluding Mexico and Canada, visited Michigan.

Libraries. In 2002 there were 381 public libraries. Total public library operating expenditures were $285·42m.; $28·72 per capita.

FURTHER READING

Michigan Manual. Dept of Management and Budget. Lansing. Biennial
Michigan Employment Security Commission. *Michigan Statistical Abstract, 1996.* Univ of Michigan Press
Browne, W. P. and Verburg, K., *Michigan Politics and Government: Facing Change in a Complex State.* Nebraska Univ. Press, 1995
Dunbar, W. F. and May, G. S., *Michigan: A History of the Wolverine State.* 3rd ed. Grand Rapids, 1995

State Library Services: Library of Michigan, Lansing 48909.

MINNESOTA

KEY HISTORICAL EVENTS

Minnesota remained an Indian territory until the middle of the 19th century, the main groups being Chippewa and Sioux, many of whom are still there. In the 17th century there had been some French exploration, but no permanent settlement. After passing under the nominal control of France, Britain and Spain, the area became part of the Louisiana Purchase and so was sold to the USA in 1803.

Fort Snelling was founded in 1819. Early settlers came from other states, especially New England, to exploit the great forests. Lumbering gave way to homesteading, and the American settlers were joined by Germans, Scandinavians and Poles. Agriculture, mining and forest industries became the mainstays of the economy. Minneapolis, founded as a village in 1856, grew first as a lumber centre, processing the logs floated down the Minnesota River, and then as a centre of flour-milling and grain marketing. St Paul, its twin city across the river, became Territorial capital in 1849 and state capital in 1858. St Paul also stands at the head of navigation on the Mississippi, which rises in Minnesota.

The Territory (1849) included parts of North and South Dakota, but at its admission to the Union in 1858, the state of Minnesota had its present boundaries.

TERRITORY AND POPULATION

Minnesota is bounded north by Canada, east by Lake Superior and Wisconsin, with the Mississippi River forming the boundary in the southeast, south by Iowa, west by South and North Dakota, with the Red River forming the boundary in the northwest. Land area, 79,610 sq. miles (206,189 sq. km). Census population, 1 April 2000, 4,919,479, an increase of 12·4% since 1990. July 2002 estimate, 5,019,720.
Population in five census years was:

	White	Black	Indian	Asiatic	Total	Per sq. mile
1910	2,059,227	7,084	9,053	344	2,075,708	25·7
1930	2,542,599	9,445	11,077	832	2,563,953	32·0
			All others			
1980	3,935,770	53,344	86,856		4,075,970	51·4
1990	4,130,395	94,944	149,760		4,375,099	55·0
2000	4,400,282	171,731	347,466		4,919,479	61·8

Of the total population in 2000, 2,483,848 were female, 3,632,585 were 18 years old or older and 3,490,059 were urban. In 2000 the Hispanic population was 143,382, up from 53,888 in 1990 (an increase of 116·1%).

The largest cities (with 2000 census population) are Minneapolis (362,618), St Paul (287,151), Duluth (86,918), Rochester (85,806) and Bloomington (85,172).

The Minneapolis–St Paul metropolitan area had a 2000 census population of 2,968,806.

SOCIAL STATISTICS

Births in 1999, 65,332 (13·7 per 1,000 population); deaths, 37,813 (7·9); (1996) infant deaths, 377 (5·9 per 1,000 live births); marriages, 33,046 (7·0 per 1,000 population); divorces, 15,254 (3·2).

CLIMATE

Duluth, Jan. 8°F (−13·3°C), July 63°F (17·2°C). Annual rainfall 29" (719 mm). Minneapolis-St. Paul, Jan. 12°F (−11·1°C), July 71°F (21·7°C). Annual rainfall 26" (656 mm). Minnesota belongs to the Great Lakes climate zone (*see* UNITED STATES: Climate).

CONSTITUTION AND GOVERNMENT

The original constitution dated from 1857; it was extensively amended and given a new structure in 1974. The Legislature consists of a Senate of 67 members, elected for four years, and a House of Representatives of 134 members, elected for two years. It meets for 120 days within each two years.

For the 108th Congress, which convened in Jan. 2003, Minnesota sends eight members to the House of Representatives. It is represented in the Senate by Mark Dayton (D. 2001–07) and Norm Coleman (R. 2003–09).

The capital is St Paul. There are 87 counties.

RECENT ELECTIONS

In the 2000 presidential election Gore polled 1,168,266 votes; Bush, 1,109,659; Nader, 126,696.

CURRENT ADMINISTRATION

Governor: Tim Pawlenty (R.), 2003–07 (salary: $120,303).
   Lieut.-Governor: Carol L. Molnau (R.), 2003–07 ($78,197).
   Secretary of State: Mary E. Kiffmeyer (R.), 2003–07 ($90,227).

Government Website: http://www.state.mn.us

ECONOMY

Per capita income (2000) was $31,913.

Budget. In 1999 total state revenue was $25,089m. Total expenditure was $20,388m. (education, $7,110m.; public welfare, $4,926m.; highways, $1,346m.; health and hospitals, $639m.; police protection, $122m.). Outstanding debt, in 1999, $5,584m.

Performance. In 2000 Gross State Product was $184,766m.

ENERGY AND NATURAL RESOURCES

Water. The total area covered by water is approximately 7,327 sq. miles.

Minerals. The iron ore and taconite industry is the most important in the USA. Production of usable iron ore in 1996 was 46m. tons, value $1,390m. Other important minerals are sand and gravel, crushed and dimension stone, clays and peat. Total value of mineral production, 1998, $1,560m.

Agriculture. In 2000 there were some 79,000 farms with a total area of 28·6m. acres; the average farm was of 362 acres. Average value of land and buildings per acre, 1995, $936. Farm income, 1996, from crops, $4,641m.; from livestock and products, $4,168m. Important products: sugarbeet, spring wheat, processing sweet corn, oats, dry milk, cheese, mink, turkeys, wild rice, butter, eggs, flaxseed, milch cows, milk, corn, barley, swine, cattle for market, soybeans, honey, potatoes, rye, chickens, sunflower seed and dry edible beans. In 1996 there were 2·9m. cattle (0·6m. milch cows) and 4·9m. hogs and pigs. In 1995 the wool clip amounted to 1·15m. lb of wool from 170,000 sheep.

Forestry. Forests of commercial timber cover 14·7m. acres, of which 55% is government-owned. The value of forest products in 1994 was $7,500m.—$2,250m. from primary processing, of which $1,687m. was from pulp and paper; and $3,100m. from secondary manufacturing. Logging, pulping, saw-mills and associated industries employed 57,200 in 1995.

INDUSTRY

Labour. Total non-agricultural employment, 1999, 2,609,000. Employees by branch, 1999 (in 1,000): services, 752; wholesale and retail trade, 619; manufacturing, 440; government, 388; finance, insurance and property, 160. In 1999 the unemployment rate was 2·8%.

COMMUNICATIONS

Roads. In 2000 there were 132,251 miles of roads (116,233 miles rural) and 4,629,940 registered motor vehicles.

Rail. There are 3 Class I and 16 Class II and smaller railroads operating, with total mileage of 4,650.

Civil Aviation. In 2000 there were 147 airports for public use and 19 public seaplane bases. There were 15,708,571 passenger enplanements statewide in 1999.

SOCIAL INSTITUTIONS

Justice. In June 2000 there were 6,219 federal and state prisoners. There is no death penalty.

Religion. The chief religious bodies are: Lutheran with 1,126,008 members in 1990; Roman Catholic, 1,110,071; Methodist, 142,771. Total membership of all denominations, 2,837,415.

Education. In 1999–2000 there were 853,267 students and 55,639 teachers in public elementary and secondary schools. In 2000–01 there were 1,755 public schools and 65 charter schools. There were 103,043 students enrolled in 564 private schools.

There are a total of 36 state colleges and universities. In 1999 enrolled students at state colleges numbered 61,491. There are seven state universities: St. Cloud, 11,962 students in 1999; Minnesota, Mankato campus, 10,946; Minnesota, Akita campus (Japan), 43; Winona, 6,426; Moorhead, 5,987; Bemidji, 3,989; Metro, 3,314; Southwest, 2,669.

Health. In 1998 the state had 140 general acute hospitals with 16,710 beds and 1,735 bassinets. Patients resident in institutions under the Department of Human Services in June 2000 included 954 people with mental illness, 52 people with mental retardation, 175 with chemical dependency and 173 in state nursing homes.

Welfare. Programmes of old age assistance, aid to the disabled, and aid to the blind are administered under the federal Supplemental Security Income (SSI) Programme. Minnesota has a supplementary programme, Minnesota Supplemental Aid (MSA), to cover individuals not eligible for SSI, to supplement SSI benefits for others whose income is below state standards, and to provide one-time payments for emergency needs such as major home repair, essential furniture or appliances, moving expenses, fuel, food and shelter.

CULTURE

Tourism. In 1995 travellers spent about $8,699m. The industry employed about 162,800.

FURTHER READING

Statistical Information: Department of Trade and Economic Development, 500 Metro Square, St Paul 55101. Publishes *Compare Minnesota: an Economic and Statistical Factbook.—Economic Report to the Governor.*
Legislative Manual. Secretary of State. St Paul. Biennial
Minnesota Agriculture Statistics. Dept. of Agric., St Paul. Annual

MISSISSIPPI

KEY HISTORICAL EVENTS
Mississippi was one of the territories claimed by France after the 17th century and ceded to Britain in 1763. The indigenous people were Choctaw and Natchez. French settlers at first traded amicably with them, but in the course of three wars (1716, 1723 and 1729) the French allied with the Choctaw to drive the Natchez out. During hostilities the Natchez massacred the settlers of Fort Rosalie, which the French had founded in 1716 and which was later renamed Natchez.

In 1783 the area became part of the USA except for Natchez which was under Spanish control until 1798. The United States then made it the capital of the Territory of Mississippi. The boundaries of the Territory were extended in 1804 and again in 1812. In 1817 it was divided into two territories, with the western part becoming the state of Mississippi. (The eastern part became the state of Alabama in 1819.) The city of Jackson was laid out in 1822 as the new state capital.

A cotton plantation economy developed, based on black slave labour, and by 1860 the majority of the population was black. Mississippi joined the Confederacy during the Civil War. After defeat and reconstruction there was a return to rigid segregation and denial of black rights. This situation lasted until the 1960s. There was a black majority until the Second World War, when out-migration began to change the pattern. By 1990 about 35% of the population was black, and manufacture (especially clothing and textiles) had become the largest single employer of labour.

TERRITORY AND POPULATION
Mississippi is bounded in the north by Tennessee, east by Alabama, south by the Gulf of Mexico and Louisiana, and west by the Mississippi River forming the boundary with Louisiana and Arkansas. Land area, 46,907 sq. miles (121,489 sq. km). Census population, 1 April 2000, 2,844,658, an increase of 10·5% since 1990. July 2002 estimate, 2,871,782.

Population of five federal census years was:

	White	Black	Indian	Asiatic	Total	Per sq. mile
1910	786,111	1,009,487	1,253	263	1,797,114	38·8
1930	998,077	1,009,718	1,458	568	2,009,821	42·4
			All others			
1980	1,615,190	887,206	18,242		2,520,638	53·0
1990	1,633,461	915,057	24,698		2,573,216	54·8
2000	1,746,099	1,033,809	63,372		2,844,658	60·6

Of the total population in 2000, 1,373,554 were male, 2,069,471 were 18 years old or older and 1,457,307 were rural (51·2% of the population). In 2000 Mississippi's Hispanic population was estimated to be 39,569, up from 15,998 in 1990 (an increase of 147%).

The largest city (2000 census) is Jackson, 184,256. Others (2000 census) are: Gulfport, 71,127; Biloxi, 50,644; Hattiesburg, 44,779; Greenville, 41,633; Meridian, 39,968; Tupelo, 34,211; Southaven, 28,977; Vicksburg, 26,407; Pascagoula, 26,200; Columbus, 25,944.

SOCIAL STATISTICS
Births occurring in the state, 2002, were 41,145 (14·9 per 1,000 population); deaths, 27,502 (9·9 per 1,000 population); infant deaths, 389; marriages, 18,605; divorces, 14,198.

CLIMATE
Jackson, Jan. 47°F (8·3°C), July 82°F (27·8°C). Annual rainfall 49" (1,221 mm). Vicksburg, Jan. 48°F (8·9°C), July 81°F (27·2°C). Annual rainfall 52" (1,311 mm). Mississippi belongs to the Central Plains climate zone (see UNITED STATES: Climate).

CONSTITUTION AND GOVERNMENT
The present constitution was adopted in 1890 without ratification by the electorate; 121 amendments by 2000.

The Legislature consists of a Senate (52 members) and a House of Representatives (122 members), both elected for four years. Electors are all citizens who have resided in the state one year, in the county one year, in the election district six months before the election and have been registered according to law.

For the 108th Congress, which convened in Jan. 2003, Mississippi sends four members to the House of Representatives. It is represented in the Senate by Thad Cochran (R. 1977–2009) and Trent Lott (R. 1989–2007).

The capital is Jackson; there are 82 counties.

RECENT ELECTIONS

In the 2000 presidential election Bush polled 572,844 votes; Gore, 404,614; Nader, 8,122.

CURRENT ADMINISTRATION

Governor: Ronnie Musgrove (D.), 2000–04 (salary: $101,800).
 Lieut.-Governor: Amy Tuck (D.), 2000–04 ($60,000).
 Secretary of State: Eric Clark (D.), 2000–04 ($75,000).

Government Website: http://www.mississippi.gov

ECONOMY

Per capita income (2000) was $20,856, the lowest in the country.

Budget. For the fiscal year ending 30 June 2002 general revenue was $12,728,690,079. General expenditures were $12,093,137,547 (education, $2,902,806,733; public welfare, including public health and health care, $1,124,086,926; highways, $882,085,028; police protection, $93,916,730). Debt outstanding, on 30 June 2002, $2,763,839,000.

Performance. Gross State Product in 2000 was $67,315m.

ENERGY AND NATURAL RESOURCES

Oil and Gas. Petroleum and natural gas account for about 90% (by value) of mineral production. Output of petroleum, 2000, was 20,091,871 bbls. and of natural gas 113,521,906,000 cu. ft. There are four oil refineries. Taxable value of oil and gas products sold in fiscal year 2002 was $518,829,528.

Minerals. The estimated value of domestic non-fuel mineral production in 2000 was $157m.

Agriculture. Agriculture is the leading industry of the state because of the semi-tropical climate and a rich productive soil. In 2001 farms numbered 42,000 with an area of 11,100,000 acres. Average size of farm was 262 acres. This compares with an average farm size of 138 acres in 1960. Average value of farm per acre in 2002 was $1,300.

Cash income from all crops and livestock during 2002 was $3,146,582,000. Cash income from crops was $871,056,000, and from livestock and products $2,275,526,000. The chief product is cotton, cash income (2001) $369,601,000 from 1,300,000 acres producing 2,366,000 bales of 480 lb. Soybeans, rice, corn, hay, wheat, oats, sorghum, peanuts, pecans, sweet potatoes, peaches, other vegetables, nursery and forest products continue to contribute.

On 1 Jan. 2001 there were 1·07m. head of cattle and calves on Mississippi farms. In Jan. 2003 milch cows totalled 33,000, beef cows, 557,000; (2002) hogs and pigs, 275,000. Of cash income from livestock and products, 2001, $1,658,846,000 was credited to cattle and calves. Cash income from poultry and eggs, 2002, totalled $1,658,846,000; dairy products, $79,695,000; swine, $63,850,000.

Forestry. In 2000 income from forestry amounted to $1·3bn.; output of pine logs was 1·66bn. bd ft; of hardwood lumber, 500m. bd ft; pulpwood, 7·31m. cords. There are about 18·5m. acres of forest (61% of the state's area). National forest area, 2000, 1·1m. acres.

INDUSTRY

In 2002 the 3,099 manufacturing establishments had average monthly employment of 222,193 workers, earning $5,922,955,074. The average annual wage was $29,376.

Labour. In 2002 total non-agricultural employment was 1,131,300. Employees by branch, 2002 (in 1,000): services, 273; wholesale and retail trade, 250; government, 244; manufacturing, 208. The unemployment rate in 2002 was 6·6%.

COMMUNICATIONS

Roads. The state as of 1 July 2002 maintained 13,590 miles of highways, of which 13,582 were paved. In fiscal year 2002, 2,367,592 passenger vehicles and pick-ups were registered.

Rail. The state in 2002 had 2,584·1 main-line and short-line miles of railway.

Civil Aviation. There were 780 public airports in 2002, 273 of them general aviation airports. There were 1,066,261 passenger enplanements statewide in 1999.

SOCIAL INSTITUTIONS

Justice. The minimum age for the death penalty is 16. There were two executions in 2002. As of Dec. 2002 the state prison system had 19,831 inmates.

Religion. In 2002: Southern Baptists in Mississippi, 713,580 members; United Methodists, 190,482; Roman Catholics, 51,347 in Biloxi and Jackson dioceses.

Education. Attendance at school is compulsory as laid down in the Education Reform Act of 1982. The public elementary and secondary schools in 2001–02 had 492,198 pupils and 29,166 classroom teachers.

In 2001–02 teachers' average salary was $33,295. The expenditure per pupil in average daily attendance, 2001–02, was $5,908.

There are 21 universities and senior colleges, of which eight are state-supported. In autumn 2002 the University of Mississippi, Oxford had 1,112 faculty and 12,323 students; Mississippi State University, Starkville, 1,437 faculty and 15,852 students; Mississippi University for Women, Columbus, 208 faculty and 2,069 students; University of Southern Mississippi, Hattiesburg, 712 faculty and 13,493 students; Jackson State University, Jackson, 471 faculty and 7,783 students; Delta State University, Cleveland, 273 faculty and 3,825 students; Alcorn State University, Lorman, 184 faculty and 3,150 students; Mississippi Valley State University, Itta Bena, 144 faculty and 3,059 students. State support for the universities (2002–03) was $314,704,985.

Community and junior colleges had (2001–02) 68,927 full-time equivalent students and 3,413 full-time instructors. The state appropriation for junior colleges, 2001–02, was $153,574,698.

Health. In 2002 the state had 112 acute general hospitals (15,376 beds) listed by the State Department of Health; 56 hospitals with facilities for the care of the mentally ill had 2,828 licensed beds. In addition, 7 rehabilitation hospital had 278 beds.

Welfare. The Division of Medicaid paid (fiscal year 2002) $2,445,523,630 for medical services, including $564,879,618 for drugs, $404,063,741 for skilled nursing home care and $383,241,958 for hospital services. There were 34,614 persons eligible for Aged Medicaid benefits as of 30 June 2002 and 124,643 persons eligible for Disabled Medicaid benefits. In June 2002, 17,695 families with 30,334 dependent children received $2,517,803 in the Temporary Assistance to Needy Families programme. The average monthly payment was $147·00 per family or $64·48 per recipient.

CULTURE

Tourism. Total receipts in 2002 amounted to $6·4bn.; an estimated 13m. overnight tourists visited the state.

Festivals. The Neshoba County Fair, Philadelphia (attendance in 2002, 125,000); Choctaw Indian Fair, Philadelphia (attendance in 2001, 21,000); USA International Ballet Competition, held in Jackson every four years (attendance in 2002, 39,309); Mississippi Delta Blues and Heritage Festival, Greenville (attendance in 2000, 15,000–17,000).

Libraries. There are 47 public library systems with 238 branches and two independent municipal public libraries. In fiscal year 2001, 1·3m. persons were registered with public libraries.

Theatre and Opera. In 2002, 15,760 persons attended the only professional theatre in Mississippi, the New Stage Theatre in Jackson. The Mississippi Opera in Jackson presents three operas a year in a season running from November to April.

Museums and Galleries. The main attractions are the Mississippi Agriculture and Forestry Museum, Jackson (123,949 visitors in 2001); Mississippi Museum of Art, Jackson (56,161 visitors in 2001); Mississippi Museum of Natural Science, Jackson (160,044 visitors in 2001); Delta Blues Museum, Clarksdale (14,876 visitors in 2001).

FURTHER READING
College of Business and Industry, Mississippi State Univ., Mississippi State 39762. Publishes *Mississippi Statistical Abstract.*

Secretary of State. *Mississippi Official and Statistical Register.* Quadrennial

Mississippi Library Commission: 1221 Ellis Avenue, Jackson, MS 39209–7328.

MISSOURI

KEY HISTORICAL EVENTS
Territory of several Indian groups, including the Missouri, the area was not settled by European immigrants until the 18th century. The French founded Ste Genevieve in 1735, partly as a lead-mining community. St Louis was founded as a fur-trading base in 1764. The area was nominally under Spanish rule from 1770 until 1800 when it passed back to France. In 1803 the USA bought it as part of the Louisiana Purchase.

St Louis was made the capital of the whole Louisiana Territory in 1805, and of a new Missouri Territory in 1812. In that year American immigration increased markedly. The Territory became a state in 1821, but there had been bitter disputes between slave-owning and anti-slavery factions, with the former succeeding in obtaining statehood without the prohibition of slavery required of all other new states north of latitude 36° 30'; this was achieved by the Missouri Compromise of 1820. The Compromise was repealed in 1854 and declared unconstitutional in 1857. During the Civil War the state held to the Union side, although St Louis was placed under martial law.

With the development of steamboat traffic on the Missouri and Mississippi rivers, and the expansion of railways, the state became the transport hub of all western movement. Lead and other mining remained important, as did livestock farming. European settlers came from Germany, Britain and Ireland.

TERRITORY AND POPULATION
Missouri is bounded north by Iowa, east by the Mississippi River forming the boundary with Illinois and Kentucky, south by Arkansas, southeast by Tennessee, southwest by Oklahoma, west by Kansas and Nebraska, with the Missouri River forming the boundary in the northwest. Land area, 68,886 sq. miles (178,414 sq. km).

Census population, 1 April 2000, 5,595,211, an increase since 1990 of 9·3%. July 2002 estimate, 5,672,579.

Population of five federal census years was:

	White	Black	Indian	Asiatic	Total	Per sq. mile
1930	3,403,876	223,840	578	1,073	3,629,367	52·4
1960	3,922,967	390,853	1,723	3,146	4,319,813	62·5
			All others			
1980	4,345,521	514,276	56,889		4,916,686	71·3
1990	4,486,228	548,208	82,637		5,117,073	74·3
2000	4,748,083	629,391	217,737		5,595,211	81·2

Of the total population in 2000, 2,875,034 were female, 4,167,519 were 18 years old or older and 3,883,442 were urban. In 2000 Missouri's Hispanic population was 118,592, up from 61,702 in 1990 (an increase of 92·2%).

The principal cities at the 2000 census were:

Kansas City	441,545	St Joseph	73,990
St Louis	348,189	Lee's Summit	70,700
Springfield	151,580	St Charles	60,321
Independence	113,288	St Peters	51,381
Columbia	84,531	Florissant	50,497

Metropolitan areas, 2000: St Louis, 2,603,607; Kansas City, 1,776,062.

SOCIAL STATISTICS
Births, 1999, were 75,376 (13·8 per 1,000 population); deaths, 55,413 (10·1). 1996 infant deaths, 7·6 pers 1,000 live births; 1997 marriages, 43,600 (8·1 per 1,000 population); divorces, 25,300 (4·7).

CLIMATE
Kansas City, Jan. 30°F (–1·1°C), July 79°F (26·1°C). Annual rainfall 38" (947 mm). St Louis, Jan. 32°F (0°C), July 79°F (26·1°C). Annual rainfall 40" (1,004 mm). Missouri belongs to the Central Plains climate zone (*see* UNITED STATES: Climate).

CONSTITUTION AND GOVERNMENT
A new constitution, the fourth, was adopted on 27 Feb. 1945; it has been revised nine times with over 100 amendments. The General Assembly consists of a Senate of 34 members elected for four years (half for re-election every two years), and a House of Representatives of 163 members elected for two years. The Governor and Lieut.-Governor are elected for four years.

For the 108th Congress, which convened in Jan. 2003, Missouri sends nine members to the House of Representatives. It is represented in the Senate by Christopher Bond (R. 1987–2005) and James Talent (R. 1993–2007).

Jefferson City is the state capital. The state is divided into 114 counties and the city of St Louis.

RECENT ELECTIONS
In the 2000 presidential election Bush polled 1,189,942 votes; Gore, 1,111,138; Nader, 38,515.

CURRENT ADMINISTRATION
Governor: Bob Holden (D.), 2001–05 (salary: $120,087).
    Lieut.-Governor: Joe Maxwell (D.), 2001–05 ($77,184).
    Secretary of State: Matt Blunt (R.), 2001–05 ($96,455).

Government Website: http://www.state.mo.us

ECONOMY
Per capita income (2000) was $27,186.

Budget. In 1999 total state revenue was $19,505m. Total expenditure was $16,525m. (education, $5,732m.; public welfare, $3,726m.; highways, $1,339m.; health and hospitals, $1,146m.; police protection, $172m.). Outstanding debt, in 1999, $8,903m.

Performance. In 2000 Gross State Product was $178,845m.

ENERGY AND NATURAL RESOURCES
Water. The total area covered by water is approximately 811 sq. miles.

Minerals. The three leading mineral commodities are lead, portland cement and crushed stone. Value of domestic non-fuel mineral production (1998) $1,360m.

Agriculture. In 2000 there were 109,000 farms in Missouri producing crops and livestock on 30m. acres; the average farm had 275 acres and in 1994 was valued at $762 per acre. Production of principal crops, 1994: corn, 273·7m. bu.; soybeans,

173·3m. bu.; wheat, 49·5m. bu.; sorghum grain, 49·5m. bu.; oats, 1·77m. bu.; rice, 6·5m. cwt; cotton, 615,000 bales (of 480 lb). Farm income 1996: $4,950m. (from crops, $2,500m.; from livestock and products, $2,450m.)

Forestry. Forest land area, 1997, 3·06m. acres.

INDUSTRY

Labour. Total non-agricultural employment, 1999, 2,725,000. Employees by branch, 1999 (in 1,000): services, 771; wholesale and retail trade, 642; government, 420; manufacturing, 411; transportation and public utilities, 172. The unemployment rate was 3·4% in 1999.

COMMUNICATIONS

Roads. In 2000 there were 123,037 miles of roads (106,668 miles rural) and 4,579,629 registered motor vehicles.

Rail. The state has eight Class I railways; approximate total mileage, 6,645. There are nine Class II and Class III railways (switching, terminal or short-line); total mileage 435 in 1993. There is a light rail line in St Louis.

Civil Aviation. In 1994 there were 114 public airports and 359 private airports. There were 20,856,722 passenger enplanements statewide in 1999.

Shipping. Two major barge lines (1993) operated on about 1,050 miles of navigable waterways including the Missouri and Mississippi Rivers. Boat shipping seasons: Missouri River, April–end Nov.; Mississippi River, all seasons.

SOCIAL INSTITUTIONS

Justice. In June 2000 there were 27,292 federal and state prisoners. The death penalty was reinstated in 1978; the minimum age is 16. There were six executions in 2002. The Missouri Law Enforcement Assistance Council was created in 1969 for law reform. With reorganization of state government in 1974 the duties of the Council were delegated to the Department of Public Safety. The Dept. of Corrections was organized as a separate department of State by an Act of the Legislature in 1981.

Religion. Chief religious bodies (1990) are Catholic, with 802,434 members, Southern Baptists (789,183), United Methodists (255,111), Christian Churches (166,412) and Lutheran (142,824). Total membership, all denominations, about 2·3m. in 1990.

Education. School attendance is compulsory for children from 7 to 16 years for the full term. In the 1993–94 school year, public schools (kindergarten through grade 12) had 851,086 pupils. Total expenditure for public schools in 1993–94, $3,563,419,000. Salaries for teachers (kindergarten through grade 12), 1993–94, averaged $30,227. Institutions for higher education include the University of Missouri, founded in 1839 with campuses at Columbia, Rolla, St Louis and Kansas City, with 3,469 accredited teachers and 48,072 students in 1994–95. Washington University at St Louis, founded in 1857, is an independent co-ed university with 11,655 students in 1994–95. St Louis University (1818) is an independent Roman Catholic co-ed university with 10,365 students in 1994–95. 17 state colleges had 129,466 students in 1994–95. Private colleges had (1994–95) 34,548 students. Church-affiliated colleges (1994–95) had 41,420 students. Public junior colleges had 66,853 students. There are about 90 secondary and post-secondary institutions offering vocational courses, and about 294 private career schools. There were 265,186 students in higher education in autumn 1994.

Health. In 1995 there were 126 community hospitals with 21,900 beds.

Welfare. The number of actual recipients of Medicaid for the last five months of 1994 averaged 346,873; eligible to receive Medicaid, 559,331. The number of recipients of Aid to Families with Dependent Children was 259,048 with an average monthly payment per family of $264·79.

CULTURE

Broadcasting. There were 196 commercial radio stations and 29 TV stations in 1995.

Press. There were (1995) 46 daily and 260 weekly newspapers.

FURTHER READING
Statistical information: Business and Public Administration Research Center, Univ. of Missouri, Columbia 65211. Publishes *Statistical Abstract for Missouri.*
Missouri Area Labor Trends, Department of Labor and Industrial Relations, monthly
Missouri Farm Facts, Department of Agriculture, annual
Report of the Public Schools of Missouri. State Board of Education, annual

MONTANA

KEY HISTORICAL EVENTS
Originally the territory of many groups of Indian hunters including the Sioux, Cheyenne and Chippewa, Montana was not settled by American colonists until the 19th century. The area passed to the USA with the Louisiana Purchase of 1803, but the area west of the Rockies was disputed with Britain until 1846. Trappers and fur-traders were the first immigrants, and the fortified trading post at Fort Benton (1846) became the first permanent settlement. Colonization increased when gold was found in 1862. Montana was created a separate Territory (out of Idaho and Dakota Territories) in 1864. In 1866 large-scale grazing of sheep and cattle was allowed, and this provoked violent confrontation with the indigenous people whose hunting lands were invaded. Indian wars led to the defeat of federal forces at Little Bighorn in 1876 and at Big Hole Basin in 1877, but the Indians could not continue the fight and they had been moved to reservations by 1880. Montana became a state in 1889.

Helena, the capital, was founded as a mining town in the 1860s. In the early 20th century there were many European immigrants who settled as farmers or in the mines, especially in copper-mining at Butte.

TERRITORY AND POPULATION
Montana is bounded north by Canada, east by North and South Dakota, south by Wyoming and west by Idaho and the Bitterroot Range of the Rocky Mountains. Land area, 145,552 sq. miles (336,978 sq. km). US Bureau of Indian Affairs (1990) administered 5,574,835 acres, of which 2,663,385 were allotted to tribes. Census population, 1 April 2000, 902,195, an increase of 12·9% since 1990. July 2002 estimate, 909,453.

Population in five census years was:

	White	Black	American Indian	Asiatic	Total	Per sq. mile
1910	360,580	1,834	10,745	2,870	376,053	2·6
1930	519,898	1,256	14,798	1,239	537,606	3·7
1980	740,148	1,786	37,270	2,503	786,690	5·3
1990	741,111	2,381	47,679	4,259	799,065	5·4
2000	817,229	2,692	56,068	5,161	902,195	6·2

Of the total population in 2000, 452,715 were female, 672,133 were 18 years old or older and 487,878 were urban. Median age, 33·8 years. Households, 306,163. In 2000 Montana's Hispanic population was estimated to be 18,081, up from 12,174 in 1990 (an increase of 48·5%).

The largest cities, 2000, are Billings, 89,847; Missoula, 57,053; Great Falls, 56,690. Others: Butte-Silver Bow, 34,606; Bozeman, 27,509; Helena (capital), 25,780; Kalispell, 14,223; Havre, 9,621; Anaconda-Deer Lodge County, 9,417.

SOCIAL STATISTICS
Births in 1999, 10,814 (12·3 per 1,000 population); deaths, 8,066 (9·1); (1996) infant mortality rate, 7·0 (per 1,000 live births). Marriages (1997), 6,600; divorces, 4,000.

CLIMATE
Helena, Jan. 18°F (−7·8°C), July 69°F (20·6°C). Annual rainfall 13" (325 mm). Montana belongs to the Mountain States climate zone (*see* UNITED STATES: Climate).

CONSTITUTION AND GOVERNMENT
A new constitution came into force on 1 July 1973. The Senate consists of 50 senators, elected for four years, one half at each biennial election. The 100 members of the House of Representatives are elected for two years.

For the 108th Congress, which convened in Jan. 2003, Montana sends one member to the House of Representatives. It is represented in the Senate by Max Baucus (D. 1978–2009) and Conrad Burns (R. 1989–2007).

The capital is Helena. The state is divided into 56 counties.

RECENT ELECTIONS
In the 2000 presidential election Bush polled 240,178 votes; Gore, 137,126; Nader, 24,437.

CURRENT ADMINISTRATION
Governor: Judy Martz (R.), 2001–05 (salary: $88,190).
  Lieut.-Governor: Karl Ohs (R.), 2001–05 ($62,471).
  Secretary of State: Bob Brown (R.), 2001–05 ($67,485).

Government Website: http://www.discoveringmontana.com

ECONOMY
Per capita income (2000) was $22,541.

Budget. In 1999 total state revenue was $3,725m. Total expenditure was $3,512m. (education, $1,107m.; public welfare, $495m.; health and hospitals, $237m.; highways, $403m.; police protection, $38m.). Outstanding debt, in 1999, $2,356m.

Performance. Gross State Product in 2000 was $21,777m.

ENERGY AND NATURAL RESOURCES
Water. The total area covered by water is approximately 1,490 sq. miles.

Minerals. 1998 domestic non-fuel mineral production value was $500m. Principal minerals include copper, gold, platinum-group metals, molybdenum and silver.

Agriculture. In 2000 there were 27,600 farms and ranches with an area of 56·7m. acres. Large-scale farming predominates; in 2000 the average size per farm was 2,054 acres, and in 1998 the average value per acre was $320. In 1997 a total of 13,267,000 acres were harvested; including 5,930,000 acres of wheat. The farm population in 1991 was 67,546.

The chief crops are wheat, barley, oats, sugarbeet, hay, potatoes, corn, dry beans and cherries. Farm income, 1996: crops, $1,230m.; livestock and products, $797m. In 1998 there were 2·6m. cattle and calves; value, $716m.

Forestry. In 1997 there were 19,106,569 acres within 11 national forests.

INDUSTRY
Labour. Total non-agricultural employment, 1999, 381,000. Employees by branch, 1999 (in 1,000): services, 112; wholesale and retail trade, 101; government, 79; manufacturing, 25. In 1999 the unemployment rate was 5·2%.

COMMUNICATIONS
Roads. In 2000 there were a total of 69,567 miles of roads and 1,026,226 registered motor vehicles.

Rail. In 1999 there were approximately 3,300 route miles of railway in the state.

Civil Aviation. There were 119 public use airports in 1999. There were nine state-owned airports and a further five-state managed. There were 1,055,884 passenger enplanements statewide in 1999.

SOCIAL INSTITUTIONS

Justice. In June 2000 there were 3,039 prison inmates. The minimum age for the death penalty is 18, which was last used in 1998.

Religion. The leading religious bodies are Roman Catholic, followed by Lutheran and Methodist.

Education. In 1995 (preliminary) public elementary and secondary schools had 165,000 pupils and (in 1994) 10,079 teachers. Expenditure on public school education by state and local governments in 1997 was $986m.

In 1996 there were 43,000 students enrolled at 26 higher education institutions. The Montana University system consists of the Montana State University, at Bozeman (autumn 1992 enrolment: 10,111 students); the University of Montana, at Missoula, founded in 1895 (10,788); the Montana College of Mineral Science and Technology, at Butte (1,881); Northern Montana College, at Havre (1,973); Eastern Montana College, at Billings (3,631); and Western Montana College, at Dillon (1,106).

Health. In 1995 there were 55 community hospitals with 4,200 beds.

Welfare. In 1994 there were 150,000 beneficiaries receiving $1,078 annual payments.

CULTURE

Press. There were 11 daily newspapers and 7 Sunday papers in 1997.

FURTHER READING

Statistical information. Census and Economic Information Center, Montana Department of Commerce, 1425 9th Ave., Helena 59620.

Lang, W. L. and Myers, R. C., *Montana, Our Land and People.* Pruett, 1979

NEBRASKA

KEY HISTORICAL EVENTS

The Nebraska region was first reached by Europeans from Mexico under the Spanish general Coronado in 1541. It was ceded by France to Spain in 1763, retroceded to France in 1801, and sold by Napoleon to the USA as part of the Louisiana Purchase in 1803. During the 1840s the Platte River valley became an established trail for thousands of pioneers' wagons heading for Oregon and California. The need to serve and protect the trail led to the creation of Nebraska as a Territory in 1854. In 1862 the Homestead Act opened the area for settlement, but colonization was not very rapid until the Union Pacific Railroad was completed in 1869. The largest city, Omaha, developed as the starting point of the Union Pacific and became one of the largest railway towns in the country.

Nebraska became a state in 1867, with approximately its present boundaries except that it later received small areas from the Dakotas. Many early settlers were from Europe, brought in by railway-company schemes, but from the late 1880s eastern Nebraska suffered catastrophic drought. Crop and stock farming recovered, but crop growing was only established in the west by means of irrigation.

TERRITORY AND POPULATION

Nebraska is bounded in the north by South Dakota, with the Missouri River forming the boundary in the northeast and the boundary with Iowa and Missouri to the east, south by Kansas, southwest by Colorado and west by Wyoming. Land area, 76,872 sq. miles (199,098 sq. km). Census population, 1 April 2000, 1,711,263, an increase of 8·4% since 1990. July 2002 estimate, 1,729,180.

Population in five census years was:

	White	Black	Indian	Asiatic	Total	Per sq. mile
1910	1,180,293	7,689	3,502	730	1,192,214	15·5
1960	1,374,764	29,262	5,545	1,195	1,411,330	18·3
				All others		
1980	1,490,381	48,390		31,054	1,569,825	20·5
1990	1,480,558	57,404		40,423	1,578,385	20·5
2000	1,533,261	68,541		109,461	1,711,263	22·3

Of the total population in 2000, 867,912 were female, 1,261,021 were 18 years old or older and 1,193,725 were urban. In 1999 the estimated Hispanic population of Nebraska was 94,425, up from 36,969 in 1990 (a rise of 155·4%). The largest cities in the state are: Omaha, with a census population, 2000, of 390,007; Lincoln, 225,581; Bellevue, 44,382; Grand Island, 42,940; Kearney, 27,431; Fremont, 25,174; Hastings, 24,064; North Platte, 23,878; Norfolk, 23,516.

The Bureau of Indian Affairs in 1990 administered 64,932 acres, of which 21,742 acres were allotted to tribal control.

SOCIAL STATISTICS
Births, 1999, were 23,592 (14·2 per 1,000 population); deaths, 15,437 (9·3); (1997) marriages, 12,500 (7·5); divorces, 6,200 (3·8); 1995, infant mortality rate, 8·7 (per 1,000 live births).

CLIMATE
Omaha, Jan. 22°F (−5·6°C), July 77°F (25°C). Annual rainfall 29" (721 mm). Nebraska belongs to the High Plains climate zone (see UNITED STATES: Climate).

CONSTITUTION AND GOVERNMENT
The present constitution was adopted in 1875; it has been amended 184 times. By an amendment of 1934 Nebraska has a single-chambered legislature (elected for four years) of 49 members elected on a non-party ballot and classed as senators—the only state in the USA to have one. It meets annually.

For the 108th Congress, which convened in Jan. 2003, Nebraska sends three members to the House of Representatives. It is represented in the Senate by Chuck Hagel (R. 1997–2009) and Ben Nelson (D. 2001–07).

The capital is Lincoln. The state has 93 counties.

RECENT ELECTIONS
In the 2000 presidential election Bush polled 433,850 votes; Gore, 231,776; Nader, 24,670.

CURRENT ADMINISTRATION
Governor: Mike Johanns (R.), 2003–07 (salary: $85,000).
 Lieut.-Governor: Dave Heineman (R.), 2003–07 ($60,000).
 Secretary of State: John Gale (R.), 2003–07 ($65,000).

Government Website: http://www.state.ne.us

ECONOMY
Per capita income (2000) was $27,658.

Budget. In 1999 total state revenue was $5,576m. Total expenditure was $5,184m. (education, $1,907m.; public welfare, $1,122m.; highways, $646m.; health and hospitals, $384m.; police protection, $57m.). Outstanding debt, in 1999, $1,820m.

Performance. Gross State Product was $56,072m. in 2000.

ENERGY AND NATURAL RESOURCES
Oil and Gas. Petroleum output, 1995: 15,934·3m. gallons; gas, 683m. cu. ft.

Water. The total area covered by water is approximately 481 sq. miles.

Minerals. Output of non-fuel minerals, 1995 (in 1,000 short tons) and value (in $1,000): clays, 243 (1,025); sand and gravel for construction, 17,637 (55·2); stone,

7,275 (39·6). Other minerals include limestone, potash, pumice, slate and shale. Total value of non-fuel mineral output in 1998 was $174m.

Agriculture. Nebraska is one of the most important agricultural states. In 2000 it contained approximately 54,000 farms, with a total area of 46·4m. acres. The average farm was 859 acres. In 1997 the total acreage harvested was 18,696,000 acres.

In 1994 net farm income was $2,264·2m. Farm income from crops (1996), $4,177m., and from livestock and products, $5,277m. Principal crops were maize, sorghum for grain, soybeans and wheat. Livestock, 1990: cattle, 6m.; pigs, 4·2m.; sheep, 0·16m.; chickens, 2·1m.; turkeys, 2·1m. Value: 1994, $656m.; dairy products, 1994: $14·3m.

Forestry. There were 346,485 acres of national forest in 1997.

INDUSTRY

In 1995 there were 2,071 manufacturing establishments with 112,951 employees, with an annual payroll of $3,121,427,000. Value added by manufacturing was $9,452·1m. The chief industry is meat-packing. Pork products were worth $878m. in 1991.

Labour. In 1999 non-agricultural employment totalled 891,000. Employees by branch in 1999 (in 1,000): services, 243; wholesale and retail trade, 215; government, 152; manufacturing, 118. In 1996 the average unemployment rate was 2·9%.

COMMUNICATIONS

Roads. In 2000 there were 92,792 miles of roads (87,606 miles rural) and 1,618,933 registered motor vehicles.

Rail. In 1996 there were 4,000 miles of railway.

Civil Aviation. Publicly owned airports in 1996 numbered 384. There were 2,007,636 passenger enplanements statewide in 1999.

SOCIAL INSTITUTIONS

Justice. A 'Civil Rights Act' revised in 1969 provides that all people are entitled to a full and equal enjoyment of public facilities. In June 2000 there were 3,663 prison inmates. The minimum age for the death penalty is 18. The last execution was in 1997.

Religion. The Roman Catholics had 337,224 members in 1992; United Methodists, 131,665; Evangelical Lutheran Church, 128,014; Lutheran Church-Missouri Synod, 115,204; Presbyterian Church (USA), 36,723.

Education. School attendance is compulsory for children from 7 to 16 years of age. Public elementary and secondary schools, in 1998–99, had 289,984 enrolled pupils and 20,099 teachers. Total enrolment in institutions of higher education, autumn 1994, was 95,560 students in public and 19,872 in independent institutions.

Opened	Institution	Students 1998–99
1867	Peru State College	1,750
	University of Nebraska (State)	45,750
1869	Lincoln	21,900
1905	Kearney	6,850
1908	Omaha	13,950
	Medical Center	2,600
	College of Technology, Agriculture, Curtis	450
1872	Doane College, Crete (United Church of Christ)	1,850
	Grace College of the Bible (Private)	600
1878	Creighton University, Omaha (Roman Catholic)	6,250
	Dana College (American Lutheran)	550
1882	Hastings College (Presbyterian)	1,150
1883	Midland Lutheran College, Fremont	
	(Lutheran Church of America)	1,050
	Nebraska Christian College (Church of Christ)	152[1]
	Nebraska Methodist College (Private)	223[1]

Opened	Institution	Students 1998–99
1887	Nebraska Wesleyan University (Private)	1,750
	Platt Valley Bible College (Private)	75[1]
1891	Union College, Lincoln (Seventh Day Adventist)	1,150
	York College[2] (Private)	500
	Nebraska Indian Community College (1994)	320
1894	Concordia Teachers' College, Seward (Lutheran)	1,200
1910	Wayne State College	3,850
	Nebraska Community Colleges (Local government)	34,442[1]
	Central Area	6,743[1]
	Metropolitan Area	11,213[1]
	Mid Plains Area	2,825[1]
	Northeast Area	4,573[1]
	Southeast Area	7,080[1]
	Western Area	2,008[1]
1911	Chardon State College	2,800
1923	College of St. Mary (Roman Catholic)	1,050
1966	Bellevue College (Private)	2,900
	Clarkson College (Private)	597[1]

[1]1997 figure. [2]Two-year college.

Health. There were 106 community hospitals in 1997.

Welfare. In 1996 public welfare provided financial aid and/or services as follows (figures and total expenditure): aid to dependent children, 14,717 families/month and \$55·2m. total expenditure; aged, blind and disabled, 6,059 persons/month and \$6·0m.; food stamps, 102,053 recipients/month and \$77·9m.; Medicaid, 120,012 recipients/month and \$645·1m.

CULTURE

Tourism. In 1995 there were an estimated 16·1m. visits. Travellers and tourists spent over \$2,000m.

FURTHER READING

Statistical information: Department of Economic Development, Box 94666, Lincoln 68509.
Nebraska Blue-Book. Legislative Council. Lincoln. Biennial
Olson, J. C., *History of Nebraska.* 3rd ed. Univ. of Nebraska Press, 1997

State Library: State Law Library, State House, Lincoln.

NEVADA

KEY HISTORICAL EVENTS

The area was part of Spanish America until 1821, when it became part of the newly independent state of Mexico. Following a war between Mexico and the USA, Nevada was ceded to the USA as part of California in 1848. Settlement began in 1849, and the area was separated from California and joined with Utah Territory in 1850. In 1859 a rich deposit of silver was found in the Comstock Lode. Virginia City was founded as a mining town and immigration increased rapidly. Nevada Territory was formed in 1861. During the Civil War the Federal government, allegedly in order to obtain the wealth of silver for the Union cause, agreed to admit Nevada to the Union in 1864 as the 36th state. Areas of Arizona and Utah Territories were added to it in 1866–67.

The mining boom lasted until 1882, by which time cattle ranching had become equally important in the valleys where the climate is less arid. Carson City, the capital, developed in association with the nearby mining industry. The largest cities, Las Vegas and Reno, grew most in the 20th century with the building of the Hoover dam, the introduction of legal gambling and of easily obtained divorce.

After 1950 much of the desert area was adopted by the Federal government for weapons testing and other military purposes.

TERRITORY AND POPULATION

Nevada is bounded north by Oregon and Idaho, east by Utah, southeast by Arizona, with the Colorado River forming most of the boundary, south and west by California. Land area, 109,889 sq. miles (284,613 sq. km). In 1999 the federal government owned 83% of the land area.

Census population on 1 April 2000, 1,998,257, an increase of 66·3% since 1990. July 2002 estimate, 2,173,491.

Population in five census years was:

	White	Black	American Indian	All others	Total	Per sq. mile
1910	74,276	513	5,240	1,846	81,875	0·7
1930	84,515	516	4,871	1,156	91,058	0·8
1980	700,360	50,999	13,308	35,841	800,508	7·2
1990	1,012,695	78,771	19,637	90,730	1,201,833	10·9
2000	1,501,886	135,477	26,420	334,474	1,998,257	18·2

Of the total population in 2000, 1,018,051 were male, 1,486,458 were 18 years old or older and 1,828,646 were urban (91·51%, the third highest of the states). In 2000 the Hispanic population was 393,970, up from 124,419 in 1990 (an increase of 216·6%). Nevada was the fastest-growing state in the USA in 2001. Its recent overall population rise has made it the fastest-growing state in the USA every year since 1986.

The largest cities in 2000 were: Las Vegas, 478,434; Reno, 180,480; Henderson, 175,381; North Las Vegas, 115,448; Sparks, 66,346; Carson City (the capital), 52,457.

SOCIAL STATISTICS

Births, 2000, were 30,477 (16·4 per 1,000); deaths, 16,080 (881·5 per 100,000); infant mortality deaths (2000) were 6·4 per 1,000 live births. Marriages (2000), 134,908; divorces, 14,084. Fertility rate, 1998, 2·5 births per woman (the second highest in the USA after Utah).

CLIMATE

Las Vegas, Jan. 57°F (14°C), July 104°F (40°C). Annual rainfall 4·13" (105 mm). Reno, Jan. 45°F (7°C), July 91°F (33°C). Annual rainfall 7·53" (191 mm). Nevada belongs to the Mountain States climate zone (see UNITED STATES: Climate).

CONSTITUTION AND GOVERNMENT

The constitution adopted in 1864 is still in force, with 145 amendments as of 2001. The Legislature meets biennially (and in special sessions) and consists of a Senate of 21 members elected for four years, half their number is elected every two years, and an Assembly of 42 members elected for two years. The Governor may be elected for two consecutive four-year terms.

For the 108th Congress, which convened in Jan. 2003, Nevada sends three members to the House of Representatives. It is represented in the Senate by Harry Reid (D. 1987–2005) and John Ensign (R. 2001–07).

The state capital is Carson City. There are 16 counties, 18 incorporated cities and 49 unincorporated communities and 1 city-county (the Capitol District of Carson City).

RECENT ELECTIONS

In the 2000 presidential election Bush polled 301,575 votes; Gore, 279,978; Nader, 15,008.

CURRENT ADMINISTRATION

Governor: Kenny C. Guinn (R.), 2003–07 (salary: $117,000).
   Lieut.-Governor: Lorraine Hunt (R.), 2003–07 ($50,000).
   Secretary of State: Dean Heller (R.), 2003–07 ($80,000).

Government Website: http://www.nv.gov

ECONOMY

Per capita personal income (2001) was $29,897.

Budget. In fiscal year 2002 the total sources of funding totalled $4,987·7m. The tax sources include $655·1m. from Sales and Use Taxes; $589·8m. from Gaming Taxes; $207·5m. from Casino Entertainment Tax; $156·3m. from Insurance Premium Tax; $78·4m. from Business Licence Tax. Total expenditure in 2002 was $4,364m. (education, $999·5m.; human services, $501·6m.; public safety, $210·4m.). Outstanding debt, in 1999, $2,997m.

Performance. Gross State Product in 2000 was $74,745m.

ENERGY AND NATURAL RESOURCES

Electricity. In 2001 there were 15 geothermal electric plants in 10 locations. Total electricity capacity in 1998 was 5·8m. kW. In 1999 total net electrical production was 26·4bn. kWh.

Oil and Gas. In 2001, 571,000 bbls. of crude oil were produced from oil fields located in Nye and Eureka Counties.

Water. The total area covered by water is approximately 761 sq. miles.

Minerals. Nevada led the nation in precious metal production in 2000, producing 76% of gold and 37% of silver. Nevada has been first in silver production since 1987 and first in gold since 1981. In 2000 Nevada produced 267,000 kg of gold and 722,000 kg of silver. Nevada was the only state in 2000 to produce magnesite, lithium minerals, brucite and mercury. Nevada also produces other minerals such as aggregates, clays, copper, diatomite, dolomite, geothermal energy, gypsum, lapidary, lime and limestone. The total value of Nevada's mineral production in 2000 was about $2·7bn.

Agriculture. In 2001 there were an estimated 3,000 farms. Farms averaged 2,267 acres; farms and ranches totalled 6·8m. acres. Average value per acre in 2000 was $460.

In 2001, 45·3% of farm income came from cattle and calves, 14·7% from dairy products, 0·6% from sheep and lambs, 3·3% from other livestock. Hay production was 22% of all farm income, potatoes 2·4%, vegetables 4·6%, wheat 0·4% and other crops 6·7%.

In 2002 there were 500,000 cattle and 100,000 sheep.

Forestry. The national forests covered an area of 6,275,439 acres in 1998.

INDUSTRY

The main industry is the service industry (42·2% of employment in 2000), especially tourism and legalized gambling. In 2000 there were 42,406 employed in manufacturing and 88,688 in construction.

Gaming industry gross revenue for 2001 was $9,220m. In 1998 there were 428 non-restricted licensed casinos and 2,700 licences in force. Nevada gets 41% of its tax revenue from the gaming industry.

Labour. In 2000 all industries employed 1,091,970 workers. The service industry employed 247,752; retail trade, 175,730; transportation and public utilities, 61,801; government, 51,920; finance, insurance and real estate, 46,580; manufacturing, 44,380; mining, 10,955. The unemployment rate in 2002 was 5·4%.

COMMUNICATIONS

Roads. In 2001 there were 44,613 miles of roads, of which the state maintained 5,447 miles. Motor vehicle registrations in 2001 numbered 679,137 with 1,420,714 licensed drivers.

Rail. In 1995 there were 1,272 miles of main-line railway. Nevada is served by the Southern Pacific, Union Pacific and Burlington Northern BPH Nevada Railroad railways, and Amtrak passenger service for Las Vegas, Elko, Reno, Caliente, Lovelock, Stateline, Winnemucca and Sparks.

Civil Aviation. There were 98 civil airports and 24 heliports in Jan. 1996. During 2001, 43,574,956 passengers arrived at Nevada's airports. McCarran International Airport (Las Vegas) handled 32,647,344 passengers and Reno-Tahoe International Airport handled 4,932,648 passengers.

SOCIAL INSTITUTIONS

Justice. Capital punishment was reintroduced in 1978, and executions began in 1979. The minimum age for the death penalty is 16. There was one execution in 2001 but none in 2002. In June 2001 there were 10,291 prison inmates in state or federal correctional institutions.

Religion. Many faiths are represented in Nevada, including Church of Jesus Christ of Latter Day Saints (Mormons), Protestantism, Roman Catholicism, Judaism and Buddhism.

Education. School attendance is compulsory for children from 7 to 17 years of age. Numbers of pupils in public schools, 2001–02: pre-kindergarten, 2,147; kindergarten, 26,877; elementary, 177,342; secondary grades 7–9, 87,538; secondary grades 10–12, 60,470; special education, 40,196. Numbers of teachers in public schools, 2001: elementary, 9,870; secondary, 6,070; special education, 2,646; occupational, 198. Numbers of pupils in private schools, 2001–02: kindergartens, 3,109; elementary, 8,281; secondary grades 7–9, 2,892; secondary grades 10–12, 2,056. Number of private school teachers, 1999, 973.

The University of Nevada System comprises campuses at Las Vegas and Reno and four community colleges. In autumn 2002 there were 54,832 students (50,527 in 2001).

Health. In 2001 the state had 24 community hospitals with nine rural hospitals and 15 urban hospitals with 4,059 beds (1·9 per 1,000). In 2000 there were 4,875 physicians and 20,495 full-time and part-time nurses, nursing assistants, aids and orderlies and other hospital personnel.

Welfare. The Nevada Women, Infants and Children (WIC) special nutrition programmes served an average of 39,000 at-risk women, infants and children each month in 2001 and 69,396 people receiving food stamps. In 2000, 5% of the population received public aid. Benefits were paid to 102,162 persons. The average per recipient monthly for TANF (Temporary Assistance for Needy Families) was $124·86.

CULTURE

Tourism. There are 24 State Parks covering 131,861 acres. In 2001, 28,216,174 people visited state and nearby national parks with 49,528,979 tourists coming to Nevada.

Festivals. Nevada hosts the Elko Cowboy Poetry Festival, the Las Vegas International Film Festival, the Reno Balloon Races, the Reno Air Races, the Reno Hot August Nights and the Winnemucca Basque Festival.

Libraries. There are 84 public libraries, 32 special libraries and 6 university libraries.

Theatre and Opera. Nevada supports the arts through a number of organizations, including the Las Vegas Civic Ballet, Las Vegas Philharmonic, Nevada Festival Ballet, Nevada Opera, Reno Philharmonic and the Carson City Symphony.

Museums and Galleries. There are over 100 museums in the state, including the Nevada State Railroad Museum, Nevada State Museum, Nevada Historical Society, Harrah's Automobile Museum, Bellagio Gallery of Fine Art, Guggenheim Hermitage Museum, Liberace Museum, Las Vegas Art Museum and the Nevada Museum of Art.

FURTHER READING

Statistical information: Budget and Planning Division, Department of Administration, Capitol Complex, Carson City, Nevada 89710. Publishes *Nevada Statistical Abstract* (Biennial).

Bowers, Michael W., *The Stagebrush State: Nevada's History, Government, and Politics.* Univ. of Nevada Press, 1996

Hulse, J. W., *The Nevada Adventure: a History.* 6th ed. Univ. of Nevada Press, 1990.—*The Silver State: Nevada's Heritage Reinterpreted.* Univ. of Nevada Press, 1998

State Government Website: http://www.nv.gov
Nevada State Library: Nevada State Library and Archives, Carson City.

NEW HAMPSHIRE

KEY HISTORICAL EVENTS

The area was part of a grant by the English crown made to John Mason and fellow-colonists, and was first settled in 1623. In 1629 an area between the Merrimack and Piscatagua rivers was called New Hampshire. More settlements followed, and in 1641 they were taken under the jurisdiction of the governor of Massachusetts. New Hampshire became a separate colony in 1679.

After the War of Independence New Hampshire became one of the 13 original states of the Union, ratifying the US constitution in 1788. The state constitution, which dates from 1776, was almost totally rewritten in 1784 and amended again in 1792.

The settlers were Protestants from Britain and Northern Ireland. They developed manufacturing industries, especially shoe-making, textiles and clothing, to which large numbers of French Canadians were attracted after the Civil War.

Portsmouth, originally a fishing settlement, was the colonial capital and is the only seaport. In 1808 the state capital was moved to Concord (having had no permanent home since 1775); Concord produced the Concord Coach which was widely used on the stagecoach routes of the West until at least 1900.

TERRITORY AND POPULATION

New Hampshire is bounded in the north by Canada, east by Maine and the Atlantic, south by Massachusetts and west by Vermont. Land area, 8,968 sq. miles (23,227 sq. km). Census population, 1 April 2000, 1,235,786, an increase of 11·4% since 1990. July 2002 estimate, 1,275,056.

Population at five federal censuses was:

	White	Black	Indian	Asiatic	Total	Per sq. mile
1910	429,906	564	34	68	430,572	47·7
1960	604,334	1,903	135	549	606,921	65·2
			All others			
1980	910,099	3,990	6,521		920,610	101·9
1990	1,087,433	7,198	14,621		1,109,252	123·7
2000	1,186,851	9,035	39,900		1,235,786	137·8

Of the total population in 2000, 628,099 were female, 926,224 were 18 years old or older and 732,335 were urban. In 2000 the Hispanic population was estimated to be 20,489, up from 11,333 in 1990 (an increase of 80·8%). The largest city in the state is Manchester, with a 2000 census population of 107,006. The capital is Concord, with 40,687. Other main cities and towns (with 2000 populations) are: Nashua, 86,605; Derry, 34,021; Rochester, 28,461; Salem, 28,112; Dover, 26,884; Merrimack, 25,119; Londonderry, 23,236; Hudson, 22,928; Keene, 22,563; Portsmouth, 20,784.

SOCIAL STATISTICS

Births, 1999, were 14,660 (12·2 per 1,000 population); deaths, 9,564 (8·0); (1996) infant mortality rate, 5·0 (per 1,000 live births); 1997, marriages, 10,100; divorces, 5,600.

CLIMATE

New Hampshire is in the New England climate zone (*see* UNITED STATES: Climate). Manchester, Jan. 22°F (−5·6°C), July 70°F (21·1°C). Annual rainfall 40" (1,003 mm).

CONSTITUTION AND GOVERNMENT

While the present constitution dates from 1784, it was extensively revised in 1792 when the state joined the Union. Since 1775 there have been 16 state conventions with 49 amendments adopted to amend the constitution.

The Legislature (called the General Court) consists of a Senate of 24 members, elected for two years, and a House of Representatives, of 400 members, elected for two years. It meets annually. The Governor and five administrative officers called 'Councillors' are also elected for two years.

For the 108th Congress, which convened in Jan. 2003, New Hampshire sends two members to the House of Representatives. It is represented in the Senate by Judd Gregg (R. 1993–2005) and John Sununu (R. 2003–09).

The capital is Concord. The state is divided into ten counties.

RECENT ELECTIONS
In the 2000 presidential election Bush polled 278,559 votes; Gore, 266,848; Nader, 22,188.

CURRENT ADMINISTRATION
Governor: Craig Benson (R.), 2003–05 (salary: $117,000).
  Secretary of State: William M. Gardner (D.), 2001–05 ($89,128).

Government Website: http://www.state.nh.us

ECONOMY
Per capita income (2000) was $33,042.

Budget. New Hampshire has no general sales tax or state income tax but does have local property taxes. Other government revenues come from rooms and meals tax, business profits tax, motor vehicle licences, fuel taxes, fishing and hunting licences, state-controlled sales of alcoholic beverages, cigarette and tobacco taxes.

In 1999 total state revenue was $4,024m. Total expenditure was $3,594m. (education, $707m.; public welfare, $947m.; highways, $346m.; health and hospitals, $164m.; police protection, $35m.). Outstanding debt, in 1999, $5,427m.

Performance. Gross State Product in 2000 was $47,708m.

ENERGY AND NATURAL RESOURCES
Water. The total area covered by water is approximately 314 sq. miles.

Minerals. Minerals are little worked; they consist mainly of sand and gravel, stone, and clay for building and highway construction. Value of domestic non-fuel mineral production, 1998, $53m.

Agriculture. In 2000 there were some 3,100 farms covering around 420,000 acres; average farm was 135 acres. Average value per acre in 1997, $2,250. Farm income 1997: from crops, $73·7m.; from livestock and products, $75·7m.

The chief field crops are hay and vegetables; the chief fruit crop is apples. Livestock, 1997: cattle, 45,115; pigs, 4,373; sheep, 6,925; poultry, 213,782.

Forestry. In 1997 there were 798,397 acres of national forest.

Fisheries. 1998 commercial fishing landings amounted to 9,394,015 lb worth $11,160,000.

INDUSTRY
Principal manufactures: electrical and electronic goods, machinery and metal products.

Labour. Total non-agricultural employment, 1999, 695,000. Employees by branch, 1999 (in 1,000): services, 178; wholesale and retail trade, 160; manufacturing, 107. In 1999 the unemployment rate was 2·7%—only Iowa, with 2·5%, had a lower rate.

COMMUNICATIONS
Roads. In 2000 there were 15,210 miles of roads (12,273 miles rural) and 1,051,751 registered motor vehicles.

Rail. In 1993 the length of operating railway in the state was 540 miles.

Civil Aviation. In 1997 there were 26 public and 21 private airports. There were 1,239,148 passenger enplanements statewide in 1999.

SOCIAL INSTITUTIONS
Justice. There were 2,254 prison inmates in June 2000. The death penalty was abolished in May 2000—the last execution had been in 1939.

Religion. The Roman Catholic Church is the largest single body. The largest Protestant churches are Congregational, Episcopal, Methodist and United Baptist Convention of N.H.

Education. School attendance is compulsory for children from 6 to 14 years of age during the whole school term, or to 16 if their district provides a high school. Employed illiterate minors between 16 and 21 years of age must attend evening or special classes, if provided by the district.

In 1995 the public elementary and secondary schools had 209,150 pupils and 12,300 teachers. Public school salaries, 1995, averaged $35,792. An average of $6,449 was spent on education per pupil.

Of the 4-year colleges, the University of New Hampshire (founded in 1866) had 14,538 students in 1998; New Hampshire College (1932), 5,653; Keene State College (1909), 4,354; Plymouth State College (1871), 3,990; Dartmouth College (1769), 5,269. Total enrolment, 1995–96, in the 30 institutions of higher education was 61,128.

Health. In 1995 the state had 29 community hospitals with 3,400 beds.

Welfare. The Division of Human Services handles public assistance for (1) aged citizens 65 years or over, (2) needy aged aliens, (3) needy blind persons, (4) needy citizens between 18 and 64 years inclusive, who are permanently and totally disabled, (5) needy children under 18 years, (6) Medicaid and the medically needy not eligible for a monthly grant.

In 1995 the annual average number of welfare cases were: 65 years or over, 8,446; disabled, 8,305; families with dependent children, 12,798.

CULTURE

Broadcasting. Across the state there were 49 radio and 6 TV stations in 1997.

Press. In 1997 there were 12 daily and 8 Sunday newspapers in circulation.

FURTHER READING

Delorme, D. (ed.) *New Hampshire Atlas and Gazetteer.* Freeport, 1983

NEW JERSEY

KEY HISTORICAL EVENTS

Originally the territory of Delaware Indians, the area was first settled by immigrant colonists in the early 17th century, when Dutch and Swedish traders established fortified posts on the Hudson and Delaware Rivers. The Dutch took control but lost it to the English in 1664. In 1676 the English divided the area in two; the eastern portion was assigned to Sir George Carteret and the western granted to Quaker settlers. This division lasted until 1702 when New Jersey was united as a colony of the Crown and placed under the jurisdiction of the governor of New York. It became a separate colony in 1738.

During the War of Independence crucial battles were fought at Trenton, Princeton and Monmouth. New Jersey became the 3rd state of the Union in 1787. Trenton, the state capital since 1790, began as a Quaker settlement and became an iron-working town. Industrial development grew rapidly, there and elsewhere in the state, after the opening of canals and railways in the 1830s. Princeton, also a Quaker settlement, became an important post on the New York road; the college of New Jersey (Princeton University) was transferred there from Newark in 1756.

The need for supplies in the Civil War stimulated industry and New Jersey became a manufacturing state. The growth beyond its borders of New York and Philadelphia, however, produced a pattern of commuting to employment in both centres. By 1980 about 60% of the state's population lived within 30 miles of New York.

TERRITORY AND POPULATION

New Jersey is bounded north by New York, east by the Atlantic with Long Island and New York City to the northeast, south by Delaware Bay and west by

Pennsylvania. Land area, 7,417 sq. miles (19,209 sq. km). Census population, 1 April 2000, 8,414,350, an increase of 8·9% since 1990. July 2002 estimate, 8,590,300. Population density, 1990, 1,042·2 per sq. mile.

Population at five federal censuses was:

	White	Black	Asiatic	Others	Total	Per sq. mile
1910	2,445,894	89,760	1,345	168	2,537,167	337·7
1930	3,829,663	208,828	2,630	213	4,041,334	537·3
1980	6,127,467	925,066	103,848	208,442	7,364,823	986·2
1990	6,130,465	1,036,825	272,521	290,377	7,730,188	1,042·0
2000	6,104,705	1,141,821	483,605	684,219	8,414,350	1,134·4

Of the total population in 2000, 4,331,537 were female, 6,326,792 were 18 years old or older and 7,939,087 were urban (94·35%, marginally less than California, the highest). In 2000 the Hispanic population was 1,117,191, up from 739,861 in 1990 (an increase of 51·0%).

Census populations of the largest cities and towns in 2000 were:

Newark	273,546	Clifton	78,672	Old Bridge	60,456
Jersey City	240,055	Brick	76,119	Lakewood	60,352
Paterson	149,222	Cherry Hill	69,965	North Bergen	58,092
Elizabeth	120,568	East Orange	69,824	Vineland	56,271
Edison	97,687	Passaic	67,861	Union Township	54,405
Woodbridge	97,203	Union City	67,088	Wayne	54,069
Dover	89,706	Middletown	66,327	Franklin	50,903
Hamilton	87,109	Gloucester	64,350	Parsippany-	
Trenton (capital)	85,403	Bayonne	61,842	Troy Hills	50,649
Camden	79,904	Irvington	60,695	Piscataway	50,482

Largest metropolitan areas (2000) are: Newark, 2,032,989; Bergen–Passaic, 1,373,167; Middlesex–Somerset–Hunterdon, 1,169,641; Monmouth–Ocean, 1,126,217; Jersey City, 608,975.

SOCIAL STATISTICS
1999 (rates per 1,000 population): births, 111,487 (13·7); deaths, 71,578 (8·8); infant deaths in 1996, 6·9 per 1,000 live births; marriages (1997), 56,400; divorces, 25,500.

CLIMATE
Jersey City, Jan. 31°F (−0·6°C), July 75°F (23·9°C). Annual rainfall 41" (1,025 mm). Trenton, Jan. 32°F (0°C), July 76°F (24·4°C). Annual rainfall 40" (1,003 mm). New Jersey belongs to the Atlantic Coast climate zone (see UNITED STATES: Climate).

CONSTITUTION AND GOVERNMENT
The present constitution, ratified by the registered voters on 4 Nov. 1947, has been amended 45 times. There is a 40-member Senate and an 80-member General Assembly. Assembly members serve two years, senators four years, except those elected at the election following each census, who serve for two years. Sessions are held throughout the year.

For the 108th Congress, which convened in Jan. 2003, New Jersey sends 13 members to the House of Representatives. It is represented in the Senate by Frank Lautenberg (D. 1982–2001, 2003–09) and Jon Corzine (D. 2001–07).

The capital is Trenton. The state is divided into 21 counties, which are subdivided into 567 municipalities—cities, towns, boroughs, villages and townships.

RECENT ELECTIONS
In the 2000 presidential election Gore polled 1,788,850 votes; Bush, 1,284,173; Nader, 94,554.

In the 2001 gubernatorial elections Democrat James E. McGreevey won with 56% of votes cast, defeating the Republican candidate Bret Schundler (42%).

CURRENT ADMINISTRATION
Governor: James E. McGreevey (D.), 2002–06 (salary: $157,000).
Secretary of State: Regena Thomas (D.), 2002–06 ($137,165).

Government Website: http://www.state.nj.us

ECONOMY
Per capita income (2000) was $37,112.

Budget. In 1999 total state revenue was $39,150m. Total expenditure was $32,058m. (education, $8,514m.; public welfare, $5,338m.; health and hospitals, $1,663m.; highways, $1,613m.; police protection, $302m.). Outstanding debt, in 1999, $27,932m.

Performance. Gross State Product in 2000 was $363,089m.

ENERGY AND NATURAL RESOURCES
Water. The total area covered by water is approximately 796 sq. miles.

Minerals. In 1992 the chief minerals were stone (17·1m. short tons, value $126m.) and sand and gravel (17·9m. short tons, value $105m.); others are clays, peat and gemstones. New Jersey is a leading producer of greensand marl, magnesium compounds and peat. Total value of domestic non-fuel mineral products, 1998, was $301m.

Agriculture. Livestock raising, market-gardening, fruit-growing, horticulture and forestry are pursued. In 2000 there were some 9,600 farms covering a total of 830,000 acres. Average value per acre in 1998 was $8,370—making it the most valuable land per acre in the USA.

Farm income 1996: crops, $605m.; livestock and products, $196m.

Leading crops are tomatoes (value, $18·9m., 1993), corn for grain ($15·1m.), peaches ($25·3m.), blueberries ($26·4m.), soybeans ($25·7m.), sweet corn ($15·9m.), peppers ($21·8m.), cranberries ($18·8m.). Livestock, 1993: 25,000 milch cows, 75,000 all cattle, 13,000 sheep and lambs and (Dec. 1992) 28,000 swine.

INDUSTRY
Labour. The unemployment rate in Sept. 2001 was 4·5%, the 22nd consecutive month in which the rate was below that of the US.

In Sept. 2001 there were 4,006,900 employees on non-agricultural payrolls; 1,340,000 in services, 934,500 in wholesale and retail trade, 598,700 in government, 438,800 in manufacturing, 266,700 in transportation and public utilities, 158,900 in construction.

COMMUNICATIONS
Roads. In 2002 there were 36,175 miles of public roads and 7,329,902 registered vehicles.

Rail. NJ Transit, the USA's third largest provider of bus, rail and light rail transit, has a fleet of 2,025 buses, 614 trains and 45 light rail vehicles, which serve more than 380,500 passengers daily on 12 rail lines (848·3 track miles) and 238 bus routes. The state is also served by 13 shortline freight railroads, two Class 1 rail carriers (Norfolk Southern and CSX), and a statewide terminal railroad (Conrail Shared Assets Carrier) which delivers freight on behalf of Class 1 rail carriers.

There is a metro link to New York (22 km), a light rail line (7 km), and extensive commuter railways around Newark.

Civil Aviation. There is an international airport at Newark. In total there are an estimated 72,000 jobs in New Jersey that are linked to the general aviation airport system. The annual payroll associated with these jobs is estimated at $2·4bn. The annual value of goods and services purchased by airport tenants, visitors and general aviation-dependent businesses exceeds $4·6bn. There were 15,392,241 passenger enplanements statewide in 1999.

Shipping. In 1999 the maritime industry contributed more than $50bn. to the state economy. The two largest ports are the Port of Newark-Elizabeth and the Port of Camden. The Port of Newark-Elizabeth, the premier port on the Eastern seaboard, employed 166,000 people in 1999.

SOCIAL INSTITUTIONS
Justice. In June 2000 there were 31,081 prison inmates. The minimum age for the death penalty is 18. It has not been used since 1963.

Religion. In 1994 the Roman Catholic population of New Jersey was 3·25m., and there were 436,000 Jews. Among Protestant sects were United Methodists, 132,000; United Presbyterians (1993), 106,700; Episcopalians, 64,200; Lutherans, 82,200; American Baptists (1992), 66,000.

Education. Elementary instruction is compulsory for all from 6 to 16 years of age and free to all from 5 to 20 years of age. 128 school districts with high concentrations of disadvantaged children must offer free pre-school education to 3- and 4-year olds. In 1999–2000 public elementary schools had 919,665 enrolled pupils and secondary schools had 369,555; public colleges in autumn 1999 had 263,576 students, including 122,882 in community colleges; independent colleges had 66,772. Average salary of approximately 90,000 elementary and secondary classroom teachers in public schools in 1999–2000 was $51,571. In 1999–2000 school expenditure totalled $13·7bn.; approximately $10,833 per pupil.

In autumn 1999: Rutgers, the State University (founded as Queen's College in 1766), had 49,465 students; Princeton University (founded in 1746) had 6,440; Fairleigh Dickinson (1941) had 8,948; Montclair State College, 13,285; Rowan University, 9,636; College of New Jersey (formerly Trenton State College), 6,747.

Health. In 1995 there were 92 community hospitals with 29,900 beds.

Welfare. In 1996, 1,314,000 beneficiaries received a total annual payment of $11,614m. Retired workers received an average monthly payment of $820; disabled workers and dependants, $744; widows and widowers, $780.

FURTHER READING

Statistical information: New Jersey State Data Center, Department of Labor, CN 388, Trenton 08625. Publishes *New Jersey Statistical Factbook.*
Legislative District Data Book. Bureau of Government Research. Annual
Manual of the Legislature of New Jersey. Trenton. Annual
Cunningham, J. T., *New Jersey: America's Main Road.* Rev. ed. New York, 1976

State Library: 185 W. State Street, Trenton, CN 520, NJ 08625.

NEW MEXICO

KEY HISTORICAL EVENTS
The first European settlement was established in 1598. Until 1771 New Mexico was the Spanish kings' 'Kingdom of New Mexico'. In 1771 it was annexed to the northern province of New Spain. When New Spain won its independence in 1821, it took the name of Republic of Mexico and established New Mexico as its northernmost department. Ceded to the USA in 1848 after war between the USA and Mexico, the area was organized as a Territory in 1850, by which time its population was Spanish and Indian. There was frequent conflict, especially between new settlers and raiding parties of Navajo and Apaches. The Indian war lasted from 1861 until 1866, and from 1864–68 about 8,000 Navajo were imprisoned at Bosque Redondo.

The boundaries were altered several times when land was taken into Texas, Utah, Colorado and lastly (1863) Arizona. New Mexico became a state in 1912.

Settlement proceeded by means of irrigated crop-growing and Mexican-style ranching. During the Second World War the desert areas were brought into use as testing zones for atomic weapons. Mineral extraction also developed, especially after the discovery of uranium and petroleum.

TERRITORY AND POPULATION
New Mexico is bounded north by Colorado, northeast by Oklahoma, east by Texas, south by Texas and Mexico and west by Arizona. Land area, 121,356 sq. miles (316,901 sq. km). Public lands, administered by federal agencies (1975) amounted to 26·7m. acres or 34% of the total area. The Bureau of Indian Affairs held 7·3m. acres; the State of New Mexico held 9·4m. acres; 34·4m. acres were privately owned.

Census population, 1 April 2000, 1,819,046, an increase of 20·1% since 1990. Of the total population in 2000, 924,729 were female, 1,310,472 were 18 years old or older and 1,363,501 were urban. July 2002 estimate, 1,855,059.

The population in five census years was:

	White	Black	American Indian	Asian and Pacific Island	Other	Total	Per sq. mile
1910	304,594	1,628	20,573	506	...	327,301	2·7
1940	492,312	4,672	34,510	324	...	531,818	4·4
1980	977,587	24,020	106,119	6,825	188,343	1,302,894	10·7
1990	1,146,028	30,210	134,355	14,124	190,352	1,515,069	12·5
2000	1,214,253	34,343	173,483	20,758	376,209	1,819,046	15·0

Before 1930 New Mexico was largely a Spanish-speaking state, but after 1945 an influx of population from other states considerably reduced the percentage of persons of Spanish origin or descent. However, in recent years the percentage of the Hispanic population has begun to rise again. In 2000 the Hispanic population was 765,386, up from 579,224 in 1990 (an increase of 32·1%). At 42·1%, New Mexico has the largest percentage of persons of Hispanic origin of any state in the USA.

The largest cities are Albuquerque, with 2000 census population of 448,607; Las Cruces, 74,267; Santa Fé, 62,203; Rio Rancho, 51,765; Roswell, 45,293.

SOCIAL STATISTICS
Statistics 1999: births, 27,855 (16·0 per 1,000 population); deaths, 13,550 (7·8); (1996) infant deaths, 169 (6·2 per 1,000 live births); marriages, 16,026 (9·4 per 1,000 population); divorces, 10,945 (6·4).

CLIMATE
Santa Fé, Jan. 26·4°F (−3·1°C), July 68·4°F (20°C). Annual rainfall 15·2" (386 mm). New Mexico belongs to the Mountain States climate zone (see UNITED STATES: Climate).

CONSTITUTION AND GOVERNMENT
The constitution of 1912 is still in force with 137 amendments. The state Legislature, which meets annually, consists of 42 members of the Senate, elected for four years, and 70 members of the House of Representatives, elected for two years.

For the 108th Congress, which convened in Jan. 2003, New Mexico sends three members to the House of Representatives. It is represented in the Senate by Pete Domenici (R. 1973–2009) and Jeff Bingaman (D. 1983–2007).

The state capital is Santa Fé. The state is divided into 33 counties.

RECENT ELECTIONS
In the 2000 presidential election Gore polled 286,783 votes; Bush, 286,417; Nader, 21,251.

CURRENT ADMINISTRATION
Governor: Bill Richardson (D.), 2003–07 (salary: $110,000).
  Lieut.-Governor: Diane Denish (D.), 2003–07 ($85,000).
  Secretary of State: Rebecca Vigil-Giron (D.), 2003–07 ($85,000).

Government Website: http://www.state.nm.us

ECONOMY
Per capita income (2000) was $21,883.

Budget. In 1999 total state revenue was $8,757m. Total expenditure was $8,089m. (education, $2,801m.; public welfare, $1,339m.; highways, $936m.; health and hospitals, $607m.; police protection, $70m.). Outstanding debt, in 1999, $3,158m.

Performance. Gross State Product in 2000 was $54,364m.

ENERGY AND NATURAL RESOURCES
Oil and Gas. 2001 production: petroleum, 68,967,000 bbls. (of 42 gallons); natural gas, 1,678bn. cu. ft. New Mexico ranks second in the USA behind Texas for natural

gas production and also has natural gas reserves second only to Texas. In late 2001, 11,500 persons were employed in the oil and gas industry.

Water. The total area covered by water is approximately 234 sq. miles.

Minerals. New Mexico is one of the largest energy producing states in the USA. Production in 2001: potash, 1,086,410 short tons; copper, 154,580 short tons; coal, 30,525,401 short tons. New Mexico is the country's leading potash producer, accounting for approximately 70% of all potash mined in the USA, and ranked third for copper production in 2001. The value of coal output in 2001 was $584·9m. and of total non-fuel mineral output $651·6m.

Agriculture. New Mexico produces grains, vegetables, hay, livestock, milk, cotton and pecans. In 2001 there were 15,000 farms covering 44·0m. acres; average farm size 2,933 acres. In 2001 average value of farmland and buildings per acre was $220.

2001 cash receipts from crops, $545m., and from livestock products, $1,670m. Principal crops are hay (1·6m. tons from 0·38m. acres), cotton (65m. lbs. from 0·70m. acres) and chilli (162m. lbs. from 0·18m. acres). Farm animals in 2001 included 290,000 milch cows, 1·6m. all cattle, 230,000 sheep and 3,000 swine.

Forestry. There were 10m. acres of national forest in 1997.

INDUSTRY

Value of manufactures shipments, 1992, $9,491·5m.; leading industries, food and kindred products, electrical and electronic equipment, petroleum and coal products.

Labour. Total non-agricultural employment, 1999, 730,000. Employees by branch, 1999 (in 1,000): services, 211; government, 180; wholesale and retail trade, 171; construction, 44.

COMMUNICATIONS

Roads. In 2000 there were 59,926 miles of roads (53,816 miles rural) and 1,528,510 registered motor vehicles.

Rail. In 1999 there were 2,027 miles of railway in operation.

Civil Aviation. There were 64 public-use airports in Nov. 1995. There were 3,048,050 passenger enplanements statewide in 1999.

SOCIAL INSTITUTIONS

Justice. In June 2000 there were 5,277 prison inmates. The death penalty is authorized (minimum age 18), and was used in 2001 (one execution) for the first time since 1960.

Since 1949 the denial of employment by reason of race, colour, religion, national origin or ancestry has been forbidden. A law of 1955 prohibits discrimination in public places because of race or colour. An 'equal rights' amendment was added to the constitution in 1972.

Religion. There were (1990) approximately 883,000 Christian Church adherents (421,868 Roman Catholics in 1996).

Education. Elementary education is free, and compulsory between 6 and 17 years or high-school graduation age. In 1995–96 the 89 school districts had an enrolment of 348,543 students in elementary and secondary schools of which private, parochial and state supported schools had 31,112. In 1994–95 there were 18,500 FTE teachers receiving an average salary of $29,074. Total revenue for public elementary and secondary schools was $1,702m. (1994–95).

In autumn 1997 there were 47,017 students attending universities and 52,736 students attending community colleges.

The state-supported four-year institutes of higher education are (autumn 1996[1]):

	Students
University of New Mexico, Albuquerque	30,534
New Mexico State University, Las Cruces	22,313
Eastern New Mexico University, Portales	7,008
New Mexico Highlands University, Las Vegas	2,787
Western New Mexico University, Silver City	2,533
New Mexico Institute of Mining and Technology, Socorro	1,467

[1]Figures include branches outside main campus in cities listed.

Health. In 1995 there were 36 community hospitals with 3,700 beds. The state had 2,009 active non-federal physicians.

Welfare. In fiscal year 1997 a monthly average of 30,280 cases received $140·4m. from aid to families with dependent children funds and 79,610 cases received $181·6m. in food stamp funds. In 1995 a total of 44,755 persons in the state were receiving federally administered payment totalling $165·6m. Among these 9,844 were receiving aid for the aged ($21·7m.), 644 were receiving aid to the blind ($2·3m.) and 34,267 were receiving aid for the disabled ($141·5m.).

CULTURE

Tourism. In 1995 there were 47,200 travel-generated jobs; total travel expenditure (domestic and international), $3,045·7m.

Festivals. In 1996, 1·7m. persons attended the New Mexico Arts and Crafts Fair, Albuquerque; and 1·5m. attended the annual Albuquerque International Balloon Fiesta.

Theatre and Opera. There is an indoor/outdoor theatre at the Santa Fé Opera in the capital.

Museums and Galleries. There were more than 150 art galleries in 1998.

FURTHER READING
Bureau of Business and Economic Research, Univ. of New Mexico—*Census in New Mexico* (Continuing series. Vols. 1–5, 1992–).—*Economic Census: New Mexico* (Continuing series. Vols. 1–3).—*New Mexico Business.* Monthly; annual review in Jan.–Feb. issue.
Etulain, R., *Contemporary New Mexico, 1940–1990.* Univ. of New Mexico Press, 1994

NEW YORK STATE

KEY HISTORICAL EVENTS
The first European immigrants came in the 17th century, when there were two powerful Indian groups in rivalry: the Iroquois confederacy (Mohawk, Oneida, Onondaga, Cayuga and Seneca) and the Algonquian-speaking Mohegan and Munsee. The Dutch made settlements at Fort Orange (now Albany) in 1624 and at New Amsterdam in 1625, trading with the Indians for furs. In the 1660s there was conflict between the Dutch and the British in the Caribbean; as part of the concluding treaty the British in 1664 received Dutch possessions in the Americas, including New Amsterdam, which they renamed New York.

In 1763 the Treaty of Paris ended war between the British and the French in North America (in which the Iroquois had allied themselves with the British). Settlers of British descent in New England then felt confident enough to expand westward into the area. The climate of northern New York being severe, most settled in the Hudson river valley. After the War of Independence New York became the 11th state of the Union (1778), having first declared itself independent of Britain in 1777.

The economy depended on manufacturing, shipping and other means of distributing goods, and trade. During the 19th century New York became the most important city in the USA. Its manufacturing industries, especially clothing, attracted thousands of European immigrants. Industrial development spread along the Hudson-Mohawk valley, which was made the route of the Erie Canal (1825) linking New York with Buffalo on Lake Erie and thus with the developing farmlands of the middle west.

On 11 Sept. 2001 New York City was attacked by hijackers when two commercial airliners were flown into the World Trade Center. The building was destroyed and 2,800 people died.

TERRITORY AND POPULATION
New York is bounded west and north by Canada with Lake Erie, Lake Ontario and the St Lawrence River forming the boundary; east by Vermont, Massachusetts and Connecticut, southeast by the Atlantic, south by New Jersey and Pennsylvania. Land

area, 47,214 sq. miles (122,284 sq. km). Census population, 1 April 2000, 18,976,457, an increase of 5·5% since 1990. July 2002 estimate, 19,157,532.

Population in five census years was:

	White	Black	Indian	Asiatic	Total	Per sq. mile
1910	8,966,845	134,191	6,046	6,532	9,113,614	191·2
1930	12,143,191	412,814	6,973	15,088	12,588,066	262·6
			All others			
1980	13,961,106	2,401,842	1,194,340		17,557,288	367·0
1990	13,385,255	2,859,055	1,746,145		17,990,455	381·0
2000	12,893,689	3,014,385	3,068,383		18,976,457	401·9

Of the total population in 2000, 9,829,709 were female, 14,286,350 were 18 years old or older and 16,602,582 were urban. In 2000 the Hispanic population was 2,867,583, up from 2,214,026 in 1990 (an increase of 29·5%). California and Texas are the only states with a higher Hispanic population.

The population of New York City, by boroughs, census of 1 April 2000 was: Manhattan, 1,537,195; Bronx, 1,332,650; Brooklyn, 2,465,326; Queens, 2,229,379; Staten Island, 443,728; total, 8,008,278. The New York–Northern New Jersey–Long Island metropolitan area had, in 2000, a population of 21,199,865.

Population of other large cities and incorporated places at the 2000 census was:

Buffalo	292,648	Niagara Falls	55,593	Elmira	30,940
Rochester	219,773	White Plains	53,077	Poughkeepsie	29,871
Yonkers	196,086	Troy	49,170	Ithaca	29,287
Syracuse	147,306	Binghampton	47,380	Auburn	28,574
Albany (capital)	95,658	Freeport	43,783	Newburgh	28,259
New Rochelle	72,182	Valley Stream	36,368	Lindenhurst	27,819
Mount Vernon	68,381	Long Beach	35,462	Watertown	26,705
Schenectady	61,821	Rome	34,950	Glen Cove	26,622
Utica	60,651	North Tonawanda	33,262	Saratoga Springs	26,186
Hempstead	56,554	Jamestown	31,730		

Other large urbanized areas, census 2000; Buffalo–Niagara Falls, 1,170,111; Rochester, 1,098,201; Albany–Schenectady–Troy, 875,583.

SOCIAL STATISTICS
Births in 1999 were 255,508 (14·0 per 1,000 population); deaths, 154,274 (8·5); (1996) infant mortality rate, 7·0 (per 1,000 live births). Marriages in 1997, 172,800; divorces, 65,500.

CLIMATE
Albany, Jan. 24°F (–4·4°C), July 73°F (22·8°C). Annual rainfall 34" (855 mm). Buffalo, Jan. 24°F (–4·4°C), July 70°F (21·1°C). Annual rainfall 36" (905 mm). New York, Jan. 30°F (–1·1°C), July 74°F (23·3°C). Annual rainfall 43" (1,087 mm). New York belongs to the Atlantic Coast climate zone (see UNITED STATES: Climate).

CONSTITUTION AND GOVERNMENT
The present constitution dates from 1894; a later constitutional convention, 1938, is now legally considered merely to have amended the 1894 constitution, which has now had 93 amendments. A proposed new constitution in 1967 was rejected by the electorate. The Senate consists of 60 members, and the Assembly of 150 members, both elected every two years. The state capital is Albany. For local government the state is divided into 62 counties, five of which constitute the city of New York. There were state parks and recreation areas covering 260,198 acres in 1990.

Each of the state's 62 cities is incorporated by charter, under special legislation. The government of New York City is vested in the mayor (Michael Bloomberg), elected for four years, and a city council, whose president and members are elected for four years. The council has a President and 51 members, each elected from a district wholly within the city. The mayor appoints all the heads of departments, except the comptroller, who is elected. Each of the five city boroughs (Manhattan, Bronx, Brooklyn, Queens and Staten Island) has a president, elected for four years. Each borough is also a county bearing the same name except Manhattan borough, which, as a county, is called New York, and Brooklyn, which is Kings County.

For the 108th Congress, which convened in Jan. 2003, New York State sends 29 members to the House of Representatives. It is represented in the Senate by Charles Schumer (D. 1999–2005) and Hillary Clinton (D. 2001–07).

RECENT ELECTIONS
In the 2000 presidential election Gore polled 4,107,697 votes; Bush, 2,403,374; Nader, 244,030.

CURRENT ADMINISTRATION
Governor: George E. Pataki (R.), 2003–07 (salary: $179,000).
  Lieut.-Governor: Mary O. Donohue (R.), 2003–07 ($151,500).
  Secretary of State: Randy A. Daniels (D.), appointed April 2001 ($120,800).

Government Website: http://www.state.ny.us

ECONOMY
Per capita income (2000) was $34,502.

Budget. In 1999 total state revenue was $102,242m. Total expenditure was $92,584m. (education, $18,748m.; public welfare, $30,487m.; health and hospitals, $5,938m.; highways, $3,215m.; police protection, $463m.). Outstanding debt, in 1999, $76,562m.

Performance. Gross State Product was $799,202m. in 2000.

ENERGY AND NATURAL RESOURCES
Water. The total area covered by water is approximately 6,766 sq. miles.

Minerals. Principal minerals are: sand and gravel, salt, titanium concentrate, talc, abrasive garnet, wollastonite and emery. Quarry products include trap rock, slate, marble, limestone and sandstone. Value of domestic non-fuel mineral output in 1998, $939m.

Agriculture. New York has large agricultural interests. In 2000 it had some 38,000 farms, with a total area of 7·9m. acres; average farm was 203 acres. Average value per acre in 1998 was $1,390.

Farm income, 1996, from crops $998m. and livestock $2,045m. Dairying is an important type of farming. Field crops comprise maize, winter wheat, oats and hay. New York ranks second in USA in the production of apples and maple syrup. Other products are grapes, tart cherries, peaches, pears, plums, strawberries, raspberries, cabbages, onions, potatoes and maple sugar. Estimated farm animals, 1990, included 1,540,000 all cattle, 966,000 milch cows, 92,000 sheep and lambs, 124,000 swine and 5·1m. chickens.

INDUSTRY
Leading industries are clothing, non-electrical machinery, printing and publishing, electrical equipment, instruments, food and allied products and fabricated metals.

Labour. Total non-agricultural employment, 1999, 8,454,000. Employees by branch, 1999 (in 1,000): services, 2,926; wholesale and retail trade, 1,710; government, 1,442; manufacturing, 893; finance, property and insurance, 748. In 1999 the unemployment rate was 5·2%.

COMMUNICATIONS
Roads. In 2000 there were 112,783 miles of roads (71,789 miles rural). The New York State Thruway extends 559 miles from New York City to Buffalo. The Northway, a 176-mile toll-free highway, is a connecting road from the Thruway at Albany to the Canadian border at Champlain, Quebec.
  Motor vehicle registrations in 2000 were 10,234,531.

Rail. There were in 1997, 2,927 miles of Class I railways. In addition the State had 626 miles of regional railway and 1,067 miles of local railway. New York City has NYCTA and PATH metro systems, and commuter railways run by Metro-North, New Jersey Transit and Long Island Rail Road.

Civil Aviation. At Jan. 1999 there were 527 aviation facilities in New York State. Of these, 147 were public use airports, 223 were private use airports, 3 were private use glider ports, 6 public use heliports, 127 private use heliports, 10 public use seaplane bases and 11 private use seaplane bases. There were 26,812,700 passenger enplanements statewide in 1999.

Shipping. The canals of the state, combined in 1918 in what is called the Improved Canal System, have a length of 524 miles, of which the Erie or Barge canal has 340 miles.

SOCIAL INSTITUTIONS

Justice. The State Human Rights Law was approved on 12 March 1945, effective on 1 July 1945. The State Division of Human Rights is charged with the responsibility of enforcing this law. The division may request and utilize the services of all governmental departments and agencies; adopt and promulgate suitable rules and regulations; test, investigate and pass judgment upon complaints alleging discrimination in employment, in places of public accommodation, resort or amusement, education, and in housing, land and commercial space; hold hearings, subpoena witnesses and require the production for examination of papers relating to matters under investigation; grant compensatory damages and require repayment of profits in certain housing cases among other provisions; apply for court injunctions to prevent frustration of orders of the Commissioner.

In June 2000 there were 71,691 federal and state prisoners.

The minimum age is 18 for the death penalty, but it has not been used since 1963.

Religion. The main religious denominations are Roman Catholics, Jews and Protestant Episcopal.

Education. Education is compulsory between the ages of 7 and 16. In 1994–95 the public elementary and secondary schools had 2,790,700 pupils and 193,000 teachers. Expenditure on education in 1996 was $27,621m.

The state's educational system, including public and private schools and secondary institutions, universities, colleges, libraries, museums, etc., constitutes (by legislative act) the 'University of the State of New York', which is governed by a Board of Regents consisting of 15 members appointed by the Legislature. Within the framework of this 'University' was established in 1948 a 'State University' which controls 64 colleges and educational centres, 30 of which are locally operated community colleges. The 'State University' is governed by a board of 16 Trustees, appointed by the Governor with the consent and advice of the Senate.

Higher education in the state is conducted in 311 institutions (1,028,000 students enrolled in 1996).

Student enrolment (Autumn 1998) and teaching faculties (Autumn 1995) of the institutions of higher education in the state included:

Founded	Name and place	Teaching faculty	Students
1754	Columbia University, New York	2,843	20,504
1795	Union College, Schenectady and Albany	202	2,484
1824	Rensselaer Polytechnic Institute, Troy	408	6,509
1831	New York University, New York	3,573	36,719
1846	Colgate University, New York	267	2,830
1846	Fordham University, New York	788	13,623
1847	University of the City of New York, New York	10,282	198,737
1848	University of Rochester, Rochester	1,000	7,830
1854	Polytechnic University	134	3,181
1856	St Lawrence University, Canton	172	1,937
1857	Cooper Union Institute of Technology, New York	124	934
1861	Vassar College, Poughkeepsie	542	2,396
1863	Manhattan College, New York	225	3,029
1865	Cornell University, Ithaca	1,810	12,505
1870	Syracuse University, Syracuse	1,083	18,293
1948	State University of New York	17,140	368,467

The Saratoga Performing Arts Centre (5,100 seats), a non-profit, tax-exempt organization, which opened in 1966, is the summer residence of the New York City Ballet and the Philadelphia Orchestra—two groups which present special educational programmes for students and teachers.

Health. In 1995 the state had 230 community hospitals (73,900 beds).

Welfare. The federal Supplemental Security Income programme covered aid to the needy aged, blind and disabled from 1 Jan. 1975. In 1996 there were 2,968,000 persons in receipt of welfare assistance: 2,103,000 retired workers received an average of $794 per month. Total annual cost for welfare assistance, in 1996, $25,268m.

FURTHER READING

Statistical information: Nelson Rockefeller Institute of Government, 411 State St., Albany 12203. Publishes *New York State Statistical Yearbook.*
New York Red Book. Albany. Biennial.
Legislative Manual. Department of State. Biennial.
The Modern New York State Legislature: Redressing the Balance. Albany, Rockefeller Institute, 1991
State Library: The New York State Library, Albany 12230.

NORTH CAROLINA

KEY HISTORICAL EVENTS

The early inhabitants were Cherokees. European settlement was attempted in 1585–87, following an exploratory visit by Sir Walter Raleigh, but this failed. Settlers from Virginia came to the shores of Albemarle Sound after 1650, and in 1663 Charles II chartered a private colony of Carolina. In 1691 the north was put under a deputy governor who ruled from Charleston in the south. The colony was formally separated into North and South Carolina in 1712. In 1729 control was taken from the private proprietors and vested in the Crown, whereupon settlement grew, and the boundary between north and south was finally fixed (1735).

After the War of Independence North Carolina became one of the original 13 states of the Union. The city of Raleigh was laid out as the new capital. Having been a plantation colony North Carolina continued to develop as a plantation state, growing tobacco with black slave labour. It was also an important source of gold before the western gold-rushes of 1848.

In 1861 at the outset of the Civil War North Carolina seceded from the Union, but General Sherman occupied the capital unopposed. A military governor was admitted in 1862, and civilian government restored with re-admission to the Union in 1868.

TERRITORY AND POPULATION

North Carolina is bounded north by Virginia, east by the Atlantic, south by South Carolina, southwest by Georgia and west by Tennessee. Land area, 48,711 sq. miles (126,161 sq. km). Census population, 1 April 2000, 8,049,313, an increase of 21·4% since 1990. July 2002 estimate, 8,320,146.

Population in five census years was:

	White	Black	Indian	Asiatic	Total	Per sq. mile
1910	1,500,511	697,843	7,851	82	2,206,287	45·3
1930	2,234,958	918,647	16,579	92	3,170,276	64·5
	White	Black	All others		Total	Per sq. mile
1980	4,453,010	1,316,050	105,369		5,874,429	111·5
1990	5,008,491	1,456,323	163,823		6,628,637	136·1
2000	5,804,656	1,737,545	507,112		8,049,313	165·2

Of the total population in 2000, 4,106,618 were female, 6,085,266 were 18 years old or older and 4,849,482 were urban. In 2000 North Carolina's Hispanic population was 378,963, up from 76,726 in 1990. This represented a rise of 393·9%, the largest increase of any state in the USA over the same period.

The principal cities (with census population in 2000) are: Charlotte, 540,828; Raleigh, 276,093; Greensboro, 223,891; Durham, 187,035; Winston-Salem, 185,776; Fayetteville, 121,015; Cary, 94,536; High Point, 85,839; Wilmington, 75,838.

SOCIAL STATISTICS
Births, 1999, were 111,720 (14·6 per 1,000 population); deaths, 68,064 (8·9); (1996) infant mortality rate, 9·2 (per 1,000 live births). Marriages (1997), 64,500; divorces, 36,800.

CLIMATE
Climate varies sharply with altitude; the warmest area is in the southeast near Southport and Wilmington; the coldest is Mount Mitchell (6,684 ft). Raleigh, Jan. 42°F (5·6°C), July 79°F (26·1°C). Annual rainfall 46" (1,158 mm). North Carolina belongs to the Atlantic Coast climate zone (*see* UNITED STATES: Climate).

CONSTITUTION AND GOVERNMENT
The present constitution dates from 1971 (previous constitution, 1776 and 1868/76); it has had 19 amendments. The General Assembly consists of a Senate of 50 members and a House of Representatives of 120 members; all are elected by districts for two years. It meets in odd-numbered years in Jan.

The Governor and Lieut.-Governor are elected for four years. The Governor may succeed himself but has no veto. There are 18 other executive heads of department, nine elected by the people and nine appointed by the Governor.

For the 108th Congress, which convened in Jan. 2003, North Carolina sends 13 members to the House of Representatives. It is represented in the Senate by John Edwards (D. 1999–2005) and Elizabeth Dole (R. 2003–09).

The capital is Raleigh. There are 100 counties.

RECENT ELECTIONS
In the 2000 presidential election Bush polled 1,631,163 votes; Gore, 1,257,692; Buchanan, 8,874.

CURRENT ADMINISTRATION
Governor: Michael F. Easley (D.), 2001–05 ($118,430).

Lieut.-Governor: Beverly Perdue (D.), 2001–05 ($104,523).

Secretary of State: Elaine Marshall (D.), 2001–05 ($104,523).

Government Website: http://www.ncgov.com

ECONOMY
Per capita income (2000) was $26,842.

Budget. In 1999 total state revenue was $34,064m. Total expenditure was $26,830m. (education, $10,584m.; public welfare, $5,113m.; highways, $2,209m.; health and hospitals, $1,836m.; police protection, $346m.). Outstanding debt, in 1999, $8,227m.

Performance. Gross State Product in 2000 was $281,741m.

ENERGY AND NATURAL RESOURCES
Water. The total area covered by water is approximately 3,954 sq. miles.

Minerals. Principal minerals are stone, sand and gravel, phosphate rock, feldspar, lithium minerals, olivine, kaolin and talc. North Carolina is a leading producer of bricks, making more than 1bn. bricks a year. Value of domestic non-fuel mineral production in 1998 was $785m.

Agriculture. In 2000 there were some 57,000 farms covering 9·2m. acres; average size of farms was 161 acres and average value per acre in 1995 was $1,749.

Farm income, 1991, from crops, $2,272m. and from livestock and products $2,554m. Main crop production: flue-cured tobacco, maize, soybeans, peanuts, wheat, sweet potatoes and apples.

Livestock, 1990: cattle, 0·9m.; pigs, 2·6m.; chickens, 19·6m.

Forestry. Commercial forest covered 18,891,000 acres in 1990. Main products are hardwood veneer and hardwood plywood, furniture woods, pulp, paper and lumber.

Fisheries. Commercial fish catch, 1998, had a value of approximately $101·1m. The catch is mainly of blue crab, menhaden, Atlantic croaker, flounder, shark, sea trout, mullet, blue fish and shrimp.

INDUSTRY

The leading industries by employment are textiles, clothing, furniture, electrical machinery and equipment, non-electrical machinery and food processing.

Labour. Total non-agricultural employment, 1999, 3,866,000. Employees by branch, 1999 (in 1,000): services, 994; wholesale and retail trade, 873; manufacturing, 803; government, 607.

COMMUNICATIONS

Roads. In 2000 there were 99,814 miles of roads (76,186 miles rural) and 6,222,503 registered motor vehicles.

Rail. The state in 1999 contained 3,682 miles of railway operating in 91 of the 100 counties. There are 22 Class II and 23 Class III rail companies.

Civil Aviation. In 1999 there were 82 public airports of which 15 are served by major airlines. There were 15,246,224 passenger enplanements statewide in 1999.

Shipping. There are two ocean ports, Wilmington and Morehead City.

SOCIAL INSTITUTIONS

Justice. Following the US Supreme Court's reinstatement of the death penalty in 1976, capital punishment has been authorized for over 17-year-olds; there were two executions in 2002. In June 2000 there were 31,110 federal and state prisoners.

Religion. Leading denominations are the Baptists (48·9% of church membership), Methodists (20·7%), Presbyterians (7·7%), Lutherans (3·0%) and Roman Catholics (2·7%). Total estimate of all denominations in 1983 was 2·6m.

Education. School attendance is compulsory between 6 and 16. In 1994–95 there were 1,146,639 pupils and 71,070 teachers. State and local government expenditure in 1996 was $7,094m.; an average of $5,623 per pupil. There were (1997) an estimated 58,000 high-school graduates.

In 1996, 373,000 students enrolled at the 121 higher education institutions. The 16 senior universities are all part of the University of North Carolina system, the largest campus being North Carolina State University and Raleigh. The university system was founded in 1789 at Chapel Hill and first opened in 1792.

Health. In 1995 the state had 119 community hospitals with 22,700 beds.

Welfare. In 1995 there were 1,232,000 persons receiving $893·4m. in social security benefits. Of that number 819,000 were retired (receiving $682 a month); 206,000 were disabled ($651 a month); and there were 206,000 others.

CULTURE

Tourism. Total receipts of the travel industry, $6,400m. in 1990.

FURTHER READING

Statistical information: Office of State Planning, 116 West Jones St., Raleigh 27603. Publishes *Statistical Abstract of North Carolina Counties.*
North Carolina Manual. Secretary of State. Raleigh. Biennial
Fleer, J. D., *North Carolina: Government and Population.* Univ. of Nebraska Press, 1995

NORTH DAKOTA

KEY HISTORICAL EVENTS

The original inhabitants were various groups of Plains Indians. French explorers and traders were active among them in the 18th century, often operating from French possessions in Canada. France claimed the area until 1803, when it passed to the USA as part of the Louisiana Purchase, except for the northeastern part which was held by the British until 1818.

Trading with the Indians, mainly for furs, continued until the 1860s, with American traders succeeding the French. In 1861 the Dakota Territory (North and

South) was established. In 1862 the Homestead Act was passed (allowing 160 acres of public land free to any family who had worked and lived on it for five years) and this greatly stimulated settlement. Farming settlers came on to the wheat lands in great numbers, many of them from Canada, Norway and Germany.

Bismarck, the capital, began as a crossing-point on the Missouri and was fortified in 1872 to protect workers building the Northern Pacific Railway. There followed a gold-rush nearby, and the town became a service centre for prospectors. In 1889 North and South Dakota were admitted to the Union as separate states, and Bismarck became the Northern capital. The largest city is Fargo which was also a railway town, named after William George Fargo the express-company founder.

The population grew rapidly until 1890 and steadily until 1930 by which time it was about one-third European in parentage. Between 1930 and 1970 there was a steady population drain, increasing whenever farming was affected by the extremes of the continental climate.

TERRITORY AND POPULATION

North Dakota is bounded north by Canada, east by the Red River (forming a boundary with Minnesota), south by South Dakota and west by Montana. Land area, 68,976 sq. miles (178,647 sq. km). The Federal Bureau of Indian Affairs administered (1992) 841,295 acres, of which 214,006 acres were assigned to tribes. Census population, 1 April 2000, 642,200, an increase of 0·5% since 1990. July 2002 estimate, 634,110.

Population at five census years was:

	White	Black	Indian	Asiatic	Total	Per sq. mile
1910	569,855	617	6,486	98	577,056	8·2
1930	671,851	377	8,617	194	680,845	9·7
			All others			
1980	625,557	2,568	24,692		652,717	9·5
1990	604,142	3,524	31,134		638,800	9·3
2000	593,182	3,916	45,102		642,200	9·3

Of the total population in 2000, 321,676 were female, 481,351 were 18 years old or older and 358,958 were urban. Estimated outward migration, 1980–90, 110 per 1,000 population. Only Vermont has fewer persons of Hispanic origin than North Dakota. In 2000 the Hispanic population was 7,786, up from 4,665 in 1990 (an increase of 66·9%).

The largest cities are Fargo with population, census 2000, of 90,599; Bismarck (capital), 55,532; Grand Forks, 49,321; and Minot, 36,567.

SOCIAL STATISTICS

Births in 1999 were 7,943 (12·5 per 1,000 population); deaths, 6,015 (9·5); (1997) infant mortality rate, 7·4 (per 1,000 live births). Marriages (1997), 4,400; divorces, 2,000.

CLIMATE

Bismarck, Jan. 8°F (−13·3°C), July 71°F (21·1°C). Annual rainfall 16" (402 mm). Fargo, Jan. 6°F (−14·4°C), July 71°F (21·1°C). Annual rainfall 20" (503 mm). North Dakota belongs to the High Plains climate zone (see UNITED STATES: Climate).

CONSTITUTION AND GOVERNMENT

The present constitution dates from 1889; it has had 95 amendments. The Legislative Assembly consists of a Senate of 53 members elected for four years, and a House of Representatives of 106 members elected for four years. The Governor and Lieut.-Governor are elected for four years.

For the 108th Congress, which convened in Jan. 2003, North Dakota sends one member to the House of Representatives. It is represented in the Senate by Kent Conrad (D. 1987–2007) and Byron Dorgan (D. 1992–2005).

The capital is Bismarck. The state has 53 organized counties.

RECENT ELECTIONS

In the 2000 presidential election Bush polled 174,852 votes; Gore, 95,284; Nader, 9,486.

CURRENT ADMINISTRATION

Governor: John Hoeven (R.), 2001–05 (salary: $87,216).
Lieut.-Governor: Jack Dalrymple (R.), 2001–05 ($67,708).
Secretary of State: Alvin A. Jaeger (R), 2001–05 ($68,018).

Government Website: http://discovernd.com

ECONOMY

Though the state is still mainly agricultural it is diversifying into high tech and information technology industries. *Per capita* income (2000) was $24,780.

Budget. In 1999 total state revenue was $2,936m. Total expenditure was $2,675m. (education, $863m.; public welfare, $589m.; highways, $306m.; health, $46m.; police protection, $13m.). Outstanding debt, in 1999, $1,329m.

Performance. Gross State Product in 2000 was $18,283m.

ENERGY AND NATURAL RESOURCES

Oil and Gas. The mineral resources of North Dakota consist chiefly of oil, which was discovered in 1951. Production of crude petroleum in 1996 was 32m. bbls. (value, $629m.); of natural gas, 50bn. cu. ft.

Water. The total area covered by water is approximately 1,710 sq. miles.

Minerals. Output of lignite coal in 1994 was 32m. tons. Total value of domestic non-fuel mineral production, 1998, $35m.

Agriculture. In 2000 there were some 30,300 farms (61,963 in 1954) with an area of 39·4m. acres. In 1998 the average value of farmland and buildings per acre was $415.

In 1994 (per farm) net farm income was $26,838. Farm income, 1996, from crops, $2,996m. and from livestock, $537m. Production, 1995: wheat (durum), 77·8m. bu.; barley, 101·3m. bu.; oats, 21·6m. bu.; flaxseed, 1·7m. bu.; dry edible beans, 7,182 cwt; sunflower (all), 17,462 cwt. Other important products are all beans, all wheat, rye and honey.

The state has also an active livestock industry, chiefly cattle raising. Livestock, 1996: cattle, 1·9m.; pigs, 0·28m.; sheep, 125,000; poultry, 270,000.

Forestry. Forest area, 1990, 0·46m. acres.

INDUSTRY

Labour. In 1999 total non-agricultural employment was 323,000. Employees by branch, 1999: services, 92,000; wholesale and retail trade, 81,000; government, 72,000. The unemployment rate in 1999 was 3·4%.

COMMUNICATIONS

Roads. In 2000 there were 86,611 miles of roads (84,776 rural) and 693,860 registered motor vehicles.

Rail. In 1994 there were 4,143 miles of railway.

Civil Aviation. In 1994 there were 100 public airports and 350 private airports. There were 481,650 passenger enplanements statewide in 1999.

Telecommunications. In 1998 there were 32,000 miles of fibre optic cable in the ground.

SOCIAL INSTITUTIONS

Justice. In June 2000 there were 1,004 federal and state prisoners. The Missouri River Correctional Center is a minimum custody institution. There is no death penalty.

Religion. Church membership totalled 484,628 in 1990. The leading religious denominations were: Combined Lutherans, 179,711 members; Roman Catholics, 173,432; Methodists, 23,850; Presbyterians, 11,960.

Education. School attendance is compulsory between the ages of 7 and 16, or until the 17th birthday if the eighth grade has not been completed. In 1995–96 the public elementary schools had 81,798 pupils; secondary schools, 36,755 pupils. State expenditure per pupil in elementary and secondary schools, 1997, $5,016. Teachers (4,208 in elementary and 2,208 in secondary schools in 1994) earned an average $25,506 in 1993–94 school year.

The University of North Dakota in Grand Forks, founded in 1883, had 10,392 students in autumn 1998; North Dakota State University in Fargo, 9,688 students (1996). Total enrolment in the 11 public institutions of higher education, autumn 1995, 35,199; in the 2 private, 2,911.

Health. In 1994 the state had 46 general hospitals (3,571 beds) and 86 nursing facilities (7,125 beds).

Welfare. In 1996, 116,000 people received $864m. in Supplemental Security Income payments.

CULTURE
Press. There were, in 1997, 10 daily and 7 Sunday newspapers in circulation.

FURTHER READING
Statistical information: Bureau of Business and Economic Research, Univ. of North Dakota, Grand Forks 58202. Publishes *Statistical Abstract of North Dakota.*
North Dakota Blue Book. Secretary of State. Bismarck
Jelliff, T. B., *North Dakota: A Living Legacy.* Fargo, 1983

OHIO

KEY HISTORICAL EVENTS
The land was inhabited by Delaware, Miami, Shawnee and Wyandot Indians. It was explored by French and British traders in the 18th century and confirmed as part of British North America in 1763. After the War of Independence it became part of the Northwest Territory of the new United States. Former American soldiers of the war came in from New England in 1788 and made the first permanent white settlement at Marietta, at the confluence of the Ohio and Muskingum rivers. In 1803 Ohio was separated from the rest of the Territory and admitted to the Union as the 17th state.

During the early 19th century there was steady immigration from Europe, mainly of Germans, Swiss, Irish and Welsh. Industrial growth began from the processing of local farm, forest and mining products; it increased rapidly with the need to supply the Union armies in the Civil War of 1861–65.

As the industrial cities grew, so immigration began again, with many whites from eastern Europe and the Balkans and blacks from the southern states looking for work in Ohio.

Cleveland, which developed rapidly as a Lake Erie port after the opening of commercial waterways to the interior and the Atlantic coast (1825, 1830 and 1855), became an iron-and-steel town during the Civil War.

TERRITORY AND POPULATION
Ohio is bounded north by Michigan and Lake Erie, east by Pennsylvania, southeast and south by the Ohio River (forming a boundary with West Virginia and Kentucky) and west by Indiana. Land area, 40,948 sq. miles (106,055 sq. km). Census population, 1 April 2000, 11,353,140, an increase of 4·7% since 1990. July 2002 estimate, 11,421,267.

Population at five census years was:

	White	Black	Indian	Asiatic	Total	Per sq. mile
1910	4,654,897	111,452	127	645	4,767,121	117·0
1930	6,335,173	309,304	435	1,785	6,646,697	161·6
			All others			
1980	9,597,458	1,076,748	123,424		10,797,630	263·2
1990	9,521,756	1,154,826	170,533		10,847,115	264·5
2000	9,645,453	1,301,307	406,380		11,353,140	277·3

Of the total population in 2000, 5,840,878 were female, 8,464,801 were 18 years old or older and 8,782,329 were urban. In 2000 the Hispanic population was 217,123, up from 139,696 in 1990 (an increase of 55·4%).

Census population of chief cities on 1 April 2000 was:

Columbus	711,470	Lorain	68,652	Cleveland Heights	49,458
Cleveland	478,403	Springfield	65,358	Cuyahoga Falls	49,374
Cincinnati	331,285	Hamilton	60,690	Mansfield	49,346
Toledo	313,619	Kettering	57,502	Warren	46,832
Akron	217,074	Lakewood	56,646	Newark	46,279
Dayton	166,179	Elyria	55,953	Strongsville	43,858
Parma	85,655	Euclid	52,717	Fairfield	42,097
Youngstown	82,026	Middletown	51,605	Lima	40,081
Canton	80,806	Mentor	50,278		

Metropolitan areas, 2000 census: Cleveland–Akron, 2,945,831; Cincinnati–Hamilton, 1,979,202; Columbus (the capital), 1,540,157; Dayton–Springfield, 950,558; Toledo, 618,203; Youngstown–Warren, 594,746; Canton–Massillon, 404,934.

SOCIAL STATISTICS
Statistics 1999 (per 1,000 population): births 151,596 (13·5); deaths, 108,034 (9·6); infant deaths 1,242 (8·2 per 1,000 live births); marriages (2000), 86,156 (7·7 per 1,000 population); divorces (2000), 47563 (4·2).

CLIMATE
Average temperatures and rainfall in 2001: Cincinnati, Jan. 30·6°F, July 74·4°F, annual rainfall 47·67"; Cleveland, Jan. 27·7°F, July 71·9°F, annual rainfall 34·38"; Columbus, Jan. 28·7°F, July 74·0°F, annual rainfall 37·11". Ohio belongs to the Great Lakes climate zone (see UNITED STATES: Climate).

CONSTITUTION AND GOVERNMENT
The question of a general revision of the constitution drafted by an elected convention is submitted to the people every 20 years. The constitution of 1851 had 142 amendments by 1994.

The Senate consists of 33 members and the House of Representatives of 99 members. The Senate is elected for four years, half every two years; the House is elected for two years; the Governor, Lieut.-Governor and Secretary of State for four years. Qualified as electors are (with necessary exceptions) all citizens 18 years of age who have the usual residential qualifications.

For the 108th Congress, which convened in Jan. 2003, Ohio sends 18 members to the House of Representatives. It is represented in the Senate by Mike DeWine (R. 1995–2007) and George Voinovich (R. 1999–2005).

The capital (since 1816) is Columbus. Ohio is divided into 88 counties.

RECENT ELECTIONS
In the 2000 presidential election Bush polled 2,350,363 votes; Gore, 2,183,628; Nader, 117,799.

CURRENT ADMINISTRATION
Governor: Bob Taft (R.), 2003–07 (salary: $130,292).
Lieut.-Governor: Jeanette Bradley (R.), 2003–07 ($68,295).
Secretary of State: J. Kenneth Blackwell (R.), 2003–07 ($97,501).

Government Website: http://www.state.oh.us

ECONOMY
Per capita income (2000) was $28,400.

Budget. In 2000–01 general state revenue was $20,929m. General expenditure was $18.580m. (public assistance and medicaid, $8,180m.; education, $5,559m.; justice and public protection, $1,738m.; health and human services, $1,089m.). Debt outstanding was $7,670m. in 2001.

Performance. In 2000 Gross State Product was $372,640m.

ENERGY AND NATURAL RESOURCES

Oil and Gas. In 2001, 6·05m. bbls. of crude oil and 98,255m. cu. ft of gas were produced. In 2001 the value of oil and gas production was $573,581,386.

Water. Lake Erie supplies northern Ohio with its water. The total area covered by water is approximately 3,877 sq. miles, of which Lake Erie covers 3,499 sq. miles.

Minerals. Ohio has extensive mineral resources, of which coal is the most important by value: estimated production (2001) 25,790,543 short tons. Coal production in 2001 was valued at $616,869,859. Production of other minerals (in short tons), 2001: limestone and dolomite, 80,998,236; sand and gravel, 56,829,272; salt, 4,261,545. Total value of non-fuel mineral production in 2001 was $802,217,295.

Agriculture. Ohio is extensively devoted to agriculture. In 2001 about 78,000 farms covered 14·8m. acres; average farm value per acre, $2,400. The average size of a farm in 2001 was 190 acres.

Cash income 2000 from total agricultural sector, $5,487·9m. Estimated crop production 2000–01: corn for grain (437·5m. bu.), soybeans (187·8m. bu.), wheat (79·9m. bu.), oats (6·8m. bu.). In 2001 there were 1·49m. pigs, 1·24m. cattle and 142,000 sheep.

Forestry. State forest area, 2001, 184,383 acres. In 2001 there were 73 state parks covering 301,681 acres.

INDUSTRY

In 2000, 17,704 manufacturing establishments employed 988,612 persons. The largest industries were manufacturing of transport equipment, fabricated metal products, and machinery.

Labour. In 2001, 5,606,000 people were in employment out of a labour force of 5,857,000, giving an unemployment rate of 4·3%.

COMMUNICATIONS

Roads. In 2001 there were 117,268 miles of roads and 11·89m. registered motor vehicles.

Rail. Ohio has about 5,800 miles of railroad track.

Civil Aviation. In 2001 there were more than 800 airports of varying sizes in the state. There are 165 public use airports and 23 public use heliports. There were 18,042,633 passenger enplanements in 1999.

Shipping. Ohio has more than 700 miles of navigable waterways, with Lake Erie having a 265-mile shoreline. There are nine deep-draft ports in the state. The busiest port is Cleveland, which handles 18m. tons of cargo annually.

SOCIAL INSTITUTIONS

Justice. In 2002 there were 45,044 inmates (93·7% males) in the 33 adult correctional institutions. The death penalty (minimum age 18) is authorized and there were three executions in 2002. There were 204 death-row inmates (all male) in 2002: 93 were white; 104 black; 3 Hispanic and 4 other.

Religion. Many religious faiths are represented, including (but not limited to) the Baptist, Jewish, Lutheran, Methodist, Muslim, Orthodox, Presbyterian and Roman Catholic.

Education. School attendance during full term is compulsory for children from 6 to 18 years of age. In 2001–02 public schools had 1,811,216 enrolled pupils. Teachers' salaries (2001–02) averaged $44,029. Estimated expenditure on elementary and secondary schools for 2002 was $7,508m., 38·8% of the total state budget. Total estimated revenue for the co-ordination of higher education in Ohio (controlled by the Board of Regents) was $2·57bn. in fiscal year 2001.

Public colleges and universities had a total enrolment (2000–01) of 445,879 students. Independent colleges and universities enrolled 122,866 students. Estimated annual operating budget for higher education institutions in 1998 was $4·4m. Average annual charge (for undergraduates in 1995) at four-year institutions: $3,405 (state); $11,782 (private).

Main campuses, 1997:

Founded	Institutions	Enrolments
1804	Ohio University, Athens (State)	19,159
1809	Miami University, Oxford (State)	15,999
1819	University of Cincinnati (State)	27,800
1826	Case Western Reserve University, Cleveland	9,569[1]
1850	University of Dayton (R.C.)	1,709[1]
1870	University of Akron (State)	21,878
1870	Ohio State University, Columbus (State)	48,004
1872	University of Toledo (State)	19,855
1908	Youngstown University (State)	12,050
1910	Bowling Green State University (State)	16,579
1910	Kent State University (State)	20,277
1964	Cleveland State University (State)	15,447
1964	Wright State University (State)	14,292
1986	Shawnee State University, Portsmouth (State)	3,163

[1]Figures for Case Western Reserve University and University of Dayton are for 1994 enrolments.

Health. In 2001 the state had 166 registered community hospitals with 33,310 beds. State facilities for the severely mentally retarded had 12 developmental centres serving 2,000 residents.

Welfare. Public assistance is administered through the Ohio Works First programme (OWS). In 2001 OWF-Combined assistance groups had 201,009 recipients and money payments totalled $317,130,119. OWF-Regular assistance groups had 186,544 recipients with $301,103,315 paid out in 2001. OWF-Unemployed had 14,465 recipients and money payments were $16,026,804 in 2001. Disability Assistance had 12,017 recipients in 2001; and food stamps, 660,446 recipients.

In 2001 Disability Assistance totalled $17,308,007; food stamps in 2001 totalled $609,479,253; and foster care totalled $144,265,957. Optional State Supplement is paid to aged, blind or disabled adults. Free social services are available to those eligible by income or circumstances.

CULTURE

Museums and Galleries. The Ohio Historical Center showcases pre-European history, and Ohio's history from the Ice Age to 1970. There is a Cincinnati Art Museum and a Columbus Museum of Art, and a Neil Armstrong Air and Space Museum.

FURTHER READING

Official Roster: Federal, State, County Officers and Department Information. Secretary of State, Columbus. Biennial

Shkurti, W. J. and Bartle, J. (eds.) *Benchmark Ohio.* Ohio State Univ. Press, 1991

OKLAHOMA

KEY HISTORICAL EVENTS

Francisco Coronado led a Spanish expedition in 1541, claiming the land for Spain. There were several Indian groups, but no strong political unit. In 1714 Juchereau de Saint Denis made the first French contact. During the 18th century French fur-traders were active, and France and Spain struggled for control, a struggle which was resolved by the French withdrawal in 1763. France returned briefly in 1800–03, and the territory then passed to the USA as part of the Louisiana Purchase.

In 1828 the Federal government set aside the area of the present state as Indian Territory, that is, a reservation and sanctuary for Indian tribes who had been driven off their lands elsewhere by white settlement. About 70 tribes came, among whom were Creeks, Choctaws and Cherokees from the southeastern states, and Plains Indians.

In 1889 the government took back about 2·5m. acres of the Territory and opened it to white settlement. About 10,000 homesteaders gathered at the site of Oklahoma

City on the Santa Fe Railway in the rush to stake their land claims. The settlers' area, and others subsequently opened to settlement, were organized as the Oklahoma Territory in 1890. In 1907 the Oklahoma and Indian Territories were combined and admitted to the Union as a state. Indian reservations were established within the state.

The economy first depended on ranching and farming, with packing stations on the railways. A mining industry grew in the 1870s attracting foreign immigration, mainly from Europe. In 1901 oil was found near Tulsa, and the industry grew rapidly.

TERRITORY AND POPULATION

Oklahoma is bounded north by Kansas, northeast by Missouri, east by Arkansas, south by Texas (the Red River forming part of the boundary) and, at the western extremity of the 'panhandle', by New Mexico and Colorado. Land area, 68,667 sq. miles (177,847 sq. km). Census population, 1 April 2000, 3,450,654, an increase of 9·7% since 1990. July 2002 estimate, 3,493,714.

The population at five federal censuses was:

	White	Black	American Indian	Other	Total	Per sq. mile
1930	2,130,778	172,198	92,725	339	2,396,040	34·6
1960	2,107,900	153,084	68,689	1,414	2,328,284	33·8
1980	2,597,783	204,658	169,292	53,557	3,025,486	43·2
1990	2,583,512	233,801	252,420	119,723	3,189,456	44·5
2000	2,628,434	260,968	273,230	288,022	3,450,654	50·3

Of the total population in 2000, 1,754,759 were female, 2,558,294 were 18 years old or older and 2,254,563 were urban. The US Bureau of Indian Affairs is responsible for 1,097,004 acres (1990), of which 96,839 acres were allotted to tribes. In 2000 Oklahoma's Hispanic population was 179,304, up from 86,160 in 1990 (an increase of 108·1%).

The most important cities with population, 2000, are Oklahoma City (capital), 506,132; Tulsa, 393,049; Norman, 95,694; Lawton, 92,757; Broken Arrow, 74,859; Edmond, 68,315; Midwest City, 54,088; Enid, 47,045; Moore, 41,138; Stillwater, 39,065; Muskogee, 38,310; Bartlesville, 34,748.

SOCIAL STATISTICS

Births, 1999, 49,424 (14·7 per 1,000 population); deaths, 34,074 (10·2) (1996) infant mortality rate, 8·5 (per 1,000 live births). Marriages (1997), 27,700; divorces, 19,100.

CLIMATE

Oklahoma City, Jan. 34°F (1°C), July 81°F (27°C). Annual rainfall 31·9" (8,113 mm). Tulsa, Jan. 34°F (1°C), July 82°F (28°C). Annual rainfall 33·2" (8,438 mm). Oklahoma belongs to the Central Plains climate zone (see UNITED STATES: Climate).

CONSTITUTION AND GOVERNMENT

The constitution, dating from 1907, provides for amendment by initiative petition and legislative referendum; it has had 155 amendments (as of Jan. 1995).

The Legislature consists of a Senate of 48 members, who are elected for four years, and a House of Representatives elected for two years and consisting of 101 members. The Governor and Lieut.-Governor are elected for four-year terms; the Governor can only be elected for two terms in succession. Electors are (with necessary exceptions) all citizens 18 years or older, with the usual qualifications.

For the 108th Congress, which convened in Jan. 2003, Oklahoma sends five members to the House of Representatives. It is represented in the Senate by Don Nickles (R. 1981–2005) and James Inhofe (R. 1994–2009).

The capital is Oklahoma City. The state has 77 counties.

RECENT ELECTIONS

In the 2000 presidential election Bush polled 744,337 votes; Gore, 474,276; Buchanan, 9,014.

CURRENT ADMINISTRATION
Governor: Brad Henry (D.), 2003–07 (salary: $101,000).
Lieut.-Governor: Mary Fallin (R.), 2003–07 ($75,530).
Secretary of State: M. Susan Savage (D.), appointed Jan. 2003 ($90,000).
Government Website: http://www.youroklahoma.com

ECONOMY
Per capita income (2000) was $23,582.

Budget. In 1999 total state revenue was $11,935m. Total expenditure was $10,665m. (education, $4,178m.; public welfare, $1,767m.; highways, $998m.; health and hospitals, $533m.; police protection, $31m.). Outstanding debt, in 1999, $5,564m.

Performance. Gross State Product in 2000 was $91,773m.

ENERGY AND NATURAL RESOURCES
Oil and Gas. Production, 1998: crude oil, 78m. bbls.; natural gas, 1,645bn. cu. ft. Oklahoma ranks third in the USA for natural gas production behind Texas and Louisiana. In 1993 there were 122,094 oil and gas wells in production.

Water. The total area covered by water is approximately 1,224 sq. miles.

Minerals. Coal production (1993), 1,796,000 tons. Principal minerals are: crushed stone, cement, sand and gravel, iodine, glass sand, gypsum. Other minerals are helium, clay and sand, zinc, lead, granite, tripoli, bentonite, lime and volcanic ash. Total value of domestic non-fuel minerals produced in 1998 was $408m.

Agriculture. In 2000 the state had some 85,000 farms and ranches with a total area of 34m. acres; average size was 400 acres; average value per acre was $494 in 1996. Area harvested, 1992, 8,272,889 acres. Livestock, 1992: cattle, 4,736,594; sheep and lambs, 103,732; hogs and pigs, 260,682.

Farm income 1996: crops, $1,126m.; livestock and products, $2,439m. The major cash grain is winter wheat (value, 1997, $579m.): 1,579m. bu. of wheat for grain were harvested from 5,400,000 acres. Other crops include barley, oats, rye, grain, corn, soybeans, grain sorghum, cotton, peanuts and peaches. Value of cattle and calves produced, 1990, $3,080m.; catfish, $1m.; racehorses, $63m.

The Oklahoma Conservation Commission works with 91 conservation districts, universities, state and federal government agencies. The early work of the conservation districts, beginning in 1937, was limited to flood and erosion control: since 1970, they include urban areas also.

Irrigated production has increased in the Oklahoma 'panhandle'. The Ogalala aquifer is the primary source of irrigation water there and in western Oklahoma, a finite source because of its isolation from major sources of recharge. Declining groundwater levels necessitate the most effective irrigation practices.

Forestry. There are 7·5m. acres of forest, one half considered commercial. The forest products industry is concentrated in the 118 eastern counties. There are 3 forest regions: Ozark (oak, hickory); Ouachita highlands (pine, oak); Cross-Timbers (post oak, black jack oak). Southern pine is the chief commercial species, at almost 80% of saw-timber harvested annually. Replanting is essential.

INDUSTRY
In 1994 there were 3,858 industrial firms: major commodities produced include transportation equipment (accounting for 15·3% of manufactured goods), petroleum and coal products (14·1%), non-electrical machinery (12·2%), food products (9·7%), electronic and electrical equipment (9·2%).

Labour. Total non-agricultural employment in 1999 was 1,462,000. Employees by branch, 1999 (in 1,000): services, 417; wholesale and retail trade, 337; government, 283; manufacturing, 184. Oklahoma's unemployment rate was 3·4% in 1999.

COMMUNICATIONS
Roads. In 2000 there were 112,634 miles of roads and 3,014,491 registered motor vehicles.

Rail. In 1995 Oklahoma had 3,867 miles of railway operated by 21 companies.

Civil Aviation. Airports in 1995 numbered 421, of which 127 were publicly owned. Five cities were served by commercial airlines. There were 3,431,736 passenger enplanements statewide in 1999.

Shipping. The McClellan-Kerr Arkansas Navigation System provides access from east central Oklahoma to New Orleans through the Verdigris, Arkansas and Mississippi rivers. In 1991, 63m. tons were shipped inbound and outbound on the Oklahoma Segment. Commodities shipped are mainly chemical fertilizer, farm produce, petroleum products, iron and steel, coal, sand and gravel.

SOCIAL INSTITUTIONS

Justice. There were 23,009 federal and state prisoners in June 2000. In 1990 there were 15 penal institutions, 8 community treatment centres and 7 probation and parole centres. The death penalty was suspended in 1966 and re-imposed in 1976. The minimum age is 16. There were 18 executions in 2001 and 7 in 2002.

Religion. The chief religious bodies are Baptists, followed by United Methodists, Roman Catholics, Churches of Christ, Assembly of God, Disciples of Christ, Presbyterian, Lutheran, Nazarene and Episcopal.

Education. In 1994–95 there were 609,800 pupils and 39,290 teachers at public elementary and secondary school. The average teacher salary per annum was $28,928. In 1997 total expenditure on the 3,257 schools was $3,033m. There were 177,000 students enrolled at the 45 higher education establishments in 1996.

Institutions of higher education include:

Founded	Name	Place	1994 Enrolment
1890	University of Oklahoma	Norman	21,373
1890	Oklahoma State University	Stillwater	18,290
1890	University of Central Oklahoma	Edmond	16,039
1894	The University of Tulsa	Tulsa	4,579
1897	Northeastern State University	Tahlequah	9,374
1897	Northwestern Oklahoma State University	Alva	1,870
1897	Southwestern Oklahoma State University	Weatherford	5,289
1908	Cameron University	Lawton	5,863
1909	East Central University	Ada	4,468
1909	Southeastern Oklahoma State University	Durant	4,104
1909	Rogers State College	Claremore	3,404
1950	Oklahoma Christian University of Science and Arts	Oklahoma City	1,505
1969	Rose State College	Midwest City	9,234
1970	Tulsa Junior College	Tulsa	21,055
1972	Oklahoma City Community College	Oklahoma City	11,185

Health. In 1995 there were 110 community hospitals with 11,500 beds.

Welfare. In 1996 there were 580,000 persons receiving welfare assistance. Of this total: 395,000 retired workers received an average of $711 per month; 106,000 widows and widowers received $680 per month; and 79,000 disabled workers and their dependants received $688 per month.

CULTURE

Broadcasting. In 1995 there were 172 radio and 25 television broadcasting stations, and 16 cable-TV companies.

Press. There were 49 daily newspapers in 1995 and 190 weeklies in 1990.

Tourism. There are 72 state parks and 10 museums and monuments. Tourists spend some $3,000m. annually.

FURTHER READING

Center for Economic and Management Research, Univ. of Oklahoma, 307 West Brooks St., Norman 73019. *Statistical Abstract of Oklahoma.*
Oklahoma Department of Libraries. *Oklahoma Almanac.* Biennial
Morris, J. W., *et al.*, *Historical Atlas of Oklahoma.* 3rd ed. Oklahoma Univ. Press, 1986

State library: Oklahoma Department of Libraries, 200 Northeast 18th Street, Oklahoma City 73105.

OREGON

KEY HISTORICAL EVENTS

The area was divided between many Indian groups including the Chinook, Tillamook, Cayuse and Modoc. In the 18th century English and Spanish visitors tried to establish national claims, based on explorations of the 16th century. The USA also laid claim by right of discovery when an expedition entered the mouth of the Columbia River in 1792.

Oregon was disputed between Britain and the USA. An American fur company established a trading settlement at Astoria in 1811, which the British took in 1812. The Hudson Bay Company were the most active force in Oregon until the 1830s when American pioneers began to migrate westwards along the Oregon Trail. The dispute between Britain and the USA was resolved in 1846 with the boundary fixed at 49°N. lat. Oregon was organized as a Territory in 1848 but with wider boundaries; it became a state with its present boundaries in 1859.

Early settlers were mainly American. They came to farm in the Willamette Valley and to exploit the western forests. Portland developed as a port for ocean-going traffic, although it was 100 miles inland at the confluence of the Willamette and Columbia rivers. Industries followed when the railways came and the rivers were exploited for hydro-electricity. The capital of the Territory from 1851 was Salem, a mission for Indians on the Willamette river; it was confirmed as state capital in 1864. Salem became the processing centre for the farming and market-gardening Willamette Valley.

TERRITORY AND POPULATION

Oregon is bounded in the north by Washington, with the Columbia River forming most of the boundary, east by Idaho, with the Snake River forming most of the boundary, south by Nevada and California and west by the Pacific. Land area, 95,997 sq. miles (248,631 sq. km). The federal government owned (1994) 32,132,581 acres (51·73% of the state area). Census population, 1 April 2000, 3,421,399, an increase of 20·4% since 1990. July 2002 estimate, 3,521,515.

Population at five federal censuses was:

	White	Black	American Indian	Asiatic	Total	Per sq. mile
1930	938,598	2,234	4,776	8,179	953,786	9·9
1960	1,732,037	18,133	8,026	9,120	1,768,687	18·4
1980	2,490,610	37,060	27,314	34,775	2,633,105	27·3
	White	Black	American Indian	All others	Total	Per sq. mile
1990	2,636,787	46,178	38,496	120,860	2,842,321	29·6
2000	2,961,623	55,662	45,211	358,903	3,421,399	35·6

Of the total population in 2000, 1,724,849 were female, 2,574,843 were 18 years old or older and 2,694,144 were urban. In 2000 the Hispanic population was 275,314, up from 112,707 in 1990 (an increase of 144·3%).

The US Bureau of Indian Affairs (area headquarters in Portland) administers (1994) 783,227·13 acres, of which 627,615·54 acres are held by the USA in trust for Indian tribes and 138,950·05 acres for individual Indians, and 16,661·54 acres of mineral tracts.

The largest cities (2000 census figures) are: Portland, 529,121: Eugene, 137,893; Salem (the capital), 136,924; Gresham, 90,205; Beaverton, 76,129; Hillsboro, 70,186; Medford, 63,154; Springfield, 52,864; Bend, 52,029. Primary statistical (metropolitan) areas: Portland–Salem, 2,265,223; Eugene-Springfield, 322,959.

SOCIAL STATISTICS

In 1999 births numbered 45,354 (13·7 per 1,000 population); deaths, 29,587 (8·9); (1996) infant mortality rate, 5·6 (per 1,000 live births). Marriages (1997), 25,800; and divorces, 14,800.

CLIMATE

Jan. 32°F (0°C), July 66°F (19°C). Annual rainfall 28" (710 mm). Oregon belongs to the Pacific coast climate zone (see UNITED STATES: Climate).

CONSTITUTION AND GOVERNMENT

The present constitution dates from 1859; some 250 items in it have been amended. The Legislative Assembly consists of a Senate of 30 members, elected for four years (half their number retiring every two years), and a House of 60 representatives, elected for two years. The Governor is elected for four years. The constitution reserves to the voters the rights of initiative and referendum and recall.

For the 108th Congress, which convened in Jan. 2003, Oregon sends five members to the House of Representatives. It is represented in the Senate by Ron Wyden (D. 1996–2005) and Gordon Smith (R. 1997–2009).

The capital is Salem. There are 36 counties in the state.

RECENT ELECTIONS

In the 2000 presidential election Gore polled 720,342 votes; Bush, 713,577; Nader, 77,357.

CURRENT ADMINISTRATION

Governor: Ted Kulongoski (D.), 2003–07 (salary: $99,200).
Secretary of State: Bill Bradbury (D.), 2001–05 ($76,300).

Government Website: http://www.oregon.gov

ECONOMY

Per capita income (2000) was $27,649.

Budget. In 1999 total state revenue was $15,666m. Total expenditure was $13,965m. (education, $4,294m.; public welfare, $2,764m.; highways, $1,010m.; health and hospitals, $950m.; police protection, $149m.). Outstanding debt, in 1999, $5,738m.

Performance. Gross State Product was $118,637m. in 2000.

ENERGY AND NATURAL RESOURCES

Water. The total area covered by water is approximately 1,129 sq. miles.

Minerals. Mineral resources include gold, silver, lead, mercury, chromite, sand and gravel, stone, clays, lime, silica, diatomite, expansible shale, scoria, pumice and uranium. There is geothermal potential. Domestic non-fuel mineral production value (1998), $272m.

Agriculture. Oregon, which has an area of 61,557,184 acres, is divided by the Cascade Range into two distinct zones as to climate. West of the Cascade Range there is a good rainfall and almost every variety of crop common to the temperate zone is grown; east of the Range stock-raising and wheat-growing are the principal industries and irrigation is needed for row crops and fruits. In 1993 the monthly average employed in agriculture was 22,500.

There were, in 2000, 40,000 farms with an acreage of 17·2m. and an average farm size of 430 acres; most are family-owned corporate farms. Average value per acre (1998), $1,030.

Farm income in 1996: from crops, $2,320m.; from livestock and products, $657m., of which cattle made most. Principal crops: greenhouse and nursery products ($415·8m.), hay ($104·4m.), farmforest products, wheat, potatoes, grass seed (ryegrass and fescue), Christmas trees, pears, onions ($255·8m.).

Livestock, 1 Jan. 1993: milch cows (1992), 0·1m.; cattle and calves, 1·4m.; sheep and lambs, 415,000; swine (1992), 75,000.

Forestry. About 28·2m. acres is forested, almost half of the state. Of this amount, 22·4m. is commercial forest land suitable for timber production; ownership is as follows (acres): US Forestry Service, 13·1m.; US Bureau of Land Management, 2·7m.; other federal, 165,000; State of Oregon, 907,000; other public (city, county), 123,000; private owners, 10·8m., of which the forest industry owns 5·8m., non-industrial private owners, 4·6m., Indians, 399,000. Oregon's commercial forest lands provided a 1992 harvest of 5,742m. bd ft of logs, as well as the benefits of recreation, water, grazing, wildlife and fish. Trees vary from the coastal forest of hemlock and spruce to the state's primary species, Douglas-fir, throughout much of western Oregon. In eastern Oregon, ponderosa pine, lodgepole pine and true firs are found.

Here, forestry is often combined with livestock grazing to provide an economic operation. Along the Cascade summit and in the mountains of northeast Oregon, alpine species are found.

Total covered payroll in lumber and wood products industry in 1991 was $1,475m.

Fisheries. All food and shellfish landings in the calendar year 1992 amounted to a value of $74·4m. The most important are: ground fish, shrimp, crab, tuna, salmon.

INDUSTRY
Forest products manufacturing is Oregon's leading industry, followed by high technology.

Labour. Total non-agricultural employment was 1,572,000 in 1999. Employees by branch, 1999 (in 1,000): services, 425; wholesale and retail trade, 388; government, 261; manufacturing, 241. The unemployment rate in 1999 was 5·7%.

COMMUNICATIONS

Roads. There were 66,904 miles of roads in 2000 (55,840 rural) and 3,021,574 registered vehicles.

Rail. The state had (1994) 21 railways with a total mileage of 2,572 (4,115 km). There is a light rail network in Portland.

Civil Aviation. In 1994 there were 1 public-use and 93 personal-use heliports; 248 personal-use and 101 public-use airports of which 34 were state-owned airports; and 2 sea-plane bases, 1 public-use and 1 personal-use. There were 7,162,856 passenger enplanements statewide in 1999.

Shipping. Portland is a major seaport for large ocean-going vessels and is 101 miles inland from the mouth of the Columbia River. In 1993 Portland handled 11·7m. short tons of cargo and other Columbia River ports 13·7m. short tons, the main commodities being grain, petroleum and wood products; the ports of Coos Bay and Newport handled 2·7m. short tons of cargo, chiefly logs, lumber and wood products.

SOCIAL INSTITUTIONS

Justice. There are 12 correctional institutions in Oregon. In June 2000 there were 10,313 federal and state prisoners. The sterilization law, originally passed in 1917, was amended in 1967 and abolished in 1993. Some categories of euthanasia were legalized in Dec. 1994.

The death penalty is authorized for over 18 year olds but there were no executions in 2002.

Religion. The chief religious bodies are Catholic, Baptist, Lutheran, Methodists, Presbyterian and Latter-day Saints (Mormons).

Education. School attendance is compulsory from 7 to 18 years of age if the twelfth year of school has not been completed; those between the ages of 16 and 18 years, if legally employed, may attend part-time or evening schools. Others may be excused under certain circumstances. In 1994–95 the public elementary and secondary schools had 521,000 students and 27,000 teachers; average salary for teachers (1993–94), $37,589. Total expenditure on elementary and secondary education (1997) was $3,769m.

Leading state-supported institutions of higher education (1993–94) included:

	Students
University of Oregon, Eugene	16,680
Oregon Health Sciences University	1,396
Oregon State University, Corvallis	14,131
Portland State University, Portland	14,428
Western Oregon State College, Monmouth	3,871
Southern Oregon State College, Ashland	4,535
Eastern Oregon State College, La Grande	1,931
Oregon Institute of Technology, Klamath Falls	2,444

Enrolment in state colleges and universities, in autumn 1996, was approximately 165,000 students. Largest of the privately endowed universities are Lewis and Clark College, Portland, with 3,132 students (1993–94); University of Portland, 2,700 students; Willamette University, Salem, 2,451 students; Reed College, Portland, 1,277 students; Linfield College, McMinnville, 2,354 students; Marylhurst College, 1,183 students; and George Fox College, 1,557 students. In 1993–94 there were 314,926 students (full-time equivalent) in community colleges.

Health. In 1995 there were 73 licensed hospitals, 2 state hospitals for the mentally ill (798 beds), 1 for the mentally retarded (400) and 1 with both programmes (133). There were 64 community hospitals with 7,200 beds.

Welfare. The State Adult and Family Services Division provides cash payments, medical care, food stamps, day care and help in finding jobs. As of July 1994 there were an estimated 495,000 people on low incomes. Many of them were children in single-parent families, benefiting from the Aid to Families with Dependent Children Programme; 282,500 people were receiving food stamps; an estimated 376,000 were below the poverty level. There is also a Children's Services Division.

A system of unemployment benefit payments, financed by employers, with administrative allotments made through a federal agency, started in 1938.

CULTURE

Broadcasting. In 1996 there were 194 commercial radio stations and 37 educational radio stations. There were 24 commercial television stations and 26 educational television stations. There were also 24 cable companies.

Cinema. The Portland Art Museum Northwest Film Center is a regional media arts resource organization. Programmes include: the Portland International Film Festival (Feb.), a survey of new world cinema; the Northwest Film and Video Festival (Nov.), a juried showcase of new work by regional artists; and the Young People's Film and Video Festival (June), featuring new work by students.

Press. In 1996 there were 21 daily newspapers with a circulation of more than 676,000 and 111 non-daily newspapers.

Tourism. The total income from tourism in 1992 was estimated to be $3,100m.

FURTHER READING

Oregon Blue Book. Issued by the Secretary of State. Salem. Biennial
Conway, F. D. L., *Timber in Oregon: History and Projected Trends.* Oregon State Univ., 1993
Friedman, R., *The Other Side of Oregon.* Caldwell (ID), 1993
McArthur, L. A., *Oregon Geographic Names.* 6th ed., rev. and enlarged. Portland, 1992
Orr, E. L., *et al., Geology of Oregon.* Dubuque (IA), 1992

State Library: The Oregon State Library, Salem.

PENNSYLVANIA

KEY HISTORICAL EVENTS

Pennsylvania was occupied by four powerful tribes in the 17th century: Delaware, Susquehannock, Shawnee and Iroquois. The first white settlers were Swedish, arriving in 1643. The British became dominant in 1664, and in 1681 William Penn, an English Quaker, was given a charter to colonize the area as a sanctuary for his fellow Quakers. Penn's ideal was peaceful co-operation with the Indians and religious toleration within the colony. Several religious groups were attracted to Pennsylvania because of this policy, including Protestant sects from Germany and France. During the 18th century, co-operation with the Indians failed as the settlers pushed into more territory and the Indians resisted.

During the War of Independence the Declaration of Independence was signed in Philadelphia, the main city. Pennsylvania became one of the original 13 states of the Union. In 1812 the state capital was moved to its current location in Harrisburg, which began as a trading post and ferry point on the Susquehanna River in the south-central part of the state. The Mason-Dixon line, the state's southern boundary, became the dividing line between free and slave states during the conflict leading to the Civil War. During the war crucial battles were fought in the state, including the battle of Gettysburg. Industrial growth was rapid after the war. Pittsburgh, founded as a British fort in 1761 during war with the French, had become an iron-making town by 1800 and grew rapidly when canal and railway links opened in the 1830s. The American Federation of Labor was founded in Pittsburgh in 1881, by which time the city was of national importance in producing coal, iron, steel and glass.

At the beginning of the 20th century, industry attracted immigration from Italy and eastern Europe. In farming areas the early sect communities survive, notably Amish and Mennonites. (The Pennsylvania 'Dutch' are of German extraction.)

TERRITORY AND POPULATION

Pennsylvania is bounded north by New York, east by New Jersey, south by Delaware and Maryland, southwest by West Virginia, west by Ohio and northwest by Lake Erie. Land area, 44,817 sq. miles (116,075 sq. km). Census population, 1 April 2000, 12,281,054, an increase of 3·4% since 1990. July 2002 estimate, 12,335,091.

Population at five census years was:

	White	Black	Indian	All others	Total	Per sq. mile
1910	7,467,713	193,919	1,503	1,976	7,665,111	171·0
1930	9,196,007	431,257	523	3,563	9,631,350	214·8
			All others			
1980	10,652,320	1,046,810	164,765		11,863,895	264·7
1990	10,520,201	1,089,795	271,647		11,881,643	265·1
2000	10,484,203	1,224,612	572,239		12,281,054	274·0

Of the total population in 2000, 6,351,391 were female, 9,358,833 were 18 years old or older and 9,464,101 were urban. In 2000 Pennsylvania's Hispanic population was 394,088, up from 232,262 in 1990 (a rise of 69·7%).

The population of the largest cities and townships, 2000 census, was:

Philadelphia	1,517,550	Upper Darby	81,821	Bethlehem	71,329
Pittsburgh	334,563	Reading	81,207	Lower Merion	59,850
Allentown	106,632	Scranton	76,415	Bensalem	58,434
Erie	103,717				

The Philadelphia–Wilmington–Atlantic City metropolitan area had a 2000 census population of 6,188,463.

SOCIAL STATISTICS

Births, 1999, 145,840 (12·2 per 1,000 population); deaths, 127,247 (10·6); (1997) infant deaths, 1,090 (7·6 per 1,000 live births). 1997 marriages, 77,300 (6·4 per 1,000 population); divorces, 38,700 (3·2).

CLIMATE

Philadelphia, Jan. 32°F (0°C), July 77°F (25°C). Annual rainfall 40" (1,006 mm). Pittsburgh, Jan. 31°F (–0·6°C), July 74°F (23·3°C). Annual rainfall 37" (914 mm). Pennsylvania belongs to the Appalachian Mountains climate zone (*see* UNITED STATES: Climate).

CONSTITUTION AND GOVERNMENT

The present constitution dates from 1968. The General Assembly consists of a Senate of 50 members chosen for four years, one-half being elected biennially, and a House of Representatives of 203 members chosen for two years. The Governor and Lieut.-Governor are elected for four years. Every citizen 18 years of age, with the usual residential qualifications, may vote. Registered voters in Nov. 1999, 7,460,339.

For the 108th Congress, which convened in Jan. 2003, Pennsylvania sends 19 members to the House of Representatives. It is represented in the Senate by Arlen Specter (R. 1981–2005) and Rick Santorum (R. 1995–2007).

The state capital is Harrisburg. The state is organized in counties (numbering 67), cities, boroughs, townships and school districts.

RECENT ELECTIONS

In the 2000 presidential election Gore polled 2,485,967 votes; Bush, 2,281,127; Nader, 103,392.

CURRENT ADMINISTRATION

Governor: Edward G. Rendell (D.), 2003–07 (salary: $144,463).

Lieut.-Governor: Catherine Baker Knoll (D.), 2003–07 ($121,349).

Secretary of the Commonwealth (acting): Pedro A. Cortés, appointed 2003 ($103,980).

Government Website: http://www.state.pa.us

ECONOMY

Per capita income (2000) was $29,533.

Budget. In 1999 total state revenue was $49,482m. Total expenditure was $44,237m. (education, $11,713m.; public welfare, $11,424m.; highways, $3,217m.; health and hospitals, $3,040m.; police protection, $765m.). Outstanding debt, in 1999, $17,658m.

Performance. Gross State Product in 2000 was $403,985m.

ENERGY AND NATURAL RESOURCES

Oil and Gas. 1998 production: crude petroleum, 1·98m. bbls.; natural gas, 68,343m. cu. ft.

Water. The total area covered by water is approximately 1,239 sq. miles.

Minerals. Pennsylvania is almost the sole producer of anthracite coal. Production, 1998: anthracite coal, 7,535,593 tons; bituminous coal, 79,544,949 tons; industrial minerals (shale, limestone, sandstone, clay, dolomite, sand and gravel), 128,332,415 tons. Non-fuel mineral production was worth $1,280m. in 1998.

Agriculture. Agriculture, market-gardening, fruit-growing, horticulture and forestry are pursued within the state. In 2000 there were 59,000 farms with a total farm area of 7·7m. acres (5·0m. acres in crops in 1997). Average number of acres per farm in 2000 was 131 and the average value per acre in 1999 was $2,440. Cash receipts, 1998, from crops, $1,282·9m., and from livestock and products, $2,913·9m.

In 1998 Pennsylvania ranked first in the production of mushrooms (379m. lb, value $258·8m.). Other production figures include: corn for grain (116·6m. bu., value $285·5m.); sweet corn (1·0m. cwt, value $30·3m.) and tomatoes (0·5m. cwt, value $13·7m.). Pennsylvania is also a major fruit producing state; in 1998 apples totalled 395m. lb (value $54·1m.), peaches, 65m. lb (value $20·6m.) and grapes, 54m. tons (value $14·4m.). Pennsylvania ranked fourth in milk production in 1998 with 10,850m. lb. Egg production totalled 5,983m., value $304m.; chicken production (excluding broilers) was 28·5m., value $48·4m. in chicken inventory, and chicken production of broilers was 135·5m., value $266m. Other products included turkey (10·5m. poults, value $88·6m.) and cheese (361m. lb).

On 1 Jan. 1999 there were on farms: 1·67m. cattle and calves, 83,000 sheep, and 1·1m. hogs and swine.

Forestry. In 1998 state forest land totalled 2,100,113 acres; state park land, 282,700 acres; state game lands, 1,392,312 acres.

INDUSTRY

In Nov. 1999 manufacturing employed 928,400 workers; services, 1,810,200; trade, 1,235,900; government, 709,200. The total workforce was 5,953,000.

COMMUNICATIONS

Roads. Highways and roads in the state (federal, local and state combined) totalled (2000) 119,642 miles. Registered motor vehicles in 2000 numbered 9,259,967.

Rail. In Jan. 1999 there were 70 freight railways operating within the state with a line mileage of 5,379. There are metro, light rail and tramway networks in Philadelphia and Pittsburgh, and commuter networks around Philadelphia.

Civil Aviation. In Jan. 1999 there were 139 public airports, 312 private and 8 public heliports, and 349 airports for personal use (includes seaplane bases). There were 19,515,998 passenger enplanements statewide in 1999.

Shipping. Trade at the ports of the Philadelphia area (Chester, Marcus Hook and Philadelphia) for 1998: imports, 50,222,884 short tons of cargo (includes bulk and general cargo); exports, 837,547 short tons of cargo.

SOCIAL INSTITUTIONS

Justice. The death penalty is authorized for 16-year-olds. The last execution was in 1999. There were 36,384 prisoners in state correctional institutions as of 31 Dec. 1999.

Religion. The principal religious bodies in 1990 were the Roman Catholics (3,675,250 members), Protestant (3,615,450) and Jewish (282,000 in 1997). The five largest Protestant denominations by adherents were the Evangelical Lutheran Church in America (682,800), the United Methodist Church (678,700), the Presbyterian Church (USA) (388,747), the United Church of Christ (286,500) and the Episcopal Church (140,050).

Education. School attendance is compulsory for children 8–17 years of age. In 1998–99 there were 1,816,566 pupils and 109,691 teachers in public elementary and secondary schools. The public kindergartens and elementary schools (Grades K-6) had 984,830 pupils and public secondary schools (Grades 7–12) had 831,736 pupils. Non-public elementary schools had 247,466 pupils and non-public secondary had 83,912 pupils. Average salary for public school professional personnel was $49,859; classroom teachers $48,457. In fiscal year 1997–98 state and local government revenues for elementary and secondary schools totalled $13,282m. Total expenditures from all funding sources (state, local, federal government and other financing sources) totalled $13,918m.

Leading senior academic institutions included:

Founded	Institutions	Faculty[1] (Autumn 1997)	Students[2] (Autumn 1998)
1740	University of Pennsylvania (non-sect.)	6,634	21,729
1787	University of Pittsburgh (all campuses)	6,142	32,292
1832	Lafayette College, Easton (Presbyterian)	264	2,244
1833	Haverford College	121	1,147
1842	Villanova University (R.C.)	1,079	9,952
1846	Bucknell University (Baptist)	285	3,726
1851	St Joseph's University, Philadelphia (R.C.)	474	6,484
1852	California University of Pennsylvania	332	5,800
1855	Pennsylvania State University (all campuses)	9,017	75,041
1855	Millersville University of Pennsylvania	440	7,466
1863	LaSalle University, Philadelphia (R.C.)	391	5,384
1864	Swarthmore College	228	1,390
1866	Lehigh University, Bethlehem (non-sect.)	909	6,363
1871	West Chester University of Pennsylvania	711	11,578
1875	Indiana University of Pennsylvania	824	13,790
1878	Duquesne University, Pittsburgh (R.C.)	1,124	9,552
1884	Temple University, Philadelphia	3,697	27,539
1885	Bryn Mawr College	283	1,796
1888	University of Scranton (R.C.)	452	4,711
1891	Drexel University, Philadelphia	1,117	11,646
1900	Carnegie-Mellon University, Pittsburgh	1,235	8,174

[1]Includes full-time and part-time.
[2]Includes undergraduate, graduate and first professional students.

Health. In June 1997 the state had 200 general/acute care hospitals with 46,528 beds licensed and approved by the Department of Health. In addition there were 80 speciality (federal, psychiatric and rehabilitation) hospitals with a licensed capacity of 10,094 beds.

Welfare. During the year ending 30 June 1999 the monthly average number of cases receiving public assistance was 383,191, including: Temporary Assistance for Needy Families (formerly Aid to Families with Dependent Children), 324,105; general assistance, 58,079; State Blind Pension, 1,007.

Payments for medical assistance (state and federal) in fiscal year 1998–99 included: outpatient care, $1,445m.; inpatient care, $948m.; capitation, $2,281m.; and long-term care, $3,184m.

CULTURE

Broadcasting. Broadcasting stations in 2000 included 50 television stations and 334 radio stations.

Press. There were (2000) 78 daily and 263 weekly newspapers.

Festivals. The leading festivals are the Festival of Fountains, Longwood; Gettysburg Civil War Heritage Days, Gettysburg; Bethlehem Musikfest, Bethlehem; and the Philadelphia Flower Show.

Theatre and Opera. Pennsylvania has an Opera Company of Philadelphia and the Pittsburgh Ballet Theatre.

Museums and Galleries. The main attractions are the Philadelphia Museum of Art; Andy Warhol Museum, Pittsburgh; and the Carnegie Museums of Art and Natural History, Pittsburgh.

FURTHER READING

Statistical information: Pennsylvania State Data Center, 777 West Harrisburg Pike, Middletown 17057. Publishes *Pennsylvania Statistical Abstract.*

Downey, D. B. and Bremer, F. (eds.) *Guide to the History of Pennsylvania.* London, 1994

RHODE ISLAND

KEY HISTORICAL EVENTS

The earliest white settlement was founded by Roger Williams, an English Puritan who was expelled from Massachusetts because of his dissident religious views and his insistence on the land-rights of the Indians. At Providence he bought land from the Narragansetts and founded a colony there in 1636. A charter was granted in 1663. The colony was governed according to policies of toleration, which attracted Jewish and nonconformist settlers; later there was French Canadian settlement also.

Shipping and fishing developed strongly, especially at Newport and Providence; these two cities were twin capitals until 1900, when the capital was fixed at Providence.

Significant actions took place in Rhode Island during the War of Independence. In 1790 the state accepted the federal constitution and was admitted to the Union.

Early farming development was most successful in dairying and poultry. Early industrialization was mainly in textiles, beginning in the 1790s, and flourishing on abundant water power. Textiles dominated until the industry began to decline after the First World War. British, Irish, Polish, Italian and Portuguese workers settled in the state, working in the mills or in the shipbuilding, shipping, fishing and naval ports. The crowding of a new population into cities led to the abolition of the property qualification for the franchise in 1888.

TERRITORY AND POPULATION

Rhode Island is bounded north and east by Massachusetts, south by the Atlantic and west by Connecticut. Land area, 1,045 sq. miles (2,707 sq. km). Census population, 1 April 2000, 1,048,319, an increase of 4·5% since 1990. July 2002 estimate, 1,069,725.

Population of five census years was:

	White	Black	Indian	Asiatic	Total	Per sq. mile
1910	532,492	9,529	284	305	542,610	508·5
1930	677,026	9,913	318	240	687,497	649·3
			All others			
1980	896,692	27,584	22,878		947,154	903·0
1990	917,375	38,861	4,071	18,325	1,003,164	960·3
2000	891,191	46,908	5,121	24,232	1,048,319	1003·2

Of the total population in 2000, 554,684 were female, 800,497 were 18 years old or older and 953,146 were urban (90·92%). In 2000 the Hispanic population was 90,820, up from 45,752 in 1990 (an increase of 98·5%).

The chief cities and their population (census, 2000) are Providence, 173,618; Warwick, 85,808; Cranston, 79,269; Pawtucket, 72,958; East Providence, 48,688.

SOCIAL STATISTICS

Births, 1999, were 12,628 (12·7 per 1,000 population); deaths, 9,769 (9·9); (1996) infant mortality rate, 5·2 (per 1,000 live births). Marriages (1997), were 8,100; divorces, 3,200.

CLIMATE
Providence, Jan. 28°F (–2·2°C), July 72°F (22·2°C). Annual rainfall 43" (1,079 mm). Rhode Island belongs to the New England climate zone (*see* UNITED STATES: Climate).

CONSTITUTION AND GOVERNMENT
The present constitution dates from 1843; it has had 42 amendments. The General Assembly consists of a Senate of 50 members and a House of Representatives of 100 members, both elected for two years. The Governor and Lieut.-Governor are now elected for four years. Every citizen, 18 years of age, who has resided in the state for 30 days, and is duly registered, is qualified to vote.

For the 108th Congress, which convened in Jan. 2003, Rhode Island sends two members to the House of Representatives. It is represented in the Senate by Jack Reed (D. 1997–2009) and Lincoln Chafee (R. 1999–2007).

The capital is Providence. The state has five counties but no county governments. There are 39 municipalities, each having its own form of local government.

RECENT ELECTIONS
In the 2000 presidential election Gore polled 249,508 votes; Bush, 130,555; Nader, 25,052.

CURRENT ADMINISTRATION
Governor: Don Carcieri (R.), 2003–07 (salary: $105,194).
  Lieut.-Gov: Charles Fogerty (D.), 2003–07 ($88,594).
  Secretary of State: Matt Brown (D), 2003–07 ($88,594).

Government Website: http://www.ri.gov

ECONOMY
Per capita income (2000) was $29,158.

Budget. In 1999 total state revenue was $5,478m. Total expenditure was $4,378m. (education, $1,078m.; public welfare, $1,061m.; health and hospitals, $238m.; highways, $232m.; police protection, $32m.). Outstanding debt, in 1999, $5,464m.

Performance. Gross State Product in 2000 was $36,453m.

ENERGY AND NATURAL RESOURCES
Water. The total area covered by water is approximately 186 sq. miles.

Minerals. The small non-fuel mineral output—mostly stone, sand and gravel—was valued (1998) at $28m.

Agriculture. In 2000 there were 700 farms with an area of some 60,000 acres. The average size of a farm was 86 acres. In 1998 the average value of land and buildings per acre was $8,200—land per acre in Rhode Island was the second most valuable in the USA, after New Jersey. Farm income 1996: from crops, $72m.; livestock and products, $11m.

Fisheries. In 1998 the catch was 133·7m. lb (mainly lobster and quahang) valued at $72·1m.

INDUSTRY
Manufacturing is the chief source of income and the largest employer. Principal industries are jewellery and silverware, electrical machinery, electronics, plastics, metal products, instruments, chemicals and boat building.

Labour. In 1999 total non-agricultural employment was 464,000. Employees by branch, 1999 (in 1,000): services, 159; wholesale and retail trade, 104; manufacturing, 75.

COMMUNICATIONS
Roads. In 2000 there were 6,053 miles of roads (1,333 miles rural) and 759,570 registered motor vehicles.

Rail. Amtrak's New York-Boston route runs through the state, serving Providence.

Civil Aviation. In 2000 there were six state-owned airports. Theodore Francis Green airport at Warwick, near Providence, is served by 15 airlines, and handled 5·1m. passengers in 2000 and 37m. lb of freight in 1995. There were 2,397,825 passenger enplanements statewide in 1999.

Shipping. Waterborne freight through the port of Providence (1988) totalled 10·6m. tons.

SOCIAL INSTITUTIONS

Justice. In June 2000 there were 3,186 federal and state prisoners. The death penalty was abolished in 1852, except that it is mandatory in the case of murder committed by a prisoner serving a life sentence.

Religion. Chief religious bodies are Roman Catholic, Protestant Episcopal (baptized persons), Jewish, Baptist, Congregational and Methodist.

Education. In 1996 there were 149,802 pupils in public elementary and secondary schools. There were 219 public elementary schools with 85,691 pupils; about 24,941 pupils were enrolled in private and parochial schools. The 38 public senior and vocational high schools had 64,111 pupils. State and local government expenditure for schools in 1991 totalled $1,212·7m. The total expenditure per pupil in 1995 was $6,634.

There are 11 institutions of higher learning (three public and eight private). The state maintains Rhode IslandCollege, at Providence, with over 350 faculty members, and 8,900 students (2,594 part-time, 1,816 graduates), and the University of Rhode Island, at South Kingstown, with over 650 faculty members and 13,707 students (2,198 part-time, 3,176 graduates). Brown University, at Providence, founded in 1764, is now non-sectarian; in 1996 it had over 500 faculty members and 7,458 students (1,786 part-time or graduate). Providence College, at Providence, founded in 1917 by the Order of Preachers (Dominican), had (1996) 300 faculty members and 5,520 students (1,911 part-time or graduate). The largest of the other colleges are Bryant College, at Smithfield, with over 200 faculty members and 3,310 students (1,100 part-time or graduate), and the Rhode Island School of Design, in Providence, with over 250 faculty members and 1,830 students (170 graduates) in 1996.

Health. In 1995 there were 11 community hospitals with 2,700 beds.

Welfare. In 1995, 190,000 people were receiving benefit totalling $1,478m. including 140,000 retired workers and dependants and 25,000 disabled workers and dependants.

CULTURE

Broadcasting. There are 24 radio stations and 5 television stations; there are 8 cable television companies.

FURTHER READING
Statistical information: Rhode Island Economic Development Corporation, 1 West Exchange Street, Providence, RI 02903. Publishes *Rhode Island Basic Economic Statistics.*
Rhode Island Manual. Prepared by the Secretary of State. Providence
Wright, M. I. and Sullivan, R. J., *Rhode Island Atlas.* Rhode Island Pubs., 1983

State Library: Rhode Island State Library, State House, Providence 02908.

SOUTH CAROLINA

KEY HISTORICAL EVENTS
Originally the territory of Yamasee Indians, the area attracted French and Spanish explorers in the 16th century. There were attempts at settlement on the coast, none of which lasted. Charles I of England made a land grant in 1629, but the first permanent white settlement began at Charles Town in 1670, moving to Charleston in 1680. This was a proprietorial colony including North Carolina until 1712; both passed to the Crown in 1729.

The coastlands developed as plantations worked by slave labour. In the hills there were small farming settlements and many trading posts, dealing with Indian suppliers.

After active campaigns during the War of Independence, South Carolina became one of the original states of the Union in 1788.

In 1793 the cotton gin was invented, enabling the speedy mechanical separation of seed and fibre. This made it possible to grow huge areas of cotton and meet the rapidly growing needs of new textile industries. Plantation farming spread widely, and South Carolina became hostile to the anti-slavery campaign which was strong in northern states. The state first attempted to secede from the Union in 1847, but was not supported by other southern states until 1860, when secession led to civil war.

At that time the population was about 703,000, of whom 413,000 were black. During the reconstruction periods there was some political power for black citizens, but control was back in white hands by 1876. The constitution was amended in 1895 to disenfranchise most black voters, and they remained with hardly any voice in government until the Civil Rights movement of the 1960s. Columbia became the capital in 1786.

TERRITORY AND POPULATION

South Carolina is bounded in the north by North Carolina, east and southeast by the Atlantic, southwest and west by Georgia. Land area, 30,109 sq. miles (77,982 sq. km). Census population, 1 April 2000, 4,012,012, an increase of 15·1% since 1990. July 2002 estimate, 4,107,183.

The population in five census years was:

	White	Black	Indian	Asiatic	Total	Per sq. mile
1910	679,161	835,843	331	65	1,515,400	49·7
1930	944,049	793,681	959	76	1,738,765	56·8
				All others		
1980	2,150,507	948,623		22,703	3,121,833	100·3
1990	2,406,974	1,039,884		39,845	3,486,703	115·8
2000	2,695,560	1,185,216		131,236	4,012,012	133·2

Of the total population in 2000, 2,063,083 were female, 3,002,371 were 18 years old or older and 2,427,124 were urban. In 2000 the Hispanic population of South Carolina was 95,076, up from 30,551 in 1990 (an increase of 211·2%).

Population estimate of large towns in 1999: Columbia (capital), 111,821; Charleston, 88,596; North Charleston, 81,989; Greenville, 56,873; Rock Hill, 48,474; Mount Pleasant, 44,785.

SOCIAL STATISTICS

Births, 1999, were 53,894 (13·9 per 1,000 population); deaths, 34,966 (9·0); (1997) marriages, 42,100 (11·7); divorces and annulments, 15,200 (4·1); (1997) infant deaths, 494 (9·5 per 1,000 live births).

CLIMATE

Columbia, Jan. 44·7°F (7°C), Aug. 80·2°F (26·9°C). Annual rainfall 49·12" (1,247·6 mm). South Carolina belongs to the Atlantic Coast climate zone (see UNITED STATES: Climate).

CONSTITUTION AND GOVERNMENT

The present constitution dates from 1895, when it went into force without ratification by the electorate. The General Assembly consists of a Senate of 46 members, elected for four years, and a House of Representatives of 124 members, elected for two years. It meets annually. The Governor and Lieut.-Governor are elected for four years.

For the 108th Congress, which convened in Jan. 2003, South Carolina sends six members to the House of Representatives. It is represented in the Senate by Ernest Hollings (D. 1966–2005) and Lindsey Graham (R. 2003–09).

The capital is Columbia. There are 46 counties.

RECENT ELECTIONS

In the 2000 presidential election Bush polled 786,892 votes; Gore, 566,037; Nader, 20,279.

CURRENT ADMINISTRATION

Governor: Mark Sanford (R.), 2003–07 (salary: $106,078).
  Lieut.-Governor: R. André Bauer (R.), 2003–07 ($44,737).
  Secretary of State: Mark Hammond (R.), 2003–07 ($92,007).

Government Website: http://www.myscgov.com

ECONOMY

Per capita income (2000) was $23,952.

Budget. In 1999 total state revenue was $14,566m. Total expenditure was $14,483m. (education, $4,424m.; public welfare, $3,126m.; health and hospitals, $1,379m.; highways, $962m.; police protection, $185m.). Outstanding debt, in 1999, $5,082m.

Performance. Gross State Product was $113,377m. in 2000.

ENERGY AND NATURAL RESOURCES

Water. The total area covered by water is approximately 1,078 sq. miles.

Minerals. Gold is found, though non-metallic minerals are of chief importance: value of non-fuel mineral output in 1998 was $589m., chiefly from cement (Portland), stone and gold. Production of kaolin, vermiculite and scrap mica is also important.

Agriculture. In 2000 there were 24,000 farms covering a farm area of 4·7m. acres. The average farm was of 196 acres. The average value of farmland and buildings per acre was $1,363 in 1996.

  Gross farm income in 1997, $1,940·2m. for livestock and products. Chief crops are tobacco, soybeans, wheat, cotton, peanuts and corn. Production, 1997: cotton, 410,000 bales; peanuts, 32·5m. lb (1996); soybeans, 13·4m. bu.; tobacco, 126·3m. lb; corn, 32m. bu.; wheat, 15m. bu. Livestock on farms, Jan. 1997: 520,000 all cattle, 300,000 swine (Dec. 1996).

Forestry. The forest industry is important; total forest land (1999), 12·7m. acres. National forests amounted to 609,000 acres in 1993.

INDUSTRY

Major sectors are business service (26·8%), textiles (23·9%), health service (22·6%), chemicals (10·2%) and apparel (8·6%). Tourism is also important.

Labour. In 1999 total non-agricultural employment was 1,833,000. Employees by branch, 1999 (in 1,000): services, 447; wholesale and retail trade, 441; manufacturing, 345; government, 315.

COMMUNICATIONS

Roads. In 2000 there were 64,920 miles of roads and 3,094,729 registered motor vehicles. The death rate in traffic accidents stood at 31·9 per 100,000 registered motor vehicles.

Rail. In 1994 the length of railway in the state was 2,306·76 miles.

Civil Aviation. In 1998 there were 1,450,844 general aviation aircraft operations in South Carolina, 116,542 taxi and commuter aircraft operations, 98,635 air carrier aircraft operations and 89,012 military aircraft operations. There were 2,177,793 passenger enplanements statewide in 1999.

Shipping. The state has three deep-water ports.

SOCIAL INSTITUTIONS

Justice. In June 2000 there were 22,154 federal and state prisoners. The minimum age for the death penalty is 16. There were three executions in 2002.

Education. In 1995–96 there were 648,677 pupils and 46,073 teachers in public elementary and secondary schools. In 1996–97 the average teaching salary was $32,830.

For higher education the state operates the University of South Carolina (USC), founded at Columbia in 1801, with (autumn 1998), 25,250 enrolled students; USC Aiken, with 3,179 students; USC Spartanburg, with 3,767 students; USC 2-year regional campuses, with 4,484 students; Clemson University, founded in 1889, with 16,685 students; the Citadel, at Charleston, with 4,015 students; Winthrop University, Rock Hill, with 5,591 students; Medical University of S. Carolina, at Charleston, with 2,353 students; S. Carolina State University, at Orangeburg, with 4,795 students; and Francis Marion University, at Florence, with 3,947 students; the College of Charleston has 11,552 students; and Lander University, Greenwood, 2,600. There are 16 technical institutions (60,343).

There are also 387 private kindergartens, elementary and high schools with total enrolment (1996–97) of 49,534 pupils, and 23 private and denominational colleges and 4 junior colleges with (autumn 1998) enrolments of 29,316 and 1,357 students respectively.

Health. In 1996 the state had 464 non-federal health facilities with 35,714 beds licensed by the South Carolina Department of Health and Environmental Control. There were 7,537 physicians and 27,770 registered nurses in 1998.

Welfare. In 1995 there were 363,362 recipients of social security benefits. The annual payment in benefits was $2,968·7m. and the average monthly benefit was $658.

CULTURE

Press. In 1997 there were 15 daily and 14 Sunday newspapers in circulation.

FURTHER READING

Statistical information: Budget and Control Board, R. C. Dennis Bldg., Columbia 29201. Publishes South Carolina Statistical Abstract.
South Carolina Legislative Manual. Columbia. Annual
Edgar, W. B., South Carolina in the Modern Age. Univ. of South Carolina Press, 1992
Graham, C. B. and Moore, W. V., South Carolina Politics and Government. Univ. of Nebraska Press, 1995

State Library: South Carolina State Library, Columbia.

SOUTH DAKOTA

KEY HISTORICAL EVENTS

The area was part of the hunting grounds of nomadic Dakota (Sioux) Indians. French explorers visited the site of Fort Pierre in 1742–43, and claimed the area for France. In 1763 the claim fell and, together with French claims to all land west of the Mississippi, passed to Spain. Spain held the Dakotas until defeated by France in the Napoleonic Wars, when France regained the area and sold it to the USA as part of the Louisiana Purchase in 1803.

Fur-traders were active, but there was no settlement until Fort Randall was founded on the Missouri river in 1856. In 1861 North and South Dakota were organized as the Dakota Territory, and the Homestead Act of 1862 stimulated settlement, mainly in the southeast until there was a gold-rush in the Black Hills of the west in 1875–76. Colonization developed as farming communities in the east, miners and ranchers in the west. Livestock farming predominated, attracting European settlers from Scandinavia, Germany and Russia.

In 1889 the North and South were separated and admitted to the Union as states. The capital of South Dakota is Pierre, founded as a railhead in 1880, chosen as a temporary capital and confirmed as permanent capital in 1904. It faces Fort Pierre, the former centre of the fur trade, across the Missouri river. During the 20th century there have been important schemes to exploit the Missouri for power and irrigation.

TERRITORY AND POPULATION

South Dakota is bounded in the north by North Dakota, east by Minnesota, southeast by the Big Sioux River (forming the boundary with Iowa), south by Nebraska (with the Missouri River forming part of the boundary) and west by Wyoming and Montana. Land area, 75,885 sq. miles (196,541 sq. km). Area administered by the Bureau of Indian Affairs, 1985, covered 5m. acres (10% of the state), of which 2·6m. acres were held by tribes. The federal government, 1994, owned 2,698,000 acres.

Census population, 1 April 2000, 754,844, an increase of 8·5% since 1990. July 2002 estimate, 761,063.

Population in five federal censuses was:

	White	Black	American Indian	Asiatic	Total	Per sq. mile
1910	563,771	817	19,137	163	583,888	7·6
1930	669,453	646	21,833	101	692,849	9·0
				All others		
1980	638,955	2,144		49,079	690,178	9·0
				Asian/ other		
1990	637,515	3,258	50,575	4,656	696,004	9·2
2000	669,404	4,685	62,283	18,472	754,844	9·9

Of the total population in 2000, 380,286 were female, 552,195 were 18 years old or older and 391,427 were urban. In 2000 the Hispanic population was 10,903, up from 5,252 in 1990 (an increase of 107·6%).

Population of the chief cities (census of 2000) was: Sioux Falls, 123,975; Rapid City, 59,607; Aberdeen, 24,658; Watertown, 20,237; Brookings, 18,507; Mitchell, 14,558; Pierre, 13,876; Yankton, 13,528; Huron, 11,893; Vermillion, 9,765; Spearfish, 8,606; Madison, 6,540; Sturgis, 6,442.

SOCIAL STATISTICS
In 1998: births, 10,300 (14·8 per 1,000 population); deaths, 6,850 (9·8); infant deaths, 92 (8·9 per 1,000 live births); marriages, 6,700 (9·6 per 1,000 population); divorces, 2,600 (3·7).

CLIMATE
Rapid City, Jan. 25°F (−3·9°C), July 73°F (22·8°C). Annual rainfall 19" (474 mm). Sioux Falls, Jan. 14°F (−10°C), July 73°F (22·8°C). Annual rainfall 25" (625 mm). South Dakota belongs to the High Plains climate zone (see UNITED STATES: Climate).

CONSTITUTION AND GOVERNMENT
Voters are all citizens 18 years of age or older. The people reserve the right of the initiative and referendum. The Senate has 35 members, and the House of Representatives 70 members, all elected for two years; the Governor and Lieut.-Governor are elected for four years.

For the 108th Congress, which convened in Jan. 2003, South Dakota sends one member to the House of Representatives. It is represented in the Senate by Thomas Daschle (D. 1987–2005) and Tim Johnson (D. 1997–2009).

The capital is Pierre. The state is divided into 66 organized counties.

RECENT ELECTIONS
In the 2000 presidential election Bush polled 190,700 votes; Gore, 118,804; Buchanan, 3,322.

CURRENT ADMINISTRATION
Governor: Michael Rounds (R.), 2003–07 (salary: $98,250).
Lieut.-Governor: Dennis Daugaard (R.), 2003–07 ($71,321).
Secretary of State: Chris Nelson (R.), 2003–07 ($66,757).

Government Website: http://www.state.sd.us

ECONOMY
Per capita income (2000) was $25,993.

Budget. In 1999 total state revenue was $2,886m. Total expenditure was $2,272m. (education, $663m.; public welfare, $434m.; highways, $310m.; health and hospitals, $106m.; police protection, $18m.). Outstanding debt, in 1999, $2,105m.

Performance. Gross State Product in 2000 was $23,192m.

ENERGY AND NATURAL RESOURCES

Water. The total area covered by water is approximately 1,225 sq. miles.

Minerals. In 1998 there was a major decline in South Dakota's production of gold, although it remained the leading mineral commodity in the state. Production dropped 26% to 389,875 oz, yielding a gross value of $115m. (a drop of 34% in gross value on the previous year). In 1998, 503 companies had active mining licences in South Dakota, with 52 permits covering the mining of non-metallic minerals. Sand and gravel was the major non-metallic industrial mineral commodity with 15·1m. tonnes produced. Other major minerals were Sioux quartzite (2·8m. tonnes); pegmatite (17,100) and granite (265,000).

Agriculture. In 2000 there were 32,500 farms, average size 1,354 acres. Average value of farmland and buildings per acre in 1998 was $350. Farm income, 1998: crops, $2,146m.; livestock and products, $1,667m.

South Dakota is a major producer of rye (1·4m. bu. in 1998), sunflower oil (1,507·2m. lb) and oats (20·1m. bu.). The other important crops are winter wheat (61m. bu.), barley (4·6m. bu.), spring wheat (59·2m. bu.), durum wheat (624,000 bu.), sorghum for grain (9·9m. bu.), corn for grain (429·5m. bu.) and soybeans (133·4m bu.). Total planted area of principal crops, including hay harvested, was 16·55m. acres with 16·11m. being harvested.

The farm livestock on 1 Jan. 1998 included 3·6m. cattle, 0·4m. sheep and lambs, and 1·25m. hogs (1 Dec 1997). In 1996, 23,280,000 lb of honey were produced.

Forestry. National forest area, 1999, 2,012,000 acres.

INDUSTRY

In 1996, 1,044 manufacturing establishments had 47,750 employees. Industrial machinery and computer equipment had 160 establishments with 13,559 workers; food and kindred products had 115 establishments with 8,590 workers. Construction had 2,925 companies with 14,646 workers. Also significant were transportation, communications and public utilities (1,811 establishments employing 15,576 workers). Mining establishments numbered 83 and employed 2,270 workers.

Labour. In 1999 total non-agricultural employment was 373,000, including 101,000 in services, 91,000 in wholesale and retail trade, and 72,000 in government. The state unemployment rate in 1999 was 2·9%.

COMMUNICATIONS

Roads. In 2000 there were 83,471 miles of roads; there were 789,783 registered cars and trucks in 2000, and 29,205 motorcycles. In 1996 there were 6,979 snowmobiles.

Rail. In 1997 there were 1,855 miles of track of which 811 miles were state-owned.

Civil Aviation. In 1996 there were 73 general aviation airports, of which nine were 'air carrier' airports with regular passenger services utilizing turbo-prop or jet aircraft. There were 514,603 passenger enplanements statewide in 1999.

SOCIAL INSTITUTIONS

Justice. On 31 Jan. 1999 there were 2,425 adults in state prisons, 429 juveniles adjudicated to the Department of Corrections and 1,141 adults on parole supervision. The minimum age for the death penalty is 16. It was last used in 1947.

Religion. The chief religious bodies are: Lutherans, Roman Catholics, Methodist, United Church of Christ, Presbyterian, Baptist and Episcopal.

Education. Elementary and secondary education are free from 6 to 21 years of age. Between the ages of 6 and 16, attendance is compulsory. In 1998–99 there were 131,117 PK-12 public school students at 763 public schools; and, in 1997, 16,792 PK-12 non-public school students at 140 schools.

Teachers' salaries (1998–99) averaged $28,386. Total expenditure on public schools was $646,930,000 ($4,934 per pupil).

Higher education (autumn 1998): the School of Mines at Rapid City, established 1885, had 2,265 students; South Dakota State University at Brookings, 8,635; the

University of South Dakota, founded at Vermillion in 1882, 7,317; Northern State University, Aberdeen, 2,873; Black Hills State University at Spearfish, 3,639; Dakota State University at Madison, 1,831. There were 9,287 students at 14 private colleges.

Health. In 1997 there were 60 licensed hospitals (3,478 beds).

Welfare. In fiscal year 1996, under Supplemental Security Income, there were on average 10,731 disabled persons receiving $42,965,196 in benefits; 131 blind persons received $505,556 and 2,462 aged persons received $4,378,038. Aid to Families with Dependent Children distributed $21,582,846 to 6,056 cases (average) involving 16,461 recipients (average) and 11,971 children (average).

FURTHER READING
Statistical information: State Data Center, Univ. of South Dakota, Vermillion 57069.
Governor's Budget Report. South Dakota Bureau of Finance and Management. Annual
South Dakota Historical Collections. 1902–82
South Dakota Legislative Manual. Secretary of State, Pierre, S.D. Biennial
Berg, F. M., *South Dakota: Land of Shining Gold.* Hettinger, 1982

State Library: South Dakota State Library, 800 Governor's Drive, Pierre, S.D. 57501–2294.

TENNESSEE

KEY HISTORICAL EVENTS
Bordered on the west by the Mississippi, Tennessee was part of an area inhabited by Cherokee. French, Spanish and British explorers penetrated the area up the Mississippi and traded with the Cherokee in the late 16th and 17th centuries. French claims were abandoned in 1763, colonists from the British colonies of Virginia and Carolina then began to cross the Appalachians westwards, but there was no organized Territory until after the War of Independence. In 1784 there was a short-lived, independent state called Franklin. In 1790 the South West Territory (including Tennessee) was formed, and Tennessee entered the Union as a state in 1796.

The state was active in the war against Britain in 1812. After the American victory, colonization increased and pressure for land mounted. The Cherokee were forcibly removed during the 1830s and taken to Oklahoma, a journey on which many died.

Tennessee was a slave state and seceded from the Union in 1861, although eastern Tennessee was against secession. There were important battles at Shiloh, Chattanooga, Stone River and Nashville. In 1866 Tennessee was re-admitted to the Union.

Nashville, the capital since 1843, Memphis, Knoxville, and Chattanooga all developed as river towns, Memphis becoming an important cotton and timber port. Growth was greatly accelerated by the creation of the Tennessee Valley Authority in the 1930s, producing power for a manufacturing economy. Industry increased to the extent that, by 1970, the normal southern pattern of emigration and population loss had been reversed.

TERRITORY AND POPULATION
Tennessee is bounded north by Kentucky and Virginia, east by North Carolina, south by Georgia, Alabama and Mississippi and west by the Mississippi River (forming the boundary with Arkansas and Missouri). Land area, 41,217 sq. miles (106,752 sq. km). Census population, 1 April 2000, 5,689,283, an increase of 16·7% since 1990. July 2002 estimate, 5,797,289.

Population in five census years was:

	White	Black	Indian	Asiatic	Total	Per sq. mile
1910	1,711,432	473,088	216	53	2,184,789	52·4
1930	2,138,644	477,646	161	105	2,616,556	62·4
			All others			
1980	3,835,452	725,942	29,726		4,591,120	111·6
1990	4,048,068	778,035	51,082		4,877,185	115·7
2000	4,563,310	932,809	193,164		5,689,283	138·0

Of the total population in 2000, 2,919,008 were female, 4,290,762 were 18 years old or older and 3,620,018 were urban. In 2000 the Hispanic population of Tennessee was 123,828, up from 32,741 in 1990 (an increase of 278·2%).

The cities, with population (2000) are Memphis, 650,100; Nashville (capital), 569,891; Knoxville, 167,535; Chattanooga, 150,425; Clarksville, 94,879; Johnson City, 55,542; Murfreesboro, 53,996; Jackson, 50,406; Kingsport, 41,335; Oak Ridge, 27,742. Metropolitan Statistical Areas, 2000: Nashville, 1,231,311; Memphis, 1,135,614; Knoxville, 687,249; Johnson City–Kingsport–Bristol, 480,091; Chattanooga, 465,161; Clarksville–Hopkinsville, 207,033; Jackson, 107,377.

SOCIAL STATISTICS

Statistics 1999: births, 77,486 (14·1 per 1,000 population); deaths, 53,545 (9·8); (1996) infant deaths, 626 (8·5 per 1,000 live births); (1997) marriages, 76,500; divorces, 29,500.

CLIMATE

Memphis, Jan. 41°F (5°C), July 82°F (27·8°C). Annual rainfall 49" (1,221 mm). Nashville, Jan. 39°F (3·9°C), July 79°F (26·1°C). Annual rainfall 48" (1,196 mm). Tennessee belongs to the Appalachian Mountains climate zone (see UNITED STATES: Climate).

CONSTITUTION AND GOVERNMENT

The state has operated under three constitutions, the last of which was adopted in 1870 and has been since amended 22 times (first in 1953). Voters at an election may authorize the calling of a convention limited to altering or abolishing one or more specified sections of the constitution. The General Assembly consists of a Senate of 33 members and a House of Representatives of 99 members, senators elected for four years and representatives for two years. Qualified as electors are all citizens (usual residential and age (18) qualifications).

For the 108th Congress, which convened in Jan. 2003, Tennessee sends nine members to the House of Representatives. It is represented in the Senate by Bill Frist (R. 1995–2007) and Lamar Alexander (R. 2003–09).

The capital is Nashville. The state is divided into 95 counties.

RECENT ELECTIONS

In the 2000 presidential election Bush polled 1,061,949 votes; Gore, 981,720; Nader, 19,781.

CURRENT ADMINISTRATION

Governor: Phil Bredesen (D.), 2003–07 (salary: $85,000, but not presently taken).
  Lieut.-Governor: John S. Wilder (D.), 2001–05 ($49,500).
  Secretary of State: Riley Darnell (D), 2003–07 ($124,200).

Government Website: http://www.tennesseeanytime.org

ECONOMY

Per capita personal income (2000) was $25,878.

Budget. In 1999 total state revenue was $16,904m. Total expenditure was $15,890m. (education, $5,224m.; public welfare, $4,602m.; highways, $1,411m.; health and hospitals, $1,146m.; police protection, $114m.). Outstanding debt, in 1999, $3,321m.

Performance. Gross State Product in 2000 was $178,362m.

ENERGY AND NATURAL RESOURCES

Water. The total area covered by water is approximately 926 sq. miles.

Minerals. Domestic non-fuel mineral production was worth $709m. in 1998.

Agriculture. In 2000, 90,000 farms covered 11·7m. acres. The average farm was of 130 acres, valued (land and buildings) at $225,088 in 1996.

Farm income (1996) from crops was $1,374m.; from livestock, $998m. Main crops were cotton, tobacco and soybeans.

On 1 Jan. 1997 the domestic animals included 115,000 milch cows, 2·4m. all cattle, 13,500 sheep, 0·4m. swine.

Forestry. Forests occupy 13,258,000 acres. The forest industry and industries dependent on it employ about 0·04m. workers. Wood products are valued at over $500m. per year. National forest system land (1999) 634,000 acres.

INDUSTRY
The manufacturing industries include iron and steel working, but the most important products are chemicals, including synthetic fibres and allied products, electrical equipment and food. In 1995 value added by manufactures was $43,126m.

Labour. In 1999 total non-agricultural employment was 2,674,000. Employees by branch, 1999 (in 1,000): services, 716; wholesale and retail trade, 628; manufacturing, 509; government, 391.

COMMUNICATIONS
Roads. In 2000 there were 87,418 miles of roads (69,679 miles rural) and 4,819,799 registered motor vehicles.

Rail. The state had (1995) 3,065 miles of track. There is a tramway in Memphis.

Civil Aviation. The state is served by 23 major and regional airlines. In 1997 Tennessee had 83 public airports; there were also 71 heliports and 2 military air bases. There were 9,660,156 passenger enplanements statewide in 1999. Memphis International handled 2,453,000 tonnes of freight in 2000—the most of any airport in the world.

SOCIAL INSTITUTIONS
Justice. The death penalty is authorized for over 18 year olds; there has been only one execution (in 2000) since 1976. In June 2000 there were 22,566 prison inmates.

Religion. In 1990 there were 1,086,680 Southern Baptists, 320,724 United Methodists, 199,698 Black Baptists, 168,933 members of the Church of Christ, 137,203 Catholics and followers of various other religions.

Education. School attendance has been compulsory since 1925 and the employment of children under 16 years of age in workshops, factories or mines is illegal.

In 1995–96 there were 1,562 public schools with a net enrolment of 948,217 pupils; 49,627 teachers earned an average salary of $33,646. Total expenditure for operating schools was $4,266m. Tennessee has 49 accredited colleges and universities, 16 two-year colleges and 27 vocational schools. The universities include the University of Tennessee, Knoxville (founded 1794), with 25,337 students in 1996–97; Vanderbilt University, Nashville (1873) with 10,253; Tennessee State University (1912) with 8,643; the University of Tennessee at Chattanooga (1886) with 8,296; University of Memphis (1912) with 19,271; and Fisk University (1866) with 812.

Health. In 1994 the state had 127 hospitals with 26,018 beds. State facilities for the mentally retarded had 1,290 resident patients and mental hospitals had 1,003 in 1996.

Welfare. In 1995 Tennessee paid $6,672m. to retired workers and their survivors and to disabled workers. Total beneficiaries: 587,940 retired; 172,110 survivors; 166,060 disabled. 1·5m. people received $2,772m. in Medicaid. Supplemental Security Income ($648m.) was paid to 179,676. In 1994, 294,733 people received aid to dependent children ($212m.).

CULTURE
Tourism. In 1994, 29·9m. out-of-state tourists spent $5,900m.

FURTHER READING
Statistical information: Center for Business and Economic Research, Univ. of Tennessee, Knoxville 37996. Publishes *Tennessee Statistical Abstract*
Tennessee Blue Book. Secretary of State, Nashville
Dykeman, W., *Tennessee.* Rev. ed., New York, 1984

State Library: State Library and Archives, Nashville.

TEXAS

KEY HISTORICAL EVENTS

A number of Indian tribes occupied the area before French and Spanish explorers arrived in the 16th century. In 1685 La Salle established a colony at Fort St Louis, but Texas was confirmed as Spanish in 1713. Spanish missions increased during the 18th century with San Antonio (1718) as their headquarters.

In 1820 a Virginian colonist, Moses Austin, obtained permission to begin a settlement in Texas. In 1821 the Spanish empire in the Americas came to an end, and Texas, together with Coahuila, formed a state of the newly independent Mexico. The Mexicans agreed to the Austin venture, and settlers of British and American descent came in.

The settlers became discontented with Mexican government and declared their independence in 1836. Warfare, including the siege of the Alamo fort, ended with the foundation of the independent Republic of Texas, which lasted until 1845. During this period the Texas Rangers were organized as a policing force and border patrol. Texas was annexed to the Union in Dec. 1845, as the Federal government feared its vulnerability to Mexican occupation. This led to war between Mexico and the USA from 1845 to 1848. In 1861 Texas left the Union and joined the southern states in the Civil War, being re-admitted in 1869. Ranching and cotton-growing were the main activities before the discovery of oil in 1901.

TERRITORY AND POPULATION

Texas is bounded north by Oklahoma, northeast by Arkansas, east by Louisiana, southeast by the Gulf of Mexico, south by Mexico and west by New Mexico. Land area, 261,797 sq. miles (678,051 sq. km). Census population, 1 April 2000, 20,851,820, an increase of 22·8% since 1990. July 2002 estimate, 21,779,893.

Population for five census years was:

	White	Black	American Indian	Asian	Total	Per sq. mile
1910	3,204,848	690,049	702	943	3,896,542	14·8
1930	4,967,172	854,964	1,001	1,578	5,824,715	22·1
			All others			
1980	11,197,663	1,710,250	1,320,470		14,228,383	54·2
				Asian/ other		
1990	12,774,762	2,021,632	65,877	2,124,239	16,986,510	64·9
2000	14,799,505	2,404,566	118,362	3,529,387	20,851,820	79·7

Of the total population in 2000, 10,498,910 were female, 14,965,061 were 18 years old or older, and 17,204,281 were urban. In 2000 the Hispanic population was 6,669,666, up from 4,339,905 in 1990 (an increase of 53·7%). This numerical increase is the second largest in the Hispanic population of any state in the USA, after California. Only New Mexico and California have a greater percentage of Hispanics in the state population.

The largest cities, with census population in 2000, are:

Houston	1,700,672	Garland	187,439	Waco	107,191
Dallas	1,036,309	Irving	166,523	Grand Prairie	103,913
San Antonio	991,861	Amarillo	163,569	Abilene	100,661
El Paso	554,496	Plano	153,624	Wichita Falls	98,356
Austin (capital)	501,637	Laredo	140,688	Midland	95,003
Fort Worth	459,085	Pasadena	127,843	Odessa	92,257
Arlington	277,939	Beaumont	118,289	McAllen	91,184
Corpus Christi	266,958	Brownsville	117,326	Carrollton	90,934
Lubbock	193,194	Mesquite	108,960	San Angelo	87,980

Metropolitan statistical areas, 2000: Dallas–Fort Worth, 5,221,801; Houston–Galveston–Brazoria, 4,669,571; San Antonio, 1,592,383; Austin–San Marcos, 1,249,763.

SOCIAL STATISTICS

Statistics 1999: births, 342,911 (17·1 per 1,000 population); deaths, 143,294 (7·2); (1997) infant deaths, 2,079 (6·3 per 1,000 live births); marriages, 183,000 (9·4 per 1,000 population); divorces, 95,185 (5·0).

CLIMATE
Dallas, Jan. 45°F (7·2°C), July 84°F (28·9°C). Annual rainfall 38" (945 mm). El Paso, Jan. 44°F (6·7°C), July 81°F (27·2°C). Annual rainfall 9" (221 mm). Galveston, Jan. 54°F (12·2°C), July 84°F (28·9°C). Annual rainfall 46" (1,159 mm). Houston, Jan. 52°F (11·1°C), July 83°F (28·3°C). Annual rainfall 48" (1,200 mm). Texas belongs to the Central Plains climate zone (*see* UNITED STATES: Climate).

CONSTITUTION AND GOVERNMENT
The present constitution dates from 1876; it has been amended 364 times since. The Legislature consists of a Senate of 31 members elected for four years (half their number retire every two years), and a House of Representatives of 150 members elected for two years. It meets in odd-numbered years in Jan. The Governor and Lieut.-Governor are elected for four years.

For the 108th Congress, which convened in Jan. 2003, Texas sends 32 members to the House of Representatives. It is represented in the Senate by Kay Hutchison (R. 1993–2007) and John Cornyn (R. 2002–09).

The capital is Austin. The state has 254 counties.

RECENT ELECTIONS
In the 2000 presidential election Bush polled 3,799,639 votes; Gore, 2,433,746; Nader, 137,994.

CURRENT ADMINISTRATION
Governor: Rick Perry (R.), 2003–07 (salary: $115,345).
  Lieut.-Governor: David Dewhurst (R.) ($7,200 plus legislature session salary).
  Secretary of State: Gwyn Shea (R.), appointed Jan. 2002 ($117,516).

Government Website: http://www.state.tx.us

ECONOMY
Per capita personal income (2000) was $27,722.

Budget. In 1999 total state revenue was $71,649m. Total expenditure was $54,761m. (education, $20,566m.; public welfare, $11,776m.; health and hospitals, $4,088m.; highways, $3,999m.; police protection, $325m.). Outstanding debt, in 1999, $14,736m.

Performance. In 2000 Gross State Product was $742,274m., the second highest after California.

ENERGY AND NATURAL RESOURCES
Oil and Gas. Texas is the leading producer in the USA of both oil and natural gas. In 2001 it produced 23% of the country's oil and 26% of its natural gas. Production, 2001: crude petroleum, 424m. bbls. (1996 value, $11,035m.); natural gas, 5,072bn. cu. ft (1996 value, $14,768m.). Natural gasoline, butane and propane gases are also produced.

Water. The total area covered by water is approximately 5,363 sq. miles.

Minerals. Minerals include helium, crude gypsum, granite and sandstone, salt and cement. Total value of domestic non-fuel mineral products in 1998 was $1,920m.

Agriculture. Texas is one of the most important agricultural states. In 2000 it had 226,000 farms covering 130m. acres; average farm was of 575 acres. Both the number of farms and the total area covered are the highest in the USA. In 1995 land and buildings were valued at $550 per acre. Large-scale commercial farms, highly mechanized, dominate in Texas; farms of 1,000 acres or more in number far exceed that of any other state, but small-scale farming persists. Soil erosion is serious in some parts. For some 97,297,000 acres drastic curative treatment has been indicated, and for 51,164,000 acres, preventive treatment.

Production: corn, barley, beans, cotton, hay, oats, peanuts, rye, sorghum, soybeans, sunflowers, wheat, oranges, grapefruit, peaches, sweet potatoes. Farm income, 1996, from crops was $5,295m.; from livestock, $7,758m.

The state has an important livestock industry, leading in the number of all cattle (15·1m.) and sheep (1·7m.), both figures for 1995; it also had 0·4m. milch cows and 0·58m. swine in 1994.

Forestry. There were (1993) 22,032,000 acres of forested land.

INDUSTRY

Labour. Texas has a labour code (adopted 1993) which includes laws concerning protection of labourers, employer-employee relations, employment services and unemployment, and workers' compensation.

In 1999 total non-agricultural employment was 9,155,000. Employees by branch, 1999 (in 1,000): services, 2,597; wholesale and retail trade, 2,179; manufacturing, 1,540; government, 1,086. The unemployment rate in 1999 was 4·6%.

COMMUNICATIONS

Roads. In 2000 there were 301,034 miles of roads and 14,070,096 registered motor vehicles.

Civil Aviation. In 1993 there were 307 public and 1,308 private airports. There were 61,758,337 passenger enplanements statewide in 1999.

Shipping. The port of Houston, connected by the Houston Ship Channel (50 miles long) with the Gulf of Mexico, is a large cotton market. Total cargo handled by all ports, 1990, 335,311,608 short tons.

SOCIAL INSTITUTIONS

Justice. In June 2000 there were 163,503 prison inmates. Between 1976 and 2002 Texas was responsible for 289 of the USA's 820 executions (three times more than any other state). In 2002, 33 people were executed in Texas; in 2000, 40 people had been executed, the highest number in a year in any state since the authorities began keeping records in 1930. The minimum age for the death penalty is 17.

Religion. Religious bodies represented include Roman Catholics, Baptists, Methodists, Churches of Christ, Lutherans, Presbyterians and Episcopalians.

Education. School attendance is compulsory from 6 to 18 years of age.

In 1995–96 public elementary and secondary schools had over 3,740,260 students; there were 240,371 teachers whose salaries averaged $31,400. State and Federal support for public schools, 1994–95, $11,256m.

In 1994 there were 138 higher education institutions (35 public, 38 independent colleges and universities, 50 public community college districts and 15 others). The largest institutions with student enrolment, 1995–96, were:

Founded	Institutions	Control	Students
1845	Baylor University, Waco	Baptist	12,202
1852	St Mary's University, San Antonio	R.C.	4,202
1869	Trinity University, San Antonio	Presb.	2,482
1873	Texas Christian University, Fort Worth	Christian	7,050
1876	Texas A. and M. Univ., College Station	State	38,636
1878	Prairie View Agr. and Mech. Coll., Prairie View	State	5,999
1879	Sam Houston State University	State	12,439
1883	University of Texas System (every campus)	State	136,597
1890	University of North Texas, Denton	State	25,122
1891	Hardin-Simmons University, Abilene	Baptist	2,373
1889	East Texas State University, Commerce	State	7,629
1899	South West Texas State University, San Marcos	State	20,929
1901	Texas Woman's University, Denton	State	9,827
1906	Abilene Christian University, Abilene	Church of Christ	4,436
1911	Southern Methodist University, Dallas	Methodist	8,986
1912	Rice University	Independent	4,099
1923	Lamar University, Beaumont	State	8,419
1923	Stephen F. Austin State University	State	11,781
1923	Texas Technical University, Lubbock	State	24,185
1925	Texas A&M University, Kingsville	State	6,061
1927	University of Houston, Houston	State	30,358
1947	Texas Southern University, Houston	State	9,458

Health. In 1995 the state had 498 hospitals (70,881 beds) listed by the American Hospital Association. In the fiscal year 1989 the average daily census of patients was: state hospitals, 3,629; state schools, 7,265; and state centres, 331.

Welfare. Aid is from state and federal sources. Number of Social Security beneficiaries in 1996 was 2,498,000, who received an average of $722 (for retired workers), $697 (for disabled workers) and $687 (for widows/widowers) per month.

FURTHER READING
Texas Almanac. Dallas. Biennial
Kingston, M., *Texas Almanac's Political History of Texas.* Austin, 1992
Kraemer, R. and Newell, C., *Essentials of Texas Politics.* 5th ed. Austin, 1992
Marten, James, *Texas.* [Bibliography] ABC-Clio, Oxford and Santa Barbara (CA), 1992

Legislative Reference Library: Box 12488, Capitol Station, Austin, Texas 78711-2488.

UTAH

KEY HISTORICAL EVENTS
Spanish Franciscan missionaries explored the area in 1776, finding Shoshoni Indians. Spain laid claim to Utah and designated it part of Spanish Mexico. As such it passed into the hands of the Mexican Republic when Mexico rebelled against Spain and gained independence in 1821.

In 1848, at the conclusion of war between the USA and Mexico, the USA received Utah along with other southwestern territory. Settlers had already arrived in 1847 when the Mormons (the Church of Jesus Christ of Latter-day Saints) arrived, having been driven on by local hostility in Ohio, Missouri and Illinois. Led by Brigham Young, they entered the Great Salt Valley and colonized it. In 1849 they applied for statehood but were refused. In 1850 Utah and Nevada were joined as one Territory. The Mormon community continued to ask for statehood but this was only granted in 1896, after they had renounced polygamy and disbanded their People's Party.

Mining, especially of copper, and livestock farming were the base of the economy. Settlement had to adapt to desert conditions, and the main centres of population were in the narrow belt between the Wasatch Mountains and the Great Salt Lake. Salt Lake City, the capital, was founded in 1847 and laid out according to Joseph Smith's plan for the city of Zion. It was the centre of the Mormons' provisional 'State of Deseret' and Territorial capital from 1856 until 1896, except briefly in 1858 when federal forces occupied it during conflict between territorial and Union governments.

TERRITORY AND POPULATION
Utah is bounded north by Idaho and Wyoming, east by Colorado, south by Arizona and west by Nevada. Land area, 82,144 sq. miles (212,752 sq. km). The Bureau of Indian Affairs in 1990 administered 2,317,604 acres, 2,284,766 acres of which were allotted to Indian tribes.

Census population, 1 April 2000, 2,233,169, an increase of 29·6% since 1990. July 2002 estimate, 2,316,256.

Population at five federal censuses was:

	White	Black	American Indian	Asiatic	Total	Per sq. mile
1910	366,583	1,144	3,123	2,501	373,851	4·5
1930	499,967	1,108	2,869	3,903	507,847	6·2
1980	1,382,550	9,225	19,256	15,076	1,461,037	17·7
1990	1,615,845	11,576	24,283	25,696	1,722,850	21·0
2000	1,992,975	17,657	29,684	37,108	2,233,169	27·2

Of the total population in 2000, 1,119,031 were male, 1,514,471 were 18 years old or older and 1,970,344 were urban. In 2000 the Hispanic population was 201,559, up from 84,597 in 1990 (an increase of 138·3%).

The largest cities are Salt Lake City, with a population (census, 2000) of 181,743; West Valley City, 108,896; Provo, 105,166; Sandy City, 88,418; Orem, 84,324; Ogden, 77,226.

SOCIAL STATISTICS
Births in 1999 were 45,261 (21·3 per 1,000 population); deaths, 11,915 (5·6); (1996) infant mortality rate, 6·0 (per 1,000 live births). Marriages (1997), 20,500; divorces, 9,200. Fertility rate, 1998, 2·7 births per woman (the highest of any American state).

CLIMATE
Salt Lake City, Jan. 29°F (−1·7°C), July 77°F (25°C). Annual rainfall 16" (401 mm). Utah belongs to the Mountain States climate region (see UNITED STATES: Climate).

CONSTITUTION AND GOVERNMENT
Utah adopted its present constitution in 1896 (now with 61 amendments). The Legislature consists of a Senate (in part renewed every two years) of 29 members, elected for four years, and of a House of Representatives of 75 members elected for two years. It sits annually in Jan. The Governor is elected for four years. The constitution provides for the initiative and referendum.

For the 108th Congress, which convened in Jan. 2003, Utah sends three members to the House of Representatives. It is represented in the Senate by Orrin Hatch (R. 1977–2007) and Robert Bennett (R. 1993–2005).

The capital is Salt Lake City. There are 29 counties in the state.

RECENT ELECTIONS
In the 2000 presidential election Bush polled 515,096 votes; Gore, 203,053; Nader, 35,850.

CURRENT ADMINISTRATION
Governor: Mike Leavitt (R.), 2001–05 (salary: $101,600).
   Lieut.-Governor: Olene S. Walker (R.), 2001–05 ($78,200).

Government Website: http://www.utah.gov

ECONOMY
Per capita income (2000) was $23,364.

Budget. In 1999 total state revenue was $8,742m. Total expenditure was $7,810m. (education, $3,395m.; public welfare, $1,303m.; highways, $603m.; health and hospitals, $588m.; police protection, $69m.). Outstanding debt, in 1999, $3,781m.

Performance. Gross State Product in 2000 was $68,549m.

ENERGY AND NATURAL RESOURCES
Water. The total area covered by water is approximately 2,736 sq. miles.

Minerals. The principal minerals are: copper, gold, magnesium, petroleum, lead, silver and zinc. The state also has natural gas, clays, tungsten, molybdenum, uranium and phosphate rock. The value of domestic non-fuel mineral production in 1998 was $1,300m.

Agriculture. In 2000 Utah had some 15,500 farms covering 11·6m. acres. Of the total surface area, 9% is severely eroded and only 9·4% is free from erosion; the balance is moderately eroded. In 1985 about 2m. acres were crop land, about 300,000 acres pasture and about 1m. acres had irrigation. In 2000 the average farm was of 748 acres and the average value per acre in 1995 was $606.

Farm income, 1996, from crops, $227m. and from livestock, $646m. The principal crops are: barley, wheat (spring and winter), oats, potatoes, hay (alfalfa, sweet clover and lespedeza) and maize. Livestock, 1990: cattle, 855,000; pigs, 34,000; sheep, 600,000; poultry, 3·8m.

Forestry. National forest area, 1999, 8,111,000 acres.

INDUSTRY
Leading manufactures by value added are primary metals, ordinances and transport, food, fabricated metals and machinery, and petroleum products.

Labour. Utah's total non-agricultural employment in 1999 was 1,050,000. Employees by branch, 1999 (in 1,000): services, 293; wholesale and retail trade, 249; government, 179; manufacturing, 133.

COMMUNICATIONS

Roads. In 2000 there were 41,855 miles of roads (34,332 miles rural) and 1,627,606 registered motor vehicles.

Rail. On 1 July 1974 the state had 1,734 miles of railways.

Civil Aviation. There is an international airport at Salt Lake City. There were 8,709,510 passenger enplanements statewide in 1999.

SOCIAL INSTITUTIONS

Justice. In June 2000 there were 5,450 prison inmates. The minimum age for the death penalty is 16; the last execution took place in 1999.

Religion. Latter-day Saints (Mormons) numbered 1,577,000 in 1998. World membership was 9,025,000. The President of the Mormon Church is Gordon B. Hinckley (born 1910). The Roman Catholic church and most Protestant denominations are represented.

Education. School attendance is compulsory for children from 6 to 18 years of age. There are 40 school districts. Teachers' salaries, 1998–99, averaged $36,030. There were 475,974 pupils and 24,514 teachers in public elementary and secondary schools in the same year. In 1999 education expenditure by state and local government was $2,432·3m.

In autumn 1999 there were 153,884 enrolled in colleges and universities. The University of Utah (1850) (25,788 students in 1999) is in Salt Lake City; the Utah State University (1890) (20,865) is in Logan; Weber State University, Ogden (15,444); Southern Utah University, Cedar City (6,025); The Mormon Church maintains the Brigham Young University at Provo (1875) with 29,217 students. Other colleges include: Westminster College, Salt Lake City (2,250); College of Eastern Utah, Price (2,688); Snow College, Ephraim (4,081); Dixie State College, St George (6,191); Utah Valley State College, Orem (20,062); Salt Lake Community College, Salt Lake City (21,273).

Health. In 1995 the state had 42 community hospital facilities (4,200 beds).

Welfare. In 1996, 228,000 beneficiaries received $1,782m. annual benefit payments.

FURTHER READING
Statistical information: Bureau of Economic and Business Research, Univ. of Utah, 401 Kendall D. Garff Bldg., Salt Lake City 84112. Publishes *Statistical Abstract of Utah.*
Utah Foundation. *Statistical Review of Government in Utah.* Salt Lake City, 1991

VERMONT

KEY HISTORICAL EVENTS
The original Indian hunting grounds of the Green Mountains and lakes was explored by the Frenchman Samuel de Champlain in 1609 who reached Lake Champlain on the northwest border. The first attempt at permanent settlement was also French, on Isle la Motte in 1666. In 1763 the British gained the area from the French by the Treaty of Paris. The Treaty, which also brought peace with the Indian allies of the French, opened the way for settlement, but in a mountain state transport was slow and difficult. Montpelier, the state capital from 1805, was chartered as a township site in 1781 to command the main pass through the Green Mountains.

During the War of Independence Vermont declared itself an independent state, to avoid being taken over by New Hampshire and New York. In 1791 it became the 14th state of the Union.

Most early settlers were New Englanders of British and Protestant descent. After 1812 a granite-quarrying industry grew around the town of Barre, attracting immigrant workers from Italy and Scandinavia. French Canadians also settled in Winooski. When textile and engineering industries developed in the 19th century these brought more European workers.

Vermont saw the only Civil War action north of Pennsylvania, when a Confederate raiding party attacked from Canada in 1864.

During the 20th century the textile and engineering industries have declined but paper and lumber industries flourish. Settlement is still mainly rural or in small towns, and farming is pastoral.

TERRITORY AND POPULATION

Vermont is bounded in the north by Canada, east by New Hampshire, south by Massachusetts and west by New York. Land area, 9,250 sq. miles (23,957 sq. km). Census population, 1 April 2000, 608,827, an increase of 8·2% since 1990. July 2002 estimate, 616,592.

Population at five census years was:

	White	Black	Indian	Asiatic	Total	Per sq. mile
1910	354,298	1,621	26	11	355,956	39·0
1930	358,966	568	36	41	359,611	38·8
1980	506,736	1,135	984	1,355	511,456	55·1
1990	555,088	1,951	1,696	3,215[1]	562,758	60·8
2000	589,208	3,063	2,420	5,358[1]	608,827	65·8

[1]Includes Pacific Islander.

Of the total population in 2000, 310,490 were female, 461,304 were 18 years old or older and 376,379 (61·8%) were rural (67·8% in 1990). Vermont still has the highest rural population percentage of any state in the USA. In 2000 the Hispanic population was 5,504, the lowest total of any state. However, this figure represents a rise of 50·3% compared to the 1990 census figure of 3,661. The largest cities are Burlington, with a population (2000 census) of 38,889; Essex, 18,626; Rutland, 17,292; Colchester, 16,986.

SOCIAL STATISTICS

Births, 2000, were 6,501 (10·9 per 1000 population); deaths, 5,127; infant deaths, 39; marriages, 6,271; civil unions, 1704; divorces, 2,526.

CLIMATE

Burlington, Jan. 17°F (−8·3°C), July 70°F (21·1°C). Annual rainfall 33" (820 mm). Vermont belongs to the New England climate zone (see UNITED STATES: Climate).

CONSTITUTION AND GOVERNMENT

The constitution was adopted in 1793 and has since been amended. Amendments are proposed by two-thirds vote of the Senate every four years, and must be accepted by two sessions of the legislature; they are then submitted to popular vote. The state Legislature, consisting of a Senate of 30 members and a House of Representatives of 150 members (both elected for two years), meets in Jan. every year. The Governor and Lieut.-Governor are elected for two years. Electors are all citizens who possess certain residential qualifications and have taken the freeman's oath set forth in the constitution.

For the 108th Congress, which convened in Jan. 2003, Vermont sends one member to the House of Representatives. It is represented in the Senate by Patrick Leahy (D. 1975–2005) and Jim Jeffords (R. 1989–2001, ind. 2001–07).

The capital is Montpelier (8,035 in 2000). There are 14 counties and 251 cities, towns and other administrative divisions.

RECENT ELECTIONS

In the 2000 presidential election Gore polled 149,022 votes; Bush, 119,775; Nader, 20,374.

CURRENT ADMINISTRATION

Governor: James Douglas (R.), 2003–05 (salary: $125,572).
  Lieut.-Governor: Brian Dubie (R.), 2003–05 ($53,303).
  Secretary of State: Deborah Markowitz (D.), 2003–05 ($79,624).

Government Website: http://vermont.gov

ECONOMY

Per capita income (2001) was $27,992.

Budget. In 2001 total state revenue was $2,777m. Total expenditure was $2,687m. (human services, $910m.; education, $895m.; transportation, $294m.; protection, $142m.). Debt outstanding in 1999 was $1,479m.

Performance. Gross State Product was $18,411m. in 2000.

Banking and Finance. In 2000 there were 26 banking institutions domiciled in Vermont, and seven out-of-state banks operating.

ENERGY AND NATURAL RESOURCES

Water. The total area covered by water is approximately 366 sq. miles. There are 46 utility-owned hydro-sites and 35 independently owned sites providing about 10% of Vermont's energy.

Minerals. Stone, chiefly granite, marble and slate, is the leading mineral produced in Vermont, contributing about 60% of the total value of mineral products. Other products include asbestos, talc, sand and gravel. Value of domestic non-fuel mineral products, 1998, approximately $96m.

Agriculture. Agriculture is the most important industry. In 2001 the state had 6,600 farms covering 1·3m. acres; the average farm was of 200 acres and the average value per acre of land and buildings was $1,750. In 2001 farm income from livestock and products, $556m.; from crops, $67m. The dairy farms produced about 2·6bn. lb of milk in 2001. The chief agricultural crops are hay, apples and silage. In 2001 Vermont had 295,000 cattle and calves and 2,500 hogs and pigs.

Forestry. The state is 80% forest, with 17% in public ownership. National forests area (2000), 350,000 acres. State-owned forests, parks, fish and game areas, 295,000 acres; municipally owned, 38,500 acres. In 2000 the harvest was 246,819m. bd ft and 356,601 cords of pulpwood and boltwood.

INDUSTRY

Labour. In 2000 service industries employed 88,212; trade, 68,306; manufacturing, 48,884; government, 47,342; construction, 14,879.

COMMUNICATIONS

Roads. The state had 14,000 miles of roads in 2000, including 12,732 miles of gravel, graded and drained, or unimproved roads. Motor vehicle registrations, 2001, 799,891 (all vehicles).

Rail. There were, in 2001, 747 miles of railway, 391 of which are state owned.

Civil Aviation. There were 17 airports in 2000, of which ten were state operated, two municipally owned and five private. Some are only open in summer. There were 520,171 passenger enplanements statewide in 2001.

Telecommunications. In 1999, 10 telephone companies provided 442,041 access lines. Total net income, $40,135,898.

SOCIAL INSTITUTIONS

Justice. Prisons and centres had on average, in 2002, 1,883 inmates (including those incarcerated in Virginia for cost-cutting reasons). The death penalty was officially abolished in 1987 but effectively in 1964.

Religion. The principal denominations are Roman Catholic, United Church of Christ, United Methodist, Protestant Episcopal, Baptist and Unitarian–Universalist.

Education. School attendance during the full school term is compulsory for children from 7 to 16 years of age, unless they have completed the 10th grade or undergo approved home instruction. In 2001–02 the public elementary and secondary schools had 100,867 pupils and 8,740 teachers. Average teacher's salary was $39,166. State and local governments expenditure on public schools, $933m.

In 2001–02 there were approximately 31,913 students in higher education. The University of Vermont (1791), in Burlington, had 8,903 students; Norwich

University (1834, founded as the American Literary, Scientific and Military Academy in 1819), had 2,512; St Michael's College (1904), 2,630; there are four other state colleges and 15 other private schools of higher education.

Health. In 2001 the state had 17 hospitals and health centres.

Welfare. Old-age assistance (Supplemental Security Income) was granted in 2001 to 3,654 Vermonters, drawing an average of $545 per month.

CULTURE

Broadcasting. In 2000 there were 56 radio stations, 7 television stations and 27 cable TV systems.

Press. There were 9 dailies and 42 weekly newspapers in 2001.

Festivals. Of particular importance are the Marlboro Music Festival (Marlboro), the Vermont Maple Festival (St Albans) and the Mozart Music Festival (Burlington).

Libraries. In 2002 there were an estimated 573 libraries.

FURTHER READING

Statistical information: Office of Policy Research and Coordination, Montpelier 05602
Legislative Directory. Secretary of State, Montpelier. Biennial
Vermont Annual Financial Report. Auditor of Accounts, Montpelier. Annual
Vermont Atlas and Gazetteer, Rev. ed., Freeport, 1983
Vermont Year-Book, formerly *Walton's Register.* Chester. Annual

State Library: Vermont Dept. of Libraries, Montpelier.

VIRGINIA

KEY HISTORICAL EVENTS

In 1607 a British colony was founded at Jamestown, on a peninsula in the James River, to grow tobacco. The area was marshy and unhealthy but the colony survived and in 1619 introduced a form of representative government. The tobacco plantations expanded and African slaves were imported. Jamestown was later abandoned, but tobacco-growing continued and spread through the eastern part of the territory.

In 1624 control of the colony passed from the Virginia Company of London to the Crown. Growth was rapid during the 17th and 18th centuries. The movement for American independence was strong in Virginia; George Washington and Thomas Jefferson were both Virginians, and crucial battles of the War of Independence were fought there.

When the Union was formed, Virginia became one of the original states, but with reservations regarding the constitution because of its attachment to slave-owning. In 1831 there was a slave rebellion. The tobacco plantations began to decline, and plantation owners turned to the breeding of slaves. While the eastern plantation lands seceded from the Union in 1861, the small farmers and miners of the western hills refused to secede and remained in the Union as West Virginia.

Richmond, the capital, became the capital of the Confederacy. Much of the Civil War's decisive conflict took place in Virginia, with considerable damage to the economy. After the war the position of the black population was little improved. Blacks remained without political or civil rights until the 1960s.

TERRITORY AND POPULATION

Virginia is bounded northwest by West Virginia, northeast by Maryland, east by the Atlantic, south by North Carolina and Tennessee and west by Kentucky. Land area, 39,594 sq. miles (102,548 sq. km). Census population, 1 April 2000, 7,078,515, an increase of 14·4% since 1990. July 2002 estimate, 7,293,542.

Population for five federal census years was:

	White	Black	Indian	Asian/Other	Total	Per sq. mile
1910	1,389,809	671,096	539	168	2,061,612	51·2
1930	1,770,441	650,165	779	466	2,421,851	60·7
			All others			
1980	4,230,000	1,008,311		108,517	5,346,818	134·7
1990	4,791,739	1,162,994	15,282	217,343	6,187,358	155·9
2000	5,120,110	1,390,293	21,172	546,940	7,078,515	178·8

Of the total population in 2000, 3,606,620 were female, 5,340,253 were 18 years old or older and 5,169,955 were urban. In 2000 the Hispanic population was 329,540, up from 160,288 in 1990 (an increase of 105·6%).

The population (2000 census) of the principal cities was: Virginia Beach, 425,257; Norfolk, 234,403; Chesapeake, 199,184; Richmond, 197,790; Newport News, 180,150; Hampton, 146,437; Alexandria, 128,283; Portsmouth, 100,565.

SOCIAL STATISTICS
In 1999 there were 94,189 births (13·7 per 1,000 population); 53,825 deaths (7·8); (1995) 712 infant deaths under 1 year (7·8 per 1,000 live births); 1997, 67,400 marriages (10·0 per 1,000 population) and 31,300 divorces (4·6).

CLIMATE
Average temperatures in Jan. are 41°F in the Tidewater coastal area and 32°F in the Blue Ridge mountains; July averages, 78°F and 68°F respectively. Precipitation averages 36" in the Shenandoah valley and 44" in the south. Snowfall is 5–10" in the Tidewater and 25–30" in the western mountains. Norfolk, Jan. 41°F (5°C), July 79°F (26·1°C). Annual rainfall 46" (1,145 mm). Virginia belongs to the Atlantic Coast climate zone (*see* UNITED STATES: Climate).

CONSTITUTION AND GOVERNMENT
The present constitution dates from 1971. The General Assembly consists of a Senate of 40 members, elected for four years, and a House of Delegates of 100 members, elected for two years. It sits annually in Jan. The Governor and Lieut.-Governor are elected for four years.

For the 108th Congress, which convened in Jan. 2003, Virginia sends 11 members to the House of Representatives. It is represented in the Senate by John Warner (R. 1979–2009) and George Allen (R. 2001–07).

The state capital is Richmond; the state contains 95 counties and 40 independent cities.

RECENT ELECTIONS
In the 2000 presidential election Bush polled 1,437,490 votes; Gore, 1,217,290; Nader, 59,398.

CURRENT ADMINISTRATION
Governor: Mark R. Warner (D.), 2002–06 (salary: $124,855).
Lieut.-Governor: Timothy M. Kaine (D.), 2002–06 ($36,321).
Secretary of the Commonwealth: Anita Rimler (D.), 2002–06 ($128,479).

Government Website: http://www.vipnet.org

ECONOMY
Per capita personal income (2000) was $31,065.

Budget. In 1999 total state revenue was $26,138m. Total expenditure was $22,739m. (education, $8,239m.; public welfare, $3,633m.; highways, $2,395m.; health and hospitals, $1,940m.; police protection, $380m.). Outstanding debt, in 1999, $11,877m.

Performance. Gross State Product in 2000 was $261,355m.

ENERGY AND NATURAL RESOURCES
Water. The total area covered by water is approximately 2,729 sq. miles.

Minerals. Coal is the most important mineral, with output (1994) of 37,129,301 short tons. Lead and zinc ores, stone, sand and gravel, lime and titanium ore are also produced. Total domestic non-fuel mineral output was valued at $679m. in 1998.

Agriculture. In 2000 there were 49,000 farms with an area of 8·7m. acres; the average farm had 178 acres, and the average value per acre was $1,771 in 1995. Farm income, 1995, from field crops, $556·2m.; from greenhouse, nursery and tree produce, $138·63m.; from vegetables, $87·8m.; from fruits, $52·19m.; and from livestock and livestock products, $1,393·18m. The chief crops are tobacco, soybeans, peanuts, winter wheat, maize, tomatoes, apples, potatoes and sweet potatoes. Livestock, 1 Jan. 1996: cattle and calves, 1·8m.; milch cows, 128,000; sheep and lambs, 84,000; 1 Dec. 1995: hogs and pigs, 0·38m.; 1995: turkeys, 23·5m.; broilers, 260·1m.

Forestry. Forests covered 16,026,874 acres in 1992 (63·1% of the total land area).

INDUSTRY

The manufacture of cigars and cigarettes, of rayon and allied products, and the building of ships lead in value of products.

Labour. In 1999 Virginia's total non-agricultural employment was 3,408,000. Employees by branch, 1999 (in 1,000): services, 1,084; wholesale and retail trade, 749; government, 610; manufacturing, 396. The unemployment rate in 1999 was 2·8%.

COMMUNICATIONS

Roads. In 2000 there were 70,391 miles of roads (51,455 miles rural) and 6,046,127 registered motor vehicles.

Rail. In 1992 there were 3,295 miles of Class I track including commuter services to Washington.

Civil Aviation. There are international airports at Norfolk, Dulles, Richmond and Newport News. There were 2,811,678 passenger enplanements statewide in 1999.

SOCIAL INSTITUTIONS

Justice. In June 2000 there were 29,890 prison inmates. The minimum age for the death penalty is 16. Between 1976 and 2002 there were 87 executions in Virginia, after Texas the most of any state. There were four executions in 2002.

Religion. The principal churches are the Baptist, Methodist, Protestant-Episcopal, Roman Catholic and Presbyterian.

Education. Elementary and secondary instruction is free, and for ages 6–17 attendance is compulsory.

In 1994–95 the 133 school districts had, in primary schools, 684,000 pupils and 43,000 teachers and in public high schools, 377,000 pupils and 28,000 teachers. Teachers' salaries averaged $32,700 (primary school) and $35,300 (high school). Total expenditure on education, 1994–95, was $6,435m.

In 1993–94 there were 87 higher education institutions (48 private) including:

Founded	Name and place of college	Staff 1994–95	Students 1994
1693	College of William and Mary, Williamsburg (State)	479	7,547
1749	Washington and Lee University, Lexington	166	1,990
1776	Hampden-Sydney College, Hampden-Sydney (Pres.)	84	970
1819	University of Virginia, Charlottesville (State)	987	21,421
1832	Randolph-Macon College, Ashland (Methodist)	79	1,093
1832	University of Richmond, Richmond (Baptist)	228	4,258
1838	Virginia Commonwealth University, Richmond	777	21,523
1839	Virginia Military Institute Lexington (State)	97	1,179
1865	Virginia Union University, Richmond	83	1,525
1868	Hampton University	303	5,769
1872	Virginia Polytechnic Institute and State University	1,466	25,842
1882	Virginia State University, Petersburg	168	4,007
1908	James Madison University, Harrisonburg	520	11,680
1910	Radford University (State)	394	9,105

Founded	Name and place of college	Staff 1994–95	Students 1994
1930	Old Dominion University, Norfolk	634	16,49
1956	George Mason University (State)	677	21,774

Health. In 1994 the state had 123 hospitals listed by the American Hospital Association.

Welfare. In 1993 there were 901,000 Social Security beneficiaries (average monthly grant $642); 118,000 Supplemental Security Income beneficiaries (average monthly grant $279); 779,000 Medicare beneficiaries (average monthly grant $259); 576,000 recipients of Medicaid; 195,000 recipients of aid to families with dependent children (average monthly payment per family $262); 11,399 persons receiving Black Lung benefits (average monthly payment $373), and 10,650 children enrolled in the Head Start programme. In 1994 there were 232,000 households (547,000 persons) participating in the federal Food Stamp programme and 601,000 students participating in the National School Lunch programme; a total of 210,116 persons received some form of state-sponsored public assistance.

Total annual payments to beneficiaries in 1996 were $7,372m.

CULTURE

Tourism. Domestic tourists spent about $9,076m. in 1993.

FURTHER READING
Statistical information: Cooper Center for Public Service, Univ. of Virginia, 918 Emmet St. N., Suite 300, Charlottesville 22903-4832. Publishes *Virginia Statistical Abstract.—Population Estimates of Virginia Cities and Counties.*
Rubin, L. D. Jr., *Virginia: a Bicentennial History.* Norris, 1977

State Library: Virginia State Library, Richmond 23219.

WASHINGTON

KEY HISTORICAL EVENTS
The strongest Indian tribes in the 18th century were Chinook, Nez Percé, Salish and Yakima. The area was designated by European colonizers as part of the Oregon Country. Between 1775 and 1800 it had been claimed by explorers for Spain, Britain and the USA; the dispute between the two latter nations was not settled until 1846.

The first small white settlements were Indian missions and fur-trading posts. In the 1840s American settlers began to push westwards along the Oregon Trail, making a speedy solution of the dispute with Britain necessary. When this was achieved the whole area was organized as the Oregon Territory in 1848, and Washington was made a separate Territory in 1853.

Apart from trapping and fishing, the important industry was logging, mainly to supply building timbers to the new settlements of California. After 1870 the westward extension of railways helped to stimulate settlement. Statehood was granted in 1889. The early population was composed mainly of Americans from neighbouring states to the east, and Canadians. Scandinavian immigrants followed. Seattle, the chief city, was laid out in 1853 as a saw-milling town and named after the Indian chief who had ceded the land and befriended the settlers. It grew as a port during the Alaskan and Yukon gold-rushes of the 1890s. The economy thrived on exploiting the Columbia River for hydro-electric power.

TERRITORY AND POPULATION
Washington is bounded north by Canada, east by Idaho, south by Oregon with the Columbia River forming most of the boundary, and west by the Pacific. Land area, 66,544 sq. miles (172,348 sq. km). Lands owned by the federal government, 1993, were 12·7m. acres or 29·8% of the total area. Census population, 1 April 2000, 5,894,121, an increase of 21·1% since 1990. July 2002 estimate, 6,068,996.

UNITED STATES OF AMERICA

Population in five federal census years was:

	White	Black	American Indian	Asian/Other	Total	Per sq. mile
1910	1,109,111	6,058	10,997	15,824	1,141,990	17·1
1930	1,521,661	6,840	11,253	23,642	1,563,396	23·3
1980	3,779,170	105,574	60,804	186,608	4,132,156	62·1
1990	4,308,937	149,801	81,483	326,471	4,866,692	73·1
2000	4,821,823	190,267	93,301	788,730	5,894,121	188·6

Of the total population in 2000, 2,959,821 were female, 4,380,278 were 18 years old or older and 4,831,106 were urban. In 2000 the Hispanic population was 441,509, up from 214,570 in 1990 (a rise of 105·8%).

There are 27 Indian reservations. Indian reservations in 1990 covered 2,718,516 acres, of which 2,250,731 acres were tribal lands.

Leading cities are Seattle, with a population in 2000 of 563,374; Spokane, 195,629; Tacoma, 193,556; Vancouver, 143,560; Bellevue, 109,569. Others: Everett, 91,488; Federal Way, 83,259; Kent, 79,524; Yakima, 71,845; Bellingham, 67,171; Lakewood, 58,211; Kennewick, 54,693; Shoreline, 53,025; Renton, 50,052. The Seattle–Tacoma–Bremerton metropolitan area had a 2000 census population of 3,554,760.

SOCIAL STATISTICS
Births, 1999, were 79,837 (13·9 per 1,000); deaths, 43,226 (7·5 per 1,000); infant mortality rate (1996), 6·0 (per 1,000 live births). Marriages, 1997, were 42,300 (7·5 per 1,000 population); divorces, 29,000 (5·2).

CLIMATE
Seattle, Jan. 40°F (4·4°C), July 63°F (17·2°C). Annual rainfall 34" (848 mm). Spokane, Jan. 27°F (−2·8°C), July 70°F (21·1°C). Annual rainfall 14" (350 mm). Washington belongs to the Pacific Coast climate zone (see UNITED STATES: Climate).

CONSTITUTION AND GOVERNMENT
The constitution, adopted in 1889, has had 63 amendments. The Legislature consists of a Senate of 49 members elected for four years, half their number retiring every two years, and a House of Representatives of 98 members, elected for two years. The Governor and Lieut.-Governor are elected for four years.

For the 108th Congress, which convened in Jan. 2003, Washington sends nine members to the House of Representatives. It is represented in the Senate by Patty Murray (D. 1993–2005) and Maria Cantwell (D. 2001–07).

The capital is Olympia. The state contains 39 counties.

RECENT ELECTIONS
In the 2000 presidential election Gore polled 1,247,652 votes; Bush, 1,108,864; Nader, 103,002.

CURRENT ADMINISTRATION
Governor: Gary Locke (D.), 2001–05 (salary: $142,286).
Lieut.-Governor: Brad Owen (D.), 2001–05 ($74,377).
Secretary of State: Sam Reed (R.), 2001–05 ($91,048).

Government Website: http://access.wa.gov

ECONOMY
Per capita personal income (2000) was $31,129.

Budget. In 1999 total state revenue was $28,737m. Total expenditure was $24,230m. (education, $8,572m.; public welfare, $4,572m.; health and hospitals, $1,753m.; highways, $1,584m.; police protection, $221m.). Outstanding debt, in 1999, $11,080m.

Performance. In 2000 Gross State Product was $219,937m.

ENERGY AND NATURAL RESOURCES

Water. The total area covered by water is approximately 4,055 sq. miles.

Minerals. Mining and quarrying are not as important as forestry, agriculture or manufacturing. Total value of non-fuel mineral production in 1998 was $583m.

Agriculture. Agriculture is constantly growing in value because of more intensive and diversified farming, and because of the 1m.-acre Columbia Basin Irrigation Project.

In 2000 there were 40,000 farms with an acreage of 15·7m.; the average farm was 393 acres. Average value of farmland and buildings per acre in 1996 was $1,117.

Apples, milk, wheat, potatoes, and cattle and calves are the top five commodities. On 1 Jan. 1997 livestock included 266,000 milch cows, 294,000 beef cows, and 50,000 sheep and lambs. Hogs and pigs as of 1 Dec. 1996 totalled 35,000 head.

Value of agricultural production in 1996 (in $1m.): field crops, 2,046·3; fruit, 1,263·7; vegetables, 299·5; livestock, poultry and their products, 1,464·8.

Forestry. Forests cover 21,856,000 acres, of which 9m. acres are national forest. In 1995 timber harvested was an estimated 4,393m. bd ft. Acres planted or seeded, 1993, 163,442, not including natural re-seeding. Production of wood residues, 1992, included 2,671,000 tons of pulp and board.

Fisheries. Salmon and shellfish are important; total fish catch, 1995, was worth an estimated $170,597,000.

INDUSTRY

Principal manufactures are aircraft, pulp and paper, lumber and plywood, aluminium, processed fruit and vegetables.

Labour. In 1999 total non-agricultural employment was 2,643,000. Employees by branch, 1999 (in 1,000): services, 736; wholesale and retail trade, 636; government, 473; manufacturing, 364.

COMMUNICATIONS

Roads. In 2000 there were 80,209 miles of roads and 5,115,866 registered motor vehicles.

Rail. In 1996 there were 3,090 route miles.

Civil Aviation. There are international airports at Seattle/Tacoma, Spokane and Boeing Field. There were 14,998,246 passenger enplanements statewide in 1999.

SOCIAL INSTITUTIONS

Justice. In June 2000 there were 14,704 prison inmates. The minimum age for the death penalty is 18. There was one execution in 2001 but none in 2002.

Religion. Religious faiths represented include the Roman Catholic, United Methodist, Lutheran, Presbyterian and Episcopalian. There were 223,000 Latter-day Saints (Mormons) in 1998.

Education. Education is given free to all children between the ages of 5 and 21 years, and is compulsory for children from 8 to 15 years of age. In Oct. 1997 there were 990,389 pupils in elementary and secondary schools. In Oct. 1995 there were 46,883 classroom teachers; average salary, $39,900.

The University of Washington, founded 1861, at Seattle, had, autumn 1997, 36,355 students; and Washington State University at Pullman, founded 1890, for science and agriculture, had 20,020 students. Eastern Washington University had 7,537; Central Washington University, 8,438; The Evergreen State College, 4,084; Western Washington University, 11,476. All counts are state-funded enrolment students. Community colleges had (1996) a total of 172,643 state-funded and excess enrolment students.

Health. In fiscal year 1997 the two state hospitals for mental illness, the one mental health facility and the child study and treatment centre had, together, a daily average of 1,278 patients.

In 1997 there were 93 accredited acute hospitals (11,484 beds) and 4 psychiatric hospitals (215 beds). In Sept. 1997 there were 16,790 doctors, 4,860 dentists, 58,120 registered nurses and 5,855 pharmacists.

Welfare. Old-age assistance is provided for persons 65 years of age or older without adequate resources (and not in need of continuing home care) who are residents of the state. In July 1997 the following assistance was provided: 916 blind persons received a monthly average of $362·07; 13,305 aged, $302·06; 80,251 disabled, $377·99. Aid was also given to 156,995 children in 88,266 families, averaging $376·90 per family monthly.

FURTHER READING
Statistical information: State Office of Financial Management, POB 43113, Olympia 98504-3113. Publishes *Washington State Data Book*
Dodds, G. B., *American North-West: a History of Oregon and Washington.* Arlington (Ill), 1986

WEST VIRGINIA

KEY HISTORICAL EVENTS
In 1861 the state of Virginia seceded from the Union over the issue of slave-owning. The 40 western counties of the state were composed of hilly country, settled by miners and small farmers who were not slave-owners, and these counties ratified an ordinance providing for the creation of a new state that same year. On 20 June 1863 West Virginia became the 35th state of the Union.

The capital, Charleston, was an 18th-century fortified post on the early westward migration routes across the Appalachians. In 1795 local brine wells were tapped and the city grew as a salt town. Coal, oil, natural gas and a variety of salt brines were all found in due course. Huntington, the next largest town, developed as a railway terminus serving the same industrial area, and also providing transport on the Ohio river. Wheeling, the original state capital, was a well established, cosmopolitan city when it hosted the statehood meetings in 1861, located on the major transportation routes of the Ohio River, Baltimore and Ohio Railroad and the National Road.

Three-quarters of the state is forest and settlement has been concentrated in the mineral-bearing Kanawha valley, along the Ohio river and in the industrial Monongahela valley of the north. More than half of the population is still classified as rural. The traditional small firms and small hill-mines, however, support few, and the majority of rural dwellers commute to industrial employment.

TERRITORY AND POPULATION
West Virginia is bounded in the north by Pennsylvania and Maryland, east and south by Virginia, southwest by the Big Sandy River (forming the boundary with Kentucky) and west by the Ohio River (forming the boundary with Ohio). Land area, 24,077 sq. miles (62,359 sq. km). Census population, 1 April 2000, 1,808,344, an increase of 0·8% since 1990. July 2002 estimate, 1,801,873.
Population in five federal census years was:

	White	Black	American Indian	Asiatic	Total	Per sq. mile
1910	1,156,817	64,173	36	93	1,221,119	50·8
1960	1,770,133	89,378	181	419	1,860,421	77·3
1980	1,874,751	65,051	1,610	5,194	1,949,644	80·3
1990	1,725,523	56,295	2,458	7,459	1,793,477	74·0
2000	1,718,777	57,232	3,606	9,834	1,808,344	75·1

Of the total population in 2000, 929,174 were female, 1,405,951 were 18 years old or older and 975,564 (53·9%) were rural (63·9% of the population in 1990). In 2000 the Hispanic population was 12,279, up from 8,489 in 1990 (an increase of 44·6%).

The 2000 census population of the principal cities was: Charleston, 53,421; Huntington, 51,475. Others: Parkersburg, 33,099; Wheeling, 31,419; Morgantown, 26,809; Weirton, 20,411; Fairmont, 19,097; Beckley, 17,254; Clarksburg, 16,743.

SOCIAL STATISTICS

Statistics 1999: births, 20,731 (11·5 per 1,000 population); deaths, 20,993 (11·6); infant deaths, 157 (7·6 per 1,000 live births); marriages, 13,705 (7·6 per 1,000 population); divorces, 9,309 (5·2).

CLIMATE

Charleston, Jan. 34°F (1·1°C), July 76°F (24·4°C). Annual rainfall 40" (1,010 mm). West Virginia belongs to the Appalachian Mountains climate zone (*see* UNITED STATES: Climate).

CONSTITUTION AND GOVERNMENT

The present constitution was adopted in 1872; it has had 70 amendments. The Legislature consists of the Senate of 34 members elected for a term of four years, one-half being elected biennially, and the House of Delegates of 100 members, elected biennially. The Governor is elected for four years and may serve one successive term.

For the 108th Congress, which convened in Jan. 2003, West Virginia sends three members to the House of Representatives. It is represented in the Senate by Robert Byrd (D. 1959–2007) and Jay Rockefeller (D. 1985–2009).

The state capital is Charleston. There are 55 counties.

RECENT ELECTIONS

In the 2000 presidential election Bush polled 336,475 votes; Gore, 295,497; Nader, 10,680.

CURRENT ADMINISTRATION

Governor: Bob Wise (D.), 2001–05 (salary: $90,000).
   Senate President-Lieut. Governor: Earl Ray Tomblin (D.), 2001–05.
   Secretary of State: Joe Manchin, III (D.), 2001–05 ($65,000).

Government Website: http://www.state.wv.us

ECONOMY

Estimated *per capita* personal income (2000) was $21,181.

Budget. Total revenues for the year ending 30 June 2000 were $6,478m.; general expenditures were $6,276m. Major areas of expenditure are (1999 figures): education, $2,413m.; public welfare, $1,581m.; highways, $761m.; health and hospitals, $266m. Outstanding debt in 1999, $3,521m.

Performance. Gross State Product in 2000 was $42,271m.

Banking and Finance. There were 56 state banks and 26 national banks with a total of $13,844m. in deposits in 2000. There were also eight federal savings and loans and federal savings banks; total deposits in 1997 were $887m.

ENERGY AND NATURAL RESOURCES

Oil and Gas. Petroleum output (2000), 1,267m. bbls.; natural gas production (2000), 233bn. cu. ft.

Water. The total area covered by water is approximately 145 sq. miles.

Minerals. 38% of the state is underlain with mineable coal; 169·3m. short tons of coal were produced in 2000. Salt, sand and gravel, sandstone and limestone are also produced. The total non-fuel mineral output in 2000 was 18·1m. tons.

Agriculture. In 2000 the state had 20,500 farms with an area of 3·6m. acres; average size of farm was 176 acres, valued at $1,060 per acre. Livestock farming predominates.

Cash income, 2000, from crops was $53·4m.; from livestock and products, $339·4m. Main crops harvested: hay (1·31m. tons); all corn (1·3m. bu.); tobacco (1·8m. lb). Area of main crops: hay, 0·61m. acres; corn, 55,000 acres. Apples (90m. lb) and peaches (19·0m. lb) are important fruit crops.

Livestock on farms, 2000, included 0·40m. cattle, of which 17,000 were milch cows; sheep, 35,000; hogs, 10,000; chickens, 1·86m. excluding broilers. Production included 91·3m broilers, 20·75m. doz. eggs; 4·1m turkeys.

Forestry. State forests, 2000, covered 79,036 acres; national forests, 1,032,000 acres; 75% of the state is woodland.

Fisheries. In 2000, nine state fish hatcheries and one federal fish hatchery sold 363,000 lb trout and stocked 815,000 lb of trout, in addition to 2·4m. fry, 507,162 fingerlings and 5,000 adults of other types of fish.

INDUSTRY

In Oct. 2001, 2,094 manufactures had 76,800 production workers. Leading manufactures are primary and fabricated metals, glass, chemicals, wood products, textiles and apparel, machinery, plastics, speciality chemicals, aerospace, electronics, medical and related technologies and industrial products recycling.

Labour. In Oct. 2001 non-agricultural employment was 741,500 of whom 162,800 were in trade, 142,000 in government and 234,300 in service industries. The state unemployment rate in 1999 was 6·6%.

INTERNATIONAL TRADE

Imports and Exports. The state's major export markets are the EU and Canada, with coal being a major export commodity. West Virginia staffs trade offices in Nagoya, Japan; Taipei, Taiwan; and Munich, Germany.

COMMUNICATIONS

Roads. In 2001 there were 37,370 miles of roads (34,610 miles rural) and 1,638,848 registered motor vehicles.

Rail. In 2001 the state had 2,659 miles of railway.

Civil Aviation. There were 37 public airports in 2001. There were 122,941 passenger enplanements statewide in 1999.

Shipping. There are some 420·5 miles of navigable rivers.

Postal Services. In 2001 there were 1,012 postal facilities.

SOCIAL INSTITUTIONS

Justice. The state court system consists of a Supreme Court, 31 circuit courts, and magistrate courts in each county. The Supreme Court of Appeals, exercising original and appellate jurisdiction, has five members elected by the people for 12-year terms. Each circuit court has from one to seven judges (as determined by the Legislature on the basis of population and case-load) chosen by the voters within each circuit for 8-year terms.

There are 11 penal and correctional institutions which had, in Dec. 2001, 3,448 inmates. There were also (Dec. 2001) eight regional jails housing 2,139 county, state and federal inmates, and seven juvenile facilities housing 271 juveniles. Capital punishment was abolished in 1965. The last execution was in 1959.

Religion. Chief denominations in 2001 were: United Methodists (115,062 members), Roman Catholics (97,232), Baptists American (94,000) and Southern (33,000).

Education. Public school education is free for all from 5 to 21 years of age, and school attendance is compulsory for all between the ages of 7 and 16 (school term, 200 days—180–185 days of actual teaching). The public schools are non-sectarian. In 2000–01 public elementary and secondary schools had 285,785 pupils and 24,507 classroom teachers. Average salary of teachers was $35,888. Total 2000–01 education expenditures, including higher education, $2,486m.

Leading institutions of higher education in the autumn of 2000:

Founded		Full-time students
1837	Marshall University, Huntington	15,640[1]
1837	West Liberty State College, West Liberty	2,606
1867	Fairmont State College, Fairmont	6,496
1868	West Virginia University, Morgantown	21,987
1872	Concord College, Athens	3,050
1872	Glenville State College, Glenville	2,198

Founded		Full-time students
1872	Shepherd College, Shepherdstown	4,703
1891	West Virginia State College, Institute	4,828
1895	West Virginia Univ. Inst. of Technology, Montgomery	2,326
1895	Bluefield State College, Bluefield	2,648
1901	Potomac State College of West Virginia Univ., Keyser	1,111
1961	West Virginia Univ. at Parkersburg, Parkersburg	3,271
1976	School of Osteopathic Medicine, Lewisburg	280

[1]Includes Marshall Univ. Graduate College, South Charleston, founded in 1972.

In addition to the universities and state-supported schools, there are 2 community colleges (4,911 students in 2000), 10 denominational and private institutions of higher education (9,808 students in 1999) and 11 business colleges (2001).

Health. In Dec. 2001 the state had 68 licensed hospitals and 64 licensed personal care homes, 141 skilled-nursing homes and five mental hospitals.

Welfare. The Department of Health Human Resources, originating in the 1930s as the Department of Public Assistance, is both state and federally financed. In 1999 expenditures for medical services totalled $1,652,769, of which $1,223,146 came from federal funds.

CULTURE

Broadcasting. In 2001 there were 156 commercial, 14 college and 14 public radio stations. Television stations numbered 14 commercial and three public.

Press. In 2001 daily newspapers numbered 19, weekly and college newspapers 78.

Tourism. There are 35 state parks, nine state forests, 58 wildlife management areas and two state trails. Visitors are attracted to the area by whitewater rafting, hiking, skiing and biking and the winter outdoor light display at Oglebay Park in Wheeling.

Festivals. Over 100 fairs and festivals occur throughout the state during the year. Some of the oldest and largest include the Mountain State Art and Craft Fair, Cedar Lakes; Mountain State Forest Festival, Elkins; West Virginia State Folk Festival, Glenville; West Virginia Italian Heritage Festival, Clarksburg; Vandalia Gathering, Charleston; Preston County Buckwheat Festival, Kingwood; Wheeling Jamboree, Wheeling; and Black Walnut Festival, Spencer.

Libraries. In 2000–01 there were 177 public libraries, 29 college and university libraries, and 68 special libraries.

Museums and Galleries. Major art museums and galleries include the Huntington Museum of Art, Huntington; Oglebay Institute, Wheeling; Sunrise Museum, Charleston. Major historical collections include the West Virginia State Museum, Charleston; Harpers Ferry National Historical Park, Harpers Ferry.

FURTHER READING

West Virginia Blue Book. Legislature, Charleston. Annual, since 1916
Statistical Handbook, 2000. West Virginia Research League, Charleston, 2000
Lewis, R. L. and Hennen, J. C., *West Virginia History: Critical Essays on the Literature.* Kendall/Hunt Publishing, Dubuque, IA, 1993
Rice, O. K., *West Virginia: A History.* 2nd ed. Univ. Press of Kentucky, Lexington, 1994
State Library: Archives and History, Division of Culture and History, Charleston.

WISCONSIN

KEY HISTORICAL EVENTS

The French were the first European explorers of the territory; Jean Nicolet landed at Green Bay in 1634, a mission was founded in 1671 and a permanent settlement at Green Bay followed. In 1763 French claims were surrendered to Britain. In 1783 Britain ceded them to the USA, which designated the Northwest Territory, of which Wisconsin was part. In 1836 a separate Territory of Wisconsin was organized, including the present Iowa, Minnesota and parts of the Dakotas.

Territorial organization was a great stimulus to settlement. In 1836 James Duane Doty founded the town site of Madison and successfully pressed its claim to be the capital of the Territory even before it was inhabited. In 1848 Wisconsin became a state, with its present boundaries.

The city of Milwaukee was founded, on Lake Michigan, when Indian tribes gave up their claims to the land in 1831–33. It grew rapidly as a port and industrial town, attracting Germans in the 1840s, Poles and Italians 50 years later. The Lake Michigan shore was developed as an industrial area; the rest of the south proved suitable for dairy farming; the north, mainly forests and lakes, has remained sparsely settled except for tourist bases.

There are 11 Indian reservations where more than 15,500 of Wisconsin's 47,000 Indians live. Since the Second World War there has been black immigration from the southern states to the industrial lake-shore cities.

TERRITORY AND POPULATION
Wisconsin is bounded north by Lake Superior and the Upper Peninsula of Michigan, east by Lake Michigan, south by Illinois, and west by Iowa and Minnesota, with the Mississippi River forming most of the boundary. Land area, 54,310 sq. miles (140,662 sq. km). Census population, 1 April 2000, 5,363,675, an increase of 9·6% since 1990. July 2002 estimate, 5,441,196.

Population in five census years was:

	White	Black	All others	Total	Per sq. mile
1910	2,320,555	2,900	10,405	2,333,860	42·2
1930	2,916,255	10,739	12,012	2,939,006	53·7
1980	4,443,035	182,592	80,015	4,705,642	86·4
1990	4,512,523	244,539	134,707	4,891,769	90·1
2000	4,769,857	304,460	289,358	5,363,675	98·8

Of the total population in 2000, 2,714,634 were female, 3,994,919 were 18 years old or older and 3,663,643 were urban. In 2000 Wisconsin's Hispanic population was 192,921, up from 93,194 in 1990 (an increase of 107·0%).

Population of the large cities, 2000 census, was as follows:

Milwaukee	596,974	Waukesha	64,825	Fond du Lac	42,203
Madison	208,054	Oshkosh	62,916	Brookfield	38,649
Green Bay	102,313	Eau Claire	61,704	Wausau	38,426
Kenosha	90,352	Janesville	59,498	New Berlin	38,220
Racine	81,855	La Crosse	51,818	Beloit	35,775
Appleton	70,087	Sheboygan	50,792	Greenfield	35,476
West Allis	61,254	Wauwatosa	47,271		

Population of largest metropolitan areas, 2000 census: Milwaukee–Racine, 1,689,572; Madison, 426,526; Appleton–Oshkosh–Neenah, 358,365; Duluth–Superior (Minn.–Wis.), 243,815; Green Bay, 226,778.

SOCIAL STATISTICS
Births in 2001 were 69,012 (12.7 per 1,000 population); deaths were 46,357 (8·6); infant deaths, 491 (6·5 per 1,000 live births). In 2001 there were 34,790 marriages (6·5 per 1,000 population); divorces and annulments, 17,457 (3·3).

CLIMATE
Milwaukee, Jan. 19°F (–7·2°C), July 70°F (21·1°C). Annual rainfall 29" (727 mm). Wisconsin belongs to the Great Lakes climate zone (see UNITED STATES: Climate).

CONSTITUTION AND GOVERNMENT
The constitution, which dates from 1848, has 138 amendments. The legislative power is vested in a Senate of 33 members elected for four years, one-half elected alternately, and an Assembly of 99 members all elected simultaneously for two years. The Governor and Lieut.-Governor are elected for four years.

For the 108th Congress, which convened in Jan. 2003, Wisconsin sends eight members to the House of Representatives. It is represented in the Senate by Herbert Kohl (D. 1989–2007) and Russell Feingold (D. 1993–2005).

The capital is Madison. The state has 72 counties.

RECENT ELECTIONS

In the 2000 presidential election Gore polled 1,242,987 votes; Bush, 1,237,279; Nader, 94,070.

CURRENT ADMINISTRATION

Governor: Jim Doyle (D.), 2003–07 (salary: $131,768).
  Lieut.-Governor: Barbara Lawton (D.), 2003–07 ($69,579).
  Secretary of State: Douglas La Follette (D.), 2003–07 ($62,549).

Government Website: http://www.wisconsin.gov

ECONOMY

Per capita personal income in 2000 was $28,066.

Overview. Wisconsin has a graduated individual income tax which ranges from 4·60% to 6·75% of gross income. Among the tax credits allowed are those for school property, working families, married couples and 60% of capital gains. Corporate income tax is 7·9% of net income. The state levies a 5% sales tax on most goods. The gasoline tax is 28·1 cents per gallon. A shared revenue programme distributes money to municipalities and the state pays for two-thirds of public school costs. The state's Department of Commerce budgeted $70·6m. for various business assistance, loan and grant programmes in 2001–02.

Budget. For the year ending 30 June 2002 total state revenue was $26,770m. ($10,020m. from state taxes); total expenditure, $31,644m. (health and human resources, $9,173m.; education, $8,863m.; transportation $2,106m.; corrections, $974m.; environmental resources, $467m.). Outstanding debt, 31 May 2000, $3,950m.

Performance. Gross State Product in 2000 was $173,478m.

Banking and Finance. On 30 Sept. 2001 there were 238 state chartered banks with assets of $60·4bn., and 52 federally chartered banks with $25·09bn. in assets. On 30 Sept. 2001, 24 state chartered savings institutions had $6·4bn. in assets and 17 federally chartered savings institutions had $14·4bn. in assets. As of 30 June 2002 there were 316 state chartered credit unions with $11·3bn. in assets.

ENERGY AND NATURAL RESOURCES

Electricity. 54,966m. kWh of electricity were produced in 2001; and 10,671m. kWh were imported. Fossil fuel plants accounted for 74·0% of state production, nuclear 20·9%, and hydropower 3·5%. Coal accounted for 64% of utility energy use in 2001; nuclear fuel, 17%; renewable sources, 2%; natural gas, 3%; and electricity imports, 14%.

Oil and Gas. Petroleum accounted for 29% of the total energy consumed in 2001 and natural gas 22%. Transportation accounted for 83% of petroleum consumption. Natural gas accounted for 51% of residential end use and petroleum 15%. There are no known petroleum or natural gas reserves in Wisconsin.

Water. The total area covered by water is approximately 11,186 sq. miles.

Minerals. Construction sand and gravel, crushed stone, industrial or specialty sand, lime, copper, gold and silver are the chief mineral products. Mineral production in 2000 was valued at over $349m. This value included $140m. for construction sand and gravel, $131m. for crushed stones, $32m. for industrial or specialty sand and $37m. for lime. The value of all other minerals including dimension (building) stone, peat and gemstones was around $9m.

Agriculture. On 1 Jan. 2002 there were 77,000 farms (17,782 dairy herds) with a total acreage of 16·3m. acres and an average size of 212 acres, compared with 142,000 farms with a total acreage of 22·4m. acres and an average of 158 acres in 1959. In 2001 the average value per acre was $2,450. Cash receipts from products sold by Wisconsin farms in 2001, $5·91bn.; $4·46bn. from livestock and livestock products; and $1·44bn. from crops.

Dairy farming is important, with 1·33m. milch cows in 2000. Production of cheese accounted for 26% of the USA's total in 2001. Production of the principal field crops in 2001 included: corn for grain, 330m. bu.; corn for silage, 11·3m. tons; oats,

12·4m. bu.; all hay, 4·8m. tons. Other crops of importance: 59·6m. bu. of soybeans, 31·9m. cwt of potatoes, 2·8m. bbls. of cranberries, 74,900 tons of carrots and the processing crops of 557,600 tons of sweet corn, 68,800 tons of green peas, 244,900 tons of snap beans, 30,100 tons of cucumbers for pickles, 13·1m. lb of tart cherries, 81,500 tons of cabbage for kraut and 81,700 cwt of cabbage for fresh market.

Wisconsin is also a major producer of mink pelts.

Forestry. Wisconsin has an estimated 16·0m. acres of forest land. Of 15·7m. acres of timberland (Oct. 1997), national forests covered 1·4m. acres; state forests, 0·7m.; county and municipal forests, 2·3m.; forest industry, 1·1m.; private land, 10·1m.

Growing stock (1996), 18,500m. cu. ft, of which 14,100m. cu. ft is hardwood and 4,400m. cu. ft softwood. Main hardwoods are maple, oak, aspen and basswood; main softwoods are red pine, white pine, northern white cedar and balsam fir. The timber industry employs 99,000, has a payroll of $3,400m. and shipments valued at $19,700m. (1996).

INDUSTRY

Wisconsin has much heavy industry, particularly in the Milwaukee area. Three-fifths of manufacturing employees work on durable goods. Industrial machinery is the major industrial group (17% of all manufacturing employment) followed by fabricated metals, food and kindred products, printing and publishing, paper and allied products, electrical equipment and transportation equipment. Manufacturing establishments in 1999 provided 23% of non-farm wage and salary workers, 26·5% of all earnings. The total number of establishments was 10,005 in 1999; the biggest concentration is in the southeast. In Dec. 2002 manufacturing employed 568,700 people out of a total civilian labour force of 3,050,600.

Labour. The civilian labour force in 2002 was 3,050,600, of whom 2,900,000 were employed. Service enterprises employed 798,800 people, manufacturing 568,700, retail 506,100 and government 423,000. Average annual pay per worker (2001) was $31,540 ($35,170 in Milwaukee metropolitan area). Median household income (2000) was $45,349. Women were 47% of the workforce in 1998. Workforce participation rates for people over 16 (1999) were 77·6% for males and 67·2% for females. Average weekly earnings ranged from $300 in the retail sector to $750 in manufacturing in 2001. Average unemployment was 5·2% in 2002.

Trade Unions. Labour union membership numbered 446,000 in 2000 compared to 465,500 in 1983. In 2000 union members were 17·6% of the workforce whereas they were 23·8% of the workforce in 1983. Union membership declined from 36% of workers in the manufacturing sector in 1983 to 22·5% in 1998.

COMMUNICATIONS

Roads. The state had, on 1 Jan. 2001, 111,905 miles of public roads. 79% of all roads in the state have a bituminous (or similar) surface. There are 11,752 miles of state and interstate highways and 19,668 miles of county highway roads.

In 2001 there were 4,964,305 registered motor vehicles.

Rail. On 31 Dec. 2000 the state had 4,596 track-miles of railway and 12 railroads that hauled 151·6m. tons of freight.

Civil Aviation. There were, in 2001, 136 public access airports. There were 4,386,021 passenger enplanements statewide in 2001.

Shipping. Lake Superior and Lake Michigan ports handled 48·3m. tons of freight in 1999; 88% of it at Superior, one of the world's biggest grain ports, and much of the rest at Milwaukee and Green Bay.

SOCIAL INSTITUTIONS

Justice. On 24 Jan. 2003 the state's penal, reformatory and correctional system held 20,068 men and 1,310 women in 14 prisons, 17 community facilities and other institutions for adult offenders, including contract beds in county jails, federal facilities, and 3,614 males in private prisons in Oklahoma, Tennessee and Minnesota; the probation and parole system was supervising 66,705 adults (56,197 on probation, 10,508 on parole). Parole for new convictions officially ended 31 Dec.

1999 (replaced by 'extended supervision'). Population in the state's five juvenile institutions on 24 Jan. 2003 was 712 males and 75 females; an additional 426 males and 47 females were under field supervision.

The death penalty was abolished in 1853.

Religion. Wisconsin church affiliation, as a percentage of the 1990 population, was estimated at 31·8% Catholic, 20·1% Lutheran, 3·2% Methodist, 9·5% other churches and 35·4% un-affiliated.

Education. All children between the ages of 6 and 18 are required to attend school full-time to the end of the school term in which they become 18 years of age. In 2001–02 the public school grades kindergarten-12 had 854,688 pupils and 60,747 (full-time equivalent) teachers. Private schools enrolled 133,246 students grades kindergarten-12. Public pre-schools enrolled 24,673 children, and private 12,866. Children taught in home schools numbered 21,134 in 1999–2000. Public elementary teachers' salaries, 2000–01, averaged $41,403; secondary, $42,175.

In 2001–02 technical colleges had an enrolment of 451,271 and 4,609 (full-time equivalent) teachers, and two Indian tribe community colleges enrolled 915 (2000–01). There is a school for the visually handicapped and a school for the deaf.

The University of Wisconsin, established in 1848, was joined by law in 1971 with the Wisconsin State Universities System to become the University of Wisconsin System with 13 degree granting campuses, 13 two-year campuses in the Center System and the University Extension. The system had, in 2001–02, 6,644 full-time professors and instructors. In autumn 2001, 159,433 students enrolled (10,643 at Eau Claire, 5,558 at Green Bay, 9,092 at La Crosse, 40,877 at Madison, 23,835 at Milwaukee, 10,929 at Oshkosh, 5,016 at Parkside, 5,511 at Platteville, 5,822 at River Falls, 8,735 at Stevens Point, 7,780 at Stout, 2,787 at Superior, 10,471 at Whitewater and 12,377 at the Center System freshman-sophomore centres).

UW-Extension enrolled 181,251 students in its continuing education programmes in 2000–01. There are also several independent institutions of higher education: Marquette University (Jesuit), in Milwaukee (11,000 in 2002); Cardinal Strich University (Franciscan), with campuses in Milwaukee, Madison and Edina, Minnesota (6,588 in 2001–02); Concordia University Wisconsin (Lutheran), in Mequon (4,810 in autumn 2001); and Lawrence University, Appleton (1,300 in 2002). There were also 17 higher education colleges, 4 technical and professional schools and 4 theological seminaries in 2000. The state's educational and broadcasting service is licensed through the UW Board of Regents.

The total expenditure, 1999–2000, for all public education (except capital outlay and debt service) was $10,932·6m. ($2,073 per capita).

Health. In 2001 the state had 121 general medical and surgical hospitals (12,524 beds), 11 psychiatric hospitals (653 beds), one treatment centre for alcohol and drug abuse (24 beds) and two physical rehabilitation hospitals (77 beds). There were two state mental hospitals (555 beds) and two US Veterans' Administration hospitals. Patients in state mental hospitals and institutions for the developmentally disabled averaged 1,864 in 2000. On 31 Dec. 2001 the state had 411 licensed nursing homes with 37,506 residents and 37 facilities for the developmentally disabled (1,869 residents).

Welfare. In Nov. 2001 there were 128,723 SSI recipients in the state; payments (2002) were $629 for a single individual, $675 for an eligible individual with an ineligible spouse, and $949 for an eligible couple. A special payment level of $725 for an individual and $1,294 for a couple may be paid with special approval for SSI recipients who are developmentally disabled or chronically mentally ill, living in a non-medical living arrangement not his or her own home. There is a monthly cash benefit for each child living with an SSI parent of $250 for the first child and $150 for each additional child. All SSI recipients receive state medical assistance coverage.

Wisconsin completed its conversion to the W-2 (Wisconsin Works) programme on 31 March 1998, ending the 62-year-old Aid to Families with Dependent Children (AFDC) programme. W-2 clients (Nov. 2002) totalled 14,049 with 10,108 receiving cash assistance. W-2 clients must be working, seeking employment, or be enrolled in job-training programmes. Recipients are limited to 60 months of financial assistance (consecutive or non-consecutive). Participants are eligible for child care assistance, a state subsidized health plan, job and transportation assistance and food stamps. In Nov. 2002 there were 285,333 food stamp recipients. Medical Assistance (Medicaid) clients, including low-income, SSI recipients and other disabled, and other elderly totalled 504,380. An additional 103,297 (Nov. 2002) are provided for under BadgerCare, a state-funded medical insurance programme for certain low-income families.

CULTURE
There are two professional opera companies in Wisconsin: the Madison Opera, and the Florentine Opera in Milwaukee.

Broadcasting. In 2000 there were 32 commercial TV stations; 8 educational TV stations; 265 commercial radio stations; and 48 non-commercial.

Press. There were 36 daily newspapers in 2001.

Tourism. The tourist-vacation industry ranks among the first three in economic importance with an estimated $11,376m. spent in 2001. The Department of Tourism budgeted $15,174,000 to promote tourism in 2002–03.

Festivals. Summer music festivals include: the Great River Jazz Fest; the River Folk Fest (both take place in La Crosse, Milwaukee); and the Peninsula Music Festival, Door County.

Museums and Galleries. Attractions include the Madison and Milwaukee Art Museums; Leigh Yawkey Woodson Art Museum, Wausau; and Wisconsin Veterans' Museum, Madison.

FURTHER READING
Wisconsin Blue Book. Wisconsin Legislative Reference Bureau, Madison. Biennial
State Historical Society of Wisconsin: *The History of Wisconsin.* Vol. IV [J. Buenker], Madison, 1999

State Information Agency: Legislative Reference Bureau, 100 N. Hamilton St., P.O. Box 2037, Madison, WI 53701-2037. *Chief:* Stephen R. Miller.
Website: http://www.legis.state.wi.us

WYOMING

KEY HISTORICAL EVENTS
The territory was inhabited by Plains Indians (Arapahoes, Sioux and Cheyenne) in the early 19th century. There was some trading between them and white Americans, but very little white settlement. In the 1840s the great western migration routes, the Oregon and the Overland Trails, ran through the territory, Wyoming offering mountain passes accessible to wagons. Once migration became a steady flow it was necessary to protect the route from Indian attack, and forts were built.

In 1867 coal was discovered. In 1868 Wyoming was organized as a separate Territory, and in 1869 the Sioux and Arapaho were confined to reservations. At the same time the route of the Union Pacific Railway was laid out, and working settlements and railway towns grew up in southern Wyoming. Settlement of the north was delayed until after the final defeat of hostile Indians in 1876.

The economy of the settlements at first depended on ranching. Cheyenne had been made Territorial capital in 1869, and also functioned as a railway town moving cattle. Casper, on the site of a fort on the Pony Express route, was also a railway town on the Chicago and North Western. Laramie started as a Union Pacific construction workers' shanty town in 1868. In 1890 oil was discovered at Casper, and Wyoming became a state in the same year. Subsequently, mineral extraction became the leading industry, as natural gas, uranium, bentonite and trona were exploited as well as oil and coal.

TERRITORY AND POPULATION
Wyoming is bounded north by Montana, east by South Dakota and Nebraska, south by Colorado, southwest by Utah and west by Idaho. Land area, 97,100 sq. miles

(251,488 sq. km). The Yellowstone National Park occupies about 2·22m. acres; the Grand Teton National Park has 307,000 acres. The federal government in 1986 owned 49,838 sq. miles (50·9% of the total area of the state). The Federal Bureau of Land Management administers 17,546,188 acres.

Census population, 1 April 2000, 493,782, an increase of 8·9% since 1990; 2002 estimate, 498,703. Wyoming has the smallest population of any of the states of the USA.

Population in five census years was:

	White	Black	American Indian	Asiatic	Total	Per sq. mile
1910	140,318	2,235	1,486	1,926	145,965	1·5
1930	221,241	1,250	1,845	1,229	225,565	2·3

	White	Black	All others	Total	Per sq. mile
1980	446,488	3,364	19,705	469,557	4·8

	White	Black	American Indian	Asian/ Pacific Islands	Other	Total	Per sq. mile
1990	427,061	3,606	9,479	2,806	10,636	453,588	4·7
2000	454,670	3,722	11,133	3,073	21,184	493,782	5·1

Of the total population in 2000, 248,374 were male, 364,909 were 18 years old or older and 321,344 were urban. At the 2000 census the Hispanic population of Wyoming was 31,669, up from 25,751 in 1990 (an increase of 23%).

The largest towns (with 2000 census population) are Cheyenne, 53,011; Casper, 49,644; Laramie, 27,204; Gillette, 19,646; Rock Springs, 18,708; Sheridan, 15,804; Green River, 11,808.

SOCIAL STATISTICS
Births in 1999 were 6,122; deaths, 4,038; marriages, 4,931; divorces, 2,818; infant deaths, 42 (6·9 per 1,000 live births). The abortion rate, at 1·0 for every 1,000 women in 2000, is the lowest of any US state.

CLIMATE
Cheyenne, Jan. 25°F (−3·9°C), July 66°F (18·9°C). Annual rainfall 15" (376 mm). Yellowstone Park, Jan. 18°F (−7·8°C), July 61°F (16·1°C). Annual rainfall 18" (444 mm). Wyoming belongs to the Mountain States climate region (see UNITED STATES: Climate).

CONSTITUTION AND GOVERNMENT
The constitution, drafted in 1890, has since had 43 amendments. The Legislature consists of a Senate of 30 members elected for four years, 15 retiring every two years, and a House of Representatives of 60 members elected for two years. It sits annually in Jan. or Feb. The Governor is elected for 4 years.

For the 108th Congress, which convened in Jan. 2003, Wyoming sends one member to the House of Representatives. It is represented in the Senate by Craig Thomas (R. 1995–2007) and Michael Enzi (R. 1997–2009).

The capital is Cheyenne. The state contains 23 counties.

RECENT ELECTIONS
In the 2000 presidential election Bush polled 147,947 votes; Gore, 60,481; Buchanan, 2,724.

CURRENT ADMINISTRATION
Governor: David Freudenthal (D.), 2003–07 (salary: $105,000).
  Secretary of State: Joe Meyer (R.), 2003–07 ($92,000).

Government Website: http://www.state.wy.us

ECONOMY
Personal income *per capita* (2000) was $27,436.

Budget. In 1999 total state revenue was $3,092m. Total expenditure was $2,373m. (education, $755m.; highways, $327m.; public welfare, $245m.; health and hospitals, $128m.; police protection, $23m.). Outstanding debt, in 1999, $1,046m.

Performance. Gross State Product was $19,294m. in 2000.

Banking and Finance. In Sept. 2001 there were 20 national and 26 state banks with a total of $6,291m. deposits.

ENERGY AND NATURAL RESOURCES

Oil and Gas. Wyoming is largely an oil-producing state. In 2001 the output of oil was 57m. bbls.; natural gas, 1,070bn. cu. ft.

Water. The total area covered by water is approximately 714 sq. miles.

Minerals. In 2000 the output of oil was 60·5m. bbs; natural gas, 1,292·6bn. cu. ft; coal (2001), 366m. short tons; trona, 17·7m. short tons; uranium, 2·1m. lbs. Wyoming is the USA's leading coal producer, accounting for 33% of the country's coal output in 2001. It also has 37% of the country's coal reserves. Total value of non-fuel mineral production, 1998, $1,060m.

Agriculture. Wyoming is semi-arid, and agriculture is carried on by irrigation and dry farming. In 2000 there were 9,200 farms and ranches; total farm area was 34·6m. acres; average size of farm in 2000 was 3,761 acres (the largest of any state). In 1999, 12,168 people were employed on farms.

Total value, 2000, of crops produced, $289m.; of livestock and products, $553m. Crop production (1,000 bu.): corn for grain, 8,184; wheat, 4,132; oats, 1,485; barley, 7,885; sugarbeet, 1,156 tons. Animals on farms included 1·55m. cattle, 530,000 sheep and 108,000 hogs and pigs. Total egg production in 2000 was 3·6m.

Forestry. National forest area, 1999, 9,238,000 acres.

INDUSTRY

In 1999 there were 559 manufacturing establishments. In 1999 there were 627 mining establishments. A large portion of the manufacturing in the state is based on natural resources, mainly oil and farm products. Leading industries are food, wood products (except furniture) and machinery (except electrical). The Wyoming Industrial Development Corporation assists in the development of small industries by providing credit.

Labour. In July 2001 the construction industry employed 19,600 wage and salary workers; mining, 19,400; transportation and public utilities, 14,600; manufacturing, 11,400. The total civilian labour force in July 2001 was 276,249, of whom 267,046 were employed; non-agricultural wage and salary employment, 252,400. The unemployment rate was 3·3% in July 2001.

Trade Unions. There were 22,900 working members in trade unions (9·1% of total employment) in 1999.

INTERNATIONAL TRADE

Imports and Exports. In 2000 total export from Wyoming was $502·5m.

COMMUNICATIONS

Roads. In 2000 there were 2,299 miles of urban roads and 25,026 miles of rural roads, the latter including (in miles): federal, 3,396; state, 6,353; county, 13,944. There were 585,690 motor vehicle registrations in 2000.

Rail. In 1999, 1,795 miles of Class I railway were operated.

Civil Aviation. There were ten towns with commuter air services and two towns on jet routes in 1995. There were 161,780 passenger enplanements statewide in 1999.

SOCIAL INSTITUTIONS

Justice. In the third quarter of 1999 there were 1,300 prisoners in state adult correctional institutions. The death penalty is authorized for over 16-year-olds, but has been used only once, in 1992, since 1976.

Religion. Chief religious bodies in 1990 were the Roman Catholic (with 59,565 members), Latter-day Saints (Mormons) (54,000 in 1998) and Protestant churches (110,375).

Education. In 2000–01 public elementary and secondary schools had 89,531 pupils and 6,743 teachers. In 1990–91 enrolment in the parochial elementary and secondary schools was about 3,500. The average expenditure per pupil for 1999–2000 was $8,046. State and local government expenditure in 1999 was $721m.

The University of Wyoming, founded at Laramie in 1887 had, in the academic year 2000–01, 11,743 students. There were seven community colleges in 2000–01 with 12,740 students.

Health. In 2000 the state had 26 general hospitals with 1,631 beds, and 40 registered nursing homes with 3,106 beds.

Welfare. In the fiscal year 2000, $18·2m. was distributed in food stamps; $1·6m. in aid to families with dependent children; and $193m. in Medicaid.

CULTURE

Broadcasting. In 2000 there were 32 AM, 38 FM radio stations and 15 television stations.

Press. In 2000 there were eight daily newspapers.

Tourism. There are over 7m. tourists annually, mainly outdoor enthusiasts. The state has large elk and pronghorn antelope herds, ten fish hatcheries and numerous wild game. In 2000, 6,134,317 people visited the six national areas; 1,925,000 people visited state parks and historic sites. In 1990, 811,183 fishing, game and bird licences were sold. In 2000 there were nine operational ski areas.

FURTHER READING

Statistical information: Department of Administration and Information, 327 E. Emerson Bldg., Cheyenne 82002. Publishes *Wyoming Data Handbook*
Equality State Almanac 1998. Wyoming Department of Administration and Information. Division of Economic Analysis. Cheyenne, WY 82002
Wyoming Official Directory. Secretary of State. Cheyenne, annual
Wyoming Data Handbook. Dept. of Administration and Information. Division of Economic Analysis. Cheyenne, annual
Treadway, T., *Wyoming.* New York, 1982

State Government Website: http://eadiv.state.wy.us

OUTLYING TERRITORIES

The outlying territories of the USA comprise the two Commonwealths of the Northern Mariana Islands and Puerto Rico, a number of unincorporated territories in the Pacific Ocean and one unincorporated territory in the Caribbean Sea.

COMMONWEALTH OF THE NORTHERN MARIANA ISLANDS

KEY HISTORICAL EVENTS

In 1889 Spain ceded Guam (largest and southernmost of the Marianas Islands) to the USA and sold the rest to Germany. Occupied by Japan in 1914, the islands were administered by Japan under a League of Nations mandate until occupied by US forces in Aug. 1944. In 1947 they became part of the US-administered Trust Territory of the Pacific Islands. On 17 June 1975 the electorate adopted a covenant to establish a Commonwealth in association with the USA; this was approved by the US government in April 1976 and came into force on 1 Jan. 1978. In Nov. 1986 the islanders were granted US citizenship. The UN terminated the Trusteeship status on 22 Dec. 1990.

TERRITORY AND POPULATION

The Northern Marianas form a single chain of 16 mountainous islands extending north of Guam for about 560 km, with a total area of 5,050 sq. km (1,950 sq. miles) of which 464 sq. km (179 sq. miles) are dry land, and with a population (2000 census) of 69,221 (female, 37,237).

The areas and populations of the islands are as follows:

Island(s)	Sq. km	1995 Census	2000 Census
Northern Group[1]	171	8	6
Saipan	122	52,698	62,392
Tinian (with Aguijan)	101[2]	2,631	3,540
Rota	83	3,509	3,283

[1]Pagan, Agrihan, Alamagan and nine uninhabited islands. [2]Including uninhabited Aguijan.

In 1980, 55% spoke Chamorro, 11% Woleaian and 13% Filipino languages, but English remains the official language. The largest town is Chalan Kanoa on Saipan.

SOCIAL STATISTICS

In 1996 the birth rate was 33 per 1,000 population and the death rate 4·6 per 1,000 population. Infant mortality was 38 per 1,000 live births.

CONSTITUTION AND GOVERNMENT

Constitution was approved by a referendum on 6 March 1977 and came into force on 9 Jan. 1978. The legislature comprises a nine-member *Senate*, with three Senators elected from each of the main three islands for a term of four years, and an 18-member *House of Representatives*, elected for a term of two years.

The Commonwealth is administered by a Governor and Lieut.-Governor, elected for four years.

RECENT ELECTIONS

At the elections of 3 Nov. 2001 the Republican Party won 12 seats in the House of Representatives (6 in the Senate), against the Democratic Party which won 5 (2 in the Senate) and the Covenant Party which won 1 seat (1 in the Senate).

In the gubernatorial elections of 3 Nov. 2001 Juan Babauta, in tandem with Diego T. Benavente, won 42·8% of votes cast, defeating Benigno Fitial (24·4%), Jesus Camacho Borja (17·5%) and Froilan Cruz Tenorio (11·3%).

CURRENT ADMINISTRATION

Governor: Juan N. Babauta (R.), 2002–04.
Lieut.-Governor: Diego T. Benavente (R.).

Government Website: http://www.saipan.com/gov

ENERGY AND NATURAL RESOURCES

Water. The total area covered by water is approximately 10 sq. miles.

Fisheries. In 1998 total catches were 518,100 lb (235 tonnes), entirely from marine waters.

INDUSTRY

Labour. In 1990 there were 7,476 workers from the indigenous population and 21,188 were foreign workers; 2,699 were unemployed.

INTERNATIONAL TRADE

Imports and Exports. In 1991 imports totalled $392·4m.; exports were $263·4m.

COMMUNICATIONS

Roads. There are about 381 km of roads.

Civil Aviation. Air Micronesia provides inter-island services. There are five airports in all. Saipan handled 1,325,000 passengers (1,048,000 on international flights) and 17,900 tonnes of freight in 2000.

Telecommunications. There were 26,800 main telephone lines in 2000. In 1995 there were 1,200 mobile phone subscribers.

SOCIAL INSTITUTIONS

Religion. The population is predominantly Roman Catholic.

Education. In 2000 there were 679 pupils enrolled in nursery school and preschool, 946 in kindergarten, 7,884 in elementary school (grades 1–8), 2,750 in high school (grades 9–12) and 1,130 in college or graduate school.

Health. In 1986 there were 23 doctors, 4 dentists, 103 nursing personnel, 2 pharmacists and 2 midwives. In 1988 there was 1 hospital with 70 beds.

CULTURE

Broadcasting. In 1989 there were 10,500 radio and 4,100 television receivers, 3 radio stations and a 15-channel cable TV station in Saipan.

Tourism. In 1998 there were 481,000 visitors bringing in revenue of US$647m.

COMMONWEALTH OF PUERTO RICO

KEY HISTORICAL EVENTS

A Spanish dependency since the 16th century, Puerto Rico was ceded to the USA in 1898 after the Spanish defeat in the Spanish-American war. In 1917 US citizenship was conferred and in 1932 there was a name change from Porto Rico to Puerto Rico. In 1952 Puerto Rico was proclaimed a commonwealth with a representative government and a directly elected governor.

TERRITORY AND POPULATION

Puerto Rico is the most easterly of the Greater Antilles and lies between the Dominican Republic and the US Virgin Islands. The total area is 13,791 sq. km (5,325 sq. miles), of which 8,871 sq. km (3,425 sq. miles) are dry land; the population, according to the census of 2000, was 3,808,610, an increase of 8·1% over 1990. The urban population was 3,595,521 in 2000, representing 94·4% (73·3% in 1995) of the total population. Population density was 1,112 per sq. mile in 2000. Of the total population in 2000, 1,975,033 were female. The UN gives a projected population for 2010 of 4·25m.

A law of April 1991 making Spanish the sole official language (which replaced a law of 1902 establishing Spanish and English as joint official languages) was reversed in 1993.

Chief towns, 1999 estimates, are: San Juan, 439,604; Bayamón, 236,688; Ponce, 193,640; Carolina, 192,088; Caguas, 145,193; Guaynabo, 104,936; Arecibo, 102,294; Mayaguez, 100,463.

The Puerto Rican island of Vieques, 10 miles to the east, has an area of 51·7 sq. miles and 9,584 (1999) inhabitants. The island of Culebra, between Puerto Rico and St Thomas, has an area of 10 sq. miles and 1,771 (1999) inhabitants. It has a good harbour.

SOCIAL STATISTICS

1999: births, 58,544 (15·1 per 1,000 population); deaths, 28,563 (7·3); marriages 26,838; infant mortality rate, 11 per 1,000 live births. Annual growth rate, 1995–99, 1·1%. In 1998 the most popular age range for marrying was 20–24 for both males and females. Fertility rate, 1990–95, 2·2 births per woman.

CLIMATE

Warm, sunny winters with hot summers. The north coast experiences more rainfall than the south coast and generally does not have a dry season as rainfall is evenly spread throughout the year. San Juan, Jan. 25°C, July 28°C. Annual rainfall 1,246 mm.

CONSTITUTION AND GOVERNMENT

Puerto Rico has representative government, the franchise being restricted to citizens 18 years of age or over, residence (one year) and such additional qualifications as may be prescribed by the Legislature of Puerto Rico, but no property qualification may be imposed. Puerto Ricans vote in presidential primary elections but not in US general elections. They have one non-voting representative in Washington. The island is given billions of dollars each year in food stamps and other federal aid from Washington and although Puerto Ricans fight in the US army, the island sends its own teams to the Olympic Games. The executive power resides in a Governor, elected directly by the people every four years. 22 heads of departments form the Governor's Council of Secretaries. The legislative functions are vested in a Senate, composed of 28 members, and the House of Representatives, composed of 51 members. Both houses meet annually in Jan. Puerto Rican men are subject to conscription in US services.

A new constitution was drafted by a Puerto Rican Constituent Assembly and approved by the electorate at a referendum on 3 March 1952. It was then submitted to Congress, which struck out Section 20 of Article 11 covering the 'right to work' and the 'right to an adequate standard of living'; the remainder was passed and proclaimed by the Governor on 25 July 1952.

RECENT ELECTIONS

At the gubernatorial election on 7 Nov. 2000 there were three candidates. Sila María Calderón (PPD) won with 48·5% of the vote, ahead of Carlos I. Pesquera (PNP) who got 45·7%.

In elections to the Chamber of Representatives on 7 Nov. 2000 the Popular Democratic Party (PPD) polled 49·2% of the vote and claimed 27 of the 51 seats; the New Progressive Party (PNP), 46·4% and 23 seats; Puerto Rican Independence Party (PIP), 4·4% and 1 seat. In the Senate elections of the same day PPD took 19 seats, PNP took 7 seats and PIP took 1.

At a plebiscite on 14 Nov. 1993 on Puerto Rico's future status, 48·6% of votes cast were for Commonwealth (status quo), 46·3% for Statehood (51st State of the USA) and 4·4% for full independence. In a further plebiscite in Dec. 1998, some 52·2% of voters backed the opposition's call for no change, while 46·5% supported statehood. Independence was supported by 2·5%, while free association received 0·3%.

CURRENT ADMINISTRATION

Governor: Sila María Calderón (Popular Democratic Party, PPD), 2001–05.
Secretary of State: Ferdinand Mercado (PPD), appointed 2001.

ECONOMY

Budget. Total consolidated budget balance as of 30 June 1996: consolidated revenues total, $16,844·6m.; consolidated budget total, $16,385·2m.; balance, $459·4m.

GNP, 1996, $30,253·7m.; GDP, 1996, $45,504·8m.; per capita GNP, 1996, $8,119; per capita GDP, 1996, $12,212.

Bonded indebtedness for the commonwealth and municipalities, 30 June 1996, was $4,968·7m.

The USA administers and finances the postal service and maintains air and naval bases. Net US federal government payments in Puerto Rico, including direct expenditures (mainly military), grants-in-aid and other payments to individuals and to business totalled: 1994, $5,998·3m.; 1995, $6,314·4m.; 1996, $6,976·7m.

Per capita personal income (1996) was $7,882.

Performance. Real GDP growth was 3·4% in 1995 and 4·3% in 1994.

Banking and Finance. Banks on 30 June 1996 had total deposits of $27,502·2m. Bank loans were $17,940·5m. This includes 15 commercial banks, 3 government banks and 1 trust company.

ENERGY AND NATURAL RESOURCES

Environment. According to the *World Bank Atlas* Puerto Rico's carbon dioxide emissions in 1998 were the equivalent of 4·6 tonnes per capita.

Electricity. Installed capacity was 5m. kW in 1997. Production in 1998 was 17·76bn. kWh. Consumption per capita in 1995 was estimated to be 4,231 kWh.

Water. The total area covered by water is approximately 81 sq. miles.

Minerals. There is stone, and some production of cement (1·54m. tons in 1995).

Agriculture. Gross income in agriculture in 1996 was $662·6m., of which $387·2m. consisted of livestock products and $71·2m. traditional crops. Production, 1997 (in 1,000 tonnes): sugarcane, 307; pineapples, 179; plantains, 76; bananas, 38; mangoes, 17; oranges, 16; pumpkins and squash, 16; coffee, 12; tomatoes, 10. Livestock (1996): cattle, 370,546; pigs, 182,247; poultry, 12,433,834.

Forestry. In 1995 the area under forests was 275,000 ha, or 31% of the total land area (down from 287,000 ha in 1990).

Fisheries. The total catch in 1999 was 2,107 tonnes, exclusively from sea fishing.

INDUSTRY

Labour. In 1997 there were 1,132,000 people in employment, of which 582,000 people were employed in community, social and personal services (including hotels), 233,000 in trade and restaurants and 163,000 in manufacturing industries. 175,000 persons were unemployed in 1996.

INTERNATIONAL TRADE

Imports and Exports. In 1998 imports amounted to $21,706m., of which $13,318m. came from the USA; exports were valued at $28,109m., of which $25,610m. went to the USA.

In 1997 main exports (in $1m.) were: chemical products, 10,627·8; machinery (except electrical), 3,490·0; food, 3,386·4. Main imports were: chemical products, 5,416·3; electrical machinery, 2,423·8; transportation equipment, 2,241·2.

Puerto Rico is not permitted to levy taxes on imports.

COMMUNICATIONS

Roads. In 2000 there were 14,871 miles of roads and 2,082,090 registered motor vehicles.

Rail. There are 96 km of railway, although no passenger service.

Civil Aviation. San Juan's Luis Muñoz Marin airport handled 10,350,000 passengers and 239,600 tonnes of freight in 2000.

Shipping. In 1996, 9,931 US and foreign vessels of 81,961,309 gross tons entered and cleared Puerto Rico.

Telecommunications. In 2000 there were 1,299,300 main telephone lines, or 331·9 for every 1,000 persons. In April 2000 there were 200,000 Internet users. Mobile phone subscribers numbered 169,000 in 1996 and there were 543,000 fax machines in 1995.

SOCIAL INSTITUTIONS

Justice. The Commonwealth judiciary system is headed by a Supreme Court of seven members, appointed by the Governor, and consists of a First Instance Court and an Appellative Court, all appointed by the Governor. The First Instance Court consists of a Superior Tribunal with 78 judges and a municipal Tribunal of 70 judges. The Appellative Court has 33 judges.

The population in penal institutions in Oct. 1998 was 14,971 (395 per 100,000 of national population).

Religion. In 1996 about 75% of the population were Roman Catholic.

Education. Education was made compulsory in 1899. The percentage of literacy in 1990 was 89·4% of those 10 years of age or older. Total enrolment in public day schools, 1999, was 613,900. All private schools had a total enrolment of 118,700 pupils in 1999. All instruction below senior high school standard is given in Spanish only.

The University of Puerto Rico, in Río Piedras, 7 miles from San Juan, had 62,340 students in 1996. Higher education is also available in the Inter-American University of Puerto Rico (39,319 students in 1996), the Pontifical Catholic University of

Puerto Rico (11,786), the Sacred Heart University (5,001) and the Fundación Ana G. Méndez (16,983). Other private colleges and universities had 35,717 students.

Health. There were 72 hospitals in 1994, with a hospital bed provision of 26 per 10,000 population.

CULTURE

Broadcasting. In 1995 there were 118 radio and 21 television stations (colour by NTSC). There were 2·7m. radio receivers and 1·02m. TV receivers in 1997.

Press. In 1996 there were three main newspapers: *El Nuevo Día* had a daily circulation of 227,661; *El Vocero*, 206,125; *San Juan Star*, 33,353.

Tourism. There were 3,396,000 foreign visitors in 1998, plus 1,243,000 cruise ship arrivals. Revenue from tourism amounted to $2,233m. in 1998.

FURTHER READING
Statistical Information: The Area of Economic Research and Social Planning of the Puerto Rico Planning Board publishes: *(a)* annual *Economic Report to the Governor; (b) External Trade Statistics* (annual report); *(c) Reports on national income and balance of payments; (d) SocioEconomic Statistics* (since 1940); *(e) Puerto Rico Monthly Economic Indicators.*
Annual Reports. Governor of Puerto Rico. Washington
Dietz, J. L., *Economic History of Puerto Rico: Institutional Change and Capital Development.* Princeton Univ. Press, 1987

Commonwealth Library: Univ. of Puerto Rico Library, Rio Piedras.

AMERICAN SAMOA

KEY HISTORICAL EVENTS
The Samoan Islands were first visited by Europeans in the 18th century; the first recorded visit was in 1722. On 14 July 1889 a treaty between the USA, Germany and Great Britain proclaimed the Samoan islands neutral territory, under a four-power government consisting of the 3 treaty powers and the local native government. By the Tripartite Treaty of 7 Nov. 1899, ratified 19 Feb. 1900, Great Britain and Germany renounced in favour of the USA all rights over the islands of the Samoan group east of 171° long. west of Greenwich, the islands to the west of that meridian being assigned to Germany (now the independent state of Samoa). The islands of Tutuila and Aunu'u were ceded to the USA by their High Chiefs on 17 April 1900, and the islands of the Manu'a group on 16 July 1904. Congress accepted the islands under a Joint Resolution approved 20 Feb. 1929. Swain's Island, 210 miles north of the Samoan Islands, was annexed in 1925 and is administered as an integral part of American Samoa.

TERRITORY AND POPULATION
The islands (Tutuila, Aunu'u, Ta'u, Olosega, Ofu and Rose) are approximately 650 miles east-northeast of the Fiji Islands. The total area is 1,511 sq. km (583 sq. miles), of which 200 sq. km (77 sq. miles) are dry land; population (2000 census), 57,291 (29,264 males), nearly all Polynesians or part-Polynesians; density 37·9 per sq. km.

In 1995 an estimated 50·3% of the population lived in urban areas. The capital is Pago Pago, which had a population of 14,000 in 1999. The island's three Districts are Eastern (population, 1980, 17,311), Western (13,227) and Manu'a (1,732). There is also Swain's Island, with an area of 1·9 sq. miles and 100 inhabitants (1994), which lies 210 miles to the northwest. Rose Island (uninhabited) is 0·4 sq. mile in area. In 1990 some 85,000 American Samoans lived in the USA.

Samoan and English are spoken.

SOCIAL STATISTICS
In 1996 the birth rate was 35·6 per 1,000 population and the death rate 4·0 per 1,000 population. Infant mortality was 18·8 per 1,000 live births. Annual growth rate, 1995–99, 4·0%.

CLIMATE

A tropical maritime climate with a small annual range of temperature and plentiful rainfall. Pago Pago, Jan. 83°F (28·3°C), July 80°F (26·7°C). Annual rainfall 194" (4,850 mm).

CONSTITUTION AND GOVERNMENT

American Samoa is constitutionally an unorganized, unincorporated territory of the USA administered under the Department of the Interior. Its indigenous inhabitants are US nationals and are classified locally as citizens of American Samoa with certain privileges under local laws not granted to non-indigenous persons. Polynesian customs (not inconsistent with US laws) are respected.

Fagatogo is the seat of the government.

The islands are organized in 15 counties grouped in 3 districts; these counties and districts correspond to the traditional political units. On 25 Feb. 1948 a bicameral legislature was established, at the request of the Samoans, to have advisory legislative functions. With the adoption of the Constitution of 22 April 1960, and the revised Constitution of 1967, the legislature was vested with limited law-making authority. The lower house, or House of Representatives, is composed of 20 members elected by universal adult suffrage and 1 non-voting member for Swain's Island. The upper house, or Senate, is comprised of 18 members elected, in the traditional Samoan manner, in meetings of the chiefs. The Governor and Lieut.-Governor have been popularly elected since 1978.

RECENT ELECTIONS

At elections to the Senate and House of Representatives on 5 and 19 Nov. 2002, only non-partisans were elected.

At gubernatorial elections on 7 Nov. 2000, Tauese P. Sunia (Democrat) won with 50·7% of the vote against 47·8% for the independent Lealaifuaneva Reid.

CURRENT ADMINISTRATION

Governor: Togiola Tulafono (D.), 2001–05 (since March 2003).

Lieut.-Governor: Vacant.

Government Website: http://www.government.as

ECONOMY

Overview. An Economic Development and Planning Office was introduced in 1971. Much has been done to promote economic expansion and outside investment interest has been stimulated. The Office has initiated the first Territorial Comprehensive Plan. This plan when completed will provide a guideline to territorial development for 20 years. The focus will be on physical development and the problems of a rapidly increasing population with limited labour resources.

Budget. The chief sources of revenue are annual federal grants from the USA, local revenues from taxes, duties, receipts from commercial operations (enterprise and special revenue funds), utilities, rents and leases, and liquor sales. In 1990–91 revenues were $97m. ($43m. in local revenue and $54m. in grant revenue).

Banking and Finance. The American Samoa branch of the Bank of Hawaii and the American Samoa Bank offer all commercial banking services. The Development Bank of American Samoa, government-owned, is concerned primarily through loans and guarantees with the economic advancement of the Territory.

ENERGY AND NATURAL RESOURCES

Environment. According to the *World Bank Atlas* American Samoa's carbon dioxide emissions in 1998 were the equivalent of 4·5 tonnes per capita.

Electricity. Installed capacity was 33,000 kW in 1993. Production in 1998 was 125m. kWh. Per capita consumption in 1995 was an estimated 1,743 kWh. All the Manu'a islands have electricity.

Water. The total area covered by water is approximately 13 sq. miles.

Agriculture. Of the 48,640 acres of land area, 11,000 acres are suitable for tropical crops; most commercial farms are in the Tafuna plains and west Tutuila. Principal crops are coconuts, taro, bread-fruit, yams and bananas.

Livestock (1996): pigs, 11,000.

Fisheries. Total catch in 2000 was 866 tonnes.

INDUSTRY
Fish canning is important, employing the second largest number of people (after government). Attempts are being made to provide a variety of light industries. Tuna fishing and local inshore fishing are both expanding. In 1990 there were 27,991 persons of employable age, of whom 14,400 were in the workforce. The unemployment rate in 1991 was 12%.

INTERNATIONAL TRADE
Imports and Exports. Imports and exports for calendar years in US$1m.:

	1993	1994	1995	1996	1997
Imports	87·4	69·0	80·2	90·9	99·7
Exports	6·4	3·5	8·7	10·1	14·6

Chief exports are canned tuna, watches, pet foods and handicrafts. Chief imports are building materials, fuel oil, food, jewellery, machines and parts, alcoholic beverages and cigarettes.

COMMUNICATIONS
Roads. There are about 150 km of paved roads and 200 km of unpaved roads in all. Motor vehicles in use, 1995, 5,900 (5,300 passenger cars and 600 commercial vehicles).

Civil Aviation. Polynesian Airlines operate daily services between American Samoa and Samoa. South Pacific Island Airways also operates between Pago Pago and Honolulu, and between Pago Pago and Tonga. The islands are also served by Air Nauru which operates between Pago Pago, Tahiti and Auckland, and Air Pacific (Fiji Islands and westward). Manu'a Air Transport runs local services. There are three airports.

Shipping. The harbour at Pago Pago, which nearly bisects the island of Tutuila, is the only good harbour for large vessels in American Samoa. By sea there is a twice-monthly service between the Fiji Islands, New Zealand and Australia and regular services between the USA, South Pacific ports, Honolulu and Japan. In 1997 vessels entering totalled 725,000 net registered tons.

Telecommunications. A commercial radiogram service is available to all parts of the world. Commercial phone and telex services are operated to all parts of the world. In Dec. 1997 there were 13,200 main telephone lines in operation and 2,550 mobile phone subscribers.

SOCIAL INSTITUTIONS
Justice. Judicial power is vested firstly in a High Court. The trial division has original jurisdiction of all criminal and civil cases. The probate division has jurisdiction of estates, guardianships, trusts and other matters. The land and title division decides cases relating to disputes involving communal land and Matai title court rules on questions and controversy over family titles. The appellate division hears appeals from trial, land and title and probate divisions as well as having original jurisdiction in selected matters. The appellate court is the court of last resort. Two American judges sit with five Samoan judges permanently. In addition there are temporary judges or assessors who sit occasionally on cases involving Samoan customs. There is also a District Court with limited jurisdiction and there are 69 village courts.

The population in penal institutions in Dec. 1997 was 102 (equivalent to 170 per 100,000 of national population).

Religion. In 1997 about 56% of the population belonged to the Congregational Church and 19% were Roman Catholics. Methodists and Latter-day Saints (Mormons) are also represented.

Education. Education is compulsory between the ages of 6 and 18. In 2000 there were 1,557 pupils enrolled in nursery school and preschool, 1,736 in kindergarten, 11,418 in elementary school (grades 1–8), 4,645 in high school (grades 9–12) and 1,474 in college or graduate school.

Welfare. In 1990 federal direct payments to individuals totalled $14·62m., of which $2·41m. were disability insurance and $4·33m. retirement insurance.

CULTURE

Broadcasting. In 1997 there were 57,000 radio and 14,000 TV (colour by NTSC) sets in use.

Tourism. In 1998 there were 21,000 tourist arrivals; receipts totalled US$10m.

FURTHER READING

Hughes, H. G. A., *Samoa: American Samoa, Western Samoa, Samoans Abroad.* [Bibliography] ABC-Clio, Oxford and Santa Barbara (CA), 1997

GUAM

KEY HISTORICAL EVENTS

Magellan is said to have discovered the island in 1521; it was ceded by Spain to the USA by the Treaty of Paris (10 Dec. 1898). The island was captured by the Japanese on 10 Dec. 1941, and retaken by American forces from 21 July 1944. Guam is of great strategic importance; substantial numbers of naval and air force personnel occupy about one-third of the usable land.

TERRITORY AND POPULATION

Guam is the largest and most southern island of the Marianas Archipelago, in 13° 26' N. lat., 144° 43' E. long. Total area, 209 sq. miles (541 sq. km). Agaña, the seat of government, is about 8 miles from the anchorage in Apra Harbor. The census in 2000 showed a population of 154,805 (79,181 males), of whom 80,737 were born in Guam; density, 286·1 per sq. km. In 1995 an estimated 61·7% of the population lived in rural areas. The Malay strain is predominant. The native language is Chamorro; English is the official language and is taught in all schools.

SOCIAL STATISTICS

Births, 1997, 4,309; deaths, 615. Birth rate, 1997, 29·5 per 1,000 population; death rate, 4·2 per 1,000 population; infant mortality rate, 8·1 per 1,000 live births. Life expectancy, 1990–95, was 72·2 years for males and 76·0 years for females. Fertility rate, 1990–95, 3·4 births per woman.

CLIMATE

Tropical maritime, with little difference in temperatures over the year. Rainfall is copious at all seasons, but is greatest from July to Oct. Agaña, Jan. 81°F (27·2°C), July 81°F (27·2°C). Annual rainfall 93" (2,325 mm).

CONSTITUTION AND GOVERNMENT

Guam's constitutional status is that of an 'unincorporated territory' of the USA. Entry of US citizens is unrestricted; foreign nationals are subject to normal regulations. In 1949–50 the President transferred the administration of the island from the Navy Department (who held it from 1899) to the Interior Department. The transfer conferred full citizenship on the Guamanians, who had previously been 'nationals' of the USA. There was a referendum on status on 30 Jan. 1982. 38% of eligible voters voted; 48·5% of those favoured Commonwealth status.

The Governor and his staff constitute the executive arm of the government. The legislature is a 21-member Senate; its powers are similar to those of an American state legislature.

RECENT ELECTIONS

At the election of 5 Nov. 2002 for the Guam Legislature the Democrats won 9 seats and the Republicans won 6. In gubernatorial elections held on the same day, Republican candidate Felix Camacho won 55·2% of the vote against 44·8% for Democrat Robert Underwood.

CURRENT ADMINISTRATION

Governor: Felix Camacho (R.), 2003–07.
  Lieut.-Governor: Kaleo Moylan (R.), 2003–07.

Government Website: http://www.gov.gu

ECONOMY

Budget. Total revenue (1991) $525m.; expenditure $395m.

Banking and Finance. Banking law makes it possible for foreign banks to operate in Guam.

ENERGY AND NATURAL RESOURCES

Environment. According to the *World Bank Atlas* Guam's carbon dioxide emissions in 1998 were the equivalent of 27·6 tonnes per capita.

Electricity. Installed capacity was 302,000 kW in 1993. Production was 800m. kWh in 1998. Consumption per capita in 1995 was estimated at 4,566 kWh.

Water. The total area covered by water is approximately 7 sq. miles. Supplies are from springs, reservoirs and groundwater; 65% comes from water-bearing limestone in the north. The Navy and Air Force conserve water in reservoirs. The Water Resources Research Centre is at Guam University.

Agriculture. The major products of the island are sweet potatoes, cucumbers, watermelons and beans. In 1998 there were approximately 6,000 acres of arable land and 6,000 acres of permanent cropland. Production (1998 estimates, in 1,000 tonnes): coconuts, 42; copra, 2; watermelons, 2. Livestock (1996) included 1,000 goats and 4,000 pigs. There is an agricultural experimental station at Inarajan.

Fisheries. In 1999 total catches were 491,631 lb (223 tonnes), exclusively from sea fishing.

INDUSTRY

Guam Economic Development Authority controls three industrial estates: Cabras Island (32 acres); Calvo estate at Tamuning (26 acres); Harmon estate (16 acres). Industries include textile manufacture, cement and petroleum distribution, warehousing, printing, plastics and ship-repair. Other main sources of income are construction and tourism.

Labour. In 1990 there were 90,990 persons of employable age, of whom 66,138 were in the workforce (54,186 civilian). 2,042 were unemployed.

INTERNATIONAL TRADE

Guam is the only American territory which has complete 'free trade'; excise duties are levied only upon imports of tobacco, liquid fuel and liquor. In 1984 imports were valued at $493m. and exports at $34m.

COMMUNICATIONS

Roads. There are 674 km of all-weather roads. In 1997 there were 79,326 passenger cars and 32,262 commercial vehicles registered.

Civil Aviation. There is an international airport at Tamuning. Seven commercial airlines serve Guam. There were 966,398 passenger enplanements in 1999.

Shipping. There is a port at Apra Harbor.

Telecommunications. Overseas telephone and radio dispatch facilities are available. Main telephone lines numbered 80,300 in 2000 (478·0 per 1,000 inhabitants). Mobile phone subscribers numbered 5,600 in 1997. Internet users in Dec. 1999 numbered 5,000.

SOCIAL INSTITUTIONS

Justice. The Organic Act established a District Court with jurisdiction in matters arising under both federal and territorial law; the judge is appointed by the President subject to Senate approval. There is also a Supreme Court and a Superior Court; all judges are locally appointed except the Federal District judge. Misdemeanours are under the jurisdiction of the police court. The Spanish law was superseded in 1933 by five civil codes based upon California law.

The population in penal institutions in Dec. 1997 was 464 (320 per 100,000 of national population).

Religion. About 98% of the Guamanians are Roman Catholics; the other 2% are Baptists, Episcopalians, Bahais, Lutherans, Latter-day Saints (Mormons), Presbyterians, Jehovah's Witnesses and members of the Church of Christ and Seventh Day Adventists.

Education. Eight years of primary education to the age of 16 are compulsory. There are Chamorro Studies courses and bi-lingual teaching programmes to integrate the Chamorro language and culture into elementary and secondary school courses. In 2000 there were 1,782 pupils enrolled in nursery school and preschool, 3,134 in kindergarten, 23,969 in elementary school (grades 1–8), 10,664 in high school (grades 9–12) and 7,279 in college or graduate school. There is a University of Guam.

Welfare. There is a hospital, eight nutrition centres, a school health programme and an extensive immunization programme. Emphasis is on disease prevention, health education and nutrition. In 1990, $83·2m. was paid in Federal direct payments for individuals, including $1·91m. Medicare, $1·91m. disability insurance and $11·37m. retirement insurance.

CULTURE

Broadcasting. There are four commercial stations, a commercial television station, a public broadcasting station and a cable television station with 24 channels. In 1997 there were 221,000 radio and 106,000 TV sets (colour by NTSC).

Press. There is one daily newspaper, a twice-weekly paper, and four weekly publications (all of which are of military or religious interest only).

Tourism. There were 1,137,000 tourist arrivals in 1998, bringing in revenue of US$1·38bn.

FURTHER READING
Report (Annual) of the Governor of Guam to the US Department of Interior
Guam Annual Economic Review. Economic Research Center, Agaña

Rogers, R. F., *Destiny's Landfall: a History of Guam.* Hawaii Univ. Press, 1995
Wuerch, W. L. and Ballendorf, D. A., *Historical Dictionary of Guam and Micronesia.* Metuchen, NJ, 1995

VIRGIN ISLANDS OF THE UNITED STATES

KEY HISTORICAL EVENTS
The Virgin Islands of the United States, formerly known as the Danish West Indies, were named and claimed for Spain by Columbus in 1493. They were later settled by Dutch and English planters, invaded by France in the mid-17th century and abandoned by the French *c.* 1700, by which time Danish influence had been established. St Croix was held by the Knights of Malta between two periods of French rule.

The Virgin Islands were purchased by the United States from Denmark for $25m. in a treaty ratified by both nations and proclaimed on 31 March 1917. Their value was wholly strategic, inasmuch as they commanded the Anegada Passage from the Atlantic Ocean to the Caribbean Sea and the approach to the Panama Canal. Although the inhabitants were made US citizens in 1927, the islands are, constitutionally, an 'unincorporated territory'.

TERRITORY AND POPULATION
The Virgin Islands group, lying about 40 miles due east of Puerto Rico, comprises the islands of St Thomas (31 sq. miles), St Croix (83 sq. miles), St John (20 sq. miles) and 65 small islets or cays, mostly uninhabited. The total area is 1,910 sq. km (738 sq. miles), of which 346 sq. km (134 sq. miles) are dry land.

The population according to the 2000 census was 108,612 (females, 56,748); density 811 per sq. mile. Official population estimate for July 2002 was 123,498. An estimated 54·9% of the population were rural in 1995.

Population (2000 census) of St Croix, 53,234; St Thomas, 51,181; St John, 4,197. In 2000, 69·8% of the population were native born.

The capital and only city, Charlotte Amalie, on St Thomas, had a population (2000 census) of 11,044. There are two towns on St Croix with 2000 census populations of: Christiansted, 2,637; Frederiksted, 732.

SOCIAL STATISTICS
1997 births, 2,017; deaths, 620. Rates, 1997 (per 1,000 population); birth, 17·6; death, 5·4; infant mortality, 12·9 per 1,000 live births.

CLIMATE
Average temperatures vary from 77°F to 82°F throughout the year; humidity is low. Average annual rainfall, about 45". The islands lie in the hurricane belt; tropical storms with heavy rainfall can occur in late summer.

CONSTITUTION AND GOVERNMENT
The Organic Act of 22 July 1954 gives the US Department of the Interior full jurisdiction; some limited legislative powers are given to a single-chambered legislature, composed of 15 senators elected for two years representing the two legislative districts of St Croix and St Thomas-St John.

The Governor is elected by the residents. Since 1954 there have been four attempts to redraft the Constitution, to provide for greater autonomy. Each has been rejected by the electorate. The latest was defeated in a referendum in Nov. 1981, 50% of the electorate participating.

For administration, there are 14 executive departments, 13 of which are under commissioners and the other, the Department of Justice, under an Attorney-General. The US Department of the Interior appoints a Federal Comptroller of government revenue and expenditure.

The franchise is vested in residents who are citizens of the United States, 18 years of age or over. In 1986 there were 34,183 voters, of whom 26,377 participated in the local elections that year. They do not participate in the US presidential election but they have a non-voting representative in Congress.

The capital is Charlotte Amalie, on St Thomas Island.

RECENT ELECTIONS
Elections for governor held on 5 Nov. 2002 were won by Charles Turnbull II (Democrat) with 50·5% of the votes, ahead of John DeJongh in second place with 24·4%. The turn-out was 62%. In Senate elections held on 7 Nov. 2000 the Democratic Party of the Virgin Islands won 8 out of 15 seats.

CURRENT ADMINISTRATION
Governor: Charles Turnbull II (D), 2003–07.
Lieut.-Governor: Vargrave A. Richards (D.), 2003–07.

Government Website: http://www.usvi.org

ECONOMY

Currency. United States currency became legal tender on 1 July 1934.

Budget. Under the 1954 Organic Act finances are provided partly from local revenues—customs, federal income tax, real and personal property tax, trade tax, excise tax, pilotage fees, etc.—and partly from Federal Matching Funds, being the excise taxes collected by the federal government on such Virgin Islands products transported to the mainland as are liable.

Per capita income, 1996, $12,393.

Budget for financial year 1999: revenues, $486·3m.; expenditures, $486·3m.

Banking and Finance. Banks are the Chase Manhattan Bank; the Bank of Nova Scotia; the First Federal Savings and Loan Association of Puerto Rico; Barclays Bank International; Citibank; First Pennsylvania Bank; Banco Popular de Puerto Rico, and the First Virgin Islands Federal Savings Bank.

ENERGY AND NATURAL RESOURCES

Environment. According to the *World Bank Atlas* carbon dioxide emissions in 1998 were the equivalent of 99·0 tonnes per capita, the highest in the world.

Electricity. The Virgin Islands Water and Power Authority provides electric power from generating plants on St Croix and St Thomas; St John is served by power cable and emergency generator. Production in 1996 was 1·02bn. kWh. Per capita consumption in 1995 was an estimated 9,565 kWh.

Water. There are six de-salinization plants with maximum daily capacity of 8·7m. gallons of fresh water. Rainwater remains the most reliable source. Every building must have a cistern to provide rainwater for drinking, even in areas served by mains (10 gallons capacity per sq. ft of roof for a single-storey house).

The total area covered by water is approximately 37 sq. miles.

Agriculture. Land for fruit, vegetables and animal feed is available on St Croix, and there are tax incentives for development. Sugar has been terminated as a commercial crop and over 4,000 acres of prime land could be utilized for food crops.

Livestock (1996): cattle, 8,000; goats, 4,000; pigs, 3,000; sheep, 3,000.

Fisheries. There is a fishermen's co-operative with a market at Christiansted. There is a shellfish-farming project at Rust-op-Twist, St Croix. The total catch in 1998 was approximately 2,006,000 lb (910 tonnes).

INDUSTRY

The main occupations on St Thomas are tourism and government service; on St Croix manufacturing is more important. Manufactures include rum (the most valuable product), watches, pharmaceuticals and fragrances. Industries in order of revenue: tourism, refining oil, watch assembly, rum distilling, construction.

Labour. In 1990 the total labour force was 45,990, of whom 13,640 were employed in government, 8,450 in retail trades, 9,030 in hotels and other lodgings, 3,550 self-employed and unpaid family workers, 2,290 in transportation and public utilities, 2,420 in manufacturing, 4,140 in construction, 930 in banking, 2,090 in finance, insurance and real estate, 970 in wholesale trades, 920 in business services, 350 in legal services, and 2,330 in gift shops. In 1995 there were 2,700 registered unemployed persons, or 5·7% of the workforce.

INTERNATIONAL TRADE

Imports and Exports. Exports, calendar year 1990, totalled $2,820·7m. and imports $3,294·6m. The main import is crude petroleum, while the principal exports are petroleum products.

COMMUNICATIONS

Roads. In 1996 the Virgin Islands had 856 km of roads.

Civil Aviation. There is a daily cargo and passenger service between St Thomas and St Croix. Alexander Hamilton Airport on St Croix can take all aircraft except Concorde. Cyril E. King Airport on St Thomas takes 727-class aircraft. There are air connections to mainland USA, other Caribbean islands, Latin America and Europe. There were 634,445 passenger enplanements in 1999.

Shipping. The whole territory has free port status. There is an hourly boat service between St Thomas and St John.

Telecommunications. All three Virgin Islands have a dial telephone system. Main telephone lines numbered 69,000 in 2000 (569·7 per 1,000 population). Direct dialling to Puerto Rico and the mainland, and internationally, is now possible. Worldwide radio telegraph service is also available. In 1998 there were 25,000 mobile phone subscribers. In Dec. 1999 there were 12,000 Internet users.

Postal Services. In 1994 there were nine post offices.

SOCIAL INSTITUTIONS

Justice. The population in penal institutions in Dec. 1997 was 417 (355 per 100,000 of national population).

Religion. There are churches of the Protestant, Roman Catholic and Jewish faiths in St Thomas and St Croix, and Protestant and Roman Catholic churches in St John.

Education. In 1997 there were 11,926 pupils in 24 public elementary schools, and 9,982 pupils in 12 public secondary schools; 38 non-public schools had 6,255 pupils. There were 777 elementary teachers and 782 secondary teachers. In autumn 1998 the University of the Virgin Islands had 1,193 full-time undergraduate students and 187 graduate students. The College is part of the United States land-grant network of higher education. The Virgin Islands has the highest proportion of female students in higher education anywhere in the world, at 77% in 1998–99.

Welfare. In 1990 federal direct payments for individuals totalled $95·4m., including: retirement insurance, $31·6m.; food stamps, $18·4m.; disability insurance, $5·69m.; medicare, $4·98m.; supplemental medical insurance, $3·72m.

CULTURE

Broadcasting. There are eight radio stations and one public and one commercial TV station. In 1997 there were 107,000 radio and 68,000 TV (colour by NTSC) receivers in use.

Press. In 1996 there were three dailies with a combined circulation of 42,000, at a rate of 437 per 1,000 inhabitants.

Tourism. Tourism accounts for some 70% of GDP. There were 485,000 foreign tourists in 1999, and 1,616,000 cruise ship arrivals in 1998. Revenue from tourism amounted to $940m. in 1999.

FURTHER READING

Moll, V. P., *Virgin Islands*. [Bibliography] ABC-Clio, Oxford and Santa Barbara (CA), 1991

OTHER UNINCORPORATED TERRITORIES

Howland, Baker and Jarvis Islands

Three small Pacific islands, the largest two of which, Howland Island and Baker Island, are 2,600 km southwest of Hawaii. Administered under the US Department of the Interior. Area 2 sq. miles; population (1995) numbered 1,168. There is a National Assembly.

Johnston Atoll

Two small Pacific islands 1,100 km southwest of Hawaii, administered by the US Air Force. Area, under 1 sq. mile; population (1996) totalled 1,200 US military and civilian contractor personnel.

OTHER UNINCORPORATED TERRITORIES

Midway Islands
Two small Pacific islands at the western end of the Hawaiian chain, administered by the US Navy. Area, 2 sq. miles; population (1995) was 453 US military personnel.

Wake Island
Three small Pacific islands 3,700 km west of Hawaii, administered by the US Air Force. Area, 3 sq. miles; population (1995) numbered 302 US military and contract personnel.

Kingman Reef
Small Pacific reef 1,500 km southwest of Hawaii, administered by the US Navy. Area one tenth of a sq. mile; uninhabited.

Navassa Island
Small Caribbean island 48 km west of Haiti, administered by US Coast Guards. Area 2 sq. miles; uninhabited.

Palmyra Atoll
Small atoll 1,500 km southwest of Hawaii, administered by the US Department of the Interior. Area 5 sq. miles; uninhabited.

URUGUAY

República Oriental
del Uruguay

Capital: Montevideo
Population estimate, 2000: 3·34m.
GDP per capita, 2000: (PPP$) 9,035
HDI/world rank: 0·831/40

KEY HISTORICAL EVENTS

Uruguay was the last colony settled by Spain in the Americas. Part of the Spanish viceroyalty of Rio de la Plata until revolutionaries expelled the Spanish in 1811 and subsequently a province of Brazil, Uruguay declared independence on 25 Aug. 1825. Conflict between two political parties, the *blancos* (conservatives) and the *colorados* (liberals), led, in 1865–70, to the War of the Triple Alliance. In 1903 peace and prosperity were restored under President José Batlle y Ordóñez. Since 1904 Uruguay has been unique in her constitutional innovations, all designed to protect her from dictatorship. A favoured device was the collegiate system of government, in which the two largest political parties were represented.

The early part of the 20th century saw the development of a welfare state in Uruguay which encouraged extensive immigration. In 1919 a new constitution was adopted providing for a *colegiado*—a plural executive based on the Swiss pattern. However, the system was abolished in 1933 and replaced by presidential government, with quadrennial elections. From 1951 to 1966 a collective form of leadership again replaced the presidency. During the 1960s, following a series of strikes and riots, the Army became increasingly influential, repressive measures were adopted and presidential government was restored in 1967. The Tupamaro, Marxist urban guerrillas, sought violent revolution but were finally defeated by the Army in 1972. The return to civilian rule came on 12 Feb. 1985.

TERRITORY AND POPULATION

Uruguay is bounded on the northeast by Brazil, on the southeast by the Atlantic, on the south by the Río de la Plata and on the west by Argentina. The area is 176,215 sq. km (68,037 sq. miles). The following table shows the area and the population of the 19 departments at census 1996:

Departments	Sq. km	Census 1996	Capital
Artigas	11,928	75,059	Artigas
Canelones	4,536	443,053	Canelones
Cerro-Largo	13,648	82,510	Melo
Colonia	6,106	120,241	Colonia
Durazno	11,643	55,716	Durazno
Flores	5,144	25,030	Trinidad
Florida	10,417	66,503	Florida
Lavalleja	10,016	61,085	Minas
Maldonado	4,793	127,502	Maldonado
Montevideo	530	1,344,839	Montevideo
Paysandú	13,922	111,509	Paysandú
Río Negro	9,282	51,713	Fray Bentos
Rivera	9,370	98,472	Rivera
Rocha	10,551	70,292	Rocha
Salto	14,163	117,597	Salto
San José	4,992	96,664	San José
Soriano	9,008	81,557	Mercedes
Tacuarembó	15,438	84,919	Tacuarembó
Treinta y Tres	9,529	49,502	Treinta y Tres

Total population, census (1996) 3,163,763 (91·0% urban, 1999). Population density, 18·0 per sq. km.

The UN gives a projected population for 2010 of 3·57m.

In 1996 Montevideo (the capital) accounted for 44·5% of the total population. It had a population in 1999 of 1,237,000. Other major cities are Salto (population of

80,323 at 1985 census) and Paysandú (76,191 at 1985 census). Uruguay has the highest percentage of urban population in South America, with 90·7% living in urban areas in 1997.

13% of the population are over 65; 24% are under 15; 63% are between 15 and 64.

The official language is Spanish.

SOCIAL STATISTICS

1998: births, 54,760; deaths, 32,082. Rates (per 1,000 population), 1998: birth, 16·6; death, 9·8. Annual population growth rate, 1990–99, 0·7%. Infant mortality, 1999 (per 1,000 live births), 14·5. Life expectancy in 1999 was 70·8 years among males and 78·3 years among females. Fertility rate, 1999, 2·4 births per woman.

CLIMATE

A warm temperate climate, with mild winters and warm summers. The wettest months are March to June, but there is really no dry season. Montevideo, Jan. 72°F (22·2°C), July 50°F (10°C). Annual rainfall 38" (950 mm).

CONSTITUTION AND GOVERNMENT

Congress consists of a *Senate* of 31 members and a *Chamber of Deputies* of 99 members, both elected by proportional representation for five-year terms. The electoral system provides that the successful presidential candidate be a member of the party which gains a parliamentary majority. Electors vote for deputies on a first-past-the-post system, and simultaneously vote for a presidential candidate of the same party. The winners of the second vote are credited with the number of votes obtained by their party in the parliamentary elections. Referendums may be called at the instigation of 10,000 signatories.

National Anthem. 'Orientales, la patria o la tumba' ('Easterners, the fatherland or the tomb'); words by F. Acuña de Figueroa, tune by F. J. Deballi.

RECENT ELECTIONS

Elections for the General Assembly were held on 31 Oct. 1999. In elections to the Chamber of Deputies 40 seats were won by the Progressive Encounter (comprised of the Uruguay Assembly, Frenteamplio Confluence, Current 78, Movement of Popular Participation, Christian-Democratic Party, Communist Party of Uruguay, Party of the Communes, Socialist Party of Uruguay and the Social Democrats) with a combined 38·5% of the vote. The Colorado Party (PC) won 32 seats (31·3%), the National Party-Whites (PN) 22 (21·3%) and New Space 4 (4·4%). A coalition government was formed between PC and PN, but in Nov. 2002 the PN withdrew from the coalition following the resignation of its five cabinet ministers. In the Senate election, PC won 10 seats, PN 7, New Space 1 and Progressive Encounter 12.

In a runoff for the presidency on 28 Nov. 1999, Jorge Batlle won 54·1% of the vote and Tabaré Vázquez 45·9%. In the first round of voting, consisting of 4 candidates, Tabaré Vázquez had polled most votes.

CURRENT ADMINISTRATION

President: Jorge Batlle; b. 1927 (PC; sworn in 1 March 2000).
  Vice-President: Luis Hierro.
  In March 2003 the government comprised:
  Minister of Agriculture and Fishing: Gonzalo González. *Defence:* Yamandú Fau. *Education, Culture, Sports and Youth:* Leonardo Guzmán. *Finance and Economy:* Alejandro Atchugarry. *Foreign Affairs:* Didier Opertti. *Health:* Conrado Bonilla. *Housing and Environment:* Saul Irureta Saralegui. *Industry, Tourism, Energy and Mining:* Pedro Bordaberry. *Interior:* Guillermo Stirling. *Labour and Social Security:* Santiago Pérez de Castillo. *Transport and Public Works:* Lucio Cáceres Behrens.

Presidency Website (Spanish only): http://www.presidencia.gub.uy/

DEFENCE

Defence expenditure totalled US$356m. in 2000 (US$107 per capita), representing 2·6% of GDP.

Army. The Army consists of volunteers who enlist for 1–2 years service. There are four military regions with divisional headquarters. Strength (1999) 17,600. In addition there are government paramilitary forces numbering 920.

Navy. The navy includes three ex-French frigates. A naval aviation service 300 strong operates anti-submarine aircraft. Personnel in 1999 totalled 5,000 including 400 naval infantry. The main base is at Montevideo.

Air Force. Organized with US aid, the Air Force had (1999) about 3,000 personnel and 27 combat aircraft.

INTERNATIONAL RELATIONS

Uruguay is a member of the UN, WTO, OAS, Inter-American Development Bank, Mercosur, LAIA, IOM and the Antarctic Treaty.

ECONOMY

In 1998 services contributed 64·0% of GDP, industry 27·5% and agriculture 8·5%.

Overview. Uruguay's small economy benefits from a favourable climate for agriculture and a substantial hydropower potential. Economic development has been restrained in recent years by high—though declining—inflation and extensive government regulation. Uruguayan trade has continued to expand and the potential for new markets continued to open through negotiations with neighbouring countries and the EU.

Currency. The unit of currency is the *Uruguayan peso* (UYP), of 100 *centésimos*, which replaced the nuevo peso in March 1993 at 1 Uruguayan peso = 1,000 nuevos pesos. In June 2002 Uruguay allowed the peso to float freely. Foreign exchange reserves were US$1,791m. and gold reserves 8,000 troy oz in May 2002 (1·8m. troy oz in Nov. 1999). Inflation, which had been over 100% in 1990, was 4·4% in 2001. Total money supply in Feb. 2002 was 12,456m. pesos.

Budget. Central government finance (1m. pesos):

	1995	1996	1997	1998	1999	2000
Revenue	33,923	45,535	60,165	70,664	67,197	68,167
Expenditure	35,390	47,914	62,363	72,673	76,079	76,489

Components of 1995 revenue: VAT, 44·9%; income tax, 10·0%; fuel tax, 7·9%; capital gains tax, 5·7%; customs duties, 5·7%. Expenditure included: social welfare and salaries, 60·8%; capital expenditure, 10·9%; interest on public debt, 7·0%.

Standard rate of VAT is 23%.

Performance. Uruguay depends heavily on its two large neighbours, Uruguay and Argentina. In 1999, as a consequence of the devaluation of the Brazilian *real* and the worst drought since 1988, Uruguay's economy shrank by 2·8%. In 2000 there was negative growth again, of 1·4%, and the general downturn in the world economy exacerbated by Argentina's crisis caused the economy to contract again in 2001, by 3·1%. Total GDP in 2001 was US$18·4bn.

Banking and Finance. The Central Bank (*President*, Julio de Brun) was inaugurated on 16 May 1967. It is the bank of issue and supreme regulatory authority. In 1994 there were 22 commercial banks, 3 state-supported and 18 foreign-owned. Savings banks deposits were 1,993,029m. pesos in 1995. The State Insurance Bank has a monopoly of new insurance business.

There is a stock exchange in Montevideo.

Weights and Measures. The metric system is in use.

ENERGY AND NATURAL RESOURCES

Environment. According to the *World Bank Atlas* Uruguay's carbon dioxide emissions in 1998 were the equivalent of 1·8 tonnes per capita. An *Environmental Sustainability Index* compiled for the World Economic Forum meeting in Feb. 2002 ranked Uruguay sixth in the world, with 66·0%. The index measured the ability of countries to maintain favourable environmental conditions and examined various factors including pollution levels and the use or abuse of natural resources.

URUGUAY

Electricity. Installed capacity was 2·14m. kW in 1995. Production in 1998 was 9·47bn. kWh, with consumption per capita 1,788 kWh.

Agriculture. Rising investment has helped agriculture, which has given a major boost to the country's economy. Some 41m. acres are devoted to farming, of which 90% to livestock and 10% to crops. Some large *estancias* have been divided up into family farms; the average farm is about 250 acres.

Main crops (in 1,000 tonnes), 2000: rice, 1,175; wheat, 310; barley, 200; sugarcane, 160; oranges, 150; grapes, 140; potatoes, 110; wine, 108; apples, 65; maize, 65; sweet potatoes, 62; tangerines and mandarins, 60; lemons and limes, 48; oats, 45. The country has some 6m. fruit trees, principally peaches, oranges, tangerines and pears.

Livestock, 2000: sheep, 13·03m.; cattle, 10·80m.; horses, 500,000; pigs, 380,000; chickens, 13m.

Livestock products, 2000 (in 1,000 tonnes): beef and veal, 453; lamb and mutton, 51; pork, bacon and ham, 26; poultry meat, 53; milk 1,422; eggs, 37; greasy wool, 55.

Forestry. In 1995 the area under forests was 814,000 ha (mainly eucalyptus and pine), representing 4·7% of the total land area. In 1999, 6·16m. cu. metres of roundwood were cut.

Fisheries. The total catch in 1999 was 103,012 tonnes, almost entirely marine fish.

INDUSTRY
Industries include meat packing, oil refining, cement manufacture, foodstuffs, beverages, leather and textile manufacture, chemicals, light engineering and transport equipment. Output (in 1,000 tonnes): cement (1997), 781; sugar (1998), 14; motor cars (1991), 11,794 units; lorries (1991), 567 units; meat-packing (1991), 1,132,000 head; petroleum (1991), 1,587,000 cu. metres; 6bn. cigarettes (1996).

Labour. In 1996 the retirement age was raised from 55 to 60 for women; it remains 60 for men. The labour force in 1996 totalled 1,444,000 (59% males). In 1995, 37.0% of the urban workforce was engaged in services and public administration, 19·6% in trade, 17·9% in manufacturing, 7·1% in building, 6·2% in financial services and 5·7% in transport and communications.

INTERNATIONAL TRADE
External debt was US$8,196m. in 2000.

Imports and Exports. Trade in US$1m.:

	1996	1997	1998	1999	2000
Imports f.o.b.	3,135·4	3,497·5	3,601·4	3,187·2	3,316·4
Exports f.o.b.	2,448·5	2,793·1	2,829·3	2,290·6	2,379·6

Principal exports in 1995 (in US$1,000): live animals and by-products, 561·8; textiles, 421·3 (including washed wool, 25·8); meat, agricultural produce, 304·1 (including rice, 163·0); leather, hides and manufactures, 250·7; footwear, 17·8.

The main import suppliers in 1996 were Brazil (22·4%), Argentina (20·8%), USA (12·0%) and Italy (5·2%). Leading export destinations in 1996 were Brazil (34·7%), Argentina (11·3%), USA (7·0%) and Germany (4·7%).

COMMUNICATIONS
Roads. In 1997 it was estimated that there were about 8,983 km of roads including 2,589 km of national roads and 5,024 km of regional roads. Uruguay has one of the densest road networks in the world. Passenger cars in 1997 numbered 517,000 (153·9 per 1,000 inhabitants). There were 737 fatalities as a result of road accidents in 1997.

Rail. The total railway system open for traffic was (1996) 2,073 km of 1,435 mm gauge; in 1997 freight tonne-km carried came to 204m. Passenger service, which had been abandoned in 1988, was resumed on a limited basis in 1993.

Civil Aviation. There is an international airport at Montevideo (Carrasco). The national carrier is Pluna. In 1998 it operated domestic services and maintained routes to Argentina, Bolivia, Brazil, Chile, Cuba, Paraguay, Spain and the USA. There were 60 airports in 1996, 45 with paved runways and 15 with unpaved runways. In 1998 Montevideo handled 1,470,000 passengers (1,198,000 on international flights) and 25,500 tonnes of freight. In 1999 scheduled airline traffic of Uruguay-based carriers flew 8·4m. km, carrying 728,000 passengers (all on international flights).

Shipping. In 1998 sea-going shipping totalled 107,000 GRT; including oil tankers 48,000 GRT. In 1997 vessels totalling 5,844,000 NRT entered ports and vessels totalling 26,844,000 NRT cleared. Navigable inland waterways total 1,270 km.

Telecommunications. The telephone system in Montevideo is controlled by the State; small companies operate in the interior. Uruguay had 929,100 main telephone lines in 2000 (278·4 for every 1,000 persons), and there were 350,000 PCs in use (104·9 for every 1,000 persons). There were 316,100 mobile phone subscribers in 1999 and 11,000 fax machines in 1995. Internet users numbered 70,000 in Dec. 2000.

Postal Services. In 1995 there were 295 post offices.

SOCIAL INSTITUTIONS

Justice. The Supreme Court is elected by Congress; it appoints all other judges. There are four courts of appeal, each with three judges. There are civil and criminal courts. Each department has its court, and there are 224 lower courts.

The population in penal institutions in 1995 was 3,190 (100 per 100,000 of national population).

Religion. State and Church are separate, and there is complete religious liberty. In 1997 there were 2·5m. Roman Catholics and 680,000 persons with other beliefs.

Education. Adult literacy in 1999 was 97·7% (male, 97·3%; female, 98·1%). The female literacy rate is the highest in South America. Primary education is obligatory; both primary and secondary education are free. In 1996 there were 1,961 pre-primary schools with 2,918 teachers for 75,580 pupils; 2,415 primary schools with 16,868 teachers for 345,573 pupils and at secondary level there were 269,826 pupils.

There is 1 state university, 1 independent Roman Catholic university and 1 private institute of technology. In 1995 there were 71,379 students and 6,683 academic staff.

In 1996 total expenditure on education came to 3·3% of GNP and represented 15·5% of total government expenditure.

Health. In 1994 there were 11,241 doctors, 3,740 dentists, 2,139 nurses, 922 pharmacists and 554 midwives. There were 112 hospitals in 1993, with a provision of 45 beds for every 10,000 persons.

Welfare. The welfare state dates from the beginning of the 1900s. In 1994 there were 0·5m. recipients of pensions and benefits. A private pension scheme inaugurated in 1996 had 315,000 members at 31 Dec. 1996. State spending on social security has been capped at 15% of GDP.

CULTURE

Broadcasting. In 1997 there were 1·97m. radio and 782,000 television receivers (colour by PAL N). There are four TV networks (three commercial) and about 100 radio stations.

Press. In 1996 there were 36 daily newspapers with a combined circulation of 950,000. There were also 62 non-daily newspapers and periodicals.

Tourism. There were 2·14m. tourists in 1999, mainly from Argentina. Receipts totalled US$653m.

DIPLOMATIC REPRESENTATIVES

Of Uruguay in the United Kingdom (2nd Floor, 140 Brompton Rd., London, SW3 1HY)
Ambassador: Miguel J. Berthet.

Of the United Kingdom in Uruguay (Calle Marco Bruto 1073, 11300 Montevideo)
Ambassador: John Everard.

Of Uruguay in the USA (2715 M. St., NW, Washington, D.C., 20007)
Ambassador: Hugo Fernández Faingold.

URUGUAY

Of the USA in Uruguay (Lauro Muller 1776, Montevideo)
Ambassador: Martin J. Silverstein.

Of Uruguay to the United Nations
Ambassador: Felipe Paolillo.

Of Uruguay to the European Union
Ambassador: Jorge Talice.

FURTHER READING

González, L. E., *Political Structures and Democracy in Uruguay.* Univ. of Notre Dame Press, 1992

Sosnowski, S. (ed.) *Repression, Exile and Democracy: Uruguayan Culture.* Duke Univ. Press, 1993

National library: Biblioteca Nacional del Uruguay, Guayabo 1793, Montevideo.
Website (Spanish only): http://www.ine.gub.uy/

UZBEKISTAN

Uzbekiston Respublikasy

Capital: Tashkent
Population estimate, 2000: 24·89m.
GDP per capita, 2000: (PPP$) 2,441
HDI/world rank: 0·727/95

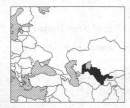

KEY HISTORICAL EVENTS

Descended from nomadic Mongol tribes who settled in Central Asia in the 13th century, the Uzbeks came under Russian control in the late 19th century. In Oct. 1917 the Tashkent Soviet assumed authority. The semi-independent Khanates of Khiva and Bokhara were first (1920) transformed into People's Republics, then (1923–24) into Soviet Socialist Republics, and finally merged in the Uzbek SSR and other republics. On 20 June 1990 the Supreme Soviet adopted a declaration of sovereignty and in Aug. 1991, following an unsuccessful coup, declared independence as the Republic of Uzbekistan. In Dec. 1991 Uzbekistan became a member of the CIS.

Islam Karimov became head of state in 1990 and was elected president in 1991 and again in 2000. In that year Uzbek border guards moved their posts 5 km into a part of neighbouring Kazakhstan. Borders with Russia and Kyrgyzstan still remain undefined, yet the chief cause for concern is the Islamist Movement of Uzbekistan's fight to create an Islamic state in the Fergana Valley. Bomb blasts in Tashkent, one of which almost killed the president in 1999, were blamed on religious extremists and the army suffered losses fighting the IMU in 2000. Central Asian governments have agreed to co-operate on the issue.

TERRITORY AND POPULATION

Uzbekistan is bordered in the north by Kazakhstan, in the east by Kyrgyzstan and Tajikistan, in the south by Afghanistan and in the west by Turkmenistan. Area, 447,400 sq. km (172,741 sq. miles). At the 1989 census the population was 19,810,077 (71·4% Uzbek, 8·4% Russian, 4·7% Tajik, 4·1% Kazakh, 3·2% Tatar and 2·1% Karakalpak). The population in 1997 was 23,467,700 (11,842,800 females); density, 52·5 per sq. km. In 1999, 62·8% of the population lived in rural areas.

The UN gives a projected population for 2010 of 28·54m.

The areas and populations of the 12 Regions and the Karakalpak Autonomous Republic (Karakalpakstan) are as follows (Uzbek spellings in brackets):

Region	Area (in sq. km)	Population (1994 estimate)	Capital	Population (1994 estimate)
Andizhan (Andijon)	4,200	1,899,000	Andizhan	303,000
Bukhara (Bukhoro)	39,400	1,262,000	Bukhara	236,000
Ferghana (Farghona)	7,100	2,338,000	Ferghana	191,000
Dzhizak (Jizzakh)	20,500	831,000	Dzhizak	116,000
Khorezm (Khorazm)	6,300	1,135,000	Urgench (Urganch)	135,000
Namangan	7,900	1,652,000	Namangan	341,000
Navoi (Nawoiy)	110,800	715,000	Nawoiy	115,000
Kashkadar (Qashqadaryo)	28,400	715,000	Karshi (Qarshi)	177,000
Karakalpakstan Autonomous Republic (Qoraqalpoghiston)	164,900	1,343,000	Nukus (Nuqus)	185,000
Samarkand (Samarqand)	16,400	2,322,000	Samarkand	368,000
Syr-Darya (Sirdaryo)	5,100	600,000	Gulistan (Guliston)	57,000[1]
Surkhan-Darya (Surkhondaryo)	20,800	1,437,000	Termez (Termiz)	90,000[1]
Tashkent (Toshkent)	15,600	4,357,000	Tashkent	2,121,000

[1]1991.

The capital is Tashkent (1999 population estimate, 2,143,000); other large towns are Namangan, Samarkand and Andizhan. There are 124 towns, 97 urban settlements and 155 rural districts.

The Roman alphabet (in use 1929–40) was reintroduced in 1994. Arabic script was in use prior to 1929, and Cyrillic, 1940–94.

Uzbek, Russian and Tajik are all spoken.

SOCIAL STATISTICS

Births, 1999, 553,745; deaths, 140,526; marriages, 1997, 181,126. Rates, 1999: birth (per 1,000 population), 23·1; death, 5·9. Life expectancy, 1999, 65·8 years for men and 71·7 for women. Annual population growth rate, 1990–99, 1·7%. In 1997 the most popular age range for marrying was 20–24 for both males and females. Infant mortality, 1999, 22·3 per 1,000 live births; fertility rate, 1999, 3·3 births per woman.

CLIMATE

The summers are warm to hot but the heat is made more bearable by the low humidity. The winters are cold but generally dry and sunny. Tashkent, Jan. −1°C, July 25°C. Annual rainfall 14·76" (375 mm).

CONSTITUTION AND GOVERNMENT

A new constitution was adopted on 8 Dec. 1992 stating that Uzbekistan is a pluralist democracy. The constitution restricts the president to standing for two five-year terms. In Jan. 2002 a referendum was held at which 91% of the electorate voted in favour of extending the presidential term from five to seven years. It was not clear whether the change would affect the current presidential term, scheduled to end in 2005. Voters were also in favour of changing from a single-chamber legislature to a bicameral parliament.

Parliament is the 250-member *Oliy Majlis* (Supreme Assembly).

RECENT ELECTIONS

Presidential elections were held on 9 Jan. 2000. Incumbent Islam Karimov was elected against a single opponent with 91·9% of the vote. Turn-out was 95%. It was the first presidential election since 1991. Elections were cancelled in 1997 after Karimov's term was extended to 2000 by referendum.

Parliamentary elections were held on 5 and 19 Dec. 1999. Turn-out was 95%. The People's Democratic Party (former Communists) won 48 of the 250 available seats; the Self Sacrifice Party won 34; Progress of the Fatherland won 20; Justice won 11; National Renaissance won 10; various initiative groups claimed 16. 110 seats went to various regional government structures and 1 seat remained vacant.

CURRENT ADMINISTRATION

President: Islam Karimov; b. 1938 (sworn in 24 March 1990).

In March 2003 the government comprised:

Prime Minister: Utkur Sultanov; b. 1939 (People's Democratic Party; sworn in 21 Dec. 1995).

First Deputy Prime Minister: Kozim Tulyaganov. *Deputy Prime Ministers:* Rustam Azimov (also *Minister of Macroeconomics and Statistics*); Rustam Yunusov; Mirabror Usmanov; Hamidulla Karamatov; Uktam Ismailov; Valeriy Otayev (also *Minister of Energy and Fuel*); Anatoliy Isayev; Nosirjon Yusupov (also *Agriculture and Water Utilization*); Elyor Ganiyev (also *Minister of Foreign Economic Relations*).

Minister of Internal Affairs: Zokirjon Almatov. *Defence:* Kodir Ghulomov. *Foreign Affairs:* Abdulaziz Komilov. *Justice:* Abdusamad Polvon-Zoda. *Finance:* Mamarizo Normuradov. *Education:* Risboy Jorayev. *Higher and Secondary Specialized Education:* Saidahror Guljamov. *Cultural Affairs:* Hairulla Juraev. *Health:* Feruz Nazirov. *Labour and Social Protection:* Oqiljon Obidov. *Emergency Situations:* Botir Parpiev.

Chairman, Oliy Majlis: Erkin Halilov.

Office of the President: http://www.gov.uz/

DEFENCE

Conscription is for 18 months. Defence expenditure in 2000 totalled US$1,481 (US$61 per capita), representing 8·0% of GDP.

Army. Personnel, 1999, 50,000. There are, in addition, paramilitary forces totalling 18,000–20,000.

Air Force. Personnel, 1999, 4,000. There were 150 combat aircraft in operation (including Su-17s, Su-24s, Su-25s, Su-27s and MiG-29s) and 42 attack helicopters.

INTERNATIONAL RELATIONS
Uzbekistan is a member of the UN, CIS, OSEC, Asian Development Bank, ECO, OIC and the NATO Partnership for Peace.

ECONOMY
Services accounted for 41·9% of GDP in 1998, agriculture 31·2% and industry 27·0%.

Currency. A coupon for a new unit of currency, the *soum* (UKS), was introduced alongside the rouble on 15 Nov. 1993. This was replaced by the *soum* proper at 1 soum = 1,000 coupons on 1 July 1994. In 1994 inflation was 1,568% but has since declined, and was 27·2% in 2001. Exchange controls were abolished on 1 July 1995.

Budget. The 1997 budget provided for revenue of 123,600m. soums and expenditure of 150,400m. soums.

Performance. Real GDP growth was 4·3% in both 1998 and 1999, 4·0% in 2000 and 4·5% in 2001; total GDP in 2001 was US$11·3bn.

Banking and Finance. The Central Bank is the bank of issue (*Chairman*, Dr Faizulla Mulladjanov). In 1996 there were ten commercial banks, the National Bank for Foreign Economic Activity (state-owned), three specialized commercial banks and one co-operative bank. Two foreign banks had representative offices.

ENERGY AND NATURAL RESOURCES

Environment. Irrigation of arid areas has caused the drying up of the Aral Sea. According to the *World Bank Atlas* Uzbekistan's carbon dioxide emissions in 1998 were the equivalent of 4·5 tonnes per capita.

Electricity. Installed capacity was 12m. kW in 1997. Production was 47·9bn. kWh in 1998 and consumption per capita 1,618 kWh. In 1997, 3,615 km of power transmission lines were conducted.

Oil and Gas. Crude oil production was 63m. bbls. in 1996; natural gas output in 1999 was 50,268m. cu. metres. In 1999 there were proven oil reserves of 0·6bn. bbls. and natural gas reserves of 1,870bn. cu. metres. In 1997, 9 oil wells, 18 gas wells and 320·4 km of gas mains lines came into operation.

Minerals. 2·89m. tonnes of lignite were produced in 1997 and 74,000 tonnes of hard coal in 1996. In 2000, 86 tonnes of gold were produced. There are also large reserves of silver, uranium, copper, lead, zinc and tungsten; all uranium mined (2,130 tonnes in 1997) is exported.

Agriculture. Farming is intensive and based on irrigation. In 1998 there were 4·48m. ha of arable land and 0·38m. ha of permanent cropland; 4·28m. ha were irrigated in 1997.

By 1996 some 97% of the 715 state farms were co-operative, private or otherwise owned, and accounted for over 98% of agricultural production.

Cotton is the main crop, accounting for more than 40% of the value of total agricultural production. In 1997 more than 3·6m. tonnes of raw cotton was laid. Fruit, vegetables and rice are also grown; sericulture and the production of astrakhan wool are also important.

Output of main agricultural products (2000, in 1,000 tonnes): seed cotton, 3,006; wheat, 2,787; cottonseed, 1,920; tomatoes, 1,000; cotton lint, 950; cabbages, 882; potatoes, 656; grapes, 625; apples, 480; watermelons, 457; sugarbeets, 380; cucumbers and gherkins, 272.

Livestock, 2000: 5·27m. cattle; 8·92m. sheep; 639,000 goats; 14m. chickens. Animal products, 2000 (in 1,000 tonnes): meat, 536; milk, 3,739; eggs, 69.

Forestry. In 1995 the area under forests was 9·12m. ha, accounting for 22% of the total land area (up from 7·99m. ha and 19·3% of the land area in 1990). This is due to new planting between 1990 and 1995, which resulted in an increase of 1·13m. ha of forest—a figure exceeded only in the USA over the same period.

Fisheries. The total catch in 1999 was 2,871 tonnes, exclusively freshwater fish.

INDUSTRY

Industrial production increased by 6·5% in 1997 owing to the growth of industrial investment in previous years. The production of consumer goods increased by 11·2%. Major industries include fertilizers, agricultural and textile machinery, aircraft, metallurgy and chemicals. Output, 1993 (in tonnes): rolled ferrous metals, 0·6m.; cement (1997), 3·3m.; mineral fertilizer, 1·3m.; chemical fibre, 22,600; paper, 13,100; fabrics, 632m. sq. metres; footwear, 39·6m. pairs; 11,500 tractors; 59,000 TV sets (1995); 19,000 refrigerators (1995); 14,000 washing machines (1995).

Labour. In 1995 the labour force was 8·2m.: agriculture and forestry, 44%; industry and construction, 20%; other, 36%. In 2000 the unemployment rate was 0·6%. Average monthly salary in 1997 was 3,681·3 soums. A minimum wage of 70,000 soum-coupons a month was imposed on 1 June 1994.

INTERNATIONAL TRADE

In Jan. 1994 an agreement to create a single economic zone was signed with Kazakhstan and Kyrgyzstan. Foreign investors are entitled to a two-year tax holiday and repatriation of hard currency. External debt was US$4,340m. in 2000. In 1997 external trade turnover was US$8,910·5m.

Imports and Exports. In 1997 imports were valued at US$3,200m. and exports at US$2,878·9m. Principal imports, 1996, were machinery (35% of the total), light industrial goods, food and raw materials; principal exports were cotton (38% of the total), textiles, machinery, chemicals, food and energy products.

The main import sources in 1996 were Russia (24·9%), South Korea (11·8%), Germany (11·0%) and USA (8·1%). Principal export markets in 1996 were Russia (22·4%), Italy (8·8%), Tajikistan (6·8%), China (5·1%) and Ukraine (also 5·1%).

COMMUNICATIONS

Roads. Length of roads, 1997, was 43,463 km (3,237 km of main roads). In 1993, 2,347m. passengers and 217·2m. tonnes of freight were carried.

Rail. The total length of railway in 1993 was 3,483 km of 1,520 mm gauge (432 km electrified). Passenger-km travelled in 1998 came to 2m. and freight tonne-km to 16m.

Civil Aviation. The main international airport is in Tashkent (Vostochny). Andizhan, Namangan and Samarkand also have airports. The national carrier is the state-owned Uzbekistan Airways, which in 1998 operated domestic services and flew to Almaty, Amsterdam, Ashgabat, Athens, Baku, Bangkok, Beijing, Chelyabinsk, Delhi, Ekaterinburg, Frankfurt, Istanbul, Kazan, Khabarovsk, Krasnoyarsk, Kuala Lumpur, London, Mineralnye Vody, Moscow, New York, Novosibirsk, Omsk, Rostov, St Petersburg, Samara, Seoul, Sharjah, Simferopol, Tel Aviv, Tyumen, Ufa and Vientiane. In 1999 it flew 36·9m. km, carrying 1,657,600 passengers (877,500 on international flights). In 2000 Tashkent handled 1,964,432 passengers (1,165,026 on international flights) and 23,167 tonnes of freight.

Shipping. The total length of inland waterways in 1990 was 1,100 km.

Telecommunications. In 1999 main telephone lines numbered 1,655,000 (67·1 per 1,000 population) and there were 40,400 mobile phone subscribers. Uzbekistan had 7,500 Internet users in Dec. 1999. There were 1,900 fax machines in 1995.

SOCIAL INSTITUTIONS

Justice. In 1994, 73,561 crimes were reported, including 1,219 murders and attempted murders. The death penalty is in force and was used in 2000. The population in penal institutions in 1996 was approximately 60,000 (260 per 100,000 of national population).

Religion. The Uzbeks are predominantly Sunni Muslims.

Education. In 1995 there were 1·07m. pre-primary pupils with 96,100 teachers, 1·9m. primary pupils with 92,400 teachers, and 3·31m. secondary pupils with 340,200 teachers. There were (1998) 55 higher educational establishments with 272,300 students, and 248 technical colleges with 240,100 students. There are universities and medical schools in Tashkent and Samarkand. Adult literacy rate in 1999 was 88·5% (93·1% among males and 84·0% among females).

Health. In 1995 there were 76,200 doctors, 249,600 nurses and 192 hospitals, with a provision of 84 beds per 10,000 population.

Welfare. In Jan. 1994 there were 1,726,000 old-age pensioners and 1,007,000 other pensioners.

CULTURE

Broadcasting. Broadcasting is under the aegis of the State Teleradio Broadcasting Company. The government-controlled Uzbek Radio transmits two national and several regional programmes, a Radio Moscow relay and a foreign service, Radio Tashkent (Uzbek, Arabic, English, Dari, Farsi, Hindi, Pushtu, Uighur). In 1997 there were 10·8m. radio and 6·4m. television receivers. Colour transmission is by SECAM H.

Press. In 1996 there were three daily newspapers with a combined circulation of 75,000.

Tourism. There were 272,000 tourists in 1998. Receipts totalled US$21m.

DIPLOMATIC REPRESENTATIVES

Of Uzbekistan in the United Kingdom (41 Holland Park, London, W11 2RP)
Ambassador: Alisher Faizullaev.

Of the United Kingdom in Uzbekistan (Ul. Gogolya 67, Tashkent 700000)
Ambassador: Craig Murray.

Of Uzbekistan in the USA (1746 Massachusetts Ave., NW, Washington, D.C., 20036)
Ambassador: Shavkat Shodiyevich Khamrakulov.

Of the USA in Uzbekistan (82 Chilanzarskaya, Tashkent)
Ambassador: John Herbst.

Of Uzbekistan to the United Nations
Ambassador: Alisher Vohidov.

Of Uzbekistan to the European Union
Ambassador: Alisher Shaykhov.

FURTHER READING

Bohr, A. (ed.) *Uzbekistan: Politics and Foreign Policy.* The Brookings Institution, Washington (D.C.), 1998

Kalter, J. and Pavaloi, M., *Uzbekistan: Heir to the Silk Road.* Thames and Hudson, London, 1997

Kangas, R. D., *Uzbekistan in the Twentieth Century: Political Development and the Evolution of Power.* New York, 1994

Melvin, N. J., *Uzbekistan: Transition to Authoritarianism on the Silk Road.* Routledge, London, 2000

KARAKALPAK AUTONOMOUS REPUBLIC (KARAKALPAKSTAN)

Area, 164,900 sq. km (63,920 sq. miles); population (Jan. 1994), 1,343,000. Capital, Nukus (1989 census population, 174,000). The Qoraqalpoghs came under Russian rule in the second half of the 19th century. On 11 May 1925 the territory was constituted within the then Kazakh Autonomous Republic (of the Russian Federation) as an Autonomous Region. On 20 March 1932 it became an Autonomous Republic within the Russian Federation, and on 5 Dec. 1936 it became part of the Uzbek SSR. At the 1989 census Qoraqalpoghs were 32·1% of the population, Uzbeks 32·8% and Kazakhs 26·3%.

Its manufactures are in the field of light industry—bricks, leather goods, furniture, canning and wine. In Jan. 1990 cattle numbered 336,000, and sheep and goats 518,100. There were 38 collective and 124 state farms in 1987. The total cultivated area in 1985 was 350,400 ha.

In 1990–91 there were 313,500 pupils at schools, 22,100 students at technical colleges, and 7,800 at Nukus University. There is a branch of the Uzbek Academy of Sciences.

There were 2,600 doctors and 12,800 hospital beds in 1987.

VANUATU

Ripablik blong Vanuatu
(Republic of Vanuatu)

Capital: Vila
Population estimate, 2000: 195,000
GDP per capita, 2000: (PPP$) 2,802
HDI/world rank: 0·542/131

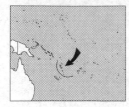

KEY HISTORICAL EVENTS

Vanuatu occupies the group of islands formerly known as the New Hebrides, in the southwestern Pacific Ocean. Captain Bligh and his companions, cast adrift by the *Bounty* mutineers, sailed through part of the island group in 1789. Sandalwood merchants and European missionaries came to the islands in the mid-19th century and were then followed by cotton planters—mostly French and British—in 1868. In response to Australian calls to annexe the islands, Britain and France agreed on joint supervision. Joint sovereignty was held over the indigenous Melanesian people but each nation retained responsibility for its own nationals according to a protocol of 1914. The island group escaped Japanese invasion during the Second World War and became an Allied base. On 30 July 1980 New Hebrides became an independent nation under the name of Vanuatu, meaning 'Our Land Forever'.

TERRITORY AND POPULATION

Vanuatu comprises 80 islands, which lie roughly 800 km west of the Fiji Islands and 400 km northeast of New Caledonia. The estimated land area is 4,706 sq. miles (12,190 sq. km). The larger islands of the group are: (Espiritu) Santo, Malekula, Epi, Pentecost, Aoba, Maewo, Paama, Ambrym, Efate, Erromanga, Tanna and Aneityum. They also claim Matthew and Hunter islands. 67 islands were inhabited in 1990. Population at the 1999 census, 186,678; density, 15·3 per sq. km.

The UN gives a projected population for 2010 of 252,000.

In 1998, 80·5% of the population lived in rural areas. Vila (the capital) has a population of 26,000 (1999 estimate), and Luganville 10,000.

40% of the population is under 15 years of age, 57% between the ages of 15 and 64 and 3% 65 or over.

The national language is Bislama (spoken by 82% of the population): English and French are also official languages; about 50,000 speak French.

SOCIAL STATISTICS

Births, 1997, 5,400; deaths, 1,600. Rates per 1,000 population, 1997: birth rate, 29·9; death rate, 8·6. Annual population growth rate, 1990–99, 2·5%. Life expectancy, 1998, was 65·8 years for males and 69·9 years for females. Infant mortality, 1998, 38 per 1,000 live births; fertility rate, 1999, 4·2 births per woman.

CLIMATE

The climate is tropical, but moderated by oceanic influences and by trade winds from May to Oct. High humidity occasionally occurs and cyclones are possible. Rainfall ranges from 90" (2,250 mm) in the south to 155" (3,875 mm) in the north. Vila, Jan. 80°F (26·7°C), July 72°F (22·2°C). Annual rainfall 84" (2,103 mm).

CONSTITUTION AND GOVERNMENT

Legislative power resides in a 50-member unicameral Parliament elected for a term of four years. The President is elected for a five-year term by an electoral college comprising Parliament and the presidents of the 11 regional councils. Executive power is vested in a Council of Ministers, responsible to Parliament, and appointed and led by a Prime Minister who is elected from and by Parliament.

There is also a *Council of Chiefs,* comprising traditional tribal leaders, to advise on matters of custom.

National Anthem. 'Yumi yumi yumi i glat blong talem se, yumi, yumi yumi i man blong Vanuatu' ('We we we are glad to tell, we we we are the people of Vanuatu'); words and tune by F. Vincent.

RECENT ELECTIONS
Parliamentary elections were held on 2 May 2002. The Union of Moderate Parties (UMP) gained 15 seats; the Party of Our Land (VP), 14; the Vanuatu National United Party (NUP), 8; the Melanesian Progressive Party (MPP), 3; the Vanuatu Republican Party (VRP), 3; the Green party, 3; and non-partisans, 5.

CURRENT ADMINISTRATION
President: Father John Bani; b. 1941 (elected on 24 March 1999).

A VP-NUP coalition government was formed following the March 1998 election. In March 2003 it consisted of the following:

Prime Minister: Edward Natapei; b. 1955 (VP; sworn in 13 April 2001).

Deputy Prime Minister, Minister of Foreign Affairs, Trade Development and Telecommunications: Serge Vohor. *Minister of Internal Affairs:* Joe Natuman. *Education:* Jacques Sese. *Finance and Management:* Sela Molisa. *Lands and Mineral Resources:* Jacklyne Reuben Titeck. *Agriculture, Forestry and Fisheries:* Steven Kalsakau. *Health:* Donald Kalpokas. *Comprehensive Reform Programme:* Philip Boedoro. *Ni-Vanuatu Business Development:* Nicolas Brown. *Industry and Commerce:* Jean Alain Mahe. *Youth and Sports:* Raphael Worwor. *Infrastructure and Public Utilities:* Willie Posen.

Government Website: http://www.vanuatugovernment.gov.vu/

DEFENCE
There is a paramilitary force with about 300 personnel. The Vanuatu Police maritime service operates one inshore patrol craft, and a former motor yacht, both lightly armed. Personnel numbered about 50 in 1996.

INTERNATIONAL RELATIONS
Vanuatu is a member of the UN, the Commonwealth, the Asian Development Bank, the Pacific Community, the Pacific Islands Forum and the International Organization of the Francophonie, and is an ACP member state of the ACP-EU relationship.

ECONOMY
Agriculture accounted for 24·7% of GDP in 1998, industry 12·2% and services 63·2%.

Currency. The unit of currency is the *vatu* (VUV) with no minor unit. There was inflation in 2001 of 2·0%. Foreign exchange reserves in June 2002 were US$34m. Total money supply in June 2002 was 11,254m. vatu.

Budget. Budget revenue and expenditure (in 1m. vatu):

	1995	1996	1997	1998	1999
Revenue	6,965	6,352	6,206	6,605	6,753
Expenditure	7,497	7,282	7,023	9,219	7,531

Performance. Real GDP growth was 3·7% in 2000, but in 2001 there was negative growth, of –0·5%. Total GDP in 2001 was US$0·2bn.

Banking and Finance. The Reserve Bank blong Vanuatu is the central bank and bank of issue. The Finance Centre in Vila consists of four international banks and six trust companies. Commercial banks' assets at 31 Dec. 1988, 20,900m. vatu.

Weights and Measures. The metric system is in force.

ENERGY AND NATURAL RESOURCES

Environment. According to the *World Bank Atlas* Vanuatu's carbon dioxide emissions in 1998 were the equivalent of 0·3 tonnes per capita.

Electricity. Electrical capacity in 1995 was 11,000 kW. Production in 1998 was 32m. kWh and consumption per capita in 1997 was 169 kWh.

Agriculture. About 65% of the labour force are employed in agriculture. The main commercial crops are copra, coconuts, cocoa and coffee. Production (2000 estimates, in 1,000 tonnes): coconuts, 364; copra, 40; bananas, 13; groundnuts, 2. 80% of the population are engaged in subsistence agriculture; yams, taro, cassava, sweet potatoes and bananas are grown for local consumption. A large number of cattle are reared on plantations, and a beef industry is developing.

Livestock (2000): cattle, 152,000; goats, 12,000; pigs, 62,000; horses, 3,000; poultry, 158,000 (1995).

Forestry. There were 900,000 ha of forest in 1995 (73·8% of the land area). In 1999, 63,000 cu. metres of roundwood were cut.

Fisheries. The principal catch is tuna, mainly exported to the USA. The total catch in 1999 was an estimated 94,581 tonnes.

INDUSTRY

Industry in 1995 employed about 3% of the workforce, with 32% employed in services. Principal industries include copra processing, meat canning and fish freezing, a saw-mill, soft drinks factories and a print works. Building materials, furniture and aluminium are also produced, and in 1984 a cement plant opened.

Contributions to GDP in 1995 (in 1m. vatu) included: wholesale and retail trade, restaurants and hotels, 8,611; agriculture, forestry and fishing, 6,051; finance and allied business services, 3,512; government services, 3,089; transport, storage and communications, 2,247; construction, 1,721; manufacturing, 1,386; electricity, gas and water, 462.

INTERNATIONAL TRADE

Foreign debt in 2000 amounted to US$69m.

Imports and Exports. In 1999 imports (f.o.b.) amounted to US$76·36m. (US$76·23m. in 1998); exports (f.o.b.) $24·91m. (US$33·78m. in 1998). Main import markets (1995): Australia (37%), New Zealand (12%), Japan (9%), France (6%) and the Fiji Islands (6%). Main export suppliers: EU (37%), Japan (24%), Australia (10%) and Bangladesh (10%).

The main exports are copra, beef, timber and cocoa.

COMMUNICATIONS

Roads. In 1996 there were 1,070 km of roads, about 250 km paved, mostly on Efate Island and Espiritu Santo. There were estimated to be 4,000 passenger cars and 2,000 commercial vehicles in use in 1996.

Civil Aviation. There is an international airport at Bauerfield Port Vila. In 1998 the state-owned Air Vanuatu provided domestic services and flew to Auckland, Brisbane, Honiara, Melbourne, Nadi, Nouméa and Sydney. In 1999 scheduled airline traffic of Vanuatu-based carriers flew 2·6m. km, carrying 86,000 passengers (all on international flights).

Shipping. Sea-going shipping totalled 1·6m. GRT in 1998, including oil tankers 11,000 GRT. Several international shipping lines serve Vanuatu, linking the country with Australia, New Zealand, other Pacific territories, China (Hong Kong), Japan, North America and Europe. The chief ports are Vila and Santo. Small vessels provide frequent inter-island services.

Telecommunications. Services are provided by the Posts and Telecommunications and Radio Departments. There are automatic telephone exchanges at Vila and Santo; rural areas are served by a network of tele-radio stations. In 2000 there were 6,600 telephone main lines, equivalent to 33·7 per 1,000 population. Mobile phone subscribers numbered around 200 in 1998, there were approximately 600 fax machines in 1995 and 3,000 Internet users in Dec. 1999.

External telephone, telegram and telex services are provided by VANITEL, through their satellite earth station at Vila. There are direct circuits to Nouméa, Sydney, Hong Kong and Paris and communications are available on a 24-hour basis to most countries. Air radio facilities are provided. Marine coast station facilities are available at Vila and Santo.

SOCIAL INSTITUTIONS

Justice. A study was begun in 1980 which could lead to unification of the judicial system. The population in penal institutions in 1995 was 89 (55 per 100,000 of national population).

Religion. Over 80% of the population are Christians, but animist beliefs are still prevalent.

Education. In 1994 there were 252 pre-primary schools and 272 primary schools with 852 teachers for 26,267 pupils. There were 4,269 secondary pupils in 1992. Tertiary education is provided at the Vanuatu Technical Institute and the Teachers College, while other technical and commercial training is through regional institutions in the Solomon Islands, the Fiji Islands and Papua New Guinea. The adult literacy rate in 1998 stood at 64%, up from 53% in 1979.

Health. In 1995 there were 12 doctors, 3 dentists, 259 nurses, 6 pharmacists and 33 midwives. There were 90 hospitals, with a provision of 22 beds per 10,000 population.

CULTURE

Broadcasting. The government-controlled Radio Vanuatu broadcasts in French, English and Bislama. In 1997 there were about 62,000 radio receivers and 2,000 television sets.

Tourism. In 1999 there were 51,000 visitors to Vanuatu. Receipts totalled US$56m.

DIPLOMATIC REPRESENTATIVES
Of Vanuatu in the United Kingdom
High Commissioner: Vacant.

Of the United Kingdom in Vanuatu (KPMG Hse., Rue Pasteur, Port Vila)
High Commissioner: Michael Hill.

Of Vanuatu in the USA
Ambassador: Vacant.

Of the USA in Vanuatu
Ambassador: Susan S. Jacobs (resides at Port Moresby, Papua New Guinea).

Of Vanuatu to the United Nations
Ambassador: Vacant.
Chargé d'Affaires a.i.: Alfred Carlot.

FURTHER READING
Miles, W, F, S., *Bridging Mental Boundaries in a Postcolonial Microcosm: Identity and Development in Vanuatu.* University of Hawaii Press, 1998

VATICAN CITY STATE

Population estimate, 2000: 900

Stato della Città del Vaticano

KEY HISTORICAL EVENTS

For many centuries the Popes bore temporal sway over a territory stretching across mid-Italy. In the 19th century the Papal States were incorporated into the Italian Kingdom. On 11 Feb. 1929 a treaty between the Italian Government and the Vatican recognized the sovereignty of the Holy See in the city of the Vatican.

TERRITORY AND POPULATION

The area of Vatican City is 44 ha (108·7 acres). It includes the Piazza di San Pietro (St Peter's Square), which is to remain normally open to the public and subject to the powers of the Italian police. It has its own railway station (for freight only), postal facilities, coins and radio. Twelve buildings in and outside Rome enjoy extra-territorial rights, including the Basilicas of St John Lateran, St Mary Major and St Paul without the Walls, the Pope's summer villa at Castel Gandolfo and a further Vatican radio station on Italian soil. *Radio Vaticana* broadcasts an extensive service in 34 languages from the transmitters in Vatican City and in Italy. The Holy See and the Vatican are not synonymous—the Holy See, referring to the primacy of the Pope, is located in Vatican City. The official language is Latin.

Vatican City has about 900 inhabitants.

CONSTITUTION AND GOVERNMENT

Vatican City State is governed by a Commission appointed by the Pope. The reason for its existence is to provide an extra-territorial, independent base for the Holy See, the government of the Roman Catholic Church. The Pope exercises sovereignty and has absolute legislative, executive and judicial powers. The judicial power is delegated to a tribunal in the first instance, to the Sacred Roman Rota in appeal and to the Supreme Tribunal of the Signature in final appeal.

The Pope is elected by the College of Cardinals, meeting in secret conclave. The election is by scrutiny and requires a two-thirds majority.

CURRENT ADMINISTRATION

Supreme Pontiff: **John Paul II** (Karol Wojtyła), born at Wadowice near Kraków, Poland, 18 May 1920. Archbishop of Kraków 1964–78, created Cardinal in 1967; elected Pope 16 Oct. 1978, inaugurated 22 Oct. 1978.

Pope John Paul II was the first non-Italian to be elected since Pope Adrian VI (a Dutchman) in 1522.

Secretary of State: Cardinal Angelo Sodano.

Secretary for Relations with Other States: H. E. Mgr Jean-Louis Tauran.

Office of the Sovereign of the Vatican City: http://www.vatican.va

ECONOMY

Currency. Since 1 Jan. 2002 the Vatican City has been using the euro. Italy has agreed that the Vatican City may mint a small part of the total Italian euro coin contingent with their own motifs. Average annual inflation in the period 1997–2001 was 11·2%.

Budget. The Vatican's budget is financed primarily by contributions from Roman Catholics around the world, various investment income, visitors to museums, and sales of souvenirs and postage stamps. Revenues in 1994 were US$175·5m. and expenditures US$175m.

Performance. Real GDP growth was 1·7% in 2001.

SOCIAL INSTITUTIONS

Justice. In 2002 the Vatican City's legal system hosted 397 civil cases and 608 criminal cases—more cases than there are inhabitants. Many of the offences are committed by outsiders, principally at St Peter's Basilica and the museums.

Roman Catholic Church. The Roman Pontiff is in orders a Bishop, but in jurisdiction held to be by divine right the centre of all Catholic unity. The Pope is the Vicar of Christ and the Successor of St Peter, who exercises universal governance over the Church. He is also the sovereign ruler of Vatican City State. He has for advisers the Sacred College of Cardinals, consisting in Jan. 2003 of 171 Cardinals from 66 countries (150 created by Pope John Paul II), of whom 112 are cardinal electors—those under the age of 80 who may enter into conclave to elect a new Pope. Cardinals, addressed by the title of 'Eminence', are appointed by the Pope from senior ecclesiastics who are either the bishops of important Sees or the heads of departments at the Roman Curia. In addition to the College of Cardinals, there is a Synod of Bishops, created by Pope Paul VI and formally instituted on 15 Sept. 1965. This consists of the Patriarchs and certain Metropolitans of the Catholic Church of Oriental Rite, of elected representatives of the national episcopal conferences and religious orders of the world, of the Cardinals in charge of the Roman Congregations and of other persons nominated by the Pope. The Synod meets in both general (global) and special (regional) assemblies. General Synods are scheduled to take place every three years. The last was held in Oct. 2001 on the theme of the mission of the local bishop in the universal church.

The central administration of the Roman Catholic Church is carried out by a number of permanent organisms called Congregations, Council, Commissions and Offices. The Congregations are composed of a number of Cardinals and diocesan bishops (both appointed for five-year periods), with Consultors and Officials. Besides the Secretariat of State (which has two sections, including the Section for Relations with States) there are now nine Congregations, viz.: Doctrine, Oriental Churches, Bishops, the Sacraments and Divine Worship, Clergy, Religious, Catholic Education, Evangelization of the Peoples and Causes of the Saints. Pontifical Councils have replaced some of the previously designated Secretariats and Prefectures and now represent the Laity, Christian Unity, the Family, Justice and Peace, Cor Unum, Migrants, Health Care Workers, Interpretation of Legislative Texts, Inter-Religious Dialogue, Culture, Preserving the Patrimony of Art and History, and a Commission, for Latin America. There are also various Offices. There are three academies: the Pontifical Academy for Sciences, the Pontifical Academy for Life and the Pontifical Academy for Social Sciences, the latter two instituted by Pope John Paul II.

CULTURE

Broadcasting. There were 3 AM, 4 FM and 2 shortwave radio broadcasting stations in 1998, and 1 television station in 1996.

DIPLOMATIC REPRESENTATIVES

In its diplomatic relations with foreign countries the Holy See is represented by the Secretariat of State and the Second Section (Relations with States) of the Council for Public Affairs of the Church. It maintains permanent observers to the UN.

Of the Holy See in the United Kingdom (54 Parkside, London, SW19 5NE) *Apostolic Nuncio:* Archbishop Pablo Puente.

Of the United Kingdom at the Holy See (91 Via Dei Condotti, 00187 Rome). *Ambassador:* Kathryn Colvin.

Of the Holy See in the USA (3339 Massachusetts Ave., NW, Washington, D.C., 20008).
Apostolic Nuncio: Gabriele Montalvo.

Of the USA at the Holy See (Villa Domiziana, Via Delle Terme Deciane 26, 00153 Rome).
Ambassador: Jim Nicholson.

Of the Holy See to the European Union
Apostolic Nuncio: Faustino Sainz Muñoz.

FURTHER READING
Reese, T., *Inside the Vatican.* Harvard Univ. Press, 1997

Permanent Observer Mission to the UN: http://www.holyseemission.org

VENEZUELA

República Bolivariana de Venezuela

Capital: Caracas
Population estimate, 2000: 24·17m.
GDP per capita, 2000: (PPP$) 5,794
HDI/world rank: 0·770/69

KEY HISTORICAL EVENTS

Columbus sighted Venezuela in 1498 and it was visited by Alonso de Ojeda and Amerigo Vespucci in 1499 who named it Venezuela (Little Venice). It was part of the Spanish colony of New Granada until 1821 when it became independent, at first in union with Colombia and then as an independent republic from 1830. Up to 1945 the country was governed mainly by dictators. In 1945 a three-day revolt against the reactionary government of Gen. Isaias Medina led to constitutional and economic reforms. In 1961 a new constitution provided for a presidential election every five years, a national congress, and state and municipal legislative assemblies. Twenty political parties participated in the 1983 elections. By now the economy was in crisis and corruption linked to drug trafficking was widespread. In Feb. 1992 there were two abortive coups. A state of emergency was declared. In Dec. 1993 Dr Rafael Caldera Rodríguez's election as president reflected disenchantment with the established political parties. He took office in the early stages of a banking crisis which cost 15% of GDP to resolve. Fiscal tightening backed by the IMF brought rapid recovery. Hugo Chávez Frías, who succeeded as president in Feb. 1999, continued with economic reforms and amended the constitution to increase presidential powers.

In Dec. 1999 the north coast of Venezuela was hit by devastating floods and mudslides which resulted in approximately 30,000 deaths.

President Chávez was deposed and arrested on 12 April 2002 in a coup following a general strike, but he was back in the presidential palace just 48 hours later.

TERRITORY AND POPULATION

Venezuela is bounded to the north by the Caribbean with a 2,813 km coastline, east by the Atlantic and Guyana, south by Brazil, and southwest and west by Colombia. The area is 916,490 sq. km (353,857 sq. miles) including 72 islands in the Caribbean. Population (1990) census, 19,455,429 (86·6% urban, 1999). Estimate (1997) 21·8m.; density, 23·9 per sq. km.

The UN gives a projected population for 2010 of 28·72m.

The official language is Spanish. English is taught as a mandatory second language in high schools.

Area, population and capitals of the 23 states and 1 federally-controlled area:

State	Area (sq. km)	1995 population estimate	Capital	Density; inhabitants per sq. km
Federal District	1,930	2,269,000	Caracas	1,175·6
Amazonas	178,895	67,000	Puerto Ayacucho	0·4
Anzoátegui	43,300	1,028,000	Barcelona	23·7
Apure	76,500	376,000	San Fernando	4·9
Aragua	7,014	1,335,000	Maracay	190·3
Barinas	35,200	517,000	Barinas	14·7
Bolívar	239,250	1,123,000	Ciudad Bolívar	4·7
Carabobo	4,650	1,808,000	Valencia	388·7
Cojedes	14,800	227,000	San Carlos	15·3
Delta Amacuro	40,200	111,000	Tucupita	2·8
Falcón	24,800	684,000	Coro	27·6
Guárico	64,986	585,000	San Juan de los Morros	9·0
Lara	19,800	1,424,000	Barquisimeto	71·9
Mérida	11,300	687,000	Mérida	60·8
Miranda	7,950	2,326,000	Los Teques	292·6
Monagas	28,900	551,000	Maturín	19·1
Nueva Esparta	1,150	326,000	La Asunción	283·4
Portuguesa	15,200	719,000	Guanare	47·3
Sucre	11,800	772,000	Cumaná	77·2

State	Area (sq. km)	1995 population estimate	Capital	Density; inhabitants per sq. km
Táchira	11,100	944,000	San Cristóbal	85·0
Trujillo	7,400	550,000	Trujillo	74·3
Yaracuy	7,100	464,000	San Felipe	65·3
Zulia	63,100	2,752,000	Maracaibo	43·6
Dependencias Federales	120	2,245[1]		

[1]1990 census figure.

37·3% of all Venezuelans are under 15 years of age, 58·7% are between the ages of 15 and 64, and 4% are over the age of 65.

SOCIAL STATISTICS
1998 births, 501,808; deaths, 98,624; marriages, 86,152; divorces (1996), 16,055. 1998 birth rate per 1,000 population, 21·6; death rate, 4·2; marriage rate, 3·7; divorce rate (1996), 0·7. Annual population growth rate, 1990–99, 2·9%. Life expectancy, 1999, was 70·2 years for males and 76·0 years for females. Infant mortality, 1999, 20 per 1,000 live births; fertility rate, 1999, 2·9 births per woman. In 1998 the most popular age for marrying was 20–24 for both men and women.

CLIMATE
The climate ranges from warm temperate to tropical. Temperatures vary little throughout the year and rainfall is plentiful. The dry season is from Dec. to April. The hottest months are July and August. Caracas, Jan. 65°F (18·3°C), July 69°F (20·6°C). Annual rainfall 32" (833 mm). Ciudad Bolívar, Jan. 79°F (26·1°C), July 81°F (27·2°C). Annual rainfall 41" (1,016 mm). Maracaibo, Jan. 81°F (27·2°C), July 85°F (29·4°C). Annual rainfall 23" (577 mm).

CONSTITUTION AND GOVERNMENT
The current constitution was approved in a referendum held on 15 Dec. 1999. Venezuela is a federal republic, comprising 34 federal dependencies, 23 states and 1 federal district. Executive power is vested in the President. The ministers, who together constitute the Council of Ministers, are appointed by the President and head various executive departments. There are 17 ministries and 7 officials who also have the rank of Minister of State.

90% of votes cast in a referendum (the first in Venezuela's history) on 25 April 1999 were in favour of the plan to rewrite the constitution proposed by President Chávez. As a result, on 25 July the public was to elect a constitutional assembly to write a new constitution, which was subsequently to be voted on in a national referendum. In Aug. 1999 the constitutional assembly declared a national state of emergency. It subsequently suspended the Supreme Court, turned the elected Congress into little more than a sub-committee, stripping it of all its powers, and assumed many of the responsibilities of government. In Dec. 1999 the President's plan to redraft the constitution was approved by over 70% of voters in a referendum. As a result presidents are able to serve two consecutive six-year-terms instead of terms of five years which cannot be consecutive, the senate is abolished and greater powers are being given to the state and the armed forces. President Chávez has effectively taken over both the executive and the judiciary. The constitution provides for procedures by which the president may reject bills passed by Congress, as well as provisions by which Congress may override such presidential veto acts.

National Anthem. 'Gloria al bravo pueblo' ('Glory to the brave people'); words by Vicente Salias, tune by Juan Landaeta.

RECENT ELECTIONS
Presidential elections were held on 30 July 2000; turn-out was 56%. Incumbent Hugo Chávez Frías (MVR) was elected President against 1 other candidate with 59% of the vote.

In elections to the Congress, held on 30 July 2000, 165 seats were contested. Movimiento V República (Movement for the Fifth Republic/MVR) won 76 seats, Accion Democrática (Democratic Action/AD) 29, Movimiento al Socialismo (Movement Towards Socialism/MAS) 21, Proyecto Venezuela (Project Venezuela/Proven) 7 and 12 other parties won 5 seats or fewer.

CURRENT ADMINISTRATION

President: Hugo Chávez Frías; b. 1953 (MVR; sworn in 2 Feb. 1999).
Executive Vice President: José Vicente Rangel.
In March 2003 the government comprised:
Minister of the Interior and Justice: Gen. Lucas Rincón. *Foreign Affairs:* Roy Chaderton. *Finance:* Tobías Nóbrega Suarez. *Defence:* José Luis Prieto. *Infrastructure:* Diosdado Cabello. *Agriculture and Lands:* Efren Andrade. *Environment and Natural Resources:* Ana Elisa Osario. *Health and Social Development:* Maria Lourdes Urbaneja. *Information and Communications:* Nora Uribe. *Education, Culture and Sports:* Aristobulo Isturiz. *Higher Education:* Héctor Navarro. *Labour:* Maria Cristina Iglesias. *Planning:* Felipe Perez Marti. *Production and Trade:* Ramon Rosales. *Social Economy:* Nelson Merentes. *Energy and Mines:* Rafael Ramírez.

Government Website: http://www.venezuela.gov.ve

DEFENCE

There is selective conscription for 30 months. Defence expenditure totalled US$1,377m. in 2000 (US$57 per capita), representing 1·5% of GDP.

Army. Equipment includes 81 main battle tanks. Army aviation comprises 24 helicopters and 14 aircraft. Strength (1999) 34,000 (27,000 conscripts). There were estimated to be an additional 8,000 reserves.

A 23,000-strong volunteer National Guard is responsible for internal security.

Navy. The combatant fleet comprises two submarines and six frigates. The Naval Air Arm, 1,000 strong, operates seven combat aircraft and eight armed helicopters. Main bases are at Caracas, Puerto Cabello and Punto Fijo.

Air Force. The Air Force was 7,000 strong in 1999 and had 124 combat aircraft and 31 armed helicopters. There are six combat squadrons. Main aircraft types include CF-5s, Mirage 50s and F-16A/Bs.

INTERNATIONAL RELATIONS

Venezuela is a member of the UN, WTO, OAS, Inter-American Development Bank, LAIA, ACS, OPEC, IOM, WTO, GATT, FAO, G-77, Interpol, Intelsat, IADB, IAEA, IMO, SELA, PAHO, UNCTAD, UNESCO, UPU, WHO and the Andean Community.

ECONOMY

In 1998 services accounted for 61·0% of GDP, industry 34·0% and agriculture 5·0%.

Overview. A stabilization programme of April 1996 introduced market-oriented reforms. An ambitious programme of privatization has stalled, with 23 companies having been privatized between 1991 and 1997.

Currency. The unit of currency is the *bolívar* (VEB) of 100 *céntimos*. Foreign exchange reserves were US$7,204m. and gold reserves 10·50m. troy oz in June 2002. Exchange controls were abolished in April 1996. The bolívar was devalued by 12·6% in 1998, and in Feb. 2002 it was floated, ending a regime that permitted the bolívar to trade only within a fixed band. However, in Feb. 2003 it was pegged to the dollar. The inflation rate in 2001 was 12·5%, the lowest in more than 15 years and down from nearly 100% in 1996. There was then a steady rise in inflation, with the annualized rate reaching 30·7% in Nov. 2002. Total money supply in May 2002 was Bs 7,232·47bn.

Budget. The fiscal year is the calendar year. Revenues and expenditures in Bs 1m.:

	1996	1997	1998	1999	2000
Revenue	5,767,795	10,240,962	9,002,797	10,738,441	16,252,235
Expenditure	4,964,167	8,894,305	10,816,958	12,169,972	17,622,501

Performance. In 2001 there was real GDP growth of 2·8%, following growth of 3·2% in 2000. In 2002, however, the economy shrank by an estimated 8·5%. Total GDP in 2001 was US$124·9bn.

Banking and Finance. A law of Dec. 1992 provided for greater autonomy for the Central Bank. Its *Governor*, currently Diego Luis Castellanos, is appointed by the

President for five-year terms. Since 1993 foreign banks have been allowed a controlling interest in domestic banks.

There is a stock exchange in Caracas.

ENERGY AND NATURAL RESOURCES

Environment. Carbon dioxide emissions in 1998 were the equivalent of 6·7 tonnes per capita according to the *World Bank Atlas*.

Electricity. Installed capacity in 1997 was 23m. kW, production was 70·39bn. kWh in 1998; consumption per capita was 2,566 kWh.

Oil and Gas. Proven resources of oil were 77·7bn. bbls. in 2001. Venezuela has the highest reserves of oil of any country outside the Middle East. The oil sector was nationalized in 1976, but private and foreign investment have again been permitted since 1992. Crude oil production in 1998 was 1·13bn. bbls. (3·1m. bbls. a day). Venezuela is the largest exporter of oil to the USA. Oil provides about 40% of Venezuela's revenues. Natural gas production (1999) 32·0bn. cu. metres. Natural gas reserves in 2000 were 4,010bn. cu. metres.

Minerals. Output (in 1,000 tonnes) in 1997: iron ore, 18,359 (23,424 in 1995); limestone, 15,130 (1996); bauxite, 4,967; coal, 3,097 (4,646 in 1995); gold, 19,661 kg (3,287 kg in 1995). Diamond production in 1998 totalled 250,000 carats.

Agriculture. Coffee, cocoa, sugarcane, maize, rice, wheat, tobacco, cotton, beans and sisal are grown. 50% of farmers are engaged in subsistence agriculture. There were 2·6m. ha of arable land in 1998 and 0·85m. ha of permanent crops. There are government price supports and tax incentives.

Production in 2000 in 1,000 tonnes: sugarcane, 6,950; bananas, 1,000; maize, 900; rice, 737; plantains, 551; cassava, 448; potatoes, 352; oranges, 332; sorghum, 320; watermelons, 261; carrots, 239; tomatoes, 188.

Livestock (2000): cattle, 15·80m.; pigs, 4·90m.; goats, 3·60m.; sheep, 781,000; horses, 500,000; chickens, 110m.

Forestry. In 1995 the area under forests was 43·99m. ha, or 49·9% of the total land area (down from 46·51m. ha in 1990). Among South American countries only Brazil lost a larger area of forests over the same five years. Timber production in 1999 was 2·71m. cu. metres.

Fisheries. In 2000 the total catch was 391,255 tonnes (346,655 tonnes from marine waters).

INDUSTRY

Production (1997, in tonnes): petrol, 19·2m.; residual fuel oil, 14·89m.; distillate fuel oil, 13·5m.; cement (1996), 7·56m.; crude steel, 4·02m.; aluminium, 662,200; sugar (1998), 590,000.

Labour. Out of 7,670,000 people in employment in 1995, 2,186,000 were in community, social and personal services, 1,739,000 in trade, restaurants and hotels, 1,047,000 in manufacturing and 1,012,000 in agriculture, fishing and forestry. In Feb. 2000 an estimated 20% of the workforce was unemployed, up from 8·6% in 1991.

In late 2002 and early 2003 a two-month long general strike intended to oust President Chávez ended in failure, instead crippling an already depressed economy.

Trade Unions. The most powerful confederation of trade unions is the CTV (*Confederación de Trabajadores de Venezuela*, formed 1947).

INTERNATIONAL TRADE

The Group of Three free trade pact with Colombia and Mexico came into effect on 1 Jan. 1995. Foreign debt was US$38,196m. in 2000.

Imports and Exports. Trade in US$1m.:

	1996	1997	1998	1999	2000
Imports f.o.b.	9,937	13,678	15,105	13,213	16,073
Exports f.o.b.	23,707	23,703	17,576	20,819	34,038

Exports of oil in 2001 were valued at US$19bn., the third highest export revenues after Saudi Arabia and Iran. The main import sources in 1995 were USA (42·6%),

Colombia (7·6%), Germany (4·8%) and Japan (4·4%). The main markets for exports in 1995 were USA (51·3%), Brazil (9·0%), Colombia (7·6%) and Netherlands Antilles (4·9%).

COMMUNICATIONS

Roads. In 1997 there were 96,155 km of roads, of which nearly 34% were paved. There were 1,520,000 passenger cars in use in 1996 (69·3 per 1,000 inhabitants) plus 434,000 trucks and vans. There were 2,900 fatalities as a result of road accidents in 1996.

Rail. Passenger-km travelled in 1995 came to 12m. and freight tonne-km to 53m. (railways 336 km—1,435 mm gauge).

There is a metro in Caracas.

Civil Aviation. The main international airport is at Caracas (Simon Bolívar), with some international flights from Maracaibo. Servivensa and Aeropostal Alas de Venezuela are the main Venezuelan carriers. In 1999 scheduled airline traffic of Venezuela-based carriers flew 75·4m. km, carrying 4,690,000 passengers (1,590,000 on international flights).

Shipping. Ocean-going shipping totalled 665,000 GRT in 1998, including oil tankers 222,000 GRT. La Guaira, Maracaibo, Puerto Cabello, Puerto Ordaz and Guanta are the chief ports. In 1995 vessels totalling 21,009,000 NRT entered ports and vessels totalling 8,461,000 NRT cleared. The principal navigable rivers are the Orinoco and its tributaries the Apure and Arauca.

Telecommunications. In 2000 Venezuela had 2,605,600 main telephone lines (107·8 per 1,000 population) and 1·1m. PCs were in use (45·5 for every 1,000 persons). Mobile phone subscribers numbered 3·4m. in 1999 and there were 70,000 fax machines in 1997. The number of Internet users in Dec. 2000 was 950,000. CANTV, the national telephone company, lost its 50-year monopoly on fixed-line telephony in 2000.

Postal Services. In 1995 there were 444 post offices, or 1 for every 49,200 persons.

SOCIAL INSTITUTIONS

Justice. A new penal code was implemented on 1 July 1999. The new, US-style system features public trials, verbal arguments, prosecutors, citizen juries and the presumption of innocence, instead of an inquisitorial system inherited from Spain which included secretive trials and long exchanges of written arguments.

In Aug. 1999 the new constitutional assembly declared a judicial emergency, granting itself sweeping new powers to dismiss judges and overhaul the court system. The assembly excluded the Supreme Court and the national Judicial Council from a commission charged with reorganizing the judiciary. President Chávez declared the assembly the supreme power in Venezuela.

The court system is plagued by chronic corruption and an astounding case backlog. Only about 9,700 of the country's 23,000 prisoners in 1999 had actually been convicted. In Oct. 1999 over 100 judges accused of corruption were suspended.

Religion. In 1997 there were 19·92m. Roman Catholics. There are 4 archbishops, 1 at Caracas, who is Primate of Venezuela, 2 at Mérida and 1 at Ciudad Bolívar. There are 19 bishops. In Feb. 2001 there were 2 Cardinals. Protestants number about 1,090,000 and those with other beliefs number 1,770,000.

Education. In 1996–97 there were 202,195 primary school teachers and 4,262,221 pupils, and 377,984 secondary school pupils.

In 1995–96 there were in the public sector 16 universities, 1 polytechnic university and 1 open (distance) university; and in the private sector, 12 universities, 2 Roman Catholic universities and 1 technological university.

Adult literacy was 92·3% in 1999 (male, 92·9%; female, 91·8%).

Health. In 1996 there were 42,725 doctors and 52,394 beds in hospitals and dispensaries.

CULTURE

Broadcasting. There are two government and four cultural radio stations; the remainder are commercial. There are four government, three commercial and three other TV channels (colour by NTSC). In 1997 there were 10·75m. radio and 4·1m. TV receivers.

Cinema. There were 213 cinemas in 1997.

Press. In 1996 there were 86 leading daily newspapers with a circulation of over 4·6m.

Tourism. In 1999 there were 587,000 foreign tourists. Tourist revenue was US$656m.

Libraries. Venezuela had 675 libraries in 1997.

Museums and Galleries. There were 144 museums in 1997.

DIPLOMATIC REPRESENTATIVES

Of Venezuela in the United Kingdom (1 Cromwell Rd., London, SW7 2HW)
Ambassador: Alfredo Toro-Hardy.

Of the United Kingdom in Venezuela (Edificio Torre Las Mercedes, piso 3, Av. La Estancia, Chuao, Caracas 1061)
Ambassador: Edgar John Hughes.

Of Venezuela in the USA (1099 30th St., NW, Washington, D.C., 20007)
Ambassador: Bernardo Alvarez-Herrera.

Of the USA in Venezuela (Calle Suapure, con calle F. Colinas de Valle Arriba, Caracas)
Ambassador: Charles S. Shapiro.

Of Venezuela to the United Nations
Ambassador: Milos Alcalay.

Of Venezuela to the European Union
Ambassador: Luis Xavier Grisanti.

FURTHER READING

Dirección General de Estadística, Ministerio de Fomento, Boletín Mensual de Estadística.—Anuario Estadístico de Venezuela. Caracas, Annual

Canache, D., *Venezuela: Public Opinion and Protest in a Fragile Democracy.* Univ. of Miami, 2002

McCoy, J., Smith, W. C., Serbin, A. and Stambouli, A., *Venezuelan Democracy Under Stress.* Univ. of Miami, 1995

Naim, M., *Paper Tigers and Minotaurs: the Politics of Venezuela's Economic Reforms.* Washington (D.C.), 1993

Rudolph, D. K. and Rudolph, G. A., *Historical Dictionary of Venezuela.* 2nd ed. Scarecrow Press, Metuchen (NJ), 1995

National statistical office: Oficina Central de Estadística e Informática.

VIETNAM

Công Hòa Xã Hôi Chu Nghĩa
Viêt Nam
(Socialist Republic of Vietnam)

Capital: Hanoi
Population estimate, 2000: 78·14m.
GDP per capita, 2000: (PPP$) 1,996
HDI/world rank: 0·688/109

KEY HISTORICAL EVENTS

By the end of the 15th century, the Vietnamese had conquered most of the Kingdom of Champa (now Vietnam's central area) and by the end of the 18th century had acquired Cochin-China (now its southern area). At the end of the 18th century, France helped to establish the Emperor Gia-Long as ruler of a unified Vietnam. Cambodia had become a French protectorate in 1863 and in 1899, after the extension of French protection to Laos in 1893, the Indo Chinese Union was proclaimed.

In 1940 Vietnam was occupied by the Japanese. In Aug. 1945 they allowed the Vietminh movement to seize power, dethrone the Emperor and establish a republic known as Vietnam. On 6 March 1946 France recognized 'the Democratic Republic of Vietnam' as a 'Free State within the Indo-Chinese Federation'. On 19 Dec. Vietminh forces made a surprise attack on Hanoi, the signal for nearly eight years of hostilities. An agreement on the cessation of hostilities was reached on 20 July 1954. The French withdrew and by the Paris Agreement of 29 Dec. 1954 completed the transfer of sovereignty to Vietnam which was divided along the 17th parallel into Communist North Vietnam and the non-Communist South. From 1959 the North promoted insurgency in the south, provoking retaliation from the USA. A full scale guerrilla war developed.

In Paris on 27 Jan. 1973 an agreement was signed ending the war in Vietnam. However, hostilities continued between the North and the South until the latter's defeat in 1975. Between 150,000 and 200,000 South Vietnamese fled the country. The unification of North and South Vietnam into the Socialist Republic of Vietnam finally took place on 2 July 1976. Vietnam invaded Cambodia in Dec. 1978 and China attacked Vietnam in consequence. In 1986 Vietnam implemented economic reforms, gradually shifting to a multi-sectoral market economy under state regulation. On 11 July 1995 Vietnam and the USA normalized relations. On 28 July 1995 Vietnam became an official member of the Association of South East Asian Nations (ASEAN) and in the same month signed a trade agreement with the European Union.

TERRITORY AND POPULATION

Vietnam is bounded in the west by Cambodia and Laos, north by China and east and south by the South China Sea. It has a total area of 332,338 sq. km and following administrative reform introduced in 1997 is divided into 60 provinces and a city under central government. Areas and populations (in 1,000):

Province	Area (sq. km)	Census population, 1999	Capital
Dac Lac	19,800	1,776	Buon Me Thoat
Gia Lai	15,662	972	Play Cu
Kon Tum	9,934	314	Kon Tum
Lam Dong	10,173	996	Da Lat
Central Highlands	55,569	4,058	
An Giang	3,424	2,049	Long Xuyen
Bac Lieu	2,485	736	Bac Lieu
Ben Tre	2,247	1,297	Ben Tre
Ca Mau	5,204	1,118	Ca Mau
Can Tho	2,951	1,811	Can Tho
Dong Thap	3,276	1,565	Cao Lamh
Kien Giang	6,243	1,494	Rach Gia
Long An	4,338	1,306	Tan An

Province	Area (sq. km)	Census population, 1999	Capital
Soc Trang	3,191	1,174	Soc Trang
Tien Giang	2,339	1,605	My Tho
Tra Vinh	2,369	966	Tra Vinh
Vinh Long	1,487	1,010	Vinh Long
Mekong River Delta	39,554	16,131	
Ha Tinh	6,054	1,269	Ha Tinh
Nghe An	16,381	2,858	Vinh
Quang Binh	7,983	794	Dong Hoi
Quang Tri	4,592	573	Dong Ha
Thanh Hoa	11,168	3,468	Thanh Hoa
North Central Coast	51,187	8,962	
Ba Ria (Vung Tau)	1,957	801	Vung Tau
Binh Duong	2,718	716	Thu Dau Mot
Binh Phuoc	6,814	654	Dong Phu
Dong Nai	5,865	1,990	Bien Hoa
Tay Ninh	4,024	965	Tay Ninh
Thanh Pho Ho Chi Minh	2,090	5,037	Ho Chi Minh City
North Eastern South Region	23,468	10,163	
Bac Can	4,796	275	Bac Can
Bac Giang	3,817	1,492	Bac Giang
Bac Ninh	797	941	Bac Ninh
Cao Bang	8,445	491	Cao Bang
Ha Giang	7,831	603	Ha Giang
Hoa Binh	4,612	758	Hoa Binh
Lai Chau	17,131	589	Lai Chau
Lang Son	8,187	705	Lang Son
Lao Cai	8,050	595	Lao Cai
Phu Tho	3,465	1,262	Phu Tho
Quang Ninh	5,939	1,004	Ha Long City
Son La	14,210	881	Son La
Thai Nguyen	3,541	1,046	Thai Nguyen
Tuyen Quang	5,801	675	Tuyen Quang
Vinh Phuc	1,371	1,092	Vinh Yen
Yen Bai	6,808	680	Yen Bai
North Mountain and Midland	104,801	13,089	
Ha Nam	827	792	Ha Nam
Ha Tay	2,147	2,387	Ha Dong
Hai Duong	1,661	1,650	Hai Duong
Hai Phong	1,504	1,673	Hai Phong
Hanoi	921	2,672	Hanoi
Hung Yen	895	1,069	Hung Yen
Nam Dinh	1,669	1,888	Nam Dinh
Ninh Binh	1,388	884	Ninh Binh
Thai Binh	1,509	1,786	Thai Binh
Red River Delta	12,521	14,801	
Binh Dinh	6,076	1,461	Quy Nhon
Binh Thuan	7,992	1,047	Phan Thiet
Da Nang	942	684	Da Nang
Khanh Hoa	5,258	1,031	Nha Trang
Ninh Thuan	3,430	503	Phan Rang
Phu Yen	5,278	787	Tuy Hoa
Quang Nam	10,406	1,372	Tam Ky
Quang Ngai	5,856	1,190	Quang Ngai
Thua Thien (Hue)	5,009	1,045	Hue
South Central Coast	45,238	9,120	

At the 1999 census the population was 76,324,753 (50·8% female); density, 230 per sq. km. 80·3% of the population lived in rural areas.

The UN gives a projected population for 2010 of 88·68m.

Cities with over 0·2m. inhabitants at the 1989 census: Ho Chi Minh City (3,169,135; 1999 population, 4,549,000), Hanoi (1,088,862), Hai Phong (456,049),

Da Nang (370,670), Long Xuyen (217,171), Nha Trang (213,687), Hue (211,085), Can Tho (208,326).

87% of the population are Vietnamese (Kinh). There are also 53 minority groups thinly spread in the extensive mountainous regions. The largest minorities are: Tay, Khmer, Thai, Muong, Nung, Meo, Dao. The last remaining 'boat people' were repatriated from Hong Kong in 1997.

The official language is Vietnamese. Chinese, French and Khmer are also spoken.

SOCIAL STATISTICS

Births, 1995, 1,992,000; deaths, 553,000. Rates (1995 per 1,000 population): birth rate, 27·0; death rate, 7·5. Life expectancy, 1999, was 65·5 years for males and 70·2 years for females. Annual population growth rate, 1990–99, 1·9%. Infant mortality, 1999, 31 per 1,000 live births (compared to an average of between 60 and 90 for most countries with a similar level of development); fertility rate, 1999, 2·5 births per woman. Vietnam has had one of the largest reductions in its fertility rate of any country in the world over the past 25 years, having had a rate of 5·8 births per woman in 1975. Sanctions are imposed on couples with more than two children. The annual abortion rate, at over 80 per 1,000 women aged 15–44, ranks among the highest in the world. The rate at which Vietnam has reduced poverty, from 58% of the population in 1993 to 37% in 1998, is among the most dramatic of any country in the world. Vietnam has a young population; 60% were born after 1975.

CLIMATE

The humid monsoon climate gives tropical conditions in the south, with a rainy season from May to Oct., and sub-tropical conditions in the north, though real winter conditions can affect the north when polar air blows south over Asia. In general, there is little variation in temperatures over the year. Hanoi, Jan. 62°F (16·7°C), July 84°F (28·9°C). Annual rainfall 72" (1,830 mm).

CONSTITUTION AND GOVERNMENT

The National Assembly unanimously approved a new constitution on 15 April 1992. Under this the Communist Party retains a monopoly of power and the responsibility for guiding the state according to the tenets of Marxism-Leninism and Ho Chi Minh, but with certain curbs on its administrative functions. The powers of the National Assembly are increased. The 450-member *National Assembly* is elected for five-year terms. Candidates may be proposed by the Communist Party or the Fatherland Front (which groups various social organizations), or they may propose themselves as individual Independents. The Assembly convenes three times a year and appoints a prime minister and cabinet. It elects the *President*, the head of state. The latter heads a *State Council* which issues decrees when the National Assembly is not in session.

The ultimate source of political power is the Communist Party of Vietnam, founded in 1930; it had 2·2m. members in 1996.

National Anthem. 'Doàn quân Viêt Nam di chung lòng cúu quóc' ('Soldiers of Vietnam, we are advancing'); words and tune by Van Cao.

RECENT ELECTIONS

In parliamentary elections held on 19 May 2002 Communist Party members won 447 of 498 seats, with 51 seats going to non-party candidates. Turn-out was 99·7%.

CURRENT ADMINISTRATION

President (titular head of state): Tran Duc Luong; b. 1937 (in office since Sept. 1997).

Vice-President: Truong My Hoa.

Full members of the Politburo of the Communist Party of Vietnam: Nong Duc Manh (b. 1940; *Secretary General*); Nguyen Van An; Pham Van Tra; Tran Duc Luong; Truong Tan Sang; Le Minh Huong; Nguyen Tan Dung; Phan Van Khai; Nguyen Phu Trong; Nguyen Minh Triet; Phan Dien; Nguyen Khoa Diem; Truong Quang Duoc; Le Hong Anh; Tran Dinh Hoan.

In March 2003 the government comprised:

Prime Minister: Phan Van Khai; b. 1933 (sworn in 25 Sept. 1997).

Deputy Prime Ministers: Nguyen Tan Dung; Vu Khoan; Pham Gia Khiem.
Minister of Foreign Affairs: Nguyen Dy Nien. *National Defence:* Pham Van Tra.
Public Security: Le Hong Anh. *Justice:* Uong Chu Luu. *Planning and Investment:*
Vo Hong Phuc. *Finance:* Nguyen Sinh Hung. *Trade:* Truong Din Tuyen. *Agriculture
and Rural Development:* Le Huy Ngo. *Communications and Transport:* Dao Dinh
Binh. *Construction:* Nguyen Hong Quan. *Industries:* Hoang Trung Hai. *Fisheries:*
Ta Quang Ngoc. *Labour, War Invalids and Social Affairs:* Nguyen Thi Hang. *Science
and Technology:* Hoang Van Phong. *Culture and Information:* Pham Quang Nghi.
Education and Training: Nguyen Minh Hien. *Public Health:* Tran Thi Trung Chien.
Resources and Environment: Mai Ai Truc. *Post and Telecommunications:* Do Trung
Ta. *Protection and Care of Children:* Le Thi Thu.
Chairman of the National Assembly: Nguyen Van An.

DEFENCE
Conscription of men and women is for two years, specialists three years. Since 1989
troops have been permitted to engage in economic activity.

In 2000 defence expenditure totalled US$931m. (US$12 per capita), representing
3·0% of GDP. In 1985 defence expenditure had been US$3,556m.

Army. There are eight military regions and two special areas. Strength (1999) was
estimated to be 412,000. Paramilitary Local Defence forces number 4m.–5m. and
consist of the Peoples' Self-Defence Force (urban), a People's Militia (rural) and a
rear force (reserves).

Navy. The fleet includes six frigates and two diesel submarines. In 1996 personnel
was estimated at 42,000 plus an additional Naval Infantry force of 27,000.

Air Force. In 1996 the Air Force had about 15,000 personnel and 189 combat
aircraft and 43 armed helicopters. Equipment included Su-22s, Su-27s and MiG-
21s.

INTERNATIONAL RELATIONS
Vietnam is a member of the UN, Asian Development Bank, Colombo Plan, APEC,
the Mekong Group, ASEAN and the International Organization of the Francophonie.

ECONOMY
Agriculture accounted for 25·9% of GDP in 1998, industry 32·6% and services
41·7%.

Overview. A reform programme (*Doi Moi*) was implemented in 1986 which resulted
in a boom in foreign investment and increased domestic economic activity. It marked
a turning point from a Stalinist, centrally planned economy to a market economy
with socialist direction. Further reforms in the 1990s failed to prevent the effects
of the Asian economic crisis. A deepening of the *Doi Moi* process, with further
economic liberalization, was scheduled in a 'Ten Year Socio-Economic
Development Strategy 2001–10'.

The 1992 constitution embodies the market-oriented reforms of recent years,
recognizing citizens' right to engage in private business. A bankruptcy law was
passed in Jan. 1994.

Currency. The unit of currency is the *dong* (VND). In March 1989 the dong was
brought into line with free market rates. The direct use of foreign currency was
made illegal in Oct. 1994. Foreign exchange reserves were US$3,888m. in March
2002. Total money supply in May 2002 was 116,936·0bn. dong. There was deflation
in 2000, of 1·7%, and inflation of just 0·1% in 2001. Gold reserves were 98,300
troy oz in June 1991.

Budget. Budget revenue and expenditure (in 1bn. dong):

	1996	1997	1998	1999	2000[1]
Revenue	60,844	62,766	70,822	76,128	79,250
Expenditure	62,889	70,749	73,419	84,817	92,101

[1]Forecast.

Performance. Real GDP growth was between 8% and 10% each year from 1994
to 1997, but has slowed since then. In 2001 the growth rate was 5·0%. GDP per

head, which was US$181 in 1993, had risen to US$368 by 2000. Vietnam's total GDP in 2001 was US$32·9bn.

Banking and Finance. The central bank and bank of issue is the State Bank of Vietnam (founded in 1951; *Governor*, Le Duc Thuy). There are 52 commercial banks (4 state run and 48 shareholding), 19 foreign branches and 4 joint ventures set up with foreign capital. Vietcombank is the foreign trade bank. 50 foreign banks had branches in 1998. Foreign direct investment in Vietnam rose from US$1bn. in 1991 to US$8·3bn. in 1996, but then declined to US$2·2bn. in 1998. In 1999 it was estimated to be only US$1·6bn.

There is a stock exchange in Ho Chi Minh City, which opened in July 2000.

ENERGY AND NATURAL RESOURCES

Environment. According to the *World Bank Atlas* Vietnam's carbon dioxide emissions were the equivalent of 0·6 tonnes per capita in 1998.

Electricity. Total capacity of power generation in 1997 was 5m. kW. In 1998, 20·62bn. kWh of electricity were produced and consumption per capita was 232 kWh. A hydro-electric power station with a capacity of 2m. kW was opened at Hoa-Binh in 1994.

Oil and Gas. Oil reserves in 1999 totalled 600m. bbls. In Aug. 2001 an offshore oil mine containing more than 400m. bbls. of petroleum were discovered. Crude oil production in 1996, 62m. bbls. Natural gas reserves in 1999 were 190bn. cu. metres. Vietnam and Thailand settled an offshore dispute in 1997 which stretched back to 1973. Demarcation allowed for petroleum exploration in the Gulf of Thailand, with each side required to give the other some revenue if an underground reservoir is discovered which straddles the border.

Minerals. Vietnam is endowed with an abundance of mineral resources such as coal (3·5bn. tonnes), bauxite (3bn. tonnes), iron ore (700m. tonnes), copper (600,000 tonnes), tin (70,000 tonnes), chromate (10m. tonnes) and apatite (1bn. tonnes): coal production was 9·97m. tonnes in 1997. There are also deposits of manganese, titanium, a little gold and marble. 1992 output (in 1,000 tonnes): sand, 13,260; limestone, 667; salt (1997 estimate), 390.

Agriculture. Agriculture employs 70% of the workforce. Ownership of land is vested in the state, but since 1992 farmers may inherit and sell plots allocated on 20-year leases. There were 5·7m. ha of arable land in 1998 and 1·5m. ha of permanent crops. Agricultural production during the period 1990–97 grew on average by 5·2% every year, giving Vietnam the fastest-growing agriculture of any Asian country. Peasants may market their produce, or deal through the co-operatives.

Production in 1,000 tonnes in 2000: rice, 32,554; sugarcane, 15,145; cassava, 2,036; maize, 1,930; sweet potatoes, 1,658; bananas, 1,270; coconuts, 940; coffee, 803; oranges, 427; groundnuts, 353. Vietnam is the second largest coffee producer in the world after Brazil, and one of the world's largest exporters of rice, having doubled its output in the past 15 years.

Livestock, 2000: cattle, 4·14m.; pigs, 20·19m.; buffaloes, 2·90m.; goats, 544,000; chickens, 196m.; ducks, 55m.

Livestock products (2000): meat, 1,968,000 tonnes; eggs, 165,000 tonnes; milk, 72,000 tonnes.

122,958 tractors were in use in 1997.

Forestry. In 1995 forests covered 9·12m. ha, or 28% of the land area (down from 9·79m. ha in 1990 and 13·5m. ha in 1943). Timber exports were prohibited in 1992. Timber production was 36·73 cu. metres in 1999, nearly all of it for fuel.

Fisheries. In 1992 there were 32 fishing vessels over 100 GRT with a total tonnage of 13,956 GRT. Total catch, 1999, approximately 1,200,000 tonnes (94% from sea fishing).

INDUSTRY

1997 production (in 1,000 tonnes): cement, 7,475; crude steel, 330; fertilizers, 137; sulphuric acid (1992), 8; dyestuffs (1992), 4·3; glass and glassware (1992), 32·3; textile fibre (1992), 42·5; processed fish (1992), 627·4; sugar (1998), 657; tea

(1992), 20·1; knitting fabric (1995), 15; (in units): bricks (1992), 3,675m.; tiles, (1992), 410m.; machine tools (1992), 2,316; hydraulic pumps (1992), 500; threshing machines (1992), 40,125; diesel motors (1992), 3,300; ventilators (1992), 257,000; batteries (1992), 68m.; lamps (1992), 9·6m.; woven fabrics, 450m. metres (1995); beer, 533m. litres; cigarettes (1992), 1,524m. packets.

Labour. In 1997 the workforce was estimated at 37m. Agriculture, forestry and fishing accounted for 25·4m. people; manufacturing, 3·3m.; trade and restaurants, 3·2m.; public administration and services, 2·2m.; transport and communications, 900,000; finance and insurance, 700,000. Official statistics put unemployment at 7·4% of the workforce in early 2000.

Trade Unions. There are 53 trade union associations.

INTERNATIONAL TRADE
In Feb. 1994 the USA lifted the trade embargo it had imposed in 1975, and in Nov. 2001 a historic trade agreement with the USA was ratified. The agreement allows Vietnam's exports access to the US market on the same terms as those enjoyed by most other countries. Foreign debt was US$12,787m. in 2000 (Vietnam had halved its foreign debt burden over the preceding five years). The 1992 constitution regulates joint ventures with western firms; full repatriation of profits and non-nationalization of investments are guaranteed.

Imports and Exports. Trade is conducted through the state import-export agencies. Value of exports in 1996, US$7,256m.; imports, US$11,144m. Earnings in 1995 from seafood exports reached US$580m. and from textiles US$700m. The main import suppliers in 1997 were Singapore (12·9%), South Korea (12·5%) and Taiwan (10·1%). Principal export markets in 1997 were Japan (22·7%), Germany (8·3%) and Singapore (5·7%). Main exports are coal, farm produce, sea produce, coffee and livestock. Imports: oil, steel, artificial fertilizers. Rice exports in 1992 were some 1·4m. tonnes, and coal 0·78m. tonnes (0·23m. in 1987), mainly to Japan and South Korea.

COMMUNICATIONS
Roads. There were about 105,000 km of roads in 1997, of which 15% are hard-surfaced. In 1995 there were 0·31m. four-wheeled vehicles and around 3m. motorcycles. 373·7m. passengers (1994) and 39·57m. tonnes of freight (1991) were transported.

Rail. There are 2,600 km of single-track line covering seven routes. Rail links with China were reopened in Feb. 1996. In 1995, 1·92m. passengers and 3·5m. tonnes of freight were carried.

Civil Aviation. There are international airports at Hanoi (Noi Bai) and Ho Chi Minh City (Tan Son Nhat) and 13 domestic airports. The national carrier is Vietnam Airlines, which provides domestic services and in 1998 had international flights to Bangkok, Dubai, Guangzhou, Hong Kong, Kaohsiung, Kuala Lumpur, Manila, Melbourne, Moscow, Osaka, Paris, Phnom Penh, Singapore, Sydney, Taipei, Vientiane and Zürich. In 1999 it flew 30·7m. km, carrying 2,600,000 passengers (994,300 on international flights). The busiest airport is Ho Chi Minh City, which in 1999 handled 3,378,081 passengers and 69,188 tonnes of freight. Hanoi handled 1,613,973 passengers and 24,567 tonnes of freight in 1999.

Shipping. In 1998 sea-going vessels totalled 784,000 GRT, including oil tankers 63,000 GRT. The major ports are Hai Phong, which can handle ships of 10,000 tons, Ho Chi Minh City and Da Nang. There are regular services to Hong Kong, Singapore, Thailand, Cambodia and Japan. There are some 19,500 km of navigable waterways.

Telecommunications. Vietnam Posts and Telecommunications and the military operate telephone systems with the assistance of foreign companies. Telephone main lines numbered 2,542,700 in 2000 (31·9 per 1,000 persons) and there were 700,000 PCs in use (8·8 for every 1,000 persons). In 1999 there were 187,000 mobile phone subscribers and in 1996 fax machines numbered 19,800. Vietnam had 100,000 Internet users in Dec. 1999.

SOCIAL INSTITUTIONS

Justice. A new penal code came into force on 1 Jan. 1986 'to complete the work of the 1980 Constitution'. Penalties (including death) are prescribed for opposition to the people's power, and for economic crimes. The judicial system comprises the Supreme People's Court, provincial courts and district courts. The president of the Supreme Court is responsible to the National Assembly, as is the Procurator-General, who heads the Supreme People's Office of Supervision and Control.

The death penalty is still in force; there were five executions in June 2002.

The population in penal institutions in 1996 was 43,000 (55 per 100,000 of national population).

Religion. Taoism is the traditional religion but Buddhism is widespread. At a Conference for Buddhist Reunification in Nov. 1981, nine sects adopted a charter for a new Buddhist church under the Council of Sangha. The Hoa Hao sect, associated with Buddhism, claimed 1·5m. adherents in 1976. Caodaism, a synthesis of Christianity, Buddhism and Confucianism founded in 1926, has some 2m. followers. In 1992 there were 38·2m. Buddhists and 6m. Roman Catholics (1997). There is an Archbishopric of Hanoi and 13 bishops. There were two seminaries in 1989.

Education. Adult literacy rate in 1999 was 93·1% (95·4% among males and 91·0% among females). Primary education consists of a 10-year course divided into 3 levels of 4, 3 and 3 years respectively. In 1993–94 there were 10,137 primary schools with 9,782,900 pupils and 278,000 teachers, and in 1995–96 there were 5,332,400 pupils and 193,814 teachers at secondary schools. In 1995–96 there were 7 universities, 2 open (distance) universities and 9 specialized universities (agriculture, 3; economics, 2; technology, 3; water resources, 1).

Health. In 1997 there were 32,900 doctors, and in 1993, 53,700 nurses, 12,000 midwives and 6,500 pharmacists. There were 12,500 hospitals in 1994.

CULTURE

Broadcasting. Broadcasting is controlled by the state Vietnam Radio and Television Committee. There are two national radio programmes from Hanoi and one from Ho Chi Minh City, 14 provincial programmes and an external service, the Voice of Vietnam (11 languages). There is a national and two provincial TV services. There were 8·2m. radio and 3·57m. TV sets in 1997 (colour by NTSC, PAL and SECAM).

Press. In 1994 there were some 350 newspaper and periodical titles. There are two national dailies, the Communist Party's *Nhan Dan* ('The People'), circulation, 0·2m., and the Army's *Quan Doi Nhan Dan*, 60,000. There are three major regional dailies with a combined circulation of 155,000. There were ten titles in English, including two dailies, in 1995. 3,043 book titles were published in 1991 totalling 62·4m. copies.

Tourism. There were 2,330,000 foreign tourists in 2001; revenue from tourists in 1998 came to US$86m.

DIPLOMATIC REPRESENTATIVES

Of Vietnam in the United Kingdom (12–14 Victoria Rd., London W8 5RD)
Ambassador: Vuong Thua Phong An.

Of the United Kingdom in Vietnam (Central Building, 31 Hai Ba Trung, Hanoi)
Ambassador: Warwick Morris.

Of Vietnam in the USA (1233 20th Street, NW, Suite 400, Washington, D.C., 20036)
Ambassador: Chiem Tam Nguyen.

Of the USA in Vietnam (7 Lang Ha, Ba Dinh District, Hanoi)
Ambassador: Raymond F. Burghardt.

Of Vietnam to the United Nations
Ambassador: Nguyen Tanh Chau.

Of Vietnam to the European Union
Ambassador: Nu Thi Ninh Ton.

FURTHER READING

Trade and Tourism Information Centre with the General Statistical Office. *Economy and Trade of Vietnam* [various 5-year periods]

Gilbert, Marc Jason, (ed.) *Why the North Won the Vietnam War.* Palgrave Macmillan, Basingstoke, 2002

Harvie, C. and Tran Van Hoa V., *Reforms and Economic Growth.* London, 1997

Karnow, S., *Vietnam: a History.* 2nd ed. London, 1992

Marr, David G., *et al.*, *Vietnam.* [Bibliography] ABC-Clio, Oxford and Santa Barbara (CA), 1992

Morley, J. W. and Nishihara M., *Vietnam Joins the World.* Armonk (NY), 1997

Norlund, I. (ed.) *Vietnam in a Changing World.* London, 1994

National statistical office: General Statistical Office, Hanoi.

YEMEN

Jamhuriya al Yamaniya
(Republic of Yemen)

Capital: Sana'a
Commercial capital: Aden
Population estimate, 2000: 18·35m.
GDP per capita, 2000: (PPP$) 893
HDI/world rank: 0·479/144

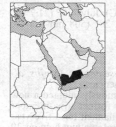

KEY HISTORICAL EVENTS

Following an agreement in Dec. 1989 on a constitution for a unified state, the (northern) Yemen Arab Republic and the (southern) People's Democratic Republic of Yemen were united as the Republic of Yemen on 22 May 1990. In Aug. 1993 Vice-President Ali Salem Albidh withdrew to Aden demanding reforms as a condition of re-joining President Saleh in Sana'a. Albidh agreed to a modified reform programme but clashes between north and south escalated into full civil war at the beginning of May. Southern officials announced their secession from Yemen on 21 May 1994. Aden was captured by northern forces on 7 June 1994. The former vice-president and government went into exile.

TERRITORY AND POPULATION

Yemen is bounded in the north by Saudi Arabia, east by Oman, south by the Gulf of Aden and west by the Red Sea. The territory includes 112 islands including Kamaran (181 sq. km) and Perim (300 sq. km) in the Red Sea and Socotra (3,500 sq. km) in the Gulf of Aden. The islands of Greater and Lesser Hanish are claimed by both Yemen and Eritrea. On 15 Dec. 1995 Eritrean troops occupied them, and Yemen retaliated with aerial bombardments. A ceasefire was agreed at presidential level on 17 Dec. On 20 Dec. the UN resolved to send a good offices mission to the area. In an agreement of 21 May 1996 brokered by France, Yemen and Eritrea renounced the use of force to settle the dispute and agreed to submit it to arbitration. The area is 555,000 sq. km excluding the desert Empty Quarter (Rub Al-Khahi). A dispute with Saudi Arabia broke out in Dec. 1994 over some 1,500–2,000 km of undemarcated desert boundary. A memorandum of understanding signed on 26 Feb. 1995 reaffirmed the border agreement reached at Taif in 1934, and on 12 June 2000 a 'final and permanent' border treaty between the two countries was signed. An agreement of June 1995 completed the demarcation of the border with Oman.

The population was estimated at 15·8m. in 1995; density, 21 persons per sq. km. The UN gives a projected population for 2010 of 27·36m.

In 1999, 75·5% of the population lived in rural areas. At the census of 1994 the population was 14,832,673. There were 1,168,199 citizens working abroad, mainly in Saudi Arabia and the United Arab Emirates, not included in the census total. Since 1990 Saudi Arabia has compulsorily repatriated almost all Yemeni workers. In 1994 there were 17 governorates plus the capital city, Sana'a:

	1994 census population		*1994 census population*
Abyan	414,543	Lahej	634,652
Aden	562,162	Mahrah	112,512
Bayd	509,265	Mahwit	403,465
Dhamar	1,050,346	Marib	167,388
Hadhrama	870,025	Sa'adah	486,059
Hajjah	1,262,590	Sana'a (city) ⎱	1,910,286
Hodeida	1,749,944	Sana'a ⎰	
Ibb	1,959,313	Shabwah	377,080
Jawf	157,096	Ta'iz	2,205,947

The population of the capital, Sana'a, was 1,231,000 in 1999. The commercial capital is the port of Aden, with a population of (1995) 562,000. Other important towns are Ta'iz, the port of Hodeida, Mukalla, Ibb and Abyan.

The national language is Arabic.

SOCIAL STATISTICS
Births, 1995, 724,000; deaths, 168,000. Birth rate, 1995, was 48·2 per 1,000 population; death rate, 11·2. Life expectancy, 1999, was 59·0 years for males and 61·2 years for females. Infant mortality, 1999, 86 per 1,000 live births. Annual population growth rate, 1990–99, 4·7%; fertility rate, 1999, 7·4 births per woman (the highest anywhere in the world).

CLIMATE
A desert climate, modified by relief. Sana'a, Jan. 57°F (13·9°C), July 71°F (21·7°C). Aden, Jan. 75°F (24°C), July 90°F (32°C). Annual rainfall 20" (508 mm) in the north, but very low in coastal areas: 1·8" (46 mm).

CONSTITUTION AND GOVERNMENT
Parliament consists of a 301-member *Assembly of Representatives* (*Majlis al-Nuwaab*), elected for a four-year term in single-seat constituencies.

On 28 Sept. 1994 the Assembly of Representatives unanimously adopted a new constitution founded on Islamic law. It abolished the former five-member Presidential Council and installed a *President* elected by parliament for a five-year term, subsequently amended to a seven-year term through a referendum held on 20 Feb. 2001. As a result of the same referendum the term for MPs was extended from four to six years.

National Anthem. 'Raddidi Ayyatuha ad Dunya nashidi' ('Repeat, O World, my song'); words by A. Noman, tune by Ayub Tarish.

RECENT ELECTIONS
The *President*, Ali Abdullah Saleh, was elected for his first term in 1990. At the election of 23 Sept. 1999 he was voted in for a third term, claiming 96·3% against the 3·7% of his sole opponent, Najeeb Qahtan Al-Sha'abi. Turn-out was 66%.

Parliamentary elections were held on 27 April 2003, in which the General People's Congress (MSA) gained 226 seats (58·0% of the vote), Yemeni Congregation for Reform (Islah) 47 seats (22·6%), Yemeni Socialist Party 7 seats (4·7%), Nasserite Unionist People's Organization (TWSN) 3 seats (1·9%), the Arab Socialist Rebirth Party (Baath) 2 seats (0·7%) and ind. 14 seats. Turn-out was 76%.

CURRENT ADMINISTRATION
President: Ali Abdullah Saleh; b. 1942 (GPC; in office since 1990, re-appointed in 1994 and 1999).

Vice-President: Abd Rabbah Mansour Hadi.

In May 2003 the government comprised:

Prime Minister: Abd al-Qadir al-Ba Jamal; b. 1946 (GPC; in office since 31 March 2001, re-appointed 10 May 2003).

Deputy Prime Minister and Minister for Finance: Alawi Salih al-Salami.

Minister of Civil Service and Insurance: Abd al-Wahab al-Raweh. *Defence:* Abdullah Ali Ulaywah. *Planning and Development:* Ahmed Mohamed Abdallah al-Sufan. *Foreign Affairs:* Abu Baker Adullah al-Kirbi. *Oil and Mineral Resources:* Rasheed Baraba'a. *Legal and Parliamentary Affairs:* Abdullah Ahmed Ghanem. *Justice:* Ahmed Akbat. *Labour and Social Affairs:* Abdul Kareem al-Arhabi. *Communications:* Abdul Malik Al-Mualimi. *Local Administration:* Sadeq Amin Husayn Aburas. *Fisheries:* Ali Hassan al-Ahmadi. *Transport and Maritime Affairs:* Saeed Yafaee. *Interior:* Rashad al-Aleemi. *Information:* Hussein Dhaif Allah al-Awahdi. *Youth and Sports:* Abd al-Rahman al-Akwa. *Electricity and Water:* Yahya al-Abyadh. *Agriculture and Water Resources:* Ahmed Salem Al-Gabali. *Trade and Industry:* Abd al-Rahman Mohamed Ali al-Uthman. *Culture:* Abdul-Wahab al-Rowhani. *Construction, Housing and Urban Planning:* Abdullah Hussein Al-Dafee. *Expatriate Affairs:* Abdu Ali al-Kubati. *Technical and Vocational Training:* Mohammed Abdullah al-Bitani. *Public Health and Population:* Abdul Nasser Mineebani. *Education:* Fadhel Abu Ghanem. *Higher Education and Scientific Research:* Dr Yahya Mohamed Abdullah Al-Shuaibi.

Awqaf and Guidance: Kassem al-Agem. *Tourism and Environment:* Abdul Malik Abdul Rahman al-Iryani.

Government Website: http://www.yemen.gov.ye

DEFENCE

Conscription is for three years. Defence expenditure in 2000 totalled US$489m. (US$27 per capita), representing 7·8% of GDP.

Estimates of the number of small arms in the country are around 70m., equivalent to nearly four firearms for every person, making Yemen arguably the world's most heavily armed country.

Army. Strength (1999) 61,000 with 40,000 reserves. There are paramilitary tribal levies numbering at least 20,000 and a Ministry of Security force of 50,000.

Navy. Navy forces are based at Aden and Hodeida, with other facilities at Mokha, Mukalla and Perim. Personnel in 1999 were estimated at 1,800.

Air Force. The unified Air Forces of the former Arab Republic and People's Democratic Republic are now under one command, although this unity was broken by the attempted secession of the south in 1994 which resulted in heavy fighting between the air forces of Sana'a and Aden. Personnel (1999) about 3,500. There were 49 combat aircraft including F-5Es, Su-20/22s, MiG-21s and MiG-29s.

INTERNATIONAL RELATIONS

Yemen is a member of the UN, the League of Arab States, IOM and the OIC.

With a view to maintaining regional stability the USA supports Yemen and its democracy both in material and moral terms.

ECONOMY

In 1998 agriculture accounted for 17·6% of GDP, industry 48·8% and services 33·6%.

Overview. Yemen's second five-year plan is from 2001 to 2005. Priorities are economic and structural reform, the improvement in living conditions, increased investment and reduction of unemployment.

Currency. The unit of currency is the *riyal* (YER) of 100 *fils*. During the transitional period to north-south unification the northern *riyal* of 100 *fils* and the southern *dinar* of 1,000 *fils* co-existed. Inflation was 11·9% in 2001. There were three foreign exchange rates operating: an internal clearing rate, an official rate and a commercial rate. In 1996 the official rate was abolished. Total money supply in May 2002 was 262,073m. riyals, gold reserves totalled 50,000 troy oz and foreign exchange reserves were US$3,722m.

Budget. The fiscal year is the calendar year. Total revenues and expenditures (in 1m. riyals):

	1996	1997	1998[1]	1999[1]
Revenue	216,053	287,347	300,791	279,418
Expenditure	215,738	285,910	309,942	310,702

[1]Estimate.

Performance. Real GDP growth was 5·1% in 2000 and 3·3% in 2001; total GDP in 2001 was US$9·1bn.

Banking and Finance. The *Governor* of the Central Bank of Yemen is Ahmed Abdul Rahman Al-Samawi. Total assets of the Central Bank were 109,497m. riyals in 1992. There were 6,616m. riyals in savings deposits.

ENERGY AND NATURAL RESOURCES

Environment. According to the *World Bank Atlas* Yemen's carbon dioxide emissions were the equivalent of 0·9 tonnes per capita in 1998.

Electricity. Installed capacity was 1m. kW in 1997. Production in 1998 was 2·24bn. kWh; consumption per capita was 96 kWh.

Oil and Gas. The first large-scale oilfield and pipeline was inaugurated in 1987. There are reserves of 4,000m. bbls. on the former north-south border. Further major oil finds were announced in 1991. Crude oil production (1996): 123m. bbls. Natural gas reserves in 1999 were 480bn. cu. metres.

Minerals. An estimated 110,000 tonnes of salt were produced in 1997. Reserves (estimate) 25m. tonnes. In 1994, 80,000 tonnes of gypsum were extracted, and in 1992, 647,000 cu. metres of stone.

Agriculture. In 1998 there were 1·45m. ha of arable land and 113,000 ha of permanent cropland; approximately 490,000 ha were irrigated in 1998. In the south, agriculture is largely of a subsistence nature, sorghum, sesame and millet being the chief crops, and wheat and barley widely grown at the higher elevations. Cash crops include cotton. Fruit is plentiful in the north.

Owing to the meagre rainfall, cultivation is largely confined to fertile valleys and flood plains on silt. Irrigation schemes with permanent installations are in progress. Estimated production (2000, in 1,000 tonnes): sorghum, 401; tomatoes, 245; potatoes, 213; oranges, 175; grapes, 157; alfalfa, 149 (1992); wheat, 137; melons and watermelons, 119; bananas, 94; onions, 71; papayas, 68; millet, 67; maize, 47; barley, 42; chick-peas, 37.

Livestock in 2000: sheep, 4·76m.; goats, 4·09m.; cattle, 1·28m.; asses, 500,000; camels, 185,000; chickens, 28m. Estimated livestock produce, 2000 (in 1,000 tonnes): meat, 163; milk, 213.

Forestry. There were 9,000 ha of forest in 1995. Timber production in 1997 was 324,000 cu. metres.

Fisheries. Fishing is a major industry. Total catch in 1999 was 123,252 tonnes, exclusively marine fish.

INDUSTRY
In 1992 there were 211 industrial firms (142 private, 48 public, 13 mixed and 8 co-operative). 64 of these were producing foodstuffs, 50 chemicals and petroleum products, 27 textiles and leather goods and 27 metal goods. Output (in 1,000 tonnes), 1997: cement, 1,229; 1995: petrol, 990; jet fuels, 350; 1992: flour, 247; edible oils, 102; asphalt, 48; cartons, 17; residual fuel oil, 1,831; distillate fuel oil, 1,399.

Labour. The labour force in 1996 totalled 4,945,000 (71% males). Approximately 57% of the economically active population in 1995 were engaged in agriculture, fisheries and forestry. Unemployment was 36% at the end of 1993.

INTERNATIONAL TRADE
Foreign debt was US$5,616m. in 2000.

Imports and Exports. Trade in US$1m.:

	1995	1996	1997	1998	1999
Imports f.o.b.	1,831·5	2,293·5	2,406·5	2,288·8	2,120·4
Exports f.o.b.	1,980·1	2,262·7	2,274·0	1,503·7	2,478·3

Main import suppliers, 1992 (in 1,000 riyals): USA, 2,858,220; UAE, 2,559,581; Saudi Arabia, 2,311,965; Japan, 2,172,044; UK, 1,713,618. Main export markets: USA, 1,396,053; Japan, 666,689; Germany, 470,723; Saudi Arabia, 268,769.

Oil, cotton and fish are major exports, the largest imports being food and live animals. Oil accounts for more than 80% of exports. A large transhipment and entrepôt trade is centred on Aden, which was made a free trade zone in May 1991.

COMMUNICATIONS

Roads. There were, in 1996, 64,725 km of roads, of which 5,240 km were paved. In 1996 there were 240,600 passenger cars, 3,400 buses and coaches, and 291,150 goods vehicles.

Rail. Passenger-km travelled in 1997 came to 2,492m.

Civil Aviation. There are international airports at Sana'a and Aden. In 2000 Sana'a handled 794,000 passengers (665,000 on international flights) and 13,000 tonnes of freight. The national carrier is Yemenia Yemen Airways, which operates internal services and in 1998 had international flights to Abu Dhabi, Addis Ababa, Amman, Bahrain, Beirut, Bombay, Cairo, Damascus, Djibouti, Doha, Dubai, Frankfurt, Jeddah, Karachi, Khartoum, London, Moroni, Nairobi, Paris, Riyadh, Rome and Sharjah. In 1999 scheduled airline traffic of Yemen-based carriers flew 14·5m. km, carrying 731,000 passengers (480,000 on international flights).

Shipping. In 1998 sea-going shipping totalled 25,000 GRT, including oil tankers 2,000 GRT. There are ports at Aden, Mokha, Hodeida, Mukalla and Nashtoon. In 1998 vessels totalling 11,210,000 NRT entered ports and vessels totalling 9,851,000 NRT cleared.

Telecommunications. Yemen had 346,700 main telephone lines in 2000, or 18·9 per 1,000 population, and there were 35,000 PCs in use (1·9 for every 1,000 persons). There were 14,000 Internet users in March 2001. Mobile phone subscribers numbered 27,000 in 1999 and there were 2,700 fax machines in 1995.

Postal Services. In 1995 there were 451 post offices.

SOCIAL INSTITUTIONS

Justice. A civil code based on Islamic law was introduced in 1992. The death penalty is still in force and there were 56 confirmed executions in 2001.

Religion. In 1997 there were some 16·47m. Muslims (mostly Sunnis) and approximately 20,000 followers of other religions.

Education. In 1994 there were 62 pre-primary schools with 680 teachers for 11,999 pupils. In 1993–94 there were 11,013 primary schools with 2,678,863 pupils and there were 212,129 pupils at secondary level. Yemen has the lowest proportion of female pupils enrolled at primary school in the world, at 28% in 1993. There are universities at Sana'a (founded 1974) and Aden (1975). The former had 3,520 students and 330 academic staff in 1994–95, the latter 4,800 and 470. The adult literacy rate in 1999 was 45·2% (66·6% among males and 23·9% among females). Yemen has the biggest difference in literacy rates between the sexes of any country in the world.

Health. In 1995 there were 3,220 doctors, and in 1994, 167 dentists, 5,772 nurses, 295 pharmacists and 385 midwives. There were 81 hospitals in 1994.

CULTURE

Broadcasting. Broadcasting is managed by the government-controlled Yemen Radio and Television Corporation. Programmes are transmitted from Sana'a and Aden. In 1997 there were 1·05m. radio and 470,000 TV receivers (colour by PAL).

Press. In 1996 there were three daily newspapers with a combined circulation of 230,000.

Tourism. There were 88,000 foreign tourists in 1998, bringing revenue of US$84m.

DIPLOMATIC REPRESENTATIVES
Of Yemen in the United Kingdom (57 Cromwell Rd., London, SW7 2ED)
Ambassador: Mutahar Abdullah Alsaeede.

Of the United Kingdom in Yemen (129 Haddah Rd., Sana'a)
Ambassador: Frances Guy.

Of Yemen in the USA (2600 Virginia Ave., NW, Washington, D.C., 20037)
Ambassador: Abdulwahab Al-Hajjiri.

Of the USA in Yemen (Dhahr Himyar Zone, Sheraton Hotel District, POB 22347, Sana'a)
Ambassador: Edmund James Hull.

Of Yemen to the United Nations
Ambassador: Abdalla Saleh Al-Ashtal.

Of Yemen to the European Union
Ambassador: Gazem Abdul Khaleq Al Aghbari.

FURTHER READING
Central Statistical Organization. *Statistical Year Book*
Auchterlonie, Paul, *Yemen.* [Bibliography] 2nd ed. ABC-Clio, Oxford and Santa Barbara (CA), 1998
Dresch, Paul, *A History of Modern Yemen.* CUP, 2001
Mackintosh-Smith, T., *Yemen—Travels in Dictionary Land.* London, 1997

National statistical office: Central Statistical Organization, Ministry of Planning and Development

ZAMBIA

Republic of Zambia

Capital: Lusaka
Population estimate, 2000: 9·87m.
GDP per capita, 2000: (PPP$) 780
HDI/world rank: 0·433/153

KEY HISTORICAL EVENTS

The majority of the population is of Bantu origin. There are more than 70 different tribes, the most important being the Bemba and the Bgoni in the northeast. One of the more successful of the invading tribes was the Lozi under Lewanika, who obtained the protection of the British government in 1891. In 1900 the British South Africa Company acquired trading and mining rights. From 1911 the territory was known as Northern Rhodesia and in 1924 the Crown took over the administration.

In 1953 the Federation of Rhodesia and Nyasaland, of which Northern Rhodesia was a part, was created. Federation brought economic benefits to Northern Rhodesia but it was from the outset opposed by African leaders. In March 1963 Britain agreed to Northern Rhodesia's right to secede from the Federation. In Jan. 1964 full internal self-government was attained. On 24 Oct. Northern Rhodesia became an independent republic within the Commonwealth, changing its name to Zambia. A highly centralized one-party state was created which suffocated the emergent economy. Living standards fell sharply and the production of copper, Zambia's biggest foreign exchange earner, almost halved. In 1991 the Movement for Multiparty Democracy (MMD) was elected on a promise to transform the economy.

TERRITORY AND POPULATION

Zambia is bounded by the Democratic Republic of the Congo in the north, Tanzania in the northeast, Malaŵi in the east, Mozambique in the southeast, Zimbabwe and Namibia in the south, and by Angola in the west. The area is 290,586 sq. miles (752,614 sq. km). Population estimate (1997), 9·35m.; population density, 11·7 per sq. km. In 1999, 60·5% of the population were rural.

The projected population for 2010 is 12·99m.

The republic is divided into nine provinces. Area, population and chief towns:

Province	Area (in sq. km)	Population (1990 census)	Chief Town
Central	94,395	725,611	Kabwe
Copperbelt	31,328	1,579,542	Ndola
Eastern	69,106	973,818	Chipata
Luapula	50,567	526,705	Mansa
Lusaka	21,898	1,207,980	Lusaka
Northern	147,826	867,795	Kasama
North-Western	125,827	383,146	Solwezi
Southern	85,283	946,353	Livingstone
Western	126,386	607,447	Mongu

The capital is Lusaka, which had a population in 1999 of 1,577,000. Other major towns (with estimated 1990 population in 1,000) are: Ndola, 329; Kitwe, 288; Kabwe, 154; Chingola, 142; Mufulira, 124; Luanshya, 118; Livingstone, 77.

The official language is English and the main ethnic groups are the Bemba (34%), Tonga (16%), Nyanja (14%) and Lozi (9%).

SOCIAL STATISTICS

Births, 1995, 351,000; deaths, 149,000. 1995 birth rate per 1,000 population, 43·4; death rate, 18·5. Zambia's life expectancy at birth in 2000 was 40 years, down from 50 in 1990. The sharp decline is largely attributed to the huge number of people in the country with HIV. Annual population growth rate, 1990–99, 2·4%. Infant mortality, 1999, 112 per 1,000 live births; fertility rate, 1999, 5·4 births per woman.

CLIMATE
The climate is tropical, but has three seasons. The cool, dry one is from May to Aug., a hot dry one follows until Nov., when the wet season commences. Frosts may occur in some areas in the cool season. Lusaka, Jan. 70°F (21·1°C), July 61°F (16·1°C). Annual rainfall 33" (836 mm). Livingstone, Jan. 75°F (23·9°C), July 61°F (16·1°C). Annual rainfall 27" (673 mm). Ndola, Jan. 70°F (21·1°C), July 59°F (15°C). Annual rainfall 52" (1,293 mm).

CONSTITUTION AND GOVERNMENT
In Aug. 1991 the National Assembly adopted a new constitution by 107 votes to 15 permitting multi-party elections for a new wholly elected parliament of 150 members. Candidates for election as president must have both parents born in Zambia (this excludes ex-president Kaunda). The constitution was amended in 1996 shortly before the parliamentary and presidential elections. The amendment restricts the president from serving more than two terms of office.

National Anthem. 'Stand and Sing of Zambia'; words collective, tune by M. E. Sontonga.

RECENT ELECTIONS
Parliamentary and presidential elections took place on 27 Dec. 2001. The elections were beset by allegations of vote rigging, prompting investigations from EU monitors. Levy Mwanawasa, former president Frederick Chiluba's chosen successor, defeated ten other candidates running for the presidency yet only won 28·8% of votes cast.

In the parliamentary elections, Levy Mwanawasa's party, the Movement for Multiparty Democracy (MMD), gained 69 seats in the 159-seat National Assembly; the United Party for National Development gained 49; the United National Independence Party, 13; the Forum for Democracy and Development, 12; and the Heritage Party, 4. Mwanawasa's inaugural speech was boycotted by all ten opposition parties.

CURRENT ADMINISTRATION
President: Levy Patrick Mwanawasa; b. 1948 (MMD; sworn in 2 Jan. 2002).
  Vice-President: Enoch Kavindele.
  In March 2003 the government comprised:
  Minister for Agriculture and Co-operatives: Mundia Sikatana. *Commerce, Trade and Industry:* Dipak Patel. *Communication and Transport:* Bates Namuyamba. *Community Development and Social Services:* Marina Nsingo. *Defence:* Michael Mabenga. *Education:* Andrew Mulenga. *Energy and Water Development:* George Mpombo. *Finance and National Planning:* Emmanuel G. Kasonde. *Foreign Affairs:* Kalombo Mwansa. *Health:* Brig.-Gen. Dr Brian Chituwo. *Home Affairs:* Ronnie Shikapwaska. *Information and Broadcasting Services:* Newstead Zimba. *Labour and Social Security:* Mutale Nalumango. *Lands:* Judith Kapijimpanga. *Legal Affairs:* George Kunda. *Local Government and Housing:* Sylvia Masebo. *Mines and Mineral Development:* Kaunda Lembalemba. *Science, Technology and Vocational Training:* Abel M. Chambeshi. *Sport, Youth and Child Development:* Gladys Nyironga. *Tourism:* Patrick Kalifungwa. *Works and Supply:* Ludwig S. Sondashi.

Government Website: http://www.state.gov.zm

DEFENCE
In 2000 defence expenditure totalled US$65m. (US$7 per capita), representing 1·8% of GDP.

Army. Strength (1999) 20,000. There are also two paramilitary police units totalling 1,400.

Air Force. In 1996 the Air Force had over 63 combat aircraft including J-6 (Chinese-built MiG-19s) and MiG-21s. Serviceability of most types is reported to be low. Personnel (1999) 1,600.

INTERNATIONAL RELATIONS

Zambia is a member of the UN, WTO, the Commonwealth, SADC, the African Union, African Development Bank, COMESA, IOM and is an ACP member state of the ACP-EU relationship.

During the 1990s Zambia received foreign aid equivalent to approximately US$900 a head, but according to the *World Bank* GNP per head declined from US$390 in 1991 to US$330 in 1999.

ECONOMY

In 1998 agriculture accounted for 17·3% of GDP, industry 26·4% and services 56·3%.

Overview. The privatization programme of 280 state-owned companies (255 had been sold by Aug. 2001) has created one of the most liberal economies in Africa. The most significant privatization has been that of the Zambia Consolidated Copper Mines Ltd (ZCCM), which previously accounted for approximately 70% of economic activity in the country.

Currency. The unit of currency is the *kwacha* (ZMK) of 100 *ngwee*. Foreign exchange reserves were US$98m. in April 2002. In Dec. 1992 the official and free market exchange rates were merged and the kwacha devalued 29%. Inflation, which was 183·3% in 1993, was brought down to 21·7% in 2001. Total money supply in May 2002 was 99,836m. kwacha.

Budget. The fiscal year is the calendar year. Budget in 1bn. kwacha:

	1996	1997	1998[1]	1999[2]
Revenue	745·3	957·0	1,097·6	1,430·4
Expenditure	842·7	1,313·6	1,717·1	1,874·3

[1]Provisional. [2]Forecast.

Performance. In 1998 there was a recession, with the economy shrinking by 1·9%. This was caused by various problems including the non-completion of the privatization of the Zambia Consolidated Copper Mines, the negative effects of the El Niño climate phenomenon and the economic crisis in East Asia which adversely affected the price of copper. There was a slight recovery in 1999, with the economy expanding by 2·4%, followed by growth of 3·6% in 2000 and 4·9% in 2001. Total GDP in 2001 was US$3·6bn.

Banking and Finance. The central bank is the Bank of Zambia (*Governor*, Dr Caleb Fundanga). In 1996, 20 banks were operating. The Bank of Zambia monitors and supervises the operations of financial institutions. Banks and building societies are governed by the Banking and Financial Services Act 1994.

There is a stock exchange in Lusaka. Its market capitalization was US$301m. in 1998, a 58% fall from 1997's figure of US$705m.

ENERGY AND NATURAL RESOURCES

Environment. According to the *World Bank Atlas* Zambia's carbon dioxide emissions in 1998 were the equivalent of 0·2 tonnes per capita.

Electricity. Installed capacity in 1997 was 2m. kW. Production in Jan.–Nov. 1998 was 6·99bn. kWh; consumption per capita (1998) was 539 kWh.

Zambia is a net exporter of hydro-electric power and has huge potential for energy growth. Between Jan. and Sept. 1998 Zambian electricity exports were worth US$3·6m. compared to US$11·9m. in the same period in 1997.

Oil and Gas. Imports of petroleum feedstock from Jan.–Nov. 1998 stood at 503,055 tonnes, a 31% increase on 1997.

Minerals. Minerals produced (in 1,000 tonnes): copper (1998), 320; cobalt (1995), 2·93; silver (1996), 8·67 tonnes; gold (1996), 2,926 troy oz. Zambia is the world's fourth leading producer of copper and produces a fifth of the world's cobalt. It is well-endowed with gemstones, especially emeralds, amethysts, aquamarine, tourmaline and garnets. In 1990 the government freed the gemstones trade from restrictions. In 1998, 192,189 tonnes of washed coal were produced (164,443 tonnes in 1997).

Agriculture. 70% of the population is dependent on agriculture. There were 5·26m. ha of arable land in 1998 and 19,000 ha of permanent crops. Principal agricultural products (2000 estimates, in 1,000 tonnes): sugarcane, 1,600; maize, 1,260; cassava, 1,020; millet, 71; seed cotton, 62; wheat, 60; groundnuts, 55.

Livestock (2000): cattle, 2·37m.; goats, 1·25m.; pigs, 330,000; sheep, 140,000; chickens, 29m.

Forestry. Forests covered 31·4m. ha in 1995, or 42·2% of the total land area (32·7m. ha and 44% in 1990). Timber production in 1999 was 8·05m. cu. metres, most of it for fuel.

Fisheries. Total catch, 1999, 67,327 tonnes (exclusively from inland waters).

INDUSTRY
In 1996 manufacturing accounted for 25·5% of GDP.

Labour. The labour force totalled 3,454,000 in 1996 (55% males). Around 74% of the economically active population in 1995 were engaged in agriculture, fisheries and forestry. Since 1992 nearly 100,000 jobs have been lost, and less than 10% of working-age Zambians work full-time in the formal sector.

Trade Unions. There is a Zambia Congress of Trade Unions.

INTERNATIONAL TRADE
In 2000 foreign debt was US$5,730m.

Imports and Exports. In 1996 exports were valued at US$1,010m. and imports at US$890m.

In 1998 the value of exports of goods and services declined by around 25%. In 1997 copper provided 80% of all exports (by value), cobalt 10%, zinc 2%. Zambia ranks 7th in the world for copper production. Since 1990 non-copper exports have increased in value from US$50m. to US$230m. The main import sources in 1995 were South Africa (27·7%), UK (11·3%), Zimbabwe (9·2%) and Japan (8·6%). Principal export markets in 1995 were Japan (17·9%), Saudi Arabia (12·9%), Thailand (12·8%) and Taiwan (7·2%).

COMMUNICATIONS

Roads. There were, in 1997, 66,781 km of roads, including 7,081 km of highway. 157,000 passenger cars were in use in 1996 (15 per 1,000 inhabitants) and there were 81,000 trucks and vans.

Rail. In 1995 there were 1,273 km of the state-owned Zambia Railways Ltd. (ZRL) and, in 1993, 891 km of the Tanzania-Zambia (Tazara) Railway, both on 1,067 mm gauge. ZRL carried 1·1m. passengers and 3·4m. tonnes of freight in 1993. Of the 66 locomotives run by Zambia Railways in 1998, 21 were non-operational.

Civil Aviation. The national carrier, Zambia Airways, went into voluntary liquidation in 1995; some of its services have been taken over by Aero Zambia, which operates internal flights and in 1998 flew to Harare, Johannesburg and Nairobi. Lusaka is the principal international airport. In 2000 Lusaka International handled 441,000 passengers (368,000 on international flights) and 14,700 tonnes of freight. In 1999 scheduled airline traffic of Zambian-based carriers flew 0·8m. km, carrying 42,000 passengers (36,000 on international flights).

Telecommunications. Main telephone lines numbered 83,300 in 2000, equivalent to 8·0 per 1,000 persons. In 1995 there were direct connections to 16 countries. Telecel (2) Ltd. has been licensed to run a mobile telecommunications service in addition to the Zambia Telecommunications Company (ZAMTEL) since 1996. Mobile phone subscribers numbered 3,700 in 1997 and there were 650 fax machines in 1996. Internet services are provided by Zambia Communications Systems (ZAMNET), a private company of ZAMTEL. There were 70,000 PCs in use (6·7 per 1,000 persons) in 2000 and approximately 15,000 Internet users.

Postal Services. In 1998 the Zambia Postal Service (ZAMPOST) operated 164 outlets of which 80% were loss making.

SOCIAL INSTITUTIONS

Justice. The Judiciary consists of the Supreme Court, the High Court and four classes of magistrates' courts; all have civil and criminal jurisdiction.

The Supreme Court hears and determines appeals from the High Court. Its seat is at Lusaka. The High Court exercises the powers vested in the High Court in England, subject to the High Court ordinance of Zambia. Its sessions are held where occasion requires, mostly at Lusaka and Ndola. All criminal cases tried by subordinate courts are subject to revision by the High Court.

The death penalty is authorized, the last execution having taken place in 1997.

Religion. In 1993 the president declared Zambia to be a Christian nation, but freedom of worship is a constitutional right. In 1992 there were 5·98m. Christians.

Education. Schooling is for nine years. In April 2002 President Mwanawasa announced the re-introduction of universal free primary education, abolished under former President Chiluba. In 1998 there were 1·7m. pupils in primary schools; secondary schools, 350,000 pupils. In 1998 expenditure on education represented 2·2% of GDP.

There are 2 universities, 3 teachers' colleges and 1 Christian college. In 1998 there were 4,797 university students. In addition the government sponsored 150 students to be trained abroad.

The adult literacy rate in 1999 was 77·2% (84·6% among males and 70·2% among females).

Health. In 1993 there were 786 doctors, and in 1990, 26 dentists, 1,503 nurses, 24 pharmacists and 311 midwives. There were 42 state, 29 mission and 11 mining company hospitals in 1987, with a total of 15,846 beds and 912 health centres with 7,081 beds.

In the period 1990–98 only 38% of the population had access to safe drinking water.

CULTURE

Broadcasting. The Zambia National Broadcasting Corporation is an independent statutory body which oversees four radio networks. There is also a religious radio station. In 1996, two privately-owned radio stations also started operations. These were Radio Phoenix and Radio Ichengelo. In 1997 there were 1·03m. radio and 277,000 TV receivers (colour by PAL). Private broadcasting stations were licensed to operate in 1996. One such company was Multi Choice Kaleidoscope (2) Ltd. which commenced operations in Aug. 1995. By Oct. 1996 the number of subscribers was 6,617.

Press. There were (1996) two state-owned daily papers, *The Times of Zambia* and *Zambia Daily Mail*, and three weeklies. There were also five privately-owned newspapers in 1995.

Tourism. Tourism-generated earnings from the 456,000 international tourists in 1999 were US$85m. There were a further 102,000 domestic tourists of which the majority were on business. Investment pledges for the industry stood at US$92·2m. including $60m. pledged for reconstructing the Livingstone Intercontinental Hotel. 865 poachers were arrested in 1998.

DIPLOMATIC REPRESENTATIVES

Of Zambia in the United Kingdom (2 Palace Gate, London, W8 5NG)
Acting High Commissioner: Geoffrey Penias Alikipo.

Of the United Kingdom in Zambia (5210 Independence Ave., 15101 Ridgeway, Lusaka)
High Commissioner: Timothy J. David.

Of Zambia in the USA (2419 Massachusetts Ave., NW, Washington, D.C., 20008)
Ambassador: Vacant.
Chargé d'Affaires a.i.: Walubita Imakando.

Of the USA in Zambia (PO Box 31617, Lusaka)
Ambassador: Martin G. Brennan.

Of Zambia to the United Nations
Ambassador: Mwelwa Musambachime.

Of Zambia to the European Union
Ambassador: Griffin Nyirongo.

FURTHER READING
Chiluba, F., *Democracy: the Challenge of Change.* Lusaka, 1995

Central Statistical Office. *Monthly Digest of Statistics.*
National statistical office: Central Statistical Office, Lusaka

ZIMBABWE

Republic of Zimbabwe

Capital: Harare
Population estimate, 2000: 12·63m.
GDP per capita, 2000: (PPP$) 2,635
HDI/world rank: 0·551/128

KEY HISTORICAL EVENTS

The territory which now forms Zimbabwe was administered by the British South Africa Company from the beginning of European colonization in 1890 until 1923 when it was granted the status of a self-governing colony. In 1911 it was divided into Southern and Northern Rhodesia (*see* Zambia). In 1953 Southern and Northern Rhodesia were again united, along with Nyasaland, to form the Federation of Rhodesia and Nyasaland. When this federation was dissolved on 31 Dec. 1963 Southern Rhodesia reverted to the status of a self-governing colony within the British Commonwealth.

On 11 Nov. 1965 the white-dominated government issued a unilateral declaration of independence (UDI). Thereupon the Governor dismissed the prime minister, Ian Smith, and his cabinet and the British government reasserted formal responsibility for Rhodesia; but effective internal government was carried on by the Smith cabinet. From 1–3 Dec. Harold Wilson, the British prime minister, met Smith on board H.M.S. *Tiger* and drafted a 'Working Document' on progress towards legal independence. This statement was rejected by the Smith government. On 2 March 1970 the Smith government declared Rhodesia a republic and adopted a new constitution. On 3 March 1978 Smith signed a constitutional agreement with the internationally-backed nationalist leaders. A draft constitution was published in Jan. 1979 and was accepted by the white electorate in a referendum. Following the Commonwealth Conference held in Lusaka in Aug. 1979, elections took place in March 1980 resulting in a victory for the Zimbabwe African National Union (ZANU). Southern Rhodesia became the Republic of Zimbabwe.

Almost immediately, the question of land redistribution became a hot political issue. In colonial days, Africans had been ejected from the best farming country. All sides recognized the need for reform but were unable to agree on the means of achieving it. In 20 years, 3·5m. ha of land have been acquired from white farmers, with the UK footing the £44m. bill for resettlement, but only 70,000 families have benefited. Another 400,000 ha went to senior colleagues in President Mugabe's government. The economy, meanwhile, suffered roaring inflation, unemployment and acute shortages. A policy of land occupation, with black settlers taking over white-owned farms, started in early 2000. Pressures on President Mugabe to restore the rule of law were ignored and violence escalated. Elections took place in June 2000, in which President Mugabe achieved a narrow victory. Violence continued during the months which followed, as support for Mugabe dwindled. In the lead-up to the 2002 presidential election, again won by Mugabe but by dubious means, the opposition leader, Morgan Tsvangirai, was charged with treason. The land reform plan, involving the redistribution of white-owned land to landless black Zimbabweans, continued in 2002 with large numbers of farms seized by war veterans. Several African countries, including Zimbabwe, faced famine in 2002.

TERRITORY AND POPULATION

Zimbabwe is bounded in the north by Zambia, east by Mozambique, south by South Africa and west by Botswana and the Caprivi Strip of Namibia. The area is 150,872 sq. miles (390,759 sq. km). The population was (1992 census) 10,401,767 (51·2% female). Estimate, 1995, 11,475,000 (50·2% female); density, 29·4 per sq. km. In 1999, 65·4% of the population were rural.

By 2010 the effects of AIDS are expected to result in the population declining to 9m.

There are eight provinces and two cities, Harare and Bulawayo, with provincial status. Area and population (1992 census):

	Area (sq. km)	Population		Area (sq. km)	Population
Bulawayo	479	620,936	Mashonaland West	57,441	1,116,928
Harare	872	1,478,810	Masvingo	56,566	1,221,845
Manicaland	36,459	1,537,676	Matabeleland North	75,025	640,957
Mashonaland Central	28,374	857,318	Matabeleland South	54,172	591,747
Mashonaland East	32,230	1,033,336	Midlands	49,166	1,302,212

Harare, the capital, had a population in 1999 of 1,686,000. Other main cities (with 1992 census populations) were Bulawayo (620,936), Chitungwiza (274,035), Mutare (131,808) and Gweru (124,735). The population is approximately 98% African, 1% mixed and Asian and there are approximately 70,000 whites. The main ethno-linguistic groups are the Shona (71%), Ndebele (16%), Ndau (3%) and Nyanja (3%). Other smaller ones include Kalanga, Manyika, Tonga and Lozi.

The official language is English.

SOCIAL STATISTICS

1995 births, 434,000; deaths, 158,000. Rates, 1995: birth, 38·8 per 1,000 population; death 14·1 per 1,000. Annual population growth rate, 1990–99, 1·7%. Zimbabwe's expectation of life at birth in 1999 was 43·2 years for males and 42·6 for females, down from (average) 54 years in 1993. The sharp decline is largely attributed to the huge number of people in the country with HIV. Researchers predict that by 2008 it will have dropped to 31 years. Approximately 25% of all adults are infected with HIV. Infant mortality, 1999, 60 per 1,000 live births; fertility rate, 1999, 3·7 births per woman.

CLIMATE

Though situated in the tropics, conditions are remarkably temperate throughout the year because of altitude, and an inland position keeps humidity low. The warmest weather occurs in the three months before the main rainy season, which starts in Nov. and lasts till March. The cool season is from mid-May to mid-Aug. and, though days are mild and sunny, nights are chilly. Harare, Jan. 69°F (20·6°C), July 57°F (13·9°C). Annual rainfall 33" (828 mm). Bulawayo, Jan. 71°F (21·7°C), July 57°F (13·9°C). Annual rainfall 24" (594 mm). Victoria Falls, Jan. 78°F (25·6°C), July 61°F (16·1°C). Annual rainfall 28" (710 mm).

CONSTITUTION AND GOVERNMENT

The Constitution provides for a single-chamber 150-member Parliament (*House of Assembly*), universal suffrage for citizens over the age of 18, an *Executive President* (elected for a six-year term of office by Parliament), an independent judiciary enjoying security of tenure and a Declaration of Rights, derogation from certain of the provisions being permitted, within specified limits, during a state of emergency. The House of Assembly is elected for five-year terms: 120 members are elected by universal suffrage, 10 are chiefs elected by all the country's tribal chiefs, 12 are appointed by the President and 8 are provincial governors. The constitution can be amended by a two-thirds parliamentary majority.

In a referendum on 12–13 Feb. 2000 on the adoption of a new constitution 697,754 (54·6%) voted against and only 578,210 in favour. Under the new constitution Zimbabwe would have had an Executive President and an Executive Prime Minister sharing power, but many people felt that it would have strengthened President Mugabe's hold on power.

National Anthem. 'Ngaikomborerwe Nyika yeZimbabwe' ('Blessed be the Land of Zimbabwe'); words by Dr Solomon M. Mutswairo; tune by Fred Changundega.

RECENT ELECTIONS

At the parliamentary elections of 24–25 June 2000 turn-out was 57%. The Zimbabwe African National Union-Patriotic Front (ZANU-PF) gained 62 of the 150 available seats (48·6% of votes cast). The Movement for Democratic Change, established in Jan. 2000, won 57 seats (47·0%) and the Zimbabwe African National Union-Ndonga gained 1 seat. 12 seats went to appointed non-constituency members, 8 went to *ex-officio* governor members and 10 to *ex-officio* chief members. The conduct of Mugabe's ZANU-PF during the pre-election campaign received widespread international condemnation. White-owned farms were illegally seized and there was a campaign of intimidation against opposition supporters that saw more than 30 people die.

Presidential elections were held between 9–11 March 2002. Incumbent Robert Mugabe was re-elected with 56·2% of votes cast, against 42·0% for Morgan Tsvangirai. There were three other candidates. Observers claimed the elections failed to meet international standards for a democratic poll.

CURRENT ADMINISTRATION

Executive President: Robert G. Mugabe; b. 1924 (ZANU-PF; sworn in on 30 Dec. 1987, having previously been prime minister from 1980 to 1987; re-elected April 1990, March 1996 and again in March 2002).

In March 2003 the council comprised:

Vice-Presidents: Simon Vengai Muzenda; Joseph Msika.

Minister of Defence: Sydney Sekeramayi. *Education, Sports and Culture:* Aeneas Chigwedere. *Energy and Power Development:* Amos Midzi. *Environment and Tourism:* Francis Nhema. *Finance and Economic Development:* Herbert Murerwa. *Foreign Affairs:* Stan Mudenge. *Health and Child Welfare:* David Parirenyatwa. *Home Affairs:* Kembo Mohadi. *Industry and International Trade:* Samuel Mumbengegwi. *Justice, Legal and Parliamentary Affairs:* Patrick Chinamasa. *Lands, Agriculture and Rural Resettlement:* Joseph Made. *Local Government, Public Works and National Housing, and Higher and Tertiary Education (acting):* Ignatius Chombo. *Mines and Mining Development:* Edward Chindori-Chininga. *Public Service, Labour and Social Welfare:* July Moyo. *Rural Resources and Water Development:* Joyce Mujuru. *Small and Medium Enterprise Development:* Sithembiso Nyoni. *Special Affairs in the President's Office:* John Nkomo. *Transport and Communications:* Witness Mangwende. *Youth Development, Gender Affairs and Employment Creation:* Elliot Manyika.

DEFENCE

In 2000 military expenditure totalled US$394m. (US$34 per capita), representing 6·1% of GDP.

Army. Strength in 1998 was estimated at 35,000. There were a further 19,500 paramilitary police and a police support unit of 2,300.

Air Force. The Air Force (ZAF) had a strength in 1999 of about 4,000 personnel and 58 combat aircraft. The headquarters of the ZAF and the main ZAF stations are in Harare; the second main base is at Gweru, with many secondary airfields throughout the country. There were 58 combat aircraft, including Hunters and F-7s (MiG-21), and 24 armed helicopters.

INTERNATIONAL RELATIONS

Zimbabwe is a member of UN, WTO, the Commonwealth, the African Union, African Development Bank, COMESA, SADC, IOM, and is an ACP member state of the ACP-EU relationship. Following the controversial presidential election of March 2002 Zimbabwe was suspended from the Commonwealth's councils for a year, extended for nine months in March 2003.

ECONOMY

Agriculture accounted for 19·5% of GDP in 1998, industry 24·4% and services 56·1%.

Robert Mugabe's 20-year rule has left the economy in a desperate situation. There is roaring inflation, heavy unemployment and shortages of food and other necessities, culminating in the authorities making an international appeal for food in July 2001. In Feb. 2000 the country ran out of gasoline because it could not pay the import bills.

Overview. The second phase of structural adjustment dubbed Zimbabwe Programme for Economic and Social Transformation (ZIMPREST) was launched in early 1998. Its goals are similar to those of the first phase (1991–95), promoting economic stabilization, liberalization of trade, deregulation, reform of the public sector and social reform. But confidence in the economy was undermined by promises to pay compensation (Z$365m.) to war veterans and to take over 1,471 privately-owned farms for resettlement. Meanwhile, inflation is beyond control and unemployment is high. Were it not for support from South Africa and other neighbouring states, the economy would collapse.

Currency. The unit of currency is the *Zimbabwe dollar* (ZWD), divided into 100 *cents*. Gold reserves were 121,000 troy oz in April 2002 and foreign exchange reserves US$72m. The currency was devalued 17% in Jan. 1994 and made fully convertible. Its value dropped by 65% in 1998. It was devalued again in Aug. 2000 by 24%. Whereas at the time of independence the Zimbabwean dollar was on a parity with the US dollar, by 2000 it was worth less than 2 cents. Inflation, which stood at 18·8% in 1997, had risen to 76·7% by 2001. Total money supply was Z$176,427m. in April 2002.

Budget. The 1999 budget forecast a budget deficit of 6%.
Revenue and expenditure (in Z$1,000):

	1996–97	1997–98
Revenue	27,289	52,152
Expenditure	32,366	63,857

The top rate of income tax is 50%; the top corporate income tax rate is 35%.

Performance. Real GDP growth was 2·5% in 1998, but in 1999 the economy contracted by 0·2%. In 2000 and 2001 it shrank further by 5·1% and 8·5% respectively. Zimbabwe's total GDP in 2001 was US$9·1bn.

Banking and Finance. The Reserve Bank of Zimbabwe is the central bank (established 1965; *Governor*, Dr Leonard Tsumba). It acts as banker to the government and to the commercial banks, is the note-issuing authority and co-ordinates the application of the government's monetary policy. The Zimbabwe Development Bank, established in 1983 as a development finance institution, is 51% government-owned. In 1997 there were seven commercial and five merchant banks. There are five registered finance houses, three of which are subsidiaries of commercial banks.

The IMF announced in June 1998 that it was to lend Zimbabwe US$175m. in the form of a 13-month standby credit which would allow Harare to draw US$52m. immediately to replenish its depleted reserves.

There is a stock exchange.

Weights and Measures. The metric system is in use but the US short ton is also used.

ENERGY AND NATURAL RESOURCES

Environment. According to the *World Bank Atlas* carbon dioxide emissions were the equivalent of 1·2 tonnes per capita in 1998.

Electricity. Installed capacity was 2m. kW in 1997. In 1997 Zimbabwe Electricity Supply Authority's (Zesa) five power stations supplied 7,323·3 GWh, and a further 3,171·5 GWh was imported via the Southern African Power Pool (SAPP). Electricity sales during the financial year 1995–96 increased by 3·6% and revenues grew by 28% from US$2,222·7m. to US$2,852·7m. Consumption per capita in 1998 was 896 kWh.

Minerals. The total value of all minerals produced in 1995 was Z$5,249·3m. 1995 production: gold, 23·9 tonnes, value Z$2,395m.; nickel, value (1993) Z$369·1m.; asbestos, 0·70m. tonnes; coal (1996), 5·2m. tonnes. Diamond production in 1998 totalled 70,000 carats.

Agriculture. Agriculture is the largest employer, providing jobs for 25% of the workforce. In 1998 there were 3·25m. ha of arable land and 0·13m. ha of permanent crops.

A constitutional amendment providing for the compulsory purchase of land for peasant resettlement came into force in March 1992. A provision to seize white-owned farmland for peasant resettlement was part of the government's new draft constitution that was rejected in the referendum of Feb. 2000. Various deadlines were given for white farmers to abandon their property during Aug. and Sept. 2002. The government claims that 300,000 landless black Zimbabweans have been resettled on seized land.

The staple food crop is maize, but 2002 production was less than a third of that in 2000. Tobacco is the most important cash crop. Production, 2000, in 1,000 tonnes: sugarcane, 4,228; maize, 2,108; seed cotton, 327; wheat, 250; tobacco, 228; cottonseed, 199; groundnuts, 191; cassava, 175; soybeans, 144; cotton lint, 128; sorghum, 103; bananas, 80; oranges, 80. Zimbabwe is the world's second largest exporter of flue-cured tobacco. In 1996 more than 201m. kg of tobacco were sold, fetching Z$5·8bn. More than 150,000 people work in the tobacco industry. Tobacco is a highly commercial crop, worth nearly 60 times as much as the same acreage planted with soya or maize.

Livestock (2000): cattle, 5·55m.; sheep, 530,000; pigs, 275,000; goats, 2·79m.; chickens, 16m. Dairy products (2000, in 1,000 tonnes): milk, 310; meat, 177.

Forestry. In 1995 forests covered 8·71m. ha, or 22·5% of the total land area (down from 8·96m. ha in 1990). Timber production in 1999 was 9·27m. cu. metres.

Fisheries. Trout, prawns and bream are farmed to supplement supplies of fish caught in dams and lakes. The catch in 1999 was 12,406 tonnes (all from inland waters).

INDUSTRY
Metal products account for over 20% of industrial output. Important agro-industries include food processing, textiles, furniture and other wood products.

Labour. The labour force in 1996 totalled 5,281,000 (56% males). Unemployment in Jan. 1998 was around 50%.

Trade Unions. There is a Zimbabwe Congress of Trade Unions which has 26 affiliated unions, representing more than 400,000 workers in 1998.

INTERNATIONAL TRADE
Foreign debt was US$4,002m. in 2000. Since 1 Jan. 1995 foreign companies have been permitted to remit 100% of after-tax profits. The Customs Agreement with South Africa was extended in 1982.

Imports and Exports. In 1996 exports totalled US$2,403m.; imports, US$2,819m.

Principal exports in 1993 (in US$1m.): tobacco, 365; ferrochrome, 142; clothing and textiles, 122; nickel, 56; cotton lint, 26; steel, 16. Main import suppliers, 1996 (% of total trade): South Africa, 38·3%; UK, 7·9%; Japan, 5·1%; USA, 5·0%; Germany, 4·9%. Main export destinations, 1996: UK, 10·1%; South Africa, 9·6%; Germany, 7·9%; USA, 6·7%; Japan, 5·1%.

Recent estimates suggest a marked deterioration in balance of payments.

Trade Fairs. The highlight of the year is the Zimbabwe International Book Fair, held in Harare in August.

COMMUNICATIONS

Roads. In 1996 the road network covered 18,338 km, of which 8,700 km were paved. Number of vehicles, 1996: passenger cars, 323,000; commercial vehicles, 32,000; motorcycles, 362,000. There were 38,777 road accidents in 1996 with 1,205 fatalities.

Rail. In 1995 the National Railways of Zimbabwe had 2,759 km (1,067 mm gauge) of route ways (313 km electrified). In 1995 the railways carried 1·9m. passengers and in 1997 freight tonne-km came to 9,122m.

Civil Aviation. There are three international airports: Harare (the main airport), Bulawayo and Victoria Falls. Air Zimbabwe, the state-owned national carrier, operates domestic services and in 1998 flew to the major centres in Africa and Europe. In 1999 it flew 11·5m. km, carrying 460,400 passengers (248,200 on international flights). Zimbabwe Express Airlines likewise operates internal services, and had flights in 1998 to Johannesburg. In 1998 Harare handled 1,262,000 passengers (905,000 on international flights).

Shipping. Zimbabwe's outlets to the sea are Maputo and Beira in Mozambique, Dar es Salaam, Tanzania and the South African ports.

Telecommunications. In 2000 Zimbabwe had 294,400 main telephone lines (18·5 for every 1,000 persons), and 160,000 PCs were in use (11·9 for every 1,000 persons). There were 256,000 mobile phone subscribers in Sept. 2000 and 30,000 Internet users in May 1999. In 1995 there were 4,100 fax machines.

Postal Services. In Aug. 1995 there were 170 post offices, 47 postal telegraph agencies and 86 postal agencies. A total of 298m. pieces of mail were handled in 1995, or 26 items per person.

SOCIAL INSTITUTIONS

Justice. The general common law of Zimbabwe is the Roman Dutch law as it applied in the Colony of the Cape of Good Hope on 10 June 1891, as subsequently modified by statute. Provision is made by statute for the application of African customary law by all courts in appropriate cases.

The death penalty is authorized. The last executions took place in May 2002.

The Supreme Court consists of the Chief Justice and at least two Supreme Court judges. It is the final court of appeal. It exercises appellate jurisdiction in appeals from the High Court and other courts and tribunals; its only original jurisdiction is that conferred on it by the Constitution to enforce the protective provisions of the Declaration of Rights. The Court's permanent seat is in Harare but it also sits regularly in Bulawayo.

The High Court is also headed by the Chief Justice, supported by the Judge President and an appropriate number of High Court judges. It has full original jurisdiction, in both Civil and Criminal cases, over all persons and all matters in Zimbabwe. The Judge President is in charge of the Court, subject to the directions of the Chief Justice. The Court has permanent seats in both Harare and Bulawayo and sittings are held three times a year in three other principal towns.

Regional courts, established in Harare and Bulawayo but also holding sittings in other centres, exercise a solely criminal jurisdiction which is intermediate between that of the High Court and the Magistrates' courts. Magistrates' courts, established in 20 centres throughout the country, and staffed by full-time professional magistrates, exercise both civil and criminal jurisdiction.

Primary courts consist of village courts and community courts. Village courts are presided over by officers selected for the purpose from the local population, sitting with two assessors. They deal with certain classes of civil cases only and have jurisdiction only where African customary law is applicable. Community courts are presided over by presiding officers in full-time public service who may be assisted by assessors. They have jurisdiction in all civil cases determinable by African customary law and also deal with appeals from village courts. They also have limited criminal jurisdiction in respect of petty offences.

The population in penal institutions in Aug. 1998 was 18,271 (155 per 100,000 of national population).

Religion. Over a third of the population adhere to traditional animist religion. In 1997 approximately 2·42m. persons were Protestants, 1·54m. African Christians, 800,000 Roman Catholics and 2·03m. followers of other religions.

Education. Education is compulsory. 'Manageable' school fees were introduced in 1991; primary education had hitherto been free to all. All instruction is given in English. There are also over 3,800 private primary schools and over 950 private secondary schools, all of which must be registered by the Ministry of Education. In 1998 there were 2,507,098 pupils at primary schools and 847,296 pupils at secondary schools. In 1999 the adult literacy rate was 88% (92·3% among males and 83·8% among females). Both the overall rate and the rate for males are the highest in Africa.

There are ten teachers' training colleges, eight of which are in association with the University of Zimbabwe. In addition, there are four special training centres for teacher trainees in the Zimbabwe Integrated National Teacher Education Course. In 1990 there were 17,873 students enrolled at teachers' training colleges, 1,003 students at agricultural colleges and 20,943 students at technical colleges. There are 4 universities and 10 technical colleges.

Health. There were 1,378 government hospitals in 1993. All mission health institutions get 100% government grants-in-aid for recurrent expenditure. In 1993 there were 1,551 doctors, 194 dentists, 22,590 nurses, 411 pharmacists and 2,894 midwives. It is estimated that one in five adults are HIV infected.

Welfare. It is a statutory responsibility of the government in many areas to provide: processing and administration of war pensions and old age pensions; protection of children; administration of remand, probation and correctional institutions; registration and supervision of welfare organizations.

CULTURE

Broadcasting. Zimbabwe Broadcasting Corporation is a statutory body broadcasting a general service in English, Shona, Ndebele, Nyanja, Tonga and Kalanga. There are three national semi-commercial services—Radio 1, 2 and 3, in English, Shona and Ndebele. Radio 4 transmits formal and informal educational programmes. Zimbabwe Television broadcasts on two channels (colour by PAL). In 1997 there were 370,000 TV and 1·14m. radio sets in use.

Press. In 1996 there were two daily newspapers with a combined circulation of 209,000, giving a rate of 19 per 1,000 inhabitants. In Jan. 2002 parliament passed an Access to Information Bill restricting press freedom, making it an offence to report from Zimbabwe unless registered by a state-appointed commission.

Tourism. There were 2,328,000 foreign tourists in 1999, bringing revenue of US$145m.

Festivals. Of particular importance are Amakhosi Inxusa Festival, a festival of soul, dance and theatre in Bulawayo (March) and the Zimbabwe National Jazz Festival in Harare (Sept.–Nov.).

Libraries. There is a City Library in Harare.

Theatre and Opera. Harare has a Repertory Theatre.

Museums and Galleries. The main attractions are the Queen Victoria Museum and the National Gallery of Zimbabwe.

DIPLOMATIC REPRESENTATIVES
Of Zimbabwe in the United Kingdom (Zimbabwe House, 429 Strand, London, WC2R 0JR)
High Commissioner: Simbarashe Simbanenduku Mumbengegwi.

Of the United Kingdom in Zimbabwe (7th Floor, Corner House, Samora Machel Ave/Leopold Takawira Street, Harare, P.O. Box 4490)
High Commissioner: Brian Donnelly, CMG.

Of Zimbabwe in the USA (1608 New Hampshire Ave., NW, Washington, D.C., 20009)
Ambassador: Simbi Veke Mubako.

Of the USA in Zimbabwe (172 Herbert Chitepo Ave., Harare)
Ambassador: Joseph Gerard Sullivan.

Of Zimbabwe to the United Nations
Ambassador: Dr Tichaona Joseph B. Jokonya.

Of Zimbabwe to the European Union
Ambassador: Kelebert Nkomani.

FURTHER READING
Central Statistical Office. *Monthly Digest of Statistics.*

Hatchard, J., *Individual Freedoms and State Security in the African Context: the Case of Zimbabwe.* Ohio Univ. Press, 1993
Potts, D., *Zimbabwe.* [Bibliography] 2nd ed. ABC-Clio, Oxford and Santa Barbara (CA), 1993
Skålnes, T., *The Politics of Economic Reform in Zimbabwe: Continuity and Change in Development.* London, 1995
Weiss, R., *Zimbabwe and the New Elite.* London, 1994

National statistical office: Central Statistical Office, POB 8063, Causeway, Harare.

ABBREVIATIONS

ACP	African Caribbean Pacific
Adm.	Admiral
a.i.	ad interim
b.	born
bbls.	barrels
bd	board
bn.	billion (one thousand million)
Brig.	Brigadier
bu.	bushel
Cdr	Commander
CFA	Communauté Financière Africaine
CFP	Comptoirs Français du Pacifique
c.i.f.	cost, insurance, freight
C.-in-C.	Commander-in-Chief
CIS	Commonwealth of Independent States
cu.	cubic
CUP	Cambridge University Press
cwt	hundredweight
D.	Democratic Party
DWT	dead weight tonnes
ECOWAS	Economic Community of West African States
EEA	European Economic Area
EEZ	Exclusive Economic Zone
EMS	European Monetary System
EMU	European Monetary Union
ERM	Exchange Rate Mechanism
f.o.b.	free on board
ft	foot/feet
FTE	full-time equivalent
G8 Group	Canada, France, Germany, Italy, Japan, UK, USA, Russia
GDP	gross domestic product
Gen.	General
GNI	gross national income
GNP	gross national product
GRT	gross registered tonnes
GW	gigawatt
GWh	gigawatt hours
ha	hectare(s)
HDI	Human Development Index
ind.	independent(s)
ISO	International Organization for Standardization (domain names)
K	kindergarten
kg	kilogramme(s)
kl	kilolitre(s)

ABBREVIATIONS

km	kilometre(s)
kW	kilowatt
kWh	kilowatt hours
lb	pound(s) (weight)
Lieut.	Lieutenant
m.	million
Maj.	Major
MW	megawatt
MWh	megawatt hours
n.e.c.	not elsewhere classified
NRT	net registered tonnes
NTSC	National Television System Committee (525 lines 60 fields)
OUP	Oxford University Press
oz	ounce(s)
PAL	Phased Alternate Line (625 lines 50 fields 4·43 MHz sub-carrier)
PAL M	Phased Alternate Line (525 lines 60 PAL 3·58 MHz sub-carrier)
PAL N	Phased Alternate Line (625 lines 50 PAL 3·58 MHz sub-carrier)
PAYE	Pay-As-You-Earn
PPP	Purchasing Power Parity
R.	Republican Party
Rt Hon.	Right Honourable
SADC	Southern African Development Community
SDR	Special Drawing Rights
SECAM H	Sequential Couleur avec Mémoire (625 lines 50 fields Horizontal)
SECAM V	Sequential Couleur avec Mémoire (625 lines 50 fields Vertical)
sq.	square
SSI	Supplemental Security Income
TAFE	technical and further education
TEU	twenty-foot equivalent units
trn.	trillion (one million million)
TV	television
Univ.	University
VAT	value-added tax
vfd	value for duty

PLACE AND INTERNATIONAL
ORGANIZATIONS INDEX

Italicized page numbers refer to extended entries
An * denotes a further reference in the addenda, pages xxxv–xxxvi

Faro (Yukon) 417, 420
Faroe Islands 73, 541, *550–2*
Farquhar 1414, 1724
Farrukhabad-Cum-Fatehgarh 878
Fars 902
Farwaniya 1015
Faryab 130
Faslane 1639
Fatehabad 844
Fatehpur 878
Fatick 1393
Fatu Hiva 668
Faya 432
Fayette 1843
Fayetteville (Arkansas) 1804
Fayetteville (North Carolina) 1754, 1896
Fayum 580
Federal Capital Territory (Nigeria) 1230, 1231
Federal Capital Territory (Pakistan) 1257
Federal District (Mexico) 1125
Federal District (Venezuela) 1985
Federal Way 1938
Feira de Santana 323
Fejér 794
Ferghana 1972
Ferkessedougou 504
Fermanagh 1701
Ferozepore 869
Ferozepur 845
Ferrara 947
Ferrol 1491
Fès 1151
Fez see Fès
Fianarantsoa 1080
Ficksburg 1476
Fier 136
Fife 1687
Figuig 1151
Fiji Islands *614–19*
—in world organizations 16, 76, 77, 92, 93, 95
Filchner Ice Shelf 1723
Fingal 916
Finke 197
Finland *620–31*
—in European organizations 52, 54, 58, 59, 61, 65, 66, 67, 69, 71, 72, 73, 74

—in other organizations 11, 14, 46, 49, 50, 81, 83, 92, 104, 112, 116
Finnmark 1238
Firozabad 878
Fitchburg 1862
Flagstaff 1801, 1802
Flamingo Bay 1508
Fleetwood 1648
Flemish Brabant 283
Flensburg 740
Flevoland 1185
Flinders 217
Flint 1754, 1863, 1865
Flint Island 995
Flintshire 1695
Florence (Italy) 947, 948, 956
Florence (South Carolina) 1920
Florencia 477
Flores (Guatemala) 767
Flores (Portugal) 1310
Flores (Uruguay) 1966
Floriancholis 325
Florianópolis 323
Florida Islands 1446
Florida (Uruguay) 1966
Florida (USA) 1752, 1762, 1764, *1822–4*
Florina 752
Florissant 1873
Focşani 1324
Foggia 947
Fogo 422
Fomboni 484
Fond du Lac 1944
Fongafale 1603
Fontana 1754, 1807
Fontvielle 1141, 1142, 1143
Food and Agricultural Organization *25–6*
Forli 947
Formentera 1488, 1490
Former Yugoslav Republic of Macedonia see Macedonia (Former Yugoslav Republic of)
Formosa 161
Fort Collins 1754, 1811, 1813

Fort-de-France 655, 656
Fort Lauderdale 1754, 1783, 1822
Fort-Liberté 783
Fort McMurray 378
Fort Providence 413
Fort Resolution 413
Fort St John 384
Fort Saskatchewan 378
Fort Simpson 413
Fort Smith (Arkansas) 1804
Fort Smith (Northwest Territories) 411, 413, 414
Fort Wayne 1754, 1839
Fort Worth 1753, 1783, 1926, 1928
Fortaleza 322, 323
Forth 1654, 1690
Framingham 1862
France *632–75*
—departmental collectivities 660–1
—dependencies 674–5
—in European organizations 52, 54, 58, 59, 61, 65, 66, 67, 69, 72, 75
—in other organizations 46, 49, 50, 81, 83, 87, 92, 95, 104, 112, 116, 123
—overseas departments 650–9
—overseas territories 668–73
—territorial collectivities 662–7
—in UN 10, 11, 12, 14, 15
Franceville 676, 679
Franche-Comté 633
Francisco de Orellano 574
Francisco Morazán 788
Francistown 317
Frankfort 1847, 1848
Frankfurt am Main 694, 695, 700, 702, 703, 720, 724
Franklin 1887
Fraserburg 1481
Fray Bentos 1966
Frederick 1857

Fredericton 388, 389, 391, 392
Frederiksberg 540, 541
Frederiksborg 540
Frederikshavn 543
Frederikstad 1239
Frederiksted 1962
Free State (South Africa) 1458, 1459, 1460, *1474–6*
Freeport (Bahamas) 255, 258
Freeport (New York) 1893
Freetown 1420, 1421, 1422, 1423
Fregate 1414
Freiburg im Breisgau 694, 704, 711
Freiburg (Switzerland) see Fribourg
Freising 704
Fremantle 186, 227, 232, 233
Fremont (California) 1754, 1807
Fremont (Nebraska) 1878, 1879
French Guiana 87, *650–2*
French Polynesia 95, 639, 650, *668–71*
Fresno 1753, 1806, 1807
Fria 772
Fribourg 1534, 1536, 1542
Friesland 1185
Friuli-Venezia Giulia 947
Frunze see Bishkek
Fuenlabrada 1488
Fuerteventura 1488, 1490
Fuglafjørdur 552
Fujairah 1620, 1623
Fujian 446, 454
Fujisawa 965
Fukui 965
Fukuoka 965, 972, 973, 974
Fukushima 965
Fukuyama 965
Fulacunda 774
Fullerton 1754, 1807
Funabashi 965
Funafuti 1603, 1604, 1605
Funchal 1310, 1315
Fürth 694
Fushun 447

Futuna *see* Wallis
and Futuna
Fuzhou 446, 447
Fyn 540
FYROM *see*
Macedonia
(Former Yugoslav
Republic of)

Gaalkacyo 1453
Gaarowe 1453
Gabés 1583, 1586
Gabon *676–80*
—in world
organizations 14,
101, 104, 106,
117, 118, 123
Gaborone 317, 320,
321
Gabú 774
Gadag-Betigeri 852
Gafsa 1583
Gagauz Yeri 1137
Gaggal 847
Gagnoa 504
Gainesville 1822,
1824
Gaithersburg 1857
Galápagos 573,
574
Galaţi 1324, 1329
Galgudug 1453
Gali 690
Galicia 1487, 1488
Galle 1500, 1503
Galveston 1926,
1927
Galway 916, 929,
930, 932
Gambella 608
Gambia *681–5*
—in world
organizations 14,
76, 104, 106, 112,
117, 118
Gambier Islands 668
Gand *see* Ghent
Gandaki 1180
Gander 392
Gandhidham 842
Gandhinagar 819,
831, 842
Gandja 249
Ganganagar 871
Gangtok 831, 873,
874
Gangwon 1000
Ganjam 867
Gansu 446, 456
Ganzourgou 343
Gao 1101, 1104
Garbahaarrey 1453
Garðabær 802
Garden Grove 1754,
1807

Gardner *see*
Nikumaroro
Garff 1708
Garissa 988, 993
Garland 1754, 1926
Garo Hills 835, 862,
863
Garoua 358, 361
Gary 1755, 1838,
1839
Gash-Setir 597
Gaspar Grande 1577
Gatineau 405
Gatwick 1653
Gauhati 828
Gauteng 1458, 1459,
1460, 1470,
1476–7
Gävle 1523
Gävleborg 1523
Gaya 814, 838
Gaza (Mozambique)
1158
Gaza (Palestine) 934,
935, 943, 944
Gaziantep 1590
Gbarnga 1047
Gdańsk 1300, 1301,
1305
Gdynia 1300, 1302,
1305
Gebze 1591
Gedaref 1506
Gedo 1453
Geelong 175, 186,
222, 226
Gelderland 1185
Geleen-Sittard 1186
Gelsenkirchen 694
General Agreement
on Tariffs and
Trade 55
General Santos 1293
Geneva 1535, 1536,
1539, 1540, 1541,
1542
Genève-Annemasse
634
Genk 284
Genoa 947, 953, 955
Gentofte 541
George 1466
George Town
(Cayman Islands)
1727, 1728, 1729
George Town
(Tasmania) 219
Georgetown
(Ascension Island)
1741
Georgetown
(Delaware) 1819
Georgetown
(Guyana) 778,
779, 780, 781

Georgetown
(Kentucky) 1850
Georgetown
(Malaysia) 1091
Georgetown (Prince
Edward Island)
405
Georgia* *686–91*
—in European
organizations 65,
66, 69, 75, 112
—in other
organizations 11,
14, 46, 79, 81, 111
Georgia (USA) 1751,
1752, 1762, 1764,
1778, *1825–7*
Gera 694
Geraldton 228, 233
Germantown 1857
Germany* *692–743*
—in European
organizations 52,
54, 58, 61, 65, 66,
67, 69, 72, 74, 75
—Länder 709–43
—in other
organizations 46,
49, 50, 81, 83, 90,
92, 104, 112, 116
—in UN 10, 11, 14,
15
Gerona 1487, 1495
Getafe 1488
Gettysburg 1915
Gezira 1506
Ghana* *744–9*
—in world
organizations 11,
14, 76, 81, 104,
106
Ghanzi 317
Gharbia 580
Ghardaia 143
Gharyan 1051
Ghaziabad 814
Ghazni 130
Ghent 283, 289, 290
Ghowr 130
Ghubriah 1253
Gia Lai 1991
Gibraltar* 78, 1639,
1717, *1733–7*
Giessen 724
Gifu 965
Gijón 1488
Gikongoro 1358
Gilan 902
Gilbert 1755, 1800
Gilbert Islands 995
Gilgit 1257
Gillette 1949
Gippsland 181, 222
Gir Forest 844
Giresun 1590

Gisborne 1203, 1204,
1208
Gisenyi 1358
Gitarama 1358
Gitega 349
Giurgiu 1324
Giza 580, 581
Gizo 1446
Gjirokastër 136
Gladstone 186, 209
Glaris *see* Glarus
Glarus 1534, 1536
Glasgow 1630, 1643,
1653, 1687, 1688,
1689, 1690, 1691,
1693, 1694
Glastonbury 1678
Glen Cove 1893
Glendale (Arizona)
1754, 1800
Glendale (California)
1754, 1807
Glenfaba 1708
Glenville 1942, 1943
Glimmerglass 1791
Gliwice 1300
Glorieuses Islands
650, *675*
Gloucester (New
Jersey) 1887
Gloucester (Ontario)
400
Gloucestershire 1681
Glücksburg 697
Glyndebourne 1678
Gmunden 246
Gnagna 343
Gniezno 1306
Goa 813, 817, 819,
827, 828, 831,
840–1
Gobabis 1171
Gode 610
Godhra 842
Godthåb *see* Nuuk
Goiânia 323
Goiás 323
Golan Heights 935
Gölcük 1592
Gold Coast 175,
209
Golden 1813
Golestan 902
Golmud 448
Goma 489, 492
Gombe 1231
Gomera 1488, 1490
Gonaïves 783
Gondiya 858
Goose Bay 392, 395
Gopalpur 868
Gorakhpur 814, 826,
879
Gorey 1714
Gorgan 902

Kalkalighat 877
Kallithea 752
Kalmar 1522, 1523
Kalmykia *1350–1*
Kalpeni Island 890
Kalyubia 580
Kamaran 1999
Kambia 1421
Kameng 833
Kamloops 381, 384
Kampala 1606, 1607, 1609, 1610
Kamsar 772
Kananga 489, 490
Kanara 851
Kanazawa 965
Kanchipuram 874
Kanchrapara 882
Kandahar 130
Kandi 297
Kandla 827, 843
Kandy 1500
Kanem 432, 434
Kangar 1091
Kangerlussuaq 554
Kanggye 1009
Kangra 846, 847
Kangwon 1009
Kankan 769, 772
Kano 1230, 1231, 1232, 1235
Kanpur 814, 879
Kansas 1752, 1762, 1764, 1785, *1844–6*
Kansas City (Kansas) 1754, 1845
Kansas City (Missouri) 1753, 1873, 1874
Kanta-Häme 620
Kanto 965
Kanton 995, 997
Kanye 317
Kaohsiung 470, 471, 475, 476
Kaolack 1393, 1396, 1397
Kapisa 130
Kaposvár 794
Kaptai 267
Kapurthala 869
Karabük 1590
Karachai-Cherkessia *1351*
Karachi 1257, 1259, 1260, 1262, 1263, 1264
Karaikal 891
Karaj 902
Karak 976
Karakalpak Autonomous Republic 1972, *1976–7*

Karamai 452
Karaman 1590
Karas 1170
Karbala 911
Karditsa 752
Karelia *1351–2*
Karen State 1164
Karimnagar 831
Karlovarský 533
Karlovy Vary 533
Karlskrone 1523
Karlsruhe 694, 710, 711
Karlstad 1523
Karnal 844
Karnataka 813, 814, 816, 817, 822, 828, 831, *851–3*
Kärnten *see* Carinthia
Karpenissi 751
Kars 1590
Karshi 1972
Kartong 683
Karuali 1180
Karuzi 348
Karwar 853
Kasai Occidental 489
Kasai Oriental 489
Kasama 2005
Kashiwa 965
Kashkadar 1972
Kashmir 1256–7 *see also* Jammu and Kashmir
Kassala 1506, 1507
Kassel 694
Kassérine 1583
Kastamonu 1590
Kastoria 752
Kasugai 965
Katerini 752
Katherine 197
Kathgodam 881
Káthmandu 1179, 1180, 1182, 1183
Katihar 837
Katima Mulilo 1170
Katiola 504
Katni 857
Katowice 1300, 1305
Katsina 1230, 1231
Katunayake 1501
Kauai 1828
Kaunas 1060, 1063, 1064
Kaustinen 630
Kavajë 136, 137
Kavaratti Island 890
Kavieng 1275
Kawagoe 965
Kawaguchi 965

Kawasaki 965
Kaya 343, 346
Kayah State 1164
Kayanza 348
Kayes 1101, 1102, 1104
Kayseri 1590
Kazakhstan 55, *982–7*
—in world organizations 14, 46, 69, 79, 81, 92, 112, 117, 118
Kazan 1354
Kaziranga 862, 866
Kearney 1878, 1879
Kebbi 1231
Kebili 1583
Kecskemét 794
Kedah 1090
Keelung 470, 475
Keene 1884, 1886
Keetmanshoop 1170, 1171
Keewatin 411, 412, 414, 416
Keflavík 802, 806
Keksholm 1352
Kelang 1091
Kelantan 1090
Kelibia 1585
Kelowna 381, 384
Kemaman 1095
Kemi 621, 630
Keminmaa 625
Kemo 427
Kenai Peninsula 1797
Kendari 893
Kénédougou 343
Kenema 1420, 1421
Kénitra 1151
Kenner 1851
Kennewick 1938
Kenosha 1834, 1944
Kensington and Chelsea 1682
Kent (England) 1681
Kent (Washington) 1938
Kentucky 1752, 1762, 1764, 1778, *1846–50*
Kentville 396
Kenya *988–94*
—in world organizations 14, 76, 104, 107, 109, 112
Kerala 813, 817, 822, 823, 828, 831, *854–5*
Kerava 621
Kerema 1275
Keren 597

Kerewan/Farafenni 681
Kerguelen Islands 671, 672
Kerkrade 1186
Kermadec Islands 1202
Kerman 902
Kermanshah 902
Kerry 916
Keshod 843
Keski-Pohjanmaa 620
Keski-Suomi 620
Ketchikan Gateway 1797
Kettering 1902
Key West 1822
Keyser 1943
Kgalagadi 317
Kgatleng 317
Khaborovsk 1334
Khajuraho 857
Khakassia *1352*
Khalid 1623
Khammam 831
Khammouane 1026
Khandwa 856, 857
Khanh Hoa 1992
Khankendi 254
Khanty-Mansi 1356
Khanty-Mansiisk 1356
Khanvel 887
Kharadpada 886
Kharagpur 81, 883
Kharkiv 1613, 1617
Kharkivska 1613
Khartoum 1506, 1507, 1508, 1509, 1510
Khasi Hills 835, 862, 863
Khatlon 1550
Khémisset 1151
Khenchela 143
Khenifra 1151
Kherson 1613, 1617
Khersonska 1613
Kheyrabad 133
Khmelnitsky 1613
Khmelnytska 1613
Khomas 1170
Khor Fakkan 1623
Khorasan 902
Khorazm *see* Khorezm
Khorezm 1972
Khorixas 1171
Khorog 1554
Khorramabad 902
Khorramshahr 902
Khouribga 1151
Khudzand 1550
Khujand 1552

Maiao (French Polynesia) 668
Maidstone 1685
Maiduguri 1230, 1231
Maikop 1346
Maine 1751, 1762, 1765, 1785, *1853–6*
Mainz 694, 707, 731, 733
Maio (Cape Verde) 422, 424
Maizuru 968
Majorca 1488
Majuro 1113, 1114, 1115
Makak 361
Makamba 348
Makati 1292
Makeni 1420
Makhachkala 1349
Makiïvka 1613
Makin 995
Makira and Ulawa 1446
Makkovik 394
Makokou 676
Makung 475
Makurdi 1230, 1231
Malabo 592, 594, 595
Malabon 1293
Malaga (Colombia) 479
Málaga (Spain) 1487, 1488, 1495
Malaita 1446
Malang 893
Malanje 152
Malatya 1590
Malawi *1085–9*
—in world organizations 14, 76, 104, 107, 108
Malaysia *1090–7*
—in world organizations 11, 14, 49, 76, 92, 93, 94, 96, 97, 117, 118
Malden 995
Maldives *1098–100*
—in world organizations 14, 76, 92, 93, 98, 117, 118
Maldonado 1966
Malé 1098
Malegaon 814
Malekula 1978
Mali *1101–5*
—in world organizations 14, 104, 105, 106,

107, 109, 112, 117, 118, 123
Malindi 993
Mallaig 1648, 1689
Mallakastër 137
Mallee 222
Mallorca 1490
Malmö 1523, 1530
Malongo 155
Małopolskie 1300
Malsi e Madhe 137
Malta *1106–12*
—in European organizations 53, 55, 58, 59, 65, 66, 69
—in other organizations 14, 76
Maluku 893
Mambere Kadéi 427
Mamou 769
Mamoudzou 660
Man (Côte d'Ivoire) 505
Man, Isle of 1660, *1707–11*
Manabi 574
Manado 898
Managua 1221, 1222, 1224, 1225
Manali 847
Manama 260, 262
Manaus 322, 323, 324, 325
Manawatu-Wanganui 1203, 1208
Manchester (England) 1630, 1643, 1653, 1668, 1681, 1682, 1684, 1685
Manchester (Jamaica) 958
Manchester (New Hampshire) 1755, 1884
Mandalay 1164, 1165
Mandaluyong 1293
Mandaue 1293
Mandeville 958
Mandi 846
Mandurah 228
Mandya 852
Mangaia 1216
Mangalia 1326
Mangalore 814, 827, 853
Mangan 873
Mangareva 668
Mangghystaü 982
Mango 1568
Manhattan (Kansas) 1846

Manhattan (New York) 1755, 1893
Manica 1158
Manicaland 2012
Maniema 489
Manihi 668
Manihiki 1216
Manila 1292, 1293, 1295, 1296, 1297
Manipur* 813, 817, 828, 831, *860–2*
Manisa 1590, 1591
Manitoba 363, 364, 365, 369, 376, 377, *385–8*
Manizales 477
Mankato 1868
Mankono 505
Manmad 860
Mannheim 694, 710, 711
Manono 1375
Manra 995
Mansa 2005
Mansfield 1902
Mansura 580
Manu'a 1956
Manuae and Te au-o-tu 1216
Manus 1275, 1277
Manzanillo 1131
Manzanillo International 1272
Manzini 1517, 1519, 1520
Mao 432
Maputo 1158, 1159, 1160, 1161, 1162, 2015
Mar del Plata 163
Mara 1555
Maracaibo 1986, 1989
Maracay 1985
Maradi 1226, 1229
Marakei 995
Maramureş 1324
Maranhão 322
Marbella 1488
Marburg/Lahn 724
Marche 947
Marcus Hook 1913
Mardin 1590
Maré Island 662
Margao 841
Margibi 1047
Mari-El *1353*
Maria Trinidad Sánchez 564
Marib 1999
Maribor 1441, 1444
Marie-Galante 652, 653, 654

Mariel 518, 520
Mariental 1170, 1171
Marigot 653
Marijampolë 1060
Marikina 1293
Marion Island 1458
Maritime 1568
Mariupol 1613, 1617
Marka 1453, 1455
Markazi 902
Markham 400
Marlboro 1934
Marlborough 1203, 1208
Marmagao 840, 841
Maroochy 175
Maroua 358
Marowijne 1512
Marquesas Islands 668
Marrakesh 1151, 1155
Marsa 1108
Marsa Alam 584
Marsabit 993
Marseilles 633, 634, 643
Marshall Islands 14, 92, 95, *1113–15*
Martin 1435
Martinique 87, 650, *655–7*
Marwar 872
Mary 1598
Maryland 1751, 1752, 1762, 1765, *1856–60*
Maryland (Liberia) 1047
Marystown 392
Masaka 1606
Masan 1005
Masaya 1221, 1222
Masbate 1292
Mascara 143
Maseru 1043, 1045, 1046
Mashhad 902
Mashonaland 2012
Mason City 1842
Massachusetts 1751, 1762, 1765, 1785, *1860–2*
Massawa 597, 598, 599, 600, 608, 609
Massilon 1902
Masuku 676, 679
Masvingo 2012
Mat 137
Mata-Utu 672, 673
Matabeleland 2012
Matadi 489, 491, 492
Matagalpa 1221, 1222

Minna 1231
Minneapolis 1753,
1783, 1866, 1867
Minnesota 1752,
1762, 1765, 1785,
1787, *1866–8*
Minorca 1488
Minot 1899
Minsk 277, 280, 281
Miquelon *see* St
Pierre and
Miquelon
Miraj 858
Miramichi 391
Miranda 1985
Mirditë 137
Miri 1091, 1095
Mirzapur-Cum-
Vindhyachal
878
Misiones (Argentina)
161
Misiones (Paraguay)
1280
Miskolc 794, 799,
800
Mission 381
Mississauga 400
Mississippi 1752,
1762, 1764, 1778,
1869–72
Missoula 1875, 1877
Missouri 1752, 1762,
1764, *1872–5*
Misurata 1055
Mitchell 1921
Mitiaro 1216
Mitú 478
Miyazaki 965
Mizoram 813, 817,
828, 831, *864–5*
Mmabatho 1483
Moanda 676
Mobaye 427
Mobile 1754, 1794,
1795
Moçâmedes *see*
Namibe
Mochudi 317
Mocoa 478
Modena 947
Modesto 1754, 1807
Modinagar 878
Moe-Yallourn 222
Moers 694
Moeskroen *see*
Mouscron
Moga 869
Mogadishu 1452,
1453, 1455
Mohale's Hoek 1043
Mohammadia-Znata
1151
Mohéli *see* Mwali
Mokha 2001, 2003

Mokhotlong 1043
Mokokchung 865
Mokpo 1005
Moldova *1136–40*
—in European
organizations 65,
66, 69, 73, 75
—in other
organizations 14,
46, 79, 123
Molepolole 317
Molise 947
Mollendo-Matarani
309
Mölndal 1523
Molokai 1828
Moluccas *see*
Maluku
Mombasa 988, 989,
990, 992, 993
Mon (India) 865
Mon (Myanmar)
1164
Monaco 14, 69, 123,
1141–4
Monaco-Ville 1141
Monagas 1985
Monaghan 916,
921
Monastir 1583, 1586
Mönchengladbach
694
Moncton 388, 391
Mongla 269
Mongo 432
Mongolia 14, 92, 93,
1145–9
Mongomo 592
Mongu 2005
Monkey Bay 1086
Monmouth 1910
Monmouth-Ocean
1887
Monmouthshire 1695
Mono 297
Mono Islands 1446
Monos 1577
Monroe 1851, 1853
Monrovia 1047,
1048, 1050
Mons 283, 284, 290
Monseñor Nouel 564
Mont-Belo 497
Montana 1752, 1762,
1764, *1875–7*
Montana (Bulgaria)
336
Montaña Clara 1488
Montbéliard 634
Monte-Carlo 1141,
1144
Monte Cristi 564
Monte Plata 564
Montego Bay 958,
961

Montenegro *1406–8*
see also Serbia
and Montenegro
Montería 478
Monterrey 1125,
1126, 1127, 1130
Montevideo 1966,
1967, 1968, 1969
Montgomery
(Alabama) 1754,
1793, 1794
Montgomery (West
Virginia) 1943
Montlhéry 637
Montpelier 1931,
1932
Montpellier 633,
634, 643
Montreal 364, 368,
371, 398, 405,
406, 407, 408, 416
Montreuil 634
Montserrado 1047
Montserrat 78, 88,
90, 91, 1717,
1737–9
Monywa 1164
Monza 947
Moore 1905
Mooréa 668
Moorhead 1868
Moose Jaw 409
Mopelia 668
Mopti 1101
Moquegua 1286
Moradabad 814
Moratuwa 1500
Moray 1687
Morazán 587
Morbi 842
Mordovia *1353*
Møre og Romsdal
1238
Morehead City 1898
Morelia 1125, 1126
Morelos 1125, 1131
Morena 856
Moreno Valley 1754,
1807
Morgantown 1940,
1942
Morioka 965
Mormugao 827
Morobe 1275
Morocco 48, *1150–7*
—and European
organizations 55,
69, 71
—in world
organizations 14,
81, 98, 99, 100,
103, 104, 112,
117, 118, 123
Morogoro 1556
Morona-Santiago 574

Moroni 484, 486
Morphou 524
Mortlock Islands
1133
Morwell 222
Moscow (Idaho)
1833
Moscow (Russia)
1332, 1334, 1335,
1337, 1342, 1343
Moss 1239
Moss Town 258
Mossel Bay 1467
Mossendjo 494
Most 533, 536, 537
Mosta 1106
Mostaganem 143
Móstoles 1488
Mosul 911, 913
Motala 1523
Mouhoun 343
Mouila 676, 679
Moulmein 1164,
1168
Moundou 432, 435
Mount Athos 751,
1343
Mount Gambier 213
Mount Hagen 1275,
1276
Mount Isa 211
Mount Pearl 392
Mount Pleasant
(Falkland Islands)
1732
Mount Pleasant
(South Carolina)
1918
Mount Vernon
(Iowa) 1843
Mount Vernon (New
York) 1893
Mouscron 284
Moxico 152
Moyamba 1421
Moyen-Chari 432
Moyen-Ogooué 676
Moyenne-Guinée 769
Moyle 1701
Moyobamba 1286
Mozambique
1158–63
—in world
organizations 11,
14, 76, 104, 108,
117, 118
M'Poko 430
Mpumalanga 1459,
1460, 1469,
1480–1
MSF *113*
M'Sila 143
Mtwara 1556, 1559
Muang Xai 1026
Muara 332, 333

—in other
organizations 11,
15, 46, 49, 50, 81,
83, 92, 104, 112,
116
Netherlands Antilles
35, 87, 1187,
1188, *1198–201*
Neuchâtel 1535,
1536, 1540, 1541,
1542
Neuenburg *see*
Neuchâtel
Neuquén 161
Neuss 694
Neutral Zone
(Kuwait-Saudi
Arabia) 1386,
1389
Neuwerk 720
Nevada 1752, 1762,
1764, *1880–3*
Neves 1384
Nevis *see* St Kitts
and Nevis
Nevşehir 1590
New Amsterdam
778, 779
New Bedford 1860,
1862
New Berlin 1944
New Bombay 814
New Britain
(Connecticut) 1815
New Brunswick 123,
363, 364, 365,
369, 376, 377,
388–92
New Caledonia 95,
639, 650, *662–6*
New Delhi 810, 814,
815, 829
New Georgia 1446,
1449
New Glasgow 396
New Hampshire
1751, 1762, 1764,
1884–6
New Haven 1754,
1814, 1815, 1816
New Ireland 1275
New Jalpaiguri 883
New Jersey 1751,
1752, 1762, 1765,
1886–9
New London 1814,
1816
New Mangalore 827
New Mexico 1752,
1762, 1765,
1889–92
New Orleans 1753,
1850, 1851, 1852,
1853
New Plymouth 1204

New Providence 255,
256, 257, 258, 259
New Rochelle 1893
New South Wales
174, 175, 176,
177, 181, *201–8*
New Territories
(Hong Kong) 459,
463
New Valley 580
New Westminster
384
New York City 1750,
1753, 1755, 1775,
1783, 1791, 1817,
1886, 1888, 1893,
1894, 1895
New York State
1751, 1752, 1762,
1765, *1892–6*
New Zealand
1202–20
—in world
organizations 15,
50, 92, 93, 94, 95,
116
—territories overseas
78, 1215–20
Newark (Delaware)
1817, 1819
Newark (New
Jersey) 1753,
1887, 1888
Newark (Ohio) 1902
Newburgh 1893
Newcastle (Australia)
175, 186, 202,
205, 207
Newcastle-under-
Lyme 1684
Newcastle upon Tyne
1653, 1660, 1684
Newfoundland 363,
364, 365, 369,
370, 376, 377,
392–6
Newham 1682
Newport (Oregon)
1910
Newport (Rhode
Island) 1915
Newport (Wales)
1635, 1685, 1695,
1698
Newport News 1754,
1935, 1936
Newry and Mourne
1635, 1701
Newton 1860
Newtownabbey
1701
Newtownards 1704
Neyagawa 965
Neyveli 874
Ngamiland 317

Ngaoundéré 358, 361
Nghe An 1992
Ngounié 676
Ngozi 348
Ngwaketse 317
Nha Trang 1992,
1993
Nhlangano 1517
Nhulunbuy 197
Niagara Falls (New
York) 1893
Niagara Falls
(Ontario) 364
Niamey 1226, 1228,
1229
Niamtougou 1571
Niari 494
Niassa 1158
Nicaragua *1221–5*
—in world
organizations 11,
15, 81, 83, 84, 85,
87, 91, 112
Nice 634, 643, 649,
1143
Nickerie 1512
Nicobar Islands *see*
Andaman and
Nicobar Islands
Nicosia 523, 524,
527, 529
Nidwalden 1534,
1536
Nieuw Amsterdam
1512, 1516
Nieuw Nickerie 1512
Nieuwegein 1186
Niğde 1590
Niger *1226–9*
—in world
organizations 15,
104, 105, 106,
107, 108, 109,
117, 118, 123
Niger (Nigeria) 1231
Niger Basin
Authority *109*
Nigeria *1230–7*
—in world
organizations 11,
15, 76, 77, 101,
104, 106, 108,
109, 112, 117
Nightingale Islands
1741
Niigata 965
Niihau 1828
Nijmegen 1186
Nikat Al-Khams
1051
Nikumaroro 995
Nikunau 995
Nile (Sudan) 1506
Nimba 1048
Nîmes 634

Nimroz 130
Ninawa 911
Ningbo 447, 455
Ningxia Hui 446,
456
Ninh Binh 1992
Ninh Thuan 1992
Nipissing 403
Nis 1400
Nishinomiya 965
Niterói 323
Nitra 1435
Niuas 1573
Niue 78, 95, 1214,
1219–20
Niulakita 1603
Niutao 1603
Nizamabad 831
Nizampatnam 833
Nizhny Novgorod
1334
Njarðvík 802
Njazídja 484
N'Kayi 494
Nkongsamba 361
Nobel Peace Prize
19–20
Nogal 1453
Nógrád 794
Noida 878
Nokia 621
Nola 427
Nome 1797
Nongkhai 1029
Nonouti 995
Nonthaburi 1561
Noord-Brabant
1186
Noord-Holland
1185
Noordwijk 1195
Noosa 175
Nord department
(Haiti) 783
Nord-Est department
(Haiti) 783
Nord-Kivu 489
Nord-Ouest
department (Haiti)
783
Nord-Ouest province
(Cameroon) 358
Nord-Pas-de-Calais
633
Nord province
(Cameroon) 358
Nord-Trøndelag 1238
Nordaustlandet 1248
Nordic Council *73*
Nordic Development
Fund *73*
Nordic Investment
Bank *73–4*
Nordjylland 540
Nordland 1238

Upper Nile 1506
Upper River region
  (Gambia) 681
Upper Volta see
  Burkina Faso
Upper West region
  (Ghana) 744
Uppsala 1522, 1523
Uqsur see Luxor
Ural district (Russia)
  1334
Urawa 965
Urbana 1834, 1837
Urbandale 1842
Urfa 1590
Urganch see
  Urgench
Urgench 1972
Uri 1534, 1536
Uruguay 1966–71
—in world
  organizations 15,
  81, 83, 85, 87, 91,
  112, 116
Urumqi 447
Uruzgan 130
USA* see United
  States of America
Uşak 1590
Ushuaia 162, 163
Ust-Orda Buryat
  1357
Ust-Ordynsk 1357
Ústecký 533
Ustí nad Labem 533
Usulatán 587, 590
Utah 1752, 1762,
  1764, 1929–31
Utena 1060
Utica 1893
Utrecht 1185, 1186,
  1192, 1195
Utsunomiya 965
Uttar Pradesh 813,
  814, 816, 817,
  828, 831,
  878–80
Uttaranchal 813, 817,
  828, 831, 880–1
Uttarpara 883
Uturoa 668
Uusimaa 620
Uva 1500
Uvéa Island (New
  Caledonia) 662
Uvéa Island (Wallis
  and Futuna) 672
Uxbridge 1684
Uyo 1231
Uzbekistan 55,
  1972–7
—in world
  organizations 15,
  46, 69, 79, 92,
  117

Vaasa 621, 628,
  629
Vacoas-Phoenix 1120
Vadarevu 833
Vadodara 814, 843
Vaduz 1056, 1057
Vágoy 551, 552
Vágur 552
Vaishali 838
Vaitupu 1603
Vakaga 427
Valais 1535, 1536
Vâlcea 1324
Valdez 1798
Valdez-Cordova 1797
Vale of Glamorgan
  1696
Valence 634
Valencia (Spain)
  1487, 1488, 1492,
  1495, 1497
Valencia (Venezuela)
  1985
Valencian
  Community 1487,
  1488
Valenciennes 634
Valenzuela 1292
Valladolid 1487,
  1488, 1495
Valle 788
Valle d'Aosta 946,
  947
Valle del Cauca 478
Valledupar 478
Vallejo 1754, 1807
Vallendar 733
Valletta 1106, 1112
Valley Stream
  1893
Valparaíso (Chile)
  437, 438, 439,
  440, 442
Valparaiso (Indiana)
  1840
Valverde 564
Van 1590
Vanadzor 169
Vancouver (British
  Columbia) 363,
  364, 368, 371,
  381, 382, 383, 384
Vancouver
  (Washington)
  1754, 1938
Vanimo 1275
Vantaa 621
Vanua Levu 614, 617
Vanuatu 15, 77, 92,
  95, 123, 1978–81
Vapi 887
Varanasi 814, 879
Varaždin 512
Varberg 1523
Vardak 130

Varkaus 621
Värmland 1523
Varna 336, 337, 338,
  341
Varsinais-Suomi 620
Vas 794
Vaslui 1324
Västerås 1523
Västerbotten 1523
Västernorrland 1523
Västmanland 1523
Västra Götalands
  1523
Vatican City 69, 81,
  953, 1982–4
Vaud 1535, 1536,
  1541
Vaughan 400
Vaupés 478
Vava'u 1573
Vavoua 505
Vavuniya 1501
Växjö 1523
Vechta 726
Veenendaal 1186
Vejle 540, 541
Vella La Vella
  Islands 1446
Vellore 874
Velsen 1186
Veneto 947
Venezuela 1985–90
—in world
  organizations 15,
  81, 83, 85, 86, 87,
  90, 91, 101, 112,
  116
Venice 947, 948,
  954, 956
Vénissieux 634
Venlo 1186
Ventspils 1031, 1035,
  1036
Veracruz 1126
Veracruz-Llave
  1126
Veraguas 1269
Verdun 406
Vermillion 1921,
  1923
Vermont 1752, 1762,
  1765, 1785,
  1931–4
Vernon 381, 384
Veroia 752
Verona 947, 956
Versailles 634
Verviers 284
Vest-Agdar 1238
Vestfold 1238
Vestmanna 551, 552
Vestmannaeyjar 802
Vestsjælland 540
Veszprém 794, 800
Viborg 540, 548

Vicenza 947
Vichada 478
Vicksburg 1869
Victoria (Australia)
  174, 175, 176,
  177, 181, 201,
  222–7
Victoria (British
  Columbia) 364,
  381, 383, 384
Victoria (Malaysia)
  1091
Victoria (Malta) 1112
Victoria (Seychelles)
  1414, 1415, 1417,
  1418
Victoria de Durango
  1125, 1126
Victoria Falls 2012,
  2015
Vidin 338
Viedma 161
Vienna 240, 241,
  244, 246, 247, 248
Vientiane 1026,
  1027, 1029
Vieques 1953
Vietnam 15, 92, 93,
  94, 96, 97, 123,
  1991–8
Vieux Fort 1367,
  1369
Vigie 1369
Vigo 1488
Viipuri 1352
Vijayawada 814,
  833
Vila 1978, 1979,
  1980
Viljandi 606
Villa Clara 516
Villach 241
Villahermosa 1126
Villavicencio 478
Villeurbanne 634
Vilnius 1060, 1061,
  1062, 1064
Viña del Mar 438
Vineland 1887
Vinh 1992
Vinh Long 1992
Vinh Phuc 1992
Vinh Yen 1992
Vinnytska 1613
Vinnytsya 1613
Virgin Gorda 1724
Virgin Islands (USA)
  1753, 1762, 1763,
  1767, 1768, 1784,
  1961–4
Virginia 1751, 1752,
  1762, 1764, 1778,
  1785, 1934–7
Virginia Beach 1753,
  1935

palgrave
macmillan

From economics to education, history to human rights, politics to accounting, Palgrave Macmillan is the reference publisher of choice.

Highlights of our programme include:

- The Statesman's Yearbook
- SYBWorld
- The Grants Register
- International Historical Statistics
- The International Handbook of Universities
- The World List of Universities and Other Institutions of Higher Education
- The World Higher Education Database
- The New Palgrave: A Dictionary of Economics
- Remembering for the Future: The Holocaust in an Age of Genocide
- British Archives
- Transnational Accounting
- The Truth and Reconciliation Commission Reports
- International Organizations
- The Finance and Capital Markets Series

For information on the full range of Palgrave Macmillan titles - including academic monographs and textbooks - visit www.palgrave.com or request a catalogue on +44 (0)1256 302929